CW00572078

2a

Collins COBUILD

English/Korean

ADVANCED

DICTIONARY

of American English

콜린스 코빌드 영영한 사전

Collins COBUILD English/Korean Advanced Dictionary of American English
콜린스 코빌드 영영한 사전

Heinle
President: *Dennis Hogan*
Publisher: *Sherrise Roehr*
Director of Content Development: *Anita Raducanu*
Development Editor: *Katherine Carroll*
Editorial Assistant: *Katherine Reilly*
Korea Regional Manager: *Kyung Han Chung*
Director of Product Marketing: *Amy Mabley*
International Marketing Manager: *Ian Martin*
Sr. Product Manager: *Michael Cahill*
Product Marketing Manager: *Katie Kelley*
Content Project Manager: *Dawn Marie Elwell*
Technology Project Manager: *Jonelle Lonergan*
Technology Project Manager: *Cara Douglas-Graff*
Sr. Frontlist Buyer: *Marybeth Hennebury*
Editors: *John Chapman, Robert Harris, Len Neufeld*
Composition: *RefineCatch Ltd, Bungay, Suffolk, Great Britain*
Illustrators: *See pg. 1744 for illustration and photo credits.*
Cover Designer: *Linda Beaupre*

Heinle
25 Thomson Place
Boston, Massachusetts 02210
USA

elt.thomson.com

Thomson Learning Korea Limited
톰슨러닝코리아 주식회사
서울 마포구 서교동 353-1, 22
서교타워빌딩 1801호

tlsg.korea@cengage.com

In-text features including: Picture Dictionary, Thesaurus, Word Links, Word Partnerships, Word Webs, and supplements including: Guide to Key Features, Brief Writer's Handbook, Words that Frequently Appear on TOEFL® and TOEIC®, USA State Names, Abbreviations, and Capitals, and Geographical Places and Nationalities

ISBN 13: 978-1-4240-0080-7
ISBN 10: 1-4240-0080-7

Photo and illustration credits can be found on page 1744, which constitutes a continuation of this copyright page.

Collins COBUILD
Founding Editor-in-Chief: *John Sinclair*
Publisher: *Lorna Knight*
Publishing Management: *Helen Forrest, Alison Macaulay, Maree Airlie, Michela Clari, Elaine Higgleton*

For the English text
Editors: *Pat Cook, Maggie Seaton*
Contributors: *Carol Braham, Carol-June Cassidy, Robert Grossmith, Orin Hargraves, Susan Norton, Elizabeth Potter, Anne Marie Radowick*

For the Korean text
Senior Advisers:
Dr. Mi-ock Cho, Senior Research Fellow, International Graduate School of English (IGSE), Seoul, Korea
Prof. Young-kuk Jeong, Deptartment of ELT Materials Development, International Graduate School of English (IGSE), Seoul, Korea
Head of the Translation Team:
Prof. Heok-Seung Kwon, Department of English Language and Literature, Seoul National University, Seoul, Korea
Consultants:
Dr. Jaehoon Yeon, Deptartment of Languages and Cultures of Japan and Korea, School of Oriental and African Studies, University of London, England
Prof. Mae-Ran Park, Department of English Language and Literature, Pukyong National University, Busan, Korea
Contributors: *You-Jin Jang, Heejae Lee, Myong-hee Oh, Hye-jin Chung, MiYoung Jin, Dongjin Kim, Shinkyu Kim, Hwa Jung Lee, Soojin Lee, Seon-A Lee, Minsu Kim, Taesun Moon, Jeong-Ah Shin, Heon-Joo Sohn, Dong Tak Yang*

Printed in China.
2 3 4 5 6 7 8 9 10   11 10 09 08

Harper Collins Publishers
Westerhill Road
Bishopbriggs
Glasgow
G64 2QT
Great Britain

www.collins.co.uk

First Edition 2008

For permission to use material from this text or product, submit all requests online at **cengage.com/permissions** or at
http://www.collins.co.uk/rights

CONTENTS

Acknowledgements iv

Benefits of a Semibilingual Dictionary v

John Sinclair Tribute vi

Guide to Key Features vii

Introduction xii

Dictionary Text A – Z 1

Brief Writer's Handbook 1680

Words that Frequently Appear on TOEFL® and TOEIC® 1694

USA State Names and Capitals 1700

Geographical Places and Nationalities 1701

Credits 1704

감사의 글

맨 처음 코빌드 사전의 개념을 형성하는 데 귀중한 공헌을 해 주신 아래 분들께 감사의 뜻을 전한다:

John Sinclair
Patrick Hanks
Gwyneth Fox
Richard Thomas

Stephen Bullion, Jeremy Clear, Rosalind Combley, Susan Hunston, Ramesh Krishnamurthy, Rosamund Moon, Elizabeth Potter

Jane Bradbury, Joanna Channell, Alice Deignan, Andrew Delahunty, Sheila Dignen, Gill Francis, Helen Liebeck, Elizabeth Manning, Carole Murphy, Michael Murphy, Jonathan Payne, Elaine Pollard, Christina Rammell, Penny Stock, John Todd, Jenny Watson, Laura Wedgeworth, John Williams

또한 Bank of English™의 자료를 사용할 수 있도록 허락해 준 많은 분들께 감사한다. 문어 자료들은 영국을 비롯한 미국, 오스트레일리아 등 여러 나라의 신문사와 잡지 및 정기 간행물 출판사에서 제공해 주었고, 광범위한 구어 자료들은 라디오와 텔레비전 방송국, 많은 대학과 기관의 연구원들, 수많은 개인 기고자들이 제공해 주었다.

편찬 고문

Paul Nation

Senior Advisers

Dr. Mi-ock Cho, Senior Research Fellow, International Graduate School of English (IGSE), Seoul, Korea

Prof. Young-kuk Jeong, Department of ELT Materials Development, International Graduate School of English (IGSE), Seoul, Korea

Head of the Translation Team

Prof. Heok-Seung Kwon, Department of English Language and Literature, Seoul National University, Seoul, Korea

Consultants

Dr. Jaehoon Yeon, Department of Languages and Cultures of Japan and Korea, School of Oriental and African Studies, University of London, England

Prof. Mae-Ran Park, Department of English Language and Literature, Pukyong National University, Busan, Korea

Benefits of a Semibilingual Dictionary

Collins COBUILD and Heinle are pleased to offer a new type of dictionary for Korean learners of English. The **Collins COBUILD English/Korean Advanced Dictionary of American English** is a semibilingual dictionary designed for high intermediate or advanced level learners of English.

- This semibilingual dictionary includes all the features of a COBUILD monolingual dictionary, such as full sentence definitions and corpus-based examples.
- Additionally, for learners who feel they would benefit from access to Korean translations, they are included for all definitions, senses, examples, and explanatory terms.
- The Korean translations are presented on the same page as the English text but in separate, parallel column for easy reference.
- Korean translations are included to complement the English material and provide additional support to the learner when they encounter a difficult word or expression.
- The index lists the translations found in the dictionary and directs the learner, in Korean, to the relevant English entry.

Thus users have all the information on meaning and usage typically found in COBUILD dictionaries, but with plenty of support in Korean.

영영한 사전의 장점

Collins COBUILD 및 Heinle에서는 한국의 영어 학습자들을 위해 새로운 유형의 사전을 발간 했습니다. **Collins COBUILD English/Korean Advanced Dictionary of American English**은 중상 급 또는 고급 수준의 영어 학습자를 위해 개발된 영영한 사전입니다.

- 이 영영한 사전에는 문장형의 정의와 방대한 언어 자료를 바탕으로 한 예문 등 COBUILD 영영 사전의 모든 기능이 포함되어 있습니다.
- 한국어 번역을 보는 것이 도움이 된다고 생각하는 학습자를 위해 사전에 모든 정의, 의미전달, 예문 및 설명문을 한국어로도 제공하고 있습니다.
- 한국어 번역은 영어 원문과 동일한 페이지에 나와 있지만 분리되어 있고 나란히 표시되어 있어 참조하기에 좋습니다.
- 한국어 번역의 수록으로 영어 자료를 보완할 뿐아니라 어려운 단어나 표현이 등장할 때 학습자가 편리하게 참조할 수 있습니다.
- 색인에는 사전에 수록된 한국어 번역이 나열되어 있으며 그와 관련된 영어 항목이 표시되어 있습니다.

따라서 사용자는 COBUILD 사전에서 일반적으로 찾을 수 있는 단어의 의미 및 용법에 대한 모든 정보와 동시에 다양한 한국어 자료도 참고할 수 있습니다.

John Sinclair
Collins COBUILD Dictionaries의 초대 편집위원장
1933–2007

John Sinclair는 일생의 대부분을 버밍햄 대학의 현대 영문과 교수로 지낸 뛰어난 학자로, 최초의 현대 뭉치언어학자 중 하나이자 동 분야에서 가장 포용력이 넓고 창조적 사고를 지닌 사람 중 하나였다. Collins 후원의 어휘 연산 관련 COBUILD 프로젝트는 1980년대 사전 편찬에 혁신을 불러 일으켰고, 그 결과 세계 영어 교재를 위한 가장 방대한 언어자료를 구축했다.

Sinclair 교수는 최초의 전자식 언어자료 구축 작업을 직접 감독하고 데이터 분석에 필요한 도구 개발에 도움을 제공하였다. Sinclair 교수와 그의 팀은 언어자료 데이터를 통해 사람들의 실제 영어 사용방법을 알아내어 사전 표제어를 구성하는 새로운 방법을 개발하였다. 예를 들어, 빈도 정보를 사용해 학습자가 느끼는 가치와 유용성에 따라 의미에 등급을 매기고(따라서 가장 일반적인 의미를 제일 먼저 표시), 언어자료가 기존의 사전에서는 대충 다루어졌던 정보를 강조표시하여 (함께 사용되는 단어를) 나란히 배열하게 된다. 또한, Sinclair 교수의 지도 하에 팀은 사용자에게 단어의 의미전달은 물론 문맥 속 문법적 용례를 보여주는 문장형 정의 스타일을 개발하였다.

1987년에 처음 발간된 *Collins COBUILD Dictionary of English*는 학습용 사전에 대변혁을 일으켰고 사전 편찬 접근법을 완전히 변화시켰으며, 영어 학습자를 위한 차세대 집적(集積)식 사전 및 참고자료의 발간을 초래했다.

Sinclair 교수는 은퇴 직전까지 Collins COBUILD 관련 직책을 역임하다가 이탈리아 피렌체로 이주한 후 과학적 언어연구 증진협회인 Tuscan Word Centre의 회장직을 맡았다. 그는 임종 직전까지 사전에 대한 열의를 불태웠으며, Collins COBUILD의 각종 사전에는 사전 편찬 및 영어학습에 대한 그의 혁신적인 접근법이 그대로 담겨 있다. 그와 함께 즐겁게 일했던 모든 이들은 Sinclair 교수를 영원히 잊지 못할 것이다.

주요 특징

콜린스 코빌드와 톰슨 영어교육사업부(ELT)가 협력하여 혁신적인 교수법과 학습자료를 제공하는 강력한 기능을 갖춘 영어사전을 출간하게 되었다.

DefinitionsPLUS와 Vocabulary Builders와 같은 혁신적인 요소들이 추가된 *Collins COBUILD English/Korean Advanced Dictionary of American English*는 단순한 참고자료로서의 기능을 뛰어넘어 학습자들에게 필수적이고 기본적인 학습도구가 될 것이다.

DefinitionsPLUS

- **DefinitionsPLUS Collocations**(연어)—각각의 정의문은 자연스럽고 간결하게 작성되어 있으며, 일반적으로 어떤 단어들이 목표 단어와 함께 사용되는지를 보여준다.
- **DefinitionsPLUS Grammar**(문법)—각각의 정의문은 가장 대표적인 문법 패턴을 포함하고 있어 학습자들이 정확한 영어 사용법을 익히는 데 도움을 줄 것이다.
- **DefinitionsPLUS Natural English**(자연스런 영어)—각각의 정의문을 통해 관용구 등 자연스러운 영어 표현법을 익힐 수 있다.

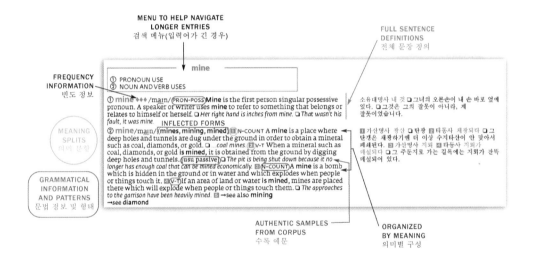

Bank of English™는 가장 최신의 정통 미국식 영어를 모아 놓은 독창적인 (전산화된) 말뭉치이다. 사전의 정의문을 작성하는 데 이 강력한 검색 툴이 사용되었으며, 모든 예문은 Bank of English™가 제공하는 풍부한 자료를 기초로 작성되었다.

Vocabulary Builders

효율적인 어휘 학습을 돕기 위해 만든 3,000여 개의 교육적 요소들이 학습자들의 호기심과 탐구심을 유발하여 실제로 학습자들의 이해력과 표현력을 향상시킬 수 있는 어휘력을 구축할 수 있게 해준다. "Vocabulary Builders"는 학습자의 어휘력과 언어 습득 능력을 향상시키고 정확한 의사소통 능력을 키워줄 것이다. 또한 학습자들이 영어에 대한 보다 폭넓고 심도 있는 지식을 체득할 수 있도록 도와줄 것이다. 한마디로 *Collins COBUILD English/Korean Advanced Dictionary of American English*는 다른 사전에서는 좀처럼 찾아볼 수 없는 참신한 내용과 구성으로 총체적인 영어 학습의 장을 제공할 것이다.

Picture Dictionary 박스에서는 단어와 그 뜻을 그림을 통해 설명한다. 여기서 선택된 단어들은 학습 환경에서 유용한 것들로서 흔히 시각적 자료를 통해 효과적으로 이해할 수 있는 개념이나 과정을 나타내는 것들이다.

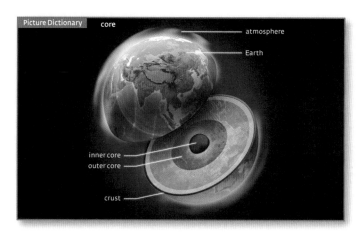

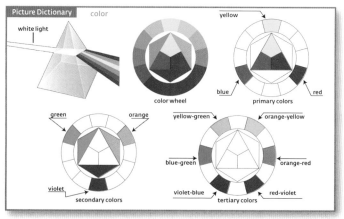

Word Webs는 단어들을 주제별로 묶어 상세한 설명과 뛰어난 그림을 통해 보여 줌으로써 개념을 더 명확히 이해할 수 있도록 도와준다. 볼드 체로 나타낸 주요 단어들은 모두 사전에 정의되어 있는 것들로, 어떤 한 단어를 찾다 보면 자연스레 다른 관련 단어들까지 익힐 수 있어 학습자들이 흥미를 갖고 영어의 매력 속으로 더 깊이 빠져들게 될 것이다. 이렇게 탐구하며 보내는 시간이 많아질수록 학습자의 어휘력은 풍부해질 것이다. Word Webs는 훌륭한 언어 탐구 자료이다.

Word Web   spice

While researching the use of **spices** in cooking, scientists discovered that many of them have strong disease-prevention properties. Bacteria can grow quickly on food and cause a variety of serious illnesses in humans. The researchers found that many spices are extremely antibacterial. For example, **garlic, onion,** allspice, and oregano kill almost all common germs. **Cinnamon,** tarragon, cumin and **chili peppers** also eliminate about 75% of bacteria. And even common, everyday **black pepper** destroys about 25% of all microbes. The research also found a connection between hot climates and **spicy** food and cold climates and **bland** food.

garlic   onion   chili pepper

ginger   black pepper   cinnamon   cloves

Word Web   wave

As **wind** blows across water, it creates **waves**. It does this by transferring energy to the water. If the waves encounter an object, they bounce off it. Light also travels in waves and behaves the same way. We are able to see an object only if light waves bounce off it. Light waves can be categorized by their **frequency**. Wave frequency is usually the measure of the number of waves per second. **Radio waves** and microwaves are examples of low-frequency light waves. **Visible light** consists of medium-frequency light waves. **Ultraviolet radiation** and **X-rays** are high-frequency light waves.

THE ELECTROMAGNETIC SPECTRUM

radio waves   microwaves   infrared light   visible light   ultraviolet light   X-rays   gamma rays

Bank of English™의 Word Partnerships는 단어가 자주 사용되는 패턴을 보여 준다. 표제어가 포함된 완전한 연어를 제시하여 그 쓰임을 분명히 보여 준다. 제시된 숫자는 표제어와 연어로 쓰이는 관련 단어의 정의문 속에서 해당하는 의미 번호를 나타낸 것이다.

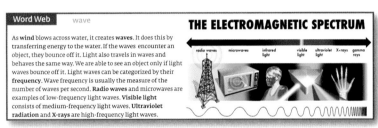

Word Partnership   *trust*의 연어

V.	**build** trust, **create** trust, **learn to** trust, **place** trust **in** *someone* **2**
ADJ.	**mutual** trust **2**
	charitable trust **10**
N.	trust *your* **instincts**, trust *someone's* **judgment** **6**
	investment trust **9**

Word Partnership   *moment*의 연어

ADV.	a moment **ago, just a** moment **1**
N.	moment **of silence,** moment **of thought** **1**
V.	**stop for a** moment, **take a** moment, **think for a** moment, **wait a** moment **1**
ADJ.	an **awkward** moment, a **critical** moment, the **right** moment **2**

Word Links는 영어 단어가 어떻게 구성되는지를 보여줌으로써 영어에 대한 기본적인 이해도를 높여준다. 이는 일상의 의사소통에서뿐만 아니라 모든 분야를 학습할 때 유용하다. 각 **Word Link**는 접두사, 접미사, 어근에 초점을 두고 각 단어의 구성요소를 간단히 설명한 다음 그것들이 포함된 예문을 세 개씩 제시한다. 세 개의 예문을 제시하는 것은 학습자들이 이 단어들을 사전에서 다시 찾아봄으로써 개념을 더욱 확실히 이해할 수 있도록 하기 위함이다.

Word Link	*port ≈ carrying* : ex*port*, im*port*, *port*able

Word Link	*geo ≈ earth* : *geo*graphy, *geo*logical, *geo*logy

Thesaurus는 특별히 사용 빈도가 높은 주요 단어들의 유의어와 반의어를 모아 놓은 것이다. 특별히 유의어를 강조하는 것은 비슷한 의미를 가진 단어들을 사전에서 찾아보는 것이 학습자들의 관심을 불러일으키고 그들의 어휘력과 표현력을 향상시키는 훌륭한 방법이 되기 때문이다. 제시된 숫자는 해당 표제어에서 해당하는 의미 번호를 나타낸다.

Thesaurus	*difficult*의 참조어
ADJ.	challenging, demanding, hard, tough; *(ant.)* easy, simple, uncomplicated **1**
	irritable, unreasonable; *(ant.)* cooperative **2**

Thesaurus	*strong*의 참조어
ADJ.	mighty, powerful, tough; *(ant.)* weak **1**
	confident, determined; *(ant.)* cowardly **2**
	solid, sturdy **3**

CD-ROM

Collins COBUILD English/Korean Advanced Dictionary of American English CD-ROM은 학습자들이 컴퓨터로 작업하면서 좀 더 빠르고 편리하게 단어를 검색할 수 있도록 해준다.

- **Search:** 정의문, 예문, Word Webs, Picture Dictionary를 검색할 수 있다.
- **Pop-Up Dictionary:** 어떤 컴퓨터 응용 프로그램의 사용 중에도 단어를 검색할 수 있다.
- 녹음과 다시 듣기가 되는 오디오 발음 기능으로 발음 연습을 할 수 있다.
- **My Dictionary:** 학습자 스스로 단어와 정의문, 예문을 추가해 가면서 자신만의 학습 자료를 만들 수 있다.
- **Bookmarks:** 단어를 체계적인 틀 속에 저장할 수 있다. 이미 만들어져 있는, 주제별 관련 단어들을 모은 75개의 북마크 폴더는 어휘 학습을 위한 훌륭한 출발점이 될 것이다.

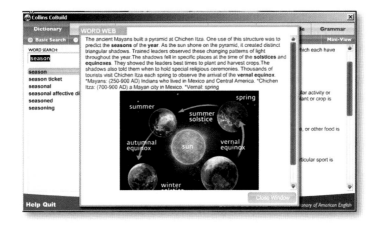

본 사전이 제공하는 학습 자료들을 이용하다 보면, *Collins COBUILD English/Korean Advanced Dictionary of American English*가 그저 빠른 답을 얻기 위해 획획 넘겨보는 흔한 영어 사전이 아니라 좀 더 깊이 파고들어 탐구하고 싶게 만드는 훌륭한 영어 교재라는 것을 알게 될 것이다. 학습자들 스스로가 의사소통에 필요한 가장 적절한 단어들을 찾아 나가면서 기존의 어떠한 참고서를 통해 경험했던 것보다 더 많은 학습 기회를 발견하게 될 것이다. *Collins COBUILD English/Korean Advanced Dictionary of American English*는 학습자들의 어휘 학습 여정에 있어서 기본적인 학습서이자 든든한 동반자가 되어 줄 것이다.

INTRODUCTION 일러두기

A dictionary is probably the single most important reference book that a learner of English can buy. At Collins we do our best to ensure that our dictionaries live up to all expectations. This **Collins Cobuild English/Korean Advanced Dictionary of American English** is a new type of dictionary. It is especially designed for Korean learners who already have a good working knowledge of English, but who may not be entirely comfortable using a monolingual English dictionary. All the features of a monolingual dictionary are included, with Korean translations provided for all senses, examples and explanatory terms. The dictionary also includes an index which lists alphabetically the translations found in the dictionary and which directs you to the relevant English entry through the medium of Korean.

사전은 아마 영어 학습자가 살 수 있는 가장 중요한 단 하나의 참고도서일 것이다. 콜린스에서는 모든 기대에 부합할 수 있는 사전을 만들기 위해 최선을 다한다. 이번 **Collins Cobuild English/Korean Advanced Dictionary of American English** 학습자 사전은 새로운 유형의 사전이다. 본 사전은 훌륭한 영어 운용 지식을 이미 지니고 있지만 영어 단일어사전(영영사전) 사용이 완전히 편안하지는 않은 한국인 학습자를 위해 특별히 고안된 것이다. 단일어사전의 특징은 모두 고수하면서 모든 의미와 용례, 설명 용어들에 대해 한글 번역을 제시했다. 또한 본 사전에 실린 역어들을 가나다순으로 정리한 색인을 덧붙여 한글을 매개로 하여 관련된 영어 표제항으로 찾아갈 수 있게 했다.

The corpus

The **Collins Cobuild English/Korean Advanced Dictionary of American English**, like all Collins dictionaries, is based on a corpus, the Bank of English ™, part of the Collins Word Web, which now contains over 650 million words of contemporary English. The corpus is central to the compilation of COBUILD dictionaries. It enables the dictionary editors to look at how the language works and make evidence-based statements about the meanings, patterns, and uses of words with confidence and accuracy.

말뭉치

모든 콜린스 사전들과 마찬가지로 Collins Cobuild English/Korean Advanced Dictionary of American English는 the Collins Word Web의 일부 말뭉치인 The Bank of English ™에 기반을 두고 만들었는데, 현재 이 말뭉치에는 6억 5천만 여개의 현대 영어 어휘가 들어 있다. 이 말뭉치는 COBUILD 사전 편찬의 중심이다. 그것은 사전 편찬자들로 하여금 영어가 어떻게 운용되고 있는지 살펴볼 수 있게 해 주고 영어 단어들의 의미와 패턴, 사용에 대해 자신감을 가지고 정확하게 증거에 입각한 진술을 할 수 있게 해 준다.

Content

A dictionary must present the most important facts about language, and dictionary compilers need good evidence to be able to make their selections. It is much easier to decide which words to include, and which to omit, when we have accurate statistical information from such a vast database of language as the Bank of English ™. This enables the compilers to look at the relative frequency of words and to identify and highlight the 2,500 most frequently used words in English. These words account for over 75% of all English usage, so it is easy to see why they are important.

내용

사전은 언어에 대해 가장 중요한 사실들을 제시해 주어야 하므로 사전 편찬자들에게는 이런 내용을 선별할 때 이용할 수 있는 훌륭한 준거가 필요하다. The Bank of English ™와 같이 방대한 언어 데이터베이스에서 나오는 정확한 통계적 정보가 있으면 어떤 어휘는 포함시키고 어떤 어휘는 제외할 것인지를 결정하기가 훨씬 수월해진다. 이를 통해 편찬자들은 어휘들의 상대적인 빈도를 살피고 영어에서 가

장 빈번히 사용되는 2500개의 어휘를 밝혀낼 수가 있다. 이 어휘들이 모든 영어 사용의 75% 이상을 차지한다. 그러니 이 어휘들이 왜 중요한지를 알기는 어렵지 않다.

Definitions
One of the most distinctive feature of all COBUILD dictionaries is the use of full English sentences in the definitions, explaining the meaning in the way that one person might explain it to another. They give the user much more than the meaning of the word they are looking up, and also contain information on usage, register, typical context, and syntax. The fullness of the definitions will give learners of English confidence as they learn what words and phrases mean and how they are used.

정의문
모든 COBUILD 사전의 가장 두드러진 특징들 중 하나는 정의문에서 완전한 영어 문장을 사용하여 한 사람이 다른 사람에게 설명을 해 주는 식으로 단어의 의미를 보여 준다는 것이다. 이런 정의문은 사용자에게 그가 찾는 단어의 의미보다 훨씬 많은 것을 보여 주어, 용법, 언어 사용역, 전형적 맥락, 통사구조에 대한 정보도 알려준다. 완전한 문장으로 된 정의문은 영어 학습자들이 단어와 구의 의미와 쓰임을 익혀 가는 동안 자신감을 가질 수 있게 해 줄 것이다.

Examples
All of the examples in this dictionary have been selected from the Bank of English ™, and have been chosen carefully to show the collocates of a word – other words that are frequently used with the word we are defining – and the patterns in which it is used. Since the examples are genuine pieces of text, you can be sure that they show the word in use in a natural context.

용례
본 사전에 실린 모든 용례는 The Bank of English ™에서 뽑은 것으로 한 단어와 연어를 이루는 단어들, 즉 정의되고 있는 그 단어와 흔히 함께 사용되는 다른 단어들과 그 단어가 사용되는 문형들을 보여 줄 수 있도록 세심히 선별한 것들이다. 이런 용례들은 실제 텍스트의 일부이므로, 그 단어가 자연스런 맥락에서 사용되는 모습을 보여 주는 것임을 확신해도 된다.

Set structures
For each definition, the word or phrase being defined is printed in **bold**. In addition, we have identified and highlighted in **bold** words which combine with the headword to make a very important or set grammatical structure or collocational pattern, for example, *A* **band of** *people is* . . . *If you* **say** *something* **to yourself**, *you think it* . . . *If you are* **unable to** *do something, it is* . . .

정형화된 구조
각 정의문에서 정의되는 단어나 구는 볼드체로 인쇄되어 있다. 뿐만 아니라, 예를 들어 *A* **band of** *people is* . . . *If you* **say** *something* **to yourself**, *you think it* . . . *If you are* **unable to** *do something, it is* . . . 처럼 표제어와 결합하여 대단히 중요하고 정형화된 문법적 구조나 영어 패턴을 형성하는 어구들도 볼드체로 뚜렷이 강조되어 있다.

Coverage
Today's learners of English need to be aware of the variation of language in different parts of the English-speaking world. The **Collins Cobuild English/Korean Advanced Dictionary of American English** includes useful notes to identify vocabulary and expressions from those parts of the world, particularly American and British English.

포괄 범위

오늘날의 영어 학습자는 영어를 사용하는 세계의 여러 다른 지역들에 존재하는 영어 변이형에 대해서도 알고 있을 필요가 있다. Collins Cobuild English/Korean Advanced Dictionary of American English에는 세계의 그런 지역들의 어휘와 표현들, 특히 미국 영어와 영국 영어를 보여주는 중요한 설명들이 들어 있다.

Usage notes

Throughout the text we have included a number of notes which give additional information about how words are used. There is a variety of useful information contained in these notes, which help to clarify important distinctions in usage and in grammar.

용법 설명

어휘의 용법에 대해 추가 정보를 제공하는 많은 설명이 본 사전 전반에 걸쳐 제시되어 있다. 이들 설명 속에는 유용한 정보가 다양하게 들어 있어서 용법과 문법상의 중요한 차이들을 명확히 하는 데 도움을 준다.

Culture notes

Extra information on culturally significant events, institutions, traditions and customs is given in the form of a note following the relevant entry. These notes are intended to help you gain a greater understanding of life and culture in English-speaking countries.

문화 설명

문화적으로 중요한 행사, 기관, 전통, 관습들에 대해서는 관련된 표제항 다음에 설명 형태로 추가 정보를 제시했다. 이들 설명은 여러분이 영어 사용 국가들의 생활과 문화를 더 잘 이해하도록 돕기 위한 것이다.

Complex entries

Entries which are long or complex are given a special treatment to make them easier to navigate. A menu shows what sections the entry is divided into, and how they are ordered, so that you can immediately go to the correct section to find the meaning you want. For example, **mean** is divided into three sections, corresponding to its verb, adjective, and noun uses. The same principle is used for **hold**, where there is an important sense distinction running through its uses.

복합 표제항

길고 복합적인 표제항은 특별히 처리하여 찾아보기 더 수월하게 했다. 그 표제항이 어떤 부분들로 나뉘져 있고 그 순서는 어떻게 되어 있는지를 보여 주는 메뉴가 있어서 원하는 의미를 찾아 알맞은 부분으로 바로 갈 수 있게 해준다. 예를 들어, **mean**은 부사, 형용사, 명사 쓰임에 해당하는 3개 부분으로 나뉘져 있다. **hold**에서도 같은 원칙을 적용하여 그 쓰임에 따라 중요한 의미 구분을 해 놓았다.

Grammatical information

Where relevant, useful information about the grammatical patterns is provided. This information appears immediately before the examples which further clarify the patterns.

문법 정보

필요할 때는 문법 구조에 대해 유용한 정보를 제공했다. 이 정보는 그 구조를 더 상세히 보여 주는 용례들 바로 앞에 나온다.

Definitions

One of the features of the **Collins Cobuild English/Korean Advanced Dictionary of American English** is that the definitions are written in full sentences, using vocabulary and grammatical structures that occur naturally with the word being explained. This enables us to give a lot of information about the way a word or meaning is used by speakers of the language. Whenever possible, words are explained using simpler and more common words. This gives us a natural defining vocabulary with most words in our definitions being among the 2,500 commonest words of English. A Korean translation is given for each sense of each word. For example, the verb **bask** has two senses, each of which has a Korean translation:

If you **bask in** the sunshine, you lie somewhere sunny and enjoy the heat.
쬐다

If you **bask in** someone's approval, favor, or admiration, you greatly enjoy their positive reaction toward you.
(은혜 등을) 입다

An individual sense of an English word may have more than one Korean translation. These translations may be interchangeable or not. For example, the noun **brother-in-law** has four different Korean translations to reflect the different relationships, for which English uses the same word:

Someone's **brother-in-law** is the brother of their husband or wife, or the man who is married to their sister.
처남; 매형; 시동생; 시아주버니

정의문

Collins Cobuild English/Korean Advanced Dictionary of American English의 특징들 중 하나는 정의문이 완전한 문장으로 되어 있어, 설명되고 있는 단어와 자연스럽게 함께 쓰이는 어휘 및 문법 구조를 활용한다는 점이다. 이런 정의문을 통해 우리는 영어 사용자들이 그 단어나 의미를 사용하는 방식에 대해 많은 정보를 제시할 수가 있다. 단어들은 가능하면 더 간단하고 일반적인 단어들을 이용하여 설명했다. 그 결과 자연스러운 정의문 어휘들은 대부분이 영어에서 가장 많이 사용되는 2500 단어 내에 속하게 되었다. 한국어 번역어는 각 단어의 각 의미에 대해 주어져 있다. 예를 들어 동사 bask는 의미가 두 가지인데 각 의미에 대해 한국어 번역어가 제시되어 있다.

If you **bask in** the sunshine, you lie somewhere sunny and enjoy the heat.
쬐다

If you **bask in** someone's approval, favor, or admiration, you greatly enjoy their positive reaction toward you.
(은혜 등을) 입다

영어 단어의 개별 의미에 해당하는 한국어가 2개 이상 있을 수도 있다. 이들 번역어들은 서로 교체 가능할 수도 있고 그렇지 않을 수도 있다. 예를 들어, 명사 brother-in-law의 경우, 관련된 여러 관계에 대해 영어에서는 모두 같은 단어를 쓰지만 한국어에서는 적어도 4 가지의 다른 단어를 쓴다.

Someone's brother-in-law is the brother of their husband or wife, or the man who is married to their sister. (누군가의 brother-in-law는 남편이나 아내의 형제, 또는 자기 여형제와 결혼한 남자이다)
처남; 매형; 시동생; 시아주버니

Information about collocates and structure

In our definitions, we show the typical collocates of a word: that is, the other words that are used with the word we are defining. For example, the definition of meaning 1 of the adjective **savory** says:

> **Savory** food has a salty or spicy flavor rather than a sweet one.

This shows that you use the adjective **savory** to describe food, rather than other things.

Meaning 1 of the verb **wag** says:

> When a dog **wags** its tail, it repeatedly waves its tail from side to side.

This shows that the subject of meaning 1 of **wag** refers to a dog, and the object of the verb is "tail".

Information about Korean collocations, if any, is given after the translation. For example, **beam** has the following definition, translation and collocational information:

A **beam** of light is a line of light that shines from an object such as a lamp.
(빛의) 한 줄기

연어를 이루는 단어들과 구조에 대한 정보

우리의 정의문은 한 단어와 전형적으로 연어를 이루는 단어들, 즉 우리가 정의하는 그 단어와 함께 쓰이는 다른 단어들을 보여준다. 예를 들어 형용사 savory의 1번 의미 정의문은 다음과 같다.

> Savory food has a salty or spicy flavor rather than a sweet one.
> (savory한 음식은 단맛보다는 짭짤하거나 매콤한 맛이 난다.)

이 정의문은 savory가 다른 무엇이 아닌 음식을 묘사하는 데 사용된다는 것을 보여 준다.

동사 wag의 1번 의미는 다음과 같다.

> When a dog wags its tail, it repeatedly waves its tail from side to side.
> (개가 꼬리를 wag할 때는, 그 꼬리를 이리저리 흔든다.)

이 정의문은 wag의 1번 의미에서는 주어가 '개'이고 동사의 목적어는 '꼬리'가 됨을 보여준다.

한국어 연어에 대한 정보도 있으면 번역어 다음에 제시했다. 예를 들어 beam에는 다음과 같은 정의문과 역어와 연어 정보가 주어져 있다.

A beam of light is a line of light that shines from an object such as a lamp.
(빛의) 한 줄기

Information about grammar

The definitions also give information about the grammatical structures in which a word is used. For example, meaning 1 of the adjective **candid** says:

> When you are **candid** about something or with someone, you speak honestly.

This shows that you use **candid** with the preposition "about" with something and "with" with someone.

Other definitions show other kinds of structure. Meaning 1 of the verb **soften** says:

> If you **soften** something or if it **softens**, it becomes less hard, stiff, or firm.

This shows that the verb is used both transitively and intransitively. In the transitive use, you have a human subject and a non-human object. In the intransitive use, you have a non-human subject.

Finally, meaning 1 of **compel** says:

> If a situation, a rule, or a person **compels** you to do something, they force you to do it.

This shows you what kinds of subject and object to use with **compel**, and it also shows that you typically use the verb in a structure with a to-infinitive.

정의문은 또한 단어가 사용되는 문법 구조에 대한 정보도 준다. 예를 들어 형용사 candid의 1번 의미는 다음과 같다.

> When you are candid about something or with someone, you speak honestly.
> (당신이 무엇에 대해서나 누군가에게 candid할 때는 정직하게 말을 한다.)

이것은 무엇에 대해 candid하다 할 때는 about을 쓰고 누구에게candid하다 할 때는 with를 쓴다는 것을 보여준다.

다른 정의문들은 다른 종류의 구조를 보여준다. 동사 soften의 의미 1번은 다음과 같다.

> If you soften something or if it softens, it becomes less hard, stiff, or firm.
> (당신이 무엇을 soften하거나 그것이soften해지면, 그것이 이전보다 덜 단단[딱딱]해지게 된다.)

이것은 이 동사가 타동사로도 쓰이고 자동사로도 쓰인다는 것을 보여준다. 타동사로 쓰일 때는 사람이 주어로 오고 사물이 목적어로 온다. 자동사로 쓰일 때는 사물이 주어로 온다.

마지막으로 compel의 1번 의미는 다음과 같다.

> If a situation, a rule, or a person compels you to do something, they force you to do it.
> (어떤 상황이나 법칙 또는 사람이 당신에게 무엇을 하도록 compel하면, 당신에게 그것을 하도록 강요하는 것이다.)

이것은 compel이 어떤 종류의 주어와 목적어와 함께 쓰이는지를 보여 주고, 또한 이 동사가 전형적으로 to 부정사가 있는 구조 속에서 쓰임을 보여주기도 한다.

Information about context and usage

In addition to information about collocation and grammar, definitions also can be used to convey your evaluation of something, for example to express your approval or disapproval. For example, here is the definition of **unhelpful**:

> If you say that someone or something is **unhelpful**, you mean that they do not help you or improve a situation, and may even make things worse.

In this definition, the expressions "if you say that", and "you mean that" indicate that these words are used subjectively, rather than objectively.

문맥과 용법에 대한 정보

정의문은 연어와 문법에 대한 정보뿐만 아니라 무엇에 대한 당신의 평가, 예를 들면 당신이 마음에 든다고 생각하는지 탐탁치 않아 하는지를 표현해 주기도 한다. 예를 들어, 다음은 unhelpful의 정의문이다.

> If you say that someone or something is **unhelpful**, you mean that they do not help you or improve a situation, and may even make things worse.
> (어떤 사람이나 무엇이 unhelpful하다고 말하는 것은, 그들이 당신을 돕지 않거나 상황을 개선하는 데 도움이 되지 않고, 심지어는 일을 더 악화시킬 수도 있음을 뜻한다.)

이 정의문에 쓰인 표현 'if you say that' 과 'you mean that'은 이들 단어가 객관적이 아니라 주관적으로 쓰임을 나타낸다.

Other kinds of definition

We sometimes explain grammatical words and other function words by paraphrasing the word in context. For example, meaning 3 of **through** says:

> To go **through** a town, area, or country means to travel across it or in it.

In many cases, it is impossible to paraphrase the word, and so we explain its function instead. For example, the definition of **unfortunately** says:

> You can use **unfortunately** to introduce or refer to a statement when you consider that it is sad or disappointing, or when you want to express regret.

Lastly, some definitions are expressed as if they are cross-references. For example:

rd. is a written abbreviation for **road**.

e-commerce is the same as **e-business**.

If you need to know more about the words **road** or **e-business**, you look at those entries.

다른 종류의 정의문들

문법어들과 다른 기능들은 종종 그 단어를 문맥 속에서 다른 말로 풀어씀으로써 설명한다. 예를 들어 through의 3번 의미는 다음과 같다.

To go through a town, area, or country means to travel across it or in it.

(어떤 도시나 지역 또는 국가를 through해서 간다는 것은 그곳을 가로질러 가거나 그 안에서 여행을 함을 뜻한다.)

많은 정의문들에서는 그 단어를 다른 말로 풀어 쓰는 것이 불가능하다. 그럴 때는 대신 그 기능을 설명한다. 예를 들어, unfortunately의 정의문은 다음과 같다.

You can use unfortunately to introduce or refer to a statement when you consider that it is sad or disappointing, or when you want to express regret.

(unfortunately는 슬프거나 실망스러운 일을 언급하거나 유감을 표현할 때, 그런 진술을 하는 서두에 쓰거나 그것을 가리키며 쓸 수 있다.)

마지막으로, 일부 정의문은 상호 참조로 표현되어 있다. 예를 들면 다음과 같다.

rd. is a written abbreviation for road.

(rd.는 road의 약어로 글에서 쓰인다.)

e-commerce is the same as e-business.

(e-commerce는 e-business와 같다.)

road나 e-business에 대해 더 알고 싶으면, 그 표제항들을 찾아보면 된다.

Style and Usage

Some words or meanings are used mainly by particular groups of people, or in particular social contexts. In this dictionary, where relevant, the definitions also give information about the kind of people who are likely to use a word or expression, and the type of social situation in which it is used.

In terms of geographical diversity, this dictionary focuses on American and British English using evidence from the Bank of English ™. Where relevant, the American or British form is shown at its equivalent word or meaning.

This information is usually placed at the end of the definition, in small capitals and within square brackets. If more than one type of information is provided, they are given in a list. The Korean translation of this information is provided after the Korean translation of the sense.

스타일과 용법

일부 단어나 의미는 특정 집단의 사람들이나 특정한 사회적 맥락 속에서만 주로 사용된다. 본 사전에서는 어떤 단어나 표현을 사용할 것 같은 사람들의 유형이나 그것이 사용될 사회적 상황의 유형들에 대한 정보도 관련이 있는 경우에는 정의문에서 제시한다.

지리적 다양성과 관련해서는 본 사전이 The Bank of English ™의 근거에 따라 미국 영어와 영국 영어에 중점을 두고 있다. 관련이 있는 경우에는 미국 영어 형태나 영국 영어 형태도 상응하는 단어나 의미에서 제시하고 있다.

이 정보는 보통 정의문 말미에 작은 대문자로 대괄호 속에 넣어 제시된다. 두 가지 이상의 정보가 제공될 때에는 목록으로 제시된다. 이런 정보에 대한 한국어 번역은 단어 의미의 한국어 번역 뒤에 나온다.

Geographical labels

AM: used mainly by speakers and writers in the US, and in other places where American English is used or taught. Where relevant the British equivalent is provided.

BRIT: used mainly by speakers and writers in Britain, and in other places where British English is used or taught. Where relevant the American equivalent is provided.

Other geographical labels are used in the text to refer to English as it is spoken in other parts of the world, e.g. AUSTRALIAN, NORTHERN ENGLISH, SCOTTISH.

지리적 표지

AM: 주로 미국 내 그리고 미국 영어가 사용되거나 가르쳐지는 다른 곳의 화자나 필자 등이 사용하는 영어

BRIT: 주로 영국 내, 그리고 영국 영어가 사용되거나 가르쳐지는 다른 곳의 화자나 필자가 사용하는 영어

지구상 다른 곳들에서 사용되는 영어를 가리키는 다른 지리적 표지들도 사전 본문 속에 나오는데, 예를 들면 Aus(오스트레일리아 영어), Northern English(잉글랜드 북부 지방 영어), Scottish(스코틀랜드 영어) 등이 있다.

Style labels

BUSINESS: used mainly when talking about the field of business, e.g. **annuity**

COMPUTING: used mainly when talking about the field of computing, e.g. **chat room**

DIALECT: used in some dialects of English, e.g. **ain't**

FORMAL: used mainly in official situations, or by political and business organizations, or when speaking or writing to people in authority, e.g. **gracious**

HUMOROUS: used mainly to indicate that a word or expression is used in a humorous way, e.g. **gents**

INFORMAL: used mainly in informal situations, conversations, and personal letters, e.g. **pep talk**

JOURNALISM: used mainly in journalism, e.g. **glass ceiling**

LEGAL: used mainly in legal documents, in law courts, and by the police in official situations, e.g. **manslaughter**

LITERARY: used mainly in novels, poetry, and other forms of literature, e.g. **plaintive**

MEDICAL: used mainly in medical texts, and by doctors in official situations, e.g. **psychosis**

MILITARY: used mainly when talking or writing about military terms, e.g. **armor**

OFFENSIVE: likely to offend people, or to insult them; words labeled OFFENSIVE should therefore usually be avoided, e.g. **cripple**

OLD-FASHIONED: generally considered to be old-fashioned, and no longer in common use, e.g. **dashing**

SPOKEN: used mainly in speech rather than in writing, e.g. **pardon**

TECHNICAL: used mainly when talking or writing about objects, events, or processes in a specialist subject, such as business, science, or music, e.g. **biotechnology**

TRADEMARK: used to show a designated trademark, e.g. **hoover**

VULGAR: used mainly to describe words which could be considered taboo by some people; words labeled VULGAR should therefore usually be avoided, e.g. **bloody**

WRITTEN: used mainly in writing rather than in speech, e.g. **avail**

사회언어적 표지

경제: 주로 경제 분야에서 사용되는 어구,
예: annuity

컴퓨터: 주로 컴퓨터 분야에서 사용되는 어구,
예: chat room

방언: 일부 영어 방언에서 사용되는 어구,
예: ain't

격식체: 주로 공식적인 상황이나 정치, 경제 분야
의 기구들에서 사용되거나 권위 있는 사람들
에게 말하거나 글을 쓸 때 사용되는 어구,
예: gracious

해학체: 주로 익살스럽게 쓰이는 어구를 나타냄,
예: gents

비격식체: 격식을 갖추지 않는 상황이나 대화 또
는 개인적인 편지에서 주로 사용하는 어구,
예: pep talk

언론: 주로 언론에서 사용되는 어구, 예: glass
ceiling

법률: 주로 법률 관련 서류나 법정에서 쓰거나 공
식적인 상황에서 경찰이 사용하는 어구,
예: manslaughter

문예체: 주로 소설, 시 그리고 다른 문학 형태에
서 쓰이는 어구, 예: plaintive

의학: 주로 의학 관련 자료에 쓰이거나 의사들이
공식적인 상황에서 사용하는 어구,
예: psychosis

군사: 군사 용어에 관해 말하거나 글을 쓸 때 사
용하는 어구, 예: armor

모욕어: 사람들의 마음을 상하게 하거나 모욕을
줄 수 있는 어구. 그러므로 OFFENSIVE 라는
표지가 붙은 어구들은 보통 사용을 피해야 한
다, 예: cripple

구식어: 대체로 고어투라고 여겨지고 더 이상 흔
히 사용되지 않는 어구, 예: dashing

구어체: 주로 글보다는 말을 할 때 사용하는 어
구, 예: pardon

과학 기술: 경제, 과학, 음악과 같은 특수한 주제
와 관련된 사물이나 행사 또는 절차에 대해 말
하거나 글을 쓸 때 주로 사용하는 어구,
예: biotechnology

상표: 특정 상표임을 나타내는 어구, 예: hoover.

비속어: 일부 사람들이 금기시하는 어구를 나타
냄. 그러므로 VULGAR라는 표지가 붙은 어구
는 보통 사용을 피해야 한다, 예: bloody

문어체: 주로 말보다는 글에서 사용되는 어구,
예: avail

PRAGMATICS LABELS 화용론적 표지

Many uses of words need more than a statement of meaning to be properly explained. People use words to do many things: give invitations, express their feelings, emphasize what they are saying, and so on. The study and description of the way in which people use language to do these things is called **pragmatics**.

In the dictionary, we draw attention to certain pragmatic aspects of words and phrases of English, paying special attention to those that, for cultural and linguistic reasons, we feel may be confusing to learners. The following labels are used:

APPROVAL: used to show that you approve of the person or thing you are talking about, e.g. **angelic**

DISAPPROVAL: used to show that you disapprove of the person or thing you are talking about, e.g. **brat**

EMPHASIS: used to emphasize the point you are making, e.g. **never-ending**

FEELINGS: used to express your feelings about something, or towards someone, e.g. **unfortunately**

FORMULAE: used in particular situations such as greeting and thanking people, or acknowledging something, e.g. **hi, congratulations**

POLITENESS: used to express politeness, sometimes even to the point of being euphemistic. e.g. **elderly**

VAGUENESS: used to show how certain you are about the truth or validity of your statements; this is sometimes called "hedging" or "modality", e.g. **presumably**

어구의 많은 사용들에 대해서는 적절히 설명을 하려면 뜻을 알려 주는 것 이상이 필요하다. 사람들은 초대를 하거나 자신의 감정을 표현하거나 자기가 하는 말을 강조하거나 등등 여러 가지 많은 것을 하기 위해 어구를 사용한다.

이런 것들을 하기 위해 사람들이 언어를 사용하는 방식을 연구하고 기술하는 것을 화용론이라고 한다. 본 사전에서는 영어의 어구가 갖는 특정한 화용론적 측면에 관심을 갖고, 문화적, 언어적 이유들로 인해 학습자들에게 혼란스러울 수도 있다고 여겨지는 것들에 특별한 주의를 기울였다. 다음은 그런 요소를 나타낸 표지들이다.

마음에 듦: 얘기되는 사람이나 사물에 대해 호감이 있음을 나타내는 어구, 예. **angelic**

탐탁찮음: 얘기되는 사람이나 사물이 탐탁찮음을 나타내는 어구, 예: **brat**

강조: 말하는 사항을 강조하기 위한 어구, 예: **never-ending**

감정 개입: 어떤 사물이나 사람에 대한 자기감정을 표현할 때 사용하는 어구, 예: **unfortunately**

의례적인 표현: 인사를 하거나 고마움을 표하거나 무엇을 인정하거나 할 때와 같은 특정한 상황에서 사용하는 어구, 예: **hi, congratulations**

공손체: 때로는 완곡할 정도로 정중한 표현을 할 때 사용하는 어구, 예: **elderly**

짐작투: 진술 내용의 진실성이나 타당성에 대한 자신의 확신 정도를 나타낼 때 사용하는 어구. 'hedging'(모호함)이나 'modality'(서법성)라고도 함, 예: **presumably**

PRONUNCIATION 발음

The basic principle underlying the suggested pronunciations is "If you pronounce it like this, most people will understand you." The pronunciations are therefore broadly based on the two most widely taught accents of English, GenAm or General American for American English, and RP or Received Pronunciation for British English.

For the majority of words, a single pronunciation is given, as most differences between American and British pronunciation are systematic. Where the usual British pronunciation differs from the usual American pronunciation more significantly, a separate transcription is given after the code BRIT. Where more than one pronunciation is common in either American or British English, alternative pronunciations are given.

The pronunciations are the result of a program of monitoring spoken English and consulting leading reference works. The transcription system has developed from original work by Dr David Brazil for the Collins COBUILD English Language Dictionary. The symbols used in the dictionary are adapted from those of the International Phonetic Alphabet (IPA), as standardized in the English Pronouncing Dictionary by Daniel Jones (14th Edition, revised by AC Gimson and SM Ramsaran 1988).

발음 제시의 배경이 된 기본 원칙은 "이렇게 발음하면 대부분의 사람들이 이해할 것이다"이다. 따라서 발음은 대체로 세계적으로 가장 널리 가르치는 영어의 두 가지 악센트에 기반을 두었는데, 그것은 미국 영어에 대해서는 GenAm(일반 미국 영어)이고 영국 영어는 RP(통용되는 발음)이다.

미국 영어와 영국 영어의 발음상의 차이는 대부분 체계적이므로 대다수의 단어에 대해서는 한 가지 발음만 제시했다. 일반적인 영국 발음이 일반적인 미국 발음과 중대한 차이가 있을 때만 BRIT라는 부호 뒤에 별도의 발음 표시를 해 두었다. 미국 영어에서든 영국 영어에서든 두 가지 이상의 발음이 일반적일 때는 대체 가능한 발음들도 제시했다.

발음들은 구어 영어를 청취하고 주요 참고서적들을 참조하는 작업을 통한 결과로 나온 것이다. 발음 전사 체계는 『콜린스 코빌드 영영사전』을 위해 만든 데이비드 브라질 박사 (Dr David Brazil)의 독창적인 연구를 발전시킨 것이다. 이 사전에 쓰인 발음 부호는 다니엘 존스(Daniel Jones)가 펴낸 『영어 발음 사전』(14판, 1988, AC Gimson과 SM Ramsaran 개정)에서 표준화된 국제음성기호(IPA)의 기호를 차용한 것이다.

IPA Symbols 국제음성기호

Vowel Sounds 모음		Consonant Sounds 자음	
ɑ	calm, ah	b	bed, rub
æ	act, mass	d	done, red
aɪ	dive, cry	f	fit, if
aʊ	out, down	g	good, dog
ɛ	met, lend, pen	h	hat, horse
eɪ	say, weight	y	yellow, you
ɪ	fit, win	k	king, pick
i	feed, me	l	lip, bill
ɒ	lot, spot	ᵊl	handle, panel
oʊ	note, coat	m	mat, ram
ɔ	claw, maul	n	not, tin
ɔɪ	boy, joint	ᵊn	hidden, written
ʊ	could, stood	p	pay, lip
u	you, use	r	run, read
ʌ	fund, must	s	soon, bus
ə	first vowel in about	t	talk, bet
i	second vowel in very	v	van, love
u	second vowel in actual	w	win, wool
		w	loch
		z	zoo, buzz
		ʃ	ship, wish
		ʒ	measure, leisure
		ŋ	sing, working
		tʃ	cheap, witch
		θ	thin, myth
		ð	then, bathe
		dʒ	joy, bridge

Notes

/æ/ or /ɑ/

There are a number of words which use the /æ/ sound in GenAm and in most accents of English, but /ɑ/ in RP, such as 'bath' which is pronounced /bæθ/ in GenAm and /bɑθ/ in RP. This affects some words in which this vowel is followed by the sounds /f/, /nd/, /ns/, /nt/, /ntʃ/, /s/, /θ/. For example, 'graph', 'command', 'answer', 'can't', 'ranch', 'class' and 'bath' are pronounced /græf/, /kəmænd/, /ænsər/, /kænt/, /ræntʃ/, /klæs/ and /bæθ/ in GenAm, but /graf/, /kəmand/, /ɑ̈nsəʳ/, /kant/, /rantʃ/, /klas/ and /baθ/ in RP. However, there are exceptions to this such as "land" /lænd/. In these cases, we show only the GenAm version as it is a common and acceptable pronunciation for British English, even though it is not RP.

/r/

In most accents of English, including GenAm, 'r' is always pronounced. One of the main ways in which RP differs is that 'r' is only pronounced as /r/ when the next sound is a vowel. Thus, in RP, 'far gone' is pronounced /fä gɒn/ but 'far out' is pronounced /fär aʊt/. Similarly, 'fire', 'flour', 'fair', 'near' and 'pure' are pronounced /faɪər/, /flaʊər/, /fɛər/, /nɪər/ and /pyʊər/ in GenAm, but /faɪə/, /flaʊə/, /fɛə/, /nɪə/ and /pyʊə/ in RP.

/oʊ/

This symbol is used to represent the sound /oʊ/ in GenAm, and also the sound /əʊ/ in RP, as these sounds are almost entirely equivalent.

/ᵊl/ and /ᵊn/

These show that /l/ and /n/ are pronounced as separate syllables:

handle /hændᵊl/
hidden /hɪdᵊn/

참고

/æ/ or /ɑ/

GenAm에서는 /bæθ/로 발음되지만 RP에서는 /bæθ/로 발음되는 'bath'처럼, GenAm과 많은 다른 악센트에서는 /æ/ 음을 쓰지만 RP에서는 /ɑ/ 음을 쓰는 단어들이 많다. 이 모음 뒤에 /f/, /nd/, /ns/, /nt/, /ntʃ/, /s/, /θ/ 같은 음이 나오는 일부 단어들에서 이런 사실이 영향을 미친다. 예를 들어, 'graph', 'command', 'answer', 'can't', 'ranch', 'class'와 'bath'가 GenAm에서는 /græf/, /kəmænd/, /ænsər/, /kænt/, /ræntʃ/, /klæs/ and /bæθ/, RP에서는 /graf/, /kəmand/, /ɑ̈nsəʳ/, /kant/, /rantʃ/, /klas/ and /baθ/이다. 그러나 'land' /lænd/처럼 예외적인 경우도 있다. 이런 경우들에는 GenAm 발음만 제시를 했는데, 그 이유는 이들 발음이 RP는 아니지만 영국 영어에서 흔하고 또 받아들여지는 발음이기도 하기 때문이다.

/r/

GenAm을 포함한 대부분의 영어 악센트에서는 'r'이 항상 발음된다. RP가 이들과 다른 주요한 점들 중 하나는 'r'이 모음 앞에 나올 때만 발음된다는 것이다. 따라서 RP에서는 'far gone'은 /fä gɒn/으로 발음되지만 'far out'은 /fä aʊt/로 발음된다. 마찬가지로 'fire', 'flour', 'fair', 'near' 그리고 'pure'가 GenAm에서는 /faɪər/, /flaʊər/, /fɛər/, /nɪər/와 /pyʊər/로 발음되지만 RP에서는 /faɪə/, /flaʊə/, /fɛə/, /nɪə/와 /pyʊə/로 발음된다.

/oʊ/

이 기호는 GenAm의 /oʊ/ 음과 RP의 /əʊ/ 음을 나티내기 위해 쓰였는데, 그 이유는 이 두 가지 음이 거의 완전히 같기 때문이다.

/ᵊl/ and /ᵊn/

이 부호들은 /l/과 /n/이 별도 음절로 발음됨을 나타낸다.

handle /hændᵊl/
hidden /hɪdᵊn/

Stress

Stress is shown by underlining the vowel in the stressed syllable:

two /tu̱/

result /rɪzʌ̱lt/

disappointing /dɪ̱səpɔ̱ɪntɪŋ/

When a word is spoken in isolation, stress falls on the syllables which have vowels which are underlined. If there is one syllable underlined, it will have primary stress.

'TWO'
'reSULT'

If two syllables are underlined, the first will have secondary stress, and the second will have primary stress:

'DISapPOINTing'

A few words are shown with three underlined syllables, for example 'disqualification' /dɪ̱skwɒ̱lɪfɪkɐ̱ɪʃᵊn/. In this case, the third underlined syllable will have primary stress, while the secondary stress may be on the first or second syllable:

'DISqualifiCAtion' or 'disQUALifiCAtion'

GenAm usually prefers 'dis-', while RP tends to prefer 'DIS-'.

In the case of compound words, where the pronunciation of each part is given separately, the stress pattern is shown by underlining the headword: '<u>off-peak</u>', '<u>first-class</u>', but 'c<u>a</u>ke pan'.

강세

강세는 강세가 있는 음절 속의 모음에 밑줄을 그어 나타내었다.

two /tu̱/

result /rɪzʌ̱lt/

disappointing /dɪ̱səpɔ̱ɪntɪŋ/

한 단어가 단독으로 발화될 때는 밑줄 친 모음이 있는 음절에 강세가 온다. 밑줄 친 음절이 하나뿐일 때는 그 음절에 제 1 강세가 온다.

'TWO'
'reSULT'

밑줄 친 음절이 둘일 때는 첫째 음절에 제 2강세가 오고 둘째 음절에 제 1강세가 온다.

'DISapPOINTing'

예를 들어 'disqualification' /dɪ̱skwɒ̱lɪfɪkɐ̱ɪʃᵊn/처럼 일부 단어들에는 세 개 음절에 밑줄이 그어져 있다. 이런 경우에는 셋째 밑줄 친 음절에 제 1 강세가 오고 제 2 강세는 첫째나 둘째 음절에 온다.

'DISqualifiCAtion' 혹은 'disQUALifiCAtion'

GenAm은 보통 'dis-'를 선호하는 반면 RP는 'DIS-'를 선호하는 경향을 보인다.

합성어에서는, 구성어들의 발음은 각 표제어에서 별도로 제시되므로, 합성어의 강세 패턴만 표제어에 밑줄을 그어 나타내었다. '<u>off-peak</u>', '<u>first-class</u>'이지만, 'c<u>a</u>ke pan'이다.

Stressed syllables

When words are used in context, the way in which they are pronounced depends upon the information units that are constructed by the speaker. For example, a speaker could say:

1   'the reSULT was disapPOINTing'
2   'it was a DISappointing reSULT'
3   'it was VERy disappointing inDEED'

In (3), neither of the two underlined syllables in disappointing /dɪsəpɔɪntɪŋ/ receives either primary or secondary stress. This shows that it is not possible for a dictionary to predict whether a particular syllable will be stressed in context.

It should be noted, however, that in the case of adjectives with two stressed syllables, the second syllable often loses its stress when it is used before a noun:

'an OFF-peak FARE'
'a FIRST-class SEAT'

Two things should be noted about the marked syllables:

1   They can take primary or secondary stress in a way that is not shared by the other syllables.
2   Whether they are stressed or not, the vowel must be pronounced distinctly; it cannot be weakened to /ə/, /ɪ/ or /ʊ/.

These features are shared by most of the one-syllable words in English, which are therefore transcribed in this dictionary as stressed syllables:

two /tu/
inn /ɪn/
tree /tri/

강세 음절

단어들이 문맥 속에 쓰이면 발음은 화자가 구성하는 정보 단위에 따라 결정된다. 예를 들어, 어떤 화자가 다음과 같이 말할 수 있을 것이다.

1   'the reSULT was disapPOINTing'
2   'it was a DISappointing reSULT'
3   'it was VERy disappointing inDEED'

(3)에서는 disappointing /dɪsəpɔɪntɪŋ/에 제시된 두 밑줄 표시 음절 중 어느 것에도 제 1 강세나 제 2 강세가 주어지지 않는다. 이것은 특정 음절이 문맥 속에서 강세를 받게 될지 아닐지를 사전이 예측하는 것은 가능하지 않음을 보여준다.

그러나 강세를 받는 음절이 두 개인 형용사들의 경우에는, 그 형용사가 명사 앞에 쓰이면 흔히 두 번째 음절이 강세를 잃게 된다는 점을 유념해야 한다.

'an OFF-peak FARE'
'a FIRST-class SEAT'

강세가 표시된 음절에 대해서는 다음의 두 가지 사항을 주의해야 한다.

1   그 음절에는 다른 음절과는 다르게 제 1 강세나 제 2 강세가 올 수 있다.
2   그 음절에 강세가 오든 안 오든 모음은 반드시 분명하게 발음해야 한다. 즉 /ə/, /ɪ/나 /ʊ/로 약하게 발음할 수 없다.

이런 사항은 대부분의 영어 단음절어에도 적용된다. 따라서 본 사전에서 단음절어는 다음과 같이 강세를 받는 음절로 표시되고 있다.

two /tu/
inn /ɪn/
tree /tri/

Unstressed syllables

It is an important characteristic of English that vowels in unstressed syllables tend not to be pronounced clearly. Many unstressed syllables contain the vowel /ə/, a neutral vowel which is not found in stressed syllables. The vowels /ɪ/ , or /ʊ/, which are relatively neutral in quality, are also common in unstressed syllables.

Single-syllable grammatical words such as 'shall' and 'at' are often pronounced with a weak vowel such as /ə/. However, some of them are pronounced with a more distinct vowel under certain circumstances, for example when they occur at the end of a sentence. This distinct pronunciation is generally referred to as the strong form, and is given in this dictionary after the word STRONG.

shall /ʃəl, STRONG ʃæl/
at /ət, STRONG æt/

비강세 음절

비강세 음절의 모음은 분명하게 발음되지 않는 경향을 띠는 것이 영어의 중요한 특징 중 하나이다. 많은 비강세 음절들에는 /ə/ 모음이 들어 있는데, 이것은 강세 음절에서는 나타나지 않는 중성모음이다. 자질 면에서 비교적 중성인 /ɪ/나 /ʊ/ 모음들도 비강세 음절들에 흔히 나온다.

shall과 at 같이 단음절어인 문법어들은 흔히 /ə/과 같은 약모음으로 발음된다. 그러나, 예를 들어 문장의 끝에 오는 것과 같은 특정한 상황에서는 그 단어들 중 일부가 더 또렷한 모음으로 발음되기도 한다. 이와 같은 또렷한 발음을 가리켜 일반적으로 강형(strong form)이라고 하는데, 본 사전에서는 이런 발음을 STRONG이라는 낱말 뒤에 제시해 놓고 있다.

shall /ʃəl, STRONG ʃæl/
at /ət, STRONG æt/

LIST OF GRAMMATICAL NOTATIONS 문법 기호 목록

Word classes 단어 분류

adjective	ADJ	형용사
adverb	ADV	부사
auxiliary verb	AUX	준조동사
color word	COLOR	색채어
combining form	COMB	연결형
conjunction	CONJ	접속사
convention	CONVENTION	관용 표현
determiner	DET	한정사
exclamation	EXCLAM	감탄사
fraction	FRACTION	분수
modal verb	MODAL	법조동사
count noun	N-COUNT	가산명사
collective count noun	N-COUNT-COLL	가산명사 - 집합
family noun	N-FAMILY	친족명사
noun in names	N-IN-NAMES	이름명사
mass noun	N-MASS	물질명사
plural noun	N-PLURAL	복수명사
proper noun	N-PROPER	고유명사
collective proper noun	N-PROPER-COLL	고유명사 - 집합
singular noun	N-SING	단수명사
collective singular noun	N-SING-COLL	단수명사 - 집합
title noun	N-TITLE	경칭명사
uncount noun	N-UNCOUNT	불가산명사
collective uncount noun	N-UNCOUNT-COLL	불가산명사 - 집합
variable noun	N-VAR	가산명사 또는 불가산명사
collective variable noun	N-VAR-COLL	가산명사 또는 불가산명사 - 집합
vocative noun	N-VOC	호격명사
negative	NEG	부정어
number	NUM	수사
ordinal	ORD	서수
phrasal verb	PHRASAL VERB	구동사
phrasal verb-link	PHRASAL VERB-LINK	연결 구동사
phrasal passive verb	PHRASAL VERB-PASSIVE	수동 구동사
phrasal reciprocal verb	PHRASAL VERB-RECIP	상호 구동사
phrase	PHRASE	구
predeterminer	PREDET	전치 한정사
preposition	PREP	전치사
pronoun	PRON	대명사
emphatic pronoun	PRON-EMPH	강조대명사
indefinite pronoun	PRON-INDEF	부정(不定)대명사
negative indefinite pronoun	PRON-INDEF-NEG	부정(不定)대명사 - 부정(否定)
negative pronoun	PRON-NEG	부정(否定)대명사
plural pronoun	PRON-PLURAL	복수대명사
possessive pronoun	PRON-POSS	소유대명사
reciprocal pronoun	PRON-RECIP	상호대명사
reflexive pronoun	PRON-REFL	재귀대명사
emphatic reflexive pronoun	PRON-REFL-EMPH	강조 재귀대명사
relative pronoun	PRON-REL	관계대명사
singular pronoun	PRON-SING	단수대명사
quantifier	QUANT	수량사
negative quantifier	QUANT-NEG	부정(否定)수량사
plural quantifier	QUANT-PLURAL	복수수량사
question word	QUEST	의문사
sound word	SOUND	소리
intransitive verb	V-I	자동사
link verb	V-LINK	연결동사
passive verb	V-PASSIVE	수동동사
reciprocal verb	V-RECIP	상호동사
passive reciprocal verb	V-RECIP-PASSIVE	상호동사 - 수동
transitive verb	V-T	타동사
passive transitive verb	V-T PASSIVE	수동 타동사
intransitive or transitive verb	V-T/V-I	타동사/자동사

Words and abbreviations used in patterns 문형에 쓰인 말들과 약어들

adjective group	**adj**	형용사구
superlative form	**adj-superl**	최상급
adverb group	**adv**	부사(구)
word or phrase indicating an amount of something	**amount**	양
broad negative	**brd-neg**	전체 부정
clause	**cl**	절
color word	**color**	색채어
comparative form	**compar**	비교급
continuous	**cont**	진행형
definite noun group	**def-n**	한정명사(구)
definite noun group with an uncount noun	**def-n-uncount**	불가산명사 포함 한정명사구
definite noun group with a noun in the plural	**def-pl-n**	복수형 포함 한정명사구
determiner	**det**	한정사
past participle of a verb	**-ed**	과거분사
noun group, adjective, adverb, or prepositional phrase	**group**	명사구, 형용사구, 부사구 또는 전치사구
imperative	**imper**	명령(문)
infinitive form of a verb	**inf**	동사 원형
present participle of a verb	**-ing**	현재 분사
interrogative	**interrog**	의문(문)
clause beginning with *like*	**like**	like로 시작하는 절
noun or noun group	**n**	명사(구)
names of places or institutions	**names**	장소 또는 기관 명칭
negative word	**neg**	부정(否定)어
proper noun	**n-proper**	고유명사
number	**num**	수
uncount noun or noun group with an uncount noun	**n-uncount**	불가산명사 또는 불가산명사 포함 명사구
ordinal	**ord**	서수
particle, part of a phrasal verb	**P**	구동사의 불변화사
passive voice	**passive**	수동태
plural	**pl**	복수(형)
noun in the plural, plural noun group, co-ordinated noun group	**pl-n**	복수 명사, 복수 명사구, 등위접속사로 연결된 명사구
plural number	**pl-num**	복수
possessive	**poss**	소유격
prepositional phrase or preposition	**prep**	전치사구 또는 전치사
pronoun	**pron**	대명사
indefinite pronoun	**pron-indef**	부정(不定) 대명사
reflexive pronoun	**pron-refl**	재귀대명사
relative pronoun	**pron-rel**	관계대명사
question word	**quest**	의문사
singular	**sing**	단수
noun in the singular	**sing-n**	단수 명사
supplementary information accompanying a noun	**supp**	명사의 부가 정보
'that'-clause	**that**	that 절
the to-infinitive form of a verb	**to-inf**	to 부정사
usually	**usu**	보통
verb or verb group	**v**	동사 또는 동사구
continuous verb	**v-cont**	진행 동사
link verb	**v-link**	연결 동사
wh-word, clause beginning with a wh-word	**wh**	wh-어, wh-어로 시작하는 절

Explanation of Grammatical Terms

Introduction

For each use of each word in this dictionary, grammar information is provided. For a very few words, such as abbreviations, contractions and some words of foreign origin, no grammar is given, because the words do not belong to any word class, or are used so freely that every example could be given a different word class, e.g. *AD, ditto, must've*.

The grammar information that is given is of three types:

1   the word class of the word: e.g. **PHRASAL VERB, N-COUNT, ADJ, QUANT**

2   restrictions or extensions to its behavior, compared to other words of that word class: e.g. **usu passive, usu sing, also no det**

3   the patterns that the word most frequently occurs in: e.g. **N** *of* **n, ADJ that, ADV with v**

For all word classes, the patterns are given immediately before the examples they accompany.

The word class of the word being explained is in CAPITAL LETTERS. The order of items in a pattern is the order in which they normally occur in a sentence. Words in *italics* are words (not word classes) that occur in the pattern. Alternatives are separated by a slash (/).

Word classes

ADJ

An **adjective** can be graded or ungraded, or be in the comparative or the superlative form, e.g. *He has been <u>absent</u> from his desk for two weeks . . . the most <u>accurate</u> description of the killer to date . . . The <u>eldest</u> child was a daughter called Fatiha.*

Adjective patterns

ADJ n The adjective is always used before a noun, e.g. . . . *a <u>governmental</u> agency.*

usu ADJ n The adjective is usually used before a noun. It is sometimes used after a link verb.

v-link ADJ The adjective is used after a link verb such as *be* or *feel*, e.g. *He felt <u>unwell</u>.* Adjectives with this label are sometimes used in other positions such as after the object of a verb such as *make* or *keep*, but never before a noun.

usu v-link ADJ The adjective is usually used after a link verb. It is sometimes used before a noun.

ADJ after v The adjective is used after a verb that is not a link verb, e.g. *I wore a white dress and was <u>barefoot</u>.*

n ADJ The adjective comes immediately after a noun, e.g. *between archaeology <u>proper</u> and science-based archaeology.*

det ADJ The adjective comes immediately after a determiner and before any other adjectives, and sometimes comes before numbers, e.g. *You owe a <u>certain</u> person a sum of money.* If the dictionary does not show that an adjective is used only or mainly in the pattern **ADJ n** and **v-link ADJ**, this means that the adjective is used freely in both patterns.

These main adjective patterns are sometimes combined with other patterns.

ADV

An **adverb** can be graded or ungraded, or be in the comparative or the superlative form. e.g. *Much of our behavior is <u>biologically</u> determined . . . I'll work <u>hard</u> . . . Inflation is below 5% and set to fall <u>further</u> . . . those areas <u>furthest</u> from the coast.*

AUX

An **auxiliary verb** is used with another verb to add particular meanings to that verb, for example, to form the continuous aspect or the passive voice, or to form negatives and interrogatives. The verbs *be, do, get* and *have* have some senses in which they are auxiliary verbs.

COLOR

A **color word** refers to a color. It is like an adjective, e.g. *the blue sky . . . The sky was blue*, and also like a noun, e.g. *She was dressed in red . . . several shades of yellow*.

COMB

A **combining form** is a word which is joined with another word, usually with a hyphen, to form compounds, e.g. *strawberry-flavored, business-speak*. The word class of the compound is also given, e.g. **COMB in ADJ, COMB in N-UNCOUNT**.

CONJ

A **conjunction** usually links elements of the same grammatical type, such as two words or two clauses, e.g. *She and Simon had already gone . . . I sat on the chair to unwrap the package while he stood by*.

CONVENTION

A **convention** is a word or a fixed phrase which is used in conversation, for example when greeting someone, apologizing, or replying, e.g. *hello, sorry, no comment*.

DET

A **determiner** is a word that is used at the beginning of a noun group, e.g. *a tray, more time, some books, this amount*. It can also be used to say who or what something belongs or relates to e.g. *his face, my house*, or to begin a question e.g. *Whose car were they in?*

EXCLAM

An **exclamation** is a word or phrase which is spoken suddenly, loudly, or emphatically in order to express a strong emotion such as shock or anger. Exclamations are often followed by exclamation marks, e.g. *good heavens! Ouch!*

FRACTION

A **fraction** is used in numbers, e.g. *five and a half, two and two thirds;* before *of* and a noun group, e.g. *half of the money, a third of the children, an eighth of Russia's grain;* after *in* or *into*, e.g. *in half, into thirds*. A fraction is also used like a count noun, e.g. *two halves, the first quarter of the year*.

MODAL

A **modal** is used before the infinitive form of a verb, e.g. *You may go*. In questions, it comes before the subject, e.g. *Must you speak?* In negatives, it comes before the negative word, e.g. *They would not like this*. It does not inflect, for example, it does not take an -*s* in the third person singular, e.g. *She can swim*.

N-COUNT

A **count noun** has a plural form, usually made by adding -*s*. When it is singular, it must have a determiner in front of it, such as *the, her*, or *such*, e.g. *My cat is getting fatter . . . She's a good friend*.

N-COUNT-COLL

A **collective count noun** is a count noun which refers to a group of people or things. It behaves like a count noun, but when it is in the singular form it can be used with either a singular or plural verb, e.g. *Their audience are much younger than the average . . . The British audience has a huge appetite for serials . . . Audiences are becoming more selective*.

N-FAMILY

A **family noun** refers to a member of a family, e.g. *father*, *mommy*, and *granny*. Family nouns are count nouns which are typically used in the singular, and usually follow a possessive determiner. They are also vocative nouns. They are also proper nouns, used with no determiner, e.g. *My mommy likes marzipan . . . Tell them I didn't do it, Mommy . . . Mommy's always telling me I'm too old for dolls.*

N-IN-NAMES

The **noun** occurs **in names** of people, things, or institutions.

N-MASS

A **mass noun** typically combines the behavior of both count and uncount nouns in the same sense. It is used like an uncount noun to refer to a substance. It is used like a count noun to refer to a brand or type, e.g. *Rinse in cold water to remove any remaining detergent . . . Wash it in hot water with a good detergent . . . We used several different detergents in our stain-removal tests.*

N-PLURAL

A **plural noun** is always plural, and is used with plural verbs. If a pronoun is used to stand for the noun, it is a plural pronoun such as *they* or *them*, e.g. *These clothes are ready to wear . . . He expressed his condolences to the families of people who died in the incident.* Plural nouns which end in -s usually lose the -s when they come in front of another noun, e.g. *pants, pants leg.* If they refer to a single object which has two main parts, such as *jeans* and *glasses*, the expression *a pair of* is sometimes used, e.g. *a pair of jeans.* This is shown as **N-PLURAL: also** *a pair of* **N**.

N-PROPER

A **proper noun** refers to one person, place, thing, or institution, and begins with a capital letter. Many proper nouns are used without a determiner, e.g. . . . *Earth*; some must be used with *the*, and this is indicated: **N-PROPER,** *the* **N**, e.g. *the UK.*

N-PROPER-COLL

A **collective proper noun** is a proper noun which refers to a group of people or things. It can be used with either a singular or a plural verb, e.g. *The Senate is expected to pass the bill shortly . . . The Houses of Parliament are the British parliament.*

N-SING

A **singular noun** is always singular, and needs a determiner, e.g. . . . *to respect the environment . . . Maureen was the epitome of sophistication.* When only *a* or *the* is used, this is indicated: **N-SING: a N** or **N-SING:** *the* **N**, e.g. *The traffic slowed to a crawl . . . We dropped to the ground.*

N-SING-COLL

A **collective singular noun** is a singular noun which refers to a group of people or things. It behaves like a singular noun, but can be used with either a singular or plural verb, e.g. *The enemy were pursued for two miles . . . Their defense has now conceded 12 goals in six games.*

N-TITLE

A **title noun** is used to refer to someone who has a particular role or position. Titles come before the name of the person and begin with a capital letter, e.g. *The Chancellor of the Exchequer.*

N-UNCOUNT

An **uncount noun** refers to things that are not normally counted or considered to

be individual items. Uncount nouns do not have a plural form, and are used with a singular verb. They do not need determiners, e.g. . . . *an area of outstanding natural beauty*.

N-UNCOUNT-COLL
A **collective uncount noun** is an uncount noun which refers to a group of people or things. It behaves like an uncount noun, but can be used with either a singular or plural verb, e.g. . . . *Hearts is one of the four suits in a pack of playing cards* . . . *Hearts are trumps*.

N-VAR
A **variable noun** typically combines the behavior of both count and uncount nouns in the same sense (see **N-COUNT, N-UNCOUNT**). The singular form occurs freely both with and without determiners. Variable nouns also have a plural form, usually made by adding -*s*. Some variable nouns when used like uncount nouns refer to abstract things like *hardship* and *technology*, and when used like count nouns refer to individual examples or instances of that thing, e.g. *Technology is changing fast* . . . *They should be allowed to wait for cheaper technologies to be developed*. Others refer to objects which can be mentioned either individually or generally, like *potato* and *salad*: you can talk about *a potato, potatoes*, or *potato*.

N-VAR-COLL
A **collective variable noun** is a variable noun which refers to a group of people or things. It behaves like a variable noun, but when it is singular it can be used with either a singular or a plural verb, e.g. *The management is doing its best to improve the situation*.

N-VOC
A **vocative noun** is used when speaking directly to someone or writing to them. Vocative nouns do not need a determiner, but some may be used with a possessive determiner, e.g. *Thank you, darling* . . . *How are you, my darling?*

NEG see PRON-INDEF-NEG, PRON-NEG, QUANT-NEG

NUM
A **number** is a word such as *three* and *hundred*. Numbers such as *one, two, three* are used like determiners, e.g. *three bears*; like adjectives, e.g. *the four horsemen*; like pronouns, e.g. *She has three cases and I have two*; and like quantifiers, e.g. *Six of the boys stayed behind*. Numbers such as *hundred, thousand, million* always follow a determiner or another number, e.g. *two hundred people, the thousand horsemen, She has a thousand dollars and I have a million, A hundred of the boys stayed behind*.

ORD
An **ordinal** is a type of number. Ordinals are used like adjectives, e.g. *He was the third victim*; like pronouns, e.g. *the second of the two teams*; like adverbs, e.g. *The other team came first*; and like determiners, e.g. *Fourth place goes to Timmy*.

PHRASAL VERB
A **phrasal verb** consists of a verb and one or more particles e.g. *look after, look back, look down on*. Some phrasal verbs are reciprocal, link or passive verbs.

PHRASE
Phrases are groups of words which are used together with little variation and which have a meaning of their own, e.g. *The emergency services were working against the clock*.

PREDET
A **predeterminer** is used in a noun group before *a, the*, or another determiner, e.g. *What a terrific idea!* . . . *both the children* . . . *all his life*.

PREFIX

A **prefix** is a letter or group of letters, such as *un-* or *multi-*, which is added to the beginning of a word in order to form another word. For example, the prefix *un-* is added to *happy* to form *unhappy*

PREP

A **preposition** begins a prepositional phrase and is followed by a noun group or a present participle. Patterns for prepositions are shown in the dictionary only if they are restricted in some way. For example, if a preposition occurs only before a present participle, it is shown as **PREP -ing**.

PREP-PHRASE

A **phrasal preposition** is a phrase which behaves like a preposition, e.g. *Prices vary according to the quantity ordered.*

PRON

Pronouns are used like noun groups, to refer to someone or something that has already been mentioned or whose identity is known, e.g. *They produced their own shampoos and hair-care products, all based on herbal recipes . . . two bedrooms, each with three beds.* Some pronouns are further classified, for example as **PRON-EMPH, PRON-INDEF**, and so on.

PRON-EMPH

Emphatic pronouns are words like *all, both,* and *each,* when they are used to emphasize another noun or pronoun, e.g. *We each have different needs and interests . . . I wish you both a good trip.*

PRON-INDEF

Indefinite pronouns are words like *anyone, anything, everyone,* and *something,* e.g. *Why would anyone want that job? . . . after everything else in his life had changed.*

PRON-INDEF-NEG

Negative indefinite pronouns are words like *none, no-one,* and *nothing,* e.g. *He searched for a sign of recognition on her face, but there was none . . . Do our years together mean nothing?*

PRON-NEG

Negative pronouns are words like *neither,* e.g. *Neither seemed likely to be aware of my absence for long.*

PRON-PLURAL

Plural pronouns are the plural personal pronouns, which include *we, us, they,* and *them,* e.g. *Neither of us forgot about it.*

PRON-POSS

A **possessive pronoun** is used to say who or what something belongs to or relates to. The possessive pronouns are *mine, yours, his, hers, ours* and *theirs,* e.g. *That wasn't his fault, it was mine . . . The author can report other people's results which more or less agree with hers.*

PRON-RECIP

The **reciprocal pronouns** are *each other* and *one another,* e.g. *We looked at each other in silence.*

PRON-REFL

Reflexive pronouns are pronouns which are used as the object of a verb or preposition when they refer to the same person or thing as the subject of the verb. They are used in the same positions as other pronouns. The reflexive pronouns are *myself, yourself, himself, herself, itself, oneself, ourselves, yourselves,* and *themselves,* e.g. *I asked myself what I would have done in such a situation . . . One must apply oneself to the present.*

PRON-REFL-EMPH
Emphatic reflexive pronouns are reflexive pronouns which are used for emphasis, often after another pronoun or at the end of a clause, e.g. *A wealthy man like yourself is bound to make an enemy or two along the way . . . The president himself is on a visit to Beijing . . . I made it myself.*

PRON-REL
Relative pronouns are words like *which* and *who*, that introduce relative clauses. They are the subject or object of the verb in the relative clause, or the object of a preposition, e.g. *. . . those who eat out for a special occasion . . . The largest asteroid is Ceres, which is about a quarter the size of the moon.*

PRON-SING
Singular pronouns are the singular personal pronouns, which include *I, me, he, him, she, her, it,* and *one*, e.g. *He didn't mean to be cruel but I cried my eyes out.*

QUANT
A **quantifier** comes before *of* and a noun group, e.g. *most of the house.* If there are any restrictions on the type of noun group, this is indicated: **QUANT** of **def-n** means that the quantifier occurs before *of* and a definite noun group, e.g. *Most of the kids have never seen the sea.*

QUANT-NEG
Negative quantifiers are words like *neither*, e.g. *Neither of us felt like going out.*

QUANT-PLURAL
Plural quantifiers are words like *billions* and *millions* which are followed by *of* and a noun group, e.g. *. . . for billions of years.*

QUEST
A **question word** is a wh-word that is used to begin a question, e.g. *Why didn't he stop me?*

SOUND
Sound words are used before or after verbs such as *go* and *say*, e.g. *Suddenly there was a loud crack.*

SUFFIX
A **suffix** is a letter or group of letters such as *–ly* or *–ness*, which is added to the end of a word in order to form a new word, usually of a different word class, e.g. *quick, quickly.*

V-I
An **intransitive verb** is one which takes an indirect object or no object, e.g. *The problems generally fall into two categories . . . As darkness fell outside, they sat down to eat.*

V-LINK
A **link verb** connects a subject and a complement. Most link verbs do not occur in the passive voice,
e.g. *be, become, taste, feel.*

V-RECIP
Reciprocal verbs describe processes in which two or more people, groups, or things interact mutually: they do the same thing to each other, or participate jointly in the same action or event. Reciprocal verbs are used where the subject is both participants, e.g. *Fred and Sally met . . .* The participants can also be referred to separately, e.g. *Fred met Sally . . . Fred argued with Sally.* These patterns are reciprocal because they also mean that *Sally met Fred* and *Sally argued with Fred.* Note that many reciprocal verbs can also be used in

a way that is not reciprocal. For example, *Fred and Sally kissed* is reciprocal, but *Fred kissed Sally* is not reciprocal (because it does not mean that Sally also kissed Fred).

V-RECIP-PASSIVE
A **passive reciprocal verb** behaves like both a passive verb and a reciprocal verb, e.g. *He never believed he and Susan would be reconciled*.

V-T
A **transitive verb** is one which takes a direct object, e.g. *He mailed me the contract*.

V-T PASSIVE
A **passive verb** occurs in the passive voice only, e.g. *The company is rumored to be a takeover target*.

V-T/V-I
Some verbs may be **transitive** or **intransitive** depending on how they are used, e.g. *He opened the window and looked out... The flower opens to reveal a bee*.

Words and abbreviations used in patterns
In a pattern, the element in capital letters represents the word in the entry. All the other elements are in small letters. Items in *italics* show the actual word that is used, such as *of*. Items in roman print show the word class or type of clause that is used. For example:

> **N** *of* **n** means that the word being explained is a noun (**N**), and it is followed in the sentence by the word *of* and another noun or noun group (**n**).
> **ADV adj/adv** means that the word being explained is an adverb (**ADV**), and it is followed in the sentence by an adjective (**adj**) or (/)
> another adverb (**adv**).

When the word in the entry occurs in a pattern, the element in capital letters is **N** for any kind of noun, **ADJ** for any kind of adjective, and so on. **PHR** is used for a phrase, and **N** is used to represent a noun in a phrase.

Words used to structure information in patterns
after: after v means after a verb. The word is used either immediately after the verb, or after the verb and another word or phrase, or in a marked position at the beginning of the clause. For example, the adverb **mildly** is used:

> immediately after a verb: *Have a nice time, dear, and drive carefully.*
> after a verb and its object: *Use a flash and position the camera carefully.*
> at the beginning of a clause: *Carefully make a cut with a small knife.*

The phrase **on hold** is used:

> immediately after a verb: *Everything is on hold until we know more.*
> after a verb and its object: *He put his retirement on hold.*

also: used with some nouns to show that the word is used in a way that is not typical of that type of noun. For example, **also N in pl** means that unlike most uncount nouns, this noun also has a plural form and use. **Also** is used with some adverbs and adjectives to show a pattern that is less common than the other patterns mentioned. For example, **usu ADV with v**, **also ADV adj** means that the adverb is usually used with a verb but is also used before an adjective.

before: before v means before a verb. The word is used before the main element in a verb group. For example, the adverb **already** is used:

> before the whole verb group: *those who already know of the delights of skiing.*
> immediately before the main element in the group: *They had already voted for him at the first ballot.*

no: used to indicate that a verb is not used in a particular way, for example **no passive**, or that a singular noun is also used without a determiner: **also no det.**

oft: used to indicate that a word or phrase often occurs in a particular pattern or behaves in a particular way.

only: used to indicate that a verb is always used in a particular way, for example **only cont.**

usu: used to indicate that a word or phrase usually occurs in a particular pattern or behaves in a particular way.

with: **with** is used when the position of a word or phrase is not fixed. This means that the word or phrase sometimes comes before the named word class and sometimes comes after it. For example, **quickly** at **quick 1** has the pattern **ADV** *with* **v.** It occurs:

> after the verb: *Cussane worked quickly and methodically;*
> before the verb: *She quickly looked away and stared down at her hands.*

In addition, **with cl** is used when the word sometimes occurs at the beginning of the clause, sometimes at the end, and sometimes in the middle. For example, **seriously** has the pattern **ADV with cl.** It occurs:

> at the beginning of the clause: *Seriously, I only watch TV in the evenings.*
> at the end of the clause: *All of us react favorably to those who take our views seriously.*
> in the middle of the clause: *This approach is now seriously out of step with the times.*

Elements used in patterns

adj: stands for **adjective group.** This may be one word, such as "happy", or a group of words, such as "very happy" or "as happy as I have ever been".

> e.g. **adj N: read** 8 . . . *Ben Okri's latest novel is a good read.*

adj-compar: stands for **comparative adjective.** This is used to indicate an adjective group with the comparative form of the adjective.

> e.g. ADJ-compar *than:* **old** 2 . . . *Bill was six years older than David.*

adj-superl: stands for **superlative adjective.** It is used to indicate an adjective group with the superlative form of the adjective.

> e.g. **ADV adj-superl: positively** 1 . . . *This is positively the last chance for the industry to establish such a system.*
> e.g. **ORD adj-superl: second** 2 . . . *the party is still the second strongest in Italy.*

adv: stands for **adverb group.** This may be one word, such as "slowly", or a group of words, such as "extremely slowly" or "more slowly than ever".

> e.g. **adv ADV: else** 1 . . . *I never wanted to live anywhere else.*

amount: means **word or phrase indicating an amount of something,** such as "a lot", "nothing", "three percent", "four hundred pounds", "more", or "much".

> e.g. **amount** *and* **ADV: above** 2 . . . *Banks have been charging 25 percent and above for unsecured loans.*

brd-neg: stands for **broad negative,** that is, a clause which is negative in meaning. It may contain a negative element such as "no-one", "never", or "hardly", or may show that it is negative in some other way.

> e.g. **oft with brd-neg: approve** 1 . . . *Not everyone approves of the festival.*

cl: stands for **clause.**

> e.g. **cl ADV: anyway** 4 . . . *What do you want from me, anyway?*

color: means **color word,** such as "red", "green", or "blue".

> e.g. **ADJ color: pastel** . . . *pastel pink, blue, peach, and green.*

compar: stands for **comparative form of an adjective or adverb**.

    e.g. **ADV compar: even** 2 . . . *On television he made an even stronger impact as an interviewer.*

cont: stands for **continuous**. It is used when indicating that a verb is always, usually, or never used in the continuous.

    e.g. **only cont: die** 4 . . . *I'm dying for a breath of fresh air.*

        no cont: adore 1 . . . *She adored her parents and would do anything to please them.*

def-n: stands for **definite noun group**. A definite noun group is a noun group that refers to a specific person or thing, or a specific group of people or things, that is known and identified.

    e.g. **QUANT** *of* **def-n: whole** 1 . . . *I was cold throughout the whole of my body.*

def-pl-n: stands for **definite noun group with a noun in the plural**.

    e.g. **QUANT** *of* **def-pl-n: many** 1 . . . *It seems there are not very many of them left in the sea.*

det: stands for **determiner**. A determiner is a word that comes at the beginning of a noun group, such as "the", "her", or "those".

    e.g. **det ADJ: following** 2 . . . *We went to dinner the following Monday evening.*

-ed: stands for **past participle of a verb,** such as "decided", "gone", or "taken".

    e.g. **ADV -ed: freshly** . . . *freshly baked bread.*

group: stands for **noun group, adjective, adverb, or prepositional phrase**.

    e.g. **ADV group: strictly** . . . *He seemed fond of her in a strictly professional way.*

imper: stands for **imperative**. It is used when indicating that a verb is always or usually used in the imperative.

    e.g. **only imper** and **inf: beware** . . . *Beware of being too impatient with others.*

inf: stands for **infinitive form of a verb,** such as "decide", "go", or "sit".

    e.g. **ADJ to-inf: duty-bound** . . . *I felt duty-bound to help.*

        ADV to-inf: yet 7: . . . *She has yet to spend a Christmas with her husband.*

-ing: stands for **present participle of a verb,** such as "deciding", "going", or "taking".

    e.g. **PREP -ing: before** 2 . . . *He spent his early life in Sri Lanka before moving to Canada.*

it: means an "introductory" or "dummy" *it*. It does not refer to anything in a previous sentence or in the world; it may refer to what is coming later in the clause or it may refer to things in general.

    e.g. **oft** *it* **v-link ADJ to-inf: nice** 7 . . . *It's nice to meet you.*

n: stands for **noun** or **noun group**. If the **n** element occurs in a pattern with something that is part of a noun group, such as an adjective or another noun, it represents a noun. If the **n** element occurs in a pattern with something that is not part of a noun group, such as a verb or preposition, it represents a noun group. The noun group can be of any kind, including a pronoun.

    e.g. **ADJ n: abiding:** . . . *He has a genuine and abiding love of the craft.*

names: means **names of places or institutions**.

    e.g. **oft in names: requiem** 2 . . . *a performance of Verdi's Requiem.*

neg: stands for **negative words,** such as "not", or "never".

    e.g. **with neg: dream** 6 . . . *I wouldn't dream of making fun of you.*

n-proper: stands for **proper noun**. A proper noun is the name of a particular person or thing.

    e.g. usu **n-proper N: lookalike** . . . a Marilyn Monroe lookalike.

num: stands for **number**.

    e.g. **num ADV: odd** 3 . . . *How many pages was it, 500 odd?*

n-uncount: stands for **uncount noun** or **noun group with an uncount noun.** An uncount noun is a noun which has no plural form and which is sometimes used with no determiner.

    e.g. **QUANT**of **n-uncount: touch** 13 . . . *She thought she just had a touch of flu.*

ord: stands for **ordinal,** such as "first", or "second".

    e.g. **ord ADJ n: generation** 4 . . . *second generation Jamaicans in New York.*

passive: stands for **passive voice.** It is used when indicating that a verb usually or never occurs in the passive voice.

    e.g. **usu passive: expel** 1 . . . *More than five-thousand high school students have been expelled for cheating.*

pl: stands for **plural.**

pl-n: stands for **noun in the plural, plural noun group,** or **co-ordinate noun group** (two or more noun groups joined by a co-ordinating conjunction).

    e.g. **PREP pl-n: between** 2 . . . *I spent a lot of time in the early Eighties travelling between Waco and El Paso.*

pl-num: stands for **plural number.** A plural number is a number which is used only in the plural.

    e.g. **PREP poss pl-num: in** 5 . . . *young people in their twenties.*

poss: stands for **possessive.** Possessives which come before the noun may be a possessive determiner, such as "my", "her", or "their", or a possessive formed from a noun group, such as "the horse's". Possessives which come after the noun are of the form "*of* n", such as "of the horse".

    e.g.**usu pl, with poss: ancestor** 1 . . . *our daily lives, so different from those of our ancestors.*

prep: stands for **prepositional phrase** or **preposition.**

    prep PRON: him 1 . . . *Is Sam there? Let me talk to him.*

pron: stands for **pronoun.** A pronoun is a word such as "I", "it", or "them" which is used like a noun group. It refers to someone or something that has already been mentioned or whose identity is known.

    e.g. **PREP pron: before** 12 . . . *Everyone in the room knew it was the single hardest task before them.*

pron-indef: stands for **indefinite pronoun.** An indefinite pronoun is a word like *anyone, anything, everyone* and *something.*

    e.g. **pron-indef ADJ: else** 2 . . . *I expect everyone else to be truthful.*

pron-refl: stands for **reflexive pronoun,** such as "yourself", "herself", or "ourselves".

    e.g. **PREP pron-refl: among** 9 . . . *The girls stood aside, talking among themselves.*

quest: stands for **question word.** A question word is a wh-word such as "what", "how", or "why" which is used to begin a question.

    e.g. **quest ADV: ever** 6 . . . *Why ever didn't you tell me?*

sing: stands for **singular.**

sing-n: stands for **noun in the singular.**

    e.g. **PREDET det sing-n: all** 2 . . . *She's worked all her life.*

supp: stands for **supplementary information accompanying a noun.** Supplementary information that comes before a noun may be given by a determiner, possessive, adjective, or noun modifier. Supplementary information that comes after the noun may be given by a prepositional phrase or a clause.

    e.g. **supp N: park** 2 . . . *a science and technology park.*

that: stands for **"that"-clause**. The clause may begin with the word "that", but does not necessarily do so.

    e.g. **usu N that: conviction** 1 . . . *It is our conviction that a step forward has been taken.*

to-inf: stands for **to-infinitive form of a verb**.

    e.g. **v-link ADJ to-inf: inclined** 2 . . . *I am inclined to agree with Alan.*

v: stands for **verb or verb group**. It is not used to represent a link verb. See also the explanations of **after, before** and **with**.

    e.g. **v PRON: her** 1 . . . *I told her I had something to say.*

      v PREP n: at 10 . . . *She opened the door and stood there, frowning at me.*

v-link: stands for **link verb**. A link verb is a verb such as "be" which connects a subject and a complement.

    e.g. **v-link ADJ: down** 3 . . . *The computer's down again.*

wh: stands for **wh-word,** or **clause beginning with a wh-word,** such as "what", "why", "when", "how", "if", or "whether".

    e.g. **ADJ** *about* **n/wh: tight-lipped** 1 . . . *Military officials are still tight-lipped about when their forces will launch a ground offensive.*

A, a /eɪ/ (**A's, a's**) N-VAR **A** is the first letter of the English alphabet. 가산명사 또는 불가산명사 영어 알파벳의 첫 번째 글자

a ♦♦♦ /ə, STRONG eɪ/ or **an** /ən, STRONG æn/

> **A** or **an** is the indefinite article. It is used at the beginning of noun groups which refer to only one person or thing. The form **an** is used in front of words that begin with vowel sounds.

> a, an은 부정관사이다. 한 명의 사람 또는 한 개의 사물을 지칭하는 명사 앞에 쓴다. an은 발음상 모음으로 시작되는 단어 앞에 쓴다.

1 DET You use **a** or **an** when you are referring to someone or something for the first time or when people may not know which particular person or thing you are talking about. ❏ *A waiter entered with a tray bearing a glass and a bottle of whiskey.* ❏ *He started eating an apple.* **2** DET You use **a** or **an** when you are referring to any person or thing of a particular type and do not want to be specific. ❏ *I suggest you leave it to an expert.* ❏ *Bring a sleeping bag.* **3** DET You use **a** or **an** in front of an uncount noun when that noun follows an adjective, or when the noun is followed by words that describe it more fully. ❏ *The islanders exhibit a constant happiness with life.* **4** DET You use **a** or **an** in front of a mass noun when you want to refer to a single type or make of something. ❏ *Bollinger "RD" is a rare, highly prized wine.* **5** DET You use **a** in quantifiers such as **a lot, a little,** and **a bit.** ❏ *I spend a lot on expensive jewelry and clothing.* **6** DET You use **a** or **an** to refer to someone or something as a typical member of a group, class, or type. ❏ *Some parents believe a boy must learn to stand up and fight like a man.* **7** DET You use **a** or **an** in front of the names of days, months, or festivals when you are referring to one particular instance of that day, month, or festival. ❏ *The interview took place on a Friday afternoon.* **8** DET You use **a** or **an** when you are saying what someone is or what job they have. ❏ *I explained that I was an artist.* **9** DET You use **a** or **an** instead of the number "one," especially with words of measurement such as "hundred," "hour," and "meter," and with fractions such as "half," "quarter," and "third." ❏ *...more than a thousand acres of land.* **10** DET You use **a** or **an** in expressions such as **eight hours a day** to express a rate or ratio. ❏ *Prices start at $13.95 a meter for printed cotton.*

1 한정사 문맥에서 사람이나 사물을 처음 지칭할 때, 혹은 지칭하는 사람이나 사물이 불분명할 때 사용하는 부정관사 ❏ 웨이터가 잔 하나와 위스키 한 병을 담은 쟁반을 들고 들어왔다. ❏ 그는 사과를 먹기 시작했다. **2** 한정사 특정한 종류의 사람이나 사물 하나를 지칭할 때 사용하는 부정관사 ❏ 그것은 전문가에게 맡겨 두는 게 좋을 것 같습니다. ❏ 침낭을 가져오너라. **3** 한정사 셀 수 없는 명사 앞에 형용사가 오거나, 그 명사를 수식하는 구가 뒤에 올 경우 명사 앞에 사용하는 부정관사 ❏ 섬주민들은 삶에 대해 끊임없이 행복해 하는 모습을 보인다. **4** 한정사 물질명사와 관련하여 어떤 종류의 사물을 지칭할 때 사용하는 부정관사 ❏ '볼린저 알디'는 희귀하고 정평 있는 와인이다. **5** 한정사 a lot 이나 a little 같은 한정구에 사용하는 부정관사 ❏ 나는 비싼 보석과 옷에 많은 돈을 쓴다. **6** 한정사 사람이나 사물이 한 집단이나 종류의 전형적인 구성원을 나타낼 때 사용하는 부정관사 ❏ 어떤 부모들은 남자 아이는 남자답게 소신을 가지고 싸우는 것을 배워야 한다고 믿는다. **7** 한정사 날짜, 축제 등의 특정한 날을 나타낼 때 사용하는 부정관사 ❏ 면접은 어느 금요일 오후에 행해졌다. **8** 한정사 사람의 직업 등을 일컬을 때 사용하는 부정관사 ❏ 나는 내가 예술가라고 설명했다. **9** 한정사 '하나'라는 숫자를 대신하여 사용하는 부정관사로서 주로 측량 단위와 사용함 ❏ 천 에이커 남짓한 땅 **10** 한정사 비율을 나타내는 표현에 사용하는 부정관사 ❏ 날염 면직물은 가격이 미터 당 13.95 달러부터이다.

A & E /eɪ ənd i/ N-COUNT In Britain, **A & E** is the part of a hospital that deals with accidents and emergencies. A & E is an abbreviation for "accident and emergency." [BRIT; AM ER]

가산명사 응급실 [영국영어; 미국영어 ER]

aback /əbæk/ PHRASE If you are **taken aback by** something, you are surprised or shocked by it and you cannot respond at once. ❏ *Roland was taken aback by our strength of feeling.*

구 놀라다, 당황하다 ❏ 롤란드는 우리의 격한 감정에 당황했다.

aban|don ♦♦◇ /əbændən/ (**abandons, abandoning, abandoned**) **1** V-T If you **abandon** a place, thing, or person, you leave the place, thing, or person permanently or for a long time, especially when you should not do so. ❏ *He claimed that his parents had abandoned him.* **2** V-T If you **abandon** an activity or piece of work, you stop doing it before it is finished. ❏ *The authorities have abandoned any attempt to distribute food in an orderly fashion.* **3** V-T If you **abandon** an idea or way of thinking, you stop having that idea or thinking in that way. ❏ *Logic had prevailed and he had abandoned the idea.* **4** →see also **abandoned** **5** PHRASE If people **abandon ship**, they get off a ship because it is sinking. ❏ *At the captain's order, they abandoned ship.*

1 타동사 버리다; 떠나다 ❏ 그는 부모가 자기를 버렸다고 주장했다. **2** 타동사 포기하다 ❏ 당국에서는 식량을 질서 정연하게 배급하려는 모든 시도를 포기했다. **3** 타동사 (생각을) 포기하다 ❏ 그는 논리적으로 따져 보고 결국 그 생각을 포기했었다. **5** 구 가라앉는 배를 떠나다 ❏ 선장의 명령에 따라 그들은 가라앉는 배를 떠났다.

Thesaurus	abandon의 참조어
v.	desert, leave; *(ant.)* stay **1**
	quit, stop; *(ant.)* continue **2**

aban|doned ♦♦◇ /əbændənd/ ADJ An **abandoned** place or building is no longer used or occupied. ❏ *All that digging had left a network of abandoned mines and tunnels.*

형용사 버려진 ❏ 그 모든 굴착 작업으로 인하여 망처럼 뚫린 갱과 터널들이 버려져 있었다.

aban|don|ment /əbændənmənt/ **1** N-UNCOUNT The **abandonment of** a place, thing, or person is the act of leaving it permanently or for a long time, especially when you should not do so. ❏ *...memories of her father's complete abandonment of her.* **2** N-UNCOUNT The **abandonment of** a piece of work or activity is the act of stopping doing it before it is finished. ❏ *Constant rain forced the abandonment of the next day's competitions.*

1 불가산명사 유기, 버림 ❏ 자기를 완전히 버린 아버지에 대한 그녀의 기억 **2** 불가산명사 포기 ❏ 계속되는 비 때문에 다음 날 경기는 포기해야 했다.

abate /əbeɪt/ (**abates, abating, abated**) V-I If something bad or undesirable **abates**, it becomes much less strong or severe. [FORMAL] ❏ *The storms had abated by the time they rounded Cape Horn.*

자동사 약해지다, 수그러지다, 잦아들다 [격식체] ❏ 그들이 케이프 혼을 돌 때쯤에는 폭풍의 기세가 수그러져 있었다.

ab|bey /æbi/ (**abbeys**) N-COUNT An **abbey** is a church with buildings attached to it in which monks or nuns live or used to live.

가산명사 대수도원

ab|bre|vi|ate /əbríːvieɪt/ (abbreviates, abbreviating, abbreviated) v-T If you **abbreviate** something, especially a word or a piece of writing, you make it shorter. ❑ *He persuaded his son to abbreviate his first name to Alec.*

타동사 줄여 쓰다 ❑ 그는 아들에게 이름을 알렉으로 줄여 쓰도록 설득했다.

ab|bre|via|tion /əbríːvieɪʃən/ (abbreviations) N-COUNT An **abbreviation** is a short form of a word or phrase, made by leaving out some of the letters or by using only the first letter of each word. ❑ *The postal abbreviation for Kansas is KS.*

가산명사 약어 ❑ 캔사스 주에 대한 우편 약어는 케이에스이다.

ab|di|cate /ǽbdɪkeɪt/ (abdicates, abdicating, abdicated) ■ v-I If a king or queen **abdicates**, he or she gives up being king or queen. ❑ *The last French king was Louis Philippe, who abdicated in 1848.* ● **ab|di|ca|tion** /ǽbdɪkéɪʃən/ N-UNCOUNT *...the most serious royal crisis since the abdication of Edward VIII.* ■ v-T If you say that someone has **abdicated** responsibility for something, you disapprove of them because they have refused to accept responsibility for it any longer. [FORMAL, DISAPPROVAL] ❑ *Many parents simply abdicate all responsibility for their children.* ● **ab|di|ca|tion** N-UNCOUNT ❑ *There had been a complete abdication of responsibility.*

■ 자동사 퇴위하다 ❑ 프랑스의 마지막 왕은 루이 필립이었는데 그는 1848년에 퇴위했다. ● 퇴위 불가산명사 ❑ 에드워드 8 세의 퇴위 이후 왕가에 닥친 가장 심각한 위기 ■ 타동사 (책임을) 유기하다 [격식체, 탐탁찮음] ❑ 많은 부모들이 자기 자식들에 대한 모든 책임을 쉽게 유기한다. ● 유기 불가산명사 ❑ 책임을 완전히 유기한 적이 있었다.

ab|do|men /ǽbdoʊmən, BRIT ǽbdəmən/ (abdomens) N-COUNT Your **abdomen** is the part of your body below your chest where your stomach and intestines are. [FORMAL] ❑ *He went into hospital to undergo tests for a pain in his abdomen.*

가산명사 복부 [격식체] ❑ 그는 복부 통증 때문에 검사를 받기 위해 병원에 입원했다.

ab|domi|nal /ǽbdɒmɪnəl/ ADJ **Abdominal** is used to describe something that is situated in the abdomen or forms part of it. [FORMAL] [ADJ n] ❑ *...vomiting, diarrhea and abdominal pain.*

형용사 복부의 [격식체] ❑ 구토, 설사 및 복통

ab|duct /ǽbdʌkt/ (abducts, abducting, abducted) v-T If someone **is abducted** by another person, he or she is taken away illegally, usually using force. ❑ *He was on his way to the airport when his car was held up and he was abducted by four gunmen.* ● **ab|duc|tion** /ǽbdʌkʃən/ (abductions) N-VAR *...the abduction of four black youths from a church hostel in Soweto.*

타동사 납치하다 ❑ 그가 공항으로 가던 도중 총을 든 괴한 네 명에게 차를 세우고 납치됐다. ● 납치 가산명사 또는 불가산명사 ❑ 소웨토 소재 교회 호스텔에서 흑인 청년 네 명이 납치된 사건

ab|er|ra|tion /ǽbəreɪʃən/ (aberrations) N-VAR An **aberration** is an incident or way of behaving that is not typical. [FORMAL] ❑ *It became very clear that the incident was not just an aberration, it was not just a single incident.*

가산명사 또는 불가산명사 이례적인 일, 정도에서 벗어남 [격식체] ❑ 그 사건이 단순히 이례적인 사건이 아니라는 것이 아주 명백해졌다. 그것은 단지 하나의 독립된 사건이 아니었다.

abide /əbáɪd/ (abides, abiding, abided) PHRASE If you **can't abide** someone or something, you dislike them very much. ❑ *I can't abide people who can't make up their minds.* →see also **abiding, law-abiding**

구 견디다, 참다 ❑ 마음을 못 정하는 사람들은 정말 싫어.

▶**abide by** PHRASAL VERB If you **abide by** a law, agreement, or decision, you do what it says you should do. ❑ *They have got to abide by the rules.*

구동사 지키다 ❑ 그들은 규칙을 지켜야 한다.

abid|ing /əbáɪdɪŋ/ ADJ An **abiding** feeling, memory, or interest is one that you have for a very long time. [ADJ n] ❑ *He has a genuine and abiding love of the craft.*

형용사 꾸준한; 오래 남는 ❑ 그는 그 기술에 대해 꾸준하고 진정한 애정을 지니고 있다.

abil|ity ♦♦◇ /əbɪ́lɪti/ (abilities) ■ N-SING Your **ability to** do something is the fact that you can do it. ❑ *The public never had faith in his ability to handle the job.* ■ N-VAR Your **ability** is the quality or skill that you have which makes it possible for you to do something. ❑ *Her drama teacher spotted her ability.* ❑ *Does the school cater to all abilities?* ■ PHRASE If you do something **to the best of** your **abilities** or **to the best of** your **ability**, you do it as well as you can. ❑ *I take care of them to the best of my abilities.*

■ 단수명사 능력 ❑ 대중은 그가 그 일을 할 수 있다고 신뢰했던 적이 없었다. ■ 가산명사 또는 불가산명사 재능 ❑ 그녀의 연기 교사가 그녀의 재능을 알아보았다. ❑ 그 학교는 모든 재능을 육성해 주나요? ■ 구 능력껏 ❑ 나는 그들을 내 능력이 닿는 한 최선을 다해 돌보고 있다.

> Do not confuse **ability** with **capability** and **capacity**. You often use **ability** to say that someone can do something well. ❑ *He had remarkable ability as a musician....the ability to bear hardship.* A person's **capability** is the amount of work they can do and how well they can do it. ❑ *...a job that was beyond the capability of one man....the director's ideas of the capability of the actor.* If someone has a particular **capacity**, a **capacity** for something, or a **capacity** to do something, they have the qualities required to do it. **Capacity** is a more formal word than **ability**. ❑ *...their capacity for hard work....his capacity to see the other person's point of view.*

> ability를 capability나 capacity와 혼동하지 않도록 하라. ability는 흔히 누가 무엇을 잘 할 수 있다고 말할 때 사용한다. ❑ 그는 음악가로서 놀라운 재능을 지니고 있었다....역경을 견디는 능력. capability는 어떤 사람이 할 수 있는 일의 양이나 그가 어떤 일을 어느 정도 잘 할 수 있는가를 나타낼 때 쓴다. ❑ ...한 사람의 역량을 넘어서는 일...그 배우의 능력에 대한 감독의 생각. 누군가가 특정한 capacity나 무엇에 대한 capacity, 무엇을 할 capacity가 있다고 하면, 그 사람이 그것을 하는 데 필요한 자질을 가지고 있다는 뜻이다. capacity가 ability보다 더 격식적이다. ❑ ...힘든 일을 할 수 있는 그들의 능력....상대방의 관점을 이해할 수 있는 그의 능력.

Thesaurus	ability의 참조어
N.	capability, competence ■
	knack, skill, talent, technique ■

Word Partnership	ability의 연어
N.	**lack of** ability ■ ■
V.	ability **to handle**, **have the** ability, **lack the** ability ■ ■
ADJ.	**natural** ability ■

ab|ject /ǽbdʒekt/ ADJ You use **abject** to emphasize that a situation or quality is extremely bad. [EMPHASIS] ❑ *Both of them died in abject poverty.*

형용사 비참한 [강조] ❑ 그들 둘 다 비참한 가난 속에서 죽었다.

ablaze /əbléɪz/ ■ ADJ Something that is **ablaze** is burning very fiercely. [v n ADJ, v-link ADJ] ❑ *Shops, houses, and vehicles were set ablaze.* ■ ADJ If a place is **ablaze with** lights or colors, it is very bright because of them. [v-link ADJ, usu ADJ with n] ❑ *The chamber was ablaze with light.*

■ 형용사 불타는 ❑ 가게, 집, 차량이 불타오르고 있었다. ■ 형용사 환히 빛나는 ❑ 그 방은 빛으로 환했다.

able ♦♦♦ /éɪbəl/ (abler) /éɪblər/ (ablest) /éɪblɪst/ ■ PHRASE If you **are able to** do something, you have skills or qualities which make it possible for you to do it. ❑ *The older child should be able to prepare a simple meal.* ❑ *The company say they're able to keep pricing competitive.*

■ 구 ~을 할 수 있다 ❑ 큰애는 간단한 식사 정도는 준비할 수 있을 것이다. ❑ 그 회사는 가격을 경쟁력 있게 유지할 수 있다고 한다.

> **Can, could,** and **be able to** are all used to talk about a person's ability to do something. They are followed by the infinitive form of a verb. You use **can** or a present form of **be able to** to refer to the present, although **can** is more common. ❑ *They can all read and write... The snake is able to catch small mammals.* You use **could** or a past form of **be able to** to refer to the past, and "will" or "shall" with **be able to** to refer to the future. **Be able to** is used if you want to refer to doing something at a particular time. ❑ *After treatment he was able*

> can, could, be able to는 모두 무엇을 할 수 있는 사람의 능력을 말할 때 쓰며, 뒤에는 동사 원형이 온다. 현재에 대해 말할 때는 can이나 be able to의 현재형을 쓰는데 can이 더 일반적이다. ❑ 그들은 모두 글을 읽고 쓸 줄 안다... 뱀은 작은 포유동물을 잡을 수 있다. 과거에 대해 말할 때는 could나 be able to의 과거형을 쓰고, 미래에 대해 말할 때는

to return to work. **Can** and **could** are used to talk about possibility. **Could** refers to a particular occasion and **can** to more general situations. ❑ *Many jobs could be lost... Too much salt can be harmful.* When talking about the past, you use **could have** and a past participle. ❑ *It could have been much worse.* You also use **can** for the present and **could** for the past to talk about rules or what people are allowed to do. ❑ *They can leave at any time.* Note that when making requests either **can** or **could** may be used. ❑ *Can I have a drink?... Could we put the fire on?* However, **could** is always used for suggestions. ❑ *You could phone her and ask.*

'will' 또는 'shall'과 함께 be able to를 쓴다. 특정한 시기에 무엇을 하는 것에 대해 말할 때는 be able to를 쓴다. ❑ 치료 후에 그는 직장으로 복귀할 수 있었다. ❑ can과 could는 모두 가능성을 얘기할 때 쓴다. could는 특정한 경우에 대해 쓰고 can은 좀 더 일반적인 상황에 대해 쓴다. ❑ 많은 일자리가 없어질 수도 있다... 염분 과다 섭취는 해로울 수 있다. 과거에 대해서 말할 때는 could have와 과거분사를 쓴다. ❑ 사정이 훨씬 더 안 좋을 수도 있었다. 규칙이나 허용되는 일에 대해 말할 때에도 현재일 때는 can을, 과거일 때는 could를 쓸 수 있다. ❑ 그들은 아무 때나 떠날 수 있다. 요청을 할 때는 can이나 could 어느 것이나 쓸 수 있음을 유의하라. ❑ 한 잔 할 수 있을까요?[한 잔 주시겠소?]... 우리 난로 피울까요? 그러나 제안에는 항상 could를 쓴다. ❑ 네가 그녀에게 전화를 해서 물어 볼 수도 있겠다.

2 PHRASE If you **are able to** do something, you have enough freedom, power, time, or money to do it. ❑ *You'll be able to read in peace.* ❑ *Have you been able to have any kind of contact?* 3 ADJ Someone who is **able** is very clever or very good at doing something. ❑ *...one of the brightest and ablest members of the government.*

2 구 -을 할 여건이 되다, -을 할 수 있다 ❑ 당신은 편안히 책을 읽을 수 있을 것이다. ❑ 어떤 형태로든 연락이 되었느냐? 3 형용사 유능한 ❑ 가장 똑똑하고 유능한 정부 각료 중 한 사람

> Note that **able** and **capable** are both used to say that someone can do something. When you say that someone is **able** to do something, you mean that they can do it either because of their knowledge or skill, or because it is possible. ❑ *He wondered if he would be able to climb over the rail... They were able to use their profits for new investments.* Note that if you use a past tense, you are saying that someone has actually done something. ❑ *We were able to reduce costs.* When you say that someone is **capable** of doing something, you mean either that they have the knowledge and skill to do it, or that they are likely to do it. ❑ *The workers are perfectly capable of running the organization themselves... She was quite capable of falling asleep.* You can say that someone is **capable** of a particular feeling or action. ❑ *He's capable of loyalty... Bowman could not believe him capable of murder.* You can also use "**capable** of" when talking about what something such as a car or machine can do. ❑ *The car was capable of 110 miles per hour.* If you describe someone as **able** or **capable**, you mean that they do things well. ❑ *He's certainly a capable gardener.*

> able과 capable은 둘 다 누가 무엇을 할 수 있다고 말할 때 쓴다. 누가 무엇을 하는 데 able하다는 것은, 그 사람이 지식이나 기술이 있어서 혹은 그 일이 가능한 일이기 때문에 그것을 할 수 있음을 의미한다. ❑ 그는 자기가 난간 위로 기어 올라갈 수 있을 것인가를 생각해 보았다... 그들은 이익금을 새 투자에 이용할 수 있었다. 과거 시제를 쓰면 누가 실제로 무엇을 했다고 말하는 것임을 유의하라. ❑ 우리는 비용을 줄일 수 있었다. 누가 무엇을 하는 데 capable하다는 것은 그가 그것을 할 지식이나 기술이 있다는 뜻이거나, 그가 그것을 할 가능성이 있어 보임을 나타낸다. ❑ 노동자들이 그 조직체를 스스로 충분히 운영할 수 있다... 그녀는 금방이라도 잠이 들어 버릴 것 같았다. 누가 특별한 감정을 갖거나 행동을 하는 것이 capable하다고 말할 수도 있다. ❑ 그는 충성을 바칠 역량이 있다... 보우먼은 그가 살인을 저지를 수도 있다고 믿어지지가 않았다. 자동차나 기계 같은 것이 할 수 있는 일에 대해 말할 때에도 'capable of'를 쓸 수가 있다. ❑ 그 차는 시속 110마일로 달릴 수 있었다. 누가 able 또는 capable하다고 말하는 것은 그 사람이 일을 잘 한다는 뜻이다. ❑ 그는 확실히 능력이 있는 원예사이다.

able-bodied /eɪbᵊl bɒdid/ ADJ An **able-bodied** person is physically strong and healthy, rather than weak or disabled. ❑ *The gym can be used by both able-bodied and disabled people.* ● N-PLURAL **The able-bodied** are people who are able-bodied. ❑ *No doubt such robots would be very useful in the homes of the able-bodied, too.*

형용사 신체 건강한; 비장애인의 ❑ 그 체육관은 장애인과 비장애인 모두 사용할 수 있다. ● 복수명사 비장애인 ❑ 의심할 여지없이 그런 로봇은 비장애인 가정에서도 아주 유용할 것이다.

ably /eɪbli/ ADV **Ably** means skillfully and successfully. [ADV with v] ❑ *He was ably assisted by a number of members from the Middlesex branches.*

부사 훌륭히 ❑ 그는 미들섹스 지점의 직원 몇 명에게서 훌륭한 도움을 받았다.

ab|nor|mal /æbnɔːrmᵊl/ ADJ Someone or something that is **abnormal** is unusual, especially in a way that is worrying. [FORMAL] ❑ *...abnormal heart rhythms and high anxiety levels.* ● **ab|nor|mal|ly** ADV ❑ *...abnormally high levels of glucose.*

형용사 비정상적인 [격식체] ❑ 비정상적인 심장 박동과 높은 불안감 ● 비정상적으로 부사 ❑ 비정상적으로 높은 포도당 수치

ab|nor|mal|ity /æbnɔːrmæliti/ (abnormalities) N-VAR An **abnormality** in something, especially in a person's body or behavior, is an unusual part or feature of it that may be worrying or dangerous. [FORMAL] ❑ *Further scans are required to confirm the diagnosis of an abnormality.*

가산명사 또는 불가산명사 이상, 비정상적인 것 [격식체] ❑ 이상이 있다는 진단을 확인하기 위해서는 더 자세한 검사가 필요합니다.

aboard /əbɔːrd/ PREP If you are **aboard** a ship or plane, you are on it or in it. ❑ *She invited 750 people aboard the luxury yacht, the "Savarona."* ● ADV **Aboard** is also an adverb. [ADV after v] ❑ *It had taken two hours to load all the people aboard.*

전치사 -을 탄, 선상의 ❑ 그녀는 호화 요트인 사바로나에 750명을 초대했다. ● 부사 승선해서, 탑승해서 ❑ 모든 사람을 태우는 데 두 시간이 걸렸다.

abol|ish /əbɒlɪʃ/ (abolishes, abolishing, abolished) V-T If someone in authority **abolishes** a system or practice, they formally put an end to it. ❑ *The following year Parliament voted to abolish the death penalty for murder.*

타동사 폐지하다 ❑ 그 이듬해에 의회는 살인에 대한 사형 제도를 폐지하기로 결의했다.

Thesaurus	abolish의 참조어
v.	eliminate, end; (ant.) continue

abo|li|tion /æbəlɪʃᵊn/ N-UNCOUNT The **abolition of** something such as a system or practice is its formal ending. ❑ *The abolition of slavery in Brazil and the Caribbean closely followed the pattern of the United States.*

불가산명사 폐지 ❑ 브라질과 카리브 제도에서 노예제 폐지는 미국과 아주 비슷한 과정을 거쳤다.

abomi|nable /əbɒmɪnəbᵊl/ ADJ Something that is **abominable** is very unpleasant or bad. ❑ *The President described the killings as an abominable crime.*

형용사 혐오스러운 ❑ 대통령은 그 살인을 두고 지탄받아 마땅한 범죄라고 했다.

abo|rigi|nal /æbərɪdʒɪnᵊl/ (aboriginals) 1 N-COUNT An **Aboriginal** is an Australian Aborigine. ❑ *He remained fascinated by the Aboriginals' tales.* 2 ADJ **Aboriginal** means belonging or relating to the Australian Aborigines. [ADJ n] ❑ *...Aboriginal art.*

1 가산명사 호주 원주민 ❑ 그는 여전히 호주 원주민들 이야기에 매료되어 있었다. 2 형용사 호주 원주민의 ❑ 호주 원주민의 예술

Abo|rigi|ne /æbərɪdʒɪni/ (Aborigines) N-COUNT **Aborigines** are members of the tribes that were living in Australia when Europeans arrived there. ❑ *Then the Aborigines entertained the crowd with an athletic display.*

가산명사 호주 원주민 ❑ 그 뒤에 호주 원주민들이 운동 경기를 펼쳐 군중을 즐겁게 했다.

abort /əbɔ:t/ (**aborts, aborting, aborted**) ◼ V-T If an unborn baby **is aborted**, the pregnancy is ended deliberately and the baby is not born alive. [FORMAL] ❑ *Ruth Ellis gunned down the lover who walked out on her after she had aborted their child.* ◼ V-T If someone **aborts** a process, plan, or activity, they stop it before it has been completed. ❑ *When the decision was made to abort the mission, there was great confusion.*

◼ 타동사 낙태하다 [격식체] ◻ 루스 엘리스는 아기를 낙태한 후 자기를 떠난 애인을 총으로 쏘아 죽였다. ◼ 타동사 중단하다 ◻ 임무를 중단한다는 결정이 내려지자 큰 혼란이 있었다.

abor|tion ◆◇◇ /əbɔ:rʃn/ (**abortions**) N-VAR If a woman has an **abortion**, she ends her pregnancy deliberately so that the baby is not born alive. ❑ *He and his girlfriend had been going out together for a year when she had an abortion.*

가산명사 또는 불가산명사 낙태 ◻ 그 남자와 그의 여자 친구가 일 년 동안 사귀고 있던 차에 그 여자 친구가 낙태 수술을 받았다.

abor|tive /əbɔ:rtɪv/ ADJ An **abortive** attempt or action is unsuccessful. [FORMAL] ❑ *...an abortive attempt to prevent the current President from taking office.*

형용사 무산된 [격식체] ◻ 현직 대통령이 재선되는 것을 방지하려 했으나 무산된 시도

abound /əbaʊnd/ (**abounds, abounding, abounded**) V-I If things **abound**, or if a place **abounds with** things, there are very large numbers of them. [FORMAL] ❑ *Stories abound about when he was in charge.*

자동사 풍부한 [격식체] ◻ 그가 그 일을 맡고 있었을 당시의 일화들이 넘쳐난다.

about ◆◆◆ /əbaʊt/ ◼ PREP You use **about** to introduce who or what something relates to or concerns. ❑ *She knew a lot about food.* ❑ *He never complains about his wife.* ◼ PREP When you mention the things that an activity or institution is **about**, you are saying what it involves or what its aims are. ❑ *Leadership is about the ability to implement change.* ◼ PREP You use **about** after some adjectives to indicate the person or thing that a feeling or state of mind relates to. ❑ *"I'm sorry about Patrick,"she said.* ◼ PREP If you do something **about** a problem, you take action in order to solve it. ❑ *Rachel was going to do something about Jacob.* ◼ PREP When you say that there is a particular quality **about** someone or something, you mean that they have this quality. ❑ *There was a warmth and passion about him I never knew existed.* ◼ ADV **About** is used in front of a number to show that the number is not exact. [ADV num] ❑ *In my local health center there are about forty parking spaces.* ◼ ADV If someone or something moves **about**, they keep moving in different directions. [ADV after v] ❑ *The house isn't big, what with three children running about.* ● PREP **About** is also a preposition. [v PREP n] ❑ *From 1879 to 1888 he wandered about Germany, Switzerland, and Italy.* ◼ PREP If you put something **about** a person or thing, you put it around them. ❑ *Helen threw her arms about him.* ◼ ADJ If someone or something is **about**, they are present or available. [v-link ADJ] ❑ *There's lots of money about these days for schemes like this.* ◼ ADJ If you are **about to** do something, you are going to do it very soon. If something is **about to** happen, it will happen very soon. [v-link ADJ to-inf] ❑ *I think he's about to leave.* ❑ *Argentina has lifted all restrictions on trade and visas are about to be abolished.* ◼ **how about** →see **how. what about** →see **what. just about** →see **just** ◼ PHRASE If someone is **out and about**, they are going out and doing things, especially after they have been unable to for a while. ❑ *Despite considerable pain she has been getting out and about almost as normal.*

◼ 전치사 -에 대해 ◻ 그녀는 음식에 대해 많은 것을 알고 있었다. ◻ 그는 아내에 대해 절대로 불평을 안 한다. ◼ 전치사 관련된 ◻ 지도력은 변화를 추진할 수 있는 능력과 관련이 있다. ◼ 전치사 -에 대해 ◻ "패트릭에 대해선 유감이야."라고 그녀가 말했다. ◼ 전치사 -에 대해 ◻ 레이첼은 제이콥에 대해서 모종의 조치를 취하려던 참이었다. ◼ 전치사 -에게, 어떤 특징이 있는 ◻ 그에게 전에는 몰랐던 따뜻함과 열정이 있었다. ◼ 부사 대략 ◻ 우리 동네의 헬스센터에는 약 40대분의 주차 공간이 있다. ◼ 부사 이리저리 ◻ 이리저리 뛰어다니는 세 명의 아이가 있다는 것을 감안하면 집이 큰 편이 아니다. ● 전치사 여기저기 ◻ 1879년부터 1888년까지 그는 독일, 스위스, 이태리 등지를 돌아다녔다. ◼ 전치사 둘레에 ◻ 헬렌이 그를 두 팔로 감싸 안았다. ◼ 형용사 이용 가능한 ◻ 요즘은 이런 계획에 이용할 수 있는 돈이 많이 있다. ◼ 형용사 -을 막 하려고 하는, -이 곧 발생하려는 ◻ 내 생각에는 그가 곧 떠나려는 것 같다. ◻ 아르헨티나는 모든 무역 관련 제재를 이미 풀었고 비자도 곧 없앨 것이다. ◼ 구 나돌아다니는 ◻ 상당한 통증에도 불구하고 그녀는 거의 정상적인 것처럼 나돌아다니고 있다.

above ◆◆◇ /əbʌv/ ◼ PREP If one thing is **above** another one, it is directly over it or higher than it. ❑ *He lifted his hands above his head.* ❑ *Apartment 46 was a quiet apartment, unlike the one above it.* ● ADV **Above** is also an adverb. ❑ *A long scream sounded from somewhere above.* ❑ *...a picture of the new plane as seen from above.* ◼ ADV In writing, you use **above** to refer to something that has already been mentioned or discussed. ❑ *Several conclusions could be drawn from the results described above.* ● N-SING-COLL **Above** is also a noun. ❑ *For additional information, contact any of the above.* ● ADJ **Above** is also an adjective. [ADJ n] ❑ *For a copy of their brochure, write to the above address.* ◼ PREP If an amount or measurement is **above** a particular level, it is greater than that level. ❑ *The temperature crept up to just above 40 degrees.* ❑ *Government spending is planned to rise 3 percent above inflation.* ● ADV **Above** is also an adverb. [amount and ADV] ❑ *Banks have been charging 25 percent and above for unsecured loans.* ◼ PREP If you hear one sound **above** another, it is louder or clearer than the second one. ❑ *Then there was a woman's voice, rising shrilly above the barking.* ◼ PREP If someone is **above** you, they are in a higher social position than you or in a position of authority over you. ❑ *I married above myself – rich county people.* ● ADV **Above** is also an adverb. [from ADV] ❑ *The policemen admitted beating the student, but said they were acting on orders from above.* ◼ PREP If you say that someone thinks they are **above** something, you mean that they act as if they are too good or important for it. [DISAPPROVAL] ❑ *This was clearly a failure by someone who thought he was above failure.* ◼ PREP If someone is **above** criticism or suspicion, they cannot be criticized or suspected because of their good qualities or their position. [v-link PREP n] ❑ *He was a respected academic and above suspicion.* ◼ PREP If you value one person or thing **above** any other, you value them more or consider that they are more important. ❑ *...his tendency to put the team above everything.* ◼ **over and above** →see **over. above the law** →see **law. above board** →see **board**

◼ 전치사 - 위에 ◻ 그는 손을 머리 위로 들었다. ◻ 46호 아파트는 그 위층의 아파트와는 달리 조용했다. ● 부사 위에서 ◻ 위쪽 어디에선가 긴 비명이 들렸다. ◻ 신형 항공기를 위에서 바라본 사진 ◼ 부사 위에서, 앞에서 ◻ 위에서 기술한 결과로부터 몇 가지 결론을 도출해 낼 수 있다. ● 단수명사-집합명사 위에 적힌 것, 상기의 것 ◻ 추가 정보가 필요하시면 위에 적힌 곳 어디로든지 연락하시기 바랍니다. ● 형용사 위의 ◻ 안내 책자가 필요하신 분은 위의 주소로 요청하시기 바랍니다. ◼ 전치사 -보다 높은 ◻ 기온이 40도보다 약간 높게까지 올라갔다. ◻ 정부 지출은 물가 상승률보다 3 퍼센트 높게 계획이다. ● 부사 -이상 ◻ 은행들은 무담보 대출에 대해 25 퍼센트 이상의 이율을 부과해 왔다. ◼ 전치사 -보다 큰 ◻ 그리고 개 짖는 소리보다 크게 여자의 날카로운 목소리가 들려왔다. ◼ 전치사 신분상으로 높은 ◻ 나는 나보다 사회 계층이 높은 지역 유지 집안과 결혼했다. ● 부사 위로부터 ◻ 경찰관들은 그 학생을 구타한 것을 시인했으나 상부의 지시에 따라 행동한 것이라고 진술했다. ◼ 전치사 -을 하기에는 너무 잘난 [탐탁잖음] ◻ 이것은 분명히 스스로 자기 실수를 저지를 사람이 아니라고 생각하는 사람이 저지른 실수이다. ◼ 전치사 -의 대상이 될 수 없는 ◻ 그는 존경받는 학자였고 의심을 살 수 있는 대상이 아니었다. ◼ 전치사 -보다 높이 ◻ 다른 어떤 것보다 팀을 중시하는 그의 성향

Above and **over** are both used to talk about position and height. If something is higher than something else and the two things are imagined as being positioned along a vertical line, you can use either **above** or **over**. ❑ *He opened a cupboard above the sink... She leaned forward until her face was over the basin.* However, if something is higher than something else but the two things are regarded as being wide or horizontal rather than tall or vertical, you have to use **above**. ❑ *The trees rose above the row of houses.* **Above** and **over** are both used to talk about measurements, for example, when you are talking about a point that is higher than another point on a scale. ❑ *Any money earned over that level is taxed....everybody above five feet eight inches in height.* You use **over** to say that a distance or period of time is longer than the one mentioned. ❑ *...a height of over twelve thousand feet... Our relationship lasted for over a year.*

above와 over는 둘 다 위치와 높이를 말할 때 쓴다. 어떤 것이 다른 것보다 높이 있고, 그 두 사물이 수직선상에 위치한 것으로 추정할 때에는 above나 over 어느 것이든 쓸 수 있다. ◻ 그는 싱크대 위의 찬장을 열었다... 그녀는 얼굴이 세면기 위까지 가도록 상체를 굽혔다. 그러나 어떤 것이 다른 것보다 높이 있기는 하지만, 그 두 사물을 그 높이나 수직선상의 관점에서가 아니라 그 너비나 수평선상의 관점에서 생각할 때에는 above를 써야 한다. ◻ 늘어선 집들 위로 나무들이 솟아올라 있었다. above와 over는 둘 다 측정 단위로, 예를 들어 눈금같은 것 위의 한 점보다 높은 것을 얘기할 때와 같은 경우에 쓰인다. ◻ 그 수준 이상으로 번 돈은 모두 과세된다....키가 5피트 8인치 이상인 모든 사람. 거리 또는 시간이 언급된 거리 또는 시간보다 길다고 말할 때는 over를 쓴다. ◻ ...일반 이천 피트가 넘는 높이... 우리 관계는 1년 이상 지속되었다.

abra|sive /əbreɪsɪv/ ■ ADJ Someone who has an **abrasive** manner is unkind and rude. ❑ *His abrasive manner has won him an unenviable notoriety.* ■ ADJ An **abrasive** substance is rough and can be used to clean hard surfaces. ❑ *...a new all-purpose, non-abrasive cleaner that cleans and polishes all metals.*

■ 형용사 거칠다 ❑ 그는 거친 태도 때문에 결코 바라지 않는 악명을 얻었다. ■ 형용사 마모성의 ❑ 모든 금속을 닦고 광을 내는 네 쓸 수 있는 새로운 다용도, 비마모성 세척제

abreast /əbrest/ ■ ADV If people or things walk or move **abreast**, they are next to each other, side by side, and facing in the same direction. ❑ *The steep sidewalk was too narrow for them to walk abreast.* ■ PHRASE If you **keep abreast of** a subject, you know all the most recent facts about it. ❑ *He will be keeping abreast of the news.*

■ 부사 (옆으로) 나란히 ❑ 가파른 인도가 너무 비좁아서 그들이 나란히 걸을 수가 없었다. ■ 구 시대의 흐름을 따라가다 ❑ 그는 새 소식에 계속 주목할 것이다.

abroad ♦◇◇ /əbrɔd/ ADV If you go **abroad**, you go to a foreign country, usually one which is separated from the country where you live by an ocean or a sea. ❑ *I would love to go abroad this year, perhaps to the South of France.* ❑ *He will stand in for Mr. Goh when he is abroad.*

부사 해외로 ❑ 나는 올해 해외로, 아마도 프랑스 남부로 갔으면 좋겠다. ❑ 고 씨가 해외에 있는 동안 그가 대신 자리를 채워줄 것이다.

ab|rupt /əbrʌpt/ ■ ADJ An **abrupt** change or action is very sudden, often in a way which is unpleasant. ❑ *Rosie's idyllic world came to an abrupt end when her parents' marriage broke up.* ● ab|rupt|ly ADV [ADV with v] ❑ *He stopped abruptly and looked my way.* ■ ADJ Someone who is **abrupt** speaks in a rather rude, unfriendly way. ❑ *He was abrupt to the point of rudeness.* ● ab|rupt|ly ADV ❑ *"Good night, then," she said abruptly.*

■ 형용사 갑작스러운 ❑ 로지의 평온한 세계는 부모님의 이혼과 함께 갑작스럽게 끝났다. ● 갑자기 부사 ❑ 그가 갑자기 멈춰 서시는 내가 있는 쪽을 쳐다봤다. ■ 형용사 퉁명스러운 ❑ 그는 무례할 정도로 퉁명스러웠다. ● 퉁명스레 부사 ❑ "그럼 잘 자."라고 그녀는 퉁명스레 말했다.

ab|sence ♦◇◇ /æbsəns/ (absences) ■ N-VAR Someone's **absence** from a place is the fact that they are not there. ❑ *a bundle of letters which had arrived for me in my absence.* ■ N-SING The **absence** of something from a place is the fact that it is not there or does not exist. ❑ *The presence or absence of clouds can have an important impact on heat transfer.*

■ 가산명사 또는 불가산명사 부재 ❑ 내가 없는 동안 내게 온 편지 한 뭉치 ■ 단수명사 부재 ❑ 구름의 존재 유무가 열전도에 큰 영향을 끼친다.

ab|sent /æbsᵊnt/ ■ ADJ If someone or something is **absent from** a place or situation where they should be or where they usually are, they are not there. ❑ *He has been absent from his desk for two weeks.* ❑ *The pictures, too, were absent from the walls.* ■ ADJ If someone appears **absent**, they are not paying attention because they are thinking about something else. ❑ *"Nothing," Rosie said in an absent way.* ● ab|sent|ly /æbsᵊntli/ ADV ❑ *He nodded absently.* ■ ADJ An **absent** parent does not live with his or her children. [ADJ n] ❑ *...absent fathers who fail to pay toward the costs of looking after their children.* ■ PREP If you say that **absent** one thing, another thing will happen, you mean that if the first thing does not happen, the second thing will happen. [AM, FORMAL] ❑ *Absent a solution, people like Sue Godfrey will just keep on fighting.*

■ 형용사 결석한, 자리를 비운 ❑ 그가 자리를 비운 지 2주일이 되었다. ❑ 그림들 또한 벽에서 사라진 상태였다. ■ 형용사 멍한 ❑ "아무것도 아냐."라고 로지는 멍한 투로 말했다. ● 멍하니 부사 ❑ 그는 멍하니 고개를 끄덕였다. ■ 형용사 부재의 ❑ 자녀들 양육비를 부담하지 않는 결혼 가정의 아버지들 ■ 전치사 …이 마땅하지 않는다면 [미국영어, 격식체] ❑ 해결책이 제시되지 않으면 수 고드프리 같은 사람은 계속 투쟁할 것이다.

ab|sen|tee /æbsᵊnti/ (absentees) ■ N-COUNT An **absentee** is a person who is expected to be in a particular place but who is not there. ❑ *At least two of the three other absentees also had justifiable reasons for being away.* ■ ADJ **Absentee** is used to describe someone who is not there to do a particular job in person. [ADJ n] ❑ *Absentee fathers will be forced to pay child support.* ■ ADJ In elections in the United States, if you vote by **absentee** ballot or if you are an **absentee** voter, you vote in advance because you will be unable to go to the polling place. [AM] [ADJ n] ❑ *He has already voted by absentee ballot.*
→see **election**

■ 가산명사 불참자 ❑ 적어도 세 명 중에 두 명의 불참자는 불참할 합당한 사유가 있었다. ■ 형용사 부재의 ❑ 가족과 함께 살지 않는 아버지는 자녀의 양육비를 부담해야만 할 것이다. ■ 형용사 부재자 [미국영어] ❑ 그는 이미 부재자 투표를 했다.

absent-minded ADJ Someone who is **absent-minded** forgets things or does not pay attention to what they are doing, often because they are thinking about something else. ❑ *In his later life he became even more absent-minded.* ● absent-mindedly ADV [ADV with v] ❑ *Elizabeth absent-mindedly picked a thread from his lapel.*

형용사 정신이 다른 곳에 팔린 ❑ 그는 인생의 말년에 더욱 정신이 다른 곳에 팔린 듯이 행동했다. ● 무심코, 멍하니 부사 ❑ 엘리자베스가 그의 옷깃에서 무심코 실을 떼어냈다.

ab|so|lute ♦◇◇ /æbsəlut/ (absolutes) ■ ADJ **Absolute** means total and complete. ❑ *It's not really suited to absolute beginners.* ■ ADJ You use **absolute** to emphasize something that you are saying. [EMPHASIS] [ADJ n] ❑ *About 12 inches wide is the absolute minimum you should consider.* ■ ADJ An **absolute** ruler has complete power and authority over his or her country. [ADJ n] ❑ *He ruled with absolute power.* ■ ADJ **Absolute** is used to say that something is definite and will not change even if circumstances change. ❑ *John brought the absolute proof that we needed.* ■ ADJ An amount that is expressed in **absolute** terms is expressed as a fixed amount rather than referring to variable factors such as what you earn or the effects of inflation. [ADJ n] ❑ *In absolute terms British wages remain low by European standards.* ■ ADJ **Absolute** rules and principles are believed to be true, right, or relevant in all situations. ❑ *There are no absolute rules.* ■ N-COUNT An **absolute** is a rule or principle that is believed to be true, right, or relevant in all situations. ❑ *This is one of the few absolutes in U.S. constitutional law.*

■ 형용사 완전한 ❑ 이것은 완전 초보들에게는 사실 적합하지 않습니다. ■ 형용사 무조건, 절대적인 [강조] ❑ 무조건 최소한 12인치 너비 정도는 돼야 한다고 생각하십시오. ■ 형용사 절대적인 ❑ 그는 절대적인 권력을 갖고 지배했다. ■ 형용사 확고한 ❑ 존이 우리가 필요로 하던 확고한 증거를 가져왔다. ■ 형용사 절대적인 ❑ 절대치로 본다면 영국의 임금 수준은 유럽에 비해 낮다. ■ 형용사 절대적인 ❑ 절대적인 규칙이란 없다. ■ 가산명사 절대적인 것 ❑ 이것은 미국 헌법에서 몇 안 되는 절대적인 조항 중 하나이다.

ab|so|lute|ly ♦◇◇ /æbsəlutli/ ■ ADV **Absolutely** means totally and completely. [EMPHASIS] ❑ *Jill is absolutely right.* ❑ *I absolutely refuse to get married.* ■ ADV Some people say **absolutely** as an emphatic way of saying yes or of agreeing with someone. They say **absolutely not** as an emphatic way of saying no or of disagreeing with someone. [EMPHASIS] [ADV as reply] ❑ *"It's worrying that they're doing things without training though, isn't it?" —"Absolutely."*

■ 부사 전적으로, 절대적으로 [강조] ❑ 질이 전적으로 옳다. ❑ 나는 결혼하는 것은 절대 반대이다. ■ 부사 당연하는, 물론 [강조] ❑ "하지만 그들이 훈련도 안 받고 일을 한다는 것이 걱정스러워, 안 그래?" "물론 그렇지."

ab|sorb /əbsɔrb, -zɔrb/ (absorbs, absorbing, absorbed) ■ V-T If something **absorbs** a liquid, gas, or other substance, it soaks it up or takes it in. ❑ *Plants absorb carbon dioxide from the air and moisture from the soil.* ■ V-T If something **absorbs** light, heat, or another form of energy, it takes it in. ❑ *A household radiator absorbs energy in the form of electric current and releases it in the form of heat.* ■ V-T If a group **is absorbed into** a larger group, it becomes part of the larger group. ❑ *The Colonial Office was absorbed into the Foreign Office.* ■ V-T If something **absorbs** a force or shock, it reduces its effect. ❑ *...footwear which does not absorb the impact of the foot striking the ground.* ■ V-T If a system or society **absorbs** changes, effects, or costs, it is able to deal with them. ❑ *The banks would be forced to absorb large losses.* ■ V-T If something **absorbs** something valuable

■ 타동사 흡수하다 ❑ 식물은 공기에서 이산화탄소를 흡수하고 흙에서 수분을 흡수한다. ■ 타동사 흡수하다 ❑ 가정용 라디에이터는 전류의 형태로 된 에너지를 흡수한 후 그것을 열의 형태로 방출한다. ■ 타동사 흡수하는, 통합하다 ❑ 식민통치국은 외무국으로 통합되었다. ■ 타동사 흡수하다 ❑ 발이 지면에 부딪힐 때 받는 충격을 흡수하지 못하는 신발 ■ 타동사 끌어안다 ❑ 은행들은 큰 손실을 끌어안도록 강요당할 것이다. ■ 타동사 (돈, 시간, 공간 등을) 잡아먹다 ❑ 그것이 투자에 사용할 수도 있었을 엄청난 액수의 자본을 잡아먹었다. ■ 타동사 흡수하다, 소화하다

A

such as money, space, or time, it uses up a great deal of it. ❑ *It absorbed vast amounts of capital that could have been used for investment.* **7** V-T If you **absorb** information, you learn and understand it. ❑ *Too often he only absorbs half the information in the manual.* **8** V-T If something **absorbs** you, it interests you a great deal and takes up all your attention and energy. ❑ *...a second career which absorbed her more completely than her acting ever had.* →see also **absorbed, absorbing**

❑ 대개 그는 지침서에 들어 있는 정보의 반밖에 소화를 못 한다. **8** 타동사 (마음을) 사로잡다 ❑ 그녀가 이전에 했던 연기보다 훨씬 더 강하게 그녀를 사로잡았던 두 번째 직업

B

C

ab|sorbed /əbsɔ̱rbd, -zɔ̱rbd/ ADJ If you are **absorbed in** something or someone, you are very interested in them and they take up all your attention and energy. [v-link ADJ, usu ADJ in/by n] ❑ *They were completely absorbed in each other.*

형용사 (마음이) 사로잡힌 ❑ 그들은 서로에게 완전히 마음이 사로잡혀 있었다.

D

ab|sor|bent /əbsɔ̱rbənt, -zɔ̱rbənt/ ADJ **Absorbent** material soaks up liquid easily. ❑ *The towels are highly absorbent.*

형용사 흡수성의 ❑ 이 수건들은 흡수성이 매우 강하다.

E

ab|sorb|ing /əbsɔ̱rbɪŋ, -zɔ̱rbɪŋ/ ADJ An **absorbing** task or activity interests you a great deal and takes up all your attention and energy. ❑ *"Two Sisters" is an absorbing book.*

형용사 (마음을) 사로잡는 ❑ '두 자매'는 흥미진진한 읽을거리이다.

F

ab|sorp|tion /əbsɔ̱rpʃ^ən, -zɔ̱rpʃ^ən/ **1** N-UNCOUNT The **absorption of** a liquid, gas, or other substance is the process of it being soaked up or taken in. ❑ *This controls the absorption of liquids.* **2** N-UNCOUNT The **absorption of** a group **into** a larger group is the process of it becoming part of the larger group. ❑ *...Serbia's absorption into the Ottoman Empire.*

1 불가산명사 흡수 ❑ 이것이 액체 흡수를 조절한다. **2** 불가산명사 합병 ❑ 오토만 제국의 세르비아 합병

G

ab|stain /æbste̱ɪn/ (**abstains, abstaining, abstained**) **1** V-I If you **abstain from** something, usually something you want to do, you deliberately do not do it. [FORMAL] ❑ *Abstain from sex or use condoms.* **2** V-I If you **abstain** during a vote, you do not use your vote. ❑ *Three Conservative MPs abstained in the vote.*

1 자동사 자제하다 [격식체] ❑ 성관계를 자제하든지 콘돔을 사용해라. **2** 자동사 기권하다 ❑ 그 표결에서 보수당 의원 세 명이 기권했다.

H

ab|sten|tion /æbste̱nʃ^ən/ (**abstentions**) N-VAR **Abstention** is a formal act of not voting either for or against a proposal. ❑ *...a vote of sixteen in favor, three against, and one abstention.*

가산명사 또는 불가산명사 기권 ❑ 찬성 열여섯 표, 반대 세 표, 기권 한 표

I

ab|sti|nence /æ̱bstɪnəns/ N-UNCOUNT **Abstinence** is the practice of abstaining from something such as alcoholic drink or sex, often for health or religious reasons. ❑ *...six months of abstinence.*

불가산명사 금욕 ❑ 육개월간의 금욕

J

K

ab|stract /æ̱bstrækt/ (**abstracts**) **1** ADJ An **abstract** idea or way of thinking is based on general ideas rather than on real things and events. ❑ *...starting with a few abstract principles.* ❑ *It's not a question of some abstract concept of justice.* **2** PHRASE When you talk or think about something **in the abstract**, you talk or think about it in a general way, rather than considering particular things or events. ❑ *Money was a commodity she never thought about except in the abstract.* **3** ADJ In grammar, an **abstract** noun refers to a quality or idea rather than to a physical object. [ADJ n] ❑ *...abstract words such as glory, honor, and courage.* **4** ADJ **Abstract** art makes use of shapes and patterns rather than showing people or things. ❑ *A modern abstract painting takes over one complete wall.* **5** N-COUNT An **abstract** is an abstract work of art. ❑ *His abstracts are held in numerous collections.* **6** N-COUNT An **abstract** of an article, document, or speech is a short piece of writing that gives the main points of it. ❑ *It might also be necessary to supply an abstract of the review of the literature as well.*

1 형용사 추상적인 ❑ 몇 가지의 추상적인 원칙에서 출발해서 ❑ 그것은 정의의 어떤 추상적 개념에 관한 문제가 아니다. **2** 구 추상적으로 ❑ 돈은 그녀가 추상적으로만 생각했던 생필품이었다. **3** 형용사 추상의 ❑ 영광, 명예, 용기와 같은 추상적인 단어들 **4** 형용사 추상의 ❑ 어떤 현대 추상화는 한 면이 벽면 하나를 완전히 덮는다. **5** 가산명사 추상화 ❑ 그의 추상화들은 여러 곳에 소장되어 있다. **6** 가산명사 개요 ❑ 문헌 연구에 대한 개요를 제공하는 것도 필요할 수 있다.

L

M

N

ab|strac|tion /æbstræ̱kʃ^ən/ (**abstractions**) N-VAR An **abstraction** is a general idea rather than one relating to a particular object, person, or situation. [FORMAL] ❑ *Is it worth fighting a big war, in the name of an abstraction like sovereignty?*

가산명사 또는 불가산명사 추상적 개념 [격식체] ❑ 주권과 같은 추상적인 개념을 명분으로 큰 전쟁을 할 가치가 있을까?

O

P

ab|surd /æbsɜ̱rd, -zɜ̱rd/ ADJ If you say that something is **absurd**, you are criticizing it because you think that it is ridiculous or that it does not make sense. [DISAPPROVAL] ❑ *That's absurd.* ❑ *It is absurd to be discussing compulsory redundancy policies for teachers.* ● N-SING The **absurd** is something that is absurd. [FORMAL] [the N] ❑ *Parkinson had a sharp eye for the absurd.* ● **ab|surd|ly** ADV ❑ *Prices were still absurdly low, in his opinion.* ● **ab|surd|ity** /æbsɜ̱rdɪti, -zɜ̱rd-/ (**absurdities**) N-VAR ❑ *I find myself growing increasingly angry at the absurdity of the situation.*

형용사 터무니없는 [탐탁잖음] ❑ 그것은 말도 안 된다. ❑ 교사에 대한 강제 해고 정책을 논의하는 것은 터무니없다. ● 단수명사 부조리한 것 [격식체] ❑ 파킨슨은 부조리한 것을 알아보는 예리한 안목이 있었다. ● 터무니없이 부사 ❑ 그의 생각에는 가격이 아직도 터무니없이 낮았다. ● 부조리 가산명사 또는 불가산명사 ❑ 상황의 부조리함을 생각하면 나는 화가 점점 더 치밀어 오른다.

Q

R

S

Thesaurus	*absurd*의 참조어
ADJ.	crazy, foolish

T

abun|dance /əbʌ̱ndəns/ N-SING-COLL An **abundance of** something is a large quantity of it. [usu N of n, also in N] ❑ *This area of France has an abundance of safe beaches and a pleasing climate.*

단수명사-집합 풍부함 ❑ 프랑스의 이 지역은 안전한 해변이 많고 기후도 쾌적하다.

U

abun|dant /əbʌ̱ndənt/ ADJ Something that is **abundant** is present in large quantities. ❑ *There is an abundant supply of cheap labor.*

형용사 풍부한 ❑ 저렴한 노동력의 공급이 풍부하다.

V

abuse ♦♦◇ (**abuses, abusing, abused**)

The noun is pronounced /əbyu̱s/. The verb is pronounced /əbyu̱z/.

명사는 /əbyu̱s /로 발음되고, 동사는 /əbyu̱z /로 발음된다.

W

1 N-UNCOUNT **Abuse of** someone is cruel and violent treatment of them. [also N in pl, usu with supp] ❑ *...investigation of alleged child abuse.* ❑ *...victims of sexual and physical abuse.* **2** N-UNCOUNT **Abuse** is extremely rude and insulting things that people say when they are angry. ❑ *I was left shouting abuse as the car sped off.* **3** N-VAR **Abuse of** something is the use of it in a wrong way or for a bad purpose. [with supp] ❑ *What went on here was an abuse of power.* **4** V-T If someone **is abused**, they are treated cruelly and violently. ❑ *Janet had been abused by her father since she was eleven.* ❑ *...parents who feel they cannot cope or might abuse their children.* **5** V-T You can say that someone **is abused** if extremely rude and insulting things are said to them. ❑ *He alleged that he was verbally abused by other soldiers.* **6** V-T If you **abuse** something, you use it in a wrong

1 불가산명사 학대 ❑ 아동 학대 혐의에 대한 조사 ❑ 성적, 신체적 학대의 피해자들 **2** 불가산명사 욕설 ❑ 폭언/욕설을 해대는 나를 내버려두고 그 차는 재빨리 달아났다. **3** 가산명사 또는 불가산명사 남용, 오용 ❑ 이곳에서 벌어진 것은 다름 아닌 권력의 남용이었다. **4** 타동사 학대하다 ❑ 재닛은 열한 살 때부터 아버지로부터 학대를 받아 왔다. ❑ 더 이상 대처할 수 없다고 생각하거나, 자식들을 학대할지도 모르는 부모들 **5** 타동사 학대하다, 욕하다 ❑ 그는 다른 병사들로부터 언어적 학대를 받았다고 주장했다. **6** 타동사 남용하다, 오용하다 ❑ 그는 돈과 권력을

X

Y

Z

way or for a bad purpose. ❏ *He showed how the rich and powerful can abuse their position.*

가진 사람들이 어떻게 그들의 지위를 남용할 수 있는지를 보여주었다.

Thesaurus *abuse*의 참조어

N.	damage, harm, injury **1**
	curse, insult; *(ant.)* compliment, flattery **2**
V.	damage, harm, injure; *(ant.)* protect, respect **4**
	insult, offend; *(ant.)* compliment, flatter, praise **5**

---

abu|sive /əbyu̱sɪv/ **1** ADJ Someone who is **abusive** behaves in a cruel and violent way toward other people. ❏ *He became violent and abusive toward Ben's mother.* **2** ADJ **Abusive** language is extremely rude and insulting. ❏ *I did not use any foul or abusive language.*

1 형용사 학대하는 ❏ 그는 벤의 어머니에 대해 폭력적이고 학대하는 태도를 취하게 되었다. **2** 형용사 욕설의 ❏ 나는 어떤 나쁜 말이나 욕설도 하지 않았다.

abys|mal /əbɪ̱zmªl/ ADJ If you describe a situation or the condition of something as **abysmal**, you think that it is very bad or poor in quality. ❏ *The general standard of racing was abysmal.* ● **abys|mal|ly** ADV ❏ *The group for the most part found the standard of education abysmally low.*

형용사 형편없는 ❏ 경주의 전반적인 수준이 형편없었다. ● 형편없게 부사 ❏ 그 단체는 교육 수준이 대체로 형편없이 낮다는 것을 발견했다.

abyss /əbɪ̱s/ (**abysses**) **1** N-COUNT An **abyss** is a very deep hole in the ground. [LITERARY] ❏ *The torrent, swollen by the melting snow, plunges into a tremendous abyss.* **2** N-COUNT If someone is on the edge or brink of an **abyss**, they are about to enter into a very frightening or threatening situation. [LITERARY] ❏ *...Downing Street's warning that the Middle East was on the brink of an abyss.*

1 가산명사 심연 [문예체] ❏ 녹는 눈으로 불어난 급류는 엄청난 심연 속으로 떨어진다. **2** 가산명사 나락, 심연 [문예체] ❏ 중동이 나락으로 빠질 위기에 처해 있다는 영국 정부의 경고

aca|dem|ic ♦◇◇ /æ̱kəde̱mɪk/ (**academics**) **1** ADJ **Academic** is used to describe things that relate to the work done in schools, colleges, and universities, especially work which involves studying and reasoning rather than practical or technical skills. [ADJ n] ❏ *Their academic standards are high.* ● **aca|dem|ical|ly** /æ̱kəde̱mɪkli/ ADV ❏ *He is academically gifted.* **2** ADJ **Academic** is used to describe things that relate to schools, colleges, and universities. [ADJ n] ❏ *...the start of the last academic year.* **3** ADJ **Academic** is used to describe work, or a school, college, or university, that places emphasis on studying and reasoning rather than on practical or technical skills. ❏ *The author has settled for a more academic approach.* **4** ADJ Someone who is **academic** is good at studying. ❏ *The system is failing most disastrously among less academic children.* **5** N-COUNT An **academic** is a member of a university or college who teaches or does research. ❏ *Welsh academics say they can predict house prices through a computer program.* **6** ADJ You can say that a discussion or situation is **academic** if you think it is not important because it has no real effect or cannot happen. ❏ *Who wants to hear about contracts and deadlines that are purely academic?*

1 형용사 학문적인 ❏ 그들의 학문 수준은 높다. ● 학문적으로 부사 ❏ 그는 학문적인 재능을 타고났다. **2** 형용사 학교의 ❏ 마지막 학년의 시작 **3** 형용사 학문적인 ❏ 저자는 보다 학문적인 접근 방식을 택했다. **4** 형용사 학구적인 ❏ 현 제도는 학구적이지 못한 아이들 사이에서 가장 크게 실패하고 있다. **5** 가산명사 학자 ❏ 웨일즈 학자들은 컴퓨터 프로그램을 통해 주택 가격을 예상할 수 있다고 한다. **6** 형용사 탁상공론의, 비현실적인 ❏ 누가 순전히 탁상공론에 불과한 계약 조건과 최종 기한 따위를 듣고 싶어 하겠는가?

acad|emy /əkæ̱dəmi/ (**academies**) **1** N-COUNT **Academy** is sometimes used in the names of schools and colleges, especially those specializing in particular subjects or skills, or private high schools in the United States. ❏ *If you want to be a musician, you go to the Royal Academy of Music.* **2** N-IN-NAMES **Academy** appears in the names of some societies formed to improve or maintain standards in a particular field. ❏ *...the American Academy of Psychotherapists.*

1 가산명사 학원 ❏ 네가 음악가가 되고 싶다면 왕립 음악원에 가거라. **2** 이름명사 학회 ❏ 미국 심리치료사 학회

ac|cel|er|ate /ækse̱ləreɪt/ (**accelerates, accelerating, accelerated**) **1** V-T/V-I If the process or rate of something **accelerates** or if something **accelerates** it, it gets faster and faster. ❏ *Growth will accelerate to 2.9 percent next year.* **2** V-I When a moving vehicle **accelerates**, it goes faster and faster. ❏ *Suddenly the car accelerated.*

1 타동사/자동사 빨라지다 ❏ 성장이 더욱 빨라져 내년에는 2.9 퍼센트가 될 것이다. **2** 자동사 가속하다 ❏ 차가 갑자기 가속했다.

ac|cel|era|tion /ækse̱ləreɪ̱ʃªn/ **1** N-UNCOUNT The **acceleration of** a process or change is the fact that it is getting faster and faster. ❏ *He has also called for an acceleration of political reforms.* **2** N-UNCOUNT **Acceleration** is the rate at which a car or other vehicle can increase its speed, often seen in terms of the time that it takes to reach a particular speed. ❏ *Acceleration to 60 mph takes a mere 5.7 seconds.* **3** N-UNCOUNT **Acceleration** is the rate at which the speed of an object increases. [TECHNICAL] →see **motion**

1 불가산명사 가속화 ❏ 그는 또한 정치 개혁을 가속화할 것을 요청했다. **2** 불가산명사 가속도 ❏ 시속 60마일로 가속하는 데 단 5.7초밖에 안 걸린다. **3** 불가산명사 가속도 [과학 기술]

ac|cel|era|tor /ækse̱ləreɪtər/ (**accelerators**) N-COUNT The **accelerator** in a car or other vehicle is the pedal which you press with your foot in order to make the vehicle go faster. ❏ *He eased his foot off the accelerator.*

가산명사 액셀러레이터 ❏ 그는 액셀러레이터에서 발을 뗐다.

ac|cent /æ̱ksɛnt/ (**accents**) **1** N-COUNT Someone who speaks with a particular **accent** pronounces the words of a language in a distinctive way that shows which country, region, or social class they come from. ❏ *He had developed a slight American accent.* **2** N-COUNT An **accent** is a short line or other mark which is written above certain letters in some languages and which indicates the way those letters are pronounced. ❏ *...an acute accent.*

1 가산명사 억양, 어투 ❏ 그에게 전에 없던 미국식 억양이 약간 생겨 있었다. **2** 가산명사 액센트 부호 ❏ 양부호

Word Partnership *accent*의 연어

| ADJ. | **American** accent, **regional** accent, **thick** accent **1** |
| V. | **have an** accent **1** |

---

ac|cen|tu|ate /ækse̱ntʃueɪt/ (**accentuates, accentuating, accentuated**) V-T To **accentuate** something means to emphasize it or make it more noticeable. ❏ *His shaven head accentuates his large round face.*

타동사 강조하다 ❏ 머리를 삭발해서 그의 크고 둥근 얼굴이 더 두드러진다.

ac|cept ♦♦♦ /æksɛ̱pt/ (**accepts, accepting, accepted**) **1** V-T/V-I If you **accept** something that you have been offered, you say yes to it or agree to take it. ❏ *Eventually Stella persuaded her to accept an offer of marriage.* ❏ *Your old clothes will be gratefully accepted by jumble sale organizers.* **2** V-T If you **accept** an idea, statement, or fact, you believe that it is true or valid. ❏ *I do not accept that there is any kind of crisis in British science.* ❏ *I don't think they would accept that view.* **3** V-T If you **accept** a plan or an intended action, you agree to it and allow it to happen. ❏ *...Britain's reluctance to accept a proposal for a single European currency.* **4** V-T If you **accept** an unpleasant fact or situation, you get used to it or recognize that it is necessary or cannot be changed. ❏ *People will accept suffering that can be shown to*

1 타동사/자동사 수락하다, 받아들이다 ❏ 마침내 스텔라는 그녀로 하여금 결혼 제안을 수락하도록 설득했다. ❏ 네 낡은 옷을 자선 바자 주최자들은 고맙게 받을 것이다. **2** 타동사 받아들이다, 동의하다 ❏ 나는 영국 과학계에 무슨 위기가 닥쳤다는 말에 동의하지 않는다. ❏ 그들이 그 견해를 받아들이리라고 나는 생각하지 않는다. **3** 타동사 받아들이다 ❏ 유럽 단일 통화안에 대한 영국의 저항 **4** 타동사 받아들이다 ❏ 사람들은 현재의 고통이 보다 큰 이득으로 이어진다는 믿음이 있으면 그 고통을 받아들인다.

a b c d e f g h i j k l m n o p q r s t u v w x y z

lead to a greater good. □ *Urban dwellers often accept noise as part of city life.* ⑤ V-T If a person, company, or organization **accepts** something such as a document, they recognize that it is genuine, correct, or satisfactory and agree to consider it or handle it. □ *We took the unusual step of contacting newspapers to advise them not to accept the advertising.* ⑥ V-T If an organization or person **accepts** you, you are allowed to join the organization or use the services that are offered. □ *All-male groups will not be accepted.* ⑦ V-T If a person or a group of people **accepts** you, they begin to be friendly toward you and are happy with who you are or what you do. □ *As far as my grandparents were concerned, they've never had a problem accepting me.* □ *Many men still have difficulty accepting a woman as a business partner.* ⑧ V-T If you **accept** the responsibility or blame for something, you recognize that you are responsible for it. □ *The company cannot accept responsibility for loss or damage.* ⑨ V-T If you **accept** someone's advice or suggestion, you agree to do what they say. □ *The army refused to accept orders from the political leadership.* ⑩ V-T If a machine **accepts** a particular kind of thing, it is designed to take it and deal with it or process it. □ *Ticket machines at stations accept only coins.* ⑪ →see also **accepted**

□ 도시민들은 흔히 소음을 도시 생활의 일부로 받아들인다. ⑤ 타동사 받아들이다 □ 그 광고를 받아들이지 말 것을 충고하기 위해 신문사들을 접촉하는 이례적인 절차를 밟았다. ⑥ 타동사 받아들이다 □ 모든 남성 단체는 사절입니다. ⑦ 타동사 받아들이다 □ 우리 조부모님의 경우는 나를 받아들이는 데 아무런 문제가 없었다. □ 많은 남성들이 아직도 여성을 사업 동반자로 받아들이는 것을 힘들어한다. ⑧ 타동사 (책임이나 비난을) 받아들이다 □ 회사는 손실이나 파손에 대한 책임을 지지 않습니다. ⑨ 타동사 (충고나 제안을) 따르다 □ 군부는 정치 수뇌부의 지시에 따르기를 거부했다. ⑩ 타동사 받아들이다 □ 역에 있는 발권기에는 동전만 사용할 수 있다.

	Thesaurus	*accept*의 참조어

v.	receive, take; *(ant.)* refuse, reject ⑴
	acknowledge, recognize; *(ant.)* object, oppose, refuse ⑵-⑤ ⑧
	endure, tolerate; *(ant.)* disallow, reject ⑷

---

ac|cept|able ◆◇◇ /æksɛptəbⁱl/ ⑴ ADJ **Acceptable** activities and situations are those that most people approve of or consider to be normal. □ *It is becoming more acceptable for women to drink.* ● **ac|cept|abil|ity** /æksɛptəbɪlɪti/ N-UNCOUNT □ *This assumption played a considerable part in increasing the social acceptability of divorce.* ● **ac|cept|ably** /æksɛptəbli/ ADV □ *The aim of discipline is to teach children to behave acceptably.* ⑵ ADJ If something is **acceptable to** someone, they agree to consider it, use it, or allow it to happen. □ *They have thrashed out a compromise formula acceptable to Moscow.* ⑶ ADJ If you describe something as **acceptable**, you mean that it is good enough or fairly good. □ *On the far side of the street was a restaurant that looked acceptable.* ● **ac|cept|ably** ADV □ *...a method that provides an acceptably accurate solution to a problem.*

⑴ 형용사 용인되는 □ 여성 음주가 점점 더 용인되고 있다. ● 용인성 불가산명사 □ 사회에서 이혼의 용인성을 증가시키는 데에 이러한 가정이 큰 역할을 했다. ● 용인될 수 있게 부사 □ 훈육의 목적은 아이들에게 사회적으로 용인되는 행동을 하도록 가르치는 것이다. ⑵ 형용사 받아들일 수 있는 □ 끈질긴 토론 끝에 그들은 러시아 정부가 받아들일 수 있는 절충안을 만들어 냈다. ⑶ 형용사 쓸 만한, 괜찮은 □ 거리의 저 멀리에 그럭저럭 쓸 만해 보이는 식당이 있었다. ● 적당히 부사 □ 문제에 대해 적당히 정확한 해결책을 제공하는 방식

	Thesaurus	*acceptable*의 참조어

ADJ.	adequate, decent, satisfactory ⑶

---

ac|cept|ance /æksɛptəns/ (**acceptances**) ⑴ N-VAR **Acceptance of** an offer or a proposal is the act of saying yes to it or agreeing to it. □ *The Party is being degraded by its acceptance of secret donations.* □ *...his acceptance speech for the Nobel Peace Prize.* ⑵ N-UNCOUNT If there is **acceptance** of an idea, most people believe or agree that it is true. □ *...a theory that is steadily gaining acceptance.* ⑶ N-UNCOUNT Your **acceptance of** a situation, especially an unpleasant or difficult one, is an attitude or feeling that you cannot change it and that you must get used to it. □ *The most impressive thing about him is his calm acceptance of whatever comes his way.* ⑷ N-UNCOUNT **Acceptance** of someone into a group means beginning to think of them as part of the group and to act in a friendly way toward them. □ *A very determined effort by society will ensure that the disabled achieve real acceptance and integration.*

⑴ 가산명사 또는 불가산명사 수락 □ 그 정당은 비밀 기부금 수락으로 위신에 타격을 입고 있다. □ 그의 노벨 평화상 수락 연설 ⑵ 불가산명사 용인, 받아들임 □ 서서히 받아들여지고 있는 이론 ⑶ 불가산명사 받아들임, 감내 □ 그에게 가장 인상적인 것은 자신에게 닥치는 모든 것을 묵묵히 감내한다는 점이다. ⑷ 불가산명사 포용 □ 사회의 확고한 노력만 있다면 장애인들을 완전히 포용하고 통합할 수 있을 것이다.

ac|cept|ed ◆◇◇ /æksɛptɪd/ ADJ **Accepted** ideas are agreed by most people to be correct or reasonable. □ *There is no generally accepted definition of life.* →see also **accept**

형용사 통용되는 □ 생명에 대해 일반적으로 통용되는 삶의 정의는 없다.

ac|cess ◆◇◇ /æksɛs/ (**accesses, accessing, accessed**) ⑴ N-UNCOUNT If you have **access to** a building or other place, you are able or allowed to go into it. □ *The facilities have been adapted to give access to wheelchair users.* □ *For logistical and political reasons, scientists have only recently been able to gain access to the area.* ⑵ N-UNCOUNT If you have **access to** something such as information or equipment, you have the opportunity or right to see it or use it. □ *...a Code of Practice that would give patients right of access to their medical records.* ⑶ N-UNCOUNT If you have **access to** a person, you have the opportunity or right to see them or meet them. □ *He was not allowed access either to a lawyer, or to officials of the British High Commission.* ⑷ V-T If you **access** something, especially information held on a computer, you succeed in finding or obtaining it. □ *You've illegally accessed and misused confidential security files.*

⑴ 불가산명사 접근 □ 휠체어 이용자도 접근할 수 있도록 시설이 개조되었다. □ 전략상 이유와 정치적인 이유로 과학자들은 최근에 들어서야 그 지역에 접근할 수 있었다. ⑵ 불가산명사 접근권 □ 환자들이 자신의 의료 기록에 접근할 수 있도록 해 주는 행동 지침 ⑶ 불가산명사 접견권 □ 그에게는 변호사나 영국 고등 판무관 접견권이 주어지지 않았다. ⑷ 타동사 접근하다 □ 당신은 보안 기밀문서에 불법으로 접근하여 이를 오용했습니다.

ac|cess course (**access courses**) N-COUNT An **access course** is an educational course which prepares adults with few or no qualifications for study at a university or other place of higher education. [BRIT]

가산명사 학력이 미달되는 성인들이 대학 혹은 고등 교육 기관에서 공부할 수 있도록 준비해 주는 교육 과정 (≒검정고시 준비 과정) [영국영어]

ac|ces|sible /æksɛsɪbⁱl/ ⑴ ADJ If a place or building is **accessible to** people, it is easy for them to reach it or get into it. If an object is **accessible**, it is easy to reach. □ *The Center is easily accessible to the general public.* ● **ac|ces|sibil|ity** /æksɛsɪbɪlɪti/ N-UNCOUNT □ *Unlike the other South Western reservoirs it has uniquely easy accessibility.* ⑵ ADJ If something is **accessible to** people, they can easily use it or obtain it. □ *The aim of any reform of legal aid should be to make the system accessible to more people.* ● **ac|ces|sibil|ity** N-UNCOUNT □ *...growing public concern about the cost, quality, and accessibility of health care.* ⑶ ADJ If you describe a book, painting, or other work of art as **accessible**, you think it is good because it is simple enough for people to understand and appreciate easily. [APPROVAL] □ *Both say they want to write literary books that are accessible to a general audience.* ● **ac|ces|sibil|ity** N-UNCOUNT □ *Seminar topics are chosen for their accessibility to a general audience.*

⑴ 형용사 접근이 용이한 □ 그 센터는 일반인들이 쉽게 갈 수 있다. ● 접근 용이성 불가산명사 □ 남서부의 다른 저수지들과는 달리 그곳은 독특하게 접근이 용이하다. ⑵ 형용사 활용이 용이한 □ 소송 경비 지원 제도 개혁은 어떤 경우든 그 제도를 더 많은 사람들이 이용할 수 있도록 하는 것을 목표로 해야 한다. ● 활용 용이성 불가산명사 □ 의료 서비스의 비용, 질, 그리고 활용 용이성에 대해 점점 커져 가는 대중의 우려 ⑶ 형용사 이해하기 쉬운 □ 그들 둘 다 일반 대중에게 쉽게 이해할 수 있는 문학적인 책을 쓰고 싶다고 말한다. ● 이해하기 쉬운 불가산명사 □ 세미나 주제는 일반 청중이 이해하기 쉬운 것으로 선정한다.

ac|ces|so|ry /æksɛsəri/ (**accessories**) ⑴ N-COUNT **Accessories** are items of equipment that are not usually essential, but which can be used with or added to something else in order to make it more efficient, useful, or

⑴ 가산명사 액세서리 □ 이곳에서만 살 수 있는 다양한 침실 및 화장실용 수제 액세서리 ⑵ 가산명사 액세서리 □ 그곳은 선글라스, 핸드백, 벨트 등의 액세서리들도

decorative. ❑ ...an exclusive range of hand-made bedroom and bathroom accessories. ❷ N-COUNT **Accessories** are articles such as belts and scarves which you wear or carry but which are not part of your main clothing. ❑ It also has a good range of accessories, including sunglasses, handbags, and belts. ❸ N-COUNT If someone is guilty of being an **accessory to** a crime, they helped the person who committed it, or knew it was being committed but did not tell the police. [LEGAL] ❑ She had been charged with being an accessory to the embezzlement of funds from a co-operative farm.

ac|cess time (access times) N-COUNT **Access time** is the time that is needed to get information that is stored in a computer. [COMPUTING] ❑ This system helps speed up access times.

ac|ci|dent ♦◇◇ /ǽksɪdənt/ (accidents) ❶ N-COUNT An **accident** happens when a vehicle hits a person, an object, or another vehicle, causing injury or damage. ❑ She was involved in a serious car accident last week. ❷ N-COUNT If someone has an **accident**, something unpleasant happens to them that was not intended, sometimes causing injury or death. ❑ 5,000 people die every year because of accidents in the home. ❸ N-VAR If something happens **by accident**, it happens completely by chance. ❑ She discovered the problem by accident during a visit to a nearby school.

패 다양하게 갖추고 있다. ❸ 가산명사 공범 [법률] ❑ 그녀는 협동 농장 기금의 횡령에 공범으로 가담한 혐의로 기소되어 있었다.

가산명사 접근 시간 [컴퓨터] ❑ 이 시스템은 접근 시간을 줄이는 것을 돕는다.

❶ 가산명사 사고 ❑ 그녀는 지난 주에 심한 자동차 사고를 겪었다. ❷ 가산명사 사고 ❑ 가정에서 발생하는 사고 때문에 매년 5천 명이 사망한다. ❸ 가산명사 또는 불가산명사 우연 ❑ 그녀는 인근의 학교를 방문하던 중 우연히 그 문제를 발견했다.

Thesaurus   accident의 참조어

| N. | mishap ❷ |
| | chance ❸ |

Word Partnership   accident의 연어

ADJ.	**bad** accident, **a tragic** accident ❶ ❷
V.	**cause an** accident, **insure against** accident, **killed in the** accident, **report an** accident ❶ ❷
N.	**car** accident ❶
	the cause of an accident ❶ ❷
PREP.	**without** accident ❷
	by accident ❸

ac|ci|den|tal /æksɪdént³l/ ADJ An **accidental** event happens by chance or as the result of an accident, and is not deliberately intended. [FORMAL] [usu ADJ n] ❑ Video evidence was shown to the inquest jury, before it returned a verdict of accidental death. ● **ac|ci|den|tal|ly** /æksɪdéntli/ ADV [ADV with v] ❑ A policeman accidentally killed his two best friends with a single bullet.

형용사 우연적 ❑ 사인 규명단은 영상 증거를 본 후 사고사라는 판정을 내렸다. ● 우연히, 실수로 부사 ❑ 한 경찰관이 실수로 자신의 가장 친한 친구 두 명을 총알 한 방으로 살해했다.

ac|ci|dent and emer|gen|cy (accident and emergencies) N-COUNT The **accident and emergency** is the room or department in a hospital where people who have severe injuries or sudden illness are taken for emergency treatment. The abbreviation **A & E** is also used. [BRIT; AM **emergency room**]

가산명사 응급실 [영국영어; 미국영어 emergency room]

Word Link   claim, clam ≈ shouting : **ac**claim, **clam**or, **ex**claim

ac|claim /əkléɪm/ (acclaims, acclaiming, acclaimed) ❶ V-T If someone or something **is acclaimed**, they are praised enthusiastically. [FORMAL] [usu passive] ❑ The restaurant has been widely acclaimed for its excellent French cuisine. ❑ He was acclaimed as England's greatest modern painter. ● **ac|claimed** ADJ ❑ She has published six highly acclaimed novels. ❷ N-UNCOUNT **Acclaim** is public praise for someone or something. [FORMAL] ❑ Angela Bassett has won critical acclaim for her excellent performance.

❶ 타동사 칭송하다, 갈채를 보내다 [격식체] ❑ 그 식당은 뛰어난 프랑스 요리로 널리 인정받아 왔다. ❑ 그는 가장 위대한 영국의 현대 화가로 칭송을 받았다. ● 갈채를 받은 형용사 ❑ 그녀는 극찬을 받은 여섯 편의 소설을 썼다. ❷ 불가산명사 갈채 [격식체] ❑ 앤젤라 배셋은 뛰어난 연기로 평단의 갈채를 받았다.

ac|cli|ma|tize /əkláɪmətaɪz/ (acclimatizes, acclimatizing, acclimatized) [BRIT also **acclimatise**] V-T/V-I When you **acclimatize** or **are acclimatized to** a new situation, place, or climate, you become used to it. [FORMAL] ❑ The athletes are acclimatizing to the heat by staying in Monte Carlo. ❑ This year he has left for St. Louis early to acclimatize himself.

[영국영어 acclimatise] 타동사/자동사 (기후 등에) 적응하다 [격식체] ❑ 선수들은 몬테카를로에 머물면서 더위에 적응하고 있다. ❑ 올해 그는 기후 적응을 위해 일찍 세인트루이스로 출발했다.

ac|co|lade /ǽkəleɪd/ (accolades) N-COUNT If someone is given an **accolade**, something is done or said about them which shows how much people admire them. [FORMAL] ❑ The Nobel prize has become the ultimate accolade in the sciences.

가산명사 찬사 [격식체] ❑ 노벨상은 과학계에서 최상의 영예가 되었다.

ac|com|mo|date /əkɒ́mədeɪt/ (accommodates, accommodating, accommodated) ❶ V-T If a building or space can **accommodate** someone or something, it has enough room for them. [no cont] ❑ The school in Poldown was not big enough to accommodate all the children. ❷ V-T To **accommodate** someone means to provide them with a place to live or stay. ❑ ...a hotel built to accommodate guests for the wedding of King Alfonso. ❸ V-T If something is planned or changed to **accommodate** a particular situation, it is planned or changed so that it takes this situation into account. [FORMAL] ❑ The roads are built to accommodate gradual temperature changes.

❶ 타동사 수용하다 ❑ 폴다운에 있는 학교는 그 아이들을 모두 수용할 수 있을 만큼 크지 못했다. ❷ 타동사 숙박시키다 ❑ 알폰소 왕 결혼식 하객들의 숙박을 위해 지은 호텔 ❸ 타동사 수용하다 [격식체] ❑ 그 도로들은 점진적인 기온 변화를 수용할 수 있도록 건설되었다.

ac|com|mo|dat|ing /əkɒ́mədeɪtɪŋ/ ADJ If you describe someone as **accommodating**, you like the fact that they are willing to do things in order to please you or help you. [APPROVAL] ❑ Eddie was among the most approachable athletes on the team, always very accommodating to me.

형용사 친절한, 싹싹한 [마음에 듦] ❑ 에디는 팀에서 가장 사귀기 쉬운 선수 중 하나였고 항상 내게 아주 싹싹했다.

ac|com|mo|da|tion /əkɒ́mədeɪʃ³n/ (accommodations) ❶ N-COUNT **Accommodations** are buildings or rooms where people live or stay. [AM; BRIT **accommodation**] [also N in pl] ❑ The government will provide temporary accommodations for up to three thousand people sleeping rough in London. ❷ N-UNCOUNT **Accommodation** is space in buildings or vehicles that is available for certain things, people, or activities. [FORMAL] ❑ The school occupies split-site accommodation on the main campus.

❶ 가산명사 숙소 [미국영어; 영국영어 accommodation] ❑ 정부는 최대 3천 명의 런던 노숙자들에게 임시 숙소를 제공할 것이다. ❷ 불가산명사 수용 공간 [격식체] ❑ 그 학교는 본 캠퍼스에 별도의 수용 시설을 두고 있다.

a b c d e f g h i j k l m n o p q r s t u v w x y z

ac|com|pa|ni|ment /əkʌmpənɪmənt/ (**accompaniments**) **1** N-COUNT The **accompaniment** to a song or tune is the music that is played at the same time as it and forms a background to it. ❏ *He sang "My Funny Valentine" and "Wanted" to musical director Jim Steffan's piano accompaniment.* **2** N-COUNT An **accompaniment** is something which goes with another thing. ❏ *This recipe makes a good accompaniment to ice cream.* ● PHRASE If one thing happens **to the accompaniment of** another, they happen at the same time.

1 가산명사 반주 ❏ 그는 음악 감독인 짐 스테판의 피아노 반주에 맞춰 '마이 퍼니 발렌타인'과 '원티드'를 불렀다. **2** 가산명사 곁들인 것 ❏ 이 요리는 아이스크림에 곁들이면 잘 어울린다. ● 구 ~와 동시에

ac|com|pa|ny /əkʌmpəni/ ◇◇ (**accompanies, accompanying, accompanied**) **1** V-T If you **accompany** someone, you go somewhere with them. [FORMAL] ❏ *Ken agreed to accompany me on a trip to Africa.* ❏ *She was accompanied by her younger brother.* **2** V-T If one thing **accompanies** another, it happens or exists at the same time, or as a result of it. [FORMAL] ❏ *This volume of essays was designed to accompany an exhibition in Cologne.* **3** V-T If you **accompany** a singer or a musician, you play one part of a piece of music while they sing or play the main tune. ❏ *On Meredith's new recording, Eddie Higgins accompanies her on all but one song.*

1 타동사 동행하다 [격식체] ❏ 켄은 아프리카 여행에 나와 동행하기로 동의했다. ❏ 그녀는 남동생과 함께 갔다. **2** 타동사 동시에 벌어지다 [격식체] ❏ 이 수필집은 쾰른에서 열린 전시회에 맞춰 발간되었다. **3** 타동사 반주하다 ❏ 메레디스의 새 음반에서는 에디 히긴스가 한 곡을 제외한 모든 곡에 반주를 한다.

ac|com|plice /əkʌmplɪs, BRIT əkʌmplɪs/ (**accomplices**) N-COUNT Someone's **accomplice** is a person who helps them to commit a crime. ❏ *Witnesses said the gunman immediately ran to a motorcycle being ridden by an accomplice.*

가산명사 공범 ❏ 증언에 따르면 총잡이가 공범이 타고 있던 오토바이로 바로 달려갔다고 한다.

ac|com|plish /əkʌmplɪʃ, BRIT əkʌmplɪʃ/ (**accomplishes, accomplishing, accomplished**) V-T If you **accomplish** something, you succeed in doing it. ❏ *If we'd all work together, I think we could accomplish our goal.*

타동사 달성하다 ❏ 만약 우리 모두가 함께 일한다면 내 생각에 우린 목표를 달성할 수 있을 것이다.

Thesaurus   *accomplish*의 참조어

   v.   achieve, complete, gain, realize, succeed

---

ac|com|plished /əkʌmplɪʃt, BRIT əkʌmplɪʃt/ ADJ If someone is **accomplished** at something, they are very good at it. [FORMAL] ❏ *She is an accomplished painter and a prolific author of stories for children.*

형용사 뛰어난 [격식체] ❏ 그녀는 뛰어난 화가이며 많은 동화를 쓴 작가이다.

ac|com|plish|ment /əkʌmplɪʃmənt, BRIT əkʌmplɪʃmənt/ (**accomplishments**) N-COUNT An **accomplishment** is something remarkable that has been done or achieved. ❏ *For a novelist, that's quite an accomplishment.*

가산명사 업적 ❏ 소설가로서 그것은 대단한 업적이다.

ac|cord ◆◆◆ /əkɔrd/ (**accords, according, accorded**) **1** N-COUNT An **accord** between countries or groups of people is a formal agreement, for example to end a war. ❏ *...UNITA, legalized as a political party under the 1991 peace accords.* **2** V-T If you **are accorded** a particular kind of treatment, people act toward you or treat you in that way. [FORMAL] ❏ *His predecessor was accorded an equally tumultuous welcome.* ❏ *On his return home, the government accorded him the rank of Colonel.* **3** →see also **according to 4** PHRASE If something happens **of its own accord**, it seems to happen by itself, without anyone making it happen. ❏ *In many cases the disease will clear up of its own accord.* **5** PHRASE If you do something **of your own accord**, you do it because you want to, without being asked or forced. ❏ *He did not quit as France's prime minister of his own accord.*

1 가산명사 협정; 합의 ❏ 1991년의 평화 협정하에 정당으로 합법화된 유니타 에이(앙골라 완전 독립 민족 동맹) **2** 타동사 주다, 허용하다 [격식체] ❏ 그의 선임자도 똑같이 떠들썩한 환영을 받았다. ❏ 그는 귀환하자마자 정부로부터 대령 계급을 수여받았다. **4** 구 저절로 ❏ 많은 경우 그 병은 저절로 낫는다. **5** 구 자진해서 ❏ 그가 자진해서 프랑스 총리직을 사임한 것은 아니었다.

ac|cord|ance /əkɔrdəns/ PHRASE If something is done **in accordance with** a particular rule or system, it is done in the way that the rule or system says that it should be done. ❏ *Entries which are illegible or otherwise not in accordance with the rules will be disqualified.*

구 ~에 맞춘 ❏ 판독이 어렵거나 여타 방식으로 규정에 맞지 않는 등록은 실격 처리됩니다.

ac|cord|ing|ly /əkɔrdɪŋli/ **1** ADV You use **accordingly** to introduce a fact or situation which is a result or consequence of something that you have just referred to. ❏ *We have a different background, a different history. Accordingly, we have the right to different futures.* **2** ADV If you consider a situation and then act **accordingly**, the way you act depends on the nature of the situation. [ADV after v] ❏ *It is a difficult job and they should be paid accordingly.*

1 부사 따라서, 그러므로 ❏ 우리는 서로 다른 배경과 역사를 가지고 있다. 따라서, 우리의 미래 또한 마땅히 서로 다를 것이다. **2** 부사 ~에 알맞게 ❏ 어려운 일이니만큼 그들은 그에 알맞은 보수를 받아야 한다.

ac|cord|ing to ◆◆◆ **1** PHRASE If someone says that something is true **according to** a particular person, book, or other source of information, they are indicating where they got their information. ❏ *Philip stayed at the hotel, according to Mr. Hemming.* **2** PHRASE If something is done **according to** a particular set of principles, these principles are used as a basis for the way it is done. ❏ *They both played the game according to the rules.* **3** PHRASE If something varies **according to** a changing factor, it varies in a way that is determined by this factor. ❏ *Prices vary according to the quantity ordered.* **4** PHRASE If something happens **according to plan**, it happens in exactly the way that it was intended to happen. ❏ *If all goes according to plan, the first concert will be Tuesday evening.*

1 구 ~에 따르면 ❏ 헤밍 씨의 말에 따르면, 필립은 그 호텔에 머물렀다. **2** 구 ~에 따라 ❏ 양측 모두 규칙에 따라 경기를 치렀다. **3** 구 ~에 따라 ❏ 가격은 주문 수량에 따라 다릅니다. **4** 구 계획대로 ❏ 모든 일이 계획대로 된다면, 첫 콘서트는 화요일 저녁이 될 거예요.

ac|count ◆◆◆ /əkaʊnt/ (**accounts, accounting, accounted**) **1** N-COUNT If you have an **account** with a bank or a similar organization, you have an arrangement to leave your money there and take some out when you need it. ❏ *Some banks make it difficult to open an account.* **2** N-COUNT In business, a regular customer of a company can be referred to as an **account**, especially when the customer is another company. [BUSINESS] ❏ *Biggart Donald, the Glasgow-based marketing agency, has won two Edinburgh accounts.* **3** N-COUNT **Accounts** are detailed records of all the money that a person or business receives and spends. [BUSINESS] ❏ *He kept detailed accounts.* **4** N-COUNT An **account** is a written or spoken report of something that has happened. ❏ *He gave a detailed account of what happened on the fateful night.* **5** →see also **accounting, bank account, current account, deposit account**

1 가산명사 계좌 ❏ 몇몇 은행들은 계좌를 개설하기가 어렵다. **2** 가산명사 고객사, 단골 거래처 [경제] ❏ 글래스고에 기반을 둔 마케팅 대행업자 비가트 도널드가 에든버러 소재 고객사 두 곳을 확보했다. **3** 가산명사 출납 장부 [경제] ❏ 그는 출납 장부를 상세하게 작성했다. **4** 가산명사 이야기; 기술 ❏ 그는 그 운명적인 날 밤에 일어난 일에 대해 자세히 이야기했다.

Do not confuse **account** and **bill**. When you have an **account** with a bank, you leave your money in the bank and take it out when you need it. When you have to pay for things such as electricity or a work done by a repairman, you get a **bill**.

account와 bill을 혼동하지 않도록 하라. 은행에 account를 가지고 있면, 그 은행에 돈을 맡겨 두고 필요할 때 찾게 된다. 전기료 또는 수선공이 한 일에 대해 돈을 지불해야 할 때에는 bill을 받는다.

6 PHRASE If you say that something is true **by all accounts** or **from all accounts**, you believe it is true because other people say so. ❑ *He is, by all accounts, a superb teacher.* **7** PHRASE If you say that someone **gave a good account** of themselves in a particular situation, you mean that they performed well, although they may not have been completely successful. ❑ *We have been hindered by our lack of preparation, but I'm sure we will give a good account of ourselves.* **8** PHRASE If you say that something is **of no account** or **of little account**, you mean that it is very unimportant and is not worth considering. [FORMAL] ❑ *These obscure groups were of little account in either national or international politics.* **9** PHRASE If you buy or pay for something **on account**, you pay nothing or only part of the cost at first, and pay the rest later. ❑ *He was ordered to pay the company £500,000 on account pending a final assessment of his liability.* **10** PHRASE You use **on account of** to introduce the reason or explanation for something. ❑ *The President declined to deliver the speech himself, on account of a sore throat.* **11** PHRASE Your feelings **on** someone's **account** are the feelings you have about what they have experienced or might experience, especially when you imagine yourself to be in their situation. ❑ *Mollie told me what she'd done and I was really scared on her account.* **12** PHRASE If you tell someone not to do something **on your account**, you mean that they should do it only if they want to, and not because they think it will please you. [SPOKEN] ❑ *Don't leave on my account.* **13** PHRASE If you say that something should **on no account** be done, you are emphasizing that it should not be done under any circumstances. [EMPHASIS] ❑ *On no account should the mixture come near boiling.* **14** PHRASE If you do something **on your own account**, you do it because you want to and without being asked, and you take responsibility for your own action. ❑ *I told him if he withdrew it was on his own account.* **15** PHRASE If you **take** something **into account**, or **take account of** something, you consider it when you are thinking about a situation or deciding what to do. ❑ *The defendant asked for 21 similar offenses to be taken into account.* **16** PHRASE If someone **is called, held,** or **brought to account** for something they have done wrong, they are made to explain why they did it, and are often criticized or punished for it. ❑ *Individuals who repeatedly provide false information should be called to account for their actions.* →see **history**

Word Partnership	*account*의 연어

N.   account **balance, bank** account, account **number, savings** account **1**

V.   **access your** account, **open an** account **1**
       give a detailed account **4**
       take *something* **into** account **15**

▶**account for** **1** PHRASAL VERB If a particular thing **accounts for** a part or proportion of something, that part or proportion consists of that thing, or is used or produced by it. ❑ *Computers account for 5% of the country's commercial electricity consumption.* **2** PHRASAL VERB If something **accounts for** a particular fact or situation, it causes or explains it. ❑ *Now, the gene they discovered today doesn't account for all those cases.* **3** PHRASAL VERB If you can **account for** something, you can explain it or give the necessary information about it. ❑ *How do you account for the company's alarmingly high staff turnover?* **4** PHRASAL VERB If someone has to **account for** an action or policy, they are responsible for it, and may be required to explain it to other people or be punished if it fails. ❑ *The President and the President alone must account for his government's reforms.* **5** PHRASAL VERB If a sum of money **is accounted for** in a budget, it has been included in that budget for a particular purpose. ❑ *The really heavy costs have been accounted for.*

ac|count|able /əkˈaʊntəbəl/ ADJ If you are **accountable to** someone **for** something that you do, you are responsible for it and must be prepared to justify your actions to that person. ❑ *Public officials can finally be held accountable for their actions.* ● **ac|count|abil|ity** /əkaʊntəbɪlɪti/ N-UNCOUNT ❑ *...an impetus toward democracy and greater accountability.*

ac|count|an|cy /əkaʊntənsi/ N-UNCOUNT **Accountancy** is the theory or practice of keeping financial accounts. ❑ *He's taking his final exams in accountancy.*

ac|count|ant /əkaʊntənt/ (**accountants**) N-COUNT An **accountant** is a person whose job is to keep financial accounts.

ac|count|ing /əkaʊntɪŋ/ N-UNCOUNT **Accounting** is the activity of keeping detailed records of the amounts of money a business or person receives and spends. ❑ *the accounting firm of Leventhal & Horwath.* →see also **account**

ac|cru|al /əkruəl/ (**accruals**) N-COUNT In finance, the **accrual** of something such as interest or investments is the adding together of interest or different investments over a period of time. [BUSINESS] ❑ *For example, the plan may provide that after an employee has 25 years of service, there is no further accrual of benefits.*

ac|crue /əkru/ (**accrues, accruing, accrued**) V-T/V-I If money or interest **accrues**, or you **accrue** it, it gradually increases in amount over a period of time. [BUSINESS] ❑ *I owed £5,000 – part of this was accrued interest.* ❑ *While they may use a credit card for convenience, affluent people never let interest charges accrue.*

ac|cu|mu|late /əkyumyəleɪt/ (**accumulates, accumulating, accumulated**) V-T/V-I When you **accumulate** things or when they **accumulate**, they collect or are gathered over a period of time. ❑ *Lead can accumulate in the body until toxic levels are reached.*

ac|cu|mu|la|tion /əkyumyəleɪʃən/ (**accumulations**) **1** N-COUNT An **accumulation of** something is a large number of things which have been collected together or acquired over a period of time. ❑ *...an accumulation of experience and knowledge* **2** N-UNCOUNT **Accumulation** is the collecting together of things over a period of time. ❑ *...the accumulation of capital and the distribution of income.*

6 구 누구 말을 들어도 ❑ 누구 말을 들어도 그 분은 훌륭한 선생님입니다. **7** 구 잘 해 내다 ❑ 준비 부족으로 지장을 받아왔지만, 우리가 잘 해 낼 것이라고 저는 확신합니다. **8** 구 하잖은, 중요하지 않은 [격식체] ❑ 이런 모호한 단체들은 국내 정치에서든 국제 정치에서든 별로 중요하지 않았다. **9** 구 할부로; 외상으로 ❑ 그 사람은 채무에 대한 최종 평가가 내려질 때까지 회사 측에 500,000 파운드를 분할 지불하라는 명령을 받았다. **10** 구 -의 이유로 ❑ 대통령은 목이 아프다는 이유로 본인이 직접 연설하는 것을 거절했다. **11** 구 -의 일을 생각하니 ❑ 몰리가 자신이 무슨 일을 저질렀는지 말했을 때 나는 그 이야기를 듣고 정말 섬뜩했다. **12** 구 - 때문에, -를 위하여 [구어체] ❑ 저 때문에 떠나지는 마세요. **13** 구 절대로 (- 하지 않다) [강조] ❑ 절대 그 혼합물을 끓을 정도로 가열하면 안 됩니다. **14** 구 자유의사에 의해; 자기 책임으로 ❑ 나는 그에게 그것을 그만두느냐 마느냐는 그 자신의 의사에 달렸다고 말했다. **15** 구 참작하여; 참작하다 ❑ 피고측은 유사한 21가지 위법 행위들을 참고해 줄 것을 요청했다. **16** 구 -의 책임을 추궁받다; 해명을 요구받다 ❑ 계속해서 그릇된 정보를 유포하는 자들은 그들의 행동에 대한 책임을 추궁해야 한다.

1 구동사 차지하다 ❑ 컴퓨터에 사용되는 전기가 그 나라 영업용 전기 사용량의 5퍼센트를 차지한다. **2** 구동사 원인이 되다; 설명하다 ❑ 한데, 그들이 오늘날 발견한 유전자로 그 모든 사례가 다 설명되는 것은 아닙니다. **3** 구동사 설명하다 ❑ 그 회사의 직원 전직률이 놀라울 정도로 높은 것을 어떻게 설명하시겠어요? **4** 구동사 책임을 지다, 떠맡다 ❑ 대통령이, 오직 대통령만이 정부 개혁에 대한 책임을 져야 한다. **5** 구동사 계상되다, 용도를 설명하다 ❑ 대단히 많은 비용이 계상되어 왔다.

형용사 책임 있는, 해명할 의무가 있는 ❑ 공무원들은 최종적으로 자신의 행동에 대해 책임을 겨야 하게 되는 수가 있다. ● 책임, 책무 불가산명사 ❑ 민주주의와 더 큰 책무를 향한 관성

불가산명사 회계학, 회계 사무 ❑ 그는 회계학 기말고사를 치르고 있다.

가산명사 회계사

불가산명사 회계; 결산 ❑ '레벤탈 앤 호워스' 회계 법인

가산명사 자연증식분 [경제] ❑ 예를 들어, 그 안은 종업원의 근무 연한이 25년을 초과하면 연금이 더 이상 자연 증식되지 않는다고 규정할 수 있다.

타동사/자동사 자연 증가로 생기다 [경제] ❑ 나는 5천 파운드의 빚을 졌다. 그 중 일부는 이자가 붙어난 것이었다. ❑ 부자들은 편의상 신용카드를 사용할 수도 있지만, 절대로 할부 이자가 쌓도록 놓아두지 않는다.

타동사/자동사 모으다, 축적하다; 모이다 ❑ 납이 체내에 축적되어 중독 수준에 도달할 수도 있다.

1 가산명사 축적물 ❑ 축적된 경험과 지식 **2** 불가산명사 축적 ❑ 자본 축적과 소득 분배

A

B

C

D

E

F

G

H

I

J

K

L

M

N

O

P

Q

R

S

T

U

V

W

X

Y

Z

ac|cu|ra|cy /ˈækyərəsi/ **1** N-UNCOUNT The **accuracy** of information or measurements is their quality of being true or correct, even in small details. ❑ Every care has been taken to ensure the accuracy of all information given in this leaflet. **2** N-UNCOUNT If someone or something performs a task, for example hitting a target, with **accuracy**, they do it in an exact way without making a mistake. ❑ ...weapons that could fire with accuracy at targets 3,000 yards away.

1 불가산명사 정확, 정밀 ❑ 이 전단지에 실린 모든 정보의 정확함을 보증하기 위해 세심한 주의를 기울여 왔다. **2** 불가산명사 정확성 ❑ 3천 야드 밖의 표적을 향해 정확하게 발사할 수 있는 무기들

ac|cu|rate ◆◇◇ /ˈækyərɪt/ **1** ADJ **Accurate** information, measurements, and statistics are correct to a very detailed level. An **accurate** instrument is able to give you information of this kind. ❑ Police have stressed that this is the most accurate description of the killer to date. ● ac|cu|rate|ly ADV ❑ The test can accurately predict what a bigger explosion would do. **2** ADJ An **accurate** statement or account gives a true or fair judgment of something. ❑ Stalin gave an accurate assessment of the utility of nuclear weapons. ● ac|cu|rate|ly ADV [ADV with v] ❑ What many people mean by the word "power" could be more accurately described as "control." **3** ADJ You can use **accurate** to describe the results of someone's actions when they do or copy something correctly or exactly. ❑ This summer's exam results are the first to be weighted for accurate spelling and punctuation. **4** ADJ An **accurate** weapon or throw reaches the exact point or target that it is intended to reach. You can also describe a person as **accurate** if they fire a weapon or throw something in this way. ❑ The rifle was extremely accurate. ● ac|cu|rate|ly ADV [ADV with v] ❑ The more accurately you can aim bombs from aircraft, the fewer civilians you will kill.

1 형용사 정밀한 ❑ 경찰은 이것이 지금까지로서는 살인자에 대한 가장 정밀한 인상착의라고 강조해 왔다. ● 정밀하게 부사 ❑ 그 실험은 더 큰 폭발이 일어나면 어떻게 될지를 정밀하게 예측할 수 있다. **2** 형용사 정확한 ❑ 스탈린은 핵무기의 효용에 대해 정확한 평가를 내렸다. ● 정확하게 부사 ❑ 많은 사람들이 '권력'이라는 말을 통해 의미하는 바는 '지배력'이라는 말로 더 정확하게 설명될 수 있을 것이다. **3** 형용사 올바른 ❑ 올 여름의 시험 결과는 처음으로 올바른 철자법과 구두법에 가중치를 두게 된다. **4** 형용사 명중률이 높은 ❑ 그 소총은 대단히 명중률이 높았다. ● 정확하게 부사 ❑ 항공기에서 폭탄 조준을 정확히 할수록, 민간인 사상자가 줄어들 것이다.

Thesaurus   accurate의 참조어

ADJ.   correct, precise, rigorous **1**
        right, true; (ant.) inaccurate **2**

ac|cu|sa|tion /ˌækyʊˈzeɪʃ³n/ (accusations) **1** N-VAR If you make an **accusation** against someone, you criticize them or express the belief that they have done something wrong. ❑ Kim rejects accusations that Country music is over-sentimental. **2** N-COUNT An **accusation** is a statement or claim by a witness or someone in authority that a particular person has committed a crime, although this has not yet been proved. ❑ ...people who have made public accusations of rape.

1 가산명사 또는 불가산명사 비난 ❑ 킴은 컨트리 음악이 지나치게 감상적이라는 비난을 받아들이지 않는다. **2** 가산명사 혐의의 제기; 고발 ❑ 공개적으로 강간 혐의를 제기한 사람들

ac|cuse ◆◇◇ /əˈkyuz/ (accuses, accusing, accused) **1** V-T If you **accuse** someone **of** doing something wrong or dishonest, you say or tell them that you believe that they did it. ❑ My mom was really upset because he was accusing her of having an affair with another man. **2** V-T If you **are accused of** a crime, a witness or someone in authority states or claims that you did it, and you may be formally charged with it and put on trial. ❑ Her assistant was accused of theft and fraud by the police. ❑ He faced a total of seven charges, all accusing him of lying in his testimony. **3** →see also **accused** **4** PHRASE If someone **stands accused of** something, they have been accused of it. ❑ The candidate stands accused of breaking promises even before he's in office.

1 타동사 비난하다, 나무라다 ❑ 다른 남자와 바람을 피웠다고 그가 비난했기 때문에 어머니는 몹시 화가 났다. **2** 타동사 고발하다, 고소하다 ❑ 그녀의 조수는 절도와 사기죄로 경찰에 의해 고발되었다. ❑ 그는 총 일곱 건의 고소를 당했는데, 전부 위증으로 고발된 것이다. **4** 구 고발된 상태이다 ❑ 그 후보자는 취임하기도 전에 공약을 어긴 혐의로 고발된 상태이다.

Thesaurus   accuse의 참조어

V.   blame, charge, implicate; (ant.) vindicate **1 2**

ac|cused /əˈkyuzd/

Accused is both the singular and the plural form.

N-COUNT You can use **the accused** to refer to a person or a group of people charged with a crime or on trial for it. [LEGAL] ❑ The accused is alleged to be a member of a right-wing gang.

accused은 단수형 및 복수형이다.

가산명사 피고인 [법률] ❑ 피고가 우익 폭력단의 일원이라는 주장이 있다.

ac|cus|tom /əˈkʌstəm/ (accustoms, accustoming, accustomed) V-T If you **accustom yourself** or another person **to** something, you make yourself or them become used to it. [FORMAL] ❑ ...while his team accustoms itself to the pace and style of first division rugby. →see also **accustomed**

타동사 익숙하게 하다 [격식체] ❑ 그의 팀이 제 1 지구 럭비 경기의 페이스와 스타일에 익숙해지는 동안

ac|cus|tomed /əˈkʌstəmd/ **1** ADJ If you are **accustomed to** something, you know it so well or have experienced it so often that it seems natural, unsurprising, or easy to deal with. [v-link ADJ to n/-ing] ❑ I was accustomed to being the only child at a table full of adults. **2** ADJ When your eyes become **accustomed to** darkness or bright light, they adjust so that you start to be able to see things, after not being able to see properly at first. [v-link ADJ to n] ❑ My eyes were becoming accustomed to the gloom and I was able to make out a door at one side of the room.

1 형용사 익숙한, 적응된 ❑ 나는 어른들로 가득 찬 식탁에서 나 혼자 어린아이인 데 익숙했다. **2** 형용사 (눈이 어둠이나 빛에) 익숙해진 ❑ 내 눈이 차츰 어둠에 익숙해지자 방 한쪽에 문이 있는 것이 보였다.

Word Partnership   accustomed의 연어

N.   accustomed **to the heat** **1**
      accustomed **to the dark** **2**
V.   **become** accustomed, **get** accustomed, **grow** accustomed **1 2**
ADV. **gradually** accustomed, **long** accustomed **1 2**

ace /eɪs/ (aces) **1** N-COUNT An **ace** is a playing card with a single symbol on it. In most card games, the ace of a particular suit has either the highest or the lowest value of the cards in that suit. ❑ ...the ace of hearts. **2** N-COUNT If you describe someone such as a sports player as an **ace**, you mean that they are very good at what they do. [JOURNALISM] ❑ ...former motor-racing ace Stirling Moss. ● ADJ **Ace** is also an adjective. [ADJ n] ❑ ...ace horror-film producer Lawrence Woolsey. **3** N-COUNT In tennis, an **ace** is a serve which is so fast that the other player cannot reach it. ❑ Henman believed he had served an ace at 5-3 (40-30) in the deciding set.

1 가산명사 (카드의) 에이스 ❑ 하트 에이스 **2** 가산명사 제 1인자, 명수 [언론] ❑ 이전 자동차 경주의 제 1인자 스털링 모스 ● 형용사 최고의 ❑ 최고의 공포 영화 제작자 로렌스 울지 **3** 가산명사 (테니스) 에이스 서브, 서브 득점 ❑ 헨만은 결승 세트 5-3 (40-30) 상황에서 자신이 에이스 서브를 넣었다고 믿었다.

ache /eɪk/ (aches, aching, ached) **1** V-I If you **ache** or a part of your body **aches**, you feel a steady, fairly strong pain. ❑ The glands in her neck were swollen, her head was throbbing and she ached all over. ❑ My leg is giving me much less pain but still aches

1 자동사 아프다 ❑ 그녀는 목의 내분비선이 붓고 머리가 쑤셨으며 온몸이 아팠다. ❑ 다리 통증이 훨씬 덜 하지만 아직도 않을 때는 아프다. **2** 가산명사 통증

when I sit down. **2** N-COUNT An **ache** is a steady, fairly strong pain in a part of your body. □ *You feel nausea and aches in your muscles.* →see also **headache**, **heartache 3** PHRASE You can use **aches and pains** to refer in a general way to any minor pains that you feel in your body. □ *It seems to ease all the aches and pains of a hectic and tiring day.*

❑ 당신은 메스꺼움과 근육통을 느낀다. **3** 구 몸의 피로 ❑ 정신없이 바쁘고 힘든 하루의 피로를 모두 덜어 주는 것 같다.

Thesaurus	*ache*의 참조어	
V.	pound, throb **1**	
N.	hurt, pain, pang **2**	
ADJ.	sore **2**	

achieve ♦♦◇ /ətʃiːv/ (**achieves**, **achieving**, **achieved**) V-T If you **achieve** a particular aim or effect, you succeed in doing it or causing it to happen, usually after a lot of effort. □ *There are many who will work hard to achieve these goals.*

타동사 이루다, 성취하다 ❑ 이러한 목표를 성취하기 위해 열심히 일할 사람들이 많이 있다.

Thesaurus	*achieve*의 참조어	
V.	accomplish, bring about, succeed; *(ant.)* fail, lose, miss	

achieve|ment ♦♦◇ /ətʃiːvmənt/ (**achievements**) **1** N-COUNT An **achievement** is something which someone has succeeded in doing, especially after a lot of effort. □ *It was a great achievement that a month later a global agreement was reached.* **2** N-UNCOUNT **Achievement** is the process of achieving something. □ *It is only the achievement of these goals that will finally bring lasting peace.*

1 가산명사 업적 ❑ 한 달 후 총체적 합의에 도달한 것은 위대한 업적이었다. **2** 불가산명사 달성, 성취 ❑ 마침내 영구적인 평화를 가져올 길은 오직 이 목표들을 달성하는 것뿐이다.

achiev|er /ətʃiːvər/ (**achievers**) N-COUNT A high **achiever** is someone who is successful in their studies or their work, usually as a result of their efforts. A low **achiever** is someone who achieves less than those around them. □ *High achievers at British Airways are in line for cash bonuses.*

가산명사 연구나 업무를 성공적으로 해낸 사람을 'high achiever,' 다른 사람보다 못한 성과를 낸 사람을 'low achiever'라고 한다. ❑ 영국 항공의 모범 근무자들이 현금 보너스를 받기 위해 줄을 서 있다.

acid ♦♦◇ /æsɪd/ (**acids**) **1** N-MASS An **acid** is a chemical substance, usually a liquid, which contains hydrogen and can react with other substances to form salts. Some acids burn or dissolve other substances that they come into contact with. □ *...citric acid.* **2** ADJ An **acid** substance contains acid. □ *These shrubs must have an acid, lime-free soil.* ● **acid|ity** /əsɪdɪti/ N-UNCOUNT [oft N of n] □ *...the acidity of rainwater.*

1 물질명사 산 ❑ 구연산 **2** 형용사 산성의 ❑ 이 관목들은 석회질이 없는 산성의 토양이 필요하다. ● 산도 불가산명사 ❑ 빗물의 산도

acid|ic /əsɪdɪk/ ADJ **Acidic** substances contain acid. □ *Dissolved carbon dioxide makes the water more acidic.*

형용사 산성의 ❑ 용해된 이산화탄소는 물을 더 산성으로 만든다.

acid rain N-UNCOUNT **Acid rain** is rain polluted by acid that has been released into the atmosphere from factories and other industrial processes. Acid rain is harmful to the environment. →see **pollution**

불가산명사 산성비

ac|knowl|edge ♦♦◇ /æknɒlɪdʒ/ (**acknowledges**, **acknowledging**, **acknowledged**) **1** V-T If you **acknowledge** a fact or a situation, you accept or admit that it is true or that it exists. [FORMAL] □ *Naylor acknowledged, in a letter to the judge, that he was a drug addict.* □ *Belatedly, the government has acknowledged the problem.* **2** V-T If someone's achievements, status, or qualities **are acknowledged**, they are known about and recognized by a lot of people, or by a particular group of people. □ *He is also acknowledged as an excellent goalkeeper.* **3** V-T If you **acknowledge** a message or letter, you write to the person who sent it in order to say that you have received it. □ *The army sent me a postcard acknowledging my request.* **4** V-T If you **acknowledge** someone, for example by moving your head or smiling, you show that you have seen and recognized them. □ *He saw her but refused to even acknowledge her.*

1 타동사 인정하다 [격식체] ❑ 네일러는 판사에게 보내는 편지에서 자신이 마약 중독자라는 것을 인정했다. ❑ 정부는 뒤늦게 그 문제를 인정했다. **2** 타동사 인정하다 ❑ 그는 또한 뛰어난 골키퍼로도 인정받고 있다. **3** 타동사 수령을 통지하다 ❑ 군대에서 내가 보낸 요구서의 수령을 통지하는 엽서를 보내왔다. **4** 타동사 아는 체를 했다 ❑ 그는 그녀를 봤지만 아는 체도 하지 않았다.

Thesaurus	*acknowledge*의 참조어	
V.	accept, admit, grant **1**	
	recognize; *(ant.)* ignore **2 4**	

ac|knowl|edg|ment /æknɒlɪdʒmənt/ (**acknowledgments**) also **acknowledgement 1** N-SING An **acknowledgment** is a statement or action which recognizes that something exists or is true. [also no det, usu with supp, oft N of n] □ *The President's resignation appears to be an acknowledgment that he has lost all hope of keeping the country together.* **2** N-PLURAL The **acknowledgments** in a book are the section in which the author thanks all the people who have helped him or her. □ *...two whole pages of acknowledgments.* **3** N-UNCOUNT A gesture of **acknowledgment**, such as a smile, shows someone that you have seen and recognized them. [also a N] □ *Farling smiled in acknowledgment and gave a bow.*

1 단수명사 인정 ❑ 대통령의 사임은 그가 국가 운영에 대한 희망을 모두 잃었음을 인정하는 것처럼 보인다. **2** 복수명사 (저자가 책에 싣는) 감사의 말 ❑ 완전 두 페이지에 걸친 감사의 말 **3** 불가산명사 알아봄, 아는 체함 ❑ 팔링이 알아보고 웃으며 머리를 숙였다.

acne /ækni/ N-UNCOUNT If someone has **acne**, they have a skin condition which causes a lot of pimples on their face and neck. □ *She wore no makeup, and her face was dotted with acne.*

불가산명사 여드름 ❑ 그녀는 화장을 하지 않았었는데 얼굴 곳곳에 여드름이 나 있었다.

acorn /eɪkɔːrn/ (**acorns**) N-COUNT An **acorn** is a pale oval nut that is the fruit of an oak tree.

가산명사 도토리

acous|tic /əkuːstɪk/ (**acoustics**) **1** ADJ An **acoustic** guitar or other instrument is one whose sound is produced without any electrical equipment. [ADJ n] **2** N-COUNT If you refer to the **acoustics** of a space, you are referring to the structural features which determine how well you can hear music or speech in it. □ *In this performance, Rattle had the acoustics of the Symphony Hall on his side.* **3** N-UNCOUNT **Acoustics** is the scientific study of sound. □ *...his work in acoustics.*

1 형용사 전자 장치를 쓰지 않은 **2** 가산명사 음향 효과 ❑ 이번 공연에서 래틀은 심포니 홀의 음향 효과 덕을 톡톡히 보았다. **3** 불가산명사 음향학 ❑ 음향학 분야에서의 그의 연구

ac|quaint /əkweɪnt/ (**acquaints**, **acquainting**, **acquainted**) V-T If you **acquaint** someone **with** something, you tell them about it so that they know it. If you **acquaint yourself with** something, you learn about it. [FORMAL] □ *Have steps been taken to acquaint breeders with their right to apply for licenses?* →see also **acquainted**

타동사 숙지시키다 [격식체] ❑ 면허를 신청할 권리가 사육자들에게 있다는 것을 숙지시키기 위한 조치가 취해졌는가?

ac|quaint|ance /əkweɪntəns/ (**acquaintances**) **1** N-COUNT An **acquaintance** is someone who you have met and know slightly, but not well. ❑ *He exchanged a few words with the proprietor, an old acquaintance of his.* **2** N-VAR If you have an **acquaintance with** someone, you have met them and you know them. ❑ *...a writer who becomes involved in a real murder mystery through his acquaintance with a police officer.* **3** PHRASE When you **make** someone's **acquaintance**, you meet them for the first time and get to know them a little. [FORMAL] ❑ *I first made his acquaintance and that of his wife and young family in the early 1960s.*

1 가산명사 아는 사람, 지인 ❑ 그는 오랫동안 아는 사이인 그 곳 주인과 몇 마디 말을 주고받았다. **2** 가산명사 또는 불가산명사 면식 ❑ 어떤 경찰관과의 면식 때문에 실제 살인 사건에 연루된 작가 **3** 구 - 와 아는 사이가 되다 [격식체] ❑ 나는 1960년대 초에 그 사람과 그의 부인 및 아이들을 처음으로 만나 알게 되었다.

ac|quaint|ed /əkweɪntɪd/ ADJ **1** If you are **acquainted with** something, you know about it because you have learned it or experienced it. [FORMAL] [v-link ADJ with n] ❑ *He was well acquainted with the literature of France, Germany and Holland.* **2** ADJ If you get or become **acquainted with** someone that you do not know, you talk to each other or do something together so that you get to know each other. You can also say that two people get or become **acquainted**. [v-link ADJ, oft ADJ with n] ❑ *At first the meetings were a way to get acquainted with each other.* **3** →see also **acquaint**

1 형용사 -을 아는 [격식체] ❑ 그는 프랑스와 독일, 네덜란드의 문학에 정통한 사람이었다. **2** 형용사 - 와 아는 사이인 ❑ 처음에는 그 회의가 서로를 알기 위한 하나의 방편이었다.

ac|quire ♦♢♢ /əkwaɪər/ (**acquires, acquiring, acquired**) **1** V-T If you **acquire** something, you buy or obtain it for yourself, or someone gives it to you. [FORMAL] ❑ *General Motors acquired a 50% stake in Saab for about $400m.* **2** V-T If you **acquire** something such as a skill or a habit, you learn it, or develop it through your daily life or experience. ❑ *I've never acquired a taste for wine.* **3** V-T If someone or something **acquires** a certain reputation, they start to have that reputation. ❑ *He has begun to acquire a reputation among some critics as perhaps this country's premier solo violinist.*

1 타동사 획득하다, 취득하다 [격식체] ❑ 제너럴 모터즈는 4억 달러에 상당하는 사브 주식 50퍼센트를 취득했다. **2** 타동사 습득하다 ❑ 나는 와인에 맛을 들여본 적이 없다. **3** 타동사 (명성 등을) 얻다 ❑ 그는 몇몇 비평가들로부터 아마도 이 나라에서 최고 바이올린 독주자일 것이라는 평을 얻기 시작했다.

ac|quir|er /əkwaɪərər/ (**acquirers**) N-COUNT In business, an **acquirer** is a company or person who buys another company. [BUSINESS] ❑ *...the ability of corporate acquirers to finance large takeovers.*

가산명사 기업 인수자 [경제] ❑ 법인 기업 인수자의 대규모 인수를 위한 자금 조달 능력

ac|qui|si|tion ♦♢♢ /ækwɪzɪʃⁿn/ (**acquisitions**) **1** N-VAR If a company or business person makes an **acquisition**, they buy another company or part of a company. [BUSINESS] ❑ *...the acquisition of a profitable paper recycling company.* **2** N-COUNT If you make an **acquisition**, you buy or obtain something, often to add to things that you already have. ❑ *How did you go about making this marvelous acquisition then?* **3** N-UNCOUNT The **acquisition** of a skill or a particular type of knowledge is the process of learning it or developing it. ❑ *...language acquisition.*

1 가산명사 또는 불가산명사 인수 [경제] ❑ 수익성 있는 종이 재생 회사 인수 **2** 가산명사 취득, 획득 ❑ 그럼 너는 어떻게 이런 놀라운 것을 얻었니? **3** 불가산명사 습득 ❑ 언어 습득

ac|quit /əkwɪt/ (**acquits, acquitting, acquitted**) V-T If someone **is acquitted of** a crime in a court of law, they are formally declared not to have committed the crime. [usu passive] ❑ *Mr. Castorina was acquitted of attempted murder.*

타동사 무죄를 선언하다 ❑ 카스토리나 씨는 살인 미수에 대해 무죄 판결을 받았다.

ac|quit|tal /əkwɪtⁿl/ (**acquittals**) N-VAR **Acquittal** is a formal declaration in a court of law that someone who has been accused of a crime is innocent. ❑ *...the acquittal of six police officers charged with the beating of an alleged drug dealer.* ❑ *The jury voted 8-to-4 in favor of acquittal.*

가산명사 또는 불가산명사 무죄 선고 ❑ 마약상으로 지정된 이를 구타로 기소된 경찰관 여섯 명에 대한 무죄 선고 ❑ 배심원단은 8 대 4로 무죄를 선고했다.

acre ♦♢♢ /eɪkər/ (**acres**) N-COUNT An **acre** is an area of land measuring 4840 square yards or 4047 square meters. ❑ *The property is set in two acres of land.*

가산명사 에이커 (면적의 단위) ❑ 그 부지는 2에이커에 걸쳐 있다.

ac|ri|mo|ni|ous /ækrɪmoʊniəs/ ADJ **Acrimonious** words or quarrels are bitter and angry. [FORMAL] ❑ *The acrimonious debate on the agenda ended indecisively.*

형용사 매서운, 신랄한 [격식체] ❑ 그 안건에 대한 매서운 논쟁은 아무런 결론을 못 내리고 끝났다.

Word Link   *onym ≈ name : acronym, anonymous, synonym*

---

ac|ro|nym /ækrənɪm/ (**acronyms**) N-COUNT An **acronym** is a word composed of the first letters of the words in a phrase, especially when this is used as a name. An example of an acronym is NATO which is made up of the first letters of the "North Atlantic Treaty Organization."

가산명사 약어, 두문자 어

across ♦♦♦ /əkrɔs, BRIT əkrɒs/

In addition to the uses shown below, **across** is used in phrasal verbs such as "come across," "get across," and "put across."

across는 아래 용법 외에도 'come across', 'get across', 'put across'와 같은 구동사에 쓰인다.

1 PREP If someone or something goes **across** a place or a boundary, they go from one side of it to the other. ❑ *She walked across the floor and lay down on the bed.* ❑ *He watched Karl run across the street to Tommy.* ● ADV **Across** is also an adverb. [ADV after v] ❑ *Richard stood up and walked across to the window.* **2** PREP If something is situated or stretched **across** something else, it is situated or stretched from one side of it to the other. ❑ *...the floating bridge across Lake Washington in Seattle.* ❑ *He scrawled his name across the bill.* ● ADV **Across** is also an adverb. [ADV after v] ❑ *Trim toenails straight across using nail clippers.* **3** PREP If something is lying **across** an object or place, it is resting on it and partly covering it. ❑ *She found her clothes lying across the chair.* **4** PREP Something that is **across** something such as a street, river, or area is on the other side of it. ❑ *Anyone from the houses across the road could see him.* ● ADV **Across** is also an adverb. ❑ *They parked across from the Castro Theater.* **5** ADV If you look **across** at a place, person, or thing, you look toward them. ❑ *He glanced across at his sleeping wife.* ❑ *She rose from the chair and gazed across at him.* **6** PREP You use **across** to say that a particular expression is shown on someone's face. ❑ *An enormous grin spread across his face.* **7** PREP If someone hits you **across** the face or head, they hit you on that part. ❑ *Graham hit him across the face with the gun, then pushed him against the wall.* **8** PREP When something happens **across** a place or organization, it happens equally everywhere within it. ❑ *The film "Hook" opens across America on December 11.* **9** PREP When something happens **across** a political, religious, or social barrier, it involves people in different groups. ❑ *...parties competing across the political spectrum.* **across the board** →see **board** **10** ADV **Across** is used in measurements to show the width of something. [amount ADV] ❑ *This hand-decorated plate measures 30cm across.*

1 전치사 -을 건너 ❑ 그녀는 방바닥 건너가 걸어가서 침대에 누웠다. ❑ 그는 칼이 길 건너에 있는 타미에게로 뛰어가는 것을 지켜보았다. ● 부사 건너편으로 ❑ 리처드는 일어나 건너편 창문 쪽으로 걸어갔다. **2** 전치사 -을 가로질러 ❑ 시애틀 워싱턴 호수를 가로지르는 부교 ❑ 그는 계산서 위에 자신의 이름을 휘갈겨 썼다. ● 부사 가로질러 ❑ 손톱깎이를 써서 발톱을 일자로 깎아 주세요. **3** 전치사 -에 걸쳐서 ❑ 그녀는 자신의 옷이 의자 위에 걸쳐져 있는 것을 발견했다. **4** 전치사 -의 건너편에 ❑ 길 건너편에 있는 집에서 누구라면지 그가 보였다. ● 부사 건너편에 ❑ 그들은 카스트로 극장 건너편에 주차했다. **5** 부사 건너편으로 ❑ 그는 잠든 아내를 흘깃 건너다보았다. ❑ 여자가 의자에서 일어서 남자 쪽을 응시했다. **6** 전치사 (얼굴) 가득히 ❑ 그의 얼굴 가득 미소가 번졌다. **7** 전치사 (머리나 얼굴) 위로 ❑ 그레이엄이 총으로 그의 얼굴을 갈긴 후, 그를 벽에다 밀어붙였다. **8** 전치사 -의 전역에서 ❑ 영화 '후크'는 12월 11일 미국 전역에서 개봉한다. **9** 전치사 -을 넘나들며, -을 초월하여 ❑ 가지각색의 정치적 색깔을 가지고 경쟁하는 정당들 **10** 부사 지름으로, 너비로 ❑ 이 수공 장식 접시는 지름이 30센티미터이다.

acryl|ic /ækrɪlɪk/ N-UNCOUNT **Acrylic** material is artificial and is manufactured by a chemical process. ❑ *...her pink acrylic sweater.*

불가산명사 아크릴 소재 ❑ 그녀의 분홍색 아크릴 스웨터

act ♦♦♦ /ækt/ (**acts**, **acting**, **acted**) **1** V-I When you **act**, you do something for a particular purpose. ❑ *The deaths occurred when police acted to stop widespread looting and vandalism.* **2** V-I If you **act on** advice or information, you do what you have been advised or suggested. ❑ *A patient will usually listen to the doctor's advice and act on it.* **3** V-I If someone **acts** in a particular way, they behave in that way. ❑ *...a gang of youths who were acting suspiciously.* ❑ *He acted as if he hadn't heard any of it.* **4** V-I If someone or something **acts as** a particular thing, they have that role or function. ❑ *Among his other duties, he acted both as the ship's surgeon and as chaplain for the men.* **5** V-I If someone **acts** in a particular way, they pretend to be something that they are not. ❑ *Chris acted astonished as he examined the note.* **6** V-I When professionals such as lawyers **act for** you, or **act on** your **behalf**, they are employed by you to deal with a particular matter. ❑ *Daniel Webster acted for Boston traders while still practicing in New Hampshire.* **7** V-I If a force or substance **acts on** someone or something, it has a certain effect on them. ❑ *He's taking a dangerous drug: it acts very fast on the central nervous system.* **8** V-I If you **act**, or **act** a part in a play or film, you have a part in it. ❑ *She confessed to her parents her desire to act.* **9** N-COUNT An **act** is a single thing that someone does. [FORMAL] [oft N of n] ❑ *Language interpretation is the whole point of the act of reading.* **10** N-SING If you say that someone's behavior is an **act**, you mean that it does not express their real feelings. ❑ *His anger was real. It wasn't an act.* **11** N-COUNT An **Act** is a law passed by the government. ❑ *...an Act of Parliament.* **12** N-COUNT An **act** in a play, opera, or ballet is one of the main parts into which it is divided. [oft N num] ❑ *Act II contained some of the funniest scenes I have ever witnessed.* **13** N-COUNT An **act** in a show is a short performance which is one of several in the show. ❑ *This year numerous bands are playing, as well as comedy acts.* **14** PHRASE If you **catch** someone **in the act**, you discover them doing something wrong or committing a crime. ❑ *The men were caught in the act of digging up buried explosives.* **15** PHRASE If someone who has been behaving badly **cleans up** their **act**, they start to behave in a more acceptable or responsible way. [INFORMAL] ❑ *The nation's advertisers need to clean up their act.* **16** PHRASE If you **get in on the act**, you take part in or take advantage of something that was started by someone else. [INFORMAL] ❑ *In the 1970s Kodak, anxious to get in on the act, launched its own instant camera.* **17** PHRASE You say that someone was **in the act of** doing something to indicate what they were doing when they were seen or interrupted. ❑ *Ken was in the act of paying his bill when Neil came up behind him.* **18** PHRASE If you **get** your **act together**, you organize your life or your affairs so that you are able to achieve what you want or to deal with something effectively. [INFORMAL] ❑ *The Government should get its act together.* **19** to **act the fool** →see **fool**

Word Partnership   *act*의 연어

PREP.	act **like** 5
N.	act **of violence**, acts **of vandalism** 9
	act **one/two/three** 12
V.	**caught in the** act 14
	get in on the act 16

act|ing /ˈæktɪŋ/ **1** N-UNCOUNT **Acting** is the activity or profession of performing in plays or films. ❑ *Saffron Burrows returned to London to pursue her acting career after four years of modeling.* **2** ADJ You use **acting** before the title of a job to indicate that someone is doing that job temporarily. [ADJ n] ❑ *The new acting President has a reputation of being someone who is independent.*

ac|tion ♦♦♦ /ˈækʃ°n/ (**actions**, **actioning**, **actioned**) **1** N-UNCOUNT **Action** is doing something for a particular purpose. ❑ *The government is taking emergency action to deal with a housing crisis.* **2** N-COUNT An **action** is something that you do on a particular occasion. ❑ *As always, Peter had a reason for his action.* **3** N-COUNT To bring a legal **action** against someone means to bring a case against them in a court of law. [LEGAL] ❑ *Two leading law firms are to prepare legal actions against tobacco companies.* **4** N-UNCOUNT The fighting which takes place in a war can be referred to as **action**. ❑ *Leaders in America have generally supported military action if it proves necessary.* **5** ADJ An **action** movie is a film in which a lot of dangerous and exciting things happen. An **action** hero is the main character in one of these films. [ADJ n] **6** V-T If you **action** something that needs to be done, you deal with it. [BUSINESS] ❑ *Documents can be actioned, or filed immediately.* **7** PHRASE If someone or something is **out of action**, they are injured or damaged and cannot work or be used. ❑ *He's been out of action for 16 months with a serious knee injury.* **8** PHRASE If someone wants to take **a piece of the action** or **a slice of the action**, they want to take part in an exciting activity or situation, usually in order to make money or become more important. ❑ *As the British rap scene grows in strength, the Americans are becoming keener to grab a slice of the action.* **9** PHRASE If you **put** an idea or policy **into action**, you begin to use it or cause it to operate. ❑ *They have excelled in learning the lessons of business management theory, and putting them into action.*

Word Partnership   *action*의 연어

N.	**course of** action, **plan of** action 1
V.	**take** action 1
ADJ.	**disciplinary** action 1
	legal action 3
	military action 4

ac|ti|vate /ˈæktɪveɪt/ (**activates**, **activating**, **activated**) V-T If a device or process **is activated**, something causes it to start working. [usu passive] ❑ *Video cameras with night vision can be activated by movement.*

---

1 자동사 행동하다 ❑ 경찰이 만연된 약탈과 파괴 행위를 막기 위해 나섰을 때 그 사망 사고들이 일어났다. **2** 자동사 -을 좇아 행동하다 ❑ 환자는 일반적으로 의사의 말을 듣고 그 말을 좇아 행동하는 법이다. **3** 자동사 행동하다 ❑ 수상한 행동을 하고 있던 한 무리의 젊은이들 ❑ 그는 그 일에 대해 아무것도 듣지 못한 것처럼 행동했다. **4** 자동사 -로서 역할을 수행하다 ❑ 다른 임무들도 있었지만, 그는 그 배의 군의관 겸 군목 역할을 수행했다. **5** 자동사 -인 체하다 ❑ 그가 그 메모를 살피자 크리스는 깜짝 놀라는 체했다. **6** 자동사 -을 위해 일하다 ❑ 다니엘 웹스터는 여전히 뉴햄프셔에 사무실을 둔 채로 보스턴의 상인들을 위해 일했다. **7** 자동사 -에 작용하다, -에 영향을 미치다 ❑ 그는 위험한 약을 먹고 있다. 그 약은 매우 빠르게 중추 신경계에 영향을 미친다. **8** 자동사 연기하다 ❑ 그녀는 부모에게 연기를 하고픈 열망을 고백했다. **9** 가산명사 행위 [격식체] ❑ 언어 해석이 읽는 행위의 전적인 목적은 언어 해석이다. **10** 단수명사 시늉, 꾸밈 ❑ 그의 분노는 진짜였다. 시늉이 아니었다. **11** 가산명사 법령, 조례 ❑ 의회법 **12** 가산명사 (연극) 막 ❑ 2막에서는 내가 지금까지 본 것 중에서 가장 재미있는 장면들이 나온다. **13** 가산명사 상연물 ❑ 올해에는 희극물은 물론 수많은 밴드들의 공연이 이루어지고 있다. **14** 구 현장을 포착하다 ❑ 그 남자들은 매장된 폭발물을 파내다가 현장에서 포착되었다. **15** 구 개과천선하다 [비격식체] ❑ 그 나라의 광고주들은 개과천선해야 한다. **16** 구 한몫 끼다 [비격식체] ❑ 1970년대에 한몫 끼고 싶어 하던 코닥이 자체 브랜드의 일회용 카메라를 시장에 내놓았다. **17** 구 -를 하고 있는 중의 ❑ 닐이 뒤에 다가갔을 때 켄은 계산을 하는 중이었다. **18** 구 일관성 있게 효율적으로 행동하다 [비격식체] ❑ 정부는 일관성을 가지고 효율적으로 움직여야 한다.

1 불가산명사 연기 ❑ 사프론 버로스는 사 년간의 모델 생활 뒤 연기 활동을 위해 런던으로 돌아왔다. **2** 형용사 임시의, 대행의 ❑ 신임 대통령 권한 대행은 독자적인 사람이라는 평을 듣는다.

1 불가산명사 조치 ❑ 정부는 주택 공급 위기를 다루기 위해 비상조치를 취하고 있다. **2** 가산명사 행위 ❑ 언제나처럼, 피터는 자신의 행위에 대한 이유가 있었다. **3** 가산명사 소송 [법의] ❑ 일류 법률 회사 두 곳이 담배 회사들을 상대로 법적 소송을 준비할 예정이다. **4** 불가산명사 교전, 전투 ❑ 일반적으로 미국의 지도자들은 필요한 것으로 입증될 경우 군사적 조치를 지지해 왔다. **5** 형용사 액션 (영화, 배우) **6** 타동사 처리하다 [경제] ❑ 서류들은 곧바로 처리하거나 정리할 수 있습니다. **7** 구 움직일 수 없는 ❑ 그는 지난 16개월 동안 심각한 무릎 부상으로 인해 움직이지를 못했다. **8** 구 한몫 ❑ 영국 랩 시장이 커지다 미국인들이 더욱더 간절히 한몫 끼고 싶어 하고 있다. **9** 구 실행하다, 실시하다 ❑ 그들은 경영 이론 수업을 배우고, 배운 것을 실행에 옮기는 데 뛰어난 실력을 보여 왔다.

타동사 작동하다 ❑ 암시(暗視) 장치가 있는 비디오카메라는 움직임에 의해 작동될 수 있다.

a b c d e f g h i j k l m n o p q r s t u v w x y z

ac|tive ♦♦◊ /ǽktɪv/ 🚹 ADJ Someone who is **active** moves around a lot or does a lot of things. ❏ *Having an active youngster about the house can be quite wearing.* 🔟 ADJ If you have an **active** mind or imagination, you are always thinking of new things. ❏ *...the tragedy of an active mind trapped by failing physical health.* 🔢 ADJ If someone is **active** in an organization, cause, or campaign, they do things for it rather than just giving it their support. ❏ *We should play an active role in politics, both at national and local level.* ● ac|tive|ly ADV ❏ *They actively campaigned for the vote.* 🔢 ADJ **Active** is used to emphasize that someone is taking action in order to achieve something, rather than just hoping for it or achieving it in an indirect way. [EMPHASIS] [ADJ n] ❏ *...if companies do not take active steps to increase exports.* ● ac|tive|ly ADV ❏ *They have never been actively encouraged to take such risks.* 🔢 ADJ If you say that a person or animal is **active** in a particular place or at a particular time, you mean that they are performing their usual activities or performing a particular activity. ❏ *Guerrilla groups are active in the province.* 🔢 ADJ An **active** volcano has erupted recently or is expected to erupt quite soon. ❏ *...molten lava from an active volcano.* 🔢 ADJ An **active** substance has a chemical or biological effect on things. ❏ *The active ingredient in some of the mouthwashes was simply detergent.* 🔢 N-SING In grammar, **the active** or **the active voice** means the forms of a verb which are used when the subject refers to a person or thing that does something. For example, in "I saw her yesterday," the verb is in the active. Compare **passive**.

Word Partnership	active의 연어
N.	active **imagination** 🔟
	active **role** 🔢
	active **ingredient** 🔢
ADV.	**politically** active 🔢

ac|tiv|ist ♦◊◊ /ǽktɪvɪst/ (activists) N-COUNT An **activist** is a person who works to bring about political or social changes by campaigning in public or working for an organization. ❏ *The police say they suspect the attack was carried out by animal rights activists.*

ac|tiv|ity ♦♦◊ /æktɪ́vɪti/ (activities) 🚹 N-UNCOUNT **Activity** is a situation in which a lot of things are happening or being done. ❏ *We will see an extraordinary level of activity in the market for UK government bonds.* 🔟 N-COUNT An **activity** is something that you spend time doing. ❏ *For lovers of the great outdoors, activities range from canoeing to bird watching.* 🔢 N-PLURAL The **activities** of a group are the things that they do in order to achieve their aims. ❏ *...a jail term for terrorist activities.*

ac|tor ♦♦◊ /ǽktər/ (actors) N-COUNT An **actor** is someone whose job is acting in plays or films. "Actor" in the singular usually refers to a man, but some women who act prefer to be called "actors" rather than "actresses." ❏ *His father was an actor in the Cantonese Opera Company.* →see **theater**

ac|tress ♦◊◊ /ǽktrɪs/ (actresses) N-COUNT An **actress** is a woman whose job is acting in plays or films. ❏ *She's not only a very great dramatic actress but she's also very funny.*

ac|tual ♦♦◊ /ǽktʃuəl/ 🚹 ADJ You use **actual** to emphasize that you are referring to something real or genuine. [EMPHASIS] [ADJ n] ❏ *The segments are filmed using either local actors or the actual people involved.* 🔟 ADJ You use **actual** to contrast the important aspect of something with a less important aspect. [EMPHASIS] [ADJ n] ❏ *She had compiled pages of notes, but she had not yet gotten down to doing the actual writing.* **in actual fact** →see **fact**

Do not confuse **actual** and **real**. You use **actual** to emphasize that what you are referring to is real or genuine, or to contrast different aspects of something. You use **real** to describe things that exist rather than being imagined or theoretical. ❏ *Robert squealed in mock terror, then in real pain.* Note that you only use **actual** in front of a noun. You do not say that something "is actual." Note also that **actual** is not used to refer to something which is happening now, at the present time. For this meaning, you need to use adjectives such as **current** or **present**.

ac|tu|al|ly ♦♦♦ /ǽktʃuəli/ 🚹 ADV You use **actually** to indicate that a situation exists or happened, or to emphasize that it is true. ❏ *One afternoon, I grew bored and actually fell asleep for a few minutes.* 🔟 ADV You use **actually** when you are correcting or contradicting someone. [EMPHASIS] [ADV with cl] ❏ *No, I'm not a student. I'm a doctor, actually.* 🔢 ADV You can use **actually** when you are politely expressing an opinion that other people might not have expected from you. [POLITENESS] [ADV with cl] ❏ *"Do you think it's a good idea to socialize with one's patients?" — "Actually, I do, I think it's a great idea."* 🔢 ADV You use **actually** to introduce a new topic into a conversation. [ADV with cl] ❏ *Well actually, John, I rang you for some advice.*

Note that **actually** and **really** are both used to emphasize statements. **Actually** is used to emphasize what is true or genuine in a situation, often when this is surprising, or a contrast with what has just been said. ❏ *All the characters in the novel actually existed... He actually began to cry.* It can also be used to be precise or to correct someone. ❏ *No one was actually drunk... We couldn't actually see the garden.* You use **really** in conversation to emphasize something that you are saying. ❏ *I really think he's sick.* When you use **really** in front of an adjective or adverb, it has a similar meaning to "very." ❏ *This is really serious.*

🚹 형용사 활동적인 ❏ 집에 활동적인 아이가 있으면 상당히 힘이 들 수 있다. 🔟 형용사 활기 있는 ❏ 쇠잔해져 가는 육체에 갇힌 활기찬 정신의 비극 🔢 형용사 적극적인 ❏ 우리는 전국적으로는 물론 지역 차원에서도 정치적으로 적극적인 역할을 해야 합니다. ● 적극적으로 부사 ❏ 그들은 적극적으로 선거권 쟁취 운동을 펼쳤다. 🔢 형용사 적극적인 [강조] ❏ 만약 회사들이 수출 증진을 위해 적극적인 조치를 취하지 않으면 ● 적극적으로 부사 ❏ 그들은 그와 같은 위험을 무릅쓰도록 적극적으로 독려받은 적이 없었다. 🔢 형용사 활동 중인 ❏ 그 지역에서는 게릴라 집단들이 활동 중입니다. 🔢 형용사 활동 중인 ❏ 활화산에서 분출되는 용암 🔢 형용사 활성이 있는 ❏ 구강 세정제들 중 일부에 든 활성 성분은 단순한 세제였다. 🔢 단수명사 능동태

가산명사 행동주의자; 운동가 ❏ 경찰은 이 공격이 동물 권익 운동가들의 소행이라는 혐의를 두고 있다고 말한다.

🚹 불가산명사 활발한 움직임 ❏ 우리는 영국 국채 시장이 대단히 활발해지는 것을 보게 될 것이다. 🔟 가산명사 활동 ❏ 야외 활동을 즐기는 사람들의 활동은 카누타기부터 조류 관찰에 이르기까지 다양하다. 🔢 복수명사 활동 ❏ 테러 행위를 이르는 감방 용어

가산명사 배우 ❏ 그의 아버지는 광동 경극단 배우였다.

가산명사 여배우 ❏ 그녀는 아주 대단한 연극 배우일 뿐만 아니라 매우 익살맞기도 하다.

🚹 형용사 실제의, 진짜 [강조] ❏ 그 부분들은 지역의 배우들이나 실제 관련 인물들을 써서 촬영된다. 🔟 형용사 실질적인 [강조] ❏ 그녀는 이미 주석 부분 편집은 마쳤지만 아직 실질적인 집필에 착수하지 않았었다.

actual과 real을 혼동하지 않도록 하라. actual은 지금 언급하고 있는 것이 진짜라는 사실을 강조하거나, 어떤 것의 다른 양상을 대조하기 위해 쓴다. real은 무엇이 상상한 것이거나 이론적인 것이 아니라 실제 존재하는 것임을 기술하기 위해 쓴다. ❏ 로버트는 거짓으로 무서운 척 비명을 지르다, 그 다음에는 진짜 고통스러워서 비명을 질렀다. actual은 명사 앞에서만 사용한다는 점을 유의하라. 즉 'something is actual'이라고는 하지 않는다. 또한 actual은 지금 현재 일어나고 있는 일을 언급하기 위해서는 쓰지 않는다는 점도 유의하라. 이런 의미로는 current나 present 같은 형용사들을 사용한다.

🚹 부사 실제로, 정말로 [강조] ❏ 어느 날 오후, 나는 싫증이 나서 실제로 몇 분 동안 잠이 들었다. 🔟 부사 사실은 [강조] ❏ 아니, 저는 학생이 아니에요. 사실은 의사입니다. 🔢 부사 사실 [공손체] ❏ "환자와 사교적으로 지내는 것이 좋은 생각이라고 보십니까?" "사실, 그렇습니다. 저는 아주 좋은 생각이라고 봅니다." 🔢 부사 사실은, 실은 ❏ 있지, 존, 실은 충고를 좀 구하려고 전화했어.

actually와 really는 둘 다 진술을 강조하기 위해 쓴다는 점에 유의하라. actually는 어떤 상황에서 진실이거나 진짜인 것을 강조하기 위해 쓰이는데, 흔히 이런 것이 놀랍거나 막 언급한 내용과 대조를 이룰 때 쓴다. ❏ 그 소설의 모든 등장인물은 실제로 존재했다... 그가 실제로 울기 시작했다. actually는 또한 정확하게 말하거나 다른 사람의 말을 정정해 줄 때도 쓴다. ❏ 정말 아무도 취하지

앉았었다... 우리는 정원을 정말 볼 수가 없었다. really는 대화에서 말하고 있는 어떤 것을 강조할 때 쓴다. □ 나는 그가 정말 아프다고 생각한다. really를 형용사 또는 부사 앞에 쓰면 'very'와 비슷한 뜻을 갖는다. □ 이건 정말 심각하다.

acu|men /əkyumən, BRIT ækyumen/ N-UNCOUNT **Acumen** is the ability to make good judgments and quick decisions. □ *His sharp business acumen meant he quickly rose to the top.*

불가산명사 판단력 □ 그의 날카로운 사업적 판단력 덕분에 그는 빨리 정상에 올랐다.

acu|punc|ture /ækyupʌŋktʃər/ N-UNCOUNT **Acupuncture** is the treatment of a person's illness or pain by sticking small needles into their body at certain places. □ *I had acupuncture in my lower back.*

불가산명사 침술, 침 치료 □ 나는 허리 아래 부분에 침을 맞았다.

acute /əkyut/ **1** ADJ You can use **acute** to indicate that an undesirable situation or feeling is very severe or intense. □ *The war has aggravated an acute economic crisis.* □ *The report has caused acute embarrassment to the government.* **2** ADJ An **acute** illness is one that becomes severe very quickly but does not last very long. Compare **chronic**. [MEDICAL] [ADJ n] □ *...a patient with acute rheumatoid arthritis.* **3** ADJ If a person's or animal's sight, hearing, or sense of smell is **acute**, it is sensitive and powerful. □ *I like how in the dark my sense of smell and hearing become so acute.* **4** ADJ An **acute** angle is less than 90°. Compare **obtuse** angle. **5** ADJ An **acute** accent is a symbol that is placed over vowels in some languages in order to indicate how that vowel is pronounced or over one letter in a word to indicate where it is stressed. You refer to a letter with this accent as, for example, e **acute**. For example, there is an acute accent over the letter "e" in the French word "café." [ADJ n, n ADJ]

1 형용사 심각한; 격심한 □ 전쟁으로 인해 심각한 경제 위기가 더 악화되었다. □ 그 보도로 인해 정부는 몹시 곤혹스러워했다. **2** 형용사 급성의 [의학] □ 급성 류머티즘 관절염 환자 **3** 형용사 예리한 □ 나는 어둠 속에 있으면 후각과 청각이 아주 예리해지는 것이 참 좋다. **4** 형용사 예각의 **5** 형용사 에음 액센트의

acute|ly /əkyutli/ ADV If you feel or notice something **acutely**, you feel or notice it very strongly. □ *He was acutely aware of the odor of cooking oil.*

부사 심하게 □ 그는 식용유 냄새가 심하게 나는 것을 느꼈다.

ad ◆◇◇ /æd/ (**ads**) N-COUNT An **ad** is an advertisement. [INFORMAL] □ *She replied to a lonely hearts ad she spotted in the New York Times.*

가산명사 광고 [비격식체] □ 그녀는 뉴욕 타임즈 지에서 발견한 애인 구함 광고에 답신을 보냈다.

AD /ˌeɪ di/ You use **AD** in dates to indicate the number of years or centuries that have passed since the year in which Jesus Christ is believed to have been born. Compare **BC**. □ *The original castle was probably built about AD 860.* □ *The cathedral was destroyed by the Great Fire of 1136 AD.*

서기 □ 원래의 성은 아마도 서기 860년경에 지어졌을 것이다. □ 그 대성당은 서기 1136년의 대화재 때 소실되었다.

ada|mant /ædəmənt/ ADJ If someone is **adamant about** something, they are determined not to change their mind about it. □ *The prime minister is adamant that he will not resign.* ● **ada|mant|ly** ADV □ *She was adamantly opposed to her husband travelling to Brussels.*

형용사 완강한; 철석 같은 □ 수상은 사임을 완강히 거부하고 있다. ● 완강히 부사 □ 그녀는 남편의 브뤼셀 여행을 완강히 반대했다.

a|dapt /ədæpt/ (**adapts, adapting, adapted**) **1** V-T/V-I If you **adapt to** a new situation or **adapt yourself to** it, you change your ideas or behavior in order to deal with it successfully. □ *The world will be different, and we will have to be prepared to adapt to the change.* **2** V-T If you **adapt** something, you change it to make it suitable for a new purpose or situation. □ *Shelves were built to adapt the library for use as an office.* **3** →see also **adapted**

1 타동사/자동사 적응하다; 적응시키다 □ 세상은 달라질 것이고, 우리는 그런 변화에 적응할 준비를 해야 할 것이다. **2** 타동사 개조하다 □ 선반들은 서재를 사무실 용도로 개조할 수 있도록 제작되었다.

Thesaurus	adapt의 참조어	
v.	adjust, assimilate, conform **1**	
	modify, revise **2**	

adapt|able /ədæptəbᵊl/ ADJ If you describe a person or animal as **adaptable**, you mean that they are able to change their ideas or behavior in order to deal with new situations. □ *By making the workforce more adaptable and skilled, he hopes to attract foreign investment.* ● **adapt|abil|ity** /ədæptəbɪlɪti/ N-UNCOUNT □ *The adaptability of wool is one of its great attractions.*

형용사 적응할 수 있는; 융통성 있는 □ 그는 직원들을 융통성 있고 숙련되게 만듦으로써 외국 투자를 유치하기를 희망한다. ● 적응성; 융통성 불가산명사 □ 적응성은 모직의 뛰어난 매력 요인 중 하나이다.

ad|ap|ta|tion /ædæptən/ (**adaptations**) **1** N-COUNT An **adaptation** of a book or play is a film or a television program that is based on it. □ *Branagh won two awards for his screen adaptation of Shakespeare's Henry the Fifth.* **2** N-UNCOUNT **Adaptation** is the act of changing something or changing your behavior to make it suitable for a new purpose or situation. □ *Most living creatures are capable of adaptation when necessary.*

1 가산명사 각색 □ 브래너는 셰익스피어의 헨리 5세를 영화로 각색하여 두 개의 상을 탔다. **2** 불가산명사 적응 □ 대부분의 생물체들은 불가피한 상황이 되면 적응을 하는 능력이 있다.

Thesaurus	adaptation의 참조어	
N.	adjustment, alteration, modification **2**	

a|dapt|ed /ədæptɪd/ ADJ If something is **adapted to** a particular situation or purpose, it is especially suitable for it. [v-link ADJ to/for n] □ *The camel's feet, well adapted for dry sand, are useless on mud.*

형용사 적합한 □ 낙타의 발은 건조한 모래땅에서는 아주 적합하지만 진흙땅에서는 쓸모가 없다.

add ◆◆◆ /æd/ (**adds, adding, added**) **1** V-T If you **add** one thing **to** another, you put it in or on the other thing, so as to increase, complete, or improve it. □ *Add the grated cheese to the sauce.* □ *Since 1908, chlorine has been added to drinking water.* **2** V-T If you **add** numbers or amounts **together**, you calculate their total. □ *Banks add all the interest and other charges together.* ● PHRASAL VERB **Add up** means the same as **add**. □ *More than a quarter of seven-year-olds cannot add up properly.* □ *We just added all the numbers up and divided one by the other.* **3** V-I If one thing **adds to** another, it makes the other thing greater in degree or amount. □ *Overnight bed-rest in a clinic adds substantially to the cost of cosmetic surgery.* **4** V-T To **add** a particular quality **to** something means to cause it to have that quality. □ *The generous amount of garlic adds flavor.* **5** V-T If you **add** something when you are speaking,

1 타동사 더하다, 첨가하다 □ 소스에 간 치즈를 첨가하세요. □ 1908년 이래로, 식수에 염소가 첨가되어 왔다. **2** 다동사 디하다, 합산하다 □ 은행은 전체 이자와 기타 수수료를 모두 합산합니다. ● 구동사 더하다 □ 일곱 살짜리 아이들 중 4분의 1 이상이 덧셈을 제대로 할 줄 모른다. □ 우리는 단지 모든 숫자를 더한 다음 한쪽 숫자를 다른 쪽 숫자로 나누었다. **3** 자동사 덧붙다, 추가하다 □ 병원에서 하룻밤 묵으며 요양하는 것이 실질적으로 성형 수술 비용에 추가된다. **4** 타동사 더하다 □ 풍부한 양의 마늘이 풍미를 더해 줍니다. **5** 타동사 덧붙이다

A

you say something more. ❑ *"You can tell that he is extremely embarrassed,"* Mr. Brigden added.

❑ "그가 매우 당황했음을 알 수 있습니다."라고 브릭든 씨는 덧붙였다.

Thesaurus add의 참조어

v.	include, put in, put on **1**
	calculate, tally, total; (ant.) reduce, subtract **2**
	augment, increase; (ant.) lessen, reduce **3**

▶**add in** PHRASAL VERB If you **add in** something, you include it as a part of something else. ❑ *Once the vegetables start to cook add in a couple of tablespoons of water.*

구동사 더하다; 포함시키다 ❑ 야채가 익기 시작하면 물 두어 숟갈을 더 넣으세요.

▶**add on** **1** PHRASAL VERB If one thing **is added on** to another, it is attached to the other thing, or is made a part of it. ❑ *Vacationers can also add on a week in Florida before or after the cruise.* **2** PHRASAL VERB If you **add on** an extra amount or item to a list or total, you include it. ❑ *Many loan application forms automatically add on insurance.*

1 구동사 덧붙이다; 곁들이다 ❑ 휴가객들은 또한 선박 여행 전후로 1주일 일정의 플로리다 여행을 추가할 수도 있다. **2** 구동사 포함하다 ❑ 많은 융자 신청 양식에는 자동적으로 보증이 포함된다.

▶**add up** **1** →see **add 2** **2** PHRASAL VERB If facts or events do not **add up**, they make you confused about a situation because they do not seem to be consistent. If something that someone has said or done **adds up**, it is reasonable and sensible. ❑ *Police said they arrested Olivia because her statements did not add up.* **3** PHRASAL VERB If small amounts of something **add up**, they gradually increase. ❑ *Even small savings, 5 pence here or 10 pence there, can add up.*

2 구동사 앞뒤가 맞다, 타당하다 ❑ 경찰은 올리비아의 진술이 앞뒤가 맞지 않아서 그녀를 구속했다고 말했다. **3** 구동사 늘어나다 ❑ 적은 액수의 저축도 여기에 5펜스, 저기에 10펜스 하는 식으로 늘어날 수 있다.

▶**add up to** PHRASAL VERB If amounts **add up to** a particular total, they result in that total when they are put together. ❑ *For a hit show, profits can add up to millions of dollars.*

구동사 총계 ~이 되다 ❑ 인기 있는 쇼의 경우에는 수익이 수백만 달러까지 될 수 있다.

add|ed /ˈædɪd/ ADJ You use **added** to say that something has more of a particular thing or quality. [ADJ n] ❑ *For added protection choose moisturising lipsticks with a sunscreen.*

형용사 추가의 ❑ 추가 보호를 위해서는 햇빛 차단 기능이 있는 수분 공급 립스틱을 선택하세요.

add|ed value N-UNCOUNT In marketing, **added value** is something which makes a product more appealing to customers. [BUSINESS] ❑ *We can create significant added value by pushing the brand into other areas.*

불가산명사 부가 가치 [경제] ❑ 우리는 브랜드를 다른 영역까지 확장함으로써 중대한 부가 가치를 창출할 수 있다.

ad|dict /ˈædɪkt/ (**addicts**) **1** N-COUNT An **addict** is someone who takes harmful drugs and cannot stop taking them. ❑ *He's only 24 years old and a drug addict.* **2** N-COUNT If you say that someone is an **addict**, you mean that they like a particular activity very much and spend as much time doing it as they can. ❑ *She is a TV addict and watches as much as she can.*

1 가산명사 중독자 ❑ 그는 겨우 스물네 살의 나이로 마약 중독자이다. **2** 가산명사 중독자 ❑ 그녀는 TV 중독자라서 시간만 나면 TV를 본다.

ad|dict|ed /əˈdɪktɪd/ **1** ADJ Someone who is **addicted to** a harmful drug cannot stop taking it. ❑ *Many of the women are addicted to heroin and cocaine.* **2** ADJ If you say that someone is **addicted to** something, you mean that they like it very much and want to spend as much time doing it as possible. ❑ *She had become addicted to golf.*

1 형용사 중독된 ❑ 그 여자들 중 다수가 헤로인과 코카인에 중독되었다. **2** 형용사 푹 빠진 ❑ 그녀는 골프에 푹 빠졌다.

ad|dic|tion /əˈdɪkʃ^ən/ (**addictions**) **1** N-VAR **Addiction** is the condition of taking harmful drugs and being unable to stop taking them. ❑ *She helped him fight his drug addiction.* **2** N-VAR An **addiction to** something is a very strong desire or need for it. ❑ *He needed money to feed his addiction to gambling.*

1 가산명사 또는 불가산명사 중독 ❑ 그녀는 그가 마약 중독과 싸우는 것을 도왔다. **2** 가산명사 또는 불가산명사 열중, 탐닉 ❑ 그는 도박에 깊이 빠져들어 돈이 필요했다.

Word Partnership addiction의 연어

N.	**drug** addiction **1**
ADJ.	**long-term** addiction **2**
V.	**fight against** addiction **2**
PREP.	addiction **to *something*** **2**

---

ad|dic|tive /əˈdɪktɪv/ **1** ADJ If a drug is **addictive**, people who take it cannot stop taking it. ❑ *Cigarettes are highly addictive.* **2** ADJ Something that is **addictive** is so enjoyable that it makes you want to do it or have it a lot. ❑ *Video movie-making can quickly become addictive.*

1 형용사 중독성이 있는 ❑ 담배는 중독성이 강하다. **2** 형용사 빠져들기 쉬운, 중독성이 있는 ❑ 비디오 영화를 제작하는 일은 급속히 빠져들기 쉽다.

ad|di|tion /əˈdɪʃ^ən/ ◆◇◇ (**additions**) **1** PHRASE You use **in addition** when you want to mention another item connected with the subject you are discussing. ❑ *The Met Office Web site provides regional reports, a shipping forecast and gale warnings. In addition, visitors can download satellite images of the UK.* **2** N-COUNT An **addition to** something is a thing which is added to it. ❑ *This is a fine book; a worthy addition to the Cambridge Encyclopedia series.* **3** N-UNCOUNT The **addition of** something is the fact that it is added to something. ❑ *It was completely refurbished in 1987, with the addition of a picnic site.* **4** N-UNCOUNT **Addition** is the process of calculating the total of two or more numbers. ❑ *...simple addition and subtraction problems using whole numbers.* →see **mathematics**

1 구 덧붙여, 게다가 ❑ 기상청 홈페이지에서는 지역 예보와 해상 통보, 폭풍 정보 등을 제공한다. 덧붙여 방문자들은 영국 지역의 위성사진을 내려받을 수 있다. **2** 가산명사 추가 사항, 부가물 ❑ 이는 케임브리지 백과사전 총서에 붙는 가치 있는 부록으로서 훌륭한 책이다. **3** 불가산명사 추가, 부가 ❑ 그곳은 1987년에 야유회장을 추가로 갖추어 전면 재단장되었다. **4** 불가산명사 덧셈 ❑ 간단한 정수 덧셈 뺄셈 문제

ad|di|tion|al ◆◇◇ /əˈdɪʃ^ən^əl/ ADJ **Additional** things are extra things apart from the ones already present. ❑ *The U.S. is sending additional troops to the region.*

형용사 추가의 ❑ 미국이 그 지역에 추가 병력을 투입하고 있다.

ad|di|tion|al|ly /əˈdɪʃ^ən^əli/ **1** ADV You use **additionally** to introduce something extra such as an extra fact or reason. [FORMAL] [ADV with cl] ❑ *All teachers are qualified to teach their native language. Additionally, we select our teachers for their engaging personalities.* **2** ADV **Additionally** is used to say that something happens to a greater extent than before. [ADV with v] ❑ *The birds are additionally protected in the reserves at Birsay.*

1 부사 그 위에, 덧붙여 [격식체] ❑ 교사들은 모두 각자의 모국어 교사 자격이 있습니다. 덧붙여, 저희는 매력적인 개성의 소유자를 교사로 선발합니다. **2** 부사 부가적으로; 특별히 ❑ 그 새들은 버세이의 보호 구역에서 특별 보호를 받는다.

ad|di|tive /ˈædɪtɪv/ (**additives**) N-COUNT An **additive** is a substance which is added in small amounts to foods or other things in order to improve them or to make them last longer. ❑ *Strict safety tests are carried out on food additives.*

가산명사 첨가물 ❑ 식품 첨가물에 대해서는 엄격한 안전 검사가 이루어진다.

add-on (**add-ons**) N-COUNT An **add-on** is an extra piece of equipment, especially computer equipment, that can be added to a larger one which you already own in order to improve its performance or its usefulness. ❑ *In most electronics shops, active speakers are sold as add-ons for personal stereos.*

가산명사 추가 기기 ❑ 대부분의 전자제품 상점에서, 앰프 내장형 스피커는 개인용 전축 추가 기기로 판매된다.

ad|dress ♦♦◇ (**addresses, addressing, addressed**)

> The noun is pronounced /ədrɛs/ or /ædrɛs/. The verb is pronounced /ədrɛs/

1 N-COUNT Your **address** is the number of the house or apartment and the name of the street and the town where you live or work. ❑ *The address is 2025 M Street, Northwest, Washington, DC, 20036.* **2** V-T If a letter, envelope, or parcel **is addressed to** you, your name and address have been written on it. [usu passive] ❑ *Applications should be addressed to: The business affairs editor.* **3** N-COUNT The **address** of a website is its location on the Internet, for example http://www.cobuild.collins.co.uk. [COMPUTING] ❑ *Full details, including the website address to log on to, are at the bottom of this page.* **4** V-T If you **address** a group of people, you make a speech to them. ❑ *He is due to address a conference on human rights next week.* ● N-COUNT **Address** is also a noun. ❑ *He had scheduled an address to the American people for the evening of May 27.*

Thesaurus   address의 참조어

V.	lecture, present, speak **4**
N.	lecture, speech, talk **4**

Word Partnership   address의 연어

ADJ.	**permanent** address **1**
	public address, **inaugural** address **4**
N.	**name and** address, **street** address **1**
	address **remarks to 4**

---

ad|dress book (**address books**) **1** N-COUNT An **address book** is a book in which you write people's names and addresses. **2** N-COUNT An **address book** is a computer file which contains a list of e-mail addresses. [COMPUTING]

adept /ædɛpt/ ADJ Someone who is **adept at** something can do it skillfully. ❑ *He's usually very adept at keeping his private life out of the media.*

ad|equa|cy /ædɪkwəsi/ N-UNCOUNT **Adequacy** is the quality of being good enough or great enough in amount to be acceptable. ❑ *...to test the adequacy of tents, sleeping bags, boots, jackets, and other gear.*

ad|equate ♦◇◇ /ædɪkwɪt/ ADJ If something is **adequate**, there is enough of it or it is good enough to be used or accepted. ❑ *One in four people worldwide are without adequate homes.* ❑ *She is prepared to offer me an amount adequate to purchase another house.* ● **ad|equate|ly** ADV [ADV with v] ❑ *Many students are not adequately prepared for higher education.*

ad|here /ædhɪər/ (**adheres, adhering, adhered**) **1** V-I If you **adhere to** a rule or agreement, you act in the way that it says you should. ❑ *All members of the association adhere to a strict code of practice.* **2** V-I If something **adheres to** something else, it sticks firmly to it. ❑ *Small particles adhere to the seed.*

ad|he|sive /ædhisɪv/ (**adhesives**) **1** N-MASS An **adhesive** is a substance such as glue, which is used to make things stick firmly together. ❑ *Glue the mirror in with a strong adhesive.* **2** ADJ An **adhesive** substance is able to stick firmly to something else. ❑ *...adhesive tape.*

ad hoc /æd hɒk/ ADJ An **ad hoc** activity or organization is done or formed only because a situation has made it necessary and is not planned in advance. ❑ *"I would accept opportunities in TV on an ad hoc basis," he said.*

ad|ja|cent /ədʒeɪsªnt/ ADJ If one thing is **adjacent to** another, the two things are next to each other. ❑ *He sat in an adjacent room and waited.* ❑ *The schools were adjacent but there were separate doors.*

ad|jec|tive /ædʒɪktɪv/ (**adjectives**) N-COUNT An **adjective** is a word such as "big," "dead," or "financial" that describes a person or thing, or gives extra information about them. Adjectives usually come before nouns or after linking verbs.

ad|join /ədʒɔɪn/ (**adjoins, adjoining, adjoined**) V-T If one room, place, or object **adjoins** another, they are next to each other. [FORMAL] ❑ *The doctor's bedroom adjoined his wife's and the door between the rooms was always open.*

ad|journ /ədʒɜrn/ (**adjourns, adjourning, adjourned**) V-T/V-I If a meeting or trial **is adjourned** or if it **adjourns**, it is stopped for a short time. ❑ *The proceedings have now been adjourned until next week.*

ad|journ|ment /ədʒɜrnmənt/ (**adjournments**) N-COUNT An **adjournment** is a temporary stopping of a trial, inquiry, or other meeting. ❑ *The court ordered a four month adjournment.*

ad|just ♦◇◇ /ədʒʌst/ (**adjusts, adjusting, adjusted**) **1** V-T/V-I When you **adjust to** a new situation, you get used to it by changing your behavior or your ideas. ❑ *We have been preparing our fighters to adjust themselves to civil society.* ❑ *I felt I had adjusted to the idea of being a mother very well.* **2** V-T If you **adjust** something, you change it so that it is more effective or appropriate. ❑ *To attract investors, Panama has adjusted its tax and labor laws.* **3** V-T If you **adjust** something such as your clothing or a machine, you correct or alter its position or setting. ❑ *Liz adjusted her mirror and then edged the car out of its parking bay.* **4** V-T/V-I If you **adjust** your vision or if your vision **adjusts**, the muscles of your eye or the pupils alter to cope with changes in light or distance. ❑ *He stopped to try to adjust his vision to the faint starlight.*

ad|just|able /ədʒʌstəbªl/ ADJ If something is **adjustable**, it can be changed to different positions or sizes. ❑ *The bags have adjustable shoulder straps.* →see **interest rate**

명사는 /ədrɛs/ 또는 /ædrɛs/로 발음되고, 동사는 /ədrɛs/로 발음된다.

1 가산명사 주소 ❑ 주소는 우편번호 20036, 워싱턴 디씨 북서부 엠가 2025번지입니다. **2** 타동사 받는 이의 주소와 성명을 쓰다 ❑ 신청서는 경제부 편집자 앞으로 보내 주십시오. **3** 가산명사 (인터넷 상의) 주소 [컴퓨터] ❑ 접속 가능한 인터넷 주소를 포함한 상세한 내용은 이 페이지 아래쪽에 있습니다. **4** 타동사 -에게 연설하다 ❑ 그는 다음 주 인권 회의에서 연설을 할 예정이다. ● 가산명사 연설 ❑ 그는 5월 27일 저녁 미국민들에게 연설을 하기로 예정되어 있었다.

1 가산명사 주소록 **2** 가산명사 이메일 주소록 [컴퓨터]

형용사 능숙한, 숙련된 ❑ 평소 그는 자신의 사생활을 언론에 노출시키지 않는 데 대단히 능숙하다.

불가산명사 타당성 ❑ 텐트, 침낭, 장화, 재킷과 다른 장비가 적절한지 시험하기

형용사 적당한, 충분한 ❑ 전세계 인구 네 명 중 한 명이 적당한 집을 가지고 있지 않다. ❑ 그녀는 집을 한 채 더 사기에 충분한 금액을 나에게 제공할 용의가 있다. ● 적절히, 충분히 부사 ❑ 많은 학생들이 고등 교육을 받을 준비가 충분히 안 되어 있다.

1 자동사 준수하다 ❑ 모든 협회원들이 엄격한 실천 요강을 준수한다. **2** 자동사 달라붙다 ❑ 작은 입자들이 씨앗에 달라붙는다.

1 물질명사 접착제 ❑ 강력 접착제로 거울을 붙여 넣으시오. **2** 형용사 접착성의 ❑ 접착 테이프

형용사 임시의, 특별한 ❑ "저는 특별 출연을 원칙으로 TV 출연을 받아들이겠습니다."라고 그가 말했다.

형용사 인접한 ❑ 그는 옆방에 앉아서 기다렸다. ❑ 그 학교들은 서로 인접해 있었지만 출입구는 달랐다.

가산명사 형용사

타동사 - 옆에 있다, 인접하다 [격식체] ❑ 그 의사의 침실은 부인의 침실 옆에 있었고 그 사이의 문은 언제나 열려 있었다.

타동사/자동사 연기하다; 휴회하다 ❑ 현재 그 소송 절차는 다음 주까지 계속 연기된 상태이다.

가산명사 휴회, 휴정 ❑ 법원은 4개월의 휴정을 명령했다.

1 타동사/자동사 적응하다 ❑ 우리는 전사들이 민간 사회에 적응할 준비를 갖추도록 해 왔다. ❑ 나는 내 자신이 엄마가 된다는 생각에 아주 잘 적응했다고 느꼈다. **2** 타동사 조정하다 ❑ 파나마는 투자자들을 유치하기 위해 조세법과 노동법을 조정해 왔다. **3** 타동사 조정하다, 바로잡다 ❑ 리즈는 거울을 조정하고 나서 차를 서서히 몰아 차고를 빠져 나왔다. **4** 타동사/자동사 초점을 맞추다; 초점이 맞다 ❑ 그는 멈춰 서서 흐릿한 별빛에 눈의 초점을 맞추려고 애썼다.

형용사 조절 가능한 ❑ 그 가방들은 조절 가능한 어깨 끈이 달려 있다.

a b c d e f g h i j k l m n o p q r s t u v w x y z

ad|just|ment /ədʒʌstmənt/ (**adjustments**) **1** N-COUNT An **adjustment** is a small change that is made to something such as a machine or a way of doing something. ❑ *Compensation could be made by adjustments to taxation.* ❑ *Investment is up by 5.7% after adjustment for inflation.* **2** N-COUNT An **adjustment** is a change in a person's behavior or thinking. ❑ *He will have to make major adjustments to his thinking if he is to survive in office.*

1 가산명사 수정, 조정 ❑ 세금을 조정하는 방법으로 보상할 수도 있다. ❑ 물가상승분을 감안한 투자 규모가 5.7퍼센트 늘었다. **2** 가산명사 변화 ❑ 그가 관직에서 살아남으려면 자신의 생각을 크게 바꿔야 할 것이다.

ad|man /ædmæn/ (**admen**) N-COUNT An **adman** is someone who works in advertising. [INFORMAL] ❑ *He was the most brilliant adman that any of us knew.*

가산명사 광고업자 [비격식체] ❑ 그는 우리가 알던 사람 중에 가장 유능한 광고업자였다.

ad|min /ædmɪn/ N-UNCOUNT **Admin** is the activity or process of organizing an institution or organization. [INFORMAL] ❑ *I have two assistants who help with the admin.*

불가산명사 [비격식체] ❑ 내게는 운영을 도와주는 조수가 두 사람이다.

ad|min|is|ter /ædmɪnɪstər/ (**administers, administering, administered**) **1** V-T If someone **administers** something such as a country, the law, or a test, they take responsibility for organizing and supervising it. ❑ *The plan calls for the UN to administer the country until elections can be held.* **2** V-T If a doctor or a nurse **administers** a drug, they give it to a patient. [FORMAL] ❑ *The physician may prescribe but not administer the drug.*

1 타동사 통치하다; 집행하다; 시행하다 ❑ 계획에 따르면 선거를 치를 수 있을 때까지 유엔이 이 나라를 통치해야 한다. **2** 타동사 투여하다 [격식체] ❑ 의사가 처방만 하고 약을 직접 투여하지 않을 수도 있다.

ad|min|is|tra|tion ♦♦◇ /ædmɪnɪstreɪʃⁿ/ (**administrations**) **1** N-UNCOUNT **Administration** is the range of activities connected with organizing and supervising the way that an organization or institution functions. ❑ *Too much time is spent on administration.* **2** N-UNCOUNT The **administration** of something is the process of organizing and supervising it. ❑ *Standards in the administration of justice have degenerated.* **3** N-SING The **administration** of a company or institution is the group of people who organize and supervise it. ❑ *They would like the college administration to exert more control over the fraternity.* **4** N-COUNT You can refer to a country's government as **the administration**; used especially in the United States. →see **government** ❑ *O'Leary served in federal energy posts in both the Ford and Carter administrations.*

1 불가산명사 행정, 운영 ❑ 행정에 너무 많은 시간이 소요된다. **2** 불가산명사 시행 ❑ 법 집행의 수준이 떨어져 왔다. **3** 단수명사 경영진, 본부; 당국 ❑ 그들은 대학 본부가 남학생 사교 클럽을 더 많이 통제해 주기를 바란다. **4** 가산명사 행정부 ❑ 오리리는 포드 행정부와 카터 행정부 시절 연방정부 에너지 부문에서 일을 했다.

ad|min|is|tra|tive /ædmɪnɪstreɪtɪv, BRIT ædmɪnɪstrətɪv/ ADJ **Administrative** work involves organizing and supervising an organization or institution. ❑ *Other industries have had to sack managers to reduce administrative costs.*

형용사 행정상의, 운영상의 ❑ 다른 업계에서도 운영 비용을 줄이기 위해 간부들을 퇴출해야만 했다.

ad|min|is|tra|tor /ædmɪnɪstreɪtər/ (**administrators**) N-COUNT An **administrator** is a person whose job involves helping to organize and supervise the way that an organization or institution functions. ❑ *On Friday the company's administrators sought permission from a Melbourne court to stay operating.*

가산명사 행정관; 경영인 ❑ 회사의 경영진은 금요일에 멜번 법원에 회사 운영을 계속해도 좋다는 허가를 요청했다.

ad|mi|rable /ædmɪrəb⁰l/ ADJ An **admirable** quality or action is one that deserves to be praised and admired. ❑ *Beyton is an admirable character.* ● **ad|mi|rably** /ædmɪrəbli/ ADV ❑ *Peter had dealt admirably with the sudden questions about Keith.*

형용사 감탄할 만한, 훌륭한 ❑ 베이튼은 훌륭한 인물이다. ● 훌륭하게 부사 ❑ 피터는 키스에 관한 갑작스러운 질문에 훌륭하게 대처했다.

ad|mi|ral /ædmərəl/ (**admirals**) N-COUNT; N-TITLE An **admiral** is a very senior officer who commands a navy. ❑ *...Admiral Hodges.*

가산명사; 경칭명사 장군 ❑ 하지스 장군

ad|mi|ra|tion /ædmɪreɪʃⁿ/ N-UNCOUNT **Admiration** is a feeling of great liking and respect for a person or thing. ❑ *I have always had the greatest admiration for him.*

불가산명사 흠모 ❑ 나는 항상 그를 가장 흠모해 왔다.

ad|mire ♦◇◇ /ədmaɪər/ (**admires, admiring, admired**) **1** V-T If you **admire** someone or something, you like and respect them very much. ❑ *I admired her when I first met her and I still think she's marvelous.* ❑ *He admired the way she had coped with life.* **2** V-T If you **admire** someone or something, you look at them with pleasure. ❑ *We took time to stop and admire the view.*

1 타동사 흠모하다 ❑ 나는 처음 만난 순간 그녀를 흠모했고, 여전히 그녀를 대단한 사람으로 여긴다. ❑ 그는 그녀가 삶을 헤쳐 나가는 모습에 탄복했다. **2** 타동사 감탄하다 ❑ 우리는 잠시 멈춰 서서 주변 경치를 감상했다.

Thesaurus   admire의 참조어

v.   esteem, honor, look up to, respect **1**

---

ad|mir|er /ədmaɪərər/ (**admirers**) N-COUNT If you are an **admirer** of someone, you like and respect them or their work very much. ❑ *He was an admirer of her grandfather's paintings.*

가산명사 흠모하는 사람 ❑ 그는 그녀 할아버지의 그림을 흠모하는 사람이었다.

ad|mis|sion /ædmɪʃⁿn/ (**admissions**) **1** N-VAR **Admission** is permission given to a person to enter a place, or permission given to a country to enter an organization. **Admission** is also the act of entering a place. ❑ *Students apply for admission to a particular college.* **2** N-PLURAL **Admissions** to a place such as a school or university are the people who are allowed to enter or join it. ❑ *Each school sets its own admissions policy.* **3** N-UNCOUNT **Admission** at a park, museum, or other place is the amount of money that you pay to enter it. ❑ *Gates open at 10.30am and admission is free.* ● N-UNCOUNT **Admission** is also used before a noun. ❑ *The admission price is $8 for adults.* **4** N-VAR An **admission** is a statement that something bad, unpleasant, or embarrassing is true. ❑ *By his own admission, he is not playing well.*

1 가산명사 또는 불가산명사 입장; 가입; 입학 ❑ 학생들은 특정 대학에 입학 지원을 한다. **2** 복수명사 입학생 ❑ 학교마다 각각 고유한 입시 정책을 세운다. **3** 가산명사 입장료 ❑ 오전 10시 30분 개장하며 입장은 무료이다. ● 불가산명사 입장 ❑ 성인 입장료는 8달러이다. **4** 가산명사 또는 불가산명사 인정 ❑ 본인도 인정하듯이, 그는 경기 성적이 좋지 않다.

ad|mit ♦♦◇ /ædmɪt/ (**admits, admitting, admitted**) **1** V-T/V-I If you **admit** that something bad, unpleasant, or embarrassing is true, you agree, often unwillingly, that it is true. ❑ *I am willing to admit that I do make mistakes.* ❑ *Up to two thirds of 14 to 16 year olds admit to buying drink illegally.* ❑ *None of these people will admit responsibility for their actions.* **2** V-T If someone **is admitted to** hospital, they are taken into hospital for treatment and kept there until they are well enough to go home. [usu passive] ❑ *She was admitted to the hospital with a soaring temperature.* **3** V-T If someone **is admitted to** an organization or group, they are allowed to join it. ❑ *He was admitted to the Académie Culinaire de France.* **4** V-T To **admit** someone **to** a place means to allow them to enter it. ❑ *Embassy security personnel refused to admit him or his wife.*

1 타동사/자동사 인정하다 ❑ 나도 내가 실수를 한다는 사실을 기꺼이 인정한다. ❑ 14~16살 청소년들 중 2/3나 불법적으로 술을 구입했다고 시인한다. ❑ 이들 중에 아무도 자신의 행동에 대한 책임을 인정하려 하지 않을 것이다. **2** 타동사 입원하다 ❑ 그녀는 갑자기 열이 심하게 올라서 입원했다. **3** 타동사 가입시키다 ❑ 그는 프랑스 요리 협회에 입회했다. **4** 타동사 들여보내다 ❑ 대사관 경비가 그 사람이나 그의 아내의 출입을 거부했다.

Word Partnership   admit의 연어

V.	ashamed to admit, be the first to admit, must admit, willing to admit **1**
N.	admit defeat **1**
CONJ.	admit that **1**

ad|mit|ted|ly /ædˈmɪtɪdli/ ADV You use **admittedly** when you are saying something which weakens the importance or force of your statement. [ADV with cl/group] □ *It's only a theory, admittedly, but the pieces fit together.*

부사 ─을 인정한다 해도 □ 이것이 단지 추측하는 걸 인정하지만, 상황이 절묘하게 들어맞는다.

ado|les|cence /ˌædəˈlɛsᵊns/ N-UNCOUNT **Adolescence** is the period of your life in which you develop from being a child into being an adult. □ *Some young people suddenly become self-conscious and tongue-tied in early adolescence.* →see **child**

불가산명사 사춘기 □ 사춘기 초반에 일부 청소년들은 갑자기 자의식이 강해지고 말이 없어진다.

ado|les|cent /ˌædəˈlɛsᵊnt/ (**adolescents**) ADJ **Adolescent** is used to describe young people who are no longer children but who have not yet become adults. It also refers to their behavior. □ *It is important that an adolescent boy should have an adult in whom he can confide.* ● N-COUNT An **adolescent** is an adolescent boy or girl. □ *Young adolescents are happiest with small groups of close friends.* →see **age, child**

형용사 사춘기의 □ 사춘기 소년에게는 마음을 터놓고 말할 수 있는 어른이 있다는 게 매우 중요하다. ● 가산명사 사춘기 청소년 □ 사춘기 청소년들은 친한 친구 몇 명과 함께 있을 때 가장 행복하다.

Word Link	opt ≈ choosing : adopt, option, optional

adopt ♦♦◇ /əˈdɒpt/ (**adopts, adopting, adopted**) ■ V-T If you **adopt** a new attitude, plan, or way of behaving, you begin to have it. □ *The United Nations General Assembly has adopted a resolution calling on all parties in the conflict to seek a political settlement.* ● **adop|tion** /əˈdɒpʃᵊn/ N-UNCOUNT □ *...the adoption of Japanese management practices by British manufacturing.* ☑ V-T/V-I If you **adopt** someone else's child, you take it into your own family and make it legally your son or daughter. □ *There are hundreds of people desperate to adopt a child.* ● **adop|tion** (**adoptions**) N-VAR □ *They gave their babies up for adoption.*

■ 타동사 채택하다, 받아들이다 □ 유엔 총회에서 분쟁 당사자들 간의 정치적 합의를 촉구하는 결의안을 채택했다. ● 채택 불가산명사 □ 영국 제조업계의 일본 경영 관행 채택 ☑ 타동사/자동사 입양하다 □ 입양을 간절히 원하는 사람이 수백 명에 달한다. ● 입양 가산명사 또는 불가산명사 □ 그들은 어린 자식들을 입양시키기로 했다.

Thesaurus	adopt의 참조어

v. approve, endorse, support; (ant.) refuse, reject ■
raise, take in; (ant.) abandon ☑

adop|tive /əˈdɒptɪv/ ADJ Someone's **adoptive** family is the family that adopted them. [ADJ n] □ *He was brought up by adoptive parents in London.*

형용사 양자 관계의 □ 그는 런던에서 양부모 밑에서 자랐다.

ador|able /əˈdɔːrəbᵊl/ ADJ If you say that someone or something is **adorable**, you are emphasizing that they are very attractive and you feel great affection for them. [EMPHASIS] □ *By the time I was 30, we had three adorable children.*

형용사 사랑스러운 [강조] □ 내가 서른 살이 되었을 무렵, 우리에겐 사랑스러운 아이가 셋 있었다.

ado|ra|tion /ˌædəˈreɪʃᵊn/ N-UNCOUNT **Adoration** is a feeling of great admiration and love for someone or something. □ *She needs and wants to be loved with overwhelming passion and adoration.* →see **emotion**

불가산명사 흠모, 동경 □ 그녀는 넘치는 열정과 흠모를 담은 사랑을 받을 필요가 있고 그것을 원하기도 한다.

adore /əˈdɔːr/ (**adores, adoring, adored**) ■ V-T If you **adore** someone, you feel great love and admiration for them. [no cont] □ *She adored her parents and would do anything to please them.* ☑ V-T If you **adore** something, you like it very much. [INFORMAL] [no cont] □ *My mother adores bananas and eats two a day.*

■ 타동사 흠모하다, 동경하다 □ 그녀는 부모님을 흠모했으며 그들을 기쁘게 하기 위해 무엇이든 하려 했다. ☑ 타동사 매우 좋아하다 [비격식체] □ 우리 어머니는 바나나를 매우 좋아하셔서 하루에 두 개씩 드신다.

adorn /əˈdɔːrn/ (**adorns, adorning, adorned**) V-T If something **adorns** a place or an object, it makes it look more beautiful. □ *His watercolor designs adorn a wide range of books.*

타동사 장식하다, 돋보이게 하다 □ 그의 수채화 문양은 다양한 종류의 책에 삽화로 들어간다.

adrena|lin /əˈdrɛnᵊlɪn/ also **adrenaline** N-UNCOUNT **Adrenalin** is a substance which your body produces when you are angry, scared, or excited. It makes your heart beat faster and gives you more energy. □ *That was my first big game in months and the adrenalin was going.*

불가산명사 아드레날린 (에너지의 원천) □ 그것은 내가 몇 달 만에 처음 갖는 큰 경기여서 에너지가 솟구쳤다.

adrift /əˈdrɪft/ ■ ADJ If a boat is **adrift**, it is floating on the water and is not tied to anything or controlled by anyone. [v-link ADJ, v n ADJ] □ *They were spotted after three hours adrift in a dinghy.* ☑ ADJ If someone is **adrift**, they feel alone with no clear idea of what they should do. [v-link ADJ, v n ADJ] □ *Amy had the growing sense that she was adrift and isolated.*

■ 형용사 표류하여 □ 그들은 구명정을 타고 세 시간 표류한 끝에 발견되었다. ☑ 형용사 방황하는 □ 에이미는 점점 더 고립감을 느끼며 방황했다.

adult ♦♦◇ /əˈdʌlt, BRIT ˈædʌlt/ (**adults**) ■ N-COUNT An **adult** is a mature, fully developed person. An adult has reached the age when they are legally responsible for their actions. □ *Becoming a father signified that he was now an adult.* ☑ N-COUNT An **adult** is a fully developed animal. □ *...a pair of adult birds.* ☒ ADJ **Adult** means relating to the time when you are an adult, or typical of adult people. [ADJ n] □ *I've lived most of my adult life in London.* ☐ ADJ You can describe things such as films or books **adult** when they deal with sex in a very clear and open way. □ *...an adult movie.* →see **age**

■ 가산명사 성인 □ 아버지가 된다는 것은 그도 이제 어른임을 뜻했다. ☑ 가산명사 다 자란 짐승 □ 다 자란 새 한 쌍 ☒ 형용사 성인의 □ 나는 성인이 된 후로 주로 런던에서 살았다. ☐ 형용사 성인용 □ 성인 영화

Thesaurus	adult의 참조어

N. grown-up, man, woman ■

adul|ter|ate /əˈdʌltəreɪt/ (**adulterates, adulterating, adulterated**) V-T If something such as food or drink **is adulterated**, someone has made its quality worse by adding water or cheaper products to it. [usu passive] □ *The food had been adulterated to increase its weight.*

타동사 이물질을 섞다, 품질을 떨어뜨리다 □ 그 식품은 중량을 늘리기 위해 이물질을 섞은 것이었다.

adul|tery /əˈdʌltəri/ N-UNCOUNT If a married person commits **adultery**, they have sex with someone who they are not married to. □ *She is going to divorce him on the grounds of adultery.*

불가산명사 간통 □ 그녀는 간통을 이유로 그와 이혼할 생각이다.

Word Link	hood ≈ state, condition : adulthood, childhood, manhood

adult|hood /əˈdʌlthʊd, BRIT ˈædʌlthʊd/ N-UNCOUNT **Adulthood** is the state of being an adult. □ *Few people nowadays are able to maintain friendships into adulthood.*

불가산명사 성인기 □ 요즘은 성인이 되어서까지 계속 우정을 유지하는 사람이 거의 없다.

ad|vance ♦♦◇ /ədˈvæns/ (**advances, advancing, advanced**) ■ V-I To **advance** means to move forward, often in order to attack someone. □ *Reports from Chad suggest that rebel forces are advancing on the capital.* □ *According to one report, the water is advancing at a rate of between 5cm and 7cm a day.* ☑ V-I To **advance** means to make progress, especially in your knowledge of something. □ *Now that medical*

■ 자동사 전진하다, 진격하다 □ 차드에서 들려오는 소식에 따르면 반군이 수도를 향해 진격하고 있다고 한다. □ 한 보도에 따르면 수위가 하루에 5─7센티미터씩 높아지고 있다고 한다. ☑ 자동사 진보하다 □ 이제 의학 기술이 현 수준까지 발전했으니

technology has advanced to its present state, more people are aware of how long one can be kept alive. →see also **advanced** 🔟 V-T If you **advance** someone a sum of money, you lend it to them, or pay it to them earlier than arranged. ❑ I advanced him some money, which he would repay on our way home. 🔟 N-COUNT An **advance** is money which is lent or paid to someone before they would normally receive it. ❑ She was paid a £100,000 advance for her next two novels. 🔟 V-T To **advance** an event, or the time or date of an event, means to bring it forward to an earlier time or date. ❑ Too much protein in the diet may advance the ageing process. 🔟 V-T If you **advance** a cause, interest, or claim, you support it and help to make it successful. ❑ When not producing art of his own, Oliver was busy advancing the work of others. 🔟 N-VAR An **advance** is a forward movement of people or vehicles, usually as part of a military operation. ❑ In an exercise designed to be as real as possible, they simulated an advance on enemy positions. 🔟 N-VAR An **advance** in a particular subject or activity is progress in understanding it or in doing it well. ❑ Air safety has not improved since the dramatic advances of the 1970s. 🔟 N-SING If something is an **advance on** what was previously available or done, it is better in some way. [usu a N on n] ❑ This could be an advance on the present situation. 🔟 ADJ **Advance** booking, notice, or warning is done or given before an event happens. [ADJ n] ❑ They don't normally give any advance notice about which building they're going to inspect. 🔟 PHRASE If you do something **in advance**, you do it before a particular date or event. ❑ The subject of the talk is announced a week in advance.

Thesaurus advance의 참조어

V.	improve 🔟
N.	allowance, credit, loan, retainer 🔟
ADV.	beforehand, previously 🔟
ADJ.	early, prior 🔟

Word Partnership advance의 연어

N.	cash advance 🔟
	advance a cause 🔟
	advance knowledge, advance notice, advance purchase, advance reservations 🔟
V.	advance and retreat 🔟
ADJ.	technological advance 🔟

---

ad|vanced ◆◇◇ /ædvænst/ 🔟 ADJ An **advanced** system, method, or design is modern and has been developed from an earlier version of the same thing. ❑ Many are afraid that, without more training or advanced technical skills, they'll lose their jobs. 🔟 ADJ A country that is **advanced** has reached a high level of industrial or technological development. ❑ Agricultural productivity remained low by comparison with advanced countries like the United States. 🔟 ADJ An **advanced** student has already learned the basic facts of a subject and is doing more difficult work. An **advanced** course of study is designed for such students. ❑ The course is suitable for beginners and advanced students. 🔟 ADJ Something that is at an **advanced** stage or level is at a late stage of development. ❑ "Medicare" is available to victims of advanced kidney disease.

Thesaurus advanced의 참조어

ADJ.	cutting-edge, foremost, latest, sophisticated 🔟

---

ad|vance|ment /ædvænsmənt/ (**advancements**) 🔟 N-UNCOUNT **Advancement** is progress in your job or in your social position. ❑ He cared little for social advancement. 🔟 N-VAR The **advancement of** something is the process of helping it to progress or the result of its progress. ❑ Her work for the advancement of the status of women in India was recognized by the whole nation.

ad|van|tage ◆◆◇ /ædvɑntɪdʒ, -væn-/ (**advantages**) 🔟 N-COUNT An **advantage** is something that puts you in a better position than other people. ❑ They are deliberately flouting the law in order to obtain an advantage over their competitors. 🔟 N-UNCOUNT **Advantage** is the state of being in a better position than others who are competing against you. ❑ Men have created a social and economic position of advantage for themselves over women. 🔟 N-COUNT An **advantage** is a way in which one thing is better than another. ❑ The great advantage of home-grown oranges is their magnificent flavor. 🔟 PHRASE If you **take advantage of** something, you make good use of it while you can. ❑ I intend to take full advantage of this trip to buy the things we need. 🔟 PHRASE If someone **takes advantage of** you, they treat you unfairly for their own benefit, especially when you are trying to be kind or to help them. ❑ She took advantage of him even after they were divorced. 🔟 PHRASE If you use or turn something **to your advantage**, you use it in order to benefit from it, especially when it might be expected to harm or damage you. ❑ The government has not been able to turn today's demonstration to its advantage.

Word Partnership advantage의 연어

V.	have an advantage 🔟
	take advantage of *something/someone* 🔟
	use to *someone's* advantage 🔟
ADJ.	competitive advantage, unfair advantage 🔟 🔟

많은 이들이 인간 생명이 얼마나 오랫동안 유지 가능한지 알고 있다. 🔟 타동사 빌려 주다; 선불하다 ❑ 내가 그에게 돈을 좀 빌려 줬고, 그는 우리가 집에 오는 길에 그 돈을 갚을 예정이었다. 🔟 가산명사 선금, 선불 ❑ 그녀는 차기 소설 두 편에 대해 선금으로 10만 파운드를 받았다. 🔟 타동사 앞당기다 ❑ 단백질이 너무 많은 식단은 노화를 앞당길 수도 있다. 🔟 타동사 주창하다 ❑ 올리버는 자신의 작품 활동은 하지 않으면서, 다른 이들의 작품을 홍보하느라 여념이 없었다. 🔟 가산명사 또는 불가산명사 진격, 진군 ❑ 그들은 최대한 실제 상황에 가깝게 계획된 훈련에서 모의로 적진을 진격했다. 🔟 가산명사 또는 불가산명사 진보, 발전 ❑ 항공 안전은 1970년대 급격히 발전한 이후로 지금까지 개선되지 않았다. 🔟 단수명사 발전, 개선 ❑ 이것은 현 상황에 대한 개선이 될 수 있다. 🔟 형용사 사전의 ❑ 그들은 보통 어떤 건물을 시찰할지에 관해 사전 통보는 하지 않는다. 🔟 구 사전에 ❑ 강연의 주제는 일주일 전에 발표된다.

🔟 형용사 발전된 ❑ 많은 사람들이 훈련을 더 받거나 고급 기술을 익히지 못하면 직장을 잃게 될지도 모른다고 걱정하고 있다. 🔟 형용사 선진의 ❑ 미국과 같은 선진국과 비교할 때 농업 생산성은 계속 저조한 수준에 머물러 있었다. 🔟 형용사 고급의 ❑ 이 과정은 입문반이나 고급반 학생에게 적합하다. 🔟 형용사 말기의 ❑ '메디케어'는 말기 신장병 환자에게 적용된다.

🔟 불가산명사 승진, 출세 ❑ 그는 사회적 출세에 별로 마음이 없었다. 🔟 가산명사 또는 불가산명사 증진, 향상 ❑ 인도 여성의 지위 향상을 위해 그녀가 해 온 일은 온 국민의 인정을 받았다.

🔟 가산명사 우위, 이점 ❑ 그들은 경쟁자들보다 우위를 점하기 위해 법을 교묘하게 어기고 있다. 🔟 불가산명사 유리한 입장 ❑ 남성은 여성보다 사회 경제적으로 유리한 입지를 창출해 왔다. 🔟 가산명사 장점 ❑ 집에서 가꾼 오렌지의 큰 장점은 풍부한 향미다. 🔟 구 활용하다 ❑ 이번 여행을 최대한 활용해서 우리가 필요한 것들을 살 생각이다. 🔟 구 이용하다 ❑ 그녀는 이혼 후에도 전 남편을 이용해 먹었다. 🔟 구 -에게 유리하게 ❑ 정부는 오늘 있었던 시위를 자기 쪽에 유리하게 이용하지 못했다.

ad|van|ta|geous /ˌædvənˈteɪdʒəs/ ADJ If something is **advantageous to** you, it is likely to benefit you. ❑ *Free exchange of goods was advantageous to all.*

형용사 유리한, 이로운 ❑ 상품의 자유로운 교역은 모두에게 유익했다.

ad|vent /ˈædvent/ N-UNCOUNT **The advent of** an important event, invention, or situation is the fact of it starting or coming into existence. [FORMAL] ❑ *The advent of the computer has brought this sort of task within the bounds of possibility.*

불가산명사 출현, 도래 [격식체] ❑ 컴퓨터의 출현으로 이 같은 종류의 작업이 가능한 일이 되었다.

ad|ven|ture /ædˈventʃər/ (**adventures**) ■ N-COUNT If someone has an **adventure**, they become involved in an unusual, exciting, and rather dangerous journey or series of events. ❑ *I set off for a new adventure in the United States on the first day of the new year.* ② N-UNCOUNT **Adventure** is excitement and willingness to do new, unusual, or rather dangerous things. ❑ *Their cultural backgrounds gave them a spirit of adventure.*

■ 가산명사 모험 ❑ 나는 새해 첫날 미국에서 맛보게 될 새로운 모험을 향해 출발했다. ② 불가산명사 모험심 ❑ 그들의 모험심은 문화적인 배경에서 나온 것이었다.

ad|ven|tur|ous /ædˈventʃərəs/ ■ ADJ Someone who is **adventurous** is willing to take risks and to try new methods. Something that is **adventurous** involves new things or ideas. ❑ *Warren was an adventurous businessman.* ② ADJ Someone who is **adventurous** is eager to visit new places and have new experiences. ❑ *He had always wanted an adventurous life in the tropics.*

■ 형용사 도전적인; 새로운 ❑ 워렌은 도전적인 사업가였다. ② 형용사 모험심이 강한 ❑ 그는 항상 열대 지방에서의 모험적인 삶을 꿈꿨었다.

ad|verb /ˈædvɜrb/ (**adverbs**) N-COUNT An **adverb** is a word such as "slowly," "now," "very," "politically," or "fortunately" which adds information about the action, event, or situation mentioned in a clause.

가산명사 부사

ad|ver|sar|ial /ˌædvərˈseəriəl/ ADJ If you describe something as **adversarial**, you mean that it involves two or more people or organizations who are opposing each other. [FORMAL] ❑ *In our country there is an adversarial relationship between government and business.*

형용사 적대적인 [격식체] ❑ 우리 나라에서는 정부와 재계 사이에 적대적인 관계가 형성되어 있다.

ad|ver|sary /ˈædvərseri, BRIT ˈædvəˈsəri/ (**adversaries**) N-COUNT Your **adversary** is someone you are competing with, or arguing or fighting against. ❑ *Elliott crossed the finish line just half a second behind his adversary.*

가산명사 상대자; 적 ❑ 엘리엇은 상대 선수보다 단 0.5초 늦게 결승선을 통과했다.

ad|verse /ˈædvɜrs, BRIT ˈædvɜːˈs/ ADJ **Adverse** decisions, conditions, or effects are unfavorable to you. ❑ *The police said Mr. Hadfield's decision would have no adverse effect on the progress of the investigation.* ● **ad|verse|ly** ADV [ADV with v] ❑ *Price changes must not adversely affect the living standards of the people.*

형용사 불리한 ❑ 경찰은 해드필드 씨의 결정이 수사 진행에 불리한 영향을 전혀 주지 않을 것이라고 말했다. ● 불리하게 부사 ❑ 가격 변동이 서민들의 생활수준에 악영향을 주어서는 안 된다.

ad|ver|sity /ædˈvɜrsiti/ (**adversities**) N-VAR **Adversity** is a very difficult or unfavorable situation. ❑ *He showed courage in adversity.*

가산명사 또는 불가산명사 역경 ❑ 그는 역경 속에서 용기를 보여 줬다.

ad|vert /ˈædvɜrt/ (**adverts**) N-COUNT An **advert** is an announcement in a newspaper, on television, or on a poster about something such as a product, event, or job. [BRIT; AM **ad**] ❑ *I saw an advert for a transport job with a large steel and engineering company.*

가산명사 광고 [영국영어; 미국영어 ad] ❑ 나는 대형 철강 회사에서 운송 직원을 한 명 채용한다는 광고를 보았다.

ad|ver|tise ♦◇◇ /ˈædvərtaɪz/ (**advertises, advertising, advertised**) ■ V-T/V-I If you **advertise** something such as a product, an event, or a job, you tell people about it in newspapers, on television, or on posters in order to encourage them to buy the product, go to the event, or apply for the job. ❑ *The players can advertise baked beans, but not rugby boots.* ❑ *In 1991, the house was advertised for sale at $49,000.* ② V-I If you **advertise for** someone to do something for you, for example to work for you or share your accommodation, you announce it in a newspaper, on television, or on a bulletin board. ❑ *We advertised for staff in a local newspaper.* →see also **advertising**

■ 타동사/자동사 광고하다 ❑ 선수들이 콩 통조림 광고는 찍을 수 있지만, 럭비화 광고는 안 된다. ❑ 1991년에 그 집은 4만 9천 달러에 내놨었다. ② 자동사 광고하여 구하다 ❑ 우리는 지역 신문에 구인 광고를 냈다.

ad|ver|tise|ment /ˌædvərˈtaɪzmənt/ (**advertisements**) ■ N-COUNT An **advertisement** is an announcement in a newspaper, on television, or on a poster about something such as a product, event, or job. [WRITTEN] ❑ *Miss Parrish recently placed an advertisement in the local newspaper.* ② N-COUNT If you say that an example of something is **an advertisement for** that thing in general, you mean that it shows how good that thing is. ❑ *The Treviso team were an effective advertisement for the improving state of Italian club rugby.* →see **advertising**

■ 가산명사 광고 [문어체] ❑ 패리쉬 씨가 최근 지역 신문에 광고를 냈다. ② 가산명사 대표적인 예 ❑ 트레비소 팀은 이탈리아 정규 럭비의 수준이 향상되고 있음을 단적으로 보여 주었다.

ad|ver|tis|er /ˈædvərtaɪzər/ (**advertisers**) N-COUNT An **advertiser** is a person or company that pays for a product, event, or job to be advertised in a newspaper, on television, or on a poster. ❑ *When will advertisers stop bombarding women with images of unattainable beauty?*

가산명사 광고주 ❑ 언제쯤 광고주들이 여성들에게 허황된 아름다움의 이미지를 쏟아 붓는 것을 그만둘까?

ad|ver|tis|ing /ˈædvərtaɪzɪŋ/ N-UNCOUNT **Advertising** is the activity of creating advertisements and making sure people see them. ❑ *I work in advertising.* →see Word Web: **advertising**

불가산명사 광고업 ❑ 저는 광고업에 종사합니다.

ad|ver|tis|ing agen|cy (**advertising agencies**) N-COUNT An **advertising agency** is a company whose business is to create advertisements for other companies or organizations. ❑ *Advertising agencies are losing their once-powerful grip on brand marketing.* →see **advertising**

가산명사 광고 대행사 ❑ 한때는 막강했던 광고 대행들의 브랜드 마케팅 장악력이 점점 미약해지고 있다.

Word Web   advertising

It's impossible to avoid **advertisements**. In our homes, **newspaper**, **magazine**, and **television** ads compete for our attention. **Posters**, **billboards**, and **flyers** greet us the moment we walk out the door. **Advertising agencies** stay busy thinking up new ways to get our attention. We have company **logos** on our clothes. Our email is full of **spam**, and pop-ups slow us down as we surf the Web. **Product placements** sneak into movies and TV shows. "Ad wrapping" turns cars into moving signboards. Advertisers have even tried **subliminal** advertising in TV **commercials**. It's no wonder that this is called the **consumer** age.

ad|ver|tis|ing cam|paign (advertising campaigns) N-COUNT An **advertising campaign** is a planned series of advertisements. ❑ *The Government has launched a mass advertising campaign to reduce the nation's electricity consumption.*

가산명사 홍보 활동 ❑ 정부가 전국적으로 전력 소비를 줄이기 위한 대대적인 홍보 활동에 들어갔다.

ad|ver|to|ri|al /ædvɜrtɔriəl/ (advertorials) N-VAR An **advertorial** is an advertisement that uses the style of newspaper or magazine articles or television documentary programs, so that it appears to be giving facts and not trying to sell a product. ❑ *Riverford could support this with press releases and advertorials in specialist health and food-related media.*

가산명사 또는 불가산명사 기사형 광고 ❑ 리버포드가 건강 및 식품 관련 전문 매체에 보도 자료도 보내고 기사형 광고도 내서 이를 후원할 수 있을 것이다.

ad|vice ♦♦◇ /ædvaɪs/ **1** N-UNCOUNT If you give someone **advice**, you tell them what you think they should do in a particular situation. ❑ *Don't be afraid to ask for advice about ordering the meal.* ❑ *Take my advice and stay away from him!* **2** PHRASE If you **take advice** or **take legal advice**, you ask a lawyer for his or her professional opinion on a situation. [mainly BRIT, FORMAL] ❑ *He requested a two-week adjournment to prepare the case and take further advice on the matter.*

1 불가산명사 조언, 충고 ❑ 식사 주문에 관해 조언이 필요하다면 주저 말고 이야기하세요. ❑ 내 말대로 그 사람 주위에 얼씬도 하지 마! **2** 구 자문을 구하다 [주로 영국영어, 격식체] ❑ 그는 변론을 준비하고 이번 사안에 관한 추가 자문을 구하기 위해 2주 동안의 휴정을 요청했다.

> Note that **advice** is an uncount noun. You can say **a piece of advice** or **some advice**, but you cannot say "an advice" or "advices". Do not confuse **advice** and **advise**. **Advise** is the verb that is connected with **advice**.

> advice는 불가산명사라는 점에 유의하라. 'a piece of advice' 또는 'some advice'라고는 할 수 있지만, 'an advice' 또는 'advices'라고는 할 수 없다. advice와 advise를 혼동하지 않도록 하라. advise는 advice와 관련된 동사이다.

Thesaurus	advice의 참조어
N.	counsel, guidance, help, information, input, opinion, recommendation, suggestion **1**

Word Partnership	advice의 연어
PREP.	**against** advice **1**
ADJ.	**bad/good** advice **1**
	expert advice **1**
V.	**ask for** advice, **give** advice, **need some** advice **1**
	take advice **1 2**

ad|vice col|umn|ist (advice columnists) N-COUNT An **advice columnist** is a person who writes a column in a newspaper or magazine in which they reply to readers who have written to them for advice on their personal problems. [AM; BRIT **agony aunt**] ❑ *...the advice columnist at the local paper.*

가산명사 고민상담 칼럼리스트 [미국영어; 영국영어 agony aunt] ❑ 지역 신문의 고민상담 칼럼리스트

ad|vis|able /ædvaɪzəbᵊl/ ADJ If you tell someone that it is **advisable to** do something, you are suggesting that they should do it, because it is sensible or is likely to achieve the result they want. [FORMAL] [v-link ADJ, oft it v-link ADJ to-inf] ❑ *Because of the popularity of the region, it is advisable to book hotels or camp sites in advance.*

형용사 타당한, 현명한 [격식체] ❑ 이 지역은 인기가 있기 때문에, 호텔이나 야영지를 미리 예약하는 것이 좋다.

ad|vise ♦◇◇ /ædvaɪz/ (advises, advising, advised) **1** V-T/V-I If you **advise** someone **to** do something, you tell them what you think they should do. ❑ *The minister advised him to leave as soon as possible.* ❑ *I would strongly advise against it.* **2** V-T/V-I If an expert **advises** people **on** a particular subject, he or she gives them help and information on that subject. ❑ *...an officer who advises undergraduates from London's City University on money matters.*

1 타동사/자동사 조언하다, 충고하다 ❑ 장관은 그에게 가능한 빠른 시일 내에 떠나라고 충고했다. ❑ 절대 그렇게 하지 말라고 충고하고 싶군요. **2** 타동사/자동사 조언하다 ❑ 런던 시티 대학 학부생들을 위한 금전 문제 상담 담당관

> Do not confuse **advise** and **advice**. **Advice** is the noun that is connected with the verb **advise**. If you **advise** someone to do something, you tell them what you think they should do. If you **suggest** something, however, you mention it as an idea or plan for someone to think about, perhaps together with other ideas or plans. You can also **suggest** doing something, or **suggest** that someone does something. ❑ *Your bank manager will probably suggest a loan... I suggested inviting Jim... I suggest that you leave this to me.*

> advise와 advice를 혼동하지 않도록 하라. advice는 advise와 관련된 명사이다. 당신이 누군가에게 무엇을 하도록 advise하면, 그가 무엇을 해야 한다고 당신이 생각하는 바를 말하는 것이다. 그러나 당신이 무엇을 suggest하면, 그것은 다른 사람이 생각해 볼 아이디어나 계획으로 언급하는 것이다. 무엇을 하는 것을 suggest할 수도 있고, 누가 무엇을 할 것을 suggest할 수도 있다. ❑ 당신의 거래 은행 지점장이 아마 대출을 제안할 것이다... 나는 짐을 초대할 것을 제안했다... 당신이 이걸 내게 맡길 것을 제안합니다.

Word Partnership	advise의 연어
PREP.	advise **against** **1**
N.	advise *someone* to **1**
ADV.	**strongly** advise **1**

ad|vis|er ♦◇◇ /ædvaɪzər/ (advisers) also advisor N-COUNT An **adviser** is an expert whose job is to give advice to another person or to a group of people. ❑ *In Washington, the President and his advisers spent the day in meetings.*

가산명사 고문, 자문관 ❑ 워싱턴에서 대통령과 대통령 자문위원들이 하루 종일 회의를 했다.

ad|vi|so|ry /ædvaɪzəri/ (advisories) **1** ADJ An **advisory** group regularly gives suggestions and help to people or organizations, especially about a particular subject or area of activity. [FORMAL] ❑ *...members of the advisory committee on the safety of nuclear installations.* **2** N-COUNT An **advisory** is an official announcement or report that warns people about bad weather, diseases, or other dangers or problems. [AM] ❑ *26 states have issued health advisories.*

1 형용사 자문의, 고문의 [격식체] ❑ 핵시설 안전에 관한 자문 위원회 위원들 **2** 가산명사 주의보 [미국영어] ❑ 26개 주가 건강 주의보를 발령한 상태이다.

ad|vo|ca|cy /ædvəkəsi/ **1** N-SING Someone's **advocacy of** a particular action or plan is their act of recommending it publicly. [FORMAL] ❑ *I support your advocacy of free trade.* **2** N-UNCOUNT An **advocacy** group or organization is one that tries to influence the decisions of a government or other authority. [AM] ❑ *Consumer advocacy groups are not so enthusiastic about removing restrictions on the telephone companies.*

1 단수명사 주장, 지지 [격식체] ❑ 저는 당신의 자유무역 주장을 지지합니다. **2** 불가산명사 옹호 [미국영어] ❑ 소비자 보호 단체들은 전화 회사에 대한 제재 철폐에 그다지 열성적이지 않다.

Word Link	voc ≈ speaking: advocate, vocabulary, vocal

ad|vo|cate ♦◇◇ (advocates, advocating, advocated)

> The verb is pronounced /ædvəkeɪt/. The noun is pronounced /ædvəkɪt/.

동사는 /ædvəkeɪt/으로 발음되고, 명사는 /ædvəkɪt/으로 발음된다.

1 V-T If you **advocate** a particular action or plan, you recommend it publicly. [FORMAL] ❑ *Mr. Williams is a conservative who advocates fewer government controls on*

1 타동사 주장하다, 지지하다 [격식체] ❑ 윌리엄 씨는 기업에 대한 정부 통제 완화를 주장하는 보수

business. ② N-COUNT An **advocate of** a particular action or plan is someone who recommends it publicly. [FORMAL] ❑ *He was a strong advocate of free market policies and a multi-party system.* ③ N-COUNT An **advocate** is a lawyer who speaks in favor of someone or defends them in a court of law. →see **lawyer** [LEGAL] ④ N-COUNT An **advocate for** a particular group is a person who works for the interests of that group. [AM] ❑ *...advocates for the homeless.*

인사이다. ② 가산명사 주장자 [격식체] ❑ 그는 자유시장 정책 및 다당제의 열렬한 주창자였다. ③ 가산명사 변호사 [법률] ④ 가산명사 대변자 [미국영어] ❑ 노숙자들의 대변자

Word Partnership		advocate의 연어
PREP.	advocate **for** *something/someone*, advocate **of** *something* ②	
ADJ.	**leading** advocate, **strong** advocate ④	

aerial /ɛəriəl/ (**aerials**) ① ADJ You talk about **aerial** attacks and **aerial** photographs to indicate that people or things on the ground are attacked or photographed by people in airplanes. [ADJ n] ❑ *Weeks of aerial bombardment had destroyed factories and highways.* ② N-COUNT An **aerial** is a device that receives television or radio signals. [BRIT; AM **antenna**] ❑ *...the radio aerials of taxis and cars.*

① 형용사 공중의, 항공기에 의한 ❑ 몇 주간 계속된 공습으로 공장과 고속도로가 파괴되어 있었다. ② 가산명사 안테나 [영국영어; 미국영어 antenna] ❑ 택시와 승용차의 무선 안테나

aerobics /ɛəroʊbɪks/ N-UNCOUNT **Aerobics** is a form of exercise which increases the amount of oxygen in your blood, and strengthens your heart and lungs. The verb that follows **aerobics** may be either singular or plural. ❑ *I'd like to join an aerobics class to improve my fitness.*

불가산명사 에어로빅 ❑ 나는 체력 단련을 위해 에어로빅 교실에 다녔으면 해요.

aerodynamic /ɛəroʊdaɪnæmɪk/ ADJ If something such as a car has an **aerodynamic** shape or design, it goes faster and uses less fuel than other cars because the air passes over it more easily. ❑ *The secret of the machine lies in the aerodynamic shape of the one-piece, carbon-fibre frame.*

형용사 기체역학적 ❑ 이 기계의 비법은 이음매 없이 탄소 섬유로 뼈대를 만들어 기체역학적으로 설계했다는 점에 있다.

aeroplane /ɛərəpleɪn/ (**aeroplanes**) N-COUNT An **aeroplane** is a vehicle with wings and one or more engines that enable it to fly through the air. [BRIT; AM **airplane**]

가산명사 비행기 [영국영어; 미국영어 airplane]

aerosol /ɛərəsɒl, BRIT ɛərəsɒl/ (**aerosols**) N-COUNT An **aerosol** is a small container in which a liquid such as paint or deodorant is kept under pressure. When you press a button, the liquid is forced out as a fine spray or foam.

가산명사 에어로졸, 분무기

aesthetic /ɛsθɛtɪk, BRIT iːsθɛtɪk/ [AM also **esthetic**] ADJ **Aesthetic** is used to talk about beauty or art, and people's appreciation of beautiful things. ❑ *...products chosen for their aesthetic appeal as well as their durability and quality.* ● N-SING The **aesthetic** of a work of art is its aesthetic quality. ❑ *He responded very strongly to the aesthetic of this particular work.* ● **aesthetically** /ɛsθɛtɪkli, BRIT iːsθɛtɪkli/ ADV *A statue which is aesthetically pleasing to one person, however, may be repulsive to another.*

[미국영어 esthetic] 형용사 심미적인, 미학의 ❑ 내구성과 품질은 물론 심미적인 매력 때문에 선택한 제품들 ● 단수명사 미적인 측면 ❑ 그는 특별히 작품의 미적인 측면에 매우 강한 반응을 보였다. ● 미학적으로 부사 ❑ 하지만 한 사람에게 아름답게 느껴지는 조상(彫像)이 다른 사람에게는 혐오감을 줄 수도 있다.

affable /æfəbl/ ADJ Someone who is **affable** is pleasant and friendly. ❑ *Mr. Brooke is an extremely affable and approachable man.*

형용사 상냥한 ❑ 브루크 씨는 매우 상냥하고 사귀기 쉬운 사람이다.

affair ◆◇◇ /əfɛər/ (**affairs**) ① N-SING If an event or a series of events has been mentioned and you want to talk about it again, you can refer to it as **the affair**. ❑ *The government has mishandled the whole affair.* ② N-SING You can refer to an important or interesting event or situation as "**the... affair**." [MAINLY JOURNALISM] ❑ *...the damage caused to the CIA and FBI in the aftermath of the Watergate affair.* ③ N-SING You can describe the main quality of an event by saying that it is a particular kind of **affair**. ❑ *Michael said that his planned 10-day visit would be a purely private affair.* ④ N-COUNT If two people who are not married to each other have an **affair**, they have a sexual relationship. ❑ *Married male supervisors were carrying on affairs with female subordinates in the office.* →see also **love affair** ⑤ N-PLURAL You can use **affairs** to refer to all the important facts or activities that are connected with a particular subject. ❑ *He does not want to interfere in the internal affairs of another country.* →see also **current affairs, state of affairs** ⑥ N-PLURAL Your **affairs** are all the matters connected with your life which you consider to be private and normally deal with yourself. ❑ *The unexpectedness of my father's death meant that his affairs were not entirely in order.*

① 단수명사 사건, 일 ❑ 정부가 이번 일을 전반적으로 잘못 처리했다. ② 단수명사 사건, 스캔들 [주로 언론] ❑ 워터게이트 사건 여파로 시아이에이와 에프비아이에 가해진 손상 ③ 단수명사 것 ❑ 마이클은 자신이 계획한 열흘 일정은 방문이 순전히 개인적인 것이라고 밝혔다. ④ 가산명사 정사, 정분 ❑ 유부남 상사들이 같은 사무실의 부하 여직원들과 불륜 관계를 맺고 있었다. ⑤ 복수명사 사항, 업무 ❑ 그는 다른 국가의 내정에 개입하는 것을 원치 않는다. ⑥ 복수명사 개인 용무 ❑ 아버지께서 갑작스럽게 돌아가시는 바람에 아버지께서 하시던 일들이 약간 뒤죽박죽이 되었다.

affect ◆◆◇ /əfɛkt/ (**affects, affecting, affected**) ① V-T If something **affects** a person or thing, it influences them or causes them to change in some way. ❑ *Nicotine adversely affects the functioning of the heart and arteries.* ❑ *More than seven million people have been affected by drought.* ② V-T If a disease **affects** someone, it causes them to become ill. ❑ *Arthritis is a crippling disease which affects people all over the world.* ③ V-T If something or someone **affects** you, they make you feel a strong emotion, especially sadness or pity. ❑ *If Jim had been more independent, the divorce would not have affected him as deeply.*

① 타동사 영향을 미치다 ❑ 니코틴은 심장과 동맥의 기능에 악영향을 미친다. ❑ 가뭄으로 7백만 명 이상이 피해를 보았다. ② 타동사 병들게 하다 ❑ 관절염은 전세계적으로 나타나는 퇴행성 질환이다. ③ 타동사 마음을 흔들어 놓다 ❑ 짐이 좀더 독립심이 강했더라면, 이혼이 그에게 그렇게 큰 충격을 주지는 않았을 것이다.

Note that the noun that comes from **affect** is **effect**. You can say that something **affects** you, or that it has an **effect** on you. ❑ *...the effect that noise has on people in factories.* You can also talk about the **effect** of something. ❑ *...the effect of the anesthetic.* **Effect** can also be a verb. If you **effect** something such as a change or a repair, you make it happen or do it. This is a fairly formal word. ❑ *She had effected a few hasty repairs.*

affect에서 온 명사는 effect이다. 어떤 것이 당신에게 영향을 준다고 할 때는 'something affects you'라고 하거나 'it has an effect on you'라고 할 수 있다. ❑ ...공장에서 소음이 사람들에게 미치는 영향. 어떤 것의 effect에 대해서 말할 수도 있다. ❑ ...마취제의 효과. effect는 동사가 될 수도 있다. 변경이나 수리 같은 것을 effect하면, 변경이 일어나게 하거나 수리를 하는 것이다. 이 단어는 상당히 격식적인 말이다. ❑ 그녀는 서둘러 몇 가지 수리를 했었다.

affection /əfɛkʃən/ (**affections**) ① N-UNCOUNT If you regard someone or something with **affection**, you like them and are fond of them. ❑ *She thought of him with affection.* ② N-PLURAL Your **affections** are your feelings of love and fondness for someone. ❑ *The distant object of his affections is Caroline.* →see **love**

① 불가산명사 애정 ❑ 그녀는 애정을 갖고 그를 생각했다. ② 복수명사 사랑, 애착 ❑ 그가 거의 애착을 못 느끼는 사람이 캐럴라인이다.

Word Link	ate ≈ filled with : affection**ate**, compassion**ate**, consider**ate**

affectionate /əfɛkʃənɪt/ ADJ If you are **affectionate**, you show your love or fondness for another person in the way that you behave toward them. ❑ *They seemed devoted to each other and were openly affectionate.* ● **affectionately** ADV [ADV with v] ❑ *He looked affectionately at his niece.*

형용사 애정어린 ❑ 그들은 서로에게 헌신적으로 보였으며 애정 표현도도 잘했다. ● 사랑스럽게 부사 ❑ 그는 조카를 사랑스런 눈으로 바라보았다.

af|fi|da|vit /ˌæfɪˈdeɪvɪt/ (affidavits) N-COUNT An affidavit is a written statement which you swear is true and which may be used as evidence in a court of law. [LEGAL] ❑ In his sworn affidavit, Roche outlined a history of actions against him by the church.

af|fili|ate (affiliates, affiliating, affiliated)

The noun is pronounced /əˈfɪliɪt/. The verb is pronounced /əˈfɪlieɪt/.

■ N-COUNT An affiliate is an organization which is officially connected with another, larger organization or is a member of it. [FORMAL] ❑ The World Chess Federation has affiliates in around 120 countries. ■ V-I If an organization affiliates with another larger organization, it forms a close connection with the larger organization or becomes a member of it. [FORMAL] ❑ He wanted to affiliate with a U.S. firm because he needed expert advice in legal affairs.

af|filia|tion /əˌfɪliˈeɪʃ°n/ (affiliations) N-VAR If one group has an affiliation with another group, it has a close or official connection with it. [FORMAL] ❑ The group has no affiliation to any political party.

af|fin|ity /əˈfɪnɪti/ (affinities) N-SING If you have an affinity with someone or something, you feel that you are similar to them or that you know and understand them very well. ❑ He has a close affinity with the landscape he knew when he was growing up.

Word Link   firm ≈ making strong : affirm, confirm, infirm

af|firm /əˈfɜrm/ (affirms, affirming, affirmed) ■ V-T If you affirm that something is true or that something exists, you state firmly and publicly that it is true or exists. [FORMAL] ❑ The European Community has repeatedly affirmed that it's in agreement with the Americans on this point. ❑ ...a speech in which he affirmed a commitment to lower taxes. ● af|fir|ma|tion /ˌæfərˈmeɪʃ°n/ (affirmations) N-VAR ❑ After the meeting, the ministers issued a robust affirmation of their faith in the European Monetary System. ■ V-T If an event affirms something, it shows that it is true or exists. [FORMAL] ❑ Everything I had accomplished seemed to affirm that opinion. ● af|fir|ma|tion N-UNCOUNT [also a N] ❑ The high turnout was an eloquent affirmation of the importance that the voters attached to the election.

af|firma|tive /əˈfɜrmətɪv/ ■ ADJ An affirmative word or gesture indicates that you agree with what someone has said or that the answer to a question is "yes." [FORMAL] ❑ Haig was desperately eager for an affirmative answer. ■ PHRASE If you reply to a question in the affirmative, you say "yes" or make a gesture that means "yes." [FORMAL] ❑ He asked me if I was ready. I answered in the affirmative. ■ ADJ In grammar, an affirmative clause is positive and does not contain a negative word.

af|firma|tive ac|tion N-UNCOUNT Affirmative action is the policy of giving jobs and other opportunities to members of groups such as racial minorities or women who might not otherwise have them. [AM; BRIT positive discrimination] ❑ Despite nearly a decade of affirmative action since apartheid was dismantled, few black sportsmen have reached the top level.

af|fix /ˈæfɪks/ (affixes) N-COUNT An affix is a letter or group of letters, for example "un-" or "-y," which is added to either the beginning or the end of a word to form a different word with a different meaning. For example, "un-" is added to "kind" to form "unkind." Compare prefix and suffix.

af|flict /əˈflɪkt/ (afflicts, afflicting, afflicted) V-T If you are afflicted by pain, illness, or disaster, it affects you badly and makes you suffer. [FORMAL] ❑ Italy has been afflicted by political corruption for decades. ❑ There are two main problems which afflict people with hearing impairments.

Word Link   flict ≈ striking : affliction, conflict, inflict

af|flic|tion /əˈflɪkʃ°n/ (afflictions) N-VAR An affliction is something which causes physical or mental suffering. [FORMAL] ❑ Hay fever is an affliction which arrives at an early age.

af|flu|ence /ˈæfluəns/ N-UNCOUNT Affluence is the state of having a lot of money or a high standard of living. [FORMAL] ❑ The postwar era was one of new affluence for the working class.

af|flu|ent /ˈæfluənt/ ADJ If you are affluent, you have a lot of money. ❑ Cigarette smoking used to be commoner among affluent people. ● N-PLURAL The affluent are people who are affluent. ❑ The diet of the affluent has not changed much over the decades.

af|ford ♦◇◇ /əˈfɔrd/ (affords, affording, afforded) ■ V-T If you cannot afford something, you do not have enough money to pay for it. ❑ My parents can't even afford a new refrigerator. ❑ The arts should be available to more people at prices they can afford. ■ V-T If you say that you cannot afford to do something or allow it to happen, you mean that you must not do it or must prevent it from happening because it would be harmful or embarrassing to you. ❑ We can't afford to wait.

Word Partnership   afford의 연어

V.	afford to buy/pay ■	
	can/could afford, can't/couldn't afford ■ ■	
	afford to lose ■	
ADJ.	able/unable to afford ■ ■	

af|ford|able /əˈfɔrdəb°l/ ADJ If something is affordable, most people have enough money to buy it. ❑ ...the availability of affordable housing.

가산명사 진술서 [법률] ❑ 선서 진술서를 통해 로쉬는 교회가 자신에게 취한 불리한 조치들을 간략하게 설명했다.

명사는 /əˈfɪliɪt/으로, 동사는 /əˈfɪlieɪt/으로 발음된다.

■ 가산명사 지부, 가맹 단체 [격식체] ❑ 세계 체스 연맹은 120여 개국에 지부를 두고 있다. ■ 자동사 가맹하다, 제휴하다 [격식체] ❑ 그는 법률문제에 전문적 조언이 필요해서 미국 회사와 제휴하고 싶어 했다.

가산명사 또는 불가산명사 연계 [격식체] ❑ 그 단체는 어떤 정당과도 연계되어 있지 않다.

단수명사 친근감 ❑ 그는 유년 시절에 알던 풍경에 강한 친근감을 느낀다.

■ 타동사 단언하다 [격식체] ❑ 유럽 공동체는 이 점에 관해선 미국에 동의한다고 거듭 확인했다. ❑ 그가 세금 삭감 의지를 분명히 한 연설 ● 확인 가산명사 또는 불가산명사 ❑ 회담 후 장관들은 유럽 통화 제도에 대한 확실한 신념을 담은 성명서를 냈다. ■ 타동사 확인하다 [격식체] ❑ 내가 이뤘던 모든 일들이 그 의견이 옳다는 것을 확인해 주는 것 같았다. ● 확인 불가산명사 ❑ 높은 투표율은 유권자들이 이번 선거에 부여하는 중요성을 단적으로 확인시켜 주었다.

■ 형용사 긍정적인 [격식체] ❑ 헤이그는 긍정적인 대답이 나오기를 간절히 바랐다. ■ 구 긍정적으로 [격식체] ❑ 그가 나에게 준비됐냐고 물었고 나는 그렇다고 대답했다. ■ 형용사 긍정문의

불가산명사 차별철폐 조치 [미국영어; 영국영어 positive discrimination] ❑ 인종 차별 철폐 이후로 근 십 년간의 차별 철폐 조치에도 불구하고, 극소수의 흑인 운동선수들만 상위권에 진입했다.

가산명사 접사

타동사 괴롭히다 [격식체] ❑ 이탈리아는 수십 년간 정치 부패에 시달려 왔다. ❑ 청각 장애가 있는 사람들을 괴롭히는 문제에는 크게 두 가지가 있다.

가산명사 또는 불가산명사 고통, 질환 [격식체] ❑ 건초열은 어린 나이에 발생하는 질환이다.

불가산명사 부유 [격식체] ❑ 전후 시대는 노동자 계층에게 새로운 부의 시대였다.

형용사 부유한 ❑ 예전에는 흡연이 부유한 사람들 사이에서 더 흔했다. ● 복수명사 부유층 ❑ 부유층의 식단은 수십 년간 크게 바뀌지 않았다.

■ 타동사 여유가 있다 ❑ 우리 부모님은 냉장고를 새로 살 여유조차 없다. ❑ 예술 작품은 더 많은 사람들이 그들이 감당할 수 있는 가격으로 이용할 수 있어야 한다. ■ 타동사 ~ 할 수 있는 입장이다 ❑ 우리가 더 이상 기다릴 수 없다.

형용사 감당할 수 있는 ❑ 구입할 수 있는 가격의 주택 구입 가능성

af|front /əfrʌnt/ (**affronts, affronting, affronted**) **1** V-T If something **affronts** you, you feel insulted and hurt because of it. [FORMAL] ❑ *One recent example, which particularly affronted Kasparov, was at the European team championship in Hungary.* **2** N-COUNT If something is an **affront to** you, it is an obvious insult to you. ❑ *It's an affront to human dignity to keep someone alive like this.*

1 타동사 모욕감을 주다 [격식체] ❑ 카스파로프에게 특히 모욕감을 주었던 최근의 사례는 헝가리에서 열렸던 유럽 팀 대항전이었다. **2** 가산명사 모욕 ❑ 이런 식으로 사람의 생명을 유지시키는 것은 인간의 존엄성을 모욕하는 일이다.

afield /əfild/ PHRASE **Further afield** or **farther afield** means in places or areas other than the nearest or most obvious one. ❑ *They enjoy participating in a wide variety of activities, both locally and further afield.*

구 멀리 떨어져 ❑ 그들은 지역 사회와 그보다 멀리 떨어진 곳에서 대단히 다양한 활동에 참여하는 것을 즐긴다.

afloat /əflout/ **1** ADV If someone or something is **afloat**, they remain partly above the surface of water and do not sink. ❑ *They talked modestly of their valiant efforts to keep the tanker afloat.* **2** ADV If a person, business, or country stays **afloat** or is kept **afloat**, they have just enough money to pay their debts and continue operating. [BUSINESS] ❑ *A number of efforts were being made to keep the company afloat.*

1 부사 떠서 ❑ 그들은 자신들이 유조선 침몰을 막기 위해 행한 용감무쌍한 노력에 대해 겸손하게 말했다. **2** 부사 파산하지 않고 [경제] ❑ 회사의 파산을 막기 위해 다양한 노력이 이루어지고 있었다.

afoot /əfut/ ADJ If you say that a plan or scheme is **afoot**, it is already happening or being planned, but you do not know much about it. [v-link ADJ] ❑ *Everybody knew that something awful was afoot.*

형용사 진행 중인 ❑ 모든 사람들이 뭔가 끔찍한 일이 일어나고 있다는 것을 알았다.

afore|men|tioned /əfɔrmɛnʃnd/ ADJ If you refer to **the aforementioned** person or subject, you mean the person or subject that has already been mentioned. [FORMAL] [det ADJ, usu *the* ADJ n] ❑ *This is the draft of a declaration that will be issued at the end of the aforementioned UN conference.*

형용사 앞서 말한 [격식체] ❑ 이는 앞서 말한 유엔 회의 끝에 발표될 선언문의 초안이다.

afore|said /əfɔrsɛd/ ADJ **Aforesaid** means the same as **aforementioned**. [FORMAL] [det ADJ, usu *the* ADJ n] ❑ *...the aforesaid organizations and institutions.*

형용사 앞서 말한 [격식체] ❑ 앞에 언급한 기관 및 기구

afraid ♦♢♢ /əfreɪd/ **1** ADJ If you are **afraid of** someone or **afraid to** do something, you are frightened because you think that something very unpleasant is going to happen to you. [v-link ADJ, oft ADJ of n, ADJ to-inf] ❑ *She did not seem at all afraid.* ❑ *I was afraid of the other boys.* **2** ADJ If you are **afraid for** someone else, you are worried that something horrible is going to happen to them. [v-link ADJ, usu ADJ for n] ❑ *She's afraid for her family in Somalia.* **3** ADJ If you are **afraid** that something unpleasant will happen, you are worried that it may happen and you want to avoid it. [v-link ADJ, ADJ that, ADJ of -ing, ADJ to-inf] ❑ *I was afraid that nobody would believe me.* **4** PHRASE If you want to apologize to someone or to disagree with them in a polite way, you can say **I'm afraid**. [SPOKEN, POLITENESS] ❑ *We don't have anything like that, I'm afraid.*

1 형용사 두려운 ❑ 그녀는 전혀 두려워하는 것 같지 않았다. ❑ 나는 다른 남자 아이들이 두려웠다. **2** 형용사 걱정하는 ❑ 그녀는 소말리아에 있는 가족을 걱정하고 있다. **3** 형용사 걱정하는 ❑ 나는 아무도 날 믿지 않을까봐 걱정이었다. **4** 구 죄송하지만 [구어체, 공손체] ❑ 죄송하지만, 저희는 그런 물건은 하나도 없어요.

Thesaurus	afraid의 참조어
ADJ.	alarmed, fearful, frightened, petrified, scared, worried **1**-**3**

Word Partnership	afraid의 연어
PREP.	afraid of *someone/something* **1**
V.	be afraid **1**-**3**

afresh /əfrɛʃ/ ADV If you do something **afresh**, you do it again in a different way. [ADV after v] ❑ *They believe that the only hope for the French left is to start afresh.*

부사 새로이 ❑ 그들은 프랑스 좌익에게 있어 유일한 희망은 새롭게 시작하는 것이라고 믿는다.

African-American /æfrɪkən əmɛrɪkən/ (**African-Americans**) N-COUNT **African-Americans** are black people living in the United States who are descended from families that originally came from Africa. ❑ *Today African-Americans are 12 percent of the population.* ● ADJ **African-American** is also an adjective. ❑ *...a group of African-American community leaders.*

가산명사 미국 흑인 ❑ 오늘날 흑인이 미국 인구의 12퍼센트를 차지한다. ● 형용사 미국 흑인의 ❑ 미국 흑인 사회 지도자 단체

The term **African-American** is used in the USA to describe people whose ancestors came from Africa. Some people prefer to use the term **black**.

미국에서 African-American(아프리카계 미국인)이란 말은 조상이 아프리카 출신인 사람들을 일컬을 때 사용된다. 어떤 사람들은 black(흑인)이란 말을 선호하기도 한다.

aft /æft/ ADV If you go **aft** in a boat or plane, you go to the back of it. If you are **aft**, you are in the back. ❑ *Clark shook hands with the pilot and walked aft to find his way off the ship.*

부사 (배나 비행기의) 뒤쪽에 ❑ 클라크는 도선사와 악수를 하고 배에서 내리는 길을 찾아 선미로 걸어갔다.

af|ter ♦♦♦ /æftər/

In addition to the uses shown below, **after** is used in phrasal verbs such as "ask after," "look after," and "take after."

after는 아래 용법 외에도 'ask after', 'look after', 'take after'와 같은 구동사에 쓰인다.

1 PREP If something happens **after** a particular date or event, it happens during the period of time that follows that date or event. ❑ *After May 19, strikes were occurring on a daily basis.* ❑ *After breakfast Amy ordered the local taxi to take her to the station.* ● CONJ **After** is also a conjunction. ❑ *After Don told me this, he spoke of his mother.* **2** PREP If you do one thing **after** doing another, you do it during the period of time that follows the other thing. [PREP -ing] ❑ *After completing and signing it, please return the form to us in the envelope provided.* **3** PREP You use **after** when you are talking about time. For example, if something is going to happen during **the day after** or **the weekend after** a particular time, it is going to happen during the following day or during the following weekend. [n PREP n] ❑ *She's leaving the day after tomorrow.* ● ADV **After** is also an adverb. [ADV after v] ❑ *Tomorrow. Or the day after.* **4** PREP If you go **after** someone, you follow or chase them. ❑ *Alice said to Gina, "Why don't you go after him, he's your son."* **5** PREP If you are **after** something, you are trying to get it. ❑ *They were after the money.* **6** PREP If you call, shout, or stare **after** someone, you call, shout, or stare at them as they move away from you. ❑ *"Come back!" he called after me.* **7** PREP If you tell someone that one place is a particular distance **after** another, you mean that it is situated beyond the other place and further away from you. ❑ *...a station 134 miles after the train starts its journey.* **8** PREP If one thing is written **after** another thing on a page, it is written following it or underneath it. ❑ *I wrote my name after Penny's at the bottom of the page.* **9** PREP You use **after** in order to give the most important aspect of something when comparing it with

1 전치사 ~이후에 ❑ 5월 19일 이후로 파업이 날마다 일어나고 있었다. ❑ 아침 식사 후에 에이미는 역까지 태워 줄 그 지역 택시를 불렀다. ● 접속사 ~한 후에 ❑ 돈은 나에게 이 말을 한 후에, 자신의 어머니 이야기를 했다. **2** 전치사 ~한 뒤에 ❑ 서식의 작성을 마치고 서명하신 다음, 동봉한 봉투에 넣어서 회송해 주시기 바랍니다. **3** 전치사 ~다음에 ❑ 그녀는 모레 떠날 예정이다. ● 부사 다음에 ❑ 내일, 아니면 그 다음날 **4** 전치사 ~을 따라서 ❑ 앨리스가 지나에게 "그를 따라가지 그래, 네 아들이잖아."라고 했다. **5** 전치사 ~을 구하여 ❑ 그들은 돈을 추구했다. **6** 전치사 ~을 향하여 ❑ "돌아와!"라고 그가 나를 향해 소리쳤다. **7** 전치사 ~뒤에 ❑ 기차가 출발한 곳에서 134마일 떨어진 역 **8** 전치사 ~뒤에, ~밑에 ❑ 나는 페이지 하단에 페니 이름 밑에 내 이름을 적었다. **9** 전치사 ~을 따라서 ❑ 독일 식당은 미국이 영국의 두 번째로 큰 고객이다. **10** 전치사 ~을 따라서 [주로 영국영어; 미국영어 대개 for] ❑ 그는 버지니아가 자신의 이름을 딴 뒤 아기의 이름을 짓도록 설득했다. **11** 관용 표현 먼저 가세요 [공손체] **12** 전치사 ~시고 지나 [미국영어]

another aspect. ❑ *After Germany, America is Britain's second-biggest customer.* ⑩ PREP To be named **after** someone means to be given the same name as them. [mainly BRIT; AM usually **for**] ❑ *He persuaded Virginia to name the baby after him.* ⑪ CONVENTION If you say "**after you**" to someone, you are being polite and allowing them to go in front of you or through a doorway before you do. [POLITENESS] ⑫ PREP **After** is used when telling the time. If it is, for example, **ten after six**, the time is ten minutes past six. [AM] ⑬ **after all** →see **all**

> You use **after**, **afterwards**, and **later** to talk about things that happen following the time when you are speaking, or following a particular event. Expressions such as "not long" and "shortly" can also be used with **after**. ❑ *After dinner she spoke to him... I returned to England after visiting India... Shortly after, she called me.* **Afterwards** can be used when you do not need to mention the particular time or event. ❑ *Afterwards we went to a night club.* You can also use words such as "soon" and "shortly" with **afterwards**. ❑ *Soon afterwards, he came to the clinic.* You can use **later** to refer to a time or situation that follows the time when you are speaking. ❑ *I'll go and see her later.* "A little," "much," and "not much" can also be used with **later**. ❑ *A little later, the lights went out... I learned all this much later.* You can use **after**, **afterwards**, or **later** following a phrase that mentions a period of time, in order to say when something happens. ❑ *...five years after his death... She wrote about it six years afterwards... Ten minutes later he left the house.*

⑭ PHRASE If you do something to several things **one after the other** or **one after another**, you do it to one, then the next, and so on, with no break between your actions. ❑ *Sybil ate three ginger biscuits, one after the other, greedily.* ⑮ PHRASE If something happens **day after day** or **year after year**, it happens every day or every year, for a long time. ❑ *...people who'd been coming here year after year.*

after- /ǽftər-/ COMB in ADJ **After-** is added to nouns to form adjectives which indicate that something takes place or exists after an event or process. [ADJ n] ❑ *...an after-dinner speech.*

after|market /ǽftərmɑrkɪt/ ▪ N-SING The **aftermarket** is all the related products that are sold after an item, especially a car, has been bought. [BUSINESS] ❑ *The company serves the national automotive aftermarket with a broad range of accessory and recreational-vehicle products.* ▪ N-SING The **aftermarket** in shares and bonds is the buying and selling of them after they have been issued. [BUSINESS] ❑ *It's illegal to get into a formal agreement with investors that they'll buy in the aftermarket.*

after|math /ǽftərmæθ/ ▪ N-SING The **aftermath of** an important event, especially a harmful one, is the situation that results from it. ❑ *In the aftermath of the coup, the troops opened fire on the demonstrators.*

after|noon ♦♦◊ /ǽftərnún/ (**afternoons**) N-VAR The **afternoon** is the part of each day which begins at lunchtime and ends at about six o'clock. ❑ *He's arriving in the afternoon.* ❑ *He had stayed in his room all afternoon.*

after|shave /ǽftərʃeɪv/ (**aftershaves**) also **after-shave** N-MASS **Aftershave** is a liquid with a pleasant smell that men sometimes put on their faces after shaving. ❑ *...a bottle of aftershave.*

after|ward ♦◊◊ /ǽftərwərd/

> The form **afterwards** is also used, mainly in British English.

ADV If you do something or if something happens **afterward**, you do it or it happens after a particular event or time that has already been mentioned. [ADV with cl] ❑ *Shortly afterward, police arrested four suspects.*

> You use **after**, **afterwards**, and **later** to talk about things that happen following the time when you are speaking, or following a particular event. Expressions such as "not long" and "shortly" can also be used with **after**. ❑ *After dinner she spoke to him... I returned to England after visiting India... Shortly after, she called me.* **Afterwards** can be used when you do not need to mention the particular time or event. ❑ *Afterwards we went to a night club.* You can also use words such as "soon" and "shortly" with **afterwards**. ❑ *Soon afterwards, he came to the clinic.* You can use **later** to refer to a time or situation that follows the time when you are speaking. ❑ *I'll go and see her later.* "A little," "much," and "not much" can also be used with **later**. ❑ *A little later, the lights went out... I learned all this much later.* You can use **after**, **afterwards**, or **later** following a phrase that mentions a period of time, in order to say when something happens. ❑ *...five years after his death... She wrote about it six years afterwards... Ten minutes later he left the house.*

again ♦♦♦ /əgɛn, əgeɪn/ ❶ ADV You use **again** to indicate that something happens a second time, or after it has already happened before. ❑ *He kissed her again.* ❑ *Again there was a short silence.* ❷ ADV You use **again** to indicate that something is now in a particular state or place that it used to be in. [ADV after v] ❑ *He opened his attaché case, removed a folder, then closed it again.* ❸ ADV You can use **again** when you want to point out that there is a similarity between the

---

말을 하는 시점 이후나 특정한 사건 이후에 일어나는 일을 얘기할 때 after, afterwards, later를 쓴다. after와 함께는 not long이나 shortly 같은 표현도 쓸 수 있다. ❑ 저녁 식사 후에 그녀는 그에게 말했다... 나는 인도를 방문하고 영국으로 돌아왔다... 바로 얼마 후에 그녀가 내게 전화를 했다. afterwards는 특정한 시간이나 사건을 언급할 필요가 없을 때 쓸 수 있다. ❑ 나중에 우리는 나이트클럽에 갔다. afterwards와 함께는 soon이나 shortly 같은 말을 쓸 수 있다. ❑ 그 뒤에 곧, 그가 진료소에 왔다. 말하는 시점 이후의 어떤 시점이나 상황을 가리킬 때는 later를 쓸 수 있다. ❑ 내가 나중에 그녀를 보러 갈게. later와 함께는 a little, much, not much를 쓸 수 있다. ❑ 조금 후에, 불이 꺼졌다... 나는 이 모든 것을 훨씬 나중에 알게 되었다. 어떤 일이 언제 일어났는지를 말하려면 일정 기간을 언급하는 구 뒤에 after, afterwards, later를 쓰면 된다. ❑ ...그가 사망한 뒤 5년 후... 그녀는 6년 후에 그것에 대한 글을 썼다... 10분 뒤에 그는 집을 떠났다.

⑭ 구 연달아 ❑ 시빌은 생강 비스킷 세 개를 연달아 게걸스럽게 먹었다. ⑮ 구 매일; 매년 ❑ 매년 이곳에 왔던 사람들

복합형-형용사 후 ❑ 식후 연설

❶ 단수명사 부품 시장 [경제] ❑ 이 회사는 다양한 종류의 부속품과 레저용 차량 용품들을 전국 자동차 부품 시장에 공급하고 있다. ❷ 단수명사 애프터마켓 [경제] ❑ 투자자들과 애프터마켓 주식 거래에 공식적으로 합의하는 것은 불법이다.

단수명사 직후 ❑ 쿠데타 직후, 군인들이 시위대를 향해 사격을 개시했다.

가산명사 또는 불가산명사 오후 ❑ 그는 오후에 도착할 겁니다. ❑ 그는 오후 내내 자기 방에 있었다.

물질명사 애프터셰이브 스킨 ❑ 애프터셰이브 스킨 한 병

afterwards도 주로 영국영어에서 쓴다.

부사 후에, 나중에 ❑ 잠시 후, 경찰이 용의자 네 명을 체포했다.

말을 하는 시점 이후나 특정한 사건 이후에 일어나는 일을 얘기할 때 after, afterwards, later를 쓴다. after와 함께는 not long이나 shortly 같은 표현도 쓸 수 있다. ❑ 저녁 식사 후에 그녀는 그에게 말했다... 나는 인도를 방문하고 영국으로 돌아왔다... 바로 얼마 후에 그녀가 내게 전화를 했다. afterwards는 특정한 시간이나 사건을 언급할 필요가 없을 때 쓸 수 있다. ❑ 나중에 우리는 나이트클럽에 갔다. afterwards와 함께는 soon이나 shortly 같은 말을 쓸 수 있다. ❑ 그 뒤에 곧, 그가 진료소에 왔다. 말하는 시점 이후의 어떤 시점이나 상황을 가리킬 때는 later를 쓸 수 있다. ❑ 내가 나중에 그녀를 보러 갈게. later와 함께는 a little, much, not much를 쓸 수 있다. ❑ 조금 후에, 불이 꺼졌다... 나는 이 모든 것을 훨씬 나중에 알게 되었다. 어떤 일이 언제 일어났는지를 말하려면 일정 기간을 언급하는 구 뒤에 after, afterwards, later를 쓰면 된다. ❑ ...그가 사망한 뒤 5년 후... 그녀는 6년 후에 그것에 대한 글을 썼다... 10분 뒤에 그는 집을 떠났다.

❶ 부사 다시 ❑ 그가 그녀에게 또 다시 키스했다. ❑ 다시 짧은 침묵이 흘렀다. ❷ 부사 다시 (원상태로) ❑ 그는 서류 가방을 열어 폴더를 꺼낸 뒤, 가방을 원상태로 닫았다. ❸ 부사 마찬가지로 ❑ 나의 이번 임신도 이전에 두 번 임신했을 때와 매우 비슷하다. ❹ 부사 하지만, 또 한편으로는 ❑ 인조 가죽을 사도

subject that you are talking about now and a previous subject. [ADV cl] ❑ *Again the pregnancy was very similar to my previous two.* **4** ADV You can use **again** in expressions such as **but again**, **then again**, and **there again** when you want to introduce a remark which contrasts with or weakens something that you have just said. [ADV with cl] ❑ *You may be happy to buy imitation leather, and then again, you may wonder what you're getting for your money.* **5** ADV You can add **again** to the end of your question when you are asking someone to tell you something that you have forgotten or that they have already told you. [SPOKEN] [cl ADV] ❑ *Sorry, what's your name again?* **6** ADV You use **again** in expressions such as **half as much again** when you are indicating how much greater one amount is than another amount you have just mentioned or are about to mention. [amount ADV] ❑ *40% of the state's general fund has to go to education. Nearly as much again is mandated to various health and welfare programs.* **7** PHRASE You can use **again and again** or **time and time again** to emphasize that something happens many times. [EMPHASIS] ❑ *He would go over his work again and again until he felt he had it right.* **8** now and again →see now. once again →see once

against ♦♦♦ /əɡɛnst, əɡeɪnst/

In addition to the uses shown below, **against** is used in phrasal verbs such as "come up against," "guard against," and "hold against."

1 PREP If one thing is leaning or pressing **against** another, it is touching it. ❑ *She leaned against him.* ❑ *On a table pushed against a wall there were bottles of beer and wine.* **2** PREP If you are **against** something such as a plan, policy, or system, you think it is wrong, bad, or stupid. ❑ *Taxes are unpopular – it is understandable that voters are against them.* ❑ *Joan was very much against commencing drug treatment.* ● ADV **Against** is also an adverb. [ADV after v] ❑ *The vote for the suspension of the party was 283 in favor with 29 against.* **3** PREP If you compete **against** someone in a game, you try to beat them. ❑ *The tour will include games against the Australian Barbarians.* **4** PREP If you take action **against** someone or something, you try to harm them. ❑ *Security forces are still using violence against opponents of the government.* **5** PREP If you take action **against** a possible future event, you try to prevent it. ❑ *Experts have been discussing how to improve the fight against crime.* **6** PREP If you do something **against** someone's wishes, advice, or orders, you do not do what they want you to do or tell you to do. ❑ *He discharged himself from the hospital against the advice of doctors.* **7** PREP If you do something in order to protect yourself **against** something unpleasant or harmful, you do something which will make its effects on you less serious if it happens. ❑ *Any business needs insurance against ordinary risks such as fire, flood, and breakage.* **8** PHRASE If you **have** something **against** someone or something, you dislike them. ❑ *Have you got something against women, Les?* **9** PREP If something is **against** the law or **against** the rules, there is a law or a rule which says that you must not do it. ❑ *It is against the law to detain you against your will for any length of time.* **10** PREP If you are moving **against** a current, tide, or wind, you are moving in the opposite direction to it. ❑ *...swimming upstream against the current.* **11** PREP If something happens or is considered **against** a particular background of events, it is considered in relation to those events, because those events are relevant to it. ❑ *The profits rise was achieved against a backdrop of falling metal prices.* **12** PREP If something is measured or valued **against** something else, it is measured or valued by comparing it with the other thing. ❑ *Our policies have to be judged against a clear test: will it improve the standard of education?* **13** PREP The odds **against** something happening are the chances or odds that it will not happen. [n PREP] ❑ *The odds against him surviving are incredible.* ● ADV **Against** is also an adverb. [n ADV] ❑ *What were the odds against?* **14** up against →see up. against the clock →see clock

age ♦♦♦ /eɪdʒ/ (ages, aging, aged)

The spelling **ageing** is also used, mainly in British English.

1 N-VAR Your **age** is the number of years that you have lived. ❑ *She has a nephew who is just ten years of age.* ❑ *At the age of sixteen he qualified for a place at the University of Hamburg.* **2** N-VAR The **age** of a thing is the number of years since it was made. ❑ *Everything in the room looks in keeping with the age of the building.* **3** N-UNCOUNT **Age** is the state of being old or the process of becoming older. ❑ *Perhaps he has grown wiser with age.* ❑ *This cologne, like wine, improves with age.* **4** V-T/V-I When someone **ages**, or when something **ages** them, they seem much older and less strong or less alert. ❑ *He had always looked so young, but he seemed to have aged in the last few months.* **5** N-COUNT An **age** is a period in history. ❑ *...the age of steam and steel.* **6** N-COUNT You can say **an age** or **ages** to mean a very long time. [INFORMAL] ❑ *He waited what seemed an age.* **7** →see also **aged, ageing, middle age** →see Picture Dictionary: **age**

aged

Pronounced /eɪdʒd/ for meaning **1**, and /eɪdʒɪd/ for meanings **2** and **3**.

1 ADJ You use **aged** followed by a number to say how old someone is. ❑ *Alan has two children, aged eleven and nine.* **2** ADJ **Aged** means very old. [ADJ n] ❑ *She has an aged parent who's capable of being very difficult.* **3** N-PLURAL You can refer to all people who are very old as **the aged**. ❑ *The American Society on Aging provides resource services to those dealing with the aged.* **4** →see also **middle-aged**

ageing →see **aging**

agency ♦♦◊ /eɪdʒənsi/ (agencies) **1** N-COUNT An **agency** is a business which provides a service on behalf of other businesses. [BUSINESS] ❑ *We had to hire maids through an agency.* →see also **advertising agency, employment agency** **2** N-COUNT An **agency** is a government organization responsible for a certain area of administration. ❑ *...the government agency which monitors health and safety at work in Britain.*

괜찮겠지만, 또 한편으로는, 지불한 돈만큼의 가치가 있을지 의문이 생길 수도 있다. **5** 부사 한 번 더 [구어체] ❑ 미안하지만 이름이 뭐라고 했죠? **6** 부사 -배 ❑ 주의 총 기금의 40퍼센트가 교육 부문에 돌아가야 한다. 이것의 거의 두 배 정도나 다양한 의료 및 복지 프로그램에 투입된다. **7** 구 되풀이하여, 거듭 [강조] ❑ 그는 일을 제대로 했다 싶을 때까지 몇 번이고 다시 검토했다.

against는 아래 용법 외에도 'come up against', 'guard against', 'hold against'와 같은 구동사에 쓰인다.

1 전치사 -에 기대어 ❑ 그녀는 그에게 몸을 기댔다. ❑ 벽에 딱 붙어 있는 테이블 위에 맥주와 와인 병들이 놓여 있었다. **2** 전치사 -에 반대하여 ❑ 세금을 반기는 사람은 별로 없다. 유권자들이 세금을 반대하는 게 이해가 간다. ❑ 조앤은 약물 치료 시작을 강력히 반대했다. ● 부사 반대하여 ❑ 그 정당의 활동 정지에 대한 투표 결과 찬성 283표에 반대 29표가 나왔다. **3** 전치사 -에 대항하여 ❑ 여행 일정에는 호주 바바리안과 대결하는 게임도 포함될 것이다. **4** 전치사 -에 불리하게 ❑ 보안군이 반정부 인사들에게 여전히 폭력을 행사하고 있다. ❑ 전문가들은 범죄 예방 노력의 개선 방안에 대해 논의해 왔다. **6** 전치사 -에 반하여, -을 듣지 않고 ❑ 그는 의료진의 충고를 무시하고 퇴원했다. **7** 전치사 -에 대비하여 ❑ 어떤 회사든 화재, 홍수, 파손 등 흔히 일어날 수 있는 위험에 대비해 보험을 들 필요가 있다. **8** 구 싫어하다 ❑ 레스야, 너는 여자들을 싫어하니? **9** 전치사 -에 어긋나 ❑ 얼마간의 기간이든 본인의 의지에 반하여 사람을 억류하는 것은 법에 어긋난다. **10** 전치사 -에 역행하여, -을 거슬러 ❑ 물살을 거슬러 상류 쪽으로 헤엄치는 **11** 전치사 -을 배경으로 ❑ 수익이 늘어난 배경에는 금속 가격의 하락이 있었다. **12** 전치사 -에 비추어 ❑ 우리는 이 정책이 과연 교육 수준을 향상시킬 수 있을 것인가를 명확한 기준에 비추어 정책을 평가해야 한다. **13** 전치사 일어나지 않을 ❑ 그의 생존 가능성은 믿기지 않을 정도이다. ● 부사 반하여 ❑ 반대의 경우는 확률이 어땠나요?

철자 ageing도 특히 영국영어에서 쓴다.

1 가산명사 또는 불가산명사 나이 ❑ 그녀에겐 이제 막 열 살 된 조카가 하나 있다. ❑ 그는 열여섯 살에 함부르크 대학에 합격했다. **2** 가산명사 또는 불가산명사 햇수 ❑ 그 방에 있는 모든 것들이 건물과 함께 나이를 먹어 가는 것 같다. **3** 불가산명사 나이, 나이가 듦 ❑ 아마도 그가 나이가 들면서 더 현명해졌을 것이다. ❑ 이 오드콜로뉴는 와인처럼 오래 묵을수록 맛이 좋아진다. **4** 타동사/자동사 늙다; 늙다 ❑ 항상 젊어 보였던 그였지만 지난 몇 달간 부쩍 늙어버린 것 같았다. **5** 가산명사 시대 ❑ 증기와 철의 시대 **6** 가산명사 오랜 시간 [비격식체] ❑ 그는 한참 동안 기다렸다.

1의 의미일 때는 /eɪdʒd/로, **2**와 **3**의 의미일 때는 /eɪdʒɪd/로 발음된다.

1 형용사 -살의 ❑ 앨런은 열한 살과 아홉 살 난 두 아이가 있다. **2** 형용사 노령의 ❑ 그녀는 굉장히 모시기 힘든 노부모를 모시고 있다. **3** 복수명사 노인 ❑ 미국 노인협회는 노인 문제를 다루는 사람들에게 필요한 재원을 제공한다.

1 가산명사 대행사, 대리점, 중개소 [경제] ❑ 우리는 직업소개소를 통해 가정부를 고용해야 했다. **2** 가산명사 정부 기관 ❑ 직장에서의 건강과 안전 문제를 감독하는 영국 정부 기관

agen|da ♦◇◇ /ədʒɛndə/ (**agendas**) **1** N-COUNT You can refer to the political issues which are important at a particular time as an **agenda**. ❑ *Does television set the agenda on foreign policy?* →see also **hidden agenda 2** N-COUNT An **agenda** is a list of the items that have to be discussed at a meeting. ❑ *This is sure to be an item on the agenda next week.*

1 가산명사 현안 ❑ 텔레비전이 외교 정책에 대한 현안을 제시하는가? **2** 가산명사 의제 ❑ 이것은 반드시 다음 주 의제에 포함될 것이다.

Word Partnership	*agenda*의 연어
ADJ.	**domestic/legislative/political** agenda, **hidden** agenda **1**
PREP.	**on the** agenda **2**
V.	**set the** agenda **1**

agent ♦◇◇ /eɪdʒənt/ (**agents**) **1** N-COUNT An **agent** is a person who looks after someone else's business affairs or does business on their behalf. [BUSINESS] ❑ *You are buying direct, rather than through an agent.* →see also **estate agent, travel agent 2** N-COUNT An **agent** in the arts world is a person who gets work for an actor or musician, or who sells the work of a writer to publishers. ❑ *My literary agent thinks it is not unreasonable to expect £500,000 in total.* **3** N-COUNT An **agent** is a person who works for a country's secret service. ❑ *All these years he's been an agent for the East.* **4** N-COUNT A chemical that has a particular effect or is used for a particular purpose can be referred to as a particular kind of **agent**. ❑ *...the bleaching agent in white flour.* →see **concert**

1 가산명사 중개인, 대리인 [경제] ❑ 당신은 중개인을 통해서가 아니라 직접 구매하고 있는 것이다. **2** 가산명사 에이전트, 대리인 ❑ 나의 문학 작품 대리인은 총 50만 파운드를 기대하는 것이 터무니없는 것은 아니라고 생각한다. **3** 가산명사 첩보원 ❑ 그는 지금까지 내내 동구권 첩보요원으로 일했다. **4** 가산명사 화학 물질 ❑ 하얀 밀가루에 함유된 표백제

age of con|sent N-SING The **age of consent** is the age at which a person can legally agree to having a sexual relationship. [the N] ❑ *He was under the age of consent.*

단수명사 승낙 연령, 법적 섹스 동의 가능 연령 ❑ 그는 합법적인 섹스 동의가 성립되는 나이 미만이었다.

age-old ADJ An **age-old** story, tradition, or problem has existed for many generations or centuries. [WRITTEN] ❑ *This age-old struggle for control had led to untold bloody wars.*

형용사 오래 동안 계속된 [문어체] ❑ 오랫동안 계속되어 이 주도권 다툼은 엄청나게 피비린내 나는 전쟁으로 치달아 있었다.

ag|gra|vate /ægrəveɪt/ (**aggravates, aggravating, aggravated**) **1** V-T If someone or something **aggravates** a situation, they make it worse. ❑ *Stress and lack of sleep can aggravate the situation.* **2** V-T If someone or something **aggravates** you, they make you annoyed. [INFORMAL] ❑ *What aggravates you most about this country?* ● **ag|gra|vat|ing** ADJ ❑ *You don't realize how aggravating you can be.* ● **ag|gra|va|tion** /ægrəveɪʃ°n/ (**aggravations**) N-VAR ❑ *I just couldn't take the aggravation.*

1 타동사 악화시키다 ❑ 스트레스와 수면 부족은 상황을 악화시킬 수 있다. **2** 타동사 화나게 하다 [비격식체] ❑ 이 나라에서 가장 짜증나는 것이 무엇입니까? ● 짜증나는 형용사 ❑ 네가 얼마나 사람을 짜증나게 만들 수 있는지 너는 몰라. ● 짜증나는 일 가산명사 또는 불가산명사 ❑ 나는 그냥 그 짜증스러운 일을 참을 수가 없었다.

ag|gre|gate /ægrɪgɪt/ ADJ An **aggregate** amount or score is made up of several smaller amounts or scores added together. [ADJ n] ❑ *The rate of growth of GNP will depend upon the rate of growth of aggregate demand.*

형용사 합산한 ❑ 지엔피 성장률은 총 수요의 증가율에 따라 달라질 것이다.

ag|gres|sion /əgrɛʃ°n/ (**aggressions**) **1** N-UNCOUNT **Aggression** is a quality of anger and determination that makes you ready to attack other people. ❑ *Aggression is by no means a male-only trait.* **2** N-VAR **Aggression** is violent and attacking behavior. ❑ *...the threat of massive military aggression.*

1 불가산명사 공격성 ❑ 공격성은 절대 남성에게서만 나타나는 성향이 아니다. **2** 가산명사 또는 불가산명사 공격 ❑ 대규모 군사 공격의 위협

Word Partnership	*aggression*의 연어
N.	**act of** aggression **1**
PREP.	aggression **against 2**
ADJ.	**military** aggression, **physical** aggression **2**

Picture Dictionary

age

infant　　toddler　　teenager / adolescent　　woman　　　　man　　senior citizen

CHILD	ADULT	

YOUNG	MIDDLE AGED	ELDERLY

a

ag|gres|sive ♦◇◇ /əgrɛsɪv/ **11** ADJ An **aggressive** person or animal has a quality of anger and determination that makes them ready to attack other people. ❑ *Some children are much more aggressive than others.* ❑ *These fish are very aggressive.* ● **ag|gres|sive|ly** ADV ❑ *They'll react aggressively.* **2** ADJ People who are **aggressive** in their work or other activities behave in a forceful way because they are very eager to succeed. ❑ *He is respected as a very aggressive and competitive executive.* ● **ag|gres|sive|ly** ADV ❑ *...countries noted for aggressively pursuing energy efficiency.*

ag|gres|sor /əgrɛsər/ (**aggressors**) N-COUNT The **aggressor** in a fight or battle is the person, group, or country that starts it. ❑ *They have been the aggressors in this conflict.*

형용사 공격적인 ❑ 어떤 아이들은 다른 아이들에 비해 훨씬 더 공격적이다. ❑ 이 물고기들은 매우 공격적이다. ● 공격적으로 부사 ❑ 그들은 공격적으로 반응할 것이다. **2** 형용사 적극적인, 의욕적인 ❑ 그는 매우 의욕적이고 경쟁심이 강한 임원으로서 존경받는다. ● 적극적으로 부사 ❑ 효율적인 에너지 소비 정책을 적극적으로 추진하는 것으로 알려진 국가들

가산명사 침략자 ❑ 이 분쟁에서 먼저 공격한 것은 그들이었다.

Word Link | griev ≈ heavy, serious : ag*griev*ed, *griev*ance, *griev*e

ag|grieved /əgriːvd/ ADJ If you feel **aggrieved**, you feel upset and angry because of the way in which you have been treated. ❑ *I really feel aggrieved at this sort of thing.*

형용사 기분이 상한 ❑ 이런 일을 겪으면 정말로 기분이 상한다.

aghast /əgɑːst, əgæst/ ADJ If you are **aghast**, you are filled with horror and surprise. [FORMAL] [ADJ after v, v-link ADJ, oft ADJ *at* n, ADJ n] ❑ *While she watched, aghast, his eyes glazed over as his life flowed away.*

형용사 아연실색한 [격식체] ❑ 그의 생명이 점점 꺼져 가면서 눈이 흐려져 가는 것을 그녀는 아연실색하여 바라봤다.

ag|ile /ædʒəl, BRIT ædʒaɪl/ **11** ADJ Someone who is **agile** can move quickly and easily. ❑ *At 20 years old he was not as strong, as fast, as agile as he is now.* ● **agil|ity** /ədʒɪlɪti/ N-UNCOUNT ❑ *She blinked in surprise at his agility.* **2** ADJ If you have an **agile** mind, you think quickly and intelligently. ❑ *She was quick-witted and had an extraordinarily agile mind.* ● **agil|ity** N-UNCOUNT ❑ *His intellect and mental agility have never been in doubt.*

11 형용사 민첩한 ❑ 그가 20살이었을 당시에도 지금만큼 강하고 빠르고 민첩하지 못했다. ● 민첩성 불가산명사 ❑ 그의 민첩성에 놀란 그녀는 눈을 깜빡였다. **2** 형용사 기민한 ❑ 그녀는 두뇌 회전이 빨라요 놀라울 정도로 기민한 머리를 가지고 있었다. ● 기민한 불가산명사 ❑ 그는 지성과 정신적 기민함이 탁월하기로 인정을 받는다.

ag|ing /eɪdʒɪŋ/ also **ageing** **11** ADJ Someone or something that is **aging** is becoming older and less healthy or efficient. ❑ *John lives with his aging mother.* **2** N-UNCOUNT **Aging** is the process of becoming old or becoming worn out. ❑ *The only signs of aging are the flecks of grey that speckle his dark hair.*

11 형용사 나이 든; 오래된 ❑ 존은 나이 든 어머니와 살고 있다. **2** 불가산명사 노화 ❑ 까만 머리에 듬성듬성 섞여 있는 흰머리만이 그가 늙어 가고 있음을 보여 준다.

agi|tate /ædʒɪteɪt/ (**agitates, agitating, agitated**) **11** V-I If people **agitate for** something, they protest or take part in political activity in order to get it. ❑ *The women who worked in these mills had begun to agitate for better conditions.* **2** V-T If you **agitate** something, you shake it so that it moves about. [FORMAL] ❑ *All you need to do is gently agitate the water with a finger or paintbrush.* **3** V-T If something **agitates** you, it worries you and makes you unable to think clearly or calmly. ❑ *Carl and Martin may inherit their grandmother's possessions when she dies. The thought agitates her.*

11 자동사 (정치적) 운동을 하다 ❑ 이 공장들에서 일한 여자들은 보다 나은 근로 조건을 위해 노동 운동을 하기 시작했다. **2** 타동사 흔들다, 긴드리다 [격식체] ❑ 물을 손가락이나 화필로 건드리기만 하면 된다. **3** 타동사 초조하게 하다 ❑ 칼과 마틴이 그들의 할머니가 돌아가실 때 재산을 물려받을지도 모른다. 그 생각은 그녀를 초조하게 한다.

agi|tat|ed /ædʒɪteɪtɪd/ ADJ If someone is **agitated**, they are very worried or upset, and show this in their behavior, movements, or voice. ❑ *Susan seemed agitated about something.*

형용사 초조한 ❑ 수잔은 뭔가에 대해 초조해 하는 것 같았다.

agi|ta|tion /ædʒɪteɪʃən/ N-UNCOUNT If someone is in a state of **agitation**, they are very worried or upset, and show this in their behavior, movements, or voice. ❑ *Danny returned to Father's house in a state of intense agitation.*

불가산명사 긴장, 초조함 ❑ 아버지의 집에 돌아왔을 때 대니가 매우 긴장해 있었다.

AGM /eɪ dʒi ɛm/ (**AGMs**) also **agm** N-COUNT The **AGM** of a company or organization is a meeting which it holds once a year in order to discuss the previous year's activities and accounts. **AGM** is an abbreviation for "Annual General Meeting." [BRIT, BUSINESS] ❑ *Uniq holds its AGM on Thursday.*

가산명사 연례 총회 [영국영어, 경제] ❑ 유니크는 목요일에 연례 총회를 연다.

ag|nos|tic /ægnɒstɪk/ (**agnostics**) N-COUNT An **agnostic** believes that it is not possible to know whether God exists or not. Compare **atheist**. ❑ *Vasari claimed with horror that he was, if not an atheist, then an agnostic.* →see **religion**

가산명사 불가지론자 ❑ 바사리는 만약 자신이 무신론자가 아니라면 불가지론자였을 것이라고 두려움에 찬 목소리로 주장했다.

ag|nos|ti|cism /ægnɒstɪsɪzəm/ N-UNCOUNT **Agnosticism** is the belief that it is not possible to say definitely whether or not there is a God. Compare **atheism**.

불가산명사 불가지론

ago ♦♦♦ /əgoʊ/ ADV You use **ago** when you are referring to past time. For example, if something happened one year **ago**, it is one year since it happened. If it happened a long time **ago**, it is a long time since it happened. ❑ *He was killed a few days ago in a skiing accident.* ❑ *The meeting is the first ever between the two sides since the war there began 14 years ago.*

부사 전에 ❑ 그는 며칠 전 스키 사고로 죽었다. ❑ 그 회의는 그 곳에서 전쟁이 발발한 지 14년 만에 양측이 맨 처음으로 가지는 회의이다.

You only use **ago** when you are talking about a period of time measured back from the present. If you are talking about a period measured back from some earlier time, you use **before** or **previously**. ❑ *He had died a month before... She had rented the apartment some fourteen months previously.* You use **for** to say how long a period lasts in the past, present, or future, or how much time passes without something happening. ❑ *She slept for eight hours... He will be away for three weeks... I hadn't seen him for four years.* You use **since** to say when a period of time started. ❑ *She has been with the group since it began....the first civilian president since the coup 17 years ago.* You also use **since** to refer to the last time that something happened, or to how much time passes without something happening. ❑ *She hadn't eaten since breakfast... It was a long time since she had been to church.*

ago는 현재 시점을 기준으로 과거의 어느 시기에 대해 말할 때에만 쓴다. 과거 시점에서 더 과거의 어느 시기에 대해 말할 때에는 before나 previously를 쓴다. ❑ 그는 그보다 한 달 전에 사망했어... 그녀는 그보다 약 14개월 전에 그 아파트에 세를 들었다. for는 과거, 현재, 미래에 어떤 기간이 얼마나 오랫동안 지속되는지, 또는 아무 일 없이 얼마나 많은 시간이 지나가는지를 말할 때 쓴다. ❑ 그녀는 8시간 동안 잤다... 그는 3주 동안 여기에 없을 것이다... 나는 그를 4년간 보지 못했다. since는 어떤 기간이 시작된 시기를 가리킬 때 쓴다. ❑ 그녀는 그 단체가 시작될 때부터 있었다....17년 전에 있은 루데타 이래 첫 민간인 대통령. since는 또 어떤 일이 일어난 마지막 시점이나 어떤 일이 일어나지 않고 지나간 시간을 언급할 때에도 쓴다. ❑ 그녀는 아침 식사 이후 아무것도 먹지 않은 상태였다... 그녀가 교회에 간 것은 오래 전 일이었다.

Word Link | agon ≈ struggling : *agon*ize, *agon*y, prot*agon*ist

ago|nize /ægənaɪz/ (**agonizes, agonizing, agonized**) [BRIT also **agonise**] V-I If you **agonize over** something, you feel very anxious about it and spend a long time thinking about it. ❑ *Perhaps he was agonizing over the moral issues involved.*

[영국영어 agonise] 자동사 괴로워하다 ❑ 어쩌면 그는 관련된 도덕적인 문제에 대해 괴로워하고 있었는지도 모르겠다.

a
b
c
d
e
f
g
h
i
j
k
l
m
n
o
p
q
r
s
t
u
v
w
x
y
z

ago|niz|ing /ǽgənaɪzɪŋ/ [BRIT also **agonising**] **1** ADJ Something that is **agonizing** causes you to feel great physical or mental pain. ❑ *He did not wish to die the agonizing death of his mother and brother.* **2** ADJ **Agonizing** decisions and choices are very difficult to make. ❑ *He now faced an agonizing decision about his immediate future.*

[영어영어 agonising] **1** 형용사 고통스러운 ❑ 그는 자신의 어머니와 형이 겪었던 고통스러운 죽음을 겪고 싶지 않았다. **2** 형용사 갈등스러운, 괴로운 ❑ 이제 그는 자신에게 당장 닥쳐올 미래와 관련된 갈등스러운 결정에 봉착했다.

Word Link	*agon* ≈ struggling : *agonize, agony, protagonist*

ago|ny /ǽgəni/ N-UNCOUNT **Agony** is great physical or mental pain. ❑ *A new machine may save thousands of animals from the agony of drug tests.*

불가산명사 심한 고통, 번민 ❑ 새로운 기계가 수천 마리의 동물을 약물 실험의 고통으로부터 해방시킬 수도 있을 것이다.

agree ◆◆◆ /əgrí/ (**agrees, agreeing, agreed**) **1** V-RECIP If people **agree with** each other about something, they have the same opinion about it or say that they have the same opinion. ❑ *Both have agreed on the need for the money.* ❑ *So we both agree there's a problem?* ❑ *I agree with you that the open system is by far the best.* ❑ *"It's appalling." — "It is. I agree."* ❑ *I agree with every word you've just said.* **2** V-T/V-I If you **agree to** do something, you say that you will do it. If you **agree to** a proposal, you accept it. ❑ *He agreed to pay me for the drawings.* **3** V-RECIP If people **agree on** something, or in British English if they **agree** something, they all decide to accept or do something. ❑ *The warring sides have agreed on an unconditional ceasefire.* ❑ *We never agreed a date.* **4** PHRASE If two people who are arguing about something **agree to disagree** or **agree to differ**, they decide to stop arguing because neither of them is going to change their opinion. ❑ *We are all going to have to agree to disagree then.* **5** V-I If you **agree with** an action or suggestion, you approve of it. ❑ *You didn't want to ask anybody whether they agreed with what you were doing.* **6** V-RECIP In grammar, if a word **agrees with** a noun or pronoun, it has a form that is appropriate to the number or gender of the noun or pronoun. For example, in "He hates it," the singular verb agrees with the singular pronoun "he." [v with n, pl-n v] **7** →see also **agreed**

1 상호동사 -와 동의하다 ❑ 둘 다 돈의 필요성에 동의했다. ❑ 그러면 우리 둘 다 문제가 있다는 것에 동의하는 거지? ❑ 열린 제도가 단연코 가장 우수하다는 당신 말에 동의합니다. ❑ "정말 질리는군." "맞아. 나도 동감이야." ❑ 네가 방금 한 말 전부에 대해 동의해. **2** 타동사/자동사 -에 동의하다, -에 승낙하다 ❑ 그는 그림에 대해 나에게 돈을 지불하기로 동의했다. **3** 상호동사 -에 동의하다 ❑ 전쟁의 당사자들은 무조건적인 휴전에 동의했다. ❑ 우리는 날짜에 동의한 적이 없다. **4** 구 서로 의견 차를 인정하고 더 이상 다투지 않기로 하다 ❑ 그럼 너와 나는 서로 의견 차이가 있다는 것에 동의하고 여기서 그만두어야 할 것 같다. **5** 자동사 -에 찬성하다 ❑ 너는 아무에게도 네가 하는 행위에 찬성하는지 묻고 싶어 하지 않았다. **6** 상호동사 일치하다

Thesaurus	*agree*의 참조어
v.	concur; (*ant.*) differ **1**
	consent, okay, refuse, reject **2**

agree|able /əgríəbᵊl/ **1** ADJ If something is **agreeable**, it is pleasant and you enjoy it. ❑ *...workers in more agreeable and better paid occupations.* **2** ADJ If someone is **agreeable**, they are pleasant and try to please people. ❑ *...sharing a bottle of wine with an agreeable companion.*

1 형용사 쾌적한 ❑ 보다 쾌적한 환경에서 더 높은 임금을 받는 직업의 노동자들 **2** 형용사 기분 좋은 ❑ 마음이 맞는 친구와 와인 한 병을 나눠 마시는 것

agreed /əgríd/ **1** ADJ If people are **agreed on** something, they have reached a joint decision on it or have the same opinion about it. [v-link ADJ, oft ADJ on n, ADJ that] ❑ *Okay, so are we agreed on going north?* **2** →see also **agree**

1 형용사 -에 동의한 ❑ 좋아, 그럼 우린 북쪽으로 가기로 합의한 것이지?

Word Link	*ment* ≈ state, condition : *agreement, management, movement*

agree|ment ◆◆◇ /əgrímənt/ (**agreements**) **1** N-COUNT An **agreement** is a formal decision about future action which is made by two or more countries, groups, or people. ❑ *It looks as though a compromise agreement has now been reached.* **2** N-UNCOUNT **Agreement on** something is a joint decision that a particular course of action should be taken. ❑ *A spokesman said, however, that the two men had not reached agreement on the issues discussed.* **3** N-UNCOUNT **Agreement** with someone means having the same opinion as they have. ❑ *The judge kept nodding in agreement.* ● PHRASE If you are **in agreement with** someone, you have the same opinion as they have. **4** N-UNCOUNT **Agreement** to a course of action means allowing it to happen or giving it your approval. ❑ *The clinic doctor will then write to your doctor to get his agreement.* ● PHRASE If you are **in agreement with** a plan or proposal, you approve of it.

1 가산명사 협정 ❑ 절충 조약에 이제 도달한 것 같다. **2** 불가산명사 합의 ❑ 그러나 대변인이 말하길 두 남자는 쟁점에 대해 합의점에 이르지를 못했다고 했다. **3** 불가산명사 동의 ❑ 판사는 동의하며 계속 고개를 끄덕였다. ● 구 -와 동의하는 **4** 불가산명사 동의 ❑ 그리고 나서 전문의는 동의를 얻기 위해 당신의 주치의에게 편지를 쓸 것이다. ● 구 -에 동의하는

Word Partnership	*agreement*의 연어
N.	**trade** agreement, **peace** agreement **1**
V.	**enter into an** agreement, **sign an** agreement **1**
	reach an agreement **1** **2** **4**

agri|busi|ness /ǽgribɪznɪs/ (**agribusinesses**) N-UNCOUNT **Agribusiness** is the various businesses that produce, sell, and distribute farm products, especially on a large scale. [BUSINESS] ❑ *Many of the old agricultural collectives are now being turned into agribusiness corporations.*

불가산명사 기업 농업 [경제] ❑ 과거에는 농업협동조합이었던 많은 곳들이 지금 기업농 회사로 바뀌고 있다.

agri|cul|tur|al ◆◆◇ /ǽgrɪkʌltʃərəl/ ADJ **Agricultural** means involving or relating to agriculture. ❑ *Farmers struggling for survival strip the forests for agricultural land.* →see **farm**

형용사 농업의 ❑ 살기 위해 발버둥치는 농부들이 농지를 위해 숲을 베고 있다.

agri|cul|ture ◆◆◇ /ǽgrɪkʌltʃər/ N-UNCOUNT **Agriculture** is farming and the methods that are used to raise and look after crops and animals. ❑ *Strong both in industry and agriculture, Ukraine produces much of the grain for the nation.* →see **industry**

불가산명사 농업 ❑ 산업과 농업 모두에 강한 우크라이나가 그 국가가 소비하는 곡물 대부분을 생산한다.

aground /əgráʊnd/ ADV If a ship runs **aground**, it touches the ground in a shallow part of a river, lake, or the sea, and gets stuck. [ADV after v] ❑ *The ship ran aground where there should have been a depth of 35ft.*

부사 좌초하여 ❑ 수심이 35 피트였던 것으로 여겨지는 곳에서 배는 좌초했다.

ah ◆◇◇ /ɑ/ EXCLAM **Ah** is used in writing to represent a noise that people make in conversation, for example to acknowledge or draw attention to something, or to express surprise or disappointment. [FEELINGS] ❑ *Ah, so many questions, so little time.*

감탄사 아 [감정 개입] ❑ 아, 질문은 많은데 시간은 너무 적구나.

ahead

① ADVERB USES
② PREPOSITION USES

① **ahead** ♦♦◇ /əhɛd/

In addition to the uses shown below, **ahead** is used in phrasal verbs such as "get ahead," "go ahead," and "press ahead."

ahead는 아래 용법 외에도 'get ahead', 'go ahead', 'press ahead'와 같은 구동사에 쓰인다.

1 ADV Something that is **ahead** is in front of you. If you look **ahead**, you look directly in front of you. ❑ *Brett looked straight ahead.* ❑ *The road ahead was now blocked solid.* 2 ADV You use **ahead** with verbs such as "push," "move," and "forge" to indicate that a plan, scheme, or organization is making fast progress. [ADV after v] ❑ *Western countries were moving ahead with plans to send financial aid to all of the former Soviet republics.* 3 ADV If you are **ahead** in your work or achievements, you have made more progress than you expected to and are performing well. ❑ *First half profits have charged ahead from £127.6m to £134.2m.* 4 ADV If a person or a team is **ahead** in a competition, they are winning. ❑ *Australia was ahead throughout the game.* ❑ *The Communists are comfortably ahead in the opinion polls.* 5 ADV **Ahead** also means in the future. ❑ *A much bigger battle is ahead for the president.* 6 ADV If you prepare or plan something **ahead**, you do it some time before a future event so that everything is ready for that event to take place. [ADV after v] ❑ *The government wants figures that help it to administer its policies and plan ahead.* 7 ADV If you go **ahead**, or if you go on **ahead**, you go in front of someone who is going to the same place so that you arrive there some time before they do. [ADV after v] ❑ *I went ahead and waited with Sean.*

1 부사 앞에, 정면으로 ❑ 브렛은 정면을 바라봤다. ❑ 앞길은 이제 완전히 막혀 있었다. 2 부사 앞으로 ❑ 서방 국가들은 구소련의 공화국들에 재정적 원조를 하려는 계획에 박차를 가하고 있었다. 3 부사 앞지른 ❑ 상반기 이익은 1억 2,760만 파운드에서 1억 3,420만 파운드로 급증했다. 4 부사 앞선 ❑ 호주는 경기 내내 앞섰다. ❑ 공산주의자들이 여론 조사에서 큰 차로 앞서 있다. 5 부사 (시간상) 앞으로 ❑ 대통령에게 훨씬 큰 싸움이 남아 있다. 6 부사 미리 ❑ 정부는 정책을 펴고 미리 계획을 짜는 데 도움이 되는 인물들을 원한다. 7 부사 먼저 ❑ 나는 먼저 가서 숀과 함께 기다렸다.

Word Partnership *ahead*의 연어

ADV.	**straight** ahead ① 1
V.	**look** ahead ① 1
	lie ahead ① 1 5
	move ahead ① 2
	get ahead ① 3
	plan ahead ① 6
	go ahead ① 7
PREP.	**in the days/months/years** ahead ① 5
	ahead **of schedule/time** ② 4

② **ahead of** ♦◇◇ →**Please look at category 6 to see if the expression you are looking for is shown under another headword.** 1 PHRASE If someone is **ahead of** you, they are directly in front of you. If someone is moving **ahead of** you, they are in front of you and moving in the same direction. ❑ *I saw a man in a blue jacket thirty meters ahead of me.* 2 PHRASE If an event or period of time lies **ahead of** you, it is going to happen or take place soon or in the future. ❑ *I tried to think about all the problems that were ahead of me tomorrow.* ❑ *Catherine had been awake all night thinking about the future that lay ahead of her.* 3 PHRASE In a competition, if a person or team does something **ahead of** someone else, they do it before the second person or team. ❑ *Robert Millar finished 1 minute and 35 seconds ahead of the Frenchman.* 4 PHRASE If something happens **ahead of** schedule or **ahead of** time, it happens earlier than was planned. ❑ *The election was held six months ahead of schedule.* 5 PHRASE If someone is **ahead of** someone else, they have made more progress and are more advanced in what they are doing. ❑ *Henry generally stayed ahead of the others in the academic subjects.* 6 **one step ahead of** someone or something →see **step. ahead of** your **time** →see **time**

1 구 앞의, 앞에서 ❑ 나는 30미터 전방에 파란 잠바를 입은 남자를 봤다. 2 구 다가올 ❑ 나는 내일 나에게 다가올 모든 문제에 대해 생각하려고 했다. ❑ 캐서린은 그녀 앞에 놓인 미래를 생각하며 밤을 지샜다. 3 구 앞서 ❑ 로버트 밀라는 프랑스인보다 1분 35초 먼저 들어왔다. 4 구 미리 ❑ 선거는 계획보다 6개월 앞당겨서 치러졌다. 5 구 앞선 ❑ 헨리는 대개 학문적 과목에선_다른 사람보다 앞섰다.

aid ♦♦♦ /eɪd/ (**aids, aiding, aided**) 1 N-UNCOUNT **Aid** is money, equipment, or services that are provided for people, countries, or organizations who need them but cannot provide them for themselves. ❑ *...regular flights carrying humanitarian aid to Cambodia.* ❑ *They have already pledged billions of dollars in aid.* 2 V-T To **aid** a country, organization, or person means to provide them with money, equipment, or services that they need. ❑ *...U.S. efforts to aid Kurdish refugees.* ● **-aided** COMB in ADJ ❑ *...state-aided schools.* 3 V-T To **aid** someone means to help or assist them. [WRITTEN] ❑ *...a software system to aid managers in advanced decision-making.* ● N-UNCOUNT **Aid** is also a noun. ❑ *He was forced to turn for aid to his former enemy.* 4 N-UNCOUNT If you perform a task **with the aid of** something, you need or use that thing to perform that task. ❑ *He succeeded with the aid of a completely new method he discovered.* 5 N-COUNT An **aid** is an object, device, or technique that makes something easier to do. ❑ *The book is an invaluable aid to teachers of literature.* 6 V-T/V-I If something **aids** a process, it makes it easier or more likely to happen. ❑ *The survey suggests that the export sector will continue to aid the economic recovery.* 7 →see also **first aid** 8 PHRASE If you **come** or **go to** someone's **aid**, you try to help them when they are in danger or difficulty. ❑ *Dr. Fox went to the aid of the dying man despite having been injured in the crash.* 9 PHRASE An activity or event **in aid of** a particular cause or charity is intended to raise money for that cause or charity. [mainly BRIT] ❑ *...a charity performance in aid of Great Ormond Street Children's Hospital.* ❑ *Most of their concerts are in aid of charity.*

1 불가산명사 원조 ❑ 인도적 원조를 캄보디아로 나르는 정기적인 항공편 ❑ 그들은 이미 수십억 달러의 원조를 약속했다. 2 타동사 돕다 ❑ 쿠르드 족 난민을 도우려는 미국의 노력 ● -의 원조를 받은 복합형-형용사 ❑ 국가 지원을 받는 학교 3 타동사 돕다 [문어체] ❑ 고도의 결정을 하는 데 있어 관리자들을 도울 소프트웨어 시스템 ● 불가산명사 원조 ❑ 그는 과거의 적에게 도움을 청할 수밖에 없었다. 4 불가산명사 도움 ❑ 그는 자신이 발견한 완전히 새로운 방법의 도움으로 성공했다. 5 가산명사 보조 기구 ❑ 그 책은 문학 교사들에게 매우 유용한 보조 교재이다. 6 타동사/자동사 돕다 ❑ 조사에 따르면 수출 부문이 경제 회복을 촉진할 것이라고 시사한다. 8 구 도우러 오다/가다 ❑ 팍스 박사는 충돌 사고에서 부상을 입었음에도 불구하고 죽어 가는 남자를 도우러 갔다. 9 구 -을 돕는 [주로 영국영어] ❑ 그레이트 오몬드 가(街) 어린이 병원을 돕기 위한 자선 공연 ❑ 그들의 콘서트 대부분은 자선 단체를 돕기 위한 것이다.

aide /eɪd/ (**aides**) N-COUNT An **aide** is an assistant to someone who has an important job, especially in government or in the armed forces. ❑ *A close aide to the Prime Minister repeated that Israel would never accept it.*

가산명사 보좌관 ❑ 이스라엘은 그것을 결코 받아들이지 않을 것이라고 수상의 가까운 보좌관이 반복했다.

AIDS ♦♦◇ /eɪdz/ N-UNCOUNT **AIDS** is a disease which destroys the natural system of protection that the body has against other diseases. **AIDS** is an

불가산명사 에이즈 ❑ 에이즈로 고통 받는 사람들

abbreviation for "acquired immune deficiency syndrome." ❑ ...people suffering from AIDS.

Word Partnership　　AIDS의 연어

N.	AIDS **activists**, AIDS **epidemic**, AIDS **patient**, AIDS **research**, **spread of** AIDS, AIDS **victims**
V.	**infected with** AIDS

---

ail|ing /ˈeɪlɪŋ/ ADJ An **ailing** organization or society is in difficulty and is becoming weaker. ❑ The rise in overseas sales is good news for the ailing American economy.

형용사 어려움에 처한 ❑ 해외 판매의 증가는 어려움에 처한 미국 경제에 희소식이다.

ail|ment /ˈeɪlmənt/ (ailments) N-COUNT An **ailment** is an illness, especially one that is not very serious. ❑ The pharmacist can assist you with the treatment of common ailments.

가산명사 (가벼운) 병 ❑ 약사는 일반적이고 가벼운 병을 치료하는 것을 도울 수 있다.

aim ♦♦♢ /eɪm/ (aims, aiming, aimed) **1** V-T/V-I If you **aim for** something or **aim to** do something, you plan or hope to achieve it. ❑ He said he would aim for the 100 meters world record at the world championships in August. ❑ Businesses will have to aim at long-term growth. **2** N-COUNT The **aim** of something that you do is the purpose for which you do it or the result that it is intended to achieve. ❑ The aim of the festival is to increase awareness of Hindu culture and traditions. **3** V-T PASSIVE If an action or plan **is aimed at** achieving something, it is intended or planned to achieve it. ❑ The new measures are aimed at tightening existing sanctions. **4** V-T If you **aim to** do something, you decide or want to do it. [AM, INFORMAL] ❑ I didn't aim to get caught. **5** V-T If your actions or remarks **are aimed at** a particular person or group, you intend that the person or group should notice them and be influenced by them. [usu passive] ❑ His message was aimed at the undecided middle ground of Israeli politics. **6** V-T/V-I If you **aim** a weapon or object **at** something or someone, you point it toward them before firing or throwing it. ❑ When he appeared again, he was aiming the rifle at Wade. ❑ ...a missile aimed at the arms factory. **7** N-SING Your **aim** is your skill or action in pointing a weapon or other object at its target. ❑ He stood with the gun gripped in his right hand and his left hand steadying his aim. **8** V-T If you **aim** a kick or punch at someone, you try to kick or punch them. ❑ They set on him, punching him in the face and aiming kicks at his shins. **9** PHRASE When you **take aim**, you point a weapon or object at someone, before firing or throwing it. ❑ She had spotted a man with a shotgun taking aim.

1 타동사/자동사 목표하다 ❑ 그는 8월에 열리는 세계 챔피언 경기에서 100미터 경주 세계 신기록을 노릴 것이라고 말했다. ❑ 기업들은 장기적 성장을 목표로 삼아야 할 것이다. **2** 가산명사 목표 ❑ 축제의 목표는 힌두교 문화와 전통에 대한 인식을 높이는 것이다. **3** 수동 타동사 -을 목표로 삼다 ❑ 새로운 방침들은 기존의 제재들을 강화하기 위한 것이다. **4** 타동사 -을 하고자 하다 [미국영어, 비격식체] ❑ 나는 잡히려고 한 것은 아니었어. **5** 타동사 -을 노리다 ❑ 그의 발언은 이스라엘 정치의 중도 부동층을 노린 것이었다. **6** 타동사/자동사 겨누다 ❑ 그가 다시 나타났을 때 그는 소총을 웨이드에게 겨누고 있었다. ❑ 무기 공장을 겨냥한 미사일 **7** 단수명사 조준 ❑ 총을 오른손에 쥐고 왼손으로는 조준을 안정시키며 그는 서 있었다. **8** 타동사 노리다 ❑ 그의 얼굴에 주먹질하고 정강이를 노려 발을 날리며 그들은 그에게 달려들었다. **9** 구 조준하다 ❑ 그녀는 산탄총을 가진 남자가 조준하는 것을 발견했다.

Word Partnership　　aim의 연어

PREP.	aim **for**, aim **to** **1**
	aim **at** **3**
	aim **of** **6**
ADJ.	**primary/sole/ultimate** aim **2**
V.	**take** aim **9**

---

aim|less /ˈeɪmləs/ ADJ A person or activity that is **aimless** has no clear purpose or plan. ❑ After several hours of aimless searching they were getting low on fuel. ● **aim|less|ly** ADV [ADV after v] ❑ I wandered around aimlessly.

형용사 목적 없는 ❑ 몇 시간 동안 목적 없이 수색하다 보니 그들의 연료가 바닥나기 시작했다. ● 목적 없이 부사 ❑ 나는 목적 없이 방황했다.

ain't /eɪnt/ People sometimes use **ain't** instead of "am not," "aren't," "isn't," "haven't," and "hasn't." Many people consider this use to be non-standard. [DIALECT, SPOKEN] ❑ Well, it's obvious, ain't it?

am이나 have 동사와 not을 결합한 축약형으로 쓰이는 비표준어 [방언, 구어체] ❑ 뭐, 당연하지 않아?

air ♦♦♦ /ɛər/ (airs, airing, aired) **1** N-UNCOUNT **Air** is the mixture of gases which forms the earth's atmosphere and which we breathe. ❑ Drafts help to circulate air. ❑ Keith opened the window and leaned out into the cold air. **2** N-SING The **air** is the space around things or above the ground. ❑ Government troops broke up the protest by firing their guns in the air. **3** N-UNCOUNT **Air** is used to refer to travel in aircraft. ❑ Air travel will continue to grow at about 6% per year. **4** V-T If a broadcasting company **airs** a television or radio program, they show it on television or broadcast it on the radio. [mainly AM] ❑ Tonight PBS will air a documentary called "Democracy In Action." ● **air|ing** N-SING ❑ Switzer said his program and his university could not tolerate the airing of this material. ❑ ...an exclusive airing of the documentary of Elizabeth II's coronation in Westminster Abbey. **5** PHRASE If you do something to **clear the air**, you do it in order to resolve any problems or disagreements that there might be. ❑ ...an inquiry just to clear the air and settle the facts of the case. **6** PHRASE If something is **in the air** it is felt to be present, but it is not talked about. ❑ There was great excitement in the air. **7** PHRASE If someone is **on the air**, they are broadcasting on radio or television. If a program is **on the air**, it is being broadcast on radio or television. If it is **off the air**, it is not being broadcast. ❑ Singer Dani Behr, 17, is going on the air as presenter of Channel 4's "The Word." **8** PHRASE If someone or something disappears **into thin air**, they disappear completely. If someone or something appears **out of thin air**, they appear suddenly and mysteriously. ❑ He had materialized out of thin air; I had not seen or heard him coming. →see **erosion, flight, respiratory, wind** →see Word Web: **air**

1 불가산명사 공기 ❑ 바람 덕분에 공기가 순환한다. ❑ 키스는 창문을 열고 차가운 공기 속으로 몸을 내밀었다. **2** 단수명사 허공 ❑ 정부군은 총을 허공에다 발포함으로써 시위를 해산시켰다. **3** 불가산명사 항공 ❑ 항공 여행은 매년 약 6%씩 성장할 것이다. **4** 타동사 방송하다 [주로 미국영어] ❑ 오늘 밤 피비에스는 '현실 속의 민주주의'라는 다큐멘터리를 방영할 것이다. ● 방송 단수명사 ❑ 스위처는 자신의 프로그램과 대학이 이 자료를 방송하는 것을 허용할 수 없다고 말했다. ❑ 웨스트민스터 사원에서 있은 엘리자베스 2세 대관식 다큐멘터리의 독점 방영 **5** 구 의혹을 없애다 ❑ 그저 의혹을 없애고 사건의 정황을 밝히기 위한 조사 **6** 구 감돌다 ❑ 엄청난 흥분이 감돌고 있었다. **7** 구 방송 중인 ❑ 17세인 가수 다니 베어는 채널 4의 '말'이라는 프로그램의 진행자로 방송에 나설 것이다. **8** 구 흔적도 없이; 난데없이 ❑ 그는 난데없이 나타났다. 나는 그가 오는 것을 보지도 듣지도 못했다.

air|bag /ˈɛərbæg/ (airbags) [AM, sometimes BRIT air bag] N-COUNT An **airbag** is a safety device in a car which automatically fills with air if the car crashes, and is designed to protect the people in the car when they are thrown forward in the crash. →see **car**

[미국영어, 가끔 영국영어 air bag] 가산명사 에어백

air base (air bases) also **airbase** N-COUNT An **air base** is a center where military aircraft take off or land and are serviced, and where many of the center's staff live. ❑ ...the largest U.S. air base in Saudi Arabia.

가산명사 공군 기지 ❑ 사우디아라비아에서 가장 큰 미국 공군 기지

Word Web   air

The **air** we breathe contains seventeen different **gases**. Surprisingly, it is composed mostly of **nitrogen**, not **oxygen**. Recently, human activities have created imbalances in the earth's **atmosphere**. The widespread burning of coal and oil increased levels of **carbon monoxide**. Scientists believe this air **pollution** may be responsible for **global warming**. Certain chemical compounds used in air conditioners, agricultural processes, and manufacturing are the problem. They break down the **ozone layer** surrounding the earth. With less protection from the sun, the air temperature rises. This leads to harmful effects on people, agriculture, animals, and the natural environment.

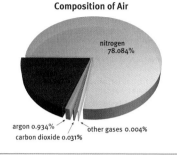

Composition of Air

nitrogen 78.084%
argon 0.934%   other gases 0.004%
carbon dioxide 0.031%

air|borne /ɛərbɔrn/ **1** ADJ If an aircraft is **airborne**, it is in the air and flying. [v-link ADJ] ❑ *The pilot did manage to get airborne.* **2** ADJ **Airborne** troops use parachutes to get into enemy territory. [ADJ n] ❑ *The allies landed thousands of airborne troops.* **3** ADJ **Airborne** means in the air or carried in the air. ❑ *Many people are allergic to airborne pollutants such as pollen.* →see **pollution**

1 형용사 이륙한 ❑ 조종사는 가까스로 이륙했다. **2** 형용사 공수된 ❑ 동맹군은 수천 명의 공수부대원을 낙하시켰다. **3** 형용사 공기로 운반되는 ❑ 많은 사람들은 꽃가루같이 공중에 날아다니는 오염원에 알레르기성 반응을 보인다.

air-conditioned ADJ If a room or vehicle is **air-conditioned**, the air in it is kept cool and dry by means of a special machine. ❑ *...our new air-conditioned trains.*

형용사 에어컨이 장착된 ❑ 에어컨이 장착된 새 기차

air-condition|ing N-UNCOUNT **Air-conditioning** is a method of providing buildings and vehicles with cool dry air.

불가산명사 냉방

air|craft ♦♦◇ /ɛərkræft/

| Aircraft is both the singular and the plural form. |

| aircraft은 단수형 및 복수형이다. |

N-COUNT An **aircraft** is a vehicle which can fly, for example an airplane or a helicopter. ❑ *The return flight of the aircraft was delayed.* →see **fly**

가산명사 항공기 ❑ 항공기의 회항은 지연되었다.

air|field /ɛərfild/ (**airfields**) N-COUNT An **airfield** is an area of ground where aircraft take off and land. It is smaller than an airport.

가산명사 비행장

air force ♦◇◇ (**air forces**) N-COUNT An **air force** is the part of a country's armed forces that is concerned with fighting in the air. ❑ *...the United States Air Force.*

가산명사 공군 ❑ 미국 공군

air host|ess (**air hostesses**) N-COUNT An **air hostess** is a woman whose job is to look after the passengers in an aircraft. [BRIT; AM **flight attendant**]

가산명사 비행기 여 승무원 [영국영어; 미국영어 flight attendant]

air|lift /ɛərlɪft/ (**airlifts, airlifting, airlifted**) **1** N-COUNT An **airlift** is an operation to move people, troops, or goods by air, especially in a war or when land routes are closed. ❑ *President Garcia has ordered an airlift of food, medicines and blankets.* **2** V-T If people, troops, or goods **are airlifted** somewhere, they are carried by air, especially in a war or when land routes are closed. ❑ *The injured were airlifted to hospital in Prestwick.*

1 가산명사 공수 ❑ 가르시아 대통령은 음식, 의약품, 담요 등을 공수할 것을 명령했다. **2** 타동사 공수되다 ❑ 부상자들은 프레스트윅의 병원으로 공수되었다.

air|line ♦♦◇ /ɛərlaɪn/ (**airlines**) N-COUNT An **airline** is a company which provides regular services carrying people or goods in airplanes. ❑ *Eleven of Europe's 15 busiest routes are controlled by only two national airlines.*

가산명사 항공사 ❑ 유럽에서 가장 이용객이 많은 15개의 노선 중 11개가 국내의 단지 두 항공사에 의해 지배되고 있다.

air|lin|er /ɛərlaɪnər/ (**airliners**) N-COUNT An **airliner** is a large airplane that is used for carrying passengers.

가산명사 대형 여객기

air|mail /ɛərmeɪl/ N-UNCOUNT **Airmail** is the system of sending letters, parcels, and goods by air. ❑ *...an airmail letter.*

불가산명사 항공 우편 ❑ 항공 우편 편지

air|man /ɛərmən/ (**airmen**) N-COUNT An **airman** is a man who flies aircraft, especially one who serves in his country's air force. ❑ *...an English airman.*

가산명사 (공군) 조종사 ❑ 영국 조종사

air|plane /ɛərpleɪn/ (**airplanes**) N-COUNT An **airplane** is a vehicle with wings and one or more engines that enable it to fly through the air. [AM; BRIT **aeroplane**] →see **fly**

가산명사 비행기 [미국영어; 영국영어 aeroplane]

air|port ♦♦◇ /ɛərpɔrt/ (**airports**) N-COUNT An **airport** is a place where aircraft land and take off, which has buildings and facilities for passengers. ❑ *...Heathrow Airport, the busiest international airport in the world.*

가산명사 공항 ❑ 세계에서 가장 붐비는 국제공항인 히드로 공항

air|port tax (**airport taxes**) N-VAR **Airport tax** is a tax that airline passengers have to pay in order to use an airport. ❑ *Overnight return flights cost from £349 including airport taxes.*

가산명사 또는 불가산명사 공항세 ❑ 1박의 왕복 항공권은 공항세를 포함하여 349파운드부터이다.

air rage N-UNCOUNT **Air rage** is aggressive or violent behavior by airline passengers. ❑ *Most air rage incidents involve heavy drinking.*

불가산명사 기내 난동 ❑ 대부분의 기내 난동 사건은 폭음과 관련이 있다.

air raid (**air raids**) N-COUNT An **air raid** is an attack by military aircraft in which bombs are dropped. This expression is usually used by the country or group that is suffering the attack. ❑ *The war began with overnight air raids on Baghdad and Kuwait.*

가산명사 공습 ❑ 그 전쟁은 바그다드와 쿠웨이트에 대한 야간 공습으로 개시되었다.

air|space /ɛərspeɪs/ also **air space** N-UNCOUNT A country's **airspace** is the part of the sky that is over that country and is considered to belong to it. ❑ *Forty minutes later, they left Colombian airspace.*

불가산명사 영공 ❑ 사십 분 후 그들은 콜롬비아 영공을 벗어났다.

air|tight /ɛərtaɪt/ also **air-tight** **1** ADJ If a container is **airtight**, its lid fits so tightly that no air can get in or out. ❑ *Store the cookies in an airtight tin.* **2** ADJ An **airtight** alibi, case, argument, or agreement is one that has been so carefully put together that nobody will be able to find a fault in it. [AM; BRIT **watertight**] ❑ *If she could just establish the time the picture had been taken, Mick would have an airtight alibi.* →see **can**

1 형용사 밀폐된 ❑ 쿠키들을 밀폐되는 깡통에 보관하세요. **2** 형용사 빈틈없는 [미국영어; 영국영어 watertight] ❑ 사진이 찍힌 시간만 입증할 수만 있다면 믹은 빈틈없는 알리바이를 갖게 될 것이다.

air traffic con|trol|ler (**air traffic controllers**) N-COUNT An **air traffic controller** is someone whose job is to organize the routes that aircraft should follow, and to tell pilots by radio which routes they should take.

가산명사 관제사

air|waves /ˈeɜrweɪvz/ also **air waves** N-PLURAL **The airwaves** is used to refer to the activity of broadcasting on radio and television. For example, if someone says something over **the airwaves**, they say it on the radio or television. [JOURNALISM] ❑ *The election campaign has been fought not in street rallies but on the airwaves.*

복수명사 방송 전파 [언론] ❑ 선거전은 길거리 집회가 아닌 방송 전파를 타고 치러져 왔다.

airy /ˈeɜri/ (**airier, airiest**) ADJ If a building or room is **airy**, it has a lot of fresh air inside, usually because it is large. ❑ *The bathroom has a light and airy feel.*

형용사 통풍이 잘 되는 ❑ 그 화장실은 분위기가 밝고 상쾌하다.

aisle /aɪl/ (**aisles**) N-COUNT An **aisle** is a long narrow gap that people can walk along between rows of seats in a public building such as a church or between rows of shelves in a supermarket. ❑ *...the frozen food aisle.*

가산명사 통로 ❑ 냉동식품 통로

aka /eɪ keɪ eɪ/

| The spelling a.k.a. is also used, especially in American English. |

| 철자 a.k.a.도 특히 미국영어에서 쓴다. |

aka is an abbreviation for "also known as." **aka** is used especially when referring to someone's nickname or stage name. ❑ *From the very beginning, Stuart Leslie Goddard, aka Adam Ant, knew he was going to be a star.*

별명; 예명 ❑ 애덤 앤트라는 예명으로 보다 잘 알려진 스튜어트 레슬리 고다드는 자신이 스타가 될 것이라는 것을 처음부터 알고 있었다.

à la carte /ɑ lɑ kɑrt/ ADJ An **à la carte** menu in a restaurant offers you a choice of individually priced dishes for each course. [ADJ n] ❑ *You could choose as much or as little as you wanted from an à la carte menu.* ● ADV **à la carte** is also an adverb. [ADV after v] ❑ *Choose a light snack in the café or eat à la carte in the elegant dining room.*

형용사 선택 요리의 일품요리의 ❑ 일품요리 메뉴에서 원하는 만큼 고를 수 있다. ● 부사 메뉴판에서 골라 ❑ 카페에서 가벼운 스낵을 먹을 수도 있고 우아한 식당에서 메뉴판을 보고 요리를 골라 먹을 수도 있습니다.

alarm ◆◇◇ /əˈlɑrm/ (**alarms, alarming, alarmed**) ■ N-UNCOUNT **Alarm** is a feeling of fear or anxiety that something unpleasant or dangerous might happen. ❑ *The news was greeted with alarm by MPs.* ② V-T If something **alarms** you, it makes you afraid or anxious that something unpleasant or dangerous might happen. ❑ *We could not see what had alarmed him.* ③ N-COUNT An **alarm** is an automatic device that warns you of danger, for example by ringing a bell. ❑ *He heard the alarm go off.* ④ N-COUNT An **alarm** is the same as an **alarm clock**. ❑ *Dad set the alarm for eight the next day.* ⑤ →see also **alarmed, alarming, car alarm, false alarm, fire alarm** ⑥ PHRASE If you say that something sets **alarm bells** ringing, you mean that it makes people feel worried or concerned about something. ❑ *This has set the alarm bells ringing in Moscow.* ⑦ PHRASE If you **raise the alarm** or **sound the alarm**, you warn people of danger. ❑ *His family raised the alarm when he had not come home by 9pm.*

■ 불가산명사 놀람 ❑ 그 소식을 듣고 하원 의원들은 놀랐다. ② 타동사 놀라게 하다 ❑ 우리는 무엇이 그를 놀라게 했는지 알 수 없었다. ③ 가산명사 경보기 ❑ 그는 경보기가 울리는 소리를 들었다. ④ 가산명사 자명종 ❑ 아버지께서는 자명종을 다음 날 8시에 맞추셨다. ⑥ 구 경각심 ❑ 이 사건으로 모스크바의 경각심이 높아졌다. ⑦ 구 위험을 알리다 ❑ 그가 저녁 9시가 되어도 집에 오지 않자 그의 가족이 위험을 알렸다.

Word Partnership	*alarm*의 연어
V.	**cause** alarm ■
	set the alarm ④
	raise/sound the alarm ⑦
N.	**alarm** system ③

alarm clock (**alarm clocks**) N-COUNT An **alarm clock** is a clock that you can set to make a noise so that it wakes you up at a particular time. ❑ *I set my alarm clock for 4:30.*

가산명사 자명종 ❑ 나는 자명종을 4시 반에 맞췄다.

alarmed /əˈlɑrmd/ ADJ If someone is **alarmed**, they feel afraid or anxious that something unpleasant or dangerous might happen. ❑ *They should not be too alarmed by the press reports.*

형용사 놀란 ❑ 그들은 언론 보도에 너무 놀랄 필요가 없다.

alarm|ing /əˈlɑrmɪŋ/ ADJ Something that is **alarming** makes you feel afraid or anxious that something unpleasant or dangerous might happen. ❑ *The disease has spread at an alarming rate.* ● **alarm|ing|ly** ADV ❑ *...the alarmingly high rate of heart disease.*

형용사 놀라운 ❑ 병은 놀라운 속도로 퍼져 나갔다. ● 놀랍게 부사 ❑ 놀라운 정도로 높은 심장 질환의 비율

alas /əˈlæs/ ADV You use **alas** to say that you think that the facts you are talking about are sad or unfortunate. [FORMAL, FEELINGS] [ADV with cl] ❑ *Such scandals have not, alas, been absent.*

부사 오호라, 애석하게도 [격식체, 감정 개입] ❑ 애석하게도 그런 비리가 없지 않았다.

al|be|it /ɔlˈbiɪt/ ADV You use **albeit** to introduce a fact or comment which reduces the force or significance of what you have just said. [FORMAL] [ADV with cl/group] ❑ *Charles's letter was indeed published, albeit in a somewhat abbreviated form.*

부사 비록 ...이지만 [격식체] ❑ 비록 약간 축약된 형태이긴 했지만 찰스의 편지는 진짜로 게재되었다.

al|bum ◆◇◇ /ˈælbəm/ (**albums**) ■ N-COUNT An **album** is a collection of songs that is available on a CD, record, or cassette. ❑ *Chris likes music and has a large collection of albums and cassettes.* ❑ *Oasis release their new album on July 1.* ② N-COUNT An **album** is a book in which you keep things such as photographs or stamps that you have collected. ❑ *Theresa showed me her photo album.*

■ 가산명사 음반 ❑ 크리스는 음악을 좋아하며 많은 음반과 카세트를 가지고 있다. ❑ 오아시스는 새 음반을 7월 1일에 발매한다. ② 가산명사 사진첩 ❑ 테레사는 나에게 자신의 사진첩을 보여 줬다.

Word Partnership	*album*의 연어
V.	**produce/release an** album ■
ADJ.	**debut/first/latest/new** album, **live** album, **solo** album ■
N.	**photo** album ②

al|co|hol ◆◇◇ /ˈælkəhɔl, BRIT ˈælkəhɒl/ ■ N-UNCOUNT Drinks that can make people drunk, such as beer, wine, and whiskey, can be referred to as **alcohol**. ❑ *Do either of you smoke cigarettes or drink alcohol?* ② N-MASS **Alcohol** is a colorless liquid that is found in drinks such as beer, wine, and whiskey. It is also used in products such as perfumes and cleaning fluids. ❑ *...low-alcohol beer.*

■ 불가산명사 술 ❑ 너희 둘 중 혹시 담배 피우거나 술 마시는 사람 있니? ② 물질명사 알코올 ❑ 알코올 함량이 낮은 맥주

al|co|hol|ic /ˌælkəˈhɔlɪk, BRIT ˌælkəˈhɒlɪk/ (**alcoholics**) ■ N-COUNT An **alcoholic** is someone who cannot stop drinking large amounts of alcohol, even when this is making them ill. ❑ *He showed great courage by admitting on television that he is an alcoholic.* ② ADJ **Alcoholic** drinks are drinks that contain alcohol. ❑ *The serving of alcoholic drinks was forbidden after six o'clock.*

■ 가산명사 알코올 중독자 ❑ 그는 텔레비전에서 자신이 알코올 중독자라는 것을 시인함으로써 굉장한 용기를 보였다. ② 형용사 알코올의 ❑ 여섯 시 이후 주류 판매는 금지되었다.

al|co|hol|ism /ˈælkəhɒlɪzəm/ N-UNCOUNT People who suffer from **alcoholism** cannot stop drinking large quantities of alcohol. ❑ *...a physician who specialized in the problems of alcoholism.*

불가산명사 알코올 중독 ❑ 알코올 중독을 전문으로 다루는 의사

ale /eɪl/ (**ales**) N-MASS **Ale** is a kind of strong beer. ❑ *...our selection of ales and spirits.*

물질명사 에일 맥주 (약간 쓰고 독한 맥주) ❑ 우리의 쓴 맥주와 증류주 선택

alert ♦♢♢ /əˈlɜːrt/ (**alerts, alerting, alerted**) ❶ ADJ If you are **alert**, you are paying full attention to things around you and are able to deal with anything that might happen. ❑ *We all have to stay alert.* ● **alert|ness** N-UNCOUNT ❑ *The drug improved mental alertness.* ❷ ADJ If you are **alert** to something, you are fully aware of it. [v-link ADJ to n] ❑ *The bank is alert to the danger.* ❸ N-COUNT An **alert** is a situation in which people prepare themselves for something dangerous that might happen soon. ❑ *Due to a security alert, this train will not be stopping at Oxford Circus.* ❹ V-T If you **alert** someone **to** a situation, especially a dangerous or unpleasant situation, you tell them about it. ❑ *He wanted to alert people to the activities of the group.* ❺ PHRASE If you are **on the alert for** something, you are ready to deal with it if it happens. ❑ *They want to be on the alert for similar buying opportunities.*
→see **hypnosis**

❶ 형용사 경계하는 ❑ 우리 모두 방심해선 안 된다. ● 경계 불가산명사 ❑ 그 약은 정신 상태를 더 맑게 해 줬다. ❷ 형용사 인지한 ❑ 은행은 그 위험을 알고 있다. ❸ 가산명사 경보 ❑ 보안 경고에 따라 본 열차는 옥스퍼드 서커스에 정차하지 않습니다. ❹ 타동사 경고하다 ❑ 그는 그 단체의 행동에 대해 사람들에게 경고하고 싶었다. ❺ 구 경계하고 있는 ❑ 그들은 비슷한 구매 기회를 포착하기 위해 경계를 늦추지 않길 바란다.

A lev|el /eɪ ˈlevᵊl/ (**A levels**) N-VAR **A levels** are British educational qualifications which students take when they are seventeen or eighteen years old. People usually need A levels if they want to go to a university in Britain. ❑ *He left school with four A levels.*

가산명사 또는 불가산명사 에이-레벨 시험 (영국에서 학생들이 17-18세 때 대학에 진학하기 위해 보는 자격시험) ❑ 그는 4과목에 대해 에이 레벨 시험 성적을 따고 고등학교를 졸업했다.

al|gae /ˈældʒiː, ˈælgaɪ/ N-PLURAL **Algae** are plants with no stems or leaves that grow in water or on damp surfaces. ❑ *If algae is infesting your garden pond, try Pond Pads, from Green Ways.*
→see **plant**

복수명사 조류 ❑ 만약 당신의 정원 연못에 조류가 끼었다면 그린 웨이즈에서 발매하는 폰드 패즈를 사용해 보십시오.

al|ge|bra /ˈældʒɪbrə/ N-UNCOUNT **Algebra** is a type of mathematics in which letters are used to represent possible quantities. →see **mathematics**

불가산명사 대수학

Word Link	*ali* ≈ *other* : *ali*as, *ali*bi, *ali*en

ali|as /ˈeɪliəs/ (**aliases**) ❶ N-COUNT An **alias** is a false name, especially one used by a criminal. ❑ *Using an alias, he had rented a house in Fleet, Hampshire.* ❷ PREP You use **alias** when you are mentioning another name that someone, especially a criminal or an actor, is known by. [n-proper PREP n-proper] ❑ *Richard Thorp, alias Alan Turner, said yesterday: "It is a sad time for both of us."*

❶ 가산명사 가명 ❑ 그는 가명을 사용하여 햄프셔 주의 플릿에 집을 빌렸었다. ❷ 전치사 가명 ❑ 앨런 터너라는 가명을 사용하는 리차드 소프는 "우리 양측 모두에게 슬픈 시기이다."라고 어제 말했다.

ali|bi /ˈælɪbaɪ/ (**alibis**) N-COUNT If you have an **alibi**, you can prove that you were somewhere else when a crime was committed. ❑ *He manages to persuade both his wife and girlfriend to provide him with an alibi.*

가산명사 알리바이 ❑ 그는 아내와 여자 친구 둘 다 그에게 알리바이를 제공하도록 겨우 설득한다.

ali|en /ˈeɪliən/ (**aliens**) ❶ ADJ **Alien** means belonging to a different country, race, or group, usually one you do not like or are frightened of. [FORMAL, DISAPPROVAL] ❑ *He said they were opposed to what he described as the presence of alien forces in the region.* ❷ ADJ If something is **alien to** you or **to** your normal feelings or behavior, it is not the way you would normally feel or behave. [FORMAL] [v-link ADJ to n] ❑ *Such an attitude is alien to most businessmen.* ❸ N-COUNT An **alien** is someone who is not a legal citizen of the country in which they live. [LEGAL] ❑ *Both women had hired illegal aliens for child care.* ❹ N-COUNT In science fiction, an **alien** is a creature from outer space. ❑ *...aliens from another planet.*

❶ 형용사 외국의, 이방의 [격식체, 탐탁찮음] ❑ 그는 그들이 그 지역에 그가 이방인 병력이라고 묘사한 집단이 주둔하는 것을 반대하고 있다고 말했다. ❷ 형용사 성질이 다른, 낯선 [격식체] ❑ 그러한 태도는 대부분의 사업가들에게서는 발견할 수 없다. ❸ 가산명사 외국인 [법률] ❑ 두 여자 다 불법 체류 외국인을 보모로 고용했었다. ❹ 가산명사 외계인 ❑ 다른 행성에서 온 외계인

ali|en|ate /ˈeɪliəneɪt/ (**alienates, alienating, alienated**) ❶ V-T If you **alienate** someone, you make them become unfriendly or unsympathetic toward you. ❑ *The government cannot afford to alienate either group.* ❷ V-T To **alienate** a person **from** someone or something that they are normally linked with means to cause them to be emotionally or intellectually separated from them. ❑ *His second wife, Alice, was determined to alienate him from his two boys.*

❶ 타동사 소원하게 만들다 ❑ 정부는 두 단체 중 어느 단체도 자신들과 소원하게 만들 여유가 없다. ❷ 타동사 멀어지게 하다 ❑ 그의 두 번째 아내인 앨리스는 그를 그의 두 아들로부터 멀어지게 하려고 작정했다.

alight /əˈlaɪt/ (**alights, alighting, alighted**) ❶ ADJ If something is **alight**, it is burning. [v n ADJ, v-link ADJ] ❑ *Several buildings were set alight.* ❷ ADJ If someone's eyes are **alight** or if their face is **alight**, the expression in their eyes or on their face shows that they are feeling a strong emotion such as excitement or happiness. [LITERARY] [v-link ADJ, oft ADJ with n] ❑ *She paused and turned, her face alight with happiness.*

❶ 형용사 불붙은 ❑ 여러 채의 건물에 불이 붙어 있었다. ❷ 형용사 빛나는 [문예체] ❑ 그녀는 잠깐 멈춰 서서 뒤를 돌아보았는데 얼굴은 행복감에 빛나고 있었다.

align /əˈlaɪn/ (**aligns, aligning, aligned**) ❶ V-T If you **align yourself with** a particular group, you support them because you have the same political aim. ❑ *Of late, though, there have been signs that the prime minister is aligning himself with the liberals.* ❷ V-T If you **align** something, you place it in a certain position in relation to something else, usually parallel to it. ❑ *A tripod will be useful to align and steady the camera.*

❶ 타동사 동조하다 ❑ 그러나 최근에는 수상이 진보 세력과 동조하는 징조가 보였다. ❷ 타동사 정렬하다 ❑ 카메라 방향을 조절하고 안정시키는 데에는 삼각대가 유용할 것이다.

align|ment /əˈlaɪnmənt/ (**alignments**) ❶ N-VAR An **alignment** is support for a particular group, especially in politics, or for a side in a quarrel or struggle. ❑ *He refused to compromise the church by a particular political alignment.* ❷ N-UNCOUNT The **alignment** of something is its position in relation to something else or to its correct position. ❑ *They shunned the belief that there is a link between the alignment of the planets and events on the Earth.*

❶ 가산명사 또는 불가산명사 동조 ❑ 그는 특정한 정치 성향을 보임으로써 교회에 누를 끼치기를 거부했다. ❷ 불가산명사 위치, 배치 ❑ 그들은 행성들의 일렬 배치와 지구에서 벌어지는 일 사이에 연관성이 있다는 믿음을 배척했다.

alike /əˈlaɪk/ ❶ ADJ If two or more things are **alike**, they are similar in some way. [v-link ADJ] ❑ *We looked very alike.* ❷ ADV **Alike** means in a similar way. [ADV after v] ❑ *They even dressed alike.*

❶ 형용사 비슷한 ❑ 우리는 외모상 많이 닮았었다. ❷ 부사 비슷하게 ❑ 그들은 심지어 옷도 비슷하게 입었다.

Thesaurus	*alike*의 참조어
ADJ.	comparable, equal, equivalent, matching, parallel, similar; *(ant.)* different ❶

a b c d e f g h i j k l m n o p q r s t u v w x y z

alive ♦♢♢ /əlaɪv/ **1** ADJ If people or animals are **alive**, they are not dead. [v-link ADJ, keep n ADJ] ❑ She does not know if he is alive or dead. **2** ADJ If you say that someone seems **alive**, you mean that they seem to be very lively and to enjoy everything that they do. ❑ She seemed more alive and looked forward to getting up in the morning. **3** ADJ If an activity, organization, or situation is **alive**, it continues to exist or function. [v-link ADJ, keep n ADJ] ❑ The big factories are trying to stay alive by cutting costs. **4** ADJ If a place is **alive with** something, there are a lot of people or things there and it seems busy or exciting. [v-link ADJ, usu ADJ with n] ❑ The river was alive with birds. **5** PHRASE If people, places, or events **come alive**, they start to be lively again after a quiet period. If someone or something **brings** them **alive**, they cause them to come alive. ❑ The doctor's voice had come alive and his small eyes shone. **6** PHRASE If a story or description **comes alive**, it becomes interesting, lively, or realistic. If someone or something **brings** it **alive**, they make it seem more interesting, lively, or realistic. ❑ She made history come alive with tales from her own memories.

Word Partnership	alive의 연어
ADJ.	**dead or** alive **1**
ADV.	alive **and well 1**
	still alive **1 3**
V.	**found** alive, **keep** *someone/something* alive **1**
	stay alive **1 3**
	feel alive **2**
	come alive **5 6**

all ♦♦♦ /ɔl/ **1** PREDET You use **all** to indicate that you are referring to the whole of a particular group or thing or to everyone or everything of a particular kind. [PREDET det pl-n/n-uncount] ❑ He felt betrayed by his mother, and this anger twisted all his later relationships. ● DET **All** is also a determiner. ❑ There is built-in storage space in all bedrooms. ● He was passionate about all literature. ● QUANT **All** is also a quantifier. [QUANT of def-pl-n/def-n-uncount] ❑ He was told to pack up all of his letters and personal belongings. ● PRON **All** is also a pronoun. ❑ Molton Brown was the only salon producing its own shampoos and hair-care products, all based on herbal recipes. ● PRON-EMPH **All** is also an emphasizing pronoun. [n PRON v] ❑ Milk, oily fish and egg all contain vitamin D.

All is often used to mean the same as **whole** but when used in front of plurals, **all** and **whole** have different meanings. For example, if you say "**All the buildings have been destroyed**," you mean that every building has been destroyed. If you say "**Whole buildings have been destroyed**," you mean that some buildings have been destroyed completely. Note that when **all** is used to consider a group, this means that the group has more than two members. To refer to two people or things, you use **both**. ❑ Tony and Bob both laughed. You use **every** to refer to all the members of a group that has more than two members. ❑ He listened to every news bulletin....an equal chance for every child. You use **each** to refer to every person or thing in a group when you are thinking about them as individuals. Note that **each** can be used to refer to both members of a pair. ❑ Each apartment has two bedrooms... We each carried a suitcase. Note that **each** and **every** are only used with singular nouns.

2 DET You use **all** to refer to the whole of a particular period of time. ❑ George had to cut grass all afternoon. ● PREDET **All** is also a predeterminer. [PREDET det sing-n] ❑ She's worked all her life. ● QUANT **All** is also a quantifier. [QUANT of def-n] ❑ He spent all of that afternoon polishing the silver. **3** PRON You use **all** to refer to a situation or to life in general. ❑ All is silent on the island now. **4** ADV You use **all** to emphasize that something is completely true, or happens everywhere or always, or on every occasion. [EMPHASIS] [ADV prep/adv] ❑ He loves animals and he knows all about them. ❑ He was doing it all by himself. **5** PRON You use **all** at the beginning of a clause when you are emphasizing that something is the only thing that is important. [EMPHASIS] ❑ He said all that remained was to agree to a time and venue. ❑ All you ever want to do is go shopping! **6** DET You use **all** in expressions such as **in all sincerity** and **in all probability** to emphasize that you are being sincere or that something is very likely. [EMPHASIS] ❑ In all fairness he had to admit that she was neither dishonest nor lazy. **7** ADV You use **all** when you are talking about an equal score in a game. For example, if the score is three **all**, both players or teams have three points. [amount ADV] **8** ADV **All** is used in structures such as **all the more** or **all the better** to mean even more or even better than before. [ADV the adv/adj-compared] ❑ The living room is decorated in pale colors that make it all the more airy. **9** PRON-EMPH You use **all** in expressions such as **seen it all** and **done it all** to emphasize that someone has had a lot of experience of something. [EMPHASIS] ❑ Pauline appeared to have it all; a happy marriage, a comfortable home and beautiful children. **10** PHRASE You say **above all** to indicate that the thing you are mentioning is the most important point. [EMPHASIS] ❑ Above all, chairs should be comfortable. **11** PHRASE You use **after all** when introducing a statement which supports or helps explain something you have just said. ❑ I thought you might know somebody. After all, you're the man with

1 형용사 살아 있는 ❑ 그녀는 그가 살았는지 죽었는지 모른다. **2** 형용사 생기 있는 ❑ 그녀는 보다 많은 생기가 도는 듯했으며 아침에 자리에서 일어나기를 고대했다. **3** 형용사 활동하는 ❑ 큰 공장들은 비용을 절감함으로써 살아남으려 하고 있다. **4** 형용사 활기찬 ❑ 강은 새들로 활기가 있었다. **5** 구 활기를 되찾다; 활기를 불어넣다 ❑ 의사의 목소리는 활기를 되찾았고 그의 작은 눈은 빛났다. **6** 구 재미있어지다; 생기를 불어넣다 ❑ 그녀는 자신의 기억에서 나온 이야기들로 역사에 생기를 불어넣었다.

1 전치한정사 전부 ❑ 그는 어머니에게 배신당함을 느꼈고 이러한 분노는 추후 그의 모든 관계를 왜곡시켰다. ● 한정사 모든 ❑ 모든 화장실에 붙박이 수납 공간이 있다. ● 그는 모든 문학에 대해 열정적이었다. ● 수량사 모든 ❑ 그는 자신의 모든 편지와 사유물을 짐 싸서 챙기라는 지시를 받았다. ● 대명사 모두 ❑ 몰튼 브라운은 샴푸와 머리 손질 용품을 자체적으로 생산하며, 그것도 모두 허브를 사용하는 유일한 미용실이었다. ● 강조대명사 모두 ❑ 우유, 기름진 생선, 계란에는 모두 비타민 디가 들어 있다.

all은 흔히 whole과 같은 뜻으로 쓰이지만 복수 앞에 쓰이면 all과 whole은 다른 뜻을 갖는다. 예를 들어, "All the buildings have been destroyed."라고 하면, 모든 건물들이 하나하나 다 파괴되었다는 뜻이다. 그런데 "Whole buildings have been destroyed."라고 하면, 일부 건물들이 완전히 파괴되었음을 의미한다. 하나의 집단을 생각하며 all을 쓸 때는 이 집단에 세 명 이상의 구성원이 있음을 의미한다는 점을 유의하라. 두 명의 사람이나 또는 두 가지 사물을 언급할 때에는 both를 쓴다. ❑ 토니와 밥은 둘 다 웃었다. every는 세 명 이상의 구성원이 있는 집단의 모든 구성원을 가리킬 때 쓴다. ❑ 그는 모든 뉴스 속보에 귀를 기울였다....모든 아이들에게 동등한 기회. each는 한 집단의 모든 구성원이나 구성체를 각각 개별적인 개체로 생각하여 언급할 때 쓴다. each는 한 쌍의 두 구성원 또는 구성체를 언급할 때에도 쓰인다는 점을 유의하라. ❑ 각 아파트에는 침실이 두 개씩 있다... 우리는 각자 여행 가방을 하나씩 들고 있었다. each와 every는 단수 명사하고만 쓰인다는 점에 유의하라.

2 한정사 내내 ❑ 조지는 오후 내내 잔디를 깎아야 했다. ● 전치한정사 내내 ❑ 그녀는 평생 일을 했다. ● 수량사 모든 ❑ 그는 오후 내내 은식기류를 닦으며 보냈다. **3** 대명사 모두 ❑ 이제 섬에는 모든 것이 조용하며. **4** 부사 모두 [강조] ❑ 그는 동물을 사랑하고 동물에 대해 모든 것을 안다. ❑ 그는 그 모든 것을 혼자 하고 있었다. **5** 대명사 오직 ~만 [강조] ❑ 그는 이제 시간과 장소만 정하면 된다고 말했다. ❑ 네가 항상 하고 싶어 하는 것이라곤 오직 쇼핑밖에 없어! **6** 한정사 모든, 전적으로 [강조] ❑ 전적으로 공평하게 따지면 그는 그녀가 부정직하지도 게으르지도 않다고 인정할 수밖에 없었다. **7** 부사 동점 **8** 부사 훨씬 더 ❑ 거실은 훨씬 공간이 넓어 보이게 하는 옅은 색깔로 장식되었다. ● 강조대명사 있는 것 [강조] ❑ 폴린은 행복한 결혼 생활, 안락한 집, 아름다운 자녀 등 모든 것을 가진 듯했다. **10** 구 무엇보다 [강조] ❑ 무엇보다 의자가 편해야 한다. **11** 구 사실 ❑ 나는 자네가 누군가를 알 줄 알았네. 사실, 연줄이 있는 사람은 자네 아닌가. **12** 구 어떻든 ❑ 어떻든 너를 집에서 찾을 수 있을까 하고 여기로 나왔지.

connections. **12** PHRASE You use **after all** when you are saying that something that you thought might not be the case is in fact the case. ❑ *I came out here on the chance of finding you at home after all.*

> Note that you do not use **after all** if you want to talk about what happens at the end of a long period, instead you use **at last, finally, in the end, lastly,** or **last of all**. You use **at last** or **finally** when you have been waiting for or expecting something for a long time. **At last** usually comes at the end of a sentence. ❑ *The storm that had threatened came at last.* **Finally** usually comes at the beginning of a sentence or before a verb. ❑ *After another search they finally located the house.* You also use **finally** to talk about something that is the last in a series of things. ❑ *He lived in Turkey, France, Norway, and finally Mexico.* You use **in the end** when talking about something that happens after a long time or a long process. ❑ *Perhaps the police got him in the end... In the end, Peter seemed quite happy.* You use **lastly** to talk about the last of a series of people or things. ❑ *I went through the bathroom, the bedroom, and lastly the living room.* You use **last of all** to emphasize that there is nobody or nothing else after the person or thing you mention. ❑ *Last of all came the cat.*

13 PHRASE You use **and all** when you want to emphasize that what you are talking about includes the thing mentioned, especially when this is surprising or unusual. [EMPHASIS] ❑ *He dropped his sausage on the pavement and someone's dog ate it, mustard and all.* **14** PHRASE You use **all in all** to introduce a summary or general statement. ❑ *We both thought that all in all it might not be a bad idea.* **15** PHRASE You use **at all** at the end of a clause to give emphasis in negative statements, conditional clauses, and questions. [EMPHASIS] ❑ *Robin never really liked him at all.* **16** PHRASE **All but** a particular person or thing means everyone or everything except that person or thing. ❑ *The general was an unattractive man to all but his most ardent admirers.* **17** PHRASE You use **all but** to say that something is almost the case. ❑ *The concrete wall that used to divide this city has now all but gone.* **18** PHRASE You use **for all** to indicate that the thing mentioned does not affect or contradict the truth of what you are saying. ❑ *For all its beauty, Prague could soon lose some of the individuality that the communist years helped to preserve.* **19** PHRASE You use **for all** in phrases such as **for all I know,** and **for all he cares,** to emphasize that you do not know something or that someone does not care about something. [EMPHASIS] ❑ *For all we know, he may even not be in this country.* **20** PHRASE **In all** means in total. ❑ *There was evidence that thirteen people in all had taken part in planning the murder.* **21** PHRASE You use **of all** to emphasize the words "first" or "last," or a superlative adjective or adverb. [EMPHASIS] ❑ *First of all, answer these questions.* **22** PHRASE You use **of all** in expressions such as **of all people** or **of all things** when you want to emphasize someone or something surprising. [EMPHASIS] ❑ *One group of women, sitting on the ground, was singing, of all things, "Greensleeves."* **23** PHRASE You use **of all** in expressions like **of all the nerve** or **of all the luck** to emphasize how angry or surprised you are at what someone else has done or said. [FEELINGS] ❑ *Of all the lazy, indifferent, unbusinesslike attitudes to have!* **24** PHRASE You use **all of** before a number to emphasize how small or large an amount is. [EMPHASIS] ❑ *It took him all of 41 minutes to score his first goal.* **25** PHRASE You use **all that** in statements with negative meaning when you want to weaken the force of what you are saying. [SPOKEN, VAGUENESS] ❑ *He wasn't all that older than we were.* **26** PHRASE You can say **that's all** at the end of a sentence when you are explaining something and want to emphasize that nothing more happens or is the case. ❑ *"Why do you want to know that?" he demanded. — "Just curious, that's all."* **27** PHRASE You use **all very well** to suggest that you do not really approve of something or you think that it is unreasonable. [DISAPPROVAL] ❑ *It is all very well to urge people to give more to charity when they have less, but is it really fair?*

Word Partnership	*all*의 연어	
N.	all **ages,** all **kinds/sorts,** all **the way** **1**	
	all **the time,** all **day/night** **2**	
V.	have it all, have seen it all **9**	
PREP.	**above** all **10**	
	after all **11**	
	at all **15**	
	in all **20**	
	of all **21**-**23**	
	all **of** **24**	

all- /ɔːl-/ **1** COMB in ADJ **All-** is added to nouns or adjectives in order to form adjectives which describe something as consisting only of the thing mentioned or as having only the quality indicated. [usu ADJ n] ❑ *An all-star cast gathered at London's Savoy Hotel for the Evening Standard Awards.* ❑ *The all-star cast includes Jeremy Irons.* **2** COMB in ADJ **All-** is added to present participles and adjectives in order to form adjectives which describe something as including or affecting everything or everyone. [usu ADJ n] ❑ *Nursing a demented person is an all-consuming task.* **3** COMB in ADJ **All-** is added to nouns in order to form adjectives which describe something as being suitable for or including all types of a particular thing. [usu ADJ n] ❑ *He wanted to form an all-party government of national unity.*

오랜 기간의 끝에 일어나는 일에 대해 얘기하고 싶으면 after all을 쓰지 않고, 그 대신 at last, finally, in the end, lastly, last of all을 쓴다는 점에 유의해야 한다. at last나 finally는 무엇을 오랫동안 기다리거나 기대해 왔을 때 쓴다. at last는 대개 문미에 온다. ❑ 잔뜩 위협하는 듯 했던 폭풍이 마침내 닥쳐왔다. finally는 대개 문두 또는 동사 뒤에 온다. ❑ 다시 한번 수색한 후에 그들은 마침내 그 집의 위치를 알아냈다. finally는 계속 이어져 나열된 것들 중 마지막 것을 얘기할 때에도 쓴다. ❑ 그는 터키, 프랑스, 노르웨이, 그리고 마지막으로 멕시코에 살았다. in the end는 긴 시간이나 긴 과정이 끝난 후에 일어나는 것에 관해 얘기할 때 쓴다. ❑ 아마 경찰이 결국에는 그를 잡았을 것이다... 마침내, 피터는 아주 행복해 보였다. lastly는 나열된 사람이나 사물 중 마지막 것을 얘기할 때 쓴다. ❑ 나는 욕실, 침실, 그리고 마지막으로 거실을 뒤졌다. last of all은 언급하고 있는 사람이나 사물이 마지막이라는 것을 강조할 때 쓴다. ❑ 맨 마지막으로 고양이가 왔다.

13 구 모조리 [강조] ❑ 그가 소시지를 보도에 떨어뜨리자 누군가의 개가 그것을 겨자까지 포함해 깨끗이 먹어 치웠다. **14** 구 요컨대 ❑ 우리 둘 다 그것이 요컨대 그다지 나쁜 생각이 아니라고 생각했다. **15** 구 전혀 [강조] ❑ 로빈은 사실 그를 한번도 진짜로 좋아한 적이 없었다. **16** 구 - 외에는 모두 ❑ 장군은 그의 가장 열렬한 추종자들을 제외하고는 모두에게 매력이 없는 인물이었다. **17** 구 거의 ❑ 이 도시를 갈라놓던 콘크리트 벽은 이제 거의 사라진 상태이다. **18** 구 -에도 불구하고 ❑ 그 모든 아름다움에도 불구하고 프라하는 곧 공산주의 획하에서 보존할 수 있었던 개성을 일부 잃을 수도 있다. **19** 구 지식이나 관심이 없는 정도를 강조함 [강조] ❑ 그가 이 나라에 있는지 없는지조차 우리는 전혀 모른다. **20** 구 총 ❑ 총 열세 명이 그 살인을 계획하는 데 가담했다는 증거가 있었다. **21** 구 최상급을 강조함 [강조] ❑ 우선 이 질문들에 답변을 해 주십시오. **22** 구 하고많은 - (놀라운 것을 강조함) [강조] ❑ 땅바닥에 앉은 한 무리의 여자들이 하고많은 노래 중에 '그린슬리브스'를 부르고 있었다. **23** 구 분노 혹은 놀라움을 강조함 [감정 개입] ❑ 참으로 게으르고 무관심하고 비사업적인 태도를 취하는군! **24** 구 숫자의 크기나 작음을 강조함 [강조] ❑ 그가 첫 번째 골을 넣는 데 무려 41분이 걸렸다. **25** 구 부정문에서 화자의 진술의 강도를 약화시킴 [구어체, 짐작투] ❑ 그는 우리보다 그다지 나이가 많은 것도 아니었다. **26** 구 그게 다야 ❑ "왜 그것을 알고 싶어 하지?" 그가 추궁했다. "그냥 궁금해서, 그게 다야." **27** 구 다 좋지만 [탐탁찮음] ❑ 별로 가지지 못한 사람들에게 자선 단체에 더 많이 기부하라고 요청하는 것도 다 좋지만 과연 그것이 정말 공평한 것일까?

1 복합형-형용사 -만으로 이뤄진 ❑ '이브닝 스탠더드 시상식'에 참석하기 위해 스타들로만 이뤄진 배우 군단이 런던의 사보이 호텔에 집결했다. ❑ 스타들로만 구성된 출연 배역에는 제레미 아이언스도 들어 있다. **2** 복합형-형용사 모든 것에 영향을 끼친다는 의미의 형용사를 만듦 ❑ 치매 환자를 돌보는 것은 전력이 소모되는 일이다. **3** 복합형-형용사 전체의 모든 종류의 것에 알맞다는 형용사를 만듦 ❑ 그는 전국 통합을 이루는 초당파적 정부를 만들고 싶어 했다.

Allah /ǽlə, ǽlɑ/ N-PROPER **Allah** is the name of God in Islam. ❑ *He praised Allah for the unexpected level of success his schemes achieved.*

고유명사 알라 ❑ 그는 자신의 계획들이 예상치 못했던 정도까지 성공한 것에 대해 알라신께 감사드렸다.

all-around [BRIT also **all-round**] **1** ADJ An **all-around** person is good at a lot of different skills, academic subjects, or sports. [ADJ n] ❑ *He is a great all-around player.* **2** ADJ **All-around** means doing or relating to all aspects of a job or activity. [ADJ n] ❑ *He demonstrated the all-around skills of a quarterback.*

[영국영어 all-round] **1** 형용사 만능의 ❑ 그는 대단한 만능선수이다. **2** 형용사 전반에 걸친 ❑ 그는 쿼터백 전반에 걸친 기술들을 시범보였다.

allay /əléɪ/ (allays, allaying, allayed) V-T If you **allay** someone's fears or doubts, you stop them feeling afraid or doubtful. [FORMAL] ❑ *He did what he could to allay his wife's myriad fears.*

타동사 진정시키다 [격식체] ❑ 그는 아내의 끝없는 공포들을 진정시키기 위해 할 수 있는 것은 다 했다.

allegation ♦◇◇ /æləgéɪʃⁿn/ (allegations) N-COUNT An **allegation** is a statement saying that someone has done something wrong. ❑ *The company has denied the allegations.*

가산명사 혐의 ❑ 회사는 그 혐의들을 부인해 왔다.

Word Partnership	allegation의 연어
V.	**deny an** allegation, **make an** allegation
PREP.	allegation **of**
CONJ.	allegation **that**

allege /əlédʒ/ (alleges, alleging, alleged) V-T If you **allege that** something bad is true, you say it but do not prove it. [FORMAL] ❑ *She alleged that there was rampant drug use among the male members of the group.* ❑ *The accused is alleged to have killed a man.*

타동사 (증거 없이) 주장하다; 혐의를 씌우다 [격식체] ❑ 그녀는 그 집단의 남성 구성원들이 약물을 마구 남용한다고 주장했다. ❑ 피고는 사람을 죽인 혐의를 받고 있습니다.

alleged ♦◇◇ /əlédʒd/ ADJ An **alleged** fact has been stated but has not been proved to be true. [FORMAL] [ADJ n] ❑ *They have begun a hunger strike in protest at the alleged beating.* ● **allegedly** /əlédʒɪdli/ ADV ❑ *His van allegedly struck the two as they were crossing a street.*

형용사 사실이 확인되지 않은 [격식체] ❑ 사실이 확인되지 않은 구타 사건에 항의하기 위해 그들은 단식 투쟁에 들어갔다. ● 사실이 확인되지 않은 주장에 의하면, 혐의에 따르면 부사 ❑ 그의 밴이 길을 건너고 있는 그들 둘을 쳤다는 혐의를 받고 있다.

Thesaurus	alleged의 참조어
ADJ.	questionable, supposed, suspicious; (ant.) certain, definite, sure

allegiance /əlíːdʒⁿns/ (allegiances) N-VAR Your **allegiance** is your support for and loyalty to a particular group, person, or belief. ❑ *My allegiance to Kendall and his company ran deep.*

가산명사 또는 불가산명사 충성 ❑ 켄달과 그의 회사에 대한 나의 충성심은 뿌리가 깊었다.

allergic /əlɜ́rdʒɪk/ **1** ADJ If you are **allergic to** something, you become ill or get a rash when you eat it, smell it, or touch it. [v-link ADJ to n] ❑ *I'm allergic to cats.* **2** ADJ If you have an **allergic** reaction to something, you become ill or get a rash when you eat it, smell it, or touch it. [ADJ n] ❑ *Soy milk can cause allergic reactions in some children.* →see **peanut**

1 형용사 알레르기가 있는 ❑ 나는 고양이가 알레르기가 있다. **2** 형용사 알레르기성 ❑ 두유가 일부 아동들에게서는 알레르기 반응을 유발할 수 있다.

allergy /ǽlərdʒi/ (allergies) N-VAR If you have a particular **allergy**, you become ill or get a rash when you eat, smell, or touch something that does not normally make people ill. ❑ *Food allergies can result in an enormous variety of different symptoms.*

가산명사 또는 불가산명사 알레르기 ❑ 음식 알레르기는 매우 다양한 종류의 다른 증상으로 나타날 수 있다.

alleviate /əlíːvieɪt/ (alleviates, alleviating, alleviated) V-T If you **alleviate** pain, suffering, or an unpleasant condition, you make it less intense or severe. [FORMAL] ❑ *Nowadays, a great deal can be done to alleviate back pain.* ● **alleviation** /əliːvieɪʃⁿn/ N-UNCOUNT [usu N of n] ❑ *Their energies were focused on the alleviation of the refugees' misery.*

타동사 경감시키다 [격식체] ❑ 오늘날에는 허리 통증을 크게 완화할 수 있다. ● 경감 불가산명사 ❑ 그들의 모든 에너지는 난민들의 고통을 경감시키는 데로 모아졌다.

alley /ǽli/ (alleys) N-COUNT An **alley** is a narrow passage or street with buildings or walls on both sides.

가산명사 골목

alliance ♦◇◇ /əláɪəns/ (alliances) **1** N-COUNT An **alliance** is a group of countries or political parties that are formally united and working together because they have similar aims. ❑ *The two parties were still too much apart to form an alliance.* **2** N-COUNT An **alliance** is a relationship in which two countries, political parties, or organizations work together for some purpose. [oft N with/between n, also in N with n] ❑ *The Socialists' electoral strategy has been based on a tactical alliance with the Communists.*

1 가산명사 동맹 ❑ 그 두 당은 동맹을 맺기에는 여전히 입장 차이가 너무 컸다. **2** 가산명사 동맹 ❑ 사회주의자들의 선거 전략은 공산주의자들과 맺은 전략적 동맹에 근거를 두고 있다.

Word Partnership	alliance의 연어
V.	**form an** alliance **1 2**
N.	**members of an** alliance **1 2**
ADJ.	**military/political** alliance **1 2**
PREP.	alliance **between**, alliance **with 2**

allied ♦◇◇ /əláɪd, BRIT ǽlaɪd/ **1** ADJ **Allied** forces or troops are armies from different countries who are fighting on the same side in a war. [ADJ n] ❑ *...the approaching Allied forces.* **2** ADJ **Allied** countries, troops, or political parties are united by a political or military agreement. [ADJ n, v-link ADJ to n] ❑ *...forces from three allied nations.* **3** ADJ If one thing or group is **allied to** another, it is related to it because the two things have particular qualities or characteristics in common. [v-link ADJ to/with n, ADJ n] ❑ *...lectures on subjects allied to health, beauty and fitness.*

1 형용사 동맹을 맺은 ❑ 다가오는 동맹군 **2** 형용사 동맹을 맺은 ❑ 세 동맹국의 병력 **3** 형용사 ...과 관련이 있는 ❑ 건강, 미용, 체력 등과 관련 있는 주제에 관한 강연

alligator /ǽlɪgeɪtər/ (alligators) N-COUNT An **alligator** is a large reptile with short legs, a long tail and very powerful jaws. ❑ *...the only place in the world where alligators and crocodiles live side by side.* ❑ *There are numerous signs warning people not to feed the alligators in the area.*

가산명사 (미국) 악어 ❑ 세계에서 미국악어와 아프리카 악어가 공존하는 유일한 곳 ❑ 악어에게 먹이를 주지 말라는 경고 안내 표지판이 많이 있다.

all-inclusive ADJ **All-inclusive** is used to indicate that a price, especially the price of a vacation, includes all the charges and all the services offered. [mainly BRIT] ❑ *An all-inclusive two-week holiday costs around £280 per person.*

형용사 모든 것을 포함한 [주로 영국영어] ❑ 모든 것을 포함한 2주간의 휴가는 한 사람당 약 2,880파운드가 든다.

allo|cate /ǽləkeɪt/ (**allocates, allocating, allocated**) V-T If one item or share of something **is allocated to** a particular person or for a particular purpose, it is given to that person or used for that purpose. ❑ *Tickets are limited and will be allocated to those who apply first.* ❑ *The 1985 federal budget allocated $7.3 billion for development programs.*

타동사 배당되다 ❑ 표는 제한되어 있으며 먼저 신청하는 사람에게 배당될 것입니다. ❑ 1985년의 연방 예산은 개발 계획에 73억 달러를 할당했다.

allo|ca|tion /ǽləkeɪʃⁿn/ (**allocations**) ◪ N-COUNT An **allocation** is an amount of something, especially money, that is given to a particular person or used for a particular purpose. ❑ *A State Department spokeswoman said that the aid allocation for Pakistan was still under review.* ◫ N-UNCOUNT The **allocation** of something is the decision that it should be given to a particular person or used for a particular purpose. ❑ *Town planning and land allocation had to be coordinated.*

◪ 가산명사 배당 ❑ 국무성 대변인이 파키스탄에 대한 지원 배당은 여전히 검토 중이라고 얘기했다. ◫ 불가산명사 배당 ❑ 도시 계획과 토지 배당을 조율해야 했다.

al|lot /əlɒt/ (**allots, allotting, allotted**) V-T If something **is allotted to** someone, it is given to them as their share. [usu passive] ❑ *The seats are allotted to the candidates who have won the most votes.*

타동사 배당되다 ❑ 가장 많은 표를 얻은 후보들에게 자리가 배당된다.

all-out also **all out** ADJ You use **all-out** to describe actions that are carried out in a very energetic and determined way, using all the resources available. [ADJ n] ❑ *He launched an all-out attack on his critics.*

형용사 전면적인 ❑ 그는 자신을 비판하는 사람들에 대한 전면 공격에 들어갔다.

al|low ♦♦♦ /əlaʊ/ (**allows, allowing, allowed**) ◪ V-T If someone **is allowed to** do something, it is all right for them to do it and they will not get into trouble. ❑ *The children are not allowed to watch violent TV programs.* ❑ *Smoking will not be allowed.* ◫ V-T If you **are allowed** something, you are given permission to have it or are given it. ❑ *Gifts like chocolates or flowers are allowed.* ◲ V-T If you **allow** something **to** happen, you do not prevent it. ❑ *He won't allow himself to fail.* ◳ V-T If one thing **allows** another thing **to** happen, the first thing creates the opportunity for the second thing to happen. ❑ *The compromise will allow him to continue his free market reforms.* ❑ *...an attempt to allow the Muslim majority a greater share of power.* ◴ V-T If you **allow** a particular length of time or a particular amount of something **for** a particular purpose, you include it in your planning. ❑ *Please allow 28 days for delivery.*

◪ 타동사 허용되다 ❑ 아이들은 폭력적인 텔레비전 프로그램을 볼 수 없다. ❑ 흡연은 허용되지 않는다. ◫ 타동사 허용되다 ❑ 초콜릿이나 꽃 같은 선물은 허용된다. ◲ 타동사 용납하다 ❑ 그는 자신이 실패하는 것을 용납하지 않을 것이다. ◳ 타동사 허용하다 ❑ 타협 덕분에 그는 자유 시장 개혁 정책을 계속할 수 있을 것이다. ❑ 회교 다수 세력에게 더 많은 권력을 부여하기 위한 시도 ◴ 타동사 (얼마의 기간이나 양을) 잡다 ❑ 배송에는 28일을 잡아 주십시오.

Thesaurus
allow의 참조어

V.　let, permit, support ◫
　　approve, consent, tolerate; (*ant.*) disallow, forbid, prevent, prohibit ◲

Word Partnership
allow의 연어

V.　allow *someone* to do *something* ◪
　　continue to allow, refuse to allow ◪ ◫ ◲
N.　allow **time** ◴

▶**allow for** PHRASAL VERB If you **allow for** certain problems or expenses, you include some extra time or money in your planning so that you can deal with them if they occur. ❑ *You have to allow for a certain amount of error.*

구동사 감안하다 ❑ 어느 정도의 실수는 감안해야 한다.

al|low|ance /əlaʊəns/ (**allowances**) ◪ N-COUNT An **allowance** is money that is given to someone, usually on a regular basis, in order to help them pay for the things that they need. ❑ *She gets an allowance for looking after Lillian.* ◫ N-COUNT A child's **allowance** is money that is given to him or her every week or every month by his or her parents. [mainly AM; BRIT **pocket money**] ❑ *When you give kids an allowance make sure they save some of it.* ◲ N-COUNT Your tax **allowance** is the amount of money that you are allowed to earn before you have to start paying income tax. [BRIT; AM **personal exemption**] ❑ *...those earning less than the basic tax allowance.* ◳ N-COUNT A particular type of **allowance** is an amount of something that you are allowed in particular circumstances. ❑ *Most of our flights have a baggage allowance of 44lbs per passenger.* ◴ PHRASE If you **make allowances for** something, you take it into account in your decisions, plans, or actions. ❑ *They'll make allowances for the fact it's affecting our performance.* ❑ *She tried to make allowances for his age.* ◵ PHRASE If you **make allowances for** someone, you accept behavior which you would not normally accept or deal with them less severely than you would normally, because of a problem that they have. ❑ *He's tired so I'll make allowances for him.*

◪ 가산명사 수당 ❑ 그녀는 릴리안을 돌보는 대가로 수당을 받는다. ◫ 가산명사 용돈 [주로 미국영어; 영국영어 pocket money] ❑ 아이들에게 용돈을 줄 때는 반드시 일부를 저축하도록 하십시오. ◲ 가산명사 소득세 기본 공제액 [영국영어; 미국영어 personal exemption] ❑ 소득세 기본 공제액보다 수입이 적은 사람들 ◳ 가산명사 허용량 ❑ 우리 비행기는 대부분 승객 한 사람당 44파운드의 수하물 한도를 두고 있다. ◴ 구 참작하다 ❑ 그것이 우리의 업무 수행 능력에 영향을 끼친다는 사실을 그들은 참작해야 할 것이다. ❑ 그녀는 그의 나이를 참작하려고 노력했다. ◵ 구 봐주다 ❑ 그는 지금 너무 지쳤으니 봐주겠다.

all right ♦♦◇ [BRIT also **alright**] ◪ ADJ If you say that someone or something is **all right**, you mean that you find them satisfactory or acceptable. [v-link ADJ] ❑ *I consider you a good friend, and if it's all right with you, I'd like to keep it that way.* ● ADJ **All right** is also used before a noun. [INFORMAL] [ADJ n] ❑ *He's an all right kind of guy really.* ◫ ADV If you say that something happens or goes **all right**, you mean that it happens in a satisfactory or acceptable manner. [ADV after v] ❑ *Things have thankfully worked out all right.* ◲ ADJ If someone or something is **all right**, they are well or safe. [v-link ADJ] ❑ *All she's worried about is whether he is all right.* ◳ CONVENTION You say "**all right**" when you are agreeing to something. [FORMULAE] ❑ *"I think you should come." — "All right."* ◴ CONVENTION You say "**all right?**" after you have given an instruction or explanation to someone when you are checking that they have understood what you have just said, or checking that they agree with or accept what you have just said. ❑ *Peter, you get half the fees. All right?* ◵ CONVENTION If someone in a position of authority says "**all right**," and suggests talking about or doing something else, they are indicating that they want you to end one activity and start another. ❑ *All right, Bob. You can go now.* ◶ CONVENTION You say "**all right**" during a discussion to show that you understand something that someone has just said, and to introduce a statement that relates to it. ❑ *I said there was no room in my mother's*

[영국영어 alright] ◪ 형용사 괜찮은 ❑ 나는 너를 좋은 친구로 생각해. 네가 괜찮다면 계속 그렇게 지내고 싶어. ● 형용사 괜찮은 [비격식체] ❑ 그 남자 정말 괜찮은 사내야. ◫ 부사 괜찮게 ❑ 고맙게도 일이 괜찮게 풀려 왔다. ◲ 형용사 괜찮은 ❑ 그녀가 걱정하는 일은 오로지 그가 괜찮은가 하는 것뿐이. ◳ 관용 표현 그래, 좋아 [의례적인 표현] ❑ "너 이제 가야 될 것 같애." "그래." ◴ 관용 표현 됐어요? (지시나 설명을 한 후 이해했는지 확인하며 물을 때 쓰는 표현) ❑ 피터, 자네가 수수료의 절반을 받는 걸세. 알겠나? ◵ 관용 표현 좋아, 됐어 (상대방에게 하던 일을 마무리하고 다른 일을 하도록 제시할 때 쓰는 표현) ❑ 좋아, 밥. 이제 가도 되네. ◶ 관용 표현 좋아요. (상대방이 한 말을 이해했음을 표시하며 그와 관련된 말을 할 때 말머리에 쓰는 표현) ❑ 내가 어머니 집에는 방이 없다고 말하자, 그가 이렇게 말했다. "좋아, 내 작업장으로 와서 그림을 그리게." ◷ 관용 표현 아니 (상대방에게 도전하거나 위협하는 느낌을 표현하는 감탄사로 말머리에 쓰는 표현) ❑ 아니,

a b c d e f g h i j k l m n o p q r s t u v w x y z

house, and he said, "All right, come to my studio and paint." ◻ CONVENTION You say **all right** before a statement or question to indicate that you are challenging or threatening someone. ◻ *All right, who are you and what are you doing in my office?*

당신은 누군데 내 사무실에서 뭘 하고 있는 거요?

all-round →see **all-around**

all-time ADJ You use **all-time** when you are comparing all the things of a particular type that there have ever been. For example, if you say that something is the **all-time** best, you mean that it is the best thing of its type that there has ever been. [ADJ n] ◻ *The president's popularity nationally is at an all-time low.*

형용사 공전의, 전례 없는 ◻ 전국적으로 대통령의 인기가 전례 없이 낮다.

al|lude /əlud/ (**alludes, alluding, alluded**) V-I If you **allude to** something, you mention it in an indirect way. [FORMAL] ◻ *With friends, she sometimes alluded to a feeling that she herself was to blame for her son's predicament.*

자동사 비추다, 암시하다 [격식체] ◻ 그녀는 아들이 곤경에 처한 것이 자기 탓이라고 느낀다는 인상을 때때로 친구들에게 내비쳤다.

al|lure /əlʊər, BRIT /əlyʊəʳ/ N-UNCOUNT The **allure** of something or someone is the pleasing or exciting quality that they have. ◻ *It's a game that has really lost its allure.*

불가산명사 매력 ◻ 그건 정말 매력을 상실한 게임이야.

al|lu|sion /əluʒ³n/ (**allusions**) N-VAR An **allusion** is an indirect reference to someone or something. ◻ *This last point was understood to be an allusion to the long-standing hostility between the two leaders.*

가산명사 또는 불가산명사 암시, 언급 ◻ 이 마지막 사항은 두 지도자 사이의 오랜 반목에 대한 암시로 이해되었다.

ally ♦♦◇ (**allies, allying, allied**)

> The noun is pronounced /ælaɪ/. The verb is pronounced /əlaɪ/.

명사는 /ælaɪ /로 발음되고, 동사는 /əlaɪ /로 발음된다.

◼ N-COUNT A country's **ally** is another country that has an agreement to support it, especially in war. ◻ *Washington would not take such a step without its allies' approval.* ◻ N-PLURAL The **Allies** were the armed forces that fought against Germany and Japan in the Second World War. ◻ *...Germany's surrender to the Allies.* ◻ N-COUNT If you describe someone as your **ally**, you mean that they help and support you, especially when other people are opposing them. ◻ *He is a close ally of the Prime Minister.* ◻ V-T If you **ally yourself with** someone or something, you give your support to them. ◻ *He will have no choice but to ally himself with the new movement.* ◻ →see also **allied**

◼ 가산명사 동맹국 ◻ 워싱턴에서 동맹국들의 찬성 없이 그와 같은 조치를 취하지는 않을 것이다. ◻ 복수명사 (제 2차 세계 대전 당시의) 연합군 ◻ 연합군에 대한 독일의 항복 ◻ 가산명사 협력자, 자기 편 ◻ 그는 국무총리의 측근이다. ◻ 타동사 -을 지지하다 ◻ 그는 새로운 운동을 지지할 수밖에 없을 것이다.

al|mighty /ɔlmaɪti/ ◼ N-PROPER The **Almighty** is another name for God. You can also refer to **Almighty God**. ◻ *Adam sought guidance from the Almighty.* ◻ EXCLAM People sometimes say **God Almighty** or **Christ Almighty** to express their surprise, anger, or horror. These expressions could cause offense. [FEELINGS]

◼ 고유명사 신 ◻ 아담은 신의 인도를 받고자 했다. ◻ 감탄사 세상에!, 저런! [감정 개입]

al|mond /ɑmənd, æm-, ælm-/ (**almonds**)

> The plural for meaning ◻ is either **almonds** or **almond**.

◻ 의미의 복수는 almonds 또는 almond이다.

◼ N-VAR **Almonds** are pale oval nuts. They are often used in cooking. ◻ *...sponge cake flavored with almonds.* ◻ N-VAR An **almond** or an **almond tree** is a tree on which almonds grow. ◻ *On the left was a plantation of almond trees.*

◼ 가산명사 또는 불가산명사 아몬드 ◻ 아몬드 맛 카스텔라 ◻ 가산명사 또는 불가산명사 아몬드 나무 ◻ 왼쪽에 아몬드 나무 농장이 있었다.

al|most ♦♦♦ /ɔlmoʊst/ ADV You use **almost** to indicate that something is not completely the case but is nearly the case. ◻ *The couple had been dating for almost three years.* ◻ *The effect is almost impossible to describe.* ◻ *He contracted Spanish flu, which almost killed him.*

부사 거의 ◻ 그 둘은 거의 3년째 사귀어 왔었다. ◻ 그 효과는 거의 말로 설명할 수 없을 정도이다. ◻ 그는 스페인 독감에 걸려서 거의 죽을 뻔 했다.

Thesaurus   *almost*의 참조어

ADV.   about, most, nearly, practically, virtually

alone ♦♦◇ /əloʊn/ ◼ ADJ When you are **alone**, you are not with any other people. [v-link ADJ] ◻ *There is nothing so fearful as to be alone in a combat situation.* ● ADV **Alone** is also an adverb. [ADV after v] ◻ *She has lived alone in this house for almost five years now.* ◻ ADJ If one person is **alone with** another person, or if two or more people are **alone**, they are together, without anyone else present. [v-link ADJ, oft ADJ with n] ◻ *I couldn't imagine why he would want to be alone with me.* ◻ ADJ If you say that you are **alone** or feel **alone**, you mean that nobody who is with you, or nobody at all, cares about you. [v-link ADJ] ◻ *Never in her life had she felt so alone, so abandoned.* ◻ ADV You say that one person or thing **alone** does something when you are emphasizing that only one person or thing is involved. [EMPHASIS] [n ADV] ◻ *You alone should determine what is right for you.* ◻ ADV If you say that one person or thing **alone** is responsible for part of an amount, you are emphasizing the size of that part and the size of the total amount. [EMPHASIS] [n ADV] ◻ *The BBC alone is sending 300 technicians, directors and commentators.* ◻ ADJ If someone is **alone in** doing something, they are the only person doing it, and so are different from other people. [v-link ADJ, oft ADJ in -ing/n] ◻ *Am I alone in recognizing that these two statistics have quite different implications?* ● ADV **Alone** is also an adverb. ◻ *I alone was sane, I thought, in a world of crazy people.* ◻ ADV When someone does something **alone**, they do it without help from other people. [ADV after v] ◻ *Bringing up a child alone should give you a sense of achievement.* ◻ PHRASE If you **go it alone**, you do something without any help from other people. [INFORMAL] ◻ *I missed the stimulation of working with others when I tried to go it alone.* ◻ to **leave** someone or something **alone** →see **leave. let alone** →see **let**

◼ 형용사 홀로인 ◻ 전투 상황에서는 홀로 되는 것만큼 무서운 것이 없다. ● 부사 홀로 ◻ 그녀는 이 집에서 이제까지 거의 5년 동안 홀로 살아왔다. ◻ 형용사 -와만 함께, -만 함께 ◻ 나는 그가 왜 나와 단둘이만 있고 싶어 하는지 상상도 할 수 없었다. ◻ 형용사 고독한 ◻ 그녀는 살아오면서 그토록 고독하고 버림받은 기분을 느낀 적이 없었다. ◻ 부사 단지 -만 [강조] ◻ 단지 너 혼자서 무엇이 스스로에게 옳은지를 결정해야 한다. ◻ 부사 혼자서만 [강조] ◻ 비비시에서만 3백 명의 기술자와 연출자, 해설자들을 보내고 있다. ◻ 형용사 유일한 ◻ 이 두 통계가 의미하는 바가 상당히 다르다는 것을 알아본 사람이 나뿐인가? ● 부사 유일하게 ◻ 광인들의 세상에서 나만이 제정신이라고 나는 생각했다. ◻ 부사 혼자 힘으로 ◻ 혼자 힘으로 아이를 키우는 일은 틀림없이 성취감을 느끼게 해 줄 것이다. ◻ 구 혼자 힘으로 행하다 [비격식체] ◻ 나 혼자 힘으로 해나가려 노력할 때, 다른 이들과 함께 일하는 데서 오는 자극이 없어서 아쉬웠다.

along ♦♦♦ /əlɔŋ, BRIT əlɒŋ/

> In addition to the uses shown below, **along** is used in phrasal verbs such as "go along with," "play along," and "string along."

along은 아래 용법 외에도 'go along with', 'play along', 'string along'과 같은 구동사에 쓰인다.

◼ PREP If you move or look **along** something such as a road, you move or look toward one end of it. ◻ *Newman walked along the street alone.* ◻ *The young man led Mark Ryle along a corridor.* ◻ PREP If something is situated **along** a road, river, or corridor, it is situated in it or beside it. ◻ *...enormous traffic jams all along the roads.* ◻ ADV When someone or something moves **along**, they keep moving in a particular direction. [ADV after v] ◻ *She skipped and danced along.* ◻ *He raised his voice a little, talking into the wind as they walked along.* ◻ ADV If you say that

◼ 전치사 -을 따라 ◻ 뉴먼은 홀로 거리를 따라 걸었다. ◻ 그 젊은 남자가 복도를 따라 마크 라일을 데리고 갔다. ◻ 전치사 -을 따라 ◻ 도로 전역에 걸친 엄청난 교통 체증 ◻ 부사 쭉 ◻ 그녀는 깡충깡충 뛰고 춤추면서 쭉 갔다. ◻ 그들이 쭉 걸어갈 때 그가 약간 목소리를 높여 바람 부는 쪽으로 이야기를 했다. ◻ 부사 쭉 ◻ 끝없이 지루하게 질질 끌어 온 협상

something is going **along** in a particular way, you mean that it is progressing in that way. [ADV after v] ❑ *...the negotiations which have been dragging along interminably.* **5** ADV If you take someone or something **along** when you go somewhere, you take them with you. [ADV after v] ❑ *This is open to women of all ages, so bring along your friends and colleagues.* **6** ADV If someone or something is coming **along** or is sent **along**, they are coming or being sent to a particular place. [ADV after v] ❑ *She invited everyone she knew to come along.* **7** PHRASE You use **along with** to mention someone or something else that is also involved in an action or situation. ❑ *The baby's mother escaped from the fire along with two other children.* **8** PHRASE If something has been true or been present **all along**, it has been true or been present throughout a period of time. ❑ *I've been fooling myself all along.* **9** **along the way** →see **way**

along|side ◆◇◇ /əlɒŋsaɪd/ **1** PREP If one thing is **alongside** another thing, the first thing is next to the second. ❑ *He crossed the street and walked alongside Central Park.* ● ADV **Alongside** is also an adverb. [ADV after v] ❑ *He waited several minutes for a car to pull up alongside.* **2** PREP If you work **alongside** other people, you all work together in the same place. ❑ *He had worked alongside Frank and Mark and they had become friends.*

aloof /əluf/ ADJ Someone who is **aloof** is not very friendly and does not like to spend time with other people. [DISAPPROVAL] ❑ *He seemed aloof and detached.*

aloud /əlaʊd/ **1** ADV When you say something, read, or laugh **aloud**, you speak or laugh so that other people can hear you. [ADV after v] ❑ *When we were children, our father read aloud to us.* **2** PHRASE If you **think aloud**, you express your thoughts as they occur to you, rather than thinking first and then speaking. ❑ *He really must be careful about thinking aloud. Who knew what he might say?*

al|pha|bet /ælfəbɛt, -bɪt/ (**alphabets**) N-COUNT An **alphabet** is a set of letters usually presented in a fixed order which is used for writing the words of a particular language or group of languages. ❑ *The modern Russian alphabet has 31 letters.*

al|pha|beti|cal /ælfəbɛtɪkᵊl/ ADJ **Alphabetical** means arranged according to the normal order of the letters in the alphabet. [ADJ n] ❑ *Their herbs and spices are arranged in alphabetical order on narrow open shelves.*

al|pine /ælpaɪn/ ADJ **Alpine** means existing in or relating to mountains, especially the ones in Switzerland. ❑ *...grassy, alpine meadows.*

al|ready ◆◆◆ /ɔlrɛdi/ **1** ADV You use **already** to show that something has happened, or that something has happened before the moment you are referring to. Some speakers of American English use **already** with the simple past tense of the verb instead of a perfect tense. Speakers of British English use **already** with a verb in a perfect tense, putting it after "have," "has," or "had," or at the end of a clause. ❑ *They had already voted for him at the first ballot.* ❑ *She says she already told the neighbors not to come over for a couple of days.* **2** ADV You use **already** to show that a situation exists at this present moment or that it exists at an earlier time than expected. You use **already** after the verb "be" or an auxiliary verb, or before a verb if there is no auxiliary. When you want add emphasis, you can put **already** at the beginning of a sentence. ❑ *The authorities believe those security measures are already paying off.* ❑ *He was already rich.*

> **Already** is often used to add emphasis or to suggest that it is surprising that something has happened so soon. ❑ *They were already eating their lunch.* If you say that something is **still** happening or is **still** the case, you are usually emphasizing your surprise that it has been happening or has been the case for so long. ❑ *She was still looking at me... There are still plenty of horses around here.* You use **yet** in negative sentences and in questions. It is often used to add emphasis, to suggest surprise that something has not happened, or to say that it will happen later. ❑ *Have you seen it yet?... The troops could not yet see the shore... It isn't dark yet.* In British English, **already** and **yet** are usually used with the present perfect tense. ❑ *I have already started knitting baby clothes... Have they said sorry yet?* In American English, a past tense is commonly used. ❑ *She already told the neighbors not to come... I didn't get any sleep yet.* This usage is becoming more common in British English.

al|right /ɔlraɪt/ →see **all right**

also ◆◆◆ /ɔlsoʊ/ **1** ADV You can use **also** to give more information about a person or thing, or to add another relevant fact. ❑ *It is the work of Ivor Roberts-Jones, who also produced the statue of Churchill in Parliament Square.* ❑ *He is an asthmatic who was also anemic three months ago.* **2** ADV You can use **also** to indicate that something you have just said about one person or thing is true of another person or thing. ❑ *General Geichenko was a survivor. His father, also a top-ranking officer, had perished during the war.* ❑ *This rule has also been applied in the case of a purchase of used tires and tubes.*

> **Also** and **too** are similar in meaning. **Also** never comes at the end of a clause, whereas **too** usually comes at the end. ❑ *He was also an artist and lived in Cleveland... He's a singer and an actor too.*

Thesaurus		*also*의 참조어
ADV.		additionally, furthermore, plus **1**
		and, likewise, too **2**

---

5 부사 함께 데리고, 함께 가지고 ❑ 이 행사는 모든 연령대의 여성에게 열려 있으니, 친구와 동료들을 데려오세요. **6** 부사 함께 (come, send 등의 동사에 덧붙여 쓰는 말이다) ❑ 그녀는 자신이 아는 모든 사람들을 초대해서 오라고 했다. **7** 구 —와 함께 ❑ 그 아기의 어머니는 다른 두 아이들과 함께 불 속에서 빠져나왔다. **8** 구 줄곧 ❑ 나는 줄곧 나 자신을 속여 왔다.

1 전치사 —와 나란히, —의 곁에 ❑ 그는 차도를 건너 센트럴 파크를 나란히 따라서 걸었다. ● 부사 나란히, 곁에 ❑ 그는 몇 분간 차가 곁에 와서 멈추기를 기다렸다. **2** 전치사 —와 함께 ❑ 그는 프랭크, 마크와 함께 일했었고 그들은 친구가 되었다.

형용사 냉담한 [탐탁찮음] ❑ 그는 냉담하고 초연해 보였다.

1 부사 소리를 내어 ❑ 우리가 어린아이였을 적에, 아버지는 우리에게 소리 내어 책을 읽어주셨다. **2** 구 생각하면서 중얼거리다 ❑ 그는 생각하면서 중얼거리는 거 정말 조심해야 돼. 무슨 말을 할지 어떻게 알아?

가산명사 알파벳, 자모 ❑ 현대 러시아어 자모는 31자로 이루어진다.

형용사 알파벳순의 ❑ 그들이 가진 향료와 양념은 덮개 없는 좁은 선반 위에 알파벳순으로 가지런히 놓여 있다.

형용사 높은 산의; 고산성의 ❑ 풀이 무성한 고산성 목초지

1 부사 이미, 벌써 ❑ 그들은 일차 투표에서 이미 그를 찍었으며, 그는 이웃들에게 이틀 동안 찾아오지 말라고 이미 말했다고 한다. **2** 부사 벌써, 이미 ❑ 당국에서는 그런 보안 조처들이 벌써 성과를 거두고 있다고 믿는다. ❑ 그는 이미 부자였다.

> already는 흔히 강조의 의미를 덧붙이거나, 어떤 일이 너무 일어난 것을 놀라움을 시사할 때 쓴다. ❑ 그들은 벌써 점심을 먹고 있었다. something is still happening이라고 하거나 something is still the case라고 하면, 대개 어떤 일이나 상황이 너무 오랫동안 계속되고 있는 데 대한 놀라움을 강조하는 것이다. ❑ 그녀가 아직도 나를 쳐다보고 있었다... 이 곳 주변에는 아직도 말이 많다. yet은 부정문과 의문문에 쓰이는데, 흔히 강조의 의미를 덧붙이거나, 어떤 일이 일어나지 않은 데 대한 놀라움을 시사하거나, 그 일이 나중에 일어날 것이라고 말할 때 쓴다. ❑ 그것을 벌써 보았나요?... 이 병력의 눈에는 아직도 해안이 보이지 않았다... 아직 어둡지 않다. 영국 영어에서는 already와 yet이 대개 현재완료 시제와 함께 쓰인다. ❑ 나는 이미 아기 옷을 뜨기 시작했다. 그들이 이미 미안하다고 했나요? 미국 영어에서는 흔히 과거시제를 쓴다. ❑ 그녀는 이미 이웃들에게 오지 말라고 말했다... 나는 아직 한잠도 못 잤다. 영국 영어에서도 이 어법이 더 일반화되고 있다.

1 부사 또한, 역시 ❑ 그것은 아이버 로버츠 존즈의 작품인데, 그는 또한 의회 광장에 있는 처칠상도 만들었다. ❑ 그는 3년 전에는 빈혈도 앓았던 천식 환자이다. **2** 부사 역시 ❑ 게이첸코 장군은 살아남았다. 역시 고위급 장교였던 그의 아버지는 전쟁 중에 사망했었다. ❑ 이 규정은 중고 타이어나 튜브를 구입하는 경우에도 역시 적용되어 왔다.

> also와 too는 뜻이 비슷하다. also는 절대로 절의 끝에 오지 않는 반면, too는 대개 절의 끝에 온다. ❑ 그도 또한 화가였고 클리블랜드에 살았다... 그는 가수이고 배우이기도 하다.

al|tar /ɔltər/ (altars) N-COUNT An **altar** is a holy table in a church or temple. □ ...the high altar at Chichester Cathedral.

가산명사 제단 □ 치체스터 대성당의 높은 제단

al|ter ♦♦♦ /ɔltər/ (alters, altering, altered) V-T/V-I If something **alters** or if you **alter** it, it changes. □ Little had altered in the village.

타동사/자동사 바뀌다; 바꾸다 □ 그 마을은 바뀐 데가 거의 없었다.

al|tera|tion /ɔltəreɪʃn/ (alterations) N-COUNT An **alteration** is a change in or to something. □ Making some simple alterations to your diet will make you feel fitter.

가산명사 변화 □ 식이 요법에 간단한 변화를 약간 주는 것만으로 더욱 건강해진 느낌을 받을 수 있을 겁니다.

al|ter|nate (alternates, alternating, alternated)

> The verb is pronounced /ɔltərneɪt/. The adjective and noun are pronounced /ɔltərnɪt/.

동사는 /ɔltərneɪt/으로 발음되고, 형용사와 명사는/ɔltərnɪt/으로 발음된다.

◼ V-RECIP When you **alternate** two things, you keep using one then the other. When one thing **alternates with** another, the first regularly occurs after the other. □ Her aggressive moods alternated with gentle or more co-operative states. □ Now you just alternate layers of that mixture and eggplant. ◼ ADJ **Alternate** actions, events, or processes regularly occur after each other. [ADJ n] □ They were streaked with alternate bands of color. ● **al|ter|nate|ly** ADV □ He could alternately bully and charm people. ◼ ADJ If something happens on **alternate** days, it happens on one day, then happens on every second day after that. In the same way, something can happen in **alternate** weeks, years, or other periods of time. [ADJ n] □ Lesley had agreed to Jim going skiing in alternate years. ◼ ADJ You use **alternate** to describe a plan, idea, or system which is different from the one already in operation and can be used instead of it. [ADJ n] □ His group was forced to turn back and take an alternate route. ◼ N-COUNT An **alternate** is a person or thing that replaces another, and can act or be used instead of them. [AM] □ In most jurisdictions, twelve jurors and two alternates are chosen.

◼ 상호동사 번갈아 사용하다; 번갈아 일어나다 □ 그녀는 호전적인 기분과 상냥하면서도 더 협조적인 기분이 번갈아 일어났다. □ 자, 이제 그냥 그 반죽을 번갈아 가며 한 켜 놓고, 가지 한 켜 놓고 하세요. ◼ 형용사 번갈아 일어나는 □ 그것들은 색줄이 번갈아 그어진 줄무늬가 있었다. ● 번갈아, 교대로 부사 □ 그는 사람들을 윽박질렀다 홀렸다 할 수 있었다. ◼ 형용사 하나 걸러의 □ 레슬리는 짐이 2년마다 한 번씩 스키 타러 가는 데 동의했었다. ◼ 형용사 기존의 것과 다른 □ 그의 무리는 되돌아서 다른 길로 갈 것을 강요당했다. ◼ 가산명사 대리인; 대체물 [미국영어] □ 대부분의 법원 관할 구역에서 열두 명의 배심원과 두 명의 대리인이 선발된다.

al|ter|na|tive ♦♦◇ /ɔltɜrnətɪv/ (alternatives) ◼ N-COUNT If one thing is an **alternative** to another, the first can be found, used, or done instead of the second. □ New ways to treat arthritis may provide an alternative to painkillers. ◼ ADJ An **alternative** plan or offer is different from the one that you already have, and can be done or used instead. [ADJ n] □ There were alternative methods of travel available. ◼ ADJ **Alternative** is used to describe something that is different from the usual things of its kind, or the usual ways of doing something, in modern Western society. For example, an **alternative** lifestyle does not follow conventional ways of living and working. [ADJ n] □ ...unconventional parents who embraced the alternative lifestyle of the Sixties. ◼ ADJ **Alternative** medicine uses traditional ways of curing people, such as medicines made from plants, massage, and acupuncture. [ADJ n] □ ...alternative health care. ◼ ADJ **Alternative** energy uses natural sources of energy such as the sun, wind, or water for power and fuel, rather than oil, coal, or nuclear power. [ADJ n]

◼ 가산명사 대안; 대체물 □ 새로운 관절염 치료법에 의해 전통제 대체물이 나올 수도 있다. ◼ 형용사 대신의 □ 이용 가능한 대체 교통 체계가 있었다. ◼ 형용사 대안적인 □ 60년대의 대안적 생활양식을 받아들였던 인습에 얽매이지 않은 부모님 ◼ 형용사 대체 (의학) □ 대체 의학적 건강관리 ◼ 형용사 대체 (에너지)

al|ter|na|tive|ly /ɔltɜrnətɪvli/ ADV You use **alternatively** to introduce a suggestion or to mention something different to what has just been stated. [ADV with cl] □ Allow about eight hours for the drive from Calais. Alternatively, you can fly to Brive.

부사 아니면, 그 대신 □ 칼레에서 자동차로 약 여덟 시간이 걸린다는 걸 고려하세요. 아니면, 브리브까지 비행기로 갈 수도 있습니다.

al|though ♦♦♦ /ɔlðoʊ/ ◼ CONJ You use **although** to introduce a subordinate clause which contains a statement which contrasts with the statement in the main clause. □ Although he is known to only a few, his reputation among them is very great. ◼ CONJ You use **although** to introduce a subordinate clause which contains a statement which makes the main clause of the sentence seem surprising or unexpected. □ Although I was only six, I can remember seeing it on TV. ◼ CONJ You use **although** to introduce a subordinate clause which gives some information that is relevant to the main clause but modifies the strength of that statement. □ He was in love with her, although a man seldom puts that name to what he feels. ◼ CONJ You use **although** when admitting a fact about something which you regard as less important than a contrasting fact. □ Although they're expensive, they last forever and never go out of style.

◼ 접속사 -이긴 하지만 □ 소수에게만 알려져 있긴 하지만, 그들 사이에서는 그에 대한 평판이 대단히 좋다. ◼ 접속사 비록 -일지라도 □ 내가 비록 겨우 여섯 살이었다 하더라도, 그것을 TV에서 봤던 일은 기억난다. ◼ 접속사 -이긴 하지만 □ 남자들은 자신이 느끼는 감정에 좀처럼 그런 이름을 붙이지 않는 법이지만, 그는 그녀를 사랑하고 있었다. ◼ 접속사 비록 -이긴 하지만 □ 비록 비싸긴 하지만, 그것들은 영구적이고 유행을 타지도 않는다.

Thesaurus		although의 참조어
PREP.	despite ◼-◼	
ADV.	still ◼-◼	
CONJ.	though, while ◼-◼	

al|ti|tude /æltɪtud, BRIT æltɪtyuːd/ (altitudes) N-VAR If something is at a particular **altitude**, it is at that height above sea level. □ The aircraft had reached its cruising altitude of about 39,000 feet.

가산명사 또는 불가산명사 고도; 해발 □ 그 비행기는 약 3만 9천 피트의 순항 고도에 도달해 있었다.

al|to|geth|er ♦♦◇ /ɔltəgeðər/ ◼ ADV You use **altogether** to emphasize that something has stopped, been done, or finished completely. [EMPHASIS] [ADV after v] □ When Artie stopped calling altogether, Julie found a new man. ◼ ADV You use **altogether** in front of an adjective or adverb to emphasize a quality that someone or something has. [EMPHASIS] [ADV adj/adv] □ The choice of language is altogether different. ◼ ADV You use **altogether** to modify a negative statement and make it less forceful. [with neg, ADV group] □ We were not altogether sure that the comet would miss the Earth. ◼ ADV You can use **altogether** to introduce a summary of what you have been saying. □ Altogether, it was a delightful town garden, peaceful and secluded. ◼ ADV If several amounts add up to a particular amount **altogether**, that amount is their total. [ADV with amount] □ Britain has a dozen warships in the area, with a total of five thousand military personnel altogether.

◼ 부사 완전히 [강조] □ 아티가 연락을 완전히 끊자, 줄리는 새 남자를 찾아냈다. ◼ 부사 아주, 전혀 [강조] □ 언어의 선택은 전혀 다르다. ◼ 부사 전적으로 □ 우리는 그 혜성이 지구를 비껴가리라고 전적으로 확신하지는 못했다. ◼ 부사 요컨대 □ 요컨대, 그곳은 평화롭고 한적한, 쾌적한 마을 공원이었다. ◼ 부사 전부, 합계하여 □ 영국은 총 5천 명의 병력과 함께 12대의 전함을 그 지역에 배치하고 있다.

al|tru|ism /æltruɪzəm/ N-UNCOUNT **Altruism** is unselfish concern for other people's happiness and welfare. □ Fortunately, volunteers and charities are not motivated by self-interest, but by altruism.

불가산명사 이타심 □ 다행스럽게도, 자원자들과 자선 단체들의 동기를 유발하는 것은 사리사욕이 아니라 이타심이다.

alu|min|ium /æljuminiəm/ → see **aluminum**

alu|mi|num /əlumɪnəm/ N-UNCOUNT **Aluminum** is a lightweight metal used, for example, for making cooking equipment and aircraft parts. [AM; BRIT **aluminium**] ❑ ...*aluminum cans*.

불가산명사 알루미늄 [미국영어; 영국영어 aluminium]
❑ 알루미늄 깡통들

al|ways ♦♦♦ /ɔlweɪz/ **1** ADV If you **always** do something, you do it whenever a particular situation occurs. If you **always** did something, you did it whenever a particular situation occurred. [ADV before v] ❑ *She's always late for everything*. ❑ *Always lock your garage*. **2** ADV If something is **always** the case, was **always** the case, or will **always** be the case, it is, was, or will be the case all the time, continuously. ❑ *We will always remember his generous hospitality*. ❑ *He has always been the family solicitor*. **3** ADV If you say that something is **always** happening, especially something which annoys you, you mean that it happens repeatedly. [ADV before v-cont] ❑ *She was always moving things around*. **4** ADV You use **always** in expressions such as **can always** or **could always** when you are making suggestions or suggesting an alternative approach or method. [can/could ADV inf] ❑ *If you can't find any decent apples, you can always try growing them yourself*. **5** ADV You can say that someone **always** was, for example, awkward or lucky to indicate that you are not surprised about what they are doing or have just done. [ADV before v] ❑ *She's going to be fine. She always was pretty strong*.

1 부사 항상 ❑ 그녀는 모든 일에 항상 늦는다. ❑ 항상 차고 문을 잠그세요. **2** 부사 늘; 죽 ❑ 우리는 그가 베푼 후한 대접을 늘 기억할 것이다. ❑ 그는 지금껏 쭉 그 집안의 가족 변호사였다. **3** 부사 줄곧, 노상 ❑ 그녀는 노상 물건들을 옮겨댔다. **4** 부사 언제든지, 언제건 ❑ 당신이 괜찮은 사과를 찾을 수 없다면, 언제든지 직접 재배해 볼 수도 있다. **5** 부사 언제나 ❑ 그녀는 괜찮을 거야. 언제나 상당히 강인했으니까.

> Do not confuse **always** and **ever**. If something **always** happens, it happens regularly or on every occasion. ❑ *I would always ask for the radio to be turned down... He's always been an active person*. If something is **always** the case, it is true at all times. ❑ *No matter what she did, she would always be forgiven*. You use **ever**, for example in negative sentences, questions, and with superlatives, to talk about any time at all when referring to the past, present, or future. ❑ *No one ever came... Will I ever see France?...the nicest thing anyone's ever said to me*.

> always와 ever를 혼동하지 않도록 하라. 어떤 일이 "항상(always)" 일어난다는 것은 그 일이 규칙적으로 또는 매번 일어남을 나타낸다. ❑ 나는 매번 라디오 소리를 줄여 달라고 부탁하곤 했다... 그는 언제나 활동적인 사람이었다. 어떤 것이 'always the case'라면, 그것이 언제나 사실이라는 뜻이다. ❑ 그녀는 무슨 짓을 해도 항상 용서받았다. ever는 예를 들면 부정문과 의문문에서, 또는 최상급과 함께 과거, 현재, 미래의 어떤 시간을 말할 때에나 다 쓴다. ❑ 아무도 오지 않았다... 내가 과연 프랑스를 보게 될까?...누가 지금까지 내게 한 말 중에서 가장 좋은 말

am /əm, STRONG æm/ **Am** is the first person singular of the present tense of **be**. **Am** is often shortened to **'m** in spoken English. The negative forms are "I am not" and "I'm not." In questions and tags in spoken English, these are usually changed to "aren't I."

be동사의 1인칭 단수 현재형

AM /eɪ ɛm/ (**AMs**) N-COUNT An **AM** is a member of the Welsh Assembly. **AM** is an abbreviation for "assembly member."

가산명사 (웨일즈) 의회의원

a.m. /eɪ ɛm/ also **am a.m.** is used after a number to show that you are referring to a particular time between midnight and noon. Compare **p.m.** ❑ *The program starts at 9 a.m.*

오전 ❑ 그 프로그램은 오전 9시에 시작한다.

amal|gam|ate /əmælɡəmeɪt/ (**amalgamates, amalgamating, amalgamated**) V-RECIP When two or more things, especially organizations, **amalgamate** or are **amalgamated**, they become one large thing. ❑ *The firm has amalgamated with an American company*. ❑ *The chemical companies had amalgamated into a vast conglomerate*. ● **amal|gama|tion** /əmælɡəmeɪʃ°n/ (**amalgamations**) N-VAR ❑ *Athletics South Africa was formed by an amalgamation of two organizations*.

상호동사 합병하다; 융합하다 ❑ 그 회사는 미국 회사와 합병했다. ❑ 그 화학 회사들은 합병을 거쳐 거대 복합기업이 되었다. ● 합병 가산명사 또는 불가산명사 ❑ 남아프리카 육상 연맹은 두 개 단체가 통합되어 만들어졌다.

amass /əmæs/ (**amasses, amassing, amassed**) V-T If you **amass** something such as money or information, you gradually get a lot of it. ❑ *It was better not to enquire too closely into how he had amassed his fortune*.

타동사 모으다; 축적하다 ❑ 그가 어떻게 재산을 모았는지에 대해 지나치게 깊이 조사하지 않는 편이 나았다.

ama|teur ♦◇◇ /æmətʃər, -tʃʊər, BRIT əmətər/ (**amateurs**) **1** N-COUNT An **amateur** is someone who does something as a hobby and not as a job. ❑ *Jerry is an amateur who dances because he feels like it*. **2** ADJ **Amateur** sports or activities are done by people as a hobby and not as a job. [ADJ n] ❑ *She'd particularly like to join the local amateur dramatics society*.

1 가산명사 아마추어 ❑ 제리는 스스로 좋아서 춤을 추는 아마추어이다. **2** 형용사 아마추어의 ❑ 그녀는 특히 지방 아마추어 연극 동호회에 가입하고 싶어 한다.

amaze /əmeɪz/ (**amazes, amazing, amazed**) V-T/V-I If something **amazes** you, it surprises you very much. ❑ *He amazed us by his knowledge of Welsh history*. ● **amazed** ADJ ❑ *He said most of the cast was amazed by the play's success*.

타동사/자동사 깜짝 놀라게 하다 ❑ 그가 웨일즈 역사를 잘 알고 있어서 우리는 깜짝 놀랐다. ● 깜짝 놀란 형용사 ❑ 그 연극의 성공에 출연진 대부분이 깜짝 놀랐다고 그가 말했다.

amaze|ment /əmeɪzmənt/ N-UNCOUNT **Amazement** is the feeling you have when something surprises you very much. [oft *in* N] ❑ *I stared at her in amazement*.

불가산명사 깜짝 놀람 ❑ 나는 깜짝 놀라서 그녀를 쳐다보았다.

amaz|ing ♦◇◇ /əmeɪzɪŋ/ ADJ You say that something is **amazing** when it is very surprising and makes you feel pleasure, approval, or wonder. ❑ *It's amazing what we can remember with a little prompting*. ● **amaz|ing|ly** ADV ❑ *She was an amazingly good cook*.

형용사 놀랄 정도의, 굉장한 ❑ 조금의 암시를 가지고 우리가 기억해 낼 수 있는 바는 놀랄 정도이다. ● 놀랄 정도로 부사 ❑ 그녀는 놀라우리만큼 훌륭한 요리사였다.

am|bas|sa|dor ♦◇◇ /æmbæsədər/ (**ambassadors**) N-COUNT An **ambassador** is an important official who lives in a foreign country and represents his or her own country's interests there. ❑ ...*the German ambassador to Poland*.

가산명사 대사 ❑ 주폴란드 독일 대사

am|ber /ǽmbər/ **1** COLOR **Amber** is used to describe things that are yellowish-brown in color. ❑ *A burst of sunshine sent a beam of amber light through the window.* **2** COLOR An **amber** traffic light is yellow. ❑ *Cars did not stop when the lights were on amber.*

❑ 색채어 호박색 ❑ 한바탕 햇빛이 쏟아져 창틈으로 호박색 빛줄기가 새어 들어왔다. ❑ 색채어 황색 (교통신호) ❑ 신호등이 노란 불일 때 차들이 멈춰 서지 않았다.

am|bi|ence /ǽmbiəns/ also **ambiance** N-SING The **ambience** of a place is the character and atmosphere that it seems to have. [LITERARY] ❑ *The overall ambience of the room is cosy.*

단수명사 분위기, 주변의 모양 [문예체] ❑ 그 방의 전반적인 분위기는 아늑하다.

am|bi|gu|ity /ǽmbɪgyúɪti/ (**ambiguities**) N-VAR If you say that there is **ambiguity** in something, you mean that it is unclear or confusing, or it can be understood in more than one way. ❑ *There is considerable ambiguity about what this part of the agreement actually means.*

가산명사 또는 불가산명사 애매함; 다의성 ❑ 협정의 이 부분이 실제로 의미하는 바에 관해 상당히 애매한 구석이 있다.

am|bigu|ous /ǽmbɪgyuəs/ ADJ If you describe something as **ambiguous**, you mean that it is unclear or confusing and can be understood in more than one way. ❑ *This agreement is very ambiguous and open to various interpretations.* ● **am|bigu|ous|ly** ADV ❑ *Zaire's national conference on democracy ended ambiguously.*

형용사 애매한; 여러 가지 해석이 가능한 ❑ 이 협약은 매우 애매하고 여러 가지로 해석할 수 있는 여지가 있다. ● 애매하게 부사 ❑ 민주주의에 대한 자이레 전국 회의는 애매하게 끝이 났다.

am|bi|tion ♦◇◇ /ǽmbɪʃ°n/ (**ambitions**) **1** N-COUNT If you have an **ambition** to do or achieve something, you want very much to do it or achieve it. ❑ *His ambition is to sail round the world.* **2** N-UNCOUNT **Ambition** is the desire to be successful, rich, or powerful. ❑ *Even when I was young I never had any ambition.*

1 가산명사 열망 ❑ 그의 열망은 배를 타고 세계를 일주하는 것이다. **2** 불가산명사 야망 ❑ 나는 어렸을 때도 야망 따위는 갖지 않았다.

am|bi|tious /ǽmbɪʃəs/ **1** ADJ Someone who is **ambitious** has a strong desire to be successful, rich, or powerful. ❑ *Chris is so ambitious, so determined to do it all.* **2** ADJ An **ambitious** idea or plan is on a large scale and needs a lot of work to be carried out successfully. ❑ *The ambitious project was completed in only nine months.*

1 형용사 야심 있는 ❑ 크리스는 그 모든 것을 해낼만한 야심도 있고 결의도 굳다. **2** 형용사 야심적인, 대규모의 ❑ 그 야심적인 사업은 단 아홉 달 만에 완료되었다.

Thesaurus	*ambitious*의 참조어
ADJ.	aspiring, determined **1**
	challenging, difficult **2**

am|biva|lent /ǽmbɪvələnt/ ADJ If you say that someone is **ambivalent** about something, they seem to be uncertain whether they really want it, or whether they really approve of it. ❑ *She remained ambivalent about her marriage.*

형용사 상반되는 태도를 가진, 양면적인 ❑ 그녀는 결혼하는 것에 대해 여전히 이도 저도 아닌 채로 있었다.

am|bu|lance /ǽmbyələns/ (**ambulances**) N-COUNT An **ambulance** is a vehicle for taking people to and from a hospital. [also *by* N]

가산명사 구급차

am|bush /ǽmbʊʃ/ (**ambushes, ambushing, ambushed**) **1** V-T If a group of people **ambush** their enemies, they attack them after hiding and waiting for them. ❑ *The Guatemalan army says rebels ambushed and killed 10 patrolmen.* **2** N-VAR An **ambush** is an attack on someone by people who have been hiding and waiting for them. ❑ *A policeman has been shot dead in an ambush in County Armagh.*

1 타동사 매복하여 습격하다 ❑ 과테말라 군은 반군의 매복 습격을 받아 순찰대원 열 명이 숨졌다고 전한다. **2** 가산명사 또는 불가산명사 매복 습격 ❑ 아르마 카운티에서 발생한 매복 습격으로 경찰관 한 명이 총격을 받아 사망했다.

amen /ɑːmɛn, eɪ-/ CONVENTION **Amen** is said by Christians at the end of a prayer. ❑ *In the name of the Father and of the Son and of the Holy Ghost, Amen.*

관용 표현 아멘 ❑ 성부와 성자와 성령의 이름으로, 아멘.

ame|nable /əmíːnəb°l, əmɛ́nə-/ ADJ If you are **amenable to** something, you are willing to do it or accept it. ❑ *The Jordanian leader seemed amenable to attending a conference.*

형용사 쾌히 받아들이는 ❑ 요르단 지도자는 회의 참석을 쾌히 수락하는 듯이 보였다.

amend /əmɛ́nd/ (**amends, amending, amended**) **1** V-T If you **amend** something that has been written such as a law, or something that is said, you change it in order to improve it or make it more accurate. ❑ *Kaunda agreed to amend the constitution and allow multi-party elections.* **2** PHRASE If you **make amends** when you have harmed someone, you show that you are sorry by doing something to please them. ❑ *He wanted to make amends for causing their marriage to fail.*

1 타동사 개정하다, 수정하다 ❑ 카운다는 헌법을 개정하고 다당제 선거를 허용하는 데 동의했다. **2** 구 보상하다 ❑ 그는 그들의 결혼을 실패로 이끈 데 대해 보상하고 싶어 했다.

amend|ment ♦◇◇ /əmɛ́ndmənt/ (**amendments**) **1** N-VAR An **amendment** is a section that is added to a law or rule in order to change it. ❑ *...an amendment to the defense bill.* **2** N-COUNT An **amendment** is a change that is made to a piece of writing. ❑ *...Chatelaine magazine, which uses the New York Times stylebook with a few amendments.*

1 가산명사 또는 불가산명사 수정안 ❑ 국방 법안 수정안 **2** 가산명사 수정 ❑ 뉴욕 타임즈 인쇄 편람을 약간 수정해서 사용하는 '샤틀렝' 지

amen|ity /əmíːnɪti, BRIT əmíːnɪti/ (**amenities**) N-COUNT **Amenities** are things such as shopping centers or sports facilities that are provided for people's convenience, enjoyment, or comfort. [usu pl] ❑ *The hotel amenities include health clubs, conference facilities, and banqueting rooms.* →see **hotel**

가산명사 부대 시설, 문화 시설 ❑ 호텔 부대 시설로는 헬스클럽, 회의 설비, 연회실 등이 있다.

Ameri|can foot|ball /əmɛ́rɪkən fʊ́tbɔl/ (**American footballs**) **1** N-UNCOUNT **American football** is a game that is played by two teams of eleven players using an oval-shaped ball. Players try to score points by carrying the ball to their opponents' end of the field, or by kicking it over a bar fixed between two posts. [BRIT; AM **football**] **2** N-COUNT An **American football** is an oval-shaped ball used for playing American football. [BRIT; AM **football**]

1 불가산명사 미식축구 [영국영어; 미국영어 football] **2** 가산명사 미식축구 공 [영국영어; 미국영어 football]

ami|able /éɪmiəb°l/ ADJ Someone who is **amiable** is friendly and pleasant to be with. [WRITTEN] ❑ *She had been surprised at how amiable and polite he had been.*

형용사 상냥한; 붙임성 있는 [문예체] ❑ 그녀는 그의 상냥함과 예의바름에 놀랐었다.

ami|cable /ǽmɪkəb°l/ ADJ When people have an **amicable** relationship, they are pleasant to each other and solve their problems without quarreling. ❑ *The meeting ended on reasonably amicable terms.* ● **ami|cably** /ǽmɪkəbli/ ADV [ADV with v] ❑ *He hoped the dispute could be settled amicably.*

형용사 우호적인, 평화적인 ❑ 회담은 상당히 우호적인 분위기 속에서 끝났다. ● 평화적으로 부사 ❑ 그는 그 싸움이 평화적으로 해결되기를 바랐다.

amid ♦◇◇ /əmɪ́d/

The form **amidst** is also used, but is more literary.

amidst도 쓰지만 더 문예체이다.

PREP If something happens **amid** noises or events of some kind, it happens while the other things are going on. ❑ *A senior leader cancelled a trip to Britain yesterday amid growing signs of a possible political crisis.*

전치사 ~의 한가운데에; 한창 ~하는 중에 ❑ 정치적 위기 조짐이 커가는 가운데 어제 원로급 지도자 한 명이 영국 출장을 취소했다.

amiss /əmɪ́s/ ADJ If you say that something is **amiss**, you mean there is something wrong. [v-link ADJ] ❑ *Their instincts warned them something was amiss.*

형용사 잘못된 ❑ 그들은 본능적으로 뭔가가 잘못되었음을 느꼈다.

am|mo|nia /əmoʊniə/ N-UNCOUNT **Ammonia** is a colorless liquid or gas with a strong, sharp smell. It is used in making household cleaning substances.

불가산명사 암모니아 (기체 혹은 액체)

am|mu|ni|tion /æmyʊnɪʃⁿn/ ■ N-UNCOUNT **Ammunition** is bullets and rockets that are made to be fired from weapons. □ *He had only seven rounds of ammunition for the revolver.* ② N-UNCOUNT You can describe information that you can use against someone in an argument or discussion as **ammunition**. □ *The improved trade figures have given the government fresh ammunition.*

■ 불가산명사 탄약 □ 그에게는 리볼버 권총 탄알이 일곱 발밖에 없었다. ② 불가산명사 (비유적) 무기; 자기주장에 유리한 정보 □ 호전된 무역 지수로 인해 정부는 새로운 무기를 손에 넣은 셈이다.

am|ne|sia /æmniʒə/ N-UNCOUNT If someone is suffering from **amnesia**, they have lost their memory. □ *People suffering from amnesia don't forget their general knowledge of objects.*

불가산명사 기억 상실증 □ 기억 상실증을 겪는 사람들은 사물에 대한 일반적인 지식을 잃지는 않는다.

am|nes|ty /æmnɪsti/ (**amnesties**) ■ N-VAR An **amnesty** is an official pardon granted to a group of prisoners by the state. □ *Activists who were involved in crimes of violence will not automatically be granted amnesty.* ② N-COUNT An **amnesty** is a period of time during which people can admit to a crime or give up weapons without being punished. □ *The government has announced an immediate amnesty for rebel fighters.*

■ 가산명사 또는 불가산명사 사면, 특사 □ 폭행에 연루되었던 운동가들은 자동적으로 사면을 받지는 못할 것이다. ② 가산명사 자진 신고 기간 (처벌받지 않고 자수나 무기 신고를 할 수 있는 기간) □ 정부는 반란군 전투원들에 대한 특별 자수 기간을 즉각 선포했다.

among ♦♦♦ /əmʌŋ/

The form **amongst** is also used, but is more literary.

amongst도 쓰지만 더 문어체이다.

■ PREP Someone or something that is situated or moving **among** a group of things or people is surrounded by them. □ *...youths in their late teens sitting among adults.* □ *They walked among the crowds in Red Square.* ② PREP If you are **among** people of a particular kind, you are with them and having contact with them. □ *Things weren't so bad, after all. I was among friends again.* ③ PREP If someone or something is **among** a group, they are a member of that group and share its characteristics. □ *A fifteen year old girl was among the injured.* ④ PREP If you want to focus on something that is happening within a particular group of people, you can say that it is happening **among** that group. □ *Homicide is the leading cause of death among black men.* ⑤ PREP If something happens **among** a group of people, it happens within the whole of that group or between the members of that group. □ *The calls for reform come as intense debate continues among the leadership over the next five-year economic plan.* ⑥ PREP If something such as a feeling, opinion, or situation exists **among** a group of people, most of them have it or experience it. □ *There was some concern among book and magazine retailers after last Wednesday's news.* ⑦ PREP If something applies to a particular person or thing **among others**, it also applies to other people or things. □ *...a news conference attended among others by our foreign affairs correspondent.* ⑧ PREP If something is shared **among** a number of people, some of it is given to all of them. □ *Most of the furniture was left to the neighbors or distributed among friends.* ⑨ PREP If people talk, fight, or agree **among themselves**, they do it together, without involving anyone else. [PREP pron-refl] □ *European farm ministers disagree among themselves.*

■ 전치사 -의 사이에, -에 둘러싸여 □ 어른들 사이에 앉아 있는 십 대 후반의 젊은이들 □ 그들은 붉은 광장의 인파들 사이를 걸어갔다. ② 전치사 -와 함께, -와 어울려 □ 어쨌든 사정이 그리 나쁘지는 않았다. 나는 다시 친구들과 어울렸다. ③ 전치사 - 중의 하나로, -에 속하여 □ 부상자들 중에는 열다섯 살 난 여자 아이가 끼어 있었다. ④ 전치사 - 사이에서 □ 흑인 남성 사이에서 살인이 가장 큰 사망 원인이다. ⑤ 전치사 - 사이 전체에 □ 지도부 내에서 향후 5년간의 경제 계획에 대한 열띤 토론이 이어짐에 따라 개혁에 대한 요구가 일어난다. ⑥ 전치사 -사이에 퍼져 □ 지난 주 수요일 보도 이후로 서적 및 잡지 소매상들 사이에 약간의 우려가 퍼져 있었다. ⑦ 전치사 -은 물론; - 중에서도 특히 □ 다른 사람들은 물론 우리 쪽 국제부 기자도 참석한 기자 회견 ⑧ 전치사 - 사이에 각자 □ 대부분의 세간은 이웃들에게 남겨 주거나 친구들에게 나눠주었다. ⑨ 전치사 -끼리 내부적으로 □ 유럽 각국의 농업부 장관들끼리 의견이 서로 달랐다.

If there are more than two people or things, you should use **among**. If there are only two people or things you should use **between** □ *...an area between Mars and Jupiter.* You can also talk about relationships **between** or **among** people or things, and discussions **between** or **among** people. □ *...an argument between his mother and another woman.* Note that if you are **between** things or people, the things or people are on either side of you. If you are **among** things or people, they are all around you □ *...the bag standing on the floor between us....the sound of a pigeon among the trees.*

among은 사람이나 사물이 셋 이상일 때 쓴다. 사람이 두 명이거나 사물이 두 개뿐일 경우에는 between을 쓴다. □ ...화성과 목성 사이의 영역. 사람이나 사물들 '사이'의 관계에 대해서나, 사람들 '사이'의 토론에 대해 말할 때도 between이나 among을 쓸 수 있다. □ ...그의 어머니와 다른 여자 사이의 언쟁. between을 써서 당신이 사물 또는 사람들 '사이'로 하면, 사물 또는 사람들이 당신의 양쪽에 있다고 하는 것임을 유의하라. among을 써서 당신이 사물 또는 사람들 '사이'나 '가운데' 있음을 나타내면, 사물 또는 사람들이 당신의 모든 주위에 다 있음을 나타낸다. □ ...우리 사이의 바닥에 세워져 있는 가방....나무 사이에서 들리는 비둘기 소리

amongst /əmʌŋst/ PREP **Amongst** means the same as **among**. [LITERARY]

전치사 among과 같은 의미 [문어체]

amor|tize /æmərtaɪz, BRIT əmɔːʳtaɪz/ (**amortizes, amortizing, amortized**) [BRIT also **amortise**] V-T In finance, if you **amortize** a debt, you pay it back in regular payments. [BUSINESS] □ *There's little advantage to amortizing the loan, especially on a 30 or 40-year basis.*

[영국영어 amortise] 타동사 분할 상환하다 [경제] □ 그 융자금을 분할 상환하는 것, 특히 30년 내지 40년 기준의 장기 분할 상환에는 이점이 별로 없다.

amount ♦♦◇ /əmaʊnt/ (**amounts, amounting, amounted**) ■ N-VAR The **amount of** something is how much there is, or how much you have, need, or get. □ *He needs that amount of money to survive.* □ *I still do a certain amount of work for them.* ② V-I If something **amounts to** a particular total, all the parts of it add up to that total. □ *Consumer spending on sports-related items amounted to £9.75 billion.*

■ 가산명사 또는 불가산명사 양; 액 □ 그는 목숨을 부지하기 위해 그만큼의 돈이 필요하다. □ 나는 아직도 그들을 위한 일을 일정량 한다. ② 자동사 총계 -이 되다 □ 스포츠 관련 용품에의 소비 지출 총계가 97억 5천만 파운드에 달했다.

You should avoid using a plural noun after **amount of**; instead you should use **number of** with a plural noun. □ *...the number of people out of work.*

amount 뒤에는 복수 명사를 쓰지 않는다. 대신에 복수 명사와는 number of을 써야 한다. □ ...일자리가 없는 사람들의 수

▶**amount to** PHRASAL VERB-LINK If you say that one thing **amounts to** something else, you consider the first thing to be the same as the second thing. □ *The banks have what amounts to a monopoly.*

연결 구동사 -에 상당하다; -나 마찬가지이다 □ 그 은행들은 독점에 상당하는 많은 양을 보유하고 있다.

amp /æmp/ (**amps**) ■ N-COUNT An **amp** is the same as an **ampere**. □ *Use a 3 amp fuse for equipment up to 720 watts.* ② N-COUNT An **amp** is the same as an **amplifier**. [INFORMAL]

■ 가산명사 앰페어 (전류의 단위) □ 720와트까지의 기구에는 3암페어짜리 퓨즈를 사용하세요. ② 가산명사 증폭기, 앰프 [비격식체]

ampere /æmpɪəʳ, æmpɪəʳ, BRIT æmpeəʳ/ (**amperes**) [BRIT also **ampère**] N-COUNT An **ampere** is a unit which is used for measuring electric current. The abbreviation **amp** is also used.

[영국영어 ampère] 가산명사 암페어 (전류의 단위)

am|pheta|mine /æmfɛtəmin/ (**amphetamines**) N-MASS **Amphetamine** is a drug which increases people's energy, makes them excited, and reduces their desire for food.

물질명사 암페타민 (중추 신경을 자극하는 각성제)

am|ple /ˈæmpəl/ (**ampler, amplest**) ADJ If there is an **ample** amount of something, there is enough of it and usually some extra. ❑ *There'll be ample opportunity to relax, swim, and soak up some sun.* ● **am|ply** ADV ❑ *This collection of his essays and journalism amply demonstrates his commitment to democracy.*

형용사 충분한, 넉넉한 ❑ 휴식을 취하고, 수영하고, 햇볕을 쬘 충분한 기회가 있을 것입니다. ● 충분히 부사 ❑ 이렇게 그가 쓴 시론과 기고문을 모아놓은 것을 보면 민주주의에 대한 그의 헌신이 충분히 드러난다.

am|pli|fi|er /ˈæmplɪfaɪər/ (**amplifiers**) N-COUNT An **amplifier** is an electronic device in a radio or stereo system which causes sounds or signals to get louder.

가산명사 증폭기, 앰프

am|pli|fy /ˈæmplɪfaɪ/ (**amplifies, amplifying, amplified**) ◼ V-T If you **amplify** a sound, you make it louder, usually by using electronic equipment. ❑ *This landscape seemed to trap and amplify sounds.* ❑ *The music was amplified with microphones.* ● **am|pli|fi|ca|tion** /ˌæmplɪfɪˈkeɪʃən/ N-UNCOUNT ❑ *...a voice that needed no amplification.* ◼ V-T To **amplify** something means to increase its strength or intensity. ❑ *The mist had been replaced by a kind of haze that seemed to amplify the heat.*

◼ 타동사 증폭하다 ❑ 이곳의 조경이 음향을 받아들여 증폭하는 것 같았다. ❑ 음악은 마이크를 통해 증폭되었다. ● 증폭; 확성 불가산명사 ❑ 확성할 필요가 없는 목소리 ◼ 타동사 증폭시키다 ❑ 안개는 더위를 증폭시키는 듯한 아지랑이 같은 것으로 바뀌어 있었다.

am|pu|tate /ˈæmpyʊteɪt/ (**amputates, amputating, amputated**) V-T To **amputate** someone's arm or leg means to cut all or part of it off in an operation because it is diseased or badly damaged. ❑ *To save his life, doctors amputated his legs.* ● **am|pu|ta|tion** /ˌæmpyʊˈteɪʃən/ (**amputations**) N-VAR ❑ *He lived only hours after the amputation.*

타동사 자르다, (사지를) 절단하다 ❑ 의사들은 그의 목숨을 구하기 위해 다리를 잘라냈다. ● 절단 수술 가산명사 또는 불가산명사 ❑ 그는 절단 수술을 받은 후 단지 몇 시간 동안만 목숨을 유지했다.

amuse /əˈmyuz/ (**amuses, amusing, amused**) ◼ V-T/V-I If something **amuses** you, it makes you want to laugh or smile. ❑ *The thought seemed to amuse him.* ◼ V-T If you **amuse yourself**, you do something in order to pass the time and not become bored. ❑ *I need distractions. I need to amuse myself so I won't keep thinking about things.* ◼ →see also **amused, amusing**

◼ 타동사/자동사 즐겁게 하다 ❑ 그 생각이 그를 즐겁게 만드는 것 같았다. ◼ 타동사 즐겁게 보내다 ❑ 기분 전환이 필요해. 자꾸만 생각에 빠져들지 않도록 뭔가 즐거운 일을 해야겠어.

amused /əˈmyuzd/ ADJ If you are **amused by** something, it makes you want to laugh or smile. ❑ *Sara was not amused by Franklin's teasing.*

형용사 즐거워하는 ❑ 사라는 프랭클린의 놀림에 즐거워하지 않았다.

amuse|ment /əˈmyuzmənt/ (**amusements**) ◼ N-UNCOUNT **Amusement** is the feeling that you have when you think that something is funny or amusing. ❑ *He stopped and watched with amusement to see the child so absorbed.* ◼ N-UNCOUNT **Amusement** is the pleasure that you get from being entertained or from doing something interesting. ❑ *I stumbled sideways before landing flat on my back, much to the amusement of the rest of the lads.* ◼ N-COUNT **Amusements** are ways of passing the time pleasantly. ❑ *People had very few amusements to choose from. There was no radio, or television.* ◼ N-PLURAL **Amusements** are games, rides, and other things that you can enjoy, for example at an amusement park or at the seashore. ❑ *...a place full of swings and amusements.*

◼ 불가산명사 즐거움 ❑ 그는 멈춰 서서 아이가 아주 열중해 있는 모습을 즐거워하며 지켜보았다. ◼ 불가산명사 재미 ❑ 나는 모로 넘어져 뒤로 벌렁 나자빠졌고, 나머지 청년들은 그런 내 모습에 매우 재미있어 했다. ◼ 가산명사 오락거리 ❑ 선택할 수 있는 오락거리가 별로 없었다. 라디오나 텔레비전도 없었다. ◼ 복수명사 오락; 놀이 기구 ❑ 그네와 놀이 기구로 가득 찬 곳

amus|ing /əˈmyuzɪŋ/ ADJ Someone or something that is **amusing** makes you laugh or smile. ❑ *He had a terrific sense of humor and could be very amusing.* ● **amus|ing|ly** ADV ❑ *It must be amusingly written.*

형용사 재미있는 ❑ 그는 유머 감각이 빼어나서 대단히 재미있었을 텐데. ● 재미있게 부사 ❑ 그것은 재미있게 써져야 한다.

an /ən, STRONG æn/ DET **An** is used instead of "a," the indefinite article, in front of words that begin with vowel sounds. →see also **a**

한정사 부정관사 에이가 모음 앞에서 변형된 형태

anaemia /əˈnimiə/ →see **anemia**

anaemic /əˈnimɪk/ →see **anemic**

an|aes|thet|ic /ˌænɪsˈθɛtɪk/ →see **anesthetic**

anaes|the|tist /əˈnɛsθətɪst/ (**anaesthetists**) N-COUNT An **anaesthetist** is a doctor who specializes in giving anaesthetics to patients. [BRIT; AM **anesthesiologist**]

가산명사 마취의(사) [영국영어; 미국영어 anesthesiologist]

anal /ˈeɪnəl/ ADJ **Anal** means relating to the anus of a person or animal. ❑ *...anal injuries.*

형용사 항문의 ❑ 항문 부상

analo|gous /əˈnæləgəs/ ADJ If one thing is **analogous to** another, the two things are similar in some way. [FORMAL] ❑ *Marine construction technology like this is very complex, somewhat analogous to trying to build a bridge under water.*

형용사 유사한 [격식체] ❑ 이와 같은 해상 건설 기술은 매우 복잡하며, 어떤 면에서는 수중에 다리를 건설하려는 시도와 유사하다.

ana|logue /ˈænəlɔg, BRIT ˈænəlɒg/ (**analogues**)

> The spelling **analog** is usually used in American English for the adjective, and also in British English for meaning ◼.

철자 analog은 대개 미국영어에서 형용사로 쓰며, 영국영어에서도 ◼ 의미로 쓴다.

◼ N-COUNT If one thing is an **analogue of** another, it is similar in some way. [FORMAL] ❑ *No model can ever be a perfect analogue of nature itself.* ◼ ADJ **Analogue** technology involves measuring, storing, or recording an infinitely variable amount of information by using physical quantities such as voltage. ❑ *The analogue signals from the videotape are converted into digital code.* ◼ ADJ An **analogue** watch or clock shows what it is measuring with a pointer on a dial rather than with a number display. Compare **digital**.

◼ 가산명사 유사물 [격식체] ❑ 어떤 모델도 자연 그 자체를 완벽하게 본뜰 수는 없다. ◼ 형용사 아날로그 ❑ 비디오테이프에서 나오는 아날로그 신호는 디지털 코드로 전환된다. ◼ 형용사 아날로그

anal|ogy /əˈnælədʒi/ (**analogies**) N-COUNT If you make or draw an **analogy** between two things, you show that they are similar in some way. ❑ *The analogy between music and fragrance has stuck.*

가산명사 유사 관계 ❑ 음악과 향기 사이의 유사 관계는 이미 확고해졌다.

Word Partnership	*analogy*의 연어
PREP.	analogy **between**
V.	**draw an** analogy, **make an** analogy
ADJ.	**false** analogy

ana|lyse /ˈænəlaɪz/ →see **analyze**

analy|sis ◆◇◇ /əˈnæləsɪs/ (**analyses**) /əˈnæləsiz/ ◼ N-VAR **Analysis** is the process of considering something carefully or using statistical methods in order to understand it or explain it. ❑ *Her criteria defy analysis.* ◼ N-VAR **Analysis** is the scientific process of examining something in order to find out what it consists of. ❑ *They collect blood samples for analysis at a national laboratory.* ◼ N-COUNT An **analysis** is an explanation or description that results from considering something carefully. ❑ *The census provides a considerable amount of detail in its analysis of internal movement in France.*

◼ 가산명사 또는 불가산명사 분석 ❑ 그녀의 기준은 분석이 불가능하다. ◼ 가산명사 또는 불가산명사 분석 ❑ 그들은 국립 연구소에서 혈액 시료를 수집했다. ◼ 가산명사 분석 ❑ 그 통계 조사는 프랑스 국내 동향 분석에 있어서 상당량의 세부 정보를 제공한다.

analyst ♦♦◇ /ǽnəlɪst/ (**analysts**) **1** N-COUNT An **analyst** is a person whose job is to analyze a subject and give opinions about it. ❑ ...*a political analyst.* **2** N-COUNT An **analyst** is someone, usually a doctor, who examines and treats people who have emotional problems. ❑ *My analyst warned me that I liked married men too much.*

1 가산명사 분석가 ❑ 정치 분석가 **2** 가산명사 정신 분석가 ❑ 내가 유부남들을 너무 좋아한다고 내 정신 치료사가 나에게 주의를 주었다.

analytic /ænəlɪ́tɪk/ ADJ **Analytic** means the same as **analytical**. [mainly AM]

형용사 분석적인 [주로 미국영어]

analytical /ænəlɪ́tɪkᵊl/ ADJ An **analytical** way of doing something involves the use of logical reasoning. ❑ *I have an analytical approach to every survey.*

형용사 분석적인 ❑ 나는 모든 조사에 분석적으로 접근한다.

analyze /ǽnəlaɪz/ (**analyzes, analyzing, analyzed**) [BRIT **analyse**] **1** V-T If you **analyze** something, you consider it carefully or use statistical methods in order to fully understand it. ❑ *McCarthy was asked to analyze the data from the first phase of trials of the vaccine.* **2** V-T If you **analyze** something, you examine it using scientific methods in order to find out what it consists of. ❑ *We haven't had time to analyze those samples yet.*

[영국영어 analyse] **1** 타동사 분석하다 ❑ 매카시는 백신 시험 첫 단계부터의 데이터를 분석해 달라는 요청을 받았다. **2** 타동사 분석하다 ❑ 아직 그 시료들을 분석할 시간이 없었습니다.

Thesaurus	*analyze*의 참조어
v.	break down, dissect, examine, inspect **1** **2**

anarchic /ænɑ́ːrkɪk/ ADJ If you describe someone or something as **anarchic**, you disapprove of them because they do not recognize or obey any rules or laws. [DISAPPROVAL] ❑ ...*anarchic attitudes and complete disrespect for authority.*

형용사 무정부 상태의; 무질서한 [탐탁잖음] ❑ 무질서한 태도와 권위에 대한 철저한 무시

anarchism /ǽnərkɪzəm/ N-UNCOUNT **Anarchism** is the belief that the laws and power of governments should be replaced by people working together freely. ❑ *He advocated anarchism as the answer to social problems.*

불가산명사 무정부주의 ❑ 그는 사회 문제에 대한 해결책으로 무정부주의를 주장했다.

anarchist /ǽnərkɪst/ (**anarchists**) **1** N-COUNT An **anarchist** is a person who believes in anarchism. [oft N n] ❑ *West Berlin always had a large anarchist community.* **2** ADJ If someone has **anarchist** beliefs or views, they believe in anarchism. [ADJ n] ❑ *He was apparently quite converted from his anarchist views.*

1 가산명사 무정부주의자 ❑ 서베를린에는 항상 큰 무정부주의자 집단이 있었다. **2** 형용사 무정부주의자적인 ❑ 분명히 그는 자신의 무정부주의자적인 관점으로부터 상당히 전향해 있었다.

anarchy /ǽnərki/ N-UNCOUNT If you describe a situation as **anarchy**, you mean that nobody seems to be paying any attention to rules or laws. [DISAPPROVAL] ❑ *The school's liberal, individualistic traditions were in danger of slipping into anarchy.*

불가산명사 무정부 상태; 무질서 상태 [탐탁잖음] ❑ 그 학교의 자유주의적이고 개인주의적인 전통이 무정부 상태로 빠질 위험에 처해 있었다.

anatomical /ænətɒ́mɪkᵊl/ ADJ **Anatomical** means relating to the structure of the bodies of people and animals. ❑ ...*minute anatomical differences between insects.*

형용사 해부의, 해부학적인 ❑ 곤충들 간의 미세한 해부학적 차이

anatomy /ənǽtəmi/ (**anatomies**) **1** N-UNCOUNT **Anatomy** is the study of the structure of the bodies of people or animals. ❑ ... *a course in anatomy.* **2** N-COUNT You can refer to your body as your **anatomy**. [HUMOROUS] ❑ *The ball hit him in the most sensitive part of his anatomy.* →see **medicine**

1 불가산명사 해부학 ❑ 해부학 강좌 **2** 가산명사 몸, 인체 [해학체] ❑ 공이 그의 몸에서 가장 민감한 부위에 맞았다.

ancestor /ǽnsestər/ (**ancestors**) **1** N-COUNT Your **ancestors** are the people from whom you are descended. [oft N poss] ❑ ...*our daily lives, so different from those of our ancestors.* **2** N-COUNT An **ancestor of** something modern is an earlier thing from which it developed. ❑ *The direct ancestor of the modern cat was the Kaffir cat of ancient Egypt.*

1 가산명사 선조, 조상 ❑ 선조들의 생활과는 너무 다른 우리들의 일상생활 **2** 가산명사 전신; 조상 ❑ 현대 고양이의 직계 조상은 고대 이집트의 카피르 고양이였다.

ancestral /ænséstrəl/ ADJ You use **ancestral** to refer to a person's family in former times, especially when the family is important and has property or land which they have had for a long time. ❑ ...*the family's ancestral home in southern Germany.*

형용사 조상 대대로의 ❑ 독일 남부에 있는 그 가문 조상 전래의 집

ancestry /ǽnsestri/ (**ancestries**) N-COUNT Your **ancestry** is the fact that you are descended from certain people. ❑ ...*a family who could trace their ancestry back to the sixteenth century.*

가산명사 가계 ❑ 16세기까지 가계를 더듬어 올라갈 수 있는 가문

anchor /ǽnkər/ (**anchors, anchoring, anchored**) **1** N-COUNT An **anchor** is a heavy hooked object that is dropped from a boat into the water at the end of a chain in order to make the boat stay in one place. **2** V-T/V-I When a boat **anchors** or when you **anchor** it, its anchor is dropped into the water in order to make it stay in one place. ❑ *We could anchor off the pier.* **3** V-T If you **anchor** an object somewhere, you fix it to something to prevent it moving from that place. ❑ *The roots anchor the plant in the earth.* **4** V-T The person who **anchors** a television or radio program, especially a news program, is the person who presents it and acts as a link between interviews and reports which come from other places or studios. [mainly AM] ❑ *Viewers saw him anchoring a five-minute summary of regional news.* **5** N-COUNT The **anchor** on a television or radio program, especially a news program, is the person who presents it. [mainly AM] ❑ *He worked in the news division of ABC – he was the anchor of its 15-minute evening newscast.* **6** PHRASE If a boat is **at anchor**, it is floating in a particular place and is prevented from moving by its anchor. ❑ *Sailing boats lay at anchor in the narrow waterway.*

1 가산명사 닻 **2** 타동사/자동사 닻을 내리다, 정박하다; 정박시키다 ❑ 우리는 부두 앞바다에 닻을 내릴 수 있었다. **3** 타동사 고정시키다 ❑ 뿌리는 식물을 흙에다 고정시킨다. **4** 타동사 앵커로 진행하다 [주로 미국영어] ❑ 시청자들은 그가 5분짜리 간추린 지역 뉴스를 앵커로 진행하는 것을 보았다. **5** 가산명사 앵커 [주로 미국영어] ❑ 그는 에이비시 뉴스국에서 일했다. 그는 15분짜리 저녁 뉴스의 앵커였다. **6** 구 정박해 있는 ❑ 돛배들이 좁은 수로에 정박해 있었다.

ancient ♦♦◇ /éɪnʃənt/ **1** ADJ **Ancient** means belonging to the distant past, especially to the period in history before the end of the Roman Empire. [ADJ n] ❑ *They believed ancient Greece and Rome were vital sources of learning.* **2** ADJ **Ancient** means very old, or having existed for a long time. ❑ ...*ancient Jewish tradition.* →see **history**

1 형용사 고대의 ❑ 그들은 고대 그리스와 로마가 지식의 중요한 원천이었다고 믿었다. **2** 형용사 아주 오래 된 ❑ 아주 오랜 유대 전통

ancillary /ǽnsɪleri, BRIT ænsɪ́ləri/ ADJ The **ancillary** workers in an institution are the people such as cleaners and cooks whose work supports the main work of the institution. [ADJ n] ❑ ...*ancillary staff.*

형용사 보조의, 부수적인 ❑ 보조 직원

and ♦♦♦ /ənd, STRONG ænd/ **1** CONJ You use **and** to link two or more words, groups, or clauses. ❑ *When he returned, she and Simon had already gone.* ❑ *I'm going to write good jokes and become a good comedian.* **2** CONJ You use **and** to link two words or phrases that are the same in order to emphasize the degree of something, or to suggest that something continues or increases over a period of time. [EMPHASIS] ❑ *Learning becomes more and more difficult as we get older.* ❑ *We talked for*

1 접속사 ~와; ~하고 ❑ 그가 돌아왔을 때, 그녀와 사이먼은 이미 떠나고 없었다. ❑ 나는 멋진 익살을 지어내서 훌륭한 코미디언이 될 거야. **2** 접속사 더하여 [강조] ❑ 배움이란 나이를 먹을수록 점점 더 어려워진다. ❑ 우리는 아주 긴 시간에 걸쳐 이야기를 나눴다. **3** 접속사 ~한 다음, ~하고 나서 ❑ 나는 손을

hours and hours. ◼ CONJ You use **and** to link two statements about events when one of the events follows the other. ❏ *I waved goodbye and went down the stone harbor steps.* ◼ CONJ You use **and** to link two statements when the second statement continues the point that has been made in the first statement. ❏ *You could only really tell the effects of the disease in the long term, and five years wasn't long enough.* ◼ CONJ You use **and** to link two clauses when the second clause is a result of the first clause. ❏ *All through yesterday crowds have been arriving and by midnight thousands of people packed the square.* ◼ CONJ You use **and** to interrupt yourself in order to make a comment on what you are saying. ❏ *As Downing claims, and as we noted above, reading is best established when the child has an intimate knowledge of the language.* ◼ CONJ You use **and** at the beginning of a sentence to introduce something else that you want to add to what you have just said. Some people think that starting a sentence with **and** is ungrammatical, but it is now quite common in both spoken and written English. ❏ *Commuter airlines fly to out-of-the-way places. And business travelers are the ones who go to those locations.* ◼ CONJ You use **and** to introduce a question which follows logically from what someone has just said. ❏ *"He used to be so handsome." — "And now?"* ◼ CONJ **And** is used by broadcasters and people making announcements to change a topic or to start talking about a topic they have just mentioned. ❏ *And now the drought in Sudan.* ◼ CONJ You use **and** to indicate that two numbers are to be added together. ❏ *What does two and two make?* ◼ CONJ **And** is used before a fraction that comes after a whole number. ❏ *McCain spent five and a half years in a prisoner of war camp in Vietnam.* ◼ CONJ You use **and** in numbers larger than one hundred, after the words "hundred" or "thousand" and before other numbers. ❏ *We printed two hundred and fifty invitations.*

an|ec|do|tal /ænɪkdoʊtᵊl/ ADJ **Anecdotal** evidence is based on individual accounts, rather than on reliable research or statistics, and so may not be valid. ❏ *Anecdotal evidence suggests that sales in Europe have slipped.*

an|ec|dote /ænɪkdoʊt/ (**anecdotes**) N-VAR An **anecdote** is a short, amusing account of something that has happened. ❏ *Pete was telling them an anecdote about their mother.*

anemia /əni̱miə/ [BRIT **anaemia**] N-UNCOUNT **Anemia** is a medical condition in which there are too few red cells in your blood, causing you to feel tired and look pale. ❏ *She suffered from anemia and even required blood transfusions.*

anemic /əni̱mɪk/ [BRIT **anaemic**] ADJ Someone who is **anemic** suffers from anemia. ❏ *Tests showed that she was very anemic.*

an|es|thesi|ol|o|gist /æ̱nɪsθiːziɒlədʒɪst/ (**anesthesiologists**) N-COUNT An **anesthesiologist** is a doctor who specializes in giving anesthetics to patients. [AM; BRIT **anaesthetist**]

an|es|thet|ic /æ̱nɪsθe̱tɪk/ (**anesthetics**) [BRIT, sometimes AM **anaesthetic**] N-MASS **Anesthetic** is a substance that doctors use to stop you feeling pain during an operation, either in the whole of your body when you are unconscious, or in a part of your body when you are awake. ❏ *The operation is carried out under a general anesthetic.*

anes|the|tist /ənɛ̱sθətɪst/ (**anesthetists**) N-COUNT An **anesthetist** is a nurse or other person who gives an anesthetic to a patient. [AM]

anew /ənu̱, BRIT ənyu̱ː/ ADV If you do something **anew**, you do it again, often in a different way from before. [WRITTEN] [ADV after v] ❏ *She's ready to start anew.*

an|gel /eɪndʒᵊl/ (**angels**) ◼ N-COUNT **Angels** are spiritual beings that some people believe are God's servants in heaven. ❏ *The artist usually painted his angels with multi-colored wings.* ◼ N-COUNT You can call someone you like very much an **angel** in order to show affection, especially when they have been kind to you or done you a favor. [FEELINGS] ❏ *Thank you a thousand times, you're an angel.* ◼ N-COUNT If you describe someone as an **angel**, you mean that they seem to be very kind and good. [APPROVAL] ❏ *Poppa thought her an angel.*

an|gel|ic /ændʒe̱lɪk/ ◼ ADJ You can describe someone as **angelic** if they are, or seem to be, very good, kind, and gentle. [APPROVAL] ❏ *...an angelic face.* ◼ ADJ **Angelic** means like angels or relating to angels. [ADJ n] ❏ *...angelic choirs.*

an|ger ◆◇◇ /æ̱ŋgər/ (**angers, angering, angered**) ◼ N-UNCOUNT **Anger** is the strong emotion that you feel when you think that someone has behaved in an unfair, cruel, or unacceptable way. ❏ *He cried with anger and frustration.* ◼ V-T If something **angers** you, it makes you feel angry. ❏ *The decision to allow more offshore oil drilling angered some Californians.* →see **emotion**
→see Word Web: **anger**

an|gle ◆◇◇ /æ̱ŋgᵊl/ (**angles**) ◼ N-COUNT An **angle** is the difference in direction between two lines or surfaces. Angles are measured in degrees. ❏ *The boat is now leaning at a 30 degree angle.* →see also **right angle** ◼ N-COUNT An **angle** is the shape that is created where two lines or surfaces join together. ❏ *...the angle of*

형용사 일화성의 ❏ 일화성 근거에 따르면 유럽에서의 판매가 감소했다는 설이 있다.

가산명사 또는 불가산명사 일화 ❏ 피트는 그 사람들에게 그들의 어머니에 대한 일화를 들려주고 있었다.

[영국영어 anaemia] 불가산명사 빈혈증 ❏ 그녀는 빈혈증을 앓아서 수혈까지 받아야 했다.

[영국영어 anaemic] 형용사 빈혈증이 있는 ❏ 검사에 의해 그 여인이 심한 빈혈을 앓고 있음이 드러났다.

가산명사 마취의 [미국영어; 영국영어 anaesthetist]

[영국영어, 미국영어 가끔 anaesthetic] 물질명사 마취제 ❏ 수술은 전신 마취하에 이루어진다.

가산명사 마취사 [미국영어]

부사 다시; 새로 [문어체] ❏ 그녀는 새로 시작할 준비가 되어 있다.

◼ 가산명사 천사 ❏ 그 화가는 평소 천사를 그릴 때 다채로운 색상의 날개를 가진 모습으로 그렸다. ◼ 가산명사 (비유적) 천사 [감정 개입] ❏ 정말 고마워. 너는 천사야. ◼ 가산명사 매우 착한 사람 [마음에 듦] ❏ 아빠는 그 여자를 천사 같은 사람으로 여겼다.

◼ 형용사 천사 같은 [마음에 듦] ❏ 천사 같은 얼굴 ◼ 형용사 천사의; 천사 같은 ❏ 천사 합창단

◼ 불가산명사 노염, 화 ❏ 그는 화가 나고 절망해서 울었다. ◼ 타동사 노하게 하다 ❏ 연해 지역 석유 추가 시추를 허용하는 결정에 일부 캘리포니아 사람들이 분노했다.

◼ 가산명사 각도 ❏ 배는 현재 30도 각도로 기울고 있다. ◼ 가산명사 각 ❏ 칼날 각 ◼ 가산명사 보는 방향, 보는 각도 ❏ 서 있는 방향 덕분에 그는 간신히 일몰을 볼 수 있었다. ◼ 가산명사 관점, 견지 ❏ 그는 그 안을

the blade. **3** N-COUNT An **angle** is the direction from which you look at something. ❑ *Thanks to the angle at which he stood, he could just see the sunset.* **4** N-COUNT You can refer to a way of presenting something or thinking about it as a particular **angle**. ❑ *He was considering the idea from all angles.* **5** PHRASE If something is **at an angle**, it is leaning in a particular direction so that it is not straight, horizontal, or vertical. ❑ *An iron bar stuck out at an angle.* →see **mathematics**

모든 각도에서 숙고하고 있었다. **5** 구 비스듬히 ❑ 쇠막대기 하나가 비스듬히 튀어나왔다.

an|gler /ˈæŋglər/ (anglers) N-COUNT An **angler** is someone who fishes with a fishing rod as a hobby.

가산명사 낚시꾼

an|gling /ˈæŋglɪŋ/ N-UNCOUNT **Angling** is the activity or sport of fishing with a fishing rod.

불가산명사 낚시질

an|gry ♦♦◇ /ˈæŋgri/ (angrier, angriest) ADJ When you are **angry**, you feel strong dislike or impatience about something. ❑ *Are you angry with me for some reason?* ❑ *I was angry about the rumors.* ❑ *An angry mob gathered outside the courthouse.*
● an|gri|ly /ˈæŋgrɪli/ ADV [ADV with v] ❑ *Officials reacted angrily to those charges.*

형용사 성난, 화가 난 ❑ 너 무슨 이유론가 나한테 화가 난 거니? ❑ 나는 그 소문에 대해 화가 났다. ❑ 성난 군중이 법원 주위에 몰려들었다. ● 성나서 부사 ❑ 관리들은 그러한 비난에 노여운 반응을 보였다.

> **Angry** is normally used to talk about someone's mood or feelings on a particular occasion. If someone is often angry, you can describe them as **bad-tempered**. ❑ *She's a bad-tempered young lady.* If someone is very angry, you can describe them as **furious**. ❑ *Senior police officers are furious at the blunder.* If they are less angry, you can describe them as **annoyed** or **irritated**. ❑ *The Premier looked annoyed but calm....a man irritated by the barking of his neighbor's dog.* Typically, someone is **irritated** by something because it happens constantly or continually. If someone is often irritated, you can describe them as **irritable**.

> angry는 보통 특정한 경우에 어떤 사람의 기분이나 감정을 얘기할 때 쓴다. 누가 자주 화를 내면, 그 사람은 bad-tempered라고 할 수 있다. ❑ 그녀는 성질이 나쁜 젊은 여자다. 누가 아주 화가 났으면, furious하다고 표현할 수 있다. ❑ 고참 경찰들이 그 중대한 실수에 격노했다. angry보다 덜한 경우에는 annoyed나 irritated를 써서 표현할 수 있다. ❑ 수상은 불쾌해 하는 것 같았으나 침착했다....이웃집 개 짖는 소리에 짜증이 난 남자. 대체로 누가 무엇에 의해 irritated되는 것은 그것이 끊임없이 계속되기 때문이다. 누가 자주 짜증을 내면, 그 사람을 irritable(짜증을 잘 내는)하다고 표현할 수 있다.

Thesaurus	*angry*의 참조어
ADJ.	bitter, mad; *(ant.)* content, happy, pleased

Word Partnership	*angry*의 연어
PREP.	angry **about** *something*, angry **at** *someone/something*, angry **with** *someone*
V.	get angry, make *someone* angry
N.	angry **mob**

angst /æŋst/ N-UNCOUNT **Angst** is a feeling of anxiety and worry. [JOURNALISM] ❑ *Many kids suffer from acne and angst.*

불가산명사 불안감; 고뇌 [언론] ❑ 많은 아이들이 여드름과 불안감 때문에 고민한다.

an|guish /ˈæŋgwɪʃ/ N-UNCOUNT **Anguish** is great mental suffering or physical pain. [WRITTEN] ❑ *Mark looked at him in anguish.*

불가산명사 고통, 괴로움 [문어체] ❑ 마크는 고통스러워하며 그를 바라보았다.

an|guished /ˈæŋgwɪʃt/ ADJ **Anguished** means showing or feeling great mental suffering or physical pain. [WRITTEN] ❑ *She let out an anguished cry.*

형용사 괴로워하는, 고통에 찬 [문어체] ❑ 그녀는 괴롭게 울부짖었다.

an|gu|lar /ˈæŋgyələr/ ADJ **Angular** things have shapes that seem to contain a lot of straight lines and sharp points. ❑ *He had an angular face with prominent cheekbones.*

형용사 각진, 모난 ❑ 그는 각진 얼굴에 광대뼈가 튀어나왔다.

an|i|mal ♦♦◇ /ˈænɪməl/ (animals) **1** N-COUNT An **animal** is a living creature such as a dog, lion, or rabbit, rather than a bird, fish, insect, or human being. ❑ *He was attacked by wild animals.* **2** N-COUNT Any living creature other than a human being can be referred to as an **animal**. ❑ *Language is something which fundamentally distinguishes humans from animals.* **3** N-COUNT Any living creature, including a human being, can be referred to as an **animal**. ❑ *Watch any young human being, or any other young animal.* **4** ADJ **Animal** products come from animals rather than from plants. ❑ *The illegal trade in animal products continues to flourish.* →see **earth**

1 가산명사 동물 ❑ 그는 야생동물의 습격을 받았다. **2** 가산명사 동물 (인간과 구분하여) ❑ 언어는 인간을 동물로부터 본질적으로 구별 짓는 요소이다. **3** 가산명사 동물 (인간까지 포함시켜) ❑ 어린 인간, 혹은 다른 어린 동물을 지켜보라. **4** 형용사 동물의 ❑ 동물성 제품의 불법 거래가 계속 성행한다.

Word Partnership	*animal*의 연어
N.	**plant and** animal **1** **3**
	cruelty to animals, animal **hide**, animal **kingdom**, animal **noises** **2**
ADJ.	**domestic** animal, **wild** animal **2**

an|i|mate (animates, animating, animated)
The adjective is pronounced /ˈænɪmət/. The verb is pronounced /ˈænɪmeɪt/.

형용사는 /ˈænɪmət/으로 발음되고, 동사는 /ˈænɪmeɪt/으로 발음된다.

1 ADJ Something that is **animate** has life, in contrast to things like stones and machines which do not. ❑ *Natural philosophy involved the study of all aspects of the material world, animate and inanimate.* **2** V-T To **animate** something means to make it lively or more cheerful. ❑ *There was precious little about the cricket to animate the crowd.*

1 형용사 생명이 있는 ❑ 자연과학은 생물과 무생물을 포함한 물질세계의 모든 측면을 탐구하는 학문이었다. **2** 타동사 생기를 불어넣다 ❑ 그 크리켓 경기는 관중을 열광시킬 만한 구석이 정말 거의 없었다.

an|i|mat|ed /ˈænɪmeɪtɪd/ **1** ADJ Someone who is **animated** or who is having an **animated** conversation is lively and is showing their feelings. ❑ *She was seen in animated conversation with the singer Yuri Marusin.* **2** ADJ An **animated** film is one in which puppets or drawings appear to move. [ADJ n] ❑ *Disney has returned to what it does best: making full-length animated feature films.*

1 형용사 활발한 ❑ 그녀가 가수 유리 마루신과 활발한 대화를 나누는 장면이 목격됐다. **2** 형용사 만화영화의 ❑ 디즈니가 주특기인 장편 애니메이션 제작으로 돌아왔다.

an|i|ma|tion /ˌænɪˈmeɪʃ°n/ (animations) **1** N-UNCOUNT **Animation** is the process of making films in which drawings or puppets appear to move. ❑ *The films are a mix of animation and full-length features.* **2** N-COUNT An **animation** is a film in which drawings or puppets appear to move. ❑ *This film is the first British animation sold to an American network.*
→see Word Web: **animation**

1 불가산명사 애니메이션 제작 ❑ 이 영화들에는 애니메이션도 있고 장편 영화도 있다. **2** 가산명사 애니메이션 ❑ 이 영화는 영국 애니메이션 최초로 미국 방송국에 판매된 작품이다.

a b c d e f g h i j k l m n o p q r s t u v w x y z

Word Web   animation

TV **cartoons** are one of the most popular forms of **animation**. Each **episode** begins with a storyline. Once the **script** is final, cartoonists make up storyboards. The director uses them to plan how the **artists** will **illustrate** the episode. First the illustrators **draw** some **sketches**. Next they draw a few key frames for each **scene**. Animators turn these into moving storyboards. This version of the cartoon looks unfinished. The producers review it and suggest changes. After they make these changes, the artists fill in the missing frames. This makes the movements of the characters look smooth and natural.

ani|mos|ity /ænɪmɒsɪti/ (**animosities**) N-UNCOUNT **Animosity** is a strong feeling of dislike and anger. **Animosities** are feelings of this kind. [also N in pl] ❑ *There's a long history of animosity between the two nations.*

불가산명사 증오, 앙심 ❑ 두 국가 사이에는 오랜 증오의 역사가 있다.

an|kle /æŋkəl/ (**ankles**) N-COUNT Your **ankle** is the joint where your foot joins your leg. ❑ *John twisted his ankle badly.* →see **body**, **foot**

가산명사 발목 ❑ 존은 발목을 심하게 삐었다.

an|nex /ænɛks/ (**annexes, annexing, annexed**) ◼ V-T If a country **annexes** another country or an area of land, it seizes it and takes control of it. ❑ *Rome annexed the Nabatean kingdom in AD 106.* ● **an|nexa|tion** /ænɛkseɪʃᵊn/ (**annexations**) N-COUNT ❑ *Indonesia's annexation of East Timor has never won the acceptance of the United Nations.* ◻ N-COUNT An **annex** is a building which is joined to or is next to a larger main building. [BRIT **annexe**] ❑ *...setting up a museum in an annex to the theater.*

◼ 타동사 합병하다 ❑ 로마는 서기 106년에 나바테아 왕국을 합병했다. ● 합병 가산명사 ❑ 인도네시아의 동티모르 합병은 유엔의 승인을 얻은 적이 없다. ◻ 가산명사 부속 건물 [영국영어 annexe] ❑ 극장 별관에 박물관을 만들기

an|ni|hi|late /ənaɪɪleɪt/ (**annihilates, annihilating, annihilated**) ◼ V-T To **annihilate** something means to destroy it completely. ❑ *There are lots of ways of annihilating the planet.* ● **an|ni|hi|la|tion** /ənaɪɪleɪʃᵊn/ N-UNCOUNT ❑ *Muslim political leaders fear the annihilation of their people.* ◻ V-T If you **annihilate** someone in a contest or argument, you totally defeat them. ❑ *The Dutch annihilated the Olympic champions 5-0.*

◼ 타동사 완전히 파괴하다, 전멸시키다 ❑ 그 행성을 완전히 파괴할 수 있는 방법은 많다. ● 전멸 불가산명사 ❑ 이슬람 정치 지도자들은 자국민의 전멸을 두려워하고 있다. ◻ 타동사 완패시키다 ❑ 네덜란드가 올림픽 우승팀을 5-0으로 완패시켰다.

Word Link   ann ≈ year : anniversary, annual, annuity

an|ni|ver|sa|ry ♦◇◇ /ænɪvɜrsəri/ (**anniversaries**) N-COUNT An **anniversary** is a date which is remembered or celebrated because a special event happened on that date in a previous year. ❑ *Vietnam is celebrating the one hundredth anniversary of the birth of Ho Chi Minh.*

가산명사 기념일 ❑ 베트남이 호치민 탄생 100주년을 기념하고 있다.

an|no|tate /ænoʊteɪt/ (**annotates, annotating, annotated**) V-T If you **annotate** written work or a diagram, you add notes to it, especially in order to explain it. ❑ *Historians annotate, check, and interpret the diary selections.*

타동사 주석을 달다 ❑ 역사가들이 선별된 그 일지에 주석을 달고, 대조 및 해석을 한다.

Word Link   nounce ≈ reporting : announce, denounce, pronounce

an|nounce ♦♦♦ /ənaʊns/ (**announces, announcing, announced**) ◼ V-T If you **announce** something, you tell people about it publicly or officially. ❑ *He will announce tonight that he is resigning from office.* ❑ *She was planning to announce her engagement to Peter.* ◻ V-T If you **announce** a piece of news or an intention, especially something that people may not like, you say it loudly and clearly, so that everyone you are with can hear it. ❑ *Peter announced that he had no intention of wasting his time at any university.* ◼ V-T If an airport or railway employee **announces** something, they tell the public about it by means of a loudspeaker system. ❑ *Station staff announced the arrival of the train over the loudspeaker.*

◼ 타동사 발표하다 ❑ 그는 오늘밤 자신의 공직 퇴임 계획을 발표할 것이다. ❑ 그녀는 피터와의 약혼식 발표를 계획하고 있었다. ◻ 타동사 선언하다 ❑ 피터는 어떤 대학에서든 대학에서 시간을 낭비할 의사가 전혀 없다고 딱 잘라 말했다. ◼ 타동사 알리다 ❑ 역 직원이 확성기를 통해 기차 도착을 알렸다.

Thesaurus   announce의 참조어

v.   advertise, declare, make public, report, reveal; (*ant.*) withhold ◼

an|nounce|ment ♦◇◇ /ənaʊnsmənt/ (**announcements**) ◼ N-COUNT An **announcement** is a statement made to the public or to the media which gives information about something that has happened or that will happen. ❑ *Sir Robert made his announcement after talks with the President.* ◻ N-SING The **announcement** of something that has happened is the act of telling people about it. ❑ *...the announcement of their engagement.* ◼ N-COUNT An **announcement** in a public place, such as a newspaper or the window of a store, is a short piece of writing telling people about something or asking for something. ❑ *He will place an announcement in the personal column of The Daily Telegraph.*

◼ 가산명사 성명서 ❑ 로버트 경이 대통령과의 면담이 끝난 후 성명서를 발표했다. ◻ 단수명사 발표 ❑ 그들의 약혼 발표 ◼ 가산명사 공고, 공지 ❑ 그는 데일리 텔레그래프 지의 개인 소식란에 공고를 낼 것이다.

Word Partnership   announcement의 연어

ADJ.   **formal** announcement, **public** announcement, **official** announcement, **surprise** announcement ◼
v.   **make an** announcement ◼

an|nounc|er /ənaʊnsər/ (**announcers**) ◼ N-COUNT An **announcer** is someone who introduces programs on radio or television or who reads the text of a radio or television advertisement. ❑ *The radio announcer said it was nine o'clock.* ◻ N-COUNT The **announcer** at a railroad station or airport is the person who makes the announcements. ❑ *The announcer apologized for the delay.*

◼ 가산명사 아나운서 ❑ 라디오 아나운서가 9시를 알렸다. ◻ 가산명사 (역이나 공항의) 방송원 ❑ 연착에 대한 사과 방송이 나왔다.

an|noy /ənɔɪ/ (annoys, annoying, annoyed) V-T If someone or something **annoys** you, it makes you fairly angry and impatient. □ *Try making a note of the things which annoy you.* □ *It annoyed me that I didn't have time to do more ironing.* →see also **annoyed**, **annoying**

타동사 짜증나게 하다 □ 당신을 짜증나게 하는 것들을 적어 보세요. □ 다림질을 더 할 시간이 없자 나는 짜증이 났다.

an|noy|ance /ənɔɪəns/ (annoyances) **1** N-UNCOUNT **Annoyance** is the feeling that you get when someone makes you feel fairly angry or impatient. □ *To her annoyance the stranger did not go away.* **2** N-COUNT An **annoyance** is something that makes you feel angry or impatient. □ *Snoring can be more than an annoyance.*

1 불가산명사 짜증 □ 짜증스럽게도 그 낯선 사람은 가지를 않았다. **2** 가산명사 짜증나는 것 □ 코를 고는 것은 단순한 골칫거리 이상일 수도 있다.

an|noyed /ənɔɪd/ ADJ If you are **annoyed**, you are fairly angry about something. □ *She is hurt and annoyed that the authorities have banned her from working with children.* →see also **annoy**

형용사 짜증이 난 □ 그녀는 관계 당국이 아이들과 함께 일하지 못하게 하자 상처를 받아서 화가 나 있다.

an|noy|ing /ənɔɪɪŋ/ ADJ Someone or something that is **annoying** makes you feel fairly angry and impatient. □ *You must have found my attitude annoying.*

형용사 신경에 거슬리는 □ 너는 내 태도가 신경에 거슬렸던 게 틀림없어.

Word Link   ann ≈ year : **ann**iversary, **ann**ual, **ann**uity

---

an|nual ♦♦◇ /ænyuəl/ (annuals) **1** ADJ **Annual** events happen once every year. [ADJ n] □ *...the annual conference of Britain's trade union movement.* ● **an|nual|ly** ADV [ADV with v] □ *Companies report to their shareholders annually.* **2** ADJ **Annual** quantities or rates relate to a period of one year. [ADJ n] □ *The electronic and printing unit has annual sales of about $80 million.* ● **an|nual|ly** ADV □ *El Salvador produces 100,000 tons of refined copper annually.* **3** N-COUNT An **annual** is a book or magazine that is published once a year. □ *I looked for Wyman's picture in my high-school annual.* **4** N-COUNT An **annual** is a plant that grows and dies within one year. □ *Maybe this year I'll sow brilliant annuals everywhere.* →see **plant**

1 형용사 해마다의 □ 영국 산별 노조운동 연례회의 ● 해마다 부사 □ 기업은 자사 주주들에게 매년 보고한다. **2** 형용사 일 년간의 □ 전자 인쇄 부문은 연간 약 8천만 달러의 매출을 올리고 있다. ● 일 년 동안에 부사 □ 엘살바도르는 연간 10만 톤의 정제 구리를 생산한다. **3** 가산명사 연감 □ 나는 고등학교 연감에서 와이먼의 사진을 찾아보았다. **4** 가산명사 일년생 식물 □ 아마 올해는 제가 여기저기에 화사한 일년생 꽃을 심을 것 같아요.

an|nu|ity /ənuɪti, BRIT ənyuːɪti/ (annuities) N-COUNT An **annuity** is an investment or insurance policy that pays someone a fixed sum of money each year. [BUSINESS] □ *He received a paltry annuity of £100.*

가산명사 연금 [경제] □ 그는 연금으로 고작 100파운드를 받는다.

an|nul /ənʌl/ (annuls, annulling, annulled) V-T If an election or a contract **is annulled**, it is declared invalid, so that legally it is considered never to have existed. [usu passive] □ *Opposition party leaders are now pressing for the entire election to be annulled.*

타동사 무효화하다 □ 야당 지도자들이 현재 총선 무효화 운동을 추진하고 있다.

an|num /ænəm/ →see **per annum**

anomaly /ənɒməli/ (anomalies) N-COUNT If something is an **anomaly**, it is different from what is usual or expected. [FORMAL] □ *The British public's wariness of opera is an anomaly in Europe.*

가산명사 이례적인 것 [격식체] □ 영국 대중의 오페라에 대한 경계심은 유럽에서는 이례적인 일이다.

Word Link   onym ≈ name : **acr**onym, **an**onym**ous**, **syn**onym

---

anony|mous /ənɒnɪməs/ **1** ADJ If you remain **anonymous** when you do something, you do not let people know that you were the person who did it. □ *You can remain anonymous if you wish.* □ *An anonymous benefactor stepped in to provide the prize money.* ● **ano|nym|ity** /ænənɪmɪti/ N-UNCOUNT □ *Both mother and daughter, who have requested anonymity, are doing fine.* ● **anony|mous|ly** ADV □ *The latest photographs were sent anonymously to the magazine's Paris headquarters.* **2** ADJ Something that is **anonymous** does not reveal who you are. □ *Of course, that would have to be by anonymous vote.* ● **ano|nym|ity** N-UNCOUNT □ *He claims many more people would support him in the anonymity of a voting booth.*

1 형용사 익명의 □ 원한다면 이름을 밝히지 않아도 됩니다. □ 한 익명의 후원자가 방문해서 상금을 제공했다. ● 익명 불가산명사 □ 익명을 요구한 어머니와 딸 모두 잘 지내고 있다. ● 익명으로 부사 □ 최근 사진들은 잡지의 파리 본사에 익명으로 보내진 것들이었다. **2** 형용사 익명의 □ 물론 이는 무기명 투표를 통해 해야 할 것이다. ● 익명성 불가산명사 □ 그는 기표소라는 익명의 공간에서는 더 많은 사람들이 그를 지지할 것이라고 주장한다.

ano|rak /ænəræk/ (anoraks) N-COUNT An **anorak** is a warm waterproof jacket, usually with a hood.

가산명사 아노락 (모자 달린 방수 재킷)

ano|rexia /ænərɛksiə/ N-UNCOUNT **Anorexia** or **anorexia nervosa** is an illness in which a person has an overwhelming fear of becoming fat, and so refuses to eat enough and becomes thinner and thinner.

불가산명사 거식증

ano|rex|ic /ænərɛksɪk/ (anorexics) ADJ If someone is **anorexic**, they are suffering from anorexia and so are very thin. □ *Claire had been anorexic for three years.* ● N-COUNT An **anorexic** is someone who is anorexic. □ *Not eating makes an anorexic feel in control.*

형용사 거식증의 □ 클레어는 3년간 거식증에 시달렸었다. ● 가산명사 거식증 환자 □ 거식증 환자는 먹지 않을 때 자신의 통제력을 느낀다.

an|other ♦♦♦ /ənʌðər/ **1** DET **Another** thing or person means an additional thing or person of the same type as one that already exists. □ *Divers this morning found the body of another American sailor drowned during yesterday's ferry disaster.* ● PRON-SING **Another** is also a pronoun. □ *The demand generated by one factory required the construction of another.* **2** DET You use **another** when you want to emphasize that an additional thing or person is different to one that already exists. □ *I think he's just going to deal with this problem another day.* ● PRON-SING **Another** is also a pronoun. □ *He didn't really believe that any human being could read another's mind.* **3** DET You use **another** at the beginning of a statement to link it to a previous statement. □ *Another time of great excitement for us boys was when war broke out.* **4** DET You use **another** before a word referring to a distance, length of time, or other amount, to indicate an additional amount. □ *Continue down the same road for another 2 kilometers until you reach the church of Santa Maria.* **5** PRON-RECIP You use **one another** to indicate that each member of a group does something to or for the other members. [V PRON, prep PRON] □ *...women learning to help themselves and one another.*

1 한정사 또 하나의 □ 오늘 아침 잠수부가 어제 여객선 참사로 익사한 또 한 명의 미국 선원의 시신을 발견했다. ● 단수대명사 또 하나의 것 □ 한 공장으로 인해 발생한 수요를 맞추기 위해 또 하나의 공장 건설이 필요했다. **2** 한정사 다른 □ 내 생각에는 그가 이 문제는 그냥 다른 날 다룰 것 같습니다. ● 단수대명사 다른 것; 다른 사람 □ 그는 사람이 다른 사람의 마음을 읽을 수 있다는 것을 진짜로 믿진 않았다. **3** 한정사 또다른, 또 한 번의 □ 또 한 번 우리 소년들에게 큰 흥분을 안겨 줬던 시기는 전쟁이 터졌을 때였다. **4** 한정사 추가의 □ 산타 마리아 교회가 나올 때까지 같은 길을 2킬로미터 더 내려가세요. **5** 상호대명사 서로 □ 자기 자신과 서로를 돕는 방법을 배우는 여성들

Do not confuse **another** and **other**. When you are talking about **another** thing or person, you often mean one more of the same type. □ *Rick's got another camera... I waited another few minutes.* You use **other** to refer to more than one type of person or thing, usually followed by a plural count noun but sometimes by an uncount noun. □ *Other boys were arriving now... There was certainly other evidence.* When you are talking about two people or things and have already referred to one of them, you refer to the second one as **the other** or **the other one**. □ *One daughter was a baby, the other a girl of twelve.* When you are talking about several people or things and have already referred to one or more of them, you usually refer to the remaining ones as **the others**. □ *Jack*

another와 other를 혼동하지 않도록 하라. another를 쓰면 동일한 유형의 사람이나 사물을 하나 더 가리킴을 나타낸다. □ 릭에게는 카메라가 하나 더 있다... 나는 몇 분을 더 기다렸다. other는 두 종류 이상의 사람이나 사물을 지칭할 때 쓰는데, 대개 복수 가산명사가 뒤에 오지만 불가산명사가 올 때도 있다. □ 이제 다른 소년들이 도착하고 있었다... 분명히 다른 증거도 있었다. 두 명의 사람이나 두 가지 사물에 대해 얘기하면서 그 중 한 사람이나 한 가지를 이미 언급한 뒤, 두 번째

and the others paid no attention. More people or things of the same type are referred to simply as **others**. ❑ *Some writers are better than others.* **Other** can also be used after words such as "the," "few," or "any," and after numbers. ❑ *...the other side of the room... I love my son, like any other mother....the Hogans and three other couples.*

사람이나 사물을 가리킬 때는 the other 또는 the other one이라고 지칭한다. ❑ 딸 하나는 아기였고, (2명 중) 다른 딸은 12살짜리 소녀였다. 여러 사람이나 사물에 대해 얘기하면서 그 중 하나 이상을 이미 언급했을 때, 나머지 사람들이나 사물은 보통 the others라고 지칭한다. ❑ 잭과 나머지 사람들은 주목하지 않았다. 같은 종류의 더 많은 사람들이나 사물은 그냥 others라고 지칭한다. ❑ 어떤 작가들은 다른 작가들보다 낫다. other는 the, few, any와 같은 단어 뒤나 숫자 뒤에도 쓰인다. ❑ ...그 방의 다른 쪽... 나는 다른 모든 엄마들과 마찬가지로 내 아들을 사랑한다....호건 부부와 다른 세 쌍의 남녀

6 PHRASE If you talk about **one** thing **after another**, you are referring to a series of repeated or continuous events. ❑ *They had faced one difficulty after another with bravery and dedication.* **7** PHRASE You use **or another** in expressions such as **one kind or another** when you do not want to be precise about which of several alternatives or possibilities you are referring to. ❑ *...family members and visiting artists of one kind or another crowding the huge kitchen.*

6 구 연달아 ❑ 그들은 어려움이 닥칠 때마다 용기와 헌신으로 맞섰었다. **7** 구 – 등의; 이러저러한 ❑ 커다란 주방에 붐비는 가족들과 이러저러한 부류의 예술가 손님들

Word Partnership	another의 연어
ADV.	**yet** another **1**
N.	another **chance**, another **day**, another **one 1 2**
	another **man/woman**, another **thing 2**
V.	**tell** one **from** another **2**
PRON.	**one** another **5**

an|swer ♦♦♦ /ǽnsər/ (answers, answering, answered) **1** V-T/V-I When you **answer** someone who has asked you something, you say something back to them. ❑ *Just answer the question.* ❑ *He paused before answering.* ❑ *Williams answered that he had no specific proposals yet.* **2** N-COUNT An **answer** is something that you say when you answer someone. [also in N to n] ❑ *Without waiting for an answer, he turned and went in through the door.* **3** PHRASE If you say that someone will not **take no for an answer**, you mean that they go on trying to make you agree to something even after you have refused. ❑ *She is tough, unwilling to take no for an answer.* **4** V-T/V-I If you **answer** a letter or advertisement, you write to the person who wrote it. ❑ *Did he answer your letter?* **5** N-COUNT An **answer** is a letter that you write to someone who has written to you. [also in N to n] ❑ *I wrote to him but I never had an answer back.* **6** V-T/V-I When you **answer** the telephone, you pick it up when it rings. When you **answer** the door, you open it when you hear a knock or the bell. ❑ *She answered her phone on the first ring.* ● N-COUNT **Answer** is also a noun. ❑ *I knocked at the front door and there was no answer.* **7** N-COUNT An **answer to** a problem is a solution to it. ❑ *There are no easy answers to the problems facing the economy.* **8** N-COUNT Someone's **answer to** a question in a test or quiz is what they write or say in an attempt to give the facts that are asked for. The **answer to** a question is the fact that was asked for. ❑ *Simply marking an answer wrong will not help the pupil to get future examples correct.* **9** V-T When you **answer** a question in a test or quiz, you write or say something in an attempt to give the facts that are asked for. ❑ *To obtain her degree, she answered 81 questions over 10 papers.* **10** N-COUNT Your **answer to** something that someone has said or done is what you say or do in response to it or in defense of yourself. [also in N to n] ❑ *In answer to speculation that she wouldn't finish the race, she boldly declared her intention of winning it.* **11** V-T/V-I If someone or something **answers** a particular description or **answers to** it, they have the characteristics described. ❑ *Two men answering the description of the suspects tried to enter Switzerland.*

1 타동사/자동사 대답하다 ❑ 질문에 대한 답변만 하세요. ❑ 그는 대답하기 전에 잠깐 멈췄다. ❑ 윌리엄스는 아직 구체적인 계획이 없다고 대답했다. **2** 가산명사 대답 ❑ 대답을 기다리지도 않고, 그는 돌아서서 문으로 들어갔다. **3** 구 거절을 받아들이지 않다 ❑ 그녀는 거절이 안 통하는 끈질긴 사람이다. **4** 타동사/자동사 답장하다 ❑ 그가 네 편지에 답장했니? **5** 가산명사 답장 ❑ 나는 그에게 편지를 썼지만 답장을 한 번도 못 받았다. **6** 타동사/자동사 전화 받다; (초인종이나 노크 소리를 듣고) 문을 열러 가다 ❑ 그녀는 벨이 한 번 울리자 전화를 받았다. ● 가산명사 받음 ❑ 내가 현관문을 두드렸지만 아무런 기척이 없었다. **7** 가산명사 해결책 ❑ 경제가 처한 문제들에 대해 쉬운 해결 방안이 없다. **8** 가산명사 해답 ❑ 단순히 답이 틀렸다고 표시만 해 주는 것은 학생들이 앞으로 문제를 정확히 푸는 데 도움이 안 될 것이다. **9** 타동사 문제를 풀다 ❑ 그녀는 학위를 따기 위해서 10장에 걸친 시험으로 81 문항을 풀었다. **10** 가산명사 해명 ❑ 그녀는 자신이 경기에서 중도 하차할 것이라는 추측에 대한 대답으로 경기 우승 의지를 당당히 밝혔다. **11** 타동사/자동사 들어맞다 ❑ 용의자들의 인상착의와 일치하는 두 남성이 스위스 입국을 시도했다.

Thesaurus	answer의 참조어
V.	reply, respond **1 4**

Word Partnership	answer의 연어
V.	**refuse to** answer **1 4**
	have an answer, **wait for an** answer **2**
	find the answer **7**
N.	answer **a question 1 9**
	answer **the door/telephone 6**
ADJ.	**correct/right** answer, **straight** answer, **wrong** answer **2**
DET.	**no** answer **2**

▶**answer back** PHRASAL VERB If someone, especially a child, **answers back**, they speak rudely to you when you speak to them. ❑ *She was beaten by teachers for answering back.*

구동사 말대꾸하다 ❑ 그녀는 말대꾸를 했다가 선생님들에게 맞았다.

▶**answer for** **1** PHRASAL VERB If you have to **answer for** something bad or wrong you have done, you are punished for it. ❑ *He must be made to answer for his terrible crimes.* **2** PHRASE If you say that someone **has a lot to answer for**, you are saying that their actions have led to problems which you think they are responsible for. ❑ *Tony Blair's Government has a lot to answer for over this foot-and-mouth crisis.*

1 구동사 –에 대한 대가를 치르다 ❑ 그가 자신이 저지른 끔찍한 범죄에 대한 대가를 치르도록 해야 한다. **2** 구 –에 대한 책임이 크다 ❑ 토니 블레어 정부는 이번 구제역 파동에 대한 책임이 크다.

an|swer|ing ma|chine (answering machines) N-COUNT An **answering machine** a device which you connect to your telephone and which records telephone calls while you are out.

가산명사 자동응답기

an|swer|phone /ɑnsərfoʊn, æn-/ (answerphones) N-COUNT An **answerphone** is the same as an **answering machine**. [mainly BRIT]

가산명사 자동응답 녹음기 [주로 영국영어]

ant /ænt/ (ants) N-COUNT **Ants** are small crawling insects that live in large groups. ❑ *Ants swarmed up out of the ground and covered her shoes and legs.*

가산명사 개미 ❑ 개미가 땅에서 떼를 지어 나와 그녀의 신발과 다리를 뒤덮었다.

an|tago|nism /æntægənɪzəm/ (antagonisms) N-UNCOUNT **Antagonism** between people is hatred or dislike between them. **Antagonisms** are instances of this. [also N in pl] ❑ *There is still much antagonism between trades unions and the oil companies.*

불가산명사 반목 ❑ 아직까지 산별 노조와 석유 회사들 사이의 반복의 골이 깊다.

an|tago|nist /æntægənɪst/ (antagonists) N-COUNT Your **antagonist** is your opponent or enemy. ❑ *Spassky had never previously lost to his antagonist.*

가산명사 적대자, 경쟁자 ❑ 스파스키는 그 이전에는 상대에게 져 본 적이 없었다.

an|tago|nize /æntægənaɪz/ (antagonizes, antagonizing, antagonized) [BRIT also **antagonise**] V-T If you **antagonize** someone, you make them feel angry or hostile toward you. ❑ *He didn't want to antagonize her.*

[영국영어 antagonise] 타동사 적대감을 느끼게 하다 ❑ 그는 그녀의 반감을 사고 싶지 않았다.

Ant|arc|tic /æntɑrktɪk/ N-PROPER The **Antarctic** is the area around the South Pole.

고유명사 남극

ante /ænti/ PHRASE If you **up the ante** or **raise the ante**, you increase your demands when you are in dispute or fighting for something. [JOURNALISM] ❑ *Whenever they reached their goal, they upped the ante, setting increasingly complex challenges for themselves.*

구 요구사항을 늘리다 [언론] ❑ 그들은 목표를 달성할 때마다 기대치를 높여 점점 더 복잡한 과제에 도전했다.

an|ten|na /æntɛnə/ (antennae) /ænteni/ or **antennas**

Antennas is the usual plural form for meaning **2**.

antennas는 **2** 의미의 일반적 복수형이다.

1 N-COUNT The **antennae** of something such as an insect or crustacean are the two long, thin parts attached to its head that it uses to feel things with. **2** N-COUNT An **antenna** is a device or a piece of wire that sends and receives television or radio signals and is usually attached to a radio, television, car, or building.

1 가산명사 더듬이 **2** 가산명사 안테나

an|them /ænθəm/ (anthems) N-COUNT An **anthem** is a song which is used to represent a particular nation, society, or group and which is sung on special occasions. ❑ *The band played the Czech anthem.*

가산명사 국가 (국가 등의 특정 집단을 대표하는 노래) ❑ 밴드는 체코 국가를 연주했다.

an|thol|ogy /ænθɒlədʒi/ (anthologies) N-COUNT An **anthology** is a collection of writings by different writers published together in one book. ❑ *...an anthology of poetry.*

가산명사 명문집 ❑ 시선집

an|thro|pol|ogy /ænθrəpɒlədʒi/ N-UNCOUNT **Anthropology** is the scientific study of people, society, and culture. ● **an|thro|polo|gist** /ænθrəpɒlədʒɪst/ (anthropologists) N-COUNT ❑ *...an anthropologist who had been in China for three years.*

불가산명사 인류학 ● 인류학자 가산명사 ❑ 3년간 중국에 체류했던 인류학자

anti|bi|ot|ic /æntibaɪɒtɪk, -taɪ-/ (antibiotics) N-COUNT **Antibiotics** are medical drugs used to kill bacteria and treat infections. ❑ *Your doctor may prescribe a course of antibiotics.* →see **medicine**

가산명사 항생제 ❑ 당신의 주치의가 일련의 항생제를 처방해 줄 것이다.

anti|body /æntibɒdi, æntaɪ-/ (antibodies) N-COUNT **Antibodies** are substances which a person's or an animal's body produces in their blood in order to destroy substances which carry disease. ❑ *Such women carry antibodies which make their blood more likely to clot during pregnancy.*

가산명사 항체 ❑ 그러한 여성들은 임신 중에 혈액이 더 잘 응고되도록 하는 항체를 지니고 있다.

an|tici|pate /æntɪsɪpeɪt/ (anticipates, anticipating, anticipated) **1** V-T If you **anticipate** an event, you realize in advance that it may happen and you are prepared for it. ❑ *At the time we couldn't have anticipated the result of our campaigning.* ❑ *It is anticipated that the equivalent of 192 full-time jobs will be lost.* **2** V-T If you **anticipate** a question, request, or need, you do what is necessary or required before the question, request, or need occurs. ❑ *What Jeff did was to anticipate my next question.*

1 타동사 예상하다 ❑ 당시에는 우리가 선거 운동 결과를 예상 못 할 수도 있었다. ❑ 정규직 192개에 해당하는 일자리가 없어질 것으로 예상된다. **2** 타동사 예상하고 준비하다 ❑ 제프는 내 다음 질문을 미리 준비하고 있었다.

an|tici|pa|tion /æntɪsɪpeɪʃⁿ/ **1** N-UNCOUNT **Anticipation** is a feeling of excitement about something pleasant or exciting that you know is going to happen. ❑ *There's been an atmosphere of anticipation around here for a few days now.* **2** PHRASE If something is done **in anticipation of** an event, it is done because people believe that event is going to happen. ❑ *Troops in the Philippines have been put on full alert in anticipation of trouble during a planned general strike.*

1 불가산명사 기대, 설렘 ❑ 요 며칠 간 이 주변이 기대감으로 들뜬 분위기였다. **2** 구 -을 예상하고 ❑ 계획된 총파업 기간 동안 발생할 문제를 예상하고 필리핀 군이 비상경계 태세에 돌입했다.

anti|clock|wise /æntiklɒkwaɪz, æntaɪ-/ also **anti-clockwise** ADV If something is moving **anticlockwise**, it is moving in the opposite direction to the direction in which the hands of a clock move. [BRIT] [ADV after v] ❑ *The cutters are opened by turning the knob anticlockwise.* ● ADJ **Anticlockwise** is also an adjective. [AM **counterclockwise**] [ADJ n] ❑ *...an anticlockwise route around the coast.*

부사 시계 반대 방향으로 [영국영어] ❑ 손잡이를 시계 반대 방향으로 돌리면 절단기가 열린다. ● 형용사 시계 반대 방향의 [미국영어 counterclockwise] ❑ 해안 주변의 시계 반대 방향 항로

an|tics /æntɪks/ N-PLURAL **Antics** are funny, silly, or unusual ways of behaving. ❑ *Elizabeth tolerated Sarah's antics.*

복수명사 엉뚱한 행동 ❑ 엘리자베스는 사라의 엉뚱한 행동을 봐줬다.

anti|dote /æntidoʊt/ (antidotes) **1** N-COUNT An **antidote** is a chemical substance that stops or controls the effect of a poison. ❑ *When he returned, he noticed their sickness and prepared an antidote.* **2** N-COUNT Something that is an **antidote to** a difficult or unpleasant situation helps you to overcome the situation. ❑ *Massage is a wonderful antidote to stress.*

1 가산명사 해독제 ❑ 그는 돌아와서 그들이 아픈 것을 발견하고 해독제를 준비했다. **2** 가산명사 해결 방안 ❑ 마사지는 스트레스 해소에 좋은 방법이다.

an|tipa|thy /æntɪpəθi/ N-UNCOUNT **Antipathy** is a strong feeling of dislike or hostility toward someone or something. [FORMAL] ❑ *She'd often spoken of her antipathy toward London.*

불가산명사 반감 [격식체] ❑ 그녀는 종종 자신이 런던에 대해 느끼는 반감에 대해 이야기했었다.

an|ti|quat|ed /æntɪkweɪtɪd/ ADJ If you describe something as **antiquated**, you are criticizing it because it is very old or old-fashioned. [DISAPPROVAL] ❑ *Many factories are so antiquated they are not worth saving.*

형용사 노후한 [탐탁찮음] ❑ 싱딩수의 공장들이 너무나 노후하기 때문에 보존할 가치가 없다.

an|tique ♦◇◇ /æntik/ (antiques) N-COUNT An **antique** is an old object such as a piece of china or furniture which is valuable because of its beauty or rarity. ❑ *...a genuine antique.*

가산명사 골동품 ❑ 진짜 골동품

an|tiq|uity /æntɪkwɪti/ (antiquities) **1** N-UNCOUNT **Antiquity** is the distant past, especially the time of the ancient Egyptians, Greeks, and Romans.

1 불가산명사 고대 ❑ 고대 시대의 유명한 유적들 **2** 가산명사 고대 유물 ❑ 고대 로마 유물 수집가

a
b
c
d
e
f
g
h
i
j
k
l
m
n
o
p
q
r
s
t
u
v
w
x
y
z

❑ *...famous monuments of classical antiquity.* ② N-COUNT **Antiquities** are things such as buildings, statues, or coins that were made in ancient times and have survived to the present day. ❑ *...collectors of Roman antiquities.*

anti|sep|tic /ˌæntəsɛptɪk/ (**antiseptics**) N-MASS **Antiseptic** is a substance that kills germs and harmful bacteria. ❑ *She bathed the cut with antiseptic.* →see **medicine**

물질명사 소독약 ❑ 그녀는 상처를 소독약으로 닦았다.

anti|so|cial /ˌæntisoʊʃ°l, ˌæntaɪ-/ ADJ Someone who is **antisocial** is unwilling to meet and be friendly with other people. ❑ *...a generation of teenagers who will become aggressive and antisocial.*

형용사 반사회적인 ❑ 공격적이고 반사회적이 될 청소년 세대

an|tith|e|sis /ænˈtɪθəsɪs/ (**antitheses**) /ænˈtɪθəsiz/ N-COUNT The **antithesis** of something is its exact opposite. [FORMAL] ❑ *The antithesis of the Middle Eastern buyer is the Japanese.*

가산명사 정반대 [격식체] ❑ 중동 바이어와 정반대되는 유형이 일본인들이다.

anti|trust /ˌæntitrʌst, ˌæntaɪ-/ ADJ In the United States, **antitrust** laws are intended to stop large firms taking over their competitors, fixing prices with their competitors, or interfering with free competition in any way. [ADJ n] ❑ *The jury found that the NFL had violated antitrust laws.*

형용사 반독점 ❑ 배심원단은 미국 미식축구 연맹이 반독점법을 위반했다는 평결을 내렸다.

anus /ˈeɪnəs/ (**anuses**) N-COUNT A person's **anus** is the hole from which feces leaves their body. [MEDICAL]

가산명사 항문 [의학]

anxi|ety ◆◇◇ /æŋˈzaɪɪti/ (**anxieties**) N-UNCOUNT **Anxiety** is a feeling of nervousness or worry. ❑ *Her voice was full of anxiety.*

불가산명사 걱정 ❑ 그녀의 목소리는 근심으로 가득했다.

anx|ious ◆◇◇ /ˈæŋkʃəs/ ① ADJ If you are **anxious to** do something or **anxious that** something should happen, you very much want to do it or you very much want it to happen. [v-link ADJ, ADJ to-inf, ADJ that, ADJ prep] ❑ *Both the Americans and the Russians are anxious to avoid conflict in South Asia.* ❑ *He is anxious that there should be no delay.* ② ADJ If you are **anxious**, you are nervous or worried about something. ❑ *The foreign minister admitted he was still anxious about the situation in the country.* ● **anx|ious|ly** ADV [ADV with v] ❑ *They are waiting anxiously to see who will succeed him.*

■ 형용사 열망하는 ❑ 미국과 러시아 모두 남아시아에서의 분쟁을 간절히 피하고 싶어 한다. ❑ 그는 지연이 안 되기를 간절히 바라고 있다. ② 형용사 걱정하는 ❑ 외무부장관은 나라 상황이 여전히 걱정스럽다고 시인했다. ● 간절히; 걱정스럽게 부사 ❑ 그들은 누가 그의 뒤를 이을지 보게 되기를 걱정스럽게 기다리고 있다.

Word Partnership	anxious의 연어
PREP.	anxious **for** *something* ■
	anxious **about** *something* ②
V.	anxious **to do** *something* ■
	become/feel/get/seem anxious, make *someone* anxious ②

any ◆◆◆ /ˈɛni/ ① DET You use **any** in statements with negative meaning to indicate that no thing or person of a particular type exists, is present, or is involved in a situation. ❑ *I'm not making any promises.* ❑ *We are doing this all without any support from the hospital.* ❑ *It is too early to say what effect, if any, there will be on the workforce.* ● QUANT **Any** is also a quantifier. [QUANT of def-n-uncount/def-pl-n] ❑ *You don't know any of my friends.* ● PRON **Any** is also a pronoun. ❑ *The children needed new school clothes and Kim couldn't afford any.* ② DET You use **any** in questions and conditional clauses to ask whether there is some of a particular thing or some of a particular group of people, or to suggest that there might be. ❑ *Do you speak any foreign languages?* ● QUANT **Any** is also a quantifier. [QUANT of def-n-uncount/def-pl-n] ❑ *Introduce foods one at a time and notice if the child is uncomfortable with any of them.* ● PRON **Any** is also a pronoun. [PRON after v] ❑ *If any bright thoughts occur to you pass them straight to me. Have you got any?* ③ DET You use **any** in positive statements when you are referring to someone or something of a particular kind that might exist, occur, or be involved in a situation, when their exact identity or nature is not important. ❑ *Any actor will tell you that it is easier to perform than to be themselves.* ● QUANT **Any** is also a quantifier. [QUANT of def-n-uncount/def-pl-n] ❑ *Nealy disappeared two days ago, several miles away from any of the fighting.* ● PRON **Any** is also a pronoun. ❑ *Clean the mussels and discard any that do not close.* ④ ADV You can also use **any** to emphasize a comparative adjective or adverb in a negative statement. [EMPHASIS] [ADV compar] ❑ *I can't see things getting any easier for graduates.*

Any is mainly used in questions and negative sentences. You use **not any** instead of **some** in negative sentences. ❑ *There isn't any money.*

■ 한정사 조금도; 아무도 ❑ 나는 어떤 약속도 하지 않을 것이다. ❑ 우리는 병원의 지원을 조금도 받지 않고 이 모든 일을 하고 있다. ❑ 노동력에 영향을 주더라도 어떤 영향이 있을지 말하기에는 너무 이르다. ● 수량사 ~ 중 아무것도; ~ 중 아무도 ❑ 너는 내 친구들 아무도 모르지. ● 대명사 아무것; 아무 사람 ❑ 아이들이 학교에 입고 갈 새 옷이 필요했는데 김은 아무것도 사 줄 수가 없었다. ② 한정사 어떠한 ~라도 ❑ 외국어 아무거나 할 수 있는 거 있어요? ● 수량사 ~중 아무거나 ❑ 음식을 한번에 하나씩 먹어 보고 그 중 입에 맞지 않는 것이 있는지 살펴보라. ● 대명사 아무것 ❑ 좋은 생각이 떠오르면 바로 저한테 전해 주세요. 좋은 생각 있어요? ③ 한정사 누구든지; 무엇이든지 ❑ 연기자라면 누구든 자기 자신이 되기보다 연기하는 것이 쉽다고 말할 것이다. ● 수량사 ~ 중 아무 ~나 ❑ 닐리는 이틀 모든 싸움을 피해 몇 마일 떨어진 곳으로 자취를 감췄다. ● 대명사 무엇이든 ~한 것 ❑ 홍합을 씻어 보고 입을 오므리지 않는 것은 모두 버려라. ④ 부사 조금 [강조] ❑ 졸업생들의 상황이 조금이라도 나아지는 기색이 안 보인다.

any는 주로 의문문과 부정문에 쓴다. 부정문에서는 some 대신에 not any를 쓴다. ❑ 돈이 조금도 없다.

⑤ PHRASE If you say that someone or something is **not just any** person or thing, you mean that they are special in some way. ❑ *Finzer is not just any East Coast businessman.* ⑥ PHRASE If something does not happen or is not true **any longer**, it has stopped happening or is no longer true. ❑ *I couldn't keep the tears hidden any longer.* ⑦ **in any case** →see **case**. **by any chance** →see **chance**. **in any event** →see **event**. **any old** →see **old**. **at any rate** →see **rate**

⑤ 구 그저 아무 ~가 아닌 ❑ 핀저는 그냥 평범한 동부 사업가가 아니다. ⑥ 구 더 이상 ❑ 나는 더 이상 눈물을 감출 수가 없었다.

Word Partnership	any의 연어
ADV.	almost any, any **better**, any **further**, hardly any, any **longer**, any **more** ■ ④
N.	any **difference**, any **good**, any **idea**, any **kind**, any **luck**, any **moment/minute (now)**, any **number of** *something*, any **questions** ③
PREP.	any **(one) of** *something*, at any **point/time**, at any **rate**, by any **chance**, by any **means**, in any **case**, in any **way**, without any ③

any|body ◆◇◇ /ˈɛnibɒdi, -bʌdi/ PRON-INDEF **Anybody** means the same as **anyone**. →see **anyone**

부정(不定)대명사 누군가, 아무도

any|how /ˈɛnihaʊ/ ① ADV **Anyhow** means the same as **anyway**. ② ADV If you do something **anyhow**, you do it in a careless or untidy way. [ADV after v] ❑ *...her long legs which she displayed all anyhow getting in and out of her car.*

■ 부사 어쨌든 ② 부사 아무렇게나, 되는대로 ❑ 차에 타고 내릴 때 아무렇게나 드러내 보이던 여자의 긴 두 다리

anymore /ɛnimɔr/

In British English, the spelling **anymore** is sometimes considered incorrect, and **any more** is used instead.

ADV If something does not happen or is not true **anymore**, it has stopped happening or is no longer true. [ADV after v] ❏ *I don't ride my motorbike much anymore.* ❏ *I couldn't trust him anymore.*

영국영어에서 anymore은 가끔 틀린 철자로 취급되며 대신 any more을 쓴다.

부사 더 이상 ❏ 나는 더 이상 오토바이를 많이 타지 않는다. ❏ 나는 더 이상 그를 믿을 수 없었다.

anyone ♦♦◊ /ɛniwʌn/

The form **anybody** is also used.

anybody도 쓴다.

1 PRON-INDEF You use **anyone** or **anybody** in statements with negative meaning to indicate in a general way that nobody is present or involved in an action. ❏ *I won't tell anyone I saw you here.* ❏ *You needn't talk to anyone if you don't want to.* **2** PRON-INDEF You use **anyone** or **anybody** in questions and conditional clauses to ask or talk about whether someone is present or doing something. ❏ *Why would anyone want that job?* ❏ *How can anyone look sad at an occasion like this?* **3** PRON-INDEF You use **anyone** or **anybody** before words which indicate the kind of person you are talking about. [PRON cl/group] ❏ *I always had been the person who achieved things before anyone else at my age.* ❏ *It's not a job for anyone who is slow with numbers.* **4** PRON-INDEF You use **anyone** or **anybody** to refer to a person when you are emphasizing that it could be any person out of a very large number of people. [EMPHASIS] ❏ *Anyone could be doing what I'm doing.* **5** PHRASE You use **anyone who is anyone** and **anybody who is anybody** to refer to people who are important or influential. ❏ *It seems anyone who's anyone in business is going to the conference.*

1 부정(不定)대명사 아무도 ❏ 내가 여기서 널 봤다고 아무한테도 말 안 할게. ❏ 네가 원하지 않으면 아무한테도 말할 필요 없어. **2** 부정(不定)대명사 누가, 누군가 ❏ 누가 왜 그 일을 원하겠니? ❏ 누가 어떻게 이런 일에 슬퍼할 수가 있겠니? **3** 부정(不定)대명사 누구든, 어떤 사람 ❏ 나는 항상 내 또래의 다른 누구보다 먼저 뭔가를 이루는 사람이었었다. ❏ 이는 누구든 숫자에 약한 사람에게 적합한 일이 아니다. **4** 부정(不定)대명사 아무나 [강조] ❏ 내가 하는 일은 아무나 할 수 있는 일이다. **5** 구 거물급 ❏ 세계에서 거물급들은 모두 이번 회의에 참석할 것으로 보인다.

Do not confuse **anyone** with **any one**. **Anyone** always refers to people. In the phrase **any one**, "one" is a pronoun or a determiner that can refer to either a person or a thing, depending on the context. It is often followed by the word **of**. ❏ *Parting from any one of you for even a short time is hard... None of us stay in any one place for a very long time.* In these examples, **any one** is a more emphatic way of saying **any**. **Anyone** or **anybody** is mainly used in questions and negative sentences. You use **not anyone** instead of **someone** in negative sentences. ❏ *There isn't anyone here... There isn't anybody here.*

anyone과 any one을 혼동하지 않도록 하라. anyone은 항상 사람을 지칭한다. any one이라는 구에서 one은 대명사나 한정사로서 문맥에 따라 사람을 가리킬 수도 있고 사물을 가리킬 수도 있다. one 뒤에는 흔히 of가 따라 나온다. ❏ 짧은 기간 동안만이라도 너희들 중 누구와도 헤어지는 것은 힘들다... 우리들 중 누구도 어느 한 장소에 아주 오랫동안 머물지는 않는다. 이들 예문에서 any one은 any라고 하는 것보다 더 강조해 쓰는 표현이다. anyone이나 anybody는 주로 의문문과 부정문에 쓴다. 부정문에서는 someone 대신 not anyone을 쓴다. ❏ 여기에는 아무도 없다... 여기에는 아무도 없다.

anyplace /ɛnipleɪs/ ADV Anyplace means the same as anywhere. [AM, INFORMAL] [ADV after v] ❏ *She didn't have anyplace to go.*

부사 어디 [미국영어, 비격식체] ❏ 그녀는 어디도 갈 곳이 없었다.

anything ♦♦♦ /ɛniθɪŋ/

1 PRON-INDEF You use **anything** in statements with negative meaning to indicate in a general way that nothing is present or that an action or event does not or cannot happen. [v PRON, oft PRON adj] ❏ *We can't do anything.* ❏ *She couldn't see or hear anything at all.* **2** PRON-INDEF You use **anything** in questions and conditional clauses to ask or talk about whether something is present or happening. ❏ *What happened, is anything wrong?* ❏ *Did you find anything?* **3** PRON-INDEF You can use **anything** before words which indicate the kind of thing you are talking about. [PRON cl/group] ❏ *More than anything else, he wanted to become a teacher.* ❏ *Anything that's cheap this year will be even cheaper next year.* **4** PRON-INDEF You use **anything** to emphasize a possible thing, event, or situation, when you are saying that it could be any one of a very large number of things. [EMPHASIS] ❏ *He is young, fresh, and ready for anything.* **5** PHRASE You use **anything** in expressions such as **anything near**, **anything close to** and **anything like** to emphasize a statement that you are making. [EMPHASIS] [PRON prep] ❏ *Doctors have decided the only way he can live anything near a normal life is to give him an operation.* **6** PRON-INDEF When you do not want to be exact, you use **anything** to talk about a particular range of things or quantities. [PRON from n to n, PRON between n and n] ❏ *Factory farming has turned the cow into a milk machine, producing anything from 25 to 40 liters of milk per day.*

1 부정(不定)대명사 아무것도 ❏ 우리는 아무 것도 할 수 없다. ❏ 그녀는 아무것도 보지도 듣지도 못했다. **2** 부정(不定)대명사 무언가 ❏ 무슨 일이야, 뭐 잘못된 거라도 있어? ❏ 뭐 좀 찾았어? **3** 부정(不定)대명사 -한 것 ❏ 무엇보다도 그는 교사가 되고 싶어 했다. ❏ 올해 싼 물건은 내년엔 훨씬 더 싸질 것이다. **4** 부정(不定)대명사 무엇이든 [강조] ❏ 그는 젊고, 신선하며 무엇이든 할 준비가 되어 있다. **5** 부정(不定)대명사 -와 비슷한 것 [강조] ❏ 의사들은 그가 일상적인 삶과 조금이나마 비슷하게 살기 위한 방법은 수술뿐이라고 결정했다. **6** 부정(不定)대명사 -정도 ❏ 공장식 축산농장은 젖소를 우유 만드는 기계로 만들어서는 하루에 우유를 25-40 리터 정도 생산하고 있다.

Anything is mainly used in questions and negative sentences. You use **not anything** instead of **something** in negative sentences. ❏ *There isn't anything here.*

anything은 주로 의문문과 부정문에 쓴다. 부정문에서는 something 대신 not anything을 쓴다. ❏ 여기에는 아무것도 없다.

7 PHRASE You use **anything but** in expressions such as **anything but quiet** and **anything but attractive** to emphasize that something is not the case. [EMPHASIS] ❏ *There's no evidence that he told anyone to say anything but the truth.* **8** PHRASE You can say that you **would not** do something **for anything** to emphasize that you definitely would not want to do or be a particular thing. [INFORMAL, SPOKEN, EMPHASIS] ❏ *I wouldn't move for anything in the world.* **9** PHRASE You use **if anything**, especially after a negative statement, to introduce a statement that adds to what you have just said. ❏ *I never had to clean up after him. If anything, he did most of the cleaning.* **10** PHRASE You can add **or anything** to the end of a clause or sentence in order to refer vaguely to other things that are or may be similar to what has just been mentioned. [INFORMAL, SPOKEN, VAGUENESS] ❏ *Listen, if you talk to him or anything make sure you let us know, will you?*

7 구 결코 -이 아닌 [강조] ❏ 그가 누군가에게 진실을 절대 이야기하지 말라고 시켰다는 증거가 없다. **8** 구 절대로 -하지 않을 것이다 [비격식체, 구어체, 강조] ❏ 난 무슨 일이 있어도 움직이고 싶지 않아. **9** 구 오히려 ❏ 그가 어지럽힌 것을 내가 치워야 했던 적은 없다. 오히려 청소는 주로 그가 했다. **10** 구 -기나 어쩌거나 [비격식체, 구어체, 짐작투] ❏ 그러니까 네가 그에게 말하게 되거나 어쩌거나 하면, 우리한테 꼭 알려줘. 알았지?

Word Partnership	*anything*의 연어	
ADJ.	anything **left**, anything **more**	**2**
	ready for anything	**4**
PREP.	anything **like**	**5**
	anything **but**	**7**

any|time /ɛnitaɪm/ ADV You use **anytime** to mean a point in time which is not fixed or set. ❑ *The college admits students anytime during the year.* ❑ *He can leave anytime he wants.*

any|way ♦♦◇ /ɛniweɪ/

> The form **anyhow** is also used.

◼ ADV You use **anyway** or **anyhow** to indicate that a statement explains or supports a previous point. [ADV with cl] ❑ *I'm certain David's told you his business troubles. Anyway, it's no secret that he owes money.* ◻ ADV You use **anyway** or **anyhow** to suggest that a statement is true or relevant in spite of other things that have been said. [ADV with cl] ❑ *I don't know why I settled on Aberdeen, but anyway I did.* ◼ ADV You use **anyway** or **anyhow** to correct or modify a statement, for example to limit it to what you definitely know to be true. [cl/group ADV] ❑ *Mary Ann doesn't want to have children. Not right now, anyway.* ◼ ADV You use **anyway** or **anyhow** to indicate that you are asking what the real situation is or what the real reason for something is. [cl ADV] ❑ *What do you want from me, anyway?* ◻ ADV You use **anyway** or **anyhow** to indicate that you are missing out some details in a story and are passing on to the next main point or event. [ADV with cl] ❑ *I was told to go to Reading for this interview. It was a very amusing affair. Anyhow, I got the job.* ◻ ADV You use **anyway** or **anyhow** to change the topic or return to a previous topic. [ADV cl] ❑ *"I've got a terrible cold." — "Have you? Oh dear. Anyway, so you're not going to go away this weekend?"* ◼ ADV You use **anyway** or **anyhow** to indicate that you want to end the conversation. [ADV cl] ❑ *"Anyway, I'd better let you have your dinner. Give our love to Francis. Bye."*

any|ways /ɛniweɪz/ ADV **Anyways** is a nonstandard or dialectal form of **anyway**. [AM, SPOKEN] ❑ *Well, anyways, she said it wasn't safe.*

any|where ♦◇◇ /ɛniweər/ ◼ ADV You use **anywhere** in statements with negative meaning to indicate that a place does not exist. ❑ *I haven't got anywhere to live.* ◻ ADV You use **anywhere** in questions and conditional clauses to ask or talk about a place without saying exactly where you mean. ❑ *Did you try to get help from anywhere?* ◼ ADV You use **anywhere** before words that indicate the kind of place you are talking about. [ADV cl/group] ❑ *He'll meet you anywhere you want.* ◼ ADV You use **anywhere** to refer to a place when you are emphasizing that it could be any of a large number of places. [EMPHASIS] ❑ *...jokes that are so funny they always work anywhere.* ◻ ADV When you do not want to be exact, you use **anywhere** to refer to a particular range of things. ❑ *His shoes cost anywhere from $200 up.* ◼ ADV You use **anywhere** in expressions such as **anywhere near** and **anywhere close to** to emphasize a statement that you are making. [EMPHASIS] [ADV adj/adv] ❑ *There weren't anywhere near enough empty boxes.*

> **Anywhere** is mainly used in questions and negative sentences. You use **not anywhere** instead of **somewhere** in negative sentences. ❑ *He isn't going anywhere.*

Word Partnership   *anywhere*의 연어

PREP.	anywhere **in the world** ◻-◼
	anywhere **near** ◼
V.	**can/could happen** anywhere, **get** anywhere, **go** anywhere ◻-◼

AOB /eɪ oʊ biː/ **AOB** is a heading on an agenda for a meeting, to show that any topics not listed separately can be discussed at this point, usually the end. **AOB** is an abbreviation for "any other business."

――――― **apart** ―――――
① POSITIONS AND STATES
② INDICATING EXCEPTIONS AND FOCUSING

① **apart** ♦♦◇ /əpɑːrt/

> In addition to the uses shown below, **apart** is used in phrasal verbs such as "grow apart" and "take apart."

◼ ADV When people or things are **apart**, they are some distance from each other. ❑ *He was standing a bit apart from the rest of us, watching us.* ❑ *Ray and sister Renee lived just 25 miles apart from each other.* ◻ ADV If two people or things move **apart** or are pulled **apart**, they move away from each other. [ADV after v] ❑ *John and Isabelle moved apart, back into the sun.* ◼ ADV If two people are **apart**, they are no longer living together or spending time together, either permanently or just for a short time. ❑ *It was the first time Jane and I had been apart for more than a few days.* ◼ ADV If you take something **apart**, you separate it into the pieces that it is made of. If it comes or falls **apart**, its parts separate from each other. [ADV after v] ❑ *When the clock stopped he took it apart, found what was wrong, and put the whole thing together again.* ◻ ADV If something such as an organization or relationship falls **apart**, or if something tears it **apart**, it can no longer continue because it has serious difficulties. [ADV after v] ❑ *Any manager knows that his company will start falling apart if his attention wanders.* ◻ ADV If something sets someone or something **apart**, it makes them different from other people or things. ❑ *What really sets Mr. Thaksin apart is that he comes not from Southern China, but from northern Thailand.* ◼ ADJ If people or groups are a long way **apart** on a particular topic or issue, they have completely different views and disagree about it. [v-link amount ADJ, oft ADJ on n] ❑ *Their concept of a performance and our concept were miles apart.* ◼ PHRASE If you can't **tell** two people or things **apart**, they look

exactly the same to you. ❑ *I can still only tell Mark and Dave apart by the color of their shoes!*

② **apart** ♦◇◇ /əpɑ̱rt/ ◼ PHRASE You use **apart from** when you are making an exception to a general statement. ❑ *The room was empty apart from one man seated beside the fire.* ◻ ADV You use **apart** when you are making an exception to a general statement. [N ADV] ❑ *This was, New York apart, the first American city I had ever been in where people actually lived downtown.* ◻ PHRASE You use **apart from** to indicate that you are aware of one aspect of a situation, but that you are going to focus on another aspect. ❑ *Illiteracy threatens Britain's industrial performance. But, quite apart from that, the individual who can't read or write is unlikely to get a job.*

apart|heid /əpɑ̱rthaɪt/ N-UNCOUNT **Apartheid** was a political system in South Africa in which people were divided into racial groups and kept apart by law. ❑ *He praised her role in the struggle against apartheid.*

apart|ment ♦◇◇ /əpɑ̱rtmənt/ (**apartments**) N-COUNT An **apartment** is a set of rooms for living in, usually on part of one floor of a large building. [mainly AM; BRIT **flat**] ❑ *Christina has her own apartment, with her own car.* →see **city**

apart|ment build|ing (**apartment buildings**) or **apartment house** N-COUNT An **apartment building** or **apartment house** is a tall building which contains different apartments on different floors. [AM; BRIT **block of flats**] ❑ *...the Manhattan apartment house where they live.*

apa|thet|ic /æpəθe̱tɪk/ ADJ If you describe someone as **apathetic**, you are criticizing them because they do not seem to be interested in or enthusiastic about doing anything. [DISAPPROVAL] ❑ *Even the most apathetic students are beginning to sit up and listen.*

apa|thy /æ̱pəθi/ N-UNCOUNT You can use **apathy** to talk about someone's state of mind if you are criticizing them because they do not seem to be interested in or enthusiastic about anything. [DISAPPROVAL] ❑ *They told me about isolation and public apathy.*

ape /e̱ɪp/ (**apes**, **aping**, **aped**) ◼ N-COUNT **Apes** are chimpanzees, gorillas, and other animals in the same family. ❑ *...the theory that man is descended from the apes.* ◻ V-T If you **ape** someone's speech or behavior, you imitate it. ❑ *Modelling yourself on someone you admire is not the same as aping all they say or do.* →see **primate**

ap|er|ture /æ̱pərtʃər/ (**apertures**) ◼ N-COUNT An **aperture** is a narrow hole or gap. [FORMAL] ❑ *Through the aperture he could see daylight.* ◻ N-COUNT In photography, the **aperture** of a camera is the size of the hole through which light passes to reach the film. ❑ *Use a small aperture and position the camera carefully.*

apex /e̱ɪpeks/ (**apexes**) ◼ N-SING The **apex of** an organization or system is the highest and most important position in it. ❑ *At the apex of the party was its central committee.* ◻ N-COUNT The **apex of** something is its pointed top or end. ❑ *Georgeanne Woods led me up a gloomy corridor to the apex of the pyramid.*

Apex also **APEX** N-SING An **Apex** or an **Apex ticket** is a ticket for a journey by air or rail which costs less than the standard ticket, but which you have to book a specified period in advance. ❑ *The Apex fare is 195 pounds.*

apiece /əpi̱s/ ◼ ADV If people have a particular number of things **apiece**, they have that number each. [amount ADV] ❑ *He and I had two fish apiece.* ◻ ADV If a number of similar things are for sale at a certain price **apiece**, that is the price for each one of them. [amount ADV] ❑ *Entire roast chickens were sixty cents apiece.*

apolo|get|ic /əpɒ̱lədʒe̱tɪk/ ADJ If you are **apologetic**, you show or say that you are sorry for causing trouble for someone, for hurting them, or for disappointing them. ❑ *The hospital staff were very apologetic but that couldn't really compensate.* ● **apolo|get|ical|ly** /əpɒ̱lədʒe̱tɪkli/ ADV [ADV with v] ❑ *"It's of no great literary merit," he said, almost apologetically.*

apolo|gize /əpɒ̱lədʒaɪz/ (**apologizes**, **apologizing**, **apologized**) [BRIT also **apologise**] V-I When you **apologize to** someone, you say that you are sorry that you have hurt them or caused trouble for them. You can say "I apologize" as a formal way of saying sorry. ❑ *I apologize for being late, but I have just had a message from the hospital.* ❑ *He apologized to the people who had been affected.*

apol|ogy /əpɒ̱lədʒi/ (**apologies**) ◼ N-VAR An **apology** is something that you say or write in order to tell someone that you are sorry that you have hurt them or caused trouble for them. ❑ *I didn't get an apology.* ❑ *We received a letter of apology.* ◻ N-PLURAL If you offer or make your **apologies**, you apologize. [FORMAL] ❑ *When Mary finally appeared, she made her apologies to Mrs. Madrigal.*

◼ 구 ~을 제외하고 ❑ 난로 옆에 앉아 있는 남자 한 명을 제외하고는 방에 아무도 없었다. ◻ 부사 제외하고 ❑ 이 도시는 내가 가 본 도시 중에서 뉴욕을 제외하고 도심에 사람들이 실제로 살았던 첫 번째 도시였다. ◳ 구 ~은 차치하고 ❑ 문맹으로 인해 영국 산업의 성과가 위협받고 있다. 하지만, 이 문제는 차치하고라도 글을 읽고 쓸 줄 모르는 개인들은 직장을 구할 가능성이 희박하다.

불가산명사 아파르트헤이트 (남아공화국의 인종 차별 정책) ❑ 그는 아파르트헤이트 철폐 운동에서 그녀가 한 역할을 높이 칭송했다.

가산명사 아파트 [주로 미국영어; 영국영어 flat] ❑ 크리스티나는 자기 자신의 아파트와 차를 가지고 있다.

가산명사 아파트 건물 [미국영어; 영국영어 block of flats] ❑ 그들이 살고 있는 맨해튼 아파트

형용사 냉담한 [탐탁찮음] ❑ 가장 냉담한 학생들조차도 똑바로 앉아 귀를 기울이기 시작하고 있다.

불가산명사 냉담, 무관심 [탐탁찮음] ❑ 그들은 나에게 소외와 대중의 무관심에 대해 이야기했다.

◼ 가산명사 원숭이 ❑ 인간이 원숭이의 후손이라는 이론 ◻ 타동사 흉내 내다 ❑ 자신이 존경하는 사람을 모델로 삼는 것은 그들의 말과 행동을 모두 흉내 내는 것과는 다른 것이다.

◼ 가산명사 틈, 균열 [격식체] ❑ 그는 틈을 통해서 햇빛을 볼 수 있었다. ◻ 가산명사 조리개 ❑ 작은 조리개를 사용하고 조심해서 카메라의 위치를 잡으세요.

◼ 단수명사 최정점 ❑ 그 당의 최정점에는 중앙위원회가 있었다. ◻ 가산명사 꼭대기 ❑ 조지앤느 우즈가 어두운 통로를 올라 피라미드 꼭대기까지 나를 안내했다.

단수명사 에이펙스 티켓 (항공 및 철도 운임의 사전 구입 할인 티켓) ❑ 에이펙스 할인 요금은 195파운드이다.

◼ 부사 각자, 각각 ❑ 그와 나는 각각 생선을 두 마리씩 먹었다. ◻ 부사 개당 ❑ 로스트 치킨 전부 조각 당 60센트였다.

형용사 미안해하는 ❑ 병원 직원들이 매우 미안해하긴 했지만 그렇다고 해서 보상이 되는 것은 아니었다. ● 미안해하며 부사 ❑ "문학적인 가치는 별로 없군요." 그가 거의 사죄하듯이 말했다.

[영국영어 apologise] 자동사 사과하다 ❑ 늦어서 죄송합니다. 실은 병원에서 방금 호출이 왔었어요. ❑ 그는 피해를 본 사람들에게 사과했다.

◼ 가산명사 또는 불가산명사 사과 ❑ 나는 사과를 받지 못했다. ❑ 우리는 사과 편지를 받았다. ◻ 복수명사 사과 [격식체] ❑ 결국 메리가 나타나 마드리갈 부인에게 사과를 했다.

apos|tro|phe /əpɒstrəfi/ (**apostrophes**) N-COUNT An **apostrophe** is the mark ' when it is written to indicate that one or more letters have been left out of a word, as in "isn't" and "we'll." It is also added to nouns to form possessives, as in "Mike's car."

가산명사 아포스트로피 (생략이나 소유를 나타내는 부호)

ap|pall /əpɔl/ (**appalls, appalling, appalled**) [BRIT **appal**] V-T If something **appalls** you, it disgusts you because it seems so bad or unpleasant. ◻ *The new-found strength of Hindu militancy appalls many observers.*

[영국영어 appal] 타동사 소름 끼치게 하다, 질리게 하다 ◻ 힌두 과격주의가 새로 힘을 얻자 많은 사람들이 섬뜩해 하고 있다.

ap|palled /əpɔld/ ADJ If you are **appalled** by something, you are shocked or disgusted because it is so bad or unpleasant. ◻ *She said that the Americans are appalled at the statements made at the conference.*

형용사 소름 끼치는, 섬뜩한 ◻ 그녀는 미국인들이 그 회담에서 발표된 성명서를 듣고 경악해 한다고 말했다.

ap|pal|ling /əpɔlɪŋ/ **1** ADJ Something that is **appalling** is so bad or unpleasant that it shocks you. ◻ *They have been living under the most appalling conditions for two months.* ● **ap|pal|ling|ly** ADV ◻ *He says that he understands why they behaved so appallingly.* **2** ADJ You can use **appalling** to emphasize that something is very great or severe. [EMPHASIS] ◻ *I developed an appalling headache.* ● **ap|pal|ling|ly** ADV ◻ *It's been an appallingly busy morning.* **3** →see also **appall**

1 형용사 소름 끼치는, 끔찍한 ◻ 그들은 두 달 동안 아주 끔찍한 환경에서 살고 있다. ● 지독하게, 끔찍하게 부사 ◻ 그는 그들이 왜 그렇게 지독하게 굴었는지 이해한다고 말한다. **2** 형용사 무지무지한 [강조] ◻ 나한테 지독한 두통이 생겼다. ● 무지무지하게 부사 ◻ 무지무지하게 바쁜 아침이었다.

ap|pa|rat|us /æpərætəs, -reɪ-/ (**apparatuses**) **1** N-VAR The **apparatus** of an organization or system is its structure and method of operation. ◻ *For many years, the country had been buried under the apparatus of the regime.* **2** N-VAR **Apparatus** is the equipment, such as tools and machines, which is used to do a particular job or activity. ◻ *One of the boys had to be rescued by firemen wearing breathing apparatus.*

1 가산명사 또는 불가산명사 기구, 조직 ◻ 이 나라는 수년 동안 그 정권의 억압을 받았었다. **2** 가산명사 또는 불가산명사 기구, 장치 ◻ 남자 아이들 중 하나를 구출하는 데는 호흡기를 낀 소방관들이 동원되어야 했다.

ap|par|ent ◆◇◇ /əpærənt/ **1** ADJ An **apparent** situation, quality, or feeling seems to exist, although you cannot be certain that it does exist. [ADJ n] ◻ *I was a bit depressed by our apparent lack of progress.* **2** ADJ If something is **apparent** to you, it is clear and obvious to you. [v-link ADJ, oft it v-link ADJ that] ◻ *It has been apparent that in other areas standards have held up well.* **3** PHRASE If you say that something happens **for no apparent reason**, you cannot understand why it happens. ◻ *The person may become dizzy for no apparent reason.*

1 형용사 명백해 보이는 ◻ 명백해 보이는 성과가 없어 나는 약간 실망했다. **2** 형용사 명백한 ◻ 분명히 다른 부문들에서는 수준이 잘 유지되어 왔다. **3** 구 특별한 이유 없이 ◻ 이런 사람은 특별한 이유 없이 어지럼증을 느낄 수도 있다.

ap|par|ent|ly ◆◆◇ /əpærəntli/ **1** ADV You use **apparently** to indicate that the information you are giving is something that you have heard, but you are not certain that it is true. [VAGUENESS] ◻ *Apparently the girls are not at all amused by the whole business.* **2** ADV You use **apparently** to refer to something that seems to be true, although you are not sure whether it is or not. ◻ *The recent deterioration has been caused by an apparently endless recession.*

1 부사 듣자하니 [짐작투] ◻ 듣자하니 여학생들은 이 일을 전혀 재미있어 하는 것 같지 않던데. **2** 부사 그냥 보기에 ◻ 최근 사태의 악화 원인은 끝이 없어 보이는 불황이다.

ap|peal ◆◆◇ /əpil/ (**appeals, appealing, appealed**) **1** V-I If you **appeal to** someone **to** do something, you make a serious and urgent request to them. ◻ *Deng Xiaoping recently appealed for students to return to China.* ◻ *He will appeal to the state for an extension of unemployment benefits.* **2** N-COUNT An **appeal** is a serious and urgent request. ◻ *He has a message from King Fahd, believed to be an appeal for Arab unity.* **3** N-COUNT An **appeal** is an attempt to raise money for a charity or for a good cause. ◻ *...an appeal to save a library containing priceless manuscripts.* **4** V-T/V-I If you **appeal to** someone in authority **against** a decision, you formally ask them to change it. In American English, you **appeal** something. In British English, you **appeal against** something. ◻ *We intend to appeal the verdict.* ◻ *He said they would appeal against the decision.* **5** N-VAR An **appeal** is a formal request for a decision to be changed. ◻ *Heath's appeal against the sentence was later successful.* **6** V-I If something **appeals** to you, you find it attractive or interesting. ◻ *On the other hand, the idea appealed to him.* **7** N-UNCOUNT The **appeal** of something is a quality that it has which people find attractive or interesting. ◻ *Its new title was meant to give the party greater public appeal.* **8** →see also **appealing** →see also **trial**

1 자동사 간청하다, 애원하다 ◻ 덩샤오핑은 최근 학생들에게 중국으로 돌아오라고 간곡히 당부했다. ◻ 그는 주 정부에 실업 수당 기한을 연장해 달라고 간청할 것이다. **2** 가산명사 호소, 간청 ◻ 그는 아랍 세계의 통합을 호소하는 것으로 보이는 파드 국왕의 메시지를 가지고 왔다. **3** 가산명사 기금 모금 ◻ 귀중한 필사본들이 소장된 도서관 살리기 모금 운동 **4** 타동사/자동사 상소하다 (항소와 상고로 나뉨) ◻ 우리는 그 평결에 상소할 생각이다. ◻ 그는 그들이 판결에 불복하여 상소할 것이라고 말했다. **5** 가산명사 또는 불가산명사 상소 ◻ 히스는 후에 판결 불복 상소심에 성공했다. **6** 자동사 호감을 주다 ◻ 반면에, 그 아이디어는 그의 마음에 들었다. **7** 불가산명사 매력 ◻ 당의 새 이름은 더 큰 대중적인 호소력을 겨냥한 것이었다.

Word Partnership	appeal의 연어
PREP.	appeal **to** *someone* **1 6**
	appeal **for** *something* **2**
	appeal **to a court** **4**
V.	**make an** appeal **2 3 5**
	appeal **a case** **5**

ap|peal|ing /əpilɪŋ/ **1** ADJ Someone or something that is **appealing** is pleasing and attractive. ◻ *There was a sense of humor to what he did that I found very appealing.* **2** ADJ An **appealing** expression or tone of voice indicates to someone that you want help, advice, or approval. ◻ *She gave him a soft appealing look that would have melted solid ice.* **3** →see also **appeal**

1 형용사 매력적인 ◻ 그의 행동엔 유머 감각이 있었는데 나에게는 참 매력적으로 보였다. **2** 형용사 호소하는 듯한 ◻ 그녀는 그에게 단단한 얼음도 녹여 버릴 것 같은 호소하는 듯한 여린 표정을 지어 보였다.

ap|pear ◆◆◆ /əpɪər/ (**appears, appearing, appeared**) **1** V-LINK If you say that something **appears to** be the way you describe it, you are reporting what you believe or what you have been told, though you cannot be sure it is true. [VAGUENESS] [no cont] ◻ *There appears to be increasing support for the leadership to take a more aggressive stance.* **2** V-LINK If someone or something **appears to** have a particular quality or characteristic, they give the impression of having that quality or characteristic. [no cont] ◻ *She did her best to appear more self-assured than she felt.* ◻ *He is anxious to appear a gentleman.* **3** V-I When someone or something **appears**, they move into a position where you can see them. ◻ *A woman appeared at the far end of the street.* **4** V-I When something new **appears**, it begins to exist or reaches a stage of development where its existence can be noticed. ◻ *...small white flowers which appear in early summer.* **5** V-I When something such as a book **appears**, it is published or becomes available for people to buy. ◻ *I could hardly wait for "Boys' World" to appear each month.* **6** V-I When someone **appears in** something such as a play, a show, or a television program, they take part in it. ◻ *Jill Bennett became John Osborne's fourth wife, and*

1 연결동사 -인 것으로 보이다 [짐작투] ◻ 지도부가 더욱 공세적인 입장을 취하는 것에 대한 지지가 높아지고 있는 것으로 보인다. **2** 연결동사 -처럼 보이다 ◻ 그녀는 자신이 느끼는 것보다 더 확신에 차 보이려고 최선을 다했다. ◻ 그는 신사처럼 보이고 싶어 안달이다. **3** 자동사 나타나다 ◻ 거리의 저 쪽 끝에 여자 한 명이 나타났다. **4** 자동사 나오다 ◻ 초여름에 피는 작고 하얀 꽃들 **5** 자동사 나오다 ◻ 나는 매달 '보이즈 월드' 발행을 손꼽아 기다린다. **6** 자동사 출연하다 ◻ 질 베넷은 존 오스본의 네 번째 아내가 되었고 그의 극작품 몇 개에 출연했다. **7** 자동사 출두하다 ◻ 다른 간부 두 명이 탈세 혐의로 워딩 법원에 출두했다.

appeared in several of his plays. ◼7 V-I When someone **appears before** a court of law or **before** an official committee, they go there in order to answer charges or to give information as a witness. ❑ *Two other executives appeared at Worthing Magistrates' Court charged with tax fraud.*

Thesaurus   appear의 참조어

v. seem ◼1
    look like, resemble, seem ◼2
    arrive, show up, turn up; (*ant.*) disappear, vanish ◼3

ap|pear|ance ♦♦◇ /əpɪərəns/ (**appearances**) ◼1 N-COUNT When someone makes an **appearance** at a public event or in a broadcast, they take part in it. ❑ *It was the president's second public appearance to date.* ◼2 N-SING Someone's or something's **appearance** is the way that they look. ❑ *She used to be so fussy about her appearance.* ◼3 N-SING The **appearance of** someone or something in a place is their arrival there, especially when it is unexpected. ❑ *The sudden appearance of a few bags of rice could start a riot.* ◼4 N-SING The **appearance of** something new is its coming into existence or use. ❑ *Flowering plants were making their first appearance, but were still a rarity.* ◼5 N-SING If something has the **appearance of** a quality, it seems to have that quality. ❑ *We tried to meet both children's needs without the appearance of favoritism or unfairness.* ◼6 PHRASE If something is true **to all appearances**, **from all appearances**, or **by all appearances**, it seems from what you observe or know about it that it is true. ❑ *He was a small and to all appearances an unassuming man.*

Word Partnership   appearance의 연어

N.   **court** appearance ◼1
ADJ. **public** appearance ◼1
     physical appearance ◼2
     sudden appearance ◼3
V.   **make an** appearance ◼1 ◼3
     change *your* appearance ◼2
     give/have an appearance of ◼5

ap|pease /əpiːz/ (**appeases, appeasing, appeased**) V-T If you try to **appease** someone, you try to stop them from being angry by giving them what they want. [DISAPPROVAL] ❑ *Gandhi was accused by some of trying to appease both factions of the electorate.*

ap|pease|ment /əpiːzmənt/ N-UNCOUNT **Appeasement** means giving people what they want to prevent them from harming you or being angry with you. [FORMAL, DISAPPROVAL] ❑ *He denied there is a policy of appeasement.*

ap|pen|dix /əpendɪks/ (**appendixes**)

The plural form **appendices** /əpendɪsiːz/ is usually used for meaning ◼2.

◼1 N-COUNT Your **appendix** is a small closed tube inside your body which is attached to your digestive system. ❑ *...a burst appendix.* ◼2 N-COUNT An **appendix to** a book is extra information that is placed after the end of the main text. ❑ *The survey results are published in full as an appendix to Mr. Barton's discussion paper.*

ap|pe|tite /æpɪtaɪt/ (**appetites**) ◼1 N-VAR Your **appetite** is your desire to eat. ❑ *He has a healthy appetite.* ◼2 N-COUNT Someone's **appetite for** something is their strong desire for it. ❑ *...his appetite for success.*

ap|pe|tiz|ing /æpɪtaɪzɪŋ/ [BRIT also **appetising**] ADJ **Appetizing** food looks and smells good, so that you want to eat it. ❑ *...the appetizing smell of freshly baked bread.*

ap|plaud /əplɔd/ (**applauds, applauding, applauded**) ◼1 V-T/V-I When a group of people **applaud**, they clap their hands in order to show approval, for example when they have enjoyed a play or concert. ❑ *The audience laughed and applauded.* ◼2 V-T When an attitude or action **is applauded**, people praise it. ❑ *He should be applauded for his courage.* ❑ *This last move can only be applauded.*

ap|plause /əplɔz/ N-UNCOUNT **Applause** is the noise made by a group of people clapping their hands to show approval. ❑ *They greeted him with thunderous applause.*

ap|ple ♦◇◇ /æpəl/ (**apples**) N-VAR An **apple** is a round fruit with smooth red, yellow, or green skin and firm white flesh. ❑ *I want an apple.* ❑ *...his ongoing search for the finest varieties of apple.*

This fruit has been used as a nickname for New York City: The Big Apple. Other nicknames include: The Windy City (Chicago), Mile High City (Denver), The Motor City (Detroit), Beantown (Boston), and Tinseltown (Hollywood).

ap|plet /æplɪt/ (**applets**) N-COUNT An **applet** is a computer program which is contained within a page on the World Wide Web, and which transfers itself to your computer and runs automatically while you are looking at that Web page.

ap|pli|ance /əplaɪəns/ (**appliances**) N-COUNT An **appliance** is a device or machine in your home that you use to do a job such as cleaning or cooking. Appliances are often electrical. [FORMAL] ❑ *He could also learn to use the vacuum cleaner, the washing machine and other household appliances.*

ap|pli|ca|ble /æplɪkəbəl, əplɪkə-/ ADJ Something that is **applicable to** a particular situation is relevant to it or can be applied to it. ❑ *What is a reasonable standard for one family is not applicable for another.*

◼1 가산명사 참석 ❑ 지금까지 대통령이 공식 석상에 모습을 드러낸 것은 그것이 두 번째였다. ◼2 단수명사 모습, 외모 ❑ 그녀는 외모에 지나치게 신경을 많이 썼었다. ◼3 단수명사 등장 ❑ 갑자기 쌀 몇 포대가 나타나면 소동이 일어날 수도 있다. ◼4 단수명사 등장, 출시 ❑ 꽃이 피는 식물이 처음 나오기 시작했지만 아직 흔하지는 않았다. ◼5 단수명사 인상 ❑ 우리는 편애한다거나 불공평하다는 인상을 주지 않고 두 아이의 필요를 충족시켜 주기 위해 노력했다. ◼6 구 어느 모로 보나 ❑ 그는 몸집이 작고 어느 모로 보나 젠체하지 않는 남자였다.

타동사 달래다 [탐탁찮음] ❑ 일각에서는 간디가 선거인단의 두 진영 모두를 달래려 한다고 비판했다.

불가산명사 유화 정책, 달래기 [격식체, 탐탁찮음] ❑ 그는 유화 정책을 편다는 것을 부인했다.

복수 appendices/əpendɪsiːz/를 대개 ◼2 의미로 쓴다.

◼1 가산명사 맹장 ❑ 맹장 파열 ◼2 가산명사 별첨, 부록 ❑ 자세한 연구 결과는 바튼 씨의 논문에 부록으로 실려 있다.

◼1 가산명사 또는 불가산명사 식욕 ❑ 그는 식욕이 왕성하다. ◼2 가산명사 욕구, 욕망 ❑ 그의 성공욕

[영국영어 appetising] 형용사 군침 도는 ❑ 갓 구운 빵의 군침 도는 냄새

◼1 타동사/자동사 박수갈채를 보내다 ❑ 관중들이 웃으며 박수갈채를 보냈다. ◼2 타동사 칭찬한다 ❑ 그의 용기는 칭찬받아 마땅하다. ❑ 이번 마지막 조치는 칭찬할 수밖에 없는 것이다.

불가산명사 박수갈채 ❑ 그들은 우레와 같은 박수로 그를 맞았다.

가산명사 또는 불가산명사 사과 ❑ 사과 하나 주세요. ❑ 최고 품종의 사과를 찾기 위한 계속되는 그의 노력

뉴욕시의 별칭인 The Big Apple에 사과가 사용되어 왔다. 도시와 관련된 다른 별칭들로는 The Windy City(시카고), Mile High City(덴버), The Motor City(디트로이트), Beantown(보스톤), Tinseltown(헐리우드)이 있다.

가산명사 애플릿 (작은 응용프로그램)

가산명사 기구, 가전 제품 [격식체] ❑ 그는 또한 진공청소기나 세탁기, 그 외 다른 가전제품 사용법을 배울 수도 있을 것이다.

형용사 적용 가능한 ❑ 한 가족에게는 합리적인 기준이 다른 가족에게는 적용이 안 될 수도 있다.

a
b
c
d
e
f
g
h
i
j
k
l
m
n
o
p
q
r
s
t
u
v
w
x
y
z

ap|pli|cant /ǽplɪkənt/ (**applicants**) N-COUNT An **applicant for** something such as a job or a place at a college is someone who makes a formal written request to be given it. ❏ *Both colleges have more than seven applicants for every place they offer.*

가산명사 지원자 ❏ 두 대학 모두 제시한 자리마다 지원자가 일곱 명이 넘는다.

ap|pli|ca|tion ♦♦◇ /æplɪkéɪʃ°n/ (**applications**) ■ N-COUNT An **application for** something such as a job or membership of an organization is a formal written request for it. [usu with supp, oft N for n, N to-inf, also on/upon N] ❏ *His application for membership of the organization was rejected.* ■ N-VAR The **application of** a rule or piece of knowledge is the use of it in a particular situation. ❏ *Students learned the practical application of the theory they had learned in the classroom.* ■ N-COUNT In computing, an **application** is a piece of software designed to carry out a particular task. ❏ *The service works as a software application that is accessed via the internet.* ■ N-UNCOUNT **Application** is hard work and concentration on what you are doing over a period of time. ❏ *...his immense talent, boundless energy and unremitting application.*

■ 가산명사 지원, 신청 ❏ 그는 그 기구에 가입 신청을 했지만 거절당했다. ■ 가산명사 또는 불가산명사 적용, 응용 ❏ 학생들은 교실에서 배운 이론을 실제로 적용하는 것을 배웠다. ■ 가산명사 컴퓨터 응용 프로그램 ❏ 이 서비스는 인터넷을 통해 접속 가능한 응용 프로그램의 역할을 한다. ■ 불가산명사 전념 ❏ 그의 방대한 재능과 끝없는 에너지와 부단한 노력

Word Partnership	application의 연어
N.	**college** application, application **form**, **grant/loan** application, **job** application, **membership** application ■
	application **software** ■
V.	**accept/reject an** application, **fill out an** application, **submit an** application ■
ADJ.	**practical** application ■

ap|plied /əpláɪd/ ADJ An **applied** subject of study has a practical use, rather than being concerned only with theory. [ADJ n] ❏ *...Applied Physics.* →see **science**

형용사 응용의 ❏ 응용 물리학

ap|ply ♦♦◇ /əpláɪ/ (**applies, applying, applied**) ■ V-T/V-I If you **apply for** something such as a job or membership of an organization, you write a letter or fill in a form in order to ask formally for it. ❏ *I am continuing to apply for jobs.* ■ V-T If you **apply yourself** to something or **apply** your mind **to** something, you concentrate hard on doing it or on thinking about it. ❏ *Faulks has applied himself to this task with considerable energy.* ■ V-I If something such as a rule or a remark **applies to** a person or in a situation, it is relevant to the person or the situation. [no cont] ❏ *The convention does not apply to us.* ❏ *The rule applies where a person owns stock in a corporation.* ■ V-T If you **apply** something such as a rule, system, or skill, you use it in a situation or activity. ❏ *The Government appears to be applying the same principle.* ■ V-T A name that **is applied** to someone or something is used to refer to them. ❏ *...a biological term which cannot be applied to a whole culture.* ■ V-T If you **apply** something **to** a surface, you put it on or rub it into the surface. ❏ *The right thing would be to apply direct pressure to the wound.* ■ →see also **applied** →see **makeup**

■ 타동사/자동사 지원하다 ❏ 나는 계속 일자리를 찾고 있다. ■ 타동사 매진하다 ❏ 폭스는 상당한 열의를 가지고 이 일에 매진하고 있다. ■ 자동사 적용되다 ❏ 그 규칙은 회사의 지분을 보유한 사람에게 적용된다. ■ 타동사 적용하다 ❏ 정부는 같은 원칙을 적용하는 듯하다. ■ 타동사 붙이다 ❏ 한 문화 전체에 갖다 붙일 수 없는 생물학적 용어 ■ 타동사 바르다, 가하다 ❏ 상처에 직접 압박을 가하는 것이 옳다.

Word Partnership	apply의 연어
PREP.	apply **for admission**, apply **for a job** ■
N.	**laws/restrictions/rules** apply ■
	apply **make-up**, apply **pressure** ■

ap|point ♦♦◇ /əpɔ́ɪnt/ (**appoints, appointing, appointed**) V-T If you **appoint** someone **to** a job or official position, you formally choose them for it. ❏ *It made sense to appoint a banker to this job.* ❏ *The Prime Minister has appointed a civilian as defence minister.* →see also **appointed**

타동사 임명하다 ❏ 이 직책에 은행원 출신을 임명하는 것이 타당했다. ❏ 수상은 민간인을 국방 장관으로 임명했다.

Word Partnership	appoint의 연어
N.	appoint **judges**, appoint **a leader**, appoint **members**

ap|point|ed /əpɔ́ɪntɪd/ ADJ If something happens at the **appointed** time, it happens at the time that was decided in advance. [FORMAL] [ADJ n] ❏ *The appointed hour of the ceremony was drawing nearer.*

형용사 예정된 [격식체] ❏ 예정된 행사 시각이 점점 다가오고 있었다.

ap|point|ment ♦♦◇ /əpɔ́ɪntmənt/ (**appointments**) ■ N-VAR The **appointment** of a person **to** a particular job is the choice of that person to do it. ❏ *His appointment to the Cabinet would please the right wing.* ■ N-COUNT An **appointment** is a job or position of responsibility. ❏ *Mr. Fay is to take up an appointment as a researcher.* ■ N-COUNT If you have an **appointment with** someone, you have arranged to see them at a particular time, usually in connection with their work or for a serious purpose. ❏ *She has an appointment with her accountant.* ■ PHRASE If something can be done **by appointment**, people can arrange in advance to do it at a particular time. ❏ *Viewing is by appointment only.*

■ 가산명사 또는 불가산명사 임명 ❏ 그가 각료로 임명된다면 우익은 좋아할 것이다. ■ 가산명사 직책 ❏ 페이 씨는 연구원 직책을 맡을 것이다. ■ 가산명사 약속 ❏ 그녀는 자신의 회계사와 약속이 있다. ■ 구 예약을 통한 ❏ 관람하려면 예약은 필수이다.

Thesaurus	appointment의 참조어
N.	date, engagement, meeting ■

Word Partnership	appointment의 연어
PREP.	appointment **to *something*** ■
	appointment **with *someone*** ■
	by appointment ■
V.	**have/make/schedule an** appointment ■

ap|prais|al /əpreɪzᵊl/ (appraisals) **1** N-VAR If you make an **appraisal** of something, you consider it carefully and form an opinion about it. ❑ *What is needed in such cases is a calm appraisal of the situation.* **2** N-VAR **Appraisal** is the official or formal assessment of the strengths and weaknesses of someone or something. Appraisal often involves observation or some kind of testing. ❑ *In Britain and many other countries appraisal is now a tool of management.*

1 가산명사 또는 불가산명사 평가 ❑ 그런 경우에는 상황을 차분하게 평가해 봐야 한다. 2 가산명사 또는 불가산명사 감정 ❑ 영국과 기타 많은 국가에서 감정은 이제 경영 도구이다.

ap|praise /əpreɪz/ (appraises, appraising, appraised) V-T If you **appraise** something or someone, you consider them carefully and form an opinion about them. [FORMAL] ❑ *This prompted many employers to appraise their selection and recruitment policies.*

타동사 평가하다, 숙고하다 [격식체] ❑ 이 때문에 많은 고용주가 선발 및 채용 정책을 숙고하게 되었다.

ap|pre|ci|ate ◆◇◇ /əprɪʃieɪt/ (appreciates, appreciating, appreciated) **1** V-T If you **appreciate** something, for example a piece of music or good food, you like it because you recognize its good qualities. ❑ *Anyone can appreciate our music.* **2** V-T If you **appreciate** a situation or problem, you understand it and know what it involves. ❑ *She never really appreciated the depth and bitterness of the Irish conflict.* **3** V-T If you **appreciate** something that someone has done for you or is going to do for you, you are grateful for it. ❑ *Peter stood by me when I most needed it. I'll always appreciate that.* **4** V-I If something that you own **appreciates** over a period of time, its value increases. ❑ *They don't have any confidence that houses will appreciate in value.*

1 타동사 감상하다, 즐기다 ❑ 누구나 우리 음악을 즐길 수 있다. 2 타동사 올바르게 인식하다, 이해하다 ❑ 그녀는 사실 아일랜드 분쟁의 깊이와 쓰라림을 제대로 인식한 적이 없었다. 3 타동사 감사하다 ❑ 피터는 내가 가장 어려울 때 내 곁을 지켜줬다. 나는 그것을 영원히 고맙게 생각할 것이다. 4 자동사 가치가 오르다 ❑ 그들은 주택 가격이 오를 것이라는 확신이 전혀 없다.

Word Partnership	*appreciate*의 연어
V.	**fail to** appreciate **1**-**3**
ADV.	**fully** appreciate **1**-**3**
N.	appreciate *someone's* **concern/support 3**
	appreciate **in value 4**

ap|pre|cia|tion /əprɪʃieɪʃᵊn/ (appreciations) **1** N-SING **Appreciation of** something is the recognition and enjoyment of its good qualities. [also no det, oft N of n] ❑ *...an investigation into children's understanding and appreciation of art.* **2** N-SING Your **appreciation for** something that someone does for you is your gratitude for it. [also no det, oft with poss, N for n] ❑ *He expressed his appreciation for what he called Saudi Arabia's moderate and realistic oil policies.* **3** N-SING An **appreciation** of a situation or problem is an understanding of what it involves. [also no det, with supp, oft N of n] ❑ *They have a stronger appreciation of the importance of economic incentives.* **4** N-UNCOUNT **Appreciation** in the value of something is an increase in its value over a period of time. ❑ *You have to take capital appreciation of the property into account.*

1 단수명사 감상, 즐김 ❑ 아동들의 예술에 대한 이해와 감상 능력에 대한 조사 2 단수명사 감사 ❑ 그는, 자신이 칭하길, 사우디아라비아의 온건하고 현실적인 석유 정책에 대해 감사를 표명했다. 3 단수명사 이해 ❑ 그들은 경제적 유인의 중요성을 그들은 더 잘 이해하고 있다. 4 불가산명사 가치 상승 ❑ 부동산의 금전적 가치 상승도 감안을 해야 한다.

ap|pre|cia|tive /əprɪʃiətɪv, -ʃətɪv/ **1** ADJ An **appreciative** reaction or comment shows the enjoyment that you are getting from something. ❑ *There is a murmur of appreciative laughter.* **2** ADJ If you are **appreciative of** something, you are grateful for it. ❑ *We have been very appreciative of their support.*

1 형용사 즐감하는 ❑ 맞장구치는 웃음이 여기저기서 터져 나온다. 2 형용사 고마워하는 ❑ 우리는 그들의 도움을 매우 고맙게 생각해 왔다.

ap|pre|hen|sion /æprɪhenʃᵊn/ (apprehensions) N-VAR **Apprehension** is a feeling of fear that something bad may happen. [FORMAL] ❑ *It reflects real anger and apprehension about the future.*

가산명사 또는 불가산명사 불안 [격식체] ❑ 그것은 미래에 대한 진정한 분노와 불안을 반영한다.

ap|pre|hen|sive /æprɪhensɪv/ ADJ Someone who is **apprehensive** is afraid that something bad may happen. ❑ *People are still terribly apprehensive about the future.*

형용사 불안한 ❑ 사람들은 아직도 미래에 대해 매우 불안해하고 있다.

ap|pren|tice /əprentɪs/ (apprentices, apprenticing, apprenticed) **1** N-COUNT An **apprentice** is a young person who works for someone in order to learn their skill. ❑ *I started off as an apprentice and worked my way up.* **2** V-T If a young person **is apprenticed to** someone, they go to work for them in order to learn their skill. [usu passive] ❑ *I was apprenticed to a builder when I was fourteen.*

1 가산명사 도제 ❑ 나는 도제로 시작해서 내 노력으로 점차 지위가 올라갔다. 2 타동사 ∼의 도제가 되다 ❑ 나는 열네 살에 건축업자의 도제로 들어갔다.

ap|pren|tice|ship /əprentɪsʃɪp/ (apprenticeships) N-VAR Someone who has an **apprenticeship** works for a fixed period of time for a person who has a particular skill in order to learn the skill. **Apprenticeship** is the system of learning a skill like this. ❑ *After serving his apprenticeship as a toolmaker, he became a manager.*

가산명사 또는불가산명사 도제살이 ❑ 공구 제작 기사로서 도제살이를 마친 후 그는 지배인이 되었다.

ap|proach ◆◆◇ /əproʊtʃ/ (approaches, approaching, approached) **1** V-T/V-I When you **approach** something, you get closer to it. ❑ *He didn't approach the front door at once.* ❑ *When I approached, they grew silent.* • N-COUNT **Approach** is also a noun. ❑ *At their approach the little boy ran away and hid.* **2** N-COUNT An **approach to** a place is a road, path, or other route that leads to it. ❑ *The path serves as an approach to the boathouse.* **3** V-T If you **approach** someone **about** something, you speak to them about it for the first time, often making an offer or request. [no cont] ❑ *When Brown approached me about the job, my first reaction was of disbelief.* ❑ *He approached me to create and design the restaurant.* • N-COUNT **Approach** is also a noun. ❑ *There had already been approaches from buyers interested in the whole of the group.* **4** V-T When you **approach** a task, problem, or situation in a particular way, you deal with it or think about it in that way. ❑ *The Bank has approached the issue in a practical way.* **5** N-COUNT Your **approach to** a task, problem, or situation is the way you deal with it or think about it. ❑ *We will be exploring different approaches to gathering information.* **6** V-I As a future time or event **approaches**, it gradually gets nearer as time passes. ❑ *As autumn approached, the plants and colors in the garden changed.* • N-SING **Approach** is also a noun. ❑ *...the festive spirit that permeated the house with the approach of Christmas.* **7** V-T As you **approach** a future time or event, time passes so that you get gradually nearer to it. ❑ *There is a need for understanding and co-operation as we approach the 21st century.* **8** V-T If something **approaches** a particular level or state, it almost reaches that level or state. ❑ *Oil prices have approached their highest level for almost ten years.*

1 타동사/자동사 다가가다 ❑ 그는 정문에 바로 다가가지 않았다. ❑ 내가 다가가자 그들은 조용해졌다. • 가산명사 접근 ❑ 그들이 다가오자 어린 소년은 도망가서 숨었다. 2 가산명사 접근로 ❑ 그 길은 보트 창고로 통한다. 3 타동사 이야기를 꺼내다 ❑ 브라운이 그 일자리에 대해 나에게 이야기를 꺼냈을 때 나는 처음에는 믿을 수가 없었다. ❑ 그가 나에게 식당을 만들어 설계해 달라는 이야기를 꺼냈다. • 가산명사 접근 ❑ 그 그룹 전체에 관심을 보인 구매자들로부터 벌써 접촉이 있었었다. 4 타동사 접근하다 ❑ 은행이 사안에 현실적으로 접근해 왔다. 5 가산명사 접근법 ❑ 우리는 여러 정보 수집 방식을 모색 중이다. 6 자동사 다가오다 ❑ 가을이 다가오자 정원의 식물과 색깔들이 변했다. • 단수명사 다가옴 ❑ 크리스마스가 다가오자 집안에 넘쳐흘렀던 축제 분위기 7 타동사 다가가다 ❑ 우리는 21세기에 들어서는 지금 이해심과 협동심이 필요하다. 8 타동사 이르다 ❑ 유가가 근 10년 만에 최고조에 달했다.

A
B
C
D
E
F
G
H
I
J
K
L
M
N
O
P
Q
R
S
T
U
V
W
X
Y
Z

Thesaurus approach의 참조어

V.	close in, near; (ant.) go away, leave **1**
N.	attitude, method, technique **5**

Word Partnership approach의 연어

N.	approach **a problem** **4**
ADJ.	**different/new/novel** approach, **hands-on** approach **5**
V.	**adopt/take an** approach **5**
PREP.	approach **to something** **5**

ap|pro|pri|ate ◆◇◇ /əproupriɪt/ ADJ Something that is **appropriate** is suitable or acceptable for a particular situation. □ *It is appropriate that Irish names dominate the list.* □ *Dress neatly and attractively in an outfit appropriate to the job.* ● **ap|pro|pri|ate|ly** ADV □ *Dress appropriately and ask intelligent questions.*

형용사 적당한, 어울리는 □ 아일랜드계 이름들이 명단에서 다수를 차지하는 것은 당연하다. □ 직책에 어울리는 단정하고 매력적인 복장을 갖춰라. ● 어울리게 부사 □ 올바른 복장을 갖추고 똑똑한 질문을 해라.

Thesaurus appropriate의 참조어

ADJ.	acceptable, correct, fitting, relevant, right, suitable; (ant.) improper, inappropriate, incorrect, unacceptable

ap|prov|al ◆◇◇ /əpruvᵊl/ (**approvals**) **1** N-UNCOUNT If you win someone's **approval** for something that you ask for or suggest, they agree to it. □ *...efforts to win congressional approval for an aid package for Moscow.* □ *The chairman has also given his approval for an investigation into the case.* **2** N-VAR **Approval** is a formal or official statement that something is acceptable. □ *The testing and approval of new drugs will be speeded up.* **3** N-UNCOUNT If someone or something has your **approval**, you like and admire them. □ *His son had an obsessive drive to gain his father's approval.*

1 불가산명사 찬성, 승인 □ 모스크바 지원 패키지에 대한 국회 승인을 얻기 위한 노력 □ 회장 또한 사건에 대한 조사를 승인했다. **2** 가산명사 또는 불가산명사 허가 □ 신약의 시험 사용과 허가 속도가 빨라질 것이다. **3** 불가산명사 인정 □ 그 아들은 아버지의 인정을 받고 싶어 하는 강박적인 욕구를 가지고 있었다.

Word Partnership approval의 연어

V.	**gain** approval, **meet with** approval, **seek** approval **1**
ADJ.	**final** approval, **subject to** approval **1** **2**
N.	approval **rating** **3**
	approval **process** **2**

ap|prove ◆◆◇ /əpruv/ (**approves, approving, approved**) **1** V-I If you **approve** of an action, event, or suggestion, you like it or are pleased about it. [oft with brd-neg] □ *Not everyone approves of the festival.* **2** V-I If you **approve of** someone or something, you like and admire them. [oft with brd-neg] □ *You've never approved of Henry, have you?* **3** V-T If someone in a position of authority **approves** a plan or idea, they formally agree to it and say that it can happen. □ *The Russian Parliament has approved a program of radical economic reforms.* **4** →see also **approved**

1 자동사 찬성하다 □ 모든 사람이 그 축제에 찬성하는 것은 아니다. **2** 자동사 인정하다 □ 너는 한번도 헨리를 인정한 적이 없었잖아? **3** 타동사 승인하다 □ 러시아 의회는 근본적인 경제 개혁 프로그램을 승인했다.

Thesaurus approve의 참조어

V.	agree to, authorize, permit; (ant.) disapprove, reject **3**

Word Partnership approve의 연어

ADJ.	**likely** to approve **1** **3**
PREP.	approve **of something/someone** **2**
N.	approve **a plan** **3**

ap|proved /əpruvd/ ADJ An **approved** method or course of action is officially accepted as appropriate in a particular situation. □ *The approved method of cleaning is industrial sand-blasting.* □ *Approved methods might include destruction of nests and eggs, and the trapping and destruction of geese.*

형용사 인정받은 □ 대개 사용되는 세척 방식은 산업 샌드블라스팅이다. □ 인가된 방식에는 둥지와 알의 파괴, 거위의 포획 및 도살 등이 포함되기도 한다.

Word Link proxim ≈ near : approximate, approximation, proximity

ap|proxi|mate (**approximates, approximating, approximated**)

The adjective is pronounced /əprɒksɪmət/. The verb is pronounced /əprɒksɪmeɪt/.

형용사는 /əprɒksɪmət/으로 발음되고, 동사는 /əprɒksɪmeɪt/으로 발음된다.

1 ADJ An **approximate** number, time, or position is close to the correct number, time, or position, but is not exact. □ *The approximate cost varies from around £150 to £250.* ● **ap|proxi|mate|ly** ADV [ADV num] □ *Approximately $150 million is to be spent on improvements.* **2** ADJ An idea or description that is **approximate** is not intended to be precise or accurate, but to give some indication of what something is like. □ *They did not have even an approximate idea what the Germans really wanted.* **3** V-T If something **approximates to** something else, it is similar to it but is not exactly the same. □ *The mixture described below will approximate it, but is not exactly the same.*

1 형용사 대략적인 □ 대략적인 가격은 150에서 250파운드 사이이다. ● 대략적으로 부사 □ 개선에 약 1.5억 달러가 사용될 것이다. **2** 형용사 개략적인 □ 그들은 독일인들이 진정 무엇을 원하는지에 대해 개략적인 개념조차 없었다. **3** 타동사 비슷하다 □ 아래에 설명된 혼합물은 그것과 비슷하기는 하겠지만 완전히 동일하지는 않다.

ap|proxi|ma|tion /əprɒksɪmeɪʃᵊn/ (**approximations**) **1** N-COUNT An **approximation** is a fact, object, or description which is similar to something else, but which is not exactly the same. □ *That is a fair approximation of the way in which the next boss is being chosen.* **2** N-COUNT An **approximation** is a number, calculation, or position that is close to a correct number, time, or position, but is not exact. □ *Clearly that's an approximation, but my guess is there'll be a reasonable balance.* □ *As we know, 365.25 is only an approximation.*

1 가산명사 근사 □ 다음 상관이 어떻게 선정되는지에 대해 개략적으로 말하자면 그렇다. **2** 가산명사 근삿값 □ 분명히 그것은 근사값이긴 하지만 내 추측에는 합당한 균형치가 있을 것 같다. □ 알다시피 365.25는 근삿값에 불과하다.

Apr. Apr. is a written abbreviation for **April**.

4월

apri|cot /ˈeɪprɪkɒt/ (apricots) **1** N-VAR An **apricot** is a small, soft, round fruit with yellowish-orange flesh and a stone inside. □ *...12 oz apricots, halved and stoned.* **2** COLOR **Apricot** is used to describe things that are yellowish-orange in color. □ *The bridesmaids wore apricot and white organza.* □ *Rose had chosen to have all her shops decorated in apricot and green.*

1 가산명사 또는 불가산명사 살구 □ 이등분해서 씨를 제거한 살구 12온스 **2** 색채어 살구색의 □ 신부 들러리들은 살구색과 흰색이 섞인 오간자 드레스를 입었다. □ 로우즈는 자신의 모든 가게를 살구색과 녹색으로 장식하기로 결정했다.

April ♦♦♦ /ˈeɪprɪl/ (Aprils) N-VAR **April** is the fourth month of the year in the Western calendar. □ *The changes will be introduced in April.*

가산명사 또는 불가산명사 4월 □ 변동 사항들은 4월부터 적용된다.

On April 1 people in Britain and America play all sorts of tricks and practical jokes on each other. People who fall for these tricks are called **April Fools**. Sometimes even the media join in the fun, inventing news stories and publishing spoof reports, for example, about spaghetti growing on trees in Italy.

4월 1일에 영미인들은 서로 온갖 짓궂은 장난을 한다. 이 장난에 걸려든 사람은 April Fools(만우절 바보)라고 불린다. 때로는 신문이나 방송도 이 장난에 가세해서 거짓 뉴스나 장난 기사를 내보내기도 하는데, 예를 들면, 이탈리아에서는 나무에 열리는 스파게티에 대한 소식 같은 것이 있었다.

apron /ˈeɪprən/ (aprons) N-COUNT An **apron** is a piece of clothing that you put on over the front of your normal clothes and tie round your waist, especially when you are cooking, in order to prevent your clothes from getting dirty.

가산명사 앞치마

apt /æpt/ ADJ An **apt** remark, description, or choice is especially suitable. □ *The words of this report are as apt today as in 1929.* ● **apt|ly** ADV □ *...the beach in the aptly named town of Oceanside.*

형용사 적절한 □ 이 보고서의 내용은 1929년 당시나 지금이나 유효하다. ● 적절하게 부사 □ 오션사이드라는 적절한 이름을 가진 마을의 해변

apti|tude /ˈæptɪtud, BRIT ˈæptɪtjuːd/ (aptitudes) N-VAR Someone's **aptitude for** a particular kind of work or activity is their ability to learn it quickly and to do it well. □ *He drifted into publishing and discovered an aptitude for working with accounts.*

가산명사 또는 불가산명사 적성 □ 그는 결국 출판업으로 흘러들어 자신에게 회계에 대한 재능이 있다는 것을 발견했다.

aquat|ic /əˈkwætɪk/ **1** ADJ An **aquatic** animal or plant lives or grows on or in water. □ *The pond is quite small but can support many aquatic plants and fish.* **2** ADJ **Aquatic** means relating to water. □ *...our aquatic resources.*

1 형용사 물 속에 사는 □ 연못은 꽤 작지만 많은 수생 식물과 물고기의 서식처가 된다. **2** 형용사 물의 □ 우리의 수자원

Arab /ˈærəb/ (Arabs) **1** N-COUNT **Arabs** are people who speak Arabic and who come from the Middle East and parts of North Africa. **2** ADJ **Arab** means belonging or relating to Arabs or to their countries or customs. □ *On the surface, it appears little has changed in the Arab world.*

1 가산명사 아랍인 **2** 형용사 아랍의 □ 표면적으로는 아랍 세계에서 변한 것이 별로 없는 것 같다.

ar|able /ˈærəbʲl/ ADJ **Arable** farming involves growing crops such as wheat and barley rather than keeping animals or growing fruit and vegetables. **Arable** land is land that is used for arable farming. □ *...arable farmers.*

형용사 (밀이나 보리 등을) 경작하는; 경작할 수 있는 □ 곡물을 기르는 농부들

ar|bi|trage /ˈɑrbɪtrɑʒ/ N-UNCOUNT In finance, **arbitrage** is the activity of buying shares or currency in one financial market and selling it at a profit in another. [BUSINESS] □ *Astute Singaporeans quickly spotted an arbitrage opportunity.*

불가산명사 차액 거래 [경제] □ 눈치 빠른 싱가포르 인들은 재빨리 차액 거래할 수 있는 기회를 발견했다.

ar|bi|trary /ˈɑrbɪtreri, BRIT ˈɑːbɪtri/ ADJ If you describe an action, rule, or decision as **arbitrary**, you think that it is not based on any principle, plan, or system. It often seems unfair because of this. [DISAPPROVAL] □ *Arbitrary arrests and detention without trial were common.* ● **ar|bi|trari|ly** /ˈɑrbɪtreərɪli/ ADV [ADV with v] □ *The victims were not chosen arbitrarily.*

형용사 임의의, 멋대로의 [탐탁찮음] □ 재판 없이 행해지는 임의의 체포와 구류가 자주 있었다. ● 임의로 부사 □ 희생자들은 임의로 선정되지 않았다.

ar|bi|trate /ˈɑrbɪtreɪt/ (arbitrates, arbitrating, arbitrated) V-I When someone in authority **arbitrates between** two people or groups who are in dispute, they consider all the facts and make an official decision about who is right. □ *He arbitrates between investors and members of the association.*

자동사 중재하다 □ 그는 협회의 투자자와 회원들 사이를 중재한다.

ar|bi|tra|tion /ˈɑrbɪtreɪʃʲn/ N-UNCOUNT **Arbitration** is the judging of a dispute between people or groups by someone who is not involved. □ *The matter is likely to go to arbitration.*

불가산명사 중재 □ 그 일은 중재 재판에 회부될 것 같다.

arc /ɑrk/ (arcs) **1** N-COUNT An **arc** is a smoothly curving line or movement. □ *His 71 offices are spread through the Thames Valley and in an arc around north London.* **2** N-COUNT In geometry, an **arc** is a part of the line that forms the outside of a circle. [TECHNICAL]

1 가산명사 호 □ 그가 보유한 사무실 71개는 템즈 유역에 분포해 있으며 런던 북부에 호의 모양을 띠고 퍼져 있다. **2** 가산명사 원호 [과학 기술]

ar|cade /ɑrˈkeɪd/ (arcades) N-COUNT An **arcade** is a covered passage where there are stores or market stalls. □ *...a shopping arcade.*

가산명사 지붕이 있는 길거리 상가, 아케이드 □ 쇼핑 아케이드

arch /ɑrtʃ/ (arches, arching, arched) **1** N-COUNT An **arch** is a structure that is curved at the top and is supported on either side by a pillar, post, or wall. □ *When she passed under the arch leading out of the park, Honoria whooped with delight.* **2** N-COUNT An **arch** is a curved line or movement. □ *...the arch of the fishing rods.* **3** N-COUNT The **arch** of your foot is the curved section at the bottom in the middle. □ *"Good girl," said Francis, winding the bandages around the arch of her foot.* **4** V-T If you **arch** a part of your body such as your back or if it **arches**, you bend it so that it forms a curve. □ *Don't arch your back, keep your spine straight.* **5** →see also **arched**

→see **architecture, foot**

1 가산명사 아치 □ 공원 밖으로 통하는 아치 아래를 지날 때 오노리아는 즐거움에 비명을 질렀다. **2** 가산명사 만곡 □ 낚싯대들의 만곡 **3** 가산명사 발바닥의 움푹 들어간 부분 □ "착하지."라며 프랜시스는 소녀의 발바닥에 붕대를 감았다. **4** 타동사 -을 둥글게 굽히다 □ 등을 굽히지 말고 척추를 꼿꼿하게 유지해라.

arch- /ɑrtʃ-/ COMB in N-COUNT **Arch-** combines with nouns referring to people to form new nouns that refer to people who are extreme examples of something. For example, your **archrival** is the rival you most want to beat. □ *Neither he nor his archrival, Giuseppe De Rita, won.*

복합형-가산명사 주요한; 최대 라이벌 □ 그나 그의 최대 라이벌인 주세페 드 리타는 이기지 못했다.

ar|chae|ol|ogy /ˌɑrkiˈɒlədʒi/ also **archeology** N-UNCOUNT **Archaeology** is the study of the societies and peoples of the past by examining the remains of their buildings, tools, and other objects. ● **ar|chaeo|logi|cal** /ˌɑrkiəˈlɒdʒɪkʲl/ ADJ [ADJ n] □ *...one of the region's most important archaeological sites.* ● **ar|chae|ol|ogist** /ˌɑrkiˈɒlədʒɪst/ (archaeologists) N-COUNT □ *The archaeologists found a house built around 300 BC, with a basement and attic.*

불가산명사 고고학 □ 고고학적인 형용사 □ 지역에서 고고학적으로 가장 중요한 유적지 중 하나 □ 고고학자 가산명사 □ 고고학자들은 지하실과 다락이 있는 기원전 300년 경 지어진 집을 발견했다.

ar|cha|ic /ɑrˈkeɪɪk/ ADJ **Archaic** means extremely old or extremely old-fashioned. □ *...archaic laws that are very seldom used.*

형용사 고풍의 □ 거의 사용되지 않는 옛날 법

arch|bishop /ˌɑrtʃˈbɪʃəp/ (archbishops) N-COUNT; N-TITLE In the Roman Catholic, Orthodox, and Anglican Churches, an **archbishop** is a bishop of the highest rank, who is in charge of all the bishops and priests in a particular country or region. □ *...the Archbishop of Canterbury.*

가산명사; 경칭명사 대주교 □ 캔터베리 대주교

a b c d e f g h i j k l m n o p q r s t u v w x y z

Word Web architecture

The Colosseum (sometimes spelled Coliseum) in Rome is a great **architectural** triumph of the ancient world. This amphitheater, built in the first century BC, could hold 50,000 spectators. It was used for animal fights, human executions, and staged combat. The elliptical shape allowed spectators to be closer to the action. It also prevented participants from hiding in the corners. The **arches** are an important part of the **building**. They are an example of a Roman improvement to the simple arch. Each arch is supported by a keystone in the top center. The **design** of the Colosseum has influenced the design of thousands of other public venues. Many modern day sports stadiums are the same shape.

arched /ɑrtʃt/ ■ ADJ An **arched** roof, window, or doorway is curved at the top. ❏ *From the television room an arched doorway leads in to the hall.* ■ ADJ An **arched** bridge has arches as part of its structure. ❏ *...a fortified arched bridge spanning the River Severn.*

■ 형용사 궁형의, 아치형의 ❏ 텔레비전이 있는 방에서 아치형 문간을 나가면 복도로 통한다. ■ 형용사 아치가 달린 ❏ 세번 강을 가로지르는 강화된 아치 다리

ar|che|ol|ogy /ɑrkiɒlədʒi/ →see **archaeology**

ar|che|typ|al /ɑrkɪtaɪpᵊl/ ADJ Someone or something that is **archetypal** has all the most important characteristics of a particular kind of person or thing and is a perfect example of it. [FORMAL] ❏ *Cricket is the archetypal English game, and probably the most arcane recreation yet invented.* →see **myth**

형용사 원형의 [격식체] ❏ 그리켓은 건청적인 영국 게임이며 어쩌면 인간이 발명한 가장 난해한 여가 활동일 수도 있다.

ar|che|type /ɑrkɪtaɪp/ (**archetypes**) N-COUNT An **archetype** is something that is considered to be a perfect or typical example of a particular kind of person or thing, because it has all their most important characteristics. [FORMAL] ❏ *He came to this country 20 years ago and is the archetype of the successful Asian businessman.*

가산명사 원형 [격식체] ❏ 그는 이 나라에서 20년 전에 왔고 성공한 아시아계 사업가의 표본이다.

ar|chi|tect /ɑrkɪtɛkt/ (**architects**) ■ N-COUNT An **architect** is a person who designs buildings. ■ N-COUNT You can use **architect** to refer to a person who plans large projects such as landscaping or rail systems. ❏ *...Paul Andreu, chief architect of French railways.*

■ 가산명사 건축가 ■ 가산명사 설계자 ❏ 프랑스 철도의 최고 설계자, 폴 앙드류

ar|chi|tec|tur|al /ɑrkɪtɛktʃərəl/ ADJ **Architectural** means relating to the design and construction of buildings. ❏ *...Tibet's architectural heritage.*
● **ar|chi|tec|tur|al|ly** ADV ❏ *The old city center is architecturally rich.* →see **architecture**

형용사 건축의 ❏ 티베트의 건축 유산 ● 건축과 관련해서 부사 ❏ 구 도시 중심은 건축물이 풍부하다.

ar|chi|tec|ture /ɑrkɪtɛktʃər/ (**architectures**) ■ N-UNCOUNT **Architecture** is the art of planning, designing, and constructing buildings. ❏ *He studied classical architecture and design in Rome.* ■ N-UNCOUNT The **architecture** of a building is the style in which it is designed and constructed. ❏ *...modern architecture.* →see Word Web: **architecture**

■ 불가산명사 건축술 ❏ 그는 로마에서 고전 건축술과 디자인을 공부했다. ■ 불가산명사 건축 양식 ❏ 현대 건축 양식

ar|chive /ɑrkaɪv/ (**archives**) ■ N-COUNT **Archives** are a collection of documents and records that contain historical information. You can also use **archives** to refer to the place where archives are stored. ❏ *...the archives of the Imperial War Museum.* [ADJ n] ■ ADJ **Archive** material is information that comes from archives. ❏ *...archive material.*

■ 가산명사 기록 문서; 기록물 보관소 ❏ 대영제국 전쟁 박물관의 역사적 문서들 ■ 형용사 고문서에 관한 ❏ 고문서 자료

arc|tic /ɑrktɪk/ ■ N-PROPER The **Arctic** is the area of the world around the North Pole. It is extremely cold and there is very little light in winter and very little darkness in summer. ❏ *...winter in the Arctic.* ■ ADJ If you describe a place or the weather as **arctic**, you are emphasizing that it is extremely cold. [INFORMAL, EMPHASIS] ❏ *The bathroom, with its spartan pre-war facilities, is positively arctic.* →see Picture Dictionary: **arctic**

■ 고유명사 북극 ❏ 북극의 겨울 ■ 형용사 매우 추운, 한대 지역 같은 [비격식체, 강조] ❏ 매우 검소하며 전쟁 이전 시설 그대로인 욕실은 한대 지역처럼 춥다.

ar|dent /ɑrdᵊnt/ ADJ **Ardent** is used to describe someone who has extremely strong feelings about something or someone. ❏ *He's been one of the most ardent supporters of the administration's policy.*

형용사 열렬한 ❏ 그는 지금까지 정부 정책의 가장 열렬한 지지자 중 1명이었다.

ar|du|ous /ɑrdʒuəs/ ADJ Something that is **arduous** is difficult and tiring, and involves a lot of effort. ❏ *...a long, hot and arduous journey.*

형용사 고된 ❏ 길고 덥고 고된 여행

are /ər, STRONG ɑr/ **Are** is the plural and the second person singular of the present tense of the verb **be**. **Are** is often shortened to **-'re** after pronouns in spoken English.

be 동사의 2인칭 단수 및 전 인칭 복수 현재형

area ♦♦♦ /ɛəriə/ (**areas**) ■ N-COUNT An **area** is a particular part of a town, a country, a region, or the world. ❏ *...the large number of community groups in the area.* ❏ *60 years ago half the French population still lived in rural areas.* ■ N-COUNT Your **area** is the part of a town, country, or region where you live. An organization's **area** is the part of a town, country, or region that it is responsible for. ❏ *Local authorities have been responsible for the running of schools in their areas.* ■ N-COUNT A particular **area** is a piece of land or part of a building that is used for a particular activity. ❏ *...a picnic area.* ■ N-COUNT An **area** is a particular place on a surface or object, for example on your body. ❏ *You will notice that your baby has*

■ 가산명사 지역 ❏ 그 지역의 많은 지역 사회 단체 ❏ 60년 전에는 프랑스 인구의 절반이 여전히 농촌 지역에 살고 있었다. ■ 가산명사 구장; 담당 구역 ❏ 지방 당국이 자신들 지역의 학교 운영에 대해 책임을 져 왔다. ■ 가산명사 구역 ❏ 소풍 구역 ■ 가산명사 부분 ❏ 당신 아기의 머리 윗부분에 부드러운 곳이 두 군데 있다는 것을 보실 겁니다. ■ 가산명사 면적 ❏ 섬들의 총 면적은 625.6 평방킬로미터이다. ■ 가산명사 분야 ❏ 노년

Picture Dictionary — Arctic

snow · polar bear · arctic fox · ice · seal · iceberg · whale · walrus · caribou · lichen · tundra

two soft areas on the top of his head. **5** N-VAR The **area** of a surface such as a piece of land is the amount of flat space or ground that it covers, measured in square units. ❏ *The islands cover a total area of 625.6 square kilometers.* **6** N-COUNT You can use **area** to refer to a particular subject or topic, or to a particular part of a larger, more general situation or activity. ❏ *...the politically sensitive area of old age pensions.* **7** →see also **gray area**
→see Picture Dictionary: **area**

연금이라는 정치적으로 민감한 분야

Thesaurus
*area*의 참조어

N.	district, place, region, vicinity **1** **2**

Word Partnership
*area*의 연어

ADJ.	**metropolitan** area, **rural/suburban/urban** area, **surrounding** area **1**
	local area, **remote** area **2**
	residential area, **restricted** area **3**
N.	**downtown** area **1** **2**
	tourist area **3**
PREP.	**throughout the** area **1** **2**
	area **of** expertise **6**

area code (**area codes**) N-COUNT The **area code** for a particular city or region is the series of numbers that you have to dial before someone's personal number if you are making a telephone call to that place from a different area. [mainly AM; BRIT **dialling code**] ❏ *The area code for western Pennsylvania is 412.*

가산명사 지역 번호 [주로 미국영어; 영국영어 dialling code] ❏ 서부 펜실베이니아의 지역번호는 412이다.

arena /əɾiːnə/ (**arenas**) **1** N-COUNT An **arena** is a place where sports, entertainments, and other public events take place. It has seats around it where people sit and watch. ❏ *...the largest indoor sports arena in the world.* **2** N-COUNT You can refer to a field of activity, especially one where there is a lot of conflict or action, as an **arena** of a particular kind. ❏ *He made it clear he had no intention of withdrawing from the political arena.*

1 가산명사 경기장 ❏ 세계에서 가장 큰 실내 경기장 **2** 가산명사 판 ❏ 그는 정치판에서 물러설 의사가 없다는 것을 분명히 했다.

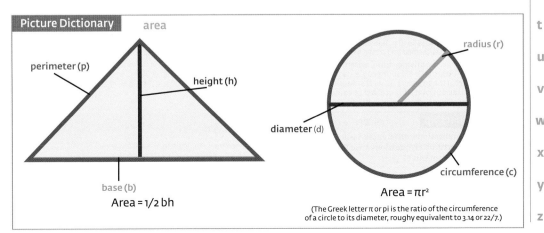

Picture Dictionary — area

perimeter (p) · height (h) · base (b)

Area = 1/2 bh

radius (r) · diameter (d) · circumference (c)

Area = πr²

(The Greek letter π or pi is the ratio of the circumference of a circle to its diameter, roughly equivalent to 3.14 or 22/7.)

A

aren't ♦♦◇ /ɑrnt, ɑrənt, BRIT ɑːˈnt/ **1** **Aren't** is the usual spoken form of "are not." **2** **Aren't** is the form of "am not" that is used in questions or tags in spoken English.

1 'are not'의 축약형 **2** 부가 의문문에서 'am not' 대신 사용되는 형태

B

ar|gu|ably /ɑrgyuəbli/ ADV You can use **arguably** when you are stating your opinion or belief, as a way of giving more authority to it. ❏ They are arguably the most important band since The Rolling Stones.

부사 거의 틀림없이 ❏ 그들은 거의 틀림없이 롤링 스톤스 이후 가장 중요한 밴드이다.

C

D

E

F

ar|gue ♦♦◇ /ɑrgyu/ (argues, arguing, argued) **1** V-RECIP If one person **argues with** another, they speak angrily to each other about something that they disagree about. You can also say that two people **argue**. ❏ The committee is concerned about players' behavior, especially arguing with referees. **2** V-I If you tell someone not to **argue with** you, you want them to do or believe what you say without protest or disagreement. [usu imper with neg] ❏ Don't argue with me. **3** V-RECIP If you **argue with** someone **about** something, you discuss it with them, with each of you giving your different opinions. ❏ He was arguing with the King about the need to maintain the cavalry at full strength. ❏ They are arguing over foreign policy. **4** V-T If you **argue that** something is true, you state it and give the reasons why you think it is true. ❏ His lawyers are arguing that he is unfit to stand trial. **5** V-T/V-I If you **argue for** something, you say why you agree with it, in order to persuade people that it is right. If you **argue against** something, you say why you disagree with it, in order to persuade people that it is wrong. ❏ The report argues against tax increases.

1 상호동사 다투다 ❏ 위원회는 선수들의 행동, 특히 심판들과 다투는 것을 우려한다. **2** 자동사 논쟁하다 ❏ 이견을 달지 마. **3** 상호동사 논쟁하다 ❏ 그는 기병대를 전원 유지하는 것의 필요성에 대해 왕과 논쟁하고 있었다. ❏ 그들은 외교 정책에 대해 논쟁하고 있다. **4** 타동사 주장하다 ❏ 그의 변호사들은 그가 재판을 받을 수 있는 여건이 안 된다고 주장하고 있다. **5** 타동사/자동사 찬성 의견을 말하다; 반대 의견을 말하다 ❏ 그 보고서는 세금 인상을 반대한다.

G

Thesaurus argue의 참조어

v.	bicker, disagree, fight, quarrel; (ant.) agree **1**
	debate, discuss, dispute **3** **5**
	allege, assert, claim **4**

H

Word Partnership argue의 연어

PREP.	argue with *someone/something* **1**-**3**
	argue about/over *something* **1** **2**
	argue against/for *something* **5**
N.	argue a **case**, **critics** argue, **officials** argue, **opponents/supporters** argue **5**

I

J

K

L

M

N

ar|gu|ment ♦♦◇ /ɑrgyəmənt/ (arguments) **1** N-VAR An **argument** is a statement or set of statements that you use in order to try to convince people that your opinion about something is correct. ❏ There's a strong argument for lowering the price. ❏ The doctors have set out their arguments against the proposals. **2** N-VAR An **argument** is a discussion or debate in which a number of people put forward different or opposing opinions. ❏ The incident has triggered fresh arguments about the role of the extreme right in France. **3** N-COUNT An **argument** is a conversation in which people disagree with each other angrily or noisily. ❏ Anny described how she got into an argument with one of the marchers. **4** N-UNCOUNT If you accept something without **argument**, you do not question it or disagree with it. ❏ He complied without argument.

1 가산명사 또는 불가산명사 주장 ❏ 가격을 인하하자는 강력한 주장이 있다. ❏ 의사들은 그 제안에 대해 반대 의견을 제출했다. **2** 가산명사 또는 불가산명사 논쟁 ❏ 그 사건은 프랑스 내 극우의 역할에 대한 새로운 논쟁을 부추겼다. **3** 가산명사 말다툼 ❏ 애니는 어떻게 자신이 시위자 중 한 명과 다투게 되었는지 설명했다. **4** 불가산명사 반대 ❏ 그는 순순히 응했다.

O

P

Q

Do not confuse **argument** and **dispute**. An **argument** is a disagreement between people who may or may not know each other. ❏ She had an argument with her father about practicing the piano... Travis got in an argument with another motorist. A **dispute** is a serious argument that can last for a long time. **Disputes** generally occur between organizations, political parties, or countries. ❏ ...a 10-year-old dispute over crude oil. Note that **dispute** can also be a verb. ❏ Opponents dispute the value of Japan's research.

argument와 dispute를 혼동하지 않도록 하라. argument는 서로 알 수도 있고 알지 못할 수도 있는 사람들 사이에 생기는 의견 차이이다. ❏ 그녀는 피아노 연습 문제를 두고 아버지와 다퉜다... 트래비스는 다른 운전자와 언쟁을 벌이게 되었다. dispute는 오랫동안 지속될 수도 있는 심각한 의견 충돌이다. dispute는 일반적으로 조직체간, 정당간, 국가간에서 발생한다. ❏ ...원유를 두고 벌인 10년간의 분쟁. dispute는 동사로도 쓸 수 있음을 유의하라. ❏ 반대자들은 일본이 한 연구의 가치를 논박하고 있다.

R

Word Partnership argument의 연어

ADJ.	persuasive argument **1**
	heated argument **3**
V.	support an argument **1**
	get into an argument, have an argument **3**
PREP.	argument against/for **1**
	without argument **4**

S

T

arid /ærɪd/ ADJ Arid land is so dry that very few plants can grow on it. ❏ ...new strains of crops that can withstand arid conditions.

형용사 척박한 ❏ 척박한 조건을 견뎌낼 수 있는 새로운 품종의 농작물

U

arise ♦♦◇ /əraɪz/ (arises, arising, arose, arisen) /ərɪzən/ **1** V-I If a situation or problem **arises**, it begins to exist or people start to become aware of it. ❏ ...if a problem arises later in the pregnancy. **2** V-I If something **arises from** a particular situation, or **arises out of** it, it is created or caused by the situation. ❏ This serenity arose in part from Rachel's religious beliefs.

1 자동사 일어나다 ❏ 만약 임신 후기에 문제가 발생하면 **2** 자동사 기인하다 ❏ 이러한 평온함은 부분적으로 레이첼의 종교적 믿음에 기인했다.

V

W

Word Partnership arise의 연어

| N. | complications/differences/issues/problems/opportunities/questions arise **1** **2** |
| PREP. | arise from/out of **1** **2** |

X

Word Link cracy ≈ rule by : aristocracy, democracy, bureaucracy

Y

aris|toc|ra|cy /ærɪstɒkrəsi/ (aristocracies) N-COUNT-COLL The **aristocracy** is a class of people in some countries who have a high social rank and special titles. ❏ ...a member of the aristocracy.

가산명사-집합 귀족 계급 ❏ 귀족 계급의 한 구성원

Z

Word Link   crat ≈ power : aristo*crat*, bureau*crat*, demo*crat*

a**ris**|to|**crat** /ǽrɪstəkræt, ərɪst-/ (**aristocrats**) N-COUNT An **aristocrat** is someone whose family has a high social rank, especially someone who has a title. ❏ ...*wealthy aristocrats such as Prince Charles.*

가산명사 귀족 ❏ 찰스 왕자와 같은 부유한 귀족

a**ris**|to|**crat**|ic /ǽrɪstəkrǽtɪk/ ADJ **Aristocratic** means belonging to or typical of the aristocracy. ❏ ...*a wealthy, aristocratic family.*

형용사 귀족적인 ❏ 부유하고 귀족적인 가족

a**rith**|me|tic /ərɪ́θmɪtɪk/ ■ N-UNCOUNT **Arithmetic** is the part of mathematics that is concerned with the addition, subtraction, multiplication, and division of numbers. ❏ ...*teaching the basics of reading, writing and arithmetic.* ② N-UNCOUNT You can use **arithmetic** to refer to the process of doing a particular sum or calculation. ❏ *4,000 women put in ten rupees each, which if my arithmetic is right adds up to 40,000 rupees.* ③ N-UNCOUNT If you refer to **the arithmetic** of a situation, you are concerned with those aspects of it that can be expressed in numbers, and how they affect the situation. ❏ *The budgetary arithmetic for 1993 suggests that government borrowing is set to surge.* →see **mathematics**

■ 불가산명사 산수 ❏ 읽기, 쓰기, 산수의 기초를 가르치기 ② 불가산명사 계산 ❏ 4천 명의 여자가 10루피씩 넣었으니 내 계산이 맞다면 합쳐서 40,000루피이다. ③ 불가산명사 계량적인 면 ❏ 1993년의 예산을 수적으로 따진다면 정부 차입이 곧 급증하리라는 예상이 나온다.

arm

① PART OF YOUR BODY OR OF SOMETHING ELSE
② WEAPONS

① **arm** ♦♦♦ /ɑ́rm/ (**arms**) ■ N-COUNT Your **arms** are the two long parts of your body that are attached to your shoulders and that have your hands at the end. ❏ *She stretched her arms out.* ② N-COUNT The **arm** of a piece of clothing is the part of it that covers your arm. ❏ ...*coats that were short in the arms.* ③ N-COUNT The **arm** of a chair is the part on which you rest your arm when you are sitting down. ❏ *Seaton gripped the arms of the chair.* ④ N-COUNT An **arm of** an object is a long thin part of it that sticks out from the main part. ❏ ...*the lever arm of the machine.* ⑤ N-COUNT An **arm** of land or water is a long thin area of it that is joined to a broader area. ❏ *At the end of the other arm of Cardigan Bay is Bardsey Island.* ⑥ N-COUNT An **arm** of an organization is a section of it that operates in a particular country or that deals with a particular activity. ❏ *Millicom Holdings is the British arm of an American company.* ⑦ PHRASE If two people are walking **arm in arm**, they are walking together with their arms linked. ❏ *He walked from the court arm in arm with his wife.* ⑧ PHRASE If you hold something **at arm's length**, you hold it away from your body with your arm straight. ❏ *He struck a match, and held it at arm's length.* ⑨ PHRASE If you **keep** someone **at arm's length**, you avoid becoming too friendly or involved with them. ❏ *She had always kept the family at arm's length.* ⑩ PHRASE If you welcome some action or change **with open arms**, you are very pleased about it. If you welcome a person **with open arms**, you are very pleased about their arrival. [APPROVAL] ❏ *They would no doubt welcome the action with open arms.* ⑪ PHRASE If you **twist** someone's **arm**, you persuade them to do something. [INFORMAL] ❏ *She had twisted his arm to get him to invite her.* →see **body**

■ 가산명사 팔 ❏ 그녀는 두 팔을 뻗었다. ② 가산명사 소매 ❏ 소매가 짧은 상의 ③ 가산명사 팔걸이 ❏ 시튼은 의자의 팔걸이를 부여잡았다. ④ 가산명사 팔과 같은 부분 ❏ 기계의 레버 ⑤ 가산명사 줄기처럼 긴게 뻗어 나온 땅덩이나 물 ❏ 카디건 만의 다른 줄기 끝에는 바지 섬이 있다. ⑥ 가산명사 지부 ❏ 밀리콤 홀딩스는 미국 회사의 영국 지부이다. ⑦ 구 팔짱을 끼고 ❏ 그는 아내와 팔짱을 끼고 법정에서 걸어 나왔다. ⑧ 구 팔을 쭉 뻗어 ❏ 그는 성냥에 불을 붙이고 그것을 팔을 쭉 뻗어 들었다. ⑨ 구 멀리하다 ❏ 그녀는 가족을 항상 멀리했었다. ⑩ 구 쌍수를 들고 [마음에 들어] ❏ 그들은 틀림없이 그 행동을 쌍수를 들고 환영할 것이다. ⑪ 구 쥐어짜다 [비격식체] ❏ 그녀는 자신을 초대하도록 그를 쥐어짜었다.

② **arm** ♦♦♦ /ɑ́rm/ (**arms, arming, armed**) ■ N-PLURAL **Arms** are weapons, especially bombs and guns. [FORMAL] ❏ *The IRA had extensive supplies of arms.* ② V-T If someone **arms** a weapon, you provide them with a weapon. ❏ *She'd been so terrified that she had armed herself with a loaded rifle.* ③ V-T If you **arm** someone **with** something that will be useful in a particular situation, you provide them with it. ❏ *She thought that if she armed herself with all the knowledge she could gather she could handle anything.* ④ →see also **armed** ⑤ PHRASE A person's right to **bear arms** is their right to own and use guns, as a means of defense. ❏ ...*a country where the right to bear arms is enshrined in the constitution.* ⑥ PHRASE If one group or country **takes up arms against** another, they prepare to attack and fight them. ❏ *They threatened to take up arms against the government if their demands were not met.* ⑦ PHRASE If people are **up in arms about** something, they are very angry about it and are protesting strongly against it. ❏ *Environmental groups are up in arms about plans to sink an oil well close to Hadrian's Wall.* →see **war**

■ 복수명사 무기 [격식체] ❏ 아일랜드 공화국 군은 폭넓은 무기를 보유하고 있었다. ② 타동사 무장시키다 ❏ 그녀는 너무나 두려운 나머지 장전된 소총으로 무장해 왔었다. ③ 타동사 제공하다 ❏ 그녀는 만약 모을 수 있는 모든 지식으로 자신을 무장한다면 무엇이든 할 수 있으리라 생각했다. ④ ⑤ 구 무기를 소유하다 ❏ 무기를 소유할 수 있는 권리가 헌법에 보장된 국가 ⑥ 구 무기를 들다 ❏ 그들은 만약 자신들의 요구 사항을 들어주지 않으면 정부에 무기를 들고 투쟁할 것이라고 협박했다. ⑦ 구 분개하여 시위하는 ❏ 환경 단체들은 하드리아누스 방벽 근처에 유전을 뚫는 계획에 대해 분개하여 시위하고 있다.

Word Partnership   *arms*의 연어

PREP.	arms **around** ① ■	
V.	arms **crossed/folded**, **hold/take in** *your* arms, **join/link** arms ① ■	
ADJ.	**open/outstretched** arms ① ■	
V.	**bear** arms ② ■	
N.	arms **control**, arms **embargo**, arms **sales** ② ■	

ar|ma|ments /ɑ́rməmənts/ N-PLURAL **Armaments** are weapons and military equipment belonging to an army or country. ❏ ...*global efforts to reduce nuclear and other armaments.*

복수명사 군비 ❏ 핵무기 및 기타 무기를 감축하려는 범세계적 노력

arm|chair /ɑ́rmtʃèər/ (**armchairs**) ■ N-COUNT An **armchair** is a big comfortable chair which has a support on each side for your arms. ❏ *She was sitting in an armchair with blankets wrapped around her.* ② ADJ An **armchair** critic, fan, or traveler knows about a particular subject from reading or hearing about it rather than from practical experience. [ADJ n] ❏ *This great book is ideal for both the traveling supporter and the armchair fan.*

■ 가산명사 안락의자 ❏ 그녀는 담요를 둘러 감고 안락의자에 앉아 있었다. ② 형용사 간접 경험의 ❏ 이 훌륭한 책은 직접적인 여행을 지지하는 사람들과 간접 경험만을 하는 팬 모두에게 이상적이다.

armed ♦♦◇ /ɑ́rmd/ ■ ADJ Someone who is **armed** is carrying a weapon, usually a gun. ❏ *City police said the man was armed with a revolver.* ❏ ...*a barbed-wire fence patrolled by armed guards.* ② ADJ An **armed** attack or conflict involves people fighting with guns or carrying weapons. [ADJ n] ❏ *They had been found guilty of armed robbery.* ③ →see also **arm**

■ 형용사 무장한 ❏ 시 경찰은 그 남자가 권총으로 무장한 상태라고 했다. ② 순찰 무장 경비들이 있는 철조망 ② 형용사 무장의 ❏ 그들은 무장 강도로 유죄 판결을 받았었다.

Word Web   army

The first Roman **army** was a poorly organized **militia band**. Its members had no **weapons** such as **swords** or **spears**. After the Etruscans, an advanced society from west-central Italy, **conquered** Rome things changed. Then the Roman army became a powerful force. They learned how to **deploy** their **troops** to **fight** more effective **battles**. By the first century BC, the Roman army realized the importance of protective equipment. They started using bronze **helmets**, **armor**, and wooden **shields**. They fought many **military campaigns** and won many **wars**.

armed forces ♦◊◊ N-PLURAL The **armed forces** or the **armed services** of a country are its military forces, usually the army, navy, marines, and air force. ❏ *Every member of the armed forces is a hero.*

복수명사 군대 ❏ 군대의 구성원 한 사람 한 사람이 영웅이다.

Word Link   or, er ≈ one who does, that which does: assess*or*, auth*or*, arm*or*

ar|mor /ɑ́rmər/ [BRIT **armour**] **1** N-UNCOUNT In former times, **armor** was special metal clothing that soldiers wore for protection in battle. ❏ *...knights in armor.* **2** N-UNCOUNT **Armor** consists of tanks and other military vehicles used in battle. [MILITARY] ❏ *...the biggest movement of heavy British armor since the Second World War.* **3** N-UNCOUNT **Armor** is a hard, usually metal, covering that protects a vehicle against attack. ❏ *...a formidable warhead that can penetrate the armor of most tanks.* **4** **knight in shining armor** →see **army**, **knight**

[영국영어 armour] **1** 불가산명사 갑옷 ❏ 갑옷을 입은 기사들 **2** 불가산명사 기갑 부대 [군사] ❏ 2차 세계 대전 이후 영국 중장비 기갑 부대의 가장 거대한 이동 **3** 불가산명사 장갑 ❏ 대부분 탱크의 장갑을 관통할 수 있는 강력한 탄두

ar|mored /ɑ́rmərd/ [BRIT **armoured**] **1** ADJ **Armored** vehicles are fitted with a hard metal covering in order to protect them from gunfire and other missiles. ❏ *More than forty armored vehicles carrying troops have been sent into the area.* **2** ADJ **Armored** troops are troops in armoured vehicles. ❏ *These front-line defenses are backed up by armored units in reserve.*

[영국영어 armoured] **1** 형용사 장갑의 ❏ 병사를 실은 40대 이상의 장갑 차량이 그 지역에 배치되었다. **2** 형용사 장갑의 ❏ 이들 전방 방어선은 예비 장갑 사단의 지원을 받는다.

ar|mory /ɑ́rməri/ (**armories**) [BRIT **armoury**] **1** N-COUNT A country's **armory** is all the weapons and military equipment that it has. ❏ *Nuclear weapons will play a less prominent part in NATO's armory in the future.* **2** N-COUNT An **armory** is a place where weapons, bombs, and other military equipment are stored. ❏ *...a failed attempt to steal weapons from an armory.* **3** N-COUNT In the United States, an **armory** is a building used by the National Guard or Army Reserve for meetings and training. ❏ *The National Guard says an armory in Fairmont has opened to shelter stranded motorists.*

[영국영어 armoury] **1** 가산명사 국가의 군비 ❏ 핵무기가 장착될 나토의 군비에서 훨씬 축소된 역할을 지닐 것이다. **2** 가산명사 무기고 ❏ 무기고에서 무기를 훔치려 했으나 실패한 시도 **3** 가산명사 부대 본부 ❏ 미국 방위군은 길 잃은 운전자들을 수용하기 위해 페어몬트에 위치한 부대 시설을 개방했다고 발표했다.

arm|pit /ɑ́rmpɪt/ (**armpits**) N-COUNT Your **armpits** are the areas of your body under your arms where your arms join your shoulders. ❏ *I shave my armpits every couple of days.*

가산명사 겨드랑이 ❏ 나는 이틀에 1번씩 겨드랑이 털을 깎는다.

army ♦♦♦ /ɑ́rmi/ (**armies**) **1** N-COUNT-COLL An **army** is a large organized group of people who are armed and trained to fight on land in a war. Most armies are organized and controlled by governments. ❏ *After returning from France, he joined the army.* **2** N-COUNT-COLL An **army of** people, animals, or things is a large number of them, especially when they are regarded as a force of some kind. ❏ *...data collected by an army of volunteers.* →see Word Web: **army**

1 가산명사-집합 육군 ❏ 프랑스에서 돌아온 후 그는 육군에 지원했다. **2** 가산명사-집합 집단, 무리 ❏ 자원 봉사단이 수집한 자료

aro|ma /əróumə/ (**aromas**) N-COUNT An **aroma** is a strong, pleasant smell. ❏ *...the wonderful aroma of freshly baked bread.*

가산명사 향기, 내음 ❏ 갓 구운 빵의 구수한 냄새

aroma|thera|py /əróuməθérəpi/ N-UNCOUNT **Aromatherapy** is a type of treatment which involves massaging the body with special fragrant oils.

불가산명사 향기 요법

aro|mat|ic /ærəmǽtɪk/ ADJ An **aromatic** plant or food has a strong, pleasant smell of herbs or spices. ❏ *...an evergreen shrub with deep green, aromatic leaves.*

형용사 향기로운 ❏ 짙은 녹색의 향기로운 잎을 가진 상록수 관목

arose /əróuz/ **Arose** is the past tense of **arise**.

arise의 과거

around ♦♦♦ /əráund/

> **Around** is an adverb and a preposition. In British English, the word "round" is often used instead. **Around** is often used with verbs of movement, such as "walk" and "drive," and also in phrasal verbs such as "get around" and "hand around."

> around는 부사, 전치사이다. 영국영어에서는 흔히 'round'가 대신 쓰인다. around는 종종 'walk', 'drive'와 같은 이동 동사와 함께 쓰며 'get around', 'hand round'와 같은 구동사에도 쓰인다.

1 PREP To be positioned **around** a place or object means to surround it or be on all sides of it. To move **around** a place means to go along its edge, back to your starting point. ❏ *She looked at the papers around her.* ❏ *Today she wore her hair down around her shoulders.* ● **Around** is also an adverb. [n ADV] ❏ *...a village with a rocky river, a ruined castle and hills all around.* **2** PREP If you move **around** a corner or obstacle, you move to the other side of it. If you look **around** a corner or obstacle, you look to see what is on the other side. ❏ *The photographer stopped clicking and hurried around the corner.* **3** ADV If you turn **around**, you turn so that you are facing in the opposite direction. [ADV after v] ❏ *I turned around and wrote the title on the blackboard.* **4** PREP If you move **around** a place, you travel through it, going to most of its parts. If you look **around** a place, you look at every part of it. ❏ *I've been walking around Moscow and the town is terribly quiet.* ● **Around** is also an adverb. [ADV after v] ❏ *He backed away from the edge, looking all around at the*

1 전치사 주위에; 둘러서 ❏ 그녀는 주위의 서류들을 쳐다봤다. ❏ 오늘 그녀는 머리를 풀어 어깨까지 내려오게 하고 다녔다. ● 부사 주위에 ❏ 바위가 많은 강과 폐허가 된 성이 있고 주위가 온통 구릉으로 둘러싸인 마을 **2** 전치사 돌아서 ❏ 사진사는 사진 찍기를 멈추고 서둘러 모퉁이를 돌아갔다. **3** 부사 돌아서 ❏ 나는 돌아서서 제목을 칠판에 썼다. **4** 전치사 둘러, 돌아 ❏ 나는 모스크바를 걸어서 돌아다녀 봤는데 도시가 너무 조용하다. ● 부사 둘러 ❏ 그는 낭떠러지에서 물러서면서 사방의 평평한 수평선을 바라봤다. **5** 전치사 여기저기에 ❏ 요즘 나는 술이 있는 파티를 여기저기 돌아다니며 내 시간 대부분을 소비하고 있다. ● 부사 여기저기에 ❏ 나는

flat horizon. **5** PREP If someone moves **around** a place, they move through various parts of that place without having any particular destination. ❑ *These days much of my time is spent weaving my way around drinks parties.* ● ADV **Around** is also an adverb. [ADV after v] ❑ *My mornings are spent rushing around after him.* **6** ADV If you go **around** to someone's house, you visit them. [ADV after v] ❑ *She helped me unpack my things and then we went around to see the other girls.* **7** ADV You use **around** in expressions such as **sit around** and **hang around** when you are saying that someone is spending time in a place and not doing anything very important. [ADV after v] ❑ *I'm just going to be hanging around twiddling my thumbs.* ● PREP **Around** is also a preposition. ❑ *He used to skip lessons and hang around the harbor with some other boys.* **8** ADV If you move things **around**, you move them so that they are in different places. [ADV after v] ❑ *Furniture in the classroom should not be changed around without warning the blind child.* **9** ADV If a wheel or object turns **around**, it turns. [ADV after v] ❑ *The boat started to spin around in the water.* **10** PREP You use **around** to say that something happens in different parts of a place or area. ❑ *Police in South Africa say ten people have died in scattered violence around the country.* ❑ *Elephants were often to be found in swamp in eastern Kenya around the Tana River.* ● ADV **Around** is also an adverb. ❑ *Giovanni has the best Parma ham for miles around.* **11** ADV If someone or something is **around**, they exist or are present in a place. ❑ *You haven't seen my publisher anywhere around, have you?* **12** PREP The people **around** you are the people who you come into contact with, especially your friends and relatives, and the people you work with. ❑ *We change our behavior by observing the behavior of those around us.* **13** PREP If something such as a film, a discussion, or a plan is based **around** something, that thing is its main theme. ❑ *...the gentle comedy based around the Larkin family.* **14** ADV You use **around** in expressions such as **this time around** or **to come around** when you are describing something that has happened before or things that happen regularly. ❑ *Senator Bentsen has declined to get involved this time around.* **15** PREP When you are giving measurements, you can use **around** to talk about the distance along the edge of something round. ❑ *She was 5 foot 4 inches, 38 around the chest, 28 around the waist and 40 around the hips.* **16** ADV **Around** means approximately. ❑ *My salary was around £19,000 plus a car and expenses.* ● PREP **Around** is also a preposition. ❑ *He expects the elections to be held around November.*

> When you are talking about movement in no particular direction, you can use **around** or **about**. **Around** is more common in American English. ❑ *It's so romantic up here, flying around in a small plane... Police officers walk about with guns on their hips.* When you are talking about something being generally present or available, you can use **around** or **about**: again, **around** is more common in American English. ❑ *There is a lot of talent around at the moment... There are not that many jobs about.*

17 PHRASE **Around about** means approximately. [SPOKEN] ❑ *There is an outright separatist party but it only scored around about 10 percent in the vote.* **18** **the other way around** →see **way**

arous|al /əraʊzᵊl/ **1** N-UNCOUNT **Arousal** is the state of being sexually excited. ❑ *...sexual arousal.* **2** N-UNCOUNT **Arousal** is a state in which you feel excited or very alert, for example as a result of fear, stress, or anger. ❑ *Thinking angry thoughts can provoke strong physiological arousal.*

arouse /əraʊz/ (**arouses, arousing, aroused**) **1** V-T If something **arouses** a particular reaction or attitude in people, it causes them to have that reaction or attitude. ❑ *His revolutionary work in linguistics has aroused intense scholarly interest.* **2** V-T If something **arouses** a particular feeling or instinct that exists in someone, it causes them to experience that feeling or instinct strongly. ❑ *There is nothing quite like a crisp, dry sherry to arouse the appetite.* **3** V-T If you **are aroused** by something, it makes you feel sexually excited. [usu passive] ❑ *Some men are aroused when their partner says erotic words to them.*

ar|range ◆◇◇ /əreɪndʒ/ (**arranges, arranging, arranged**) **1** V-T If you **arrange** an event or meeting, you make plans for it to happen. ❑ *She arranged an appointment for Friday afternoon at four-fifteen.* **2** V-T/V-I If you **arrange** with someone **to** do something, you make plans with them to do it. ❑ *I've arranged to see him on Friday morning.* ❑ *It was arranged that the party would gather for lunch in the Royal Garden Hotel.* **3** V-T/V-I If you **arrange** something **for** someone, you make it possible for them to have it or to do it. ❑ *I will arrange for someone to take you around.* ❑ *The hotel manager will arrange for a baby-sitter.* **4** V-T If you **arrange** things somewhere, you place them in a particular position, usually in order to make them look attractive or neat. ❑ *When she has a little spare time she enjoys arranging dried flowers.* **5** V-T If a piece of music **is arranged by** someone, it is changed or adapted so that it is suitable for particular instruments or voices, or for a particular performance. [usu passive] ❑ *The songs were arranged by another well-known bass player, Ron Carter.*

ar|range|ment ◆◇◇ /əreɪndʒmənt/ (**arrangements**) **1** N-COUNT **Arrangements** are plans and preparations which you make so that something will happen or be possible. ❑ *The staff is working frantically on final arrangements for the summit.* ❑ *She telephoned Ellen, but made no arrangements to see her.* **2** N-COUNT An **arrangement** is an agreement that you make with someone to do something. [also by N] ❑ *The caves can be visited only by prior arrangement.* **3** N-COUNT An **arrangement** of things, for example flowers or furniture, is a group of them displayed in a particular way. ❑ *The house was always decorated with imaginative flower arrangements.* **4** N-COUNT If someone makes an **arrangement** of a piece of music, they change it so that it is suitable for

여기저기 그의 뒤를 쫓아다니며 아침을 보낸다. **6** 부사 들러 ❑ 그녀가 내 짐을 푸는 것을 도와준 후 우리는 다른 여자 아이들을 만나러 돌아다녔다. **7** 부사 하릴없이; 하릴없이 앉아 있다; 하릴없이 머물다 ❑ 나는 그저 손가락이나 만지작거리며 여기에 당분간 죽치고 있을 것이다. ● 전치사 하릴없이 ❑ 그는 수업을 빼먹고 그 다른 남자 아이들과 항구 주위에서 어슬렁거리곤 했다. **8** 부사 이리저리 ❑ 교실의 가구는 맹인 아이에게 주의를 주지 않은 상태에서 이리저리 옮겨선 안 된다. **9** 부사 빙글빙글 ❑ 배는 물 속에서 빙글빙글 돌기 시작했다. **10** 전치사 여기저기서 ❑ 남아프리카의 경찰 발표에 따르면 전국 곳곳에서 발생한 폭력 사태로 열 명이 사망했다고 한다. ❑ 동부 케냐 타나 강 유역의 늪지대에서 코끼리들을 종종 볼 수 있었다. ● 부사 근처에 ❑ 지오바니가 주변 수마일 내에서는 최고의 파르마 햄을 생산한다. **11** 부사 존재하여 ❑ 혹시 제 출판 담당자를 어디서 보지 못하셨나요? **12** 전치사 주변의 ❑ 우리는 주변 사람들의 행동을 관찰함으로써 스스로의 행동을 바꾼다. **13** 전치사 ~을 중심으로 한 ❑ 라킨 가족을 중심으로 한 잔잔한 코미디 **14** 부사 돌아와는; 이번에는; 닥쳐오는 ❑ 벤트슨 상원 의원은 이번에는 개입하지 않기로 거부했다. **15** 전치사 둘레에 ❑ 그녀는 키가 5피트 4인치에 가슴둘레 38, 허리둘레 28, 히프 둘레는 40인치였다. **16** 부사 약 ❑ 내 연봉은 자동차와 경비를 별도로 약 19,000파운드였다. ● 전치사 약 ❑ 그는 선거가 11월쯤에 치러지리라 예상한다.

특정한 방향이 없이 움직이는 것에 대해 말할 때는, around나 about을 쓸 수 있다. 미국 영어에서는 around가 더 일반적이다. ❑ 저기 위에서 작은 비행기를 타고 돌아다니는 것은 너무도 낭만적이다... 경찰관들은 허리에 총을 차고 이리저리 두어 시간 동안 차를 몰고 돌아 다녔다... 경찰관들은 허리에 총을 차고 이리저리 걸어 다닌다. 일반적으로 주변에 있거나 이용 가능한 것을 얘기할 때 around나 about을 쓴다. 다시 말하지만, 미국 영어에서는 around가 더 일반적이다. ❑ 현재 주변에 재능 있는 사람들이 많이 있다... 그렇게 많은 일자리가 주변에 있는 것은 아니다.

17 구 약 [구어체] ❑ 공개적으로 분리주의를 표방하는 당이 있는데 투표에서 10퍼센트 정도밖에 득표하지 못했다.

1 불가산명사 흥분 **2** 성적 흥분 **3** 불가산명사 흥분 ❑ 분노에 찬 생각을 하면 강한 생리적 흥분을 야기할 수 있다.

1 타동사 불러일으키다 ❑ 언어학에서 그의 혁명적인 연구는 뜨거운 학문적 관심을 불러일으켰다. **2** 타동사 돋우다 ❑ 산뜻하고 담백한 셰리주만큼 식욕을 돋우는 것은 없다. **3** 타동사 성적으로 흥분시키다 ❑ 어떤 남자들은 파트너가 자신에게 야한 말을 할 때 성적으로 흥분한다.

1 타동사 준비하다 ❑ 그녀는 금요일 약속을 오후 4시 15분으로 잡았다. **2** 타동사/자동사 약속하다 ❑ 나는 그와 금요일 오전에 만나기로 약속했다. ❑ 일행이 점심 식사하러 '로열 가든 호텔'에서 만나기로 일정이 잡혀 있었다. **3** 타동사/자동사 마련하다 ❑ 누군가가 당신을 모시고 다니도록 조치하겠습니다. ❑ 호텔 지배인이 보모를 마련해 줄 것이다. **4** 타동사 배열하다 ❑ 시간 여유가 좀 있으면 그녀는 말린 꽃으로 꽃꽂이 하는 것을 좋아한다. **5** 타동사 편곡되다 ❑ 그 곡들은 또 다른 유명한 베이스 연주자인 론 카터에 의해 편곡되었다.

1 가산명사 준비 ❑ 직원들은 정상 회담의 막바지 준비에 모든 힘을 다하고 있다. ❑ 그녀는 엘렌에게 전화를 했지만 만날 약속은 하지 않았다. **2** 가산명사 약속 ❑ 그 동굴들은 사전 예약으로 이해서만 방문이 가능하다. **3** 가산명사 배열 ❑ 집은 항상 상상력이 풍부한 꽃꽂이들로 장식되어 있었다. **4** 가산명사 편곡 ❑ 모차르트의 잘 알려진 곡의 편곡

A

particular voices or instruments, or for a particular performance. ❑ ...*an arrangement of a well-known piece by Mozart.*

B

Word Partnership	*arrangement*의 연어
ADJ.	**informal/formal, special** arrangement, **temporary/permanent** arrangement 1 2 3
N.	**flower** arrangement, **seating** arrangement 3

C

D

ar|ray /ərei/ (arrays) 1 N-COUNT-COLL An **array of** different things or people is a large number or wide range of them. ❑ *As the deadline approached she experienced a bewildering array of emotions.* 2 N-COUNT An **array of** objects is a collection of them that is displayed or arranged in a particular way. ❑ *We visited the local markets and saw wonderful arrays of fruit and vegetables.*

1 가산명사-집합 다수 ❑ 마감 일자가 임박하자 그녀는 당황스러울 정도로 복잡한 감정들을 겪었다. 2 가산명사 정렬 ❑ 우리는 지역 시장에 들러서 놀랄 만큼 다양한 과일과 야채들이 진열되어 있는 것을 보았다.

E

Word Partnership	*array*의 연어
ADJ.	**broad/vast/wide** array, **impressive** array 1 2
PREP.	array **of** *something* 1 2

F

ar|rears /əriərz/ 1 N-PLURAL **Arrears** are amounts of money that you owe, especially regular payments that you should have made earlier. ❑ *They promised to pay the arrears over the next five years.* 2 PHRASE If someone is **in arrears** with their payments, or falls **into arrears**, they have not paid the regular amounts of money that they should have paid. ❑ *...the 300,000 households who are more than six months in arrears with their mortgages.* 3 PHRASE If sums of money such as wages or taxes are paid **in arrears**, they are paid at the end of the period of time to which they relate, for example after a job has been done and the wages have been earned. ❑ *Interest is paid in arrears after you use the money.*

G

1 복수명사 연체금 ❑ 그들은 다음 5년 동안 연체금을 지불하기로 약속했다. 2 구 연체된 ❑ 주택 담보 융자금을 육 개월 이상 연체한 30만 가구 3 구 후불의 ❑ 이자는 돈을 쓰고 나서 후불로 낸다.

H

I

ar|rest ♦♦◇ /ərest/ (arrests, arresting, arrested) 1 V-T If the police **arrest** you, they take charge of you and take you to a police station, because they believe you may have committed a crime. ❑ *Police arrested five young men in connection with one of the attacks.* ● N-VAR **Arrest** is also a noun. [oft under N] ❑ *...a substantial reward for information leading to the arrest of the bombers.* ❑ *Police chased the fleeing terrorists and later made two arrests.* 2 V-T If something or someone **arrests** a process, they stop it from continuing. [FORMAL] ❑ *The sufferer may have to make major changes in his or her life to arrest the disease.* 3 →see also **house arrest**

J

K

1 타동사 체포하다 ❑ 경찰은 그 폭행 사건 중 한 건과 관련하여 다섯 명의 청년을 체포했다. ● 가산명사 또는 불가산명사 체포 ❑ 폭파범들의 체포를 도울 수 있는 정보에 대한 상당한 보상 ❑ 경찰늘은 도망가는 테러범들을 쫓아가 결국 두 명을 체포했다. 2 타동사 중단시키다, 저지하다 [격식체] ❑ 환자는 질병의 진행을 막기 위해 자신의 삶에 중대한 변화를 시도해야 할지도 모른다. 3

L

ar|ri|val ♦◇◇ /əraɪvəl/ (arrivals) 1 N-VAR When a person or vehicle **arrives** at a place, you can refer to their **arrival**. ❑ *...the day after his arrival in England.* ❑ *He was dead on arrival at the nearby hospital.* 2 N-VAR When someone starts a new job, you can refer to their **arrival** in that job. ❑ *...the power vacuum created by the arrival of a new president.* 3 N-SING When something is brought to you or becomes available, you can refer to its **arrival**. ❑ *I was flicking idly through a newspaper while awaiting the arrival of orange juice and coffee.* 4 N-SING When a particular time comes or a particular event happens, you can refer to its **arrival**. ❑ *He celebrated the arrival of the New Year with a bout of drinking that nearly killed him.* 5 N-COUNT You can refer to someone who has just arrived at a place as a new **arrival**. ❑ *A high proportion of the new arrivals are skilled professionals.*

M

N

1 가산명사 또는 불가산명사 도착 ❑ 그가 영국에 도착한 다음 날 ❑ 인근 병원에 도착했을 때 그는 이미 사망했다. 2 가산명사 또는 불가산명사 부임, 취임 ❑ 새 대통령 취임에 따른 권력 공백 3 단수명사 도래 ❑ 나는 오렌지 주스와 커피가 나오길 기다리며 한가로이 신문을 뒤적이고 있었다. 4 단수명사 도래 ❑ 그는 새해의 도래를 폭주로 축하하다가 거의 죽을 뻔했다. 5 가산명사 신참 ❑ 신입 사원의 상당 부분이 유능한 전문가이다.

O

Word Partnership	*arrival*의 연어
N.	**time of** arrival 1
PREP.	arrival **at** *someplace*, **on** arrival 1
	arrival **of** *something* 2 3 4
ADJ.	**early/late** arrival 1
	new arrival, **recent** arrival 5
V.	**awaiting the** arrival 1 3 4

P

Q

R

ar|rive ♦♦◇ /əraɪv/ (arrives, arriving, arrived) 1 V-I When a person or vehicle **arrives** at a place, they come to it at the end of a journey. ❑ *Fresh groups of guests arrived.* ❑ *...a small group of commuters waiting for their train, which arrived on time.* 2 V-I When you **arrive** at a place, you come to it for the first time in order to stay, live, or work there. ❑ *...in the old days before the European settlers arrived in the country.* 3 V-I When something such as a letter or meal **arrives**, it is brought or delivered to you. ❑ *Breakfast arrived while he was in the bathroom.* 4 V-I When something such as a new product or invention **arrives**, it becomes available. ❑ *Several long-awaited movies will finally arrive in the stores this month.* 5 V-I When a particular moment or event **arrives**, it happens, especially after you have been waiting for it or expecting it. ❑ *The time has arrived when I need to give up smoking.* 6 V-I When you **arrive at** something such as a decision, you decide something after thinking about it or discussing it. ❑ *...if the jury cannot arrive at a unanimous decision.*

S

T

U

1 자동사 도착하다 ❑ 새로운 손님들이 도착했다. ❑ 제때에 도착한 기차를 기다리던 소수의 통근자들 2 자동사 정착하다, 도래하다 ❑ 유럽 이주민들이 이 나라에 정착하기 전인 옛날 3 자동사 배달되다 ❑ 그가 화장실에 있을 때 아침 식사가 배달되었다. 4 자동사 출시되다, 나오다 ❑ 오랫동안 기다려 온 영화 몇 편이 드디어 이번 달에 출시될 것이다. 5 자동사 도래하다, 이르다 ❑ 내가 금연해야 할 때가 드디어 왔다. 6 자동사 도달하다 ❑ 만약 배심원이 만장일치의 결정에 도달하지 못한다면

V

You use both **arrive** and **reach** to talk about coming to a particular place. You can use **arrive** to emphasize being in a place rather than traveling to it. ❑ *When I arrived in England I was exhausted.* **Reach** is always followed by a noun or pronoun referring to a place and you can use it to emphasize the effort required to get there. ❑ *To reach the capital might not be easy.* **Arrive at** and **reach** can also be used to say that someone eventually makes a decision or finds the answer to something. ❑ *It took hours to arrive at a decision... They were unable to reach a decision.*

W

특정한 장소에 도착하는 것을 얘기할 때는 arrive와 reach를 둘 다 쓸 수 있다. arrive는 어떤 장소까지 가는 과정보다 거기에 가 있는 것을 강조할 때 쓴다. ❑ 내가 영국에 도착했을 때에는 기진맥진한 상태였다. reach는 항상 뒤에 장소를 지칭하는 명사나 대명사가 나온다. reach는 거기에 도달하는 데 소요되는 노력을 강조하기 위해 쓸 수 있다. ❑ 그 수도에 도달하는 것이 쉽지 않을 수도 있다. arrive at과 reach는 누가 마침내 어떤 결정을 내리게 되었거나 무엇에 대한 답을 찾게 되었을 때에도 쓸 수 있다. ❑ 결정을 내리는 데 몇 시간이나 걸렸다... 그들은 결정에 이를 수 없었다.

X

Y

Thesaurus	*arrive*의 참조어
V.	enter, land, pull into, reach; *(ant.)* depart 1

Z

ar|ro|gant /ǽrəgənt/ ADJ Someone who is **arrogant** behaves in a proud, unpleasant way toward other people because they believe that they are more important than others. [DISAPPROVAL] ❑ *He was so arrogant.* ❑ *That sounds arrogant, doesn't it?* ● **ar|ro|gance** N-UNCOUNT ❑ *At times the arrogance of those in power is quite blatant.*

형용사 거만한 [탐탁잖음] ❑ 그는 너무 거만했다. ❑ 참 거만하게 들리지 않아? ● 거만함 불가산명사 ❑ 권력을 잡은 자들의 거만함은 때론 너무 노골적이다.

ar|row /ǽroʊ/ (arrows) **1** N-COUNT An **arrow** is a long thin weapon which is sharp and pointed at one end and which often has feathers at the other end. An arrow is shot from a bow. ❑ *Warriors armed with bows and arrows and spears have invaded their villages.* **2** N-COUNT An **arrow** is a written or printed sign that consists of a straight line with another line bent at a sharp angle at one end. This is a printed arrow: →. The arrow points in a particular direction to indicate where something is. ❑ *A series of arrows points the way to the modest grave of Andrei Sakharov.*

1 가산명사 화살 ❑ 활, 화살, 창 등으로 무장한 무사들이 그들의 마을을 침략했다. **2** 가산명사 화살표 ❑ 일련의 화살표를 따라가면 안드레이 사하로프의 검소한 무덤에 이른다.

arse /ɑrs/ (arses) N-COUNT Your **arse** is your bottom. [BRIT, INFORMAL, VULGAR; AM **ass**] ❑ *She's the one that fell on her arse the other week.* **a pain in the arse** →see **pain**

가산명사 엉덩이 [영국영어, 비격식체, 비속어; 미국영어 ass] ❑ 그녀가 저번 주에 엉덩방아를 찧은 사람이다.

ar|se|nal /ɑ́rsənəl/ (arsenals) **1** N-COUNT An **arsenal** is a large collection of weapons and military equipment held by a country, group, or person. ❑ *Russia and the other republics are committed to destroying most of their nuclear arsenals.* **2** N-COUNT An **arsenal** is a building where weapons and military equipment are stored.

1 가산명사 군비 ❑ 러시아와 기타 공화국들은 자신들의 핵보유고 대부분을 폐기한다는 약속을 했다. **2** 가산명사 무기고

ar|son /ɑ́rsən/ N-UNCOUNT **Arson** is the crime of deliberately setting fire to a building or vehicle. ❑ *...a terrible wave of rioting, theft and arson.*

불가산명사 방화 ❑ 폭동, 절도, 방화의 끔찍한 증가

art ♦♦♦ /ɑrt/ (arts) **1** N-UNCOUNT **Art** consists of paintings, sculpture, and other pictures or objects which are created for people to look at and admire or think deeply about. ❑ *...the first exhibition of such art in the West.* ❑ *...contemporary and modern American art.* **2** N-UNCOUNT **Art** is the activity or educational subject that consists of creating paintings, sculptures, and other pictures or objects for people to look at and admire or think deeply about. ❑ *...a painter, content to be left alone with her all-absorbing art.* ❑ *...Plymouth College of Art and Design.* **3** N-VAR **The arts** are activities such as music, painting, literature, film, and dance, which people can take part in for enjoyment, or to create works which express certain meanings or ideas of beauty. ❑ *Catherine the Great was a patron of the arts and sciences.* **4** N-PLURAL At a university or college, **arts** are subjects such as history, literature, or languages in contrast to scientific subjects. ❑ *...arts and social science graduates.* **5** ADJ **Arts** or **art** is used in the names of theaters which show plays or films that are intended to make the audience think deeply about the content, and not just to entertain them. [ADJ n] ❑ *...the Cambridge Arts Cinema.* **6** N-COUNT If you describe an activity as an **art**, you mean that it requires skill and that people learn to do it by instinct or experience, rather than by learning facts or rules. ❑ *...pioneers who transformed clinical medicine from an art to a science.* **7** →see also **fine art, martial art, state-of-the-art, work of art** →see **culture, drawing**

1 불가산명사 미술 ❑ 서방에서 열린 그러한 미술 작품의 첫번째 전시회 ❑ 현대 및 근대 미국 미술 **2** 불가산명사 미술 활동, 미술 ❑ 완전히 자기 몰두적인 미술 활동과 더불어 홀로 있는 것에 만족하는 화가 ❑ 플리머스 미술과 디자인 대학 **3** 가산명사 또는 불가산명사 예술 ❑ 캐서린 대제는 예술과 과학의 후원자였다. **4** 복수명사 인문학 ❑ 인문 및 사회 과학 졸업생 **5** 형용사 예술 영화, 순수 연극 ❑ 케임브리지 예술 영화 상영관 **6** 가산명사 기술 ❑ 임상 의학을 기술에서 과학으로 발전시킨 개척자들

ar|te|fact /ɑ́rtɪfækt/ →see **artifact**

ar|tery /ɑ́rtəri/ (arteries) **1** N-COUNT **Arteries** are the tubes in your body that carry blood from your heart to the rest of your body. Compare **vein**. ❑ *...patients suffering from blocked arteries.* **2** N-COUNT You can refer to an important main route through a complex road, railroad, or river system as an **artery**. ❑ *Clarence Street was one of the north-bound arteries of the central business district.*

1 가산명사 동맥 ❑ 동맥 폐쇄를 앓고 있는 환자들 **2** 가산명사 간선 ❑ 클래런스 거리는 상업 중심가의 북행 간선 도로 중 하나였다.

ar|thrit|ic /ɑrθrɪ́tɪk/ **1** ADJ **Arthritic** is used to describe the condition, the pain, or the symptoms of arthritis. [ADJ n] ❑ *I developed serious arthritic symptoms and chronic sinusitis.* **2** ADJ An **arthritic** person is suffering from arthritis, and cannot move very easily. **Arthritic** joints or hands are affected by arthritis. ❑ *...an elderly lady who suffered with arthritic hands.*

1 형용사 관절염의 ❑ 심각한 관절염 증세와 만성 정맥동염 증세가 내게 나타났다. **2** 형용사 관절염의 ❑ 관절염에 걸린, 관절염의 ❑ 관절염에 걸린 손 때문에 고통 받던 할머니

ar|thri|tis /ɑrθráɪtɪs/ N-UNCOUNT **Arthritis** is a medical condition in which the joints in someone's body are swollen and painful. ❑ *I have a touch of arthritis in the wrist.*

불가산명사 관절염 ❑ 나는 손목에 약간 관절염 증상이 있다.

ar|ti|choke /ɑ́rtɪtʃoʊk/ (artichokes) N-VAR **Artichokes** or **globe artichokes** are round green vegetables that have fleshy leaves arranged like the petals of a flower.

가산명사 또는 불가산명사 아티초크

Word Link	cle ≈ small : article, cubicle, particle

ar|ti|cle ♦♦◊ /ɑ́rtɪkəl/ (articles) **1** N-COUNT An **article** is a piece of writing that is published in a newspaper or magazine. ❑ *...a newspaper article.* ❑ *According to an article in The Economist the drug could have side effects.* **2** N-COUNT You can refer to objects as **articles** of some kind. ❑ *...articles of clothing.* ❑ *He had stripped the house of all articles of value.* **3** PHRASE If you describe something as **the genuine article**, you are emphasizing that it is genuine, and often that it is very good. [EMPHASIS] ❑ *The vodka was the genuine article.* **4** N-COUNT An **article of** a formal agreement or document is a section of it which deals with a particular point. ❑ *The country appears to be violating several articles of the convention.* **5** N-COUNT In grammar, an **article** is a kind of determiner. In English, "a" and "an" are called **the indefinite article**, and "the" is called **the definite article**. **6** N-PLURAL Someone who is in **articles** is being trained as a lawyer or accountant by a firm with whom they have a written agreement. [BRIT] ❑ *Students spent the rest of the day in articles at a law firm.* →see **newspaper**

1 가산명사 기사 ❑ 신문 기사 ❑ 이코노미스트 지의 기사에 따르면 그 약은 부작용이 있을 수 있었다. **2** 가산명사 (물품) 한 개; 물품 ❑ 의류 여러 점 ❑ 그는 그 집에서 값나가는 물품들을 모조리 빼앗아 가 버렸다. **3** 구 진품 [강조] ❑ 그 보드카는 진품이었다. **4** 가산명사 조항 ❑ 그 나라가 협정의 몇몇 조항을 어기고 있는 것으로 보인다. **5** 가산명사 관사 **6** 복수명사 수습 [영국영어] ❑ 학생들은 나머지 낮 시간 동안에 법률 회사에서 수습 교육을 받았다.

ar|ticu|late (articulates, articulating, articulated)

The adjective is pronounced /ɑrtɪ́kyəlɪt/. The verb is pronounced /ɑrtɪ́kyəleɪt/.

형용사는 /ɑrtɪ́kyəlɪt/으로 발음되고, 동사는 /ɑrtɪ́kyəleɪt/으로 발음된다.

1 ADJ If you describe someone as **articulate**, you mean that they are able to express their thoughts and ideas easily and well. [APPROVAL] ❑ *She is an*

1 형용사 분명한 [마음에 듦] ❑ 그녀는 자기주장이 분명한 젊은 여성이다. **2** 타동사 분명히 말하다

articulate young woman. **2** V-T When you **articulate** your ideas or feelings, you express them clearly in words. [FORMAL] ❑ *The president has been accused of failing to articulate an overall vision in foreign affairs.* **3** V-T If you **articulate** something, you say it very clearly, so that each word or syllable can be heard. ❑ *He articulated each syllable.*

[격식체] **2** 대통령은 외교 문제에 대해 종합적인 비전을 명확히 제시하지 못한다는 비난을 받아 왔다. **3** 타동사 똑똑히 말하다 ❑ 그는 한 음절 한 음절을 똑똑히 말했다.

ar|ticu|lat|ed /ɑrtɪkyəleɪtɪd/ ADJ An **articulated** vehicle, especially a truck, is made in two or more sections which are joined together by metal bars, so that the vehicle can turn more easily. [BRIT; AM usually **rig, trailer truck**]

형용사 굴절형의 (차량) [영국영어; 미국영어 대개 rig, trailer truck]

Word Link   *fact, fic ≈ making : artifact, artificial, factor*

---

ar|ti|fact /ɑrtɪfækt/ (artifacts) [BRIT usually **artefact**] N-COUNT An **artifact** is an ornament, tool, or other object that is made by a human being, especially one that is historically or culturally interesting. ❑ *They also repair broken religious artifacts.* →see **history**

[영국영어 대개 artefact] 가산명사 유물, 인공물 ❑ 그들은 또한 부서진 종교 유물을 수리한다.

ar|ti|fi|cial /ɑrtɪfɪʃl/ **1** ADJ **Artificial** objects, materials, or processes do not occur naturally and are created by human beings, for example using science or technology. ❑ *The city is dotted with small lakes, natural and artificial.* ❑ *...a wholefood diet free from artificial additives, colors and flavors.* ● ar|ti|fi|cial|ly ADV ❑ *...artificially sweetened lemonade.* **2** ADJ An **artificial** state or situation exists only because someone has created it, and therefore often seems unnatural or unnecessary. ❑ *Even in the artificial environment of an office, our body rhythms continue to affect us.* ● ar|ti|fi|cial|ly ADV ❑ *...state subsidies that have kept retail prices artificially low.*

1 형용사 인공의 ❑ 그 도시에는 작은 천연 및 인공 호수들이 점재해 있다. ❑ 인공 첨가물과 색소, 조미료가 함유되지 않은 건강식 ● 인공적으로 부사 ❑ 인공 가당 레모네이드 ❑ 그의 어머니가 인위적인, 부자연스러운 ❑ 인위적인 사무실 환경에서조차도 우리는 계속 신체 리듬의 영향을 받는다. ● 인위적으로 부사 ❑ 소매 물가를 인위적으로 낮게 억제해 온 국가 보조금

Thesaurus   *artificial*의 참조어

ADJ.   synthetic, unnatural; *(ant.)* natural **1** **2**

---

ar|ti|fi|cial in|tel|li|gence N-UNCOUNT **Artificial intelligence** is a type of computer technology which is concerned with making machines work in an intelligent way, similar to the way that the human mind works.

불가산명사 인공 지능

ar|til|lery /ɑrtɪləri/ **1** N-UNCOUNT **Artillery** consists of large, powerful guns which are transported on wheels and used by an army. ❑ *Using tanks and heavy artillery, they seized the town.* **2** N-SING-COLL **The artillery** is the section of an army which is trained to use large, powerful guns. ❑ *From 1935 to 1937 he completed his compulsory national service in the artillery.*

1 불가산명사 포, 대포 ❑ 그들은 탱크와 중포를 써서 그 마을을 장악했다. **2** 단수명사-집합 포병대 ❑ 그는 1935년부터 1937년까지 포병대에서 의무 병역을 이행했다.

art|ist ♦♦◇ /ɑrtɪst/ (artists) **1** N-COUNT An **artist** is someone who draws or paints pictures or creates sculptures as a job or a hobby. ❑ *...the studio of a great artist.* ❑ *Each poster is signed by the artist.* **2** N-COUNT An **artist** is a person who creates novels, poems, films, or other things which can be considered as works of art. ❑ *His books are enormously easy to read, yet he is a serious artist.* **3** N-COUNT An **artist** is a performer such as a musician, actor, or dancer. ❑ *...a popular artist who has sold millions of records.* →see **animation**

1 가산명사 미술가 ❑ 위대한 미술가의 작업장 ❑ 모든 포스터에는 그 미술가의 서명이 들어 있다. **2** 가산명사 예술가 ❑ 그의 저서들은 무척 읽기 쉽지만, 그는 진지한 예술가이다. **3** 가산명사 연예인, 공연 예술가 ❑ 수백만 장의 음반이 팔린 인기 연예인

ar|tis|tic /ɑrtɪstɪk/ **1** ADJ Someone who is **artistic** is good at drawing or painting, or arranging things in a beautiful way. ❑ *They encourage boys to be sensitive and artistic.* **2** ADJ **Artistic** means relating to art or artists. ❑ *...the campaign for artistic freedom.* ● ar|tis|ti|cal|ly /ɑrtɪstɪkli/ ADV ❑ *...artistically gifted children.* **3** ADJ An **artistic** design or arrangement is beautiful. ❑ *...an artistic arrangement of stone paving.* ● ar|tis|ti|cal|ly ADV ❑ *...artistically carved vessels.*

1 형용사 예술적인 ❑ 그들은 남자 아이들의 감수성과 예술적 소양을 장려한다. **2** 형용사 예술의 ❑ 예술 자유 운동 ● 예술적으로 부사 ❑ 예술적 재능이 있는 아이들 **3** 형용사 멋진, 예술적인 ❑ 멋지게 깔린 돌 포장도로 ● 멋지게, 예술적으로 부사 ❑ 멋진 조각이 새겨진 그릇들

art|ist|ry /ɑrtɪstri/ N-UNCOUNT **Artistry** is the creative skill of an artist, writer, actor, or musician. ❑ *...his artistry as a cellist.*

불가산명사 예술성 ❑ 그의 첼로 연주자로서의 예술성

---

                     as

① CONJUNCTION AND PREPOSITION USES
② USED WITH OTHER PREPOSITIONS AND CONJUNCTIONS

---

① **as** ♦♦♦ /əz, STRONG æz/ →Please look at category **12** to see if the expression you are looking for is shown under another headword. **1** CONJ If something happens **as** something else happens, it happens at the same time. ❑ *Another policeman has been injured as fighting continued this morning.* ❑ *All the jury's eyes were on him as he continued.* **2** PHRASE You use the structure **as...as** when you are comparing things. ❑ *I never went through a final exam that was as difficult as that one.* ● PHRASE **As** is also a conjunction. ❑ *Being a mother isn't as bad as I thought at first!* **3** PHRASE You use **as...as** to emphasize amounts of something. [EMPHASIS] ❑ *She gets as many as eight thousand letters a month.* **4** PREP You use **as** when you are indicating what someone or something is or is thought to be, or what function they have. ❑ *He has worked as a diplomat in the U.S., Sudan and Saudi Arabia.* ❑ *The news apparently came as a complete surprise.* **5** PREP If you do something **as** a child or **as** a teenager, for example, you do it when you are a child or a teenager. ❑ *She loved singing as a child and started vocal training at 12.* **6** CONJ You use **as** to say how something happens or is done, or to indicate that something happens or is done in the same way as something else. ❑ *I'll behave toward them as I would like to be treated.* ❑ *Today, as usual, he was wearing a three-piece suit.* **7** PREP You use **as** in expressions like **as a result** and **as a consequence** to indicate how two situations or events are related to each other. ❑ *As a result of the growing fears about home security, more people are arranging for someone to stay in their home when they're away.* **8** CONJ You use **as** to introduce short clauses which comment on the truth of what you are saying. ❑ *As you can see, we're still working.* **9** CONJ You can use **as** to mean "because" when you are explaining the reason for something. ❑ *Enjoy the first hour of the day. This is important as it sets the mood for the rest of the day.*

1 접속사 ~할 때, ~하면서 ❑ 오늘 아침 싸움이 계속되면서 또 한 명의 경찰관이 부상당했다. ❑ 그가 계속 말을 이을 때 모든 배심원들의 눈이 그를 향했다. **2** 구 ~만큼...한 ❑ 그 시험만큼 어려운 기말 고사는 처음 본 적이 없었다. ● 구 ~만큼...한 ❑ 어머니가 되는 일은 내가 처음에 생각했던 것만큼 나쁘지 않다! **3** 구 ~만큼이나 되는 (양의 많거나 적음을 강조함) [강조] ❑ 그녀는 1달에 자그마치 8천 통이나 되는 편지를 받는다. **4** 전치사 ~로서 ❑ 그는 미국과 수단, 사우디아라비아에서 외교관으로 일해 왔다. ❑ 언뜻 보기에 그 소식은 대단히 놀라운 일로 다가왔다. **5** 전치사 ~일 때 ❑ 그녀는 아이 적에 노래 부르기를 좋아해서 열두 살 때 가장 훈련을 시작했다. **6** 접속사 ~대로, ~와 같이 ❑ 나는 내 자신이 대우받기를 원하는 대로 그들을 대할 것이다. ❑ 그는 오늘, 평소와 같이 스리피스 정장을 입고 있었다. **7** 전치사 ~의 결과로'라는 뜻의 표현 ❑ 가정 보안에 대한 두려움이 점점 더 커져 가는 탓에, 더 많은 사람들이 집을 떠나 있는 동안 누군가를 집에 머물도록 하고 있다. **8** 접속사 ~처럼 ❑ 보다시피 우리는 아직 일하고 있다. **9** 접속사 ~이기 때문에 ❑ 하루의 첫 시간을 즐겁게 보내라. 이 시간이 나머지 하루의 기분을 결정하기 때문에 그와 같은 일은 중요하다.

You can use **as**, **because**, **since**, or **for** to give an explanation for something. **Because** is the commonest of these, and is used when answering a question beginning with 'why'. You can use **as** or **since** instead of **because** to introduce a clause containing a reason for something, especially in writing. ❏ *The size of the room is important as it will dictate the type of desk you choose... Since the juice is quite strong, you should always dilute it.* In stories, **for** is sometimes used to explain or justify something. ❏ *He seemed to be in need of company, for he suddenly went back into the house.* Note that **because** is a conjunction, and is used to link two ideas within one sentence. ❏ *I just forgot because I was nervous.*

as, because, since, for는 무엇에 대한 이유를 설명할 때 쓴다. 이들 중 because가 가장 일반적이며, why로 시작하는 질문에 대한 대답을 할 때 쓴다. as나 since는 특히 문어체에서 이유를 포함하는 절을 도입할 때 because 대신 쓰인다. ❏ 방의 크기에 따라 책상의 종류가 달라질 테니까 방의 크기가 중요하다... 그 주스는 상당히 진하니까 항상 희석시켜야 한다. for는 이야기에서 가끔 무엇을 설명하거나 정당화할 때 쓴다. ❏ 그는 함께 갈 사람이 필요했던 모양이다. 갑자기 다시 집으로 들어간 것을 보면. because는 접속사로서 한 문장 내에서 두 가지 생각을 연결하기 위해 쓴다는 점을 유의하라. ❏ 나는 긴장해서 그냥 잊어버렸다.

⑩ PHRASE You say **as it were** in order to make what you are saying sound less definite. [VAGUENESS] ❏ *I'd understood the words, but I didn't, as it were, understand the question.* ⑪ PHRASE You use expressions such as **as it is**, **as it turns out**, and **as things stand** when you are making a contrast between a possible situation and what actually happened or is the case. ❏ *I want to work at home on a Tuesday but as it turns out sometimes it's a Wednesday or a Thursday.* ⑫ **as ever** →see **ever**. **as a matter of fact** →see **fact**. **as follows** →see **follow**. **as long as** →see **long**. **as opposed to** →see **opposed**. **as regards** →see **regard**. **as soon as** →see **soon**. **as such** →see **such**. **as well** →see **well**. **as well as** →see **well**. **as yet** →see **yet**

⑩ 구 말하자면 [점잖투] ❏ 내가 그 단어들은 이해했었지만, 말하자면 질문은 이해하지 못했다. ⑪ 구 실제로는 ❏ 나는 화요일에 재택근무를 하고 싶지만, 실제로는 때때로 수요일이나 목요일에 하게 된다.

② **as** ♦♦♦ /əz, STRONG æz/ ❶ PHRASE You use **as for** and **as to** at the beginning of a sentence in order to introduce a slightly different subject that is still connected to the previous one. ❏ *I feel that there's a lot of pressure put on policemen. And as for putting guns in their hands, I don't think that's a very good idea at all.* ❷ PHRASE You use **as to** to indicate what something refers to. ❏ *They should make decisions as to whether the student needs more help.* ❸ PHRASE If you say that something will happen **as of**, or in British English **as from**, a particular date or time, you mean that it will happen from that time on. ❏ *The border, effectively closed since 1981, will be opened as of January the 1st.* ❹ PHRASE You use **as if** and **as though** when you are giving a possible explanation for something or saying that something appears to be the case when it is not. ❏ *Anne shrugged, as if she didn't know.*

❶ 구 ~로 ~은 어떠냐 하면, ~로 말하자면 ❏ 경찰관들은 많은 압박감을 받는 것 같다. 때문에 그들의 손에 총을 쥐어 주는 것에 대해 말하자면, 나는 그것이 전혀 좋은 생각이 아니라고 본다. ❷ 구 ~에 대해서 ❏ 그들은 그 학생에게 더 많은 도움이 필요한지에 대해 결정을 내려야 한다. ❸ 구 ~을 기해, ~ 이래로 ❏ 1981년 이후 사실상 폐쇄되었던 국경은 1월 1일을 기해 개방될 것이다. ❹ 구 마치 ~처럼 ❏ 앤은 마치 모르는 것처럼 어깨를 으쓱했다.

Word Partnership   *as*의 연어

ADJ.	as **good** ① ②
V.	**act** as, (also) **known** as, **describe** as, **perceived/seen** as, **serve/use** as, **treat** as ① ⑥
N.	**reputation** as ① ④
	as a **result** ① ⑦
PREP.	as **for/to** *something* ② ❶
	as **of** ② ❸
CONJ.	as **if/though** ② ❹

asap /eɪ ɛs eɪ pi/ ADV **asap** is an abbreviation for "as soon as possible." [ADV after v] ❏ *The colonel ordered, "I want two good engines down here asap."*

부사 가능한 한 빨리 ❏ 대령은 명령했다. "가능한 한 빨리 상태가 좋은 엔진 두 개를 여기로 가져오게."

as|bes|tos /æsbɛstəs, æz-/ N-UNCOUNT **Asbestos** is a gray material which does not burn and which was used in the past as a protection against fire or heat. Clothing and mats are sometimes made from it. ❏ *...asbestos gloves.*

불가산명사 석면 ❏ 석면 장갑

Word Link   scend ≈ climbing : a*scend*, conde*scend*, de*scend*

as|cend /əsɛnd/ (ascends, ascending, ascended) ❶ V-T If you **ascend** a hill or staircase, you go up it. [WRITTEN] ❏ *Mrs. Clayton had to hold Lizzie's hand as they ascended the steps.* ❷ V-I If a staircase or path **ascends**, it leads up to a higher position. [WRITTEN] ❏ *A number of staircases ascend from the cobbled streets onto the ramparts.* ❸ V-I If something **ascends**, it moves up, usually vertically or into the air. [WRITTEN] ❏ *Keep the drill centered in the borehole while it ascends and descends.* ❹ →see also **ascending**

❶ 타동사 올라가다 [문어체] ❏ 층계를 올라갈 때 클레이턴 부인은 리지의 손을 붙잡아야 했다. ❷ 자동사 올라가다 [문어체] ❏ 자갈이 깔린 거리에서 성벽 위로 여러 개의 계단이 올라간다. ❸ 자동사 올라가다 [문어체] ❏ 드릴이 오르내릴 때 계속 시추공의 중심에 있도록 하시오.

as|cend|ing /əsɛndɪŋ/ ADJ If a group of things is arranged in **ascending** order, each thing is bigger, greater, or more important than the thing before it. [ADJ n] ❏ *Now draw or trace ten dinosaurs in ascending order of size.* →see also **ascend**

형용사 오름차순의 ❏ 이제 크기가 작은 것부터 차례대로 열 마리의 공룡을 그려 보세요.

as|cent /əsɛnt/ (ascents) ❶ N-COUNT An **ascent** is an upward journey, especially when you are walking or climbing. ❏ *In 1955 he led the first ascent of Kangchenjunga, the world's third highest mountain.* ❷ N-COUNT An **ascent** is an upward slope or path, especially when you are walking or climbing. ❏ *It was a tough course over a gradual ascent before the big climb of Bluebell Hill.* ❸ N-COUNT An **ascent** is an upward, vertical movement. ❏ *Burke pushed the button and the elevator began its slow ascent.*

❶ 가산명사 등반 ❏ 1955년에 그는 세계에서 세 번째로 높은 봉우리인 캉첸중가 등반을 최초로 이끌었다. ❷ 가산명사 비탈, 오르막 ❏ 그것은 블루벨 힐의 가파른 등성이 앞에서 점점 오르막이 되는 까다로운 코스였다. ❸ 가산명사 상승 ❏ 버크가 단추를 누르자 엘리베이터는 천천히 올라가기 시작했다.

Word Link   cert ≈ determined, true : as*cert*ain, *cert*ificate, *cert*ify

as|cer|tain /æsərteɪn/ (ascertains, ascertaining, ascertained) V-T If you **ascertain** the truth about something, you find out what it is, especially by making a deliberate effort to do so. [FORMAL] ❏ *Through doing this, the teacher will be able to ascertain the extent to which the child understands what he is reading.* ❏ *Once they had ascertained that he was not a spy, they agreed to release him.*

타동사 확인하다, 조사하다 [격식체] ❏ 이렇게 함으로써, 선생님은 아이가 자신이 읽고 있는 것을 얼마만큼 이해하는지 확인할 수 있을 것이다. ❏ 일단 그들이 그가 스파이가 아니라는 사실을 확인하자, 그들은 그를 풀어주는 데 동의했다.

as|cribe /əskraɪb/ (ascribes, ascribing, ascribed) ❶ V-T If you **ascribe** an event or condition **to** a particular cause, you say or consider that it was caused by

❶ 타동사 ~의 탓으로 돌리다 [격식체] ❏ 부검 결과 그 아기의 사인은 결국 유아 돌연사 증후군으로 나왔다.

a b c d e f g h i j k l m n o p q r s t u v w x y z

that thing. [FORMAL] ☐ *An autopsy eventually ascribed the baby's death to sudden infant death syndrome.* **2** V-T If you **ascribe** a quality **to** someone, you consider that they possess it. [FORMAL] ☐ *We do not ascribe a superior wisdom to government or the state.*

2 타동사 —에 속하다고 생각하다 [격식체] ● 우리는 국가나 정부가 월등히 현명하고 생각하지 않는다.

ash /æʃ/ (**ashes**) **1** N-UNCOUNT **Ash** is the gray or black powdery substance that is left after something is burnt. You can also refer to this substance as **ashes**. [also N in pl] ☐ *A cloud of volcanic ash is spreading across wide areas of the Philippines.* ☐ *He brushed the cigarette ash from his sleeve.* **2** N-PLURAL A dead person's **ashes** are their remains after their body has been cremated. ☐ *And she asks him to go back there after her death and scatter her ashes on the lake.* **3** N-VAR An **ash** is a tree that has smooth gray bark and loses its leaves in winter. ● N-UNCOUNT **Ash** is the wood from this tree. ☐ *The rafters are made from ash.* →see **fire, volcano**

1 불가산명사 재 ☐ 화산재 구름이 필리핀 군도의 광범위한 지역으로 퍼지고 있다. ☐ 그는 소매에 묻은 담뱃재를 털어 냈다. **2** 복수명사 유골 ☐ 그리고 그녀는 그에게 자신이 죽은 다음 그 곳에 돌아가 호수에 유골을 뿌려 달라고 부탁한다. **3** 가산명사 또는 불가산명사 양물푸레나무 ● 불가산명사 양물푸레나무 재목 ☐ 그 서까래들은 양물푸레나무로 만들어진다.

ashamed /əʃeɪmd/ **1** ADJ If someone is **ashamed**, they feel embarrassed or guilty because of something they do or they have done, or because of their appearance. [v-link ADJ, usu ADJ of/about n, ADJ that] ☐ *I felt incredibly ashamed of myself for getting so angry.* **2** ADJ If you are **ashamed of** someone, you feel embarrassed to be connected with them, often because of their appearance or because you disapprove of something they have done. [v-link ADJ of n] ☐ *I've never told this to anyone, but it's true, I was terribly ashamed of my mom.*

1 형용사 부끄러워하는 ☐ 나는 그렇게 화를 내는 내 자신이 몹시 부끄러웠다. **2** 형용사 -를 부끄럽게 여기는 ☐ 이런 말을 누구한테도 한 적 없지만, 내가 엄마를 대단히 부끄럽게 여겼던 것은 사실이다.

ashore /əʃɔːr/ ADV Someone or something that comes **ashore** comes from the sea onto the shore. ☐ *Oil has come ashore on a ten mile stretch to the east of Plymouth.*

부사 해변으로, 물가로 ☐ 플리머스 동부 10마일에 걸친 해안에 기름이 떠내려왔다.

ash|tray /æʃtreɪ/ (**ashtrays**) N-COUNT An **ashtray** is a small dish in which smokers can put the ash from their cigarettes and cigars.

가산명사 재떨이

Asian ♦♦◇ /eɪʒ³n/ (**Asians**) ADJ Someone or something that is **Asian** comes from or is associated with Asia. Americans use this term especially to refer to China, Korea, Thailand, Japan, or Vietnam. British people use this term especially to refer to India, Pakistan, and Bangladesh. ☐ *...Asian music.* ● N-COUNT An **Asian** is a person who comes from or is associated with a country or region in Asia. ☐ *Many of the shops were run by Asians.*

형용사 아시아의 ☐ 아시아 음악 ● 가산명사 아시아 사람 ☐ 그 상점들 중 다수가 아시아인이 운영하는 것이었다.

The word **Asian** is used to describe people from Asia, but the word **Oriental** is considered a derogatory term, and should be used only to refer to inanimate objects such as art, music, or history.

Asian(아시아인)이란 말은 아시아 출신 사람을 일컬을 때 사용하지만, Oriental(동양인)은 경멸적인 말로 여겨지므로 미술, 음악, 역사와 같은 무생물 대상에만 사용해야 한다.

aside ♦◇◇ /əsaɪd/

In addition to the uses shown below, **aside** is used in phrasal verbs such as "cast aside," "stand aside," and "step aside."

aside는 아래 용법 외에도 'cast aside', 'stand aside', 'step aside'와 같은 구동사에 쓰인다.

1 ADV If you move something **aside**, you move it to one side of you. [ADV after v] ☐ *Sarah closed the book and laid it aside.* **2** ADV If you take or draw someone **aside**, you take them a little way away from a group of people in order to talk to them in private. [ADV after v] ☐ *Billy Ewing grabbed him by the elbow and took him aside.* **3** ADV If you move something **aside**, you get out of someone's way. [ADV after v] ☐ *She had been standing in the doorway, but now she stepped aside to let them pass.* **4** ADV If you set something such as time, money, or space **aside** for a particular purpose, you save it and do not use it for anything else. [ADV after v] ☐ *She wants to put her pocket-money aside for holidays.* **5** ADV If you brush or sweep **aside** a feeling or suggestion, you reject it. [ADV after v] ☐ *Talk to a friend who will really listen and not brush aside your feelings.* **6** ADV You use **aside** to indicate that you have finished talking about something, or that you are leaving it out of your discussion, and that you are about to talk about something else. ☐ *Leaving aside the tiny minority who are clinically depressed, most people who have bad moods also have very good moods.*

1 부사 한 쪽으로 ☐ 세라는 책을 덮어 한 쪽에 놓았다. **2** 부사 한쪽으로 (데려가다) ☐ 빌리 유잉은 그의 팔꿈치를 잡고 그를 한쪽으로 데려갔다. **3** 부사 한쪽으로 비켜 ☐ 그녀는 문간에 서 있었지만, 이제는 그들이 지나가도록 한쪽으로 비켜섰다. **4** 부사 따로 ☐ 그녀는 휴가를 위해 쌈짓돈을 따로 모아 두고 싶어 한다. **5** 부사 떨치 버리고 ☐ 진정으로 말을 들어주고 당신의 감정을 떨쳐 내지 않을 친구와 얘기를 나누세요. **6** 부사 제쳐두고 ☐ 병적 우울 증세가 있는 극소수는 제쳐두고, 우울한 기분을 갖는 사람들도 대부분은 아주 쾌활한 기분 또한 느낀다.

ask ♦♦♦ /ɑːsk, æsk/ (**asks, asking, asked**) **1** V-T/V-I If you **ask** someone something, you say something to them in the form of a question because you want to know the answer. ☐ *"How is Frank?" he asked.* ☐ *I asked him his name.* ☐ *She asked me if I'd enjoyed my dinner.* **2** V-T If you **ask** someone **to** do something, you tell them that you want them to do it. ☐ *We had to ask him to leave.* **3** V-T If you **ask to** do something, you tell someone that you want to do it. ☐ *I asked to see the Director.* **4** V-I If you **ask for** something, you say that you would like it. ☐ *I decided to go to the next house and ask for food.* **5** V-I If you **ask for** someone, you say that you would like to speak to them. ☐ *There's a man at the gate asking for you.* **6** V-T If you **ask** someone's permission, opinion, or forgiveness, you try to obtain it by making a request. ☐ *Please ask permission from whoever pays the phone bill before making your call.* **7** V-T If you **ask** someone **to** an event or place, you invite them to go there. ☐ *Couldn't you ask Jon to the party?* **8** V-T If someone **is asking** a particular price **for** something, they are selling it for that price. ☐ *Mr. Pantelaras was asking £6,000 for his collection.* **9** CONVENTION You reply "**don't ask me**" when you do not know the answer to a question, usually when you are annoyed or surprised that you have been asked. [FEELINGS] ☐ *"She's got other things on her mind, wouldn't you think?" "Don't ask me," murmured Chris. "I've never met her."* **10** PHRASE You can say "**if you ask me**" to emphasize that you are stating your personal opinion. [EMPHASIS] ☐ *He was nuts, if you ask me.* **11** PHRASE If you say that someone **is asking for trouble** or **is asking for it**, you mean that they are behaving in a way that makes it very likely that they will get into trouble. ☐ *To go ahead with the match after such clear advice had been asking for trouble.*

1 타동사/자동사 묻다 ☐ "프랭크는 어때?"라고 그가 물었다. ☐ 나는 그 남자에게 이름을 물었다. ☐ 저녁 식사는 맛있고 물었다. **2** 타동사 요구하다 ☐ 우리는 그 사람에게 떠나라고 해야 했다. **3** 타동사 부탁하다 ☐ 나는 감독을 만나 보게 해 달라고 부탁했다. **4** 자동사 -을 달라고 부탁하다 ☐ 나는 다음 집으로 가서 음식을 달라고 하기로 결심했다. **5** 자동사 면회를 요청하다 ☐ 입구에 너를 찾아온 사람이 있다. **6** 타동사 요청하다 ☐ 전화를 걸기 전에 그 전화 요금을 내는 사람에게 허락을 받도록 하세요. **7** 타동사 초대하다 ☐ 존을 그 파티에 초대할 수 없을까요? **8** 타동사 얼마의 가격에 내놓다 ☐ 판텔라라스 씨는 자신의 소장품을 6,000파운드에 내놓았다. **9** 관용 표현 몰라, 묻지 마 [감정 개입] ☐ "그녀는 다른 생각을 하고 있는 것 같아. 그렇게 생각 안 해?" "모르겠어. "라고 크리스가 나지막이 말했다. "나는 그녀를 만나 본 적이 없어." **10** 구 내 생각에는 [강조] ☐ 내 생각에, 그는 미치광이였다. **11** 구 사서 고생을 하다 ☐ 그렇게 분명한 조언을 받고서도 시합을 계속 추진한다면 사서 고생을 하는 것일 터였다.

Thesaurus	ask의 참조어
v.	demand, interrogate, question, quiz; (ant.) answer, reply, respond **1**
	beg, petition, plead, request; (ant.) command, insist **6**

Word Partnership ask의 연어

PREP.	ask **about** 🔟
	ask **for** 4️⃣ 5️⃣
	ask **to** 2️⃣ 3️⃣ 7️⃣
ADJ.	**afraid to** ask 🔟
DET.	ask **how/what/when/where/who/why** 🔟
CONJ.	ask **if/whether** 🔟
N.	ask **a question** 🔟
	ask **for help** 4️⃣
	ask **forgiveness**, ask *someone's* **opinion**, ask **permission** 6️⃣
V.	**come to** ask, **have to** ask 🔟
	don't ask **me** 9️⃣

ask|ing price (**asking prices**) N-COUNT The **asking price** of something is the price which the person selling it says that they want for it, although they may accept less. ❏ *Offers 15% below the asking price are unlikely to be accepted.*

가산명사 제시 가격 ❏ 제시 가격보다 15퍼센트 낮은 값을 제안하는 것은 받아들여질 것 같지 않다.

asleep /əsli̱p/ 🔟 ADJ Someone who is **asleep** is sleeping. [v-link ADJ] ❏ *My four-year-old daughter was asleep on the sofa.* 2️⃣ PHRASE When you **fall asleep**, you start sleeping. ❏ *Sam snuggled down in his pillow and fell asleep.* 3️⃣ PHRASE Someone who is **fast asleep** or **sound asleep** is sleeping deeply. ❏ *They were both fast asleep in their beds.* →see **sleep**

🔟 형용사 잠든 ❏ 나의 네 살짜리 딸은 소파에서 잠들어 있었다. 2️⃣ 구 잠들다 ❏ 샘은 베개에 머리를 묻고 잠이 들었다. 3️⃣ 구 깊이 잠든 ❏ 그들은 둘 다 침대 속에서 깊이 잠들어 있었다.

as|para|gus /əspæ̱rəgəs/ N-UNCOUNT **Asparagus** is a vegetable that is long and green and has small shoots at one end. It is cooked and served whole.

불가산명사 아스파라거스

as|pect ♦♦◇ /æ̱spɛkt/ (**aspects**) 🔟 N-COUNT An **aspect** of something is one of the parts of its character or nature. ❏ *Climate and weather affect every aspect of our lives.* ❏ *He was interested in all aspects of the work here.* 2️⃣ N-COUNT The **aspect** of a building or window is the direction in which it faces. [FORMAL] ❏ *The house had a southwest aspect.*

🔟 가산명사 측면 ❏ 기후와 날씨는 우리 생활의 모든 측면에 영향을 끼친다. ❏ 그는 여기 일의 모든 측면에 관심이 있었다. 2️⃣ 가산명사 (집이나 건물의) 방향 [격식체] ❏ 그 집은 남서쪽을 향하고 있었다.

Word Partnership aspect의 연어

DET.	**another/any/every** aspect 🔟
ADJ.	**most important** aspect, **particular** aspect 🔟
PREP.	aspect **of** *something* 🔟 2️⃣

as|pi|ra|tion /æ̱spəre̱ɪʃ⁰n/ (**aspirations**) N-VAR Someone's **aspirations** are their desire to achieve things. ❏ *...the needs and aspirations of our pupils.* ❏ *He is unlikely to send in the army to quell nationalist aspirations.*

가산명사 또는 불가산명사 열망 ❏ 우리 학생들의 필요와 열망 ❏ 그가 민족주의 열망을 잠재우기 위해 군대를 투입할 것 같지는 않다.

Word Link spir ≈ breath : a*spire*, in*spire*, re*spir*atory

as|pire /əspa̱ɪər/ (**aspires, aspiring, aspired**) V-T/V-I If you **aspire to** something such as an important job, you have a strong desire to achieve it. ❏ *...people who aspire to public office.* →see also **aspiring**

타동사/자동사 열망하다 ❏ 관직을 열망하는 사람들

as|pi|rin /æ̱spərɪn, -prɪn/ (**aspirins**)

The form **aspirin** can also be used for the plural.

N-VAR **Aspirin** is a mild drug which reduces pain and fever.

aspirin도 복수에 쓸 수 있다.

가산명사 또는 불가산명사 아스피린

as|pir|ing /əspa̱ɪərɪŋ/ ADJ If you use **aspiring** to describe someone who is starting a particular career, you mean that they are trying to become successful in it. [ADJ n] ❏ *Many aspiring young artists are advised to learn by copying the masters.* →see **aspire**

형용사 야심이 있는 ❏ 다수의 야심 있는 젊은 미술가들은 대가들의 작품을 모사하면서 연습하라는 충고를 받는다.

ass /æ̱s/ (**asses**) 🔟 N-COUNT An **ass** is an animal which is related to a horse but which is smaller and has long ears. 2️⃣ N-COUNT If you describe someone as an **ass**, you think that they are silly or do silly things. [INFORMAL, DISAPPROVAL] ❏ *He was generally disliked and regarded as a pompous ass.* 3️⃣ N-COUNT Your **ass** is your bottom. [AM, INFORMAL, VULGAR; BRIT **arse, bum**] ❏ *...those fat legs and that big ass.* 4️⃣ **a pain in the ass** →see **pain**

🔟 가산명사 당나귀 2️⃣ 가산명사 바보 [비격식체, 탐탁찮음] ❏ 사람들은 대체로 그 남자를 미워했고 또 건방진 바보로 여겼다. 3️⃣ 가산명사 엉덩이 [미국영어, 비격식체, 비속어; 영국영어 arse, bum] ❏ 저 살찐 다리와 커다란 엉덩이

as|sail|ant /əse̱ɪlənt/ (**assailants**) N-COUNT Someone's **assailant** is a person who has physically attacked them. [FORMAL] ❏ *Other party-goers rescued the injured man from his assailant.*

가산명사 공격자, 가해자 [격식체] ❏ 다른 파티 손님들이 다친 남자를 가해자로부터 구해 냈다.

as|sas|sin /əsæ̱sɪn/ (**assassins**) N-COUNT An **assassin** is a person who assassinates someone. ❏ *He saw the shooting and memorized the license plate of the assassin's car.*

가산명사 암살자 ❏ 그는 총격을 목격했고 암살자의 차 번호를 외워 두었다.

as|sas|si|nate /əsæ̱sɪneɪt/ (**assassinates, assassinating, assassinated**) V-T When someone important **is assassinated**, they are murdered as a political act. ❏ *Would the U.S. be radically different today if Kennedy had not been assassinated?* ● **as|sas|si|na|tion** /əsæ̱sɪne̱ɪʃⁿn/ (**assassinations**) N-VAR ❏ *She would like an investigation into the assassination of her husband.* ❏ *He lives in constant fear of assassination.* →see **kill**

타동사 암살당하다 ❏ 만약 케네디가 암살당하지 않았더라면 오늘날 미국이 완전히 다를까? ● 암살 가산명사 또는 불가산명사 ❏ 그녀는 남편의 암살 사건에 대해 조사가 이루어지기를 바란다. ❏ 그는 끊임없이 암살을 두려워하며 산다.

as|sault ♦◇◇ /əsɔ̱lt/ (**assaults, assaulting, assaulted**) 🔟 N-COUNT An **assault** by an army is a strong attack made on an area held by the enemy. ❏ *The rebels are poised for a new assault on the government garrisons.* 2️⃣ ADJ **Assault** weapons such as rifles are intended for soldiers to use in battle rather than for purposes such as hunting. [ADJ n] 3️⃣ N-VAR An **assault on** a person is a physical attack on them. [oft N on/upon n] ❏ *The attack is one of a series of savage sexual assaults on women in the university area.* 4️⃣ V-T To **assault** someone means to physically attack them. ❏ *The gang assaulted him with iron bars.*

🔟 가산명사 공습 ❏ 반란군은 정부군 주둔지에 대해 새로운 공습을 벌일 태세를 갖추고 있다. 2️⃣ 형용사 전투용의 3️⃣ 가산명사 또는 불가산명사 폭행 ❏ 그 습격 사건은 대학가에서 발생한 일련의 잔인한 부녀자 성폭행 사건 중 하나였다. 4️⃣ 타동사 폭행하다 ❏ 깡패들이 그를 쇠막대기로 폭행했다.

as|sem|ble /əsɛ̱mb⁰l/ (**assembles, assembling, assembled**) 🔟 V-I When people **assemble** or when someone **assembles** them, they come together in a group,

🔟 자동사 모이다; 모으다 ❏ 학생들이 쉬는 시간에 모이기 좋은 장소조차도 없었다. 2️⃣ 타동사 조직하다;

usually for a particular purpose such as a meeting. ❏ *There wasn't even a convenient place for students to assemble between classes.* **2** V-T To **assemble** something means to collect it together or to fit the different parts of it together. ❏ *Greenpeace managed to assemble a small flotilla of inflatable boats to waylay the ship at sea.* →see **industry**

조립하다 ❏ 그린피스는 해상에서 그 배를 가로막기 위해 소규모의 고무보트 선단을 조직해 냈다.

as|sem|bly ♦♦♢ /əsɛmbli/ (**assemblies**) **1** N-COUNT An **assembly** is a large group of people who meet regularly to make decisions or laws for a particular region or country. ❏ *...the campaign for the first free election to the National Assembly.* **2** N-COUNT An **assembly** is a group of people gathered together for a particular purpose. ❏ *He waited until complete quiet settled on the assembly.* **3** N-UNCOUNT When you refer to rights of **assembly** or restrictions on **assembly**, you are referring to the legal right that people have to gather together. [FORMAL] ❏ *The U.S. Constitution guarantees free speech, freedom of assembly and equal protection.* **4** N-VAR In a school, **assembly** is a gathering of all the teachers and pupils at the beginning of each school day. ❏ *By 9, the juniors are in the hall for assembly.* **5** N-UNCOUNT The **assembly** of a machine, device, or object is the process of fitting its different parts together. ❏ *For the rest of the day, he worked on the assembly of an explosive device.*

1 가산명사 집회, 회합 ❏ 최초의 국회의원 자유선거를 위한 운동 **2** 가산명사 집회자, 회합자 ❏ 그는 집회 군중이 완전히 조용해질 때까지 기다렸다. **3** 불가산명사 집회 [격식체] ❏ 미국 헌법은 표현과 집회의 자유, 그리고 평등한 보호를 보장한다. **4** 가산명사 또는 불가산명사 조회 ❏ 9시면 저학년 학생들은 조회를 위해 강당에 있다. **5** 불가산명사 조립 ❏ 그 날의 나머지 시간 동안, 그는 폭발 장치를 조립하는 일에 매달렸다.

as|sent /əsɛnt/ (**assents, assenting, assented**) **1** N-UNCOUNT If someone gives their **assent to** something that has been suggested, they formally agree to it. ❏ *He gave his assent to the proposed legislation.* **2** V-I If you **assent to** something, you agree to it or agree with it. ❏ *I assented to the request of the American publishers to write this book.*

1 불가산명사 동의, 찬성 ❏ 그는 제안된 법률 제정에 찬성했다. **2** 자동사 동의하다, 승낙하다 ❏ 나는 이 책을 써 달라는 미국 출판사들의 요청을 승낙했다.

as|sert /əsɜrt/ (**asserts, asserting, asserted**) **1** V-T If someone **asserts** a fact or belief, they state it firmly. [FORMAL] ❏ *Mr. Helm plans to assert that the bill violates the First Amendment.* ❏ *The defendants, who continue to assert their innocence, are expected to appeal.* ● **as|ser|tion** /əsɜrʃᵊn/ (**assertions**) N-VAR ❏ *There is no concrete evidence to support assertions that the recession is truly over.* **2** V-T If you **assert** your authority, you make it clear by your behavior that you have authority. ❏ *After the war, the army made an attempt to assert its authority in the south of the country.* ● **as|ser|tion** N-UNCOUNT ❏ *The decision is seen as an assertion of his authority within the company.* **3** V-T If you **assert** your right or claim to something, you insist that you have the right to it. ❏ *The republics began asserting their right to govern themselves.* ● **as|ser|tion** N-UNCOUNT ❏ *These institutions have made the assertion of ethnic identity possible.* **4** V-T If you **assert yourself**, you speak and act in a forceful way, so that people take notice of you. ❏ *He's speaking up and asserting himself and doing things he enjoys.*

1 타동사 주장하다, 단언하다 [격식체] ❏ 헬름 씨는 그 법안이 헌법 수정 제 1항을 위반한다고 주장할 계획이다. ❏ 계속해서 무죄를 주장하는 피고측은 상소할 것으로 예상된다. ● 주장 가산명사 또는 불가산명사 ❏ 경기 후퇴가 확실히 끝났다는 주장을 뒷받침하는 구체적인 증거는 없다. **2** 타동사 시위하다 ❏ 전쟁 이후, 그 군대는 그 나라 남부에서 지배력을 가지고 요구하고자 했다. ● 시위 불가산명사 ❏ 그 결정은 그가 회사 내에서 지닌 권위의 시위처럼 보인다. **3** 타동사 주장하다 ❏ 공화국들은 자치권을 주장하기 시작했다. ● 주장 불가산명사 ❏ 이 단체들에 의해 민족적 정체성을 주장하는 것이 가능해졌다. **4** 타동사 (자기주장을) 뚜렷이 내세우다 ❏ 그는 목소리를 높여 자기주장을 내세우며 자신이 좋아하는 일들을 하고 있다.

as|ser|tive /əsɜrtɪv/ ADJ Someone who is **assertive** states their needs and opinions clearly, so that people take notice. ❏ *Women have become more assertive in the past decade.* ● **as|ser|tive|ness** N-UNCOUNT ❏ *Clare's assertiveness stirred up his deep-seated sense of inadequacy.*

형용사 자기주장을 뚜렷이 내세우는 ❏ 지난 십 년 동안에 여성들은 자신들의 주장을 더 뚜렷이 내세우게 되었다. ● 자기주장을 뚜렷이 내세움 불가산명사 ❏ 클레어의 자기주장을 뚜렷이 내세우는 태도가 그의 고질적인 무능력감을 자극했다.

as|sess ♦♢♢ /əsɛs/ (**assesses, assessing, assessed**) **1** V-T When you **assess** a person, thing, or situation, you consider them in order to make a judgment about them. ❏ *Our correspondent has been assessing the impact of the sanctions.* ❏ *The test was to assess aptitude rather than academic achievement.* **2** V-T When you **assess** the amount of money that something is worth or should be paid, you calculate or estimate it. ❏ *Ask them to send you information on how to assess the value of your belongings.*

1 타동사 진단하다, 평가하다 ❏ 우리 쪽 특파원은 그와 같은 제재의 영향을 진단해 왔다. ❏ 그 시험은 학문적 성취보다는 적성을 평가하기 위한 것이었다. **2** 타동사 평가하다, 사정하다 ❏ 당신의 재산 가치를 평가하는 방법에 대한 정보를 보내 달라고 그들에게 요청하세요.

as|sess|ment ♦♢♢ /əsɛsmənt/ (**assessments**) **1** N-VAR An **assessment** is a consideration of someone or something and a judgment about them. ❏ *There is little assessment of the damage to the natural environment.* **2** N-VAR An **assessment** of the amount of money that something is worth or that should be paid is a calculation or estimate of the amount. ❏ *Price Waterhouse have traced the losses to lenders' inflated assessments of mortgaged property.*

1 가산명사 또는 불가산명사 진단, 평가 ❏ 자연 환경에 미칠 피해에 대한 평가가 거의 없다. **2** 가산명사 또는 불가산명사 평가, 사정 ❏ 프라이스 워터하우스 사는 저당 자산에 대한 대부업자들의 부풀려진 평가에서부터 손실이 기인한 것으로 추적해 냈다.

Word Link	or, er ≈ one who does, that which does: **assessor, author, armor**

---

as|ses|sor /əsɛsər/ (**assessors**) N-COUNT An **assessor** is a person who is employed to calculate the value of something, or the amount of money that should be paid, for example in tax. [BUSINESS]

가산명사 평가인; 사정인 [경제]

as|set ♦♦♢ /æsɛt/ (**assets**) **1** N-COUNT Something or someone that is an **asset** is considered useful or helps a person or organization to be successful. ❏ *Her leadership qualities were the greatest asset of the Conservative Party.* **2** N-PLURAL The **assets** of a company or a person are all the things that they own. [BUSINESS] ❏ *By the end of 2003 the group had assets of 3.5 billion euros.*

1 가산명사 자산 ❏ 그녀의 지도자로서의 자질은 보수당이 가진 최고의 자산이었다. **2** 복수명사 자산 [경제] ❏ 2003년 말경 그 기업의 자산 가치는 35억 유로였다.

asset-stripping N-UNCOUNT If a person or company is involved in **asset-stripping**, they buy companies cheaply, sell off their assets to make a profit, and then close the companies down. [BUSINESS, DISAPPROVAL]

불가산명사 자산 박탈 (부실 회사 정리) [경제, 탐탁찮음]

as|sign /əsaɪn/ (**assigns, assigning, assigned**) **1** V-T If you **assign** a piece of work **to** someone, you give them the work to do. ❏ *When I taught, I would assign a topic to children which they would write about.* ❏ *Later in the year, she'll assign them research papers.* **2** V-T If you **assign** something **to** someone, you say that it is for their use. ❏ *The selling broker is then required to assign a portion of the commission to the buyer broker.* **3** V-T If someone **is assigned to** a particular place, group, or person, they are sent there, usually in order to work at that place or for that person. [usu passive] ❏ *I was assigned to Troop A of the 10th Cavalry.* ❏ *Did you choose Russia or were you simply assigned there?* **4** V-T If you **assign** a particular function or value **to** someone or something, you say they have it. ❏ *Under the system, each business must assign a value to each job.*

1 타동사 주다, 할당하다 ❏ 아이들을 가르칠 때, 나는 글을 쓸 주제를 아이들에게 주곤 했다. ❏ 그녀는 올해 후반에 그들에게 연구 보고서를 써 내도록 할 것이다. **2** 타동사 양도하다 ❏ 그리고 나서 매도 중개인은 커미션의 일부를 매수 중개인에게 양도해야 한다. **3** 타동사 배치되다, 배속되다 ❏ 나는 10 기갑부대 에이 중대에 배속되었다. ❏ 네가 러시아를 택한 거니, 아니면 그냥 거기 배치된 거니? **4** 타동사 -의 것으로 하다 ❏ 그 시스템 하에서는, 모든 사업이 각 직무에 가치를 부여해야 한다.

as|sign|ment /əsaɪnmənt/ (**assignments**) N-COUNT An **assignment** is a task or piece of work that you are given to do, especially as part of your job or

가산명사 임무; 과제 ❏ 그 과목의 평가는 필기 과제와 실기 시험으로 이루어진다.

studies. ❑ *The assessment for the course involves written assignments and practical tests.*

Thesaurus   *assignment*의 참조어

N.   chore, duty, job, task

as|simi|late /əsɪmɪleɪt/ (**assimilates, assimilating, assimilated**) ◾ V-T/V-I When people such as immigrants **assimilate into** a community or when that community **assimilates** them, they become an accepted part of it. ❑ *There is every sign that new Asian-Americans are just as willing to assimilate.* ❑ *His family tried to assimilate into the white and Hispanic communities.* ● **as|simi|la|tion** /əsɪmɪleɪʃᵊn/ N-UNCOUNT ❑ *They promote social integration and assimilation of minority ethnic groups into the culture.* ◾ V-T If you **assimilate** new ideas, customs, or techniques, you learn them or adopt them. ❑ *My mind could only assimilate one impossibility at a time.* ● **as|simi|la|tion** N-UNCOUNT ❑ *This technique brings life to instruction and eases assimilation of knowledge.*

as|sist ◆◇◇ /əsɪst/ (**assists, assisting, assisted**) ◾ V-T If you **assist** someone, you help them to do a job or task by doing part of the work for them. ❑ *The family decided to assist me with my chores.* ◾ V-T/V-I If you **assist** someone, you give them information, advice, or money. ❑ *The public is urgently requested to assist police in tracing this man.* ❑ *Foreign Office officials assisted with transport and finance problems.* ◾ V-T/V-I If something **assists in** doing a task, it makes the task easier to do. ❑ *...a chemical that assists in the manufacture of proteins.*

as|sis|tance ◆◇◇ /əsɪstəns/ ◾ N-UNCOUNT If you give someone **assistance**, you help them do a job or task by doing part of the work for them. [oft with poss] ❑ *Since 1976 he has been operating the shop with the assistance of volunteers.* ◾ N-UNCOUNT If you give someone **assistance**, you give them information or advice. ❑ *Any assistance you could give the police will be greatly appreciated.* ◾ N-UNCOUNT If someone gives a person or country **assistance**, they help them by giving them money. [oft supp N] ❑ *...a viable program of economic assistance.* ◾ N-UNCOUNT If something is done **with the assistance of** a particular thing, that thing is helpful or necessary for doing it. ❑ *The translations were carried out with the assistance of a medical dictionary.* ◾ PHRASE Someone or something that **is of assistance** to you is helpful or useful to you. ❑ *Can I be of any assistance?* ◾ PHRASE If you **come to** someone's **assistance**, you take action to help them. ❑ *They are appealing to the world community to come to Jordan's assistance.*

Word Partnership   *assistance*의 연어

V.   **need/require** assistance ◾ ◾
     provide assistance ◾ ◾ ◾
ADJ.   **emergency** assistance, **medical** assistance, **technical** assistance ◾
     financial assistance ◾

as|sis|tant ◆◇◇ /əsɪstənt/ (**assistants**) ◾ ADJ **Assistant** is used in front of titles or jobs to indicate a slightly lower rank. For example, an assistant director is one rank lower than a director in an organization. [ADJ n] ❑ *...the assistant secretary of defense.* ◾ N-COUNT Someone's **assistant** is a person who helps them in their work. ❑ *Kalan called his assistant, Hashim, to take over while he went out.* ◾ N-COUNT An **assistant** is a person who works in a store selling things to customers. ❑ *The assistant took the book and checked the price on the back cover.*

Word Link   *soci* ≈ companion : as**soci**ate, **soci**al, **soci**ology

as|so|ci|ate ◆◇◇ (**associates, associating, associated**)

The verb is pronounced /əsoʊʃieɪt/. The noun and adjective are pronounced /əsoʊʃiɪt, -siɪt/.

◾ V-T If you **associate** someone or something **with** another thing, the two are connected in your mind. ❑ *Through science we've got the idea of associating progress with the future.* ◾ V-T If you **are associated with** a particular organization, cause, or point of view, or if you **associate yourself with** it, you support it publicly. ❑ *I haven't been associated with the project over the last year.* ◾ V-I If you say that someone **is associating with** another person or group of people, you mean they are spending a lot of time in the company of people you do not approve of. ❑ *What would they think if they knew that they were associating with a murderer?* ◾ N-COUNT Your **associates** are the people you are closely connected with, especially at work. ❑ *...the restaurant owner's business associates.* ◾ ADJ **Associate** is used before a rank or title to indicate a slightly different or lower rank or title. [ADJ n] ❑ *Mr. Lin is associate director of the Institute.*

as|so|ci|at|ed ◆◇◇ /əsoʊʃieɪtɪd, -siei-/ ◾ ADJ If one thing is **associated with** another, the two things are connected with each other. ❑ *These symptoms are particularly associated with migraine headaches.* ◾ ADJ **Associated** is used in the name of a company that is made up of a number of smaller companies which have joined together. [ADJ n] ❑ *...the Associated Press.*

as|so|cia|tion ◆◆◇ /əsoʊʃieɪ-, -sieɪ-/ (**associations**) ◾ N-COUNT An **association** is an official group of people who have the same job, aim, or interest. ❑ *...the British Olympic Association.* ◾ N-COUNT Your **association with** a person or a thing such as an organization is the connection that you have with them. ❑ *...the company's six-year association with retailer J.C. Penney Co.* ◾ N-COUNT If something has particular **associations** for you, it is connected in your mind with a particular memory, idea, or feeling. ❑ *He has a shelf full of*

◾ 타동사/자동사 동화되다; 동화시키다 ❑ 새로운 아시아계 미국인들이 자발적으로 동화되려 한다는 여러 가지 조짐이 있다. ❑ 그의 가족은 백인 사회와 히스패닉계 사회에 동화되려고 노력했다. ● 동화 불가산명사 ❑ 그들은 사회 통합과 소수 인종 집단의 문화적 동화를 장려한다. ◾ 타동사 받아들이다, 흡수하다 ❑ 내 마음은 불가능한 일을 한 번에 1가지씩만 받아들일 수 있을 것이다. ● 흡수 불가산명사 ❑ 이 기법은 교육에 활기를 불어넣고 지식의 흡수 속도를 조절해 줍니다.

◾ 타동사 돕다, 거들다 ❑ 그 가족은 내 허드렛일을 거들어 주기로 결정했다. ◾ 타동사/자동사 협조하다 ❑ 경찰에서는 이 사내의 행방을 찾아내는 데 있어 일반 국민들의 협조를 긴급히 요청합니다. ❑ 운송과 재정 문제에 관해 협조를 받는 외무성 직원들 ◾ 타동사/자동사 도움이 되다 ❑ 단백질 생산을 돕는 화학 약품

◾ 불가산명사 도움, 지원 ❑ 1976년 이래로 그는 자원 봉사자들의 도움을 받아 그 가게를 운영해 오고 있다. ◾ 불가산명사 원조 ❑ 경찰에 어떤 형태의 협조라도 해 주시면 대단히 감사하겠습니다. ◾ 불가산명사 원조 ❑ 실행 가능한 경제 원조 프로그램 ◾ 불가산명사 도움 ❑ 그 번역은 의학 사전의 도움을 받아 이루어졌다. ◾ 구 도움이 되다 ❑ 제가 도움이 될까요? ◾ 구 -를 돕다 ❑ 그들은 세계 사회에 요르단을 도와 달라고 호소하고 있다.

◾ 형용사 부(副)-, -보(補) ❑ 국방 차관보 ◾ 가산명사 조수 ❑ 케일런은 자기가 나가 있는 동안 일을 맡도록 조수 하심을 불렀다. ◾ 가산명사 점원 ❑ 점원이 책을 집어 들고 뒤표지에 있는 가격을 확인했다.

동사는 /əsoʊʃieɪt, -sieɪt/으로 발음되고, 명사와 형용사는 /əsoʊʃiɪt, -siɪt/으로 발음된다.

◾ 타동사 관련시키다, 연상하다 ❑ 과학을 통해 우리는 진보와 미래를 관련짓는 생각을 하게 되었다. ◾ 타동사 찬동하다; 참여하다 ❑ 나는 지난 한 해 동안 그 프로젝트에 참여하지 않았다. ◾ 자동사 어울려 다니다 ❑ 자기들이 살인자와 어울리고 있다는 걸 안다면 그들이 무슨 생각을 할까? ◾ 가산명사 동료, 한패 ❑ 식당 주인의 사업 동료들 ◾ 형용사 준-, 부- ❑ 린 씨는 그 연구소 부소장이다.

◾ 형용사 관련된 ❑ 이런 증상들은 특히 편두통과 관련이 있다. ◾ 형용사 연합된 ❑ 연합 통신

◾ 가산명사 협회, 조합 ❑ 영국 올림픽 협회 ◾ 가산명사 제휴; 친밀한 관계 ❑ 소매상인 J. C. 페니 사와 그 회사의 6년에 걸친 제휴 ◾ 가산명사 연상 ❑ 그에게는 물건들로 가득 찬 선반이 있는데, 그는 그 물건 하나하나마다 연상되는 것이 있다. ◾ 구 -와 공동으로 ❑ 18개월 전에 내가 이사회와 함께 변화를 촉구했던 것은 이 회사를 사랑하기 때문이었다.

things, each of which has associations for him. ◳ PHRASE If you do something **in association with** someone else, you do it together. ◳ *The changes I instigated in association with the board 18 months ago were because I love this company.* →see **memory**

as|sort|ed /əsˈɔrtɪd/ ADJ A group of **assorted** things is a group of similar things that are of different sizes or colors or have different qualities. ◳ *It should be a great week, with overnight stops in assorted hotels in the West Highlands.*

형용사 여러 종류로 된, 다채로운 ◳ 웨스트 하일랜드의 다양한 호텔을 거쳐 가며 하룻밤씩 묵는 멋진 한 주가 될 것입니다.

as|sort|ment /əsˈɔrtmənt/ (**assortments**) N-COUNT An **assortment** is a group of similar things that are of different sizes or colors or have different qualities. ◳ *...an assortment of cheese.*

가산명사 갖가지 물건, 각종 모음 ◳ 각종 치즈 모음

Word Link   *sume ≈ taking : as*sume, con*sume, pre*sume

---

as|sume ♦♦◇ /əsˈum, BRIT əsyuːm/ (**assumes, assuming, assumed**) ◼ V-T If you **assume that** something is true, you imagine that it is true, sometimes wrongly. ◳ *It is a misconception to assume that the two continents are similar.* ◳ *If mistakes occurred, they were assumed to be the fault of the commander on the spot.* ◿ V-T If someone **assumes** power or responsibility, they take power or responsibility. ◳ *Mr. Cross will assume the role of Chief Executive with a team of four directors.*

◼ 타동사 추정하다 ◳ 그 두 대륙이 비슷하다고 추정하는 것은 잘못된 생각이다. ◳ 실수가 발생하면, 그것은 현지 지휘관의 과실로 추정되었다. ◿ 타동사 취하다, 떠맡다 ◳ 크로스 씨는 네 명의 이사진을 거느리고 최고 경영자 역할을 맡을 것이다.

Word Partnership   *assume의 연어*

V.	let's assume *that*, tend to assume ◼
ADV.	assume so ◼
N.	assume the worst ◼
	assume power/control, assume responsibility, assume a role ◿

---

as|sum|ing /əsˈumɪŋ, BRIT əsyuːmɪŋ/ CONJ You use **assuming** or **assuming that** when you are considering a possible situation or event, so that you can think about the consequences. ◳ *"Assuming you're right," he said, "there's not much I can do about it, is there?"*

접속사 ﹏라고 가정한다면 ◳ "내가 옳다고 한다면,"하고 그는 말했다. "그것에 대해 내가 할 수 있는 일은 많지 않아. 그렇지?"

Word Link   *sumpt ≈ taking : as*sumption, con*sumption, pre*sumption

---

as|sump|tion ♦◇◇ /əsˈʌmpʃən/ (**assumptions**) N-COUNT If you make an **assumption that** something is true or will happen, you accept that it is true or will happen, often without any real proof. ◳ *They have taken a wrong turning in their assumption that all men and women think alike.*

가산명사 가정 ◳ 그들은 모든 남녀가 똑같은 생각을 하리라고 가정한 것에서 방향을 잘못 잡았다.

Word Partnership   *assumption의 연어*

ADJ.	assumption based on, common assumption, underlying assumption
V.	challenge an assumption, make an assumption

---

as|sur|ance /əʃˈʊərəns/ (**assurances**) ◼ N-VAR If you give someone an **assurance that** something is true or will happen, you say that it is definitely true or will definitely happen, in order to make them feel less worried. ◳ *He would like an assurance that other forces will not move into the territory that his forces vacate.* ◿ N-UNCOUNT If you do something **with assurance**, you do it with a feeling of confidence and certainty. ◳ *Masur led the orchestra with assurance.* ◾ N-UNCOUNT **Assurance** is insurance that provides a guarantee of payment in the event of death. [BRIT] ◳ *...endowment assurance.* →see also **life assurance**

◼ 가산명사 또는 불가산명사 보증 ◳ 그는 자신의 병력이 철수하는 지역에 다른 병력이 들어오지 않는다는 보증을 원한다. ◿ 불가산명사 확신; 자신 ◳ 마주르는 확신을 가지고 관현악단을 이끌었다. ◾ 불가산명사 보험 [영국영어] ◳ 양로 보험

as|sure /əʃˈʊər/ (**assures, assuring, assured**) ◼ V-T If you **assure** someone **that** something is true or will happen, you tell them that it is definitely true or will definitely happen, often in order to make them less worried. ◳ *He hastened to assure me that there was nothing traumatic to report.* ◳ *"Are you sure the raft is safe?" she asked anxiously. "Couldn't be safer," Max assured her confidently.* →see also **assured** ◿ V-T To **assure** someone of something means to make certain that they will get it. ◳ *Last night's resounding victory over Birmingham City has virtually assured them of promotion.* ◾ PHRASE You use phrases such as **I can assure you** or **let me assure you** to emphasize the truth of what you are saying. [EMPHASIS] ◳ *I can assure you that the animals are well cared for.*

◼ 타동사 보증하다 ◳ 그는 이야기할 만한 깊은 상처가 아무것도 없다고 서둘러 내게 보증했다. ◳ "그 뗏목이 안전하다고 확신하세요?"라고 그녀는 걱정스레 물었다. "그 이상 안전할 수가 없지요."라고 맥스가 자신 있게 그녀에게 보증했다. ◿ 타동사 보장하다 ◳ 지난 밤 버밍엄 시에 대해 완벽한 승리를 거둠으로써 그들은 사실상 승진을 보장받았다. ◾ 구 틀림없이 [강조] ◳ 틀림없이 그 동물들은 잘 보호받고 있습니다.

as|sured ♦◇◇ /əʃˈʊərd/ ◼ ADJ Someone who is **assured** is very confident and relaxed. ◳ *He was infinitely more assured than in his more recent parliamentary appearances.* ◿ ADJ If something is **assured**, it is certain to happen. [V-LINK ADJ] ◳ *Our victory is assured; nothing can stop us.* ◾ ADJ If you are **assured of** something, you are certain to get it or achieve it. [V-LINK ADJ of n] ◳ *Laura Davies is assured of a place in Europe's team.* ◳ PHRASE If you say that someone **can rest assured that** something is the case, you mean that it is definitely the case, so they do not need to worry about it. [EMPHASIS] ◳ *Their parents can rest assured that their children's safety will be of paramount importance.*

◼ 형용사 자신 있는 ◳ 그는 최근에 의회에 출석했을 때보다 훨씬 더 자신 있었다. ◿ 형용사 확실한 ◳ 우리의 승리는 확실하다. 그 무엇도 우리를 막을 수 없다. ◾ 형용사 확신이 있는 ◳ 로라 데이비스는 유럽 조에서 순위에 들 것을 확신하고 있다. ◳ 구 믿고 안심하다 [강조] ◳ 자녀들의 안전이 가장 중요하게 여겨지리라는 것에 대해 부모들은 믿고 안심할 수 있다.

as|ter|isk /æstərɪsk/ (**asterisks**) N-COUNT An **asterisk** is the sign *. It is used especially to indicate that there is further information about something in another part of the text.

가산명사 별표

asth|ma /æzmə, BRIT æsmə/ N-UNCOUNT **Asthma** is a lung condition which causes difficulty in breathing.

불가산명사 천식

asth|mat|ic /æzmætɪk, BRIT æsmætɪk/ (**asthmatics**) ◼ N-COUNT People who suffer from asthma are sometimes referred to as **asthmatics**. ◳ *I have been an asthmatic from childhood and was never able to play any sports.* ● ADJ **Asthmatic** is also an adjective. ◳ *One child in ten is asthmatic.* ◿ ADJ **Asthmatic** means relating to asthma. [ADJ n] ◳ *...asthmatic breathing.*

◼ 가산명사 천식 환자 ◳ 나는 어린 시절부터 천식을 앓아 와서 어떤 운동도 할 수가 없었다. ● 형용사 천식의 ◳ 열 명의 아이 중 한 명이 천식 환자이다. ◿ 형용사 천식의 ◳ 천식성 호흡

Word Web   astronomer

The Italian **astronomer** Galileo Galilei did not invent the telescope. However, he used it to do the first complete survey of **celestial** bodies. He also made a complete record of his findings. Galileo proposed the theory that the **planet** Earth is not the center of the universe. He said that all the planets in the universe revolve around the **sun**. In 1609, Galileo used a telescope to observe the **craters** on Earth's **moon**. He also discovered the four largest **satellites** of the planet Jupiter. These four bodies are called the Galilean moons.

aston|ish /əstɒnɪʃ/ (**astonishes, astonishing, astonished**) v-т If something or someone **astonishes** you, they surprise you very much. ❑ *My news will astonish you.*

타동사 깜짝 놀라게 하다 ❑ 내가 가져온 소식을 들으면 깜짝 놀랄 거야.

aston|ished /əstɒnɪʃt/ ADJ If you are **astonished** by something, you are very surprised about it. ❑ *They were astonished to find the driver was a six-year-old boy.*

형용사 깜짝 놀란 ❑ 그들은 운전사가 여섯 살짜리 사내애라는 것을 알고 깜짝 놀랐다.

aston|ish|ing /əstɒnɪʃɪŋ/ ADJ Something that is **astonishing** is very surprising. ❑ *It's astonishing, he's learned Latin in three hours!* ● **aston|ish|ing|ly** ADV ❑ *Isabella was an astonishingly beautiful young woman.*

형용사 매우 놀라운 ❑ 대단히 놀랍습니다. 그는 세 시간 만에 라틴어를 배웠어요! ● 놀랄 만큼; 대단히 부사 ❑ 이사벨라는 대단히 아름다운 젊은 여자였다.

aston|ish|ment /əstɒnɪʃmənt/ N-UNCOUNT **Astonishment** is a feeling of great surprise. ❑ *I spotted a shooting star which, to my astonishment, was bright green in color.*

불가산명사 경악, 놀람 ❑ 나는 정말 놀랍게도 색깔이 밝은 초록빛인 유성을 발견했다.

astound /əstaʊnd/ (**astounds, astounding, astounded**) v-т If something **astounds** you, you are very surprised by it. ❑ *He used to astound his friends with feats of physical endurance.*

타동사 깜짝 놀라게 하다 ❑ 그는 놀라운 지구력으로 친구들을 놀라게 하곤 했다.

astound|ing /əstaʊndɪŋ/ ADJ If something is **astounding**, you are shocked or amazed that it could exist or happen. ❑ *The results are quite astounding.*

형용사 깜짝 놀랄 만한 ❑ 그 결과는 대단히 놀랄 만했다.

astray /əstreɪ/ 1 PHRASE If you **are led astray** by someone or something, you behave badly or foolishly because of them. ❑ *The judge thought he'd been led astray by older children.* 2 PHRASE If someone or something **leads** you **astray**, they make you believe something which is not true, causing you to make a wrong decision. ❑ *The testimony would inflame the jurors, and lead them astray from the facts of the case.* 3 PHRASE If something **goes astray**, it gets lost while it is being taken or sent somewhere. ❑ *Many items of mail being sent to her have gone astray.*

1 구 나쁜 길로 이끌리다 ❑ 판사는 나이 많은 아이들이 그를 나쁜 길로 이끌었다고 생각했다. 2 구 잘못된 판단을 하게 만들다 ❑ 그 증언은 배심원들을 흥분시켜서 사건의 진실과 동떨어진 판단을 하게 만들 것이다. 3 구 없어지다; 길을 잃다 ❑ 그녀 앞으로 가고 있던 많은 편지들이 없어졌다.

astride /əstraɪd/ ADV If you sit or stand **astride** something, you sit or stand with one leg on each side of it. ❑ *...three youths who stood astride their bicycles and stared.*

부사 걸터앉아, 올라서서 ❑ 자전거에 올라서서 쳐다보던 젊은이 세 명

as|trolo|ger /əstrɒlədʒər/ (**astrologers**) N-COUNT An **astrologer** is a person who uses astrology to try to tell you things about your character and your future.

가산명사 점성가

as|trol|ogy /əstrɒlədʒi/ N-UNCOUNT **Astrology** is the study of the movements of the planets, sun, moon, and stars in the belief that these movements can have an influence on people's lives. →see **star**

불가산명사 점성학

Word Link   aster, astro ≈ star : asterisk, astronaut, astronomy

as|tro|naut /æstrənɔt/ (**astronauts**) N-COUNT An **astronaut** is a person who is trained for traveling in a spacecraft.

가산명사 우주 비행사

as|trono|mer /əstrɒnəmər/ (**astronomers**) N-COUNT An **astronomer** is a scientist who studies the stars, planets, and other natural objects in space. →see **galaxy**
→see Word Web: **astronomer**

가산명사 천문학자

as|tro|nomi|cal /æstrənɒmɪkˀl/ 1 ADJ If you describe an amount, especially the cost of something as **astronomical**, you are emphasizing that it is very large indeed. [EMPHASIS] ❑ *Houses in the village are going for astronomical prices.* 2 ADJ **Astronomical** means relating to astronomy. ❑ *...the British Astronomical Association.*

1 형용사 천문학적인 [강조] ❑ 그 마을의 집들은 천문학적인 가격에 거래되고 있다. 2 형용사 천문학의 ❑ 영국 천문학 협회

as|trono|my /əstrɒnəmi/ N-UNCOUNT **Astronomy** is the scientific study of the stars, planets, and other natural objects in space. →see **star**

불가산명사 천문학

as|tute /əstut, BRIT əstyuːt/ ADJ If you describe someone as **astute**, you think they show an understanding of behavior and situations, and are skillful at using this knowledge to your own advantage. ❑ *She was politically astute.*

형용사 기민한, 눈치 빠른 ❑ 그녀는 정치적으로 기민했다.

asy|lum /əsaɪləm/ (**asylums**) 1 N-UNCOUNT If a government gives a person from another country **asylum**, they allow them to stay, usually because they are unable to return home safely for political reasons. ❑ *He applied for asylum in 1987 after fleeing the police back home.* 2 N-COUNT An **asylum** is a psychiatric hospital. [OLD-FASHIONED]

1 불가산명사 망명 ❑ 그는 1987년 고국에서 경찰을 피해 달아난 이후 망명을 신청했다. 2 가산명사 정신 병원 [구식어]

asy|lum seek|er (**asylum seekers**) N-COUNT An **asylum seeker** is a person who is trying to get asylum in a foreign country. ❑ *Fewer than 7% of asylum seekers are accepted as political refugees.*

가산명사 망명 희망자 ❑ 망명 희망자들 중 7퍼센트 미만이 정치적 난민으로 인정된다.

at ♦♦♦ /ət, STRONG æt/

In addition to the uses shown below, **at** is used after some verbs, nouns, and adjectives to introduce extra information. **At** is also used in phrasal verbs such as "keep on at" and "play at."

at은 아래 용법 외에도 추가 정보를 나타내기 위해 일부의 동사, 명사, 형용사 뒤에 쓴다. 또한 'keep on at', 'play at'과 같은 구동사에도 쓰인다.

1 PREP You use **at** to indicate the place or event where something happens or is situated. ❑ *He will be at the airport to meet her.* ❑ *I didn't like being alone at home.* ❑ *They agreed to meet at a restaurant in Soho.* **2** PREP If someone is **at** school or college, or at a particular school or college, they go there regularly to study. ❑ *He was shy and nervous as a boy, and unhappy at school.* ❑ *It was at university that he first encountered Hopkins.* **3** PREP If you are **at** something such as a table, a door, or someone's side, you are next to it or them. ❑ *An assistant sat typing away at a table beside him.* ❑ *At his side was a beautiful young woman.* **4** PREP When you are describing where someone or something is, you can say that they are **at** a certain distance. You can also say that one thing is at an angle in relation to another thing. ❑ *The two journalists followed at a discreet distance.* **5** PREP If something happens **at** a particular time, that is the time when it happens or begins to happen. ❑ *The funeral will be carried out this afternoon at 3:00.* **6** PREP If you do something **at** a particular age, you do it when you are that age. ❑ *Blake emigrated to Australia with his family at 13.* **7** PREP You use **at** to express a rate, frequency, level, or price. ❑ *I drove back down the highway at normal speed.* ❑ *Check the oil at regular intervals, and have the car serviced regularly.* **8** PREP You use **at** before a number or amount to indicate a measurement. [PREP amount] ❑ *...as unemployment stays pegged at three million.* **9** PREP If you look **at** someone or something, you look toward them. If you direct an object or a comment **at** someone, you direct it toward them. ❑ *He looked at Michael and laughed.* **10** PREP You can use **at** after verbs such as "smile" or "wave" and before nouns referring to people to indicate that you have put on an expression or made a gesture which someone is meant to see or understand. [V PREP n] ❑ *She opened the door and stood there, frowning at me.* **11** PREP If you point or gesture **at** something, you move your arm or head in its direction so that it will be noticed by someone you are with. [V PREP n] ❑ *He pointed at the empty bottle and the waitress quickly replaced it.* **12** PREP If you are working **at** something, you are dealing with it. If you are aiming **at** something, you are trying to achieve it. ❑ *She has worked hard at her marriage.* **13** PREP If something is done **at** someone's invitation or request, it is done as a result of it. [PREP n with poss] ❑ *She left the light on in the bathroom at his request.* **14** PREP You use **at** to say that someone or something is in a particular state or condition. [v-link PREP n] ❑ *I am afraid we are not at liberty to disclose that information.* **15** PREP You use **at** before a possessive pronoun and a superlative adjective to say that someone or something has more of a particular quality than at any other time. [PREP poss adj-superl] ❑ *He was at his happiest whilst playing cricket.* **16** PREP You use **at** to say how something is being done. ❑ *Three people were killed by shots fired at random from a minibus.* **17** PREP You use **at** to show that someone is doing something repeatedly. [V PREP n] ❑ *She lowered the handkerchief which she had kept dabbing at her eyes.* **18** PREP You use **at** to indicate an activity or task when saying how well someone does it. [adj PREP n, n PREP n, v PREP n] ❑ *I'm good at my work.* **19** PREP You use **at** to indicate what someone is reacting to. [adj PREP n, n PREP n, v PREP n] ❑ *Eleanor was annoyed at having had to wait so long for him.* **at all** →see **all**

ate /eɪt/ **Ate** is the past tense of **eat**.

athe|ism /ˈeɪθiɪzəm/ N-UNCOUNT **Atheism** is the belief that there is no God. Compare **agnosticism**. ❑ *Marlowe courted notoriety by professing atheism.*

athe|ist /ˈeɪθiɪst/ (**atheists**) N-COUNT An **atheist** is a person who believes that there is no God. Compare **agnostic**.

ath|lete ◆◇◇ /ˈæθliːt/ (**athletes**) **1** N-COUNT An **athlete** is a person who does any kind of physical sports, exercise, or games, especially in competitions. ❑ *Daley Thompson was a great athlete.* **2** N-COUNT You can refer to someone who is fit and athletic as an **athlete**. ❑ *I was no athlete.*

ath|let|ic /æθˈletɪk/ **1** ADJ **Athletic** means relating to athletes and athletics. [ADJ n] ❑ *They have been given college scholarships purely on athletic ability.* **2** ADJ An **athletic** person is fit, and able to perform energetic movements easily. ❑ *Xandra is an athletic 36-year-old with a 21-year-old's body.*

ath|let|ics /æθˈletɪks/ **1** N-UNCOUNT **Athletics** refers to any kind of physical sports, exercise, or games. [AM] ❑ *...students who play intercollegiate athletics.* **2** N-UNCOUNT **Athletics** refers to track and field sports such as running, the high jump, and the javelin. [mainly BRIT; AM **track field**] ❑ *As the modern Olympics grew in stature, so too did athletics.*

at|las /ˈætləs/ (**atlases**) N-COUNT An **atlas** is a book of maps.

ATM /eɪ tiː em/ (**ATMs**) N-COUNT An **ATM** is a machine built into the wall of a bank or other building, which allows you to take out money from your bank account by using a special card. **ATM** is an abbreviation for "automated teller machine." [mainly AM; BRIT **cash dispenser**] ❑ *Keep your ATM card in a safe place.* →see **bank**

at|mos|phere ◆◇◇ /ˈætməsfɪər/ (**atmospheres**) **1** N-COUNT A planet's **atmosphere** is the layer of air or other gases around it. ❑ *The shuttle Columbia will re-enter Earth's atmosphere tomorrow morning.* **2** N-COUNT The **atmosphere** of a place is the air that you breathe there. ❑ *These gases pollute the atmosphere of towns and cities.* **3** N-SING The **atmosphere** of a place is the general impression that you get of it. ❑ *There's still an atmosphere of great hostility and tension in the city.* **4** N-UNCOUNT If a place or an event has **atmosphere**, it is interesting. ❑ *The old harbor is still full of atmosphere and well worth visiting.* →see **core**, **earth**, **greenhouse effect**, **meteor**, **moon**, **water**

at|mos|pher|ic /ætməsˈferɪk/ **1** ADJ **Atmospheric** is used to describe something which relates to the earth's atmosphere. ❑ *...atmospheric gases.* **2** ADJ If you describe a place or a piece of music as **atmospheric**, you like it because it has a particular quality which is interesting or exciting and makes you feel a particular emotion. [APPROVAL] ❑ *...wonderfully atmospheric electronic music.*

---

1 전치사 -에, -에서 ❑ 그는 그녀를 만나러 공항에 갈 것이다. ❑ 나는 집에 혼자 있기 싫었다. ❑ 그들은 소호에 있는 식당에서 만나기로 합의했다. **2** 전치사 -에, -에서 ❑ 그는 어렸을 때 숫기가 없고 소심해서, 학교에서 잘못 어울렸다. ❑ 그가 홉킨스를 처음 만난 것은 대학에서였다. **3** 전치사 -에, -에서 (위치) ❑ 조수 한 명이 멀찍이 그 남자 옆의 탁자에 앉아 타자를 치고 있었다. ❑ 그 남자 옆에는 아름다운 젊은 여자가 있었다. **4** 전치사 거리나 각도를 나타낼 때 쓴다. ❑ 두 기자는 신중하게 거리를 두고 따라갔다. **5** 전치사 -에 (특정한 시각) ❑ 장례식은 오늘 오후 3시에 거행될 예정이다. **6** 전치사 나이를 나타낼 때 쓴다. ❑ 블레이크는 열세 살 때 가족들과 호주로 이민을 갔다. **7** 전치사 비율, 빈도, 수준, 가격 등을 나타낼 때 쓴다. ❑ 나는 보통 속도로 차를 몰아 고속도로로 다시 내려왔다. ❑ 규칙적인 간격으로 오일을 확인하고, 정기적으로 자동차 정비를 받으세요. **8** 전치사 수량을 나타낼 때 쓴다. ❑ 실업자 수가 3백만에 고정되어 있을 ... **9** 전치사 -에, 방향을 나타낼 때 쓴다. ❑ 그는 마이클을 보고 웃었다. **10** 전치사 -를 향해 ❑ 그녀는 문을 열고 거기 서서 나를 향해 인상을 쓰며 ... **11** 전치사 -에 ❑ 그가 빈 병 쪽을 가리키자 여종업원이 재빨리 그것 대신에 새 병을 갖다 놓았다. **12** 전치사 목표하는 대상을 나타낸다 ❑ 그녀는 혼자에게 무척 애를 써 왔다. **13** 전치사 -에 의하여, -에 따라 ❑ 그녀는 그의 요청에 따라 욕실의 불을 켜 두었다. **14** 전치사 상태를 나타낼 때 쓴다. ❑ 내 생각에 우리 마음대로 그 정보를 발표할 수는 없을 것 같다. **15** 전치사 'at+소유격+최상급'의 형태로 '가장 -한 상태에'라는 의미로 쓴다. ❑ 그는 크리켓을 하는 동안에 가장 행복했다. **16** 전치사 상황, 조건을 나타낼 때 쓴다. ❑ 소형 버스에서 무작위로 발사된 총알에 맞아 세 명이 목숨을 잃었다. **17** 전치사 동작이 반복되는 것을 나타내는 용도로 쓴다. ❑ 그녀는 눈가를 꼭꼭 닦던 손수건을 내렸다. **18** 전치사 능력, 성질의 대상을 나타낼 때 쓴다. ❑ 나는 내 일을 잘한다. **19** 전치사 감정의 원인을 나타낼 때 쓴다. ❑ 엘리노어는 그토록 오랫동안 그를 기다려야 했던 것이 불쾌했다.

eat의 과거형

불가산명사 무신론 ❑ 말로는 무신론자임을 고백함으로써 악명을 자초했다.

가산명사 무신론자

1 가산명사 운동선수; 육상선수 ❑ 데일리 톰프슨은 위대한 육상 선수였다. **2** 가산명사 강건한 사람 ❑ 나는 결코 강건한 사람은 아니었다.

1 형용사 운동의, 체육의 ❑ 그들은 순전히 운동 재능에 의해 대학 장학금을 받아 왔다. **2** 형용사 강건한 ❑ 산드라는 21살의 신체를 가진 강건한 36살이다.

1 불가산명사 운동, 체육 [미국영어] ❑ 대학 대항 운동 경기를 하는 학생들 ... **2** 불가산명사 육상 [주로 영국영어; 미국영어 track field] ❑ 근대 올림픽의 규모가 성장함에 따라 육상의 규모도 성장했다.

가산명사 지도책

가산명사 자동 현금 인출기 [주로 미국영어; 영국영어 cash dispenser] ❑ 현금 카드를 안전한 곳에 보관하세요.

1 가산명사 대기 ❑ 컬럼비아 호는 내일 아침 지구 대기권으로 재진입할 것이다. **2** 가산명사 공기 ❑ 이런 가스들이 도시의 공기를 오염시킨다. **3** 단수명사 분위기 ❑ 그 도시에는 아직도 엄청나게 적대적이고 긴장된 분위기가 감돈다. **4** 불가산명사 운치; 정취 ❑ 그 옛 항구는 여전히 운치가 가득해서 방문할 가치가 충분히 있다.

1 형용사 대기의 ❑ 대기 가스 **2** 형용사 운치 있는 [마음에 듦] ❑ 놀랄 만큼 운치 있는 전자 음악

atom /ˈætəm/ (**atoms**) N-COUNT An **atom** is the smallest amount of a substance that can take part in a chemical reaction. ❑ ...the news that Einstein's former colleagues Otto Hahn and Fritz Strassmann had split the atom. →see **element**

가산명사 원자 ❑ 아인슈타인의 이전 동료였던 오토 한과 프리츠 슈트라스만이 원자 분열에 성공했다는 소식

atom|ic /əˈtɒmɪk/ ❶ ADJ **Atomic** means relating to power that is produced from the energy released by splitting atoms. ❑ ...atomic energy. ❷ ADJ **Atomic** means relating to the atoms of substances. [ADJ n] ❑ ...the atomic number of an element.

❶ 형용사 원자력의 ❑ 원자력 에너지 ❷ 형용사 원자의 ❑ 원소의 원자 번호

atro|cious /əˈtroʊʃəs/ ❶ ADJ If you describe something as **atrocious**, you are emphasizing that its quality is very bad. [EMPHASIS] ❑ I remain to this day fluent in Hebrew, while my Arabic is atrocious. ❷ ADJ If you describe someone's behavior or their actions as **atrocious**, you mean that it is unacceptable because it is extremely violent or cruel. ❑ The judge said he had committed atrocious crimes against women.

❶ 형용사 형편없는 [강조] ❑ 나는 아랍어 실력은 형편없지만 히브리어는 요즘도 여전히 유창하다. ❷ 형용사 흉악한 ❑ 재판관은 그가 여자들을 상대로 흉악한 범죄를 저질러 왔다고 말했다.

atro|city /əˈtrɒsɪti/ (**atrocities**) N-VAR An **atrocity** is a very cruel, shocking action. ❑ The killing was cold-blooded, and those who committed this atrocity should be tried and punished.

가산명사 또는 불가산명사 잔학 행위 ❑ 그 학살은 비정한 것이었고, 그런 잔학한 일을 저지른 자들은 재판을 받고 벌을 받아야만 한다.

at|tach ♦♢♢ /əˈtætʃ/ (**attaches, attaching, attached**) ❶ V-T If you **attach** something **to** an object, you join it or fasten it to the object. ❑ We attach labels to things before we file them away. ❑ For further information, please contact us on the attached form. ❷ V-T In computing, if you **attach** a file **to** a message that you send to someone, you send it with the message but separate it from it. ❑ It is possible to attach executable program files to e-mail. ❸ →see also **attached**. **no strings attached** →see **string**

❶ 타동사 붙이다, 부착하다 ❑ 우리는 물건들을 철을 해서 정리하기 전에 라벨을 붙인다. ❑ 더 자세한 정보를 원하시면, 첨부된 양식에 따라 저희에게 연락 주세요. ❷ 타동사 첨부하다 ❑ 이메일에 실행 가능한 프로그램 파일을 첨부할 수 있다.

at|tached /əˈtætʃt/ ❶ ADJ If you are **attached to** someone or something, you like them very much. [v-link ADJ to n] ❑ She is very attached to her family and friends. ❷ ADJ If someone is **attached to** an organization or group of people, they are working with them, often only for a short time. [v-link ADJ to n] ❑ Ford was attached to the battalion's first line of transport.

❶ 형용사 애착이 강한 ❑ 그녀는 가족과 친구들에게 강한 애착을 가지고 있다. ❷ 형용사 ~에 소속된 ❑ 포드는 대대의 제1수송대에 속해 있었다.

at|tach|ment /əˈtætʃmənt/ (**attachments**) ❶ N-VAR If you have an **attachment** to someone or something, you are fond of or loyal to them. ❑ As a teenager she formed a strong attachment to one of her teachers. ❷ N-COUNT An **attachment** is a device that can be fixed onto a machine in order to enable it to do different jobs. ❑ Some models come with attachments for dusting. ❸ N-COUNT In computing, an **attachment** is a file which is attached separately to a message that you send to someone. ❑ When you send an e-mail you can also send a file as an attachment and that file can be a graphic, a program, a sound or whatever.

❶ 가산명사 또는 불가산명사 애착, 애정 ❑ 그녀는 10대 때 선생님 중 한 분을 몹시 사모하게 되었다. ❷ 가산명사 부속물 ❑ 몇몇 모델은 먼지털이용 부품도 딸려 나온다. ❸ 가산명사 첨부 파일 ❑ 이메일 전송 시 파일도 첨부해서 보낼 수 있는데 그래픽이나 프로그램, 사운드 파일 등 파일 종류는 상관이 없다.

at|tack ♦♦♦ /əˈtæk/ (**attacks, attacking, attacked**) ❶ V-T/V-I To **attack** a person or place means to try to hurt or damage them using physical violence. ❑ Fifty civilians in Masawa were killed when government planes attacked the town. ❑ He bundled the old lady into her hallway and brutally attacked her. ● N-VAR **Attack** is also a noun. ❑ ...a campaign of air attacks on strategic targets. ❷ V-T If you **attack** a person, belief, idea, or act, you criticize them strongly. ❑ He publicly attacked the people who've been calling for secret ballot nominations. ● N-VAR **Attack** is also a noun. [usu with supp] ❑ The role of the state as a prime mover in planning social change has been under attack. ❸ V-T If something such as a disease, a chemical, or an insect **attacks** something, it harms or spoils it. ❑ The virus seems to have attacked his throat. ● N-UNCOUNT **Attack** is also a noun. [also N in pl] ❑ The virus can actually destroy those white blood cells, leaving the body wide open to attack from other infections. ❹ V-T If you **attack** a job or a problem, you start to deal with it in an energetic way. ❑ Any attempt to attack the budget problem is going to have to in some way deal with those issues. ❺ V-T/V-I In games such as soccer, when one team **attacks** the opponent's goal, they try to score a goal. ❑ Now the U.S. is controlling the ball and attacking the opponent's goal. ● N-COUNT **Attack** is also a noun. ❑ Lee was at the hub of some incisive attacks in the second half. ❻ N-COUNT An **attack of** an illness is a short period in which you suffer badly from it. ❑ It had brought on an attack of asthma. ❼ →see also **counterattack, heart attack** →see **war**

❶ 타동사/자동사 공격하다, 폭행하다 ❑ 정부군 비행기가 마사와를 공격했을 때 민간인 50명이 사망했다. ❑ 그는 중년 여성을 그녀의 집 현관 안으로 밀어붙인 다음 잔인하게 폭행했다. ● 가산명사 또는 불가산명사 공격 ❑ 전략적 목표물을 겨냥한 공습 작전 ❷ 타동사 비난하다, 공격하다 ❑ 그는 비밀 투표를 통한 공천을 주장해 온 사람들을 공개적으로 비난했다. ● 가산명사 또는 불가산명사 비판, 공격 ❑ 사회 변화 계획에 있어서 정부의 주도적인 역할이 비판을 받아 왔다. ❸ 타동사 감염시키다, 침범하다 ❑ 그의 목이 바이러스에 감염된 것 같다. ● 불가산명사 감염 ❑ 이 바이러스는 사실상 백혈구를 파괴해서 인체를 다른 병원균에 의한 감염에 무방비 상태로 노출시킨다. ❹ 타동사 착수하다 ❑ 예산 문제 해결에 착수하기 위해서는 어떤 식으로든 반드시 이 문제들을 짚고 넘어가야 할 것이다. ❺ 타동사/자동사 공격하다 (골문을) ❑ 이제 미국 팀이 공을 주도하며 상대편 골문을 공격하고 있다. ● 가산명사 공격 ❑ 후반전의 몇몇 예리한 공격의 중심에 리가 있었다. ❻ 가산명사 발병, 발작 ❑ 이것이 천식 발작을 일으켰다.

Thesaurus
*attack*의 참조어

V.	assault, hit, invade; (ant.) defend ❶
	abuse, blame, criticize; (ant.) defend, praise ❷
	tackle; (ant.) avoid, ignore, put off ❹
N.	assault, invasion ❶
	abuse, criticism, libel, slander; (ant.) defense ❷
	bout, fit ❻

Word Partnership
*attack*의 연어

N.	**terrorist** attack ❶
V.	**launch/lead/plan an** attack ❶ ❷
ADJ.	**sudden/surprise** attack ❶
	personal attack ❷
PREP.	attack **on/against, under** attack ❶ ❷
	attack *of something* ❻

---

at|tack|er /əˈtækər/ (**attackers**) N-COUNT You can refer to a person who attacks someone as their **attacker**. ❑ There were signs that she struggled with her attacker before she was repeatedly stabbed.

가산명사 괴한, 가해자 ❑ 그녀가 칼에 여러 번 찔리기 전에 가해자와 몸싸움을 벌인 흔적이 보였다.

at|tain /əˈteɪn/ (**attains, attaining, attained**) V-T If you **attain** something, you gain it or achieve it, often after a lot of effort. [FORMAL] ❑ Jim is halfway to attaining his pilot's license.

타동사 획득하다, 달성하다 [격식체] ❑ 짐은 조종사 면허증을 반 정도 딴 상태이다.

at|tain|ment /ət<u>eɪ</u>nmənt/ (**attainments**) **1** N-UNCOUNT The **attainment** of an aim is the achieving of it. [FORMAL] ❏ ...the attainment of independence. **2** N-COUNT An **attainment** is a skill you have learned or something you have achieved. [FORMAL] ❏ ...their educational attainments.

Word Link	tempt ≈ trying : at**tempt**, temp**t**ation, temp**t**ed

1 불가산명사 획득, 달성 [격식체] ❏ 독립 획득
2 가산명사 기술, 학식 [격식체] ❏ 그들의 학력

at|tempt ♦♦♦ /ət<u>e</u>mpt/ (**attempts**, **attempting**, **attempted**) **1** V-T If you **attempt to** do something, especially something difficult, you try to do it. ❏ The only time that we attempted to do something like that was in the city of Philadelphia. **2** N-COUNT If you make an **attempt to** do something, you try to do it, often without success. ❏ ...a deliberate attempt to destabilize the defense. **3** N-COUNT An **attempt on** someone's life is an attempt to kill them. ❏ ...an attempt on the life of the former Iranian Prime Minister.

1 타동사 시도하다 ❏ 우리가 유일하게 그러한 일을 시도했던 때는 필라델피아에서였다. **2** 가산명사 시도 ❏ 방어 태세를 흩뜨리기 위한 의도적인 시도 **3** 가산명사 (암살) 기도 ❏ 전 이란 총리의 암살 기도

Thesaurus	attempt의 참조어
V.	strive, tackle, take on, try **1**
N.	effort, try, venture **2**

Word Partnership	attempt의 연어
ADJ.	**any** attempt, **desperate** attempt, **failed/successful** attempt **1** **2**
V.	attempt **to control/find/prevent/solve 1**
	make an attempt **1** **2**
N.	attempt **suicide 3**

at|tempt|ed /ət<u>e</u>mptɪd/ ADJ An **attempted** crime or unlawful action is an unsuccessful effort to commit the crime or action. [ADJ n] ❏ ...a case of attempted murder.

형용사 미수의 ❏ 살인 미수 사건

at|tend ♦♦◇ /ət<u>e</u>nd/ (**attends**, **attending**, **attended**) **1** V-T/V-I If you **attend** a meeting or other event, you are present at it. ❏ Thousands of people attended the funeral. ❏ The meeting will be attended by finance ministers from many countries. **2** V-T If you **attend** an institution such as a school, college, or church, you go there regularly. ❏ They attended college together at the University of Pennsylvania. **3** V-I If you **attend to** something, you deal with it. If you **attend to** someone who is hurt or injured, you care for them. ❏ The staff will helpfully attend to your needs.

1 타동사/자동사 참석하다 ❏ 수천 명의 사람들이 장례식에 참석했다. ❏ 이번 회담에는 각국 재무장관들이 참석할 것이다. **2** 타동사 다니다 ❏ 그들은 펜실베니아 대학교에 함께 다녔다. **3** 자동사 돌보다, 간호하다 ❏ 직원들이 여러분들의 필요를 보살피고 도울 것입니다.

at|tend|ance /ət<u>e</u>ndəns/ (**attendances**) **1** N-UNCOUNT Someone's **attendance** at an event or an institution is the fact that they are present at the event or go regularly to the institution. ❏ Her attendance at school was sporadic. **2** N-VAR The **attendance** at an event is the number of people who are present at it. ❏ Rain played a big part in the air show's drop in attendance.

1 불가산명사 참석, 출석 ❏ 그녀는 학교에 나왔다 안 나왔다 했다. **2** 가산명사 또는 불가산명사 참석자 수 ❏ 비로 인해 에어쇼의 관람자 수가 아주 적었다.

at|tend|ant /ət<u>e</u>ndənt/ (**attendants**) N-COUNT An **attendant** is someone whose job is to serve or help people in a place such as a gas station or a parking lot. ❏ Tony Williams was working as a parking lot attendant in Los Angeles.

가산명사 안내원 ❏ 토니 윌리엄스는 로스앤젤레스에서 주차장 안내원으로 일하고 있었다.

at|ten|tion ♦♦◇ /ət<u>e</u>nʃ³n/ (**attentions**) **1** N-UNCOUNT If you give someone or something your **attention**, you look at it, listen to it, or think about it carefully. ❏ You have my undivided attention. ❏ Later he turned his attention to the desperate state of housing in the province. **2** N-UNCOUNT **Attention** is great interest that is shown in someone or something, particularly by the general public. ❏ Volume Two, sub-titled "The Lawyers," will also attract considerable attention. **3** N-UNCOUNT If someone or something is getting **attention**, they are being dealt with or cared for. ❏ Each year more than two million household injuries need medical attention. **4** N-UNCOUNT If you **bring** something to someone's **attention** or **draw** their **attention** to it, you tell them about it or make them notice it. ❏ If we don't keep bringing this to the attention of the people, nothing will be done. **5** PHRASE If someone or something **attracts** your **attention** or **catches** your **attention**, you suddenly notice them. ❏ A faint aroma of coffee attracted his attention. **6** PHRASE If you **pay attention to** someone, you watch them, listen to them, or take notice of them. If you **pay no attention to** someone, you behave as if you are not aware of them or as if they are not important. ❏ More than ever before, the food industry is paying attention to young consumers. **7** PHRASE When people **stand to attention** or **stand at attention**, they stand straight with their feet together and their arms at their sides. ❏ Soldiers in full combat gear stood at attention.

1 불가산명사 주목 ❏ 당신에게만 전념하고 있습니다. ❏ 그리고 나서 그는 그 지역의 절박한 주택 문제에 주목했다. **2** 불가산명사 관심 ❏ '변호사'라는 제목의 두 번째 권 역시 상당한 관심을 끌 것이다. **3** 불가산명사 대처, 돌봄 ❏ 매년 집안에서 입는 부상 200만 건 이상이 치료가 필요하다. **4** 불가산명사 주목 ❏ 우리가 이 문제에 관해 계속 사람들의 주의를 환기시키지 못한다면, 아무것도 되지 않을 것이다. **5** 구 주의를 끌다 ❏ 은은한 커피향이 그의 주의를 끌었다. **6** 구 주목하다; 무시하다 ❏ 그 어느 때보다도 많이 식품업계가 젊은 소비자들을 주목하고 있다. **7** 구 차려 자세를 취하다 ❏ 완전 무장을 한 군인들이 차려 자세로 서 있었다.

Word Partnership	attention의 연어
ADJ.	**careful/close** attention **1**
	special attention **1** **3**
	unwanted attention **2**
	medical attention **3**
PREP.	attention **to detail 1**
V.	**catch someone's** attention, **focus** attention, **turn** attention **to** something/someone **1** **5**
	call/direct *someone's* attention **4**
	draw attention **4**
	attract attention **5**
	pay attention **6**
N.	**center of** attention **2**

at|ten|tive /ət<u>e</u>ntɪv/ **1** ADJ If you are **attentive**, you are paying close attention to what is being said or done. ❏ He wishes the government would be more attentive to detail in their response. ● **at|ten|tive|ly** ADV ❏ He questioned Chrissie, and

1 형용사 주의 깊은, 세심한 ❏ 그는 정부가 답변의 세부 사항에 조금 더 신경을 써 주기를 바란다. ● 주의 깊게, 세심하게 부사 ❏ 그는 크리시에게 질문한 후

listened attentively to what she told him. **2** ADJ Someone who is **attentive** is helpful and polite. ❑ *At society parties he is attentive to his wife.*

그녀의 이야기를 경청했다. **2** 형용사 상냥한, 정중한 ❑ 그는 사교 모임에서 아내에게 정중한 남편이다.

at|test /ətɛst/ (attests, attesting, attested) V-T/V-I To **attest** something or **attest to** something means to say, show, or prove that it is true. [FORMAL] ❑ *Police records attest to his long history of violence.*

타동사/자동사 증명하다, 증언하다 [격식체] ❑ 그가 오래전부터 폭력을 행사한 사실을 경찰 기록이 증명한다.

at|tic /ætɪk/ (attics) N-COUNT An **attic** is a room at the top of a house just below the roof. →see **house**

가산명사 다락방

at|ti|tude ◆◇◇ /ætɪtud, BRIT ætɪtyuːd/ (attitudes) N-VAR Your **attitude** to something is the way that you think and feel about it, especially when this shows in the way you behave. ❑ *...the general change in attitude toward handicapped people.* ❑ *Being unemployed produces negative attitudes to work.*

가산명사 또는 불가산명사 태도 ❑ 장애인에 대한 태도의 전반적인 변화 ❑ 실업 상태는 일에 대한 부정적인 태도를 낳는다.

Word Partnership	*attitude*의 연어
PREP.	attitude **toward**/**about**
ADJ.	**bad** attitude, **new** attitude, **positive**/**negative** attitude, **progressive** attitude
V.	**change** your attitude

at|tor|ney ◆◇◇ /ətɜrni/ (attorneys) N-COUNT In the United States, an **attorney** or **attorney-at-law** is a lawyer. ❑ *...a prosecuting attorney.* →see **lawyer** →see **trial**

가산명사 변호사 ❑ 검사

Attorney General (Attorneys General) N-COUNT A country's **Attorney General** is its chief law officer, who advises its government or ruler.

가산명사 법무 장관

at|tract ◆◆◇ /ətrækt/ (attracts, attracting, attracted) **1** V-T If something **attracts** people or animals, it has features that cause them to come to it. ❑ *The Cardiff Bay project is attracting many visitors.* **2** V-T If someone or something **attracts** you, they have particular qualities which cause you to like or admire them. If a particular quality **attracts** you **to** a person or thing, it is the reason why you like them. ❑ *He wasn't sure he'd got it right, although the theory attracted him by its logic.* **3** V-T If you **are attracted to** someone, you are interested in them sexually. ❑ *In spite of her hostility, she was attracted to him.* ● at|tract|ed ADJ [v-link ADJ, usu ADJ to n] ❑ *He was nice looking, but I wasn't deeply attracted to him.* **4** V-T If something **attracts** support, publicity, or money, it receives support, publicity, or money. ❑ *President Mwinyi said his country would also like to attract investment from private companies.* **5** to **attract** someone's **attention** →see **attention** →see **magnet**

1 타동사 끌다 ❑ 카디프 베이 프로젝트가 많은 방문객들을 끌어 모으고 있다. **2** 타동사 사로잡다, 매혹시키다 ❑ 그는 그 이론의 논리에는 매력을 느꼈지만, 자신이 제대로 이해했는지는 확신하지 못했다. **3** 타동사 매력을 느끼다 ❑ 쌀쌀맞게 굴기는 했어도 그녀는 그에게 매력을 느꼈다. ● 끌리는 형용사 ❑ 그가 잘생기긴 했어도 나는 그에게 깊이 끌리지는 않았다. **4** 타동사 받다 ❑ 음위니 대통령은 자기 나라가 민간 기업으로부터의 투자 유치도 바라고 있다고 말했다.

at|trac|tion /ətrækʃn/ (attractions) **1** N-UNCOUNT **Attraction** is a feeling of liking someone, and often of being sexually interested in them. ❑ *Our level of attraction to the opposite sex has more to do with our inner confidence than how we look.* **2** N-COUNT An **attraction** is a feature which makes something interesting or desirable. ❑ *...the attractions of living on the waterfront.* **3** N-COUNT An **attraction** is something that people can go to for interest or enjoyment, for example a famous building. ❑ *The walled city is an important tourist attraction.*

1 불가산명사 매력 ❑ 이성이 우리에게 느끼는 매력의 정도는 외모보다는 내면의 자신감과 관련이 있다. **2** 가산명사 매력 ❑ 해안가에서의 삶이 가지는 매력 **3** 가산명사 명소 ❑ 성벽으로 둘러싸인 이 도시는 중요한 관광 명소이다.

at|trac|tive ◆◇◇ /ətræktɪv/ **1** ADJ A person who is **attractive** is pleasant to look at. ❑ *She's a very attractive woman.* ❑ *I thought he was very attractive and obviously very intelligent.* ● at|trac|tive|ness N-UNCOUNT ❑ *Most of us would maintain that physical attractiveness does not play a major part in how we react to the people we meet.*

1 형용사 매력적인 ❑ 그녀는 매우 매력적인 여성이다. ❑ 나는 그가 아주 매력적이고 지성미가 넘치는 사람이라고 생각했다. ● 매력 불가산명사 ❑ 우리 대부분은 우리가 만나는 사람들에게 우리가 보이는 반응에 신체적인 매력이 큰 역할을 하지 않는다고 주장할 것이다.

When you are describing someone's appearance, you generally use **pretty** and **beautiful** to describe women, girls, and babies. **Beautiful** is a much stronger word than **pretty**. The equivalent word for a man is **handsome**. **Good-looking** and **attractive** can be used to describe people of either sex. **Pretty** can also be used to modify adjectives and adverbs but is less strong than **very**. In this sense, **pretty** is informal.

사람의 외모를 묘사할 때, 여성, 소녀, 아기에 대해서는 대개 pretty와 beautiful을 쓴다. beautiful은 pretty보다 훨씬 더 강한 말이다. 이에 상응하는 말로 남성에게 쓸 수 있는 것이 handsome이다. good-looking과 attractive는 남녀 모두에 대해 쓸 수 있다. pretty는 형용사와 부사를 수식하기 위해서도 쓸 수 있으나 very 보다는 강도가 약하다. 이런 의미에서의 pretty는 비격식체이다.

2 ADJ Something that is **attractive** has a pleasant appearance or sound. ❑ *The apartment was small but attractive, if rather shabby.* **3** ADJ You can describe something as **attractive** when it seems worth having or doing. ❑ *Smoking is still attractive to many young people who see it as glamorous.*

2 형용사 매력적인 ❑ 좀 낡고 작긴 했지만 그 아파트는 매력적이었다. **3** 형용사 매력적인 ❑ 흡연이 멋있다고 생각하는 많은 젊은이들에게 흡연은 여전히 매력적이다.

Thesaurus	*attractive*의 참조어
ADJ.	appealing, charming, good-looking, pleasant; *(ant.)* repulsive, ugly, unattractive **1**

Word Link	*tribute ≈ giving:* at**tribute**, con**tribute**, dis**tribute**

at|trib|ute (attributes, attributing, attributed)
The verb is pronounced /ətrɪbyut/. The noun is pronounced /ætrɪbyut/.

동사는 /ətrɪbyut /으로 발음되고, 명사는 /ætrɪbyut /으로 발음된다.

1 V-T If you **attribute** something **to** an event or situation, you think that it was caused by that event or situation. ❑ *Women tend to attribute their success to external causes such as luck.* **2** V-T If you **attribute** a particular quality or feature **to** someone or something, you think that they have it. ❑ *People were beginning to attribute superhuman qualities to him.* **3** V-T If a piece of writing, a work of art, or a remark **is attributed to** someone, people say that they wrote it, created it, or said it. [usu passive] ❑ *This, and the remaining frescoes, are not attributed to Giotto.* **4** N-COUNT An **attribute** is a quality or feature that someone or something has. ❑ *Cruelty is a normal attribute of human behavior.*

1 타동사 -에 원인을 돌리다 ❑ 여성들은 자신의 성공을 운과 같은 외부적인 요인에 돌리는 경향이 있다. **2** 타동사 -한 특징이 있다고 생각하다 ❑ 사람들이 그에게 초인적인 능력이 있다고 생각하기 시작했다. **3** 타동사 -의 것이라고 하다 ❑ 이를 비롯해 나머지 프레스코 벽화는 지오토의 작품이 아니라고 한다. **4** 가산명사 특성, 특징 ❑ 잔인함은 인간 행동의 정상적인 특성이다.

a b c d e f g h i j k l m n o p q r s t u v w x y z

auber|gine /<u>ou</u>bərʒin/ (aubergines) N-VAR An **aubergine** is a vegetable with a smooth, dark purple skin. [BRIT; AM **eggplant**]

가산명사 또는 불가산명사 가지 [영국영어; 미국영어 eggplant]

auburn /<u>ɔ</u>bərn/ COLOR **Auburn** hair is reddish brown. □ ...a tall woman with long auburn hair.

색채어 적갈색 □ 긴 적갈색 머리의 키가 큰 여성

auc|tion ♦♦◊ /<u>ɔ</u>kʃ°n/ (auctions, auctioning, auctioned) **1** N-VAR An **auction** is a public sale where goods are sold to the person who offers the highest price. □ Lord Salisbury bought the picture at auction in London some years ago. **2** V-T If something **is auctioned**, it is sold in an auction. □ Eight drawings by French artist Jean Cocteau will be auctioned next week.

1 가산명사 또는 불가산명사 경매 □ 솔즈베리 경은 그 그림을 몇 년 전 런던 경매에서 샀다. **2** 타동사 경매되다 □ 프랑스 화가 장 콕토의 작품 8점이 다음 주에 경매될 것이다.

▶**auction off** PHRASAL VERB If you **auction off** something, you sell it to the person who offers the most money for it, often at an auction. □ Any fool could auction off a factory full of engineering machinery.

구동사 경매로 팔다 □ 기계가 완비된 공장은 바보라도 경매에 붙여 팔 수 있을 것이다.

Word Link   eer ≈ one who does : auction**eer**, mountain**eer**, volunt**eer**

---

auc|tion|eer /ɔkʃənɪər/ (auctioneers) N-COUNT An **auctioneer** is a person in charge of an auction.

가산명사 경매인

auda|cious /ɔde<u>ɪ</u>ʃəs/ ADJ Someone who is **audacious** takes risks in order to achieve something. □ ...an audacious plan to win the presidency.

형용사 대담한 □ 대통령 당선을 위한 대담한 계획

auda|city /ɔdæsiti/ N-UNCOUNT **Audacity** is audacious behavior. □ I was shocked at the audacity and brazenness of the gangsters.

불가산명사 대담함, 무모함 □ 나는 폭력배들의 무모함과 뻔뻔스러움에 충격을 받았다.

Word Link   ible ≈ able to be : aud**ible**, flex**ible**, poss**ible**

---

audible /<u>ɔ</u>dɪb°l/ ADJ A sound that is **audible** is loud enough to be heard. □ The Colonel's voice was barely audible. ● **audibly** /ɔdɪbli/ ADV □ Hugh sighed audibly.

형용사 들리는 □ 대령의 목소리는 겨우 들을 수 있는 정도였다. ● 들리도록 부사 □ 휴는 소리가 들리도록 한숨을 쉬었다.

Word Link   audi ≈ hearing : **audi**ence, **audi**tion, **audi**torium

---

audi|ence ♦♦◊ /<u>ɔ</u>diəns/ (audiences) **1** N-COUNT-COLL The **audience** at a play, concert, film, or public meeting is the group of people watching or listening to it. □ The entire audience broke into loud applause. **2** N-COUNT-COLL The **audience** for a television or radio program consists of all the people who watch or listen to it. □ The concert will be relayed to a worldwide television audience estimated at one thousand million. **3** N-COUNT-COLL The **audience** of a writer or artist is the people who read their books or look at their work. □ Say's writings reached a wide audience during his lifetime. →see **concert**, **theater**

1 가산명사-집합 관객, 관중 □ 전 관객이 큰 박수를 치기 시작했다. **2** 가산명사-집합 시청자; 청취자 □ 그 콘서트는 1억 명으로 추산되는 전 세계 시청자들에게 중계 방송될 것이다. **3** 가산명사-집합 독자; 감상자 □ 세이의 글은 그의 생전에 다양한 독자들에게 읽혔다.

Word Partnership   audience의 연어

PREP.	**before/in front of an** audience **1**
N.	**studio** audience **2**
	television audience **2**
ADJ.	**captive** audience, **live** audience **1**
	large audience **1**-**3**
	general audience, **target** audience, **wide** audience **1**-**3**
V.	**reach an** audience **2** **3**

---

audio /<u>ɔ</u>dioʊ/ ADJ **Audio** equipment is used for recording and reproducing sound. [ADJ n] □ She uses her vocal training to record audio tapes of books for blind people.

형용사 오디오의 □ 그녀는 맹인들을 위한 오디오 북을 녹음하기 위해 발성 연습을 한다.

audio|tape /<u>ɔ</u>dioʊteɪp/ (audiotapes, audiotaping, audiotaped) also audio tape N-UNCOUNT **Audiotape** is magnetic tape which is used to record sound. □ Unfortunately, fewer than 5 percent of books are now available in Braille or audiotape.

불가산명사 오디오 테이프 □ 안타깝게도 점자나 오디오 테이프로 나와 있는 책이 5%도 되지 않는다.

Word Link   vid, vis ≈ seeing : **audio**visual, **vid**eotape, **vis**ible

---

audio|visual /<u>ɔ</u>dioʊvɪʒuəl/ also audio-visual ADJ **Audio-visual** equipment and materials involve both recorded sound and pictures. [ADJ n]

형용사 음향 영상의

audit /<u>ɔ</u>dɪt/ (audits, auditing, audited) V-T When an accountant **audits** an organization's accounts, he or she examines the accounts officially in order to make sure that they have been done correctly. □ Each year they audit our accounts and certify them as being true and fair. ● N-COUNT **Audit** is also a noun. □ The bank first learned of the problem when it carried out an internal audit.

타동사 감사하다 □ 그들은 매년 회계 감사를 통해 우리의 회계 장부가 정확하고 공정함을 증명한다. ● 가산명사 감사 □ 그 은행은 내부 감사를 실시하면서 처음으로 그 문제를 발견하게 되었다.

audi|tion /ɔdɪʃ°n/ (auditions, auditioning, auditioned) **1** N-COUNT An **audition** is a short performance given by an actor, dancer, or musician so that a director or conductor can decide if they are good enough to be in a play, film, or orchestra. □ ...an audition for a West End musical. **2** V-I If you **audition** or if someone **auditions** you, you do an audition. □ I was auditioning for the part of a jealous girlfriend. □ They're auditioning for new members of the cast for "Miss Saigon" today.

1 가산명사 오디션 □ 웨스트 엔드 뮤지컬을 위한 오디션 **2** 자동사 오디션을 보다 □ 나는 질투심 많은 여자 친구 역할의 오디션을 보고 있었다. □ 그들은 오늘 '미스 사이공' 출연진의 새 멤버들을 뽑기 위해 오디션 중이다.

audi|tor /<u>ɔ</u>dɪtər/ (auditors) N-COUNT An **auditor** is an accountant who officially examines the accounts of organizations.

가산명사 회계 감사원

audi|to|rium /ɔdɪt<u>ɔ</u>riəm/ (auditoriums or auditoria) /ɔdɪt<u>ɔ</u>riə/ **1** N-COUNT An **auditorium** is the part of a theater or concert hall where the audience sits. □ The Albert Hall is a huge auditorium. **2** N-COUNT An **auditorium** is a large room, hall, or building which is used for events such as meetings and concerts. [AM] □ ...a high school auditorium.

1 가산명사 관중석, 객석 □ 앨버트 홀은 하나의 거대한 객석이다. **2** 가산명사 강당, 회관, 공연장 [미국영어] □ 고등학교 강당

Aug. **Aug.** is a written abbreviation for **August**.

8월

augment /ɔgmɛnt/ (augments, augmenting, augmented) v-τ To **augment** something means to make it larger, stronger, or more effective by adding something to it. [FORMAL] ❑ *While searching for a way to augment the family income, she began making dolls.*

타동사 증가시키다, 증대시키다 [격식체] ❑ 그녀는 가계 수입을 높이기 위한 방법을 찾던 중에 인형 만드는 일을 시작했다.

August ♦♦♦ /ɔgəst/ (Augusts) N-VAR **August** is the eighth month of the year in the Western calendar. ❑ *The world premiere took place in August 1956.* ❑ *The trial will resume on August the twenty-second.*

가산명사 또는 불가산명사 8월 ❑ 세계 초연은 1956년 8월에 있었다. ❑ 재판이 8월 22일 재개될 것이다.

aunt ♦♦◊ /ænt, ɑnt/ (aunts) N-FAMILY; N-TITLE Someone's **aunt** is the sister of their mother or father, or the wife of their uncle. ❑ *She wrote to her aunt in America.* →see **family**

친족명사; 경칭명사 이모, 고모, 숙모 ❑ 그녀는 미국에 있는 숙모에게 편지를 썼다.

auntie /ænti, ɑnti/ (aunties) also **aunty** N-FAMILY; N-TITLE Someone's **auntie** is their aunt. [INFORMAL] ❑ *His uncle is dead, but his auntie still lives here.*

친족명사; 경칭명사 이모, 고모, 숙모 [비격식체] ❑ 그의 삼촌은 돌아가셨지만, 숙모는 아직 여기에 사신다.

au pair /ou pɛər, BRIT ou peəʳ/ (au pairs) N-COUNT An **au pair** is a young person from a foreign country who lives with a family in order to learn the language and who helps to look after the children.

가산명사 오페어 (말을 배우기 위해 가정집에 살면서 아이도 돌봐주는 젊은 외국인)

aura /ɔrə/ (auras) N-COUNT An **aura** is a quality or feeling that seems to surround a person or place or to come from them. ❑ *She had an aura of authority.*

가산명사 기운, 분위기 ❑ 그녀는 권위적인 분위기를 풍겼다.

auspices /ɔspɪsɪz/ PHRASE If something is done **under the auspices of** a particular person or organization, or **under** someone's **auspices**, it is done with their support and approval. [FORMAL] ❑ *.... to meet and discuss peace under the auspices of the United Nations.*

구 ∼의 후원하에, ∼의 승인하에 [격식체] ❑ 유엔의 후원하에 회담을 갖고 평화를 논의하다.

austere /ɔstɪəʳ/ **1** ADJ If you describe something as **austere**, you approve of its plain and simple appearance. [APPROVAL] ❑ *a cream linen suit and austere black blouse.* **2** ADJ If you describe someone as **austere**, you disapprove of them because they are strict and serious. [DISAPPROVAL] ❑ *I found her a rather austere, distant, somewhat cold person.* **3** ADJ An **austere** way of life is one that is simple and without luxuries. ❑ *The life of the troops was still comparatively austere.* **4** ADJ An **austere** economic policy is one which reduces people's living standards sharply. ❑ *...a set of very austere economic measures to control inflation.*

1 형용사 깔끔한 [마음에 듦] ❑ 크림 색 리넨 정장과 깔끔한 검정 블라우스 **2** 형용사 엄격한 [탐탁찮음] ❑ 나는 그녀가 다소 엄격하고 쌀쌀하며 약간 냉정한 사람이란 인상을 받았다. **3** 형용사 간소한 ❑ 군인들의 삶은 여전히 비교적 간소했다. **4** 형용사 긴축의 ❑ 인플레이션 통제를 위한 일련의 강력한 경제 긴축 정책

austerity /ɔstɛrɪti/ N-UNCOUNT **Austerity** is a situation in which people's living standards are reduced because of economic difficulties. ❑ *...the years of austerity which followed the war.*

불가산명사 내핍 ❑ 전쟁 뒤에 이어진 내핍의 세월들

authentic /ɔθɛntɪk/ **1** ADJ An **authentic** person, object, or emotion is genuine. ❑ *...authentic Italian food.* ❑ *She has authentic charm whereas most people simply have nice manners.* ● **authenticity** /ɔθɛntɪsɪti/ N-UNCOUNT ❑ *There are factors, however, that have cast doubt on the statue's authenticity.* **2** ADJ If you describe something as **authentic**, you mean that it is such a good imitation that it is almost the same as or as good as the original. [APPROVAL] ❑ *...patterns for making authentic frontier-style clothing.* **3** ADJ An **authentic** piece of information or account of something is reliable and accurate. ❑ *I had obtained the authentic details about the birth of the organization.*

1 형용사 진짜의, 진통의 ❑ 정통 이탈리아 음식 ❑ 대부분의 사람들이 단순히 매너가 좋은 것과는 달리, 그녀에게는 진정한 매력이 있다. ● 진품 불가산명사 ❑ 하지만 그 동상이 진품이 아니라고 생각할 만한 요소들이 있다. **2** 형용사 진짜 같은, 진품 같은 [마음에 듦] ❑ 진짜 프런티어 스타일의 옷처럼 만들기 위한 패턴들 **3** 형용사 믿을 만한 ❑ 나는 그 기구의 탄생에 관한 믿을 만한 세부 정보를 얻었다.

Word Link	or, er ≈ one who does, that which does: assessor, author, armor

author ♦♦◊ /ɔθəʳ/ (authors) **1** N-COUNT The **author of** a piece of writing is the person who wrote it. [oft N of n] ❑ *...Jill Phillips, author of the book "Give Your Child Music".* **2** N-COUNT An **author** is a person whose job is writing books. ❑ *Haruki Murakami is Japan's best-selling author.*

1 가산명사 저자 ❑ '자녀에게 음악을 선물하세요'라는 책의 저자 질 필립스 **2** 가산명사 작가 ❑ 무라카미 하루키는 일본의 베스트셀러 작가이다.

authorise /ɔθəraɪz/ →see **authorize**

authoritarian /əθɔrɪtɛəriən, BRIT ɔːθɒrɪtɛəriən/ ADJ If you describe a person or an organization as **authoritarian**, you are critical of them controlling everything rather than letting people decide things for themselves. [DISAPPROVAL] ❑ *Senior officers could be considering a coup to restore authoritarian rule.*

형용사 독재적인, 권위적인 [탐탁찮음] ❑ 고급 장교들이 독재 정권 회복을 위한 쿠데타를 고려하고 있을 수도 있다.

authoritative /əθɔrɪteɪtɪv, BRIT ɔːθɒrɪtətɪv/ **1** ADJ Someone or something that is **authoritative** gives an impression of power and importance and is likely to be obeyed. ❑ *He has a commanding presence and deep, authoritative voice.* **2** ADJ Someone or something that is **authoritative** has a lot of knowledge of a particular subject. ❑ *The first authoritative study of polio was published in 1840.*

1 형용사 권위 있는 ❑ 그는 당당한 풍채와 깊고 권위 있는 목소리를 지녔다. **2** 형용사 권위 있는 ❑ 소아마비에 관한 권위 있는 첫 번째 연구는 1840년에 발표되었다.

authority ♦♦♦ /əθɔrɪti, BRIT ɔːθɒrɪti/ (authorities) **1** N-PLURAL The **authorities** are the people who have the power to make decisions and to make sure that laws are obeyed. ❑ *This provided a pretext for the authorities to cancel the elections.* **2** N-COUNT An **authority** is an official organization or government department that has the power to make decisions. ❑ *...the Health Education Authority.* →see also **local authority** **3** N-UNCOUNT **Authority** is the right to command and control other people. ❑ *Local police chiefs should re-emerge as figures of authority and reassurance in their areas.* **4** N-UNCOUNT If someone has **authority**, they have a quality which makes other people take notice of what they say. ❑ *He had no natural authority and no capacity for imposing his will on others.* **5** N-UNCOUNT **Authority** is official permission to do something. ❑ *The prison governor has refused to let him go, saying he must first be given authority from his own superiors.* **6** N-COUNT Someone who is an **authority on** a particular subject knows a lot about it. ❑ *He's universally recognized as an authority on Russian affairs.*

1 복수명사 당국 ❑ 이는 당국이 선거를 취소할 수 있는 구실이 되었다. **2** 가산명사 기관, ∼부 ❑ 보건 교육부 **3** 불가산명사 권한, 권위 ❑ 지역 경찰청장은 담당 지역의 권위와 평안을 상징하는 인물로 거듭나야 한다. **4** 불가산명사 권위 ❑ 그는 자신의 의지를 다른 사람에게 관철시킬 수 있는 권위나 능력을 타고나지 못했다. **5** 불가산명사 허가 ❑ 교도소장은 상관의 허락을 먼저 받아야 한다고 말하면서 그를 못 가게 했다. **6** 가산명사 권위자, 대가 ❑ 그는 러시아 문제에 관한 권위자로 널리 인정받는다.

authorize /ɔθəraɪz/ (authorizes, authorizing, authorized) [BRIT also **authorise**] v-τ If someone in a position of authority **authorizes** something, they give their official permission for it to happen. ❑ *It would certainly be within his power to authorize a police raid like that.* ● **authorization** /ɔθəraɪzeɪʃᵊn/ (authorizations) N-VAR ❑ *The United Nations will approve his request for authorization to use military force to deliver aid.*

[영국영어 authorise] 타동사 허가하다 ❑ 틀림없이 그의 권한으로 그 같은 경찰 단속을 허락할 수 있을 것이다. ● 허가, 인증 가산명사 또는 불가산명사 ❑ 유엔은 구호물자 전달을 위한 병력 사용을 허가해 달라는 그의 요청을 승인할 것이다.

a
b
c
d
e
f
g
h
i
j
k
l
m
n
o
p
q
r
s
t
u
v
w
x
y
z

autism /ɔ́tɪzəm/ N-UNCOUNT **Autism** is a severe mental disorder that affects children and makes them unable to respond to other people.

불가산명사 자폐증

auto ♦♢♢ /ɔ́toʊ/ (**autos**) N-COUNT An **auto** is a car. [AM] ❑ ...*the auto industry.*

가산명사 자동차 [미국영어] ❑ 자동차 산업

auto|bio|graphi|cal /ɔ̀toʊbaɪəgrǽfɪkᵊl/ ADJ An **autobiographical** piece of writing relates to events in the life of the person who has written it. ❑ ...*a highly autobiographical novel of a woman's search for identity.*

형용사 자전적인, 자전적인 ❑ 한 여성의 자아 발견 과정을 담은, 대단히 자전적인 소설

auto|bi|og|ra|phy /ɔ̀tɔbaɪɔ́grəfi/ (**autobiographies**) N-COUNT Your **autobiography** is an account of your life, which you write yourself. ❑ *He published his autobiography last autumn.*

가산명사 자서전 ❑ 그는 지난 가을 자서전을 출판했다.

Word Link   *graph ≈ writing : auto*graph, *bio*graph*y*, *graph*

---

auto|graph /ɔ́təgræf/ (**autographs, autographing, autographed**) 🔢 N-COUNT An **autograph** is the signature of someone famous which is specially written for a fan to keep. ❑ *He went backstage and asked for her autograph.* 🔢 V-T If someone famous **autographs** something, they put their signature on it. ❑ *I autographed a copy of one of my books.*

🔢 가산명사 사인 ❑ 그는 무대 뒤로 가서 그녀에게 사인해 달라고 했다. 🔢 타동사 -에 사인하다 ❑ 나는 내 책 중 한 권에 사인을 했다.

auto|mate /ɔ́təmeɪt/ (**automates, automating, automated**) V-T To **automate** a factory, office, or industrial process means to put in machines which can do the work instead of people. ❑ *He wanted to use computers to automate the process.* ● **auto|ma|tion** /ɔ̀təmeɪʃᵊn/ N-UNCOUNT ❑ *In the last ten years automation has reduced the work force here by half.*

타동사 자동화하다 ❑ 그는 컴퓨터를 사용해서 그 과정을 자동화하기를 원했다. ● 자동화 불가산명사 ❑ 자동화 때문에 지난 10년 동안 여기 직원 수가 반으로 줄었다.

auto|mat|ed /ɔ́təmeɪtɪd/ ADJ An **automated** factory, office, or industrial process uses machines to do the work instead of people. ❑ *The equipment was made on highly automated production lines.*

형용사 자동화된 ❑ 그 장비는 고도로 자동화된 생산 라인을 통해 만들어졌다.

Word Link   *auto ≈ self : auto*matic, *auto*mobile, *auto*nomy*

---

auto|mat|ic ♦♢♢ /ɔ̀təmǽtɪk/ (**automatics**) 🔢 ADJ An **automatic** machine or device is one which has controls that enable it to perform a task without needing to be constantly operated by a person. **Automatic** methods and processes involve the use of such machines. ❑ *Modern trains have automatic doors.* 🔢 ADJ An **automatic** weapon is one which keeps firing shots until you stop pulling the trigger. [ADJ n] ❑ *Three gunmen with automatic rifles opened fire.* ● N-COUNT **Automatic** is also a noun. ❑ *He drew his automatic and began running in the direction of the sounds.* 🔢 N-COUNT An **automatic** is a car in which the gears change automatically as the car's speed increases or decreases. 🔢 ADJ An **automatic** action is one that you do without thinking about it. ❑ *All of the automatic body functions, even breathing, are affected.* ● **auto|mati|cal|ly** /ɔ̀təmǽtɪkli/ ADV ❑ *Strangely enough, you will automatically wake up after this length of time.*

🔢 형용사 자동의, 자동적인 ❑ 요즘 기차에는 자동문이 달려 있다. 🔢 형용사 자동의 ❑ 자동 소총을 든 괴한 세 명이 사격을 시작했다. ● 가산명사 자동 권총 ❑ 그는 자동 권총을 꺼내 들고 소리가 나는 쪽을 향해 뛰기 시작했다. 🔢 가산명사 오토매틱 자동차 🔢 형용사 무의식적인 ❑ 모든 무의식적인 신체 기능이, 심지어 호흡까지도, 영향을 받는다. ● 자동적으로 부사 ❑ 신기하게도 당신은 이 정도의 시간이 지나면 자동적으로 깨어날 것이다.

auto|mo|bile /ɔ́təmoʊbil, BRIT ɔ̀təməbiːl/ (**automobiles**) N-COUNT An **automobile** is a car. [mainly AM] ❑ ...*the automobile industry.* →see **car**

가산명사 자동차 [주로 미국영어] ❑ 자동차 산업

auto|no|mous /ɔtɔ́nəməs/ 🔢 ADJ An **autonomous** country, organization, or group governs or controls itself rather than being controlled by anyone else. ❑ *They proudly declared themselves part of a new autonomous province.* 🔢 ADJ An **autonomous** person makes their own decisions rather than being influenced by someone else. ❑ *He treated us as autonomous individuals who had to learn to make up our own minds about important issues.*

🔢 형용사 자치의 ❑ 그들은 그들 자신도 새 자치 지역의 일부분이라는 사실을 자랑스럽게 선포했다. 🔢 형용사 자율적인 ❑ 그는 중요한 일은 스스로 결정을 내리는 법을 터득해야 하는 자율적인 인간으로 우리를 대했다.

auto|no|my /ɔtɔ́nəmi/ 🔢 N-UNCOUNT **Autonomy** is the control or government of a country, organization, or group by itself rather than by others. ❑ *Activists stepped up their demands for local autonomy last month.* 🔢 N-UNCOUNT **Autonomy** is the ability to make your own decisions about what to do rather than being influenced by someone else or told what to do. [FORMAL] ❑ *Each of the area managers enjoys considerable autonomy in the running of his own area.*

🔢 불가산명사 자치 ❑ 지난달 지방 자치를 요구하는 목소리가 높아졌다. 🔢 불가산명사 자율 [격식체] ❑ 지역 매니저들은 각 지역을 운영하는 데 있어 상당한 자율성을 누리고 있다.

autop|sy /ɔ́tɔpsi/ (**autopsies**) N-COUNT An **autopsy** is an examination of a dead body by a doctor who cuts it open in order to try to discover the cause of death. ❑ *Macklin had the grim task of carrying out an autopsy on his friend.*

가산명사 부검 ❑ 맥클린은 자신의 친구를 부검하는 끔찍한 일을 해야 했다.

autumn ♦♢♢ /ɔ́təm/ (**autumns**) N-VAR **Autumn** is the season between summer and winter when the weather becomes cooler and the leaves fall off the trees. [mainly BRIT; AM usually **fall**] ❑ *We are always plagued by wasps in autumn.*

가산명사 또는 불가산명사 가을 [주로 영국영어; 미국영어 대개 fall] ❑ 가을이 되면 항상 말벌이 극성이다.

aux|il|ia|ry /ɔgzɪ́lyəri, -zɪ́ləri, BRIT ɔːgzɪ́lyəri/ (**auxiliaries**) 🔢 N-COUNT An **auxiliary** is a person who is employed to assist other people in their work. Auxiliaries are often medical workers or members of the armed forces. ❑ *Nursing auxiliaries provide basic care, but are not qualified nurses.* 🔢 ADJ **Auxiliary** staff and troops assist other staff and troops. [ADJ n] ❑ *The government's first concern was to augment the army and auxiliary forces.* 🔢 ADJ **Auxiliary** equipment is extra equipment that is available for use when necessary. [ADJ n] ❑ ...*an auxiliary motor.* 🔢 N-COUNT In grammar, an **auxiliary** or **auxiliary verb** is a verb which is used with a main verb, for example to form different tenses or to make the verb passive. In English, the basic auxiliary verbs are "be," "have," and "do." Modal verbs such as "can" and "will" are also sometimes called auxiliaries.

🔢 가산명사 조수, 보조 ❑ 간호조무사는 기본적인 치료는 하지만 정식 간호사는 아니다. 🔢 형용사 보조의 ❑ 정부의 첫 번째 관심사는 군과 보충병의 증원이었다. 🔢 형용사 예비용의, 보조의 ❑ 보조 모터 🔢 가산명사 조동사

avail /əveɪl/ PHRASE If you do something **to no avail** or **to little avail**, what you do fails to achieve what you want. [WRITTEN] ❑ *His efforts were to no avail.*

구 무익하게, 보람 없이 [문어체] ❑ 그의 노력은 수포로 돌아갔다.

avail|able ♦♦♦ /əveɪləbᵊl/ 🔢 ADJ If something you want or need is **available**, you can find it or obtain it. ❑ *Since 1978, the amount of money available to buy books has fallen by 17%.* ❑ *There are three small boats available for hire.* ● **avail|abil|ity** /əveɪləbɪ́lɪti/ N-UNCOUNT ❑ ...*the easy availability of guns.* 🔢 ADJ Someone who is **available** is not busy and is therefore free to talk to you or to do a

🔢 형용사 이용 가능한, 구할 수 있는 ❑ 1978년 이후로 서적 구입에 사용할 수 있는 돈의 액수가 17% 떨어졌다. ❑ 빌릴 수 있는 작은 배가 3척 있다. ● 이용 가능함, 구할 수 있음 불가산명사 ❑ 총기를 쉽게 구할 수 있음 🔢 형용사 한가한 ❑ 리치는 휴가

particular task. [v-link ADJ] ❏ *Mr. Leach is on holiday and was not available for comment.*

중이어서 그의 의견을 들어 보려 했지만 연락이 닿지 않았다.

Thesaurus   *available*의 참조어

ADJ.	accessible, handy, usable **1**
	accessible, free; (*ant.*) busy **2**

Word Partnership   *available*의 연어

N.	available **information**, available **opportunities/options**, available **resources** **1**
ADV.	**readily** available **1**
	now available **1 2**
PREP.	available **on request** **1**
	available **for** *something* **2**
V.	**make** *yourself* available **2**

ava|lanche /ˈævəlæntʃ/ (**avalanches**) N-COUNT An **avalanche** is a large mass of snow that falls down the side of a mountain.

가산명사 눈사태

avant-garde /ˌævɒŋ ˈɡɑrd/ ADJ **Avant-garde** art, music, theater, and literature is very modern and experimental. ❏ *...avant-garde concert music.*

형용사 전위적인, 아방가르드의 ❏ 전위적인 콘서트 음악

avenge /əˈvɛndʒ/ (**avenges, avenging, avenged**) V-T If you **avenge** a wrong or harmful act, you hurt or punish the person who is responsible for it. ❏ *He has devoted the past five years to avenging his daughter's death.*

타동사 복수하다 ❏ 그는 딸의 죽음에 대한 복수를 하는 데 지난 5년의 세월을 바쳤다.

av|enue /ˈævɪnyu, -nu, BRIT ˈævɪnyuː/ (**avenues**) N-IN-NAMES **Avenue** is sometimes used in the names of streets. The written abbreviation **Ave.** is also used. ❏ *...the most expensive apartments on Park Avenue.* **2** N-COUNT An **avenue** is a wide, straight road, especially one with trees on either side.

1 이름명사 애비뉴 (거리), Ave.는 축약형임. ❏ 파크 애비뉴의 최고가 아파트들 **2** 가산명사 대로

av|er|age ♦♦◇ /ˈævərɪdʒ, ˈævrɪdʒ/ (**averages, averaging, averaged**) **1** N-COUNT An **average** is the result that you get when you add two or more numbers together and divide the total by the number of numbers you added together. ❏ *Take the average of those ratios and multiply by a hundred.* ● ADJ **Average** is also an adjective. [ADJ n] ❏ *The average price of goods rose by just 2.2%.* **2** N-SING You use **average** to refer to a number or size that varies but is always approximately the same. ❏ *It takes an average of ten weeks for a house sale to be completed.* **3** ADJ An **average** person or thing is typical or normal. [ADJ n] ❏ *The average adult man burns 1,500 to 2,000 calories per day.* **4** N-SING An amount or quality that is **the average** is the normal amount or quality for a particular group of things or people. ❏ *35% of staff time was being spent on repeating work, about the average for a service industry.* ● ADJ **Average** is also an adjective. ❏ *£2.20 for a beer is average.* **5** ADJ Something that is **average** is neither very good nor very bad, usually when you had hoped it would be better. ❏ *I was only average academically.* **6** V-T To **average** a particular amount means to do, get, or produce that amount as an average over a period of time. ❏ *We averaged 42 miles per hour.* **7** PHRASE You say **on average** or **on an average** to indicate that a number is the average of several numbers. ❏ *American shares rose, on average, by 38%.*

1 가산명사 평균 ❏ 그 비율들의 평균을 낸 후 100을 곱하시오. ● 형용사 평균의 ❏ 제화의 평균가가 2.2%밖에 오르지 않았다. **2** 단수명사 평균치 ❏ 집을 내놓고 완전히 팔기까지 평균 10주 정도 걸린다. **3** 형용사 보통의, 평균의 ❏ 보통 성인 남성은 하루 1,500–2,000칼로리를 소비한다. **4** 단수명사 평균, 보통 수준 ❏ 근무 시간의 35%가 같은 일을 반복하는 데 사용되었다는데, 이는 서비스 업종에서는 보통 수준이다. ● 형용사 평균의 ❏ 맥주 한 잔당 평균 2.2파운드이다. **5** 형용사 평균의, 중간의 ❏ 나의 학교 성적은 겨우 평균 정도에 그쳤다. **6** 타동사 평균 –이다 ❏ 우리는 시간당 평균 42마일을 갔다. **7** 구 평균적으로 ❏ 미국 증시가 평균 38% 올랐다.

aver|sion /əˈvɜrʒ³n, BRIT əˈvɜːʃ³n/ (**aversions**) N-VAR If you have an **aversion to** someone or something, you dislike them very much. ❏ *Many people have a natural and emotional aversion to insects.*

가산명사 또는 불가산명사 혐오 ❏ 많은 사람이 천성적으로 또 감정적으로 곤충을 매우 싫어한다.

avert /əˈvɜrt/ (**averts, averting, averted**) **1** V-T If you **avert** something unpleasant, you prevent it from happening. ❏ *Talks with the teachers' union over the weekend have averted a strike.* **2** V-T If you **avert** your eyes or gaze **from** someone or something, you look away from them. ❏ *He avoids any eye contact, quickly averting his gaze when anyone approaches.*

1 타동사 막다, 피하다 ❏ 주말에 있었던 교원 노조와의 협상으로 파업을 피할 수 있게 됐다. **2** 타동사 (눈길을) 돌리다 ❏ 그는 누군가 다가서면 재빨리 시선을 돌려 누구와도 눈을 맞추려 하지 않는다.

aviary /ˈeɪviɛri/ (**aviaries**) N-COUNT An **aviary** is a large cage or covered area in which birds are kept.

가산명사 새 사육장

avia|tion /ˌeɪviˈeɪʃ³n/ N-UNCOUNT **Aviation** is the operation and production of aircraft. ❏ *...the aviation industry.*

불가산명사 항공 ❏ 항공 산업

avid /ˈævɪd/ ADJ You use **avid** to describe someone who is very enthusiastic about something that they do. ❏ *He misses not having enough books because he's an avid reader.* ● **av|id|ly** ADV [ADV with v] ❏ *Thank you for a most entertaining magazine, which I read avidly each month.*

형용사 열심인, 열렬한 ❏ 그는 열렬한 독서가라서 책이 충분히 없으면 아쉬워한다. ● 열심히 부사 ❏ 재미있는 잡지를 만들어 주셔서 감사합니다. 매달 열심히 읽고 있어요.

avo|ca|do /ˌævəˈkɑdoʊ/ (**avocados**) [BRIT also **avocado pear**] N-VAR **Avocados** are pear-shaped vegetables, with hard skins and large stones, which are usually eaten raw.

[영국영어 avocado pear] 가산명사 또는 불가산명사 아보카도

avoid ♦♦◇ /əˈvɔɪd/ (**avoids, avoiding, avoided**) **1** V-T If you **avoid** something unpleasant that might happen, you take action in order to prevent it from happening. ❏ *The pilots had to take emergency action to avoid a disaster.* **2** V-T If you **avoid** doing something, you choose not to do it, or you put yourself in a situation where you do not have to do it. ❏ *By borrowing from dozens of banks, he managed to avoid giving any of them an overall picture of what he was up to.* **3** V-T If you **avoid** a person or thing, you keep away from them. When talking to someone, if you **avoid** the subject, you keep the conversation away from a particular topic. ❏ *She eventually had to lock herself in the toilets to avoid him.* **4** V-T If a person or vehicle **avoids** someone or something, they change the direction they are moving in, so that they do not hit them. ❏ *The driver had ample time to brake or swerve and avoid the woman.*

1 타동사 피하다, 막다 ❏ 조종사들은 재난을 피하기 위해 비상조치를 취해야 했다. **2** 타동사 피하다 ❏ 그는 수십 개의 은행에서 돈을 빌림으로써 어떤 은행도 자신이 무슨 일을 꾸미고 있는지 알아채지 못하게 했다. **3** 타동사 피하다, 회피하다 ❏ 그녀는 그를 피하기 위해 결국엔 화장실에 틀어박혀 있어야 했다. **4** 타동사 피하다 ❏ 운전사가 브레이크를 밟거나 차를 틀어서 그 여자를 피할 수 있는 시간이 충분히 있었다.

Thesaurus   *avoid*의 참조어

V.	abstain, bypass, evade, shun; (*ant.*) confront, embrace, face, seek **1**-**3**

await ♦♢♢ /əweɪt/ (awaits, awaiting, awaited) **1** V-T If you **await** someone or something, you wait for them. [FORMAL] ❑ *Very little was said as we awaited the arrival of the chairman.* **2** V-T Something that **awaits** you is going to happen or come to you in the future. [FORMAL] ❑ *A nasty surprise awaited them in Rosemary Lane.*

1 타동사 기다리다 [격식체] ❑ 회장님이 도착하기를 기다리는 동안 우리는 거의 말을 하지 않았다. **2** 타동사 기다리다 [격식체] ❑ 로즈마리 레인에서는 뜻밖의 불쾌한 사건이 그들을 기다리고 있었다.

Thesaurus		await의 참조어
v.	anticipate, count on, expect, hope **1**	

Word Link	wak ≈ being awake : awake, wake, wakeful

awake /əweɪk/ **1** ADJ Someone who is **awake** is not sleeping. [v-link ADJ, ADJ after v] ❑ *I don't stay awake at night worrying about that.* **2** PHRASE Someone who is **wide awake** is fully awake and unable to sleep. ❑ *I could not relax and still felt wide awake.* →see **sleep**

1 형용사 깨어 있는 ❑ 나는 그런 일로 걱정하면서 밤잠을 설치지는 않는다. **2** 구 정신이 또렷한, 전혀 잠이 안 오는 ❑ 나는 긴장도 안 풀리고 정신도 계속 또렷했다.

Word Partnership		awake의 연어
V.	keep *someone* awake, lie awake, stay awake **1**	
ADV.	half awake **1**	
	fully awake, wide awake **2**	

awak|en|ing /əweɪkənɪŋ/ (awakenings) **1** N-COUNT The **awakening** of a feeling or realization is the start of it. ❑ *...the awakening of national consciousness in people.* **2** PHRASE If you have a **rude awakening**, you are suddenly made aware of an unpleasant fact. ❑ *It was a rude awakening to learn after I left home that I wasn't so special anymore.*

1 가산명사 각성, 자각 ❑ 국민들의 국가 의식 각성 **2** 구 엄연한 현실의 자각 ❑ 고향을 떠난 후 내가 더 이상 그렇게 특별하지 않다는 것을 알게 되면서 정신을 번쩍 차리게 됐다.

award ♦♦♢ /əwɔːrd/ (awards, awarding, awarded) **1** N-COUNT An **award** is a prize or certificate that a person is given for doing something well. ❑ *...the Booker Award, Britain's top award for fiction.* **2** N-COUNT In law, an **award** is a sum of money that a court decides should be given to someone. ❑ *...worker's compensation awards.* **3** V-T If someone **is awarded** something such as a prize or an examination mark, it is given to them. ❑ *She was awarded the prize for both films.* **4** V-T To **award** something **to** someone means to decide that it will be given to that person. ❑ *We have awarded the contract to a British shipyard.* **5** N-COUNT A pay **award** is an increase in pay for a particular group of workers. [BRIT] ❑ *...this year's average pay award for teachers of just under 8%.*

1 가산명사 상 ❑ 소설 부문에 대한 영국 최고의 상인 부커상 **2** 가산명사 배상금 ❑ 노동자 배상금 **3** 타동사 수여받다 ❑ 그녀는 두 영화 모두에 대해 상을 받았다. **4** 타동사 주다 ❑ 우리는 영국 조선소와 계약을 체결했다. **5** 가산명사 급여 인상 [영국영어] ❑ 8%를 약간 밑도는 올해 교사들의 평균 급여 인상액

aware ♦♦♢ /əweər/ **1** ADJ If you are **aware of** something, you know about it. [v-link ADJ, ADJ of n, ADJ that] ❑ *Smokers are well aware of the dangers to their own health.* ❑ *He should have been aware of what his junior officers were doing.* ● **aware|ness** N-UNCOUNT ❑ *The 1980s brought an awareness of green issues.* **2** ADJ If you are **aware of** something, you realize that it is present or is happening because you hear it, see it, smell it, or feel it. [v-link ADJ, ADJ of n, ADJ that] ❑ *She was acutely aware of the noise of the city.*

1 형용사 인식하고 있는, 알고 있는 ❑ 흡연자들은 자신의 건강에 미치는 폐해를 잘 알고 있다. ❑ 그는 자기 밑의 하급 장교들이 무슨 일을 하고 있는지 알고 있었어야 했다. ● 인식 불가산명사 ❑ 1980년대에 환경 문제에 관한 인식이 싹텄다. **2** 형용사 알고 있는, 인식하고 있는 ❑ 그녀는 도시의 소음에 관해 예민하게 인식하고 있었다.

Word Partnership		aware의 연어
ADV.	painfully aware, well aware **1** **2**	
	acutely/vaguely aware, fully aware **1** **2**	
PREP.	aware of *something/someone*, aware that **1** **2**	
V.	become aware **1** **2**	

awash /əwɒʃ/ **1** ADJ If the ground or a floor is **awash**, it is covered in water, often because of heavy rain or as the result of an accident. [v-link ADJ] ❑ *The bathroom floor was awash.* **2** ADJ If a place is **awash with** something, it contains a large amount of it. [v-link ADJ, usu ADJ with n] ❑ *This, after all, is a company which is awash with cash.*

1 형용사 물에 잠긴 ❑ 화장실 바닥이 온통 물투성이였다. **2** 형용사 ~로 가득하여 ❑ 결국 이 회사는 현금이 넘쳐나는 곳이다.

away ♦♦♦ /əweɪ/

Away is often used with verbs of movement, such as "go" and "drive," and also in phrasal verbs such as "do away with" and "fade away."

away는 종종 'go', 'drive'와 같은 이동 동사와 함께 쓰이며 'do away with', 'fade away'와 같은 구동사에도 쓰인다.

1 ADV If someone or something moves or is moved **away from** a place, they move or are moved so that they are no longer there. If you are **away from** a place, you are not in the place where people expect you to be. ❑ *An injured policeman was led away by colleagues.* ❑ *He walked away from his car.* ❑ *Jason was away on a business trip.* **2** ADV If you look or turn **away from** something, you move your head so that you are no longer looking at it. ❑ *She quickly looked away and stared down at her hands.* **3** ADV If you put something **away**, you put it where it should be. If you hide someone or something **away**, you put them in a place where nobody can see them or find them. [ADV after v] ❑ *I put my journal away and prepared for bed.* ❑ *All her letters were carefully filed away in folders.* **4** PHRASE If something is **away from** a person or place, it is at a distance from that person or place. ❑ *The two women were sitting as far away from each other as possible.* **5** ADV You use **away** to talk about future events. For example, if an event is a week **away**, it will happen after a week. [be amount ADV] ❑ *...the Washington summit, now only just over two weeks away.* **6** ADV When a sports team plays **away**, it plays on its opponents' playing field. [ADV after v] ❑ *...a sensational 4-3 victory for the team playing away.* ● ADJ **Away** is also an adjective. [ADJ n] ❑ *Charlton are about to play an important away match.* **7** ADV You can use **away** to say that something slowly disappears, becomes less significant, or changes so that it is no longer the same. [ADV after v] ❑ *So much snow has already melted away.* ❑ *His voice died away in a whisper.* **8** ADV You use **away** to show that there has been a change or development from one state or situation to another. ❑ *British courts are*

1 부사 멀리 ❑ 부상을 당한 경찰관 한 명이 동료들에 의해 실려 나갔다. ❑ 그는 차에서 멀리 걸어갔다. ❑ 제이슨은 출장차 멀리 나가 있었다. **2** 부사 다른 곳으로 ❑ 그녀는 재빨리 시선을 돌려 자신의 손을 내려다보았다. **3** 부사 치워서, 보이지 않게 ❑ 나는 일기를 치운 후에 잘 준비를 했다. ❑ 그녀의 편지는 전부 폴더에 꼼꼼하게 정리되어 있었다. **4** 구 떨어져 ❑ 두 여성은 서로에게서 되도록 멀리 떨어져 앉아 있었다. **5** 부사 후에 ❑ 이제 겨우 2주 정도 남은 다가온 워싱턴 정상회담 **6** 부사 원정 경기에서 ❑ 원정 경기에 나선 팀이 거둔 4:3의 선풍적인 승리 ● 형용사 원정 경기의 ❑ 찰튼은 이제 곧 중요한 원정 경기를 하게 된다. **7** 부사 점점 사라져, 점점 약해져 ❑ 너무나도 많던 눈이 벌써 녹아 버렸다. ❑ 그의 목소리가 점점 작아져 속삭임이 되었다. **8** 부사 변화하여 ❑ 영국 법원은 청소년 범죄자들을 감옥으로 보내는 관행에서 점점 더 벗어나고 있다. **9** 부사 계속해서 [강조] ❑ 그는 자주 한밤중까지 워드 프로세서로 계속 작업을 하곤 했었다. **10** 부사 없어져 ❑ 만약 당신이 내 일을 가져가 버린다면 나는 더 이상 행복하지 못할 것이다.

increasingly moving away from sending young offenders to prison. **9** ADV You can use **away** to emphasize a continuous or repeated action. [EMPHASIS] [ADV after v] ❑ *He would often be working away on his word processor late into the night.* **10** ADV You use **away** to show that something is removed. [ADV after v] ❑ *If you take my work away I can't be happy anymore.* **11** **right away** →see **right**

Word Partnership	*away*의 연어
V.	back away, blow away, chase *someone* away, drive away, hide away, get away, go away, move away, pull/take/wash *something* away, stay away, walk away **1**
	look/turn away **2**
	put away, throw away **3**
ADJ.	far away **4**
N.	away from home **4**

awe /ɔ/ (**awes, awed**) **1** N-UNCOUNT **Awe** is the feeling of respect and amazement that you have when you are faced with something wonderful and often rather frightening. ❑ *She gazed in awe at the great stones.* **2** V-T If you **are awed by** someone or something, they make you feel respectful and amazed, though often rather frightened. [usu passive, no cont] ❑ *I am still awed by David's courage.*

Word Link	*some ≈ causing: awesome, fearsome, troublesome*

awe|some /ɔsəm/ ADJ An **awesome** person or thing is very impressive and often frightening. ❑ *...the awesome responsibility of sending men into combat.*

aw|ful ◆◇◇ /ɔfəl/ **1** ADJ If you say that someone or something is **awful**, you dislike that person or thing or you think that they are not very good. ❑ *We met and I thought he was awful.* ❑ *...an awful smell of paint.* **2** ADJ If you say that something is **awful**, you mean that it is extremely unpleasant, shocking, or bad. ❑ *Her injuries were massive. It was awful.* **3** ADJ If you look or feel **awful**, you look or feel ill. [v-link] ❑ *I hardly slept at all and felt pretty awful.* **4** ADJ You can use **awful** with noun groups that refer to an amount in order to emphasize how large that amount is. [EMPHASIS] [ADJ n] ❑ *I've got an awful lot of work to do.* ● **aw|ful|ly** ADV ❑ *The caramel looks awfully good.*

Thesaurus	*awful*의 참조어
ADJ.	bad, dreadful, horrible, terrible; (ant.) good, nice, pleasing **1** **2**

awhile /əwaɪl/ ADV **Awhile** means for a short time. It is more commonly spelled "a while," which is considered more correct, especially in British English. ❑ *He worked awhile as a pharmacist in Cincinnati.*

awk|ward /ɔkwərd/ **1** ADJ An **awkward** situation is embarrassing and difficult to deal with. ❑ *I was the first to ask him awkward questions but there'll be harder ones to come.* ● **awk|ward|ly** ADV [ADV adj/-ed] ❑ *There was an awkwardly long silence.* **2** ADJ Something that is **awkward** to use or carry is difficult to use or carry because of its design. A job that is **awkward** is difficult to do. ❑ *It was small but heavy enough to make it awkward to carry.* ● **awk|ward|ly** ADV [ADV -ed] ❑ *The autoexposure button is awkwardly placed under the lens release button.* **3** ADJ An **awkward** movement or position is uncomfortable or clumsy. ❑ *Amy made an awkward gesture with her hands.* ● **awk|ward|ly** ADV [ADV with v] ❑ *He fell awkwardly and went down in agony clutching his right knee.* **4** ADJ Someone who feels **awkward** behaves in a shy or embarrassed way. ❑ *Women frequently say that they feel awkward taking the initiative in sex.* ● **awk|ward|ly** ADV [ADV with v] ❑ *"This is Malcolm," the girl said awkwardly, to fill the silence.*

Thesaurus	*awkward*의 참조어
ADJ.	delicate, embarrassing, uncomfortable **1**
	bulky, cumbersome, difficult **2**

awoke /əwoʊk/ **Awoke** is the past tense of **awake**.

awok|en /əwoʊkən/ **Awoken** is the past participle of **awake**.

ax /æks/ (**axes, axing, axed**) [BRIT, sometimes AM **axe**] **1** N-COUNT An **ax** is a tool used for cutting wood. It consists of a heavy metal blade which is sharp at one edge and attached by its other edge to the end of a long handle. **2** V-T If someone's job or something such as a public service or a television program **is axed**, it is ended suddenly and without discussion. [usu passive] ❑ *Community projects are being axed by hard-pressed social services departments.*

axes
Pronounced /æksɪz/ for meaning **1**, and /æksiz/ for meaning **2**.

1 **Axes** is the plural of **ax**. **2** **Axes** is the plural of **axis**.

axis /æksɪs/ (**axes**) **1** N-COUNT An **axis** is an imaginary line through the middle of something. ❑ *...the tilt of the earth's axis.* **2** N-COUNT An **axis** of a graph is one of the two lines on which the scales of measurement are marked. ❑ *The level of spiritual achievement is plotted along the Y axis, and the degree of physical health is plotted along the X axis.* →see **graph, moon**

1 불가산명사 경외 ❑ 그녀는 거대한 석상들을 경외의 눈으로 바라보았다. **2** 타동사 경외심을 느끼다 ❑ 나는 아직도 데이빗의 용기에 경외심을 느낀다.

형용사 장엄한 ❑ 전투병 파병이라는 막중한 책임

1 형용사 끔찍한, 지독한 ❑ 우리는 만났고, 나는 그가 정말 싫었다. ❑ 지독한 페인트 냄새 **2** 형용사 끔찍한 ❑ 그녀가 부상을 크게 입었다. 너무 끔찍했다. **3** 형용사 찌뿌드드한 ❑ 나는 거의 잠을 못 자서 몸이 찌뿌드드했다. **4** 형용사 엄청난 [강조] ❑ 나는 할 일이 엄청 많다. ● 대단히, 엄청 부사 ❑ 캐러멜이 엄청 맛있어 보인다.

부사 잠깐 ❑ 그는 신시내티에서 잠깐 동안 약사로 일했다.

1 형용사 곤란한, 난처한 ❑ 그에게 처음으로 곤란한 질문을 한 사람은 나였지만 앞으로 더 난처한 질문들이 나올 것이다. ● 곤란하게, 난처하게 부사 ❑ 난처할 정도로 긴 침묵이 흘렀다. **2** 형용사 힘든, 불편한 ❑ 그것은 작지만 무거워 들고 다니기 힘들 정도였다. ● 불편하게, 어색하게 부사 ❑ 자동 노출 버튼이 셔터 릴리스 버튼 밑에 어설프게 배치되어 있다. **3** 형용사 서투른, 어설픈 ❑ 에이미가 손으로 어설픈 제스처를 취했다. ● 서투르게, 어설프게 부사 ❑ 그는 어설프게 떨어져 괴로워하며 오른쪽 무릎을 움켜쥐고 걸어 내려갔다. **4** 형용사 어색한, 지척은 ❑ 여성들은 자신이 성관계를 먼저 요구할 때 어색함을 느낀다고 흔히 말한다. ● 어색하게 부사 ❑ "이 분은 말콤 씨예요."라고 소녀가 침묵을 메우려고 어색하게 말했다.

awake의 과거형

awake의 과거 분사

[영국영어, 미국영어 가끔 axe] **1** 가산명사 도끼 **2** 타동사 싹둑 자르다 ❑ 재정난에 처한 사회 복지 부처들이 지역 사회 프로젝트를 중단하고 있다.

1의 의미일 때는 /æksɪz/로 발음하고, **2**의 의미일 때는 /æksiz/로 발음된다.

1 ax의 복수형 **2** axis의 복수형

1 가산명사 축 ❑ 지구 자전축의 기울기 **2** 가산명사 축 ❑ Y축은 정신적인 성취도를, X축은 신체 건강 정도를 나타낸다.

Bb

B, b /biː/ (**B's, b's**) N-VAR B is the second letter of the English alphabet.

가산명사 또는 불가산명사 영어 알파벳의 두 번째 글자

B2B /biː tə biː/ N-UNCOUNT B2B is the selling of goods and services by one company to another using the Internet. **B2B** is an abbreviation for "business to business." [BUSINESS] ❑ *American analysts have been somewhat cautious in estimating the size of the B2B market.*

불가산명사 기업 대 기업 [경제] ❑ 비투비 시장 규모를 추정함에 있어서 미국 분석가들은 다소 진중을 기해 왔다.

B2C /biː tə siː/ N-UNCOUNT B2C is the selling of goods and services by businesses to consumers using the Internet. **B2C** is an abbreviation for "business to consumer." [BUSINESS] ❑ *B2C companies look particularly vulnerable with 19 percent of them now worth little more than the cash on their balance sheets.*

불가산명사 기업 대 고객 [경제] ❑ 비투씨 기업의 19퍼센트가 대차 대조표의 현금 잔고 남짓한 가치를 가지고 있기 때문에 이들은 특히 불안해 보인다.

bab|ble /bæbᵊl/ (**babbles, babbling, babbled**) **1** V-I If someone **babbles**, they talk in a confused or excited way. ❑ *Momma babbled on and on about how he was ruining me.* ❑ *They all babbled simultaneously.* **2** N-SING You can refer to people's voices as a **babble of** sound when they are excited and confused, preventing you from understanding what they are saying. ❑ *Kemp knocked loudly so as to be heard above the high babble of voices.*

1 타동사/자동사 횡설수설하다, 주절대다 ❑ 그가 어떻게 나를 망치고 있는지에 대해 엄마는 끝도 없이 횡설수설했다. ❑ 그들은 동시에 주절댔다. **2** 단수명사 횡설수설 ❑ 켐프는 사람들이 시끄럽게 떠드는 와중에도 들리도록 노크를 크게 했다.

baby ♦♦◇ /beɪbi/ (**babies**) **1** N-COUNT A **baby** is a very young child, especially one that cannot yet walk or talk. ❑ *She used to take care of me when I was a baby.* ❑ *My wife has just had a baby.* **2** N-COUNT A **baby** animal is a very young animal. ❑ *...a baby elephant.* **3** ADJ **Baby** vegetables are vegetables picked when they are very small. [ADJ n] ❑ *Cook the baby potatoes in their skins.* **4** N-VOC; N-COUNT Some people use **baby** as an affectionate way of addressing someone, especially a young woman, or referring to them. [INFORMAL] ❑ *You have to wake up now, baby.* →see **child**

1 가산명사 아기 ❑ 내가 아기였을 때 그 분이 나를 돌보곤 했다. ❑ 아내가 막 아기를 낳았다. **2** 가산명사 새끼 ❑ 새끼 코끼리 **3** 형용사 어린 ❑ 어린 감자를 껍질째 익혀라. **4** 호격명사; 가산명사 사람에 대한 애칭 [비격식체] ❑ 이제 일어나야지, 자기.

Word Partnership | baby의 연어

N.	baby **boy/girl/sister**, baby **names** **1**
V.	**deliver a** baby, **have a** baby **1**
ADJ.	**new/newborn** baby, **unborn** baby **1**

---

baby car|riage (**baby carriages**) N-COUNT A **baby carriage** is a small vehicle in which a baby can lie as it is pushed along. [AM; BRIT **pram**]

가산명사 유모차 [미국영어; 영국영어 pram]

baby|sit /beɪbisɪt/ (**babysits, babysitting, babysat**) V-T/V-I If you **babysit for** someone or **babysit** their children, you look after their children while they are out. ❑ *I promised to babysit for Mrs. Plunkett.* ❑ *She had been babysitting him and his four-year-old sister.* ● **baby|sitter** N-COUNT ❑ *It can be difficult to find a good babysitter.*

타동사/자동사 아이를 봐 주다 ❑ 플렁켓 부인의 아이를 돌봐 주기로 약속했다. ❑ 그녀는 그 남자 아이와 그의 네 살짜리 여동생을 돌보고 있었다. ● 애를 봐 주는 사람 가산명사 ❑ 애를 잘 돌봐 줄 사람을 찾기란 어려울 수 있다.

bach|elor /bætʃələr/ (**bachelors**) N-COUNT A **bachelor** is a man who has never married. ❑ *...Britain's most eligible bachelor.*

가산명사 총각 ❑ 영국에서 가장 근사한 신랑감

---

back

① ADVERB USES
② OPPOSITE OF FRONT; NOUN AND ADJECTIVE USES
③ VERB USES

① back ♦♦♦ /bæk/

In addition to the uses shown below, **back** is also used in phrasal verbs such as "date back" and "fall back on."

back은 아래 용법 외에도 'date back', 'fall back on'과 같은 구동사에 쓰인다.

→Please look at category **17** to see if the expression you are looking for is shown under another headword. **1** ADV If you move **back**, you move in the opposite direction to the one in which you are facing or in which you were moving before. ❑ *She stepped back from the door expectantly.* ❑ *He pushed her away and she fell back on the wooden bench.* **2** ADV If you go **back** somewhere, you return to where you were before. ❑ *I'll be back as soon as I can.* **3** ADV If someone or something is **back** in a particular state, they were in that state before and are now in it again. ❑ *The rail company said it expected services to get slowly back to normal.* **4** ADV If you give or put something **back**, you return it to the person who had it or to the place where it was before you took it. If you get or take something **back**, you then have it again after not having it for a while. ❑ *She handed the knife back.* ❑ *Put it back in the freezer.* **5** ADV If you put a clock or watch **back**, you change the time shown on it so that it shows an earlier time, for example when the time changes to standard time. [ADV after v] ❑ *The clocks go back at 2 o'clock tomorrow morning.* **6** ADV If you write or call **back**, you write to or telephone someone after they have written to or telephoned you. If you look **back** at someone, you look at them after they have started looking at you. ❑ *They wrote back to me and they told me that I didn't have to do it.* **7** If the phone rings

1 부사 뒤로 ❑ 그녀는 기대를 하며 문에서 뒤로 물러섰다. ❑ 그가 그녀를 밀치자 그녀는 뒤의 나무 벤치로 넘어졌다. **2** 부사 다시, 돌아 ❑ 나는 침대로 돌아갔다. ❑ 가능한 빨리 돌아오겠다. **3** 부사 다시, 원상태로 ❑ 철도 회사는 서비스가 서서히 정상으로 돌아오리라 기대한다고 했다. **4** 부사 되돌리, 되돌아 ❑ 그녀는 칼을 되돌려 줬다. ❑ 그것을 다시 냉동고에 넣어라. **5** 부사 늦춰 ❑ 시계는 내일 아침 2시에 늦춰진다. **6** 부사 답례로, 되받아 ❑ 그들은 나에게 답장을 보내 내가 그것을 할 필요는 없다고 얘기했다. ❑ 전화가 울리면 네가 저녁 식사 이후에 다시 전화하겠다고 해라. **7** 부사 다시, 돌아 ❑ 치안 유지의 문제로 다시 돌아가도 될까요? **8** 부사 다시 유행하는 ❑ 짧은 치마가 다시 유행한다. **9** 부사 넘찍이, 떨어져 ❑ 승강장 가장자리에서 떨어져 계세요. ❑ 나는 국경에서 몇 마일 떨어져 있다. **10** 부사 고정되어 ❑ 커튼은 장식용 술로 묶여 있었다. **11** 부사 뒤로 ❑ 그녀는 뒤로 누워 천장을 쳐다봤다. **12** 부사

say you'll call back after dinner. **7** ADV You can say that you go or come **back to** a particular point in a conversation to show that you are mentioning or discussing it again. ❑ Can I come back to the question of policing once again? **8** ADV If something is or comes **back**, it is fashionable again after it has been unfashionable for some time. ❑ Short skirts are back. **9** ADV If someone or something is kept or situated **back from** a place, they are at a distance away from it. ❑ Keep back from the edge of the platform. ❑ two miles back from the border. **10** ADV If something is held or tied **back**, it is held or tied so that it does not hang loosely over something. [ADV after v] ❑ The curtains were held back by tassels. **11** ADV If you lie or sit **back**, you move your body backward into a relaxed sloping or flat position, with your head and body resting on something. [ADV after v] ❑ She lay back and stared at the ceiling. **12** ADV If you look or shout **back** at someone or something, you turn to look or shout at them when they are behind you. ❑ Nick looked back over his shoulder and then stopped, frowning. **13** ADV You use **back** in expressions like **back in Chicago** or **back at the house** when you are giving an account, to show that you are going to start talking about what happened or was happening in the place you mention. ❑ Meanwhile, back in London, Palace Pictures was collapsing. **14** ADV If you talk about something that happened **back** in the past or several years ago, you are emphasizing that it happened quite a long time ago. [EMPHASIS] ❑ The story starts back in 1950, when I was five. **15** ADV If you think **back to** something that happened in the past, you remember it or try to remember it. ❑ I thought back to the time in 1975 when my son was desperately ill. **16** PHRASE If someone moves **back and forth**, they repeatedly move in one direction and then in the opposite direction. ❑ He paced back and forth. **17** to **cast** your **mind back** →see **mind**

② **back** ♦♦♦ /bæk/ (backs) →Please look at category **17** to see if the expression you are looking for is shown under another headword. **1** N-COUNT A person's or animal's **back** is the part of their body between their head and their legs that is on the opposite side to their chest and stomach. ❑ Her son was lying peacefully on his back. ❑ She turned her back to the audience. **2** N-COUNT The **back of** something is the side or part of it that is toward the rear or farthest from the front. The back of something is normally not used or seen as much as the front. ❑ ...a room at the back of the shop. ❑ She raised her hands to the back of her neck. **3** ADJ **Back** is used to refer to the side or part of something that is toward the rear or farthest from the front. [ADJ n] ❑ He opened the back door. ❑ Ann could remember sitting in the back seat of their car. **4** N-COUNT The **back** of a chair or sofa is the part that you lean against when you sit on it. ❑ There was a neatly folded pink sweater on the back of the chair. **5** N-COUNT The **back** of something such as a piece of paper or an envelope is the side which is less important. ❑ Send your answers on the back of a postcard or sealed, empty envelope. **6** N-COUNT The **back** of a book is the part nearest the end, where you can find the index or the notes, for example. ❑ The index at the back of the book lists both brand and generic names. **7** N-UNCOUNT You use **out back** to refer to the area behind a house or other building. You also use **in back** to refer to the rear part of something, especially a car or building. [AM] ❑ Dan informed her that he would be out back on the patio cleaning his shoes. **8** N-SING You can use **back** in expressions such as **round the back** and **out the back** to refer generally to the area behind a house or other building. [BRIT, SPOKEN] ❑ He had chickens and things round the back. **9** PHRASE If you say that something was done **behind** someone's **back**, you disapprove of it because it was done without them knowing about it, in an unfair or dishonest way. [DISAPPROVAL] ❑ You eat her food, enjoy her hospitality and then criticize her behind her back. **10** PHRASE If you are wearing something **back to front**, you are wearing it with the back of it at the front of your body. If you do something **back to front**, you do it the wrong way around, starting with the part that should come last. [mainly BRIT; AM usually **backward**] ❑ He wears his baseball cap back to front. **11** to **take a back seat** →see **seat** →see **body**

③ **back** ♦♦♦ /bæk/ (backs, backing, backed) **1** V-I If a building **backs onto** something, the back of it faces in the direction of that thing or touches the edge of that thing. ❑ We live in a ground floor flat which backs onto a busy street. **2** V-T/V-I When you **back** a car or other vehicle somewhere or when it **backs** somewhere, it moves backward. ❑ He backed his car out of the drive. **3** V-T If you **back** a person or a course of action, you support them, for example by voting for them or giving them money. ❑ His defense says it has found a new witness to back his claim that he is a victim of mistaken identity. **4** V-T If you **back** a particular person, team, or horse in a competition, you predict that they will win, and usually you bet money that they will win. ❑ Roland Nilsson last night backed Sheffield Wednesday to win the UEFA Cup. **5** V-T If a singer **is backed by** a band or by other singers, they provide the musical background for the singer. [usu passive] ❑ She chose to be backed by a classy trio of acoustic guitar, bass and congas. **6** →see also **backing**

▶**back away** **1** PHRASAL VERB If you **back away from** a commitment that you made or something that you were involved with in the past, you try to show that you are no longer committed to it or involved with it. ❑ The company backed away from plans to cut their pay by 15%. **2** PHRASAL VERB If you **back away**, you walk backward away from someone or something, often because you are frightened of them. ❑ James got to his feet and started to come over, but the girls hastily backed away.

▶**back down** PHRASAL VERB If you **back down**, you withdraw a claim, demand, or commitment that you made earlier, because other people are strongly opposed to it. ❑ It's too late to back down now.

▶**back off** **1** PHRASAL VERB If you **back off**, you move away in order to avoid problems or a fight. ❑ They backed off in horror. **2** PHRASAL VERB If you **back off** from a claim, demand, or commitment that you made earlier, or if you **back off** it, you withdraw it. ❑ A spokesman says the President has backed off from his threat to boycott the conference.

뒤로 ❑ 닉은 어깨 뒤로 돌아보고 인상을 찌푸리며 멈춰 섰다. **13** 부사 멀리 (시간이나 거리상으로 떨어져 있는 장소 등을 지칭할 때 쓰임) ❑ 한편 멀리 런던에서는 팰러스 영화사가 망하고 있었다. **14** 부사 과거에, 옛날 [강조] ❑ 이야기는 옛날 내가 다섯 살이던 1950년에서 시작한다. **15** 부사 과거로, 예전에 ❑ 나는 예전에 내 아들이 매우 아팠던 1975년 당시로 기억을 거슬러 올라갔다. **16** 구 앞뒤로 ❑ 그는 앞뒤로 왔다 갔다 했다.

1 가산명사 등 ❑ 그녀의 아들은 평화롭게 등을 대고 누워 있었다. ❑ 그녀는 관객에게 등을 돌렸다. **2** 가산명사 후미, 뒤 ❑ 가게의 뒤쪽에 있는 방 ❑ 그녀는 자신의 목덜미로 손을 올렸다. **3** 형용사 뒤 ❑ 그는 뒷문을 열었다. ❑ 앤은 그들 차의 뒷좌석에 앉았던 것을 기억할 수 있었다. **4** 가산명사 등받이 ❑ 곱게 접힌 분홍색 스웨터가 의자의 등받이에 걸쳐져 있었다. **5** 가산명사 뒷면 ❑ 엽서나 봉해진 빈 봉투의 뒷면에 답을 적어 보내 주세요. **6** 가산명사 뒷부분 ❑ 책 뒷부분의 색인은 상품명과 일반 명칭이 열거되어 있다. **7** 불가산명사 (건물의) 뒤에; 후미에 [미국영어] ❑ 자신은 뒷마당에서 신발을 닦고 있을 것이라고 댄은 그녀에게 알려 줬다. **8** 단수명사 뒤 [영국영어, 구어체] ❑ 뒤로 돌아가면 그는 닭과 기타 잡동사니를 두고 있었다. **9** 구 몰래, 등 뒤에서 [탐탁찮음] ❑ 너는 그녀의 음식을 먹고 그녀의 환대를 받으면서도 그녀를 등 뒤에서 험담한다. **10** 구 (앞뒤를) 거꾸로 [주로 영국영어; 미국영어 대개 backward] ❑ 그는 야구 모자를 거꾸로 쓴다.

1 자동사 뒷면이 인접하다 ❑ 우리는 뒤가 복잡한 도로와 인접해 있는 1층 아파트에 산다. **2** 타동사/자동사 후진하다 ❑ 그는 후진해서 차를 집의 차도에서 뺐다. **3** 타동사 후원하다 ❑ 피고의 변호인단은 그가 신원 착오로 인한 희생자라는 주장을 뒷받침할 새로운 증인을 찾았다고 한다. **4** 타동사 (돈, 희망 등을) 걸다 ❑ 로랜드 닐슨은 어젯밤 셰필드 웬즈데이가 '유이에파 컵'을 차지할 것이라는 쪽에 돈을 걸었다. **5** 타동사 -의 반주를 받다 ❑ 어쿠스틱 기타, 베이스, 콩가 등 우아한 세 악기의 반주를 쓰기로 그녀는 결정했다.

1 구동사 꽁무니 빼다, 손을 떼다 ❑ 회사는 봉급을 15퍼센트 줄이려는 계획에서 손을 뗐다. **2** 구동사 뒷걸음질치다 ❑ 제임스가 일어서서 다가오기 시작했으나 여자 아이들은 서둘러 뒷걸음질을 쳤다.

구동사 물러서다 ❑ 이제 물러서기에는 너무 늦었다.

1 구동사 물러나다 ❑ 그들은 공포에 질려 물러났다. **2** 구동사 철회하다 ❑ 대변인은 대통령은 회담을 보이콧하겠다던 협박을 철회했다고 한다.

▶**back out** PHRASAL VERB If you **back out**, you decide not to do something that you previously agreed to do. ❑ *The Hungarians backed out of the project in 1989 on environmental grounds.*

구동사 손을 떼다 ❑ 헝가리 사람들은 환경을 이유로 1989년에 그 프로젝트에서 손을 뗐다.

▶**back up** **1** PHRASAL VERB If someone or something **backs up** a statement, they supply evidence to suggest that it is true. ❑ *Radio signals received from the galaxy's center back up the black hole theory.* **2** PHRASAL VERB If you **back up** a computer file, you make a copy of it which you can use if the original file is damaged or lost. [COMPUTING] ❑ *Make a point of backing up your files at regular intervals.* **3** PHRASAL VERB If an idea or intention **is backed up** by action, action is taken to support or confirm it. ❑ *The Secretary General says the declaration must now be backed up by concrete and effective actions.* **4** PHRASAL VERB If you **back** someone **up**, you show your support for them. ❑ *His employers, Norfolk Social Services, backed him up.* **5** PHRASAL VERB If you **back** someone **up**, you help them by confirming that what they are saying is true. ❑ *The girl denied being there, and the man backed her up.* **6** PHRASAL VERB If you **back up**, the car or other vehicle that you are driving moves back a short distance. ❑ *Back up, Hans.* **7** PHRASAL VERB If you **back up**, you move backward a short distance. ❑ *I backed up carefully until I felt the wall against my back.* **8** PHRASAL VERB When a car **backs up** or when you **back** it **up**, the car is driven backwards. [AM; BRIT usually **reverse**] **9** →see also **backup**

1 구동사 뒷받침하다 ❑ 은하계의 중심에서부터 잡히는 무선 신호는 블랙홀 이론을 뒷받침한다. **2** 구동사 (컴퓨터를) 백업하다 [컴퓨터] ❑ 파일을 주기적으로 백업하도록 해라. **3** 구동사 뒷받침되다 ❑ 이제 선언을 구체적이고 효과적인 행동으로 뒷받침해야 한다고 사무총장은 말한다. **4** 구동사 지지하다 ❑ 그의 고용주인 노포크 사회 서비스는 그를 지지했다. **5** 구동사 뒷받침하다 ❑ 소녀는 그곳에 있었다는 것을 부인했고 그 남자가 그녀의 말을 뒷받침해 주었다. **6** 구동사 후진하다 ❑ 후진해라, 한스. **7** 구동사 뒤로 물러서다 ❑ 등이 벽에 닿을 때까지 나는 조심스럽게 뒤로 물러섰다. **8** 구동사 후진하다 [미국영어; 영국영어 대개 reverse]

back|bench /bǽkbɛntʃ/ ADJ A **backbench** MP is a Member of Parliament who is not a minister and who does not hold an official position in his or her political party. [BRIT, AUSTRALIAN] [ADJ n] ❑ *...the Conservative backbench MP Sir Teddy Taylor.*

형용사 (영국 의회) 뒷자석의, 평의원의 [영국, 호주영어] ❑ 보수당 평의원 테디 테일러 경

back|bone /bǽkboʊn/ (**backbones**) N-COUNT Your **backbone** is the column of small linked bones down the middle of your back.

가산명사 척추

back|date /bǽkdeɪt/ (**backdates, backdating, backdated**) also **back-date** V-T If a document or an arrangement **is backdated**, it is valid from a date before the date when it is completed or signed. ❑ *The contract that was signed on Thursday morning was backdated to March 11.*

타동사 소급되다 ❑ 목요일 아침에 체결한 계약은 3월 11일로 소급 적용되었다.

back|er /bǽkər/ (**backers**) N-COUNT A **backer** is someone who helps or supports a project, organization, or person, often by giving or lending money. ❑ *I was looking for a backer to assist me in the attempted buy-out.*

가산명사 후원자 ❑ 나는 내가 시도하는 소유권 완전 매입을 도와줄 후원자를 찾고 있었다.

back|fire /bǽkfaɪər, BRIT bækfáɪəʳ/ (**backfires, backfiring, backfired**) **1** V-I If a plan or project **backfires**, it has the opposite result to the one that was intended. ❑ *The President's tactics could backfire.* **2** V-I When a motor vehicle or its engine **backfires**, it produces an explosion in the exhaust pipe. ❑ *The car backfired.*

1 자동사 역효과를 가져오다 ❑ 대통령의 전략이 역효과를 가져올 수도 있다. **2** 자동사 역화하다 ❑ 그 자동차는 역화했다.

Word Link	ground ≈ bottom : background, foreground, groundwork

back|ground ♦♢♢ /bǽkgraʊnd/ (**backgrounds**) **1** N-COUNT Your **background** is the kind of family you come from and the kind of education you have had. It can also refer to such things as your social and racial origins, your financial status, or the type of work experience that you have. ❑ *She came from a working-class Yorkshire background.* **2** N-COUNT The **background** to an event or situation consists of the facts that explain what caused it. ❑ *The background to the current troubles is provided by the dire state of the country's economy.* ❑ *The meeting takes place against a background of continuing political violence.* **3** N-SING The **background** is sounds, such as music, which you can hear but which you are not listening to with your full attention. ❑ *I kept hearing the sound of applause in the background.* **4** N-COUNT You can use **background** to refer to the things in a picture or scene that are less noticeable or important than the main things or people in it. ❑ *...roses patterned on a blue background.*

1 가산명사 출신 배경, 신원 ❑ 그녀는 출신 배경이 요크셔 노동자 계급이었다. **2** 가산명사 배경 ❑ 현 문제들의 배경은 암울한 상태의 국가 경제에서 찾을 수 있다. ❑ 그 회담은 끊임없는 정치적 폭력을 배경으로 개최된다. **3** 단수명사 배경음 ❑ 박수 소리가 배경음으로 계속 들렸다. **4** 가산명사 배경 ❑ 파란색 바탕에 찍힌 장미 문양

Word Partnership	background의 연어
N.	background **check** **1**
	background **information/knowledge** **1** **2**
	background **story** **2**
	background **music/noise** **3**
ADJ.	**cultural/ethnic/family** background, **educational** background **1**
PREP.	**in the** background **3** **4**
	against a background **4**

back|ing ♦♢♢ /bǽkɪŋ/ (**backings**) **1** N-UNCOUNT If someone has the **backing of** an organization or an important person, they receive support or money from that organization or person in order to do something. ❑ *He said the president had the full backing of his government to negotiate a deal.* **2** N-VAR A **backing** is a layer of something such as cloth that is put onto the back of something in order to strengthen or protect it. ❑ *The table mats and coasters have a non-slip, soft green backing.* **3** N-COUNT The **backing** of a popular song is the music which is sung or played to accompany the main tune. ❑ *Sharon also sang backing vocals for Barry Manilow.*

1 불가산명사 지지, 후원 ❑ 대통령의 협상을 정부가 전적으로 지지하고 있다고 그는 얘기했다. **2** 가산명사 또는 불가산명사 안감, 뒷바닥 ❑ 식탁 깔개와 컵받침의 뒷바닥은 미끄러지지 않는 부드러운 녹색의 재료로 만들어졌다. **3** 가산명사 반주 ❑ 샤론은 또한 배리 매닐로우의 백보컬도 했다.

back|lash /bǽklæʃ/ N-SING A **backlash against** a tendency or recent development in society or politics is a sudden, strong reaction against it. ❑ *...the male backlash against feminism.*

단수명사 반발 ❑ 페미니즘에 대한 남성의 반발

back|log /bǽklɔg/ (**backlogs**) N-COUNT A **backlog** is a number of things which have not yet been done but which need to be done. ❑ *There is a backlog of repairs and maintenance in schools.*

가산명사 잔여 업무 ❑ 학교들에서 처리해야 할 유지 보수 업무가 남아 있다.

back pay N-UNCOUNT **Back pay** is money which an employer owes an employee for work that he or she did in the past. [BUSINESS] ❑ *He will receive $6,000 in back pay.*

불가산명사 체불 임금 [경제] ❑ 그는 체불 임금 6,000달러를 받을 것이다.

back|side /bæksaɪd/ (**backsides**) N-COUNT Your **backside** is the part of your body that you sit on. [INFORMAL] ❑ *The lad fell backwards, landing on his backside.*

가산명사 엉덩이 [비격식체] ❑ 소년은 뒤로 넘어져 엉덩방아를 찧었다.

back|stage /bæksteɪdʒ/ ADV In a theater, **backstage** refers to the areas behind the stage. [ADV after v] ❑ *He went backstage and asked for her autograph.* ● ADJ **Backstage** is also an adjective. [ADJ n] ❑ *...a backstage pass.* →see **theater**

부사 무대 뒤로 ❑ 그는 무대 뒤로 가서 그녀의 사인을 요청했다. ● 형용사 무대 뒤의 ❑ 무대 뒤 출입증

back|stroke /bækstroʊk/ N-UNCOUNT **Backstroke** is a swimming stroke that you do lying on your back. [also the N] ❑ *"I see you know how to swim very well," she said, watching him do the backstroke.*

불가산명사 배영 ❑ "당신이 수영을 아주 잘한다는 것을 알겠네요."라고 그녀는 그가 배영을 하는 것을 바라보며 말했다.

back|up /bækʌp/ (**backups**) also **back-up** ▌1 N-VAR **Backup** consists of extra equipment, resources, or people that you can get help or support from if necessary. ❑ *There is no emergency back-up immediately available.* ▌2 N-VAR If you have something such as a second piece of equipment or set of plans as **backup**, you have arranged for them to be available for use in case the first one does not work. ❑ *Every part of the system has a backup.*

▌1 가산명사 또는 불가산명사 예비 자원 ❑ 당장 조달 가능한 응급용 자원이 없다. ▌2 가산명사 또는 불가산명사 예비 장치 ❑ 시스템의 모든 부분은 예비 장치를 갖추고 있다.

Word Link   *ward* ≈ *in the direction of* : *back**ward**, for**ward**, in**ward***

back|ward /bækwərd/

> In American English, **backward** is usually used as an adverb and almost always used as an adjective instead of **backwards**. **Backward** is also sometimes used in this way in formal British English, although **backwards** is much more common.

> backward는 미국영어에서 대개 backwards 대신 부사로 쓰이며, 거의 항상 형용사로 쓰인다. backward는 격식체 영국영어에서도 backwards가 훨씬 더 일반적이지만 때때로 위와 같은 방식으로 쓰인다.

▌1 ADJ A **backward** movement or look is in the direction that your back is facing. [ADJ n] ❑ *He unlocked the door of apartment two and disappeared inside after a backward glance at Larry.* ▌2 ADJ If someone takes a **backward** step, they do something that does not change or improve their situation, but causes them to go back a stage. [ADJ n] ❑ *At a certain age, it's not viable for men to take a backward step into unskilled work.* ▌3 ADJ A **backward** country or society does not have modern industries and machines. ❑ *We need to accelerate the pace of change in our backward country.* ▌4 ADJ A **backward** child has difficulty in learning. ❑ *...research into teaching techniques to help backward children.* ▌5 ADV If you move or look **backward**, you move or look in the direction that your back is facing. [ADV after v] ❑ *The diver flipped over backward into the water.* ❑ *He took two steps backward.* [ADJ n] ▌6 ADV If you do something **backward**, you do it in the opposite way to the usual way. [ADV after v] ❑ *He works backward, building a house from the top downward.* ▌7 ADV You use **backward** to indicate that something changes or develops in a way that is not an improvement, but is a return to old ideas or methods. ❑ *Greater government intervention in businesses would represent a step backward.* ▌8 PHRASE If someone or something moves **backward and forward**, they move repeatedly first in one direction and then in the opposite direction. ❑ *Using a gentle, sawing motion, draw the floss backward and forward between the teeth.*

▌1 형용사 뒤로의 ❑ 그는 아파트 2호의 문을 열쇠로 연후 래리를 힐끗 뒤돌아보고는 안으로 사라졌다. ▌2 형용사 후퇴하는 ❑ 일정 나이가 되면 남자들이 단순 노동으로 후퇴하는 것은 어렵다. ▌3 형용사 뒤떨어진 ❑ 후진국인 우리나라의 변화 속도를 높일 필요가 있다. ▌4 형용사 뒤떨어진 ❑ 학습 부진아들을 돕기 위한 교수법에 관한 연구 ▌5 부사 뒤로 ❑ 잠수부는 몸을 뒤로 책 제치며 물속으로 들어갔다. ❑ 그는 뒤로 두 걸음 물러섰다. ▌6 부사 거꾸로 ❑ 그는 일을 거꾸로 해서 집을 꼭대기부터 짓는다. ▌7 부사 악행하는 ❑ 기업들에 대한 정부의 관여가 증가한다면 그것은 진보에 역행하는 것이다. ▌8 구 앞뒤로 ❑ 부드럽게 톱질하듯이 치실을 이빨 사이에 넣고 앞뒤로 움직여라.

back|water /bækwɔtər/ (**backwaters**) ▌1 N-COUNT A **backwater** is a place that is isolated. ❑ *...a quiet rural backwater.* ▌2 N-COUNT If you refer to a place or institution as a **backwater**, you think it is not developing properly because it is isolated from ideas and events in other places and institutions. [DISAPPROVAL] ❑ *Britain could become a political backwater with no serious influence in the world.* ❑ *This agency will be relegated to the backwaters of Washington.*

▌1 가산명사 벽촌 ❑ 조용하고 전원적인 벽촌 ▌2 가산명사 침체된 곳, 한촌 [탐탁찮음] ❑ 영국이 세계에서 어떤 중요한 영향력도 없는 정치적 후진국이 될 수도 있다. ❑ 이 부서는 워싱턴의 한촌으로 좌천당할 것이다.

back|yard /bækyɑrd/ (**backyards**) also **back yard** ▌1 N-COUNT A **backyard** is an area of land at the back of a house. ▌2 N-COUNT If you refer to a country's own **backyard**, you are referring to its own territory or to somewhere that is very close and where that country wants to influence events. ❑ *Economics will not stop Europe's politicians complaining when jobs are lost in their own backyard.*

▌1 가산명사 뒷마당 ▌2 가산명사 터전 ❑ 자신들의 터전에서 일자리가 없어진다면 경제의 논리로 유럽 정치인들의 불평을 막을 수는 없을 것이다.

ba|con /beɪkən/ N-UNCOUNT **Bacon** is salted or smoked meat which comes from the back or sides of a pig. ❑ *...bacon and eggs.*

불가산명사 베이컨 ❑ 베이컨과 계란

bac|te|ria /bæktɪəriə/ N-PLURAL **Bacteria** are very small organisms. Some bacteria can cause disease. ❑ *Chlorine is added to kill bacteria.* →see **can**

복수명사 박테리아 ❑ 염소는 박테리아를 죽이기 위해 첨가한다.

bac|te|rial /bæktɪəriəl/ ADJ **Bacterial** is used to describe things that relate to or are caused by bacteria. [ADJ n] ❑ *Cholera is a bacterial infection.*

형용사 박테리아의 ❑ 콜레라는 박테리아에 의해 감염된다.

bad ♦♦♦ /bæd/ (**worse, worst**) ▌1 ADJ Something that is **bad** is unpleasant, harmful, or undesirable. ❑ *The bad weather conditions prevented the plane from landing.* ❑ *Divorce is bad for children.* ▌2 You use **bad** to indicate that something unpleasant is severe or great in degree. ❑ *Glick had a bad accident two years ago and had to give up farming.* ❑ *The floods are described as the worst in nearly fifty years.* ▌3 ADJ A **bad** idea, decision, or method is not sensible or not correct. ❑ *Giving your address to a man you don't know is a bad idea.* ❑ *The worst thing you can do is underestimate an opponent.* ▌4 ADJ If you describe a piece of news, an action, or a sign as **bad**, you mean that it is unlikely to result in benefit or success. ❑ *The closure of the project is bad news for her staff.* ❑ *It was a bad start in my relationship with Warr.* ▌5 ADJ Something that is **bad** is of an unacceptably low standard, quality, or amount. ❑ *Many old people in Britain are living in bad housing.* ❑ *The state schools' main problem is that teachers' pay is so bad.* ▌6 ADJ Someone who is **bad at** doing something is not skillful or successful at it. [v-link ADJ at -ing /n, ADJ n] ❑ *He had increased Britain's reputation for being bad at languages.* ❑ *He was a bad driver.* ▌7 ADJ If you say that it is **bad** that something happens, you mean it is unacceptable, unfortunate, or wrong. [v-link ADJ that] ❑ *Not being able to hear doesn't seem as bad to the rest of us as not being able to see.* ▌8 ADJ You can say that something is **not bad** to mean that it is quite good or acceptable, especially when you are rather surprised about this. [with neg] ❑ *"How much is he paying you?" — "Oh, five thousand." — "Not bad."* ❑ *That's not a bad idea.* ▌9 ADJ A **bad** person has morally unacceptable attitudes and behavior. ❑ *I was selling drugs, but I didn't think I was a bad person.* ▌10 ADJ A **bad** child disobeys rules and

▌1 형용사 나쁜 ❑ 악천후 때문에 비행기가 착륙하지 못했다. ❑ 이혼은 아이들에게 좋지 않다. ▌2 형용사 심한 ❑ 글릭은 이 년 전 심한 사고를 당해 농사를 포기해야 했다. ❑ 근 50년 만에 최악의 홍수라고 한다. ▌3 형용사 나쁜, 좋지 않은 ❑ 모르는 남자에게 자신의 주소를 주는 것은 현명하지 못한 것이다. ❑ 적을 얕잡아 보는 것은 최악의 판단이다. ▌4 형용사 좋지 않은 ❑ 프로젝트의 중단은 그녀의 직원들에게 좋지 않은 소식이다. ❑ 그것은 나와 와르 사이의 관계에 있어서 평탄치 못한 출발이었다. ▌5 형용사 열악한, 나쁜 ❑ 영국의 많은 노인들이 열악한 주거 환경에서 거주하고 있다. ❑ 국립 학교의 가장 큰 문제는 교사들의 보수가 열악하다는 것이다. ▌6 형용사 미숙한, 잘 못하는 ❑ 그는 영국인들이 언어를 잘 배우지 못한다는 인식을 강화시켰다. ❑ 그는 미숙한 운전자였다. ▌7 형용사 나쁜 ❑ 우리 정상인들에게 듣지 못하는 것은 보지 못하는 것만큼 불행하게 비치지 않는다. ▌8 형용사 괜찮은 ❑ "그는 너에게 얼마를 주고 있냐?" "어, 오천." "괜찮은데." ❑ 괜찮은 생각이다. ▌9 형용사 나쁜 ❑ 나는 마약을 팔고 있었지만 스스로 나쁜 사람이라고 생각하진 않았다. ▌10 형용사 나쁜 ❑ 내가 말한 것을 그대로 따라 하다니, 너는 나쁜 아이야. ▌11 형용사 좋지 않은 ❑ 갓 금연을 시작했기

a b c d e f g h i j k l m n o p q r s t u v w x y z

instructions or does not behave in a polite and correct way. ❑ *You are a bad boy for repeating what I told you.* **11** ADJ If you are in a **bad** mood, you are angry and behave unpleasantly to people. ❑ *She is in a bit of a bad mood because she's just given up smoking.* **12** ADJ If you **feel bad about** something, you feel rather sorry or guilty about it. [feel ADJ, oft ADJ about n, ADJ that] ❑ *You don't have to feel bad about relaxing.* ❑ *I feel bad that he's doing most of the work.* **13** ADJ If you have a **bad** back, heart, leg, or eye, it is injured, diseased, or weak. ❑ *Alastair has a bad back so we have a hard bed.* **14** ADJ Food that has **gone bad** is not suitable to eat because it has started to decay. ❑ *They bought so much beef that some went bad.* **15** ADJ **Bad** language is language that contains offensive words such as swear words. ❑ *I don't like to hear bad language in the street.* **16** →see also **worse, worst** **17** **bad blood** →see **blood**. **bad luck** →see **luck**. to **get a bad press** →see **press**

Thesaurus	*bad*의 참조어
ADJ.	dangerous, harmful; (*ant.*) good **11** inferior, poor, unsatisfactory; (*ant.*) acceptable, good, satisfactory **3** **5** naughty; (*ant.*) nice, obedient, well-behaved **10** rotten; (*ant.*) fresh, good **14**

때문에 그녀는 기분이 좀 좋지 않다. **12** 형용사 안 좋은, 미안해 하는 ❑ 쉬는 것에 대해 죄책감을 가질 필요는 없다. ❑ 그가 일 대부분을 하고 있어서 미안하다. **13** 형용사 좋지 않은 ❑ 앨리스터의 허리가 좋지 않아서 우리는 딱딱한 침대를 쓴다. **14** 형용사 상한 ❑ 그들이 쇠고기를 너무 많이 사는 바람에 일부는 상했다. **15** 형용사 상스러운 ❑ 나는 거리의 상스러운 말을 듣는 것을 좋아하지 않는다.

bad debt (**bad debts**) N-COUNT A **bad debt** is a sum of money that has been lent but is not likely to be repaid. ❑ *The bank set aside £1.1 billion to cover bad debts from business failures.*

가산명사 부실 채권 ❑ 기업 실패로 인한 부실 채권을 처리하기 위해 그 은행은 11억 파운드를 따로 마련했다.

badge /bædʒ/ (**badges**) N-COUNT A **badge** is a piece of metal or cloth which you wear to show that you belong to an organization or support a cause. American English usually uses **button** to refer to a small round metal badge. ❑ *He is wearing a badge on his shirt that reads "Real Men Love Jesus."*

가산명사 배지 ❑ 그는 '진정한 사나이는 예수를 사랑한다'고 적힌 배지를 셔츠에 달고 있다.

badger /bædʒər/ (**badgers, badgering, badgered**) **11** N-COUNT A **badger** is a wild animal which has a white head with two wide black stripes on it. Badgers live underground and usually come up to feed at night. **2** V-T If you **badger** someone, you repeatedly tell them to do something or repeatedly ask them questions. ❑ *She badgered her doctor time and again, pleading with him to do something.* ❑ *They kept phoning and writing, badgering me to go back.*

11 가산명사 오소리 **2** 타동사 닦달하다 ❑ 그녀는 의사에게 뭐라도 해 보라며 애원하며 계속 닦달했다. ❑ 그들은 나에게 돌아가라고 닦달하는 전화와 서신을 계속 보냈다.

badly ◆◇◇ /bædli/ (**worse, worst**) **11** ADV If something is done **badly** or goes **badly**, it is not very successful or effective. [ADV with v] ❑ *I was angry because I played so badly.* ❑ *The whole project was badly managed.* **2** ADV If someone or something is **badly** hurt or **badly** affected, they are severely hurt or affected. ❑ *The bomb destroyed a police station and badly damaged a church.* ❑ *One man was killed and another badly injured.* **3** ADV If you want or need something **badly**, you want or need it very much. [ADV with v] ❑ *Why do you want to go so badly?* **4** ADV If someone behaves **badly** or treats other people **badly**, they act in an unkind, unpleasant, or unacceptable way. [ADV with v] ❑ *They have both behaved very badly and I am very hurt.* **5** ADV If something reflects **badly** on someone or makes others think **badly** of them, it harms their reputation. [ADV after v] ❑ *Teachers know that low exam results will reflect badly on them.* **6** ADV If a person or their job is **badly** paid, they are not paid very much for what they do. ❑ *You may have to work part-time, in a badly paid job with unsociable hours.* **7** →see also **worse, worst**

11 부사 나쁘게, 좋지 않게 ❑ 너무나도 엉망으로 게임을 처리 나는 화가 났었다. ❑ 프로젝트 전체가 미숙하게 관리되었다. **2** 부사 심하게 ❑ 폭탄은 경찰서를 파괴하였고 교회를 심하게 파손했다. ❑ 한 남자는 사망하고 또 한 명은 심하게 다쳤다. **3** 부사 몹시 ❑ 왜 그렇게 몹시 가고 싶어 하니? **4** 부사 나쁘게 ❑ 그들은 모두 너무 나쁘게 굴었고 나는 크게 상처 입었다. **5** 부사 부정적으로 ❑ 교사들은 나쁜 시험 결과가 자신들에게 부정적으로 반영되리라는 것을 안다. **6** 부사 낮은 ❑ 업무 시간도 불편한 박봉의 직장에서 시간제로 근무해야 할지도 모른다.

badly off (**worse off, worst off**) [AM also **bad off**] **11** ADJ If you are **badly off**, you are in a bad situation. ❑ *The average working week in Japan is 42.3 hours, compared with 41.6 in the UK, so they are not too badly off.* **2** ADJ If you are **badly off**, you do not have much money. ❑ *It is outrageous that people doing well-paid jobs should moan about how badly off they are.*

[미국영어 bad off] **11** 형용사 상황이 좋지 않은 ❑ 일본의 주당 평균 근로 시간은 42.3시간이며 영국의 41.6시간과 비교했을 때 그다지 나쁜 것은 아니다. **2** 형용사 돈이 부족한, 형편이 어려운 ❑ 고소득 직업을 가진 사람들이 자신들의 경제적 어려움을 호소한다는 것은 분통 터질 일이다.

bad off (**worse off, worst off**) [BRIT also **badly off**] **11** ADJ If you are **bad off**, you are in a bad situation. [usu v-link ADJ] ❑ *But there were other people worse off than me at the hospital, linked up to respirators and unable to walk.* **2** ADJ If you are **bad off**, you do not have much money. [usu v-link ADJ] ❑ *But an independent study by Forbes magazine said the owners are not nearly as bad off as they say, and most are making money.*

[영국영어 badly off] **11** 형용사 불우한 ❑ 하지만 병원에는 인공호흡기에 연결된 채 걷지 못하는 나보다 처지가 불우한 사람들이 있었다. **2** 형용사 돈이 부족한 ❑ 그러나 포브스 지의 독자적인 조사에 의하면 소유주들은 그들이 말하는 만큼 경제적으로 어렵지 않으며 대부분은 오히려 돈을 벌고 있다고 한다.

bad-tempered ADJ Someone who is **bad-tempered** is not very cheerful and gets angry easily. ❑ *When his headaches developed Nick became bad-tempered and even violent.*

형용사 성질이 나쁜 ❑ 두통이 심해지자 닉은 성질이 나빠졌으며 심지어는 폭력적으로 변했다.

Angry is normally used to talk about someone's mood or feelings on a particular occasion. If someone is often angry, you can describe them as **bad-tempered**. ❑ *She's a bad-tempered young lady.* If someone is very angry, you can describe them as **furious**. ❑ *Senior police officers are furious at the blunder.* If they are less angry, you can describe them as **annoyed** or **irritated**. ❑ *The Premier looked annoyed but calm.* ... *a man irritated by the barking of his neighbor's dog.* Typically, someone is **irritated** by something because it happens constantly or continually. If someone is often irritated, you can describe them as **irritable**.

---

angry는 보통 특정한 경우에 어떤 사람의 기분이나 감정을 얘기할 때 쓴다. 누가 자주 화를 내면, 그 사람은 bad-tempered라고 할 수 있다. ❑ 그녀는 성질이 나쁜 젊은 여자다. 누가 아주 화가 나면, furious하다고 표현할 수 있다. ❑ 고참 경찰들이 그 중대한 실수에 격노했다. angry보다 덜한 경우에는 annoyed나 irritated를 써서 표현할 수 있다. ❑ 수상은 불쾌해 하는 것 같았으나 침착했다....이웃집 개 짖는 소리에 짜증이 난 남자. 대체로 누가 무엇에 의해 irritated되는 것은 그것이 끊임없이 계속 일어나기 때문이다. 누가 자주 짜증을 내면, 그 사람을 irritable(짜증을 잘 내는)하다고 표현할 수 있다.

---

baffle /bæfl/ (**baffles, baffling, baffled**) V-T If something **baffles** you, you cannot understand it or explain it. ❑ *An apple tree producing square fruit is baffling experts.* ● **baffling** ADJ ❑ *I was constantly ill, with a baffling array of symptoms.*

타동사 당혹하게 하다 ❑ 네모난 과일이 나는 사과나무가 있어 전문가들을 당혹케 하고 있다. ● 당혹하게 하는 형용사 ❑ 나는 당혹스럽도록 다양한 증상을 보이며 항상 아팠다.

bag ◆◆◇ /bæg/ (**bags**) **11** N-COUNT A **bag** is a container made of thin paper or plastic, for example one that is used in stores to put things in that a customer has bought. ● N-COUNT A **bag** of things is the amount of things contained in a bag. ❑ *...a bag of sweets.* **2** N-COUNT A **bag** is a strong container with one or two

11 가산명사 봉지 ● 가산명사 봉지 ❑ 사탕 한 봉지 **2** 가산명사 봉투, 가방 ❑ 그녀는 쇼핑백을 하나 들고 호텔을 떠났다. ● 가산명사 봉투 ❑ 그는 쇼핑한 물건이 든 봉투를 3층까지 낑낑대며 가지고 올라갔다.

handles, used to carry things in. ❑ *She left the hotel carrying a shopping bag.* ● N-COUNT A **bag** of things is the amount of things contained in a bag. ❑ *He was hauling a bag of shopping up to the third floor.* ❸ N-COUNT A **bag** is the same as a **handbag.** →see **baggage** ❹ N-PLURAL If you have **bags** under your eyes, you have folds of skin there, usually because you have not had enough sleep. ❑ *The bags under his eyes have grown darker.* ❺ →see also **sleeping bag**

bag|gage /bǽgɪdʒ/ ❶ N-UNCOUNT Your **baggage** consists of the bags that you take with you when you travel. ❑ *The passengers went through immigration control and collected their baggage.* ❷ N-UNCOUNT You can use **baggage** to refer to someone's emotional problems, fixed ideas, or prejudices. ❑ *How much emotional baggage is he bringing with him into the relationship?*

> **Baggage** is an uncount noun. You can have **a piece of baggage** or **some baggage** but you cannot have "a baggage" or "some baggages." Both British and American speakers can refer to everything that travelers carry as their **bags.** American speakers can also call an individual suitcase a **bag.** In British English, people normally use **luggage** when they are talking about everything that travelers carry. **Baggage** is a more technical word and is used for example when discussing airports or travel insurance. In American English, **luggage** refers to empty bags and suitcases and **baggage** refers to bags and suitcases with their contents.

bag|gage car (**baggage cars**) N-COUNT A **baggage car** is a railroad car, often without windows, which is used to carry luggage, goods, or mail. [AM; BRIT **van**] ❑ *The coffin was loaded into the baggage car of the train.*

bag|gy /bǽgi/ (**baggier, baggiest**) ADJ If a piece of clothing is **baggy,** it hangs loosely on your body. ❑ *...a baggy jumper.*

bail /beɪl/ (**bails, bailing, bailed**)

> The spelling **bale** is also used for meaning ❹, and for meanings ❶ and ❸ of the phrasal verb.

❶ N-UNCOUNT **Bail** is a sum of money that an arrested person or someone else puts forward as a guarantee that the arrested person will attend their trial in a law court. If the arrested person does not attend it, the money will be lost. ❑ *He was freed on bail pending an appeal.* ❷ N-UNCOUNT **Bail** is permission for an arrested person to be released after bail has been paid. ❑ *He was yesterday given bail by South Yorkshire magistrates.* ❸ V-T If someone **is bailed,** they are released while they are waiting for their trial, after paying an amount of money to the court. [usu passive] ❑ *He was bailed to appear before local magistrates on 5 November.* ❹ V-I If you **bail,** you use a container to remove water from a boat or from a place which is flooded. ❑ *We kept her afloat for a couple of hours by bailing frantically.* ● PHRASAL VERB **Bail out** means the same as **bail.** ❑ *A crew was sent down the shaft to close it off and bail out all the water.* ❺ PHRASE If a prisoner **jumps bail,** he or she does not come back for his or her trial after being released on bail. ❑ *He had jumped bail last year while being tried on drug charges.*

▶**bail out** ❶ PHRASAL VERB If you **bail** someone **out,** you help them out of a difficult situation, often by giving them money. ❑ *They will discuss how to bail the economy out of its slump.* ❷ PHRASAL VERB If you **bail** someone **out,** you pay bail on their behalf. ❑ *He has been jailed eight times. Each time, friends bailed him out.* ❸ PHRASAL VERB If a pilot **bails out** of an aircraft that is crashing, he or she jumps from it, using a parachute to land safely. ❑ *Reid was forced to bail out of the crippled aircraft.* ❹ →see **bail 4**

bai|liff /béɪlɪf/ (**bailiffs**) ❶ N-COUNT A **bailiff** is an official in a court of law who deals with tasks such as keeping control in court. [AM] ❑ *The court bailiff said jurors did not wish to speak to news media until the sentencing.* ❷ N-COUNT A **bailiff** is a law officer who makes sure that the decisions of a court are obeyed. Bailiffs can take a person's furniture or possessions away if the person owes money. [BRIT] ❸ N-COUNT A **bailiff** is a person who is employed to look after land or property for the owner. [BRIT]

bait /beɪt/ (**baits, baiting, baited**) ❶ N-VAR **Bait** is food which you put on a hook or in a trap in order to catch fish or animals. ❑ *Vivien refuses to put down bait to tempt wildlife to the waterhole.* ❷ V-T If you **bait** a hook or trap, you put bait on it or in it. ❑ *He baited his hook with pie.* ❑ *The boys dug pits and baited them so that they could spear their prey.* ❸ N-UNCOUNT To use something as **bait** means to use it to trick or persuade someone to do something. [also a N] ❑ *Television programs are essentially bait to attract an audience for commercials.* ❹ V-T If you **bait** someone, you deliberately try to make them angry by teasing them. ❑ *He delighted in baiting his mother.*

bake ♦◇◇ /beɪk/ (**bakes, baking, baked**) ❶ V-T/V-I If you **bake,** you spend some time preparing and mixing together ingredients to make bread, cakes, pies, or other food which is cooked in the oven. [no passive] ❑ *How did you learn to bake cakes?* ● **bak|ing** N-UNCOUNT [also the N] ❑ *On a Thursday she used to do all the baking.* ❷ V-T/V-I When a cake or bread **bakes** or when you **bake** it, it cooks in the oven without any extra liquid or fat. ❑ *Bake the cake for 35 to 50 minutes.* ❑ *The batter rises as it bakes.* →see **cook** →see also **baking** →see **cook**

bak|er /béɪkər/ (**bakers**) ❶ N-COUNT A **baker** is a person whose job is to bake and sell bread, pastries, and cakes. ❷ N-COUNT A **baker** or a **baker's** is a store where bread and cakes are sold. ❑ *They're freshly baked. I fetched them from the baker's this morning.*

bak|ery /béɪkəri, béɪkri/ (**bakeries**) N-COUNT A **bakery** is a building where bread, pastries, and cakes are baked, or the store where they are sold. ❑ *A smell of bread drifted from some distant bakery.*

❸ 가산명사 핸드백 ❹ 복수명사 (눈 밑의) 처진 살 ❑ 그의 눈 아래의 처진 살이 더욱 두드러졌다.

❶ 불가산명사 짐 ❑ 승객들은 입국 심사대를 통과한 후 짐을 찾았다. ❷ 불가산명사 짐 ❑ 그는 얼마나 많은 감정적 짐을 지닌 채 그 관계를 시작하는 거지?

> baggage는 불가산 명사이다. 그래서 a piece of baggage나 some baggage라고 할 수는 있지만 a baggage나 some baggages라 할 수는 없다. 영국 영어에서든 미국 영어에서든 여행자가 가지고 다니는 모든 짐을 다 가리켜 bags라고 할 수 있다. 미국인들은 개별 여행가방을 bag이라고 하기도 한다. 영국 영어에서는 여행자가 가지고 다니는 짐을 통틀어 가리킬 때는 보통 luggage라고 하고, baggage는 좀 더 전문적인 용어로서 공항이나 여행 보험 등과 관련된 논의를 할 때 쓴다. 미국 영어에서 luggage는 빈 가방을 가리키고 baggage는 내용물이 든 가방을 가리킨다.

가산명사 화물칸 [미국영어; 영국영어 van] ❑ 관은 기차의 화물칸에 실렸다.

형용사 부대자루 같은 ❑ 부대자루 같은 잠바

철자 bale도 ❹ 의미 및 구동사 ❶과 ❸ 의미로 쓴다.

❶ 불가산명사 보석금 ❑ 항소심을 기다리는 중 남자는 보석금을 내고 풀려났다. ❷ 불가산명사 보석 ❑ 그는 어제 남요크셔 판사들로부터 보석을 허가받았다. ❸ 타동사 보석되다 ❑ 지방 판사들 앞에 11월 5일 출두할 수 있도록 그는 보석되었다. ❹ 타동사/자동사 물을 퍼내다 ❑ 우리는 미친 듯이 물을 퍼냄으로써 배가 두어 시간 동안 계속 떠 있게 했다. ● 구동사 물을 퍼내다 ❑ 수직 통로 아래로 선원들을 보내 그것을 막고 모든 물을 퍼내도록 했다. ❺ 구 보석 중에 잠적하다 ❑ 그는 작년에 마약 관련 혐의로 재판을 받던 중 보석 상태에서 잠적했다.

❶ 구동사 구제하다 ❑ 그들은 경제를 침체에서 어떻게 구할지에 대해 의논할 것이다. ❷ 구동사 보석금을 내 주다 ❑ 그는 감옥에 여덟 번 갔다 왔다. 매번 친구들이 그를 위해 보석금을 내주었다. ❸ 구동사 (낙하산으로) 뛰어내리다 ❑ 레이드는 고장 난 파손된 비행기에서 낙하산을 메고 뛰어내려야 했다.

❶ 가산명사 집행관 [미국영어] ❑ 법정 집행관의 말에 따르면 배심원들은 선고가 있을 때까지는 언론과 말하고 싶어 하지 않는다고 했다. ❷ 가산명사 집행관 [영국영어] ❸ 가산명사 토지 관리인 [영국영어]

❶ 가산명사 또는 불가산명사 미끼 ❑ 비비언은 물구덩이로 야생 동물들을 유혹하기 위한 미끼를 설치하기를 거부한다. ❷ 타동사 미끼를 놓다 ❑ 그는 낚싯바늘에 파이를 미끼로 달았다. ❑ 소년들은 사냥감을 창으로 잡기 위해 구덩이를 판 후 미끼를 놓았다. ❸ 불가산명사 미끼 ❑ 텔레비전 프로는 본질적으로 시청자들이 광고를 보도록 끌어들이기 위한 미끼다. ❹ 타동사 (일부러) 지분거리다 ❑ 그는 어머니를 지분거리는 것에서 쾌감을 느꼈다.

❶ 타동사/자동사 굽다 ❑ 케이크 굽는 것은 어떻게 배웠니? ● 빵 굽기 불가산명사 ❑ 목요일이면 그녀는 빵 굽기를 도맡아 하곤 했다. ❷ 타동사/자동사 굽히다; 굽다 ❑ 케이크를 35분에서 50분 동안 구우세요. ❑ 반죽은 굽히면서 부풀어 오른다.

❶ 가산명사 제빵사 ❷ 가산명사 빵집 ❑ 그 빵들은 갓 구운 것이다. 오늘 아침 내가 빵집에서 가져온 것이다.

가산명사 빵집 ❑ 어느 먼 빵집에서 빵 냄새가 풍겨 왔다.

bak|ing /ˈbeɪkɪŋ/ ADJ You can use **baking** to describe weather or a place that is very hot indeed. ❏ *...a baking July day.* ❏ *The coffins stood in the baking heat surrounded by mourners.* [ADV adj]

형용사 찌는 듯이 더운 ❏ 찌는 듯이 더운 7월의 하루 ❏ 관들은 찌는 더위 속에 애도자들에게 둘러싸여 있었다.

Word Link   ance ≈ quality, state : bal*ance*, perform*ance*, resist*ance*

---

bal|ance ♦♦◇ /ˈbæləns/ (balances, balancing, balanced) **1** V-T/V-I If you **balance** something somewhere, or if it **balances** there, it remains steady and does not fall. ❏ *I balanced on the ledge.* **2** N-UNCOUNT **Balance** is the ability to remain steady when you are standing up. ❏ *The medicines you are currently taking could be affecting your balance.* **3** V-RECIP If you **balance** one thing **with** something different, each of the things has the same strength or importance. ❏ *Balance spicy dishes with mild ones.* ❏ *The government has got to find some way to balance these two needs.* ❏ *Supply and demand on the currency market will generally balance.* ● **bal|anced** ADJ ❏ *This book is a well balanced biography.* **4** N-SING A **balance** is a situation in which all the different parts are equal in strength or importance. ❏ *...the ecological balance of the forest.* **5** N-SING If you say that **the balance** tips in your favor, you start winning or succeeding, especially in a conflict or contest. ❏ *...a powerful new gun which could tip the balance of the war in their favor.* **6** V-T If you **balance** one thing **against** another, you consider its importance in relation to the other one. ❏ *She carefully tried to balance religious sensitivities against democratic freedom.* **7** V-T If someone **balances** their budget or if a government **balances** the economy of a country, they make sure that the amount of money that is spent is not greater than the amount that is received. ❏ *He balanced his budgets by rigid control over public expenditure.* **8** V-T/V-I If you **balance** your books or make them **balance**, you prove by calculation that the amount of money you have received is equal to the amount that you have spent. ❏ *...teaching them to balance the books.* **9** N-COUNT The **balance** in your bank account is the amount of money you have in it. ❏ *I'd like to check the balance in my account please.* **10** N-SING The **balance** of an amount of money is what remains to be paid for something or what remains when part of the amount has been spent. ❏ *They were due to pay the balance on delivery.* **11** →see also **bank balance** **12** PHRASE If you **keep** your **balance**, for example when standing in a moving vehicle, you remain steady and do not fall over. If you **lose** your **balance**, you become unsteady and fall over. ❏ *She was holding onto the rail to keep her balance.* **13** PHRASE If you are **off balance**, you are in an unsteady position and about to fall. ❏ *A gust of wind knocked him off balance and he fell face down in the mud.* **14** PHRASE You can say **on balance** to indicate that you are stating an opinion after considering all the relevant facts or arguments. ❏ *On balance he agreed with Christine.* →see **bank**

1 타동사/자동사 균형 잡다; 균형 잡히다 ❏ 나는 가장자리에서 균형을 잡고 섰다. **2** 불가산명사 균형 감각 ❏ 현재 당신이 먹고 있는 약은 당신의 균형 감각에 영향을 미칠 수 있습니다. **3** 상호동사 균형을 맞추다 ❏ 매운 요리와 순한 요리의 균형을 맞춰라. ❏ 정부는 이 두 요구 사항 사이에서 균형을 맞출 방도를 찾아야 한다. ❏ 화폐 시장에서의 수요와 공급은 일반적으로 균형을 이룬다. ● 균형 잡힌 형용사 ❏ 이 책은 균형이 잘 잡힌 전기이다. **4** 단수명사 균형 ❏ 숲의 생태적 균형 **5** 단수명사 저울추, 우세 ❏ 그들에게 유리하도록 전황을 돌릴 수 있는 새로 개발된 강력한 총 **6** 타동사 저울질하다 ❏ 그녀는 신중하게 종교적 민감성과 민감한 사안을 민주적 자유를 저울질해 보았다. **7** 타동사 균형을 유지하다 ❏ 공공 지출을 철저하게 관리함으로써 그는 예산의 균형을 유지했다. **8** 타동사/자동사 맞아떨어지도록 하다 ❏ 장부를 정리하는 방식을 가르치는 것 **9** 가산명사 잔고 ❏ 계좌의 잔고를 확인하고 싶습니다. **10** 단수명사 잔금 ❏ 그들은 배달을 받고 잔금을 치르기로 되어 있었다. **12** 구 균형을 유지하다; 균형을 잃다 ❏ 그녀는 균형을 잡기 위해 난간을 붙잡고 있었다. **13** 구 균형을 잃은 ❏ 한바탕 돌풍에 그는 균형을 잃고 진창에 엎어졌다. **14** 구 모든 것을 고려하여 ❏ 모든 것을 고려한 후 그는 크리스틴에게 동의했다.

Word Partnership   balance의 연어

ADJ.	**delicate** balance **4**
	balance **due, outstanding** balance **10**
N.	balance **a budget 7**
	account balance **9**
V.	**check a** balance, **maintain a** balance **9**
	pay a balance **10**
	keep/lose your balance, **restore** balance **12**

---

bal|anced /ˈbælənst/ **1** ADJ A **balanced** report, book, or other document takes into account all the different opinions on something and presents information in a fair and reasonable way. [APPROVAL] ❏ *...a fair, balanced, comprehensive report.* **2** ADJ Something that is **balanced** is pleasing or useful because its different parts or elements are in the correct proportions. [APPROVAL] ❏ *...a balanced diet.* **3** ADJ Someone who is **balanced** remains calm and thinks clearly, even in a difficult situation. [APPROVAL] ❏ *I have to prove myself as a respectable, balanced, person.* **4** →see also **balance**

1 형용사 균형 잡힌 [마음에 듦] ❏ 공정하고 균형 잡힌 포괄적인 보고서 **2** 형용사 균형 잡힌 [마음에 듦] ❏ 균형 잡힌 식사 **3** 형용사 평정을 잃지 않는 [마음에 듦] ❏ 나는 내가 품행이 방정하고 평정을 잃지 않는 사람이라는 것을 증명해야 한다.

bal|ance of pay|ments (**balances of payments**) N-COUNT A country's **balance of payments** is the difference, over a period of time, between the payments it makes to other countries for imports and the payments it receives from other countries for exports. [BUSINESS] ❏ *Britain's balance of payments deficit has improved slightly.*

가산명사 국제 수지 [경제] ❏ 영국의 국제 수지 적자는 약간 개선되었다.

bal|ance of trade (**balances of trade**) N-COUNT A country's **balance of trade** is the difference in value, over a period of time, between the goods it imports and the goods it exports. [BUSINESS] [usu sing] ❏ *The deficit in Britain's balance of trade in March rose to more than 2100 million pounds.*

가산명사 무역 수지 [경제] ❏ 영국의 3월 무역 수지 적자가 21억 파운드 이상으로 증가했다.

bal|ance sheet (**balance sheets**) N-COUNT A **balance sheet** is a written statement of the amount of money and property that a company or person has, including amounts of money that are owed or are owing. **Balance sheet** is also used to refer to the general financial state of a company. [BUSINESS] ❏ *Rolls-Royce needed a strong balance sheet.*

가산명사 대차 대조표; 재정 상태 [경제] ❏ 롤스로이스는 건실한 대차 대조표가 필요했다.

bal|co|ny /ˈbælkəni/ (**balconies**) N-COUNT A **balcony** is a platform on the outside of a building, above ground level, with a wall or railing around it.

가산명사 발코니

bald /bɔld/ (**balder, baldest**) **1** ADJ Someone who is **bald** has little or no hair on the top of their head. ❏ *The man's bald head was beaded with sweat.* ● **bald|ness** N-UNCOUNT ❏ *He wears a cap to cover a spot of baldness.* **2** ADJ If a tire is **bald**, its surface has worn down and it is no longer safe to use. **3** ADJ A **bald** statement is in plain language and contains no extra explanation or information. [ADJ n] ❏ *The bald truth is he's just not happy.* ● **bald|ly** ADV [ADV with v] ❏ *"The leaders are outdated," he stated baldly. "They don't relate to young people."*

1 형용사 대머리의 ❏ 남자의 대머리에는 땀이 방울져 있었다. ● 대머리 불가산명사 ❏ 그는 머리가 벗겨진 부분을 가리기 위해 모자를 쓴다. **2** 형용사 마모된 **3** 형용사 노골적인 ❏ 사실을 노골적으로 말하자면 그는 전혀 행복하지 않다. ● 노골적으로 부사 ❏ "지도자들은 구시대적이다. 그들은 젊은 사람들과 소통하지 못한다."라고 그는 노골적으로 선언했다.

bald|ing /bɔ́ldɪŋ/ ADJ Someone who is **balding** is beginning to lose the hair on the top of their head. ❑ *He wore a straw hat to keep his balding head from getting sunburned.*

형용사 머리가 벗겨지는 ❑ 그는 대머리가 되어 가는 머리가 햇볕에 타는 것을 막기 위해 밀짚모자를 썼다.

bale /beɪl/ (**bales, baling, baled**) **1** N-COUNT A **bale** is a large quantity of something such as hay, cloth, or paper, tied together tightly. ❑ *...bales of hay.* **2** V-T If something such as hay, cloth, or paper **is baled**, it is tied together tightly. ❑ *Once hay has been cut and baled it has to go through some chemical processes.* **3** →see also **bail**

1 가산명사 꾸러미, 더미 ❑ 건초 더미들 **2** 타동사 세게 묶다, 더미로 묶다 ❑ 건초를 일단 자르고 더미로 묶은 다음 화학적 처리를 거쳐야 한다.

ball ♦♦◇ /bɔl/ (**balls, balling, balled**) **1** N-COUNT A **ball** is a round object that is used in games such as tennis, baseball, football, basketball, and cricket. ❑ *...a golf ball.* **2** N-COUNT A **ball** is something or an amount of something that has a round shape. ❑ *Thomas screwed the letter up into a ball.* **3** V-T/V-I When you **ball** something or when it **balls**, it becomes round. ❑ *He picked up the sheets of paper, and balled them tightly in his fists.* **4** N-COUNT The **ball of** your foot or **the ball of** your thumb is the rounded part where your toes join your foot or where your thumb joins your hand. **5** N-COUNT A **ball** is a large formal social event at which people dance. ❑ *My Mama and Daddy used to have a grand Christmas Ball every year.* →see **foot, soccer**

1 가산명사 공 ❑ 골프공 **2** 가산명사 구체 ❑ 토머스는 편지를 공 모양으로 구겼다. **3** 타동사/자동사 둥글게 만들다; 둥글어지다 ❑ 그는 종잇장들을 집은 후 주먹을 쥐고 둥글게 세게 구겼다. **4** 가산명사 (발바닥이나 엄지 손가락의) 동그랗게 볼록한 부분 **5** 가산명사 무도회 ❑ 우리 엄마와 아빠는 매년 화려한 크리스마스 무도회를 열곤 하셨다.

Word Partnership	ball의 연어
N.	bowling/golf/tennis/soccer ball, ball **field**, ball **game** **1**
V.	bounce/catch/hit/kick/throw a ball **1**
	roll into a ball **3**
PREP.	ball of *something* **2**

bal|lad /bǽləd/ (**ballads**) **1** N-COUNT A **ballad** is a long song or poem which tells a story in simple language. ❑ *...an eighteenth century ballad about some lost children called the Babes in the Wood.* **2** N-COUNT A **ballad** is a slow, romantic, popular song. ❑ *"You Don't Know Paris" is one of the most beautiful ballads that he ever sang.*

1 가산명사 발라드 ❑ '숲 속의 아기들'이라고 불린 미아들에 관한 18세기의 발라드 **2** 가산명사 발라드 ❑ '당신은 파리를 몰라'는 그가 쓴 가장 아름다운 발라드 중 하나이다.

bal|let /bǽleɪ, BRIT bǽleɪ/ (**ballets**) **1** N-UNCOUNT **Ballet** is a type of very skilled and artistic dancing with carefully planned movements. [also the N, oft N n] ❑ *I trained as a ballet dancer.* **2** N-COUNT A **ballet** is an artistic work that is performed by ballet dancers. ❑ *The performance will include the premiere of three new ballets.*

1 불가산명사 발레 ❑ 나는 발레 무용수로서 훈련을 했다. **2** 가산명사 발레 ❑ 공연에는 세 가지 새로운 발레의 초연이 포함된다.

bal|loon /bəlún/ (**balloons, ballooning, ballooned**) **1** N-COUNT A **balloon** is a small, thin, rubber bag that you blow air into so that it becomes larger and rounder or longer. Balloons are used as toys or decorations. ❑ *She popped a balloon with her fork.* **2** N-COUNT A **balloon** is a large, strong bag filled with gas or hot air, which can carry passengers in a container that hangs underneath it. [also by N] ❑ *They are to attempt to be the first to circle the Earth non-stop by balloon.* **3** V-I When something **balloons**, it increases rapidly in amount. ❑ *In London, the use of the Tube has ballooned.* →see **fly**

1 가산명사 풍선 ❑ 그녀는 포크로 풍선을 터뜨렸다. **2** 가산명사 열기구 ❑ 그들은 열기구로 쉬지 않고 지구를 한 바퀴 도는 최초의 시도를 할 것이다. **3** 자동사 급증하다 ❑ 런던에서는 지하철 사용량이 급증했다.

bal|lot ♦◇◇ /bǽlət/ (**ballots, balloting, balloted**) **1** N-COUNT A **ballot** is a secret vote in which people select a candidate in an election, or express their opinion about something. [also by N] ❑ *The result of the ballot will not be known for two weeks.* **2** N-COUNT A **ballot** is a piece of paper on which you indicate your choice or opinion in a secret vote. ❑ *Election boards will count the ballots by hand.* **3** V-T If you **ballot** a group of people, you find out what they think about a subject by organizing a secret vote. ❑ *The union said they will ballot members on whether to strike.* →see **election, vote**

1 가산명사 투표 ❑ 투표의 결과는 2주 안에는 알 수 없다. **2** 가산명사 투표용지 ❑ 선거 위원회는 투표용지를 손으로 셀 것이다. **3** 타동사 투표에 부치다 ❑ 노조는 파업 여부를 조합원들의 투표를 통해 결정하겠다고 했다.

ball|park /bɔ́lpɑrk/ (**ballparks**) also **ball park** **1** N-COUNT A **ballpark** is a park or stadium where baseball is played. ❑ *...one of the oldest and most beautiful ballparks in baseball.* **2** ADJ A **ballpark** figure or **ballpark** estimate is an approximate figure or estimate. [ADJ n] ❑ *I can't give you anything more than just sort of a ballpark figure.*

1 가산명사 야구장 ❑ 야구계에 있어서 가장 오래되고 아름다운 구장 중 하나 **2** 형용사 대략적인 ❑ 그냥 대략적인 수치 이상의 것은 말할 수 없을 것 같습니다.

balm /bɑm/ (**balms**) **1** N-MASS **Balm** is a sweet-smelling oil that is obtained from some tropical trees and used to make creams that heal wounds or reduce pain. ❑ *...a pot of lip balm.* **2** N-UNCOUNT If you refer to something as **balm**, you mean that it makes you feel better. [APPROVAL] [also a N] ❑ *The place is balm to the soul.*

1 물질명사 향유, 연고 ❑ 입술 연고 한 통 **2** 불가산명사 위안제 [마음에 듦] ❑ 그곳은 영혼의 안식처이다.

bam|boo /bæmbú/ (**bamboos**) N-VAR **Bamboo** is a tall tropical plant with hard, hollow stems. The young shoots of the plant can be eaten and the stems are used to make furniture. ❑ *...huts with walls of bamboo.*

가산명사 또는 불가산명사 대나무 ❑ 벽을 대나무로 만든 오두막

ban ♦♦◇ /bæn/ (**bans, banning, banned**) **1** V-T To **ban** something means to state officially that it must not be done, shown, or used. ❑ *Canada will ban smoking in all offices later this year.* ❑ *Last year arms sales were banned.* **2** N-COUNT A **ban** is an official ruling that something must not be done, shown, or used. ❑ *The General also lifted a ban on political parties.* **3** V-T If you **are banned from** doing something, you are officially prevented from doing it. ❑ *He was banned from driving for three years.*

1 타동사 금지하다 ❑ 캐나다는 올해 후반에 모든 사무실에서 흡연을 금지할 것이다. ❑ 작년에는 무기 판매가 금지되었다. **2** 가산명사 금지 ❑ 장군은 또한 정당에 대한 금지를 해제했다. **3** 타동사 ~이 금지되다 ❑ 그는 삼 년 동안 운전면허를 정지당했다.

Thesaurus	ban의 침조어
V.	bar, forbid, prohibit; (*ant.*) allow, legalize, permit **1**
N.	prohibition; (*ant.*) approval, sanction **2**

ba|nal /bənɔ́l, -nǽl, beɪnᵊl/ ADJ If you describe something as **banal**, you do not like it because you think that it is so ordinary that it is not at all effective or interesting. [DISAPPROVAL] ❑ *The text is banal.*

형용사 진부한 [탐탁찮음] ❑ 진부한 글이다.

a
b
c
d
e
f
g
h
i
j
k
l
m
n
o
p
q
r
s
t
u
v
w
x
y
z

ba|na|na /bənǽnə/ (bananas) N-VAR **Bananas** are long curved fruit with yellow skins. ❑ ...a bunch of bananas.

가산명사 또는 불가산명사 바나나 ❑ 바나나 한 뭉치

band ♦♦◇ /bǽnd/ (bands, banding, banded) **1** N-COUNT-COLL A **band** is a small group of musicians who play popular music such as jazz, rock, or pop. ❑ He was a drummer in a rock band. **2** N-COUNT-COLL A **band** is a group of musicians who play brass and percussion instruments. ❑ Bands played German marches. **3** N-COUNT-COLL A **band of** people is a group of people who have joined together because they share an interest or belief. ❑ Bands of government soldiers, rebels, and just plain criminals have been roaming some neighborhoods. **4** N-COUNT A **band** is a flat, narrow strip of cloth which you wear around your head or wrists, or which forms part of a piece of clothing. ❑ Almost all hospitals use a wrist-band of some kind with your name and details on it. **5** N-COUNT A **band** is a strip of something such as color, light, land, or cloth which contrasts with the areas on either side of it. ❑ ...bands of natural vegetation between strips of crops. **6** N-COUNT A **band** is a strip or loop of metal or other strong material which strengthens something, or which holds several things together. ❑ Surgeon Geoffrey Horne placed a metal band around the kneecap to help it knit back together. →see also **elastic band, rubber band 7** N-COUNT A **band** is a range of numbers or values within a system of measurement. ❑ For an initial service, a 10 megahertz-wide band of frequencies will be needed. **8**
→see army, concert

1 가산명사-집합 밴드 ❑ 그는 록밴드의 드러머였다. **2** 가산명사-집합 악대 ❑ 악대들은 독일 행진곡을 연주했다. **3** 가산명사-집합 무리 ❑ 정부군, 반군, 그리고 단순 범죄인들의 무리가 일부 동네에서 배회하고 있다. **4** 가산명사 띠, 팔찌 ❑ 거의 모든 병원이 환자의 이름과 신상 정보가 적힌 팔찌를 쓴다. **5** 가산명사 띠, 띠같이 생긴 것 ❑ 기다란 경작지 사이사이에 위치한 띠 모양의 자연 목초지 **6** 가산명사 밴드, 묶는 줄 ❑ 제프리 혼 의사는 재접합을 돕도록 슬개골 주위에 철제 밴드를 둘렀다. **7** 가산명사 대역 ❑ 최초 서비스에는 10메가헤르츠 대역폭의 주파수가 필요할 것이다.

▶**band together** PHRASAL VERB If people **band together**, they meet and act as a group in order to try and achieve something. ❑ Women banded together to protect each other.

구동사 뭉치다, 단결하다 ❑ 여자들은 서로를 돕기 위해 함께 뭉쳤다.

band|age /bǽndɪdʒ/ (bandages, bandaging, bandaged) **1** N-COUNT A **bandage** is a long strip of cloth which is wrapped around a wounded part of someone's body to protect or support it. ❑ We put some ointment and a bandage on his knee. **2** V-T If you **bandage** a wound or part of someone's body, you tie a bandage around it. ❑ Apply a dressing to the wound and bandage it. ● PHRASAL VERB **Bandage up** means the same as **bandage**. ❑ I bandaged the leg up and gave her aspirin for the pain.

1 가산명사 붕대 ❑ 우리는 그의 무릎에 연고를 바르고 붕대를 감았다. **2** 타동사 붕대를 감다 ❑ 상처 부위에 약을 바른 후 붕대를 감아라. ● 구동사 붕대를 감다 ❑ 나는 다리에 붕대를 감은 후 그녀에게 진통제로 아스피린을 줬다.

Band-Aid (Band-Aids) also band-aid **1** N-VAR A **Band-Aid** is a small piece of sticky tape that you use to cover small cuts or wounds on your body. [mainly AM, TRADEMARK; BRIT **plaster**] **2** ADJ If you refer to a **Band-Aid** solution to a problem, you mean that you disapprove of it because you think that it will only be effective for a short period. [DISAPPROVAL] [ADJ n] ❑ We need long-term solutions, not short-term Band-Aid ones.

1 가산명사 또는 불가산명사 일회용 반창고, 밴드 [주로 미국영어, 상표; 영국영어 plaster] **2** 형용사 미봉책 [탐탁찮음] ❑ 우리에겐 미봉책이 아닌 장기적인 해결책이 필요하다.

B & B /bíː ən bíː/ (B&Bs) also b&b **1** N-UNCOUNT **B&B** is the same as **bed and breakfast**. ❑ ...three nights b&b. **2** N-COUNT A **B&B** is the same as a **bed and breakfast**. ❑ There are B&Bs all over the islands.

1 불가산명사 잠자리와 아침 식사 ❑ 3일간의 숙박과 아침 식사 **2** 가산명사 아침 식사를 제공하는 숙소 ❑ 섬들 전역에 아침 식사를 제공하는 숙소가 있다.

ban|dit /bǽndɪt/ (bandits) N-COUNT Robbers are sometimes called **bandits**, especially if they are found in areas where the law has broken down. ❑ This is real bandit country.

가산명사 도적 ❑ 여기는 완전 도둑놈 세상이다.

band|wagon /bǽndwægən/ (bandwagons) **1** N-COUNT You can refer to an activity or movement that has suddenly become fashionable or popular as a **bandwagon**. ❑ ...the environmental bandwagon. **2** N-COUNT If someone, especially a politician, jumps or climbs **on the bandwagon**, they become involved in an activity or movement because it is fashionable or likely to succeed and not because they are really interested in it. [DISAPPROVAL] ❑ In recent months many conservative politicians have jumped on the anti-immigrant bandwagon.

1 가산명사 풍조 ❑ 환경 보호주의적 풍조 **2** 가산명사 시류 [탐탁찮음] ❑ 최근 몇 달간에 많은 보수적 정치가들이 반이민주의 시류에 편승했다.

band|width /bǽndwɪdθ/ (bandwidths) N-VAR A **bandwidth** is the range of frequencies used for a particular telecommunications signal, radio transmission, or computer network. ❑ To cope with this amount of data, the system will need a bandwidth of around 100mhz.

가산명사 또는 불가산명사 대역폭 ❑ 이 정도 양의 데이터를 다루려면 시스템이 약 100메가헤르츠의 대역폭을 필요로 할 것이다.

bang /bǽŋ/ (bangs, banging, banged) **1** N-COUNT; SOUND A **bang** is a sudden loud noise such as the noise of an explosion. ❑ I heard four or five loud bangs. ❑ She slammed the door with a bang. **2** V-I If something **bangs**, it makes a sudden loud noise, once or several times. ❑ The engine spat and banged. **3** V-T/V-I If you **bang** a door or if it **bangs**, it closes suddenly with a loud noise. ❑ ...the sound of doors banging. ❑ All up and down the street the windows bang shut. **4** V-T/V-I If you **bang on** something or if you **bang** it, you hit it hard, making a loud noise. ❑ We could bang on the desks and shout till they let us out. **5** V-T If you **bang** something on something or if you **bang** it down, you quickly and violently put it on a surface, because you are angry. ❑ She banged his dinner on the table. **6** V-T If you **bang** a part of your body, you accidentally knock it against something and hurt yourself. ❑ She'd fainted and banged her head. ● N-COUNT **Bang** is also a noun. ❑ ...a nasty bang on the head. **7** V-I If you **bang into** something or someone, you bump into them hard, usually because you are not looking where you are going. ❑ I didn't mean to bang into you. **8** N-PLURAL **Bangs** are hair which is cut so that it hangs over your forehead. [AM; BRIT **fringe**] ❑ My bangs were cut short, but the rest of my hair was long. **9** ADV You can use **bang** to emphasize expressions that indicate an exact position or an exact time. [EMPHASIS] [ADV prep] ❑ ...bang in the middle of the track.

1 가산명사; 소리 쾅 하는 소리, 탕 하는 소리 ❑ 크게 쾅 하는 소리가 너댓 번 들렸다. **2** 자동사 쾅 하는 소리를 내다 ❑ 엔진은 픽픽거리는 소리와 쿵쿵거리는 소리를 냈다. **3** 타동사/자동사 쾅 닫다, 쾅 하며 닫히다 ❑ 문들이 쾅 닫히는 소리 ❑ 길거리 위 아래 모든 곳에서 창문들이 쾅 닫혔다. **4** 타동사/자동사 쾅 치다 ❑ 그들이 우리를 내보내 줄 때까지 책상을 두드리고 소리를 지를 수 있겠지. **5** 타동사 쾅 내려놓다 ❑ 그녀는 그의 저녁 식사를 탁자 위에 탕 하고 내려놨다. **6** 타동사 쿵 하고 부딪치다 ❑ 그녀는 기절하며 머리를 쿵 하고 부딪혔다. ● 가산명사 부딪침 ❑ 머리를 심하게 부딪힘 **7** 자동사 부딪치다 ❑ 당신에게 부딪힐 의도는 아니었습니다. **8** 복수명사 가지런히 짧게 자른 앞머리 [미국영어; 영국영어 fringe] ❑ 나는 앞머리는 짧게 잘랐지만 나머지 머리는 길었다. **9** 부사 바로 [강조] ❑ 트랙의 바로 한가운데에서

Word Partnership	bang의 연어	
V.	**hear a bang** **1**	
ADJ.	**loud** bang **1**	
PREP.	**with a** bang **1**	
	bang **on** *something* **4**	
	bang **into** **7**	
ADV.	bang **down** **5**	
N.	bang *your* head **6**	

ban|ish /bǽnɪʃ/ (banishes, banishing, banished) ◼ v-т If someone or something **is banished from** a place or area of activity, they are sent away from it and prevented from entering it. ❑ *John was banished from England.* ❑ *I was banished to the small bedroom upstairs.* ◻ v-т If you **banish** something unpleasant, you get rid of it. ❑ *...a public investment program intended to banish the recession.*

◼ 타동사 추방당하다, 쫓기나다 ❑ 존은 영국에서 추방됐다. ❑ 나는 위층의 작은 침실로 쫓겨났다. ◻ 타동사 멀쳐 버리다 ❑ 경기 후퇴를 떨쳐 버리기 위해 마련된 공적 투자 프로그램

Thesaurus	banish의 참조어

    v.   ban, deport, evict, exile; (*ant.*) embrace, invite, welcome ◼

---

bank

① FINANCE AND STORAGE
② AREAS AND MASSES
③ OTHER VERB USES

---

① **bank** ♦♦♦ /bǽŋk/ (banks, banking, banked) ◼ N-COUNT A **bank** is an institution where people or businesses can keep their money. ❑ *Students should look to see which bank offers them the service that best suits their financial needs.* ◻ N-COUNT A **bank** is a building where a bank offers its services. ◼ v-ı If you **bank with** a particular bank, you have an account with that bank. ❑ *My husband has banked with the Co-op since before the war.* ◼ N-COUNT You use **bank** to refer to a store of something. For example, a blood **bank** is a store of blood that is kept ready for use. ❑ *...Britain's National Police Computer, one of the largest data banks in the world.*
→see Word Web: bank

◼ 가산명사 은행 ❑ 학생들은 어느 은행이 자신들의 재정적 필요에 가장 적합한 서비스를 제공하는지 살펴봐야 한다. ◻ 가산명사 은행 건물 ◼ 자동사 은행에 계좌를 개설하고 이용하다 ❑ 내 남편은 전쟁 이전부터 쭉 생활 협동 조합 은행을 이용해 왔다. ◼ 가산명사 저장소, 은행 ❑ 세계 최대의 데이터 은행 중 하나인 영국 경찰청 컴퓨터

② **bank** /bǽŋk/ (banks) ◼ N-COUNT The **banks of** a river, canal, or lake are the raised areas of ground along its edge. ❑ *...30 miles of new developments along both banks of the Thames.* ◻ N-COUNT A **bank** of ground is a raised area of it with a flat top and one or two sloping sides. ❑ *...resting indolently upon a grassy bank.* ◼ N-COUNT A **bank of** something is a long high mass of it. ❑ *On their journey south they hit a bank of fog off the north-east coast of Scotland.* ◼ N-COUNT A **bank of** things, especially machines, switches, or dials, is a row of them, or a series of rows. ❑ *The typical laborer now sits in front of a bank of dials.*

◼ 가산명사 둑, 제방 ❑ 템스 강 양쪽 강둑을 따라 30마일에 걸쳐 새로 조성된 단지 ◻ 가산명사 둔덕 ❑ 풀이 무성한 둔덕 위에서의 나른한 휴식 ◼ 가산명사 둑처럼 쌓인 것 ❑ 남쪽으로 향하는 길에 그들은 스코틀랜드 북동쪽 연안에서 깊고 높게 덮인 안개와 마주쳤다. ◼ 가산명사 늘어선 열 ❑ 오늘날의 전형적인 노동자는 늘어선 눈금판 앞에 앉아 있다.

③ **bank** /bǽŋk/ (banks, banking, banked) v-ı When an aircraft **banks**, one of its wings rises higher than the other, usually when it is changing direction. ❑ *A single-engine plane took off and banked above the highway in front of him.*

자동사 한쪽 옆으로 기울다 ❑ 단발 비행기가 이륙하더니 그 남자 앞에 있는 고속도로 상공에서 날개를 한쪽으로 기울였다.

▶**bank on** PHRASAL VERB If you **bank on** something happening, you expect it to happen and rely on it happening. ❑ *The Berlin government is banking on the Olympics to save the city money.*

구동사 ~을 기대하다, ~에 의지하다 ❑ 베를린 정부는 올림픽 대회를 통해 시 재정을 부양할 수 있을 것으로 기대하고 있다.

bank ac|count (bank accounts) N-COUNT A **bank account** is an arrangement with a bank which allows you to keep your money in the bank and to take some out when you need it. ❑ *Paul had at least 17 different bank accounts.*

가산명사 은행 예금 계좌 ❑ 폴은 은행 예금 계좌를 최소한 17개 가지고 있었다.

bank bal|ance (bank balances) N-COUNT Your **bank balance** is the amount of money that you have in your bank account at a particular time. ❑ *Do you wish to use the Internet simply to check your bank balance?*

가산명사 은행 예금 잔고 ❑ 인터넷으로 간단하게 은행 예금 잔고를 확인하고 싶으십니까?

bank card (bank cards) also **bank|card** ◼ N-COUNT A **bank card** is a plastic card which your bank gives you so you can get money from your bank account using a cash machine. It is also called an **ATM card** in American English. In Britain, you can use bank cards to prove who you are when you pay for something by check. ◻ N-COUNT A **bank card** is a credit card that is supplied by a bank. [AM] →see bank

◼ 가산명사 현금 카드 ◻ 가산명사 은행 발행 신용 카드 [미국영어]

bank draft (bank drafts) N-COUNT A **bank draft** is a check which you can buy from a bank in order to pay someone who is not willing to accept a personal check. ❑ *Payments should be made by credit card or bank draft in U.S. dollars.*

가산명사 은행 환어음 ❑ 미국 달러화로 신용 카드나 은행 환어음을 사용해서 지불해야 한다.

bank|er ♦◌◌ /bǽŋkər/ (bankers) N-COUNT A **banker** is someone who works in banking at a senior level. ❑ *...an investment banker.*

가산명사 은행 간부 직원, 금융인 ❑ 투자 상담사

banker's draft (banker's drafts) N-COUNT A **banker's draft** is the same as a **bank draft**. ❑ *You pay for the car by banker's draft in the local currency.*

가산명사 은행 환어음 ❑ 차 값은 현지 통화로 은행 환어음을 사용하여 결제한다.

bank holi|day (bank holidays) N-COUNT A **bank holiday** is a public holiday. [BRIT; AM usually **national holiday**] ❑ *Some hypermarkets and shops are closed on Sundays and bank holidays.*

가산명사 일반 공휴일 [영국영어; 미국영어 대개 national holiday] ❑ 일부 대형 슈퍼마켓과 상점들은 일요일과 일반 공휴일에 문을 닫는다.

Word Web   bank

Most people deposit **money** into **checking accounts** and savings accounts. Money can be **withdrawn** from a checking account by writing a **check** or using a **bank card** at an automated teller machine (**ATM**). People record these **transactions** in a check register. People **balance** their accounts using their monthly **bank statements**. Customers can also **bank online** at their bank's website. When people **deposit** money into a savings account they earn **interest** from the bank for the use of the money. A bank uses its customers' money to make **loans**. Banks **lend** money for mortgages, car loans, student loans, and business loans. The **borrower** pays back the **principal** amount borrowed, plus interest.

bank|ing ◆◇◇ /bǽŋkɪŋ/ N-UNCOUNT **Banking** is the business activity of banks and similar institutions. ❑ ...the online banking revolution. →see **industry**

불가산명사 은행 업무 ❑ 온라인 뱅킹의 혁명

bank|note /bǽŋknoʊt/ (banknotes) also bank note N-COUNT **Banknotes** are pieces of paper money. ❑ ...a shopping bag full of banknotes.

가산명사 은행권, 지폐 ❑ 지폐가 가득 담긴 쇼핑백

bank rate (bank rates) N-COUNT The **bank rate** is the rate of interest at which a bank lends money, especially the minimum rate of interest that banks are allowed to charge, which is decided from time to time by the country's central bank. ❑ ...a sterling crisis that forced the bank rate up.

가산명사 은행의 할인율 ❑ 은행 할인율을 상승시킨 영국 화폐 위기

bank|roll /bǽŋkroʊl/ (bankrolls, bankrolling, bankrolled) V-T To **bankroll** a person, organization, or project means to provide the financial resources that they need. [mainly AM, INFORMAL] ❑ The company has bankrolled a couple of local movies.

타동사 자금을 지원하다 [주로 미국영어, 비격식체] ❑ 그 회사는 현지에서 제작되는 두 편의 영화에 자금을 지원한 바 있다.

bank|rupt /bǽŋkrʌpt/ (bankrupts, bankrupting, bankrupted) **1** ADJ People or organizations that go **bankrupt** do not have enough money to pay their debts. [BUSINESS] ❑ If the firm cannot sell its products, it will go bankrupt. **2** V-T To **bankrupt** a person or organization means to make them go bankrupt. [BUSINESS] ❑ The move to the market nearly bankrupted the firm and its director. **3** N-COUNT A **bankrupt** is a person who has been declared bankrupt by a court of law. ❑ In total, 80% of bankrupts are men. **4** ADJ If you say that something is **bankrupt**, you are emphasizing that it lacks any value or worth. [BUSINESS, EMPHASIS] ❑ He really thinks that European civilisation is morally bankrupt.

1 형용사 파산한 [경제] ❑ 만약 상품을 팔지 못하면, 그 회사는 파산할 것이다. **2** 타동사 파산시키다 [경제] ❑ 시장 경제로의 전환 때문에 회사와 그 관리자는 파산할 지경에 이르렀다. **3** 가산명사 파산자 ❑ 합계하여, 파산자의 80퍼센트가 남성이다. **4** 형용사 파탄에 이른 [경제, 강조] ❑ 그는 정말 유럽 문명이 도덕적 파탄에 이르렀다고 생각한다.

bank|rupt|cy /bǽŋkrʌptsi/ (bankruptcies) **1** N-UNCOUNT **Bankruptcy** is the state of being bankrupt. [BUSINESS] ❑ Pan Am is the second airline in two months to file for bankruptcy. **2** N-COUNT A **bankruptcy** is an instance of an organization or person going bankrupt. [BUSINESS] ❑ The number of corporate bankruptcies climbed in August.

1 불가산명사 파산 [경제] ❑ 팬암은 두 달 동안 두 번째로 파산을 신청한 항공사이다. **2** 가산명사 파산 [경제] ❑ 8월 들어 법인 파산 수가 증가했다.

Word Partnership   bankruptcy의 연어

V.	**declare** bankruptcy, **force into** bankruptcy **1**
	avoid bankruptcy **1** **2**
N.	bankruptcy **law**, bankruptcy **protection** **1** **2**

---

bank state|ment (bank statements) N-COUNT A **bank statement** is a printed document showing all the money paid into and taken out of a bank account. Bank statements are usually sent by a bank to a customer at regular intervals. →see **bank**

가산명사 은행 잔고 증명서

ban|ner /bǽnər/ (banners) **1** N-COUNT A **banner** is a long strip of cloth with something written on it. Banners are usually attached to two poles and carried during a protest or rally. ❑ A large crowd of students followed the coffin, carrying banners and shouting slogans denouncing the government. **2** PHRASE If someone does something **under the banner of** a particular cause, idea, or belief, they do it saying that they support that cause, idea, or belief. ❑ Russia was the first country to forge a new economic system under the banner of Marxism.

1 가산명사 기 ❑ 많은 수의 학생들이 기를 들고 정부를 비난하는 구호를 외치며 관을 따라갔다. **2** 구 ...의 기치 아래 ❑ 러시아는 처음으로 마르크시즘의 기치 아래 새로운 경제 체제를 세워 낸 나라였다.

ban|quet /bǽŋkwɪt/ (banquets) N-COUNT A **banquet** is a grand formal dinner. ❑ Last night he attended a state banquet at Buckingham Palace.

가산명사 연회 ❑ 지난밤 그는 버킹엄 궁전에서 열린 공식 연회에 참석했다.

ban|ter /bǽntər/ (banters) N-UNCOUNT **Banter** is teasing or joking talk that is amusing and friendly. ❑ As she closed the door, she heard Tom exchanging good-natured banter with Jane.

불가산명사 희롱, 농지거리 ❑ 그녀는 문을 닫으면서 톰이 제인과 유쾌한 농담을 주고받는 것을 들었다.

bap|tism /bǽptɪzəm/ (baptisms) N-VAR A **baptism** is a Christian ceremony in which a person is baptized. Compare **christening**. ❑ Infants prepared for baptism should be dressed in pure white.

가산명사 또는 불가산명사 세례, 침례 ❑ 세례를 받을 준비가 된 유아들은 순백색의 옷을 입어야 한다.

bap|tize /bǽptaɪz/ (baptizes, baptizing, baptized) [BRIT also **baptise**] V-T When someone **is baptized**, water is put on their heads or they are covered with water as a sign that their sins have been forgiven and that they have become a member of the Christian Church. Compare **christen**. [usu passive] ❑ At this time she decided to become a Christian and was baptized.

[영국영어 baptise] 타동사 세례를 받다 ❑ 그녀는 이번에는 기독교인이 되기로 결심하고 세례를 받았다.

bar ◆◆◇ /bɑr/ (bars, barring, barred) **1** N-COUNT A **bar** is a place where you can buy and drink alcoholic drinks. [mainly AM] ❑ ...Devil's Herd, the city's most popular country-western bar. **2** N-COUNT A **bar** is a room in a hotel or other establishment where alcoholic drinks are served. [BRIT] ❑ Last night in the hotel there was some talk in the bar about drugs. **3** N-COUNT A **bar** is a counter on which alcoholic drinks are served. ❑ Michael was standing alone by the bar when Brian rejoined him. →see also **snack bar, wine bar**

1 가산명사 술집 [주로 미국영어] ❑ 그 도시에서 가장 인기 있는 컨트리 웨스턴 바 '데블스 허드' **2** 가산명사 바 [영국영어] ❑ 어젯밤 호텔 바에서 마약에 대한 이야기가 오갔다. **3** 가산명사 바, 카운터 ❑ 브라이언이 다시 합류했을 때 마이클은 바 옆에 홀로 서 있었다.

There are a number of names that can be applied to businesses serving alcohol. The most common is **bar**. In the UK, these are **pubs**, which sometimes also serve light meals. **Nightclubs** also serve drinks along with music or entertainment. However, a **snack bar** does not serve alcohol, just food and soft drinks.

주류를 판매하는 업체에 적용할 수 있는 이름은 여러가지다. 가장 흔한 것으로는 bar(바)가 있다. 영국에는 pub(펍)이 있는데 가벼운 식사도 제공한다. nightclub(나이트클럽)에서도 음악이나 여흥과 함께 주류를 판매한다. 그러나 snackbar(스낵바)에는 음식과 음료수만 있지 주류는 판매하지 않는다.

---

4 N-COUNT A **bar** is a long, straight, stiff piece of metal. ❑ ...a brick building with bars across the ground floor windows. **5** PHRASE If you say that someone is **behind bars**, you mean that they are in prison. ❑ Fisher was behind bars last night, charged with attempted murder. **6** N-COUNT A **bar of** something is a piece of it which is roughly rectangular. ❑ What is your favorite chocolate bar? **7** V-T If you **bar** a door, you place something in front of it or a piece of wood or metal across it in order to prevent it from being opened. ❑ For added safety, bar the door to the kitchen. **8** V-T If you **bar** someone's way, you prevent them from going somewhere or entering a place, by blocking their path. ❑ Harry moved to bar his way. **9** V-T If someone **is barred from** a place or **from** doing something, they are officially forbidden to go there or to do it. [usu passive]

4 가산명사 살 ❑ 1층 창문에 창살이 달린 벽돌 건물 **5** 구 감옥에 갇힌 ❑ 피셔는 어젯밤 살인 미수 혐의로 감옥에 갇혀 있었다. **6** 가산명사 직사각형의 물건 ❑ 네가 좋아하는 초콜릿은 뭐니? **7** 타동사 -에 빗장을 질러 잠그다 ❑ 안전을 더하기 위해 부엌문을 빗장을 질러 잠그세요. **8** 타동사 막다 ❑ 해리는 움직여서 그 남자의 길을 막았다. **9** 타동사 금지당하다 ❑ 국제사면위원회 직원들은 1982년 이래로 스리랑카 입국이 금지되어 왔다. **10** 가산명사 장애, 장벽 ❑ 의사소통에 있어서 근본적인 장벽 중 한 가지는 전 세계적으로 사용되는 공통의 언어가 없다는 점이다.

Amnesty workers have been barred from Sri Lanka since 1982. ⑩ N-COUNT If something is a **bar to** doing a particular thing, it prevents someone from doing it. ❑ *One of the fundamental bars to communication is the lack of a universally spoken, common language.* ⑪ PREP You can use **bar** when you mean "except." For example, all the work **bar** the washing means all the work except the washing. [mainly BRIT] ❑ *Bar a plateau in 1989, there has been a rise in inflation ever since the mid-1980's.* →see also **barring** ⑫ N-PROPER The **bar** is used to refer to the profession of any kind of lawyer in the United States, or of a barrister in England. [BRIT **Bar**] ❑ *Less than a quarter of graduates from the law school pass the bar exam on the first try.* ⑬ N-COUNT In music, a **bar** is one of the several short parts of the same length into which a piece of music is divided. [mainly BRIT; AM **measure**] ❑ *She sat down at the piano and played a few bars of a Chopin Polonaise.* →see **soap**

Word Partnership		bar의 연어
ADJ.	**gay** bar, **local** bar ①	
	candy/chocolate bar ⑥	
N.	bar **and grill**, bar **and lounge**, bar **owner**, **restaurant and** bar, bar **stool** ①	
	bar **of soap** ⑥	
	bar **a door** ⑦	
	bar **exam** ⑫	
PREP.	**behind a** bar ③	
	bar *someone* **from** ⑨	

bar|bar|ic /bɑrbǽrɪk/ ADJ If you describe someone's behavior as **barbaric**, you strongly disapprove of it because you think that it is extremely cruel or uncivilized. [DISAPPROVAL] ❑ *This barbaric treatment of animals has no place in any decent society.*

형용사 야만적인 [탐탁잖음] ❑ 동물에 대한 이런 야만적인 대우는 제대로 된 사회에서는 결코 있을 수 없다.

bar|ba|rism /bɑrbərɪzəm/ N-UNCOUNT If you refer to someone's behavior as **barbarism**, you strongly disapprove of it because you think that it is extremely cruel or uncivilized. [DISAPPROVAL] ❑ *We do not ask for the death penalty: barbarism must not be met with barbarism.*

불가산명사 야만, 미개 [탐탁잖음] ❑ 우리는 사형을 요구하지 않는다. 야만을 야만으로 다스려서는 안 된다.

bar|be|cue /bɑrbɪkyu/ (**barbecues, barbecuing, barbecued**) [AM also **barbeque, Bar-B-Q**] ① N-COUNT A **barbecue** is a piece of equipment which you use for cooking on in the open air. ② N-COUNT If someone has a **barbecue**, they cook food on a barbecue in the open air. ❑ *On New Year's Eve we had a barbecue on the beach.* ③ V-T If you **barbecue** food, especially meat, you cook it on a barbecue. ❑ *Tuna can be grilled, fried or barbecued.* ❑ *Here's a way of barbecuing corn-on-the-cob that I learned in the States.* →see **cook**

[미국영어 barbeque, BAR-B-Q] ① 가산명사 야외 바비큐용 기구 ② 가산명사 야외 바비큐 파티 ❑ 새해 전날 우리는 해변에서 바비큐 파티를 벌였다. ③ 타동사/자동사 바비큐 하다 ❑ 참치는 석쇠에 굽거나, 기름에 튀기거나, 바비큐로 할 수도 있다. ❑ 이것이 내가 미국에서 배운 통옥수수를 바비큐 하는 방법이다.

A **barbecue** is a popular style of cooking during the summer. Meat with a spicy sauce is cooked on a metal grill over an open fire. Some food may not be spiced, such as hamburgers, hot dogs, or corn on the cob, and this is cooked over the fire as well. North Americans may also call this event a **cookout**. In South Africa a barbecue is called a **braai** (pronounced like the word "cry"), and is a very common social or family gathering.

barbecue(바비큐)는 여름에 많이 즐기는 요리법이다. 양념을 한 고기를 바로 불 위에 석쇠를 얹어 굽는다. 양념을 하지 않은 햄버거, 핫도그, 통옥수수와 같은 음식도 바로 불 위에 대고 굽는다. 북미에서는 이것을 cookout이라고도 한다. 남아프리카 공화국에서는 braai(cry처럼 발음됨)라고 하며 가족 또는 친목 모임에서 즐겨 한다.

barbed wire /bɑrbd waɪər/ N-UNCOUNT **Barbed wire** is strong wire with sharp points sticking out of it, and is used to make fences. ❑ *The factory was surrounded by barbed wire.*

불가산명사 가시철사 ❑ 그 공장 주위에는 가시철사가 둘러쳐져 있었다.

bar|ber /bɑrbər/ (**barbers**) ① N-COUNT A **barber** is a man whose job is cutting men's hair. ❑ *My father marched me over to Otto, the local barber, to have my hair cut short.* ② N-SING A **barber's** is a store where a barber works. [mainly BRIT; AM usually **barber shop**] ❑ *My Mum took me to the barber's.*

① 가산명사 이발사 ❑ 우리 아버지가 내 머리를 짧게 자르려고 나를 동네 이발사 오토에게 끌고 갔다. ② 단수명사 이발소 [주로 영국영어; 미국영어 대개 barber shop] ❑ 엄마가 나를 이발소에 데려갔다.

bar chart (**bar charts**) N-COUNT A **bar chart** is the same as a **bar graph**. [mainly BRIT; AM usually **bar graph**] ❑ *The bar chart below shows the huge growth of UK car exports over the past few years.*

가산명사 막대그래프 [주로 영국영어; 미국영어 대개 bar graph] ❑ 아래의 막대그래프는 영국의 자동차 수출이 지난 수년간에 걸쳐 매우 크게 성장했음을 보여준다.

bar code (**bar codes**) also **barcode** N-COUNT A **bar code** is an arrangement of numbers and parallel lines that is printed on products to be sold in shops. The bar code can be read by computers. →see **laser**

가산명사 바코드

bare ◇◇◇ /beər/ (**barer, barest, bares, baring, bared**) ① ADJ If a part of your body is **bare**, it is not covered by any clothing. ❑ *She was wearing only a thin robe over a flimsy nightdress, and her feet were bare.* ② ADJ A **bare** surface is not covered or decorated with anything. ❑ *They would have liked bare wooden floors throughout the house.* ③ ADJ If a tree or a branch is **bare**, it has no leaves on it. ❑ *...an old, twisted tree, its bark shaggy, many of its limbs brittle and bare.* ④ ADJ If a room, cupboard, or shelf is **bare**, it is empty. ❑ *His fridge was bare apart from three very withered tomatoes.* ⑤ ADJ An area of ground that is **bare** has no plants growing on it. ❑ *That's probably the most bare, bleak, barren and inhospitable island I've ever seen.* ⑥ ADJ If someone gives you the **bare** facts or the **barest** details of something, they tell you only the most basic and important things. [det ADJ] ❑ *Newspaper reporters were given nothing but the bare facts by the Superintendent in charge of the investigation.* ⑦ ADJ If you talk about the **bare** minimum or the **bare** essentials, you mean the very least that is necessary. [det ADJ] ❑ *The army would try to hold the western desert with a bare minimum of forces.* ⑧ ADJ **Bare** is used in front of an amount to emphasize how small it is. [EMPHASIS] [a ADJ amount] ❑ *Sales are growing for premium wines, but at a bare 2 percent a year.* ⑨ V-T If you **bare** something, you uncover it and show it. [WRITTEN] ❑ *Walsh bared his teeth in a grin.* ⑩ **bare bones** →see **bone** ⑪ PHRASE If someone does something **with their**

① 형용사 벌거벗은 ❑ 그녀는 아주 얇은 잠옷 위에 얇은 가운만 걸치고 있었고 맨발이었다. ② 형용사 가리지 않은; 꾸미지 않은 ❑ 그들은 집 전체의 마룻바닥이 그냥 나무로만 되어 있는 것을 좋아했을 것이다. ③ 형용사 잎이 없는 ❑ 껍질은 우둘투둘하고 가지는 바삭바삭하고 잎이 없는, 늙고 뒤틀린 나무 ④ 형용사 텅 빈, 횅댕그렁한 ❑ 그의 냉장고는 아주 시든 토마토 세 개를 제외하고는 텅 비어 있었다. ⑤ 형용사 불모의 ❑ 저 섬은 아마도 내가 지금껏 본 중에서 가장 척박하고 황폐하며 메마르고 황량한 섬일 것이다. ⑥ 형용사 사실 그대로의, 가장 기본적인 ❑ 신문 기자들은 조사를 담당하고 있는 총경으로부터 가장 기본적인 사실 외에는 아무것도 전해 받지 못했다. ⑦ 형용사 그저-뿐인 ❑ 군대는 그저 최소한의 병력만으로 서부 사막 방어를 시도하고자 했다. ⑧ 형용사 겨우-한 [강조] ❑ 고급 와인 판매가 증가하고 있지만, 증가율은 겨우 일 년에 2퍼센트에 불과하다. ⑨ 타동사 드러내다 [문어체] ❑ 월시는 이빨을 드러내며 씩 웃었다. ⑪ 구 맨손으로 ❑ 경찰은

① 전치사 —을 제외하고 [주로 영국영어] ❑ 1989년의 한 번의 안정기를 제외하고, 1980년대 중반 이래로 축 물가가 상승해 왔다. ⑫ 고유명사 변호사업; 법조계 [영국영어 Bar] ❑ 법학대학원 졸업생의 4분의 1도 안 되는 숫자가 첫 도전에 변호사 시험에 합격한다. ⑬ 가산명사 마디; 세로줄 [주로 영국영어; 미국영어 measure] ❑ 그녀는 피아노 앞에 앉더니 쇼팽의 폴로네즈 몇 마디를 연주했다.

bare hands, they do it without using any weapons or tools. ◻ *Police believe the killer punched her to death with his bare hands.*

살인자가 그녀를 맨손으로 때려죽였다고 믿는다.

Thesaurus	*bare*의 참조어
ADJ.	naked, nude, undressed; *(ant.)* clothed, dressed **1**
	arid, barren, bleak; *(ant.)* lush **5**
V.	disclose, expose, reveal, show; *(ant.)* cover, hide **9**

bare|foot /bɛərfʊt/ also **barefooted** ADJ Someone who is **barefoot** or **barefooted** is not wearing anything on their feet. [v-link ADJ, ADJ after v, ADJ n] ◻ *I wore a white dress and was barefoot.*

형용사 맨발의 ◻ 나는 흰 드레스에 맨발 차림이었다.

bare|ly ♦◇◇ /bɛərli/ **1** ADV You use **barely** to say that something is only just true or only just the case. ◻ *Anastasia could barely remember the ride to the hospital.* ◻ *It was 90 degrees and the air conditioning barely cooled the room.* **2** ADV If you say that one thing had **barely** happened when something else happened, you mean that the first event was followed immediately by the second. [ADV before v] ◻ *The water had barely come to a simmer when she cracked four eggs into it.*

1 부사 가까스로, 겨우 ◻ 아나스타샤는 겨우 병원까지 실려 간 것만 기억했다. ◻ 기온이 90도까지 올라가서, 냉방 장치가 그 방 안을 간신히 식혀 주는 정도였다. **2** 부사 ―하자마자 ◻ 물이 끓자마자 그녀는 계란 네 개를 깨 넣었다.

bar|gain ♦◇◇ /bɑːrgɪn/ (**bargains, bargaining, bargained**) **1** N-COUNT Something that is a **bargain** is good value for money, usually because it has been sold at a lower price than normal. ◻ *At this price the wine is a bargain.* **2** N-COUNT A **bargain** is an agreement, especially a formal business agreement, in which two people or groups agree what each of them will do, pay, or receive. ◻ *I'll make a bargain with you. I'll play hostess if you'll include Matthew in your guest-list.* **3** V-I When people **bargain with** each other, they discuss what each of them will do, pay, or receive. ◻ *They prefer to bargain with individual clients, for cash.* ● **bar|gain|ing** N-UNCOUNT ◻ *The government has called for sensible pay bargaining.* **4** PHRASE You use **into the bargain** when mentioning an additional quantity, feature, fact, or action, to emphasize the fact that it is also involved. You can also say **in the bargain** in American English. [EMPHASIS] ◻ *This machine is designed to save you effort, and keep your work surfaces tidy into the bargain.*

1 가산명사 싸게 삼 ◻ 이 가격이면 그 와인을 싸게 사시는 겁니다. **2** 가산명사 거래, 계약 ◻ 당신과 거래를 하겠어요.. 당신이 손님 명부에 매슈를 올려 주면 제가 여주인 역할을 하도록 하지요. **3** 자동사 거래하다; 흥정을 하다 ◻ 그들은 개인 고객과 현찰로 거래하는 것을 선호한다. ● 거래, 교섭 불가산명사 ◻ 정부는 분별 있는 임금 교섭을 요청해 왔다. **4** 게다가 [강조] ◻ 이 기계는 당신의 수고를 덜어 주고, 게다가 당신의 작품 표면을 매끈하게 해 주도록 고안되었습니다.

Thesaurus	*bargain*의 참조어
N.	deal, discount **1**
	agreement, deal, understanding **2**
V.	barter, haggle, negotiate **3**

Word Partnership	*bargain*의 연어
V.	**find/get a** bargain **1**
	make/strike a bargain **2**
N.	bargain **price**, bargain **rate 1**
	part of the bargain **2**
PREP.	bargain **with *someone* 3**

▶**bargain for** or **bargain on** PHRASAL VERB If you have not **bargained for** or **bargained on** something that happens, you did not expect it to happen and so feel surprised or worried by it. ◻ *The effects of this policy were more than the government had bargained for.*

구동사 기대하다 ◻ 이 정책의 효과는 정부가 기대했던 것 이상이었다.

barge /bɑːrdʒ/ (**barges, barging, barged**) **1** N-COUNT A **barge** is a long, narrow boat with a flat bottom. Barges are used for carrying heavy loads, especially on canals. ◻ *Carrying goods by train costs nearly three times more than carrying them by barge.* **2** V-I If you **barge into** a place or **barge through** it, you rush or push into it in a rough and rude way. [INFORMAL] ◻ *Students tried to barge into the secretariat buildings.* **3** V-I If you **barge into** someone or **barge past** them, you bump against them roughly and rudely. [INFORMAL] ◻ *He would barge into them and kick them in the shins.* →see **ship**

1 가산명사 거룻배, 마지선 ◻ 열차로 상품을 수송하는 것은 거룻배로 수송하는 것보다 거의 세 배의 비용이 든다. **2** 자동사 난입하다 [비격식체] ◻ 학생들은 서 사무처 공관에 난입하려고 시도했다. **3** 자동사 난폭하게 부딪치다 [비격식체] ◻ 그는 그들에게 난폭하게 부딪치고 정강이를 차곤 했다.

▶**barge in** PHRASAL VERB If you **barge in** or **barge in on** someone, you rudely interrupt what they are doing or saying. [INFORMAL] ◻ *I'm sorry to barge in like this, but I have a problem I hope you can solve.*

구동사 끼어들다 [비격식체] ◻ 이렇게 끼어들어서 미안하지만, 네가 해결해 줬으면 하는 문제가 있어.

bar graph (**bar graphs**) N-COUNT A **bar graph** is a graph which uses parallel rectangular shapes to represent changes in the size, value, or rate of something or to compare the amount of something relating to a number of different countries or groups. [mainly AM; BRIT usually **bar chart**] ◻ *They made a bar graph to display the results.* →see **graph**

가산명사 막대그래프 [주로 미국영어; 영국영어 대개 bar chart] ◻ 그들은 결과를 보여주려고 막대그래프를 그렸다.

bari|tone /bærɪtoʊn/ (**baritones**) N-COUNT In music, a **baritone** is a man with a fairly deep singing voice that is lower than that of a tenor but higher than that of a bass. ◻ *...the young American baritone Monte Pederson.*

가산명사 바리톤 ◻ 젊은 미국인 바리톤 가수 몬테 페더슨

bark /bɑːrk/ (**barks, barking, barked**) **1** V-I When a dog **barks**, it makes a short, loud noise, once or several times. ◻ *Don't let the dogs bark.* ● N-COUNT **Bark** is also a noun. ◻ *The Doberman let out a string of roaring barks.* **2** V-I If you **bark at** someone, you shout at them aggressively in a loud, rough voice. ◻ *I didn't mean to bark at you.* **3** N-UNCOUNT **Bark** is the tough material that covers the outside of a tree. **4** to **be barking up the wrong tree** →see **tree**

1 자동사 짖다 ◻ 개를 짖지 못하게 해라. ● 가산명사 짖는 소리 ◻ 그 도베르만은 길게 포효하며 울부짖었다. **2** 타동사/자동사 고함치다 ◻ 네게 고함치려는 생각은 없었어. **3** 불가산명사 나무 껍질

bar|ley /bɑːrli/ N-UNCOUNT **Barley** is a grain that is used to make food, beer, and whisky. ◻ *...fields of ripening wheat and barley.*

불가산명사 보리 ◻ 밀과 보리가 익어 가는 들판

bar|maid /bɑːrmeɪd/ (**barmaids**) N-COUNT A **barmaid** is a woman who serves drinks behind a bar. [mainly BRIT; AM **bartender**]

가산명사 바 여급, 여자 바텐더 [주로 영국영어; 미국영어 bartender]

bar|man /bɑːrmən/ (**barmen**) N-COUNT A **barman** is a man who serves drinks behind a bar. [mainly BRIT; AM **bartender**]

가산명사 바텐더 [주로 영국영어; 미국영어 bartender]

barn /bɑrn/ (**barns**) N-COUNT A **barn** is a building on a farm in which animals, animal food, or crops can be kept. →see Picture Dictionary: barn

가산명사 헛간

ba|rom|eter /bərɒmɪtər/ (**barometers**) **1** N-COUNT A **barometer** is an instrument that measures air pressure and shows when the weather is changing. ❑ *A man in camp took a barometer reading at half-hour intervals.* **2** N-COUNT If something is a **barometer of** a particular situation, it indicates how things are changing or how things are likely to develop. ❑ *In past presidential elections, Missouri has been a barometer of the rest of the country.*

1 가산명사 기압계 ❑ 야영지에 있는 어떤 사람이 30분 간격으로 측정되는 기압계를 가져갔다. **2** 가산명사 지표, 척도 ❑ 과거의 대통령 선거에서, 미주리 주는 미국 내 나머지 지역들의 척도가 되어 왔다.

bar|on /bærən/ (**barons**) **1** N-COUNT; N-TITLE A **baron** is a man who is a member of the lowest rank of the nobility. [BRIT] ❑ *...their stepfather, Baron Michael Distemple.* **2** N-COUNT You can use **baron** to refer to someone who controls a large amount of a particular industry or activity and who is therefore extremely powerful. ❑ *...the battle against the drug barons.*

1 가산명사; 경칭명사 남작 [영국영어] ❑ 그들의 의붓아버지인 마이클 디스템플 남작 **2** 가산명사 대실업가; 거물 ❑ 마약 왕들과의 전투

bar|on|ess /bærənɛs/ (**baronesses**) N-COUNT; N-TITLE A **baroness** is a woman who is a member of the lowest rank of the nobility, or who is the wife of a baron. [BRIT] ❑ *...Baroness Blatch.*

가산명사; 경칭명사 남작 부인; 여남작 [영국영어] ❑ 블래치 남작 부인

bar|rage /bərɑʒ, BRIT bærɑːʒ/ (**barrages, barraging, barraged**)

Pronounced /bɑrɪdʒ/ for meaning **4** in American English.

미국 영어에서는 **4**의 의미일 때는 /bɑrɪdʒ/로 발음된다.

1 N-COUNT A **barrage** is continuous firing on an area with large guns and tanks. ❑ *The artillery barrage on the city center was the heaviest since the ceasefire.* **2** N-COUNT A **barrage of** something such as criticism or complaints is a large number of them directed at someone, often in an aggressive way. ❑ *He was faced with a barrage of angry questions from the floor.* **3** V-T If you **are barraged** by people or things, you have to deal with a great number of people or things you would rather avoid. [usu passive] ❑ *Doctors are complaining about being barraged by drug-company salesmen.* **4** N-COUNT A **barrage** is a structure that is built across a river to control the level of the water. ❑ *...a hydro-electric tidal barrage.*

1 가산명사 집중 사격, 탄막 ❑ 도시 중심부에 퍼부어진 포병대의 집중 사격은 정전 이후 가장 강력한 것이었다. **2** 가산명사 집중 공격 ❑ 의원석으로부터 그에게 성난 질문 공세가 쏟아졌다. **3** 타동사 -의 집중 공격을 받다 ❑ 의사들은 제약 회사 외판원들의 집중 공격에 대해 불평을 털어놓고 있다. **4** 가산명사 댐 ❑ 조력 발전 댐

bar|rel ♦◇◇ /bærəl/ (**barrels, barreling, barreled**) [BRIT, sometimes AM **barrelling, barrelled**] **1** N-COUNT A **barrel** is a large, round container for liquids or food. ❑ *The wine is aged for almost a year in oak barrels.* **2** N-COUNT In the oil industry, a **barrel** is a unit of measurement equal to 42 gallons (159 litres). ❑ *In 1989, Kuwait was exporting 1.5 million barrels of oil a day.* **3** N-COUNT The **barrel** of a gun is the tube through which the bullet moves when the gun is fired. ❑ *He pushed the barrel of the gun into the other man's open mouth.* **4** V-I If a vehicle or person **is barreling** in a particular direction, they are moving very quickly in that direction. [mainly AM] ❑ *The car was barreling down the street at a crazy speed.* **5** PHRASE If you say, for example, that someone moves or buys something **lock, stock, and barrel**, you are emphasizing that they move or buy every part or item of it. [EMPHASIS] ❑ *They dug up their New Jersey garden and moved it lock, stock, and barrel back home.*

[영국영어, 미국영어 가끔 barrelling] **1** 가산명사 통 ❑ 그 와인은 참나무통에 담겨 일 년 가까이 숙성되었다. **2** 가산명사 (159 리터에 해당하는 원유 계량 단위) 배럴 ❑ 1989년에 쿠웨이트는 하루에 원유 1백 5십만 배럴을 수출했다. **3** 가산명사 총열, 총신 ❑ 그는 다른 사내의 벌린 입 속에 총신을 밀어넣었다. **4** 자동사 -의 집중 공격을 받다 [주로 미국영어] ❑ 그 차는 미친 듯이 빠르게 차도를 질주해 내려가고 있었다. **5** 구 완전히, 모조리 [강조] ❑ 그들은 뉴저지의 정원을 파내서 모조리 집으로 옮겨왔다.

Word Partnership	barrel의 연어
N.	**wine** barrel **1**
	barrel **of oil 2**
	barrel **of a gun 3**
PREP.	barrel **down toward** *somewhere* **4**

Picture Dictionary   **barn**

barn
hay
pasture
orchard
greenhouse
livestock
plow
tractor

bar|ren /bǽrən/ ■ ADJ A **barren** landscape is dry and bare, and has very few plants and no trees. □ ...the Tibetan landscape of high barren mountains. ② ADJ **Barren** land consists of soil that is so poor that plants cannot grow in it. □ He also wants to use the water to irrigate barren desert land. ③ ADJ If you describe something such as an activity or a period of your life as **barren**, you mean that you achieve no success during it or that it has no useful results. [WRITTEN] □ ...an empty exercise barren of utility. ④ ADJ If you describe a room or a place as **barren**, you do not like it because it has almost no furniture or other objects in it. [WRITTEN, DISAPPROVAL] □ The room was austere, nearly barren of furniture or decoration.

■ 형용사 불모의, 메마른 □ 높은 불모의 산들이 펼쳐진 티베트의 경관 ② 형용사 척박한 □ 그 역시 그 물을 이용하여 척박한 황무지에 물을 대기를 원한다. ③ 형용사 무익한, 헛된 [문예체] □ 쓸모없는 헛된 훈련 ④ 형용사 휑뎅그렁한 [문예체, 탐탁찮음] □ 그 방은 간소하고, 가구나 장식이 거의 없이 휑뎅그렁하였다.

Thesaurus   barren의 참조어

ADJ.   desolate, empty, infertile, sparse, sterile; (ant.) fertile, lush, rich ■ ②

---

bar|ri|cade /bǽrɪkeɪd, BRIT bǽrɪkeɪd/ (**barricades, barricading, barricaded**) ■ N-COUNT A **barricade** is a line of vehicles or other objects placed across a road or open space to stop people getting past, for example during street fighting or as a protest. □ Large areas of the city have been closed off by barricades set up by the demonstrators. ② V-T If you **barricade** something such as a road or an entrance, you place a barricade or barrier across it, usually to stop someone getting in. □ The rioters barricaded streets with piles of blazing tyres. ③ V-T If you **barricade** yourself inside a room or building, you place barriers across the door or entrance so that other people cannot get in. □ The students have barricaded themselves into their dormitory building.

■ 가산명사 바리케이드 □ 도시 내 광범위한 지역들이 시위자들이 세운 바리케이드에 의해 통행이 차단되어 왔다. ② 타동사 -에 바리케이드를 치다 □ 폭도들은 타이어 더미에 불을 붙여 도로에 바리케이드를 쳤다. ③ 타동사 점거하여 입구를 봉쇄하다 □ 학생들은 기숙사 건물을 점거하고 입구를 봉쇄해 왔다.

bar|ri|er ♦◇◇ /bǽriər/ (**barriers**) ■ N-COUNT A **barrier** is something such as a rule, law, or policy that makes it difficult or impossible for something to happen or be achieved. □ Duties and taxes are the most obvious barrier to free trade. ② N-COUNT A **barrier** is a problem that prevents two people or groups from agreeing, communicating, or working with each other. □ There is no reason why love shouldn't cross the age barrier. □ She had been waiting for Simon to break down the barrier between them. ③ N-COUNT A **barrier** is something such as a fence or wall that is put in place to prevent people from moving easily from one area to another. □ The demonstrators broke through heavy police barriers. ④ N-COUNT A **barrier** is an object or layer that physically prevents something from moving from one place to another. □ ...a severe storm, which destroyed a natural barrier between the house and the lake. ⑤ N-SING You can refer to a particular number or amount as a **barrier** when you think it is significant, because it is difficult or unusual to go above it. □ They are fearful that unemployment will soon break the barrier of three million.

■ 가산명사 장애, 방해 □ 관세와 세금은 자유 무역의 가장 명백한 장애 요인이다. ② 가산명사 장벽 □ 사랑이 나이의 장벽을 넘어설 수는 없다. □ 그녀는 사이먼이 그들 사이의 장벽을 허물기를 기다려 왔다. ③ 가산명사 장벽 □ 시위자들은 두터운 경찰 저지선을 돌파했다. ④ 가산명사 장애물; 방벽 □ 집과 호수 사이의 자연 방벽을 파괴한, 격심한 폭풍 ⑤ 단수명사 관문 □ 그들은 실업자 수가 곧 3백만 관문을 돌파할 것을 두려워하고 있다.

Word Partnership   barrier의 연어

ADJ.   **psychological** barrier, **racial** barrier ②
N.   **language** barrier ②
     police barrier ③
PREP.   barrier **between** ② ③ ④
V.   **break down** a barrier, **cross a** barrier ② ③ ④

---

bar|ring /bɑ́rɪŋ/ PREP You use **barring** to indicate that the person, thing, or event that you are mentioning is an exception to your statement. □ Barring accidents, I believe they will succeed.

전치사 -이 없다면, -을 제외하고는 □ 사고만 없다면 그들이 성공하리라고 나는 믿는다.

bar|ris|ter /bǽrɪstər/ (**barristers**) N-COUNT In England and Wales, a **barrister** is a lawyer who represents clients in the higher courts of law. Compare **solicitor**. →see **lawyer**

가산명사 법정 변호사

bar|room /bɑ́rum/ (**barrooms**) also bar-room N-COUNT A **barroom** is a room or building in which alcoholic drinks are served over a counter. [mainly AM; BRIT usually **bar, pub**] □ ...a barroom brawl.

가산명사 바 [주로 미국영어; 영국영어 대개 bar, pub] □ 바에서 벌어지는 떠들썩한 싸움

bar|tender /bɑ́rtɛndər/ (**bartenders**) N-COUNT A **bartender** is a person who serves drinks behind a bar. [AM; BRIT **barman, barmaid**]

가산명사 바텐더 [미국영어; 영국영어 barman, barmaid]

bar|ter /bɑ́rtər/ (**barters, bartering, bartered**) V-T/V-I If you **barter** goods, you exchange them for other goods, rather than selling them for money. □ They have been bartering wheat for cotton and timber. □ The market-place and street were crowded with those who'd come to barter. ● N-UNCOUNT **Barter** is also a noun. □ Overall, barter is a very inefficient means of organizing transactions. →see **money**

타동사/자동사 물물교환하다, 교역하다 □ 그들은 밀을 면화와 목재로 교환해 왔다. □ 장터와 거리는 물물교환하러 온 사람들로 붐볐다. ● 불가산명사 물물 교환, 교역 □ 전반적으로, 물물 교환은 매우 비효율적인 상거래 조직 방식이다.

base ♦♦♦ /beɪs/ (**bases, basing, based, baser, basest**) ■ N-COUNT The **base** of something is its lowest edge or part. □ There was a cycle path running along this side of the wall, right at its base. ② N-COUNT The **base** of something is the lowest part of it, where it is attached to something else. □ The surgeon placed catheters through the veins and arteries near the base of the head. ③ N-COUNT The **base** of an object such as a box or vase is the lower surface of it that touches the surface it rests on. □ Remove from the heat and plunge the base of the pan into a bowl of very cold water. ④ N-COUNT The **base** of an object that has several sections and that rests on a surface is the lower section of it. □ The mattress is best on a solid bed base. ⑤ N-COUNT A **base** is a layer of something which will have another layer added to it. □ Spoon the mixture on to the biscuit base and cook in a pre-heated oven. ⑥ N-COUNT A position or thing that is a **base** for something is one from which that thing can be developed or achieved. □ The post will give him a powerful political base from which to challenge the Kremlin. ⑦ V-T If you **base** one thing **on** another thing, the first thing develops from the second thing. □ He based his

■ 가산명사 맨 아래 부분 □ 담의 이쪽 편을 따라 바로 그 맨 아래 부분에 자전거 길이 있었다. ② 가산명사 맨 아래 부분 □ 의사는 머리와 목이 닿는 부분 근처의 정맥과 동맥 사이에 도관을 꽂았다. ③ 가산명사 바닥 □ 냄비를 불 위에서 들어내서 아주 찬 물이 담긴 그릇에 바닥을 담그세요. ④ 가산명사 받침 부위 □ 그 매트리스는 받침대가 딱딱한 침대에 최고로 좋습니다. ⑤ 가산명사 층, 켜 □ 섞은 재료를 숟갈로 떠서 비스킷 위에 얇은 다음 미리 가열된 오븐에 넣고 구우세요. ⑥ 가산명사 기초; 토대 □ 그 직위를 통해 그는 크렘린에 도전하기 위한 유력한 정치적 토대를 확보할 것이다. ⑦ 타동사 -의 근거를 두다 □ 그는 붙잡힌 죄수들이 내놓은 증언에 근거하여 자신의 결론을 내렸다. ● 기초를 둔 형용사 □ 신상품 중 세 가지가 한약을 기초로 하여 만들어진 것입니다. ⑧ 가산명사

conclusions on the evidence given by the captured prisoners. ● **based** ADJ [v-link ADJ on/upon n] ❑ *Three of the new products are based on traditional herbal medicines.* **⑧** N-COUNT A company's client **base** or customer **base** is the group of regular clients or customers that the company gets most of its income from. [BUSINESS] ❑ *The company has been expanding its customer base using trade magazine advertising.* **⑨** N-COUNT A military **base** is a place which part of the armed forces works from. ❑ *Gunfire was heard at an army base close to the airport.* **⑩** N-COUNT Your **base** is the main place where you work, stay, or live. ❑ *For most of the spring and early summer her base was her home in Scotland.* **⑪** N-COUNT If a place is a **base** for a certain activity, the activity can be carried out at that place or from that place. ❑ *The two hotel-restaurants are attractive bases from which to explore southeast Tuscany.* **⑫** N-COUNT The **base** of a substance such as paint or food is the main ingredient of it, to which other substances can be added. ❑ *Just before cooking, drain off any excess marinade and use it as a base for a pouring sauce.* **⑬** N-COUNT A **base** is a system of counting and expressing numbers. The decimal system uses base 10, and the binary system uses base 2. [also N num] **⑭** N-COUNT A **base** in baseball or softball is one of the places at each corner of the diamond on the field. ❑ *The first runner to reach second base in the game was John Flaherty.* →see **area**

Word Partnership　　　base의 연어

N.	**knowledge** base, **tax** base **⑥**
	client/customer base, **fan** base **⑧**
	base **camp**, **home** base, base **of operation** **⑩ ⑪**
ADJ	**military/naval** base **⑨**
	stolen base **⑭**

---

base|ball ♦♢♢ /beɪsbɔl/ (**baseballs**) **①** N-UNCOUNT **Baseball** is a game played by two teams of nine players. Each player from one team hits a ball with a bat and then tries to run around three bases and get to home plate before the other team can get the ball back. **②** N-COUNT A **baseball** is a small hard ball which is used in the game of baseball. →see **park**

> Although it isn't the most watched sport anymore, **baseball** is still called "America's Pastime." A player who wants to reach his goal usually dreams of playing in the Major League and winning the World Series.

based ♦♦♦ /beɪst/ ADJ If you are **based** in a particular place, that is the place where you live or do most of your work. See also **base**. [v-link ADJ] ❑ *Both firms are based in Kent.*

base|ment /beɪsmənt/ (**basements**) N-COUNT The **basement** of a building is a floor built partly or completely below ground level. ❑ *They bought an old schoolhouse to live in and built a workshop in the basement.* →see **house**

base rate (**base rates**) N-COUNT In Britain, the **base rate** is the rate of interest that banks use as a basis when they are calculating the rates that they charge on loans. [BUSINESS] ❑ *Bank base rates of 7 percent are too high.*

bases

> Pronounced /beɪsɪz/ for meaning **①**. Pronounced /beɪsiz/ and hyphenated ba|ses for meaning **②**.

① **Bases** is the plural of **base**. **②** **Bases** is the plural of **basis**.

bash /bæʃ/ (**bashes**, **bashing**, **bashed**) **①** N-COUNT A **bash** is a party or celebration, especially a large one held by an official organization or attended by famous people. [INFORMAL] ❑ *He threw one of the biggest showbiz bashes of the year as a 36th birthday party for Jerry Hall.* **②** V-T If someone **bashes** you, they attack you by hitting or punching you hard. [INFORMAL] ❑ *If someone tried to bash my best friend they would have to bash me as well.* ❑ *I bashed him on the head and dumped him in the cold, cold water.* **③** V-T If you **bash** something, you hit it hard in a rough or careless way. [INFORMAL] ❑ *Too many golfers try to bash the ball out of sand. That spells disaster.*

ba|sic ♦♦♢ /beɪsɪk/ **①** ADJ You use **basic** to describe things, activities, and principles that are very important or necessary, and on which others depend. ❑ *...the basic skills of reading, writing, and communicating.* ❑ *Access to justice is a basic right.* **②** ADJ **Basic** goods and services are very simple ones which every human being needs. You can also refer to people's **basic** needs for such goods and services. ❑ *...shortages of even the most basic foodstuffs.* ❑ *Hospitals lack even basic drugs for surgical operations.* **③** ADJ If one thing is **basic to** another, it is absolutely necessary to it, and the second thing cannot exist, succeed, or be imagined without it. [v-link ADJ to n] ❑ *...an oily liquid, basic to the manufacture of a host of other chemical substances.* **④** ADJ You can use **basic** to emphasize that you are referring to what you consider to be the most important aspect of a situation, and that you are not concerned with less important details. [EMPHASIS] [ADJ n] ❑ *There are three basic types of tea.* ❑ *The basic design changed little from that patented by Edison more than 100 years ago.* **⑤** ADJ You can use **basic** to describe something that is very simple in style and has only the most necessary features, without any luxuries. ❑ *We provide 2-person tents and basic cooking and camping equipment.* **⑥** ADJ **Basic** is used to describe a price or someone's income when this does not include any additional amounts. [ADJ n] ❑ *...an increase of more than twenty percent on the basic pay of a typical worker.* ❑ *The basic retirement pension will go up by £1.95 a week.* **⑦** ADJ The **basic** rate of income tax is the lowest or most common

---

주된 요소 [경제] ❑ 그 회사는 업계 잡지 광고를 활용하여 주 고객층을 확장해 오고 있다. **⑨** 가산명사 기지 ❑ 공항 근처의 육군 기지에서 총격 소리가 들렸다. **⑩** 가산명사 근거지 ❑ 봄부터 초여름까지 대부분의 기간 동안 그녀의 근거지는 스코틀랜드의 자택이었다. **⑪** 가산명사 기지 ❑ 그 2곳의 호텔 레스토랑은 토스카나 동남부 답사를 위한 기지로서 매력적인 장소이다. **⑫** 가산명사 주성분 ❑ 요리하기 직전에, 여분의 양념장을 따라 내어 소스의 주성분으로 쓰시오. **⑬** 가산명사 진법 **⑭** 가산명사 누, 베이스 ❑ 그 경기에서 처음으로 2루를 밟은 주자는 존 플래허티였다.

① 불가산명사 야구 **②** 가산명사 야구공

야구는 이제 더 이상 사람들이 가장 많이 관람하는 운동 경기가 아니지만 여전히 '미국의 취미'라고 불린다. 야구 선수들은 대개 메이저 리그에서 뛰고 월드 시리즈에서 우승하게 되길 꿈꾼다.

형용사 근거를 둔 ❑ 두 회사 모두 켄트에 근거를 두고 있다.

가산명사 지하층 ❑ 그들은 들어가 살 집으로 오래된 교사를 사들여 지하층에 작업장을 꾸몄다.

가산명사 기본 금리 [경제] ❑ 은행 기본 금리로 7퍼센트는 너무 높다.

①의 의미일 때는 /beɪsɪz/로 발음된다. **②**의 의미일 때는 /beɪsiz/로 발음되고, balses로 분철된다.

① base의 복수형 **②** basis의 복수형

① 가산명사 성대한 파티 [비격식체] ❑ 그는 제리 홀의 36번째 생일 파티로 그 해 가장 성대한 연예계 파티 중 하나를 열었다. **②** 타동사 후려갈기다 [비격식체] ❑ 만약 누가 내 가장 친한 친구를 두들겨 패려면, 그 사람은 나 또한 두들겨 패야 할 것이다. ❑ 나는 그의 머리를 후려갈긴 다음 차디찬 물 속에 던져 넣었다. **③** 타동사/자동사 강타하다 [비격식체] ❑ 아주 많은 골퍼들이 모래에 묻힌 공을 세게 쳐내려 한다. 이는 큰 실패를 가져온다.

① 형용사 기본적인 ❑ 읽고, 쓰고, 의사 소통하는 기본적 기술 ❑ 사법 접근권은 기본권이다. **②** 형용사 기초적인 ❑ 심지어 가장 기초적인 식료품까지 부족함 ❑ 병원들에는 외과 수술에 필요한 기초 약품조차 없다. **③** 형용사 필수적인 ❑ 다른 많은 화학 물질의 제조에 필수적인 유성 액체 **④** 형용사 주요한, 주된 [강조] ❑ 차의 주요 종류로 세 가지가 있다. ❑ 주된 설계는 100년 전에 에디슨이 특허를 낸 것에서 거의 바뀌지 않았다. **⑤** 형용사 기본적인, 간단한 ❑ 2인용 텐트와 간단한 취사 용품 및 야영 장비가 제공됩니다. **⑥** 형용사 기본적인 ❑ 보통 노동자 기본급의 20퍼센트 이상 인상 ❑ 기본 퇴직 연금이 주당 1.95파운드 오를 것이다. **⑦** 형용사 기본적인 (세율) ❑ 이 모든 것은 커다란 증가 없이 기본 과세 수준으로 이루어질 예정이다.

rate, which applies to people who earn average incomes. [ADJ n] ❑ *All this is to be done without big rises in the basic level of taxation.*

Thesaurus   *basic*의 참조어

ADJ.   essential, fundamental, key, main, necessary, principal, vital; *(ant.)* secondary **1**-**4**

Word Partnership   *basic*의 연어

N.   basic **right** **1**
basic **idea**, basic **principles/values**, basic **problem**, basic **questions**, basic **skills**, basic **understanding** **1** **4**
basic **needs** **2**

ADJ.   **most** basic, basic **types of** *something* **1**-**5**

---

ba∙si∙cal∙ly ♦♦◇ /beɪsɪkli/ **1** ADV You use **basically** for emphasis when you are stating an opinion, or when you are making an important statement about something. [EMPHASIS] [ADV with cl/group] ❑ *This gun is designed for one purpose – it's basically to kill people.* **2** ADV You use **basically** to show that you are describing a situation in a simple, general way, and that you are not concerned with less important details. ❑ *Basically you've got two choices.*

ba∙sics /beɪsɪks/ **1** N-PLURAL The **basics** of something are its simplest, most important elements, ideas, or principles, in contrast to more complicated or detailed ones. ❑ *They will concentrate on teaching the basics of reading, writing, and arithmetic.* ❑ *A strong community cannot be built until the basics are in place.* **2** N-PLURAL **Basics** are things such as simple food, clothes, or equipment that people need in order to live or to deal with a particular situation. ❑ *...supplies of basics such as bread and milk.*

ba∙sin /beɪsⁿn/ (basins) **1** N-COUNT A **basin** is a large or deep bowl that you use for holding liquids. ❑ *Water dripped into a basin at the back of the room.* ● N-COUNT A **basin of** something such as water is an amount of it that is contained in a basin. ❑ *We were given a basin of water to wash our hands in.* **2** N-COUNT A **basin** is a sink. ❑ *...a cast-iron bath with a matching basin.* **3** N-COUNT The **basin** of a large river is the area of land around it from which streams run down into it. ❑ *...the Amazon basin.* **4** N-COUNT In geography, a **basin** is a particular region of the world where the earth's surface is lower than in other places. [TECHNICAL] ❑ *...countries around the Pacific Basin.* →see **lake, plumbing**

ba∙sis ♦♦◇ /beɪsɪs/ (bases/beɪsiːz/) **1** N-SING If something is done **on** a particular **basis**, it is done according to that method, system, or principle. ❑ *We're going to be meeting there on a regular basis.* ❑ *They want all groups to be treated on an equal basis.* **2** N-SING If you say that you are acting **on the basis of** something, you are giving that as the reason for your action. ❑ *McGregor must remain confined, on the basis of the medical reports we have received.* **3** N-COUNT The **basis** of something is its starting point or an important part of it from which it can be further developed. ❑ *Both factions have broadly agreed that the UN plan is a possible basis for negotiation.* **4** N-COUNT The **basis** for something is a fact or argument that you can use to prove or justify it. ❑ *...Japan's attempt to secure the legal basis to send troops overseas.*

Word Partnership   *basis*의 연어

ADJ.   **equal** basis, on a **daily/weekly/regular** basis, on a **voluntary** basis **1**

PREP.   **on the** basis of *something* **2**
basis **for** *something* **3** **4**

V.   **serve as a** basis **3** **4**

---

ba∙sis point (basis points) N-COUNT In finance, a **basis point** is one hundredth of a percent (.01%). [BUSINESS] ❑ *The dollar climbed about 30 basis points during the morning session.*

bask /bɑːsk, bæsk/ (basks, basking, basked) **1** V-I If you **bask in** the sunshine, you lie somewhere sunny and enjoy the heat. ❑ *All through the hot, still days of their holiday Amy basked in the sun.* **2** V-I If you **bask in** someone's approval, favor, or admiration, you greatly enjoy their positive reaction toward you. ❑ *He has spent a month basking in the adulation of the fans back in Jamaica.*

bas∙ket /bɑːskɪt, bæs-/ (baskets) **1** N-COUNT A **basket** is a stiff container that is used for carrying or storing objects. Baskets are made from thin strips of materials such as straw, plastic, or wire woven together. ❑ *...big wicker picnic baskets filled with sandwiches.* ● N-COUNT A **basket of** things is a number of things contained in a basket. ❑ *...a small basket of fruit and snacks.* **2** N-COUNT In economics, a **basket of** currencies or goods is the average or total value of a number of different currencies or goods. [BUSINESS] ❑ *The pound's value against a basket of currencies hit a new low of 76.9.*

bas∙ket∙ball /bɑːskɪtbɔːl, bæs-/ (basketballs) **1** N-UNCOUNT **Basketball** is a game in which two teams of five players each try to score goals by throwing a large ball through a circular net fixed to a metal ring at each end of the court. **2** N-COUNT A **basketball** is a large ball which is used in the game of basketball.
→see Picture Dictionary: **basketball**

---

1 부사 기본적으로 [강조] ❑ 이 총은 한 가지 목적을 위해 설계되는데, 기본적으로 인명을 살상하는 것이다. **2** 부사 기본적으로 ❑ 기본적으로 당신에겐 두 가지 선택의 여지가 있다.

1 복수명사 기초, 기본 ❑ 그들은 읽기와 쓰기, 산수 등의 기초 교육에 집중할 것이다. ❑ 기초가 제대로 세워져야만 튼튼한 사회를 건설할 수 있다. **2** 복수명사 필수품 ❑ 빵과 우유 같은 생필품의 공급

1 가산명사 대야; 큰 그릇 ❑ 물이 방 안쪽에 있는 대야에 똑똑 떨어졌다. ● 가산명사 한 대야 가득한 분량 ❑ 우리는 손 씻을 물 한 대야를 받았다. **2** 가산명사 세면대 ❑ 주철 욕조와 그와 짝이 맞는 세면대 **3** 가산명사 유역 ❑ 아마존 강 유역 **4** 가산명사 분지 [과학 기술] ❑ 태평양 연안의 국가들

1 단수명사 기준, 원칙 ❑ 우리는 그곳에서 정기적으로 만날 것이다. ❑ 그들은 모든 집단이 동등한 대우를 받기를 원한다. **2** 단수명사 ~을 근거로 ❑ 우리가 입수한 건강 진단 보고서를 근거로 볼 때, 맥그레거는 계속 외출을 삼가야 한다. **3** 가산명사 토대 ❑ 유엔의 계획이 가능한 협상의 토대라는 것에 양 당파가 대체로 합의를 이루었다. **4** 가산명사 근거 ❑ 해외 파병의 합법적 근거를 확보하려는 일본의 시도

가산명사 (증권) 1/100퍼센트 [경제] ❑ 전장 동안 달러화가 0.3퍼센트 정도 상승했다.

1 자동사 쬐다 ❑ 에이미는 휴가 기간 중의 무덥고 고요한 나날들 내내 햇볕을 쬐었다. **2** 자동사 (은혜 등을) 입다 ❑ 그는 고국 자메이카에 있는 팬들의 찬사를 받으며 한 달을 보냈다.

1 가산명사 바구니 ❑ 샌드위치가 가득 들어 있는, 가는 가지로 엮어 만든 커다란 소풍 바구니 ● 가산명사 한 바구니 분량 ❑ 작은 바구니 하나 분량의 과일과 간단한 음식 **2** 가산명사 평균 가치 [경제] ❑ 평균 통화 가치 대비 파운드화 가치가 76.9로 최저 시세 기록을 갱신했다.

1 불가산명사 농구 **2** 가산명사 농구공

basketball

basketball

sideline

referee

uniform

player

---

bass ♦◇◇ (**basses**)

Pronounced /beɪs/ for meanings ① to ④, and /bæs/ for meaning ⑤. The plural of the noun in meaning ⑤ is **bass**.

① N-COUNT A **bass** is a man with a very deep singing voice. ❏ ...*the great Russian bass Chaliapin.* ② ADJ A **bass** drum, guitar, or other musical instrument is one that produces a very deep sound. [ADJ n] ❏ ...*bass guitarist Dee Murray.* ③ N-VAR In popular music, a **bass** is a bass guitar or a **double bass**. ❏ ...*Dave Ranson on bass and Kenneth Blevins on drums.* ④ N-UNCOUNT On a stereo system or radio, the **bass** is the ability to reproduce the lower musical notes. The **bass** is also the knob which controls this. ❏ ...*larger models which will then give more bass.* ⑤ N-VAR **Bass** are edible fish that are found in rivers and the sea. There are several types of bass. ❏ *They unloaded their catch of cod and bass.* ● N-UNCOUNT **Bass** is a piece of this fish eaten as food. ❏ ...*a large fresh fillet of sea bass.*

bas|ti|on /bæstʃən, BRIT bæstiən/ (**bastions**) N-COUNT If a system or organization is described as a **bastion of** a particular way of life, it is seen as being important and effective in defending that way of life. **Bastion** can be used both when you think that this way of life should be ended and when you think it should be defended. [FORMAL] ❏ ...*a town which had been a bastion of white prejudice.* ❏ ...*a bastion of spiritual freedom.*

bat ♦◇◇ /bæt/ (**bats, batting, batted**) ① N-COUNT A **bat** is a specially shaped piece of wood that is used for hitting the ball in baseball, softball, cricket, or table tennis. ❏ ...*a baseball bat.* ② V-I When you **bat**, you have a turn at hitting the ball with a bat in baseball, softball, or cricket. ❏ *Australia, put in to bat, made a cautious start.* ③ N-COUNT A **bat** is a small flying animal that looks like a mouse with wings made of skin. Bats are active at night. ④ PHRASE If someone does something **off** their **own bat**, they do it without anyone else suggesting it. [BRIT] ❏ *Whatever she did she did off her own bat. Whatever she did was nothing to do with me.* ⑤ PHRASE If something happens **right off the bat**, it happens immediately. [AM] ❏ *He learned right off the bat that you can't count on anything in this business.* →see **flower**
→see Word Web: **bat**

---

①부터 ④까지의 의미일 때는 /beɪs/로, ⑤의 의미일 때는 /bæs/로 발음된다. ⑤의 의미일 때 명사 복수형은 bass이다.

① 가산명사 베이스 가수 ❏ 위대한 러시아 베이스 가수 살리아핀 ② 형용사 저음의, 베이스의 ❏ 베이스 기타리스트 디 머리 ③ 가산명사 또는 불가산명사 베이스 기타 ❏ 베이스에 데이브 랜슨, 드럼에 케네스 블레빈스 ④ 불가산명사 저음의; 저음 조절 손잡이 ❏ 더 풍부한 저음을 내는 대형 모델들 ⑤ 가산명사 또는 불가산명사 베스 (농어의 일종) ❏ 그들은 자기들이 잡은 대구와 농어를 내렸다. ● 불가산명사 베스 요리 ❏ 뼈를 바른 커다랗고 신선한 베스 고기

가산명사 요새 [격식체] ❏ 백인들의 인종적 편견의 요새였던 마을 ❏ 영적 자유의 요새

① 가산명사 베트 ❏ 야구 베트 ② 자동사 타석에 서다; 공격하다 ❏ 공격에 나선 호주는 신중한 출발을 했다. ③ 가산명사 박쥐 ④ 구 자발적으로 [영국영어] ❏ 그녀가 무엇을 하건 그건 그녀가 자발적으로 하는 것이었다. 뭘 하든 나하고는 상관없었다. ⑤ 구 즉시 [미국영어] ❏ 그는 이 사업에서는 어떤 것도 의지할 수 없다는 것을 즉시 깨달았다.

Word Web   bat

Bats fly like birds, but they are **mammals**. Female bats give birth to live young and produce milk. Bats are **nocturnal**, searching for food at night and sleeping during the day. They **roost** upside down in dark, quiet places such as caves and attics. People think that bats drink blood, but only vampire bats do this. Most bats eat fruit or insects. As bats fly they make high-pitched sounds that bounce off objects. This echolocation is a kind of **radar** that guides them.

---

batch /bætʃ/ (batches) N-COUNT A **batch of** things or people is a group of things or people of the same kind, especially a group that is dealt with at the same time or is sent to a particular place at the same time. ❏ ...the current batch of trainee priests. ❏ She brought a large batch of newspaper clippings.

가산명사 한 묶음; 한 때 ❏ 현재의 견습 사제 무리 ❏ 그녀는 신문에서 오려 낸 기사 한 묶음을 가져왔다.

bath ♦◇◇ /bæθ/ (baths, bathing, bathed)

When the form **baths** is the plural of the noun it is pronounced /bæðz/ in American English and /bɑːðz/ or /bæθs/ in British English. When it is used in the present tense of the verb, it is pronounced /bɑːθs/ or /bæθs/.

baths가 명사의 복수형일 때는 미국 영어에서는 /bæðz/로 발음되고, 영국 영어에서는 /bɑːðz/ 나 /bæθs/로 발음된다. 이것이 동사의 현재 시제형일 때에는 /bɑːθs/나 /bæθs/로 발음된다.

1 N-COUNT A **bath** is the process of washing your body in a bathtub. ❏ The midwife gave him a warm bath. **2** N-COUNT When you take a **bath**, or when you are in the **bath**, you sit or lie in a bathtub filled with water in order to wash your body. [BRIT also **have a bath**] ❏ ...if you have a bath every morning. ❏ Take a shower instead of a bath. **3** V-T If you **bath** someone, especially a child, you wash them in a bath. [BRIT; AM **bathe**] ❏ Don't feel you have to bath your child every day. **4** N-COUNT A **bath** is a container, usually a long rectangular one, which you fill with water and sit in while you wash your body. [BRIT; AM **bathtub**] ❏ In those days, only quite wealthy families had baths of their own. **5** V-I When you **bath**, you have a bath. [BRIT; AM **bathe**] ❏ The three children all bath in the same bath water. **6** N-COUNT A **bath** or a **baths** is a public building containing a swimming pool, and sometimes other facilities that people can use to wash or take a bath. ❏ ...a thriving town with houses, government buildings and public baths. **7** N-COUNT A **bath** is a container filled with a particular liquid, such as a dye or an acid, in which particular objects are placed, usually as part of a manufacturing or chemical process. ❏ ...a developing photograph placed in a bath of fixer.

1 가산명사 목욕시키기 ❏ 산파가 그를 따뜻한 물에 목욕시켰다. **2** 가산명사 목욕, 입욕 [영국영어 have a bath] ❏ 만약 매일 아침 목욕을 한다면 ❏ 목욕 대신 샤워를 해라. **3** 타동사 목욕시키다 [영국영어; 미국영어 bathe] ❏ 아이를 매일같이 목욕시켜야 한다고 생각하지 마세요. **4** 가산명사 욕조 [영국영어; 미국영어 bathtub] ❏ 그 시절에는, 제법 부유한 가정에서만 자기들만의 욕조를 가지고 있었다. **5** 자동사 목욕하다 [영국영어; 미국영어 bathe] ❏ 세 아이 모두 같은 목욕물에 목욕을 했다. **6** 가산명사 목욕탕 ❏ 집들과 관공서 건물, 공중목욕탕 등이 있는 번영하는 마을 **7** 가산명사 용액조 ❏ 정착액조에 넣어져 현상 중인 사진

bathe /beɪð/ (bathes, bathing, bathed) **1** V-I When you **bathe**, you take a bath. [AM, also BRIT, FORMAL] ❏ At least 60% of us now bathe or shower once a day. **2** V-T If you **bathe** someone, especially a child, you wash them in a bathtub. [AM, also BRIT, FORMAL] ❏ Back home, Shirley plays with, feeds, and bathes the baby. **3** V-I If you **bathe** in a sea, river, or lake, you swim, play, or wash yourself in it. Birds and animals can also **bathe**. ❏ The police have warned the city's inhabitants not to bathe in the polluted river. ● N-SING **Bathe** is also a noun. [mainly BRIT] ❏ Fifty soldiers were taking an early morning bathe in a nearby lake. ● **bath|ing** N-UNCOUNT ❏ Nude bathing is not allowed. **4** V-T If you **bathe** a part of your body or a wound, you wash it gently or soak it in a liquid. ❏ Bathe the infected area in a salt solution. **5** V-T If a place **is bathed in** light, it is covered with light, especially a gentle, pleasant light. ❏ The arena was bathed in warm sunshine. ❏ I was led to a small room bathed in soft red light. **6** →see also **sunbathe**

1 자동사 목욕하다 [미국, 영국영어, 격식체] ❏ 요즘은 우리들 중 최소한 60퍼센트가 하루에 한 번 목욕이나 샤워를 한다. **2** 타동사 목욕시키다 [미국, 영국영어, 격식체] ❏ 집으로 돌아와서, 셜리는 아기와 함께 놀고, 젖을 먹이고 목욕을 시킨다. **3** 자동사 목욕하다; 해엄치다 ❏ 경찰은 그 도시의 주민들에게 오염된 강물에 목욕하지 말라고 경고해 왔다. ● 단수명사 미역 감기, 해수욕 [주로 영국영어] ❏ 군인 50명이 인근 호수에서 이른 아침에 미역을 감고 있었다. ● 미역 감기, 수영 불가산명사 ❏ 발가벗고 미역 감는 것은 금지되어 있다. **4** 타동사 씻다 ❏ 감염 부위를 소금물로 씻으세요. **5** 타동사 (빛으로) 가득 차다 ❏ 그 경기장에는 온통 따뜻한 햇살이 내리쬐었다. ❏ 나는 부드러운 붉은 빛으로 가득 찬 작은 방으로 인도되었다.

bath|room ♦◇◇ /bæθrum/ (bathrooms) **1** N-COUNT A **bathroom** is a room in a house that contains a bathtub or shower, a sink, and sometimes a toilet. **2** N-SING A **bathroom** is a room in a house or public building that contains a sink and toilet. [AM; BRIT usually **toilet**] ❏ She had gone in to use the bathroom. **3** PHRASE People say that they **are going to the bathroom** when they want to say that they are going to use the toilet. [POLITENESS] ❏ Although he had been treated with antibiotics, he went to the bathroom repeatedly.
→see **house, plumbing**

1 가산명사 욕실 **2** 단수명사 화장실 [미국영어; 영국영어 usually toilet] ❏ 그녀는 화장실을 쓰기 위해 안으로 들어갔다. **3** 구용면을 보다 [공손체] ❏ 그는 항생제 치료를 받아 왔었음에도 불구하고, 계속해서 화장실에 갔다.

Thesaurus   bathroom의 참조어

N.   lavatory, restroom, toilet **2**

bath|tub /bæθtʌb/ (bathtubs) N-COUNT A **bathtub** is a long, usually rectangular container which you fill with water and sit in to wash your body. [AM; BRIT **bath**] ❏ ...a gigantic pink marble bathtub.

가산명사 욕조 [미국영어; 영국영어 bath] ❏ 거대한 분홍색 대리석 욕조

ba|ton /bætɒn, BRIT bætɒn/ (batons) **1** N-COUNT A **baton** is a light, thin stick used by a conductor to conduct an orchestra or a choir. ❏ The maestro raises his baton. **2** N-COUNT In track and field or track events, a **baton** is a short stick that is passed from one runner to another in a relay race. ❏ ...their biggest relay outing since dropping the baton in Edmonton last August. **3** N-COUNT A **baton** is a short heavy stick which is sometimes used as a weapon by the police. [BRIT; AM **billy, billy club**] ❏ The man was beaten with a baton.

1 가산명사 지휘봉 ❏ 지휘자가 지휘봉을 들어올린다. **2** 가산명사 (릴레이 경주의) 배턴 ❏ 그들이 작년 8월 에드먼턴에서 배턴을 떨어뜨린 이후 가장 큰 계주 경주 출전 **3** 가산명사 곤봉 [영국영어; 미국영어 billy, billy club] ❏ 그 남자는 곤봉으로 두드려 맞았다.

bat|tal|ion /bətælyən/ (battalions) **1** N-COUNT A **battalion** is a large group of soldiers that consists of three or more companies. ❏ Ten hours later Anthony was ordered to return to his battalion. **2** N-COUNT A **battalion of** people is a large group of them, especially a well-organized, efficient group that has a particular task to do. ❏ There were battalions of highly paid publicists to see that such news didn't make the press.

1 가산명사 대대 ❏ 열 시간 후 앤서니는 소속 대대로 돌아가라는 명령을 받았다. **2** 가산명사 대부대, 집단 ❏ 그와 같은 소식이 기사화되지 않도록 지켜보는, 높은 보수를 받는 정치 평론가 집단이 있었다.

bat|ter /bǽtər/ (**batters, battering, battered**) ■ V-T To **batter** someone means to hit them many times, using fists or a heavy object. ❑ *He battered her around the head.* ❑ *A karate expert battered a man to death.* ● **bat|tered** ADJ ❑ *Her battered body was discovered in a field.* ❷ V-T If someone **is battered**, they are regularly hit and badly hurt by a member of their family or by their partner. ❑ *...evidence that the child was being battered.* ❑ *...boys who witness fathers battering their mothers.* ● **bat|ter|ing** N-UNCOUNT ❑ *Leaving the relationship does not mean that the battering will stop.* ❸ V-T If a place **is battered by** wind, rain, or storms, it is seriously damaged or affected by very bad weather. [usu passive] ❑ *The country has been battered by winds of between fifty and seventy miles an hour.* ❹ V-T If you **batter** something, you hit it many times, using your fists or a heavy object. ❑ *They were battering the door, they were breaking in.* ❺ N-VAR **Batter** is a mixture of flour, eggs, and milk that is used in cooking. ❑ *...pancake batter.* ❻ N-COUNT In sports such as baseball and softball, a **batter** is a person who hits the ball with a wooden bat. ❑ *...batters and pitchers.* ❼ →see also **battered, battering**

bat|tered /bǽtərd/ ADJ Something that is **battered** is old and in poor condition because it has been used a lot. ❑ *He drove up in a battered old car.*

bat|ter|ing /bǽtəriŋ/ (**batterings**) N-COUNT If something takes a **battering**, it suffers very badly as a result of a particular event or action. ❑ *Sterling took a battering yesterday as worries grew about the state of Britain's economy.*

bat|tery /bǽtəri/ (**batteries**) ■ N-COUNT **Batteries** are small devices that provide the power for electrical items such as radios and children's toys. ❑ *The shavers come complete with batteries.* ❑ *...a battery-operated cassette player.* ❷ N-COUNT A car **battery** is a rectangular box containing acid that is found in a car engine. It provides the electricity needed to start the car. ❑ *...a car with a dead battery.* ❸ N-COUNT A **battery of** equipment such as guns, lights, or computers is a large set of it kept together in one place. ❑ *They stopped beside a battery of abandoned guns.* ❹ N-COUNT A **battery of** people or things is a very large number of them. ❑ *...a battery of journalists and television cameras.* ❺ ADJ **Battery** farming is a system of breeding chickens and hens in which large numbers of them are kept in small cages, and used for their meat and eggs. [BRIT] [ADJ n] ❑ *...battery hens being raised in dark, cramped conditions.* →see **cellphone**

Word Partnership	battery의 연어	
N.	battery **charger**, battery **pack** ■	
	car battery ❷	
	missile battery ❸	
ADJ.	**dead** battery ■ ❷	

bat|tle ♦♦◇ /bǽtəl/ (**battles, battling, battled**) ■ N-VAR A **battle** is a violent fight between groups of people, especially one between military forces during a war. ❑ *...the victory of King William III at the Battle of the Boyne.* ❑ *...after a gun battle between police and drug traffickers.* ❷ N-COUNT A **battle** is a conflict in which different people or groups compete in order to achieve success or control. ❑ *...a renewed political battle over Britain's attitude to Europe.* ❑ *...the eternal battle between good and evil in the world.* ❸ N-COUNT You can use **battle** to refer to someone's efforts to achieve something in spite of very difficult circumstances. ❑ *...the battle against crime.* ❑ *She has fought a constant battle with her weight.* ❹ V-RECIP To **battle with** an opposing group means to take part in a fight or contest against them. In American English, you can also say that one group or person **is battling** another. ❑ *In one town thousands of people battled with police and several were reportedly wounded.* ❑ *The sides must battle again for a quarter-final place on December 16.* ❺ V-T/V-I To **battle** means to try hard to do something in spite of very difficult circumstances. In American English, you **battle** something. In British English and sometimes in American English, you **battle against** something or **with** something. ❑ *Doctors battled throughout the night to save her life.* ❑ *Firefighters are still battling the two blazes.* ❻ PHRASE If one group or person **battles it out with** another, they take part in a fight or contest against each other until one of them wins or a definite result is reached. You can say that two groups or two people **battle it out**. ❑ *In the Cup Final, Leeds battled it out with the old enemy, Manchester United.* →see **army**

Word Partnership	battle의 연어	
ADJ.	**bloody** battle, **major** battle ■	
	legal battle ❷	
	constant battle, **uphill** battle ❷ ❸	
V.	**prepare for** battle ■	
	fight a battle ■ ❷ ❸	
	win/lose a battle ■ ❷ ❸	
N.	battle **of wills** ❷	

battle|field /bǽtəlfild/ (**battlefields**) ■ N-COUNT A **battlefield** is a place where a battle is fought. ❑ *...the battlefields of the Somme.* ❷ N-COUNT You can refer to an issue or field of activity over which people disagree or compete as a **battlefield**. ❑ *...the domestic battlefield of family life.*

battle|ground /bǽtəlgraund/ (**battlegrounds**) ■ N-COUNT A **battleground** is the same as a **battlefield**. ❷ N-COUNT You can refer to an issue or field of activity over which people disagree or compete as a **battleground**. ❑ *...the battleground of education.*

■ 타동사 구타하다 ❑ 그는 그녀의 머리 부위를 구타했다. ● 구타당한 형용사 ❑ 그녀의 구타당한 시체가 들판에서 발견되었다. ❷ 타동사 매를 맞다, 가정 폭력을 당하다 ❑ 그 아이가 매를 맞고 있다는 증거 ❑ 아버지가 어머니에게 폭력을 행사하는 것을 목격하는 남자 아이들 ● 가정 폭력 불가산명사 ❑ 관계를 끊는다고 해서 가정 폭력이 사라지는 것은 아니다. ❸ 타동사 (악천후로) 심각한 피해를 입다 ❑ 그 나라는 시속 50 내지 70마일의 강풍에 의해 심각한 피해를 입어 왔다. ❹ 타동사 난타하다 ❑ 그들은 문을 난타하며 돌파해 들어가고 있었다. ❺ 가산명사 또는 불가산명사 (우유, 달걀, 밀가루 등의) 반죽 ❑ 팬케이크 반죽 ❻ 가산명사 타자 ❑ 타자와 투수

형용사 낡을 대로 낡은 ❑ 그는 낡은 고물차를 몰고 갔다.

가산명사 후폭풍 ❑ 영국의 경제 사정에 대한 우려가 커 감에 따라 영국 화폐가 어제 심각한 난조를 겪었다.

■ 가산명사 건전지 ❑ 그 면도기는 건전지를 포함하여 공급된다. ❑ 건전지로 작동되는 카세트 플레이어 ❷ 가산명사 자동차 배터리 ❑ 배터리가 다된 자동차 ❸ 가산명사 한 벌의 기구 ❑ 그들은 버려진 포대 옆에 멈춰 섰다. ❹ 가산명사 다수 ❑ 다수의 기자들과 텔레비전 카메라들 ❺ 형용사 집단 사육의 [영국영어] ❑ 어둡고 비좁은 환경 속에서 집단 사육되는 암탉들

■ 가산명사 또는 불가산명사 전투, 싸움 ❑ 윌리엄 3세의 보인 전투에서의 승리 ❑ 경찰과 마약상 간의 총격전 이후 ❷ 가산명사 경쟁; 투쟁 ❑ 유럽에 대한 영국의 태도를 놓고 재개된 정쟁 ❑ 세상의 선과 악 사이의 영원한 투쟁 ❸ 가산명사 (비유적) 전쟁 ❑ 범죄와의 전쟁 ❑ 그녀는 끊임없이 몸무게와의 전쟁을 해 왔다. ❹ 상호동사 싸우다 ❑ 한 마을에서 수천 명의 사람들이 경찰과 싸워 소식에 의하면 몇 명이 부상당했다고 한다. ❑ 그 팀들은 12월 16일에 4강 진출을 놓고 다시 싸워야 한다. ❺ 타동사/자동사 고투하다 ❑ 의사들은 그녀의 생명을 구하기 위해 밤새 고투했다. ❑ 소방관들이 아직도 두 개의 불길과 고투하고 있다. ❻ 구 싸워서 결론을 짓다 ❑ 영국 축구 연맹배 결승전에서, 리즈는 숙적 맨체스터 유나이티드와 맞붙어 결판을 냈다.

■ 가산명사 전장 ❑ 솜 전장 ❷ 가산명사 (비유적) 전쟁터 ❑ 가정 내의 전쟁터 같은 가족생활

■ 가산명사 전쟁터 ❷ 가산명사 (비유적) 전쟁터 ❑ 교육의 전쟁터

a
b
c
d
e
f
g
h
i
j
k
l
m
n
o
p
q
r
s
t
u
v
w
x
y
z

battle|ship /bæt^əlʃɪp/ (**battleships**) N-COUNT A **battleship** is a very large, heavily armed warship.

bawl /bɔl/ (**bawls, bawling, bawled**) **1** V-I If you say that a child **is bawling**, you are annoyed because it is crying loudly. ❑ *One of the toddlers was bawling, and the other had a runny nose.* **2** V-T/V-I If you **bawl**, you shout in a very loud voice, for example because you are angry or you want people to hear you. ❑ *When I came back to the hotel Laura and Peter were shouting and bawling at each other.* ❑ *Then a voice bawled: "Lay off! I'll kill you, you little rascal!"* ● PHRASAL VERB **Bawl out** means the same as **bawl.** ❑ *Someone in the audience bawled out "Not him again!"*

bay ◆◇◇ /beɪ/ (**bays, baying, bayed**) **1** N-COUNT A **bay** is a part of a coast where the land curves inward. ❑ *...a short ferry ride across the bay.* ❑ *...the Bay of Bengal.* **2** N-COUNT A **bay** is a partly enclosed area, inside or outside a building, that is used for a particular purpose. ❑ *The animals are herded into a bay, then butchered.* **3** N-COUNT A **bay** is an area of a room which extends beyond the main walls of a house, especially an area with a large window at the front of a house. **4** ADJ A **bay** horse is reddish-brown in color. ❑ *...a 10-year-old bay mare.* **5** V-I If a number of people are **baying for** something, they are demanding something angrily, usually that someone should be punished. [usu cont] ❑ *The referee ignored voices baying for a penalty.* ❑ *Opposition politicians have been baying for his blood.* **6** V-I If a dog or wolf **bays**, it makes loud, long cries. ❑ *A dog suddenly howled, baying at the moon.* **7** PHRASE If you **keep** something or someone **at bay**, or **hold** them **at bay**, you prevent them from reaching, attacking, or affecting you. ❑ *Eating oranges keeps colds at bay.*

bayo|net /beɪənɪt, beɪənɛt/ (**bayonets**) N-COUNT A **bayonet** is a long, sharp blade that can be fixed to the end of a rifle and used as a weapon.

ba|zaar /bəzɑr/ (**bazaars**) **1** N-COUNT In areas such as the Middle East and India, a **bazaar** is a place where there are many small stores and stalls. ❑ *Kamal was a vendor in Egypt's open-air bazaar.* **2** N-COUNT A **bazaar** is a sale to raise money for charity. ❑ *...a church bazaar.*

BBC ◆◆◇ /bi bi si/ N-PROPER The **BBC** is a British organization which broadcasts programs on radio and television. **BBC** is an abbreviation for "British Broadcasting Corporation." [the N] ❑ *The concert will be broadcast live by the BBC.*

BC /bi si/ You use **BC** in dates to indicate a number of years or centuries before the year in which Jesus Christ is believed to have been born. Compare **AD.** ❑ *The brooch dates back to the fourth century BC.*

---
                    be
---

① AUXILIARY VERB USES
② OTHER VERB USES

① **be** ◆◆◆ /bi, STRONG bi/ (**am, are, is, being, was, were, been**)

> In spoken English, forms of **be** are often shortened, for example "I am" is shortened to "I'm" and "was not" is shortened to "wasn't."

1 AUX You use **be** with a present participle to form the continuous tenses of verbs. ❑ *This is happening in every school throughout the country.* ❑ *She didn't always think carefully about what she was doing.* **be going to** →see **going 2** AUX You use **be** with a past participle to form the passive voice. ❑ *Her husband was killed in a car crash.* ❑ *Similar action is being taken by the U.S. government.* **3** AUX You use **be** with an infinitive to indicate that something is planned to happen, that it will definitely happen, or that it must happen. ❑ *The talks are to begin tomorrow.* ❑ *It was to be Johnson's first meeting with the board in nearly a month.* **be about to** →see **about 4** AUX You use **be** with an infinitive to say or ask what should happen or be done in a particular situation, how it should happen, or who should do it. ❑ *What am I to do without him?* ❑ *Who is to say which of them had more power?* **5** AUX You use **was** and **were** with an infinitive to talk about something that happened later than the time you are discussing, and was not planned or certain at that time. ❑ *He started something that was to change the face of China.* **6** AUX You can say that something is **to be** seen, heard, or found in a particular place to mean that people can see it, hear it, or find it in that place. ❑ *Little traffic was to be seen on the streets.*

② **be** ◆◆◆ /bi, STRONG bi/ (**am, are, is, being, was, were, been**)

> In spoken English, forms of **be** are often shortened, for example "I am" is shortened to "I'm" and "was not" is shortened to "wasn't."

1 V-LINK You use **be** to introduce more information about the subject, such as its identity, nature, qualities, or position. ❑ *She's my mother.* ❑ *He's a very attractive man.* ❑ *He is fifty and has been through two marriages.* ❑ *The sky was black.* ❑ *His house is next door.* ❑ *He's still alive, isn't he?* **2** V-LINK You use **be**, with "it" as the subject, in clauses where you are describing something or giving your judgment of a situation. ❑ *It was too chilly for swimming.* ❑ *Sometimes it is necessary to say no.* ❑ *It is likely that investors will face losses.* ❑ *It's nice having friends to chat to.* **3** V-LINK You use **be** with the impersonal pronoun "there" in expressions like **there is** and **there are** to say that something exists or happens. ❑ *Clearly there is a problem here.* ❑ *There are very few cars on this street.* **4** V-LINK You use **be** as a link between a subject and a clause and in certain other clause structures, as shown below. ❑ *Our greatest problem is convincing them.* ❑ *All she knew was that I'd had a broken marriage.* ❑ *Local residents said it was as if there had been a nuclear explosion.* **5** V-LINK You use **be** in expressions like **the thing is** and **the point is** to introduce a clause in which you make a statement or give your opinion. [SPOKEN] ❑ *The fact is, the players gave everything they had.* **6** V-LINK The form "**be**" is used occasionally instead of the normal forms of the present tense,

---

가산명사 전함

1 자동사 큰 소리로 울다 ❑ 겨우 걸음마를 걷는 아기들 중 하나는 큰 소리로 울어댔고, 다른 하나는 콧물을 질질 흘렸다. **2** 타동사/자동사 고함치다, 악을 쓰다 ❑ 내가 호텔에 돌아왔을 때 로라와 피터가 서로에게 고래고래 악을 쓰고 있었다. ❑ 그러자 고함 소리가 들려왔다: "떨어져! 죽여 버리겠어, 이 악당 새끼!" ● 구동사 고함처럼 ❑ 관객 중 누군가가 소리쳤다. "그 사람은 다시는 안 돼!"

1 가산명사 만, 내포 ❑ 만을 가로질러 잠깐 동안 나룻배를 타고 가기 ❑ 벵골 만 **2** 가산명사 특정한 목적으로 사용하기 위해 부분적으로 둘러쳐진 공간을 bay라고 한다. ❑ 동물들은 한쪽 터로 몰려가서 도살된다. **3** 가산명사 방에서 주변보다 뒤로 물러난 공간 **4** 형용사 적갈색의 ❑ 열 살짜리 적갈색 암말 **5** 자동사 소리 높여 요구하다 ❑ 주심은 반칙 선언을 요구하는 목소리를 무시했다. ❑ 야당 정치인들은 그의 숙청을 강하게 요구해 왔다. **6** 자동사 울부짖다 ❑ 개 한 마리가 갑자기 달을 보고 울부짖었다. **7** 구 - 을 멀리하다; 견제하다 ❑ 오렌지를 먹으면 감기가 예방된다.

가산명사 총검

1 가산명사 시장 ❑ 카말은 이집트 노천 시장의 상인이었다. **2** 가산명사 자선 바자회 ❑ 교회 바자회

고유명사 비비시 방송 ❑ 그 콘서트는 비비시에서 생중계될 것이다.

기원전 ❑ 그 브로치는 기원전 4세기 것이다.

구어체 영어에서 be의 형태는 종종 축약된다. 예를 들면, 'I am'은 'I'm'으로 'was not'은 'wasn't'로 쓴다.

1 준조동사 현재 분사와 함께 진행 시제 형성 ❑ 이는 전국의 모든 학교에서 일어나고 있다. ❑ 그녀는 자신이 무엇을 하고 있는지 신중하게 생각하지 않았다. **2** 준조동사 과거 분사와 함께 수동태 형성 ❑ 그녀의 남편은 자동차 충돌 사고로 죽었다. ❑ 미국 정부가 비슷한 조치를 취하고 있다. **3** 준조동사 to 부정사와 함께 예정된 일이나 확실히 일어날 사건 등을 나타냄 ❑ 회담이 내일 시작된다. ❑ 그것은 존슨이 이사회와 거의 한 달 만에 갖게 되는 회담이었다. **4** 준조동사 to 부정사와 함께 의무를 나타냄 ❑ 그 사람 없이 내가 어떻게 하지? ❑ 그들 중 어느 쪽이 더 막강한 권력을 가졌는지 누가 말해야 하나요? **5** 준조동사 to 부정사와 함께 과거 시점 기준에서 그 후에 일어날 일 설명 ❑ 그는 후에 중국의 모습을 바꾸게 될 어떤 일을 시작했다. **6** 준조동사 - 할 수 있는 ❑ 거리에서 차를 별로 볼 수 없었다.

구어체 영어에서 be의 형태는 종종 축약된다. 예를 들면, 'I am'은 'I'm'으로 'was not'은 'wasn't'로 쓴다.

1 연결동사 이다 ❑ 그 분은 우리 어머니이시다. ❑ 그는 매우 매력적인 남자이다. ❑ 그는 50세이고 두 번 결혼했다. ❑ 하늘이 까맸다. ❑ 그의 집은 옆집이다. ❑ 그 남자 아직 살아 있는 거 맞죠? **2** 연결동사 이다 ❑ 수영하기에는 너무 추웠다. ❑ 때로는 아니라고 말할 필요가 있다. ❑ 투자자들이 손실을 볼 가능성이 있다. ❑ 수다 떨 친구가 있다는 것은 좋은 일이다. **3** 연결동사 있다 ❑ 분명히 여기에 문제가 있어. ❑ 거리에 차가 거의 없다. **4** 연결동사 이다 ❑ 우리의 가장 큰 문제는 그들을 설득하는 것이다. ❑ 그녀가 아는 것은 내가 결혼에 실패했다는 것뿐이었다. ❑ 지역 주민들은 마치 핵폭발이 일어난 것 같았다고 말했다. **5** 연결동사 - 은, - 는 [구어체] ❑ 사실은 선수들이 가진 것 전부를 주었다는 것이야. **6** 연결동사 whether 등과 함께 현재형 대신에 쓰이기도 함 [격식체] ❑ 그리고 나면 그들이 당신이 주치의든 치과 의사든 안과 의사든 적절한

especially after "whether." [FORMAL] ❑ *They should then be able to refer you to the appropriate type of practitioner, whether it be your GP, dentist, or optician.* ◻ PHRASE If you talk about what would happen **if it wasn't for** someone or something, you mean that they are the only thing that is preventing it from happening. ❑ *I could happily move back into a flat if it wasn't for the fact that I'd miss my garden.*

beach ♦◇◇ /biːtʃ/ (**beaches, beaching, beached**) ◼ N-COUNT A **beach** is an area of sand or stones beside the sea. ❑ *...a beautiful sandy beach.* ◻ V-T/V-I If something such as a boat **beaches**, or if it **is beached**, it is pulled or forced out of the water and onto land. ❑ *We beached the canoe, running it right up the bank.* ❑ *The boat beached on a mud flat.*
→see Word Web: **beach**

> You can use **beach**, **coast**, and **shore** to talk about the piece of land beside a stretch of water. A **beach** is a flat area of sand or pebbles next to the sea. The **coast** is the area of land that lies alongside the sea. You may be referring just to the land close to the sea, or to a wider area that extends further inland. The **shore** is the area of land along the edge of the sea, a lake, or a wide river.

Word Partnership   beach의 연어

PREP.	**along the** beach, **at/on the** beach ◼
N.	beach **chair**, beach **club/resort**, beach **vacation** ◼
V.	**lie on the** beach, **walk on the** beach ◼
ADJ.	**nude** beach, **private** beach, **rocky** beach, **sandy** beach ◼

bea|con /biːkən/ (**beacons**) ◼ N-COUNT A **beacon** is a light or a fire, usually on a hill or tower, which acts as a signal or a warning. ❑ *The Queen will light the final beacon, which is 5 meters tall.* ◻ N-COUNT If someone acts as a **beacon to** other people, they inspire or encourage them. ❑ *Our Parliament has been a beacon of hope to the peoples of Europe.*

bead /biːd/ (**beads**) ◼ N-COUNT **Beads** are small pieces of colored glass, wood, or plastic with a hole through the middle. Beads are often put together on a piece of string or wire to make jewelry. ◻ N-COUNT A **bead of** liquid or moisture is a small drop of it. ❑ *...beads of blood.*

beak /biːk/ (**beaks**) N-COUNT A bird's **beak** is the hard curved or pointed part of its mouth. ❑ *...a black bird with a yellow beak.* →see **bird**

beak|er /biːkər/ (**beakers**) ◼ N-COUNT A **beaker** is a large cup or glass. [AM] ◻ N-COUNT A **beaker** is a plastic cup used for drinking, usually one with no handle. [BRIT] ◼ N-COUNT A **beaker** is a glass or plastic jar which is used in chemistry.

beam /biːm/ (**beams, beaming, beamed**) ◼ V-T/V-I If you say that someone **is beaming**, you mean that they have a big smile on their face because they are happy, pleased, or proud about something. [WRITTEN] ❑ *Frances beamed at her friend with undisguised admiration.* ❑ *"Welcome back," she beamed.* ◻ N-COUNT A **beam** is a line of energy, radiation, or particles sent in a particular direction. ❑ *...high-energy laser beams.* ◼ V-T/V-I If radio signals or television pictures **are beamed** somewhere, they are sent there by means of electronic equipment. ❑ *The interview was beamed live across America.* ❑ *Soon, CMTV will be beaming into British homes via the Astra satellite.* ◼ N-COUNT A **beam of** light is a line of light that shines from an object such as a lamp. ❑ *A beam of light slices through the darkness.* ◼ N-COUNT A **beam** is a long thick bar of wood, metal, or concrete, especially one used to support the roof of a building. ❑ *The ceilings are supported by oak beams.* →see **laser**

Word Partnership   beam의 연어

PREP.	beam **at** *someone* ◼
	beam **down** *(on something)* ◼
N.	**laser** beam ◻
	beam **of light** ◼
ADJ.	**steel/wooden** beam ◼

bean ♦◇◇ /biːn/ (**beans**) ◼ N-COUNT Beans such as green **beans**, French **beans**, or broad **beans** are the seeds of a climbing plant or the long thin cases which contain those seeds. ◻ N-COUNT Beans such as soy **beans** and kidney **beans** are the dried seeds of other types of bean plants. ◼ N-COUNT Beans such as coffee **beans** or cocoa **beans** are the seeds of plants that are used to produce coffee, cocoa, and chocolate.

Word Web   beach

Beaches have a natural cycle of build-up and **erosion**. **Ocean currents**, wind, and **waves** move **sand** along the **coast**. In certain spots, some of the sand gets left behind. The **surf** deposits it on the beach. Then the wind blows it into **dunes**. As currents change, they **erode** sand from the beach. High waves carry beach sand seaward. This process raises the seafloor. As the water gets shallower, the waves become smaller. Then they begin depositing sand on the beach. At the same time, small **pebbles** smash into each other. They break up and form new sand.

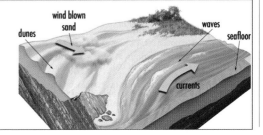

wind blown sand   dunes   waves   seafloor   currents

a b c d e f g h i j k l m n o p q r s t u v w x y z

bear

① VERB USES
② NOUN USES

Word Partnership bear의 연어

N.	bear **a burden/weight** ① ⒈ ⒊ ⒌
	bear **responsibility** ① ⒏
	bear **fruit** ① ⒑
	bear **interest** ① ⒒
ADV.	bear **left/right** ① ⒓

① **bear** ♦♦◇◇ /beər/ (bears, bearing, bore, borne) →Please look at category ⒔ to see if the expression you are looking for is shown under another headword. ⒈ V-T If you **bear** something somewhere, you carry it there or take it there. [LITERARY] ❑ They bore the oblong hardwood box into the kitchen and put it on the table. ⒉ V-T If you **bear** something such as a weapon, you hold it or carry it with you. [FORMAL] ❑ ...the constitutional right to bear arms. ⒊ V-T If one thing **bears** the weight of something else, it supports the weight of that thing. ❑ The ice was not thick enough to bear the weight of marching men. ⒋ V-T If something **bears** a particular mark or characteristic, it has that mark or characteristic. ❑ The houses bears the marks of bullet holes and the streets are practically deserted. ❑ ...note paper bearing the Presidential seal. ⒌ V-T If you **bear** an unpleasant experience, you accept it because you are unable to do anything about it. ❑ They will have to bear the misery of living in constant fear of war. ⒍ V-T If you can't **bear** someone or something, you dislike them very much. [with neg] ❑ I can't bear people who make judgements and label me. ⒎ V-T If someone **bears** the cost of something, they pay for it. ❑ Patients should not have to bear the costs of their own treatment. ⒏ V-T If you **bear** the responsibility for something, you accept responsibility for it. ❑ If a woman makes a decision to have a child alone, she should bear that responsibility alone. ⒐ V-T If one thing **bears** no resemblance or no relationship to another thing, they are not at all similar. [usu with brd-neg] ❑ Their daily menus bore no resemblance whatsoever to what they were actually fed. ⒑ V-T When a plant or tree **bears** flowers, fruit, or leaves, it produces them. ❑ As the plants grow and start to bear fruit they will need a lot of water. ⒒ V-T If something such as a bank account or an investment **bears** interest, interest is paid on it. [BUSINESS] ❑ The eight-year bond will bear annual interest of 10.5%. ⒓ V-I If you **bear** left or **bear** right when you are driving or walking along, you turn and continue in that direction. ❑ Go left onto the A107 and bear left into Seven Sisters Road. ⒔ →see also **bore, borne** ⒕ to **bear the brunt of** →see **brunt**. to **bear fruit** →see **fruit**. to **grin and bear it** →see **grin**. to **bear in mind** →see **mind**

Thesaurus bear의 참조어

V.	carry, lug, move, transport ① ⒈
	endure, put up with, stand, tolerate ① ⒌
	produce, yield ① ⒑

▶**bear out** PHRASAL VERB If someone or something **bears** a person **out** or **bears out** what that person is saying, they support what that person is saying. ❑ Recent studies have borne out claims that certain perfumes can bring about profound psychological changes.

▶**bear with** PHRASAL VERB If you ask someone to **bear with** you, you are asking them to be patient. ❑ If you'll bear with me, Frank, just let me try to explain.

② **bear** /beər/ (bears) ⒈ N-COUNT A **bear** is a large, strong wild animal with thick fur and sharp claws. ⒉ N-COUNT In the stock market, **bears** are people who sell shares in expectation of a drop in price, in order to make a profit by buying them back again after a short time. Compare **bull**. [BUSINESS]

bear|able /beərəbəl/ ADJ If something is **bearable**, you feel that you can accept it or deal with it. ❑ A cool breeze made the heat pleasantly bearable.

beard /bɪərd/ (beards) N-COUNT A man's **beard** is the hair that grows on his chin and cheeks. ❑ He's decided to grow a beard.

beard|ed /bɪərdɪd/ ADJ A **bearded** man has a beard. ❑ ...a bearded 40-year-old sociology professor.

bear|er /beərər/ (bearers) ⒈ N-COUNT The **bearer** of something such as a message is the person who brings it to you. ❑ I hate to be the bearer of bad news. ⒉ N-COUNT A **bearer** of a particular thing is a person who carries it, especially in a ceremony. [FORMAL] ❑ ...Britain's flag bearer at the Olympic Games opening ceremony. ⒊ N-COUNT The **bearer** of something such as a document, a right, or an official position is the person who possesses it or holds it. [FORMAL] ❑ ...the traditional bourgeois notion of the citizen as a bearer of rights.

bear|ing ♦◇◇ /beərɪŋ/ (bearings) ⒈ N-COUNT If something **has a bearing on** a situation or event, it is relevant to it. ❑ Experts generally agree that diet has an important bearing on your general health. ⒉ N-SING Someone's **bearing** is the way in which they move or stand. [LITERARY] ❑ She later wrote warmly of his bearing and behaviour. ⒊ PHRASE If you **get** your **bearings** or **find** your **bearings**, you find out where you are or what you should do next. If you **lose** your **bearings**, you do not know where you are or what you should do next. ❑ A sightseeing tour of the city is included to help you get your bearings.

⒈ 타동사 나르다 [문예체] ❑ 그들은 장방형의 나무 상자를 부엌으로 날라 테이블 위에 올려놓았다. ⒉ 타동사 몸에 지니다 [격식체] ❑ 헌법에 보장된 총기 소지권 ⒊ 타동사 지탱하다 ❑ 얼음이 지나가는 사람들의 무게를 견딜 만큼 두껍지 않았다. ⒋ 타동사 지니다 ❑ 집들에는 총알 자국이 나 있고 거리는 사실상 텅 비어 있다. ❑ 대통령 직인이 찍힌 메모지 ⒌ 타동사 견디다 ❑ 그들은 끝없는 전쟁의 공포 속에서 살아야 하는 비극을 견뎌야 할 것이다. ⒍ 타동사 참다 ❑ 나는 나를 재단하고 특정한 유형으로 분류하는 사람들을 못 참는다. ⒎ 타동사 부담하다 ❑ 환자들이 치료비를 부담해야만 하는 상황이 되어서는 안 된다. ⒏ 타동사 책임지다 ❑ 만약 한 여성이 출산을 혼자서 결정한다면, 그에 대한 책임은 그 여성 혼자서 져야 한다. ⒐ 타동사 가지다 ❑ 그들의 일일 식단은 그들이 실제로 먹게 되는 것과 조금도 비슷하지 않았다. ⒑ 타동사 피우다; 맺다 ❑ 나무가 자라고 열매를 맺으면서 많은 물이 필요할 것이다. ⒒ 타동사 이자가 붙다 [경제] ❑ 8년 만기 채권은 연 10.5퍼센트의 이자가 붙는다. ⒓ 자동사 향하다 ❑ 왼쪽으로 가서 에이 107 도로를 타고 가다 '세븐 시스터즈 로드'로 좌회전하세요.

구동사 뒷받침하다 ❑ 최근 잇따른 연구 결과가 특정 향수가 큰 심리적 변화를 유발한다는 주장을 뒷받침한다.

구동사 참아 주다, 봐주다 ❑ 프랭크, 네가 날 좀 봐줄 거면, 그냥 내 설명 좀 들어 봐.

⒈ 가산명사 곰 ⒉ 가산명사 매도인 [경제]

형용사 견딜 만한 ❑ 시원한 바람 덕택에 더위도 견딜 만큼 쾌적해졌다.

가산명사 턱수염 ❑ 그는 턱수염을 기르기로 결심했다.

형용사 턱수염을 기른 ❑ 턱수염을 기른 40세의 사회학 교수

⒈ 가산명사 전달자 ❑ 나쁜 소식을 전하게 되어서 유감이군요. ⒉ 가산명사 행사에서 특정한 물건을 나르는 사람 [격식체] ❑ 올림픽 개막식의 영국 기수 ⒊ 가산명사 소유자; 보유자 [격식체] ❑ 시민은 권리를 가진다는 전통적인 부르주아적 개념

⒈ 구 관련이 있다 ❑ 전문가들은 음식이 전반적인 건강과 밀접한 관련이 있다는 데 대체로 동의한다. ⒉ 단수명사 태도, 행동 [문예체] ❑ 그녀는 후에 그의 태도와 행동에 대해 좋게 썼다. ⒊ 구 방향 감각을 찾다; 방향 감각을 얻다 ❑ 시내 관광은 여러분들이 방향감을 얻는 데 도움을 드리기 위해서 포함되었습니다.

bear|ish /ˈbeərɪʃ/ ADJ In the stock market, if there is a **bearish** mood, prices are expected to fall. Compare **bullish**. [BUSINESS] ❑ *Dealers said investors remain bearish.*

형용사 약세의, 소극적인 [경제] ❑ 중권사들이 투자자들이 여전히 소극적이라고 말했다.

bear mar|ket (bear markets) N-COUNT A **bear market** is a situation in the stock market when people are selling a lot of shares because they expect that the shares will decrease in value and that they will be able to make a profit by buying them again after a short time. Compare **bull market**. [BUSINESS] ❑ *Is the bear market in equities over?*

가산명사 주식 시장 약세 [경제] ❑ 주식 시장 약세가 끝난 것일까?

beast /biːst/ (beasts) N-COUNT You can refer to an animal as a **beast**, especially if it is a large, dangerous, or unusual one. [LITERARY] ❑ *...the threats our ancestors faced from wild beasts.*

가산명사 짐승 [문예체] ❑ 우리 조상들이 야생 동물로부터 받았던 위협

beat ♦♦♦ /biːt/ (beats, beating, beaten)

> The form **beat** is used in the present tense and is the past tense.

> beat은 현재 및 과거로 쓴다.

1 V-T If you **beat** someone or something, you hit them very hard. ❑ *My wife tried to stop them and they beat her.* **2** V-I To **beat on, at,** or **against** something means to hit it hard, usually several times or continuously for a period of time. ❑ *There was dead silence but for a fly beating against the glass.* ❑ *Nina managed to free herself and began beating at the flames with a pillow.* ● N-SING **Beat** is also a noun. ❑ *...the rhythmic beat of the surf.* ● **beat|ing** N-SING *...the silence broken only by the beating of the rain.* **3** V-I When your heart or pulse **beats**, it continually makes regular rhythmic movements. ❑ *I felt my heart beating faster.* ● N-COUNT **Beat** is also a noun. ❑ *He could hear the beat of his heart.* ● **beat|ing** N-SING ❑ *I could hear the beating of my heart.* **4** V-T If you **beat** a drum or similar instrument, you hit it in order to make a sound. ❑ *When you beat the drum, you feel good.* ● N-SING **Beat** is also a noun. ❑ *...the rhythmical beat of the drum.* **5** N-COUNT The **beat** of a piece of music is the main rhythm that it has. ❑ *...the thumping beat of rock music.* **6** N-COUNT In music, a **beat** is a unit of measurement. The number of beats in a bar of a piece of music is indicated by two numbers at the beginning of the piece. ❑ *It's got four beats to a bar.* →see also **upbeat** **7** V-T If you **beat** eggs, cream, or butter, you mix them thoroughly using a fork or beater. ❑ *Beat the eggs and sugar until they start to thicken.* **8** V-T/V-I When a bird or insect **beats** its wings or when its wings **beat**, its wings move up and down. ❑ *Beating their wings they flew off.* **9** V-T If you **beat** someone in a competition or election, you defeat them. ❑ *In yesterday's games, Switzerland beat the United States two-one.* **10** V-T If someone **beats** a record or achievement, they do better than it. ❑ *He was as eager as his Captain to beat the record.* **11** V-T If you **beat** something that you are fighting against, for example an organization, a problem, or a disease, you defeat it. ❑ *It became clear that the Union was not going to beat the government.* **12** V-T If an attack or an attempt **is beaten off** or **is beaten back**, it is stopped, often temporarily. [usu passive] ❑ *The rescuers were beaten back by strong winds and currents.* **13** V-T If you say that one thing **beats** another, you mean that it is better than it. [INFORMAL] [no cont] ❑ *Being boss of a software firm beats selling insurance.* **14** V-T To **beat** a time limit or an event means to achieve something before that time or event. ❑ *They were trying to beat the midnight deadline.* **15** N-COUNT A police officer's or journalist's **beat** is the area for which he or she is responsible. ❑ *A policeman was patrolling his regular beat, when he saw a group of boys milling about the street.* **16** →see also **beating** **17** PHRASE If you intend to do something but someone **beats** you **to it,** they do it before you do. ❑ *Don't be too long about it or you'll find someone has beaten you to it.* **18** to **beat** someone **at their own game** →see **game** →see **drum**

beat은 현재 및 과거로 쓴다.

1 타동사 때리다 ❑ 아내가 그들을 막으려 하자 그들은 아내를 때렸다. **2** 자동사 두드리다, 치다 ❑ 파리가 유리창에 부딪혀 파닥거리는 소리를 빼고는 쥐 죽은 듯 조용했다. ❑ 니나는 간신히 빠져 나와 베개로 불길을 두드려 끄기 시작했다. ● 단수명사 때림, 박자 ❑ 리듬 있게 부딪치는 파도 ● 때림 단수명사 ❑ 비가 부딪치는 소리만 들리는 가운데 흐르는 침묵 **3** 자동사 뛰다 ❑ 나는 심장이 더 빨리 뛰는 것을 느꼈다. ● 가산명사 맥박, 고동 ❑ 그는 자기 심장이 뛰는 소리를 들을 수 있었다. ● 맥박, 고동 단수명사 ❑ 나는 내 심장의 고동 소리를 들을 수 있었다. **4** 자동사 치다 ❑ 드럼을 치면, 기분이 좋아진다. ● 단수명사 비트, 장단 ❑ 리듬 있는 드럼 소리 **5** 가산명사 리듬, 비트 ❑ 록 음악의 강렬한 비트 **6** 가산명사 박자 ❑ 그것은 4박자로 되어 있다. **7** 타동사 섞다, 휘젓다 ❑ 달걀과 설탕을 걸쭉해질 때까지 휘젓는다. **8** 타동사/자동사 푸드덕거리다 ❑ 그들은 날개 치며 날아올랐다. **9** 타동사 이기다 ❑ 어제 경기에서 스위스가 미국을 2 대 1로 이겼다. **10** 타동사 깨다 ❑ 그는 팀의 주장만큼이나 기록을 깨고 싶어 했다. **11** 타동사 이기다, 무찌르다 ❑ 노조가 정부를 이기지 못할 것이라는 점이 분명해졌다. **12** 타동사 중단되다 ❑ 강풍과 급류로 구조 작업이 일시 중단되었다. **13** 타동사 더 낫다 [비격식체] ❑ 소프트웨어 사의 사장이 되는 것이 보험을 파는 것보다 낫다. **14** 타동사 – 전에 일을 끝내다 ❑ 그들은 마감 시간인 자정 전에 일을 끝내려고 애쓰고 있었다. **15** 가산명사 담당 구역 ❑ 한 경찰관이 순찰을 돌다가 한 무리의 남자 아이들이 거리에 몰려다니는 것을 목격했다. **17** 구 선수를 치다 ❑ 너무 오래 걸리지는 마. 그렇지 않으면 다른 사람이 너보다 선수를 칠 거야.

<table>
<tr><td colspan="2">**Thesaurus**   beat의 참조어</td></tr>
<tr><td>V.</td><td>hit, pound, punch; (ant.) caress, pat, pet **1**</td></tr>
<tr><td></td><td>flutter, quiver, vibrate **3** **8**</td></tr>
<tr><td></td><td>mix, stir, whip **7**</td></tr>
</table>

<table>
<tr><td colspan="2">**Word Partnership**   beat의 연어</td></tr>
<tr><td>N.</td><td>beat **a rug** **1**</td></tr>
<tr><td></td><td>**heart** beat **3**</td></tr>
<tr><td></td><td>beat **a drum** **4**</td></tr>
<tr><td></td><td>beat **eggs** **7**</td></tr>
<tr><td></td><td>beat **a deadline** **14**</td></tr>
<tr><td>PREP.</td><td>beat **against**, beat **on** **2**</td></tr>
<tr><td></td><td>**on/to a** beat **6**</td></tr>
<tr><td>PRON.</td><td>beat **its/their wings** **8**</td></tr>
</table>

▶**beat up** PHRASAL VERB If someone **beats** a person **up,** they hit or kick the person many times. ❑ *Then they actually beat her up as well.*

구동사 구타하다 ❑ 그리고 나서 그들은 사실상 그녀도 구타했다.

beat|en ♦♢♢ /ˈbiːtən/ PHRASE A place that is **off the beaten track** is in an area where not many people live or go. ❑ *Tiny secluded beaches can be found off the beaten track.*

구 인적이 드문 ❑ 인적이 드문 곳에서 작고 한적한 해변들을 발견할 수 있다.

beat|ing ♦♢♢ /ˈbiːtɪŋ/ (beatings) **1** N-COUNT If someone is given a **beating,** they are hit hard many times, often with something such as a stick. ❑ *...the savage beating of a black motorist by white police officers.* **2** N-SING If something such as a business, a political party, or a team takes a **beating,** it is defeated by a large amount in a competition or election. ❑ *Our firm has taken a terrible beating in recent years.*

1 가산명사 구타 ❑ 흑인 운전자에 대한 백인 경찰들의 무지막지한 구타 **2** 단수명사 완패, 참패 ❑ 최근 몇 년간 우리 회사는 무참한 패배를 보아 왔다.

beau|ti|ful ♦♦◇ /byˈuːtɪfəl/ 🔲 ADJ A **beautiful** person is very attractive to look at. 🔲 *She was a very beautiful woman.* 🔲 ADJ If you describe something as **beautiful**, you mean that it is very attractive or pleasing. 🔲 *New England is beautiful.* 🔲 *It was a beautiful morning.* ● **beau|ti|ful|ly** /byˈuːtɪfli/ ADV 🔲 *The children behaved beautifully.* 🔲 ADJ You can describe something that someone does as **beautiful** when they do it very skilfully. 🔲 *That's a beautiful shot!* ● **beau|ti|ful|ly** ADV 🔲 *Arsenal played beautifully.*

🔲 형용사 아름다운 🔲 그녀는 매우 아름다운 여자였다. 🔲 형용사 아름다운 🔲 뉴잉글랜드는 아름답다. 🔲 아름다운 아침이었다. ● 아름답게, 훌륭하게 부사 🔲 아이들은 훌륭하게 행동했다. 🔲 형용사 훌륭한, 멋진 🔲 멋지게 맞혔어! ● 훌륭하게, 멋지게 부사 🔲 아스날은 멋진 경기를 펼쳤다.

> When you are describing someone's appearance, you usually use **beautiful** and **pretty** to describe women, girls, and babies. **Beautiful** is a much stronger word than **pretty**. The equivalent word for a man is **handsome**. **Good-looking** and **attractive** can be used to describe people of either sex.

> 사람의 외모를 묘사할 때, 여성, 소녀, 아기에 대해서는 대개 pretty와 beautiful을 쓴다. beautiful은 pretty보다 훨씬 더 강한 말이다. 이에 상응하는 말로 남성에게 쓸 수 있는 것이 handsome이다. good-looking과 attractive는 남녀 모두에 대해 쓸 수 있다.

Thesaurus   *beautiful*의 참조어

ADJ.   attractive, gorgeous, lovely, pretty, stunning; (ant.) grotesque, hideous, homely, ugly 🔲

beau|ty ♦◇◇ /byˈuːti/ (**beauties**) 🔲 N-UNCOUNT **Beauty** is the state or quality of being beautiful. 🔲 *...an area of outstanding natural beauty.* 🔲 N-COUNT A **beauty** is a beautiful woman. [JOURNALISM] 🔲 *She is known as a great beauty.* 🔲 N-COUNT You can say that something is a **beauty** when you think it is very good. [INFORMAL] 🔲 *It was the one opportunity in the game – the pass was a real beauty, but the shot was poor.* 🔲 N-COUNT The **beauties** of something are its attractive qualities or features. [LITERARY] 🔲 *He was beginning to enjoy the beauties of nature.* 🔲 ADJ **Beauty** is used to describe people, products, and activities that are concerned with making women look beautiful. [ADJ n] 🔲 *Additional beauty treatments can be booked in advance.* 🔲 N-COUNT If you say that a particular feature is **the beauty of** something, you mean that this feature is what makes the thing so good. 🔲 *There would be no effect on animals – that's the beauty of such water-based materials.*

🔲 불가산명사 아름다움, 미 🔲 특출한 자연미를 자랑하는 지역 🔲 가산명사 미인 [언론] 🔲 그녀는 절세미인으로 알려져 있다. 🔲 가산명사 훌륭한 것 [비격식체] 🔲 그때가 게임의 유일한 기회였습니다. 패스는 아주 훌륭했지만 슈팅이 안 좋았어요. 🔲 가산명사 매력, 특징 [문예체] 🔲 그는 자연의 매력을 즐기기 시작하고 있었다. 🔲 형용사 미용의 🔲 추가 미용 시술을 미리 예약할 수 있다. 🔲 가산명사 장점 🔲 동물에게는 아무런 영향도 주지 않을 것이다. 이것이 바로 그러한 수성 재료의 장점이다.

bea|ver /bˈiːvər/ (**beavers, beavering, beavered**) 🔲 N-COUNT A **beaver** is a furry animal with a big flat tail and large teeth. Beavers use their teeth to cut wood and build dams in rivers. 🔲 N-UNCOUNT **Beaver** is the fur of a beaver. 🔲 *...a coat with a huge beaver collar.*

🔲 가산명사 비버 🔲 불가산명사 비버 털 🔲 큰 비버 털목도리가 달린 코트

▶ **beaver away** PHRASAL VERB If you **are beavering away at** something, you are working very hard at it. 🔲 *They had a team of architects beavering away at a scheme for the rehabilitation of District 6.*

구동사 부지런히 일하다 🔲 그들에게는 6번가 재건 계획을 부지런히 작성 중인 건축가 팀이 있었다.

be|came /bɪkˈeɪm/ **Became** is the past tense of **become**.

became의 과거형

be|cause ♦♦♦ /bɪkˈɔːz, bɪkˈʌz/ 🔲 CONJ You use **because** when stating the reason for something. 🔲 *He is called Mitch, because his name is Mitchell.* 🔲 *Because it is an area of outstanding natural beauty, the number of boats available for hire on the river is limited.* 🔲 CONJ You use **because** when stating the explanation for a statement you have just made. 🔲 *Maybe they just didn't want to ask too many questions, because they rented us a room without even asking to see our papers.* 🔲 *The President has played a shrewd diplomatic game because from the outset he called for direct talks with the United States.* 🔲 PHRASE If an event or situation occurs **because of** something, that thing is the reason or cause. 🔲 *Many families break up because of a lack of money.*

🔲 접속사 – 때문에 🔲 그는 이름이 미첼이라서 미치로 불린다. 🔲 이곳은 뛰어난 자연 경관을 자랑하는 지역이기 때문에, 강에서 빌릴 수 있는 보트의 숫자가 제한되어 있다. 🔲 접속사 왜냐하면 🔲 신분증을 보여 달라고 하지도 않고 우리에게 방을 빌려 준 것을 보면, 그들이 그냥 질문을 너무 많이 하기 싫었던 것인지도 모른다. 🔲 처음부터 미국과의 직접 회담을 요구한 점으로 미루어 보면, 대통령은 능수능란한 외교전을 펼쳤다. 🔲 구 – 때문에 🔲 돈이 없어서 깨지는 가정이 많다.

beck|on /bˈɛkən/ (**beckons, beckoning, beckoned**) 🔲 V-T/V-I If you **beckon to** someone, you signal to them to come to you. 🔲 *He beckoned to the waiter.* 🔲 *I beckoned her over.* 🔲 V-I If something **beckons**, it is so attractive to someone that they feel they must become involved in it. 🔲 *All the attractions of the peninsula beckon.* 🔲 V-I If something **beckons for** someone, it is very likely to happen to them. 🔲 *The big time beckons for Billy Dodds.*

🔲 타동사/자동사 손짓으로[고갯짓으로] 부르다 🔲 그는 웨이터를 불렀다. 🔲 나는 그녀에게 오라고 손짓했다. 🔲 자동사 유인하다, 유혹하다 🔲 반도의 온갖 매력이 유혹을 한다. 🔲 자동사 다가오다 🔲 빌리 도즈에게 전성기가 다가오고 있다.

be|come ♦♦♦ /bɪkˈʌm/ (**becomes, becoming, became**)

> The form **become** is used in the present tense and is the past participle.

> become은 현재 및 과거 분사로 쓴다.

🔲 V-LINK If someone or something **becomes** a particular thing, they start to change and develop into that thing, or start to develop the characteristics mentioned. 🔲 *I first became interested in Islam while I was doing my nursing training.* 🔲 V-T If something **becomes** someone, it makes them look attractive or it seems right for them. [no passive, no cont] 🔲 *Does khaki become you?* 🔲 PHRASE If you wonder **what** has **become of** someone or something, you wonder where they are and what has happened to them. 🔲 *She thought constantly about her family; she might never know what had become of them.*

🔲 연결동사 되다 🔲 나는 간호사 훈련을 받는 동안 처음으로 이슬람교에 관심을 가지게 되었다. 🔲 타동사 어울리다 🔲 너한테 카키색이 어울리니? 🔲 구 어떻게 되다 🔲 그녀는 계속 가족을 생각했다. 그녀는 식구들이 어떻게 됐는지 결코 모르게 될지도 몰랐다.

bed ♦♦◇ /bˈɛd/ (**beds**) 🔲 N-COUNT A **bed** is a piece of furniture that you lie on when you sleep. [also prep N] 🔲 *We finally went to bed at about 4am.* 🔲 *By the time we got back from dinner, Nona was already in bed.* 🔲 N-COUNT If a place such as a hospital or a hotel has a particular number of **beds**, it is able to hold that number of patients or guests. 🔲 *... a large hospital with more than eight hundred beds.* 🔲 N-COUNT A **bed** in a garden or park is an area of ground that has been specially prepared so that plants can be grown in it. 🔲 *...beds of strawberries and rhubarb.* 🔲 N-COUNT A **bed** of shellfish or plants is an area in the sea or in a lake where a particular type of shellfish or plant is found in large quantities. 🔲 *The whole lake was rimmed with thick beds of reeds.* 🔲 N-COUNT The sea **bed** or a river **bed** is the ground at the bottom of the sea or a river. 🔲 *For three weeks a big operation went on to recover the wreckage from the sea bed.* 🔲 N-COUNT A **bed** of rock is a layer of rock that is found within a larger area of rock. 🔲 *Between the white limestone and the greyish pink limestone is a thin bed of clay.* 🔲 N-COUNT If a recipe or a menu says that something is served on a **bed of** a food such as rice or vegetables, it means it is served on a layer of that food. 🔲 *Heat the curry thoroughly and serve it on a bed of rice.* 🔲 →see also **bedding** 🔲 PHRASE To **go to bed**

🔲 가산명사 침대, 잠자리 🔲 우리는 마침내 4시쯤 잠자리에 들었다. 🔲 우리가 저녁 식사를 마치고 돌아왔을 때, 노나는 벌써 자고 있었다. 🔲 가산명사 병상, 침상 🔲 800개 이상의 병상을 갖춘 큰 병원 🔲 가산명사 화단, 작은 밭 🔲 딸기와 대황이 심겨진 밭 🔲 가산명사 밭, 양식장 🔲 호수 전체가 두터운 갈대밭으로 둘러싸여 있었다. 🔲 가산명사 바닥 🔲 3주 동안 해저로부터 잔해를 회수하기 위한 대규모 작업이 진행됐다. 🔲 가산명사 지층 🔲 백색 석회석과 잿빛이 도는 분홍색 석회석 사이에 얇은 점토층이 있다. 🔲 가산명사 바닥에 깔린 음식 🔲 카레를 완전히 데워서 밥을 밑에 깔고 그 위에 끼얹는다. 🔲 구 성관계를 갖다 🔲 내가 그와 관계를 가진 것은 딱 한번뿐이다. 🔲 구 잠자리를 정돈하다 🔲 그는 훌륭한 공군답게 아침 식사 후에 침대를 정리했다.

with someone means to have sex with them. ❑ *I went to bed with him once, just once.* 🔟 PHRASE When you **make** the **bed**, you neatly arrange the sheets and covers of a bed so that it is ready to sleep in. ❑ *He had made the bed after breakfast, as a good airman should.* 🔟 **bed of roses** →see **rose**
→see lake, sleep

bed and break|fast (bed and breakfasts) also **bed-and-breakfast**
🔟 N-UNCOUNT **Bed and breakfast** is a system of accommodations in a hotel or guest house, in which you pay for a room for the night and for breakfast the following morning. The abbreviation **B&B** is also used. [mainly BRIT] ❑ *Bed and breakfast costs from £30 per person per night.* 🔟 N-COUNT A **bed and breakfast** is a guest house that provides bed and breakfast accommodations. The abbreviation **B&B** is also used. [mainly BRIT] ❑ *Accommodation can be arranged at local bed and breakfasts.*

🔟 불가산명사 아침 식사 포함 숙박 [주로 영국영어] ❑ 아침 식사를 포함한 숙박은 하룻밤에 일 인당 30 파운드부터입니다. 🔟 가산명사 숙박 업소, 여관 [주로 영국영어] ❑ 숙박은 현지 숙소에서 해결할 수 있습니다.

bed|clothes /bɛdkloʊz, -kloʊðz/ N-PLURAL **Bedclothes** are the sheets and covers which you put put over yourself when you get into bed. ❑ *Momma was cleaning inside, changing the bedclothes.*

복수명사 침대 커버, 침구 ❑ 엄마가 안에서 청소를 하시면서 침대 커버를 갈고 있었다.

bed|ding /bɛdɪŋ/ N-UNCOUNT **Bedding** is sheets, blankets, and covers that are used on beds. ❑ *...a crib with two full sets of bedding.*

불가산명사 침구 ❑ 침구 두 세트가 다 갖춰진 아기 침대

bed|room ♦◇◇ /bɛdrum/ (bedrooms) N-COUNT A **bedroom** is a room used for sleeping in. ❑ *...the spare bedroom.* →see **house**

가산명사 침실 ❑ 예비 침실

bed|side /bɛdsaɪd/ 🔟 N-SING Your **bedside** is the area beside your bed. ❑ *She put a cup of tea down on the bedside table.* 🔟 N-SING If you talk about being at someone's **bedside**, you are talking about being near them when they are ill in bed. ❑ *She kept vigil at the bedside of her critically ill son.*

🔟 단수명사 침대맡 ❑ 그녀는 침대 옆 탁자에 차가 담긴 잔을 놓았다. 🔟 단수명사 아픈 사람의 곁 병상 ❑ 그녀는 중태에 빠져 누워 있는 아들 곁을 지켰다.

bee /bi/ (bees) N-COUNT A **bee** is an insect with a yellow-and-black striped body that makes a buzzing noise as it flies. Bees make honey, and can sting. ❑ *A bee buzzed in the flowers.* →see **flower**

가산명사 벌 ❑ 벌 한 마리가 꽃들 사이에서 윙윙거렸다.

beef /bif/ (beefs, beefing, beefed) N-UNCOUNT **Beef** is the meat of a cow, bull, or ox. ❑ *...roast beef.* ❑ *...beef stew.* →see **meat**

불가산명사 쇠고기 ❑ 쇠고기 로스트 ❑ 쇠고기 스튜

▶**beef up** PHRASAL VERB If you **beef up** something, you increase, strengthen, or improve it. ❑ *...a campaign to beef up security.* ❑ *Both sides are still beefing up their military strength.*

구동사 강화하다, 증강시키다 ❑ 안보 강화를 위한 작전 ❑ 양쪽 진영이 여전히 군사력을 강화하고 있다.

been /bɪn/ 🔟 **Been** is the past participle of **be**. 🔟 V-I If you have **been** to a place, you have gone to it or visited it. ❑ *He's already been to Tunisia, and is to go on to Morocco and Mauritania.*

🔟 be의 과거 분사 🔟 자동사 가 본 적이 있다 ❑ 그는 튀니지에는 이미 가 본 적이 있고, 앞으로 모로코와 모리타니아에 가 볼 생각이다.

beep|er /bipər/ (beepers) N-COUNT A **beeper** is a portable device that makes a beeping noise, usually to tell you to phone someone or to remind you to do something. ❑ *His beeper sounded and he picked up the telephone.*

가산명사 무선 호출기, 삐삐 ❑ 호출이 오자 그가 수화기를 들었다.

beer ♦◇◇ /bɪər/ (beers) N-MASS **Beer** is a bitter alcoholic drink made from grain. ❑ *He sat in the kitchen drinking beer.* ● N-COUNT A glass of beer can be referred to as a **beer**. ❑ *Would you like a beer?*

물질명사 맥주 ❑ 그는 맥주를 마시며 주방에 앉아 있었다. ● 가산명사 맥주 한 잔 ❑ 맥주 한 잔 하실래요?

Word Partnership	beer의 연어
N.	**bottle of** beer, beer **bottle/can, glass/pint of** beer
ADJ.	**cold** beer
V.	**drink/sip (a)** beer

beet /bit/ (beets) 🔟 N-UNCOUNT **Beet** is a crop with a thick round root. ❑ *...fields of sweet corn and beet.* 🔟 N-VAR **Beets** are dark red roots that are eaten as a vegetable. They are often preserved in vinegar. [AM; BRIT **beetroot**] ❑ *It comes with a garnish of red beets, white cottage cheese, and blueberries.* →see **sugar**

🔟 불가산명사 사탕무 ❑ 옥수수와 사탕무 밭 🔟 가산명사 또는 불가산명사 홍당무 [미국영어; 영국영어 beetroot] ❑ 이 음식은 홍당무와 백색 연치즈, 블루베리가 곁들여져 나온다.

bee|tle /bitᵊl/ (beetles) N-COUNT A **beetle** is an insect with a hard covering to its body.

가산명사 딱정벌레

beet|root /bitrut/ (beetroots) N-VAR **Beetroot** is a dark red root that is eaten as a vegetable. It is often preserved in vinegar. [BRIT; AM **beet**]

가산명사 또는 불가산명사 홍당무 [영국영어; 미국영어 beet]

be|fit /bɪfɪt/ (befits, befitting, befitted) V-T If something **befits** a person or thing, it is suitable or appropriate for them. [FORMAL] ❑ *They offered him a post befitting his seniority and experience.*

타동사 적합하다, 어울리다 [격식체] ❑ 그들은 그에게 그의 경륜과 경험에 어울리는 자리를 제안했다.

be|fore ♦♦♦ /bɪfɔr/

In addition to the uses shown below, **before** is used in the phrasal verbs "go before" and "lay before."

before는 아래 용법 외에도 'go before', 'lay before'와 같은 구동사에 쓰인다.

🔟 PREP If something happens **before** a particular date, time, or event, it happens earlier than that date, time, or event. ❑ *Annie was born a few weeks before Christmas.* ❑ *Before World War II, women were not recruited as intelligence officers.* ● CONJ **Before** is also a conjunction. ❑ *Stock prices have climbed close to the peak they'd registered before the stock market crashed in 1987.* 🔟 PREP If you do one thing **before** doing something else, you do it earlier than the other thing. [PREP -ing] ❑ *He spent his early life in Sri Lanka before moving to England.* ● CONJ **Before** is also a conjunction. ❑ *He took a cold shower and then towelled off before he put on fresh clothes.* 🔟 ADV You use **before** when you are talking about time. For example, if something happened the day **before** a particular date or event, it happened during the previous day. [n ADV] ❑ *The war had ended only a month or so before.* ● PREP **Before** is also a preposition. [n PREP n] ❑ *It's interesting that he sent me the book twenty days before the deadline for my book.* ● CONJ **Before** is also a conjunction. ❑ *Kelman had a book published in the U.S. more than a decade before a British publisher*

🔟 전치사 - 전에, - 이전에 ❑ 애니는 크리스마스 몇 주 전에 태어났다. ❑ 2차 세계대전 이전에는 여성들이 첩보 요원으로 선발되지 않았다. ● 접속사 - 전에 ❑ 주가가 1987년 주식 시장이 폭락하기 이전에 기록한 최고치에 가깝게 올라갔다. 🔟 전치사 - 전에 ❑ 그는 영국으로 이사 오기 전에 스리랑카에서 유년시절을 보냈다. ● 접속사 - 전에 ❑ 그는 차가운 물로 샤워를 하고 보송보송한 옷을 입기 전에 수건으로 몸을 닦았다. 🔟 부사 - 전에 ❑ 전쟁이 겨우 한 달 정도 전에 끝났었다. ● 전치사 - 전에 ❑ 내 책의 마감일 20일 전에 그가 나에게 그 책을 보내 준 점이 흥미롭다. ● 접속사 - 전에 ❑ 켈만은 영국 출판사가 그와 접촉하기 십 년도 더 전에 미국에서 책을 한 권 출판했다. 🔟 접속사 -보다 먼저 ❑ 갈라쳐가 공을

a b c d e f g h i j k l m n o p q r s t u v w x y z

would touch him. ◢ CONJ If you do something **before** someone else can do something, you do it when they have not yet done it. ❑ *Before Gallacher could catch up with the ball, Nadlovu had beaten him to it.* ◤ ADV If someone has done something **before**, they have done it on a previous occasion. If someone has not done something **before**, they have never done it. [ADV after v] ❑ *I've been here before.* ❑ *I had met Professor Lown before.* ◥ CONJ If there is a period of time or if several things are done **before** something happens, it takes that amount of time or effort for this thing to happen. ❑ *It was some time before the door opened in response to his ring.* ◧ CONJ If a particular situation has to happen **before** something else happens, the first situation must happen or exist in order for the other thing to happen. ❑ *There was additional work to be done before all the troops would be ready.* ◨ PREP If someone is **before** something, they are in front of it. [FORMAL] ❑ *They drove through a tall iron gate and stopped before a large white villa.* ◩ PREP If you tell someone that one place is a certain distance **before** another, you mean that they will come to the first place first. ❑ *The station is on the right, one mile before downtown Romney.* ◪ PREP If you appear or come **before** an official person or group, you go there and answer questions. ❑ *The Governor will appear before the committee next Tuesday.* ⬛ PREP If something happens **before** a particular person or group, it is seen by or happens while this person or this group is present. ❑ *The game followed a colorful opening ceremony before a crowd of seventy-four thousand.* ⬛ PREP If you have something such as a journey, a task, or a stage of your life **before** you, you must do it or live through it in the future. [PREP pron] ❑ *Everyone in the room knew it was the single hardest task before them.* ⬛ PREP When you want to say that one person or thing is more important than another, you can say that they come **before** the other person or thing. [V PREP n] ❑ *Her husband, her children, and the Church came before her needs.* ⬛ **before long** →see **long**

Thesaurus	before의 참조어
ADV.	already, earlier, previously; *(ant.)* after ◥

before|hand /bɪfɔ̱rhænd/ ADV If you do something **beforehand**, you do it earlier than a particular event. ❑ *How could she tell beforehand that I was going to go out?*

be|friend /bɪfre̱nd/ (**befriends, befriending, befriended**) V-T If you **befriend** someone, especially someone who is lonely or far from home, you make friends with them. ❑ *The film's about an elderly woman and a young nurse who befriends her.*

beg /be̱g/ (**begs, begging, begged**) ◢ V-T/V-I If you **beg** someone **to** do something, you ask them very anxiously or eagerly to do it. ❑ *I begged him to come back to England with me.* ❑ *We are not going to beg for help any more.* ◤ V-I If someone who is poor **is begging**, they are asking people to give them food or money. [oft cont] ❑ *I was surrounded by people begging for food.* ❑ *There are thousands like him in Los Angeles, begging on the streets and sleeping rough.* ◥ **I beg your pardon** →see **pardon**

Word Partnership	beg의 연어
V.	beg and plead ◢
PREP.	beg for *something* ◢ ◤
N.	beg for help/mercy ◢ ◤
	beg for food/money ◤
	beg *(someone's)* pardon/forgiveness ◥

be|gan /bɪgæ̱n/ **Began** is the past tense of **begin**.

beg|gar /be̱gər/ (**beggars**) N-COUNT A **beggar** is someone who lives by asking people for money or food. ❑ *There are no beggars on the street in Vienna.*

be|gin ♦♦♦ /bɪgɪ̱n/ (**begins, beginning, began, begun**) ◢ V-T To **begin** to do something means to start doing it. ❑ *He stood up and began to move around the room.* ❑ *The weight loss began to look more serious.* ◤ V-T/V-I When something **begins** or when you **begin** it, it takes place from a particular time onward. ❑ *The problems began last November.* ❑ *He has just begun his fourth year in hiding.* ◥ V-I If you **begin with** something, or **begin by** doing something, this is the first thing you do. ❑ *Could I begin with a few formalities?* ❑ *...a businessman who began by selling golf shirts from the trunk of his car.* ◧ V-T You use **begin** to mention the first thing that someone says. [no cont] ❑ *"Professor Theron," he began, "I'm very pleased to see you."* ◨ V-I If one thing **began as** another, it first existed in the form of the second thing. [no cont] ❑ *What began as a local festival has blossomed into an international event.* ◩ V-I If you say that a thing or place **begins** somewhere, you are talking about one of its limits or edges. [no cont] ❑ *The fate line begins close to the wrist.* ◪ V-I If a word **begins with** a particular letter, that is the first letter of that word. [no cont] ❑ *The first word begins with an F.* ⬛ PHRASE You use **to begin with** when you are talking about the first stage of a situation, event, or process. ❑ *It was great to begin with but now it's difficult.* ⬛ PHRASE You use **to begin with** to introduce the first of several things that you want to say. ❑ *"What do scientists you've spoken with think about that?" — "Well, to begin with, they doubt it's going to work."*

Begin, start, and **commence** all have a similar meaning, although **commence** is more formal and is not normally used in conversation. ❑ *The meeting is ready to begin... He tore the list up and started a fresh one... an alternative to*

따라잡기 전에, 나드로브가 먼저 공을 낚아챘다. ⑤ 부사 전에 ❑ 전에 여기 온 적이 있다. ❑ 전에 로운 교수를 만난 적이 있었다. ⑥ 접속사 -까지 ❑ 그가 벨을 누르고 문이 열리기까지 시간이 좀 걸렸다. ⑦ 접속사 -에 앞서 ❑ 장병 전원을 준비시키기에 앞서 해야 할 일이 또 있었다. ⑧ 전치사 - 앞에 [격식체] ❑ 그들은 차를 몰고 높은 철문을 통과해 커다란 흰색 빌라 앞에 멈췄다. ⑨ 전치사 -보다 앞에 ❑ 역은 롬니 시내에서 1마일 못 미쳐서 오른쪽에 있다. ⑩ 전치사 - 앞에 ❑ 주지사가 다음 주 화요일 위원회에 출석할 것이다. ⑪ 전치사 - 앞에서 ❑ 화려한 개막식이 7만 4천 관중들 앞에서 펼쳐진 후 경기가 이어졌다. ⑫ 전치사 - 앞에 놓인 ❑ 그 방의 모든 사람들은 그것이 그들 앞에 놓인 가장 힘든 일이라는 것을 알았다. ⑬ 전치사 -보다 먼저 ❑ 남편과 아이들과 교회가 그녀의 필요보다 먼저였다.

부사 미리 ❑ 어떻게 그녀가 내가 나갈 걸 미리 알 수 있었지?

타동사 친구가 되다 ❑ 이 영화는 한 할머니 그리고 그 할머니와 우정을 나누는 젊은 간호사에 대한 이야기이다.

◢ 타동사/자동사 간청하다 ❑ 나는 그에게 같이 영국으로 돌아오자고 애원했다. ❑ 우리는 더 이상 도움을 구걸하지 않을 것이다. ◤ 자동사 구걸하다 ❑ 나는 음식을 구걸하는 사람들에게 둘러싸였다. ❑ 로스앤젤레스에는 그처럼 거리에서 구걸하고 한데서 잠을 자는 사람들이 수천 명 있다.

begin의 과거형

가산명사 거지, 걸인 ❑ 비엔나 거리에는 걸인이 없다.

◢ 타동사 시작하다 ❑ 그는 일어서서 방에서 이리저리 움직이기 시작했다. ❑ 체중 감소가 더 심각해 보이기 시작했다. ◤ 타동사/자동사 시작하다 ❑ 문제는 지난 11월에 시작됐다. ❑ 그의 은둔 생활은 이제 막 4년째 접어들었다. ◥ 자동사 -로 시작하다 ❑ 몇 가지 공식 절차로 시작해도 되겠습니까? ❑ 차 트렁크를 열고 골프 셔츠를 팔면서 사업을 시작한 사람 ◧ 타동사 말을 시작하다 ❑ "테론 교수님,"하고 그가 말을 시작했다. "만나 뵙게 되어서 정말 반갑습니다." ◨ 자동사 -로 시작되다 ❑ 지역 축제로 시작된 것이 국제적인 행사로 꽃피게 되었다. ◩ 자동사 -에서 시작되다 ❑ 운명선은 팔목 근처에서 시작된다. ◪ 자동사 -로 시작되다 ❑ 첫 단어는 에프로 시작된다. ⬛ 구 처음에는 ❑ 처음에는 아주 좋았지만 지금은 어렵다. ⬛ 구 먼저, 우선 ❑ "같이 이야기를 나눈 과학자들은 그 문제에 대해 어떻게 생각합니까?" "글쎄요, 먼저, 실현 가능성에 대해 회의적입니다."

commence가 더 격식적이고 대화에서 잘 쓰이지 않기는 하지만, begin, start, commence는 모두 비슷한 뜻을 갖는다. ❑ 회의를 시작할 준비가

commencing the process of European integration. Note that **begin**, **start**, and **commence** can all be followed by an -ing form or a noun, but only **begin** and **start** can be followed by a "to" infinitive.

Thesaurus   *begin의 참조어*

V.	commence, kick off, start; (ant.) end, stop 🔟

Word Partnership   *begin의 연어*

ADJ.	**ready to** begin 🔟 🔢
ADV.	begin **again/anew**, begin **immediately/soon**, **suddenly** begin 🔟 🔢
V.	begin **to show**, begin **to understand** 🔟 🔢
N.	begin **a process** 🔢
PREP.	begin **by doing** *something* 🔢
	to begin with 🔢 🔢

be|gin|ner /bɪgɪnər/ (**beginners**) N-COUNT A **beginner** is someone who has just started learning to do something and cannot do it very well yet. ❏ *The course is suitable for beginners and advanced students.*

be|gin|ning ♦♢♢ /bɪgɪnɪŋ/ (**beginnings**) 🔟 N-COUNT The **beginning of** an event or process is the first part of it. ❏ *This was also the beginning of her recording career.* 🔢 N-PLURAL The **beginnings of** something are the signs or events which form the first part of it. ❏ *The discussions were the beginnings of a dialogue with Moscow.* 🔢 N-SING The **beginning of** a period of time is the time at which it starts. ❏ *The wedding will be at the beginning of March.* 🔢 N-COUNT The **beginning of** a piece of written material is the first words or sentences of it. ❏ *...the question which was raised at the beginning of this chapter.* 🔢 N-PLURAL If you talk about the **beginnings** of a person, company, or group, you are referring to their backgrounds or origins. ❏ *His views come from his own humble beginnings.*

Thesaurus   *beginning의 참조어*

N.	birth; (ant.) conclusion, end 🔟
	start; (ant.) conclusion, end 🔢

Word Partnership   *beginning의 연어*

PREP.	beginning **of** *something*, **from/since the** beginning 🔟 🔢 🔢
ADV.	**just the** beginning 🔟 🔢 🔢
ADJ.	**a new** beginning 🔟 🔢 🔢

be|gun /bɪgʌn/ **Begun** is the past participle of **begin**.

be|half ♦♢♢ /bɪhæf/ 🔟 PHRASE If you do something **on** someone's **behalf**, you do it for that person as their representative. The form **in** someone's **behalf** is also used, mainly in American English. ❏ *She made an emotional public appeal on her son's behalf.* 🔢 PHRASE If you feel, for example, embarrassed or angry **on** someone's **behalf**, you feel embarrassed or angry for them. ❏ *"What do you mean?" I asked, offended on Liddie's behalf.*

be|have ♦♢♢ /bɪheɪv/ (**behaves, behaving, behaved**) 🔟 V-I The way that you **behave** is the way that you do and say things, and the things that you do and say. ❏ *I couldn't believe these people were behaving in this way.* 🔢 V-T/V-I If you **behave** or **behave yourself**, you act in the way that people think is correct and proper. ❏ *You have to behave.* 🔢 V-I In science, the way that something **behaves** is the things that it does. ❏ *Under certain conditions, electrons can behave like waves rather than particles.*

Word Partnership   *behave의 연어*

ADV.	behave **badly/well** 🔟
PRON.	behave *themselves/yourself* 🔢
PREP.	behave **toward** *someone* 🔟

be|hav|ior ♦♢♢ /bɪheɪvyər/ (**behaviors**) [BRIT **behaviour**] 🔟 N-VAR People's or animals' **behavior** is the way that they behave. You can refer to a typical and repeated way of behaving as a **behavior**. ❏ *Make sure that good behavior is rewarded.* ❏ *...human sexual behavior.* 🔢 N-UNCOUNT In science, the **behavior** of something is the way that it behaves. ❏ *It will be many years before anyone can predict a hurricane's behavior with much accuracy.* 🔢 PHRASE If someone is **on** their **best behavior**, they are trying very hard to behave well. ❏ *The 1,400 fans were on their best behavior and filed out peacefully at the end.*

Thesaurus   *behavior의 참조어*

N.	action, conduct 🔟

Word Partnership   *behavior의 연어*

ADJ.	**aggressive/criminal** behavior, **bad/good** behavior 🔟
V.	**change** *someone's* behavior 🔟
N.	**human** behavior, behavior **pattern**, behavior **problems** 🔟

되었다... 그는 리스트를 찢어 버리고 새 것을 쓰기 시작했다....유럽 통합 과정 착수에 대한 대안. begin, start, commence 모두 그 뒤에 -ing 형이나 명사가 올 수 있으나, begin과 start 다음에만 to 부정사가 올 수 있다.

가산명사 초보자 🔟 이 강좌는 초급반과 고급반 학생에게 적합합니다.

🔟 가산명사 시작 🔟 이는 또한 그녀의 음반 제작 인생의 시작이었다. 🔢 복수명사 조짐, 초기 🔟 그 논의가 구소련 정부와의 대화의 시초였다. 🔢 단수명사 초기, 시작 🔟 결혼식은 3월 초에 있을 것이다. 🔢 가산명사 도입부 🔟 이 장 도입부에 제기된 문제 🔢 복수명사 어린 시절; 기원; 발단 🔟 그의 견해는 불우했던 어린 시절의 경험에서 나온 것이다.

begin의 과거 분사

🔟 구 - 대표해서, - 대신에 🔟 그녀는 아들을 대신해서 사람들의 감정에 호소했다. 🔢 구 - 대신에 🔟 "무슨 뜻이야?"라고 리디 대신에 내가 화가 나서 물었다.

🔟 자동사 행동하다, 처신하다 🔟 이 사람들이 이런 식으로 행동하는 것이 믿겨지지 않았다. 🔢 타동사/자동사 예절 바르게 처신하다 🔟 똑바로 처신해야 해. 🔢 자동사 움직이다, 작용하다 🔟 특정 조건하에서는 전자가 입자가 아닌 파장처럼 작용할 수 있다.

[영국영어 behaviour] 🔟 가산명사 또는 불가산명사 행동, 태도 🔟 착한 일에 대해선 꼭 보상을 하도록 한다. 🔢 인간의 성적 행동 🔢 불가산명사 움직임, 작용 🔟 허리케인의 움직임을 아주 정확히 예측할 수 있기까지는 수년이 걸릴 것이다. 🔢 구 아주 성숙한 태도 🔟 1,400명의 팬들은 아주 성숙한 태도를 보였으며 마지막에는 조용히 줄지어 빠져나갔다.

a
b
c
d
e
f
g
h
i
j
k
l
m
n
o
p
q
r
s
t
u
v
w
x
y
z

be|hav|ior|al /bɪheɪvyərəl/ [BRIT **behavioural**] ADJ **Behavioral** means relating to the behavior of a person or animal, or to the study of their behavior. [ADJ n] ❏ ...*emotional and behavioral problems.*

[영국영어 **behavioural**] 형용사 행동의, 행동 연구의 ❏ 정서와 행동상의 문제

be|hind ♦♦♦ /bɪhaɪnd/

> In addition to the uses shown below, **behind** is also used in a few phrasal verbs, such as "fall behind" and "lie behind."

> behind는 아래 용법 외에도 'fall behind', 'lie behind'와 같은 몇몇 구동사에 쓰인다.

1 PREP If something is **behind** a thing or person, it is on the other side of them from you, or nearer their back rather than their front. ❏ *I put one of the cushions behind his head.* ● ADV **Behind** is also an adverb. ❏ *They were parked behind the truck.* ❏ *Rising into the hills behind are 800 acres of parkland.* **2** PREP If you are walking or traveling **behind** someone or something, you are following them. ❏ *Keith wandered along behind him.* ● ADV **Behind** is also an adverb. [ADV after v] ❏ *The troopers followed behind, every muscle tensed for the sudden gunfire.* **3** PREP If someone is **behind** a desk, counter, or bar, they are on the other side of it from where you are. ❏ *The colonel was sitting behind a cheap wooden desk.* **4** PREP When you shut a door or gate **behind** you, you shut it after you have gone through it. [PREP pron] ❏ *I walked out and closed the door behind me.* **5** PREP The people, reason, or events **behind** a situation are the causes of it or are responsible for it. ❏ *It is still not clear who was behind the killing.* **6** PREP If something or someone is **behind** you, they support you and help you. [PREP pron] ❏ *He had the state's judicial power behind him.* **7** PREP If you refer to what is **behind** someone's outside appearance, you are referring to a characteristic which you cannot immediately see or is not obvious, but which you think is there. ❏ *What lay behind his anger was really the hurt he felt at Grace's refusal.* **8** PREP If you are **behind** someone, you are less successful than them, or have done less or advanced less. ❏ *She finished second behind the American, Ann Cody, in the 800 meters.* ● ADV **Behind** is also an adverb. ❏ *The rapid development of technology means that she is now far behind, and will need retraining.* **9** PREP If an experience is **behind** you, it happened in your past and will not happen again, or no longer affects you. [PREP pron] ❏ *Maureen put the nightmare behind her.* **10** PREP If you have a particular achievement **behind** you, you have managed to reach this achievement, and other people consider it to be important or valuable. [have/with n PREP pron] ❏ *He has 20 years of loyal service to Barclays Bank behind him.* **11** PREP If something is **behind** schedule, it is not as far advanced as people had planned. If someone is **behind** schedule, they are not progressing as quickly at something as they had planned. ❏ *The work is 22 weeks behind schedule.* **12** ADV If you stay **behind**, you remain in a place after other people have gone. [ADV after v] ❏ *About 1,200 personnel will remain behind to take care of the air base.* **13** ADV If you leave something or someone **behind**, you do not take them with you when you go. [ADV after v] ❏ *The rebels fled into the mountains, leaving behind their weapons and supplies.* **14** to do something **behind** someone's **back** →see **back**. **behind bars** →see **bar**. **behind the scenes** →see **scene**. **behind the times** →see **time**

1 전치사 - 뒤에 ❏ 나는 쿠션 하나를 그의 머리 뒤에 받쳐 주었다. ❏ 그 차들은 트럭 뒤에 주차되어 있었다. ❏ 부사 뒤에 ❏ 뒤쪽 언덕에는 800에이커의 녹지가 펼쳐져 있다. **2** 전치사 -의 뒤를 따라 ❏ 키스는 그의 뒤를 따라 떠돌았다. ● 부사 뒤따라 ❏ 기병들이 갑작스러운 총격에 잔뜩 긴장을 한 채 뒤를 따랐다. **3** 전치사 - 뒤에 ❏ 대령은 싸구려 나무 책상 뒤에 앉아 있었다. **4** 전치사 - 뒤로 ❏ 나는 걸어 나와서 등 뒤로 문을 닫았다. **5** 전치사 - 배후에 ❏ 암살 사건 배후에 누가 있었는지 아직 확실치 않다. **6** 전치사 -을 지지하여 ❏ 주 사법부는 그의 편이었다. **7** 전치사 - 이면에 ❏ 그의 분노 이면에는 사실 그레이스가 거절했을 때 그가 받은 상처가 있었다. **8** 전치사 -보다 뒤떨어져 ❏ 그녀는 800미터 경주에서 미국의 앤 코디에 이어 2위로 들어왔다. ● 부사 뒤떨어져 ❏ 기술의 급격한 발전으로 그녀는 이제 한참 뒤떨어졌으며, 재훈련이 필요할 것이다. **9** 전치사 이미 지나간 ❏ 모린은 지난날의 악몽을 잊어둘 수 있었다. **10** 전치사 -라는 배경을 지닌 ❏ 그는 20년 동안 바클리 은행에서 성실히 일한 든든한 배경이 있다. **11** 전치사 -보다 뒤처져 ❏ 작업이 예정보다 22주 늦어지고 있다. **12** 부사 남아서 ❏ 1,200명 정도 남아서 공군 기지를 지킬 것이다. **13** 부사 남기고 ❏ 반군은 무기와 보급품을 남겨둔 채 산속으로 도주했다.

beige /beɪʒ/ COLOR Something that is **beige** is pale brown in color. ❏ *The walls are beige.*

색채어 베이지색 ❏ 벽은 베이지색이다.

be|ing ♦♦◇ /biɪŋ/ (**beings**) **1** **Being** is the present participle of **be**. **2** V-LINK **Being** is used in nonfinite clauses where you are giving the reason for something. ❏ *It being a Sunday, the old men had the day off.* ❏ *Little boys, being what they are, might decide to play on it.* **3** N-COUNT You can refer to any real or imaginary creature as a **being**. ❏ *People expect a horse to perform like a car, with no thought for its feelings as a living being.* →see also **human being** **4** N-UNCOUNT **Being** is existence. Something that is **in being** or comes **into being** exists. ❏ *Abraham Maslow described psychology as "the science of being."* **5** PHRASE You can use **being as** to introduce a reason for what you are saying. [mainly BRIT, INFORMAL, SPOKEN] ❏ *I used to go everywhere with my mother, you know, being as I was the youngest.* **6** →see also **well-being**. **other things being equal** →see **equal**. **for the time being** →see **time**

1 be의 현재 분사 **2** 연결동사 이유를 설명할 때 사용 ❏ 일요일이기 때문에, 노인들은 그날 쉬었다. ❏ 꼬마 남자 아이들은 꼬마 아이들인지라 그것을 갖고 놀려고 할지도 모른다. **3** 가산명사 생물 ❏ 사람들은 생명체로서 말이 느끼는 것은 전혀 생각하지 않고, 말이 자동차처럼 움직여 주기만을 바란다. →see also **human being** **4** 불가산명사 존재 ❏ 에이브럼 매슬로는 심리학을 '존재의 과학'이라고 묘사했다. **5** 구 -이기 때문에 [주로 영국영어, 비격식체, 구어체] ❏ 난 어디를 가든 엄마랑 함께 다녔는데, 너도 알다시피 내가 막내라서 그랬지.

be|lat|ed /bɪleɪtɪd/ ADJ A **belated** action happens later than it should have. [FORMAL] ❏ *...the government's belated attempts to alleviate the plight of the poor.*

형용사 뒤늦은 [격식체] ❏ 빈민층의 고통을 줄이기 위한 정부의 뒤늦은 시도

belch /beltʃ/ (**belches, belching, belched**) **1** V-I If someone **belches**, they make a sudden noise in their throat because air has risen up from their stomach. ❏ *Garland covered his mouth with his hand and belched discreetly.* ● N-COUNT **Belch** is also a noun. ❏ *He drank and stifled a belch.* **2** V-T/V-I If a machine or chimney **belches** smoke or fire or if smoke or fire **belches** from it, large amounts of smoke or fire come from it. ❏ *Tired old trucks were struggling up the road below us, belching black smoke.* ● PHRASAL VERB **Belch out** means the same as **belch**. ❏ *The power-generation plant belched out five tonnes of ash an hour.*

1 자동사 트림하다 ❏ 갈런드는 손으로 입을 가리고 조심스럽게 트림했다. ● 가산명사 트림 ❏ 그는 술을 마신 후 트림을 참았다. **2** 타동사/자동사 내뿜다 ❏ 지친 낡은 트럭들이 시꺼먼 연기를 내뿜으며 우리 아래에 있는 길을 힘겹게 오르고 있었다. ● 구동사 내뿜다 ❏ 발전소는 시간당 5톤의 먼지를 내뿜었다.

be|lea|guered /bɪliɡərd/ ADJ A **beleaguered** person, organization, or project is experiencing a lot of difficulties, opposition, or criticism. [FORMAL] ❏ *There have been several coup attempts against the beleaguered government.*

형용사 궁지에 몰린 [격식체] ❏ 지금까지 궁지에 몰린 정부를 타도하기 위한 쿠데타가 일곱 번 시도되었다.

be|lie /bɪlaɪ/ (**belies, belying, belied**) **1** V-T If one thing **belies** another, it hides the true situation and so creates a false idea or image of someone or something. ❏ *Her looks belie her 50 years.* **2** V-T If one thing **belies** another, it proves that the other thing is not true or genuine. ❏ *The facts of the situation belie his testimony.*

1 타동사 -와 딴판이다 ❏ 그녀는 모습으로 봐서는 50세가 아닌 것처럼 보인다. **2** 타동사 거짓임을 드러내다 ❏ 사건 당시의 사실은 그의 증언이 거짓임을 증명한다.

be|lief ♦♦◇ /bɪli:f/ (**beliefs**) **1** N-UNCOUNT **Belief** is a feeling of certainty that something exists, is true, or is good. ❏ *One billion people throughout the world are Muslims, united by their belief in one god.* **2** N-PLURAL Your religious or political **beliefs** are your views on religious or political matters. ❏ *He refuses to compete on Sundays because of his religious beliefs.* **3** N-SING If it is your **belief** that something is the case, it is your opinion that it is the case. ❏ *It is our belief that improvements in health care will lead to a stronger, more prosperous economy.* **4** PHRASE You use **beyond belief** to emphasize that something is true to a very great degree or that it happened to a very great degree. [EMPHASIS] ❏ *We are devastated, shocked beyond belief.* **5** PHRASE If you do one thing **in the belief that**

1 불가산명사 믿음 ❏ 전 세계 10억 명의 사람들이 유일신에 대한 믿음으로 결속된 회교도들이다. **2** 복수명사 믿음, 신조 ❏ 그는 종교적인 믿음 때문에 일요일에는 경기를 하지 않는다. **3** 단수명사 신념 ❏ 우리는 의료 제도 개선이 경제 발전과 번영으로 이어질 것으로 믿는다. **4** 구 -할 수 없을 정도로 [강조] ❏ 우리는 믿을 수 없을 정도로 충격을 받아 망연자실한 상태이다. **5** 구 -라고 생각하여 ❏ 민간인들은 분명히 음식이 있을 것으로 생각하고 그 건물 안으로 난입했던 것 같다.

another thing is true or will happen, you do it because you think, usually wrongly, that it is true or will happen. ❑ *Civilians had broken into the building, apparently in the belief that it contained food.* →see **religion**

Thesaurus   *belief*의 참조어

N.   dogma, faith, ideology, principle **2**
       assumption, opinion **3**

Word Partnership   *belief*의 연어

N.   belief **in God 1 2**
ADJ.   **religious/spiritual** belief **1 2**
       firm belief, **strong** belief, **widespread** belief **1 3**
       (contrary to) popular belief **1 3**
V.   **hold a** belief **1 3**
PREP.   belief **in** *something* **1**
       beyond belief **4**

---

be|liev|able /bɪlivəbᵊl/ ADJ Something that is **believable** makes you think that it could be true or real. ❑ *...believable evidence.*

형용사 믿을 만한 ❑ 믿을 만한 증거

be|lieve ♦♦♦ /bɪliv/ (believes, believing, believed) **1** V-T If you **believe** that something is true, you think that it is true, but you are not sure. [FORMAL] ❑ *Experts believe that the coming drought will be extensive.* ❑ *We believe them to be hidden here in this apartment.* **2** V-T If you **believe** someone or if you **believe** what they say or write, you accept that they are telling the truth. ❑ *He did not sound as if he believed her.* ❑ *Never believe anything a married man says about his wife.* **3** V-I If you **believe** in fairies, ghosts, or miracles, you are sure that they exist or happen. If you **believe in** a god, you are sure of the existence of that god. ❑ *I don't believe in ghosts.* **4** V-I If you **believe in** a way of life or an idea, you are in favor of it because you think it is good or right. ❑ *He believed in marital fidelity.* **5** V-I If you **believe in** someone or what they are doing, you have confidence in them and think that they will be successful. ❑ *If you believe in yourself you can succeed.*

1 타동사 생각하다 [격식체] ❑ 전문가들은 다가오는 가뭄이 광범위할 것으로 보고 있다. ❑ 우리는 그들이 이 아파트에 숨어 있다고 생각합니다. **2** 타동사 믿다 ❑ 그가 그녀를 믿는 것처럼 들리지 않았다. ❑ 유부남이 아내에 대해 말하는 것은 절대 믿지 말라. **3** 자동사 믿다 ❑ 난 귀신을 믿지 않아. **4** 자동사 믿다 ❑ 그는 부부의 정절을 믿었다. **5** 자동사 믿다 ❑ 네가 네 자신을 믿는다면 성공할 수 있다.

> Note that when you are using the verb **believe** with a **that**-clause in order to state a negative opinion or belief, you normally make **believe** negative, rather than the verb in the **that**-clause. For instance, it is more usual to say *"He didn't believe that she could do it..."* than *"He believed that she couldn't do it."* The same applies to other verbs with a similar meaning, such as **consider, suppose,** and **think.** ❑ *I don't consider that you kept your promise... I don't suppose he ever saw it... I don't think he saw me.*

부정적인 의견이나 믿음을 표현하기 위해서 동사 believe를 that 절과 함께 쓸 때는, 대개 that 절 속의 동사가 아니라 believe를 부정형으로 만든다. 예를 들면, "He believed that she couldn't do it."이라고 말하는 것보다 "He didn't believe she could do it."이라고 하는 것이 더 일반적이다. 뜻이 비슷한 consider, suppose, think와 같은 동사도 마찬가지다. ❑ 나는 네가 약속을 지키지 않았다고 생각한다... 나는 그가 그것을 보지 않았다고 생각한다... 나는 그가 나를 못 보았다고 생각한다.

Thesaurus   *believe*의 참조어

V.   consider, guess, speculate, think **1**
      accept, buy, trust; (ant.) doubt **2**

---

be|liev|er /bɪlivər/ (believers) **1** N-COUNT If you are a great **believer in** something, you think that it is good, right, or useful. ❑ *Mom was a great believer in herbal medicines.* **2** N-COUNT A **believer** is someone who is sure that God exists or that their religion is true. ❑ *I made no secret of the fact that I was not a believer.*

1 가산명사 신봉자 ❑ 엄마는 한약 신봉자였다. **2** 가산명사 신자 ❑ 나는 내가 종교가 없다는 사실을 숨기지 않았다.

bell ♦♦◇ /bɛl/ (bells) **1** N-COUNT A **bell** is a device that makes a ringing sound and is used to give a signal or to attract people's attention. ❑ *I had just enough time to finish eating before the bell rang and I was off to my first class.* **2** N-COUNT A **bell** is a hollow metal object shaped like a cup which has a piece hanging inside it that hits the sides and makes a sound. ❑ *My brother, Neville, was born on a Sunday, when all the church bells were ringing.* **3** PHRASE If you say that something **rings a bell**, you mean that it reminds you of something, but you cannot remember exactly what it is. [INFORMAL] ❑ *The description of one of the lads is definitely familiar. It rings a bell.*

1 가산명사 종 ❑ 식사를 마치자마자 종이 울려서 나는 1교시 수업을 받으러 갔다. **2** 가산명사 종, 방울 ❑ 내 남동생 네빌은 어느 일요일, 교회 종이 모두 울릴 때 태어났다. **3** 구 어렴풋이 생각나다 [비격식체] ❑ 남자들 중 한 사람의 인상착의가 아주 친숙하다. 어디서 본 듯하다.

bel|lig|er|ent /bɪlɪdʒərənt/ ADJ A **belligerent** person is hostile and aggressive. ❑ *...the belligerent statements from both sides which have led to fears of war.* ● bel|lig|er|ence N-UNCOUNT ❑ *He could be accused of passion, but never belligerence.*

형용사 공격적인 ❑ 전쟁의 우려를 낳은 양측의 공격적인 발언 ● 공격성 불가산명사 ❑ 그가 열정이 지나칠지는 모르지만 결코 공격적이지는 않다.

bel|low /bɛloʊ/ (bellows, bellowing, bellowed) **1** V-T/V-I If someone **bellows,** they shout angrily in a loud, deep voice. ❑ *"I didn't ask to be born!" she bellowed.* ❑ *She prayed she wouldn't come in and find them there, bellowing at each other.* ● **Bellow** is also a noun. ❑ *I was distraught and let out a bellow of tearful rage.* **2** V-I When a large animal such as a bull or an elephant **bellows,** it makes a loud and deep noise. ❑ *A heifer bellowed in her stall.* **3** N-COUNT A **bellows** is or **bellows** are a device used for blowing air into a fire in order to make it burn more fiercely. [also *a pair of* N]

1 타동사/자동사 고함지르다 ❑ "누가 낳아 달라고 했어!"라고 그녀가 소리쳤다. ❑ 그녀는 자신이 들어갔을 때 그들이 서로 으르렁거리고 있지 않기를 기도했다. ● 가산명사 고함, 호통 ❑ 나는 이성을 잃고 눈물을 흘리며 분노에 차 소리질렀다. **2** 자동사 음매하고 울다 ❑ 암소가 외양간에서 울었다. **3** 가산명사 풀무

bell pep|per (bell peppers) N-COUNT A **bell pepper** is a hollow green, red, or yellow vegetable with seeds. [mainly AM; BRIT, AM often **pepper**]

가산명사 피망 [주로 미국영어; 영국영어, 미국영어 종종 pepper]

bel|ly /bɛli/ (bellies) N-COUNT The **belly** of a person or animal is their stomach or abdomen. In British English, this is an informal or literary use. ❑ *She laid her hands on her swollen belly.* ❑ *...a horse with its belly ripped open.*

가산명사 배 ❑ 그녀는 자신의 불룩한 배에 손을 얹었다. ❑ 복부가 크게 찢어진 말

be|long ♦♦◇ /bɪlɔŋ, BRIT bɪlɒŋ/ (belongs, belonging, belonged) **1** V-I If something **belongs to** you, you own it. [no cont] ❑ *The house had belonged to her family for three or four generations.* **2** V-I You say that something **belongs to** a particular person when you are guessing, discovering, or explaining that it

1 자동사 -의 소유이다 ❑ 집은 서너 세대에 걸쳐 그녀의 집안에서 소유하고 있었다. **2** 자동사 -의 것이다 ❑ 이 글씨는 남자 글씨이다. **3** 자동사 -에 속하다 ❑ 나는 전에 청년 단체에 속해 있었다.

belongings 122

was produced by or is part of that person. [no cont] ❑ *The handwriting belongs to a male.* ◼ V-I If someone **belongs to** a particular group, they are a member of that group. [no cont] ❑ *I used to belong to a youth club.* ◼ V-I If something or someone **belongs** in or **to** a particular category, type, or group, they are of that category, type, or group. [no cont] ❑ *The judges could not decide which category it belonged in.* ◼ V-I If something **belongs to** a particular time, it comes from that time. [no cont] ❑ *The pictures belong to an era when there was a preoccupation with high society.* ◼ V-I If you say that something **belongs to** someone, you mean that person has the right to it. [no cont] ❑ *...but the last word belonged to Rosanne.* ◼ V-I If you say that a time **belongs to** a particular system or way of doing something, you mean that that time is or will be characterized by it. [no cont] ❑ *The future belongs to democracy.* ◼ V-I If a baby or child **belongs to** a particular adult, that adult is his or her parent or the person who is looking after him or her. [no cont] ❑ *He deduced that the two children belonged to the couple.* ◼ V-I If a person or thing **belongs** in a particular place or situation, that is where they should be. [no cont] ❑ *You don't belong here.* ❑ *They need to feel they belong.*

Word Partnership   belong의 연어

PREP.	belong **to** *someone* ◼ ◼ ◼ ◼
	belong **to a club/group/organization** ◼
V.	*someone/something* doesn't belong ◼

be|long|ings /bɪlɒŋɪŋz, BRIT bɪlɒŋɪŋz/ N-PLURAL Your **belongings** are the things that you own, especially things that are small enough to be carried. ❑ *I collected my belongings and left.*

be|lov|ed /bɪlʌvɪd/

When the adjective is not followed by a noun it is pronounced /bɪlʌvd/ and is hyphenated be**loved**.

ADJ A **beloved** person, thing, or place is one that you feel great affection for. ❑ *He lost his beloved wife last year.*

be|low ♦♦◇ /bɪloʊ/ ◼ PREP If something is **below** something else, it is in a lower position. ❑ *He appeared from the apartment directly below Leonard's.* ❑ *The sun had already sunk below the horizon.* ● ADV **Below** is also an adverb. ❑ *We climbed rather perilously down a rope-ladder to the boat below.* ❑ *...a view to the street below.* ◼ PHRASE If something is **below ground** or **below the ground**, it is in the ground. ❑ *They have designed a system which pumps up water from 70m below ground.* ◼ ADV You use **below** in a piece of writing to refer to something that is mentioned later. ❑ *Please write to me at the address below.* ◼ PREP If something is **below** a particular amount, rate, or level, it is less than that amount, rate, or level. ❑ *Night temperatures can drop below 15 degrees Celsius.* ● ADV **Below** is also an adverb. ❑ *...temperatures at zero or below.* ◼ PREP If someone is **below** you in an organization, they are lower in rank. ❑ *Such people often experience less stress than those in the ranks immediately below them.* ◼ **below par →**see **par**

Word Partnership   below의 연어

ADV.	**directly** below, **far/substantially/well** below, **just/slightly** below ◼
N.	below **the surface** ◼
	below **ground** ◼
	below **the waist**, below **cost**, below **freezing**, below **the poverty level**, below **zero** ◼
V.	**dip/drop/fall** below ◼ ◼
	described below, **see** below ◼
ADJ.	below **average**, below **normal** ◼

below-the-belt →see **belt**

belt ♦◇◇ /bɛlt/ (**belts, belting, belted**) ◼ N-COUNT A **belt** is a strip of leather or cloth that you fasten round your waist. ❑ *He wore a belt with a large brass buckle.* →see also **safety belt, seat belt** ◼ N-COUNT A **belt** in a machine is a circular strip of rubber that is used to drive moving parts or to move objects along. ❑ *The turning disc is connected by a drive belt to an electric motor.* →see also **conveyor belt** ◼ N-COUNT A **belt** of land or sea is a long, narrow area of it that has some special feature. ❑ *Miners in Zambia's northern copper belt have gone on strike.* →see also **commuter belt, green belt** ◼ V-T If someone **belts** you, they hit you very hard. [INFORMAL] ❑ *"Is it right she belted old George in the gut?" she asked.* ● N-COUNT **Belt** is also a noun. ❑ *Father would give you a belt over the head with the scrubbing brush.* ◼ V-I If you **belt** somewhere, you move or travel there very fast. [INFORMAL] ❑ *Darren and I belted down the stairs and ran out of the house.* ◼ PHRASE Something that is **below the belt** is cruel and unfair. ❑ *Do you think it's a bit below the belt what they're doing?* ◼ PHRASE If you have to **tighten** your **belt**, you have to spend less money and manage without things because you have less money than you used to have. ❑ *Clearly, if you are spending more than your income, you'll need to tighten your belt.* ◼ PHRASE If you have something **under** your **belt**, you have already achieved it or done it. ❑ *Clare is now a full-time author with six books, including four novels, under her belt.*

belt|way /bɛltweɪ/ (**beltways**) N-COUNT A **beltway** is a road that goes around a city or town, to keep traffic away from the center. [AM; BRIT **ring road**] ❑ *Interstate 295 is a 20-mile beltway that bypasses Jacksonville's busy downtown area.*

be|mused /bɪmyuzd/ ADJ If you are **bemused**, you are puzzled or confused. ❑ *He was rather bemused by children.*

bench /bɛntʃ/ (**benches**) **1** N-COUNT A **bench** is a long seat of wood or metal that two or more people can sit on. ❏ *He sat down on a park bench.* **2** N-COUNT A **bench** is a long, narrow table in a factory or laboratory. ❏ *...the laboratory bench.* **3** N-PLURAL In parliament, different groups sit on different **benches**. For example, the government sits on the government **benches**. [BRIT] ❏ *Members of Hungary's former ruling Communist party watched the day's proceedings from the opposition benches.* →see also **backbench 4** N-SING-COLL In a court of law, **the bench** is the judge or magistrates. ❏ *The chairman of the bench adjourned the case until October 27.*

1 가산명사 벤치 ❏ 그는 공원 벤치에 앉았다. **2** 가산명사 작업용 탁자 ❏ 실험실의 작업 탁자 **3** 복수명사 의석 [영국영어] ❏ 헝가리의 전 여당인 공산당의 의원들은 그 날의 의사 진행을 야당 의석에 앉아서 지켜보았다. **4** 단수명사·집합 재판관석 ❏ 재판장이 10월 27일까지 심리를 연기했다.

bench|mark /bɛntʃmɑrk/ (**benchmarks**) also **bench mark** N-COUNT A **benchmark** is something whose quality or quantity is known and which can therefore be used as a standard with which other things can be compared. ❏ *The truck industry is a benchmark for the economy.*

가산명사 지표 ❏ 트럭 산업은 경제의 지표 역할을 한다.

bend ♦◇◇ /bɛnd/ (**bends, bending, bent**) **1** V-I When you **bend**, you move the top part of your body downward and forward. Plants and trees also **bend**. ❏ *I bent over and kissed her cheek.* ❏ *She bent and picked up a plastic bucket.* **2** V-T When you **bend** your head, you move your head forward and downward. ❏ *Rick appeared, bending his head a little to clear the top of the door.* **3** V-T/V-I When you **bend** a part of your body such as your arm or leg, or when it **bends**, you change its position so that it is no longer straight. ❏ *These cruel devices are designed to stop prisoners bending their legs.* ● **bent** ADJ ❏ *Keep your knees slightly bent.* **4** V-T If you **bend** something that is flat or straight, you use force to make it curved or to put an angle in it. ❏ *Bend the bar into a horseshoe.* ● **bent** ADJ ❏ *...a length of bent wire.* **5** V-T/V-I When a road, beam of light, or other long thin thing **bends**, or when something **bends** it, it changes direction to form a curve or angle. ❏ *The road bent slightly to the right.* **6** N-COUNT A **bend** in a road, pipe, or other long thin object is a curve or angle in it. ❏ *The crash occurred on a sharp bend.* **7** V-T If you **bend** rules or laws, you interpret them in a way that allows you to do something they would not normally allow you to do. ❏ *A minority of officers were prepared to bend the rules.* **8** →see also **bent**

1 자동사 굽히다 ❏ 나는 앞으로 몸을 굽혀 그녀의 볼에 입맞춤을 했다. 그녀는 몸을 굽혀 플라스틱 양동이를 집어들었다. **2** 타동사 숙이다 ❏ 출입구의 윗부분에 머리가 닿지 않게 고개를 약간 숙이며 릭이 나타났다. **3** 타동사/자동사 구부리다; 구부러지다 ❏ 이 잔인한 기기들은 죄수들이 다리를 구부리는 것을 막도록 고안되었다. ● 구부러진 형용사 ❏ 무릎을 살짝 구부린 채로 있어라. **4** 타동사 구부리다 ❏ 쇠막대기를 말발굽 모양으로 구부려라. ● 구부러진 형용사 ❏ 구부러진 철사 한 토막 **5** 타동사/자동사 굽어지다 ❏ 길이 오른쪽으로 살짝 굽어졌다. **6** 가산명사 굽이 ❏ 사고는 길이 심하게 꺾어지는 곳에서 발생했다. **7** 타동사 악용하다 ❏ 소수의 장교들은 규칙을 악용할 의지를 가지고 있었다.

be|neath ♦◇◇ /bɪniθ/ **1** PREP Something that is **beneath** another thing is under the other thing. ❏ *She could see the muscles of his shoulders beneath his T-shirt.* ❏ *Four levels of parking beneath the theater was not enough.* ● ADV **Beneath** is also an adverb. ❏ *On a shelf beneath he spotted a photo album.* **2** PREP If you talk about what is **beneath** the surface of something, you are talking about the aspects of it which are hidden or not obvious. ❏ *...emotional strains beneath the surface.* ❏ *Somewhere deep beneath the surface lay a caring character.* **3** PREP If you say that someone or something is **beneath** you, you feel that they are not good enough for you or not suitable for you. ❏ *They decided she was marrying beneath her.*

1 전치사 밑의 ❏ 남자의 티셔츠 밑의 어깨 근육을 여자는 볼 수 있었다. 극장 밑에 주차 공간 네 개 층을 둔 것도 충분하지 않았다. ● 부사 밑에 ❏ 밑의 선반에서 그는 사진첩을 발견했다. **2** 전치사 밑의 ❏ 겉으로 드러나지 않는 감정적 긴장 ❏ 겉보기로는 드러나지 않는 내면 깊은 곳 어딘가에 남을 배려하는 성격이 숨어 있었다. **3** 전치사 자기보다 못한 ❏ 그들은 그녀가 자신보다 못한 사람과 결혼한다고 여겼다.

ben|efac|tor /bɛnɪfæktər/ (**benefactors**) N-COUNT A **benefactor** is a person who helps a person or organization by giving them money. ❏ *In his old age he became a benefactor of the arts.*

가산명사 후원자 ❏ 그는 노년에 예술의 후원자가 되었다.

ben|efi|cial /bɛnɪfɪʃ°l/ ADJ Something that is **beneficial** helps people or improves their lives. ❏ *...vitamins which are beneficial to our health.*

형용사 유익한 ❏ 우리의 건강에 유익한 비타민

bene|fi|ciary /bɛnɪfɪʃieri, BRIT bɛnɪfɪʃəri/ (**beneficiaries**) **1** N-COUNT Someone who is a **beneficiary of** something is helped by it. ❏ *One of the main beneficiaries of the early election is thought to be the former president.* **2** N-COUNT The **beneficiaries** of a will are legally entitled to receive money or property from someone when that person dies. ❏ *...one of the beneficiaries of the will made by the late Mr. Steil.*

1 가산명사 수혜자 ❏ 조기 선거의 주된 수혜자 중 한 명이 전 대통령으로 여겨진다. **2** 가산명사 상속인 ❏ 고(故) 스타일 씨가 쓴 유서의 상속자 중 1명

ben|efit ♦◇◇ /bɛnɪfɪt/ (**benefits, benefiting, benefited**)

The forms **benefitting** and **benefitted** are also used.

benefitting 또는 benefitted도 쓴다.

1 N-VAR The **benefit of** something is the help that you get from it or the advantage that results from it. ❏ *Each family farms individually and reaps the benefit of its labor.* ❏ *I'm a great believer in the benefits of this form of therapy.* **2** N-UNCOUNT If something is **to** your **benefit** or is **of benefit to** you, it helps you or improves your life. ❏ *This could now work to Albania's benefit.* **3** V-T/V-I If you **benefit** from something or if it **benefits** you, it helps you or improves your life. ❏ *Both sides have benefited from the talks.* **4** N-UNCOUNT If you have the **benefit of** some information, knowledge, or equipment, you are able to use it so that you can achieve something. ❏ *Steve didn't have the benefit of a formal college education.* **5** N-VAR **Benefit** is money that is given by the government to people who are poor, ill, or unemployed. ❏ *In order to get benefit payments I would have to answer some questions.* **6** →see also **fringe benefit, unemployment benefit 7** PHRASE If you give someone **the benefit of the doubt**, you treat them as if they are telling the truth or as if they have behaved properly, even though you are not

1 가산명사 또는 불가산명사 이익 ❏ 모든 가족은 각자 농사를 지어 노동의 수익을 거둔다. ❏ 나는 이 치료 방식의 이점에 대해 큰 믿음을 가지고 있다. **2** 불가산명사 ~에게 이익인 ❏ 이것은 이제 알바니아에게 이익이 될 수도 있다. **3** 타동사/자동사 이익을 얻다; 이익을 주다 ❏ 양측 모두 대화를 통해 이익을 얻었다. **4** 불가산명사 ~의 혜택 ❏ 스티브는 정규 대학 교육의 혜택을 받지 못했다. **5** 가산명사 또는 불가산명사 (빈민 등을 위한) 보조금 ❏ 보조금을 받으려면 나는 몇 가지 질문에 대답해야 할 것이다. **7** 구 좋은 쪽으로 생각하려고 하다 ❏ 처음에는 내가 그를 좋게 생각하려고 하였다. **8** 구 ~를 위해 ❏ 공동체를 위해 일하는 사람들이 필요하다.

sure that this is the case. ❑ *At first I gave him the benefit of the doubt.* ⑥ PHRASE If you say that someone is doing something **for the benefit of** a particular person, you mean that they are doing it for that person. ❑ *You need people working for the benefit of the community.*

Word Partnership   *benefit*의 연어

PREP.	benefit **of** *something* ① ④
	benefit **from** *something* ③
	to *someone's* benefit ②
N.	benefit **programs** ⑤

Word Link   *vol ≈ will : bene*vol*ent, in*vol*untary, *vol*unteer*

be|nevo|lent /bɪnɛvələnt/ ❶ ADJ If you describe a person in authority as **benevolent**, you mean that they are kind and fair. ❑ *The company has proved to be a most benevolent employer.* ● **be|nevo|lence** N-UNCOUNT ❑ *A bit of benevolence from people in power is not what we need.* ❷ ADJ **Benevolent** is used in the names of some organizations that give money and help to people who need it. [mainly BRIT] [ADJ n] ❑ *...the Army Benevolent Fund.*

be|nign /bɪnaɪn/ ❶ ADJ You use **benign** to describe someone who is kind, gentle, and harmless. ❑ *They are normally a more benign audience.* ● **be|nign|ly** ADV ❑ *I just smiled benignly and stood back.* ❷ ADJ A **benign** substance or process does not have any harmful effects. ❑ *We're taking relatively benign medicines and we're turning them into poisons.* ❸ ADJ A **benign** tumour will not cause death or serious harm. [MEDICAL] ❑ *It wasn't cancer, only a benign tumor.* ❹ ADJ **Benign** conditions are pleasant or make it easy for something to happen. ❑ *They enjoyed an especially benign climate.*

bent /bɛnt/ ❶ **Bent** is the past tense and past participle of **bend**. ❷ ADJ If an object is **bent**, it is damaged and no longer has its correct shape. ❑ *The trees were all bent and twisted from the wind.* ❸ ADJ If a person is **bent**, their body has become curved because of old age or disease. [WRITTEN] ❑ *...a bent, frail, old man.* ❹ ADJ If someone is **bent on** doing something, especially something harmful, they are determined to do it. [DISAPPROVAL] [v-link ADJ on/upon n/-ing] ❑ *He's bent on suicide.* ❺ N-SING If you have a **bent for** something, you have a natural ability to do it or a natural interest in it. ❑ *His bent for natural history directed him toward his first job.* ❻ N-SING If someone is **of** a particular **bent**, they hold a particular set of beliefs. ❑ *...economists of a socialist bent.* ❼ ADJ If you say that someone in a position of responsibility is **bent**, you mean that they are dishonest or do illegal things. [BRIT, INFORMAL] ❑ *...this bent accountant.* ❽ PHRASE If someone is **bent double**, the top part of their body is leaning forward toward their legs, usually because they are in great pain or because they are laughing a lot. In American English, you can also say that someone is **bent over double**. ❑ *He left the courtroom on the first day bent double with stomach pain.*

be|queath /bɪkwɪð/ (bequeaths, bequeathing, bequeathed) V-T If you **bequeath** your money or property **to** someone, you legally state that they should have it when you die. [FORMAL] ❑ *He bequeathed all his silver to his children.*

be|reaved /bɪriːvd/ ADJ A **bereaved** person is one who has a relative or close friend who has recently died. ❑ *Mr. Dinkins visited the bereaved family to offer comfort.*

be|reave|ment /bɪriːvmənt/ (bereavements) N-VAR **Bereavement** is the sorrow you feel or the state you are in when a relative or close friend dies. ❑ *When Mary died Anne did not share her brother's sense of bereavement.*

be|reft /bɪrɛft/ ADJ If a person or thing is **bereft** of something, they no longer have it. [FORMAL] ❑ *The place seemed to be utterly bereft of human life.*

ber|ry /bɛri/ (berries) N-COUNT **Berries** are small, round fruit that grow on a bush or a tree. Some berries are edible, for example blackberries and raspberries.

berth /bɜːθ/ (berths, berthing, berthed) ❶ PHRASE If you **give** someone or something **a wide berth**, you avoid them because you think they are unpleasant or dangerous, or simply because you do not like them. ❑ *She gives showbiz parties a wide berth.* ❷ N-COUNT A **berth** is a bed on a ship or train. ❑ *Goldring booked a berth on the first boat he could.* ❸ N-COUNT A **berth** is a space in a harbor where a ship stays for a period of time. ❑ *...the slow passage through the docks to the ship's berth.* ❹ V-I When a ship **berths**, it sails into harbour and stops at the quay. ❑ *As the ship berthed in New York, McClintock was with the first immigration officers aboard.*

be|set /bɪsɛt/ (besets, besetting)

The form **beset** is used in the present tense and is the past tense and past participle.

V-T If someone or something **is beset by** problems or fears, they have many problems or fears which affect them severely. ❑ *The country is beset by severe economic problems.* ❑ *The discussions were beset with difficulties.*

be|side ♦♢♢ /bɪsaɪd/ ❶ PREP Something that is **beside** something else is at the side of it or next to it. ❑ *On the table beside an empty plate was a pile of books.* →see also **besides** ❷ PHRASE If you are **beside yourself with** anger or excitement, you are extremely angry or excited. ❑ *He had shouted down the phone at her, beside himself with anxiety.* **beside the point** →see **point**

---

❶ 형용사 너그러운 ❑ 그 회사는 알고 보니 매우 너그러운 고용주이다. ● 너그러움 불가산명사 ❑ 권력을 가진 자들이 베푸는 약간의 너그러움을 우리가 필요로 하는 건 아니다. ❷ 형용사 자선 단체임을 나타내기 위해 조직명을 씀 [주로 영국영어] ❑ 군대 자선기금

❶ 형용사 친절한 ❑ 그들이 평상시에는 이보다 친절한 청중이다. ● 친절하게 부사 ❑ 나는 그저 굼은 허약한 웃으 뒤 뒤로 물러섰다. ❷ 형용사 무해한 ❑ 우리가 비교적 무해한 약을 가지고 독약을 만들고 있다. ❸ 형용사 양성의 [의학] ❑ 그것은 암이 아닌 양성 종양에 불과했다. ❹ 형용사 유리한; 온화한 ❑ 그들은 특별히 온화한 날씨를 즐겼다.

❶ bend의 과거 및 과거 분사 ❷ 형용사 구부러진 ❑ 나무들은 바람 때문에 모두 구부러지고 휘었다. ❸ 형용사 등이 굽은 [문어체] ❑ 등이 굽은 허약한 노인 ❹ 형용사 -하려고 결심한 [탐탁찮음] ❑ 그는 자살할 결심을 하고 있다. ❺ 단수명사 소질이 있는, 성향이 있는 ❑ 그는 첫 번째 직장은 자연사에 대한 소질 때문으로 선택하게 되었다. ❻ 단수명사 신념 ❑ 사회주의적 신념을 지닌 경제학자들 ❼ 형용사 부정직한, 비뚤어진 [영국영어, 비격식체] ❑ 이 부정직한 회계사 ❽ 구 몸을 제대로 펴지 못하는 ❑ 그는 첫날에 복통 때문에 몸을 제대로 못 펴고 법정을 떠났다.

타동사 유언으로 증여하다 [격식체] ❑ 그는 자신의 모든 은 제품을 아이들에게 유언으로 남겼다.

형용사 상을 당한 ❑ 딘킨스 씨는 유족을 조문하기 위해 방문했다.

가산명사 또는 불가산명사 사별의 슬픔 ❑ 메리가 죽었을 때 앤은 오빠가 느끼는 슬픔에 공감하지 않았다.

형용사 -을 상실한 [격식체] ❑ 그곳에서는 인간의 삶의 흔적을 전혀 찾을 수 없었다.

가산명사 장과(漿果)

❶ 구 피하다 ❑ 그녀는 연예계의 파티를 피한다. ❷ 가산명사 침대 ❑ 골드링은 가장 빨리 잡을 수 있는 배에 침실을 예약했다. ❸ 가산명사 정박 위치 ❑ 배의 정박 위치를 향해 선창들을 느리게 통과하 ❹ 자동사 정박하다 ❑ 배가 뉴욕에 정박하자 맥클린톡이 맨 먼저 승선한 이민국 직원들과 만났다.

beset은 동사의 현재, 과거, 과거 분사로 쓴다.

타동사 시달리다 ❑ 그 나라는 많은 심각한 경제 문제에 시달리고 있다. ❑ 토론은 많은 문제에 부딪혔다.

❶ 전치사 옆에 ❑ 탁자 위 빈 접시 옆에 책 한 더미가 쌓여 있었다. ❷ 구 제 정신이 아닌, 이성을 잃은 ❑ 남자는 불안하여 이성을 잃고 전화에 대고 여자에게 고함을 질렀다.

be|sides ♦◇◇ /bɪsaɪdz/ **1** PREP **Besides** something or **beside** something means in addition to it. ❑ *I think she has many good qualities besides being very beautiful.* ● ADV **Besides** is also an adverb. [cl ADV] ❑ *You get to sample lots of baked things and take home masses of cookies besides.* **2** ADV **Besides** is used to emphasize an additional point that you are making, especially one that you consider to be important. [ADV with cl] ❑ *The house was out of our price range and too big anyway. Besides, I'd grown fond of our little rented house.*

> Do not confuse **besides**, **except**, **except for**, and **unless**. You use **besides** to introduce extra things in addition to the ones you are mentioning already. ❑ *Fruit will give you, besides enjoyment, a source of vitamins.* However, note that if you talk about "the only thing" or "the only person" **besides** means the same as "apart from." ❑ *He was the only person besides Gertrude who talked to Guy.* You use **except** to introduce the only things, situations, people, or ideas that a statement does not apply to. ❑ *All of his body relaxed except his right hand... Travelling was impossible, except in the cool of the morning.* You use **except for** before something that prevents a statement from being completely true. ❑ *The classrooms were silent, except for the scratching of pens on paper... I had absolutely no friends except for Tom.* **Unless** is used to introduce the only situation in which something will take place or be true. ❑ *In the 1940s, unless she wore gloves a woman was not properly dressed... You must not give compliments unless you mean them.*

be|siege /bɪsidʒ/ (besieges, besieging, besieged) **1** V-T If you **are besieged by** people, many people want something from you and continually bother you. [usu passive] ❑ *She was besieged by the press and the public.* **2** V-T If soldiers **besiege** a place, they surround it and wait for the people in it to stop fighting or resisting. ❑ *The main part of the army moved to Sevastopol to besiege the town.*

best ♦♦♦ /bɛst/ **1** **Best** is the superlative of **good**. ❑ *If you want further information the best thing to do is have a word with the driver as you get on the bus.* **2** **Best** is the superlative of **well**. ❑ *James Fox is best known as the author of White Mischief, and he is currently working on a new book.* **3** N-SING **The best** is used to refer to things of the highest quality or standard. ❑ *We offer only the best to our clients.* **4** N-SING Someone's **best** is the greatest effort or highest achievement or standard that they are capable of. ❑ *Miss Blockey was at her best when she played the piano.* **5** N-SING If you say that something is **the best** that can be done or hoped for, you think it is the most pleasant, successful, or useful thing that can be done or hoped for. ❑ *A draw seems the best they can hope for.* **6** ADV If you like something **best** or like it **the best**, you prefer it. ❑ *The thing I liked best about the show was the music.* ❑ *Mother liked it best when Daniel got money.* **7** **Best** is used to form the superlative of compound adjectives beginning with "good" and "well." For example, the superlative of "well-known" is "best-known." **8** →see also **second best** **9** PHRASE You use **best of all** to indicate that what you are about to mention is the thing that you prefer or that has most advantages out of all the things you have mentioned. ❑ *It was comfortable and cheap: best of all, most of the rent was being paid by two American friends.* **10** PHRASE If someone does something **as best** they **can**, they do it as well as they can, although it is very difficult. ❑ *Let's leave people to get on with their jobs and do them as best they can.* **11** PHRASE You use **at best** to indicate that even if you describe something as favorably as possible or if it performs as well as it possibly can, it is still not very good. ❑ *This policy, they say, is at best confused and at worst non-existent.* **12** PHRASE If you **do** your **best** or **try** your **best** to do something, you try as hard as you can to do it, or do it as well as you can. ❑ *I'll do my best to find out.* **13** PHRASE If you say that something is **for the best**, you mean it is the most desirable or helpful thing that could have happened or could be done, considering all the circumstances. ❑ *Whatever the circumstances, parents are supposed to know what to do for the best.* **14** PHRASE If you say that a particular person **knows best**, you mean that they have a lot of experience and should therefore be trusted to make decisions for other people. ❑ *He was convinced that doctors and dentists knew best.* **15 to the best of** your **ability** →see **ability**. **to hope for the best** →see **hope**. **to the best of** your **knowledge** →see **knowledge**. **best of luck** →see **luck**. **the best of both worlds** →see **world**

be|stow /bɪstoʊ/ (bestows, bestowing, bestowed) V-T To **bestow** something **on** someone means to give or present it to them. [FORMAL] ❑ *The Queen has bestowed a knighthood on him.*

best|seller /bɛstsɛlər/ (bestsellers) N-COUNT A **bestseller** is a book of which a great number of copies has been sold. ❑ *By mid-August the book was a bestseller.*

best-selling also **bestselling** **1** ADJ A **best-selling** product such as a book is very popular and a large quantity of it has been sold. [ADJ n] **2** ADJ A **best-selling** author is an author who has sold a very large number of copies of his or her book. [ADJ n]

bet ♦◇◇ /bɛt/ (bets, betting)

> The form **bet** is used in the present tense and is the past tense and past participle.

1 V-I If you **bet on** the result of a horse race, football game, or other event, you give someone a sum of money which they give you back with extra money if the result is what you predicted, or which they keep if it is not. ❑ *Jockeys are forbidden to bet on the outcome of races.* ❑ *I bet £10 on a horse called Premonition.* ● N-COUNT **Bet** is also a noun. ❑ *Do you always have a bet on the Grand National?* ● **bet|ting** N-UNCOUNT ❑ *...his thousand-pound fine for illegal betting.* **2** N-COUNT A

---

1 전치사 ~에 더하여 ❑ 내 생각에 그녀는 매우 아름답다는 것 외에도 많은 장점을 지닌 것 같다. ● 부사 게다가 ❑ 구운 음식들을 많이 맛볼 수 있고 게다가 과자를 집으로 많이 가지고 갈 수도 있다. **2** 부사 게다가 ❑ 그 집은 우리의 가격대를 벗어났었고 어쨌든 너무 컸다. 게다가 나는 우리의 작은 임대 주택에 정이 든 상태였다.

> besides, except, except for, unless을 혼동하지 않도록 하라. besides는 이미 언급된 것에 더하여 추가로 다른 것을 소개할 때 쓴다. ❑ 과일은 즐거움뿐만 아니라 비타민도 제공한다. 그러나 특정한 사람이나 물건 이외(besides)의 the only thing 또는 the only person이라고 하면, 이 때 besides는 apart from과 같은 뜻이다. ❑ 그는 거트루드를 제외하고는 가이에게 말을 건 유일한 사람이었다. except는 진술이 적용되지 않는 유일한 사물, 상황, 사람, 생각을 말할 때 쓴다. ❑ 그는 오른손을 제외한 몸 전체가 긴장이 풀렸다... 아침에 서늘한 때를 제외하면 여행은 불가능했다. except for는 진술이 완벽한 진실이 되지 못하게 하는 것 앞에 쓴다. ❑ 교실은 고요했고 종이 위에 펜 긁히는 소리만 들렸다... 나는 톰을 빼면 친구가 한 명도 없었다. unless는 어떤 일이 발생하거나 사실이 될 수 있는 유일한 상황을 언급할 때 쓴다. ❑ 1940년대에는 여자가 장갑을 끼지 않으면 복장을 갖추어 입지 않은 것이었다... 진심이 아니면 칭찬을 하면 안 된다.

1 타동사 괴롭힘을 당하다 ❑ 그녀는 언론과 대중에게 시달렸다. **2** 타동사 포위하다 ❑ 군대의 주력 부대는 마을을 포위하기 위해 세바스토폴로 이동했다.

1 최고의 ❑ 더 많은 정보를 원한다면 최선책은 버스에 타자마자 기사와 대화를 나누는 것이다. **2** 최고 ❑ 제임스 폭스는 '화이트 미스치프'의 저자로서 가장 유명하며 현재 새로운 책을 쓰고 있다. **3** 단수명사 최선 ❑ 저희는 고객들에게 최고만을 제공합니다. **4** 단수명사 최선, 최고의 기량 ❑ 블록키 양은 피아노를 칠 때 최고의 기량을 보여 줬다. **5** 단수명사 최선 ❑ 비길 수 있는 것이 최상인가 보다. **6** 부사 최고로, 가장 ❑ 그 쇼에서 가장 내 마음에 들었던 것은 음악이다. ❑ 어머니는 다니엘이 돈을 받을 때를 가장 좋아하셨다. **7** 'good'나 'well'로 붙은 복합 형용사에서 최상급을 만들 때 사용 **8** 구 무엇보다 ❑ 그곳은 편하고 저렴했다. 무엇보다 임대료의 대부분을 2명의 미국인 친구가 부담하고 있었다. **9** 구 할 수 있는 대로 ❑ 사람들이 자기들이 할 수 있는 한 일을 해 나가도록 놔두자. **10** 구 좋아 봤자 ❑ 그들의 말에 의하면 이 정책은 좋아 봤자 혼란스러울 뿐이고 최악의 경우엔 없는 것이나 마찬가지다. **11** 구 최선을 다하다 ❑ 최선을 다해 알아보겠다. **12** 구 최선을 위해 ❑ 상황이 어떻든 간에, 어떻게 하는 게 최선인지를 부모는 안다. **13** 구 가장 잘 안다 ❑ 그는 의사와 치과의사들이 가장 잘 안다고 확신하고 있었다.

타동사 수여하다 [격식체] ❑ 여왕은 그에게 작위를 수여했다.

가산명사 베스트셀러 ❑ 8월 중순이 되자 그 책은 베스트셀러가 되었다.

1 형용사 베스트셀러의, 가장 잘 나가는 **2** 형용사 베스트셀러의

> bet은 동사의 현재, 과거, 과거 분사로 쓴다.

1 타동사/자동사 내기하다, 걸다 ❑ 기수들은 경기의 결과에 내기를 걸지 못하도록 되어 있다. ❑ 프리모니션이라는 말에 10파운드를 걸었다. ● 가산명사 내기 ❑ '그랜드 내셔널' 경마에 항상 돈을 거십니까? ● 내기 도박 불가산명사 ❑ 불법 내기 도박 때문에 그가 문 천 파운드 벌금 **2** 가산명사 내기에

bet is a sum of money which you give to someone when you bet. □ *You can put a bet on almost anything these days.* ◨ V-T/V-I If someone **is betting** that something will happen, they are hoping or expecting that it will happen. [JOURNALISM] [only cont] □ *The party is betting that the presidential race will turn into a battle for younger voters.* ◪ PHRASE You use expressions such as "**I bet**," "**I'll bet**," and "**you can bet**" to indicate that you are sure something is true. [INFORMAL] □ *I bet you were good at games when you were at school.* □ *I'll bet they'll taste out of this world.* ◫ PHRASE If you tell someone that something is a **good bet**, you are suggesting that it is the thing or course of action that they should choose. [INFORMAL] □ *Your best bet is to choose a guest house.* ◬ PHRASE If you say that it is **a good bet** or **a safe bet** that something is true or will happen, you are saying that it is extremely likely to be true or to happen. [INFORMAL] □ *It is a safe bet that the current owners will not sell.* ◭ PHRASE You use **I bet** or **I'll bet** in reply to a statement to show that you agree with it or that you expected it to be true, usually when you are annoyed or amused by it. [INFORMAL, SPOKEN, FEELINGS] □ *"I'd like to ask you something," I said. "I bet you would," she grinned.* ◮ PHRASE You can use **my bet is** or **it's my bet** to give your personal opinion about something, when you are fairly sure that you are right. [INFORMAL] □ *My bet is that next year will be different.* →see **lottery**

Word Partnership   bet의 연어

N.	bet **money** ◨
V.	lose/win a bet ◨ ◪
	make a bet, place a bet ◨ ◪
PREP.	bet **against** *someone/something*, bet on *something* ◨ ◪
ADJ.	willing to bet ◬
	best bet, good bet, safe bet ◭ ◮

be|tray /bɪtreɪ/ (betrays, betraying, betrayed) ◨ V-T If you **betray** someone who loves or trusts you, your actions hurt and disappoint them. □ *When I tell someone I will not betray his confidence I keep my word.* ◪ V-T If someone **betrays** their country or their friends, they give information to an enemy, putting their country's security or their friends' safety at risk. □ *They offered me money if I would betray my associates.* ◫ V-T If you **betray** an ideal or your principles, you say or do something which goes against those beliefs. □ *We betray the ideals of our country when we support capital punishment.* ◬ V-T If you **betray** a feeling or quality, you show it without intending to. □ *She studied his face, but it betrayed nothing.*

be|tray|al /bɪtreɪəl/ (betrayals) N-VAR A **betrayal** is an action which betrays someone or something, or the fact of being betrayed. □ *She felt that what she had done was a betrayal of Patrick.*

bet|ter ♦♦♦ /betər/ (betters, bettering, bettered) ◨ **Better** is the comparative of **good**. ◪ **Better** is the comparative of **well**. ◫ ADV If you like one thing **better than** another, you like it more. [ADV after v] □ *I like your interpretation better than the one I was taught.* □ *They liked it better when it rained.* ◬ ADJ If you are **better** after an illness or injury, you have recovered from it. If you feel **better**, you no longer feel so ill. [v-link ADJ] □ *He is much better now, he's fine.* ◭ PHRASE You use **had better** or **'d better** when you are advising, warning, or threatening someone, or expressing an opinion about what should happen. □ *It's half past two. I think we had better go home.* □ *You'd better run if you're going to get your ticket.* ● In spoken English, people sometimes use **better** without "had" or "be" before it. It has the same meaning. □ *Better not say too much aloud.* ◮ PRON If you say that you expect or deserve **better**, you mean that you expect or deserve a higher standard of achievement, behavior, or treatment from people than they have shown you. □ *We expect better of you in the future.* ◯ V-T If someone **betters** a high achievement or standard, they achieve something higher. □ *He recorded a time of 4 minutes 23, bettering the old record of 4-24.* ◰ V-T If you **better** your situation, you improve your social status or the quality of your life. If you **better yourself**, you improve your social status. □ *He had dedicated his life to bettering the lot of the oppressed people of South Africa.* ◱ **Better** is used to form the comparative of compound adjectives beginning with "good" and "well." For example, the comparative of "well-off" is "better-off." ◲ PHRASE You can say that someone **is better** doing one thing than another, or **it is better** doing one thing than another, to advise someone about what they should do. □ *Wouldn't it be better putting a time-limit on the task?* ◳ PHRASE If something changes **for the better**, it improves. □ *He dreams of changing the world for the better.* ◴ PHRASE If a feeling such as jealousy, curiosity, or anger **gets the better of** you, it becomes too strong for you to hide or control. □ *She didn't allow her emotions to get the better of her.* ◵ PHRASE If you **get the better of** someone, you defeat them in a contest, fight, or argument. □ *He is used to tough defenders, and he usually gets the better of them.* ◶ PHRASE If someone **knows better than to** do something, they are old enough or experienced enough to know it is the wrong thing to do. □ *She knew better than to argue with Adeline.* ◷ PHRASE If you **know better than** someone, you have more information, knowledge, or experience than them. □ *He thought he knew better than I did, though he was much less experienced.* ◸ PHRASE If you say that someone would **be better off** doing something, you are advising them to do it or expressing the opinion that it would benefit them to do it. □ *If you've got bags you're better off taking a taxi.* ◹ CONVENTION You say "**That's better**" in order to express your approval of what someone has said or done, or to praise or encourage them. □ *"I came to ask your advice – no, to ask for your help." — "That's better. And how can I help you?"* ◺ PHRASE You can say "**so much the better**" or "**all the better**" to indicate that it is desirable that a particular thing is used, done, or available. □ *Make sure that you use strong white flour, and if you can get hold of durum wheat flour, then so much the better.* ◻ PHRASE If you intend to do something

and then **think better of it**, you decide not to do it because you realize it would not be sensible. ❑ *Alberg opened his mouth, as if to protest. But he thought better of it.* ⑳ to **be better than nothing** →see **nothing**

→see **nothing**

Word Partnership		*better*의 연어
V.	make *something* better ①	
	look better ① ④	
	feel better, get better ② ④	
	deserve better ⑥	
ADV.	any better, even better, better than ① ②	
	much better ① ③ ④	
N.	better idea, nothing better ③	

be|tween ♦♦♦ /bɪtwin/

In addition to the uses shown below, **between** is used in a few phrasal verbs, such as "come between."

between은 아래 용법 외에도 'come between'과 같은 몇몇 구동사에 쓰인다.

① PREP If something is **between** two things or is **in between** them, it has one of the things on one side of it and the other thing on the other side. ❑ *She left the table to stand between the two men.* ② PREP If people or things travel **between** two places, they travel regularly from one place to the other and back again. [PREP pl-n] ❑ *I spent a lot of time in the early Eighties travelling between London and Bradford.* ③ PREP A relationship, discussion, or difference **between** two people, groups, or things is one that involves them both or relates to them both. [PREP pl-n] ❑ *I think the relationship between patients and doctors has got a lot less personal.* ❑ *There have been intensive discussions between the two governments in recent days.* ④ PREP If something stands **between** you and what you want, it prevents you from having it. [PREP n and n] ❑ *His sense of duty often stood between him and the enjoyment of life.* ⑤ PREP If something is **between** two amounts or ages, it is greater or older than the first one and smaller or younger than the second one. [PREP num and num] ❑ *Increase the amount of time you spend exercising by walking between 15 and 20 minutes.* ⑥ PREP If something happens **between** or **in between** two times or events, it happens after the first time or event and before the second one. [PREP pl-n, PREP num and num] ❑ *The canal was built between 1793 and 1797.* ● ADV **Between** is also an adverb. [ADV with cl/group] ❑ *Henry had to endure a journey by jetfoil, coach and two aircraft, with a four-hour wait in Bangkok in between.* ⑦ PREP If you must choose **between** two or more things, you must choose just one of them. [PREP pl-n] ❑ *Students will be able to choose between English, French, and Russian as their first foreign language.* ⑧ PREP If people or places have a particular amount of something **between** them, this is the total amount that they have. [PREP pron] ❑ *The three sites employ 12,500 people between them.* ⑨ PREP When something is divided or shared **between** people, they each have a share of it. [PREP pl-n] ❑ *There is only one bathroom shared between eight bedrooms.*

If there are only two people or things you should use **between**. If there are more than two people or things, you should use **among**. You can also talk about relationships **between** or **among** people or things, and discussions **between** or **among** people. ❑ *...an argument between his mother and another woman....an opportunity to discuss these issues among themselves.* Note that if you are **between** things or people, the things or people are on either side of you. If you are **among** things or people, they are all around you. ❑ *...the bag standing on the floor between us....the sound of a pigeon among the trees.*

① 전치사 사이에 ❑ 그녀는 두 남자 사이의 탁자를 있는 그대로 놔뒀다. ② 전치사 사이로 ❑ 나는 80년대 초반에 런던과 브래드포드 사이를 오가며 많은 시간을 보냈다. ③ 전치사 사이의 ❑ 환자와 의사 사이의 관계가 내 생각엔 훨씬 비인간적이 된 것 같아. ❑ 최근 두 정부 사이에 집중적인 논의가 있었다. ④ 전치사 사이에 ❑ 그의 의무감이 종종 그가 삶을 즐기는 데 장애물이 되었다. ⑤ 전치사 사이의 ❑ 15분에서 20분 동안 걸음으로써 운동하는 시간을 늘이세요. ⑥ 전치사 사이에 ❑ 그 운하는 1793년과 1797년 사이에 지어졌다. ● 부사 사이의 ❑ 헨리는 중간에 방콕에서 4시간을 기다리는 것을 포함하여 제트 수중익선, 버스, 두 차례의 비행기를 타는 여행을 견뎌야 했다. ⑦ 전치사 중에서 ❑ 학생들은 제1외국어로 영어, 불어, 혹은 러시아어 중에서 선택할 수 있을 것이다. ⑧ 전치사 합쳐 ❑ 그 세 현장에서 모두 합쳐 12,500명을 고용한다. ⑨ 전치사 공유된 ❑ 여덟 개의 침실에 화장실은 하나뿐이다.

사람이 두 명이거나 사물이 두 개뿐일 경우에는 between을 쓴다. among은 사람이나 사물이 셋 이상일 때 쓴다. 사람이나 사물들 '사이'의 관계에 대해서나, 사람들 '사이'의 토론에 대해 말할 때도 between이나 among을 쓸 수 있다. ❑ ...그의 어머니와 다른 여자 사이의 언쟁....그들 사이에서 그 문제에 대해서 논의할 수 있는 기회. between을 써서 당신이 사물 또는 사람들 '사이'에 있다고 하면, 사물 또는 사람들이 당신의 양쪽에 있다고 하는 것임을 유의하라. among을 써서 당신이 사물 또는 사람들 '사이'나 '가운데' 있음을 나타내면, 사물 또는 사람들이 당신의 모든 주위에 있음을 나타낸다. ❑ ...우리 사이의 바닥에 세워져 있는 가방....나무 사이에서 들리는 비둘기 소리

Word Partnership		*between*의 연어
N.	line between, link between ① ③	
	between countries/nations, difference between, relationship between ③	
	choice between ⑦	
ADV.	*somewhere* in between ⑥	
V.	caught between ①	
	choose/decide/distinguish between ⑦	

bev|er|age /bɛvərɪdʒ/ (**beverages**) N-COUNT **Beverages** are drinks. [FORMAL] ❑ *Alcoholic beverages are served in the hotel lounge.* ❑ *...artificially sweetened beverages.* →see **sugar**

가산명사 음료 [격식체] ❑ 알코올음료는 호텔 라운지에서 판매한다. ❑ 인공 감미료 첨가 음료

be|ware /bɪweər/ V-I If you tell someone to **beware of** a person or thing, you are warning them that the person or thing may harm them or be dangerous. [only imper and inf] ❑ *Beware of being too impatient with others.* ❑ *Motorists were warned to beware of slippery conditions.*

자동사 주의하다 ❑ 사람들에게 너무 성급하게 굴지 않도록 해라. ❑ 운전자들은 미끄러운 길을 주의하라는 경고를 받았다.

be|wil|dered /bɪwɪldərd/ ADJ If you are **bewildered**, you are very confused and cannot understand something or decide what you should do. ❑ *Some shoppers looked bewildered by the sheer variety of goods on offer.*

형용사 어찌할 바를 모르는 ❑ 어떤 쇼핑객들은 그저 제공되는 상품의 종류에만도 어찌할 바를 모르는 것 같았다.

be|wil|der|ing /bɪwɪldərɪŋ/ ADJ A **bewildering** thing or situation is very confusing and difficult to understand or to make a decision about. ❑ *A glance along his bookshelves reveals a bewildering array of interests.*

형용사 당혹스러운, 아찔한 정도의 ❑ 그의 책장을 훑어보면 아찔할 정도로 다양한 관심 분야가 드러난다.

be|wil|der|ment /bɪwɪldərmənt/ N-UNCOUNT **Bewilderment** is the feeling of being bewildered. ❑ *He shook his head in bewilderment.*

불가산명사 당혹감 ❑ 그는 당황하여 고개를 저었다.

be|witch /bɪwɪtʃ/ (**bewitches, bewitching, bewitched**) V-T If someone or something **bewitches** you, you are so attracted to them that you cannot think about anything else. ❑ *She was not moving, as if someone had bewitched her.* ● **be|witch|ing** ADJ ❑ *Frank was a quiet young man with bewitching brown eyes.*

타동사 홀리다 ❑ 그녀는 마치 홀린 듯이 움직이지 않았다. ● 홀리는 형용사 ❑ 프랭크는 사람을 홀릴 정도로 매력적인 갈색 눈을 가진 조용한 젊은이였다.

A
B
C
D
E
F

be|yond ♦♦◇ /bɪyɒnd/ **1** PREP If something is **beyond** a place or barrier, it is on the other side of it. ❑ *On his right was a thriving vegetable garden and beyond it a small orchard of apple trees.* ● ADV **Beyond** is also an adverb. ❑ *The house had a fabulous view out to the Strait of Georgia and the Rockies beyond.* **2** PREP If something happens **beyond** a particular time or date, it continues after that time or date has passed. ❑ *Few jockeys continue race-riding beyond the age of 40.* ● ADV **Beyond** is also an adverb. [and ADV] ❑ *The financing of home ownership will continue through the 1990s and beyond.* **3** PREP If something extends **beyond** a particular thing, it affects or includes other things. ❑ *His interests extended beyond the fine arts to international politics and philosophy.* **4** PREP You use **beyond** to introduce an exception to what you are saying. ❑ *He appears to have almost no personal staff, beyond a secretary who can't make coffee.* **5** PREP If something goes **beyond** a particular point or stage, it progresses or increases so that it passes that point or stage. ❑ *Their five-year relationship was strained beyond breaking point.* **6** PREP If something is, for example, **beyond** understanding or **beyond** belief, it is so extreme in some way that it cannot be understood or believed. ❑ *What Jock had done was beyond my comprehension.* **7** PREP If you say that something is **beyond** someone, you mean that they cannot deal with it. ❑ *The situation was beyond her control.* **8 beyond** your **wildest dreams** →see **dream**. **beyond a joke** →see **joke**

1 전치사 너머 ❑ 그의 오른쪽으로는 무성한 채소밭이 있었고 그 너머에는 작은 사과나무 과수원이 있었다. ● 부사 너머 ❑ 그 집은 조지아 해협과 그 너머의 록키 산맥이 보이는 멋진 전망이 기가 막혔다. **2** 전치사 이후까지 ❑ 마흔 살 이후까지 경주마를 노는 기수는 거의 없다. ● 부사 이후 ❑ 주택 소유에 대한 금융 지원은 1990년대와 그 이후에도 계속될 것이다. **3** 전치사 넘어 ❑ 그의 관심사는 미술을 넘어서 국제 정치와 철학에까지 미쳤다. **4** 전치사 제외하고 ❑ 커피도 탈 줄 모르는 비서를 제외하고는 그에겐 개인 직원이 거의 없는 것 같다. **5** 전치사 넘어선 ❑ 5년 동안 이어진 그들의 관계는 한계점을 넘을 정도로 힘들어져 있었다. **6** 전치사 넘어선, 초월한 ❑ 잭이 한 것은 내가 도무지 이해할 수 없는 것이었다. **7** 전치사 벗어난 ❑ 상황은 그녀의 통제를 벗어나 있었다.

Word Link bi ≈ two : biannual, bicycle, bilateral

G
H
I
J
K
L
M
N
O
P
Q
R
S
T
U

bi|an|nual /baɪænyuəl/ ADJ A **biannual** event happens twice a year. ❑ *You will need to have a routine biannual examination.* ● **bi|an|nu|al|ly** ADV [ADV after v] ❑ *Only since 1962 has the show been held biannually.*

형용사 반 년마다의 ❑ 반 년마다 정기적인 검진을 받아야 합니다. ● 반년마다 부사 ❑ 1962년이 되어서야 그 때부터 그 쇼는 반 년마다 열렸다.

bias /baɪəs/ (**biases, biasing, biased**) **1** N-VAR **Bias** is a tendency to prefer one person or thing to another, and to favor that person or thing. ❑ *Bias against women permeates every level of the judicial system.* **2** V-T To **bias** someone means to influence them in favor of a particular choice. ❑ *We mustn't allow it to bias our teaching.*

1 가산명사 또는 불가산명사 편견 ❑ 여성에 대한 편견은 법률 체계의 모든 부문에 도사리고 있다. **2** 타동사 치우치게 하다, 편견을 갖게 하다 ❑ 그것 때문에 우리가 학생을 가르칠 때 편견을 가져선 안 됩니다.

bi|ased /baɪəst/ **1** ADJ If someone is **biased**, they prefer one group of people to another, and behave unfairly as a result. You can also say that a process or system is **biased**. ❑ *He seemed a bit biased against women in my opinion.* **2** ADJ If something is **biased toward** one thing, it is more concerned with it than with other things. [v-link ADJ toward n] ❑ *University funding was tremendously biased toward scientists.*

1 형용사 편견을 가진 ❑ 내 생각에 그는 여자에 대해 약간 편견을 가진 듯 했어. **2** 형용사 -쪽으로 치우친 ❑ 대학 자금은 과학자들에게 너무 많이 치우쳐 있었다.

Bi|ble /baɪbəl/ (**Bibles**) **1** N-PROPER **The Bible** is the holy book on which the Jewish and Christian religions are based. **2** N-COUNT A **Bible** is a copy of the Bible. ❑ *...a publisher of Bibles and hymn books.* →see **religion**

1 고유명사 성경 **2** 가산명사 성경 ❑ 성경 및 성가집 출판사

bib|li|cal /bɪblɪkəl/ ADJ **Biblical** means contained in or relating to the Bible. ❑ *The community, whose links with Syria date back to biblical times, is mainly elderly.*

형용사 성경의 ❑ 시리아와의 관계가 성경 시대까지 거슬러 올라가는 그 곳의 주민 대다수는 노인이다.

bib|li|og|ra|phy /bɪbliɒɡrəfi/ (**bibliographies**) **1** N-COUNT A **bibliography** is a list of books on a particular subject. ❑ *At the end of this chapter there is a select bibliography of useful books.* **2** N-COUNT A **bibliography** is a list of the books and articles that are referred to in a particular book. ❑ *...the full bibliography printed at the end of the second volume.*

1 가산명사 관계 서적 목록 ❑ 이 장의 끝에 유용한 책을 선별한 관계 서적 목록이 있다. **2** 가산명사 참고 문헌 목록 ❑ 둘째 권의 끝에 인쇄되어 있는 참고 문헌 목록

bick|er /bɪkər/ (**bickers, bickering, bickered**) V-RECIP When people **bicker**, they argue or quarrel about unimportant things. ❑ *I went into medicine to care for patients, not to waste time bickering over budgets.* ❑ *...as states bicker over territory.* ● **bick|er|ing** N-UNCOUNT ❑ *The election will end months of political bickering.*

상호동사 말다툼하다 ❑ 나는 환자를 돌보기 위해 의학을 선택했지 예산 가지고 말다툼하면서 시간이나 낭비하려고 그런 것이 아니다. ❑ 국가들이 영토를 두고 다투면서 ● 말다툼 불가산명사 ❑ 선거가 수개월의 정치적 다툼을 종결지을 것이다.

bi|cy|cle /baɪsɪkəl/ (**bicycles**) N-COUNT A **bicycle** is a vehicle with two wheels which you ride by sitting on it and pushing two pedals with your feet. You steer it by turning a bar that is connected to the front wheel. →see Word Web: **bicycle**

가산명사 자전거

bid ♦♦◇ /bɪd/ (**bids, bidding**)

The form **bid** is used in the present tense and is the past tense and past participle.	bid는 동사의 현재, 과거, 과거 분사로 쓴다.

1 N-COUNT A **bid for** something or a **bid to** do something is an attempt to obtain it or do it. [JOURNALISM] ❑ *...Sydney's successful bid for the 2000 Olympic Games.* **2** N-COUNT A **bid** is an offer to pay a particular amount of money for something that is being sold. ❑ *Hanson made an agreed takeover bid of £351 million.* **3** V-T/V-I If you **bid** for something or **bid to** do something, you try to obtain it or do it. ❑ *Singapore Airlines is rumored to be bidding for a management contract to run both airports.* **4** V-T/V-I If you **bid for** something that is being sold, you offer to pay a particular amount of money for it. ❑ *She wanted to bid for it.* ❑ *The bank announced its intention to bid.*

1 가산명사 시도 [언론] ❑ 시드니의 성공적인 2000년 올림픽 유치 시도 **2** 가산명사 입찰 ❑ 핸슨은 351백만 파운드의 합의된 주식의 공개매수를 했다. **3** 타동사/자동사 (얻으려고) 시도하다 ❑ 싱가포르 항공이 두 공항 모두를 운영하기 위한 경영권 계약을 따내려고 한다는 소문이 있다. **4** 타동사/자동사 입찰하다 ❑ 그녀는 그것을 위해 입찰하고 싶어 했다. ❑ 그 은행은 입찰하겠다는 의도를 발표했다.

V
W
X
Y
Z

Word Web bicycle

A Scotsman named Kirkpatrick MacMillan invented the first **bicycle** with **pedals** around 1840. Early bicycles had wooden or metal **wheels**. However, by the mid-1800s **tires** with tubes appeared. Modern racing bikes are very lightweight and aerodynamic. The wheels have fewer spokes and the tires are very thin and smooth. Mountain bikes allow riders to ride up and down steep hills on dirt trails. These bikes have fat, knobby tires for extra traction. The **tandem** is a bicycle for two people. It has about the same **wind resistance** as a one-person bike. But with twice the power, it goes faster.

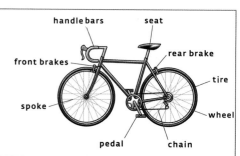

handle bars · seat · rear brake · front brakes · tire · wheel · chain · pedal · spoke

bid|der /bɪdər/ (bidders) **1** N-COUNT A **bidder** is someone who offers to pay a certain amount of money for something that is being sold. If you sell something to the highest **bidder**, you sell it to the person who offers the most money for it. ❑ *The sale will be made to the highest bidder subject to a reserve price being attained.* **2** N-COUNT A **bidder for** something is someone who is trying to obtain it or do it. ❑ *Vodafone is among successful bidders for two licenses to develop cellphone systems in Greece.*

1 가산명사 입찰자 ❑ 최저 경매 가격이 확보되면 그 이후 최고 입찰자에게 매물을 할 것이다. **2** 가산명사 지원자 ❑ 보다폰은 그리스에서 이동 전화 시스템을 개발하는 두 개의 허가권을 성공적으로 따낸 회사 중 하나이다.

bid price (bid prices) N-COUNT The **bid price** of a particular stock or share is the price that investors are willing to pay for it. [BUSINESS] ❑ *Speculation centered on a likely bid price of 380p a share.*

가산명사 매수 호가 [경제] ❑ 주당 매수 호가가 380펜스가 될 가능성이 높다는 것이 대체적인 추측이었다.

big ♦♦♦ /bɪg/ (bigger, biggest) **1** ADJ A **big** person or thing is large in physical size. ❑ *Australia's a big country.* ❑ *Her husband was a big man.* **2** ADJ Something that is **big** consists of many people or things. ❑ *The crowd included a big contingent from Ipswich.* **3** ADJ If you describe something such as a problem, increase, or change as a **big** one, you mean it is great in degree, extent, or importance. ❑ *Her problem was just too big for her to tackle on her own.* **4** ADJ A **big** organization, activity, or place, you mean that they have a lot of influence or employs many people and has many customers. ❑ *...one of the biggest companies in Italy.* **5** ADJ If you say that someone is **big in** a particular organization, activity, or place, you mean that they have a lot of influence or authority in it. [INFORMAL] [ADJ n, v-link ADJ in n] ❑ *Their father was very big in the army.* **6** ADJ If you call someone a **big** bully or a **big** coward, you are emphasizing your disapproval of them. [INFORMAL, EMPHASIS] [ADJ n] ❑ *His personality changed. He turned into a big bully.* **7** ADJ Children often refer to their older brother or sister as their **big** brother or sister. [ADJ n] ❑ *She always introduces me as her big sister.* **8** ADJ **Big** words are long or rare words which have meanings that are difficult to understand. [INFORMAL] ❑ *They use a lot of big words.* **9** PHRASE If you **make it big**, you become successful or famous. [INFORMAL] ❑ *We're not just looking at making it big in the UK, we want to be big internationally.* **10** PHRASE If you **think big**, you make plans on a large scale, often using a lot of time, effort, or money. ❑ *Maybe we're not thinking big enough.*

1 형용사 큰 ❑ 호주는 큰 나라이다. ❑ 그녀의 남편은 덩치가 큰 남자였다. **2** 형용사 큰 ❑ 군중에는 입스위치에서 온 대규모 파견단도 포함되어 있었다. **3** 형용사 큰 ❑ 그녀의 문제는 스스로 해결하기에는 너무 컸다. **4** 형용사 큰 ❑ 이탈리아에서 가장 큰 회사 중 하나 **5** 형용사 중요한 [비격식체] ❑ 그들의 아버지는 군대에서 중요한 인물이었다. **6** 형용사 혐오감 등을 강조하는 표현 [비격식체, 강조] ❑ 그는 성격이 변해 있었다. 약한 사람들을 괴롭히는 나쁜 인간으로 변해 있었다. **7** 형용사 손위의 ❑ 그 애는 항상 나를 자신의 언니라고 소개한다. **8** 형용사 거창한 [비격식체] ❑ 그들은 거창한 말들을 많이 쓴다. **9** 구 크게 되다 [비격식체] ❑ 우리는 단지 영국 내에서만 크게 되려는 것이 아니라 국제적으로 성공하고 싶다. **10** 구 크게 생각하다 ❑ 어쩌면 우리가 너무 작게 생각하고 있는지도 모르겠다.

Big, **large**, and **great** are all used to talk about size. In general, **large** is more formal than **big**, and **great** is more formal than **large**. **Big** and **large** are normally used to describe objects, but you can also use **big** to suggest that something is important or impressive. ❑ *...his influence over the big advertisers.* You normally use **great** to emphasize the importance of someone or something. ❑ *...the great English architect, Inigo Jones.* However, you can also use **great** to suggest that something is impressive because of its size. ❑ *The great bird of prey was a dark smudge against the sun.* You can use **large** or **great**, but not **big**, to describe amounts. ❑ *...a large amount of blood on the floor....the coming of tourists in great numbers.* Both **big** and **great** can be used to emphasize the intensity of something, although **great** is more formal. ❑ *It gives me great pleasure to welcome you... Most of them act like big fools.* Remember that **great** has several other meanings, when it does not refer to size, but to something that is remarkable, very good, or enjoyable.

big, large, great은 모두 크기를 말할 때 쓴다. 일반적으로 large가 big보다, great이 large보다 더 격식체이다. big과 large는 보통 사물을 묘사할 때 쓰지만, big은 무엇이 중요하거나 인상적임을 시사할 때에도 쓴다. ❑ ...주요 광고주들에 대한 그의 영향력. 사람이나 사물의 중요성을 강조할 때는 보통 great을 쓴다. ❑ ...위대한 영국 건축가 이니고 존스. 그러나 great은 사물이 그 크기 때문에 인상적임을 시사할 때도 쓸 수 있다. ❑ 그 거대한 맹금은 햇빛을 배경으로 하나의 흐릿한 검은 점처럼 보였다. 양을 나타낼 때는 large나 great은 쓸 수 있지만 big은 못 쓴다. ❑ ...바닥 위의 많은 양의 피.... 수많은 여행객의 방문. big과 great은 어떤 것의 강도를 강조할 때에도 쓸 수 있는데 great이 더 격식체이다. ❑ 이렇게 환영 인사를 드리게 되어 정말 기쁩니다. ... 그들 대부분은 엄청난 바보처럼 행동한다. great에는 다른 뜻도 몇 가지가 있어서 크기를 가리키지 않고 놀랄 만하거나, 아주 좋거나, 유쾌한 무엇을 가리키는 경우도 있음을 기억하라.

Thesaurus   big의 참조어

ADJ.	enormous, huge, large, massive; (ant.) little, small, tiny **1**
	considerable, significant, substantial; (ant.) insignificant, unimportant **3**
	important, influential, prominent; (ant.) obscure **5**

big busi|ness **1** N-UNCOUNT **Big business** is business which involves very large companies and very large sums of money. ❑ *Big business will never let petty nationalism get in the way of a good deal.* **2** N-UNCOUNT Something that is **big business** is something which people spend a lot of money on, and which has become an important commercial activity. ❑ *Britain's railways are big business.*

1 불가산명사 대기업 ❑ 대기업들이 절대 사소한 국수주의 때문에 좋은 거래를 놓치지는 않을 것이다. **2** 불가산명사 큰 사업 ❑ 영국의 철도는 큰 사업이다.

big deal **1** N-SING If you say that something is a **big deal**, you mean that it is important or significant in some way. [INFORMAL] ❑ *I felt the pressure on me, winning was such a big deal for the whole family.* **2** PHRASE If someone **makes a big deal out of** something, they make a fuss about it or treat it as if it were very important. [INFORMAL] ❑ *The Joneses make a big deal out of being "different."* **3** CONVENTION You can say "**big deal**" to someone to show that you are not impressed by something that they consider important or impressive. [INFORMAL, FEELINGS] ❑ *So the Queen has finally got her own mobile phone. Big deal!*

1 단수명사 큰 일 [비격식체] ❑ 이기는 것이 우리 가족 전체에게 너무 중요한 일이어서 나는 엄청난 압박감을 느꼈다. **2** 구 야단을 피우다 [비격식체] ❑ 존스 가족은 '다르다'는 것에 대해 굉장한 의미를 부여한다. **3** 관용 표현 남에게 중요한 것이 자신에게는 별 의미가 없다는 것을 나타내는 표현 [비격식체, 감정 개입] ❑ 여왕께서 드디어 핸드폰을 한 대 장만하셨다는 거지. 그게 뭐 대수라고.

big|ot /bɪgət/ (bigots) N-COUNT If you describe someone as a **bigot**, you mean that they are bigoted. [DISAPPROVAL] ❑ *Anyone who opposes them is branded a racist, a bigot, or a homophobe.*

가산명사 편협한 사람 [탐탁찮음] ❑ 그들을 반대하는 사람은 모두 인종차별주의자, 편협한 인간, 혹은 동성애 혐오자로 낙인찍힌다.

big|ot|ed /bɪgətɪd/ ADJ Someone who is **bigoted** has strong, unreasonable prejudices or opinions and will not change them, even when they are proved to be wrong. [DISAPPROVAL] ❑ *He was bigoted and racist.*

형용사 편협한 [탐탁찮음] ❑ 그는 편협한 인종차별주의자였다.

big|ot|ry /bɪgətri/ N-UNCOUNT **Bigotry** is the possession or expression of strong, unreasonable prejudices or opinions. ❑ *He deplored religious bigotry.*

불가산명사 편협함 ❑ 그는 종교적 편협함을 개탄했다.

big time also **big-time** **1** ADJ You can use **big time** to refer to the highest level of an activity or sport where you can achieve the greatest amount of success or importance. If you describe a person as **big time**, you mean they are successful and important. [INFORMAL] ❑ *He took a long time to settle in to big-time*

1 형용사 일류의; 성공한 [비격식체] ❑ 그는 프로 축구에 적응하는 데 오랜 시간이 걸렸다. **2** 단수명사 대박 [비격식체] ❑ 그는 '사랑과 영혼,' '더티 댄싱' 등의 영화로 대박을 터뜨렸다. **3** 부사 크게 [미국영어,

football. **2** N-SING If someone hits **the big time**, they become famous or successful in a particular area of activity. [INFORMAL] ❑ *He hit the big time with films such as "Ghost" and "Dirty Dancing."* **3** ADV You can use **big time** if you want to emphasize the importance or extent of something that has happened. [AM, INFORMAL, EMPHASIS] [ADV after v] ❑ *Mike Edwards has tasted success big time.*

비격식체, 강조] ❑ 마이크 에드워즈는 성공을 크게 맛봤다.

bike ♦♢♢ /baɪk/ (**bikes, biking, biked**) **1** N-COUNT A **bike** is a bicycle, motorcycle, or motorbike. [INFORMAL] ❑ *When you ride a bike, you exercise all of the leg muscles.* **2** V-I To **bike** somewhere means to go there on a bicycle. [INFORMAL] ❑ *I biked home from the beach.*

1 가산명사 자전거 [비격식체] ❑ 자전거를 타면 모든 다리 근육에 운동이 된다. **2** 자동사 자전거를 타다 [비격식체] ❑ 나는 해변에서 집까지 자전거를 타고 왔다.

bik|er /baɪkər/ (**bikers**) **1** N-COUNT **Bikers** are people who ride around on motorcycles or motorbikes, usually in groups. ❑ *There are always fights going on between rival bikers.* **2** N-COUNT People who ride bicycles are called **bikers**. [AM; BRIT **cyclist**] ❑ *And as the morning begins moving toward noon, look out for more bikers and pedestrians.*

1 가산명사 오토바이 폭주족 ❑ 라이벌 폭주족 집단들 간에 항상 싸움이 붙는다. **2** 가산명사 자전거 이용자 [미국영어; 영국영어 cyclist] ❑ 아침이 지나 정오가 될 쯤에는 많아지는 자전거 이용자와 보행자들을 조심해라.

bi|ki|ni /bɪkini/ (**bikinis**) N-COUNT A **bikini** is a two-piece swimsuit worn by women.

가산명사 비키니

Word Link   bi ≈ two : *bi*annual, *bi*cycle, *bi*lateral

bi|lat|er|al /baɪlætərəl/ ADJ **Bilateral** negotiations, meetings, or agreements, involve only the two groups or countries that are directly concerned. [FORMAL] [ADJ n] ❑ *...bilateral talks between Britain and America.* ● **bi|lat|er|al|ly** ADV ❑ *The Agreement provided for disputes and differences between the two neighbors to be solved bilaterally.*

형용사 쌍방의 [격식체] ❑ 영국과 미국 사이의 양자 회담 ● 쌍방에서 부사 ❑ 그 두 이웃 나라 사이의 분쟁과 이견은 양자 협의를 통해 해결하도록 협정에 규정되어 있었다.

bi|lin|gual /baɪlɪŋgwəl/ **1** ADJ **Bilingual** means involving or using two languages. [ADJ n] ❑ *...bilingual education.* **2** ADJ Someone who is **bilingual** can speak two languages equally well, usually because they learned both languages as a child. [v-link ADJ] ❑ *He is bilingual in an Asian language and English.*

1 형용사 두 개 언어의 ❑ 두 개 언어 교육 **2** 형용사 두 나라 말을 하는 ❑ 그는 아시아의 언어 하나와 영어를 하는 이중 언어 사용자이다.

bill ♦♦♢ /bɪl/ (**bills, billing, billed**) **1** N-COUNT A **bill** is a written statement of money that you owe for goods or services. ❑ *They couldn't afford to pay the bills.* ❑ *He paid his bill for the newspapers promptly.*

1 가산명사 청구서 ❑ 그들은 각종 공과금을 낼 돈이 없었다. ❑ 그는 신문 대금을 곧바로 냈다.

Do not confuse **account** and **bill**. When you have an **account** with a bank, you leave your money in the bank and take it out when you need it. When you have to pay for things such as electricity or a work done by a repairman, you get a **bill**.

account와 bill을 혼동하지 않도록 하라. 은행에 account를 가지고 있으면, 그 은행에 돈을 맡겨 두고 필요할 때 찾는다. 전기료 또는 수선공이 한 일에 대해 돈을 지불해야 할 때에는 bill을 받는다.

2 V-T If you **bill** someone **for** goods or services you have provided them with, you give or send them a bill stating how much money they owe you for these goods or services. [no cont] ❑ *Are you going to bill me for this?* **3** N-SING **The bill** in a restaurant is a piece of paper on which the price of the meal you have just eaten is written and which you are given before you pay. [mainly BRIT; AM usually **check**] ❑ *Now call over the waiter and ask for the bill.* **4** N-COUNT A **bill** is a piece of paper money. [AM; BRIT **note**] ❑ *The case contained a large quantity of U.S. dollar bills.* **5** N-COUNT In government, a **bill** is a formal statement of a proposed new law that is discussed and then voted on. ❑ *This is the toughest crime bill that Congress has passed in a decade.* **6** N-SING The **bill** of a show or concert is a list of the entertainers who will take part in it. ❑ *Bob Dylan topped the bill.* **7** V-T If someone **is billed to** appear in a particular show, it has been advertised that they are going to be in it. [usu passive] ❑ *She was billed to play the Red Queen in Snow White.* ● **bill|ing** N-UNCOUNT ❑ *...their quarrels over star billing.* **8** V-T If you **bill** a person or event **as** a particular thing, you advertise them in a way that makes people think they have particular qualities or abilities. ❑ *They bill it as Britain's most exciting museum.* **9** N-COUNT A bird's **bill** is its beak. **10** PHRASE If you say that someone or something **fits the bill** or **fills the bill**, you mean that they are suitable for a particular job or purpose. ❑ *If you fit the bill, send a CV to Rebecca Rees.*

2 타동사 청구하다 ❑ 이것에 대해 저에게 비용을 청구하실 건가요? **3** 단수명사 계산서 [주로 영국영어; 미국영어 대개 check] ❑ 이제 웨이터를 불러서 계산서를 달라고 해라. **4** 가산명사 지폐 [미국영어; 영국영어 note] ❑ 그 상자에는 상당한 미국 달러 지폐가 들어 있었다. **5** 가산명사 법안 ❑ 이것은 하원이 10년 동안 통과시킨 것 중 가장 강력한 범죄 대처 법안이다. **6** 단수명사 출연자 명단 ❑ 출연자 명단 맨 위에 밥 딜런이 있었다. **7** 타동사 출연이 예정되다 ❑ 그녀는 백설공주에서 붉은 여왕 역할을 하도록 출연이 낙점되어 있었다. ● 출연자 홍보 우선순위 불가산명사 ❑ 출연자들 홍보 우선순위를 두고 벌이는 그들의 다툼 **8** 타동사 ─으로 선전하다 ❑ 그들은 그곳을 영국에서 가장 신기한 박물관이라고 선전한다. **9** 가산명사 (새의) 부리 **10** 구 자격이 되다 ❑ 본인의 자격이 된다고 생각하시면 레베카 리스에게 이력서를 보내십시오.

Word Partnership   bill의 연어

N.   **electricity/gas/phone** bill, **hospital/hotel** bill **1**
        dollar bill **4**
V.   **pay a** bill **1** **3**
        pass a bill, **vote on a** bill **5**

bill|board /bɪlbɔrd/ (**billboards**) N-COUNT A **billboard** is a very large board on which posters are displayed. →see **advertising**

가산명사 광고 게시판

bill|fold /bɪlfoʊld/ (**billfolds**) N-COUNT A **billfold** is a small wallet, usually made of leather or plastic, where you can keep paper money and credit cards. [AM] ❑ *...a billfold containing fifteen dollars.*

가산명사 (접을 수 있는) 지갑 [미국영어] ❑ 15달러가 든 지갑

bil|liards /bɪliərdz/

The form **billiard** is used as a modifier.

billiard은 수식어구로 쓴다.

1 N-UNCOUNT **Billiards** is a game played on a large table, in which you use a long stick called a cue to hit balls against each other or into pockets around the sides of the table. [BRIT; AM **pocket billiards, pool**] **2** N-UNCOUNT **Billiards** is a game played on a large table, in which you use a long stick called a cue to hit balls against each other or against the walls around the sides of the table. [AM]

1 불가산명사 포켓볼 [영국영어; 미국영어 pocket billiards, pool] **2** 불가산명사 당구 [미국영어]

bil|lion ♦♦♦ /bɪlyən/ (billions)

> The plural form is **billion** after a number, or after a word or expression referring to a number, such as "several" or "a few."

‖ NUM A **billion** is a thousand million. ❑ *The Ethiopian foreign debt stands at 3 billion dollars.* ‖ QUANT-PLURAL If you talk about **billions of** people or things, you mean that there is a very large number of them but you do not know or do not want to say exactly how many. [QUANT of pl-n] ❑ *Biological systems have been doing this for billions of years.* ● PRON You can also use **billions** as a pronoun. ❑ *He thought that it must be worth billions.*

숫자 또는 'several', 'a few'와 같이 수를 지칭하는 단어나 표현 뒤에서 복수형은 billion이다.

‖ 수사 10억 ❑ 에티오피아의 외채는 현재 30억 달러이다. ‖ 복수수량사 수십억 개의 ❑ 생물학적 시스템들은 이 일을 수십억 년 동안 해 왔다. ● 대명사 수십억 ❑ 그는 그것의 가치가 수십억은 된다고 생각했다.

bil|lion|aire /bɪlyəneər/ (billionaires) N-COUNT A **billionaire** is an extremely rich person who has money or property worth at least a thousand million dollars or pounds.

가산명사 억만장자

Bill of Rights N-SING A **Bill of Rights** is a written list of citizens' rights which is usually part of the constitution of a country. ❑ *And what are your rights according to the Bill of Rights?*

단수명사 국민 기본 인권 선언 ❑ 그러면 국민 기본 인권 선언에 따른 당신의 권리는 뭐죠?

bil|low /bɪloʊ/ (billows, billowing, billowed) ‖ V-I When something made of cloth **billows**, it swells out and moves slowly in the wind. ❑ *The curtains billowed in the breeze.* ❑ *Her pink dress billowed out around her.* ‖ V-I When smoke or cloud **billows**, it moves slowly upward or across the sky. ❑ *...thick plumes of smoke billowing from factory chimneys.* ❑ *Steam billowed out from under the hood.* ‖ N-COUNT A **billow** of smoke or dust is a large mass of it rising slowly into the air. ❑ *...smoke stacks belching billows of almost solid black smoke.*

‖ 자동사 하늘거리다, 펄럭이다 ❑ 커튼이 바람에 하늘거렸다. ❑ 그녀의 분홍색 드레스가 그녀의 몸을 감으며 하늘거렸다. ‖ 자동사 피어 오르다 ❑ 공장 굴뚝에서 피어오르는 짙은 연기 ❑ 자동차 보닛 안에서 연기가 피어올랐다. ‖ 가산명사 (연기, 먼지 등의) 넝쿨 ❑ 거의 숯덩이 같은 시커먼 연기를 내뿜는 굴뚝

bil|ly /bɪli/ (billies) N-COUNT A **billy** or **billy club** is a short heavy stick which is sometimes used as a weapon by the police. [AM; BRIT **baton**]

가산명사 경찰봉 [미국영어; 영국영어 baton]

bi|month|ly /baɪmʌnθli/ ADJ A **bimonthly** event or publication happens or appears every two months. [BRIT also **bi-monthly**] [usu ADJ n] ❑ *...bimonthly assemblies.* ❑ *...bimonthly newsletters.*

형용사 두 달에 한 번씩의 [영국영어 bi-monthly] ❑ 격월간 집회 ❑ 격월 소식지

bin /bɪn/ (bins, binning, binned) ‖ N-COUNT A **bin** is a container that you keep or store things in. ❑ *...a bread bin.* ‖ N-COUNT A **bin** is a container that you put garbage or trash in. [mainly BRIT; AM usually **garbage can, trash can**] ❑ *He screwed the paper small and chucked it in the bin.* ‖ V-T If you **bin** something, you throw it away. [BRIT, INFORMAL] ❑ *He decided to bin his paintings.*

‖ 가산명사 보관 통 ❑ 빵 보관용 통 ‖ 가산명사 쓰레기통 [주로 영국영어; 미국영어 대개 garbage can, trash can] ❑ 그는 종이를 작게 꾸긴 다음 쓰레기통에 집어던졌다. ‖ 타동사 버리다 [영국영어, 비격식체] ❑ 그는 자신의 그림들을 버리기로 결심했다.

bi|na|ry /baɪnəri/ ‖ ADJ The **binary** system expresses numbers using only the two digits 0 and 1. It is used especially in computing. [usu ADJ n] ❑ *The genetic code is not a binary code as in computers.* ‖ N-UNCOUNT **Binary** is the binary system of expressing numbers. ❑ *The machine does the calculations in binary.*

‖ 형용사 2진법의 ❑ 유전 코드는 컴퓨터에서와 같은 2진 코드가 아니다. ‖ 불가산명사 2진법 ❑ 그 기계는 2진법으로 계산을 한다.

bi|na|ry code (binary codes) N-VAR **Binary code** is a computer code that uses the binary number system. [COMPUTING] ❑ *The instructions are translated into binary code, a form that computers can easily handle.*

가산명사 또는 불가산명사 2진 코드 [컴퓨터] ❑ 명령은 컴퓨터가 쉽게 처리할 수 있는 형식인 2진 코드로 변환된다.

bind /baɪnd/ (binds, binding, bound) ‖ V-T If something **binds** people **together**, it makes them feel as if they are all part of the same group or have something in common. ❑ *It is the memory and threat of persecution that binds them together.* ❑ *...the social and political ties that bind the U.S. to Britain.* ‖ V-T If you **are bound** by something such as a rule, agreement, or restriction, you are forced or required to act in a certain way. ❑ *The Luxembourg-based satellite service is not bound by the same strict rules as the BBC.* ❑ *The authorities will be legally bound to arrest any suspects.* ● **bound** ADJ [v-link ADJ by n] ❑ *The world of advertising is obviously less bound by convention than the world of banking.* ‖ V-T If you **bind** something or someone, you tie rope, string, tape, or other material around them so that they are held firmly. ❑ *Bind the ends of the cord together with thread.* ❑ *...the red tape which was used to bind the files.* ‖ V-T When a book **is bound**, the pages are joined together and the cover is put on. ❑ *Each volume is bound in bright-colored cloth.* ❑ *Their business came from a few big publishers, all of whose books they bound.*

‖ 타동사 한데 묶다, 단결시키다 ❑ 그들을 한데 묶는 것은 바로 그러한 박해의 기억과 위협이다. ❑ 미국과 영국을 묶는 사회적 정치적 유대 ‖ 타동사 매이다, ~을 따르다 ❑ 룩셈부르크에 근거를 둔 위성 방송 서비스는 비비시와 같은 엄격한 규정에 매이지 않는다. ❑ 당국은 법에 따라 모든 혐의자를 체포해야만 할 것이다. ● 매이는 형용사 ❑ 광고업계는 분명히 은행 업계보다는 인습에 덜 얽매인다. ‖ 타동사 묶다, 동이다 ❑ 실을 끈의 양쪽 끝을 함께 동여매세요. ❑ 서류철을 묶는 데 쓰였던 붉은색 테이프 ‖ 타동사 제본되다, 장정되다 ❑ 각 권의 장정은 밝은 색 천으로 되어 있습니다. ❑ 그들의 일거리는 몇몇 대형 출판사에서 왔는데, 그 출판사들에서 내는 책 전부를 제본하는 것이었다.

bind|ing /baɪndɪŋ/ (bindings) ‖ ADJ A **binding** promise, agreement, or decision must be obeyed or carried out. ❑ *...proposals for a legally binding commitment on nations to stabilize emissions of carbon dioxide.* ‖ N-VAR The **binding** of a book is its cover. ❑ *Its books are noted for the quality of their paper and bindings.* ‖ N-COUNT **Binding** is a strip of material that you put around the edge of a piece of cloth or other object in order to protect or decorate it. ❑ *...the Regency mahogany dining table with satinwood binding.* ‖ →see also **bind**

‖ 형용사 구속력 있는 ❑ 각국의 탄산가스 배출을 안정화하기 위한 법적 구속력 있는 서약 제안 ‖ 가산명사 또는 불가산명사 표지, 장정 ❑ 그 회사의 책은 질 좋은 용지와 장정으로 유명하다. ‖ 가산명사 또는 불가산명사 선 두르는 재료; 마감재 ❑ 새틴우드로 가장자리가 처리되어 있는 리전시 풍의 마호가니 식탁

binge /bɪndʒ/ (binges, bingeing, binged) ‖ N-COUNT If you go on a **binge**, you do too much of something, such as drinking alcohol, eating, or spending money. [INFORMAL] ❑ *She went on occasional drinking binges.* ‖ V-I If you **binge**, you do too much of something, such as drinking alcohol, eating, or spending money. [INFORMAL] ❑ *I haven't binged since 1986.*

‖ 가산명사 과도; 탐닉 [비격식체] ❑ 그녀는 이따금씩 과음을 했다. ‖ 자동사 과식하다; 과음하다; 과소비하다 [비격식체] ❑ 나는 1986년 이후로 과음을 자제해 왔다.

bin|go /bɪŋgoʊ/ N-UNCOUNT **Bingo** is a game in which each player has a card with numbers on it. Someone calls out numbers and if you are the first person to have all your numbers called out, you win the game. ❑ *...a bingo hall.*

불가산명사 빙고 (게임) ❑ 빙고장

bin|ocu|lars /bɪnɒkyələrz/ N-PLURAL **Binoculars** consist of two small telescopes joined together side by side, which you look through in order to look at things that are a long distance away. [also **a pair of** n]

복수명사 쌍안경

bio|chemi|cal /baɪoʊkemɪkəl/ ADJ **Biochemical** changes, reactions, and mechanisms relate to the chemical processes that happen in living things. [ADJ n] ❑ *Starvation brings biochemical changes in the body.*

형용사 생화학적인 ❑ 기아는 체내에 생화학적 변화를 일으킨다.

bio|chem|ist /baɪoʊkemɪst/ (biochemists) N-COUNT A **biochemist** is a scientist or student who studies biochemistry.

가산명사 생화학자

bio|chem|is|try /baɪoʊkemɪstri/ ‖ N-UNCOUNT **Biochemistry** is the study of the chemical processes that occur in living things. ‖ N-UNCOUNT The **biochemistry** of a living thing is the chemical processes that occur in it or

‖ 불가산명사 생화학 ‖ 불가산명사 생화학 작용 ❑ 대기 오염 물질이 동식물의 생화학 작용에 미치는 영향

A

are involved in it. ❑ ...*the effects of air pollutants on the biochemistry of plants or animals.*

B

Word Link　　bio ≈ life : *biodegradable, biography, biology*

bio|degrad|able /baɪoʊdɪgreɪdəbəl/ ADJ Something that is **biodegradable** breaks down or decays naturally without any special scientific treatment, and can therefore be thrown away without causing pollution. ❑ ...*a natural and totally biodegradable plastic.*

형용사 생분해성의 ❑ 완전 생분해성 천연 플라스틱

C

bi|og|raph|er /baɪɒgrəfər/ (biographers) N-COUNT Someone's **biographer** is a person who writes an account of their life. ❑ ...*Picasso's biographer.*

가산명사 전기 작가 ❑ 피카소의 전기 작가

D

bio|graphi|cal /baɪəgræfɪkəl/ ADJ **Biographical** facts, notes, or details are concerned with the events in someone's life. ❑ *The book contains few biographical details.*

형용사 전기적인 ❑ 그 책에는 전기적인 세부 사항이 거의 없다.

E

Word Link　　graph ≈ writing : *autograph, biography, graph*

F

bi|og|ra|phy /baɪɒgrəfi/ (biographies) **1** N-COUNT A **biography** of someone is an account of their life, written by someone else. ❑ ...*recent biographies of Stalin.* **2** N-UNCOUNT **Biography** is the branch of literature which deals with accounts of people's lives. ❑ ...*a volume of biography and criticism.* →see **library**

1 가산명사 전기 ❑ 최근에 나온 스탈린 전기 **2** 불가산명사 전기 문학 ❑ 전기와 비평으로 이루어진 책

G

bio|logi|cal /baɪəlɒdʒɪkəl/ **1** ADJ **Biological** is used to describe processes and states that occur in the bodies and cells of living things. ❑ *The living organisms somehow concentrated the minerals by biological processes.* ● **bio|logi|cal|ly** /baɪəlɒdʒɪkli/ ADV ❑ *Much of our behavior is biologically determined.* **2** ADJ **Biological** is used to describe activities concerned with the study of living things. [ADJ n] ❑ ...*all aspects of biological research associated with leprosy.* **3** ADJ **Biological** weapons and **biological** warfare involve the use of bacteria or other living organisms in order to attack human beings, animals, or plants. ❑ *Such a war could result in the use of chemical and biological weapons.* **4** ADJ **Biological** pest control is the use of bacteria or other living organisms in order to destroy other organisms which are harmful to plants or crops. [ADJ n] ❑ ...*a consultant on biological control of agricultural pests.* **5** ADJ A child's **biological** parents are the man and woman who caused him or her to be born, rather than other adults who look after him or her. [ADJ n] ❑ ...*foster parents for young teenagers whose biological parents have rejected them.* →see **war**, **zoo**

H

1 형용사 생물학적인 ❑ 그 생물체는 생물학적 작용에 의하여 어떤 식으로든 무기물을 농축했다. ● 생물학적으로 부사 ❑ 우리의 행동 중 많은 부분은 생물학적으로 결정된다. **2** 형용사 생물의 ❑ 한센병과 관련된 생물학적 연구의 모든 국면 **3** 형용사 생물학적 (무기, 전투) ❑ 그와 같은 전쟁은 결국 화학 무기와 생물학 무기의 사용으로 이어질 수도 있다. **4** 형용사 생물학적인 ❑ 농작물 병해충의 생물학적 방제 ❑ 생물학적인 방제에 대한 자문역 **5** 형용사 생물학적인 ❑ 친부모에게 버림받은 어린 십대 아이들을 돌보는 수양부모들

I

J

K

L

Word Link　　logy, ology ≈ study of : *anthropology, biology, geology*

M

bi|ol|ogy /baɪɒlədʒi/ N-UNCOUNT **Biology** is the science which is concerned with the study of living things. ● **bi|olo|gist** /baɪɒlədʒɪst/ (biologists) N-COUNT ❑ ...*biologists studying the fruit fly.* **2** N-UNCOUNT The **biology** of a living thing is the way in which its body or cells behave. ❑ *The biology of these diseases is terribly complicated.*

1 불가산명사 생물학 ● 생물학자 가산명사 ❑ 과실파리를 연구하는 생물학자들 **2** 불가산명사 생태; 양상 ❑ 이들 질병의 양상은 대단히 복잡하다.

N

bi|op|sy /baɪɒpsi/ (biopsies) N-VAR A **biopsy** is the removal and examination of fluids or tissue from a patient's body in order to discover why they are ill. ❑ *James had had a biopsy of the tumor over his right ear.*

가산명사 또는 불가산명사 생체 검사 ❑ 제임스는 오른쪽 귀의 종기에 대해 생체 검사를 받았었다.

O

bio|tech|nol|ogy /baɪoʊtɛknɒlədʒi/ N-UNCOUNT **Biotechnology** is the use of living parts such as cells or bacteria in industry and technology. [TECHNICAL] ❑ ...*the Scottish biotechnology company that developed Dolly the cloned sheep.* →see **technology**

불가산명사 생명 공학 [과학 기술] ❑ 복제 양 돌리를 탄생시킨 스코틀랜드 생명 공학 회사

P

birch /bɜrtʃ/ (birches) N-VAR A **birch** is a type of tall tree with thin branches.

가산명사 또는 불가산명사 자작나무

Q

bird ♦♦♢ /bɜrd/ (birds) **1** N-COUNT A **bird** is a creature with feathers and wings. Female birds lay eggs. Most birds can fly. **2** N-COUNT Some men refer to young women as **birds**. This use could cause offense. [BRIT, INFORMAL] ❑ *Russell Crowe snogged his bird Danielle on the sofa all night.* **3** →see also **early bird** **4** PHRASE If you refer to two people as **birds of a feather**, you mean that they have the same interests or are very similar. ❑ *We're birds of a feather, you and me, Mr. Plimpton.* **5** PHRASE A **bird in the hand** is something that you already have and do not want to risk losing by trying to get something else. ❑ *Another temporary discount may not be what you want, but at least it is a bird in the hand.* **6** PHRASE If you say that a **little bird** told you about something, you mean that someone has told you it, but you do not want to say who it was. ❑ *Incidentally, a little bird tells me that your birthday's coming up.* **7** PHRASE If you say that doing something will **kill two birds with one stone**, you mean that it will enable you to achieve two things that you want to achieve, rather than just one. ❑ *We can talk about Union Hill while I get this business over with. Kill two birds with one stone, so to speak.* →see **pet**
→see Word Web: **bird**

1 가산명사 새 **2** 가산명사 아가씨, 연인 [영국영어, 비격식체] ❑ 러셀 크로는 밤새도록 소파 위에서 연인 다니엘과 뒹굴었다. **4** 구 비슷한 유형, 동류 ❑ 너나 나나 플림턴 씨나 모두 비슷한 사람들이다. **5** 구 수중에 든 새, 확실히 쥔 이득 ❑ 또 한 번의 임시 할인이 당신이 원하는 게 아닐 수도 있지만, 최소한 그건 확실히 이득을 먹고 들어가는 것이다. **6** 구 (소문의) 바람결에 ❑ 말이 나왔으니 말인데, 네 생일이 다가오고 있다는 소리를 바람결에 들었어. **7** 구 일석이조의 효과를 보다 ❑ 내가 이 일을 끝낼 동안 우리는 유니언 힐에 대해 이야기를 나눌 수 있다. 말하자면 일석이조인 거지.

R

S

T

U

V

W

Word Web　　bird

Many scientists today believe that birds evolved from avian dinosaurs. Recently many links have been found. Like birds, these dinosaurs laid their **eggs** in **nests**. Some had **wings**, **beaks**, and **claws** similar to modern birds. But perhaps the most dramatic link was found in 2001. Scientists in China discovered a well-preserved *Sinornithosaurus*, a bird-like dinosaur with **feathers**. This dinosaur is believed to be related to a prehistoric bird, the *Archaeopteryx*.

Sinornithosaurus

X

Y

Z

Biro /ba͟ɪroʊ/ (**Biros**) N-COUNT A **Biro** is a pen with a small metal ball at its tip which transfers the ink onto the paper. [BRIT, TRADEMARK; AM **ballpoint**]

birth ◆◇◇ /bɜ͟ːθ/ (**births**) **1** N-VAR When a baby is born, you refer to this event as his or her **birth**. ❑ *It was the birth of his grandchildren which gave him greatest pleasure.* ❑ *She weighed 5lb 7oz at birth.* **2** N-UNCOUNT You can refer to the beginning or origin of something as its **birth**. ❑ *...the birth of popular democracy.* **3** N-UNCOUNT Some people talk about a person's **birth** when they are referring to the social position of the person's family. ❑ *...men of low birth.* **4** →see also **date of birth** **5** PHRASE If, for example, you are French **by birth**, you are French because your parents are French, or because you were born in France. ❑ *Sadrudin was an Iranian by birth.* **6** PHRASE When a woman **gives birth**, she produces a baby from her body. ❑ *She's just given birth to a baby girl.* **7** PHRASE To **give birth to** something such as an idea means to cause it to start to exist. ❑ *In 1980, strikes at the Lenin shipyards gave birth to the Solidarity trade union.* **8** PHRASE The country, town, or village **of** your **birth** is the place where you were born. ❑ *He left the town of his birth five years later for Australia.*

Word Partnership		*birth*의 연어
ADJ.	**premature** birth **1**	
N.	birth **of a** baby/child, birth **and** death, birth **defect**, birth **rate 1**	
	date of birth **1 4**	
	birth **of a** nation **2**	
PREP.	**at** birth, **before** birth **1**	
	by birth **5**	
V.	**give** birth **6 7**	

birth cer|tifi|cate (**birth certificates**) N-COUNT Your **birth certificate** is an official document which gives details of your birth, such as the date and place of your birth, and the names of your parents.

birth con|trol N-UNCOUNT **Birth control** means planning whether to have children, and using contraception to prevent having them when they are not wanted. ❑ *Today's methods of birth control make it possible for a couple to choose whether or not to have a child.*

birth|day ◆◇◇ /bɜ͟ːθdeɪ, -di/ (**birthdays**) N-COUNT Your **birthday** is the anniversary of the date on which you were born. ❑ *On his birthday she sent him presents.*

birth|place /bɜ͟ːθpleɪs/ (**birthplaces**) **1** N-COUNT Your **birthplace** is the place where you were born. [WRITTEN] ❑ *...Bob Marley's birthplace in the village of Nine Mile.* **2** N-COUNT The **birthplace** of something is the place where it began. ❑ *...Athens, the birthplace of the ancient Olympics.*

birth rate (**birth rates**) also **birth-rate** N-COUNT The **birth rate** in a place is the number of babies born there for every 1000 people during a particular period of time. ❑ *The UK has the highest birth rate among 15 to 19-year-olds in Western Europe.* →see **population**

bis|cuit /bɪ͟skɪt/ (**biscuits**) **1** N-COUNT A **biscuit** is a small round dry cake that is made with baking powder, baking soda, or yeast. [AM] **2** N-COUNT A **biscuit** is a small flat cake that is crisp and usually sweet. [BRIT; AM **cookie**] **3** PHRASE If someone has done something very stupid, rude, or selfish, you can say that they **take the biscuit** or that what they have done **takes the biscuit**, to emphasize your surprise at their behavior. [BRIT, EMPHASIS] [AM **take the cake**] ❑ *This ban takes the biscuit. The whole idea is ridiculous.*

bi|sex|ual /ba͟ɪse͟kʃuəl/ (**bisexuals**) ADJ Someone who is **bisexual** is sexually attracted to both men and women. ● N-COUNT **Bisexual** is also a noun. ❑ *He was an active bisexual.*

bish|op /bɪ͟ʃəp/ (**bishops**) **1** N-COUNT; N-TITLE; N-VOC A **bishop** is a clergyman of high rank in the Roman Catholic, Anglican, and Orthodox churches. **2** N-COUNT In chess a **bishop** is a piece that can be moved diagonally across the board on squares that are the same color. →see **chess**

bis|tro /bi͟ːstroʊ/ (**bistros**) N-COUNT A **bistro** is a small, informal restaurant or a bar where food is served.

bit ◆◆◆ /bɪ͟t/ (**bits**) **1** QUANT A **bit of** something is a small amount of it. [QUANT of n-uncount] ❑ *All it required was a bit of work.* **2** PHRASE A **bit** means to a small extent or degree. It is sometimes used to make a statement less extreme. [VAGUENESS] ❑ *This girl was a bit strange.* ❑ *I think people feel a bit more confident.* **3** PHRASE You can use **a bit of** to make a statement less forceful. For example, the statement "It's a bit of a nuisance" is less forceful than "It's a nuisance." [VAGUENESS] ❑ *It's all a bit of a mess.* ❑ *Students have always been portrayed as a bit of a joke.* **4** PHRASE **Quite a bit** means quite a lot. ❑ *They're worth quite a bit of money.* ❑ *Things have changed quite a bit.* **5** PHRASE You use **a bit** before "more" or "less" to mean a small amount more or a small amount less. ❑ *I still think I have a bit more to offer.* ❑ *Maybe we'll hear a little bit less noise.* **6** PHRASE If you do something **a bit** or do something **for a bit**, you do it for a short time. ❑ *Let's wait a bit.* ❑ *I hope there will be time to talk a bit — or at least ask you about one or two things this evening.* **7** N-COUNT A **bit** of something is a small part or section of it. ❑ *It's the bit of the meeting that I missed.* ❑ *Now comes the really important bit.* **8** N-COUNT A **bit of** something is a small piece of it. ❑ *Only a bit of string looped round a nail in the doorpost held it shut.* **9** N-COUNT You can use **bit** to refer to a particular item or to one of a group or set of things. For example, a **bit of** information is an item of information. ❑ *There was one bit of vital evidence which helped win the case.* **10** N-COUNT In computing, a **bit** is the smallest unit of information that is held

---

가산명사 (상표명) 볼펜의 일종 [영국영어, 상표; 미국영어 ballpoint]

1 가산명사 또는 불가산명사 탄생, 출생 ❑ 그에게 커다란 기쁨을 안겨 준 일은 바로 손자의 탄생이었다. ❑ 그녀는 출생 시 몸무게가 5파운드 7온스 나갔다. **2** 불가산명사 기원, 시초 ❑ 대중 민주주의의 기원 **3** 불가산명사 태생, 집안 ❑ 태생이 미천한 사람들 **5** 구 태생의 ❑ 사드루딘은 이란 태생이었다. **6** 구 낳다, 출산하다 ❑ 그녀는 방금 막 딸아이를 출산했다. **7** 구 -을 생겨나게 하다 ❑ 1980년, 레닌 조선소에서 일어난 파업을 통해 폴란드 자유 노조가 탄생했다. **8** 구 -가 태어난 ❑ 그는 5년 후 자신이 태어난 마을을 떠나 호주로 갔다.

가산명사 출생 증명서

불가산명사 가족계획, 산아 제한 ❑ 오늘날의 가족계획 방식은 아이를 가질 것인지 말 것인지를 각 부부들 스스로 선택할 수 있도록 한다.

가산명사 생일 ❑ 그의 생일날, 그녀가 그에게 선물을 보냈다.

1 가산명사 출생지, 고향 [문어체] ❑ 나인 마일 마을에 있는 밥 말리의 출생지 **2** 가산명사 발생지 ❑ 고대 올림픽의 발생지인 아테네

가산명사 출산율 ❑ 영국은 열다섯 살에서 열아홉 살 사이의 출산율이 서유럽 전체에서 가장 높다.

1 가산명사 소형 빵 [미국영어] **2** 가산명사 비스킷 [영국영어; 미국영어 cookie] **3** 구 (비꼬는 투로) take the cake ❑ 이와 같은 금지령은 기가 찬다. 전체적인 발상 자체가 터무니없었다.

형용사 양성애의 ● 가산명사 양성애자 ❑ 그는 적극적인 양성애자였다.

1 가산명사; 경칭명사; 호격명사 주교 **2** 가산명사 (체스) 비숍

가산명사 작은 식당이나 술집

1 수량사 소량, 조금 ❑ 거기에 필요한 것은 약간의 노력뿐이었다. **2** 구 약간, 조금 [완곡투] ❑ 이 소녀는 약간 이상했다. ❑ 사람들이 조금 더 자신감을 가지는 것 같다. **3** 구 약간 [완곡투] ❑ 모든 게 약간 어수선하다. ❑ 학생들은 언제나 웃음거리 비슷하게 그려져 왔다. **4** 구 꽤 많은, 상당한 ❑ 그것들은 상당한 값어치가 있다. ❑ 사정이 꽤 많이 변해 버렸다. **5** 구 약간, 조금 ❑ 미국적으로 내가 제공할 수 있는 것이 조금 더 남아 있다고 생각한다. ❑ 아마도 소음을 조금은 덜 듣게 될 거야. **6** 구 잠깐 ❑ 잠깐 기다리자. ❑ 오늘 저녁에 잠깐 얘기를 하거나, 그것도 안 되면 한두 가지만이라도 물어 볼 수 있는 시간이 있기를 바랍니다. **7** 가산명사 작은 부분 ❑ 그것이 내가 회의에서 놓친 부분이다. ❑ 이제 정말 중요한 부분이 나옵니다. **8** 가산명사 작은 조각 ❑ 그 문은 문설주에 박힌 못에 감긴 작은 끈 쪼가리 하나에 의해 닫혀져 있었다. **9** 가산명사 (단위를 나타내는) 가지 ❑ 그 소송에서 이기는 데 도움이 된 결정적인 증거 하나가 있었다. **10** 가산명사 (컴퓨터) 비트 **11** 가산명사 12센트 반 [미국영어, 비격식체 또는 구식어]

in a computer's memory. It is either 1 or 0. Several bits form a byte. **11** N-COUNT A **bit** is 12½ cents; mainly used in expressions such as **two bits**, which means 25 cents, or **four bits**, which means 50 cents. [AM, INFORMAL or OLD-FASHIONED] □ *They weren't worth four bits.* **12** **Bit** is the past tense of **bite**. **13** PHRASE If something happens **bit by bit**, it happens in stages. □ *Bit by bit I began to understand what they were trying to do.* **14** PHRASE If you **do your bit**, you do something that, to a small or limited extent, helps to achieve something. □ *Marcie always tried to do her bit.* **15** PHRASE You say that one thing is **every bit as** good, interesting, or important **as** another to emphasize that the first thing is just as good, interesting, or important as the second. [EMPHASIS] □ *My dinner jacket is every bit as good as his.* **16** PHRASE If you say that something is **a bit much**, you are annoyed because you think someone has behaved in an unreasonable way. [INFORMAL, FEELINGS] □ *It's a bit much expecting young people to carry the can for lenders' past mistakes.* **17** PHRASE You use **not a bit** when you want to make a strong negative statement. [EMPHASIS] □ *I'm really not a bit surprised.* **18** PHRASE You can use **bits and pieces** to refer to a collection of different things. The form **bits and bobs** is also used, mainly in British English. [INFORMAL] □ *The drawers are full of bits and pieces of armour.*

bitch /bɪtʃ/ (**bitches**, **bitching**, **bitched**) **11** N-COUNT If someone calls a woman a **bitch**, they are saying in a very rude way that they think she behaves in a very mean or unkind way. →see also **son of a bitch** [INFORMAL, VULGAR, DISAPPROVAL] **2** V-I If you say that someone **is bitching about** something, you mean that you disapprove of the fact that they are complaining about it in an unpleasant way. [INFORMAL, DISAPPROVAL] [oft cont] □ *They're forever bitching about everybody else.* **3** N-COUNT A **bitch** is a female dog.

bite ♦♦♦ /baɪt/ (**bites**, **biting**, **bit**, **bitten**) **11** V-T/V-I If you **bite** something, you use your teeth to cut into it, for example in order to eat it or break it. If an animal or person **bites** you, they use their teeth to hurt or injure you. □ *Both sisters bit their nails as children.* □ *He bit into his sandwich.* □ *Every year in this country more than 50,000 children are bitten by dogs.* **2** N-COUNT A **bite** of something, especially food, is the action of biting it. □ *He took another bite of apple.* ● N-COUNT A **bite** is also the amount of food you take into your mouth when you bite it. □ *Look forward to eating the food and enjoy every bite.* **3** N-SING If you have **a bite** to eat, you have a small meal or a snack. [INFORMAL] □ *It was time to go home for a little rest and a bite to eat.* **4** V-T If a snake or a small insect **bites** you, it makes a mark or hole in your skin, and often causes the surrounding area of your skin to become painful or itchy. □ *When an infected mosquito bites a human, spores are injected into the blood.* **5** N-COUNT A **bite** is an injury or a mark on your body where an animal, snake, or small insect has bitten you. □ *Any dog bite, no matter how small, needs immediate medical attention.* **6** V-I When an action or policy begins to **bite**, it begins to have a serious or harmful effect. □ *As the sanctions begin to bite there will be more political difficulties ahead.* **7** V-I If an object **bites** into a surface, it presses hard against it or cuts into it. □ *There may even be some wire or nylon biting into the flesh.* **8** V-I If a fish **bites** when you are fishing, it takes the hook or bait at the end of your fishing line in its mouth. □ *After half an hour, the fish stopped biting and we moved on.* ● N-COUNT **Bite** is also a noun. □ *If I don't get a bite in a few minutes I lift the rod and twitch the bait.* **9** PHRASE If someone **bites the hand that feeds** them, they behave badly or in an ungrateful way toward someone who they depend on. □ *She may be cynical about the film industry, but ultimately she has no intention of biting the hand that feeds her.* **10** PHRASE If you **bite your lip** or your **tongue**, you stop yourself from saying something that you want to say, because it would be the wrong thing to say in the circumstances. □ *I must learn to bite my lip.* **11** to **bite the bullet** →see **bullet**. to **bite the dust** →see **dust**

bit|ing /baɪtɪŋ/ **11** ADJ **Biting** wind or cold is extremely cold. □ *...a raw, biting northerly wind.* **2** ADJ **Biting** criticism or wit is very harsh or unkind, and is often caused by such feelings as anger or dislike. □ *...a furor caused by the author's biting satire on the Church.*

bit|map /bɪtmæp/ (**bitmaps**, **bitmapping**, **bitmapped**) N-COUNT A **bitmap** is a type of graphics file on a computer. [COMPUTING] □ *...bitmap graphics for representing complex images such as photographs.* ● V-T **Bitmap** is also a verb. □ *Bitmapped maps require huge storage space.*

bit|ten /bɪt'n/ **Bitten** is the past participle of **bite**.

bit|ter ♦♦♦ /bɪtər/ (**bitterest**, **bitters**) **11** ADJ In a **bitter** argument or conflict, people argue very angrily or fight very fiercely. □ *...the scene of bitter fighting during the Second World War.* □ *...a bitter attack on the Government's failure to support manufacturing.* ● **bit|ter|ly** ADV □ *Any such thing would be bitterly opposed by most of the world's democracies.* ● **bit|ter|ness** N-UNCOUNT □ *The rift within the organization reflects the growing bitterness of the dispute.* **2** ADJ If someone is **bitter** after a disappointing experience or after being treated unfairly, they continue to feel angry about it. □ *She is said to be very bitter about the way she was sacked.* ● **bit|ter|ly** ADV □ *"And he sure didn't help us," Grant said bitterly.* ● **bit|ter|ness** N-UNCOUNT □ *I still feel bitterness and anger toward the person who knocked me down.* **3** ADJ A **bitter** experience makes you feel very disappointed. You can also use **bitter** to emphasize feelings of disappointment. □ *I think the decision was a bitter blow from which he never quite recovered.* □ *A great deal of bitter experience had taught him how to lose gracefully.* ● **bit|ter|ly** ADV □ *I was bitterly disappointed to have lost yet another race so near the finish.* **4** ADJ **Bitter** weather, or a **bitter** wind, is extremely cold. □ *Outside, a bitter east wind was accompanied by flurries of snow.* ● **bit|ter|ly** ADV [ADV adj] □ *It's been bitterly cold here in Moscow.* **5** ADJ A **bitter** taste is sharp, not sweet, and often slightly unpleasant. □ *The leaves taste rather bitter.* **6** N-MASS **Bitter** is a kind of beer that is light brown in color. [BRIT] □ *...a pint of bitter.* **7** a **bitter pill** →see **pill** →see **taste**

□ 그것들은 50센트의 가치도 없었다. **12** bite의 과거형 **13** 구 조금씩; 점차 □ 나는 그들이 뭘 하려고 하는지 조금씩 이해하기 시작했다. **14** 구 본분을 다하다 □ 마시는 언제나 자신의 본분을 다하려 노력했다. **15** 구 어느 모로나 [강조] □ 내 야회복은 어느 모로 보나 그의 것만큼 좋다. **16** 구 지나친, 너무한 [비격식체, 감정 개입] □ 대부업자들의 지난 잘못에 대한 책임까지 짊어질 것을 젊은이들에게 기대하는 것은 도가 지나친 일이다. **17** 구 조금도 –하지 않다 [강조] □ 나는 정말 조금도 놀랍지 않다. **18** 구 잡동사니 [비격식체] □ 서랍은 갖은 잡동사니로 가득 차 있다.

1 가산명사 잡년 [비격식체, 비속어, 탐탁찮음] **2** 자동사 씹다 [비격식체, 탐탁찮음] □ 그들은 다른 모든 사람들을 끊임없이 씹어 댄다. **3** 가산명사 암캐

1 타동사/자동사 물다, 깨물다, 물어뜯다 □ 두 자매 모두 어린아이일 때 손톱을 깨물었다. □ 그는 샌드위치를 베어 물었다. □ 이 나라에서는 매년 5만 명 이상의 아이들이 개에게 물린다. **2** 가산명사 묾 □ 그는 사과를 한 입 더 깨물었다. ● 한 입에 넣는 음식 □ 그 음식을 먹으며 한 입 한 입 맛있게 즐기기를 기대하세요. **3** 단수명사 가볍게 먹을거리 [비격식체] □ 집에 가서 잠깐 쉬며 가볍게 뭘 좀 먹을 때였다. **4** 타동사 쏘다, 물다 □ 감염된 모기가 사람을 쏘면, 포자가 피 속으로 주입된다. **5** 가산명사 물린 상처 □ 개에게 물린 상처는 아무리 작은 것이라도 즉시 응급 처치를 해야 한다. **6** 자동사 나쁘게 작용하다 □ 그런 제재가 나쁘게 작용하기 시작함에 따라 앞으로 더 큰 정치적 어려움이 있을 것이다. **7** 자동사 파고들다; 파고들다 □ 심지어는 철사나 나일론 따위가 살 속으로 파고들 수도 있답니다. **8** 자동사 미끼를 물다 □ 30분 뒤, 고기가 물지 않아서 우리는 계속 이동을 했다. ● 가산명사 입질, 미끼를 묾 □ 몇 분 안에 입질이 오지 않으면 나는 낚싯대를 들어올려 미끼를 뺀다. **9** 구 은혜를 원수로 갚다 □ 그녀가 영화 업계에 대해 냉소적일 수도 있지만, 궁극적으로 은혜를 원수로 갚을 의도는 없다. **10** 구 입을 다물다 □ 나는 입을 다물 줄 알아야 한다.

1 형용사 살을 에는 듯이 추운 □ 살을 에는 듯이 차가운 북풍 **2** 형용사 신랄한 □ 그 작가의 교회에 대한 신랄한 풍자로 말미암은 일대 소동

가산명사 비트맵 (컴퓨터 그래픽 파일 형식) [컴퓨터] □ 사진과 같은 복잡한 이미지 구현을 위한 비트맵 그래픽 ● 타동사 비트맵 형식으로 만들다 □ 비트맵 형식으로 만들어진 지도는 대단히 큰 저장 공간이 필요하다.

bite의 과거 분사

1 형용사 모진, 격렬한 □ 제2차 세계 대전 중 격전의 현장 □ 정부의 제조업 지원 불이행에 대한 모진 비난 ● 격렬하게 부사 □ 그와 같은 어떠한 것도 전 세계 대부분의 민주국가들로부터 격렬한 반대를 받을 것이다. ● 격렬함 불가산명사 □ 그 기구 내의 불화는 점점 더 커져 가는 분쟁의 격렬함을 반영한다. **2** 형용사 원통한; 몹시 괴로운 □ 그녀는 그렇게 해고당했던 것에 대해 몹시 원통해 한다고 사람들이 말한다. ● 원통하게 부사 □ "그리고 그는 물론 우리를 돕지 않았지."라고 그랜트가 원통한 듯이 말했다. ● 원통함 불가산명사 □ 나는 나를 때려눕혔던 그 사람에게 아직도 원통함과 분노를 느낀다. **3** 형용사 쓰라린, 괴로운 □ 그로서는 그 결정이 회복하기 힘든 쓰라린 일격이었다고 생각한다. □ 수많은 쓰라린 경험들은 그에게 명예롭게 지는 법을 가르쳐 주었다. ● 쓰게, 몹시 부사 □ 나는 또 한 번 결승선을 코앞에 두고 패한 것에 몹시 낙담하였다. **4** 형용사 매서운 □ 밖에는 눈보라를 동반한 몹시 차가운 동풍이 불었다. ● 매섭게 부사 □ 이곳 모스크바에서는 몹시 추운 날씨가 계속되어 왔다. **5** 형용사 쓴 □ 이 이파리는 다소 쓴맛이 난다. **6** 물질명사 비터 (맛이 쓴 맥주) [영국영어] □ 비터 1파인트

bit|ter|ly /bɪtərli/ ADV You use **bitterly** when you are describing an attitude which involves strong, unpleasant emotions such as anger or dislike. [ADV adj] ❑ *We are bitterly upset at what has happened.*

bi|week|ly /baɪwiːkli/ ADJ A **biweekly** event or publication happens or appears once every two weeks. [AM; BRIT **fortnightly**] [ADJ n] ❑ *He used to see them at the biweekly meetings.* ❑ *...Beverage Digest, the industry's biweekly newsletter.* ● ADV **Biweekly** is also an adverb. [ADV with v] ❑ *The group meets on a regular basis, usually weekly or biweekly.*

bi|zarre /bɪzɑːr/ ADJ Something that is **bizarre** is very odd and strange. ❑ *The game was also notable for the bizarre behavior of the team's manager.* ● **bi|zarre|ly** ADV ❑ *She dressed bizarrely.*

black ♦♦♦ /blæk/ (**blacker, blackest, blacks, blacking, blacked**) ◼ COLOR Something that is **black** is of the darkest color that there is, the color of the sky at night when there is no light at all. ❑ *She was wearing a black coat with a white collar.* ❑ *He had thick black hair.* ◻ ADJ A **black** person belongs to a race of people with dark skins, especially a race originally from Africa. ❑ *He worked for the rights of black people.* ❑ *Sherry is black, tall, slender and soft-spoken.* ◼ N-COUNT **Black** people are sometimes referred to as **blacks**. This use could cause offense. ❑ *There are about thirty-one million blacks in the U.S.* ◻ ADJ **Black** coffee or tea has no milk or cream added to it. [ADJ n, v n ADJ] ❑ *A cup of black tea or black coffee contains no calories.* ◻ ADJ If you describe a situation as **black**, you are emphasizing that it is very bad indeed. [EMPHASIS] ❑ *It was, he said later, one of the blackest days of his political career.* ◻ ADJ If someone is in a **black** mood, they feel very miserable and depressed. ❑ *In late 1975, she fell into a black depression.* ◼ PHRASE If a person or an organization is in the **black**, they do not owe anyone any money. ❑ *Remington's operations in Japan are now in the black.*
→see **spice**

▶**black out** ◼ PHRASAL VERB If you **black out**, you lose consciousness for a short time. ❑ *I could feel blood draining from my face. I wondered whether I was about to black out.* ◻ PHRASAL VERB If a place is **blacked out**, it is in darkness, usually because it has no electricity supply. ❑ *Large parts of Lima and other areas south of the capital were blacked out after electricity pylons were blown up.* ◼ PHRASAL VERB If a film or a piece of writing is **blacked out**, it is prevented from being broadcast or published, usually because it contains information which is secret or offensive. ❑ *TV pictures of the demonstration were blacked out.* ◻ PHRASAL VERB If you **black out** a piece of writing, you color over it in black so that it cannot be seen. ❑ *U.S. government specialists went through each page, blacking out any information a foreign intelligence expert could use.* ◼ PHRASAL VERB If you **black out** the memory of something, you try not to remember it because it upsets you. ❑ *I tried not to think about it. I blacked it out. It was the easiest way of coping.* →see also **blackout**

black and white also **black-and-white** ◼ COLOR In a **black and white** photograph or film, everything is shown in black, white, and gray. ❑ *...a black-and-white photo of the two of us together.* ❑ *...old black and white film footage.* ◻ ADJ A **black and white** television set shows only black-and-white pictures. ◼ ADJ A **black and white** issue or situation is one which involves issues which seem simple and therefore easy to make decisions about. ❑ *But this isn't a simple black and white affair, Marianne.* ◻ PHRASE You say that something is in **black and white** when it has been written or printed, and not just said. ❑ *He'd seen the proof in black and white.*

black|ber|ry /blækbɛri, BRIT blækbəri/ (**blackberries**) N-COUNT A **blackberry** is a small, soft black or dark purple fruit.

black|board /blækbɔːrd/ (**blackboards**) N-COUNT A **blackboard** is a dark-colored board that you can write on with chalk. Blackboards are often used by teachers in the classroom. [AM also **chalkboard**]

black|cur|rant /blækkʌrənt, BRIT blækkʌrənt/ (**blackcurrants**) N-COUNT In Europe, a **blackcurrant** is a type of very small, dark purple fruit that grows in bunches on bushes. [BRIT] ❑ *Place the blackcurrants in a pan.*

black econo|my N-SING The **black economy** consists of the buying, selling, and producing of goods or services that goes on without the government being informed, so that people can avoid paying tax on them. [BRIT] ❑ *...an attempt to clamp down on the black economy.*

black|en /blækən/ (**blackens, blackening, blackened**) ◼ V-T/V-I To **blacken** something means to make it black or very dark in color. Something that **blackens** becomes black or very dark in color. ❑ *The married women of Shitamachi maintained the custom of blackening their teeth.* ◻ V-T If someone **blackens** your character, they make other people believe that you are a bad person. ❑ *They're trying to blacken our name.*

black eye (**black eyes**) N-COUNT If someone has a **black eye**, they have a dark-colored bruise around their eye. ❑ *He punched her in the face at least once giving her a black eye.*

black|list /blæklɪst/ (**blacklists, blacklisting, blacklisted**) ◼ N-COUNT If someone is on a **blacklist**, they are seen by a government or other organization as being one of a number of people who cannot be trusted or who have done something wrong. ❑ *A government official disclosed that they were on a secret blacklist.* ◻ V-T If someone is **blacklisted** by a government or organization, they are put on a blacklist. [usu passive] ❑ *He has been blacklisted since being convicted of possessing marijuana in 1969.*

black|mail /blækmeɪl/ (**blackmails, blackmailing, blackmailed**) ◼ N-UNCOUNT **Blackmail** is the action of threatening to reveal a secret about someone, unless they do something you tell them to do, such as giving you money. ❑ *It looks like the pictures were being used for blackmail.* ◻ N-UNCOUNT If you describe an

부사 몹시 ❑ 벌어져 왔던 일에 우리는 몹시 당황했다.

형용사 격주의 [미국영어; 영국영어 fortnightly] ❑ 그는 격주로 벌어지는 회의에서 그들을 보곤 했다. ❑ 음료 업계 격주간 소식지 '베버리지 다이제스트' ● 부사 격주로 ❑ 그 단체는 일반적으로 매주 혹은 2주에 한 번씩 정기적으로 만난다.

형용사 기괴한 ❑ 그 시합은 또한 그 팀 매니저의 기행으로도 유명했다. ● 기괴하게 부사 ❑ 그녀는 기괴한 옷차림을 하고 있었다.

◼ 색채어 검은 ❑ 그녀는 흰 깃이 달린 검은색 코트를 입고 있었다. ❑ 그의 머리칼은 숱이 많고 검은색이었다. ◻ 형용사 흑인의 ❑ 그는 흑인들의 인권을 위해 일했다. ❑ 셰리는 흑인으로 키가 크고 날씬하며 말씨가 상냥하다. ◼ 가산명사 흑인 ❑ 미국에는 약 삼천 백만 명의 흑인이 있다. ◻ 형용사 우유나 크림을 넣지 않은, 블랙의 ❑ 우유나 크림을 넣지 않은 홍차나 커피 한 잔은 열량이 전혀 없다. ◻ 형용사 어두운, 암담한 [강조] ❑ 그것은 그의 정치 생애에서 가장 암담한 날들 중 하나였다고 나중에 그가 말했다. ◻ 형용사 우울한, 음울한 ❑ 1975년 후반, 그녀는 깊은 우울증에 빠졌다. ◼ 구 흑자의 ❑ 레밍턴의 일본 사업은 이제 흑자를 내고 있다.

◼ 구동사 잠깐 동안 의식을 잃다 ❑ 나는 얼굴에서 핏기가 가시는 것을 느낄 수 있었다. 의식을 잃는 게 아닌가 하고 생각했다. ◻ 구동사 캄캄하게 되다, 정전되다 ❑ 송전탑이 폭파된 이후 리마 대부분과 그 남쪽의 다른 지역들은 암흑 속에 묻혔다. ◼ 구동사 보도 규제되다 ❑ 시위 장면의 텔레비전 방영은 통제되었다. ◻ 구동사 검은 잉크로 지우다 ❑ 미국 정부 측 전문가는 매 페이지를 꼼꼼히 살피며 외국 첩보 전문가가 이용할 만한 정보를 모두 검은색으로 덧칠해 지웠다. ◻ 구동사 (기억을) 지우다 ❑ 나는 그 일을 생각하지 않으려 했다. 아예 그 기억을 지워 버렸다. 그렇게 하는 것이 가장 쉬운 대처 방법이었다.

◼ 색채어 흑백 ❑ 우리 둘이 함께 찍은 흑백 사진 ❑ 남은 흑백 영화 필름 ◻ 형용사 흑백의 ◼ 형용사 흑백이 분명한 ❑ 하지만 이건 흑백이 분명한 단순한 사안이 아니라고, 메리앤. ◻ 구 인쇄된, 기록된 ❑ 그는 기록된 증거를 보았다.

가산명사 검은 딸기

가산명사 칠판 [미국영어 chalkboard]

가산명사 까막까치밥 나무 열매 [영국영어] ❑ 까막까치밥 나무 열매를 냄비에 넣으세요.

단수명사 지하 경제 [영국영어] ❑ 지하 경제를 단속하려는 시도

◼ 타동사/자동사 검게 하다, 어둡게 하다 ❑ 시타마치의 기혼 여성들은 이빨을 검게 칠하는 풍습을 계속 지켰다. ◻ 타동사 (이름을) 먹칠하다 ❑ 그들은 우리의 이름에 먹칠을 하려 한다.

가산명사 눈 주위의 멍, 멍든 눈 ❑ 그는 그녀의 얼굴을 때려서 최소한 한 번 이상 그녀의 눈에 멍이 들게 했다.

◼ 가산명사 블랙리스트, 요시찰인 명부 ❑ 그들이 비밀 블랙리스트에 올라 있음을 한 정부 관리가 밝혔다. ◻ 타동사 블랙리스트에 오르다 ❑ 그는 1969년에 마리화나 소지죄로 유죄 선고를 받은 이후 죽 블랙리스트에 올라 있었다.

◼ 불가산명사 공갈 협박 ❑ 그 사진들이 공갈 협박용으로 쓰이고 있는 것 같다. ◻ 불가산명사 감정 자극; 도덕적 자극 [탐탁치않음] ❑ 사용되는 책략은 공공연한 협박에서부터 미묘한 감정 자극에

action as emotional or moral **blackmail**, you disapprove of it because someone is using a person's emotions or moral values to persuade them to do something against their will. [DISAPPROVAL] ❑ *The tactics employed can range from overt bullying to subtle emotional blackmail.* **3** V-T If one person **blackmails** another person, they use blackmail against them. ❑ *He told her their affair would have to stop, because Jack Smith was blackmailing him.* ❑ *The government insisted that it would not be blackmailed by violence.* ● **black|mail|er** (**blackmailers**) N-COUNT ❑ *The nasty thing about a blackmailer is that his starting point is usually the truth.*

이르기까지 다양하다. **3** 타동사 공갈 협박하다 ❑ 그는 잭 스미스로부터 공갈 협박을 받고 있으니 관계를 끝내야 할 것 같다고 그녀에게 말했다. ❑ 정부는 폭력에 의한 공갈 협박에 굴복하지 않겠다고 주장했다. ● 공갈 협박자 가산명사 ❑ 공갈 협박자에 관해 골치 아픈 일은, 그런 공갈의 출발점이 대개의 경우 사실에 기인한다는 것이다.

black mar|ket (**black markets**) N-COUNT If something is bought or sold **on the black market**, it is bought or sold illegally. ❑ *There is a plentiful supply of arms on the black market.*

가산명사 암시장 ❑ 암시장에는 무기가 풍부하게 공급되고 있다.

black|out /blǽkaʊt/ (**blackouts**) also **black-out** **1** N-COUNT A **blackout** is a period of time during a war in which towns and buildings are made dark so that they cannot be seen by enemy planes. ❑ *...blackout curtains.* **2** N-COUNT If a **blackout** is imposed on a particular piece of news, journalists are prevented from broadcasting or publishing it. ❑ *...a media blackout imposed by the Imperial Palace.* **3** N-COUNT If there is a power **blackout**, the electricity supply to a place is temporarily cut off. ❑ *There was an electricity black-out in a large area in the north of the country.* **4** N-COUNT If you have a **blackout**, you temporarily lose consciousness. ❑ *I suffered a black-out which lasted for several minutes.*

1 가산명사 등화관제 ❑ 등화관제용 커튼 **2** 가산명사 보도 관제 ❑ 제정에 의해 강제된 언론 통제 **3** 가산명사 정전 ❑ 그 나라 북부의 광범위한 지역에서 정전이 되었다. **4** 가산명사 일시적 의식 상실 ❑ 나는 일시적으로 수 분 동안 의식을 잃었다.

black|smith /blǽksmɪθ/ (**blacksmiths**) N-COUNT A **blacksmith** is a person whose job is making things by hand out of metal that has been heated to a high temperature.

가산명사 대장장이

black|top /blǽktɒp/ N-UNCOUNT **Blacktop** is a hard black substance which is used as a surface for roads. [AM; BRIT **tarmac**] ❑ *...waves of heat rising from the blacktop.*

불가산명사 아스팔트 포장 [미국영어; 영국영어 tarmac] ❑ 아스팔트로부터 올라오는 열기

blad|der /blǽdər/ (**bladders**) N-COUNT Your **bladder** is the part of your body where urine is stored until it leaves your body. See also **gall bladder**. ❑ *...an opportunity to empty a full bladder.*

가산명사 방광 ❑ 꽉 찬 오줌보를 비울 기회

blade /bleɪd/ **1** N-COUNT The **blade** of a knife, ax, or saw is the edge, which is used for cutting. ❑ *Many of them will have sharp blades.* **2** N-COUNT The **blades** of a propeller are the long, flat parts that turn around. **3** N-COUNT The **blade** of an oar is the thin flat part that you put into the water. **4** N-COUNT A **blade** of grass is a single piece of grass. ❑ *Brian began to tear blades of grass from between the bricks.* →see **silverware**

1 가산명사 날 ❑ 그것들 중 여럿에 날카로운 날이 달릴 것이다. **2** 가산명사 (프로펠러) 날개 **3** 가산명사 (노의) 날 **4** 가산명사 (풀의) 잎 ❑ 브라이언은 벽돌 사이의 풀잎들을 잡아 뽑기 시작했다.

blame ♦♦◇ /bleɪm/ (**blames, blaming, blamed**) **1** V-T If you **blame** a person or thing **for** something bad, you believe or say that they are responsible for it or that they caused it. ❑ *The commission is expected to blame the army for many of the atrocities.* ❑ *Ms. Carey appeared to blame her breakdown on EMI's punishing work schedule.* ● N-UNCOUNT **Blame** is also a noun. ❑ *Nothing could relieve my terrible sense of blame.* **2** N-UNCOUNT The **blame for** something bad that has happened is the responsibility for causing it or letting it happen. ❑ *Some of the blame for the miscarriage of justice must be borne by the solicitors.* **3** V-T If you say that you do not **blame** someone **for** doing something, you mean that you consider it was a reasonable thing to do in the circumstances. [usu with brd-neg] ❑ *I do not blame them for trying to make some money.* **4** PHRASE If someone is **to blame for** something bad that has happened, they are responsible for causing it. ❑ *If their forces were not involved, then who is to blame?* **5** PHRASE If you say that someone **has only** themselves **to blame** or **has no one but** themselves **to blame**, you mean that they are responsible for something bad that has happened to them and that you have no sympathy for them. ❑ *My life is ruined and I suppose I only have myself to blame.*

1 타동사 -의 책임으로 돌리다 ❑ 위원회는 잔학 행위의 많은 부분을 군의 책임으로 돌릴 것으로 예상된다. ❑ 케리 양은 자신의 건강 쇠약을 이엠아이 측의 고된 작업 스케줄 탓으로 돌리는 것처럼 보였다. ● 불가산명사 책임, 죄 ❑ 그 어떤 것도 내가 느끼는 심한 죄책감을 덜어 주지 못할 것이다. **2** 불가산명사 책임 ❑ 오심에 대한 책임 일부는 변호사들이 져야 한다. **3** 타동사 나무라다, 비난하다 ❑ 나는 그들이 돈을 벌어 보려고 했던 것을 나무라지 않는다. **4** 구 책임을 져야 마땅하다 ❑ 그들의 병력이 관련되지 않았다면, 대체 누가 책임을 져야 하나? **5** 구 오로지 본인 탓이다 ❑ 내 삶은 망쳐졌는데, 나 자신 말고는 탓할 사람이 없는 것 같다.

blanch /blɑːntʃ/ (**blanches, blanching, blanched**) **1** V-I If you **blanch**, you suddenly become very pale. ❑ *Simon's face blanched as he looked at Sharpe's frayed and blood-drenched uniform.* **2** V-I If you say that someone **blanches at** something, you mean that they find it unpleasant and do not want to be involved with it. ❑ *Everything he had said had been a mistake. He blanched at his miscalculations.*

1 자동사 새파래지다 ❑ 샤프의 피에 흠뻑 젖은 닳아빠진 유니폼을 보자 사이먼의 얼굴이 새파래졌다. **2** 자동사 몹쓸하게 여겨 받을 빼다; 치를 떨다 ❑ 그가 했던 말은 모두 실언이었다. 그는 자신의 오산에 치를 떨었다.

bland /blænd/ (**blander, blandest**) **1** ADJ If you describe someone or something as **bland**, you mean that they are rather dull and unexciting. ❑ *Serle has a blander personality than Howard.* ❑ *It sounds like a commercial: easy on the ear but bland and forgettable.* **2** ADJ Food that is **bland** has very little flavor. ❑ *It tasted bland and insipid, like warmed cardboard.* →see **spice**

1 형용사 재미없는, 지루한 ❑ 설은 하워드보다 재미없는 성격이다. ❑ 그것은 광고 같다: 듣기에 편안하지만 지루하고 쉽게 잊혀진다. **2** 형용사 맛이 없는, 싱거운 ❑ 그것은 마분지를 데운 것처럼 맛없고 싱거웠다.

blank /blæŋk/ (**blanks**) **1** ADJ Something that is **blank** has nothing on it. ❑ *We could put some of the pictures over on that blank wall over there.* ❑ *He tore a blank page from his notebook.* **2** N-COUNT A **blank** is a space which is left in a piece of writing or on a printed form for you to fill in particular information. ❑ *Put a word in each blank to complete the sentence.* **3** ADJ If you look **blank**, your face shows no feeling, understanding, or interest. ❑ *Abbot looked blank. "I don't quite follow, sir."* ● **blank|ly** ADV [ADV with v] ❑ *She stared at him blankly.* **4** N-SING If your mind or memory is **a blank**, you cannot think of anything or remember anything. ❑ *I'm sorry, but my mind is a blank.* **5** N-COUNT **Blanks** are gun cartridges which contain explosive but do not contain a bullet, so that they cause no harm when the gun is fired. ❑ *...a starter pistol which only fires blanks.* **6** →see also **point-blank** **7** PHRASE If your mind **goes blank**, you are suddenly unable

1 형용사 공백의; 빈 ❑ 저쪽의 빈 벽에 그 그림 몇 점을 걸 수도 있을 것 같다. ❑ 그는 공책에서 아무것도 적히지 않은 면을 한 장 찢어 냈다. **2** 가산명사 빈칸 ❑ 빈칸에 단어를 하나씩 넣어 문장을 완성하시오. **3** 형용사 멍청한, 표정 없는 ❑ 애벗은 멍청한 표정이었다. "잘 이해 못 하겠는데요, 선생님." ● 멍청하게 부사 ❑ 그녀는 그를 멍청히 바라보았다. **4** 단수명사 멍한 상태, 백지 상태 ❑ 미안하지만, 제가 아무 생각이 안 나요. **5** 가산명사 공포탄 ❑ 공포탄만 쏴지는 출발 신호용 권총 **6** 구 갑자기 멍해지다, 백지 상태가 되다 ❑ 정신이 완전히 백지 상태가 되었다.

to think of anything appropriate to say, for example in reply to a question. ❑ *My mind went totally blank.*

blank check (blank checks) [BRIT **blank cheque**] **1** N-COUNT If someone is given a **blank check**, they are given the authority to spend as much money as they need or want. [JOURNALISM] ❑ *We are not prepared to write a blank check for companies that have run into trouble.* **2** N-COUNT If someone is given a **blank check**, they are given the authority to do what they think is best in a particular situation. [JOURNALISM] ❑ *He has, in a sense, been given a blank check to negotiate the new South Africa.*

blan|ket /blǽŋkɪt/ (blankets, blanketing, blanketed) **1** N-COUNT A **blanket** is a large square or rectangular piece of thick cloth, especially one which you put on a bed to keep you warm. **2** N-COUNT A **blanket of** something such as snow is a continuous layer of it which hides what is below or beyond it. ❑ *The mud disappeared under a blanket of snow.* **3** V-T If something such as snow **blankets** an area, it covers it. ❑ *More than a foot of snow blanketed parts of Michigan.* **4** ADJ You use **blanket** to describe something when you want to emphasize that it affects or refers to every person or thing in a group, without any exceptions. [EMPHASIS] ❑ *There's already a blanket ban on foreign unskilled labour in Japan.*

blare /bleər/ (blares, blaring, blared) V-I If something such as a siren or radio **blares**, it makes a loud, unpleasant noise. ❑ *The fire engines were just pulling up, sirens blaring.* ❑ *Music blared from the apartment behind me.* ● N-COUNT **Blare** is also a noun. ❑ *...the blare of a radio through a thin wall.* ● PHRASAL VERB **Blare out** means the same as **blare.** ❑ *Music blares out from every cafe.*

blas|phe|my /blǽsfəmi/ (blasphemies) N-VAR You can describe something that shows disrespect for God or a religion as **blasphemy**. ❑ *He was found guilty of blasphemy and seditious libel and sentenced to three years in jail.*

blast ♦◇◇ /blǽst/ (blasts, blasting, blasted) **1** N-COUNT A **blast** is a big explosion, especially one caused by a bomb. ❑ *250 people were killed in the blast.* **2** V-T If something is **blasted** into a particular place or state, an explosion causes it to be in that place or state. If a hole **is blasted** in something, it is created by an explosion. ❑ *There is a risk that toxic chemicals might be blasted into the atmosphere.* ❑ *The explosion which followed blasted out the external supporting wall of her apartment.* **3** V-T If workers **are blasting** rock, they are using explosives to make holes in it or destroy it, for example so that a road or tunnel can be built. ❑ *Their work was taken up with boring and blasting rock with gelignite.* **4** V-T To **blast** someone means to shoot them with a gun. [JOURNALISM] ❑ *A son blasted his father to death after a lifetime of bullying, a court was told yesterday.* ● N-COUNT **Blast** is also a noun. ❑ *...the man who killed Nigel Davies with a shotgun blast.* **5** V-T If someone **blasts** their way somewhere, they get there by shooting at people or causing an explosion. ❑ *The police were reported to have blasted their way into the house using explosives.* **6** V-T If something **blasts** water or air somewhere, it sends out a sudden, powerful stream of it. ❑ *Blasting cold air over it makes the water evaporate.* ● N-COUNT **Blast** is also a noun. ❑ *Blasts of cold air swept down from the mountains.* **7** V-T/V-I If you **blast** something such as a car horn, or if it **blasts**, it makes a sudden, loud sound. If something **blasts** music or music **blasts**, the music is very loud. ❑ *...drivers who do not blast their horns.* ● N-COUNT **Blast** is also a noun. ❑ *The buzzer suddenly responded in a long blast of sound.* **8** PHRASE If something such as a radio or a heater is on **full blast**, or on **at full blast**, it is producing as much sound or power as it is able to. ❑ *In many of those homes the television is on full blast 24 hours a day.*

▶**blast off** PHRASAL VERB When a space rocket **blasts off**, it leaves the ground at the start of its journey. ❑ *Columbia is set to blast off at 1:20 a.m. Eastern Time tomorrow.*

bla|tant /bleɪtᵊnt/ ADJ You use **blatant** to describe something bad that is done in an open or very obvious way. [EMPHASIS] ❑ *Outsiders will continue to suffer the most blatant discrimination.* ❑ *...a blatant attempt to spread the blame for the fiasco.* ● **bla|tant|ly** ADV ❑ *...a blatantly sexist question.*

bla|tant|ly /bleɪtᵊntli/ ADV **Blatantly** is used to add emphasis when you are describing states or situations which you think are bad. [EMPHASIS] ❑ *It became blatantly obvious to me that the band wasn't going to last.* ❑ *For years, blatantly false assertions have gone unchallenged.*

blaze /bleɪz/ (blazes, blazing, blazed) **1** V-I When a fire **blazes**, it burns strongly and brightly. ❑ *Three people died as wreckage blazed, and rescuers fought to release trapped drivers.* ❑ *The log fire was blazing merrily.* **2** N-COUNT A **blaze** is a large fire which is difficult to control and which destroys a lot of things. [JOURNALISM] ❑ *Two firemen were hurt in a blaze which swept through a tower block last night.* **3** V-I If something **blazes with** light or color, it is extremely bright. [LITERARY] ❑ *The gardens blazed with color.* ● N-COUNT **Blaze** is also a noun. ❑ *I wanted the front garden to be a blaze of color.* **4** N-SING A **blaze of** publicity or attention is a great amount of it. ❑ *He was arrested in a blaze of publicity.* **5** V-I If guns **blaze**, or **blaze away**, they fire continuously, making a lot of noise. ❑ *Guns were blazing, flares going up and the sky was lit up all around.* **6** with all guns blazing →see gun

blaz|er /bleɪzər/ (blazers) N-COUNT A **blazer** is a kind of light jacket for men or women which is also often worn by members of a particular group, especially schoolchildren and members of a sports team.

blaz|ing /bleɪzɪŋ/ ADJ The **blazing** sun or **blazing** hot weather is very hot. [ADJ n] ❑ *Quite a few people were eating outside in the blazing sun.*

bleach /bliːtʃ/ (bleaches, bleaching, bleached) **1** V-T If you **bleach** something, you use a chemical to make it white or pale in color. ❑ *These products don't bleach the hair.* ❑ *...bleached pine tables.* **2** V-T/V-I If the sun **bleaches** something, or something **bleaches**, its color gets paler until it is almost white. ❑ *The tree's*

[영국영어 blank cheque] **1** 가산명사 백지 수표 [언론] ❑ 우리는 곤경에 빠진 회사들을 위해 백지 수표를 쓸 준비가 되어 있지 않다. **2** 가산명사 무제한의 권한, 자유 행동권 [언론] ❑ 어떤 면에서, 그는 새로운 남아프리카 공화국과 자유롭게 교섭할 수 있는 전권을 얻은 것이었다.

1 가산명사 담요 **2** 가산명사 전면을 덮는 것 ❑ 진흙이 온통 눈으로 덮여 보이지 않았다. **3** 타동사 온통 덮다 ❑ 1피트 이상의 눈이 내려 미시간 일부 지역이 온통 눈으로 덮였다. **4** 형용사 포괄적인 [강조] ❑ 일본에서는 이미 미숙련 외국인 노동에 대한 포괄적 금지가 이루어지고 있다.

자동사 울려 퍼지다 ❑ 소방차가 막 사이렌을 울리며 멈춰 서고 있었다. ❑ 내 뒤에 있는 집에서 음악이 울려 퍼졌다. ● 단수명사 울림; 큰 소리 ❑ 얇은 벽을 통해 들려오는 라디오 소리 ● 구동사 울려 퍼지다 ❑ 모든 카페에서 음악이 울려 퍼져 나왔다.

가산명사 또는 불가산명사 신에 대한 불경, 신성 모독 ❑ 그는 신성 모독죄와 선동적 명예 훼손으로 유죄 판결을 받고 3년간의 징역을 선고받았다.

1 가산명사 폭발, 폭파 ❑ 그 폭발로 250명이 목숨을 잃었다. **2** 타동사 폭발하다, 폭발로 생기다 ❑ 유독한 화학 약품이 폭발로 인해 대기 중에 퍼질 위험이 있다. ❑ 뒤이은 폭발로 그녀가 사는 아파트의 외부 지지벽이 날아가 버렸다. **3** 타동사 발파하다 ❑ 그들의 작업은 젤리그나이트로 바위에 구멍을 뚫고 발파하는 일에 집중되어 있었다. **4** 타동사 총으로 쏘다 [언론] ❑ 어제 법원에서는, 어떤 아들이 일생 동안 자신을 괴롭히던 그 아버지를 총으로 쏘아 죽인 사건에 대한 재판이 있었다. ● 가산명사 총격 ❑ 나이젤 데이비스를 엽총으로 쏘아 죽인 남자 **5** 타동사 뚫고 들어가다 ❑ 보도에 따르면 경찰은 폭약을 사용하여 그 집 내부로 진입했다고 했다. **6** 타동사 일으켜 보내다; 몰아치게 하다 ❑ 그 위로 찬바람을 일으켜 보내면 물이 증발한다. ● 가산명사 몰아침; 돌풍 ❑ 차가운 돌풍이 산맥을 타고 휘몰아쳐 내려왔다. **7** 타동사/자동사 시끄럽게 울리다; 시끄럽게 울다 ❑ 경적을 시끄럽게 울리지 않는 운전자들 ● 가산명사 시끄럽게 울림 ❑ 버저가 갑자기 반응하며 길고 시끄러운 소리를 울려 댔다. **8** 구 최대 출력 ❑ 그 가정들 중 많은 집에서 볼륨을 최대로 해서 하루 24시간 내내 텔레비전을 틀어 놓는다.

구동사 발진하다 ❑ 컬럼비아호는 내일 동부 시간으로 오전 1시 20분에 발진하기로 되어 있다.

형용사 노골적인 [강조] ❑ 국외자들은 계속해서 가장 노골적인 차별을 받을 것이다. ❑ 그 대실패에 대한 비난을 유포시키려는 노골적인 시도 ● 부사 노골적으로 ❑ 노골적으로 성차별주의적인 질문

부사 아주, 몹시 [강조] ❑ 그 밴드가 지속되지 않으리라는 사실이 내게는 아주 명백해졌다. ❑ 수년 동안, 어처구니없이 잘못된 주장들이 아무런 도전도 받지 않고 제기되어 왔다.

1 자동사 타오르다 ❑ 잔해가 타오르면서 3명이 숨졌고, 구조원들은 갇힌 운전자들을 구출하려고 애썼다. ❑ 화톳불이 보기 좋게 타오르고 있었다. **2** 가산명사 큰 불 [언론] ❑ 지난밤 한 고층 빌딩을 휩쓴 큰 불로 소방수 2명이 부상당했다. **3** 자동사 밝게 빛나다; 번쩍거리다 [문예체] ❑ 정원들은 찬연히 빛났다. ● 가산명사 번쩍거림, 광휘 ❑ 나는 앞 정원이 찬란하게 빛나기를 원했다. **4** 단수명사 엄청난 양 ❑ 그는 엄청난 유명세를 치렀다. **5** 자동사 요란하게 발사되다 ❑ 요란하게 총이 발사되었고, 조명탄이 쏘아 올려져 온 하늘이 밝아졌다.

가산명사 블레이저 (바지와 색깔이 다른 상의)

형용사 타는 듯이 더운 ❑ 꽤 많은 사람들이 야외에서 뜨거운 태양 아래 식사를 하고 있었다.

1 타동사 표백하다; 탈색하다 ❑ 이 제품들은 머리카락을 탈색시키지 않는다. ❑ 탈색된 소나무 탁자 **2** 타동사/자동사 탈색하다; 탈색되다 ❑ 그 나무뿌리는 껍질을 벗긴 채 매달아서 말리고

roots are stripped and hung to season and bleach. □ *He has hair which is naturally black but which has been bleached by the sun.* 🔟 N-MASS **Bleach** is a chemical that is used to make cloth white, or to clean things thoroughly and kill germs.

탈색시킨다. □ 그의 머리카락은 원래 검은색이지만 햇볕에 탈색되었다. 🔟 물질명사 표백제

bleak /bliːk/ (**bleaker, bleakest**) 🔟 ADJ If a situation is **bleak**, it is bad, and seems unlikely to improve. □ *The immediate outlook remains bleak.* ● **bleak|ness** N-UNCOUNT □ *The continued bleakness of the American job market was blamed.* 🔟 ADJ If you describe a place as **bleak**, you mean that it looks cold, empty, and unattractive. □ *The island's pretty bleak.* 🔟 ADJ When the weather is **bleak**, it is cold, dull, and unpleasant. □ *The weather can be quite bleak on the coast.* 🔟 ADJ If someone looks or sounds **bleak**, they look or sound depressed, as if they have no hope or energy. □ *His face was bleak.* ● **bleak|ly** ADV □ *"There is nothing left,"* she says bleakly.

🔟 형용사 가망 없는 □ 당장의 전망은 여전히 어둡다. ● 가망 없음 불가산명사 □ 미국 인력 시장의 지속적인 어두운 전망이 원인으로 지목되었다. 🔟 형용사 황량한 □ 그 섬은 아주 황량하다. 🔟 형용사 스산한 □ 해안 지방의 날씨는 상당히 스산할 수도 있겠습니다. 🔟 형용사 스산한 □ 그는 스산한 얼굴이었다. ● 스산하게 부사 □ "아무것도 남지 않았어."라고 그녀는 스산하게 말한다.

bleed /bliːd/ (**bleeds, bleeding, bled**) 🔟 V-I When you **bleed**, you lose blood from your body as a result of injury or illness. □ *His head had struck the sink and was bleeding.* ● **bleed|ing** N-UNCOUNT □ *This results in internal bleeding.* 🔟 V-I If the color of one substance **bleeds into** the color of another substance that it is touching, it goes into the other thing so that its color changes in an undesirable way. □ *The coloring pigments from the skins are not allowed to bleed into the grape juice.* 🔟 V-T If someone **is being bled**, money or other resources are gradually being taken away from them. [DISAPPROVAL] □ *We have been gradually bled for twelve years.*

🔟 자동사 피를 흘리다 □ 그는 머리를 싱크대에 부딪치며 피를 흘리고 있었다. □ 그 사람은 심하게 피를 흘리고 있었다. ● 출혈 불가산명사 □ 이것은 내출혈을 유발한다. 🔟 자동사 번지다 □ 포도 주스에 껍질의 색소가 번져 들어가서는 안 된다. 🔟 타동사 착취당하다 [탈탈잃음] □ 우리는 12년 동안 차츰차츰 착취당해 왔다.

blem|ish /blɛmɪʃ/ (**blemishes, blemishing, blemished**) 🔟 N-COUNT A **blemish** is a small mark on something that spoils its appearance. □ *Every piece is closely scrutinised, and if there is the slightest blemish on it, it is rejected.* 🔟 N-COUNT A **blemish on** something is a small fault in it. □ *This is the one blemish on an otherwise resounding success.* 🔟 V-T If something **blemishes** someone's character or reputation, it spoils it or makes it seem less good than it was in the past. □ *He wasn't about to blemish that pristine record.*

🔟 가산명사 흠 □ 모든 물건이 철저한 검사를 거치며, 아주 작은 흠이라도 있을 때는 퇴짜를 맞는다. 🔟 가산명사 오점 □ 이것이, 대성공일 뻔했던 일의 유일한 오점이다. 🔟 타동사 -에 흠을 내다 □ 그는 그 깨끗한 경력에 오점을 남길 마음이 없었다.

blend /blɛnd/ (**blends, blending, blended**) 🔟 V-RECIP If you **blend** substances together or if they **blend**, you mix them together so that they become one substance. □ *Blend the butter with the sugar and beat until light and creamy.* □ *Blend the ingredients until you have a smooth cream.* 🔟 N-COUNT A **blend** of things is a mixture or combination of them that is useful or pleasant. □ *The public areas offer a subtle blend of traditional charm with modern amenities.* □ *...a blend of wine and sparkling water.* 🔟 V-RECIP When colors, sounds, or styles **blend**, they come together or are combined in a pleasing way. □ *You could paint the walls and ceilings the same color so they blend together.* 🔟 V-T If you **blend** ideas, policies, or styles, you use them together in order to achieve something. □ *His "cosmic vision" is to blend Christianity with "the wisdom of all world religions."*

🔟 상호동사 섞다; 섞이다 □ 버터와 설탕을 섞은 다음 연한 크림처럼 될 때까지 휘저으세요. □ 부드러운 크림처럼 될 때까지 재료를 섞으세요. 🔟 가산명사 혼합 □ 공공 지역에는 전통적 매력과 현대적 설비가 미묘하게 한데 뒤섞여 있습니다. □ 와인과 탄산수를 섞은 것 🔟 상호동사 한데 어우러지다; 조화를 이루다 □ 벽과 천장이 서로 어우러지도록 같은 색상으로 칠하실 수도 있습니다. 🔟 타동사 아우르다 □ 그의 '우주적 비전'은 기독교 신앙과 '전 세계 모든 종교의 지혜'를 아우르는 것이다.

bless /blɛs/ (**blesses, blessing, blessed**) 🔟 V-T When someone such as a priest **blesses** people or things, he asks for God's favor and protection for them. □ *...asking for all present to bless this couple and their loving commitment to one another.* 🔟 CONVENTION **Bless** is used in expressions such as "God bless" or "bless you" to express affection, thanks, or good wishes. [INFORMAL, SPOKEN, FEELINGS] □ *"Bless you, Eva,"* he whispered. 🔟 CONVENTION You can say **"bless you"** to someone who has just sneezed. [SPOKEN, FORMULAE] 🔟 →see also **blessed, blessing**

🔟 타동사 축복하다 □ 참석하신 모든 분들께서 이 한 쌍과 이들의 서로에 대한 깊은 어린 언약을 축복해 주시길 바라며 🔟 관용 표현 애정, 감사, 호의 등을 나타내는 'God bless' 등의 관용적 표현에, bless을 쓴다. [비격식체, 구어체, 감정 개입] □ "신의 가호가 있기를, 에바."라고 그가 속삭였다. 🔟 관용 표현 상대방이 재채기를 했을 때 "조심하세요."라는 뜻으로 하는 말 [구어체, 의례적인 표현]

bless|ed

Pronounced /blɛst/ for meaning 🔟, and /blɛsɪd/ for meaning 🔟.

🔟 ADJ If someone is **blessed with** a particular good quality or skill, they have that good quality or skill. [v-link ADJ with n] □ *Both are blessed with uncommon ability to fix things.* 🔟 ADJ You use **blessed** to describe something that you think is wonderful, and that you are grateful for or relieved about. [APPROVAL] [ADJ n] □ *The birth of a live healthy baby is a truly blessed event.* ● **bless|ed|ly** ADV □ *Most British election campaigns are blessedly brief.* 🔟 →see also **bless**

🔟 🔟의 의미일 때는 /blɛst/로, 🔟의 의미일 때는 /blɛsɪd/로 발음된다.

🔟 형용사 -을 지닌 □ 둘 다 물건을 수선하는 비범한 능력을 지니고 있다. 🔟 형용사 기쁜; 다행스러운 [마음에 듦] □ 건강한 아기의 탄생은 정말로 기쁜 일이다. ● 다행히; 기쁘게 부사 □ 대부분의 영국 선거 운동은 다행히도 짧다. 🔟 →see also **bless**

bless|ing /blɛsɪŋ/ (**blessings**) 🔟 N-COUNT A **blessing** is something good that you are grateful for. □ *Rivers are a blessing for an agricultural country.* 🔟 N-COUNT If something is done with someone's **blessing**, it is done with their approval and support. □ *With the blessing of the White House, a group of Democrats in Congress is meeting to find additional budget cuts.* 🔟 N-COUNT A **blessing** is a prayer asking God to look kindly upon the people who are present or the event that is taking place. □ *The Bishop of Oxford led the prayers and pronounced the blessing.* 🔟 →see also **bless**

🔟 가산명사 축복; 고마운 것 □ 농경 국가에 있어서 강은 고마운 존재이다. 🔟 가산명사 동조, 찬동 □ 백악관의 동조를 등에 업고, 의회 내 일군의 민주당의원들이 추가 예산 삭감을 위해 회합을 가질 예정이다. 🔟 가산명사 축원 □ 옥스퍼드 주교는 기도를 인도한 후 축도를 했다.

blew /bluː/ **Blew** is the past tense of **blow**.

blow의 과거형

blight /blaɪt/ (**blights, blighting, blighted**) 🔟 N-VAR You can refer to something as a **blight** when it causes great difficulties, and damages or spoils other things. □ *This discriminatory policy has really been a blight on America.* 🔟 V-T If something **blights** your life or your hopes, it damages and spoils them. If something **blights** an area, it spoils it and makes it unattractive. □ *An embarrassing blunder nearly blighted his career before it got off the ground.* □ *...thousands of families whose lives were blighted by unemployment.* 🔟 N-UNCOUNT **Blight** is a disease which makes plants dry up and die. □ *All you can do to prevent potato blight is keep an eye on your crops.*

🔟 가산명사 또는 불가산명사 해치는 것; 재앙 □ 이 차별 정책은 지금껏 미국에 커다란 재앙이었다. 🔟 타동사 파괴하다; 꺾다; 황폐화시키다 □ 곤란한 큰 실수 때문에 그는 첫발을 내딛기도 전에 앞길이 막힐 뻔했다. □ 실업으로 인해 삶이 황폐해진 수천 가구의 가정 🔟 불가산명사 마름병 □ 감자 마름병을 예방하기 위해 할 수 있는 일은 작물에서 눈을 떼지 않는 것뿐이다.

blind /blaɪnd/ (**blinds, blinding, blinded**) 🔟 ADJ Someone who is **blind** is unable to see because their eyes are damaged. □ *I started helping him run the business when he went blind.* □ **The blind** are people who are blind. □ *He was a teacher of the blind.* ● **blind|ness** N-UNCOUNT □ *Early diagnosis and treatment can usually prevent blindness.* 🔟 V-T If something **blinds** you, it makes you unable to see, either for a short time or permanently. □ *The sun hit the windshield, momentarily blinding him.* 🔟 ADJ If you are **blind with** something such as tears or a bright light, you are unable to see for a short time because of the tears or light. [v-link ADJ, usu ADJ with n] □ *Her mother groped for the back of the chair, her eyes*

🔟 형용사 눈이 먼 □ 나는 그가 실명하던 때부터 그의 사업 운영을 돕기 시작했다. ● 복수명사 시각 장애인 □ 그 사람은 시각 장애인들의 스승이었다. ● 눈이 멂, 실명 불가산명사 □ 초기에 진단과 치료를 받으면 대개는 실명을 막을 수 있다. 🔟 타동사 눈멀게 하다 □ 햇빛이 차 앞 유리에 쏟아져 그는 순간적으로 앞을 볼 수 없었다. 🔟 형용사 -로 앞이 안 보이는 □ 눈물로 앞을 가려, 그녀의 어머니는 의자 등받이를 더듬어 찾았다 ● 앞이 보이지 않아 부사 □ 레티는 앞이 안 보여

blind with tears. • **blind|ly** ADV ❏ *Lettie groped blindly for the glass.* **4** ADJ If you say that someone is **blind to** a fact or a situation, you mean that they ignore it or are unaware of it, although you think that they should take notice of it or be aware of it. [DISAPPROVAL] [v-link ADJ *to* n] ❏ *David's good looks and impeccable manners had always made her blind to his faults.* • **blind|ness** N-UNCOUNT ❏ *...blindness in government policy to the very existence of the unemployed.* **5** V-T If something **blinds** you **to** the real situation, it prevents you from realizing that it exists or from understanding it properly. ❏ *He never allowed his love of Australia to blind him to his countrymen's faults.* **6** ADJ You can describe someone's beliefs or actions as **blind** when you think that they seem to take no notice of important facts or behave in an unreasonable way. [DISAPPROVAL] ❏ *...her blind faith in the wisdom of the Church.* **7** N-COUNT A **blind** is a roll of cloth or paper which you can pull down over a window as a covering. ❏ *Pulling the blinds up, she let some of the bright sunlight in.* **8** →see also **blinding, blindly** **9** PHRASE If you say that someone **is turning a blind eye to** something bad or illegal that is happening, you mean that you think they are pretending not to notice that it is happening so that they will not have to do anything about it. [DISAPPROVAL] ❏ *Teachers are turning a blind eye to pupils smoking at school, a report reveals today.*

잔을 더듬어 찾았다. **4** 형용사 ~을 못 보는; ~에 몰이해한 [탐탁찮음] ❏ 데이비드의 잘생긴 외모와 나무랄 데 없는 매너 때문에, 그녀에게는 언제나 그의 잘못이 눈에 들어오지 않았다. • 무지, 몰이해 불가산명사 ❏ 실업자의 존재 자체에 대한 정부 정책의 몰이해 **5** 타동사 (비유적) 눈멀게 하다; 판단력을 흐리다 ❏ 그가 호주에 대한 사랑 때문에 동포의 잘못을 눈감아 주는 일은 결코 없었다. **6** 형용사 맹목적인 [탐탁찮음] ❏ 교회의 현명함에 대한 그녀의 맹목적인 믿음 **7** 가산명사 발, 블라인드 ❏ 그녀는 블라인드를 걷어 올려 화창한 햇빛이 약간 들어오게 했다. **9** 구 ~을 보고도 못 본 체하다 [탐탁찮음] ❏ 교사들이 학생들의 학교 내 흡연을 보고도 못 본 체하고 있다고, 오늘 어떤 기사가 폭로했다.

Word Partnership *blind*의 연어

ADJ.	blind **and deaf** 1
ADV.	**partially** blind 1
N.	blind **person** 1
	blind **faith** 6

blind|fold /blaɪndfoʊld/ (**blindfolds, blindfolding, blindfolded**) **1** N-COUNT A **blindfold** is a strip of cloth that is tied over someone's eyes so that they cannot see. **2** V-T If you **blindfold** someone, you tie a blindfold over their eyes. ❏ *His abductors blindfolded him and drove him to a flat in southern Beirut.*

1 가산명사 눈가리개 **2** 타동사 눈을 가리다 ❏ 납치범들은 그의 눈을 가린 후 그를 베이루트 남부의 한 아파트로 끌고 갔다.

blind|ing /blaɪndɪŋ/ **1** ADJ A **blinding** light is extremely bright. ❏ *The doctor worked busily beneath the blinding lights of the delivery room.* **2** ADJ You use **blinding** to emphasize that something is very obvious. [EMPHASIS] [ADJ n] ❏ *The miseries I went through made me suddenly realise with a blinding flash what life was all about.* **3** ADJ **Blinding** pain is very strong pain. ❏ *There was a pain then, a quick, blinding agony that jumped along Danlo's spine.*

1 형용사 눈부신 ❏ 의사는 분만실의 강렬한 불빛 아래서 바쁘게 움직였다. **2** 형용사 명확한 [강조] ❏ 나는 그 고난을 겪으면서 문득 삶이 과연 무엇인지 명확하게 깨닫게 되었다. **3** 형용사 강렬한 ❏ 조금 통증이 오더니 다음엔 강렬한 고통이 단로의 등골을 따라 빠르게 밀려왔다.

blind|ly /blaɪndli/ ADV If you say that someone does something **blindly**, you mean that they do it without having enough information, or without thinking about it. [DISAPPROVAL] ❏ *Don't just blindly follow what the banker says.* ❏ *Without adequate information, many students choose a college almost blindly.* →see also **blind**

부사 맹목적으로 [탐탁찮음] ❏ 은행원이 하는 말을 그냥 맹목적으로 따르지 말라. ❏ 많은 학생들이 충분한 정보 없이 거의 맹목적으로 대학을 선택한다.

blind trust (**blind trusts**) N-COUNT A **blind trust** is a financial arrangement in which someone's investments are managed without the person knowing where the money is invested. **Blind trusts** are used especially by people in public office, so that they cannot be accused of using their position to make money unfairly. [BUSINESS] ❏ *His shares were placed in a blind trust when he became a government minister.*

가산명사 백지 신탁 [경제] ❏ 그가 정부 각료가 되었을 때, 그의 주식은 백지 신탁으로 관리되기 시작했다.

blink /blɪŋk/ (**blinks, blinking, blinked**) **1** V-T/V-I When you **blink** or when you **blink** your eyes, you shut your eyes and very quickly open them again. ❏ *Kathryn blinked and forced a smile.* ❏ *She was blinking her eyes rapidly.* • N-COUNT **Blink** is also a noun. ❏ *He kept giving quick blinks.* **2** V-I When a light **blinks**, it flashes on and off. ❏ *Green and yellow lights blinked on the surface of the harbor.* ❏ *The plane was flying normally for about 15 minutes before a warning light blinked on.*

1 타동사/자동사 눈을 깜박이다 ❏ 캐서린이 눈을 깜박이며 억지로 미소를 지었다. ❏ 그녀는 빠르게 눈을 깜박거리고 있었다. • 가산명사 깜박거림 ❏ 그는 계속 재빨리 눈을 깜박였다. **2** 자동사 깜박이다 ❏ 초록색과 노란색의 불빛이 항구의 수면 위에 깜박였다. ❏ 비행기는 경고등이 깜박이기 전까지 15분간 정상적으로 날고 있었다.

bliss /blɪs/ N-UNCOUNT **Bliss** is a state of complete happiness. ❏ *It was a scene of such domestic bliss.*

불가산명사 지극한 행복 ❏ 그것은 아주 행복한 가족의 모습이었다.

bliss|ful /blɪsfəl/ **1** ADJ A **blissful** situation or period of time is one in which you are extremely happy. ❏ *We spent a blissful week together.* • **bliss|ful|ly** /blɪsfəli/ ADV ❏ *We're blissfully happy.* **2** ADJ If someone is in **blissful** ignorance of something unpleasant or serious, they are totally unaware of it. [ADJ n] ❏ *Many country parishes were still living in blissful ignorance of the post-war crime wave.* • **bliss|ful|ly** ADV ❏ *At first, he was blissfully unaware of the conspiracy against him.*

1 형용사 더없이 행복한 ❏ 우리는 함께 더없이 행복한 1주를 보냈다. • 더없이 행복하게 부사 ❏ 우리는 더없이 행복하다. **2** 형용사 전혀 모르는 ❏ 그때까지도 전후 범죄 물결이 전혀 알려지지 않았던 시골 교구가 많이 있었다. • 전혀 부사 ❏ 처음에 그는 자신을 타도하려는 음모를 전혀 모르고 있었다.

blis|ter /blɪstər/ (**blisters, blistering, blistered**) **1** N-COUNT A **blister** is a painful swelling on the surface of your skin. Blisters contain a clear liquid and are usually caused by heat or by something repeatedly rubbing your skin. **2** V-T/V-I When your skin **blisters** or when something **blisters** it, blisters appear on it. ❏ *The affected skin turns red and may blister.* ❏ *The sap of this plant blisters the skin.*

1 가산명사 물집, 수포 **2** 타동사/자동사 물집이 생기다, 물집이 생기게 하다 ❏ 환부가 빨갛게 변하고 물집이 생길 수도 있다. ❏ 이 식물의 수액은 피부에 물집이 생기게 한다.

blis|ter|ing /blɪstərɪŋ/ **1** ADJ **Blistering** heat is very great heat. ❏ *...a blistering summer day.* **2** ADJ A **blistering** remark expresses great anger or dislike. ❏ *The president responded to this with a blistering attack on his critics.* **3** ADJ **Blistering** is used to describe actions in sport to emphasize that they are done with great speed or force. [JOURNALISM, EMPHASIS] [ADJ n] ❏ *Sharon Wild set a blistering pace to take the lead.*

1 형용사 찌는 듯한 ❏ 찌는 듯한 여름날 **2** 형용사 신랄한, 통렬한 ❏ 대통령은 이에 대해 그의 비평가들에 대한 통렬한 비난으로 대응했다. **3** 형용사 맹렬한 [언론, 강조] ❏ 샤론 와일드는 선두로 나서기 위해 맹렬한 속도로 달렸다.

blithe /blaɪð/ ADJ You use **blithe** to indicate that something is done casually, without serious or careful thought. [DISAPPROVAL] ❏ *Acts of trespass and petty theft often grew out of the blithe disregard that boys had for private property.* • **blithe|ly** ADV ❏ *Your editorial blithely ignores the hard facts.*

형용사 심상한, 무심한 [탐탁찮음] ❏ 무단 침입과 좀도둑질 행위는 종종 사내아이들이 사유 재산을 대수롭지 않게 생각한 데서 발생했다. • 평범하게, 대수롭지 않게 부사 ❏ 귀사의 사설은 엄연한 사실을 아무렇지도 않은 듯 간과하고 있습니다.

blitz /blɪts/ (**blitzes, blitzing, blitzed**) **1** V-T If a city or building **is blitzed** during a war, it is attacked by bombs dropped by enemy aircraft. ❏ *In the autumn of 1940 London was blitzed by an average of two hundred aircraft a night.* **2** N-PROPER The heavy bombing of British cities by German aircraft in 1940

1 타동사 공습을 받다 ❏ 1940년 가을 런던은 밤마다 평균 200대의 비행기로부터 공습을 받았다. **2** 고유명사 1940년부터 1941년까지의 독일의 영국 도시 공습 **3** 가산명사 대대적인 캠페인 [비격식체]

a b c d e f g h i j k l m n o p q r s t u v w x y z

and 1941 is referred to as **the Blitz**. ◼ N-COUNT If you have a **blitz on** something, you make a big effort to deal with it or to improve it. [INFORMAL] ❑ *Regional accents are still acceptable but there is to be a blitz on incorrect grammar.*

bliz|zard /blɪzərd/ (**blizzards**) N-COUNT A **blizzard** is a very bad snowstorm with strong winds. →see **storm**, **weather**

bloat|ed /bloʊtɪd/ ◼ ADJ If someone's body or a part of their body is **bloated**, it is much larger than normal, usually because it has a lot of liquid or gas inside it. ❑ *...the bloated body of a dead bullock.* ◻ ADJ If you feel **bloated** after eating a large meal, you feel very full and uncomfortable. [v-link ADJ] ❑ *Diners do not want to leave the table feeling bloated.*

blob /blɒb/ (**blobs**) ◼ N-COUNT A **blob of** thick or sticky liquid is a small, often round, amount of it. [INFORMAL] ❑ *...a blob of chocolate mousse.* ◻ N-COUNT You can use **blob** to refer to something that you cannot see very clearly, for example because it is in the distance. [INFORMAL] ❑ *You could just see vague blobs of faces.*

bloc /blɒk/ (**blocs**) N-COUNT A **bloc** is a group of countries which have similar political aims and interests and that act together over some issues. ❑ *...the former Soviet bloc.*

block ◆◆◇ /blɒk/ (**blocks, blocking, blocked**) ◼ N-COUNT A **block of** a substance is a large rectangular piece of it. ❑ *a block of ice.* ◻ N-COUNT A **block** of apartments or offices is a large building containing them. ❑ *...a white-painted apartment block.* ◾ N-COUNT A **block** in a town or city is an area of land with streets on all its sides, or the area or distance between such streets. ❑ *He walked around the block three times.* ❑ *She walked four blocks down High Street.* ◗ V-T To **block** a road, channel, or pipe means to put an object across it or in it so that nothing can pass through it or along it. ❑ *Some students today blocked a highway that cuts through the center of the city.* ◙ V-T If something **blocks** your view, it prevents you from seeing something because it is between you and that thing. ❑ *...a row of spruce trees that blocked his view of the long north slope of the mountain.* ◚ V-T If you **block** someone's way, you prevent them from going somewhere or entering a place by standing in front of them. ❑ *I started to move round him, but he blocked my way.* ◛ V-T If you **block** something that is being arranged, you prevent it from being done. ❑ *For years the country has tried to block imports of various cheap foreign products.* ◜ N-COUNT If you have a **mental block** or a **block**, you are temporarily unable to do something that you can normally do which involves using, thinking about, or remembering something. ❑ *I cannot do maths. I've got a mental block about it.* ◝ →see also **stumbling block**

▸**block out** ◼ PHRASAL VERB If someone **blocks out** a thought, they try not to think about it. ❑ *She accuses me of having blocked out the past.* ◻ PHRASAL VERB Something that **blocks out** light prevents it from reaching a place. ❑ *Thick chipboard across the window frames blocked out the daylight.*

block|ade /blɒkeɪd/ (**blockades, blockading, blockaded**) ◼ N-COUNT A **blockade** of a place is an action that is taken to prevent goods or people from entering or leaving it. ❑ *It's not yet clear who will actually enforce the blockade.* ◻ V-T If a group of people **blockade** a place, they stop goods or people from reaching that place. If they **blockade** a road or a port, they stop people using that road or port. ❑ *About 50,000 people are trapped in the town, which has been blockaded for more than 40 days.*

block|age /blɒkɪdʒ/ (**blockages**) N-COUNT A **blockage in** a pipe, tube, or tunnel is an object which blocks it, or the state of being blocked. ❑ *The logical treatment is to remove this blockage.*

block|bust|er /blɒkbʌstər/ (**blockbusters**) N-COUNT A **blockbuster** is a movie or book that is very popular and successful, usually because it is very exciting. [INFORMAL] ❑ *...the latest Hollywood blockbuster.*

bloke /bloʊk/ (**blokes**) N-COUNT A **bloke** is a man. [BRIT, INFORMAL] ❑ *He is a really nice bloke.*

blonde /blɒnd/ (**blondes, blonder, blondest**)

> The form **blonde** is usually used to refer to women, and **blond** to refer to men.

◼ COLOR A woman who has **blonde** hair has pale-colored hair. Blonde hair can be very light brown or light yellow. The form **blond** is used when describing men. ❑ *There were two little girls, one Asian and one with blonde hair.* ◻ ADJ Someone who is **blonde** has blonde hair. ❑ *He was blonder than his brother.* ◾ N-COUNT A **blonde** is a woman who has blonde hair. ❑ *...a stunning blonde in her early thirties.*

blood ◆◆◇ /blʌd/ ◼ N-UNCOUNT **Blood** is the red liquid that flows inside your body, which you can see if you cut yourself. ❑ *His shirt was covered in blood.* ◻ N-UNCOUNT You can use **blood** to refer to the race or social class of someone's parents or ancestors. ❑ *There was Greek blood in his veins: his ancestors originally bore the name Karajannis.* ◾ PHRASE If you say that there is **bad blood between** people, you mean that they have argued about something and dislike each other. ❑ *There is, it seems, some bad blood between Mills and the Baldwins.* ◗ PHRASE If something violent and cruel is done **in cold blood**, it is done deliberately and in an unemotional way. [DISAPPROVAL] ❑ *The crime had been committed in cold blood.* →see also **cold-blooded** ◙ PHRASE If you say that someone has a person's **blood** on their **hands**, you mean that they are responsible for that person's death. ❑ *He has my son's blood on his hands. I hope it haunts him for the rest of his days.* ◚ PHRASE If a quality or talent is **in** your **blood**, it is part of your nature, and other members of your family have it too. ❑ *Diplomacy was in his blood: his ancestors had been feudal lords.* ◛ PHRASE You can use the expressions **new blood, fresh blood,** or **young blood** to refer to people

---

❑ 지역 사투리는 아직 용납되지만, 문법 오류에 관해서는 대대적인 캠페인이 펼쳐질 것이다.

가산명사 눈보라

◼ 형용사 부은 ❑ 어린 수소의 부은 사체 ◻ 형용사 배가 잔뜩 부른, 과식한 ❑ 사람들이 식사 후 지나친 포만감을 갖고 싶어 하지 않는다.

◼ 가산명사 한 방울 [비격식체] ❑ 초콜릿 무스 한 방울 ◻ 가산명사 흐릿한 형상 [비격식체] ❑ 당신은 단지 얼굴들을 흐릿하게만 볼 수 있을 것이다.

가산명사 블록 ❑ 구소련 블록

◼ 가산명사 토막, 덩어리 ❑ 얼음 한 덩어리 ◻ 가산명사 (큰 건물) 한 동 ❑ 흰색으로 페인트칠한 아파트 한 동 ◾ 가산명사 구역, 블록 ❑ 그는 그 구역을 걸어서 세 번 돌았다. ❑ 그녀는 시내 중심가를 따라 네 블록을 걸어 내려갔다. ◗ 타동사 막다, 봉쇄하다 ❑ 몇몇 학생들이 오늘 도시 중심부를 관통하는 고속도로를 봉쇄했다. ◙ 타동사 막다, 가리다 ❑ 그에게서 길게 이어지는 산의 북쪽 경사면 시야를 막는 죽 늘어선 가문비나무들 ◚ 타동사 막다 ❑ 나는 그를 비켜 가려고 했지만, 그가 내 길을 막아섰다. ◛ 타동사 막다 ❑ 수년간 이 국가는 저가의 다양한 외제 수입품을 막기 위해 노력해 왔다. ◜ 가산명사 정신적 단절, 사고력 차단 ❑ 계산이 안돼. 하나도 생각이 안나.

◼ 구동사 생각하지 않으려 하다, 생각을 묻어 두다 ❑ 그녀는 내가 과거를 묻어 두려 한다고 비난했다. ◻ 구동사 들어오지 못하게 하다, 차단하다 ❑ 창틀에 가로질러 놓은 두꺼운 합판 때문에 햇빛이 들어오지 않았다.

◼ 가산명사 봉쇄 ❑ 누가 실제적으로 봉쇄를 강행할지 아직 확실치 않다. ◻ 타동사 봉쇄하다 ❑ 40여 일 동안 봉쇄된 그 마을에 대략 5만 명이 갇혀 있다.

가산명사 막혀 있는 것; 막힘 ❑ 논리적인 조치는 이 막힌 부분을 제거하는 것이다.

가산명사 블록버스터, 초대형 히트작 [비격식체] ❑ 최신 할리우드 블록버스터

가산명사 놈, 녀석 [영국영어, 비격식체] ❑ 걔 정말 괜찮은 녀석이야.

> blonde는 대개 여성을, blond는 남성을 지칭할 때 쓴다.

◼ 색채어 금발 ❑ 꼬마 여자 아이 둘이 있었는데, 한 명은 동양인, 또 한 명은 금발이었다. ◻ 형용사 금발의 ❑ 그는 동생보다 머리가 더 금발이다. ◾ 가산명사 금발의 여인 ❑ 30대 초반의 매력적인 금발 여인

◼ 불가산명사 피 ❑ 그의 셔츠는 피투성이였다. ◻ 불가산명사 피, 혈통 ❑ 그에게는 그리스 인의 피가 흘렀다. 그의 조상들은 원래 카라자니스라는 이름을 썼다. ◾ 구 악감정, 불화 ❑ 밀스와 볼드윈 가 사이에 약간의 불화가 있는 것으로 보인다. ◗ 구 냉정하게, 냉혹하게 [탐탁찮음] ❑ 냉혹하게 자행된 범행이었다. ◙ 구 -의 죽음에 책임이 있다 ❑ 내 아들은 그 사람 때문에 죽었다. 이 사실이 여생 동안 그를 따라다니며 괴롭히길 바란다. ◚ 구 집안 내력이다 ❑ 그의 외교적 기질은 집안 내력이다. 선조들이 봉건 시대 군주였던 것이다. ◛ 구 새 얼굴, 젊은 피 ❑ 젊은 피를 수혈하기 위한 대대적인 개각이 단행되었다.

who are brought into an organization to improve it by thinking of new ideas or new ways of doing things. ❑ *There's been a major reshuffle of the cabinet to bring in new blood.* ◳ **flesh and blood** →see **flesh. own flesh and blood** →see **flesh** →see **donor**

	Word Partnership	*blood*의 연어
V.	**donate/give** blood ◳	
N.	**white** blood **cells,** blood **clot,** blood **disease,** blood **loss, pool of** blood, blood **sample,** blood **supply,** blood **test,** blood **transfusion** ◳	
ADJ.	**covered in** blood, blood **stained** ◳ **related by** blood ◳ **bad** blood ◳	
PREP.	**in** *someone's* blood ◳	

blood pres|sure N-UNCOUNT Your **blood pressure** is the amount of force with which your blood flows around your body. ❑ *Your doctor will monitor your blood pressure.* →see **diagnosis**

blood|shed /blʌdʃɛd/ N-UNCOUNT **Bloodshed** is violence in which people are killed or wounded. ❑ *The government must increase the pace of reforms to avoid further bloodshed.*

blood|stream /blʌdstrim/ (**bloodstreams**) N-COUNT Your **bloodstream** is the blood that flows around your body. ❑ *The disease releases toxins into the bloodstream.*

blood test (**blood tests**) N-COUNT A **blood test** is a medical examination of a small amount of your blood.

blood ves|sel (**blood vessels**) N-COUNT **Blood vessels** are the narrow tubes through which your blood flows.

bloody ◆◇◇ /blʌdi/ (**bloodier, bloodiest, bloodies, bloodying, bloodied**) ◳ ADJ If you describe a situation or event as **bloody**, you mean that it is very violent and a lot of people are killed. ❑ *Forty-three demonstrators were killed in bloody clashes.* ◳ ADJ You can describe someone or something as **bloody** if they are covered in a lot of blood. ❑ *He was arrested last October still carrying a bloody knife.* ◳ V-T If you have **bloodied** part of your body, there is blood on it, usually because you have had an accident or you have been attacked. ❑ *One of our children fell and bloodied his knee.* ◳ ADJ **Bloody** is used by some people to emphasize what they are saying, especially when they are angry. [BRIT, VULGAR, EMPHASIS] ❑ *"Don't be such a bloody fool," Baird growled.*

bloom /blum/ (**blooms, blooming, bloomed**) ◳ N-COUNT A **bloom** is the flower on a plant. [LITERARY] ❑ *The sweet fragrance of the white blooms makes this climber a favorite.* ◳ PHRASE A plant or tree that is **in bloom** has flowers on it. ❑ *...a pink climbing rose in full bloom.* ◳ V-I When a plant or tree **blooms**, it produces flowers. When a flower **blooms**, it opens. ❑ *This plant blooms between May and June.* ◳ V-I If someone or something **blooms**, they develop good, attractive, or successful qualities. ❑ *Not many economies bloomed in 1990, least of all gold exporters like Australia.* ◳ N-UNCOUNT If something such as someone's skin has a **bloom**, it has a fresh and healthy appearance. [also a N] ❑ *The skin loses its youthful bloom.*

blos|som /blɒsəm/ (**blossoms, blossoming, blossomed**) ◳ N-VAR **Blossom** is the flowers that appear on a tree before the fruit. ❑ *The cherry blossom came out early in Washington this year.* ◳ V-I If someone or something **blossoms**, they develop good, attractive, or successful qualities. ❑ *Why do some people take longer than others to blossom?* ❑ *What began as a local festival has blossomed into an international event.* ◳ V-I When a tree **blossoms**, it produces blossom. ❑ *Rain begins to fall and peach trees blossom.*

blot /blɒt/ (**blots, blotting, blotted**) ◳ N-COUNT If something is a **blot on** a person's or thing's reputation, it spoils their reputation. ❑ *...a blot on the reputation of the architectural profession.* ◳ N-COUNT A **blot** is a drop of liquid that has fallen on to a surface and has dried. ❑ *...an ink blot.* ◳ V-T If you **blot** a surface, you remove liquid from it by pressing a piece of soft paper or cloth onto it. ❑ *Before applying makeup, blot the face with a tissue to remove any excess oils.*

▶ **blot out** ◳ PHRASAL VERB If one thing **blots out** another thing, it is in front of the other thing and prevents it from being seen. ❑ *About the time the three climbers were halfway down, clouds blotted out the sun.* ❑ *...the victim, whose face was blotted out by a camera blur.* ◳ PHRASAL VERB If you try to **blot out** a memory, you try to forget it. If one thought or memory **blots out** other thoughts or memories, it becomes the only one that you can think about. ❑ *Are you saying that she's trying to blot out all memory of the incident?* ❑ *The boy has gaps in his mind about it. He is blotting certain things out.*

blotch /blɒtʃ/ (**blotches**) N-COUNT A **blotch** is a small unpleasant-looking area of color, for example on someone's skin. ❑ *His face was covered in red blotches, seemingly a nasty case of acne.*

blouse /blaʊs, BRIT blaʊz/ (**blouses**) N-COUNT A **blouse** is a kind of shirt worn by a girl or woman. →see **clothing**

blow	
①	VERB USES
②	NOUN USES

① **blow** ◆◆◇ /bloʊ/ (**blows, blowing, blew, blown**) →Please look at

불가산명사 혈압 ❑ 주치의가 당신의 혈압을 계속 살필 것이다.

불가산명사 유혈 사태 ❑ 정부는 더 이상의 유혈 사태를 막기 위해 개혁의 속도를 높여야 한다.

가산명사 혈류 ❑ 이 병에 걸리면 독소가 혈류 속으로 분비된다.

가산명사 혈액 검사

가산명사 혈관

◳ 형용사 피비린내 나는, 유혈의 ❑ 유혈 충돌로 시위자 43명이 사망했다. ◳ 형용사 피투성이의 ❑ 그는 지난 10월 피 묻은 칼을 든 채 체포되었다. ◳ 타동사 -에 피가 났다 ❑ 우리 아이 중 하나가 넘어져서 무릎에 피가 났다. ◳ 형용사 빌어먹을 [영국영어, 비속어, 강조] ❑ "그놈의 빌어먹을 바보짓 좀 그만해."라고 베어드가 투덜거렸다.

◳ 가산명사 꽃 [문예체] ❑ 이 덩굴 식물은 그 하얀 꽃의 달콤한 향기 때문에 사람들의 사랑을 받는다. ◳ 구 꽃이 피어 ❑ 활짝 핀 핑크색 덩굴장미 ◳ 자동사 꽃을 피우다; 꽃이 피다 ❑ 이 식물은 5월과 6월 사이에 꽃을 피운다. ◳ 자동사 번영하다 ❑ 1990년에 호황을 맞은 국가들은 많지 않다. 특히 호주 같은 금 수출국의 경기가 가장 안 좋았다. ◳ 불가산명사 혈색, 홍조 ❑ 피부가 젊은 시절의 혈색을 잃는다.

◳ 가산명사 또는 불가산명사 꽃 ❑ 올해 워싱턴에서는 벚꽃이 일찍 폈다. ◳ 자동사 꽃을 피우다, 번창하다 ❑ 왜 어떤 사람들은 꽃을 피우는 데 다른 사람들보다 시간이 더 오래 걸리는 것일까? ❑ 지역 축제로 시작된 것이 국제적인 행사로 발전했다. ◳ 자동사 꽃을 피우다 ❑ 비가 내리기 시작하면서 복숭아나무는 꽃을 피운다.

◳ 가산명사 오점 ❑ 전문 건축가로서의 명성에 오점 ◳ 가산명사 얼룩 ❑ 잉크 얼룩 ◳ 타동사 눌러서 닦아내다 ❑ 메이크업을 시작하기 전에, 티슈로 얼굴을 눌러 주면서 지나친 유분기를 제거한다.

◳ 구동사 가리다 ❑ 3명의 등반객이 반쯤 내려왔을 때, 구름이 해를 가렸다. ❑ 모자이크 처리로 얼굴을 가린 피해자 ◳ 구동사 지우다 ❑ 지금 그녀가 그 사건에 대한 모든 기억을 지워 버리려 한다는 거야? ❑ 소년은 이에 대해 군데군데 기억을 못 한다. 특정한 기억을 지우고 있는 것이다.

가산명사 얼룩, 반점 ❑ 그의 얼굴은 온통 악성 여드름처럼 보이는 붉은 반점투성이였다.

가산명사 블라우스

◳ 자동사 불다 ❑ 언덕 꼭대기에는 차가운 바람이

category ⓚ to see if the expression you are looking for is shown under another **headword**. ◨ V-I When a wind or breeze **blows**, the air moves. ❏ *A chill wind blew at the top of the hill.* ◪ V-T/V-I If the wind **blows** something somewhere or if it **blows** there, the wind moves it there. ❏ *The wind blew her hair back from her forehead.* ❏ *Sand blew in our eyes.* ◫ V-I If you **blow**, you send out a stream of air from your mouth. ❏ *Danny rubbed his arms and blew on his fingers to warm them.* ◬ V-T If you **blow** something somewhere, you move it by sending out a stream of air from your mouth. ❏ *He picked up his mug and blew off the steam.* ◭ V-T If you **blow** bubbles or smoke rings, you make them by blowing air out of your mouth through liquid or smoke. ❏ *He blew a ring of blue smoke.* ◮ V-T/V-I When a whistle or horn **blows** or someone **blows** it, they make a sound by blowing into it. ❏ *The whistle blew and the train slid forward.* ◯ V-T When you **blow** your nose, you force air out of it through your nostrils in order to clear it. ❏ *He took out a handkerchief and blew his nose.* ◰ V-T To **blow** something **out**, **off**, or **away** means to remove or destroy it violently with an explosion. ❏ *The can exploded, wrecking the kitchen and bathroom and blowing out windows.* ◱ V-T If you say that something **blows** an event, situation, or argument into a particular extreme state, especially an uncertain or unpleasant state, you mean that it causes it to be in that state. ❏ *Someone took an inappropriate use of words on my part and tried to blow it into a major controversy.* ◲ V-T If you **blow** a large amount of money, you spend it quickly on luxuries. [INFORMAL] ❏ *My brother lent me some money and I went and blew the lot.* ⓚ →see also **full-blown**. to **blow hot and cold** →see **hot**. to **blow a kiss** →see **kiss**. to **blow the whistle** →see **whistle** →see **wind**

Word Partnership	*blow*의 연어	
N.	blow **bubbles**, blow **smoke**	①◭
	blow **a whistle**	①◮
	blow *your* **nose**	①◯
ADV.	blow **away**	①◰
PREP.	blow **to the head**	②◨
	blow to *someone*	②◪
V.	**deliver/strike** a blow	②◨ ◪
	cushion/soften a blow, **suffer** a blow	②◨ ◪
ADJ.	**crushing/devastating/heavy** blow	②◨ ◪

▶**blow out** PHRASAL VERB If you **blow out** a flame or a candle, you blow at it so that it stops burning. ❏ *I blew out the candle.*

▶**blow over** PHRASAL VERB If something such as trouble or an argument **blows over**, it ends without any serious consequences. ❏ *Wait, and it'll all blow over.*

▶**blow up** ◨ PHRASAL VERB If someone **blows** something **up** or if it **blows up**, it is destroyed by an explosion. ❏ *He was jailed for 45 years for trying to blow up a plane.* ◪ PHRASAL VERB If you **blow up** something such as a balloon or a tire, you fill it with air. ❏ *Other than blowing up a tire I hadn't done any car maintenance.* ◫ PHRASAL VERB If a wind or a storm **blows up**, the weather becomes very windy or stormy. ❏ *A storm blew up over the mountains.* ◬ PHRASAL VERB If you **blow up at** someone, you lose your temper and shout at them. [INFORMAL] ❏ *I'm sorry I blew up at you.* ◭ PHRASAL VERB If someone **blows** an incident **up** or if it **blows up**, it is made to seem more serious or important than it really is. ❏ *Newspapers blew up the story.* ❏ *The media may be blowing it up out of proportion.* ◮ PHRASAL VERB If a photographic image **is blown up**, a large copy is made of it. ❏ *The image is blown up on a large screen.*

② **blow** ◆◇◇ /bloʊ/ (**blows**) ◨ N-COUNT If someone receives a **blow**, they are hit with a fist or weapon. ❏ *He went to the hospital after a blow to the face.* ◪ N-COUNT If something that happens is a **blow to** someone or something, it is very upsetting, disappointing, or damaging to them. ❏ *That ruling comes as a blow to environmentalists.*

bludg|eon /blʌdʒ°n/ (**bludgeons**, **bludgeoning**, **bludgeoned**) V-T To **bludgeon** someone means to hit them several times with a heavy object. ❏ *He broke into the old man's house and bludgeoned him with a hammer.*

blue ◆◆◆ /bluː/ (**bluer**, **bluest**, **blues**) ◨ COLOR Something that is **blue** is the color of the sky on a sunny day. ❏ *There were swallows in the cloudless blue sky.* ❏ *She fixed her pale blue eyes on her father's.* ◪ N-PLURAL **The blues** is a type of music which was developed by African American musicians in the southern United States. It is characterized by a slow tempo and a strong rhythm. ❏ *Can white girls sing the blues?* ◫ ADJ If you are feeling **blue**, you are feeling sad or depressed, often when there is no particular reason. [INFORMAL] [v-link ADJ] ❏ *There's no earthly reason for me to feel so blue.* →see **rainbow**

blue|berry /bluːbɛri, BRIT bluːbəri/ (**blueberries**) N-COUNT A **blueberry** is a small dark blue fruit that is found in North America. Blueberries are often cooked before they are eaten.

blue chip (**blue chips**) N-COUNT **Blue chip** stocks and shares are an investment which are considered fairly safe to invest in while also being profitable. [BUSINESS] ❏ *Blue chip issues were sharply higher, but the rest of the market actually declined slightly by the end of the day.*

blue-collar ADJ **Blue-collar** workers work in industry, doing physical work, rather than in offices. [ADJ n] ❏ *It wasn't just the blue collar workers who lost their jobs, it was everyone.*

불었다. ◪ 타동사/자동사 날리다 ❏ 바람에 그녀의 머리가 이마 뒤로 날렸다. ❏ 모래가 바람에 날려 우리 눈에 들어왔다. ◫ 자동사 입김을 불다 ❏ 대니가 팔을 문지르고 손가락에 입김을 불어 따뜻하게 했다. ◬ 타동사 불어 날리다 ❏ 그는 머그잔을 들고 김을 불어 날렸다. ◭ 타동사 불어서 만들다 ❏ 그는 담배 연기를 뿜어 파란색 고리를 만들었다. ◮ 타동사/자동사 울리다; 불다 ❏ 호루라기가 울리자 기차가 미끄러지듯 앞으로 나아갔다. ◯ 타동사 코를 풀다 ❏ 그는 손수건을 꺼내 코를 풀었다. ◰ 타동사 폭파하다 ❏ 깡통이 터지면서 부엌과 욕실이 부서지고 창문은 산산조각이 났다. ◱ 타동사 -로 확대하다, -로 일을 만들다 ❏ 어떤 사람이 내가 단어를 부적절하게 사용한 점을 꼬투리 잡아서 주요 논쟁으로 확대하려고 했다. ⓚ 타동사 탕진하다 [비격식체] ❏ 형이 나에게 돈을 조금 빌려 줬는데 내가 가서 돈을 다 써 버렸다.

구동사 불어 끄다 ❏ 나는 촛불을 불어 껐다.

구동사 무사히 끝나다 ❏ 기다리면 모두 무사히 끝날 거야.

◨ 구동사 폭파하다; 폭파되다 ❏ 그는 비행기 폭파 시도 혐의로 45년 동안 수감되었다. ◪ 구동사 불다, 부풀리다 ❏ 타이어에 바람 넣는 일 빼고는 내가 차량 정비를 해본 적이 없었다. ◫ 구동사 바람이 거세지다 ◬ 폭풍이 산 위로 거세게 불기 시작했다. ◬ 구동사 호통치다, 화내다 [비격식체] ❏ 너한테 큰 소리쳐서 미안해. ◭ 구동사 과장하다, 부풀리다 ❏ 신문이 이야기를 부풀렸다. ❏ 언론이 이를 실제보다 과장하고 있는 것인지도 모른다. ◮ 구동사 확대되다 ❏ 그 이미지는 대형 스크린에 확대된다.

◨ 가산명사 강타, 구타 ❏ 그는 얼굴을 강타당한 뒤 병원으로 갔다. ◪ 가산명사 충격, 타격 ❏ 그 판결이 환경론자들에게는 충격이다.

타동사 둔기로 때리다 ❏ 그는 노인 집에 침입해서 노인을 망치로 때렸다.

◨ 색채어 파랑 ❏ 구름 한 점 없는 파란 하늘에는 제비들이 있었다. ❏ 그녀는 담청색 눈으로 아버지의 눈을 응시했다. ◪ 복수명사 블루스 ❏ 백인 여학생들이 블루스를 부를 수 있나요? ◫ 형용사 우울한 [비격식체] ❏ 내가 이렇게 우울할 이유가 전혀 없다.

가산명사 블루베리

가산명사 우량주 [경제] ❏ 우량주는 급등했지만 나머지는 사실상 약간 떨어진 상태에서 장을 마감했다.

형용사 블루칼라의 ❏ 블루칼라 노동자들만 일자리를 잃은 것이 아니었다. 모든 사람들이 직장을 잃었다.

a
b
c
d
e
f
g
h
i
j
k
l
m
n
o
p
q
r
s
t
u
v
w
x
y
z

blue|print /bluːprɪnt/ (blueprints) **1** N-COUNT A **blueprint for** something is a plan or set of proposals that shows how it is expected to work. ❑ *The country's president will offer delegates his blueprint for the country's future.* **2** N-COUNT A **blueprint** of an architect's building plans or a designer's pattern is a photographic print consisting of white lines on a blue background. Blueprints contain all of the information that is needed to build or make something. ❑ *...a blueprint of the whole place, complete with heating ducts and wiring.* **3** N-COUNT A genetic **blueprint** is a pattern which is contained within all living cells. This pattern decides how the organism develops and what it looks like. ❑ *The offspring contain a mixture of the genetic blueprint of each parent.* →see **copy**

1 가산명사 청사진, 계획 ❑ 대통령은 외교 사절들에게 나라의 미래에 대한 청사진을 제시할 것이다. **2** 가산명사 청사진, 설계도 ❑ 난방용 덕트와 전선 배선까지 포함한 건물 전체의 설계도 **3** 가산명사 유전자 지도 ❑ 자식에게는 각 부모의 유전자가 섞여 있다.

bluff /blʌf/ (bluffs, bluffing, bluffed) **1** N-VAR A **bluff** is an attempt to make someone believe that you will do something when you do not really intend to do it. ❑ *The letter was a bluff.* ❑ *It is essential to build up the military option and show that this is not a bluff.* **2** PHRASE If you **call** someone's **bluff**, you tell them to do what they have been threatening to do, because you are sure that they will not really do it. ❑ *The Socialists have decided to call the opposition's bluff.* **3** V-T/V-I If you **bluff**, you make someone believe that you will do something when you do not really intend to do it, or that you know something when you do not really know it. ❑ *Either side, or both, could be bluffing.* ❑ *In each case the hijackers bluffed the crew using fake grenades.*

1 가산명사 또는 불가산명사 엄포 ❑ 편지는 엄포에 불과했다. ❑ 군사적인 수단을 강화하고 이것이 단순한 엄포가 아님을 보여 주는 것이 중요하다. **2** 구 해볼 테면 해보라고 하다 ❑ 사회당원들은 야당의 엄포에 해볼 테면 해보라는 자세로 맞서기로 했다. **3** 타동사/자동사 엄포를 놓다 ❑ 둘 중 하나, 아니면 양쪽 모두 엄포만 놓고 있는 것인지도 모른다. ❑ 각각의 경우 납치범들이 가짜 수류탄을 사용해 승무원들에게 엄포를 놓았다.

blun|der /blʌndər/ (blunders, blundering, blundered) **1** N-COUNT A **blunder** is a stupid or careless mistake. ❑ *I think he made a tactical blunder by announcing it so far ahead of time.* **2** V-I If you **blunder**, you make a stupid or careless mistake. ❑ *No doubt I had blundered again.* **3** V-I If you **blunder into** a dangerous or difficult situation, you get involved in it by mistake. ❑ *People wanted to know how they had blundered into war, and how to avoid it in the future.* **4** V-I If you **blunder** somewhere, you move there in a clumsy and careless way. ❑ *He had blundered into the table, upsetting the flowers.*

1 가산명사 어처구니없는 실수 ❑ 나는 그가 너무 이르게 이를 발표해서 전술상 어처구니없는 실수를 범했다고 생각한다. **2** 자동사 어처구니없는 실수를 하다 ❑ 틀림없이 내가 또 어처구니없는 실수를 했던 것이다. **3** 자동사 -에 빠지다 ❑ 사람들은 어떻게 그들이 전쟁에 빠지게 되었는지, 어떻게 하면 앞으로 전쟁을 피할 수 있는지 알고 싶어 했다. **4** 자동사 아무렇게나 걷다 ❑ 그는 아무렇게나 식탁으로 걸어와서 꽃을 엎었다.

blunt /blʌnt/ (blunter, bluntest, blunts, blunting, blunted) **1** ADJ If you are **blunt**, you say exactly what you think without trying to be polite. ❑ *She is blunt about her personal life.* ● **blunt|ly** ADV [ADV with v] ❑ *"I don't believe you!" Jeanne said bluntly.* ● **blunt|ness** N-UNCOUNT ❑ *His bluntness got him into trouble.* **2** ADJ A **blunt** object has a rounded or flat end rather than a sharp one. [ADJ n] ❑ *One of them had been struck 13 times over the head with a blunt object.* **3** ADJ A **blunt** knife or blade is no longer sharp and does not cut well. ❑ *Use a sharp knife as a blunt blade can damage the skin.* **4** V-T If something **blunts** an emotion, a feeling or a need, it weakens it. ❑ *The constant repetition of violence has blunted the human response to it.*

1 형용사 직설적인, 솔직한, 퉁명스러운 ❑ 그녀는 자신의 사생활에 대해 솔직하다. ● 직설적으로, 퉁명스럽게 부사 ❑ "난 널 믿지 않아!"라고 진이 퉁명스럽게 말했다. ● 직설적임, 솔직함 불가산명사 ❑ 그는 직설적인 성격 때문에 곤란을 겪었다. **2** 형용사 뭉툭한 ❑ 그들 중 1명은 둔기로 머리를 13번 맞았었다. **3** 형용사 무딘 ❑ 날이 무디면 피부를 손상시킬 수 있으므로 잘 드는 칼을 사용한다. **4** 타동사 무디게 하다 ❑ 폭력이 끊임없이 되풀이되면서 사람들은 폭력에 대해 무디다.

blur /blɜr/ (blurs, blurring, blurred) **1** N-COUNT A **blur** is a shape or area which you cannot see clearly because it has no distinct outline or because it is moving very fast. ❑ *Out of the corner of my eye I saw a blur of movement on the other side of the glass.* **2** V-T/V-I When a thing **blurs** or when something **blurs** it, you cannot see it clearly because its edges are no longer distinct. ❑ *This creates a spectrum of colors at the edges of objects which blurs the image.* ● **blurred** ADJ ❑ *...blurred black and white photographs.* **3** V-T If something **blurs** an idea or a distinction between things, that idea or distinction no longer seems clear. ❑ *...her belief that scientists are trying to blur the distinction between "how" and "why" questions.* ● **blurred** ADJ ❑ *The line between fact and fiction is becoming blurred.* **4** V-T/V-I If your vision **blurs**, or if something **blurs** it, you cannot see things clearly. ❑ *Her eyes, behind her glasses, began to blur.* ● **blurred** ADJ ❑ *...visual disturbances like eye-strain and blurred vision.*

1 가산명사 흐릿하게 보이는 것 ❑ 나는 유리창 건너편에서 뭔가 흐릿하게 움직이는 것을 곁눈으로 보았다. **2** 타동사/자동사 흐릿해지다; 흐리게 하다 ❑ 이는 사물 가장자리에서 빛의 스펙트럼을 분산시켜 이미지를 흐릿하게 만든다. ● 흐릿한 형용사 ❑ 흐릿한 흑백 사진 **3** 타동사 흐리게 하다 ❑ 과학자들이 방법과 이유에 관한 질문 사이의 경계를 흐리려 한다는 그녀의 믿음 ● 흐려진 형용사 ❑ 사실과 허구 사이의 경계가 흐려지고 있다. **4** 타동사/자동사 시야가 흐려지다, 침침해지다 ❑ 안경을 쓴 그녀의 눈이 흐릿해지기 시작했다. ● 침침한 형용사 ❑ 눈의 피로나 침침함 같은 시력 저하

blurt /blɜrt/ (blurts, blurting, blurted) V-T If someone **blurts** something, they say it suddenly, after trying hard to keep quiet or to keep it secret. ❑ *"I was looking for Sally," he blurted, and his eyes filled with tears.*

▶ **blurt out** PHRASAL VERB If someone **blurts** something **out**, they blurt it. [INFORMAL] ❑ *"You're mad," the driver blurted out.*

타동사 불쑥 말하다 ❑ "나는 샐리를 찾고 있었어."라고 그는 불쑥 그렇게 말하고는 눈에 눈물이 그렁그렁해졌다.

구동사 불쑥 말하다 [비격식체] ❑ "당신 미쳤군."라고 운전기사가 불쑥 말했다.

blush /blʌʃ/ (blushes, blushing, blushed) V-I When you **blush**, your face becomes redder than usual because you are ashamed or embarrassed. ❑ *"Hello, Maria," he said, and she blushed again.* ● N-COUNT **Blush** is also a noun. ❑ *"The most important thing is to be honest," she says, without the trace of a blush.*

자동사 얼굴을 붉히다 ❑ "안녕, 마리아."라고 그가 말하자 그녀는 다시 얼굴을 붉혔다. ● 가산명사 홍조 ❑ "가장 중요한 것은 정직이다."라고 그녀는 전혀 당황한 기색 없이 말했다.

boar /bɔr/ (boars)

The plural **boar** can also be used for meaning **1**.

1 N-COUNT A **boar** or a **wild boar** is a wild pig. ❑ *Wild boar are numerous in the valleys.* **2** N-COUNT A **boar** is a male pig.

복수 boar도 **1** 의미로 쓸 수 있다.

1 가산명사 멧돼지 ❑ 그 계곡에는 멧돼지가 많다. **2** 가산명사 수퇘지

board ♦♦◇ /bɔrd/ (boards, boarding, boarded) **1** N-COUNT A **board** is a flat, thin, rectangular piece of wood or plastic which is used for a particular purpose. ❑ *...a chopping board.* **2** N-COUNT A **board** is a square piece of wood or stiff cardboard that you use for playing games such as chess. ❑ *...a checkers board.* **3** N-COUNT You can refer to a blackboard or a bulletin board as a **board**. ❑ *He wrote a few more notes on the board.* **4** N-COUNT **Boards** are long flat pieces of wood which are used, for example, to make floors or walls. ❑ *The floor was draughty bare boards.* **5** N-COUNT The **board** of a company or organization is the group of people who control it and direct it. [BUSINESS] ❑ *Arthur has made a recommendation, which he wants her to put before the board at a special meeting scheduled for tomorrow afternoon.* →see also **board of directors** **6** N-COUNT **Board** is used in the names of various organizations which are involved in dealing with a particular kind of activity. ❑ *The Scottish Tourist Board said 33,000 Japanese visited Scotland last year.* **7** V-T When you **board** a train, ship, or aircraft, you get on it in order to travel somewhere. [FORMAL] ❑ *I boarded the plane bound for England.* **8** N-UNCOUNT **Board** is the food which is provided when you stay somewhere, for example in a hotel. ❑ *Free room and board are provided for all hotel*

1 가산명사 판 ❑ 도마 **2** 가산명사 게임판 ❑ 체스판 **3** 가산명사 칠판; 게시판 ❑ 그는 칠판에 몇 가지를 더 적었다. **4** 가산명사 판자 ❑ 바닥은 거친 맨 판자로 되어 있었다. **5** 가산명사 이사회 [경제] ❑ 아서가 제안을 하나 했는데, 이 제안을 그녀가 내일 오후에 있을 특별 회의 때 이사회에 제출하기를 바란다. **6** 가산명사 특정 기구나 기관의 이름에 사용 ❑ 스코틀랜드 관광청은 작년에 일본인 33,000명이 스코틀랜드를 방문했다고 말했다. **7** 타동사 타다 [격식체] ❑ 나는 영국행 비행기를 탔다. **8** 불가산명사 식사 [경제] 호텔 직원 모두에게 무료 숙식이 제공된다. **9** 구 공명정대하게 ❑ 내가 아는 전부는 앤토니의 금융 거래에 관한 것인데, 이는 항상 공명정대하게 이루어졌다. **10** 구 일률적으로, 전반적으로 ❑ 편도 임대료가 전반적으로 높다. **11** 구 무시되다 ❑ 요즘 세상에서 중요한 것은 무엇을 아느냐가 아니라 누구를 아느냐이며 자격이나 능력은 무시되기

A

B

staff. ⓽ PHRASE An arrangement or deal that is **above board** is legal and is being carried out honestly and openly. ☐ *All I knew about were Antony's own financial dealings, which were always above board.* ⓾ PHRASE If a policy or a situation applies **across the board**, it affects everything or everyone in a particular group. ☐ *There are hefty charges across the board for one-way rental.* ⓫ PHRASE If something **goes by the board**, it is rejected or ignored, or is no longer possible. ☐ *It's a case of not what you know but who you know in this world today and qualifications quite go by the board.* ⓬ PHRASE When you are **on board** a train, ship, or aircraft, you are on it or in it. ☐ *They arrived at Gatwick airport on board a plane chartered by the Italian government.* ⓭ PHRASE If someone **sweeps the board** in a competition or election, they win nearly everything that it is possible to win. ☐ *Spain swept the board in boys' team competitions.* ⓮ PHRASE If you **take on board** an idea or a problem, you begin to accept it or understand it. ☐ *You may have to accept their point of view, but hope that they will take on board some of what you have said.*

C

D

E

F

G

Word Partnership   *board*의 연어

N.	
	diving board ⓵
	board **game** ⓶
	bulletin board, **message** board ⓷
	chair/member of the board, board **of directors**, board **meeting** ⓹
	board **a flight/plane/ship** ⓻
	room and board ⓼

H

▶**board up** PHRASAL VERB If you **board up** a door or window, you fix pieces of wood over it so that it is covered up. ☐ *Shopkeepers have boarded up their windows.*

구동사 판자로 막다 ☐ 가게 주인들은 가게 창문을 판자로 막았다.

I

board|ing card (**boarding cards**) N-COUNT A **boarding card** is a card which a passenger must have when boarding a plane or a boat.

가산명사 탑승권; 승선권

J

board|ing school (**boarding schools**) also **boarding-school** N-VAR A **boarding school** is a school which some or all of the students live in during the school term. Compare **day school**.

가산명사 또는 불가산명사 기숙학교

K

board of di|rec|tors (**boards of directors**) N-COUNT A company's **board of directors** is the group of people elected by its shareholders to manage the company. [BUSINESS] ☐ *The Board of Directors has approved the decision unanimously.*

가산명사 이사회 [경제] ☐ 이사회가 그 결정을 만장일치로 통과시켰다.

L

board|room /bɔrdruːm/ (**boardrooms**) also **board room** N-COUNT The **boardroom** is a room where the board of a company meets. [BUSINESS] ☐ *Everyone had already assembled in the boardroom for the 9:00 a.m. session.*

가산명사 회의실 [경제] ☐ 전원이 오전 9시 회의를 위해 회의실에 이미 모여 있었다.

M

boast /boʊst/ (**boasts, boasting, boasted**) ⓵ V-T/V-I If someone **boasts** about something that they have done or that they own, they talk about it very proudly, in a way that other people may find irritating or offensive. [DISAPPROVAL] ☐ *Witnesses said Furci boasted that he took part in killing them.* ☐ *Carol boasted about her costume.* ● N-COUNT **Boast** is also a noun. ☐ *It is the charity's proud boast that it has never yet turned anyone away.* ⓶ V-T If someone or something can **boast** a particular achievement or possession, they have achieved or possess that thing. ☐ *The houses will boast the latest energy-saving technology.*

N

O

⓵ 타동사/자동사 떠벌리다, 자랑하다 [탐탁찮음] ☐ 증인들은 퍼치가 살인에 가담한 것을 떠벌렸다고 말했다. ☐ 캐롤은 자신의 복장에 대해 자랑했다. ● 가산명사 자랑 ☐ 지금까지 단 한 사람도 돌려보낸 일이 없다는 것이 이 자선 단체의 자랑이다. ⓶ 타동사 자랑하다 ☐ 이 주택들은 최신 에너지 절약 기술을 자랑할 것이다.

boat ♦♦◇ /boʊt/ (**boats**) ⓵ N-COUNT A **boat** is something in which people can travel across water. [also by N] ☐ *One of the best ways to see the area is in a small boat.* ⓶ N-COUNT You can refer to a passenger ship as a **boat**. ☐ *When the boat reached Cape Town, we said a temporary goodbye.* ⓷ PHRASE If you say that someone has **missed the boat**, you mean that they have missed an opportunity and may not get another. ☐ *If you don't want to miss the boat, the auction is scheduled for 2.30 pm on June 26.* →see **ship**

P

Q

⓵ 가산명사 보트 ☐ 그 지역을 가장 잘 볼 수 있는 방법 중의 하나는 작은 배를 타는 것이다. ⓶ 가산명사 여객선 ☐ 여객선이 케이프타운에 도착했을 때, 우리는 잠깐 작별인사를 나눴다. ⓷ 구 좋은 기회를 놓치다 ☐ 절호의 기회를 놓치고 싶지 않으시다면, 경매는 6월 26일 오후 2시 30분으로 잡혀 있습니다.

Thesaurus   *boat*의 참조어

N.	
	craft, ship, vessel ⓵ ⓶

R

S

boat|ing /boʊtɪŋ/ N-UNCOUNT **Boating** is travelling on a lake or river in a small boat for pleasure. ☐ *You can go boating or play tennis.*

불가산명사 뱃놀이 ☐ 뱃놀이를 가거나 테니스를 칠 수 있다.

T

bob /bɒb/ (**bobs, bobbing, bobbed**) ⓵ V-I If something **bobs**, it moves up and down, like something does when it is floating on water. ☐ *Huge balloons bobbed about in the sky above.* ⓶ V-I If you **bob** somewhere, you move there quickly so that you disappear from view or come into view. ☐ *She handed over a form, then bobbed down again behind a typewriter.* ⓷ PHRASE **Bits and bobs** are small objects or parts of something. [mainly BRIT, INFORMAL] ☐ *The microscope contains a few hundred dollars-worth of electronic bits and bobs.*

⓵ 자동사 둥둥 떠다니다 ☐ 대형 풍선이 상공에서 둥둥 떠다녔다. ⓶ 자동사 휙 움직이다 ☐ 그녀는 양식을 하나 건네주고 다시 타자기 뒤로 휙 몸을 숙였다. ⓷ 구 자잘한 물건들, 잡동사니 [주로 영국영어, 비격식체] ☐ 현미경에는 수백 달러어치의 작은 전자 부품들이 들어 있다.

U

V

bob|by pin (**bobby pins**) N-COUNT A **bobby pin** is a small piece of metal or plastic bent back on itself, which someone uses to hold their hair in position. [AM; BRIT **hairgrip**]

가산명사 머리핀 [미국영어; 영국영어 hairgrip]

W

bode /boʊd/ (**bodes, boding, boded**) V-I If something **bodes** ill, it makes you think that something bad will happen in the future. If something **bodes** well, it makes you think that something good will happen. [FORMAL] ☐ *She says the way the bill was passed bodes ill for democracy.*

자동사 징조를 보이다 [격식체] ☐ 그녀는 그 법안이 통과된 방식이 민주주의에 대한 불길한 징조를 보인다고 말한다.

X

bod|i|ly /bɒdɪli/ ⓵ ADJ Your **bodily** needs and functions are the needs and functions of your body. [ADJ n] ☐ *...descriptions of natural bodily functions.* ⓶ ADV You use **bodily** to indicate that an action involves the whole of someone's body. [ADV with v] ☐ *I was hurled bodily to the deck.*

Y

⓵ 형용사 육체의, 신체의 ☐ 신체의 자연 기능에 대한 묘사 ⓶ 부사 온몸으로 ☐ 나는 갑판으로 송두리째 내동댕이쳐졌다.

body ♦♦♦ /bɒdi/ (**bodies**) ⓵ N-COUNT Your **body** is all your physical parts, including your head, arms, and legs. ☐ *The largest organ in the body is the liver.* ⓶ N-COUNT You can also refer to the main part of your body, except for your

Z

⓵ 가산명사 인체 ☐ 인체에서 가장 큰 기관은 간이다. ⓶ 가산명사 몸 ☐ 바닥에 똑바로 누운 후, 한쪽 골반 쪽으로 몸을 튼 다음 위쪽 다리를 몸 위로 교차시킨다.

십상이다. ⓬ 구 타고 있는 ☐ 그들은 이탈리아 정부의 전세기를 타고 개트윅 공항에 도착했다. ⓭ 구 휩쓸다 ☐ 스페인이 청소년 팀 대항전을 휩쓸었다. ⓮ 구 받아들이다, 이해하다 ☐ 당신이 그들의 견해를 수용해야 할지도 모르지만, 그들도 당신 말을 일부 받아들이기를 바란다.

arms, head, and legs, as your **body**. ❏ *Lying flat on the floor, twist your body on to one hip and cross your upper leg over your body.* ❸ N-COUNT You can refer to a person's dead body as a **body**. ❏ *Officials said they had found no traces of violence on the body of the politician.* ❹ N-COUNT A **body** is an organized group of people who deal with something officially. ❏ *...the Chairman of the policemen's representative body, the Police Federation.* ❺ N-COUNT A **body of** people is a group of people who are together or who are connected in some way. ❏ *...that large body of people which teaches other people how to teach.* ❻ N-SING The **body of** something such as a building or a document is the main part of it or the largest part of it. ❏ *The main body of the church had been turned into a massive television studio.* ❼ N-COUNT The **body** of a car or airplane is the main part of it, not including its engine, wheels, or wings. ❏ *The only shade was under the body of the plane.* ❽ N-COUNT A **body of** water is a large area of water, such as a lake or a sea. ❏ *It is probably the most polluted body of water in the world.* ❾ N-COUNT A **body of** information is a large amount of it. ❏ *An increasing body of evidence suggests that all of us have cancer cells in our bodies at times during our lives.* ❿ N-UNCOUNT If you say that an alcoholic drink has **body**, you mean that it has a full and strong flavor. ❏ *...a dry wine with good body.*
→see Picture Dictionary: **body**

body|guard /bɒdigɑrd/ (**bodyguards**) N-COUNT A **bodyguard** is a person or a group of people employed to protect someone. ❏ *Three of his bodyguards were injured in the attack.*

body lan|guage also body-language N-UNCOUNT Your **body language** is the way in which you show your feelings or thoughts to other people by means of the position or movements of your body, rather than with words. ❏ *I can tell by your body language that you're happy with the decision.*

bog /bɒg/ (**bogs**) N-COUNT A **bog** is an area of land which is very wet and muddy.
→see **wetland**

bogged down ADJ If you get **bogged down in** something, it prevents you from making progress or getting something done. [v-link ADJ, usu ADJ in n] ❏ *But why get bogged down in legal details?*

bog|gle /bɒgᵊl/ (**boggles, boggling, boggled**) V-T/V-I If you say that the mind **boggles at** something, or that something **boggles** the mind, you mean that it is so strange or amazing that it is difficult to imagine or understand. ❏ *The mind boggles at the possibilities that could be in store for us.* ❏ *The good grace and humor with which they face the latest privations makes the mind boggle.*

bo|gus /boʊgəs/ ADJ If you describe something as **bogus**, you mean that it is not genuine. ❏ *...their bogus insurance claim.*

boil ♦◇◇ /bɔɪl/ (**boils, boiling, boiled**) ❶ V-T/V-I When a hot liquid **boils** or when you **boil** it, bubbles appear in it and it starts to change into steam or vapor. ❏ *I stood in the kitchen, waiting for the water to boil.* ❏ *Boil the water in the saucepan and add the sage.* ❷ V-T/V-I When you **boil** a kettle or pot, or put it on to **boil**, you heat the water inside it until it boils. ❏ *He had nothing to do but boil the kettle and make the tea.* ❸ V-I When a kettle or pot **is boiling**, the water inside it has reached boiling point. [only cont] ❏ *Is the kettle boiling?* ❹ V-T/V-I When you **boil** food, or when it **boils**, it is cooked in boiling water. ❏ *Boil the chick peas, add garlic and lemon juice.* ❏ *I'd peel potatoes and put them on to boil.* →see **cook** ❺ V-I If you **are boiling with** anger, you are very angry. [usu cont] ❏ *I used to be all sweetness and light on the outside, but inside I would be boiling with rage.* ❻ N-COUNT A **boil** is a red, painful swelling on your skin, which contains a thick yellow liquid called pus. ❼ →see also **boiling** ❽ PHRASE When you **bring** a liquid **to a boil** or **to the boil**, you heat it until it boils. When it **comes to a boil** or **comes to the boil**, it begins to boil. ❏ *Put water, butter and lard into a saucepan and bring slowly to the boil.*
→see **cook**

▶**boil down to** PHRASAL VERB If you say that a situation or problem **boils down to** a particular thing or can **be boiled down to** a particular thing, you mean that this is the most important or the most basic aspect of it. ❏ *What they want boils down to just one thing. It is land.*

❸ 가산명사 시체, 시신 ❏ 관계자에 따르면 그 정치가의 시신에서 폭력의 흔적은 발견되지 않았다고 한다. ❹ 가산명사 기구 ❏ 경찰관들의 대표 기구인 경찰 연합의 위원장 ❺ 가산명사 일단의 ❏ 다른 사람들에게 교수 방법을 가르치는 일단의 사람들 ❻ 단수명사 본관; 본문 ❏ 교회 본관은 거대한 텔레비전 스튜디오로 개조되어 있었다. ❼ 가산명사 본체, 동체 ❏ 유일한 그늘은 비행기 동체 아래뿐이었다. ❽ 가산명사 수역 ❏ 이는 아마도 세계에서 가장 오염이 심한 수역일 것이다. ❾ 가산명사 많은 ❏ 우리 모두가 살면서 한번쯤은 몸 안에 암세포를 지니게 된다는 것을 시사하는 증거가 점점 증가하고 있다. ❿ 불가산명사 맛과 향이 강함 ❏ 단맛이 없는 향취가 강한 와인

가산명사 경호원 ❏ 그 공격으로 그의 경호원 중 3명이 부상을 입었다.

불가산명사 바디랭귀지 ❏ 나는 네가 그 결정에 만족한다는 것을 너의 바디랭귀지를 보고 알 수 있다.

가산명사 습지

형용사 얽매인, 꼼짝달싹 못 하는 ❏ 하지만 뭐 하러 법적인 세부 사항에 얽매이는 거야?

타동사/자동사 상상할 수도 없는 일이다 ❏ 우리 앞에 놓여 있는 가능성은 상상할 수 없을 정도로 많다. ❏ 그들이 최근에 어려움을 겪으면서 보여 준 인격과 유머 감각은 상상할 수 없을 정도이다.

형용사 가짜의, 거짓의 ❏ 그들의 허위 보험 청구

❶ 타동사/자동사 끓다; 끓이다 ❏ 나는 물이 끓기를 기다리며 부엌에 서 있었다. ❏ 냄비에 물을 끓이고 세이지를 넣는다. ❷ 타동사/자동사 물을 끓이다 ❏ 그는 물을 끓여야 차를 만드는 일 외에 할 일이 없었다. ❸ 자동사 끓다 ❏ 주전자가 끓고 있어? ❹ 타동사/자동사 삶다, 익히다 ❏ 이집트 콩을 삶아 마늘과 레몬즙을 첨가한다. ❏ 나는 토마토의 껍질을 벗겨 익히곤 했다. ❺ 자동사 부글부글 끓다 ❏ 나는 겉으로는 아주 친절하고 밝아 보였지만 속으로는 분노로 들끓곤 했다. ❻ 가산명사 종기 ❽ 구 끓이다; 끓다 ❏ 물과 버터, 라드를 자루 달린 냄비에 넣고 천천히 끓인다.

구동사 —로 귀결되다, 결국 ― 문제이다 ❏ 그들이 원하는 것은 결국 하나로 귀착된다. 그것은 땅이다.

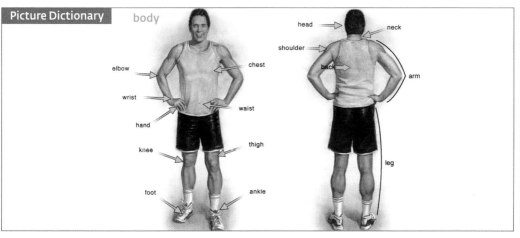

Picture Dictionary body

head → neck
shoulder →
elbow
chest
back → arm
wrist
waist
hand
knee
thigh
leg
foot ankle

▶**boil over** [1] PHRASAL VERB When a liquid that is being heated **boils over**, it rises and flows over the edge of the container. ❏ *Heat the liquid in a large, wide container rather than a high narrow one, or it can boil over.* [2] PHRASAL VERB When someone's feelings **boil over**, they lose their temper or become violent. ❏ *Sometimes frustration and anger can boil over into direct and violent action.*

boil|er /bɔɪlər/ (**boilers**) N-COUNT A **boiler** is a device which burns gas, oil, electricity, or coal in order to provide hot water, especially for the central heating in a building.

boil|ing /bɔɪlɪŋ/ [1] ADJ Something that is **boiling** or **boiling hot** is very hot. ❏ *"It's boiling in here," complained Miriam.* [2] ADJ If you say that you are **boiling** or **boiling hot**, you mean that you feel very hot, usually unpleasantly hot. [v-link ADJ] ❏ *When everybody else is boiling hot, I'm freezing!*

> In informal English, if you want to emphasize how hot the weather is, you can say that it is **boiling** or **scorching**. In winter, if the temperature is above average, you can say that it is **mild**. In general, **hot** suggests a higher temperature than **warm**, and **warm** things are usually pleasant. ❏ *...a warm evening.*

bois|ter|ous /bɔɪstərəs, -strəs/ ADJ Someone who is **boisterous** is noisy, lively, and full of energy. ❏ *...a boisterous but good-natured crowd.*

bold /boʊld/ (**bolder, boldest**) [1] ADJ Someone who is **bold** is not afraid to do things which involve risk or danger. ❏ *Amrita becomes a bold, daring rebel.* ❏ *In 1960 this was a bold move.* ● **bold|ly** ADV [ADV with v] ❏ *You can and must act boldly and confidently.* ● **bold|ness** N-UNCOUNT ❏ *Don't forget the boldness of his economic program.* [2] ADJ Someone who is **bold** is not shy or embarrassed in the company of other people. ❏ *I don't feel I'm being bold, because it's always been natural for me to just speak out about whatever disturbs me.* ● **bold|ly** ADV ❏ *"You should do it," the girl said, boldly.* [3] ADJ A **bold** color or pattern is very bright and noticeable. ❏ *...bold flowers in various shades of red, blue or white.* [4] ADJ **Bold** lines or designs are drawn in a clear, strong way. ❏ *Each picture is shown in color on one page and as a bold outline on the opposite page.* [5] N-UNCOUNT **Bold** is print which is thicker and looks blacker than ordinary printed letters. [TECHNICAL] ❏ *When a candidate is elected his or her name will be highlighted in bold.*

bol|ster /boʊlstər/ (**bolsters, bolstering, bolstered**) [1] V-T If you **bolster** something such as someone's confidence or courage, you increase it. ❏ *Hopes of an early cut in interest rates bolstered confidence.* [2] V-T If someone tries to **bolster** their position in a situation, they try to strengthen it. ❏ *Britain is free to adopt policies to bolster its economy.* [3] N-COUNT A **bolster** is a firm pillow shaped like a long tube which is sometimes put across a bed under the ordinary pillows.

bolt /boʊlt/ (**bolts, bolting, bolted**) [1] N-COUNT A **bolt** is a long metal object which screws into a nut and is used to fasten things together. [2] V-T When you **bolt** one thing to another, you fasten them firmly together, using a bolt. ❏ *The safety belt is easy to fit as there's no need to bolt it to seat belt anchorage points.* ❏ *Bolt the components together.* [3] N-COUNT A **bolt** on a door or window is a metal bar that you can slide across in order to fasten the door or window. ❏ *I heard the sound of a bolt being slowly and reluctantly slid open.* [4] V-T When you **bolt** a door or window, you slide the bolt across to fasten it. ❏ *He reminded her that he would have to lock and bolt the kitchen door after her.* [5] V-I If a person or animal **bolts**, they suddenly start to run very fast, often because something has frightened them. ❏ *The pig rose squealing and bolted.* [6] V-T If you **bolt** your food, you eat it so quickly that you hardly chew it or taste it. ❏ *Being under stress can cause you to miss meals, eat on the move, or bolt your food.* ● PHRASAL VERB **Bolt down** means the same as **bolt**. ❏ *I like to think back to high school, when I could bolt down three or four burgers and a pile of French fries.* [7] N-COUNT A **bolt** of lightning is a flash of lightning that is seen as a white line in the sky. ❏ *Suddenly a bolt of lightning crackled through the sky.* [8] PHRASE If someone is sitting or standing **bolt upright**, they are sitting or standing very straight. ❏ *When I pushed his door open, Trevor was sitting bolt upright in bed.* →see **lightning**

bomb /bɒm/ (**bombs, bombing, bombed**) [1] N-COUNT A **bomb** is a device which explodes and damages or destroys a large area. ❏ *Bombs went off at two London train stations.* ❏ *It's not known who planted the bomb.* [2] N-SING Nuclear weapons are sometimes referred to as **the bomb**. ❏ *They are generally thought to have the bomb.* [3] V-T When people **bomb** a place, they attack it with bombs. ❏ *Airforce jets bombed the airport.* ● **bomb|ing** (**bombings**) N-VAR ❏ *Aerial bombing of rebel positions is continuing.*

Word Partnership	*bomb의 연어*	
ADJ.	**atomic/nuclear** bomb [1] [2]	
N.	bomb **blast**, bomb **shelter**, bomb **squad**, bomb **threat** [1]	
V.	**drop/plant** a bomb, **set off** a bomb [1]	

bom|bard /bɒmbɑːrd/ (**bombards, bombarding, bombarded**) [1] V-T If you **bombard** someone **with** something, you make them face a great deal of it. For example, if you **bombard** them **with** questions or criticism, you keep asking them a lot of questions or you keep criticizing them. ❏ *He bombarded Catherine with questions to which he should have known the answers.* [2] V-T When soldiers **bombard** a place, they attack it with continuous heavy gunfire or bombs. ❏ *Rebel artillery units have regularly bombarded the airport.*

---

[1] 구동사 끓어 넘치다 ❏ 액체를 좁고 높은 용기보다 크고 넓은 용기에 넣어야 가열해야 끓어 넘치지 않는다. [2] 구동사 분출되다 ❏ 때로는 좌절과 분노가 직접적이고 폭력적인 행동으로 분출될 수 있다.

가산명사 보일러

[1] 형용사 매우 뜨거운, 찌는 듯한 ❏ "이 안은 푹푹 찌는군."라고 미리암이 불평했다. [2] 형용사 찌는 듯이 더운 ❏ 다른 사람들은 모두 너무 덥다지만, 나는 추워서 얼 정도이다.

비격식체 영어에서는, 날씨가 얼마나 더운지를 강조하고 싶으면, boiling이나 scorching을 쓸 수 있다. 겨울에 기온이 평균보다 높으면, 날씨가 mild하다고 할 수 있다. 대체로, hot은 warm보다 더 기온이 높은 것을 나타내고, warm한 것은 대개 쾌적하다. ❏ ...따스한 저녁

형용사 명랑한, 떠들썩한 ❏ 시끄럽긴 하지만 친절한 사람들

[1] 형용사 대담한, 배짱 있는, 도전적인 ❏ 암리타는 대담하고 도전적인 반항아가 된다. ❏ 1960년 당시 이는 대담한 조치였다. ● 대담하게 부사 ❏ 너는 배짱 있고 자신 있게 행동할 수 있으며 또 그렇게 해야 한다. ● 대담함, 과감함 불가산명사 ❏ 그의 경제 계획의 대담성을 잊지 마라. [2] 형용사 당돌한, 대담한 ❏ 나는 뭔가 거슬리는 것이 있으면 항상 솔직히 말하는 것이 자연스럽기 때문에, 지금 내가 당돌하게 행동한다고 생각하지 않는다. ● 당돌하게 부사 ❏ "네가 해야 해."라고 소녀가 당돌하게 말했다. [3] 형용사 두드러진, 뚜렷한 ❏ 빨강, 파랑, 하양 등의 다양한 색조의 눈에 띄는 꽃들 [4] 형용사 또렷한 ❏ 각 그림이 한 면에는 칼라로, 반대 면에는 굵은 선으로 나와 있다. [5] 불가산명사 볼드체 [과학 기술] ❏ 당선된 후보의 이름은 볼드체로 강조된다.

[1] 타동사 높이다, 북돋우다 ❏ 금리 인하의 조기 단행이 기대되면서 신용도가 높아졌다. [2] 타동사 강화하다 ❏ 영국은 경제를 강화하기 위한 정책을 자유로이 채택할 수 있다. [3] 가산명사 베개 받침대

[1] 가산명사 볼트, 나사 [2] 타동사 나사로 고정시키다 ❏ 이 안전벨트는 안전벨트 고정점에 나사로 고정시킬 필요가 없기 때문에 장착하기 쉽다. ❏ 부품을 나사로 조립하세요. [3] 가산명사 빗장 ❏ 나는 빗장이 천천히 힘겹게 열리는 소리를 들었다. [4] 타동사 빗장을 걷다 ❏ 그는 그녀가 나간 다음 자신이 부엌문을 잠그고 빗장을 걸어야 한다는 것을 그녀에게 일러 주었다. [5] 자동사 뛰어나가다 ❏ 돼지가 꽥꽥거리며 일어나 뛰어 나갔다. [6] 타동사 급히 먹다, 통째로 삼키다 ❏ 스트레스를 받으면 식사를 거르거나 돌아다니면서 먹거나 음식을 급히 먹게 된다. ● 구동사 급히 먹다, 통째로 삼키다 ❏ 나는 고등학교 시절을 회상하는 것을 좋아하는데, 그때만 해도 햄버거 서너 개와 감자칩한 무더기를 순식간에 해치울 수 있었다. [7] 가산명사 섬광 ❏ 갑자기 하늘에 번쩍하고 번개가 쳤다. [8] 구 꼿꼿하게, 똑바로 ❏ 내가 그의 방문을 열었을 때, 트레버는 침대에 꼿꼿이 앉아 있었다.

[1] 가산명사 폭탄 ❏ 런던의 기차역 두 곳에서 폭탄이 터졌다. ❏ 누가 폭탄을 설치했는지는 알려지지 않았다. [2] 단수명사 핵무기 ❏ 그들은 대체로 핵무기를 보유하고 있다는 것으로 생각된다. [3] 타동사 폭격하다 ❏ 공군 제트기가 그 공항을 폭파시켰다. ● 폭격 가산명사 또는 불가산명사 ❏ 반군 진영에 대한 공습이 계속되고 있다.

[1] 타동사 퍼붓다 ❏ 그는 캐서린에게 자신이 답을 알았어야 했던 질문들을 퍼부었다. [2] 타동사 연속 폭격을 가하다 ❏ 반군의 포병대가 주기적으로 공항에 연속 폭격을 가했다.

bom|bard|ment /bɒmbˈɑːʳdmənt/ (bombardments) **1** N-VAR A **bombardment** is a strong and continuous attack of gunfire or bombing. □ *The city has been flattened by heavy artillery bombardments.* **2** N-VAR A **bombardment of** ideas, demands, questions, or criticisms is an aggressive and exhausting stream of them. □ *...the constant bombardment of images urging that work was important.*

1 가산명사 또는 불가산명사 포격, 폭격 **2** 대규모 포격으로 그 도시는 초토화되었다. **2** 가산명사 또는 불가산명사 퍼부음, 쇄도 □ 끊임없이 쏟아지는 노동의 중요성을 역설하는 이미지

bomb|er /bɒmər/ (bombers) **1** N-COUNT A **bomber** is a military aircraft which drops bombs. □ *...a high speed bomber with twin engines.* **2** N-COUNT **Bombers** are people who cause bombs to explode in public places. □ *Detectives hunting the London bombers will be keen to interview him.*

1 가산명사 폭격기 □ 엔진 두 개가 달린 고속 폭격기 **2** 가산명사 폭파범 □ 런던 폭파범을 추적 중인 탐정들은 그를 무척이나 인터뷰하고 싶을 것이다.

bomb|shell /bɒmʃel/ (bombshells) N-COUNT A **bombshell** is a sudden piece of bad or unexpected news. □ *His resignation after thirteen years is a political bombshell.* ● PHRASE If someone **drops a bombshell**, they give you a sudden piece of bad or unexpected news.

가산명사 충격적인 소식, 폭탄선언 □ 13년 연임한 후의 그의 사퇴는 정치계에 큰 충격이었다. ● 구 폭탄선언 하다

bo|nan|za /bənænzə/ (bonanzas) N-COUNT You can refer to a sudden great increase in wealth, success, or luck as a **bonanza**. □ *The expected sales bonanza hadn't materialised.*

가산명사 노다지; 대성공; 우수행동 □ 예상했던 매출 급증은 일어나지 않았었다.

bond ♦♦◇ /bɒnd/ (bonds, bonding, bonded) **1** N-COUNT A **bond between** people is a strong feeling of friendship, love, or shared beliefs and experiences that unites them. □ *The experience created a very special bond between us.* **2** V-RECIP When people **bond with** each other, they form a relationship based on love or shared beliefs and experiences. You can also say that people **bond** or that something **bonds** them. □ *Belinda was having difficulty bonding with the baby.* □ *They all bonded while writing graffiti together.* **3** N-COUNT A **bond between** people or groups is a close connection that they have with each other, for example because they have a special agreement. □ *...the strong bond between church and nation.* **4** N-COUNT A **bond between** two things is the way in which they stick to one another or are joined in some way. □ *If you experience difficulty with the superglue not creating a bond with dry wood, moisten the surfaces with water.* **5** V-RECIP When one thing **bonds with** another, it sticks to it or becomes joined to it in some way. You can also say that two things **bond together**, or that something **bonds** them **together**. □ *Diamond may be strong in itself, but it does not bond well with other materials.* □ *In graphite sheets, carbon atoms bond together in rings.* **6** N-COUNT When a government or company issues a **bond**, it borrows money from investors. The certificate which is issued to investors who lend money is also called a **bond**. [BUSINESS] □ *Most of it will be financed by government bonds.*
→see also **junk bond**
→see **love**

1 가산명사 연대감, 유대감 □ 그 경험으로 우리 사이에 아주 특별한 유대감이 생겼다. **2** 상호동사 유대 관계를 형성하다; 하나로 이어 주다 □ 벨린다는 아이와 유대 관계를 형성하는 데 어려움을 겪고 있었다. □ 그들은 낙서를 함께 하면서 모두 친해졌다. **3** 가산명사 관계 □ 교회와 국가 간의 밀접한 관계 **4** 가산명사 접착 □ 강력 접착제가 마른 나무에 잘 붙지 않으면, 나무 표면에 물을 바르세요. **5** 상호동사 결합하다; 결합시키다 □ 다이아몬드가 그 자체로는 강할지 모르지만 다른 물질과는 잘 결합되지 않는다. □ 흑연판에서 탄소 원자는 고리형태로 서로 결합한다. **6** 가산명사 채권 [경제] □ 그것에 대해서는 대부분 국채로 자금이 조달될 것이다.

bond|age /bɒndɪdʒ/ **1** N-UNCOUNT **Bondage** is the condition of being someone's property and having to work for them. □ *Masters often hired out their slaves and sometimes allowed them to share in earnings and to buy their way out of bondage.* **2** N-UNCOUNT **Bondage** is the condition of not being free because you are strongly influenced by something or someone. [FORMAL] □ *All people, she said, lived their lives in bondage to hunger, pain and lust.*

1 불가산명사 노예의 신분 □ 주인은 자신의 노예를 빌려 주기도 했고, 때때로 노예들이 수입을 나눠 갖거나 돈으로 노예 신분에서 벗어나도록 허락해 주었다. **2** 불가산명사 속박, 구속 [격식체] □ 그녀는 모든 사람들이 배고픔과 고통 그리고 욕정에 사로잡혀 산다고 말했다.

bond|ed /bɒndɪd/ ADJ A **bonded** company has entered into a legal agreement which offers its customers some protection if the company does not fulfill its contract with them. [BUSINESS] □ *The company is a fully bonded member of the Association of British Travel Agents.*

형용사 채권보증으로 보증되는, 담보가 붙은 [경제] □ 이 회사는 영국 여행 대행사 협회 보증 정회원이다.

bond|holder /bɒndhoʊldəʳ/ (bondholders) also bond holder N-COUNT A **bondholder** is a person who owns one or more investment bonds. [BUSINESS]

가산명사 채권 소유자 [경제]

bone ♦♦◇ /boʊn/ (bones, boning, boned) **1** N-VAR Your **bones** are the hard parts inside your body which together form your skeleton. □ *Many passengers suffered broken bones.* □ *The body is made up primarily of bone, muscle, and fat.* **2** V-T If you **bone** a piece of meat or fish, you remove the bones from it before cooking it. □ *Make sure that you do not pierce the skin when boning the chicken thighs.* **3** ADJ A **bone** tool or ornament is made of bone. □ *...a small, expensive pocketknife with a bone handle.* **4** PHRASE The **bare bones** of something are its most basic parts or details. □ *There are not even the bare bones of a garden here – I've got nothing.* **5** PHRASE If something such as costs are cut **to the bone**, they are reduced to the minimum possible. □ *It has survived by cutting its costs to the bone.*
→see **skeleton**

1 가산명사 또는 불가산명사 뼈 □ 많은 승객들이 뼈가 부러졌다. □ 인체는 주로 뼈와 근육, 지방으로 이뤄진다. **2** 타동사 뼈를 발라내다 □ 닭의 넓적다리뼈를 발라낼 때 닭 껍질을 절개하지 않도록 해야 한다. **3** 형용사 뼈로 만든, 골재로 만든 □ 상아 손잡이가 달린 작고 비싼 주머니칼 **4** 구 기본, 골자 □ 여기는 정원의 기본도 갖추고 있지 않다. 나에게는 아무것도 없다. **5** 구 줄이고 줄여 □ 비용을 줄일 수 있는 대로 절감해서 살아남았다.

bone of con|ten|tion (bones of contention) N-COUNT If a particular matter or issue is a **bone of contention**, it is the subject of a disagreement or argument. □ *The main bone of contention is the temperature level of the air-conditioners.*

가산명사 논쟁점 □ 주요 논쟁점은 에어컨의 온도 수준이다.

bon|fire /bɒnfaɪəʳ/ (bonfires) N-COUNT A **bonfire** is a fire that is made outdoors, usually to burn waste. Bonfires are also sometimes lit as part of a celebration. □ *With bonfires outlawed in urban areas, gardeners must cart their refuse to a dump.*

가산명사 모닥불 □ 도시에서 쓰레기 소각은 불법이기 때문에, 정원사들은 쓰레기를 폐기장으로 실어 날라야 한다.

bon|net /bɒnɪt/ (bonnets) **1** N-COUNT A **bonnet** is a hat with ribbons that are tied under the chin. Bonnets are now worn by babies. In the past, they were also worn by women. **2** N-COUNT The **bonnet** of a car is the metal cover over the engine at the front. [BRIT; AM **hood**] □ *When I eventually stopped and lifted the bonnet, the noise seemed to be coming from the alternator.*

1 가산명사 보닛 **2** 가산명사 보닛 [영국영어; 미국영어 hood] □ 결국 차를 세우고 보닛을 열어 보니 소리가 발전기에서 나는 것 같았다.

bo|nus /boʊnəs/ (bonuses) **1** N-COUNT A **bonus** is an extra amount of money that is added to someone's pay, usually because they have worked very hard. □ *Workers in big firms receive a substantial part of their pay in the form of bonuses and overtime.* □ *...a £15 bonus.* **2** N-COUNT A **bonus** is something good that you get in addition to something else, and which you would not usually expect. □ *We felt we might finish third. Any better would be a bonus.* **3** N-COUNT A **bonus** is a sum of

1 가산명사 상여금, 보너스 □ 대기업의 근로자들은 봉급의 상당 부분을 상여금과 초과근무수당의 형태로 받는다. □ 15파운드의 보너스 **2** 가산명사 보너스, 기대 이상의 것 □ 우리는 3등을 할 수 있을 것이라고 생각했다. 그 이상의 결과는 보너스일 것이라고 생각했다. **3** 가산명사 이익 배당금 □ 이 정도

a b c d e f g h i j k l m n o p q r s t u v w x y z

money that an insurance company pays to its policyholders, for example a percentage of the company's profits. ❏ *These returns will not be enough to meet the payment of annual bonuses to policyholders.*

bony /boʊni/ **1** ADJ Someone who has a **bony** face or **bony** hands, for example, has a very thin face or very thin hands, with very little flesh covering their bones. ❏ *...an old man with a bony face and white hair.* **2** ADJ The **bony** parts of a person's or animal's body are the parts made of bone. ❏ *...the bony ridge of the eye socket.*

수익으로는 보험 계약자들에게 약정된 금년 이익 배당금을 맞춰서 지급하기에 부족하다.

1 형용사 뼈가 앙상한 ❏ 뼈가 앙상한 얼굴에 머리가 허연 노인 **2** 형용사 뼈가 있는 ❏ 눈구멍 주위의 뼈

boo /buː/ (**boos, booing, booed**) **1** V-T/V-I If you **boo** a speaker or performer, you shout "boo" or make other loud sounds to indicate that you do not like them, their opinions, or their performance. ❏ *People were booing and throwing things at them.* ❏ *Demonstrators booed and jeered him.* ● N-COUNT **Boo** is also a noun. ❏ *She was greeted with boos and hisses.* ● **booing** N-UNCOUNT ❏ *The fans are entitled to their opinion but booing doesn't help anyone.* **2** EXCLAM You say "**Boo!**" loudly and suddenly when you want to surprise someone who does not know that you are there.

1 타동사/자동사 야유하다 ❏ 사람들은 그들에게 야유하며 물건을 집어던지고 있었다. ❏ 시위자들은 그를 야유하고 조롱했다. ● 가산명사 야유 ❏ 그녀를 맞이한 것은 야유와 '에이씨'하는 소리들이었다. ● 야유 불가산명사 ❏ 팬들의 의견은 자유지만 야유한다고 해서 상황이 나아지는 것은 아니다. **2** 감탄사 쾅! (놀래키려고 내는 소리)

book ♦♦♦ /bʊk/ (**books, booking, booked**) **1** N-COUNT A **book** is a number of pieces of paper, usually with words printed on them, which are fastened together and fixed inside a cover of stronger paper or cardboard. Books contain information, stories, or poetry, for example. ❏ *His eighth book came out earlier this year and was an instant bestseller.* ❏ *...the author of a book on politics.* ❏ *...a new book by Rosella Brown.* **2** N-COUNT A **book** of something such as stamps, matches, or tickets is a small number of them fastened together between thin cardboard covers. ❏ *Can I have a book of first class stamps please?* **3** V-T When you **book** something such as a hotel room or a ticket, you arrange to have it or use it at a particular time. ❏ *British officials have booked hotel rooms for the women and children.* ❏ *Laurie revealed she had booked herself a flight home last night.* **4** N-PLURAL A company's or organization's **books** are its records of money that has been spent and earned or of the names of people who belong to it. [BUSINESS] ❏ *For the most part he left the books to his managers and accountants.* **5** V-T When a police officer **books** someone, he or she officially records their name and the offense that they may be charged with. ❏ *They took him to the station and booked him for assault with a deadly weapon.* **6** N-COUNT In a very long written work such as the Bible, a **book** is one of the sections into which it is divided. ❏ *...the last book of the Bible.* **7** V-T When a referee **books** a player who has seriously broken the rules of the game, he or she officially writes down the player's name. [mainly BRIT] ❏ *League referee Keith Cooper booked him in the first half for a tussle with the goalie.* **8** →see also **booking, checkbook, phone book** **9** PHRASE If you **bring** someone **to book**, you punish them for an offence or make them explain their behaviour officially. ❏ *Police should be asked to investigate so that the guilty can be brought to book soon.* **10** PHRASE If you say that someone or something is a **closed book**, you mean that you do not know anything about them. ❏ *Frank Spriggs was a very able man but something of a closed book.* **11** PHRASE If transportation or a hotel, restaurant, or theater is **fully booked**, or **booked solid**, it is booked up. ❏ *The car ferries from the mainland are often fully booked by February.* →see **concert, library**

1 가산명사 책 ❏ 그의 여덟 번째 책이 올해 초에 나왔는데 즉각 베스트셀러가 되었다. ❏ 정치에 관한 책의 저자 ❏ 로젤라 브라운의 새 책 **2** 가산명사 쪽 ❏ 1등 우표첩 한 개 주실래요? **3** 타동사 예약하다 ❏ 영국 관리들이 여자들과 아이들을 위해 호텔방을 예약해 두었다. ❏ 로리는 어젯밤에 자신이 집으로 갈 비행기 편을 예약했다고 밝혔다. **4** 복수명사 장부; 명부 [경제] ❏ 그는 대개 중간 관리자들과 회계사들에게 장부를 맡겼다. **5** 타동사 입건하다 ❏ 그들은 그를 경찰서로 끌고 가서 살상무기를 이용한 폭행죄로 입건했다. **6** 가산명사 편(篇), 서(書) ❏ 성경의 마지막 서에는 **7** 타동사 이름을 적다 ❏ 리그 심판인 키스 쿠퍼가 전반에 골키퍼와 싸웠다는 이유로 그의 이름을 적었다. **9** 구 책임을 묻다, 추궁하다 ❏ 죄를 지은 사람들에게 이른 시일 안에 책임을 물을 수 있도록 경찰들에게 조사를 요청해야 한다. **10** 구 베일에 싸여 있는 것[사람] ❏ 프랭크 스프리스는 매우 유능한 사람이었지만 그는 좀 베일에 싸여 있는 인물이었다. **11** 구 예약이 꽉 찬 ❏ 대륙에서 오는 자동차 연락선은 대개 2월이 되면 예약이 꽉 찬다.

Word Partnership		*book*의 연어
N.	address book, book award, children's book, book club, comic book, copy of a book, book cover, library book, phone book, book review, subject of a book, title of a book **1**	
ADJ.	latest/new/recent book **1**	
V.	publish a book, read a book, write a book **1**	

---

book|case /bʊkkeɪs/ (**bookcases**) N-COUNT A **bookcase** is a piece of furniture with shelves that you keep books on.

가산명사 책장

booked up **1** ADJ If transportation or a hotel, restaurant, or theater is **booked up**, it has no seats, rooms, tables, or tickets left for a time or date. [mainly BRIT] [v-link ADJ] ❏ *Friday and Saturday dinner tables are already booked up several weeks in advance.* **2** ADJ If someone is **booked up**, they have made so many arrangements that they have no more time to do things. [mainly BRIT] [v-link ADJ] ❏ *Mr. Wilson's diary is booked up for months ahead.*

1 형용사 예약이 꽉 찬 [주로 영국영어] ❏ 금요일과 토요일의 저녁 테이블은 몇 주 전에 이미 예약이 꽉 찬다. **2** 형용사 일정이 꽉 찬 [주로 영국영어] ❏ 윌슨 씨의 일정은 몇 달 뒤까지 빈틈없이 잡혀 있다.

book|ing /bʊkɪŋ/ (**bookings**) N-COUNT A **booking** is the arrangement that you make when you book something such as a hotel room, a table at a restaurant, a theater seat, or a place on public transportation. ❏ *I suggest you tell him there was a mistake over his late booking.*

가산명사 예약 ❏ 그가 지난번에 늦게 한 예약에 실수가 있었다고 네가 그에게 말하는 것이 좋을 것 같다.

book|keeper /bʊkkiːpər/ (**bookkeepers**) also **book-keeper** N-COUNT A **bookkeeper** is a person whose job is to keep an accurate record of the money that is spent and received by a business or other organization. [BUSINESS]

가산명사 부기 계원, 장부 작성자 [경제]

book|keeping /bʊkkiːpɪŋ/ also **book-keeping** N-UNCOUNT Bookkeeping is the job or activity of keeping an accurate record of the money that is spent and received by a business or other organization. [BUSINESS]

불가산명사 부기 [경제]

Word Link	*let* ≈ little : book*let*, drop*let*, in*let*

---

book|let /bʊklɪt/ (**booklets**) N-COUNT A **booklet** is a very thin book that has a paper cover and that gives you information about something. ❏ *...a 48-page booklet of notes for the completion of the form.*

가산명사 소책자 ❏ 서류를 작성하는 데 필요한 내용을 담은 48쪽짜리 소책자

book|maker /bʊkmeɪkər/ (**bookmakers**) N-COUNT A **bookmaker** is a person whose job is to take your money when you bet and to pay you money if you win. ❏ *...the country's largest chain of bookmakers.*

가산명사 도박업자 ❏ 나라의 가장 큰 도박업자 체인

book|mark /bʊkmɑrk/ (**bookmarks**) ◼ N-COUNT A **bookmark** is a narrow piece of card or leather that you put between the pages of a book so that you can find a particular page easily. ◼ N-COUNT In computing, a **bookmark** is the address of an Internet site that you put into a list on your computer so that you can return to it easily. [COMPUTING] ❑ *This makes it extremely simple to save what you find with an electronic bookmark so you can return to it later.*

◼ 가산명사 책갈피표 ◼ 가산명사 즐겨찾기 [컴퓨터] ❑ 이를 이용하면 찾은 것을 컴퓨터에서 즐겨찾기로 아주 쉽게 저장해서 나중에 다시 이용할 수 있다.

book|store /bʊkstɔr/ (**bookstores**) N-COUNT A **bookstore** is a store where books are sold. [mainly AM; BRIT usually **bookshop**]

가산명사 서점 [주로 미국영어; 영국영어 대개 bookshop]

book value (**book values**) N-COUNT In business, the **book value** of an asset is the value it is given in the account books of the company that owns it. [BUSINESS] ❑ *The insured value of the airplane was greater than its book value, so the airline made a profit of $1.7 million.*

가산명사 장부 가격 [경제] ❑ 비행기의 보험 가격이 장부 가격보다 높았기 때문에 항공사는 천철백만 달러의 이익을 거뒀다.

boom ◆◇◇ /bum/ (**booms, booming, boomed**) ◼ N-COUNT If there is a **boom** in the economy, there is an increase in economic activity, for example in the amount of things that are being bought and sold. ❑ *An economic boom followed, especially in housing and construction.* ❑ *The 1980s were indeed boom years.* ◼ N-COUNT A **boom in** something is an increase in its amount, frequency, or success. ❑ *The boom in the sport's popularity has meant more calls for stricter safety regulations.* ◼ V-I If the economy or a business **is booming**, the amount of things being bought or sold is increasing. ❑ *By 1988 the economy was booming.* ❑ *Sales are booming.* ◼ V-T/V-I When something such as someone's voice, a cannon, or a big drum **booms**, it makes a loud, deep sound that lasts for several seconds. ❑ *"Ladies," boomed Helena, without a microphone, "we all know why we're here tonight."* ● PHRASAL VERB **Boom out** means the same as **boom**. ❑ *Music boomed out from loudspeakers.* ❑ *A megaphone boomed out, "This is the police."* ● N-COUNT; SOUND **Boom** is also a noun. ❑ *The stillness of night was broken by the boom of a cannon.*

◼ 가산명사 경기 활성, 호황 ❑ 특히 주택과 건설 분야에서 경제적 호황이 뒤따랐다. ❑ 1980년대는 참으로 호황기였다. ◼ 가산명사 증가 ❑ 그 스포츠의 인기 증가로 인하여 보다 철저한 안전 규제에 대한 요청이 늘어났다. ◼ 자동사 호황을 타다, (경기가) 활성화되다 ❑ 1988년에 이르러 경기는 호황을 타고 있었다. ❑ 판매가 증가하고 있다. ◼ 타동사/자동사 쿵 소리를 내다, 우렁찬 소리로 말하다 ❑ "숙녀 여러분, 오늘 밤 우리가 여기 모인 이유는 모두 잘 아실 것입니다."라고 헬레나는 마이크 없이 우렁차게 말했다. ● 구동사 크게 울리다 ❑ 확성기에서 음악이 크게 울려 나왔다. ❑ 메가폰에서 "경찰이다."라고 큰 소리로 울렸다. ● 가산명사; 소리 쿵 하는 소리 ❑ 밤의 고요함은 대포의 포효에 의해 깨졌다.

Thesaurus   *boom*의 참조어

v.	flourish, prosper, succeed, thrive; *(ant.)* fail ◼
N.	explosion, roar ◼

---

boom-bust cycle (**boom-bust cycles**) N-COUNT A **boom-bust cycle** is a series of events in which a rapid increase in business activity in the economy is followed by a rapid decrease in business activity, and this process is repeated again and again. [BUSINESS] ❑ *We must avoid the damaging boom-bust cycles which characterised the 1980s.*

가산명사 호황과 불황의 반복 [경제] ❑ 1980년의 특징이었던 해로운 호황과 불황의 반복을 피해야 한다.

boon /bun/ (**boons**) N-COUNT You can describe something as a **boon** when it makes life better or easier for someone. ❑ *It is for this reason that television proves such a boon to so many people.*

가산명사 혜택 ❑ 이 때문에 텔레비전이 그처럼 많은 사람들에게 그러한 축복이 되는 것이다.

boost ◆◇◇ /bust/ (**boosts, boosting, boosted**) ◼ V-T If one thing **boosts** another, it causes it to increase, improve, or be more successful. ❑ *Lower interest rates can boost the economy by reducing borrowing costs for consumers and businesses.* ● N-COUNT **Boost** is also a noun. ❑ *It would get the economy going and give us the boost that we need.* ◼ V-T If something **boosts** your confidence or morale, it improves it. ❑ *We need a big win to boost our confidence.* ● N-COUNT **Boost** is also a noun. ❑ *It did give me a boost to win such a big event.*

◼ 타동사 부양하다, 개선하다 ❑ 낮은 금리로 소비자와 기업들의 대출 비용을 줄임으로써 경제를 부양할 수 있다. ● 가산명사 부양, 활성화 ❑ 그러면 경제가 활기를 찾을 것이고 우리는 필요한 지원을 받게 될 것이다. ◼ 타동사 북돋우다 ❑ 우리의 자신감을 북돋우기 위해선 큰 승리가 필요하다. ● 가산명사 북돋움 ❑ 그런 큰 경기에서 이기게 되어 자신감에 큰 도움이 되었다.

boot ◆◇◇ /but/ (**boots, booting, booted**) ◼ N-COUNT **Boots** are shoes that cover your whole foot and the lower part of your leg. ❑ *He sat in a kitchen chair, reached down and pulled off his boots.* ◼ N-COUNT **Boots** are strong, heavy shoes which cover your ankle and which have thick soles. You wear them to protect your feet, for example when you are walking or taking part in sports. ❑ *The soldiers' boots resounded in the street.* ◼ V-T If you **boot** something such as a ball, you kick it hard. [INFORMAL] ❑ *He booted the ball 40 yards back up field.* ◼ N-COUNT The **boot** of a car is a covered space at the back or front, in which you carry things such as luggage and groceries. [BRIT; AM **trunk**] ❑ *He opened the boot to put my bags in.* ◼ PHRASE If you **get the boot** or **are given the boot**, you are told that you are not wanted any more, either in your job or by someone you are having a relationship with. [INFORMAL] ❑ *She was a disruptive influence, and after a year or two she got the boot.* ◼ PHRASE If someone **puts the boot in**, they attack another person by saying something cruel, often when the person is already feeling weak or upset. [BRIT, INFORMAL] ❑ *And Montoya put the boot in again on Schumacher by insisting "You'll never be the best."* →see **clothing**

◼ 가산명사 장화, 부츠 ❑ 그는 부엌 의자에 앉아 손을 내려 장화를 벗었다. ◼ 가산명사 워커 ❑ 군인들의 군화 소리가 길에 울려 퍼졌다. ◼ 타동사 세게 차다 [비격식체] ❑ 그는 공을 40야드 멀리 필드 위쪽으로 세게 찼다. ◼ 가산명사 트렁크 [영국영어; 미국영어 trunk] ❑ 그는 나의 가방을 넣기 위해 트렁크를 열었다. ◼ 구 잘리다 [비격식체] ❑ 그녀는 분위기를 해쳤으며 결국 1, 2년 뒤 잘렸다. ◼ 구 불 난 집에 부채질하다 [영국영어, 비격식체] ❑ "자넨 결코 최고가 될 수 없어,"라고 주장하며 몬토야는 슈마허에게 또 불난 집에 부채질을 해댔다.

booth /buθ/ (**booths**) ◼ N-COUNT A **booth** is a small area separated from a larger public area by screens or thin walls where, for example, people can make a telephone call or vote in private. ❑ *I called her from a public phone booth near the entrance to the bar.* ◼ N-COUNT A **booth** in a restaurant or café consists of a table with long fixed seats on two or sometimes three sides of it. ❑ *They sat in a corner booth, away from other diners.*

◼ 가산명사 부스 ❑ 나는 술집의 입구 근처에 있는 공중전화 부스에서 그녀에게 전화를 걸었다. ◼ 가산명사 (측면에 긴 의자가 있는) 테이블 ❑ 그들은 다른 손님들과 떨어진 구석의 테이블에 앉았다.

booze /buz/ (**boozes, boozing, boozed**) ◼ N-UNCOUNT **Booze** is alcoholic drink. [INFORMAL] [also the N] ❑ *...booze and cigarettes.* ◼ V-I If people **booze**, they drink alcohol. [INFORMAL] ❑ *...a load of drunken businessmen who had been boozing all afternoon.*

◼ 불가산명사 술 [비격식체] ❑ 술과 담배 ◼ 자동사 술을 마시다 [비격식체] ❑ 오후 내내 술을 마셨던 취한 사업가들 무리

bor|der ◆◆◇ /bɔrdər/ (**borders, bordering, bordered**) ◼ N-COUNT The **border** between two countries or regions is the dividing line between them. Sometimes the **border** also refers to the land close to this line. ❑ *They fled across the border.* ❑ *Soldiers had temporarily closed the border between the two countries.* ◼ V-T A country that **borders** another country, a sea, or a river is next to it. ❑ *...the European and Arab countries bordering the Mediterranean.* ● PHRASAL VERB **Border on**

◼ 가산명사 국경, 변경 ❑ 그들은 국경을 넘어 도망갔다. ❑ 군인들이 두 나라 사이의 국경을 임시 폐쇄했다. ◼ 타동사 인접하다, 접경하다 ❑ 지중해에 인접한 유럽 및 아랍 국가들 ● 구동사 인접하다, 접경하다 ❑ 두 공화국 모두 흑해에 인접해 있다. ◼ 가산명사 테두리, 가장자리 ❑ 손으로 테두리에

means the same as **border**. ❑ *Both republics border on the Black Sea.* **3** N-COUNT A **border** is a strip or band around the edge of something. ❑ *...pillowcases trimmed with a hand-crocheted border.* **4** N-COUNT In a garden, a **border** is a long strip of ground along the edge planted with flowers. ❑ *...a lawn flanked by wide herbaceous borders.* **5** V-T If something **is bordered** by another thing, the other thing forms a line along the edge of it. ❑ *...the mile of white sand beach bordered by palm trees and tropical flowers.*

크로세 뜨개질을 한 베갯잇 **4** 가산명사 테두리, 가장자리 ❑ 테두리에 넓게 화초를 심어 놓은 잔디밭 **5** 타동사 ~로 테가 둘러진 ❑ 야자수와 열대성 꽃이 둘러싸고 있는 1마일 길이의 흰 모래 사장

Thesaurus	border의 참조어
N.	boundary, end, perimeter; *(ant.)* center, inside, middle **1**
V.	enclose, surround, touch **5**

bor|der|line /bɔ̩rdərlaɪn/ (**borderlines**) **1** N-COUNT The **borderline between** two different or opposite things is the division between them. ❑ *...a task which involves exploring the borderline between painting and photography.* **2** ADJ Something that is **borderline** is only just acceptable as a member of a class or group. ❑ *Some were obviously unsuitable and could be ruled out at once. Others were borderline cases.*

1 가산명사 경계선 ❑ 회화와 사진 사이의 경계를 탐색하게 되는 작업 **2** 형용사 경계선상의 ❑ 어떤 것들은 눈에 띄게 부적합했기 때문에 바로 제거할 수 있었다. 다른 것들은 결정하기가 애매했다.

bore ♦◇◇ /bɔ̩r/ (**bores, boring, bored**) **1** V-T If someone or something **bores** you, you find them dull and uninteresting. ❑ *Dickie bored him all through the meal with stories of the Navy.* **2** PHRASE If someone or something **bores you to tears**, **bores you to death**, or **bores you stiff**, they bore you very much indeed. [INFORMAL, EMPHASIS] ❑ *...a handsome engineer who bored me to tears with his tales of motorway maintenance.* **3** N-COUNT You describe someone as a **bore** when you think that they talk in a very uninteresting way. ❑ *There is every reason why I shouldn't enjoy his company – he's a bore and a fool.* **4** N-SING You can describe a situation as a **bore** when you find it annoying. ❑ *It's a bore to be sick, and the novelty of lying in bed all day wears off quickly.* **5** V-T If you **bore** a hole in something, you make a deep round hole in it using a special tool. ❑ *Get the special drill bit to bore the correct-size hole for the job.* **6** **Bore** is the past tense of **bear**. **7** →see also **bored, boring**

1 타동사 지루하게 하다 ❑ 디키는 해군에 대한 이야기로 식사 내내 그를 지루하게 했다. **2** 구 지루해서 죽을 지경이 되게 하다 [비격식체, 강조] ❑ 고속도로 유지에 대한 이야기를 하면서 나를 하품 나도록 지루하게 만들었던 잘생긴 기술자 **3** 가산명사 지루한 사람 ❑ 내가 그와 같이 있는 것을 꺼려할 이유는 무궁무진해. 그는 지루한데다 바보야. **4** 단수명사 귀찮은 것, 싱가신 것 ❑ 아프다는 것은 싱가신 일이고 하루 종일 침대에 누워 있는 것의 신선함은 금방 사라진다. **5** 타동사 뚫다 ❑ 특수 드릴 날을 가지고 작업하기에 올바른 크기의 구멍을 뚫으세요. **6** bear의 과거

bored /bɔ̩rd/ ADJ If you are **bored**, you feel tired and impatient because you have lost interest in something or because you have nothing to do. ❑ *I am getting very bored with this entire business.*

형용사 지루한 ❑ 나는 이 일 전체가 굉장히 지루해지기 시작한다.

bore|dom /bɔ̩rdəm/ N-UNCOUNT **Boredom** is the state of being bored. ❑ *He had given up attending lectures out of sheer boredom.*

불가산명사 지루함 ❑ 그는 단순히 지루함 때문에 강의에 출석하는 것을 그만뒀다.

bor|ing /bɔ̩rɪŋ/ ADJ Someone or something **boring** is so dull and uninteresting that they make people tired and impatient. ❑ *Not only are mothers not paid but also most of their boring or difficult work is unnoticed.*

형용사 지루한 ❑ 어머니들은 임금을 못 받을 뿐더러 그들의 지루하거나 힘겨운 일은 대부분 인정조차 못 받는다.

Thesaurus	boring의 참조어
ADJ.	dull, tedious; *(ant.)* exciting, fun, interesting, lively

born ♦♦◇ /bɔ̩rn/ **1** V-T PASSIVE When a baby **is born**, it comes out of its mother's body at the beginning of its life. In formal English, if you say that someone **is born of** someone or **to** someone, you mean that person is their parent. ❑ *She was born in London on April 29, 1923.* ❑ *He was born of German parents and lived most of his life abroad.* **2** V-T PASSIVE If someone **is born with** a particular disease, problem, or characteristic, they have it from the time they are born. [no cont] ❑ *He was born with only one lung.* ❑ *Some people are born brainy.* **3** V-T PASSIVE You can use **be born** in front of a particular name to show that a person was given this name at birth, although they may be better known by another name. [FORMAL] [no cont] ❑ *She was born Jenny Harvey on June 11, 1946.* **4** ADJ You use **born** to describe someone who has a natural ability to do a particular activity or job. For example, if you are a **born** cook, you have a natural ability to cook well. [ADJ n] ❑ *Jack was a born teacher.* **5** V-T PASSIVE When an idea or organization **is born**, it comes into existence. If something **is born of** a particular emotion or activity, it exists as a result of that emotion or activity. [FORMAL] ❑ *The idea for the show was born in his hospital room.* ❑ *Congress passed the National Security Act, and the CIA was born.* **6** →see also **newborn**

1 수동 타동사 태어나다; ~의 자식이다 ❑ 그녀는 1923년 4월 29일 런던에서 태어났다. ❑ 그는 독일계 부모에게서 태어나 삶의 대부분을 해외에서 보냈다. **2** 수동 타동사 ~을 가지고 태어나다 ❑ 그는 한 쪽 폐만 지니고 태어났다. ❑ 어떤 사람들은 머리를 타고난다. **3** 수동 타동사 ~의 이름을 얻으며 태어나다 [격식체] ❑ 그녀는 1946년 6월 11일 제니 하비라는 이름을 얻으며 태어났다. **4** 형용사 타고난 ❑ 잭은 타고난 교사였다. **5** 수동 타동사 탄생하다 [격식체] ❑ 쇼에 대한 아이디어는 그의 병실에서 탄생했다. ❑ 하원이 국가보안법을 통과시켰고 그렇게 시아이에이는 탄생했다.

borne /bɔ̩rn/ **Borne** is the past participle of **bear**.

bear의 과거 분사

bor|ough /bɜ̩roʊ, BRIT bʌ̩rə/ (**boroughs**) N-COUNT A **borough** is a town, or a district within a large town, which has its own council. ❑ *...the South London borough of Lambeth.* ❑ *...the New York City borough of Brooklyn.*

가산명사 자치 도시, 자치구, 독립구 ❑ 남부 런던의 자치구 램베스 ❑ 뉴욕 시의 독립구인 브루클린

bor|row ♦◇◇ /bɒ̩roʊ/ (**borrows, borrowing, borrowed**) **1** V-T If you **borrow** something that belongs to someone else, you use it for a period of time, usually with their permission. ❑ *Can I borrow a pen please?* **2** V-T/V-I If you **borrow** money **from** someone or **from** a bank, they give it to you and you agree to pay it back at some time in the future. ❑ *Morgan borrowed £5,000 from his father to form the company 20 years ago.* ❑ *It's so expensive to borrow from finance companies.* **3** V-T If you **borrow** a book **from** a library, you take it away for a fixed period of time. ❑ *I couldn't afford to buy any, so I borrowed them from the library.* **4** V-T When you **borrow** something such as a word or an idea from another language or from another person's work, you use it in your own language or work. ❑ *I borrowed his words for my book's title.*

1 타동사 빌리다 ❑ 펜 하나 빌려 주시겠어요? **2** 타동사/자동사 빌리다 ❑ 모건은 20년 전에 회사를 설립하기 위해 아버지로부터 5천 파운드를 빌렸다. ❑ 일부 금융사로부터 대출받는 것은 너무 비싸다. **3** 타동사 빌리다 ❑ 그것들을 살 돈이 없어서 도서관에서 빌렸다. **4** 타동사 빌리다 ❑ 내 책의 제목에 쓰기 위해 그의 말을 가져왔다.

Do not confuse **borrow** and **lend**. You say that you **borrow** something **from** another person. However, if you allow someone to **borrow** something that belongs to you, you say that you **lend** it **to** them. **Lend** is often followed by two objects. ❑ *Betty lent him some blankets... He lent Tim the money.* Both **borrow**

borrow와 lend를 혼동하지 않도록 하라. borrow는 다른 사람으로부터 무엇을 "빌리는" 것이다. 그러나 누가 당신의 것을 빌리도록(borrow)허락하는 경우에는, 당신이

and **lend** can be used without objects. ❑ *The poor had to borrow from the rich... Banks will not lend to them.* The noun related to **lend** is **loan**. ❑ *...a government loan of $3m.* **Loan** can also be used as a verb in the same way as **lend**, especially in American English. ❑ *I'll loan you fifty dollars.*

그에게 그것을 "빌려주는(lend)" 것이다. lend 뒤에는 흔히 목적어가 두 개 온다. ❑ 베티가 그에게 담요를 좀 빌려 주었다... 그는 팀에게 그 돈을 빌려주었다. borrow와 lend 둘 다 목적어 없이 쓸 수 있다. ❑ 가난한 사람들은 부자들에게서 돈을 빌려야 했다... 은행에서 그들에게 돈을 빌려주지 않을 것이다. lend와 관련된 명사는 loan이다. ❑ ...공채 300만 달러. loan은 특히 미국 영어에서 lend와 마찬가지로 동사로도 쓸 수 있다. ❑ 내가 50달러를 빌려줄게.

Word Partnership borrow의 연어

PREP.	borrow **from** 1-4
V.	forced to borrow 1 2
N.	**ability to** borrow, borrow **cash/money** 2
	borrow **a phrase** 4

bor|row|er /bɒrouər/ (borrowers) N-COUNT A **borrower** is a person or organization that borrows money. ❑ *Borrowers with a big mortgage should go for a fixed rate even though it may not be the cheapest.* →see bank, interest rate, library

가산명사 차용자 ❑ 주택 담보 대출을 크게 받는 사람들은 비록 그것이 가장 싸지 못하더라도 고정 금리를 택해야 한다.

bor|row|ing /bɒrouɪŋ/ (borrowings) N-UNCOUNT **Borrowing** is the activity of borrowing money. [also N in pl] ❑ *We have allowed spending and borrowing to rise in this recession.*

불가산명사 융자 대출 ❑ 이번 불황 때 소비와 대출이 증가하도록 허용해 왔다.

bos|om /bʊzəm/ (bosoms) 1 N-COUNT A woman's breasts are sometimes referred to as her **bosom** or her **bosoms**. [OLD-FASHIONED] ❑ *...a large young mother with a baby resting against her ample bosom.* 2 ADJ A **bosom** friend is a friend who you know very well and like very much indeed. [ADJ n] ❑ *They were bosom friends.*

1 가산명사 여성의 가슴 [구식어] ❑ 풍만한 가슴에 아기를 안고 있는 젊고 체격 좋은 어머니 2 형용사 흉금을 털어놓는 ❑ 그들은 흉금을 털어놓는 친구였다.

boss ♦♦◇ /bɒs/ (bosses, bossing, bossed) 1 N-COUNT Your **boss** is the person in charge of the organization or department where you work. ❑ *He cannot stand his boss.* 2 N-COUNT If you are **the boss** in a group or relationship, you are the person who makes all the decisions. [INFORMAL] ❑ *He thinks he's the boss.* 3 V-T If you say that someone **bosses** you, you mean that they keep telling you what to do in a way that is irritating. ❑ *We cannot boss them into doing more.* • PHRASAL VERB **Boss around**, or in British English **boss about**, means the same as **boss**. ❑ *He started bossing people around and I didn't like what was happening.*

1 가산명사 상사, 사장 ❑ 그는 자기 상사를 굉장히 싫어한다. 2 가산명사 보스 [비격식체] ❑ 그는 자기가 보스인 줄 착각하나 봐. 3 타동사 시키다, 부려먹다 ❑ 그들보고 더 하라고 시킬 수 없다. • 구동사 시키다, 부려먹다 ❑ 그가 사람들을 부려먹기 시작했는데 그런 것이 내 마음에 들지 않았다.

Thesaurus boss의 참조어

N.	chief, director, employer, foreman, manager, owner, superintendent, supervisor 1

bossy /bɒsi/ ADJ If you describe someone as **bossy**, you mean that they enjoy telling people what to do. [DISAPPROVAL] ❑ *She remembers being a rather bossy little girl.*

형용사 부려먹는, 보스 행세하는 [탐탁찮음] ❑ 그녀의 기억에 자신은 남들에게 이래라 저래라 잘 하는 어린 소녀였다.

Word Link botan ≈ plant : botanical, botanist, botany

bo|tani|cal /bətænɪkᵊl/ ADJ **Botanical** books, research, and activities relate to the scientific study of plants. [ADJ n] ❑ *The area is of great botanical interest.*

형용사 식물학의 ❑ 이 지역은 식물학적으로 매우 흥미로운 곳이다.

bota|nist /bɒtənɪst/ (botanists) N-COUNT A **botanist** is a scientist who studies plants.

가산명사 식물학자

bota|ny /bɒtəni/ N-UNCOUNT **Botany** is the scientific study of plants.

불가산명사 식물학

botch /bɒtʃ/ (botches, botching, botched) V-T If you **botch** something that you are doing, you do it badly or clumsily. [INFORMAL] ❑ *...a botched job.* • PHRASAL VERB **Botch up** means the same as **botch**. ❑ *I hate having builders botch up repairs on my house.*

타동사 망치다, 실패하다 [비격식체] ❑ 실패한 일 • 구동사 망치다, 실패하다 ❑ 건축업자들이 내 집 수리를 엉망으로 하는 것이 싫다.

both ♦♦♦ /bouθ/ 1 DET You use **both** when you are referring to two people or things and saying that something is true about each of them. ❑ *She cried out in fear and flung both arms up to protect her face.* • QUANT **Both** is also a quantifier. [QUANT of pl-n] ❑ *Both of these women have strong memories of the Vietnam War.* • PRON **Both** is also a pronoun. ❑ *Miss Brown and her friend, both from Stoke, were arrested on the 8th of June.* • PRON-EMPH **Both** is also an emphasizing pronoun. [n PRON] ❑ *He visited the Institute of Neurology in Havana where they both worked.* • PREDET **Both** is also a predeterminer. [EMPHASIS] [PREDET det pl-n] ❑ *Both the horses were out, tacked up and ready to ride.* 2 CONJ You use the structure **both...and** when you are giving two facts or alternatives and emphasizing that each of them is true or possible. ❑ *Now women work both before and after having their children.*

1 한정사 둘 다 ❑ 그녀는 두려움에 소리를 지르며 두 팔을 위로 들어 얼굴을 가렸다. • 수량사 둘 다 ❑ 이 두 여성 모두 베트남 전에 대해 강하게 각인된 기억을 지니고 있다. • 대명사 둘 다 ❑ 둘 모두 스토우크 출신인 브라운 양과 그녀의 친구는 6월 8일에 체포되었다. • 강조대명사 둘 다 ❑ 그는 그들 둘의 근무지인 아바나의 신경학 연구소를 방문했다. • 전치 한정사 둘 다 [강조] ❑ 두 마리 말 모두 마구를 갖춘 채 밖에 나와 있었고 타기만 하면 되었다. 2 접속사 두 개의 진술 모두가 참이거나 가능함을 나타낼 때 쓰임 ❑ 이제는 여성들이 아이를 가지기 전뿐만 아니라 가진 뒤에도 일을 한다.

> Notice that all these sentences mean the same thing: "**Both boys have been ill**," "**Both the boys have been ill**," "**Both of the boys have been ill**," "**The boys have both been ill**." You cannot say "**Both of boys have been ill**," although when a pronoun is used, you can say "**Both of them have been ill**." See also note at **all**.

> 다음 문장이 모두 같은 뜻임을 유의하라. "Both boys have been ill," "Both the boys have been ill," "Both of the boys have been ill," "The boys have both been ill." 대명사를 쓸 때는 "Both of them have been ill."이라고 할 수 있지만, "Both of boys have been ill."이라고는 하지 않는다. all의 주석도 참고하라.

both|er ♦◇◇ /bɒðər/ (bothers, bothering, bothered) 1 V-T/V-I If you do not **bother to** do something or if you do not **bother with** it, you do not do it, consider it, or use it because you think it is unnecessary or because you are too lazy, [with brd-neg] ❑ *Lots of people don't bother to go through a marriage ceremony these days.* ❑ *Nothing I do makes any difference anyway, so why bother?* 2 N-UNCOUNT **Bother** means trouble or difficulty. You can also use **bother** to refer to an activity which causes this, especially when you would prefer not to do it or get involved with it. [also a N] ❑ *I usually buy sliced bread - it's less bother.* ❑ *The courts take too long and going to the police is a bother.* 3 V-T/V-I If something **bothers** you, or if you **bother** about it, it worries, annoys, or upsets you. ❑ *Is something bothering you?* ❑ *It bothered me that boys weren't interested in me.* • **both|ered** ADJ [v-link ADJ, oft ADJ about n] ❑ *I was bothered about the blister on my hand.* 4 V-T If

1 타동사/자동사 일부러 -하다 ❑ 요즘에는 많은 사람들이 굳이 결혼식을 올리는 번거로움을 치르지 않는다. ❑ 내가 무엇을 하든 달라지는 것은 없는데 귀찮게 그럴 필요가 있나? 2 불가산명사 번거로운 일 ❑ 나는 대개 잘라 놓은 식빵을 산다. 그것이 덜 번거롭다. ❑ 법정으로 가면 너무 오래 걸리고 경찰에게 가는 것은 성가시다. 3 타동사/자동사 괴롭히다 ❑ 무슨 괴로운 일이라도 있나? ❑ 남자애들이 나에게 관심이 없다는 것이 괴로웠다. • -때문에 고민하는 형용사 ❑ 나는 내 손에 난 물집 때문에 성가셨다. 4 타동사 귀찮게 하다 ❑ 나를 자꾸 귀찮게 하는 남자에게 골탕을 먹이려고 하는 중이다. 5 구 -라고

a b c d e f g h i j k l m n o p q r s t u v w x y z

A

someone **bothers** you, they talk to you when you want to be left alone or interrupt you when you are busy. ❑ *We are playing a trick on a man who keeps bothering me.* ⑤ PHRASE If you say that you **can't be bothered to** do something, you mean that you are not going to do it because you think it is unnecessary or because you are too lazy. ❑ *I just can't be bothered to look after the house.* ⑥ **hot and bothered** →see **hot**

강요당하기 싫다 ❑ 나보고 집을 돌보라고 귀찮게 하지 말아라.

B

bot|tle ♦♦◇ /bɒtªl/ (**bottles, bottling, bottled**) ❶ N-COUNT A **bottle** is a glass or plastic container in which drinks and other liquids are kept. Bottles are usually round with straight sides and a narrow top. ❑ *There were two empty bottles on the table.* ❑ *...a plastic water bottle.* ● N-COUNT A **bottle of** something is an amount of it contained in a bottle. ❑ *...a bottle of soda.* ❷ V-T To **bottle** a drink or other liquid means to put it into bottles after it has been made. ❑ *...allowing the company to bottle water at the site.* ❸ N-COUNT A **bottle** is a drinking container used by babies. It has a special rubber part at the top through which they can suck their drink. ❑ *Gary was holding a bottle to the baby's lips.* ❹ →see also **bottled**

C
D
E

❶ 가산명사 병 ❑ 테이블 위에 빈 병 두개가 있었다. ❑ 플라스틱 물통 ● 가산명사 병 ❑ 소다수 한 병 ❷ 타동사 병에 담다 ❑ 회사가 현장에서 물을 용기에 담아 포장하는 것을 허락하는 ❸ 가산명사 젖병 ❑ 게리는 아기의 입술에 젖병을 대어 주고 있었다.

bot|tled /bɒtªld/ ADJ **Bottled** gas is kept under pressure in special metal cylinders which can be moved from one place to another.

F

형용사 병에 담긴

bot|tom ♦♦◇ /bɒtəm/ (**bottoms, bottoming, bottomed**) ❶ N-COUNT The **bottom of** something is the lowest or deepest part of it. ❑ *He sat at the bottom of the stairs.* ❑ *Answers can be found at the bottom of page 8.* ❷ ADJ The **bottom** thing or layer in a series of things or layers is the lowest one. [ADJ n] ❑ *There's an extra duvet in the bottom drawer of the cupboard.* ❸ N-COUNT The **bottom of** an object is the flat surface at its lowest point. You can also refer to the inside or outside of this surface as the **bottom**. ❑ *Spread the onion slices on the bottom of the dish.* ❑ *...the bottom of their shoes.* ❹ N-SING If you say that the **bottom** has dropped or fallen out of a market or industry, you mean that people have stopped buying the products it sells. [BUSINESS, JOURNALISM] ❑ *The bottom had fallen out of the city's property market.* ❺ N-SING The **bottom of** a street or yard is the end farthest away from you or from your house. [mainly BRIT; AM usually **end**] ❑ *...the Cathedral at the bottom of the street.* ❻ N-SING The **bottom of** a table is the end farthest away from where you are sitting. The **bottom of** a bed is the end where you usually rest your feet. [mainly BRIT; AM usually **end**] ❑ *Malone sat down on the bottom of the bed.* ❼ N-SING The **bottom of** an organization or career structure is the lowest level in it, where new employees often start. [the N, oft N of n] ❑ *He had worked in the theater for many years, starting at the bottom.* ❽ N-SING If someone is **bottom** or at the **bottom** in a survey, test, or league their performance is worse than that of all the other people involved. [the N, also no det] ❑ *He was always bottom of the class.* ❾ N-COUNT Your **bottom** is the part of your body that you sit on. ❑ *If there was one thing she could change about her body it would be her bottom.* ❿ N-COUNT The lower part of a swimsuit, tracksuit, or pair of pajamas can be referred to as the **bottoms** or the **bottom**. ❑ *She wore blue tracksuit bottoms.* ⓫ →see also **rock bottom** ⓬ PHRASE You use **at bottom** to emphasize that you are stating what you think is the real nature of something or the real truth about a situation. [EMPHASIS] ❑ *The two systems are, at bottom, conceptual models.* ⓭ PHRASE If something is **at the bottom of** a problem or unpleasant situation, it is the real cause of it. ❑ *Often I find that anger and resentment are at the bottom of the problem.* ⓮ PHRASE If you want to **get to the bottom of** a problem, you want to solve it by finding out its real cause. ❑ *I have to get to the bottom of this mess.*

G
H
I
J
K
L
M
N
O

❶ 가산명사 하단 ❑ 그는 계단 맨 아래에 앉았다. ❑ 해답은 8페이지 하단에 있습니다. ❷ 형용사 하단의 ❑ 찬장의 아래 서랍에 여분의 이불이 있다. ❸ 가산명사 바닥 ❑ 접시의 바닥에 썬 양파 조각을 깔라라. ❑ 그들 신발의 바닥 ❹ 단수명사 바닥 [경제, 언론] ❑ 도시의 부동산 시장에서는 더 이상 구매자가 나타나지 않았다. ❺ 단수명사 저쪽 끝 [주로 영국영어; 미국영어 대개 end] ❑ 길 저쪽 끝의 성당 ❻ 단수명사 발치 [주로 영국영어; 미국영어 대개 end] ❑ 멜론은 침대의 발치에 앉았다. ❼ 단수명사 밑바닥 ❑ 그는 밑바닥부터 시작해서 연극계에서 오랫동안 일했다. ❽ 단수명사 밑바닥 ❑ 그는 항상 성적이 반에서 밑바닥이었다. ❾ 가산명사 엉덩이 ❑ 만약 여자가 자신의 몸에서 단 한 군데를 바꾼다면 그것은 자신의 둔부일 것이다. ❿ 가산명사 하의 ❑ 그녀는 파란색 육상복 하의를 입고 있었다. ⓬ 구 사실 [강조] ❑ 두 시스템은 사실 개념적 모형이다. ⓭구 -의 기저에는 ❑ 그 문제의 기저에는 보통 분노와 원한이 있는 것으로 알고 있다. ⓮구 진상을 밝히다 ❑ 이 난리의 진상을 밝혀야 한다.

P
Q

Thesaurus   bottom의 참조어

N.	base, floor, foundation, ground; *(ant.)* peak, top ❶

R

Word Partnership   bottom의 연어

N.	bottom **of a hill**, bottom **of the page/screen** ❶
	bottom **of the sea**, bottom **of the pool**, river bottom ❶ ❸
	bottom **drawer** ❷
	bottom **lip**, bottom **rung** ❸
V.	**reach** the bottom, **sink to** the bottom ❶ ❽
PREP.	**along** the bottom, **on** the bottom ❶-❸
	at/near the bottom ❶-❸ ❺-❽

S
T

U
V

bot|tom line (**bottom lines**) ❶ N-COUNT The **bottom line** in a decision or situation is the most important factor that you have to consider. ❑ *The bottom line is that it's not profitable.* ❷ N-COUNT The **bottom line** in a business deal is the least a person is willing to accept. ❑ *She says £95,000 is her bottom line.* ❸ N-COUNT The **bottom line** is the total amount of money that a company has made or lost over a particular period of time. [BUSINESS] ❑ *...to force chief executives to look beyond the next quarter's bottom line.*

❶ 가산명사 결정적인 요소 ❑ 결정적으로 수익이 없다는 것이다. ❷ 가산명사 하한선 ❑ 그녀는 9만 5천 파운드가 하한선이라고 말한다. ❸ 가산명사 결산 [경제] ❑ 대표 임원들로 하여금 다음 분기의 결산 이후까지 바라보도록 하기 위해

bought /bɔt/ **Bought** is the past tense and past participle of **buy**.

W

buy의 과거 및 과거 분사

boul|der /boʊldər/ (**boulders**) N-COUNT A **boulder** is a large rounded rock. ❑ *It is thought that the train hit a boulder that had fallen down a cliff on to the track.*

X

가산명사 바위 ❑ 절벽에서 철길로 떨어지는 바위에 기차가 부딪힌 것으로 추정되고 있다.

boule|vard /buləvɑrd, BRIT buːləvɑːd/ (**boulevards**) N-COUNT A **boulevard** is a wide street in a city, usually with trees along each side. ❑ *...Lenton Boulevard.*

Y

가산명사 대로 ❑ 렌턴 대로

bounce /baʊns/ (**bounces, bouncing, bounced**) ❶ V-T/V-I When an object such as a ball **bounces** or when you **bounce** it, it moves upward from a surface or away from it immediately after hitting it. ❑ *My father would burst into the kitchen bouncing a football.* ❑ *...a falling pebble, bouncing down the eroded cliff.* ● N-COUNT

Z

❶ 타동사/자동사 튀게 하다, 튀다 ❑ 아버지께서는 축구공을 퉁기며 부엌으로 뛰쳐들어오곤 하셨다. ❑ 침식된 절벽에서 퉁기듯 떨어지는 자갈 ● 가산명사 바운드, 퉁김 ❑ 휠체어를 탄 테니스 선수는 공을 두 번

Bounce is also a noun. ❑ *The wheelchair tennis player is allowed two bounces of the ball.* ② V-T/V-I If sound or light **bounces off** a surface or **is bounced off** it, it reaches the surface and is reflected back. ❑ *Your arms and legs need protection from light bouncing off glass.* ③ V-T/V-I If something **bounces** or if something **bounces** it, it swings or moves up and down. ❑ *Her long black hair bounced as she walked.* ❑ *Then I noticed the car was bouncing up and down as if someone were jumping on it.* ④ V-I If you **bounce** on a soft surface, you jump up and down on it repeatedly. ❑ *She lets us do anything, even bounce on our beds.* ⑤ V-I If someone **bounces** somewhere, they move there in an energetic way, because they are feeling happy. ❑ *Moira bounced into the office.* ⑥ V-T If you **bounce** your ideas **off** someone, you tell them to that person, in order to find out what they think about them. ❑ *It was good to bounce ideas off another mind.* ⑦ V-T/V-I If a check **bounces** or if a bank **bounces** it, the bank refuses to accept it and pay out the money, because the person who wrote it does not have enough money in their account. ❑ *Our only complaint would be if the check bounced.* ⑧ V-I If an e-mail or other electronic message **bounces**, it is returned to the person who sent it because the address was wrong or because of a problem with one of the computers involved in sending it. [COMPUTING] ❑ *...a message saying that your mail has "bounced" or was unable to be delivered.*

튀게 해도 된다. ② 자동사/자동사 반사되다
❑ 유리에서 반사되는 빛으로부터 팔과 다리를 보호할 필요가 있다. ③ 타동사/자동사 위아래로 움직이다
❑ 그녀가 걸을 때마다 기다란 검은 머리가 출렁거렸다.
❑ 그때 누군가가 그 위에서 뛰고 있는 것처럼 차가 위아래로 출렁이는 것이 보였다. ④ 자동사 위아래로 뛰다 ❑ 그녀는 우리가 뭘 해도 놔둔다. 심지어는 침대에서 뛰는 것도 허용한다. ⑤ 자동사 (활기 차게) 움직이다 ❑ 모이라가 활기차게 사무실로 들어왔다. ⑥ 타동사 의사를 타진하다 ❑ 다른 사람의 의사를 타진할 수 있어서 좋았다. ⑦ 타동사/자동사 (수표의) 지불을 거절당하다 ❑ 우리의 유일한 불평은 수표가 거부당할 경우에만 생길 것이다. ⑧ 자동사 되돌아오다 [컴퓨터] ❑ 메일이 '되돌아왔다'는, 즉 배달할 수 없었다는 메시지

Word Partnership   bounce의 연어

ADJ.	**a big/high/little** bounce ①
ADV.	bounce **around** ① ③-⑤
	bounce **along** ① ③ ⑤
	bounce **off** ② ⑥
N.	bounce **a ball** ①
	bounce **ideas off** *someone* ⑥
	bounce **a check** ⑦

---

bounc|er /ˈbaʊnsər/ (**bouncers**) N-COUNT A **bouncer** is a man who stands at the door of a club, prevents unwanted people from coming in, and makes people leave if they cause trouble.

가산명사 (술집의) 경비원

bouncy /ˈbaʊnsi/ ① ADJ Someone or something that is **bouncy** is very lively. ❑ *She was bouncy and full of energy.* ② ADJ A **bouncy** thing can bounce very well or makes other things bounce well. ❑ *...a children's paradise filled with bouncy toys.*

① 형용사 활기찬 ❑ 그녀는 활기차고 에너지가 충만했다. ② 형용사 통통 튀는 ❑ 통통 튀는 장난감들로 가득한 아이들의 천국

---

bound

① BE BOUND
② OTHER USES

Word Partnership   bound의 연어

V.	bound **to fail** ① ② ③
PREP.	bound **together**, bound **up with** ① ④
N.	**feet/hands/wrists** bound, **leather** bound ① ①
	bound **with tape** ① ①
	a flight/train/plane/ship bound **for** ① ⑤
N.	bound **by duty** ② ③

---

① **bound** ♦♢♢ /baʊnd/ ① **Bound** is the past tense and past participle of **bind**. ② PHRASE If you say that something **is bound to** happen, you mean that you are sure it will happen, because it is a natural consequence of something that is already known or exists. ❑ *There are bound to be price increases next year.* ③ PHRASE If you say that something **is bound to** happen or be true, you feel confident and certain of it, although you have no definite knowledge or evidence. [SPOKEN] ❑ *I'll show it to Benjamin. He's bound to know.* ④ ADJ If one person, thing, or situation is **bound** to another, they are closely associated with each other, and it is difficult for them to be separated or to escape from each other. [v-link ADJ to n] ❑ *We are as tightly bound to the people we dislike as to the people we love.* ⑤ ADJ If a vehicle or person is **bound for** a particular place, they are traveling toward it. [v-link ADJ for n] ❑ *The ship was bound for Italy.* ● COMB in ADJ **Bound** is also a combining form. ❑ *...a Texas-bound oil freighter.*

① bind의 과거 및 과거 분사 ② 구 -이 반드시 일어날 것이다 ❑ 내년에 분명히 물가 인상이 있을 것이다. ③ 구 반드시 -일 것이다 [구어체] ❑ 벤자민에게 보여 주겠다. 그라면 반드시 알 것이다. ④ 형용사 -에 얽매인 ❑ 우리는 우리가 사랑하는 사람들에게 만큼이나 싫어하는 사람들에게도 강하게 얽매여 있다. ⑤ 형용사 -을 향하는 ❑ 배는 이탈리아로 가고 있었다. ● 복합형-형용사 -행 ❑ 텍사스 행 유조선

② **bound** ♦♢♢ /baʊnd/ (**bounds, bounding, bounded**) ① N-PLURAL **Bounds** are limits which normally restrict what can happen or what people can do. ❑ *Changes in temperature occur slowly and are constrained within relatively tight bounds.* ❑ *...a forceful personality willing to go beyond the bounds of convention.* ② V-T If an area of land **is bounded by** something, that thing is situated around its edge. ❑ *Kirgizia is bounded by Uzbekistan, Kazakhstan and Tajikistan.* ❑ *...the trees that bounded the car park.* ③ V-T PASSIVE If someone's life or situation **is bounded by** certain things, those are its most important aspects and it is limited or restricted by them. ❑ *Our lives are bounded by work, family and television.* ④ V-I If a person or animal **bounds** in a particular direction, they move quickly with large steps or jumps. ❑ *He bounded up the steps and pushed the bell of the door.* ⑤ N-COUNT A **bound** is a long or high jump. [LITERARY] ❑ *With one bound Jack was free.* ⑥ V-I If the quantity or performance of something **bounds** ahead, it increases or improves something suddenly and suddenly. ❑ *The shares bounded ahead a further 11p to 311p.* ⑦ PHRASE If a place is **out of bounds**, people are not allowed to go there. ❑ *For the last few days the area has been out of bounds to foreign journalists.* ⑧ PHRASE If something is **out of bounds**, people are not allowed to do it, use it, see it, or know about it. ❑ *American parents may soon be able to rule violent TV programs out of bounds.*

① 복수명사 범위, 도 ❑ 온도 변화는 서서히 일어나며 비교적 엄격한 범위 내에서 통제된다. ❑ 관습의 한계를 벗어나려는 의지가 있는 강한 개성을 지닌 인물 ② 타동사 -에 둘러싸이다 ❑ 키르기지아는 우즈베키스탄, 카자흐스탄, 타지키스탄에 둘러싸여 있다. ❑ 주차장을 둘러싼 나무들 ③ 수동 타동사 -으로 정의되다 ❑ 우리의 삶은 일, 가족, 텔레비전으로 정의된다. ④ 자동사 성큼성큼 뛰다, 약진하다 ❑ 그는 계단을 성큼성큼 뛰어올라가 문의 초인종을 눌렀다. ⑤ 가산명사 도약 [문예체] ❑ 한 번의 도약으로 잭은 자유를 찾았다. ⑥ 자동사 약진하다 ❑ 주가는 11포인트 더 약진해서 311포인트가 되었다. ⑦ 구 출입이 금지된 ❑ 지난 며칠간 그 지역은 외국 기자들의 출입이 금지되어 왔다. ⑧ 구 접근이 금지된 ❑ 미국의 부모들은 곧 폭력적인 텔레비전 프로그램을 차단할 수 있을지도 모른다.

boun|da|ry /ˈbaʊndəri/ (**boundaries**) ◼ N-COUNT The **boundary of** an area of land is an imaginary line that separates it from other areas. ❑ ...*the Bow Brook which forms the western boundary of the wood.* ◼ N-COUNT The **boundaries of** something such as a subject or activity are the limits that people think that it has. ❑ *The boundaries between history and storytelling are always being blurred and muddled.*

◼ 가산명사 경계 ❑ 숲의 서쪽 경계를 형성하는 보우 개천 ◼ 가산명사 경계 ❑ 역사와 이야기 사이의 경계는 항상 흐려지고 애매해진다.

Word Partnership		boundary의 연어
N.	boundary **dispute**, boundary **line** ◼	
PREP.	boundary **around places/things**, boundary **between places/things**, **beyond a** boundary, boundary **of someplace/something**, ◼	
V.	**cross a** boundary, **mark/set a** boundary ◼	

boun|ty /ˈbaʊnti/ (**bounties**) ◼ N-VAR You can refer to something that is provided in large amounts as **bounty**. [LITERARY] ❑ ...*autumn's bounty of fruits, seeds, and berries.* ◼ N-COUNT A **bounty** is money that is offered as a reward for doing something, especially for finding or killing a particular person. ❑ *A bounty of $50,000 was put on Dr. Alvarez's head.*

◼ 가산명사 또는 불가산명사 풍성함, 풍요로움 [문예체] ❑ 과일, 곡물, 장과 등 가을이 주는 풍요 ◼ 가산명사 보상금, 현상금 ❑ 알바레즈 박사의 머리에 5만 달러의 보상금이 걸려 있었다.

bou|quet /boʊˈkeɪ, buː-/ (**bouquets**) ◼ N-COUNT A **bouquet** is a bunch of flowers which is attractively arranged. ❑ *The woman carried a bouquet of dried violets.* ◼ N-VAR The **bouquet** of something, especially wine, is the pleasant smell that it has. ❑ ...*a Sicilian wine with a light red color and a bouquet of cloves.*

◼ 가산명사 부케 ❑ 그 여자는 말린 제비꽃 부케를 들고 있었다. ◼ 가산명사 또는 불가산명사 향기 ❑ 엷은 붉은 색을 띠면서 정향나무의 향기가 나는 시칠리아산 와인

bour|geois /ˈbʊərʒwɑ/ ADJ If you describe people, their way of life, or their attitudes as **bourgeois**, you disapprove of them because you consider them typical of conventional middle-class people. [DISAPPROVAL] ❑ *He's accusing them of having a bourgeois and limited vision.*

형용사 소시민의 [탐탁찮음] ❑ 그는 그들이 소시민적이고 편협한 시야를 가졌다고 비난하고 있다.

bout /baʊt/ (**bouts**) ◼ N-COUNT If you have a **bout of** an illness or of an unpleasant feeling, you have it for a short period. ❑ *He was recovering from a severe bout of flu.* ◼ N-COUNT A **bout of** something that is unpleasant is a short time during which it occurs a great deal. ❑ *The latest bout of violence has claimed twenty four lives.* ◼ N-COUNT A **bout** is a boxing or wrestling match. ❑ *This will be his eighth title bout in 19 months.*

◼ 가산명사 한 바탕 ❑ 그는 한 바탕 심한 독감을 앓고 회복하는 중이었다. ◼ 가산명사 한 바탕 ❑ 최근에 있은 한 바탕 폭력 사태로 24명이 사망했습니다. ◼ 가산명사 시합 ❑ 이번 시합은 그가 19개월 동안 여덟 번째 치르는 타이틀전이 될 것이다.

bou|tique /buːˈtik/ (**boutiques**) N-COUNT A **boutique** is a small store that sells fashionable clothes, shoes, or jewelry.

가산명사 부티크

bow
① BENDING OR SUBMITTING
② PART OF A SHIP
③ OBJECTS

① **bow** /baʊ/ (**bows, bowing, bowed**) ◼ V-I When you **bow to** someone, you briefly bend your body toward them as a formal way of greeting them or showing respect. ❑ *They bowed low to Louis and hastened out of his way.* ● N-COUNT **Bow** is also a noun. ❑ *I gave a theatrical bow and waved.* ◼ V-T If you **bow** your head, you bend it downward so that you are looking toward the ground, for example because you want to show respect or because you are thinking deeply about something. ❑ *The Colonel bowed his head and whispered a prayer of thanksgiving.* ◼ V-I If you **bow to** pressure or to someone's wishes, you agree to do what they want you to do. ❑ *Some shops are bowing to consumer pressure and stocking organically grown vegetables.*

◼ 자동사 (고개 숙여) 인사하다, 절하다 ❑ 그들은 루이스에게 허리를 굽혀 인사한 다음 그의 면전에서 서둘러 물러났다. ● 가산명사 (고개를 숙이는) 인사, 절 ❑ 나는 배우처럼 고개를 숙여 절을 한 다음 손을 흔들었다. ◼ 타동사 (고개를) 숙이다 ❑ 대령은 고개를 숙이고 감사의 기도를 속삭였다. ◼ 자동사 굴복하다 ❑ 일부 가게들이 소비자들의 압력에 굴복해서 유기농 채소를 갖다 놓고 있다.

▶ **bow out** PHRASAL VERB If you **bow out** of something, you stop taking part in it. [WRITTEN] ❑ *He had bowed out gracefully when his successor had been appointed.*

구동사 물러나다 [문어체] ❑ 후임자가 임명되자 그는 품위 있게 물러났다.

② **bow** /baʊ/ (**bows**) N-COUNT The front part of a ship is called **the bow** or **the bows**. The plural **bows** can be used to refer either to one or to more than one of these parts. ❑ *The waves were about five feet now, and the bow of the boat was leaping up and down.*

가산명사 이물, 뱃머리 ❑ 파도 높이가 이제는 5피트 정도 되었으며 뱃머리가 아래위로 춤추고 있었다.

③ **bow** /boʊ/ (**bows**) ◼ N-COUNT A **bow** is a knot with two loops and two loose ends that is used in tying shoelaces and ribbons. ❑ *Add a length of ribbon tied in a bow.* ◼ N-COUNT A **bow** is a weapon for shooting arrows which consists of a long piece of curved wood with a string attached to both its ends. ❑ *Some of the raiders were armed with bows and arrows.* ◼ N-COUNT The **bow** of a violin or other stringed instrument is a long thin piece of wood with fibers stretched along it, which you move across the strings of the instrument in order to play it.

◼ 가산명사 나비매듭 ❑ 나비 매듭으로 묶은 리본을 달아라. ◼ 가산명사 활 ❑ 침략자 몇은 활과 화살로 무장하고 있었다. ◼ 가산명사 활

bowed
Pronounced /boʊd/ for meaning ◼, and /baʊd/ for meaning ◼.

◼의 의미일 때는 /boʊd/로, ◼의 의미일 때는 /baʊd/로 발음된다.

◼ ADJ Something that is **bowed** is curved. ❑ ...*an old lady with bowed legs.* ◼ ADJ If a person's body is **bowed**, it is bent forward. ❑ *He walked aimlessly along street after street, head down and shoulders bowed.*

◼ 형용사 휘어진 ❑ 다리가 휘어진 할머니 ◼ 형용사 구부정한 ❑ 그는 고개를 숙이고 어깨가 축 처진 채 정처 없이 길거리를 배회했다.

bow|el /ˈbaʊəl/ (**bowels**) N-COUNT Your **bowels** are the tubes in your body through which digested food passes from your stomach to your anus. ❑ *Symptoms such as stomach pains and irritable bowels can be signs of bowel cancer.*

가산명사 내장 ❑ 복통이나 뱃속이 불편한 것과 같은 증상은 내장에 암이 있다는 징후일 수 있다.

bowl ♦◇◇ /boʊl/ (**bowls, bowling, bowled**) ◼ N-COUNT A **bowl** is a round container with a wide uncovered top. Some kinds of bowl are used, for example, for serving or eating food from, or in cooking, while other larger kinds are used for washing or cleaning. ❑ *Put all the ingredients into a large bowl.* ◼ N-COUNT The contents of a bowl can be referred to as a **bowl of** something. ❑ ...*a bowl of soup.* ◼ N-COUNT You can refer to the hollow rounded part of an object as its **bowl**. ❑ *He smacked the bowl of his pipe into his hand.* ◼ V-T/V-I In a sport such as cricket, when a bowler **bowls** a ball, he or she sends it down the

◼ 가산명사 사발 ❑ 모든 재료를 큰 사발에 담으세요. ◼ 가산명사 사발 ❑ 수프 한 사발 ◼ 가산명사 사발처럼 생긴 부분 ❑ 그는 파이프 윗부분을 손에 대고 털었다. ◼ 타동사/자동사 투구하다 ❑ 공을 저렇게 던지는 이유를 모르겠다. ◼ 자동사 앞으로 볼나 ❑ 차가

field toward a batsman. ❑ *I can't see the point of bowling a ball like that.* **5** V-I If you **bowl along** in a car or on a boat, you move along very quickly, especially when you are enjoying yourself. ❑ *Veronica looked at him, smiling, as they bowled along.* **6** →see also **bowling**

달려나가자 베로니카가 그를 웃으며 바라봤다.

bow|ler /ˈboʊlər/ (**bowlers**) N-COUNT The **bowler** in a sport such as cricket is the player who is bowling the ball. ❑ *He's a rather good fast bowler.*

가산명사 투수 ❑ 그는 상당히 빠르고 좋은 투수이다.

bowl|ing /ˈboʊlɪŋ/ **1** N-UNCOUNT **Bowling** is a game in which you roll a heavy ball down a narrow track toward a group of wooden objects and try to knock down as many of them as possible. ❑ *I go bowling for relaxation.* **2** N-UNCOUNT In a sport such as cricket, **bowling** is the action or activity of bowling the ball toward the batsman. ❑ *Much of the bowling today will be done by Phil Tufnell.*

1 불가산명사 볼링 ❑ 나는 휴식을 위해 볼링을 하러 간다. **2** 불가산명사 투구 ❑ 오늘의 투구 대부분은 필 터프넬이 할 것입니다.

box ♦♦♢ /bɒks/ (**boxes, boxing, boxed**) **1** N-COUNT A **box** is a square or rectangular container with hard or stiff sides. Boxes often have lids. ❑ *He reached into the cardboard box beside him.* ❑ *They sat on wooden boxes.* ● N-COUNT A **box** of something is an amount of it contained in a box. ❑ *She ate two boxes of chocolates.* **2** N-COUNT A **box** is a square or rectangle that is printed or drawn on a piece of paper, a road, or on some other surface. ❑ *For more information, just tick the box and send us the form overleaf.* **3** N-COUNT A **box** is a small separate area in a theater or at a sports ground or stadium, where a small number of people can sit to watch the performance or game. ❑ *The entire Manchester United team, plus wives and girlfriends, have hired a private box.* **4** N-COUNT **Box** is used before a number as a mailing address by people or organizations that receive a lot of mail. ❑ *...Country Crafts, Box 111, Landisville.* **5** N-SING Television is sometimes referred to as **the box**. [BRIT, INFORMAL] ❑ *Do you watch it live at all or do you watch it on the box?* **6** V-I To **box** means to fight someone according to the rules of boxing. ❑ *At school I boxed and played rugby.* **7** →see also **boxing, post office box**

1 가산명사 상자 ❑ 그는 옆에 있는 종이 상자 안으로 손을 넣었다. ❑ 그들은 나무 상자 위에 앉아 있었다. ● 가산명사 상자 ❑ 그녀는 초콜릿 두 상자를 먹었다. **2** 가산명사 네모 ❑ 정보가 더 필요하시면 네모 부분에 표시를 하신 후 뒷면의 양식을 보내주십시오. **3** 가산명사 특별석 구역, 박스 ❑ 부인들과 여자 친구들까지 포함한 맨체스터 유나이티드 팀 전체가 전용 특별석 구역을 빌렸다. **4** 가산명사 사서함 ❑ 랜디스빌, 사서함 111, 컨트리 공예 **5** 단수명사 텔레비전 [영국영어, 비격식체] ❑ 혹시 현장에서 직접 보나 아니면 텔레비전으로 보나 **6** 자동사 권투 하다 ❑ 학교에서 나는 권투와 럭비를 했다.

▶**box in** **1** PHRASAL VERB If you **are boxed in**, you are unable to move from a particular place because you are surrounded by other people or cars. ❑ *The black cabs cut in front of them, trying to box them in.* **2** PHRASAL VERB If something **boxes** you **in**, it puts you in a situation where you have very little choice about what you can do. ❑ *We are not trying to box anybody in, we are trying to find a satisfactory way forward.*

1 구동사 간히다 ❑ 검은색 택시들이 그들을 가두기 위해 앞으로 끼어들었다. **2** 구동사 제한하다 ❑ 우리는 어느 누구의 자유도 제한할 생각은 없으며 단지 만족스럽게 진전할 수 있는 방법을 찾고자 하는 것뿐입니다.

box|er /ˈbɒksər/ (**boxers**) N-COUNT A **boxer** is someone who takes part in the sport of boxing.

가산명사 권투 선수

box|ing /ˈbɒksɪŋ/ N-UNCOUNT **Boxing** is a sport in which two people wearing large leather gloves fight according to special rules.

불가산명사 권투

box lunch (**box lunches**) N-COUNT A **box lunch** is food packed in a box, for example a sandwich, which you buy and eat as your lunch. [AM; BRIT **packed lunch**] ❑ *Box lunches can be arranged to take with you on day trips into the Valley.*

가산명사 도시락 [미국영어; 영국영어 packed lunch] ❑ 그 계곡을 하루 동안 여행할 때는 가지고 갈 수 있는 도시락을 마련해 드릴 수 있습니다.

box num|ber (**box numbers**) N-COUNT A **box number** is a number used as an address, for example one given by a newspaper for replies to a private advertisement, or one used by an organization for the letters sent to it. ❑ *In a print shop, he produced 1000 leaflets tagged with his phone number and a post office box number.*

가산명사 사서함 번호 ❑ 인쇄소에서 그는 자신의 전화번호와 사서함 번호가 찍힌 전단을 1,000 장 뽑았다.

box of|fice (**box offices**) also **box-office** **1** N-COUNT The **box office** in a theater or concert hall is the place where the tickets are sold. ❑ *...the long line of people outside the box-office.* **2** N-SING When people talk about **the box office**, they are referring to the degree of success of a film or play in terms of the number of people who go to watch it or the amount of money it makes. ❑ *The film has taken £180 million at the box office.*

1 가산명사 매표소 ❑ 매표소 밖의 장사진 **2** 단수명사 박스 오피스 ❑ 그 영화의 박스 오피스 수익은 1억 8천만 파운드이다.

boy ♦♦♦ /bɔɪ/ (**boys**) **1** N-COUNT A **boy** is a child who will grow up to be a man. ❑ *He was still just a boy.* **2** N-COUNT You can refer to a young man as a **boy**, especially when talking about relationships between boys and girls. ❑ *...the age when girls get interested in boys.* **3** N-COUNT Someone's **boy** is their son. [INFORMAL] ❑ *Eric was my cousin Edward's boy.* **4** N-COUNT You can refer to a man as a **boy**, especially when you are talking about him in an affectionate way. [INFORMAL, FEELINGS] ❑ *...the local boy who made President.* **5** EXCLAM Some people say "**boy**" or "**oh boy**" in order to express feelings of excitement or admiration. [mainly AM, INFORMAL, FEELINGS] ❑ *Oh boy! what resourceful children I have.*

1 가산명사 소년, 남자애 ❑ 그는 아직도 소년에 불과했다. **2** 가산명사 남자애 ❑ 여자애들이 남자애들에게 관심을 갖기 시작하는 나이 **3** 가산명사 아들 [비격식체] ❑ 에릭은 내 사촌 에드워드의 아들이었다. **4** 가산명사 남자 [비격식체, 감정 개입] ❑ 대통령이 된 이 고장 출신 남자 **5** 감탄사 아 [주로 미국영어, 비격식체, 감정 개입] ❑ 와! 내 아이들은 정말 기지가 풍부한 것 같아.

boy|cott /ˈbɔɪkɒt/ (**boycotts, boycotting, boycotted**) V-T If a country, group, or person **boycotts** a country, organization, or activity, they refuse to be involved with it in any way because they disapprove of it. ❑ *The main opposition parties are boycotting the elections.* ● N-COUNT **Boycott** is also a noun. ❑ *Opposition leaders had called for a boycott of the vote.*

타동사 보이콧하다 ❑ 주요 야당들이 선거를 보이콧하고 있다. ● 가산명사 보이콧 ❑ 야당 지도자들이 투표에 대한 보이콧을 요청했었다.

boy|friend /ˈbɔɪfrɛnd/ (**boyfriends**) N-COUNT Someone's **boyfriend** is a man or boy with whom they are having a romantic or sexual relationship. ❑ *...Brenda and her boyfriend Anthony.*

가산명사 남자 친구 ❑ 브렌다와 그녀의 남자 친구 앤터니

A **boyfriend** is the male person in a romantic relationship. It is not used to describe friendship between men. This is different from **girlfriend**, which can describe either a friendship or a romance.

boyfriend는 애인 사이인 남자를 가리킨다. 이 단어는 남자끼리의 친구 사이에는 쓰지 않는다. 이 점이 girlfriend의 경우와는 다른데, girlfriend는 친구 사이에든 연인 사이에든 쓸 수 있다.

boy|hood /ˈbɔɪhʊd/ N-UNCOUNT **Boyhood** is the period of a male person's life during which he is a boy. ❑ *He has been a Derby County supporter since boyhood.*

불가산명사 소년기, 어릴 때 ❑ 그는 어릴 적부터 더비 지역 팀의 지지자였다.

boy|ish /ˈbɔɪɪʃ/ **1** ADJ If you describe a man as **boyish**, you mean that he is like a boy in his appearance or behavior, and you find this characteristic quite attractive. [APPROVAL] ❑ *She was relieved to see his face light up with a boyish grin.* ● **boy|ish|ly** ADV ❑ *John grinned boyishly.* **2** ADJ If you describe a girl or woman as **boyish**, you mean that she looks like a boy, for example because she has short hair or small breasts. ❑ *...her tall, boyish figure.*

1 형용사 소년 같은 [마음에 듦] ❑ 그의 얼굴이 소년 같이 천진한 미소로 밝아지는 것을 보고 그녀는 안도했다. ● 소년 같이 부사 ❑ 존은 소년처럼 씩 웃었다. **2** 형용사 사내아이 같은 ❑ 그녀의 중성적인 장신의 체구

a
b
c
d
e
f
g
h
i
j
k
l
m
n
o
p
q
r
s
t
u
v
w
x
y
z

bps /ˌbiː piː ˈɛs/ **bps** is a measurement of the speed at which computer data is transferred, for example by a modem. **bps** is an abbreviation for "bits per second." [COMPUTING] ❑ *A minimum 28,800 bps modem is probably the slowest you'll want to put up with.*

비피시, 초당 비트 전송율 [컴퓨터] ❑ 28,800비피에스 모뎀이 일반적으로 견딜 수 있는 최소한의 속도의 장비이다.

bra /brɑ/ (**bras**) A bra is a piece of underwear that women wear to support their breasts.

브래지어

brace /breɪs/ (**braces, bracing, braced**) **1** V-T If you **brace yourself for** something unpleasant or difficult, you prepare yourself for it. ❑ *He braced himself for the icy plunge into the black water.* **2** V-T If you **brace yourself against** something or **brace** part of your body **against** it, you press against something in order to steady your body or to avoid falling. ❑ *Elaine braced herself against the dresser and looked in the mirror.* **3** V-T If you **brace** your shoulders or knees, you keep them stiffly in a particular position. ❑ *He braced his shoulders defiantly as another squall of wet snow slashed across his face.* **4** V-T To **brace** something means to strengthen or support it with something else. ❑ *Overhead, the lights showed the old timbers, used to brace the roof.* **5** N-COUNT A **brace** is a device attached to a part of a person's body, for example to a weak leg, in order to strengthen or support it. ❑ *He wore leg braces after polio in childhood.* **6** N-COUNT A **brace** is a metal device that can be fastened to a child's teeth in order to help them grow straight. ❑ *Her parents should've made her wear a brace.* **7** N-COUNT **Braces** or **curly braces** are a pair of written marks {} that you place around words, numbers, or parts of a computer code, for example to indicate that they are connected in some way or are separate from other parts of the writing or code. [AM; BRIT usually **curly brackets**] **8** N-PLURAL **Braces** are a pair of straps that pass over your shoulders and fasten to your pants at the front and back in order to stop them from falling down. [BRIT; AM **suspenders**] ❑ *...a thin bald man in braces and shirtsleeves.* →see **teeth**

1 타동사 마음의 준비를 하다 ❑ 그는 얼음처럼 차가운 검은 물 속으로 들어가기 위해 마음의 준비를 했다. **2** 타동사 -에 대고 몸을 지탱하다 ❑ 일레인은 화장대에 몸을 기대고 거울을 들여다보았다. **3** 타동사 꼿꼿이 하다 ❑ 젖은 눈을 실은 돌풍이 또 한 차례 얼굴을 스치고 지나가자 남자는 반항하듯이 어깨에 힘을 주었다. **4** 타동사 보강하다 ❑ 머리 위로 불빛 속에 지붕을 받치고 있는 오래된 목재들이 보였다. **5** 가산명사 보호대 ❑ 그는 어렸을 때 소아마비에 걸린 이후 다리에 보호대를 찼다. **6** 가산명사 치열 교정기 ❑ 부모들이 그녀가 교정기를 쓰도록 했어야 했다. **7** 가산명사 중괄호 [미국영어; 영국영어 대개 curly brackets] **8** 복수명사 멜빵 [영국영어; 미국영어 suspenders] ❑ 셔츠만 입고 멜빵을 멘 머리가 벗겨진 여윈 남자

brace|let /breɪslɪt/ (**bracelets**) N-COUNT A **bracelet** is a chain or band, usually made of metal, which you wear around your wrist as jewelry. →see **jewelry**

가산명사 팔찌

brac|ing /breɪsɪŋ/ ADJ If you describe something, especially a place, climate, or activity as **bracing**, you mean that it makes you feel fresh and full of energy. ❑ *...a bracing walk.*

형용사 상쾌한 ❑ 상쾌한 산책

brack|et /brækɪt/ (**brackets, bracketing, bracketed**) **1** N-COUNT If you say that someone or something is in a particular **bracket**, you mean that they come within a particular range, for example a range of incomes, ages, or prices. ❑ *...a 33% tax rate on everyone in these high-income brackets.* **2** N-COUNT **Brackets** are pieces of metal, wood, or plastic that are fastened to a wall in order to support something such as a shelf. ❑ *Fix the beam with the brackets and screws.* **3** V-T If two or more people or things **are bracketed together**, they are considered to be similar or related in some way. ❑ *The Magi, Bramins, and Druids were bracketed together as men of wisdom.* **4** N-COUNT **Brackets** are a pair of written marks that you place around a word, expression, or sentence in order to indicate that you are giving extra information. In British English, curved marks used in this way are called **brackets**, but in American English, they are called **parentheses**. ❑ *The prices in brackets are special rates for the under 18s.* **5** N-COUNT **Brackets** are pair of marks that are placed around a series of symbols in a mathematical expression to indicate that those symbols function as one item within the expression.

1 가산명사 집단 ❑ 이런 고소득 집단에 속하는 사람들에 대한 33퍼센트의 최고 세율 **2** 가산명사 까치발, 브래킷 ❑ 까치발과 나사로 들보를 고정하세요. **3** 타동사 (동류로) 분류되다 ❑ 마기족, 브라민, 드루이드 등은 현자로 분류되었다. **4** 가산명사 괄호 ❑ 괄호 안의 가격은 열여덟 살 미만을 위한 특별 가격이다. **5** 가산명사 괄호

brag /bræɡ/ (**brags, bragging, bragged**) V-I If you **brag**, you say in a very proud way that you have something or have done something. [DISAPPROVAL] ❑ *He's always bragging about his prowess as a cricketer.* ❑ *He'll probably go around bragging to his friends.*

타동사/자동사 자랑하다 [탐탁잖음] ❑ 그는 자신이 얼마나 크리켓을 잘하는지 항상 자랑하고 다닌다. ❑ 그는 아마도 친구들에게 자랑하고 다닐 것이다.

braid /breɪd/ (**braids, braiding, braided**) **1** N-UNCOUNT **Braid** is a narrow piece of decorated cloth or twisted threads, which is used to decorate clothes or curtains. ❑ *...a plum-colored uniform with lots of gold braid.* **2** V-T If you **braid** hair or a group of threads, you twist three or more lengths of the hair or threads over and under each other to make one thick length. [AM; BRIT **plait**] ❑ *She had almost finished braiding Louisa's hair.* **3** N-COUNT A **braid** is a length of hair which has been divided into three or more lengths and then braided. [AM; BRIT **plait**] ❑ *...a short, energetic woman with her hair in braids.*

1 불가산명사 노끈, 끈 ❑ 금빛 끈 장식이 많이 달린 자두색 제복 **2** 타동사 땋다 [미국영어; 영국영어 plait] ❑ 그녀가 루이사의 머리를 땋는 것을 거의 마친 상태였다. **3** 가산명사 땋은 머리 [미국영어; 영국영어 plait] ❑ 머리를 땋은 작은 키의 활동적인 여자

brain ♦♦◇ /breɪn/ (**brains**) **1** N-COUNT Your **brain** is the organ inside your head that controls your body's activities and enables you to think and to feel things such as heat and pain. ❑ *Her father died of a brain tumor.* **2** N-COUNT Your **brain** is your mind and the way that you think. ❑ *Once you stop using your brain you soon go stale.* **3** N-COUNT If someone has **brains** or a good **brain**, they have the ability to learn and understand things quickly, to solve problems, and to make good decisions. ❑ *They were not the only ones to have brains and ambition.* **4** N-COUNT If someone is **the brains** behind an idea or an organization, he or she had that idea or makes the important decisions about how that organization is managed. [INFORMAL] ❑ *Mr. White was the brains behind the scheme.* **5** to **rack** your **brains** →see **rack** →see **nervous system** →see Word Web: **brain**

1 가산명사 뇌 ❑ 그녀의 아버지는 뇌종양으로 사망했다. **2** 가산명사 머리 ❑ 머리 쓰기를 멈추는 순간 창의력이 곧 사라진다. **3** 가산명사 머리 ❑ 좋은 머리와 야망을 가진 사람들은 그들뿐이 아니었다. **4** 가산명사 두뇌 [비격식체] ❑ 화이트 씨가 그 계획 뒤의 두뇌 역할을 했다.

brain|child /breɪntʃaɪld/ also **brain-child** N-SING Someone's **brainchild** is an idea or invention that they have thought up or created. ❑ *The record was the brainchild of rock star Bob Geldof.*

단수명사 창작물 ❑ 그 음반은 록 가수 밥 겔도프의 아이디어가 낳은 것이었다.

brain|storm /breɪnstɔrm/ (**brainstorms, brainstorming, brainstormed**) **1** N-COUNT If you have a **brainstorm**, you suddenly have a clever idea. [AM; BRIT usually **brainwave**] ❑ *"Look," she said, getting a brainstorm, "Why don't you invite them here?"* **2** V-T/V-I If a group of people **brainstorm**, they have a meeting in which they all put forward as many ideas and suggestions as they can think of. ❑ *The women meet twice a month to brainstorm and set business goals for each other.* ● **brain|storming** N-UNCOUNT ❑ *Le Shuttle was chosen after hundreds of other ideas*

1 가산명사 (갑자기 떠오른) 좋은 생각 [미국영어; 영국영어 대개 brainwave] ❑ "그들을 여기로 초대하는 게 어때?"라고 좋은 생각이 났다는 듯 그녀가 말했다. **2** 타동사/자동사 브레인스토밍 하다 ❑ 여자들은 한 달에 두 번 만나 브레인스토밍을 하며 서로에 대한 사업 목표를 수립한다. ● 브레인스토밍 불가산명사 ❑ 2년간의 브레인스토밍 끝에 수백 개의 아이디어가

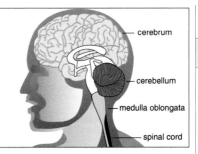

Word Web brain

The human **brain** weighs about three pounds. It contains seven distinct sections. The largest are the cerebrum, the cerebellum, and the medulla oblongata. The cerebrum wraps around the outside of the brain. It handles **learning**, **communication**, and voluntary **movement**. The cerebellum controls **balance**, **posture**, and movement. The medulla oblongata links the spinal cord with other parts of the brain. This part of the brain controls automatic actions such as breathing, heartbeat, and swallowing. It also tells us when we are hungry and when we need to sleep.

had been tried and discarded during two years of brainstorming. **3** N-COUNT If you have a **brainstorm**, you suddenly become unable to think clearly. [BRIT] ❑ *I can have a brainstorm and be very extravagant.*

brain|wash /breɪnwɒʃ/ (**brainwashes, brainwashing, brainwashed**) V-T If you **brainwash** someone, you force them to believe something by continually telling them that it is true, and preventing them from thinking about it properly. ❑ *They brainwash people into giving up all their money.*

brain|wave /breɪnweɪv/ (**brainwaves**) N-COUNT If you have a **brainwave**, you suddenly have a clever idea. [BRIT; AM **brainstorm**] ❑ *In 1980 she had a brainwave that changed her life.*

brake /breɪk/ (**brakes, braking, braked**) **1** N-COUNT **Brakes** are devices in a vehicle that make it go slower or stop. ❑ *A seagull swooped down in front of her car, causing her to slam on the brakes.* **2** V-T/V-I When a vehicle or its driver **brakes**, or when a driver **brakes** a vehicle, the driver makes it slow down or stop by using the brakes. ❑ *He heard tires squeal as the car braked to avoid a collision.* ❑ *He lit a cigarette and braked the car slightly.* **3** N-COUNT You can use **brake** in a number of expressions to indicate that something has slowed down or stopped. ❑ *Illness had put a brake on his progress.*

bran /bræn/ N-UNCOUNT **Bran** is the outer skin of grain that is left when the grain has been used to make flour. ❑ *...oat bran.*

branch ◆◇◇ /brɑːntʃ/ (**branches, branching, branched**) **1** N-COUNT The **branches** of a tree are the parts that grow out from its trunk and have leaves, flowers, or fruit growing on them. ❑ *...the upper branches of a row of pines.* **2** N-COUNT A **branch** of a business or other organization is one of the offices, stores, or groups which belong to it and which are located in different places. ❑ *The local branch of Bank of America is handling the accounts.* **3** N-COUNT A **branch of** an organization such as the government or the police force is a department that has a particular function. ❑ *Senate employees could take their employment grievances to another branch of government.* ❑ *He had a fascination for submarines and joined this branch of the service.* **4** N-COUNT A **branch of** a subject is a part or type of it. ❑ *Whole branches of science may not receive any grants.* **5** N-COUNT A **branch of** your family is a group of its members who are descended from one particular person. ❑ *This is one of the branches of the Roosevelt family.*

▶**branch off** PHRASAL VERB A road or path that **branches off** from another one starts from it and goes in a slightly different direction. If you **branch off** somewhere, you change the direction in which you are going. ❑ *After a few miles, a small road branched off to the right.*

▶**branch out** PHRASAL VERB If a person or an organization **branches out**, they do something that is different from their normal activities or work. ❑ *I continued studying moths, and branched out to other insects.*

brand ◆◇◇ /brænd/ (**brands, branding, branded**) **1** N-COUNT A **brand** of a product is the version of it that is made by one particular manufacturer. ❑ *Winston is a brand of cigarette.* ❑ *I bought one of the leading brands.* **2** N-COUNT A **brand** of something such as a way of thinking or behaving is a particular kind of it. ❑ *The British brand of socialism was more interested in reform than revolution.* **3** V-T If someone **is branded** as something bad, people think they are that thing. ❑ *I was instantly branded as a rebel.* ❑ *The company has been branded racist by some of its own staff.* **4** V-T When you **brand** an animal, you put a permanent mark on its skin in order to show who it belongs to, usually by burning a mark onto its skin. ❑ *The owner couldn't be bothered to brand the cattle.* ● N-COUNT **Brand** is also a noun. ❑ *A brand was a mark of ownership burned into the hide of an animal with a hot iron.*

The **brand** of a product such as jeans, tea, or soap is its name, which can also be the name of the company that makes or sells it. The **make** of a car or electrical appliance such as a radio or washing machine is the name of the company that produces it. If you talk about what **type** of product or service you want, you are talking about its quality and what features it should have. You can also talk about **types** of people or of abstract things. ❑ *...which type of coffeemaker to choose....a new type of bank account....looking for a certain type of actor.* A **model** of car or of some other devices is a name that is given to a particular type, for example, Ford Escort or Nissan Micra. Note that **type** can also be used informally to mean either **make** or **model**. For example, if someone asks what **type** of car you have got, you could reply "an SUV," "a Ford," or perhaps "an Escort."

시도되고 버려진 이후 '르 셔틀'이 선정되었다. **3** 가산명사 정신 착란 [영국영어] ❑ 나는 갑자기 정신 착란을 일으켜서 심한 낭비를 하는 경우가 있다.

타동사 세뇌하다 ❑ 그들은 사람들이 모든 돈을 내놓도록 세뇌한다.

가산명사 영감 [영국영어; 미국영어 brainstorm] ❑ 1980년에 그녀는 자신의 인생을 바꿔 버린 영감을 얻었다.

1 가산명사 브레이크 ❑ 갈매기들이 차 앞으로 날아 내려와서 그녀는 급히 브레이크를 밟아야 했다. **2** 타동사/자동사 브레이크를 밟다 ❑ 충돌을 피하기 위해 브레이크를 밟자 타이어가 끼익하는 소리가 들렸다. ❑ 그는 담배에 불을 붙이고 차의 브레이크를 살짝 밟았다. **3** 가산명사 제동 ❑ 병이 그의 진로에 제동을 걸었었다.

불가산명사 겨 ❑ 귀리의 겨

1 가산명사 가지 ❑ 늘어선 소나무의 위쪽 가지들 **2** 가산명사 지국, 지점 ❑ 아메리카 은행 지점에서 그 계좌들을 취급하고 있다. **3** 가산명사 분과, 부문 ❑ 상원에 고용된 사람들은 고용상의 불만을 정부의 다른 분과로 가져갈 수 있다. ❑ 그는 잠수함에 매료되어 이 병과에 입대했다. **4** 가산명사 분야 ❑ 모든 과학 분야가 어떤 보조금도 받지 못할 수도 있다. **5** 가산명사 분가 ❑ 이것은 루즈벨트 집안의 분가 중 하나이다.

구동사 갈라져 나오다; 다른 길로 들다 ❑ 몇 마일 지나자, 길이 갈라지면서 오른쪽으로 작은 길이 나 있었다.

구동사 다른 일을 벌이다 ❑ 나는 계속 나방을 연구하며, 다른 곤충들로도 손을 뻗쳤다.

1 가산명사 특정 상표의 제품, 브랜드 ❑ 윈스턴은 담배 브랜드이다. ❑ 나는 일류 브랜드 중 한 곳의 제품을 샀다. **2** 가산명사 특정 종류 ❑ 영국식 사회주의는 혁명보다 개혁에 더 관심을 두었다. **3** 타동사 오명을 뒤집어 쓰다 ❑ 나는 즉각 반역자라는 오명을 뒤집어썼다. ❑ 그 회사는 직원들 일부로부터 인종 차별적이라는 오명을 들어왔다. **4** 타동사 낙인을 찍다 ❑ 가축에 낙인을 찍으라고 주인에게 강요할 수는 없었다. ● 가산명사 낙인 ❑ 낙인은 뜨거운 인두로 짐승의 가죽을 지져 소유를 나타내는 표시였다.

청바지, 차, 비누와 같은 상품의 brand는 그 상품의 이름인데, 상품명이 그것을 만들거나 파는 회사명일 수도 있다. 자동차 또는 라디오나 세탁기 같은 전기제품의 make는 그것을 생산하는 회사명이다. 원하는 상품이나 서비스의 type을 얘기하는 것은 그 상품이나 서비스가 지녀야 할 품질이나 특성을 말하는 것이다. 사람이나 추상적 사물에 대해서도 type을 말할 수 있다. ❑ ...어떤 종류의 커피 메이커를 선택할지....새로운 종류의 은행 계좌....어떤 특정한 유형의 배우를 찾는. 자동차나 다른 일부 장치의 model은 특정 type에 붙여진 이름으로, 예를 들면 포드 에스코트나 니산 마이크라와 같은 것이다. type은 또한 비격식체로 make나 model을 뜻할 수도 있다. 예를 들어 어떤 type의 자동차를 가지고 있느냐고 누가 물으면, "스포츠 유틸리티 차량," 또는 "포드," 또는 "에스코트"라고 대답할 수 있다.

A

brand|ed /brǽndɪd/ ADJ A **branded** product is one which is made by a well-known manufacturer and has the manufacturer's label on it. [BUSINESS] [ADJ n] ❏ *Supermarket lines are often cheaper than branded goods.*

형용사 유명 상표의 [경제] ❏ 슈퍼마켓에서 파는 물건들은 유명 상표보다 싼 경우가 많다.

B

brand im|age (**brand images**) N-COUNT The **brand image** of a particular brand of a product is the image or impression that people have of it, usually created by advertising. [BUSINESS] ❏ *Few products have brand images anywhere near as strong as Levi's.*

가산명사 브랜드 이미지 [경제] ❏ 리바이스에 비견될 만큼 강력한 브랜드 이미지를 가진 상품은 거의 없다.

C

bran|dish /brǽndɪʃ/ (**brandishes, brandishing, brandished**) V-T If you **brandish** something, especially a weapon, you hold it in a threatening way. ❏ *He appeared in the lounge brandishing a knife.*

타동사 휘두르다, 쳐들다 ❏ 그는 칼을 휘두르며 휴게실에 나타났다.

D

brand lead|er (**brand leaders**) N-COUNT The **brand leader** of a particular product is the brand of it that most people choose to buy. [BUSINESS] ❏ *In office supplies, we're the brand leader.*

가산명사 (특정 상품 분야의) 선두 주자 [경제] ❏ 사무용품 분야에서는, 우리 회사가 선두 주자이다.

E

brand name (**brand names**) N-COUNT The **brand name** of a product is the name the manufacturer gives it and under which it is sold. [BUSINESS] ❏ *When it comes to soft drinks Coca-Cola is the biggest selling brand name in Britain.*

가산명사 상표명 [경제] ❏ 청량음료 분야에서는 코카콜라가 영국에서 가장 많이 팔리는 상표이다.

F

The maker of a product may come to be identified so closely with it that all products of that sort are called by the same name. For example, tissue paper for blowing your nose is branded as Kleenex and so people often call all brands of tissue "Kleenex" rather than "tissue." "My nose is running. Please give me a Kleenex." The "Trademark" label in this dictionary will show you brands which are commonly used in this way.

한 상품의 제조사가 그 상품 자체와 동일시되어 그런 종류의 모든 상품이 그 제조사의 이름으로 불리는 경우가 있다. 예를 들면, 코를 푸는 데 사용하는 화장지가 '클리넥스(Kleenex)'라는 상표로 불리자 사람들이 흔히 다른 모든 상표의 화장지를 '화장지'라고 하지 않고 '클리넥스'라고 부른다. "세가 코가 나오네. 크리넥스 좀 주세요."처럼, 이 사전에서 'Trademark'라는 표시는 이런 식으로 흔히 사용되는 상표를 가리킨다.

G

H

I

brand-name prod|uct /brǽndŋeɪm/ (**brand-name product**) N-COUNT A **brand-name product** is one which is made by a well-known manufacturer and has the manufacturer's label on it. [BUSINESS] ❏ *In buying footwear, 66% prefer brand-name products.*

가산명사 유명 상품 [경제] ❏ 신발류를 구입할 때, 66퍼센트가 유명 상품을 선호한다.

J

brand-new ADJ A **brand-new** object is completely new. ❏ *Yesterday he went off to buy himself a brand-new car.*

형용사 신품의 ❏ 어제 그는 말없이 사라져 새 차를 샀다.

brandy /brǽndi/ (**brandies**) **1** N-MASS **Brandy** is a strong alcoholic drink. It is often drunk after a meal. **2** N-COUNT A **brandy** is a glass of brandy. ❏ *After a couple of brandies Michael started telling me his life story.*

1 물질명사 브랜디 **2** 가산명사 브랜디 한 잔 ❏ 브랜디를 두 잔 마신 다음 마이클은 내게 자신이 살아온 이야기를 해 주기 시작했다.

K

brash /brǽʃ/ (**brasher, brashest**) ADJ If you describe someone or their behavior as **brash**, you disapprove of them because you think that they are too confident and aggressive. [DISAPPROVAL] ❏ *On stage she seems hard, brash and uncompromising.* • **brash|ly** ADV ❏ *I brashly announced to the group that NATO needed to be turned around.*

형용사 성마른, 경솔한 [탐탁잖음] ❏ 무대 위의 그녀는 엄하고 성마르면 완고해 보인다. • 경솔하게, 무모하게 부사 ❏ 나는 그 단체에게 무모하게 북대서양조약기구가 태도를 바꾸도록 할 필요가 있다고 공표했다.

L

brass /brǽs/ **1** N-UNCOUNT **Brass** is a yellow-colored metal made from copper and zinc. It is used especially for making ornaments and musical instruments. ❏ *The instrument is beautifully made in brass.* **2** N-SING The **brass** is the section of an orchestra which consists of brass wind instruments such as trumpets and horns. ❏ *Consequently even this vast chorus was occasionally overwhelmed by the brass.* →see **orchestra**

1 불가산명사 놋쇠 ❏ 그 악기는 놋쇠로 멋지게 만들어졌다. **2** 단수명사 금관 악기부 ❏ 그 결과 이토록 방대한 합창단마저도 이따금씩 금관 악기부에 압도되었다.

M

N

brat /brǽt/ (**brats**) N-COUNT If you call someone, especially a child, a **brat**, you mean that he or she behaves badly or annoys you. [INFORMAL, DISAPPROVAL] ❏ *He's a spoiled brat.*

가산명사 버릇없는 놈 [비격식체, 탐탁잖음] ❏ 그 녀석은 버릇없는 망나니이다.

O

bra|va|do /brəvάdoʊ/ N-UNCOUNT **Bravado** is an appearance of courage or confidence that someone shows in order to impress other people. ❏ *"You won't get away with this," he said with unexpected bravado.*

불가산명사 허세 ❏ "너는 여기서 빠져 나갈 수 없을 거야."라고 그가 뜻밖의 허세를 부리며 말했다.

P

brave ♦◇◇ /breɪv/ (**braver, bravest, braves, braving, braved**) **1** ADJ Someone who is **brave** is willing to do things which are dangerous, and does not show fear in difficult or dangerous situations. ❏ *He was not brave enough to report the loss of the documents.* • **brave|ly** ADV ❏ *Our men wiped them out, but the enemy fought bravely and well.* **2** V-T If you **brave** unpleasant or dangerous conditions, you deliberately expose yourself to them, usually in order to achieve something. [WRITTEN] ❏ *Thousands have braved icy rain to demonstrate their support.* →see **hero**

1 형용사 용감한 ❏ 그는 그 서류들을 분실했다고 보고할 만큼 용감하지 못했다. • 용감하게 부사 ❏ 우리 병사들이 적들을 소탕했지만, 적들도 용감하게 잘 싸웠다. **2** 타동사 (위험) 따위를 무릅쓰다 [문어체] ❏ 수천 명의 사람들이 찬비를 무릅쓰고 지지 시위를 벌였다.

Q

R

S

Thesaurus	brave의 참조어	
ADJ.	courageous, fearless; (ant.) afraid, cowardly **1**	
V.	dare, endure, risk **2**	

T

U

bra|very /breɪvəri/ N-UNCOUNT **Bravery** is brave behavior or the quality of being brave. ❏ *He deserves the highest praise for his bravery.*

불가산명사 용감한 행위; 용기 ❏ 그의 용기는 최고의 찬사를 받을 만하다.

V

brawl /brɔl/ (**brawls, brawling, brawled**) **1** N-COUNT A **brawl** is a rough or violent fight. ❏ *He had been in a drunken street brawl.* **2** V-RECIP If someone **brawls**, they fight in a very rough or violent way. ❏ *He was suspended for a year from the university after brawling with police over a speeding ticket.*

1 가산명사 난투극 ❏ 그는 술에 취해 길거리에서 벌어진 싸움판에 끼어 있었다. **2** 상호동사 난투극을 벌이다 ❏ 그는 과속 단속을 놓고 경찰과 난투극을 벌인 후 대학에서 1년간 정학을 당했다.

W

bra|zen /breɪz°n/ ADJ If you describe a person or their behavior as **brazen**, you mean that they are very bold and do not care what other people think about them or their behavior. ❏ *They're quite brazen about their bisexuality, it doesn't worry them.* • **bra|zen|ly** ADV ❏ *He was brazenly running a $400,000-a-month drug operation from the prison.*

형용사 뻔뻔스러운, 매우 당당한 ❏ 그들은 자신들의 양성애 취향에 대해 상당히 당당하며, 그것에 개의치 않는다. • 뻔뻔스럽게 부사 ❏ 그는 뻔뻔스럽게도 감옥에서 한 달에 40만 달러 규모의 마약 거래를 지휘하고 있었다.

X

Y

breach /britʃ/ (**breaches, breaching, breached**) **1** V-T If you **breach** an agreement, a law, or a promise, you break it. ❏ *The newspaper breached the code of conduct on privacy.* **2** N-VAR A **breach of** an agreement, a law, or a promise is an act of breaking it. ❏ *The congressman was accused of a breach of secrecy rules.* **3** N-COUNT A **breach in** a relationship is a serious disagreement which often

1 타동사 어기다 ❏ 그 신문은 사생활에 대한 규정을 어겼다. **2** 가산명사 또는 불가산명사 위반, 어김 ❏ 그 하원 의원은 비밀 엄수 규칙을 어겼다는 비난을 받았다. **3** 가산명사 불화 [격식체] ❏ 그들의 행동은 양국 간에 심각한 불화를 초래할 염려가 있었다.

Z

results in the relationship ending. [FORMAL] ❑ *Their actions threatened a serious breach in relations between the two countries.* ❹ V-T If someone or something **breaches** a barrier, they make an opening in it, usually leaving it weakened or destroyed. [FORMAL] ❑ *The limestone is sufficiently fissured for tree roots to have breached the roof of the cave.* ❺ V-T If you **breach** someone's security or their defenses, you manage to get through and attack an area that is heavily guarded and protected. ❑ *The bomber had breached security by hurling his dynamite from a roof overlooking the building.* ● N-COUNT **Breach** is also a noun. ❑ *...widespread breaches of security at Ministry of Defence bases.*

bread ♦♢♢ /brɛd/ (**breads**) N-MASS **Bread** is a very common food made from flour, water, and usually yeast. ❑ *...a loaf of bread.* ❑ *...bread and butter.*

breadth /brɛtθ, BRIT brɛdθ/ ❶ N-UNCOUNT The **breadth** of something is the distance between its two sides. ❑ *The breadth of the whole camp was 400 paces.* ❷ N-UNCOUNT The **breadth** of something is its quality of consisting of or involving many different things. ❑ *Older people have a tremendous breadth of experience.*

bread|winner /brɛdwɪnər/ (**breadwinners**) also **bread-winner** N-COUNT The **breadwinner** in a family is the person in it who earns the money that the family needs for essential things. ❑ *I've always paid the bills and been the breadwinner.*

break ♦♦♦ /breɪk/ (**breaks**, **breaking**, **broke**, **broken**) ❶ V-T/V-I When an object **breaks** or when you **break** it, it suddenly separates into two or more pieces, often because it has been hit or dropped. ❑ *He fell through the window, breaking the glass.* ❑ *The plate broke.* ❑ *The plane broke into three pieces.* ❷ V-T/V-I If you **break** a part of your body such as your leg, your arm, or your nose, or if a bone **breaks**, you are injured because a bone cracks or splits. ❑ *She broke a leg in a skiing accident.* ❑ *Old bones break easily.* ● N-COUNT **Break** is also a noun. ❑ *It has caused a bad break to Gabriella's leg.* ❸ V-T/V-I If a surface, cover, or seal **breaks** or if something **breaks** it, a hole or tear is made in it, so that a substance can pass through. ❑ *Once you've broken the seal of a bottle there's no way you can put it back together again.* ❑ *The bandage must be put on when the blister breaks.* ❹ V-T/V-I When a tool or piece of machinery **breaks** or when you **break** it, it is damaged and no longer works. ❑ *When the clutch broke, the car was locked into second gear.* ❺ V-T If you **break** a rule, promise, or agreement, you do something that you should not do according to that rule, promise, or agreement. ❑ *We didn't know we were breaking the law.* ❑ *The company has consistently denied it had knowingly broken arms embargoes.* ❻ V-I If you **break** free or loose, you free yourself from something or escape from it. ❑ *She broke free by thrusting her elbow into his chest.* ❼ V-T If someone **breaks** something, especially a difficult or unpleasant situation that has existed for some time, they end it or change it. ❑ *The Home Secretary aims to break the vicious circle between disadvantage and crime.* ❑ *New proposals have been put forward to break the deadlock among rival factions.* ● N-COUNT **Break** is also a noun. ❑ *Nothing that might lead to a break in the deadlock has been discussed yet.* ❽ V-T If someone or something **breaks** a silence, they say something or make a noise after a long period of silence. ❑ *Hugh broke the silence. "Is she always late?" he asked.* ❾ V-T/V-I If you **break with** a group of people or a traditional way of doing things, or you **break** your connection with them, you stop being involved with that group or stop doing things in that way. ❑ *In 1959, Akihito broke with imperial tradition by marrying a commoner.* ❑ *They were determined to break from precedent.* ● N-COUNT **Break** is also a noun. ❑ *Making a completely clean break with the past, the couple got rid of all their old furniture.* ❿ V-T If you **break** a habit or if someone **breaks** you **of** it, you no longer have that habit. ❑ *If you continue to smoke, keep trying to break the habit.* ⓫ V-I If someone **breaks for** a short period of time, they rest or change from what they are doing for a short period. ❑ *They broke for lunch.* ⓬ N-COUNT A **break** is a short period of time when you have a rest or a change from what you are doing, especially if you are working or if you are in a boring or unpleasant situation. ❑ *They may be able to help with childcare so that you can have a break.* ❑ *I thought a 15 minute break from his work would do him good.* ⓭ N-COUNT A **break** is a short vacation. ❑ *They are currently taking a short break in Spain.* ⓮ V-T If you **break** your journey somewhere, you stop there for a short time so that you can have a rest. ❑ *Because of the heat we broke our journey at a small country hotel.* ⓯ V-T To **break** the force of something such as a blow or fall means to weaken its effect, for example by getting in the way of it. ❑ *He sustained serious neck injuries after he broke someone's fall.* ⓰ V-I When a piece of news **breaks**, people hear about it from the newspapers, television, or radio. ❑ *The news broke that the Prime Minister had resigned.* ⓱ V-T When you **break** a piece of bad news to someone, you tell it to them, usually in a kind way. ❑ *Then Louise broke the news that she was leaving me.* ⓲ N-COUNT A **break** is a lucky opportunity that someone gets to achieve something. [INFORMAL] ❑ *He went into TV and got his first break playing opposite Sid James in the series "Citizen James".* ⓳ V-T If you **break** a record, you beat the previous record for a particular achievement. ❑ *Carl Lewis has broken the world record in the 100 meters.* ⓴ V-I When day or dawn **breaks**, it starts to grow light after the night has ended. ❑ *They continued the search as dawn broke.* ㉑ V-I When a wave **breaks**, it passes its highest point and turns downward, for example when it reaches the shore. ❑ *Danny listened to the waves breaking against the shore.* ㉒ V-T If you **break** a secret code, you work out how to understand it. ❑ *It was hoped they could break the Allies' codes.* ㉓ V-I If someone's voice **breaks** when they are speaking, it changes its sound, for example because they are sad or afraid. ❑ *Godfrey's voice broke, and halted.* ㉔ V-I When a boy's voice **breaks**, it becomes deeper and sounds more like a man's voice. ❑ *He sings with the strained discomfort of someone whose voice hasn't quite broken.* ㉕ V-I If the weather **breaks** or a storm **breaks**, it suddenly becomes rainy or stormy after a period of sunshine. ❑ *I've been waiting for the weather to break.* ㉖ →see also **broke, broken, heartbreak, heartbreaking, heartbroken, outbreak** ㉗ to **break even** →see **even**. to **break new ground** →see **ground**. to **break** someone's **heart** →see **heart**. all hell **breaks loose** →see **hell**. to break the

❹ 타동사 구멍내다, 뚫다 [격식체] ❑ 그 석회암은 나무뿌리가 동굴의 천장에 구멍을 내기에 충분할 만큼 벌어져 있다. ❺ 타동사 뚫고 들어가다 ❑ 폭파범은 그 건물이 내려다보이는 지붕에서 다이너마이트를 집어 던져 방어를 뚫었었다. ● 가산명사 돌파 공격 ❑ 국방부 기지에 감행된 광범위한 돌파 공격

물질명사 빵 ❑ 빵 한 덩어리 ❑ 버터 바른 빵

❶ 불가산명사 너비 ❑ 야영지 전체의 너비는 4백 걸음이었다. ❷ 불가산명사 폭 ❑ 노인들은 대단히 폭넓은 경험을 갖고 있다.

가산명사 한 집안의 생계를 책임진 사람 ❑ 내가 항상 각종 공과금을 내고 밥벌이를 해 왔다.

❶ 타동사/자동사 깨뜨리다, 쪼개다, 부수다; 깨어지다 ❑ 그가 창문 쪽으로 넘어지면서 유리창이 깨졌다. ❑ 그 접시는 깨졌다. ❑ 그 비행기는 세 조각이 났다. ❷ 타동사/자동사 부러뜨리다; 부러지다 ❑ 그녀는 스키를 타다 사고를 당해 다리가 부러졌다. ❑ 노화한 뼈는 쉽게 부러진다. ● 가산명사 골절 ❑ 그 때문에 가브리엘라는 다리에 심한 골절을 입었다. ❸ 타동사/자동사 뜯다, 트다, 뜯기다, 터지다 ❑ 병의 봉인을 한 번 뜯고 나면 다시 원상태로 해 놓을 수 없다. ❑ 물집이 터지면 붕대를 감아 줘야 한다. ❹ 타동사/자동사 부수다, 고장내다; 고장나다 ❑ 클러치가 고장 났을 때, 그 차는 기어가 2단에 걸려 있었다. ❺ 타동사 어기다 ❑ 우리는 우리가 법을 어기고 있는지 몰랐다. ❑ 그 회사는 무기 수출 금지를 알고도 어겨 왔었다는 사실을 시종일관 부인해 왔다. ❻ 자동사 벗어나다 ❑ 그녀는 팔꿈치로 그의 가슴을 질러서 빠져 나왔다. ❼ 타동사 타개하다; 해소하다 ❑ 내무장관은 불우한 환경과 범죄 사이의 악순환을 타개하고자 한다. ❑ 경쟁 당파들 사이의 교착 상태를 타개하기 위해 새로운 안들이 제기되어 왔다. ● 가산명사 타개 ❑ 아직까지 그러한 교착 상태를 타개할 수 있을 만한 것은 논의된 바가 없다. ❽ 타동사 (침묵을) 깨뜨리다 ❑ 휴가 침묵을 깨뜨렸다. "그녀가 항상 늦니?"라고 그가 물었다. ❾ 타동사/자동사 결별하다, 관계를 끊다 ❑ 1959년, 아키히토는 평민 출신과 결혼함으로써 황가의 전통과 결별했다. ❑ 그들은 선례로부터 벗어나기로 결심을 굳혔다. ● 가산명사 결별, 절연 ❑ 과거와 완전히 깨끗하게 결별하면서 그 부부는 낡은 가구를 모두 없앴다. ❿ 타동사 (버릇을) 버리다; ―의 습관을 고치다 ❑ 계속 담배를 피우신다면, 그 습관을 버리려고 계속 시도해 보세요. ⓫ 자동사 휴식하다, 쉬다 ❑ 그들은 점심 식사를 위해 휴식을 가졌다. ⓬ 가산명사 휴식 ❑ 네가 잠시 쉴 수 있도록 그들이 아이 돌보는 일을 도와줄 수 있을지도 모른다. ❑ 15분간 일에서 벗어나 휴식을 취하는 것이 그에게 좋으리라고 생각했다. ⓭ 가산명사 짧은 휴가 ❑ 현재 그들은 스페인에서 짧은 휴가를 보내고 있다. ⓮ 타동사 (여행 등을) 잠시 중단하다 ❑ 더위 때문에 우리는 여행을 잠시 중단하고 작은 지방 호텔에 머물렀다. ⓯ 타동사 (충격이나 추락 등을) 막다 ❑ 그는 어떤 사람이 떨어지는 것을 막은 후 목에 심각한 부상을 입었다. ⓰ 자동사 알려지다 ❑ 수상이 사임했다는 뉴스가 공표되었다. ⓱ 타동사 알리다, 공표하다 ❑ 그러고 나서 루이즈는 나를 떠나간 얘기를 꺼내 놓았다. ⓲ 가산명사 좋은 기회 [비격식체] ❑ 그는 텔레비전에 진출하여 연속극 '시티즌 제임스'에서 시드 제임스의 상대역을 연기하는 것으로 첫 번째 좋은 기회를 얻었다. ⓳ 타동사 (기록을) 깨다, 갱신하다 ❑ 칼 루이스가 100미터 달리기에서 세계 기록을 갱신했다. ⓴ 자동사 (날이) 새다 ❑ 그들은 날이 새자 수색을 계속했다. ㉑ 자동사 (파도가) 부서지다 ❑ 대니는 파도가 해안에 부딪혀 부서지는 소리에 귀를 기울였다. ㉒ 타동사 해독하다 ❑ 그들이 연합군의 암호를 풀 수 있을지도 모른다는 두려움이 있었다. ㉓ 자동사 (목소리가) 갈라지다 ❑ 고드프리의 목소리가 갈라지더니 말을 멈췄다. ㉔ 자동사 (변성기를) 변하다 ❑ 그는 아직 변성기를 거치지 않은 사람처럼 불편하게 쥐어짜듯 노래한다. ㉕ 자동사 (날씨가) 바뀌다 ❑ 나는 날씨가 바뀌기를 기다려 왔다.

ice →see ice. to break ranks →see rank. to break wind →see wind →see factory

---

Word Partnership   *break의 연어*

N.	break **a bone**, break **your arm/leg/neck** ②
	break **the silence** ⑧
	break **a habit** ⑩
	coffee/lunch break ⑫
	break **the law**, break **a promise**, break **a rule** ⑤
	break **a record** ⑲
V.	need **a break**, take **a** break ⑫ ⑬ ⑱

▶**break down** ① PHRASAL VERB If a machine or a vehicle **breaks down**, it stops working. ❏ *Their car broke down.* ② PHRASAL VERB If a discussion, relationship, or system **breaks down**, it fails because of a problem or disagreement. ❏ *Talks with business leaders broke down last night.* ③ PHRASAL VERB To **break down** something such as an idea or statement means to separate it into smaller parts in order to make it easier to understand or deal with. ❏ *The report breaks down the results region by region.* ④ PHRASAL VERB When a substance **breaks down** or when something **breaks** it **down**, a biological or chemical process causes it to separate into the substances which make it up. ❏ *Over time, the protein in the eggshell breaks down into its constituent amino acids.* ⑤ PHRASAL VERB If someone **breaks down**, they lose control of themselves and start crying. ❏ *Because he was being so kind and concerned, I broke down and cried.* ⑥ PHRASAL VERB If you **break down** a door or barrier, you hit it so hard that it falls to the ground. ❏ *An unruly mob broke down police barricades and stormed the courtroom.* ⑦ PHRASAL VERB To **break down** barriers or prejudices that separate people or restrict their freedom means to change society's attitudes so that the barriers or prejudices no longer exist. [APPROVAL] ❏ *His early experience enabled him to break down barriers between Scottish Catholics and Protestants.* ⑧ →see also **breakdown**

▶**break in** ① PHRASAL VERB If someone, usually a thief, **breaks in**, they get into a building by force. ❏ *Masked robbers broke in and made off with $8,000.* →see also **break-in** ② PHRASAL VERB If you **break in** on someone's conversation or activity, you interrupt them. ❏ *O'Leary broke in on his thoughts.* ❏ *Mrs. Southern listened keenly, occasionally breaking in with pertinent questions.* ③ PHRASAL VERB If you **break** someone **in**, you get them used to a new job or situation. ❏ *The band is breaking in a new backing vocalist.* ④ PHRASAL VERB If you **break in** something new, you gradually use or wear it for longer and longer periods until it is ready to be used or worn all the time. ❏ *When breaking in an engine, you probably should refrain from high speed for the first thousand miles.*

▶**break into** ① PHRASAL VERB If someone **breaks into** a building, they get into it by force. ❏ *There was no one nearby who might see him trying to break into the house.* ② PHRASAL VERB If someone **breaks into** something they suddenly start doing it. For example if someone **breaks into** a run they suddenly start running, and if they **break into** song they suddenly start singing. ❏ *The moment she was out of sight she broke into a run.* ③ PHRASAL VERB If you **break into** a profession or area of business, especially one that is difficult to succeed in, you manage to have some success in it. ❏ *She finally broke into films after an acclaimed stage career.*

▶**break off** ① PHRASAL VERB If part of something **breaks off** or if you **break** it **off**, it comes off or is removed by force. ❏ *The two wings of the aircraft broke off on impact.* ❏ *Grace broke off a large piece of the clay.* ② PHRASAL VERB If you **break off** when you are doing or saying something, you suddenly stop doing it or saying it. ❏ *Barry broke off in mid-sentence.* ③ PHRASAL VERB-RECIP If someone **breaks off** a relationship, they end it. ❏ *The two West African states had broken off relations two years ago.*

▶**break out** ① PHRASAL VERB If something such as war, fighting, or disease **breaks out**, it begins suddenly. ❏ *He was 29 when war broke out.* ② PHRASAL VERB If a prisoner **breaks out of** a prison, they escape from it. ❏ *The two men broke out of their cells and cut through a perimeter fence.* →see also **breakout** ③ PHRASAL VERB If you **break out of** a dull situation or routine, you manage to change it or escape from it. ❏ *It's taken a long time to break out of my own conventional training.* ④ PHRASAL VERB If you **break out in** a rash or a sweat, a rash or sweat appears on your skin. ❏ *A person who is allergic to cashews may break out in a rash when he consumes these nuts.*

▶**break through** ① PHRASAL VERB If you **break through** a barrier, you succeed in forcing your way through it. ❏ *Protesters tried to break through a police cordon.* ② PHRASAL VERB If you **break through**, you achieve success even though there are difficulties and obstacles. ❏ *There is still scope for new writers to break through.* ③ →see also **breakthrough**

▶**break up** ① PHRASAL VERB When something **breaks up** or when you **break** it **up**, it separates or is divided into several smaller parts. ❏ *Civil war could come if the country breaks up.* ❏ *Break up the chocolate and melt it.* ② PHRASAL VERB If a marriage **breaks up** or if someone **breaks** it **up**, the marriage ends and the partners separate. ❏ *MPs say they work too hard and that is why so many of their marriages break up.* ③ PHRASAL VERB When a meeting or gathering **breaks up** or when someone **breaks** it **up**, it is brought to an end and the people involved in it leave. ❏ *A neighbor asked for the music to be turned down and the party broke up.* ❏ *Police used tear gas to break up a demonstration.*

break│away /ˈbreɪkweɪ/ ADJ A **breakaway** group is a group of people who have separated from a larger group, for example because of a disagreement. [ADJ n] ❏ *Sixteen members of Parliament have formed a breakaway group.*

---

① 구동사 고장나다 ❏ 그들의 차가 고장 났다. ② 구동사 결렬되다; 깨지다 ❏ 지난밤 경제 지도자들과의 회담은 결렬되었다. ③ 구동사 분석하다; 분해하다 ❏ 그 기사는 결과를 지역별로 분석한다. ④ 구동사 (화학적으로) 분해하다, 분해되다 ❏ 시간의 흐름에 따라, 달걀 껍데기에 있는 단백질은 그 성분을 이루는 아미노산으로 분해된다. ⑤ 구동사 자제력을 잃다 ❏ 그가 아주 친절하고 사려 깊게 대해 주었기에, 나는 자제력을 잃고 울음을 터뜨렸다. ⑥ 구동사 무너뜨리다 ❏ 사나운 폭도들이 경찰의 바리케이드를 무너뜨리고 법정에 난입했다. ⑦ 구동사 무너뜨리다, 폐기하다 [마음에 둠] ❏ 어릴 때 경험 덕분에 그는 스코틀랜드 가톨릭교도와 개신교도 사이의 장벽을 무너뜨릴 수 있었다.

① 구동사 난입하다 ❏ 복면을 쓴 강도들이 난입하여 8천 달러를 갖고 도망쳤다. ② 구동사 끼어들다, 말참견하다 ❏ 그가 생각을 하고 있을 때 오리어리가 끼어들었다. ❏ 서던 부인은 열심히 귀를 기울였고, 이따금씩 적절한 질문을 던지며 끼어들었다. ③ 구동사 적응시키다 ❏ 그 밴드는 새로 들어온 백보컬을 적응시키는 중이다. ④ 구동사 길들이다 ❏ 엔진을 길들일 때는, 첫 1,000마일 동안은 고속 주행을 삼가야 할 것이다.

① 구동사 침입하다 ❏ 그가 그 집에 침입을 시도하는 것을 볼 만한 사람은 근처에 아무도 없었다. ② 구동사 갑자기 ~하기 시작하다 ❏ 시야를 벗어나자마자 그녀는 갑자기 달리기 시작했다. ③ 구동사 ~에 진입하다 ❏ 그녀는 연극 무대에서의 화려한 활약 후 마침내 영화계에 진입했다.

① 구동사 떨어지다; 떼어 내다 ❏ 충돌 순간 비행기의 양 날개가 떨어져 나갔다. ❏ 그레이스는 커다란 점토 조각을 떼어냈다. ② 구동사 그만두다, 멈추다 ❏ 배리는 말을 하다 말고 끊었다. ③ 상호 구동사 (관계를) 끊다, 절교하다 ❏ 서아프리카의 그 두 나라는 2년 전에 국교를 단절했다.

① 구동사 일어나다, 터지다 ❏ 전쟁이 터졌을 때 그는 스물아홉 살이었다. ② 구동사 탈옥하다 ❏ 그 두 남자는 감방에서 탈옥하여 경계 울타리를 빠져나갔다. ③ 구동사 벗어나다 ❏ 나 자신의 판에 박힌 훈련에서 벗어나는 데는 오랜 시간이 걸렸다. ④ 구동사 (뾰루지나 땀 등이) 나다 ❏ 캐슈에 알레르기가 있는 사람은 이런 견과를 먹으면 뾰루지가 날 수도 있다.

① 구동사 ~을 헤치고 나아가다, 돌파하다 ❏ 시위자들은 경찰 경계선 돌파를 시도했다. ② 구동사 난관을 뚫고 성공하다 ❏ 신인 작가들이 난관을 뚫고 성공할 수 있는 여지가 여전히 있다.

① 구동사 갈라지다; 분해하다 ❏ 나라가 분열되면 내란이 일어날 수도 있다. ❏ 초콜릿을 쪼개서 녹이세요. ② 구동사 파탄 나다, 파탄을 초래하다 ❏ 업무가 너무 고되고 또 그 때문에 그들의 결혼 생활이 많이 파탄 난다고 의회의원들은 말한다. ③ 구동사 해산하다; 해산시키다 ❏ 이웃 사람이 음악을 줄여 달라고 요구하자 파티는 끝났다. ❏ 경찰은 시위를 해산시키기 위해 최루 가스를 사용했다.

형용사 이탈한 ❏ 하원 의원 16명이 이탈 집단을 형성했다.

break|down /breɪkdaʊn/ (breakdowns) **1** N-COUNT The **breakdown** of something such as a relationship, plan, or discussion is its failure or ending. ❑ ...the breakdown of talks between the U.S. and EU officials. ❑ ...the irretrievable breakdown of a marriage. **2** N-COUNT If you have a **breakdown**, you become very depressed, so that you are unable to cope with your life. ❑ My personal life was terrible. My mother had died, and a couple of years later I had a breakdown. →see also **nervous breakdown 3** N-COUNT If a car or a piece of machinery has a **breakdown**, it stops working. ❑ Her old car was unreliable, so the trip was plagued by breakdowns. **4** N-COUNT A **breakdown** of something is a list of its separate parts. ❑ The organisers were given a breakdown of the costs. →see **traffic**

break|fast ♦♢♢ /brɛkfəst/ (breakfasts, breakfasting, breakfasted) **1** N-VAR **Breakfast** is the first meal of the day. It is usually eaten in the early part of the morning. ❑ What's for breakfast? →see also **bed and breakfast 2** V-I When you **breakfast**, you have breakfast. [FORMAL] ❑ All the ladies breakfasted in their rooms. →see **meal**

break-in (break-ins) N-COUNT If there has been a **break-in**, someone has got into a building by force. ❑ The break-in had occurred just before midnight.

break|ing point N-UNCOUNT If something or someone has reached **breaking point**, they have so many problems or difficulties that they can no longer cope with them, and may soon collapse or be unable to continue. [also the/a N] ❑ The report on the riot exposed a prison system stretched to breaking point.

break|neck /brɛknɛk/ ADJ If you say that something happens or travels at **breakneck** speed, you mean that it happens or travels very fast. [ADJ n] ❑ Jack drove to Mayfair at breakneck speed.

break|out /breɪkaʊt/ (breakouts) also **break-out** N-COUNT If there has been a **breakout**, someone has escaped from prison. ❑ High Point prison had the highest number of breakouts of any jail in Britain.

break|through /breɪkθruː/ (breakthroughs) N-COUNT A **breakthrough** is an important development or achievement. ❑ The company looks poised to make a significant breakthrough in China.

break|up /breɪkʌp/ (breakups) also **break-up 1** N-COUNT The **breakup** of a marriage, relationship, or association is the act of it finishing or coming to an end because the people involved decide that it is not working successfully. ❑ ...the acrimonious breakup of the meeting's first session. **2** N-COUNT The **breakup** of an organization or a country is the act of it separating or dividing into several parts. ❑ ...the breakup of British Rail for privatization.

breast ♦♢♢ /brɛst/ (breasts) **1** N-COUNT A woman's **breasts** are the two soft, round parts on her chest that can produce milk to feed a baby. ❑ She wears a low-cut dress which reveals her breasts. **2** N-COUNT A person's **breast** is the upper part of his or her chest. [LITERARY] ❑ He struck his breast, asking blessed Mary ever Virgin to pray for him. **3** N-COUNT A bird's **breast** is the front part of its body. ❑ The cock's breast is tinged with chestnut and narrowly barred with white. **4** N-SING The **breast** of a shirt, jacket, or coat is the part which covers the top part of the chest. ❑ He reached into his breast pocket for his cigar case. **5** N-VAR You can refer to piece of meat that is cut from the front of a bird or lamb as **breast**. ❑ ...a chicken breast with vegetables.

breast|stroke /brɛststroʊk, brɛs-/ N-UNCOUNT **Breaststroke** is a swimming stroke which you do lying on your front, moving your arms and legs horizontally in a circular motion. [also the N] ❑ I do not yet know how to swim breaststroke effectively.

breath ♦♦♢ /brɛθ/ (breaths) **1** N-VAR Your **breath** is the air that you let out through your mouth when you breathe. If someone has **bad breath**, their breath smells unpleasant. ❑ I could smell the whisky on his breath. **2** N-VAR When you take a **breath**, you breathe in once. ❑ He took a deep breath, and began to climb the stairs. ❑ Gasping for breath, she leaned against the door. **3** PHRASE If you go outside **for a breath of fresh air** or **for a breath of air**, you go outside because it is unpleasantly warm indoors. ❑ I had to step outside for a breath of fresh air. **4** PHRASE If you describe something new or different as **a breath of fresh air**, you mean that it makes a situation or subject more interesting or exciting. [APPROVAL] ❑ Her brisk treatment of an almost taboo subject was a breath of fresh air. **5** PHRASE When you **get** your **breath back** after doing something energetic, you start breathing normally again. ❑ I reached out a hand to steady myself against the house while I got my breath back. **6** PHRASE If you are **out of breath**, you are breathing very quickly and with difficulty because you have been doing something energetic. ❑ There she was, slightly out of breath from running. **7** PHRASE You can use **in the same breath** or **in the next breath** to indicate that someone says two very different or contradictory things, especially when you are criticizing them. [DISAPPROVAL] ❑ He hailed this week's arms agreement but in the same breath expressed suspicion about the motivations of the United States. **8** PHRASE If you are **short of breath**, you find it difficult to breathe properly, for example because you are ill. You can also say that someone suffers from **shortness of breath**. ❑ She felt short of breath and flushed. **9** PHRASE If you say something **under** your **breath**, you say it in a very quiet voice, often because you do not want other people to hear what you are saying. ❑ Walsh muttered something under his breath.

Word Partnership	breath의 연어
ADJ.	bad breath, fresh breath 1
	deep breath 2
V.	hold *your* breath 1
	gasp for breath, take a breath 2

1 가산명사 결렬; 파탄 ❑ 미국과 유럽 연합 임원들 간에 열린 회담의 결렬 ❑ 돌이킬 수 없이 파탄 난 결혼 **2** 가산명사 (건강상의) 쇠약 ❑ 내 생활은 끔찍했다. 어머니가 돌아가셨고, 2년 후 나는 쇠약해졌다. **3** 가산명사 고장 ❑ 그녀의 낡은 자동차는 믿지 못할 상태였고, 따라서 잦은 고장 때문에 여행은 엉망이 되었다. **4** 가산명사 명세, 내역 ❑ 주최자들은 경비 내역을 전달받았다.

1 N-VAR 또는 불가산명사 아침밥 ❑ 아침밥은 뭐야? **2** 자동사 아침밥을 먹다 [격식체] ❑ 숙녀들은 모두 자기 방에서 아침밥을 먹었다.

가산명사 가택 침입 ❑ 그 가택 침입은 자정 직전에 일어났다.

불가산명사 극한 상황, 한계점 ❑ 그 폭동에 대한 보고서는 한계점에 도달한 교도소 시스템을 폭로했다.

형용사 무서운 속도로 ❑ 잭은 메이페어를 향해 무서운 속력으로 차를 몰았다.

가산명사 탈옥 ❑ 하이 포인트 교도소는 영국 내 모든 교도소 중에서 탈옥 건수가 가장 많았다.

가산명사 획기적인 진전, 돌파구 ❑ 그 회사는 중국에서 중요한 돌파구를 마련한 가오를 한 것 같다.

1 가산명사 와해; 결별 ❑ 회담 중 가진 첫 번째 회의의 쓰라린 결렬 **2** 가산명사 분리, 분할 ❑ 영국 국철의 민영화를 위한 기업 분할

1 가산명사 젖가슴, 유방 ❑ 그녀는 젖가슴이 드러나도록 깊게 패인 드레스를 입고 있다. **2** 가산명사 가슴 [문예체] ❑ 그는 가슴을 치면서 성모 마리아께 자신을 위해 기도해 달라고 간구했다. **3** 가산명사 (새의) 가슴 ❑ 그 수탉의 가슴은 밤색을 띠고 있고 그 위로 흰색 줄무늬가 가늘게 쳐져 있다. **4** 단수명사 (의복의) 가슴 부분 ❑ 그는 가슴 쪽 주머니에 손을 넣어 담뱃갑을 찾았다. **5** 가산명사 또는 불가산명사 가슴살 ❑ 야채를 곁들인 닭 가슴살

불가산명사 평영 ❑ 아직 평영을 잘 하는 방법을 모르겠다.

1 가산명사 또는 불가산명사 (날) 숨, 숨김 ❑ 그 남자의 입에서 위스키 냄새가 났다. **2** 가산명사 또는 불가산명사 (들) 숨 ❑ 그는 숨을 깊게 들이마시고 계단을 오르기 시작했다. **3** 구 신선한 공기를 마시러 ❑ 나는 신선한 공기를 마시러 바깥으로 나가야 했다. **4** 구 청량제 [마음에 듦] ❑ 금기나 다름없는 주제를 활기 있게 다루는 그녀의 모습은 일종의 청량제와 같았다. **5** 구 호흡을 가다듬다 ❑ 나는 호흡을 가다듬는 동안 몸이 흔들리지 않도록 손을 뻗어 그 집에 기댔다. **6** 구 숨을 헐떡이며 ❑ 저만치에서 그녀가 달리기를 하고 나서 약간 숨을 헐떡거리고 있었다. **7** 구 한 입에 (두말하는) [탐탁찮음] ❑ 그는 이번 주 있었던 무기 협정을 환영하면서, 또 미국의 동기에 대한 의구심을 나타냈다. **8** 구 숨이 가쁜 ❑ 그녀는 숨이 가쁘고 얼굴이 붉어지는 것을 느꼈다. **9** 구 낮은 목소리로, 숨을 죽여 ❑ 월시는 숨을 죽여 뭐라고 중얼거렸다.

A

breatha|lyze / brɛθəlaɪz/ (breathalyzes, breathalyzing, breathalyzed) v-T If the driver of a car **is breathalyzed** by the police, they ask him or her to breathe into a special bag or device in order to test whether he or she has drunk too much alcohol. [mainly BRIT; BRIT also **breathalyse**] [usu passive] ❑ *She was breathalysed and found to be over the limit.*

타동사 음주측정을 하다 [주로 영국영어; 영국영어 breathalyse] ❑ 그녀는 음주 측정을 당했고 단속 기준치를 넘긴 것으로 드러났다.

B

Breatha|lyz|er /brɛθəlaɪzər/ (Breathalyzers) N-COUNT A **Breathalyzer** is a bag or electronic device that the police use to test whether a driver has drunk too much alcohol. [TRADEMARK; BRIT also **Breathalyser**] ❑ *Luckily I was never stopped for a breathalyzer.*

가산명사 음주측정기 [상표; 영국영어 breathalyser] ❑ 다행히 나는 한번도 음주 측정을 당해 보지 않았다.

C

breathe ♦◇◇ /briːð/ (breathes, breathing, breathed) **1** v-T/v-I When people or animals **breathe**, they take air into their lungs and let it out again. When they **breathe** smoke or a particular kind of air, they take it into their lungs and let it out again as they breathe. ❑ *He stood there breathing deeply and evenly.* ❑ *No American should have to drive out of town to breathe clean air.* ● **breath|ing** N-UNCOUNT ❑ *Her breathing became slow and heavy.* **2** to **be breathing down** someone's **neck** →see **neck**. to breathe a **sigh of relief** →see **sigh** →see **respiratory system**

D

1 타동사/자동사 호흡하다, 숨쉬다 ❑ 그는 깊고 고른 호흡을 하면서 거기에 서 있었다. ❑ 미국인이라면 그 누구도 깨끗한 공기를 마시기 위해 도시 밖까지 갈 필요가 없게 될 것이다. ● 호흡 불가산명사 ❑ 그녀는 호흡이 느리고 힘겨워졌다.

E

▶**breathe in** PHRASAL VERB When you **breathe in**, you take some air into your lungs. ❑ *She breathed in deeply.*

구동사 숨을 들이쉬다 ❑ 그녀는 깊이 숨을 들이쉬었다.

F

▶**breathe out** PHRASAL VERB When you **breathe out**, you send air out of your lungs through your nose or mouth. ❑ *Breathe out and ease your knees in toward your chest.*

구동사 숨을 내쉬다 ❑ 숨을 내쉬고 천천히 무릎을 가슴 쪽으로 가져오세요.

G

breath|er /briːðər/ (breathers) N-COUNT If you take a **breather**, you stop what you are doing for a short time in order to rest. [INFORMAL] ❑ *Relax and take a breather whenever you feel that you need one.*

가산명사 한숨 돌리기 [비격식체] ❑ 언제든지 필요하다 싶으면 긴장을 풀고 한숨 돌리세요.

H

breath|ing space (breathing spaces) N-VAR A **breathing space** is a short period of time between two activities in which you can recover from the first activity and prepare for the second one. ❑ *Firms need a breathing space if they are to recover.*

가산명사 또는 불가산명사 숨 돌릴 여유 ❑ 기업들이 회복하려면 숨 돌릴 여유가 필요하다.

I

breath|less /brɛθlɪs/ ADJ If you are **breathless**, you have difficulty in breathing properly, for example because you have been running or because you are afraid or excited. ❑ *I was a little breathless and my heartbeat was bumpy and fast.* ● **breath|less|ly** ADV ❑ *"I'll go in," he said breathlessly.* ● **breath|less|ness** N-UNCOUNT ❑ *Asthma causes wheezing and breathlessness.*

J

형용사 숨찬; 숨막히는 ❑ 나는 약간 숨이 찼으며 심장 박동이 불규칙하고 빨랐다. ● 숨을 헐떡이며 부사 ❑ "내가 들어가겠어."라고 그가 헐떡거리며 말했다. ● 숨이 참, 호흡 곤란 불가산명사 ❑ 천식은 씨근거림과 호흡 곤란을 일으킨다.

K

breath|taking /brɛθteɪkɪŋ/ also **breath-taking** ADJ If you say that something is **breathtaking**, you are emphasizing that it is extremely beautiful or amazing. [EMPHASIS] ❑ *The house has breathtaking views from every room.* ❑ *Some of their football was breathtaking, a delight to watch.*

L

형용사 숨 막힐 정도의 [강조] ❑ 그 집의 모든 방이 숨 막힐 정도로 전망이 좋다. ❑ 그들이 벌이는 축구 경기 중 어떤 것들은 숨 막힐 정도로 흥미진진하여, 아주 볼만했다.

M

breed ♦◇◇ /briːd/ (breeds, breeding, bred) **1** N-COUNT A **breed** of a pet animal or farm animal is a particular type of it. For example, terriers are a breed of dog. ❑ *...rare breeds of cattle.* **2** v-T If you **breed** animals or plants, you keep them for the purpose of producing more animals or plants with particular qualities, in a controlled way. ❑ *He lived alone, breeding horses and dogs.* ❑ *He used to breed dogs for the police.* ● **breed|ing** N-UNCOUNT ❑ *There is potential for selective breeding for better yields.* **3** v-I When animals **breed**, they have babies. ❑ *Frogs will usually breed in any convenient pond.* ● **breed|ing** N-UNCOUNT ❑ *During the breeding season the birds come ashore.* **4** v-T If you say that something **breeds** bad feeling or bad behavior, you mean that it causes bad feeling or bad behavior to develop. ❑ *If they are unemployed it's bound to breed resentment.* **5** →see also **breeding**

N

1 가산명사 품종 ❑ 희귀한 품종의 소 **2** 타동사 기르다 ❑ 그는 말과 개를 기르며 혼자 살았다. ❑ 예전에 그는 경찰견을 길렀었다. ● 사육, 교배 불가산명사 ❑ 보다 나은 수확을 위한 선택적 교배 가능성이 있다. **3** 자동사 새끼를 낳다 ❑ 개구리는 일반적으로 아무 곳이나 편리한 연못에 알을 낳는다. ● 번식 불가산명사 ❑ 번식기 동안에 그 새들은 뭍으로 올라온다. **4** 타동사 ~을 생기게 하다 ❑ 그들이 실직 상태라면 분개심이 생기기 마련이다.

O

P

breed|er /briːdər/ (breeders) N-COUNT **Breeders** are people who breed animals or plants. ❑ *Her father was a well-known racehorse breeder.*

가산명사 사육자 ❑ 그녀의 아버지는 잘 알려진 경주마 사육자였다.

Q

breed|ing /briːdɪŋ/ N-UNCOUNT If someone says that a person has **breeding**, they mean that they think the person is from a good social background and has good manners. ❑ *It's a sign of good breeding to know the names of all your staff.* →see also **breed** →see **zoo**

불가산명사 교양, 예의범절 ❑ 직원들의 이름을 모두 안다는 것은 훌륭한 교양의 표시입니다.

R

breeze /briːz/ (breezes, breezing, breezed) **1** N-COUNT A **breeze** is a gentle wind. ❑ *...a cool summer breeze.* **2** v-I If you **breeze into** a place or a position, you enter it in a very casual or relaxed manner. ❑ *Lopez breezed into the quarter-finals of the tournament.* **3** v-I If you **breeze through** something such as a game or test, you cope with it easily. ❑ *John seems to breeze effortlessly through his many commitments at work.* →see **wind**

S

1 가산명사 산들바람 ❑ 시원한 여름 산들바람 **2** 자동사 수월하게 들어가다 ❑ 로페즈는 수월하게 대회 준준결승에 진출했다. **3** 자동사 어렵지 않게 해치우다 ❑ 존은 그 많은 일거리들을 전혀 힘들이지 않고 쉽게 해치우는 것 같다.

T

breezy /briːzi/ ADJ If you describe someone as **breezy**, you mean that they behave in a casual, cheerful, and confident manner. ❑ *...his bright and breezy personality.*

형용사 시원시원한 ❑ 그의 밝고 시원시원한 성격

U

breth|ren /brɛðrɪn/ N-PLURAL You can refer to the members of a particular organization or group, especially a religious group, as **brethren**. [OLD-FASHIONED] ❑ *We must help our brethren, it is our duty.*

복수명사 (종교 단체 등에서) 형제 [구식어] ❑ 우리는 형제를 도와야 하며, 이는 우리의 의무이다.

V

brew /bruː/ (brews, brewing, brewed) **1** v-T If you **brew** tea or coffee, you make it by pouring hot water over tea leaves or ground coffee. ❑ *He brewed a pot of coffee.* **2** N-COUNT A **brew** is a particular kind of tea or coffee. It can also be a particular pot of tea or coffee. ❑ *She swallowed a mouthful of the hot strong brew, and wiped her eyes.* **3** v-T If a person or company **brews** beer, they make it. ❑ *I brew my own beer.* **4** v-I If a storm **is brewing**, large clouds are beginning to form and the sky is becoming dark because there is going to be a storm. [usu cont] ❑ *We'd seen the storm brewing when we were out in the boat.* **5** v-I If an unpleasant or difficult situation **is brewing**, it is starting to develop. [usu cont] ❑ *At home a crisis was brewing.* →see **tea**

W

1 타동사 우리다 ❑ 그는 커피를 한 주전자 우렸다. **2** 가산명사 우려낸 차 ❑ 그녀는 그 뜨겁고 진하게 우린 차를 한 모금 가득 삼키고 나서 눈물을 닦았다. **3** 타동사 (맥주 등을) 양조하다 ❑ 나는 내 맥주를 직접 양조한다. **4** 자동사 (폭풍우가) 일어나려고 하다 ❑ 보트를 타고 나가 있을 때 우리는 폭풍우가 잔뜩 몰려와 채비를 하는 것을 보았다. **5** 자동사 (안 좋은 일이) 일어나려고 하다 ❑ 집에서는 위기가 발생하려는 중이다.

X

Y

brew|er /bruːər/ (brewers) N-COUNT **Brewers** are people or companies who make beer.

가산명사 양조자, 양조 회사

Z

brew|ery /brʊəri/ (**breweries**) N-COUNT A **brewery** is a place where beer is made.

가산명사 양조장

bribe /braɪb/ (**bribes, bribing, bribed**) **1** N-COUNT A **bribe** is a sum of money or something valuable that one person offers or gives to another in order to persuade him or her to do something. ❑ *He was being investigated for receiving bribes.* **2** V-T If one person **bribes** another, they give them a bribe. ❑ *He was accused of bribing a senior bank official.*

1 가산명사 뇌물 ❑ 그는 수뢰 혐의로 조사를 받고 있었다. **2** 타동사 뇌물을 주다 ❑ 그는 은행 고위직 임원에게 뇌물을 준 혐의로 기소되었다.

brib|ery /braɪbəri/ N-UNCOUNT **Bribery** is the act of offering someone money or something valuable in order to persuade them to do something for you. ❑ *He was jailed on charges of bribery.*

불가산명사 뇌물 증여, 매수 ❑ 그는 뇌물 증여 혐의로 투옥되었다.

brick /brɪk/ (**bricks**) **1** N-VAR **Bricks** are rectangular blocks of baked clay used for building walls, which are usually red or brown. **Brick** is the material made up of these blocks. ❑ *She built bookshelves out of bricks and planks.* **2** PHRASE If you **hit a brick wall** or **come up against a brick wall**, you are unable to continue or make progress because something stops you. [INFORMAL] ❑ *After that my career just seemed to hit a brick wall.*

1 가산명사 또는 불가산명사 벽돌 ❑ 그녀는 벽돌과 판자로 서가를 만들었다. **2** 구 (비유적) 벽에 부닥치다 [비격식체] ❑ 그 이후 내 앞길은 그저 벽에 부닥친 것처럼 보였다.

brid|al /braɪdᵊl/ ADJ **Bridal** is used to describe something that belongs or relates to a bride, or to both a bride and her bridegroom. [ADJ n] ❑ *She wore a floor length bridal gown.*

형용사 신부의; 혼례의 ❑ 그녀는 바닥에 닿을 듯 말 듯한 길이의 신부 드레스를 입었다.

bride /braɪd/ (**brides**) N-COUNT A **bride** is a woman who is getting married or who has just gotten married. ❑ *Guests toasted the bride and groom with champagne.* →see **wedding**

가산명사 신부, 새색시 ❑ 하객들은 신랑 신부를 위해 샴페인으로 축배를 들었다.

bride|groom /braɪdgrum/ (**bridegrooms**) N-COUNT A **bridegroom** is a man who is getting married.

가산명사 신랑

brides|maid /braɪdzmeɪd/ (**bridesmaids**) N-COUNT A **bridesmaid** is a woman or a girl who helps and accompanies a bride on her wedding day. →see **wedding**

가산명사 신부 들러리

bridge ♦♦◇ /brɪdʒ/ (**bridges, bridging, bridged**) **1** N-COUNT A **bridge** is a structure that is built over a railroad, river, or road so that people or vehicles can cross from one side to the other. ❑ *He walked back over the railway bridge.* **2** N-COUNT A **bridge** between two places is a piece of land that joins or connects them. ❑ *...a land bridge linking Serbian territories.* **3** V-T To **bridge** the gap between two people or things means to reduce it or get rid of it. ❑ *It is unlikely that the two sides will be able to bridge their differences.* **4** V-T Something that **bridges** the gap between two very different things has some of the qualities of each of these things. ❑ *...the singer who bridged the gap between pop music and opera.* **5** N-COUNT If something or someone acts as a **bridge** between two people, groups, or things, they connect them. ❑ *We hope this book will act as a bridge between doctor and patient.* **6** N-COUNT The **bridge** is the place on a ship from which it is steered. ❑ *Captain Ronald Warwick was on the bridge with four crewmen when the wave hit.* **7** N-COUNT The **bridge** of your nose is the thin top part of it, between your eyes. ❑ *On the bridge of his hooked nose was a pair of gold rimless spectacles.* **8** N-COUNT The **bridge** of a pair of glasses is the part that rests on your nose. **9** N-COUNT The **bridge** of a violin, guitar, or other stringed instrument is the small piece of wood under the strings that holds them up. →see **ship**

1 가산명사 다리 ❑ 그는 철교 위로 걸어서 돌아갔다. **2** 가산명사 다른 두 지역을 잇는 땅덩어리 ❑ 세르비아의 영토를 이어 주는 지역 **3** 타동사 다리를 놓다; 간극을 메우다 ❑ 양쪽이 서로의 의견 차이를 해소할 수 없을 듯하다. **4** 타동사 간극을 좁히다 ❑ 대중음악과 오페라 사이의 간극을 좁힌 가수 **5** 가산명사 가교, 연결 고리 ❑ 우리는 이 책이 의사와 환자 사이를 연결하는 가교 역할을 해 주길 희망한다. **6** 가산명사 함교 ❑ 파도가 쳤을 때 로널드 워릭 함장은 승무원 4명과 함께 함교 위에 있었다. **7** 가산명사 콧대 ❑ 그의 매부리코 위에는 금으로 된 테 없는 안경이 얹혀져 있었다. **8** 가산명사 안경테의 가운데 연결 부위 **9** 가산명사 (기타나 바이올린 등의) 브리지

bridge loan (**bridge loans**) N-COUNT A **bridge loan** is money that a bank lends you for a short time, for example so that you can buy a new house before you have sold the one you already own. [AM; BRIT **bridging loan**]

가산명사 단기 융자 [미국영어; 영국영어 bridging loan]

bri|dle /braɪdᵊl/ (**bridles**) N-COUNT A **bridle** is a set of straps that is put around a horse's head and mouth so that the person riding or driving the horse can control it. →see **horse**

가산명사 고삐

brief ♦♦◇ /brif/ (**briefer, briefest, briefs, briefing, briefed**) **1** ADJ Something that is **brief** lasts for only a short time. ❑ *She once made a brief appearance on television.* **2** ADJ A **brief** speech or piece of writing does not contain too many words or details. ❑ *In a brief statement, he concentrated on international affairs.* **3** ADJ If you are **brief**, you say what you want to say in as few words as possible. [v-link ADJ] ❑ *Now please be brief – my time is valuable.* **4** ADJ You can describe a period of time as **brief** if you want to emphasize that it is very short. [EMPHASIS] ❑ *For a few brief minutes we forgot the anxiety and anguish.* **5** N-PLURAL Men's or women's underpants can be referred to as **briefs**. [also *a pair of N*] ❑ *A bra and a pair of briefs lay on the floor.* **6** V-T If someone **briefs** you, especially about a piece of work or a serious matter, they give you information that you need before you do it or consider it. ❑ *A Defense Department spokesman briefed reporters.* **7** N-COUNT If someone gives you a **brief**, they officially give you responsibility and instructions for dealing with a particular thing. [mainly BRIT, FORMAL] ❑ *...customs officials with a brief to stop foreign porn coming into Britain.* **8** →see also **briefing** **9** PHRASE You can say **in brief** to indicate that you are about to say something in as few words as possible or to give a summary of what you have just said. ❑ *In brief, take no risks.*

1 형용사 잠깐 동안의 ❑ 그녀는 언젠가 한 번 텔레비전에 잠깐 출연했다. **2** 형용사 간결한 ❑ 간결한 성명서에서, 그는 전적으로 국제 문제에 초점을 맞췄다. **3** 형용사 간결히 말하는 ❑ 부디 간결히 말해 주게. 나는 시간이 귀하니까. **4** 형용사 아주 짧은 [강조] ❑ 아주 짧은 몇 분 동안 우리는 걱정과 고민을 잊었다. **5** 복수명사 팬티 ❑ 바닥에 브래지어와 팬티가 하나씩 놓여 있었다. **6** 타동사 요약 설명하다, 브리핑을 하다 ❑ 국방부 대변인이 기자들에게 브리핑을 했다. **7** 가산명사 임무, 권한 (주로 영국영어, 격식체) ❑ 외국 포르노물이 영국에 들어오는 것을 막는 임무를 띤 세관원들 **9** 구 요컨대 ❑ 요컨대, 모험을 하지 마세요.

Word Partnership	brief의 연어
N.	brief **appearance**, brief **conversation**, brief **pause** **1** brief **description**, brief **explanation**, brief **history**, brief **speech**, brief **statement** **2**

brief|case /brifkeɪs/ (**briefcases**) N-COUNT A **briefcase** is a case used for carrying documents in.

가산명사 서류 가방

brief|ing /brifɪŋ/ (**briefings**) N-VAR A **briefing** is a meeting at which information or instructions are given to people, especially before they do something. ❑ *They're holding a press briefing tomorrow.* →see also **brief**

가산명사 또는 불가산명사 요약 보고, 브리핑 ❑ 그들은 내일 언론 브리핑을 가질 예정이다.

A

brief|ly /bríːfli/ ➊ ADV Something that happens or is done **briefly** happens or is done for a very short period of time. [ADV with v] ❑ He smiled briefly. ➋ ADV If you say or write something **briefly**, you use very few words or give very few details. [ADV with v] ❑ There are four basic alternatives; they are described briefly below. ➌ ADV You can say **briefly** to indicate that you are about to say something in as few words as possible. [ADV with cl] ❑ Briefly, no less than nine of our agents have passed information to us.

B

➊ 부사 잠시 ❑ 그는 잠시 미소 지었다. ➋ 부사 간결하게 ❑ 기본적인 대안이 네 가지 있다. 아래 그것들을 간결하게 설명해 놓았다. ➌ 부사 간단히 말하면 ❑ 간단히 말하면, 우리 쪽 요원들이 9명 이상이 우리에게 정보를 넘겨 왔다.

C

bri|gade /brɪɡéɪd/ (brigades) N-COUNT-COLL A **brigade** is one of the groups which an army is divided into. ❑ ...the men of the Seventh Armoured Brigade. →see also **fire brigade**

가산명사-집합 여단 ❑ 제 7기갑 여단 병사들

D

bri|ga|dier /brɪɡədɪər/ (brigadiers) N-COUNT; N-TITLE A **brigadier** is a senior officer in the British armed forces who is in charge of a brigade and has the rank above colonel and below major general.

가산명사; 경칭명사 여단장, 육군 준장

E

bright ♦♦◇ /braɪt/ (brighter, brightest) ➊ ADJ A **bright** color is strong and noticeable, and not dark. ❑ ...a bright red dress. ● **bright|ly** ADV ❑ ...a display of brightly colored flowers. ● **bright|ness** N-UNCOUNT ❑ You'll be impressed with the brightness and the beauty of the colors. ➋ ADJ A **bright** light, object, or place is shining strongly or is full of light. ❑ ...a bright October day. ● **bright|ly** ADV [ADV with v] ❑ ...a warm, brightly lit room. ● **bright|ness** N-UNCOUNT ❑ An astronomer can determine the brightness of each star. ➌ ADJ If you describe someone as **bright**, you mean that they are quick at learning things. ❑ I was convinced that he was brighter than average. ➍ ADJ A **bright** idea is clever and original. ❑ There are lots of books crammed with bright ideas. ➎ ADJ If someone looks or sounds **bright**, they look or sound cheerful and lively. ❑ The boy was so bright and animated. ● **bright|ly** ADV [ADV with v] ❑ He smiled brightly as Ben approached. ➏ ADJ If the future is **bright**, it is likely to be pleasant or successful. ❑ Both had successful careers and the future looked bright.

F

G

➊ 형용사 밝은; 선명한 ❑ 선홍색 드레스 ● 밝게; 선명하게 부사 ❑ 밝은 색 꽃들의 진열 ● 밝음; 선명함 불가산명사 ❑ 그 색채의 선명함과 아름다움에 강한 인상을 받으실 겁니다. ➋ 형용사 빛나는, 광채 나는 ❑ 빛나는 10월의 하루 ● 밝게, 빛나게 부사 ❑ 따뜻하고 조명이 밝은 방 ● 빛남, 밝기 불가산명사 ❑ 천문학자는 각 별의 밝기 등급을 결정할 수 있다. ➌ 형용사 머리가 좋은, 영리한 ❑ 나는 그가 보통 이상으로 머리가 좋다고 확신했다. ➍ 형용사 영리한 ❑ 영리한 생각들이 가득 들어 있는 책들이 많이 있다. ➎ 형용사 밝은, 명랑한 ❑ 소년은 아주 명랑하고 생기발랄했다. ● 밝게, 명랑하게 부사 ❑ 벤이 다가오자 그는 밝게 미소 지었다. ➏ 형용사 (전망이) 밝은 ❑ 둘 다 화려한 경력의 소유자였고 앞날의 전망은 밝았다.

H

bright|en /bráɪtən/ (brightens, brightening, brightened) ➊ V-I If someone **brightens** or their face **brightens**, they suddenly look happier. ❑ Seeing him, she seemed to brighten a little. ● PHRASAL VERB **Brighten up** means the same as **brighten**. ❑ He brightened up a bit. ➋ V-I If your eyes **brighten**, you suddenly look interested or excited. ❑ His eyes brightened and he laughed. ➌ V-T If someone or something **brightens** a place, they make it more colorful and attractive. ❑ Tubs planted with wallflowers brightened the area outside the door. ● PHRASAL VERB **Brighten up** means the same as **brighten**. ❑ David spotted the pink silk lampshade in a shop and thought it would brighten up the room. ➍ V-T/V-I If someone or something **brightens** a situation or the situation **brightens**, it becomes more pleasant, enjoyable, or favorable. ❑ That does not do much to brighten the prospects of kids in the city. ➎ V-T/V-I When a light **brightens** a place or when a place **brightens**, it becomes brighter or lighter. ❑ The sky above the ridge of mountains brightened. ➏ V-I If the weather **brightens**, it becomes less cloudy or rainy, and the sun starts to shine. ❑ By early afternoon the weather had brightened.

I

J

K

L

M

➊ 자동사 (얼굴이) 밝아지다 ❑ 그를 보자, 그녀는 얼굴이 약간 밝아지다 ❑ 그는 얼굴이 약간 밝아졌다. ➋ 자동사 (눈이) 반짝이다 ❑ 그가 두 눈을 반짝이며 웃었다. ➌ 타동사 빛내다, 환하게 하다 ❑ 향꽃무를 심어 놓은 통 덕분에 문 바깥쪽이 환해졌다. ● 구동사 빛내다, 환하게 하다 ❑ 데이비드는 상점에서 분홍색 실크 램프갓을 발견하고는 그걸 가져다 놓으면 방이 환해지리라 생각했다. ➍ 타동사/자동사 밝히다; 밝아지다 ❑ 그것은 도시 아이들의 성공 가능성을 밝히는 데 크게 도움이 되지 않는다. ➎ 타동사/자동사 밝히다; 밝아지다 ❑ 산맥 능선 위의 하늘이 환해졌다. ➏ 자동사 개다 ❑ 이른 오후가 되자 날씨가 개었다.

N

bril|liant ♦◇◇ /brɪliənt/ ➊ ADJ A **brilliant** person, idea, or performance is extremely clever or skillful. ❑ She had a brilliant mind. ● **bril|liant|ly** ADV ❑ It is a very high quality production, brilliantly written and acted. ● **bril|liance** N-UNCOUNT ❑ He was a deeply serious musician who had shown his brilliance very early. ➋ ADJ You can say that something is **brilliant** when you are very pleased with it or think that it is very good. [mainly BRIT, INFORMAL, SPOKEN] ❑ If you get a chance to see the show, do go – it's brilliant. ● **bril|liant|ly** ADV ❑ It's extremely hard working together but on the whole it works brilliantly and we're still good friends. ➌ ADJ A **brilliant** career or success is very successful. ❑ He served four years in prison, emerging to find his brilliant career in ruins. ● **bril|liant|ly** ADV ❑ The strategy worked brilliantly. ➍ ADJ A **brilliant** color is extremely bright. [ADJ n] ❑ The woman had brilliant green eyes. ● **bril|liant|ly** ADV [ADV adj/-ed] ❑ Many of the patterns show brilliantly colored flowers. ● **bril|liance** N-UNCOUNT ❑ ...an iridescent blue butterfly in all its brilliance. ➎ ADJ You describe light, or something that reflects light, as **brilliant** when it shines very brightly. ❑ The event was held in brilliant sunshine. ● **bril|liant|ly** ADV ❑ It's a brilliantly sunny morning. ● **bril|liance** N-UNCOUNT ❑ His eyes became accustomed to the dark after the brilliance of the sun outside.

O

P

Q

R

S

➊ 형용사 재기 넘치는 ❑ 그녀는 재기가 넘치는 사람이었다. ● 재기 넘치게; 훌륭히 부사 ❑ 그 작품은 각본과 연기가 훌륭한, 대단히 좋은 작품이다. ● 재기 발랄; 명민함 불가산명사 ❑ 그는 아주 일찍이 재기 발랄함을 과시했던 대단히 진지한 음악가였다. ➋ 형용사 훌륭한 [주로 영국영어, 비격식체, 구어체] ❑ 기회가 된다면 그 공연을 꼭 보러 가세요. 아주 멋집니다. ● 훌륭히 부사 ❑ 함께 작업한다는 건 대단히 어려운 일이지만, 대체로 잘 되고 있고 우리는 여전히 좋은 친구 사이이다. ➌ 형용사 훌륭한, 매우 성공적인 ❑ 그는 4년간 옥살이를 한 뒤 나타나 파국 속에서 매우 성공적인 출셋길을 발견했다. ● 훌륭하게 부사 ❑ 그 전략은 훌륭하게 먹혀들었다. ➍ 형용사 매우 밝은 ❑ 그 여인의 눈은 아주 밝은 초록색이었다. ● 매우 밝게 부사 ❑ 그 무늬들 중 여럿은 매우 밝은 색으로 빛나는 꽃무늬이다. ● 매우 밝음 불가산명사 ❑ 아주 무지개 빛깔로 휘황찬란히 빛나는 푸른 나비 한 마리 ➎ 형용사 찬란하게 빛나는 ❑ 그 행사는 찬란한 태양이 빛나는 속에서 거행되었다. ● 번쩍번쩍, 찬연히 부사 ❑ 햇살이 눈부시게 빛나는 아침이다. ● 광휘 불가산명사 ❑ 바깥의 밝은 태양빛 속에 있다가 들어온 그의 두 눈이 차츰 어둠에 익숙해졌다.

T

brim /brɪm/ (brims, brimming, brimmed) ➊ N-COUNT The **brim** of a hat is the wide part that sticks outward at the bottom. ❑ Rain dripped from the brim of his baseball cap. ➋ V-I If someone or something **is brimming with** a particular quality, they are full of that quality. [usu cont] ❑ The team is brimming with confidence after two straight wins in the tournament. ➌ V-I When your eyes **are brimming with** tears, they are full of fluid because you are upset, although you are not actually crying. ❑ Michael looked at him imploringly, eyes brimming with tears. ➍ V-I If something **brims** with particular things, it is packed full of them. ❑ The flowerbeds brim with a mixture of lilies and roses.

U

V

➊ 가산명사 챙 ❑ 그의 야구 모자챙에서 빗물이 방울져 떨어졌다. ➋ 자동사 넘칠 정도로 가득 차다 ❑ 그 팀은 토너먼트에서 두 번 연승한 뒤라서 자신감이 넘쳐 흐른다. ➌ 자동사 그렁그렁하다 ❑ 마이클은 눈물이 그렁그렁한 눈으로 애원하듯이 그를 바라보았다. ➍ 자동사 가득 차다 ❑ 백합과 장미가 뒤섞여 꽃밭 가득 피어 있다.

W

bring ♦♦♦ /brɪŋ/ (brings, bringing, brought) ➊ V-T If you **bring** someone or something **with** you when you come to a place, they come with you or you have them with you. ❑ Remember to bring an apron or an old shirt to protect your clothes. ❑ Someone went upstairs and brought down a huge kettle. ➋ V-T If you **bring** something somewhere, you move it there. ❑ Reaching into her pocket, she brought out a cigarette. ➌ V-T If you **bring** something that someone wants or needs, you get it for them or carry it to them. ❑ He went and poured a brandy for Dena and brought it to her. ➍ V-T To **bring** something or someone to a place or position means to cause them to come to the place or move into that position. ❑ I told you about what brought me here. ❑ The shock of her husband's arrival brought her to her feet.

X

Y

Z

➊ 타동사 가져오다, 데려오다 ❑ 옷 버리지 않게 앞치마나 낡은 셔츠를 잊지 말고 가져오세요. ❑ 누군가가 위층으로 올라가서 커다란 주전자를 가지고 내려왔다. ➋ 타동사 움직이다; 옮기다 ❑ 그녀는 주머니에 손을 넣더니 담배 하나를 꺼냈다. ➌ 타동사 가져다주다 ❑ 그는 가서 브랜디를 한 잔 따른 다음 디나에게 가져다 주었다. ➍ 타동사 오게 하다 ❑ 내가 여기 온 이유에 대해 네게 말했다. ❑ 그녀는 남편의 등장에 충격을 받아 벌떡 일어났다.

Bring and **take** are both used to talk about carrying something or accompanying someone somewhere, but **bring** is used to suggest movement toward the speaker and **take** is used to suggest movement away from the speaker. ❑ *Bring your calculator to every lesson... Anna took the book to school with her.* In the first sentence, **bring** suggests that the person and the calculator should come to the place where the speaker is. In the second sentence, ❑ *took* suggests that Anna left the speaker when she went to school. You could also say "take your calculator to every lesson" to suggest that the speaker will not be present at the lesson, and "Anna brought the book to school with her" to suggest that Anna and the speaker were both at school.

bring과 take는 둘 다 무엇을 옮기거나 누구를 동행하는 것을 말할 때 쓰지만, bring은 화자 쪽으로 가는 이동을, take는 화자로부터 멀어져 가는 이동을 나타낼 때 쓴다. ❑ 수업 때마다 계산기를 가지고 오시오... 안나가 그 책을 학교에 가지고 갔다. 첫 번째 문장에서 bring은 화자가 있는 곳으로 사람과 계산기가 와야 함을 말한다. 두 번째 문장에서 took은 안나가 학교에 가면서 화자로부터 떠났음을 나타낸다. 화자가 수업 현장에 있지 않음을 시사할 때에는 "수업마다 계산기를 가지고 가시오"라고 하고, 안나와 화자가 모두 학교에 있음을 시사할 때에는 "안나가 그 책을 학교에 가지고 왔다"고 말할 수 있다.

5 V-T If you **bring** something new **to** a place or group of people, you introduce it to that place or cause those people to hear or know about it. ❑ *...the drive to bring art to the public.* **6** V-T To **bring** someone or something into a particular state or condition means to cause them to be in that state or condition. ❑ *He brought the car to a stop in front of the square.* ❑ *They have brought down income taxes.* **7** V-T If something **brings** a particular feeling, situation, or quality, it makes people experience it or have it. ❑ *He called on the United States to play a more effective role in bringing peace to the region.* ❑ *Her three children brought her joy.* **8** V-T If a period of time **brings** a particular thing, it happens during that time. ❑ *For Sandro, the new year brought disaster.* **9** V-T When you are talking, you can say that something **brings** you **to** a particular point in order to indicate that you have now reached that point and are going to talk about a new subject. ❑ *And that brings us to the end of this special report from Germany.* **10** V-T If you cannot **bring yourself to** do something, you cannot do it because you find it too upsetting, embarrassing, or disgusting. [with brd-neg] ❑ *It is all very tragic and I am afraid I just cannot bring myself to talk about it at the moment.* **11** to **bring** something **alive** →see **alive**. to **bring the house down** →see **house**. to **bring up the rear** →see **rear**

5 타동사 소개하다, 알리다 ❑ 대중에게 미술을 알리기 위한 운동 **6** 타동사 (상대나 현상을) 오래하다 ❑ 그는 광장 앞에 차를 세웠다. ❑ 그들은 소득세를 낮추었다. **7** 타동사 가져다 주다 ❑ 그는 미국이 그 지역에 평화를 가져다주는 데 있어서 보다 효과적인 역할을 수행해 줄 것을 요청했다. ❑ 3명의 자식들이 그녀에게 기쁨을 주었다. **8** 타동사 (어떤 일이) 일어나게 하다 ❑ 산드로에게, 그 새해에는 재난이 찾아왔다. **9** 타동사 이끌다 ❑ 그럼 그것으로써 독일로부터 본 특별 보도를 마치겠습니다. **10** 타동사 -하도록 하다 ❑ 그 일은 너무나 비극적이어서 내가 지금은 그저 그 일에 대해 말하기 힘들 것 같다.

Thesaurus bring의 참조어

v.   bear, carry, take; (*ant.*) drop, leave **1**
      move, take, transfer **2** **3**

Word Partnership bring의 연어

N.   bring *something/someone* home **4**
      bring **to a boil**, bring **to life**, bring **together** **6**
      bring **bad/good luck**, bring **to** *someone's* **attention**, bring **to justice** **7**

Do not confuse the verbs **bring up** and **grow up**. **Bring up** is a transitive verb, and describes the process of looking after and socializing a child. ❑ *...we both felt the town was the perfect place to bring up a family.* **Grow up** is an intransitive verb, and describes the process of becoming an adult. ❑ *I grew up in rural southern Colorado.* Note then, that parents do not "grow up" their children, they "bring them up." See also note at **educate**.

bring up과 grow up을 혼동하지 않도록 하라. bring up은 타동사이며, 아이를 돌보고 가르치는 과정을 나타낸다. ❑ ...우리는 둘 다 그 마을이 아이들을 키우기에 완벽한 곳이라고 생각했다. grow up은 자동사이며, 성인이 되는 과정을 나타낸다. ❑ 나는 콜로라도 남부 시골에서 성장했다. 그러니까 부모가 자녀들을 기르는 것은 grow up their children이 아니라 bring them up 또는 bring up their children임을 유의하라. educate의 주석도 참고하라.

▶**bring about** PHRASAL VERB To **bring** something **about** means to cause it to happen. ❑ *The only way they can bring about political change is by putting pressure on the country.*

구동사 일으키다 ❑ 그들이 정치적 변화를 일으킬 수 있는 유일한 방법은 그 나라에 압력을 가하는 것뿐이다.

▶**bring along** PHRASAL VERB If you **bring** someone or something **along**, you bring them with you when you come to a place. ❑ *They brought along Laura Jane in a pram.*

구동사 가지고 오다; 데리고 오다 ❑ 그들은 로라 제인을 유모차에 태워 데리고 왔다.

▶**bring back** **1** PHRASAL VERB Something that **brings back** a memory makes you think about it. ❑ *Your article brought back sad memories for me.* **2** PHRASAL VERB When people **bring back** a practice or fashion that existed at an earlier time, they introduce it again. ❑ *The House of Commons is to debate once again whether to bring back the death penalty.*

1 구동사 상기시키다 ❑ 당신의 기사를 보고 슬픈 기억이 떠올랐다. **2** 구동사 되살리다 ❑ 하원에서는 사형 제도를 되살릴 것인지에 대해 다시 한 번 논의할 예정이다.

▶**bring down** **1** PHRASAL VERB When people or events **bring down** a government or ruler, they cause the government or ruler to lose power. ❑ *They were threatening to bring down the government by withdrawing from the ruling coalition.* **2** PHRASAL VERB If someone or something **brings down** a person or airplane, they cause them to fall, usually by shooting them. ❑ *Military historians may never know what brought down the jet.*

1 구동사 전복시키다 ❑ 그들은 연립 정부에서 발을 뺌으로써 정부를 전복시키겠다고 협박하고 있었다. **2** 구동사 격추하다; 낚이뜨리다 ❑ 군사 역사학자들은 무엇이 그 제트기를 추락시켰는지 결코 알 수 없을지도 모른다.

▶**bring forward** PHRASAL VERB If you **bring forward** a meeting or event, you arrange for it to take place at an earlier date or time than had been planned. ❑ *He had to bring forward an 11 o'clock meeting so that he could get to the funeral on time.*

구동사 앞당기다 ❑ 그는 장례식에 늦지 않기 위해 11시 회의를 앞당겨야 했다.

▶**bring in** **1** PHRASAL VERB When a government or organization **brings in** a new law or system, they introduce it. ❑ *The government brought in a controversial law under which it could take any land it wanted.* **2** PHRASAL VERB Someone or something that **brings in** money makes or earns it. ❑ *I have three part-time jobs, which bring in about £14,000 a year.* **3** PHRASAL VERB If you **bring in** someone from outside a team or organization, you invite them to do a job or join in an activity or discussion. ❑ *The firm decided to bring in a new management team.*

1 구동사 도입하다 ❑ 정부는 정부가 원하는 토지를 마음대로 취할 수 있도록 하는, 논란의 여지가 있는 법률을 도입했다. **2** 구동사 수입이 생기다 ❑ 나는 파트타임 일을 세 개 하는데, 그걸로 버는 수입이 1년에 14,000파운드 정도 된다. **3** 구동사 영입하다 ❑ 그 회사는 새로운 경영진을 영입하기로 결정했다.

▶**bring out** **1** PHRASAL VERB When a person or company **brings out** a new product, especially a new book or CD, they produce it and put it on sale. ❑ *A*

1 구동사 발표하다; 출시하다 ❑ 일생을 저널리스트로 살아온 그가 이번에 책을 한 권 발표했다. **2** 구동사

journalist all his life, he's now brought out a book. ◨ PHRASAL VERB Something that **brings out** a particular kind of behaviour or feeling in you causes you to show it, especially when it is something you do not normally show. ◻ *He is totally dedicated and brings out the best in his pupils.*

▶**bring up** ◨ PHRASAL VERB When someone **brings up** a child, they look after it until it is an adult. If someone has **been brought up** in a certain place or with certain attitudes, they grew up in that place or were taught those attitudes when they were growing up. ◻ *She brought up four children.* ◻ *He was brought up in North Yorkshire.* ◨ PHRASAL VERB If you **bring up** a particular subject, you introduce it into a discussion or conversation. ◻ *He brought up a subject rarely raised during the course of this campaign.*

brink /brɪŋk/ N-SING If you are **on the brink of** something, usually something important, terrible, or exciting, you are just about to do it or experience it. ◻ *Their economy is teetering on the brink of collapse.*

brisk /brɪsk/ (brisker, briskest) ◨ ADJ A **brisk** activity or action is done quickly and in an energetic way. ◻ *Taking a brisk walk can often induce a feeling of well-being.* ● **brisk|ly** ADV [ADV with v] ◻ *Eve walked briskly down the corridor to her son's room.* ◨ ADJ If trade or business is **brisk**, things are being sold very quickly and a lot of money is being made. [BUSINESS] ◻ *Vendors were doing a brisk trade in souvenirs.* ● **brisk|ly** ADV [ADV after v] ◻ *A trader said gold sold briskly on the local market.* ◨ ADJ If the weather is **brisk**, it is cold and fresh. ◻ *...a typically brisk winter's day on the South Coast.* ◨ ADJ Someone who is **brisk** behaves in a busy, confident way which shows that they want to get things done quickly. ◻ *The Chief summoned me downstairs. He was brisk and businesslike.* ● **brisk|ly** ADV [ADV with v] ◻ *"Anyhow," she added briskly, "it's none of my business."*

bris|tle /brɪsᵊl/ (bristles) ◨ N-COUNT **Bristles** are the short hairs that grow on a man's face after he has shaved. The hairs on the top of a man's head can also be called **bristles** when they are cut very short. ◻ *...two days' growth of bristles.* ◨ N-COUNT The **bristles** of a brush are the thick hairs or hairlike pieces of plastic which are attached to it. ◻ *As soon as the bristles on your toothbrush begin to wear, throw it out.* ◨ N-COUNT **Bristles** are thick, strong animal hairs that feel hard and rough. ◻ *It has a short stumpy tail covered with bristles.*

Brit|on /brɪtᵊn/ (Britons) N-COUNT A **Briton** is a British citizen, or a person of British origin. [FORMAL] ◻ *The role is played by seventeen-year-old Briton Jane March.*

brit|tle /brɪtᵊl/ ADJ An object or substance that is **brittle** is hard but easily broken. ◻ *Pine is brittle and breaks.*

broach /broʊtʃ/ (broaches, broaching, broached) V-T When you **broach** a subject, especially a sensitive one, you mention it in order to start a discussion on it. ◻ *Eventually I broached the subject of her early life.*

broad ♦♦◇ /brɔd/ (broader, broadest) ◨ ADJ Something that is **broad** is wide. ◻ *His shoulders were broad and his waist narrow.* ◻ *The hills rise green and sheer above the broad river.* ◨ ADJ A **broad** smile is one in which your mouth is stretched very wide because you are very pleased or amused. ◻ *He greeted them with a wave and a broad smile.* ● **broad|ly** ADV ◻ *Charles grinned broadly.* ◨ ADJ You use **broad** to describe something that includes a large number of different things or people. ◻ *A broad range of issues was discussed.* ● **broad|ly** ADV [ADV with v] ◻ *This gives children a more broadly based education.* ◨ ADJ You use **broad** to describe a word or meaning which covers or refers to a wide range of different things. ◻ *...restructuring in the broad sense of the word.* ● **broad|ly** ADV [ADV with v] ◻ *We define education very broadly and students can study any aspect of its consequences for society.* ◨ ADJ You use **broad** to describe a feeling or opinion that is shared by many people, or by people of many different kinds. [ADJ n] ◻ *The agreement won broad support in the U.S. Congress.* ● **broad|ly** ADV [ADV with v] ◻ *The new law has been broadly welcomed by road safety organisations.* ◨ **in broad daylight** →see **daylight**

Word Partnership	broad의 연어
N.	broad **expanse**, broad **shoulders** ◨
	broad **smile** ◨
	broad **range**, broad **spectrum** ◨
	broad **definition**, broad **view** ◨

broad|band /brɔdbænd/ N-UNCOUNT **Broadband** is a method of sending many electronic messages at the same time by using a wide range of frequencies. [COMPUTING] ◻ *The two companies said they planned to develop new broadband services for customers in the UK and Ireland jointly.*

broad|cast ♦◇◇ /brɔdkæst/ (broadcasts, broadcasting)

The form **broadcast** is used in the present tense and is the past tense and past participle of the verb.

◨ N-COUNT A **broadcast** is a program, performance, or speech on the radio or on television. ◻ *In a broadcast on state radio the government also announced that it was willing to resume peace negotiations.* ◨ V-T To **broadcast** a program means to send it out by radio waves, wires, or satellites so that it can be heard on the radio or seen on television. ◻ *The concert will be broadcast live on television and radio.*

broad|cast|er /brɔdkæstər/ (broadcasters) N-COUNT A **broadcaster** is someone who gives talks or takes part in interviews and discussions on radio or television programs. ◻ *...the prominent naturalist and broadcaster, Sir David Attenborough.*

broad|cast|ing ♦◇◇ /brɔdkæstɪŋ/ N-UNCOUNT **Broadcasting** is the making and sending out of television and radio programs. ◻ *If this happens it will change the face of religious broadcasting.*

이끌어 내다 ◻ 그는 대단히 헌신적이며 자신이 가르치는 학생들에게서 최상의 것을 이끌어 낸다.

◨ 구동사 기르다, 가르치다 ◻ 그녀는 4명의 아이를 길렀다. ◻ 그는 노스 요크셔에서 자랐다. ◨ 구동사 (화제 등을) 내놓다 ◻ 이번 선거 운동 과정에서 좀처럼 제기되지 않았던 문제를 그가 제기했다.

단수명사 –하기 직전인 ◻ 경제가 붕괴 직전에서 허덕이고 있다.

◨ 형용사 활기찬, 경쾌한 ◻ 활기차게 걸으면 흔히 행복한 느낌을 받을 수 있다. ● 활기차게, 기운차게 부사 ◻ 이브는 복도를 따라 아들의 방으로 활기차게 걸어갔다. ◨ 형용사 활발한 [경제] ◻ 상인들이 기념품을 활발하게 매매하고 있었다. ● 활발히 부사 ◻ 한 거래원에 따르면 금이 현지 시장에서 활발히 거래되고 있다고 한다. ◨ 형용사 차고 건조한 ◻ 전형적인 차고 건조한 사우스 코스트의 어느 겨울날 ◨ 형용사 사무적인, 딱 부러지는 ◻ 사장이 나를 아래층으로 불렀다. 그는 딱 부러지고 사무적이었다. ● 딱 부러지게 부사 ◻ "어쨌든, 내가 상관할 바가 아니야."라고 그녀가 딱 부러지게 덧붙였다.

◨ 가산명사 꺼끌꺼끌한 수염; 뻣뻣한 털 ◻ 면도 후이틀 동안 자라난 꺼끌꺼끌한 수염 ◨ 가산명사 센 털, 플라스틱 솔 ◻ 칫솔모가 닳기 시작하면 바로 버려라. ◨ 가산명사 억센 털 ◻ 그것은 짤막한 꼬리가 억센 털로 덮여 있다.

가산명사 영국인 [격식체] ◻ 이 역은 17세의 영국 배우인 제인 마치가 맡았다.

형용사 부서지기 쉬운 ◻ 소나무는 잘 부러지고 쪼개진다.

타동사 (화제를) 꺼내다 ◻ 결국 나는 그녀의 젊은 시절 이야기를 꺼냈다.

◨ 형용사 넓은 ◻ 그는 어깨가 넓고 허리가 가늘었다. ◻ 푸르고 가파른 언덕이 드넓은 강을 내려다보고 있다. ◨ 형용사 활짝 웃는 ◻ 그는 손을 흔들고 활짝 웃으며 그들을 맞았다. ● 활짝 부사 ◻ 찰스가 활짝 웃었다. ◨ 형용사 다양한, 폭넓은 ◻ 다양한 문제가 논의되었다. ● 다양하게, 폭넓게 부사 ◻ 이는 아이들에게 더욱 폭넓은 교육을 제공한다. ◨ 형용사 폭넓은 의미의 ◻ 폭넓은 의미의 구조 조정 ● 넓은 의미로 부사 ◻ 우리는 교육을 매우 폭넓게 정의하고 있으며 학생들은 교육이 사회에 미치는 영향의 어떤 측면이든 연구할 수 있다. ◨ 형용사 폭넓은 ◻ 이 협정은 미국 의회의 폭넓은 지지를 얻었다. ● 폭넓게 부사 ◻ 새 법률은 도로 안전 기관들로부터 폭넓은 환영을 받았다.

불가산명사 광대역 [컴퓨터] ◻ 두 기업은 영국과 아일랜드 고객을 위한 새로운 광대역 서비스를 합작 개발하기로 했다고 밝혔다.

broadcast은 동사의 현재, 과거, 과거 분사로 쓴다.

◨ 가산명사 방송 ◻ 정부는 또한 평화 협상을 재개할 의사가 있다고 국영 라디오 방송을 통해 발표했다. ◨ 타동사/자동사 방송하다 ◻ 콘서트는 텔레비전과 라디오를 통해서 생방송될 것이다.

가산명사 방송인 ◻ 유명한 박물학자이자 방송인인 데이비드 아텐보로 경

불가산명사 방송 ◻ 그렇게 된다면, 이는 종교 방송의 면모를 바꿔 놓을 것이다.

broad|en /brɔ́dən/ (broadens, broadening, broadened) ◾ V-I When something **broadens**, it becomes wider. ❑ *The trails broadened into roads.* ◾ V-T/V-I When you **broaden** something such as your experience or popularity or when it **broadens**, the number of things or people that it includes becomes greater. ❑ *We must broaden our appeal.* ❑ *I thought you wanted to broaden your horizons.*

broad|ly /brɔ́dli/ ADV You can use **broadly** to indicate that something is generally true. [ADV with cl] ❑ *The President broadly got what he wanted out of his meeting.* →see also **broad**

broad|sheet /brɔ́dʃit/ (broadsheets) N-COUNT A **broadsheet** is a newspaper that is printed on large sheets of paper. Broadsheets are generally considered to be more serious than other newspapers. Compare **tabloid**. ❑ *Even the broadsheets made it their lead story.*

broc|co|li /brɒ́kəli/ N-UNCOUNT **Broccoli** is a vegetable with green stalks and green or purple tops. →see **vegetable**

bro|chure /broʊʃʊr, BRIT broʊʃəʳ/ (brochures) N-COUNT A **brochure** is a magazine or thin book with pictures that gives you information about a product or service. ❑ *...travel brochures.*

broil /brɔ́ɪl/ (broils, broiling, broiled) V-T When you **broil** food, you cook it using very strong heat directly above or below it. [AM; BRIT **grill**] ❑ *I'll broil the lobster.* →see **cook**

broil|er /brɔ́ɪlər/ (broilers) N-COUNT A **broiler** is a part of a stove which produces strong heat and cooks food placed underneath it. [AM; BRIT **grill**] ❑ *Remove from heat and finish off under the broiler until cheese melts.*

broke /broʊk/ ◾ **Broke** is the past tense of **break**. ◾ ADJ If you are **broke**, you have no money. [INFORMAL] [v-link ADJ] ❑ *What do you mean, I've got enough money? I'm as broke as you are.* ◾ PHRASE If a company or person **goes broke**, they lose money and are unable to continue in business or to pay their debts. [INFORMAL, BUSINESS] ❑ *Balton went broke twice in his career.*

Thesaurus	broke의 참조어
ADJ.	bankrupt, destitute, penniless, poor; (ant.) rich, wealthy, well-to-do ◾

bro|ken /broʊkən/ ◾ **Broken** is the past participle of **break**. ◾ ADJ A **broken** line is not continuous but has gaps or spaces in it. [ADJ n] ❑ *A broken blue line means the course of a waterless valley.* ◾ ADJ You can use **broken** to describe a marriage that has ended in divorce, or a home in which the parents of the family are divorced, when you think this is a sad or bad thing. [DISAPPROVAL] [ADJ n] ❑ *She spoke for the first time about the traumas of a broken marriage.* ◾ ADJ If someone talks in **broken** English, for example, or in **broken** French, they speak slowly and make a lot of mistakes because they do not know the language very well. [ADJ n] ❑ *Eric could only respond in broken English.*

bro|ker ◆◇◇ /broʊkər/ (brokers, brokering, brokered) ◾ N-COUNT A **broker** is a person whose job is to buy and sell shares, foreign money, or goods for other people. [BUSINESS] ◾ V-T If a country or government **brokers** an agreement, a ceasefire, or a round of talks, they try to negotiate or arrange it. ❑ *The United Nations brokered a peace in Mogadishu at the end of March.*

bro|ker|age /broʊkərɪdʒ/ (brokerages) N-COUNT A **brokerage** or a **brokerage** firm is a company of brokers. [BUSINESS] ❑ *...Japan's four biggest brokerages.*

bronze /brɒ́nz/ ◾ N-UNCOUNT **Bronze** is a yellowish-brown metal which is a mixture of copper and tin. ❑ *...a bronze statue of Giorgi Dimitrov.* ◾ COLOR Something that is **bronze** is yellowish-brown in color. ❑ *Her hair shone bronze and gold.*

bronze med|al (bronze medals) N-COUNT A **bronze medal** is a medal made of bronze or bronze-colored metal that is given as a prize to the person who comes third in a competition, especially a sports contest.

brooch /broʊtʃ/ (brooches) N-COUNT A **brooch** is a small piece of jewelry which has a pin at the back so it can be fastened on a dress, blouse, or coat. →see **jewelry**

brood /brúd/ (broods, brooding, brooded) ◾ N-COUNT A **brood** is a group of baby birds that were born at the same time to the same mother. ❑ *...a hungry brood of fledglings.* ◾ N-COUNT You can refer to someone's young children as their **brood** when you want to emphasize that there are a lot of them. [EMPHASIS] ❑ *...a large brood of children.* ◾ V-I If someone **broods** over something, they think about it a lot, seriously and often unhappily. ❑ *She constantly broods about her family.*

brood|ing /brúdɪŋ/ ADJ **Brooding** is used to describe an atmosphere or feeling that makes you feel anxious or slightly afraid. [LITERARY] ❑ *The same heavy, brooding silence descended on them.*

broom /brúm/ (brooms) ◾ N-COUNT A **broom** is a kind of brush with a long handle. You use a broom for sweeping the floor. ◾ N-UNCOUNT **Broom** is a wild bush with a lot of tiny yellow flowers.

Bros. **Bros.** is an abbreviation for **brothers**. It is usually used as part of the name of a company. [BUSINESS]

broth /brɔ́θ, BRIT brɒ́θ/ (broths) N-VAR **Broth** is a kind of soup made by boiling meat or vegetables.

broth|el /brɒ́θəl/ (brothels) N-COUNT A **brothel** is a building where men can go to pay to have sex with prostitutes.

◾ 자동사 넓어지다, 벌어지다 ❑ 오솔길이 넓어져 도로가 되었다. ◾ 타동사/자동사 넓히다 ❑ 우리는 더 많은 사람들에게 매력 있게 보여야 한다. ❑ 나는 내가 시야를 넓히고 싶어 한다고 생각했어.

부사 대체적으로 ❑ 대통령은 그가 회담에서 바라던 것을 대체적으로 얻었다.

가산명사 (타블로이드판이 아닌) 일반 판형의 신문 ❑ 주요 일간지조차도 이를 머리기사로 썼다.

불가산명사 브로콜리

가산명사 책자, 팸플릿 ❑ 여행 안내 책자

타동사 굽다 [미국영어; 영국영어 grill] ❑ 내가 바닷가재를 구울게.

가산명사 브로일러 [미국영어; 영국영어 grill] ❑ 불에서 꺼내서 브로일러 밑에서 치즈를 녹여 완성하라.

◾ break의 과거형 ◾ 형용사 빈털터리의 [비격식체] ❑ 내가 돈이 충분하다니, 도대체 무슨 소리야? 나도 너처럼 빈털터리야. ◾ 구 파산하다 [비격식체, 경제] ❑ 발튼은 일을 하는 동안 두 번 파산했다.

◾ break의 과거 분사 ◾ 형용사 끊어진, 점선으로 된 ❑ 파란색 점선은 물이 없는 계곡을 나타낸다. ◾ 형용사 파탄난, 결손의 [탐탁잖음] ❑ 그녀는 처음으로 실패한 결혼 생활의 상처에 대해 이야기했다. ◾ 형용사 엉터리의 ❑ 에릭은 엉터리 영어로만 대답할 수 있었다.

◾ 가산명사 중개인, 브로커 [경제] ◾ 타동사 중재하다 ❑ 미국은 3월 말 모가디슈에서 평화 협상을 중재했다.

가산명사 중개업체 [경제] ❑ 일본의 4대 중개업체

◾ 불가산명사 청동 ❑ 조르지 디미트로프의 청동상 ◾ 색채어 청동색 ❑ 그녀의 머리는 청동색과 금빛으로 빛났다.

가산명사 동메달

가산명사 브로치

◾ 가산명사 어린 새들 ❑ 배가 고픈 어린 새들 ◾ 가산명사 자식들 [강조] ❑ 많은 자식들 ◾ 자동사 노심초사하다, 고심하다 ❑ 그녀는 끊임없이 식구들 때문에 노심초사한다.

형용사 불길한, 답답한 [문예체] ❑ 똑같이 무겁고 답답한 침묵이 그들을 감쌌다.

◾ 가산명사 빗자루 ◾ 불가산명사 금작화

brothers의 약어로 보통 회사 이름에 사용 [경제]

가산명사 또는 불가산명사 수프

가산명사 사창가

A

broth|er ♦♦♦ /brʌðər/ (brothers)

B

| The old-fashioned form **brethren** is still sometimes used as the plural for meanings **2** and **3**. | 구식어인 brethren은 여전히 가끔 **2**와 **3** 의미의 복수로 쓴다. |

1 N-COUNT Your **brother** is a boy or a man who has the same parents as you. ❑ *Oh, so you're Peter's younger brother.* →see also **half-brother, stepbrother** **2** N-COUNT You can describe a man as your **brother** if he belongs to the same race, religion, country, or profession as you, or if he has similar ideas to you.

C

❑ *He told reporters he'd come to be with his Latvian brothers.* **3** N-TITLE; N-COUNT; N-VOC **Brother** is a title given to a man who belongs to a religious community such as a monastery. ❑ *...Brother Otto.* **4** N-IN-NAMES **Brothers** is used in the names of some companies and stores. ❑ *...the film company Warner Brothers.*

D

broth|er|hood /brʌðərhʊd/ (brotherhoods) **1** N-UNCOUNT **Brotherhood** is the affection and loyalty that you feel for people who you have something in common with. ❑ *People threw flowers into the river between the two countries as a symbolic act of brotherhood.* **2** N-COUNT A **brotherhood** is an organization whose

E

members all have the same political aims and beliefs or the same job or profession. ❑ *...the Brotherhood of Locomotive Engineers.*

brother-in-law (brothers-in-law) N-COUNT Someone's **brother-in-law** is the brother of their husband or wife, or the man who is married to their sister. →see **family**

F

brought /brɔːt/ **Brought** is the past tense and past participle of **bring**.

G

brow /braʊ/ (brows) **1** N-COUNT Your **brow** is your forehead. ❑ *He wiped his brow with the back of his hand.* **2** N-COUNT Your **brows** are your eyebrows. ❑ *He had thick brown hair and shaggy brows.* **3** N-COUNT The **brow** of a hill is the top part of it. ❑ *He was on the look-out just below the brow of the hill.*

H

brown ♦♦♦ /braʊn/ (browner, brownest, browns, browning, browned) **1** COLOR Something that is **brown** is the color of earth or of wood. ❑ *...her deep brown eyes.* **2** ADJ You can describe a white-skinned person as **brown** when they have been sitting in the sun until their skin has become darker than usual. ❑ *I don't want to be really really brown, just have a nice light golden color.* **3** ADJ A **brown** person is someone who belongs to a race of people who have brown-colored skins.

I

❑ *...a slim brown man with a speckled turban.* **4** ADJ **Brown** is used to describe grains that have not had their outer layers removed, and foods made from these grains. ❑ *...brown bread.* **5** V-T/V-I When food **browns** or when you **brown** food, you cook it, usually for a short time on a high flame. ❑ *Cook for ten minutes until the sugar browns.*

J

K

brown|field /braʊnfiːld/ ADJ **Brownfield** land is land in a town or city where houses or factories have been built in the past, but which is not being used at the present time. [ADJ n]

L

brown goods N-PLURAL **Brown goods** are electrical appliances such as televisions and audio equipment. Compare **white goods**. ❑ *Revenue from brown goods, including televisions and hi-fis, rose nearly 12 percent.*

M

browse /braʊz/ (browses, browsing, browsed) **1** V-I If you **browse** in a store, you look at things in a fairly casual way, in the hope that you might find something you like. ❑ *I stopped in several bookstores to browse.* ❑ *She browsed in an up-market antiques shop.* ● N-COUNT **Browse** is also a noun. ❑ *...a browse around the shops.* **2** V-I If you **browse through** a book or magazine, you look through it in a fairly casual way. ❑ *...sitting on the sofa browsing through the TV pages of the paper.*

N

O

P

3 V-I If you **browse** on a computer, you search for information in computer files or on the Internet, especially on the World Wide Web. [COMPUTING] ❑ *Try browsing around in the network bulletin boards.* **4** V-T/V-I When animals **browse**, they feed on plants. ❑ *...the three red deer stags browsing 50 yards from my lodge on the fringes of the forest.*

Q

brows|er /braʊzər/ (browsers) **1** N-COUNT A **browser** is a piece of computer software that you use to search for information on the Internet, especially on the World Wide Web. [COMPUTING] ❑ *You need an up-to-date web browser, such as Internet Explorer version 5.1 or above.* **2** N-COUNT A **browser** is someone who browses in a store. ❑ *...a casual browser.*

R

bruise /bruːz/ (bruises, bruising, bruised) **1** N-COUNT A **bruise** is an injury which appears as a purple mark on your body, although the skin is not broken. ❑ *How did you get that bruise on your cheek?* **2** V-T/V-I If you **bruise** a part of your body, a bruise appears on it, for example because something hits you. If you **bruise** easily, bruises appear when something hits you only slightly. ❑ *I had only bruised my knee.* ● **bruised** ADJ ❑ *I escaped with severely bruised legs.*

S

T

3 V-T/V-I If a fruit, vegetable, or plant **bruises** or is **bruised**, it is damaged by being handled roughly, making a mark on the skin. ❑ *Choose a warm, dry day to cut them off the plants, being careful not to bruise them.* ❑ *...bruised tomatoes and cucumbers.* ● N-COUNT **Bruise** is also a noun. ❑ *...bruises on the fruit's skin.* **4** V-T If you **are bruised** by an unpleasant experience, it makes you feel unhappy or upset. [usu passive] ❑ *The government will be severely bruised by yesterday's events.*

U

V

brunt /brʌnt/ PHRASE To **bear the brunt** or **take the brunt** of something unpleasant means to suffer the main part or force of it. ❑ *Young people are bearing the brunt of unemployment.*

W

brush ♦♦♦ /brʌʃ/ (brushes, brushing, brushed) **1** N-COUNT A **brush** is an object which has a large number of bristles or hairs fixed to it. You use brushes for painting, for cleaning things, and for making your hair neat. ❑ *We gave him paint and brushes.* **2** V-T If you **brush** something or **brush** something such as dirt off it, you clean it or make it neat using a brush. ❑ *Have you brushed your teeth?* ❑ *She brushed the powder out of her hair.* ● N-SING **Brush** is also a noun. ❑ *I gave it a quick brush with my hairbrush.* **3** V-T If you **brush** something **with** a liquid, you apply a layer of that liquid using a brush. ❑ *Brush the dough with beaten egg yolk.* **4** V-T If you **brush** something somewhere, you remove it with quick light movements

X

Y

Z

---

1 가산명사 형제 ❑ 아, 네가 피터 동생이구나. **2** 가산명사 동료; 동포 ❑ 그는 기자들에게 라트비아 동포들과 함께 하기위해서 왔다고 말했다. **3** 경칭명사; 가산명사; 호격명사 수사 ❑ 오토 수사 **4** 이름명사 회사나 가게 이름에 사용 ❑ 워너 브라더스 영화사

1 불가산명사 형제애 ❑ 사람들이 형제애를 상징하는 행위로 두 나라 사이를 흐르는 강에 꽃을 던졌다. **2** 가산명사 조합, 협회 ❑ 로코모티브 엔지니어 조합

가산명사 처남; 매형; 시동생, 시아주버니

bring의 과거형과 과거 분사

1 가산명사 이마 ❑ 그는 손등으로 이마를 훔쳤다. **2** 가산명사 눈썹 ❑ 그는 숱이 많은 갈색 머리에 눈썹이 덥수룩했다. **3** 가산명사 꼭대기 ❑ 그는 언덕 꼭대기 바로 밑에서 망을 보고 있었다.

1 색채어 갈색 ❑ 그녀의 깊은 갈색 눈 **2** 형용사 볕에 탄, 구릿빛의 ❑ 정말 너무 많이 태운 구릿빛 말고, 그냥 멋지게 약간만 태운 황금색 피부를 갖고 싶다. **3** 형용사 갈색 피부의 ❑ 점무늬 터번을 쓴 호리호리하고 까무잡잡한 남자 **4** 형용사 현미로 된; 통밀로 된 ❑ 통밀빵 **5** 타동사/자동사 갈색이 되다; 갈색으로 만들다 ❑ 설탕이 갈색으로 변할 때까지 10분간 가열한다.

형용사 옛 공장 지대, 옛 주택 지대

복수명사 (텔레비전이나 오디오 같은) 갈색 가전제품 ❑ 텔레비전과 오디오 같은 갈색 가전제품 매출이 거의 12퍼센트 올랐다.

1 자동사 둘러보다 ❑ 서점 몇 군데를 둘러보았다. ❑ 그녀는 고급 앤티크 숍에서 물건을 둘러보았다. ● 단수명사 둘러보기 ❑ 상가를 둘러보기 **2** 자동사 훑어보다 ❑ 신문의 TV면을 훑어보며 소파에 앉아서 **3** 자동사 검색하다 [컴퓨터] ❑ 게시판 네트워크에서 검색해 봐. **4** 타동사/자동사 풀을 뜯어 먹다 ❑ 숲 가장자리에 있는 내 숙소에서 50야드 떨어진 곳에서 풀을 뜯고 있는 붉은 수사슴 세 마리

1 가산명사 브라우저 [컴퓨터] ❑ 인터넷 익스플로러 5.01버전 이상의 최신 웹브라우저가 필요하다. **2** 가산명사 둘러보는 손님 ❑ 그냥 둘러보는 손님

1 가산명사 멍, 타박상 ❑ 어쩌다가 뺨에 멍이 든 거야? **2** 타동사/자동사 멍들다 ❑ 그냥 무릎에 멍이 들었을 뿐이다. ● 멍든 형용사 ❑ 나는 다리에 심하게 타박상을 입으며 빠져 나갔다. **3** 타동사/자동사 멍들다, 상처나다 ❑ 열매는 포근하고 건조한 날을 골라 멍이 들지 않도록 조심하며 딴다. ● 상처 난 토마토와 오이 ● 가산명사 멍, 상처 ❑ 과일 껍질에 난 상처 **4** 타동사 상처 받다, 타격받다 ❑ 정부는 어제 일로 심한 타격을 받을 것이다.

구 가장 큰 피해를 보다 ❑ 젊은이들이 가장 큰 실업난을 겪고 있다.

1 가산명사 붓; 솔; 빗 ❑ 우리는 그에게 페인트와 붓을 주었다. **2** 타동사 털다, 닦다 ❑ 양치질 했니? ❑ 그녀는 머리에 묻은 가루를 빗으로 빗어 냈다. ● 단수명사 솔질, 빗질 ❑ 나는 재빨리 빗으로 손질했다. **3** 타동사 붓으로 칠하다 ❑ 계란 노른자를 풀어서 반죽에 바르세요. **4** 타동사 쓸어 내다, 빗어 내리다 ❑ 그는 그녀 양손으로 머리를 뒤로 빗었다. ❑ 그녀는 그에 대해 이야기하면서 눈물을 훔쳤다. **5** 타동사/자동사 스치다 ❑ 뭔가 그녀의 다리를 스치고 지나갔다. ❑ 나는

of your hands. ❑ *He brushed his hair back with both hands.* ❑ *She brushed away tears as she spoke of him.* **5** V-T/V-I If one thing **brushes against** another or if you **brush** one thing **against** another, the first thing touches the second thing lightly while passing it. ❑ *Something brushed against her leg.* ❑ *I felt her dark brown hair brushing the back of my shoulder.* **6** N-COUNT If you have a **brush with** a particular situation, usually an unpleasant one, you almost experience it. ❑ *...the trauma of a brush with death.* **7** N-UNCOUNT **Brush** is an area of rough open land covered with small bushes and trees. You also use **brush** to refer to the bushes and trees on this land. ❑ *...the brush fire that destroyed nearly 500 acres.*
→see **hair**, **teeth**

▶**brush aside** or **brush away** PHRASAL VERB If you **brush aside** or **brush away** an idea, remark, or feeling, you refuse to consider it because you think it is not important or useful, even though it may be. ❑ *Perhaps you shouldn't brush the idea aside too hastily.*

그녀의 짙은 갈색 머리가 내 어깨 뒤로 스치는 것을 느꼈다. **5** 가산명사 거의 - 할 뻔함 ❑ 죽을 뻔한 경험에서 받은 충격 **7** 불가산명사 덤불 ❑ 거의 500에이커를 태운 산불

구동사 무시하다 ❑ 어쩌면 그 아이디어를 너무 서둘러 제외시키지 말아야 할지도 모른다.

▶**brush up** or **brush up on** PHRASAL VERB If you **brush up** something or **brush up on** it, you practice it or improve your knowledge of it. ❑ *I had hoped to brush up my Spanish.*

구동사 향상시키다, 더 공부하다 ❑ 나는 스페인어를 더 공부하고 싶어 했었다.

brusque /brʌsk/ ADJ If you describe a person or their behavior as **brusque**, you mean that they deal with things, or say things, quickly and shortly, so that they seem to be rude. ❑ *The doctors are brusque and busy.*

형용사 퉁명스러운, 쌀쌀맞은 ❑ 의사들은 쌀쌀맞고 바쁘다.

brus|sels sprout /brʌsəlz spraʊt/ (**brussels sprouts**) also **Brussels sprout** N-COUNT **Brussels sprouts** are vegetables that look like tiny cabbages.

가산명사 브러셀 스프라우트 (통째로 먹는 아주 작은 양배추)

bru|tal /brut°l/ **1** ADJ A **brutal** act or person is cruel and violent. ❑ *He was the victim of a very brutal murder.* ❑ *...the brutal suppression of anti-government protests.* ● **bru|tal|ly** ADV *Her real parents had been brutally murdered.* **2** ADJ If someone expresses something unpleasant with **brutal** honesty or frankness, they express it in a clear and accurate way, without attempting to disguise its unpleasantness. ❑ *It was refreshing to talk about themselves and their feelings with brutal honesty.* ● **bru|tal|ly** ADV ❑ *The talks had been brutally frank.*

1 형용사 잔인한, 난폭한 ❑ 그는 매우 잔인한 살인의 희생자였다. ❑ 반정부 시위에 대한 폭력 진압 ● 잔인하게 부사 그녀의 친부모는 잔인하게 살해되었다. **2** 형용사 솔직 담백한 ❑ 그들 자신과 그들의 생각을 솔직 담백하게 이야기한 것은 매우 신선했다. ● 솔직 담백하게 부사 ❑ 진솔한 회담들이었다.

bru|tal|ity /brutǽlɪti/ (**brutalities**) N-VAR **Brutality** is cruel and violent treatment or behavior. A **brutality** is an instance of cruel and violent treatment or behavior. ❑ *Her experience of men was of domination and brutality.* ❑ *...police brutality.*

가산명사 또는 불가산명사 무자비함, 야만성, 만행 ❑ 그녀가 만난 남자들은 권위적이고 잔혹한 사람들이었다. ❑ 경찰의 만행

brute /brut/ (**brutes**) N-COUNT If you call someone, usually a man, a **brute**, you mean that they are rough, violent, and insensitive. [DISAPPROVAL] ❑ *Custer was an idiot and a brute and he deserved his fate.*

가산명사 짐승 같은 사람 [탐탁찮음] ❑ 커스터는 짐승 같은 얼간이였으며 그런 운명을 맞아도 쌌다.

BSE /bi ɛs i/ N-UNCOUNT **BSE** is a disease which affects the nervous system of cattle and kills them. **BSE** is an abbreviation for "bovine spongiform encephalopathy." ❑ *...meat from cattle infected with BSE, or mad cow disease.*

불가산명사 광우병 ❑ 광우병에 감염된 소의 고기

BTW **BTW** is the written abbreviation for "by the way," often used in e-mail. ❑ *BTW, the machine is simply amazing.*

by the way의 약어 ❑ 그건 그렇고, 이 기계는 정말 놀랍다.

bub|ble /bʌb°l/ (**bubbles, bubbling, bubbled**) **1** N-COUNT **Bubbles** are small balls of air or gas in a liquid. ❑ *Ink particles attach themselves to air bubbles and rise to the surface.* **2** N-COUNT A **bubble** is a hollow ball of soapy liquid that is floating in the air or standing on a surface. ❑ *With soap and water, bubbles and boats, children love bathtime.* **3** N-COUNT In a cartoon, a speech **bubble** is the shape which surrounds the words which a character is thinking or saying. ❑ *All that was missing were speech bubbles saying, "Golly!" and "Wow!"* **4** V-I When a liquid **bubbles**, bubbles move in it, for example because it is boiling or moving quickly. ❑ *Heat the seasoned stock until it is bubbling.* ❑ *The fermenting wine has bubbled up and over the top.* **5** V-I A feeling, influence, or activity that **is bubbling** away continues to occur. [usu cont] ❑ *...political tensions that have been bubbling away for years.* →see **soap**

1 가산명사 기포 ❑ 잉크 입자가 기포에 붙어서 표면 위로 떠오른다. **2** 가산명사 거품 ❑ 비누와 물, 거품과 보트가 있으면, 아이들은 목욕 시간을 좋아한다. **3** 가산명사 말풍선 ❑ 빠진 것이라곤 "저런!"과 "와!" 등의 말풍선 뿐이었다. **4** 자동사 거품이 일다, 기포가 생기다 ❑ 양념한 재료를 보글보글 끓을 때까지 끓인다. ❑ 와인이 발효되면서 거품이 일어 넘쳐흘렀다. **5** 자동사 계속되다 ❑ 수년 동안 계속된 정치적 긴장

bub|bly /bʌbli/ **1** ADJ Someone who is **bubbly** is very lively and cheerful and talks a lot. [APPROVAL] ❑ *...a bubbly girl who loves to laugh.* **2** ADJ If something is **bubbly**, it has a lot of bubbles in it. ❑ *Melt the butter over a medium-low heat. When it is melted and bubbly, put in the flour.*

1 형용사 발랄한 [마음에 듦] ❑ 잘 웃고 발랄한 소녀 **2** 형용사 거품이 많은 ❑ 중간 불과 약한 불 사이에서 버터를 녹인다. 버터가 녹고 거품이 일면, 밀가루를 넣는다.

buck /bʌk/ (**bucks, bucking, bucked**) **1** N-COUNT A **buck** is a U.S. or Australian dollar. [INFORMAL] ❑ *That would probably cost you about fifty bucks.* ❑ *Why can't you spend a few bucks on a coat?* **2** N-COUNT A **buck** is the male of various animals, including the deer, antelope, rabbit, and kangaroo. **3** ADJ If someone has **buck** teeth, their upper front teeth stick forward out of their mouth. [ADJ n] **4** V-I If a horse **bucks**, it kicks both of its back legs wildly into the air, or jumps into the air wildly with all four feet off the ground. ❑ *The stallion bucked as he fought against the reins holding him tightly in.* **5** V-T If you **buck** the trend, you obtain different results from others in the same area. If you **buck** the system, you get what you want by breaking or ignoring the rules. ❑ *While other newspapers are losing circulation, we are bucking the trend.* ❑ *He wants to be the tough rebel who bucks the system.* **6** PHRASE If you **pass the buck**, you refuse to accept responsibility for something, and say that someone else is responsible. [INFORMAL] ❑ *David says the responsibility is Mr. Smith's and it's no good trying to pass the buck.*

1 가산명사 달러 [비격식체] ❑ 아마 50달러 정도 들 거야. ❑ 코트에 돈 좀 쓰지 그래? **2** 가산명사 수컷 **3** 형용사 돌출된, 뻐드러진 **4** 자동사 날뛰다 ❑ 그가 말을 꽉 붙들면서 고삐를 잡고 씨름하는 와중에 그 종마는 날뛰었다. **5** 타동사 맞서다, 거스르다 ❑ 다른 신문들은 판매 부수가 떨어지고 있지만, 우리는 딴판이다. ❑ 그는 체제를 거스르는 강인한 반항아가 되고 싶어 한다. **6** 구 책임을 전가하다 [비격식체] ❑ 데이비드는 책임이 스미스 씨에게 있으며 책임을 전가하려 해도 소용이 없다고 말한다.

buck|et /bʌkɪt/ (**buckets**) N-COUNT A **bucket** is a round metal or plastic container with a handle attached to its sides. Buckets are often used for holding and carrying water. ❑ *We drew water in a bucket from the well outside the door.* ● N-COUNT A **bucket of** water is the amount of water contained in a bucket. ❑ *She threw a bucket of water over them.*

가산명사 들통, 물통 ❑ 우리는 문 밖에 있는 우물에서 두레박으로 물을 길렀다. ● 가산명사 물 한 통 ❑ 그녀는 그들에게 물을 한 통 퍼부었다.

buck|le /bʌk°l/ (**buckles, buckling, buckled**) **1** N-COUNT A **buckle** is a piece of metal or plastic attached to one end of a belt or strap, which is used to fasten it. ❑ *He wore a belt with a large brass buckle.* **2** V-T When you **buckle** a belt or strap, you fasten it. ❑ *A door slammed in the house and a man came out buckling his belt.* **3** V-T/V-I If an object **buckles** or if something **buckles** it, it becomes bent as a result of very great heat or force. ❑ *The door was beginning to buckle from the intense heat.* **4** V-I If your legs or knees **buckle**, they bend because they have

1 가산명사 버클 ❑ 그는 큰 놋쇠 버클이 달린 벨트를 하고 있었다. **2** 타동사 버클을 채우다 ❑ 집 안에서 문이 쾅 닫힌 후 한 남자가 벨트를 채우며 나왔다. **3** 타동사/자동사 휘어지다, 구부러다 ❑ 강한 열기 때문에 문이 휘어지기 시작했다. **4** 자동사 힘이 풀리다 ❑ 무릎에 힘이 풀리면서 맥카날리는 바닥으로 쓰러졌다.

a b c d e f g h i j k l m n o p q r s t u v w x y z

become very weak or tired. ☐ *Mcanally's knees buckled and he crumpled down onto the floor.*

bud /bʌd/ (buds) ■ N-COUNT A **bud** is a small pointed lump that appears on a tree or plant and develops into a leaf or flower. ☐ *Rosanna's favorite time is early summer, just before the buds open.* ■ →see also **budding** ■ PHRASE If you **nip** something such as bad behavior **in the bud**, you stop it before it can develop very far. [INFORMAL] ☐ *It is important to recognize jealousy and to nip it in the bud before it gets out of hand.*

■ 가산명사 눈, 꽃봉오리 ☐ 로잔나는 꽃봉오리가 열리기 직전의 초여름을 가장 좋아한다. ■ 구 싹을 잘라 버리다, 초반에 막다 [비격식체] ☐ 질투심을 인식하고 걷잡을 수 없어지기 전에 아예 싹을 잘라 버리는 것이 중요하다.

Bud|dhism /bʊdɪzəm, bʊd-/ N-UNCOUNT **Buddhism** is a religion which teaches that the way to end suffering is by overcoming your desires. →see **religion**

불가산명사 불교

Bud|dhist /bʊdɪst, bʊd-/ (Buddhists) ■ N-COUNT A **Buddhist** is a person whose religion is Buddhism. ■ ADJ **Buddhist** means relating or referring to Buddhism. ☐ *...Buddhist monks.*

■ 가산명사 불교도 ■ 형용사 불교의 ☐ 스님

bud|ding /bʌdɪŋ/ ■ ADJ If you describe someone as, for example, a **budding** businessman or a **budding** artist, you mean that they are starting to succeed or become interested in business or art. [ADJ n] ☐ *The forum is now open to all budding entrepreneurs.* ■ ADJ You use **budding** to describe a situation that is just beginning. [ADJ n] ☐ *Our budding romance was over.*

■ 형용사 떠오르는; 신예의 ☐ 이 포럼은 신예 사업가 모두에게 열려 있다. ■ 형용사 막 싹트기 시작한 ☐ 막 싹트기 시작한 우리의 사랑이 끝났다.

bud|dy /bʌdi/ (buddies) N-COUNT A **buddy** is a close friend, usually a male friend of a man. [mainly AM] ☐ *We became great buddies.*

가산명사 친구 [주로 미국영어] ☐ 우리는 절친한 친구가 되었다.

budge /bʌdʒ/ (budges, budging, budged) ■ V-T/V-I If someone will not **budge** on a matter, or if nothing **budges** them, they refuse to change their mind or to come to an agreement. [with brd-neg] ☐ *The Americans are adamant that they will not budge on this point.* ■ V-T/V-I If someone or something will not **budge**, they will not move. If you cannot **budge** them, you cannot make them move. [with brd-neg] ☐ *Her mother refused to budge from London.* ☐ *The window refused to budge.*

■ 타동사/자동사 양보하다; 움직이다 ☐ 미국인들이 이 점에 관해서는 양보하지 않겠다며 단호하게 나온다. ■ 타동사/자동사 꼼짝이다; 꼼짝하게 하다 ☐ 그녀의 어머니는 런던에서 꼼짝도 하지 않으려 했다. ☐ 창문이 꼼짝도 하지 않았다.

bud|get ♦♢♢ /bʌdʒɪt/ (budgets, budgeting, budgeted) ■ N-COUNT Your **budget** is the amount of money that you have available to spend. The **budget** for something is the amount of money that a person, organization, or country has available to spend on it. [BUSINESS] ☐ *She will design a fantastic new kitchen for you – and all within your budget.* ☐ *Someone had furnished the place on a tight budget.* ■ N-COUNT The **budget** of an organization or country is its financial situation, considered as the difference between the money it receives and the money it spends. [BUSINESS] ☐ *The hospital obviously needs to balance the budget each year.* ■ N-PROPER In Britain, the **Budget** is the financial plan in which the government states how much money it intends to raise through taxes and how it intends to spend it. The **Budget** is also the speech in which this plan is announced. ☐ *The Chancellor could use the Budget to bring in taxation reforms.* ■ V-T If you **budget** certain amounts of money for particular things, you decide that you can afford to spend those amounts on those things. ☐ *The company has budgeted $10 million for advertising.* ☐ *The movie is only budgeted at $10 million.* ● **bud|get|ing** N-UNCOUNT ☐ *We have continued to exercise caution in our budgeting for the current year.* ■ ADJ **Budget** is used in advertising to suggest that something is being sold cheaply. [ADJ n] ☐ *Cheap flights are available from budget travel agents from £240.*

■ 가산명사 경비, 예산 [경제] ☐ 그녀는 모두 당신의 예산 내에서 당신에게 멋진 새 부엌을 설계해 줄 것이다. ■ 가산명사 재무 상태, 수지 타산 [경제] ☐ 병원은 분명 해마다 수지 타산을 맞출 필요가 있다. ■ 고유명사 정부 예산안; 예산안 발표 ☐ 재무 장관이 세제 개혁 도입을 위해 정부 예산안을 사용할 수도 있다. ■ 타동사/자동사 예산을 세우다 ☐ 회사는 광고에 천만 달러의 예산을 할당해 왔다. ☐ 그 영화의 예산은 겨우 천만 달러밖에 되지 않는다. ● 예산 세우기 불가산명사 ☐ 우리는 당해 연도의 예산을 세우면서 항상 신중하려 해 왔다. ■ 형용사 저렴한, 저가의 ☐ 저가 여행사가 제공하는 최저 240파운드의 저렴한 비행기 편을 이용할 수 있다.

Word Partnership	budget의 연어
V.	**balance a** budget ■ ■
PREP.	**over** budget, **under** budget ■ ■
N.	budget **crunch** ■ ■
	budget **crisis**, budget **cuts**, budget **deficit** ■
ADJ.	**tight** budget ■ ■
	federal budget ■

▶**budget for** PHRASAL VERB If you **budget for** something, you take account of it when you are deciding how much you can afford to spend on different things. ☐ *The authorities had budgeted for some non-payment.*

구동사 예산에 감안하다 ☐ 관계 당국은 일정액의 미납금을 예산에 감안했었다.

budg|et|ary /bʌdʒɪteri, BRIT bʌdʒɪtəri/ ADJ A **budgetary** matter or policy is concerned with the amount of money that is available to a country or organization, and how it is to be spent. [FORMAL] [ADJ n] ☐ *There are huge budgetary pressures on all governments in Europe to reduce their armed forces.*

형용사 예산상의 [격식체] ☐ 유럽의 모든 정부가 막대한 예산상의 압박으로 자국의 병력을 줄여야 하는 상황에 처해 있다.

buff /bʌf/ (buffs) ■ COLOR Something that is **buff** is pale brown in color. ☐ *He took a largish buff envelope from his pocket.* ■ N-COUNT You use **buff** to describe someone who knows a lot about a particular subject. For example, if you describe someone as a film **buff**, you mean that they know a lot about films. [INFORMAL] ☐ *Judge Lanier is a real film buff.*

■ 색채어 담황색, 황갈색 ☐ 그가 주머니에서 큼직한 누런 봉투를 꺼냈다. ■ 가산명사 -광, -꾼 [비격식체] ☐ 래니어 판사는 진정한 영화 팬이다.

buf|fa|lo /bʌfəloʊ/

The plural can be either **buffaloes** or **buffalo**.

복수는 buffaloes 또는 buffalo이다.

N-COUNT A **buffalo** is a wild animal like a large cow with horns that curve upwards. Buffalo are usually found in southern and eastern Africa. →see **grassland**

가산명사 버팔로

buff|er /bʌfər/ (buffers, buffering, buffered) ■ N-COUNT A **buffer** is something that prevents something else from being harmed or that prevents two things from harming each other. ☐ *Keep savings as a buffer against unexpected cash needs.* ■ V-T If something **is buffered**, it is protected from harm. ☐ *The company is buffered by long-term contracts with growers.* ■ N-COUNT The **buffers** on a train or at the end of a rail line are two metal discs on springs that reduce the shock when a train hits them. [mainly BRIT] ☐ *...when a train hit the buffers at Edinburgh's*

■ 가산명사 완충 장치 ☐ 갑자기 돈이 필요할 때를 대비하여 저축을 해 두세요. ■ 타동사 피해로부터 보호받다 ☐ 회사는 재배 농가와의 장기 계약을 완충 장치로 삼고 있다. ■ 가산명사 (기차나 철도의) 버퍼 [주로 영국영어] ☐ 기차가 에든버러의 웨이벌리 역에서 버퍼에 닿았을 때 ■ 가산명사 (컴퓨터) 버퍼 [컴퓨터]

Waverley station. ❹ N-COUNT A **buffer** is an area in a computer's memory where information can be stored for a short time. [COMPUTING]

buf|fet (buffets, buffeting, buffeted)

> Pronounced /ˈbʊfeɪ, BRIT ˈbʌfeɪ/ for meanings ❶ and ❷, and /ˈbʌfɪt/ for meaning ❸.

❶ N-COUNT A **buffet** is a meal of cold food that is displayed on a long table at a party or public occasion. Guests usually serve themselves from the table. ❑ *...a buffet lunch.* ❷ N-COUNT A **buffet** is a café, usually in a hotel or station. ❑ *We sat in the station buffet sipping tea.* ❸ V-T If something **is buffeted** by strong winds or by stormy seas, it is repeatedly struck or blown around by them. ❑ *Their plane had been severely buffeted by storms.*

bug /bʌg/ (bugs, bugging, bugged) ❶ N-COUNT A **bug** is an insect or similar small creature. [INFORMAL] ❑ *We noticed tiny bugs that were all over the walls.* ❷ N-COUNT A **bug** is an illness which is caused by small organisms such as bacteria. [INFORMAL] ❑ *I think I've got a bit of a stomach bug.* ❸ N-COUNT If there is a **bug** in a computer program, there is a mistake in it. [COMPUTING] ❑ *There is a bug in the software.* ❹ N-COUNT A **bug** is a tiny hidden microphone which transmits what people are saying. ❑ *There was a bug on the phone.* ❺ V-T If someone **bugs** a place, they hide tiny microphones in it which transmit what people are saying. ❑ *He heard that they were planning to bug his office.*

Thesaurus	*bug*의 참조어
N.	disease, germ, infection, microorganism, virus ❷
	breakdown, defect, error, hitch, malfunction ❸

bug|ger /ˈbʌgər/ (buggers, buggering, buggered) ❶ N-COUNT Some people use **bugger** to describe a person who has done something annoying or stupid. [mainly BRIT, INFORMAL, VULGAR, DISAPPROVAL] [oft adj N] ❷ N-SING Some people say that a job or task is a **bugger** when it is difficult to do. [BRIT, INFORMAL, VULGAR] [a N] ❸ EXCLAM Some people say **bugger it** or **bugger** when they are angry that something has gone wrong.

▶**bugger off** [BRIT, INFORMAL, VULGAR, FEELINGS] PHRASAL VERB If someone **buggers off**, they go away quickly and suddenly. People often say **bugger off** as a rude way of telling someone to go away. [V P] ❑ *She should bugger off back to where she came from.*

bug|ger all also **bugger-all** PRON **Bugger all** is a rude way of saying "nothing." [BRIT, INFORMAL, VULGAR] ❑ *Chadha admits she knows "bugger all" about the sport.*

build ♦♦♦ /bɪld/ (builds, building, built) ❶ V-T If you **build** something, you make it by joining things together. ❑ *Developers are now proposing to build a hotel on the site. The house was built in the early 19th century.* ● **building** N-UNCOUNT ❑ *In Japan, the building of Kansai airport continues.* ● **built** ADJ [adv ADJ, ADJ for n, ADJ to-inf] ❑ *Even newly built houses can need repairs.* ❑ *It's a product built for safety.* ❷ V-T If you **build** something **into** a wall or object, you make it in such a way that it is in the wall or object, or is part of it. ❑ *If the TV was built into the ceiling, you could lie there while watching your favorite program.* ❸ V-T If people **build** an organization, a society, or a relationship, they gradually form it. ❑ *He and a partner set up on their own and built a successful fashion company.* ❑ *Their purpose is to build a fair society and a strong economy.* ● **building** N-UNCOUNT ❑ *...the building of the great civilizations of the ancient world.* ❹ V-T If you **build** an organization, system, or product **on** something, you base it on it. ❑ *We will then have a firmer foundation of fact on which to build theories.* ❺ V-T If you **build** something **into** a policy, system, or product, you make it part of it. ❑ *We have to build computers into the school curriculum.* ❻ V-T To **build** someone's confidence or trust means to increase it gradually. ❑ *Diplomats hope the meetings will build mutual trust.* ● PHRASAL VERB **Build up** means the same as **build**. ❑ *The delegations had begun to build up some trust in one another.* ❼ V-I If you **build on** the success of something, you take advantage of this success in order to make further progress. ❑ *The new regime has no successful economic reforms on which to build.* ❽ V-I If pressure, speed, sound, or excitement **builds**, it gradually becomes greater. ❑ *Pressure built yesterday for postponement of the ceremony.* ● PHRASAL VERB **Build up** means the same as **build**. ❑ *We can build up the speed gradually and safely.* ❾ N-VAR Someone's **build** is the shape that their bones and muscles give to their body. ❑ *He's described as around thirty years old, six feet tall and of medium build.* ❿ →see also **building, built** →see **muscle**

Thesaurus	*build*의 참조어
V.	assemble, make, manufacture, produce, put together, set up; (ant.) demolish, destroy, knock down ❶

Word Partnership	*build*의 연어
V.	**plan to** build ❶
N.	build **bridges**, build **roads**, build **schools** ❶
	build **confidence** ❻
	build **momentum** ❽
ADJ.	**athletic** build, **slender** build, **strong** build ❾

❶과 ❷의 의미일 때는 /ˈbʊfeɪ, 영국 영어 bʌfeɪ/로, ❸의 의미일 때는 /ˈbʌfɪt/으로 발음된다.

❶ 가산명사 뷔페 ❷ 점심 뷔페 ❷ 가산명사 카페 ❑ 우리는 역 카페에 앉아 차를 마셨다. ❸ 타동사 시달리다, 이리저리 치이다 ❑ 그들이 탄 비행기는 폭풍에 심하게 시달렸었다.

❶ 가산명사 곤충, 벌레 [비격식체] ❑ 우리는 조그만 벌레들이 온 벽을 뒤덮고 있는 것을 발견했다. ❷ 가산명사 병 [비격식체] ❑ 내가 배탈이 좀 난 것 같다. ❸ 가산명사 (컴퓨터) 버그, 오류 [컴퓨터] ❑ 소프트웨어에 오류가 있다. ❹ 가산명사 도청기 ❑ 전화에 도청기가 있었다. ❺ 타동사 도청하다 ❑ 그는 그들이 자기 사무실을 도청하려 한다는 이야기를 들었다.

❶ 가산명사 귀찮은 놈, 멍청이 [주로 영국영어, 비격식체, 비속어, 탐탁찮음] ❷ 단수명사 굳이 어려운 일 [영국영어, 비격식체, 비속어] ❸ 감탄사 빌어먹을

[영국영어, 비격식체, 비속어, 감정 개입] 구동사 꺼지다 ❑ 그녀는 전에 있던 곳으로 꺼져 버려야 해.

대명사 쥐뿔도 (없는) [영국영어, 비격식체, 비속어] ❑ 차다는 그 경기에 대해 쥐뿔도 아는 것이 없다고 인정한다.

❶ 타동사 짓다, 조립하다, 만들다 ❑ 개발업자들이 지금 그 장소에 호텔을 지을 것을 제안하고 있다. ❑ 그 집은 19세기 초반에 지어졌다. ● 건설 불가산명사 ❑ 일본에서는 간사이 공항 건설이 진행 중이다. ● 지은, 만든 형용사 ❑ 새로 지은 집들도 수리가 필요할 수 있다. ❑ 이는 안전을 위해 만든 제품이다. ❷ 타동사 –에 만들어 넣다, 붙박이로 만들다 ❑ 텔레비전이 천장에 붙박이로 박혀 있으면, 누워서 좋아하는 프로를 볼 수 있을 텐데. ❸ 타동사 만들다, 구축하다 ❑ 그와 동업자는 자력으로 시작해서 성공적인 의류 회사를 만들어 냈다. ❑ 그들의 목적은 공평한 사회와 튼튼한 경제를 이룩하는 것이다. ● 건설 불가산명사 ❑ 고대의 위대한 문명 건설 ❹ 타동사 –을 토대로 하다 ❑ 그렇게 되면 우리는 이론의 토대가 될 사실적 기반을 더욱 확고히 갖추게 될 것이다. ❺ 타동사 –에 포함시키다 ❑ 우리는 컴퓨터를 교과 과정에 포함시켜야 한다. ❻ 타동사 구축하다 ❑ 외교관들은 이 회담들이 상호 신뢰를 구축하는 계기가 되기를 바란다. ● 구동사 구축하다 ❑ 대표단들이 서로에 대해 약간의 신뢰를 구축하기 시작했다. ❼ 자동사 –을 기반으로 발전시키다 ❑ 새 정권은 계승하여 발전시킬 만한 성공적인 경제 개혁안을 물려받지 못했다. ❽ 자동사 고조되다, 높아지다 ❑ 어제 행사 지연에 대한 압력이 고조되었다. ● 구동사 높이다 ❑ 우리는 점진적이고 안전하게 속도를 높일 수 있다. ❾ 가산명사 또는 불가산명사 체격 ❑ 그는 인상착의가 키 6피트에 중간 체구, 나이는 서른 정도이다.

a
b
c
d
e
f
g
h
i
j
k
l
m
n
o
p
q
r
s
t
u
v
w
x
y
z

A

B

▶build up ❶ PHRASAL VERB If you **build up** something or if it **builds up**, it gradually becomes bigger, for example because more is added to it. ❑ *The regime built up the largest army in Africa.* ❑ *The collection has been built up over the last seventeen years.* ❷ PHRASAL VERB If you **build** someone **up**, you help them to feel stronger or more confident, especially when they have had a bad experience or have been ill. ❑ *Build her up with kindness and a sympathetic ear.* ❸ PHRASAL VERB If you **build** someone or something **up**, you make them seem important or exciting, for example by talking about them a lot. ❑ *The media will report on it and the tabloids will build it up.* ❑ *Historians built him up as the champion of parliament.* ❹ →see also **build 6, 8, build-up, built-up**

❶ 구동사 키우다, 강화하다, 쌓다 ❑ 그 정권은 아프리카에서 가장 큰 병력을 키웠다. ❑ 그 수집품은 지난 17년간 모은 것이다. ❷ 구동사 기를 살리다 ❑ 친절하게 대하고 말을 경청하면서 그녀의 기를 살려 주어라. ❸ 구동사 치켜세우다, 칭찬하다 ❑ 언론이 이에 대해 보도할 것이고, 타블로이드 신문이 이를 치켜세울 것이다. ❑ 역사학자들은 그를 의회의 승리자로 치켜세웠다.

C

build|er /bɪldər/ (**builders**) N-COUNT A **builder** is a person whose job is to build or repair houses and other buildings. ❑ *The builders have finished the roof.*

가산명사 건축업자 ❑ 건축업자들이 지붕 공사를 마쳤다.

D

build|ing ♦♦♦ /bɪldɪŋ/ (**buildings**) N-COUNT A **building** is a structure that has a roof and walls, for example a house or a factory. ❑ *They were on the upper floor of the building.*
→see **architecture**

가산명사 건물, 빌딩 ❑ 그들은 그 건물 위층에 있었다.

E

build|ing so|ci|ety (**building societies**) N-COUNT In Britain, a **building society** is a business which will lend you money when you want to buy a house. You can also invest money in a building society, where it will earn interest. Compare **savings and loan**.

가산명사 영국 건축 조합

F

build-up (**build-ups**) also **buildup**, **build up** ❶ N-COUNT A **build-up** is a gradual increase in something. ❑ *There has been a build-up of troops on both sides of the border.* ❷ N-COUNT The **build-up** to an event is the way that journalists, advertisers, or other people talk about it a lot in the period of time immediately before it, and try to make it seem important and exciting. ❑ *The exams came, almost an anti-climax after the build-up that the students had given them.*

❶ 가산명사 증가, 강화 ❑ 국경 양편 모두에서 병력이 증가되어 왔다. ❷ 가산명사 잔뜩 술렁거림 ❑ 시험 치기 전에 학생들이 잔뜩 술렁거렸던 것에 비하면, 시험은 약간 맥이 빠지는 것이었다.

G

H

built /bɪlt/ ❶ **Built** is the past tense and past participle of **build**. ❷ ADJ If you say that someone is **built** in a particular way, you are describing the kind of body they have. [adv ADJ, ADJ like n, ADJ for n/-ing] ❑ *...a strong, powerfully-built man of 60.* →see also **well-built**

❶ build의 과거 및 과거 분사 ❷ 형용사 -한 체격의 ❑ 튼튼하고 강인한 체격의 60세 남성

I

built-in ADJ **Built-in** devices or features are included in something as a part of it, rather than being separate. [ADJ n] ❑ *...modern cameras with built-in flash units.*

형용사 내장된 ❑ 플래시 장치가 내장된 최신 카메라

J

built-up ADJ A **built-up** area is an area such as a town or city which has a lot of buildings in it. ❑ *A speed limit of 30 mph was introduced in built-up areas.*

형용사 건물이 밀집된 ❑ 건물이 밀집된 지역에서 시속 30마일의 속도 제한이 도입되었다.

K

bulb /bʌlb/ (**bulbs**) ❶ N-COUNT A **bulb** is the glass part of an electric lamp, which gives out light when electricity passes through it. ❑ *The stairwell was lit by a single bulb.* ❷ N-COUNT A **bulb** is a root shaped like an onion that grows into a flower or plant. ❑ *...tulip bulbs.*

❶ 가산명사 전구 ❑ 단 한 개의 전구가 계단을 밝히고 있었다. ❷ 가산명사 구근 ❑ 튤립 구근

L

bulge /bʌldʒ/ (**bulges, bulging, bulged**) ❶ V-I If something such as a person's stomach **bulges**, it sticks out. ❑ *Jiro waddled closer, his belly bulging and distended.* ❑ *He bulges out of his black T-shirt.* ❷ V-I If someone's eyes or veins **are bulging**, they seem to stick out a lot, often because the person is making a strong physical effort or is experiencing a strong emotion. ❑ 불£ 오다 ❑ *He shouted at his brother, his neck veins bulging.* ❸ V-I If you say that something **is bulging with** things, you are emphasizing that it is full of them. [EMPHASIS] [oft cont] ❑ *They returned home with the car bulging with boxes.* ❹ N-COUNT **Bulges** are lumps that stick out from a surface which is otherwise flat or smooth. ❑ *Why won't those bulges on your hips and thighs go?* ❺ N-COUNT If there is a **bulge in** something, there is a sudden large increase in it. ❑ *...a bulge in aircraft sales.*

❶ 자동사 불룩하다 ❑ 배가 잔뜩 불러 툭 튀어나온 지로가 뒤뚱거리며 다가왔다. ❑ 그는 검정 티셔츠 밖으로 튀어나올 듯 배가 불렀다. ❷ 자동사 튀어 나오다 ❑ 그는 목에 핏대를 세우며 형[동생]을 향해 소리쳤다. ❸ 자동사 -로 가득 차다 [강조] ❑ 그들은 차에 박스를 가득 싣고 집으로 돌아왔다. ❹ 가산명사 불룩한 부분 ❑ 네 엉덩이와 허벅지에 불룩 튀어나온 것들이 왜 없어지지 않을까? ❺ 가산명사 급증 ❑ 비행기 판매 급증

M

N

O

bu|limia /bulɪmiə, -lɪm-/ N-UNCOUNT **Bulimia** or **bulimia nervosa** is an illness in which a person has a very great fear of becoming fat, and so they make themselves vomit after eating.

불가산명사 게걸증, 병적 과식

P

Q

bu|lim|ic /bulɪmɪk, -lɪm-/ (**bulimics**) ADJ If someone is **bulimic**, they are suffering from bulimia. ❑ *...bulimic patients.* ● N-COUNT A **bulimic** is someone who is bulimic. ❑ *...a former bulimic.*

형용사 폭식하는 ❑ 폭식증 환자 ● 가산명사 폭식증 환자 ❑ 전에 폭식증을 앓았던 사람

R

bulk /bʌlk/ ❶ N-SING You can refer to something's **bulk** when you want to emphasize that it is very large. [WRITTEN, EMPHASIS] ❑ *The truck pulled out of the lot, its bulk unnerving against the dawn.* ❷ N-SING You can refer to a person's body or their weight or size as their **bulk**. ❑ *Bannol lowered his bulk carefully into the chair.* ❸ QUANT The **bulk of** something is most of it. [QUANT of def-n] ❑ *The bulk of the text is essentially a review of these original documents.* ● PRON **Bulk** is also a pronoun. ❑ *They come from all over the world, though the bulk is from the Indian subcontinent.* ❹ N-UNCOUNT If you buy or sell something **in bulk**, you buy or sell it in large quantities. ❑ *Buying in bulk is more economical than shopping for small quantities.*

❶ 단수명사 크기나 부피가 큼을 강조 [문어체, 강조] ❑ 새벽녘 하늘을 배경으로 걱정스러울 정도로 커 보이는 트럭이 주차장을 빠져 나왔다. ❷ 단수명사 큰 체구 ❑ 배놀은 조심스럽게 큰 체구를 낮춰 의자에 앉았다. ❸ 수량사 대부분 ❑ 글의 태반이 사실상 원전들에 대한 평론이다. ● 대명사 대다수, 대부분 ❑ 비록 대다수가 인도 아대륙 출신이지만, 그들은 전 세계 곳곳에서 온 사람들이다. ❹ 불가산명사 대량으로 ❑ 한꺼번에 많이 사는 것이 조금씩 사는 것보다 경제적이다.

S

T

bulky /bʌlki/ (**bulkier, bulkiest**) ADJ Something that is **bulky** is large and heavy. Bulky things are often difficult to move or deal with. ❑ *...bulky items like lawn mowers.*

형용사 육중한 ❑ 잔디 깎는 기계 같은 육중한 물건들

U

V

bull /bʊl/ (**bulls**) ❶ N-COUNT A **bull** is a male animal of the cow family. ❷ N-COUNT Some other male animals, including elephants and whales, are called **bulls**. ❑ *Suddenly a massive bull elephant with huge tusks charged us.* ❸ N-COUNT In the stock market, **bulls** are people who buy shares in expectation of a price rise, in order to make a profit by selling the shares again after a short time. Compare **bear**. [BUSINESS] ❑ *The bulls argue stock prices are low and there are bargains to be had.* ❹ N-COUNT In the Roman Catholic church, a papal **bull** is an official statement on a particular subject that is issued by the Pope.

❶ 가산명사 황소 ❷ 가산명사 (코끼리, 고래 등의) 수컷 ❑ 갑자기 큰 송곳니를 가진 거대한 수코끼리가 우리를 향해 달려왔다. ❸ 가산명사 매수인 [경제] ❑ 매수인들은 주가가 낮으며 헐값에 괜찮은 주식을 살 수 있다고 주장한다. ❹ 가산명사 로마 교황의 교서

W

X

Y

bull|doze /bʊldoʊz/ (**bulldozes, bulldozing, bulldozed**) ❶ V-T If people **bulldoze** something such as a building, they knock it down using a bulldozer. ❑ *She defeated developers who wanted to bulldoze her home to build a supermarket.* ❷ V-T If people **bulldoze** earth, stone, or other heavy material, they move it using a bulldozer. ❑ *Last week, the department's road builders began to bulldoze a water*

❶ 타동사 불도저로 밀다 ❑ 그녀는 자기 집을 불도저로 밀어 버리고 슈퍼마켓을 지으려던 개발업자들을 이겼다. ❷ 타동사 불도저로 퍼 나르다 ❑ 지난 주 백화점 도로 건설자들이 트위포드다운에 있는 범람원의 흙을 퍼 나르기 시작했다. ❸ 타동사

Z

meadow on Twyford Down. ❸ V-T If someone **bulldozes** a plan **through** or **bulldozes** another person **into** doing something, they get what they want in an unpleasantly forceful way. [DISAPPROVAL] ❏ The party in power planned to bulldoze through a full socialist program. ❏ The coalition bulldozed the resolution through the plenary session.

밀어붙이다, 강행하다 [탐탁찮음] ❏ 집권당은 완전히 사회주의적인 프로그램을 밀어붙이기로 계획했다. ❏ 연합 세력이 총회에서 결의안을 억지로 통과시켰다.

bull|doz|er /ˈbʊldoʊzər/ (**bulldozers**) N-COUNT A **bulldozer** is a large vehicle with a broad metal blade at the front, which is used for knocking down buildings or moving large amounts of earth.

가산명사 불도저

bul|let /ˈbʊlɪt/ (**bullets**) ❶ N-COUNT A **bullet** is a small piece of metal with a pointed or rounded end, which is fired out of a gun. ❏ Two of the police fired 16 bullets each. ❷ PHRASE If someone **bites the bullet**, they accept that they have to do something unpleasant but necessary. [JOURNALISM] ❏ Tour operators may be forced to bite the bullet and cut prices.

❶ 가산명사 총알 ❏ 경찰 두 명이 각각 16발을 쐈다. ❷ 구 이를 악물고 참다 [언론] ❏ 관광 업자들은 꾹 참고 가격을 내려야 할 수밖에 없을지도 모른다.

bul|le|tin /ˈbʊlɪtɪn/ (**bulletins**) ❶ N-COUNT A **bulletin** is a short news report on the radio or television. ❏ ...the early morning news bulletin. ❷ N-COUNT A **bulletin** is a short official announcement made publicly to inform people about an important matter. ❏ At 3.30 p.m. a bulletin was released announcing that the president was out of immediate danger. ❸ N-COUNT A **bulletin** is a regular newspaper or leaflet that is produced by an organization or group such as a school or church.

❶ 가산명사 뉴스 단신 ❏ 새벽 뉴스 단신 ❷ 가산명사 공고, 공보 ❏ 오후 3시 30분에 대통령이 큰 위험은 벗어났다는 공식 발표가 있었다. ❸ 가산명사 소식지

bul|le|tin board (**bulletin boards**) N-COUNT In computing, a **bulletin board** is a system that enables users to send and receive messages of general interest. ❏ The Internet is the largest computer bulletin board in the world, and it's growing.

가산명사 게시판 ❏ 인터넷은 전 세계에서 가장 큰 컴퓨터 게시판인데, 점점 더 커지고 있다.

bul|let point (**bullet points**) N-COUNT A **bullet point** is one of a series of important items for discussion or action in a document, usually marked by a square or round symbol. ❏ Use bold type for headings and bullet points for noteworthy achievements.

가산명사 논점, 주안점 ❏ 제목이나 주요 논의 사항은 볼드체를 사용하여 눈에 띄도록 하라.

bullet-proof [AM, sometimes BRIT **bulletproof**] ADJ Something that is **bullet-proof** is made of a strong material that bullets cannot pass through. ❏ ...bullet-proof glass.

[미국영어, 가끔 영국영어 bulletproof] 형용사 방탄의 ❏ 방탄유리

bull|horn /ˈbʊlhɔrn/ (**bullhorns**) N-COUNT A **bullhorn** is a device for making your voice sound louder in the open air. [AM; BRIT **loudhailer**, **megaphone**] ❏ A bullhorn blared warnings of a bomb scare.

가산명사 확성기 [미국영어; 영국영어 loudhailer, megaphone] ❏ 확성기에서 공습 경고 방송이 흘러나왔다.

bul|lion /ˈbʊliən/ N-UNCOUNT **Bullion** is gold or silver, usually in the form of bars. ❏ The Japanese are busy buying up gold bullion.

불가산명사 금괴; 은괴 ❏ 일본인들이 금괴를 사재느라 바쁘다.

bull|ish /ˈbʊlɪʃ/ ADJ On the stock market, if there is a **bullish** mood, prices are expected to rise. Compare **bearish**. [BUSINESS] ❏ The market opened in a bullish mood.

형용사 강세의, 상승세의 [경제] ❏ 시장이 상승세로 출발했다.

bull mar|ket (**bull markets**) N-COUNT A **bull market** is a situation on the stock market when people are buying a lot of shares because they expect that the shares will increase in value and that they will be able to make a profit by selling them again after a short time. Compare **bear market**. [BUSINESS] ❏ ...the decline in prices after the bull market peaked in April 2000.

가산명사 주식 시장 강세 [경제] ❏ 2000년 4월 주식 시장이 정점을 친 후의 주가 하락

bull|ock /ˈbʊlək/ (**bullocks**) N-COUNT A **bullock** is a young bull that has been castrated.

가산명사 거세된 어린 수소

bul|ly /ˈbʊli/ (**bullies, bullying, bullied**) ❶ N-COUNT A **bully** is someone who uses their strength or power to hurt or frighten other people. ❏ I fell victim to the office bully. ❷ V-T If someone **bullies** you, they use their strength or power to hurt or frighten you. ❏ I wasn't going to let him bully me. ● **bully|ing** N-UNCOUNT ❏ ...schoolchildren who were victims of bullying. ❸ V-T If someone **bullies** you **into** something, they make you do it by using force or threats. ❏ We think an attempt to bully them into submission would be counterproductive. ❏ She used to bully me into doing my schoolwork.

❶ 가산명사 깡패, 불량배 ❏ 나는 사무실 깡패의 희생양이 되었다. ❷ 타동사 괴롭히다 ❏ 나는 그가 나를 괴롭히도록 놔두지 않을 참이었다. ● 괴롭힘 불가산명사 ❏ 괴롭힘을 당했던 학생들 ❸ 타동사 협박하다 ❏ 우리는 협박을 통해 그들을 굴복시키려는 시도가 역효과를 낼지도 모른다고 생각한다. ❏ 그녀는 나를 윽박질러 공부를 시키곤 했다.

bum /bʌm/ (**bums, bumming, bummed**) ❶ N-COUNT A **bum** is a person who has no permanent home or job and who gets money by working occasionally or by asking people for money. [AM, INFORMAL] ❏ ...the bums on the corner fighting over beers. ❷ N-COUNT If someone refers to another person as a **bum**, they think that person is worthless or irresponsible. [INFORMAL, DISAPPROVAL] ❏ You're all a bunch of bums. ❸ ADJ Some people use **bum** to describe a situation that they find unpleasant or annoying. [INFORMAL] [ADJ n] ❏ You know you're getting a bum deal. ❹ V-T If you **bum** something off someone, you ask them for it and they give it to you. [INFORMAL] ❏ Mind if I bum a cigarette? ❺ N-COUNT Someone's **bum** is the part of their body which they sit on. [BRIT, INFORMAL, VULGAR] ❏ My husband got a tattoo on his bum.

❶ 가산명사 백수 [미국영어, 비격식체] ❏ 모퉁이에서 맥주를 마시다 싸우는 백수들 ❷ 가산명사 무능한 사람, 무책임한 사람 [비격식체, 탐탁찮음] ❏ 너희는 전부 쓸모없는 녀석들이야. ❸ 형용사 재수 없는, 부당한 [비격식체] ❏ 그는 네가 부당한 대우를 받고 있다는 것을 안다. ❹ 타동사 빌리다 [비격식체] ❏ 담배 하나 빌려도 될까요? ❺ 가산명사 엉덩이 [영국영어, 비격식체, 비속어] ❏ 우리 남편은 엉덩이에 문신이 있다.

bump /bʌmp/ (**bumps, bumping, bumped**) ❶ V-I If you **bump into** something or someone, you accidentally hit them while you are moving. ❏ They stopped walking and he almost bumped into them. ❏ There was a jerk as the boat bumped against something. ● N-COUNT **Bump** is also a noun. ❏ Small children often cry after a minor bump. ❷ N-COUNT A **bump** is the action or the dull sound of two heavy objects hitting each other. ❏ I felt a little bump and I knew instantly what had happened. ❸ N-COUNT A **bump** is a minor injury or swelling that you get if you bump into something or if something hits you. ❏ She fell against our coffee table and got a large bump on her forehead. ❹ N-COUNT A **bump** on a road is a raised, uneven part. ❏ The truck hit a bump and bounced. ❺ V-I If a vehicle **bumps over** a surface, it travels in a rough, bouncing way because the surface is very uneven. ❏ We left the road, and again bumped over the mountainside.

❶ 타동사/자동사 우연히 부딪치다 ❏ 그들이 걸음을 멈춰서 그가 거의 그들에게 부딪칠 뻔했다. ❏ 배가 뭔가에 부딪치면서 덜컹거렸다. ● 가산명사 충돌 ❏ 어린아이들은 조금만 부딪쳐도 자주 운다. ❷ 가산명사 쿵, 쾅 ❏ 나는 뭔가 쿵 하고 부딪치는 걸 느꼈고 즉각 무슨 일이 났는지 알았다. ❸ 가산명사 혹 ❏ 그녀는 커피 탁자에 부딪치면서 넘어져 이마에 큰 혹이 생겼다. ❹ 가산명사 융기, 돌출된 부분 ❏ 트럭이 도로의 돌출된 부분에 걸려 덜커덕거렸다. ❺ 자동사 덜커덕거리며 가다 ❏ 우리는 도로를 벗어나 또다시 산 중턱을 덜커덕거리며 갔다.

▶**bump into** PHRASAL VERB If you **bump into** someone you know, you meet them unexpectedly. [INFORMAL] ❏ I happened to bump into Mervyn Johns in the hallway.

구동사 우연히 만나다 [비격식체] ❏ 나는 복도에서 머빈 존스를 우연히 만났다.

bump|er /ˈbʌmpər/ (**bumpers**) ❶ N-COUNT **Bumpers** are bars at the front and back of a vehicle which protect it if it bumps into something. ❏ What stickers do you have on the bumper or the back windshield? ❷ ADJ A **bumper** crop or harvest is one that is larger than usual. [ADJ n] ❏ ...a bumper crop of rice. ❸ ADJ If you say that something is **bumper** size, you mean that it is very large. [ADJ n]

❶ 가산명사 범퍼, 완충기 ❏ 범퍼나 뒷유리에 어떤 스티커를 붙이고 다닙니까? ❷ 형용사 풍작의 ❏ 쌀 풍년 ❸ 형용사 막대한 ❏ 막대한 이익 ❹ 구 (자동차가) 꼬리에 꼬리를 물 ❏ 출퇴근 시간에 꼬리를 물고 늘어선 차량들

a b c d e f g h i j k l m n o p q r s t u v w x y z

A

B
□ ...bumper profits. ❹ PHRASE If traffic is **bumper-to-bumper**, the vehicles are so close to one another that they are almost touching and are moving very slowly. [v-link PHR, PHR n, PHR after v] □ ...bumper-to-bumper rush-hour traffic.

bumpy /bʌmpi/ (**bumpier, bumpiest**) ❶ ADJ A **bumpy** road or path has a lot of bumps on it. □ ...bumpy cobbled streets. ❷ ADJ A **bumpy** journey is uncomfortable and rough, usually because you are traveling over an uneven surface. □ ...a hot and bumpy ride across the desert.

C
bun /bʌn/ (**buns**) ❶ N-COUNT **Buns** are small bread rolls. They are sometimes sweet and may contain dried fruit or spices. □ ...a currant bun. ❷ N-COUNT **Buns** are small sweet cakes. They often have icing on the top. [BRIT]

D
bunch ◆◇◇ /bʌntʃ/ (**bunches, bunching, bunched**) ❶ N-COUNT A **bunch of** people is a group of people who share one or more characteristics or who are doing something together. [INFORMAL] □ My neighbors are a bunch of busybodies. □ We were a pretty inexperienced bunch of people really. ❷ N-COUNT A **bunch of** flowers is a number of flowers with their stalks held or tied together. □ He had left a huge bunch of flowers in her hotel room. ❸ N-COUNT A **bunch of** bananas or grapes is a group of them growing on the same stem. □ Lili had fallen asleep clutching a fat bunch of grapes. ❹ N-COUNT A **bunch of** keys is a set of keys kept together on a metal ring. □ George took out a bunch of keys and went to work on the complicated lock.

E

F

G
▶**bunch up** or **bunch together** PHRASAL VERB If people or things **bunch up** or if you **bunch** them **up**, they move close to each other so that they form a small tight group. **Bunch together** means the same as **bunch up**. □ They were bunching up, almost touching upon each other's heels. □ People were bunched up at all the exits.

H
bun|dle /bʌndəl/ (**bundles, bundling, bundled**) ❶ N-COUNT A **bundle of** things is a number of them that are tied together or wrapped in a cloth or bag so that they can be carried or stored. □ She produced a bundle of notes and proceeded to count out one hundred and ninety-five pounds. □ He gathered the bundles of clothing into his arms. ❷ N-SING If you describe someone as, for example, a **bundle of** fun, you are emphasizing that they are full of fun. If you describe someone as a **bundle** of nerves, you are emphasizing that they are very nervous. [EMPHASIS] □ I remember Mickey as a bundle of fun, great to have around. □ Life at high school wasn't a bundle of laughs, either. ❸ V-T If someone **is bundled** somewhere, someone pushes them there in a rough and hurried way. □ He was bundled into a car and driven 50 miles to a police station. ❹ V-T To **bundle** software means to sell it together with a computer, or with other hardware or software, as part of a set. [COMPUTING] □ It's cheaper to buy software bundled with a PC than separately.

I

J

K

L
bun|ga|low /bʌŋgəloʊ/ (**bungalows**) N-COUNT A **bungalow** is a house which has only one level, and no stairs.

M
bun|gle /bʌŋgəl/ (**bungles, bungling, bungled**) V-T If you **bungle** something, you fail to do it properly, because you make mistakes or are clumsy. □ Two prisoners bungled an escape bid after running either side of a lamp-post while handcuffed. ● N-COUNT **Bungle** is also a noun. □ ...an appalling administrative bungle. ● **bun|gling** ADJ □ ...a bungling burglar.

N
bunk /bʌŋk/ (**bunks**) N-COUNT A **bunk** is a narrow bed that is usually fixed to a wall, especially in a ship. □ He left his bunk and went up on deck again.

O
bun|ker /bʌŋkər/ (**bunkers**) ❶ N-COUNT A **bunker** is a place, usually underground, that has been built with strong walls to protect it against heavy gunfire and bombing. □ ...an extensive network of fortified underground bunkers. ❷ N-COUNT A **bunker** is a container for coal or other fuel. ❸ N-COUNT On a golf course, a **bunker** is a large area filled with sand, which is deliberately put there as an obstacle that golfers must try to avoid. □ He put his second shot in a bunker to the left of the green.

P

Q
bun|ny /bʌni/ (**bunnies**) N-COUNT A **bunny** or a **bunny rabbit** is a child's word for a rabbit. [INFORMAL]

R
buoy /bui, BRIT bɔɪ/ (**buoys, buoying, buoyed**) ❶ N-COUNT A **buoy** is a floating object that is used to show ships and boats where they can go and to warn them of danger. ❷ V-T If someone in a difficult situation **is buoyed** by something, it makes them feel more cheerful and optimistic. □ In May they danced in the streets, buoyed by their victory. ● PHRASAL VERB **Buoy up** means the same as **buoy**. □ They are buoyed up by a sense of hope.

S

T
buoy|an|cy /bɔɪənsi/ ❶ N-UNCOUNT **Buoyancy** is the ability that something has to float on a liquid or in the air. □ Air can be pumped into the diving suit to increase buoyancy. ❷ N-UNCOUNT **Buoyancy** is a feeling of cheerfulness. □ ...a mood of buoyancy and optimism. ❸ N-UNCOUNT There is economic **buoyancy** when the economy is growing. □ The likelihood is that the slump will be followed by a period of buoyancy.

U
buoy|ant /bɔɪənt/ ❶ ADJ If you are in a **buoyant** mood, you feel cheerful and behave in a lively way. □ You will feel more buoyant and optimistic about the future than you have for a long time. ❷ ADJ A **buoyant** economy is a successful one in which there is a lot of trade and economic activity. □ We have a buoyant economy and unemployment is considerably lower than the regional average. ❸ ADJ A **buoyant** object floats on a liquid. □ While there is still sufficient trapped air within the container to keep it buoyant, it will float.

V

W

X
bur|den ◆◇◇ /bɜrdən/ (**burdens, burdening, burdened**) ❶ N-COUNT If you describe a problem or a responsibility as a **burden**, you mean that it causes someone a lot of difficulty, worry, or hard work. □ The developing countries bear the burden of an enormous external debt. □ Her death will be an impossible burden on Paul. ❷ N-COUNT A **burden** is a heavy load that is difficult to carry. [FORMAL] □ ...African women carrying burdens on their heads. ❸ V-T If someone **burdens** you **with** something that is likely to worry you, for example a problem or a difficult decision, they tell you about it. □ We decided not to burden him with the news.

Y

Z

---

❶ 형용사 울퉁불퉁한 □ 울퉁불퉁한 자갈길 ❷ 형용사 덜컹거리는 □ 덥고 험난한 사막 횡단

❶ 가산명사 마른 과일이나 향료가 든 작고 둥근 빵 □ 건포도 빵 ❷ 가산명사 다반 □ 작고 달콤한 케이크의 일종 [영국영어]

❶ 가산명사 한패 [비격식체] □ 내 이웃들은 모두 남의 일에 참견하는 것을 너무 좋아해. □ 우리는 사실 꽤나 경험이 미숙한 사람들이었다. ❷ 가산명사 다발 □ 그는 그녀의 호텔 방에 큰 꽃다발을 남겨놓았다. ❸ 가산명사 송이 □ 릴리는 덩치 큰 포도 한 송이를 끌어안고 잠든 상태였다. ❹ 가산명사 묶음 □ 조지는 열쇠 한 묶음을 꺼내 들고는 복잡한 자물쇠를 열어 보러 갔다.

구동사 뭉치다 □ 그들은 서로의 발등을 밟을 정도로 잔뜩 뭉쳐 있었다. □ 사람들이 출구에 잔뜩 몰려 있었다.

❶ 가산명사 다발, 뭉치 □ 그녀는 지폐 다발을 꺼내 195파운드에 달하는 금액을 세기 시작했다. □ 그는 옷 뭉치들을 두 팔로 끌어 모았다. ❷ 단수명사 -덩이, -넝어리 [강조] □ 내 기억에 미키는 같이 있기에 너무 좋은, 매우 재간둥이었다. □ 고등학교 생활도 사실상 그다지 웃을 거리가 넘치진 않았다. ❸ 타동사 떠밀다 □ 그는 차 안으로 떠밀어 넣어져 경찰서까지 50마일을 실려 갔다. ❹ 타동사 번들 [컴퓨터] □ 소프트웨어를 따로 사는 것보다 피시와 함께 번들로 사는 것이 싸다.

가산명사 방갈로

타동사 (어처구니 없이) 실패하다 □ 죄수 둘이 수갑을 찬 상태에서 서로 전봇대를 사이에 두고 달려 나가는 바람에 탈출 시도를 어처구니없게 망쳤다. ● 가산명사 (어처구니 없는) 실수, 실패 □ 정부의 어처구니없는 실수 ● 실수투성이의 형용사 □ 실수투성이의 도둑

가산명사 침대 □ 그는 침대에서 일어나 다시 갑판으로 나갔다.

❶ 가산명사 벙커 □ 광대한 네트워크를 이루는 지하 요새 같은 벙커들 ❷ 가산명사 연료 창고 ❸ 가산명사 벙커 □ 그의 두 번째 샷은 그린 왼편에 있는 벙커로 빠졌다.

가산명사 토끼 [비격식체]

❶ 가산명사 부표 ❷ 타동사 들뜨다, 부풀다 □ 5월에 승리에 들뜬 그들은 거리에서 춤을 췄다. ● 구동사 들뜨게 하다, 부풀게 하다 □ 그들은 희망감에 마음이 부풀었다.

❶ 불가산명사 부력 □ 잠수복에 공기를 불어넣어서 부력을 높일 수 있다. ❷ 불가산명사 들뜬 기분 □ 희망적이고 들뜬 기분 ❸ 불가산명사 경기 활성 □ 침체 이후에 경기 활성의 시기가 뒤따르리라는 전망이다.

❶ 형용사 들뜬, 부푼 □ 오랜만에 미래에 대해 훨씬 희망적이고 부푼 기분을 갖게 될 것이다. ❷ 형용사 활발한 □ 우리의 경제는 활발하고 실업률은 지역 평균을 훨씬 밑돈다. ❸ 형용사 부력이 있는 □ 부력을 유지할 수 있을 정도의 공기가 통 안에 있는 동안은 그것은 뜰 것이다.

❶ 가산명사 짐 □ 개발 도상 국가들은 엄청난 대외 부채를 지고 있다. □ 그녀의 죽음은 폴에게 견딜 수 없는 짐이 될 것이다. ❷ 가산명사 짐 [격식체] □ 머리에 짐을 이고 나르는 아프리카 여자들 ❸ 타동사 짐을 지우다 □ 우리는 그 소식으로 그를 짐스럽게 하지 않기로 했다.

bur|dened /bɜrdᵊnd/ ■ ADJ If you are **burdened** with something, it causes you a lot of worry or hard work. [v-link ADJ with/by n] ❑ *Nicaragua was burdened with a foreign debt of $11 billion.* ② ADJ If you describe someone as **burdened** with a heavy load, you are emphasizing that it is very heavy and that they are holding it or carrying it with difficulty. [EMPHASIS] [v-link ADJ with/by n] ❑ *Anna and Rosemary arrived burdened by bags and food baskets.*

bu|reau /byʊəroʊ/

> The usual plural in British English is **bureaux**. The usual plural in American English is **bureaus**.

■ N-COUNT; N-IN-NAMES A **bureau** is an office, organization, or government department that collects and distributes information. ❑ *...the Federal Bureau of Investigation.* ② N-COUNT A **bureau** is an office of a company or organization which has its main office in another town or country. [mainly AM, BUSINESS] ❑ *...the Wall Street Journal's Washington bureau.* ③ N-COUNT A **bureau** is a chest of drawers. [AM] ④ N-COUNT A **bureau** is a writing desk with shelves and drawers and a lid that opens to form the writing surface. [BRIT]

Word Link   cracy ≈ rule by : aristo*cracy*, demo*cracy*, bureau*cracy*
---

bu|reau|cra|cy /byʊrɒkrəsi/ (**bureaucracies**) ■ N-COUNT A **bureaucracy** is an administrative system operated by a large number of officials. ❑ *State bureaucracies can tend to stifle enterprise and initiative.* ② N-UNCOUNT **Bureaucracy** refers to all the rules and procedures followed by government departments and similar organizations, especially when you think that these are complicated and cause long delays. [DISAPPROVAL] ❑ *People usually complain about having to deal with too much bureaucracy.*

Word Link   crat ≈ power : aristo*crat*, bureau*crat*, demo*crat*
---

bu|reau|crat /byʊərəkræt/ (**bureaucrats**) N-COUNT **Bureaucrats** are officials who work in a large administrative system. You can refer to officials as bureaucrats especially if you disapprove of them because they seem to follow rules and procedures too strictly. [DISAPPROVAL] ❑ *The economy is still controlled by bureaucrats.*

bu|reau|crat|ic /byʊərəkrætɪk/ ADJ **Bureaucratic** means involving complicated rules and procedures which can cause long delays. ❑ *Diplomats believe that bureaucratic delays are inevitable.*

bu|reaux /byʊərouz/ **Bureaux** is a plural form of **bureau**.

bur|geon /bɜrdʒᵊn/ (**burgeons, burgeoning, burgeoned**) V-I If something **burgeons**, it grows or develops rapidly. [LITERARY] ❑ *Plants burgeon from every available space.* ❑ *My confidence began to burgeon later in life.*

burg|er /bɜrgər/ (**burgers**) N-COUNT A **burger** is a flat round mass of ground meat or minced vegetables, which is fried and often eaten in a bread roll. ❑ *...burger and chips.*

bur|glar /bɜrglər/ (**burglars**) N-COUNT A **burglar** is a thief who enters a house or other building by force. ❑ *Burglars broke into their home.*

bur|glar|ize /bɜrgləraɪz/ (**burglarizes, burglarizing, burglarized**) V-T If a building is **burglarized**, a thief enters it by force and steals things. [AM; BRIT **burgle**] [usu passive] ❑ *Her home was burglarized.*

bur|gla|ry /bɜrgləri/ (**burglaries**) N-VAR If someone commits a **burglary**, they enter a building by force and steal things. **Burglary** is the act of doing this. ❑ *An 11-year-old boy committed a burglary.*

bur|gle /bɜrgᵊl/ (**burgles, burgling, burgled**) V-T If a building is **burgled**, a thief enters it by force and steals things. [BRIT; AM **burglarize**] ❑ *I found that my flat had been burgled.* ❑ *I thought we had been burgled.*

bur|ial /bɛriəl/ (**burials**) N-VAR A **burial** is the act or ceremony of putting a dead body into a grave in the ground. ❑ *The priest prepared the body for burial.*

bur|ly /bɜrli/ (**burlier, burliest**) ADJ A **burly** man has a broad body and strong muscles. ❑ *He was a big, burly man.*

burn ♦♦◇ /bɜrn/ (**burns, burning, burned, burnt**)

> The past tense and past participle is usually **burned** in American English, and usually **burnt** in British English.

■ V-I If there is a fire or a flame somewhere, you say that there is a fire or flame **burning** there. ❑ *Fires were burning out of control in the center of the city.* ❑ *There was a fire burning in the large fireplace.* ② V-I If something is **burning**, it is on fire. ❑ *When I arrived one of the vehicles was still burning.* ❑ *The building housed 1,500 refugees and it burned for hours.* ● **burning** N-UNCOUNT ❑ *When we arrived in our village there was a terrible smell of burning.* ③ V-T If you **burn** something, you destroy or damage it with fire. ❑ *Protesters set cars on fire and burned a building.* ❑ *Incineration plants should be built to burn household waste.* ● **burning** N-UNCOUNT ❑ *The French government has criticized the burning of a U.S. flag outside the American Embassy.* ④ V-T/V-I If you **burn** a fuel or if it **burns**, it is used to produce heat, light, or energy. ❑ *The power stations burn coal from the Ruhr region.* ⑤ V-T/V-I If you **burn** something that you are cooking or if it **burns**, you spoil it by using too much heat or cooking it for too long. ❑ *I burned the toast.* ● **burnt** ADJ ❑ *...the smell of burnt toast.* ⑥ V-T If you **burn** part of your body, **burn yourself**, or are **burned** or **burnt**, you are injured by fire or by something very hot. ❑ *Take care not to burn your fingers.* ● N-COUNT **Burn** is also a noun. ❑ *She suffered appalling burns to her back.* ⑦ V-T If someone is **burned** or **burned** to death, they are killed by fire. [usu passive] ❑ *Women were burned as witches in the middle ages.* ⑧ V-I If a light **is burning**, it is shining. [LITERARY] ❑ *The building was darkened except for a single light burning in a third-story window.* ⑨ V-T/V-I If you **burn** or get **burned** in

---

■ 형용사 짐을 진 ❑ 니카라과는 110억 달러의 외채를 지고 있었다. ② 형용사 짐을 진 [강조] ❑ 애너와 로즈마리는 봉지들과 음식 바구니를 잔뜩 들고 왔다.

> 복수형으로 대개 영국영어에서는 bureaux, 미국영어에서는 bureaus를 쓴다.

■ 가산명사; 이름명사 국 ❑ 연방 수사국 ② 가산명사 지부 [주로 미국영어, 경제] ❑ 월스트리트 저널의 워싱턴 지부 ③ 가산명사 서랍장 [미국영어] ④ 가산명사 (뚜껑 달린) 책상 [영국영어]

■ 가산명사 행정 체계 ❑ 주 행정 체제가 진취성과 자발성을 억제하는 경향을 띨 수 있다. ② 불가산명사 요식 행위 [탐탁찮음] ❑ 사람들은 대개 지나친 요식 행위를 거쳐야 하는 것을 불평한다.

가산명사 관료 [탐탁찮음] ❑ 경제는 여전히 관료들의 통제를 받고 있다.

형용사 요식에 따른 ❑ 외교관들은 요식에 따른 지연이 불가피하다고 생각한다.

bureau의 복수

자동사 (쑥쑥) 자라다 [문예체] ❑ 식물들은 클 수 있는 모든 곳에서 쑥쑥 자란다. ❑ 나의 자신감이 뒤늦게 쑥쑥 커지기 시작했다.

가산명사 버거 ❑ 버거와 감자 칩

가산명사 도둑 ❑ 그들의 집에 도둑이 들었다.

타동사 도둑이 들다 [미국영어; 영국영어 burgle] ❑ 그녀의 집에 도둑이 들었다.

가산명사 또는 불가산명사 도둑질 ❑ 열한 살짜리 소년이 도둑질을 했다.

타동사 도둑이 들다 [영국영어; 미국영어 burglarize] ❑ 내 아파트에 도둑이 들었다는 것을 알았다. ❑ 나는 우리 집에 도둑이 들었다고 생각했다.

가산명사 또는 불가산명사 장례 ❑ 신부는 시신을 장례 치를 준비를 했다.

형용사 건장한, 떡 벌어진 ❑ 그는 크고 건장한 남자였다.

> 과거 및 과거 분사는 대개 미국영어에서 burned, 영국영어에서 burnt이다.

■ 자동사 타오르는 ❑ 도시의 중심에서 불이 걷잡을 수 없이 번지고 있었다. ❑ 큰 벽난로에 불이 타오르고 있었다. ② 자동사 타고 있는 ❑ 내가 도착했을 때 차량 중 하나는 아직도 불에 타고 있었다. ❑ 1,500명의 난민을 수용한 그 건물은 여러 시간 동안 탔다. ● 타고 있는 것 불가산명사 ❑ 우리가 마을에 도착했을 때 뭔가가 불타는 악취가 풍겼다. ③ 타동사 태우다 ❑ 시위대는 차에 불을 지르고 건물한 채를 태웠다. ❑ 가정용 폐기물을 태울 수 있도록 소각장을 지어야 한다. ● 소각 불가산명사 ❑ 프랑스 정부는 미국 대사관 밖에서 미국 국기를 소각한 행위를 비난했다. ④ 타동사/자동사 태우다, 타다 ❑ 발전소들은 루르 지방에서 난 석탄을 태운다. ⑤ 타동사/자동사 태우다; 타다 ❑ 내가 토스트를 태웠다. ● 탄 형용사 ❑ 토스트 탄 냄새 ⑥ 타동사 데다 ❑ 손가락을 데지 않도록 조심해라. ● 가산명사 화상 ❑ 그녀는 등에 심한 화상을 입었다. ⑦ 타동사 화형당하다 ❑ 여자들은 마녀로 화형을 당했다. ⑧ 자동사 빛나다 [문예체] ❑ 3층 창문에서 나는 하나의 불빛을 제외하고는 그 건물은 컴컴했다. ⑨ 타동사/자동사 살갗을 태우다

a b c d e f g h i j k l m n o p q r s t u v w x y z

the sun, the sun makes your skin become red and sore. ☐ *Build up your tan slowly and don't allow your skin to burn.* ⑩ V-T/V-I If a part of your body **burns** or if something **burns** it, it has a painful hot or stinging feeling. ☐ *My eyes burn from staring at the needle.* ☐ *His face was burning with cold.* ⑪ V-T To **burn** a CD means to write or copy data onto it. [INFORMAL, COMPUTING] ☐ *You can use this software to burn custom compilations of your favorite tunes.* ⑫ →see also **burning** ⑬ to **burn** something **to the ground** →see **ground**. to **burn the midnight oil**, →see **midnight**. to **have money to burn**, →see **money**, →see **calories**, →see **fire**

썬탠을 서서히 하도록 하고 피부를 햇볕에 태우지 말아라. ⑩ 타동사/자동사 화끈거리다 ☐ 바늘을 쳐다봐서 눈이 따끔거린다. ☐ 그는 추위에 얼굴이 화끈거렸다. ⑪ 타동사 굽다 [비격식체, 컴퓨터] ☐ 이 소프트웨어를 이용해서 가장 선호하는 곡들의 모음을 시디에 구울 수 있습니다.

▶**burn down** PHRASAL VERB If a building **burns down** or if someone **burns** it **down**, it is completely destroyed by fire. ☐ *Six months after Bud died, the house burned down.*

구동사 소실되다; 다 태우다 ☐ 버드가 죽은 지 육개월 뒤에, 집은 화재로 소실되었다.

burned-out [BRIT also **burnt-out**] ① ADJ **Burned-out** vehicles or buildings have been so badly damaged by fire that they can no longer be used. ☐ *...a burned-out car.* ② ADJ If someone is **burned-out**, they exhaust themselves at an early stage in their life or career because they have achieved too much too quickly. [INFORMAL] ☐ *But everyone I know who kept it up at that intensity is burned-out.*

[영국영어 burnt-out] ① 형용사 불타 버린 ☐ 불타 버린 차 ② 형용사 일찌감치 나가떨어진 [비격식체] ☐ 내가 아는 사람 중에 그 정도의 강도로 계속한 사람은 모두 일찌감치 나가떨어졌다.

burn|er /bɜʳnəʳ/ (**burners**) N-COUNT A **burner** is a device which produces heat or a flame, especially as part of a stove or heater. ☐ *He put the frying pan on the gas burner.*

가산명사 버너 ☐ 그는 프라이팬을 가스버너 위에 올렸다.

burn|ing /bɜʳnɪŋ/ ① ADJ You use **burning** to describe something that is extremely hot. ☐ *...the burning desert of Central Asia.* ● ADV **Burning** is also an adverb. [ADV adj] ☐ *He touched the boy's forehead. It was burning hot.* ② ADJ If you have a **burning** interest in something or a **burning** desire to do something, you are extremely interested in it or want to do it very much. [ADJ n] ☐ *I had a burning ambition to become a journalist.* ③ ADJ A **burning** issue or question is a very important or urgent one that people feel very strongly about. [ADJ n] ☐ *The burning question in this year's debate over the federal budget is: whose taxes should be raised?*

① 형용사 타는 듯한 ☐ 중앙아시아의 타는 듯한 사막 ● 부사 타는 듯이 ☐ 그는 소년의 이마를 짚어 보았다. 이마가 타는 듯이 뜨거웠다. ② 형용사 불타는, 타오르는 ☐ 나는 기자가 되고자 하는 불타는 야망을 지니고 있었다. ③ 형용사 초미의 ☐ 연방 예산에 관한 올해 논쟁의 초미의 문제는 이것이다: 누구의 세금을 올릴 것인가?

burnt /bɜʳnt/ **Burnt** is a past tense and past participle of **burn**.

*burn*의 과거 및 과거 분사형

burnt-out →see **burned-out**

bur|row /bɜroʊ, BRIT bʌroʊ/ (**burrows**, **burrowing**, **burrowed**) ① N-COUNT A **burrow** is a tunnel or hole in the ground that is dug by an animal such as a rabbit. ☐ *Normally timid, they rarely stray from their burrows.* ② V-I If an animal **burrows** into the ground or into a surface, it moves through it by making a tunnel or hole. ☐ *The larvae burrow into cracks in the floor.* ③ V-I If you **burrow** in a container or pile of things, you search there for something using your hands. ☐ *...the enthusiasm with which he burrowed through old records in search of facts.* ④ V-I If you **burrow** into something, you move underneath it or press against it, usually in order to feel warmer or safer. ☐ *She turned her face away from him, burrowing into her heap of covers.*

① 가산명사 굴 ☐ 그들은 대개 소심해서 굴에서 멀리 벗어나지 않는다. ② 자동사 굴을 파다, 파고들다 ☐ 유충들은 바닥의 틈새로 굴을 파고든다. ③ 자동사 헤집다, 헤집고, 파고들다 ☐ 사실들을 알아내기 위해 옛 기록들을 파고드는 그의 열정 ④ 자동사 파고들다 ☐ 그녀는 그로부터 얼굴을 돌려 이불 더미 속으로 파고들었다.

burst ◆◇◇ /bɜʳst/ (**bursts**, **bursting**)

The form **burst** is used in the present tense and is the past tense and past participle.

burst은 동사의 현재, 과거, 과거 분사로 쓴다.

① V-T/V-I If something **bursts** or if you **burst** it, it suddenly breaks open or splits open and the air or other substance inside it comes out. ☐ *The driver lost control when a tire burst.* ☐ *It is not a good idea to burst a blister.* ② V-T/V-I If a dam **bursts**, or if something **bursts** it, it breaks apart because the force of the river is too great. ☐ *A dam burst and flooded their villages.* ③ V-T If a river **bursts** its banks, the water rises and goes on to the land. ☐ *Monsoons caused the river to burst its banks.* ④ V-I When a door or lid **bursts** open, it opens very suddenly and violently because someone pushes it or there is great pressure behind it. ☐ *The door burst open and an angry young nurse appeared.* ⑤ V-I To **burst into** or **out** of a place means to enter or leave it suddenly with a lot of energy or force. ☐ *Gunmen burst into his home and opened fire.* ⑥ V-I If you say that something **bursts** onto the scene, you mean that it suddenly starts or becomes active, usually after developing quietly for some time. [JOURNALISM] ☐ *He burst onto the fashion scene in the early 1980s.* ⑦ N-COUNT A **burst of** something is a sudden short period of it. ☐ *...a burst of machine-gun fire.*

① 타동사/자동사 터지다; 터뜨리다 ☐ 타이어가 터지자 운전자는 자제력을 잃었다. ☐ 물집을 터뜨리는 것은 좋은 생각이 아니다. ② 타동사/자동사 터지다; 터뜨리다 ☐ 댐이 터져 그들의 마을이 물에 잠겼다. ③ 타동사 범람하다 ☐ 몬순 폭우 때문에 강이 범람해 제방을 넘었다. ④ 자동사 벌컥 열리다 ☐ 문이 벌컥 열리면서 화난 젊은 간호사가 나타났다. ⑤ 자동사 불쑥 들어오다; 불쑥 나가다 ☐ 총을 든 사람들이 그의 집에 불쑥 들어와 총을 갈겼다. ⑥ 자동사 혜성처럼 나타나다 [언론] ☐ 그는 1980년대 초기에 패션 업계에 혜성처럼 나타났다. ⑦ 가산명사 분출, 격발 ☐ 갑자기 쏟아지는 기관총 발사

▶**burst into** ◼ PHRASAL VERB If you **burst into** tears, laughter, or song, you suddenly begin to cry, laugh, or sing. ❑ *She burst into tears and ran from the kitchen.* ◼ PHRASAL VERB If you say that something **bursts into** a particular situation or state, you mean that it suddenly changes into that situation or state. ❑ *This weekend's fighting is threatening to burst into full-scale war.* ◼ to **burst into flames**
→see **flame**
→see **cry, laugh**

▶**burst out** PHRASAL VERB If someone **bursts out** laughing, crying, or making another noise, they suddenly start making that noise. You can also say that a noise **bursts out.** ❑ *The class burst out laughing.* ❑ *Then the applause burst out.*

burst|ing /ˈbɜːrstɪŋ/ ◼ ADJ If a place is **bursting with** people or things, it is full of them. [v-link ADJ, usu ADJ with n] ❑ *The place appears to be bursting with women directors.* ◼ ADJ If you say that someone is **bursting with** a feeling or quality, you mean that they have a great deal of it. [v-link ADJ with n] ❑ *I was bursting with curiosity.* ◼ →see also **burst**

bury ♦◇◇ /ˈbɛri/ (**buries, burying, buried**) ◼ V-T To **bury** something means to put it into a hole in the ground and cover it up with earth. ❑ *They make the charcoal by burying wood in the ground and then slowly burning it.* ❑ *...squirrels who bury nuts and seeds.* ◼ V-T To **bury** a dead person means to put their body into a grave and cover it with earth. ❑ *...soldiers who helped to bury the dead in large communal graves.* ❑ *I was horrified that people would think I was dead and bury me alive.* ◼ V-T If someone says they **have buried** one of their relatives, they mean that one of their relatives has died. ❑ *He had buried his wife some two years before he retired.* ◼ V-T If you **bury** something under a large quantity of things, you put it there, often in order to hide it. ❑ *She buried it under some leaves.* ◼ V-T If something **buries** a place or person, it falls on top of them so that it completely covers them and often harms them in some way. ❑ *Latest reports say that mud slides buried entire villages.* ❑ *Their house was buried by a landslide.* ◼ V-T If you **bury** your head or face in something, you press your head or face against it, often because you are unhappy. ❑ *She buried her face in the pillows.* ◼ V-T If something **buries itself** somewhere, or if you **bury** it there, it is pushed very deeply in there. ❑ *The missile buried itself deep in the grassy hillside.* ◼ to **bury the hatchet**
→see **hatchet**

bus ♦◇◇ /bʌs/ (**buses, busing, bused**)

> The plural form of the noun is **buses**. In American English, the third person singular of the verb is **buses** and sometimes **busses**, but British English uses the spellings **busses, bussing, bussed** for the verb.

◼ N-COUNT A **bus** is a large motor vehicle which carries passengers from one place to another. Buses drive along particular routes, and you have to pay to travel in them. [also by N] ❑ *He missed his last bus home.* ◼ V-T/V-I When someone is **bused** to a particular place or when they **bus** there, they travel there on a bus. ❑ *On May Day hundreds of thousands used to be bused in to parade through East Berlin.* ❑ *To get our Colombian visas we bused back to Medellin.* →see **transportation**

bush /bʊʃ/ (**bushes**) ◼ N-COUNT A **bush** is a large plant which is smaller than a tree and has a lot of branches. ❑ *Trees and bushes grew down to the water's edge.* ◼ N-SING The wild, uncultivated parts of some hot countries are referred to as **the bush.** ❑ *They walked through the dense Mozambican bush for thirty-six hours.*

bushy /ˈbʊʃi/ (**bushier, bushiest**) ◼ ADJ **Bushy** hair or fur is very thick. ❑ *...bushy eyebrows.* ◼ ADJ A **bushy** plant has a lot of leaves very close together. ❑ *...strong, sturdy, bushy plants.*

busi|ly /ˈbɪzɪli/ ADV If you do something **busily**, you do it in a very active way. [ADV with v] ❑ *The two saleswomen were busily trying to keep up with the demand.*

busi|ness ♦♦♦ /ˈbɪznɪs/ (**businesses**) ◼ N-UNCOUNT **Business** is work relating to the production, buying, and selling of goods or services. ❑ *Jennifer has an impressive academic and business background.* ❑ *...Harvard Business School.* ◼ N-UNCOUNT **Business** is used when talking about how many products or services a company is able to sell. If **business** is good, a lot of products or services are being sold and if **business** is bad, few of them are being sold. ❑ *They worried that German companies would lose business.* ◼ N-COUNT A **business** is an organization which produces and sells goods or which provides a service. ❑ *The company was a family business.* ❑ *The majority of small businesses go broke within the first twenty-four hours.* ◼ N-UNCOUNT **Business** is work or some other activity that you do as part of your job and not for pleasure. ❑ *I'm here on business.* ❑ *You can't mix business with pleasure.* ◼ N-SING You can use **business** to refer to a particular area of work or activity in which the aim is to make a profit. ❑ *May I ask you what business you're in?* ◼ N-SING You can use **business** to refer to something that you are doing or concerning yourself with. ❑ *...recording Ben as he goes about his business.* ◼ N-UNCOUNT You can use **business** to refer to important matters that you have to deal with. ❑ *The most important business was left to the last.* ◼ N-UNCOUNT If you say that something is your **business**, you mean that it concerns you personally and that other people have no right to ask questions about it or disagree with it. ❑ *My sex life is my business.* ❑ *If she doesn't want the police involved, that's her business.* ◼ N-SING You can use **business** to refer in a general way to an event, situation, or activity. For example, you can say something is "a wretched business" or you can refer to "this assassination business." ❑ *We have sorted out this wretched business at last.* ◼ →see also **big business, show business** ◼ PHRASE If two people or companies **do business with** each other, one sells goods or services to the other. ❑ *I was fascinated by the different people who did business with me.* ◼ PHRASE If you say that someone **has no business** to be in a place or to do something, you mean that they have no right to be there or to do it. ❑ *Really I had no business to be there at all.* ◼ PHRASE A company that is **in business** is operating and trading. ❑ *You can't*

◼ 구동사 터뜨리다 ❑ 그녀가 눈물을 터뜨리며 부엌에서 뛰쳐나갔다. ◼ 구동사 격변하다 ❑ 이번 주말의 싸움은 전면전으로 치달을 위험이 있다.

구동사 (웃음, 울음, 소음 등을) 터뜨리다 ❑ 반 학생들이 웃음을 터뜨렸다. ❑ 그러자 갑자기 박수가 터졌다.

◼ 형용사 ~으로 터질 듯한, ~천지의 ❑ 그곳은 여성 감독 천지인 것 같았다. ◼ 형용사 ~으로 터질 듯한 ❑ 나는 터질 듯한 호기심에 가득 차 있었다.

◼ 타동사 묻다 ❑ 그들은 나무를 땅에 묻은 다음 그것을 천천히 태워서 숯을 만든다. ❑ 견과와 씨앗을 묻어 두는 다람쥐 ◼ 타동사 묻다, 매장하다 ❑ 사망자들을 큰 공동묘지에 묻는 것을 도운 군인들 ❑ 나는 사람들이 내가 죽었다고 생각해서 나를 산 채로 묻을 것 같아 무서웠다. ◼ 타동사 여의다 ❑ 그는 은퇴하기 2년 전쯤에 아내를 여의었다. ◼ 타동사 파묻다 ❑ 그녀는 그것을 나뭇잎들 밑에 파묻었다. ◼ 타동사 매몰하다 ❑ 최근 보도에 따르면 진흙 사태에 마을들이 통째로 매몰되었다고 한다. ❑ 그들의 집은 산사태에 매몰되었다. ◼ 타동사 파묻다 ❑ 그녀는 얼굴을 베개에 파묻었다. ◼ 타동사 박히다; 박다 ❑ 미사일은 풀이 무성한 언덕 비탈에 깊이 박혔다.

이 명사의 복수형은 buses이다. 미국영어에서 동사의 3인칭 단수는 buses 또는 가끔 busses를 쓰지만, 영국영어에서는 동사로 철자 busses, bussing, bussed를 쓴다.

◼ 가산명사 버스 ❑ 그는 집으로 가는 마지막 버스를 놓쳤다. ◼ 타동사/자동사 버스로 옮기다[가다]; 버스로 가다 ❑ 노동절에는 동베를린에서 하는 행진에 수십만 명이 버스로 동원되곤 했다. ❑ 콜롬비아 비자를 얻기 위해 우리는 버스를 타고 다시 메델린으로 갔다.

◼ 가산명사 관목 ❑ 나무와 관목이 물가까지 자라 있었다. ◼ 단수명사 오지, 밀림 ❑ 그들은 36시간 동안 모잠비크의 짙은 숲을 헤치고 걸었다.

◼ 형용사 무성한 ❑ 짙은 눈썹 ◼ 형용사 잎이 무성한 ❑ 잎이 무성한 강하고 억센 식물들

부사 부지런히 ❑ 두 여성 판매원들은 그 요구를 들어주기 위해 부지런히 움직이고 있었다.

◼ 불가산명사 경영, 사업 ❑ 제니퍼는 학문적으로 그리고 실무적으로 화려한 이력을 가지고 있다. ❑ 하버드 경영 대학원 ◼ 불가산명사 사업 ❑ 그들은 독일 회사들의 사업이 잘 안될까 봐 걱정했다. ◼ 가산명사 업체 ❑ 그 회사는 가족 기업이었다. ❑ 대부분의 소규모 업체는 첫 24개월 안에 파산한다. ◼ 불가산명사 업무 ❑ 나는 일 때문에 여기 왔다. ❑ 공과 사를 구분해라. ◼ 단수명사 사업, 업종 ❑ 어떤 사업을 하시는지 여쭤 봐도 될까요? ◼ 단수명사 용무, 일 ❑ 벤이 일하는 모습을 기록하는 ◼ 불가산명사 중요한 일 ❑ 가장 중요한 일은 마지막으로 남겨졌다. ◼ 불가산명사 개인적인 일 ❑ 내 성생활은 내 일이다. ❑ 만약 그녀가 경찰이 관여하는 것을 원치 않는다면 그것은 그녀가 알아서 할 일이다. ◼ 단수명사 일 ❑ 드디어 이 불쾌한 일을 해결했다. ◼ 구 거래하다 ❑ 나는 나와 거래한 여러 사람들이 너무 신기했다. ◼ 구 권리가 없다 ❑ 진짜로 나는 그곳에 있을 권리가 전혀 없었다. ◼ 구 영업 중인 ❑ 현금 없이는 사업을 계속할 수 없다. ◼ 구 도산한 ◼ 구 수천 개의 기업이 도산할 수 있다. ◼ 구 아무 일도 없다는 듯 ❑ 여왕은 아무 일도 없다는 듯이 행동하기로 작심했다.

a b c d e f g h i j k l m n o p q r s t u v w x y z

stay in business without cash. ■ PHRASE If a store or company goes **out of business** or is put **out of business**, it has to stop trading because it is not making enough money. ❏ *Thousands of firms could go out of business.* ■ PHRASE In a difficult situation, if you say it is **business as usual**, you mean that people will continue doing what they normally do. ❏ *The Queen was determined to show it was business as usual.* →see **city**

Thesaurus   business의 참조어

N.   company, corporation, firm, organization ❸

Word Partnership   business의 연어

N.   business **school**, business **opportunity** ❶ ❺
business **administration**, business **decision**, business **expenses**,
business **hours**, business **owner**, business **partner**,
business **practices** ❶-❺
V.   **go out of** business ❹
ADJ.   **family** business, **online** business, **small** business ❶
unfinished business ❻
your own business ❻ ❼ ❽

---

busi|ness card (business cards) N-COUNT A person's **business card** or their **card** is a small card which they give to other people, and which has their name and details of their job and company printed on it. ❏ *When we met, he gave me his business card.*

busi|ness class ADJ **Business class** seating on an airplane costs less than first class but more than economy class. [ADJ n] ❏ *You can pay to be upgraded to a business class seat.* ● ADV **Business class** is also an adverb. [ADV after v] ❏ *They flew business class.* ● N-UNCOUNT **Business class** is the business class seating on an airplane. ❏ *The Australian team will be seated in business class.*

busi|ness hours N-PLURAL **Business hours** are the hours of the day in which a store or a company is open for business. ❏ *All showrooms are staffed during business hours.*

business|like /bɪznɪslaɪk/ ADJ If you describe someone as **businesslike**, you mean that they deal with things in an efficient way without wasting time. ❏ *Mr. Penn sounds quite businesslike.*

business|man ♦◇◇ /bɪznɪsmæn/ (businessmen) N-COUNT A **businessman** is a man who works in business. ❏ *...a wealthy businessman who owns a printing business in north London.*

business|person /bɪznɪspɜrsᵊn/ (businesspeople) also **business person** N-COUNT **Businesspeople** are people who work in business. ❏ *...businesspeople who serve or supply the security forces.*

busi|ness plan (business plans) N-COUNT A **business plan** is a detailed plan for setting up or developing a business, especially one that is written in order to borrow money. ❏ *She learned how to write a business plan for the catering business she wanted to launch.*

busi|ness school (business schools) N-COUNT A **business school** is a school or college which teaches business subjects such as economics and management.

business|woman /bɪznɪswʊmən/ (businesswomen) N-COUNT A **businesswoman** is a woman who works in business. ❏ *...a successful businesswoman who runs her own international cosmetic company.*

busk /bʌsk/ (busks, busking, busked) V-I People who **busk** play music or sing for money in the streets or other public places. [BRIT] ❏ *They spent their free time in Glasgow busking in Argyle Street.* ● **busk|ing** N-UNCOUNT ❏ *Passers-by in the area have been treated to some high-quality busking.*

bust /bʌst/ (busts, busting, busted)

The form **bust** is used as the present tense of the verb, and can also be used as the past tense and past participle.

■ V-T If you **bust** something, you break it or damage it so badly that it cannot be used. [INFORMAL] ❏ *They will have to bust the door to get him out.* ■ V-T If someone **is busted**, the police arrest them. [INFORMAL] [usu passive] ❏ *They were busted for possession of cannabis.* ■ V-T If police **bust** a place, they go to it in order to arrest people who are doing something illegal. [INFORMAL] ❏ *...police success in busting UK-based drug factories.* ● N-COUNT ❏ *Six tons of cocaine were seized last week in Panama's biggest drug bust.* ■ ADJ A company or fund that is **bust** has no money left and is being forced to close down. [INFORMAL, BUSINESS] ❏ *It is taxpayers who will pay most of the bill for bailing out bust banks.* ■ PHRASE If a company **goes bust**, it loses so much money that it is forced to close down. [INFORMAL, BUSINESS] ❏ *...a Swiss company which went bust last May.* ■ N-COUNT A **bust** is a statue of the head and shoulders of a person. ❏ *...a bronze bust of the Queen.* ■ N-COUNT You can use **bust** to refer to a woman's breasts, especially when you are describing their size. ❏ *Good posture also helps your bust look bigger.*

bus|tle /bʌsᵊl/ (bustles, bustling, bustled) ■ V-I If someone **bustles** somewhere, they move there in a hurried way, often because they are very busy. ❏ *My mother bustled around the kitchen.* ■ V-I A place that **is bustling with** people or activity is full of people who are very busy or lively. ❏ *The sidewalks are bustling with people.* ■ N-UNCOUNT **Bustle** is busy, noisy activity. ❏ *...the hustle and bustle of modern life.*

가산명사 명함 ❏ 우리가 만났을 때 그는 나에게 명함을 줬다.

형용사 비즈니스 석의 ❏ 돈을 내시면 비즈니스 석으로 승급해 드릴 수 있습니다. ● 부사 비즈니스 석으로 ❏ 그들은 비행기의 비즈니스 석을 타고 갔다. ● 불가산명사 비즈니스 석 ❏ 호주 팀은 비즈니스 석에 앉을 것이다.

복수명사 영업시간 ❏ 영업 시간 중에는 모든 전시실에 직원이 있습니다.

형용사 사무적인 ❏ 말하는 것을 들어 보면 펜 씨는 상당히 사무적인 사람인 것 같다.

가산명사 사업가 ❏ 북부 런던에서 인쇄 사업을 하는 부유한 사업가

가산명사 사업가 ❏ 치안 유지군에게 서비스를 제공하거나 물자를 공급하는 사업가들

가산명사 사업 계획 ❏ 그녀는 자신이 창업하고자 하는 출장 요리 사업을 위한 사업 계획서를 짜는 것을 배웠다.

가산명사 경영 대학원

가산명사 여성 사업가 ❏ 자기 소유의 국제적인 화장품 회사를 운영하는 성공한 여성 사업가

자동사 음악을 연주하다 [영국영어] ❏ 그들은 아가일 거리에서 음악을 연주하며 글래스고에서 남는 시간을 보냈다. ● 음악 연주 불가산명사 ❏ 그 지역의 보행자들은 상당히 수준 높은 음악 연주를 듣는 대접을 받아 왔다.

bust은 동사의 현재, 과거 및 과거분사로 쓸 수 있다.

■ 타동사 때려부수다 [비격식체] ❏ 그를 꺼내기 위해 그들은 문을 때려 부숴야 할 것이다. ■ 타동사 체포되다 [비격식체] ❏ 그들은 대마초를 소지한 죄로 체포되었다. ■ 타동사 급습하다, 단속하다 [비격식체] ❏ 영국에 근거지를 둔 마약 공장을 급습한 경찰들의 성과 ● 가산명사 단속 ❏ 파나마 최대 마약 단속에서 코카인 6톤을 압수했다. ■ 형용사 망한 [비격식체, 경제] ❏ 망한 은행을 구제하는 데 드는 비용의 대부분을 납세자들이 부담할 것이다. ■ 구 망하다 [비격식체, 경제] ❏ 지난 5월에 망한 스위스 회사 ■ 가산명사 흉상 ■ 가산명사 가슴 ❏ 자세가 올바르면 가슴도 커 보인다.

■ 자동사 부산히 움직이다 ❏ 어머님께서 부엌에서 부산히 움직이셨다. ■ 자동사 부산하다 ❏ 보도가 사람들로 부산하다. ■ 불가산명사 부산함 ❏ 현대 생활의 바쁘고 부산함

bust-up (**bust-ups**) **1** N-COUNT A **bust-up** is a serious quarrel, often resulting in the end of a relationship. [INFORMAL] ❑ *She had had this bust-up with her family.* **2** N-COUNT A **bust-up** is a fight. [BRIT, INFORMAL] ❑ *...a bust-up which she says left her seriously hurt.*

1 가산명사 (결별할 정도의) 대판 싸움 [비격식체] ❑ 그녀는 자기 가족과 대판 싸웠다. **2** 가산명사 싸움 [영국영어, 비격식체] ❑ 그녀의 말에 의하면 자신을 크게 다치게 한 싸움

busy ♦♢♢ /bɪzi/ (**busier, busiest, busies, busying, busied**) **1** ADJ When you are **busy**, you are working hard or concentrating on a task, so that you are not free to do anything else. ❑ *What is it? I'm busy.* ❑ *They are busy preparing for a hectic day's activity on Saturday.* **2** ADJ A **busy** time is a period of time during which you have a lot of things to do. ❑ *It'll have to wait. This is our busiest time.* ❑ *Even with her busy schedule she finds time to watch TV.* **3** ADJ If you say that someone is **busy** thinking or worrying about something, you mean that it is taking all their attention, often to such an extent that they are unable to think about anything else. [v-link ADJ, oft ADJ -ing] ❑ *Companies are so busy analysing the financial implications that they overlook the effect on workers.* **4** V-T If you **busy yourself** with something, you occupy yourself by dealing with it. ❑ *He busied himself with the camera.* ❑ *She busied herself getting towels ready.* **5** ADJ A **busy** place is full of people who are doing things or moving around. ❑ *The Strand is one of London's busiest and most affluent streets.* **6** ADJ When a telephone line is **busy**, you cannot make your call because the line is already being used by someone else. [mainly AM] ❑ *I tried to reach him, but the line was busy.* **7** →see also **busily**

1 형용사 바쁜 ❑ 뭐야? 나 바빠. ❑ 그들은 토요일의 정신없는 바쁜 일정 때문에 준비하느라 바쁘다. **2** 형용사 바쁜 ❑ 그것은 미루어야 한다. 지금이 우리에겐 가장 바쁜 시기이다. 하지만 내가 지적하고자 하는 또 하나는 이 나라의 교도소 상당 부분이 19세기에 지어졌다는 것이다. ❑ 일정이 바쁜 와중에도 그녀는 시간을 내서 텔레비전을 본다. **3** 형용사 몰입한, 바쁜 ❑ 회사들은 재정적인 의미를 분석하는 데 너무 바쁜 나머지 그것이 근로자들에게 미치는 영향을 간과한다. **4** 타동사 ~하느라 바빠다 ❑ 그는 카메라에 신경 쓰느라 바빴다. ❑ 그녀는 수건을 마련하느라 바빴다. **5** 형용사 붐비는 ❑ 스트랜드는 런던에서 가장 붐비고 번화한 거리 중 하나이다. **6** 형용사 통화 중인 [주로 미국영어] ❑ 그에게 연락하려 했으나 전화가 통화 중이었다.

but ♦♦♦ /bət, STRONG bʌt/ **1** CONJ You use **but** to introduce something which contrasts with what you have just said, or to introduce something which adds to what you have just said. ❑ *"You said you'd stay till tomorrow." — "I know, Bel, but I think I would rather go back."* ❑ *Place the saucepan over moderate heat until the cider is very hot but not boiling.* **2** CONJ You use **but** when you are about to add something further in a discussion or to change the subject. ❑ *They need to change the image because they need to recruit more people into the prison service. But another point I'd like to make is that a large proportion of the prisons in this country were built in the nineteenth century.* **3** CONJ You use **but** after you have made an excuse or apologized for what you are just about to say. ❑ *Please excuse me, but there is something I must say.* ❑ *I'm sorry, but it's nothing to do with you.* **4** CONJ You use **but** to introduce a reply to someone when you want to indicate surprise, disbelief, refusal, or protest. [FEELINGS] ❑ *"I don't think I should stay in this house." — "But why?"* **5** PREP **But** is used to mean "except." [n PREP n] ❑ *Europe will be represented in all but two of the seven races.* ❑ *He didn't speak anything but Greek.* **6** ADV **But** is used to mean "only." [FORMAL] ❑ *This is but one of the methods used to try and get through to the patients that alcohol, as far as they are concerned, should be a thing of the past.* **7** PHRASE You use **but for** to introduce the only factor that causes a particular thing not to happen or not to be completely true. ❑ *...the small square below, empty but for a delivery van and a clump of palm trees.* **8** PHRASE You use **but then** or **but then again** before a remark which slightly contradicts what you have just said. ❑ *The house is probably unsaleable because the bathroom extension has been built to contravene building regulations. But then again the estate agent thinks that the surveyor is wrong.* **9** PHRASE You use **but then** before a remark which suggests that what you have just said should not be regarded as surprising. ❑ *He was a fine young man, but then so had his father been.* **10** **all but**→see **all. anything but** →see **anything**

1 접속사 그러나, 하지만 ❑ "내일까지 있겠다고 했잖아." "알아, 벨, 하지만 나는 돌아가고 싶어." ❑ 중불에 자루 달린 냄비를 올려놓고 사이다를 끓지 않을 정도로 뜨겁게 데우세요. **2** 접속사 하지만 ❑ 교도소들이 사람들을 더 채용하기 위해선 이미지를 개선할 필요가 있다. 하지만 내가 지적하고자 하는 또 하나는 이 나라의 교도소 상당 부분이 19세기에 지어졌다는 것이다. **3** 접속사 하지만 ❑ 최송하지만 꼭 드릴 말씀이 있습니다. ❑ 미안하지만 너와는 아무 상관이 없어. **4** 접속사 하지만 [감정 개입] ❑ "내가 이 집에서 머물러서는 안 될 것 같아." "그런데 왜?" **5** 전치사 ~을 제외하고 ❑ 유럽은 7개의 경주 중 2개를 제외하고는 모두 출전할 것이다. ❑ 그는 그리스 어를 제외하고는 아는 언어가 없었다. **6** 부사 ~에 불과한 [격식체] ❑ 이것은 환자들에게, 최소한 그들의 경우엔, 더 이상 술을 마시면 안 된다는 것을 납득시키기 위한 여러 방법 중 하나일 뿐이다. **7** 구 ~만 빼고 ❑ 배달용 소형 트럭 한 대와 야자수 무리를 빼곤 딩 비어 있는 아래의 작은 광장 **8** 구 그러나 한편으로는 ❑ 증축된 화장실이 건축 규정에 어긋나게 지어졌기 때문에 이 집은 아마 팔릴 수 없을지도 모른다. 하지만 또 한편으론 부동산 중개인은 건물 검사관이 틀렸다고 생각한다. **9** 구 그도 그럴 것이 ❑ 그는 훌륭한 젊은이었다. 그도 그럴 것이 그의 아버지도 그랬으니까.

butch|er /bʊtʃər/ (**butchers, butchering, butchered**) **1** N-COUNT A **butcher** is a storekeeper who cuts up and sells meat. Some butchers also kill animals for meat and make foods such as sausages and meat pies. **2** N-COUNT A **butcher** or a **butcher's** is a store where meat is sold. ❑ *He worked in a butcher's.* **3** V-T To **butcher** an animal means to kill it and cut it up for meat. ❑ *Pigs were butchered, hams were hung to dry from the ceiling.* **4** V-T You can say that someone **has butchered** people when they have killed a lot of people in a very cruel way, and you want to express your horror and disgust. [DISAPPROVAL] ❑ *...rebels who butchered eight tourists in Bwindi national park.*

1 가산명사 정육점 주인; 푸주한 **2** 가산명사 정육점 ❑ 그는 정육점에서 일했다. **3** 타동사 도살하다 ❑ 돼지를 도살한 후 넓적다리를 천장에 매달아 건조시켰다. **4** 타동사 학살하다 [탐탁찮음] ❑ 브윈디 국립공원에서 여덟 명의 관광객을 도살한 반군들

but|ler /bʌtlər/ (**butlers**) N-COUNT A **butler** is the most important male servant in a wealthy house. ❑ *...Paul Burrell, the former butler to Diana, Princess of Wales.*

가산명사 집사 ❑ 영국 황태자비 다이애나의 전 집사인 폴 버렐

butt /bʌt/ (**butts, butting, butted**) **1** N-COUNT Someone's **butt** is their bottom. [AM, INFORMAL, VULGAR] ❑ *Frieda grinned, pinching him on the butt.* **2** N-COUNT The **butt** or the **butt end of** a weapon or tool is the thick end of its handle. ❑ *Troops used tear gas and rifle butts to break up the protests.* **3** N-COUNT The **butt of** a cigarette or cigar is the small part of it that is left when someone has finished smoking it. ❑ *He dropped his cigarette butt into the street below.* **4** N-COUNT A **butt** is a large barrel used for collecting or storing liquid. ❑ *Make sure your water butt has a top to exclude sunlight.* **5** N-SING If someone or something is **the butt of** jokes or criticism, people often make fun of them or criticize them. ❑ *He is still the butt of cruel jokes about his humble origins.* **6** V-T If a person or animal **butts** you, they hit you with the top of their head. ❑ *Lawrence kept on butting me but the referee did not warn him.*

1 가산명사 엉덩이 [미국영어, 비격식체, 비속어] ❑ 프리다는 미소를 지으며 그의 엉덩이를 꼬집었다. **2** 가산명사 손잡이의 굵은 쪽 끝, 개머리판 ❑ 군인들은 최루탄과 총의 개머리판을 휘둘러 시위를 해산시켰다. **3** 가산명사 꽁초 ❑ 그는 담배 꽁초를 아래의 길거리에 버렸다. **4** 가산명사 큰 통 ❑ 큰 물통에 햇빛을 차단할 수 있는 뚜껑이 있는지 확인하세요. **5** 단수명사 대상 ❑ 그는 아직도 미천한 출생 신분 때문에 잔인한 농담의 놀림감이 된다. **6** 타동사 머리로 들이받다 ❑ 로렌스는 계속 나를 머리로 들이받았으나 심판은 그에게 경고를 주지 않았다.

▶**butt in** PHRASAL VERB If you say that someone **is butting in**, you are criticizing the fact that they are joining in a conversation or activity without being asked to. [DISAPPROVAL] ❑ *Sorry, I don't mean to butt in.*

구동사 끼어들다 [탐탁찮음] ❑ 최송해요, 끼어들고 싶지는 않지만.

but|ter ♦♢♢ /bʌtər/ (**butters, buttering, buttered**) **1** N-MASS **Butter** is a soft yellow substance made from cream. You spread it on bread or use it in cooking. ❑ *...bread and butter.* **2** V-T If you **butter** something such as bread or toast, you spread butter on it. ❑ *She spread pieces of bread on the counter and began buttering them.*

1 물질명사 버터 ❑ 버터 바른 빵 **2** 타동사 버터를 바르다 ❑ 그녀는 카운터에 빵 여러 조각을 펼친 다음 버터를 바르기 시작했다.

but|ter|fly /bʌtərflaɪ/ (**butterflies**) N-COUNT A **butterfly** is an insect with large colorful wings and a thin body. ❑ *Butterflies and moths are attracted to the wild flowers.* →see **flower**

가산명사 나비 ❑ 나비와 나방은 야생화에 이끌린다.

but|tock /bʌtək/ (buttocks) N-COUNT Your **buttocks** are the two rounded fleshy parts of your body that you sit on. ❑ There were marks on his buttocks I hadn't seen before.

가산명사 엉덩이 ❑ 내가 전에 보지 못한 자국들이 그의 엉덩이에 나 있었다.

but|ton ♦◇◇ /bʌtªn/ (buttons, buttoning, buttoned) **1** N-COUNT **Buttons** are small hard objects sewn on to shirts, coats, or other pieces of clothing. You fasten the clothing by pushing the buttons through holes called buttonholes. ❑ ...a coat with brass buttons. **2** V-T If you **button** a shirt, coat, or other piece of clothing, you fasten it by pushing its buttons through the buttonholes. ❑ Ferguson stood up and buttoned his coat. ● PHRASAL VERB **Button up** means the same as **button**. ❑ I buttoned up my coat; it was chilly. ❑ The young man slipped on the shirt and buttoned it up. **3** N-COUNT A **button** is a small object on a machine or electrical device that you press in order to operate it. ❑ He reached for the remote control and pressed the "play" button. **4** N-COUNT A **button** is a small piece of metal or plastic which you wear to show that you support a particular movement, organization, or person. You fasten a button to your clothes with a pin. [AM; BRIT **badge**] ❑ Wear a Campaign button to show support for mothers in prison. →see **photography**

1 가산명사 단추 ❑ 황동 단추가 달린 코트 **2** 타동사 단추를 잠그다 ❑ 퍼거슨은 일어서서 코트의 단추를 잠갔다. ● 구동사 단추를 잠그다 ❑ 나는 코트의 단추를 잠갔다. 날이 추웠다. ❑ 청년은 셔츠를 걸친 후 단추를 잠갔다. **3** 가산명사 단추 ❑ 그는 리모콘을 집어 들고 '재생' 단추를 눌렀다. **4** 가산명사 배지 [미국영어; 영국영어 badge] ❑ 감옥에 갇힌 어머니들에 대한 지지를 나타낼 수 있도록 캠페인 배지를 달아 주십시오.

Word Partnership	button의 연어
N.	**shirt** button **1**
V.	**sew on** a button **1**
	press a button, **push** a button **3**
PREP.	button **up something 2**

▶**button up** →see **button 2**

button|hole /bʌtªnhoʊl/ (buttonholes) **1** N-COUNT A **buttonhole** is a hole that you push a button through in order to fasten a shirt, coat, or other piece of clothing. **2** N-COUNT A **buttonhole** is a flower that you wear on your coat or dress. [BRIT]

1 가산명사 단추 구멍 **2** 가산명사 (옷에 꽂는) 장식용 꽃 [영국영어]

but|tress /bʌtrɪs/ (buttresses) N-COUNT **Buttresses** are supports, usually made of stone or brick, that support a wall. ❑ ...the neo-Gothic buttresses of Riverside Church in Manhattan.

가산명사 부벽 ❑ 맨해튼 리버사이드 교회의 신고딕 양식 부벽

buy ♦♦♦ /baɪ/ (buys, buying, bought) **1** V-T If you **buy** something, you obtain it by paying money for it. ❑ He could not afford to buy a house. ❑ Lizzie bought herself a mountain bike. **2** V-T If you talk about the quantity or standard of goods an amount of money **buys**, you are referring to the price of the goods or the value of the money. ❑ About £35,000 buys a habitable house. **3** V-T If you **buy** something like time, freedom, or victory, you obtain it but only by offering or giving up something in return. ❑ It was a risky operation, but might buy more time. **4** V-T If you say that a person can **be bought**, you are criticizing the fact that they will give their help or loyalty to someone in return for money. [DISAPPROVAL] [usu passive] ❑ Any number of our military and government officials can be bought. **5** V-T If you **buy** an idea or a theory, you believe and accept it. [INFORMAL] ❑ I'm not buying any of that nonsense. ● PHRASAL VERB **Buy into** means the same as **buy**. ❑ I bought into the popular myth that when I got the new car or the next house, I'd finally be happy. **6** N-COUNT If something is a good **buy**, it is of good quality and not very expensive. ❑ This was still a good buy even at the higher price.

1 타동사 사다 ❑ 그는 집을 살 돈이 없었다. ❑ 리지는 산악자전거를 샀다. **2** 타동사 -의 값이 되다 ❑ 35,000파운드면 살 만한 집을 구할 수 있다. **3** 타동사 벌다, 얻다 ❑ 위험한 수술이긴 했으나 그것으로 시간을 더 벌 수 있을지도 몰랐다. **4** 타동사 매수되다 [탐탁찮음] ❑ 우리나라의 군인과 공무원 어느 누구든 매수할 수 있다. **5** 타동사 동의하다, 믿다 [비격식체] ❑ 그런 터무니없는 것에 동의할 수 없다. ● 구동사 동의하다, 믿다 ❑ 나는 새 차나 새 집을 갖게 되면 마침내 행복해질 것이라는 대중적인 믿음에 빠져 있었다. **6** 가산명사 잘 산 물건 ❑ 좀 더 오른 가격에 사긴 했지만 그래도 이건 잘 샀다.

Do not confuse **buy** and **pay**. If you **buy** something, you obtain it by paying money for it. ❑ Gary's bought a bicycle. If you **pay** someone, **pay** them money, or **pay for** something, you give someone money for something they are selling to you. ❑ I paid the taxi driver... I need some money to pay the window cleaner... Some people are forced to pay for their own health insurance. If you **pay** a bill or debt, you pay the amount of money that is owed. ❑ He paid his bill and left... We were paying $50 for a single room.

buy와 pay를 혼동하지 않도록 하라. 무엇을 buy하면, 그것에 대해 돈을 지불하고 그것을 얻는 것이다. ❑ 개리는 자전거를 샀다. 누구에게 pay하면, 그에게 돈을 pay하는 것이고, 무엇에 대해 pay for하면, 당신에게 파는 물건 값으로 누구에게 돈을 지불하는 것이다. ❑ 나는 택시 기사에게 돈을 지불했다...나는 창문 닦는 사람에게 줄 돈이 좀 필요하다... 어떤 사람들은 자신의 건강 보험료를 직접 내야만 한다. pay a bill(고지서) or debt(빚)이라고 하면 당신이 지불하거나 갚아야 할 액수의 돈을 주는 것이다. ❑ 그는 자기 계산서대로 계산을 하고 떠났다... 우리는 일인용 방 하나에 50달러를 내고 있었다.

Thesaurus	buy의 참조어
V.	acquire, get, obtain, pay, purchase; (ant.) sell **1**

Word Partnership	buy의 연어
V.	**afford to** buy, buy **and/or sell 1**
N.	buy **in bulk**, buy **a house**, buy **clothes**, buy **food**, buy **shares/stocks**, buy **tickets 1**
ADV.	buy **direct**, buy **online**, buy **retail**, buy **secondhand**, buy **wholesale 1**

▶**buy into** PHRASAL VERB If you **buy into** a company or an organization, you buy part of it, often in order to gain some control over it. [BUSINESS] ❑ Other companies could buy into the firm. →see also **buy 5**

구동사 지분을 사다 [경제] ❑ 다른 회사들이 그 회사의 지분을 살 수도 있다.

▶**buy out** PHRASAL VERB If you **buy** someone **out**, you buy their share of something such as a company or piece of property that you previously owned together. ❑ The bank had to pay to buy out most of the 200 former partners. →see also **buyout**

구동사 (공동 지분을 단독 소유로) 사들이다 ❑ 은행은 200명의 이전 파트너들의 공동 지분을 사들이기 위해 돈을 지불해야 했다.

▶**buy up** PHRASAL VERB If you **buy up** land, property, or a commodity, you buy large amounts of it, or all that is available. ❑ The mention of price increases sent citizens out to buy up as much as they could.

구동사 사재기하다, 매점하다 ❑ 가격 인상 소식에 시민들은 마구 사재기를 하러 나섰다.

buy-back (buy-backs) N-COUNT A **buy-back** is a situation in which a company buys shares back from its investors. [BUSINESS] ❑ ...a share buy-back scheme.

가산명사 되사기 [경제] ❑ 주식 환매 계획

Word Link　　*ar, er ≈ one who acts as : buyer, liar, seller*

buy|er ♦◇◇ /ˈbaɪr/ (buyers) **1** N-COUNT A **buyer** is a person who is buying something or who intends to buy it. ❏ *Car buyers are more interested in safety and reliability than speed.* **2** N-COUNT A **buyer** is a person who works for a large store deciding what goods will be bought from manufacturers to be sold in the store. ❏ *...Diana, a forty-four-year-old buyer for a chain of furniture stores.*

buy|er's mar|ket N-SING When there is a **buyer's market** for a particular product, there are more of the products for sale than there are people who want to buy them, so buyers have a lot of choice and can make prices come down. [BUSINESS] ❏ *Real estate remains a buyer's market.*

buy|out /ˈbaɪaʊt/ (buyouts) N-COUNT A **buyout** is the buying of a company, especially by its managers or employees. [BUSINESS] ❏ *It is thought that a management buyout is one option.* →see also **MBO**

buzz /bʌz/ (buzzes, buzzing, buzzed) **1** V-I If something **buzzes** or **buzzes** somewhere, it makes a long continuous sound, like the noise a bee makes when it is flying. ❏ *The intercom buzzed and he pressed down the appropriate switch.* ● N-COUNT; SOUND **Buzz** is also a noun. ❏ *...the irritating buzz of an insect.* **2** V-I If people **are buzzing around**, they are moving around quickly and busily. [WRITTEN] ❏ *A few tourists were buzzing around.* **3** V-I If questions or ideas **are buzzing around** your head, or if your head **is buzzing with** questions or ideas, you are thinking about a lot of things, often in a confused way. ❏ *Many more questions were buzzing around in my head.* **4** V-I If a place **is buzzing with** activity or conversation, there is a lot of activity or conversation there, especially because something important or exciting is about to happen. [usu cont] ❏ *The rehearsal studio is buzzing with lunchtime activity.* **5** N-SING You can use **buzz** to refer to a long continuous sound, usually caused by lots of people talking at once. ❏ *A buzz of excitement filled the courtroom as the defendant was led in.* **6** ADJ You can use **buzz** to refer to a word, idea, or activity which has recently become extremely popular. [ADJ n] ❏ *...the latest buzz phrase in garden design circles.* **7** V-T If an aircraft **buzzes** a place, it flies low over it, usually in a threatening way. ❏ *American fighter planes buzzed the city.*

buzz|er /ˈbʌzər/ (buzzers) N-COUNT A **buzzer** is an electrical device that is used to make a buzzing sound, for example to attract someone's attention. ❏ *She rang a buzzer at the information desk.*

buzz|word /ˈbʌzwɜrd/ (buzzwords) also **buzz word** N-COUNT A **buzzword** is a word or expression that has become fashionable in a particular field and is being used a lot by the media. ❏ *Biodiversity was the buzzword of the Rio Earth Summit.*

by ♦♦♦

The preposition is pronounced /baɪ/. The adverb is pronounced /baɪ/.

In addition to the uses shown below, **by** is used in phrasal verbs such as "abide by," "put by," and "stand by."

1 PREP If something is done **by** a person or thing, that person or thing does it. ❏ *The feast was served by his mother and sisters.* ❏ *I was amazed by their discourtesy and lack of professionalism.* **2** PREP If you say that something such as a book, a piece of music, or a painting is **by** a particular person, you mean that this person wrote it or created it. ❏ *A painting by Van Gogh has been sold in New York for more than eighty-two million dollars.*

When you are talking about the author of a book or play, the composer of a piece of music, or the painter of a painting, you say that the piece of work is **by** that person or is written or painted **by** him or her. *... three books by Michael Moorcock... a collection of piano pieces by Mozart.* When you are talking about the person who has written you a letter or sent a message to you, you say that the letter or message is **from** that person. ❏ *He received a message from Vito Corleone.*

3 PREP If you do something **by** a particular means, you do it using that thing. ❏ *If you're travelling by car, ask whether there are parking facilities nearby.* **4** PREP If you achieve one thing **by** doing another thing, your action enables you to achieve the first thing. [PREP -ing] ❏ *Make the sauce by boiling the cream and stock together in a pan.* ❏ *The all-female yacht crew made history by becoming the first to sail round the world.* **5** PREP You use **by** in phrases such as "by chance" or "by accident" to indicate whether or not an event was planned. ❏ *I met him by chance out walking yesterday.* ❏ *He opened Ingrid's letter by mistake.* **6** PREP If someone is a particular type of person **by** nature, **by** profession, or **by** birth, they are that type of person because of their nature, their profession, or the family they were born into. [adj/n PREP n] ❏ *I am certainly lucky to have a kind wife who is loving by nature.* ❏ *She's a nurse by profession and now runs a counselling service for women.* **7** PREP If something must be done **by** law, it happens according to the law. If something is the case **by** particular standards, it is the case according to the standards. ❏ *Pharmacists are required by law to give the medicine prescribed by the doctor.* **8** PREP If you say what someone means **by** a particular word or expression, you are saying what they intend the word or expression to refer to. ❏ *Stella knew what he meant by "start again."* **9** PREP If you hold someone or something **by** a particular part of them, you hold that part. ❏ *He caught her by the shoulder and turned her around.* ❏ *She was led by the arm to a small room at the far end of the corridor.* **10** PREP Someone or something that is **by** something else is beside it and close to it. ❏ *Judith was sitting in a rocking-chair by the window.* ❏ *Felicity Maxwell stood by the bar and ordered a glass of wine.* ● ADV **By** is also an adverb. [ADV after v] ❏ *Large numbers of security police stood by.* **11** PREP If a person or

1 가산명사 구매자 ❏ 차량 구매자들은 속도보다는 안전성과 신뢰도에 더 관심을 가진다. **2** 가산명사 구매 담당자 ❏ 가구점 체인에서 구매 담당자로 일하는 44세의 다이애나

단수명사 구매자 시장 [경제] ❏ 부동산 시장은 여전히 구매자 시장이다.

가산명사 주식 매점 [경제] ❏ 경영진에 의한 주식 매점이 하나의 가능성으로 여겨지고 있다.

1 자동사 윙윙거리다 ❏ 인터컴이 울리자 그가 관련된 스위치를 눌렀다. ● 가산명사; 소리 윙윙거림; 소리 ❏ 신경에 거슬리게 벌레가 윙윙거리는 소리 **2** 자동사 부산히 움직이다 [문어체] ❏ 몇 명의 관광객들이 부산히 돌아다니고 있었다. **3** 자동사 (생각이) 맴돌다 ❏ 훨씬 많은 질문들이 내 머릿속을 맴돌았다. **4** 자동사 부산하다 ❏ 연습실은 점심시간을 맞아 부산했다. **5** 단수명사 웅성거림, 윙윙거림 ❏ 피고가 들어오자 법정 안이 흥분하는 사람들의 웅성거림으로 가득 찼다. **6** 형용사 최신 유행 ❏ 정원 디자인 관계자들 사이에서 최근에 가장 자주 언급되는 단어 **7** 타동사 낮게 난다 ❏ 미군 전투기들이 도시 위를 낮게 날았다.

가산명사 버저 ❏ 그녀는 안내 데스크의 버저를 눌렀다.

가산명사 유행어 ❏ 지구를 위한 리오 정상 회담에서는 생물학적 다양성이 유행어였다.

전치사는 /baɪ /로 발음되고, 부사는 /baɪ /로 발음된다.

by는 아래 용법 외에도 'abide by', 'put by', 'stand by'와 같은 구동사에 쓰인다.

1 전치사 -에 의해, -에 ❏ 그 만찬은 그의 어머니와 누이들이 차렸다. ❏ 나는 그들의 불친절과 전문성 결여에 놀랐다. **2** 전치사 -의 ❏ 뉴욕에서 반 고흐의 그림이 8천 2백만 달러를 웃도는 가격으로 팔렸다.

책이나 희곡의 저자, 음악 작품의 작곡가, 회화의 화가를 얘기할 때, 그 작품이 그 사람의 의해서(by him/her) 쓰여졌거나 그려졌다고 말한다. ❏ ...마이클 무어콕이 쓴 책 세 권...모차르트가 작곡한 피아노 소품 모음. 당신에게 편지나 메시지를 보낸 사람을 얘기할 때는, 그 편지나 메시지가 그 사람한테서(from that person) 온 것이라고 말한다. ❏ 그는 비토 콜레오네로부터 메시지를 받았다.

3 전치사 -로 ❏ 차로 여행할 것이면 근처에 주차 시설이 있는지 물어 보세요. **4** 전치사 -함으로써 ❏ 크림과 육수를 냄비에서 같이 삶아 소스를 만드세요. ❏ 여성 선원으로만 구성된 요트가 최초로 세계를 순항하는 역사적인 일을 해냈다. **5** 전치사 by chance나 by accident 등의 표현에 쓰임 ❏ 나는 어제 산책하다 우연히 그를 만났다. ❏ 그는 실수로 잉그리드의 편지를 열었다. **6** 전치사 by nature, by profession 등의 표현에 쓰임 ❏ 천성적으로 애정이 많고 착한 아내를 가진 나는 정말 운이 좋다. ❏ 그녀는 간호사가 직업인데 지금은 여성들을 위한 상담소를 운영한다. **7** 전치사 -에 따라 ❏ 약사들은 법에 따라 의사가 처방한 약을 주어야 한다. **8** 전치사 -의 의미 ❏ '다시 시작한다'는 그의 말이 무슨 뜻인지 스텔라는 알고 있었다. **9** 전치사 -을 ❏ 그는 그녀의 어깨를 잡고 돌려세웠다. ❏ 그녀는 팔이 잡힌 채 복도의 맨 끝 쪽에 있는 작은 방으로 인도되었다. **10** 전치사 옆에 ❏ 주디스는 창가의 흔들의자에 앉아 있었다. ❏ 펠리시티 맥스웰은 바 옆에 서서 와인 한 잔을 주문했다. ● 부사 옆에 ❏ 다수의 치안 유지 경찰이 근처에 대기해 있었다. **11** 전치사 옆으로 ❏ 여러 차들이 내 옆으로 아슬아슬하게 지나갔다. ● 부사 옆으로 ❏ 경찰 순찰차량이 지나갈 때 폭탄이 터졌다. **12** 전치사 -에 ❏ 우리는 퍼시픽 그로브에 있는 그녀의 집에 잠깐 들르도록 일정을 잡았었다. ● 부사

vehicle goes **by** you, they move past you without stopping. [v PREP n] ❑ *A few cars passed close by me.* ● ADV **By** is also an adverb. [ADV after v] ❑ *The bomb went off as a police patrol went by.* **12** PREP If you stop **by** a place, you visit it for a short time. ❑ *We had made arrangements to stop by her house in Pacific Grove.* ● ADV **By** is also an adverb. [ADV after v] ❑ *I'll stop by after dinner and we'll have that talk.* **13** PREP If something happens **by** a particular time, it happens at or before that time. ❑ *By eight o'clock he had arrived at my hotel.* **14** PREP If you do something **by** day, you do it during the day. If you do it **by** night, you do it during the night. ❑ *By day a woman could safely walk the streets, but at night the pavements became dangerous.* **15** PREP In arithmetic, you use **by** before the second number in a multiplication or division sum. [PREP num] ❑ *...an apparent annual rate of 22.8 percent (1.9 multiplied by 12).* **16** PREP You use **by** to talk about measurements of area. For example, if a room is twenty feet **by** fourteen feet, it measures twenty feet in one direction and fourteen feet in the other direction. [PREP num] ❑ *Three prisoners were sharing one small cell 3 meters by 2½ meters.* **17** PREP If something increases or decreases **by** a particular amount, that amount is gained or lost. [PREP amount] ❑ *Violent crime has increased by 10 percent since last year.* **18** PREP Things that are made or sold **by** the million or **by** the dozen are made or sold in those quantities. [PREP the n] ❑ *Parcels arrived by the dozen from America.* **19** PREP You use **by** in expressions such as "minute by minute" and "drop by drop" to talk about things that happen gradually, not all at once. [n PREP n] ❑ *His father began to lose his memory bit by bit, becoming increasingly forgetful.* **20** PHRASE If you are **by yourself**, you are alone. ❑ *...a dark-haired man sitting by himself in a corner.* **21** PHRASE If you do something **by yourself**, you succeed in doing it without anyone helping you. ❑ *I didn't know if I could raise a child by myself.*

bye ◆◇◇ /baɪ/ CONVENTION **Bye** and **bye-bye** are informal ways of saying goodbye. ❑ *Bye, Daddy.*

by-election (**by-elections**) N-COUNT A **by-election** is an election that is held to choose a new member of parliament or another legislature when a member has resigned or died. [mainly BRIT] ❑ *...the by-election for Leeds Central.*

by|gone /baɪgɒn, BRIT baɪgɒn/ (**bygones**) ADJ **Bygone** means happening or existing a very long time ago. [ADJ n] ❑ *The book recalls other memories of a bygone age.*

by|pass /baɪpæs/ (**bypasses**, **bypassing**, **bypassed**) **1** V-T If you **bypass** someone or something that you would normally have to get involved with, you ignore them, often because you want to achieve something more quickly. ❑ *A growing number of employers are trying to bypass the unions altogether.* **2** N-COUNT A **bypass** is a surgical operation performed on or near the heart, in which the flow of blood is redirected so that it does not flow through a part of the heart which is diseased or blocked. ❑ *...heart bypass surgery.* **3** N-COUNT A **bypass** is a main road which takes traffic around the edge of a town or city rather than through its center. ❑ *A new bypass around the city is being built.* **4** V-T If a road **bypasses** a place, it goes around it rather than through it. ❑ *...money for new roads to bypass cities.* **5** V-T If you **bypass** a place when you are travelling, you avoid going through it. ❑ *The rebel forces simply bypassed the town on their way further south.*

by-product (**by-products**) [AM, sometimes BRIT **byproduct**] N-COUNT A **by-product** is something which is produced during the manufacture or processing of another product. ❑ *The raw material for the tire is a by-product of gasoline refining.*

by|stander /baɪstændər/ (**bystanders**) N-COUNT A **bystander** is a person who is present when something happens and who sees it but does not take part in it. ❑ *It looks like an innocent bystander was killed instead of you.*

byte /baɪt/ (**bytes**) N-COUNT In computing, a **byte** is a unit of storage approximately equivalent to one printed character. ❑ *...two million bytes of data.*

_에 ❑ 저녁 식사 후에 잠깐 들를 테니까 그 얘기를 하자. **13** 전치사 시에 ❑ 8시에 그가 내가 묵는 호텔에 도착했다. **14** 전치사 에 ❑ 낮에는 여자들이 안전하게 거리를 다닐 수 있었지만 밤에는 길이 위험해졌다. **15** 전치사 곱셈이나 나눗셈에서 둘째 숫자 앞에 쓰임 ❑ 22.8퍼센트의 두드러진 연 이자율 (1.9 곱하기 12) **16** 전치사 면적의 수치를 나타내는 데 쓰임 ❑ 세 명의 죄수가 길이 3미터 너비 2½미터의 작은 방을 함께 쓰고 있었다. **17** 전치사 만큼 ❑ 폭력 범죄가 작년 이후 10퍼센트 증가했다. **18** 전치사 단위로 ❑ 소포가 12개 단위로 미국에서 도착했다. **19** 전치사 씩 ❑ 그의 아버지는 기억력을 조금씩 상실해 가며 점점 건망증이 심해졌다. **20** 구 혼자 ❑ 구석에 혼자 앉아 있는 짙은 머리색의 남자 **21** 구 혼자 힘으로 ❑ 나 혼자만의 힘으로 아이를 기를 수 있을지 의문이었다.

관용 표현 안녕 ❑ 아빠, 안녕.

가산명사 보궐 선거 [주로 영국영어] ❑ 리즈 센트럴 지역의 보궐 선거

형용사 지나간 ❑ 그 책은 지나간 시절에 대한 다른 추억들도 떠오르게 한다.

1 타동사 피해 가다, 회피하다 ❑ 점점 많은 고용주들이 노동조합을 아예 회피하려고 하고 있다. **2** 가산명사 우회수술 ❑ 심장 우회수술 **3** 가산명사 우회로 ❑ 도시 주위로 새로운 우회로가 건설되고 있다. **4** 타동사 우회하다 ❑ 도시를 우회할 새 도로들에 드는 돈 **5** 타동사 피해 가다 ❑ 반란군은 남쪽으로 더 내려가는 길에 그 마을은 그냥 피해 갔다.

[미국영어, 가끔 영국영어 byproduct] 가산명사 부산물 ❑ 타이어에 쓰이는 원자재는 휘발유를 정제하면서 생긴 부산물이다.

가산명사 구경꾼, 방관자 ❑ 너 대신에 죄 없는 구경꾼이 죽은 것 같다.

가산명사 바이트 ❑ 2백만 바이트의 데이터

Cc

C, c /siː/ (**C's, c's**) N-VAR C is the third letter of the English alphabet.

가산명사 또는 불가산명사 영어 알파벳의 세 번째 글자

cab /kæb/ (**cabs**) ◆ N-COUNT A **cab** is a taxi. ▢ Could I use your phone to call a cab? ◆ N-COUNT The **cab** of a truck or train is the front part in which the driver sits. ▢ A Luton van has additional load space over the driver's cab.

◆ 가산명사 택시 ▢ 네 전화를 써서 택시를 불러도 될까? ◆ 가산명사 운전석 ▢ 루튼 밴에는 운전석 위에 추가 적재 공간이 있다.

caba|ret /kæbəreɪ, BRIT -reɪ/ N-UNCOUNT **Cabaret** is live entertainment consisting of dancing, singing, or comedy acts that are performed in the evening in restaurants or nightclubs. [oft N n] ▢ Helen made a successful career in cabaret.

불가산명사 카바레 ▢ 헬렌은 카바레 무대에서 성공적인 경력을 쌓았다.

cab|bage /kæbɪdʒ/ (**cabbages**) N-VAR A **cabbage** is a round vegetable with white, green or purple leaves that is usually eaten cooked. →see **vegetable**

가산명사 또는 불가산명사 양배추

cab|in /kæbɪn/ (**cabins**) ◆ N-COUNT A **cabin** is a small room in a ship or boat. ▢ He showed her to a small cabin. ◆ N-COUNT A **cabin** is one of the areas inside a plane. ▢ He sat quietly in the First Class cabin of the British Airways flight looking tired. ◆ N-COUNT A **cabin** is a small wooden house, especially one in an area of forests or mountains. ▢ ...a log cabin.

◆ 가산명사 선실 ▢ 그는 그녀를 작은 선실로 안내했다. ◆ 가산명사 (비행기의) 객실 ▢ 그는 피곤해 보이는 모습으로 영국 항공편 일등석에 조용히 앉아 있었다. ◆ 가산명사 오두막 ▢ 통나무 오두막

cabi|net ◆◇◇ /kæbɪnɪt/ (**cabinets**) ◆ N-COUNT A **cabinet** is a cupboard used for storing things such as medicine or alcoholic drinks or for displaying decorative things in. ▢ The star of my medicine cabinet is the humble aspirin. ◆ N-COUNT The **Cabinet** is a group of the most senior advisers or ministers in a government, who meet regularly to discuss policies. ▢ The announcement came after a three-hour Cabinet meeting. →see **government**

◆ 가산명사 진열장, 캐비닛 ▢ 내 약 진열장의 인기 품목은 소박한 아스피린이다. ◆ 가산명사 내각 ▢ 그 성명은 세 시간에 걸친 내각 회의 이후에 나왔다.

ca|ble ◆◇◇ /keɪbəl/ (**cables**) ◆ N-VAR A **cable** is a kind of very strong, thick rope, made of wires twisted together. ▢ The miners rode a conveyance attached to a cable made of braided steel wire. ◆ N-VAR A **cable** is a thick wire, or a group of wires inside a rubber or plastic covering, which is used to carry electricity or electronic signals. ▢ ...overhead power cables. ◆ N-UNCOUNT **Cable** is used to refer to television systems in which the signals are sent along underground wires rather than by radio waves. ▢ They ran commercials on cable systems across the country. →see **laser**, **television**

◆ 가산명사 또는 불가산명사 케이블 ▢ 광부들은 철선을 꼬아 만든 케이블에 달린 수송 기구를 탔다. ◆ 가산명사 또는 불가산명사 전선 ▢ 고가 전력선 ◆ 불가산명사 케이블 방송 ▢ 그들은 전국 케이블 방송망을 통해 광고를 내보냈다.

cache /kæʃ/ (**caches**) ◆ N-COUNT A **cache** is a quantity of things such as weapons that have been hidden. ▢ A huge arms cache was discovered by police. ◆ N-COUNT A **cache** or **cache memory** is an area of computer memory that is used for temporary storage of data and can be accessed more quickly than the main memory. [COMPUTING] ▢ In your Web browser's cache are the most recent Web files that you have downloaded.

◆ 가산명사 은닉물 ▢ 막대한 양의 은닉 무기가 경찰에 의해 발견되었다. ◆ 가산명사 (컴퓨터) 캐시 메모리 [컴퓨터] ▢ 웹 브라우저의 캐시 메모리에는 가장 최근에 내려 받은 웹 파일들이 들어 있습니다.

cac|tus /kæktəs/ (**cactuses** or **cacti**) /kæktaɪ/ N-COUNT A **cactus** is a thick fleshy plant that grows in many hot, dry parts of the world. Cacti have no leaves and many of them are covered in prickles. →see **desert**

가산명사 선인장

CAD /kæd/ N-UNCOUNT **CAD** refers to the use of computer software in the design of things such as cars, buildings, and machines. **CAD** is an abbreviation for "computer aided design." [COMPUTING] ▢ ...CAD software.

불가산명사 캐드, 컴퓨터 설계 [컴퓨터] ▢ 캐드 소프트웨어

ca|det /kədet/ (**cadets**) N-COUNT A **cadet** is a young man or woman who is being trained in the armed services or the police force. ▢ ...army cadets.

가산명사 생도 ▢ 육군 사관생도

café /kæfeɪ, BRIT kæfeɪ/ (**cafés**) also **cafe** N-COUNT A **café** is a place where you can buy drinks, simple meals, and snacks, but, in Britain, not usually alcoholic drinks.

가산명사 카페, 커피집

A **café** serves tea, coffee, soft drinks, and light meals, but not usually alcoholic drinks. If you want an alcoholic drink, you can go to a **pub**. In American English, a **pub** is usually called a **bar**. Many pubs serve food, especially at lunchtime, but for a larger or more special meal, you might go to a **restaurant**.

café에서는 차, 커피, 음료, 가벼운 식사를 제공하지만 보통 술은 팔지 않는다. 주류를 원하면 pub에 갈 수 있다. 미국 영어에서는 pub을 흔히 bar라고 한다. 많은 pub에서는 특히 점심시간에 음식을 제공한다. 하지만 더 거창하게 특별한 식사를 하려면 restaurant에 갈 수 있다.

caf|eteria /kæfɪtɪəriə/ (**cafeterias**) N-COUNT A **cafeteria** is a restaurant where you choose your food from a counter and take it to your table after paying for it. Cafeterias are usually found in public buildings such as hospitals, colleges, and offices. →see **restaurant**

가산명사 카페테리아

caf|feine /kæfiːn, BRIT kæfiːn/ N-UNCOUNT **Caffeine** is a chemical substance found in coffee, tea, and cocoa, which affects your brain and body and makes you more active.

불가산명사 카페인

cage /keɪdʒ/ (**cages**) N-COUNT A **cage** is a structure of wire or metal bars in which birds or animals are kept. ▢ I hate to see birds in cages.

가산명사 새장; 우리 ▢ 나는 새장 속에 갇힌 새를 보는 것이 싫다.

caged /keɪdʒd/ ADJ A **caged** bird or animal is inside a cage. ▢ Mark was still pacing like a caged animal.

형용사 우리에 갇힌, 새장에 갇힌 ▢ 마크는 여전히 우리에 갇힌 짐승처럼 서성거리고 있었다.

ca|jole /kədʒoʊl/ (**cajoles, cajoling, cajoled**) V-T If you **cajole** someone **into** doing something, you get them to do it after persuading them for some time. ▢ It was he who had cajoled Garland into doing the film.

타동사 구슬리다, 구워삶다 ▢ 갈런드를 구슬려 그 영화를 찍도록 한 것은 바로 그 사람이었다.

cake ♦◇◇ /keɪk/ (**cakes**) **1** N-VAR A **cake** is a sweet food made by baking a mixture of flour, eggs, sugar, and fat in an oven. Cakes may be large and cut into slices or small and intended for one person only. □ ...*a piece of cake.* □ *Would you like some chocolate cake?* **2** N-COUNT Food that is formed into flat round shapes before it is cooked can be referred to as **cakes**. □ ...*fish cakes.* **3** N-COUNT A **cake of soap** is a small block of it. □ ...*a small cake of lime-scented soap.* **4** PHRASE If someone has done something very stupid, rude, or selfish, you can say that they **take the cake** or that what they have done **takes the cake**, to emphasize your surprise at their behavior. [AM, EMPHASIS] [BRIT **take the biscuit**] →see **icing** →see **dessert**

1 가산명사 또는 불가산명사 케이크 □ 케이크 한 조각 □ 초콜릿 케이크 좀 드시겠어요? **2** 가산명사 납작하고 둥근 케이크 형태의 음식 □ 어육 완자 **3** 가산명사 (비누 단위) □ 작은 라임향 비누 한 개 **4** 구 어리석은 짓을 하다, 무례한 짓을 하다, 얌체 짓을 하다 [미국영어, 강조] [영국영어 take the biscuit]

cake pan (**cake pans**) N-COUNT A **cake pan** is a metal container that you bake a cake in. [AM; BRIT **cake tin**] □ *Lightly grease and flour a 13-by-9-inch cake pan.*

가산명사 케이크 팬 [미국영어; 영국영어 cake tin] □ 가로 13인치 세로 9인치 크기의 케이크 팬에 기름을 약간 두르고 가루를 뿌리세요.

ca|lam|ity /kəlæmɪti/ (**calamities**) N-VAR A **calamity** is an event that causes a great deal of damage, destruction, or personal distress. [FORMAL] □ *He described drugs as the greatest calamity of the age.*

가산명사 또는 불가산명사 재난, 재앙 [격식체] □ 그는 마약을 이 시대 최대의 재앙이라고 말했다.

cal|cium /kælsiəm/ N-UNCOUNT **Calcium** is a soft white chemical element which is found in bones and teeth, and also in limestone, chalk, and marble.

불가산명사 칼슘

cal|cu|late /kælkyəleɪt/ (**calculates, calculating, calculated**) **1** V-T If you **calculate** a number or amount, you discover it from information that you already have, by using arithmetic, mathematics, or a special machine. □ *From this you can calculate the total mass in the Galaxy.* □ *We calculate that the average size farm in Lancaster County is 65 acres.* **2** V-T If you **calculate** the effects of something, especially a possible course of action, you think about them in order to form an opinion or decide what to do. □ *I believe I am capable of calculating the political consequences accurately.*

1 타동사 계산하다, 산정하다 □ 이로부터 은하계의 전체 질량을 계산할 수 있다. □ 랭커스터 카운티 내 농장의 평균 면적은 65에이커로 산정된다. **2** 타동사 추정하다; 예측하다 □ 내가 그 정치적 결과를 정확히 예측할 수 있다고 믿는다.

cal|cu|lat|ed /kælkyəleɪtɪd/ **1** ADJ If something is **calculated** to have a particular effect, it is specially done or arranged in order to have that effect. [v-link ADJ to-inf] □ *Their movements through the region were calculated to terrify landowners into abandoning their holdings.* **2** ADJ If you say that something is not **calculated** to have a particular effect, you mean that it is unlikely to have that effect. [with brd-neg, v-link ADJ to-inf] □ *His views seem so extreme, so calculated to offend the left-liberal establishment.* **3** ADJ You can describe a clever or dishonest action as **calculated** when it is very carefully planned or arranged. □ *Irene's use of the mop had been a calculated attempt to cover up her crime.* **4** ADJ If you take a **calculated** risk, you do something which you think might be successful, although you have fully considered the possible bad consequences of your action. [ADJ n] □ *The President took a calculated political risk in throwing his full support behind the rebels.*

1 형용사 계산된 □ 그들이 그 지역을 통해 이동한 것은 지주들로 하여금 겁을 먹고 보유지를 포기하게 하도록 계산된 것이었다. **2** 형용사 – 할 것 같은 □ 그의 견해는 대단히 과격하고 좌파-자유주의 진영의 신경을 거스를 공산이 큰 것 같다. **3** 형용사 계산된 □ 아이린이 대걸레를 쓴 것은 자신의 범죄를 감추려는 계산된 행위였다. **4** 형용사 계산된 □ 대통령은 반란군에게 전적인 지지를 보내며 계산된 정치적 모험을 했다.

cal|cu|lat|ing /kælkyəleɪtɪŋ/ ADJ If you describe someone as **calculating**, you disapprove of the fact that they deliberately plan to get what they want, often by hurting or harming other people. [DISAPPROVAL] □ *Northbridge is a cool, calculating and clever criminal who could strike again.*

형용사 계산적인 [탐탁찮음] □ 노스브리지는 재범 가능성이 있는, 냉정하고 계산적이며 영리한 범죄자이다.

cal|cu|la|tion /kælkyəleɪʃ[o]n/ (**calculations**) N-VAR A **calculation** is something that you think about and work out mathematically. **Calculation** is the process of working something out mathematically. □ *Leonard made a rapid calculation: he'd never make it in time.* →see **mathematics**

가산명사 또는 불가산명사 계산 □ 레너드는 서둘러 계산을 해 봤다. 그는 결코 시간 내에 그 일을 마칠 수 없을 것이었다.

cal|cu|la|tor /kælkyəleɪtər/ (**calculators**) N-COUNT A **calculator** is a small electronic device that you use for making mathematical calculations. □ ...*a pocket calculator.* →see **office**

가산명사 계산기 □ 소형 계산기

cal|en|dar /kælɪndər/ (**calendars**) **1** N-COUNT A **calendar** is a chart or device which displays the date and the day of the week, and often the whole of a particular year divided up into months, weeks, and days. □ *There was a calendar on the wall above, with large squares around the dates.* **2** N-COUNT A **calendar** is a particular system for dividing time into periods such as years, months, and weeks, often starting from a particular point in history. □ *The Christian calendar was originally based on the Julian calendar of the Romans.* **3** N-COUNT You can use **calendar** to refer to a series or list of events and activities which take place on particular dates, and which are important for a particular organization, community, or person. □ *It is one of the British sporting calendar's most prestigious events.* →see **year**

1 가산명사 달력 □ 위쪽 벽에는, 커다란 네모 안에 날짜가 적힌 달력이 있었다. **2** 가산명사 역법 □ 기독교력은 본래 로마인들의 율리우스력에 기초한 것이었다. **3** 가산명사 일련의 연중행사 □ 그것은 영국의 가장 유명한 연중 체육 행사 중 하나이다.

cal|en|dar year (**calendar years**) N-COUNT A **calendar year** is a period of twelve months from January 1 to December 31. **Calendar year** is often used in business to compare with the **financial year**. □ *In the last calendar year Eurostar had a turnover of £426m.*

가산명사 역년 □ 그 전 한 해 동안에 유로스타는 4억 2천 6백만 파운드의 총매상을 올렸다.

calf /kæf, BRIT kɑːf/ (**calves**) /kævz, BRIT kɑːvz/ **1** N-COUNT A **calf** is a young cow. **2** N-COUNT Some other young animals, including elephants and whales, are called **calves**. **3** N-COUNT Your **calf** is the thick part at the back of your leg, between your ankle and your knee. □ ...*a calf injury.*

1 가산명사 송아지 **2** 가산명사 (코끼리, 고래 등의) 새끼 **3** 가산명사 종아리 □ 종아리 부상

cal|iber /kælɪbər/ (**calibers**) [BRIT **calibre**] **1** N-UNCOUNT The **caliber of** a person is the quality or standard of their ability or intelligence, especially when this is high. □ *I was impressed by the high caliber of the researchers and analysts.* **2** N-UNCOUNT The **caliber of** something is its quality, especially when it is good. □ *The caliber of teaching was very high.*

[영국영어 calibre] **1** 불가산명사 자질; 재간 □ 나는 연구원과 분석자들의 뛰어난 자질에 감동을 받았다. **2** 불가산명사 품질 □ 수업의 질이 매우 높았다.

cal|i|brate /kælɪbreɪt/ (**calibrates, calibrating, calibrated**) V-T If you **calibrate** an instrument or tool, you mark or adjust it so that you can use it to measure something accurately. [TECHNICAL] □ ...*instructions on how to calibrate a thermometer.*

타동사 (계측기 눈금을) 조정하다 [과학 기술] □ 온도계를 조정하는 방법에 대한 설명서

cal|i|bre /kælɪbər/ →see **caliber**

call ♦♦♦ /kɔl/ (**calls, calling, called**) **1** V-T If you **call** someone or something **by** a particular name or title, you give them that name or title. □ *I always wanted to call the dog Mufty for some reason.* □ "*Doctor...*" — "*Will you please call me Sarah?*" **2** V-T

1 타동사 –라고 부르다, –라고 이름 짓다 □ 나는 언제나 그 개를 왠지 머프티라고 부르고 싶었다. □ "박사님... 저를 새러라고 불러 주시겠어요?"

If you **call** someone or something a particular thing, you suggest they are that thing or describe them as that thing. ❏ *The speech was interrupted by members of the Conservative Party, who called him a traitor.* ❏ *She calls me lazy and selfish.* ◆ V-T If you **call** something, you say it in a loud voice, because you are trying to attract someone's attention. ❏ *He could hear the others downstairs in different parts of the house calling his name.* ● PHRASAL VERB **Call out** means the same as **call**. ❏ *The butcher's son called out a greeting.* ◆ V-T/V-I If you **call** someone, you telephone them. ❏ *Would you call me as soon as you find out? My number's in the phone book.* ❏ *A friend of mine gave me this number to call.* ◆ V-T If you **call** someone such as a doctor or the police, you ask them to come to you, usually by telephoning them. ❏ *He screamed for his wife to call an ambulance.* ◆ V-T If you **call** someone, you ask them to come to you by shouting to them. ❏ *She called her young son: "Here, Stephen, come and look at this!"* ◆ N-COUNT When you make a telephone **call**, you telephone someone. ❏ *I made a phone call to the United States to talk to a friend.* ❏ *I've had hundreds of calls from other victims.* ◆ V-T If someone in authority **calls** something such as a meeting, rehearsal, or election, they arrange for it to take place at a particular time. ❏ *The Committee decided to call a meeting of the All India Congress.* ◆ V-T If someone **is called** before a court or committee, they are ordered to appear there, usually to give evidence. ❏ *The child waited two hours before she was called to give evidence.* ◆ V-I If you **call** somewhere, you make a short visit there. ❏ *A market researcher called at the house where he was living.* ● N-COUNT **Call** is also a noun. ❏ *He decided to pay a call on Tommy Cummings.* ◆ V-I When a train, bus, or ship **calls** somewhere, it stops there for a short time to allow people to get on or off. ❏ *The steamer calls at several palm-fringed ports along the way.* ◆ V-T To **call** a game or sporting event means to cancel it, for example because of rain or bad light. [AM] ❏ *We called the next game.* ◆ N-COUNT If there is a **call for** something, someone demands that it should happen. ❏ *There have been calls for a new kind of security arrangement.* ◆ N-UNCOUNT If there is little or no **call for** something, very few people want it to be done or provided. ❏ *"Have you got just plain chocolate?" — "No, I'm afraid there's not much call for that."* ◆ N-SING The **call** of something such as a place is the way it attracts or interests you strongly. ❏ *But the call of the wild was simply too strong and so he set off once more.* ◆ N-COUNT The **call** of a particular bird or animal is the characteristic sound that it makes. ❏ *...a wide range of animal noises and bird calls.* ◆ →see also **so-called** ◆ PHRASE If someone is **on call**, they are ready to go to work at any time if they are needed, especially if there is an emergency. ❏ *In theory I'm on call day and night.* ◆ to **call** someone's **bluff** →see **bluff**. to **call a halt** →see **halt**. to **call** something your **own** →see **own**. to **call** something **into question** →see **question**. to **call it quits** →see **quit**. to **call the tune** →see **tune**

Thesaurus   call의 참조어

v.   cry, holler, scream, shout ◆

Word Partnership   call의 연어

N.   call *someone* names ◆
    (tele)phone call ◆
    call an ambulance, call a doctor, call the police ◆
    call a meeting ◆
v.   call collect, make a call, receive a call, return a call, take a call, wait for a call ◆

If you **cancel** or **call off** an arrangement or an appointment, you stop it from happening. ❏ *His failing health forced him to cancel the meeting... The European Community has threatened to call off peace talks.* If you **postpone** or **put off** an arrangement or an appointment, you make another arrangement for it to happen at a later time. ❏ *Elections have been postponed until next year... The Senate put off a vote on the nomination for one week.* If you **delay** something that has been arranged, you make it happen later than planned. ❏ *Space agency managers decided to delay the launch of the space shuttle.* If something **delays** you or **holds you up**, you start or finish what you are doing later than you planned. ❏ *He was delayed in traffic... Delivery of equipment had been held up by delays and disputes.*

▶**call around** PHRASAL VERB If you **call around**, you phone several people, usually when you are trying to organize something or to find some information. [mainly AM] ❏ *Call around to find the keenest bargains.*

▶**call back** PHRASAL VERB If you **call** someone **back**, you telephone them again or in return for a telephone call that they have made to you. [BRIT usually **ring round**, **ring around**] ❏ *If we're not around she'll take a message and we'll call you back.*

▶**call for** ◆ PHRASAL VERB If you **call for** someone, you go to the building where they are, so that you can both go somewhere. ❏ *I shall be calling for you at seven o'clock.* ◆ PHRASAL VERB If you **call for** something, you demand that it should happen. ❏ *They angrily called for Robinson's resignation.* ◆ PHRASAL VERB If something **calls for** a particular action or quality, it needs it or makes it necessary. ❏ *It's a situation that calls for a blend of delicacy and force.*

▶**call in** ◆ PHRASAL VERB If you **call** someone **in**, you ask them to come and help you or do something for you. ❏ *Call in an architect or surveyor to oversee the work.*

◆ 타동사 ~라고 일컫는다, ~으로 간주하다 ❏ 그를 배신자라고 일컫는 보수당원들에 의해 연설이 중단되었다. ❏ 그녀는 나를 보고 게으르고 이기적이라고 했다. ◆ 타동사 부르다, 소리 내어 부르다 ❏ 그는 집의 아래층 여기저기에서 사람들이 자신의 이름을 부르는 것을 들을 수 있었다. ● 구동사 부르다, 소리 내어 부르다 ❏ 정육점 주인의 아들이 소리 내어 인사를 했다. ◆ 타동사/자동사 ~에게 전화를 걸다 ❏ 찾는 대로 제게 전화를 해 주시겠어요? 제 번호는 전화번호부에 있어요. ❏ 내 친구 하나가 전화하라고 이 번호를 알려 주었다. ◆ 타동사 전화로 부르다 ❏ 그는 아내에게 구급차를 부르라고 소리쳤다. ◆ 타동사 부르다, ~을 오라고 하다 ❏ 그녀는 어린 아들을 불렀다. "이리 와, 스티븐, 와서 이것 좀 봐!" ◆ 가산명사 통화, 전화를 걺 ❏ 나는 미국에 있는 친구에게 전화를 걸었다. ❏ 나는 다른 피해자들로부터 수백 통의 전화를 받아 왔다. ◆ 타동사 소집하다 ❏ 위원회는 전 인도 의회 모임을 소집하기로 결정했다. ◆ 타동사 소환되다 ❏ 그 아이는 증언하기 위해 두 시간을 기다렸다. ◆ 자동사 들르다, 방문하다 ❏ 시장 조사원이 그가 살고 있는 집을 방문했다. ● 가산명사 방문 ❏ 그는 토미 커밍스를 방문하기로 결정했다. ◆ 자동사 정차하다, 기항하다 ❏ 그 기선은 항로를 따라가며 해안에 야자수가 심어져 있는 몇몇 항구에 정차한다. ◆ 타동사 취소하다 ❏ 우리는 다음 경기를 취소했다. ◆ 가산명사 요구 ❏ 새로운 방식의 보안 계획에 대한 요구가 있어 왔다. ◆ 불가산명사 ~에 대한 요구 ❏ "그냥 보통 초콜릿 있어요?" "아니요, 그건 별로 찾는 사람이 없는 것 같은데요." ◆ 단수명사 매력, 유혹 ❏ 하지만 야생의 유혹이 그저 너무나 강했기에 그는 다시 한 번 길을 나섰다. ◆ 가산명사 (새 등의) 우는 소리 ❏ 대단히 다양한 짐승 소리와 새소리들 ◆ 구 대기 중인 ❏ 이론상으로는 나는 밤낮으로 대기 중이다.

합의나 약속을 cancel 또는 call off하면, 그것이 일어나지 않도록 하는 것이다. ❏ 그는 건강이 나빠져서 회의를 취소해야 했다... 유럽 공동체가 평화 협상을 취소하겠다고 협박해 왔다. 어떤 조치나 약속을 postpone 또는 put off하면, 그것이 더 뒤의 어느 시기에 일어날 수 있도록 새로운 약속을 하는 것이다. ❏ 선거가 내년으로 연기되었다... 상원은 지명 투표를 일주일 동안 연기했다. 이미 약속된 것을 delay하면, 그것이 계획했던 것보다 나중에 일어나도록 하는 것이다. ❏ 우주항공 센터 관리자들이 우주선 발사를 연기하기로 결정했다. 무슨 일이 당신을 delay하거나 당신을 hold up하면, 일의 시작이나 마무리를 계획보다 늦게 하는 것이다. ❏ 그 사람은 차가 막혀서 늦었다... 장비 배달이 일정 연기와 의견 충돌 때문에 지연되었다.

구동사 전화 연락을 돌리다 [주로 미국영어] ❏ 가장 싼 물건을 찾아서 여기저기 전화를 돌려 보세요.

구동사 ~에게 화답의 전화를 걸다; 다시 전화하다 [영국영어 대개 ring round, ring around] ❏ 우리가 부재 중일 때 그녀가 메시지를 받아 놓으면 우리가 나중에 전화를 드릴 겁니다.

◆ 구동사 데리러 가다 ❏ 7시에 데리러 갈게. ◆ 구동사 요구하다 ❏ 그들은 성이 나서 로빈슨의 사임을 요구했다. ◆ 구동사 ~을 필요로 하다 ❏ 지금은 섬세함과 힘을 아울러 필요로 하는 상황이다.

◆ 구동사 불러들이다 ❏ 건축 기사나 측량 기사를 불러서 작업을 감독하게 하세요.

a b c d e f g h i j k l m n o p q r s t u v w x y z

A

B

C

D

E

F

G

H

I

J

K

L

M

N

O

P

Q

R

S

T

U

V

W

X

Y

Z

2 PHRASAL VERB If you **call in** somewhere, you make a short visit there. ❑ *He just calls in occasionally.*

▶**call in** PHRASAL VERB If you **call in**, you phone a place, such as the place where you work. [mainly AM] ❑ *She reached for the phone to call in sick.*

▶**call off** [BRIT usually **ring in**] PHRASAL VERB If you **call off** an event that has been planned, you cancel it. ❑ *He has called off the trip.*

▶**call on** or **call upon** **1** PHRASAL VERB If you **call on** someone **to** do something or **call upon** them **to** do it, you say publicly that you want them to do it. ❑ *One of Kenya's leading churchmen has called on the government to resign.* **2** PHRASAL VERB If you **call on** someone or **call upon** someone, you pay them a short visit. ❑ *Sofia was intending to call on Miss Kitts.*

▶**call out** PHRASAL VERB If you **call** someone **out**, you order or request that they come to help, especially in an emergency. ❑ *Colombia has called out the army and imposed emergency measures.* ❑ *I called the doctor out.* →see also **call 3**

▶**call up** **1** PHRASAL VERB If you **call** someone **up**, you telephone them. [mainly AM] ❑ *When I'm in Pittsburgh, I call him up.* ❑ *He called up the museum.* **2** PHRASAL VERB If someone **is called up**, they are ordered to join the army, navy, or air force. ❑ *The United States has called up some 150,000 military reservists.*

▶**call upon** →see **call on**

call cen|ter (**call centers**) [BRIT **call centre**] N-COUNT A call centrt is an office where people work answering or making telephone calls for a particular company.

call|er /kɔlər/ (**callers**) **1** N-COUNT A **caller** is a person who is making a telephone call. ❑ *An anonymous caller told police what had happened.* **2** N-COUNT A **caller** is a person who comes to see you for a short visit. ❑ *She ushered her callers into a cluttered living-room.*

call-in (**call-ins**) N-COUNT A **call-in** is a program on radio or television in which people telephone with questions or opinions and their calls are broadcast. [AM; BRIT **phone-in**] ❑ *...a call-in show on Los Angeles radio station KABC.*

call|ing card (**calling cards**) N-COUNT A **calling card** is a small card with personal information about you on it, such as your name and address, which you can give to people when you go to visit them. [OLD-FASHIONED] ❑ *...and don't forget to give your calling card to those you'd like to see again.*

cal|lous /kæləs/ ADJ A **callous** person or action is very cruel and shows no concern for other people or their feelings. ❑ *...his callous disregard for human life.* ● **cal|lous|ness** N-UNCOUNT ❑ *...the callousness of Raymond's murder.* ● **cal|lous|ly** ADV [ADV with v] ❑ *He is accused of consistently and callously ill-treating his wife.*

call wait|ing N-UNCOUNT **Call waiting** is a telephone service that sends you a signal if another call arrives while you are already on the phone. ❑ *ICM is an internationally patented call waiting service suited to the domestic market.*

calm ♦♢♢ /kɑm/ (**calmer, calmest, calms, calming, calmed**) **1** ADJ A **calm** person does not show or feel any worry, anger, or excitement. ❑ *She is usually a calm and diplomatic woman.* ❑ *Try to keep calm and just tell me what happened.* ● N-UNCOUNT **Calm** is also a noun. [also a N] ❑ *He felt a sudden sense of calm, of contentment.* ● **calm|ly** ADV ❑ *Alan looked at him and said calmly, "I don't believe you."* **2** V-T If you **calm** someone, you do something to make them feel less angry, worried, or excited. ❑ *The ruling party's veterans know how to calm their critics.* ❑ *She was breathing quickly and tried to calm herself.* ● **calm|ing** ADJ ❑ *...a fresh, cool fragrance which produces a very calming effect on the mind.* **3** N-UNCOUNT **Calm** is used to refer to a quiet, still, or peaceful atmosphere in a place. ❑ *The house projects an atmosphere of neoclassical calm and order.* **4** ADJ If someone says that a place is **calm**, they mean that it is free from fighting or public disorder, when trouble has recently occurred there or had been expected. [JOURNALISM] ❑ *The city of Sarajevo appears relatively calm today.* ● N-UNCOUNT **Calm** is also a noun. [also a N] ❑ *Community and church leaders have appealed for calm and no retaliation.* **5** V-T To **calm** a situation is to reduce the amount of trouble, violence, or panic there is. ❑ *Officials hoped admitting fewer foreigners would calm the situation.* **6** ADJ If the sea or a lake is **calm**, the water is not moving very much and there are no big waves. ❑ *...as we slid into the calm waters of Cowes Harbour.* **7** ADJ **Calm** weather is pleasant weather with little or no wind. ❑ *Tuesday was a fine, clear and calm day.* **8** V-I When the sea **calms**, it becomes still because the wind stops blowing strongly. When the wind **calms**, it stops blowing strongly. ❑ *Dawn came, the sea calmed but the cold was as bitter as ever.* →see **hypnosis**

Thesaurus		calm의 참조어
ADJ.	laid-back, relaxed; (ant.) excited, upset **1**	
	mild, peaceful, placid, serene, tranquil; (ant.) rough **1**-**3** **6**	

▶**calm down** **1** PHRASAL VERB If you **calm down**, or if someone **calms** you **down**, you become less angry, upset, or excited. ❑ *Calm down for a minute and listen to me.* ❑ *I'll try a herbal remedy to calm him down.* **2** PHRASAL VERB If things **calm down**, or someone or something **calms** things **down**, the amount of activity, trouble, or panic is reduced. ❑ *We will go back to normal when things calm down.*

Word Link	**cal, caul ≈ hot, heat : cauldron, calorie, scald**

calo|rie /kæləri/ (**calories**) N-COUNT **Calories** are units used to measure the energy value of food. People who are on diets try to eat food that does not contain many calories. ❑ *A glass of wine does have quite a lot of calories.* →see **diet**

2 구동사 들르다, 방문하다 ❑ 그는 다만 가끔씩 들를 뿐이다.

구동사 (근무처에) 전화하다 [주로 미국영어] ❑ 그녀는 병결을 알리기 위해 전화기에 손을 뻗었다.

[영국영어 대개 ring in] 구동사 취소하다 ❑ 그는 여행을 취소했다.

1 구동사 요구하다, 부탁하다 ❑ 케냐의 지도적 위치에 있는 성직자 한 명이 정부에게 물러날 것을 요구했다. **2** 구동사 들르다, 방문하다 ❑ 소피아는 키츠 양을 방문할 생각을 하고 있었다.

구동사 불러내다; 출동시키다 ❑ 컬럼비아는 군대를 출동시키고 비상 조처를 취했다. ❑ 나는 의사를 불렀다.

1 구동사 ～에게 전화를 걸다 [주로 미국영어] ❑ 나는 피츠버그에 있을 때 그에게 전화를 한다. ❑ 그는 박물관에 전화를 걸었다. **2** 구동사 징집되다 ❑ 미국은 약 15만 명의 예비군을 소집했다.

[영국영어 call centre] 가산명사 콜 센터

1 가산명사 전화 거는 사람 ❑ 익명의 제보자가 경찰에 전화를 걸어 무슨 일이 일어났었는지 알렸다. **2** 가산명사 방문자 ❑ 그녀는 어수선한 거실로 방문객들을 안내했다.

가산명사 시청자 전화 참여 프로 [미국영어; 영국영어 phone-in] ❑ 로스엔젤레스 케이에이비시 라디오 방송국의 시청자 전화 참여 프로그램

가산명사 명함 [구식어] ❑ 그리고 다시 만나고 싶은 사람들에게는 잊지 말고 명함을 건네세요.

형용사 냉혹한, 비정한 ❑ 냉혹하게 인명을 경시하는 그의 태도 ● 냉혹함, 비정함 불가산명사 ❑ 레이먼드 살인 사건의 냉혹함 ● 냉혹하게, 비정하게 부사 ❑ 그는 시종일관 냉혹하게 아내를 학대한다는 비난을 받는다.

불가산명사 통화 중 대기 ❑ 아이엠은 국내 시장에 적합하게 맞춘, 국제 특허된 통화 중 대기 서비스이다.

1 형용사 침착한 ❑ 그녀는 평소 침착하고 사교적인 여자이다. ❑ 침착하고, 무슨 일이 일어났는지 나한테 얘기해 봐. ● 불가산명사 침착함, 평온함 ❑ 그는 갑자기 평온함과 만족감을 느꼈다. ● 침착하게 부사 ❑ 앨런은 그를 보고 침착하게 말했다. "나는 널 믿지 않아." **2** 타동사 진정시키다, 달래다 ❑ 집권당의 고참 의원들은 이 비판자들을 진정시킬 방법을 알고 있다. ❑ 그녀는 급하게 숨을 쉬며 마음을 가라앉히려고 했다. ● 진정시키는, 달래는 형용사 ❑ 마음을 아주 진정시켜 주는 효과를 내는 맑고 시원한 향기 **3** 불가산명사 평온 ❑ 그 집은 신고전주의풍의 고요하고 정돈된 분위기를 풍긴다. **4** 형용사 평온한 [언론] ❑ 오늘 사라예보 시는 비교적 평온해 보인다. ● 불가산명사 평온 ❑ 사회와 교회의 지도자들은 평온과 보복 금지를 호소해 왔다. **5** 타동사 진정시키다 ❑ 관리들은 외국인들의 입국 제한을 통해 사태를 진정시킬 수 있기를 희망했다. **6** 형용사 잔잔한 ❑ 우리가 카우즈 항의 잔잔한 수면으로 미끄러져 들어갈 때 **7** 형용사 잔잔한, 바람이 없는 ❑ 화요일은 맑고 화창하며 맑고 바람이 잔잔한 날이었다. **8** 자동사 잔잔해지다 ❑ 새벽이 오자, 바다는 잔잔해졌으나 추위는 변함없이 살을 에는 듯했다.

1 구동사 진정시키다; 진정하다 ❑ 잠깐만 진정하고 내 말을 들어봐. ❑ 그 사람을 진정시키기 위해 약초 치료법을 시도해 보겠다. **2** 구동사 안정시키다; 안정되다 ❑ 사태가 안정되면 보통 상태로 돌아갈 것이다.

가산명사 칼로리 ❑ 와인 한 잔에는 상당히 높은 칼로리가 들어 있다.

Word Web calories

Calories are a measure of **energy**. One calorie of heat raises the **temperature** of 1 gram of water by 1°C*. However, we usually think of calories in relation to food and exercise. A person eating a cup of vanilla ice cream **takes in** 270 calories. Walking a mile **burns** 66 calories. Different types of foods store different amounts of energy. **Proteins** and **carbohydrates** contain 4 calories per gram. However **fat** contains 9 calories per gram. Our bodies store extra calories in the form of fat. For every 3,500 excess calories we take in, we gain a pound of fat.

* 0°Celsius = 32° Fahrenheit

---

cam|cord|er /kǽmkɔːrdər/ (**camcorders**) N-COUNT A **camcorder** is a portable video camera which records both pictures and sound.

가산명사 캠코더

came /keɪm/ **Came** is the past tense of **come**.

come의 과거형

cam|el /kǽmᵊl/ (**camels**) N-COUNT A **camel** is a large animal that lives in deserts and is used for carrying goods and people. Camels have long necks and one or two lumps on their backs called humps. **the straw that broke the camel's back** →see **straw**

가산명사 낙타

cameo /kǽmioʊ/ (**cameos**) **1** N-COUNT A **cameo** is a short description or piece of acting which expresses cleverly and neatly the nature of a situation, event, or person's character. ❑ *...a succession of memorable cameos of Scottish history.* **2** N-COUNT A **cameo** is a piece of jewelry, usually oval in shape, consisting of a raised stone figure or design fixed on to a flat stone of another color. ❑ *...a cameo brooch.*

1 가산명사 명장면; 카메오 출연 ❑ 일련의 스코틀랜드 역사 속 명장면들 **2** 가산명사 카메오. (가공 보석류의 일종) ❑ 카메오 브로치

cam|era ◆◆◇ /kǽmrə/ (**cameras**) **1** N-COUNT A **camera** is a piece of equipment that is used for taking photographs, making movies, or producing television pictures. ❑ *Her gran lent her a camera for a school trip to Venice and Egypt.* **2** PHRASE If someone or something is **on camera**, they are being filmed. ❑ *Fay was so impressive on camera that a special part was written in for her.* **3** PHRASE If you do something or if something happens **off camera**, you do it or it happens when not being filmed. ❑ *They were anything but friendly off-camera, refusing even to take the same lift.* **4** PHRASE If a trial is held **in camera**, the public and the press are not allowed to attend. [FORMAL] ❑ *This morning's appeal was held in camera.* →see **photography**

1 가산명사 카메라 ❑ 그 여자 아이의 할머니는 베니스와 이집트로 수학여행을 가는 손녀에게 카메라를 빌려 주었다. **2** 구 촬영 카메라 앞에서; 촬영되고 있는 ❑ 페이는 카메라 앞에서 대단히 인상적인 모습을 보여 주었기에 그녀를 위한 역할이 특별히 써 넣어졌다. **3** 구 카메라 앞에서 벗어나 ❑ 카메라 앞을 벗어나면 그들은 결코 사이가 좋지 않았고, 심지어는 승강기조차 같이 타려 하지 않았다. **4** 구 비공개로, 방청 금지로 [격식체] ❑ 오늘 아침의 항소심은 비공개로 열렸다.

cam|era|man /kǽmrəmæn/ (**cameramen**) N-COUNT A **cameraman** is a person who operates a camera for television or movies.

가산명사 촬영 기사, 카메라 맨

camou|flage /kǽməflɑːʒ/ (**camouflages, camouflaging, camouflaged**) **1** N-UNCOUNT **Camouflage** consists of things such as leaves, branches, or brown and green paint, which are used to make it difficult for an enemy to see military forces and equipment. [also *a n*, oft N n] ❑ *They were dressed in camouflage and carried automatic rifles.* ❑ *...a camouflage jacket.* **2** V-T If military buildings or vehicles **are camouflaged**, things such as leaves, branches, or brown and green paint are used to make it difficult for an enemy to see them. [usu passive] ❑ *You won't see them from the air. They'd be very well camouflaged.* **3** V-T If you **camouflage** something such as a feeling or a situation, you hide it or make it appear to be something different. ❑ *He has never camouflaged his desire to better himself.* ● N-UNCOUNT **Camouflage** is also a noun. [also *a n*] ❑ *The frenzied merrymaking of her later years was a desperate camouflage for her grief.* **4** N-UNCOUNT **Camouflage** is the way in which some animals are colored and shaped so that they cannot easily be seen in their natural surroundings. [also *a n*] ❑ *Confident in its camouflage, being the same color as the rocks, the lizard stands still when it feels danger.*

1 불가산명사 위장 ❑ 그들은 위장을 하고 자동 소총을 휴대했다. ❑ 위장 재킷 **2** 타동사 위장하다 ❑ 공중에서 그것들을 볼 수는 없을 겁니다. 위장을 아주 잘해 놓았을 테니까요. **3** 타동사 감추다, 위장하다 ❑ 그는 출세하고자 하는 욕망을 숨긴 적이 없다. ● 불가산명사 감춤, 위장 ❑ 말년에 그녀가 미친 듯이 유쾌하게 떠들어댔던 것은 자신의 슬픔을 필사적으로 감추기 위함이었다. **4** 불가산명사 보호색 ❑ 몸 색깔이 바위와 같기 때문에 위장에 자신이 있는 도마뱀은, 위험을 감지하면 움직임을 멈추고 가만히 있는다.

camp ◆◆◇ /kæmp/ (**camps, camping, camped**) **1** N-COUNT A **camp** is a collection of huts and other buildings that is provided for a particular group of people, such as refugees, prisoners, or soldiers, as a place to live or stay. ❑ *...a refugee camp.* **2** N-VAR A **camp** is an outdoor area with cabins, tents, or trailers where people stay on vacation. **3** N-VAR A **camp** is a collection of tents or trailers where people are living or staying, usually temporarily while they are traveling. ❑ *...gypsy camps.* **4** V-I If you **camp** somewhere, you stay or live there for a short time in a tent or trailer, or in the open air. ❑ *We camped near the beach.* ● PHRASAL VERB **Camp out** means the same as **camp**. ❑ *For six months they camped out in a meadow at the back of the house.* ● **camping** N-UNCOUNT ❑ *They went camping in the wilds.* **5** N-COUNT You can refer to a group of people who all support a particular person, policy, or idea as a particular **camp**. ❑ *The press release provoked furious protests from the Gore camp and other top Democrats.* **6** →see also **concentration camp**

1 가산명사 주둔지, 막사 ❑ 난민 주둔지 **2** 가산명사 또는 불가산명사 캠프장 **3** 가산명사 또는 불가산명사 야영단 ❑ 집시 야영단 **4** 자동사 야영하다 ❑ 우리는 해변 근처에서 야영을 했다. ● 구동사 야영하다 ❑ 그들은 여섯 달 동안 집 뒤의 풀밭에서 야영을 했다. ● 야영, 캠핑 불가산명사 ❑ 그들은 광야로 캠핑을 갔다. **5** 가산명사 진영 ❑ 그 보도 자료는 고어 진영과 다른 민주당 고위 인사들의 격렬한 항의를 불러일으켰다.

cam|paign ◆◆◆ /kæmpéɪn/ (**campaigns, campaigning, campaigned**) **1** N-COUNT A **campaign** is a planned set of activities that people carry out over a period of time in order to achieve something such as social or political change. ❑ *During his election campaign he promised to put the economy back on its feet.* ❑ *...a campaign to improve the training of staff.* **2** V-T/V-I If someone **campaigns for** something, they carry out a planned set of activities over a period of time in order to achieve their aim. ❑ *We are campaigning for law reform.* **3** N-COUNT In a war, a **campaign** is a series of planned movements carried out by armed forces. ❑ *The allies are intensifying their air campaign.* **4** →see also **advertising campaign** →see **army, election**

1 가산명사 운동 ❑ 선거 운동 기간 동안 그는 경제를 되살리겠다고 약속했다. ❑ 직원 훈련을 개선하기 위한 캠페인 **2** 타동사/자동사 운동을 하다 ❑ 우리는 법률 개혁 운동을 하고 있다. **3** 가산명사 일련의 군사 행동, 전역 ❑ 연합군들은 공습을 강화하고 있다.

a b c d e f g h i j k l m n o p q r s t u v w x y z

Word Partnership	*campaign*의 연어
N.	**advertising/marketing** campaign, **election** campaign, campaign **slogan** ∎
PREP.	campaign **against** *someone/something*, campaign **for** *something* ∎

cam|paign|er /kæmpeɪnər/ (**campaigners**) N-COUNT A **campaigner** is a person who campaigns for social or political change. ❑ *...anti-hunting campaigners.*

가산명사 운동가 ❑ 사냥 반대 운동가

camp|er /kæmpər/ (**campers**) ∎ N-COUNT A **camper** is someone who is camping somewhere. ❑ *My fellow campers were already packing up their tents.* ∎ N-COUNT A **camper** is a motor vehicle which is equipped with beds and cooking equipment so that you can live, cook, and sleep in it. [BRIT; AM **camper van**]

∎ 가산명사 야영자 ❑ 내 동료 야영자들은 이미 천막을 걷어서 챙기고 있었다. ∎ 가산명사 캠프용 트레일러 [영국영어; 미국영어 camper van]

camp|er van (**camper vans**) N-COUNT A **camper van** is the same as a **camper**.

가산명사 야영용 자동차

camp|site /kæmpsaɪt/ (**campsites**) N-COUNT A **campsite** is a place where people who are on vacation can stay in tents.

가산명사 캠프장

cam|pus /kæmpəs/ (**campuses**) N-COUNT A **campus** is an area of land that contains the main buildings of a university or college. [also prep N] ❑ *...during a rally at the campus.*

가산명사 대학 교정 ❑ 대학 교정에서의 집회 중

---
can
---

① MODAL USES
② CONTAINER

① can ♦♦♦ /kən, STRONG kæn/

Can is a modal verb. It is used with the base form of a verb. The form **cannot** is used in negative statements. The usual spoken form of **cannot** is **can't**, pronounced /kænt/, BRIT /kɑːnt/.

can은 조동사이며 동사 원형과 함께 쓴다. cannot은 부정문에 쓴다. 보통 cannot의 구어체 형태는 can't이며 /kænt /로, 영국영어는 /kɑːnt /로 발음된다.

∎ MODAL You use **can** when you are mentioning a quality or fact about something which people may make use of if they want to. ❑ *Pork is also the most versatile of meats. It can be roasted whole or in pieces.* ❑ *A central reservation number operated by the resort can direct you to accommodations that best suit your needs.* ∎ MODAL You use **can** to indicate that someone has the ability or opportunity to do something. ❑ *Don't worry yourself about me, I can take care of myself.* ❑ *I can't give you details because I don't actually have any details.* ❑ *The United States will do whatever it can to help Greece.* ∎ MODAL You use **cannot** to indicate that someone is not able to do something because circumstances make it impossible for them to do it. ❑ *We cannot buy food, clothes and pay for rent and utilities on $20 a week.* ∎ MODAL You use **can** to indicate that something is true sometimes or is true in some circumstances. ❑ *...long-term therapy that can last five years or more.* ❑ *Exercising alone can be boring.* ∎ MODAL You use **cannot** and **can't** to state that you are certain that something is not the case or will not happen. ❑ *From her knowledge of Douglas's habits, she feels sure that that person can't have been Douglas.* ❑ *Things can't be that bad.* ∎ MODAL You use **can** to indicate that someone is allowed to do something. You use **cannot** or **can't** to indicate that someone is not allowed to do something. ❑ *Here, can I really have your jeans when you go?* ❑ *We can't answer any questions, I'm afraid.* ∎ MODAL You use **cannot** or **can't** when you think it is very important that something should not happen or that someone should not do something. [EMPHASIS] ❑ *It is an intolerable situation and it can't be allowed to go on.* ∎ MODAL You use **can**, usually in questions, in order to make suggestions or to offer to do something. ❑ *What can I do around here?* ❑ *This old lady was struggling out of the train and I said, "Oh, can I help you?"* ∎ MODAL You use **can** in questions in order to make polite requests. You use **can't** in questions in order to request strongly that someone does something. [POLITENESS] ❑ *Can I have a look at that?* ❑ *Can you fill in some of the details of your career?* ∎ MODAL You use **can** as a polite way of interrupting someone or of introducing what you are going to say next. [FORMAL, SPOKEN] ❑ *Can I interrupt you just for a minute?* ❑ *But if I can interrupt, Joe, I don't think anybody here is personally blaming you.* ∎ MODAL You use **can** with verbs such as "imagine," "think," and "believe" in order to emphasize how you feel about a particular situation. [INFORMAL or SPOKEN, EMPHASIS] ❑ *You can imagine he was terribly upset.* ❑ *You can't think how glad I was to see them all go.* ∎ MODAL You use **can** in questions with "how" to indicate that you feel strongly about something. [SPOKEN, EMPHASIS] ❑ *How can millions of dollars go astray?* ❑ *How can you say such a thing?*

∎ 법조동사 - 할 수 있다 ❑ 돼지고기는 또한 육류 중에서 가장 용도가 다양하다. 통째로 혹은 썰어서 구울 수 있다. ❑ 리조트에서 운영하는 대표 예약 번호를 이용하시면 원하시는 것에 가장 부합하는 숙박 시설에 대해 안내를 받으실 수 있습니다. ∎ 법조동사 - 할 수 있다 ❑ 내 걱정 하지 마. 내가 알아서 할 수 있어. ❑ 사실 나도 아는 것이 없기 때문에 너에게 자세한 사항을 알려줄 수가 없다. ❑ 미국은 그리스를 돕기 위해 할 수 있는 일이라면 무슨 일이든 할 것이다. ∎ 법조동사 - 할 수 없다 ❑ 일주일에 20달러 가지고는 식료품 값, 옷값, 집세와 공공요금을 치를 수가 없다. ∎ 법조동사 - 할 수도 있다 ❑ 5년 이상 지속될 수도 있는 장기 요법 ❑ 운동만으로는 지루할 수도 있다. ∎ 법조동사 -하지 못하다, - 할 수 없다 ❑ 미국은 그리스를 돕기 위해 할 수 있는... 더글러스의 습성에 비추어 볼 때, 그녀는 그 사람이 더글러스였으리는 없다는 확신이 든다. ❑ 사태가 그 정도로 나쁠 리가 없다. ∎ 법조동사 -해도 된다, - 할 수 있다 ❑ 있잖아, 네가 가면 내가 정말 네 청바지를 가져도 되니? ❑ 안됐지만 어떤 질문에도 답변을 해 줄 수 없을 것 같다. ∎ 법조동사 -해서는 안 된다 [강조] ❑ 그것은 용납될 수 없는 상황이므로 계속되도록 두어서는 안 된다. ∎ 법조동사 주로 의문문 형식으로 제안이나 제의를 할 때 쓰는 조동사 ❑ 제가 뭘 할까요? ❑ 이 나이 든 아주머니가 열차에서 나오려고 애쓰고 있길래 내가 말했다. "아, 도와 드릴까요?" ∎ 법조동사 공손하게 부탁하는 의문문에서 쓰는 조동사 [공손체] ❑ 저걸 좀 볼 수 있을까요? ❑ 당신의 경력에 대해서 좀 자세하게 적어 넣어 주시겠어요? ∎ 법조동사 공손히 상대방의 말에 끼어들 때 [격식체, 구어체] ❑ 말씀 중에 잠깐 실례해도 될까요? ❑ 조, 이야기하는 중에 미안하지만, 나는 여기 있는 사람 누구도 개인적으로 너를 비난하고 있다고 생각지 않아. ∎ 법조동사 느낌을 강조하기 위해 쓰는 조동사 [비격식체 또는 구어체, 강조] ❑ 그 사람이 몹시 당황했음을 상상할 수 있을 거다. ❑ 그들이 모두 가는 것을 보고 내가 얼마나 기뻤는지 너는 상상도 못할 거야. ∎ 법조동사 how와 함께 씌어 강한 감정을 나타낸다. [구어체, 강조] ❑ 어떻게 수백만 달러의 돈이 잘못될 수 있어? ❑ 네가 어떻게 그런 말을 할 수가 있지?

Can, could, and **be able to** are all used to talk about a person's ability to do something. They are followed by the infinitive form of a verb. You use **can** or a present form of **be able to** to refer to the present, although **can** is more common. ❑ *They can all read and write... The snake is able to catch small mammals.* You use **could** or a past form of **be able to** to refer to the past, and "will" or "shall" with **be able to** to refer to the future. **Be able to** is used if you want refer to doing something at a particular time. ❑ *After treatment he was able to return to work.* **Can** and **could** are used to talk about possibility. **Could** refers to a particular occasion and **can** to more general situations. ❑ *Many jobs could be lost... Too much salt can be harmful.* When talking about the past, you use **could have** and a past participle. ❑ *It could have been much worse.* You also use **can** for the present and **could** for the past to talk about rules or what

can, could, be able to는 모두 무엇을 할 수 있는 사람의 능력을 말할 때 쓰며, 뒤에는 동사 원형이 온다. 현재에 대해 말할 때는 can이나 be able to의 현재형을 쓰는데 can이 더 일반적이다. ❑ 그들은 모두 글을 읽고 쓸 줄 안다... 뱀은 작은 포유동물을 잡을 수 있다. 과거에 대해 말할 때는 could나 be able to의 과거형을 쓰고, 미래에 대해 말할 때는 'will' 또는 'shall'과 함께 be able to를 쓴다. 특정한 시기에 무엇을 한다는 것에 대해 말할 때는 be able to를 쓴다. ❑ 치료 후에 그는 직장으로 복귀할 수 있었다. can과 could는 모두 가능성을 얘기할 때 쓴다. could는 특정한 경우에 대해 쓰고 can은 좀

people are allowed to do. ❑ *They can leave at any time.* Note that when making requests either **can** or **could** may be used. ❑ *Can I have a drink?... Could we put the fire on?* However, **could** is always used for suggestions. ❑ *You could phone her and ask.*

더 일반적인 상황에 대해 쓴다. ❑ 많은 일자리가 없어질 수도 있다... 염분 과다 섭취는 해로울 수 있다. 과거에 대해서 말할 때는 could have와 과거분사를 쓴다. ❑ 사정이 훨씬 더 안 좋을 수도 있었다. 규칙이나 허용되는 일에 대해 말할 때에도 현재일 때는 can을, 과거일 때는 could를 쓸 수 있다. ❑ 그들은 아무 때나 떠날 수 있다. 요청을 할 때는 can이나 could 어느 것이나 쓸 수 있음을 유의하라. ❑ 한 잔 할 수 있을까요?[한 잔 주시겠소?]... 우리 난로 피울까요? 그러나 제안에는 항상 could를 쓴다. ❑ 네가 그녀에게 전화를 해서 물어 볼 수도 있겠지.

② **can**/kæn/ (**cans, canning, canned**) **1** N-COUNT A **can** is a metal container in which something such as food, drink, or paint is put. The container is usually sealed to keep the contents fresh. ❑ *Several young men were kicking a tin can along the middle of the road.* ❑ *...empty beer cans.* **2** V-T When food or drink **is canned**, it is put into a metal container and sealed so that it will remain fresh. [usu passive] ❑ *...fruits and vegetables that will be canned, skinned, diced or otherwise processed.* **3** N-SING **The can** is the toilet. [AM, INFORMAL] **4** V-T If you **are canned**, you are dismissed from your job. [AM, INFORMAL] ❑ *The extremists prevailed, and the security minister was canned.* →see Word Web: **can**

1 가산명사 깡통 ❑ 젊은이들 몇 명이 길 가운데를 따라가며 양철 깡통을 발로 차고 있었다. ❑ 빈 맥주 깡통 **2** 타동사 통조림으로 만들다 ❑ 통조림으로 만들거나, 껍질을 벗기거나, 네모꼴로 썰거나, 기타 방식으로 가공 처리될 과일과 야채 **3** 단수명사 화장실 [미국영어, 비격식체] **4** 타동사 해고당하다, 잘리다 [미국영어, 비격식체] ❑ 극단론자들이 득세하자, 안보 장관은 해임되었다.

ca|nal/kənæl/ (**canals**) **1** N-COUNT A **canal** is a long, narrow stretch of water that has been made for boats to travel along or to bring water to a particular area. ❑ *...the Grand Union Canal.* **2** N-COUNT A **canal** is a narrow tube inside your body for carrying food, air, or other substances. ❑ *...delaying its progress through the alimentary canal.*

1 가산명사 운하, 수로 ❑ 그랜드 유니언 운하 **2** 가산명사 관 ❑ 그것이 소화관을 거쳐 진행하는 것을 지체시키며

can|cel ◆◇◇ /kænsᵊl/ (**cancels, canceling, canceled**) [BRIT, sometimes AM **cancelling, cancelled**] **1** V-T/V-I If you **cancel** something that has been arranged, you stop it from happening. If you **cancel** an order for goods or services, you tell the person or organization supplying them that you no longer wish to receive them. ❑ *The Russian foreign minister yesterday canceled his visit to Washington.* ❑ *Many trains have been cancelled and a limited service is operating on other lines.* ● **can|cel|la|tion** /kænsəleɪʃᵊn/ (**cancellations**) N-VAR ❑ *Outbursts of violence forced the cancellation of Haiti's first free elections in 1987.* **2** V-T If someone in authority **cancels** a document, an insurance policy, or a debt, they officially declare that it is no longer valid or no longer legally exists. ❑ *He intends to try to leave the country, in spite of a government order canceling his passport.* ● **can|cel|la|tion** N-UNCOUNT ❑ *...a march by groups calling for cancellation of Third World debt.* **3** V-T To **cancel** a stamp or a check means to mark it to show that it has already been used and cannot be used again. ❑ *The new device can also cancel the check after the transaction is complete.*

[영국영어, 미국영어 가끔 cancelling] **1** 타동사/자동사 취소하다 ❑ 러시아 외무 장관이 어제 워싱턴 방문을 취소했다. ❑ 많은 기차 편이 취소되었으며 다른 노선들에서는 제한적으로 운행이 이루어지고 있다. ● 취소 가산명사 또는 불가산명사 ❑ 폭력 사태의 발발로 인해 1987년 아이티 최초의 자유선거는 취소될 수밖에 없었다. **2** 타동사 소멸시키다, 말소하다 ❑ 그는 정부 명령에 의해 여권이 말소되었음에도 불구하고 출국을 시도하려 한다. ● 소멸, 말소 불가산명사 ❑ 제 3세계 부채 탕감을 요구하는 단체들의 행진 **3** 타동사 (우표에) 소인을 찍다; (사용된 수표에) 무효 표시를 하다 ❑ 새 장비는 거래가 완료된 후 사용 수표에 무효 표시를 하는 기능도 있다.

If you **cancel** or **call off** an arrangement or an appointment, you stop it from happening. ❑ *His failing health forced him to cancel the meeting... The European Community has threatened to call off peace talks.* If you **postpone** or **put off** an arrangement or an appointment, you make another arrangement for it to happen at a later time. ❑ *Elections have been postponed until next year... The Senate put off a vote on the nomination for one week.* If you **delay** something that has been arranged, you make it happen later than planned. ❑ *Space agency managers decided to delay the launch of the space shuttle.* If something **delays** you or **holds** you **up**, you start or finish what you are doing later than you planned. ❑ *He was delayed in traffic... Delivery of equipment had been held up by delays and disputes.*

합의나 약속을 cancel 또는 call off하면, 그것이 일어나지 않도록 하는 것이다. ❑ 그는 건강이 나빠져서 회의를 취소해야 했다... 유럽 공동체가 평화 협상을 취소하겠다고 협박해 왔다. 어떤 조치나 약속을 연기(postpone 또는 put off)하면, 그것이 더 뒤의 어느 시기에 일어날 수 있도록 새로운 약속을 하는 것이다. ❑ 선거가 내년으로 연기되었다... 상원은 지명 투표를 일주일 동안 연기했다. 이미 약속된 것을 delay하면, 그것이 계획했던 것보다 나중에 일어나도록 하는 것이다. ❑ 우주항공 센터 관리자들이 우주선 발사를 연기하기로 결정했다. 무슨 일이 당신을 delay하거나 당신을 hold up하면, 일의 시작이나 마무리를 계획보다 늦게 하는 것이다. ❑ 그 사람은 차가 막혀서 늦었다... 장비 배달이 일정 연기와 의견 충돌 때문에 지연되었다.

Thesaurus　　　　*cancel*의 참조어

v.　　　annul, call off, scrap, undo **1**

▶**cancel out** PHRASAL VERB If one thing **cancels out** another thing, the two things have opposite effects, so that when they are combined no real effect is produced. ❑ *He wonders if the different influences might not cancel each other out.*

구동사 상쇄하다 ❑ 그는 서로 다른 영향력이 서로를 상쇄하지 않을까 하고 생각한다.

can|cer ◆◆◇ /kænsər/ (**cancers**) N-VAR **Cancer** is a serious disease in which cells in a person's body increase rapidly in an uncontrolled way, producing abnormal growths. ❑ *Her mother died of breast cancer.* ❑ *Jane was just 25 when she learned she had cancer.* →see Word Web: **cancer**

가산명사 또는 불가산명사 암 ❑ 그녀의 어머니는 유방암으로 돌아가셨다. ❑ 제인은 암에 걸렸다는 것을 알았을 때 겨우 스물다섯 살이었다.

can|cer|ous /kænsərəs/ ADJ **Cancerous** cells or growths are cells or growths that are the result of cancer. ❑ *The production of these cancerous cells suppresses the production of normal white blood cells.*

형용사 암의 ❑ 이런 암세포들이 생기면 정상적인 백혈구의 생성이 억제된다.

can|did /kændɪd/ **1** ADJ When you are **candid** about something or with someone, you speak honestly. ❑ *Nat is candid about the problems she is having with Steve.* ❑ *I haven't been completely candid with him.* **2** ADJ A **candid** photograph of someone is one that was taken when the person did not know they were being photographed. [ADJ n] ❑ *...candid snaps of off-duty royals.*

1 형용사 정직한, 솔직한 ❑ 냇은 스티브와의 문제에 대해 솔직하다. ❑ 나는 그에게 완전히 솔직하지 못해 왔어. **2** 형용사 꾸밈없는 ❑ 휴식 중인 왕족들의 꾸밈없는 모습을 담은 스냅 사진들

Word Web　　　can

A Frenchman named Nicholas Appert* invented the process of **canning** in 1795. First he pre-**cooked** the food. Then he placed it in glass **jars** with cork **lids** to make an **airtight seal**. The final step was a boiling water bath to kill **bacteria**. Food **preserved** in this way lasted for a least a year. In 1804, Appert opened the world's first factory to produce **vacuum-packed** foods. In 1810, an Englishman, Peter Durance, began to use **metal containers** to can food. Today's canning factories use steel cans covered with a thin coating of **tin**.

Nicholas Appert (1750-1840): a confectioner.

Word Web cancer

The traditional **treatments** for **cancer** are **surgery**, **radiation therapy**, and chemotherapy. However, a new type of treatment called targeted therapy has emerged in the past few years. This treatment uses new drugs that target specific types of cancer cells. Targeted therapy also eliminates many of the **toxic** effects on healthy **tissue** that often result from traditional chemotherapy. One of these drugs helps prevent blood vessels that feed a tumor from growing. Another drug kills cancer cells.

can|di|da|cy /kændɪdəsi/ (candidacies) N-VAR Someone's **candidacy** is their position of being a candidate in an election. ❑ *Today he is formally announcing his candidacy for President.*

가산명사 또는 불가산명사 입후보 ❑ 그는 오늘 대통령 입후보를 공식적으로 선언할 것이다.

can|di|date ♦♦◇ /kændɪdeɪt/ (candidates) **1** N-COUNT A **candidate** is someone who is being considered for a position, for example someone who is running in an election or applying for a job. ❑ *The Democratic candidate is still leading in the polls.* ❑ *He is a candidate for the office of Governor.* **2** N-COUNT A **candidate** is someone who is studying for a degree at a college. [AM] ❑ *He is now a candidate for a Master's degree in Social Work at San Francisco State University.* **3** N-COUNT A **candidate** is a person or thing that is regarded as being suitable for a particular purpose or as being likely to do or be a particular thing. ❑ *Those who are overweight or indulge in high-salt diets are candidates for hypertension.* **4** N-COUNT A **candidate** is someone who is taking an examination. [BRIT] ❑ *Subject to satisfactory performance in this examination, candidates are permitted to write a dissertation for the MSc degree.* →see **election, vote**

1 가산명사 후보자 ❑ 민주당 후보가 여전히 여론 조사에서 앞서고 있다. ❑ 그는 주지사직 후보자이다. **2** 가산명사 학위 취득 희망자 [미국영어] ❑ 그는 현재 샌프란시스코 주립 대학에서 사회 복지 사업 전공 석사 과정을 밟고 있다. **3** 가산명사 -이 될 듯한 사람; -에 적합한 물건 ❑ 체중이 많이 나가거나 고염분 식품을 많이 섭취하는 사람들은 고혈압에 걸리기 쉽다. **4** 가산명사 수험생 [영국영어] ❑ 이 시험에서 만족할 만한 성적을 받으면, 수험생들은 이학 석사 논문을 쓸 자격을 얻게 된다.

can|dle /kænd³l/ (candles) N-COUNT A **candle** is a stick of hard wax with a piece of string called a wick through the middle. You light the wick in order to give a steady flame that provides light. ❑ *The bedroom was lit by a single candle.*

가산명사 양초 ❑ 촛불 하나가 침실을 밝히고 있었다.

can|dor /kændər/ [BRIT **candour**] N-UNCOUNT **Candor** is the quality of speaking honestly and openly about things. ❑ *...a brash, forceful man, noted both for his candor and his quick temper.*

[영국영어 candour] 불가산명사 정직함, 솔직함 ❑ 솔직함과 동시에 급한 성미로 이름난, 거만하고 강압적인 사내

can|dy /kændi/ (candies) N-VAR **Candy** is sweet foods such as chocolate or taffy. [AM; BRIT usually **sweets**] ❑ *...a piece of candy.*

가산명사 또는 불가산명사 사탕 [미국영어; 영국영어 대개 sweets] ❑ 사탕 한 개

cane /keɪn/ (canes) **1** N-VAR **Cane** is used to refer to the long, hollow, hard stems of plants such as bamboo. Strips of cane are often used to make furniture, and some types of cane can be crushed and processed to make sugar. ❑ *...cane furniture.* ❑ *...cane sugar.* **2** N-COUNT A **cane** is a long thin stick with a curved or round top which you can use to support yourself when you are walking, or which in the past was fashionable to carry with you. ❑ *He wore a grey suit and leaned heavily on his cane.*

1 가산명사 또는 불가산명사 (대나무 등의) 줄기 ❑ 등가구 ❑ 사탕수수 설탕 **2** 가산명사 지팡이, 단장 ❑ 그는 회색 정장을 입고 지팡이에 크게 의지하고 있었다.

ca|nine /keɪnaɪn/ (canines) ADJ **Canine** means relating to dogs. [ADJ n] ❑ *...research into canine diseases.*

형용사 개의 ❑ 개의 질병에 대한 연구

can|is|ter /kænɪstər/ (canisters) **1** N-COUNT A **canister** is a strong metal container. It used to hold gases or chemical substances. ❑ *Riot police hurled tear gas canisters and smoke bombs into the crowd.* **2** N-COUNT A **canister** is a metal, plastic, or china container with a lid. It is used for storing food such as sugar and flour. ❑ *...a canister of tea.* **3** N-COUNT A **canister** is a flat round container. It is usually made of metal and is used to store photographic film. ❑ *She bought a travel-bag large enough to contain the film canisters.*

1 가산명사 (가스 등의) 금속 용기 ❑ 전투 경찰이 군중들 속으로 최루탄과 연막탄을 집어 던졌다. **2** 가산명사 (거피 등의) 깡통 ❑ 차 통 **3** 가산명사 필름통 ❑ 그녀는 필름통을 담을 만큼 넉넉하게 큰 여행 가방을 샀다.

can|na|bis /kænəbɪs/ N-UNCOUNT **Cannabis** is the hemp plant when it is used as a drug. ❑ *...cannabis smokers.*

불가산명사 마리화나 ❑ 마리화나 흡연자들

canned /kænd/ ADJ **Canned** music, laughter, or applause on a television or radio program has been recorded beforehand and is added to the program to make it sound as if there is a live audience. [usu ADJ n] ❑ *However, the temptation is always there to add canned laughter in the editing.* →see also **can**

형용사 효과음으로 녹음된 ❑ 하지만 효과음으로 녹음된 웃음소리를 넣고 싶은 유혹이 편집 과정에서는 항상 따른다.

can|ni|bal /kænɪb³l/ (cannibals) N-COUNT **Cannibals** are people who eat the flesh of other human beings. ❑ *...a tropical island inhabited by cannibals.*

가산명사 식인종 ❑ 식인종이 사는 열대의 섬

can|ni|bal|ism /kænɪbəlɪzəm/ N-UNCOUNT If a group of people practice **cannibalism**, they eat the flesh of other people. ❑ *They were forced to practice cannibalism in order to survive.*

불가산명사 식인 풍습 ❑ 그들은 살아남기 위해 사람을 잡아먹어야 했다.

can|non /kænən/ (cannons) **1** N-COUNT A **cannon** is a large gun, usually on wheels, which used to be used in battles. ❑ *The cannons boom, the band plays.* **2** N-COUNT A **cannon** is a heavy automatic gun, especially one that is fired from an aircraft. ❑ *Others carried huge cannons plundered from Russian aircraft.* **3** PHRASE If someone is a **loose cannon**, they do whatever they want and nobody can predict what they are going to do. ❑ *Max is a loose cannon politically.*

1 가산명사 대포 ❑ 대포가 울리고, 밴드가 연주를 한다. **2** 가산명사 기관포 ❑ 다른 사람들은 러시아 비행기에서 훔쳐낸 커다란 기관총을 들고 있었다. **3** 구 통제 불능인 사람, 어디로 튈지 모르는 사람 ❑ 맥스는 정치적으로 통제 불능이다.

can|not /kænɒt, kənɒt/ **Cannot** is the negative form of **can**.

can의 부정형

ca|noe /kənu/ (canoes) N-COUNT A **canoe** is a small, narrow boat that you move through the water using a stick with a wide end called a paddle.

가산명사 카누

can|on /kænən/ (canons) N-COUNT A **canon** is a member of the clergy who is on the staff of a cathedral.

가산명사 대성당 참사회 의원

cano|py /kænəpi/ (canopies) **1** N-COUNT A **canopy** is a decorated cover, often made of cloth, which is placed above something such as a bed or a seat. **2** N-COUNT A **canopy** is a layer of something that spreads out and covers an area, for example the branches and leaves that spread out at the top of trees in a forest. ❑ *The trees formed such a dense canopy that all beneath was a deep carpet of pine-needles.*

1 가산명사 닫집 모양의 차양 **2** 가산명사 넓게 모양의 깃 ❑ 그 나무들은 아주 조밀한 덮개를 이루어서 그 밑에는 온통 융단을 깔아 놓은 것처럼 솔잎이 수북이 쌓여 있었다.

can't /kænt, BRIT kɑːnt/ **Can't** is the usual spoken form of "cannot."

cannot의 단축형

can|teen /kænˈtiːn/ (canteens) **1** N-COUNT A **canteen** is a place in a factory, hospital, or college where meals are served to the people who work or study there. ❑ *Rennie had eaten his tea in the canteen.* ❑ *...a school canteen.* **2** N-COUNT A **canteen** is a small metal or plastic bottle for carrying water and other drinks. Canteens are used by soldiers. ❑ *...a full canteen of water.*

can|ter /kæntər/ (canters, cantering, cantered) V-I When a horse **canters**, it moves at a speed that is slower than a gallop but faster than a trot. ❑ *The competitors cantered into the arena to conclude the closing ceremony.* ● N-COUNT **Canter** is also a noun. ❑ *Carnac set off at a canter.*

can|vas /kænvəs/ (canvases) **1** N-UNCOUNT **Canvas** is a strong, heavy cloth that is used for making things such as tents, sails, and bags. ❑ *...a canvas bag.* **2** N-VAR A **canvas** is a piece of canvas or similar material on which an oil painting can be done. **3** N-COUNT A **canvas** is a painting that has been done on canvas. ❑ *The show includes canvases by masters like Carpaccio, Canaletto, and Guardi.* → see **painting**

can|vass /kænvəs/ (canvasses, canvassing, canvassed) **1** V-I If you **canvass for** a particular person or political party, you go around an area trying to persuade people to vote for that person or party. ❑ *I'm canvassing for the Conservative Party.* **2** V-T If you **canvass** public opinion, you find out how people feel about a particular subject. ❑ *Members of Parliament are spending the weekend canvassing opinion in their constituencies.*

can|yon /kænyən/ (canyons) N-COUNT; N-IN-NAMES A **canyon** is a long, narrow valley with very steep sides. ❑ *...the Grand Canyon.*

cap ♦♢♢ /kæp/ (caps, capping, capped) **1** N-COUNT A **cap** is a soft, flat hat with a curved part at the front which is called a visor. Caps are usually worn by men and boys. ❑ *...a dark blue baseball cap.* **2** N-COUNT A **cap** is a special hat which is worn as part of a uniform. ❑ *...a frontier guard in olive-gray uniform and a cap.* **3** N-COUNT The **cap** of a bottle is its lid. ❑ *She unscrewed the cap of her water bottle and gave him a drink.* **4** N-COUNT If a sports player represents their country in a team game such as soccer, rugby, or cricket, you can say that they have been awarded a **cap**. [BRIT] ❑ *Mark Davis will win his first cap for Wales in Sunday's Test match against Australia.* **5** V-T If someone says that a good or bad event **caps** a series of events, they mean it is the final event in the series, and the other events were also good or bad. [JOURNALISM] ❑ *The unrest capped a weekend of right-wing attacks on foreigners.* → see **clothing**

ca|pa|bil|ity /keɪpəˈbɪlɪti/ (capabilities) **1** N-VAR If you have the **capability** or the **capabilities** to do something, you have the ability or the qualities that are necessary to do it. ❑ *People experience differences in physical and mental capability depending on the time of day.* **2** N-VAR A country's military **capability** is its ability to fight in a war. ❑ *Their military capability has gone down because their air force has proved not to be an effective force.*

Do not confuse **capability** with **ability** and **capacity**. A person's **capability** is the amount of work they can do and how well they can do it. ❑ *...a job that was beyond the capability of one man....the director's ideas of the capability of the actor.* You often use **ability** to say that someone can do something well. ❑ *He had remarkable ability as a musician....the ability to bear hardship.* If someone has a particular **capacity**, a **capacity** for something, or a **capacity** to do something, they have the qualities required to do it. **Capacity** is a more formal word than **ability** .❑ *...their capacity for hard work....his capacity to see the other person's point of view.*

ca|pable ♦♢♢ /keɪpəbəl/ **1** ADJ If a person or thing is **capable of** doing something, they have the ability to do it. [v-link ADJ of -ing/n] ❑ *He appeared hardly capable of conducting a coherent conversation.* ❑ *The kitchen is capable of catering for several hundred people.* **2** ADJ Someone who is **capable** has the skill or qualities necessary to do a particular thing, and can do most things well. ❑ *She's a very capable speaker.* ● **ca|pably** /keɪpəbli/ ADV [ADV with v] ❑ *Happily it was all dealt with very capably by the police and security people.*

Note that **capable** and **able** are both used to say that someone can do something. When you say that someone is **able** to do something, you mean that they can do it either because of their knowledge or skill, or because it is possible. ❑ *He wondered if he would be able to climb over the rail... They were able to use their profits for new investments.* Note that if you use a past tense, you are saying that someone has actually done something. ❑ *We were able to reduce costs.* When you say that someone is **capable** of doing something, you mean either that they have the knowledge and skill to do it, or that they are likely to do it. ❑ *The workers are perfectly capable of running the organization themselves... She was quite capable of falling asleep.* You can say that someone is **capable** of a particular feeling or action. ❑ *He's capable of loyalty... Bowman could not believe him capable of murder.* You can also use "**capable of**" when talking about what something such as a car or machine can do. ❑ *The car was capable of 110 miles per hour.* If you describe someone as **able** or **capable**, you mean that they do things well. ❑ *He's certainly a capable gardener.*

Thesaurus *capable*의 참조어

ADJ. able, competent, skillful, talented; (ant.) incapable, incompetent **2**

1 가산명사 구내식당 ❑ 레니는 구내식당에서 이미 차를 마신 참이었다. ❑ 학교 식당 **2** 가산명사 수통 ❑ 수통 하나 가득 담긴 물

자동사 느린 구보로 나아가다 ❑ 경쟁마들은 폐회식을 마무리 짓기 위해 느린 구보로 경기장 안으로 들어갔다. ● 가산명사 느린 구보 ❑ 카낙은 느린 구보로 출발했다.

1 불가산명사 범포, 캔버스 천 ❑ 캔버스 천으로 만든 가방 **2** 가산명사 또는 불가산명사 캔버스, 화포 **3** 가산명사 유화 ❑ 그 전시회에는 카파초와 카날레토, 과르디 등 거장들의 유화가 포함되어 있다.

1 자동사 선거 운동을 하다 ❑ 나는 보수당 선거 운동을 하고 있다. **2** 타동사 (여론을) 수렴하다 ❑ 하원 의원들은 자신들의 선거구에서 여론을 수렴하며 주말을 보내고 있다.

가산명사; 이름명사 협곡 ❑ 그랜드 캐년

1 가산명사 모자 ❑ 짙은 파란색 야구 모자 **2** 가산명사 제모 ❑ 회녹색 제복을 입고 제모를 쓴 국경 수비 대원 **3** 가산명사 뚜껑 ❑ 그녀는 물병 뚜껑을 돌려서 연 다음 그에게 한 모금 주었다. **4** 가산명사 국가 대표 마크 [영국영어] ❑ 마크 데이비스는 일요일 열리는 호주와의 크리켓 결승전에서 처음으로 웨일스 국가 대표 마크를 달 것이다. **5** 타동사 대미를 장식하다 [언론] ❑ 그 소요 사태가 우파의 외국인 습격으로 벌어졌던 주말의 대미를 이루었다.

1 가산명사 또는 불가산명사 능력, 역량 ❑ 사람들은 하루 중 시간대에 따라 신체적 또는 정신적 능력이 달라짐을 경험한다. **2** 가산명사 또는 불가산명사 (군사) 능력 ❑ 공군이 실전에 동원될 수 없음이 밝혀졌기 때문에 그들의 군사 능력은 저하되었다.

capabilty를 ability나 capacity와 혼동하지 않도록 하라. capability는 어떤 사람이 할 수 있는 일의 양이나 그가 어떤 일을 어느 정도 잘할 수 있는가를 나타낼 때에 쓴다. ❑ ...한 사람의 역량은 넘어서는 일...그 배우의 능력에 대한 감독의 생각. ability는 흔히 누가 무엇을 잘할수 있다고 말할 때 사용한다. ❑ 그는 음악가로서 놀라운 재능을 지니고 있었다....역경을 견디는 능력. 누군가가 특정한 capacity나 무엇에 대한 capacity, 무엇을 할 capacity가 있다고 하면, 그 사람이 그것을 하는 데 필요한 자질을 가지고 있다는 뜻이다. capacity가 ability보다 더 격식적이다. ❑ ...힘든 일을 할 수 있는 그들의 능력....상대방의 관점을 이해할 수 있는 그의 능력

1 형용사 -할 수 있는 ❑ 그는 일관성 있게 대화를 진행해 나갈 능력이 별로 없어 보였다. ❑ 그 주방은 수백 명분의 음식을 제공할 수 있다. **2** 형용사 유능한, 역량 있는 ❑ 그녀는 대단히 유능한 강연자이다. ● 유능하게, 잘 부사 ❑ 다행히 경찰과 보호 요원들이 모든 일을 잘 처리했다.

capable과 able은 둘 다 누가 무엇을 할 수 있다고 말할 때 쓴다. 누가 무엇을 하는 데 able하다는 것은, 그 사람이 지식이나 기술이 있어서 혹은 그 일이 가능한 일이기 때문에 그것을 할 수 있음을 의미한다. ❑ 그는 자기 라인 위로 기어 올라갈 수 있을 것인가를 생각하고 있었다... 그들은 이익금을 새 투자에 이용할 수 있었다. 과거 시제를 쓰면 누가 실제로 무엇을 했다고 말하는 것임을 유의하라. ❑ 우리는 비용을 줄일 수 있었다. 누가 무엇을 하는 데 capable하다는 것은 그가 그것을 할 지식이나 기술이 있다는 뜻이거나, 그가 그것을 할 가능성이 있어 보임을 나타낸다. ❑ 노동자들이 그 조직체를 스스로 충분히 운영할 수 있다... 그녀는 금방이라도 잠이 들어 버릴것 같았다. 누가 특별한 감정을 갖거나 행동을 하는 것이 capable하다고 말할 수도 있다. ❑ 그는 충성을 바칠 역량이 있다... 보우먼은 그가 살인을 저지를 수도 있다고 믿어지지가 않았다. 자동차나 기계 같은 것이 할 수 있는 일에 대해 말할 때에도 capable을 쓸 수가 있다. ❑ 그 차는 시속 110 마일로 달릴 수 있었다. 누가 able 또는 capable 하다고 말하는 것은 그 사람이 일을 잘 한다는 뜻이다. ❑ 그는 확실히 능력이 있는 원예사이다.

ca|pac|ity ♦◇◇ /kəpæsɪti/ (capacities) **1** N-VAR Your **capacity for** something is your ability to do it, or the amount of it that you are able to do. ❑ *Our capacity for giving care, love and attention is limited.* ❑ *Her mental capacity and temperament are as remarkable as his.* **2** N-UNCOUNT The **capacity** of something such as a factory, industry, or region is the quantity of things that it can produce or deliver with the equipment or resources that are available. ❑ *...the amount of spare capacity in the economy.* ❑ *Bread factories are working at full capacity.* **3** N-COUNT The **capacity** of a piece of equipment is its size or power, often measured in particular units. ❑ *...an aircraft with a bomb-carrying capacity of 454 kg.* **4** N-VAR The **capacity** of a container is its volume, or the amount of liquid it can hold, measured in units such as quarts or gallons. ❑ *...containers with a maximum capacity of 200 gallons of water.* **5** N-SING The **capacity** of a building, place, or vehicle is the number of people or things that it can hold. If a place is filled **to capacity**, it is as full as it can possibly be. [also no det, oft to N] ❑ *Each stadium had a seating capacity of about 50,000.* **6** ADJ A **capacity** crowd or audience completely fills a theater, sports stadium, or other place. [ADJ n] ❑ *A capacity crowd of 76,000 people was at Wembley football stadium for the event.* **7** N-COUNT If you do something **in** a particular **capacity**, you do it as part of a particular job or duty, or because you are representing a particular organization or person. [WRITTEN] ❑ *Ms. Halliwell visited the Philippines in her capacity as a Special Representative of Unicef.*

Do not confuse **capacity** with **ability** and **capability**. If someone has a particular **capacity**, a **capacity** for something, or a **capacity** to do something, they have the qualities required to do it. **Capacity** is a more formal word than **ability**. ❑ *...their capacity for hard work....his capacity to see the other person's point of view.* You often use **ability** to say that someone can do something well. ❑ *He had remarkable ability as a musician....the ability to bear hardship.* A person's **capability** is the amount of work they can do and how well they can do it. ❑ *...a job that was beyond the capability of one man....the director's ideas of the capability of the actor.*

cape /keɪp/ (capes) **1** N-COUNT; N-IN-NAMES A **cape** is a large piece of land that sticks out into the sea from the coast. ❑ *In 1978, Naomi James became the first woman to sail solo around the world via Cape Horn.* **2** N-COUNT A **cape** is a short cloak. ❑ *...a woolen cape.*

Word Link	cap ≈ head : capital, capitulate, captain

cap|ital ♦♦♦ /kæpɪtᵊl/ (capitals) **1** N-UNCOUNT **Capital** is a large sum of money which you use to start a business, or which you invest in order to make more money. [BUSINESS] ❑ *Companies are having difficulty in raising capital.* **2** N-UNCOUNT You can use **capital** to refer to buildings or machinery which are necessary to produce goods or to make companies more efficient, but which do not make money directly. [BUSINESS] ❑ *...capital equipment that could have served to increase production.* **3** N-UNCOUNT **Capital** is the part of an amount of money borrowed or invested which does not include interest. [BUSINESS] ❑ *With a conventional repayment mortgage, the repayments consist of both capital and interest.* **4** N-COUNT The **capital** of a country is the city or town where its government or legislature meets. ❑ *...Kathmandu, the capital of Nepal.* **5** N-COUNT If a place is **the capital of** a particular industry or activity, it is the place that is most famous for it, because it happens in that place more than anywhere else. ❑ *Colmar has long been considered the capital of the wine trade.* **6** N-COUNT **Capitals** or **capital letters** are written or printed letters in the form which is used at the beginning of sentences or names. "T," "B," and "F" are capitals. ❑ *The name and address are written in capitals.* **7** ADJ A **capital** offense is one that is so serious that the person who commits it can be punished by death. [ADJ n] ❑ *Espionage is a capital offense in this country.* **8** →see also **working capital**

Note that you must always use a capital letter with days of the week, months of the year, and festivals. ❑ *...on Monday the 13th of January....at Christmas.* Names of seasons, however, usually begin with a small letter. ❑ *...in spring.* Capitals must also be used with the names of countries and other places, as well with the adjectives and nouns derived from them, such as those which refer to their inhabitants or languages. ❑ *...in Portugal....the Swiss police....thousands of Germans... He spoke fluent Arabic.*

9 PHRASE If you say that someone **is making capital out of** a situation, you disapprove of the way they are gaining an advantage for themselves through other people's efforts or bad luck. [FORMAL, DISAPPROVAL] ❑ *He rebuked the President for trying to make political capital out of the hostage situation.* →see **city**, **economics**, **stock market**

cap|ital ac|count (capital accounts) **1** N-COUNT A country's **capital account** is the part of its balance of payments that is concerned with the movement of capital. ❑ *...restrictions that affect the capital account of a country's balance of payments.* **2** N-COUNT A **capital account** is a financial statement showing the capital value of a company on a particular date. [BUSINESS] ❑ *No business can survive without a capital account.*

cap|ital gains N-PLURAL **Capital gains** are the profits that you make when you buy something and then sell it again at a higher price. [BUSINESS] ❑ *He called for the reform of capital gains tax.*

---

1 가산명사 또는 불가산명사 능력, 재능 ❑관심과 애정, 배려를 베풀 수 있는 우리의 능력은 제한되어 있다. ❑그녀의 이지적 능력과 기질은 그 남자만큼이나 놀랍다. **2** 불가산명사 생산 능력 ❑경제상 여유 생산 능력의 양 ❑빵 공장들은 풀가동되고 있다. **3** 가산명사 (장비의) 능력 ❑454킬로그램의 폭탄 수송 능력을 갖춘 비행기 **4** 가산명사 또는 불가산명사 용적, 용량 ❑최대 용량이 물 200갤런인 저장용기들 **5** 단수명사 수용 능력 ❑각 경기장의 관중 수용 능력은 약 5만 명이었다. **6** 형용사 최대한의 ❑웸블리 축구 경기장에 최대 수용 인원인 7만 6천 명의 관중이 그 행사를 위해 운집해 있었다. **7** 가산명사 자격 [문어체] ❑헬리웰 씨는 유니세프 특사 자격으로 필리핀을 방문했다.

capacity와 ability나 capability를 혼동하지 않도록 하라. 누군가가 특정한 capacity나 무엇에 대한 capacity, 무엇을 할 capacity가 있다고 하면, 그 사람이 그것을 하는 데 필요한 자질을 가지고 있다는 뜻이다. capacity가 ability보다 더 격식적이다. ❑...힘든 일을 할 수 있는 그들의 능력....상대방의 관점을 이해할 수 있는 그의 능력. ability는 흔히 누가 무엇을 잘할 수 있다고 말할 때 사용한다. ❑그는 음악가로서 놀라운 재능을 지니고 있었다.... 역경을 견디는 능력. capability는 어떤 사람이 할 수 있는 일의 양이나 그가 어떤 일을 어느 정도 잘 할 수 있는가를 나타낼 때 쓴다. ❑...한 사람의 역량을 넘어서는 일....그 배우의 능력에 대한 감독의 생각.

1 가산명사; 이름명사 곶, 갑 ❑1978년, 나오미 제임스는 케이프혼을 거쳐 단독 세계 일주 항해를 한 최초의 여성이 되었다. **2** 가산명사 케이프, 어깨 망토 ❑모직 케이프

1 불가산명사 자본금, 밑천 [경제] ❑기업체들은 자본금을 조달하는 데 어려움을 겪고 있다. **2** 불가산명사 자본 [경제] ❑생산량 증대에 도움이 되었을 수도 있는 자본 설비 **3** 불가산명사 원금 [경제] ❑통상적인 상환 융자의 경우, 상환은 원금과 이자 모두로 이루어진다. **4** 가산명사 수도 ❑네팔의 수도인 카트만두 **5** 가산명사 중심지 ❑콜마르는 오랫동안 와인 판매의 중심지로 여겨져 왔다. **6** 가산명사 대문자 ❑이름과 주소는 대문자로 쓴다. **7** 형용사 사형에 처할 만한 ❑간첩 행위는 이 나라에서는 사형에 해당하는 중범죄이다.

요일, 월, 축일에는 항상 대문자를 써야 함을 유의하라. ❑...1월 13일, 월요일에...성탄절에. 그러나 계절명은 대개 소문자로 시작한다. ❑...봄에. 대문자는 국가명, 지명, 또한 거기서 파생되어 거주하나 언어를 가리키는 형용사와 명사에도 쓰인다. ❑...포르투갈에....스위스 경찰...수천 명의 독일인... 그는 아랍어가 유창했다.

9 구 -을 이용하다 [격식체, 탐탁잖음] ❑그는 대통령이 인질 사태를 정치적으로 이용하려 한다고 비난했다.

1 가산명사 자본 수지 ❑한 국가의 국제 수지 중 자본 수지에 영향을 미치는 규제 **2** 가산명사 자본 계정 [경제] ❑어떤 사업도 자본 계정 없이는 살아남을 수 없다.

복수명사 자본 이득; 양도 소득 [경제] ❑그는 양도 소득세의 개정을 요구했다.

capi|tal goods N-PLURAL **Capital goods** are used to make other products. Compare **consumer goods**. [BUSINESS] ❑ *Most imports into Korea are raw materials and capital goods.*

복수명사 자본재 [경제] ❑ 한국으로 들어오는 수입품은 대부분 원자재와 자본재이다.

capital-intensive ADJ **Capital-intensive** industries and businesses need the investment of large sums of money. Compare **labor-intensive**. [BUSINESS] ❑ *...highly capital-intensive industries like auto manufacturing or petrochemicals.*

형용사 자본 집약적 [경제] ❑ 자동차 제조 공업이나 석유 화학 산업 같은 고도의 자본 집약적 산업

capi|tal|ise /kǽpɪtªlaɪz/, →see **capitalize**

capi|tal|ism /kǽpɪtªlɪzəm/ N-UNCOUNT **Capitalism** is an economic and political system in which property, business, and industry are owned by private individuals and not by the state. ❑ *...the two fundamentally opposed social systems, capitalism and socialism.*

불가산명사 자본주의 ❑ 본질적으로 대립하는 두 가지 사회 체제인 자본주의와 사회주의

capi|tal|ist /kǽpɪtªlɪst/ (**capitalists**) ■ ADJ A **capitalist** country or system supports or is based on the principles of capitalism. ❑ *China has pledged to retain Hong Kong's capitalist system for 50 years.* ☑ N-COUNT A **capitalist** is someone who believes in and supports the principles of capitalism. ❑ *Lenin had hoped to even have a working relationship with the capitalists.* ☒ N-COUNT A **capitalist** is someone who owns a business which they run in order to make a profit for themselves. ❑ *They argue that only private capitalists can remake Poland's economy.*

■ 형용사 자본주의의 ❑ 중국은 홍콩의 자본주의 체제를 50년 동안 유지하겠다고 서약했다. ☑ 가산명사 자본주의자 ❑ 레닌은 심지어 자본주의자들과 업무적인 관계를 맺기까지도 희망했다. ☒ 가산명사 자본가 ❑ 그들은 민간 자본가들만이 폴란드 경제를 개조할 수 있다고 주장한다.

capi|tal|ize /kǽpɪtªlaɪz/ (**capitalizes, capitalizing, capitalized**) [BRIT also **capitalise**] ■ V-I If you **capitalize on** a situation, you use it to gain some advantage for yourself. ❑ *The rebels seem to be trying to capitalize on the public's discontent with the government.* ☑ V-T In business, if you **capitalize** something that belongs to you, you sell it in order to make money. [BUSINESS] ❑ *Our intention is to capitalize the company by any means we can.*

[영국영어 capitalise] ■ 자동사 이용하다 ❑ 반란 세력은 정부에 대한 대중의 불만을 이용하려고 하고 있는 것 같다. ☑ 타동사 자본화하다 [경제] ❑ 우리의 의도는 무슨 수단을 써서라도 회사를 매각하는 것이다.

capi|tal pun|ish|ment N-UNCOUNT **Capital punishment** is punishment which involves the legal killing of a person who has committed a serious crime such as murder. ❑ *Most democracies have abolished capital punishment.*

불가산명사 사형, 극형 ❑ 대부분의 민주주의 국가는 사형을 폐지했다.

Word Link　　*cap ≈ head : capital, capitulate, captain*

---

ca|pitu|late /kəpɪ́tʃəleɪt/ (**capitulates, capitulating, capitulated**) V-I If you **capitulate**, you stop resisting and do what someone else wants you to do. ❑ *The club eventually capitulated and now grants equal rights to women.*

자동사 항복하다 ❑ 그 클럽은 결국 항복했고 이제는 여성에게 동등한 권리를 부여한다.

cap|size /kǽpsaɪz, BRIT kæpsáɪz/ (**capsizes, capsizing, capsized**) V-T/V-I If you **capsize** a boat or if it **capsizes**, it turns upside down in the water. ❑ *The sea got very rough and the boat capsized.*

타동사/자동사 전복시키다; 전복하다 ❑ 바다가 몹시 거칠어져 배가 전복했다.

cap|sule /kǽpsªl, BRIT kǽpsjuːl/ (**capsules**) ■ N-COUNT A **capsule** is a very small tube containing powdered or liquid medicine, which you swallow. ❑ *...cod liver oil capsules.* ☑ N-COUNT A **capsule** is a small container with a drug or other substance inside it, which is used for medical or scientific purposes. ❑ *They first implanted capsules into the animals' brains.* ☒ N-COUNT A space **capsule** is the part of a spacecraft in which people travel, and which often separates from the main rocket. ❑ *A Russian space capsule is currently orbiting the Earth.*

■ 가산명사 캡슐 ❑ 대구 간유 캡슐 ☑ 가산명사 캡슐 ❑ 그들은 먼저 동물들의 뇌에 캡슐을 심어 넣었다. ☒ 가산명사 (우주) 캡슐 ❑ 러시아의 우주 캡슐이 현재 지구 궤도를 돌고 있다.

cap|tain ♦♦◇ /kǽptɪn/ (**captains, captaining, captained**) ■ N-TITLE; N-COUNT; N-VOC In the army, navy, and some other armed forces, a **captain** is an officer of middle rank. ❑ *...Captain Mark Phillips.* ❑ *...a captain in the British army.* ☑ N-COUNT The **captain of** a sports team is the player in charge of it. ❑ *...Mickey Thomas, the captain of the tennis team.* ☒ N-COUNT The **captain** of a ship is the sailor in charge of it. ❑ *...the captain of an excursion boat.* ◢ N-COUNT; N-TITLE The **captain** of an airplane is the pilot in charge of it. ◤ N-COUNT; N-TITLE In the United States and some other countries, a **captain** is a police officer or firefighter of fairly senior rank. ❑ *...a former Honolulu police captain.* ◥ V-T If you **captain** a team or a ship, you are the captain of it. ❑ *...Murdo McLeod, who captained Hibernian's League-Cup-winning team in 1991.* →see **ship**

■ 경칭명사; 가산명사; 호격명사 (중간급) 장교, 대령, 대위 ❑ 마크 필립스 대령 ❑ 영국 육군 대위 ☑ 가산명사 주장 ❑ 그 테니스팀 주장 미키 토머스 ☒ 가산명사 선장 ❑ 유람선 선장 ◢ 가산명사; 경칭명사 기장 ◤ 가산명사; 경칭명사 경감, 소방대장 ❑ 전 호놀룰루 경찰 경감 ◥ 타동사 이끌다; 주장이 되다; 선장이 되다 ❑ 1991년 하이버니언 리그 우승 팀의 주장이었던 머도 맥리오드

cap|tain|cy /kǽptɪnsi/ N-UNCOUNT The **captaincy** of a team is the position of being captain. ❑ *His captaincy of the team was ended by mild eye trouble.*

불가산명사 주장 지위, 주장 임기 ❑ 그는 가벼운 안과 질환으로 팀의 주장을 그만두었다.

cap|tion ♦♦◇ /kǽpʃªn/ (**captions**) N-COUNT A **caption** is the words printed underneath a picture or cartoon which explain what it is about. ❑ *The local paper featured me standing on a stepladder with a caption, "Wendy climbs the ladder to success."*

가산명사 사진 설명, 캡션 ❑ 지역 신문에 '웬디, 성공의 사다리를 오르다'라는 설명과 함께 집사다리에 올라가 있는 내 사진이 실렸다.

cap|ti|vate /kǽptɪveɪt/ (**captivates, captivating, captivated**) V-T If you **are captivated** by someone or something, you find them fascinating and attractive. ❑ *I was captivated by her brilliant mind.*

타동사 사로잡히다 ❑ 나는 그녀의 총명함에 사로잡혔다.

cap|tive /kǽptɪv/ (**captives**) ■ ADJ A **captive** person or animal is being kept imprisoned or enclosed. [LITERARY] ❑ *Her heart had begun to pound inside her chest like a captive animal.* ● N-COUNT A **captive** is someone who is captive. ❑ *He described the difficulties of surviving for four months as a captive.* ☑ ADJ A **captive** audience is a group of people who are not free to leave a certain place and so have to watch or listen. A **captive** market is a group of people who cannot choose whether or where to buy things. [ADJ n] ❑ *We all performed action songs, sketches and dances before a captive audience of parents and patrons.* ☒ PHRASE If you **take** someone **captive** or **hold** someone **captive**, you take or keep them as a prisoner. ❑ *Richard was finally released on February 4, one year and six weeks after he'd been taken captive.*

■ 형용사 사로잡힌, 갇혀 있는 [문예체] ❑ 그녀의 심장이 갇혀 있는 짐승처럼 가슴 속에서 쿵쾅대기 시작했다. ● 가산명사 포로 ❑ 그는 넉 달간의 포로 생활에서 살아남기 위해 겪었던 고충을 자세히 설명했다. ☑ 형용사 선택의 여지가 없는, 싫어도 –한 수밖에 없는 ❑ 싫어도 공연을 볼 수밖에 없는 부모님들과 후원자들 앞에서 안무를 곁들인 노래와 촌극, 춤을 선보였다. ☒ 구 가두다, 포로로 잡다; 가두어 놓다, 포로로 잡아 두다 ❑ 리처드는 포로로 잡힌 지 1년 6주 만인 2월 4일에 마침내 풀려났다.

cap|tiv|ity /kæptɪ́vɪti/ N-UNCOUNT **Captivity** is the state of being kept imprisoned or enclosed. ❑ *The great majority of barn owls are reared in captivity.*

불가산명사 갇힌 상태 ❑ 원숭이 올빼미의 대다수가 갇힌 상태에서 사육된다.

cap|ture ♦◇◇ /kǽptʃər/ (**captures, capturing, captured**) ■ V-T If you **capture** someone or something, you catch them, especially in a war. ❑ *The guerrillas shot down one aeroplane and captured the pilot.* ❑ *The Russians now appear ready to capture more territory from the Chechens.* ● N-UNCOUNT **Capture** is also a noun. ❑ *...the final battles which led to the army's capture of the town.* ☑ V-T If something or someone **captures** a particular quality, feeling, or atmosphere, they represent or express it successfully. [no cont] ❑ *Chef Idris Caldora offers an inspired menu that*

■ 타동사 생포하다; 점령하다 ❑ 게릴라들이 비행기 한 대를 추격해서 기장을 생포했다. ❑ 러시아는 현재 체첸의 영토를 더 빼앗을 준비가 되어 있는 것처럼 보인다. ● 불가산명사 생포; 점령 ❑ 부대가 마을을 점령한 계기가 된 최종 전투 ☑ 타동사 잘 살리다, 보여주다 ❑ 이드리스 칼도라 주방장은 지중해의 정취를 가득 담은 요리를 선보인다. ☒ 타동사

a b c d e f g h i j k l m n o p q r s t u v w x y z

A

captures the spirit of the Mediterranean. **3** V-T If something **captures** your attention or imagination, you begin to be interested or excited by it. If someone or something **captures** your heart, you begin to love them or like them very much. ❑ *...the great names of the Tory party who usually capture the historian's attention.* **4** V-T If an event **is captured** in a photograph or on film, it is photographed or filmed. ❑ *The incident was captured on videotape.* ❑ *The images were captured by TV crews filming outside the base.*

사로잡다 ❑ 늘 역사가들의 관심의 대상이었던 토리당의 유명 인사들 **4** 타동사 찍히다 ❑ 그 사건은 비디오로 찍혔다. ❑ 이 영상은 기지 밖에서 촬영 중이던 텔레비전 제작진들이 포착한 것이다.

B

C

Word Partnership   *capture*의 연어

V.	**avoid** capture, **escape** capture, **fail to** capture **1**
N.	capture **territory 1**
	capture **your** *attention*, capture *your* imagination **3**

D

car ◆◆◆ /kɑr/ (**cars**) **1** N-COUNT A **car** is a motor vehicle with room for a small number of passengers. [also by N] ❑ *He had left his tickets in his car.* **2** N-COUNT A **car** is one of the separate, long sections of a train that carries passengers. [mainly AM; BRIT usually **carriage**] ❑ *The company manufactured elegant railroad sleeper cars.* **3** N-COUNT The separate sections of a train are called **cars** when they are used for a particular purpose. ❑ *He made his way into the dining car for breakfast.*
→see Word Web: car

1 가산명사 차, 자동차 ❑ 그는 티켓을 자기 차에 놓고 내렸다. **2** 가산명사 차, 차량 [주로 미국영어; 영국영어 대개 carriage] ❑ 그 회사는 격조 높은 침대 열차를 제조했다. **3** 가산명사 (기차의) -차 ❑ 그는 아침 식사를 하기 위해 식당차로 갔다.

E

F

G

car alarm (**car alarms**) N-COUNT A **car alarm** is a device in a car which makes a loud noise if anyone tries to break into the vehicle. ❑ *He returned to the airport to find his car alarm going off.*

가산명사 차량 경보기 ❑ 그가 공항으로 돌아오니 그의 차의 경보기가 울리고 있었다.

H

car|a|mel /kærəmɛl, -məl, kɑrməl/ (**caramels**) **1** N-VAR A **caramel** is a chewy sweet food made from sugar, butter, and milk. **2** N-UNCOUNT **Caramel** is burnt sugar used for coloring and flavoring food.

1 가산명사 또는 불가산명사 캐러멜 **2** 불가산명사 캐러멜, 설탕엿

I

car|at /kærət/ (**carats**) **1** N-COUNT A **carat** is a unit for measuring the weight of diamonds and other precious stones. It is equal to 0.2 grams. ❑ *The gemstone is 28.6 millimeters high and weighs 139.43 carats.* **2** COMB IN ADJ **Carat** is used after a number to indicate how pure gold is. The purest gold is 24-carat gold. ❑ *...a 14-carat gold fountain pen.* →see **diamond**

1 가산명사 캐럿 ❑ 원석의 높이는 28.6밀리미터, 무게는 139.43캐럿이다. **2** 복합형-형용사 캐럿, 케이 ❑ 14케이 금으로 된 만년필

J

K

car|a|van /kærəvæn/ (**caravans**) **1** N-COUNT A **caravan** is a group of people and animals or vehicles who travel together. ❑ *...the old caravan routes from Central Asia to China.* **2** N-COUNT A **caravan** is a vehicle without an engine that can be pulled by a car or van. It contains beds and cooking equipment so that people can live or spend their vacations in it. [BRIT; AM **trailer**]

1 가산명사 대상(隊商) ❑ 중앙아시아에서 중국에 이르는 옛날 대상 이동로 **2** 가산명사 이동 주택, 트레일러 [영국영어; 미국영어 trailer]

L

car|a|van site (**caravan sites**) N-COUNT A **caravan site** is an area of land where people can stay in a trailer on vacation, or where people live in trailers. [BRIT; AM **trailer park**]

가산명사 이동 주택 주차장 [영국영어; 미국영어 trailer park]

M

car|bo|hy|drate /kɑrbouhaɪdreɪt/ (**carbohydrates**) N-VAR **Carbohydrates** are substances, found in certain kinds of food, that provide you with energy. Foods such as sugar and bread that contain these substances can also be referred to as **carbohydrates**. ❑ *...carbohydrates such as bread, pasta or chips.* →see **calories, diet**

가산명사 또는 불가산명사 탄수화물, 탄수화물 식품 ❑ 빵, 파스타, 포테이토칩 같은 탄수화물 식품

N

car|bon ◆◇◇ /kɑrbən/ N-UNCOUNT **Carbon** is a chemical element that diamonds and coal are made up of. →see **diamond**

불가산명사 탄소

O

car|bon|at|ed /kɑrbəneɪtɪd/ ADJ **Carbonated** drinks are drinks that contain small bubbles of carbon dioxide. [usu ADJ n] ❑ *...colas and other carbonated soft drinks.*

형용사 탄산의 ❑ 콜라와 다른 탄산음료들

P

car|bon di|ox|ide /kɑrbən daɪɒksaɪd/ N-UNCOUNT **Carbon dioxide** is a gas. It is produced by animals and people breathing out, and by chemical reactions. →see **dry cleaning, greenhouse effect, respiratory**

불가산명사 이산화탄소

Q

car|bon mon|ox|ide /kɑrbən mənɒksaɪd/ N-UNCOUNT **Carbon monoxide** is a poisonous gas that is produced especially by the engines of vehicles. ❑ *The limit for carbon monoxide is 4.5 per cent of the exhaust gas.*

불가산명사 일산화탄소 ❑ 일산화탄소 배출량은 총 배출 가스의 4.5퍼센트로 제한되어 있다.

R

car|cass /kɑrkəs/ (**carcasses**) [BRIT also **carcase**] N-COUNT A **carcass** is the body of a dead animal. ❑ *A cluster of vultures crouched on the carcass of a dead buffalo.*

[영국영어 carcase] 가산명사 시체 ❑ 한 떼의 독수리가 버팔로 시체 위에 웅크리고 앉아 있었다.

S

card ◆◆◇ /kɑrd/ (**cards**) **1** N-COUNT A **card** is a piece of stiff paper or thin cardboard on which something is written or printed. ❑ *Check the numbers below against the numbers on your card.* **2** N-COUNT A **card** is a piece of cardboard or plastic, or a small document, which shows information about you and which

1 가산명사 카드 ❑ 당신의 카드 번호와 아래에 있는 번호를 대조해 보시오. **2** 가산명사 카드, -증 ❑ 그들은 내 가방과 기자증을 확인한다. ❑ 그녀의 회원 카드 **3** 가산명사 카드 ❑ 그는 모든 대금을 아메리칸

T

U

Word Web   car

The first mass-produced **automobile** in the U.S. was the Model T. In 1909, Ford sold over 10,000 of these **vehicles**. They all had the same basic **engine** and **chassis**. For years the only color choice was black. Three different bodies were available—roadster, **sedan**, and coupe. Today manufacturers offer many more options. These include **convertibles, sports cars, station wagons, vans,** pickups, and **SUVs**. Laws now require devices such as **seat belts** and **airbags** to make **driving** safer. Some car makers now offer **hybrid** vehicles. They combine an electrical engine with an internal combustion **engine** to improve **fuel** economy.

V

W

X

Y

Z

a
b
c
d
e
f
g
h
i
j
k
l
m
n
o
p
q
r
s
t
u
v
w
x
y
z

you carry with you, for example to prove your identity. ❑ ...they check my bag and press card. ❑ ...her membership card. ❸ N-COUNT A **card** is a rectangular piece of plastic, issued by a bank, company, or store, which you can use to buy things or obtain money. ❑ He paid the whole bill with an American Express card. ❹ N-COUNT A **card** is a folded piece of stiff paper with a picture and sometimes a message printed on it, which you send to someone on a special occasion. ❑ She sends me a card on my birthday. ❺ N-COUNT A **card** is the same as a **postcard**. ❑ Send your details on a card to the following address. ❻ N-COUNT A **card** is a piece of thin cardboard carried by someone such as a businessperson in order to give to other people. A card shows the name, address, telephone number, and other details of the person who carries it. [BUSINESS] ❑ Here's my card. You may need me. ❼ N-COUNT **Cards** are thin pieces of cardboard with numbers or pictures printed on them which are used to play various games. ❑ ...a pack of cards. ❽ N-UNCOUNT If you are playing **cards**, you are playing a game using cards. ❑ They enjoy themselves drinking wine, smoking and playing cards. ❾ N-UNCOUNT **Card** is strong, stiff paper or thin cardboard. ❑ She put the pieces of card in her pocket. ❿ →see also **bank card, business card, calling card, cash card, credit card, gold card, identity card, playing card, smart card, wild card** ⓫ PHRASE If you say that something is **in the cards** in American English, or **on the cards** in British English, you mean that it is very likely to happen. ❑ Last summer she began telling friends that a New Year marriage was in the cards.

card|board /kɑrdbɔrd/ N-UNCOUNT **Cardboard** is thick, stiff paper that is used, for example, to make boxes and models. ❑ ...a cardboard box.

car|di|ac /kɑrdiæk/ ADJ **Cardiac** means relating to the heart. [MEDICAL] [ADJ n] ❑ The king was suffering from cardiac weakness. →see **muscle**

car|di|gan /kɑrdɪgən/ (**cardigans**) N-COUNT A **cardigan** is a knitted woolen sweater that you can fasten at the front with buttons or a zipper.

car|di|nal /kɑrd°n°l/ (**cardinals**) ❶ N-COUNT; N-TITLE A **cardinal** is a high-ranking priest in the Catholic church. ❑ In 1448, Nicholas was appointed a cardinal. ❷ ADJ A **cardinal** rule or quality is the one that is considered to be the most important. [FORMAL] [ADJ n] ❑ As a salesman, your cardinal rule is to do everything you can to satisfy a customer.

card in|dex (**card indexes**) N-COUNT A **card index** is a number of cards with information written on them which are arranged in a particular order, usually alphabetical, so that you can find the information you want easily. ❑ Then he turned to the card index and tore out the entry for Matthew Holmwood.

care ♦♦♦ /keər/ (**cares, caring, cared**) ❶ V-T/V-I If you **care about** something, you feel that it is important and are concerned about it. [no cont] ❑ ...a company that cares about the environment. ❑ ...young men who did not care whether they lived or died. ❷ V-I If you **care for** someone, you feel a lot of affection for them. [APPROVAL] [no cont] ❑ He wanted me to know that he still cared for me. ● **car|ing** N-UNCOUNT ❑ ...the "feminine" traits of caring and compassion. ❸ V-T/V-I If you **care for** someone or something, you look after them and keep them in a good state or condition. ❑ They hired a nurse to care for her. ❑ ...these distinctive cars, lovingly cared for by private owners. ● N-UNCOUNT **Care** is also a noun. ❑ Most of the staff specialise in the care of children. ❑ ...sensitive teeth which need special care. ❹ N-UNCOUNT Children who are **in care** are looked after by the state because their parents are dead or unable to look after them properly. [BRIT] ❑ ...a home for children in care. ❺ V-T/V-I You can ask someone if they would **care for** something or if they would **care to** do something as a polite way of asking if they would like to have or do something. [POLITENESS] [no cont] ❑ Would you care for some orange juice? ❻ N-UNCOUNT If you do something **with care**, you give careful attention to it because you do not want to make any mistakes or cause any damage. ❑ Condoms are an effective method of birth control if used with care. ❼ N-COUNT Your **cares** are your worries, anxieties, or fears. ❑ Lean back in a hot bath and forget all the cares of the day. ❽ →see also **caring, day care, intensive care** ❾ PHRASE You can use **for all I care** to emphasize that it does not matter at all to you what someone does. [EMPHASIS] ❑ You can go right now for all I care. ❿ PHRASE If you say that you **couldn't care less about** someone or something, you are emphasizing that you are not interested in them or worried about them. In American English, you can also say that you **could care less**, with the same meaning. [EMPHASIS] ❑ I couldn't care less about the bloody woman. ⓫ PHRASE If someone sends you a letter or package **care of** a particular person or place, they send it to that person or place, and it is then passed on to you. In American English, you can also say **in care of**. ❑ Please write to me care of the publishers. ⓬ PHRASE If you **take care of** someone or something, you look after them and prevent them from being harmed or damaged. ❑ There was no one else to take care of their children. ⓭ PHRASE If you **take care to** do something, you make sure that you do it. ❑ Foley followed Albert through the gate, taking care to close the latch. ⓮ PHRASE To **take care of** a problem, task, or situation means to deal with it. ❑ They leave it to the system to try and take care of the problem. ⓯ PHRASE You can say "**Who cares?**" to emphasize that something does not matter to you at all. [EMPHASIS] ❑ "But we might ruin the stove." — "Who cares?"

Word Partnership	care의 연어
ADJ.	**good** care, **loving** care ❸
V.	**provide** care, **receive** care ❸

ca|reer ♦♦◇ /kərɪər/ (**careers, careering, careered**) ❶ N-COUNT A **career** is the job or profession that someone does for a long period of their life. ❑ She is now concentrating on a career as a fashion designer. ❑ ...a career in journalism. ❷ N-COUNT Your **career** is the part of your life that you spend working. ❑ During his career, he wrote more than fifty plays. ❸ ADJ **Career** advice or guidance in American English, or **careers** advice or guidance in British English, consists of

익스프레스 카드로 지불했다. ❹ 가산명사 카드 ❑ 그녀는 나에게 생일 카드를 보낸다. ❺ 가산명사 엽서 ❑ 엽서에 당신의 세부 정보를 적어서 다음 주소로 보내세요. ❻ 가산명사 명함 [경제] ❑ 제 명함입니다. 제가 필요하실지도 모르잖아요. ❼ 가산명사 게임카드 ❑ 카드 한 벌 ❽ 불가산명사 카드놀이 ❑ 그들은 와인을 마시고, 담배도 피우고, 카드놀이도 하면서 즐거운 시간을 보낸다. ❾ 불가산명사 판지 ❑ 그녀는 판지 조각을 주머니에 넣었다. ❿ 구 →참고 가능성이 크다 ⓫ 지난여름에 그녀는 연초에 결혼할 가능성이 크다고 친구들에게 말하고 다니기 시작했다.

불가산명사 판지, 마분지 ❑ 마분지 상자

형용사 심장의 [의학] ❑ 왕은 심장이 약해서 고생하고 있었다.

가산명사 카디건

❶ 가산명사; 경칭명사 추기경 ❑ 1448년에 니콜라스는 추기경으로 임명됐다. ❷ 형용사 가장 중요한 [격식체] ❑ 판매 사원으로서 당신이 가장 중요하게 지켜야 할 것은 고객 만족을 위해 할 수 있는 것은 모두 하는 것이다.

가산명사 카드식 색인 ❑ 그리곤 그가 카드 색인을 보더니 매튜 홈우드의 참가증을 찢어 주었다.

❶ 타동사/자동사 관심을 갖다, 중요하게 여기다 ❑ 환경을 생각하는 기업 ❑ 자신이 살든 죽든 상관하지 않던 젊은이들 ❷ 자동사 좋아하다 [마음에 들다] ❑ 그는, 자기가 나를 여전히 좋아한다는 사실을 내가 알아주길 바랐다. ● 관심, 사랑 불가산명사 관심과 동정심이라는 여성적 자질 ❸ 타동사/자동사 돌보다; 관리하다 ❑ 그들은 그녀를 돌볼 간호사를 고용했다. ❑ 주인들이 애지중지 관리한 특별한 이 차들 ● 불가산명사 돌봄, 관리 ❑ 직원 대부분이 육아를 전문으로 하고 있다. ❑ 특별한 관리가 필요한 민감한 치아 ❹ 불가산명사 국가의 보호를 받고 있는 [영국영어] 국가의 보호 대상인 아이들을 위한 집 ❺ 타동사/자동사 -을 갖고 싶다; -을 하고 싶다 [공손체] ❑ 오렌지 주스 좀 드실래요? ❻ 불가산명사 신경 써서, 조심하여 ❑ 콘돔은 조심해서 사용하면 피임에 효과적인 방법이다. ❼ 가산명사 걱정, 근심 ❑ 따뜻한 물이 담긴 욕조에서 몸을 뒤로 기대고 그날의 걱정은 모두 잊으세요. ❾ 구 상관할 바 아니다 [강조] ❑ 네가 당장 가든 말든 내가 상관할 바 아니다. ❿ 구 전혀 관심 없다 [강조] ❑ 그 빌어먹을 여자 따윈 전혀 관심 없어. ⓫ 구 -을 통해서, -로 ❑ 저에게 편지를 주실 땐 출판사로 보내 주세요. ⓬ 구 보살피다 ❑ 그들의 아이를 돌볼 만한 다른 사람이 없었다. ⓭ 구 -하도록 각별히 신경 쓰다 ❑ 폴리가 앨버트를 따라 문을 나오면서 잊지 않고 빗장을 채웠다. ⓮ 구 처리하다, 다루다 ❑ 그들은 문제의 처리를 시스템에 맡겨두고 있다. ⓯ 구 알게 뭐야 [강조] ❑ "하지만 우리가 스토브를 망가뜨릴지도 몰라." "알게 뭐야?"

❶ 가산명사 직업, 일, 경력 ❑ 그녀는 현재 패션 디자이너로 집중하고 있다. ❷ 가산명사 활동 기간 ❑ 그는 활동 기간 동안 50편이 넘는 희곡을 썼다. ❸ 형용사 진로의, 직업의 ❑ 그녀는 어릴 적에 진로 지도를 거의 받지 못했다. ❹ 자동사 질주하다 ❑ 그의 차가 강 속으로 질주한다.

A

information about different jobs and help with deciding what kind of job you want to do. [ADJ n] ❑ *She received very little career guidance when young.* ◪ V-I If a person or vehicle **careers** somewhere, they move fast and in an uncontrolled way. [oft cont] ❑ *His car careered into a river.*

B

Thesaurus   career의 참조어

N.   field, job, profession, specialty, vocation, work ◫

C

Word Partnership   career의 연어

N.   career **advancement**, career **goals**, career **opportunities**,
       career **path** ◫ ◪
ADJ.   **political** career, **professional** career ◫ ◪
V.   **pursue** a career ◫ ◪

D

E

F

ca|reer wom|an (career women) N-COUNT A **career woman** is a woman with a career who is interested in working and progressing in her job, rather than staying at home taking care of the house and children.

가산명사 직장 여성

G

Word Link   free ≈ without : care*free*, duty-*free*, tax-*free*

care|free /kɛərfri/ ADJ A **carefree** person or period of time doesn't have or involve any problems, worries, or responsibilities. ❑ *Chantal remembered carefree past summers at the beach.*

형용사 걱정 없는, 태평스러운 ❑ 샨탈은 해변에서 걱정 없이 보낸 예전의 여름들을 떠올렸다.

H

I

Word Link   ful ≈ filled with : beauti*ful*, care*ful*, dread*ful*

care|ful ♦♦◇ /kɛərfəl/ ◫ ADJ If you are **careful**, you give serious attention to what you are doing, in order to avoid harm, damage, or mistakes. If you are **careful to** do something, you make sure that you do it. ❑ *Be very careful with this stuff, it can be dangerous if it isn't handled properly.* ❑ *Careful on those stairs!* ● **care|ful|ly** ADV [ADV with v] ❑ *Have a nice time, dear, and drive carefully.* ◪ ADJ **Careful** work, thought, or examination is thorough and shows a concern for details. ❑ *He has decided to prosecute her after careful consideration of all the relevant facts.* ● **care|ful|ly** ADV [ADV with v] ❑ *...a vast series of deliberate and carefully planned thefts.* ◫ ADJ If you tell someone to be **careful about** doing something, you think that what they intend to do is probably wrong, and that they should think seriously before they do it. [v-link ADJ about/of -ing] ❑ *I think you should be careful about talking of the rebels as heroes.* ● **care|ful|ly** ADV [ADV after v] ❑ *He should think carefully about actions like this which play into the hands of his opponents.* ◪ ADJ If you are **careful with** something such as money or resources, you use or spend only what is necessary. ❑ *It would force industries to be more careful with natural resources.*

❶ 형용사 조심스러운 ❑ 이 물질은 제대로 사용하지 않으면 위험할 수도 있으므로 아주 조심해서 다루어야 한다. ❑ 그 계단에서는 조심해야 해! ● 조심스럽게 부사 ❑ 좋은 시간 되고 운전 조심해서 해. ❷ 형용사 철저한, 꼼꼼한 ❑ 그는 관련된 모든 사실을 철저하게 고려한 후에 그녀를 기소하기로 결정했다. ● 철저하게, 꼼꼼하게 부사 ❑ 치밀하고 철저하게 계획된 대규모 연쇄 절도 사건 ❸ 형용사 신중한 ❑ 나는 반군을 영웅시하는 발언은 신중하게 해야 한다고 생각한다. ● 신중하게 부사 ❑ 그는 반대 세력의 계략에 걸려드는 이 같은 행동에 대해 신중하게 생각해야 한다. ❹ 형용사 아끼는 ❑ 이렇게 되면 산업 전반에서 천연 자원을 더욱 아껴서 사용할 수밖에 없을 것이다.

J

K

L

M

N

Word Partnership   careful의 연어

N.   careful **attention**, careful **consideration**, careful **observation**,
       careful **planning** ◪
ADV.   **very** careful, **extremely** careful ◫ ◫ ◪

O

P

care|giv|er /kɛərgɪvər/ (caregivers) also care giver N-COUNT A **caregiver** is someone who is responsible for taking care of another person, for example, a person who is disabled, ill, or very young. [mainly AM] ❑ *It is nearly always women who are the primary care givers.*

가산명사 간병인, 돌보는 사람 [주로 미국영어] ❑ 다른 사람을 주로 돌보는 사람은 거의 항상 여자들이다.

Q

care|less /kɛərlɪs/ ◫ ADJ If you are **careless**, you do not pay enough attention to what you are doing, and so you make mistakes, or cause harm or damage. ❑ *I'm sorry. How careless of me.* ❑ *Some parents are accused of being careless with their children's health.* ● **care|less|ly** ADV [ADV with v] ❑ *She was fined £100 for driving carelessly.* ● **care|less|ness** N-UNCOUNT ❑ *The defense conceded stupid goals through sheer carelessness.* ◪ ADJ If you say that someone is **careless of** something such as their health or appearance, you mean that they do not seem to be concerned about it, or do nothing to keep it in a good condition. ❑ *He had shown himself careless of personal safety where the life of his colleagues might be at risk.*

❶ 형용사 부주의한, 경솔한 ❑ 죄송해요. 제가 너무 경솔했어요. ❑ 어떤 부모들은 아이들의 건강에 신경을 쓰지 않아 비난을 받는다. ● 부주의하게, 경솔하게 부사 ❑ 그녀는 운전 부주의로 100파운드의 벌금형을 받았다. ● 부주의, 경솔함 불가산명사 ❑ 수비측이 완전한 부주의로 터무니없는 골을 허용하고 말았다. ❷ 형용사 소홀한, 무관심한 ❑ 그는 동료들의 목숨이 걸려 있는 개인 안전 문제에 대해 소홀한 모습을 보였었다.

R

S

T

Thesaurus   careless의 참조어

ADJ.   absent-minded, forgetful, irresponsible, reckless, sloppy; (ant.)
       attentive, careful, cautious ◫

U

V

car|er /kɛərər/ (carers) N-COUNT A **carer** is someone who is responsible for taking care of another person, for example, a person who is disabled, ill, or very young. [BRIT; AM **caregiver**, **caretaker**] ❑ *Women are more likely than men to be carers of elderly dependent relatives.*

가산명사 간병인, 돌보는 사람 [영국영어; 미국영어 caregiver, caretaker] ❑ 여성이 남성보다 연로한 가족들을 돌보는 경우가 많다.

W

ca|ress /kərɛs/ (caresses, caressing, caressed) V-T If you **caress** someone, you stroke them gently and affectionately. [WRITTEN] ❑ *He was gently caressing her golden hair.* ● N-COUNT **Caress** is also a noun. ❑ *Margaret took me to one side, holding my arm in a gentle caress.*

타동사 쓰다듬다, 어루만지다 [문어체] ❑ 그는 그녀의 금발 머리를 부드럽게 쓰다듬고 있었다. ● 가산명사 어루만짐 ❑ 마가렛은 내 팔을 부드럽게 잡으며 나를 한쪽으로 데려갔다.

X

Y

care|taker /kɛərteɪkər/ (caretakers) ◫ N-COUNT A **caretaker** is a person whose job it is to take care of a house or property when the owner is not there. ❑ *Sligo remained at St. Ives House, acting as its caretaker when the family was not in residence.*

❶ 가산명사 관리인, 대리인 ❑ 슬라이고는 주인집 식구들이 저택에 없을 때 대리인 자격으로 세인트 아이브즈 저택에 남았다. ❷ 형용사 임시의, 과도기의

Z

2 ADJ A **caretaker** government or leader is in charge temporarily until a new government or leader is appointed. [ADJ n] ❑ *The military intends to hand over power to a caretaker government and hold elections within six months.* **3** N-COUNT A **caretaker** is someone who is responsible for looking after another person, for example, a person who is disabled, ill, or very young. [mainly AM; BRIT **carer**] ❑ *His caretakers labeled him severely disabled.* **4** N-COUNT A **caretaker** is a person whose job it is to take care of a large building such as a school or an apartment house, and deal with small repairs to it. [BRIT; AM **janitor**]

군은 과도 정부에 전권을 넘기고 6개월 안으로 선거를 열 생각이다. **3** 가산명사 간병인, 돌보는 사람 [주로 미국영어; 영국영어 carer] ❑ 그의 간병인들은 그를 중증 장애인으로 불렸다. **4** 가산명사 관리인 [영국영어; 미국영어 janitor]

car‖go /kɑ́ːrgoʊ/ (**cargoes**) N-VAR The **cargo** of a ship or plane is the goods that it is carrying. ❑ *The boat calls at the main port to load its regular cargo of bananas.* →see **ship, train**

가산명사 또는 불가산명사 화물 ❑ 배는 정기적으로 싣는 바나나를 선적하기 위해 중앙 항구에 들른다.

Ca‖rib‖bean ◇◇◇ /kǽrəbiən, kərɪ́biən, BRIT kærəbíːən/ (**Caribbeans**)
1 N-PROPER The **Caribbean** is the sea which is between the West Indies, Central America and the north coast of South America. **2** ADJ **Caribbean** means belonging or relating to the Caribbean Sea and its islands, or to its people. ❑ *...the Caribbean island of St. Thomas.* ● N-COUNT A **Caribbean** is a person from a Caribbean island. ❑ *Caribbeans settled in Sheffield in the early '50s.*

1 고유명사 카리브 해 **2** 형용사 카리브 해의; 카리브 제도의; 카리브 사람의 ❑ 카리브 해의 세인트 토머스 섬 ● 가산명사 카리브 사람 ❑ 카리브 사람들은 50년대 초에 셰필드에 정착했다.

cari‖ca‖ture /kǽrɪkətʃər, -tʃʊər, BRIT -tʃʊǝr/ (**caricatures, caricaturing, caricatured**) **1** N-COUNT A **caricature** of someone is a drawing or description of them that exaggerates their appearance or behavior in a humorous or critical way. ❑ *The poster showed a caricature of Hitler with a devil's horns and tail.* **2** V-T If you **caricature** someone, you draw or describe them in an exaggerated way in order to be humorous or critical. ❑ *Her political career has been caricatured in headlines.* **3** N-COUNT If you describe something as a **caricature of** an event or situation, you mean that it is a very exaggerated account of it. [DISAPPROVAL] ❑ *Hall is angry at what he sees as a caricature of the training offered to modern-day social workers.*

1 가산명사 캐리커처, 희화(戱畵) ❑ 포스터에는 악마의 뿔과 꼬리를 단 히틀러의 캐리커처가 그려져 있었다. **2** 타동사 희화하다, 우스꽝스럽게 묘사하다 ❑ 그녀의 정치 인생은 머리기사에서 희화화되어 왔다. **3** 가산명사 희화, 과장된 묘사 [탐탁잖음] ❑ 홀은 오늘날의 사회 복지사들에게 제공되는 연수가 과장되게 희화화된 것을 보고 화가 나 있다.

car‖ing ◇◇◇ /kéərɪŋ/ **1** ADJ If someone is **caring**, they are affectionate, helpful, and sympathetic. ❑ *He is a lovely boy, very gentle and caring.* **2** ADJ The **caring** professions are those such as nursing and social work that are involved with looking after people who are ill or who need help in coping with their lives. [ADJ n] ❑ *The course is also suitable for those in the caring professions.*

1 형용사 상냥한, 친절한 ❑ 그는 아주 상냥하고 친절한 사랑스런 아이다. **2** 형용사 돌보는, 봉사하는 ❑ 이 과정은 간호 및 사회복지업 종사자들에게도 적합하다.

car‖nage /kɑ́ːrnɪdʒ/ N-UNCOUNT **Carnage** is the violent killing of large numbers of people, especially in a war. [LITERARY] ❑ *...his strategy for stopping the carnage in Kosovo.*

불가산명사 대학살 [문예체] ❑ 그가 코소보 대학살을 중단시키기 위해 내놓은 전략

car‖na‖tion /kɑːrnéɪʃⁿn/ (**carnations**) N-COUNT A **carnation** is a plant with white, pink, or red flowers.

가산명사 카네이션

car‖ni‖val /kɑ́ːrnɪvⁿl/ (**carnivals**) **1** N-COUNT A **carnival** is a public festival during which people play music and sometimes dance in the streets. **2** N-COUNT A **carnival** is a traveling show which is held in a park or field and at which there are machines to ride on, entertainments, and games. [AM; BRIT **funfair**]

1 가산명사 카니발, 사육제 **2** 가산명사 이동 유원지 [미국영어; 영국영어 funfair]

car‖ol /kǽrəl/ (**carols**) N-COUNT **Carols** are Christian religious songs that are sung at Christmas. ❑ *The singing of Christmas carols is a custom derived from early dance routines of pagan origin.*

가산명사 캐럴 ❑ 크리스마스 캐럴을 부르는 관습은 초기 이교도들이 춤을 추던 관행에서 파생된 것이다.

carou‖sel /kǽrəsel/ (**carousels**) N-COUNT At an airport, a **carousel** is a moving surface from which passengers can collect their luggage. →see **park**

가산명사 회전식 원형 컨베이어

car park (**car parks**) also **carpark** N-COUNT A **car park** is an area or building where people can leave their cars. [BRIT; AM **parking lot**]

가산명사 주차장 [영국영어; 미국영어 parking lot]

car‖pen‖ter /kɑ́ːrpɪntər/ (**carpenters**) N-COUNT A **carpenter** is a person whose job is making and repairing wooden things.

가산명사 목수

car‖pet /kɑ́ːrpɪt/ (**carpets, carpeting, carpeted**) **1** N-VAR A **carpet** is a thick covering of soft material which is laid over a floor or a staircase. ❑ *They put down wooden boards, and laid new carpets on top.* **2** V-T If a floor or a room is **carpeted**, a carpet is laid on the floor. [usu passive] ❑ *The room had been carpeted and the windows glazed with colored glass.* **3** to **sweep** something **under the carpet** →see **sweep**

1 가산명사 또는 불가산명사 카펫, 양탄자 ❑ 그들은 나무판자를 놓고 그 위에 새 카펫을 깔았다. **2** 타동사 카펫이 깔리다 ❑ 방에는 카펫이 깔려 있었고 창문은 색유리로 되어 있었다.

car phone (**car phones**) N-COUNT A **car phone** is a cellular phone which is designed to be used in a car.

가산명사 카폰

car‖pool /kɑ́ːrpuːl/ (**carpools**) also **car-pool** also **car pool** **1** N-COUNT A **carpool** is an arrangement where a group of people take turns driving each other to work, or driving each other's children to school. In American English, **carpool** is sometimes used to refer simply to people traveling together in a car. ❑ *His wife stays home to drive the children to school in the carpool.* **2** N-COUNT A **carpool** is a number of cars that are owned by a company or organization for the use of its employees or members. [BUSINESS]

1 가산명사 카풀, 자동차 함께 다니기; 한 차에 탄 사람들 ❑ 그의 아내는 아이들을 카풀로 학교에 데려다 주기 위해 집에 있다. **2** 가산명사 보유 차량 [경제]

car‖riage /kǽrɪdʒ/ (**carriages**) **1** N-COUNT A **carriage** is an old-fashioned vehicle, usually for a small number of passengers, which is pulled by horses. [also by n] ❑ *The President-elect followed in an open carriage drawn by six beautiful gray horses.* **2** N-COUNT A **carriage** is one of the separate, long sections of a train that carries passengers. [mainly BRIT; AM usually **car**] ❑ *The fire broke out in the last two carriages of the train.* **3** N-UNCOUNT **Carriage** is the cost or action of transporting or delivering goods. [BRIT, FORMAL; AM **delivery**] ❑ *It costs £10.86 for one litre including carriage.*

1 가산명사 4륜 마차 ❑ 대통령 당선자가 멋진 회색 말 여섯 마리가 끄는 무개마차를 타고 뒤따랐다. **2** 가산명사 객차, 차량 [주로 영국영어; 미국영어 대개 car] ❑ 그 불은 기차 맨 끝에 있는 차량 두 개에서 발생했다. **3** 불가산명사 운송료; 운송 [영국영어, 격식체; 미국영어 delivery] ❑ 운송료까지 포함해서 1리터당 10.86파운드가 든다.

car‖riage‖way /kǽrɪdʒweɪ/ (**carriageways**) N-COUNT A **carriageway** is one side of a road on which traffic traveling in opposite directions is separated by a barrier. [BRIT] ❑ *The southbound carriageway was reopened to traffic shortly after 2pm.*

가산명사 차도, 차선 [영국영어] ❑ 오후 2시 직후에 남쪽 방향 차선이 다시 개통되었다.

car‖ri‖er ◇◇◇ /kǽriər/ (**carriers**) **1** N-COUNT A **carrier** is a vehicle that is used for carrying people, especially soldiers, or things. ❑ *There were armored personnel carriers and tanks on the streets.* **2** N-COUNT A **carrier** is a passenger airline.

1 가산명사 수송차 ❑ 길거리에는 병사 수송용 장갑차와 탱크가 있었다. **2** 가산명사 여객 항공사 ❑ 스위스 국유 항공사인 스위스에어가 최근 들어

a b c d e f g h i j k l m n o p q r s t u v w x y z

A

❏ *Switzerland's national carrier, Swissair, has been having a hard time recently.* **B** N-COUNT A **carrier** is a person or an animal that is infected with a disease and so can make other people or animals ill. ❏ *...an AIDS carrier.*

어려움을 겪고 있다. **B** 가산명사 보균자, 감염자 ❏ 에이즈 보균자

B

car|rot /kǽrət/ (**carrots**) **1** N-VAR **Carrots** are long, thin, orange-colored vegetables. They grow under the ground, and have green shoots above the ground. **2** N-COUNT Something that is offered to people in order to persuade them to do something can be referred to as a **carrot**. Something that is meant to persuade people not to do something can be referred to in the same sentence as a "stick." ❏ *Why the new emphasis on sticks instead of diplomatic carrots?* →see **vegetable**

C

1 가산명사 또는 불가산명사 당근 **2** 가산명사 당근, 회유책 ❏ 외교적인 회유책 대신에 강경책을 새로이 강조하는 이유는 무엇일까?

D

car|ry ♦♦♦ /kǽri/ (**carries, carrying, carried**) **1** V-T If you **carry** something, you take it with you, holding it so that it does not touch the ground. ❏ *He was carrying a briefcase.* ❏ *She carried her son to the car.* **2** V-T If you **carry** something, you have it with you wherever you go. ❏ *You have to carry a pager so that they can call you in at any time.* **3** V-T If something **carries** a person or thing somewhere, it takes them there. ❏ *Flowers are designed to attract insects which then carry the pollen from plant to plant.* ❏ *The delegation was carrying a message of thanks to President Mubarak.* **4** V-T If a person or animal **is carrying** a disease, they are infected with it and can pass it on to other people or animals. ❏ *The official number of people carrying the AIDS virus is low.* **5** V-T If an action or situation has a particular quality or consequence, you can say that it **carries** it. [no passive, no cont] ❏ *Check that any medication you're taking carries no risk for your developing baby.* **6** V-T If a quality or advantage **carries** someone into a particular position or through a difficult situation, it helps them to achieve that position or deal with that situation. ❏ *He had the ruthless streak necessary to carry him into the Cabinet.* **7** V-T If you **carry** an idea or a method to a particular extent, you use or develop it to that extent. ❏ *It's not such a new idea, but I carried it to extremes.* **8** V-T If a newspaper or poster **carries** a picture or a piece of writing, it contains it or displays it. ❏ *Several papers carry the photograph of Mr. Anderson.* **9** V-T In a debate, if a proposal or motion **is carried**, a majority of people vote in favor of it. [usu passive] ❏ *A motion backing its economic policy was carried by 322 votes to 296.* **10** V-T If a crime **carries** a particular punishment, a person who is found guilty of that crime will receive that punishment. [no cont] ❏ *It was a crime of espionage and carried the death penalty.* **11** V-I If a sound **carries**, it can be heard a long way away. ❏ *Even in this stillness Leaphorn doubted if the sound would carry far.* **12** V-T If you **carry yourself** in a particular way, you walk and move in that way. ❏ *They carried themselves with great pride and dignity.* **13** PHRASE If you **get carried away** or **are carried away**, you are so eager or excited about something that you do something hasty or foolish. ❏ *I got completely carried away and almost cried.* **14** to **carry weight** →see **weight**

E

1 타동사 들다, 나르다 ❏ 그는 서류 가방을 들고 있었다. ❏ 그녀는 아들을 안고 차로 갔다. **2** 타동사 가지고 다니다 ❏ 당신은 그들이 언제든지 부를 수 있도록 항상 호출기를 가지고 다녀야 한다. **3** 타동사 데리고 가다; 나르다, 전하다 ❏ 꽃은 식물로 꽃가루를 날라주는 곤충을 유인하도록 되어 있다. ❏ 대표단은 무바라크 대통령에게 전할 감사의 메시지를 지니고 있었다. **4** 타동사 감염된 상태이다 ❏ 공식적인 에이즈 바이러스 감염자 수가 적다. **5** 타동사 지니다, 수반하다 ❏ 당신이 복용하고 있는 약이 태아에게 전혀 해가 되지 않는지 확인하라. **6** 타동사 ─하는 데 힘이 되다 ❏ 그는 내각에 진출하는 데 필요한 냉혹한 면을 지니고 있었다. **7** 타동사 확대하다, 발전시키다 ❏ 이는 그다지 새로운 생각은 아니지만 내가 극단적으로 발전시킨 것이다 **8** 타동사 싣다 ❏ 몇몇 일간지가 앤더슨 씨의 사진을 싣고 있다. **9** 타동사 통과되다 ❏ 그 경제 정책을 지지하는 동의안이 투표 결과 322 대 296으로 통과되었다. **10** 타동사 ─을 수반하다 ❏ 이는 간첩죄였고 사형으로 처벌되는 범죄였다. **11** 자동사 퍼지다 ❏ 이처럼 고요한 가운데서도 립혼은 소리가 멀리까지 퍼질지 의심스러웠다. **12** 타동사 거동하다, 처신하다 ❏ 그들은 자신만만하고 위엄 있게 처신했다. **13** 구 쑥 빠지다, 넋이 나가다 ❏ 나는 완전히 넋이 나가서 거의 울 뻔했다.

F

G

H

I

J

K

L

M

Do not confuse **carry** and **lift**. When you **carry** something, you move it from one place to another without letting it touch the ground. When you **lift** something, you move it upwards using your hands or a machine. After you have lifted it, you may **carry** it to a different place.

carry와 lift를 혼동하지 않도록 하라. 무엇을 **carry**하는 것은, 그것을 땅에 닿지 않게 해서 한 장소에서 다른 장소로 옮기는 것이다. 무엇을 **lift**하면 손이나 기계로 그것을 위로 들어올리는 것이다. 무엇을 들어올린(lift) 다음에, 그것을 다른 장소로 **carry**할 수 있다.

N

Thesaurus carry의 참조어

v. bear, bring, cart, haul, lug, move, transport **1** **3**

O

▶**carry on 1** PHRASAL VERB If you **carry on** doing something, you continue to do it. ❏ *The assistant carried on talking.* ❏ *Her bravery has given him the will to carry on with his life and his work.* ❏ *His eldest son Joseph carried on his father's traditions.* **2** PHRASAL VERB If you **carry on** an activity, you do it or take part in it for a period of time. ❏ *The consulate will carry on a political dialogue with Indonesia.*

P

1 구동사 계속하다, 잇다 ❏ 조수가 계속 말했다. ❏ 그녀의 용기를 보고 그는 계속해서 살아가고 일할 의지를 얻었다. ❏ 그의 장남 조셉이 아버지가 하던 일을 이어서 했다. **2** 구동사 지속하다 ❏ 영사관은 인도네시아와의 정치적 대화를 지속할 방침이다.

Q

▶**carry out** PHRASAL VERB If you **carry out** a threat, task, or instruction, you do it or act according to it. ❏ *The Social Democrats could still carry out their threat to leave the government.* ❏ *Police say they believe the attacks were carried out by nationalists.*

R

구동사 실행으로 옮기다, 감행하다 ❏ 사회 민주당원들은 정부를 떠나겠다는 협박을 여전히 실행으로 옮길 수도 있다. ❏ 경찰은 민족주의자들이 그 공격들을 감행한 것으로 생각한다고 밝혔다.

▶**carry through** PHRASAL VERB If you **carry** something **through**, you do it or complete it, often in spite of difficulties. ❏ *We don't have the confidence that the UN will carry it through a sustained program.*

S

구동사 완수하다, 관철시키다 ❏ 우리에게는 유엔의 지속적인 프로그램 완수에 대한 확신이 없다.

carry|all /kǽriɔl/ (**carryalls**) N-COUNT A **carryall** is a large bag made of nylon, canvas, or leather, which you use to carry your clothes and other possessions, for example when you are traveling. [mainly AM; BRIT usually **holdall**] ❏ *He shivered, humping his canvas carryall higher onto his shoulder.*

T

가산명사 여행용 대형 가방 [주로 미국영어; 영국영어 대개 holdall] ❏ 그는 커다란 캔버스 가방을 어깨 높이 메고 나르면서 몸을 부들부들 떨었다.

U

cart /kɑrt/ (**carts, carting, carted**) **1** N-COUNT A **cart** is an old-fashioned wooden vehicle that is used for transporting goods or people. Some carts are pulled by animals. ❏ *...a country where horse-drawn carts far outnumber cars.* **2** V-T If you **cart** things or people somewhere, you carry them or transport them, often with difficulty. [INFORMAL] ❏ *After both their parents died, one of their father's relatives carted off the entire contents of the house.* **3** N-COUNT A **cart** is a small vehicle with a motor. [AM] ❏ *Cars are prohibited, so transportation is by electric cart or by horse and buggy.* **4** N-COUNT A **cart** or a **shopping cart** is a large metal basket on wheels which is provided by stores such as supermarkets for customers to use while they are in the store. [AM; BRIT **trolley**]

V

W

1 가산명사 수레 ❏ 말이 끄는 수레가 자동차보다 훨씬 많은 국가 **2** 타동사 실어 나르다 [비격식체] ❏ 양친이 모두 사망한 후에, 아버지의 친척 중 한 명이 집안에 있던 물건을 전부 실어 갔다. **3** 가산명사 소형 전동차, 카트 [미국영어] ❏ 차가 금지되어 있어서 운송은 작은 전동차나 말, 경마차로 한다. **4** 가산명사 쇼핑용 카트 [미국영어; 영국영어 trolley]

X

carte blanche /kɑrt blɒnʃ/ N-UNCOUNT If someone gives you **carte blanche**, they give you the authority to do whatever you think is right. ❏ *They gave him carte blanche to make decisions.*

Y

불가산명사 백지위임, 전권 위임 ❏ 그들은 그에게 의사 결정에 관한 전권을 위임했다.

car|tel /kɑrtɛl/ (**cartels**) N-COUNT A **cartel** is an association of similar companies or businesses that have grouped together in order to prevent competition and to control prices. [BUSINESS] ❏ *...a drug cartel.*

Z

가산명사 카르텔 [경제] ❏ 의약품 카르텔

car|ti|lage /kɑrtɪlɪdʒ/ (**cartilages**) N-VAR Cartilage is a strong, flexible substance in your body, especially around your joints and in your nose. ❑ *Andre Agassi has pulled out of next week's Grand Slam Cup after tearing a cartilage in his chest.* →see **shark**

car|ton /kɑrt³n/ (**cartons**) ◼ N-COUNT A **carton** is a plastic or cardboard container in which food or drink is sold. ❑ *A two-pint carton of milk comes cheaper than two single pints.* ◻ N-COUNT A **carton** is a large, strong cardboard box in which goods are stored and transported. [AM] ❑ *Those cartons contain the archives of The New Yorker for the years 1925 to 1980.*

car|toon /kɑrtun/ (**cartoons**) ◼ N-COUNT A **cartoon** is a humorous drawing or series of drawings in a newspaper or magazine. ❑ *One of Britain's best-loved cartoon characters, Rupert the Bear, celebrates his seventieth birthday today.* ◻ N-COUNT A **cartoon** is a film in which all the characters and scenes are drawn rather than being real people or objects. ❑ *...a TV set blares out a cartoon comedy.* →see **animation**

car|toon|ist /kɑrtunɪst/ (**cartoonists**) N-COUNT A **cartoonist** is a person whose job is to draw cartoons for newspapers and magazines.

car|tridge /kɑrtrɪdʒ/ (**cartridges**) ◼ N-COUNT A **cartridge** is a metal or cardboard tube containing a bullet and an explosive substance. Cartridges are used in guns. ❑ *Only four of the five spent cartridges were recovered by police.* ◻ N-COUNT A **cartridge** is part of a machine or device that can be easily removed and replaced when it is worn out or empty. ❑ *Change the filter cartridge as often as instructed by the manufacturer.*

carve /kɑrv/ (**carves, carving, carved**) ◼ V-T/V-I If you **carve** an object, you make it by cutting it out of a substance such as wood or stone. If you **carve** something such as wood or stone into an object, you make the object by cutting it out. ❑ *One of the prisoners has carved a beautiful wooden chess set.* ❑ *I picked up a piece of wood and started carving.* →see also **carving** ◻ V-T If you **carve** writing or a design on an object, you cut it into the surface of the object. ❑ *He carved his name on his desk.* ◾ V-T If you **carve** a piece of cooked meat, you cut slices from it so that you can eat it. ❑ *Andrew began to carve the chicken.*

▶ **carve up** PHRASAL VERB If you say that someone **carves** something **up**, you disapprove of the way they have divided it into small parts. [DISAPPROVAL] ❑ *He has set about carving up the company which Hammer created from almost nothing.*

carv|ing /kɑrvɪŋ/ (**carvings**) ◼ N-COUNT A **carving** is an object or a design that has been cut out of a material such as stone or wood. ❑ *...a wood carving of a human hand.* ◻ N-UNCOUNT **Carving** is the art of carving objects, or of carving designs or writing on objects. ❑ *I found wood carving satisfying and painting fun.*

cas|cade /kæskeɪd/ (**cascades, cascading, cascaded**) ◼ N-COUNT If you refer to a **cascade** of something, you mean that there is a large amount of it. [LITERARY] ❑ *The women have lustrous cascades of black hair.* ◻ V-I If water **cascades** somewhere, it pours or flows downward very fast and in large quantities. ❑ *She hung on as the freezing, rushing water cascaded past her.*

| Word Link | cas ≈ box, hold : case, encase, suitcase |

------

case

① INSTANCES AND OTHER ABSTRACT MEANINGS
② CONTAINERS
③ GRAMMAR TERM

------

①**case** ♦♦♢ /keɪs/ (**cases**) ◼ N-COUNT A particular **case** is a particular situation or incident, especially one that you are using as an individual example or instance of something. ❑ *Surgical training takes at least nine years, or 11 in the case of obstetrics.* ❑ *In extreme cases, insurance companies can prosecute for fraud.* ◻ N-COUNT A **case** is a person or their particular problem that a doctor, social worker, or other professional is dealing with. ❑ *Dr. Thomas Bracken describes the case of a 45-year-old Catholic priest much given to prayer whose left knee became painful.* ❑ *Some cases of arthritis respond to a gluten-free diet.* ◾ N-COUNT If you say that someone is a sad **case** or a hopeless **case**, you mean that they are in a sad situation or a hopeless situation. ❑ *I knew I was going to make it – that I wasn't a hopeless case.* ◽ N-COUNT A **case** is a crime or mystery that the police are investigating. ❑ *The police have several suspects in the case of five murders committed in Gainesville, Florida.* ◾ N-COUNT The **case for** or **against** a plan or idea consists of the facts and reasons used to support it or oppose it. ❑ *He sat there while I made the case for his dismissal.* ❑ *Both these facts strengthen the case against hanging.* ◾ N-COUNT In law, a **case** is a trial or other legal inquiry. ❑ *It can be difficult for public figures to win a libel case.* →see also **test case** ◼ PHRASE You say **in any case** when you are adding something which is more important than what you have just said, but which supports or corrects it. [EMPHASIS] ❑ *The concert was booked out, and in any case, most of the people gathered in the square could not afford the price of a ticket.* ◼ PHRASE If you do something **in case** or **just in case** a particular thing happens, you do it because that thing might happen. ❑ *In case anyone was following me, I made an elaborate detour.* ◾ PHRASE If you do something or have something **in case of** a particular thing, you do it or have it because that thing might happen or be true. ❑ *Many shops along the route have been boarded up in case of trouble.* ◾ PHRASE You use **in case** in expressions like "in case you didn't know" or "in case you've forgotten" when you are telling someone in a rather irritated way something that you think is either obvious or none of their business. [FEELINGS] ❑ *She's nervous about something, in case you didn't notice.* ◾ PHRASE You say **in that case** or **in which case** to indicate that what you are going to say is true if the possible situation that has just been mentioned actually exists. ❑ *Perhaps you've some doubts about the attack. In that case it may*

가산명사 또는 불가산명사 연골 ❑안드레 아가시가 가슴 연골 부상을 입은 후에 다음 주 그랜드슬램에 출전하지 않기로 했다.

◼ 가산명사 곽, 용기 ❑2파인트짜리 우유가 1파인트짜리 우유 두 개보다 더 싸게 나온다. ◻ 가산명사 상자 [미국영어] ❑이 상자에는 1925년부터 1980년까지의 시사 주간지 '뉴요커'의 과월호가 들어 있다.

◼ 가산명사 시사만화 ❑영국인들이 가장 사랑하는 시사만화 캐릭터 중 하나인 루퍼트가 오늘 70번째 생일을 맞았다. ◻ 가산명사 만화 영화 ❑텔레비전에서 코미디 만화 영화 소리가 요란하게 난다.

가산명사 만화가

◼ 가산명사 단약동, 화약통 ❑탄피 5개 중 4개만 경찰에 의해 회수되었다. ◻ 가산명사 카트리지 ❑제조사에서 지시한 만큼 자주 필터 카트리지를 가세요.

◼ 타동사/자동사 깎다, 조각하다 ❑죄수 중 한 명이 나무를 깎아서 멋진 체스 세트를 만들었다. ❑나는 나무 조각 하나를 집어 들고 깎기 시작했다. ◻ 타동사 새기다 ❑그는 책상에 자신의 이름을 새겨 넣었다. ◾ 타동사 썰다, 저미다 ❑앤드류가 닭고기를 썰기 시작했다.

구동사 분할하다, 조각내다 [탐탁않음] ❑그는 해머가 무일푼에서 일궈낸 회사를 조각내기 시작했다.

◼ 가산명사 조각상 ❑사람의 손을 묘사한 나무 조각상 ◻ 불가산명사 조각 ❑나의 경우 목조는 보람 있었고 회화는 재미있었다.

◼ 가산명사 상당한 양, 다량 [문예체] ❑그 여인들은 윤기 있고 숱이 많은 검은 머리를 가졌다. ◻ 자동사 폭포처럼 쏟아지다 ❑그녀는 얼음장 같은 급류를 맞으면서도 버텨 냈다.

◼ 가산명사 사례, 경우 ❑외과 훈련은 최소 9년, 산과의 경우엔 11년이 걸린다. ❑극단적인 경우엔 보험 회사가 사기로 기소할 수도 있다. ◻ 가산명사 환자, 사례 ❑토머스 브래켄 박사는, 너무나 기도를 많이 한 나머지 왼쪽 무릎이 아프게 된 45세의 천주교 신부 환자를 묘사한다. ❑글루텐이 없는 식단에 차도를 보이는 관절염 환자들이 있다. ◾ 가산명사 신세, 처지 ❑나는 내가 해낼 것을, 내 처지가 희망이 없지는 않다는 것을 알았다. ◽ 가산명사 사건 ❑경찰은 플로리다 게인즈빌에서 발생한 5건의 살인 사건의 용의자로 몇 명을 지목하고 있다. ◾ 가산명사 논거, 논리, 주장 ❑내가 그의 해고에 대한 논리를 펼치는 동안 그는 거기에 앉아 있었다. ❑이 두 가지 사실 모두 교수형 반대 논거를 탄탄하게 해 준다. ◾ 가산명사 소송 사건 ❑공인이 명예 훼손 사건에서 승소하기가 힘들 수 있다. ◼ 구 어쨌 됐건 [강조] ❑콘서트 표가 매진되었다. 어쨌 됐건 광장에 모인 사람 대부분은 티켓 값이 너무 비싸 살 수도 없었다. ◼ 구 만일의 경우를 대비하여 ❑누가 나를 따라올 경우를 대비하여 나는 애써 길을 돌아왔다. ◾ 구 -을 대비해서 ❑그 길에 있는 많은 가게들은 문제가 발생할 경우를 대비해 판자로 건물을 막아 놓았다. ◾ 구 뻔한 사실이나 상대와 관계없는 일임을 신경질적으로 전할 때 사용 [감정 개입] ❑네가 눈치 채지 못한 것 같은데, 그 여자는 뭔가 걱정이 있어. ◾ 구 그러한 경우에는, 그렇다면 ❑그 공격에 관해 완전히 믿지 못하는 것 같군요. 그렇다면 우즈 양이 그 사건을 목격했다면 어때요일까? ◾ 구 혹시 모르니까, 만일을 위하여 ❑이 문제는 우리가 이미 이야기한 것 같습니다만, 혹시 모르니까 다시 묻겠습니다. ◾ 구 -한 것, -의 문제 ❑이는 누군가가 눈치를 채느냐 마느냐의 문제가 아니다. ◾ 구 사실이다, 그렇다 ❑당신은 그녀가 삼킬 때 힘들어하는

interest you to know that Miss Woods witnessed it. **12** PHRASE You can say that you are doing something **just in case** to refer vaguely to the possibility that a thing might happen or be true, without saying exactly what it is. ❑ *I guess we've already talked about this but I'll ask you again just in case.* **13** PHRASE If you say that a task or situation is **a case of** a particular thing, you mean that it consists of that thing or can be described as that thing. ❑ *It's not a case of whether anyone would notice or not.* **14** PHRASE If you say that something **is the case**, you mean that it is true or correct. ❑ *You'll probably notice her having difficulty swallowing. If this is the case, give her plenty of liquids.*
→see **hospital**

것을 발견할지도 모른다. 만약 그렇다면, 물을 많이 먹여라.

Word Partnership   *case*의 연어

V.	**make a** case **5**
	argue a case **5 6**
	lose/win a case **6**
N.	**court** case **6**
PREP.	**in any** case **7**
	just in case **8 12**
	in that case, **in which** case **11**

---

② **case**/keɪs/ (cases) **1** N-COUNT A **case** is a container that is specially designed to hold or protect something. ❑ *...a black case for his spectacles.* →see also **bookcase, briefcase** **2** N-COUNT A **case** is a suitcase. ❑ *I caught Paul and Steve packing their cases.*

1 가산명사 용기, 케이스 ❑ 그의 까만 안경집
2 가산명사 여행 가방 ❑ 나는 폴과 스티브가 가방을 싸고 있는 현장을 잡았다.

③ **case**/keɪs/ (cases) **1** N-COUNT In the grammar of many languages, the **case** of a group such as a noun group or adjective group is the form it has which shows its relationship to other groups in the sentence. **2** →see also **lowercase, uppercase.**

1 가산명사 격

case study (case studies) N-COUNT A **case study** is a written account that gives detailed information about a person, group, or thing and their development over a period of time. ❑ *...a large case study of malaria in West African children.*

가산명사 사례 연구 ❑ 서아프리카 어린이 말라리아 환자를 대상으로 한 대규모 사례 연구

cash ♦♦◇ /kæʃ/ (cashes, cashing, cashed) **1** N-UNCOUNT **Cash** is money in the form of bills and coins rather than checks. ❑ *...two thousand pounds in cash.* →see also **hard cash, petty cash** **2** N-UNCOUNT **Cash** means the same as money, especially money which is immediately available. [INFORMAL] ❑ *...a state-owned financial-services group with plenty of cash.* **3** V-T If you **cash** a check, you exchange it at a bank for the amount of money that it is worth. ❑ *There are similar charges if you want to cash a check or withdraw money at a branch other than your own.*

1 불가산명사 현금, 현찰 ❑ 현금 2,000파운드
2 불가산명사 자금, 현금 [비격식체] ❑ 자금 사정이 좋은 국유 금융 서비스 업체 **3** 타동사 현금으로 바꾸다 ❑ 거래 지점 말고 다른 지점에서 수표를 현금화하거나 돈을 인출할 때도 수수료가 비슷하다.

▶**cash in** **1** PHRASAL VERB If you say that someone **cashes in on** a situation, you are criticizing them for using it to gain an advantage, often in an unfair or dishonest way. [DISAPPROVAL] ❑ *Residents said local gang leaders had cashed in on the violence to seize valuable land.* **2** PHRASAL VERB If you **cash in** something such as an insurance policy, you exchange it for money. ❑ *Avoid cashing in a policy early as you could lose out heavily.*

1 구동사 이용하다 [탐탁잖음] ❑ 주민들은 지역 폭력배 두목들이 폭력을 이용해서 고가의 땅을 차지했다고 말했다. **2** 구동사 현금화하다, 환금하다 ❑ 큰 손해를 볼 수 있으므로 보험을 일찍 해약하는 것은 피하라.

cash-and-carry (cash-and-carries) N-COUNT A **cash-and-carry** is a large store where you can buy goods in larger quantities and at lower prices than in ordinary stores. Cash-and-carries are mainly used by people in business to buy goods for their stores or companies.

가산명사 대형 도매 매장

cash card (cash cards) also **cashcard** N-COUNT A **cash card** is a card that banks give to their customers so that they can get money out of a cash dispenser. [BRIT]

가산명사 현금 인출 카드 [영국영어]

cash cow (cash cows) N-COUNT In business, a **cash cow** is a product or investment that steadily continues to be profitable. [BUSINESS] ❑ *The retail division is BT's cash cow.*

가산명사 효자 상품, 재원 [경제] ❑ 소매 부문이 비티의 재원이다.

cash desk (cash desks) N-COUNT A **cash desk** is the same as a **cashier's desk.** [BRIT]

가산명사 계산대 [영국영어]

cash dis|pens|er (cash dispensers) N-COUNT A **cash dispenser** is a machine built into the wall of a bank or other building, which allows people to take out money from their bank account using a special card. [BRIT; AM **ATM**]

가산명사 현금 지급기 [영국영어; 미국영어 ATM]

cash flow also **cashflow** N-UNCOUNT The **cash flow** of a firm or business is the movement of money into and out of it. [BUSINESS] ❑ *A French-based pharmaceuticals company ran into cash-flow problems and faced liquidation.*

불가산명사 자금 흐름, 캐시플로 [경제] ❑ 프랑스에 본사를 둔 제약 회사가 자금 흐름 문제로 파산 위기를 맞았다.

cash|ier /kæʃɪər/ (cashiers) N-COUNT A **cashier** is a person who customers pay money to or get money from in places such as stores or banks.

가산명사 출납원

cash|ier's desk (cashier's desks) N-COUNT A **cashier's desk** is a place in a large store where you pay for the things you want to buy. [AM]

가산명사 계산대 [미국영어]

cash|mere /kæʒmɪər, BRIT kæʃmɪəʳ/ N-UNCOUNT **Cashmere** is a kind of very fine, soft wool. ❑ *...a big soft cashmere sweater.*

불가산명사 캐시미어 ❑ 크고 부드러운 캐시미어 스웨터

cash|point /kæʃpɔɪnt/ (cashpoints) N-COUNT A **cashpoint** is the same as a **cash dispenser.** [BRIT; AM ATM]

가산명사 현금 지급기 [영국영어; 미국영어 ATM]

cash reg|is|ter (cash registers) N-COUNT A **cash register** is a machine in a store, bar, or restaurant that is used to add up and record how much money people pay, and in which the money is kept. ❑ *At the cash registers, most of those buying booze are English.*

가산명사 금전 등록기 ❑ 금전 등록기에서 술을 구입한 사람 대부분은 잉글랜드 출신이다.

cash-starved ADJ A **cash-starved** company or organization does not have enough money to operate properly, usually because another organization, such as the government, is not giving them the money that they need. [BUSINESS, JOURNALISM] ❑ *We are heading for a crisis, with cash-starved councils forced to cut back on vital community services.*

형용사 자금난을 겪고 있는 [경제, 언론] ❑ 자금난에 봉착한 지방 의회들이 주요 지역 사회 서비스에 대한 지원을 줄일 수밖에 없게 되면서, 우리는 위기로 치닫고 있다.

ca|si|no /kəsiːnoʊ/ (**casinos**) N-COUNT A **casino** is a building or room where people play gambling games such as roulette.

가산명사 카지노

cas|se|role /kæsəroʊl/ (**casseroles**) ■ N-COUNT A **casserole** is a dish made of meat and vegetables that have been cooked slowly in a liquid. □ ...*a huge beef casserole, full of herbs, vegetables and wine.* ■ N-COUNT A **casserole** or a **casserole dish** is a large heavy container with a lid. You cook casseroles and other dishes in it. □ *Place all the chopped vegetables into a casserole dish.*

■ 가산명사 캐서롤 (고기와 야채를 넣은 요리) □ 허브와 야채, 와인이 듬뿍 든 소고기 캐서롤 ■ 가산명사 큰 냄비 □ 다진 야채를 전부 큰 냄비에 넣으세요.

cas|sette /kəset/ (**cassettes**) ■ N-COUNT A **cassette** is a small, flat, rectangular plastic case containing magnetic tape which is used for recording and playing back sound or film. [also on N] □ *His two albums released on cassette have sold more than 10 million copies.* ■ N-COUNT A **cassette** is the container or case for the film that you load into a camera.

■ 가산명사 녹음테이프 □ 테이프로 발매된 그의 두 앨범은 천만 개 이상 팔렸다. ■ 가산명사 필름통

cast ♦♦◇ /kæst/ (**casts, casting**)

> The form **cast** is used in the present tense and is the past tense and past participle.

> cast은 동사의 현재, 과거, 과거 분사로 쓴다.

■ N-COUNT-COLL The **cast** of a play or movie is all the people who act in it. □ *The show is very amusing and the cast is very good.* ■ V-T To **cast** an actor **in** a play or film means to choose them to act a particular role in it. □ *The world premiere of Harold Pinter's new play casts Ian Holm in the lead role.* □ *He was cast as a college professor.* ■ V-T If you **cast** your eyes or **cast** a look in a particular direction, you look quickly in that direction. [WRITTEN] □ *He cast a stern glance at the two men.* □ *I cast my eyes down briefly.* ■ V-T If something **casts** a light or shadow somewhere, it causes it to appear there. [WRITTEN] □ *The moon cast a bright light over the yard.* ■ V-T To **cast** doubt on something means to cause people to be unsure about it. □ *Last night a top criminal psychologist cast doubt on the theory.* ■ V-T When you **cast** your vote in an election, you vote. □ *About ninety-five per cent of those who cast their votes approve the new constitution.* ■ V-T To **cast** an object means to make it by pouring a liquid such as hot metal into a specially shaped container and leaving it there until it becomes hard. □ *The stair grips, cast in either brass or bronze, resemble exotic sea shells.* ■ N-COUNT A **cast** is a model that has been made by pouring a liquid such as plaster or hot metal onto something or into something, so that when it hardens it has the same shape as that thing. □ *An orthodontist took a cast of the inside of Billy's mouth to make a dental plate.* ■ to **cast** your **mind back** →see **mind**
→see **election, vote**

■ 가산명사·집합 출연진 □ 공연이 매우 재미있고 출연진도 아주 훌륭하다. ■ 타동사 캐스팅하다, 출연시키다 □ 해롤드 핀터 신작의 세계적인 초연에 이안 홀름이 주연으로 출연한다. □ 그는 대학 교수로 출연했다. ■ 타동사 시선을 던지다, 눈길을 보내다 [문어체] □ 그는 그 두 남자에게 엄한 시선을 보냈다. □ 나는 잠깐 동안 눈을 내리깔았다. ■ 타동사 비추다 [문어체] □ 달이 마당 위로 밝은 빛을 비췄다. ■ 타동사 의문을 제기하다 □ 어젯밤 한 유명 범죄 심리학자가 그 이론에 의문을 제기했다. ■ 타동사 투표하다 □ 투표자들 가운데 95퍼센트 정도가 새 헌법을 찬성하고 있다. ■ 타동사 주조하다 □ 놋쇠나 청동으로 주조된 계단 손잡이가 이국적인 조개껍질 모양을 하고 있다. ■ 가산명사 주물 □ 치열 교정 전문의가 의치상을 만들기 위해 빌리의 구강 내부를 본떴다.

►**cast aside** PHRASAL VERB If you **cast aside** someone or something, you get rid of them because they are no longer necessary or useful to you. □ *Sweden needs to cast aside outdated policies and thinking.*

구동사 버리다 □ 스웨덴은 시대에 뒤진 정책과 생각을 버릴 필요가 있다.

caste /kæst/ (**castes**) ■ N-COUNT A **caste** is one of the traditional social classes into which people are divided in a Hindu society. □ *Most of the upper castes worship the Goddess Kali.* ■ N-UNCOUNT **Caste** is the system of dividing people in a society into different social classes. □ *Caste is defined primarily by social honour attained through personal life-style.*

■ 가산명사 카스트 □ 상류 카스트의 대부분은 칼리 여신을 숭배한다. ■ 불가산명사 카스트 제도, 신분 제도 □ 카스트 제도는 개인의 생활양식을 통해 얻은 사회적인 명예로 규정된다.

cas|ti|gate /kæstɪgeɪt/ (**castigates, castigating, castigated**) V-T If you **castigate** someone or something, you speak to them angrily or criticize them severely. [FORMAL] □ *Marx never lost an opportunity to castigate colonialism.*

타동사 혹평하다 [격식체] □ 마르크스는 기회가 생길 때마다 식민주의를 혹평했다.

cast|ing vote (**casting votes**) N-COUNT When a committee has given an equal number of votes for and against a proposal, the chairperson can give a **casting vote**. This vote decides whether or not the proposal will be passed. □ *The vote was tied and a local union leader used his casting vote in favor of the return to work.*

가산명사 캐스팅보트, 결정권 □ 찬반 동수인 상태에서 현지 노조 지도자가 캐스팅보트를 행사해 업무 복귀를 결정했다.

cast iron ■ N-UNCOUNT **Cast iron** is iron which contains a small amount of carbon. It is hard and cannot be bent so it has to be made into objects by casting. □ *Made from cast iron, it is finished in graphite enamel.* ■ ADJ A **cast-iron** guarantee or alibi is one that is absolutely certain to be effective and will not fail you. □ *They would have to offer cast-iron guarantees to invest in long-term projects.*
→see **pan**

■ 불가산명사 무쇠 □ 이는 무쇠로 만들어졌으며 마감재로 흑연 에나멜을 사용했다. ■ 형용사 확실한 □ 그들은 장기 프로젝트에 투자하겠다는 확실한 보증을 제공해야 할 것이다.

cas|tle ♦♦◇ /kæsəl/ (**castles**) N-COUNT A **castle** is a large building with thick, high walls. Castles were built by important people, such as kings, in former times, especially for protection during wars and battles.

가산명사 성, 요새

cas|trate /kæstreɪt, BRIT kæstreɪt/ (**castrates, castrating, castrated**) V-T To **castrate** a male animal or a man means to remove his testicles. □ *In the ancient world, it was probably rare to castrate a dog or cat.* ● **cas|tra|tion** /kæstreɪʃən/ (**castrations**) N-VAR □ ...*the castration of male farm animals.*

타동사 거세하다 □ 고대에는 개나 고양이를 거세하는 경우가 드물었을 것이다. ● 거세 가산명사 또는 불가산명사 □ 농장 동물 수컷의 거세

cas|ual /kæʒuəl/ ■ ADJ If you are **casual**, you are, or you pretend to be, relaxed and not very concerned about what is happening or what you are doing. □ *It's difficult for me to be casual about anything.* ● **casu|al|ly** ADV [ADV with v] □ *"No need to hurry," Ben said casually.* ■ ADJ A **casual** event or situation happens by chance or without planning. [ADJ n] □ *What you mean as a casual remark could be misinterpreted.* ■ ADJ **Casual** clothes are ones that you normally wear at home or on vacation, and not on formal occasions. [ADJ n] □ *I also bought some casual clothes for the weekend.* ● **casu|al|ly** ADV □ *They were smartly but casually dressed.* ■ ADJ **Casual** work is done for short periods and not on a permanent or regular basis. [ADJ n] □ ...*establishments which employ people on a casual basis, such as pubs and restaurants.*

■ 형용사 심상한, 편안하게 생각하는 □ 나는 무슨 일이고 그냥 편안하게 생각하는 것이 어렵다. ● 심상하게 부사 □ "서두를 필요 없어,"라고 벤이 심상하게 말했다. ■ 형용사 무심결의, 뜻하지 않은 □ 네가 무심코 한 말이 잘못 해석될 수도 있다. ■ 형용사 평상복의, 캐주얼의 □ 나는 주말에 입을 평상복도 몇 벌 샀다. ● 편안하게, 캐주얼하게 부사 □ 그들은 단정하지만 편안한 차림이었다. ■ 형용사 그때그때의, 임시의 □ 주점이나 식당같이 그때그때 직원을 뽑는 곳들

casu|al|ize /kæʒuəlaɪz/ (**casualizes, casualizing, casualized**) [BRIT also **casualise**] V-T If a business **casualizes** its employees or **casualizes** their labor, it replaces employees with permanent contracts and full rights with employees with temporary contracts and few rights. [BUSINESS] □ ...*a casualized workforce.* ● **casu|ali|za|tion** /kæʒuəlaɪzeɪʃən/ N-UNCOUNT □ ...*the casualization of employment.*

[영국영어 casualise] 타동사 비정규직으로 대체하다 [경제] □ 비정규직으로 대체된 노동력 ● 비정규직화 불가산명사 □ 고용의 비정규직화

casu|al|ty ◆◇◇ /kǽʒuəlti/ (**casualties**) **1** N-COUNT A **casualty** is a person who is injured or killed in a war or in an accident. ❑ *Troops fired on demonstrators near the Royal Palace causing many casualties.* **2** N-COUNT A **casualty of** a particular event or situation is a person or a thing that has suffered badly as a result of that event or situation. ❑ *Fiat has been one of the greatest casualties of the recession.* **3** N-UNCOUNT **Casualty** is the part of a hospital where people who have severe injuries or sudden illnesses are taken for emergency treatment. [BRIT; AM **emergency room**] ❑ *I was taken to casualty at St Thomas's Hospital.*

1 가산명사 사상자 ❑ 군이 왕궁 근처의 시위대들을 향해 발포해 많은 사상자가 발생했다. **2** 가산명사 희생자, 피해자 ❑ 피아트는 지금까지 경기 침체에서 가장 큰 피해를 본 기업 중에 하나이다. **3** 불가산명사 응급실 [영국영어; 미국영어 emergency room] ❑ 나는 세인트 토머스 병원의 응급실로 실려 갔다.

cat ◆◇◇ /kǽt/ (**cats**) **1** N-COUNT A **cat** is a furry animal that has a long tail and sharp claws. Cats are often kept as pets. **2** N-COUNT **Cats** are lions, tigers, and other wild animals in the same family. ❑ *The lion is perhaps the most famous member of the cat family.* **3** →see also **fat cat** →see **pet**

1 가산명사 고양이 **2** 가산명사 고양이과 동물 ❑ 사자가 고양이과 동물 중에서 가장 유명할 것이다.

cata|log /kǽtˀlɒg/ (**catalogs**) [BRIT, sometimes AM **catalogue**] **1** N-COUNT A **catalog** is a list of things such as the goods you can buy from a particular company, the objects in a museum, or the books in a library. ❑ *...the world's biggest seed catalog.* **2** N-COUNT A **catalog of** similar things, especially bad things, is a number of them considered or discussed one after another. ❑ *His story is a catalog of misfortune.* →see **library**

[영국영어, 미국영어 가끔 catalogue] **1** 가산명사 카탈로그, 목록 ❑ 세계에서 가장 큰 종자 목록 **2** 가산명사 연속 ❑ 그의 이야기는 불행의 연속이다.

cata|lyst /kǽtˀlɪst/ (**catalysts**) **1** N-COUNT You can describe a person or thing that causes a change or event to happen as a **catalyst**. ❑ *I very much hope that this case will prove to be a catalyst for change.* **2** N-COUNT In chemistry, a **catalyst** is a substance that causes a chemical reaction to take place more quickly.

1 가산명사 촉매, 계기 ❑ 나는 이번 사건이 변화의 계기가 되기를 간절히 바란다. **2** 가산명사 촉매제

cata|pult /kǽtəpʌlt/ (**catapults, catapulting, catapulted**) **1** V-T/V-I If someone or something **catapults** or **is catapulted** through the air, they are thrown very suddenly, quickly, and violently through it. ❑ *We've all seen enough dummies catapulting through windscreens in TV warnings to know the dangers of not wearing seat belts.* **2** N-COUNT A **catapult** is the same as a **slingshot**. [BRIT] **3** V-T/V-I If something **catapults** you into a particular state or situation, or if you **catapult** there, you are suddenly and unexpectedly caused to be in that state or situation. ❑ *"Basic Instinct" catapulted her to top status among Hollywood's glamor goddesses.*

1 타동사/자동사 튕겨 나가다 ❑ 우리는 모두 경고성 텔레비전 방송에서 인체 대용 인형들이 앞 유리를 통해 튕겨 나가는 장면을 많이 봐서 안전벨트 미착용이 발생하는 위험을 안다. **2** 가산명사 새총 [영국영어] **3** 타동사/자동사 급부상시키다; 급부상하다 ❑ 영화 '원초적 본능'으로 그녀는 매혹적인 할리우드 여배우 중에서도 최고의 자리로 급부상했다.

cata|ract /kǽtərækt/ (**cataracts**) N-COUNT **Cataracts** are layers over a person's eyes that prevent them from seeing properly. Cataracts usually develop because of old age or illness. ❑ *In one study, light smokers were found to be more than twice as likely to get cataracts as non-smokers.*

가산명사 백내장 ❑ 한 연구 결과에 따르면 담배를 조금 피우는 사람들이 담배를 피우지 않는 사람들보다 백내장에 걸릴 가능성이 두 배가 높다고 한다.

catas|tro|phe /kətǽstrəfi/ (**catastrophes**) N-COUNT A **catastrophe** is an unexpected event that causes great suffering or damage. ❑ *From all points of view, war would be a catastrophe.*

가산명사 재앙, 대참사 ❑ 어느 모로 보아도 전쟁은 큰 재앙을 몰고 올 것이다.

cata|stroph|ic /kætəstrɒfɪk/ **1** ADJ Something that is **catastrophic** involves or causes a sudden terrible disaster. ❑ *A tidal wave caused by the earthquake hit the coast causing catastrophic damage.* ❑ *The water shortage in this country is potentially catastrophic.* **2** ADJ If you describe something as **catastrophic**, you mean that it is very bad or unsuccessful. ❑ *...another catastrophic attempt to arrest control from a rival Christian militia.*

1 형용사 재앙의, 끔찍한 ❑ 지진으로 인한 해일이 해안을 덮치면서 끔찍한 피해를 낳았다. ❑ 이 나라의 물 부족 사태는 재앙으로 이어질 가능성이 있다. **2** 형용사 처참한 ❑ 적수인 기독교 민병대의 통제력을 저지하려던 처참하게 끝난 또 한 번의 시도

catch ◆◆◇ /kǽtʃ/ (**catches, catching, caught**) **1** V-T If you **catch** a person or animal, you capture them after chasing them, or by using a trap, net, or other device. ❑ *Police say they are confident of catching the gunman.* ❑ *Where did you catch the fish?* **2** V-T If you **catch** an object that is moving through the air, you seize it with your hands. ❑ *I jumped up to catch a ball and fell over.* ● N-COUNT **Catch** is also a noun. ❑ *He missed the catch and the match was lost.* **3** V-T If you **catch** a part of someone's body, you take or seize it with your hand, often in order to stop them going somewhere. ❑ *Liz caught his arm.* ❑ *He knelt beside her and caught her hand in both of his.* **4** V-T If one thing **catches** another, it hits it accidentally or manages to hit it. ❑ *The stinging slap almost caught his face.* ❑ *I may have caught him with my elbow but it was just an accident.* **5** V-T/V-I If something **catches on** or in an object, it accidentally becomes attached to the object or stuck in it. ❑ *Her ankle caught on a root, and she almost lost her balance.* **6** V-T When you **catch** a bus, train, or plane, you get on it in order to travel somewhere. ❑ *We were in plenty of time for Anthony to catch the ferry.* **7** V-T If you **catch** someone doing something wrong, you see or find them doing it. ❑ *He caught a youth breaking into a car.* ❑ *I don't want to catch you pushing yourself into the picture to get some personal publicity.* **8** V-T If you **catch yourself** doing something, especially something surprising, you suddenly become aware that you are doing it. ❑ *I caught myself feeling almost sorry for poor Mr. Laurence.* **9** V-T If you **catch** a glimpse of it, you notice it or manage to see it briefly. ❑ *As she turned back she caught the puzzled look on her mother's face.* **10** V-T If you **catch** something that someone has said, you manage to hear it. ❑ *His ears caught a faint cry.* ❑ *I do not believe I caught your name.* **11** V-T If you **catch** a TV or radio program or an event, you manage to see or listen to it. ❑ *Bill turns on the radio to catch the local news.* **12** V-T If you **catch** someone, you manage to contact or meet them to talk to them, especially when they are just about to go somewhere else. ❑ *I dialed Elizabeth's number thinking I might catch her before she left for work.* **13** V-T If something or someone **catches** you by surprise or at a bad time, you were not expecting them or do not feel able to deal with them. ❑ *She looked as if the photographer had caught her by surprise.* ❑ *I'm sorry but I just cannot say anything. You've caught me at a bad time.* **14** V-T If something **catches** your attention or your eye, you notice it or become interested in it. ❑ *My shoes caught his attention.* **15** V-T PASSIVE If you **are caught** in a storm or other unpleasant situation, it happens when you cannot avoid its effects. ❑ *When he was fishing off the island he was caught in a storm and almost drowned.* **16** V-T PASSIVE If you **are caught between** two alternatives or two people, you do not know which one to choose or follow. ❑ *The Jordanian leader is caught between both sides in the dispute.* **17** V-T If you **catch** a cold or a disease, you become ill with it. ❑ *The more stress you are under, the more likely you are to catch a cold.* **18** V-T If something **catches** the light or if the light **catches** it, it reflects the light and looks bright or shiny. ❑ *They saw the ship's*

1 타동사 잡다 ❑ 경찰은 저격범의 검거를 자신한다고 말한다. ❑ 그 물고기 어디서 잡았어요? **2** 타동사 잡다, 받다 ❑ 나는 공을 잡기 위해 뛰어올랐다가 넘어졌다. ● 가산명사 잡기 ❑ 그가 공을 놓쳐서 경기에서 지고 말았다. **3** 타동사 붙들다, 잡다 ❑ 리즈가 그의 팔을 붙들었다. ❑ 그는 그녀 옆에 무릎을 꿇고 그녀의 손을 두 손으로 감쌌다. **4** 타동사 치다 ❑ 그는 얼굴을 세게 맞을 뻔했다. ❑ 내가 팔꿈치로 그를 쳤을지는 모르지만 그건 단순한 사고였다. **5** 타동사/자동사 -에 걸리다, -에 끼이다 ❑ 그녀는 발목이 뿌리에 걸려서 거의 균형을 잃을 뻔했다. **6** 타동사 타다 ❑ 우리는 앤소니가 배를 타기 전까지 시간이 넉넉했다. **7** 타동사 목격하다, 발견하다 ❑ 그는 한 젊은이의 자동차 절도 장면을 목격했다. ❑ 나는 네가 얼굴을 알리려고 그 사진에 억지로 찍히려는 모습을 보고 싶지 않아. **8** 타동사 자신이 -하고 있는 것을 깨닫다 ❑ 나는 가난한 로렌 씨를 거의 딱하게 여기고 있는 내 자신을 발견했다. **9** 타동사 알아채다, 얼핏 보다 ❑ 뒤로 돌아서며 그녀는 어머니의 얼굴에서 어리둥절해 하는 기색을 알았다. **10** 타동사 알아듣다 ❑ 그의 귀에 희미한 울음소리가 들렸다. ❑ 당신의 이름을 못 들은 것 같아요. **11** 타동사 보다; 듣다 ❑ 빌은 지방 뉴스를 듣기 위해 라디오를 켰다. **12** 타동사 만나다, 연락하다 ❑ 나는 그녀가 출근하기 전에 연락이 될지도 모른다는 생각에 엘리자베스에게 전화를 걸었다. **13** 타동사 갑자기 나타나다 ❑ 그녀는 사진 기사가 갑자기 나타나 깜짝 놀란 것처럼 보였다. ❑ 죄송하지만 어떤 말도 할 수가 없네요. 때를 잘못 택해서 오셨어요. **14** 타동사 사로잡다 ❑ 내 신발에 그의 시선이 꽂혔다. **15** 수동 타동사 갇히다 ❑ 그는 섬 근처 바다에서 낚시를 하다가 폭풍우를 만나 거의 익사할 뻔했다. **16** 수동 타동사 -사이에서 이러지도 저러지도 못하다 ❑ 요르단 지도자는 분쟁의 양 진영 사이에 끼어 이러지도 저러지도 못하고 있다. **17** 타동사 걸리다 ❑ 스트레스를 많이 받을수록 감기에 걸릴 확률이 높아진다. **18** 타동사 빛을 받다 ❑ 그들은 배에 있는 대포가 달빛을 받아 반짝이는 것을 보았다. **19** 가산명사 잠금장치 ❑ 그녀는 가방의 잠금장치를 만지작거렸다. **20** 가산명사 함정 ❑ 여기서 함정은 저녁값은 직접 벌어야 하고, 숙식이 매우 기본적인 수준에 머물 수도 있다는 것이다.

guns, catching the light of the moon. ◼ N-COUNT A **catch** on a window, door, or container is a device that fastens it. ❑ *She fiddled with the catch of her bag.*
◼ N-COUNT A **catch** is a hidden problem or difficulty in a plan or an offer that seems surprisingly good. ❑ *The catch is that you work for your supper, and the food and accommodations can be very basic.* ◼ to **catch fire** →see **fire**. to **catch hold of** something →see **hold**. to **catch sight of** something →see **sight**

Thesaurus   catch의 참조어

v.   arrest, capture, grab, seize, snatch, trap; *(ant.)* free, let go, release ◼·◼

Word Partnership   catch의 연어

N.   catch **a fish** ◼
      catch **a thief** ◼ ◼
      catch **a ball** ◼
      catch **a bus/ flight/plane/train** ◼
      catch **your attention**, catch **your eye** ◼
      ❑ *The songs were both catchy and cutting.*
v.   **play** catch ◼

▶**catch on** ◼ PHRASAL VERB If you **catch on to** something, you understand it, or realize that it is happening. ❑ *He got what he could out of me before I caught on to the kind of person he'd turned into.* ◼ PHRASAL VERB If something **catches on**, it becomes popular. ❑ *The idea has been around for ages without catching on.*

▶**catch out** PHRASAL VERB To **catch** someone **out** means to cause them to make a mistake that reveals that they are lying about something, do not know something, or cannot do something. [mainly BRIT] ❑ *Detectives followed him for months hoping to catch him out in some deception.* ❑ *He did not like to be caught out on details.*

▶**catch up** ◼ PHRASAL VERB If you **catch up with** someone who is in front of you, you reach them by walking faster than they are walking. ❑ *I stopped and waited for her to catch up.* ◼ PHRASAL VERB To **catch up with** someone means to reach the same standard, stage, or level that they have reached. ❑ *Most late developers will catch up with their friends.* ❑ *John began the season better than me but I have fought to catch up.* ◼ PHRASAL VERB If you **catch up on** an activity that you have not had much time to do recently, you spend time doing it. ❑ *I was catching up on a bit of reading.* ◼ PHRASAL VERB If you **catch up** on friends who you have not seen for some time or on their lives, you talk to them and find out what has happened in their lives since you last talked together. ❑ *The ladies spent some time catching up on each other's health and families.* ◼ PHRASAL VERB-PASSIVE If you **are caught up in** something, you are involved in it, usually unwillingly. ❑ *The people themselves weren't part of the conflict; they were just caught up in it.*

▶**catch up with** ◼ PHRASAL VERB When people **catch up with** someone who has done something wrong, they succeed in finding them in order to arrest or punish them. ❑ *The law caught up with him yesterday.* ◼ PHRASAL VERB If something **catches up with** you, you are forced to deal with something unpleasant that happened or that you did in the past, which you have been able to avoid until now. ❑ *Although he subsequently became a successful businessman, his criminal past caught up with him.*

catchy /kǽtʃi/ (**catchier, catchiest**) ADJ If you describe a tune, name, or advertisement as **catchy**, you mean that it is attractive and easy to remember. ❑ *The songs were both catchy and cutting.*

cat|egori|cal /kæ̀tɪgɒ́rɪkʰl, BRIT kæ̀tɪgɒ́rɪkʰl/ ADJ If you are **categorical** about something, you state your views very definitely and firmly. ❑ *...his categorical denial of the charges of sexual harassment.* ● **cat|egori|cal|ly** /kæ̀tɪgɒ́rɪkli, BRIT kæ̀tɪgɒ́rɪkli/ ADV [ADV with v] ❑ *They totally and categorically deny the charges.*

cat|ego|rize /kǽtɪgəraɪz/ (**categorizes, categorizing, categorized**) [BRIT also **categorise**] V-T If you **categorize** people or things, you divide them into sets or you say which set they belong to. ❑ *Lindsay, like his peers, is hard to categorize.* ❑ *Make a list of your child's toys and then categorize them as sociable or antisocial.* ● **cat|ego|ri|za|tion** /kæ̀tɪgəraɪzéɪʃʰn/ (**categorizations**) N-VAR ❑ *Her first novel defies easy categorization.*

cat|ego|ry ♦◇◇ /kǽtɪgɔri, BRIT kǽtɪgri/ (**categories**) N-COUNT If people or things are divided into **categories**, they are divided into groups in such a way that the members of each group are similar to each other in some way. ❑ *This book clearly falls into the category of fictionalized autobiography.*

Thesaurus   category의 참조어

N.   class, classification, grouping, kind, rank, sort, type

---

ca|ter /kéɪtər/ (**caters, catering, catered**) ◼ V-I In American English, to **cater to** a group of people means to provide all the things that they need or want. In British English, you say you **cater for** a person or group of people. ❑ *We cater to an exclusive clientele.* ◼ V-I In American English, to **cater to** something means to take it into account. In British English, you say you **cater for** something. ❑ *Exercise classes cater to all levels of fitness.* ❑ *...shops that cater for the needs of men.* ◼ V-I If a person or company **caters for** an occasion such as a wedding or a party, they provide food and drink for all the people there. ❑ *The chef is pleased to cater for vegetarian diets.* →see also **catering, self-catering**

◼ 구동사 이해하다, 깨닫다 ❑ 내가 그의 변한 모습을 깨닫기 전에 그는 내게서 얻을 수 있는 것을 가져갔다. ◼ 구동사 유행하다, 인기를 얻다 ❑ 이 아이디어는 오래전부터 있었지만 유행한 적은 없다.

구동사 본색을 드러내게 만들다, 꼬투리를 잡히게 만들다 [주로 영국영어] ❑ 탐정들은 그가 사기를 치면서 본색을 드러내기를 바라며 몇 달 동안 그의 뒤를 쫓았다. ❑ 그는 세부 사항에서 꼬투리 잡히고 싶지 않았다.

◼ 구동사 따라잡다 ❑ 나는 멈춰 서서 그녀가 따라오기를 기다렸다. ◼ 구동사 따라잡다 ❑ 발육이 늦은 아이들 대부분이 친구들을 따라잡을 것이다. ◼ 시즌 초에는 존이 나보다 나았지만 나는 따라잡기 위해서 분투해 왔다. ◼ 구동사 못했던 일을 하다 ❑ 밀린 독서 좀 하고 있었어. ◼ 구동사 친구와 밀린 이야기를 하다 ❑ 그 여인들은 서로의 건강과 가족에 대해 그간 밀린 이야기를 나누며 시간을 좀 보냈다. ◼ 수동 구동사 말려들다 ❑ 그 사람들 자체는 분쟁 당사자가 아니었다. 그들은 다만 분쟁에 말려든 것이었다.

◼ 구동사 찾아내다, 붙잡다 ❑ 어제 그는 법의 심판을 받았다. ◼ 구동사 옭아매기 시작하다 ❑ 그는 후에 성공적인 사업가가 되기는 했지만, 전과가 그를 옭아매기 시작했다.

형용사 눈에 잘 띄는, 귀에 쏙쏙 들어오는 ❑ 그 노래들은 귀에 잘 들어오고 신랄했다.

형용사 단호한 ❑ 성희롱 혐의에 대한 그의 단호한 부인 ● 단호히 부사 ❑ 그들은 단호하게 또 전적으로 혐의를 부인했다.

[영국영어 categorise] 타동사 분류하다, 유별하다 ❑ 린지는, 그의 영화와 마찬가지로 분류하기가 힘들다. ❑ 아이들의 장난감 목록을 만든 다음 친목적인 것과 그렇지 않은 것으로 분류하세요. ● 분류 가산명사 또는 불가산명사 ❑ 그녀의 첫 번째 소설은 쉽게 분류할 수가 없다.

가산명사 범주, 분류 ❑ 이 책은 분명히 허구를 가미한 자서전 범주에 들어간다.

가산명사 범주, 분류, 집단, 종류, 등급, 유형, 형

◼ 자동사 ―에게 제반 편의를 제공하다 ❑ 우리는 특수층 고객만을 대상으로 한다. ◼ 자동사 (요구에) 부응하다, 고려하다 ❑ 체육 수업들은 모든 체력수준에 다 맞추어 마련되어 있다. ❑ 남성들의 필요에 부응하는 상점들 ◼ 자동사 음식을 제공하다 ❑ 조리사는 기꺼이 채식주의 식단을 제공합니다.

ca|ter|er /keɪtərər/ (caterers) N-COUNT **Caterers** are people or companies that provide food and drink for a place such as an office or for special occasions such as weddings and parties. □ *The caterers were already laying out the tables for lunch.*

가산명사 요리 조달자, 연회 담당자 □ 연회 담당자들이 점심 식탁을 차리고 있었다.

ca|ter|ing /keɪtərɪŋ/ N-UNCOUNT **Catering** is the activity of providing food and drink for a large number of people, for example at weddings and parties. [also *the N, oft N n*] □ *His catering business made him a millionaire at 41.*

불가산명사 케이터링 (행사에 음식을 제공하는 업무) □ 그는 케이터링 사업을 통해 마흔 살에 백만장자가 되었다.

cat|er|pil|lar /kætərpɪlər/ (caterpillars) N-COUNT A **caterpillar** is a small, worm-like animal that feeds on plants and eventually develops into a butterfly or moth.

가산명사 모충, 애벌레

ca|thedral /kəθiːdrəl/ (cathedrals) N-COUNT A **cathedral** is a very large and important church which has a bishop in charge of it. □ *...St. Paul's Cathedral.*

가산명사 대성당 □ 세인트 폴 대성당

Catho|lic ◆◇◇ /kæθlɪk/ (Catholics) **1** ADJ The **Catholic** Church is the branch of the Christian Church that accepts the Pope as its leader and is based in the Vatican in Rome. □ *...the Catholic Church.* □ *...Catholic priests.* **2** N-COUNT A **Catholic** is a member of the Catholic Church. □ *At least nine out of ten Mexicans are baptised Catholics.* **3** ADJ If you describe a collection of things or people as **catholic**, you are emphasizing that they are very varied. □ *He was a man of catholic tastes, a lover of grand opera, history and the fine arts.*

1 형용사 가톨릭교의, 천주교의 □ 가톨릭교회 □ 가톨릭 사제 **2** 가산명사 가톨릭교도 □ 멕시코인들은 최소한 열에 아홉이 세례를 받은 가톨릭교도이다. **3** 형용사 매우 다양한, 광범위한 □ 그는 아주 다양한 취미를 가진 사람으로, 그랜드 오페라와 역사, 미술의 애호가였다.

Catho|li|cism /kəθɒlɪsɪzəm/ N-UNCOUNT **Catholicism** is the traditions, the behavior, and the set of Christian beliefs that are held by Catholics. □ *...her conversion to Catholicism.*

불가산명사 가톨릭교, 천주교 □ 그녀의 가톨릭교로의 개종

cat|tle /kætᵊl/ N-PLURAL **Cattle** are cows and bulls. □ *...the finest herd of beef cattle for two hundred miles.* →see **dairy**

복수명사 소, 축우 □ 2백 마일 내에서 가장 질 좋은 육우 무리

cat|walk /kætwɔːk/ (catwalks) **1** N-COUNT At a fashion show, the **catwalk** is a narrow platform that models walk along to display clothes. □ *On the catwalk the models stomped around in thigh-high leather boots.* **2** N-COUNT A **catwalk** is a narrow bridge high in the air, for example between two parts of a tall building, on the outside of a large structure, or over a stage. □ *...a catwalk overlooking a vast room.*

1 가산명사 패션쇼의 돌출 무대 □ 패션쇼 무대 위에서는 모델들이 허벅지까지 올라오는 가죽 부츠를 신고 처벅처벅 걸어 다녔다. **2** 가산명사 캣워크, 좁은 통로 다리 □ 커다란 방이 내려다보이는 좁은 통로

Cau|ca|sian /kɔːkeɪʒən/ (Caucasians) ADJ A **Caucasian** person is a white person. [FORMAL] □ *...a 25-year-old Caucasian male.* ● N-COUNT A **Caucasian** is someone who is Caucasian. □ *Ann Hamilton was a Caucasian from New England.*

형용사 백색 인종의 [격식체] □ 25세의 백인 남성 ● 가산명사 백인 □ 앤 해밀턴은 뉴잉글랜드 출신의 백인이었다.

cau|cus /kɔːkəs/ (caucuses) N-COUNT A **caucus** is a group of people within an organization who share similar aims and interests or who have a lot of influence. [FORMAL] □ *...the Black Caucus of minority congressmen.*

가산명사 이익 단체, 압력 단체, 대의원회 [격식체] □ 소수 인종 국회의원들 중의 흑인 의원 모임

caught /kɔːt/ **Caught** is the past tense and past participle of **catch**.

catch의 과거 및 과거 분사

Word Link   **cal, caul ≈ hot, heat : cauldron, calorie, scald**

caul|dron /kɔːldrən/ (cauldrons) N-COUNT A **cauldron** is a very large, round metal pot used for cooking over a fire. [LITERARY] □ *...a witch's cauldron.*

가산명사 큰 솥 [문예체] □ 마녀의 솥

cau|li|flow|er /kɒliflaʊər, BRIT kɒliflaʊəʳ/ (cauliflowers) N-VAR **Cauliflower** is a large round vegetable that has a hard white center surrounded by green leaves.

가산명사 또는 불가산명사 콜리플라워, 꽃양배추

cause ◆◆◆ /kɔːz/ (causes, causing, caused) **1** N-COUNT The **cause of** an event, usually a bad event, is the thing that makes it happen. □ *Smoking is the biggest preventable cause of death and disease.* **2** V-T To **cause** something, usually something bad, means to make it happen. □ *Attempts to limit family size among some minorities are likely to cause problems.* □ *This was a genuine mistake, but it did cause me some worry.* **3** N-UNCOUNT If you have **cause for** a particular feeling or action, you have good reasons for feeling it or doing it. □ *Only a few people can find any cause for celebration.* **4** N-COUNT A **cause** is an aim or principle which a group of people supports or is fighting for. □ *Refusing to have one leader has not helped the cause.* **5** PHRASE If you say that something is **for a good cause** or **in a good cause**, you mean that it is worth doing or giving to because it will help other people, for example by raising money for charity. □ *The Raleigh International Bike Ride is open to anyone who wants to raise money for a good cause.*

1 가산명사 원인 □ 흡연은 예방 가능성이 가장 큰, 사망과 질병의 원인이다. **2** 타동사 -의 원인이 되다, 일으키다 □ 몇몇 소수 집단 내에서 가족의 규모를 제한하려는 시도는 문제를 일으킬 것 같다. □ 이 일은 진짜 실수였지만 나는 그 때문에 정말 걱정을 좀 했다. **3** 불가산명사 동기 □ 오직 소수의 사람들만이 축하의 동기를 찾을 수 있다. **4** 가산명사 대의, 목적 □ 일인 지도 체제를 거부하는 것은 지금까지 대의에 도움이 되지 않았다. **5** 구 좋은 뜻으로, 유익한 목적으로 □ 롤리 국제 자전거 타기 운동은 좋은 뜻으로 모금 운동을 원하는 사람은 누구나 참가 가능하다.

Thesaurus   cause의 참조어

v.   generate, make, produce, provoke; (ant.) deter, prevent, stop **2**

Word Partnership   cause의 연어

N.   cause **of death 1**
cause **an accident**, cause **cancer**, cause **problems**, cause **a reaction 2**
cause **for concern 3**
v.   **determine the** cause **1**
support a cause **4**

'cause /kʌz, kɒz/ also **cause** CONJ **'Cause** is an informal way of saying **because**. □ *30 families are suffering 'cause they're out of work.*

접속사 because의 구어체 형태 □ 30가구가 실직 때문에 괴로움을 겪고 있다.

Word Link   **caut ≈ taking care : caution, cautious, precaution**

cau|tion /kɔːʃᵊn/ (cautions, cautioning, cautioned) **1** N-UNCOUNT **Caution** is great care which you take in order to avoid possible danger. □ *Extreme caution should be exercised when buying part-worn tyres.* **2** V-T If someone **cautions** you, they warn you about problems or danger. □ *Tony cautioned against misrepresenting the situation.* □ *The statement clearly was intended to caution Seoul against attempting to block the council's action again.* ● N-UNCOUNT **Caution** is also a

1 불가산명사 조심, 신중 □ 중고 타이어를 살 때는 극히 조심해야 한다. **2** 타동사 주의시키다, 경고하다 □ 토니는 상황을 와전하지 말도록 주의를 주었다. □ 그 성명은 또다시 서울시가 시의회의 활동을 방해하지 못하도록 경고하려는 의도를 명백히 담고 있었다. ● 불가산명사 주의, 경고 □ 그 수치들 속에는 재무부의

noun. ❑ *There was a note of caution for the Treasury in the figures.* ❸ V-T If someone who has broken the law **is cautioned** by the police, they are warned that if they break the law again official action will be taken against them. [BRIT] [usu passive] ❑ *The two men were cautioned but police say they will not be charged.* ● N-COUNT **Caution** is also a noun. ❑ *In November 1987 Paula escaped with a caution. In October 1988 she was fined.* ❹ V-T If someone who has been arrested **is cautioned**, the police warn them that anything they say may be used as evidence in a trial. [BRIT] [usu passive] ❑ *Nobody was cautioned after arrest.* ❺ to **err on the side of caution** →see **err**

대한 경고의 의미가 들어 있었다. ❸ 타동사 경고를 받다 [영국영어] ❑ 그 두 남자가 경고는 받았지만 고발되지는 않을 것이라고 경찰은 말한다. ● 가산명사 경고, 경고 ❑ 폴라는 1987년 11월에는 경고만 받고 풀려났다. 1988년 10월에는 벌금을 징수당했다. ❹ 타동사 경고하다 [영국영어] ❑ 체포된 후에 자신이 말하는 것들이 재판에서 증거로 쓰일 수 있다는 주의를 받은 사람은 아무도 없었다.

cau|tion|ary /kɔ́ʃənɛri, BRIT kɔ́ːʃənri/ ADJ A **cautionary** story or a **cautionary** note to a story is one that is intended to give a warning to people. ❑ *Barely fifteen months later, it has become a cautionary tale of the pitfalls of international mergers and acquisitions.*

형용사 경계의, 주의의 ❑ 겨우 열다섯 달 뒤, 그 일은 국제적 인수 및 합병의 함정을 경계하는 일화가 되었다.

Word Link | caut ≈ taking care : **caut**ion, **caut**ious, pre**caut**ion
---

cau|tious ♦◇◇ /kɔ́ʃəs/ ADJ Someone who is **cautious** acts very carefully in order to avoid possible danger. ❑ *The scientists are cautious about using enzyme therapy on humans.* ● **cau|tious|ly** ADV ❑ *David moved cautiously forward and looked over the edge.*

형용사 조심하는, 신중한 ❑ 그 과학자들은 사람에게 효소 요법을 쓰는 것에 대해 매우 조심스럽다. ● 조심스럽게, 신중하게 부사 ❑ 데이비드는 조심스럽게 나아가서 가장자리를 살펴보았다.

Thesaurus   cautious의 참조어

ADJ.   alert, careful, guarded, watchful; (ant.) careless, rash, reckless
---

cava|lier /kæ̀vəlíər/ ADJ If you describe a person or their behavior as **cavalier**, you are criticizing them because you think that they do not consider other people's feelings or take account of the seriousness of a situation. [DISAPPROVAL] ❑ *The Editor takes a cavalier attitude to the concept of fact checking.*

형용사 안중에도 없는 [탐탁잖음] ❑ 그 편집자는 사실 확인 원칙은 안중에도 없는 듯한 태도를 취한다.

cav|al|ry /kǽvəlri/ ❶ N-SING **The cavalry** is the part of an army that uses armored vehicles for fighting. ❑ *The Cavalry were exercising on Salisbury Plain.* ❷ N-SING **The cavalry** is the group of soldiers in an army who ride horses. ❑ *...a young cavalry officer.*

❶ 단수명사 기갑 부대 ❑ 기갑 부대는 솔즈베리 평원에서 훈련 중이었다. ❷ 단수명사 기병대 ❑ 젊은 기병대 장교

Word Link | cav ≈ hollow : **cav**e, **cav**ity, ex**cav**ate
---

cave ♦◇◇ /keɪv/ (**caves, caving, caved**) N-COUNT A **cave** is a large hole in the side of a cliff or hill, or one that is under the ground. ❑ *Outside the cave mouth the blackness of night was like a curtain.*

가산명사 굴, 동굴 ❑ 동굴 입구 바깥쪽에는 칠흑 같은 밤이 장막처럼 덮여 있었다.

▶**cave in** ❶ PHRASAL VERB If something such as a roof or a ceiling **caves in**, it collapses inward. ❑ *Part of the roof has caved in.* ❷ PHRASAL VERB If you **cave in**, you suddenly stop arguing or resisting, especially when people put pressure on you to stop. ❑ *After a ruinous strike, the union caved in.* ❑ *The Prime Minister has caved in to backbench pressure.*

❶ 구동사 꺼지다, 움푹 내려앉다 ❑ 지붕 일부가 내려앉았다. ❷ 구동사 굴복하다, 수그러들다 ❑ 파업이 처참한 실패로 돌아가자, 노조측은 수그러들었다. ❑ 수상은 하원 평의원들의 압력에 수그러들다.

cav|ern /kǽvərn/ (**caverns**) N-COUNT A **cavern** is a large deep cave.

가산명사 큰 동굴

cav|ern|ous /kǽvərnəs/ ADJ A **cavernous** room or building is very large inside, and so it reminds you of a cave. ❑ *Climbing steep stairs to the choir gallery you peer into a cavernous interior.*

형용사 동굴같이 내부가 넓은 ❑ 성가대석으로 가는 가파른 계단을 오르면 동굴처럼 넓은 내부가 들여다보입니다.

cavi|ar /kǽviɑr/ (**caviars**) also **caviare** N-MASS **Caviar** is the salted eggs of a fish called a sturgeon.

물질명사 캐비아 (철갑상어의 알젓)

cav|ity /kǽviti/ (**cavities**) ❶ N-COUNT A **cavity** is a space or hole in something such as a solid object or a person's body. [FORMAL] ❑ *...a cavity in the roof.* ❷ N-COUNT In dentistry, a **cavity** is a hole in a tooth, caused by decay. [TECHNICAL] →see **teeth**

❶ 가산명사 구멍, 공동 [격식체] ❑ 지붕에 난 구멍 ❷ 가산명사 (치아의) 구멍 [과학 기술]

cc /sí síː/ ❶ You use **cc** when referring to the volume or capacity of something such as the size of a car engine. **cc** is an abbreviation for "cubic centimeters." ❑ *...1,500 cc sports cars.* ❷ **cc** is used at the end of a business letter to indicate that a copy is being sent to another person. [BUSINESS] ❑ *...cc J. Chater, S. Cooper.*

❶ 시시 (부피의 단위) ❑ 1,500시시짜리 스포츠카 ❷ 참조 [경제] ❑ 참조 : J. 체이터, S. 쿠퍼

CCTV /sí sí tí ví/ N-UNCOUNT **CCTV** is an abbreviation for "closed-circuit television." ❑ *...a CCTV camera.*

불가산명사 폐쇄 회로 텔레비전 ❑ 폐쇄 회로 텔레비전 카메라

CD ♦◇◇ /sí díː/ (**CDs**) N-COUNT **CDs** are small plastic discs on which sound, especially music, is recorded. **CDs** can also be used to store information which can be read by a computer. **CD** is an abbreviation for **compact disc**. ❑ *The Beatles' Red and Blue compilations are issued on CD for the first time next month.* →see **DVD, laser**

가산명사 시디, 콤팩트디스크 ❑ 다음 달에 비틀즈의 '레드 앤 블루' 편집 앨범이 최초로 시디판으로 발매된다.

CD burn|er (**CD burners**) N-COUNT A **CD burner** is the same as a **CD writer**. [COMPUTING]

가산명사 (컴퓨터) 시디라이터 [컴퓨터]

CD play|er (**CD players**) N-COUNT A **CD player** is a machine on which you can play CDs.

가산명사 시디플레이어

CD-ROM /sí di rɒ́m/ (**CD-ROMs**) N-COUNT A **CD-ROM** is a CD on which a very large amount of information can be stored and then read using a computer. **CD-ROM** is an abbreviation for "compact disc read-only memory." [COMPUTING] ❑ *A single CD-ROM can hold more than 500 megabytes of data.*

가산명사 (컴퓨터) 시디롬 [컴퓨터] ❑ 시디롬 하나에 500메가바이트 이상의 데이터를 저장할 수 있다.

CD-ROM drive /sí di rɒ́m draɪv/ (**CD-ROM drives**) N-COUNT A **CD-ROM drive** is the device that you use with a computer to play CD-ROMs. [COMPUTING]

가산명사 (컴퓨터) 시디롬 드라이브 [컴퓨터]

CD writ|er (**CD writers**) N-COUNT A **CD writer** is a piece of computer equipment that you use for copying data from a computer onto a CD. [COMPUTING] ❑ *Users can download MP3 music files and record them directly onto a CD audio disc using a PC CD writer.*

가산명사 시디라이터 [컴퓨터] ❑ 사용자들은 엠피스리 음악 파일을 내려받은 다음 개인용 컴퓨터의 시디라이터를 사용해서 음악 시디에 바로 녹음할 수 있다.

a
b
c
d
e
f
g
h
i
j
k
l
m
n
o
p
q
r
s
t
u
v
w
x
y
z

cease ◆◇◇ /siːs/ (ceases, ceasing, ceased) **1** v-i If something **ceases**, it stops happening or existing. [FORMAL] ❑ *At one o'clock the rain had ceased.* **2** v-t If you **cease to** do something, you stop doing it. [FORMAL] ❑ *He never ceases to amaze me.* The secrecy about the President's condition had ceased to matter. **3** v-t If you **cease** something, you stop it happening or working. [FORMAL] ❑ *The Tundra Times, a weekly newspaper in Alaska, ceased publication this week.*

1 자동사 그치다, 끝나다 [격식체] ❑ 1시에 비가 그쳤다. **2** 타동사 그만두다, -하지 않게 되다 [격식체] ❑ 그는 끊임없이 나를 놀라게 한다. ● 대통령의 건강 상태에 대해 비밀을 엄수하는 것은 이미 의미가 없는 상태였다. **3** 타동사 중단하다 [격식체] ❑ 알래스카의 주간 신문인 툰드라 타임스가 이번 주에 발행을 중단했다.

Thesaurus	*cease*의 참조어
v.	end, finish, halt, quit, shut down, stop; (ant.) begin, continue, start **1**

cease|fire ◆◇◇ /siːsfaɪər/ (ceasefires) also **cease-fire** N-COUNT A **ceasefire** is an arrangement in which countries or groups of people that are fighting each other agree to stop fighting. ❑ *They have agreed to a ceasefire after three years of conflict.*

가산명사 정전 ❑ 그들은 삼 년간의 전투 끝에 정전에 합의했다.

ce|dar /siːdər/ (cedars) N-COUNT A **cedar** is a large evergreen tree with wide branches and small thin leaves called needles. ● N-UNCOUNT **Cedar** is the wood of this tree. ❑ *The yacht is built of cedar strip planking.*

가산명사 삼목 ● 불가산명사 삼목재 ❑ 그 요트는 삼목 판자로 만들어졌다.

cede /siːd/ (cedes, ceding, ceded) v-t If someone in a position of authority **cedes** land or power **to** someone else, they let them have the land or power, often as a result of military or political pressure. [FORMAL] ❑ *Only a short campaign took place in Puerto Rico, but after the war Spain ceded the island to America.*

타동사 (권력을) 양도하다; (영토를) 할양하다 [격식체] ❑ 푸에르토리코에서는 아주 짧은 교전만이 일어났지만, 전쟁이 끝난 후 스페인은 미국에 그 섬을 할양했다.

ceil|ing /siːlɪŋ/ (ceilings) **1** N-COUNT A **ceiling** is the horizontal surface that forms the top part or roof inside a room. ❑ *The rooms were spacious, with tall windows and high ceilings.* **2** N-COUNT A **ceiling on** something such as prices or wages is an official upper limit that cannot be broken. ❑ *...an informal agreement to put a ceiling on salaries.*

1 가산명사 천장 ❑ 그 방들은 널찍했고, 창문과 천장이 높았다. **2** 가산명사 최고 한도 ❑ 봉급에 최고 한도를 두기로 하는 비공식 합의

cel|e|brate ◆◇◇ /sɛlɪbreɪt/ (celebrates, celebrating, celebrated) **1** v-t/v-i If you **celebrate**, you do something enjoyable because of a special occasion or to mark someone's success. ❑ *I was in a mood to celebrate.* **2** v-t If an organization or country **is celebrating** an anniversary, it has existed for that length of time and is doing something special because of it. ❑ *The Society is celebrating its tenth anniversary this year.* **3** v-t When priests **celebrate** Holy Communion or Mass, they officially perform the actions and ceremonies that are involved. ❑ *Pope John Paul celebrated mass today in a city in central Poland.*

1 타동사/자동사 축하하다 ❑ 나는 축하하고 싶은 기분이었다. **2** 타동사 경축하다 ❑ 그 단체는 올해 10주년을 맞이했다. **3** 타동사 (의식 또는 제전을) 집전하다 ❑ 교황 요한 바오로는 오늘 폴란드 중부의 한 도시에서 미사를 집전했다.

cel|e|brat|ed /sɛlɪbreɪtɪd/ ADJ A **celebrated** person or thing is famous and much admired. ❑ *He was soon one of the most celebrated young painters in England.*

형용사 유명한, 고명한 ❑ 그는 곧 영국에서 가장 유명한 젊은 화가들 중 한 사람이 되었다.

cel|e|bra|tion ◆◇◇ /sɛlɪbreɪʃən/ (celebrations) **1** N-COUNT A **celebration** is a special enjoyable event that people organize because something pleasant has happened or because it is someone's birthday or anniversary. ❑ *I can tell you, there was a celebration in our house that night.* **2** N-SING The **celebration of** something is praise and appreciation which is given to it. ❑ *This was not a memorial service but a celebration of his life.*

1 가산명사 축전, 축하 행사 ❑ 정말로 그날 밤 우리 집에서는 잔치가 벌어졌어요. **2** 단수명사 칭송; 찬사 ❑ 이는 추도식이 아니라 그의 생애에 보내는 찬사였다.

ce|leb|rity /sɪlɛbrɪti/ (celebrities) **1** N-COUNT A **celebrity** is someone who is famous, especially in areas of entertainment such as movies, music, writing, or sports. ❑ *In 1944, at the age of 30, Hersey suddenly became a celebrity.* **2** N-UNCOUNT If a person or thing achieves **celebrity**, they become famous, especially in areas of entertainment such as movies, music, writing, or sports. ❑ *Joanna has finally made it to the first rank of celebrity after 25 years as an actress.*

1 가산명사 명사, 유명인 ❑ 1944년 30세의 나이에, 허시는 갑자기 명사가 되었다. **2** 불가산명사 명성 ❑ 조안나는 여배우로서 25년을 보낸 끝에 마침내 최고의 명성을 획득했다.

cel|ery /sɛləri/ N-UNCOUNT **Celery** is a vegetable with long pale green stalks. It is eaten raw in salads. ❑ *...a stick of celery.*

불가산명사 샐러리 ❑ 셀러리 한 줄기

ce|les|tial /sɪlɛstiəl/ ADJ **Celestial** is used to describe things relating to heaven or to the sky. [LITERARY] ❑ *...the clusters of celestial bodies in the ever-expanding universe.*

형용사 하늘의; 천체의 [문예체] ❑ 끝없이 팽창하는 우주 속의 천체 성단들

celi|ba|cy /sɛlɪbəsi/ N-UNCOUNT **Celibacy** is the state of being celibate. ❑ *...priests who violate their vows of celibacy.*

불가산명사 독신, 금욕 ❑ 금욕 서약을 어긴 성직자들

celi|bate /sɛlɪbɪt/ (celibates) **1** ADJ Someone who is **celibate** does not marry or have sex, because of their religious beliefs. ❑ *The Pope bluntly told the world's priests yesterday to stay celibate.* ● N-COUNT A **celibate** is someone who is celibate. ❑ *...the USA's biggest group of celibates.* **2** ADJ Someone who is **celibate** does not have sex during a particular period of their life. ❑ *I was celibate for two years.*

1 형용사 순결주의의 ❑ 교황은 어제 전 세계의 성직자들에게 순결주의를 지키라고 단도직입적으로 말했다. ● 가산명사 독신주의자 ❑ 미국 최대의 독신주의자 단체 **2** 형용사 (일정 기간 동안) 성관계를 갖지 않는 ❑ 나는 이 년 동안 성관계를 갖지 않았다.

cell ◆◆◇ /sɛl/ (cells) **1** N-COUNT A **cell** is the smallest part of an animal or plant that is able to function independently. Every animal or plant is made up of millions of cells. ❑ *Those cells divide and give many other different types of cells.* ❑ *...blood cells.* **2** N-COUNT A **cell** is a small room in which a prisoner is locked. A **cell** is also a small room in which a monk or nun lives. ❑ *Do you recall how many prisoners were placed in each cell?* →see **clone**, **skin**

1 가산명사 세포 ❑ 그 세포들은 분열하여 다양한 형태의 다른 세포들을 생성한다. ❑ 혈구 **2** 가산명사 작은 감방, 수도원의 작은 방 ❑ 좁은 감방 하나마다 몇 명의 죄수들이 갇혀 있었는지 생각나세요?

cel|lar /sɛlər/ (cellars) **1** N-COUNT A **cellar** is a room underneath a building, which is often used for storing things in. ❑ *The box of papers had been stored in a cellar at the family home.* **2** N-COUNT A person's or restaurant's **cellar** is the collection of different wines that they have. ❑ *Choose a superb wine to complement your meal from our extensive wine cellar.*

1 가산명사 지하실 ❑ 그 서류 상자는 가족 자택의 지하실에 보관되어 왔다. **2** 가산명사 포도주 저장실 ❑ 방대한 저희 포도주 저장실에서 당신의 식사에 곁들일 훌륭한 포도주를 골라 보세요.

cel|list /tʃɛlɪst/ (cellists) N-COUNT A **cellist** is someone who plays the cello.

가산명사 첼로 연주자

cel|lo /tʃɛloʊ/ (cellos) N-VAR A **cello** is a musical instrument with four strings that looks like a large violin. You play the cello with a bow while sitting down and holding it upright between your legs. →see **orchestra**

가산명사 또는 불가산명사 첼로

cell|phone /sɛlfoʊn/ (cellphones) also **cell-phone** N-COUNT A **cellphone** is the same as a **cellular phone**. [mainly AM] →see Word Web: **cellphone**

가산명사 휴대 전화 [주로 미국영어]

Word Web   cellphone

The word **"cell"** does not refer to something inside the **cellular phone** itself. It describes the area around a **wireless transmitter**. The electrical system and **battery** in today's **mobile** phones are tiny. This makes their electronic **signals** weak. They can't travel very far. Therefore today's **cellular** phone systems need a lot of closely-spaced cells. When you make a call, your phone connects to the transmitter with the strongest signal. Then it chooses a **channel** and connects you to the number you dialed. If you are driving, **stations** in several different cells may handle your call.

cel|lu|lar /sɛlyələr/ ADJ **Cellular** means relating to the cells of animals or plants. ❑ *Many toxic effects can be studied at the cellular level.* →see **cellphone**

형용사 세포의 ❑ 다양한 독성 효과를 세포 단계에서 연구할 수 있다.

cel|lu|lar phone (**cellular phones**) N-COUNT A **cellular phone** or **cellular telephone** is a type of telephone which does not need wires to connect it to a telephone system. [mainly AM; BRIT **mobile phone**] →see **cellphone**

가산명사 휴대 전화 [주로 미국영어; 영국영어 mobile phone]

cel|lu|lite /sɛlyəlaɪt/ N-UNCOUNT **Cellulite** is lumpy fat which people may get under their skin, especially on their thighs. ❑ *...an Italian-made product that is said to eradicate cellulite within weeks.*

불가산명사 셀룰라이트 (피하 지방) ❑ 수 주 내에 셀룰라이트를 완전 제거한다는 이탈리아산 제품

Celsius /sɛlsiəs/ ADJ **Celsius** is a scale for measuring temperature, in which water freezes at 0 degrees and boils at 100 degrees. It is represented by the symbol °C. [n/num ADJ] ❑ *...Highest temperature 11° Celsius, that's 52° Fahrenheit.* ● N-UNCOUNT **Celsius** is also a noun. ❑ *The thermometer shows the temperature in Celsius and Fahrenheit.* →see **temperature**

형용사 섭씨의 ❑ 최고 기온은 섭씨 11도, 즉 화씨 52도. ● 불가산명사 섭씨 ❑ 그 온도계는 온도를 섭씨와 화씨로 나타내 줍니다.

ce|ment /sɪmɛnt/ (**cements, cementing, cemented**) **1** N-UNCOUNT **Cement** is a gray powder which is mixed with sand and water in order to make concrete. ❑ *Builders have trouble getting the right amount of cement into their concrete.* **2** N-UNCOUNT **Cement** is the same as **concrete**. ❑ *...the hard cold cement floor.* **3** N-UNCOUNT Glue that is made for sticking particular substances together is sometimes called **cement**. ❑ *Stick the pieces on with tile cement.* **4** V-T Something that **cements** a relationship or agreement makes it stronger. ❑ *Nothing cements a friendship between countries so much as trade.* **5** V-T If things **are cemented** together, they are stuck or fastened together. [usu passive] ❑ *Most artificial joints are cemented into place.*

1 불가산명사 시멘트 ❑ 건설 인부들은 콘크리트에 적정한 양의 시멘트를 넣는 데 어려움을 겪는다. **2** 불가산명사 콘크리트 ❑ 딱딱하고 차가운 콘크리트 바닥 **3** 불가산명사 접착제 ❑ 조각들을 타일 접착제로 붙이세요. **4** 타동사 공고히 하다 ❑ 무역만큼 나라 간의 친선을 공고히 하는 것은 없다. **5** 타동사 접합되다 ❑ 대부분의 인공 관절들은 제자리에 접합된다.

cem|etery /sɛmətɛri, BRIT sɛmətri/ (**cemeteries**) N-COUNT A **cemetery** is a place where dead people's bodies or their ashes are buried.

가산명사 묘지

cen|sor /sɛnsər/ (**censors, censoring, censored**) **1** V-T If someone in authority **censors** letters or the media, they officially examine them and cut out any information that is regarded as secret. ❑ *The military-backed government has heavily censored the news.* **2** N-COUNT A **censor** is a person who has been officially appointed to examine letters or the media and to cut out any parts that are regarded as secret. ❑ *The report was cleared by the American military censors.* **3** V-T If someone in authority **censors** a book, play, or movie, they officially examine it and cut out any parts that are considered to be immoral or inappropriate. ❑ *The Late Show censored the band's live version of "Bullet in the Head".* **4** N-COUNT A **censor** is a person who has been officially appointed to examine plays, movies, and books and to cut out any parts that are considered to be immoral. ❑ *...the British Board of Film Censors.*

1 타동사 검열하다 ❑ 군대를 등에 업은 정부가 뉴스를 심하게 검열해 왔다. **2** 가산명사 검열관 ❑ 그 보고서는 미국 군사 검열관의 검열을 거쳤다. **3** 타동사 삭제하다, 잘라내다 ❑ '레이트 쇼'에서는 그 밴드가 라이브로 연주하는 '머리에 박힌 총알'을 삭제했다. **4** 가산명사 검열관 ❑ 영국 영화 검열관 회의

Word Link   ship ≈ condition or state : censor**ship**, citizen**ship**, friend**ship**

cen|sor|ship /sɛnsərʃɪp/ N-UNCOUNT **Censorship** is the censoring of books, plays, movies, or reports, especially by government officials, because they are considered immoral or secret in some way. ❑ *The government today announced that press censorship was being lifted.*

불가산명사 검열 ❑ 정부는 오늘 언론 검열이 해제되고 있다고 발표했다.

cen|sure /sɛnʃər/ (**censures, censuring, censured**) V-T If you **censure** someone **for** something that they have done, you tell them that you strongly disapprove of it. [FORMAL] ❑ *The ethics committee may take a decision to admonish him or to censure him.* ● N-UNCOUNT **Censure** is also a noun. ❑ *It is a controversial policy which has attracted international censure.*

타동사 책망하다, 견책하다 [격식체] ❑ 윤리 위원회가 그에게 경고나 견책 결정을 내릴지도 모른다. ● 불가산명사 책망, 견책 ❑ 그것은 국제적인 책망을 받아 온, 논란의 여지가 있는 정책이다.

cen|sus /sɛnsəs/ (**censuses**) N-COUNT A **census** is an official survey of the population of a country that is carried out in order to find out how many people live there and to obtain details of such things as people's ages and jobs. ❑ *...the first analysis of the 2001 census.* →see Word Web: **census**

가산명사 인구 조사 ❑ 2001년 인구 조사에 대한 첫 분석

cent /sɛnt/ (**cents**) N-COUNT A **cent** is a small unit of money worth one hundredth of some currencies, for example the dollar and the euro. ❑ *A cup of rice which cost thirty cents a few weeks ago is now being sold for up to one dollar.*

가산명사 센트 ❑ 몇 주 전에 30센트였던 쌀 1컵이 지금은 최고 1달러에 팔리고 있다.

cen|te|nary /sɛntɛnəri, BRIT sɛntiːnəri/ (**centenaries**) N-COUNT A **centenary** is the same as a **centennial**. [mainly BRIT; AM **centennial**] ❑ *This week is the centenary of the death of the world-famous Dutch painter, Vincent Van Gogh.*

가산명사 100주기 [주로 영국영어; 미국영어 centennial] ❑ 이번 주는 세계적으로 유명한 네덜란드 화가 빈센트 반 고흐의 사망 100주기이다.

Word Link   enn ≈ year : cent**enn**ial, mill**enn**ium, per**enn**ial

cen|ten|nial /sɛntɛniəl/ N-SING The **centennial of** an event such as someone's birth is the 100th anniversary of that event. [mainly AM, also BRIT, FORMAL] [oft N n] ❑ *The centennial Olympics will be in Atlanta, Georgia.*

단수명사 100주년 [주로 미국영어, 영국영어, 격식체] ❑ 100주년을 맞는 올림픽 대회가 조지아 주 애틀랜타에서 열릴 것이다.

cen|ter ♦♦♦ /sɛntər/ (**centers, centering, centered**) [BRIT **centre**] **1** N-COUNT A **center** is a building where people have meetings, take part in a particular

[영국영어 centre] **1** 가산명사 센터, 종합 시설 ❑ 그녀는 현재 지역 문화 회관에서 도예 강좌를 한다.

Word Web   census

Every 10 years the U.S. government conducts a **census**. This **survey counts** the number of people and provides details about the way they live. It determines how many delegates each state sends to the House of Representatives. It also affects how the federal government spends its money. The census takes months to complete. In March, the Census Bureau* mails out around 100 million **questionnaires**. Government employees also deliver about 22 million more forms in person. In April, census workers visit people who haven't returned their forms. All the information must be pulled together by December 31 of that year.

Census Bureau: a part of the government that collects and reports data about the population and economy.

activity, or get help of some kind. ❑ *She now also does pottery classes at a community center.* **2** N-COUNT If an area or town is a **center** for an industry or activity, that industry or activity is very important there. ❑ *London is also the major international insurance center.* **3** N-COUNT The **center** of something is the middle of it. ❑ *A large wooden table dominates the center of the room.* **4** N-COUNT The **center** of a town or city is the part where there are the most stores and businesses and where a lot of people come from other areas to work or shop. ❑ *...the city center.* **5** N-COUNT If something or someone is at the **center of** a situation, they are the most important thing or person involved. ❑ *...the man at the center of the controversy.* **6** N-COUNT If someone or something is the **center of** attention or interest, people are giving them a lot of attention. ❑ *The rest of the cast was used to her being the center of attention.* **7** N-SING In politics, **the center** refers to groups and their beliefs, when they are considered to be neither left-wing nor right-wing. ❑ *The Democrats have become a party of the center.* **8** V-T/V-I If something **centers** or is **centered on** a particular thing or person, that thing or person is the main subject of attention. ❑ *...the improvement was the result of a plan which centered on academic achievement and personal motivation.* ❑ *All his concerns were centered around himself rather than Rachel.* ● **-centered** COMB in ADJ ❑ *...a child-centered approach to teaching.* **9** V-T/V-I If an industry or event **is centered** in a place, or if it **centers** there, it takes place to the greatest extent there. ❑ *The fighting has been centered around the town of Vucovar.* ❑ *The disturbances have centered round the two main university areas.* **10** →see also **community center, shopping center**

Word Partnership   center의 연어

N.	**research** center **1**
	center **of a circle** **3**
	city/town center **4**
	center **of attention** **6**

-centered /-sɛntərd/ [BRIT **-centred**] COMB in ADJ **-centered** can be added to adjectives and nouns to indicate what kind of a center something has. ❑ *...lemon-centered white chocolates.* →see also **center, self-centered**

center|piece /sɛntərpis/ (**centerpieces**) [BRIT **centrepiece**] N-COUNT The **centerpiece** of something is the best or most interesting part of it. ❑ *The centerpiece of the plan is the idea of regular referendums, initiated by voters.*

cen|ti|grade /sɛntɪgreɪd/ ADJ **Centigrade** is a scale for measuring temperature, in which water freezes at 0 degrees and boils at 100 degrees. It is represented by the symbol °C. ❑ *...daytime temperatures of up to forty degrees centigrade.* ● N-UNCOUNT **Centigrade** is also a noun. ❑ *The number at the bottom is the recommended water temperature in Centigrade.* →see **temperature**

cen|ti|me|ter /sɛntɪmitər/ (**centimeters**) [BRIT **centimetre**] N-COUNT A **centimeter** is a unit of length in the metric system equal to ten millimeters or one-hundredth of a meter. ❑ *...a tiny fossil plant, only a few centimeters high.*

cen|tral ♦♦♦ /sɛntrəl/ **1** ADJ Something that is **central** is in the middle of a place or area. ❑ *...Central America's Caribbean coast.* ❑ *The disruption has now spread and is affecting a large part of central Liberia.* ● **cen|tral|ly** ADV ❑ *The main cabin has its full-sized double bed centrally placed with plenty of room around it.* **2** ADJ A place that is **central** is easy to reach because it is in the center of a city, town, or particular area. ❑ *...a central location in the capital.* ● **cen|tral|ly** ADV ❑ *...this centrally located hotel, situated on the banks of the Marne Canal.* **3** ADJ A **central** group or organization makes all the important decisions throughout a larger organization or a country. [ADJ n] ❑ *There is a lack of trust towards the central government in Rome.* ● **cen|tral|ly** ADV ❑ *This is a centrally planned economy.* **4** ADJ The **central** person or thing in a particular situation is the most important one. ❑ *Black dance music has been central to mainstream pop since the early '60s.*

Word Partnership   central의 연어

N.	central **location** **2**
	central **government** **3**

2 가산명사 중심지 ❑ 런던은 또한 국제 보험의 주요 중심지이기도 하다. **3** 가산명사 가운데, 중앙 ❑ 커다란 나무 탁자가 그 방 한가운데 떡 하니 놓여 있다. **4** 가산명사 중심가 ❑ 도시 중심가 **5** 가산명사 (사건 등의) 중심 ❑ 논란의 중심에 있는 남자 **6** 가산명사 (흥미 또는 관심 등의) 중심 ❑ 나머지 출연진들은 그녀에게 이목이 집중되는 것에 익숙했다. **7** 단수명사 중도파 ❑ 민주당은 중도 정당이 되었다. **8** 타동사/자동사 중심을 두다; 집중되다 ❑ 그러한 개선은 계획을 학문적 성취와 개인의 동기 부여에 중점을 둔 결과였다. ❑ 그의 모든 관심은 레이첼보다는 자기 자신에게 집중되어 있었다. ● - 중심의 복합형-형용사 ❑ 아동 중심 교수법 **9** 타동사/자동사 집중되다 ❑ 전투는 부코바르 읍 주위에서 집중적으로 진행되어 왔다. ❑ 그와 같은 소동은 두 곳의 주요 대학 지역 주변에 집중되어 왔다.

[영국영어 -centred] 복합형-형용사 -이 속에 든 ❑ 속에 레몬이 들어 있는 화이트 초콜릿

[영국영어 centrepiece] 가산명사 핵심 ❑ 그 계획의 핵심은 유권자들이 발의한 정기적 국민 투표 제안이다.

형용사 섭씨의 ❑ 섭씨 사실 도까지 이르는 주간 기온 ● 불가산명사 섭씨 ❑ 아래쪽에 적힌 숫자는 권장 수온을 섭씨로 표시한 것입니다.

[영국영어 centimetre] 가산명사 센티미터 ❑ 키가 몇 센티미터밖에 안 되는 작은 화석 식물

1 형용사 중앙의 ❑ 중앙아메리카의 카리브 해안 ❑ 그와 같은 혼란은 이제 널리 퍼졌고 라이베리아 중부의 넓은 지역에 영향을 미치고 있다. ● 중심으로, 중앙에 부사 ❑ 주 객실에는 풀사이즈의 2인용 침대가 주변에 충분한 공간을 두고 중앙에 놓여 있다. **2** 형용사 중심부의 ❑ 수도에서도 중심부의 입지 ● 중심부에 부사 ❑ 마른 운하 기슭에 자리한, 중심부에 위치한 이 호텔 **3** 형용사 중앙의, 중심적인 ❑ 로마에서는 중앙 정부에 대한 신뢰가 결여되어 있다. ● 중앙 집권적으로 부사 ❑ 이것은 중앙 집권적 계획 경제이다. **4** 형용사 중심 되는 ❑ 흑인 댄스 음악은 60년대 초 이래로 주류 대중음악의 중심을 차지해 왔다.

cen|tral heat|ing N-UNCOUNT **Central heating** is a heating system for buildings. Air or water is heated in one place and travels around a building through pipes and radiators. ❑ *I am thinking of installing central heating before I sell the flat.*

불가산명사 중앙난방 ❑아파트를 팔기 전에 중앙난방 설비를 갖추는 것을 생각하고 있다.

cen|tral|ize /sɛntrəlaɪz/ (**centralizes, centralizing, centralized**) [BRIT also **centralise**] V-T To **centralize** a country, state, or organization means to create a system in which one central group of people gives instructions to regional groups. ❑ *In the mass production era multinational firms tended to centralize their operations.* ● **cen|tral|iza|tion** /sɛntrəlaɪzeɪʃⁿn/ N-UNCOUNT *Nowhere in Britain has bureaucratic centralization proceeded with more pace than in Scotland.*

[영국영어 centralise] 타동사 중앙 집권화하다 ❑ 대량 생산 시대에 다국적 기업들은 운영권을 중앙 집중화하는 경향이 있었다. ● 중앙 집권 불가산명사 ❑영국 내 어느 곳도 관료 정치의 중앙 집권화가 스코틀랜드보다 빠른 속도로 진행된 곳이 없다.

cen|tre /sɛntər/ →see **center**

cen|tu|ry ♦♦♦ /sɛntʃəri/ (**centuries**) **1** N-COUNT A **century** is a period of a hundred years that is used when stating a date. For example, the 19th century was the period from 1801 to 1900. ❑ *The material position of the Church had been declining since the late eighteenth century.* **2** N-COUNT A **century** is any period of a hundred years. ❑ *The drought there is the worst in a century.* **3** N-COUNT In cricket, a **century** is a score of one hundred runs or more by one batsman. ❑ *Bassano scored a century in each innings.*

1 가산명사 세기 ❑18세기 후반 이래로 교회의 세속적 지위는 계속 쇠퇴해 가고 있었다. **2** 가산명사 백 년 ❑그곳의 가뭄은 100년 만에 최악이었다. **3** 가산명사 (크리켓에서) 100점 ❑바사노는 매 이닝마다 100점을 득점했다.

CEO /siː iː oʊ/ (**CEOs**) N-COUNT **CEO** is an abbreviation for **chief executive officer**.

가산명사 최고 경영자

ce|ram|ic /sɪræmɪk/ (**ceramics**) **1** N-MASS **Ceramic** is clay that has been heated to a very high temperature so that it becomes hard. ❑ *...ceramic tiles.* **2** N-COUNT **Ceramics** are ceramic ornaments or objects. ❑ *...a collection of Chinese ceramics.* **3** N-UNCOUNT **Ceramics** is the art of making artistic objects out of clay. ❑ *He did a degree in ceramics at Middlesex University.* →see **pottery**

1 물질명사 세라믹 ❑세라믹 타일 **2** 가산명사 도자 제품; 도자 장신구 ❑중국 도자품 수집물 **3** 불가산명사 도예 ❑그는 미들섹스 대학에서 도예 전공으로 학위를 취득했다.

ce|real /sɪəriəl/ (**cereals**) **1** N-MASS **Cereal** or **breakfast cereal** is a food made from grain. It is mixed with milk and eaten for breakfast. ❑ *I have a glass of fruit juice and a bowl of cereal every morning.* **2** N-COUNT **Cereals** are plants such as wheat, corn, or rice that produce grain. ❑ *...the rich cereal-growing districts of the Paris Basin.*

1 물질명사 시리얼 ❑나는 매일 아침 과일 주스 한 잔과 시리얼 한 그릇을 먹는다. **2** 가산명사 곡류 ❑풍부한 곡류가 자라는 파리 바쟁 지구

cere|bral /sɛrɪbrəl, BRIT sɪriːbrəl/ ADJ If you describe someone or something as **cerebral**, you mean that they are intellectual rather than emotional. [FORMAL] ❑ *Washington struck me as a precarious place from which to publish such a cerebral newspaper.* **2** ADJ **Cerebral** means relating to the brain. [MEDICAL] [ADJ n] ❑ *...a cerebral hemorrhage.*

1 형용사 지적인; 지성에 호소하는 [격식체] ❑나는 워싱턴이 그와 같은 지적인 신문을 발간하기는 불안정한 곳이라는 인상을 받았다. **2** 형용사 뇌의 [의학] ❑뇌출혈

cer|emo|nial /sɛrɪmoʊniəl/ **1** ADJ Something that is **ceremonial** relates to a ceremony or is used in a ceremony. [ADJ n] ❑ *He represented the nation on ceremonial occasions.* **2** ADJ A position, function, or event that is **ceremonial** is considered to be representative of an institution, but has very little authority or influence. ❑ *Up to now the post of president has been largely ceremonial.* →see **funeral**

1 형용사 의식의, 공식적인 ❑그는 공식 행사에서 국가를 대표했다. **2** 형용사 의례적인, 형식적인 ❑지금까지 대통령직은 주로 상징적이었다.

cer|emo|ny ♦♦◇ /sɛrɪmoʊni, BRIT sɛrɪməni/ (**ceremonies**) **1** N-COUNT A **ceremony** is a formal event such as a wedding. ❑ *...his grandmother's funeral, a private ceremony attended only by the family.* **2** N-UNCOUNT **Ceremony** consists of the special things that are said and done on very formal occasions. ❑ *The Republic was proclaimed in public with great ceremony.* →see **graduation, wedding**

1 가산명사 의식 ❑가족들만 참석하여 사적으로 치러진 그의 할머니의 장례식 **2** 불가산명사 의식, 예식 ❑성대한 의식과 함께 공화국이 공포되었다.

---

certain

① BEING SURE
② REFERRING AND INDICATING AMOUNT

---

① cer|tain ♦◇◇ /sɜrtⁿn/ **1** ADJ If you are **certain** about something, you firmly believe it is true and have no doubt about it. If you are not **certain** about something, you do not have definite knowledge about it. [v-link ADJ, oft ADJ that/wh, ADJ of/about n] ❑ *She's absolutely certain she's going to make it in the world.* ❑ *We are not certain whether the appendix had already burst or not.* **2** ADJ If you say that something is **certain** to happen, you mean that it will definitely happen. ❑ *However, the scheme is certain to meet opposition from fishermen's leaders.* ❑ *It's not certain they'll accept that candidate if he wins.* ❑ *The Prime Minister is heading for certain defeat if he forces a vote.* **3** ADJ If you say that something is **certain**, you firmly believe that it is true, or have definite knowledge about it. [v-link ADJ, oft v-link ADJ that/wh] ❑ *One thing is certain, both have the utmost respect for each other.* **4** PHRASE If you know something **for certain**, you have no doubt at all about it. ❑ *She couldn't know what time he'd go, or even for certain that he'd go at all.* **5** PHRASE If you **make certain that** something is the way you want or expect it to be, you take action to ensure that it is. ❑ *Parents should make certain that the children spend enough time doing homework.*

1 형용사 확신하는 ❑그녀는 자신이 그 일을 해 내리라고 절대적으로 확신한다. ❑맹장이 이미 터졌는지 아닌지는 잘 모르겠습니다. **2** 형용사 확실한 ❑하지만 그 계획은 어민 지도자들로부터의 반대에 부닥칠 것이 확실하다. ❑만약 그 후보가 승리한다고 해도 그들이 받아들일지는 확실치 않다. ❑만약 수상이 투표를 강행한다면, 그는 틀림없이 패배하고 말 것이다. **3** 형용사 확실한 ❑한 가지 확실한 것은, 양쪽 모두 상대방을 극도로 존중한다는 것이다. **4** 구 확실히 ❑그가 몇 시에 갈지, 심지어는 그가 확실히 가긴 가는 건지조차 그녀는 알 수 없었다. **5** 구 확실하게 하다, 확인하다 ❑부모는 아이들이 충분히 시간을 들여 숙제를 하는지 확인해야 한다.

Thesaurus   certain의 참조어

ADJ.   definite, known, positive, sure, true, unmistakable ①**3**

---

② cer|tain ♦♦◇ /sɜrtⁿn/ **1** ADJ You use **certain** to indicate that you are referring to one particular thing, person, or group, although you are not saying exactly which it is. [det ADJ, ADJ n] ❑ *There will be certain people who'll say "I told you so!"* ❑ *You owe a certain person a sum of money.* **2** QUANT When you refer to **certain of** a group of people or things, you are referring to some particular members of that group. [FORMAL] [QUANT of def-pl-n] ❑ *They'll have to give up completely on certain of their studies.* **3** ADJ You use **a certain** to indicate that something such as a quality or condition exists, and often to suggest that it is not great in amount or degree. [a ADJ sing-n/n-uncount] ❑ *That was the very reason why he felt a certain bitterness.*

1 형용사 어떤 ❑"내가 그렇게 말했지!"라고 할 사람들이 있을 것이다. ❑당신은 어떤 사람에게 얼마간의 빚이 있다. **2** 수량사 몇몇, 일부 [격식체] ❑그들이 연구 중 일부는 완전히 포기해야만 할 것이다. **3** 형용사 어느 정도의, 다소의 ❑그것이 바로 그가 다소 씁쓸해 하는 이유였다.

a b c d e f g h i j k l m n o p q r s t u v w x y z

cer|tain|ly ♦♦◇ /sɜ́rt³nli/ ■ ADV You use **certainly** to emphasize what you are saying when you are making a statement. [EMPHASIS] [ADV with cl/group] ❑ *The public is certainly getting tired of hearing about it.* ❑ *The bombs are almost certainly part of a much bigger conspiracy.* ② ADV You use **certainly** when you are agreeing with what someone has said. [ADV as reply] ❑ *"In any case you remained friends."* — *"Certainly."* ③ ADV You say **certainly not** when you want to say "no" in a strong way. [EMPHASIS] [ADV as reply] ❑ *"Perhaps it would be better if I withdrew altogether."* — *"Certainly not!"*

> You use **certainly** to emphasize that what you say is definitely true. ❑ *His death was certainly not an accident.* You use **surely** to express disagreement or surprise. ❑ *Surely you care about what happens to her.* Both British and American speakers use **certainly** to agree with requests and statements. Note that American speakers also use **surely** in this way. ❑ *"Can I have a drink?"* — *"Why, surely."*

■ 부사 확실히 [강조] ❑ 대중은 확실히 그것에 대해 듣는 걸 지겨워하고 있다. ❑ 폭탄이 훨씬 더 커다란 음모의 일부임은 거의 확실하다. ② 부사 물론, 그럼 ❑ "어떤 요청이든 너희들은 계속 친구가 되어 주겠지." "암, 그래야지." ③ 부사 천만에 [강조] ❑ "아마도 내가 완전히 물러나는 편이 더 나을 거야." "천만에!"

> certainly는 말하는 내용이 분명히 사실임을 강조할 때 쓴다. ❑ 그의 죽음은 분명히 사고가 아니었다. surely는 동의하지 않음 또는 놀람을 표현할 때 쓴다. ❑ 확실히 당신은 그녀에게 일어나는 일을 걱정하는군요. 영국인과 미국인 모두 요청이나 진술에 동의할 때도 certainly를 쓴다. 미국인들은 surely도 이런 식으로 쓴다는 점을 유의하라. ❑ "한 잔 주시겠어요?" — "아, 그럼요."

cer|tain|ty /sɜ́rt³nti/ (**certainties**) ■ N-UNCOUNT **Certainty** is the state of being definite or of having no doubts at all about something. ❑ *I have told them with absolute certainty there'll be no change of policy.* ② N-VAR **Certainty** is the fact that something is certain to happen. [also a N] ❑ *A general election became a certainty three weeks ago.* ❑ *...the certainty of more violence and bloodshed.* ③ N-COUNT **Certainties** are things that nobody has any doubts about. [usu pl] ❑ *There are no certainties in modern Europe.*

■ 불가산명사 확신 ❑ 나는 절대적인 확신을 가지고 어떠한 정책 변화도 없으리라고 그들에게 말해 왔다. ② 가산명사 또는 불가산명사 확실한 일 ❑ 3주 전에 총선거 실시가 확정되었다. ❑ 반드시 더 많은 폭력과 유혈 사태가 일어나리라는 사실 ③ 가산명사 확실한 것 ❑ 현대 유럽에서 확실한 것이라고는 없다.

> ### Word Link
> cert ≈ determined, true : ascertain, certificate, certify

cer|tifi|cate /sərtífɪkɪt/ (**certificates**) ■ N-COUNT A **certificate** is an official document stating that particular facts are true. ❑ *...birth certificates.* ② N-COUNT A **certificate** is an official document that you receive when you have completed a course of study or training. The qualification that you receive is sometimes also called a **certificate**. ❑ *To the right of the fireplace are various framed certificates.* →see **wedding**

■ 가산명사 증명서 ❑ 출생증명서 ② 가산명사 수료증; 면허증 ❑ 벽난로 오른쪽에는 각종 수료증이 든 액자들이 놓여 있었다.

cer|ti|fy /sɜ́rtɪfaɪ/ (**certifies**, **certifying**, **certified**) ■ V-T If someone in an official position **certifies** something, they officially state that it is true. ❑ *...if the president certified that the project would receive at least $650m from overseas sources.* ❑ *The National Election Council is supposed to certify the results of the election.* ● **cer|ti|fi|ca|tion** /sɜ́rtɪfɪkéɪʃ³n/ (**certifications**) N-VAR ❑ *An employer can demand written certification that the relative is really ill.* ② V-T If someone **is certified as** a particular kind of worker, they are given a certificate stating that they have successfully completed a course of training in their profession. [usu passive] ❑ *They wanted to get certified as divers.* ❑ *...a certified accountant.* ● **cer|ti|fi|ca|tion** N-UNCOUNT ❑ *Pupils would be offered on-the-job training leading to the certification of their skill in a particular field.*

■ 타동사 보증하다, 공인하다 ❑ 그 계획이 해외 재원으로부터 최소한 6억 5천만 달러를 받으리라고 대통령이 보증한다면 ❑ 국가 선거 위원회에서 선거 결과를 공인하기로 되어 있다. ● 보증, 증명 가산명사 또는 불가산명사 ❑ 고용주는 친척이 정말로 아프다는 서면 증명을 요구할 수 있다. ② 타동사 공인을 받다 ❑ 그들은 잠수부 공인을 받기를 원했다. ❑ 공인 회계사 ● 공인, 검정 불가산명사 ❑ 학생들은 특정 분야의 기술 검정으로 이어지는 현장 연수를 받을 수도 있을 것이다.

cer|vi|cal /sɜ́rvɪk³l/ ■ ADJ **Cervical** means relating to the cervix. [MEDICAL] [ADJ n] ❑ *Doctors aim to cut the number of women dying from cervical cancer by half this decade.* ② ADJ **Cervical** means relating to the neck. [MEDICAL] [ADJ n] ❑ *Making a circle so your head leans back could damage the cervical spine.*

■ 형용사 자궁 경부의 [의학] ❑ 의사들은 이번 10년간 자궁 경부암으로 사망하는 여성의 수를 절반으로 줄이는 것을 목표로 삼고 있다. ② 형용사 목의 [의학] ❑ 머리를 뒤로 젖혀지도록 원을 그리며 고개를 돌리는 것이 경추에 손상을 입힐 수도 있다.

cer|vix /sɜ́rvɪks/ (**cervixes** or **cervices**) /sərvaɪsɪz, sɜ́rvɪsiz/ N-COUNT The **cervix** is the entrance to the womb. [MEDICAL]

가산명사 자궁 경부 [의학]

cf. **cf.** is used in writing to introduce something that should be considered in connection with the subject you are discussing. ❑ *For the more salient remarks on the matter, cf. Isis Unveiled, Vol. I.*

참조 ❑ 그 문제에 관하여 보다 뚜렷한 소견에 대해서는 '베일을 벗은 이시스' 1권 참조.

CFC /sí ɛf sí/ (**CFCs**) N-COUNT **CFCs** are gases that are used in things such as aerosols and refrigerators and can cause damage to the ozone layer. **CFC** is an abbreviation for "chlorofluorocarbon." ❑ *...the continued drop in CFC emissions.*

가산명사 염화불화탄소 ❑ 염화불화탄소 배출량의 지속적인 감소

chain ♦◇◇ /tʃéɪn/ (**chains**, **chaining**, **chained**) ■ N-COUNT A **chain** consists of metal rings connected together in a line. ❑ *His open shirt revealed a fat gold chain.* ② N-PLURAL If prisoners are **in chains**, they have thick rings of metal round their wrists or ankles to prevent them from escaping. ❑ *He'd spent four and a half years in windowless cells, much of the time in chains.* ③ V-T If a person or thing **is chained** to something, they are fastened to it with a chain. ❑ *The dog was chained to the leg of the one solid garden seat.* ❑ *We were sitting together in our cell, chained to the wall.* ● PHRASAL VERB **Chain up** means the same as **chain**. ❑ *I'll lock the doors and chain you up.* ❑ *They kept me chained up every night and released me each day.* ④ N-COUNT A **chain of** things is a group of them existing or arranged in a line. ❑ *...a chain of islands known as the Windward Islands.* ⑤ N-COUNT A **chain of** stores, hotels, or other businesses is a number of them owned by the same person or company. ❑ *...a large supermarket chain.* ⑥ N-SING A **chain of** events is a series of them happening one after another. ❑ *...the bizarre chain of events that led to his departure in January 1938.*

■ 가산명사 사슬; 목걸이 ❑ 그의 열린 셔츠 안으로 굵은 금목걸이가 보였다. ② 복수명사 사슬, 족쇄 ❑ 그는 대부분의 시간 동안 족쇄를 찬 채 창문도 없는 감방에서 사 년 반을 보냈다. ③ 타동사 사슬로 매이다 ❑ 그 개는 튼튼한 정원 의자 다리에 사슬로 매여 있었다. ❑ 우리는 벽에 달린 사슬에 묶인 채 감방 안에 같이 앉아 있었다. ● 구동사 사슬로 매다 ❑ 나는 문을 잠그고 너를 사슬에 매어 둘 것이다. ❑ 그들은 밤마다 나를 사슬로 묶었다가 낮에는 풀어 주었다. ④ 가산명사 한 줄로 늘어선 것 ❑ 윈드워드 제도로 알려진 한 줄로 늘어선 섬들 ⑤ 가산명사 체인 ❑ 대형 슈퍼마켓 체인 ⑥ 단수명사 일련, 연속 ❑ 1938년 1월에 그로 하여금 떠나게 만든 기괴한 일련의 사건들

> ### Word Partnership
> chain의 연어
>
> | | |
> |---|---|
> | ADJ. | **gold** chain, **silver** chain ■ |
> | V. | **break a** chain ■ |
> | N. | **department store** chain, **hotel** chain, **restaurant** chain, **supermarket** chain ⑤ |

chair ♦◇◇ /tʃéər/ (**chairs**, **chairing**, **chaired**) ■ N-COUNT A **chair** is a piece of furniture for one person to sit on, with a back and four legs. ❑ *He rose from his*

■ 가산명사 의자 ❑ 그는 의자에서 일어나 창문 쪽으로 걸어갔다. ② 가산명사 대학 교수의 직 ❑ 그는

chair and walked to the window. **2** N-COUNT At a university, a **chair** is the position or job of professor. ❑ *He has been appointed to the chair of sociology at Southampton University.* **3** N-COUNT The person who is the **chair of** a committee or meeting is the person in charge of it. ❑ *She is the chair of the Defense Advisory Committee on Women in the Military.* **4** V-T If you **chair** a meeting or a committee, you are the person in charge of it. ❑ *He was about to chair a meeting in Venice of EU foreign ministers.* **5** N-SING **The chair** is the same as the **electric chair**. [AM]

chair|man ♦♦◇ /tʃɛərmən/ (**chairmen**) **1** N-COUNT The **chairman** of a committee, organization, or company is the head of it. ❑ *Glyn Ford is chairman of the Committee which produced the report.* **2** N-COUNT; N-VOC The **chairman** of a meeting or debate is the person in charge, who decides when each person is allowed to speak. ❑ *The chairman declared the meeting open.*

chair|man|ship /tʃɛərmənʃɪp/ (**chairmanships**) N-VAR The **chairmanship** of a committee or organization is the fact of being its chairperson. Someone's **chairmanship** can also mean the period during which they are chairperson. ❑ *The Government has set up a committee under the chairmanship of Professor Roy Goode.*

chair|person /tʃɛərpɜrsən/ (**chairpersons**) N-COUNT The **chairperson** of a meeting, committee, or organization is the person in charge of it. ❑ *She's the chairperson of the safety committee.*

chair|woman /tʃɛərwʊmən/ (**chairwomen**) N-COUNT The **chairwoman** of a meeting, committee, or organization is the woman in charge of it. ❑ *Primakov was in Japan meeting with the chairwoman of the Socialist Party there.*

cha|let /ʃæleɪ, BRIT ʃæleɪ/ (**chalets**) N-COUNT A **chalet** is a small wooden house, especially in a mountain area. ❑ *...Swiss ski chalets.*

chalk /tʃɔk/ (**chalks, chalking, chalked**) **1** N-UNCOUNT **Chalk** is a type of soft white rock. You can use small pieces of it for writing or drawing with. ❑ *...the highest chalk cliffs in Britain.* **2** N-UNCOUNT **Chalk** is small sticks of chalk, or a substance similar to chalk, used for writing or drawing with. [also N in pl] ❑ *...somebody writing with a piece of chalk.* **3** V-T If you **chalk** something, you draw or write it using a piece of chalk. ❑ *He chalked the message on the blackboard.*

▶**chalk up** PHRASAL VERB If you **chalk up** a success, a victory, or a number of points in a game, you achieve it. ❑ *For almost 11 months, the Bosnian army chalked up one victory after another.*

chalk|board /tʃɔkbɔrd/ (**chalkboards**) N-COUNT A **chalkboard** is a dark-colored board that you can write on with chalk. Chalkboards are often used by teachers in the classroom. [mainly AM; BRIT **blackboard**] ❑ *The menu was on a chalkboard.*

chal|lenge ♦♦◇ /tʃælɪndʒ/ (**challenges, challenging, challenged**) **1** N-VAR A **challenge** is something new and difficult which requires great effort and determination. ❑ *The new government's first challenge is the economy.* **2** PHRASE If someone **rises to the challenge**, they act in response to a difficult situation which is new to them and are successful. ❑ *The new Germany must rise to the challenge of its enhanced responsibilities.* **3** N-VAR A **challenge to** something is a questioning of its truth or value. A **challenge** to someone is a questioning of their authority. ❑ *The demonstrators have now made a direct challenge to the authority of the government.* **4** V-T If you **challenge** ideas or people, you question their truth, value, or authority. ❑ *Democratic leaders have challenged the president to sign the bill.* ❑ *The move was immediately challenged by two of the republics.* **5** V-T If you **challenge** someone, you invite them to fight or compete with you in some way. ❑ *Marsyas thought he could play the flute better than Apollo and challenged the god to a contest.* ❑ *He left a note at the scene of the crime, challenging detectives to catch him.* ● N-COUNT **Challenge** is also a noun. ❑ *A third presidential candidate emerged to mount a serious challenge and throw the campaign wide open.* **6** →see also **challenging**

Word Partnership	*challenge*의 연어
V.	**accept a** challenge, **present a** challenge **1** **3** **5**
	dare to challenge **4** **5**
ADJ.	**biggest** challenge, **new** challenge **1** **3** **5**
	legal challenge **3**

chal|leng|er /tʃælɪndʒər/ (**challengers**) N-COUNT A **challenger** is someone who competes with you for a position or title that you already have, for example being a sports champion or a political leader. ❑ *Draskovic has emerged as the strongest challenger to the leader of the Serbian government.*

chal|leng|ing /tʃælɪndʒɪŋ/ **1** ADJ A **challenging** task or job requires great effort and determination. ❑ *Mike found a challenging job as a computer programmer.* **2** ADJ If you do something in a **challenging** way, you seem to be inviting people to argue with you or compete against you in some way. ❑ *Mona gave him a challenging look.*

cham|ber ♦◇◇ /tʃeɪmbər/ (**chambers**) **1** N-COUNT A **chamber** is a large room, especially one that is used for formal meetings. ❑ *We are going to be in the council chamber every time he speaks.* **2** N-COUNT You can refer to a country's legislature or to one section of it as a **chamber**. ❑ *More than 80 parties are contesting seats in the two-chamber parliament.* **3** N-COUNT A **chamber** is a room designed and equipped for a particular purpose. ❑ *For many, the dentist's office remains a torture chamber.*

cham|ber of com|merce (**chambers of commerce**) N-COUNT A **chamber of commerce** is an organization of businesspeople that promotes local commercial interests. [BUSINESS]

사우샘프턴 대학 사회학과 교수직에 임명되었다.
3 가산명사 의장, 위원장 ❑ 그녀는 국방부 여군 자문위원회 위원장이다. **4** 자동사 (회의 등을) 주재하다; ~의 의장직을 맡다 ❑ 그는 베니스에서 열릴 유럽 연합 외무 장관 회의를 주재하려던 참이었다. **5** 단수명사 (사형용) 전기의자 [미국영어]

1 가산명사 의장, 위원장 ❑ 글린 포드는 그 보고서를 작성한 위원회의 위원장이다. **2** 가산명사; 호격명사 사회자 ❑ 사회자가 회의 개회를 선포했다.

가산명사 또는 불가산명사 의장직; 의장 임기 ❑ 정부는 로이 구드 교수를 위원장으로 하는 위원회를 구성했다.

가산명사 의장, 위원장 ❑ 그녀는 안전 위원회 위원장이다.

가산명사 여자 의장 ❑ 프리마코프는 일본의 사회당 의장과 회의를 하느라 그곳에 있었다.

가산명사 샬레, 산장 ❑ 스위스의 스키 산장

1 불가산명사 백악 ❑ 영국에서 가장 높은 백악 절벽 **2** 불가산명사 분필 ❑ 분필로 글을 쓰고 있는 어떤 사람 **3** 타동사 ~을 분필로 쓰다 ❑ 그는 그 전갈을 칠판에 분필로 썼다.

구동사 거두다, 획득하다 ❑ 거의 11개월 동안, 보스니아 육군은 연이어 승리를 거두었다.

가산명사 칠판 [주로 미국영어; 영국영어 blackboard] ❑ 메뉴는 칠판에 적혀 있었다.

1 가산명사 또는 불가산명사 과제, 난제; 도전 ❑ 새 정부의 첫 번째 과제는 경제이다. **2** 구 난국을 타개하다 ❑ 새로운 독일은 더 커진 책무라는 난국을 타개해야만 한다. **3** 가산명사 또는 불가산명사 도전, 이의 제기 ❑ 시위자들은 지금 정부의 권위에 직접적인 도전을 했다. **4** 타동사 (정당성 또는 가치 등에) 도전하다, 이의를 제기하다 ❑ 민주당 지도자들은 대통령에게 도전적으로 그 법안에 서명할 것을 요구해 왔다. ❑ 그 조처에 대해 두 개 공화국이 즉각 이의를 제기했다. **5** 타동사 도전하다; (결투 또는 시합 등을) 신청하다 ❑ 마르시아스는 자신이 아폴로보다 더 피리를 잘 분다고 생각하여 그에게 경연을 신청했다. ❑ 그는 범죄 현장에 쪽지를 남겨 형사들에게 자신을 잡아 보라고 했다. ● 가산명사 도전; 결투 신청 ❑ 세 번째 대통령 후보가 출현하여 도전장을 내밀고 선거 운동을 대대적으로 벌였다.

가산명사 도전자 ❑ 드라스코비치가 세르비아 정부 수반의 가장 유력한 도전자로 떠올랐다.

1 형용사 큰 노력과 결심을 요하는, 만만찮은 ❑ 마이크는 만만찮은 컴퓨터 프로그래머 일자리를 얻었다. **2** 형용사 도전적인; 도발적인 ❑ 모나는 그를 도전적으로 바라보았다.

1 가산명사 방; 회의장 ❑ 우리는 그가 연설할 때마다 회의장에 갈 것이다. **2** 가산명사 의회, 원 (상하 양원 중 한 쪽) ❑ 80개 이상의 정당들이 상하 양원의 의석을 두고 다투고 있다. **3** 가산명사 (특정한 용도의) 방 ❑ 많은 사람에게 치과는 고문실로 기억된다.

가산명사 상공 회의소 [경제]

a
b
c
d
e
f
g
h
i
j
k
l
m
n
o
p
q
r
s
t
u
v
w
x
y
z

A

champ /tʃæmp/ (**champs**) N-COUNT A **champ** is the same as a **champion**. [INFORMAL] [oft n n] ❑ *...boxing champ Mike Tyson.*

가산명사 챔피언 [비격식체] ❑ 권투 챔피언 마이크 타이슨

B

cham|pagne /ʃæmpeɪn/ (**champagnes**) N-MASS **Champagne** is an expensive French white wine with bubbles in. It is often drunk to celebrate something.

물질명사 샴페인

C

cham|pi|on ♦♦♢ /tʃæmpiən/ (**champions, championing, championed**)
1 N-COUNT A **champion** is someone who has won the first prize in a competition, contest, or fight. ❑ *...a former Olympic champion.* ❑ *Kasparov became world champion.* **2** N-COUNT If you are a **champion of** a person, a cause, or a principle, you support or defend them. ❑ *He received acclaim as a champion of the oppressed.* **3** V-T If you **champion** a person, a cause, or a principle, you support or defend them. ❑ *He passionately championed the poor.*

D

1 가산명사 챔피언, 선수권 보유자 ❑ 이전 올림픽 챔피언 ❑ 카스파로프는 세계 챔피언이 되었다. **2** 가산명사 투사, 옹호자 ❑ 그는 억압받는 이들의 투사로서 갈채를 받았다. **3** 타동사 투사로서 활동하다, 옹호하다 ❑ 그는 가난한 사람들을 위해 열정적으로 싸웠다.

E

Word Partnership   champion의 연어

ADJ.	**former** champion, **world** champion **1**
N.	champion **a cause** **3**

F

cham|pi|on|ship ♦♦♢ /tʃæmpiənʃɪp/ (**championships**) **1** N-COUNT A **championship** is a competition to find the best player or team in a particular sport. ❑ *...the world chess championship.* **2** N-SING **The championship** refers to the title or status of being a sports champion. ❑ *He went on to take the championship.*

G

1 가산명사 선수권 대회 ❑ 세계 체스 선수권 대회 **2** 단수명사 선수권, 우승 ❑ 그는 우승을 향해 나아갔다.

H

chance ♦♦♦ /tʃæns/ (**chances, chancing, chanced**) **1** N-VAR If there is a **chance** of something happening, it is possible that it will happen. ❑ *Do you think they have a chance of beating Australia?* ❑ *There was really very little chance that Ben would ever have led a normal life.* **2** N-SING If you have a **chance to** do something, you have the opportunity to do it. ❑ *The electoral council announced that all eligible people would get a chance to vote.* ❑ *Most refugee doctors never get the chance to practice medicine in British hospitals.* **3** ADJ A **chance** meeting or event is one that is not planned or expected. [ADJ n] ❑ *...a chance meeting.* ● N-UNCOUNT **Chance** is also a noun. ❑ *...a victim of chance and circumstance.* **4** V-T If you **chance** something, you do it even though there is a risk that you may not succeed or that something bad may happen. ❑ *Andy knew the risks. I cannot believe he would have chanced it.* **5** PHRASE Something that happens **by chance** was not planned by anyone. ❑ *He had met Mr. Maude by chance.* **6** PHRASE You can use **by any chance** when you are asking questions in order to find out whether something that you think might be true is actually true. ❑ *Are they by any chance related?* **7** PHRASE If you say that someone **stands a chance** of achieving something, you mean that they are likely to achieve it. If you say that someone doesn't **stand a chance of** achieving something, you mean that they cannot possibly achieve it. ❑ *Being very good at science subjects, I stood a good chance of gaining high grades.* **8** PHRASE When you **take a chance**, you try to do something although there is a large risk of danger or failure. ❑ *You take a chance on the weather if you holiday in the UK.* ❑ *From then on, the Chinese were taking no chances.*

I

J

K

L

M

1 가산명사 또는 불가산명사 가망, 가능성 ❑ 그들이 호주를 이길 가망이 있다고 생각하세요? ❑ 벤이 평범한 삶을 살았을 가능성은 정말이지 매우 적었다. **2** 단수명사 기회 ❑ 선거 관리 위원회는 자격이 있는 모든 사람들에게 선거할 수 있는 기회가 돌아갈 것이라고 공표했다. ❑ 망명 의사들 대부분은 영국 병원에서 의술을 펼칠 기회를 결코 얻지 못한다. **3** 형용사 우연한 ❑ 우연한 만남 ● 불가산명사 우연 ❑ 우연과 상황이 낳은 희생자 **4** 타동사 (운에 맡기고) 해 보다 ❑ 앤디는 그 위험들을 알고 있었다. 그가 그걸 어떻게 되겠지 하고 그 일을 했으리라고는 생각할 수가 없다. **5** 구 우연히 ❑ 그는 모드 씨를 우연히 만난 적이 있었다. **6** 구 정말 ❑ 그들이 정말 관련이 있을까? **7** 구 _할 가망이 있다; _할 가망이 없다 ❑ 나는 과학 과목에 아주 뛰어났기 때문에, 좋은 성적을 받을 가망이 충분히 있었다. **8** 구 운에 맡기고 해 보다 ❑ 영국에서 휴일을 보내는 것은 날씨를 가지고 도박을 하는 것이나 다름없다. ❑ 그때 이후로 중국인들은 요행수를 바라는 일이 없었다.

N

O

Word Partnership   chance의 연어

N.	chance **of survival**, chance **of success**, chance **of winning** **1**
	chance **encounter**, chance **meeting** **3**
ADJ.	**fair** chance, **good** chance, **slight** chance **1 2**
V.	**get** a chance, **give** *someone/something* a chance, **have a** chance, **miss a** chance **2**

P

Q

Chan|cel|lor ♦♦♢ /tʃɑnslər, tʃæns-/ (**Chancellors**) **1** N-TITLE; N-COUNT **Chancellor** is the title of the head of government in Germany and Austria. ❑ *...Chancellor Gerhard Schröder of Germany.* **2** N-COUNT In Britain, the **Chancellor** is the Chancellor of the Exchequer.

R

1 경칭명사; 가산명사 (독일과 오스트리아의) 수상 ❑ 수상 게르하르트 슈뢰더 **2** 가산명사 재무 장관

Chan|cel|lor of the Ex|cheq|uer (**Chancellors of the Exchequer**) N-COUNT The **Chancellor of the Exchequer** is the minister in the British government who makes decisions about finance and taxes.

가산명사 재무 장관

S

chan|de|lier /ʃændəlɪər/ (**chandeliers**) N-COUNT A **chandelier** is a large, decorative frame which holds light bulbs or candles and hangs from the ceiling. ❑ *A crystal chandelier lit the room.*

가산명사 상들리에 ❑ 크리스털 상들리에가 그 방을 밝혔다.

T

change ♦♦♦ /tʃeɪndʒ/ (**changes, changing, changed**) **1** N-VAR If there is a **change** in something, it becomes different. ❑ *The ambassador appealed for a change in U.S. policy.* ❑ *There are going to have to be some drastic changes.* →see also **sea change** **2** N-SING If you say that something is a **change** or makes a **change**, you mean that it is enjoyable because it is different from what you are used to. [APPROVAL] ❑ *It is a complex system, but it certainly makes a change.* **3** V-I If you **change from** one thing **to** another, you stop using or doing the first one and start using or doing the second. ❑ *His physician modified the dosage but did not change to a different medication.* **4** V-T/V-I When something **changes** or when you **change** it, it becomes different. ❑ *We are trying to detect and understand how the climates change.* ❑ *In the union office, the mood gradually changed from resignation to rage.* ❑ *She has now changed into a happy, self-confident woman.* ❑ *They should change the law to make it illegal to own replica weapons.* **5** V-T To **change** something means to replace it with something new or different. ❑ *I paid £80 to have my car radio fixed and I bet all they did was change a fuse.* ● N-COUNT **Change** is also a noun. ❑ *A change of leadership alone will not be enough.* **6** V-T/V-I When you **change** your clothes or **change**, you take some or all of your clothes off and put on different ones. ❑ *Ben had merely changed his shirt.* ❑ *They had allowed her to shower and change.* →see **wear** **7** N-COUNT A **change of** clothes is an extra set of clothes that you take with you when you go to stay somewhere or to take part in an activity. [N

U

V

W

X

Y

Z

1 가산명사 또는 불가산명사 변화 ❑ 특사는 미국 정책의 변화를 간청했다. ❑ 어떤 과감한 변화가 필요하게 될 것이다. **2** 단수명사 새로운 것, 신선한 것 [마음에 듦] ❑ 그것은 복잡한 체계지만, 확실히 신선한 면이 있다. **3** 자동사 바꾸다, 갈다 ❑ 그의 주치의는 복용량은 수정했지만 약의 종류는 바꾸지 않았다. **4** 타동사/자동사 바꾸다; 변하다 ❑ 우리는 기후가 어떻게 변하는지 알아내어 이해하려고 하고 있다. ❑ 노조 사무실 내의 분위기는 체념에서 점점 분노로 바뀌어 갔다. ❑ 그녀는 이제 즐겁고 자신감에 넘친 여성으로 바뀌었다. ❑ 모형 무기를 소지하는 것을 불법화하려면 법을 고쳐야 한다. **5** 타동사 교체하다 ❑ 내 차 라디오를 수리하는 데 80파운드를 치렀는데, 장담하지만 수리점에서 한 일이라고는 퓨즈를 간 것밖에 없었다. ● 가산명사 교환, 교체 ❑ 지도부 교체만으로는 충분하지 못할 것이다. **6** 타동사/자동사 갈아입다 ❑ 벤은 단순히 셔츠를 갈아입었을 뿐이었다. ❑ 그들은 그녀에게 샤워를 하고 옷을 갈아입도록 허락했다. **7** 가산명사 갈아입을 옷 ❑ 그는 가방 하나에 갈아입을 옷 몇 벌을 채워 넣었다.

of n] ❑ *He stuffed a bag with a few changes of clothing.* ❽ v-t When you **change** a bed or **change** the sheets, you take off the dirty sheets and put on clean ones. ❑ *After changing the bed, I would fall asleep quickly.* ❾ v-t When you **change** a baby or **change** its diaper, you take off the dirty one and put on a clean one. ❑ *She criticizes me for the way I feed or change him.* ❿ v-t/v-i When you **change** buses, trains, or planes or **change**, you get off one bus, train, or plane and get on to another in order to continue your journey. ❑ *At Glasgow I changed trains for Greenock.* ⓫ v-t/v-i When you **change** gear or **change** into another gear, you move the gear lever on a car, bicycle, or other vehicle in order to use a different gear. [mainly BRIT; AM usually **shift**] ❑ *There were other sounds: a dog barking, a lorry changing gear.* ⓬ N-UNCOUNT Your **change** is the money that you receive when you pay for something with more money than it costs because you do not have exactly the right amount of money. ❑ *"There's your change." — "Thanks very much."* ⓭ N-UNCOUNT **Change** is coins, rather than paper money. ❑ *Thieves ransacked the office, taking a sack of loose change.* ⓮ N-UNCOUNT If you have **change for** larger bills or coins, you have the same value in smaller bills or coins, which you can give to someone in exchange. ❑ *The courier had change for a £10 note.* ● PHRASE If you **make change**, you give someone smaller bills or coins, in exchange for the same value of larger ones. [AM] ⓯ v-t When you **change** money, you exchange it for the same amount of money in a different currency, or in smaller bills or coins. ❑ *You can expect to pay the bank a fee of around 1% to 2% every time you change money.* ⓰ PHRASE If you say that you are doing something or something is happening **for a change**, you mean that you do not usually do it or it does not usually happen, and you are happy to be doing it or that it is happening. ❑ *Now let me ask you a question, for a change.* ⓱ to change **for the better** →see **better**. to **change hands** →see **hand**. a **change of heart** →see **heart**. to **change** your **mind** →see **mind**. to **change places** →see **place**. to **change the subject** →see **subject**. to **change tack** →see **tack**. to **change** your **tune** →see **tune**. to change **for the worse** →see **worse**

Thesaurus		*change*의 참조어
N.	adjustment, alteration ❶	
V.	adapt, alter, modify, transform, vary; (*ant.*) preserve ❹	

Word Partnership		*change*의 연어
V.	**adapt to** change, **resist** change ❶	
	make a change ❷	
ADJ.	**gradual** change, **social** change, **sudden** change ❶	
	loose change, **spare** change ⓭ ⓮	
N.	**policy** change ❶	
	change **of pace** ❸	
	change **direction** ❹	
	change **of address**, change **color**, change **the subject** ❺	
	change **clothes** ❻	

▶**change over** PHRASAL VERB If you **change over from** one thing **to** another, you stop doing one thing and start doing the other. ❑ *We are gradually changing over to a completely metric system.*

change purse (**change purses**) N-COUNT A **change purse** is a very small bag that people, especially women, keep their coins in. [AM; BRIT **purse**] ❑ *Eve searched her change purse and found thirty cents.*

chan|nel ♦♦◇ /tʃænᵊl/ (**channels, channeling, channeled**) [BRIT, sometimes AM **channelling, channelled**] ❶ N-COUNT; N-IN-NAMES A **channel** is a television station. ❑ *...the only serious current affairs program on either channel.* ❑ *...the proliferating number of television channels in America.* ❷ N-COUNT A **channel** is a band of radio waves on which radio messages can be sent and received. ❑ *The radio channels were filled with the excited, jabbering voices of men going to war.* ❸ N-COUNT If you do something through a particular **channel**, or particular **channels**, that is the system or organization that you use to achieve your aims or to communicate. ❑ *The government will surely use the diplomatic channels available.* ❑ *The Americans recognize that the UN can be the channel for greater diplomatic activity.* ❹ v-t If you **channel** money or resources into something, you arrange for them to be used for that thing, rather than for a wider range of things. ❑ *Jacques Delors wants a system set up to channel funds to the poor countries.* ❺ v-t If you **channel** your energies or emotions **into** something, you concentrate on or do that one thing, rather than a range of things. ❑ *Stephen is channeling his energies into a novel called Blue.* ❻ N-COUNT A **channel** is a passage along which water flows. ❑ *Keep the drainage channel clear.* ❼ N-COUNT A **channel** is a route used by boats. ❑ *...the busy shipping channels of the harbour.* →see **cellphone**

chant /tʃænt/ (**chants, chanting, chanted**) ❶ N-COUNT A **chant** is a word or group of words that is repeated over and over again. ❑ *He was greeted by the chant of "Judas! Judas!"* ❷ N-COUNT A **chant** is a religious song or prayer that is sung on only a few notes. ❑ *...a Gregorian chant.* ❸ v-t/v-i If you **chant** something or if you **chant**, you repeat the same words over and over again. ❑ *Demonstrators chanted slogans.* ❑ *The crowd chanted "We are with you."* ● **chant|ing** N-UNCOUNT ❑ *A lot of the chanting was in support of the deputy Prime Minister.* ❹ v-t/v-i If you **chant** or if you **chant** something, you sing a religious song or prayer. ❑ *Muslims chanted and prayed.* ● **chant|ing** N-UNCOUNT ❑ *The chanting inside the temple stopped.*

❽ 타동사 (침대의) 시트를 갈다 ❑ 침대 시트를 간 다음, 나는 곧 잠들곤 했다. ❾ 타동사 기저귀를 갈다 ❑ 그녀는 아기에게 젖을 먹이거나 기저귀를 가는 방식을 가지고 나를 나무란다. ❿ 타동사/자동사 갈아타다 ❑ 글래스고에서 나는 그리녹 행 열차로 갈아탔다. ⓫ 타동사/자동사 기어를 바꾸다 [주로 영국영어; 미국영어 대개 shift] ❑ 다른 소리들도 있었다. 개 짖는 소리, 트럭이 기어를 바꾸는 소리. ⓬ 불가산명사 거스름돈 ❑ "거스름돈 여기 있습니다." "감사합니다." ⓭ 불가산명사 동전 ❑ 도둑들이 사무실을 약탈하고, 동전 한 부대를 가져갔다. ⓮ 불가산명사 잔돈 ❑ 급사는 10파운드짜리 지폐를 바꿀 잔돈을 가지고 있었다. ● 구 잔돈으로 바꾸어 주다 [미국영어] ⓯ 타동사 환전하다 ❑ 환전할 때마다 1퍼센트에서 2퍼센트 정도의 수수료를 은행에 지불한다고 예상할 수 있다. ⓰ 구 변화를 위해; 기분 전환을 위해 ❑ 자, 변화를 주기 위해서 질문 하나 할게요.

구동사 바꾸다, 전환하다 ❑ 우리는 차차 미터법으로 완전히 전환하고 있다.

가산명사 동전지갑 [미국영어; 영국영어 purse] ❑ 이브는 동전지갑을 뒤져 30센트를 찾았다.

[영국영어, 미국영어 가끔 channelling] ❶ 가산명사; 이름명사 방송국 ❑ 양 방송국에서 유일하게 진지한 시사 프로그램 ❑ 미국 내 텔레비전 방송국 급증 ❷ 가산명사 주파수대, 채널 ❑ 라디오 채널마다 전쟁터로 향하는 젊은이들의 빠르고 상기된 목소리가 들렸다. ❸ 가산명사 수단, 통로 ❑ 정부는 분명 사용할 수 있는 외교적 수단을 이용할 것이다. ❑ 미국인들은 유엔이 더 큰 외교 활동의 통로가 될 수 있다는 점을 인식하고 있다. ❹ 타동사 -에 쏟다 ❑ 자크 들로르는 빈국들에 자금을 지원할 수 있는 시스템 도입을 원한다. ❺ 타동사 -에 쏟다 ❑ 스티븐은 '블루'라는 제목의 소설에 에너지를 쏟아붓고 있다. ❻ 가산명사 수로 ❑ 배수로를 깨끗하게 유지하라. ❼ 가산명사 항로 ❑ 항구의 붐비는 항로들

❶ 가산명사 챈트 (반복되는 단어나 구문) ❑ "배신자! 배신자!"라는 함성이 그를 맞이했다. ❷ 가산명사 성가 ❑ 그레고리언 성가 ❸ 타동사/자동사 되풀이하여 외치다, 연호하다 ❑ 시위자들이 연신 구호를 외쳤다. ❑ 군중들이 일제히 "우리는 당신을 지지합니다."라고 외쳐 댔다. ● 연호 소리 불가산명사 ❑ 연호 소리의 대부분은 부총리를 지지하는 것이었다. ❹ 타동사/자동사 성가를 부르다 ❑ 이슬람교도들이 성가를 부르고 기도를 했다. ● 성가 소리 불가산명사 ❑ 사원 안에서 성가 소리가 멈췄다.

a b c d e f g h i j k l m n o p q r s t u v w x y z

cha|os ♦◇◇ /ˈkeɪɒs/ N-UNCOUNT **Chaos** is a state of complete disorder and confusion. ❑ *The world's first transatlantic balloon race ended in chaos last night.*

불가산명사 무질서, 대혼란, 카오스 ❑ 사상 최초의 대서양 횡단 기구 경주가 어젯밤 대혼란으로 끝나고 말았다.

Word Partnership	chaos의 연어
V.	**bring** chaos, **cause** chaos
N.	chaos **and confusion**
ADJ.	**complete** chaos, **total** chaos

cha|ot|ic /keɪˈɒtɪk/ ADJ Something that is **chaotic** is in a state of complete disorder and confusion. ❑ *My own house feels as filthy and chaotic as a bus terminal.*

형용사 무질서한, 혼란스러운 ❑ 내 집은 꼭 버스터미널만큼이나 더럽고 복잡한 느낌을 준다.

chap /tʃæp/ (**chaps**) N-COUNT A **chap** is a man or boy. [mainly BRIT, INFORMAL] ❑ *"I am a very lucky chap," he commented. "The doctors were surprised that I was not paralyzed."*

가산명사 놈, 녀석 [주로 영국영어, 비격식체] ❑ "나는 참 운 좋은 놈이다."라고 그가 말했다. "의사들은 내 몸이 마비되지 않은 것이 기적이라고 했다."

chap|el /tʃæpˀl/ (**chapels**) **1** N-COUNT A **chapel** is a part of a church which has its own altar and which is used for private prayer. ❑ *...the chapel of the Virgin Mary.* **2** N-COUNT A **chapel** is a small church attached to a hospital, school, or prison. ❑ *We married in the chapel of Charing Cross Hospital in London.* **3** N-VAR A **chapel** is a building used for worship by members of some Christian churches. **Chapel** refers to the religious services that take place there. ❑ *...a Methodist chapel.*

1 가산명사 예배당 ❑ 성모마리아 예배당 **2** 가산명사 부속 예배당 ❑ 우리는 런던에 있는 채링 크로스 병원 부속 예배당에서 결혼했다. **3** 가산명사 또는 불가산명사 예배당; 예배 ❑ 감리교 예배당

chap|lain /tʃæplɪn/ (**chaplains**) N-COUNT A **chaplain** is a member of the Christian clergy who does religious work in a place such as a hospital, school, prison, or in the armed forces. ❑ *He joined the 40th Division as an army chaplain.*

가산명사 부속 예배당 신부 ❑ 그는 군목 자격으로 육군 40사단에 합류했다.

chapped /tʃæpt/ ADJ If your skin is **chapped**, it is dry, cracked, and sore. ❑ *...chapped hands.*

형용사 살갗이 튼, 갈라진 ❑ 튼 손

chap|ter ♦♦◇ /tʃæptər/ (**chapters**) **1** N-COUNT A **chapter** is one of the parts that a book is divided into. Each chapter has a number, and sometimes a title. [also N num] ❑ *Chromium supplements were used successfully in the treatment of diabetes (see Chapter 4).* **2** N-COUNT A **chapter** in someone's life or in history is a period of time during which a major event or series of related events takes place. [WRITTEN] ❑ *This had been a particularly difficult chapter in Lebanon's recent history.*

1 가산명사 장(章) ❑ 크롬 보충제 사용이 당뇨병 치료에 효과적이었다(4장 참고). **2** 가산명사 시기 [문어체] ❑ 이때는 근대 레바논 역사에서 특히나 어려웠던 시기였다.

char|ac|ter ♦♦◇ /kærɪktər/ (**characters**) **1** N-COUNT The **character** of a person or place consists of all the qualities they have that make them distinct from other people or places. ❑ *Perhaps there is a negative side to his character that you haven't seen yet.* **2** N-SING If something has a particular **character**, it has a particular quality. [usu supp N, also in N] ❑ *The financial concessions granted to British Aerospace were, he said, of a precarious character.* **3** N-SING You can use **character** to refer to the qualities that people from a particular place are believed to have. ❑ *Individuality is a valued and inherent part of the British character.* **4** N-COUNT You use **character** to say what kind of person someone is. For example, if you say that someone is a strange **character**, you mean they are strange. ❑ *It's that kind of courage and determination that makes him such a remarkable character.* **5** N-VAR Your **character** is your personality, especially how reliable and honest you are. If someone is of good **character**, they are reliable and honest. If they are of bad **character**, they are unreliable and dishonest. ❑ *He's begun a series of personal attacks on my character.* **6** N-UNCOUNT If you say that someone has **character**, you mean that they have the ability to deal effectively with difficult, unpleasant, or dangerous situations. [APPROVAL] ❑ *She showed real character in her attempts to win over the crowd.* **7** N-UNCOUNT If you say that a place has **character**, you mean that it has an interesting or unusual quality which makes you notice it and like it. [APPROVAL] ❑ *A soulless shopping center stands across from one of the few buildings with character, the Town Hall.* **8** N-COUNT The **characters** in a movie, book, or play are the people that it is about. ❑ *The film is autobiographical and the central character is played by Collard himself.* **9** N-COUNT A **character** is a letter, number, or other symbol that is written or printed. ❑ *...a shopping list written in Chinese characters.* →see **printing**, **theater**

1 가산명사 성격, 기질 ❑ 어쩌면 그의 성격에 네가 아직 보지 못한 어두운 면이 있을지도 몰라. **2** 단수명사 특징 ❑ 영국 항공 우주국이 제공받은 재정 지원은 불안정한 성격의 것이었다고 그가 말했다. **3** 단수명사 민족성, 국민성 ❑ 개인주의는 영국 국민성 중에 소중하며 내재적인 부분이다. **4** 가산명사 사람, 인물 ❑ 그 같은 용기와 의지가 있기 때문에 그가 훌륭한 인물이라는 것이다. **5** 가산명사 또는 불가산명사 인격, 품성 ❑ 그는 나를 인신공격하기 시작했다. **6** 불가산명사 인격 [마음에 듦] ❑ 그녀는 군중들의 마음을 사로잡기 위한 시도에서 진정한 인격을 보여 주었다. **7** 불가산명사 특색 [마음에 듦] ❑ 특색 있는 몇 안 되는 건물 중 하나인 타운홀 건너편에는 활기를 느낄 수 없는 쇼핑센터가 있다. **8** 가산명사 등장인물 ❑ 영화는 자서전적 성격을 띠고 있으며 주인공은 콜라드 자신이 연기했다. **9** 가산명사 문자, 기호, 부호 ❑ 한자로 적힌 쇼핑 리스트

Word Partnership	character의 연어
N.	character **flaw**, character **trait** **1**
	character **in a book/movie**, **cartoon** character, character **development** **8**
ADJ.	**moral** character **4** **5**
	fictional character, **main** character, **minor** character **8**

char|ac|ter|is|tic ♦◇◇ /kærɪktərɪstɪk/ (**characteristics**) **1** N-COUNT The **characteristics** of a person or thing are the qualities or features that belong to them and make them recognizable. ❑ *Genes determine the characteristics of every living thing.* **2** ADJ A quality or feature that is **characteristic of** someone or something is one which is often seen in them and seems typical of them. ❑ *...the absence of strife between the generations that was so characteristic of such societies.* ❑ *Windmills are a characteristic feature of the Mallorcan landscape.* ● **char|ac|ter|is|ti|cal|ly** /kærɪktərɪstɪkli/ ADV ❑ *He replied in characteristically robust style.*

1 가산명사 특성 ❑ 유전자는 모든 생물의 특성을 결정한다. **2** 형용사 -에 특징적인, -에 전형적인 ❑ 그와 같은 사회에서는 너무나 전형적으로 세대 간 갈등의 부재 ❑ 풍차는 마요르카 풍경에서 빠지지 않는 명물이다. ● -답게 부사 ❑ 그는 특유의 힘찬 말투로 대답했다.

char|ac|teri|za|tion /kærɪktəraɪzeɪʃˀn/ (**characterizations**) [BRIT also **characterisation**] N-VAR **Characterization** is the way an author or an actor describes or shows what a character is like. ❑ *As a writer I am interested in characterization.*

[영국영어 characterisation] 가산명사 또는 불가산명사 성격 묘사 ❑ 작가로서 나는 성격 묘사에 흥미를 느낀다.

char|ac|ter|ize /kærɪktəraɪz/ (**characterizes, characterizing, characterized**) [BRIT also **characterise**] **1** V-T If something **is characterized by** a particular feature or quality, that feature or quality is an obvious part of it. [FORMAL] ❑ *This election campaign has been characterized by violence.* **2** V-T If you **characterize** someone or something **as** a particular thing, you describe them as that thing. [FORMAL] ❑ *Both companies have characterized the relationship as friendly.*

[영국영어 characterise] **1** 타동사 ~을 특징으로 하다 [격식체] ❑ 이번 선거에서는 폭력이 두드러지게 나타났다. **2** 타동사 ~라고 묘사하다 [격식체] ❑ 두 회사는 둘 사이의 관계를 우호적이라고 묘사해 왔다.

char|ac|ter rec|og|ni|tion N-UNCOUNT **Character recognition** is a process which allows computers to recognize written or printed characters such as numbers or letters and to change them into a form that the computer can use. [COMPUTING] ❑ *...optical character recognition software that allows you to convert a scanned document to an electronic file.*

불가산명사 문자 인식 [컴퓨터] ❑ 스캔한 문서를 컴퓨터 파일로 바꿔 주는 광문자 인식 소프트웨어

cha|rade /ʃəreɪd, BRIT ʃərɑːd/ (**charades**) **1** N-COUNT If you describe someone's actions as a **charade**, you mean that their actions are so obviously false that they do not convince anyone. [DISAPPROVAL] ❑ *I wondered why he had gone through the elaborate charade.* **2** N-UNCOUNT **Charades** is a game for teams of players in which one team acts a word or phrase, syllable by syllable, until other players guess the whole word or phrase. ❑ *We are all going to play charades in the library.*

1 가산명사 뻔한 속임수 [탐탁찮음] ❑ 나는 그가 왜 굳이 공을 들여서 뻔한 수작을 부렸는지 궁금했다. **2** 불가산명사 제스처를 사용해 낱말이 구문을 표현하는 게임 ❑ 우리는 도서관에서는 모두 몸짓으로 말을 대신할 거다.

char|coal /tʃɑrkoʊl/ N-UNCOUNT **Charcoal** is a black substance obtained by burning wood without much air. It can be burned as a fuel, and small sticks of it are used for drawing with. →see **drawing**

불가산명사 숯, 목탄

charge ♦♦♦ /tʃɑrdʒ/ (**charges, charging, charged**) **1** V-T/V-I If you **charge** someone an amount of money, you ask them to pay that amount for something that you have sold to them or done for them. ❑ *Even local nurseries charge £100 a week.* ❑ *Some banks charge if you access your account to determine your balance.* ❑ *...the architect who charged us a fee of seven hundred and fifty pounds.* **2** V-T To **charge** something **to** a person or organization means to tell the people providing it to send the bill to that person or organization. To **charge** something **to** someone's account means to add it to their account so they can pay for it later. ❑ *Go out and buy a pair of glasses, and charge it to us.* **3** N-COUNT A **charge** is an amount of money that you have to pay for a service. ❑ *We can arrange this for a small charge.* **4** N-COUNT A **charge** is a formal accusation that someone has committed a crime. ❑ *He may still face criminal charges.* **5** V-T When the police **charge** someone, they formally accuse them of having done something illegal. ❑ *They have the evidence to charge him.* **6** N-UNCOUNT If you take **charge of** someone or something, you make yourself responsible for them and take control over them. If someone or something is **in** your **charge**, you are responsible for them. ❑ *A few years ago Bacryl took charge of the company.* ❑ *I have been given charge of this class.* **7** PHRASE If you are **in charge** in a particular situation, you are the most senior person and have control over something or someone. ❑ *Who's in charge here?* **8** N-COUNT If you describe someone as your **charge**, they have been given to you to be looked after and you are responsible for them. ❑ *The coach tried to get his charges motivated.* **9** V-I If you **charge** toward someone or something, you move quickly and aggressively toward them. ❑ *He charged through the door to my mother's office.* ❑ *He ordered us to charge.* ● N-COUNT **Charge** is also a noun. ❑ *...a bayonet charge.* **10** V-T To **charge** a battery means to pass an electrical current through it in order to make it more powerful or to make it last longer. ❑ *Alex had forgotten to charge the battery.* ● PHRASAL VERB **Charge up** means the same as **charge**. ❑ *There was nothing in the brochure about having to drive it every day to charge up the battery.* **11** N-COUNT An electrical **charge** is an amount of electricity that is held in or carried by something. [TECHNICAL] ❑ *A tiny wire - sending an electrical charge - was then fitted, leading to her heart.* **12** →see also **service charge** **13** PHRASE If something is **free of charge**, it does not cost anything. ❑ *The leaflet is available free of charge from post offices.* →see **lightning**, **magnet**, **trial**

1 타동사/자동사 청구하다 ❑ 지방 놀이방도 일주일 이용에 100파운드가 든다. ❑ 몇몇 은행에서는 통장 잔액을 확인할 때도 수수료를 청구한다. ❑ 우리에게 750파운드를 청구한 건축가 ❑ 가서 안경 하나 사, 돈은 우리한테 청구하고. **2** 타동사 요금, 비용 ❑ 우리는 저렴한 가격에 이를 준비해 줄 수 있다. **4** 가산명사 고발, 고소; 죄 ❑ 그는 여전히 형사죄로 처벌받을 수 있다. **5** 타동사 고발하다 ❑ 그들은 그를 고발할 수 있는 증거를 갖고 있다. **6** 불가산명사 담당, 책임짐 ❑ 몇 년 전 바크릴이 회사의 책임자가 되었다. ❑ 내가 이 수업을 맡게 되었다. **7** 구 책임지고 있는 ❑ 여기 책임자가 누굽니까? **8** 가산명사 맡은 사람 ❑ 코치는 그가 맡은 팀원들에게 의욕을 불어넣기 위해 노력했다. **9** 자동사 돌진하다, 돌격하다 ❑ 그는 문으로 재빨리 나가 내 어머니의 사무실로 향했다. ❑ 그는 우리에게 돌격 명령을 내렸다. ● 가산명사 돌진, 돌격 ❑ 총검 돌격 **10** 타동사 충전시키다 ❑ 알렉스는 배터리 충전을 깜박했었다. ● 구동사 충전시키다 ❑ 안내 책자에는 배터리를 충전시키려면 그것을 매일 가동시켜야 한다는 데 대해서는 아무런 설명이 없었다. **11** 가산명사 전하 [과학 기술] ❑ 작은 전선을 그녀의 심장으로 연결시킨다. **13** 구 무료로 ❑ 그 전단지는 우체국에서 무료로 받을 수 있다.

Word Partnership   charge의 연어

N.	charge **a fee** **1**
	charge **a battery** **10**
V.	deny a charge **4**
	lead a charge **9**
ADJ.	**criminal** charge, **guilty of a** charge **4**
	electrical charge **11**

charge|able /tʃɑrdʒəbᵊl/ **1** ADJ If something is **chargeable**, you have to pay a sum of money for it. [FORMAL] ❑ *The day of discharge is not chargeable if rooms are vacated by 12:00 noon.* **2** ADJ If something is **chargeable**, you have to pay tax on it. [FORMAL] ❑ *...the taxpayer's chargeable gain.*

1 형용사 요금이 부과되는 [격식체] ❑ 퇴실 당일은 방을 정오 이전에만 비우면 요금이 부과되지 않는다. **2** 형용사 과세 대상의 [격식체] ❑ 납세자의 과세 대상 이득

charge card (**charge cards**) also **chargecard** **1** N-COUNT A **charge card** is a plastic card that you use to buy goods on credit from a particular store or group of stores. Compare **credit card**. **2** N-COUNT A **charge card** is the same as a **credit card**. [AM]

1 가산명사 (특정 백화점 등의) 차지 카드 **2** 가산명사 신용 카드 [미국영어]

charg|er /tʃɑrdʒər/ (**chargers**) N-COUNT A **charger** is a device used for charging or recharging batteries. ❑ *He forgot the charger for his mobile phone.*

가산명사 충전기 ❑ 그는 휴대폰 충전기를 깜박하고 놓고 왔다.

cha|ris|ma /kərɪzmə/ N-UNCOUNT You say that someone has **charisma** when they can attract, influence, and inspire people by their personal qualities. ❑ *He has neither the policies nor the personal charisma to inspire people.*

불가산명사 카리스마 ❑ 그는 이렇다 할 정책도 없고 사람들을 끄는 개인적인 카리스마도 없다.

char|is|mat|ic /kærɪzmætɪk/ ADJ A **charismatic** person attracts, influences, and inspires people by their personal qualities. ❑ *With her striking looks and charismatic personality, she was noticed far and wide.*

형용사 카리스마 있는 ❑ 그녀는 빼어난 미모와 카리스마 있는 개성으로 멀리서도 눈에 띄었다.

A B C D E F G H I J K L M N O P Q R S T U V W X Y Z

charitable /tʃærɪtəbᵊl/ ■ ADJ A **charitable** organization or activity helps and supports people who are ill, disabled, or very poor. [ADJ n] □ ...charitable work for the handicapped. ② ADJ Someone who is **charitable** to people is kind or understanding toward them. □ They were rather less than charitable towards the referee.

■ 형용사 자선의 □ 장애인을 위한 자선 활동 ② 형용사 자비로운, 관대한 □ 그들은 심판에게 관대하지 않은 편이었다.

charity ♦♦◇ /tʃærɪti/ (**charities**) ■ N-COUNT A **charity** is an organization which raises money in order to help people who are ill, disabled, or very poor. □ The National Trust is a registered charity. ② N-UNCOUNT If you give money **to charity**, you give it to one or more charitable organizations. If you do something **for charity**, you do it in order to raise money for one or more charitable organizations. □ He made substantial donations to charity. □ Gooch will be raising money for charity. ③ N-UNCOUNT People who live on **charity** live on money or goods which other people give them because they are poor. □ Her husband is unemployed and the family depends on charity.

■ 가산명사 자선 단체 □ 내셔널트러스트는 정식 자선 단체이다. ② 불가산명사 자선 사업, 구호 활동 □ 그는 자선 사업에 상당한 액수의 돈을 기부했다. □ 구치가 자선 사업 기금을 모으게 될 것이다. ③ 불가산명사 구호금, 구호물자 □ 그녀의 남편이 실직 상태여서 식구들이 구호물자에 의존하고 있다.

Word Partnership	charity의 연어
ADJ.	**local** charity, **private** charity ■
N.	charity **organization** ■
	donation to charity, charity **event**, **money for** charity, charity **work** ②
V.	**collect for** charity, **donate to** charity, **give to** charity ②

charm /tʃɑrm/ (**charms, charming, charmed**) ■ N-VAR **Charm** is the quality of being pleasant or attractive. □ "Snow White and the Seven Dwarfs," the 1937 Disney classic, has lost none of its original charm. ② N-UNCOUNT Someone who has **charm** behaves in a friendly, pleasant way that makes people like them. □ He was a man of great charm and distinction. ③ V-T If you **charm** someone, you please them, especially by using your charm. □ He even charmed Mrs. Prichard, carrying her shopping and flirting with her, though she's 83. ④ N-COUNT A **charm** is a small ornament that is fixed to a bracelet or necklace. □ Inside was a gold charm bracelet, with one charm on it - a star. ⑤ N-COUNT A **charm** is an act, saying, or object that is believed to have magic powers. □ They cross their fingers and spit over their shoulders as charms against the evil eye. →see **jewelry**

■ 가산명사 또는 불가산명사 매력 □ 1937년 제작된 디즈니의 고전인 '백설 공주와 일곱 난장이'는 본래의 매력을 하나도 잃지 않았다. ② 불가산명사 매력 □ 그는 뛰어난 매력과 남다른 면을 가진 남자였다. ③ 타동사 매혹하다 □ 그는 쇼핑 가방도 들어주고 농담도 걸면서 83세나 된 프리차드 부인의 환심도 샀다. ④ 가산명사 작은 장식물 □ 안에는 별 모양 장식이 있는 금팔찌가 들어 있었다. ⑤ 가산명사 주술적 행위; 주문; 부적 □ 그들은 악마의 눈을 피하기 위한 주술적 행위로 손가락을 꼬고 어깨 너머로 침을 뱉었다.

charming /tʃɑrmɪŋ/ ■ ADJ If you say that something is **charming**, you mean that it is very pleasant or attractive. □ ...a charming little fishing village. ● **charmingly** ADV □ There's something charmingly old-fashioned about his brand of entertainment. ② ADJ If you describe someone as **charming**, you mean they behave in a friendly, pleasant way that makes people like them. □ ...a charming young man. □ He found her as smart and beautiful as she is charming. ● **charmingly** ADV [ADV after v] □ Calder smiled charmingly and put out his hand. "A pleasure, Mrs. Talbot."

■ 형용사 매력적인 □ 매력적인 작은 어촌 ● 매력적으로 부사 □ 그의 손님 접대 방식에는 뭔가 고풍스러운 멋이 있다. ② 형용사 매력적인 □ 매력적인 젊은이 □ 그는 그녀가 매력적일 뿐만 아니라 영리하고 아름답다는 것을 알았다. ● 매력적으로 부사 □ 칼더는 매력적인 미소를 지으며 손을 내밀었다. "탈보트 부인, 영광입니다."

charred /tʃɑrd/ ADJ **Charred** plants, buildings, or vehicles have been badly burned and have become black because of fire. □ ...the charred remains of a tank.

형용사 까맣게 탄 □ 까맣게 탄 탱크 잔해

chart ♦♦◇ /tʃɑrt/ (**charts, charting, charted**) ■ N-COUNT A **chart** is a diagram, picture, or graph which is intended to make information easier to understand. □ Male unemployment was 14.2%, compared with 5.8% for women (see chart on next page). →see also **bar chart, flow chart, pie chart** ② N-COUNT A **chart** is a map of the sea or stars. □ ...charts of Greek waters. ③ V-T If you **chart** an area of land, sea, or sky, or a feature in that area, you make a map of the area or show the feature in it. □ Ptolemy charted more than 1000 stars in 48 constellations. ④ V-T If you **chart** the development or progress of something, you observe it and record or show it. You can also say that a report or graph **charts** the development or progress of something. □ One GP has charted a dramatic rise in local childhood asthma since the M25 was built nearby.

■ 가산명사 차트, 도표 □ 남성 실업률은 14.2퍼센트, 그에 비해 여성 실업률은 5.8퍼센트이다(다음 페이지의 차트 참고). ② 가산명사 해도; 천체도 □ 그리스 해역 지도 ③ 타동사 지도를 만들다 □ 폴레미는 48개 성좌의 별 1,000개 이상을 포함한 천체도를 만들었다. ④ 타동사 기록하다, 보여 주다 □ 한 일반의가 조사한 바에 따르면 인근에 엠25 고속도로가 건설된 이후로 지역 어린이들의 천식 발생률이 급격히 증가한 것으로 드러났다.

charter ♦♦◇ /tʃɑrtər/ (**charters, chartering, chartered**) ■ N-COUNT A **charter** is a formal document describing the rights, aims, or principles of an organization or group of people. □ ...Article 50 of the United Nations Charter. ② ADJ A **charter** plane or boat is one which is hired for use by a particular person or group and which is not part of a regular service. [ADJ n] □ ...the last charter plane carrying out foreign nationals. ③ V-T If a person or organization **charters** a plane, boat, or other vehicle, they hire it for their own use. □ He chartered a jet to fly her home from California to Switzerland.

■ 가산명사 헌장 □ 유엔 헌장 50조 ② 형용사 전세의 □ 출국 외국인을 실은 마지막 전세 비행기 ③ 타동사 전세 내다 □ 그녀는 캘리포니아에서 고향 스위스까지 타고 갈 제트기를 전세냈다.

chartered /tʃɑrtərd/ ADJ **Chartered** is used to indicate that someone, such as an accountant or a surveyor, has formally qualified in their profession. [BRIT; AM **certified**] [ADJ n] □ ...a firm of chartered accountants.

형용사 공인된 [영국영어; 미국영어 certified] □ 공인 회계 법인

chase ♦♦◇ /tʃeɪs/ (**chases, chasing, chased**) ■ V-T If you **chase** someone, or **chase after** them, you run after them or follow them quickly in order to catch or reach them. □ She chased the thief for 100 yards. ● N-COUNT **Chase** is also a noun. □ He was reluctant to give up the chase. ② V-T/V-I If you **are chasing** something you want, such as work or money, you are trying hard to get it. □ In Wales, 14 people are chasing every job. □ There are too many schools chasing too few pupils. ● N-SING **Chase** is also a noun. [N for n] □ They took an invincible lead in the chase for the championship. ③ V-T/V-I If someone **chases** someone that they are attracted to, or **chases after** them, they try hard to persuade them to have a sexual relationship with them. □ Women also have another reason for not chasing men too hard, of course. ● N-SING **Chase** is also a noun. □ The chase is always much more exciting than the conquest anyway. ④ V-T If someone **chases** you from a place, they force you to leave by using threats or violence. □ Many farmers will then chase you off their land quite aggressively. ⑤ PHRASE If someone **cuts to the chase**, they start talking about or dealing with what is important, instead of less important things. □ Hi everyone, we all know why we are here today, so let's cut to the chase. ⑥ V-T To **chase** someone **from** a job or a position or **from** power means to

■ 타동사 뒤쫓다 □ 그녀는 도둑을 100야드나 뒤쫓았다. ● 가산명사 추적, 추격 □ 그는 추적을 포기하려 하지 않았다. ② 타동사/자동사 추구하다 □ 웨일스의 평균 취업 경쟁률은 14:1이다. □ 학생 수는 적은데 이들을 원하는 학교는 너무 많다. ● 단수명사 추구 □ 그들은 우승을 향한 대결에서 절대적인 선두 자리를 굳혔다. ③ 타동사/자동사 (이성을) 열심히 쫓아다니다 □ 물론 여자들이 남자를 그렇게 열심히 쫓아다니지 않는 또 다른 이유가 있다. ● 단수명사 (이성을) 쫓아다님 □ 어쨌든 그런 연인을 차지하는 것보다 차지하기까지의 과정이 항상 훨씬 더 흥미진진하다. ④ 타동사 쫓아내다 □ 그렇게 되면 상당수의 농장주가 꽤 공격적으로 당신을 자기 땅에서 쫓아낼 것이다. ⑤ 구 본론으로 들어가다 □ 안녕하세요. 우리가 오늘 왜 이 자리에 모였는지 모두들 아실 테니까 본론으로 들어갑시다. ⑥ 타동사 쫓아내다, 몰아내다 □ 그가 한결같이 유럽 연합을 추구한 것이 대처를 물러나게

force them to leave it. ❑ *His single-minded pursuit of European union helped chase Mrs. Thatcher from power.* ◻ v-ɪ If you **chase** somewhere, you run or rush there. ❑ *They chased down the stairs into the narrow, dirty street.*

하는 데 도움이 되었다. ◻ 자동사 뛰어가다 ❑ 그들은 계단을 뛰어내려와 좁고 더러운 거리로 향했다.

Word Partnership   chase의 연어

ADJ.	chase after *someone/something*, car chase ◻

---

chasm /kǽzəm/ (**chasms**) ◻ N-COUNT A **chasm** is a very deep crack in rock, earth, or ice. ◻ *A yawning fourteen-foot-deep chasm which inexplicably had opened up in the riverbed.* ◻ N-COUNT If you say that there is a **chasm** between two things or between two groups of people, you mean that there is a very large difference between them. ❑ *...the chasm that divides the worlds of university and industry.*

◻ 가산명사 깊게 갈라진 틈, 균열 ❑ 뚜렷한 원인 없이 강바닥에 생긴, 14피트 깊이로 입을 쩍 벌리고 있는 균열 ◻ 가산명사 차이, 단절 ❑ 학계와 산업계 간의 단절

chas|sis /tʃǽsi, ʃǽsi/

Chassis /ʃǽsiz/ can also be used as the plural form.

chassis /ʃǽsiz/ 는 복수형으로도 쓸 수 있다.

N-COUNT A **chassis** is the framework that a vehicle is built on. →see **car**

가산명사 차대, 섀시

chat ◆◇◇ /tʃǽt/ (**chats, chatting, chatted**) V-RECIP When people **chat**, they talk to each other in an informal and friendly way. ◻ *The women were chatting.* ❑ *I was chatting to him the other day.* ● N-COUNT **Chat** is also a noun. ❑ *I had a chat with John.*

상호동사 수다 떨다, 한담을 나누다 ❑ 여자들이 수다를 떨고 있었다. ◻ 나는 요전 날 그와 한담을 나누고 있었다. ● 가산명사 수다, 한담 ❑ 나는 존과 이런저런 이야기를 나눴다.

▶**chat up** PHRASAL VERB If you **chat** someone **up**, usually someone you do not know very well, you talk to them in a friendly way because you are sexually attracted to them. [BRIT, INFORMAL] ❑ *He'd spent most of that evening chatting up one of my friends.*

구동사 말을 걸다, 수작을 걸다 [영국영어, 비격식체] ❑ 그는 그날 저녁 대부분을 내 친구 중 한 명에게 수작을 걸며 보냈다.

Word Partnership   chat의 연어

V.	**have a** chat
ADJ.	**online** chat
N.	chat **site**

---

châ|teau /ʃǽtou/ (**châteaux**) /ʃǽtouz/ also **chateau** N-COUNT A **château** is a large country house or castle in France.

가산명사 저택, 성

chat|line /tʃǽtlaɪn/ (**chatlines**) also **chat line** N-COUNT People phone in to **chatlines** to have conversations with other people who have also phoned in. [BRIT] ❑ *She started using chat lines basically for someone to talk to.*

가산명사 대화방 [영국영어] ❑ 그녀는 그저 누군가 이야기할 사람이 필요해서 대화방을 이용하기 시작했다.

chat room (**chat rooms**) N-COUNT A **chat room** is a site on the Internet where people can exchange messages about a particular subject. [COMPUTING] ❑ *...a woman I met in a chat room.*

가산명사 채팅방 [컴퓨터] ❑ 채팅하다 만난 여성

chat show (**chat shows**) N-COUNT A **chat show** is a television or radio show in which people talk in a friendly, informal way about different topics. [BRIT; AM **talk show**]

가산명사 토크 쇼 [영국영어; 미국영어 talk show]

chat|ter /tʃǽtər/ (**chatters, chattering, chattered**) ◻ V-ɪ If you **chatter**, you talk quickly and continuously, usually about things which are not important. ❑ *Everyone's chattering away in different languages.* ❑ *Erica was friendly and chattered about Andrew's children.* ● N-UNCOUNT **Chatter** is also a noun. ❑ *...idle chatter.* ◻ V-ɪ If your teeth **chatter**, they keep knocking together because you are very cold or very nervous. ❑ *She was so cold her teeth chattered.* ◻ V-ɪ When birds or animals **chatter**, they make high-pitched noises. [LITERARY] ❑ *Birds were chattering somewhere, and occasionally he could hear a vehicle pass by.* ● N-UNCOUNT **Chatter** is also a noun. ❑ *...almond trees vibrating with the chatter of crickets.*

◻ 자동사 재잘거리다 ❑ 모두들 다른 언어로 떠들고 있었다. ❑ 에리카는 친절하고 앤드류의 아이들에 대해 이런저런 이야기를 했다. ● 불가산명사 수다, 잡담 ❑ 쓸데없는 잡담 ◻ 자동사 (이가) 딱딱 부딪치다 ❑ 그녀는 너무 추워서 이가 딱딱 부딪혔다. ◻ 자동사 지저귀다, (큰소리로) 울다 [문예체] ❑ 새들이 어디선가 지저귀고 있었고 가끔씩 지나가는 차 소리도 그의 귀에 들렸다. ● 불가산명사 지저귐, 울음소리 ❑ 귀뚜라미 울음소리에 흔들리는 아몬드나무

Word Link   eur ≈ one who does : amateur, chauffeur, entrepreneur

---

chauf|feur /ʃóufər, ʃoufɜ́r/ (**chauffeurs, chauffeuring, chauffeured**) ◻ N-COUNT The **chauffeur** of a rich or important person is the man or woman who is employed to take care of their car and drive them around in it. ◻ V-T If you **chauffeur** someone somewhere, you drive them there in a car, usually as part of your job. ❑ *It was certainly useful to have her there to chauffeur him around.*

◻ 가산명사 전속 기사 ◻ 타동사 자가용으로 데려다 주다 ❑ 그녀가 차로 그를 여기저기 데려다 주도록 하면 분명히 편리할 것이었다.

chau|vin|ism /ʃóuvɪnɪzəm/ N-UNCOUNT **Chauvinism** is a strong, unreasonable belief that your own country is more important and morally better than other people's. [DISAPPROVAL] ❑ *It may also appeal to the latent chauvinism of many ordinary people.* ● **chau|vin|ist** (**chauvinists**) N-COUNT ❑ *Antwerpers are so convinced that their city is best that other Belgians think them chauvinists.*

불가산명사 국수주의, 쇼비니즘 [탐탁찮음] ❑ 이는 또한 많은 보통 사람들 속에 잠재되어 있는 국수주의에 호소할 수도 있다. ● 국수주의자, 쇼비니스트 가산명사 ❑ 앤트워프 사람들이 지나치게 자기 도시가 최고라고 확신하는 바람에 다른 벨기에 인들은 그들을 쇼비니스트라고 생각한다.

cheap ◆◆◇ /tʃíp/ (**cheaper, cheapest**) ◻ ADJ Goods or services that are **cheap** cost less money than usual or than you expected. [v-link ADJ, ADJ n, v n ADJ] ❑ *I'm going to live off campus if I can find somewhere cheap enough.* ❑ *Running costs are coming down because of cheaper fuel.* ● **cheap|ly** ADV [ADV after v] ❑ *It will produce electricity more cheaply than a nuclear plant.* ◻ ADJ If you describe goods as **cheap**, you mean they cost less than similar products but their quality is poor. [ADJ n] ❑ *Don't resort to cheap copies; save up for the real thing.* ◻ ADJ If you describe someone's remarks or actions as **cheap**, you mean that they are unkindly or insincerely using a situation to benefit themselves or to harm someone else. [DISAPPROVAL] [ADJ n] ❑ *These tests will inevitably be used by politicians to make cheap political points.* ◻ ADJ If you describe someone as **cheap**, you are criticizing them for being unwilling to spend money. [AM, DISAPPROVAL] ❑ *Oh, please, Dad, just this once don't be cheap.*

◻ 형용사 저렴한, 싼 ❑ 나는 가격이 웬만큼 저렴한 곳을 찾을 수 있다면 캠퍼스를 벗어나 살 것이다. ❑ 연료값이 떨어져서 운영비가 내려가고 있다. ● 싼값하게, 싸게 부사 ❑ 이는 원자력 발전소보다 더 저렴하게 전기를 생산할 것이다. ◻ 형용사 싸구려의 ❑ 싸구려 복제품을 사용하지 말고 돈을 모아서 진품을 구입하라. ◻ 형용사 치사한, 천박한, 저속한 [탐탁찮음] ❑ 정치인들은 분명 이번 실험 결과를 천박한 정치적 주장을 펼치는 데 사용할 것이다. ◻ 형용사 인색한 [미국영어, 탐탁찮음] ❑ 아빠, 제발 이번 한 번만큼은 인색하게 그러지 마세요.

Thesaurus   cheap의 참조어

ADJ.	budget, economical, reasonable; (ant.) costly, expensive ◻
	second-rate, shoddy ◻

cheat /tʃiːt/ (cheats, cheating, cheated) **1** v-ı When someone **cheats**, they do not obey a set of rules which they should be obeying, for example in a game or exam. ❑ *Students may be tempted to cheat in order to get into top schools.* ● **cheat**|ing N-UNCOUNT ❑ *In an election in 1988, he was accused of cheating by his opponent.* **2** N-COUNT Someone who is a **cheat** does not obey a set of rules which they should be obeying. ❑ *Cheats will be disqualified.* **3** v-T If someone **cheats** you **out of** something, they get it from you by behaving dishonestly. ❑ *The company engaged in a deliberate effort to cheat them out of their pensions.*

▶**cheat on 1** PHRASAL VERB If someone **cheats on** their husband, wife, or partner, they have a sexual relationship with another person. [INFORMAL] ❑ *I'd found Philippe was cheating on me and I was angry and hurt.* **2** PHRASAL VERB If someone **cheats on** something such as an agreement or their taxes, they do not do what they should do under a set of rules. [mainly AM] ❑ *Their job is to check that none of the signatory countries is cheating on the agreement.*

1 자동사 부정행위를 하다 ❑ 학생들은 명문 학교에 들어가기 위해 부정행위를 할 마음이 생길 지도 모른다. ● 부정행위 불가산명사 ❑ 1988년 선거에서 상대 후보가 그를 부정 선거 혐의로 고발했다. 2 가산명사 부정행위자 ❑ 부정행위자는 자격이 박탈될 것이다. 3 타동사 속여서 빼앗다 ❑ 회사는 그들의 연금을 사취하기 위한 치밀한 노력을 펼쳤다.

1 구동사 배우자 몰래 바람을 피우다 [비격식체] ❑ 나는 필립이 나 몰래 바람을 피우고 있다는 것을 알고 화도 났고 속도 상했다. 2 구동사 어기다 [주로 미국영어] ❑ 그들이 하는 일은 조인국 중에 협약을 어기는 나라가 없는지 확인하는 것이다.

check ♦♦♢ /tʃɛk/ (checks, checking, checked) **1** v-T/v-ı If you **check** something such as a piece of information or a document, you make sure that it is correct or satisfactory. ❑ *Check the accuracy of everything in your CV.* ❑ *I think there is an age limit, but I have to check.* ❑ *She hadn't checked whether she had a clean ironed shirt.* ● N-COUNT **Check** is also a noun. ❑ *He is being constantly monitored with regular checks on his blood pressure.* **2** v-ı If you **check on** someone or something, you make sure they are in a safe or satisfactory condition. ❑ *Stephen checked on her several times during the night.* **3** v-T If you **check** something that is written on a piece of paper, you put a mark, like a V with the right side extended, next to it to show that something is correct or has been selected or dealt with. [mainly AM; BRIT usually **tick**] ❑ *Frequently, men who check answer (b) have not actually had the experience of being repeatedly rejected by women.* **4** v-T To **check** something, usually something bad, means to stop it from spreading or continuing. ❑ *Sex education is also expected to help check the spread of AIDS.* **5** v-T When you **check** your luggage at an airport, you give it to an official so that it can be taken on to your plane. ❑ *We arrived at the airport, checked our baggage and wandered around the gift shops.* ● PHRASAL VERB To **check in** your luggage means the same as to **check** it. ❑ *They checked in their luggage and found seats in the departure lounge.* **6** N-COUNT The **check** in a restaurant is a piece of paper on which the price of your meal is written and which you are given before you pay. [mainly AM; BRIT usually **bill**] ❑ *After coffee, Gastler asked for the check.* **7** N-COUNT A pattern of squares, usually of two colors, can be referred to as **checks** or a **check**. ❑ *Styles include stripes and checks.* **8** PHRASE If something or someone **is held in check** or **is kept in check**, they are controlled and prevented from becoming too great or powerful. ❑ *Life on Earth will become unsustainable unless population growth is held in check.* **9** N-COUNT A **check** is a printed form on which you write an amount of money and who it is to be paid to. Your bank then pays the money to that person from your account. ❑ *He handed me an envelope with a check for $1,500.* →see also **blank check, traveler's check 10** A **check** is the same as a **cheque**. [AM] **11** →see also **double-check, rain check** →see **bank**

1 타동사/자동사 확인하다, 점검하다 ❑ 자신의 이력서 내용이 모두 정확한지 확인하라. ❑ 나이 제한이 있는 것 같은데 확인해 봐야 해. ❑ 그녀는 깨끗이 다림질한 셔츠가 있는지 확인하지 않았었다. ● 가산명사 확인, 점검 ❑ 혈압을 정기적으로 체크하면서 그를 계속 지켜보고 있는 중이다. 2 자동사 잘 있나 확인하다, 들여다보다 ❑ 스티븐은 밤새 여러 번 그녀가 잘 자고 있는지 확인했다. 3 타동사 답을 표시하다, 체크하다 [주로 미국영어; 영국영어 대개 tick] ❑ (b)라고 답한 남성이 실제로는 여성으로부터 여러 번 거절당한 경험이 없는 경우가 흔하다. 4 타동사 저지하다, 억제하다 ❑ 성교육은 또한 에이즈 확산 저지에도 도움이 될 것으로 기대된다. 5 타동사 (물품을 받고) 맡기다 ❑ 우리는 공항에 도착해서 짐을 맡기고 선물 가게를 돌아다녔다. ● 구동사 (물품을 받고) 맡기다 ❑ 그들은 짐을 맡기고 출국 라운지에 자리를 잡고 앉았다. 6 가산명사 계산서 [주로 미국영어; 영국영어 대개 bill] ❑ 커피를 마신 후에, 개슬러는 계산서를 달라고 했다. 7 가산명사 체크무늬 ❑ 줄무늬와 체크무늬 스타일도 있다. 8 구 견제되다, 억제되다 ❑ 인구 증가를 억제하지 않으면 지구에서의 삶이 지속 불가능하게 될 것이다. 9 가산명사 수표 ❑ 그는 내게 1,500달러짜리 수표가 든 봉투를 건네주었다. 10 수표 [미국영어]

Thesaurus
check의 참조어

v. confirm, find out, make sure, verify; (ant.) ignore, overlook **1**

Word Partnership
check의 연어

PREP. **background** check, **credit** check, **security** check **1**
check **your baggage/luggage 5**
N. check **for/that** *something*, check **with** *someone* **1**
V. **cash a** check, **deposit a** check, **pay with a** check, **write a** check **9**

▶**check in 1** PHRASAL VERB When you **check in** or **check into** a hotel or clinic, or if someone **checks** you **in**, you arrive and go through the necessary procedures before you stay there. ❑ *I'll ring the hotel. I'll tell them we'll check in tomorrow.* ❑ *He has checked into an alcohol treatment center.* **2** PHRASAL VERB When you **check in** at an airport, you arrive and show your ticket before going on a flight. ❑ *He had checked in at Amsterdam's Schiphol airport for a flight to Manchester.* →see also **check 5** →see **hotel**

1 구동사 체크인하다 ❑ 내가 호텔에 전화해서 내일 체크인하겠다고 말할게. ❑ 그는 알코올 중독 치료 센터에 입원했다. 2 구동사 탑승 수속을 밟다 ❑ 그는 암스테르담 스키폴 공항에서 맨체스터 행 비행기 탑승 수속을 마친 참이었다.

▶**check off** When you **check** things **off**, you check or count them while referring to a list of them, to make sure you have considered all of them. PHRASAL VERB ❑ *Once you've checked off the items you ordered, put this record in your file.* ❑ *I haven't checked them off but I would say that's about the number.*

하나하나 확인하다 구동사 ❑ 주문한 물건을 하나하나 확인한 다음, 그 기록을 파일에 보관해라. ❑ 일일이 확인해 보진 않았지만 숫자가 대충 맞는 것 같아.

▶**check out 1** PHRASAL VERB When you **check out of** a hotel or clinic where you have been staying, or if someone **checks** you **out**, you pay the bill and leave. ❑ *They packed and checked out of the hotel.* ❑ *I was disappointed to miss Bryan, who had just checked out.* **2** PHRASAL VERB If you **check out** something or someone, you find out information about them to make sure that everything is correct or satisfactory. ❑ *Maybe we ought to go down to the library and check it out.* ❑ *We ought to check him out on the computer.* **3** PHRASAL VERB If something **checks out**, it is correct or satisfactory. ❑ *She was in San Diego the weekend Jensen got killed. It checked out.* **4** →see also **checkout**

1 구동사 체크아웃하다 ❑ 그들은 짐을 싼 후 호텔을 나왔다. ❑ 나는 브라이언이 체크아웃하는 바람에 간발의 차로 만나지 못해서 아쉬웠다. 2 구동사 확인해 보다, 찾아보다 ❑ 우리가 도서관에 가서 한번 확인해 봐야겠어. ❑ 우리가 컴퓨터에서 그에 대해 찾아봐야 해. 3 구동사 확인되다 ❑ 그녀는 옌센이 살해된 주말에 샌디에고에 있었다. 확인된 사실이다.

▶**check up 1** PHRASAL VERB If you **check up on** something, you find out information about it. ❑ *It is certainly worth checking up on your benefit entitlements.* →see also **checkup 2** PHRASAL VERB If you **check up on** someone, you obtain information about them, usually secretly. ❑ *I'm sure he knew I was checking up on him.*

1 구동사 조사하다, 알아보다 ❑ 자신이 받을 수 있는 혜택이 있는지 확실히 알아볼 만하다. 2 구동사 뒷조사하다 ❑ 그는 분명히 내가 자기 뒷조사를 하고 있는 것을 알았을 것이다.

check|**book** /tʃɛkbʊk/ (checkbooks) N-COUNT A **checkbook** is a book of checks which your bank gives you so that you can pay for things by check. [AM; BRIT **cheque book**]

가산명사 수표책 [미국영어; 영국영어 cheque book]

checked /tʃɛkt/ ADJ Something that is **checked** has a pattern of small squares, usually of two colors. ❑ *He was wearing blue jeans and checked shirt.*

check|er /tʃɛkər/ (**checkers**) **1** N-UNCOUNT **Checkers** is a game for two people, played with 24 round pieces on a board. [AM; BRIT **draughts**] ❑ *...a game of checkers.* **2** N-COUNT A **checker** is a person or machine that has the job of checking something. ❑ *Modern word processors usually have spelling checkers and even grammar checkers.*

check-in (**check-ins**) N-COUNT At an airport, a **check-in** is the counter or desk where you check in. ❑ *The line at the check-in was already dispersing.*

check|ing ac|count (**checking accounts**) N-COUNT A **checking account** is a personal bank account which you can take money out of at any time using your check book or bank card. [mainly AM; BRIT usually **current account**] ❑ *...Commonwealth Bank, where he has his checking account.* →see **bank**

check|out /tʃɛkaʊt/ (**checkouts**) also **check-out** N-COUNT In a supermarket, a **checkout** is a counter where you pay for things you are buying. ❑ *...queuing at the checkout in Sainsbury's.*

check|point /tʃɛkpɔɪnt/ (**checkpoints**) N-COUNT A **checkpoint** is a place where traffic is stopped so that it can be checked. ❑ *...a bomb explosion close to an army checkpoint.*

check|up /tʃɛkʌp/ (**checkups**) also **check-up** N-COUNT A **checkup** is a medical examination by your doctor or dentist to make sure that there is nothing wrong with your health. ❑ *The disease was detected during a routine checkup.*

cheek /tʃiːk/ (**cheeks**) **1** N-COUNT Your **cheeks** are the sides of your face below your eyes. ❑ *Tears were running down her cheeks.* **2** N-SING You say that someone has a **cheek** when you are annoyed or shocked at something unreasonable that they have done. [mainly BRIT, INFORMAL] [also no det, oft the N to-inf] ❑ *I'm amazed they had the cheek to ask in the first place.* ❑ *I still think it's a bit of a cheek sending a voucher rather than a refund.* →see **face, kiss**

cheek|bone /tʃiːkboʊn/ (**cheekbones**) N-COUNT Your **cheekbones** are the two bones in your face just below your eyes. ❑ *She was very beautiful, with high cheekbones.*

cheeky /tʃiːki/ (**cheekier, cheekiest**) ADJ If you describe a person or their behavior as **cheeky**, you think that they are slightly rude or disrespectful but in a charming or amusing way. [mainly BRIT] ❑ *The boy was cheeky and casual.*

cheer ♦◇◇ /tʃɪər/ (**cheers, cheering, cheered**) **1** V-T/V-I When people **cheer**, they shout loudly to show their approval or to encourage someone who is doing something such as taking part in a game. ❑ *The crowd cheered as Premier Wayne Goss unveiled a lifesize statue of poet Banjo Paterson.* ❑ *Swiss fans cheered Jakob Hlasek during yesterday's match with Courier.* N-COUNT **Cheer** is also a noun. ❑ *The colonel was rewarded with a resounding cheer from the men.* **2** V-T If you **are cheered** by something, it makes you happier or less worried. ❑ *Stephen noticed that the people around him looked cheered by his presence.* ● **cheer|ing** ADJ ❑ *...very cheering news.* **3** CONVENTION People sometimes say "**Cheers**" to each other just before they drink an alcoholic drink.

▶**cheer on** [mainly BRIT, FORMULAE] PHRASAL VERB When you **cheer** someone **on**, you shout loudly in order to encourage them, for example when they are taking part in a game. ❑ *A thousand supporters packed into the stadium to cheer them on.*

▶**cheer up** PHRASAL VERB When you **cheer up** or when something **cheers** you **up**, you stop feeling depressed and become more cheerful. ❑ *I think he misses her terribly. You might cheer him up.* ❑ *I wrote that song just to cheer myself up.*

cheer|ful /tʃɪərfəl/ **1** ADJ Someone who is **cheerful** is happy and shows this in their behavior. ❑ *They are both very cheerful in spite of their colds.* ● **cheer|ful|ly** ADV [ADV with v] ❑ *"We've come with good news," Pat said cheerfully.* ● **cheer|ful|ness** N-UNCOUNT ❑ *I remember this extraordinary man with particular affection for his unfailing cheerfulness.* **2** ADJ Something that is **cheerful** is pleasant and makes you feel happy. ❑ *The nursery is bright and cheerful, with plenty of toys.*

cheery /tʃɪəri/ (**cheerier, cheeriest**) ADJ If you describe a person or their behavior as **cheery**, you mean that they are cheerful and happy. ❑ *She was cheery and talked to them about their problems.* ● **cheer|i|ly** ADV ❑ *"Come on in," she said cheerily.*

cheese ♦◇◇ /tʃiːz/ (**cheeses**) N-MASS **Cheese** is a solid food made from milk. It is usually white or yellow. ❑ *...bread and cheese.* ❑ *...delicious French cheeses.*

cheese|burg|er /tʃiːzbɜːrgər/ (**cheeseburgers**) N-COUNT A **cheeseburger** is a flat round piece of ground meat called a hamburger with a slice of cheese on top, served in a bread roll.

chef /ʃɛf/ (**chefs**) N-COUNT A **chef** is a cook in a restaurant or hotel. ❑ *...some of Australia's leading chefs.*

chemi|cal ♦♦◇ /kɛmɪkəl/ (**chemicals**) **1** ADJ **Chemical** means involving or resulting from a reaction between two or more substances, or relating to the substances that something consists of. [ADJ n] ❑ *...chemical reactions that cause ozone destruction.* ❑ *...the chemical composition of the ocean.* ● **chemi|cal|ly** /kɛmɪkli/ ADV ❑ *...chemically treated foods.* **2** N-COUNT **Chemicals** are substances that are used in a chemical process or made by a chemical process. ❑ *The whole food chain is affected by the over-use of chemicals in agriculture.* ❑ *...a chemicals company.* →see **farm, war**

chem|ist /kɛmɪst/ (**chemists**) **1** N-COUNT A **chemist** is a person who does research connected with chemistry or who studies chemistry. ❑ *She worked as a research chemist.* **2** N-COUNT A **chemist** or a **chemist's** is a store where drugs and medicines are sold or given out, and where you can buy cosmetics and some household goods. [BRIT; AM **drugstore, pharmacy**] ❑ *There are many creams*

형용사 체크무늬의 ❑ 그는 청바지와 체크무늬 셔츠를 입고 있었다.

1 불가산명사 체커 [미국영어; 영국영어 draughts] ❑ 체커 한 판 **2** 가산명사 검사인, 검사기 ❑ 요즘 워드프로세서에는 보통 맞춤법 및 문법 검사 기능이 포함되어 있다.

가산명사 탑승 수속대 ❑ 탑승 수속대의 줄이 벌써 흩어지고 있었다.

가산명사 당좌 예금 구좌 [주로 미국영어; 영국영어 대개 current account] ❑ 그가 당좌 예금 구좌를 갖고 있는 커먼웰스 뱅크

가산명사 계산대 ❑ 세인스베리스 슈퍼마켓 계산대에서 줄을 서서

가산명사 검문소 ❑ 육군 검문소 근처에서 발생한 폭파 사건

가산명사 건강 진단 ❑ 그 병은 정기 검진을 하는 동안 발견되었다.

1 가산명사 볼, 뺨 ❑ 눈물이 그녀의 뺨 위로 흘러내렸다. **2** 단수명사 뻔뻔스러움, 건방짐 [주로 영국영어, 비격식체] ❑ 뻔뻔스럽게 물어 볼 생각을 했다는 것부터가 놀랍기 그지없다. ❑ 나는 아직까지도 환불이 아니라 교환권을 보냈다는 것이 뻔뻔스럽게 느껴진다.

가산명사 광대뼈 ❑ 그녀는 도드라진 광대뼈를 가진 매우 아름다운 여인이었다.

형용사 당돌한 [주로 영국영어] ❑ 꼬마는 당돌하고 거리낌이 없었다.

1 타동사/자동사 응원하다, 갈채를 보내다 ❑ 웨인 고스 주지사가 실물 크기의 시인 반조 패티슨 동상의 베일을 걷어내자 시민들은 갈채를 보냈다. ❑ 스위스 팬들은 어제 쿠리어와의 경기에서 제이콥 하섹을 응원했다. 가산명사 응원, 갈채 ❑ 대령은 부하들의 열렬한 응원을 받고 보람을 느꼈다. **2** 타동사 기분 좋다, 힘이 나다 ❑ 스티븐은 주변 사람들이 자신이 와서 기분이 좋아진 것을 알아챘다. ● 힘이 되는, 기운을 돋우는 형용사 ❑ 매우 기분 좋은 소식 **3** 관용 표현 건배

[주로 영국영어, 의례적인 표현] 구동사 응원하다 ❑ 그들을 응원하기 위한 서포터 천 명이 경기장을 가득 메웠다.

구동사 격려하다 ❑ 그가 그녀를 미치도록 그리워하는 것 같아. 네가 격려 좀 해 줘. ❑ 나는 그냥 우울한 기분을 떨치기 위해 그 곡을 썼다.

1 형용사 명랑한, 발랄한 ❑ 감기에도 불구하고 둘 다 매우 명랑해 보였다. ● 명랑하게, 발랄하게 부사 ❑ "좋은 소식을 갖고 왔어요."라고 팻이 발랄하게 말했다. ● 명랑함 쾌활 불가산명사 ❑ 나는 이 멋진 남자를 기억한다. 특히 한결같이 명랑한 성격이 마음에 드는 사람이다. **2** 형용사 쾌적한 ❑ 놀이방은 밝고 쾌적한 곳으로 장난감도 많다.

형용사 발랄한 ❑ 그녀는 생기발랄했으며 그들에게 그들의 문제점에 대해 이야기했다. ● 발랄하게 부사 ❑ "들어오세요."라고 그녀가 발랄하게 말했다.

물질명사 치즈 ❑ 빵과 치즈 ❑ 맛있는 프랑스산 치즈

가산명사 치즈버거

가산명사 요리사, 주방장 ❑ 호주의 일류 요리사 몇 명

1 형용사 화학의; 화학적인; 화학 작용의 ❑ 오존층 파괴를 일으키는 화학 반응 ❑ 해양의 화학 성분비 ● 화학적으로, 화학 작용으로 부사 ❑ 화학 처리된 식품 **2** 가산명사 화학 물질; 화학 약품 ❑ 농업에서의 과다한 화학 물질 사용으로 먹이 사슬 전체가 영향을 빚는다. ❑ 화학 회사

1 가산명사 화학자 ❑ 그녀는 화학 연구원으로 일했다. **2** 가산명사 약국 [영국영어; 미국영어 drugstore, pharmacy] ❑ 감염 부위를 소독해 주는 연고가 약국에 많이 나와 있다. **3** 가산명사 약사 [영국영어; 미국영어 druggist, pharmacist]

a b c d e f g h i j k l m n o p q r s t u v w x y z

available from the chemist which should clear the infection. ⑤ N-COUNT A **chemist** is someone who works in a chemist's and is qualified to prepare and sell medicines.
[BRIT; AM **druggist, pharmacist**]

> In American English, the usual way of referring to a store where medicines are sold is a **drugstore**. ❑ *She went into a drugstore and bought some aspirin.* **Pharmacy** refers specifically to a part of the drugstore where you get prescription medicines. Pharmacies are often located in stores that mainly sell other merchandise, such as food supermarkets and discount centers. In Britain, the nearest equivalent of a drugstore is a **chemist's**.

> 미국 영어에서는 약을 파는 상점을 흔히 drugstore라고 한다. ❑ 그녀는 약국에 들어가서 아스피린을 좀 샀다. pharmacy는 약국에서 특별히 처방약을 사는 곳을 지칭한다. pharmacy는 흔히 식료품 슈퍼마켓이나 할인점과 같이 주로 다른 상품을 파는 상점 안에 있다. 영국에서 drugstore와 가장 비슷한 것은 chemist's이다.

chem|is|try /kɛmɪstri/ ❶ N-UNCOUNT **Chemistry** is the scientific study of the structure of substances and of the way that they react with other substances. ❷ N-UNCOUNT The **chemistry** of an organism or a material is the chemical substances that make it up and the chemical reactions that go on inside it. ❑ *We have literally altered the chemistry of our planet's atmosphere.* ❸ N-UNCOUNT If you say that there is **chemistry** between two people, you mean that is obvious they are attracted to each other or like each other very much. ❑ *...the extraordinary chemistry between Ingrid and Bogart.*

❶ 불가산명사 화학 ❷ 불가산명사 화학적 성격 ❑ 우리는 말 그대로 지구 대기의 화학적 성격을 바꿔 놓았다. ❸ 불가산명사 공감대, 손발이 맞음 ❑ 잉그리드와 보가트 사이의 특별한 공감대

cheque /tʃɛk/ A **cheque** is the same as a **check**. [BRIT]

수표 [영국영어]

cheque book (**cheque books**) also **chequebook** N-COUNT A **cheque book** is the same as a **checkbook**. [BRIT]

가산명사 수표책 [영국영어]

cheque card (**cheque cards**) N-COUNT In Britain, a **cheque card** or a **cheque guarantee card** is a small plastic card given to you by your bank and which you have to show when you are paying for something by cheque or when you are cashing a cheque at another bank.

가산명사 수표 보증 카드

cher|ish /tʃɛrɪʃ/ (**cherishes, cherishing, cherished**) ❶ V-T If you **cherish** something such as a hope or a pleasant memory, you keep it in your mind for a long period of time. ❑ *The president will cherish the memory of this visit to Ohio.* ● **cher|ished** ADJ [ADJ n] ❑ *...the cherished dream of a world without wars.* ❷ V-T If you **cherish** someone or something, you take good care of them because you love them. ❑ *He genuinely loved and cherished her.* ● **cher|ished** ADJ [ADJ n] ❑ *He described the picture as his most cherished possession.* ❸ V-T If you **cherish** a right, a privilege, or a principle, you regard it as important and try hard to keep it. ❑ *Chinese people cherish their independence and sovereignty.* ● **cher|ished** ADJ [ADJ n] ❑ *Freud called into question some deeply cherished beliefs.*

❶ 타동사 간직하다 ❑ 대통령은 이번 오하이오 방문을 기억 속에 간직할 것이다. ● 고이 간직한 형용사 ❑ 전쟁 없는 세상에 대한 오랜 꿈 ❷ 타동사 소중히 여기다 ❑ 그는 진정으로 그녀를 사랑하며 소중히 여겼다. ● 소중한 형용사 ❑ 그는 그 그림을 그가 가장 아끼는 물건이라고 했다. ❸ 타동사 소중히 받들다, 신봉하다 ❑ 중국인들은 그들의 독립과 주권을 소중히 받든다. ● 신봉되어 온 형용사 ❑ 프로이드는 오랫동안 신봉되어 온 몇 가지 믿음들에 의문을 던졌다.

cher|ry /tʃɛri/ (**cherries**) ❶ N-COUNT **Cherries** are small, round fruit with red skins. ❷ N-COUNT A **cherry** or a **cherry tree** is a tree that cherries grow on.

❶ 가산명사 체리 ❷ 가산명사 체리나무

cherry-pick /tʃɛripɪk/ (**cherry-picks, cherry-picking, cherry-picked**) V-T If someone **cherry-picks** people or things, they choose the best ones from a group of them, often in a way that other people consider unfair. ❑ *The club is in debt while others are queuing to cherry-pick their best players.*

타동사 선별하다 ❑ 구단이 빚더미에 앉아 있는 동안 다른 구단에서는 서로 최고 선수들을 데려가려고 줄을 서 있다.

chess /tʃɛs/ N-UNCOUNT **Chess** is a game for two people, played on a chessboard. Each player has 16 pieces, including a king. Your aim is to move your pieces so that your opponent's king cannot escape being taken. ❑ *...the world chess championships.*
→see Word Web: **chess**

불가산명사 체스 ❑ 세계 체스 선수권 대회

chest ♦♢♢ /tʃɛst/ (**chests**) ❶ N-COUNT Your **chest** is the top part of the front of your body where your ribs, lungs, and heart are. ❑ *He crossed his arms over his chest.* ❑ *He was shot in the chest.* ❷ N-COUNT A **chest** is a large, heavy box used for storing things. ❑ *At the very bottom of the chest were his carving tools.* ❑ *...a treasure chest.* →see **body**

❶ 가산명사 가슴 ❑ 그는 가슴 위로 팔짱을 꼈다. ❑ 그는 가슴에 총격을 입었다. ❷ 가산명사 상자 ❑ 상자 맨 아래에 그의 조각칼이 있었다. ❑ 보물 상자

chest|nut /tʃɛsnʌt, -nət/ (**chestnuts**) ❶ N-COUNT A **chestnut** or **chestnut tree** is a tall tree with broad leaves. ❷ N-COUNT **Chestnuts** are the reddish-brown nuts that grow on chestnut trees. You can eat chestnuts. ❸ COLOR Something that is **chestnut** is dark reddish-brown in color. ❑ *...a woman with chestnut hair.*

❶ 가산명사 밤나무 ❷ 가산명사 밤 ❸ 색채어 밤색 ❑ 밤색 머리의 여인

chew /tʃu/ (**chews, chewing, chewed**) ❶ V-T/V-I When you **chew** food, you use your teeth to break it up in your mouth so that it becomes easier to swallow. ❑ *Be certain to eat slowly and chew your food extremely well.* ❑ *Daniel leaned back on the sofa, still chewing on his apple.* ❷ V-T If you **chew** gum or tobacco, you keep biting it and moving it around your mouth to taste the flavor of it. You do not

❶ 타동사/자동사 씹다 ❑ 음식은 항상 천천히 꼭꼭 씹어 먹어야 한다. ❑ 다니엘은 계속 사과를 씹으면서 소파 뒤로 몸을 기댔다. ❷ 타동사 씹다 ❑ 여자 애 하나가 껌을 씹고 있었다. ❸ 타동사 물어뜯다, 깨물다 ❑ 그는 불안한 듯 아랫입술을 깨물었다.

Word Web · chess

Scholars disagree on the origin of **chess**. Some say it started in China around 570 AD. Others say it was invented in India sometime later. In early versions of the **game**, the **king** was the most powerful **chess piece**. But when the game was brought to Europe in the Middle Ages, a new form appeared. It was called Queen's Chess. Modern chess is based on this game. The king is the most important piece, but the **queen** is the most powerful. Chess **players** use rooks, **bishops**, **knights**, and **pawns** to protect their king and to put their **opponent** in checkmate.

a

swallow it. ❑ *One girl was chewing gum.* ❸ V-T If you **chew** your lips or your fingernails, you keep biting them because you are nervous. ❑ *He chewed his lower lip nervously.* ❹ V-T/V-I If a person or animal **chews** an object, they bite it with their teeth. ❑ *They pause and chew their pencils.*

chic /ʃiːk/ ❶ ADJ Something or someone that is **chic** is fashionable and sophisticated. ❑ *Her gown was very French and very chic.* ❷ N-UNCOUNT **Chic** is used to refer to a particular style or to the quality of being chic. ❑ *...French designer chic.*

chick /tʃɪk/ (**chicks**) N-COUNT A **chick** is a baby bird. ❑ *...newly-hatched chicks.*

chick|en ◆◇◇ /tʃɪkɪn/ (**chickens**) ❶ N-COUNT **Chickens** are birds which are kept on a farm for their eggs and for their meat. ❑ *Lionel built a coop so that they could raise chickens and have a supply of fresh eggs.* ● N-UNCOUNT **Chicken** is the flesh of this bird eaten as food. ❑ *...roast chicken with wild mushrooms.* ❷ N-COUNT If someone calls you a **chicken**, they mean that you are afraid to do something. [INFORMAL, DISAPPROVAL] ❑ *I'm scared of the dark. I'm a big chicken.* ● ADJ **Chicken** is also an adjective. [v-link ADJ] ❑ *Why are you so chicken, Gregory?* ❸ PHRASE If you say that someone **is counting** their **chickens**, you mean that they are assuming that they will be successful or get something, when this is not certain. ❑ *I don't want to count my chickens before they are hatched.* ❹ **chickens come home to roost** →see **roost**
→see **meat**

chide /tʃaɪd/ (**chides**, **chiding**, **chided**) V-T If you **chide** someone, you speak to them angrily because they have done something bad or foolish. [OLD-FASHIONED] ❑ *Cross chided himself for worrying.*

chief ◆◆◆ /tʃiːf/ (**chiefs**) ❶ N-COUNT The **chief** of an organization is the person who is in charge of it. ❑ *...a commission appointed by the police chief.* ❷ N-COUNT; N-TITLE The **chief** of a tribe is its leader. ❑ *...Sitting Bull, chief of the Sioux tribes of the Great Plains.* ❸ ADJ **Chief** is used in the job titles of the most senior worker or workers of a particular kind in an organization. [ADJ n] ❑ *...the chief test pilot.* ❹ ADJ The **chief** cause, part, or member of something is the most important one. [ADJ n] ❑ *Financial stress is well established as a chief reason for divorce.*

Thesaurus	*chief*의 참조어
N.	boss, director, head, leader; subordinate ❶
ADJ.	key, main, major, primary; (*ant.*) minor, unimportant ❹

Chief Constable (**Chief Constables**) N-COUNT; N-TITLE A **Chief Constable** is the officer who is in charge of the police force in a particular county or area in Britain.

chief ex|ec|u|tive of|fic|er (**chief executive officers**) N-COUNT The **chief executive officer** of a company is the person who has overall responsibility for the management of that company. The abbreviation **CEO** is often used. [BUSINESS]

Chief Jus|tice (**Chief Justices**) N-COUNT; N-TITLE A **Chief Justice** is the most important judge in a court of law, especially a supreme court.

chief|ly /tʃiːfli/ ADV You use **chiefly** to indicate that a particular reason, emotion, method, or feature is the main or most important one. ❑ *He joined the consular service in China, chiefly because this was one of the few job vacancies.*

Chief of Staff (**Chiefs of Staff**) N-COUNT The **Chiefs of Staff** are the highest-ranking officers of each service of the armed forces.

chif|fon /ʃɪfɒn, BRIT ʃɪfɒn/ (**chiffons**) N-MASS **Chiffon** is a kind of very thin silk or nylon cloth that you can see through. ❑ *...floaty chiffon skirts.*

child ◆◆◆ /tʃaɪld/ (**children**) ❶ N-COUNT A **child** is a human being who is not yet an adult. ❑ *When I was a child I lived in a country village.* ❑ *...a child of six.* ❷ N-COUNT Someone's **children** are their sons and daughters of any age. ❑ *How are the children?* ❑ *His children have left home.* →see **age**
→see Word Web: **child**

Word Partnership	*child*의 연어
V.	adopt a child, have a child, raise a child ❶
N.	child abuse ❶
ADJ.	difficult child, happy child, small/young child, unborn child ❶

❹ 타동사/자동사 깨물다 ❑ 그들이 잠시 멈춰서 연필을 깨문다.

❶ 형용사 세련된, 우아한 ❑ 그녀의 드레스는 아주 프랑스풍이었고 매우 우아했다. ❷ 불가산명사 독특한 스타일, 세련미 ❑ 프랑스 디자이너 스타일

가산명사 병아리, 새끼 새 ❑ 갓 깨어난 병아리들

❶ 가산명사 닭 ❑ 라이오넬은 닭을 키워서 신선한 계란을 얻을 생각으로 닭장을 만들었다. ● 불가산명사 닭고기 ❑ 자연산 버섯을 곁들인 닭구이 ❷ 가산명사 겁쟁이 [비격식체, 탐탁찮음] ❑ 나는 어두운 걸 무서워해. 진짜 겁이 많지. ● 형용사 겁 많은 ❑ 그레고리, 너 왜 그렇게 겁쟁이냐? ❸ 구 김칫국부터 마신다 ❑ 김칫국부터 마시긴 싫어.

타동사 꾸짖다, 나무라다 [구식어] ❑ 크로스는 걱정하고 있는 자신을 꾸짖었다.

❶ 가산명사 우두머리 ❑ 경찰서장이 임명한 위원회 ❷ 가산명사; 경칭명사 족장, 추장 ❑ 대초원 지대의 수우 부족 추장 시팅불 ❸ 형용사 최고의 ❑ 일등 시험비행 조종사 ❹ 형용사 가장 중요한 ❑ 경제적인 문제가 가장 큰 이혼 사유로 꼽히고 있다.

가산명사; 경칭명사 경찰서장

가산명사 최고 경영자 [경제]

가산명사; 경칭명사 재판장; 대법원장

부사 주로, 대개 ❑ 그는 중국에 있는 영사관에 들어갔다. 주된 이유는 그곳이 사람을 뽑는 몇 안 되는 곳 중 하나였기 때문이다.

가산명사 참모총장

물질명사 시폰 ❑ 하늘하늘한 시폰 스커트

❶ 가산명사 어린이, 아이 ❑ 나는 어릴 적에 시골 마을에서 살았다. ❑ 여섯 살 난 아이 ❷ 가산명사 자녀 ❑ 자녀들은 어떻게 지내요? ❑ 그의 아이들은 이제 집에 함께 살지 않는다.

b
c
d
e
f
g
h
i
j
k
l
m
n
o
p
q
r
s
t
u
v
w
x
y
z

Word Web	child

In the Middle Ages, only **infants** and **toddlers** enjoyed the freedoms of **childhood**. A **child** of seven or eight was important to the survival of the family. In the countryside, **sons** started working on the family's farm. **Daughters** did essential housework. In cities, children became laborers and worked along with adults. Today **parents** treat children with special care. The toys **babies** play with help them learn. There are educational programs for preschoolers. The idea of **adolescence** as a separate phase of life appeared about 100 years ago. Today **teenagers** often have part-time jobs while they go to school.

child|birth /tʃaɪldbɜrθ/ N-UNCOUNT **Childbirth** is the act of giving birth to a child. ❑ *She died in childbirth.*

불가산명사 분만, 해산 ❑ 그녀는 아이를 분만하다 죽었다.

child|care /tʃaɪldkɛər/ N-UNCOUNT **Childcare** refers to taking care of children, and to the facilities which help parents to do so. ❑ *Both partners shared childcare.*

불가산명사 양육, 육아 시설 ❑ 아이는 부부가 함께 봤다.

Word Link   hood ≈ state, condition : adulthood, childhood, manhood

---

child|hood ♦◇◇ /tʃaɪldhʊd/ (**childhoods**) N-VAR A person's **childhood** is the period of their life when they are a child. ❑ *She had a happy childhood.* ❑ *He was remembering a story heard in childhood.* →see **child**

가산명사 또는 불가산명사 어린 시절 ❑ 그녀는 행복한 어린 시절을 보냈다. ❑ 그는 어릴 때 들었던 이야기를 떠올리고 있었다.

child|ish /tʃaɪldɪʃ/ 1 ADJ **Childish** means relating to or typical of a child. ❑ *...childish enthusiasm.* 2 ADJ If you describe someone, especially an adult, as **childish**, you disapprove of them because they behave in an immature way. [DISAPPROVAL] ❑ *...Penny's selfish and childish behaviour.*

1 형용사 어린애 같은 ❑ 어린애 같은 열광 2 형용사 유치한 [탐탁찮음] ❑ 페니의 이기적이고 유치한 행동

child|less /tʃaɪldlɪs/ ADJ Someone who is **childless** has no children. ❑ *...childless couples.*

형용사 아이가 없는 ❑ 아이 없는 부부

child|like /tʃaɪldlaɪk/ ADJ You describe someone as **childlike** when they seem like a child in their character, appearance, or behavior. ❑ *His most enduring quality is his childlike innocence.*

형용사 어린애 같은, 천진한, 순진한 ❑ 그의 특징 중 가장 변치 않는 것은 어린애 같은 순수함이다.

child|minder /tʃaɪldmaɪndər/ (**childminders**) N-COUNT A **childminder** is someone whose job it is to take care of children when the children's parents are away or are at work. Childminders usually work in their own homes. [BRIT]

가산명사 보모, 애 봐 주는 사람 [영국영어]

chil|dren /tʃɪldrən/ **Children** is the plural of **child**.

child의 복수형

chili /tʃɪli/ (**chilies** or **chilis**) also **chilli** N-VAR **Chilies** are small red or green peppers. They have a very hot taste and are used in cooking. →see **spice**

가산명사 또는 불가산명사 칠리

chill /tʃɪl/ (**chills**, **chilling**, **chilled**) 1 V-T/V-I When you **chill** something or when it **chills**, you lower its temperature so that it becomes colder but does not freeze. ❑ *Chill the fruit salad until serving time.* ❑ *These doughs can be rolled out while you wait for the pastry to chill.* 2 V-T When cold weather or something cold **chills** a person or a place, it makes that person or that place feel very cold. ❑ *The marble floor was beginning to chill me.* ❑ *Wade placed his chilled hands on the radiator and warmed them.* 3 N-COUNT If something sends a **chill** through you, it gives you a sudden feeling of fear or anxiety. ❑ *The violence used against the students sent a chill through Indonesia.* 4 N-COUNT A **chill** is a mild illness which can give you a slight fever and headache. ❑ *He caught a chill while performing at a rain-soaked open-air venue.* 5 ADJ **Chill** weather is cold and unpleasant. [ADJ n] ❑ *...chill winds, rain and choppy seas.* 6 N-SING **Chill** is also a noun. ❑ *September is here, bringing with it a chill in the mornings.*
→see **illness**, **refrigerator**

1 타동사/자동사 차게 하다, 식히다; 식다 ❑ 과일 샐러드는 식탁에 내기 전까지 냉장 보관한다. ❑ 페스트리가 식기를 기다리는 동안 반죽을 밀면 된다. 2 타동사 춥게 하다 ❑ 나는 대리석 바닥 때문에 추워지기 시작하고 있었다. ❑ 웨이드는 차가워진 손을 라디에이터에 얹고 녹였다. 3 가산명사 간담을 서늘하게 하다 ❑ 학생들을 상대로 자행된 그 폭력은 인도네시아 전 국민의 간담을 서늘하게 만들었다. 4 가산명사 오한 ❑ 그는 비에 흠뻑 젖는 야외 공연장에서 공연을 하다가 오한이 들었다. 5 형용사 쌀쌀한, 으스스한 ❑ 쌀쌀한 바람, 비 그리고 거친 바다 ● 단수명사 냉기, 한기 ❑ 아침에는 쌀쌀한 것이, 이제 완연한 9월이다.

▶**chill out** PHRASAL VERB To **chill out** means to relax after you have done something tiring or stressful. [INFORMAL] ❑ *After raves, we used to chill out in each others' bedrooms.*

구동사 열을 식히다 [비격식체] ❑ 우리는 한바탕 파티를 한 후에 서로 다른 친구들의 침실에서 열을 식히곤 했다.

chil|li /tʃɪli/ (**chillies** or **chillis**) →see **chili**

chill|ing /tʃɪlɪŋ/ ADJ If you describe something as **chilling**, you mean it is frightening. ❑ *He described in chilling detail how he attacked her.* ● **chill|ing|ly** ADV ❑ *...since the murder of a London teenager in chillingly similar circumstances in February.*

형용사 오싹한, 간담이 서늘한 ❑ 그는 자기가 그녀를 어떻게 폭행했는지 오싹할 만큼 자세히 말했다. ● 오싹하게 부사 ❑ 오싹할 정도로 비슷한 상황에서 런던의 십대 한 명이 살해된 이후에

chilly /tʃɪli/ (**chillier**, **chilliest**) 1 ADJ Something that is **chilly** is unpleasantly cold. ❑ *It was a chilly afternoon.* 2 ADJ If you feel **chilly**, you feel rather cold. [v-link ADJ] ❑ *I'm a bit chilly.*

1 형용사 쌀쌀한 ❑ 쌀쌀한 오후였다. 2 형용사 추운 ❑ 약간 춥다

If you want to emphasize how cold the weather is, you can say that it is **freezing**, especially in winter when there is ice or frost. In summer, if the temperature is below average, you can say that it is **cool**. In general, **cold** suggests a lower temperature than **cool**, and **cool** things may be pleasant or refreshing. ❑ *A cool breeze swept off the sea; it was pleasant out there.* If it is very **cool** or too **cool**, you can also say that it is **chilly**.

특히 얼음이 얼거나 서리가 내리는 겨울에 날씨가 추운 것을 강조하고 싶으면, 날씨가 freezing하다고 할 수 있다. 여름에 기온이 평균 이하면, 날씨가 cool하다고 할 수 있다. 일반적으로 cold는 cool보다 낮은 기온을 의미하고, cool한 것은 쾌적하거나 상쾌할 수 있다. ❑ 시원한 미풍이 바다에서 불어 왔다; 거기에 나가 있으니 쾌적했다. 날씨가 아주 cool하거나 너무 cool하면, 날씨가 chilly하다고도 말할 수 있다.

---

chime /tʃaɪm/ (**chimes**, **chiming**, **chimed**) 1 V-T/V-I When a bell or a clock **chimes**, it makes ringing sounds. ❑ *He heard the front doorbell chime.* ❑ *...as the Guildhall clock chimed three o'clock.* 2 N-COUNT A **chime** is a ringing sound made by a bell, especially when it is part of a clock. ❑ *At that moment a chime sounded from the front of the house.* 3 N-PLURAL **Chimes** are a set of small objects which make a ringing sound when they are blown by the wind. ❑ *...the haunting sound of the wind chimes.*

1 타동사/자동사 울리다 ❑ 그는 초인종이 울리는 것을 들었다. ❑ 런던 시청 시계가 세 시임을 알릴 때 2 가산명사 차임벨 ❑ 그때 집 앞에서 차임벨 소리가 들려왔다. 3 복수명사 풍경 ❑ 으스스한 풍경 소리

▶**chime in** PHRASAL VERB If you **chime in**, you say something just after someone else has spoken. ❑ *"Why?" Pete asked impatiently. — "Yes, why?" Bob chimed in. "It seems like a good idea to me."*

구동사 바로 되받아 말하다 ❑ "왜?"라고 피트가 짜증난다는 듯이 물었다. "그래, 왜?"라고 밥이 바로 되받았다. "내가 볼 때에는 괜찮은 생각 같은데."

chim|ney /tʃɪmni/ (**chimneys**) N-COUNT A **chimney** is a pipe through which smoke goes up into the air, usually through the roof of a building. ❑ *Thick, yellow smoke pours constantly out of the chimneys at the steelworks in Katowice.*

가산명사 굴뚝 ❑ 카토비체의 제철소 굴뚝에서는 짙은 노란색 연기가 끊임없이 뿜어져 나온다.

chim|pan|zee /tʃɪmpænzi/ (**chimpanzees**) N-COUNT A **chimpanzee** is a kind of small African ape. →see **primate**, **zoo**

가산명사 침팬지

chin /tʃɪn/ (**chins**) N-COUNT Your **chin** is the part of your face that is below your mouth and above your neck. ❑ *...a double chin.*

가산명사 턱 ❑ 이중 턱

chi|na /tʃaɪnə/ 1 N-UNCOUNT **China** is a hard white substance made from clay. It is used to make things such as cups, bowls, plates, and ornaments. ❑ *...a small boat made of china.* 2 N-UNCOUNT Cups, bowls, plates, and ornaments made of china are referred to as **china**. ❑ *Judy collects blue and white china.* →see **pottery**

1 불가산명사 자기 ❑ 자기로 만들어진 작은 배 2 불가산명사 자기 ❑ 주디는 파랗고 하얀 색의 자기를 수집한다.

chink /tʃɪŋk/ (**chinks**) **1** N-COUNT A **chink** in a surface is a very narrow crack or opening in it. ❑ ...*a chink in the wall*. **2** N-COUNT A **chink of** light is a small patch of light that shines through a small opening in something. ❑ *I noticed a chink of light at the end of the corridor.*

chip ◆◇◇ /tʃɪp/ (**chips, chipping, chipped**) **1** N-COUNT **Chips** or **potato chips** are very thin slices of fried potato that are eaten cold as a snack. [AM; BRIT **crisps**] ❑ ...*a package of onion-flavored potato chips.* **2** N-COUNT **Chips** are long, thin pieces of potato fried in oil or fat and eaten hot, usually with a meal. [BRIT; AM **French fries**] ❑ *I had fish and chips in a cafe.* **3** N-COUNT A silicon **chip** is a very small piece of silicon with electronic circuits on it which is part of a computer or other piece of machinery. ❑ ...*an electronic card containing a chip.* **4** N-COUNT A **chip** is a small piece of something or a small piece which has been broken off something. ❑ *It contains real chocolate chips.* **5** N-COUNT A **chip** in something such as a piece of china or furniture is where a small piece has been broken off it. ❑ *The washbasin had a small chip.* **6** V-T/V-I If you **chip** something or if it **chips**, a small piece is broken off it. ❑ *The blow chipped the woman's tooth.* ● **chipped** ADJ ❑ *The wagon's paint was badly chipped on the outside.* **7** N-COUNT **Chips** are plastic counters used in gambling to represent money. ❑ *He put the pile of chips in the center of the table and drew a card.* **8** N-COUNT In discussions between people or governments, a **chip** or a **bargaining chip** is something of value which one side holds, which can be exchanged for something they want from the other side. ❑ *The information could be used as a bargaining chip to extract some parallel information from Britain.* **9** →see also **blue chip** →see **computer**

▶**chip in** PHRASAL VERB When a number of people **chip in**, each person gives some money so that they can pay for something together. [INFORMAL] ❑ *They chip in for the gas.*

chis|el /tʃɪzᵊl/ (**chisels, chiseling, chiseled**) [BRIT, sometimes AM **chiselling, chiselled**] **1** N-COUNT A **chisel** is a tool that has a long metal blade with a sharp edge at the end. It is used for cutting and shaping wood and stone. ❑ ...*a hammer and chisel.* **2** V-T If you **chisel** wood or stone, you cut and shape it using a chisel. ❑ *He set out to chisel a dog out of sandstone.*

chlo|rine /klɔrin/ N-UNCOUNT **Chlorine** is a strong-smelling gas that is used to clean water and in making cleaning products.

choco|late ◆◇◇ /tʃɒkəlɪt, tʃɒklɪt, BRIT tʃɒklɪt/ (**chocolates**) **1** N-MASS **Chocolate** is a sweet hard food made from cocoa beans. It is usually brown in color and is eaten as a candy. ❑ ...*a bar of chocolate.* ❑ *Do you want some chocolate?* **2** N-UNCOUNT **Chocolate** or **hot chocolate** is a drink made from a powder containing chocolate. It is usually made with hot milk. ❑ ...*a small cafeteria where the visitors can buy tea, coffee and chocolate.* ● N-COUNT A cup of chocolate can be referred to as a **chocolate** or a **hot chocolate**. ❑ *I'll have a hot chocolate please.* **3** N-COUNT **Chocolates** are small candies or nuts covered with a layer of chocolate. They are usually sold in a box. ❑ ...*a box of chocolates.* **4** COLOR **Chocolate** is used to describe things that are dark brown in color. ❑ *The curtains and the coverlet of the bed were chocolate velvet.*

choice ◆◆◇ /tʃɔɪs/ (**choices, choicer, choicest**) **1** N-COUNT If there is a **choice of** things, there are several of them and you can choose the one you want. ❑ *It's available in a choice of colors.* ❑ *At lunchtime, there's a choice between the buffet or the set menu.* **2** N-COUNT Your **choice** is someone or something that you choose from a range of things. ❑ *Although he was only grumbling, his choice of words made Rodney angry.* **3** ADJ **Choice** means of very high quality. [FORMAL] [ADJ n] ❑ ...*Fortnum and Mason's choicest chocolates.* **4** PHRASE If you **have no choice but** to do something or **have little choice but** to do it, you cannot avoid doing it. ❑ *They had little choice but to agree to what he suggested.* **5** PHRASE The thing or person **of** your **choice** is the one that you choose. ❑ ...*tickets to see the football team of your choice.* **6** PHRASE The item **of choice** is the one that most people prefer. ❑ *The drug is set to become the treatment of choice for asthma worldwide.*

Word Partnership		choice의 연어
N.	choice **of *something*, freedom of** choice **1 2**	
V.	**given a** choice, **have a** choice, **make a** choice **1 2**	
ADJ.	**best/good** choice, **wide** choice **1**	

choir /kwaɪər/ (**choirs**) N-COUNT A **choir** is a group of people who sing together, for example in a church or school. ❑ *He has been singing in his church choir since he was six.*

choke /tʃoʊk/ (**chokes, choking, choked**) **1** V-T/V-I When you **choke** or when something **chokes** you, you cannot breathe properly or get enough air into your lungs. ❑ *A small child could choke on the doll's hair.* ❑ *Dense smoke swirled and billowed, its rank fumes choking her.* ❑ *The girl choked to death after breathing in smoke.* **2** V-T To **choke** someone means to squeeze their neck until they are dead. ❑ *The men pushed him into the entrance of a nearby building where they choked him with his tie.* **3** V-T If a place **is choked with** things or people, it is full of them and they prevent movement in it. [usu passive] ❑ *The village's roads are choked with traffic.* **4** N-COUNT The **choke** in a car, truck, or other vehicle is a device that reduces the amount of air going into the engine and makes it easier to start. ❑ *It is like driving your car with the choke out all the time.*

Word Partnership		choke의 연어
N.	choke **on *something* 1**	
V.	choke ***someone* 2**	
	make *someone* choke **1**	

1 가산명사 금, 틈 ❑ 벽에 난 금 **2** 가산명사 새어 나오는 (불빛) ❑ 복도 끝에서 한 줄기 불빛이 새어 나오는 게 보였다.

1 가산명사 감자칩 [미국영어; 영국영어 crisps] ❑ 양파맛 감자칩 한 봉 **2** 가산명사 얇게 썬 감자튀김 [영국영어; 미국영어 french fries] ❑ 식당에서 생선과 감자튀김을 먹었다. **3** 가산명사 칩 ❑ 칩이 든 전자 카드 **4** 가산명사 부스러기 ❑ 거기엔 진짜 초콜릿 칩이 들어 있다. **5** 가산명사 홈 ❑ 세면대에 작은 홈이 있었다. **6** 타동사/자동사 한쪽 끝을 깨뜨리다; 한쪽 끝이 떨어져 나가다 ❑ 그 타격에 여자의 이빨 끝이 떨어져 나갔다. ● 이가 빠진, 조각이 떨어져 나간 형용사 ❑ 짐마차 외부의 페인트칠이 심하게 벗겨져 있었다. **7** 가산명사 (도박용) 칩 ❑ 그는 칩 더미를 탁자 한가운데 쌓아 놓은 뒤 카드를 뽑았다. **8** 가산명사 협상용 대상 ❑ 이 정보를 협상용으로 활용해서 영국으로부터 그에 상응하는 정보를 얻을 수 있을 것이다.

구동사 돈을 추렴하다 [비격식체] ❑ 그들은 기름값을 추렴해서 낸다.

[영국영어, 미국영어 가끔 chiselling] **1** 가산명사 끌 ❑ 망치와 끌 **2** 타동사 끌로 다듬다 ❑ 그는 끌로 사암을 다듬어 개를 조각하기 시작했다.

불가산명사 염소

1 물질명사 초콜릿 ❑ 초콜릿 바 ❑ 초콜릿 좀 먹을래? **2** 불가산명사 핫초코 ❑ 손님들이 차, 커피, 핫초코 등을 사 마실 수 있는 찻집 ● 가산명사 핫초코 ❑ 핫초코 한 잔 주세요. **3** 가산명사 초콜릿 ❑ 초콜릿 한 상자 **4** 색채어 초콜릿빛 ❑ 커튼과 침대 덮개는 초콜릿색 벨벳이었다.

1 가산명사 선택의 폭 ❑ 그것은 색깔을 선택할 수 있게 몇 가지 색깔로 나온다. ❑ 점심시간에는 뷔페와 정식 사이에서 고를 수 있다. **2** 가산명사 선택 ❑ 그가 그냥 투덜댄 것이긴 했으나 그의 단어 선택이 로드니를 화나게 했다. **3** 형용사 엄선된 것 [격식체] ❑ 포트넘과 메이슨즈의 가장 엄선된 초콜릿 **4** 구 선택의 여지가 없다 ❑ 그들은 그의 제안에 동의하는 수밖에는 선택의 여지가 없었다. **5** 구 -가 원하는 ❑ 당신이 원하는 축구 팀을 볼 수 있는 표 **6** 구 선호되는 ❑ 천식을 치료하는 데 그 약이 가장 널리 쓰일 전망이다.

가산명사 합창단 ❑ 그는 여섯 살 때부터 교회 성가대에서 노래를 불렀다.

1 타동사/자동사 질식하다; 질식시키다 ❑ 작은 아이는 인형의 머리카락에 질식할 수도 있다. ❑ 짙은 연기가 소용돌이치며 뿜어져 나왔고 그 악취 나는 연기에 그녀는 숨이 막혔다. ❑ 소녀는 연기 흡입으로 질식사했다. **2** 타동사 목 졸라 죽이다 ❑ 남자들은 그를 인근 건물의 입구로 밀어 넣은 뒤 넥타이로 목 졸라 죽였다. **3** 타동사 -으로 가득 차다 ❑ 마을 도로는 차량으로 꽉 막혔다. **4** 가산명사 초크 ❑ 그것은 늘 초크가 없는 상태에서 차를 운전하는 것과 같다.

chol|era /kɒlərə/ N-UNCOUNT **Cholera** is a serious disease that often kills people. It is caused by drinking infected water or by eating infected food. ❑ *...a cholera epidemic.*

불가산명사 콜레라 ❑ 콜레라의 대규모 발병

cho|les|ter|ol /kəlestərɒl, BRIT kəlestərɒl/ N-UNCOUNT **Cholesterol** is a substance that exists in the fat, tissues, and blood of all animals. Too much cholesterol in a person's blood can cause heart disease. ❑ *...a dangerously high cholesterol level.*

불가산명사 콜레스테롤 ❑ 위험하게 높은 콜레스테롤 수치

choose ♦♦◇ /tʃuːz/ (**chooses, choosing, chose, chosen**) ◼ V-T/V-I If you **choose** someone or something **from** several people or things that are available, you decide which person or thing you want to have. ❑ *They will be able to choose their own leaders in democratic elections.* ❑ *There are several patchwork cushions to choose from.* ◼ V-T/V-I If you **choose to** do something, you do it because you want to or because you feel that it is right. ❑ *They knew that discrimination was going on, but chose to ignore it.*

◼ 타동사/자동사 고르다, 선출하다 ❑ 그들은 민주적 선거로 자신들의 지도자를 선출할 수 있을 것이다. ❑ 여러 가지 조각보 쿠션 중에서 고를 수 있다. ◼ 타동사/자동사 선택하다 ❑ 그들은 차별이 행해진다는 것을 알았으나 그것을 무시하기로 했다.

Thesaurus		*choose*의 참조어
v.		decide on, opt for, prefer, settle on; *(ant.)* refuse, reject ◼

chop ♦◇◇ /tʃɒp/ (**chops, chopping, chopped**) ◼ V-T If you **chop** something, you cut it into pieces with strong downward movements of a knife or an ax. ❑ *Chop the butter into small pieces.* ❑ *Visitors were set to work chopping wood.* ◼ N-COUNT A **chop** is a small piece of meat cut from the ribs of a sheep or pig. ❑ *...grilled lamb chops.* ◼ PHRASE If something is **for the chop** or is going to **get the chop**, it is going to be stopped or closed. If someone is **for the chop**, they are going to lose their job or position. [BRIT, INFORMAL] ❑ *He won't say which programmes are for the chop.*

◼ 타동사 자르다 ❑ 버터를 잘게 다지세요. ❑ 방문자들에게 장작을 패도록 했다. ◼ 가산명사 갈비 ❑ 양갈비구이 ◼ 구 정리 대상의; 해고 대상의 [영국영어, 비격식체] ❑ 그는 어떤 프로그램들이 정리 대상인지 말하지 않으려 한다.

▶**chop down** PHRASAL VERB If you **chop down** a tree, you cut through its trunk with an ax so that it falls to the ground. ❑ *Sometimes they have to chop down a tree for firewood.*

구동사 (나무를) 베다 ❑ 때로는 그들이 나무를 베어 장작을 마련해야 한다.

▶**chop off** PHRASAL VERB To **chop off** something such as a part of someone's body means to cut it off. ❑ *She chopped off her golden, waist-length hair.*

구동사 싹둑 자르다, 절단하다 ❑ 그녀는 허리까지 오는 금발을 싹둑 잘랐다.

▶**chop up** PHRASAL VERB If you **chop** something **up**, you chop it into small pieces. ❑ *Chop up three firm tomatoes.*

구동사 다지다 ❑ 단단한 토마토 세 개를 다지세요.

chop|per /tʃɒpər/ (**choppers**) N-COUNT A **chopper** is a helicopter. [INFORMAL] ❑ *Overhead, the chopper roared and the big blades churned the air.*

가산명사 헬리콥터 [비격식체] ❑ 머리 위에서는 헬리콥터가 큰 소리를 내며 거대한 날을 허공에 저어대고 있었다.

cho|ral /kɔːrəl/ ADJ **Choral** music is sung by a choir. ❑ *His collection of choral music from around the world is called "Voices".*

형용사 합창의 ❑ 그가 전 세계 합창 음악을 모아 만든 음반 제목은 '목소리들'이다.

chord /kɔːrd/ (**chords**) ◼ N-COUNT A **chord** is a number of musical notes played or sung at the same time with a pleasing effect. ❑ *I could play a few chords on the guitar and sing a song.* ◼ PHRASE If something **strikes a chord with** you, it makes you feel sympathy or enthusiasm. ❑ *Mr. Jenkins' arguments for stability struck a chord with Europe's two most powerful politicians.*

◼ 가산명사 화음; (기타 연주의) 코드 ❑ 기타로 몇 개의 코드를 연주하면서 노래할 줄은 알았다. ◼ 구 심금을 울리다, 마음을 움직이다 ❑ 안정을 호소하는 젠킨스 씨의 주장은 유럽의 가장 강력한 정치인 두 명의 마음을 움직였다.

chore /tʃɔːr/ (**chores**) N-COUNT A **chore** is a task that you must do but that you find unpleasant or boring. ❑ *She sees exercise primarily as an unavoidable chore.*

가산명사 허드렛일 ❑ 그녀의 눈에 운동은 기본적으로 어쩔 수 없이 하는 허드렛일이다.

cho|reo|graph /kɔːriəgræf, BRIT kɒriəgrɑːf/ (**choreographs, choreographing, choreographed**) V-T/V-I When someone **choreographs** a ballet or other dance, they invent the steps and movements and tell the dancers how to perform them. ❑ *Achim had choreographed the dance in Act II himself.*

타동사/자동사 안무하다 ❑ 아킴이 직접 2막의 춤을 안무했다.

cho|reog|ra|phy /kɔːriɒgrəfi, BRIT kɒriɒgrəfi/ N-UNCOUNT **Choreography** is the inventing of steps and movements for ballets and other dances. ❑ *The choreography of Eric Hawkins is considered radical by ballet audiences.*

불가산명사 안무 ❑ 에릭 호킨스의 안무는 발레 관객들의 눈에 과격하게 비친다.

cho|rus /kɔːrəs/ (**choruses, chorusing, chorused**) ◼ N-COUNT A **chorus** is a part of a song which is repeated after each verse. ❑ *Caroline sang two verses and the chorus of her song.* ◼ N-COUNT A **chorus** is a large group of people who sing together. ❑ *The chorus was singing "The Ode to Joy".* ◼ N-COUNT A **chorus** is a piece of music written to be sung by a large group of people. ❑ *...the Hallelujah Chorus.* ◼ N-COUNT A **chorus** is a group of singers or dancers who perform together in a show, in contrast to the soloists. ❑ *Students played the lesser parts and sang in the chorus.* ◼ N-COUNT When there is a **chorus** of criticism, disapproval, or praise, that attitude is expressed by a lot of people at the same time. ❑ *The government is defending its economic policies against a growing chorus of criticism.* ◼ V-T When people **chorus** something, they say it or sing it together. [WRITTEN] ❑ *"Hi," they chorused.*

◼ 가산명사 후렴 ❑ 캐롤라인은 자신의 노래에서 가사 두 절과 후렴을 불렀다. ◼ 가산명사 합창단 ❑ 합창단은 '환희의 송가'를 부르고 있었다. ◼ 가산명사 합창곡 ❑ 할렐루야 합창곡 ◼ 가산명사 합창단 ❑ 학생들은 소역을 맡거나 합창대에서 노래를 불렀다. ◼ 가산명사 합창, 한 목소리로 말함 ❑ 정부는 점점 커가는 비판의 목소리에 대응해서 그들의 경제 정책을 옹호하고 있다. ◼ 타동사 동시에 말하다, 합창을 하다 [문어체] ❑ "안녕."하고 그들은 동시에 말했다.

chose /tʃoʊz/ **Chose** is the past tense of **choose**.

choose의 과거형

cho|sen /tʃoʊzən/ **Chosen** is the past participle of **choose**.

choose의 과거 분사형

Christ /kraɪst/ N-PROPER **Christ** is one of the names of Jesus, whom Christians believe to be the son of God and whose teachings are the basis of Christianity. ❑ *...the teachings of Christ.*

고유명사 예수 ❑ 예수의 가르침

chris|ten /krɪsən/ (**christens, christening, christened**) V-T When a baby **is christened**, he or she is given a name during the Christian ceremony of baptism. Compare **baptize**. [usu passive] ❑ *She was born in March and christened in June.*

타동사 세례를 받다 ❑ 그 여자 아이는 3월에 태어나 6월에 세례를 받았다.

chris|ten|ing /krɪsənɪŋ/ (**christenings**) N-COUNT A **christening** is a Christian ceremony in which a baby is made a member of the Christian church and is officially given his or her name. Compare **baptism**. ❑ *...my granddaughter's christening.*

가산명사 (기독교의) 세례식 ❑ 나의 손녀의 세례식

a b c d e f g h i j k l m n o p q r s t u v w x y z

Word Link | *an, ian ≈ one of, relating to : Christian, pedestrian, vegan*

Christian ♦♦◇ /krɪstʃən/ (Christians) **1** N-COUNT A **Christian** is someone who follows the teachings of Jesus Christ. ❑ *He was a devout Christian.* **2** ADJ **Christian** means relating to Christianity or Christians. ❑ *...the Christian Church.* ❑ *Most of my friends are Christian.* →see **religion**

1 가산명사 기독교인 ❑ 그는 독실한 기독교인이었다. **2** 형용사 기독교의 ❑ 기독교 교회 ❑ 내 친구들 대부분은 기독교인이다.

Chris|ti|an|ity /krɪstʃiænɪti/ N-UNCOUNT **Christianity** is a religion that is based on the teachings of Jesus Christ and the belief that he was the son of God. ❑ *He converted to Christianity that day.*

불가산명사 기독교 ❑ 그는 그날 기독교로 개종했다.

Christian name (Christian names) N-COUNT Some people refer to their first names as their **Christian names**. ❑ *Despite my attempts to get him to call me by my Christian name he insisted on addressing me as "Mr. Kennedy."*

가산명사 이름 ❑ 그는 내가 이름을 부르라고 했는데도 불구하고 계속 나를 '케네디 씨'라고 불렀다.

Christ|mas ♦♦◇ /krɪsməs/ (Christmases) **1** N-VAR **Christmas** is a Christian festival when the birth of Jesus Christ is celebrated. Christmas is celebrated on the 25th of December. ❑ *The day after Christmas is generally a busy one for retailers.* **2** N-VAR **Christmas** is the period of several days around and including Christmas Day. ❑ *During the Christmas holidays there's a tremendous amount of traffic between the Northeast and Florida.*

1 가산명사 또는 불가산명사 크리스마스 ❑ 소매업자들에게 크리스마스 다음 날은 대체로 바쁜 날이다. **2** 가산명사 또는 불가산명사 크리스마스 기간 ❑ 크리스마스 연휴 동안 동북부와 플로리다 사이는 교통량이 엄청나다.

Christ|mas Day N-UNCOUNT **Christmas Day** is the 25th of December, when Christmas is celebrated.

불가산명사 크리스마스 ❑

Christ|mas Eve N-UNCOUNT **Christmas Eve** is the 24th of December, the day before Christmas Day.

불가산명사 크리스마스 전야 ❑

chrome /kroʊm/ N-UNCOUNT **Chrome** is metal plated with chromium. ❑ *...old-fashioned chrome taps.*

불가산명사 크롬 ❑ 구식 크롬 수도꼭지

chro|mium /kroʊmiəm/ N-UNCOUNT **Chromium** is a hard, shiny metallic element, used to make steel alloys and to coat other metals. ❑ *...chromium-plated fire accessories.*

불가산명사 크로뮴 ❑ 크로뮴으로 도금된 화재용 기구

chro|mo|some /kroʊməsoʊm/ (chromosomes) N-COUNT A **chromosome** is a part of a cell in an animal or plant. It contains genes which determine what characteristics the animal or plant will have. ❑ *Each cell of our bodies contains 46 chromosomes.*

가산명사 염색체 ❑ 우리 몸의 모든 세포는 46개의 염색체를 가지고 있다.

chron|ic /krɒnɪk/ **1** ADJ A **chronic** illness or disability lasts for a very long time. Compare **acute**. ❑ *...chronic back pain.* ● **chroni|cal|ly** /krɒnɪkli/ ADV [ADV adj/-ed] ❑ *Most of them were chronically ill.* **2** ADJ You can describe someone's bad habits or behavior as **chronic** when they have behaved like that for a long time and do not seem to be able to stop themselves. [ADJ n] ❑ *...a chronic worrier.* **3** ADJ A **chronic** situation or problem is very severe and unpleasant. ❑ *One cause of the artist's suicide seems to have been chronic poverty.* ● **chroni|cal|ly** ADV [ADV adj/-ed] ❑ *Research and technology are said to be chronically underfunded.*

1 형용사 만성적인 ❑ 만성 요통 ● 만성적으로 부사 ❑ 그들 대부분은 만성 환자였다. **2** 형용사 상습적인 ❑ 걱정을 달고 사는 사람 **3** 형용사 극심한 ❑ 그 예술가의 자살 원인의 한 가지 원인은 극심한 가난이었던 것 같다. ● 극심하게 부사 ❑ 연구 개발은 극심하게 자금이 부족하다고 한다.

chron|icle /krɒnɪkᵊl/ (chronicles, chronicling, chronicled) **1** V-T To **chronicle** a series of events means to write about them or show them in broadcasts in the order in which they happened. ❑ *The series chronicles the everyday adventures of two eternal bachelors.* **2** N-COUNT A **chronicle** is an account or record of a series of events. ❑ *...this vast chronicle of Napoleonic times.* **3** N-IN-NAMES **Chronicle** is sometimes used as part of the name of a newspaper. ❑ *...the San Francisco Chronicle.* →see **diary**

1 타동사 연대순으로 기록하다 ❑ 그 시리즈물은 영원한 독신자인 두 남자의 일상적인 모험담을 시간 순으로 서술한다. **2** 가산명사 연대기 ❑ 나폴레옹 시대에 대한 방대한 연대기 **3** 이름명사 신문 이름으로 쓰이는 단어 ❑ 샌프란시스코 크로니클

chrono|logi|cal /krɒnᵊlɒdʒɪkᵊl/ ADJ If things are described or shown in **chronological** order, they are described or shown in the order in which they happened. ❑ *I have arranged these stories in chronological order.* ● **chrono|logi|cal|ly** ADV ❑ *The exhibition is organised chronologically.*

형용사 연대순의 ❑ 나는 이 이야기들을 연대순으로 정리했다. ● 연대순으로 부사 ❑ 전시회는 연대순으로 짜였다.

chub|by /tʃʌbi/ (chubbier, chubbiest) ADJ A **chubby** person is rather fat. ❑ *Do you think I'm too chubby?* →see **fat**

형용사 통통한 ❑ 내가 너무 통통한 것 같니?

chuck /tʃʌk/ (chucks, chucking, chucked) **1** V-T When you **chuck** something somewhere, you throw it there in a casual or careless way. [INFORMAL] ❑ *I took a great dislike to the clock, so I chucked it in the trash.* **2** V-T If you **chuck** your job or some other activity, you stop doing it. [INFORMAL] ❑ *Last summer, he chucked his 10-year career as a London stockbroker and headed for the mountains.* **3** PHRASE If someone **chucks it all**, they stop doing their job, and usually move somewhere else. In British English, you can also say that someone **chucks it all up** or **chucks it all in**. ❑ *Sometimes I'd like to chuck it all and go fishing.* **4** V-T If your girlfriend or boyfriend **chucks** you, they end the relationship. [INFORMAL] ❑ *There wasn't a great hoo-ha when I chucked her.* **5** N-COUNT A **chuck** is a device for holding a tool in a machine such as a drill.

1 타동사 팽개치다 [비격식체] ❑ 나는 그 시계가 너무 싫어져서 쓰레기통에 팽개쳐 버렸다. **2** 타동사 때려치우다 [비격식체] ❑ 지난 여름, 그는 런던 증권 중개인으로서의 10년 생활을 때려치우고 산으로 향했다. **3** 구 일을 그만두고 떠나다 ❑ 때때로 나는 일을 때려치우고 낚시하러 가고 싶다. **4** 타동사 차다 [비격식체] ❑ 내가 그녀를 찼을 때 그다지 큰 소란은 없었다. **5** 가산명사 척

chuck|le /tʃʌkᵊl/ (chuckles, chuckling, chuckled) V-I When you **chuckle**, you laugh quietly. ❑ *The banker chuckled and said, "Of course not."* ● N-COUNT **Chuckle** is also a noun. ❑ *He gave a little chuckle.*

자동사 킥 하고 웃다 ❑ 은행원이 킥 웃고는 "물론 아니죠."라고 했다. ● 가산명사 킥 웃음 ❑ 그가 킥킥거리며 웃었다.

chug /tʃʌg/ (chugs, chugging, chugged) V-I When a vehicle **chugs** somewhere, it goes there slowly, noisily, and with difficulty. ❑ *The train chugs down the track.*

자동사 칙칙 소리를 내며 가다 ❑ 기차가 철로를 따라 칙칙거리며 간다.

chunk /tʃʌŋk/ (chunks) **1** N-COUNT **Chunks** of something are thick solid pieces of it. ❑ *They had to be careful of floating chunks of ice.* ❑ *...a chunk of meat.* **2** N-COUNT A **chunk of** something is a large amount or large part of it. [INFORMAL] ❑ *The company owns a chunk of farmland near Gatwick Airport.*

1 가산명사 덩어리 ❑ 그들은 떠다니는 얼음 덩어리를 조심해야 했다. ❑ 고깃덩어리 **2** 가산명사 상당한 양의 것 [비격식체] ❑ 그 회사는 개트윅 공항 근처에 상당한 규모의 농지를 소유하고 있다.

chunky /tʃʌŋki/ (chunkier, chunkiest) **1** ADJ A **chunky** person is broad and heavy. ❑ *The soprano was a chunky girl from California.* **2** ADJ A **chunky** object is large and thick. ❑ *Her taste in fiction was for chunky historical romances.* ❑ *...a chunky sweater.*

1 형용사 땅딸막한 ❑ 소프라노는 캘리포니아 출신의 땅딸막한 여자였다. **2** 형용사 두툼한 ❑ 그녀는 두툼한 역사적인 낭만 소설을 선호했다. ❑ 두툼한 스웨터

A

church ◆◆◇ /tʃɜrtʃ/ (churches) **1** N-VAR A **church** is a building in which Christians worship. You usually refer to this place as **church** when you are talking about the time that people spend there. □ ...one of Britain's most historic churches. □ ...St Helen's Church. **2** N-COUNT A **Church** is one of the groups of people within the Christian religion, for example Catholics or Methodists, that have their own beliefs, clergy, and forms of worship. □ ...cooperation with the Catholic Church. □ Church leaders said he was welcome to return.

1 가산명사 또는 불가산명사 교회 □ 영국에서 역사적으로 가장 중요한 교회 중 한 곳 □ 성 헬렌 교회 **2** 가산명사 교파 □ 천주교와의 협력 □ 교회 지도자들은 그의 귀환을 환영한다고 했다.

B

C

churn /tʃɜrn/ (churns, churning, churned) **1** N-COUNT A **churn** is a container which is used for making butter. **2** V-T If something **churns** water, mud, or dust, it moves it about violently. □ Ferries churn the waters of Howe Sound from Langdale to Horseshoe Bay. ● PHRASAL VERB **Churn up** means the same as **churn**. □ The recent rain had churned up the waterfall into a muddy whirlpool. □ Occasionally they slap the water with their tails or churn it up in play. **3** V-I If you say that your stomach **is churning**, you mean that you feel sick. You can also say that something **churns** your stomach. □ My stomach churned as I stood up.

1 가산명사 버터를 만드는 통 **2** 타동사 휘젓다 □ 하우 해협의 랭데일과 호스슈 만 사이를 연락선들이 파도를 일으키며 다닌다. ● 구동사 휘젓다 □ 최근 내린 비로 폭포는 소용돌이치는 흙탕물 같았다. □ 간혹 그들은 꼬리로 물을 치거나 휘저으며 논다. **3** 자동사 울렁거리다; 울렁거리게 하다 □ 일어서자 속이 울렁거렸다.

D

E

►**churn out** PHRASAL VERB To **churn out** something means to produce large quantities of it very quickly. [INFORMAL] □ He began to churn out literary compositions in English.

구동사 속속 만들어 내다 [비격식체] □ 그는 영어로 문학 작품을 속속 써내기 시작했다.

F

►**churn up** →see **churn 2**

chute /ʃut/ (chutes) **1** N-COUNT A **chute** is a steep, narrow slope down which people or things can slide. □ Passengers escaped from the plane's front four exits by sliding down emergency chutes. **2** N-COUNT A **chute** is a parachute. [INFORMAL] □ You can release the chute with either hand, but it is easier to do it with the left.

1 가산명사 활강로 □ 승객들은 비행기의 전방 4개 출구에서 비상 활강로를 타고 탈출했다. **2** 가산명사 낙하산 [비격식체] □ 아무 손으로나 낙하산을 펼 수 있으나 왼손으로 하는 것이 더 쉽다.

G

H

chut|ney /tʃʌtni/ (chutneys) N-MASS **Chutney** is a cold sauce made from fruit, vinegar, sugar, and spices. It is sold in jars and you eat it with meat or cheese. □ ...mango chutney.

물질명사 인도의 양념장 □ 망고 처트니

I

ci|der /saɪdər/ (ciders) N-MASS **Cider** is a drink made from apples which in Britain usually contains alcohol. In the United States, **cider** does not usually contain alcohol, and if it does contain alcohol, it is usually called **hard cider**. ● N-COUNT A glass of cider can be referred to as a **cider**. □ Inside, he ordered a cider, the alcoholic English variety.

물질명사 사과주; 사과 주스 ● 가산명사 사과주 한 잔 □ 안에서 그는 영국식 주류인 사과주 한 잔을 시켰다.

J

K

ci|gar /sɪgɑr/ (cigars) N-COUNT **Cigars** are rolls of dried tobacco leaves which people smoke. □ He was sitting alone smoking a big cigar.

가산명사 시가 □ 그는 혼자 앉아 큰 시가를 피우고 있었다.

L

ciga|rette ◆◇◇ /sɪgəret/ (cigarettes) N-COUNT **Cigarettes** are small tubes of paper containing tobacco which people smoke. □ He went out to buy a packet of cigarettes.

가산명사 담배 □ 그는 담배 한 갑을 사러 나갔다.

M

cin|ema ◆◇◇ /sɪnɪmə/ (cinemas) **1** N-UNCOUNT **Cinema** is the business and art of making movies. □ Contemporary African cinema has much to offer in its vitality and freshness. **2** N-COUNT A **cinema** is a place where people go to watch movies for entertainment. [mainly BRIT; AM usually **movie theater**, **movie house**] □ The country has relatively few cinemas. **3** N-SING You can talk about **the cinema** when you are talking about seeing a movie. [mainly BRIT; AM usually **the movies**] □ I can't remember the last time we went to the cinema.

1 불가산명사 영화 □ 현대 아프리카 영화는 생동감과 신선함이 넘친다. **2** 가산명사 영화관 [주로 영국영어; 미국영어 대개 movie theater, movie house] □ 그 나라에는 영화관이 별로 없다. **3** 단수명사 영화 관람 [주로 영국영어; 미국영어 대개 the movies] □ 마지막으로 영화 보러 간 것이 언제인지 기억이 안 난다.

N

O

cin|emat|ic /sɪnɪmætɪk/ ADJ **Cinematic** means relating to movies made for movie theaters. □ ...a genuine cinematic masterpiece.

형용사 영화의 □ 진정한 명화

cin|na|mon /sɪnəmən/ N-UNCOUNT **Cinnamon** is a sweet spice used for flavoring food. →see **spice**

불가산명사 계피

P

cir|ca /sɜrkə/ PREP **Circa** is used in front of a particular year to say that this is the approximate date when something happened or was made. [FORMAL] □ The story tells of a runaway slave girl in Louisiana, circa 1850.

전치사 −경 [격식체] □ 그 소설은 1850년 경의 루이지애나 주 도망 노예 소녀 이야기를 다룬다.

Q

R

Word Link	circ ≈ around : circle, circuit, circulate

cir|cle ◆◆◇ /sɜrkəl/ (circles, circling, circled) **1** N-COUNT A **circle** is a shape consisting of a curved line completely surrounding an area. Every part of the line is the same distance from the center of the area. □ The flag was red, with a large white circle in the center. **2** N-COUNT A **circle of** something is a round flat piece or area of it. □ Cut out 4 circles of pastry. **3** N-COUNT A **circle of** objects or people is a group of them arranged in the shape of a circle. □ ...a circle of gigantic stones. **4** V-T/V-I If something **circles** an object or a place, or **circles around** it, it forms a circle around it. □ This is the ring road that circles the city. **5** V-T/V-I If an aircraft or a bird **circles** or **circles** something, it moves around in a circle in the air. □ The plane circled, awaiting permission to land. □ There were two helicopters circling around. **6** V-T If you **circle** something on a piece of paper, you draw a circle around it. □ Circle the correct answers on the coupon below. **7** N-COUNT You can refer to a group of people as a **circle** when they meet each other regularly because they are friends or because they belong to the same profession or share the same interests. □ He has a small circle of friends. **8** N-SING In a theater, **the circle** is an area of seats on the upper floor. □ ...the best seats in the stalls and circle. **9** →see also **inner circle**, **vicious circle** →see Word Web: **circle**

1 가산명사 원, 동그라미 □ 깃발은 붉은색이었는데 가운데에 큰 흰색 원이 있었다. **2** 가산명사 원 모양의 가루 반죽 네 개를 잘라 내라. **3** 가산명사 원 □ 거대한 돌들의 원 **4** 타동사/자동사 둘러싸다, 빙 두르다 □ 이것은 도시 순환 도로이다. **5** 타동사/자동사 선회하다 □ 비행기는 착륙 허가를 기다리며 하늘을 선회했다. □ 두 대의 헬리콥터가 주위를 선회하고 있었다. **6** 타동사 동그라미를 치다 □ 아래 쿠폰에서 정답에 동그라미를 치세요. **7** 가산명사 패, 집단 □ 그는 작은 친구 집단과 어울린다. **8** 단수명사 상층 원형 관람석 □ 무대 바로 앞 좌석과 상층 관람석에서 가장 좋은 자리들

S

T

U

V

W

X

Y

Word Partnership		circle의 연어
V.	draw a circle	**1**
	form a circle, make a circle	**1**-**4**
ADJ.	big/large/small circle	**1 2 3 7**
PREP.	circle around, inside/within/outside a circle	**1 3**

Z

Word Web   circle

During the 1970s crop **circles** began to appear in England and the U.S. Something creates these mysterious **rings** in fields of crops such as wheat or corn. Are they messages left by visitors from other worlds? Most people think they are made by humans. The **diameter** of each crop circle ranges from a few inches to a few hundred feet. Sometimes the patterns contain **shapes** that are not **circular**, such as **ovals**, **triangles**, and **spirals**. Occasionally the shapes seem to represent something, such as a face or a flower. One design even contained a written message: *We are not alone.*

Word Link   circ ≈ around : circle, circuit, circulate

cir|cuit ♦○○ /sɜrkɪt/ (circuits) **1** N-COUNT An electrical **circuit** is a complete route which an electric current can flow around. ❑ *Any attempts to cut through the cabling will break the electrical circuit.* →see also **closed-circuit 2** N-COUNT A **circuit** is a series of places that are visited regularly by a person or group, especially as a part of their job. ❑ *It's a common problem, the one I'm asked about most when I'm on the lecture circuit.* **3** N-COUNT A racing **circuit** is a track on which cars, motorcycles, or bicycles race. [mainly BRIT] ❑ *An extra 1,500 policemen will also be stationed around the circuit to search the 160,000 fans.*

1 가산명사 회로 ❑ 전선을 자르려고 시도하기만 하면 전자 회로가 고장 날 것이다. **2** 가산명사 순회, 순회지 ❑ 흔히 있는 문제죠. 제가 순회강연을 돌 때 가장 많은 질문을 받는 문제입니다. **3** 가산명사 경주로 [주로 영국영어] ❑ 16만 명의 팬들을 살피기 위해 1,500명의 경찰이 추가로 경주로 주위에 배치될 것이다.

cir|cu|lar /sɜrkyələr/ (circulars) **1** ADJ Something that is **circular** is shaped like a circle. ❑ *...a circular hole twelve feet wide and two feet deep.* **2** ADJ A **circular** journey or route is one in which you go to a place and return by a different route. ❑ *Both sides of the river can be explored on this circular walk.* **3** N-COUNT A **circular** is an official letter or advertisement that is sent to a large number of people at the same time. ❑ *The proposal has been widely publicised in BBC-TV press information circulars sent to 1,800 newspapers.* →see **circle**

1 형용사 원형의 ❑ 지름 12피트, 깊이 2피트의 둥근 구멍 **2** 형용사 순환하는 ❑ 이 순환 도로를 걸어가면 강의 양쪽 모두를 구경할 수 있다. **3** 가산명사 안내장, 광고 전단 ❑ 그 제안은 1,800개의 신문에 보낸 비비시 텔레비전의 보도 자료 안내장을 통해 널리 홍보되었다.

cir|cu|late /sɜrkyəleɪt/ (circulates, circulating, circulated) **1** V-T/V-I If a piece of writing **circulates** or **is circulated**, copies of it are passed around among a group of people. ❑ *The document was previously circulated in New York at the United Nations.* ❑ *Public employees, teachers and liberals are circulating a petition for his recall.* ● cir|cu|la|tion /sɜrkyəleɪʃ°n/ N-UNCOUNT ❑ *...an inquiry into the circulation of "unacceptable literature."* **2** V-T/V-I If something such as a rumor **circulates** or **is circulated**, the people in a place tell it to each other. ❑ *Rumors were already beginning to circulate that the project might have to be abandoned.* **3** V-I When something **circulates**, it moves easily and freely within a closed place or system. ❑ *...a virus which circulates via the bloodstream and causes ill health in a variety of organs.* ● cir|cu|la|tion N-UNCOUNT ❑ *The north pole is warmer than the south and the circulation of air around it is less well contained.* **4** V-I If you **circulate** at a party, you move among the guests and talk to different people. ❑ *Let me get you something to drink, then I must circulate.*

1 타동사/자동사 회람되다 ❑ 그 문서는 이전에 뉴욕의 국제 연합에서 회람되었다. ❑ 공공 근로자, 교사, 그리고 진보 인사들이 그의 복귀를 위한 서명 운동을 벌이고 있다. ● 순람, 유포 불가산명사 ❑ '용납할 수 없는 문학'의 유포에 대한 조사 **2** 타동사/자동사 (소문이) 돌다; 유포되다 ❑ 프로젝트를 포기해야 할지도 모른다는 소문이 벌써 돌고 있었다. **3** 자동사 돌다 ❑ 피를 따라 돌면서 여러 장기의 건강을 해치는 바이러스 ● 순환 불가산명사 ❑ 북극이 남극보다 따뜻하며 그 주변의 공기 순환이 남극의 경우보다 더 활발하다. **4** 자동사 돌아다니다 ❑ 당신께 마실 것을 갖다 주고 나서 좀 둘러봐야겠어요.

cir|cu|la|tion /sɜrkyəleɪʃ°n/ (circulations) **1** N-COUNT The **circulation** of a newspaper or magazine is the number of copies that are sold each time it is produced. ❑ *The Daily News once had the highest circulation of any daily in the country.* **2** N-UNCOUNT Your **circulation** is the movement of blood through your body. ❑ *Anyone with heart, lung or circulation problems should seek medical advice before flying.* **3** →see also **circulate 4** PHRASE If something such as money is **in circulation**, it is being used by the public. If something is **out of circulation** or has been **withdrawn from circulation**, it is no longer available for use by the public. ❑ *The supply of money in circulation was drastically reduced overnight.* ❑ *...a society like America, with perhaps 180 million guns in circulation.*

1 가산명사 발행 부수 ❑ 데일리 뉴스가 한때는 전국에서 일간지 중 발행 부수가 가장 많았다. **2** 불가산명사 혈액 순환 ❑ 심장, 폐, 혹은 순환 계통에 문제가 있으신 분은 비행기를 타기 전에 의료 자문을 구하셔야 합니다. **4** 구 유통되는; 유통되지 않는 ❑ 유통되는 현금의 공급이 하룻밤 새에 급격히 줄어들었다. ❑ 약 1억 8천억 정 정도의 총기가 돌아다니는 미국과 같은 사회

Word Link   circum ≈ around : circumcise, circumference, circumstance

cir|cum|cise /sɜrkəmsaɪz/ (circumcises, circumcising, circumcised) **1** V-T If a boy or man **is circumcised**, the loose skin at the end of his penis is cut off. [usu passive] ❑ *He had been circumcised within eight days of birth as required by Jewish law.* ● cir|cum|ci|sion /sɜrkəmsɪʒ°n/ N-UNCOUNT [also a N] ❑ *Jews and Moslems practise circumcision for religious reasons.* **2** V-T In some cultures, if a girl or woman **is circumcised**, her clitoris is cut or cut off. [usu passive] ❑ *An estimated number of 90 to 100 million women around the world living today have been circumcised.* ● cir|cum|ci|sion N-UNCOUNT ❑ *...a campaigner against female circumcision.*

1 타동사 할례를 받다 ❑ 그는 유대교 율법에 따라 출생 후 8일 안에 할례를 받았다. ● 할례 불가산명사 ❑ 유대인들과 회교도들은 종교적인 이유로 할례를 한다. **2** 타동사 할례를 받다 ❑ 전 세계적으로 지금 살아 있는 여성 중 9천만에서 1억 명 정도가 할례를 받은 것으로 추정된다. ● 할례 불가산명사 ❑ 여성 할례를 반대하는 운동가

cir|cum|fer|ence /sərkʌmfrəns/ **1** N-UNCOUNT The **circumference** of a circle, place, or round object is the distance around its edge. ❑ *...a scientist calculating the earth's circumference.* **2** N-UNCOUNT The **circumference** of a circle, place, or round object is its edge. ❑ *Cut the salmon into long strips and wrap it round the circumference of the bread.* →see **area**

1 불가산명사 둘레 ❑ 지구의 둘레를 계산하는 과학자 **2** 불가산명사 테두리 ❑ 연어를 길게 잘라 그것을 빵의 테두리에 감아라.

cir|cum|stance ♦○○ /sɜrkəmstæns/ (circumstances) **1** N-COUNT The **circumstances** of a particular situation are the conditions which affect what happens. ❑ *Recent opinion polls show that 60 percent favor abortion under certain circumstances.* ❑ *The strategy was too dangerous in the explosive circumstances of the times.* **2** N-PLURAL The **circumstances** of an event are the way it happened or the causes of it. ❑ *I'm making inquiries about the circumstances of Mary Dean's murder.* **3** N-PLURAL Your **circumstances** are the conditions of your life, especially the amount of money that you have. ❑ *...help and support for the single mother, whatever her circumstances.* **4** N-UNCOUNT Events and situations which

1 가산명사 상황 ❑ 최근의 여론 조사에 따르면 60퍼센트가 특정 상황에서는 낙태를 선호한다고 한다. ❑ 당시의 일촉즉발의 상황에서 그 전략은 너무 위험했다. **2** 복수명사 정황 ❑ 나는 메리 딘의 살인에 얽힌 정황에 대한 조사를 하고 있다. **3** 복수명사 처지 ❑ 처지에 상관없이 편모에게 제공되는 원조와 지원 **4** 불가산명사 불가항력 ❑ 불가항력에 의해서 노숙자 신세로 전락하는 그런 사람들도 있거든. **5** 구 어떤 상황에서도 [강조] ❑ 인종 차별은 어떤 상황에서도

cannot be controlled are sometimes referred to as **circumstance**. ❑ *There are those, you know, who, by circumstance, end up homeless.* **5** PHRASE You can emphasize that something must not or will not happen by saying that it must not or will not happen under any **circumstances**. [EMPHASIS] ❑ *Racism is wholly unacceptable under any circumstances.* **6** PHRASE You can use **in the circumstances** or **under the circumstances** before or after a statement to indicate that you have considered the conditions affecting the situation before making the statement. ❑ *In the circumstances, Paisley's plans looked highly appropriate.*

용납할 수 없다. **6** 구 그 상황에서는, 상황이 그러하니 ❑ 그런 상황에서는 페이슬리의 계획이 매우 적절해 보였다.

Word Partnership   *circumstances*의 연어

PREP.	**under the** circumstances **1 2**
ADJ.	**certain** circumstances, **different/similar** circumstances, **difficult** circumstances, **exceptional** circumstances **1 - 3**

cir|cus /sɜrkəs/ (**circuses**) **1** N-COUNT A **circus** is a group that consists of clowns, acrobats, and animals which travels around to different places and performs shows. ❑ *My real ambition was to work in a circus.* ● N-SING **The circus** is the show performed by these people. ❑ *My dad took me to the circus.* **2** N-SING If you describe a group of people or an event as a **circus**, you disapprove of them because they attract a lot of attention but do not achieve anything useful. [DISAPPROVAL] ❑ *It could well turn into some kind of a media circus.*

1 가산명사 서커스 ❑ 나의 진정한 꿈은 서커스에서 일하는 것이었다. ● 단수명사 서커스 ❑ 아버지께서 나를 서커스에 데려가셨다. **2** 단수명사 떠들썩하기만 한 일 [탐탁잖음] ❑ 그것이 일종의 대중 매체용 잔치로 변질될 수도 있다.

ci|ta|tion /saɪteɪʃⁿn/ (**citations**) **1** N-COUNT A **citation** is an official document or speech which praises a person for something brave or special that they have done. ❑ *His citation says he showed outstanding and exemplary courage.* **2** N-COUNT A **citation** from a book or other piece of writing is a passage or phrase from it. [FORMAL] ❑ *...a 50-minute manifesto with citations from the Koran.* **3** N-COUNT A **citation** is the same as a **summons**. [AM] ❑ *The court could issue a citation and fine Ms. Robbins.*

1 가산명사 표창장, 감사장 ❑ 그의 표창장에는 그가 훌륭하고 모범적인 용맹을 보였다고 쓰여 있다. **2** 가산명사 인용 [격식체] ❑ 코란의 인용문이 포함된 50분짜리 선언문 **3** 가산명사 소환장 [미국영어] ❑ 법원은 로빈스 씨에게 소환장을 발부하고 벌금을 부과할 수도 있다.

cite ♦♢♢ /saɪt/ (**cites, citing, cited**) **1** V-T If you **cite** something, you quote it or mention it, especially as an example or proof of what you are saying. [FORMAL] ❑ *She cites a favorite poem by George Herbert.* ❑ *Domestic interest rates are often cited as a major factor affecting exchange rates.* **2** V-T To **cite** a person means to officially name them in a legal case. To **cite** a reason or cause means to state it as the official reason for your case. ❑ *They cited Alex's refusal to return to the marital home.* **3** V-T If someone **is cited**, they are officially ordered to appear before a court. [AM, LEGAL; BRIT **be summonsed**] ❑ *The judge ruled a mistrial and cited the prosecutors for outrageous misconduct.*

1 타동사 인용하다, 언급하다 [격식체] ❑ 그녀는 조지 허버트가 쓴 애송시를 인용한다. ❑ 국내 금리가 종종 환율에 영향을 끼치는 주요 요인으로 언급된다. **2** 타동사 인용하다 ❑ 그들은 알렉스가 결혼 생활을 꾸려나가는 집으로 돌아가기를 거부한 것을 소송 사유로 밝혔다. **3** 타동사 소환당하다 [미국영어, 법률; 영국영어 be summonsed] ❑ 판사는 심리 무효를 선언하고 검사들의 지나친 직권 남용을 그 사유로 밝혔다.

citi|zen ♦♦♢ /sɪtɪzⁿn/ (**citizens**) **1** N-COUNT Someone who is a **citizen** of a particular country is legally accepted as belonging to that country. ❑ *...American citizens.* **2** N-COUNT The **citizens of** a town or city are the people who live there. ❑ *...the citizens of Buenos Aires.* **3** →see also **senior citizen** →see **election**

1 가산명사 시민, 국민 ❑ 미국 시민 **2** 가산명사 시민 ❑ 부에노스아이레스의 시민들

Word Link   *ship* ≈ *condition or state* : *censor*ship, *citizen*ship, *friend*ship

citi|zen|ship /sɪtɪzⁿʃɪp/ **1** N-UNCOUNT If you have **citizenship** of a country, you are legally accepted as belonging to it. ❑ *After 15 years in the U.S., he has finally decided to apply for American citizenship.* **2** N-UNCOUNT **Citizenship** is the fact of belonging to a community because you live in it, and the duties and responsibilities that this brings. ❑ *Their German peers had a more developed sense of citizenship.*

1 불가산명사 시민권 ❑ 미국에서 지낸 지 15년 만에 그는 드디어 미국 시민권 취득 절차를 밟기로 결심했다. **2** 불가산명사 시민임 ❑ 그들과는 달리 독일인들은 보다 발달된 시민 의식을 지니고 있었다.

cit|rus /sɪtrəs/ ADJ A **citrus** fruit is a juicy fruit with a sharp taste such as an orange, lemon, or grapefruit. [ADJ n] ❑ *...citrus groves.*

형용사 감귤류 ❑ 감귤류를 기르는 과수원

city ♦♦♦ /sɪti/ (**cities**) N-COUNT A **city** is a large town. ❑ *...the city of Bologna.* →see Word Web: **city**

가산명사 도시 ❑ 볼로냐 시

City ♦♦♢ N-PROPER **The City** is the part of London where many important financial institutions have their main offices. People often refer to these financial institutions as **the City**. ❑ *...a foreign bank in the City.*

고유명사 런던의 금융 중심가 ❑ 런던 금융 중심가의 외국계 은행

Word Link   *civ* ≈ *citizen* : *civ*ic, *civ*il, *civ*ilian

civ|ic /sɪvɪk/ **1** ADJ You use **civic** to describe people or things that have an official status in a town or city. [ADJ n] ❑ *...the businessmen and civic leaders of Manchester.* **2** ADJ You use **civic** to describe the duties or feelings that people have because they belong to a particular community. [ADJ n] ❑ *...a sense of civic pride.*

1 형용사 시민의, 공민의 ❑ 맨체스터의 사업가와 시민 지도자들 **2** 형용사 시민으로서의 ❑ 시민으로서의 자부심

Word Web   city

For the past 6,000 years people have been moving from the **countryside** to **urban** centers. The world's oldest **capital** is Damascus, Syria. People have lived there for over 2,500 years. Cities are usually economic, commercial, cultural, political, social, and transportation centers. **Tourists** travel to cities for shopping and **sightseeing**. In some big cities, **skyscrapers** contain **apartments, businesses, restaurants, theaters,** and **retail stores**. People never have to leave their building. Sometimes cities become overpopulated and **crime rates** soar. Then people move to the **suburbs**. In recent decades this trend has been reversed in some places and **inner cities** are being rebuilt.

Word Link   civ ≈ citizen : civic, civil, civilian

civ|il ♦♦◇ /sɪvᵊl/ **1** ADJ You use **civil** to describe events that happen within a country and that involve the different groups of people in it. [ADJ n] ❑ ...civil unrest. **2** ADJ You use **civil** to describe people or things in a country that are not connected with its armed forces. ❑ ...the U.S. civil aviation industry. **3** ADJ You use **civil** to describe things that are connected with the state rather than with a religion. [ADJ n] ❑ They were married on August 9 in a civil ceremony in Venice. **4** ADJ You use **civil** to describe the rights that people have within a society. [ADJ n] ❑ ...a United Nations covenant on civil and political rights. **5** ADJ Someone who is **civil** is polite in a formal way, but not particularly friendly. [FORMAL] ❑ As visitors, the least we can do is be civil to the people in their own land. ● **ci|vil|ity** /sɪvɪlɪti/ N-UNCOUNT ❑ ...civility to underlings.

Word Partnership   civil의 연어

N.   civil **disobedience**, civil **unrest** **1**
civil **rights** **1** **4**
civil **court** (law)**suit/trial** **3**

ci|vil|ian ♦◇◇ /sɪvɪliən/ (**civilians**) **1** N-COUNT In a military situation, a **civilian** is anyone who is not a member of the armed forces. ❑ The safety of civilians caught up in the fighting must be guaranteed. **2** ADJ In a military situation, **civilian** is used to describe people or things that are not military. ❑ ...the country's civilian population. ❑ ...civilian casualties. →see war

ci|vil|ity /sɪvɪlɪti/ →see civil

civ|i|li|za|tion /sɪvɪlɪzeɪʃᵊn/ (**civilizations**) [BRIT also **civilisation**] **1** N-VAR A **civilization** is a human society with its own social organization and culture. ❑ The ancient civilizations of Central and Latin America were founded upon corn. **2** N-UNCOUNT **Civilization** is the state of having an advanced level of social organization and a comfortable way of life. ❑ ...our advanced state of civilization. →see history

civ|i|lize /sɪvɪlaɪz/ (**civilizes, civilizing, civilized**) [BRIT also **civilise**] V-T To **civilize** a person or society means to educate them and improve their way of life. ❑ ...a comedy about a man who tries to civilize a woman – but she ends up civilizing him.

civ|i|lized /sɪvɪlaɪzd/ [BRIT also **civilised**] **1** ADJ If you describe a society as **civilized**, you mean that it is advanced and has established laws and customs. [APPROVAL] ❑ I believed that in civilized countries, torture had ended long ago. **2** ADJ If you describe a person or their behavior as **civilized**, you mean that they are polite and reasonable. ❑ I wrote to my ex-wife. She was very civilized about it.

civ|il rights N-PLURAL **Civil rights** are the rights that people have in a society to equal treatment and equal opportunities, whatever their race, sex, or religion. ❑ ...the civil rights movement.

civ|il serv|ant (**civil servants**) N-COUNT A **civil servant** is a person who works in the Civil Service in Britain and some other countries, or for the local, state, or federal government in the United States. ❑ ...two senior civil servants.

Civ|il Ser|vice also **civil service** N-SING The **Civil Service** of a country consists of its government departments and all the people who work in them. In many countries, the departments concerned with military and legal affairs are not part of the Civil Service. ❑ ...a job in the Civil Service.

civ|il war ♦◇◇ (**civil wars**) N-COUNT A **civil war** is a war which is fought between different groups of people who live in the same country. ❑ ...the Spanish Civil War.

CJD /si dʒeɪ di/ N-UNCOUNT **CJD** is an incurable brain disease that affects human beings and is believed to be caused by eating beef from cows with BSE. **CJD** is an abbreviation for "Creutzfeldt-Jakob disease."

clad /klæd/ **1** ADJ If you are **clad in** particular clothes, you are wearing them. [LITERARY] [v-link ADJ in n, adv ADJ] ❑ The figure of a woman, clad in black. ❑ Johnson was clad casually in slacks and a light blue golf shirt. ● COMB in ADJ **Clad** is also a combining form. ❑ ...the leather-clad biker. **2** ADJ A building, part of a building, or mountain that is **clad** with something is covered by that thing. [LITERARY] [v-link ADJ in/with n] ❑ The walls and floors are clad with ceramic tiles. ● COMB in ADJ **Clad** is also a combining form. ❑ ...the distant shapes of snow-clad mountains.

claim ♦♦♦ /kleɪm/ (**claims, claiming, claimed**) **1** V-T If you say that someone **claims that** something is true, you mean they say that it is true but you are not sure whether or not they are telling the truth. ❑ He claimed that it was all a conspiracy against him. ❑ A man claiming to be a journalist threatened to reveal details about her private life. **2** N-COUNT A **claim** is something someone says which they cannot prove and which may be false. ❑ He repeated his claim that the people of Trinidad and Tobago backed his action. **3** V-T If you say that someone **claims** responsibility or credit for something, you mean they say that they are responsible for it, but you are not sure whether or not they are telling the truth. ❑ An underground organization has claimed responsibility for the bomb explosion. **4** V-T If you **claim** something, you try to get it because you think you have a right to it. ❑ Now they are returning to claim what was theirs. **5** N-COUNT A **claim** is a demand for something that you think you have a right to. ❑ Rival claims to Macedonian territory caused conflict in the Balkans. **6** V-T If you **claim** a record, title, or prize, they gain or win it. [JOURNALISM] ❑ Zhuang claimed the record in 54.64 seconds. **7** N-COUNT If you have a **claim on** someone or their attention, you have the right to demand things from them or to demand their attention. ❑ She'd no claims on him now. **8** V-T If something or someone **claims** your attention, they need you to spend your time and effort on them. ❑ There is already a long list of people claiming her attention. **9** V-T/V-I If you **claim** money from

1 형용사 국내의 ❑ 국내의 불안 **2** 형용사 민간의 ❑ 미국의 민간 항공 산업 **3** 형용사 공공의 ❑ 그들은 8월 9일 베니스의 공공 기관에서 결혼했다. **4** 형용사 시민의 ❑ 시민적 및 정치적 권리에 관한 국가 연합의 계약 **5** 형용사 정중한 [격식체] ❑ 방문자로서는 원래 주민들에게 정중하게 대하는 것이 최소한의 의무이다. ● 예의 불가산명사 ❑ 아랫사람들에 대한 예의

1 가산명사 민간인 ❑ 싸움의 틈바구니에 낀 민간인의 안전이 보장되어야 한다. **2** 형용사 민간의 ❑ 국가의 민간인 인구 ❑ 민간인 사상자

[영국영어 civilisation] **1** 가산명사 또는 불가산명사 문명 ❑ 중남미의 고대 문명들은 옥수수를 기반으로 세워졌다. **2** 불가산명사 문명 ❑ 우리의 고도로 발달한 문명

[영국영어 civilise] 타동사 개화시키다 ❑ 여자를 개화시키려고 하지만 결국 도리어 여자에게 개화당하는 남자에 관한 코미디

[영국영어 civilised] **1** 형용사 개화된, 문명화된 [마음에 듦] ❑ 나는 문명국가에서는 고문이 옛날에 종식되었으리라고 믿었다. **2** 형용사 정중하고 합리적인 ❑ 나는 전처에게 편지를 썼다. 그녀는 매우 정중하고 합리적으로 반응했다.

복수명사 민권 ❑ 민권 운동

가산명사 공복, 공무원 ❑ 두 명의 고위 공무원

단수명사 (군부와 사법부를 제외한) 행정부 ❑ 행정부에서의 일자리

가산명사 내전 ❑ 스페인 내전

불가산명사 '크로이츠펠트-야콥병'의 약자

1 형용사 -을 입고 있는 [문예체] ❑ 검은 옷을 입은 여자의 모습 ❑ 존슨은 캐주얼하게 일상복 바지와 옅은 푸른색의 골프 셔츠를 입고 있었다. ● 복합명-형용사 -을 입은 ❑ 가죽옷을 입은 오토바이 운전자 **2** 형용사 -으로 덮인 [문예체] ❑ 벽과 바닥은 세라믹 타일로 덮여 있었다. ● 복합명-형용사 -으로 덮인 ❑ 눈 덮인 산의 아련한 모습

1 타동사 주장하다 ❑ 그는 모든 것이 자신에 대한 모함이라고 주장했다. ❑ 기자라고 주장하는 남자가 그녀의 사생활에 대한 정보를 폭로하겠다고 협박했다. **2** 가산명사 주장 ❑ 그는 트리니다드 토바고 시민들은 자기 행동을 지지한다는 주장을 되풀이했다. **3** 타동사 주장하다 ❑ 한 지하 조직이 자기들이 그 폭발 사건을 일으켰다고 주장했다. **4** 타동사 소유권을 주장하다 ❑ 이제 그들은 자신들의 것이었던 것을 되찾기 위해 돌아오고 있다. **5** 가산명사 소유권 주장 ❑ 마케도니아 땅에 대한 상반되는 소유권 주장에 발칸 반도에서 분쟁이 일어났다. **6** 타동사 차지하다 [언론] ❑ 장은 54.64초로 기록을 세웠다. **7** 가산명사 권리 ❑ 그녀가 관심을 기울여야 할 사람들은 이미 많이 있다. **8** 타동사 차지하다 ❑ 그녀의 관심을 끌려고 하는 사람들이 줄을 섰다. **9** 타동사/자동사 청구하다 ❑ 국가 보조금을 청구할 권리를 가진 사람 중 약 25퍼센트가 이를 행사하고 있다. ❑ 존은 실업 보험에 가입한 상태였으나 보험금을 청구하자 지급을 거부당했다. ● 가산명사 청구 ❑ 지난번 우리가 보험금을 청구했을 때 그들은 정말 빨리 지불해

the government, an insurance company, or another organization, you officially apply to them for it, because you think you are entitled to it according to their rules. ❏ *Some 25 percent of the people who are entitled to claim State benefits do not do so.* ❏ *John had taken out redundancy insurance but when he tried to claim, he was refused payment.* ● N-COUNT **Claim** is also a noun. ❏ *Last time we made a claim on our insurance they paid up really quickly.* ⑩ V-T If you **claim** money or other benefits from your employers, you demand them because you think you deserve or need them. ❏ *The union claimed a raise worth four times the rate of inflation.* ● N-COUNT **Claim** is also a noun. ❏ *They are making substantial claims for improved working conditions.* ⑪ V-T If you say that a war, disease, or accident **claims** someone's life, you mean that they are killed in it or by it. [FORMAL] ❏ *The civil war claimed the life of a U.N. interpreter yesterday.* ⑫ to **stake a claim** →see **stake**

주었다. ⑩ 타동사 요구하다 ❏ 노동조합은 물가 인상률보다 네 배 높은 임금 인상을 요구했다. ● 가산명사 요구 ❏ 그들은 근로 조건 개선을 위한 실질적인 요구를 하고 있다. ⑪ 타동사 빼앗다 [격식체] ❏ 국제 연합 통역관 한 명이 어제 내전에서 목숨을 잃었다.

claim|ant /kleɪmənt/ (**claimants**) ■ N-COUNT A **claimant** is someone who asks to be given something which they think they are entitled to. ❏ *The claimants allege that manufacturers failed to warn doctors that their drugs should only be used only in limited circumstances.* ❷ N-COUNT A **claimant** is someone who is receiving money from the state because they are unemployed or they are unable to work because they are ill. [BRIT] ❏ *...benefit claimants.*

■ 가산명사 요구자 ❏ 제조업자들이 그들이 제조한 약을 제한된 상황에서만 사용해야 한다는 것을 의사들에게 경고하지 않았다고 원고들은 주장한다. ❷ 가산명사 (정부 보조금) 수혜자, 대상자 [영국영어] ❏ 보조금 대상자

claims ad|just|er (**claims adjusters**) also **claims adjustor** N-COUNT A **claims adjuster** is someone who is employed by an insurance company to decide how much money a person making a claim should receive. [AM, BUSINESS; BRIT **loss adjuster**]

가산명사 손해 사정인 [미국영어, 경제; 영국영어 loss adjuster]

clair|voy|ant /kleərvɔɪənt/ ADJ Someone who is believed to be **clairvoyant** is believed to know about future events or to be able to communicate with dead people. ❏ *...clairvoyant powers.*

형용사 신통력이 있는 ❏ 신통력

clam /klæm/ (**clams**) N-COUNT **Clams** are a kind of shellfish which can be eaten.

가산명사 조개

clam|ber /klæmbər/ (**clambers, clambering, clambered**) V-I If you **clamber** somewhere, you climb there with difficulty, usually using your hands as well as your feet. ❏ *They clambered up the stone walls of a steeply terraced olive grove.*

자동사 기어오르다 ❏ 그들은 계단식으로 가파르게 조성된 올리브 과수원의 돌담을 힘겹게 기어 올랐다.

Word Link	claim, clam ≈ shouting : ac*claim*, *clam*or, ex*claim*

clam|or /klæmər/ (**clamors, clamoring, clamored**) N-SING If people **are clamoring for** something, they are demanding it in a noisy or angry way. [JOURNALISM; BRIT **clamour**] ❏ *...competing parties clamoring for the attention of the voter.*

단수명사 ~을 시끄럽게 주장하는 [언론; 영국영어 clamour] ❏ 유권자의 관심을 끌려고 시끄럽게 떠들어대는 경쟁 관계에 있는 정당들

clamp /klæmp/ (**clamps, clamping, clamped**) ■ N-COUNT A **clamp** is a device that holds two things firmly together. ❏ *Many openers have a magnet or set of clamps to grip the open lid.* ❷ V-T When you **clamp** one thing to another, you fasten the two things together with a clamp. ❏ *Somebody forgot to bring along the U-bolts to clamp the microphones to the pole.* ❸ V-T To **clamp** something in a particular place means to put it or hold it there firmly and tightly. ❏ *Simon finished dialing and clamped the phone to his ear.* ❏ *He clamped his lips together.* ❹ N-COUNT A **clamp** is a large metal device which is fitted to the wheel of an illegally parked car or other vehicle in order to prevent it from being driven away. The driver has to pay to have the clamp removed. [BRIT; AM **Denver boot**] ❺ V-T To **clamp** a car means to fit a clamp to one of its wheels so that it cannot be driven away. [BRIT; AM **boot**] ❏ *Courts in Scotland have ruled it illegal to clamp a car parked on private ground and then to demand a fine.*

■ 가산명사 죔쇠 ❏ 많은 병따개들에는 열린 뚜껑이 달아나지 않게 자석이나 죔쇠가 붙어 있다. ❷ 타동사 죄어 붙이다 ❏ 누군가가 잊어버리고 마이크를 기둥에 조일 유자 볼트를 안 가져왔다. ❸ 타동사 꽉 붙이다 ❏ 사이먼은 번호를 다 누르고 수화기를 귀에 꽉 갖다 댔다. ❏ 그는 입을 꾹 다물어 버렸다. ❹ 가산명사 바퀴 자물쇠 [영국영어; 미국영어 Denver boot] ❺ 타동사 바퀴 자물쇠를 걸다 [영국영어; 미국영어 boot] ❏ 스코틀랜드의 법원들은 사유지에서 차에 바퀴 자물쇠를 건 후 벌금을 물리는 행위는 불법이라고 판정했다.

▶**clamp down** PHRASAL VERB To **clamp down on** people or activities means to take strong official action to stop or control them. [JOURNALISM] ❏ *If the government clamps down on the movement, that will only serve to strengthen it in the long run.*

구동사 억압하다 [언론] ❏ 만약 정부가 그 운동을 억압한다면 그것은 장기적으로 그것을 더욱 강하게 키우는 것밖에 안 된다.

clan /klæn/ (**clans**) ■ N-COUNT A **clan** is a group which consists of families that are related to each other. ❏ *...rival clans.* ❷ N-COUNT You can refer to a group of people who share the same interests as a **clan**. [INFORMAL] ❏ *...a powerful clan of industrialists from Monterrey.*

■ 가산명사 씨족, 일가 ❏ 경쟁 관계에 있는 집안 ❷ 가산명사 일당, 한패 [비격식체] ❏ 몬터레이 출신의 세력 있는 사업가 일당

clan|des|tine /klændestɪn/ ADJ Something that is **clandestine** is hidden or kept secret, often because it is illegal. [FORMAL] ❏ *...their clandestine meetings.*

형용사 비밀의 [격식체] ❏ 그들의 비밀 만남

clap /klæp/ (**claps, clapping, clapped**) ■ V-T/V-I When you **clap**, you hit your hands together to express appreciation or attract attention. ❏ *The men danced and the women clapped.* ❏ *Midge clapped her hands, calling them back to order.* ● N-SING **Clap** is also a noun. ❏ *As long as the crowd give them a clap, they're quite happy.* ❷ V-T If you **clap** your hand or an object onto something, you put it there quickly and firmly. ❏ *I clapped a hand over her mouth.* ❸ N-COUNT A **clap of thunder** is a sudden and loud noise of thunder.

■ 타동사/자동사 박수를 치다, 손뼉을 치다 ❏ 남자들은 춤추고 여자들은 박수를 쳤다. ❏ 미지는 손뼉을 치면서 그들을 다시 정숙하게 했다. ● 단수명사 박수 ❏ 관중이 박수를 쳐 주기만 한다면 그들은 지극히 행복하다. ❷ 타동사 (손을) 급히 대다 ❏ 나는 손으로 그녀의 입을 급히 막았다. ❸ 가산명사 뇌성

Word Link	clar ≈ clear : *clar*ify, *clar*ity, de*clar*e

Word Link	ify ≈ making : clar*ify*, divers*ify*, intens*ify*

clari|fy /klærɪfaɪ/ (**clarifies, clarifying, clarified**) V-T To **clarify** something means to make it easier to understand, usually by explaining it in more detail. [FORMAL] ❏ *Thank you for writing and allowing me to clarify the present position.* ● **clari|fi|ca|tion** /klærɪfɪkeɪʃ°n/ (**clarifications**) N-VAR ❏ *The union has written to Zurich asking for clarification of the situation.*

타동사 분명히 하다, 설명하다 [격식체] ❏ 이렇게 서신을 보내서 제게 현재의 입장을 분명히 말씀하실 기회를 주셔서 감사합니다. ● 해명 가산명사 또는 불가산명사 ❏ 노동조합은 상황에 대한 해명을 요구하며 취리히로 서신을 보냈다.

clari|net /klærɪnet/ (**clarinets**) N-VAR A **clarinet** is a musical instrument in the shape of a pipe. You play the clarinet by blowing into it and covering and uncovering the holes with your fingers. →see **orchestra**

가산명사 또는 불가산명사 클라리넷

Word Link
clar ≈ clear : clarify, clarity, declare

clar|ity /klǽriti/ **1** N-UNCOUNT The **clarity** of something such as a book or argument is its quality of being well explained and easy to understand. □ ...the ease and clarity with which the author explains difficult technical and scientific subjects. **2** N-UNCOUNT **Clarity** is the ability to think clearly. □ In business circles he is noted for his flair and clarity of vision. **3** N-UNCOUNT **Clarity** is the quality of being clear in outline or sound. □ This remarkable technology provides far greater clarity than conventional x-rays.

1 불가산명사 명료함 □ 저자가 기술적이고 과학적인 어려운 주제들을 설명하면서 보이는 평이함과 명료함 **2** 불가산명사 명석함 □ 업계에서 그는 안목이 예리하고 명석하기로 유명하다. **3** 불가산명사 밝음, 깨끗함 □ 이 놀라운 기술은 기존의 엑스선보다 훨씬 깨끗한 사진을 제공한다.

clash ♦♢♢ /klǽʃ/ (**clashes, clashing, clashed**) **1** V-RECIP When people **clash**, they fight, argue, or disagree with each other. [JOURNALISM] □ A group of 400 demonstrators ripped down the state Parliament's front gate and clashed with police. □ Behind the scenes, Parsons clashed with almost everyone on the show. ● N-COUNT **Clash** is also a noun. [oft N between/with n] □ There have been a number of clashes between police in riot gear and demonstrators. **2** V-RECIP Beliefs, ideas, or qualities that **clash with** each other are very different from each other and therefore are opposed. □ Don't make any policy decisions which clash with official company thinking. ● N-COUNT **Clash** is also a noun. □ Inside government, there was a clash of views. **3** V-I If one event **clashes with** another, the two events happen at the same time so that you cannot attend both of them. □ The detective changed his holiday dates when his flight was brought forward and it now clashed with the trial. **4** V-RECIP If one color or style **clashes with** another, the colors or styles look ugly together. You can also say that two colors or styles **clash**. □ The red door clashed with the soft, natural tones of the stone walls.

1 상호동사 부딪치다, 충돌하다 [언론] □ 400명의 시위자가 주 의회의 정문을 부수고 경찰과 충돌했다. □ 무대 뒤에서는 파슨스가 쇼에 나오는 거의 모든 사람들과 부딪쳤다. ● 가산명사 충돌 □ 진압용 장비를 갖춘 경찰들과 시위자들 사이에 몇 번의 충돌이 있었다. **2** 상호동사 배치되다, 충돌하다 □ 회사의 공식적 입장과 배치되는 정책 결정을 내리지 말아라. ● 가산명사 충돌, 배치 □ 정부 내에서 의견 충돌이 있었다. **3** 자동사 겹치다 □ 비행 일정이 앞당겨지자 형사는 휴가 날짜를 바꿨으나 이제는 그것이 재판과 겹치게 되었다. **4** 상호동사 어울리지 않다 □ 붉은 문은 돌담의 부드러운 자연색과 어울리지 않았다.

clasp /klǽsp/ (**clasps, clasping, clasped**) **1** V-T If you **clasp** someone or something, you hold them tightly in your hands or arms. □ She clasped the children to her. **2** N-COUNT A **clasp** is a small device that fastens something. □ ...the clasp of her handbag.

1 타동사 단단히 붙잡다 □ 그녀는 아이들을 꼭 붙잡았다. **2** 가산명사 걸쇠, 버클 □ 그녀 핸드백의 걸쇠

class ♦♦♦ /klǽs/ (**classes, classing, classed**) **1** N-COUNT A **class** is a group of pupils or students who are taught together. □ He had to spend about six months in a class with younger students. **2** N-COUNT A **class** is a course of teaching in a particular subject. □ He acquired a law degree by taking classes at night. **3** N-UNCOUNT If you do something **in class**, you do it during a lesson in school. □ There is lots of reading in class. **4** N-SING The students in a school or college who finish their course in a particular year are sometimes referred to as the **class** of that year. □ These two members of Yale's Class of '57 never miss a reunion. **5** N-VAR **Class** refers to the division of people in a society into groups according to their social status. □ ...the relationship between social classes. □ What it will do is create a whole new ruling class. →see also **middle class, upper class, working class** **6** N-COUNT A **class of** things is a group of them with similar characteristics. □ Harbor staff noticed that measurements given for the same class of boats often varied. **7** V-T If someone or something **is classed as** a particular thing, they are regarded as belonging to that group of things. □ Since they can and do successfully inter-breed they cannot be classed as different species. □ I class myself as an ordinary working person. **8** N-UNCOUNT If you say that someone or something has **class**, you mean that they are elegant and sophisticated. [INFORMAL, APPROVAL] □ The most elegant woman I've ever met – she had class in every sense of the word. **9** →see also **business class, first-class, second-class, world-class**

1 가산명사 학급, 반 □ 그는 약 여섯 달 동안 자기보다 어린 학생들과 한 반을 해야 했다. **2** 가산명사 강좌 □ 그는 야간 강좌를 듣고 법학 학위를 취득했다. **3** 불가산명사 수업 중에 □ 수업 중에는 읽기를 많이 한다. **4** 단수명사 동기생 □ 예일 57년도 동기생들 중 이 두 사람은 동창회에 절대 빠지지 않는다. **5** 가산명사 또는 불가산명사 계급 □ 사회 계급 간의 관계 □ 그것이 할 일은 전혀 새로운 지배 계급을 만들어 내는 것이다. **6** 가산명사 종류, 부류 □ 항구 직원들은 같은 종류의 배들의 제원이 가끔 다르다는 사실을 알아차렸다. **7** 타동사 -로 분류되다 □ 그것들은 성공적으로 이종 교배가 될 수 있으며 또 실제로 그러하기 때문에 다른 종으로 분류할 수 없다. □ 나는 내 자신이 평범한 노동자에 속한다고 생각한다. **8** 불가산명사 기품, 세련미 [비격식체, 마음에 듦] □ 내가 만나 본 중에 가장 우아한 여성인 그녀는 문자 그대로 기품이 있었다.

Word Partnership   class의 연어

N.	class **for beginners, senior** class, class **size, students in a** class **1**
	leisure class, class **struggle, working** class **5**
V.	**take a** class, **teach a** class **1 2**
ORD.	**first/second** class **9**
ADJ.	**social** class **5**

clas|sic ♦♦♢ /klǽsɪk/ (**classics**) **1** ADJ A **classic** example of a thing or situation has all the features which you expect such a thing or situation to have. □ The debate in the mainstream press has been a classic example of British hypocrisy. ● N-COUNT **Classic** is also a noun. □ It was a classic of interrogation: first the bully, then the kind one who offers sympathy. **2** ADJ A **classic** movie, piece of writing, or piece of music is of very high quality and has become a standard against which similar things are judged. [ADJ n] □ ...the classic children's film Huckleberry Finn. ● N-COUNT **Classic** is also a noun. □ The record won a gold award and remains one of the classics of modern popular music. **3** N-COUNT A **classic** is a book which is well-known and considered to be of a high literary standard. You can refer to such books generally as **the classics**. □ As I grow older, I like to reread the classics regularly. **4** N-UNCOUNT **Classics** is the study of the ancient Greek and Roman civilizations, especially their languages, literature, and philosophy. □ ...a Classics degree.

1 형용사 전형적인 □ 주류 언론에서 벌어져 온 그 논쟁은 영국적 위선의 전형적인 표본이다. ● 가산명사 전형 □ 그것은 전형적인 심문 방식이었다. 처음엔 위협적인 사람의 역할, 그 다음엔 동정심을 보이는 친절한 사람을 내세우는. **2** 형용사 고전의 반열에 오른 □ 아동 영화의 고전 허클베리 핀 ● 가산명사 고전 □ 그 음반은 금상을 수상했고 현대 대중음악의 고전으로 남아 있다. **3** 가산명사 고전 문학 □ 나이가 들면서, 나는 규칙적으로 고전 작품을 다시 읽는 것을 즐긴다. **4** 불가산명사 (그리스와 로마에 대한) 고전학 □ 고전학 학위

clas|si|cal ♦♢♢ /klǽsɪkᵊl/ **1** ADJ You use **classical** to describe something that is traditional in form, style, or content. □ Fokine did not change the steps of classical ballet; instead he found new ways of using them. **2** ADJ **Classical** music is music that is considered to be serious and of lasting value. □ ...a classical composer like Beethoven. **3** ADJ **Classical** is used to describe things which relate to the ancient Greek or Roman civilizations. □ ...the healers of ancient Egypt and classical Greece.

1 형용사 고전적인 □ 포킨은 고전 발레 스텝을 바꾸지 않았다. 대신 그는 그것의 새로운 활용법을 발견했다. **2** 형용사 고전 (음악) □ 베토벤 같은 고전 음악 작곡가 **3** 형용사 그리스 또는 로마 문명의 □ 고대 이집트와 고대 그리스의 의사들

clas|si|cal|ly /klǽsɪkli/ **1** ADV Someone who has been **classically** trained in something such as art, music, or ballet has learned the traditional skills and methods of that subject. [ADV -ed] □ Peter is a classically trained pianist. **2** ADV **Classically** is used to indicate that something is based on or reminds people of the culture of ancient Greece and Rome. [ADV adj/-ed] □ ...the classically inspired church of S. Francesco.

1 부사 정통적으로 □ 피터는 정통적으로 훈련을 받은 피아니스트이다. **2** 부사 그리스와 로마풍의 □ 고대 그리스와 로마풍의 영향을 받은 성 프란체스코 성당

a b c d e f g h i j k l m n o p q r s t u v w x y z

clas|si|fi|ca|tion /klæsɪfɪkeɪʃ⁰n/ (**classifications**) N-COUNT A **classification** is a division or category in a system which divides things into groups or types. ❑ *Bottom of the league come engineering companies, a classification that includes the car companies.* →see also **classify**

가산명사 계열, 범주 ❑ 연맹의 맨 밑에는 자동차 회사를 포함하는 계열인 엔지니어링 회사들이 온다.

clas|si|fied /klæsɪfaɪd/ ADJ **Classified** information or documents are officially secret. ❑ *He has a security clearance that allows him access to classified information.*

형용사 기밀의 ❑ 그는 기밀 정보에 접근할 수 있는 보안 허가를 받았다.

clas|si|fied ad (**classified ads**) N-COUNT **Classified ads** or **classified advertisements** are small advertisements in a newspaper or magazine. They are usually from a person or company.

가산명사 항목별 광고

clas|si|fieds /klæsɪfaɪdz/ N-PLURAL The **classifieds** are the same as **classified ads**. ❑ *It's common for companies to post job openings on their Web sites and in newspaper classifieds.*

복수명사 항목별 광고 ❑ 회사에서는 보통 자기 웹사이트나 신문 광고란에 구인 광고를 낸다.

clas|si|fy /klæsɪfaɪ/ (**classifies, classifying, classified**) V-T To **classify** things means to divide them into groups or types so that things with similar characteristics are in the same group. ❑ *It is necessary initially to classify the headaches into certain types.* ● **clas|si|fi|ca|tion** /klæsɪfɪkeɪʃ⁰n/ (**classifications**) N-VAR ❑ *...the arbitrary classification of knowledge into fields of study.*

타동사 분류하다 ❑ 우선 두통을 특정 유형별로 분류하는 일이 필요하다. ● 분류 가산명사 또는 불가산명사 ❑ 학문을 여러 개의 연구 분야로 임의 분류하는 것

class|less /klɑːsləs, klæs-/ ADJ When politicians talk about a **classless** society, they mean a society in which people are not affected by social status. [APPROVAL] ❑ *...the new Prime Minister's vision of a classless society.*

형용사 계급 차별이 없는 [마음에 듦] ❑ 신임 수상의 계급 차별 없는 사회에 대한 비전

class|mate /klæsmeɪt/ (**classmates**) N-COUNT Your **classmates** are students who are in the same class as you at school or college.

가산명사 급우

class|room /klæsrʊm/ (**classrooms**) N-COUNT A **classroom** is a room in a school where lessons take place.

가산명사 교실

class sched|ule (**class schedules**) N-COUNT In a school or college, a **class schedule** is a list that shows the times in the week at which particular subjects are taught. You can also refer to the range of subjects that a student learns or the classes that a teacher teaches as their **class schedule**. [AM; BRIT usually **timetable**] ❑ *They had to be back at their American colleges this week to enroll and work out class schedules for the new term.*

가산명사 수업 시간표 [미국영어; 영국영어 대개 timetable] ❑ 그들은 새 학기 등록과 수업 시간표 작성을 위해 이번 주에 미국 대학으로 돌아가야 했다.

classy /klæsi/ (**classier, classiest**) ADJ If you describe someone or something as **classy**, you mean they are stylish and sophisticated. [INFORMAL] ❑ *The German star put in a classy performance.*

형용사 세련된, 멋진 [비격식체] ❑ 그 독일 선수는 멋진 경기를 펼쳤다.

clat|ter /klætər/ (**clatters, clattering, clattered**) V-I If you say that people or things **clatter** somewhere, you mean that they move there noisily. ❑ *He turned and clattered down the stairs.*

자동사 시끄러운 소리를 내며 가다 ❑ 그는 몸을 돌려 쿵쿵거리며 층계를 내려갔다.

clause /klɔːz/ (**clauses**) **1** N-COUNT A **clause** is a section of a legal document. ❑ *He has a clause in his contract which entitles him to a percentage of the profits.* ❑ *...a compromise document sprinkled with escape clauses.* **2** N-COUNT In grammar, a **clause** is a group of words containing a verb. Sentences contain one or more clauses. There are finite clauses and nonfinite clauses.

1 가산명사 조목, 조항 ❑ 그는 자신에게 수익의 1퍼센트를 부여하게 하는 조항을 계약서에 넣어 놓았다. ❑ 면책 조항들이 여기저기 들어 있는 타협안 **2** 가산명사 절

claw /klɔː/ (**claws, clawing, clawed**) **1** N-COUNT The **claws** of a bird or animal are the thin, hard, curved nails at the end of its feet. ❑ *The cat tried to cling to the edge by its claws.* **2** N-COUNT The **claws** of a lobster, crab, or scorpion are the two pointed parts at the end of its legs which are used for holding things. **3** V-I If an animal **claws at** something, it scratches or damages it with its claws. ❑ *The wolf clawed at the tree and howled the whole night.* **4** V-I To **claw at** something means to try very hard to get hold of it. ❑ *His fingers clawed at Blake's wrist.* **5** V-T If you **claw** your **way** somewhere, you move there with great difficulty, trying desperately to find things to hold on to. ❑ *From the flooded depths of the ship some did manage to claw their way up iron ladders to the safety of the upper deck.* →see **bird**

1 가산명사 발톱 ❑ 고양이는 발톱으로 모서리에 매달리려 애썼다. **2** 가산명사 집게발 **3** 자동사 발톱으로 할퀴다 ❑ 늑대는 나무를 발톱으로 할퀴며 밤새도록 울부짖었다. **4** 자동사 움켜잡으려고 하다 ❑ 그는 손가락으로 블레이크의 손목을 움켜잡으려 했다. **5** 타동사 기듯이 간신히 나아가다 ❑ 그 배의 침수된 안쪽에서 몇몇 사람이 철 사다리를 가까스로 기어 올라 상갑판에 있는 안전한 장소로 갔다.

clay /kleɪ/ (**clays**) **1** N-MASS **Clay** is a kind of earth that is soft when it is wet and hard when it is dry. Clay is shaped and baked to make things such as pots and bricks. ❑ *...the heavy clay soils of Cambridgeshire.* ❑ *As the wheel turned, the potter shaped and squeezed the lump of clay into a graceful shape.* **2** N-UNCOUNT In tennis, matches played on **clay** are played on courts whose surface is covered with finely crushed stones or brick. ❑ *Most tennis is played on hard courts, but a substantial amount is played on clay.* →see **pottery**

1 물질명사 점토, 찰흙 ❑ 케임브리지셔의 중점토 ❑ 물레가 돌아가면, 도공은 점토 덩어리를 우아한 모양으로 빚어내었다. **2** 불가산명사 (테니스) 클레이 코트 ❑ 대부분의 테니스 경기는 하드 코트에서 치러지지만, 상당히 많은 경기가 클레이 코트에서 치러진다.

clean ♦♦◇ /kliːn/ (**cleaner, cleanest, cleans, cleaning, cleaned**) **1** ADJ Something that is **clean** is free from dirt or unwanted marks. ❑ *The metro is efficient and spotlessly clean.* ❑ *Tiled kitchen floors are easy to keep clean.* **2** ADJ You say that people or animals are **clean** when they keep themselves or their surroundings clean. ❑ *We like pigs, they're very clean.* **3** ADJ A **clean** fuel or chemical process does not create many harmful or polluting substances. ❑ *Fans of electric cars say they are clean, quiet and economical.* **4** V-T/V-I If you **clean** something or **clean** dirt off it, you make it free from dirt and unwanted marks, for example by washing or wiping it. If something **cleans** easily, it is easy to clean. ❑ *Her father cleaned his glasses with a paper napkin.* ❑ *It took half an hour to clean the orange powder off the bathtub.* ● N-SING **Clean** is also a noun. ❑ *Give the cooker a good clean.* **5** V-T/V-I If you **clean** a room or house, you make the inside of it and the furniture in it free from dirt and dust. ❑ *With them also lived Mary, who cooked and cleaned.* ● **clean|ing** N-UNCOUNT ❑ *I do the cleaning myself.* **6** ADJ If you describe something such as a book, joke, or lifestyle as **clean**, you think that they are not sexually immoral or offensive. [APPROVAL] ❑ *They're trying to show clean, wholesome, decent movies.* ❑ *Flirting is good clean fun.* **7** ADJ If someone has a **clean** reputation or record, they have never done anything illegal or wrong. ❑ *Accusations of tax evasion have tarnished his clean image.* **8** ADJ A **clean** game or fight is carried out fairly, according to the rules. ❑ *He called for a clean fight in the election and an end to "negative campaigning".* ● **cleanly** ADV ❑ *The game had been cleanly fought.* **9** ADJ A **clean** sheet of paper has no writing or drawing on it. ❑ *Take a clean sheet of paper and down the left-hand side make a list.* **10** ADV **Clean** is used to emphasize that something was done completely. [INFORMAL,

1 형용사 깨끗한 ❑ 지하철은 효율적이고 흠 하나 없이 깨끗하다. ❑ 타일을 붙인 부엌 바닥은 깨끗이 유지하기가 쉽다. **2** 형용사 깔끔한, 깨끗한 것을 좋아하는 ❑ 우리는 돼지를 좋아한다. 그것들은 매우 깔끔하다. **3** 형용사 오염 물질을 배출하지 않는 ❑ 전기 자동차 애호가들은 전기 자동차가 오염 물질을 배출하지 않고 조용하며 경제적이라고 말한다. **4** 타동사/자동사 깨끗하게 하다, 닦다 ❑ 그녀의 아버지는 종이 냅킨으로 안경을 닦았다. ❑ 목욕통에서 그 오렌지색 가루를 닦아 내는 데 30분이 걸렸다. ● 단수명사 청소 ❑ 조리 기구를 잘 닦아라. **5** 타동사/자동사 청소하다 ❑ 메리도 그들과 함께 살았는데, 그녀는 요리와 청소를 했다. ● 청소 불가산명사 ❑ 나는 청소를 직접 한다. **6** 형용사 건전한, 음란하지 않은 [마음에 듦] ❑ 그들은 깨끗하고 건전하며 점잖은 영화들을 보여 주려고 노력하고 있다. ❑ 시시덕거리는 즐겁고 건전한 놀이다. **7** 형용사 깨끗한, 부정이 없는 ❑ 탈세 혐의로 인해 깨끗한 이미지에 손상을 입었다. **8** 형용사 공정한 ❑ 그는 선거에서 공정한 경쟁과 '네거티브 캠페인'의 종식을 요구했다. ● 공정하게 부사 ❑ 그 경기는 공정하게 치러졌다. **9** 형용사 아무것도 씌어 있지 않은 ❑ 백지를 한 장 꺼내서 왼편으로 목록을 작성해 내려가라. **10** 부사 완전히; 깨끗이 [비격식체,

EMPHASIS] ❑ *It burned clean through the seat of my overalls.* ❑ *The thief got clean away with the money.* ⬛ to **clean up** your **act** →see **act**. to keep your **nose clean**, →see **nose**. a **clean slate**, →see **slate**. a **clean sweep**, →see **sweep**. **clean as a whistle**, →see **whistle**
→see **dry cleaning**, **soap**

Thesaurus	*clean*의 참조어
ADJ.	neat, pure; (*ant.*) dirty, filthy ⬛
V.	launder, rinse, wash; (*ant.*) dirty, soil, stain ⬜

▶**clean out** PHRASAL VERB If you **clean out** something such as a closet, room, or container, you take everything out of it and clean the inside of it thoroughly. ❑ *Mr. Wall asked if I would help him clean out the bins.*

▶**clean up** PHRASAL VERB If you **clean up** a mess or **clean up** a place where there is a mess, you make things neat and free of dirt again. ❑ *Police in the city have been cleaning up the debris left by a day of violent confrontation.* ⬛ PHRASAL VERB To **clean up** something such as the environment or an industrial process means to make it free from substances or processes that cause pollution. ❑ *Under pressure from the public, many regional governments cleaned up their beaches.* ⬛ PHRASAL VERB If the police or authorities **clean up** a place or area of activity, they make it free from crime, corruption, and other unacceptable forms of behavior. ❑ *After years of neglect and decline the city was cleaning itself up.* ⬜ PHRASAL VERB If you go and **clean up**, you make yourself clean and neat, especially after doing something that has made you dirty. ❑ *Johnny, go inside and get cleaned up.*

clean|er /klínər/ (**cleaners**) ⬛ N-COUNT A **cleaner** is someone who is employed to clean the rooms and furniture inside a building. ❑ *...the prison hospital where Sid worked as a cleaner.* ⬛ N-COUNT A **cleaner** is someone whose job is to clean a particular type of thing. ❑ *He was a window cleaner.* ⬛ N-MASS A **cleaner** is a substance used for cleaning things. ❑ *...oven cleaner.* ⬜ N-COUNT A **cleaner** is a device used for cleaning things. ❑ *...an air cleaner.* →see also **vacuum cleaner** ⬛ N-COUNT A **cleaner** or a **cleaner's** is a store where things such as clothes are dry-cleaned. ❑ *He was wearing his cassock, which had clearly been on a visit to the cleaner's.*

clean|li|ness /klɛnlinɪs/ N-UNCOUNT **Cleanliness** is the degree to which people keep themselves and their surroundings clean. ❑ *Many of Britain's beaches fail to meet minimum standards of cleanliness.*

cleanse /klɛnz/ (**cleanses, cleansing, cleansed**) ⬛ V-T To **cleanse** a place, person, or organization **of** something dirty, unpleasant, or evil means to make them free from it. ❑ *Straight after your last cigarette your body will begin to cleanse itself of tobacco toxins.* ⬛ V-T If you **cleanse** your skin or a wound, you clean it. ❑ *Catherine demonstrated the proper way to cleanse the face.* →see also **ethnic cleansing**

cleans|er /klɛnzər/ (**cleansers**) ⬛ N-MASS A **cleanser** is a liquid or cream that you use for cleaning your skin. ❑ *...an extremely effective cleanser for dry and sensitive skins.* ⬛ N-MASS A **cleanser** is a liquid or powder that you use in cleaning kitchens and bathrooms. [mainly AM] ❑ *...a certain kind of bathroom cleanser.*

clear ♦♦♦ /klɪər/ (**clearer, clearest, clears, clearing, cleared**) ⬛ ADJ Something that is **clear** is easy to understand, see, or hear. ❑ *The book is clear, readable and adequately illustrated.* ❑ *The space telescope has taken the clearest pictures ever of Pluto.* ● **clear|ly** ADV ❑ *Whales journey up the coast of Africa, clearly visible from the beach.* ⬛ ADJ Something that is **clear** is obvious and impossible to be mistaken about. ❑ *It was a clear case of homicide.* ❑ *It became clear that I hadn't been able to convince Mike.* ● **clear|ly** ADV [ADV with cl/group] ❑ *Clearly, the police cannot break the law in order to enforce it.* ⬛ ADJ If you are **clear about** something, you understand it completely. ❑ *It is important to be clear about what Chomsky is doing here.* ❑ *He is not entirely clear on how he will go about it.* ⬜ ADJ If your mind or your way of thinking is **clear**, you are able to think sensibly and reasonably, and are not affected by confusion or by a drug such as alcohol. ❑ *She needed a clear head to carry out her instructions.* ● **clear|ly** ADV [ADV after v] ❑ *The only time I can think clearly is when I'm alone.* ⬛ V-T To **clear** your mind or your head means to free it from confused thoughts or from the effects of a drug such as alcohol. ❑ *He walked up Fifth Avenue to clear his head.* ⬛ ADJ A **clear** substance is one you can see through and which has no color, like clean water. ❑ *...a clear glass panel.* ❑ *...a clear gel.* ⬛ ADJ If a surface, place, or view is **clear**, it is free of unwanted objects or obstacles. ❑ *The runway is clear – go ahead and land.* ❑ *Caroline prefers her worktops to be clear of clutter.* ⬛ V-T When you **clear** an area or place or **clear** something **from** it, you remove things from it that you do not want to be there. ❑ *To clear the land and harvest the bananas they decided they needed a male workforce.* ❑ *Workers could not clear the tunnels of smoke.* ⬛ V-T If something or someone **clears** the way or the path **for** something to happen, they make it possible. ❑ *The Prime Minister resigned today, clearing the way for the formation of a new government.* ⬛ ADJ If it is a **clear** day or if the sky is **clear**, there is no mist, rain, or cloud. ❑ *On a clear day you can see the French coast.* ⬛ V-I When fog or mist **clears**, it gradually disappears. ❑ *The early morning mist had cleared.* ⬛ ADJ **Clear** eyes look healthy, attractive, and shining. ❑ *...clear blue eyes.* ⬛ ADJ If your skin is **clear**, it is healthy and free from blemishes. ❑ *No amount of cleansing or mineral water consumption can guarantee a clear skin.* ⬛ ADJ If you say that your conscience is **clear**, you mean you do not think you have done anything wrong. ❑ *Mr. Garcia said his conscience was clear over the jail incidents.* ⬛ ADJ If something or someone is **clear of** something else, it is not touching it or is a safe distance away from it. [v-link ADJ of n, v n ADJ] ❑ *As soon as he was clear of the terminal building he looked around.* ⬛ V-T/V-I When a bank **clears** a check or when a check **clears**, the bank agrees to pay the sum of money mentioned on it. ❑ *Polish banks can still take two*

강조] ❑ 그것은 내 작업복의 엉덩이 부분을 완전히 태워 버렸다. ❑ 그 도둑은 돈을 가지고 깨끗이 빠져나갔다.

구동사 깨끗이 비우다 ❑ 월 씨가 나에게 쓰레기통 비우는 것을 도와 주겠냐고 물었다.

⬛ 구동사 청소하다, 말끔히 치우다 ❑ 하루 동안의 격렬한 대치 끝에 남겨진 잔해를 시 경찰이 계속 치우고 있는 중이다. ⬛ 구동사 오염 요인을 없애다 ❑ 대중들로부터 압력을 받고, 많은 지방 정부들이 관할 해변의 오염 요인을 제거했다. ⬛ 구동사 (범죄, 부패 등을) 정화하다 ❑ 그 도시에서는 수년 간의 무관심과 쇠락 후에 자정 작용이 일어나고 있었다. ⬜ 구동사 몸을 씻다 ❑ 조니, 안에 들어가서 몸을 씻으렴.

⬛ 가산명사 청소부 ❑ 시드가 청소부로 일했던 교도소 병원 ⬛ 가산명사 ~ 닦는 사람 ❑ 그는 창문 닦는 사람이었다. ⬛ 물질명사 세제 ❑ 오븐 세척제 ⬜ 가산명사 청소기; 깨끗하게 하는 기구 ❑ 공기 정화기 ⬛ 가산명사 세탁소 ❑ 그는 자신의 성직자복을 입고 있었는데, 그 옷은 분명히 세탁소에 갔다 온 것이었다.

불가산명사 청결; 깔끔함 ❑ 영국의 많은 해변들이 최소한의 청결 기준치를 충족시키지 못한다.

⬛ 타동사 깨끗이 하다, 정화하다 ❑ 마지막 담배를 피운 직후에 당신의 몸은 담배의 독소를 정화하기 시작합니다. ⬛ 타동사 세척하다 ❑ 캐서린은 얼굴을 씻는 올바른 방법의 시범을 보여 주었다.

⬛ 물질명사 세안제 ❑ 건성, 민감성 피부에 대단히 효과적인 세안제 ⬛ 물질명사 세제제 [주로 미국영어] ❑ 특정 종류의 욕실 세척제

⬛ 형용사 알기 쉬운, 또렷한 ❑ 그 책은 이해하기 쉽고 읽기도 쉬우며 적절한 삽화도 곁들여져 있다. ❑ 그 천체 망원경이 명왕성의 모습을 이제껏 가장 또렷하게 잡아 왔다. ● 또렷한 부사 ❑ 고래들은 아프리카 해안을 따라 올라가는데, 그 모습은 해변에서도 또렷이 보인다. ⬛ 형용사 명백한, 의심할 여지없는 ❑ 그것은 명백한 살인 사건이었다. ❑ 내가 마이크를 납득시키지 못했다는 사실이 명백해졌다. ● 명백히 부사 ❑ 명백히, 경찰이 그 일을 집행하기 위해 법을 어길 수는 없다. ⬛ 형용사 확실히 이해한 ❑ 촘스키가 여기서 무엇을 하고 있는지 확실히 아는 것이 중요하다. ❑ 그는 그 일을 어떻게 해야 할지에 대해 생각이 완전히 확실한 것은 아니다. ⬜ 형용사 명료한, 명료한 ❑ 그녀는 자신의 지시를 실행에 옮기 명석한 두뇌가 필요했다. ● 명석하게, 명료하게 부사 ❑ 내가 명료하게 생각할 수 있는 유일한 시간은 혼자 있을 때뿐이다. ⬛ 타동사 머리를 맑게 하다 ❑ 그는 머리를 맑게 하기 위해 5번가를 걸어 올라갔다. ⬛ 형용사 투명한 ❑ 투명한 유리판 ❑ 투명한 젤 ⬛ 형용사 장애물이 없는, 깨끗한 ❑ 활주로는 깨끗하다. 계속 진행하여 착륙하라. ❑ 캐럴라인은 작업대에 물건들이 어수선하게 널려 있는 것을 좋아하지 않는다. ⬛ 타동사 정리하다, 제거하다 ❑ 경지를 정리하고 바나나를 수확하기 위해서 그들은 남자 일꾼이 필요하다고 결정했다. ❑ 인부들은 그을음을 치울 수가 없었다. ⬛ 타동사 길을 열다 ❑ 수상이 오늘 사임하면서, 새 정부 구성을 위한 길이 열렸다. ⬛ 형용사 맑은, 갠 ❑ 맑은 날에는 프랑스 해안을 볼 수 있다. ⬛ 자동사 개다, 걷히다 ❑ 이른 아침의 안개는 걷혀 있었다. ⬛ 형용사 맑은 ❑ 맑고 푸른 눈 ⬛ 형용사 깨끗한 ❑ 아무리 많은 양의 세안액이나 광천수를 쓰더라도 깨끗한 피부가 보장되는 것은 아니다. ⬛ 형용사 결백한 ❑ 가르시아 씨는 교도소 사건에 대해 자신의 양심은 결백하다고 말했다. ⬛ 형용사 ~에서 벗어난 ❑ 그는 터미널 건물로부터 어느 정도 벗어나자 주위를 둘러보았다. ⬛ 타동사/자동사 (수표의) 지불을 승인하다; 지불 승인을 받다 ❑ 그래도 폴란드 은행이 수표 지불 승인을

or three weeks to clear a check. **17** V-T If a course of action **is cleared**, people in authority give permission for it to happen. [usu passive] ◻ *Linda Gradstein has this report from Jerusalem, which was cleared by an Israeli censor.* **18** V-T If someone **is cleared**, they are proved to be not guilty of a crime or mistake. ◻ *She was cleared of murder and jailed for just five years for manslaughter.* **19** →see also **clearing, crystal clear 20** CONVENTION You can say "**Is that clear?**" or "**Do I make myself clear?**" after you have told someone your wishes or instructions, to make sure that they have understood you, and to emphasize your authority. ◻ *We're only going for half an hour, and you're not going to buy anything. Is that clear?* **21** PHRASE If someone is **in the clear**, they are not in danger, or are not blamed or suspected of anything. ◻ *The Audit Commission said that the ministry was in the clear.* **22** PHRASE If you **make** something **clear**, you say something in a way that makes it impossible for there to be any doubt about your meaning, wishes, or intentions. ◻ *Mr. O'Friel made it clear that further insults of this kind would not be tolerated.* **23** to **clear the air** →see **air**. to **clear** your **throat** →see **throat**

Thesaurus   clear의 참조어

ADJ.	obvious, plain, straightforward; (*ant.*) confusing **1** **2** bright, sunny; cloudy **10**

Word Partnership   clear의 연어

V.	be clear, **seem** clear **1**-**4**
	make it clear **1** **2**
N.	clear **goals/purpose**, clear **picture** **1**
	clear **idea**, clear **understanding** **1** **2**
	clear *someone's* **head** **5**
	clear **the way** **3** **9** **17**
ADJ.	**crystal** clear **1** **2** **3**

▶**clear away** PHRASAL VERB When you **clear** things **away** or **clear away**, you put away the things that you have been using, especially for eating or cooking. ◻ *The waitress had cleared away the plates and brought coffee.*

▶**clear off** PHRASAL VERB If you tell someone to **clear off**, you are telling them rather rudely to go away. [INFORMAL, DISAPPROVAL] ◻ *They looked at me as if I was nuts and told me to clear off.*

▶**clear out** **1** PHRASAL VERB If you tell someone to **clear out** of a place or to **clear out**, you are telling them rather rudely to leave the place. [INFORMAL, DISAPPROVAL] ◻ *She turned to the others in the room. "The rest of you clear out of here."* **2** PHRASAL VERB If you **clear out** a container, room, or house, you make it neat and throw away the things in it that you no longer want. ◻ *I took the precaution of clearing out my desk before I left.*

▶**clear up** **1** PHRASAL VERB When you **clear up** or **clear** a place **up**, you make things neat and put them away. ◻ *After breakfast they played while I cleared up.* **2** PHRASAL VERB To **clear up** a problem, misunderstanding, or mystery means to settle it or find a satisfactory explanation for it. ◻ *There should be someone to whom you can turn for any advice or to clear up any problems.* **3** PHRASAL VERB To **clear up** a medical problem, infection, or disease means to cure it or get rid of it. If a medical problem **clears up**, it goes away. ◻ *Antibiotics should be used to clear up the infection.* **4** PHRASAL VERB When the weather **clears up**, it stops raining or being cloudy. ◻ *It all depends on the weather clearing up.*

clear|ance /klɪ̯ərəns/ (**clearances**) **1** N-VAR **Clearance** is the removal of old buildings, trees, or other things that are not wanted from an area. ◻ *...a slum clearance operation in Nairobi.* ◻ *The UN pledged to help supervise the clearance of mines.* **2** N-VAR If you get **clearance** to do or have something, you get official approval or permission to do or have it. ◻ *Thai Airways said the plane had been given clearance to land.*

clear-cut also **clear cut** ADJ Something that is **clear-cut** is easy to recognize and quite distinct. ◻ *This was a clear-cut case of the original land owner being in the right.*

clear|ing /klɪ̯ərɪŋ/ (**clearings**) N-COUNT A **clearing** is a small area in a forest where there are no trees or bushes. ◻ *A helicopter landed in a clearing in the dense jungle.*

clear|ing bank (**clearing banks**) N-COUNT The **clearing banks** are the main banks in Britain. Clearing banks use the central clearing house in London to deal with other banks. [BUSINESS]

clear|ing|house /klɪ̯ərɪŋhaʊs/ (**clearinghouses**) [BRIT also **clearing house, clearing-house**] **1** N-COUNT If an organization acts as a **clearinghouse**, it collects, sorts, and distributes specialized information. ◻ *The center will act as a clearinghouse for research projects for former nuclear scientists.* **2** N-COUNT A **clearinghouse** is a central bank which deals with all the business between the banks that use its services. [BUSINESS]

clench /klɛntʃ/ (**clenches, clenching, clenched**) **1** V-T/V-I When you **clench** your fist or your fists **clenches**, you curl your fingers up tightly, usually because you are very angry. ◻ *Alex clenched her fists and gritted her teeth.* ◻ *She pulled at his sleeve and he turned on her, fists clenching again before he saw who it was.* **2** V-T/V-I When you **clench** your teeth or they **clench**, you squeeze your teeth together firmly, usually because you are angry or upset. ◻ *Patsy had to clench her jaw to suppress her anger.* **3** V-T If you **clench** something in your hand or in your teeth, you hold it tightly with your hand or your teeth. ◻ *I clenched the arms of my chair.*

하는 데 이삼 주가 걸릴 수 있다. **17** 타동사 허가를 받다, 검열을 통과하다 ◻ 린다 그래드스타인은 이 보고서를 예루살렘으로부터 받았는데, 그것은 이스라엘 검열관의 검열을 통과한 것이었다. **18** 타동사 무죄임이 밝혀지다 ◻ 그녀는 살인 혐의에 대해서는 무죄 선고를 받고 과실 치사 혐의에 대해서만 5년형에 처해졌다. **20** 관용 표현 알겠니? ◻ 우리는 30분 동안만 가는 거고, 너는 아무것도 사지 않을 거야. 알겠어? **21** 구 자유로위; 결백하여 ◻ 감사 위원회는 교단이 결백하다고 말했다. **22** 구 확실히 말하면, 분명히 하다 ◻ 오프릴 씨는 이와 같은 무례한 짓을 더 이상은 용인하지 않겠다고 확실히 말했다.

구동사 치우다 ◻ 종업원이 그릇을 치우고 커피를 가져왔다.

구동사 꺼져 버리다 [비격식체, 탐탁찮음] ◻ 그들은 마치 내가 바보라도 되는 것처럼 나를 쳐다보며 꺼져 버리라고 말했다.

1 구동사 꺼져 버리다 [비격식체, 탐탁찮음] ◻ 그녀는 방 안에 있는 다른 사람들을 돌아보며 말했다. "너희들 나머지는 여기서 꺼져." **2** 구동사 비우다, 소제하다 ◻ 나는 떠나기 전에 예방 차원에서 책상을 비웠다.

1 구동사 청소하다, 치우다 ◻ 아침 식사 후 내가 청소를 하는 동안 그들은 놀았다. **2** 구동사 풀다, 해결하다 ◻ 네가 조언을 받거나 문제를 해결하기 위해 의지할 수 있는 사람이 있어야 한다. **3** 구동사 고치다, 낫다 ◻ 감염을 방지하기 위해서는 항생제를 써야 한다. **4** 구동사 개다 ◻ 모든 일이 날씨가 개는 것에 달렸다.

1 가산명사 또는 불가산명사 제거; 정리 ◻ 나이로비에서의 빈민굴 정리 사업 ◻ 유엔은 광산 정리를 감독하는 일을 지원하겠다고 약속했다. **2** 가산명사 또는 불가산명사 허가 ◻ 타이 항공은 그 비행기가 착륙 허가를 받았었다고 말했다.

형용사 뚜렷한, 명백한 ◻ 이 일은 원래 땅 임자 쪽이 옳은 명백한 경우였다.

가산명사 (숲속의) 공터 ◻ 헬리콥터 한 대가 울창한 정글 속의 공터에 착륙했다.

가산명사 어음 교환 은행 [경제]

[영국영어 clearing house, clearing-house] **1** 가산명사 정보 센터 ◻ 그 센터는 이전 핵 과학자들에 대한 연구 프로젝트의 정보 센터 역할을 할 것이다. **2** 가산명사 어음 교환소 [경제]

1 타동사/자동사 꽉 쥐다; 꽉 쥐어지다 ◻ 알렉스는 주먹을 꽉 쥐고 이를 악물었다. ◻ 그녀가 그의 소매를 당기자 그는 그녀를 향해 돌아섰는데, 누구인지 알아보기 전까지 주먹을 다시 꽉 쥔 채였다. **2** 타동사/자동사 악물다; 악물리다 ◻ 팻시는 화를 억누르기 위해 이를 악물어야만 했다. **3** 타동사 단단히 잡다; 단단히 물다 ◻ 나는 의자 팔걸이를 단단히 잡았다.

cler|gy /klɜrdʒi/ N-PLURAL The **clergy** are the official leaders of the religious activities of a particular group of believers. ❑ *Stalin deported Catholic clergy to Siberia.*

복수명사 성직자들 ❑ 스탈린은 가톨릭 신부들을 시베리아로 추방했다.

cler|gy|man /klɜrdʒimən/ (clergymen) N-COUNT A **clergyman** is a male member of the clergy.

가산명사 성직자

cler|ic /klɛrɪk/ (clerics) N-COUNT A **cleric** is a member of the clergy. ❑ *His grandfather was a Muslim cleric.*

가산명사 성직자 ❑ 그의 할아버지는 이슬람교 성직자였다.

cler|i|cal /klɛrɪkəl/ **1** ADJ **Clerical** jobs, skills, and workers are concerned with routine work that is done in an office. [ADJ n] ❑ *...a strike by clerical staff in all government departments.* **2** ADJ **Clerical** means relating to the clergy. [ADJ n] ❑ *...Iran's clerical leadership.*

1 형용사 사무직의 ❑ 정부 전 부처 사무직 직원들의 파업 **2** 형용사 성직자의 ❑ 이란의 성직자 지도부

clerk /klɜrk, BRIT klɑːk/ (clerks, clerking, clerked) **1** N-COUNT A **clerk** is a person who works in an office, bank, or law court and whose job is to keep the records or accounts. ❑ *She was offered a job as an accounts clerk with a travel firm.* **2** N-COUNT In a hotel, office, or hospital, a **clerk** is the person whose job is to answer the telephone and deal with people when they arrive. [mainly AM] ❑ *...a hotel clerk.* **3** N-COUNT A **clerk** is someone who sells things to customers in a store. [AM] ❑ *Now Thomas was working as a clerk in a West Berlin shop that sold leather goods.* **4** V-I To **clerk** means to work as a clerk. [mainly AM] ❑ *Gene clerked at the auction.* →see **hotel**

1 가산명사 사무원 ❑ 그녀는 한 여행사의 경리 사무원 자리를 제의받았다. **2** 가산명사 점원, 종업원 [주로 미국영어] ❑ 호텔 종업원 **3** 가산명사 판매원 [미국영어] ❑ 그때 토머스는 가죽 제품을 파는 서베를린의 한 상점에서 판매원으로 일하고 있었다. **4** 자동사 사무원으로 근무하다 [주로 미국영어] ❑ 진은 경매장에서 사무원으로 근무했다.

clev|er ♦◇◇ /klɛvər/ (cleverer, cleverest) **1** ADJ Someone who is **clever** is intelligent and able to understand things easily or plan things well. ❑ *He's a very clever man.* ● **clev|er|ly** ADV ❑ *She would cleverly pick up on what I said.* ● **clev|er|ness** N-UNCOUNT ❑ *Her cleverness seems to get in the way of her emotions.* **2** ADJ A **clever** idea, book, or invention is extremely effective and shows the skill of the people involved. ❑ *It is a clever and gripping novel, yet something is missing from its heart.* ● **clev|er|ly** ADV [ADV -ed] ❑ *...a cleverly designed swimsuit.*

1 형용사 영리한, 똑똑한 ❑ 그는 매우 똑똑한 사람이다. ● 영리하게 부사 ❑ 그녀는 내가 말하는 것을 영리하게 알아차리곤 했다. ● 영리함 불가산명사 ❑ 그녀의 영리함이 그녀 자신의 감정을 방해하는 것처럼 보인다. **2** 형용사 독창적인 ❑ 그것은 독창적이고 흥미로운 소설이지만, 그 핵심에 뭔가가 빠져 있다. ● 독창적으로 부사 ❑ 독창적인 디자인의 수영복

Thesaurus	*clever*의 참조어
ADJ.	bright, ingenious, smart; *(ant.)* dumb, stupid **1**

cli|ché /kliʃeɪ, BRIT kliːʃeɪ/ (clichés) [BRIT also cliche] N-COUNT A **cliché** is an idea or phrase which has been used so much that it is no longer interesting or effective or no longer has much meaning. [DISAPPROVAL] ❑ *I've learned that the cliché about life not being fair is true.*

[영국영어 cliche] 가산명사 진부한 생각, 상투적인 문구 [탐탁찮음] ❑ 삶이 공평하지 못하다는 진부한 표현이 참이라는 사실을 알았다.

click /klɪk/ (clicks, clicking, clicked) **1** V-T/V-I If something **clicks** or if you **click** it, it makes a short, sharp sound. ❑ *The applause rose to a crescendo and cameras clicked.* ❑ *He clicked off the radio.* ● N-COUNT **Click** is also a noun. ❑ *The telephone rang three times before I heard a click and then her recorded voice.* **2** V-T/V-I If you **click on** an area of a computer screen, you point the cursor at that area and press one of the buttons on the mouse in order to make something happen. [COMPUTING] [no passive] ❑ *I clicked on a link and recent reviews of the production came up.* ● N-COUNT **Click** is also a noun. ❑ *You can check your email with a click of your mouse.* **3** V-I When you suddenly understand something, you can say that it **clicks**. [INFORMAL] ❑ *When I saw the television report it all clicked.* **4** to **click into place** →see **place**

1 타동사/자동사 딱 소리 나다; 찰칵 하고 울리게 하다 ❑ 박수 갈채는 점점 커져 갔고 카메라들은 찰칵거렸다. ❑ 그는 라디오를 찰칵 껐다. ● 가산명사 찰칵 하는 소리 ❑ 전화 신호음이 세 번 울리고 찰칵 하는 소리가 나더니 녹음된 그녀의 음성이 들렸다. **2** 타동사/자동사 (컴퓨터) 마우스 버튼을 누르다, 클릭하다 [컴퓨터] ❑ 링크를 클릭하자 그 제품에 대한 최근의 논평들이 나왔다. ● 가산명사 (컴퓨터) 클릭 ❑ 마우스를 한 번 클릭하면 이메일을 확인할 수 있다. **3** 자동사 불현듯이 이해되다 [비격식체] ❑ 텔레비전 보도를 보자 모든 것이 불현듯 이해되었다.

click|able /klɪkəbəl/ ADJ A **clickable** image on a computer screen is one that you can point the cursor at and click on, in order to make something happen. [COMPUTING] ❑ *...a Web site with clickable maps showing hotel locations.*

형용사 (컴퓨터) 활성화된 [컴퓨터] ❑ 활성화된 호텔 위치 지도가 있는 웹 사이트

cli|ent ♦◇◇ /klaɪənt/ (clients) N-COUNT A **client** of a professional person or organization is a person or company that receives a service from them in return for payment. [BUSINESS] ❑ *...a solicitor and his client.* →see **trial**

가산명사 고객 [경제] ❑ 변호사와 그의 고객

If you use the professional services of someone such as a lawyer or an accountant, you are one of their **clients**. When you buy goods from a particular shop or company, you are one of its **customers**. Doctors and hospitals have **patients**, while hotels have **guests**. People who travel on public transportation are referred to as **passengers**.

변호사나 회계사 같은 전문가의 서비스를 이용하면, 그들의 client가 된다. 특정한 상점이나 회사에서 상품을 사면, 그 상점이나 회사의 customer가 된다. 의사와 병원은 patient를 받고, 호텔은 guest를 받는다. 대중 교통수단으로 이동하는 사람들은 passenger라고 일컫는다.

cli|en|tele /klaɪəntɛl, kliːɒn-/ N-SING-COLL The **clientele** of a place or organization are its customers or clients. ❑ *This pub had a mixed clientele.*

단수명사-집합 (집합적) 고객 ❑ 이 술집에는 잡다한 고객들이 드나들었다.

cliff /klɪf/ (cliffs) N-COUNT A **cliff** is a high area of land with a very steep side, especially one next to the sea. ❑ *The car rolled over the edge of a cliff.*

가산명사 낭떠러지, 벼랑 ❑ 그 차가 굴러서 벼랑 끝을 넘어갔다.

cli|mate ♦◇◇ /klaɪmɪt/ (climates) **1** N-VAR The **climate** of a place is the general weather conditions that are typical of it. ❑ *...the hot and humid climate of Cyprus.* **2** N-COUNT You can use **climate** to refer to the general atmosphere or situation somewhere. ❑ *The economic climate remains uncertain.* ❑ *...the existing climate of violence and intimidation.* →see Word Web: **climate**

1 가산명사 또는 불가산명사 기후 ❑ 덥고 습한 사이프러스의 기후 **2** 가산명사 분위기, 환경 ❑ 경제적 환경은 여전히 불확실하다. ❑ 폭력적이고 위협적인 현재 분위기

cli|max /klaɪmæks/ (climaxes, climaxing, climaxed) **1** N-COUNT The **climax of** something is the most exciting or important moment in it, usually near the end. ❑ *For Pritchard, reaching an Olympics was the climax of her career.* ❑ *It was the climax to 24 hours of growing anxiety.* **2** V-T/V-I The event that **climaxes** a sequence of events is an exciting or important event that comes at the end. You can also say that a sequence of events **climaxes with** a particular event. [JOURNALISM] ❑ *The demonstration climaxed two weeks of strikes.*

1 가산명사 최고조, 절정 ❑ 프리처드로서는 올림픽 경기에 나간 것이 생애의 정점이었다. ❑ 그때가 24시간 커져 가던 불안감이 최고조에 달한 때였다. **2** 타동사/자동사 정점에 달하게 하다; 정점에 달하다 [언론] ❑ 그 시위로 2주 간의 파업은 정점에 달했다.

climb ♦◇◇ /klaɪm/ (climbs, climbing, climbed) **1** V-T/V-I If you **climb** something such as a tree, mountain, or ladder, or **climb up** it, you move toward the top of it. If you **climb down** it, you move toward the bottom of it. ❑ *Climbing the first hill took half an hour.* ❑ *I told her about him climbing up the drainpipe.* ● N-COUNT **Climb** is also a noun. ❑ *...an hour's leisurely climb through olive*

1 타동사/자동사 오르다, 기어오르다; 기어 내려오다 ❑ 첫 번째 언덕을 오르는 데 30분이 걸렸다. ❑ 나는 그녀에게 그가 배수관을 타고 기어 올라가는 것에 대해 말해 주었다. ● 가산명사 오름, 등반 ❑ 올리브 과수원과 포도밭 사이로 한 시간 동안 한가로이 올라감

Word Web climate

During the past 100 years, the surface air **temperature** of the earth has increased by about 1° **Fahrenheit** (F). Alaska has warmed by about 4° F. At the same time, precipitation over the northern hemisphere increased by 10%. The global sea level also rose 4-8 inches. The years 1998, 2001, and 2002 were the three hottest ever recorded. This warm period followed what some scientists call the "Little Ice Age." Researchers found that from the 1400s to the 1800s the Earth cooled by about 6° F. Air and water temperatures were lower, **glaciers** grew quickly, and ice floes came further south than usual.

St. Mark's Square in Venice flooded 111 times in 2002.

groves and vineyards. **2** V-I If you **climb** somewhere, you move there carefully, for example because you are moving in a small space or trying to avoid falling. ❑ *The girls hurried outside, climbed into the car, and drove off.* ❑ *He must have climbed out of his bed.* **3** V-I When something such as an aeroplane **climbs**, it moves upwards to a higher position. When the sun **climbs**, it moves higher in the sky. ❑ *The plane took off for LA, lost an engine as it climbed, and crashed just off the runway.* **4** V-I When something **climbs**, it increases in value or amount. ❑ *The nation's unemployment rate has been climbing steadily since last June.* ❑ *Prices have climbed by 21% since the beginning of the year.* **5** →see also **climbing. a mountain to climb** →see **mountain**

Word Partnership   climb의 연어

PREP.	climb **up/down**, climb **in/on** ■
V.	**begin/continue to** climb ■-■
N.	climb **the stairs** ■
	prices climb ■

▶**climb down** PHRASAL VERB If you **climb down** in an argument or dispute, you admit that you are wrong, or change your intentions or demands. ❑ *If Lafontaine is forced to climb down, he may wish to reconsider his position.*

climb|er /klaɪmər/ (**climbers**) **1** N-COUNT A **climber** is someone who climbs rocks or mountains as a sport or a hobby. ❑ *He was, from childhood, a keen climber and hill walker.* **2** N-COUNT A **climber** is a plant that grows upwards by attaching itself to other plants or objects. ❑ *All good garden centers carry a selection of climbers.*

climb|ing /klaɪmɪŋ/ N-UNCOUNT **Climbing** is the activity of climbing rocks or mountains. ❑ *I had done no skiing, no climbing and no hill walking.*

clinch /klɪntʃ/ (**clinches, clinching, clinched**) **1** V-T If you **clinch** something you are trying to achieve, such as a business deal or victory in a contest, you succeed in obtaining it. ❑ *Hibernian clinched the First Division title when they beat Hamilton 2-0.* **2** V-T The thing that **clinches** an uncertain matter settles it or provides a definite answer. ❑ *Evidently this information clinched the matter.*

cling /klɪŋ/ (**clings, clinging, clung**) **1** V-I If you **cling to** someone or something, you hold onto them tightly. ❑ *Another man was rescued as he clung to the riverbank.* ❑ *She had to cling onto the door handle until the pain passed.* **2** V-I If someone **clings to** a position or a possession they have, they do everything they can to keep it even though this may be very difficult. ❑ *Instead, he appears determined to cling to power.* ❑ *Another minister clung on with a majority of only 18.*

clin|ic ◆◇◇ /klɪnɪk/ (**clinics**) N-COUNT A **clinic** is a building where people go to receive medical advice or treatment. ❑ *...a family planning clinic.*

Word Partnership   clinic의 연어

| N. | **abortion/family planning** clinic |
| ADJ. | **free** clinic, **medical** clinic |

clini|cal /klɪnɪkᵊl/ ADJ **Clinical** means involving or relating to the direct medical treatment or testing of patients. [MEDICAL] [ADJ n] ❑ *The first clinical trials were expected to begin next year.* ● **clini|cal|ly** /klɪnɪkli/ ADV ❑ *She was diagnosed as being clinically depressed.*

clip /klɪp/ (**clips, clipping, clipped**) **1** N-COUNT A **clip** is a small device, usually made of metal or plastic, that is specially shaped for holding things together. ❑ *She took the clip out of her hair.* **2** V-T/V-I When you **clip** things together or when things **clip** together, you fasten them together using a clip or clips. ❑ *He clipped his safety belt to a fitting on the deck.* **3** N-COUNT A **clip** from a movie or a radio or television program is a short piece of it that is broadcast separately. ❑ *...an historical film clip of Lenin speaking.* **4** V-T If you **clip** something, you cut small pieces from it, especially in order to shape it. ❑ *I saw an old man out clipping his hedge.* **5** V-T If you **clip** something out of a newspaper or magazine, you cut it

2 자동사 좁은 공간으로 들어가거나 떨어지는 것을 피하려 할 때처럼 조심스럽게 이동할 때 climb이라는 표현을 쓴다. ❑ 그 여자 아이들은 서둘러 밖으로 나가서 차를 타고는 떠나 버렸다. ❑ 그가 자신의 침대에서 빠져나간 게 틀림없다. **3** 자동사 솟다, 상승하다 ❑ 그 비행기는 로스앤젤레스를 향해 이륙하여 상승하던 중에 엔진 하나를 잃고 활주로를 벗어나자마자 바로 추락했다. **4** 자동사 (가치나 수량이) 오르다 ❑ 전국 실업률이 작년 6월 이래로 꾸준히 증가해 오고 있다. ❑ 연초 이후 물가가 21퍼센트 상승했다.

구동사 물러나다, 주장을 철회하다 ❑ 만약 라퐁텐이 강요에 의해 주장을 굽힌다면, 그가 자신의 위치를 재고하고자 할지도 모른다.

1 가산명사 등산가 ❑ 그는 어렸을 때부터 등산과 힐 워킹에 열심이었다. **2** 가산명사 덩굴 식물 ❑ 괜찮은 원예 센터는 어느 곳이나 정선된 덩굴 식물을 구비하고 있다.

불가산명사 등반, 등산 ❑ 나는 스키, 등산, 힐 워킹 중 어떤 것도 해 본 적이 없었다.

1 타동사 손에 넣다 ❑ 하이버니언 팀이 해밀턴 팀을 2대0으로 누르고 제1 디비전 타이틀을 손에 쥐었다. **2** 타동사 매듭을 짓다, 결말을 내다 ❑ 분명히 이 정보로 인해 그 일이 매듭지어졌다.

1 자동사 매달리다, 붙들고 늘어지다 ❑ 다른 남자는 강둑에 매달려 있다가 구조되었다. ❑ 그녀는 통증이 가라앉을 때까지 문고리를 붙들고 있어야 했다. **2** 자동사 -을 지켜내기 위해 무슨 일이든 다 하다 ❑ 대신, 그는 권력을 지켜내기 위해 무슨 일이든 하기로 결심한 것처럼 보인다. ❑ 또 다른 장관은 겨우 18명밖에 안 되는 다수파를 거느리고 온 힘을 다해 버텼다.

가산명사 진료소, 진료 상담소 ❑ 가족계획 상담소

형용사 임상의, 진료의 [의학] ❑ 첫 번째 임상 시험이 내년에 시작될 예정이었다. ● 임상적으로 부사 ❑ 그녀는 임상적으로 우울증에 빠진 것으로 진단을 받았다.

1 가산명사 클립, 집게 ❑ 그녀는 머리에서 클립을 빼냈다. **2** 타동사/자동사 클립으로 고정시키다 ❑ 그는 안전띠를 데크 연결 부분에 클립으로 고정시켰다. **3** 가산명사 클립 (영화 등의 장면) ❑ 레닌의 연설 장면이 담긴 역사적 영화 클립 **4** 타동사 깎다, 다듬다 ❑ 바깥에서 한 늙은 남자가 생울타리를 깎는 것을 보았다. **5** 타동사 오려 내다 ❑ 이웃에 사는 아이들이 신문에서 그의 사진을 오려 내어 가지고 다녔다. **6** 타동사 치다, 치고 지나가다

out. ❑ *Kids in his neighborhood clipped his picture from the newspaper and carried it around.* ⑥ V-T If something **clips** something else, it hits it accidentally at an angle before moving off in a different direction. ❑ *The truck clipped the rear of a tanker and then crashed into a second truck.* ⑦ →see also **clipping, clipped, paper clip**

❑ 그 트럭은 유조차의 뒤를 치고 나가서 두 번째 트럭에 충돌했다.

Word Partnership   *clip*의 연어

N.   **audio/film/movie/music/video** clip, a clip **from a tape** ③
     clip **coupons** ⑤
V.   **play a** clip ③

---

clip|board /klɪpbɔrd/ (**clipboards**) ① N-COUNT A **clipboard** is a board with a clip at the top. It is used to hold together pieces of paper that you need to carry around, and provides a firm base for writing. ② N-COUNT In computing, a **clipboard** is a file where you can temporarily store text or images from one document until you are ready to use them again. [COMPUTING]

① 가산명사 (종이를 끼워 쓸 수 있는) 받침판 ② 가산명사 (컴퓨터) 클립보드 [컴퓨터]

clipped /klɪpt/ ① ADJ **Clipped** means neatly cut. ❑ *...a quiet street of clipped hedges and flowering gardens.* ② ADJ If you say that someone has a **clipped** way of speaking, you mean they speak with quick, short sounds, and usually that they sound upper-class. ❑ *The Chief Constable's clipped tones crackled over the telephone line.*

① 형용사 깔끔하게 잘라 다듬은 ❑ 울타리가 잘 다듬어지고 정원에는 꽃이 피어 있는 조용한 거리 ② 형용사 딱 부러지는 말투의 ❑ 전화기 너머에서 경찰서장의 딱 부러지는 듯한 말투가 들려왔다.

clip|ping /klɪpɪŋ/ (**clippings**) ① N-COUNT A **clipping** is an article, picture, or advertisement that has been cut from a newspaper or magazine. ❑ *...bulletin boards crowded with newspaper clippings.* ② N-COUNT **Clippings** are small pieces of something that have been cut from something larger. ❑ *Having mown the lawn, there are all those grass clippings to get rid of.*

① 가산명사 오려 낸 기사나 사진 ❑ 오려 낸 신문 기사로 꽉 채워진 게시판 ② 가산명사 깎아낸 조각 ❑ 잔디를 깎아서, 치워야 할 잔디 쓰레기가 널렸다.

clique /klik/ (**cliques**) N-COUNT If you describe a group of people as a **clique**, you mean that they spend a lot of time together and seem unfriendly towards people who are not in the group. [DISAPPROVAL] ❑ *Anna Ford recently hit out at the male clique which she believes holds back women in television.*

가산명사 파벌 [탐탁찮음] ❑ 애너 포드는 텔레비전에 종사하는 여성들을 방해한다고 생각되는 남성 파벌을 최근 맹렬히 비난했다.

cloak /kloʊk/ (**cloaks**) ① N-COUNT A **cloak** is a long, loose, sleeveless piece of clothing which people used to wear over their other clothes when they went out. ② N-SING A **cloak of** something such as mist or snow completely covers and hides something. ❑ *Today most of England will be under a cloak of thick mist.* ③ N-SING If you refer to something as a **cloak**, you mean that it is intended to hide the truth about something. ❑ *Preparations for the wedding were made under a cloak of secrecy.*

① 가산명사 망토 ② 단수명사 덮어 가리는 것 ❑ 오늘 영국 대부분 지역이 짙은 안개에 덮이겠습니다. ③ 단수명사 은폐 수단 ❑ 결혼식 준비는 비밀리에 이루어졌다.

cloak|room /kloʊkrum/ (**cloakrooms**) ① N-COUNT In a public building, the **cloakroom** is the place where people can leave their coats, umbrellas, and so on. ❑ *...a cloakroom attendant.* ② N-COUNT A **cloakroom** is a room containing toilets in a public building or a room containing a toilet on the ground floor of someone's house. [BRIT]

① 가산명사 휴대품 보관소 ❑ 휴대품 보관소 안내원 ② 가산명사 화장실 [영국영어]

clock ♦♢♢ /klɒk/ (**clocks, clocking, clocked**) ① N-COUNT A **clock** is an instrument, usually in a room or on the outside of a building, that shows what time of day it is. ❑ *He was conscious of a clock ticking.* ❑ *...a digital clock.* ② N-COUNT A time **clock** in a factory or office is a device that is used to record the hours that people work. Each worker puts a special card into the device when they arrive and leave, and the times are recorded on the card. ❑ *Government workers were made to punch time clocks morning, noon and night.* ③ N-COUNT In a car, the **clock** is the instrument that shows the speed of the car or the distance it has traveled. [mainly BRIT] ❑ *The car had 160,000 miles on the clock.* ④ V-T To **clock** a particular time or speed in a race means to reach that time or speed. ❑ *Elliott clocked the fastest time this year for the 800 meters.* ⑤ V-T If something or someone **is clocked at** a particular time or speed, their time or speed is measured at that level. [usu passive] ❑ *He has been clocked at 11 seconds for 100 meters.* ⑥ →see also **alarm clock, o'clock** ⑦ PHRASE If you are doing something **against the clock**, you are doing it in a great hurry, because there is very little time. ❑ *The emergency services were working against the clock as the tide began to rise.* ⑧ PHRASE If something is done **around the clock** or **round the clock**, it is done all day and all night without stopping. ❑ *Rescue services have been working round the clock to free stranded motorists.* →see **time zone**

① 가산명사 시계 ❑ 그는 시계가 똑딱거리는 것을 의식하고 있었다. ❑ 디지털 시계 ② 가산명사 (출퇴근용) 시간 기록계 ❑ 행정부 직원들은 아침과 정오, 그리고 밤에 시간 기록계에 카드를 찍어야 하게 되었다. ③ 가산명사 속도계; 미터기 [주로 영국영어] ❑ 그 자동차의 미터기에는 총 주행 거리가 16만 마일로 적혀 있었다. ④ 타동사 -의 기록을 내다 ❑ 엘리어트는 800미터 경주의 올해 최고 기록을 냈다. ⑤ 타동사 -의 기록을 내다 ❑ 그는 100미터를 11초에 주파해 왔다. ⑦ 구 시간을 다투어 ❑ 밀물이 올라오기 시작함에 따라, 응급 구조대는 시간을 다투며 작업을 하고 있었다. ⑧ 구 24시간 내내 ❑ 꼼짝 못하게 된 운전자들을 구해 주기 위해 구조 서비스는 24시간 가동하고 있다.

Word Partnership   *clock*의 연어

N.   **clock radio, hands of a** clock ①
V.   **look at a** clock, **put/turn the** clock **forward/back, set a** clock,
     clock **strikes,** clock **ticks** ①

▶**clock in** PHRASAL VERB When you **clock in** at work, you arrive there or put a special card into a device to show what time you arrived. ❑ *I have to clock in by eight.*

구동사 출근하다, 출근 카드를 찍다 ❑ 나는 8시까지 출근해야 한다.

▶**clock off** PHRASAL VERB When you **clock off** at work, you leave work or put a special card into a device to show what time you left. ❑ *The Night Duty Officer was ready to clock off.*

구동사 퇴근하다, 카드를 찍고 퇴근하다 ❑ 야간 당직 사령은 퇴근할 준비가 되어 있었다.

▶**clock on** PHRASAL VERB When workers **clock on** at a factory or office, they put a special card into a device to show what time they arrived. ❑ *They arrived to clock on and found the factory gates locked.*

구동사 (시간 기록계로) 출근 시각을 기록하다 ❑ 그들은 출근 카드를 찍으려고 도착해서야 공장 문이 잠겨 있는 것을 발견했다.

▶**clock out** PHRASAL VERB **Clock out** means the same as **clock off**. ❑ *She had clocked out of her bank at 5:02pm using her plastic card.*

구동사 (시간 기록계로) 퇴근 시각을 기록하다 ❑ 그녀는 오후 5시 2분에 기록계에 카드를 찍고서 은행에서 퇴근했다.

▶**clock up** PHRASAL VERB If you **clock up** a large number or total of things, you reach that number or total. ❑ *In two years, he clocked up over 100 victories.*

구동사 기록을 올리다 ❑ 2년 만에, 그는 100승이 넘는 기록을 올렸다.

a
b
c
d
e
f
g
h
i
j
k
l
m
n
o
p
q
r
s
t
u
v
w
x
y
z

A

Word Link

wise ≈ in the direction or manner of : clockwise, likewise, otherwise

B

clock|wise /klɒkwaɪz/ ADV When something is moving **clockwise**, it is moving in a circle in the same direction as the hands on a clock. [ADV after v] ❏ *He told the children to start moving clockwise around the room.* ● ADJ **Clockwise** is also an adjective. [ADJ n] ❏ *Gently swing your right arm in a clockwise direction.*

부사 시계 방향으로 ❏ 그는 아이들에게 방 안을 시계 방향으로 돌기 시작하라고 말했다. ● 형용사 시계 방향의 ❏ 오른팔을 시계 방향으로 천천히 돌리세요.

C

clock|work /klɒkwɜrk/ ① ADJ A **clockwork** toy or device has machinery inside it which makes it move or operate when it is wound up with a key. [ADJ n] ❏ *...a clockwork train-set.* ② PHRASE If you say that something happens **like clockwork**, you mean that it happens without any problems or delays, or happens regularly. ❏ *The Queen's trip is arranged to go like clockwork, everything pre-planned to the minute.*

① 형용사 태엽 장치 ❏ 태엽 장치가 붙은 기차 세트 ② 구 시계같이, 정확히 ❏ 여왕의 여행은 시계처럼 정확하게 만사가 분 단위까지 미리 계획된다.

D

clog /klɒg/ (clogs, clogging, clogged) ① V-T When something **clogs** a hole or place, it blocks it so that nothing can pass through. ❏ *Dirt clogs the pores, causing blemishes.* ② N-COUNT **Clogs** are heavy leather or wooden shoes with thick wooden soles.

① 타동사 막다 ❏ 먼지가 모공을 막아서 점이 생기게 만듭니다. ② 가산명사 나막신

E

clone /kloʊn/ (clones, cloning, cloned) ① N-COUNT If someone or something is a **clone** of another person or thing, they are so similar to this person or thing that they seem to be exactly the same as them. ❏ *Tom was in some ways a younger clone of his handsome father.* ② N-COUNT A **clone** is an animal or plant that has been produced artificially, for example in a laboratory, from the cells of another animal or plant. A clone is exactly the same as the original animal or plant. ❏ *...the world's first human clone.* ③ V-T To **clone** an animal or plant means to produce it as a clone. ❏ *The idea of cloning extinct life forms still belongs to science fiction.*
→see Word Web: **clone**

① 가산명사 꼭 닮은 사람, 꼭 닮은 것 ❏ 탐은 어떤 면에서 보면 잘생긴 아버지를 쏙 빼닮았다. ② 가산명사 복제 생물 ❏ 세계 최초의 복제 인간 ③ 타동사 복제하다 ❏ 멸종된 생물 종을 복제한다는 생각은 아직까지는 공상 과학 소설에나 나오는 것이다.

F

G

H

I

Word Partnership

*close*의 연어

N.	close **a door** ① ①
	close *your* **eyes** ① ④
	close **friend**, close **to** *someone* ② ②
	close **family/relative** ② ② ③
	close **attention/scrutiny** ② ⑦
	close **election**, close **race** ② ⑧
ADV.	close **enough**, **so/too/very** close ② ① ⑨

J

K

L

---

close

① SHUTTING OR COMPLETING
② NEARNESS; ADJECTIVE USES
③ NEARNESS; VERB USES
④ USED AS A ROAD NAME

M

N

① **close** ♦♦♦ /kloʊz/ (closes, closing, closed) →Please look at category ⑩ to see if the expression you are looking for is shown under another headword.
① V-T/V-I When you **close** something such as a door or lid or when it **closes**, it moves so that a hole, gap, or opening is covered. ❏ *If you are cold, close the window.* ❏ *Zacharias heard the door close.* ② V-T When you **close** something such as an open book or umbrella, you move the different parts of it together. ❏ *Slowly he closed the book.* ③ V-T If you **close** something such as a computer file or window, you give the computer an instruction to remove it from the screen. [COMPUTING] ❏ *To close your document, press CTRL+W on your keyboard.* ④ V-T/V-I When you **close** your eyes or your eyes **close**, your eyelids move downward, so that you can no longer see. ❏ *Bess closed her eyes and fell asleep.* ⑤ V-T/V-I When a place **closes** or **is closed**, work or activity stops there for a short period. ❏ *Shops close only on Christmas Day and New Year's Day.* ❏ *Government troops closed the airport.* ⑥ V-T/V-I If a place such as a factory, store, or school **closes**, or if it **is closed**, all work or activity stops there permanently. ❏ *Many enterprises will be forced to close.* ● PHRASAL VERB **Close down** means the same as **close**. ❏ *Minford closed down the business and went into politics.* ● **clos|ing** N-SING ❏ *...since the closing of the steelworks in 1984.* ⑦ V-T To **close** a road or border means to block it in order to prevent people from using it. ❏ *They were cut off from the West in 1948 when their government closed that border crossing.* ⑧ V-T To **close** a conversation, event, or matter means to bring it to an end or to complete it. ❏ *Judge Isabel Oliva said last night: "I have closed the case. There was no foul play." ❏ *The Prime Minister is said to now consider the matter closed.* ⑨ V-T If you **close** a bank account, you take all your money out of it and inform the bank that you will no longer be using the account. ❏ *He had closed his account with the bank five years earlier.* ⑩ V-I On the stock market or the

① 타동사/자동사 닫다; 닫히다 ❏ 추우면 창문을 닫아. ❏ 차하리아스는 문이 닫히는 소리를 들었다. ② 타동사 (책을) 덮다; (우산을) 접다 ❏ 그는 천천히 책을 덮었다. ③ 타동사 (컴퓨터 파일이나 창을) 닫다 [컴퓨터] ❏ 서류 창을 닫으려면, CTRL+W 키를 누르세요. ④ 타동사/자동사 (눈을) 감다; 감기다 ❏ 베스는 눈을 감고 잠들었다. ⑤ 타동사/자동사 (상점이나 시설 따위가 잠시) 문을 닫다 ❏ 상점들은 성탄절과 설날에만 문을 닫는다. ❏ 정부군이 공항을 임시 폐쇄했다. ⑥ 타동사/자동사 폐업하다, 폐점하다 ❏ 다수의 기업체들이 폐쇄당할 것이다. ● 구동사 폐업하다 ❏ 민포드는 사업을 접고 정계에 입문했다. ● 폐업, 폐쇄 단수명사 ❏ 1984년에 제철소가 문을 닫은 이래로 ⑦ 타동사 막다, 차단하다 ❏ 1948년 정부가 국경을 봉쇄하자 그들은 서방 세계로부터 고립되었다. ⑧ 타동사 종결하다, 끝내다 ❏ 이사벨 올리바 판사가 지난밤 말했다. "나는 그 사건을 종결했습니다. 부정행위는 없었어요." ❏ 종결된 그 사안에 대해 수상이 숙고 중이라는 말이 있다. ⑨ 타동사 (은행 계좌를) 폐쇄하다 ❏ 그는 5년 앞서 그 은행 계좌를 폐쇄했다. ⑩ 자동사 (증권) 종가가 -이 되다 [경제] ❏ 미국 달러가 오늘 동경에서 강세로 마감했다.

O

P

Q

R

S

T

U

V

W

Word Web

clone

Clones have always existed. For example, plant propagation using a leaf cutting produces an **identical** new plant. Identical **twins** are also natural clones of each other. Recently however, scientists have started using **genetic engineering** to produce artificial clones of animals. The first step involves removing the **DNA** from a **cell**. Next, a technician places this genetic information into an egg cell. The egg then matures into a **copy** of the donor animal. The first animal experiments in the 1970s involved tadpoles. In 1997 a sheep named Dolly became the first successfully cloned mammal.

X

Y

Z

currency markets, if a share price or a currency **closes** at a particular value, that is its value at the end of the day's business. [BUSINESS] ❑ *The US dollar closed higher in Tokyo today.* **11** →see also **closing**. to **close** your **eyes** to something →see **eye**. to **close ranks**, →see **rank**

Thesaurus	*close*의 참조어
v.	fasten, seal, shut, slam; (ant.) open ① **11**

▶**close down** →see **close 6**

② **close** ♦♦♦ /kloʊs/ (closer, closest) →Please look at category **13** to see if the expression you are looking for is shown under another headword. **1** ADJ If one thing or person is **close to** another, there is only a very small distance between them. [v-link ADJ, ADJ after v, oft ADJ prep/adv] ❑ *Her lips were close to his head and her breath tickled his ear.* ❑ *The man moved closer, lowering his voice.* ● **close|ly** ADV ❑ *They crowded more closely around the stretcher.* **2** ADJ You say that people are **close to** each other when they like each other very much and know each other very well. ❑ *She and Linda became very close.* ❑ *I shared a house with a close friend from school.* ● **close|ness** N-UNCOUNT ❑ *I asked whether her closeness to her mother ever posed any problems.* **3** ADJ Your **close** relatives are the members of your family who are most directly related to you, for example your parents and your brothers or sisters. [ADJ n] ❑ *...large changes such as the birth of a child or death of a close relative.* **4** ADJ A **close** ally or partner of someone knows them well and is very involved in their work. ❑ *He was once regarded as one of Mr. Brown's closest political advisers.* **5** ADJ **Close** contact or cooperation involves seeing or communicating with someone often. [ADJ n] ❑ *Both nations are seeking closer links with the West.* ● **close|ly** ADV [ADV after v] ❑ *Our agencies work closely with local groups in developing countries.* **6** ADJ If there is a **close** connection or resemblance between two things, they are strongly connected or are very similar. ❑ *There is a close connection between pain and tension.* ● **close|ly** ADV ❑ *...a pattern closely resembling a cross.* **7** ADJ **Close** inspection or observation of something is careful and thorough. ❑ *He discovered, on closer inspection, that the rocks contained gold.* ● **close|ly** ADV [ADV with v] ❑ *If you look closely at many of the problems in society, you'll see evidence of racial discrimination.* **8** ADJ A **close** competition or election is won or seems likely to be won by only a small amount. ❑ *It is still a close contest between two leading opposition parties.* ● **close|ly** ADV ❑ *This will be a closely fought race.* **9** ADJ If you are **close** to something or if it is **close**, it is likely to happen or come soon. If you are **close to** doing something, you are likely to do it soon. [v-link ADJ, usu ADJ to n/-ing] ❑ *She sounded close to tears.* ❑ *A senior White House official said the agreement is close.* **10** ADJ If something is **close** or comes **close to** something else, it almost is, does, or experiences that thing. [v-link ADJ, usu ADJ to n] ❑ *An airliner came close to disaster while approaching Heathrow Airport.* **11** ADJ If the atmosphere somewhere is **close**, it is unpleasantly warm with not enough air. **12** PHRASE Something that is **close by** or **close at hand** is near to you. ❑ *Did a new hair salon open close by?* **13** PHRASE **Close to** a particular amount or distance means slightly less than that amount or distance. In British English, you can also say **close on** a particular amount or distance. ❑ *Sisulu spent close to 30 years in prison.* **14** PHRASE If you look at something **close up**, you look at it when you are very near to it. ❑ *They always look smaller close up.* →see also **close-up 13** **at close quarters**, →see **quarter**. **at close range**, →see **range**

③ **close** ♦♢♢ /kloʊz/ (closes, closing, closed) V-I If you **are closing on** someone or something that you are following, you are getting nearer and nearer to them. ❑ *I was within 15 seconds of the guy in second place and closing on him.*

▶**close in** PHRASAL VERB If a group of people **close in on** a person or place, they come nearer and nearer and gradually surround them. ❑ *Hitler himself committed suicide as Soviet forces were closing in on Berlin.*

④ **Close** /kloʊs/ (Closes) N-IN-NAMES **Close** is used in the names of some streets in Britain. ❑ *...116 Dendridge Close.*

closed-circuit ADJ A **closed-circuit** television or video system is one that operates within a limited area such as a building. [ADJ n] ❑ *There's a closed-circuit television camera in the reception area.*

closed shop (closed shops) N-COUNT If a factory, store, or other business is a **closed shop**, the employees must be members of a particular trade union. [BUSINESS] ❑ *...the trade union which they are required to join under the closed shop agreement.*

clos|et /klɒzɪt/ (closets) N-COUNT A **closet** is a piece of furniture with one or two doors at the front and shelves inside, which is used for storing things. [AM; BRIT **cupboard**] →see **house**

close-up /kloʊs ʌp/ (close-ups) N-COUNT A **close-up** is a photograph or a picture in a film that shows a lot of detail because it is taken very near to the subject. ❑ *...a close-up of Harvey's face.* ● PHRASE If you see something **in close-up**, you see it in great detail in a photograph or piece of film which has been taken very near to the subject.

clos|ing /kloʊzɪŋ/ ADJ The **closing** part of an activity or period of time is the final part of it. [ADJ n] ❑ *He entered RAF service in the closing stages of the war.*

closing price (closing prices) N-COUNT On the stock exchange, the **closing price** of a share is its price at the end of a day's business. [BUSINESS] ❑ *The price is slightly above yesterday's closing price.*

clo|sure /kloʊʒər/ (closures) **1** N-VAR The **closure** of a place such as a business or factory is the permanent ending of the work or activity there. ❑ *...the closure of the Ravenscraig steelworks.* ❑ *...British Coal's proposed pit closures.* **2** N-COUNT The **closure** of a road or border is the blocking of it in order to prevent people from using it. ❑ *Overnight storms left Belgian streets underwater and forced the closure of*

1 형용사 가까운 ❑ 그녀의 입술은 그의 머리 가까이에 있었고 그녀의 숨결이 그의 귀를 간지럽혔다. ❑ 사내는 더 가까이 다가서며 목소리를 낮추었다. ● 가까이 부사 ❑ 그들은 들것 주위로 더 가까이 모여들었다. **2** 형용사 친밀한, 가까운 ❑ 그녀와 린다는 매우 친밀해졌다. ❑ 나는 친한 학교 친구와 한집에 같이 살았다. ● 친밀함 불가산명사 ❑ 나는 그녀에게 어머니와의 친밀함 때문에 무슨 문제가 있었던 적이 있냐고 물었다. **3** 형용사 가까운 ❑ 아이의 탄생이나 근친의 사망 같은 큰 변화 **4** 형용사 가까운 ❑ 그는 한때 브라운 씨의 가장 가까운 정치적 조언자로 여겨졌다. **5** 형용사 긴밀한 ❑ 양국 모두 서방과의 보다 긴밀한 유대 관계를 추구하고 있다. ● 긴밀하게 부사 ❑ 우리 사무소들은 개발도상국에서 지역 단체들과 긴밀하게 공조한다. **6** 형용사 밀접한 ❑ 통증과 긴장 사이에는 밀접한 연관이 있다. ● 밀접하게 부사 ❑ 십자가를 아주 많이 닮은 무늬 **7** 형용사 정밀한, 면밀한 ❑ 그는 더욱 정밀한 조사를 통해 그 암석에 금이 함유되어 있음을 발견했다. ● 면밀히 부사 ❑ 만약 사회 문제를 면밀히 들여다보면, 인종 차별의 흔적이 보일 것이다. **8** 형용사 근소한 차이, 거의 호각의 ❑ 여전히 두 주요 야당 간의 접전이다. ● 거의 호각으로 부사 ❑ 이 경주는 접전이 될 것이다. **9** 형용사 (시각적으로) 가까운 ❑ 그녀의 목소리는 곧 눈물을 흘릴 것처럼 들렸다. ❑ 백악관의 선임 관리가 그 협정이 이루어질 것이라고 말했다. **10** 형용사 유사한, 다름없는 ❑ 여객기 한 대가 히드로 공항에 접근하던 중에 대참사를 만날 뻔했다. **11** 형용사 답답한, 밀폐된 **12** 구 옆에, 가까이에 ❑ 근처에 새 미용실이 생겼습니까? **13** 구 거의 ❑ 시술루는 30년 가까운 세월을 감옥에서 보냈다. **14** 구 가까이에서 ❑ 그것들은 항상 가까이에서 보면 더 작아 보인다.

자동사 다가서다, 따라잡다 ❑ 나와 2등 선수와의 격차는 15초 이내였고 나는 그를 따라잡고 있었다.

구동사 포위하다 ❑ 히틀러 자신은 소련군이 베를린을 포위해 들어오자 자살했다.

이름명사 클로즈 (영국에서 한쪽 길이 막힌 길) ❑ 덴드리지 클로즈 116번지

형용사 폐쇄 회로 ❑ 접수 구역에는 폐쇄 회로 텔레비전 카메라가 있다.

가산명사 클로즈드 숍 (노동 조합원만을 고용하는 사업장) [경제] ❑ 클로즈드 숍 협정에 따라 그들이 가입해야 하는 노동조합

가산명사 벽장, 찬장 [미국영어; 영국영어 cupboard]

가산명사 근접 촬영, 클로즈업 ❑ 하비의 얼굴을 클로즈업으로 찍은 사진 ● 구 클로즈업으로

형용사 마지막의 ❑ 그는 전쟁이 끝나갈 무렵에 영국 공군에 입대했다.

가산명사 종가 [경제] ❑ 가격이 어제 종가보다 약간 높다.

1 가산명사 또는 불가산명사 폐업, 폐쇄 ❑ 레이븐스크레이그 제철소의 폐업 ❑ 영국 석탄의 탄갱 폐쇄 기도 **2** 가산명사 폐쇄 ❑ 간밤의 폭풍우로 인해 벨기에의 도로들은 침수되었고 수도의 도로 터널은 폐쇄되었다. **3** 불가산명사 종결 [주로

A

road tunnels in the capital. **3** N-UNCOUNT If someone achieves **closure**, they succeed in accepting something bad that has happened to them. [mainly AM] ❑ *I asked McKean if the reunion was meant to achieve closure.*

미국영어] ❑ 나는 그 재결합의 목적이 종결을 짓기 위한 것인지 맥킨에게 물었다.

B

clot /klɒt/ (**clots, clotting, clotted**) **1** N-COUNT A **clot** is a sticky lump that forms when blood dries up or becomes thick. ❑ *He needed emergency surgery to remove a blood clot from his brain.* **2** V-I When blood **clots**, it becomes thick and forms a lump. ❑ *The patient's blood refused to clot.*

1 가산명사 (피가 엉긴) 덩어리 ❑ 그는 뇌의 혈괴를 제거하기 위해 응급 수술을 받아야 했다. **2** 자동사 응고하다 ❑ 그 환자는 피가 응고되지 않았다.

C

cloth /klɔθ, BRIT klɒθ/ (**cloths**) **1** N-MASS **Cloth** is fabric which is made by weaving or knitting a substance such as cotton, wool, silk, or nylon. Cloth is used especially for making clothes. ❑ *She began cleaning the wound with a piece of cloth.* →see **clothes** **2** N-COUNT A **cloth** is a piece of cloth which you use for a particular purpose, such as cleaning something or covering something. ❑ *Clean the surface with a damp cloth.*

1 물질명사 천, 헝겊 ❑ 그녀는 천 조각으로 상처를 닦기 시작했다. **2** 가산명사 보자기; 행주 ❑ 젖은 행주로 표면을 닦으세요.

D

E

clothed /kloʊðd/ ADJ If you are **clothed** in a certain way, you are dressed in that way. [adv ADJ, v-link ADJ in n] ❑ *He lay down on the bed fully clothed.* ❑ *She was clothed in a flowered dress.*

형용사 옷을 입은 ❑ 그는 옷을 다 입고 침대 위에 누웠다. ❑ 그녀는 꽃무늬 원피스를 입고 있었다.

F

clothes ♦♦♢ /kloʊz, kloʊðz/ N-PLURAL **Clothes** are the things that people wear, such as shirts, coats, pants, and dresses. ❑ *Moira walked upstairs to change her clothes.*
→see **dry cleaning**

복수명사 옷 ❑ 모이라는 옷을 갈아입기 위해 위층으로 올라갔다.

G

> Note that there is no singular form of **clothes**, so you cannot talk about "a clothe." In formal English, you can talk about a **garment**. **Clothing** is a more formal word that is used to refer to a person's clothes. ❑ *He took off his wet clothing....prison clothing.* You can refer to a **garment** less formally as a **piece of clothing**, an **article of clothing**, or an **item of clothing**, but in ordinary conversation you usually just name the piece of clothing you are talking about. **Cloth** is material made from something such as cotton, wool, or nylon. A **cloth** is a piece of **cloth** that is used, for example, for cleaning or wiping things. Note that the plural, **cloths**, is used only for this sense. For the different verbs associated with clothes, see the note at **wear**.

> clothes는 단수형이 없어 a clothe라고 말할 수 없음을 유의하라. 격식체 영어에서는 a garment라고 할 수 있다. clothing은 어떤 사람이 입은 옷을 가리킬 때 쓰는 더 격식체 단어이다. ❑ 그는 젖은 옷을 벗었다....수형자의 옷[죄수복]. garment를 보다 덜 격식체로 a piece of clothing, an article of clothing, an item of clothing이라고 할 수 있으나, 보통 대화에서는 대개 언급하고 있는 옷의 이름을 바로 부른다. cloth는 면, 모, 나일론과 같은 것으로 만든 직물이다. a cloth는 예를 들면 물건을 닦는 데 사용하는 한 조각의 천(cloth)이다. 복수형인 cloths는 이런 의미로만 쓰임을 유의하라. 옷과 관련된 여러 동사에 관해서는 wear의 주석을 보라.

H

I

J

K

clothes peg (**clothes pegs**) N-COUNT A **clothes peg** is the same as a **clothespin**. [BRIT]

가산명사 빨래집게 [영국영어]

clothes|pin /kloʊzpɪn, kloʊðz-/ (**clothespins**) N-COUNT A **clothespin** is a small device which you use to fasten clothes to a washing line. [AM; BRIT **clothes peg**]

가산명사 빨래집게 [미국영어; 영국영어 clothes peg]

L

cloth|ing ♦♢♢ /kloʊðɪŋ/ N-UNCOUNT **Clothing** is the things that people wear. ❑ *Some locals offered food and clothing to the refugees.* ❑ *...the clothing industry.* →see **clothes**
→see Picture Dictionary: **clothing**

불가산명사 의류, 옷 ❑ 지역 주민 일부가 난민들에게 식량과 옷을 제공했다. ❑ 의류 산업

M

cloud ♦♢♢ /klaʊd/ (**clouds, clouding, clouded**) **1** N-VAR A **cloud** is a mass of water vapor that floats in the sky. Clouds are usually white or gray in color. ❑ *...the varied shapes of the clouds.* ❑ *The sky was almost entirely obscured by cloud.* **2** N-COUNT A **cloud of** something such as smoke or dust is a mass of it floating in the air. ❑ *The hens darted away on all sides, raising a cloud of dust.* **3** V-T If you say that something **clouds** your view of a situation, you mean that it makes you unable to understand the situation or judge it properly. ❑ *Perhaps anger had clouded his vision, perhaps his judgment had been faulty.* **4** V-T If you say that something **clouds** a situation, you mean that it makes it unpleasant. ❑ *The atmosphere has already been clouded by the BJP's anger at the media.* **5** V-T/V-I If glass **clouds** or if moisture **clouds** it, tiny drops of water cover the glass, making it difficult to see through. ❑ *The mirror clouded beside her cheek.* →see **water**

1 가산명사 또는 불가산명사 구름 ❑ 다양한 모양의 구름 ❑ 하늘이 거의 전부 구름에 뒤덮여 있었다. **2** 가산명사 – 구름 ❑ 암탉들이 잔뜩 흙먼지를 날리며 사방으로 달아났다. **3** 타동사 흐리다 ❑ 분노가 그의 시야를 흐렸을 수도, 그의 판단이 잘못된 것이었을 수도 있다. **4** 타동사 흐리다 ❑ 바라티야자나타당(BJP)의 언론에 대한 분노가 분위기를 이미 흐려놓은 상태이다. **5** 타동사/자동사 김이 서리다 ❑ 그녀의 뺨 옆에 있는 거울에 김이 서렸다.

N

O

P

Q

Word Partnership	cloud의 연어
ADJ.	**black/dark** cloud, **white** cloud **1**
N.	cloud **of dust**, cloud **of smoke 2**

R

S

cloudy /klaʊdi/ (**cloudier, cloudiest**) **1** ADJ If it is **cloudy**, there are a lot of clouds in the sky. ❑ *...a windy, cloudy day.* **2** ADJ A **cloudy** liquid is less clear than it should be. ❑ *If the water's cloudy like that, it'll be hard to see anyone underwater.*

1 형용사 흐린 ❑ 바람 불고 흐린 날 **2** 형용사 탁한 ❑ 물이 그렇게 탁하면, 물속에서 누군가를 보기가 어려울 것이다.

T

clout /klaʊt/ (**clouts, clouting, clouted**) **1** V-T If you **clout** someone, you hit them. [INFORMAL] ❑ *Rachel clouted him.* ● N-COUNT **Clout** is also a noun. ❑ *I was half tempted to give one of them a clout myself.* **2** N-UNCOUNT A person or institution that has **clout** has influence and power. [INFORMAL] ❑ *Mr. Sutherland may have the clout needed to push the two trading giants into a deal.*

1 타동사 때리다, 치다 [비격식체] ❑ 레이첼이 그를 때렸다. ● 가산명사 때림, 강타 ❑ 나는 그들 중 한 명을 내가 직접 갈겨주고 싶은 마음이 반쯤 들었다. **2** 불가산명사 영향력 [비격식체] ❑ 두 거물급 무역 회사의 계약 체결에 필요한 영향력이 서더랜드 씨에게 있을지도 모른다.

U

V

Picture Dictionary   clothing

W

X

Y

Z

clove /kloʊv/ (cloves) **1** N-VAR **Cloves** are small dried flower buds which are used as a spice. ❑ ...chicken soup with cloves. **2** N-COUNT A **clove of** garlic is one of the sections of a garlic bulb.

1 가산명사 또는 불가산명사 정향 ❑ 정향을 가미한 닭고기 수프 **2** 가산명사 (마늘) 한 쪽

clown /klaʊn/ (clowns, clowning, clowned) **1** N-COUNT A **clown** is a performer in a circus who wears funny clothes and bright makeup, and does silly things in order to make people laugh. **2** V-I If you **clown**, you do silly things in order to make people laugh. ❑ He clowned with John Belushi and Bill Murray in National Lampoon shows. ● PHRASAL VERB **Clown around** and **clown about** mean the same as **clown**. ❑ Bev made her laugh, the way she was always clowning around. **3** N-COUNT If you say that someone is a **clown**, you mean that they say funny things or do silly things to amuse people. ❑ Chapman was the family clown, with a knack for making a joke out of any situation.

1 가산명사 어릿광대 **2** 자동사 어릿광대짓을 하다, 익살부리다 ❑ 그는 내셔널 램푼 쇼들에서 존 벨루쉬와 빌 머레이와 함께 익살스런 연기를 했다. ● 구동사 어릿광대짓을 하다, 익살부리다 ❑ 베브는 자신이 항상 익살부릴 때 쓰는 방법으로 그녀를 웃게 만들었다. **3** 가산명사 익살꾼 ❑ 챕맨은 집안의 익살꾼이었다. 어떤 상황도 재미있게 풀어나가는 재주가 있었다.

club ♦♦♦ /klʌb/ (clubs, clubbing, clubbed) **1** N-COUNT A **club** is an organization of people interested in a particular activity or subject who usually meet on a regular basis. ❑ ...the Chorlton Conservative Club. **2** N-COUNT A **club** is a place where the members of a club meet. ❑ I stopped in at the club for a drink. **3** N-COUNT A **club** is a team which competes in sports competitions. ❑ ...the New York Yankees baseball club. **4** N-COUNT A **club** is the same as a **nightclub**. ❑ It's a big dance hit in the clubs. **5** N-COUNT A **club** is a long, thin, metal stick with a piece of wood or metal at one end that you use to hit the ball in golf. ❑ ...a six-iron club. **6** N-COUNT A **club** is a thick heavy stick that can be used as a weapon. ❑ Men armed with knives and clubs attacked his home. **7** V-T To **club** a person or animal means to hit them hard with a thick heavy stick or a similar weapon. ❑ Two thugs clubbed him with baseball bats. **8** N-UNCOUNT-COLL **Clubs** is one of the four suits in a pack of playing cards. Each card in the suit is marked with one or more black symbols: ♣. ❑ ...the ace of clubs. ● N-COUNT A **club** is a playing card of this suit. ❑ The next player discarded a club.

1 가산명사 클럽 ❑ 콜튼 보수 클럽 **2** 청소년클럽 **2** 가산명사 클럽 회관, 클럽 ❑ 나는 술 한 잔 하러 클럽에 들렀다. **3** 가산명사 구단 ❑ 뉴욕 양키 구단 **4** 가산명사 나이트클럽 ❑ 그것은 나이트클럽에서 대히트치고 있는 댄스곡이다. **5** 가산명사 골프 클럽, 골프채 ❑ 6번 아이언 골프채 **6** 가산명사 곤봉, 둔기 ❑ 칼과 둔기로 무장한 괴한들이 그의 집을 습격했다. **7** 타동사 둔기로 때리다 ❑ 흉악범 두 명이 그를 야구방망이로 때렸다. **8** 불가산명사-집합 (카드의) 클럽 ❑ 클럽 에이스 ● 가산명사 클럽 한 장 ❑ 그 다음 사람이 클럽 한 장을 버렸다.

club|house /klʌbhaʊs/ (clubhouses) N-COUNT A **clubhouse** is a place where the members of a club, especially a sports club, meet.

가산명사 클럽 회관

clue /klu/ (clues) **1** N-COUNT A **clue to** a problem or mystery is something that helps you to find the answer to it. ❑ Geneticists in Canada have discovered a clue to the puzzle of why our cells get old and die. **2** N-COUNT A **clue** is an object or piece of information that helps someone solve a crime. ❑ The vital clue to the killer's identity was his nickname, Peanuts. **3** N-COUNT A **clue** in a crossword or game is information which is given to help you to find the answer to a question. ❑ Give me a clue. What's it begin with? **4** PHRASE If you **haven't a clue** about something, you do not know anything about it or you have no idea what to do about it. [INFORMAL] ❑ I haven't a clue what I'll give Carl for his birthday next year.

1 가산명사 실마리, 단서 ❑ 캐나다의 유전학자들이 인간의 세포가 노화하고 죽는 이유에 관한 중요한 단서를 풀 실마리를 발견했다. **2** 가산명사 단서 ❑ 살인자의 신원에 대한 중요한 단서는 피너츠라는 애명이었다. **3** 가산명사 힌트 ❑ 힌트 하나만 줘. 첫 글자가 뭐야? **4** 구 전혀 모르다 [비격식체] ❑ 내년 칼의 생일 선물로 뭘 사줘야 할 지 도무지 모르겠다.

clump /klʌmp/ (clumps) **1** N-COUNT A **clump of** things such as trees or plants is a small group of them growing together. ❑ ...a clump of trees bordering a side road. **2** N-COUNT A **clump of** things such as wires or hair is a group of them collected together in one place. ❑ I was combing my hair and it was just falling out in clumps.

1 가산명사 수풀, 덤불 ❑ 샛길을 따라 난 나무 수풀 **2** 가산명사 뭉치 ❑ 내가 머리를 빗을 때 머리카락이 뭉텅이로 빠졌다.

clum|sy /klʌmzi/ (clumsier, clumsiest) **1** ADJ A **clumsy** person moves or handles things in a careless, awkward way, often so that things are knocked over or broken. ❑ I'd never seen a clumsier, less coordinated boxer. ● **clum|si|ly** /klʌmzɪli/ ADV [ADV with v] ❑ The rooks flew clumsily towards their nests. ● **clum|si|ness** N-UNCOUNT ❑ His clumsiness and ineptitude with the wooden sticks did not embarrass him. **2** ADJ A **clumsy** action or statement is not skillful or is likely to upset people. ❑ The action seemed a clumsy attempt to topple the Janata Dal government. ● **clum|si|ly** ADV ❑ If the matter were handled clumsily, it could cost Miriam her life. ● **clum|si|ness** N-UNCOUNT ❑ I was ashamed at my clumsiness and insensitivity.

1 형용사 서투른, 어설픈 ❑ 나는 그보다 더 서투르고 동작이 안 맞는 권투 선수를 본 적이 없었다. ● 서투르게, 어설프게 부사 ❑ 당까마귀들이 그들의 보금자리로 서투르게 날아갔다. ● 서투름, 어설픔 불가산명사 ❑ 그는 나무젓가락 사용이 서투르고 어설펐지만 이에 개의치 않았다. **2** 형용사 어설픈 ❑ 그 조치는 자나타 달 정부를 타도하기 위한 어설픈 시도처럼 보였다. ● 어설프게 부사 ❑ 문제를 어설프게 처리하면, 미리암이 목숨을 잃을 수도 있다. ● 어설픔 불가산명사 ❑ 나는 어설프고 둔감했던 것이 부끄러웠다.

clung /klʌŋ/ **Clung** is the past tense and past participle of **cling**.

cling의 과거와 과거 분사

clus|ter /klʌstər/ (clusters, clustering, clustered) **1** N-COUNT A **cluster of** people or things is a small group of them close together. ❑ ...clusters of men in formal clothes. **2** V-I If people **cluster together**, they gather in a small group. ❑ The passengers clustered together in small groups.

1 가산명사 떼, 무리, 집단 ❑ 삼삼오오 모여 있는 정장을 입은 남자들 **2** 자동사 삼삼오오 모이다 ❑ 승객들이 삼삼오오 모여들었다.

clutch /klʌtʃ/ (clutches, clutching, clutched) **1** V-T/V-I If you **clutch at** something or **clutch** something, you hold it tightly, usually because you are afraid or anxious. ❑ I staggered and had to clutch at a chair for support. **2** N-PLURAL If someone is in another person's **clutches**, that person has captured them or has power over them. ❑ Tony fell into the clutches of an attractive American who introduced him to drugs. **3** N-COUNT In a vehicle, the **clutch** is the pedal that you press before you change gear. ❑ Laura let out the clutch and pulled slowly away down the drive. **4** to **clutch at straws** →see **straw**

1 타동사/자동사 붙잡다 ❑ 나는 휘청거리는 바람에 몸을 지탱하기 위해 의자를 붙잡아야 했다. **2** 복수명사 수중, 마수 ❑ 토니는 그를 마약의 세계로 끌어 들인 한 매력적인 미국인의 마수에게 걸려들었다. **3** 가산명사 클러치 ❑ 로라는 클러치를 풀고 진입로에서 천천히 차를 뺐다.

clut|ter /klʌtər/ (clutters, cluttering, cluttered) **1** N-UNCOUNT **Clutter** is a lot of things in a messy state, especially things that are not useful or necessary. ❑ Caroline prefers her worktops to be clear of clutter. **2** V-T If things or people **clutter** a place, they fill it in a messy way. ❑ Empty soft-drink cans lie everywhere. They clutter the desks and are strewn across the floor. ● PHRASAL VERB **Clutter up** means the same as **clutter**. ❑ The vehicles cluttered up the car park.

1 불가산명사 어질러 놓은 물건, 잡동사니 ❑ 캐럴라인은 작업대에 물건들이 어수선하게 널려 있는 것을 좋아하지 않는다. **2** 타동사 어지럽히다, 어지럽게 메우다 ❑ 빈 음료수 캔들이 여기저기 놓여 있다. 그것들이 책상들에도 어지럽게 널려 있고 바닥에도 흩어져 있다. ● 구동사 어지럽히다, 어지럽게 메우다 ❑ 차들이 주차장을 어지럽게 메우고 있었다.

cm **cm** is the written abbreviation for **centimeter** or **centimeters**. ❑ His height had increased by 2.5 cm.

센티미터 ❑ 그는 키가 2.5센티미터 커 있었다.

c/o You write **c/o** before an address on an envelope when you are sending it to someone who is staying or working at that address, often for only a short time. **c/o** is an abbreviation for "care of."

~ 전교

Co. ♦♦♦ **Co.** is used as an abbreviation for **company** when it is part of the name of an organization. [BUSINESS] ❑ ...the Blue Star Amusement Co.

company의 축약형 [경제] ❑ 블루 스타 어뮤즈먼트사

coach ♦♦◇ /koʊtʃ/ (coaches, coaching, coached) **1** N-COUNT A **coach** is someone who trains a person or team in a particular sport. ❑ Tony

1 가산명사 코치 ❑ 토니 우드록이 독일 아마추어팀 에스시 브루엑에 코치로 합류했다. **2** 타동사 코치하다

a
b
c
d
e
f
g
h
i
j
k
l
m
n
o
p
q
r
s
t
u
v
w
x
y
z

A

Woodcock has joined German amateur team SC Brueck as coach. **2** V-T When someone **coaches** a person or a team, they help them to become better at a particular sport. ❑ *Beckenbauer coached the West Germans to success in the World Cup final in Italy.* **3** N-COUNT A **coach** is a person who is in charge of a sports team. [mainly AM; BRIT usually **manager**] ❑ *...the women's soccer coach at Rowan University.*

B

4 N-COUNT In baseball, a **coach** is a member of a team who stands near the first or third base, and gives signals to other members of the team who are on bases and are trying to score. [AM] **5** N-COUNT A **coach** is someone who gives people special teaching in a particular subject, especially in order to prepare them for an examination. ❑ *What you need is a drama coach.* **6** V-T If you **coach**

C

someone, you give them special teaching in a particular subject, especially in order to prepare them for an examination. ❑ *He gently coached me in French.* **7** N-COUNT A **coach** is an enclosed vehicle with four wheels which is pulled by horses, and in which people used to travel. Coaches are still used for

D

ceremonial events in some countries, such as Britain. ❑ *...a coach pulled by six black horses.* **8** N-COUNT A **coach** is a large, comfortable bus that carries passengers on long trips. [AM **bus**] [also *by* n] ❑ *As we headed back to Calais, the coach was badly delayed by roadworks.* **9** N-COUNT A **coach** is one of the separate

E

sections of a train that carries passengers. [BRIT; AM **car**] ❑ *The train was an elaborate affair of sixteen coaches.*

F

coal ♦♢♢ /koʊl/ (**coals**) **1** N-UNCOUNT **Coal** is a hard black substance that is extracted from the ground and burned as fuel. ❑ *Gas-fired electricity is cheaper than coal.* **2** N-PLURAL **Coals** are burning pieces of coal. ❑ *The iron teakettle was hissing splendidly over live coals.* →see **energy**

G

coa|li|tion ♦♢♢ /koʊəlɪʃ³n/ (**coalitions**) **1** N-COUNT A **coalition** is a government consisting of people from two or more political parties. ❑ *Since June the country has had a coalition government.* **2** N-COUNT A **coalition** is a group consisting of people from different political or social groups who are cooperating to

H

achieve a particular aim. ❑ *He had been opposed by a coalition of about 50 civil rights, women's and Latino organizations.*

I

coarse /kɔrs/ (**coarser, coarsest**) **1** ADJ **Coarse** things have a rough texture because they consist of thick threads or large pieces. ❑ *...a jacket made of very coarse cloth.* ● **coarse|ly** ADV ❑ *...coarsely ground black pepper.* **2** ADJ If you describe

J

someone as **coarse**, you mean that he or she talks and behaves in a rude and offensive way. [DISAPPROVAL] ❑ *The soldiers did not bother to moderate their coarse humor in her presence.* ● **coarse|ly** ADV [ADV with v] ❑ *The women laughed coarsely at some vulgar joke.*

K

coast ♦♦♢ /koʊst/ (**coasts, coasting, coasted**) **1** N-COUNT The **coast** is an area of land that is next to the sea. ❑ *Camp sites are usually situated along the coast, close to beaches.* **2** V-I If a vehicle **coasts** somewhere, it continues to move there with the motor switched off, or without being pushed or pedaled. ❑ *My*

L

gearbox broke with a crunch and I coasted into the pits to retire. →see **beach**

M

You can use **beach, coast,** and **shore** to talk about the piece of land beside a stretch of water. The **coast** is the area of land that lies alongside the sea. You may be referring just to the land close to the sea, or to a wider area that extends further inland. A **beach** is a flat area of sand or pebbles next to the sea. The **shore** is the area of land along the edge of the sea, a lake, or a wide river.

N

O

coast|al /koʊst³l/ ADJ **Coastal** is used to refer to things that are in the sea or on the land near a coast. [ADJ n] ❑ *Local radio stations serving coastal areas often broadcast forecasts for yachtsmen.*

P

Coast Guard (**Coast Guards**) [BRIT, sometimes AM **coastguard**] **1** N-COUNT The **Coast Guard** is a part of a country's military forces and is responsible for

Q

protecting the coast, carrying out rescues, and doing police work along the coast. [AM] ❑ *The U.S. Coast Guard says it rescued more than 100 Haitian refugees.* ● N-COUNT A **Coast Guard** is a member of the Coast Guard. [AM] ❑ *The boat was intercepted by U.S. Coast Guards.* **2** N-COUNT A **coastguard** is an official who

R

watches the sea near a coast in order to get help for sailors when they need it and to stop illegal activities. [mainly BRIT] ❑ *My father was a coastguard.* ● N-SING The **coastguard** is the organization to which coastguards belong. [BRIT] ❑ *The survivors were lifted off by two helicopters, one from the Coastguard and one from the RAF.*

S

coast|line /koʊstlaɪn/ (**coastlines**) N-VAR A country's **coastline** is the outline of its coast. ❑ *This is some of the most exposed coastline in the world.*

T

coat ♦♢♢ /koʊt/ (**coats, coating, coated**) **1** N-COUNT A **coat** is a piece of clothing with long sleeves which you wear over your other clothes when you go outside. ❑ *He turned off the television, put on his coat and walked out.* **2** N-COUNT

U

An animal's **coat** is the fur or hair on its body. ❑ *Vitamin B6 is great for improving the condition of dogs' and horses' coats.* **3** V-T If you **coat** something **with** a substance or **in** a substance, you cover it with a thin layer of the substance. ❑ *Coat the fish with seasoned flour.* **4** N-COUNT A **coat of** paint or varnish is a thin

V

layer of it on a surface. ❑ *The front door needs a new coat of paint.* →see **clothing, painting**

W

-coated /koʊtɪd/ **1** COMB in ADJ **-coated** combines with color adjectives such as "white" and "red," or words for types of coat like "fur," to form adjectives that describe someone as wearing a certain sort of coat. [ADJ n] ❑ *At the top of the stairs stood the white-coated doctors.* **2** COMB in ADJ **-coated** combines with

X

names of substances such as "sugar" and "plastic" to form adjectives that describe something as being covered with a thin layer of that substance. ❑ *...chocolate-coated sweets.*

Y

coat hang|er (**coat hangers**) also **coathanger** N-COUNT A **coat hanger** is a curved piece of wood, metal, or plastic that you hang a piece of clothing on.

Z

❑ 베켄바우어 코치는 이탈리아에서 열린 월드컵 결승전에서 서독을 승리로 이끌었다. **3** 가산명사 감독 [주로 미국영어; 영국영어 대개 manager] ❑ 로완 대학교 여자 축구팀 감독 **4** 가산명사 주루 코치 [미국영어] **5** 가산명사 개인 교사 ❑ 네가 필요한 것은 연극 개인 교사이다. **6** 타동사 개인 교습을 하다 ❑ 그는 나에게 친절하게 프랑스어를 개인 교습해 주었다. **7** 가산명사 마차 ❑ 흑마 여섯 마리가 끄는 마차 **8** 가산명사 장거리 버스 [미국영어 bus] ❑ 우리가 칼레로 돌아가는 길에 도로 공사 때문에 버스가 심하게 지연되었다. **9** 가산명사 객차 [영국영어; 미국영어 car] ❑ 기차는 16개의 객차를 연결해 공들여 만든 것이었다.

1 불가산명사 석탄 ❑ 휘발유로 생산한 전기가 석탄보다 싸다. **2** 복수명사 숯 ❑ 철제 찻주전자가 숯불 위에서 쌕쌕거리며 맹렬히 끓고 있었다.

1 가산명사 연립 정부 ❑ 6월 이래로 그 나라는 연립 정부 체제로 들어갔다. **2** 가산명사 연합 ❑ 50개의 민권 및 여성, 중남미 단체로 구성된 연합 세력이 그를 반대해 왔었다.

1 형용사 결이 거친, 올이 굵은 ❑ 아주 거친 천으로 만든 재킷 ● 거칠게, 굵게 부사 ❑ 굵게 간 후춧가루 **2** 형용사 거친, 무례한, 상스러운 [탐탁찮음] ❑ 군인들은 그녀가 있어도 거친 농담을 굳이 삼가려 하지 않았다. ● 거칠게, 무례하게, 상스럽게 부사 ❑ 여자들이 저속한 농담을 듣고, 상스럽게 웃었다.

1 가산명사 해안 ❑ 야영장은 보통 해변 근처에 해안을 따라 위치해 있다. **2** 자동사 관성의 힘으로 달리다 ❑ 차의 변속 장치가 우두둑 소리와 함께 고장이 나, 나는 퇴장하기 위해 피트로 미끄러져 갔다.

물가에 펼쳐진 땅을 얘기할 때 beach, coast, shore를 쓸 수 있다. coast는 바닷가를 따라 길게 펼쳐져 있는 지역인데, 바다에 인접한 땅만을 가리킬 수도 있고 내륙으로 더 확장된 넓은 지역을 가리킬 수도 있다. beach는 바닷가로 모래나 자갈이 있는 평평한 지역이다. shore는 바닷가, 호숫가, 넓은 강가를 따라 나 있는 땅을 가리킨다.

형용사 연해의, 해안의 ❑ 해안 지역의 지방 라디오 방송국들은 흔히 요트 이용객들을 위해 일기 예보를 한다.

[영국영어, 미국영어 가끔 coastguard] **1** 가산명사 해안 수비대 [미국영어] ❑ 미국 해안 수비대는 100명이 넘는 아이티 난민을 구출했다고 한다. ● 가산명사 해안 수비 대원 [미국영어] ❑ 미국 해안 수비 대원들이 그 배를 가로막았다. **2** 가산명사 해안 경비 대원 [주로 영국영어] ❑ 우리 아버지는 해안 경비 대원이었다. ● 단수명사 해안 수비대 [영국영어] ❑ 생존자들은 해안 경비대와 영국 공군에서 보낸 헬기 두 대로 구조되었다.

가산명사 또는 불가산명사 해안선 ❑ 이곳은 세계에서 가장 공격받기 쉬운 해안선 중 하나이다.

1 가산명사 코트 ❑ 그는 텔레비전을 끈 후 코트를 입고 걸어 나갔다. **2** 가산명사 털 ❑ 비타민 B6은 개와 말의 털 상태를 개선시키는 데 아주 좋다. **3** 타동사 입히다 ❑ 생선에 간이 된 밀가루로 옷을 입히세요. **4** 가산명사 한 번 입힌 막, 한 번 바른 것 ❑ 앞문에 새로 페인트칠을 한 번 해야겠다.

1 복합형-형용사 -을 입은 ❑ 계단 꼭대기에는 하얀 옷을 입은 의사들이 서 있었다. **2** 복합형-형용사 -을 입힌 ❑ 초콜릿을 입힌 사탕

가산명사 옷걸이

coat|ing /kóʊtɪŋ/ (**coatings**) N-COUNT A **coating of** a substance is a thin layer of it spread over a surface. ❑ *Under the coating of dust and cobwebs, he discovered a fine French Louis XVI clock.*

coax /kóʊks/ (**coaxes, coaxing, coaxed**) 1 V-T If you **coax** someone **into** doing something, you gently try to persuade them to do it. ❑ *After lunch, she watched, listened and coaxed Bobby into talking about himself.* 2 V-T If you **coax** something such as information out of someone, you gently persuade them to give it to you. ❑ *The WPC talked yesterday of her role in trying to coax vital information from the young victim.*

cob|ble /kɒ́bᵊl/ (**cobbles, cobbling, cobbled**) N-COUNT **Cobbles** are the same as **cobblestones**. ❑ *They found Trish sitting on the cobbles of the stable yard.*

▶**cobble together** PHRASAL VERB If you say that someone has **cobbled** something **together**, you mean that they have made or produced it roughly or quickly. [DISAPPROVAL] ❑ *The group had cobbled together a few decent songs.*

cobble|stone /kɒ́bᵊlstoʊn/ (**cobblestones**) N-COUNT **Cobblestones** are stones with a rounded upper surface which used to be used for making streets. ❑ *...the narrow, cobblestone streets of the Left Bank.*

co|bra /kóʊbrə/ (**cobras**) N-COUNT A **cobra** is a kind of poisonous snake that can make the skin on the back of its neck into a hood.

cob|web /kɒ́bweb/ (**cobwebs**) N-COUNT A **cobweb** is the net which a spider makes for catching insects. ❑ *The windows are cracked and covered in cobwebs.*

co|caine /koʊkéɪn/ N-UNCOUNT **Cocaine** is a powerful drug which some people take for pleasure, but which they can become addicted to.

cock /kɒ́k/ (**cocks**) 1 N-COUNT A **cock** is an adult male chicken. [mainly BRIT; AM **rooster**] ❑ *The cock was announcing the start of a new day.* 2 N-COUNT You refer to a male bird, especially a male game bird, as a **cock** when you want to distinguish it from a female bird. [mainly BRIT] ❑ *...a cock pheasant.*

cock|pit /kɒ́kpɪt/ (**cockpits**) N-COUNT In an airplane or racing car, the **cockpit** is the part where the pilot or driver sits.

cock|roach /kɒ́kroʊtʃ/ (**cockroaches**) N-COUNT A **cockroach** is a large brown insect that is sometimes found in warm places or where food is kept.

cock|tail /kɒ́kteɪl/ (**cocktails**) 1 N-COUNT A **cocktail** is an alcoholic drink which contains several ingredients. ❑ *On arrival, guests are offered wine or a champagne cocktail.* ❑ *A cocktail party was thrown at the British Officers Club.* 2 N-COUNT A **cocktail** is a mixture of a number of different things, especially ones that do not go together well. ❑ *The court was told she had taken a cocktail of drugs and alcohol.*

cocky /kɒ́ki/ (**cockier, cockiest**) ADJ Someone who is **cocky** is so confident and sure of their abilities that they annoy other people. [INFORMAL, DISAPPROVAL] ❑ *He was a little bit cocky when he was about 11 because he was winning everything.*

co|coa /kóʊkoʊ/ 1 N-UNCOUNT **Cocoa** is a brown powder made from the seeds of a tropical tree. It is used in making chocolate. ❑ *The Ivory Coast became the world's leading cocoa producer.* 2 N-UNCOUNT **Cocoa** is a hot drink made from cocoa powder and milk or water. ❑ *...a cup of cocoa*

coco|nut /kóʊkənʌt/ (**coconuts**) 1 N-COUNT A **coconut** is a very large nut with a hairy shell, which has white flesh and milky juice inside it. ❑ *...the smell of roasted meats mingled with spices, coconut oil and ripe tropical fruits.* 2 N-UNCOUNT **Coconut** is the white flesh of a coconut. ❑ *Desiccated coconut is used by confectioners and cake makers for its flavor.*

co|coon /kəkúːn/ (**cocoons, cocooning, cocooned**) 1 N-COUNT A **cocoon** is a covering of silky threads that the larvae of moths and other insects make for themselves before they grow into adults. ❑ *...like a butterfly emerging from a cocoon.* 2 N-COUNT If you are in a **cocoon of** something, you are wrapped up in it or surrounded by it. ❑ *He stood there in a cocoon of golden light.* 3 N-COUNT If you are living in a **cocoon**, you are in an environment in which you feel protected and safe, and sometimes isolated from everyday life. ❑ *...her innocent desire to envelop her beloved in a cocoon of love.* 4 V-T If something **cocoons** you **from** something, it protects you or isolates you from it. ❑ *There is nowhere to hide when things go wrong, no organisation to cocoon you from blame.*

cod /kɒ́d/

The plural can be either **cod** or **cods**.

N-VAR **Cod** are a type of large edible fish. ● N-UNCOUNT **Cod** is this fish eaten as food. ❑ *A Catalan speciality is to serve salt cod cold.*

Word Link   cod ≈ writing : code, decode, encode

code ♦♢♢ /kóʊd/ (**codes, coding, coded**) 1 N-COUNT A **code** is a set of rules about how people should behave or about how something must be done. ❑ *...Article 159 of the Turkish penal code.* 2 N-COUNT A **code** is a system of replacing the words in a message with other words or symbols, so that nobody can understand it unless they know the system. [also in N] ❑ *They used elaborate secret codes, as when the names of trees stood for letters.* 3 N-COUNT A **code** is a group of numbers or letters which is used to identify something, such as a mailing address or part of a telephone system. ❑ *Callers dialing the wrong area code will not get through.* 4 N-COUNT A **code** is any system of signs or symbols that has a meaning. ❑ *It will need more chips to reconvert the digital code back into normal TV signals.* 5 N-COUNT The genetic **code** of a person, animal or plant is the information contained in DNA which determines the structure and function of cells, and the inherited characteristics of all living things. ❑ *Scientists provided the key to understanding the genetic code that determines every bodily feature.*

가산명사 칠, 입힌 것 ❑그는 먼지와 거미줄 밑에서 프랑스 루이 16세 당시의 멋진 시계를 발견했다.

1 타동사 구슬리다 ❑점심 식사 후, 그녀는 바비의 행동과 말을 살피면서 그를 구슬려 자신에 대해 이야기하도록 했다. 2 타동사 살살 달래어 알아내다 ❑여성 경관이 어린 희생자를 달래 중요한 정보를 얻어낸 과정에서 자신이 한 역할에 대해 어제 이야기했다.

가산명사 자갈 ❑그들은 트리시가 마구간의 자갈 위에 앉아 있는 것을 발견했다.

구동사 급조하다 [탐탁잖음] ❑그 그룹은 괜찮은 곡 몇 개를 급조해 냈었다.

가산명사 자갈 ❑레프트뱅크의 좁은 자갈길

가산명사 코브라

가산명사 거미줄 ❑창문은 금이 가고 거미줄로 덮여 있다.

불가산명사 코카인

1 가산명사 수탉 [주로 영국영어; 미국영어 rooster] ❑수탉이 새로운 하루의 시작을 알리고 있었다. 2 가산명사 새의 수컷 [주로 영국영어] ❑수꿩

가산명사 조정실, 조종석

가산명사 바퀴벌레

1 가산명사 칵테일 ❑도착하자마자 손님들에게 와인이나 샴페인 칵테일이 제공되었다. ❑영국 장교 클럽에서 칵테일파티가 열렸다. 2 가산명사 혼합물 ❑법정에서는 그녀가 각종 약물과 술을 섞어서 마셨다는 진술이 있었다.

형용사 잘난 체하는, 건방진 [비격식체, 탐탁잖음] ❑그는 11살 무렵에 어디에서건 항상 이겼기 때문에 약간 건방진 편이었다.

1 불가산명사 코코아 ❑아이보리 해안은 세계 제일의 코코아 생산지가 되었다. 2 불가산명사 코코아 ❑코코아 한 잔

1 가산명사 코코넛 ❑각종 향신료와 코코넛 오일, 잘 익은 열대 과일을 가미해 오븐에서 구운 고기 냄새 2 불가산명사 코코넛 ❑코코넛 분말은 그 독특한 향미 때문에 과자나 케이크를 만들 때 사용된다.

1 가산명사 고치 ❑고치를 빠져 나오는 한 마리 나비처럼 2 가산명사 둘러싸는 것, 고치 같은 것 ❑그는 황금색 빛 속에 둘러싸여 거기에 서 있었다. 3 가산명사 보호막; 단절체 ❑자신이 사랑하는 사람을 사랑의 보호막으로 감싸고 싶은 그녀의 순수한 소망 4 타동사 보호하다; 단절시키다 ❑일이 잘못되면 숨을 곳이 없어. 너한테 쏟아지는 비난을 막아줄 기관이 하나도 없다고.

복수는 cod 또는 cods이다.

가산명사 또는 불가산명사 대구 ● 불가산명사 대구 ❑소금에 절인 찬 대구 요리가 카탈로니아의 별미 중 하나이다.

1 가산명사 규범, 법전 ❑터키 형법 159조 2 가산명사 암호 ❑그들은 정교한 비밀 암호를 사용했다. 나무 이름이 글자 하나를 상징하는 식이었다. 3 가산명사 번호, 코드 번호 ❑지역 번호를 잘못 누른 사람들의 경우 전화 연결이 안 될 것이다. 4 가산명사 부호, 코드 ❑디지털 코드를 다시 일반 텔레비전 신호로 바꾸기 위해서는 다른 칩이 필요할 것이다. 5 가산명사 (유전자) 정보 ❑과학자들이 모든 신체적 특징을 결정하는 유전자 정보 이해에 중요한 열쇠를 제공했다. 6 타동사 코드로 표시하다 ❑그는 모든 발언을 독특한 코드로 표시할 수 있는 방법을 고안했다. 7 불가산명사 코드 [컴퓨터] ❑분명히 그 컴퓨터 두 대가 양쪽 모두 해독할 수 있는 코드를 찾아냈을 것이다.

a b c d e f g h i j k l m n o p q r s t u v w x y z

6 V-T To **code** something means to give it a code or to mark it with its code. ❑ *He devised a way of coding every statement uniquely.* **7** N-UNCOUNT Computer **code** is a system or language for expressing information and instructions in a form which can be understood by a computer. [COMPUTING] ❑ *Obviously the two computers had found a code they both could translate.* **8** →see also **bar code, postcode, zip code**

Word Partnership   *code*의 연어

N.	code **of conduct**, **dress** code **1**
	code **name**, code **word** **2**
ADJ.	**secret** code **2**

---

cod|ed /kóʊdɪd/ **1** ADJ **Coded** messages have words or symbols which represent other words, so that the message is secret unless you know the system behind the code. ❑ *In a coded telephone warning, Scotland Yard were told four bombs had been planted in the area.* **2** ADJ If someone is using **coded** language, they are expressing their opinion in an indirect way, usually because that opinion is likely to offend people. ❑ *They have sent barely coded messages to the Education Secretary endorsing this criticism.* **3** ADJ **Coded** electronic signals use a binary system of digits which can be decoded by an appropriate machine. [TECHNICAL] [ADJ n] ❑ *The coded signal is received by satellite dishes.*

1 형용사 암호화된 ❑ 런던 경찰청은 런던에 폭탄 네 개가 설치되었다는 암호화된 경고를 전화를 통해 받았다. **2** 형용사 간접적인 ❑ 그들은 교육부 장관에게 이러한 비판에 동의하는 메시지를 간접적으로 간신히 전달했다. **3** 형용사 코드화된 [과학 기술] ❑ 코드화된 신호는 위성 안테나로 수신된다.

cod|ing /kóʊdɪŋ/ N-UNCOUNT **Coding** is a method of making something easy to recognize or distinct, for example by coloring it. ❑ *...a color coding that will ensure easy reference for potential users.*

불가산명사 코드화 ❑ 앞으로 사용할 사람들이 찾아보기 편하도록 색깔을 써서 구분하는 방법

co|erce /koʊɜ́rs/ (**coerces, coercing, coerced**) V-T If you **coerce** someone **into** doing something, you make them do it, although they do not want to. [FORMAL] ❑ *Potter had argued that the government coerced him into pleading guilty.*

타동사 강요하다 [격식체] ❑ 포터는 정부가 유죄 시인을 강요했다고 주장했다.

co|er|cion /koʊɜ́rʃⁿn/ N-UNCOUNT **Coercion** is the act or process of persuading someone forcefully to do something that they do not want to do. ❑ *It was vital that the elections should be free of coercion or intimidation.*

불가산명사 강제, 강요 ❑ 강요와 협박이 없는 선거를 치르는 것이 중요했다.

cof|fee ♦♢♢ /kɔ́fi, BRIT kɒ́fi/ (**coffees**) **1** N-UNCOUNT **Coffee** is a hot drink made with water and ground or powdered coffee beans. ❑ *Would you like some coffee?* ● N-COUNT A **coffee** is a cup of coffee. ❑ *I made a coffee.* **2** N-MASS **Coffee** is the roasted beans or powder from which the drink is made. ❑ *Brazil harvested 28m bags of coffee in 1991, the biggest crop for four years.* →see Word Web: **coffee**

1 불가산명사 커피 ❑ 커피 좀 드실래요? ● 가산명사 커피 한 잔 ❑ 나는 커피를 한 잔 만들었다. **2** 물질명사 커피 ❑ 브라질은 1991년 2800만 부대의 커피를 생산해 4년 만에 최대의 수확을 거두었다.

cof|fee shop (**coffee shops**) also **coffee-shop** N-COUNT A **coffee shop** is a kind of restaurant that sells coffee, tea, cakes, and sometimes sandwiches and light meals. →see **restaurant**

가산명사 커피숍

cof|fin /kɔ́fɪn, BRIT kɒ́fɪn/ (**coffins**) **1** N-COUNT A **coffin** is a box in which a dead body is buried or cremated. **2** PHRASE If you say that one thing is **a nail in the coffin of** another thing, you mean that it will help bring about its end or failure. ❑ *A fine would be the final nail in the coffin of the airline.*

1 가산명사 관 **2** 구 파멸이나 실패를 재촉하는 요인 ❑ 벌금까지 받게 되면 항공사는 아예 끝장이 나고 말 것이다.

cog|nac /kóʊnyæk, BRIT kɒ́nyæk/ (**cognacs**) also **Cognac** N-MASS **Cognac** is a type of brandy made in the southwest of France. ❑ *...a bottle of Cognac.* ● N-COUNT A **cognac** is a glass of cognac. ❑ *Phillips ordered a cognac.*

물질명사 코냑 ❑ 코냑 한 병 ● 가산명사 코냑 한 잔 ❑ 필립스가 코냑 한 잔을 시켰다.

cog|ni|tive /kɒ́gnɪtɪv/ ADJ **Cognitive** means relating to the mental process involved in knowing, learning, and understanding things. [TECHNICAL] [ADJ n] ❑ *As children grow older, their cognitive processes become sharper.*

형용사 인지의, 인식의 [과학 기술] ❑ 아이들은 성장하면서 인지적 처리능력이 더욱 날카로워진다.

co|her|ence /koʊhɪ́ərəns, -hɛ́rəns/ N-UNCOUNT **Coherence** is a state or situation in which all the parts or ideas fit together well so that they form a united whole. ❑ *The anthology has a surprising sense of coherence.*

불가산명사 통일성, 일관성 ❑ 이 명문집은 놀라운 일관성을 갖추고 있다.

co|her|ent /koʊhɪ́ərənt, -hɛ́rənt/ **1** ADJ If something is **coherent**, it is well planned, so that it is clear and sensible and all its parts go well with each other. ❑ *He has failed to work out a coherent strategy for modernizing the service.* ● **co|her|ence** N-UNCOUNT ❑ *The campaign was widely criticized for making tactical mistakes and for a lack of coherence.* **2** ADJ If someone is **coherent**, they express their thoughts in a clear and calm way, so that other people can understand what they are saying. [v-link ADJ] ❑ *He's so calm when he answers questions in interviews. I wish I could be that coherent.* ● **co|her|ence** N-UNCOUNT ❑ *This was debated eagerly at first, but with diminishing coherence as the champagne took hold.*

1 형용사 일관성 있는 ❑ 그는 서비스의 현대화를 위한 일관성 있는 전략 도출에 실패했다. ● 일관성 불가산명사 ❑ 이 캠페인은 전술상의 착오와 일관성 부족으로 여러 사람들로부터 비판을 받았다. **2** 형용사 조리 있는 ❑ 그는 인터뷰에서 질문에 대답할 때 매우 침착하다. 나도 그렇게 조리가 있었으면 좋겠다. ● 조리, 일관성 불가산명사 ❑ 처음에는 이에 대해 활발한 이야기가 오고 갔지만, 샴페인을 마시고 술기운이 돌면서 말에 일관성이 없어졌다.

Word Web   coffee

Coffee plants produce a bright red fruit. Inside each fruit is a single coffee **bean**. Workers pick the beans and dry the beans in the sun. Then the beans are roasted at 550°F* to bring out the true coffee flavor. Next the coffee is **ground**. It can be either **coarse** or **fine**. Many people **brew** coffee by putting it in a **filter** and pouring boiling water over it. Some people add **cream** or **sugar**, while others like it **black**. Many people drink coffee in the morning because the **caffeine** in it wakes them up. Others drink decaffeinated coffee, or decaf, which has little or no caffeine.

550°F= 287.8°C

co|he|sion /koʊhiːʒ³n/ N-UNCOUNT If there is **cohesion** within a society, organization, or group, the different members fit together well and form a united whole. ❑ *By 1990, it was clear that the cohesion of the armed forces was rapidly breaking down.*

불가산명사 응집력, 결속력 ❑ 1990년에 와서는 군대의 결속력이 급속히 와해되고 있음이 분명해졌다.

co|he|sive /koʊhiːsɪv/ ADJ Something that is **cohesive** consists of parts that fit together well and form a united whole. ❑ *"Daring Adventures" from '86 is a far more cohesive and successful album.*

형용사 통일된, 일관성 있는 ❑ '86년의 '데어링 어드벤처'가 훨씬 더 통일성 있고 성공적인 앨범이다.

coil /kɔɪl/ (**coils**) **1** N-COUNT A **coil of** rope or wire is a length of it that has been wound into a series of loops. ❑ *Tod shook his head angrily and slung the coil of rope over his shoulder.* **2** N-COUNT A **coil** is one loop in a series of loops. ❑ *Pythons kill by tightening their coils so that their victim cannot breathe.* **3** N-COUNT A **coil** is a thick spiral of wire through which an electrical current passes. **4** N-COUNT The **coil** is a contraceptive device used by women. It is fitted inside a woman's womb, usually for several months or years.

1 가산명사 둥글게 감아 놓은 것 ❑ 토드는 화가 난 듯 머리를 흔들며 둥글게 감은 로프를 어깨에 걸쳐 멨다. **2** 가산명사 고리, 사리 ❑ 비단 뱀은 먹이를 휘감아 조이면서 숨을 쉬지 못하게 해서 죽인다. **3** 가산명사 코일 **4** 가산명사 피임 링

coin /kɔɪn/ (**coins, coining, coined**) **1** N-COUNT A **coin** is a small piece of metal which is used as money. ❑ *...50 pence coins.* **2** V-T If you **coin** a word or a phrase, you are the first person to say it. ❑ *Jaron Lanier coined the term "virtual reality" and pioneered its early development.* **3** PHRASE You say **"to coin a phrase"** to show that you realize you are making a pun or using a cliché. ❑ *Fifty local musicians have, to coin a phrase, banded together to form the Jazz Umbrella.* **4** PHRASE You use **the other side of the coin** to mention a different aspect of a situation. ❑ *These findings are a reminder that poverty pay is the other side of the coin of falling unemployment.* →see **English, money**

1 가산명사 동전 ❑ 페니 50개 **2** 타동사 신조어를 만들다 ❑ 제론 레니어가 '가상현실'이라는 말을 만들고 그것의 초기 개발에 선도적인 역할을 했다. **3** 구 하자면, 말하자면 ❑ 지역 음악가 50명이 시쳇말로 의기투합해서 재즈 엄브렐러를 결성했다. **4** 구 다른 측면, 이면 ❑ 이번 조사 결과는 실업률 하락의 이면에는 턱없이 낮은 임금이 있다는 사실을 상기시켜 준다.

coin|age /kɔɪnɪdʒ/ **1** N-UNCOUNT **Coinage** is the coins which are used in a country. ❑ *The city produced its own coinage from 1325 to 1864.* **2** N-UNCOUNT **Coinage** is the system of money used in a country. ❑ *It took four years for Britain just to decimalise its own coinage.*

1 불가산명사 한 나라에서 쓰이는 동전 ❑ 이 도시는 1325년부터 1864년까지 자체 동전을 만들어 썼다. **2** 불가산명사 화폐제도 ❑ 영국이 화폐 제도를 십진법으로 바꾸는 데만도 4년이 걸렸다.

co|in|cide /koʊɪnsaɪd/ (**coincides, coinciding, coincided**) **1** V-RECIP If one event **coincides with** another, they happen at the same time. ❑ *The exhibition coincides with the 50th anniversary of his death.* **2** V-RECIP If the ideas or interests of two or more people **coincide**, they are the same. ❑ *The kids' views on life don't always coincide, but they're not afraid of voicing their opinions.*

1 상호동사 동시에 일어나다 ❑ 전시회는 그의 사망 50주기에 맞춰 열린다. **2** 상호동사 일치하나 ❑ 아이들의 인생관이 항상 일치하지는 않지만, 아이들은 자신의 의견을 밝히는 것을 두려워하지 않는다.

co|in|ci|dence /koʊɪnsɪdəns/ (**coincidences**) N-VAR A **coincidence** is when two or more similar or related events occur at the same time by chance and without any planning. ❑ *Mr. Berry said the timing was a coincidence and that his decision was unrelated to Mr. Roman's departure.*

가산명사 또는 불가산명사 우연의 일치 ❑ 베리는 시간상 우연히 맞아떨어진 것일 뿐 자신의 결정이 로만이 떠난 것과는 관련이 없다고 말했다.

co|in|ci|den|tal /koʊɪnsɪdent³l/ ADJ Something that is **coincidental** is the result of a coincidence and has not been deliberately arranged. ❑ *Any resemblance to actual persons, places or events is purely coincidental.*

형용사 우연의 일치인 ❑ 실제 인물이나 장소, 사건과 닮았다면 그건 순전히 우연의 일치일 뿐이다.

co|in|ci|dent|al|ly /koʊɪnsɪdentli/ ADV You use **coincidentally** when you want to draw attention to a coincidence. ❑ *Coincidentally, I had once found myself in a similar situation.*

부사 우연히도 ❑ 우연히도 나 역시 비슷한 상황에 처한 적이 있었다.

coke /koʊk/ **1** N-UNCOUNT **Coke** is a solid black substance that is produced from coal and is burned as a fuel. ❑ *...a coke-burning stove.* **2** N-UNCOUNT **Coke** is the same as **cocaine**. [INFORMAL]

1 불가산명사 코크스 ❑ 코크스 난로 **2** 불가산명사 코카인 [비격식체]

cola /koʊlə/ (**colas**) N-MASS **Cola** is a sweet brown nonalcoholic carbonated drink. ❑ *...a can of cola.*

물질명사 콜라 ❑ 콜라 한 캔

Word Link	er ≈ more : **cold**er, high**er**, larg**er**

Word Link	est ≈ most : **cold**est, high**est**, larg**est**

cold ♦♦◇ /koʊld/ (**colder, coldest, colds**) **1** ADJ Something that is **cold** has a very low temperature or a lower temperature than is normal or acceptable. ❑ *Rinse the vegetables under cold running water.* ❑ *He likes his tea neither too hot nor too cold.* ● **cold|ness** N-UNCOUNT ❑ *She complained about the coldness of his hands.* **2** ADJ If it is **cold**, or if a place is **cold**, the temperature of the air is very low. ❑ *It was bitterly cold.* ❑ *The house is cold because I can't afford to turn the heat on.* ● **cold|ness** N-UNCOUNT ❑ *Within quarter of an hour the coldness of the night had gone.* **3** N-UNCOUNT Cold weather or low temperatures can be referred to as **the cold**. [also the N] ❑ *He must have come inside to get out of the cold.* **4** ADJ If you are **cold**, your body is at an unpleasantly low temperature. ❑ *I was freezing cold.*

1 형용사 차가운 ❑ 차가운 수돗물에 야채를 헹구세요. ❑ 그는 차가 너무 뜨겁지도 차갑지도 않은 걸 좋아한다. ● 차가움 불가산명사 ❑ 그녀는 그의 손이 차갑다고 불평했다. **2** 형용사 추운 ❑ 몹시 추웠다. ❑ 내가 난방을 가동할 만한 형편이 못 되기 때문에 집이 춥다. ● 냉기 불가산명사 ❑ 15분 안에 밤의 냉기가 가셨다. **3** 불가산명사 추위 ❑ 그가 추위를 피하기 위해 안으로 들어온 것이 틀림없다. **4** 형용사 추운 ❑ 나는 몸이 얼 정도로 추웠다.

> If you want to emphasize how cold the weather is, you can say that it is **freezing**, especially in winter when there is ice or frost. In summer, if the temperature is below average, you can say that it is **cool**. In general, **cold** suggests a lower temperature than **cool**, and **cool** things may be pleasant or refreshing. ❑ *A cool breeze swept off the sea; it was pleasant out there.* If it is very **cool** or too **cool**, you can also say that it is **chilly**.

> 특히 얼음이 얼거나 서리가 내리는 겨울에 날씨가 추운 것을 강조하고 싶으면, 날씨가 freezing하다고 할 수 있다. 여름에 기온이 평균 이하면, 날씨가 cool하다고 할 수 있다. 일반적으로 cold는 cool보다 낮은 기온을 의미하고, cool한 것은 쾌적하거나 상쾌할 수 있다. ❑ 시원한 미풍이 바다에서 불어 왔다; 거기에 나가 있으니 쾌적했다. 날씨가 아주 cool하거나 너무 cool하면, 날씨가 chilly하다고도 할 수 있다.

5 ADJ **Cold** colors or **cold** light give an impression of coldness. ❑ *Generally, warm colors advance in painting and cold colors recede.* **6** ADJ A **cold** person does not show much emotion, especially affection, and therefore seems unfriendly and unsympathetic. If someone's voice is **cold**, they speak in an unfriendly unsympathetic way. [DISAPPROVAL] ❑ *What a cold, unfeeling woman she was.* ● **cold|ly** ADV ❑ *"I'll see you in the morning," Hugh said coldly.* ● **cold|ness** N-UNCOUNT ❑ *His coldness angered her.* **7** N-COUNT If you have a **cold**, you have a mild, very common illness which makes you sneeze a lot and gives you a sore throat or a cough. ❑ *I had a pretty bad cold.* **8** PHRASE If you **catch cold**, or **catch a cold**, you become ill with a cold. ❑ *Let's dry our hair so we don't catch cold.* **9** PHRASE If someone is **out cold**, they are unconscious or sleeping very heavily. ❑ *She*

5 형용사 차가운 ❑ 보통 그림에서 따뜻한 색은 튀어나와 보이고 차가운 색은 안으로 들어가 보인다. **6** 형용사 냉정한, 차가운 [탐탁찮음] ❑ 정말 냉정하고 감정이라고는 없는 여자야. ● 냉정하게, 차갑게 부사 ❑ "내일 아침에 봅시다."라고 휴가 차갑게 말했다. ● 냉정함 불가산명사 ❑ 그의 냉정한 태도가 그녀를 화나게 했다. **7** 가산명사 감기 ❑ 나는 지독한 감기에 걸려 있었다. **8** 구 감기에 걸리다 ❑ 감기에 걸리지 않도록 머리를 말리자. **9** 구 의식이 없는 ❑ 그녀는 의식은 없었지만 숨은 쉬고 있었다.

a b c d e f g h i j k l m n o p q r s t u v w x y z

A
was out cold but still breathing. ⑩ **in cold blood** →see **blood**. to get **cold feet** →see **foot**. to **blow hot and cold** →see **hot**. to **pour cold water on** something →see **water**

B

Thesaurus cold의 참조어

ADJ. bitter, chilly, cool, freezing, frozen, raw; *(ant.)* hot, warm ① ② ④
cool, distant, unfriendly; *(ant.)* friendly, warm ⑤ ⑥

C

D

Word Partnership cold의 연어

ADV. **bitterly** cold ① ②
freezing cold ① ②

E
N. cold **air**, **dark and** cold, cold **night**, cold **rain**,
cold **water**, cold **weather**, cold **wind** ① ②

F
V. **feel** cold, **get** cold ① ④
catch a cold ⑧

G
cold-blooded ① ADJ Someone who is **cold-blooded** does not show any pity or emotion. [DISAPPROVAL] ❑ *...a cold-blooded murderer.* ② ADJ **Cold-blooded** animals have a body temperature that changes according to the surrounding temperature. Reptiles, for example, are cold-blooded.

① 형용사 피도 눈물도 없는, 냉혈의 [탐탁찮음] ❑ 피도 눈물도 없는 살인마 ② 형용사 냉혈 동물의

H
cold call (**cold calls**, **cold calling**, **cold called**) ① N-COUNT If someone makes a **cold call**, they telephone or visit someone they have never contacted, without making an appointment, in order to try and sell something. ❑ *She had worked as a call center operator making cold calls for time-share holidays.* ② V-T/V-I To **cold call** means to make a cold call. ❑ *You should refuse to meet anyone who cold calls with an offer of financial advice.* ● **cold-calling** N-UNCOUNT ❑ *We will adhere to strict sales ethics, with none of the cold-calling that has given the industry such a bad name.*

① 가산명사 물건 판매용 방문이나 전화 ❑ 그녀는 타임쉐어 숙박 시설 전화 판매원으로 콜센터에서 일했었다. ② 타동사/자동사 물건 판매를 목적으로 전화나 방문을 하다 ❑ 금융 상담을 해 주겠다며 무작정 전화를 건 사람이 만나자고 하면 거절해야 한다. ● 물건 판매용 방문이나 전화 불가산명사 ❑ 우리는 지금까지 업계를 먹칠했던 영업용 방문이나 전화 판매를 떨쳐버리고, 엄격한 판매 윤리를 고수할 것이다.

I

J

K

Word Link co ≈ together : coauthor, codependent, collaborate

Word Link labor ≈ working : collaborate, elaborate, laboratory

L
col|labo|rate /kəlǽbəreɪt/ (**collaborates**, **collaborating**, **collaborated**) ① V-RECIP When one person or group **collaborates with** another, they work together, especially on a book or on some research. ❑ *Much later he collaborated with his son Michael on the English translation of a text on food production.* ❑ *He turned his country house into a place where professionals and amateurs collaborated in the making of music.* ② V-I If someone **collaborates with** an enemy that is occupying their country during a war, they help them. [DISAPPROVAL] ❑ *He was accused of having collaborated with the Communist secret police.*

① 상호동사 공동으로 일하다, 협력하다 ❑ 그보다 훨씬 뒤에 그는 아들 마이클과 함께 공동으로 식품 생산에 대한 책을 영어로 번역했다. ❑ 그는 자신의 별장을 프로와 아마추어가 함께 음악 작업을 할 수 있는 곳으로 바꿨다. ② 자동사 적에게 협력하다 [탐탁찮음] ❑ 그는 공산당 비밀경찰에 협력한 혐의로 기소되었다.

M

N
col|labo|ra|tion /kəlæbəreɪʃⁿn/ (**collaborations**) ① N-VAR **Collaboration** is the act of working together to produce a piece of work, especially a book or some research. ❑ *There is substantial collaboration with neighboring departments.* ❑ *...scientific collaborations.* ② N-COUNT A **collaboration** is a piece of work that has been produced as the result of people or groups working together. ❑ *He was also a writer of beautiful stories, some of which are collaborations with his fiancee.* ③ N-UNCOUNT **Collaboration** is the act of helping an enemy who is occupying your country during a war. [DISAPPROVAL] ❑ *...rumors of his collaboration with the occupying forces during the war.*

① 가산명사 또는 불가산명사 협력, 합작, 공동 작업 ❑ 인근 부서와 실질적으로 협력이 이뤄지고 있다. ② 과학부문의 공동 작업 ② 가산명사 합작품 ❑ 그는 또한 아름다운 이야기를 쓴 작가이기도 했다. 그 중 몇몇은 그의 약혼녀와 함께 쓴 작품이다. ③ 불가산명사 이적 행위 [탐탁찮음] ❑ 그가 전쟁 중 점령군 편에서 이적 행위를 했다는 소문

O

P

Q
col|labo|ra|tive /kəlǽbəreɪtɪv, -ərətɪv, BRIT kəlǽbərətɪv/ ADJ A **collaborative** piece of work is done by two or more people or groups working together. [FORMAL] [ADJ n] ❑ *...a collaborative research project.*

형용사 공동 제작의 [격식체] ❑ 공동 연구 프로젝트

R
col|labo|ra|tor /kəlǽbəreɪtər/ (**collaborators**) ① N-COUNT A **collaborator** is someone that you work with to produce a piece of work, especially a book or some research. ❑ *The Irvine group and their collaborators are testing whether lasers do the job better.* ② N-COUNT A **collaborator** is someone who helps an enemy who is occupying their country during a war. [DISAPPROVAL] ❑ *Two alleged collaborators were shot dead by masked activists.*

① 가산명사 공동 제작자, 협력자 ❑ 어빈 팀과 공동 연구원들이 레이저가 성능이 더 뛰어난 지 시험하고 있다. ② 가산명사 이적 행위자 [탐탁찮음] ❑ 이적 행위 혐의를 받고 있던 두 명이 복면을 한 활동가들의 총에 맞아 사망했다.

S

T
col|lage /kəlɑ́ʒ, BRIT kɒlɑːʒ/ (**collages**) ① N-COUNT A **collage** is a picture that has been made by sticking pieces of colored paper and cloth onto paper. ❑ *... a collage of words and pictures from magazines.* ② N-UNCOUNT **Collage** is the method of making pictures by sticking pieces of colored paper and cloth onto paper. ❑ *The illustrations make use of collage, watercolor and other media.*

① 가산명사 콜라주 ❑ 잡지에서 오린 단어와 사진으로 만든 콜라주 ② 불가산명사 콜라주 ❑ 이 삽화들은 콜라주와 수채화법을 비롯한 다른 기법들을 사용하고 있다.

U

V

Word Link lapse ≈ falling : collapse, elapse, lapse

W
col|lapse ◆◆◇ /kəlǽps/ (**collapses**, **collapsing**, **collapsed**) ① V-I If a building or other structure **collapses**, it falls down very suddenly. ❑ *A section of the Bay Bridge had collapsed.* ● N-UNCOUNT **Collapse** is also a noun. ❑ *Governor Deukmejian called for an inquiry into the freeway's collapse.* ② V-I If something, for example a system or institution, **collapses**, it fails or comes to an end completely and suddenly. ❑ *His business empire collapsed under a massive burden of debt.* ● N-UNCOUNT **Collapse** is also a noun. ❑ *The coup's collapse has speeded up the drive to independence.* ③ V-I If you **collapse**, you suddenly faint or fall down because you are very ill or weak. ❑ *He collapsed following a vigorous exercise session at his home.* ● N-UNCOUNT **Collapse** is also a noun. ❑ *A few days after his collapse he was sitting up in bed.* ④ V-I If you **collapse** onto something, you sit or lie down suddenly because you are very tired. ❑ *She arrived home exhausted and barely capable of showering before collapsing on her bed.*

① 자동사 무너지다 ❑ 베이 브리지의 한 구역이 무너져 버렸다. ● 불가산명사 붕괴 ❑ 듀크메지안 주지사가 고속도로 붕괴사고 조사를 촉구했다. ② 자동사 좌절되다, 곤두박질치다 ❑ 그의 기업 왕국이 막대한 부채에 허덕이다 쓰러지고 말았다. ● 불가산명사 좌절, 곤두박질 ❑ 쿠데타가 좌절되면서 독립을 향한 움직임이 빨라졌다. ③ 자동사 쓰러지다 ❑ 그는 자택에서 격렬한 운동을 하다가 쓰러졌다. ● 불가산명사 쓰러짐 ❑ 쓰러지고 나서 며칠 후에 그는 침대에 일어나 앉아 있었다. ④ 자동사 쓰러지다, 주저앉다 ❑ 그녀는 녹초가 되어 집에 도착해서 겨우 샤워를 하고 침대 위로 쓰러졌다.

X

Y

Z

col|lar /kɒlər/ (collars) **1** N-COUNT The **collar** of a shirt or coat is the part which fits round the neck and is usually folded over. ❑ *His tie was pulled loose and his collar hung open.* →see also **blue-collar, white-collar 2** N-COUNT A **collar** is a band of leather or plastic which is put round the neck of a dog or cat.

col|lar|bone /kɒlərboʊn/ (collarbones) N-COUNT Your **collarbones** are the two long bones which run from throat to your shoulders. [BRIT also **collar bone**] ❑ *Harold had a broken collarbone.*

col|late /kəleɪt/ (collates, collating, collated) V-T When you **collate** pieces of information, you gather them all together and examine them. ❑ *Roberts has spent much of his working life collating the data on which the study was based.*

col|lat|er|al /kəlætərəl/ N-UNCOUNT **Collateral** is money or property which is used as a guarantee that someone will repay a loan. [FORMAL] ❑ *Many people use personal assets as collateral for small business loans.*

col|lat|er|al dam|age N-UNCOUNT **Collateral damage** is accidental injury to nonmilitary people or damage to nonmilitary buildings which occurs during a military operation. ❑ *To minimize collateral damage maximum precision in bombing was required.*

col|league ♦♦◇ /kɒliːg/ (colleagues) N-COUNT Your **colleagues** are the people you work with, especially in a professional job. ❑ *Without consulting his colleagues he flew from Lisbon to Split.*

col|lect ♦♦◇ /kəlɛkt/ (collects, collecting, collected) **1** V-T If you **collect** a number of things, you bring them together from several places or from several people. ❑ *Two young girls were collecting firewood.* ❑ *Elizabeth had been collecting snails for a school project.* **2** V-T If you **collect** things, such as stamps or books, as a hobby, you get a large number of them over a period of time because they interest you. ❑ *I used to collect stamps.* ● **col|lect|ing** N-UNCOUNT ❑ *...hobbies like stamp collecting and fishing.* **3** V-T When you **collect** someone or something, you go and get them from the place where they are waiting for you or have been left for you. [mainly BRIT; AM usually **pick up**] ❑ *David always collects Alistair from school on Wednesdays.* ❑ *She had just collected her pension from the post office.* **4** V-T/V-I If a substance **collects** somewhere, or if something **collects** it, it keeps arriving over a period of time and is held in that place or thing. ❑ *Methane gas does collect in the mines around here.* **5** V-T If something **collects** light, energy, or heat, it attracts it. ❑ *Like a telescope it has a curved mirror to collect the sunlight.* **6** V-T/V-I If you **collect for** a charity or **for** a present for someone, you ask people to give you money for it. ❑ *Are you collecting for charity?* **7** PHRASE If you **call collect** when you make a telephone call, the person who you are phoning pays the cost of the call and not you. [AM; BRIT usually **reverse the charges**]

Thesaurus	collect의 참조어
v.	accumulate, compile, gather; (ant.) scatter **1**

col|lect call (collect calls) N-COUNT A **collect call** is a telephone call which is paid for by the person who receives the call, rather than the person who makes the call. [AM; BRIT **reverse charge call**] ❑ *"I want to make a collect call," she said as soon as a voice came on the line.*

col|lec|tion ♦♦◇ /kəlɛkʃ°n/ (collections) **1** N-COUNT A **collection of** things is a group of similar things that you have deliberately acquired, usually over a period of time. ❑ *Robert's collection of prints and paintings has been bought over the years.* ❑ *The Art Gallery of Ontario has the world's largest collection of sculptures by Henry Moore.* **2** N-COUNT A **collection of** stories, poems, or articles is a number of them published in one book. ❑ *Two years ago he published a collection of short stories called "Facing The Music".* **3** N-COUNT A **collection of** things is a group of things. ❑ *Wye Lea is a collection of farm buildings that have been converted into an attractive complex.* **4** N-COUNT A fashion designer's new **collection** consists of the new clothes they have designed for the next season. ❑ *Her spring/summer collection 1993 deliberately used both simple and rich fabrics.* **5** N-UNCOUNT **Collection** is the act of collecting something from a place or from people. ❑ *Money can be sent to any one of 22,000 agents worldwide for collection.* ❑ *...computer systems to speed up collection of information.* **6** N-COUNT If you organize a **collection for** charity, you collect money from people to give to charity. ❑ *I asked my headmaster if he could arrange a collection for a refugee charity.* **7** N-COUNT A **collection** is money that is given by people in church during some Christian services.

col|lec|tive ♦◇◇ /kəlɛktɪv/ (collectives) **1** ADJ **Collective** actions, situations, or feelings involve or are shared by every member of a group of people. [ADJ n] ❑ *It was a collective decision.* ● **col|lec|tive|ly** ADV ❑ *They collectively decided to recognize the changed situation.* **2** ADJ A **collective** amount of something is the total obtained by adding together the amounts that each person or thing in a group has. [ADJ n] ❑ *Their collective volume wasn't very large.* ● **col|lec|tive|ly** ADV [ADV with v] ❑ *In 1968 the states collectively spent $2 billion on it.* **3** ADJ The **collective** term for two or more types of thing is a general word or expression which refers to all of them. [ADJ n] ❑ *Social science is a collective name, covering a series of individual sciences.* ● **col|lec|tive|ly** ADV [ADV with v] ❑ *...other sorts of cells (known collectively as white corpuscles).* **4** N-COUNT A **collective** is a business or farm which is run, and often owned, by a group of people. [BUSINESS] ❑ *He will see that he is participating in all the decisions of the collective.*

col|lec|tive bar|gain|ing N-UNCOUNT When a labor union engages in **collective bargaining**, it has talks with an employer about its members' pay and working conditions. [BUSINESS] ❑ *...a new collective-bargaining agreement.*

---

1 가산명사 칼라, 깃 ❑ 그는 넥타이를 느슨하게 풀고 깃을 열어젖히고 있었다. **2** 가산명사 개 목걸이

가산명사 쇄골 [영국영어 collar bone] ❑ 해럴드는 쇄골골절상을 입었다.

타동사 맞추어 보다, 대조하다 ❑ 로버츠는 일하면서 보낸 시간의 많은 부분을 그 연구의 기반이 된 데이터를 모으고 대조하는 데 사용했다.

불가산명사 담보 [격식체] ❑ 많은 사람들이 중소기업 대출을 받을 때 개인 자산을 담보로 이용한다.

불가산명사 민간 피해 ❑ 민간 피해를 최소화하기 위해 폭격 시에 최대한의 정확성이 요구되었다.

가산명사 동료 ❑ 동료들과 상의하지 않고 그는 리스본을 떠나 스플리트로 갔다.

1 타동사 모으다, 걷다 ❑ 어린 소녀 두 명이 땔감을 모으고 있었다. ❑ 엘리자베스는 학교 프로젝트에 필요한 달팽이를 채집하고 있었다. **2** 타동사 수집하다 ❑ 나는 예전에 우표를 수집했었다. ● 수집 불가산명사 ❑ 우표 수집이나 낚시 같은 취미 **3** 타동사 데리러 가다, 데리오다, 찾으러 가다, 찾아오다 [주로 영국영어; 미국영어 대개 pick up] ❑ 데이비드는 수요일마다 알리스테어를 데리러 학교에 간다. ❑ 그녀가 우체국에서 막 연금을 찾아온 상태였다. **4** 타동사/자동사 모이다, 쌓이다; 모으다 ❑ 이 주변에 있는 광산에 확실히 메탄가스가 모여든다. **5** 타동사 끌어당기다, 모으다 ❑ 망원경처럼 이것의 굴절 렌즈가 태양 광선을 모은다. **6** 타동사/자동사 모금하다 ❑ 자선기금을 모금하고 있습니까? **7** 구 수신자 부담 전화를 하다 [미국영어; 영국영어 대개 reverse the charges]

가산명사 수신자 부담 전화 [미국영어; 영국영어 reverse charge call] ❑ "수신자 부담 전화를 하고 싶은데요."라고 전화에서 목소리가 들리자 받자마자 그녀가 말했다.

1 가산명사 수집물, 소장품 ❑ 로버트의 복사본과 진품 그림으로 구성된 소장품은 몇 년에 걸쳐 모은 것이다. ❑ 온타리오 미술관이 헨리 무어의 조각 작품을 세계에서 가장 많이 소장하고 있다. **2** 가산명사 문집 ❑ 2년 전 그는 '페이싱 더 뮤직'이라는 단편 소설집을 냈다. **3** 가산명사 집단 ❑ 와이레아는 여러 농장 건물들이 모인 곳으로 관광객이 많이 찾는 단지로 변모한 장소이다. **4** 가산명사 컬렉션 ❑ 그녀의 1993 봄여름 컬렉션은 의도적으로 심플한 옷감과 화려한 옷감을 모두 사용하고 있다. **5** 불가산명사 수집, 수금, 수거 ❑ 전 세계 22,000명의 에이전트 중 누구를 통해서도 수금이 가능하다. ❑ 정보 수집 속도를 높이기 위한 컴퓨터 시스템들 **6** 가산명사 모금 운동 ❑ 나는 교장 선생님께 난민 구호 단체를 위한 모금 운동을 조직할 수 있는지 여쭤 보았다. **7** 가산명사 헌금

1 형용사 공동의, 집단의 ❑ 이는 모두가 함께 내린 결정이었다. ● 공동으로, 집단으로 부사 ❑ 그들은 변화된 상황을 인정하기로 공동 결정을 내렸다. **2** 형용사 합치, 총 ❑ 이들의 총 부피는 그다지 크지 않다. ● 합계로 부사 ❑ 1968년에 이들 주에서는 그것에 총 20억 달러를 사용했다. **3** 형용사 총칭의, 집합의, 아우르는 ❑ 사회과학이란 일련의 개별적인 학문들을 아우르는 총칭이다. ● 총칭하여 부사 ❑ 총칭하여 백혈구로 알려진 다른 종류의 세포들 **4** 가산명사 집단, 공동체 [경제] ❑ 그는 자신이 공동체의 모든 의사 결정에 참여하게 된다는 걸 알게 될 것이다.

불가산명사 단체 협상 [경제] ❑ 새 단체 협상 합의

col|lec|tor /kəlɛktər/ (**collectors**) **1** N-COUNT A **collector** is a person who collects things of a particular type as a hobby. □ ...a stamp-collector. □ ...a respected collector of Indian art. **2** N-COUNT You can use **collector** to refer to someone whose job is to take something such as money, tickets, or garbage from people. For example, a rent **collector** collects rent from people. □ He earned his living as a tax collector.

1 가산명사 수집가 □ 우표 수집가 □ 저명한 인디안 공예품 수집가 **2** 가산명사 수금원, 징수원 □ 그는 세금 징수원으로 생계를 유지했다.

col|lege ♦♦◇ /kɒlɪdʒ/ (**colleges**) **1** N-VAR; N-IN-NAMES A **college** is an institution where students study after they have left secondary school. □ Their daughter Joanna is doing business studies at a local college. □ Stephanie took up making jewelry after leaving art college this summer.

1 가산명사 또는 불가산명사; 이름명사 대학 □ 그들의 딸 조안나는 지방의 한 대학에서 경영학을 공부하고 있다. □ 스테파니는 이번 여름 미대를 졸업하고 보석 만드는 일을 시작했다.

In North American education, students who have finished secondary school may go on to **college**, **university**, or **technical school**. College and university both offer baccalaureate degrees. Universities also have graduate schools for post-graduate education. Technical school provides training in a very specific area. In everyday speech a person will say they **go to college** regardless of which type of institution they attend.

북미 교육제도에서 중등교육을 마친 학생들은 college(단과대학)나, university(종합대학교)나, technical school(기술전문대학)로 진학할 수 있다. 단과대학과 종합대학교에서는 학사 학위를 수여한다. 종합대학교에서는 대학원 교육을 위한 대학원을 두기도 한다. 기술전문대학에서는 아주 전문적인 분야의 훈련을 제공한다. 일상 대화에서는 이들 중 어떤 교육기관에 다니든지 go to college(대학에 다닌다)라고 말한다.

2 N-COUNT; N-IN-NAMES At some universities in the United States, **colleges** are divisions which offer degrees in particular subjects. □ ...a professor at the University of Florida College of Law. **3** N-COUNT A **college** is one of the institutions which some British universities are divided into. □ He was educated at Balliol College, Oxford. **4** N-IN-NAMES **College** is used in Britain in the names of some secondary schools which charge fees. □ In 1854, Cheltenham Ladies' College became the first girls' public school. →see **graduation**

2 가산명사; 이름명사 단과 대학 □ 플로리다 법대 교수 **3** 가산명사 칼리지 □ 그는 옥스퍼드 밸리올 칼리지에서 수학했다. **4** 이름명사 사립 중등학교 □ 1854년 최초의 여학생 전용 사립 중등학교인 체트넘 여학교가 설립되었다.

col|lide /kəlaɪd/ (**collides**, **colliding**, **collided**) **1** V-RECIP If two or more moving people or objects **collide**, they crash into one another. If a moving person or object **collides with** a person or object that is not moving, they crash into them. □ Two trains collided head-on in north-eastern Germany early this morning. □ Racing up the stairs, he almost collided with Daisy. **2** V-RECIP If the aims, opinions, or interests of one person or group **collide with** those of another person or group, they are very different from each other and are therefore opposed. □ The aims of the negotiators in New York again seem likely to collide with the aims of the warriors in the field.

1 상호동사 충돌하다, 부딪치다 □ 오늘 새벽 독일 동북지방에서 열차 두 대가 정면으로 충돌했다. □ 그는 계단을 뛰어올라 가다가 데이지와 부딪칠 뻔했다. **2** 상호동사 상충하다 □ 뉴욕 협상가들의 목표가 전투 중인 전사들의 목표와 다시 한 번 상충할 것으로 보인다.

Thesaurus collide의 참조어

v. bump, clash, crash, hit, smash; (ant.) avoid **1**

col|liery /kɒlyəri/ (**collieries**) N-COUNT A **colliery** is a coal mine and all the buildings and equipment which are connected with it. [BRIT]

가산명사 탄갱 [영국영어]

col|li|sion /kəlɪʒ³n/ (**collisions**) **1** N-VAR A **collision** occurs when a moving object crashes into something. □ They were on their way to the Shropshire Union Canal when their van was involved in a collision with a car. **2** N-COUNT A **collision of** cultures or ideas occurs when two very different cultures or people meet and conflict. □ The play represents the collision of three generations.

1 가산명사 또는 불가산명사 충돌 □ 그들은 밴을 타고 슈롭셔 유니온 운하로 가던 중에 다른 차와 충돌하는 사고를 당했다. **2** 가산명사 상충, 대립 □ 이 연극은 세 세대간의 충돌을 그리고 있다.

Thesaurus collision의 참조어

N. accident, crash **1**

col|lo|quial /kəloʊkwiəl/ ADJ **Colloquial** words and phrases are informal and are used mainly in conversation. □ ...a colloquial expression.

형용사 구어체의 □ 구어체 표현

col|lude /kəlud/ (**colludes**, **colluding**, **colluded**) V-RECIP If one person **colludes with** another, they cooperate with them secretly or illegally. [DISAPPROVAL] □ Several local officials are in jail on charges of colluding with the Mafia. □ My mother colluded in the myth of him as the swanky businessman.

상호동사 결탁하다, 공모하다 [탐탁찮음] □ 몇몇 지방 공무원들이 마피아와 결탁한 혐의로 수감된 상태이다. □ 우리 어머니는 그가 세련된 사업가라는 환상을 만드는 데 한몫했다.

col|lu|sion /kəluʒ³n/ N-UNCOUNT **Collusion** is secret or illegal cooperation, especially between countries or organizations. [FORMAL, DISAPPROVAL] [usu N between pl-n, N with n, in N] □ He found no evidence of collusion between record companies and retailers.

불가산명사 결탁, 공모 [격식체, 탐탁찮음] □ 그는 음반사와 소매업자의 결탁에 관한 어떤 증거도 발견하지 못했다.

co|lon /koʊlən/ (**colons**) **1** N-COUNT A **colon** is the punctuation mark : which you can use in several ways. For example, you can put it before a list of things or before reported speech. **2** N-COUNT Your **colon** is the part of your intestine above your rectum. □ In the U.S., there are 60,000 deaths a year from cancer of the colon.

1 가산명사 콜론 **2** 가산명사 결장 □ 매년 미국인 6만 명이 결장암으로 사망한다.

colo|nel ♦♦◇ /kɜrn³l/ (**colonels**) N-COUNT; N-TITLE; N-VOC A **colonel** is a senior officer in an army, air force, or the marines. □ This particular place was run by an ex-Army colonel.

가산명사; 경칭명사; 호격명사 대령 □ 이 특별한 곳의 책임자는 전 육군 대령이었다.

co|lo|nial /kəloʊniəl/ **1** ADJ **Colonial** means relating to countries that are colonies, or to colonialism. [ADJ n] □ ...the 31st anniversary of Jamaica's independence from British colonial rule. **2** ADJ A **Colonial** building or piece of furniture was built or made in a style that was popular in America in the 17th and 18th centuries. [mainly AM] □ ...the white colonial houses on the north side of the campus.

1 형용사 식민지의, 식민지 시대의 □ 자메이카가 영국 식민 통치로부터 독립한 지 31주년 **2** 형용사 식민지 시대 풍의 [주로 미국영어] □ 캠퍼스 북쪽의 하얀 식민지 시대풍의 가옥들

co|lo|ni|al|ism /kəloʊniəlɪzəm/ N-UNCOUNT **Colonialism** is the practice by which a powerful country directly controls less powerful countries and uses their resources to increase its own power and wealth. □ ...the bitter oppression of slavery and colonialism.

불가산명사 식민통치, 식민지주의 □ 노예제와 식민통치의 쓰라린 탄압

colo|nist /kɒlənɪst/ (**colonists**) N-COUNT **Colonists** are the people who start a colony or the people who are among the first to live in a particular colony. □ The apple was brought over here by the colonists when they came.

가산명사 식민지 개척자 □ 사과는 식민지 개척자들이 이주 당시 이곳으로 가져온 것이었다.

colo|nize /kɒlənaɪz/ (colonizes, colonizing, colonized) [BRIT also **colonise**] ■ V-T If people **colonize** a foreign country, they go to live there and take control of it. ❑ *The first British attempt to colonize Ireland was in the twelfth century.* ❑ *Liberia was never colonised by the European powers.* ■ V-T When large numbers of animals **colonize** a place, they go to live there and make it their home. ❑ *Toads are colonizing the whole place.* ■ V-T When an area **is colonized by** a type of plant, the plant grows there in large amounts. [usu passive] ❑ *The area was then colonized by scrub.*

[영국영어 colonise] ❶ 타동사 식민지로 만들다 ❑ 영국이 처음으로 아일랜드를 식민지로 만들고자 했던 때는 12세기였다. ❑ 라이베리아는 유럽 강국의 식민 지배를 받은 적이 없다. ❷ 타동사 서식하다 ❑ 두꺼비가 지역 전체에 서식하고 있다. ❸ 타동사 -로 뒤덮이다, -의 군락지이다 ❑ 그 당시에는 그 지역이 덤불로 뒤덮여 있었다.

colo|ny /kɒləni/ (colonies) ■ N-COUNT A **colony** is a country which is controlled by a more powerful country. ❑ *In France's former North African colonies, anti-French feeling is growing.* ■ N-COUNT You can refer to a place where a particular group of people lives as a particular kind of **colony**. ❑ *In 1932, he established a school and artists' colony in Stone City, Iowa.* ❑ *...a penal colony.* ■ N-COUNT A **colony** of birds, insects, or animals is a group of them that live together. ❑ *The Shetlands are famed for their colonies of sea birds.*

❶ 가산명사 식민지 ❑ 북부 아프리카의 전 프랑스령 식민지들에서 프랑스에 대한 반감이 커지고 있다. ❷ 가산명사 거류지, 집단 거주지 ❑ 그는 1932년 아이오와 주 스톤 시티에 학교와 예술인 마을을 세웠다. ❑ 범죄자 유배지 ❸ 가산명사 집단, 떼, 무리 ❑ 셔틀랜드 제도는 바닷새 무리들로 유명하다.

col|or ♦♦♦ /kʌlər/ (colors, coloring, colored) [BRIT **colour**] ■ N-COUNT The **color** of something is the appearance that it has as a result of the way in which it reflects light. Red, blue, and green are colors. ❑ *"What color is the car?" — "Red."* ❑ *Judi's favorite color is pink.* ■ N-VAR A **color** is a substance you use to give something a particular color. Dyes and makeup are sometimes referred to as **colors**. ❑ *It is better to avoid all food colors.* ❑ *...The Body Shop Herbal Hair Color.* ■ V-T If you **color** something, you use something such as dyes or paint to change its color. ❑ *Many women begin coloring their hair in their mid-30s.* ❑ *We'd been making cakes and coloring the posters.* ● **col|or|ing** N-UNCOUNT ❑ *They could not afford to spoil those maps by careless coloring.* ■ V-I If someone **colors**, their face becomes redder than it normally is, usually because they are embarrassed. ❑ *Andrew couldn't help noticing that she colored slightly.* ■ N-COUNT Someone's **color** is the color of their skin. People often use **color** in this way to refer to a person's race. [POLITENESS] ❑ *I don't care what color she is.* ■ ADJ A **color** television, photograph, or picture is one that shows things in all their colors, and not just in black, white, and gray. ❑ *In Japan 99 per cent of all households now have a color television set.* ■ N-UNCOUNT **Color** is a quality that makes something especially interesting or exciting. ❑ *She had resumed the travel necessary to add depth and color to her novels.* ■ V-T If something **colors** your opinion, it affects the way that you think about something. ❑ *All too often it is only the negative images of Ireland that are portrayed, coloring opinions and hiding the true nature of the country.* ■ N-PLURAL A country's national **colors** are the colors of its national flag. ❑ *The Opera House is decorated with the Hungarian national colors: green, red and white.* ■ N-PLURAL People sometimes refer to the flag of a particular part of an army, navy, or air force, or the flag of a particular country as its **colors**. ❑ *Troops raised the country's colors in a special ceremony.* ■ N-PLURAL A sports team's **colors** are the colors of the clothes they wear when they play. ❑ *I was wearing the team's colors.* ■ →see also **colored, coloring** ■ PHRASE If a movie or television program is **in color**, it has been made so that you see the picture in all its colors, and not just in black, white, or gray. ❑ *Was he going to show the movie? Was it in color?* ■ PHRASE People **of color** are people who belong to a race with dark skins. [POLITENESS] ❑ *Black communities spoke up to defend the rights of all people of color.*
→see **flower**, **painting**
→see Picture Dictionary: **color**

[영국영어 colour] ❶ 가산명사 색 ❑ "차는 무슨 색이야?" "빨간색이야." ❑ 주디가 가장 좋아하는 색은 분홍색이다. ❷ 가산명사 유색물, 집단 거주지 ❑ 그는 1932년 착색제는 아예 피하는 것이 상책이다. ❑ 바디샵의 허브 염색약 ❸ 타동사 염색하다, 색칠하다 ❑ 많은 여성들은 머리를 30대 중반부터 염색하기 시작한다. ❑ 우리는 케이크를 만들고 포스터를 색칠하고 있었다. ● 염색, 색칠 불가산명사 ❑ 그들은 색칠을 잘못해서 그 지도들을 망치면 안 되는 형편이었다. ❹ 자동사 얼굴을 붉히다 ❑ 그녀의 얼굴이 약간 붉어지는 것을 앤드류가 보고야 알았다. ❺ 가산명사 피부색; 인종 (공손체) ❑ 그녀가 어떤 인종인지 상관없다. ❻ 형용사 컬러 ❑ 일본에서는 모든 가구의 99퍼센트가 컬러텔레비전을 가지고 있다. ❼ 불가산명사 색채 ❑ 그녀는 자신의 소설에 깊이와 색채를 더하기 위해 필요한 여행을 재개했다. ❽ 타동사 영향을 미치다 ❑ 아일랜드의 부정적인 이미지들만 자주 부각되기 때문에 사람들의 인식이 영향을 받고 그 나라의 참모습이 드러나지 않는다. ❾ 복수명사 국기에 사용된 색 ❑ 오페라 극장은 헝가리 국기의 색깔들인 초록, 빨강, 하양으로 장식되어 있다. ❿ 복수명사 국기, 깃발 ❑ 군대는 특별 행사 때 그 나라의 국기를 게양했다. ⓫ 복수명사 (팀 유니폼의) 색 ❑ 나는 그 팀의 유니폼과 동일한 색깔의 옷을 입고 있었다. ⓬ 구 컬러로 ❑ 그는 그 영화를 상영하려고 했나요? 컬러로 된 것이었나요? ⓮ 구 유색 인종의 [공손체] ❑ 흑인 사회는 모든 유색 인종의 권리를 변호하기 위해 목소리를 높였다.

▶**color in** PHRASAL VERB If you **color in** a drawing, you give it different colors using crayons or paints. ❑ *Someone had colored in all the black and white pictures.*

구동사 색칠하다 ❑ 누군가 모든 흑백 그림에 색깔을 칠해 놓은 상태였다.

col|ored ♦♢♢ /kʌlərd/ [BRIT **coloured**] ■ ADJ Something that is **colored** a particular color is that color. ❑ *The illustration shows a cluster of five roses colored apricot orange.* ■ ADJ Something that is **colored** is a particular color or combination of colors, rather than being just white, black, or the color that it is naturally. ❑ *You can often choose between plain white or colored and patterned scarves.* ■ ADJ A **colored** person belongs to a race of people with dark skins. [OFFENSIVE, OLD-FASHIONED]

[영국영어 coloured] ❶ 형용사 -한 색의 ❑ 그 삽화에는 주황색으로 색칠된 다섯 송이의 장미 묶음이 나와 있다. ❷ 형용사 채색된 ❑ 흔히 순백색 스카프와 색깔과 문양이 있는 스카프 중에서 고를 수 있다. ❸ 형용사 유색 인종의 [모욕어, 구식어]

col|or|ful /kʌlərfəl/ [BRIT **colourful**] ■ ADJ Something that is **colorful** has bright colors or a lot of different colors. ❑ *The flowers were colorful and the scenery magnificent.* ■ ADJ A **colorful** story is full of exciting details. ❑ *The story she told was certainly colorful, and extended over her life in England, Germany and Spain.* ■ ADJ A **colorful** character is a person who behaves in an interesting and amusing way. ❑ *Casey Stengel was probably the most colorful character in baseball.*
→see **flower**

[영국영어 colourful] ❶ 형용사 다채로운, 색색의 ❑ 색색의 꽃들이 피어 있었고 경치는 훌륭했다. ❷ 형용사 다채로운 ❑ 그녀가 해 준 이야기는 다채로운 내용에 그녀가 영국, 독일, 스페인에서 지낸 삶을 아울렀다. ❸ 형용사 이채로운 ❑ 캐시 스텡겔은 아마 야구계에서 가장 이채로운 인물이었을 것이다.

col|or|ing /kʌlərɪŋ/ [BRIT **colouring**] ■ N-UNCOUNT The **coloring** of something is the color or colors that it is. ❑ *Other countries vary the coloring of their bank notes as well as their size.* ■ N-UNCOUNT Someone's **coloring** is the color of their hair,

[영국영어 colouring] ❶ 불가산명사 색깔 ❑ 다른 국가들은 지폐의 색깔뿐만 아니라 크기도 다양하게 만든다. ❷ 불가산명사 피부색, 머리카락 색 ❑ 그들 중

Picture Dictionary color

white light

color wheel

yellow

blue   red

primary colors

green   orange

secondary colors

violet

yellow-green   orange-yellow

blue-green   orange-red

violet-blue   red-violet

tertiary colors

---

skin, and eyes. ❑ *None of them had their father's dark coloring.* ❸ N-UNCOUNT **Coloring** is a substance that is used to give color to food. ❑ *A few drops of green food coloring were added.* ❹ →see also **colour**

col|or|less /kʌlərlɪs/ [BRIT **colourless**] ❶ ADJ Something that is **colorless** has no color at all. ❑ *...a colorless, almost odorless liquid with a sharp, sweetish taste.* ❷ ADJ If someone's face is **colorless**, it is very pale, usually because they are frightened, shocked, or ill. ❑ *Her face was colorless, and she was shaking.* ❸ ADJ **Colorless** people or places are dull and uninteresting. ❑ *...the much more experienced but colorless General.*

co|los|sal /kəlɒsəl/ ADJ If you describe something as **colossal**, you are emphasizing that it is very large. [EMPHASIS] ❑ *There has been a colossal waste of public money.*

col|our /kʌlər/ →see **color**

colt /koʊlt/ (**colts**) N-COUNT A **colt** is a young male horse.

col|umn ♦♢♢ /kɒləm/ (**columns**) ❶ N-COUNT A **column** is a tall, often decorated cylinder of stone which is built to honor someone or forms part of a building. ❑ *...a London landmark, Nelson's Column in Trafalgar Square.* ❷ N-COUNT A **column** is something that has a tall narrow shape. ❑ *The explosion sent a column of smoke thousands of feet into the air.* ❸ N-COUNT A **column** is a group of people or animals which moves in a long line. ❑ *There were reports of columns of military vehicles appearing on the streets.* ❹ N-COUNT On a printed page such as a page of a dictionary, newspaper, or printed chart, a **column** is one of two or more vertical sections which are read downward. ❑ *We had stupidly been looking at the wrong column of figures.* ❺ N-COUNT In a newspaper or magazine, a **column** is a section that is always written by the same person or is always about the same topic. ❑ *His name features frequently in the social columns of the tabloid newspapers.*

col|umn|ist /kɒləmɪst/ (**columnists**) N-COUNT A **columnist** is a journalist who regularly writes a particular kind of article in a newspaper or magazine. ❑ *Clarence Page is a columnist for the Chicago Tribune.*

coma /koʊmə/ (**comas**) N-COUNT Someone who is in a **coma** is in a state of deep unconsciousness. ❑ *She was in a coma for seven weeks.*

comb /koʊm/ (**combs, combing, combed**) ❶ N-COUNT A **comb** is a flat piece of plastic or metal with narrow pointed teeth along one side, which you use to make your hair neat. ❷ V-T When you **comb** your hair, you make it neat using a comb. ❑ *Salvatore combed his hair carefully.* ❸ V-T If you **comb** a place, you search everywhere in it in order to find someone or something. ❑ *Officers combed the woods for the murder weapon.* ❹ V-I If you **comb through** information, you look at it very carefully in order to find something. ❑ *Eight policemen then spent two years combing through the evidence.* →see **hair**

com|bat ♦♢♢ (**combats, combating** or **combatting, combated** or **combatted**)

The noun is pronounced /kɒmbæt/. The verb is pronounced /kəmbæt/.

❶ N-UNCOUNT **Combat** is fighting that takes place in a war. ❑ *Over 16 million men had died in combat.* ❑ *Yesterday saw hand-to-hand combat in the city.* ❷ N-COUNT A **combat** is a battle, or a fight between two people. ❑ *It was the end of a long*

누구도 아버지의 짙은 피부색을 물려받지 않았다. ❸ 불가산명사 착색제 ❑ 녹색 착색제 몇 방울이 첨가되었다.

[영국영어 colourless] ❶ 형용사 무색의 ❑ 강렬하면서도 달콤한 맛을 가진 무색의 그리고 거의 무취의 액체 ❷ 형용사 창백한 ❑ 그녀는 얼굴이 창백했고 떨고 있었다. ❸ 형용사 개성 없는 ❑ 경험은 훨씬 더 많지만 개성이 없는 장군

형용사 거대한, 엄청난 [강조] ❑ 공공 자금이 엄청나게 낭비되어 왔다.

가산명사 망아지

❶ 가산명사 기둥 ❑ 런던의 명물인 트라팔가 광장의 넬슨 제독의 기둥 ❷ 가산명사 기둥 ❑ 폭발로 인해 거대한 연기 기둥이 수천 피트 상공까지 뻗어 올라갔다. ❸ 가산명사 행렬 ❑ 군용 차량들이 열을 지어 거리에 나타나고 있다는 보도가 있었다. ❹ 가산명사 난 ❑ 우리는 멍청하게도 엉뚱한 단의 숫자를 쳐다보고 있었다. ❺ 가산명사 난 ❑ 그의 이름은 타블로이드 지의 사교난에 자주 등장한다.

가산명사 기고가, 칼럼니스트 ❑ 클래런스 페이지는 시카고 트리뷴 지의 기고가이다.

가산명사 혼수 ❑ 그녀는 7주 동안 혼수상태에 빠져 있었다.

❶ 가산명사 빗 ❷ 타동사 빗다 ❑ 살바토레는 머리를 조심스레 빗었다. ❸ 타동사 샅샅이 훑다 ❑ 경관들은 살인 무기를 찾기 위해 숲을 샅샅이 뒤졌다. ❹ 자동사 꼼꼼히 찾다 ❑ 그리고선 여덟 명의 경관이 꼼꼼히 증거를 찾느라 2년을 보냈다.

명사는 /kɒmbæt/으로 발음되고, 동사는 /kəmbæt/으로 발음된다.

❶ 불가산명사 전투 ❑ 천 6백만 명 이상이 전투에서 사망했었다. ❑ 그 도시에서 어제 백병전이 벌어졌다. ❷ 가산명사 (일 대 일의) 싸움 ❑ 그것은 오랜 싸움의

combat. 3 V-T If people in authority **combat** something, they try to stop it from happening. ❏ *Congress has criticized new government measures to combat crime.* →see **war**

Word Partnership	*combat의 연어*
N.	combat **forces/troops/units**, combat **gear** 1
	combat **crime**, combat **disease**, combat **terrorism** 3
ADJ.	**heavy** combat 1 2

com|bat|ant /kəmbætªnt, BRIT kɒmbətªnt/ (**combatants**) N-COUNT A **combatant** is a person, group, or country that takes part in the fighting in a war. ❏ *I have never suggested that UN forces could physically separate the combatants in the region.*

가산명사 전투원 ❏ 나는 유엔군이 그 지역의 전투원들을 물리적으로 격리시킬 수 있을 것이라고 시사한 적이 없다.

com|bat|ive /kəmbætɪv, BRIT kɒmbətɪv/ ADJ A person who is **combative** is aggressive and eager to fight or argue. ❏ *He conducted the meeting in his usual combative style, refusing to admit any mistakes.*

형용사 호전적인 ❏ 그는 평상시의 호전적인 태도로 회의를 지휘하며 어떤 실수도 인정하지 않았다.

com|bi|na|tion ◆◇◇ /kɒmbɪneɪʃ°n/ (**combinations**) N-COUNT A **combination of** things is a mixture of them. ❏ *...a fantastic combination of colors.*

가산명사 혼합 ❏ 색깔의 놀라운 혼합

Word Link	com ≈ with, together : *companion*, *compact*, *combine*

com|bine ◆◇◇ /kəmbaɪn/ (**combines, combining, combined**) 1 V-RECIP If you **combine** two or more things or if they **combine**, they exist together. ❏ *The Church has something to say on how to combine freedom with responsibility.* ❏ *Relief workers say it's worse than ever as disease and starvation combine to kill thousands.* 2 V-RECIP If you **combine** two or more things or if they **combine**, they join together to make a single thing. ❏ *David Jacobs was given the job of combining the data from these 19 studies into one giant study.* ❏ *Combine the flour with 3 tablespoons water to make a paste.* 3 V-T If someone or something **combines** two qualities or features, they have both those qualities or features at the same time. ❏ *Their system seems to combine the two ideals of strong government and proportional representation.* ❏ *...a clever, far-sighted lawyer who combines legal expertise with social concern.* 4 V-T If someone **combines** two activities, they do them both at the same time. ❏ *It is possible to combine a career with being a mother.* 5 V-RECIP If two or more groups or organizations **combine** or if someone **combines** them, they join to form a single group or organization. ❏ *...an announcement by Steetley and Tarmac of a joint venture that would combine their brick, tile, and concrete operations.*

1 상호동사 결합하다; 결합되다 ❏ 교회는 자유와 책임을 어떻게 결합시킬 수 있는지에 대해 할 말이 있다. ❏ 구호 요원들은 질병과 기아가 합쳐져 수천 명이 죽으니 상황은 전보다 악화되었다고 한다. 2 상호동사 합치다; 합쳐지다 ❏ 19개 연구의 자료를 합쳐 하나의 거대한 연구로 결합하는 일이 데이비드 제이컵스에게 주어졌다. ❏ 밀가루에 물 3테이블 스푼을 넣어 밀가루 반죽을 만들어라. 3 타동사 겸비하다 ❏ 그들의 체계는 강력한 정부와 비례 대표제라는 두 개의 이상을 겸비한 것처럼 보인다. ❏ 법률적 전문성과 사회적 관심을 겸비한 똑똑하고 멀리 내다볼 줄 아는 변호사 4 타동사 겸하다 ❏ 직장과 어머니로서의 임무를 겸하는 것이 가능하다. 5 상호동사 합병하다 ❏ 벽돌, 타일, 콘크리트 사업부를 합병하는 스티틀리와 타맥의 공동 사업 발표

Thesaurus	*combine의 참조어*
V.	blend, fuse, incorporate, join, mix, unite; *(ant.)* detach, disconnect, divide, separate 1 2 3 5

com|bined /kəmbaɪnd/ 1 ADJ A **combined** effort or attack is made by two or more groups of people at the same time. [ADJ n] ❏ *These refugees are looked after by the combined efforts of the host countries and non-governmental organizations.* 2 ADJ The **combined** size or quantity of two or more things is the total of their sizes or quantities added together. [ADJ n] ❏ *Such a merger would be the largest in U.S. banking history, giving the two banks combined assets of some $146 billion.*

1 형용사 합동의 ❏ 난민 수용 국가들과 비정부 기관의 합동 노력을 통해서 이 난민들이 보살핌을 받고 있다. 2 형용사 합계의 ❏ 그 합병은 미국 금융 사상 가장 대규모로 두 은행의 통합 자산은 약 1460억 달러가 될 것이다.

com|bus|tion /kəmbʌstʃən/ N-UNCOUNT **Combustion** is the act of burning something or the process of burning. [TECHNICAL] ❏ *The energy is released by combustion on the application of a match.* →see **engine**

불가산명사 연소 [과학 기술] ❏ 성냥을 대면 연소를 통하여 에너지가 방출된다.

come ◆◆◆ /kʌm/ (**comes, coming, came**)

The form **come** is used in the present tense and is the past participle.

Come is used in a large number of expressions which are explained under other words in this dictionary. For example, the expression "to come to terms with something" is explained at "term."

come은 현재 및 과거 분사로 쓴다.

이 사전에서 come이 포함된 많은 표현들이 다른 표제어에서 설명된다. 예를 들어, 'to come to terms with something'은 'terms'에서 설명된다.

1 V-I When a person or thing **comes** to a particular place, especially to a place where you are, they move there. ❏ *Two police officers came into the hall.* ❏ *Come here, Tom.* ❏ *We heard the train coming.* ❏ *The impact blew out some of the windows and the sea came rushing in.* 2 V-T When someone **comes** to do something, they move to the place where someone else is in order to do it, and they do it. In American English, someone can also **come** do something and in British English, someone can **come and** do something. However, you always say that someone **came and** did something. ❏ *Eleanor had come to see her.* ❏ *I want you to come visit me.* 3 V-I When you **come to** a place, you reach it. ❏ *He came to a door that led into a passageway.* 4 V-I If something **comes up** to a particular point or **down** to it, it is tall enough, deep enough, or long enough to reach that point. ❏ *The water came up to my chest.* 5 V-I If something **comes apart** or **comes to pieces**, it breaks into pieces. If something **comes off** or **comes away**, it becomes detached from something else. ❏ *The pistol came to pieces, easily and quickly.* 6 V-LINK You use **come** in expressions such as **come to an end** or **come into operation** to indicate that someone or something enters or reaches a particular state or situation. ❏ *The summer came to an end.* ❏ *Their worst fears may be coming true.* 7 V-T If someone **comes to** do something, they do it at the end of a long process or period of time. ❏ *She said it so many times that she came to believe it.* 8 V-T You can ask how something **came to** happen when you want to know what caused it to happen or made it possible. ❏ *How did you come to meet him?* 9 V-T/V-I When a particular event or time **comes**, it arrives or happens. ❏ *The announcement came after a meeting at the Home Office.* ❏ *There will come a time when the crisis will occur.* ● **com|ing** N-SING ❏ *Most of my patients welcome the coming of summer.* 10 PREP You can use **come** before a date, time, or event to mean when that date, time, or event arrives. For example, you can say **come the spring** to

끝이었다. 3 타동사 -에 대항해 싸우다 ❏ 의회는 범죄와 싸우기 위한 정부의 새로운 조치들을 비판했다.

1 자동사 오다 ❏ 두 명의 경관이 복도로 들어왔다. ❏ 이리와, 탐. ❏ 우리는 기차가 오는 소리를 들었다. ❏ 그 충격에 창문 몇 개가 터져 나가 바닷물이 쏟아져 들어왔다. ❏ 나는 네가 날 보러 왔으면 좋겠어. 3 자동사 도착하다 ❏ 그는 통로로 이어지는 문에 도착했다. 4 자동사 -까지 올라오다; -까지 내려오다 ❏ 물이 내 가슴까지 올라왔다. 5 자동사 분해되다; 분리되다 ❏ 권총은 쉽고 빠르게 분해되었다. 6 연결동사 막되다에 이르다; 작동하다 ❏ 여름이 막바지에 이르렀다. ❏ 그들이 생각하는 최악의 우려가 현실화되는 것일 수도 있다. 7 타동사 -하게 되어버리다 ❏ 그녀는 그것을 너무도 자주 말해 결국 스스로도 그것을 믿어버리게 되었다. 8 타동사 -하게 되다 ❏ 그를 어떻게 해서 만나게 되었니? 9 자동사/타동사 도래하다 ❏ 내무부에서의 회의 이후 그 발표가 나왔다. ❏ 위기가 발생하는 시기가 올 것이다. ● 도래 단수명사 ❏ 내 환자들 대부분은 여름의 도래를 환영한다. 10 전치사 -이 되면 ❏ 5월 20일 선거일이 되면 우리는 결정을 해야 한다. 11 자동사 떠오르다 ❏ 그가 문을 닫으려는 순간 그에게 한 가지 생각이 떠올랐다. 12 자동사 -의 것이 되다 ❏ 공장에서 문을 닫았을 때 그는 받을 연금이 있긴 했다. 13 자동사 -에 회부되다 ❏ 가입 신청이 9월에 각료 회의에 회부되었다. 14 자동사 -에 달하다 ❏ 점심값은 총 80달러였다. 15 자동사 -의 출신이다 ❏ 학생 거의

mean "when the spring arrives." □ *Come the election on the 20th of May, we will have to decide.* ◼ᴸ v-ɪ If a thought, idea, or memory **comes to** you, you suddenly think of it or remember it. □ *He was about to shut the door when an idea came to him.* ◼ᴸ v-ɪ If money or property is going to **come to** you, you are going to inherit or receive it. □ *He did pay pension money coming to him when the factory shut down.* ◼ᴸ v-ɪ If a case **comes before** a court or tribunal or **comes to** court, it is presented there so that the court or tribunal can examine it. □ *The membership application came before the Council of Ministers in September.* ◼ᴸ v-ɪ If something **comes to** a particular number or amount, it adds up to it. □ *Lunch came to $80.* ◼ᴸ v-ɪ If someone or something **comes from** a particular place or thing, that place or thing is their origin, source, or starting point. □ *Nearly half the students come from abroad.* □ *Chocolate comes from the cacao tree.* ◼ᴸ v-ɪ Something that **comes from** something else or **comes of** it is the result of it. □ *There is a feeling of power that comes from driving fast.* □ *Some good might come of all this gloomy business.* ◼ᴸ v-ᴛ If someone or something **comes** first, next, or last, they are first, next, or last in a series, list, or competition. □ *The two countries have been unable to agree which step should come next.* □ *The alphabet might be more rational if all the vowels came first.* ◼ᴸ v-ɪ If a type of thing **comes in** a particular range of colors, forms, styles, or sizes, it can have any of those colors, forms, styles, or sizes. □ *Bikes come in all shapes and sizes.* ◼ᴸ v-ɪ The next subject in a discussion that you **come to** is the one that you talk about next. □ *Finally in the programme, we come to the news that the American composer and conductor, Leonard Bernstein, has died.* ◼ᴸ →see also **coming** ◼ᴸ PHRASE You can use the expression **when it comes down to it** or **when you come down to it** for emphasis, when you are giving a general statement or conclusion. [EMPHASIS] □ *When you come down to it, however, the basic problems of life have not changed.* ◼ᴸ PHRASE You use the expression **come to think of it** to indicate that you have suddenly realized something, often something obvious. □ *He was his distant relative, an unknown someone else on the island, come to think of it.* ◼ᴸ PHRASE When you refer to a time or an event **to come** or one that is still **to come**, you are referring to a future time or event. □ *I hope in years to come he will reflect on his decision.* ◼ᴸ PHRASE You can use expressions like **I know where you're coming from** or **you can see where she's coming from** to say that you understand someone's attitude or point of view. □ *To understand why they are doing it, it is necessary to know where they are coming from.*

▶**come about** PHRASAL VERB When you say how or when something **came about**, you say how or when it happened. □ *Any possible solution to the Irish question can only come about through dialogue.* □ *That came about when we went to New York last year.*

▶**come across** ◼ᴸ PHRASAL VERB If you **come across** something or someone, you find them or meet them by chance. □ *He came across the jawbone of a 4.5 million-year-old marsupial.* ◼ᴸ PHRASAL VERB If someone or what they are saying **comes across** in a particular way, they make that impression on people who meet them or are listening to them. □ *When sober he can come across as an extremely pleasant and charming young man.*

▶**come along** ◼ᴸ PHRASAL VERB You tell someone to **come along** to encourage them in a friendly way to do something, especially to attend something. □ *There's a big press launch today and you're most welcome to come along.* ◼ᴸ PHRASAL VERB When something or someone **comes along**, they occur or arrive by chance. □ *I waited a long time until a script came along that I thought was genuinely funny.* ◼ᴸ PHRASAL VERB If something **is coming along**, it is developing or making progress. [BRIT also **come round**] □ *Pentagon spokesman Williams says those talks are coming along quite well.*

▶**come around** ◼ᴸ PHRASAL VERB If someone **comes around** or **comes round** to your house, they call there to see you. □ *Beryl came around this morning to apologize.* ◼ᴸ PHRASAL VERB If you **come around** or **come round** to an idea, you eventually change your mind and accept it or agree with it. □ *It looks like they're coming around to our way of thinking.* ◼ᴸ PHRASAL VERB When something **comes around** or **comes round**, it happens as a regular or predictable event. □ *I hope still to be in the side when the World Cup comes around next year.* ◼ᴸ PHRASAL VERB When someone who is unconscious **comes around** or **comes round**, they recover consciousness. □ *When I came round I was on the kitchen floor.*

▶**come at** PHRASAL VERB If a person or animal **comes at** you, they move towards you in a threatening way and try to attack you. □ *He maintained that he was protecting himself from Mr. Cox, who came at him with an axe.*

▶**come back** ◼ᴸ PHRASAL VERB If something that you had forgotten **comes back** to you, you remember it. □ *He was also an MP – I'll think of his name in a moment when it comes back to me.* ◼ᴸ PHRASAL VERB When something **comes back**, it becomes fashionable again. □ *I'm glad hats are coming back.* ◼ᴸ →see also **comeback**

▶**come by** PHRASAL VERB To **come by** something means to obtain it or find it. □ *How did you come by that check?*

▶**come down** ◼ᴸ PHRASAL VERB If the cost, level, or amount of something **comes down**, it becomes less than it was before. □ *Interest rates should come down.* □ *If you buy three bottles, the bottle price comes down to £2.42.* ◼ᴸ PHRASAL VERB If something **comes down**, it falls to the ground. □ *The cold rain came down.*

▶**come down on** ◼ᴸ PHRASAL VERB If you **come down on** one side of an argument, you declare that you support that side. □ *He clearly and decisively came down on the side of President Rafsanjani.* ◼ᴸ PHRASAL VERB If you **come down on** someone, you criticize them severely or treat them strictly. □ *If Douglas came down hard enough on him, Dale would rebel.*

▶**come down to** PHRASAL VERB If a problem, decision, or question **comes down to** a particular thing, that thing is the most important factor involved. □ *Walter Crowley says the problem comes down to money.* □ *I think that it comes down to the fact that people do feel very dependent on their automobile.*

절반이 해외 출신이다. □ 초콜릿은 카카오나무에서 나온다. ◼ᴸ 자동사 –의 결과이다 □ 빨리 운전을 하면 힘이 생기는 것 같은 느낌이 든다. □ 이 암울하기만 한 일에서 무슨 좋은 일이 생길지도 모르는 일이다. ◼ᴸ 타동사 –한 순서에 오다 □ 이 다음에 어떤 절차를 밟아야 할지에 대해서 두 나라는 합의를 보지 못하고 있다. □ 모든 모음이 먼저 온다면 알파벳이 더 합리적이 될지도 모르겠다. ◼ᴸ 자동사 –한 종류로 나오다 □ 자전거는 온갖 모양과 크기로 나온다. ◼ᴸ 자동사 –에 이르다 □ 이제 본 프로그램 마지막 순서로, 미국의 작곡가이자 지휘자인 레너드 번스타인이 사망했다는 소식입니다. ◼ᴸ 구 결국 [강조] □ 그러나 결국 삶의 근본적인 문제들은 변한 게 없다. ◼ᴸ 구 생각해 보면 □ 생각해 보면 그는 섬의 다른 모든 사람과 마찬가지로 남자의 먼 친척이었다. ◼ᴸ 구 다가올 □ 그가 자신의 결정을 돌이켜 보기를 바란다. ◼ᴸ 구 누군가의 입장을 이해한다는 의미로 사용 □ 그들이 왜 그렇게 하는지 이해하기 위해선 그들이 어떤 입장인지를 알 필요가 있다.

구동사 발생하다 □ 아일랜드 문제에 어떤 가능한 해결책이 있다면 이는 대화를 통해서만 얻을 수 있다. □ 그 일은 우리가 작년에 뉴욕에 갔을 때 일어났다.

◼ᴸ 구동사 (우연히) 발견하다, 조우하다 □ 그는 우연히 4백 5십만 년 된 유대류 동물의 턱뼈를 발견했다. ◼ᴸ 구동사 인상을 주다 □ 술에 취하지 않았을 때 그는 굉장히 친근하고 매력적인 젊은이라는 인상을 준다.

◼ᴸ 구동사 동행하다 □ 오늘 큰 언론 발표회가 있는데 같이 가주시면 매우 고맙겠습니다. ◼ᴸ 구동사 우연히 발생하다, 접하게 되다 □ 정말 재미있다고 생각되는 대본을 접하게 될 때까지 나는 매우 오래 기다렸다. ◼ᴸ 구동사 진전되다 [영국영어 come round] □ 국방성 대변인 윌리엄스는 대화가 상당히 잘 진척되고 있다고 한다.

◼ᴸ 구동사 방문하다 □ 베릴이 오늘 아침 사과하러 왔다. ◼ᴸ 구동사 마음을 돌리다 □ 그들이 드디어 우리의 사고방식 쪽으로 마음을 돌리는 것 같다. ◼ᴸ 구동사 정기적으로 돌아오다 □ 나는 내년 월드컵 때에도 팀에 남아 있기를 바란다. ◼ᴸ 구동사 의식을 차리다 □ 의식을 차렸을 때 나는 부엌 바닥에 누워있었다.

구동사 공격하다, 덤벼들다 □ 그는 자기에게 도끼를 들고 덤벼드는 콕스 씨로부터 자신을 방어하고 있었다는 주장을 계속했다.

◼ᴸ 구동사 기억이 되살아나다 □ 그는 또한 하원의원이었다. 기억이 되살아나기만 한다면 그의 이름을 생각해낼 수 있을 것이다. ◼ᴸ 구동사 유행이 돌아오다 □ 모자 유행이 돌아오다니 기쁘다.

구동사 취득하다, 손에 넣다 □ 그 수표를 어떻게 손에 넣었습니까?

◼ᴸ 구동사 줄어들다, 떨어지다 □ 금리가 하락할 것이다. □ 세 병을 구입하면 병당 가격이 2.42파운드로 떨어집니다. ◼ᴸ 구동사 떨어지다 □ 차가운 비가 내렸다.

◼ᴸ 구동사 (한쪽을) 지지하다 □ 그는 분명히 그리고 결단력 있게 라프산자니 대통령을 지지하고 나섰다. ◼ᴸ 구동사 심하게 꾸짖다, 심하게 대하다 □ 만약 더글러스가 그를 너무 심하게 대한다면 데일도 반항할 것이다.

구동사 –에 귀착되다 □ 월터 크롤리는 근본적인 문제는 돈이라고 한다. □ 내 생각에 문제는 사람들이 자신들의 자가용에 심리적으로 굉장히 의지한다는 사실로 귀착되는 것 같다.

▶**come down with** PHRASAL VERB If you **come down with** an illness, you get it. ❑ *Thomas came down with chickenpox.*

▶**come for** PHRASAL VERB If people such as soldiers or police **come for** you, they come to find you, usually in order to harm you or take you away, for example to prison. ❑ *Lotte was getting ready to fight if they came for her.*

▶**come forward** PHRASAL VERB If someone **comes forward**, they offer to do something or to give some information in response to a request for help. ❑ *A vital witness came forward to say that she saw Tanner wearing the boots.*

▶**come in** **1** PHRASAL VERB If information, a report, or a telephone call **comes in**, it is received. ❑ *Reports are now coming in of trouble at yet another jail.* **2** PHRASAL VERB If you have some money **coming in**, you receive it regularly as your income. ❑ *She had no money coming in and no funds.* **3** PHRASAL VERB If someone **comes in on** a discussion, arrangement, or task, they join it. ❑ *Can I come in here too, on both points?* **4** PHRASAL VERB When a new idea, fashion, or product **comes in**, it becomes popular or available. ❑ *It was just when geography was really beginning to change and lots of new ideas were coming in.* **5** PHRASAL VERB If you ask where something or someone **comes in**, you are asking what their role is in a particular matter. ❑ *Rose asked again, "But where do we come in, Henry?"* **6** PHRASAL VERB When the tide **comes in**, the water in the sea gradually moves so that it covers more of the land. [V P] ❑ *...after she became trapped on a mudflat as the tide came in.*

▶**come in for** PHRASAL VERB If someone or something **comes in for** criticism or blame, they receive it. ❑ *The plans have already come in for fierce criticism in many quarters of the country.*

▶**come into** **1** PHRASAL VERB If someone **comes into** some money, some property, or a title, they inherit it. [no passive] ❑ *My father has just come into a fortune in diamonds.* **2** PHRASAL VERB If someone or something **comes into** a situation, they have a role in it. [no passive] ❑ *We don't really know where Hortense comes into all this, Inspector.*

▶**come off** **1** PHRASAL VERB If something **comes off**, it is successful or effective. ❑ *It was a good try but it didn't quite come off.* **2** PHRASAL VERB If someone **comes off** worst in a contest or conflict, they are in the worst position after it. If they **come off** best, they are in the best position. ❑ *Some Democrats still have bitter memories of how, against all odds, they came off worst during the inquiry.*

▶**come on** **1** CONVENTION You say **"Come on"** to someone to encourage them to do something they do not much want to do. [SPOKEN] ❑ *Come on Doreen, let's dance.* **2** CONVENTION You say **"Come on"** to someone to encourage them to hurry up. [SPOKEN] ❑ *Come on, darling, we'll be late.* **3** PHRASAL VERB If you have an illness or a headache **coming on**, you can feel it starting. ❑ *Tiredness and fever are much more likely to be a sign of flu coming on.* **4** PHRASAL VERB If something or someone **is coming on** well, they are developing well or making good progress. ❑ *Lee is coming on very well now and it's a matter of deciding how to fit him into the team.* **5** PHRASAL VERB When something such as a machine or system **comes on**, it starts working or functioning. ❑ *The central heating was coming on and the ancient wooden boards creaked.*

▶**come on to** PHRASAL VERB When you **come on to** a particular topic, you start discussing it. ❑ *We're now looking at a smaller system but I'll come on to that later.*

▶**come out** **1** PHRASAL VERB When a new product such as a book or CD **comes out**, it becomes available to the public. ❑ *The book comes out this week.* **2** PHRASAL VERB If a fact **comes out**, it becomes known to people. ❑ *The truth is beginning to come out about what happened.* **3** PHRASAL VERB When a gay person **comes out**, they let people know that they are gay. ❑ *...the few gay men there who dare to come out.* **4** PHRASAL VERB To **come out** in a particular way means to be in the position or state described at the end of a process or event. ❑ *In this grim little episode of recent American history, few people come out well.* ❑ *So what makes a good marriage? Faithfulness comes out top of the list.* **5** PHRASAL VERB If you **come out for** something, you declare that you support it. If you **come out against** something, you declare that you do not support it. ❑ *Its members had come out virtually unanimously against the tests.* **6** PHRASAL VERB When the sun, moon, or stars **come out**, they appear in the sky. ❑ *Oh, look. The sun's come out.* **7** PHRASAL VERB When a group of workers **comes out** on strike, they go on strike. [BRIT; AM **go out on strike**] ❑ *On September 18 the dockers again came out on strike.*

▶**come over** **1** PHRASAL VERB If a feeling or desire, especially a strange or surprising one, **comes over** you, it affects you strongly. [no passive] ❑ *As I entered the corridor which led to my room that eerie feeling came over me.* **2** PHRASAL VERB-LINK If someone **comes over all** dizzy or shy, for example, they suddenly start feeling or acting in that way. ❑ *When Connie pours her troubles out to him, Joe comes over all sensitive.* **3** PHRASAL VERB If someone or what they are saying **comes over** in a particular way, they make that impression on people who meet them or are listening to them. ❑ *You come over as a capable and amusing companion.*

▶**come round** →see **come around**

▶**come through** **1** PHRASAL VERB To **come through** a dangerous or difficult situation means to survive it and recover from it. [no passive] ❑ *The city had faced racial crisis and come through it.* **2** PHRASAL VERB If a feeling or message **comes through**, it is clearly shown in what is said or done. ❑ *I hope my love for the material came through, because it is a great script.* **3** PHRASAL VERB If something **comes through**, it arrives, especially after some procedure has been carried out. ❑ *The father of the baby was waiting for his divorce to come through.* **4** PHRASAL VERB If you **come through** with what is expected or needed from you, you succeed in doing or providing it. ❑ *He puts his administration at risk if he doesn't come through on these promises for reform.*

구동사 ~에 걸리다 ❑ 토머스는 수두에 걸렸다.

구동사 ~을 잡으러 오다 ❑ 롯데는 그들이 자기를 잡으러 오면 싸울 준비를 하고 있었다.

구동사 나서다 ❑ 중요한 목격자가 나타나 태너가 그 부츠를 신고 있는 것을 봤다고 증언했다.

1 구동사 들어오다 ❑ 또 다른 감옥에서도 문제가 발생했다는 보고가 지금 들어오고 있다. **2** 구동사 (돈이) 정기적으로 들어오다 ❑ 그녀에게 정기적으로 들어오는 돈도 없었으며 자금도 없었다. **3** 구동사 참가하다 ❑ 두 가지 사항 모두에 대해 저도 몇 마디 해도 될까요? **4** 구동사 유행하게 되다, 나오다 ❑ 그 때는 지리학이 진정한 변화를 겪기 시작하고 많은 새로운 생각들이 나오는 바로 그런 시기였다. **5** 구동사 관여하다 ❑ "하지만 우리가 할 일은 뭐야. 헨리?"라고 로즈가 다시 물었다. **6** 구동사 들어오다 ❑ 조수가 밀려들어와 그녀가 개펄에 갇힌 후

구동사 (비난을) 받다 ❑ 그 계획들은 나라의 여러 곳에서 이미 강한 비판을 받아 왔다.

1 구동사 ~을 상속하다 ❑ 아버지께서 최근에 큰 재산을 다이아몬드로 상속받으셨다. **2** 구동사 관여하게 되다 ❑ 형사님, 우리는 정말 호텐스가 이 모든 것과 어떤 관계가 있는지 모르겠습니다.

1 구동사 성공하다, 효과가 있다 ❑ 시도는 좋았으나 별로 성공하지는 못했다. **2** 구동사 처지에 처하다 ❑ 일부 민주당원들은 그들이 그 조사에서 어떻게 모든 불리한 조건들에 맞서 최악의 처지에 처하게 되었는지에 대해 아직도 쓰라린 기억을 가지고 있다.

1 관용 표현 어서 [구어체] ❑ 어서, 도린, 우리 춤추자. **2** 관용 표현 서둘러 [구어체] ❑ 서둘러, 여보, 우리 늦겠다. **3** 구동사 기미가 나타나다 ❑ 피로와 열은 독감이 오려는 징조일 가능성이 훨씬 더 높다. **4** 구동사 발전하다 ❑ 리는 이제 많이 발전했고 남은 문제는 그를 팀에 어떻게 편입시키느냐이다. **5** 구동사 커지다, 작동하다 ❑ 중앙난방이 들어오고 있었고 오래된 마루장들은 삐걱거렸다.

구동사 다루기 시작하다 ❑ 우리는 더 작은 시스템을 살펴보고 있는데 이것은 나중에 다루기로 하죠.

1 구동사 발매되다 ❑ 그 책은 이번 주에 발매된다. **2** 구동사 드러나다 ❑ 무슨 일이 일어났는지 드러나기 시작하고 있다. **3** 구동사 커밍아웃 하다 ❑ 커밍아웃할 용기가 있는 소수의 남성 동성애자들 **4** 구동사 진취적으로 ~하게 되다 ❑ 미국 역사상 발전했던 이 우울한 작은 사건에서 상처를 받지 않은 사람은 극소수이다. ❑ 그렇다면 좋은 결혼의 조건은 무엇인가? 부부간의 정절이 제일 중요하게 꼽힌다. **5** 구동사 (지지나 반대를) 선언하다 ❑ 회원들은 거의 이구동성으로 그 실험들을 반대하고 나섰다. **6** 구동사 나오다 ❑ 야, 봐. 해가 나오고 있어. **7** 구동사 파업하다 [영국영어; 미국영어 **go out on strike**] ❑ 9월 18일에 부두 노동자들은 다시 파업에 들어갔다.

1 구동사 ~을 사로잡다 ❑ 내 방으로 이어지는 통로에 들어서자 으스스한 기운이 나를 사로잡았다. **2** 연결 구동사 ~을 느끼다 ❑ 코니가 그에게 자신의 고민을 털어놓을 때 조는 굉장히 민감해진다. **3** 구동사 ~한 인상을 주다 ❑ 당신은 유능하고 재미있는 동료라는 인상을 줍니다.

1 구동사 ~을 극복하다 ❑ 그 도시는 인종적 위기를 겪었고 그것을 극복했었다. **2** 구동사 ~이 드러나다 ❑ 그것에 대한 나의 애정이 드러났으면 좋겠다. 그것은 너무나 좋은 대본이니까. **3** 구동사 도달하다 ❑ 아기의 아버지는 이혼이 이루어지기를 기다리고 있었다. **4** 구동사 ~에 성공하다 ❑ 그가 개혁에 대한 이 약속들을 실현하지 못한다면 그의 정부가 위기에 빠질 것이다.

a
b
c
d
e
f
g
h
i
j
k
l
m
n
o
p
q
r
s
t
u
v
w
x
y
z

▶**come to** PHRASAL VERB When someone who is unconscious **comes to**, they recover consciousness. ❑ *When he came to and raised his head he saw Barney.*

구동사 의식을 찾다 ❑ 의식을 차리고 고개를 들었을 때 그는 바니를 봤다.

▶**come under** **1** PHRASAL VERB If you **come under** attack or pressure, for example, people attack you or put pressure on you. [no passive] ❑ *The police came under attack from angry crowds.* **2** PHRASAL VERB If something **comes under** a particular authority, it is managed or controlled by that authority. [no passive] ❑ *They were neglected before because they did not come under the Ministry of Defence.* **3** PHRASAL VERB If something **comes under** a particular heading, it is in the category mentioned. [no passive] ❑ *There was more news about Britain, but it came under the heading of human interest.*

1 구동사 –을 받다 ❑ 경찰이 분개한 군중들의 공격을 받았다. **2** 구동사 –의 통제를 받다 ❑ 그들은 국방부의 관할에 들어가지 않았기 때문에 이전에는 소홀히 대해졌다. **3** 구동사 –의 항목에 들다 ❑ 영국에 대한 더 많은 기사가 있었으나 사람들의 관심사라는 항목 밑에 들어 있었다.

▶**come up** **1** PHRASAL VERB If someone **comes up** or **comes up to** you, they approach you until they are standing close to you. ❑ *Her cat came up and rubbed itself against their legs.* **2** PHRASAL VERB If something **comes up** in a conversation or meeting, it is mentioned or discussed. ❑ *The subject came up at a news conference in Peking today.* **3** PHRASAL VERB If something **is coming up**, it is about to happen or take place. ❑ *We do have elections coming up.* **4** PHRASAL VERB If something **comes up**, it happens unexpectedly. ❑ *I was delayed – something came up at home.* **5** PHRASAL VERB If a job **comes up** or if something **comes up for** sale, it becomes available. ❑ *A research fellowship came up at Girton and I applied for it and got it.* **6** PHRASAL VERB When the sun or moon **comes up**, it rises. ❑ *It will be so great watching the sun come up.* **7** PHRASAL VERB In law, when a case **comes up**, it is heard in a court of law. ❑ *He is one of the reservists who will plead not guilty when their cases come up.*

1 구동사 다가오다 ❑ 그녀의 고양이가 다가와 그들의 다리에 몸을 비볐다. **2** 구동사 논의에 오르다 ❑ 그 주제는 오늘 북경의 기자 회견에서 논의에 올랐다. **3** 구동사 다가오다 ❑ 선거가 곧 다가올 것이다. **4** 구동사 갑자기 일어나다 ❑ 지체할 일이 있었어. 집에서 갑자기 일이 생겨서. **5** 구동사 나오다, 나타나다 ❑ 거튼에 연구원 자리가 생겨서 내가 지원을 했고 그 자리를 얻었다. **6** 구동사 떠오르다 ❑ 태양이 떠오르는 것을 보면 너무 멋질 것이다. **7** 구동사 회부되다 ❑ 그는 그들의 사건이 법정에 회부되면 무죄를 주장할 예비역들 중 한 명이다.

▶**come up against** PHRASAL VERB If you **come up against** a problem or difficulty, you are faced with it and have to deal with it. ❑ *We came up against a great deal of resistance in dealing with the case.*

구동사 –에 부딪히다, –에 직면하다 ❑ 이 사건을 다루면서 우리는 엄청난 저항에 부딪혔다.

come|back (**comebacks**) **1** N-COUNT If someone such as an entertainer or sports personality makes a **comeback**, they return to their profession or sport after a period away. ❑ *Sixties singing star Petula Clark is making a comeback.* **2** N-COUNT If something makes a **comeback**, it becomes fashionable again. ❑ *Tight fitting T-shirts are making a comeback.*

1 가산명사 복귀, 컴백 ❑ 60년대의 유명 가수 페툴라 클락이 컴백에 성공하고 있다. **2** 가산명사 다시 유행하다 ❑ 꽉 끼는 티셔츠가 다시 유행을 타고 있다.

co|median /kəmiːdiən/ (**comedians**) N-COUNT A **comedian** is an entertainer whose job is to make people laugh, by telling jokes or funny stories.

가산명사 코미디언

com|edy ◆◇◇ /kɒmədi/ (**comedies**) **1** N-UNCOUNT **Comedy** consists of types of entertainment, such as plays and movies, or particular scenes in them, that are intended to make people laugh. ❑ *Actor Dom Deluise talks about his career in comedy.* **2** N-COUNT A **comedy** is a play, movie, or television program that is intended to make people laugh. ❑ *...the new BBC1 romantic comedy Rescue Me.* →see **theater**

1 불가산명사 코미디 ❑ 배우 돔 들루이즈가 코미디계에서 자신이 걸어온 길에 대해 이야기한다. **2** 가산명사 코미디 ❑ 비비시1의 새 로맨틱 코미디 '레스큐 미'

com|et /kɒmɪt/ (**comets**) N-COUNT A **comet** is a bright object with a long tail that travels around the sun. ❑ *Halley's Comet is going to come back in 2061.* →see **solar system**

가산명사 혜성 ❑ 핼리 혜성은 2061년에 돌아올 것이다.

com|fort ◆◇◇ /kʌmfərt/ (**comforts, comforting, comforted**) **1** N-UNCOUNT If you are doing something in **comfort**, you are physically relaxed and contented, and are not feeling any pain or other unpleasant sensations. ❑ *This will enable the audience to sit in comfort while watching the shows.* **2** N-UNCOUNT **Comfort** is a style of life in which you have enough money to have everything you need. ❑ *Surely there is some way of ordering our busy lives so that we can live in comfort and find spiritual harmony too.* **3** N-UNCOUNT **Comfort** is what you feel when worries or unhappiness stop. ❑ *He welcomed the truce, but pointed out it was of little comfort to families spending Christmas without a loved one.* ❑ *He will be able to take some comfort from inflation figures due on Friday.* **4** N-COUNT If you refer to a person, thing, or idea as a **comfort**, you mean that it helps you to stop worrying or makes you feel less unhappy. ❑ *It's a comfort talking to you.* **5** V-T If you **comfort** someone, you make them feel less worried, unhappy, or upset, for example by saying kind things to them. ❑ *Ned put his arm around her, trying to comfort her.* **6** N-COUNT **Comforts** are things which make your life easier and more pleasant, such as electrical devices you have in your home. ❑ *She enjoys the material comforts married life has brought her.* **7** PHRASE If you say that something is, for example, **too close for comfort**, you mean you are worried because it is closer than you would like it to be. ❑ *The bombs fell in the sea, many too close for comfort.*

1 불가산명사 편안함 ❑ 이 덕분에 관중이 쇼를 보는 동안 편안하게 앉아 있을 수 있다. **2** 불가산명사 안락 ❑ 우리의 바쁜 인생을 정리해서 안락하면서도 정신적으로 조화를 이룬 삶을 찾을 수 있는 길이 분명히 어딘가에 있을 것이다. **3** 불가산명사 위안 ❑ 그는 정전을 반겼으나 사랑하는 사람들이 없는 크리스마스를 보내야 하는 가족들에게는 별다른 위안이 되지 못한다는 점을 지적했다. ❑ 금요일에 나올 물가 인상 수치에서 그는 어느 정도의 위안을 받을 수 있을 것이다. **4** 가산명사 위로 ❑ 너와 이야기하니 위로가 된다. **5** 타동사 위로하다 ❑ 네드는 그녀를 팔로 감싸고 위로를 하려 했다. **6** 가산명사 생활용품, 편하게 하는 것들 ❑ 그녀는 결혼 생활이 가져다 줄 물질적인 편리함을 즐긴다. **7** 구 불안할 정도로 가까운 ❑ 폭탄들은 바다에 떨어졌는데 그 것은 불안한 정도로 너무 가까운 거리였다.

Word Partnership	comfort의 연어
V.	find/take comfort, give/offer/provide comfort **3**
N.	source of comfort **4**
	comfort *someone* **5**

com|fort|able ◆◇◇ /kʌmftəbəl, -fərtəbəl/ **1** ADJ If a piece of furniture or an item of clothing is **comfortable**, it makes you feel physically relaxed when you use it, for example because it is soft. ❑ *...a comfortable fireside chair.* **2** ADJ If a building or room is **comfortable**, it makes you feel physically relaxed when you spend time in it, for example because it is warm and has nice furniture. ❑ *A home should be comfortable and friendly.* ● **com|fort|ably** /kʌmftəbli, -fərtəbli/ ADV ❑ *...the comfortably furnished living room.* **3** ADJ If you are **comfortable**, you are physically relaxed because of the place or position you are sitting or lying in. ❑ *Lie down on your bed and make yourself comfortable.* ● **com|fort|ably** ADV [ADV with v] ❑ *Are you sitting comfortably?* **4** ADJ If you say that someone is **comfortable**, you mean that they have enough money to be able to live without financial problems. ❑ *"Is he rich?" — "He's comfortable."* ● **com|fort|ably** ADV ❑ *Cayton describes himself as comfortably well-off.* **5** ADJ In a race, competition, or election, if you have a **comfortable** lead, you are likely to win it easily. If you gain a **comfortable** victory or majority, you win easily.

1 형용사 편안한 ❑ 벽난로 옆의 편안한 의자 **2** 형용사 편안한 ❑ 집은 편안하고 친근감이 있어야 한다. ● 편안하게 부사 ❑ 편안하게 가구가 갖춰진 거실 **3** 형용사 편안한 ❑ 침대에 편안하게 누우세요. ● 편안하게 부사 ❑ 앉은 자리가 편하신가요? **4** 형용사 수입이 충분한 ❑ "그 남자 부자야?" "먹고 살 만해." ● 수입이 충분하게 부사 ❑ 케이튼은 본인의 말로는 처지가 그럭저럭 풍족하다고 한다. **5** 형용사 여유 있는, 쉬운 ❑ 중반쯤 가자 우리는 다른 선수들을 여유 있게 두 바퀴 앞서 있었다. ● 여유 있게 부사 ❑ 시즌 초에 베이스를 여유 있게 이긴 로스앤젤레스의 레이더스 ❑ 형용사 편한 ❑ 불안한 정치인들에게는 단계별로 밟아 나가는 접근법이 편할 수도 있다. ❑ 그는 나를 좋아했고 나는 그가 편했다. ● 편하게 부사 ❑ 그들은 자신들의 계획에 대해 편하게 이야기했다.

[ADJ n] ❑ *By half distance we held a comfortable two-lap lead.* ● **com|fort|ably** ADV [ADV with v] ❑ *...the Los Angeles Raiders, who comfortably beat the Bears earlier in the season.* ⑥ ADJ If you feel **comfortable with** a particular situation or person, you feel confident and relaxed with them. [v-link ADJ, oft ADJ prep] ❑ *Nervous politicians might well feel more comfortable with a step-by-step approach.* ❑ *He liked me and I felt comfortable with him.* ● **com|fort|ably** ADV [ADV after v] ❑ *They talked comfortably of their plans.* ⑦ ADJ When a sick or injured person is said to be **comfortable**, they are in a stable physical condition. ❑ *He was described as comfortable in hospital last night.*

Thesaurus	*comfortable*의 참조어
ADV.	comfy, cozy, soft; (ant.) uncomfortable ① ②
	relaxed ③
	well-off ④

com|fort|ably /kʌmftəbli, -fərtəbli/ ADV If you do something **comfortably**, you do it easily. [ADV with v] ❑ *Only take upon yourself those things that you know you can manage comfortably.* →see also **comfortable**

com|fort|er /kʌmfərtər/ (**comforters**) ① N-COUNT A **comforter** is a person or thing that comforts you. ❑ *He became Vivien Leigh's devoted friend and comforter.* ② N-COUNT A **comforter** is a large cover filled with feathers or similar material which you put over yourself in bed instead of a sheet and blankets. [AM; BRIT **duvet, quilt**]

com|fort|ing /kʌmfərtɪŋ/ ADJ If you say that something is **comforting**, you mean it makes you feel less worried or unhappy. ❑ *My mother had just died and I found the book very comforting.*

com|fy /kʌmfi/ (**comfier, comfiest**) ADJ A **comfy** item of clothing, piece of furniture, room, or position is a comfortable one. [INFORMAL] ❑ *...a comfy chair.*

com|ic /kɒmɪk/ (**comics**) ① ADJ If you describe something as **comic**, you mean that it makes you laugh, and is often intended to make you laugh. ❑ *The novel is comic and tragic.* ② ADJ **Comic** is used to describe comedy as a form of entertainment, and the actors and entertainers who perform it. [ADJ n] ❑ *Grodin is a fine comic actor.* ③ N-COUNT A **comic** is an entertainer who tells jokes in order to make people laugh. ❑ *...the funniest comic in America.* ④ N-COUNT A **comic** is a magazine that contains stories told in pictures. [mainly BRIT; AM usually **comic book**] ❑ *Joe loved to read "Superman" comics.*

com|i|cal /kɒmɪkəl/ ADJ If you describe something as **comical**, you mean that it makes you want to laugh because it seems funny or silly. ❑ *Her expression is almost comical.*

com|ic book (**comic books**) N-COUNT A **comic book** is a magazine that contains stories told in pictures. [mainly AM; BRIT usually **comic**] ❑ *...comic-book heroes such as Spider-Man.*

com|ing ♦◇◇ /kʌmɪŋ/ ADJ A **coming** event or time is an event or time that will happen soon. [ADJ n] ❑ *This obviously depends on the weather in the coming months.* →see also **come**

com|ma /kɒmə/ (**commas**) N-COUNT A **comma** is the punctuation mark , which is used to separate parts of a sentence or items in a list.

com|mand ♦◇◇ /kəmænd/ (**commands, commanding, commanded**) ① V-T/V-I If someone in authority **commands** you to do something, they tell you that you must do it. [mainly WRITTEN] ❑ *He commanded his troops to attack.* ❑ *"Get in your car and follow me," he commanded.* ● N-VAR **Command** is also a noun. ❑ *The tanker failed to respond to a command to stop.* ❑ *I closed my eyes at his command.* ② V-T If you **command** something such as respect or obedience, you obtain it because you are popular, famous, or important. [no cont] ❑ *...an excellent physician who commanded the respect of all his colleagues.* ③ V-T If an army or country **commands** a place, they have total control over it. ❑ *Yemen commands the strait at the southern end of the Red Sea.* ● N-UNCOUNT **Command** is also a noun. ❑ *...the struggle for command of the air.* ④ V-T An officer who **commands** part of an army, navy, or air force is responsible for controlling and organizing it. ❑ *...the French general who commands the UN troops in the region.* ● N-UNCOUNT **Command** is also a noun. ❑ *...a small garrison under the command of Major James Craig.* ⑤ N-COUNT-COLL In the armed forces, a **command** is a group of officers who are responsible for organizing and controlling part of an army, navy, or air force. ❑ *He had authorization from the military command to retaliate.* ⑥ N-COUNT In computing, a **command** is an instruction that you give to a computer. ❑ *He entered the command into his navigational computer.* ⑦ N-UNCOUNT If someone has **command** of a situation, they have control of it because they have, or seem to have, power or authority. ❑ *Mr. Baker would take command of the campaign.* ⑧ N-UNCOUNT Your **command of** something, such as a foreign language, is your knowledge of it and your ability to use this knowledge. ❑ *His command of English was excellent.* ⑨ PHRASE If you have a particular skill or particular resources **at** your **command**, you have them and can use them fully. [FORMAL] ❑ *The country should have the right to defend itself with all legal means at its command.*

com|man|dant /kɒməndænt/ (**commandants**) N-COUNT; N-TITLE A **commandant** is an army officer in charge of a particular place or group of people.

com|mand econo|my (**command economies**) N-COUNT In a **command economy**, business activities and the use of resources are decided by the government, and not by market forces. [BUSINESS] ❑ *...the Czech Republic's transition from a command economy to a market system.*

---

⑦ 형용사 안정된 ❑ 그는 어제 저녁 병원에서 상태가 안정되었다고 전해졌다.

부사 쉽게 ❑ 네 자신이 쉽게 다룰 수 있는 그런 것들만 맡으세요.

① 가산명사 위로자, 위로감 주는 것 ❑ 그는 비비언 리의 충실한 친구이자 위로자가 되었다. ② 가산명사 푹신한 이불 [미국영어; 영국영어 duvet, quilt]

형용사 위로가 되는 ❑ 나의 어머니가 돌아가신 지 얼마 안 된 상태에서 그 책은 나에게 큰 위로가 되었다.

형용사 편안한 [비격식체] ❑ 편안한 의자

① 형용사 희극적인 ❑ 그 소설은 희극적이면서도 비극적이다. ② 형용사 코미디의, 희극의 ❑ 그로딘은 훌륭한 희극 배우이다. ③ 가산명사 만담꾼 ❑ 미국에서 가장 웃기는 만담꾼 ④ 가산명사 만화책 [주로 영국영어; 미국영어 대개 comic book] ❑ 조는 슈퍼맨 만화책 읽는 것을 정말 좋아했다.

형용사 우스운 ❑ 그녀의 표정은 거의 우스꽝스러울 정도이다.

가산명사 만화책 [주로 미국영어; 영국영어 대개 comic] ❑ 스파이더맨 같은 만화 주인공들

형용사 다가올 ❑ 이는 분명히 다음 몇 달 간의 날씨에 달려 있다.

가산명사 쉼표

① 타동사/자동사 명령하다 [주로 문어체] ❑ 그는 자신의 부하들에게 공격 명령을 내렸다. ❑ "당신 차를 타고 나를 따라와."라고 그는 명령했다. ● 가산명사 또는 불가산명사 명령 ❑ 유조선은 정지하라는 명령에 따르지 않았다. ❑ 나는 그의 명령대로 눈을 감았다. ② 타동사 (존경, 복종 등을) 얻다 ❑ 동료들의 존경을 한 몸에 받고 있던 훌륭한 의사 ③ 타동사 지배하다, 장악하다 ❑ 홍해 남단의 해협을 예멘이 장악하고 있다. ● 불가산명사 장악 ❑ 하늘을 장악하기 위한 투쟁 ④ 타동사 지휘하다 ❑ 그 지역의 유엔군을 지휘하는 프랑스 장군 ● 불가산명사 지휘 ❑ 제임스 크레이그 소령의 지휘 하에 있는 소규모 수비대 ⑤ 가산명사-집합 지휘부 ❑ 그는 군 지휘부로부터 대응해도 된다는 허가를 받은 상태였다. ⑥ 가산명사 명령어 ❑ 남자는 자신의 항법용 컴퓨터에 명령어를 입력했다. ⑦ 불가산명사 지휘, 지휘권 ❑ 베이커 씨가 운동의 지휘를 맡을 것이다. ⑧ 불가산명사 ~의 구사력 ❑ 그는 영어를 아주 잘했다. ⑨ 구 완벽하게 활용하는 [격식체] ❑ 그 나라는 가지고 있는 모든 법적 수단을 활용해서 스스로를 보호할 수 있는 권한을 가져야 한다.

가산명사; 경칭명사 지휘관

가산명사 국가 지배 경제 [경제] ❑ 체크 공화국의 국가 지배 경제에서 시장 지배 경제로의 전환

a b c d e f g h i j k l m n o p q r s t u v w x y z

com|mand|er ◆◇◇ /kəmændər, -mænd-/ (**commanders**) **1** N-COUNT; N-TITLE; N-VOC A **commander** is an officer in charge of a military operation or organization. ❑ *The commander and some of the men had been released.* **2** N-COUNT; N-TITLE; N-VOC A **commander** is an officer in the U.S. Navy or the Royal Navy.

1 가산명사; 경칭명사; 호격명사 지휘관 ❑ 지휘관과 일부 부하들이 석방되었다. **2** 가산명사; 경칭명사; 호격명사 (해군) 장교

com|mand|ing /kəmændɪŋ/ **1** ADJ If you are in a **commanding** position or situation, you are in a strong or powerful position or situation. ❑ *Right now you're in a more commanding position than you have been for ages.* **2** ADJ If you describe someone as **commanding**, you mean that they are powerful and confident. [APPROVAL] ❑ *Lovett was a tall, commanding man with a waxed gray mustache.* **3** →see also **command**

1 형용사 지휘하는 ❑ 지금 당신은 몇 년 간 가졌던 것보다 더 강한 지휘권을 가진 상태이다. **2** 형용사 위풍당당한 [마음에 듦] ❑ 러벳은 허연 콧수염을 빳빳하게 세운 키가 크고 위풍당당한 남자였다.

com|man|do /kəmændoʊ/ (**commandos** or **commandoes**) **1** N-COUNT A **commando** is a group of soldiers who have been specially trained to carry out surprise attacks. ❑ *...a small commando of marines.* **2** N-COUNT A **commando** is a soldier who is a member of a commando. ❑ *...small groups of American commandos.*

1 가산명사 특공대 ❑ 소규모 해병 특공대 **2** 가산명사 특공대원 ❑ 미국 특공대원으로 이루어진 소규모 무리들

Word Link | memor ≈ memory : com**memor**ate, **memor**ial, **memor**y

---

com|memo|rate /kəmɛməreɪt/ (**commemorates, commemorating, commemorated**) V-T To **commemorate** an important event or person means to remember them by means of a special action, ceremony, or specially created object. ❑ *One room contained a gallery of paintings commemorating great moments in baseball history.* ● **com|memo|ra|tion** /kəmɛməreɪʃən/ (**commemorations**) N-VAR ❑ *...a march in commemoration of Malcolm X.*

타동사 기리다 ❑ 방 하나에는 야구 역사상 위대한 순간들을 기리는 그림들이 화랑처럼 전시되어 있었다. ● 기념, 가산명사 또는 불가산명사 ❑ 말콤 엑스를 추도하는 행렬

com|memo|ra|tive /kəmɛmərətɪv, -əreɪtɪv/ ADJ A **commemorative** object or event is intended to make people remember a particular event or person. [ADJ n] ❑ *The Queen unveiled a commemorative plaque.*

형용사 기념하는 ❑ 여왕이 기념 명판의 덮개를 벗겼다.

com|mence /kəmɛns/ (**commences, commencing, commenced**) V-T/V-I When something **commences** or you **commence** it, it begins. [FORMAL] ❑ *The academic year commences at the beginning of October.* ❑ *They commenced a systematic search.*

타동사/자동사 시작하다 [격식체] ❑ 새 학년은 10월 초에 시작한다. ❑ 그들은 체계적인 조사를 개시했다.

> Commence, start, and begin all have a similar meaning, although commence is more formal and is not normally used in conversation. ❑ *The meeting is ready to begin... He tore the list up and started a fresh one....an alternative to commencing the process of European integration.* Note that **begin, start**, and **commence** can all be followed by an -ing form or a noun, but only **begin** and **start** can be followed by a "to" infinitive.

> commence가 더 격식적이고 대화에서 잘 쓰이지 않기는 하지만, commence, start, begin은 모두 비슷한 뜻을 갖는다. ❑ 회의를 시작할 준비가 되었다... 그는 리스트를 찢어 버리고 새 것을 쓰기 시작했다....유럽 통합 과정 착수의 대안. begin, start, commence 모두 그 뒤에 -ing 형이나 명사가 올 수 있으나, begin과 start 다음에만 to 부정사가 올 수 있다.

com|mence|ment /kəmɛnsmənt/ (**commencements**) **1** N-UNCOUNT The **commencement** of something is its beginning. [FORMAL] ❑ *All applicants should be at least 16 years of age at the commencement of this course.* **2** N-VAR **Commencement** is a ceremony at a university, college, or high school at which students formally receive their degrees or diplomas. [AM; BRIT **graduation**] ❑ *President Bush gave the commencement address today at the University of Notre Dame.*

1 불가산명사 시작 [격식체] ❑ 모든 지원자들은 과정 시작 시점에 최소한 만 열여섯 살이어야 한다. **2** 가산명사 또는 불가산명사 학위 수여식, 졸업식 [미국영어; 영국영어 graduation] ❑ 부시 대통령은 오늘 노트르담대학 학위 수여식에서 연설을 했다.

com|mend /kəmɛnd/ (**commends, commending, commended**) **1** V-T If you **commend** someone or something, you praise them formally. [FORMAL] ❑ *I commended her for that action.* ❑ *The reports commend her bravery.* ● **com|men|da|tion** /kɒmɛndeɪʃən/ (**commendations**) N-COUNT ❑ *Clare won a commendation for bravery in 1998 after risking his life at the scene of a gas blast.* **2** V-T If someone **commends** a person or thing **to** you, they tell you that you will find them good or useful. [FORMAL] ❑ *I can commend it to him as a realistic course of action.*

1 타동사 칭찬하다 [격식체] ❑ 나는 그녀의 그런 행동을 칭찬했다. ❑ 보고서들은 그녀의 용맹을 찬양한다. ● 칭찬 가산명사 ❑ 클레어는 1998년 가스 폭발 현장에서 자신의 목숨을 내놓고 용기를 발휘하여 훈장을 받았다. **2** 타동사 추천하다 [격식체] ❑ 나는 그것이 현실적인 방안이라고 그에게 추천할 수 있다.

com|mend|able /kəmɛndəbəl/ ADJ If you describe someone's behavior as **commendable**, you approve of it or are praising it. [FORMAL, APPROVAL] ❑ *Mr. Sparrow has acted with commendable speed.*

형용사 칭찬할 만한 [격식체, 마음에 듦] ❑ 스패로우 씨는 훌륭할 정도로 신속하게 행동했다.

com|ment ◆◆◇ /kɒmɛnt/ (**comments, commenting, commented**) **1** V-T/V-I If you **comment on** something, you give your opinion about it or you give an explanation for it. ❑ *So far, Mr. Cook has not commented on these reports.* ❑ *You really can't comment till you know the facts.* **2** N-VAR A **comment** is something that you say which expresses your opinion of something or which gives an explanation for it. ❑ *He made his comments at a news conference in Amsterdam.* ❑ *There's been no comment so far from police about the allegations.* **3** CONVENTION People say "**no comment**" as a way of refusing to answer a question, usually when it is asked by a journalist. ❑ *No comment. I don't know anything.*

1 타동사/자동사 논평하다 ❑ 아직까지 쿡 씨는 이 보도들에 대해 논평하지 않았다. ❑ 사실을 알기 전까지 논평하기란 어렵다. **2** 가산명사 또는 불가산명사 논평, 의견 ❑ 그는 자신의 의견을 암스테르담의 기자 회견에서 발표했다. ❑ 그 의혹에 대해 여태껏 경찰로부터 어떠한 코멘트도 없었다. **3** 관용 표현 노 코멘트 ❑ 노 코멘트. 저는 아무것도 모릅니다.

> If you **comment** on a situation, or make a **comment** about it, you give your opinion on it. ❑ *Mr. Cook has not commented on these reports... I was wondering whether you had any comments.* If you **mention** something, you say it, but only briefly, especially when you have not talked about it before. ❑ *He mentioned that he might go to New York.* If you **remark** on something, or make a **remark** about it, you say what you think or what you have noticed, often in a casual way. ❑ *Visitors remark on how well the children look... General Sutton's remarks about the conflict.*

> 어떤 상황에 대해서 comment하거나 make a comment하면, 그것에 대한 의견을 말하는 것이다. ❑ 쿡 씨는 이 보고서들에 대해 논평을 하지 않았다... 논평할 것이 있으신지 궁금해 하던 참이었습니다. 특히 이전에 무엇에 대해 이야기한 적이 없으면서 그것을 mention하면, 그것에 대해 간략하게 얘기하는 것이다. ❑ 그는 뉴욕에 갈지도 모른다고 언급했다. 무엇에 대해 remark한다고 하면, 생각하는 바나 인지한 바를 흔히 가볍게 말하는 것이다. ❑ 방문객들은 그 아이들이 얼마나 좋아 보이는지에 대해 말한다... 그 분쟁에 대한 서튼 장군의 발언

Word Partnership | comment의 연어

PREP.	comment **on** *someone/something* **1**
	comment **about** *something* **2**
ADJ.	**further** comment **2**
V.	**make a** comment, **refuse to** comment **2**

com|men|tary /kɒmənteri, BRIT kɒməntri/ (commentaries) **1** N-VAR A **commentary** is a description of an event that is broadcast on radio or television while the event is taking place. □ *He gave the listening crowd a running commentary.* **2** N-COUNT A **commentary** is an article or book which explains or discusses something. □ *Mr. Rich will be writing a twice-weekly commentary on American society and culture.* **3** N-UNCOUNT **Commentary** is discussion or criticism of something. [also a N, with supp] □ *The show mixed comedy with social commentary.*

com|men|tate /kɒmənteɪt/ (commentates, commentating, commentated) V-I To **commentate** means to give a radio or television commentary on an event. □ *They are in Sweden to commentate on the European Championships.*

com|men|ta|tor ♦♢◇ /kɒmənteɪtər/ (commentators) **1** N-COUNT A **commentator** is a broadcaster who gives a radio or television commentary on an event. □ *...a sports commentator.* **2** N-COUNT A **commentator** is also someone who often writes or broadcasts about a particular subject. □ *...a political commentator.*

com|merce ♦♢◇ /kɒmɜrs/ N-UNCOUNT **Commerce** is the activities and procedures involved in buying and selling things. □ *They have made their fortunes from industry and commerce.* →see also **chamber of commerce** →see **stock market**

com|mer|cial ♦♦◇ /kəmɜrʃ°l/ (commercials) **1** ADJ **Commercial** means involving or relating to the buying and selling of goods. □ *Docklands in its heyday was a major center of industrial and commercial activity.* **2** ADJ **Commercial** organizations and activities are concerned with making money or profits, rather than, for example, with scientific research or providing a public service. □ *The company has indeed become more commercial over the past decade.* □ *Conservationists in Chile are concerned over the effect of commercial exploitation of forests.* ● **com|mer|cial|ly** ADV □ *The plane will be commercially viable if 400 can be sold.* **3** ADJ A **commercial** product is made to be sold to the public. [ADJ n] □ *They are the leading manufacturer in both defense and commercial products.* ● **com|mer|cial|ly** ADV □ *It was the first commercially available machine to employ artificial intelligence.* **4** ADJ A **commercial** vehicle is a vehicle used for carrying goods, or passengers who pay. □ *The route is used every day not just by private motorists and public transport vehicles but by many hundreds of commercial vehicles.* **5** ADJ **Commercial** television and radio are paid for by the broadcasting of advertisements, rather than by the government. □ *...Classic FM, the first national commercial radio station.* **6** ADJ **Commercial** is used to describe something such as a movie or a type of music that it is intended to be popular with the public, and is not very original or of high quality. □ *There's a feeling among a lot of people that music has become too commercial.* **7** N-COUNT A **commercial** is an advertisement that is broadcast on television or radio. □ *The government has launched a campaign of television commercials and leaflets.* →see **advertising**

A **commercial** is a form of advertising done on the radio or television. **Advertisements** that appear in newspapers, magazines or on the internet are not called commercials. Newspapers allow individuals to post notices for selling items or announcing job vacancies. These are called **classified ads** or (in the US only) **want ads**.

com|mer|cial bank (commercial banks) N-COUNT A **commercial bank** is a bank which makes short-term loans using money from checking accounts. [BUSINESS]

com|mer|cial break (commercial breaks) N-COUNT A **commercial break** is the interval during a commercial television program, or between programs, during which advertisements are shown. □ *As you would expect, this is a distressing programme, and ITV has decided to screen it without commercial breaks.*

com|mer|cial|ism /kəmɜrʃəlɪzəm/ N-UNCOUNT **Commercialism** is the practice of making a lot of money from things without caring about their quality. [DISAPPROVAL] □ *Koons has engrossed himself in a world of commercialism that most modern artists disdain.*

com|mer|cial|ize /kəmɜrʃəlaɪz/ (commercializes, commercializing, commercialized) [BRIT also **commercialise**] V-T If something **is commercialized**, it is used or changed in such a way that it makes money or profits, often in a way that people disapprove of. [DISAPPROVAL] □ *It seems such a pity that a distinguished and honored name should be commercialized in such a manner.* ● **com|mer|cial|ized** ADJ □ *Rock'n'roll has become so commercialized and safe since punk.* ● **com|mer|cial|iza|tion** /kəmɜrʃəlɪzeɪʃ°n/ N-UNCOUNT □ *...the commercialization of Christmas.*

com|mis|sion ♦♦◇ /kəmɪʃ°n/ (commissions, commissioning, commissioned) **1** V-T If you **commission** something or **commission** someone **to** do something, you formally arrange for someone to do a piece of work for you. □ *The Ministry of Agriculture commissioned a study into low-input farming.* □ *You can commission them to paint something especially for you.* ● N-VAR **Commission** is also a noun. □ *Our china can be bought off the shelf or by commission.* **2** N-COUNT A **commission** is a piece of work that someone is asked to do and is paid for. □ *Just a few days ago, I finished a commission.* **3** N-VAR **Commission** is a sum of money paid to a salesperson for every sale that he or she makes. If a salesperson is paid **on commission**, the amount they receive depends on the amount they sell. □ *The salesmen work on commission only.* **4** N-UNCOUNT If a bank or other company charges **commission**, they charge a fee for providing a service, for example for exchanging money or issuing an insurance policy. [BUSINESS] □ *Travel agents charge 1 per cent commission on sterling cheques.* **5** N-COUNT-COLL A **commission** is a group of people who have been appointed to find out about something or to control something. □ *The authorities have been asked to set up a commission to investigate the murders.*

com|mis|sion|er ♦♢♢ /kəmɪʃənər/ (**commissioners**) also Commissioner
N-COUNT A **commissioner** is an important official in a government department or other organization. ❏ ...the European Commissioner for External Affairs.

가산명사 위원, 이사; 국장 ❏ 유럽 연합 대외 업무 담당 위원

com|mit ♦♦♢ /kəmɪt/ (**commits, committing, committed**) **1** V-T If someone **commits** a crime or a sin, they do something illegal or bad. ❏ I have never committed any crime. ❏ This is a man who has committed murder. **2** V-T If someone **commits suicide**, they deliberately kill themselves. ❏ There are unconfirmed reports he tried to commit suicide. **3** V-T If you **commit** money or resources to something, you decide to use them for a particular purpose. ❏ They called on Western nations to commit more money to the poorest nations. ❏ The government had committed billions of pounds for a programme to reduce acid rain. **4** V-T/V-I If you **commit yourself to** something, you say that you will definitely do it. If you **commit yourself to** someone, you decide that you want to have a long-term relationship with them. ❏ I would advise people to think very carefully about committing themselves to working Sundays. ❏ I'd like a friendship that might lead to something deeper, but I wouldn't want to commit myself too soon. **5** V-T If you do not want to **commit yourself** on something, you do not want to say what you really think about it or what you are going to do. [with brd-neg] ❏ It isn't their diplomatic style to commit themselves on such a delicate issue. **6** V-T If someone **is committed to** a mental hospital, prison, or other institution, they are officially sent there for a period of time. [usu passive] ❏ Arthur's drinking caused him to be committed to a psychiatric hospital. **7** V-T If you **commit** something **to** paper or **to** writing, you record it by writing it down. If you **commit** something **to** memory, you learn it so that you will remember it. ❏ She had not committed anything to paper about it. **8** V-T In the British legal system, if someone **is committed for trial**, they are sent by magistrates to stand trial in a crown court. [usu passive] ❏ He is expected to be committed for trial at Liverpool Crown Court.

1 타동사 (죄 또는 과실 등을) 범하다, 저지르다 ❏ 나는 범죄를 저지른 적이 없다. ❏ 이 사람은 살인을 저지른 사람이다. **2** 타동사 자살하다 ❏ 그가 자살을 시도했다는 미확인 보도가 있다. **3** 타동사 할애하다 ❏ 그들은 극빈국들에 더 많은 돈을 할애할 것을 서방 국가들에게 요구했다. ❏ 정부는 산성비 방지 계획에 수십억 파운드를 할애했었다. **4** 타동사/자동사 확약하다 ❏ 일요일 근무를 확약하는 것에 대해 매우 조심스럽게 생각해야 한다고 사람들에게 충고하고 싶다. ❏ 나는 더 깊은 관계로 발전할 수도 있는 우정을 바라지만, 너무 일찍 깊은 관계에 접어들고 싶지는 않다. **5** 타동사 언명하다, 입장을 분명히 하다 ❏ 그렇게 민감한 사안에 대해 입장을 분명히 하는 것은 그들의 외교 스타일이 아니다. **6** 타동사 (병원 또는 시설 등에) 보내지다, 수용되다 ❏ 아서는 주벽 때문에 정신과 병원에 보내졌다. **7** 타동사 적어 두다; 기억해 두다 ❏ 그녀는 그 일에 대해 아무것도 적어 두지 않았었다. **8** 타동사 재판을 받다 ❏ 그는 리버풀 중범죄 재판소에서 재판을 받을 것으로 예상된다.

Word Partnership   commit의 연어

N.	commit **a crime** **1**
	commit **suicide** **2**
	commit **resources** **3**
	commit **to** *something* **4**
	commit **to memory** **7**

---

com|mit|ment ♦♦♢ /kəmɪtmənt/ (**commitments**) **1** N-UNCOUNT **Commitment** is a strong belief in an idea or system. ❏ ...commitment to the ideals of Bolshevism. **2** N-COUNT A **commitment** is something which regularly takes up some of your time because of an agreement you have made or because of responsibilities that you have. ❏ I've got a lot of commitments. **3** N-COUNT If you make a **commitment to** do something, you promise that you will do it. [FORMAL] ❏ We made a commitment to keep working together.

1 불가산명사 강한 신념 ❏ 볼셰비즘 이념에 대한 강한 신념 **2** 가산명사 책무, (해야 할) 일 ❏ 나는 해야 할 일이 아주 많다. **3** 가산명사 시약, 약속 [격식체] ❏ 우리는 계속 함께 일하기로 약속했다.

Word Partnership   commitment의 연어

ADJ.	**deep/firm/strong** commitment **1**
	long-term commitment, **prior** commitment **2**
N.	*someone's* commitment **2**
PREP.	commitment **to** *someone/something* **1** **3**
V.	**make a** commitment **3**

---

com|mit|tee ♦♦♢ /kəmɪti/ (**committees**) N-COUNT-COLL A **committee** is a group of people who meet to make decisions or plans for a larger group or organization that they represent. ❏ ...a committee of ministers.

가산명사-집합 위원회 ❏ 각료 위원회

com|mod|ity /kəmɒdɪti/ (**commodities**) N-COUNT A **commodity** is something that is sold for money. [BUSINESS] ❏ The government increased prices on several basic commodities like bread and meat. →see **economics, stock market**

가산명사 상품 [경제] ❏ 정부는 빵과 고기 같은 몇 가지 종류의 생필품 가격을 올렸다.

com|mon ♦♦♦ /kɒmən/ (**commoner, commonest, commons**) **1** ADJ If something is **common**, it is found in large numbers or it happens often. ❏ His name was Hansen, a common name in Norway. ❏ Oil pollution is the commonest cause of death for seabirds. ● **com|mon|ly** ADV [ADV with v] ❏ Parsley is probably the most commonly used of all herbs. **2** ADJ If something is **common to** two or more people or groups, it is done, possessed, or used by them all. ❏ Moldavians and Romanians share a common language. **3** ADJ When there are more animals or plants of a particular species than there are of related species, then the first species is called **common**. [ADJ n] ❏ ...the common house fly. **4** ADJ **Common** is used to indicate that someone or something is of the ordinary kind and not special in any way. [ADJ n] ❏ Democracy might elevate the common man to a position of political superiority. **5** ADJ **Common** decency or **common** courtesy is the decency or courtesy which most people have. You usually talk about this when someone has not shown these characteristics in their behavior to show your disapproval of them. [DISAPPROVAL] ❏ It is common decency to give your seat to anyone in greater need. **6** ADJ You can use **common** to describe knowledge, an opinion, or a feeling that is shared by people in general. [ADJ n] ❏ It is common knowledge that swimming is one of the best forms of exercise. ● **com|mon|ly** ADV [ADV -ed] ❏ A little adolescent rebellion is commonly believed to be healthy. **7** ADJ If you describe someone or their behavior as **common**, you mean that they show a lack of taste, education, and good manners. [DISAPPROVAL] ❏ She might be a little common at times, but she was certainly not boring. **8** N-COUNT; N-IN-NAMES A **common** is an area of grassy land, usually in or near a village or small town, where the public is allowed to go. ❏ We are warning women not to go out on to the common alone. **9** N-PROPER-COLL **The Commons** is the same as the **House of Commons**. The members of the House of Commons can also be referred to as

1 형용사 흔한, 자주 일어나는 ❏ 그의 이름은 노르웨이에서는 흔한 이름인 한센이었다. ❏ 기름에 의한 오염은 바닷새들을 죽게 만드는 가장 흔한 원인이다. ● 흔히 부사 ❏ 파슬리는 아마도 모든 종류의 허브 중에서 가장 흔히 쓰이는 종류일 것이다. **2** 형용사 공통의, 공유의 ❏ 몰다비아 인과 루마니아 인은 공통의 언어를 사용한다. **3** 형용사 보통의 ❏ 보통 집파리 **4** 형용사 평범한, 보통의 ❏ 민주주의는 평범한 사람을 정치적으로 우월한 지위로 격상시킬 수도 있다. **5** 형용사 기본적인 (예의 또는 예절) [탐탁찮음] ❏ 더 필요한 사람에게 자리를 양보하는 것은 기본적인 예의이다. **6** 형용사 일반적인 ❏ 수영이 가장 좋은 운동 중 한 가지라는 것은 상식이다. ● 일반적으로 부사 ❏ 사춘기의 약간의 반항은 일반적으로 건강한 것으로 생각된다. **7** 형용사 품위 없는, 천박한 [탐탁찮음] ❏ 그녀는 때로는 약간 천박할 수도 있지만, 분명히 따분하지는 않다. **8** 가산명사; 이름명사 공유지 ❏ 우리는 여자들에게 혼자서 그 공원에 나가지 말라고 주의를 주고 있다. **9** 고유명사 하원; 하원의원 ❏ 하원은 오늘 성명을 발표할 예정이다. **10** 구 공통으로 ❏ 오보에와 클라리넷에는 어떤 공통적인 특성이 있다. **11** 구 공유의 ❏ 그는 자기 누이와 공유하는 바가 거의 없었다.

the Commons. ❑ *The Prime Minister is to make a statement in the Commons this afternoon.* 🔟 PHRASE If two or more things have something **in common**, they have the same characteristic or feature. ❑ *The oboe and the clarinet have certain features in common.* 🔟 PHRASE If two or more people have something **in common**, they share the same interests or experiences. ❑ *He had very little in common with his sister.* 🔟 **common ground** →see **ground**

→see **ground**

Thesaurus	*common*의 참조어
ADJ.	frequent, typical, usual; *(ant.)* unusual 🔟
	commonplace, everyday; *(ant.)* special 🔟
	accepted, standard, universal; *(ant.)* rare 🔟

Word Partnership	*common*의 연어
ADV.	**fairly/increasingly/more/most** common 🔟
N.	common **belief**, common **language**, common **practice**, common **problem** 🔟
V.	**have** *something* **in** common 🔟 🔟

---

com|mon law also **common-law** 🔟 N-UNCOUNT **Common law** is the system of law which is based on judges' decisions and on custom rather than on written laws. ❑ *Canadian libel law is based on English common law.* 🔟 ADJ A **common law** relationship is regarded as a marriage because it has lasted a long time, although no official marriage contract has been signed. [ADJ n] ❑ *...his common law wife.*

🔟 불가산명사 관습법 ❑ 캐나다의 명예 훼손 관련법은 영국 관습법에 근거를 두고 있다. 🔟 형용사 사실혼의, 내연의 ❑ 그의 내연의 처

com|mon noun (**common nouns**) N-COUNT A **common noun** is a noun such as "tree," "water," or "beauty" that is not the name of one particular person or thing. Compare **proper noun**.

가산명사 보통 명사

com|mon|place /kɒmənpleɪs/ (**commonplaces**) 🔟 ADJ If something is **commonplace**, it happens often or is often found, and is therefore not surprising. ❑ *Foreign vacations have become commonplace.* 🔟 N-COUNT A **commonplace** is a remark or opinion that is often expressed and is therefore not original or interesting. ❑ *It is a commonplace to say that Northern Ireland is a backwater in modern Europe.*

🔟 형용사 평범한, 흔한 ❑ 해외로 휴가 여행을 가는 것은 평범한 일이 되어 버렸다. 🔟 가산명사 진부한 말, 상투어 ❑ 북아일랜드가 현대 유럽에서 침체된 지역이라고 말하는 것은 진부한 말이다.

com|mon sense also **commonsense** N-UNCOUNT Your **common sense** is your natural ability to make good judgments and to behave in a practical and sensible way. ❑ *Use your common sense.* ❑ *She always had a lot of common sense.*

불가산명사 상식, 양식 ❑ 상식을 발휘하세요. ❑ 그녀는 언제나 상식이 풍부했다.

com|mon stock N-UNCOUNT **Common stock** refers to the shares in a company that are owned by people who have a right to vote at the company's meetings and to receive part of the company's profits after the holders of preferred stock have been paid. [AM, BUSINESS; BRIT **ordinary shares**] ❑ *The company priced its offering of 2.7 million shares of common stock at 20 cents a share.* →see also **preferred stock**

불가산명사 보통주 [미국영어, 경제; 영국영어 ordinary shares] ❑ 그 회사는 2백 7십만 주의 보통주 매물에 주당 20센트의 값을 매겼다.

com|mon|wealth /kɒmənwelθ/ 🔟 N-PROPER The **Commonwealth** is an organization consisting of the United Kingdom and most of the countries that were previously under its rule. ❑ *...the Asian, Caribbean, and African members of the Commonwealth.* 🔟 N-IN-NAMES **Commonwealth** is used in the official names of some countries, groups of countries, or parts of countries. ❑ *...the Commonwealth of Australia.*

🔟 고유명사 영국 연방 ❑ 아시아와 카리브 해 지역, 그리고 아프리카의 영연방 국가들 🔟 이름명사 연방; 공화국 ❑ 오스트레일리아 연방

com|mo|tion /kəmoʊʃ°n/ (**commotions**) N-VAR A **commotion** is a lot of noise, confusion, and excitement. ❑ *He heard a commotion outside.*

가산명사 또는 불가산명사 동요, 소동 ❑ 그는 바깥에서 소동이 벌어지는 소리를 들었다.

com|mu|nal /kəmyun°l, BRIT kɒmyun°l/ 🔟 ADJ **Communal** means relating to particular groups in a country or society. [ADJ n] ❑ *Communal violence broke out in different parts of the country.* 🔟 ADJ You use **communal** to describe something that is shared by a group of people. ❑ *The inmates ate in a communal dining room.*

🔟 형용사 (특정) 집단의 ❑ 그 나라의 여러 지역에서 집단 폭력이 발생했다. 🔟 형용사 공동의 ❑ 피수용자들은 공동 식당에서 식사를 했다.

com|mune /kɒmyun/ (**communes**) N-COUNT A **commune** is a group of people who live together and share everything. ❑ *Mack lived in a commune.*

가산명사 공동 생활체 ❑ 맥은 공동 생활체 안에서 살았다.

Word Link	commun ≈ sharing : commun**icate**, commun**ism**, commun**ity**

---

com|mu|ni|cate ♦◇◇ /kəmyunɪkeɪt/ (**communicates**, **communicating**, **communicated**) 🔟 V-RECIP If you **communicate with** someone, you share or exchange information with them, for example by speaking, writing, or using equipment. You can also say that two people **communicate**. ❑ *My natural mother has never communicated with me.* ❑ *Officials of the CIA depend heavily on electronic mail to communicate with each other.* ● **com|mu|ni|ca|tion** N-UNCOUNT [oft with/between n] ❑ *Lithuania hasn't had any direct communication with Moscow.* ❑ *...use of the radio telephone for communication between controllers and pilots.* 🔟 V-T If you **communicate** information, a feeling, or an idea **to** someone, you let them know about it. ❑ *They successfully communicate their knowledge to others.* 🔟 V-RECIP If one person **communicates with** another, they successfully make each other aware of their feelings and ideas. You can also say that two people **communicate**. ❑ *He was never good at communicating with the players.* ❑ *Family therapy showed us how to communicate with each other.* ● **com|mu|ni|ca|tion** N-UNCOUNT ❑ *There was a tremendous lack of communication between us.* ❑ *Good communication with people around you could prove difficult.*

🔟 상호동사 연락을 주고받다; 교통하다 ❑ 내 친엄마는 나와 연락을 주고받은 적이 없다. ❑ 시아이에이 직원들은 서로 연락을 주고받는 데 있어 이메일에 크게 의존한다. ● 연락, 교통, 교신 불가산명사 ❑ 리투아니아와 모스크바 사이에는 지금껏 직접적인 연락이 없었다. ❑ 관제사와 조종사 간의 교신을 위한 무선 전화의 사용 🔟 타동사 전달하다, 통보하다 ❑ 그들은 성공적으로 자신들의 지식을 다른 이들에게 전달한다. 🔟 상호동사 의사소통하다 ❑ 그는 선수들과 의사 소통을 잘 하지 못했다. ❑ 가족 요법은 우리에게 서로 의사 소통하는 법을 보여 주었다. ● 의사 소통 불가산명사 ❑ 우리 사이에는 의사 소통이 엄청나게 결여되어 있었다. ❑ 주변 사람들과 잘 의사 소통하는 것은 어려운 일일 수도 있다.

com|mu|ni|ca|tion ♦◇◇ /kəmyunɪkeɪʃ°n/ (**communications**) 🔟 N-PLURAL **Communications** are the systems and processes that are used to communicate or broadcast information, especially by means of electricity or radio waves. ❑ *...a communications satellite.* 🔟 N-COUNT A **communication** is a message. [FORMAL] ❑ *The ambassador has brought with him a communication from the President.* 🔟 →see also **communicate** →see **radio**

🔟 복수명사 통신 ❑ 통신 위성 🔟 가산명사 전언, 소식 [격식체] ❑ 그 대사가 대통령의 전언을 가지고 왔다.

→see **radio**

A

com|mun|ion /kəmyunyən/ (communions) **1** N-UNCOUNT **Communion** with nature or with a person is the feeling that you are sharing thoughts or feelings with them. [also *a* N, oft *N* with n] ❑ ...*communion with nature.* **2** N-UNCOUNT **Communion** is the Christian ceremony in which people eat bread and drink wine in memory of Christ's death. ❑ *Most villagers took communion only at Easter.*

B

1 불가산명사 교감 ❑ 자연과의 교감 **2** 불가산명사 성찬식 ❑ 대부분의 마을 사람들은 부활절에만 성찬식을 갖는다.

C

com|mu|ni|qué /kəmyunɪkeɪ, BRIT kəmyuːnɪkeɪ/ (communiqués) N-COUNT A **communiqué** is an official statement or announcement. [FORMAL] ❑ *Representatives of Jordan, Syria, and Lebanon issued a joint communiqué today after a two-day meeting in Amman.*

가산명사 공식 발표, 성명 [격식체] ❑ 요르단과 시리아, 레바논의 대표자들은 암만에서 이틀간 회의를 가진 후 오늘 공동 성명을 발표했다.

D

Word Link | commun ≈ sharing : communicate, communism, community

E

Word Link | ism ≈ action or state : communism, optimism, patriotism

com|mun|ism /kɒmyənɪzəm/ also Communism N-UNCOUNT **Communism** is the political belief that all people are equal and that workers should control the means of producing things. ❑ ...*the ultimate triumph of communism in the world.*

F

불가산명사 공산주의 ❑ 세계에서 공산주의의 궁극적인 승리

com|mun|ist ♦♦◇ /kɒmyənɪst/ (communists) also Communist **1** N-COUNT A **communist** is someone who believes in communism. ❑ *Her family fled Czechoslovakia when the communists seized power in 1947.* **2** ADJ **Communist** means relating to communism. ❑ ...*the Communist Party.*

G

1 가산명사 공산주의자 ❑ 그녀의 가족은 1947년 공산주의자들이 권력을 장악했을 때 체코슬로바키아를 빠져나갔다. **2** 형용사 공산주의의 ❑ 공산당

com|mu|nity ♦♦♦ /kəmyunɪti/ (communities) **1** N-SING-COLL The **community** is all the people who live in a particular area or place. ❑ *He's well liked by people in the community.* **2** N-COUNT-COLL A particular **community** is a group of people who are similar in some way. ❑ *The police haven't really done anything for the black community in particular.* **3** N-UNCOUNT **Community** is friendship between different people or groups, and a sense of having something in common. ❑ *Two of our greatest strengths are diversity and community.*

H

I

1 단수명사-집합 지역 사회; 지역 사람들 ❑ 그는 그 지역에 사는 사람들로부터 많은 사랑을 받는다. **2** 가산명사-집합 (특정한) 사회, 집단 ❑ 경찰이 사실 특별히 흑인 사회를 위해 한 일은 아무것도 없다. **3** 불가산명사 친교, 친목 ❑ 우리의 가장 큰 장점 두 가지는 다양성과 친목이다.

J

Thesaurus | community의 참조어

K

N. neighborhood, public, society **1**

com|mu|nity cen|ter (community centers) [BRIT community centre] N-COUNT A **community center** is a place that specially provided for the people, groups, and organizations in a particular area, where they can go in order to meet one another and do things.

L

[영국영어 community centre] 가산명사 지역 문화회관

M

com|mu|nity ser|vice N-UNCOUNT **Community service** is unpaid work that criminals sometimes do as a punishment instead of being sent to prison. ❑ *He was sentenced to 140 hours community service.*

N

불가산명사 사회봉사 ❑ 그는 사회봉사 140시간을 선고받았다.

com|mute /kəmyut/ (commutes, commuting, commuted) **1** V-I If you **commute**, you travel a long distance every day between your home and your place of work. ❑ *Mike commutes to London every day.* ❑ *McLaren began commuting between Paris and London.* ● **com|mut|er** (commuters) N-COUNT ❑ *The number of commuters to London has dropped by 100,000.* **2** N-COUNT A **commute** is the journey that you make when you commute. [mainly AM] ❑ *The average Los Angeles commute is over 60 miles a day.* →see **traffic, transportation**

O

1 자동사 통근하다 ❑ 마이크는 매일 런던으로 통근한다. ❑ 매클래런은 파리와 런던 사이를 통근하기 시작했다. ● 통근자 가산명사 ❑ 런던 통근자 수가 10만 명 감소했다. **2** 가산명사 통근 거리 [주로 미국영어] ❑ 로스앤젤레스 평균 통근 거리는 하루 60 마일이 넘는다.

P

com|mut|er belt (commuter belts) N-COUNT A **commuter belt** is the area surrounding a large city, where many people who work in the city live. ❑ ...*people who live in the commuter belt around the capital.*

Q

가산명사 통근권 ❑ 수도 주위의 통근권에 사는 사람들

Word Link | com ≈ with, together : companion, compact, combine

R

com|pact /kəmpækt/ **1** ADJ **Compact** things are small or take up very little space. You use this word when you think this is a good quality. [APPROVAL] ❑ ...*my compact office in Washington.* **2** ADJ A **compact** person is small but strong. ❑ *He was compact, probably no taller than me.*

S

1 형용사 아담한, 소형이고 경제적인 [마음에 듦] ❑ 워싱턴에 있는 나의 아담한 사무실 **2** 형용사 작지만 단단한 ❑ 그는 작지만 단단한 체구였고, 아마 키는 나보다 작은 듯했다.

com|pact disc (compact discs) [AM also compact disk] N-COUNT **Compact discs** are small shiny discs that contain music or computer information. The abbreviation **CD** is also used. [also AM -] →see **DVD**

T

[미국영어 compact disk] 가산명사 콤팩트디스크

com|pan|ion /kəmpænyən/ (companions) N-COUNT A **companion** is someone who you spend time with or who you are traveling with. ❑ *Fred had been her constant companion for the last six years of her life.*

U

가산명사 동료 ❑ 그녀 삶의 마지막 6년 동안 프레드는 그녀의 충실한 동반자였었다.

com|pan|ion|ship /kəmpænyənʃɪp/ N-UNCOUNT **Companionship** is having someone you know and like with you, rather than being on your own. ❑ *I depended on his companionship and on his judgment.*

V

불가산명사 교우 관계, 동반자 정신 ❑ 나는 그의 동반자 정신과 그의 판단력에 의존했다.

W

com|pa|ny ♦♦♦ /kʌmpəni/ (companies) **1** N-COUNT-COLL; N-IN-NAMES A **company** is a business organization that makes money by selling goods or services. ❑ *Sheila found some work as a secretary in an insurance company.* **2** N-COUNT-COLL; N-IN-NAMES A **company** is a group of opera singers, dancers, or actors who work together. ❑ ...*the Phoenix Dance Company.* **3** N-COUNT; N-IN-NAMES A **company** is a group of soldiers that is usually part of a battalion or regiment, and that is divided into two or more platoons. ❑ *The division will consist of two tank companies and one infantry company.* **4** N-UNCOUNT **Company** is having another person or other people with you, usually when this is pleasant or stops you feeling lonely. ❑ *"I won't stay long." — "No, please. I need the company."* ❑ *Ross had always enjoyed the company of women.* **5** →see also **joint-stock company, public company** **6** PHRASE If you **keep** someone **company**, you

X

Y

Z

1 가산명사-집합; 이름명사 회사 ❑ 실라는 보험 회사 비서로 일자리를 구했다. **2** 가산명사-집합; 이름명사 극단; 합창단; 무용단 ❑ 피닉스 무용단 **3** 가산명사; 이름명사 중대 ❑ 당 사단은 2개 탱크 중대와 1개 보병 중대로 이루어질 것이다. **4** 불가산명사 동석, 동행 ❑ "난 오래 있지 않을 거야." "안 돼, 제발. 나는 사람이 필요해." ❑ 로스는 언제나 여자들과 함께 있는 것을 즐겼다. **6** 구 -와 함께 있어 주다 ❑ 여기 있으면서 에마의 말벗이 되어 주는 게 어때요?

spend time with them and stop them from feeling lonely or bored. ❑ *Why don't you stay here and keep Emma company?* →see **electricity**
→see Word Web: **company**

→see Word Web: company

Word Partnership   *company*의 연어

ADJ.	**foreign** company, **parent** company **1**
V.	**buy/own/sell/start a** company, company **employs**, company **makes** **1**
	have company, **keep** company, **part** company **4** **6**

---

com|pa|ny car (**company cars**) N-COUNT A **company car** is a car which an employer gives to an employee to use as their own, usually as a benefit of having a particular job, or because their job involves a lot of traveling. [BUSINESS] ❑ *...changes to tax laws for company cars.*

가산명사 회사 차량, 업무용 차량 [경제] ❑ 회사 차에 대한 조세법의 변화

com|pa|ny sec|re|tary (**company secretaries**) N-COUNT A **company secretary** is a person whose job within a company is to keep the legal affairs, accounts, and administration in order. [BRIT, BUSINESS]

가산명사 총무부장 [영국영어, 경제]

com|pa|rable /kɒmpərəbᵊl/ **1** ADJ Something that is **comparable** to something else is roughly similar, for example in amount or importance. ❑ *...paying the same wages to men and women for work of comparable value.* ❑ *Farmers were meant to get an income comparable to that of townspeople.* **2** ADJ If two or more things are **comparable**, they are of the same kind or are in the same situation, and so they can reasonably be compared. ❑ *In other comparable countries real wages increased much more rapidly.* ❑ *By contrast, the comparable figure for the Netherlands is 16 per cent.*

1 형용사 엇비슷한 ❑ 엇비슷한 중요도를 가진 업무를 하는 남녀에게 동일한 임금을 지급하는 것 ❑ 농부들도 도시 사람들과 엇비슷한 소득을 벌어야 한다. **2** 형용사 비교되는, 비슷가는 ❑ 다른 비교 대상 국가들에서는 실질 임금이 훨씬 더 급격하게 증가한다. ❑ 대조적으로, 네덜란드의 비교 수치는 16퍼센트이다.

com|para|tive /kəmpærətɪv/ (**comparatives**) **1** ADJ You use **comparative** to show that you are judging something against a previous or different situation. For example, **comparative** calm is a situation which is calmer than before or calmer than the situation in other places. [ADJ n] ❑ *The task was accomplished with comparative ease.* ● **com|para|tive|ly** ADV [ADV adj/adv] ❑ *...a comparatively small nation.* **2** ADJ A **comparative** study is a study that involves the comparison of two or more things of the same kind. [ADJ n] ❑ *...a comparative study of the dietary practices of people from various regions of India.* **3** ADJ In grammar, the **comparative** form of an adjective or adverb shows that something has more of a quality than something else has. For example, "bigger" is the comparative form of "big," and "more quickly" is the comparative form of "quickly." Compare **superlative**. [ADJ n] ● N-COUNT **Comparative** is also a noun. ❑ *The comparative of "pretty" is "prettier."*

1 형용사 비교적인 ❑ 그 임무는 비교적 쉽게 달성되었다. ● 비교적 부사 ❑ 비교적 작은 나라 **2** 형용사 비교에 의한 ❑ 인도의 다양한 지역 사람들의 식습관에 대한 비교 연구 **3** 형용사 비교급의 ● 가산명사 비교급 ❑ 'pretty'의 비교급은 'prettier'이다.

Word Link   *par ≈ equal : com*par*e, dis*par*ate, *par*t*

---

com|pare ◆◇◇ /kəmpɛər/ (**compares, comparing, compared**) **1** V-T When you **compare** things, you consider them and discover the differences or similarities between them. ❑ *Compare the two illustrations in Fig 60.* ❑ *Managers analyze their company's data and compare it with data on their competitors.* **2** V-T If you **compare** one person or thing **to** another, you say that they are like the other person or thing. ❑ *Some commentators compared his work to that of James Joyce.* **3** V-RECIP If one thing **compares** favorably **with** another, it is better than the other thing. If it **compares** unfavorably, it is worse than the other thing. ❑ *Our road safety record compares favorably with that of other European countries.* **4** V-I If you say that something does not **compare with** something else, you mean that it is much worse. [usu with neg] ❑ *The flowers here do not compare with those at home.* **5** →see also **compared**

1 타동사 비교하다 ❑ 그림 60에 나와 있는 두 개의 도해를 비교하시오. ❑ 경영자들은 자기 회사의 자료를 분석하고 이를 자기 경쟁사들의 자료와 비교한다. **2** 타동사 비유하다, 비기다 ❑ 어떤 주석자들은 그의 작품을 제임스 조이스의 작품에 비유했다. **3** 상호동사 ~보다 낫다; ~보다 못하다 ❑ 우리 나라의 도로 안전 기록은 다른 유럽 국가들보다 낫다. **4** 자동사 ~과 비교가 되다, ~과 견줄 만하다 ❑ 여기 있는 꽃들은 집에 있는 꽃들과 비교도 안 된다.

Thesaurus   *compare*의 참조어

V.	analyze, consider, contrast, examine **1**
	equate, match **2**

---

com|pared ◆◆◇ /kəmpɛərd/ **1** PHRASE If you say, for example, that one thing is large or small **compared with** another or **compared to** another, you mean that it is larger or smaller than the other thing. ❑ *The room was light and lofty compared with our Tudor ones.* **2** PHRASE You talk about one situation or thing **compared with** another or **compared to** another when contrasting the two situations or things. ❑ *In 1800 Ireland's population was nine million, compared to Britain's 16 million.*

1 구 ~와 비교하여, ~에 비해 ❑ 그 방은 우리의 튜더 양식 방들에 비해 밝고 높았다. **2** 구 ~에 비해 ❑ 1800년 당시, 영국 인구가 1천 6백만이었던 데 비해 아일랜드의 인구는 9백만이었다.

Word Web   company

In the United States most **companies** are **privately held corporations**. All of the **stock** in the company goes to the people who organized it. All the **profits** go to the same people. Some companies have publicly traded **stock**. This means that some or all of the start-up money came from **shares** of stock sold to the public. Such shares are **traded** on the **stock market**. People who own stock in a company receive **dividends**. They usually also have voting rights. This allows them to play a role in guiding the corporation.

com|par|i|son ♦♢♢ /kəmpǽrɪsən/ (comparisons) **1** N-VAR When you make a **comparison**, you consider two or more things and discover the differences between them. ☐ ...a comparison of the British and German economies. ☐ Its recommendations are based on detailed comparisons between the public and private sectors. **2** N-COUNT When you make a **comparison**, you say that one thing is like another in some way. ☐ It is demonstrably an unfair comparison. **3** PHRASE If you say, for example, that something is large or small **in comparison with, in comparison to**, or **by comparison with** something else, you mean that it is larger or smaller than the other thing. ☐ The amount of carbon dioxide released by human activities such as burning coal and oil is small in comparison.

1 가산명사 또는 불가산명사 비교 ☐ 영국과 독일 경제의 비교 ☐ 그것의 장점은 공공 부문과 민간 부문 사이의 정밀한 비교에 의거해 나온 것이다. **2** 가산명사 비교 ☐ 그것은 명백히 부당한 비유이다. **3** 구 -와 비교하여 ☐ 석탄과 석유 연소 같은 인간 활동에 의해 배출되는 이산화탄소의 양은 상대적으로 적다.

Word Partnership   comparison의 연어

PREP.	comparison **between/of/with** *something* **1** **2**
	by/in comparison, in comparison **3**

---

com|part|ment /kəmpɑ́rtmənt/ (compartments) **1** N-COUNT A **compartment** is one of the separate spaces into which a railroad car is divided. ☐ On the way home we shared our first-class compartment with a group of businessmen. **2** N-COUNT A **compartment** is one of the separate parts of an object that is used for keeping things in. ☐ I put a bottle of Sainsbury's champagne in the freezer compartment.

1 가산명사 (객차 내의) 칸(막이) ☐ 집으로 올 때 우리는 한 무리의 실업가들과 일등석 칸에 함께 타고 왔다. **2** 가산명사 적재 공간 ☐ 나는 세인스베리스 샴페인 한 병을 냉동칸에 넣었다.

com|pass /kʌ́mpəs/ (compasses) N-COUNT A **compass** is an instrument that you use for finding directions. It has a dial and a magnetic needle that always points to the north. ☐ We had to rely on a compass and a lot of luck to get here. →see **magnet, navigation**

가산명사 나침반 ☐ 우리는 여기 도달하기 위해 나침반 하나와 운에 많이 의지해야 했다.

com|pas|sion /kəmpǽʃən/ N-UNCOUNT **Compassion** is a feeling of pity, sympathy, and understanding for someone who is suffering. ☐ Elderly people need time and compassion from their physicians.

불가산명사 연민, 측은지심 ☐ 나이가 지긋한 사람들에게는 담당 의사가 시간과 연민을 베풀어야 한다.

Word Link   ate ≈ filled with : affectionate, compassionate, considerate

---

com|pas|sion|ate /kəmpǽʃnɪt/ ADJ If you describe someone or something as **compassionate**, you mean that they feel or show pity, sympathy, and understanding for people who are suffering. [APPROVAL] ☐ My father was a deeply compassionate man. ☐ She has a wise, compassionate face.

형용사 자애로운, 측은해하는 [마음에 듦] ☐ 우리 아버지는 매우 자애로운 분이었다. ☐ 그녀는 현명하고 자애로운 얼굴을 지니고 있다.

com|pas|sion|ate leave N-UNCOUNT **Compassionate leave** is time away from your work that your employer allows you for personal reasons, especially when a member of your family dies or is seriously ill. [BUSINESS] ☐ ...plans for compassionate leave for employees faced with family crises.

불가산명사 청원휴가 [경제] ☐ 가족 내 위기에 직면한 고용인들을 위한 청원 휴가에 대한 계획

com|pat|ible /kəmpǽtɪbʰl/ **1** ADJ If things, for example systems, ideas, and beliefs, are **compatible**, they work well together or can exist together successfully. ☐ Free enterprise, he argued, was compatible with Russian values and traditions. ● **com|pat|ibil|ity** /kəmpǽtɪbɪ́lɪti/ N-UNCOUNT ☐ National courts can freeze any law while its compatibility with European legislation is being tested. **2** ADJ If you say that you are **compatible** with someone, you mean that you have a good relationship with them because you have similar opinions and interests. ☐ Mildred and I are very compatible. She's interested in the things that interest me. ● **com|pat|ibil|ity** N-UNCOUNT ☐ As a result of their compatibility, Haig and Fraser were able to bring about wide-ranging reforms. **3** ADJ If one make of computer or computer equipment is **compatible with** another make, they can be used together and can use the same software. ☐ Fujitsu took over another American firm, Amdal, to help it to make and sell machines compatible with IBM in the United States.

1 형용사 양립하는, 모순되지 않는 ☐ 자유 기업이 러시아적인 가치와 전통에 모순되지 않는다고 그는 주장했다. ● 양립성 불가산명사 ☐ 국가 법원은 어떤 법이든 유럽 연합 법률과의 양립성을 시험하는 동안은 그 효력을 정지시킬 수 있다. **2** 형용사 마음이 잘 통하는, 호흡이 잘 맞는 ☐ 밀드러드와 나는 마음이 아주 잘 맞는다. 내가 관심을 갖는 일들에 그녀도 관심을 갖는다. ● 마음이 잘 통한 불가산명사 ☐ 헤이그와 프레이저는 서로 호흡이 잘 맞아 함께 광범위한 개혁을 이뤄 낼 수 있었다. **3** 형용사 호환성 있는 ☐ 후지쯔는 미국에서 IBM과 호환성 있는 제품을 만들어 판매하도록 지원하기 위해 또 다른 미국 회사인 암달을 인수했다.

com|pat|ri|ot /kəmpéɪtriət, BRIT kəmpǽtriət/ (compatriots) N-COUNT Your **compatriots** are people from your own country. ☐ Chris Robertson of Australia beat his compatriot Chris Dittmar in the final.

가산명사 동포 ☐ 호주의 크리스 로버트슨은 결승에서 자국 동료인 크리스 디트마를 이겼다.

Word Link   pel ≈ driving, forcing : compel, expel, propel

---

com|pel /kəmpɛ́l/ (compels, compelling, compelled) **1** V-T If a situation, a rule, or a person **compels** you to do something, they force you to do it. ☐ ...the introduction of legislation to compel cyclists to wear a helmet. ☐ Leonie's mother was compelled to take in washing to help support her family. **2** PHRASE If you **feel compelled** to do something, you feel that you must do it, because it is the right thing to do. ☐ Dickens felt compelled to return to the stage for a final good-bye.

1 타동사 강제하다, 강요하다 ☐ 자전거 타는 사람들에게 헬멧을 쓸 것을 강제하는 법안의 도입 ☐ 레오니의 어머니는 가족을 부양하는 데 도움이 되기 위해 빨래 일을 해야만 했다. **2** 구 -해야 할 것처럼 느끼다 ☐ 디킨스는 마지막 작별 인사를 하기 위해 무대로 돌아가야 할 것처럼 느꼈다.

com|pel|ling /kəmpɛ́lɪŋ/ **1** ADJ A **compelling** argument or reason is one that convinces you that something is true or that something should be done. ☐ Factual and forensic evidence makes a suicide verdict the most compelling answer to the mystery of his death. **2** ADJ If you describe something such as a film or book, or someone's appearance, as **compelling**, you mean you want to keep looking at it or reading it because you find it so interesting. ☐ ...a frighteningly violent yet compelling film.

1 형용사 설득력 있는 ☐ 사실에 입각한 증거와 법의학적 증거를 고려할 때, 자살 평결이 그의 비밀스러운 죽음에 대한 가장 설득력 있는 답이다. **2** 형용사 흡인력 있는 ☐ 굉장히 폭력적이지만 흡인력 있는 영화

com|pen|sate /kɒ́mpənseɪt/ (compensates, compensating, compensated) **1** V-T To **compensate** someone **for** money or things that they have lost means to pay them money or give them something to replace that money or those things. ☐ The official promise to compensate people for the price rise clearly hadn't been worked out properly. **2** V-I If you **compensate for** a lack of something or **for** something you have done wrong, you do something to make the situation better. ☐ The company agreed to keep up high levels of output in order to compensate for supplies lost. **3** V-I Something that **compensates for** something else balances it or reduces its effects. ☐ MPs say it is crucial that a mechanism is found to compensate for inflation. **4** V-I If you try to **compensate for** something that is wrong or missing in your life, you try to do something that removes or reduces the

1 타동사 보상하다, 변상하다 ☐ 국민들에게 물가 인상분을 보상해 준다는 공약은 분명히 제대로 지켜져 오지 않았었다. **2** 자동사 벌충하다 ☐ 그 회사는 공급량의 손실분을 벌충하기 위해 생산량을 높은 수준으로 유지하는 데 합의했다. **3** 자동사 보완하다 ☐ 국회의원들은 인플레이션을 보완할 수 있는 기제가 발견된 것이 중요하다고 말한다. **4** 자동사 (결점 또는 약점 등을) 메우다, 보완하다 ☐ 그들은 특히 자신들의 유머 감각과 사람들과 잘 어울리는 능력에 만족한다. 이 두 가지는 그들이 스스로 인식하고 있는 역량 부족을 보완하는 특질이다.

harmful effects. ❑ *They are particularly pleased with their sense of humor and ability to get on with people, two characteristics which might compensate for their perceived inadequacies.*

com|pen|sa|tion ◆◇◇ /kɒmpənseɪʃⁿn/ (**compensations**) **1** N-UNCOUNT **Compensation** is money that someone who has experienced loss or suffering claims from the person or organization responsible, or from the state. ❑ *He received one year's salary as compensation for loss of office.* ❑ *There should be compensation for British farmers hit by the slump in demand.* **2** N-VAR If something is some **compensation** for something bad that has happened, it makes you feel better. ❑ *Helen gained some compensation for her earlier defeat by winning the final open class.*

com|pete ◆◇◇ /kəmpiːt/ (**competes, competing, competed**) **1** V-RECIP When one firm or country **competes with** another, it tries to get people to buy its own goods in preference to those of the other firm or country. You can also say that two firms or countries **compete**. ❑ *The banks have long competed with American Express's charge cards and various store cards.* ❑ *Banks and building societies are competing fiercely for business.* **2** V-RECIP If you **compete with** someone **for** something, you try to get it for yourself and stop the other person from getting it. You can also say that two people **compete** for something. ❑ *Kangaroos compete with sheep and cattle for sparse supplies of food and water.* ❑ *Schools should not compete with each other or attempt to poach pupils.* **3** V-I If you **compete** in a contest or a game, you take part in it. ❑ *He will be competing in the London-Calais-London race.*

com|pe|tence /kɒmpɪtəns/ N-UNCOUNT **Competence** is the ability to do something well or effectively. ❑ *His competence as an economist had been reinforced by his successful fight against inflation.*

com|pe|tent /kɒmpɪtənt/ **1** ADJ Someone who is **competent** is efficient and effective. ❑ *He was a loyal, distinguished, and very competent civil servant.* ● **com|pe|tent|ly** ADV ❑ *The government performed competently in the face of multiple challenges.* **2** ADJ If you are **competent to** do something, you have the skills, abilities, or experience necessary to do it well. ❑ *Most adults do not feel competent to deal with a medical emergency involving a child.*

com|pe|ti|tion ◆◆◇ /kɒmpɪtɪʃⁿn/ (**competitions**) **1** N-UNCOUNT **Competition** is a situation in which two or more people or groups are trying to get something which not everyone can have. ❑ *There's been some fierce competition for the title.* **2** N-SING **The competition** is the person or people you are competing with. ❑ *I have to change my approach: the competition is too good now.* **3** N-UNCOUNT **Competition** is an activity involving two or more firms, in which each firm tries to get people to buy its own goods in preference to the other firms' goods. ❑ *The deal would have reduced competition in the commuter-aircraft market.* ❑ *The farmers have been seeking higher prices as better protection from foreign competition.* **4** N-UNCOUNT The **competition** is the goods that a rival organization is selling. ❑ *Microsoft faces stiff competition from Sony's Playstation 2.* **5** N-VAR A **competition** is an event in which many people take part in order to find out who is best at a particular activity. ❑ *...a surfing competition.*

Word Partnership	*competition의 연어*
ADJ.	**unfair** competition **1**
	stiff competition **1**-**5**
PREP.	competition **between** *something*, competition **for** *something*, competition **in** *something* **1** **3**

com|peti|tive ◆◇◇ /kəmpetɪtɪv/ **1** ADJ **Competitive** is used to describe situations or activities in which people or firms compete with each other. ❑ *Only by keeping down costs will America maintain its competitive advantage over other countries.* ❑ *Japan is a highly competitive market system.* ● **com|peti|tive|ly** ADV [ADV after v] ❑ *He's now back up on the slopes again, skiing competitively in events for the disabled.* **2** ADJ A **competitive** person is eager to be more successful than other people. ❑ *He has always been ambitious and fiercely competitive.* ● **com|peti|tive|ly** ADV [ADV after v] ❑ *They worked hard together, competitively and under pressure.* ● **com|peti|tive|ness** N-UNCOUNT ❑ *I can't stand the pace, I suppose, and the competitiveness, and the unfriendliness.* **3** ADJ Goods or services that are at a **competitive** price or rate are likely to be bought, because they are less expensive than other goods of the same kind. ❑ *Only those homes offered for sale at competitive prices will secure interest from serious purchasers.* ● **com|peti|tive|ly** ADV ❑ *...a number of early Martin and Gibson guitars, which were competitively priced.* ● **com|peti|tive|ness** N-UNCOUNT ❑ *It is only on the world market that we can prove the competitiveness and quality of our goods.*

Word Partnership	*competitive의 연어*
N.	competitive **advantage**, competitive **sport** **1**
	competitive **person** **2**
ADV.	**highly** competitive, **more** competitive **1** **2**

com|peti|tor ◆◇◇ /kəmpetɪtər/ (**competitors**) **1** N-COUNT A company's **competitors** are companies who are trying to sell similar goods or services to the same people. ❑ *The bank isn't performing as well as some of its competitors.* **2** N-COUNT A **competitor** is a person who takes part in a competition or contest. ❑ *Herbert Blocker of Germany, one of the oldest competitors, won the individual silver medal.*

1 불가산명사 보상금, 배상금 ❑ 그는 사무실을 잃은 데 대한 보상금으로 1년치 봉급을 받았다. ❑ 수요 침체로 타격을 받은 영국 농부들에게 보상금을 지불해야 한다. **2** 가산명사 또는 불가산명사 보상 ❑ 헬렌은 마지막 무제한급 경기에서 우승함으로써 이전의 패배를 조금이나마 보상받았다.

1 상호동사 경쟁하다 ❑ 은행들은 아메리칸 익스프레스의 신용카드와 다양한 상점 카드를 상대로 오랫동안 경쟁해 왔다. ❑ 은행 측과 주택 조합 은행 측이 치열한 영업 경쟁을 벌이고 있다. **2** 상호동사 (~을 얻기 위해) 경쟁하다, 다투다 ❑ 캥거루들은 부족한 먹이와 물을 두고 양이나 소 떼와 다툰다. ❑ 학교들이 서로 경쟁하거나 학생들을 가로채려고 해서는 안 된다. **3** 자동사 (대회 또는 시합 등에) 참가하다 ❑ 그는 런던-칼레-런던 경주에 참가할 것이다.

불가산명사 능력, 자질 ❑ 인플레이션에 맞서 훌륭하게 대처함으로써 그의 경제 전문가로서의 능력이 강화되었다.

1 형용사 유능한 ❑ 그는 성실하고 출중하며 매우 유능한 공직자였다. ● 유능하게 부사 ❑ 정부는 복잡한 난국에 직면하여 유능하게 대처했다. **2** 형용사 적임의, ~의 역량이 있는 ❑ 대부분의 성인들은 어린이가 관련된 의료적 응급 사태에 대응할 역량이 없다고 느낀다.

1 불가산명사 경쟁 ❑ 선수권을 두고 치열한 경쟁이 벌어져 왔다. **2** 단수명사 경쟁자 ❑ 나는 접근법을 바꿔야 한다. 현재 경쟁자가 너무 뛰어나다. **3** 불가산명사 경쟁 ❑ 그 협정이 통근 항공기 시장에서의 경쟁을 감소시킬 수도 있었다. ❑ 농부들은 외국의 경쟁으로부터 보다 안전하게 보호받는 방편으로 더 높은 가격을 추구해 오고 있다. **4** 불가산명사 경쟁 상품 ❑ 마이크로소프트사는 소니의 플레이스테이션 2에서 나온 만만찮은 경쟁 상품들과 맞선다. **5** 가산명사 또는 불가산명사 시합, 경기, 대회 ❑ 서핑 대회

1 형용사 경쟁의, 경쟁에 의한 ❑ 가격을 낮게 유지해야만 미국이 다른 나라들에 대해 경쟁 우위를 유지할 것이다. ❑ 일본은 고도의 자유 경쟁 시장 체제이다. ● 경쟁하여 부사 ❑ 그는 이제 장애인들을 대상으로 한 스키 경기에 참가하여 다시 슬로프에 돌아와 섰다. **2** 형용사 경쟁심이 강한 ❑ 그는 언제나 야심만만하고 대단히 경쟁심이 강했다. ● 경쟁적으로 부사 ❑ 그들은 경쟁적으로, 또 압력을 받으며 함께 열심히 일했다. ● 경쟁심 불가산명사 ❑ 나는 그 속도와 경쟁심, 그리고 비우호적인 것을 견딜 수 없을 것 같다. **3** 형용사 경쟁력 있는 ❑ 경쟁력 있는 가격에 내어놓은 집들만이 진지한 구매자들의 관심을 얻을 것이다. ● 경쟁력 있게 부사 ❑ 경쟁력 있는 가격을 갖추었던 마틴 사나 깁슨 사의 많은 모델 기타들 ● 경쟁력 불가산명사 ❑ 우리 제품의 경쟁력과 품질을 증명할 수 있는 것은 오로지 세계 시장에서뿐이다.

1 가산명사 경쟁사 ❑ 그 은행은 몇몇 경쟁 은행들만큼 잘 운영되지 않고 있다. **2** 가산명사 (경기 또는 시합 능의) 참가자 ❑ 가장 나이 많은 참가자 중 한 명인 독일 선수 헤르베르트 블로커가 개인전 은메달을 땄다.

A

com·pi·la·tion /kɒmpɪleɪʃ³n/ (compilations) N-COUNT A **compilation** is a book, CD, or program that contains many different items that have been gathered together, usually ones which have already appeared in other places. ❑ *His latest album release is a compilation of his jazz works over the past decade.*

가산명사 편집물, 편찬물 ❑ 가장 최근에 발표된 그의 앨범은 지난 10년 동안 발표한 재즈곡을 모은 편집 앨범이다.

B

com·pile /kəmpaɪl/ (compiles, compiling, compiled) V-T When you **compile** something such as a report, book, or program, you produce it by collecting and putting together many pieces of information. ❑ *The book took 10 years to compile.*

타동사 편찬하다, 편집하다 ❑ 그 책은 편찬하는 데 10년이 걸렸다.

C

com·pla·cen·cy /kəmpleɪsʰnsi/ N-UNCOUNT **Complacency** is being complacent about a situation. [DISAPPROVAL] ❑ *...a worrying level of complacency about the risks of infection from AIDS.*

불가산명사 태평스러움, 안심 [탐탁찮음] ❑ 에이즈 감염 위험에 대한 걱정될 만큼의 태평스러움

D

com·pla·cent /kəmpleɪsʰnt/ ADJ A **complacent** person is very pleased with themselves or feels that they do not need to do anything about a situation, even though the situation may be uncertain or dangerous. [DISAPPROVAL] ❑ *We cannot afford to be complacent about our health.*

형용사 안심하는, 태평한 [탐탁찮음] ❑ 우리는 스스로의 건강에 대해 태평할 수가 없다.

E

com·plain ♦♦◇ /kəmpleɪn/ (complains, complaining, complained) ◼ V-T/V-I If you **complain about** a situation, you say that you are not satisfied with it. ❑ *Miners have complained bitterly that the government did not fulfill their promises.* ❑ *The American couple complained about the high cost of visiting Europe.* ❑ *People should complain when they consider an advert offensive.* ◻ V-I If you **complain of** pain or illness, you say that you are feeling pain or feeling ill. ❑ *He complained of a headache.*

F

◼ 타동사/자동사 불평하다, 불만을 제기하다 ❑ 광부들은 정부가 약속을 이행하지 않았다고 몹시 불평했다. ❑ 그 미국인 부부는 유럽 방문에 비용이 많이 든다고 불평했다. ❑ 어떤 광고가 불건전하다고 여겨질 때는 불만을 제기해야 한다. ◻ 자동사 (통증을) 호소하다 ❑ 그는 두통을 호소했다.

G

com·plaint ♦◇◇ /kəmpleɪnt/ (complaints) ◼ N-VAR A **complaint** is a statement in which you express your dissatisfaction with a particular situation. ❑ *There's been a record number of complaints about the standard of service on Britain's railways.* ❑ *People have been reluctant to make formal complaints to the police.* ◻ N-COUNT A **complaint** is a reason for complaining. ❑ *My main complaint is that we can't go out on the racecourse anymore.* ◼ N-COUNT You can refer to an illness as a **complaint**, especially if it is not very serious. ❑ *Eczema is a common skin complaint which often runs in families.*

H

◼ 가산명사 또는 불가산명사 불평, 불만 제기 ❑ 영국 철도의 서비스 수준에 대해 기록적인 숫자의 불만이 제기되어 왔다. ❑ 사람들은 경찰에 대해 정식으로 불만을 제기하기를 꺼려 왔다. ◻ 가산명사 불평거리, 고충 ❑ 나의 주된 고충은 더 이상 경마장에 나갈 수 없다는 것이다. ◼ 가산명사 (소소한) 병 ❑ 습진은 종종 유전되는 흔한 피부병이다.

I

J

Word Partnership   complaint의 연어

PREP.	complaint **about** *something*, complaint **against** *someone*, complaint **from** *someone* ◼
V.	**deal with** complaints, **file a** complaint, **make a formal** complaint ◼

K

L

Word Link   ple ≈ filling : complement, complete, deplete

M

com·ple·ment (complements, complementing, complemented)

The verb is pronounced /kɒmplɪmɛnt/. The noun is pronounced /kɒmplɪmənt/.

동사는 /kɒmplɪmɛnt/로 발음되고, 명사는 /kɒmplɪmənt/로 발음된다.

N

◼ V-T If one thing **complements** another, it goes well with the other thing and makes its good qualities more noticeable. ❑ *Nutmeg, parsley, and cider all complement the flavor of these beans well.* ◻ V-T If people or things **complement** each other, they are different or do something different, which makes them a good combination. ❑ *There will be a written examination to complement the practical test.* ◼ N-COUNT Something that is a **complement** to something else complements it. ❑ *The green wallpaper is the perfect complement to the old pine of the dresser.*

O

◼ 타동사 ~와 잘 어울리다 ❑ 너트멕과 파슬리, 그리고 사과즙 모두 이런 콩의 풍미와 잘 어울린다. ◻ 타동사 보완하다 ❑ 실기 시험을 보완하기 위한 필기 고사가 시행될 것이다. ◼ 가산명사 보완물; 잘 어울리는 것 ❑ 그 녹색 벽지는 소나무 재목으로 된 그 오래된 찬장과 완벽하게 어울린다.

P

com·ple·men·tary /kɒmplɪmɛntəri, -mɛntri/ ◼ ADJ **Complementary** things are different from each other but make a good combination. [FORMAL] ❑ *To improve the quality of life through work, two complementary strategies are necessary.* ❑ *He has done experiments complementary to those of Eigen.* ◻ ADJ **Complementary** medicine refers to ways of treating patients which are different from the ones used by most Western doctors, for example acupuncture and homoeopathy. [ADJ n] ❑ *...combining orthodox treatment with a wide range of complementary therapies.*

Q

◼ 형용사 보완적인 [격식체] ❑ 일을 통해 삶의 질을 개선하려면, 두 가지의 상호 보완적인 전략이 필요하다. ❑ 그는 아이겐의 실험을 보완하는 실험을 해 왔다. ◻ 형용사 보완 의학의, 대안 의학의 ❑ 정통 의학의 치료법과 광범위한 대안 의학 요법을 결합하는 일

R

S

Word Link   ple ≈ filling : complement, complete, deplete

T

com·plete ♦♦♦ /kəmpliːt/ (completes, completing, completed) ◼ ADJ You use **complete** to emphasize that something is as great in extent, degree, or amount as it possibly can be. [EMPHASIS] ❑ *The rebels had taken complete control.* ❑ *The resignation came as a complete surprise.* ● **com·plete·ly** ADV ❑ *Dozens of flats had been completely destroyed.* ❑ *Make sure that you defrost it completely.* ◻ ADJ You can use **complete** to emphasize that you are referring to the whole of something and not just part of it. [EMPHASIS] [ADJ n] ❑ *A complete tenement block was burnt to the ground.* ◼ ADJ If something is **complete**, it contains all the parts that it should contain. ❑ *The list may not be complete.* ❑ *...a complete dinner service.* ◼ V-T To **complete** a set or group means to provide the last item that is needed to make it a full set or group. [no cont] ❑ *Children don't complete their set of 20 baby teeth until they are two to three years old.* ◼ ADJ The **complete** works of a writer are all their books or poems published together in one book or as a set of books. [ADJ n] ❑ *...the Complete Works of William Shakespeare.* ◼ PHRASE If one thing comes **complete** with another, it has that thing as an extra or additional part. ❑ *The diary comes complete with a gold-colored ballpoint pen.* ◼ ADJ If something is **complete**, it has been finished. [v-link ADJ] ❑ *The work of restoring the farmhouse is complete.* ◼ V-T To **complete** something, you finish doing, making, or producing it. ❑ *Peter Mayle has just completed his first novel.* ● **com·ple·tion** /kəmpliːʃ³n/ (completions) N-VAR ❑ *The project is nearing completion.* ◼ V-T If you **complete** something, you do all of it. [no cont] ❑ *She completed her degree in two*

U

◼ 형용사 완전한 [강조] ❑ 반란자들이 완전히 지휘권을 장악했다. ❑ 그의 사직은 완전히 뜻밖의 일이었다. ● 완전히 부사 ❑ 수십 채의 아파트가 완전히 파괴되었다. ❑ 반드시 서리를 완전히 제거해라. ◻ 형용사 전부의 [강조] ❑ 한 아파트 구역 전체가 전소되었다. ◼ 형용사 완전한, 완비된 ❑ 그 리스트는 완전하지 않을 수도 있다. ❑ 제대로 갖추어진 정찬 서비스 ◼ 타동사 전부 갖추다, 다 채우다 ❑ 어린이들은 두세 살이 될 때까지 20개의 젖니가 다 나지 않는다. ◼ 형용사 전부 갖춘, 전집 ❑ 윌리엄 셰익스피어 전집 ◼ 구 ~까지 갖춰진 채로 ❑ 그 다이어리는 금색 볼펜까지 곁들여진 채로 제공된다. ◼ 형용사 완료된 ❑ 농가를 복원하는 작업은 완료되었다. ◼ 타동사 완성하다 ❑ 피터 메일은 첫 소설을 막 완성했다. ● 완성 가산명사 또는 불가산명사 ❑ 그 프로젝트는 거의 완성되어 가고 있다. ◼ 타동사 끝마치다, 완결하다 ❑ 그녀는 2년 만에 학위를 마쳤다. ◼ 타동사 작성하다, (빈칸을) 채우다 ❑ 아래 있는 쿠폰을 작성하기만 하면 됩니다.

V

W

X

Y

Z

years. **10** V-T If you **complete** a form or questionnaire, you write the answers or information asked for in it. ☐ *Simply complete the coupon below.*

Thesaurus　　　*complete*의 참조어

ADJ.　　total, utter **1**
　　　　entire, whole; (*ant.*) partial **2**

---

com|plex ♦♦◇ /kɒmplɛks/ (**complexes**)

The adjective is pronounced /kəmplɛks/ or sometimes /kɒmplɛks/. The noun is pronounced /kɒmplɛks/.

1 ADJ Something that is **complex** has many different parts, and is therefore often difficult to understand. ☐ *...in-depth coverage of today's complex issues.* ☐ *...a complex system of voting.* **2** N-COUNT A **complex** is a group of buildings designed for a particular purpose, or one large building divided into several smaller areas. ☐ *...plans for constructing a new stadium and leisure complex.*

Thesaurus　　　*complex*의 참조어

ADJ.　　complicated, intricate, involved; (*ant.*) obvious, plain, simple **1**

Word Partnership　　　*complex*의 연어

N.　　complex **issues**, complex **personality**, complex **problem/situation**, complex **process**, complex **system** **1**

---

com|plex|ion /kəmplɛkʃn/ (**complexions**) N-COUNT When you refer to someone's **complexion**, you are referring to the natural color or condition of the skin on their face. ☐ *She had short brown hair and a pale complexion.* →see **makeup**

com|plex|ities /kəmplɛksɪtiz/ N-PLURAL The **complexities** of something are the many complicated factors involved in it. ☐ *...those who find it hardest to cope with the complexities of modern life.*

com|plex|ity /kəmplɛksɪti/ N-UNCOUNT **Complexity** is the state of having many different parts connected or related to each other in a complicated way. ☐ *...a diplomatic tangle of great complexity.*

com|pli|ance /kəmplaɪəns/ N-UNCOUNT **Compliance with** something, for example a law, treaty, or agreement, means doing what you are required or expected to do. [FORMAL] ☐ *Inspectors were sent to visit nuclear sites and verify compliance with the treaty.*

Word Link　　　ate ≈ causing to be : complic*ate*, humili*ate*, motiv*ate*

---

com|pli|cate /kɒmplɪkeɪt/ (**complicates, complicating, complicated**) V-T To **complicate** something means to make it more difficult to understand or deal with. ☐ *What complicates the issue is the burden of history.* ☐ *The day's events, he said, would only complicate the task of the peacekeeping forces.*

com|pli|cat|ed ♦◇◇ /kɒmplɪkeɪtɪd/ ADJ If you say that something is **complicated**, you mean it has so many parts or aspects that it is difficult to understand or deal with. ☐ *The situation in Lebanon is very complicated.*

com|pli|ca|tion /kɒmplɪkeɪʃn/ (**complications**) **1** N-COUNT A **complication** is a problem or difficulty that makes a situation harder to deal with. ☐ *The age difference was a complication to the relationship.* **2** N-COUNT A **complication** is a medical problem that occurs as a result of another illness or disease. ☐ *Blindness is a common complication of diabetes.*

com|plic|ity /kəmplɪsɪti/ N-UNCOUNT **Complicity** is involvement with other people in an illegal activity or plan. [FORMAL] ☐ *Recently a number of policemen were sentenced to death for their complicity in the murder.*

com|pli|ment (**compliments, complimenting, complimented**)

The verb is pronounced /kɒmplɪment/. The noun is pronounced /kɒmplɪmənt/.

1 N-COUNT A **compliment** is a polite remark that you say to someone to show that you like their appearance, appreciate their qualities, or approve of what they have done. ☐ *You can do no harm by paying a woman compliments.* **2** V-T If you **compliment** someone, you pay them a compliment. ☐ *They complimented me on the way I looked each time they saw me.*

com|pli|men|tary /kɒmplɪmentəri, -mentri/ **1** ADJ If you are **complimentary** about something, you express admiration for it. ☐ *The staff have been very complimentary, and so have the customers.* **2** ADJ A **complimentary** seat, ticket, or book is given to you free. ☐ *He had complimentary tickets to take his wife to see the movie.*

com|ply /kəmplaɪ/ (**complies, complying, complied**) V-I If someone or something **complies with** an order or set of rules, they are in accordance with what is required or expected. ☐ *The commander said that the army would comply with the ceasefire.* ☐ *Some beaches had failed to comply with European directives on bathing water.*

com|po|nent ♦◇◇ /kəmpoʊnənt/ (**components**) **1** N-COUNT The **components** of something are the parts that it is made of. ☐ *Enriched uranium is a key component of a nuclear weapon.* ☐ *The management plan has four main components.*

형용사는 보통 /kəmplɛks /로 발음되지만, 때때로 /kɒmplɛks /로 발음되고, 명사는 /kɒmplɛks /로 발음된다.

1 형용사 복잡한 ☐ 오늘의 복잡한 사안들에 대한 심층 보도 ☐ 복잡한 선거 시스템 **2** 가산명사 복합 건물 ☐ 새 경기장과 종합 레저 센터를 건설하는 계획

가산명사 안색, 피부색 ☐ 그녀의 머리는 짧은 갈색이었고 안색은 창백했다.

복수명사 복잡한 일들 ☐ 현대 생활의 복잡한 일들에 대처하는 것을 가장 어렵게 생각하는 사람들

불가산명사 복잡성 ☐ 대단히 복잡하게 뒤얽힌 외교 상황

불가산명사 순응; 준수 [격식체] ☐ 핵 기지를 방문하여 조약이 준수되고 있는지 검증하도록 조사관들이 파견되었다.

타동사 복잡하게 만들다, 까다롭게 만들다 ☐ 그 문제를 복잡하게 만드는 것은 역사의 짐이다. ☐ 그 날의 사건은 평화유지군의 임무를 까다롭게 만들 뿐이라고 그가 말했다.

형용사 복잡한, 까다로운 ☐ 레바논의 상황은 매우 복잡하다.

1 가산명사 문제거리, 말썽거리 ☐ 나이 차가 그 관계에 문제거리였다. **2** 가산명사 합병증 ☐ 실명은 당뇨병의 흔한 합병증이다.

불가산명사 공모, 연루 [격식체] ☐ 최근 다수의 경찰관들이 그 살인 사건에 연루되어 사형을 선고받았다.

동사는 /kɒmplɪment /로 발음된다. 명사는 /kɒmplɪmənt /로 발음된다.

1 가산명사 찬사, 칭찬 ☐ 여성에게 칭찬의 말을 해서 나쁠 건 없다. **2** 타동사 칭찬하다 ☐ 그들은 매번 나를 만날 때마다 내 모습에 대해 칭찬을 했다.

1 형용사 칭찬의, 찬양하는 ☐ 직원들은 아주 칭찬을 많이 해 왔고, 고객들도 마찬가지였다. **2** 형용사 무료의, 우대의 ☐ 그는 그 영화에 아내를 데리고 갈 수 있는 무료 티켓을 가지고 있었다.

자동사 좇다, 따르다 ☐ 사령관은 군이 정전 명령을 따르리라고 말했다. ☐ 몇몇 해변들은 해수욕장에 대한 유럽 연합 지침을 따르지 못했다.

1 가산명사 성분, 구성 요소 ☐ 농축 우라늄은 핵무기의 주요 성분이다. ☐ 그 관리 계획은 네 가지 주요 부분으로 이루어져 있다. **2** 형용사 구성하고

A

2 ADJ The **component** parts of something are the parts that make it up. [ADJ n] ❑ *Gorbachev failed to keep the component parts of the Soviet Union together.* →see **mass production**

있는, 성분을 이루는 ❑ 고르바초프는 소비에트 연방의 소속국들을 한데 묶어 두는 데 실패했다.

B

Word Partnership	*component*의 연어
ADJ.	**key** component, **main** components, **separate** components **1**
N.	component **parts 2**

C

com|pose /kəmpo͞oz/ (composes, composing, composed) **1** V-T The things that something **is composed of** are its parts or members. The separate things that **compose** something are the parts or members that form it. ❑ *The force would be composed of troops from NATO countries.* ❑ *Protein molecules compose all the complex working parts of living cells.* **2** V-T/V-I When someone **composes** a piece of music, they write it. ❑ *Vivaldi composed a large number of very fine concertos.* **3** V-T If you **compose** something such as a letter, poem, or speech, you write it, often using a lot of concentration or skill. [FORMAL] ❑ *He started at once to compose a reply to Anna.* →see **music**

1 타동사 조립하다, 조직하다, 구성하다 ❑ 그 부대는 나토 국가들에서 보내 온 병력들로 구성될 것이었다. ❑ 단백질 분자가 살아 있는 세포의 모든 복잡한 작동 부위들을 구성한다. **2** 타동사/자동사 작곡하다 ❑ 비발디는 대단히 멋진 협주곡을 많이 작곡했다. **3** 타동사 (시 또는 글 등을) 쓰다, 작문하다 [격식체] ❑ 그는 즉각 애너에게 보내는 답장을 쓰기 시작했다.

D

E

com|pos|er /kəmpo͞ozər/ (composers) N-COUNT A **composer** is a person who writes music, especially classical music. ❑ *...music by Tchaikovsky, Strauss, Mozart, Puccini, Grieg, and other great composers.* →see **music**

가산명사 작곡가 ❑ 차이코프스키, 슈트라우스, 모차르트, 푸치니, 그리그와 그 밖의 위대한 작곡가들의 음악

F

com|po|site /kɒmpəzɪt, BRIT kɒmpəzaɪt/ (composites) ADJ A **composite** object or item is made up of several different things, parts, or substances. ❑ *Galton devised a method of creating composite pictures in which the features of different faces were superimposed over one another.* ● N-COUNT **Composite** is also a noun. [usu sing, oft N of n] ❑ *Spain is a composite of diverse traditions and people.*

형용사 혼성의, 합성의 ❑ 골턴은 여러 다른 얼굴 형태가 서로 겹쳐지는 합성 사진을 만드는 방법을 고안해 냈다. ● 가산명사 혼합물, 합성물 ❑ 스페인은 다양한 전통과 민족이 혼합된 나라이다.

G

H

com|po|si|tion /kɒmpəzɪʃᵊn/ (compositions) **1** N-UNCOUNT When you talk about the **composition** of something, you are referring to the way in which its various parts are put together and arranged. ❑ *Television has transformed the size and social composition of the audience at great sporting occasions.* **2** N-COUNT The **compositions** of a composer, painter, or other artist are the works of art that they have produced. ❑ *Mozart's compositions are undoubtedly amongst the world's greatest.* →see **orchestra**

1 불가산명사 구성, 조직 ❑ 텔레비전은 대형 스포츠 행사에서 관객의 규모와 사회적 구성을 변화시켜 왔다. **2** 가산명사 (음악 또는 미술 등의) 작품 ❑ 모차르트의 작품들은 의심의 여지이 세계 최고에 속한다.

I

J

com|post /kɒmpo͞ost, BRIT kɒmpɒst/ (composts) **1** N-UNCOUNT **Compost** is a mixture of decayed plants and vegetable waste which is added to the soil to help plants grow. ❑ *...a small compost heap.* **2** N-MASS **Compost** is specially treated soil that you buy and use to grow seeds and plants in pots. ❑ *...a 75-litre bag of compost.*

1 불가산명사 퇴비, 혼합 비료 ❑ 작은 퇴비 더미 **2** 물질명사 배양토 ❑ 배양토 75리터들이 한 자루

K

L

com|po|sure /kəmpo͞oʒər/ N-UNCOUNT **Composure** is the appearance or feeling of calm and the ability to control your feelings. [FORMAL] ❑ *For once Dimbleby lost his composure. It was all he could do to stop tears of mirth falling down his cheeks.*

불가산명사 침착, 평정 [격식체] ❑ 딤블비는 단 한 번 평정을 잃었다. 기쁨의 눈물이 뺨을 타고 흘러내리는 것을 막기 위해 그렇게 할 수밖에 없었다.

M

com|pound /kɒmpaʊnd/ (compounds) **1** N-COUNT A **compound** is an enclosed area of land that is used for a particular purpose. ❑ *Police fired on them as they fled into the embassy compound.* **2** N-COUNT In chemistry, a **compound** is a substance that consists of two or more elements. ❑ *Organic compounds contain carbon in their molecules.* **3** N-COUNT If something is a **compound of** different things, it consists of those things. [FORMAL] ❑ *Honey is basically a compound of water, two types of sugar, vitamins, and enzymes.* **4** ADJ **Compound** is used to indicate that something consists of two or more parts or things. [ADJ n] ❑ *...a tall shrub with shiny compound leaves.* **5** ADJ In grammar, a **compound** noun, adjective, or verb is one that is made up of two or more words, for example "fire engine," "bottle-green," and "force-feed." [ADJ n] →see **element**

1 가산명사 (특정 용도의) 부지, 구내 ❑ 그들이 대사관 관내로 달아나자 경찰이 발포했다. **2** 가산명사 화합물 ❑ 유기 화합물은 분자 속에 탄소를 함유한다. **3** 가산명사 혼합물 [격식체] ❑ 꿀은 기본적으로 물과 두 가지 종류의 당, 비타민, 그리고 효소의 혼합물이다. **4** 형용사 합성의, 복합의 ❑ 윤기가 흐르는 겹잎을 가진 키 큰 관목 **5** 형용사 합성의

N

O

P

com|pound in|ter|est N-UNCOUNT **Compound interest** is interest that is calculated both on an original sum of money and on interest which has previously been added to the sum. Compare **simple interest**. [BUSINESS]

불가산명사 복리 [경제]

Q

com|pre|hend /kɒmprɪhend/ (comprehends, comprehending, comprehended) V-T/V-I If you cannot **comprehend** something, you cannot understand it. [FORMAL] [with brd-neg] ❑ *I just cannot comprehend your attitude.*

타동사/자동사 이해하다 [격식체] ❑ 네 태도를 이해할 수가 없다.

R

com|pre|hen|sion /kɒmprɪhenʃᵊn/ (comprehensions) **1** N-UNCOUNT **Comprehension** is the ability to understand something. [FORMAL] ❑ *This was utterly beyond her comprehension.* **2** N-UNCOUNT **Comprehension** is full knowledge and understanding of the meaning of something. [FORMAL] ❑ *They turned to one another with the same expression of dawning comprehension, surprise, and relief.* **3** N-VAR When students do **comprehension**, they do an exercise to find out how well they understand a piece of spoken or written language.

1 불가산명사 이해력 [격식체] ❑ 이것은 완전히 그녀의 이해력을 넘어서는 것이었다. **2** 불가산명사 이해 [격식체] ❑ 그들은 점점 분명해지는 이해와 놀라움, 안도감을 담은 똑같은 표정을 지으며 서로를 향해 눈길을 돌렸다. **3** 가산명사 또는 불가산명사 독해 문제, 청해 문제

S

T

com|pre|hen|sive ♦◇◇ /kɒmprɪhensɪv/ (comprehensives) **1** ADJ Something that is **comprehensive** includes everything that is needed or relevant. ❑ *The Rough Guide to Nepal is a comprehensive guide to the region.* **2** N-COUNT; N-IN-NAMES In Britain, a **comprehensive** is a state school in which children of all abilities are taught together. ❑ *...Birmingham's inner-city comprehensives.* ● ADJ **Comprehensive** is also an adjective. [ADJ n] ❑ *He left comprehensive school at the age of 16.*

1 형용사 포괄적인 ❑ '네팔 길잡이'는 그 지역에 대한 포괄적인 여행 안내서이다. **2** 가산명사; 이름명사 일반 공립학교 ❑ 버밍엄 도심의 일반 공립학교들 ● 형용사 일반 공립학교의 ❑ 그는 16세 때 학교를 마쳤다.

U

V

com|pre|hen|sive|ly /kɒmprɪhensɪvli/ ADV Something that is done **comprehensively** is done thoroughly. ❑ *She was comprehensively outplayed by Coetzer.*

부사 철저히, 완전히 ❑ 그녀는 쿠처에게 완패했다.

W

com|press /kəmpres/ (compresses, compressing, compressed) **1** V-T/V-I When you **compress** something or when it **compresses**, it is pressed or squeezed so that it takes up less space. ❑ *Poor posture, sitting or walking slouched over, compresses the body's organs.* ● **com|pres|sion** /kəmpreʃᵊn/ N-UNCOUNT ❑ *The compression of the wood is easily achieved.* **2** V-T If you **compress** something such as a piece of writing or a description, you make it shorter. ❑ *He never understood how to organize or compress large masses of material.* **3** V-T If an event **is compressed into** a short space of time, it is given less time to happen than normal or

1 타동사/자동사 압축하다; 압축되다 ❑ 구부정하게 앉거나 걷는 나쁜 자세는 신체 기관을 압박한다. ● 불가산명사 ❑ 목재의 압축은 쉽게 이루어진다. **2** 타동사 압축하다, 줄이다 ❑ 그는 방대한 양의 자료를 체계화하거나 압축하는 방법을 절대로 이해하지 못했다. **3** 타동사 단축되다 ❑ 네 번에 걸친 토론회는 유례없이 짧은 8일이라는 기간으로 단축될 것이다.

X

Y

Z

previously. [usu passive] ❑ *The four debates will be compressed into an unprecedentedly short eight-day period.*

com|prise /kəmpraɪz/ (**comprises, comprising, comprised**) v-t If you say that something **comprises** or **is comprised of** a number of things or people, you mean it has them as its parts or members. [FORMAL] ❑ *The special cabinet committee comprises Mr. Brown, Mr. Mandelson, and Mr. Straw.* ❑ *The task force is comprised of congressional leaders, cabinet heads, and administration officials.*

타동사 포함하다; 구성되다 [격식체] ❑ 특별 각료 위원회는 브라운 씨와 멘델슨 씨, 그리고 스트로 씨로 이루어져 있다. ❑ 대책 위원회는 국회 지도자들과 정부 각료들, 그리고 정부 공직자들로 구성된다.

com|pro|mise ♦◇◇ /kɒmprəmaɪz/ (**compromises, compromising, compromised**) **1** N-VAR A **compromise** is a situation in which people accept something slightly different from what they really want, because of circumstances or because they are considering the wishes of other people. ❑ *Encourage your child to reach a compromise between what he wants and what you want.* **2** V-RECIP If you **compromise with** someone, you reach an agreement with them in which you both give up something that you originally wanted. You can also say that two people or groups **compromise**. ❑ *The government has compromised with its critics over monetary policies.* ❑ *"Nine," said I. "Nine thirty," tried he. We compromised on 9.15.* **3** V-T If someone **compromises** themselves or **compromises** their beliefs, they do something which damages their reputation for honesty, loyalty, or high moral principles. [DISAPPROVAL] ❑ *...members of the government who have compromised themselves by co-operating with the emergency committee.*

1 가산명사 또는 불가산명사 타협, 양보 ❑ 아이로 하여금 자기가 원하는 것과 당신이 원하는 것 사이에서 타협을 보도록 장려하세요. **2** 상호동사 타협하다, 절충하다 ❑ 정부는 재정 정책에 있어서 비판자들과 타협을 해 왔다. ❑ "9"라고 내가 말했다. "9.3"이라고 그가 말했다. 우리는 9.15에 타협했다. **3** 타동사 더럽히다, 훼손하다 [탐탁잖음] ❑ 비상 대책 위원회에 협력함으로써 스스로의 명예를 더럽힌 공직자들

com|pro|mis|ing /kɒmprəmaɪzɪŋ/ ADJ If you describe information or a situation as **compromising**, you mean that it reveals an embarrassing or guilty secret about someone. ❑ *How had this compromising picture come into the possession of the press?*

형용사 명예를 훼손하는 ❑ 이런 명예를 훼손할 만한 사진이 어떻게 언론의 손에 들어갔을까?

comp|trol|ler /kəntroʊlər, kɒmp-/ (**comptrollers**) N-COUNT A **comptroller** is someone who is in charge of the accounts of a business or a government department; used mainly in official titles. [BUSINESS] ❑ *...Robert Clarke, U.S. Comptroller of the Currency.*

가산명사 감사원장, 감사관 [경제] ❑ 미국 통화 감사원장 로버트 클라크

com|pul|sion /kəmpʌlʃ°n/ (**compulsions**) **1** N-COUNT A **compulsion** is a strong desire to do something, which you find difficult to control. ❑ *He felt a sudden compulsion to drop the bucket and run.* **2** N-UNCOUNT If someone uses **compulsion** in order to get you to do something, they force you to do it, for example by threatening to punish you if you do not do it. ❑ *Many universities argued that students learned more when they were in classes out of choice rather than compulsion.*

1 가산명사 강한 충동 ❑ 그는 갑자기 양동이를 떨어뜨리고 뛰고 싶은 강한 충동을 느꼈다. **2** 불가산명사 강요, 강제 ❑ 다수의 대학들이 학생들이 강요가 아닌 선택에 의해 수업을 받을 때 더 많은 것을 배운다고 주장했다.

com|pul|sive /kəmpʌlsɪv/ **1** ADJ You use **compulsive** to describe people or their behavior when they cannot stop doing something wrong, harmful, or unnecessary. [ADJ n] ❑ *...a compulsive liar.* ❑ *He was a compulsive gambler and often heavily in debt.* **2** ADJ If a book or television program is **compulsive**, it is so interesting that you do not want to stop reading or watching it. ❑ *The BBC series Hot Chefs is compulsive viewing.*

1 형용사 강박감에 사로잡힌 ❑ 거짓말을 하지 않고는 못 배기는 사람 ❑ 그는 도박을 하지 않고는 못 배기는 사람이었고 종종 큰 빚을 졌다. **2** 형용사 눈을 뗄 수 없는, 매우 재미있는 ❑ 비비시의 시리즈물 '멋진 요리사들'은 눈을 떼지 못하고 보게 만든다.

com|pul|so|ry /kəmpʌlsəri/ ADJ If something is **compulsory**, you must do it or accept it, because it is the law or because someone in a position of authority says you must. ❑ *In East Germany learning Russian was compulsory.*

형용사 의무적인; 강제적인 ❑ 동독에서는 러시아 어를 의무적으로 배워야 했다.

com|pu|ta|tion|al /kɒmpyuteɪʃən°l/ ADJ **Computational** means using computers. ❑ *Students may pursue research in any aspect of computational linguistics.*

형용사 컴퓨터를 사용하는 ❑ 학생들은 컴퓨터 언어학의 모든 측면에 대해 연구를 수행할 수 있다.

com|put|er ♦♦◇ /kəmpyutər/ (**computers**) N-COUNT A **computer** is an electronic machine that can store and deal with large amounts of information. [also by/on N] ❑ *The data are then fed into a computer.* ❑ *The company installed a $650,000 computer system.* →see also **personal computer**, **office** →see Word Web: **computer**

가산명사 컴퓨터 ❑ 그런 다음 데이터가 컴퓨터에 입력된다. ❑ 그 회사는 650,000달러짜리 컴퓨터 시스템을 설치했다.

com|put|er|ate /kəmpyutərət/ ADJ If someone is **computerate**, they have enough skill and knowledge to be able to use a computer.

형용사 컴퓨터 사용 능력이 있는

Word Web   computer

Computers have revolutionized the way we live. Particularly exciting are the advances in the field of medicine. Computer **chips** allow deaf people to hear. Doctors recently placed an implant in the brain of a paralyzed man who could not speak. Soon he learned to move a **cursor** on a computer **screen** just by thinking. By pointing to letters and icons, he was able to express his ideas. Voice recognition **software** allows handicapped people to use a computer without a **keyboard**. Scientists are now experimenting with **devices** that will permit blind people to see.

a b c d e f g h i j k l m n o p q r s t u v w x y z

com|put|er game (computer games) N-COUNT A **computer game** is a game that you play on a computer or on a small portable piece of electronic equipment.

가산명사 컴퓨터 게임

com|put|er|ize /kəmpyutəraɪz/ (**computerizes, computerizing, computerized**) [BRIT also **computerise**] V-T/V-I To **computerize** a system, process, or type of work means to arrange for a lot of the work to be done by computer. ❏ *I'm trying to make a spreadsheet up to computerize everything that's done by hand at the moment.*

[영국영어 computerise] 타동사/자동사 컴퓨터로 처리하다; 전산화하다 ❏ 나는 현재 수작업으로 이루어지고 있는 모든 것들을 전산화하기 위해 스프레드시트를 작성하려 하고 있다.

com|put|er|ized /kəmpyutəraɪzd/ [BRIT also **computerised**] **1** ADJ A **computerized** system, process, or business is one in which the work is done by computer. ❏ *The National Cancer Institute now has a computerized system that can quickly provide information.* **2** ADJ **Computerized** information is stored on a computer. ❏ *Computerized data bases are proliferating fast.*

[영국영어 computerised] **1** 형용사 전산화된 ❏ 현재 국립 암 연구소는 신속히 정보를 제공할 수 있는 전산화된 시스템을 갖추고 있다. **2** 형용사 컴퓨터에 저장된 ❏ 컴퓨터에 저장된 데이터베이스가 급격히 증가하고 있다.

computer-literate ADJ If someone is **computer-literate**, they have enough skill and knowledge to be able to use a computer. ❏ *We look for applicants who are numerate, computer-literate, and energetic self-starters.*

형용사 컴퓨터 사용 능력이 있는 ❏ 계산 능력이 있고, 컴퓨터를 사용할 줄 아는 자발적이고 활동적인 지원자를 찾습니다.

com|put|ing /kəmpyutɪŋ/ **1** N-UNCOUNT **Computing** is the activity of using a computer and writing programs for it. ❏ *Courses range from cookery to computing.* **2** ADJ **Computing** means relating to computers and their use. [ADJ n] ❏ *Many graduates are employed in the electronics and computing industries.*

1 불가산명사 컴퓨터 사용 ❏ 강좌는 요리법 강좌에서 컴퓨터 사용 강좌까지 다양하다. **2** 형용사 컴퓨터의 ❏ 많은 졸업생들이 전자 산업이나 컴퓨터 산업에 고용된다.

com|rade /kɒmræd, BRIT kɒmreɪd/ (**comrades**) N-COUNT Your **comrades** are your friends, especially friends that you share a difficult or dangerous situation with. [LITERARY] ❏ *Unlike so many of his comrades he survived the war.*

가산명사 동료, 동지 [문예체] ❏ 그 많은 동료들과는 달리 그 자신은 전쟁에서 살아남았다.

con /kɒn/ (**cons, conning, conned**) **1** V-T If someone **cons** you, they persuade you to do something or believe something by telling you things that are not true. [INFORMAL] ❏ *He claimed that the businessman had conned him of £10,000.* ❏ *White conned his way into a job as a warehouseman with Dutch airline, KLM.* **2** N-COUNT A **con** is a trick in which someone deceives you by telling you something that is not true. [INFORMAL] ❏ *Snacks that offer miraculous weight loss are a con.* **3 pros and cons** →see **pro**

1 타동사 속이다, 사기치다 [비격식체] ❏ 그는 그 사업가가 자신에게서 1만 파운드를 사기쳤다고 주장했다. **2** 화이트는 신분을 감추고 네덜란드 항공사 케이엘엠에 창고 계원으로 잠입해 들어갔다. **2** 가산명사 사기, 협잡 [비격식체] ❏ 기적적으로 체중을 줄여 준다고 하는 간편식은 사기다.

con|ceal /kənsil/ (**conceals, concealing, concealed**) **1** V-T If you **conceal** something, you cover it or hide it carefully. ❏ *Frances decided to conceal the machine behind a hinged panel.* **2** V-T If you **conceal** a piece of information or a feeling, you do not let other people know about it. ❏ *Robert could not conceal his relief.* **3** V-T If something **conceals** something else, it covers it and prevents it from being seen. ❏ *...a pair of carved Indian doors which conceal a built-in cupboard.*

1 타동사 숨기다, 비밀로 하다 ❏ 프랜시스는 돌쩌귀가 달린 벽널 뒤에 그 기계를 숨기로 결심했다. **2** 타동사 감추다, 드러내지 않다 ❏ 로버트는 안도감을 감출 수가 없었다. **3** 타동사 덮어 가리다, 숨기다 ❏ 붙박이 찬장을 가리고 있는 한 쌍의 인도식 새김문

con|ceal|ment /kənsilmənt/ N-UNCOUNT **Concealment** is the state of being hidden or the act of hiding something. ❏ *The criminals vainly sought concealment from the searchlight.*

불가산명사 숨김, 은폐; 숨음 ❏ 범인들은 탐조등을 피해 몸을 숨기려 했지만 허사였다.

con|cede ◆◇◇ /kənsid/ (**concedes, conceding, conceded**) **1** V-T If you **concede** something, you admit, often unwillingly, that it is true or correct. ❏ *Bess finally conceded that Nancy was right.* ❏ *"Well," he conceded, "I do sometimes mumble a bit."* **2** V-T If you **concede** something to someone, you allow them to have it as a right or privilege. ❏ *Poland's Communist government conceded the right to establish independent trade unions.* **3** V-T If you **concede** something, you give it to the person who has been trying to get it from you. ❏ *A strike by some ten thousand bank employees has ended after the government conceded some of their demands.* **4** V-T If you **concede** a game, contest, or argument, you end it by admitting that you can no longer win. ❏ *Reiner, 56, has all but conceded the race to his rival.* **5** V-T If you **concede** defeat, you accept that you have lost a struggle. ❏ *Airtours conceded defeat in its attempt to take control of holiday industry rival Owners Abroad.*

1 타동사 인정하다, 시인하다 ❏ 베스가 마침내 낸시가 옳다는 것을 인정했다. ❏ "뭐 내가 가끔씩 조금 중얼거리기는 하지."라고 그가 시인했다. **2** 타동사 주다, 부여하다 ❏ 폴란드 공산당 정부가 독립된 산별 노조 결성권을 주었다. **3** 타동사 양보하다, 허용하다 ❏ 대략 만여 명이 참가한 은행 파업이 정부가 요구를 일부 수용하면서 일단락됐다. **4** 타동사 패배를 선언하다 ❏ 56세의 레이너가 상대에게 거의 패배를 선언했다. **5** 타동사 패배를 인정하다 ❏ 에어투어스가 여행업 라이벌 오너스 어브로드의 경영권을 쥐려다 실패했음을 인정했다.

con|ceiv|able /kənsivəb³l/ ADJ If something is **conceivable**, you can imagine it or believe it. ❏ *Without their support the project would not have been conceivable.*

형용사 상상할 수 있는, 생각할 수 있는 ❏ 그들의 지지가 없었더라면, 프로젝트는 상상할 수 없었을 것이다.

con|ceive /kənsiv/ (**conceives, conceiving, conceived**) **1** V-T/V-I If you cannot **conceive of** something, you cannot imagine it or believe it. [usu with brd-neg] ❏ *I just can't even conceive of that quantity of money.* **2** V-T/V-I If you **conceive** something **as** a particular thing, you consider it to be that thing. ❏ *The ancients conceived the earth as afloat in water.* ❏ *We conceive of the family as being in a constant state of change.* **3** V-T/V-I If you **conceive** a plan or idea, you think of it and work out how it can be done. ❏ *She had conceived the idea of a series of novels, each of which would reveal some aspect of Chinese life.* **4** V-T/V-I When a woman **conceives**, she becomes pregnant. ❏ *Women, he says, should give up alcohol before they plan to conceive.*

1 타동사/자동사 상상하다 ❏ 돈의 액수가 상상조차 안 될 정도로 어마어마하다. **2** 타동사/자동사 생각하다 ❏ 고대인들은 지구가 물 위에 떠 있는 것으로 생각했다. ❏ 우리는 가족의 형태가 끊임없이 변한다고 생각한다. **3** 타동사/자동사 품다, 생각해 내다 ❏ 그녀는 소설 시리즈를 펴내 각각 중국인의 삶의 특정한 모습을 그릴 생각을 품어 왔었다. **4** 타동사/자동사 임신하다 ❏ 그는 여성들이 아이를 갖기 이전에 술을 끊어야 한다고 말한다.

con|cen|trate ◆◇◇ /kɒnsⁿntreɪt/ (**concentrates, concentrating, concentrated**) **1** V-T/V-I If you **concentrate on** something, or **concentrate** your mind **on** it, you give all your attention to it. ❏ *It was up to him to concentrate on his studies and make something of himself.* ❏ *At work you need to be able to concentrate.* **2** V-T If something **is concentrated in** an area, it is all there rather than being spread around. [usu passive] ❏ *Italy's industrial districts are concentrated in its north-central and north-eastern regions.*

1 타동사/자동사 집중하다 ❏ 공부에 집중해서 성공하는 것은 전적으로 그에게 달려 있었다. ❏ 일할 때는 집중할 수 있어야 해. **2** 타동사 집중되어 있다 ❏ 이탈리아의 산업 단지는 중북부 지방과 동북 지방에 집중되어 있다.

con|cen|trat|ed /kɒnsⁿntreɪtɪd/ **1** ADJ A **concentrated** liquid has been increased in strength by having water removed from it. ❏ *Sweeten dishes sparingly with honey, or concentrated apple or pear juice.* **2** ADJ A **concentrated** activity is directed with great intensity in one place. ❏ *...a more concentrated effort to reach out to troubled kids.*

1 형용사 농축된 ❏ 꿀 또는 농축 사과즙이나 배즙을 약간만 사용해서 음식의 단맛을 내세요. **2** 형용사 집중된 ❏ 어려운 아이들을 돕기 위한 좀 더 집중된 노력

con|cen|tra|tion ◆◇◇ /kɒnsⁿntreɪʃ³n/ (**concentrations**) **1** N-UNCOUNT **Concentration on** something involves giving all your attention to it. ❏ *Neal kept interrupting, breaking my concentration.* **2** N-VAR A **concentration of** something is a large amount of it or large numbers of it in a small area. ❏ *The area has one of the world's greatest concentrations of wildlife.* **3** N-VAR The **concentration of** a substance is the proportion of essential ingredients or substances in it. ❏ *pH is a measure of the concentration of free hydrogen atoms in a solution.*

1 불가산명사 집중, 전념 ❏ 닐이 계속해서 방해해서 나는 집중할 수가 없었다. **2** 가산명사 또는 불가산명사 집중, 집결 ❏ 이 지역은 세계에서 야생동물이 가장 많이 집중되어 있는 곳 중 하나이다. **3** 가산명사 또는 불가산명사 농도 ❏ pH는 용액의 수소 이온 농도 측정 단위이다.

con|cen|tra|tion camp (concentration camps) N-COUNT A **concentration camp** is a prison in which large numbers of ordinary people are kept in very bad conditions, usually during a war. □ ...the ruins of the Nazi concentration camp at Buchenwald.

가산명사 수용소 □ 부헨발트의 나치 수용소 잔해

con|cept ◆◇◇ /kɒnsept/ (concepts) N-COUNT A **concept** is an idea or abstract principle. □ She added that the concept of arranged marriages is misunderstood in the west.

가산명사 개념 □ 그녀는 서양에서 중매결혼의 개념이 잘못 이해되고 있다고 덧붙였다.

con|cep|tion /kənsepʃən/ (conceptions) **1** N-VAR A **conception of** something is an idea that you have of it in your mind. □ My conception of a garden was based on gardens I had visited in England. **2** N-VAR **Conception** is the process in which the egg in a woman is fertilized and she becomes pregnant. □ Six weeks after conception your baby is the size of your little fingernail.

1 가산명사 또는 불가산명사 개념, 생각 □ 내가 생각하는 정원의 개념은 영국에서 방문한 여러 정원에서 나온 것이다. **2** 가산명사 또는 불가산명사 임신, 수태 □ 임신 6주된 태아의 크기는 새끼손가락 손톱만하다.

con|cern ◆◆◆ /kənsɜrn/ (concerns, concerning, concerned) **1** N-UNCOUNT **Concern** is worry about a situation. □ The group has expressed concern about reports of political violence in Africa. □ The move follows growing public concern over the spread of the disease. **2** V-T If something **concerns** you, it worries you. [no cont] □ The growing number of people seeking refuge in Thailand is beginning to concern Western aid agencies. ● **con|cerned** ADJ □ Academics and employers are deeply concerned that students are not sufficiently prepared mathematically for university courses. **3** N-COUNT A **concern** is a fact or situation that worries you. □ His concern was that people would know that he was responsible. **4** N-VAR **Concern for** someone is a feeling that you want them to be happy, safe, and well. If you do something out of **concern for** someone, you do it because you want them to be happy, safe, and well. □ Without her care and concern, he had no chance at all. **5** V-T If you **concern yourself with** something, you give it attention because you think that it is important. □ I didn't concern myself with politics. ● **con|cerned** ADJ [v-link ADJ with n] □ The agency is more concerned with making arty ads than understanding its clients' businesses. **6** V-T If something such as a book or a piece of information **concerns** a particular subject, it is about that subject. [no cont] □ The bulk of the book concerns Sandy's two middle-aged children. ● **con|cerned** ADJ [v-link ADJ with n] □ Randolph's work was exclusively concerned with the effects of pollution on health. **7** V-T If a situation, event, or activity **concerns** you, it affects or involves you. [no cont] □ It was just a little unfinished business from my past, and it doesn't concern you at all. ● **con|cerned** ADJ [n ADJ, v-link ADJ in/with n] □ It's a very stressful situation for everyone concerned. **8** N-SING If a situation or problem is your **concern**, it is something that you have a duty or responsibility to be involved with. □ The technical aspects were the concern of the Army. **9** N-COUNT You can refer to a company or business as a **concern**, usually when you are describing what type of company or business it is. [FORMAL, BUSINESS] □ If not a large concern, Queensbury Nursery was at least a successful one. **10** PHRASE If a company is a **going concern**, it is actually doing business, rather than having stopped trading or not yet having started trading. [BUSINESS] □ The receivers will always prefer to sell a business as a going concern.

1 불가산명사 근심, 우려 □ 그 단체는 아프리카 정치 폭력에 관한 보고서에 대해 우려를 표명해 왔다. □ 이번 조치는 질병 확산에 대한 국민들의 우려가 커지면서 나왔다. **2** 타동사 걱정하다 □ 태국으로 피신하는 사람들이 증가하면서 서방 구호 단체의 우려를 낳기 시작했다. ● 근심하는, 염려하는 형용사 □ 학생들이 대학 과정에 적합한 수학 능력을 충분히 갖추고 있지 않아 대학과 기업이 크게 염려하고 있다. **3** 가산명사 걱정거리 □ 그는 사람들이 자기에게 책임이 있다는 사실을 알아 봐 걱정이었다. **4** 가산명사 또는 불가산명사 관심, 배려 □ 그녀의 보살핌과 관심 없이는 그에게 기회가 전혀 없었다. **5** 타동사 관심을 가지다, 관여하다 □ 나는 정치에는 관심이 없었다. ● 관심 있는, 신경 쓰는 형용사 □ 그 광고 업체는 고객의 사업 특성에 대한 이해보다 예술 같은 광고를 만드는 데 더 신경을 쓴다. **6** 타동사 ~을 주제로 하다, ~에 관하다 □ 이 두꺼운 책은 이제 모두 중년이 된 샌디의 두 자녀에 대한 이야기이다. ● ~에 관한 형용사 □ 랜돌프의 작품은 전적으로 환경오염이 건강에 미치는 영향을 다루었다. **7** 타동사 ~와 관계가 있다 □ 그건 아직 정리 안 된 사소한 내 과거 문제야, 너와는 전혀 관계없어. ● 관계된 형용사 □ 이는 관계자 모두에게 매우 스트레스를 주는 상황이다. **8** 단수명사 일, 소관 □ 기술적인 문제는 육군 소관이었다. **9** 가산명사 ~한 유형의 회사 [격식체, 경제] □ 퀸스베리 너서리는 비록 큰 회사는 아니지만 적어도 성공한 기업이었다. **10** 구 영업 중인 회사 [경제] □ 법정 관리인은 기업 매각 시 항상 영업 중인 회사로 팔고 싶어 할 것이다.

con|cerned ◆◇◇ /kənsɜrnd/ **1** →see concern **2** ADJ If you are **concerned to** do something, you want to do it because you think it is important. [v-link ADJ to-inf] □ We were very concerned to keep the staff informed about what we were doing.

2 형용사 ~하기를 바라는 □ 우리는 직원들이 우리가 어떤 일을 하는지 알고 있기를 많이 바랐다.

con|cern|ing /kənsɜrnɪŋ/ PREP You use **concerning** to indicate what a question or piece of information is about. [FORMAL] □ For more information concerning the club contact I. Coldwell.

전치사 ~에 관해 [격식체] □ 클럽에 관해 더 문의할 사항이 있으면 아이 콜드웰에게 연락하세요.

con|cert ◆◇◇ /kɒnsɜrt/ (concerts) **1** N-COUNT A **concert** is a performance of music. □ ...a short concert of piano music. □ I've been to plenty of live rock concerts. **2** PHRASE If a musician or group of musicians appears **in concert**, they are giving a live performance. □ I want people to remember Elvis in concert.
→see Word Web: concert

1 가산명사 콘서트 □ 소규모 피아노 콘서트 □ 나는 라이브 록 콘서트에 많이 가봤다. **2** 구 라이브 공연의 □ 사람들이 라이브 공연 중인 엘비스의 모습을 기억하길 바란다.

a
b
c
d
e
f
g
h
i
j
k
l
m
n
o
p
q
r
s
t
u
v
w
x
y
z

A
B
C
D
E
F
G
H
I
J
K
L
M
N
O
P
Q
R
S
T
U
V
W
X
Y
Z

con|cert|ed /kənsɜrtɪd/ 🔟 ADJ A **concerted** action is done by several people or groups working together. [ADJ n] ❑ *Martin Parry, author of the report, says it's time for concerted action by world leaders.* 🔟 ADJ If you make a **concerted** effort to do something, you try very hard to do it. [ADJ n] ❑ *He made a concerted effort to win me away from my steady, sweet but boring boyfriend.*

🔟 형용사 공동의, 함께하는 ❑ 전세계 지도자들이 함께 행동해야 할 때라고 보고서 저자 마틴 패리는 말한다. 🔟 형용사 집중적인 ❑ 그는 한결같고 사랑스럽지만 지루한 남자친구에게서 나를 빼앗기 위해 갖은 노력을 다했다.

con|cer|to /kəntʃɛərtoʊ/ (concertos) N-COUNT A **concerto** is a piece of music written for one or more solo instruments and an orchestra. ❑ *...Tchaikovsky's First Piano Concerto.* →see **music**

가산명사 콘체르토, 협주곡 ❑ 차이코프스키 피아노 협주곡 1번

con|ces|sion ♦◇◇ /kənsɛʃ³n/ (concessions) 🔟 N-COUNT If you make a **concession to** someone, you agree to let them do or have something, especially in order to end an argument or conflict. ❑ *It appears that Britain has made sweeping concessions to China in order to reach a settlement.* 🔟 N-COUNT A **concession** is a special right or privilege that is given to someone. ❑ *The government has granted concessions to three private telephone companies.* 🔟 N-COUNT A **concession** is an arrangement where someone is given the right to sell a product or to run a business, especially in a building belonging to another business. [mainly AM, BUSINESS; BRIT usually **franchise**] ❑ *...the man who ran the catering concession at the Rob Roy Links in Palominas.* 🔟 N-COUNT A **concession** is a special price which is lower than the usual price and which is often given to old people, students, and the unemployed. [BRIT] ❑ *Open daily; admission £1.10 with concessions for children and OAPs.*

🔟 가산명사 양보 ❑ 타협에 이르기 위해 영국이 중국에 대폭 양보한 것으로 보인다. 🔟 가산명사 허가, 사업권 ❑ 정부가 민간 통신 업체 세 곳에 허가를 내주었다. 🔟 가산명사 구내 영업 허가 [주로 미국영어, 경제; 영국영어 대개 franchise] ❑ 팔로미나스의 롭로이 링크스에서 음식 조달 사업을 하는 사람 🔟 가산명사 특별 할인가 [영국영어] ❑ 주간 영업; 입장료 1.1파운드, 어린이 및 연금 생활자 할인

Word Partnership	concession의 연어
V.	**make a** concession 🔟 🔟
PREP.	concessions **for** *someone* 🔟 🔟
N.	**tax** concessions 🔟

con|ces|sion|aire /kənsɛʃənɛər/ (concessionaires) N-COUNT A **concessionaire** is a person or company that has the right to sell a product or to run a business, especially in a building belonging to another business. [AM, BUSINESS; BRIT **franchisee, franchise-holder**] ❑ *Concessionaires and shop owners report retail sales are up.*

가산명사 허가 소유자 [미국영어, 경제; 영국영어 franchisee, franchise-holder] ❑ 허가 소유자와 상점 주인들이 매출 신장 소식을 전하고 있다.

con|cili|ation /kənsɪlieɪʃ³n/ N-UNCOUNT **Conciliation** is willingness to end a disagreement or the process of ending a disagreement. ❑ *Resolving the dispute will require a mood of conciliation on both sides.*

불가산명사 화해, 타협 ❑ 분쟁 해결을 위해서 양쪽 모두 화해 분위기를 조성할 필요가 있다.

con|cilia|tory /kənsɪliətɔri, BRIT kənsɪliətri/ ADJ When you are **conciliatory** in your actions or behavior, you show that you are willing to end a disagreement with someone. ❑ *The next time he spoke he used a more conciliatory tone.*

형용사 타협적인, 달래는 ❑ 그는 다음번에 조금 더 타협적인 어조로 말했다.

con|cise /kənsaɪs/ 🔟 ADJ Something that is **concise** says everything that is necessary without using any unnecessary words. ❑ *Burton's text is concise and informative.* ● con|cise|ly ADV [ADV with v] ❑ *He'd delivered his report clearly and concisely.* 🔟 ADJ A **concise** edition of a book, especially a dictionary, is shorter than the original edition. [ADJ n] ❑ *...Sotheby's Concise Encyclopedia of Porcelain.*

🔟 형용사 간단명료한 ❑ 버튼의 글은 간단명료하고 유익하다. ● 간단명료하게 부사 ❑ 그는 명확하고 간결하게 보고서 내용을 전달했다. 🔟 형용사 축약판의 ❑ 소더비에서 낸 "자기 백과사전 축약판"

con|clude ♦◇◇ /kənklud/ (concludes, concluding, concluded) 🔟 V-T If you **conclude** that something is true, you decide that it is true using the facts you know as a basis. ❑ *Larry had concluded that he had no choice but to accept Paul's words as the truth.* ❑ *So what can we conclude from this debate?* 🔟 V-T/V-I When you **conclude**, you say the last thing that you are going to say. [FORMAL] ❑ *"It's a waste of time," he concluded.* 🔟 V-T/V-I When something **concludes**, or when you **conclude** it, you end it. [FORMAL] ❑ *The evening concluded with dinner and speeches.* 🔟 V-RECIP If one person or group **concludes** an agreement, such as a treaty or business deal, **with** another, they arrange it. You can also say that two people or groups **conclude** an agreement. [FORMAL] ❑ *Mexico and the Philippines have both concluded agreements with their commercial bank creditors.*

🔟 타동사 결론짓다 ❑ 래리는 폴이 한 말을 사실로 받아들일 수밖에 없다고 결론지었다. ❑ 우리가 이 토론에서 얻을 수 있는 결론이 무엇입니까? 🔟 타동사/자동사 끝냈다 [격식체] ❑ "시간 낭비야."라는 말로 그가 끝을 맺었다. 🔟 타동사/자동사 끝나다; 끝내다 [격식체] ❑ 저녁 행사는 만찬과 연설로 끝이 났다. 🔟 상호동사 마무리 짓다 [격식체] ❑ 멕시코와 필리핀 모두 자국 상업은행 채권자들과 협약을 마무리 지었다.

Word Partnership	conclude의 연어
N.	conclude *something*, conclude **that** *something* 🔟 🔟
	conclude **a deal** 🔟
PRON.	**he/she** concluded 🔟

con|clu|sion ♦◇◇ /kənkluʒ³n/ (conclusions) 🔟 N-COUNT When you come to a **conclusion**, you decide that something is true after you have thought about it carefully and have considered all the relevant facts. ❑ *Over the years I've come to the conclusion that she's a very great musician.* 🔟 N-SING The **conclusion** of something is its ending. [also no det, usu with supp] ❑ *At the conclusion of the programme, I asked the children if they had any questions they wanted to ask me.* 🔟 N-SING The **conclusion** of a treaty or a business deal is the act of arranging it or agreeing on it. ❑ *...the expected conclusion of a free-trade agreement between Mexico and the United States.* 🔟 PHRASE You say "**in conclusion**" to indicate that what you are about to say is the last thing that you want to say. ❑ *In conclusion, walking is a cheap, safe, enjoyable, and readily available form of exercise.*

🔟 가산명사 결론 ❑ 나는 몇 년간 지켜보면서 그녀가 매우 훌륭한 음악가라는 결론을 내리게 되었다. 🔟 단수명사 결말, 끝 ❑ 프로그램 끝 무렵 나는 아이들에게 하고 싶은 질문이 있는지 물었다. 🔟 단수명사 체결, 마무리 ❑ 멕시코와 미국 간에 예상되는 자유 무역 협정 체결 🔟 구 마지막으로, 결론으로 ❑ 결론적으로 걷기는 싸고 안전하며 재미있고 언제나 쉽게 할 수 있는 운동이다.

Word Partnership	conclusion의 연어
V.	**come to a** conclusion, **draw a** conclusion, **reach a** conclusion 🔟
PREP.	conclusion **of** *something* 🔟 🔟
	in conclusion 🔟

con|clu|sive /kənklusɪv/ ADJ **Conclusive** evidence shows that something is certainly true. ❑ *Her attorneys claim there is no conclusive evidence that any murders took place.*

형용사 결정적인 ❑ 그녀의 변호인단은 살인이 일어났다는 결정적인 증거가 없다고 주장한다.

con|coct /kənkɒkt/ (concocts, concocting, concocted) **1** V-T If you **concoct** an excuse or explanation, you invent one that is not true. ❑ *Mr. Ferguson said the prisoner concocted the story to get a lighter sentence.* **2** V-T If you **concoct** something, especially something unusual, you make it by mixing several things together. ❑ *Eugene was concocting Rossini Cocktails from champagne and pureed raspberries.*

con|coc|tion /kənkɒkʃn/ (concoctions) N-COUNT A **concoction** is something that has been made out of several things mixed together. ❑ *...a concoction of honey, yogurt, oats, and apples.*

con|crete ◆◇◇ /kɒŋkriːt/ (concretes, concreting, concreted) **1** N-UNCOUNT **Concrete** is a substance used for building which is made by mixing together cement, sand, small stones, and water. ❑ *The posts have to be set in concrete.* ❑ *They had lain on sleeping bags on the concrete floor.* **2** V-T When you **concrete** something such as a path, you cover it with concrete. ❑ *He merely cleared and concreted the floors.* **3** ADJ You use **concrete** to indicate that something is definite and specific. ❑ *He had no concrete evidence.* ❑ *There were no concrete proposals on the table.* **4** ADJ A **concrete** object is a real, physical object. ❑ *...using concrete objects to teach addition and subtraction.* **5** ADJ A **concrete** noun is a noun that refers to a physical object rather than to a quality or idea. [ADJ n]

con|cur /kənkɜr/ (concurs, concurring, concurred) V-RECIP If one person **concurs** with another person, the two people agree. You can also say that two people **concur**. [FORMAL] ❑ *Local feeling does not necessarily concur with the press.* ❑ *Daniels and Franklin concurred in an investigator's suggestion that the police be commended.*

con|cur|rent /kənkɜrənt, BRIT kənkʌrənt/ ADJ **Concurrent** events or situations happen at the same time. ❑ *Galerie St. Etienne is holding three concurrent exhibitions.* ❑ *He will actually be serving three concurrent five-year sentences.* ● **con|cur|rent|ly** ADV [ADV with v] ❑ *He was jailed for 33 months to run concurrently with a sentence he is already serving for burglary.*

con|cus|sion /kənkʌʃn/ (concussions) N-VAR If you suffer **concussion** after a blow to your head, you lose consciousness or feel sick or confused. ❑ *Nicky was rushed to the hospital with concussion.*

con|demn ◆◇◇ /kəndem/ (condemns, condemning, condemned) **1** V-T If you **condemn** something, you say that it is very bad and unacceptable. ❑ *Political leaders united yesterday to condemn the latest wave of violence.* ❑ *Graham was right to condemn his players for lack of ability, attitude and application.* **2** V-T If someone **is condemned to** a punishment, they are given this punishment. [usu passive] ❑ *He was condemned to life imprisonment.* **3** V-T If circumstances **condemn** you to an unpleasant situation, they make it certain that you will suffer in that way. ❑ *Their lack of qualifications condemned them to a lifetime of boring, usually poorly-paid work.* **4** V-T If authorities **condemn** a building, they officially decide that it is not safe and must be pulled down or repaired. ❑ *State officials said the court's ruling clears the way for proceedings to condemn buildings in the area.* **5** →see also **condemned**

con|dem|na|tion /kɒndemneɪʃn/ (condemnations) N-VAR **Condemnation** is the act of saying that something or someone is very bad and unacceptable. ❑ *There was widespread condemnation of Saturday's killings.*

con|demned /kəndemd/ ADJ A **condemned** man or woman is going to be executed. ❑ *...prison officers who had sat with the condemned man during his last days.*

con|dense /kəndens/ (condenses, condensing, condensed) **1** V-T If you **condense** something, especially a piece of writing or speech, you make it shorter, usually by including only the most important parts. ❑ *We have learnt how to condense serious messages into short, self-contained sentences.* **2** V-I When a gas or vapor **condenses**, or **is condensed**, it changes into a liquid. ❑ *Water vapour condenses to form clouds.* →see **matter**, **water**

> **Word Link** *scend ≈ climbing : a*scend, *conde*scend, *de*scend

con|de|scend /kɒndɪsend/ (condescends, condescending, condescended) **1** V-T If someone **condescends** to do something, they agree to do it, but in a way which shows that they think they are better than other people and should not have to do it. [DISAPPROVAL] ❑ *When he condescended to speak, he contradicted himself three or four times in the space of half an hour.* **2** V-I If you say that someone **condescends to** other people, you are showing your disapproval of the fact that they behave in a way which shows that they think they are superior to other people. [DISAPPROVAL] ❑ *Don't condescend to me.*

con|de|scend|ing /kɒndɪsendɪŋ/ ADJ If you say that someone is **condescending**, you are showing your disapproval of the fact that they talk or behave in a way which shows that they think they are superior to other people. [DISAPPROVAL] ❑ *I'm fed up with your money and your whole condescending attitude.*

con|di|tion ◆◆◆ /kəndɪʃn/ (conditions, conditioning, conditioned) **1** N-SING If you talk about the **condition** of a person or thing, you are talking about the state that they are in, especially how good or bad their physical state is. [also no det, with suppl] ❑ *He remains in a critical condition in a California hospital.* ❑ *I received several compliments on the condition of my skin.* ❑ *The two-bedroom chalet is in good condition.* **2** N-PLURAL The **conditions** under which something is done or happens are all the factors or circumstances which directly affect it. ❑ *In ideal conditions, a devaluation will work by putting up the prices of imported goods while boosting exports.* **3** N-PLURAL The **conditions** in which people live or work are the factors which affect their comfort, safety, or health. ❑ *People are living in appalling conditions.* ❑ *He could not work in these conditions any longer.* **4** N-COUNT A **condition** is something which must happen or be done in order for something else to be possible, especially when this is written into a contract

---

1 타동사 꾸미다, 날조하다 ❑ 퍼거슨은 적은 형량을 받기 위해 수감자가 이야기를 날조했다고 말했다. **2** 타동사 섞어서 만들다 ❑ 유진은 샴페인과 산딸기 퓨레를 가지고 로시니 칵테일을 만들고 있었다.

가산명사 혼합물 ❑ 꿀과 요구르트, 귀리, 사과를 혼합해서 만든 음식

1 불가산명사 콘크리트 ❑ 푯말을 콘크리트에 고정시켜야 한다. ❑ 그들은 콘크리트 바닥에 침낭을 깔고 누운 터였다. **2** 타동사 콘크리트를 깔다 ❑ 그는 바닥만 겨우 치우고 콘크리트를 깔았다. **3** 형용사 구체적인 ❑ 그는 구체적인 증거가 하나도 없었다. ❑ 논의할 만한 구체적인 제안이 하나도 없었다. **4** 형용사 실제의 ❑ 실제 물건을 사용해서 덧셈과 뺄셈을 가르치기 **5** 형용사 구상 명사의

상호동사 일치하다 [격식체] ❑ 지역 정서가 언론과 항상 일치하는 것은 아니다. ❑ 다니엘과 프랭클린은 경찰을 칭찬해야 한다는 수사관의 제안에 동의했다.

형용사 동시에 일어나는 ❑ 세인트 에띠엔느 미술관이 전시회 세 개를 동시에 열고 있다. ❑ 그는 사실상 5년형 세 개를 동시에 살게 될 것이다. ● 동시에 부사 ❑ 그는 빈집털이로 이미 살고 있는 형기와 동시에 형을 살도록 징역 33개월 형에 처해졌다.

가산명사 또는 불가산명사 뇌진탕 ❑ 니키가 뇌진탕으로 병원에 실려 갔다.

1 타동사 비난하다 ❑ 경찰 지도부가 어제 한 목소리로 최근 폭력 사태를 비난했다. ❑ 선수들이 실력이나 정신 상태, 전력투구 면에서 부족하다고 비난한 그레이엄의 말이 맞다. **2** 타동사 선고받다 ❑ 그는 종신형을 선고받았다. **3** 타동사 비참하게 ~하게 되다 ❑ 그들은 능력 부족으로 따분하고 보통 보수가 적은 일을 평생 할 수밖에 없었다. **4** 타동사 철거하기로 결정하다 ❑ 법원의 결정으로 그 지역 건물 철거가 쉬워졌다고 주 관계자들이 밝혔다.

가산명사 또는 불가산명사 비난, 규탄 ❑ 지난 토요일의 살인 사건들에 대한 비난이 확산되었다.

형용사 사형을 선고받은 ❑ 사형 집행 전 며칠 동안 사형수와 함께 이야기를 나눴던 교관들

1 타동사 요약하다 ❑ 우리는 중요한 내용을 짧고 군더더기 없이 완벽한 문장으로 요약하는 방법을 배웠다. **2** 자동사 응축되다 ❑ 수증기가 응축되어 구름을 만든다.

1 타동사 잘난 체 하며 ~해 주다 [탐탁찮음] ❑ 그는 잘난 체하며 연설을 해 주면서 30분 동안 서너 번씩이나 자신의 말과 모순되는 이야기를 했다. **2** 자동사 잘난 체하다, 으스대다 [탐탁찮음] ❑ 내 앞에서 잘난 체하지 마.

형용사 잘난 체하는, 으스대는 [탐탁찮음] ❑ 난 네 돈이나 잘난 체하는 태도에 딱 질렸어.

1 단수명사 상태 ❑ 그는 아직 중태로 캘리포니아 병원에 입원해 있다. ❑ 나는 피부 상태가 좋다는 칭찬을 몇 번 받았다. ❑ 방 두 개짜리 별장은 상태가 아주 좋다. **2** 복수명사 조건, 사정, 상황 ❑ 이상적인 조건에서는 수입품 가격은 오르고 수출은 신장되면서 평가 절하가 일어날 것이다. **3** 복수명사 조건, 상황 ❑ 사람들이 아주 열악한 조건에서 생활하고 있다. ❑ 그는 이 같은 상황에서 더 이상 일할 수 없었다. **4** 가산명사 조건 ❑ 북한티나가 차관 지급 조건으로 제시된 경제 관련 목표 달성에 실패했다. ● 고용 계약 조건 **5** 가산명사 병, 이상 ❑ 의사들은 그가 심장 이상이 있을지도 모른다고 말한다. **6** 타동사 ~의 영향을 받다 ❑ 우리는 어릴 적에 받은 인상과 경험의

or law. ❑ *Argentina failed to hit the economic targets set as a condition for loan payments.* ❑ *...terms and conditions of employment.* **5** N-COUNT If someone has a particular **condition**, they have an illness or other medical problem. ❑ *Doctors suspect he may have a heart condition.* **6** V-T If someone **is conditioned** by their experiences or environment, they are influenced by them over a period of time so that they do certain things or think in a particular way. [usu passive] ❑ *We are all conditioned by early impressions and experiences.* ❑ *I just feel women are conditioned into doing housework.* ● **con|di|tion|ing** N-UNCOUNT ❑ *Because of social conditioning, men don't expect themselves to be managed by women.* **7** PHRASE When you agree to do something **on condition that** something else happens, you mean that you will only do it if this other thing also happens. ❑ *He spoke to reporters on condition that he was not identified.*
→see **factory**

영향을 받는다. ❑ 나는 여성이 집안일을 해야 한다는 인식을 갖도록 교육받았다고 생각한다. ● 조건 형성 불가산명사 ❑ 사회적 조건 형성 때문에 남성은 여성의 관리를 받으리라는 생각을 못한다. **7** 구 ~을 조건으로 ❑ 그는 익명을 조건으로 기자들에게 말했다.

Word Partnership	condition의 연어
ADJ.	**critical** condition **5**
N.	**weather** conditions, **working** conditions **2** **3**

con|di|tion|al /kəndɪʃənᵊl/ **1** ADJ If a situation or agreement is **conditional on** something, it will only happen or continue if this happens. ❑ *Their support is conditional on his proposals meeting their approval.* ❑ *...a conditional offer.* **2** ADJ In grammar, a **conditional** clause is a subordinate clause which refers to a situation which may exist or whose possible consequences you are considering. Most conditional clauses begin with "if" or "unless," for example "If that happens, we'll be in big trouble" and "You don't have to come unless you want to." [ADJ n]

1 형용사 ~을 조건으로 한 ❑ 그들은 그가 내놓은 제안이 마음에 들 때에만 지원하기로 했다. ❑ 조건부 제안 **2** 형용사 조건절의

con|do|lence /kəndoʊləns/ (**condolences**) **1** N-UNCOUNT A message of **condolence** is a message in which you express your sympathy for someone because one of their friends or relatives has died recently. ❑ *Neil sent him a letter of condolence.* **2** N-PLURAL When you offer or express your **condolences** to someone, you express your sympathy for them because one of their friends or relatives has died recently. ❑ *He expressed his condolences to the families of the people who died in the incident.*

1 불가산명사 조문, 애도 ❑ 닐은 그에게 조문 편지를 보냈다. **2** 복수명사 조의, 애도 ❑ 그는 사고로 목숨을 잃은 사람들의 가족에게 조의를 표했다.

con|dom /kɒndəm/ (**condoms**) N-COUNT A **condom** is a covering made of thin rubber which a man can wear on his penis as a contraceptive or as protection against disease during sexual intercourse.

가산명사 콘돔

con|done /kəndoʊn/ (**condones**, **condoning**, **condoned**) V-T If someone **condones** behavior that is morally wrong, they accept it and allow it to happen. [oft with brd-neg] ❑ *I have never encouraged nor condoned violence.*

타동사 묵인하다 ❑ 나는 결코 폭력을 조장하거나 묵인한 적이 없다.

con|du|cive /kəndusɪv, BRIT kəndyuːsɪv/ ADJ If one thing is **conducive to** another thing, it makes the other thing likely to happen. ❑ *Make your bedroom as conducive to sleep as possible.*

형용사 ~에 이바지하는, ~에 도움이 되는 ❑ 침실을 수면에 최대한 적합하게 꾸미세요.

con|duct ♦♦◇ (**conducts**, **conducting**, **conducted**)

The verb is pronounced /kəndʌkt/. The noun is pronounced /kɒndʌkt/.

동사는 /kəndʌkt/로 발음되고, 명사는 /kɒndʌkt/로 발음된다.

1 V-T When you **conduct** an activity or task, you organize it and carry it out. ❑ *I decided to conduct an experiment.* **2** N-SING The **conduct of** a task or activity is the way in which it is organized and carried out. ❑ *Also up for discussion will be the conduct of free and fair elections.* **3** V-T If you **conduct** yourself in a particular way, you behave in that way. ❑ *The way he conducts himself reflects on the party and will increase criticisms against him.* **4** N-UNCOUNT Someone's **conduct** is the way they behave in particular situations. ❑ *For Europeans, the law is a statement of basic principles of civilised conduct.* **5** V-T/V-I When someone **conducts** an orchestra or choir, they stand in front of it and direct its performance. ❑ *Dennis had recently begun a successful career conducting opera in Europe.* ❑ *Solti will continue to conduct here and abroad.* **6** V-T If something **conducts** heat or electricity, it allows heat or electricity to pass through it or along it. [no cont] ❑ *Water conducts heat faster than air.*

1 타동사 수행하다, 진행하다 ❑ 나는 실험을 하기로 결정했다. **2** 단수명사 수행 방법, 진행 방법 ❑ 공명정대한 선거 진행 방법 역시 논의의 대상이다. **3** 타동사 행동하다, 처신하다 ❑ 그의 행동거지 때문에 당의 이미지가 나빠지고 그에 대한 비난의 소리가 높아질 것이다. **4** 불가산명사 행실 ❑ 유럽인들에게 법은 교양 있는 행실의 기본 원칙을 명확히 표현한 것이다. **5** 타동사/자동사 지휘하다 ❑ 데니스는 최근 유럽 오페라 지휘자로서 성공을 거두기 시작한 터였다. ❑ 솔티는 국내외에서 지휘 활동을 계속할 것이다. **6** 타동사 전도하다 ❑ 물은 공기보다 열을 빨리 전도한다.

Thesaurus	conduct의 참조어
v.	control, direct, manage **1**
N.	attitude, behavior, manner **4**

Word Partnership	conduct의 연어
N.	conduct **business**, conduct **an experiment** **1**
	code of conduct **4**

con|duc|tor /kəndʌktər/ (**conductors**) **1** N-COUNT A **conductor** is a person who stands in front of an orchestra or choir and directs its performance. **2** N-COUNT On a train, a **conductor** is a person whose job is to travel on the train in order to help passengers and check tickets. [AM; BRIT **guard**] **3** N-COUNT On a streetcar or a bus, the **conductor** is the person whose job is to sell tickets to the passengers. **4** N-COUNT A **conductor** is a substance that heat or electricity can pass through or along. ❑ *Graphite is a highly efficient conductor of electricity.* →see also **semiconductor** →see **metal**

1 가산명사 지휘자 **2** 가산명사 기차 차장 [미국영어; 영국영어 guard] **3** 가산명사 버스 차장 **4** 가산명사 전도체 ❑ 흑연은 전기 전도율이 높은 전도체이다.

cone /koʊn/ (**cones**) **1** N-COUNT A **cone** is a shape with a circular base and smooth curved sides ending in a point at the top. ❑ *...the streetlight's yellow cone of light.* **2** N-COUNT A **cone** is the fruit of a tree such as a pine or fir. ❑ *...a bowl of fir cones.* **3** N-COUNT A **cone** is a thin, cone-shaped cookie that is used for holding ice cream. You can also refer to an ice cream that you eat in this way as a **cone**. ❑ *She stopped by the ice-cream shop and had a chocolate cone.* →see **volcano**, **volume**

1 가산명사 원뿔, 원뿔형 ❑ 원추형 모양의 노란 가로등 불빛 **2** 가산명사 뾰족한 방울 모양의 열매 ❑ 전나무 열매 한 사발 **3** 가산명사 아이스크림콘 ❑ 그녀는 아이스크림 가게에 들러서 초콜릿 아이스크림콘을 먹었다.

con|fec|tion|ers' sug|ar N-UNCOUNT **Confectioners' sugar** is very fine white sugar that is used for making frosting and candy. [AM; BRIT **icing sugar**]

불가산명사 정제 설탕 [미국영어; 영국영어 icing sugar]

con|fed|era|tion /kənfɛdəreɪʃ°n/ (**confederations**) N-COUNT; N-IN-NAMES A **confederation** is an organization or group consisting of smaller groups or states, especially one that exists for business or political purposes. □ ...the Confederation of Indian Industry.

가산명사; 이름명사 연합 □ 인도 산업 연합

con|fer /kənfɜr/ (**confers, conferring, conferred**) **1** V-RECIP When you **confer with** someone, you discuss something with them in order to make a decision. You can also say that two people **confer**. □ He conferred with Hill and the others in his office. **2** V-T To **confer** something such as power or an honor **on** someone means to give it to them. [FORMAL] □ The constitution also confers large powers on Brazil's 25 constituent states.

1 상호동사 논의하다, 협의하다 □ 그는 사무실의 힐을 비롯한 다른 사람들과 논의했다. **2** 타동사 부여하다, 수여하다, 주다 [격식체] □ 헌법은 또한 브라질 25개 주에 막대한 권한을 부여하고 있다.

con|fer|ence ◆◆◆ /kɒnfərəns, -frəns/ (**conferences**) **1** N-COUNT A **conference** is a meeting, often lasting a few days, which is organized on a particular subject or to bring together people who have a common interest. □ The President took the unprecedented step of summoning all the state governors to a conference on education. □ ...the Conservative Party conference. **2** N-COUNT A **conference** is a meeting at which formal discussions take place. [also in N] □ They sat down at the dinner table, as they always did, before the meal, for a conference. **3** →see also **press conference**

1 가산명사 회의 □ 대통령은 이례적으로 주지사 전원을 불러 교육 문제에 관한 회의를 열었다. □ 보수당 회의 **2** 가산명사 협의 □ 그들은 관례대로 식전 협의를 위해 만찬 테이블에 앉았다.

con|fer|ence call (**conference calls**) N-COUNT A **conference call** is a phone call in which more than two people take part. [BUSINESS] □ There are daily conference calls with Washington.

가산명사 전화 회의 [경제] □ 매일 워싱턴과 전화 회의가 있다.

con|fess /kənfɛs/ (**confesses, confessing, confessed**) **1** V-T/V-I If someone **confesses** to doing something wrong, they admit that they did it. □ He had confessed to seventeen murders. □ I had expected her to confess that she only wrote these books for the money. □ Ray changed his mind, claiming that he had been forced into confessing. **2** V-T If someone **confesses** or **confesses** their sins, they tell God or a priest about their sins so that they can be forgiven. □ You just go to the church and confess your sins.

1 타동사/자동사 자백하다, 고백하다 □ 그는 17건의 살인을 저질렀다고 자백했다. □ 나는 그녀가 오직 돈을 목적으로 이런 책을 쓴다고 고백하리라고 예상했었다. □ 레이는 마음을 바꿔 자백하도록 강요받았다고 주장했다. **2** 타동사 고백하다, 고해하다 □ 너는 교회에 가서 죄를 고백하기만 하면 된다.

con|fes|sion /kənfɛʃ°n/ (**confessions**) **1** N-COUNT A **confession** is a signed statement by someone in which they admit that they have committed a particular crime. □ They forced him to sign a confession. **2** N-VAR **Confession** is the act of admitting that you have done something that you are ashamed of or embarrassed about. □ The diaries are a mixture of confession and observation. **3** N-VAR If you make a **confession of** your beliefs or feelings, you publicly tell people that this is what you believe or feel. □ ...Tatyana's confession of love. **4** N-VAR In the Catholic church and in some other churches, if you go to **confession**, you privately tell a priest about your sins and ask for forgiveness. □ He never went to Father Porter for confession again.

1 가산명사 자술서 □ 그들은 그에게 자술서 서명을 강요했다. **2** 가산명사 또는 불가산명사 자백, 고백 □ 그 일기는 고백과 관찰을 담고 있다. **3** 가산명사 또는 불가산명사 고백 □ 타티아나의 사랑 고백 **4** 가산명사 또는 불가산명사 고해 □ 그는 이후로 다시는 포터신부에게 고해를 하지 않았다.

con|fide /kənfaɪd/ (**confides, confiding, confided**) V-T/V-I If you **confide in** someone, you tell them a secret. □ I knew she had some fundamental problems in her marriage because she had confided in me a year earlier. □ He confided to me that he felt like he was being punished.

타동사/자동사 비밀을 털어놓다 □ 그보다 일년 전에 나에게 속마음을 털어놓았기 때문에 그녀가 결혼 생활에 근본적인 문제를 안고 있다는 것을 나는 알고 있었다. □ 그는 벌을 받고 있는 것 같다고 나에게 털어놓았다.

con|fi|dence ◆◆◇ /kɒnfɪdəns/ **1** N-UNCOUNT If you have **confidence in** someone, you feel that you can trust them. □ I have every confidence in you. □ This has contributed to the lack of confidence in the police. **2** N-UNCOUNT If you have **confidence**, you feel sure about your abilities, qualities, or ideas. □ The band is in excellent form and brimming with confidence. **3** N-UNCOUNT If you can say something **with confidence**, you feel certain it is correct. □ I can say with confidence that such rumors were totally groundless. **4** N-UNCOUNT If you tell someone something **in confidence**, you tell them a secret. □ We told you all these things in confidence. □ Even telling Lois seemed a betrayal of confidence. ● PHRASE If you **take** someone **into** your **confidence**, you tell them a secret. →see **stock market**

1 불가산명사 신뢰 □ 나는 너를 전적으로 신뢰해. □ 이 역시 경찰에 대한 신뢰가 떨어지는 데 한몫 했다. **2** 불가산명사 자신감 □ 밴드는 최상의 컨디션에 자신감이 넘친다. **3** 불가산명사 확신 □ 나는 그것들이 전혀 근거 없는 소문이라고 확실하게 말할 수 있다. **4** 불가산명사 비밀 □ 우리가 너에게 모두 비밀로 이야기한 거야. □ 로이스에게 이야기하는 것조차 비밀 누설로 보였다. ● 구 -에게 비밀을 이야기하다

con|fi|dent ◆◇◇ /kɒnfɪdənt/ **1** ADJ If you are **confident** about something, you are certain that it will happen in the way you want it to. □ I am confident that everything will come out right in time. □ Mr. Ryan is confident of success. ● **con|fi|dent|ly** ADV [ADV with v] □ I can confidently promise that this year is going to be very different. **2** ADJ If a person or their manner is **confident**, they feel sure about their own abilities, qualities, or ideas. □ In time he became more confident and relaxed. ● **con|fi|dent|ly** ADV □ She walked confidently across the hall. **3** ADJ If you are **confident that** something is true, you are sure that it is true. A **confident** statement is one that the speaker is sure is true. □ She is confident that everybody is on her side. ● **con|fi|dent|ly** ADV [ADV with v] □ I can confidently say that none of them were or are racist.

1 형용사 자신하는, 확신하는 □ 나는 때가 되면 모든 일이 잘 될 거라고 확신해. □ 라이언 씨는 성공을 자신했다. ● 자신 있게, 확실히 부사 □ 저는 올해가 상당히 다르리라고 자신 있게 약속할 수 있습니다. **2** 형용사 자신만만한 □ 시간이 흐르자 그는 자신감과 여유가 더 생겼다. ● 자신만만하게 부사 □ 그녀는 자신만만하게 복도를 가로질러 걸어갔다. **3** 형용사 확신하는 □ 그녀는 모든 사람이 자기편이라고 확신한다. ● 자신 있게 부사 □ 그들 중 어느 누구도 인종 차별주의자가 아니었고 지금도 아니라고 자신 있게 말할 수 있다.

con|fi|den|tial /kɒnfɪdɛnʃ°l/ **1** ADJ Information that is **confidential** is meant to be kept secret or private. □ She accused them of leaking confidential information about her private life. ● **con|fi|den|tial|ly** ADV □ People can phone in the knowledge that any information they give will be treated confidentially. ● **con|fi|den|ti|al|ity** /kɒnfɪdɛnʃiæliti/ N-UNCOUNT □ ...the confidentiality of the client-solicitor relationship. **2** ADJ If you talk to someone in a **confidential** way, you talk to them quietly because what you are saying is secret or private. □ "Look," he said in a confidential tone, "I want you to know that me and Joey are cops." ● **con|fi|den|tial|ly** ADV □ Nash hadn't raised his voice, still spoke rather softly, confidentially.

1 형용사 비밀의, 기밀의 □ 그녀는 자신의 사생활에 관한 비밀 정보를 유출한 혐의로 그들을 고소했다. ● 비밀로, 기밀로 부사 □ 전화로 말하는 정보는 모두 비밀에 부치기 때문에 사람들은 전화를 할 수 있다. ● 기밀성 불가산명사 □ 의뢰인과 변호인 간의 비밀 유지 **2** 형용사 다른 사람에게는 들리지 않는 □ "이봐, 나와 조이가 경찰이라는 사실을 명심하라고."라고 그가 다른 사람에게는 들리지 않게 말했다. ● 작은 소리로 부사 □ 내쉬는 목소리를 높이지 않고 여전히 다소 부드럽고 조용한 소리로 말했다.

Thesaurus confidential의 참조어

ADJ. private, restricted, secret; (ant.) public **1**

con|fi|den|tial|ly /kɒnfɪdɛnʃəli/ ADV **Confidentially** is used to say that what you are telling someone is a secret and should not be discussed with anyone else. [ADV with cl] ❑ *Confidentially, I am not sure that it wasn't above their heads.*

부사 비밀인데 ❑비밀인데, 그게 그들이 이해할 수 없는 수준은 아니었을 거야.

con|fig|u|ra|tion /kənfɪgyəreɪʃⁿn, BRIT kənfɪgʊreɪʃⁿn/ (**configurations**)
■ N-COUNT A **configuration** is an arrangement of a group of things. [FORMAL] ❑ ...*Stonehenge, in south-western England, an ancient configuration of giant stones.* ■ N-UNCOUNT The **configuration** of a computer system is way in which all its parts, such as the hardware and software, are connected together in order for the computer to work. [COMPUTING] ❑ *Prices range from $119 to $199, depending on the particular configuration.*

■ 가산명사 배치 [격식체] ❑잉글랜드 남서부의 스톤헨지는 거석을 배치해 놓은 고대 유적지이다. ■ 불가산명사 구성 [컴퓨터] ❑시스템 구성 형태에 따라 가격이 119달러에서 199달러까지 다양하다.

con|fig|ure /kənfɪgyər, BRIT kənfɪgə⁰/ (**configures, configuring, configured**) V-T If you **configure** a piece of computer equipment, you set it up so that it is ready for use. [COMPUTING] ❑ *How easy was it to configure the software?*

타동사 구성하다 [컴퓨터] ❑소프트웨어 구성이 얼마나 쉬웠나?

con|fine /kənfaɪn/ (**confines, confining, confined**) ■ V-T To **confine** something **to** a particular place or group means to prevent it from spreading beyond that place or group. ❑ *Health officials have successfully confined the epidemic to the Tabatinga area.* ■ V-T If you **confine yourself** or your activities **to** something, you do only that thing and are involved with nothing else. ❑ *He did not confine himself to the one language.*

■ 타동사 제한하다, 국한시키다 ❑보건 관계자들이 전염병이 타바팅가 지역을 벗어나지 않도록 하는 데 성공했다. ■ 타동사 -만 하다 ❑그는 한 가지 언어만 사용하지 않았다.

con|fined /kənfaɪnd/ ■ ADJ If something is **confined to** a particular place, it exists only in that place. If it is **confined to** a particular group, only members of that group have it. [v-link ADJ to n] ❑ *The problem is not confined to Germany.* ■ ADJ A **confined** space or area is small and enclosed by walls. ❑ *His long legs bent up in the confined space.* ■ ADJ If someone is **confined to** a wheelchair, bed, or house, they have to stay there, because they are disabled or ill. [v-link ADJ to n] ❑ *He had been confined to a wheelchair since childhood.*

■ 형용사 -에 국한된 ❑독일에 국한된 문제가 아니다. ■ 형용사 제한된, 비좁은 ❑그는 비좁은 공간에서 다리를 구부리고 있었다. ■ 형용사 -에 갇힌, -에 매인 ❑그는 어릴 때부터 휠체어 신세를 져 왔다.

con|fine|ment /kənfaɪnmənt/ N-UNCOUNT **Confinement** is the state of being forced to stay in a prison or another place which you cannot leave. ❑ *She had been held in solitary confinement for four months.*

불가산명사 감금 ❑그녀는 넉 달 동안 독방에 갇혔었다.

> #### Word Link
> firm ≈ making strong : af**firm**, con**firm**, in**firm**

con|firm ♦♦◊ /kənfɜrm/ (**confirms, confirming, confirmed**) ■ V-T If something **confirms** what you believe, suspect, or fear, it shows that it is definitely true. [no cont] ❑ *X-rays have confirmed that he has not broken any bones.* ● **con|fir|ma|tion** /kɒnfərmeɪʃⁿn/ N-UNCOUNT ❑ *They took her resignation from Bendix as confirmation of their suspicions.* ■ V-T If you **confirm** something that has been stated or suggested, you say that it is true because you know about it. ❑ *The spokesman confirmed that the area was now in rebel hands.* ● **con|fir|ma|tion** N-UNCOUNT ❑ *She glanced over at James for confirmation.* ■ V-T If you **confirm** an arrangement or appointment, you say that it is definite, usually in a letter or on the telephone. ❑ *You make the reservation, and I'll confirm it in writing.* ● **con|fir|ma|tion** N-UNCOUNT ❑ *Travel arrangements are subject to confirmation by State Tourist Organisations.* ■ V-T If someone **is confirmed**, they are formally accepted as a member of a Christian church during a ceremony in which they say they believe what the church teaches. [usu passive] ❑ *He was confirmed as a member of the Church of England.* ● **con|fir|ma|tion** (**confirmations**) N-VAR ❑ ...*when I was being prepared for Confirmation.* ■ V-T If something **confirms** you in your decision, belief, or opinion, it makes you think that you are definitely right. [no cont] ❑ *It has confirmed me in my decision not to become a nun.* ■ V-T If something **confirms** you **as** something, it shows that you definitely deserve a name, role, or position. ❑ *His new role could confirm him as one of our leading actors.*

■ 타동사 확증하다, 확인하다 ❑엑스레이로 그의 뼈가 하나도 부러지지 않았다는 사실이 확인되었다. ● 확인 불가산명사 ❑그들은 그녀가 벤딕스를 그만둔 것을 보고 추측이 맞았음을 확인했다. ■ 타동사 확인하다, 확인해 주다 ❑대변인의 발언으로 그 지역이 현재 반군 수중에 있다는 사실이 확인됐다. ● 확인, 확인 불가산명사 ❑그녀는 확인차 제임스를 힐끗 보았다. ■ 타동사 확정하다 ❑네가 예약하면 내가 서면으로 예약을 확정할게. ● 확인, 확정 불가산명사 ❑여행 계획은 주 여행 기구의 확인을 받아야 한다. ■ 타동사 견진 성사를 받다 ❑그는 영국 국교회 견진 성사를 받았다. ● 견진 성사 가산명사 또는 불가산명사 ❑내가 견진 성사를 받을 준비를 하고 있을 때 ■ 타동사 굳히다 ❑이를 계기로 나는 수녀가 되지 않기로 마음을 굳혔다. ■ 타동사 굳히다 ❑그는 새로 맡은 역할로 일류 배우 자리를 굳힐 수 있을 것이다.

con|fis|cate /kɒnfɪskeɪt/ (**confiscates, confiscating, confiscated**) V-T If you **confiscate** something **from** someone, you take it away from them, usually as a punishment. ❑ *There is concern that police use the law to confiscate assets from people who have committed minor offences.* ● **con|fis|ca|tion** /kɒnfɪskeɪʃⁿn/ (**confiscations**) N-VAR ❑ *The new laws allow the confiscation of assets purchased with proceeds of the drugs trade.*

타동사 몰수하다, 압수하다 ❑경찰이 그 법을 이용해서, 경범죄를 범한 사람들로부터 재산을 몰수한다는 우려가 있다. ● 몰수, 압수 가산명사 또는 불가산명사 ❑새 법에 따라 마약 매매 수익으로 사들인 재산 압수가 허용된다.

> #### Word Link
> flict ≈ striking : af**flict**ion, con**flict**, in**flict**

con|flict ♦♦◊ (**conflicts, conflicting, conflicted**)

> The noun is pronounced /kɒnflɪkt/. The verb is pronounced /kənflɪkt/.

명사는 /kɒnflɪkt/로 발음되고, 동사는 /kənflɪkt/로 발음된다.

■ N-UNCOUNT **Conflict** is serious disagreement and argument about something important. If two people or groups are **in conflict**, they have had a serious disagreement or argument and have not yet reached agreement. [oft in/into n] ❑ *Try to keep any conflict between you and your ex-partner to a minimum.* ■ N-UNCOUNT **Conflict** is a state of mind in which you find it impossible to make a decision. ❑ ...*the anguish of his own inner conflict.* ■ N-VAR **Conflict** is fighting between countries or groups of people. [JOURNALISM] ❑ ...*talks aimed at ending four decades of conflict.* ■ N-VAR A **conflict** is a serious difference between two or more beliefs, ideas, or interests. If two beliefs, ideas, or interests are **in conflict**, they are very different. ❑ *There is a conflict between what they are doing and what you want.* ■ V-RECIP If ideas, beliefs, or accounts **conflict**, they are very different from each other and it seems impossible for them to exist together or to each be true. ❑ *Personal ethics and professional ethics sometimes conflict.* ❑ *He held firm opinions which usually conflicted with my own.* →see **war**

■ 불가산명사 갈등, 분쟁 ❑당신과 이혼한 배우자 사이의 모든 갈등을 최소화하도록 노력하세요. ■ 불가산명사 갈등 ❑그 자신의 내적 갈등으로 인한 고뇌 ■ 가산명사 또는 불가산명사 분쟁, 다툼 [언론] ❑40년간의 분쟁 종식을 목표로 한 회담 ■ 가산명사 또는 불가산명사 큰 차이, 충돌, 모순 ❑그들이 하는 일과 네가 원하는 것 사이에 큰 차이가 있다. ■ 상호동사 충돌하다, 대립하다 ❑개인 윤리와 직업윤리가 때때로 충돌하기도 한다. ❑그는 보통 나의 견해와 대립되는 확고한 견해를 지니고 있었다.

> #### Word Partnership
> conflict의 연어
>
> | | |
> |---|---|
> | N. | conflict **resolution**, **source of** conflict ■ |
> | V. | **avoid** conflict ■ ■ ■ |
> | | **end/resolve/settle a** conflict ■ ■ |
> | ADJ. | **military** conflict ■ |

con|form /kənf_ɔ_rm/ (conforms, conforming, conformed) **1** V-I If something **conforms to** something such as a law or someone's wishes, it is of the required type or quality. ❑ *The lamp has been designed to conform to new British Standard safety requirements.* **2** V-I If you **conform**, you behave in the way that you are expected or supposed to behave. ❑ *Many children who can't or don't conform are often bullied.*

1 자동사 _에 부합하다, _에 따르다 ❑ 이 전등은 새로운 영국 표준 안전 기준에 맞게 설계되었다. **2** 자동사 규범에 맞게 행동하다 ❑ 자의든 타의든 튀는 아이들은 괴롭힘을 당한다.

con|form|ity /kənf_ɔ_rmɪti/ N-UNCOUNT If something happens **in conformity with** something such as a law or someone's wishes, it happens as the law says it should, or as the person wants it to. ❑ *The prime minister is, in conformity with the constitution, chosen by the president.* **2** N-UNCOUNT **Conformity** means behaving in the same way as most other people. ❑ *Excessive conformity is usually caused by fear of disapproval.*

1 불가산명사 _에 따라, _에 부합하이 ❑ 수상은 헌법에 따라 대통령이 임명한다. **2** 불가산명사 획일적인 행동 ❑ 지나치게 획일적인 행동은 보통 비난에 대한 두려움 때문에 나타난다.

con|found /kənf_au_nd/ (confounds, confounding, confounded) V-T If someone or something **confounds** you, they make you feel surprised or confused, often by showing you that your opinions or expectations of them were wrong. ❑ *He momentarily confounded his critics by his cool handling of the hostage crisis.*

타동사 당황하게 하다, 난처하게 하다 ❑ 그는 인질극을 멋지게 처리함으로써 잠시나마 비판가들을 난처하게 했다.

con|front ◆◇◇ /kənf_rʌ_nt/ (confronts, confronting, confronted) **1** V-T If you **are confronted with** a problem, task, or difficulty, you have to deal with it. ❑ *She was confronted with severe money problems.* **2** V-T If you **confront** a difficult situation or issue, you accept the fact that it exists and try to deal with it. ❑ *We are learning how to confront death.* **3** V-T If you **are confronted** by something that you find threatening or difficult to deal with, it is there in front of you. [usu passive] ❑ *I was confronted with an array of knobs, levers, and switches.* **4** V-T If you **confront** someone, you stand or sit in front of them, especially when you are going to fight, argue, or compete with them. ❑ *She pushed her way through the mob and confronted him face to face.* ❑ *They don't hesitate to open fire when confronted by police.* **5** V-T If you **confront** someone **with** something, you present facts or evidence to them in order to accuse them of something. ❑ *She had decided to confront Kathryn with what she had learnt.* ❑ *I could not bring myself to confront him about it.*

1 타동사 직면하다 ❑ 그녀는 심각한 금전 문제에 직면했다. **2** 타동사 맞서다 ❑ 우리는 죽음에 맞서는 법을 배우고 있다. **3** 타동사 직면하다 ❑ 내 눈앞에 손잡이와 레버, 스위치가 늘어서 있었다. **4** 타동사 맞서다, 대결하다 ❑ 그는 군중을 밀치고 나아가 그와 정면으로 맞섰다. **5** 경찰과 맞서게 되면 그들은 주저하지 않고 발포한다. **5** 타동사 _을 가지고 따지다 ❑ 그녀는 자신이 알게 된 사실을 가지고 캐더린에게 따지려고 했다. ❑ 나는 그 문제에 관해 그에게 따질 용기가 나지 않았다.

con|fron|ta|tion ◆◇◇ /k_ɒ_nfrʌnt_eɪ_ʃ°n/ (confrontations) N-VAR A **confrontation** is a dispute, fight, or battle between two groups of people. ❑ *The commission remains so weak that it will continue to avoid confrontation with governments.*

가산명사 또는 불가산명사 대립 ❑ 그 위원회는 힘이 워낙 약하기 때문에 정부와의 대립을 계속 피할 것이다.

con|fron|ta|tion|al /k_ɒ_nfrʌnt_eɪ_ʃən°l/ ADJ If you describe the way that someone behaves as **confrontational**, you are showing your disapproval of the fact that they are aggressive and likely to cause an argument or dispute. [DISAPPROVAL] ❑ *The committee's confrontational style of campaigning has made it unpopular.*

형용사 공격적인 [탐탁찮은] ❑ 공격적인 활동 방식 때문에 그 위원회의 인기가 떨어졌다.

con|fuse /kənf_yu_z/ (confuses, confusing, confused) **1** V-T If you **confuse** two things, you get them mixed up, so that you think one of them is the other one. ❑ *Great care is taken to avoid confusing the two types of projects.* ● **con|fu|sion** /kənf_yu_ʒ°n/ *Use different colors of felt pen on your sketch to avoid confusion.* **2** V-T To **confuse** someone means to make it difficult for them to know exactly what is happening or what to do. ❑ *German politics surprised and confused him.* **3** V-T To **confuse** a situation means to make it complicated or difficult to understand. ❑ *To further confuse the issue, there is an enormous variation in the amount of sleep people feel happy with.*

1 타동사 혼동하다 ❑ 그 두 종류의 프로젝트를 혼동하지 않기 위해서 각별한 주의를 기울이고 있다. ● 혼동 불가산명사 ❑ 혼동을 피할 수 있도록 스케치할 때 서로 다른 색의 매직펜을 사용하라. **2** 타동사 혼란스럽게 하다 ❑ 독일 정치가 그에게 놀라움과 혼란을 안겨 주었다. **3** 타동사 복잡하게 하다 ❑ 사람마다 충분하다고 느끼는 수면 시간이 크게 다르기 때문에 그 문제가 더욱 복잡해진다.

con|fused /kənf_yu_zd/ **1** ADJ If you are **confused**, you do not know exactly what is happening or what to do. ❑ *A survey showed people were confused about what they should eat to stay healthy.* **2** ADJ Something that is **confused** does not have any order or pattern and is difficult to understand. ❑ *The situation remains confused as both sides claim success.*

1 형용사 혼란스러운, 어리둥절한 ❑ 한 조사에서 사람들이 건강 유지를 위해 무엇을 먹어야 할지 혼란스러워 한다는 결과가 나왔다. **2** 형용사 혼란스러운, 복잡한 ❑ 양쪽 모두 성공을 주장하면서 상황이 여전히 혼란스러운 상태이다.

con|fus|ing /kənf_yu_zɪŋ/ ADJ Something that is **confusing** makes it difficult for people to know exactly what is happening or what to do. ❑ *The statement is highly confusing.*

형용사 애매모호한, 헷갈리는 ❑ 발언이 상당히 모호했다.

con|fu|sion /kənf_yu_ʒ°n/ (confusions) N-VAR **1** If there is **confusion** about something, it is not clear what the true situation is, especially because people believe different things. ❑ *There's still confusion about the number of casualties.* **2** N-UNCOUNT **Confusion** is a situation in which everything is in disorder, especially because there are lots of things happening at the same time. ❑ *There was confusion when a man fired shots.* **3** →see also **confuse**

1 가산명사 또는 불가산명사 애매모호 ❑ 사상자 숫자가 아직도 모호한 상태이다. **2** 불가산명사 혼란, 혼동 ❑ 한 남성이 총을 쏘자 혼란이 빚어졌다.

con|gen|ial /kənd_ʒi_nyəl/ ADJ A **congenial** person, place, or environment is pleasant. [FORMAL] ❑ *He is back in more congenial company.*

형용사 친절한; 기분 좋은; 쾌적한 [격식체] ❑ 그는 다시 더욱 친절한 사람들과 함께했다.

con|gest|ed /kənd_ʒe_stɪd/ ADJ A **congested** road or area is extremely crowded and blocked with traffic or people. ❑ *He first promised two weeks ago to clear Britain's congested roads.*

형용사 혼잡이 심한, 혼잡한 ❑ 2주 전 그는 먼저 영국의 교통 체증을 해소하겠다고 약속했다.

con|ges|tion /kənd_ʒe_stʃ°n/ N-UNCOUNT If there is **congestion** in a place, the place is extremely crowded and blocked with traffic or people. ❑ *The problems of traffic congestion will not disappear in a hurry.* →see **traffic**

불가산명사 체증, 혼잡 ❑ 교통 체증 문제는 단번에 사라지지 않을 것이다.

con|glom|er|ate /kəngl_ɒ_mərɪt/ (conglomerates) N-COUNT A **conglomerate** is a large business firm consisting of several different companies. [BUSINESS] ❑ *Fiat is Italy's largest industrial conglomerate.*

가산명사 대기업 [경제] ❑ 피아트는 이탈리아의 가장 큰 대기업이다.

Word Link	grat ≈ pleasing : con**grat**ulate, **grat**ify, **grat**itude

con|gratu|late /kəngr_æ_tʃəleɪt/ (congratulates, congratulating, congratulated) **1** V-T If you **congratulate** someone, you say something to show you are pleased that something nice has happened to them. ❑ *She congratulated him on the birth of his son.* ● **con|gratu|la|tion** /kəngr_æ_tʃəl_eɪ_ʃ°n/ N-UNCOUNT ❑ *We have received many letters of congratulation.* **2** V-T If you **congratulate** someone, you praise them for something good that they have done. ❑ *I really must congratulate the organisers for a well run and enjoyable event.*

1 타동사 축하하다 ❑ 그녀는 아들을 얻은 그를 축하했다. ● 축하 불가산명사 ❑ 우리는 축하 편지를 많이 받았다. **2** 타동사 찬사를 보내다 ❑ 순조롭고 즐거운 행사를 마련해 주신 조직위원 여러분들께 진심으로 찬사를 보냅니다.

a
b
c
d
e
f
g
h
i
j
k
l
m
n
o
p
q
r
s
t
u
v
w
x
y
z

congratulations /kəngrætʃəleɪʃnz/ **1** CONVENTION You say "**Congratulations**" to someone in order to congratulate them on something nice that has happened to them or something good that they have done. [FORMULAE] ❑ *Congratulations, you have a healthy baby boy.* ❑ *Congratulations on your interesting article.* **2** N-PLURAL If you offer someone your **congratulations**, you congratulate them on something nice that has happened to them or on something good that they have done. ❑ *The club also offers its congratulations to D. Brown on his appointment as president.*

1 관용 표현 축하합니다 [의례적인 표현] ❑ 축하합니다. 건강한 아드님을 얻으셨어요. ❑ 축하합니다. 재미있는 글을 쓰셨군요. **2** 복수명사 축하인사 ❑ 클럽은 회장으로 임명된 디 브라운에게도 축하인사를 보냅니다.

congregate /kɒŋgrɪgeɪt/ (**congregates, congregating, congregated**) V-I When people **congregate**, they gather together and form a group. ❑ *Visitors congregated on Sunday afternoons to view public exhibitions.*

자동사 모이다 ❑ 일요일 오후 방문객들이 공공 전시회 관람을 위해 모여들었다.

congregation /kɒŋgrɪgeɪʃn/ (**congregations**) N-COUNT-COLL The people who are attending a religious service or who regularly attend a religious service are referred to as the **congregation**. ❑ *Most members of the congregation begin arriving a few minutes before services.*

가산명사-집합 회중 ❑ 교인 대부분이 예배 시작 몇 분 전에 도착하기 시작했다.

congress /kɒŋgrɪs/ (**congresses**) N-COUNT-COLL A **congress** is a large meeting that is held to discuss ideas and policies. ❑ *A lot has changed after the party congress.*

가산명사-집합 대회 ❑ 당대회 이후로 많은 것이 바뀌었다.

Congress ♦♦◇ N-PROPER-COLL **Congress** is the elected group of politicians that is responsible for making laws in the United States. It consists of two parts: the House of Representatives and the Senate. ❑ *We want to cooperate with both the administration and Congress.* →see **government**

고유명사-집합 의회 ❑ 우리는 행정부와 의회 둘 다와 협력하기를 원한다.

congressional ♦◇◇ /kəngreʃənl/ also **Congressional** ADJ A **congressional** policy, action, or person relates to the U.S. Congress. [ADJ n] ❑ *The president explained his plans to congressional leaders.*

형용사 의회의 ❑ 대통령이 의회 지도자들에게 그의 계획을 설명했다.

congressman /kɒŋgrɪsmən/ (**congressmen**) N-COUNT; N-TITLE A **congressman** is a male member of the U.S. Congress, especially of the House of Representatives. →see **government**

가산명사; 경칭명사 남성 하원의원

congresswoman /kɒŋgrɪswʊmən/ (**congresswomen**) N-COUNT; N-TITLE A **congresswoman** is a female member of the U.S. Congress, especially of the House of Representatives. ❑ *The meeting was organised by Congresswoman Maxine Waters.* →see **government**

가산명사; 경칭명사 이성 하원의원 ❑ 맥신 워터스 하원의원이 회의를 조직을 맡았다.

conjecture /kəndʒektʃər/ (**conjectures, conjecturing, conjectured**) **1** N-VAR A **conjecture** is a conclusion that is based on information that is not certain or complete. [FORMAL] ❑ *That was a conjecture, not a fact.* ❑ *There are several conjectures.* **2** V-T/V-I When you **conjecture**, you form an opinion or reach a conclusion on the basis of information that is not certain or complete. [FORMAL] ❑ *He conjectured that some individuals may be able to detect major calamities.*

1 가산명사 또는 불가산명사 추측, 억측 [격식체] ❑ 그것은 사실이 아닌 추측이었다. ❑ 몇 가지 추측이 가능하다. **2** 타동사/자동사 추측하다, 억측하다 [격식체] ❑ 주요 재난을 감지하는 능력을 지닌 사람들이 있을지도 모른다고 그가 추측했다.

conjunction /kəndʒʌŋkʃn/ (**conjunctions**) **1** N-COUNT A **conjunction of** two or more things is the occurrence of them at the same time or place. [FORMAL] ❑ *...the conjunction of two events.* **2** N-COUNT In grammar, a **conjunction** is a word or group of words that joins together words, groups, or clauses. In English, there are coordinating conjunctions such as "and" and "but," and subordinating conjunctions such as "although," "because," and "when."

1 가산명사 동시 발생 [격식체] ❑ 두 사건이 동시에 발생한 사실 **2** 가산명사 접속사

conjure /kʌndʒər, BRIT kʌndʒəʳ/ (**conjures, conjuring, conjured**) V-T If you **conjure** something out of nothing, you make it appear as if by magic. ❑ *Thirteen years ago she found herself having to conjure a career from thin air.* ● PHRASAL VERB **Conjure up** means the same as **conjure**. ❑ *Every day a different chef will be conjuring up delicious dishes in the restaurant.*

타동사 요술을 부리듯 생기게 하다 ❑ 13년 전 그녀는 아무것도 없는 상태에서 요술을 부리듯 직장을 구해야만 했다. ● 구동사 요술을 부리듯 생기게 하다 ❑ 레스토랑에서 매일 다른 주방장이 요술을 부리듯 맛있는 음식을 만들어 낼 것이다.

▶**conjure up** PHRASAL VERB **1** If you **conjure up** a memory, picture, or idea, you create it in your mind. ❑ *When he closed his eyes, he could conjure up in exact color almost every event of his life.* **2** →see **conjure**

1 구동사 떠올리다 ❑ 눈을 감으면, 그는 인생의 거의 모든 일들을 생생하게 떠올릴 수 있었다.

connect /kənekt/ (**connects, connecting, connected**) **1** V-RECIP If something or someone **connects** one thing **to** another, or if one thing **connects to** another, the two things are joined together. ❑ *You can connect the machine to your hi-fi.* ❑ *The adrenaline was rushing through me as I fumbled to connect the wires.* **2** V-T If a piece of equipment or a place **is connected to** a source of power or water, it is joined to that source so that it has power or water. ❑ *These appliances should not be connected to power supplies.* ● PHRASAL VERB **Connect up** means the same as **connect**. ❑ *The shower is easy to install – it needs only to be connected up to the hot and cold water supply.* **3** V-RECIP If two things or places **connect** or if something **connects** them, they are joined and people or things can pass between them. ❑ *...the long hallway that connects the rooms.* ❑ *The fallopian tubes connect the ovaries with the uterus.* **4** V-RECIP If one train or plane, for example, **connects with** another, it arrives at a time which allows passengers to change to the other one in order to continue their trip. ❑ *...a train connecting with a ferry to Ireland.* **5** V-T If you **connect** a person or thing **with** something, you realize that there is a link or relationship between them. ❑ *I hoped he would not connect me with that now-embarrassing review I'd written seven years earlier.* **6** V-T Something that **connects** a person or thing **with** something else shows or provides a link or relationship between them. ❑ *A search of Brady's house revealed nothing that could connect him with the robberies.*

1 상호동사 연결하다; 연결되다 ❑ 그 기계를 오디오에 연결할 수 있다. ❑ 전선을 연결하려고 더듬거리고 있자니 온몸에 긴장감이 감돌았다. **2** 타동사 연결되다 ❑ 이들 장비는 전원에 연결시키면 안 된다. ● 구동사 연결하다 ❑ 샤워기 설치는 쉽다. 샤워기를 뜨거운 물과 차가운 물 공급원에 연결시키기만 하면 된다. **3** 상호동사 연결하다, 잇다 ❑ 방 사이를 연결하는 긴 복도 ❑ 나팔관이 난소와 자궁을 연결하다 **4** 상호동사 -와 연계되다 ❑ -와 연결되는 아일랜드 행 여객선과 연계된 기차 **5** 타동사 -와 ...을 연결시키다, -을 보고 ... 을 떠올리다 ❑ 그가 나를 보고 내가 7년 전에 쓴, 지금 생각하면 창피한 평론을 떠올리지 않기를 바랐다. **6** 타동사 -와 ... 의 관계를 보여 주다 ❑ 브래디의 자택 수색 결과 그와 강도 사건들 간의 관계를 증명할 만한 것을 하나도 찾지 못했다.

connected /kənektɪd/ ADJ If one thing is **connected with** another, there is a link or relationship between them. ❑ *Have you ever had any skin problems connected with exposure to the sun?* ❑ *The dispute is not directly connected to the negotiations.* →see also **connect, well-connected**

형용사 -와 관련된, -와 관계 있는 ❑ 태양 광선 노출과 관련된 피부 질환을 앓은 적이 있습니까? ❑ 논쟁이 협상과 직접적으로 관계된 것은 아니다.

connection ♦◇◇ /kənekʃn/ (**connections**) [BRIT also **connexion**] **1** N-VAR A **connection** is a relationship between two things, people, or groups. ❑ *There was no evidence of a connection between BSE and the brain diseases recently confirmed in cats.* **2** N-COUNT A **connection** is a point where two wires or pipes are joined together. ❑ *Check all radiators for small leaks, especially round pipework connections.* **3** N-COUNT If a place has good road, rail, or air **connections**, many places can be directly reached from there by car, train, or plane. ❑ *Fukuoka has excellent air*

[영국영어 connexion] **1** 가산명사 또는 불가산명사 관계, 관련 ❑ 광우병과 최근 고양이에서 확인된 뇌질환 사이의 관계를 뒷받침할 증거가 없었다. **2** 가산명사 연결 부분, 접합 부분 ❑ 동그란 파이프 연결 부분을 중심으로 라디에이터에 조금이라도 새는 부분이 있나 찾아보세요. **3** 가산명사 연결, 연계 ❑ 후쿠오카는 비행기나 기차로 다른 지역과 잘 연결되어 있다.

and rail connections to the rest of the country. ◳ N-COUNT If you get a **connection** at a station or airport, you catch a train, bus, or plane, after getting off another train, bus, or plane, in order to continue your trip. ❑ *My flight was late and I missed the connection.* ◳ PHRASE If you write or talk to someone **in connection with** something, you write or talk to them about that thing. [FORMAL] ❑ *I am writing in connection with Michael Shower's letter.*

con|nec|tiv|ity /kɒnɛktɪvəti/ N-UNCOUNT **Connectivity** is the ability of a computing device to connect to other computers or to the Internet. [COMPUTING] ❑ *...a DVD video and CD player with Internet connectivity.*

con|nois|seur /kɒnəsɜr, -sʊər/ (**connoisseurs**) N-COUNT A **connoisseur** is someone who knows a lot about the arts, food, drink, or some other subject. ❑ *Sarah tells me you're something of an art connoisseur.*

con|no|ta|tion /kɒnəteɪʃ³n/ (**connotations**) N-COUNT The **connotations** of a particular word or name are the ideas or qualities which it makes you think of. ❑ *It's just one of those words that's got so many negative connotations.*

con|quer /kɒŋkər/ (**conquers, conquering, conquered**) ◳ V-T If one country or group of people **conquers** another, they take complete control of their land. ❑ *During 1936, Mussolini conquered Abyssinia.* ◲ V-T If you **conquer** something such as a problem, you succeed in ending it or dealing with it successfully. ❑ *I was certain that love was quite enough to conquer our differences.* ❑ *He has never conquered his addiction to smoking.* →see **army, empire**

con|quer|or /kɒŋkərər/ (**conquerors**) N-COUNT The **conquerors** of a country or group of people are the people who have taken complete control of that country or group's land. ❑ *The people of an oppressed country obey their conquerors because they want to go on living.*

con|quest /kɒŋkwɛst/ (**conquests**) ◳ N-UNCOUNT **Conquest** is the act of conquering a country or group of people. [also N in pl, oft N of n] ❑ *He had led the conquest of southern Poland in 1939.* ❑ *After the Norman Conquest the forest became a royal hunting preserve.* ◲ N-COUNT **Conquests** are lands that have been conquered in war. ❑ *He had realized that Britain could not have peace unless she returned at least some of her former conquests.* ◳ N-SING **The conquest of** something such as a problem is success in ending it or dealing with it. ❑ *The conquest of inflation has been the Government's overriding economic priority for nearly 15 years.*

Word Link	sci ≈ knowing : con*science*, con*scious*, *science*

con|science /kɒnʃns/ (**consciences**) ◳ N-COUNT Your **conscience** is the part of your mind that tells you whether what you are doing is right or wrong. If you have a **guilty conscience**, you feel guilty about something because you know it was wrong. If you have a **clear conscience**, you do not feel guilty because you know you have done nothing wrong. ❑ *I have battled with my conscience over whether I should actually send this letter.* ❑ *What if he got a guilty conscience and brought it back?* ◲ N-UNCOUNT **Conscience** is doing what you believe is right even though it might be unpopular, difficult, or dangerous. ❑ *He refused for reasons of conscience to sign a new law legalizing abortion.* ◳ N-UNCOUNT **Conscience** is a feeling of guilt because you know you have done something that is wrong. ❑ *I'm so glad he had a pang of conscience.* ◴ PHRASE If you have something **on** your **conscience**, you feel guilty because you know you have done something wrong. ❑ *Now the murderer has two deaths on his conscience.*

con|sci|en|tious /kɒnʃiɛnʃəs/ ADJ Someone who is **conscientious** is very careful to do their work properly. ❑ *We are generally very conscientious about our work.* ● con|sci|en|tious|ly ADV ❑ *He studied conscientiously and enthusiastically.*

con|scious ◆◇◇ /kɒnʃəs/ ◳ ADJ If you are **conscious of** something, you notice it or realize that it is happening. [v-link ADJ of n/-ing, v-link ADJ that] ❑ *He was conscious of the faint, musky aroma of aftershave.* ❑ *She was very conscious of Max studying her.* ◲ ADJ If you are **conscious of** something, you think about it a lot, especially because you are unhappy about it or because you think it is important. [v-link ADJ of n/-ing, v-link ADJ that] ❑ *I'm very conscious of my weight.* ◳ ADJ A **conscious** decision or action is made or done deliberately with you giving your full attention to it. ❑ *I don't think we ever made a conscious decision to have a big family.* ● con|scious|ly ADV [ADV with v] ❑ *Sophie was not consciously seeking a replacement after her father died.* ◴ ADJ Someone who is **conscious** is awake rather than asleep or unconscious. ❑ *She was fully conscious all the time and knew what was going on.* ◵ ADJ **Conscious** memories or thoughts are ones that you are aware of. [ADJ n] ❑ *He had no conscious memory of his four-week stay in the hospital.* ● con|scious|ly ADV ❑ *Most people cannot consciously remember much before the ages of 5 to 7 years.* →see **hypnosis**

Thesaurus	conscious의 참조어
ADJ.	calculated, deliberate, intentional, rational; (ant.) unintentional ◳ awake, aware, responsive; (ant.) unaware, unconscious ◴

-conscious /kɒnʃəs/ COMB in ADJ **-conscious** combines with words such as "health," "fashion," "politically," and "environmentally" to form adjectives which describe someone who believes that the aspect of life indicated is important. ❑ *We're all becoming increasingly health-conscious these days.*

Word Link	ness ≈ state, condition : conscious*ness*, happi*ness*, kind*ness*

con|scious|ness ◆◇◇ /kɒnʃəsnəs/ (**consciousnesses**) ◳ N-COUNT Your

---

◳ 가산명사 갈아탐, 연결편 ❑ 비행기가 연착되는 바람에 연결편을 놓쳤다. ◵ 구 -과 관련해 [격식체] ❑ 저는 마이클 샤워의 편지와 관련해 이 글을 드립니다.

불가산명사 접속 [컴퓨터] ❑ 인터넷 접속이 가능한 디브이디 및 시디플레이어

가산명사 감식가 ❑ 당신이 훌륭한 미술 감식가라고 사라에게 들었어요.

가산명사 함축적 의미, 내포된 의미 ❑ 이는 부정적인 의미를 함축하는 아주 많은 단어 중 하나일 뿐이다.

◳ 타동사 정복하다 ❑ 1936년 무솔리니가 아비시니아를 정복했다. ◲ 타동사 극복하다, 공략하다 ❑ 사랑이면 우리 사이의 차이점을 극복하는 데 충분하다고 나는 확신했다. ❑ 그는 단 한번도 담배를 끊지 못했다.

가산명사 정복자 ❑ 압제를 받던 사람들은 생계를 이어 가기 위해 정복자에게 복종했다.

◳ 불가산명사 정복 ❑ 그는 1939년 폴란드 남부 정복의 주역이었다. ❑ 노르만 정복 이후 그 숲이 왕족의 사냥터가 되었다. ◲ 가산명사 점령지 ❑ 영국이 점령지의 최소한 일부라도 반환하지 않는 한 영국의 평화는 불가능하다는 것을 그는 깨달았다. ◳ 단수명사 극복 ❑ 근 15년 동안 정부의 최우선 경제 과제는 인플레이션 극복이었다.

◳ 가산명사 양심; 양심의 가책; 떳떳한 마음 ❑ 이 편지를 정말 보내야 할지를 두고 나는 양심의 갈등을 느꼈다. ❑ 그가 양심의 가책을 느끼고 돌려준다면 어떨까? ◲ 불가산명사 양심 ❑ 그는 양심상의 이유를 들어 낙태를 허용하는 새 법안의 서명을 거부했다. ◳ 불가산명사 양심 ❑ 그가 양심의 가책을 느껴서 정말 다행이야. ◴ 구 양심에 걸리는 ❑ 살인자는 이제 두 사람의 죽음이 양심에 걸렸다.

형용사 꼼꼼한 ❑ 우리는 대체로 일을 굉장히 꼼꼼하게 한다. ● 꼼꼼하게 부사 ❑ 그는 꼼꼼하게 그리고 열성적으로 공부했다.

◳ 형용사 의식하고 있는 ❑ 그는 애프터세이브의 열은 사향 냄새를 의식하고 있었다. ❑ 맥스가 자신을 유심히 관찰한다는 것을 그녀는 크게 의식하고 있었다. ◲ 형용사 의식하고 있는 ❑ 나는 내 몸무게를 굉장히 의식한다. ◳ 형용사 의식적인, 의도적인 ❑ 우리가 대가족을 꾸리겠다고 의식적으로 결정한 적은 없는 것 같아. ● 의식적으로, 의도적으로 부사 ❑ 소피가 아버지가 돌아가신 이후로 의식적으로 그를 대체할 사람을 찾은 것은 아니었다. ◴ 형용사 의식이 깨어 있는 ❑ 그녀의 의식은 시종 완전히 깨어 있었고 무슨 일이 벌어지는지 알고 있었다. ◵ 형용사 의식하는 ❑ 그의 의식에 병원에서 지낸 4주에 대한 기억이 남아 있지 않았다. ● 의식적으로 부사 ❑ 대부분의 사람들은 5세부터 7세 훨씬 이전의 기억이 의식에 남아 있지 않다.

복합형-형용사 -에 신경을 쓰는 ❑ 요즘 우리는 모두 건강에 대해 점점 더 신경을 많이 쓴다.

◳ 가산명사 의식 ❑ 그 생각이 우리의 의식으로

consciousness is your mind and your thoughts. □ *That idea has been creeping into our consciousness for some time.* **2** N-UNCOUNT The **consciousness** of a group of people is their set of ideas, attitudes, and beliefs. □ *The Greens were the catalysts of a necessary change in the European consciousness.* **3** N-UNCOUNT You use **consciousness** to refer to an interest in and knowledge of a particular subject or idea. □ *Her political consciousness sprang from her upbringing when her father's illness left the family short of money.* **4** N-UNCOUNT **Consciousness** is the state of being awake rather than being asleep or unconscious. If someone **loses consciousness**, they become unconscious, and if they **regain consciousness**, they become conscious after being unconscious. □ *She banged her head and lost consciousness.*

con|script (**conscripts**, **conscripting**, **conscripted**)

The noun is pronounced /ˈkɒnskrɪpt/. The verb is pronounced /kənˈskrɪpt/.

1 N-COUNT A **conscript** is a person who has been made to join the armed forces of a country. □ *Most of the soldiers are reluctant conscripts.* **2** V-T If someone **is conscripted**, they are officially made to join the armed forces of a country. [usu passive] □ *He was conscripted into the German army.*

con|scrip|tion /kənˈskrɪpʃᵊn/ N-UNCOUNT **Conscription** is officially making people in a particular country join the armed forces. □ *All adult males will be liable for conscription.*

con|se|crate /ˈkɒnsɪkreɪt/ (**consecrates**, **consecrating**, **consecrated**) V-T When a building, place, or object **is consecrated**, it is officially declared to be holy. When a person **is consecrated**, they are officially declared to be a bishop. □ *The church was consecrated in 1234.*

con|secu|tive /kənˈsekyətɪv/ ADJ **Consecutive** periods of time or events happen one after the other without interruption. □ *The Cup was won for the third consecutive year by the Toronto Maple Leafs.*

Word Link   con ≈ together, with : consensus, contemporary, convene

con|sen|sus /kənˈsensəs/ N-SING A **consensus** is general agreement among a group of people. [also no det] □ *The consensus amongst the world's scientists is that the world is likely to warm up over the next few decades.*

con|sent /kənˈsent/ (**consents**, **consenting**, **consented**) **1** N-UNCOUNT If you give your **consent to** something, you give someone permission to do it. [FORMAL] □ *At approximately 11:30 p.m., Pollard finally gave his consent to the search.* **2** V-T/V-I If you **consent to** something, you agree to do it or to allow it to be done. [FORMAL] □ *He finally consented to go.* □ *He asked Ginny if she would consent to a small celebration after the christening.* **3** →see also **age of consent**

Word Link   sequ ≈ following : consequence, sequel, sequence

con|se|quence ♦◊◊ /ˈkɒnsɪkwens, -kwəns/ (**consequences**) **1** N-COUNT The **consequences of** something are the results or effects of it. □ *Her lawyer said she understood the consequences of her actions and was prepared to go to jail.* **2** PHRASE If one thing happens and then another thing happens **in consequence** or **as a consequence**, the second thing happens as a result of the first. □ *His death was totally unexpected and, in consequence, no plans had been made for his replacement.* □ *Maternity services were to be reduced in consequence of falling birth rates.*

Word Partnership   consequence의 연어

PREP.	consequences **for/of something** **1**
ADJ.	**disastrous** consequence, **unfortunate** consequence **1**
V.	**suffer the** consequences **1**

con|se|quent /ˈkɒnsɪkwent, -kwənt/ ADJ **Consequent** means happening as a direct result of an event or situation. [FORMAL] □ *The warming of the Earth and the consequent climatic changes affect us all.*

con|se|quent|ly /ˈkɒnsɪkwentli, -kwəntli/ ADV **Consequently** means as a result. [FORMAL] [ADV with cl] □ *Grandfather Dingsdale had sustained a broken back while working in the mines. Consequently, he spent the rest of his life in a wheelchair.*

con|ser|va|tion /ˌkɒnsərˈveɪʃᵊn/ **1** N-UNCOUNT **Conservation** is saving and protecting the environment. □ *...a four-nation regional meeting on elephant conservation.* **2** N-UNCOUNT **Conservation** is saving and protecting historical objects or works of art such as paintings, buildings, or buildings. □ *Then he began his most famous work, the conservation and rebinding of the Book of Kells.* **3** N-UNCOUNT The **conservation** of a supply of something is the careful use of it so that it lasts for a long time. □ *...projects aimed at promoting energy conservation.*

con|ser|va|tion|ist /ˌkɒnsərˈveɪʃənɪst/ (**conservationists**) N-COUNT A **conservationist** is someone who cares greatly about the conservation of the environment and who works to protect it. □ *Conservationists say the law must be strengthened.*

con|ser|va|tism /kənˈsɜrvətɪzəm/

The spelling **Conservatism** is also used for meaning **1**.

1 N-UNCOUNT **Conservatism** is a political philosophy which believes that if changes need to be made to society, they should be made gradually. You can also refer to the political beliefs of a conservative party in a particular country

---

스며들기 시작한 지는 꽤 되었다. **2** 불가산명사 의식 구조 □ 녹색당은 유럽의 의식 구조에 필요한 변화를 이끈 촉매 역할을 했다. **3** 불가산명사 의식, 인식 □ 그녀의 정치의식은 아버지의 질병 때문에 가족이 금전적으로 궁핍하게 된 성장 배경에서 싹텄다. **4** 불가산명사 의식; 의식을 잃다; 의식을 되찾다 □ 그녀는 머리를 부딪치고 의식을 잃었다.

명사는 /ˈkɒnskrɪpt/로 발음되고, 동사는 /kənˈskrɪpt/로 발음된다.

1 가산명사 징집병 □ 군인 대부분은 마지못해 끌려온 징집병이었다. **2** 타동사 징집되다 □ 그는 독일 육군으로 징집되었다.

불가산명사 징집 □ 모든 성인 남성은 징집 대상이 된다.

타동사 축성되다; 주교에 임명되다 □ 교회는 1234년에 축성되었다.

형용사 연속의 □ 토론토의 메이플 리프스가 3년 연속 컵을 차지했다.

단수명사 의견의 일치 □ 전 세계 과학자들이 대체로 동의하는 바는 앞으로 몇십 년에 걸쳐 지구가 온난화되리라는 것이다.

1 불가산명사 허락 [격식체] □ 저녁 11시 30분 경에 폴라드는 드디어 수색을 허락했다. **2** 타동사/자동사 동의하다 [격식체] □ 그는 드디어 가기로 동의했다. □ 그는 지니에게 세례식 이후 작은 축하연을 하는 것에 동의하겠냐고 물었다.

1 가산명사 결과 □ 그녀의 변호사는 그녀가 자신의 행동의 결과를 이해하고 있으며 감옥에 갈 준비가 되어 있다고 말했다. **2** 구 결과적으로 □ 그의 죽음은 전혀 뜻밖이었으며 결과적으로 그를 대체할 사람에 대한 준비가 전혀 되어 있지 않은 상태였다. □ 출산율에 따른 감소 결과로 출산 서비스가 축소될 계획이었다.

형용사 결과적인 [격식체] □ 지구의 온난화와 그 결과로 생기는 기후 변화는 우리 모두에게 영향을 끼친다.

부사 결과적으로 [격식체] □ 딩스데일 할아버지께서는 광산에서 일하면서 허리를 다쳤다. 그 결과 그 분은 여생 동안 휠체어를 타셨다.

1 불가산명사 환경 보호 □ 인근 4개 국가의 코끼리 보호에 관한 회의 **2** 불가산명사 보존 □ 그리고 그는 그가 한 일 중 가장 널리 알려진 작업, 즉 켈스서의 보존 및 재제본 작업을 시작했다. **3** 불가산명사 절약 □ 에너지 절약을 권장하는 것이 목표인 사업들

가산명사 환경 보호주의자 □ 환경 보호주의자들은 법이 더 강화되어야 한다고 한다.

철자 Conservatism도 **1** 의미로 쓴다.

1 불가산명사 보수주의 □ 현대 보수주의 철학 **2** 불가산명사 보수주의 □ 이 나라 문인 사회의 보수주의는 놀라울 뿐이다.

as **Conservatism**. ❑ *...the philosophy of modern Conservatism.* ◳ N-UNCOUNT **Conservatism** is unwillingness to accept changes and new ideas. ❑ *The conservatism of the literary establishment in this country is astounding.*

con|serva|tive ♦♦◇ /kənsɜrvətɪv/ (**conservatives**)

> The spelling **Conservative** is also used for meaning ◳.

◳ ADJ A **Conservative** politician or voter is a member of or votes for the Conservative Party in Britain and in various other countries. ❑ *Most Conservative MPs appear happy with the government's reassurances.* ● N-COUNT **Conservative** is also a noun. ❑ *In 1951 the Conservatives were returned to power.* ◱ ADJ Someone who is **conservative** has right-wing views. ❑ *...counties whose citizens invariably support the most conservative candidate in any election.* ● N-COUNT **Conservative** is also a noun. ❑ *The new judge is 50-year-old David Suitor who's regarded as a conservative.* ◳ ADJ Someone who is **conservative** or has **conservative** ideas is unwilling to accept changes and new ideas. ❑ *People tend to be more aggressive when they're young and more conservative as they get older.* ◴ ADJ If someone dresses in a **conservative** way, their clothes are conventional in style. ❑ *The girl was well dressed, as usual, though in a more conservative style.* ● **con|serva|tive|ly** ADV [ADV with v] ❑ *She was always very conservatively dressed when we went out.* ◵ ADJ A **conservative** estimate or guess is one in which you are cautious and estimate or guess a low amount which is probably less that the real amount. ❑ *The average fan spends $25 – a conservative estimate based on ticket price and souvenirs.* ● **con|serva|tive|ly** ADV [ADV with v] ❑ *The bequest is conservatively estimated at £30 million.*

> **Thesaurus**   conservative의 참조어
>
> ADJ.   conventional, right-wing, traditional; (ant.) left-wing, liberal, radical ◱ ◳

Con|serva|tive Party N-PROPER The **Conservative Party** is the main right of center party in Britain. In various other countries, the **Conservative Party** is a political party generally opposing change.

con|serva|tory /kənsɜrvətɔri, BRIT kənsɜːˈvətri/ (**conservatories**) ◳ N-COUNT A **conservatory** is a room with glass walls and a glass roof, which is attached to a house. People often grow plants in a conservatory. ◱ N-COUNT; N-IN-NAMES A **conservatory** is an institution where musicians are trained. ❑ *...the New England Conservatory of Music.*

> **Word Link**   serv ≈ keeping : conserve, observe, preserve

con|serve /kənsɜrv/ (**conserves, conserving, conserved**) ◳ V-T If you **conserve** a supply of something, you use it carefully so that it lasts for a long time. ❑ *The republic's factories have closed for the weekend to conserve energy.* ◱ V-T To **conserve** something means to protect it from harm, loss, or change. ❑ *...a big increase in U.S. aid to help developing countries conserve their forests.*

con|sid|er ♦♦♦ /kənsɪdər/ (**considers, considering, considered**) ◳ V-T If you **consider** a person or thing **to** be something, you have the opinion that this is what they are. ❑ *We don't consider our customers to be mere consumers; we consider them to be our friends.* ❑ *I had always considered myself a strong, competent woman.* ◱ V-T If you **consider** something, you think about it carefully. ❑ *The government is being asked to consider a plan to fix the date of the Easter break.* ❑ *You do have to consider the feelings of those around you.* ◳ V-T If you **are considering** doing something, you intend to do it, but have not yet made a final decision whether to do it. ❑ *I had seriously considered telling the story from the point of view of the wives.* ◴ →see also **considering**

> Note that when you are using the verb **consider** with a "that"-clause in order to state a negative opinion or belief, you normally make **consider** negative, rather than the verb in the "that"-clause. For instance, it is more usual to say "I don't consider that you kept your promise." than "I consider that you didn't keep your promise." The same pattern applies to other verbs with a similar meaning, such as **believe**, **suppose**, and **think**.

> **Thesaurus**   consider의 참조어
>
> V.   contemplate, examine, study, think about, think over; (ant.) dismiss, forget, ignore ◱

con|sid|er|able ♦♦◇ /kənsɪdərəbᵊl/ ADJ **Considerable** means great in amount or degree. [FORMAL] ❑ *To be without Pearce would be a considerable blow.* ❑ *Doing it properly makes considerable demands on our time.* ● **con|sid|er|ably** ADV ❑ *Children vary considerably in the rate at which they learn these lessons.*

> **Word Link**   ate ≈ filled with : affectionate, compassionate, considerate

con|sid|er|ate /kənsɪdərɪt/ ADJ Someone who is **considerate** pays attention to the needs, wishes, or feelings of other people. [APPROVAL] ❑ *I think he's the most charming, most considerate man I've ever known.*

con|sid|er|ation ♦♦◇ /kənsɪdəreɪʃᵊn/ (**considerations**) ◳ N-UNCOUNT **Consideration** is careful thought about something. ❑ *He said there should be careful consideration of the future role of the BBC.* ◱ N-UNCOUNT If something is **under consideration**, it is being discussed. ❑ *Several proposals are under consideration by the state assembly.* ◳ N-UNCOUNT If you show **consideration**, you pay attention to the needs, wishes, or feelings of other people. ❑ *Show*

철자 Conservative도 ◳ 의미로 쓴다.

◳ 형용사 보수정당의 ❑ 대부분의 보수 국회의원들은 정부의 안심시키려는 노력에 만족하는 것 같다. ● 가산명사 보수주의자 ❑ 1951년에 보수주의자들이 권력을 다시 쥐었다. ◱ 형용사 우익의 ❑ 어느 선거에서든 변함없이 가장 우경화된 후보를 지지하는 구들 ● 가산명사 우익 인사, 보수주의자 ❑ 새 판사는 보수주의자로 알려져 있는 50세의 데이비드 수터이다. ◳ 형용사 보수적인 ❑ 사람들은 젊었을 때 보다 적극적이다가 나이가 들수록 보수적으로 변하는 경향이 있다. ◴ 형용사 점잖은 ❑ 그 처녀는 평상시보다 차림이 더 점잖긴 했지만 늘 그렇듯 옷을 잘 입고 있었다. ● 점잖게 부사 ❑ 그녀는 우리가 같이 외출을 할 때 항상 옷을 아주 점잖게 입었다. ◵ 형용사 조심스러운 ❑ 보통의 팬은 25달러를 쓰는데, 입장료와 기념품에 근거한 신중한 추산이다. ● 조심스럽게 부사 ❑ 유산은 적게 잡아도 3천만 파운드 정도는 될 것이다.

고유명사 (영국의) 보수당

◳ 가산명사 온실 ◱ 가산명사; 이름명사 음악 학교 ❑ 뉴잉글랜드 음악 학교

◳ 타동사 절약하다, 아끼다 ❑ 공화국의 공장들은 에너지를 아끼기 위해 주말 동안 문을 닫았다. ◱ 타동사 보호하다 ❑ 개발 도상 국가들의 삼림 보호를 돕는 미국 지원금의 대규모 증가

◳ 타동사 ...라고 여기다 ❑ 우리는 고객을 단순한 고객이라고 생각하지 않는다. 우리는 그들을 우리의 친구라고 생각한다. ❑ 나는 항상 나 자신을 강하고 유능한 여자라고 생각했었다. ◱ 타동사 고려하다 ❑ 부활절 연휴 날짜를 정하는 계획을 고려하라는 요청을 정부는 받았다. ❑ 반드시 네 주변 사람들의 기분을 고려해야 한다. ◳ 타동사 고려하다 ❑ 나는 그 이야기를 아내들의 시점에서 서술하는 것도 심각하게 고려했었다.

부정적인 의견이나 믿음을 표현하기 위해서 동사 consider를 that 절과 함께 쓸 때는, 대개 that 절 속의 동사가 아니라 consider를 부정형으로 만든다. 예를 들면, "I don't consider that you kept your promise."라고 말하는 것이 "I consider that you didn't keep your promise."라고 하는 것보다 더 일반적이다. 뜻이 비슷한 believe, suppose, think와 같은 동사도 마찬가지다.

형용사 상당한 [격식체] ❑ 피어스가 없으면 타격이 상당할 것이다. ❑ 그 일을 제대로 하려면 우리가 상당한 시간을 투자해야 한다. ● 상당하게 부사 ❑ 이 과정들을 배우는 속도에 있어 아이들은 상당한 편차를 보인다.

형용사 사려 깊은, 배려하는 [마음에 듦] ❑ 그는 내가 아는 사람 중에 가장 매력적이고 사려 깊은 남자인 것 같다.

◳ 불가산명사 고려 ❑ 비비시의 앞날의 역할에 대해 심각하게 고려해 봐야 한다고 그는 이야기했다. ◱ 불가산명사 고려 중인 ❑ 주 의회가 여러 개의 안을 고려하는 중이다. ◳ 불가산명사 배려 ❑ 다른 기차 승객들에 대해 배려를 보이세요. ◴ 가산명사 고려 사항 ❑ 불황 전에 비해 어느 가게에 가느냐를 정하는

consideration for other rail travellers. ◢ N-COUNT A **consideration** is something that should be thought about, especially when you are planning or deciding something. ❏ *Price has become a more important consideration for shoppers in choosing which store to visit than it was before the recession.* ◣ PHRASE If you **take** something **into consideration**, you think about it because it is relevant to what you are doing. ❏ *Safe driving is good driving because it takes into consideration the lives of other people.*

데 있어서 가격이 더 중요한 고려 사항이 되었다. ◣ 구 -을 고려하다 ❏ 안전 운전은 타인의 목숨을 고려하는 것이므로 좋은 운전이라고 할 수 있다.

Word Partnership	consideration의 연어
ADJ.	**careful** consideration, **an important** consideration ◢
PREP.	**in** consideration of ◢
	under consideration ◢
V.	**show** consideration ◢
	take into consideration ◣

con|sid|er|ing ♦◇◇ /kənsɪdərɪŋ/ ◢ PREP You use **considering** to indicate that you are thinking about a particular fact when making a judgment or giving an opinion. ❏ *He must be hoping, but considering the situation in June he may be hoping for too much too soon.* ◢ CONJ You use **considering that** to indicate that you are thinking about a particular fact when making a judgment or giving an opinion. ❏ *Considering that you are no longer involved with this man, your response is a little extreme.* ◢ ADV When you are giving an opinion or making a judgment, you can use **considering** to suggest that you have thought about all the circumstances, and often that something has succeeded in spite of these circumstances. [SPOKEN] [cl ADV] ❏ *I think you're pretty safe, considering.*

◢ 전치사 -을 고려하면 ❏ 그는 희망을 걸고 있을지 모르나 6월의 상황을 생각하면 그는 너무 많은 것을 너무 빨리 바라는지도 모르겠다. ◢ 접속사 -을 고려하면 ❏ 네가 이 남자와 더 이상 관련이 없다는 것을 고려한다면 네 반응은 조금 지나치다. ◢ 부사 모든 점을 고려해 볼 때 [구어체] ❏ 모든 것을 고려해 볼 때 너는 꽤 안전한 것 같다.

con|sign /kənsaɪn/ (consigns, consigning, consigned) V-T To **consign** something or someone **to** a place where they will be forgotten about, or **to** an unpleasant situation or place, means to put them there. [FORMAL] ❏ *For decades, many of Malevich's works were consigned to the basements of Soviet museums.*

타동사 -에 내버려 두다 [격식체] ❏ 수십 년간, 말레비치의 많은 작품들이 소련 박물관의 지하실에 내버려져 있었다.

con|sign|ment /kənsaɪnmənt/ (consignments) N-COUNT A **consignment of** goods is a load that is being delivered to a place or person. ❏ *The first consignment of food has already left Bologna.*

가산명사 탁송품 ❏ 첫 번째 수송 분량 식품이 볼로냐에서 출발했다.

con|sist ♦◇◇ /kənsɪst/ (consists, consisting, consisted) ◢ V-I Something that **consists of** particular things or people is formed from them. ❏ *My diet consisted almost exclusively of chocolate-covered cookies and glasses of milk.* ◢ V-I Something that **consists in** something else has that thing as its main or only part. ❏ *His work as a consultant consisted in advising foreign companies on the siting of new factories.*

◢ 자동사 -으로 구성되다 ❏ 내 식사는 거의 전적으로 초콜릿을 입힌 비스킷과 우유로 이루어진다. ◢ 자동사 -이 주를 이루다 ❏ 컨설턴트로서의 그의 업무는 외국 회사들에게 새로운 공장 부지를 선정하는 것에 자문을 제공하는 것이 주를 이루었다.

con|sist|en|cy /kənsɪstənsi/ ◢ N-UNCOUNT **Consistency** is the quality or condition of being consistent. ❏ *He scores goals with remarkable consistency.* ◢ N-UNCOUNT The **consistency** of a substance is how thick or smooth it is. ❏ *Dilute the paint with water until it is the consistency of milk.*

◢ 불가산명사 일관성 ❏ 그는 놀라운 일관성을 가지고 득점을 기록했다. ◢ 불가산명사 밀도 ❏ 페인트가 우유와 비슷한 밀도를 가질 때까지 물로 희석하세요.

con|sist|ent ♦◇◇ /kənsɪstənt/ ◢ ADJ Someone who is **consistent** always behaves in the same way, has the same attitudes towards people or things, or achieves the same level of success in something. ❏ *Becker has never been the most consistent of players anyway.* ● con|sist|ent|ly ADV ❏ *It's something I have consistently denied.* ◢ ADJ If one fact or idea is **consistent with** another, they do not contradict each other. [v-link ADJ, usu ADJ with n] ❏ *This result is consistent with the findings of Garnett & Tobin.* ◢ ADJ An argument or set of ideas that is **consistent** is one in which no part contradicts or conflicts with any other part. ❏ *A theory should be internally consistent.*

◢ 형용사 일관성 있는 ❏ 어쨌든 베커는 실력이 가장 기복이 없는 선수인 적이 없었다. ● 일관성 있게 부사 ❏ 그것은 내가 꾸준히 부정해 왔다. ◢ 형용사 일치하다, 부합하다 ❏ 이 결과는 가넷과 토빈의 연구 결과와 일치한다. ◢ 형용사 모순이 없는 ❏ 이론은 내적으로 모순이 없어야 한다.

con|sole (consoles, consoling, consoled)

The verb is pronounced /kənsoʊl/. The noun is pronounced /kɒnsoʊl/.

동사는 /kənsoʊl/로 발음되고, 명사는 /kɒnsoʊl/로 발음된다.

◢ V-T If you **console** someone who is unhappy about something, you try to make them feel more cheerful. ❏ *"Never mind, Ned," he consoled me.* ❏ *I can console myself with the fact that I'm not alone.* ● con|so|la|tion /kɒnsəleɪʃ°n/ (consolations) N-VAR ❏ *The only consolation for the Scottish theater community is that they look likely to get another chance.* ◢ N-COUNT A **console** is a panel with a number of switches or knobs that is used to operate a machine. ❏ *Several nurses sat before a console of flickering lights and bleeping monitors.*

◢ 타동사 위로하다 ❏ "신경 쓰지 마, 네드."라고 그가 나를 위로했다. ❏ 나는 내가 혼자가 아니라는 사실에서 위안을 얻는다. ● 위안 가산명사 또는 불가산명사 ❏ 스코틀랜드 연극계의 유일한 위안은 그들에게 기회가 한번 더 있을 것 같다는 것뿐이다. ◢ 가산명사 콘솔 ❏ 빛이 깜박이고 삑삑 소리가 나는 모니터로 구성된 콘솔 앞에 여러 명의 간호사가 앉아 있었다.

con|soli|date /kənsɒlɪdeɪt/ (consolidates, consolidating, consolidated) ◢ V-T If you **consolidate** something that you have, for example power or success, you strengthen it so that it becomes more effective or secure. ❏ *The question is: will the junta consolidate its power by force?* ◢ V-T To **consolidate** a number of small groups or firms means to make them into one large organization. ❏ *Judge Charles Schwartz is giving the state 60 days to disband and consolidate Louisiana's four higher education boards.*

◢ 타동사 공고히 하다, 강화하다 ❏ 문제는 쿠데타 정권이 무력으로 권력을 공고히 할 것이냐이다. ◢ 타동사 통합하다 ❏ 판사 찰스 스와르츠는 루이지애나의 4개 고등 교육 위원회를 해산한 후 통폐합하도록 주에 60일의 기한을 주었다.

con|so|nant /kɒnsənənt/ (consonants) N-COUNT A **consonant** is a sound such as "p", "f", "n", or "t" which you pronounce by stopping the air flowing freely through your mouth. Compare **vowel**.

가산명사 자음

con|sor|tium /kənsɔːrʃiəm, -ti-/ (consortia) /kənsɔːrʃiə, -ti-/ or consortiums N-COUNT-COLL A **consortium** is a group of people or firms who have agreed to cooperate with each other. ❏ *The consortium includes some of the biggest building contractors in Britain.*

가산명사-집합 컨소시엄 ❏ 그 컨소시엄에는 영국에서 가장 큰 건설업체들 몇 군데가 속해 있다.

con|spic|u|ous /kənspɪkyuəs/ ADJ If someone or something is **conspicuous**, people can see or notice them very easily. ❏ *The most conspicuous way in which the old politics is changing is in the growing use of referendums.* ● con|spic|u|ous|ly ADV ❏ *Britain continues to follow U.S. policy in this and other areas where American policies have most conspicuously failed.*

형용사 눈에 띄는 ❏ 구시대의 정치가 가장 눈에 띄게 바뀌고 있는 부분은 국민 투표제를 점점 많이 사용한다는 것이다. ● 눈에 띄게 부사 ❏ 영국은 이것을 포함해 미국의 정책이 가장 눈에 띄게 실패한 영역에서 계속 미국의 정책을 따르고 있다.

con|spira|cy /kənspɪrəsi/ (**conspiracies**) ◼ N-VAR **Conspiracy** is the secret planning by a group of people to do something illegal. ❑ *Seven men, all from Bristol, admitted conspiracy to commit arson.* ◻ N-COUNT A **conspiracy** is an agreement between a group of people which other people think is wrong or is likely to be harmful. ❑ *It's all part of a conspiracy to dispense with the town center all together and move everything out to Meadowhall.*

◼ 가산명사 또는 불가산명사 공모 ❑ 모두 브리스톨 출신인 일곱 명의 남자가 방화를 공모했음을 시인했다. ◻ 가산명사 음모 ❑ 이것은 모두 도시 중심을 아예 없애고 모든 것을 메도우홀로 옮기려는 음모의 일부이고.

con|spira|tor /kənspɪrətər/ (**conspirators**) N-COUNT A **conspirator** is a person who joins a conspiracy. ❑ *Julius Caesar was murdered by a group of conspirators famously headed by Marcus Junius Brutus.*

가산명사 공모자, 음모 가담자 ❑ 줄리어스 시저는 널리 알려졌다시피 마르쿠스 유니우스 브루투스가 이끄는 일단의 공모자들에 의해 살해되었다.

con|spire /kənspaɪər/ (**conspires, conspiring, conspired**) ◼ V-RECIP If two or more people or groups **conspire to** do something illegal or harmful, they make a secret agreement to do it. ❑ *They'd conspired to overthrow the government.* ❑ *...a defendant convicted of conspiring with his brother to commit robberies.* ◻ V-T/V-I If events **conspire to** produce a particular result, they seem to work together to cause this result. ❑ *History and geography have conspired to bring Greece to a moment of decision.*

◼ 상호동사 공모하다 ❑ 그들은 정부를 전복시킬 음모를 했다. ❑ 형과 강도짓을 공모하여 유죄 판결을 받은 피고 ◻ 타동사/자동사 맞물리다 ❑ 역사와 지리가 맞물려 그리스를 결정의 순간으로 몰고 갔다.

con|sta|ble /kʌnstəb'l, kɒn-/ (**constables**) ◼ N-COUNT; N-TITLE In the United States, a **constable** is an official who helps keep the peace in a town. They are lower in rank than a sheriff. ❑ *Courts and magistrates may be set up but they cannot function without sheriffs and constables.* ◻ N-COUNT; N-TITLE; N-VOC In Britain and some other countries, a **constable** is a police officer of the lowest rank. ❑ *He was a constable at Sutton police station.* ❑ *...Constable Stuart Clark.* →see also **Chief Constable**

◼ 가산명사; 경칭명사 치안관 ❑ 법원과 재판관들을 둘 수는 있지만 그들은 보안관과 치안관 없이는 제 역할을 하지 못한다. ◻ 가산명사; 경칭명사; 호격명사 순경 ❑ 그는 서튼 경찰서의 순경이었다. ❑ 스튜어트 클라크 순경

con|stant ♦♦◇ /kɒnstənt/ ◼ ADJ You use **constant** to describe something that happens all the time or is always there. ❑ *She suggests that women are under constant pressure to be abnormally slim.* ❑ *Inflation is a constant threat.* ● **con|stant|ly** ADV ❑ *The direction of the wind is constantly changing.* ◻ ADJ If an amount or level is **constant**, it stays the same over a particular period of time. ❑ *The body feels hot and the temperature remains more or less constant at the new elevated level.*

◼ 형용사 지속적인 ❑ 여성들이 비정상적으로 말라야 한다는 끊임없는 압박감에 시달리는 것 같다고 그녀가 시사했다. ❑ 물가 인상은 항상 존재하는 위협이다. ● 지속적으로 부사 ❑ 바람의 방향이 계속 바뀌고 있다. ◻ 형용사 일정한 ❑ 몸은 덥게 느껴지고 체온은 새로 상승한 상태에서 어느 정도 일정하게 유지된다.

You can use **constant**, **continual**, and **continuous** to describe things that happen or exist without stopping. You describe something as **constant** when it happens all the time or never goes away. ❑ *He was in constant pain....Eva's constant criticism.* **Continual** is usually used to describe something that happens often over a period of time, especially something undesirable. ❑ *...his continual drinking....continual demands to cut costs.* If something is **continuous**, it happens all the time without stopping, or seems to do so. ❑ *...days of continuous rain....a continuous background noise.*

끊임없이 계속 일어나거나 존재하는 것을 묘사할 때 constant, continual, continuous를 쓸 수 있다. 항상 일어나고 없어지지 않을는 것을 constant로 묘사한다. ❑ 그는 통증이 계속되었다....에바의 계속된 비난. continual은 흔히 일정 기간에 걸쳐 일어나는, 특히 바람직하지 않은 것을 묘사할 때 쓴다. ❑ ...그의 계속된 음주....비용을 줄이라는 계속된 요구. 어떤 것이 continuous하다는 것은, 그것이 그치지 않고 내내 계속되거나 그런 것처럼 여겨짐을 나타낸다. ❑ ...계속 비가 내리는 나날....계속되는 배경의 소음

Thesaurus constant의 참조어

ADJ. continual, continuous, uninterrupted; (ant.) occasional ◼
consistent, permanent, stable; (ant.) variable ◻

con|stel|la|tion /kɒnstəleɪʃ'n/ (**constellations**) N-COUNT A **constellation** is a group of stars which form a pattern and have a name. ❑ *...a planet orbiting a star in the constellation of Cepheus.* →see **star**

가산명사 별자리 ❑ 케페우스 자리의 별을 공전하는 행성

con|ster|na|tion /kɒnstərneɪʃ'n/ N-UNCOUNT **Consternation** is a feeling of anxiety or fear. [FORMAL] ❑ *His decision caused consternation in the art photography community.*

불가산명사 경악, 당혹 [격식체] ❑ 그의 결정은 예술 사진가 사회에 당혹감을 불러일으켰다.

con|sti|pa|tion /kɒnstɪpeɪʃ'n/ N-UNCOUNT **Constipation** is a medical condition which causes people to have difficulty getting rid of solid waste from their body. ❑ *Do you suffer from constipation?*

불가산명사 변비 ❑ 변비로 고생하십니까?

con|stitu|en|cy /kənstɪtʃuənsi/ (**constituencies**) ◼ N-COUNT A **constituency** is an area for which someone is elected as the representative in a legislature or government. ❑ *...one of Britain's poorest constituencies.* ◻ N-COUNT A particular **constituency** is a section of society that may give political support to a particular party or politician. ❑ *In France, farmers are a powerful political constituency.*

◼ 가산명사 선거구 ❑ 영국에서 가장 가난한 선거구 중 하나 ◻ 가산명사 지지층 ❑ 프랑스에선 농민들이 매우 강력한 지지층을 구성한다.

con|stitu|ent /kənstɪtʃuənt/ (**constituents**) ◼ N-COUNT A **constituent** is someone who lives in a particular constituency, especially someone who is able to vote in an election. ❑ *He told his constituents that he would continue to represent them to the best of his ability.* ◻ N-COUNT A **constituent of** a mixture, substance, or system is one of the things from which it is formed. ❑ *Caffeine is the active constituent of drinks such as tea and coffee.* ◾ ADJ The **constituent** parts of something are the things from which it is formed. [FORMAL] [ADJ n] ❑ *...a plan to split the company into its constituent parts and sell them separately.*

◼ 가산명사 선거구민 ❑ 그는 선거구민들에게 계속 최선을 다해서 그들을 대표하겠다고 말했다. ◻ 가산명사 성분 ❑ 카페인은 차나 커피와 같은 음료의 활성 성분이다. ◾ 형용사 구성 요소 [격식체] ❑ 회사를 부문별로 분리한 후 그것들을 따로 매각하려는 계획

con|sti|tute /kɒnstɪtut, BRIT kɒnstɪtjuːt/ (**constitutes, constituting, constituted**) ◼ V-LINK If something **constitutes** a particular thing, it can be regarded as being that thing. [no cont] ❑ *Testing patients without their consent would constitute a professional and legal offence.* ◻ V-LINK If a number of things or people **constitute** something, they are the parts or members that form it. [no cont] ❑ *China's ethnic minorities constitute less than 7 percent of its total population.*

◼ 연결동사 설립시키다, ~하는 것과 마찬가지이다 ❑ 환자들의 동의 없이 그들에게 실험을 행하는 것은 직업상 윤리와 일반 법률을 위반하는 것이다. ◻ 연결동사 구성하다 ❑ 중국에서 소수 민족은 전체 인구의 7퍼센트 미만을 구성한다.

con|sti|tu|tion ♦◇◇ /kɒnstɪtuʃ'n, BRIT kɒnstɪtjuːʃ'n/ (**constitutions**) ◼ N-COUNT The **constitution** of a country or organization is the system of laws which formally states people's rights and duties. ❑ *The king was forced to adopt a new constitution which reduced his powers.* ◻ N-COUNT Your **constitution** is your health. ❑ *He must have an extremely strong constitution.*

◼ 가산명사 헌법 ❑ 왕은 자신의 권한을 줄이는 새로운 헌법을 채택하도록 강요당했다. ◻ 가산명사 건강 ❑ 그는 건강이 아주 좋은가 보다.

con|sti|tu|tion|al ♦◇◇ /kɒnstɪtuʃən'l, BRIT kɒnstɪtjuːʃən'l/ ADJ **Constitutional** means relating to the constitution of a particular country or organization. ❑ *Political leaders are making no progress in their efforts to resolve the country's constitutional crisis.*

형용사 헌법의 ❑ 국가의 헌법적 위기를 극복하려는 정치 지도자들의 노력은 어떠한 진척도 거두지 못하고 있다.

A

con|strain /kənstreɪn/ (constrains, constraining, constrained) v-t To **constrain** someone or something means to limit their development or force them to behave in a particular way. [FORMAL] ❑ *Women are too often constrained by family commitments and by low expectations.*

타동사 제약하다 [격식체] ❑ 여성들은 너무나 자주 가족에 대한 의무와 낮은 기대치로 인해 제약을 받는다.

B

con|straint /kənstreɪnt/ (constraints) 1 N-COUNT A **constraint** is something that limits or controls what you can do. ❑ *Their decision to abandon the trip was made because of financial constraints.* 2 N-UNCOUNT **Constraint** is control over the way you behave which prevents you from doing what you want to do. ❑ *The networks have decided to exercise constraint when it comes to showing the planes hitting the Twin Towers.*

1 가산명사 제약 ❑ 경제적 제약 때문에 그들은 여행을 포기하기로 결심했다. 2 불가산명사 절제, 제한 ❑ 방송사들은 비행기들이 두 쌍둥이 건물에 부딪치는 장면을 보여 주는 것은 절제하기로 결정했다.

C

con|strict /kənstrɪkt/ (constricts, constricting, constricted) 1 v-t/v-i If a part of your body, especially your throat, **is constricted** or if it **constricts**, something causes it to become narrower. ❑ *Severe migraine can be treated with a drug which constricts the blood vessels.* 2 v-t If something **constricts** you, it limits your actions so that you cannot do what you want to do. ❑ *She objects to the tests the Government's advisers have devised because they constrict her teaching style.*

1 타동사/자동사 수축되다; 수축하다 ❑ 심한 편두통은 혈관을 수축시키는 약으로 치료할 수 있다. 2 타동사 제한하다 ❑ 그녀는 자신의 교육 방식을 제한한다는 이유로 정부 자문들이 고안한 시험에 반대한다.

D

E

F

con|struct /kənstrʌkt/ (constructs, constructing, constructed) 1 v-t If you **construct** something such as a building, road, or machine, you build it or make it. ❑ *The French constructed a series of fortresses from Dunkirk on the Channel coast to Douai.* ❑ *The boxes should be constructed from rough-sawn timber.* 2 v-t If you **construct** something such as an idea, a piece of writing, or a system, you create it by putting different parts together. ❑ *He eventually constructed a business empire which ran to Thailand and Singapore.* ❑ *The novel is constructed from a series of on-the-spot reports.*

1 타동사 건설하다, 제작하다 ❑ 프랑스는 영국 해협의 됭케르크에서 듀에까지 일련의 성채를 구축했다. ❑ 그 박스들은 거칠게 톱질한 목재로 만들어야 한다. 2 타동사 구성하다 ❑ 그는 마침내 태국에서 싱가포르까지 이어지는 기업 왕국을 일궜다. ❑ 그 소설은 일련의 현장 보고서에서 구성한 것이다.

G

H

con|struc|tion ♦♢♢ /kənstrʌkʃⁿn/ (constructions) 1 N-UNCOUNT **Construction** is the building of things such as houses, factories, roads, and bridges. ❑ *He'd already started construction on a hunting lodge.* ❑ *...the downturn in the construction industry.* 2 N-UNCOUNT The **construction** of something such as a vehicle or machine is the making of it. ❑ *...companies who have long experience in the construction of those types of equipment.* 3 N-UNCOUNT The **construction** of something such as a system is the creation of it. ❑ *...the construction of a just system of criminal justice.* 4 N-COUNT You can refer to an object that has been built or made as a **construction**. ❑ *The British pavilion is an impressive steel and glass construction the size of Westminster Abbey.* 5 N-UNCOUNT You use **construction** to refer to the structure of something and the way it has been built or made. ❑ *The Shakers believed that furniture should be plain, simple, useful, practical, and of sound construction.* 6 N-COUNT A grammatical **construction** is a particular arrangement of words in a sentence, clause, or phrase. ❑ *Avoid complex verbal constructions.*

1 불가산명사 건설 ❑ 그는 벌써 사냥용 오두막을 짓기 시작한 상태였다. ❑ 건설 부문의 침체 2 불가산명사 제작, 조립 ❑ 이런 종류의 장비를 오랫동안 제작한 경험이 있는 회사들 3 불가산명사 수립 ❑ 공정한 형법 체계의 수립 4 가산명사 구조물 ❑ 영국의 전시장은 웨스트민스터 성당 정도 크기의 유리와 철골로 이루어진 인상적인 구조물이다. 5 불가산명사 구조 ❑ 셰이커교도들은 가구가 소박하며 단순하며 유용하고 실용적이면서도 단단해야 한다고 생각했다. 6 가산명사 구문 ❑ 복잡한 구문을 피하세요.

I

J

K

L

M

con|struc|tive /kənstrʌktɪv/ ADJ A **constructive** discussion, comment, or approach is useful and helpful rather than negative and unhelpful. ❑ *She welcomes constructive criticism.* ❑ *After their meeting, both men described the talks as frank, friendly and constructive.*

형용사 건설적인 ❑ 그녀는 건설적인 비평을 환영한다. ❑ 회의 이후 두 남자 다 대화가 솔직하고 우호적이면서도 건설적이었다고 말했다.

N

con|strue /kənstruː/ (construes, construing, construed) v-t If something **is construed** in a particular way, its nature or meaning is interpreted in that way. [FORMAL] ❑ *What may seem helpful behavior to you can be construed as interference by others.* ❑ *He may construe the approach as a hostile act.*

타동사 이해되다 [격식체] ❑ 네가 보기엔 도와주는 것 같은 것이 남들이 보기엔 참견으로 받아들여질 수도 있다. ❑ 그는 그 접근 행위를 위협적인 행동으로 이해할 수도 있다.

O

con|sul /kɒnsⁿl/ (consuls) N-COUNT; N-TITLE A **consul** is an official who is sent by his or her government to live in a foreign city in order to help all the people there that belong to his or her own country. ❑ *...Stephanie Sweet, the British Consul in Tangier.*

가산명사; 경칭명사 영사 ❑ 탕헤르 주재 영국 영사인 스테파니 스위트

P

Q

con|su|lar /kɒnsələr, BRIT kɒnsyʊlɑⁱr/ ADJ **Consular** means involving or relating to a consul or the work of a consul. [ADJ n] ❑ *If you need to return to the UK quickly, British Consular officials may be able to arrange it.*

형용사 영사의 ❑ 당신이 영국으로 속히 돌아가야 한다면 영국 영사관 직원들이 주선해 줄 수 있을지도 모릅니다.

R

con|su|late /kɒnsəlɪt, BRIT kɒnsyʊlət/ (consulates) N-COUNT A **consulate** is the place where a consul works. ❑ *They managed to make contact with the British consulate in Lyons.*

가산명사 영사관 ❑ 그들은 간신히 리용의 영국 영사관과 접촉할 수 있었다.

S

con|sult ♦♢♢ /kənsʌlt/ (consults, consulting, consulted) 1 v-t/v-i If you **consult** an expert or someone senior to you or **consult with** them, you ask them for their opinion and advice about what you should do or their permission to do something. ❑ *Consult your doctor about how much exercise you should attempt.* ❑ *He needed to consult with an attorney.* 2 v-RECIP If a person or group of people **consults with** other people or **consults** them, they talk and exchange ideas and opinions about what they might decide to do. ❑ *After consulting with her daughter and manager she decided to take on the part, on her terms.* ❑ *The two countries will have to consult their allies.* 3 v-t If you **consult** a book or a map, you look in it or look at it in order to find some information. ❑ *Consult the chart on page 44 for the correct cooking times.*

1 타동사/자동사 -의 자문을 구하다 ❑ 얼마나 많은 운동을 해야 할지에 대해 담당 의사에게 자문을 구해라. ❑ 그는 변호사의 자문을 구해야 했다. 2 상호동사 -와 의견을 교환하다 ❑ 딸과 부장의 의견을 들은 뒤 그녀는 자신이 제시하는 조건으로 그 일을 맡기로 결정했다. ❑ 두 나라는 동맹국들의 의견을 들어야 할 것이다. 3 타동사 -을 참조하다 ❑ 올바른 요리 시간에 대해서는 44페이지의 표를 참조하세요.

T

U

V

con|sul|tan|cy /kənsʌltənsi/ (consultancies) 1 N-COUNT A **consultancy** is a company that gives expert advice on a particular subject. ❑ *A survey of 57 hospitals by Newchurch, a consultancy, reveals striking improvements.* 2 N-UNCOUNT **Consultancy** is expert advice on a particular subject which a person or group is paid to provide to a company or organization. ❑ *The project provides both consultancy and training.*

1 가산명사 컨설팅 회사 ❑ 컨설팅 회사인 뉴처치가 행한 57개 병원에 대한 조사는 눈에 띄는 개선이 있었음을 보여준다. 2 불가산명사 컨설팅 ❑ 그 프로젝트는 컨설팅과 연수 두 가지를 다 제공한다.

W

X

con|sul|tant ♦♢♢ /kənsʌltənt/ (consultants) 1 N-COUNT A **consultant** is a person who gives expert advice to a person or organization on a particular subject. ❑ *He was a consultant to the Swedish government.* 2 N-COUNT A **consultant** is an experienced doctor with a high position, who specializes in one area of medicine. [mainly BRIT; AM usually **specialist**] ❑ *Shirley's brother is now a consultant heart surgeon in Sweden.*

1 가산명사 고문 ❑ 그는 스웨덴 정부의 고문이었다. 2 가산명사 고문 의사 [주로 영국영어; 미국영어 대개 specialist] ❑ 셜리의 오빠는 지금 스웨덴에서 심장 외과 고문 의사로 일하고 있다.

Y

Z

con|sul|ta|tion /kɒnsəlteɪᵊn/ (consultations) 1 N-VAR A consultation is a meeting which is held to discuss something. Consultation is discussion about something. ❑ Next week he'll be in Florida for consultations with President Mitterrand. 2 N-COUNT A consultation is a meeting where several doctors discuss a patient and his or her condition and treatment. [AM] ❑ I had to call in a medical specialist for a consultation. 3 N-VAR A consultation with a doctor or other expert is a meeting with them to discuss a particular problem and get their advice. Consultation is the process of getting advice from a doctor or other expert. [mainly BRIT] ❑ A personal diet plan is devised after a consultation with a nutritionist.

1 가산명사 또는 불가산명사 회의; 토론 ❑ 다음 주 그는 미테랑 대통령과의 회담을 위해 플로리다를 방문할 것이다. 2 가산명사 진료 자문 회의 [미국영어] ❑ 나는 치료 자문 회의에 의학 전문가를 불러야 했다. 3 가산명사 또는 불가산명사 상담, 자문을 구함 [주로 영국영어] ❑ 영양사와 상담한 후 개인 식사 계획을 세운다.

con|sul|ta|tive /kənsʌltətɪv/ ADJ A consultative committee or document gives advice or makes proposals about a particular problem or subject. ❑ ...the consultative committee on local government finance.

형용사 자문의 ❑ 지방 정부 재정 자문 위원회

con|sum|able /kənsuːməbᵊl, BRIT kənsyuːməbᵊl/ (consumables) ADJ Consumable goods are items which are intended to be bought, used, and then replaced. ❑ ...demand for consumable articles. ● N-COUNT Consumable is also a noun. ❑ Suppliers add computer consumables, office equipment, and furniture to their product range.

형용사 소모성의 ❑ 소모성 물품에 대한 수요 ● 가산명사 소모품 ❑ 공급자들은 자신들의 물품 내역에 컴퓨터 소모품, 사무 기구, 가구 등을 추가한다.

Word Link	sume ≈ taking : assume, consume, presume

con|sume /kənsuːm, BRIT kənsyuːm/ (consumes, consuming, consumed) 1 V-T If you consume something, you eat or drink it. [FORMAL] ❑ Martha would consume nearly a pound of cheese per day. 2 V-T To consume an amount of fuel, energy, or time means to use it up. ❑ Some of the most efficient refrigerators consume 70 percent less electricity than traditional models. 3 →see also consuming

1 타동사 섭취하다 [격식체] ❑ 마사는 매일 거의 1파운드의 치즈를 섭취하곤 했다. 2 타동사 소비하다 ❑ 가장 효율적인 냉장고들 중 일부는 기존의 모델보다 전기를 70퍼센트 적게 소비한다.

con|sum|er ♦♦◇ /kənsuːmər, BRIT kənsyuːməʳ/ (consumers) N-COUNT A consumer is a person who buys things or uses services. ❑ ...claims that tobacco companies failed to warn consumers about the dangers of smoking. →see advertising

가산명사 소비자 ❑ 담배 회사들이 소비자들에게 흡연의 해로움을 경고하지 않았다는 주장

con|sum|er cred|it N-UNCOUNT Consumer credit is money that is lent to people by organizations such as banks and stores so that they can buy things. ❑ New consumer credit fell to $3.7 billion in August.

불가산명사 소비자 대출 ❑ 8월에 신규 소비자 대출이 37억 달러로 줄었다.

con|sum|er du|rable (consumer durables) N-COUNT Consumer durables are goods which are expected to last a long time, and are bought infrequently. [BRIT; AM durable goods] ❑ Consumer durables such as refrigerators, television sets, bicycles and so on were produced in large quantities.

가산명사 내구재 [영국영어; 미국영어 durable goods] ❑ 냉장고, 텔레비전, 자전거 등의 내구재가 대량으로 생산되었다.

con|sum|er goods N-PLURAL Consumer goods are items bought by people for their own use, rather than by businesses. Compare capital goods. [BUSINESS] ❑ The choice of consumer goods available in local shops is small.

복수명사 소비재 [경제] ❑ 지역 상점들에 있는 소비재의 종류는 한정되어 있다.

con|sum|er so|ci|ety (consumer societies) N-COUNT You can use consumer society to refer to a society where people think that spending money on goods and services is very important. ❑ We live in a consumer society in which money is a massive preoccupation.

가산명사 소비 중심 사회 ❑ 우리는 돈이 최대 관심사인 소비 중심 사회에 살고 있다.

con|sum|ing /kənsuːmɪŋ, BRIT kənsyuːmɪŋ/ ADJ A consuming passion or interest is more important to you than anything else. ❑ He has developed a consuming passion for chess. →see also consume, time-consuming

형용사 사람을 사로잡는 ❑ 그는 최근 체스에 완전히 푹 빠져 지낸다.

con|sum|mate /kɒnsəmeɪt/ (consummates, consummating, consummated) 1 ADJ You use consummate to describe someone who is extremely skillful. [FORMAL] ❑ He acted the part with consummate skill. 2 V-T If two people consummate a marriage or relationship, they make it complete by having sex. [FORMAL] ❑ His beautiful wife divorces him for failing to consummate their marriage.

1 형용사 최고로 숙련된 [격식체] ❑ 그는 최고로 숙련된 연기로 그 역할을 연기했다. 2 타동사 (성관계를 통해 결혼이나 관계를) 완성시키다 [격식체] ❑ 그의 아름다운 아내는 결혼 생활 중에 성관계를 할 수 없어서 그와 이혼을 했다.

Word Link	sumpt ≈ taking : assumption, consumption, presumption

con|sump|tion /kənsʌmpᵊn/ 1 N-UNCOUNT The consumption of fuel or natural resources is the amount of them that is used or the act of using them. ❑ The laws have led to a reduction in fuel consumption in the U.S. 2 N-UNCOUNT The consumption of food or drink is the act of eating or drinking something, or the amount that is eaten or drunk. [FORMAL] ❑ Most of the wine was unfit for human consumption. 3 N-UNCOUNT Consumption is the act of buying and using things. ❑ They were prepared to put people out of work and reduce consumption by strangling the whole economy.

1 불가산명사 소비 ❑ 그 법률들로 인하여 미국의 연료 소비가 줄었다. 2 불가산명사 섭취 [격식체] ❑ 대부분의 와인이 사람이 마시기엔 부적합했다. 3 불가산명사 소비 ❑ 그들은 경제 전체의 목을 죔으로써 사람들의 일자리를 없애고 소비를 줄일 각오가 되어 있었다.

cont. Cont. is an abbreviation for 'continued,' which is used at the bottom of a page to indicate that a letter or text continues on another page.

'다음 페이지에 계속됨'을 나타내는 약어

con|tact ♦♦◇ /kɒntækt/ (contacts, contacting, contacted) 1 N-UNCOUNT Contact involves meeting or communicating with someone, especially regularly. [also N in pl, oft N with/between n] ❑ Opposition leaders are denying any contact with the government in Kabul. 2 PHRASE If you are in contact with someone, you regularly meet them or communicate with them. ❑ He was in direct contact with the kidnappers. 3 V-T If you contact someone, you telephone them, write to them, or go to see them in order to tell or ask them something. ❑ Contact the Tourist Information Bureau for further details. 4 N-UNCOUNT If you come into contact with someone or something, you meet that person or thing in the course of your work or other activities. ❑ Doctors I came into contact with voiced their concern. 5 PHRASE If you make contact with someone, you find out where they are and talk or write to them. ❑ How did you make contact with the terrorists? 6 PHRASE If you lose contact with someone who you have been friendly with, you no longer see them, speak to them, or write to them. ❑ Though they all live nearby, I lost contact with them really quickly. 7 N-UNCOUNT When people or things are in contact, they are touching each other. ❑ They compared how these organisms behaved when left in contact with different materials.

1 불가산명사 (정기적인) 접촉 ❑ 야당 지도자들은 카불 정부와의 어떤 접촉도 부인하고 있다. 2 구 -와 접촉 중인 ❑ 그는 납치범들과 직접 접촉하고 있었다. 3 타동사 연락하다 ❑ 추가 정보가 필요하시면 관광 안내 사무소에 연락하세요. 4 불가산명사 -와 접촉하게 된 ❑ 내가 접촉하게 된 의사들은 우려를 표시했다. 5 구 -와 연락하다 ❑ 테러리스트들과는 어떻게 연락했나? 6 구 -와 연락이 두절되다 ❑ -와 접촉이 없어지다 ❑ 그들 모두 인근에 살고 있지만 나는 곧 그들과 연락을 끊고 지냈다. 7 불가산명사 접촉 ❑ 다른 물질들과 접촉하게 될 경우 이 유기체들이 어떻게 반응을 보이는지를 그들은 비교했다. ❑ 공기가 아기의 후두와 접촉할 때 울음소리가 난다. 8 가산명사 연락처 ❑ 미국 대사관에 있는 그들의 연락책의 이름은 필이었다.

A

The cry occurs when air is brought into contact with the baby's larynx. ◼ N-COUNT A **contact** is someone you know in an organization or profession who helps you or gives you information. ❑ *Their contact in the United States Embassy was called Phil.*

B

con|tact lens (**contact lenses**) N-COUNT **Contact lenses** are small plastic lenses that you put on the surface of your eyes to help you see better, instead of wearing glasses. →see **eye**

가산명사 콘택트렌즈

C

con|ta|gious /kənteɪdʒəs/ ◼ ADJ A disease that is **contagious** can be caught by touching people or things that are infected with it. Compare **infectious**. ❑ *...a highly contagious disease of the lungs.* ◼ ADJ A feeling or attitude that is **contagious** spreads quickly among a group of people. ❑ *Laughing is contagious.*

◼ 형용사 (접촉) 전염성의 ❑ 전염성이 굉장히 높은 폐질환 ◼ 형용사 전염성이 강한 ❑ 웃음은 전염성이 강하다.

D

con|tain ◆◆◇ /kəntɛɪn/ (**contains, containing, contained**) ◼ V-T If something such as a box, bag, room, or place **contains** things, those things are inside it. [no cont] ❑ *The bag contained a Christmas card.* ❑ *Factory shops contain a wide range of cheap furnishings.* ◼ V-T If a substance **contains** something, that thing is a part of it. [no cont] ❑ *Watermelon contains vitamins and also potassium.* ◼ V-T If writing, speech, or film **contains** particular information, ideas, or images, it includes them. [no cont] ❑ *This sheet contained a list of problems a patient might like to raise with the doctor.* ◼ V-T If a group or organization **contains** a certain number of people, those are the people that are in it. [no cont] ❑ *The committee contains 11 Democrats and nine Republicans.* ◼ V-T If you **contain** something, you control it and prevent it from spreading or increasing. ❑ *More than a hundred firemen are still trying to contain the fire at the plant.* ◼ →see also **self-contained**

◼ 타동사 ~을 담고 있다 ❑ 봉투에는 크리스마스카드가 들어 있었다. ❑ 공장 도매 상점은 다양한 종류의 저렴한 가구를 갖추고 있다. ◼ 타동사 함유하다 ❑ 수박은 비타민과 칼륨을 함유하고 있다. ◼ 타동사 포함하다 ❑ 이 종이에는 환자가 의사에게 제기할 수 있는 문제들의 목록이 들어있었다. ◼ 타동사 포함하다 ❑ 그 위원회에는 11명의 민주당원과 9명의 공화당원이 있다. ◼ 타동사 제어하다, 진압하다 ❑ 공장의 불을 진압하기 위해 백 명 이상의 소방관이 아직도 애를 쓰고 있다.

G

H

con|tain|er /kənteɪnər/ (**containers**) ◼ N-COUNT A **container** is something such as a box or bottle that is used to hold or store things in. ❑ *...the plastic containers in which fish are stored and sold.* ◼ N-COUNT A **container** is a very large metal or wooden box used for transporting goods so that they can be loaded easily onto ships and trucks. ❑ *The train, carrying loaded containers on flatcars, was 1.2 miles long.* →see **can, ship**

◼ 가산명사 용기 ❑ 생선을 담아서 파는 플라스틱 용기 ◼ 가산명사 컨테이너 ❑ 가득 찬 컨테이너를 무개화차로 나르는 그 기차는 길이가 1.2마일이었다.

I

J

con|tami|nate /kəntæmɪneɪt/ (**contaminates, contaminating, contaminated**) V-T If something **is contaminated by** dirt, chemicals, or radiation, they make it dirty or harmful. ❑ *Have any fish been contaminated in the Arctic Ocean?* ● **con|tami|na|tion** /kəntæmɪneɪʃⁿn/ N-UNCOUNT ❑ *The contamination of the sea around Capri may be just the beginning.*

타동사 오염된 ❑ 북극해에 오염된 어류가 있습니까? ● 오염 불가산명사 ❑ 카프리 주변 해역의 오염은 시작에 불과할지도 모른다.

K

con|tem|plate /kɒntəmpleɪt/ (**contemplates, contemplating, contemplated**) ◼ V-T If you **contemplate** an action, you think about whether to do it or not. ❑ *For a time he contemplated a career as an army medical doctor.* ◼ V-T If you **contemplate** an idea or subject, you think about it carefully for a long time. ❑ *As he lay in his hospital bed that night, he cried as he contemplated his future.* ● **con|tem|pla|tion** /kɒntəmpleɪʃⁿn/ N-UNCOUNT ❑ *It is a place of quiet contemplation.* ◼ V-T If you **contemplate** something or someone, you look at them for a long time. ❑ *He contemplated his hands, still frowning.* ● **con|tem|pla|tion** N-UNCOUNT ❑ *He was lost in the contemplation of the landscape for a while.*

◼ 타동사 고려하다 ❑ 한동안 그는 군의관의 길을 고려했다. ◼ 타동사 심사숙고하다 ❑ 그는 그 날 밤 병원 침대에 누워서 자신의 미래를 생각하며 울었다. ● 심사숙고 불가산명사 ❑ 조용히 생각할 수 있는 곳이다. ◼ 타동사 응시하다 ❑ 그는 여전히 인상을 찡그린 채 자신의 손을 응시했다. ● 응시 불가산명사 ❑ 그는 한동안 풍경을 응시하며 넋을 잃고 있었다.

L

M

N

Word Link	con ≈ together, with : con*sensus*, con*temporary*, con*vene*

Word Link	tempo ≈ time : con*temporary*, *temporal*, *temporary*

P

con|tem|po|rary ◆◇◇ /kəntɛmpəreri, BRIT kəntɛmpərəri/ (**contemporaries**) ◼ ADJ **Contemporary** things are modern and relate to the present time. ❑ *She writes a lot of contemporary music for people like Whitney Houston.* ◼ ADJ **Contemporary** people or things were alive or happened at the same time as something else you are talking about. ❑ *...drawing upon official records and the reports of contemporary witnesses.* ◼ N-COUNT Someone's **contemporary** is a person who is or was alive at the same time as them. ❑ *Like most of my contemporaries, I grew up in a vastly different world.*

◼ 형용사 현대적인 ❑ 그녀는 휘트니 휴스턴 같은 사람들을 위해 현대적인 곡을 쓴다. ◼ 형용사 동시대의 ❑ 공식 문서와 동시대 목격자의 보고를 근거로 하여 ◼ 가산명사 동시대의 ❑ 내 또래 대부분처럼 나는 확연히 다른 세계에서 성장했다.

Q

R

con|tempt /kəntɛmpt/ N-UNCOUNT If you have **contempt for** someone or something, you have no respect for them or think that they are unimportant. ❑ *He has contempt for those beyond his immediate family circle.*

불가산명사 경멸 ❑ 그는 자신의 직계 친척을 제외하고는 모두를 경멸한다.

S

con|temp|tu|ous /kəntɛmptʃuəs/ ADJ If you are **contemptuous of** someone or something, you do not like or respect them at all. ❑ *He was contemptuous of private farmers.* ❑ *He's openly contemptuous of all the major political parties.*

형용사 경멸하는 ❑ 그는 개인 농부들을 경멸했다. ❑ 그는 모든 주요 정당들을 공개적으로 경멸한다.

T

con|tend /kəntɛnd/ (**contends, contending, contended**) ◼ V-I If you have to **contend with** a problem or difficulty, you have to deal with it or overcome it. ❑ *It is time, once again, to contend with racism.* ◼ V-T If you **contend that** something is true, you state or argue that it is true. [FORMAL] ❑ *The government contends that he is fundamentalist.* ◼ V-RECIP If you **contend with** someone **for** something such as power, you compete with them to try to get it. ❑ *...the two main groups contending for power.* ❑ *...with 10 UK construction yards contending with rivals from Norway, Holland, Italy, and Spain.*

◼ 자동사 ~와 대적하다 ❑ 다시 한번 인종 차별주의와 대적해야 할 때이다. ◼ 타동사 주장하다 [격식체] ❑ 정부는 그가 원리주의자라고 주장한다. ◼ 상호동사 다투다 ❑ 권력을 위해 다투는 두 개의 주요 집단 ❑ 10개의 영국 제작소들이 노르웨이, 네덜란드, 이탈리아, 스페인의 경쟁자들과 다투는 상황에서

U

V

con|tend|er /kəntɛndər/ (**contenders**) N-COUNT A **contender** is someone who takes part in a competition. [JOURNALISM] ❑ *Her trainer said yesterday that she would be a strong contender for a place in Britain's Olympic squad.*

가산명사 경쟁자 [언론] ❑ 그녀의 트레이너는 어제 그녀가 영국의 올림픽 팀에 합류할 가능성이 높은 경쟁자라고 했다.

W

content
① NOUN USES
② ADJECTIVE USES

X

Y

Z

① **con|tent** ◆◇◇ /kɒntɛnt/ (**contents**) ◼ N-PLURAL The **contents** of a container such as a bottle, box, or room are the things that are inside it. ❑ *Empty the*

◼ 복수명사 내용물 ❑ 냄비의 내용물을 체에 부으세요. ◼ 불가산명사 내용 ❑ 그녀는 그 연극의 내용을

a

b

c

d

e

f

g

h

i

j

k

l

m

n

o

p

q

r

s

t

u

v

w

x

y

z

contents of the pan into the sieve. ② N-UNCOUNT If you refer to the **content** or **contents** of something such as a book, speech, or television program, you are referring to the subject that it deals with, the story that it tells, or the ideas that it expresses. [also N in pl, usu N of n] ❑ *She is reluctant to discuss the content of the play.* ❑ *Stricter controls were placed on the content of video films.* ③ N-PLURAL The **contents** of a book are its different chapters and sections, usually shown in a list at the beginning of the book. ❑ *There is no initial list of contents.* ④ N-UNCOUNT The **content** of something such as an educational course or a program of action is the elements that it consists of. ❑ *Previous students have had nothing but praise for the course content and staff.* ⑤ N-SING You can use **content** to refer to the amount or proportion of something that a substance contains. ❑ *Sunflower margarine has the same fat content as butter.*

② con|tent/kəntɛnt/ →Please look at category ③ to see if the expression you are looking for is shown under another headword. ① ADJ If you are **content with** something, you are willing to accept it, rather than wanting something more or something better. [v-link ADJ, ADJ to-inf, ADJ with n/-ing] ❑ *I am content to admire the mountains from below.* ❑ *I'm perfectly content with the way the campaign has gone.* ② ADJ If you are **content**, you are fairly happy or satisfied. [v-link ADJ] ❑ *He says his daughter is quite content.* ③ **to** your **heart's content** →see **heart**

con|tent|ed /kəntɛntɪd/ ADJ If you are **contented**, you are satisfied with your life or the situation you are in. ❑ *Whenever he returns to this place he is happy and contented.*

con|ten|tion /kəntɛnʃ'n/ (**contentions**) ① N-COUNT Someone's **contention** is the idea or opinion that they are expressing in an argument or discussion. ❑ *It is my contention that death and murder always lurk as potentials in violent relationships.* ② N-UNCOUNT If something is a cause **of contention**, it is a cause of disagreement or argument. ❑ *A particular source of contention are plans to privatise state-run companies.* →see also **bone of contention**

con|ten|tious /kəntɛnʃəs/ ADJ A **contentious** issue causes a lot of disagreement or arguments. [FORMAL] ❑ *Sanctions are expected to be among the most contentious issues.*

con|tent|ment /kəntɛntmənt/ N-UNCOUNT **Contentment** is a feeling of quiet happiness and satisfaction. ❑ *I cannot describe the feeling of contentment that was with me at that time.*

con|test ◆◇◇ (**contests, contesting, contested**)

The noun is pronounced /kɒntɛst/. The verb is pronounced /kəntɛst/.

① N-COUNT A **contest** is a competition or game in which people try to win. ❑ *Few contests in the recent history of British boxing have been as thrilling.* ② N-COUNT A **contest** is a struggle to win power or control. ❑ *The state election due in November will be the last such ballot before next year's presidential contest.* ③ V-T If you **contest** a statement or decision, you object to it formally because you think it is wrong or unreasonable. ❑ *Your former employer has to reply within 14 days in order to contest the case.* ④ V-T If someone **contests** an election or competition, they take part in it and try to win it. [mainly BRIT] ❑ *He quickly won his party's nomination to contest the elections.*

Thesaurus　　　*contest*의 참조어

N.　competition, game, match ①
　　fight, struggle ②

con|test|ant /kəntɛstənt/ (**contestants**) N-COUNT A **contestant** in a competition or quiz is a person who takes part in it. ❑ *Later he applied to be a contestant on the BBC television show*

con|text ◆◇◇ /kɒntɛkst/ (**contexts**) ① N-VAR The **context of** an idea or event is the general situation that relates to it, and which helps it to be understood. ❑ *We are doing this work in the context of reforms in the economic, social and cultural spheres.* ❑ *...the historical context in which Chaucer wrote.* ② N-VAR The **context** of a word, sentence, or text consists of the words, sentences, or text before and after it which help to make its meaning clear. ❑ *Without a context, I would have assumed it was written by a man.* ③ PHRASE If something is seen **in context** or if it is put **into context**, it is considered together with all the factors that relate to it. ❑ *Taxation is not popular in principle, merely acceptable in context.* ④ PHRASE If a statement or remark is quoted **out of context**, the circumstances in which it was said are not correctly reported, so that it seems to mean something different from the meaning that was intended. ❑ *Thomas says that he has been taken out of context on the issue.*

con|ti|nent ◆◇◇ /kɒntɪnənt/ (**continents**) ① N-COUNT A **continent** is a very large area of land, such as Africa or Asia, that consists of several countries. ❑ *She loved the African continent.* ② N-PROPER People sometimes use **the Continent** to refer to the whole of Europe except for Britain. [mainly BRIT] ❑ *Its shops are among the most stylish on the Continent.* →see **earth** →see Word Web: **continents**

con|ti|nen|tal /kɒntɪnɛnt'l/ (**continentals**) ① ADJ **Continental** is used to refer to something that belongs to or relates to a continent. [ADJ n] ❑ *The most ancient parts of the continental crust are 4000 million years old.* ② ADJ The **continental** United States consists of all the states which are situated on the continent of North America, as opposed to Hawaii and territories such as the Virgin Islands. [mainly AM] ❑ *Shipping is included on orders sent within the continental U.S.* ③ ADJ **Continental** means situated on or belonging to the continent of Europe except for Britain. [mainly BRIT] [ADJ n] ❑ *He sees no signs of improvement in the UK*

이야기하기를 꺼린다. ❑ 비디오 영화의 내용에 대해 보다 강력한 제재가 가해졌다. ③ 복수명사 목차 ❑ 목차가 없다. ④ 불가산명사 내용 ❑ 이전 학생들은 과정의 내용과 강사진에 대해 칭찬 일색이었다. ⑤ 단수명사 함유량 ❑ 해바라기 씨 마가린은 지방 함유량이 버터와 동일하다.

① 형용사 만족한 ❑ 나는 아래에서 산을 구경하는 것만으로도 만족한다. ❑ 선거 운동이 이루어진 방식에 대해 나는 전적으로 만족한다. ② 형용사 만족스러워하는 ❑ 그는 자신의 딸이 꽤 만족스러워 한다고 한다.

형용사 만족한 ❑ 그는 집으로 돌아올 때마다 행복하고 만족스럽다.

① 가산명사 논점, 주장의 요지 ❑ 폭력이 수반된 관계에서는 죽음과 살인의 가능성이 항상 잠재해 있다는 것이 내 주장의 요지이다. ② 불가산명사 분쟁 ❑ 국영 기업을 민영화하려는 계획이 분쟁의 특정 요인이다.

형용사 첨예한 [격식체] ❑ 여러 가지 제재 조치가 가장 첨예한 쟁점 중 하나가 되리라 예상된다.

불가산명사 만족 ❑ 그 당시 내가 느꼈던 만족감은 말로 형용할 수 없다.

명사는 /kɒntɛst/로 발음되고, 동사는 /kəntɛst/로 발음된다.

① 가산명사 대회, 경기 ❑ 최근 영국 권투 경기 중 이만큼 흥미진진한 경기는 드물었다. ② 가산명사 다툼 ❑ 11월의 주 선거는 내년의 대통령 선거전 이전에 행해지는 마지막 선거가 될 것이다. ③ 타동사 이의를 제기하다 ❑ 본건에 이의를 제기하기 위해서는 당신의 전 고용주가 14일 이내에 답변을 해야 한다. ④ 타동사 경쟁에 참가하다 [주로 영국영어] ❑ 그는 선거에 나설 수 있도록 당의 후보 지명을 신속히 받았다.

가산명사 경쟁자 ❑ 후에 그는 비비시 텔레비전 프로에 경쟁자로 참가하기 위해 지원했다.

① 가산명사 또는 불가산명사 맥락, 상황 ❑ 우리는 경제, 사회, 문화 부문 개혁의 맥락 안에서 이 일을 하고 있다. ❑ 초서가 작품을 쓸 당시의 역사적 상황 ② 가산명사 또는 불가산명사 문맥 ❑ 문맥이 없다면 나는 그것을 남자가 쓴 것이라고 짐작했을 것이다. ③ 구 맥락 안에서 ❑ 과세가 원칙상으로는 그다지 인기가 없으나 맥락 안에서 파악하면 받아들일 만하다. ④ 구 문맥 없이 ❑ 그 사안에 대한 자신의 발언이 문맥에 대한 고려 없이 인용되었다고 토머스는 말한다.

① 가산명사 대륙 ❑ 그녀는 아프리카 대륙을 사랑했다. ② 고유명사 유럽 본토 [주로 영국영어] ❑ 그 상점들은 유럽 본토에서 가장 화려한 축에 속한다.

① 형용사 대륙의 ❑ 대륙 지각의 가장 오래된 부분은 40억 년 되었다. ② 형용사 미국 본토의 [주로 미국영어] ❑ 미국 본토 내의 주문에 대해선 배송료가 포함됩니다. ③ 형용사 유럽 본토의 [주로 영국영어] ❑ 영국과 유럽 본토의 경제가 개선되고 있다는 어떠한 징표도 그는 찾지 못하고 있다. ④ 가산명사 유럽 본토 출신의 [영국영어, 비격식체] ❑ 유럽 본토 사람들과 미국인들은 왜 우측으로 운전을 하지?

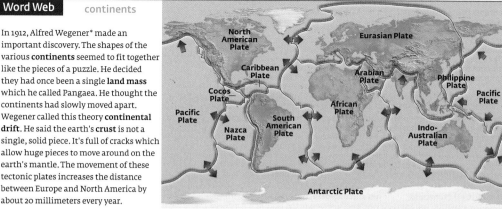

Word Web — continents

In 1912, Alfred Wegener* made an important discovery. The shapes of the various **continents** seemed to fit together like the pieces of a puzzle. He decided they had once been a single **land mass** which he called Pangaea. He thought the continents had slowly moved apart. Wegener called this theory **continental drift**. He said the earth's **crust** is not a single, solid piece. It's full of cracks which allow huge pieces to move around on the earth's mantle. The movement of these tectonic plates increases the distance between Europe and North America by about 20 millimeters every year.

Alfred Wegener (1880-1930): a German scientist.

Major Plates of the Earth's Crust

and continental economy. ◳ N-COUNT A **continental** is someone who comes from the continent of Europe. [BRIT, INFORMAL] ❑ *Why do Continentals and Americans drive on the right?*

con|tin|gen|cy /kəntɪndʒ³nsi/ (**contingencies**) ◱ N-VAR A **contingency** is something that might happen in the future. [FORMAL] ❑ *I need to examine all possible contingencies.* ◲ ADJ A **contingency** plan or measure is one that is intended to be used if a possible situation actually occurs. [FORMAL] [ADJ n] ❑ *We have contingency plans.*

◱ 가산명사 또는 불가산명사 가능성 [격식체] ❑ 모든 가능성을 점검해야 한다. ◲ 형용사 가능성에 대비한, 예비 [격식체] ❑ 예비 대책을 갖추었습니다.

con|tin|gent /kəntɪndʒ³nt/ (**contingents**) ◱ N-COUNT A **contingent** of police, soldiers, or military vehicles is a group of them. [FORMAL] ❑ *Nigeria provided a large contingent of troops to the West African Peacekeeping Force.* ◲ N-COUNT A **contingent** is a group of people representing a country or organization at a meeting or other event. [FORMAL] ❑ *The strong British contingent suffered mixed fortunes.*

◱ 가산명사 부대 [격식체] ❑ 나이지리아는 서아프리카 평화 유지군에 대규모의 병력을 제공했다. ◲ 가산명사 대표단 [격식체] ❑ 강력한 영국의 대표단은 좋고 나쁜 것을 다 겪었다.

con|tin|ual /kəntɪnyuəl/ ◱ ADJ A **continual** process or situation happens or exists without stopping. [ADJ n] ❑ *The school has been in continual use since 1883.* ❑ *They felt continual pressure to perform well.* ● **con|tin|ual|ly** ADV ❑ *She cried almost continually and threw temper tantrums.* ◲ ADJ **Continual** events happen again and again. [ADJ n] ❑ *...the government's continual demands for cash to finance its chronic deficit.* ● **con|tin|ual|ly** ADV ❑ *Malcolm was continually changing his mind.*

◱ 형용사 지속적인 ❑ 그 학교는 1883년 이래 지속적으로 사용되어 왔다. ❑ 그들은 잘해야 한다는 압력을 끊임없이 받았다. ● 지속적으로 부사 ❑ 그 애는 거의 끊임없이 울었고 심한 투정을 부렸다. ◲ 형용사 잇따른, 거듭되는 ❑ 만성적인 부채를 지탱할 수 있는 자금에 대한 정부의 잇따른 요청 ● 거듭 부사 ❑ 말콤은 계속 마음을 바꾸고 있었다.

You can use **continual**, **continuous**, and **constant** to describe things that happen or exist without stopping. **Continual** is usually used to describe something that happens often over a period of time, especially something undesirable. ❑ *...his continual drinking....continual demands to cut costs.* If something is **continuous**, it happens all the time without stopping, or seems to do so. ❑ *...days of continuous rain...a continuous background noise.* You describe something as **constant** when it happens all the time or never goes away. ❑ *He was in constant pain....Eva's constant criticism.*

끊임없이 계속 일어나거나 존재하는 것을 묘사할 때 continual, continuous, constant를 쓸 수 있다. continual은 흔히 일정 기간에 걸쳐 일어나는, 특히 바람직하지 않은 것을 묘사할 때 쓴다. ❑ ...그의 계속된 음주....비용을 줄이라는 계속된 요구. 어떤 것이 continuous하다는 것은, 그것이 그치지 않고 내내 계속되거나 그런 것처럼 여겨짐을 나타낸다. ❑ ...계속 비가 내리는 나날....계속되는 배경의 소음. 항상 일어나며 없어지지 않는 것은 constant로 묘사한다. ❑ 그는 통증이 계속되었다....에바의 계속된 비난

Thesaurus — *continual*의 참조어

ADJ. constant; (ant.) intermittent ◱
ongoing, repeated ◲

con|tinu|ation /kəntɪnyueɪ∫³n/ (**continuations**) ◱ N-VAR The **continuation of** something is the fact that it continues, rather than stopping. ❑ *It's the coalition forces who are to blame for the continuation of the war.* ◲ N-COUNT Something that is a **continuation of** something else is closely connected with it or forms part of it. ❑ *...since this chapter is a continuation of Chapter 8.*

◱ 가산명사 또는 불가산명사 지속 ❑ 전쟁의 지속에 대한 책임을 져야 할 사람들은 연합군들이다. ◲ 가산명사 -의 연장 ❑ 이 장은 8장의 연장인 관계로

con|tinue ♦♦♦ /kəntɪnyu/ (**continues, continuing, continued**) ◱ V-T/V-I If someone or something **continues to** do something, they keep doing it and do not stop. ❑ *I hope they continue to fight for equal justice after I'm gone.* ❑ *Diana and Roy Jarvis are determined to continue working when they reach retirement age.* ◲ V-T/V-I If something **continues** or if you **continue** it, it does not stop happening. ❑ *He insisted that the conflict would continue until conditions were met for a ceasefire.* ❑ *Outside the building people continue their vigil, huddling around bonfires.* ◳ V-T/V-I If you **continue** with something, you start doing it again after a break or interruption. ❑ *I went up to my room to continue with my packing.* ◴ V-T/V-I If something **continues** or if you **continue** it, it starts again after a break or interruption. ❑ *He denies 18 charges. The trial continues today.* ◵ V-T/V-I If you **continue**, you begin speaking again after a pause or interruption. ❑ *"You have no right to intimidate this man," Alison continued.* ❑ *Tony drank some coffee before he continued.* ◶ V-I If you **continue as** something or **continue** in a particular state, you remain in a particular job or state. ❑ *He had hoped to continue as a full-time career officer.* ◷ V-I If you **continue** in a particular direction, you keep walking

◱ 타동사/자동사 계속하다 ❑ 내가 떠난 이후에도 그들이 평등한 정의를 위해 계속 싸우길 바란다. ❑ 다이애나와 로이는 정년이 되도 계속 일할 결심을 가지고 있다. ◲ 타동사/자동사 계속되다 ❑ 정전 조건이 충족될 때까지 분쟁은 계속될 것이라고 그는 주장했다. ❑ 건물 밖에서는 사람들이 모닥불 주위에 바짝 모여 철야를 계속했다. ◳ 타동사/자동사 속행하다 ❑ 짐 싸는 것을 계속하기 위해 나는 방으로 올라갔다. ◴ 타동사/자동사 속행되다 ❑ 그는 18가지의 혐의를 부인한다. 재판은 오늘 계속된다. ◵ 타동사/자동사 말을 계속하다 ❑ "이 남자를 위협할 어떠한 권한도 당신에겐 없어요." 라고 앨리슨은 계속 얘기했다. ❑ 토니는 커피를 좀 마신 다음 말을 이었다. ◶ 자동사 계속하다 ❑ 그는 정식 장교로 계속 근무하기를 희망했었다. ◷ 자동사 계속 나아가다 ❑ 그는

or traveling in that direction. ❏ *He continued rapidly up the path, not pausing until he neared the Chapter House.*

집회소에 도달할 때까지 멈추지 않고 길을 따라 계속 빨리 올라갔다.

Thesaurus   *continue*의 참조어

v.   go on, persist; (*ant.*) stop **1**
          carry on, resume **3**

---

con|tinu|ing edu|ca|tion N-UNCOUNT **Continuing education** is education for adults in a variety of subjects, most of which are practical, not academic.

불가산명사 평생 교육

con|ti|nu|ity /kɒntɪnuːɪti, BRIT kɒntɪnyuːɪti/ (**continuities**) N-VAR **Continuity** is the fact that something continues to happen or exist, with no great changes or interruptions. ❏ *...a tank designed to ensure continuity of fuel supply during aerobatics.*

가산명사 또는 불가산명사 연속 ❏ 곡예비행 도중에 연료 공급이 꾸준히 유지되도록 설계된 연료 탱크

con|tinu|ous /kəntɪnyuəs/ **1** ADJ A **continuous** process or event continues for a period of time without stopping. ❏ *Residents report that they heard continuous gunfire.* ● con|tinu|ous|ly ADV ❏ *The civil war has raged almost continuously since 1976.* **2** ADJ A **continuous** line or surface has no gaps or holes in it. ❏ *...a continuous line of boats.* **3** ADJ In English grammar, **continuous** verb groups are formed using the auxiliary "be" and the present participle of a verb, as in "I'm feeling a bit tired" and "She had been watching them for some time." Continuous verb groups are used especially when you are focusing on a particular moment. Compare **simple**.

1 형용사 끊임없이 이어지는 ❏ 주민들은 끊임없이 이어지는 총성을 들었다고 한다. ● 끊임없이 부사 ❏ 내전은 1976년 이후로 거의 끊임없이 벌어졌다. **2** 형용사 계속 이어지는 ❏ 쭉 이어진 보트의 행렬 **3** 형용사 진행형의

You can use **continual**, **continuous**, and **constant** to describe things that happen or exist without stopping. **Continual** is usually used to describe something that happens often over a period of time, especially something undesirable. ❏ *...his continual drinking....continual demands to cut costs.* If something is **continuous**, it happens all the time without stopping, or seems to do so. ❏ *...days of continuous rain...a continuous background noise.* You describe something as **constant** when it happens all the time or never goes away. ❏ *He was in constant pain....Eva's constant criticism.*

끊임없이 계속 일어나거나 존재하는 것을 묘사할 때 continual, continuous, constant를 쓸 수 있다. continual은 흔히 일정 기간에 걸쳐 일어나는, 특히 바람직하지 않은 것을 묘사할 때 쓴다. ❏ ...그의 계속된 음주....비용을 줄이라는 계속된 요구. 어떤 것이 continuous하다는 것은, 그것이 그치지 않고 내내 계속되거나 그런 것처럼 여겨짐을 나타낸다. ❏ ...계속 비가 내리는 나날....계속되는 배경의 소음. 항상 일어나며 없어지지 않는 것은 constant로 묘사한다. ❏ 그는 통증이 계속되었다....에바의 계속되는 비난

---

con|tinu|ous as|sess|ment N-UNCOUNT If pupils or students undergo **continuous assessment**, they get qualifications partly or entirely based on the work they do during the year, rather than on exam results. [BRIT]

불가산명사 상시 평가 [영국영어]

con|tort /kəntɔrt/ (**contorts, contorting, contorted**) V-T/V-I If someone's face or body **contorts** or is **contorted**, it moves into an unnatural and unattractive shape or position. ❏ *His face contorts as he screams out the lyrics.* ❏ *The gentlest of her caresses would contort his already tense body.*

타동사/자동사 일그러지다 ❏ 소리 지르며 가사를 뱉어낼 때 그는 얼굴이 일그러진다. ❏ 그녀가 조금만 애무를 해도 이미 긴장한 그는 온 몸이 뒤틀릴 것이다.

con|tour /kɒntʊər/ (**contours**) **1** N-COUNT You can refer to the general shape or outline of an object as its **contours**. [LITERARY] ❏ *...the texture and color of the skin, the contours of the body.* **2** N-COUNT A **contour** on a map is a line joining points of equal height and indicating hills, valleys, and the steepness of slopes. ❏ *...a contour map showing two hills and this large mountain in the middle.*

1 가산명사 윤곽 [문예체] ❏ 피부의 질감과 색깔, 몸의 윤곽 **2** 가산명사 등고선 ❏ 두 개의 언덕과 그 사이의 큰 산을 나타내는 등고선 지도

Word Link   contra ≈ against : contraband, contraception, contradict

---

contra|cep|tion /kɒntrəsɛpʃ°n/ N-UNCOUNT **Contraception** refers to methods of preventing pregnancy. ❏ *Use a reliable method of contraception.*

불가산명사 피임 ❏ 믿을 수 있는 피임 방식을 사용하세요.

contra|cep|tive /kɒntrəsɛptɪv/ (**contraceptives**) **1** ADJ A **contraceptive** method or device is a method or a device which a woman uses to prevent herself from becoming pregnant. [ADJ n] ❏ *It was at that time she started taking the contraceptive pill.* **2** N-COUNT A **contraceptive** is a device or drug that prevents a woman from becoming pregnant. ❏ *...oral contraceptives.*

1 형용사 피임의 ❏ 그녀가 피임약을 복용하기 시작한 것이 그때였다. **2** 가산명사 피임제 ❏ 구강 피임제

Word Link   tract ≈ dragging, drawing : contract, subtract, tractor

---

con|tract ♦♦◇ (**contracts, contracting, contracted**)

The noun is pronounced /kɒntrækt/. The verb is pronounced /kəntrækt/.

명사는 /kɒntrækt/로 발음되고, 동사는 /kəntrækt/로 발음된다.

---

1 N-COUNT A **contract** is a legal agreement, usually between two companies or between an employer and employee, which involves doing work for a stated sum of money. ❏ *The company won a prestigious contract for work on Europe's tallest building.* **2** V-T If you **contract with** someone **to** do something, you legally agree to do it for them or for them to do it for you. [FORMAL] ❏ *You can contract with us to deliver your cargo.* **3** V-T/V-I When something **contracts** or when something **contracts** in, it becomes smaller or shorter. ❏ *Blood is only expelled from the heart when it contracts.* ● con|trac|tion /kəntrækʃ°n/ (**contractions**) N-VAR ❏ *...the contraction and expansion of blood vessels.* **4** V-I When something such as an economy or market **contracts**, it becomes smaller. ❏ *The manufacturing economy contracted in October for the sixth consecutive month.* **5** V-T If you **contract** a serious illness, you become ill with it. [FORMAL] [no cont] ❏ *He contracted AIDS from a blood transfusion.* **6** PHRASE If you are **under contract** to someone, you have signed a contract agreeing to work for them, and for no one else, during a fixed period of time. ❏ *The director wanted Olivia de Havilland, then under contract to Warner Brothers.* →see **illness, muscle**

1 가산명사 계약 ❏ 회사는 유럽의 가장 높은 건물을 작업하는, 명망 있는 계약을 따냈다. **2** 자동사 계약하다 [격식체] ❏ 우리가 당신의 화물을 배송하도록 계약할 수 있습니다. **3** 타동사/자동사 수축하다; 수축시키다 ❏ 심장이 수축할 때에만 피가 심장에서 방출된다. ● 수축 가산명사 또는 불가산명사 ❏ 혈관의 수축과 팽창 **4** 자동사 위축되다 ❏ 제조 분야는 10월에 6개월 연속 위축되었다. **5** 타동사 걸리다 [격식체] ❏ 그는 수혈을 통해 에이즈에 감염되었다. **6** 구 전속되어 있는, 도급을 맡은 ❏ 감독은 당시에 워너 브러더스에게 전속되어 있던 올리비아 드 하빌랜드를 원했다.

Word Partnership   *contract*의 연어

V.   **sign a contract** **1**
N.   **terms of a contract** **1**
        contract **a disease** **5**
PREP.   contract **with** *someone* **2**

▶**contract out** PHRASAL VERB If a company **contracts out** work, they employ other companies to do it. [BUSINESS] ❑ *Firms can contract out work to one another.* ❑ *When Barclays Bank contracted out its cleaning, the new company was cheaper.*

구동사 외주를 주다 [경제] ❑ 회사들은 서로에게 일을 외주 줄 수 있다. ❑ 바클레이스 은행이 청소를 외주로 줄 때 새 회사가 더 저렴했다.

con|trac|tion /kəntrækʃən/ (**contractions**) **1** N-COUNT When a woman who is about to give birth has **contractions**, she experiences a very strong, painful tightening of the muscles of her womb. ❑ *The contractions were getting stronger.* **2** N-COUNT A **contraction** is a shortened form of a word or words. ❑ *"It's" (with an apostrophe) should be used only as a contraction for "it is."* **3** →see also **contract**

1 가산명사 자궁 수축 ❑ 자궁 수축의 강도가 더 심해지고 있었다. **2** 가산명사 단축형 ❑ 'it's' (아포스트로피가 붙은)는 'it is'의 단축형으로만 쓰여야 한다.

con|trac|tor /kɒntræktər, kəntræk-/ (**contractors**) N-COUNT A **contractor** is a person or company that does work for other people or organizations. [BUSINESS] ❑ *We told the building contractor that we wanted a garage big enough for two cars.*

가산명사 도급자, 청부인 [경제] ❑ 우리는 건축 도급업자에게 차 두 대가 들어갈 만큼 큰 차고를 원한다고 말했다.

con|trac|tual /kəntræktʃuəl/ ADJ A **contractual** arrangement or relationship involves a legal agreement between people. [FORMAL] ❑ *The company has not fulfilled certain contractual obligations.* ● con|trac|tu|al|ly ADV ❑ *Rank was contractually obliged to hand him a check for $30 million.*

형용사 계약상의, 계약적인 [격식체] ❑ 그 회사는 정해진 계약상의 의무를 이행하지 않았다. ● 계약상으로 부사 ❑ 랭크는 계약상 그에게 3천만 달러짜리 수표를 주어야만 했다.

Word Link	contra ≈ against : contraband, contraception, contradict

Word Link	dict ≈ speaking : contradict, dictate, predict

contra|dict /kɒntrədɪkt/ (**contradicts, contradicting, contradicted**) **1** V-T If you **contradict** someone, you say that what they have just said is wrong, or suggest that it is wrong by saying something different. ❑ *She dared not contradict him.* ❑ *His comments appeared to contradict remarks made earlier in the day by the chairman.* **2** V-T If one statement or piece of evidence **contradicts** another, the first one makes the second one appear to be wrong. ❑ *Her version contradicted the Government's claim that they were shot after being challenged.*

1 타동사 반박하다 ❑ 그녀는 감히 그의 말을 반박하지 못했다. ❑ 그의 논평은 의장이 그날 앞서 제시했던 소견을 반박하는 것 같았다. **2** 타동사 -에 반하다, 모순되다 ❑ 그녀의 설명은 그들을 수하를 한 후에 발포했다는 정부 측의 주장에 반하는 것이었다.

contra|dic|tion /kɒntrədɪkʃən/ (**contradictions**) N-COUNT If you describe an aspect of a situation as a **contradiction**, you mean that it is completely different from other aspects, and so makes the situation confused or difficult to understand. ❑ *The militants see no contradiction in using violence to bring about a religious state.*

가산명사 모순 ❑ 호전주의자들은 종교 국가를 이룩하기 위해 폭력을 쓰는 것에서 아무런 모순을 느끼지 않는다.

contra|dic|tory /kɒntrədɪktəri, BRIT kɒntrədɪktəri/ ADJ If two or more facts, ideas, or statements are **contradictory**, they state or imply that opposite things are true. ❑ *Customs officials have made a series of contradictory statements about the equipment.*

형용사 모순된, 양립되지 않는 ❑ 세관원들은 그 장비에 대해 일련의 모순된 진술들을 해 왔다.

con|tra|ry /kɒntreri, BRIT kɒntrəri/ **1** ADJ Ideas, attitudes, or reactions that are **contrary to** each other are completely different from each other. ❑ *This view is contrary to the aims of critical social research for a number of reasons.* **2** PHRASE If you say that something is true **contrary to** other people's beliefs or opinions, you are emphasizing that it is true and that they are wrong. [EMPHASIS] ❑ *Contrary to popular belief, moderate exercise actually decreases your appetite.* **3** PHRASE You use **on the contrary** when you have just said or implied that something is not true and are going to say that the opposite is true. ❑ *It is not an idea around which the Community can unite. On the contrary, I see it as one that will divide us.* **4** PHRASE You can use **on the contrary** when you are disagreeing strongly with something that has just been said or implied, or are making a strong negative reply. [EMPHASIS] ❑ *"People just don't do things like that." — "On the contrary, they do them all the time."*

1 형용사 -에 반하는, 반대되는 ❑ 이 견해는 여러 가지 이유로 정밀한 사회적 연구의 목적에 반한다. **2** 구 -에 반하여, 반대되는 [강조] ❑ 통속적인 믿음과는 반대로, 적당한 운동은 사실상 식욕을 감퇴시킨다. **3** 구 도리어 ❑ 그것은 공동체를 결속시킬 수 있는 사상이 아니다. 도리어, 내가 보기에 그것은 분열시킬 사상이다. **4** 구 도리어, 반대로 [강조] ❑ "사람들은 그런 일을 하지 않아." "그 반대로야, 항상 그런 일을 해."

> Do not confuse **on the contrary** with **on the other hand**. **On the contrary** is used to contradict someone, to say that they are wrong. **On the other hand** is used to state a different, often contrasting aspect of the situation you are considering. ❑ *Prices of other foods and consumer goods fell. Wages on the other hand increased.*

> on the contrary와 on the other hand를 혼동하지 않도록 하라. on the contrary는 누구의 말을 반박해서 틀렸다고 말하기 위해 쓴다. on the other hand는 현재 고려하고 있는 상황에서 다르거나, 흔히 대조되는 면을 말하기 위해 쓴다. ❑ 다른 식품과 소비재 가격은 떨어졌다. 반면 임금은 올랐다.

5 PHRASE When a particular idea is being considered, evidence or statements **to the contrary** suggest that this idea is not true or that the opposite is true. ❑ *That does not automatically mean, however, that the money supply has been curbed, and there is considerable evidence to the contrary.*

5 구 그에 반하는 ❑ 하지만 그것이 필연적으로 통화 공급량이 억제되어 왔다는 것을 의미하지는 않으며, 그에 반하는 상당한 증거가 있다.

con|trast ♦◇◇ (**contrasts, contrasting, contrasted**)

> The noun is pronounced /kɒntræst/. The verb is pronounced /kəntræst/.

> 명사는 /kɒntræst /로 발음되고, 동사는 /kəntræst/로 발음된다.

1 N-VAR A **contrast** is a great difference between two or more things which is clear when you compare them. ❑ *...the contrast between town and country.* ❑ *The two visitors provided a startling contrast in appearance.* **2** PHRASE You say **by contrast** or **in contrast**, or **in contrast to** something, to show that you are mentioning a very different situation from the one you have just mentioned. ❑ *The private sector, by contrast, has plenty of money to spend.* ❑ *In contrast, the lives of girls in well-to-do families were often very sheltered.* **3** PHRASE If one thing is **in contrast to** another, it is very different from it. ❑ *His public statements have always been in marked contrast to those of his son.* **4** V-T If you **contrast** one thing **with** another, you point out or consider the differences between those things. ❑ *She contrasted the situation then with the present crisis.* ❑ *Contrast that approach with what goes on in most organizations.* **5** V-RECIP If one thing **contrasts with** another, it is very different from it. ❑ *Johnson's easy charm contrasted sharply with the prickliness of his boss.* **6** N-UNCOUNT **Contrast** is the degree of difference between the darker and lighter parts of a photograph, television picture, or painting. ❑ *...a television with brighter colors, better contrast, and digital sound.*

1 가산명사 또는 불가산명사 대조 ❑ 도회지와 시골 사이의 대조 ❑ 그 두 명의 방문객은 겉모습이 놀랄 만큼 대조를 보였다. **2** 구 대조적으로; 대비하여 ❑ 대조적으로, 민간 부문은 쓸 수 있는 자금을 풍부하게 가지고 있다. ❑ 대조적으로, 유복한 가정에 사는 여자 아이들의 생활은 흔히 너무 엄한 보호를 받았다. **3** 구 -와는 현저히 다른 ❑ 그의 공개 성명은 언제나 그 아들의 성명과는 현저히 달랐다. **4** 타동사 대조시키다, 대비시키다 ❑ 그녀는 당시 상황을 현재의 위기와 대비시켰다. ❑ 그 접근법을 대부분의 조직 내에서 일어나는 일과 대비해 보세요. **5** 상호동사 대조를 이루다, 차이를 보이다 ❑ 존슨의 부드러운 매력은 그 상관의 성마른 성격과 뚜렷한 대조를 이루었다. **6** 불가산명사 명암 대비 ❑ 더 밝은 색상과 더 나은 명암 대비, 디지털 사운드 기능을 갖춘 텔레비전

contra|vene /kɒntrəviːn/ (**contravenes, contravening, contravened**) v-т To **contravene** a law or rule means to do something that is forbidden by the law or rule. [FORMAL] ❑ *The Board has banned the film on the grounds that it contravenes criminal libel laws.* ● **contra|ven|tion** /kɒntrəvɛnʃən/ (**contraventions**) N-VAR ❑ *The government has lent millions of pounds to debt-ridden banks in contravention of local banking laws.*

타동사 위반하다 [격식체] ❑ 위원회는 형사상 명예 훼손법을 위반한다는 이유로 그 영화의 상영을 금지했다. ● 위반 가산명사 또는 불가산명사 ❑ 정부는 지방 은행법을 위반하며 부채에 시달리는 은행들에 수백만 파운드를 대출해 주었다.

---

con|trib|ute ♦♢♢ /kəntrɪbjuːt/ (**contributes, contributing, contributed**) **1** v-т/v-ı If you **contribute to** something, you say or do things to help to make it successful. ❑ *The three sons also contribute to the family business.* ❑ *I believe that each of us can contribute to the future of the world.* **2** v-т/v-ı To **contribute** money or resources **to** something means to give money or resources to help pay for something or to help achieve a particular purpose. ❑ *The U.S. is contributing $4 billion in loans, credits, and grants.* ● **con|tribu|tor** /kəntrɪbjətər/ (**contributors**) N-COUNT ❑ *...the largest net contributors to EU funds.* **3** v-ı If something **contributes to** an event or situation, it is one of the causes of it. ❑ *The report says design faults in both the vessels contributed to the tragedy.*

1 타동사/자동사 기여하다, 공헌하다 ❑ 세 아들 역시 가업에 힘을 보태고 있다. ❑ 나는 우리들 각자가 세계의 미래에 기여할 수 있다고 믿는다. **2** 타동사/자동사 기부하다, 기증하다 ❑ 미국은 차관과 채권, 보조금 등의 형태로 40억 달러를 기부하고 있다. ● 기부자 가산명사 ❑ 유럽 연합 기금 최대 순기부국 **3** 자동사 한 가지 원인이 되다 ❑ 보도에 따르면 두 선박 모두의 설계 결함이 그 비극적 사고의 원인이었다고 한다.

Thesaurus	contribute의 참조어

v.	aid, assist, chip in, commit, donate, give, grant, help, support; *(ant.)* neglect, take away **2**

con|tri|bu|tion ♦♢♢ /kɒntrɪbjuːʃən/ (**contributions**) **1** N-COUNT If you make a **contribution to** something, you do something to help make it successful or to produce it. ❑ *American economists have made important contributions to the field of financial and corporate economics.* **2** N-COUNT A **contribution** is a sum of money that you give in order to help pay for something. ❑ *This list ranked companies that make charitable contributions of a half million dollars or more.*

1 가산명사 기여, 공헌 ❑ 미국 경제학자들은 금융 경제학과 기업 경제학 부문에 중요한 공헌을 해 왔다. **2** 가산명사 기부금 ❑ 이 리스트에는 5십만 달러 이상의 자선 기부금을 낸 회사들이 나란히 올라 있다.

Word Partnership	contribution의 연어

V.	**make a** contribution, **send a** contribution **1 2**
ADJ.	**important** contribution, **significant** contribution **1 2**

con|tribu|tor /kəntrɪbjətər/ (**contributors**) N-COUNT You can use **contributor** to refer to one of the causes of an event or situation, especially if that event or situation is an unpleasant one. ❑ *Old buses are major contributors to pollution in British cities.* →see also **contribute**

가산명사 하나의 원인 ❑ 낡은 버스는 영국 시내 오염의 주된 원인이다.

con|trive /kəntraɪv/ (**contrives, contriving, contrived**) v-т If you **contrive** an event or situation, you succeed in making it happen, often by tricking someone. [FORMAL] ❑ *The oil companies were accused of contriving a shortage of gasoline to justify price increases.*

타동사 획책하다 [격식체] ❑ 그 석유 회사들은 가격 상승을 정당화하기 위해 가솔린 부족 사태를 획책했다는 비난을 받았다.

con|trived /kəntraɪvd/ ADJ If you say that something someone says or does is **contrived**, you think it is false and deliberate, rather than natural and not planned. [DISAPPROVAL] ❑ *There was nothing contrived or calculated about what he said.*

형용사 인위적인 [탐탁찮음] ❑ 그가 한 말에는 인위적이거나 계산된 것이 아무 것도 없었다.

con|trol ♦♦♦ /kəntroʊl/ (**controls, controlling, controlled**) **1** N-UNCOUNT **Control of** an organization, place, or system is the power to make all the important decisions about the way that it is run. ❑ *The restructuring involves Mr. Ronson giving up control of the company.* ● PHRASE If you are **in control of** something, you have the power to make all the important decisions about the way it is run. ❑ *Nobody knows who is in control of the club.* ● PHRASE If something is **under** your **control**, you have the power to make all the important decisions about the way that it is run. ❑ *All the newspapers were taken under government control.* **2** N-UNCOUNT If you have **control** of something or someone, you are able to make them do what you want them to do. [oft N of/over n] ❑ *He lost control of his car.* **3** N-UNCOUNT If you show **control**, you prevent yourself behaving in an angry or emotional way. ❑ *He had a terrible temper, and sometimes he would completely lose control.* **4** v-т The people who **control** an organization or place have the power to take all the important decisions about the way that it is run. ❑ *He now controls the largest retail development empire in southern California.* **5** v-т To **control** a piece of equipment, process, or system means to make it work in the way that you want it to work. ❑ *...a computerized system to control the gates.* ❑ *Scientists would soon be able to manipulate human genes to control the ageing process.* **6** v-т When a government **controls** prices, wages, or the activity of a particular group, it uses its power to restrict them. ❑ *The federal government tried to control rising health-care costs.* ● N-UNCOUNT **Control** is also a noun. ❑ *Control of inflation remains the government's absolute priority.* **7** v-т If you **control yourself**, or if you **control** your feelings, voice, or expression, you make yourself behave calmly even though you are feeling angry, excited, or upset. ❑ *Jo was advised to learn to control herself.* ● **con|trolled** ADJ ❑ *Her manner was quiet and very controlled.* **8** v-т To **control** something dangerous means to prevent it from becoming worse or from spreading. ❑ *...the need to control environmental pollution.* **9** N-COUNT A **control** is a device such as a switch or lever which you use in order to operate a machine or other piece of equipment. ❑ *I practised operating the controls.* **10** N-VAR **Controls** are the methods that a government uses to restrict increases, for example in prices, wages, or weapons. ❑ *Critics question whether price controls would do any good.* **11** N-VAR **Control** is used to refer to a place where your documents or luggage are officially checked when you enter a foreign country. ❑ *He went straight through Passport Control without incident.* **12** →see also **birth control, quality control, remote control, stock control**

1 불가산명사 지배권 ❑ 구조 조정에는 론슨 씨가 회사의 지배권을 포기하는 것이 포함된다. ● 구 -에 대한 지배권을 가진 ❑ 누가 그 클럽의 지배권을 갖고 있는지 아무도 모른다. ● 구 -의 통제를 받고 있는 ❑ 모든 신문이 정부의 통제 하에 있었다. **2** 불가산명사 제어 ❑ 그는 자동차를 제어할 수 없었다. **3** 불가산명사 자제력 ❑ 그는 엄청나게 성미가 급해서, 때때로 자제력을 완전히 잃곤 했다. **4** 타동사 지배하다, 관리하다 ❑ 그는 현재 캘리포니아 남부 최대의 소매상 제국을 지배하고 있다. **5** 타동사 제어하다 ❑ 자동화된 출입구 제어 시스템 ❑ 과학자들이 머지않아 노화 작용을 제어하기 위해 인간의 유전자를 조작할 수 있게 될지도 모른다. **6** 타동사 제어하다, 억제하다 ❑ 연방 정부는 상승하는 건강 관리 비용을 억제하기 위해 애썼다. ● 불가산명사 제어, 억제 ❑ 인플레이션 억제가 여전히 정부의 절대적 급선무이다. **7** 타동사 자제하다 ❑ 조는 자제심을 기르라는 충고를 받았다. ● 자제된, 조심스런 형용사 ❑ 그녀의 거동은 조용하고 아주 조심스러웠다. **8** 타동사 제어하다, 억제하다 ❑ 환경오염을 억제해야 할 필요 ❑ 가산명사 조종 장치 ❑ 나는 조종 장치를 작동하는 것을 연습했다. **10** 가산명사 또는 불가산명사 억제책, 제한 조치 ❑ 평론가들은 가격 억제책이 과연 도움이 될지 의문시한다. **11** 가산명사 또는 불가산명사 검사소 ❑ 그는 무사히 여권 검사소를 곧장 통과했다.

A

You do not use **control** as a verb to talk about inspecting documents. The verb you use is **check**. ❑ *Police were searching cars and checking identity documents.* However, at an airport or port, the place where passports are checked is called **passport control**.

서류를 점검하는 것에 대해 말할 때는 동사 control을 쓰지 않는다. 이 때 쓰는 동사는 check이다. ❑ 경찰이 자동차들을 수색하고 신분증명서를 확인하고 있었다. 그러나 공항이나 항구에서 여권을 검사하는 곳은 passport control이라고 한다.

B

C

🔃 PHRASE If something is **out of control**, no one has any power over it. ❑ *The fire is burning out of control.* 🔃 PHRASE If something harmful is **under control**, it is being dealt with successfully and is unlikely to cause any more harm. ❑ *The situation is under control.*

🔃 구 제어할 수 없는 ❑ 불이 걷잡을 수 없이 타오르고 있다. 🔃 구 통제되는 ❑ 그 사태는 통제 하에 있다.

Word Partnership   control의 연어

N.	**self**-control 🔢
	air traffic control 🔢
	birth control 🔢
V.	**gain** control, **lose** control 🔢 🔢 🔢
	have control **of/over** *something* 🔢 🔢 🔢
PREP.	**out of** control 🔢
	under control 🔢

D

E

F

G

con|trol|ler /kəntroʊlər/ (**controllers**) 🔢 N-COUNT A **controller** is a person who has responsibility for a particular organization or for a particular part of an organization. [mainly BRIT] ❑ *...the job of controller of BBC1.* →see also **air traffic controller** 🔢 N-COUNT A **controller** is the same as a **comptroller**.

🔢 가산명사 책임자, 지배인 [주로 영국영어] ❑ 비비시 1 방송 책임자 직 🔢 가산명사 검사관, 감사관

H

con|tro|ver|sial ♦◇◇ /kɒntrəvɜːrʃəl/ ADJ If you describe something or someone as **controversial**, you mean that they are the subject of intense public argument, disagreement, or disapproval. ❑ *Immigration is a controversial issue in many countries.*

형용사 논쟁의 소지가 많은, 물의를 일으키는 ❑ 많은 나라에서 이민은 논쟁의 소지가 많은 문제이다.

I

Word Partnership   controversial의 연어

N.	controversial **bill**, controversial **drug**, controversial **issue/subject/topic**, controversial **law**, controversial **measure**, controversial **policy**
ADV.	**highly** controversial

J

K

L

con|tro|ver|sy ♦◇◇ /kɒntrəvɜːrsi, kəntrɒvərsi/ (**controversies**) N-VAR **Controversy** is a lot of discussion and argument about something, often involving strong feelings of anger or disapproval. ❑ *The proposed cuts have caused considerable controversy.*

가산명사 또는 불가산명사 논쟁, 논전 ❑ 그런 삭감 제안은 상당한 논쟁을 불러일으켜 왔다.

M

Word Partnership   controversy의 연어

N.	**center of the** controversy
V.	**create** controversy
ADJ.	**major** controversy, **political** controversy
PREP.	controversy **over/surrounding** *something*

N

O

con|va|lesce /kɒnvəlɛs/ (**convalesces, convalescing, convalesced**) V-I If you **are convalescing**, you are resting and getting your health back after an illness or operation. [FORMAL] ❑ *After two weeks, I was allowed home, where I convalesced for three months.*

자동사 건강을 회복하다, 요양하다 [격식체] ❑ 두 주일 후 나는 집에 가도 좋다는 허락을 받았고, 집에서 석 달 동안 요양했다.

P

con|va|les|cence /kɒnvəlɛsᵊns/ N-UNCOUNT **Convalescence** is the period or process of becoming healthy and well again after an illness or operation. [FORMAL] ❑ *Also thanks to Lucy and Guthrie Scott for inviting me to stay with them during my convalescence.*

불가산명사 회복 (기), 요양 (기간) [격식체] ❑ 루시 스코트와 거스리 스코트 부부에게도, 요양 기간 동안 함께 머물도록 초대해 준 것에 대해 감사를 드린다.

Q

R

con|vene /kənviːn/ (**convenes, convening, convened**) V-T/V-I If someone **convenes** a meeting or conference, they arrange for it to take place. You can also say that people **convene** or that a meeting **convenes**. [FORMAL] ❑ *Last August he convened a meeting of his closest advisers at Camp David.*

타동사/자동사 (모임 또는 회의를) 소집하다; 모이다, 회합하다 [격식체] ❑ 지난 8월 그는 캠프 데이비드에서 자신의 최측근 고문들을 소집해서 회의를 가졌다.

S

con|veni|ence /kənviːnjəns/ (**conveniences**) 🔢 N-UNCOUNT If something is done for your **convenience**, it is done in a way that is useful or suitable for you. ❑ *He was happy to make a detour for her convenience.* 🔢 N-COUNT If you describe something as a **convenience**, you mean that it is very useful. ❑ *Mail order is a convenience for buyers who are too busy to shop.* 🔢 N-COUNT **Conveniences** are pieces of equipment designed to make your life easier. ❑ *...an apartment with all the modern conveniences.* 🔢 →see also **convenient**

🔢 불가산명사 편의; 형편, 편의 ❑ 그는 그녀의 편의를 위해 기뻐 멀리 우회했다. 🔢 가산명사 편리한 것, (문명의) 이기 ❑ 통신 판매는 너무 바빠서 쇼핑할 시간이 없는 소비자들에게 매우 편리한 제도이다. 🔢 가산명사 (편리한) 설비 ❑ 모든 현대적 설비를 갖춘 아파트

T

U

V

con|veni|ent /kənviːnjənt/ 🔢 ADJ If a way of doing something is **convenient**, it is easy, or very useful or suitable for a particular purpose. ❑ *...a flexible and convenient way of paying for business expenses.* ● **con|veni|ence** N-UNCOUNT ❑ *They may use a credit card for convenience.* ❑ *The body spray slips conveniently into your sports bag for freshening up after a game.* 🔢 ADJ If you describe a place as **convenient**, you are pleased because it is near to where you are, or because you can reach another place from there quickly and easily. [APPROVAL] ❑ *The town is well placed for easy access to London and convenient for Heathrow Airport.* ● **con|veni|ent|ly** ADV ❑ *It was very conveniently situated just across the road from the City Reference Library.* 🔢 ADJ A **convenient** time to do something, for example to meet someone, is a time when you are free to do it or would like to do it. ❑ *She will try to arrange a mutually convenient time and place for an interview.*

🔢 형용사 편리한 ❑ 사업 비용을 치르는 융통성 있고 편리한 방법 ● 편리, 편의 불가산명사 ❑ 그들은 편의상 신용 카드를 사용할 수도 있다. ● 편리하게 부사 ❑ 그 바디스프레이는 운동 경기 후 기분을 상쾌하게 하는 데 쓸 수 있도록 스포츠백에 간편하게 쏙 들어갑니다. 🔢 형용사 가까이에 있는; 입지가 편리한 [마음에 듦] ❑ 그 읍은 입지가 좋아 런던까지 쉽게 갈 수 있고 히스로 공항에서도 가깝다. ● 가까이에, 가기 쉽게 부사 ❑ 그곳은 시립 도서관에서 아주 가까이 바로 길 건너에 위치하고 있었다. 🔢 형용사 편한, 형편 좋은 ❑ 그녀는 인터뷰를 위해 서로가 편한 시간과 장소를 잡으려고 노력할 것이다.

W

X

Y

con|vent /kɒnvɛnt, -vᵊnt/ (**convents**) N-COUNT A **convent** is a building in which a community of nuns live.

가산명사 수녀원

Z

con|ven|tion ♦♦◇ /kənvɛnʃ³n/ (**conventions**) ◼ N-VAR A **convention** is a way of behaving that is considered to be correct or polite by most people in a society. ❑ *It's just a social convention that men don't wear skirts.* ◻ N-COUNT In art, literature, or the theater, a **convention** is a traditional method or style. ❑ *We go offstage and come back for the convention of the encore.* ◼ N-COUNT A **convention** is an official agreement between countries or groups of people. ❑ *...the UN convention on climate change.* ◼ N-COUNT A **convention** is a large meeting of an organization or political group. ❑ *...the annual convention of the Society of Professional Journalists.*

◼ 가산명사 또는 불가산명사 관습 ❑ 남자들이 치마를 입지 않는 것은 그저 사회적 관습일 뿐이다. ◻ 가산명사 (예술상의) 관례 ❑ 우리는 무대 뒤로 갔다가 관례적인 앙코르를 위해 돌아온다. ◼ 가산명사 협정, 협약 ❑ 유엔 기후 변화 협약 ◼ 가산명사 집회, 대회 ❑ 전문 언론인 협회 연례 대회

con|ven|tion|al ♦◇◇ /kənvɛnʃən³l/ ◼ ADJ Someone who is **conventional** has behavior or opinions that are ordinary and normal. ❑ *...a respectable married woman with conventional opinions.* ● **con|ven|tion|al|ly** ADV ❑ *People still wore their hair short and dressed conventionally.* ◻ ADJ A **conventional** method or product is one that is usually used or that has been in use for a long time. ❑ *...the risks and drawbacks of conventional family planning methods.* ● **con|ven|tion|al|ly** ADV [ADV with v] ❑ *Organically grown produce does not differ greatly in appearance from conventionally grown crops.* ◼ ADJ **Conventional** weapons and wars do not involve nuclear explosives. ❑ *We must reduce the danger of war by controlling nuclear, chemical, and conventional arms.*

◼ 형용사 (행실이나 견해가) 평범한 ❑ 평범한 견해를 가진 번듯한 기혼 여성 ● 평범하게 부사 ❑ 사람들은 여전히 짧은 머리를 하고 평범한 옷차림을 했다. ◻ 형용사 통상의; 전통적인 ❑ 전통적 가족계획 방식의 위험과 결점 ● 통상적으로 부사 ❑ 유기농 재배 작물은 겉보기에는 통상적으로 기른 작품과 크게 다르지 않다. ◼ 형용사 (병기가) 재래식의, 비핵의 ❑ 핵무기와 화학 무기, 재래식 무기를 억제해서 전쟁의 위험을 줄여야 한다.

Word Link   verg, vert ≈ turning : con**verge**, di**verge**, sub**vert**

---

con|verge /kənvɜrdʒ/ (**converges, converging, converged**) ◼ V-I If people or vehicles **converge on** a place, they move toward it from different directions. ❑ *Hundreds of coaches will converge on the capital.* ◻ V-I If roads or lines **converge**, they meet or join at a particular place. [FORMAL] ❑ *As they flow south, the five rivers converge.*

◼ 자동사 한데 모이다 ❑ 수백 명의 코치가 수도에 모일 것이다. ◻ 자동사 한 점에 모이다 [격식체] ❑ 그 다섯 개의 강은 남쪽으로 흘러가면서 한곳으로 모인다.

con|ver|gence /kənvɜrdʒ³ns/ (**convergences**) N-VAR The **convergence** of different ideas, groups, or societies is the process by which they stop being different and become more similar. [FORMAL] ❑ *...the need to move towards greater economic convergence.*

가산명사 또는 불가산명사 수렴 [격식체] ❑ 경제적으로 더욱 수렴되는 방향으로 가야 할 필요

con|ver|sa|tion ♦♦◇ /kɒnvərseɪʃ³n/ (**conversations**) N-COUNT If you have a **conversation with** someone, you talk with them, usually in an informal situation. ❑ *He's a talkative guy, and I struck up a conversation with him.*

가산명사 대화 ❑ 그는 말이 많은 남자인데, 나는 그와 대화를 시작했다.

con|ver|sa|tion|al /kɒnvərseɪʃ³n³l/ ADJ **Conversational** means relating to, or similar to, casual and informal talk. ❑ *What is refreshing is the author's easy, conversational style.*

형용사 대화의, 대화체의 ❑ 참신한 점은 작가의 편안한 대화체의 문체이다.

con|verse (**converses, conversing, conversed**)

The verb is pronounced /kənvɜrs/. The noun is pronounced /kɒnvɜrs/.

동사는 /kənvɜrs/로 발음되고, 명사는 /kɒnvɜrs/로 발음된다.

◼ V-RECIP If you **converse with** someone, you talk to them. You can also say that two people **converse**. [FORMAL] ❑ *Luke sat directly behind the pilot and conversed with him.* ◻ N-SING The **converse** of a statement is its opposite or reverse. [FORMAL] ❑ *What you do for a living is critical to where you settle and how you live – and the converse is also true.*

◼ 상호동사 대화하다; 서로 이야기하다 [격식체] ❑ 루크는 조종사 바로 뒤에 앉아서 그와 이야기를 나누었다. ◻ 단수명사 역, 반대 [격식체] ❑ 네가 생계를 위해 하는 일은 어디에 정착해서 어떻게 사는가 하는 데 매우 중요하다. 그리고 그 반대의 경우도 마찬가지이다.

con|verse|ly /kɒnvɜrsli, kən-/ ADV You say **conversely** to indicate that the situation you are about to describe is the opposite or reverse of the one you have just described. [FORMAL] [ADV with cl] ❑ *Malaysia and Indonesia rely on open markets for forest and fishery products. Conversely, some Asian countries are highly protectionist.*

부사 거꾸로, 반대로 [격식체] ❑ 말레이시아와 인도네시아는 임산물과 수산물을 개방 시장에 의존한다. 반대로 몇몇 아시아 국가들은 강력한 보호 무역주의 체제이다.

con|ver|sion /kənvɜrʒ³n/ (**conversions**) ◼ N-VAR **Conversion** is the act or process of changing something into a different state or form. ❑ *...the conversion of disused rail lines into cycle routes.* ◻ N-VAR If someone changes their religion or beliefs, you can refer to their **conversion to** their new religion or beliefs. ❑ *...his conversion to Christianity.*

◼ 가산명사 또는 불가산명사 변화, 전환 ❑ 쓰이지 않고 있는 철도 노선을 자전거 도로로 전환하는 것 ◻ 가산명사 또는 불가산명사 개종; 전향 ❑ 그의 기독교로의 개종

Word Link   vert ≈ turning : con**vert**, in**vert**, re**vert**

---

con|vert ♦♦◇ (**converts, converting, converted**)

The verb is pronounced /kənvɜrt/. The noun is pronounced /kɒnvɜrt/.

동사는 /kənvɜrt/로 발음되고, 명사는 /kɒnvɜrt/로 발음된다.

◼ V-T/V-I If one thing **is converted** or **converts into** another, it is changed into a different form. ❑ *The signal will be converted into digital code.* ❑ *...naturally occurring substances which the body can convert into vitamins.* ◻ V-T If someone **converts** a room or building, they alter it in order to use it for a different purpose. ❑ *By converting the loft, they were able to have two extra bedrooms.* ❑ *...the entrepreneur who wants to convert County Hall into an hotel.* ◼ V-T If you **convert** a vehicle or piece of equipment, you change it so that it can use a different fuel. ❑ *Save money by converting your car to unleaded.* ◼ V-T If you **convert** a quantity **from** one system of measurement **to** another, you calculate what the quantity is in the second system. ❑ *Converting metric measurements to U.S. equivalents is easy.* ◼ V-T/V-I If someone **converts** you, they persuade you to change your religious or political beliefs. You can also say that someone **converts to** a different religion. ❑ *If you try to convert him, you could find he just walks away.* ❑ *He was a major influence in converting Godwin to political radicalism.* ◼ N-COUNT A **convert** is someone who has changed their religious or political beliefs. [oft N to n] ❑ *She, too, was a convert to Roman Catholicism.* ◼ N-COUNT If you describe someone as a **convert** to something, you mean that they have recently become very enthusiastic about it. [usu N to n] ❑ *As recent converts to vegetarianism and animal rights, they now live with a menagerie of stray animals.*

◼ 타동사/자동사 변환하다; 바뀌다 ❑ 그 신호는 디지털 코드로 변환될 것이다. ❑ 신체가 비타민으로 바꿀 수 있는 자연 발생 물질 ◻ 타동사 개조하다 ❑ 다락을 개조함으로써 그들은 침실 두 개를 추가로 얻을 수 있었다. ❑ 군립 회관을 호텔로 개조하기 원하는 실업가 ◼ 타동사 개조하다 ❑ 자가용을 무연차로 개조해서 돈을 절약하세요. ◼ 타동사 환산하다 ❑ 미터법을 미국식 도량형으로 환산하는 것은 쉽다. ◼ 타동사/자동사 개종시키다; 전향시키다 ❑ 만약 네가 그 사람을 개종시키려고 하면, 그 사람은 그냥 무시하고 가 버릴 거야. ❑ 그는 고드윈을 정치적 급진주의로 전향시키는 데 있어 큰 영향을 끼친 사람이었다. ◼ 가산명사 개종자; 전향자 ❑ 그녀 역시 천주교로 개종한 사람이었다. ◼ 가산명사 어떤 것에 열중하게 된 사람 ❑ 최근 채식주의와 동물 보호에 열중하게 된 그들은 현재 주인 잃은 동물들을 모아 놓은 동물원을 운영하고 있다.

Thesaurus   convert의 참조어

v.   adapt, alter, change, modify, transform ◼-◼

a b c d e f g h i j k l m n o p q r s t u v w x y z

con|vert|ible /kənvɜrtɪb²l/ (**convertibles**) **1** N-COUNT A **convertible** is a car with a soft roof that can be folded down or removed. ❑ *Her own car is a convertible Golf.* **2** ADJ In finance, **convertible** investments or money can be easily exchanged for other forms of investments or money. [BUSINESS] ❑ *...the introduction of a convertible currency.* ● **con|vert|ibil|ity** /kənvɜrtɪbɪlɪti/ N-UNCOUNT ❑ *...the convertibility of the rouble.* →see **car**

1 가산명사 컨버터블 (접는 포장이 있는 자동차) ❑ 그녀의 자가용은 컨버터블 골프이다. **2** 형용사 (금융) 태환할 수 있는 [경제] ❑ 태환 통화의 도입 ● 태환성 불가산명사 ❑ 루블화의 태환성

con|vey /kənveɪ/ (**conveys, conveying, conveyed**) V-T To **convey** information or feelings means to cause them to be known or understood by someone. ❑ *When I returned home, I tried to convey the wonder of this machine to my husband.* ❑ *In every one of her pictures she conveys a sense of immediacy.*

타동사 전하다 ❑ 집에 돌아와서, 나는 이 기계의 놀라움을 남편에게 전하려 했다. ❑ 그녀는 자신의 모든 그림 작품에 현장감을 담는다.

con|vey|or belt /kənveɪər bɛlt/ (**conveyor belts**) N-COUNT A **conveyor belt** or a **conveyor** is a continuously moving strip of rubber or metal which is used in factories for moving objects along so that they can be dealt with as quickly as possible. ❑ *The damp bricks went along a conveyor belt into another shed to dry.*

가산명사 운반 장치; 컨베이어 벨트 ❑ 젖은 벽돌들은 건조를 위해 컨베이어 벨트를 타고 다른 창고로 들어갔다.

Word Link	vict, vinc ≈ conquering : convict, convince, invincible

con|vict ♦◇◇ (**convicts, convicting, convicted**)

The verb is pronounced /kənvɪkt/. The noun is pronounced /kɒnvɪkt/.

동사는 /kənvɪkt/로 발음되고, 명사는 /kɒnvɪkt/로 발음된다

1 V-T If someone **is convicted of** a crime, they are found guilty of that crime in a law court. ❑ *In 1977 he was convicted of murder and sentenced to life imprisonment.* ❑ *There was insufficient evidence to convict him.* **2** N-COUNT A **convict** is someone who is in prison. [JOURNALISM] ❑ *...Neil Jordan's tale of two escaped convicts who get mistaken for priests.*

1 타동사 유죄 선고를 받다, 유죄가 입증되다 ❑ 1977년에 그는 살인 혐의로 유죄 선고를 받고 무기 징역형에 처해졌다. ❑ 그의 유죄를 입증할 만한 증거가 불충분했다. **2** 가산명사 죄수 [언론] ❑ 닐 조던의 성직자로 오인된 두 명의 탈옥 죄수에 대한 이야기

con|vic|tion ♦◇◇ /kənvɪkʃⁿn/ (**convictions**) **1** N-COUNT A **conviction** is a strong belief or opinion. [usu N that] ❑ *It is our firm conviction that a step forward has been taken.* **2** N-UNCOUNT If you have **conviction**, you have great confidence in your beliefs or opinions. ❑ *"We shall, sir," said Thorne, with conviction.* **3** N-COUNT If someone has a **conviction**, they have been found guilty of a crime in a court of law. ❑ *He will appeal against his conviction.*

1 가산명사 강한 신념 ❑ 우리는 일보 전진을 이루었다고 굳게 믿는다. **2** 불가산명사 확신 ❑ "그렇게 하겠습니다."라고 손이 확신을 가지고 말했다. **3** 가산명사 유죄 선고 ❑ 그는 유죄 선고에 대해 항소할 것이다.

con|vince ♦◇◇ /kənvɪns/ (**convinces, convincing, convinced**) **1** V-T If someone or something **convinces** you **of** something, they make you believe that it is true or that it exists. ❑ *Although I soon convinced him of my innocence, I think he still has serious doubts about my sanity.* **2** V-T If someone or something **convinces** you **to** do something, they persuade you to do it. [mainly AM] ❑ *That weekend in Plattsburgh, he convinced her to go ahead and marry Bud.*

1 타동사 납득시키다, 확신시키다 ❑ 내가 곧 그에게 나의 결백을 납득시켰음에도 불구하고, 그는 아직도 내가 제정신인가는 데 대해 심각한 의심을 품고 있는 것 같다. **2** 타동사 설득하다 [주로 미국영어] ❑ 플래츠버그에서 보낸 그 주말에, 그는 계속 밀고 나가서 버드와 결혼하라고 그녀를 설득했다.

Thesaurus		convince의 참조어
v.	argue, brainwash, persuade, sell, talk into, win over; (ant.) discourage **1** **2**	

con|vinced ♦◇◇ /kənvɪnst/ ADJ If you are **convinced that** something is true, you feel sure that it is true. ❑ *He was convinced that I was part of the problem.* ❑ *He became convinced of the need for cheap editions of good quality writing.*

형용사 확신을 가진 ❑ 그는 내가 문제의 일부라고 확신하고 있었다. ❑ 그는 질 좋은 저서의 보급판이 필요하다는 것을 확신하게 되었다.

con|vinc|ing /kənvɪnsɪŋ/ ADJ If you describe someone or something as **convincing**, you mean that they make you believe that a particular thing is true, correct, or genuine. ❑ *Scientists say there is no convincing evidence that power lines have anything to do with cancer.* ● **con|vinc|ing|ly** ADV [usu ADV with v, also ADV adj] ❑ *He argued forcefully and convincingly that they were likely to bankrupt the budget.*

형용사 설득력 있는, 납득이 가는 ❑ 과학자들은 송전선이 암과 관계가 있다는 설득력 있는 증거가 없다고 말한다. ● 설득력 있게, 납득이 가도록 부사 ❑ 그는 그들이 예산을 바닥낼 것이라고 강력하고 설득력 있게 주장했다.

con|voy /kɒnvɔɪ/ (**convoys**) N-COUNT A **convoy** is a group of vehicles or ships traveling together. [also in N] ❑ *...a U.N. convoy carrying food and medical supplies.* ❑ *...humanitarian relief convoys.*

가산명사 (자동차나 배의) 호송 대열 ❑ 식량과 의약품을 수송하는 유엔의 호송 차량 ❑ 인도주의적 원조 호송 대열

con|vul|sion /kənvʌlʃⁿn/ (**convulsions**) N-COUNT If someone has **convulsions**, they suffer uncontrollable movements of their muscles. ❑ *Thirteen per cent said they became unconscious at night and 5 per cent suffered convulsions.*

가산명사 (근육의) 경련 ❑ 13퍼센트의 사람들은 밤에 의식을 잃는다고 말했고, 5퍼센트는 근육 경련을 겪었다.

cook ♦◇◇ /kʊk/ (**cooks, cooking, cooked**) **1** V-T/V-I When you **cook** a meal, you prepare food for eating by heating it. ❑ *I have to go and cook the dinner.* ❑ *Chefs at the St James Court restaurant have cooked for the Queen.* ● **cook|ing** N-UNCOUNT ❑ *Her hobbies include music, dancing, sport, and cooking.* **2** V-T/V-I When you **cook** food, or when food **cooks**, it is heated until it is ready to be eaten. ❑ *...some basic instructions on how to cook a turkey.* ❑ *Let the vegetables cook gently for about 10 minutes.* **3** N-COUNT A **cook** is a person whose job is to prepare and cook food, especially in someone's home or in an institution. ❑ *They had a butler, a cook, and a maid.* **4** N-COUNT If you say that someone is a good **cook**, you mean they are good at preparing and cooking food. ❑ *I'm a lousy cook.* →see **can** →see Picture Dictionary: **cook**

1 타동사/자동사 요리하다, 조리하다 ❑ 나는 가서 저녁을 해야 한다. ❑ 성 제임스 궁정 식당의 요리사들이 여왕을 위해 요리를 해 왔다. ● 요리 불가산명사 ❑ 그녀의 취미로는 음악, 춤, 운동과 요리 등이 있다. **2** 타동사/자동사 굽다; 익히다; 구워지다, 익다 ❑ 칠면조를 굽는 방법에 대한 기초적인 설명 몇 가지 ❑ 약 10분 동안 서서히 야채를 익히세요. **3** 가산명사 요리사 ❑ 그들은 집사 한 명과 요리사 한 명, 그리고 하녀 한 명을 거느렸다. **4** 가산명사 요리하는 사람 ❑ 나는 요리 솜씨가 엉망이다.

You often use a more specific verb instead of **cook** when you are talking about preparing food using heat. For example, you **roast** meat in an oven, but you **bake** bread and cakes. You can **boil** vegetables in hot water, or you can **steam** them over a pan of boiling water. You can **fry** meat and vegetables in oil or fat. You can also **broil** or, in British English, **grill** them directly under or over a flame. You do not normally talk about **grilling** bread. Instead, you **toast** it.

열을 이용하여 음식을 준비하는 것에 대해 말할 때는 흔히 cook 대신에 더 구체적인 동사를 쓴다. 예를 들면, 오븐에 육류를 roast하거나, 빵과 케이크는 bake할 수 있다. 뜨거운 물에 야채를 넣어 boil하거나 끓는 물이 든 냄비 위에 대고 야채를 steam할 수도 있다. 식물성이나 동물성 기름에 육류나 야채를 fry할 수도 있다. 불 바로 위에 직접 대고 육류나 야채를 broil(영국 영어에서는 grill)할 수도 있다. 보통 빵을 grill한다고는 하지 않고, 대신 빵은 toast한다고 한다.

Thesaurus		cook의 참조어
v.	heat up, make, prepare **1** **2**	
n.	chef **3**	

Picture Dictionary · cook

boil · steam · roast · fry · stir fry · bake · microwave · toast · barbecue · broil

▶**cook up** **1** PHRASAL VERB If someone **cooks up** a dishonest scheme, they plan it. [INFORMAL] ❑ *He must have cooked up his scheme on the spur of the moment.* **2** PHRASAL VERB If someone **cooks up** an explanation or a story, they make it up. [INFORMAL] ❑ *She'll cook up a convincing explanation.*

cook|book /ku̱kbʊk/ (**cookbooks**) N-COUNT A **cookbook** is a book that contains recipes for preparing food.

cook|er /ku̱kər/ (**cookers**) N-COUNT A **cooker** is a large metal device for cooking food using gas or electricity. A cooker usually consists of an oven, a broiler, and some gas burners or electric rings. [BRIT; AM **stove**] ❑ *...a gas cooker.*

cook|ery /ku̱kəri/ N-UNCOUNT **Cookery** is the activity of preparing and cooking food. ❑ *The school runs cookery classes throughout the year.*

cook|ie /ku̱ki/ (**cookies**) **1** N-COUNT A **cookie** is a small sweet cake. [mainly AM] **2** N-COUNT A **cookie** is a piece of computer software which enables a website you have visited to recognize you if you visit it again. [COMPUTING] →see **dessert**

cook|ing ♦♢♢ /ku̱kɪŋ/ **1** N-UNCOUNT **Cooking** is food which has been cooked. ❑ *The menu is based on classic French cooking.* **2** ADJ **Cooking** ingredients or equipment are used in cookery. [ADJ n] ❑ *...Finely slice the cooking apples.* ❑ *...cooking chocolate.* **3** →see also **cook** →see Word Web: **cooking**

cool ♦♦♢ /ku̱l/ (**cooler**, **coolest**, **cools**, **cooling**, **cooled**) **1** ADJ Something that is **cool** has a temperature which is low but not very low. ❑ *I felt a current of cool air.* ❑ *The water was slightly cooler than a child's bath.*

> If you want to emphasize how cold the weather is, you can say that it is **freezing**, especially in winter when there is ice or frost. In summer, if the temperature is below average, you can say that it is **cool**. In general, **cold** suggests a lower temperature than **cool**, and **cool** things may be pleasant or refreshing. ❑ *A cool breeze swept off the sea; it was pleasant out there.* If it is very **cool** or too **cool**, you can also say that it is **chilly**.

2 ADJ If it is **cool**, or if a place is **cool**, the temperature of the air is low but not very low. ❑ *Thank goodness it's cool in here.* ❑ *Store grains and cereals in a cool, dry place.* ❑ N-SING **Cool** is also a noun. ❑ *She walked into the cool of the hallway.* **3** ADJ Clothing that is **cool** is made of thin material so that you do not become too hot in hot weather. ❑ *In warm weather, you should wear clothing that is cool and comfortable.* **4** ADJ **Cool** colors are light colors which give an impression of coolness. [ADJ n] ❑ *Choose a cool color such as cream.* **5** V-T/V-I When something **cools** or when you **cool** it, it becomes lower in temperature. ❑ *Drain the meat and allow it to cool.* ❑ *Huge fans will have to cool the concrete floor to keep it below 150 degrees.* ● PHRASAL VERB To **cool down** means the same as to **cool**. ❑ *Avoid putting your car away until the engine has cooled down.* **6** V-T/V-I When a feeling or emotion **cools**, or when you **cool** it, it becomes less powerful. ❑ *Within a few minutes tempers had cooled.* **7** ADJ If you say that a person or their behavior is **cool**, you mean that they are calm and unemotional, especially in a difficult situation. [APPROVAL] ❑ *He was marvelously cool again, smiling as if nothing had happened.*

1 구동사 (계략을) 꾸미다 [비격식체] ❑ 그는 앞뒤 생각 없이 계략을 꾸몄음에 틀림없다. **2** 구동사 꾸며 내다, 날조하다 [비격식체] ❑ 그녀는 설득력 있는 변명을 꾸며 낼 것이다.

가산명사 요리책

가산명사 (레인지나 오븐 등) 요리 기구 [영국영어; 미국영어 stove] ❑ 가스레인지

불가산명사 요리, 조리 ❑ 그 학교는 연중 요리 수업을 진행한다.

1 가산명사 쿠키 [주로 미국영어] **2** 가산명사 (컴퓨터) 쿠키 [컴퓨터]

1 불가산명사 요리 ❑ 그 식단은 고전 프랑스 요리에 기초를 두고 있다. **2** 형용사 요리용의 ❑ 요리용 사과를 얇게 써세요. ❑ 요리용 초콜릿

1 형용사 시원한, 시늘한 ❑ 시원한 바람 한 줄기가 불어오는 게 느껴졌다. ❑ 그 물은 어린아이 목욕물보다 약간 서늘했다.

> 특히 얼음이 얼거나 서리가 내리는 겨울에 날씨가 추운 것을 강조하고 싶으면, 날씨가 freezing하다고 할 수 있다. 여름에 기온이 평균 이하면, 날씨가 cool하다고 할 수 있다. 일반적으로 cold는 cool보다 낮은 기온을 의미하고, cool한 것은 쾌적하거나 상쾌할 수 있다. ❑ 시원한 미풍이 바다에서 불어 왔다; 거기에 나가 있으니 쾌적했다. 날씨가 아주 cool하거나 너무 cool하면, 날씨가 chilly하다고도 말할 수 있다.

2 형용사 시원한, 시늘한 ❑ 고맙게도 이 안은 시원하군. ❑ 곡물류는 서늘하고 건조한 장소에 보관하세요. ● 단수명사 서늘한 장소 ❑ 그녀는 복도의 서늘한 곳으로 걸어 들어갔다. **3** 형용사 (의복 등이) 시원한 ❑ 더운 날씨에는 시원하고 편한 옷을 입어야 한다. **4** 형용사 (색깔이) 시원스러운 ❑ 크림색 같은 시원한 색을 고르세요. **5** 타동사/자동사 식히다; 시원해지다 ❑ 고기의 물기를 빼고 식혀라. ❑ 콘크리트 바닥의 온도를 150도 아래로 유지하기 위해서는 거대한 선풍기들로 식혀야 할 것이다. ● 구동사 식히다; 시원해지다 ❑ 엔진이 냉각될 때까지 차를 치우지 말도록 하세요. **6** 타동사/자동사 식다, 약해지다 ❑ 몇 분 안에 화가 식어 버렸다. **7** 형용사 냉정한, 침착한 [마음에 듦] ❑ 그는 다시 놀랍도록 냉정해져서, 아무 일도 일어나지 않았었던 듯 웃고

Word Web · cooking

Anthropologists believe our ancestors began to experiment with cooking about 1.5 million years ago. Cooking made some toxic or **inedible** plants safe to **eat**. It made tough meat **tender** and easier to **digest**. It also improved the flavor of the food they ate. **Heating up food** to a high **temperature** killed dangerous bacteria. Cooked food could be stored longer. This all helped increase the amount of food available to our ancestors.

a b c d e f g h i j k l m n o p q r s t u v w x y z

• **cool|ly** ADV ❑ *Everyone must think this situation through calmly and coolly.* ◪ ADJ If you say that a person or their behavior is **cool**, you mean that they are unfriendly or not enthusiastic. ❑ *I didn't like him at all. I thought he was cool, aloof, and arrogant.* • **cool|ly** ADV ❑ *"It's your choice, Nina," David said coolly.* ◪ ADJ If you say that a person or their behavior is **cool**, you mean that they are fashionable and attractive. [INFORMAL, APPROVAL] ❑ *He was trying to be really cool and trendy.* →see **refrigerator**

있었다. • 냉정하게 부사 ❑ 모두 침착하고 냉정하게 이 상황에 대해 충분히 생각해야 한다. ◪ 형용사 냉담한 ❑ 나는 그가 전혀 마음에 들지 않았다. 내 생각에 그는 냉담하고 무관심하며 건방졌다. • 냉담하게 부사 ❑ "그건 너한테 달려 있어, 니나." 라고 데이비드가 냉담하게 말했다. ◪ 형용사 멋들어진, 근사한 [비격식체, 마음에 듦] ❑ 그는 정말 멋지게 최신 유행을 따르려고 애쓰고 있었다.

Thesaurus   *cool*의 참조어

ADJ.	chilly, cold; *(ant.)* warm ◪ ◪
	easygoing, serene, tranquil ◪
	distant, unfriendly ◪

Word Partnership   *cool*의 연어

N.	cool air, cool breeze ◪ ◪
V.	stay cool ◪

▶**cool down** ◪ →see **cool** 5 ◪ PHRASAL VERB If someone **cools down** or if you **cool** them **down**, they become less angry than they were. ❑ *He has had time to cool down and look at what happened more objectively.*

◪ 구동사 진정하다; 진정시키다 ❑ 그는 마음을 가라앉히고 일어난 일을 더 객관적으로 보기 위한 시간을 가져 왔다.

▶**cool off** PHRASAL VERB If someone or something **cools off**, or if you **cool** them **off**, they become cooler after having been hot. ❑ *Maybe he's trying to cool off out there in the rain.* ❑ *She made a fanning motion, pretending to cool herself off.*

구동사 (열을) 식히다; 식다 ❑ 아마도 그가 바깥의 빗속에서 열을 식히려 하고 있는 것 같다. ❑ 그녀는 열을 식히는 체하며 부채질하는 시늉을 했다.

Word Link   *oper ≈ work : cooperate, opera, operation*

---

cooperate ♦◇◇ /koʊɒpəreɪt/ (**cooperates, cooperating, cooperated**) [BRIT also **co-operate**] ◪ V-RECIP If you **cooperate with** someone, you work with them or help them for a particular purpose. You can also say that two people **co-operate**. ❑ *The UN had been cooperating with the State Department on a plan to find countries willing to take the refugees.* • **cooperation** /koʊɒpəreɪʃⁿn/ N-UNCOUNT ❑ *A deal with Japan could indeed open the door to economic cooperation with East Asia.* ◪ V-I If you **cooperate**, you do what someone has asked or told you to do. ❑ *He agreed to cooperate with the police investigation.* • **cooperation** N-UNCOUNT ❑ *The police underlined the importance of the public's cooperation in the hunt for the bombers.*

[영국영어 co-operate] ◪ 상호동사 협력하다, 제휴하다 ❑ 유엔은 국무부와 협력해서 난민들을 받아들일 국가를 찾는 계획을 세우고 있는 중이다. • 협력, 제휴 불가산명사 ❑ 일본과의 협정을 통해 실제로 동아시아와의 경제적 제휴로 가는 문을 열 수 있을 것이다. ◪ 자동사 협조하다 ❑ 그는 경찰 조사에 협조하는 데 동의했다. • 협조 불가산명사 ❑ 경찰은 폭파범 추적에 있어서 일반 국민의 협조의 중요성을 강조했다.

Word Partnership   *cooperate*의 연어

V.	**agree to** cooperate, **continue to** cooperate, **fail to** cooperate, **refuse to** cooperate ◪ ◪
ADV.	cooperate **fully** ◪ ◪
N.	**willingness to** cooperate ◪ ◪

Word Partnership   *cooperation*의 연어

ADJ.	**close** cooperation, **full** cooperation ◪ ◪
N.	**lack of** cooperation ◪ ◪

---

cooperative /koʊɒpərətɪv/ (**cooperatives**) [BRIT also **co-operative**] ◪ N-COUNT A **cooperative** is a business or organization run by the people who work for it, or owned by the people who use it. These people share its benefits and profits. [BUSINESS] ❑ *They decided a housing cooperative was the way to regenerate Ormiston Road.* ◪ ADJ A **cooperative** activity is done by people working together. ❑ *He was transferred to FBI custody in a smooth cooperative effort between Egyptian and U.S. authorities.* • **cooperatively** ADV [ADV after v] ❑ *They agreed to work cooperatively to ease tensions wherever possible.* ◪ ADJ If you say that someone is **cooperative**, you mean that they do what you ask them to without complaining or arguing. ❑ *I made every effort to be cooperative.*

[영국영어 co-operative] ◪ 가산명사 협동조합 [경제] ❑ 그들은 주택 조합이 오미스턴 도로를 되살리는 길이라고 결정했다. ◪ 형용사 협력적인, 협동의 ❑ 이집트와 미국 당국 간의 원활한 협력 속에 그는 에프비아이의 보호 관리로 넘겨졌다. • 협력하여 부사 ❑ 그들은 가능한 곳이라면 어디서든 긴장 완화를 위해 협력하기로 합의했다. ◪ 형용사 협조적인, 협력하는 ❑ 나는 협조하기 위해 갖은 애를 썼다.

Thesaurus   *cooperative*의 참조어

ADJ.	combined, shared, united; *(ant.)* independent, private, separate ◪
	accommodating ◪

---

coordinate (**coordinates, coordinating, coordinated**)

The verb is pronounced /koʊɔːrdɪneɪt/. The noun is pronounced /koʊɔːrdɪnət/.

동사는 /koʊɔːrdɪneɪt /, 명사는 /koʊɔːrdɪnət/로 발음된다.

[BRIT also **co-ordinate**] ◪ V-T If you **coordinate** an activity, you organize the various people and things involved in it. ❑ *Government officials visited the earthquake zone on Thursday morning to coordinate the relief effort.* • **coordinator** (**coordinators**) N-COUNT ❑ *...the party's campaign coordinator, Mr. Peter Mandelson.* ◪ V-RECIP If you **coordinate** clothes or furnishings that are used together, or if they **coordinate**, they are similar in some way and look nice together. ❑ *She'll show you how to coordinate pattern and colors.* ❑ *Tie it with fabric bows that coordinate with other furnishings.* ◪ V-T If you **coordinate** the different parts of your body, you make them work together efficiently to perform particular movements. ❑ *They spend several weeks each year undergoing intensive treatment which enables them to coordinate their limbs better.* ◪ N-COUNT The **coordinates** of a point on a map or

[영국영어 co-ordinate] ◪ 타동사 조직하다; 조정하다 ❑ 정부 공무원들이 구조 작업을 조직하기 위해 목요일 아침 지진 사고 현장을 방문했다. • 조직책, 조정자 가산명사 ❑ 그 정당의 선거 운동 조직책 피터 맨들슨 씨 ◪ 상호동사 어울리다; 어우러지다 ❑ 무늬와 색깔을 조화시키는 방법을 그녀가 보여 드릴 겁니다. ❑ 다른 소품과 어울리는 천 리본으로 묶으세요. ◪ 타동사 조화롭게 움직이도록 하다 ❑ 매년 그들은 몇 주간에 걸쳐 팔다리를 조화롭게 움직일 수 있도록 해 주는 집중 치료를 받는다. ◪ 가산명사 좌표 [과학 기술] ❑ 당신의 좌표를 내게 알려주겠소?

graph are the two sets of numbers or letters that you need in order to find that point. [TECHNICAL] ❏ *Can you give me your coordinates?*

Thesaurus
                    coordinate의 참조어

v.   direct, manage, organize **1**

coordination /koʊɔːrdˈneɪᵊn/ [BRIT also **co-ordination**] **1** N-UNCOUNT **Coordination** means organizing the activities of two or more groups so that they work together efficiently and know what the others are doing. ❏ *...the lack of coordination between the civilian and military authorities.* ❏ *...the coordination of economic policy.* ● PHRASE If you do something **in coordination** with someone else, you both organize your activities so that you work together efficiently. **2** N-UNCOUNT **Coordination** is the ability to use the different parts of your body together efficiently. ❏ *...clumsiness and lack of coordination.*

cop /kɒp/ (**cops**) N-COUNT A **cop** is a policeman or policewoman. [INFORMAL] ❏ *Frank didn't like having the cops know where to find him.*

cope ♦◇◇ /koʊp/ (**copes, coping, coped**) **1** V-I If you **cope with** a problem or task, you deal with it successfully. ❏ *It was amazing how my mother coped with bringing up three children on less than three pounds a week.* **2** V-I If you have to **cope with** an unpleasant situation, you have to accept it or bear it. ❏ *Never before has the industry had to cope with war and recession at the same time.* **3** V-I If a machine or a system can **cope with** something, it is large enough or complex enough to deal with it satisfactorily. ❏ *A giant American washing machine copes with the mountain of laundry created by their nine boys and five girls.*

Word Partnership
                    cope의 연어

ADV.   **how to** cope **1 2**
V.   **learn to** cope, **manage to** cope **1 2**
N.   cope **with loss 1 2**
        ability to cope **1 2 3**
ADJ.   **unable to** cope **1 2 3**

co|pi|ous /koʊpiəs/ ADJ A **copious** amount of something is a large amount of it. ❏ *I went out for a meal last night and drank copious amounts of red wine.* ● **co|pi|ous|ly** ADV ❏ *The victims were bleeding copiously.*

cop|per /kɒpər/ (**coppers**) **1** N-UNCOUNT **Copper** is reddish brown metal that is used to make things such as coins and electrical wires. ❏ *Chile is the world's largest producer of copper.* **2** ADJ **Copper** is sometimes used to describe things that are reddish-brown in color. [LITERARY] ❏ *His hair has reverted back to its original copper hue.* **3** N-COUNT A **copper** is a policeman or a policewoman. [BRIT, INFORMAL] ❏ *...your friendly neighborhood copper.* →see **metal, mineral, pan, plumbing**

copy ♦♦◇ /kɒpi/ (**copies, copying, copied**) **1** N-COUNT If you make a **copy of** something, you produce something that looks like the original thing. ❏ *The reporter apparently obtained a copy of Steve's resignation letter.* **2** V-T If you **copy** something, you produce something that looks like the original thing. ❏ *...lawsuits against companies who have unlawfully copied computer programs.* ❏ *He copied the chart from a book.* **3** V-T/V-I If you **copy** a piece of writing, you write it again exactly. ❏ *He would allow John slyly to copy his answers to impossibly difficult algebra questions.* ❏ *He copied the data into a notebook.* ● PHRASAL VERB **Copy out** means the same as **copy**. ❏ *He wrote the title on the blackboard, then copied out the text sentence by sentence.* **4** V-T If you **copy** a person or what they do, you try to do what they do or try to be like them, usually because you admire them or what they have done. ❏ *Children can be seen to copy the behavior of others whom they admire or identify with.* ❏ *He can claim to have been defeated by opponents copying his own tactics.* **5** N-COUNT A **copy of** a book, newspaper, or CD is one of many that are exactly the same. ❏ *I bought a copy of "U.S. Today" from a street-corner machine.* **6** →see also **hard copy** →see **clone** →see Word Web: **copy**

Thesaurus
                    copy의 참조어

N.   likeness, photocopy, replica, reprint; (ant.) master, original **1**
V.   replicate, reproduce; (ant.) originate **2**
        imitate, mimic **4**

[영국영어 co-ordination] **1** 불가산명사 조정 ❏ 민간 당국과 군 당국 간의 조정 부족 ❏ 경제 정책의 조정 ● 구 ―와 조화를 이루어, ―와 보조를 맞추어 **2** 불가산명사 신체의 각 부위를 조화롭게 사용하는 능력 ❏ 신체의 조화로운 운용 능력의 부족함과 서투름

가산명사 경찰관 [비격식체] ❏ 프랭크는 경찰에 자신의 소재를 알리기 싫어했다.

1 자동사 극복하다 ❏ 우리 어머니가 일주일에 3파운드도 안 되는 돈으로 자식 셋을 길러 낸 것은 놀라운 일이었다. **2** 자동사 맞닥뜨리다, 만나다 ❏ 산업이 전쟁과 불경기를 동시에 맞닥뜨려야 했던 적이 이전에는 한 번도 없었다. **3** 자동사 감당하다; 처리하다 ❏ 대용량의 미국 산 세탁기가 사내아이 아홉 명과 여자 아이 다섯 명에게서 나오는 산더미 같은 빨랫감을 처리해 낸다.

형용사 매우 많은, 풍부한 ❏ 나는 지난밤에 식사를 하러 나가서 적포도주를 아주 많이 마셨다. ● 매우 많이 부사 ❏ 희생자들은 매우 많은 양의 피를 흘리고 있었다.

1 불가산명사 구리, 동 ❏ 칠레는 세계 최대 구리 생산국이다. **2** 형용사 구릿빛의, 적갈색의 [문예체] ❏ 그의 머리칼은 원래의 적갈색 빛으로 되돌아갔다. **3** 가산명사 경찰 [영국영어, 비격식체] ❏ 여러분의 친근한 이웃 경찰

1 가산명사 사본; 모사 ❏ 그 기자가 스티브의 사직서 사본을 입수한 것 같다. **2** 타동사 복사하다; 모사하다 ❏ 컴퓨터 프로그램을 불법 복제해 온 회사들에 대한 소송 ❏ 그는 그 도표를 책에서 복사했다. **3** 타동사/자동사 베껴 쓰다 ❏ 그는 존에게 아주 어려운 대수학 문제 답안을 몰래 베껴 쓰도록 허락해 주곤 했다. ❏ 그는 그 자료를 공책에 베껴 적었다. ● 구동사 베껴 쓰다 ❏ 그는 칠판에 제목을 쓰고 나서 본문을 한 문장 한 문장 베껴 썼다. **4** 타동사 모방하다, 흉내내다 ❏ 아이들이 자기가 좋아하거나 동질감을 갖는 사람들의 행동을 모방하는 것을 볼 수 있다. ❏ 그는 상대가 자신의 작전을 모방했기 때문에 자신이 패배했다고 주장할 수 있다. **5** 가산명사 부, 권 ❏ 나는 길모퉁이에 있는 가판기에서 '유에스에이 투데이'를 한 부 샀다.

Word Web
                    copy

Making **copies** used to be difficult. Typists used sheets of carbon paper to make **multiple** copies. But the process was messy and the copies weren't very clear. Architects made photographic **blueprints**. But it was complicated and expensive. Modern **photocopiers** are completely different. You place your **document** on the glass and press a button. A bright light helps transfer the **image** from the paper onto a drum. Toner is spread over the drum. It sticks only to the image on the drum, not the blank spaces. A sheet of paper then passes over the drum and picks up the image.

copy|right /kɒpiraɪt/ (**copyrights**) N-VAR If someone has **copyright** on a piece of writing or music, it is illegal to reproduce or perform it without their permission. ❑ *To order a book one first had to get permission from the monastery that held the copyright.*

가산명사 또는 불가산명사 저작권, 판권 ❑ 책을 주문하려면 우선 판권을 가지고 있는 수도원 측의 허가를 받아야 했다.

cor|al /kɒrəl, BRIT kɒrəl/ (**corals**) **1** N-VAR **Coral** is a hard substance formed from the bones of very small sea animals. It is often used to make jewelry. ❑ *The women have elaborate necklaces of turquoise and pink coral.* **2** N-COUNT **Corals** are very small sea animals. ❑ *The seas around Bermuda are full of colorful corals and fantastic fish.* **3** COLOR Something that is **coral** is dark orangey-pink in color. ❑ *...coral lipstick.*

1 가산명사 또는 불가산명사 산호 ❑ 그 여인들은 터키석과 분홍색 산호로 된 정교한 목걸이를 가지고 있다. **2** 가산명사 산호 ❑ 버뮤다 주변의 바다는 색색의 산호와 환상적인 물고기들로 가득하다. **3** 색채어 산호빛 ❑ 산호빛 립스틱

cord /kɔrd/ (**cords**) **1** N-VAR **Cord** is strong, thick string. ❑ *The door had been tied shut with a length of nylon cord.* **2** N-VAR **Cord** is wire covered in rubber or plastic which connects electrical equipment to an electricity supply. ❑ *...electrical cord.* →see **rope**

1 가산명사 또는 불가산명사 끈, 줄 ❑ 그 문은 기다란 나일론 줄로 매어 닫혀져 있었다. **2** 가산명사 또는 불가산명사 (전기) 코드 ❑ 전깃줄

cor|dial /kɔrdʒəl, BRIT kɔːrdiəl/ ADJ **Cordial** means friendly. [FORMAL] ❑ *He had never known him to be so chatty and cordial.* ● **cor|di|al|ly** ADV [ADV with v] ❑ *They all greeted me very cordially and were eager to talk about the new project.*

형용사 친절한, 따뜻한 [격식체] ❑ 그는 그 사람이 그토록 이야기를 잘하고 친절한 것을 본 적이 없었다. ● 친절하게, 따뜻하게 부사 ❑ 그들은 모두 나를 아주 따뜻하게 맞아 주었고 새 프로젝트에 대해 몹시 이야기하고 싶어 했다.

cor|don /kɔrdⁿn/ (**cordons**) N-COUNT A **cordon** is a line or ring of police, soldiers, or vehicles preventing people from entering or leaving an area. ❑ *Police formed a cordon between the two crowds.*

가산명사 비상 경계선; 교통 차단선 ❑ 경찰이 두 패의 군중들 사이에 비상 경계선을 쳤다.

core ♦◇◇ /kɔr/ (**cores, coring, cored**) **1** N-COUNT The **core** of a fruit is the central part of it. It contains seeds or pips. ❑ *Someone threw an apple core.* **2** V-T If you **core** a fruit, you remove its core. ❑ *...machines for peeling and coring apples.* **3** N-COUNT The **core** of an object, building, or city is the central part of it. [usu with poss] ❑ *...the earth's core.* **4** N-SING The **core of** something such as a problem or an issue is the part of it that has to be understood or accepted before the whole thing can be understood or dealt with. ❑ *...the ability to get straight to the core of a problem.* **5** N-SING A **core** team or a **core** group is a group of people who do the main part of a job or piece of work. Other people may also help, but only for limited periods of time. ❑ *We already have our core team in place.* **6** N-SING In a school or college, **core** subjects are a group of subjects that have to be studied. ❑ *The core subjects are English, mathematics, and science.* ❑ *I'm not opposed to a core curriculum in principle, but I think requiring a foreign language is unrealistic.* **7** N-SING The **core** businesses or the **core** activities of a company or organization are their most important ones. ❑ *The core activities of local authorities were reorganised.* ❑ *The group plans to concentrate on six core businesses.* →see Picture Dictionary: **core**

1 가산명사 (과일의) 속 ❑ 누군가가 사과 속을 던졌다. **2** 타동사 (과일의) 속을 빼다 ❑ 사과의 껍질을 벗기고 속을 빼내는 기계 **3** 가산명사 중심부 ❑ 지구의 중심부 **4** 단수명사 핵심 ❑ 곧바로 문제의 핵심에 다가가는 능력 **5** 단수명사 핵심 (집단) ❑ 우리는 이미 핵심 팀을 적소에 배치해 두고 있다. **6** 단수명사 핵심 (과목) ❑ 핵심 과목은 영어, 수학, 그리고 과학이다. ❑ 원칙적으로는 핵심 교과 과정에 반대하지 않지만, 외국어를 요구하는 것은 비현실적이라고 생각한다. **7** 단수명사 핵심 (사업) ❑ 지방 행정 당국의 핵심 사업이 재편성되었다. ❑ 그 기업은 여섯 개의 핵심 사업에 집중할 작정이다.

Word Partnership   core의 연어

N.   apple core **1**
     Earth's core **3**
     core **beliefs** **4**
     core **group** **5**
     core **curriculum** **6**

Picture Dictionary   core

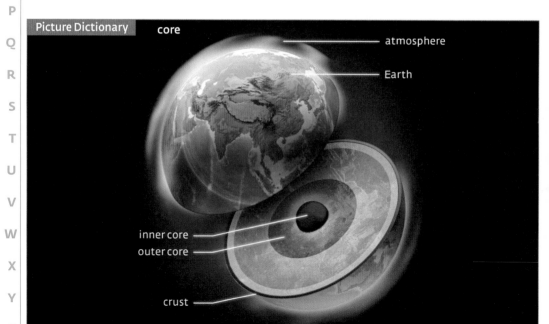

atmosphere
Earth
inner core
outer core
crust

cork /kɔrk/ (**corks**) 1 N-UNCOUNT **Cork** is a soft, light substance which forms the bark of a type of Mediterranean tree. ❑ *...cork floors.* 2 N-COUNT A **cork** is a piece of cork or plastic that is pushed into the opening of a bottle to close it. ❑ *He popped the cork and the champagne fizzed out over the bottle.*

1 불가산명사 코르크 ❑ 코르크 바닥 2 가산명사 코르크 마개 ❑ 그가 코르크 마개를 따자 샴페인이 쉬잇 하고 거품이 일며 병 밖으로 터져 나왔다.

cork|screw /kɔrkskru/ (**corkscrews**) N-COUNT A **corkscrew** is a device for pulling corks out of bottles.

가산명사 코르크 마개 따개

corn /kɔrn/ 1 N-UNCOUNT **Corn** is used to refer to tall plants which produce long vegetables covered with yellow seeds. It can also be used to refer to the seeds or the vegetables from these plants. ❑ *...rows of corn in an Iowa field.* 2 N-UNCOUNT **Corn** is used to refer to crops such as wheat and barley. It can also be used to refer to the seeds from these plants. [BRIT; AM **grain**] ❑ *...fields of corn.* 3 →see also **popcorn, sweetcorn** →see **grain**

1 불가산명사 옥수수 ❑ 아이오와 들판에 줄지어 자란 옥수수 2 불가산명사 잡곡 [영국영어; 미국영어 grain] ❑ 잡곡 밭

cor|ner ♦♦◊ /kɔrnər/ (**corners, cornering, cornered**) 1 N-COUNT A **corner** is a point or an area where two or more edges, sides, or surfaces of something join. ❑ *He saw the corner of a magazine sticking out from under the blanket.* 2 N-COUNT The **corner** of a room, box, or similar space is the area inside it where its edges or walls meet. ❑ *...a card table in the corner of the living room.* ❑ *The ball hurtled into the far corner of the net.* 3 N-COUNT The **corner of** your mouth or eye is the side of it. ❑ *She flicked a crumb off the corner of her mouth.* 4 N-COUNT The **corner** of a street is the place where one of its sides ends as it joins another street. ❑ *She would spend the day hanging round street corners.* ❑ *We can't have police officers on every corner.* 5 N-COUNT A **corner** is a bend in a road. ❑ *...a sharp corner.* 6 N-COUNT In soccer, hockey, and some other sports, a **corner** is a free shot or kick taken from the corner of the field. ❑ *McPherson took the corner and James crashed his header off the crossbar and over the line.* 7 V-T If you **corner** a person or animal, you force them into a place they cannot escape from. ❑ *A police motor-cycle chased his car twelve miles, and cornered him near Rome.* 8 V-T If you **corner** someone, you force them to speak to you when they have been trying to avoid you. ❑ *Golan managed to corner the young producer-director for an interview.* 9 V-T If a company or place **corners** an area of trade, they gain control over it so that no one else can have any success in that area. [BUSINESS] ❑ *Sony has cornered the market in chic-looking mp3 players.* 10 V-I If a car, or the person driving it, **corners** in a particular way, the car goes around bends in roads in this way. ❑ *Peter drove jerkily, cornering too fast and fumbling the gears.* 11 PHRASE If you say that something is **around the corner**, you mean that it will happen very soon. In British English, you can also say that something is **round the corner.** ❑ *The Chancellor of the Exchequer says that economic recovery is just around the corner.* 12 PHRASE If you say that something is **around the corner**, you mean that it is very near. In British English, you can also say that something is **round the corner.** ❑ *My new place is just around the corner.* 13 PHRASE If you **cut corners**, you do something quickly by doing it in a less thorough way than you should. [DISAPPROVAL] ❑ *Take your time, don't cut corners and follow instructions to the letter.*

1 가산명사 모서리, 귀퉁이 ❑ 그는 잡지책 모서리가 담요 아래로 삐져나온 것을 보았다. 2 가산명사 귀퉁이, 구석 ❑ 거실 구석에 놓여 있는 카드놀이용 탁자 ❑ 공은 그물의 저쪽 귀퉁이에 날아가 꽂혔다. 3 가산명사 (눈이나 입의) 가 ❑ 그녀는 입가에 묻은 빵 부스러기를 털어 냈다. 4 가산명사 모퉁이, 길모퉁이 ❑ 그녀는 길모퉁이를 어슬렁거리며 낮 시간을 보내곤 했다. ❑ 길모퉁이마다 경찰관을 둘 수는 없다. 5 가산명사 굽은 길, 커브 ❑ 급커브 6 가산명사 코너킥; 코너 히트 ❑ 맥퍼슨이 코너킥을 찼고, 제임스가 헤딩슛을 날렸으나 크로스바를 넘어가 아웃되었다. 7 타동사 구석에 몰아넣다; 궁지에 빠뜨리다 ❑ 경찰 오토바이가 그의 자동차를 12 마일에 걸쳐 추격해서 로마 인근으로 몰아갔다. 8 타동사 강제로 말하게 하다 ❑ 골란은 젊은 제작자 겸 감독에게서 강제로 인터뷰를 따냈다. 9 타동사 매점하다; 장악하다 [경제] ❑ 소니는 세련된 외양의 엠피3 플레이어 시장을 장악해 왔다. 10 자동사 커브를 돌다 ❑ 피터는 지나치게 빠르게 커브를 돌고 기어를 헛잡으며, 거칠게 차를 몰았다. 11 구 임박하여 ❑ 재무장관은 경제가 곧 회복되리라고 말한다. 12 구 바로 근처에 ❑ 내 새로운 거처는 아주 가깝다. 13 구 대충 해치우다 [탐탁찮음] ❑ 느긋하게 여유를 가지고, 대충대충 해치우지 말고 지시를 엄수하세요.

Word Partnership *corner*의 연어

ADJ.	**far** corner 1 2 4
	sharp corner 4 5
V.	**sit in a** corner 2
	round/turn a corner 2 4 5
N.	corner **of a room** 2
	street corner 4 5
PREP.	**in a** corner 2
	around the corner 2 4 5 11 12

corner|stone /kɔrnərstoʊn/ (**cornerstones**) N-COUNT The **cornerstone of** something is the basic part of it on which its existence, success, or truth depends. [FORMAL] ❑ *Research is the cornerstone of the profession.*

가산명사 초석, 기초 [격식체] ❑ 연구는 그 직업의 기초이다.

corny /kɔrni/ (**cornier, corniest**) ADJ If you describe something as **corny**, you mean that it is obvious or sentimental and not at all original. [DISAPPROVAL] ❑ *I know it sounds corny, but I'm not really motivated by money.*

형용사 뻔한; 감상적인; 진부한 [탐탁찮음] ❑ 진부하게 들리리라는 걸 알지만, 정말이지 나는 돈에 의해 움직이는 사람이 아니다.

coro|nary /kɔrənɛri, BRIT kɒrənri/ ADJ **Coronary** means belonging or relating to the heart. [MEDICAL] [ADJ n] ❑ *If all the coronary arteries are free of significant obstructions, all parts of the heart will receive equal amounts of oxygen.*

형용사 심장의 [의학] ❑ 심장 동맥 전체에 중한 장애가 없다면, 심장의 전체 부위는 동일한 양의 산소를 공급 받을 것이다.

coro|na|tion /kɔrəneɪʃən, BRIT kɒrəneɪʃən/ (**coronations**) N-COUNT A **coronation** is the ceremony at which a king or queen is crowned. ❑ *...the coronation of Her Majesty Queen Elizabeth II.*

가산명사 대관식, 즉위식 ❑ 엘리자베스 2세 여왕의 대관식

coro|ner /kɔrənər, BRIT kɒrənəʳ/ (**coroners**) N-COUNT A **coroner** is an official who is responsible for investigating the deaths of people who have died in a sudden, violent, or unusual way. ❑ *The coroner recorded a verdict of accidental death.*

가산명사 검시관 ❑ 검시관은 사고사 판정을 내렸다.

Corp. ♦♦◊ **Corp.** is a written abbreviation for **corporation.** [BUSINESS] ❑ *...Sony Corp. of Japan.*

주식회사; 법인 [경제] ❑ 일본 소니 주식회사

cor|po|ral /kɔrpərəl, -prəl/ (**corporals**) N-COUNT; N-TITLE A **corporal** is a noncommissioned officer in the army or United States Marines. ❑ *The corporal shouted an order at the men.*

가산명사; 경칭명사 상등병 ❑ 상등병이 병사들을 향해 구령을 외쳤다.

cor|po|ral pun|ish|ment N-UNCOUNT **Corporal punishment** is the punishment of people by hitting them. ❑ *Now, of course, corporal punishment in schools is forbidden.*

불가산명사 체형, 태형 ❑ 물론, 현재는 학교에서의 체벌이 금지되어 있다.

A

cor|po|rate ♦◇◇ /kɔ́rpərɪt, -prɪt/ ADJ **Corporate** means relating to business corporations or to a particular business corporation. [BUSINESS] [ADJ n] ❑ ...top U.S. corporate executives. ❑ ...a corporate lawyer.

형용사 법인의, 회사의 [경제] ❑ 미국 기업계 최고 간부들 ❑ 법인 고문 변호사

B

Word Partnership	corporate의 연어
N.	corporate **clients**, corporate **culture**, corporate **hospitality**, corporate **image**, corporate **lawyer**, corporate **sector**, corporate **structure**

C

D

cor|po|rate raid|er (**corporate raiders**) N-COUNT A **corporate raider** is a person or organization that tries to take control of a company by buying a large number of its shares. [BUSINESS] ❑ Your present company could be taken over by corporate raiders.

가산명사 기업 매수자 [경제] ❑ 당신의 현 회사가 기업 매수자들에게 인수될 수도 있습니다.

E

cor|po|ra|tion ♦◇◇ /kɔ́rpəreɪʃn/ (**corporations**) N-COUNT; N-IN-NAMES A **corporation** is a large business or company. [BUSINESS] ❑ ...multinational corporations. →see **company**

가산명사; 이름명사 법인, 회사 [경제] ❑ 다국적 기업들

F

cor|po|ra|tion tax N-UNCOUNT **Corporation tax** is a tax that companies have to pay on the profits they make. [BUSINESS]

불가산명사 법인세 [경제]

G

corps /kɔr/

Corps is both the singular and the plural form.

corps는 단수형 및 복수형이다.

H

1 N-COUNT; N-IN-NAMES A **corps** is a part of the army which has special duties. ❑ ...the Army Medical Corps. **2** N-COUNT **The Corps** is the United States Marine Corps. [AM] ❑ ...seventy-five men, all combat veterans, all members of The Corps' most exclusive unit. **3** N-COUNT A **corps** is a small group of people who do a special job. ❑ ...the diplomatic corps.

1 가산명사; 이름명사 특수 병과, 부대 ❑ 육군 의무 부대 **2** 가산명사 미 해병대 [미국영어] ❑ 전원 전투의 베테랑이자 해병대 최정예 부대원인 79명의 병사들 **3** 가산명사 (특수 임무를 띤) 단체, 단 ❑ 외교단

I

corpse /kɔrps/ (**corpses**) N-COUNT A **corpse** is a dead body, especially the body of a human being. ❑ ...when he first received permission to dissect the corpses of pregnant women.

가산명사 시체, 송장 ❑ 그가 임신한 여성의 시신을 해부해도 좋다는 허가를 처음으로 받았을 때

J

Word Link	rect ≈ right, straight : correct, rectangle, rectify

K

cor|rect ♦♦◇ /kərékt/ (**corrects, correcting, corrected**) **1** ADJ If something is **correct**, it is in accordance with the facts and has no mistakes. [FORMAL] ❑ The correct answers can be found at the bottom of page 8. ❑ The following information was correct at time of going to press. ❑ Did I pronounce your name correctly? ● **cor|rect|ly** ADV [ADV with v] ❑ Did I pronounce your name correctly? ● **cor|rect|ness** N-UNCOUNT ❑ Ask the investor to check the correctness of what he has written. **2** ADJ If someone is **correct**, what they have said or thought is true. [FORMAL] [v-link ADJ] ❑ You are absolutely correct. The leaves are from a bay tree. **3** ADJ The **correct** thing or method is the thing or method that is required or is most suitable in a particular situation. [ADJ n] ❑ The use of the correct materials was crucial. ❑ White was in no doubt the referee made the correct decision. ● **cor|rect|ly** ADV [ADV with v] ❑ If correctly executed, this shot will give them a better chance of getting the ball close to the hole. **4** ADJ If you say that someone is **correct in** doing something, you approve of their action. ❑ You are perfectly correct in trying to steer your mother towards increased independence. ● **cor|rect|ly** ADV [ADV with cl] ❑ When an accident happens, quite correctly questions are asked. **5** V-T If you **correct** a problem, mistake, or fault, you do something which puts it right. ❑ He may need surgery to correct the problem. ● **cor|rec|tion** /kərékʃn/ (**corrections**) N-VAR ❑ ...legislation to require the correction of factual errors. **6** V-T If you **correct** someone, you say something which you think is more accurate or appropriate than what they have just said. ❑ "Actually, that isn't what happened," George corrects me. **7** V-T When someone **corrects** a piece of writing, they look at it and mark the mistakes in it. ❑ It took an extraordinary effort to focus on preparing his classes or correcting his students' work. **8** ADJ If a person or their behavior is **correct**, their behavior is in accordance with social or other rules. ❑ I think English men are very polite and very correct. ● **cor|rect|ly** ADV [ADV with v] ❑ The High Court of Parliament began very correctly with a prayer for the Queen. ● **cor|rect|ness** N-UNCOUNT ❑ ...his stiff-legged gait and formal correctness.

1 형용사 정확한 [격식체] ❑ 정답은 8페이지 아래쪽에 있습니다. ❑ 다음 정보는 인쇄 당시 기준으로 정확한 것입니다. ● 정확히 부사 ❑ 제가 당신 이름을 정확히 발음했나요? ● 정확함 불가산명사 ❑ 투자자에게 자신이 작성한 내용이 정확한지 확인하도록 요청하세요. **2** 형용사 옳은, 맞는 [격식체] ❑ 네가 전적으로 옳아. 그 잎사귀들은 월계수 잎이야. **3** 형용사 적절한, 온당한 ❑ 적절한 재료를 사용한 것이 결정적이었다. ❑ 화이트는 주심이 온당한 판정을 내렸다는 것을 전혀 의심하지 않았다. ● 적절히, 제대로 부사 ❑ 제대로 쳐낸다면, 이번 타로 그들은 홀 가까이에 공을 가져다 놓을 수 있는 더 좋은 기회를 얻을 것이다. **4** 형용사 옳은, 온당한 ❑ 네가 어머니께서 독립심을 가지시도록 하려고 노력하는 것은 전적으로 옳다. ● 온당하게 부사 ❑ 사고가 발생하면, 지극히 온당하게 심문이 행해진다. **5** 타동사 바로잡다, 고치다 ❑ 그는 문제를 바로잡기 위해 수술을 해야 할지도 모른다. ● 정정, 교정 가산명사 또는 불가산명사 ❑ 실제적인 오류를 바로잡을 것을 규정하는 입법 조치 **6** 타동사 (다른 사람의 말을) 정정하다 ❑ "사실, 실제 일어났던 일은 그렇지 않아."라고 조지가 내 말을 정정한다. **7** 타동사 교정하다 ❑ 수업 준비나 학생들의 과제를 교정하는 일에 집중하는 데는 엄청난 노력이 필요했다. **8** 형용사 격식을 갖춘 ❑ 영국 남성들은 매우 예의바르고 격식을 갖추는 것 같다. ● 격식에 맞추어 부사 ❑ 국회 회원은 여왕을 위한 기도로 대단히 격식을 갖추며 개원했다. ● 격식을 갖춘 불가산명사 ❑ 그 사람의 다리를 빳빳이 세운 걸음걸이와 딱딱하게 격식을 갖추는 태도

Thesaurus	correct의 참조어
ADJ.	accurate, legitimate, precise, right, true; (ant.) false, inaccurate, incorrect, wrong **1 2**
V.	fix, rectify, repair; (ant.) damage, hurt **5**

Word Partnership	correct의 연어
N.	correct **answer**, correct **response** **1 2**
	correct **a situation** **5**
	correct **a mistake** **5 6 7**
	correct **someone** **6**

X

cor|rec|tion /kərékʃn/ (**corrections**) **1** N-COUNT **Corrections** are marks or comments made on a piece of work, especially school work, which indicate where there are mistakes and what are the right answers. ❑ In a group, compare your corrections to Exercise 2A. **2** N-UNCOUNT **Correction** is the punishment of criminals. [mainly AM] ❑ ...jails and other parts of the correction system. **3** →see also **correct**

1 가산명사 수정; 첨삭 ❑ 모둠끼리 연습 문제 2에이 번에 대한 여러분들의 수정 사항을 비교하세요. **2** 불가산명사 교정; 징계 [주로 미국영어] ❑ 교도소와 기타 교정 제도들

Z

cor|rec|tive /kəréktɪv/ (**correctives**) **1** ADJ **Corrective** measures or techniques are intended to put right something that is wrong. ❑ Scientific institutions have

1 형용사 바로잡는, 교정의 ❑ 과학 단체들은 교정 방침을 받아들이기를 꺼려 왔다. **2** 가산명사 개선책,

been reluctant to take corrective action. ② N-COUNT If something is a **corrective to** a particular view or account, it gives a more accurate or fairer picture than there would have been without it. [FORMAL] ❏ ...a useful corrective to the mistaken view that all psychologists are behaviorists.

조정책 [격식체] ❏ 모든 심리학자들이 행동주의자라는 그릇된 견해에 대한 유용한 조정안

Word Link   cor ≈ with : correlate, correspond, corroborate

cor|re|late /kɔrəleɪt, BRIT kɒrəleɪt/ (correlates, correlating, correlated)
■ V-RECIP If one thing **correlates with** another, there is a close similarity or connection between them, often because one thing causes the other. You can also say that two things **correlate**. [FORMAL] ❏ Obesity correlates with increased risk for hypertension and stroke. ❏ The political opinions of spouses correlate more closely than their heights. ② V-T If you **correlate** things, you work out the way in which they are connected or the way they influence each other. [FORMAL] ❏ Attempts to correlate specific language functions with particular parts of the brain have not advanced very far.

■ 상호동사 서로 관련되다, 상관하다 [격식체] ❏ 비만은 고혈압과 뇌졸중 위험 증가와 관련이 있다. ❏ 배우자들의 지위보다는 정치적 견해가 더 밀접하게 상호 관련이 있다. ② 타동사 서로 관련시키다 [격식체] ❏ 특정 언어 기능을 뇌의 특정 부위와 연관짓는 시도는 아주 많이 진척되지는 못했다.

cor|re|la|tion /kɔrəleɪʃⁿn, BRIT kɒrəleɪʃⁿn/ (correlations) N-COUNT A **correlation between** things is a connection or link between them. [FORMAL] ❏ ...the correlation between smoking and disease.

가산명사 상관관계 [격식체] ❏ 흡연과 질병 간의 상관관계

Word Partnership   correlation의 연어

V.	**find a** correlation
ADJ.	**direct** correlation, **negative** correlation, **significant** correlation, **strong** correlation

---

cor|re|spond /kɔrɪspɒnd, BRIT kɒrɪspɒnd/ (corresponds, corresponding, corresponded) ■ V-RECIP If one thing **corresponds to** another, there is a close similarity or connection between them. You can also say that two things **correspond**. ❏ Racegoers will be given a number which will correspond to a horse running in a race. ❏ The two maps of London correspond closely. ● **cor|re|spond|ing** ADJ [ADJ n] ❏ March and April sales this year were up 8 percent on the corresponding period in 1992. ② V-RECIP If you **correspond with** someone, you write letters to them. You can also say that two people **correspond**. ❏ She still corresponds with American friends she met in Majorca nine years ago.

■ 상호동사 해당하다, 상응하다; 일치하다 ❏ 경마 팬은 경주마 중 하나에 해당하는 번호를 받을 것이다. ❏ 그 런던 지도 두 개가 거의 일치한다. ● 상응하는 형용사 ❏ 올해 3, 4월 매출이 1992년 같은 기간에 비해 8퍼센트 증가했다. ② 상호동사 -와 편지를 주고받다 ❏ 그녀는 아직도 9년 전 마요르카에서 만난 미국 친구들과 편지를 주고받는다.

cor|re|spond|ence /kɔrɪspɒndəns, BRIT kɒrɪspɒndəns/ (correspondences) ■ N-UNCOUNT **Correspondence** is the act of writing letters to someone. [also a N, oft N with n] ❏ The judges' decision is final and no correspondence will be entered into. ② N-UNCOUNT Someone's **correspondence** is the letters that they receive or send. ❏ He always replied to his correspondence. ③ N-COUNT If there is a **correspondence between** two things, there is a close similarity or connection between them. ❏ In African languages there is a close correspondence between sounds and letters.

■ 불가산명사 편지 쓰기 ❏ 재판관의 결정은 최종적인 것이다. 어떤 서신도 고려되지 않을 것이다. ② 불가산명사 편지, 서신 ❏ 그는 편지를 받으면 항상 답장했다. ③ 가산명사 부합, 일치 ❏ 아프리카 언어는 소리와 문자가 거의 일치한다.

cor|re|spond|ence course (correspondence courses) N-COUNT A **correspondence course** is a course in which you study at home, receiving your work by mail and sending it back by mail. ❏ I took a correspondence course in computing.

가산명사 통신 교육 ❏ 나는 컴퓨터 과정을 통신 교육으로 이수했다.

cor|re|spond|ent ♦♦◇ /kɔrɪspɒndənt, BRIT kɒrɪspɒndənt/ (correspondents) N-COUNT A **correspondent** is a newspaper or television journalist, especially one who specializes in a particular type of news. ❏ As our Diplomatic Correspondent Mark Brayne reports, the president was given a sympathetic hearing.

가산명사 기자, 특파원 ❏ 외교부 기자 마크 브라인에 따르면 대통령의 발언이 호의적인 반응을 얻었다고 한다.

cor|re|spond|ing|ly /kɔrɪspɒndɪŋli, BRIT kɒrɪspɒndɪŋli/ ADV You use **correspondingly** when describing a situation which is closely connected with one you have just mentioned or is similar to it. ❏ As his political stature has shrunk, he has grown correspondingly more dependent on the army.

부사 그에 상응하여 ❏ 그는 정치적인 위상이 위축되면서 그가 그만큼 더 군대에 의존하게 됐다.

cor|ri|dor /kɔrɪdər, -dɔr, BRIT kɒrɪdɔːʳ/ (corridors) ■ N-COUNT A **corridor** is a long passage in a building or train, with doors and rooms on one or both sides. ❏ There were doors on both sides of the corridor. ② N-COUNT A **corridor** is a strip of land that connects one country to another or gives it a route to the sea through another country. ❏ East Prussia and the rest of Germany were separated, in 1919, by the Polish corridor.

■ 가산명사 복도 ❏ 복도 양편에 문이 늘어서 있었다. ② 가산명사 회랑 지대 ❏ 1919년 동프러시아와 나머지 독일 지역이 폴란드 회랑에 의해 분리되었다.

cor|robo|rate /kɔrɒbəreɪt, BRIT kɒrɒbəreɪt/ (corroborates, corroborating, corroborated) V-T To **corroborate** something that has been said or reported means to provide evidence or information that supports it. [FORMAL] ❏ I had access to a wide range of documents which corroborated the story. ● **cor|robo|ra|tion** /kɔrɒbəreɪʃⁿn/ N-UNCOUNT ❏ He could not get a single witness to establish independent corroboration of his version of the accident.

타동사 입증하다 [격식체] ❏ 나는 그 이야기를 입증하는 다양한 문서를 접했다. ● 입증 불가산명사 ❏ 그는 그 사고에 대한 자신의 설명을 객관적으로 입증시켜 줄 증인을 단 한 명도 확보하지 못했다.

cor|rode /kərɔʊd/ (corrodes, corroding, corroded) V-T/V-I If metal or stone **corrodes**, or **is corroded**, it is gradually destroyed by a chemical or by rust. ❏ He has devised a process for making gold wires which neither corrode nor oxidise. ❏ Engineers found the structure had been corroded by moisture. ● **cor|rod|ed** ADJ ❏ The investigators found that the underground pipes were badly corroded.

타동사/자동사 부식되다 ❏ 그는 부식되거나 녹슬지 않는 금철사 제조법을 개발했다. ❏ 기술자들은 그 구조물이 습기로 부식된 것을 발견했다. ● 부식된 형용사 ❏ 조사 팀은 지하 파이프가 심하게 부식된 것을 발견했다.

cor|ro|sion /kərɒʊʒⁿn/ N-UNCOUNT **Corrosion** is the damage that is caused when something is corroded. ❏ Zinc is used to protect other metals from corrosion.

불가산명사 부식 ❏ 아연은 다른 금속의 부식을 막는 데 사용된다.

cor|ru|gat|ed /kɔrəgeɪtɪd, BRIT kɒrəgeɪtɪd/ ADJ **Corrugated** metal or cardboard has been folded into a series of small parallel folds to make it stronger. ❏ ...a hut with a corrugated iron roof.

형용사 물결 모양의, 골판지의 ❏ 물결 모양의 철제 지붕을 올린 오두막집

cor|rupt /kərʌpt/ (corrupts, corrupting, corrupted) ■ ADJ Someone who is **corrupt** behaves in a way that is morally wrong, especially by doing dishonest

■ 형용사 부패한, 타락한 ❏ 양 당의 부패 정치인으로부터 나라를 구하기 위해 ② 타동사 -

a
b
c
d
e
f
g
h
i
j
k
l
m
n
o
p
q
r
s
t
u
v
w
x
y
z

A

or illegal things in return for money or power. ❑ ...*to save the nation from corrupt politicians of both parties.* ❷ V-T If someone **is corrupted by** something, it causes them to become dishonest and unjust and unable to be trusted. [usu passive] ❑ *It is sad to see a man so corrupted by the desire for money and power.* ❸ V-T/V-I To **corrupt** someone means to cause them to stop caring about moral standards. ❑ ...*warning that television will corrupt us all.*

때문에 타락하다 ❑ 돈과 권력에 대한 욕망 때문에 사람이 그렇게 타락하다니 안타깝다. ❸ 타동사/자동사 타락시키다 ❑ 텔레비전이 우리 모두를 타락시키리라는 경고

B

cor|rup|tion ♦♢♢ /kərʌpʃⁿn/ N-UNCOUNT **Corruption** is dishonesty and illegal behavior by people in positions of authority or power. ❑ *The President faces 54 charges of corruption and tax evasion.*

불가산명사 부패, 타락 ❑ 대통령은 54가지의 부패 및 탈세 혐의를 받고 있다.

'**cos** ♦♢♢ /kəz, STRONG kʌz/ also **cos** CONJ '**Cos** is an informal way of saying **because.** [BRIT, SPOKEN; AM '**cause**] ❑ *It was absolutely horrible going up the hills 'cos they were really, really steep.*

접속사 왜냐면 [영국영어, 구어체; 미국영어 'cause] ❑ 언덕이 너무나 가팔라서 올라갈 때 정말이지 무시무시했다.

C

cos|met|ic /kɒzmɛtɪk/ (**cosmetics**) ❶ N-COUNT **Cosmetics** are substances such as lipstick or powder, which people put on their face to make themselves look more attractive. ❑ ...*the cosmetics counter of a department store.* ❷ ADJ If you describe measures or changes as **cosmetic,** you mean they improve the appearance of a situation or thing but do not change its basic nature, and you are usually implying that they are inadequate. [DISAPPROVAL] ❑ *It is a cosmetic measure which will do nothing to help the situation long term.* →see **makeup**

❶ 가산명사 화장품 ❑ 백화점 화장품 코너 ❷ 형용사 표면상의 [탐탁잖음] ❑ 장기적인 상황 개선에는 아무런 도움도 안 되는 표면적인 대책이다.

D

E

F

cos|met|ic sur|gery N-UNCOUNT **Cosmetic surgery** is surgery done to make a person look more attractive. ❑ *Singing star Cher, 56, is rumored to have had cosmetic surgery on nine different parts of her body.*

불가산명사 성형 수술 ❑ 올해 56세의 팝 가수 셰어는 지금까지 몸 아홉 군데에 성형 수술을 받았다는 소문이 있다.

G

cos|mic /kɒzmɪk/ ❶ ADJ **Cosmic** means occurring in, or coming from, the part of space that lies outside Earth and its atmosphere. ❑ ...*cosmic radiation.* ❷ ADJ **Cosmic** means belonging or relating to the universe. ❑ ...*the cosmic laws governing our world.*

❶ 형용사 우주의 ❑ 우주 복사 ❷ 형용사 보편적인 ❑ 세상을 지배하는 보편법

H

I

cos|mo|poli|tan /kɒzməpɒlɪtən/ ❶ ADJ A **cosmopolitan** place or society is full of people from many different countries and cultures. [APPROVAL] ❑ *London has always been a cosmopolitan city.* ❷ ADJ Someone who is **cosmopolitan** has had a lot of contact with people and things from many different countries and as a result is very open to different ideas and ways of doing things. [APPROVAL] ❑ *The family are rich, and extremely sophisticated and cosmopolitan.*

❶ 형용사 국제적인 [마음에 듦] ❑ 런던은 지금까지 항상 국제도시였다. ❷ 형용사 국제적인, 시야가 넓은 [마음에 듦] ❑ 그 가족은 부유하고 상당히 세련된 데다가 국제적이다.

J

K

cos|mos /kɒzməs, -mɒʊs, BRIT kɒzmɒs/ N-SING The **cosmos** is the universe. [LITERARY] ❑ ...*the natural laws of the cosmos.*

단수명사 우주 [문예체] ❑ 우주의 자연 법칙

L

cost ♦♦♦ /kɔst, BRIT kɒst/ (**costs, costing**)

> The form **cost** is used in the present tense, and is also the past tense and past participle, except for meaning ❹, where the form **costed** is used.

cost는 동사의 현재, 과거, 과거 분사로 쓰는데, ❹ 의미에서만은 costed를 쓴다.

M

❶ N-COUNT The **cost of** something is the amount of money that is needed in order to buy, do, or make it. ❑ *The cost of a loaf of bread has increased five-fold.* ❑ *In 1989 the price of coffee fell so low that in many countries it did not even cover the cost of production.* ❷ V-T If something **costs** a particular amount of money, you can buy, do, or make it for that amount. ❑ *This course is limited to 12 people and costs £50.* ❑ *Painted walls look much more interesting and don't cost much.* ❸ N-PLURAL Your **costs** are the total amount of money that you must spend on running your home or business. ❑ *Costs have been cut by 30 to 50 percent.* ❹ V-T When something that you plan to do or make **is costed,** the amount of money you need is calculated in advance. [usu passive] ❑ *Everything that goes into making a program, staff, rent, lighting, is now costed.* ❺ N-PLURAL If someone is ordered by a court of law to pay **costs,** they have to pay a sum of money towards the expenses of a court case they are involved in. ❑ *He was jailed for 18 months and ordered to pay £550 costs.* ❻ N-UNCOUNT If something is sold **at cost,** it is sold for the same price as it cost the seller to buy it. ❑ ...*a store that provided cigarettes and candy bars at cost.* ❼ N-SING The **cost of** something is the loss, damage, or injury that is involved in trying to achieve it. ❑ *In March Mr. Salinas shut down the city's oil refinery at a cost of $500 million and 5,000 jobs.* ❽ V-T If an event or mistake **costs** you something, you lose that thing as the result of it. ❑ ...*a six-year-old boy whose life was saved by an operation that cost him his sight.*

❶ 가산명사 가격, 비용 ❑ 빵 한 덩이 가격이 다섯 배나 증가했다. ❑ 1989년 커피 가격이 급격히 떨어지면서 상당수 국가에서는 생산 원가도 뽑아내지 못했다. ❷ 타동사 비용이 들다, 가격이 ~이다 ❑ 이 강좌의 최대 정원은 12명이고 수강료는 50파운드이다. ❑ 그림을 그린 벽이 더 재미있어 보이고 비용도 많이 들지 않는다. ❸ 복수명사 경비 ❑ 경비가 30~50퍼센트 줄어들었다. ❹ 타동사 견적이 나오다 ❑ 프로그램 제작과 스태프, 임대료, 조명 등에 들어가는 비용의 견적이 나와 있다. ❺ 복수명사 소송 비용 ❑ 그는 징역 18개월에 소송 비용 550파운드 지불을 명령받았다. ❻ 불가산명사 원가 ❑ 담배와 캔디바를 원가에 파는 가게 ❼ 단수명사 희생, 손실 ❑ 3월에 살리나스 씨는 시내 원유 정제소의 문을 닫으면서 5억 달러를 손해보고 직원 5천 명을 해고해야 했다. ❽ 타동사 희생시키다, 앗아가다 ❑ 수술로 목숨을 건졌지만 그 과정에서 시력을 잃은 여섯 살 난 소년

N

O

P

Q

R

S

> Do not confuse **cost** and **costs.** The **cost** of something is the amount of money that you need in order to buy it, do it, or make it. ❑ ...*the cost of the telephone call....the total cost was over a million pounds.* The **costs** of a business or a home are the sums of money that have to be spent on running it. They include money spent on electricity, repairs, and taxes. ❑ ...*attempts to cut costs and boost profits.* See also note at **price.**

cost와 costs를 혼동하지 않도록 하라. 무엇의 cost는 그것을 사거나, 하거나, 만들기 위해 필요한 만큼의 돈이다. ❑ ...전화 통화료....총 비용이 백만 파운드가 넘었다. 한 사업체나 가구의 costs는 그것을 운영하는 데 써야 할 비용이다. 여기에는 전기, 보수, 세금에 드는 돈이 포함된다. ❑ ...비용을 줄이고 수익을 높이려는 시도들. price의 주석도 보라.

T

U

V

❾ PHRASE If you say that something must be avoided **at all costs,** you are emphasizing that it must not be allowed to happen under any circumstances. [EMPHASIS] ❑ *They told Jacques Delors a disastrous world trade war must be avoided at all costs.* ❿ PHRASE If you say that something must be done **at any cost,** you are emphasizing that it must be done, even if this requires a lot of effort or money. [EMPHASIS] ❑ *This book is of such importance that it must be published at any cost.*

❾ 구 어떻게 해서든 [강조] ❑ 그들은 자크 들로르에게 어떻게 해서든 막대한 피해를 동반하는 무역 전쟁을 막아야 한다고 말했다. ❿ 구 어떻게 해서든, 어떤 대가를 치르고서라도 [강조] ❑ 이 책은 그 중요성이 매우 크기 때문에 어떻게 해서든 출판해야 한다.

W

X

Y

Z

> **Thesaurus** cost의 참조어
>
> N.   fee, price ❶
>   harm, loss, sacrifice ❼

Word Partnership	cost의 연어
ADJ.	additional costs ■
V.	cover the cost, cut costs, keep costs down ② ⑤

cost ac|count|ing N-UNCOUNT **Cost accounting** is the recording and analysis of all the various costs of running a business. [BUSINESS] ❑ But full cost accounting will be introduced without delay.

co|star /koʊstɑr/ (costars, costarring, costarred) [BRIT also **co-star**] ■ N-COUNT An actor's or actress's **costars** are the other actors or actresses who also have one of the main parts in a particular movie. ❑ During the filming, Curtis fell in love with his costar, Christine Kaufmann. ② V-T If a movie **costars** particular actors, they have the main parts in it. ❑ Produced by Oliver Stone, "Wild Palms" costars Dana Delaney, Jim Belushi and Angie Dickinson.

cost-effective ADJ Something that is **cost-effective** saves or makes a lot of money in comparison with the costs involved. ❑ The bank must be run in a cost-effective way. ● **cost-effectively** ADV ❑ The management tries to produce the magazine as cost-effectively as possible. ● **cost-effectiveness** N-UNCOUNT ❑ A Home Office report has raised doubts about the cost-effectiveness of the proposals.

cost|ing /kɒstɪŋ, BRIT kɒstɪŋ/ (costings) N-VAR A **costing** is an estimate of all the costs involved in a project or a business venture. [mainly BRIT, BUSINESS] ❑ We'll put together a proposal, including detailed costings, free of charge.

cost|ly /kɒstli, BRIT kɒstli/ (costlier, costliest) ADJ If you say that something is **costly**, you mean that it costs a lot of money, often more than you would want to pay. ❑ Having professionally made curtains can be costly, so why not make your own?

cost of liv|ing N-SING The **cost of living** is the average amount of money that people in a particular place need in order to be able to afford basic food, housing, and clothing. ❑ The cost of living has increased dramatically.

cost of liv|ing in|dex N-PROPER The **cost-of-living index** is a list of the prices of typical goods which shows how much the cost of living changes from one month to the next. [AM, BUSINESS; AM **retail price index**] [the n] ❑ Switzerland's cost-of-living index in July fell 0.2% from June.

cost-plus ADJ A **cost-plus** basis for a contract about work to be done is one in which the buyer agrees to pay the seller or contractor all the cost plus a profit. [ADJ n] ❑ All vessels were to be built on a cost-plus basis.

cost price (cost prices) N-VAR If something is sold **at cost price**, it is sold for the same price as it cost the seller to buy it. [BRIT] ❑ ...a factory shop where you can buy very fashionable shoes at cost price.

cos|tume /kɒstum, BRIT kɒstyu:m/ (costumes) ■ N-VAR An actor's or performer's **costume** is the set of clothes they wear while they are performing. ❑ Even from a distance the effect of his fox costume was stunning. ❑ The performers, in costume and makeup, were walking up and down backstage. ② N-UNCOUNT The clothes worn by people at a particular time in history, or in a particular country, are referred to as a particular type of **costume**. ❑ ...men and women in eighteenth-century costume. ③ ADJ A **costume** play or drama is one which is set in the past and in which the actors wear the type of clothes that were worn in that period. [ADJ n] ❑ ...a lavish costume drama set in Ireland and the U.S. in the 1890s. →see **theater**

cosy /koʊzi/ →see **cozy**

cot /kɒt/ (cots) ■ N-COUNT A **cot** is a narrow bed, usually made of canvas fitted over a frame which can be folded up. [AM; BRIT **camp bed**] ② N-COUNT A **cot** is a bed for a baby. [BRIT; AM **crib**]

cot|tage ♦◇◇ /kɒtɪdʒ/ (cottages) N-COUNT; N-IN-NAMES A **cottage** is a small house, usually in the country. ❑ They used to have a cottage in N.W. Scotland.

cot|tage in|dus|try (cottage industries) N-COUNT A **cottage industry** is a small business that is run from someone's home, especially one that involves a craft such as knitting or pottery. [BUSINESS] ❑ Bookbinding is largely a cottage industry.

cot|ton ♦◇◇ /kɒtⁿn/ (cottons, cottoning, cottoned) ■ N-MASS **Cotton** is a type of cloth made from soft fibers from a particular plant. ❑ ...a cotton shirt. ② N-UNCOUNT **Cotton** is a plant which is grown in warm countries and which produces soft fibers used in making cotton cloth. ❑ ...a large cotton plantation in Tennessee. ③ N-MASS **Cotton** is thread that is used for sewing, especially thread that is made from cotton. [mainly BRIT; AM **thread**] ❑ There's a needle and cotton there. ④ N-UNCOUNT **Cotton** or **absorbent cotton** is a soft mass of cotton, used especially for applying liquids or creams to your skin. [AM; BRIT **cotton wool**] →see Word Web: **cotton**

cot|ton can|dy N-UNCOUNT **Cotton candy** is a large pink or white mass of sugar threads that is eaten from a stick. It is sold at fairs or other outdoor events. [AM; BRIT **candyfloss**]

cot|ton wool N-UNCOUNT **Cotton wool** is a soft mass of cotton, used especially for applying liquids or creams to your skin. [BRIT; AM **cotton**]

couch /kaʊtʃ/ (couches) ■ N-COUNT A **couch** is a long, comfortable seat for two or three people. ② N-COUNT A **couch** is a narrow bed which patients lie on while they are being examined or treated by a doctor. ❑ Between films he often winds up spending every single morning on his psychiatrist's couch.

cough ♦◇◇ /kɒf, BRIT kɒf/ (coughs, coughing, coughed) ■ V-I When you **cough**, you force air out of your throat with a sudden, harsh noise. You often cough

불가산명사 원가 계산 [경제] ❑ 그러나 종합 원가 계산 방식이 지체 없이 도입될 것이다.

[영국영어 co-star] ■ 가산명사 공동 주연 ❑ 커티스는 촬영 기간 동안 같이 주연을 맡은 크리스틴 카우프만과 사랑에 빠졌다. ② 타동사 공동 주연시키다 ❑ 올리버 스톤이 제작한 '와일드 팜'에는 다나 딜래니, 짐 벨루쉬, 앤지 디킨슨이 공동 주연으로 나온다.

형용사 비용 효율이 높은 ❑ 비용 효율이 높은 방식으로 은행 경영을 해야 한다. ● 비용 효율적으로 부사 ❑ 경영진은 최대한 비용 효율적으로 잡지를 만들기 위해 노력한다. ● 비용 효율성 불가산명사 ❑ 한 내무부 보고서에서 이 제안의 비용 효율성에 대한 의문을 제기한다.

가산명사 또는 불가산명사 원가 계산, 견적 [주로 영국영어, 경제] ❑ 우리는 자세한 원가 내역을 포함한 기획안을 수수료 없이 마련해 드립니다.

형용사 비싼 ❑ 전문가가 만든 커튼은 비쌀 수도 있으므로, 스스로 만드는 것은 어떨까요?

단수명사 생활비, 생계비 ❑ 생활비가 급격히 증가했다.

고유명사 생계비 지수 [미국영어, 경제; 미국영어 retail price index] ❑ 7월 스위스 생계비 지수가 6월보다 0.2퍼센트 하락했다.

형용사 이익 가산의 ❑ 모든 배는 이익 가산 방식으로 건조된다.

가산명사 또는 불가산명사 원가 [영국영어] ❑ 최신 유행 신발을 원가에 살 수 있는 공장

■ 가산명사 또는 불가산명사 의상, 복장 ❑ 멀리서 봤을 때에도 그의 여우 복장의 효과는 놀라웠다. ❑ 의상을 입고 분장을 한 연기자들이 무대 뒤를 왔다 갔다 했다. ② 불가산명사 복장, 전통의상 ❑ 18세기 복장을 한 남녀 ③ 형용사 시대극의 ❑ 1890년대 아일랜드와 미국을 배경으로 한 화려한 시대극

■ 가산명사 간이침대 [미국영어; 영국영어 camp bed] ② 가산명사 유아용 침대 [영국영어; 미국영어 crib]

가산명사; 이름명사 작은 시골집 ❑ 그들은 예전에 스코틀랜드 서북 지역에 시골집을 가지고 있었다.

가산명사 가내 수공업 [경제] ❑ 제본은 대개 가내 수공업 형태로 이뤄진다.

■ 물질명사 면직물 ❑ 면 셔츠 ② 불가산명사 목화 ❑ 테네시에 위치한 대규모 목화 농장 ③ 물질명사 면사 [주로 영국영어; 미국영어 thread] ❑ 바늘과 면사가 저기 있다. ④ 불가산명사 탈지면 [미국영어; 영국영어 cotton wool]

불가산명사 솜사탕 [미국영어; 영국영어 candyfloss]

불가산명사 탈지면 [영국영어; 미국영어 cotton]

■ 가산명사 소파 ② 가산명사 진찰대 ❑ 그는 영화 촬영이 없을 때는 아침마다 정신과 전문의의 상담을 받곤 한다.

■ 자동사 기침하다 ❑ 그레이엄이 격렬하게 기침을 하기 시작했다. ● 가산명사 기침 ❑ 기침이나 재채기를

Word Web   cotton

Some historians believe that **cotton** was first used in Egypt around 12,000 BC. Pieces of **fabric** containing a mixture of cotton and fur have been found in Mexico. They date back to about 5000 BC. Today's cotton **crop** in the U.S. totals about 20 billion dollars a year. The **textile industry** uses most of this cotton to make things like **denim** clothing, T-shirts, and bed sheets. However, many other products contain some cotton. For example, cotton fiber is used to make coffee filters, tents, stationery, and even U.S. currency.

when you are ill, or when you are nervous or want to attract someone's attention. • N-COUNT **Cough** is also a noun. ❑ *Coughs and sneezes spread infections much faster in a warm atmosphere.* • **cough|ing** N-UNCOUNT ❑ *He was then overcome by a terrible fit of coughing.* ❷ N-COUNT A **cough** is an illness in which you cough often and your chest or throat hurts. ❑ *...if you have a persistent cough for over a month.* ❸ V-T If you **cough** blood or mucus, it comes up out of your throat or mouth when you cough. ❑ *I started coughing blood so they transferred me to a hospital.* • PHRASAL VERB **Cough up** means the same as **cough.** ❑ *On the chilly seas, Keats became feverish, continually coughing up blood.*
→see **illness**

▶**cough up** PHRASAL VERB If you **cough up** an amount of money, you pay or spend that amount, usually when you would prefer not to. [INFORMAL] ❑ *I'll have to cough up $10,000 a year for tuition.* →see also **cough 3**

could ♦♦♦ /kəd, STRONG kʊd/

Could is a modal verb. It is used with the base form of a verb. **Could** is sometimes considered to be the past form of **can**, but in this dictionary the two words are dealt with separately.

❶ MODAL You use **could** to indicate that someone had the ability to do something. You use **could not** or **couldn't** to say that someone was unable to do something. ❑ *I could see that something was terribly wrong.* ❑ *When I left school at 16, I couldn't read or write.*

Can, **could**, and **be able to** are all used to talk about a person's ability to do something. They are followed by the infinitive form of a verb. You use **can** or a present form of **be able to** to refer to the present, although **can** is more common. ❑ *They can all read and write... The snake is able to catch small mammals.* You use **could** or a past form of **be able to** to refer to the past, and "will" or "shall" with **be able to** to refer to the future. **Be able to** is used if you want refer to doing something at a particular time. ❑ *After treatment he was able to return to work.* **Can** and **could** are used to talk about possibility. **Could** refers to a particular occasion and **can** to more general situations. ❑ *Many jobs could be lost... Too much salt can be harmful.* When talking about the past, you use **could have** and a past participle. ❑ *It could have been much worse.* You also use **can** for the present and **could** for the past to talk about rules or what people are allowed to do. ❑ *They can leave at any time.* Note that when making requests either **can** or **could** may be used. ❑ *Can I have a drink?... Could we put the fire on?* However, **could** is always used for suggestions. ❑ *You could phone her and ask.*

❷ MODAL You use **could** to indicate that something sometimes happened. ❑ *Though he had a temper and could be nasty, it never lasted.* ❸ MODAL You use **could have** to indicate that something was a possibility in the past, although it did not actually happen. ❑ *He could have made a fortune as a lawyer.* ❑ *You could have been killed!* ❹ MODAL You use **could** to indicate that something is possibly true, or that it may possibly happen. ❑ *Doctors told him the disease could have been caused by years of working in smokey clubs.* ❑ *An improvement in living standards could be years away.* ❺ MODAL You use **could not** or **couldn't** to indicate that it is not possible that something is true. ❑ *They argued all the time and thought it couldn't be good for the baby.* ❑ *Anne couldn't be expected to understand the situation.* ❻ MODAL You use **could** to talk about a possibility, ability, or opportunity that depends on other conditions. ❑ *Their hope was that a new and better East Germany could be born.* ❼ MODAL You use **could** when you are saying that one thing or situation resembles another. ❑ *The charming characters she draws look like they could have walked out of the 1920s.* ❽ MODAL You use **could**, or **couldn't** in questions, when you are making offers and suggestions. ❑ *I could call the local doctor.* ❑ *You could look for a career abroad where environmental jobs are better paid and more secure.* ❾ MODAL You use **could** in questions when you are making a polite request or asking for permission to do something. Speakers sometimes use **couldn't** instead of "could" to show that they realize that their request may be refused. [POLITENESS] ❑ *Could I stay tonight?* ❑ *He asked if he could have a cup of coffee.* ❑ *Couldn't I watch you do it?* ❿ MODAL You use **could** to say emphatically that someone ought to do the thing mentioned, especially when you are annoyed because they have not done it. You use **why couldn't** in questions to express your surprise or annoyance that someone has not done something. [EMPHASIS] ❑ *We've come to see you, so you could at least stand and greet us properly.* ❑ *Why couldn't she have said something?* ⓫ MODAL You use **could** when you are

하면, 따뜻한 공기 속에서는 바이러스가 훨씬 빨리 퍼진다. ❑ 기침 불가산명사 그리고 나서 그는 심한 기침 발작으로 맥을 못 췄다. ❷ 가산명사 기침 감기 ❑ 한 달 이상 기침 감기를 앓을 경우 ❸ 타동사 기침하면서 토해 내다 ❑ 내가 각혈을 하기 시작하자 그들은 나를 병원으로 옮겼다. ● 구동사 기침하며 토해 내다 ❑ 키츠는 차가운 바다에서 열병에 걸려 계속 콜록거리며 피를 토해 냈다.

구동사 마지못해 내놓다 [비격식체] ❑ 나는 등록금으로 한 해에 1만 달러를 내야 할 것이다.

could은 조동사이며 동사 원형과 함께 쓴다. could은 가끔 can의 과거형으로 취급되지만 이 사전에서는 두 단어를 별개로 다룬다.

❶ 법조동사 -할 수 있었다; -할 수 없었다 ❑ 뭔가 단단히 잘못된 것을 알 수 있었다. ❑ 열여섯 살에 학교를 졸업했을 때, 나는 읽지도 쓰지도 못했다.

can, could, be able to는 모두 무엇을 할 수 있는 사람의 능력을 말할 때 쓰며, 뒤에는 동사 원형이 온다. 현재에 대해 말할 때는 can이나 be able to의 현재형을 쓰는데 can이 더 일반적이다. ❑ 그들은 모두 읽고 쓸 줄 안다... 뱀은 작은 포유동물을 잡을 수 있다. 과거에 대해 말할 때는 could나 be able to의 과거형을 쓰고, 미래에 대해 말할 때는 'will' 또는 'shall'과 함께 be able to를 쓴다. 특정한 시기에 무엇을 하는 것에 대해 말할 때는 be able to를 쓴다. ❑ 치료 후에 그는 직장으로 복귀할 수 있었다. can과 could는 모두 가능성을 얘기할 때 쓴다. could는 특정한 경우에 대해 쓰고 can은 좀 더 일반적인 상황에 대해 쓴다. ❑ 많은 일자리가 없어질 수도 있다... 염분과다 섭취는 해로울 수 있다. 과거에 대해서 말할 때는 could have와 과거분사를 쓴다. ❑ 사정이 훨씬 더 안 좋을 수도 있었다. 규칙이나 허용되는 일에 대해 말할 때에도 현재일 때는 can을, 과거일 때는 could를 쓸 수 있다. ❑ 그들은 아무 때나 떠날 수 있다. 요청을 할 때는 can이나 could에 어느 것이나 쓸 수 있음을 유의하라. ❑ 한 잔 할 수 있을까요?[한 잔 주시겠소?]... 우리 난로 피울까요? 그러나 제안에는 항상 could를 쓴다. ❑ 네가 그녀에게 전화를 해서 물어 볼 수도 있겠지.

❷ 법조동사 -하기도 했다 ❑ 그가 성깔도 있고 심술을 부릴 때도 있었지만, 오래가지는 않았다. ❸ 법조동사 -할 수도 있었다 ❑ 그는 변호사가 되어 일확천금을 벌 수도 있었다. ❑ 너 죽을 수도 있었어! ❹ 법조동사 -일 수도 있다, -할 수도 있다 ❑ 의사들은 그에게 담배 연기가 자욱한 클럽에서 수년간 일하면서 병이 생겼을 수도 있다고 말했다. ❑ 몇 년 후에나 생활수준이 나아질지도 모른다. ❺ 법조동사 -일 리가 없다 ❑ 그들은 항상 다투면서 자신들의 싸움이 아이에게 좋을 리가 없다고 생각했다. ❑ 앤이 상황을 이해했을 리가 없다. ❻ 법조동사 -할 수도 있다 ❑ 그들의 희망은 더 나은 새 동독이 탄생할 수도 있다는 희망이 있었다. ❼ 법조동사 마치 -와 같다 ❑ 그녀가 그리는 매력적인 캐릭터들은 마치 1920년대에서 걸어 나온 것처럼 보인다. ❽ 법조동사 -할 수도 있다 ❑ 동네 의사를 불러 드릴 수 있어요. ❑ 환경 보호와 관련된 직업이 보수도 좋고 안정적 때 그녀는 해외로 일자리를 찾아볼 수도 있다. ❾ 법조동사 -해도 될까요, -해 주시겠습니까 [공손체] ❑ 오늘밤 여기 있어도 될까요? ❑ 그는 커피 한 잔을 부탁했다. ❑ 일하시는 모습을 지켜봐도 될까요? ❿ 법조동사 -할 수는 있잖아; 왜 - 안 한 거야 [강조] ❑ 우리가 널 보러 왔으니, 최소한 일어서서 제대로 인사는 한 거야? ⓫ 법조동사 -라도 하고 싶다 [강조] ❑ 마음 같아선 널 죽이고 싶어! 정말 죽이고 싶어! ❑ 그들은 돌아온 걸 환영한다는 말도 했다. 뽀뽀라도 해 주고 싶었다. ⓬ 법조동사 -할 수 있다면 ❑ 살 수만 있다면,

expressing strong feelings about something by saying that you feel as if you want to do the thing mentioned, although you do not do it. [EMPHASIS] ❑ *I could kill you! I swear I could! "Welcome back" was all they said. I could have kissed them!* **12 MODAL** You use **could** after "if" when talking about something that you do not have the ability or opportunity to do, but which you are imagining in order to consider what the likely consequences might be. ❑ *If I could afford it I'd have four television sets.* **13 MODAL** You use **could not** or **couldn't** with comparatives to emphasize that someone or something has as much as is possible of a particular quality. For example, if you say "I couldn't be happier," you mean that you are extremely happy. [EMPHASIS] ❑ *The rest of the players are a great bunch of lads and I couldn't be happier.* **14 MODAL** In speech, you use **how could** in questions to emphasize that you feel strongly about something bad that has happened. [EMPHASIS] ❑ *How could you allow him to do something like that?* ❑ *How could I have been so stupid?* **15 could do with →see do**

나는 텔레비전을 네 대 갖고 싶다. **13** 법조동사 이보다 -할 수 없다, 가장 -하다 [강조] ❑ 나머지 선수들이 아주 뛰어나기 때문에 나는 더 이상 바랄 게 없다. **14** 법조동사 어떻게 -할 수 있어? [강조] ❑ 그가 그런 짓을 하도록 어떻게 내버려 둘 수 있어? ❑ 내가 어쩜 그렇게 바보 같았을까?

couldn't /ˈkʊdnt/ **Couldn't** is the usual spoken form of "could not."

could not의 축약형

could've /ˈkʊdəv/ **Could've** is the usual spoken form of "could have," when "have" is an auxiliary verb.

could have의 축약형

coun|cil ♦♦♦ /ˈkaʊnsəl/ (**councils**) **1** N-COUNT-COLL; N-IN-NAMES A **council** is a group of people who are elected to govern a local area such as a city or, in Britain, a county. ❑ *...Cheshire County Council.* ❑ *The city council has voted almost unanimously in favor.* **2** ADJ **Council** houses or flats are owned by the local council, and people pay rent to live in them. [BRIT] [ADJ n] ❑ *There is a shortage of council housing.* **3** N-COUNT-COLL **Council** is used in the names of some organizations. ❑ *...the National Council for Civil Liberties.* ❑ *...the Arts Council.* **4** N-COUNT-COLL In some organizations, the **council** is the group of people that controls or governs it. ❑ *The permanent council of the Organization of American States meets today here in Washington.* **5** N-COUNT A **council** is a specially organized, formal meeting that is attended by a particular group of people. ❑ *President Najibullah said he would call a grand council of all Afghans.*

1 가산명사-집합; 이름명사 지방 의회 ❑ 체셔카운티 의회 ❑ 시의회가 거의 만장일치로 찬성표를 던졌다. **2** 형용사 공영의 [영국영어] ❑ 공영 주택이 부족하다. **3** 가산명사-집합 일부 기관 이름에 사용 ❑ 시민 자유 전국 협회 ❑ 예술원 **4** 가산명사-집합 위원회 ❑ 미주 기구 상임 위원회가 오늘 이곳 워싱턴에서 회의를 연다. **5** 가산명사 회의 ❑ 나지불라 대통령이 아프가니스탄 전국민회의를 소집하겠다고 밝혔다.

coun|cil|lor /ˈkaʊnsələr/ (**councilors**) N-COUNT; N-TITLE A **councilor** is a member of a local council. [BRIT **councillor**] ❑ *...Councilor Michael Poulter.*

가산명사; 경칭명사 지방 의회 의원 [영국영어 councillor] ❑ 마이클 폴터 의원

coun|sel ♦◇◇ /ˈkaʊnsəl/ (**counsels, counseling, counseled**) [BRIT, sometimes AM **counselling, counselled**] **1** N-UNCOUNT **Counsel** is advice. [FORMAL] ❑ *He had always been able to count on her wise counsel.* **2** V-T If you **counsel** someone **to** take a course of action, or if you **counsel** a course of action, you advise that course of action. [FORMAL] ❑ *My advisers counseled me to do nothing.* **3** V-T If you **counsel** people, you give them advice about their problems. ❑ *...a psychologist who counsels people with eating disorders.* **4** N-COUNT Someone's **counsel** is the lawyer who gives them advice on a legal case and speaks on their behalf in court. ❑ *Singleton's counsel said after the trial that he would appeal.*

[영국영어, 미국영어 가끔 counselling] **1** 불가산명사 조언 [격식체] ❑ 그는 항상 그녀의 현명한 조언에 의지할 수 있었다. **2** 타동사 권하다 [격식체] ❑ 내 조언자들이 내게 아무것도 하지 말라는 권고를 했다. **3** 타동사 조언하다, 상담하다 ❑ 식이 장애 환자 상담 전문 정신과 의사 **4** 가산명사 법률 고문, 변호사 ❑ 싱글턴 측 고문 변호사가 재판 후에 항소하겠다고 밝혔다.

coun|sel|ing /ˈkaʊnsəlɪŋ/ [BRIT, sometimes AM **counselling**] N-UNCOUNT **Counseling** is advice which a therapist or other expert gives to someone about a particular problem. ❑ *She will need medical help and counseling to overcome the tragedy.*

[영국영어, 미국영어 가끔 counselling] 불가산명사 상담, 조언 ❑ 그녀가 그 비극을 극복하려면 의학 치료와 상담이 필요할 것이다.

coun|se|lor /ˈkaʊnsələr/ (**counselors**) [BRIT, sometimes AM **counsellor**] **1** N-COUNT A **counselor** is a person whose job is to give advice to people who need it, especially advice on their personal problems. ❑ *Children who have suffered like this should see a counselor experienced in bereavement.* **2** N-COUNT A **counselor** is a young person who supervises children at a summer camp. ❑ *Hicks worked with children as a camp counselor.*

[영국영어, 미국영어 가끔 counsellor] **1** 가산명사 상담원, 카운슬러 ❑ 이와 같은 일을 겪은 아이들은 가족 구성원 사망 문제에 경험이 있는 전문가의 상담을 받아야 한다. **2** 가산명사 캠프 지도원 ❑ 힉스는 캠프 지도원으로 어린이들과 일했다.

count ♦♦◇ /ˈkaʊnt/ (**counts, counting, counted**) **1** V-I When you **count**, you say all the numbers one after another up to a particular number. ❑ *He was counting slowly under his breath.* **2** V-T/V-I If you **count** all the things in a group, you add them up in order to find how many there are. ❑ *I counted the money. It was more than five hundred pounds.* ❑ *I counted 34 wild goats grazing.* ● PHRASAL VERB **Count up** means the same as **count**. ❑ *Couldn't we just count up our ballots and bring them to the courthouse?* **3** N-COUNT A **count** is the action of counting a particular set of things, or the number that you get when you have counted them. ❑ *The final count in last month's referendum showed 56.7 per cent in favor.* **4** N-COUNT You use **count** when referring to the level or amount of something that someone or something has. ❑ *A glass or two of wine will not significantly add to the calorie count.* **5** V-I If something or someone **counts for** something or **counts**, they are important or valuable. ❑ *Surely it doesn't matter where charities get their money from: what counts is what they do with it.* **6** V-I If something **counts** or **is counted as** a particular thing, it is regarded as being that thing, especially in particular circumstances or under particular rules. ❑ *No one agrees on what counts as a desert.* **7** V-T If you **count** something when you are making a calculation, you include it in that calculation. ❑ *It's under 7 percent who say statistics don't count the people who aren't qualified to be in the work force.* **8** N-COUNT In law, a **count** is one of a number of charges brought against someone in court. ❑ *He was indicted by a grand jury on two counts of murder.* **9** PHRASE If you **keep count of** a number of things, you note or keep a record of how many have occurred. If you **lose count of** a number of things, you cannot remember how many have occurred. ❑ *The authorities say they are not able to keep count of the bodies still being found as bulldozers clear the rubble.*
→see **census, mathematics, zero**

1 자동사 세다 ❑ 그는 작은 소리로 천천히 숫자를 셌다. **2** 타동사/자동사 세다, 계산하다 ❑ 나는 돈을 셌다. 500파운드가 넘었다. ❑ 세어 보니 풀을 뜯는 야생 염소가 34마리였다. ● 구동사 세다, 계산하다 ❑ 그냥 개표한 후 법원에 제출하면 안 될까요? **3** 가산명사 계산, 셈; 총계 ❑ 지난달 국민 투표 최종 집계 결과 56.7퍼센트가 찬성한 것으로 나타났다. **4** 가산명사 수치 ❑ 와인 한두 잔을 마신다고 해서 칼로리 섭취량이 크게 증가하지는 않는다. **5** 자동사 중요하다 ❑ 자선 단체가 돈을 어디서 구하는지는 결코 중요하지 않다. 중요한 것은 그 돈을 가지고 무엇을 하느냐이다. **6** 자동사 -로 간주되다 ❑ 사막의 정의에 관해서는 의견이 분분하다. **7** 타동사 포함되다 ❑ 수치가 7퍼센트 이하인 이유는, 단지 노동 인구로 분류되지 않는 사람들이 통계에 포함되지 않기 때문일 뿐이다. **8** 가산명사 죄목 ❑ 대배심이 살인 관련 죄목 두 개로 그를 기소했다. **9** 구 계속하여 세다; 몇 개인지 까먹다 ❑ 불도저가 잔해를 치우면서 아직도 시신이 발견되고 있어서 사망자 수를 계속 집계할 수 없다고 관계 당국이 말한다.

▶**count against** PHRASAL VERB If something **counts against** you, it may cause you to be rejected or punished, or cause people to have a lower opinion of you. ❑ *He is highly regarded, but his youth might count against him.*

구동사 불리하게 작용하다 ❑ 그에 대한 평판은 좋지만, 나이가 적다는 것이 불리하게 작용할지도 모른다.

▶**count on** or **count upon** **1** PHRASAL VERB If you **count on** something or **count upon** it, you expect it to happen and include it in your plans. ❑ *The government thought it could count on the support of the trades unions.* **2** PHRASAL VERB If you **count on** someone or **count upon** them, you rely on them to support you or help you. ❑ *Don't count on Lillian.*

1 구동사 기대하다 ❑ 정부는 산별 노조의 지지를 기대할 수 있다고 생각했다. **2** 구동사 의지하다, 기대다 ❑ 릴리안에게 기대지 않는 편이 좋아.

a b c d e f g h i j k l m n o p q r s t u v w x y z

▶**count out** PHRASAL VERB If you **count out** a sum of money, you count the notes or coins as you put them in a pile one by one. ❏ *Mr. Rohmbauer counted out the money and put it in an envelope.*

구동사 세어 놓다 ❏ 롬바우어 씨는 돈을 세어서 봉투에 넣었다.

▶**count up** →see **count 2**

▶**count upon** →see **count on**

count|able noun /ka͟ʊntəbᵊl na͟ʊn/ (**countable nouns**) N-COUNT A **countable noun** is the same as a **count noun**.

가산명사 가산 명사

count|down /ka͟ʊntdaʊn/ N-SING A **countdown** is the counting aloud of numbers in reverse order before something happens, especially before a spacecraft is launched. [also no det] ❏ *The countdown has begun for the launch later today of the American space shuttle.*

단수명사 카운트다운, 초읽기 ❏ 오늘 오후 미국 우주 왕복선 발사 카운트다운이 시작됐다.

coun|te|nance /ka͟ʊntɪnəns/ (**countenances, countenancing, countenanced**) V-T If someone will not **countenance** something, they do not agree with it and will not allow it to happen. [FORMAL] [usu with brd-neg] ❏ *Jake would not countenance Janis's marrying while still a student.*

타동사 찬성하다, 묵인하다 [격식체] ❏ 제이크는 재니스가 아직 학생일 때 결혼하는 것을 허락하지 않을 것이다.

coun|ter ◆◇◇ /ka͟ʊntər/ (**counters, countering, countered**) ■ N-COUNT In a place such as a store or café, a **counter** is a long narrow table or flat surface at which customers are served. ❏ *...those fellows we see working behind the counter at our local video rental store.* ❷ V-T/V-I If you do something to **counter** a particular action or process, you do something which has an opposite effect to it or makes it less effective. ❏ *The leadership discussed a plan of economic measures to counter the effects of such a blockade.* ❸ N-SING Something that is a **counter to** something else has an opposite effect to it or makes it less effective. ❏ *...NATO's traditional role as a counter to the military might of the Warsaw pact.* ❹ N-COUNT A **counter** is a mechanical or electronic device which keeps a count of something and displays the total. ❏ *...an answerphone with one-touch playback and LED display call counter.* ❺ N-COUNT A **counter** is a small, flat, round object used in board games. ❏ *...a versatile book which provides boards and counters for fifteen different games.* ❻ PHRASE If a medicine can be bought **over the counter**, you do not need a prescription to buy it. ❏ *Are you taking any other medicines whether on prescription or bought over the counter?* ❼ PHRASE **Over-the-counter** shares are bought and sold directly rather than on a stock exchange. [BUSINESS] ❏ *In national over-the-counter trading yesterday, Clarcor shares tumbled $6.125 to close at $35.625.*

■ 가산명사 카운터 ❏ 지역 동네 비디오 가게 카운터에서 일하는 그런 녀석들 ❷ 타동사/자동사 막다, 대항하다, 상쇄시키다 ❏ 지도부는 그와 같은 봉쇄의 효과를 상쇄시키기 위한 경제 정책 마련을 논의했다. ❸ 단수명사 균형추, 대응책 ❏ 바르샤바 조약의 군사력에 대한 대응책으로서 나토의 전통적인 역할 ❹ 가산명사 측정기 ❏ 재생 기능 및 엘이디 전화 횟수 측정 기능이 있는 자동 응답기 ❺ 가산명사 (보드게임용) 말 ❏ 열다섯 가지 게임에 필요한 게임판과 모조 화폐를 제공하는 다용도 서적 ❻ 구 처방전 없이, 일반 판매 약의 ❏ 처방약이나 일반 판매 약 중 현재 복용 중인 약이 있습니까? ❼ 구 장외의, 점두의 [경제] ❏ 어제 국내 장외 시장에서 클라르코르 주가가 6.125달러 폭락해 35.625달러로 마감했다.

Word Partnership	*counter*의 연어
PREP.	**behind the** counter, **on the** counter ■
	over the counter ❻
N.	counter **an argument** ❷

counter|act /ka͟ʊntəræ͟kt/ (**counteracts, counteracting, counteracted**) V-T To **counteract** something means to reduce its effect by doing something that produces an opposite effect. ❏ *My husband has to take several pills to counteract high blood pressure.*

타동사 막다 ❏ 남편은 혈압을 낮추는 약을 몇 알씩 먹어야 한다.

counter|attack /ka͟ʊntərətæk/ (**counterattacks, counterattacking, counterattacked**) [BRIT also **counter-attack**] V-I If you **counterattack**, you attack someone who has attacked you. ❏ *The security forces counterattacked the following day and quelled the unrest.* • N-COUNT **Counterattack** is also a noun. ❏ *The army began its counterattack this morning.*

[영국영어 counter-attack] 자동사 반격하다 ❏ 보안대가 다음날 반격하면서 소요 사태를 진압했다. • 가산명사 반격 ❏ 육군이 오늘 아침 반격을 시작했다.

counter|clockwise /ka͟ʊntərklɒ͟kwaɪz/ ADV If something is moving **counterclockwise**, it is moving in the opposite direction to the direction in which the hands of a clock move. [AM] [ADV after v] ❏ *Rotate the head clockwise and counterclockwise.* • ADJ **Counterclockwise** is also an adjective. [BRIT **anticlockwise**] [ADJ n] ❏ *The dance moves in a counter-clockwise direction.*

부사 반시계 방향으로 [미국영어] ❏ 고개를 시계 방향과 반시계 방향으로 돌려라. • 형용사 반시계 방향의 [영국영어 anticlockwise] ❏ 춤은 반시계 방향으로 진행된다.

counter|feit /ka͟ʊntərfɪt/ (**counterfeits, counterfeiting, counterfeited**) ■ ADJ **Counterfeit** money, goods, or documents are not genuine, but have been made to look exactly like genuine ones in order to deceive people. ❏ *He admitted possessing and delivering counterfeit currency.* • N-COUNT **Counterfeit** is also a noun. ❏ *Levi Strauss says counterfeits of the company's jeans are flooding Europe.* ❷ V-T If someone **counterfeits** something, they make a version of it that is not genuine but has been made to look genuine in order to deceive people. ❏ *...the coins Davies is alleged to have counterfeited.*

■ 형용사 위조된 ❏ 그는 위조지폐 소지 및 운반 사실을 시인했다. • 가산명사 위조돈, 모조품 ❏ 레비 스트라우스는 리바이스 청바지 모조품이 유럽 시장에 넘쳐 난다고 말한다. ❷ 타동사 위조하다 ❏ 데이비스가 위조했다는 동전

counter|part ◆◇◇ /ka͟ʊntərpɑrt/ (**counterparts**) N-COUNT Someone's or something's **counterpart** is another person or thing that has a similar function or position in a different place. ❏ *As soon as he heard what was afoot, the Foreign Secretary telephoned his German and Italian counterparts to protest.*

가산명사 상대편 사람; 상대되는 것 ❏ 무슨 일이 진행 중인지 듣자마자 외무 장관은 독일과 이탈리아 외무 장관에게 항의 전화를 했다.

counter|pro|duc|tive /ka͟ʊntərprədʌ͟ktɪv/ [BRIT also **counter-productive**] ADJ Something that is **counterproductive** achieves the opposite result from the one that you want to achieve. ❏ *In practice, however, such an attitude is counterproductive.*

[영국영어 counter-productive] 형용사 역효과의 ❏ 하지만 실제로 그와 같은 태도는 역효과를 낳을 뿐이다.

counter|top /ka͟ʊntərtɒp/ (**countertops**) N-COUNT A **countertop** is a flat surface in a kitchen which is easily cleaned and on which you can prepare food. [AM; BRIT **worktop, work surface**] ❏ *She reached for a cloth and began scouring the countertop.*

가산명사 조리대 [미국영어; 영국영어 worktop, work surface] ❏ 그녀는 행주를 들고 조리대를 문질러 닦기 시작했다.

count|less /ka͟ʊntlɪs/ ADJ **Countless** means very many. [ADJ n] ❏ *She brought joy to countless people through her music.*

형용사 무수한 ❏ 그녀는 음악을 통해 수없이 많은 사람들에게 기쁨을 줬다.

count noun (**count nouns**) N-COUNT A **count noun** is a noun such as "bird," "chair," or "year" which has a singular and a plural form and is always used after a determiner in the singular.

가산명사 가산 명사

coun|try ◆◆◆ /kʌ͟ntri/ (**countries**) ■ N-COUNT A **country** is one of the political units which the world is divided into, covering a particular area of land. ❏ *Indonesia is the fifth most populous country in the world.* ❏ *...that disputed boundary*

■ 가산명사 나라, 국가 ❏ 인도네시아는 세계에서 다섯 번째로 인구가 많은 국가이다. ❏ 양국의 분쟁 대상인 국경 ❷ 단수명사 국민 ❏ 국민들이 네 번 연속 토리당

between the two countries. ◨ N-SING **The people** who live in a particular country can be referred to as **the country**. ❑ *The country had confounded the pundits by electing a fourth-term Tory government.* ◨ N-SING **The country** consists of places such as farms, open fields, and villages which are away from towns and cities. ❑ *...a healthy life in the country.* ❑ *She was cycling along a country road near Compiegne.* ◪ N-UNCOUNT A particular kind of **country** is an area of land which has particular characteristics or is connected with a particular well-known person. ❑ *Varese Ligure is a small town in mountainous country east of Genoa.* ◫ N-UNCOUNT **Country** music is popular music from the southern United States. ❑ *For a long time I just wanted to play country music.* ◬ PHRASE If you travel **across country**, you travel through country areas, avoiding major roads and towns. ❑ *From here we walked across country to Covington.*
→see Word Web: **country**

정부를 선출하면서 전문가들의 예상을 뒤엎었다. ◨ 단수명사 시골, 전원 ❑ 건강한 전원생활 ❑ 그녀는 자전거를 타고 콩피에뉴 근처 시골 도로를 달리고 있었다. ◪ 불가산명사 지역, 지방 ❑ 바레세 리구레는 제노바 동쪽 산악 지방에 자리한 작은 마을이다. ◫ 불가산명사 컨트리 뮤직 ❑ 오랫동안 나는 그냥 컨트리 뮤직을 하고 싶었다. ◬ 구 들판으로, 큰 도로를 이용하지 않고 ❑ 우리는 이곳에서부터 큰 도로를 피해 코빙턴까지 걸었다.

Country is the most usual word to use when you are talking about the major political units that the world is divided into. **State** is used when you are talking about politics or government institutions. ❑ *...the new German state created by the unification process....Italy's state-controlled telecommunications company.* **State** can also refer to a political unit within a particular country. ❑ *...the state of California.* **Nation** is often used when you are talking about a country's inhabitants, and their cultural or ethnic background. ❑ *Wales is a proud nation with its own traditions... A senior government spokesman will address the nation.* **Land** is a less precise and more literary word, which you can use, for example, to talk about the feelings you have for a particular country. ❑ *She was fascinated to learn about this strange land at the edge of Europe.*

country는 세계를 나누는 주요 정치 단위에 대해 얘기할 때 쓰는 가장 일반적인 말이다. state는 정치나 정부 기관에 대해 얘기할 때 쓴다. ❑ ...통일 과정에 의해 만들어진 새 독일 정부.... 정부가 관장하는 이태리 통신 회사. state는 특정 국가 내의 정치 단위를 가리킬 수도 있다. ❑ ...캘리포니아 주. nation은 한 나라의 거주자, 거주자의 문화적 또는 인종적 배경을 얘기할 때 흔히 쓴다. ❑ 웨일스는 고유의 전통을 통해 자부심을 지닌 나라이다... 정부 고위 대변인이 국민들에게 연설할 것이다. land는 덜 정확하고 더 문학적인 말이며, 예를 들면 특정 국가에 대한 감정을 얘기할 때 쓸 수 있다. ❑ 그녀는 유럽의 가장자리에 있는 이 낯선 땅에 대해 배우는 데 매료되었다.

---

country|man /kʌntrimən/ (**countrymen**) N-COUNT Your **countrymen** are people from your own country. ❑ *He beat his fellow countryman, Andre Agassi, 6-4, 6-3, 6-2.*

가산명사 같은 나라 사람, 동포 ❑ 그는 같은 나라 출신인 안드레 아가시를 6-4, 6-3, 6-2로 꺾었다.

country|side ◆◇◇ /kʌntrisaɪd/ N-UNCOUNT **The countryside** is land which is away from towns and cities. ❑ *I've always loved the English countryside.*
→see **city**

불가산명사 시골 ❑ 나는 잉글랜드 시골 지방이 항상 좋았다.

Do not confuse **countryside**, **scenery**, **landscape**, and **nature**. **Countryside** is land which is away from towns and cities. ❑ *...3,500 acres of mostly flat countryside.* With **landscape**, the emphasis is on the physical features of the land, while **scenery** includes everything you can see when you look out over an area of land. ❑ *...the landscape of steep woods and distant mountains....unattractive urban scenery.* **Nature** includes the landscape, the weather, animals, and plants. ❑ *These creatures roamed the Earth as the finest and rarest wonders of nature.*

countryside, scenery, landscape, nature를 혼동하지 않도록 하라. countryside는 중소 도시나 대도시에서 떨어져 있는 땅이다. ❑ ... 대부분이 평지인 3,500에이커의 시골 지역. scenery는 어떤 지역에서 눈에 보이는 모든 것을 포함하는 반면, landscape는 땅의 물리적 특징을 강조한다. ❑ ...우뚝 서 있는 숲과 멀리 산이 보이는 경치...볼품없는 도회지 풍경. nature는 경치, 날씨, 동물, 식물을 포함한다. ❑ 이 생물체들은 가장 멋지고 가장 희귀한 자연의 경이로서 지구상을 활보했다.

---

coun|ty ◆◆◇ /kaʊnti/ (**counties**) N-COUNT A **county** is a region of the U.S., Britain, or Ireland, which has its own local government. ❑ *He is living now in his mother's home county of Oxfordshire.*

가산명사 카운티, 지역구 ❑ 그는 현재 옥스퍼드 주에 있는 어머니의 고향인 지역구에서 살고 있다.

coup ◆◇◇ /ku/ (**coups**) ◨ N-COUNT When there is a **coup**, a group of people seize power in a country. ❑ *...a military coup.* ◨ N-COUNT A **coup** is an achievement which is thought to be especially good because it was very difficult. ❑ *The sale is a big coup for the auction house.*

◨ 가산명사 쿠데타 ❑ 군사 쿠데타 ◨ 가산명사 성과, 성공 ❑ 이번 낙찰은 경매소에게 큰 성과였다.

Word Partnership　coup의 연어

N.	coup **attempt**, **leader of the** coup ◨
V.	**plot a** coup, **support the** coup ◨
ADJ.	**military** coup ◨
	big coup ◨

---

coup d'état /ku deɪtɑ/ (**coups d'état**) N-COUNT When there is a **coup d'état**, a group of people seize power in a country.

가산명사 쿠데타

cou|ple ◆◆◇ /kʌpᵊl/ (**couples, coupling, coupled**) ◨ QUANT If you refer to **a couple of** people or things, you mean two or approximately two of them, although the exact number is not important or you are not sure of it. [QUANT of pl-n] ❑ *Across the street from me there are a couple of police officers standing guard.* ❑ *I think the trouble will clear up in a couple of days.* ● DET **Couple** is also a

◨ 수량사 두어 개의 ❑ 길 건너 내 반대편에 경찰 두어 명이 보초를 서고 있다. ❑ 이틀 정도만 지나면 문제가 사라질 거라고 생각한다. ● 한정사 두어 개의 ❑ 선거 전 2주 정도 ● 대명사 두어 개 ❑ 상태가 그다지 나쁘지 않은 물건 두어 개가 있다. ◨ 가산명사-집합 커플, 부부

Word Web　country

The largest **country** in the world geographically is Russia. It has an area of six million square miles and a **population** of more than 142 million people. Russia is a federal state with a republican form of **government**. The government is based in Russia's **capital** city, Moscow.

One of the smallest countries in the world is Naru. This tiny island **nation** in the South Pacific Ocean is 8.1 square miles in size. Many of Naru's more than 13,00 **residents** live in Yaren, which is the largest city, but not the capital. The Republic of Naru is the only nation in the world without an official capital.

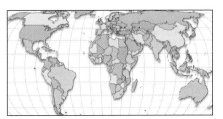

determiner in spoken American English, and before "more" and "less." ❑ *...a couple weeks before the election.* ● PRON **Couple** is also a pronoun. ❑ *I've got a couple that don't look too bad.* **2** N-COUNT-COLL A **couple** is two people who are married, living together, or having a sexual relationship. ❑ *The couple have no children.* ❑ *...after burglars ransacked an elderly couple's home.* **3** N-COUNT-COLL A **couple** is two people that you see together on a particular occasion or that have some association. ❑ *...as the four couples began the opening dance.* **4** V-T If you say that one thing produces a particular effect when it **is coupled with** another, you mean that the two things combine to produce that effect. [usu passive] ❑ *...a problem that is coupled with lower demand for the machines themselves.*

❑ 그 부부는 아이가 없다. ❑ 강도가 한 노부부의 집을 턴 후에 **2** 가산명사-집합 쌍 ❑ 네 쌍이 오프닝 댄스를 시작하자 **4** 타동사 ~와 결부되다, ~와 겹치다 **4** 기계 자체에 대한 수요 하락과 겹쳐 나타난 문제

cou|pon /kuːpɒn, kyuː-/ (**coupons**) **1** N-COUNT A **coupon** is a piece of printed paper which allows you to pay less money than usual for a product, or to get it free. ❑ *...a money-saving coupon.* **2** N-COUNT A **coupon** is a small form, for example in a newspaper or magazine, which you send off to ask for information, to order something, or to enter a competition. ❑ *Mail this coupon with your check or money order.*

1 가산명사 쿠폰 ❑ 돈을 절약하는 쿠폰 **2** 가산명사 (신문이나 잡지에 포함된) 우편엽서, 응모권 ❑ 이 응모권을 수표나 우편환과 함께 우편으로 보내세요.

cour|age ◆◇◇ /kɜːrɪdʒ, BRIT kʌrɪdʒ/ N-UNCOUNT **Courage** is the quality shown by someone who decides to do something difficult or dangerous, even though they may be afraid. ❑ *General Lewis Mackenzie has impressed everyone with his authority and personal courage.* **2** to **pluck up the courage** →see pluck

1 불가산명사 용기 ❑ 루이스 매켄지 장군은 권위와 용기로 모든 이에게 감명을 주었다.

Word Partnership	courage의 연어
v.	courage **to do** *something*, **find the** courage, **have the** courage, **show** courage **1**
ADJ.	**great** courage **1**

cour|ageous /kəreɪdʒəs/ ADJ Someone who is **courageous** shows courage. ❑ *It was a very frightening experience and they were very courageous.*

형용사 용기 있는 ❑ 매우 무서운 일이었지만 그들은 아주 용기 있게 맞섰다.

cour|gette /kʊrʒet/ (**courgettes**) N-VAR **Courgettes** are long thin vegetables with dark green skin. [BRIT; AM zucchini]

가산명사 또는 불가산명사 서양 호박 [영국영어; 미국영어 zucchini]

cou|ri|er /kʊəriər, kɜːr-/ (**couriers**, **couriering**, **couriered**) **1** N-COUNT A **courier** is a person who is paid to take letters and parcels direct from one place to another. ❑ *He worked as a motorcycle courier.* **2** V-T If you **courier** something somewhere, you send it there by courier. ❑ *I couriered it to Darren in New York.*

1 가산명사 배달원 ❑ 그는 퀵서비스 배달원으로 일했다. **2** 타동사 퀵서비스로 보내다 ❑ 나는 뉴욕에 있는 다른에게 그것을 택배로 보냈다.

course ◆◆◆ /kɔːrs/ (**courses**, **coursing**, **coursed**) **1** **Course** is often used in the expression "of course," or instead of "of course" in informal spoken English. See **of course**. **2** N-UNCOUNT The **course** of a vehicle, especially a ship or aircraft, is the route along which it is traveling. [also a N] ❑ *Aircraft can avoid each other by going up and down, as well as by altering course to left or right.* **3** N-COUNT A **course of** action is an action or a series of actions that you can do in a particular situation. ❑ *My best course of action was to help Gill by being loyal, loving and endlessly sympathetic.* **4** V-T A **course** is a series of lessons or lectures on a particular subject. ❑ *...a course in business administration.* →see also **correspondence course, refresher course 5** N-COUNT A **course of** medical treatment is a series of treatments that a doctor gives someone. ❑ *Treatment is supplemented with a course of antibiotics to kill the bacterium.* **6** N-COUNT A **course** is one part of a meal. ❑ *The lunch was excellent, especially the first course.* **7** N-COUNT In sports, a **course** is an area of land where races are held or golf is played, or the land over which a race takes place. ❑ *Only 12 seconds separated the first three riders on the Bickerstaffe course.* **8** N-COUNT The **course** of a river is the channel along which it flows. ❑ *Romantic chateaux and castles overlook the river's twisting course.* **9** PHRASE If something happens **in the course of** a particular period of time, it happens during that period of time. ❑ *In the course of the 1930s steel production in Britain approximately doubled.* **10** PHRASE If you do something **as a matter of course**, you do it as part of your normal work or way of life. ❑ *If police are carrying arms as a matter of course then doesn't it encourage criminals to carry them?* **11** PHRASE If a ship or aircraft is **on course**, it is traveling along the correct route. If it is **off course**, it is no longer traveling along the correct course. ❑ *The ill fated ship was sent off course into shallow waters and rammed by another vessel.* **12** PHRASE If you are **on course for** something, you are likely to achieve it. ❑ *The company is on course for profits of $20m.* **13** **in due course** →see due

1 물론 **2** 불가산명사 운항로, 항로 ❑ 비행기는 좌우 항로 변경은 물론 위아래로 움직여서 다른 비행기와의 충돌을 피할 수 있다. **3** 가산명사 방침, 노선 ❑ 나의 최선의 행동 방침은 한결 같은 사랑과 따뜻한 마음으로 질을 돕는 것이었다. **4** 가산명사 과정, 강좌 ❑ 경영학 과정 **5** 가산명사 일련의 치료 ❑ 치료와 함께 세균을 없애기 위해 항생제도 투여한다. **6** 가산명사 코스 요리 ❑ 오찬은 훌륭했다. 특히 첫 번째 요리가 맛있었다. **7** 가산명사 코스, 경기장 ❑ 비커스테프 경기장에서 겨우 12초 만에 세 명의 선두가 들어왔다. **8** 가산명사 수로 ❑ 로맨틱한 저택과 성들이 구불구불 흐르는 강을 내려다보고 있다. **9** 구 - 중에 ❑ 1930년대에 영국 철강 생산량이 대략 두 배로 뛰었다. **10** 구 아무렇지도 않게, 당연하다는 듯이 ❑ 경찰이 당연하다는 듯이 총기를 소지하게 되면 범죄자의 무기 소지도 부추기지 않을까? **11** 구 침로대로; 침로를 벗어나 ❑ 그 비운의 배가 얕은 물 쪽으로 침로를 벗어난 후 다른 배에 부딪혔다. **12** 구 순조로운, 착착 진행 중인 ❑ 그 회사는 2천만 달러의 이익을 향해 순조롭게 진행 중이다.

Word Partnership	course의 연어
N.	course **of** *something* **2 3 5**
	course **of action 3**
	golf course **7**
ADJ.	**full-time** course **4**
	main course **6**

course book (**course books**) also **coursebook** N-COUNT A **course book** is a textbook that students and teachers use as the basis of a course.

가산명사 교과서

course work also **coursework** N-UNCOUNT **Course work** is work that students do during a course, rather than in exams, especially work that counts towards a student's final grade. ❑ *Some 20 per cent of marks are awarded for coursework.*

불가산명사 수업 ❑ 수업이 점수의 20퍼센트 정도를 차지한다.

Word Partnership	court의 연어
v.	**appear in** court, **hold** court ① **1**
	go to court ① **1 5**

```
court
① NOUN USES
② VERB USES
```

① **court** ◆◆◆ /kɔrt/ (**courts**) ■ N-COUNT A **court** is a place where legal matters are decided by a judge and jury or by a magistrate. [oft N N, N N, also in/at N] ❑ At this rate, we could find ourselves in the divorce courts! ❑ ...a county court judge. ② N-COUNT You can refer to the people in a court, especially the judge, jury, or magistrates, as a **court**. ❑ A court at Tampa, Florida has convicted five officials on charges of handling millions of dollars earned from illegal drugs deals. ③ N-COUNT A **court** is an area in which you play a game such as tennis, basketball, badminton, or squash. [usu supp N, also on/off N] ❑ The hotel has several tennis and squash courts. ④ N-COUNT The **court** of a king or queen is the place where he or she lives and carries out ceremonial or administrative duties. [oft with poss, also at N] ❑ She came to visit England, where she was presented at the court of James I. ⑤ PHRASE If you **go to court** or **take** someone **to court**, you take legal action against them. ❑ They have received at least twenty thousand pounds each but had gone to court to demand more. ⑥ PHRASE If a legal matter is decided or settled **out of court**, it is decided without legal action being taken in a court of law. ❑ The Government is anxious to keep the whole case out of court.
→see park

② **court** /kɔrt/ (**courts, courting, courted**) ■ V-T To **court** a particular person, group, or country means to try to please them or improve your relations with them, often so that they will do something that you want them to do. [JOURNALISM] ❑ Both Democratic and Republican parties are courting former supporters of Ross Perot. ② V-T If you **court** something such as publicity or popularity, you try to attract it. ❑ Having spent a lifetime avidly courting publicity, Paul has suddenly become secretive. ③ V-T If you **court** something unpleasant such as disaster or unpopularity, you act in a way that makes it likely to happen. ❑ If he thinks he can remain in power by force he is courting disaster.

cour|teous /kɜrtiəs/ ADJ Someone who is **courteous** is polite and respectful to other people. ❑ He was a kind and courteous man. ● **cour|teous|ly** ADV ❑ Then he nodded courteously to me and walked off to perform his unpleasant duty.

cour|tesy /kɜrtisi/ ■ N-UNCOUNT **Courtesy** is politeness, respect, and consideration for others. [FORMAL] ❑ ...a gentleman who behaves with the utmost courtesy towards ladies. ② N-SING If you refer to **the courtesy of** doing something, you are referring to a polite action. [FORMAL] ❑ By extending the courtesy of a phone call to my clients, I was building a personal relationship with them. ③ ADJ **Courtesy** is used to describe services that are provided free of charge by an organization to its customers, or to the general public. [ADJ n] ❑ A courtesy shuttle bus operates between the hotel and the town. ④ ADJ A **courtesy** call or a **courtesy** visit is a formal visit that you pay someone as a way of showing them politeness or respect. [ADJ n] ❑ The President paid a courtesy call on Emperor Akihito. ⑤ PHRASE If something is provided **courtesy of** someone or **by courtesy of** someone, they provide it. You often use this expression in order to thank them. ❑ The waitress brings over some congratulatory glasses of champagne, courtesy of the restaurant.

court|house /kɔrthaʊs/ (**courthouses**) ■ N-COUNT A **courthouse** is a building in which a court of law meets. [AM; BRIT **court**] ❑ The two were tried in the same courthouse at the same time, on separate floors. ② N-COUNT A **courthouse** is a building used by the government of a county. [AM] ❑ They were married at the Los Angeles County Courthouse.

court|ier /kɔrtiər/ (**courtiers**) N-COUNT **Courtiers** were noblemen and women who spent a lot of time at the court of a king or queen.

court martial (**court martials, court martialing, court martialed**) also **court-martial**

> The spellings **court martialling** and **court martialled** are used in British English and sometimes in American English. **Courts martial** is also used as a plural form for the noun.

■ N-VAR A **court martial** is a trial in a military court of a member of the armed forces who is charged with breaking a military law. ❑ He is due to face a court martial on drugs charges. ② V-T If a member of the armed forces **is court martialed**, he or she is tried in a military court. [usu passive] ❑ I was court martialed and sentenced to six months in a military prison.

court|room /kɔrtrum/ (**courtrooms**) N-COUNT A **courtroom** is a room in which a legal court meets.

court|yard /kɔrtyɑrd/ (**courtyards**) N-COUNT A **courtyard** is an open area of ground which is surrounded by buildings or walls. ❑ They walked through the arch and into the cobbled courtyard.

cous|in ◆◇◇ /kʌzⁿn/ (**cousins**) N-COUNT Your **cousin** is the child of your uncle or aunt. ❑ My cousin Mark helped me.

cove /koʊv/ (**coves**) N-COUNT; N-IN-NAMES A **cove** is a part of a coast where the land curves inward so that the sea is partly enclosed. ❑ ...a hillside overlooking Fairview Cove.

cov|enant /kʌvənənt/ (**covenants**) ■ N-COUNT A **covenant** is a formal written agreement between two or more people or groups of people which is recognized in law. ❑ ...the International Covenant on Civil and Political Rights. ② N-COUNT A **covenant** is a formal written promise to pay a sum of money each year for a fixed period, especially to a charity. [mainly BRIT; AM usually

■ 가산명사 법정, 법원 ❑ 우리가 이런 식으로 가면 이혼 법정에까지 서게 될 수도 있어! ❑ 카운티 법원 판사 ② 가산명사 법원 ❑ 플로리다 탐파의 한 법원이 불법 마약 거래로 번 수백만 달러에 손댄 혐의로 공무원 5명에게 유죄 판결을 내렸다. ③ 가산명사 코트, 경기장 ❑ 그 호텔에는 테니스와 스쿼시 경기장 몇 개가 있다. ④ 가산명사 왕실, 궁정 ❑ 그녀는 영국을 방문해 제임스 1세 왕실에서 배알했다. ⑤ 구 소송을 제기하다 ❑ 그들은 각각 최소한 2만 파운드씩 받았지만 원래는 더 높은 액수를 받기 위해 소송을 제기했었다. ⑥ 구 법정 밖에서, 합의로 ❑ 정부는 그 사건을 모두 법정 밖에서 해결하길 바란다.

■ 타동사 비위 맞추다 [언론] ❑ 민주 공화 양당이 이전에 로스 페로를 지지한 사람들의 비위를 맞추고 있다. ② 타동사 추구하다 ❑ 평생 화려한 스포트라이트를 쫓으며 살아온 폴이 어느 순간부터 모습을 감추고 있다. ③ 타동사 자초하다 ❑ 그가 만약 힘으로 권력을 유지할 수 있다고 생각한다면, 재앙을 자초하는 것이다.

형용사 예의 바른, 정중한 ❑ 그는 친절하고 예의 바른 사람이었다. ● 깍듯이, 정중히 부사 ❑ 그리고 나서 그는 나에게 깍듯이 인사를 하고 재미있는 임무를 수행하러 걸어갔다.

■ 불가산명사 예의 [격식체] ❑ 최대한 예의를 갖추고 숙녀를 대하는 신사 ② 단수명사 호의, 정중한 행동 [격식체] ❑ 나는 직접 전화를 거는 호의를 베풀어서 고객과의 인간적인 관계를 형성하고 있었다. ③ 형용사 무료의 ❑ 호텔과 읍내 간에 무료 버스를 운행 중이다. ④ 형용사 예의를 표하는 ❑ 대통령이 아키히토 일왕을 예방했다. ⑤ 구 – 제공 ❑ 웨이트리스가 레스토랑이 서비스로 제공하는 축하 샴페인 몇 잔을 갖다 준다.

■ 가산명사 법원 청사, 재판소 [미국영어; 영국영어 court] ❑ 그 둘은 같은 시간 같은 재판소의 서로 다른 층에서 재판을 받았다. ② 가산명사 지방 정부 청사 [미국영어] ❑ 그들은 로스앤젤레스 카운티 청사에서 결혼했다.

가산명사 왕실 사람들

> 철자 court martialling과 court martialled는 영국영어에서 쓰며, 가끔 미국영어에서도 쓴다. courts martial은 명사의 복수형으로도 쓴다.

■ 가산명사 또는 불가산명사 군법 회의 ❑ 그는 마약 복용 혐의로 군법 회의에 회부되기로 되어 있다. ② 타동사 군법 회의에 회부되다 ❑ 나는 군법 회의에 회부되어 영창에서 6개월을 선고받았다.

가산명사 법정

가산명사 안마당, 안뜰 ❑ 그들은 아치형 문을 걸어 나가 자갈이 깔린 안뜰로 향했다.

가산명사 사촌 ❑ 사촌 마크가 나를 도왔다.

가산명사; 이름명사 만 ❑ 페어뷰 만이 내려다보이는 산허리

■ 가산명사 계약, 규약 ❑ 시민적·정치적 권리에 관한 국제 규약 ② 가산명사 기부서약 [주로 영국영어; 미국영어 대개 pledge] ❑ 기부 서약을 통해 정기적으로 기부를 하시면, 귀하가 그 금액에 관해 이미 지급한 소득세를 저희가 이중으로 지불하지 않아도 됩니다.

A

B

C

D

E

F

G

H

I

J

K

L

M

N

O

pledge] [also by N] *If you make regular gifts through a covenant we can reclaim the income tax which you have already paid on this money.*

cov|er ♦♦♦ /kʌvər/ (covers, covering, covered) **1** V-T If you **cover** something, you place something else over it in order to protect it, hide it, or close it. ❑ *Cover the casserole with a tight-fitting lid.* ❑ *He whimpered and covered his face.* **2** V-T If one thing **covers** another, it has been placed over it in order to protect it, hide it, or close it. ❑ *His finger went up to touch the black patch which covered his left eye.* **3** V-T If one thing **covers** another, it forms a layer over its surface. ❑ *The clouds had spread and nearly covered the entire sky.* ❑ *The desk was covered with papers.* **4** V-T To **cover** something **with** or **in** something else means to put a layer of the second thing over its surface. ❑ *The trees in your garden may have covered the ground with apples, pears or plums.* **5** V-T If you **cover** a particular distance, you travel that distance. ❑ *It would not be easy to cover ten miles on that amount of petrol.* **6** N-UNCOUNT **Cover** is protection from enemy attack that is provided for troops or ships carrying out a particular operation, for example by aircraft. ❑ *They said they could not provide adequate air cover for ground operations.* **7** N-UNCOUNT **Cover** is trees, rocks, or other places where you shelter from the weather or from an attack, or hide from someone. ❑ *Charles lit the fuses and they ran for cover.* **8** V-T An insurance policy that **covers** a person or thing guarantees that money will be paid by the insurance company in relation to that person or thing. ❑ *Their insurer paid the £900 bill, even though the policy did not strictly cover it.* **9** N-UNCOUNT Insurance **cover** is a guarantee from an insurance company that money will be paid if it is needed. ❑ *Make sure that the firm's insurance cover is adequate.* **10** V-T If a law **covers** a particular set of people, things, or situations, it applies to them. ❑ *The law covers four categories of experiments.* **11** V-T If you **cover** a particular topic, you discuss it in a lecture, course, or book. ❑ *The Oxford Chemistry Primers aim to cover important topics in organic chemistry.* **12** V-T If a sum of money **covers** something, it is enough to pay for it. ❑ *Send it to the address given with £1.50 to cover postage and administration.* **13** N-COUNT A **cover** is something which is put over an object, usually in order to protect it. ❑ *...a family room with washable covers on the furniture.* **14** N-PLURAL The **covers** on your bed are the things such as sheets and blankets that you have on top of you. ❑ *She set her glass down and slid farther under the covers.* **15** N-COUNT The **cover** of a book or a magazine is the outside part of it. ❑ *...a small spiral-bound booklet with a green cover.* **16** N-COUNT Something that is a **cover** for secret or illegal activities seems respectable or normal, and is intended to hide the activities. ❑ *They set up a spurious temple that was a cover for sexual debauchery.* **17** V-I If you **cover for** someone who is doing something secret or illegal, you give false information or do not give all the information you have, in order to protect them. ❑ *Why would she cover for someone who was trying to kill her?* **18** V-I If you **cover for** someone who is ill or away, you do their work for them while they are not there. ❑ *She did not have enough nurses to cover for those who were sick.* **19** →see also **covering** **20** PHRASE If you **take cover**, you shelter from gunfire, bombs, or the weather. ❑ *Shoppers took cover behind cars as police marksmen returned fire.* **21** PHRASE If you do something **under cover of** a particular situation, you are able to do it without being noticed because of that situation. ❑ *They move under cover of darkness.* **22** PHRASE If you **cover** your **back** or **cover** your **rear**, you do something in order to protect yourself, for example against criticism or against accusations of doing something wrong. ❑ *The canny Premier covered his back by pointing out that he was of Scottish stock.*

P

Thesaurus   cover의 참조어

v.   conceal, drape, hide, screen; (ant.) uncover **1** **2** **3**
      guard, insure, protect **8**

Q

Word Partnership   cover의 연어

N.	cover *your* face **1** **2**
V.	run for cover **6**
	take cover **20**
PREP.	covered in *something* **4**
	under cover **21**

R

S

▶**cover up** **1** PHRASAL VERB If you **cover** something or someone **up**, you put something over them in order to protect or hide them. ❑ *He fell asleep in the front room so I covered him up with a duvet.* **2** PHRASAL VERB If you **cover up** something that you do not want people to know about, you hide the truth about it. ❑ *He suspects there's a conspiracy to cover up the crime.* ❑ *They knew they had done something terribly wrong and lied to cover it up.* →see also **cover-up**

T

cov|er|age ♦♦♦ /kʌvərɪdʒ/ N-UNCOUNT The **coverage** of something in the news is the reporting of it. ❑ *Now a special TV network gives live coverage of most races.*

U

V

cov|er|ing /kʌvərɪŋ/ (coverings) N-COUNT A **covering** is a layer of something that protects or hides something else. ❑ *Leave a thin covering of fat.*

W

cov|er|ing let|ter (covering letters) N-COUNT A **covering letter** is the same as a **cover letter**. [BRIT] ❑ *Tailor your covering letter and CV to each job you apply for.*

X

cov|er let|ter (cover letters) N-COUNT A **cover letter** is a letter that you send with a package or with another letter in order to provide extra information. [AM; BRIT **covering letter**]

Y

cov|er|mount /kʌvərmaʊnt/ (covermounts) N-COUNT A **covermount** is a small gift attached to the front cover of a magazine. ❑ *The covermount with this week's mag is a handy guide to family holidays.*

Z

---

1 타동사 덮다, 가리다, 감추다 ❑ 캐서롤 냄비에 꼭 맞는 뚜껑을 덮으세요. ❑ 그는 훌쩍이며 얼굴을 가렸다. **2** 타동사 덮다, 가리다, 감추다 ❑ 그는 손가락을 올려 왼쪽 눈을 가리고 있는 검은 천 조각을 만졌다. **3** 타동사 뒤덮다 ❑ 구름이 퍼져서 거의 온 하늘을 뒤덮었고 책상이 서류로 뒤덮여 있었다. **4** 타동사 -로 뒤덮다 ❑ 당신의 정원에 있는 나무들이 사과, 배, 서양자두 등으로 땅을 뒤덮었을지도 모른다. **5** 타동사 가다 ❑ 휘발유 그만큼을 가지고 10마일을 가기가 쉽지 않을 것이다. **6** 불가산명사 엄호 ❑ 지상군을 공중에서 충분히 엄호할 수 없다고 그들이 말했다. **7** 불가산명사 피신처, 숨을 곳 ❑ 찰스가 도화선에 불을 붙이자 그들은 몸을 피해 달렸다. **8** 타동사 보험에 적용하다 ❑ 엄밀하게 보험 처리 대상은 아니었지만, 보험 회사가 900파운드를 지급했다. **9** 불가산명사 보험 적용 ❑ 기업의 보험 적용 내용이 충실한지 확인하세요. **10** 타동사 적용되다 ❑ 그 법은 네 가지 종류의 실험에 적용된다. **11** 타동사 다루다 ❑ 옥스퍼드 화학 입문서는 유기 화학에서 중요한 주제들을 다루기 위한 책이다. **12** 타동사 충당하다 ❑ 이것을 우편 요금 및 처리 비용 1.5파운드와 함께 다음 주소로 보내세요. **13** 가산명사 커버 ❑ 세탁 가능한 커버로 덮인 가구가 있는 거실 **14** 복수명사 침대 커버 ❑ 그녀는 유리컵을 내려놓고 이불 속으로 더 미끄러져 들어갔다. **15** 가산명사 표지 ❑ 초록색 표지의 작은 스프링 책 **16** 가산명사 위장, 구실 ❑ 그들은 가짜 사원을 세워 방탕한 성생활을 위장하는 데 사용했다. **17** 자동사 감싸다 ❑ 그녀가 왜 자신을 죽이려 한 사람을 감싸 주려 하겠어? **18** 자동사 대신 일하다 ❑ 그녀는 아픈 간호사들 대신 일할 간호사를 충분히 확보하지 못했다. **20** 구 숨다, 대피하다 ❑ 사격 경찰이 응사하자 쇼핑을 하던 시민들이 차 뒤로 몸을 피했다. **21** 구 - 을 틈타 ❑ 그들은 어둠을 틈타 움직인다. **22** 구 방패막이로 만들다 ❑ 빈틈없는 총리는 자신이 스코틀랜드 출신이라는 점을 방패막이로 사용했다.

1 구동사 덮어주다 ❑ 나는 거실에서 잠든 그에게 이불을 덮어 주었다. **2** 구동사 은폐하다 ❑ 그는 범죄를 은폐하기 위한 음모가 있을지도 모른다고 의심하고 있다. ❑ 그들은 자신들이 뭔가 단단히 잘못했다는 사실을 알고 이를 은폐하기 위해 거짓말을 했다.

불가산명사 보도 ❑ 이제 전문 TV 네트워크가 경기 대부분을 생방송한다.

가산명사 막 ❑ 얇은 지방 막을 남겨 두세요.

가산명사 신청서, 소개서 [영국영어] ❑ 자기소개서와 이력서를 지원하는 직업에 맞게 작성하세요.

가산명사 신청서, 소개서 [미국영어; 영국영어 covering letter]

가산명사 책 속 부록 ❑ 이번 주 잡지 책 속 부록은 편리한 가족여행 안내서이다.

cov|ert /koʊvɜrt, kʌvərt/ ADJ **Covert** activities or situations are secret or hidden. [FORMAL] ❏ *They have been supplying covert military aid to the rebels.* ● **cov|ert|ly** ADV ❏ *They covertly observed Lauren, who was sitting between Ned and Algie at a nearby table.*

형용사 비밀의, 은밀한 [격식체] ❏ 그들은 근거에게 군사적인 지원을 해왔다. ● 비밀리에, 암암리에 부사 ❏ 그들은 근처 테이블에 네드와 앨지 사이에 앉아 있는 로렌을 은밀히 지켜봤다.

cover-up /ˈkʌvər ʌp/ (**cover-ups**) [AM also **coverup**] N-COUNT A **cover-up** is an attempt to hide a crime or mistake. ❏ *General Schwarzkopf denied there'd been any cover-up.*

[미국영어 coverup] 가산명사 은폐 ❏ 슈바르츠코프 장군이 은폐 사실을 전면 부인했다.

cov|et /kʌvɪt/ (**covets, coveting, coveted**) V-T If you **covet** something, you strongly want to have it for yourself. [FORMAL] ❏ *She coveted his job so openly that conversations between them were tense.*

타동사 몹시 탐내다 [격식체] ❏ 그녀는 드러내 놓고 그의 자리를 탐내는 바람에 둘 사이의 대화에 긴장감이 돌았다.

cov|et|ed /kʌvɪtɪd/ ADJ You use **coveted** to describe something that very many people would like to have. ❏ *Allan Little from Radio 4 took the coveted title of reporter of the year.* ❏ *...one of sport's most coveted trophies.*

형용사 선망의 대상인, 영예의 ❏ 라디오4의 앨런 리틀이 올해의 기자로 뽑히는 영예를 차지했다. ❏ 스포츠 계의 가장 영예로운 트로피 중의 하나

cow /kaʊ/ (**cows, cowing, cowed**) **1** N-COUNT A **cow** is a large female animal that is kept on farms for its milk. People sometimes refer to male and female animals of this species as **cows**. ❏ *He kept a few dairy cows.* ❏ *Dad went out to milk the cows.* **2** N-COUNT Some female animals, including elephants and whales, are called **cows**. ❏ *...a cow elephant.* **3** V-T If someone **is cowed**, they are made afraid, or made to behave in a particular way because they have been frightened or badly treated. [FORMAL] ❏ *The government, far from being cowed by these threats, has vowed to continue its policy.* ● **cowed** ADJ ❏ *By this time she was so cowed by the beatings that she meekly obeyed.* →see **dairy**, **meat**

1 가산명사 젖소 ❏ 그는 젖소 몇 마리를 키웠다. ❏ 아빠가 소젖을 짜려고 나가셨다. **2** 가산명사 (코끼리나 고래의) 암컷 ❏ 코끼리 암컷 **3** 타동사 겁먹다, 위협을 느끼다 [격식체] ❏ 정부는 이와 같은 위협에 겁을 먹기는커녕 정책을 계속 추진하겠다고 선언했다. ● 겁먹은 형용사 ❏ 이때쯤 그녀는 구타로 너무 겁을 먹었기 때문에 순순히 복종했다.

cow|ard /kaʊərd/ (**cowards**) N-COUNT If you call someone a **coward**, you disapprove of them because they are easily frightened and avoid dangerous or difficult situations. [DISAPPROVAL] ❏ *She accused her husband of being a coward.*

가산명사 겁쟁이 [탐탁찮음] ❏ 그녀는 남편을 겁쟁이라고 비난했다.

cow|ard|ice /kaʊərdɪs/ N-UNCOUNT **Cowardice** is cowardly behavior. ❏ *He openly accused his opponents of cowardice.*

불가산명사 비겁함 ❏ 그는 상대방의 비겁함을 공개적으로 비난했다.

cow|ard|ly /kaʊərdli/ ADJ If you describe someone as **cowardly**, you disapprove of them because they are easily frightened and avoid doing dangerous and difficult things. [DISAPPROVAL] ❏ *I was too cowardly to complain.*

형용사 비겁한 [탐탁찮음] ❏ 나는 비겁해서 불평도 하지 못했다.

cow|boy /kaʊbɔɪ/ (**cowboys**) **1** N-COUNT A **cowboy** is a male character in a western. ❏ *Boys used to play at cowboys and Indians.* **2** N-COUNT A **cowboy** is a man employed to look after cattle in North America, especially in former times. ❏ *In his twenties Roosevelt had sought work as a cowboy on a ranch in the Dakota Territory.* **3** N-COUNT You can refer to someone who runs a business as a **cowboy** if they run it dishonestly or are not experienced, skillful, or careful in their work. [BRIT, DISAPPROVAL] ❏ *We don't want to look like a bunch of cowboys.* →see **horse**

1 가산명사 카우보이 ❏ 남자 아이들이 카우보이와 인디언으로 나눠 서부극 놀이를 하곤 했다. **2** 가산명사 카우보이, 목동 ❏ 루즈벨트는 이십대에 다코타 지역에 있는 목장에서 목동 일을 찾아다녔다. **3** 가산명사 막가는 사람 [영국영어, 탐탁찮음] ❏ 우리가 막가는 사람들처럼 보이기는 싫다.

coy /kɔɪ/ **1** ADJ A **coy** person is shy, or pretends to be shy, about love and sex. ❏ *I was sickened by the way Carol charmed all the men by turning coy.* ● **coy|ly** ADV [ADV with v] ❏ *She smiled coyly at Algie as he took her hand and raised it to his lips.* **2** ADJ If someone is **coy**, they are unwilling to talk about something that they feel guilty or embarrassed about. ❏ *Mr. Alexander is not the slightest bit coy about his ambitions.* ● **coy|ly** ADV [ADV with v] ❏ *The administration coyly refused to put a firm figure on the war's costs.*

1 형용사 내숭떠는 ❏ 나는 캐롤이 내숭을 떨면서 모든 남자들을 꼬시는 것에 신물이 났다. ● 부끄러운 척하며, 내숭을 떨며 부사 ❏ 앨지가 그녀의 손을 들어 입을 맞추자 그녀는 부끄러운 척 웃었다. **2** 형용사 말하기 꺼리는 ❏ 알렉산더 씨는 조금도 꺼리지 않고 자신의 야망에 대해 말한다. ● 말하기 꺼려하며 부사 ❏ 행정부는 전쟁 비용에 대한 확실한 수치를 알리기 꺼려했다.

cozy /koʊzi/ (**cozier, coziest**) [BRIT **cosy**] **1** ADJ A house or room that is **cozy** is comfortable and warm. ❏ *Downstairs there's a breakfast room and guests can relax in the cozy bar.* **2** ADJ If you are **cozy**, you are comfortable and warm. [v-link ADJ] ❏ *They like to make sure their guests are comfortable and cozy.* **3** ADJ You use **cozy** to describe activities that are pleasant and friendly, and involve people who know each other well. ❏ *...a cozy chat between friends.*

[영국영어 cosy] **1** 형용사 아늑한 ❏ 아래층에 조반용 식당이 있으며 손님들은 아늑한 바에서 쉴 수 있다. **2** 형용사 편안한, 아늑한 ❏ 그들은 손님들에게 편안하고 아늑한 공간을 제공하고 싶어 한다. **3** 형용사 편안한 ❏ 친구 사이의 편안한 대화

CPU /si pi yu/ (**CPUs**) N-COUNT In a computer, the **CPU** is the part that processes all the data and makes the computer work. **CPU** is an abbreviation for "central processing unit." [COMPUTING]

가산명사 (컴퓨터) 중앙 처리 장치 [컴퓨터]

crab /kræb/ (**crabs**) N-COUNT A **crab** is a sea creature with a flat round body covered by a shell, and five pairs of legs with large claws on the front pair. Crabs usually move sideways. ● N-UNCOUNT **Crab** is the flesh of this creature eaten as food. ❏ *I can't remember when I last had crab.*

가산명사 게 ● 불가산명사 게살 ❏ 내가 게요리를 마지막으로 먹었던 때가 언제였는지 모르겠다.

Word Partnership	crack의 연어		
ADJ.	crack **open** ① **1** **4**		
N.	crack **a code**, crack **the system** ① **5**		
	crack **jokes** ① **8**		
V.	**have a** crack ② **1** **3**		
ADJ.	**deep** crack ② **1** **3**		

--- **crack** ---

① VERB USES
② NOUN AND ADJECTIVE USES

① **crack** ♦♢♢ /kræk/ (**cracks, cracking, cracked**) **1** V-T/V-I If something hard **cracks**, or if you **crack** it, it becomes slightly damaged, with lines appearing on its surface. ❏ *A gas main had cracked under my neighbor's garage and gas had seeped into our homes.* **2** V-T/V-I If something **cracks**, or if you **crack** it, it makes a sharp sound like the sound of a piece of wood breaking. ❏ *Thunder cracked in the sky.* **3** V-T If you **crack** a hard part of your body, such as your knee or your head, you hurt it by accidentally hitting it hard against something. ❏ *He cracked his head on the pavement and was knocked cold.* **4** V-T When you **crack** something that has a shell, such as an egg or a nut, you break the shell in order to reach the inside part. ❏ *Crack the eggs into a bowl.* **5** V-T If you **crack** a problem or a code, you solve

1 타동사/자동사 금이 가다; 금이 가게 하다 ❏ 이웃집 차고 밑에 있는 가스 파이프에 금이 가서 우리 집으로 가스가 새어 들어왔다. **2** 타동사/자동사 날카로운 소리가 나다; 요란한 소리를 내다 ❏ 하늘에서 천둥소리가 요란하게 났다. **3** 타동사 (몸의 단단한 부분을) 부딪치다 ❏ 그는 보도에 머리를 부딪쳐서 기절했다. **4** 타동사 (껍질을) 깨다 ❏ 계란을 풀어서 그릇에 담으세요. **5** 타동사 (문제나 암호를) 풀다 ❏ 그는 수 년간의 피나는 연구 끝에 드디어 그 시스템의 문제점을 풀었다. **6** 자동사 신경 쇠약에

it, especially after a lot of thought. ❑ *He has finally cracked the system after years of painstaking research.* ⑥ V-I If someone **cracks**, they lose control of their emotions or actions because they are under a lot of pressure. [INFORMAL] ❑ *She's calm and strong, and she is just not going to crack.* ⑦ V-I If your voice **cracks** when you are speaking or singing, it changes in pitch because you are feeling a strong emotion. ❑ *Her voice cracked and she began to cry.* ⑧ V-T If you **crack** a joke, you tell it. ❑ *He drove a Volkswagen, cracked jokes, and talked about beer and girls.*

▶**crack down** PHRASAL VERB If people in authority **crack down on** a group of people, they become stricter in making the group obey rules or laws. ❑ *The government has cracked down hard on those campaigning for greater democracy.* →see also **crackdown**

▶**crack up** ❶ PHRASAL VERB If someone **cracks up**, they are under such a lot of emotional strain that they become mentally ill. [INFORMAL] ❑ *She would have cracked up if she hadn't allowed herself some fun.* ❷ PHRASAL VERB If you **crack up** or if someone or something **cracks** you **up**, you laugh a lot. [INFORMAL] ❑ *She told stories that cracked me up and I swore to write them down so you could enjoy them too.*

② **crack** /kræk/ (**cracks**) ❶ N-COUNT A **crack** is a very narrow gap between two things, or between two parts of a thing. ❑ *Kathryn had seen him through a crack in the curtains.* ❷ N-SING If you open something such as a door, window, or curtain **a crack**, you open it only a small amount. ❑ *He went to the door, opened it a crack, and listened.* ❸ N-COUNT A **crack** is a line that appears on the surface of something when it is slightly damaged. ❑ *The plate had a crack in it.* ❹ N-COUNT; SOUND A **crack** is a sharp sound, like the sound of a piece of wood breaking. ❑ *Suddenly there was a loud crack and glass flew into the car.* ❺ N-UNCOUNT **Crack** is a very pure form of the drug cocaine. ❻ ADJ A **crack** soldier or sportsman is highly trained and very skillful. [ADJ n] ❑ *...a crack undercover police officer.*

crack|down /krækdaʊn/ (**crackdowns**) N-COUNT A **crackdown** is strong official action that is taken to punish people who break laws. ❑ *...anti-government unrest that ended with the violent army crackdown.*

crack|er /krækər/ (**crackers**) N-COUNT A **cracker** is a thin, crisp piece of baked bread which is often eaten with cheese.

crack|le /kræk³l/ (**crackles, crackling, crackled**) V-I If something **crackles**, it makes a rapid series of short, harsh noises. ❑ *The radio crackled again.* ● N-COUNT **Crackle** is also a noun. ❑ *...the crackle of flames and gunfire.*

cra|dle /kreɪd³l/ (**cradles, cradling, cradled**) ❶ N-COUNT A **cradle** is a baby's bed with high sides. Cradles often have curved bases so that they rock from side to side. ❷ V-T If you **cradle** someone or something **in** your arms or hands, you hold them carefully and gently. ❑ *I cradled her in my arms.*

craft ◆◇◇ /kræft/ (**crafts, crafting, crafted**)

Craft is both the singular and the plural form for meaning ❶.

❶ N-COUNT You can refer to a boat, a spacecraft, or an aircraft as a **craft**. ❑ *With great difficulty, the fisherman manoeuvred his small craft close to the reef.* ❷ N-COUNT A **craft** is an activity such as weaving, carving, or pottery that involves making things skillfully with your hands. ❑ *...the arts and crafts of the North American Indians.* ❸ N-COUNT You can use **craft** to refer to any activity or job that involves doing something skillfully. ❑ *...the craft of writing.* ❹ V-T If something **is crafted**, it is made skillfully. ❑ *The windows would probably have been crafted in the latter part of the Middle Ages.* ❑ *...original, hand-crafted bags at affordable prices.* →see **ship**

crafts|man /kræftsmən/ (**craftsmen**) N-COUNT A **craftsman** is a man who makes things skillfully with his hands. ❑ *The table in the kitchen was made by a local craftsman.*

crafts|man|ship /kræftsmənʃɪp/ N-UNCOUNT **Craftsmanship** is the skill that someone uses when they make beautiful things with their hands. ❑ *It is easy to appreciate the craftsmanship of Armani.*

crafty /kræfti/ (**craftier, craftiest**) ADJ If you describe someone as **crafty**, you mean that they achieve what they want in a clever way, often by deceiving people. ❑ *...a crafty, lying character who enjoys plotting against others.* ❑ *A crafty look came to his eyes.*

cram /kræm/ (**crams, cramming, crammed**) ❶ V-T If you **cram** things or people **into** a container or place, you put them into it, although there is hardly enough room for them. ❑ *While nobody was looking, she squashed her school hat and crammed it into a wastebasket.* ❑ *She crammed her mouth with caviar.* ❷ V-T/V-I If people **cram into** a place or vehicle or **cram** a place or vehicle, so many of them enter it at one time that it is completely full.. ❑ *We crammed into my car and set off.* ❸ V-I If you **are cramming for** an examination, you are learning as much as possible in a short time just before you take the examination. ❑ *She was cramming for her Economics exam.* ● **cram|ming** N-UNCOUNT ❑ *It would take two or three months of cramming to prepare for Vermont's bar exam.*

crammed /kræmd/ ❶ ADJ If a place is **crammed with** things or people, it is full of them, so that there is hardly room for anything or anyone else. ❑ *The house is crammed with priceless furniture and works of art.* ❷ ADJ If people or things are **crammed into** a place or vehicle, it is full of them. [v-link ADJ prep/adv] ❑ *Between two and three thousand refugees were crammed into the church buildings.*

cramp /kræmp/ (**cramps, cramping, cramped**) ❶ N-UNCOUNT **Cramp** is a sudden strong pain caused by a muscle suddenly contracting. You sometimes get cramp in a muscle after you have been making a physical effort over a long period of time. [also N in pl] ❑ *Hillsden was complaining of cramp in his calf muscles.* ❑ *...muscle cramp.* ❷ PHRASE If someone or something **cramps** your **style**, their presence or existence restricts your behavior in some way. [INFORMAL] ❑ *Like more and more women, she believes wedlock would cramp her style.*

걸리다 [비격식체] ❑ 그녀는 침착하고 강인해서 신경 쇠약에 걸리지 않을 것이다. ⑦ 자동사 (목소리가) 갈라지다 ❑ 그녀는 목이 메어 울기 시작했다. ⑧ 타동사 (농담을) 지껄이다 ❑ 그는 폭스바겐을 타고 농담을 지껄이며 술과 여자에 대해서 얘기했다.

구동사 엄하게 다스리다, 엄중히 단속하다 ❑ 정부는 더 강력한 민주주의를 요구하는 사람들을 엄중 단속해 왔다.

❶ 구동사 미치다, 돌아버리다 [비격식체] ❑ 그녀는 그때 좀 놀지 않았었더라면 돌아 버렸을 것이다. ❷ 구동사 파안대소하다; 파안대소하게 하다 [비격식체] ❑ 그녀가 나를 파안대소하게 한 얘기를 해 줘서 네게도 해 주려고 꼭 적어 두리라 다짐했다.

❶ 가산명사 틈 ❑ 캐서린은 커튼 사이로 난 작은 틈을 통해서 그를 보았었다. ❷ 단수명사 조금, 약간 ❑ 그는 문 쪽으로 다가가 문을 조금 열고 귀를 기울였다. ❸ 가산명사 금 ❑ 그 접시에 금이 가 있었다. ❹ 가산명사; 소리 날카로운 소리, 우지끈 하는 소리 ❑ 갑자기 우지끈 소리가 크게 나더니 유리 조각이 차 안쪽으로 날아 들어왔다. ❺ 불가산명사 코카인 마약 ❻ 형용사 잘 훈련된, 능숙한 ❑ 잘 훈련된 비밀경찰관

가산명사 엄정 단속 ❑ 군의 폭력적이고도 엄정한 단속으로 끝난 반정부 시위

가산명사 크래커

자동사 지직 소리 나다 ❑ 라디오가 다시 지지직거렸다. ● 가산명사 타다다닥 하는 소리 ❑ 타다거리는 화염과 포격 소리

❶ 가산명사 요람 ❷ 타동사 보듬다 ❑ 나는 두 팔로 그녀를 안아 주었다.

craft는 ❶ 의미로 단수형과 복수형으로 다 쓸 수 있다.

❶ 가산명사 선박, 우주선, 항공기 ❑ 그 어부는 아주 어렵게 자신의 작은 배를 그 암초 가까이로 요령껏 몰았다. ❷ 가산명사 수공예 ❑ 북미 인디언들의 미술과 공예품 ❸ 가산명사 기술, 재주 ❑ 글 쓰는 재주 ❹ 타동사 정교하게 만들어지다 ❑ 아마도 중세 후반기였을지라도 그 창문들이 정교하게 만들어졌을 것이다. ❑ 수공예로 만든 독창적이면서 적당한 가격의 가방들

가산명사 장인 ❑ 부엌에 있는 그 식탁은 그 지방의 장인이 만든 것이었다.

불가산명사 장인의 솜씨 ❑ 아르마니의 장인적 솜씨를 쉽게 느낄 수 있다.

형용사 교활한 ❑ 다른 사람을 해칠 계략 짜기를 즐겨 하는 교활하고 거짓말 잘하는 인물 ❑ 그의 두 눈에 교활한 빛이 돌았다.

❶ 타동사 쑤셔 넣다 ❑ 아무도 안 보는 사이, 그녀는 학교 모자를 구겨서 쓰레기통에 쑤셔 넣었다. ❑ 그녀는 캐비아를 입 안 가득 쑤셔 넣었다. ❷ 타동사/자동사 (장소나 차에) 빽빽이 들어가다; (장소나 차를) 빽빽이 채우다 ❑ 우리는 모두 내 차에 빽빽이 들어탔다. ❸ 자동사 벼락치기 공부하다 ❑ 그녀는 경제학 시험에 대비해 벼락치기 공부를 하고 있었다. ● 벼락치기 공부 불가산명사 ❑ 버몬트 변호사 시험을 준비하려면 두세 달 정도의 벼락치기 공부를 해야 할 것이다.

❶ 형용사 빽빽이 들어찬 ❑ 그 집에는 값을 매길 수 없는 귀중한 가구와 예술품들이 빽빽이 들어차 있다. ❷ 형용사 가득 채운 ❑ 이 삼천 명의 피난민들이 그 교회 건물을 가득 채웠다.

❶ 불가산명사 (근육의 갑작스러운) 경련, 쥐 ❑ 힐스덴이 정강이의 근육 경련을 호소하고 있었다. ❑ 근육 경련 ❷ 구 (행동을) 구속하다 [비격식체] ❑ 점점 더 많은 여자들이 그러는 것처럼 그녀도 결혼 생활이 자기를 구속할 것이라고 생각한다.

cramped /krǽmpt/ ADJ A **cramped** room or building is not big enough for the people or things in it. ❏ *There are hundreds of families living in cramped conditions on the floor of the airport lounge.*

형용사 비좁은 ❏ 수백 가족이 공항 라운지 바닥에서 비좁게 생활하고 있다.

crane /kreɪn/ (**cranes, craning, craned**) **1** N-COUNT A **crane** is a large machine that moves heavy things by lifting them in the air. ❏ *The little prefabricated hut was lifted away by a huge crane.* **2** N-COUNT A **crane** is a kind of large bird with a long neck and long legs. **3** V-T/V-I If you **crane** your neck or head, you stretch your neck in a particular direction in order to see or hear something better. ❏ *She craned her neck to get a better view.* ❏ *Children craned to get close to him.*

1 가산명사 기중기 ❏ 자그마한 조립식 막사를 거대한 기중기가 들어냈다. **2** 가산명사 학, 두루미 **3** 타동사/자동사 (목을) 길게 빼다 ❏ 그녀는 더 잘 보려고 목을 길게 뺐다. ❏ 아이들이 그에게 가까이 가려고 목을 쭉 내밀었다.

crank /krǽŋk/ (**cranks, cranking, cranked**) **1** N-COUNT If you call someone a **crank**, you think their ideas or behavior are strange. [INFORMAL, DISAPPROVAL] ❏ *The Prime Minister called Councillor Marshall "a crank."* **2** N-COUNT A **crank** is a device that you turn in order to make something move. ❏ *He was idly turning a crank on a strange mechanism strapped to his chest.* **3** V-T If you **crank** an engine or machine, you make it move or function, especially by turning a handle. ❏ *The chauffeur got out to crank the motor.*

1 가산명사 괴짜 [비격식체, 탐탁찮음] ❏ 그 수상은 마샬 의원을 괴짜라고 불렀다. **2** 가산명사 크랭크 (기계 장치) ❏ 그는 하릴없이 가슴에 붙어 있는 이상한 장치의 크랭크를 돌리고 있었다. **3** 타동사 시동시키다 ❏ 운전사가 차에 시동을 걸려고 밖으로 나갔다.

crap /krǽp/ **1** ADJ If you describe something as **crap**, you think that it is wrong or of very poor quality. [INFORMAL, VULGAR, DISAPPROVAL] ❏ *She later said the book was "crap."* ● N-UNCOUNT **Crap** is also a noun. ❏ *It is a tedious, humorless load of crap.* **2** N-UNCOUNT **Crap** is sometimes used to refer to feces. [INFORMAL, VULGAR] ❏ *I look down and I'm standing next to a pile of crap!*

1 형용사 쓰레기 같은, (품질이) 엉망인 [비격식체, 비속어, 탐탁찮음] ❏ 후에 그녀는 그 책을 쓰레기라고 말했다. ● 불가산명사 쓰레기 ❏ 그것은 지루하고 재미없는 쓰레기 같은 작품이다. **2** 불가산명사 똥, 배설물 [비격식체, 비속어] ❏ 아래를 내려다 봤더니 내가 똥 더미 옆에 서 있더라구.

crash ♦♦♢ /krǽʃ/ (**crashes, crashing, crashed**) **1** N-COUNT A **crash** is an accident in which a moving vehicle hits something and is damaged or destroyed. ❏ *His elder son was killed in a car crash a few years ago.* **2** V-T/V-I If a moving vehicle **crashes** or if the driver **crashes** it, it hits something and is damaged or destroyed. ❏ *The plane crashed mysteriously near the island of Ustica.* ❏ *...when his car crashed into the rear of a van.* **3** V-I If something **crashes** somewhere, it moves and hits something else violently, making a loud noise. ❏ *The door swung inwards to crash against a chest of drawers behind it.* ❏ *My words were lost as the walls above us crashed down, filling the cellar with brick dust.* **4** N-COUNT A **crash** is a sudden, loud noise. ❏ *Two people in the flat recalled hearing a loud crash about 1.30 a.m.* **5** V-I If a business or financial system **crashes**, it fails suddenly, often with serious effects. [BUSINESS] ❏ *When the market crashed, they assumed the deal would be cancelled.* ● N-COUNT **Crash** is also a noun. ❏ *He predicted correctly that there was going to be a stock market crash.* **6** V-I If a computer or a computer program **crashes**, it fails suddenly. ❏ *...after the computer crashed for the second time in 10 days.* →see **stock market**
→see Word Web: **crash**

1 가산명사 자동차 사고 ❏ 그의 큰 아들이 자동차 사고로 몇 년 전 사망했다. **2** 타동사/자동사 (비행기가) 추락하다, (자동차가) 충돌하다 ❏ 그 비행기가 우스티카 섬 근처에서 원인을 알 수 없이 추락했다. ❏ 그의 차가 트럭 뒷부분과 충돌했을 때 **3** 타동사 세차게 부딪치다 ❏ 그 문이 안쪽으로 닫히면서 그 뒤에 있었던 서랍장과 세차게 부딪쳤다. ❏ 우리 위에 있던 담이 와르르 무너지는 소리에 내 말은 들리지도 않았고, 지하실이 벽돌 먼지로 가득 찼다. **4** 가산명사 꽝음 ❏ 그 아파트에 있었던 두 사람이 새벽 1시 30분 경에 꽝음이 들렸던 것을 기억했다. **5** 자동사 대폭락하다 [경제] ❏ 주식 시장이 대폭락했을 때, 그들은 거래가 취소될 것이라고 생각했다. ● 가산명사 대폭락 ❏ 그는 주식 시장에 대폭락이 있을 것을 정확하게 예상했다. **6** 자동사 (컴퓨터가) 갑자기 작동을 멈추다 ❏ 10일 만에 두 번째로 갑자기 컴퓨터가 작동을 멈춘 후에

Thesaurus	*crash*의 참조어
N.	collision, wreck **1**
	collide, hit, smash **2**
	bang **3**
	fail **5 6**

crass /krǽs/ (**crasser, crassest**) ADJ **Crass** behavior is stupid and does not show consideration for other people. ❏ *The government has behaved with crass insensitivity.*

형용사 세멋대로의 ❏ 정부는 제멋대로의 밀어붙이기식으로 대응했고 오고 있다.

crate /kreɪt/ (**crates, crating, crated**) **1** N-COUNT A **crate** is a large box used for transporting or storing things. ❏ *...a pile of wooden crates.* **2** V-T If something **is crated**, it is packed in a crate so that it can be transported or stored somewhere safely. [usu passive] ❏ *The much repaired plane was crated for the return journey.* **3** N-COUNT A **crate** is a plastic or wire box divided into sections which is used for carrying bottles. ● N-COUNT A **crate of** something is the amount of it that is contained in a crate. ❏ *We've also got a bonus quiz with crates of beer as prizes!*

1 가산명사 상자, (보관용) 틀 ❏ 나무 상자 더미 **2** 타동사 상자에 넣다, 틀에 넣다 ❏ 상당 부분 수선한 비행기를 돌려보내기 위해 수송용 틀에 넣었다. **3** 가산명사 (운반용) 상자 ● 가산명사 상자(의 양) ❏ 우리는 상으로 맥주 몇 상자를 주는 보너스 퀴즈도 맞췄다.

crater /kreɪtər/ (**craters**) N-COUNT A **crater** is a very large hole in the ground, which has been caused by something hitting it or by an explosion. ❏ *The explosion, believed to be a car bomb, left a ten foot crater in the street.* →see **lake, meteor, moon, solar system**

가산명사 (땅이 패어 생긴) 큰 구멍 ❏ 자동차에 장착된 폭탄 때문으로 보이는 폭발로 인해 그 도로에 10피트 깊이의 구멍이 생겼다.

crave /kreɪv/ (**craves, craving, craved**) V-T/V-I If you **crave** something, you want to have it very much. ❏ *There may be certain times of day when smokers crave their cigarette.* ● **crav|ing** (**cravings**) N-COUNT ❏ *...a craving for sugar.*

타동사/자동사 몹시 원하다, 갈망하다 ❏ 하루 중에 흡연자들이 담배를 피우고 싶어 못 견딜 것 같은 때가 몇 번 있을 것이다. ● 갈구, 갈망 가산명사 ❏ 설탕을 몹시 원함

Word Web   crash

Every year the National Highway Traffic Safety Administration* conducts crash tests on new cars. They evaluate exactly what happens during an accident. How fast do you have to be going to **buckle** a bumper during a collision? Does the gas tank **rupture**? Do the tires **burst**? What happens when the windshield **breaks**? Does it **crack**, or does it **shatter** into a thousand pieces? Does the force of the **impact crush** the front of the car completely? This is actually a good thing. It means that the engine and hood would protect the passengers during the crash.

National Highway Traffic Safety Administration: a U.S. government agency that sets safety standards.

crawl /krɔl/ (crawls, crawling, crawled) **1** V-I When you **crawl**, you move forward on your hands and knees. ❑ Don't worry if your baby seems a little reluctant to crawl or walk. ❑ I began to crawl on my hands and knees towards the door. **2** V-I When an insect **crawls** somewhere, it moves there quite slowly. ❑ I watched the moth crawl up the outside of the lampshade. **3** V-I If someone or something **crawls** somewhere, they move or progress slowly or with great difficulty. ❑ I crawled out of bed at nine-thirty. ● N-SING **Crawl** is also a noun. [a n] ❑ The traffic on the approach road slowed to a crawl. **4** V-I If you say that a place **is crawling with** people or animals, you are emphasizing that it is full of them. [INFORMAL, EMPHASIS] [only cont] ❑ This place is crawling with police. **5** N-SING **The crawl** is a kind of swimming stroke which you do lying on your front, swinging one arm over your head, and then the other arm. ❑ I expected him to do 50 lengths of the crawl.

cray|on /kreɪɒn/ (crayons) N-COUNT A **crayon** is a pencil containing colored wax or clay, or a rod of colored wax used for drawing.

craze /kreɪz/ (crazes) N-COUNT If there is a **craze** for something, it is very popular for a short time. ❑ ...the craze for Mutant Ninja Turtles.

crazed /kreɪzd/ ADJ **Crazed** people are wild and uncontrolled, and perhaps insane. ❑ A crazed gunman slaughtered five people last night.

cra|zy ♦◇◇ /kreɪzi/ (crazier, craziest, crazies) **1** ADJ If you describe someone or something as **crazy**, you think they are very foolish or strange. [INFORMAL, DISAPPROVAL] ❑ People thought they were all crazy to try to make money from manufacturing. ● **cra|zi|ly** ADV ❑ The teenagers shook their long, black hair and gesticulated crazily. **2** ADJ Someone who is **crazy** is insane. [INFORMAL] ❑ If I sat home and worried about all this stuff, I'd go crazy. ● N-COUNT **Crazy** is also a noun. ❑ Outside, mumbling, was one of New York's ever-present crazies. **3** ADJ If you are **crazy about** something, you are very enthusiastic about it. If you are **not crazy about** something, you do not like it. [INFORMAL] [v-link ADJ about n] ❑ He's still crazy about both his work and his hobbies. ● COMB in ADJ **Crazy** is also a combining form. ❑ Every football-crazy schoolboy in Europe dreams of one day being involved in the championships. **4** ADJ If you are **crazy about** someone, you are deeply in love with them. [INFORMAL] [v-link ADJ about n] ❑ None of that matters, because we're crazy about each other.

creak /kriːk/ (creaks, creaking, creaked) V-I If something **creaks**, it makes a short, high-pitched sound when it moves. ❑ The bed-springs creaked. ❑ The door creaked open. ● N-COUNT **Creak** is also a noun. ❑ The door was pulled open with a creak.

cream ♦♦◇ /kriːm/ (creams, creaming, creamed) **1** N-UNCOUNT **Cream** is a thick yellowish-white liquid taken from milk. You can use it in cooking or put it on fruit or desserts. ❑ ...strawberries and cream. **2** N-UNCOUNT **Cream** is used in the names of soups that contain cream or milk. ❑ ...cream of mushroom soup. **3** N-VAR A **cream** is a substance that you rub into your skin, for example to keep it soft or to heal or protect it. ❑ Gently apply the cream to the affected areas. **4** COLOR Something that is **cream** is yellowish-white in color. ❑ ...cream silk stockings. **5** →see also **ice cream**

▶**cream off** **1** PHRASAL VERB To **cream off** part of a group of people means to take them away and treat them in a special way, because they are better than the others. [DISAPPROVAL] ❑ The private schools cream off many of the best pupils. **2** PHRASAL VERB If a person or organization **creams off** a large amount of money, they take it and use it for themselves. [INFORMAL, DISAPPROVAL] ❑ This means smaller banks can cream off big profits during lending booms.

creamy /kriːmi/ (creamier, creamiest) **1** ADJ Food or drink that is **creamy** contains a lot of cream or milk. ❑ ...rich, creamy coffee. **2** ADJ Food that is **creamy** has a soft smooth texture and appearance. ❑ ...creamy mashed potato.

crease /kriːs/ (creases, creasing, creased) **1** N-COUNT **Creases** are lines that are made in cloth or paper when it is crushed or folded. ❑ She stood up, frowning at the creases in her silk dress. **2** V-T/V-I If cloth or paper **creases** or if you **crease** it, lines form in it when it is crushed or folded. ❑ Most outfits crease a bit when you are travelling. ● **creased** ADJ ❑ His clothes were creased, as if he had slept in them. **3** N-COUNT **Creases** in someone's skin are lines which form where their skin folds when they move. ❑ ...the tiny creases at the corners of his eyes. ● **creased** ADJ ❑ ...Jock's creased drunken face.

cre|ate ♦♦♦ /krieɪt/ (creates, creating, created) **1** V-T To **create** something means to cause it to happen or exist. ❑ We set business free to create more jobs in Britain. ❑ She could create a fight out of anything. ● **cre|ation** /krieɪʃⁿn/ N-UNCOUNT ❑ These businesses stimulate the creation of local jobs. **2** V-T When someone **creates** a new product or process, they invent it or design it. ❑ It is really great for a radio producer to create a show like this.

Thesaurus	create의 참조어
v.	make, produce; (ant.) destroy **1**
	compose, craft, design, invent **2**

Word Link	creat ≈ making : creation, creature, recreate

cre|ation /krieɪʃⁿn/ (creations) **1** N-UNCOUNT In many religions, **creation** is the making of the universe, earth, and creatures by God. [also the N] ❑ ...the

자동사 기다 ❑당신 얘기가 잘 기거나 걸으려 하지 않아도 걱정하지 마세요. ❑나는 문 쪽을 향해서 양손과 두 무릎으로 기어가기 시작했다. **2** 자동사 기다 ❑나는 그 나방이 전등갓 밖을 기어 올라가는 것을 지켜보았다. **3** 자동사 기어가다 ❑나는 9시 30분에 겨우 침대에서 기어 나왔다. ● 단수명사 서행, 기어감 ❑진입로에 들어선 차량들이 속도가 떨어져 기어갔다. **4** 자동사 득실거리다 [비격식체, 강조] ❑이곳에는 경찰들이 득실거린다. **5** 단수명사 (수영) 크롤 ❑나는 그가 50미터 크롤에 나오리라 기대했다.

가산명사 크레용

가산명사 대유행 ❑돌연변이 닌자 거북이의 대유행

형용사 정신 나간, 발광한 [문어체] ❑어젯밤 발광한 총잡이 한 명이 다섯 사람을 무자비하게 살해했다.

1 형용사 멍청한 [비격식체, 탐탁찮음] ❑사람들은 그들이 제조업으로 돈을 벌려 하는 건 참 멍청한 짓이라고 생각했다. ● 미친 듯이 부사 ❑그 십대들은 그들의 길고 검은 머리칼을 흔들며 미친 듯이 몸을 움직였다. **2** 형용사 미친 [비격식체] ❑내가 집안에 앉아서 이 일에만 신경을 쓴다면 나는 미쳐 버릴 것이다. ● 가산명사 미친 사람 ❑뉴욕에 늘 존재하는 미치광이들이 하는 일 중 하나가 밖에 나가서 중얼거리는 것이었다. **3** 형용사 좋아서 미치는 [비격식체] ❑그는 여전히 일과 취미 생활 둘 다를 미치도록 좋아한다. ● 복합형 형용사 열광하는 ❑유럽에서 축구에 미쳐 있는 남학생들은 하나같이 언젠가는 자기가 선수권 대회에 나가게 되기를 꿈꾼다. **4** 형용사 -에게 푹 빠지다, -에 미치다 [비격식체] ❑우리가 서로에게 미쳐 있기 때문에 그 어떤 것도 문제가 되지 않는다.

자동사 삐거덕거리다 ❑그 침대 스프링이 삐거덕거렸다. ❑그 문이 삐거덕거리며 열렸다. ● 가산명사 삐거덕거리는 소리 ❑누군가가 삐거덕거리는 소리를 내며 문을 당겨 열었다.

1 불가산명사 크림 ❑크림을 끼얹은 딸기 **2** 불가산명사 크림 성분이 들어 있는 것 ❑버섯 크림 스프 **3** 가산명사 또는 불가산명사 (바르는) 크림 ❑환부에 그 크림을 부드럽게 바르세요. **4** 색채어 크림색의 ❑크림색의 실크 스타킹

1 구동사 (소수 정예를 뽑아) 특별 지도하다 [탐탁찮음] ❑사립학교들에서는 우수한 학생들 여러 명을 뽑아 특별 지도한다. **2** 구동사 착복하다 [비격식체, 탐탁찮음] ❑이것은 대출 붐이 있을 때 소규모의 은행들이 큰 이윤을 착복할 수 있다는 것을 의미한다.

1 형용사 크림을 함유한 ❑크림이 들어간 진한 커피 **2** 형용사 크림 같은, 부드러운 ❑부드러운 으깬 감자 요리

1 가산명사 (종이나 천의) 접힌 자국, 구김 ❑그녀는 자신의 실크 드레스가 구겨진 것에 인상을 쓰며 일어섰다. **2** 타동사/자동사 구겨지다; -을 구기다 ❑여행을 할 때는 옷이 대부분 구겨진다. ● 구겨진 형용사 ❑마치 그 옷을 입은 채로 잠을 잔 것처럼 그 남자의 옷은 구겨져 있었다. **3** 가산명사 주름 ❑그의 두 눈가에 생긴 잔주름 ● 주름진 형용사 ❑술에 취한 조크의 주름진 얼굴

1 타동사 창조하다, 창출하다; 유발시키다 ❑영국에 더 많은 일자리를 창출하기 위해서 우리는 사업을 자유화했다. ❑그녀는 아무 것도 아닌 일도 싸움이 되게 할 수 있다. ● 창조 불가산명사 ❑이런 사업들이 그 지역의 일자리 창출을 촉진한다. **2** 타동사 (새로운 것을) 제작하다, 창작하다 ❑라디오 프로듀서가 이런 쇼를 제작한다는 것은 정말로 대단한 일이다.

1 불가산명사 창조 ❑창세기 1장에 나오는 우주 창조 **2** 불가산명사 우주 [문예체] ❑전 우주는 에너지로

Creation of the universe as told in Genesis Chapter One. **2** N-UNCOUNT People sometimes refer to the whole universe as **creation**. [LITERARY] ❑ *The whole of creation is made up of energy.* **3** N-COUNT You can refer to something that someone has made as a **creation**, especially if it shows skill, imagination, or artistic ability. ❑ *The bathroom is entirely my own creation.* **4** →see also **create**

구성되어 있다. **3** 가산명사 창작물 ❑ 그 목욕탕은 완전히 나 혼자 만든 창작물이다.

crea|tive ♦♦◇◇ /kriˈeɪtɪv/ **1** ADJ A **creative** person has the ability to invent and develop original ideas, especially in the arts. ❑ *Like so many creative people he was never satisfied.* ● **crea|tiv|ity** /kriˌeɪˈtɪvɪti/ N-UNCOUNT ❑ *American art reached a peak of creativity in the '50s and 60s.* **2** ADJ **Creative** activities involve the inventing and making of new kinds of things. ❑ *...creative writing.* ❑ *...creative arts.* **3** ADJ If you use something in a **creative** way, you use it in a new way that produces interesting and unusual results. ❑ *...his creative use of words.*

1 형용사 창의력이 있는 ❑ 창의력이 있는 다른 많은 사람들처럼 그도 결코 만족하는 법이 없었다. ● 창의력 불가산명사 ❑ 1950년대와 1960년대에 미국 미술은 그 창의력에 있어서 최고조에 달했다. **2** 형용사 창의적인 ❑ 창의적인 글쓰기 활동 ❑ 창의적인 예술품 **3** 형용사 창의적인 ❑ 그 사람의 창의적인 어휘 사용

crea|tive ac|count|ing N-UNCOUNT **Creative accounting** is when companies present or organize their accounts in such a way that they gain money for themselves or give a false impression of their profits. [DISAPPROVAL] ❑ *Much of the apparent growth in profits that occurred in the 1980s was the result of creative accounting.*

불가산명사 분식 회계 [탐탁잖음] ❑ 1980년대에 이룬 것으로 보였던 수익 증가는 상당 부분 분식 회계의 결과였다.

crea|tor /kriˈeɪtər/ (**creators**) N-COUNT The **creator** of something is the person who made it or invented it. ❑ *...Ian Fleming, the creator of James Bond.*

가산명사 창조자 ❑ 제임스 본드의 창조자인 이안 플레밍

Word Link	creat ≈ making : creation, creature, recreate

crea|ture /kriˈtʃər/ (**creatures**) N-COUNT You can refer to any living thing that is not a plant as a **creature**, especially when it is of an unknown or unfamiliar kind. People also refer to imaginary animals and beings as **creatures**. ❑ *Alaskan Eskimos believe that every living creature possesses a spirit.*

가산명사 생명체 ❑ 알래스카의 에스키모들은 모든 생명체가 영혼을 가지고 있다고 믿고 있다.

crèche /krɛʃ/ (**crèches**) also **creche** N-COUNT A **crèche** is a place where small children can be left to be cared for while their parents are working or doing something else. [BRIT; AM **day care center**]

가산명사 유아원 [영국영어; 미국영어 day care center]

cre|dence /kriˈdns/ **1** N-UNCOUNT If something lends or gives **credence to** a theory or story, it makes it easier to believe. [FORMAL] ❑ *Good studies are needed to lend credence to the notion that genuine progress can be made in this important field.* **2** N-UNCOUNT If you give **credence to** a theory or story, you believe it. [FORMAL] ❑ *You're surely not giving any credence to this story of Hythe's?*

1 불가산명사 뒷받침 [격식체] ❑ 이 중요한 분야가 진정으로 발전할 것이라는 생각을 뒷받침할 수 있는 훌륭한 연구들이 필요하다. **2** 불가산명사 신뢰 [격식체] ❑ 너는 히데의 이 이야기를 전혀 신뢰하지 않는구나?

Word Link	cred ≈ to believe : credentials, credibility, incredible

cre|den|tials /krɪdɛnʃ^əlz/ **1** N-PLURAL Someone's **credentials** are their previous achievements, training, and general background, which indicate that they are qualified to do something. ❑ *...her credentials as a Bach specialist.* **2** N-PLURAL Someone's **credentials** are a letter or certificate that proves their identity or qualifications. ❑ *Britain's new ambassador to Lebanon has presented his credentials to the President.*

1 복수명사 자기 증명, 이력 ❑ 그녀가 바흐 전문가임을 보여주는 이력들 **2** 복수명사 신임장 ❑ 레바논으로 파견된 영국 대사가 그곳 대통령께 신임장을 제출했다.

cred|ibil|ity /krɛdɪbɪlɪti/ N-UNCOUNT If someone or something has **credibility**, people believe in them and trust them. ❑ *The police have lost their credibility.*

불가산명사 신임 ❑ 경찰은 신임을 잃었다.

cred|ible /krɛdɪb^əl/ **1** ADJ **Credible** means able to be trusted or believed. ❑ *Baroness Thatcher's claims seem credible to many.* **2** ADJ A **credible** candidate, policy, or system, for example, is one that appears to have a chance of being successful. ❑ *Mr. Robertson would be a credible candidate.*

1 형용사 믿을 수 있는, 신뢰할 수 있는 ❑ 대처 남작 부인의 주장은 많은 사람들에게 믿을 만해 보인다. **2** 형용사 성공 가능성이 있는 ❑ 로버슨 씨는 당선 가능성이 있는 후보자가 될 것이다.

cred|it ♦♦◇ /krɛdɪt/ (**credits, crediting, credited**) **1** N-UNCOUNT If you are given **credit**, you are allowed to pay for goods or services several weeks or months after you have received them. ❑ *The group can't get credit to buy farming machinery.* **2** V-T When a sum of money **is credited to** an account, the bank adds that sum of money to the total in the account. ❑ *She noticed that only $80,000 had been credited to her account.* ❑ *Midland decided to change the way it credited payments to accounts.* **3** N-UNCOUNT If someone or their bank account is **in credit**, their bank account has money in it. [mainly BRIT] ❑ *The idea that I could be charged when I'm in credit makes me very angry.* **4** N-COUNT A **credit** is a sum of money which is added to an account. ❑ *The statement of total debits and credits is known as a balance.* **5** N-COUNT A **credit** is an amount of money that is given to someone. ❑ *Senator Bill Bradley outlined his own tax cut, giving families $350 in tax credits per child.* **6** N-UNCOUNT If you get **the credit for** something good, you are praised because you are responsible for it, or are thought to be responsible for it. ❑ *We don't mind who gets the credit so long as we don't get the blame.* ❑ *It would be wrong for us to take all the credit.* **7** V-T If people **credit** someone **with** an achievement or if it **is credited** to them, people say or believe that they were responsible for it. ❑ *The staff are crediting him with having saved Hythe's life.* ❑ *The 74-year-old mayor is credited with helping make Los Angeles the financial capital of the West Coast.* **8** N-SING If you say that someone is **a credit to** someone or something, you mean that their qualities or achievements will make people have a good opinion of the person or thing mentioned. ❑ *He is one of the greatest British players of recent times and is a credit to his profession.* **9** N-COUNT The list of people who helped to make a movie, a CD, or a television program is called **the credits**. ❑ *It was fantastic seeing my name in the credits.* **10** N-COUNT A **credit** is a successfully completed part of a higher education course. At some universities and colleges you need a certain number of credits to be awarded a degree. ❑ *Smedley stayed three years at Duntroon and took credits in commerce and economics back to the University of Western Australia.* **11** PHRASE To **give** someone **credit for** a good quality means to believe that they have it. ❑ *Bratbakk had more ability than the media gave him credit for.*

1 불가산명사 외상 거래 ❑ 그 사람들은 농기계를 외상으로 살 수 없다. **2** 타동사 입금하다, 입금되다 ❑ 그녀는 자신의 구좌에 단지 8만 달러밖에 기록되어 있지 않다는 것을 알았다. ❑ 미들랜드 사는 급여 입금 방식을 바꾸기로 결정했다. **3** 불가산명사 구좌에 돈이 들어 있는 [주로 영국영어] ❑ 내 구좌에 돈이 들어 있으면 내게 요금을 청구할 수도 있다는 생각에 나는 매우 화가 난다. **4** 가산명사 대변 액수, 입금액 ❑ 총 입출금 내역서를 'balance'라 한다. **5** 가산명사 공제액 ❑ 빌 브래들리 상원 의원은 자녀 한 명당 350달러의 세금 공제라는 자신의 감세안을 설명했다. **6** 불가산명사 찬사 ❑ 우리가 비난만 받지 않는다면 누가 찬사를 받든 상관하지 않는다. ❑ 모든 찬사를 우리가 받는다는 것은 이치에 맞지 않을 것 같다. **7** 타동사 …덕분이라 생각하다, 공로로 인정하다 ❑ 직원들은 히드가 생명을 구할 수 있었던 것이 그 사람 덕분이라고 믿고 있다. ❑ 로스앤젤레스가 서부 지역의 금융 도시로 발전할 수 있었던 것은 74세 된 그 시장의 공로라고 여겨진다. **8** 단수명사 자랑거리, 명예 ❑ 그는 근래 영국의 가장 훌륭한 배우 중 한 명이며 연극계의 자랑이다. **9** 가산명사 제작에 참여한 사람들, 크레디트 ❑ 내 이름이 크레디트에 오른 걸 보다니 정말 멋졌어. **10** 가산명사 (이수) 학점 ❑ 스메들리는 삼 년간 던트룬에 머물렀고 '웨스턴 오스트레일리아' 대학에서 상업과 경제학을 이수했다. **11** 구 …자질을) 지니고 있다고 믿다 ❑ 브라트박은 매스컴이 믿고 있었던 것보다 더 많은 능력을 지니고 있었다. **12** 구 대견하게도 ❑ 그녀는 간신히 자신을 추스렸고, 대견하게도 삶을 여전히 긍정적으로 바라보며 지냈다.

a b c d e f g h i j k l m n o p q r s t u v w x y z

⓬ PHRASE If something is **to** someone's **credit**, they deserve praise for it. ❑ *She had managed to pull herself together and, to her credit, continued to look upon life as a positive experience.*

Word Partnership		*credit*의 연어
N.	credit **history** ❶	
	letter of credit ❶ ❹ ❺	
	credit **an account** ❷	
ADJ.	**personal** credit ❶ ❺	
V.	**provide** credit ❶ ❺	
	deserve credit, **take** credit ❻	

cred|it|able /krɛdɪtəbəl/ ❶ ADJ A **creditable** performance or achievement is of a reasonably high standard. ❑ *They turned out a quite creditable performance.* ❷ ADJ If you describe someone's actions or aims as **creditable**, you mean that they are morally good. ❑ *Not a very creditable attitude, I'm afraid.*

❶ 형용사 수준 높은 ❑ 그들은 상당히 수준 높은 공연을 선보였다. ❷ 형용사 존경할 만한 ❑ 그렇게 존경할 만한 태도는 아닌 것 같다.

cred|it card (**credit cards**) N-COUNT A **credit card** is a plastic card that you use to buy goods on credit. Compare **charge card**.

가산명사 신용 카드

cred|it note (**credit notes**) N-COUNT A **credit note** is the same as a **credit slip**. [BRIT]

가산명사 환불증 [영국영어]

cred|itor /krɛdɪtər/ (**creditors**) N-COUNT Your **creditors** are the people who you owe money to. ❑ *The company said it would pay in full all its creditors except Credit Suisse.*

가산명사 채권자 ❑ 그 회사는 '크레디트 스위스'를 제외한 모든 채권자들에게 전액을 지불할 것이라고 말했다.

cred|it rat|ing N-SING Your **credit rating** is a judgment of how likely you are to pay money back if you borrow it or buy things on credit. ❑ *But Cahoot's overdraft rate depends on your credit rating.*

단수명사 신용 등급 ❑ 그러나 카후트의 당좌 차월 등급은 당신의 신용 등급에 달려 있다.

cred|it slip (**credit slips**) N-COUNT A **credit slip** is a piece of paper that a shop gives you when you return goods that you have bought from it. It states that you are entitled to take goods of the same value without paying for them. [AM; BRIT **credit note**]

가산명사 환불증 [미국영어; 영국영어 credit note]

cred|it trans|fer (**credit transfers**) N-COUNT A **credit transfer** is a direct payment of money from one bank account into another. [BRIT; AM **money transfer**] [also *by* N]

가산명사 계좌 이체, 자금 이체 [영국영어; 미국영어 money transfer]

credit|worthy /krɛdɪtwɜrði/ also **credit-worthy** ADJ A **creditworthy** person or organization is one who can safely be lent money or allowed to have goods on credit, for example because in the past they have always paid back what they owe. ❑ *Building societies make loans to creditworthy customers.* ● **credit|worthi|ness** N-UNCOUNT ❑ *They now take extra steps to verify the creditworthiness of customers.*

형용사 신용도가 좋은 ❑ 주택 금융 조합에서는 신용도가 좋은 고객에게 대출을 해 준다. ● 신용 상태, 신용도 불가산명사 ❑ 이제 그들은 고객의 신용 상태를 확인할 수 있는 추가 조치를 취하고 있다.

creed /krid/ (**creeds**) ❶ N-COUNT A **creed** is a set of beliefs, principles, or opinions that strongly influence the way people live or work. [FORMAL] ❑ *...their devotion to their creed of self-help.* ❷ N-COUNT A **creed** is a religion. [FORMAL] ❑ *The center is open to all, no matter what race or creed.*

❶ 가산명사 신조 [격식체] ❑ 그들의 신조인 자립에 대한 강한 애착 ❷ 가산명사 종교 [격식체] ❑ 그 센터는 인종과 종교에 상관없이 모든 사람이 이용할 수 있다.

creek /krik/ (**creeks**) ❶ N-COUNT A **creek** is a small stream or river. [AM] ❑ *Follow Austin Creek for a few miles.* ❷ N-COUNT A **creek** is a narrow place where the sea comes a long way into the land. [BRIT] ❑ *Our particular pleasure was to find a quiet anchorage in some sheltered creek.*

❶ 가산명사 작은 시내, 샛강 [미국영어] ❑ 오스틴 강을 따라 몇 마일을 가세요. ❷ 가산명사 작은 만 [영국영어] ❑ 아늑한 작은 만에 있는 조용한 정박지를 찾을 수 있어러 우리는 특히 즐거웠다.

creep /krip/ (**creeps, creeping, crept**) ❶ V-I When people or animals **creep** somewhere, they move very quietly and slowly. ❑ *Back I go to the hotel and creep up to my room.* ❷ V-I If something **creeps** somewhere, it moves very slowly. ❑ *Mist had crept in again from the sea.* ❸ V-I If something **creeps** in or **creeps** back, it begins to occur or becomes part of something without people realizing or without them wanting it. ❑ *Insecurity might creep in.* ❑ *An increasing ratio of mistakes, perhaps induced by tiredness, crept into her game.* ❹ V-I If a rate or number **creeps up** to a higher level, it gradually reaches that level. ❑ *The inflation rate has been creeping up to 9.5 per cent.* ❺ to **make** someone's **flesh creep** →see **flesh**

❶ 자동사 살금살금 걷다 ❑ 나는 호텔로 돌아가서 살금살금 내 방으로 걸어 올라간다. ❷ 자동사 느리게 나아가다 ❑ 바다에서 안개가 또다시 슬며시 밀려왔다. ❸ 자동사 슬며시 나타나다 ❑ 불안감이 슬며시 밀려올지도 모른다. ❑ 아마도 피곤해서 그랬겠지만 그녀가 게임에서 실수하는 횟수가 점점 늘고 있었다. ❹ 자동사 (비율이나 수치가) 달하다 ❑ 인플레이션율이 점점 올라가서 9.5퍼센트에 달하고 있다.

Word Partnership		*creep*의 연어
PREP.	creep **toward** ❶ ❷	
	creep **into** ❶ ❷ ❸	
	creep **in** ❷ ❸	
	creep **up** ❷ ❹	

creepy /kripi/ (**creepier, creepiest**) ADJ If you say that something or someone is **creepy**, you mean they make you feel very nervous or frightened. [INFORMAL] ❑ *There were certain places that were really creepy at night.*

형용사 소름끼치게 하는 [비격식체] ❑ 밤이면 정말로 소름 끼치게 하는 몇몇 장소들이 있었다.

cre|mate /krimeɪt, BRIT krɪmeɪt/ (**cremates, cremating, cremated**) V-T When someone **is cremated**, their dead body is burned, usually as part of a funeral service. [usu passive] ❑ *She wants Chris to be cremated.* ● **cre|ma|tion** /krɪmeɪʃən/ (**cremations**) N-VAR ❑ *At Miss Garbo's request there was a cremation after a private ceremony.*

타동사 화장(火葬)되다 ❑ 그녀는 크리스를 화장시키기를 원한다. ● 화장(火葬) 가산명사 또는 불가산명사 ❑ 가르보 양의 요청에 따라 비공개 의식 이후에 화장이 거행되었다.

crept /krɛpt/ **Crept** is the past tense and past participle of **creep**.

creep의 과거, 과거 분사

cre|scen|do /krɪʃɛndoʊ/ (**crescendos**) ❶ N-COUNT A **crescendo** is a noise that gets louder and louder. Some people also use **crescendo** to refer to the point when a noise is at its loudest. ❑ *She spoke in a crescendo: "You are a bad girl! You are a wicked girl! You are evil!"* ❷ N-COUNT People sometimes describe an increase in

❶ 가산명사 점점 커지는 소리 ❑ 그녀는 점점 더 소리 높여 말했다. "너는 나쁜 애야! 정말 못된 애야! 악마야!" ❷ 가산명사 (이야기 사건의) 최고조 [언론] ❑ 의회와 언론에서의 비난이 최고조에 이르렀다.

the intensity of something, or its most intense point, as a **crescendo**. [JOURNALISM] ❑ *There was a crescendo of parliamentary and press criticism.*

Word Link   cresc, creas ≈ growing : cresc*ent*, de*crease*, in*crease*

---

cres|cent /krɛsᵊnt/ (**crescents**) **1** N-COUNT A **crescent** is a curved shape that is wider in the middle than at its ends, like the shape of the moon during its first and last quarters. It is the most important symbol of the Islamic faith. ❑ *A glittering Islamic crescent tops the mosque.* ❑ *...a narrow crescent of sand dunes.* **2** N-IN-NAMES **Crescent** is sometimes used as part of the name of a street or row of houses that is usually built in a curve. [mainly BRIT] ❑ *...44 Colville Crescent.*

crest /krɛst/ (**crests**) **1** N-COUNT The **crest** of a hill or a wave is the top of it. ● PHRASE If you say that you are **on the crest of a wave**, you mean that you are feeling very happy and confident because things are going well for you. ❑ *The band are riding on the crest of a wave with the worldwide success of their number one selling single.* **2** N-COUNT A bird's **crest** is a group of upright feathers on the top of its head. ❑ *Both birds had a dark blue crest.* **3** N-COUNT A **crest** is a design that is the symbol of a noble family, a town, or an organization. ❑ *On the wall is the family crest.* →see **sound**

crev|ice /krɛvɪs/ (**crevices**) N-COUNT A **crevice** is a narrow crack or gap, especially in a rock. ❑ *...a huge boulder with rare ferns growing in every crevice.*

crew ♦◇◇ /kru/ (**crews, crewing, crewed**) **1** N-COUNT-COLL The **crew** of a ship, an aircraft, or a spacecraft is the people who work on and operate it. ❑ *The mission for the crew of the space shuttle Endeavour is essentially over.* ❑ *Despite their size, these vessels carry small crews, usually of around twenty men.* **2** N-COUNT A **crew** is a group of people with special technical skills who work together on a task or project. ❑ *...a two-man film crew making a documentary.* **3** V-T/V-I If you **crew** a boat, you work on it as part of the crew. ❑ *She was already a keen and experienced sailor, having crewed in both Merlin and Grayling.* ❑ *There were to be five teams of three crewing the boat.*

crib /krɪb/ (**cribs**) N-COUNT A **crib** is a bed for a baby. [mainly AM; BRIT usually **cot**]

crick|et ♦◇◇ /krɪkɪt/ (**crickets**) **1** N-UNCOUNT **Cricket** is an outdoor game played between two teams. Players try to score points, called runs, by hitting a ball with a wooden bat. ❑ *During the summer term we would play cricket at the village ground.* **2** N-COUNT A **cricket** is a small jumping insect that produces short, loud sounds by rubbing its wings together.

crick|et|er /krɪkɪtər/ (**cricketers**) N-COUNT A **cricketer** is a person who plays cricket.

crime ♦♦◇ /kraɪm/ (**crimes**) **1** N-VAR A **crime** is an illegal action or activity for which a person can be punished by law. ❑ *He and Lieutenant Cassidy were checking the scene of the crime.* ❑ *...the growing problem of organized crime.* **2** N-COUNT If you say that doing something is a **crime**, you think it is very wrong or a serious mistake. [DISAPPROVAL] ❑ *It would be a crime to travel all the way to Australia and not stop in Sydney.* →see **city**

Word Partnership   crime의 연어

V.	**commit a** crime, **fight against** crime **1**
ADJ.	**organized** crime, **terrible** crime, **violent** crime **1**
N.	**partner in** crime, crime **prevention**, crime **scene**, crime **wave 1**

---

crimi|nal ♦♦◇ /krɪmɪnᵊl/ (**criminals**) **1** N-COUNT A **criminal** is a person who has committed a crime. ❑ *A group of gunmen attacked a prison and set free nine criminals in Moroto.* **2** ADJ **Criminal** means connected with crime. ❑ *Her husband faces various criminal charges.* **3** ADJ If you describe an action as **criminal**, you think it is very wrong or a serious mistake. [DISAPPROVAL] ❑ *He said a full-scale dispute involving strikes would be criminal.*

crim|son /krɪmzᵊn/ (**crimsons**) COLOR Something that is **crimson** is deep red in color. ❑ *...a mass of crimson flowers.*

cringe /krɪndʒ/ (**cringes, cringing, cringed**) V-I If you **cringe at** something, you feel embarrassed or disgusted, and perhaps show this feeling in your expression or by making a slight movement. ❑ *Molly had cringed when Ann started picking up the guitar.* ❑ *Chris had cringed at the thought of using her own family for publicity.*

crip|ple /krɪpᵊl/ (**cripples, crippling, crippled**) **1** N-COUNT A person with a physical disability or a serious permanent injury is sometimes referred to as a **cripple**. [OFFENSIVE] ❑ *She has gone from being a healthy, fit, and sporty young woman to being a cripple.* **2** V-T If someone **is crippled** by an injury, it is so serious that they can never move their body properly again. ❑ *Mr. Easton was seriously crippled in an accident and had to leave his job.* ❑ *He had been warned that another bad fall could cripple him for life.*

crip|pling /krɪplɪŋ/ **1** ADJ A **crippling** illness or disability is one that severely damages your health or your body. [ADJ n] ❑ *Arthritis and rheumatism are prominent crippling diseases.* **2** ADJ If you say that an action, policy, or situation has a **crippling** effect on something, you mean it has a very serious, harmful effect. ❑ *The high cost of capital has a crippling effect on many small American high-tech firms.*

cri|sis ♦♦◇ /kraɪsɪs/ (**crises**) /kraɪsiz/ N-VAR A **crisis** is a situation in which something or someone is affected by one or more very serious problems.

---

1 가산명사 초승달 모양 ❑ 이슬람교의 반짝이는 초승달 문양이 예배당에 높이 걸려 있다. ❑ 가는 초승달 모양의 모래 언덕 **2** 이름명사 크레센트 (초승달 모양의 거리) [주로 영국영어] ❑ 콜빌 크레센트 44번가

1 가산명사 산마루, 물마루 ● 구 의기양양한, 최고조에 오른 ❑ 그 밴드는 전 세계적으로 싱글 음반 판매의 1위를 차지하면서 최고의 인기를 구가하고 있다. **2** 가산명사 (새나 닭의) 볏슬 ❑ 두 마리 새 모두 볏슬이 진한 청색이었다. **3** 가산명사 (가문이나 조직 등의) 문장(紋章) ❑ 벽에는 그 집안의 문장(紋章)이 걸려 있다.

가산명사 (바위나 벽 등의) 갈라진 틈, 크레바스 ❑ 갈라진 틈마다 희귀한 고비 식물이 자라고 있는 큰 바위

1 가산명사-집합 선원, 승무원 ❑ 우주 왕복선 '인데버'호의 승무원들이 해야 할 임무는 대체로 끝났다. ❑ 큰 크기에도 불구하고 이런 선박에는 보통 이십여 명의 소수 승무원들만이 탑승한다. **2** 가산명사 팀원들 ❑ 기록물을 찍고 있는 두 명으로 구성된 영화 제작 팀 **3** 타동사/자동사 승무원으로 일하다 ❑ 그녀는 이미 멀린과 그레이링에서 일해 본 적이 있는 의욕과 경험이 많은 선원이었다. ❑ 그 배에서 일하는 승무원은 세 명씩 다섯 팀이 조직될 예정이었다.

가산명사 아기 침대 [주로 미국영어; 영국영어 대개 cot]

1 불가산명사 크리켓 ❑ 그 여름 학기 동안 우리는 동네 운동장에서 크리켓 경기를 하곤 했었다. **2** 가산명사 귀뚜라미

가산명사 크리켓 선수

1 가산명사 또는 불가산명사 범죄 ❑ 그와 캐시디 부서장은 그 범죄 현장을 조사하고 있었다. ❑ 점점 늘어나는 조직범죄의 문제 **2** 가산명사 큰 실수 [탐탁찮음] ❑ 호주까지 그 먼 길을 여행하면서 시드니에 들리지 않는 것은 큰 실수를 하는 것이다.

1 가산명사 죄인 ❑ 모로토에서는 한 무리의 총잡이들이 감옥을 습격해서 죄수 아홉 명을 풀어 주었다. **2** 형용사 범죄의 ❑ 그녀의 남편은 여러 가지 범죄 혐의를 받고 있다. **3** 형용사 심각하게 잘못된 [탐탁찮음] ❑ 파업을 동반한 전면적인 분쟁은 매우 잘못된 것이라고 그는 말했다.

색채어 진홍색 ❑ 수많은 진홍색 꽃들

자동사 움찔하다 ❑ 몰리는 앤이 그 기타를 집으려 하자 움찔했었다. ❑ 크리스는 자신의 가족을 선전에 이용한다는 생각에 움찔했었다.

1 가산명사 불구자 [모욕어] ❑ 건강하고 튼튼하며 운동을 좋아하는 젊은 여자였던 그녀가 이제는 불구자가 되었다. **2** 타동사 불구가 되다 ❑ 이스턴 씨는 사고로 심한 불구가 되어 직장을 떠나야 했다. ❑ 그는 한 번 더 심하게 추락하게 되면 영원히 불구가 될 수도 있다는 경고를 들었었다.

1 형용사 불구로 만드는 ❑ 관절염과 류머티즘은 불구가 되게 만드는 잘 알려진 병이다. **2** 형용사 심한 손상을 입히는, 못 쓰게 만드는 ❑ 높은 자본 비용 때문에 소규모의 많은 미국 하이테크 회사들이 제대로 기능을 못하게 되었다.

가산명사 또는 불가산명사 위기 ❑ 자연 재해가 분명히 그 대륙의 경제 위기를 초래한 한 요인으로

❑ *Natural disasters have obviously contributed to the continent's economic crisis.* ❑ *...someone to turn to in moments of crisis.*

작용해 왔다. ❑ 위기의 순간에 의지할 수 있는 사람

Word Partnership crisis의 연어

N.	**housing** crisis, crisis **management**, **solution to a** crisis
V.	**solve a** crisis
ADJ.	**major** crisis, **political** crisis

crisp /krɪsp/ (**crisper**, **crispest**, **crisps**, **crisping**, **crisped**) ■ ADJ Food that is **crisp** is pleasantly hard, or has a pleasantly hard surface. [APPROVAL] ❑ *Bake the potatoes for 15 minutes, till they're nice and crisp.* ❑ *...crisp bacon.* ■ V-T/V-I If food **crisps** or if you **crisp** it, it becomes pleasantly hard, for example because you have heated it at a high temperature. ❑ *Cook the bacon until it begins to crisp.* ■ N-COUNT **Crisps** are very thin slices of fried potato that are eaten cold as a snack. [BRIT; AM **chips**, **potato chips**] ❑ *...a packet of crisps.* ■ ADJ Weather that is pleasantly fresh, cold, and dry can be described as **crisp**. [APPROVAL] ❑ *...a crisp autumn day.* ■ ADJ **Crisp** cloth or paper is clean and has no creases in it. ❑ *He wore a panama hat and a crisp white suit.* ❑ *I slipped between the crisp clean sheets.*

■ 형용사 바삭바삭한, 아삭아삭한 [마음에 듦] ❑ 감자가 잘 구워져서 바삭바삭할 때까지 15분간 굽는다. ❑ 바삭바삭한 베이컨 ■ 타동사/자동사 바삭하게 구워지다; 바삭하게 굽다 ❑ 베이컨이 바삭해질 때까지 익힌다. ■ 가산명사 포테이토칩 [영국영어; 미국영어 chips, potato chips] ❑ 포테이토칩 한 봉지 ■ 형용사 (날씨가) 상쾌한, 보송보송한 [마음에 듦] ❑ 상쾌한 어느 가을날 ■ 형용사 까실까실한, 보송보송한 ❑ 그는 파나마모자를 쓰고 까실까실한 흰색 정장을 입고 있었다. ❑ 나는 보송보송하고 깨끗한 시트 안으로 미끄러져 들어갔다.

criss-cross /krɪs krɒs, BRIT -krɒs/ (**criss-crosses**, **criss-crossing**, **criss-crossed**) also **crisscross** ■ V-T If a person or thing **criss-crosses** an area, they travel from one side to the other and back again many times, following different routes. If a number of things **criss-cross** an area, they cross it, and cross over each other. ❑ *They criss-crossed the country by bus.* ■ V-RECIP If two sets of lines or things **criss-cross**, they cross over each other. ❑ *Wires criss-cross between the tops of the poles, forming a grid.* ■ ADJ A **criss-cross** pattern or design consists of lines crossing each other. [ADJ n] ❑ *Slash the tops of the loaves with a sharp serrated knife in a criss-cross pattern.*

■ 타동사 누비고 다니다 ❑ 그들은 버스를 타고 그 지역을 누비고 다녔다. ■ 상호동사 교차하다 ❑ 전선들이 기둥 꼭대기 사이에 격자 모양을 이루면서 교차한다. ■ 형용사 십자의, 교차된 ❑ 빵의 윗부분에 잘 드는 톱니칼로 십자 모양을 낸다.

cri|teri|on /kraɪtɪəriən/ (**criteria**) /kraɪtɪəriə/ N-COUNT A **criterion** is a factor on which you judge or decide something. ❑ *The most important criterion for entry is that applicants must design and make their own work.*

가산명사 기준, 표준 ❑ 가장 중요한 참가 기준은 신청자들이 자신들의 작품을 직접 디자인하고 만들어야 하는 것이다.

Word Link crit ≈ to judge : critic, critical, criticize

crit|ic ♦♦◇ /krɪtɪk/ (**critics**) ■ N-COUNT A **critic** is a person who writes about and expresses opinions about things such as books, movies, music, or art. ❑ *Mather was film critic on the Daily Telegraph for many years.* ■ N-COUNT Someone who is a **critic** of a person or system disapproves of them and criticizes them publicly. ❑ *The newspaper has been the most consistent critic of the government.*

■ 가산명사 평론가 ❑ 매더는 오랜 세월 동안 데일리 텔레그라프의 영화 평론가였다. ■ 가산명사 비평가 ❑ 그 신문은 정부에 대해 가장 일관된 비평가의 역할을 해 왔다.

criti|cal ♦♦◇ /krɪtɪk'l/ ■ ADJ A **critical** time, factor, or situation is extremely important. ❑ *The incident happened at a critical point in the campaign.* ❑ *He says setting priorities is of critical importance.* ● **criti|cal|ly** /krɪtɪkli/ ADV ❑ *Economic prosperity depends critically on an open world trading system.* ■ ADJ A **critical** situation is very serious and dangerous. ❑ *The German authorities are considering an airlift if the situation becomes critical.* ● **criti|cal|ly** ADV ❑ *Moscow is running critically low on food supplies.* ■ ADJ If a person is **critical** or in a **critical** condition in a hospital, they are seriously ill. ❑ *Ten of the injured are said to be in critical condition.* ● **criti|cal|ly** ADV ❑ *She was critically ill.* ■ ADJ To be **critical of** someone or something means to criticize them. ❑ *His report is highly critical of the trial judge.* ● **criti|cal|ly** ADV ❑ *She spoke critically of Lara.* ■ ADJ A **critical** approach to something involves examining and judging it carefully. [ADJ n] ❑ *We need to become critical text-readers.* ● **criti|cal|ly** ADV ❑ *Wyman watched them critically.* ■ ADJ If something or someone receives **critical** acclaim, critics say that they are very good. [ADJ n] ❑ *The film met with considerable critical and public acclaim.*

■ 형용사 결정적인, 중대한 ❑ 그 사건은 선거 유세에서 결정적인 순간에 발생했다. ❑ 그는 일의 우선 순위를 정하는 것이 가장 중요하다고 말했다. ● 결정적으로, 아주 중요하게 부사 ❑ 경제 번영은 결정적으로 개방적인 세계 무역 구조에 달려 있다. ■ 형용사 심각한 ❑ 독일 당국은 사태가 심각해질 경우 공수 작전을 고려하고 있다. ● 심각하게 부사 ❑ 모스크바는 식량 공급이 심각하게 줄어들고 있다. ■ 형용사 위독한 ❑ 부상자들 중 열 명이 현재 중태라고 한다. ● 위독하여 부사 ❑ 그녀는 병이 위독했다. ■ 형용사 비판하는 ❑ 그의 보고서는 그 심리 판사를 강하게 비판하고 있다. ● 비판적으로 부사 ❑ 그녀는 라라에 관해서 비판적으로 말했다. ■ 형용사 비판적인, 분석적인 ❑ 우리는 비판적인 독자가 될 필요가 있다. ● 비판적으로, 분석하듯 부사 ❑ 와이먼은 그들을 분석하듯 쳐다보았다. ■ 형용사 평론가들의 ❑ 그 영화는 평론가들과 일반인들로부터 상당한 호평을 받았다.

Word Partnership critical의 연어

N.	critical **issue**, critical **role** ■
	critical **state** ■ ■
	critical **condition** ■
	critical **acclaim** ■
V.	**become** critical ■
PREP.	critical **of** *someone*, critical **of** *something* ■

criti|cism ♦♦◇ /krɪtɪsɪzəm/ (**criticisms**) ■ N-VAR **Criticism** is the action of expressing disapproval of something or someone. A **criticism** is a statement that expresses disapproval. ❑ *This policy has repeatedly come under strong criticism on Capitol Hill.* ■ N-UNCOUNT **Criticism** is a serious examination and judgment of something such as a book or play. ❑ *She has published more than 20 books including novels, poetry and literary criticism.*

■ 가산명사 또는 불가산명사 비난, 비판 ❑ 이 정책과 함께 의회는 여러 번 혹독한 비판을 받았다. ■ 불가산명사 비평 ❑ 그녀는 소설책, 시집, 문학 비평서를 포함해서 20여 권의 책을 출판했다.

Thesaurus criticism의 참조어

N.	disapproval, judgment; (ant.) approval, praise ■
	commentary, critique, review ■

Word Partnership criticism의 연어

PREP.	criticism **against** *something*, criticism **from** *something*, criticism **of** *something* ■
N.	**public** criticism ■
	constructive criticism, **open to** criticism ■ ■
	literary criticism ■

Word Link
crit ≈ to judge : critic, critical, criticize

criti|cize ◆◇◇ /krɪtɪsaɪz/ (criticizes, criticizing, criticized) [BRIT also **criticise**] V-T
If you **criticize** someone or something, you express your disapproval of them by saying what you think is wrong with them. ❑ *His mother had rarely criticized him or any of her children.*

[영국영어 criticise] 타동사 나무라다 ❑ 그의 어머니는 그나 다른 자식들을 거의 나무라지 않으셨다.

Thesaurus
criticize의 참조어

v.   condemn, denounce, knock; (ant.) applaud, praise

Word Partnership
criticize의 연어

N.   criticize **the government**
PREP. *be* criticized **about/by/for**

cri|tique /krɪtik/ (critiques) N-COUNT A **critique** is a written examination and judgment of a situation or of a person's work or ideas. [FORMAL] ❑ *She had brought a book, a feminist critique of Victorian lady novelists.*

가산명사 평론, 비평 [격식체] ❑ 그녀는 빅토리아 시대의 여성 작가들에 대한 페미니스트적 평론서를 한 권 가져왔다.

croak /krouk/ (croaks, croaking, croaked) ❶ V-I When a frog or bird **croaks**, it makes a harsh, low sound. ❑ *Thousands of frogs croaked in the reeds by the riverbank.* ● N-COUNT **Croak** is also a noun. ❑ *...the guttural croak of the frogs.* ❷ V-T If someone **croaks** something, they say it in a low, rough voice. ❑ *Tiller moaned and managed to croak, "Help me."* ● N-COUNT **Croak** is also a noun. ❑ *His voice was just a croak.*

❶ 자동사 개굴개굴 울다 ❑ 수천 마리의 개구리들이 강둑 옆에 있는 갈대숲에서 개굴개굴 울었다. ● 가산명사 개굴개굴 우는 소리 ❑ 개구리들이 개굴개굴 우는 소리 ❷ 타동사 잠긴 목소리로 말하다 ❑ 틸러는 잠긴 목소리로 "도와줘요."라고 겨우 울부짖었다. ● 가산명사 잠긴 목소리 ❑ 그의 목소리는 딱 잠긴 목소리였다.

crock|ery /krɒkəri/ N-UNCOUNT **Crockery** is the plates, cups, saucers, and dishes that you use at meals. [mainly BRIT] ❑ *We had no fridge, cooker, cutlery, or crockery.*

불가산명사 식기류 [주로 영국영어] ❑ 우리는 냉장고도 요리 기구도 수저도 식기류 아무것도 없었다.

croco|dile /krɒkədaɪl/ (crocodiles) N-COUNT A **crocodile** is a large reptile with a long body and strong jaws. Crocodiles live in rivers and eat meat.

가산명사 악어

crois|sant /krwɑsɒn, krəsɒnt, BRIT kwæsɒn/ (croissants) N-VAR **Croissants** are small, sweet bread rolls in the shape of a crescent that are eaten for breakfast. ❑ *...coffee and croissants.*

가산명사 또는 불가산명사 크로와상 (빵) ❑ 커피와 크로와상

cro|ny /krouni/ (cronies) N-COUNT You can refer to friends that someone spends a lot of time with as their **cronies**, especially when you disapprove of them. [INFORMAL, DISAPPROVAL] ❑ *Daily he returned, tired and maudlin from lunchtime drinking sessions with his business cronies.*

가산명사 패거리들 [비격식체, 탐탁찮음] ❑ 그는 매일 사업을 같이하는 패거리들과 낮술을 마신 후 울적하고 지친 상태로 돌아왔다.

crook /krʊk/ (crooks, crooking, crooked) ❶ N-COUNT A **crook** is a dishonest person or a criminal. [INFORMAL] ❑ *The man is a crook and a liar.* ❷ N-COUNT **The crook of** your arm or leg is the soft inside part where you bend your elbow or knee. ❑ *She hid her face in the crook of her arm.* ❸ V-T If you **crook** your arm or finger, you bend it. ❑ *He crooked his finger. "Come forward," he said.* ❹ N-COUNT A **crook** is a long pole with a large hook at the end. A crook is carried by a bishop in religious ceremonies, or by a shepherd. ❑ *...a shepherd's crook.*

❶ 가산명사 사기꾼 [비격식체] ❑ 그 남자는 사기꾼이고 거짓말쟁이다. ❷ 가산명사 (팔, 다리의 접히는) 안쪽 부분 ❑ 그녀는 팔에 얼굴을 묻었다. ❸ 타동사 구부리다 ❑ 그는 손가락을 구부리며 "이리 와."라고 말했다. ❹ 가산명사 (기다란) 지팡이 ❑ 양치기의 지팡이

crook|ed /krʊkɪd/ ❶ ADJ If you describe something as **crooked**, especially something that is usually straight, you mean that it is bent or twisted. ❑ *...the crooked line of his broken nose.* ❷ ADJ A **crooked** smile is uneven and bigger on one side than the other. ❑ *Polly gave her a crooked grin.* ❸ ADJ If you describe a person or an activity as **crooked**, you mean that they are dishonest or criminal. [INFORMAL] ❑ *...a crooked cop.*

❶ 형용사 비뚤어진 ❑ 코가 부러져서 생긴 그의 비뚤어진 콧대 ❷ 형용사 비뚤어진 ❑ 폴리는 그녀에게 입을 비틀어 씩 웃었다. ❸ 형용사 부정직한 [비격식체] ❑ 부정직한 경찰관

croon /krun/ (croons, crooning, crooned) ❶ V-T/V-I If you **croon**, you sing or hum quietly and gently. ❑ *He would much rather have been crooning in a smoky bar.* ❷ V-T/V-I If one person talks to another in a soft gentle voice, you can describe them as **crooning**, especially if you think they are being sentimental or insincere. ❑ *"Dear boy," she crooned, hugging him heartily.*

❶ 타동사/자동사 흥얼거리다 ❑ 그는 담배 연기 자욱한 술집에서 흥얼거리는 걸 훨씬 더 좋아했을 텐데. ❷ 타동사/자동사 부드럽게 말하다 ❑ 그녀는 아이를 꼭 끌어안으며, "아가야." 하고 부드럽게 말했다

crop ◆◇◇ /krɒp/ (crops, cropping, cropped) ❶ N-COUNT **Crops** are plants such as wheat and potatoes that are grown in large quantities for food. ❑ *Rice farmers here still plant and harvest their crops by hand.* ❷ N-COUNT The plants or fruits that are collected at harvest time are referred to as a **crop**. ❑ *Each year it produces a fine crop of fruit.* ❑ *The U.S. government says that this year's corn crop should be about 8 percent more than last year.* ❸ N-SING You can refer to a group of people or things that have appeared together as a **crop of** people or things. [INFORMAL] ❑ *The present crop of books and documentaries about Marilyn Monroe exploit the thirtieth anniversary of her death.* ❹ V-I When a plant **crops**, it produces fruits or parts which people want. ❑ *Although these vegetables adapt well to our temperate climate, they tend to crop poorly.* ❺ V-T To **crop** someone's hair means to cut it short. ❑ *She cropped her hair and dyed it blonde.* ❻ N-COUNT A **crop** is a short hairstyle. ❑ *She had her long hair cut into a boyish crop.* ❼ V-T If you **crop** a photograph, you cut part of it off, in order to get rid of part of the picture or to be able to frame it. ❑ *I decided to crop the picture just above the water line.*
→see **farm**, **grain**, **photography**

❶ 가산명사 농작물 ❑ 벼농사를 짓는 이곳 농부들은 아직도 직접 손으로 농작물을 재배하고 수확한다. ❷ 가산명사 수확물 ❑ 매년 그곳은 양질의 과일을 생산한다. ❑ 미국 정부는 올해 옥수수 수확량이 작년보다 약 8퍼센트 정도 많아질 것이라고 말한다. ❸ 단수명사 일련의 무리 [비격식체] ❑ 최근 마릴린 먼로의 사망 삼십 주년을 이용해 한꺼 벌어는, 그녀에 대한 일련의 책들과 기록물들이 쏟아져 나오고 있다. ❹ 자동사 (농작물이) 잘 되다, (알이) 영글다 ❑ 이 채소들이 이곳 온화한 기후에 잘 적응하고 있지만 잘 되지는 않을 것 같다. ❺ 타동사 (머리를) 짧게 자르다 ❑ 그녀는 머리를 짧게 자르고 금발로 염색했다. ❻ 가산명사 짧은 헤어스타일 ❑ 그녀는 긴 머리를 사내아이 같은 짧은 머리로 잘랐다. ❼ 타동사 (사진을) 자르다 ❑ 나는 그 사진에서 해안선 바로 윗부분만 잘라 내기로 결심했다.

▶crop up PHRASAL VERB If something **crops up**, it appears or happens, usually unexpectedly. ❑ *His name has cropped up at every selection meeting this season.*

구동사 불쑥 나타나다 ❑ 이번 시즌 선발 회의 때마다 그의 이름이 불쑥불쑥 거론되었다.

cro|quet /kroukeɪ, BRIT kroukeɪ/ N-UNCOUNT **Croquet** is a game played on grass in which the players use long wooden sticks called mallets to hit balls through metal arches. ❑ *During the summer, staff play croquet in the impeccably maintained garden outside the office.*

불가산명사 크로켓 (운동 경기) ❑ 여름 내내 직원들은 사무실 바깥에 있는, 완벽하게 보수가 된 정원에서 크로켓 경기를 한다.

a
b
c
d
e
f
g
h
i
j
k
l
m
n
o
p
q
r
s
t
u
v
w
x
y
z

cross

① VERB AND NOUN USES
② ADJECTIVE USE

① **cross** ♦♦◊ /krɒs, BRIT krɒs/ (crosses, crossing, crossed) →Please look at category ⑬ to see if the expression you are looking for is shown under another headword. **1** V-T/V-I If you **cross** something such as a room, a road, or an area of land or water, you move or travel to the other side of it. If you **cross to** a place, you move or travel over a room, road, or area of land or water in order to reach that place. ☐ *She was partly to blame for failing to look as she crossed the road.* ☐ *Egan crossed to the drinks cabinet and poured a Scotch.* **2** V-T A road, railroad, or bridge that **crosses** an area of land or water passes over it. ☐ *The Defford to Eckington road crosses the river half a mile outside Eckington.* **3** V-RECIP Lines or roads that **cross** meet and go across each other. ☐ *...the intersection where Main and Center streets cross.* **4** V-T If someone or something **crosses** a limit or boundary, for example the limit of acceptable behavior, they go beyond it. ☐ *I normally never write into magazines but Mr. Stubbs has finally crossed the line.* **5** V-T If an expression **crosses** someone's face, it appears briefly on their face. [WRITTEN] ☐ *Berg tilts his head and a mischievous look crosses his face.* **6** N-COUNT A **cross** is a shape that consists of a vertical line or piece with a shorter horizontal line or piece across it. It is the most important Christian symbol. ☐ *Round her neck was a cross on a silver chain.* **7** N-COUNT A **cross** is a written mark in the shape of an X. You can use it, for example, to indicate that an answer to a question is wrong, to mark the position of something on a map, or to indicate your vote on a ballot paper. ☐ *Put a cross next to those activities you like.* **8** V-T If a check **is crossed**, two parallel lines are drawn across it or printed on it to indicate that it must be paid into a bank account and cannot be cashed. [BRIT] [usu passive] ☐ *Cheques/postal orders should be crossed and made payable to Newmarket Promotions.* **9** V-T If you **cross** your arms, legs, or fingers, you put one of them on top of the other. ☐ *Jill crossed her legs and rested her chin on one fist, as if lost in deep thought.* **10** N-SING Something that is a **cross between** two things is neither one thing nor the other, but a mixture of both. ☐ *"Ha!" It was a cross between a laugh and a bark.* **11** N-COUNT In some team sports such as soccer and hockey, a **cross** is the passing of the ball from the side of the field to a player in the center, usually in front of the goal. ☐ *Le Tissier hit an accurate cross to Groves.* **12** ADJ A **cross** street is a road that crosses another more important road. [AM] [ADJ n] ☐ *The Army boys had personnel carriers blocking the cross streets.* **13** →see also **crossing.** to **cross** your **fingers** →see **finger. cross** my **heart** →see **heart.** to **cross** your **mind** →see **mind.** to **cross swords** →see **sword.**

Word Partnership   cross의 연어

N. cross **a street** ① ③
    cross *your* **legs** ⑨
    cross *someone's* **mind** ⑬

▶**cross out** PHRASAL VERB If you **cross out** words on a page, you draw a line through them, because they are wrong or because you want to change them. ☐ *He crossed out "fellow subjects," and instead inserted "fellow citizens."*

② **cross** /krɒs, BRIT krɒs/ (crosser, crossest) ADJ Someone who is **cross** is rather angry or irritated. ☐ *The women are cross and bored.* ☐ *I'm terribly cross with him.* ● **cross|ly** ADV [ADV with v] ☐ *"No, no, no," Morris said crossly.*

cross-country **1** N-UNCOUNT **Cross-country** is the sport of running, riding, or skiing across open countryside rather than along roads or around a running track. ☐ *She finished third in the world cross-country championships in Antwerp.* **2** ADJ A **cross-country** journey involves less important roads or rail lines, or takes you from one side of a country to the other. [ADJ n] ☐ *...cross-country rail services.* ● ADV **Cross-country** is also an adverb. [ADV after v] ☐ *I drove cross-country in his van.*

cross-examine (cross-examines, cross-examining, cross-examined) V-T When a lawyer **cross-examines** someone during a trial or hearing, he or she questions them about the evidence that they have already given. ☐ *The accused's lawyers will get a chance to cross-examine him.* ● **cross-examination** (cross-examinations) N-VAR ☐ *...during the cross-examination of a witness in a murder case.* →see **trial**

cross|ing /krɒsɪŋ, BRIT krɒsɪŋ/ (crossings) **1** N-COUNT A **crossing** is a journey by boat or ship to a place on the other side of a sea, river, or lake. ☐ *He made the crossing from Cape Town to Sydney in just over twenty-six days.* **2** N-COUNT A **crossing** is a place where two roads, paths, or lines cross. ☐ *She sighed and squatted down next to the crossing of the two trails.* **3** N-COUNT A **crossing** is the same as a **pedestrian crossing.** [BRIT] ☐ *A car hit her on a crossing.* **4** N-COUNT A **crossing** is the same as a **grade crossing** or a **level crossing.**

cross|over /krɒsoʊvər, BRIT krɒsoʊvər/ (crossovers) **1** N-VAR A **crossover** of one style and another, especially in music or fashion, is a combination of the two different styles. ☐ *...the contemporary crossover of pop, jazz, and funk.* **2** N-SING In music or fashion, if someone makes a **crossover from** one style **to** another, they become successful outside the style they were originally known for. ☐ *I told her the crossover from actress to singer is easier than singer to actress.*

cross-reference (cross-references) N-COUNT A **cross-reference** is a note in a book which tells you that there is relevant or more detailed information in another part of the book. ☐ *It concludes with a very useful summary of key points, with cross-references to where each key point is dealt with in the book.*

---

1 타동사/자동사 가로질러 가다, 건너다 ☐ 그녀가 길을 건너면서 쳐다보지 않았던 것은 부분적으로 그녀의 잘못이었다. ☐ 이건은 주류 선반 쪽으로 가로 건너가서 스카치를 한 잔 따랐다. **2** 타동사 통과하다, 넘나 ☐ 데포드에서 에킹턴으로 뻗은 도로는 에킹턴 외곽으로 반 마일 떨어진 강을 통과한다. **3** 상호동사 교차하다 ☐ 메인 가와 센터 가가 교차하는 교차로 **4** 타동사 (한계 등을) 넘다, 넘어서다 ☐ 나는 보통 잡지사에 기고하지 않지만 스팁스 씨가 마침내 선을 넘었다. **5** 타동사 (표정이) 스치다 [문어체] ☐ 버그는 고개를 갸우뚱하더니 장난기 어린 표정이 얼굴에 스친다. **6** 가산명사 십자형 ☐ 그녀는 십자가 달린 목걸이를 걸고 있었다. **7** 가산명사 엑스표 ☐ 당신이 좋아하는 활동에 엑스표를 하시오. **8** 타동사 (수표에) 두 줄로 횡선을 긋다 [영국영어] ☐ 수표/우편환은 횡선을 긋고, '마켓 프로모션즈' 앞으로 지급되게 명시해야 한다. **9** 타동사 (팔, 다리 등을) 꼬다, (팔짱을) 끼다 ☐ 질은 마치 깊은 생각에 빠져 있는 것처럼 다리를 꼬고 턱을 괴었다. **10** 단수명사 중간 ☐ "하." 하는 그 소리는 웃음과 호령의 중간이었다. **11** 가산명사 (축구나 하키의) 크로스 ☐ 레티시에르는 그로브즈에게 정확히 크로스했다. **12** 형용사 (큰 길과 교차하는) 골목, 교차 도로의 [미국영어] ☐ 그 군인들에게는 그 골목길을 차단한 병사 수송차가 있었다.

구동사 삭제하다 ☐ 그는 '동료 백성'이란 말을 삭제하고 그 대신 '동료 시민'이란 말을 써 넣었다.

형용사 짜증을 내는 ☐ 여자들이 짜증을 내며 따분해한다. ☐ 나는 그에게 몹시 짜증이 난다. ● 짜증을 내며 부사 ☐ "아, 아냐, 아니라니까." 라고 모리스가 짜증을 내며 말했다.

1 불가산명사 크로스컨트리 경주 ☐ 그녀는 앤트워프에서 열린 크로스컨트리 세계 선수권 대회에서 3등을 했다. **2** 형용사 국토를 횡단하는 ☐ 전국 횡단 철도편 ● 부사 국토를 횡단하여 ☐ 나는 그의 밴을 몰고 국토를 횡단했다.

타동사 반대 심문하다 ☐ 피고인의 변호사가 그를 반대 심문할 기회를 가질 것이다. ● 반대 심문 가산명사 또는 불가산명사 ☐ 살인 사건의 증인을 반대 심문하는 동안

1 가산명사 횡단 여행 ☐ 그는 겨우 26일 만에 케이프타운에서 시드니까지 횡단했다. **2** 가산명사 교차점 ☐ 그녀가 두 길의 교차점 옆에서 한숨을 내쉬며 쪼그려 앉았다. **3** 가산명사 횡단보도 [영국영어] ☐ 어떤 차가 횡단보도에서 그녀를 치었다. **4** 가산명사 건널목

1 가산명사 또는 불가산명사 크로스오버 (음악, 패션), 장르 혼합 ☐ 요즘 유행하는 팝, 재즈, 펑크 음악의 크로스오버 **2** 단수명사 기존 분야에서 다른 분야로의 진출 ☐ 배우에서 가수로 진출하는 것이 가수에서 배우로 진출하는 것보다 쉽다고 내가 그녀에게 말했다.

가산명사 책 속의 상호 참조 ☐ 그 책은 매우 유용하게 주요 항목을 요약하여 끝맺고 있는데, 책 안에서 다루어진 각 주요 항목의 위치를 상호 참조할 수 있도록 표기되어 있다.

a b c d e f g h i j k l m n o p q r s t u v w x y z

cross|roads /krɔ́sroʊdz, BRIT krɒ́sroʊdz/

> **Crossroads** is both the singular and the plural form.

■ N-COUNT A **crossroads** is a place where two roads meet and cross each other. ❑ *Turn right at the first crossroads.* ■ N-SING If you say that something is **at a crossroads**, you mean that it has reached a very important stage in its development where it could go one way or another. ❑ *The company was clearly at a crossroads.*

cross-section (**cross-sections**) also **cross section** ■ N-COUNT If you refer to a **cross-section of** particular things or people, you mean a group of them that you think is typical or representative of all of them. ❑ *I was surprised at the cross-section of people there.* ■ N-COUNT A **cross-section** of an object is what you would see if you could cut straight through the middle of it. [also *in* N] ❑ *...a cross-section of an airplane.*

cross|word /krɔ́sw3rd, BRIT krɒ́sw3ːʳd/ (**crosswords**) N-COUNT A **crossword** or **crossword puzzle** is a word game in which you work out the answers and write them in the white squares of a pattern of small black and white squares. ❑ *He could do the Times crossword in 15 minutes.*

crotch /krɒtʃ/ (**crotches**) ■ N-COUNT Your **crotch** is the part of your body between the tops of your legs. ❑ *Glover kicked him hard in the crotch.* ■ N-COUNT The **crotch** of something such as a pair of pants is the part that covers the area between the tops of your legs. ❑ *They were too long in the crotch.*

crouch /kraʊtʃ/ (**crouches, crouching, crouched**) V-I If you **are crouching**, your legs are bent under you so that you are close to the ground and leaning forward slightly. ❑ *We were crouching in the bushes.* ❑ *I crouched on the ground.* ● N-SING **Crouch** is also a noun. ❑ *They walked in a crouch, each bent over close to the ground.* ● PHRASAL VERB **Crouch down** means the same as **crouch**. ❑ *He crouched down and reached under the mattress.*

crow /kroʊ/ (**crows, crowing, crowed**) ■ N-COUNT A **crow** is a large black bird which makes a loud, harsh noise. ❑ *The crows roosted in Fonsa's Tower.* ■ V-I When a cock **crows**, it makes a loud sound, often early in the morning. ❑ *The cock crows and the dawn chorus begins.*

crowd ♦♦◇ /kraʊd/ (**crowds, crowding, crowded**) ■ N-COUNT-COLL A **crowd** is a large group of people who have gathered together, for example to watch or listen to something interesting, or to protest about something. ❑ *A huge crowd gathered in a square outside the Kremlin walls.* ❑ *It took some two hours before the crowd was fully dispersed.* ■ N-COUNT A particular **crowd** is a group of friends, or a set of people who share the same interests or job. [INFORMAL] ❑ *All the old crowd have come out for this occasion.* ■ V-I When people **crowd around** someone or something, they gather closely together around them. ❑ *The hungry refugees crowded around the tractors.* ■ V-T/V-I If people **crowd into** a place or **are crowded into** a place, large numbers of them enter it so that it becomes very full. ❑ *Hundreds of thousands of people have crowded into the center of the Lithuanian capital, Vilnius.* ❑ *One group of journalists were crowded into a minibus.* ■ V-T If a group of people **crowd** a place, there are so many of them there that it is full. ❑ *Thousands of demonstrators crowded the streets shouting slogans.*

Word Partnership	*crowd의 연어*
ADJ.	**enthusiastic** crowd, **small** crowd ■
V.	**attract** a crowd, **avoid** the crowd, crowd **gathers** ■
PREP.	crowd **around** *something* ■
	crowd **into** *something* ■

crowd|ed /kraʊdɪd/ ■ ADJ If a place is **crowded**, it is full of people. ❑ *He peered slowly around the small crowded room.* ■ ADJ If a place is **crowded**, a lot of people live there. ❑ *...a crowded city of 2 million.* ■ ADJ If your schedule, your life, or your mind is **crowded**, it is full of events, activities, or thoughts. ❑ *Never before has a summit had such a crowded agenda.*

crown ♦♦◇ /kraʊn/ (**crowns, crowning, crowned**) ■ N-COUNT A **crown** is a circular ornament, usually made of gold and jewels, which a king or queen wears on their head at official ceremonies. You can also use **crown** to refer to anything circular that is worn on someone's head. ❑ *...a crown of flowers.* ■ N-PROPER The government of a country that has a king or queen is sometimes referred to as **the Crown**. In British criminal cases the prosecutor is **the Crown**. ❑ *She says the sovereignty of the Crown must be preserved.* ❑ *...a Minister of the Crown.* ■ V-T When a king or queen **is crowned**, a crown is placed on their head as part of a ceremony in which they are officially made king or queen. [usu passive] ❑ *Elizabeth was crowned in Westminster Abbey on 2 June 1953.* ❑ *Two days later, Juan Carlos was crowned king.* ■ N-COUNT Your **crown** is the top part of your head, at the back. ❑ *He laid his hand gently on the crown of her head.* ■ N-COUNT A **crown** is an artificial top piece fixed over a broken or decayed tooth. ❑ *How long does it take to have crowns fitted?* →see **teeth**

Word Link	*cruc ≈ cross : crucial, crucifixion, crucify*

cru|cial ♦♦◇ /krúʃ°l/ ADJ If you describe something as **crucial**, you mean it is extremely important. ❑ *He had administrators under him but took the crucial decisions himself.* ● **cru|cial|ly** ADV ❑ *Chewing properly is crucially important.*

Word Partnership	*crucial의 연어*
N.	crucial **decision**, crucial **development**, crucial **role**, crucial **skill**, crucial **stage**, crucial **to** *something*

crossroads은 단수형 및 복수형이다.

■ 가산명사 네거리, 십자로 ❑ 첫 번째 네거리에서 우회전하세요. ■ 단수명사 기로, 중대한 갈림길 ❑ 분명히 그 회사는 기로에 서 있었다.

■ 가산명사 특징적인 면, 대표적인 단면 ❑ 나는 그곳 사람들의 특징적인 면을 보고 놀랐다. ■ 가산명사 단면도 ❑ 비행기의 단면도

가산명사 십자말풀이 ❑ 그는 타임스에 실린 십자말풀이를 15분 안에 풀 수 있었다.

■ 가산명사 (인체의) 샅, 가랑이 ❑ 글로버가 그의 가랑이를 세게 걷어찼다. ■ 가산명사 (바지의) 아랫 ❑ 그 바지는 하단 부분이 너무 길었다.

자동사 쪼그려 앉아 있다 ❑ 우리는 덤불 속에 쪼그려 앉아 있었다. ❑ 나는 땅 바닥에 쪼그려 앉았다. ● 단수명사 쪼그림 ❑ 그들은 몸을 땅바닥 위로 바짝 굽혀 쪼그려 앉은 채 걸어갔다. ● 구동사 쪼그려 앉다, 웅크리다 ❑ 그가 몸을 웅크려서 매트리스 밑으로 다가갔다.

■ 가산명사 까마귀 ❑ 까마귀들이 폰사의 탑에 자리를 틀고 있었다. ■ 자동사 (수탉이) 울다 ❑ 수탉이 울면 새들이 함께 지저귀기 시작한다.

■ 가산명사-집합 군중 ❑ 엄청난 수의 군중이 크렘린 밖 광장에 모였다. ❑ 군중이 완전히 해산하기까지 두 시간 정도가 걸렸다. ■ 가산명사 패거리 [비격식체] ❑ 옛날 그 패거리들이 이번 일에 모두 나섰다. ■ 자동사 떼 지어 모여들다 ❑ 굶주린 난민들이 트랙터 주위로 떼 지어 모여 들었다. ■ 타동사/자동사 가득 몰려들다 ❑ 수십만 명의 사람들이 리투아니아 공화국의 수도인 빌뉴스의 중심지로 몰려들었다. ❑ 언론인 한 무리가 소형 버스 한 대에 가득 탔다. ■ 타동사 가득 메우다 ❑ 수천 명의 시위자들이 거리를 가득 메우고 슬로건들을 외쳐 댔다.

■ 형용사 사람들로 가득 찬 ❑ 그는 사람들로 가득 찬 그 작은 방을 천천히 살펴며 둘러보았다. ■ 형용사 인구가 많은 ❑ 2백만의 인구로 북적거리는 도시 ■ 형용사 꽉 짜인, 가득 찬 ❑ 그렇게 많은 의제로 꽉 짜인 정상 회담은 처음이다.

■ 가산명사 왕관, 머리에 쓰는 관 ❑ 화관 ■ 고유명사 군주국의 정부 ❑ 그녀는 군주국 정부의 통치권이 유지되어야 한다고 말한다. ❑ 군주국 정부의 장관 ■ 타동사 즉위하다, 왕위에 오르다 ❑ 엘리자베스 여왕은 1953년 6월 2일에 웨스트민스터 성당에서 즉위했다. ❑ 이틀 후에 후안 카를로스가 왕위에 올랐다. ■ 가산명사 정수리 ❑ 그가 살포시 한 손을 그녀의 정수리에 얹었다. ■ 가산명사 인공 치관 ❑ 치관을 끼우는 데 얼마나 오래 걸립니까?

형용사 중대한 ❑ 그 밑으로 관리자들이 있었지만 중대한 결정은 자신이 직접 내렸다. ● 아주, 결정적으로 부사 ❑ 음식물을 제대로 씹는 것이 아주 중요하다.

Word Link   cruc ≈ cross : crucial, crucifixion, crucify

cru|ci|fix|ion /krusɪfɪkʃ°n/ (**crucifixions**) **1** N-VAR **Crucifixion** is a way of killing people which was common in the Roman Empire, in which they were tied or nailed to a cross and left to die. ❏ *...her historical novel about the crucifixion of Christians in Rome.* **2** N-PROPER **The Crucifixion** is the crucifixion of Christ. ❏ *...the central message of the Crucifixion.*

1 가산명사 또는 불가산명사 십자가에 못 박음 ❏ 로마에서 기독교인들을 십자가에 못 박은 것에 관해 그녀가 쓴 역사 소설 **2** 고유명사 그리스도를 십자가에 못 박음 ❏ 그리스도가 십자가에 못 박히신 일이 지닌 주된 의미

cru|ci|fy /krusɪfaɪ/ (**crucifies, crucifying, crucified**) **1** V-T If someone **is crucified**, they are killed by being tied or nailed to a cross and left to die. [usu passive] ❏ *...the day that Christ was crucified.* **2** V-T To **crucify** someone means to criticize or punish them severely. [INFORMAL] ❏ *She'll crucify me if she finds you still here.*

1 타동사 십자가에 못 박히다 ❏ 그리스도가 십자가에 못 박히시던 그 날 **2** 타동사 혹평하다, 호내 주다 [비격식체] ❏ 아직 네가 여기 있는 걸 그녀가 발견하면 나를 가만 안 둘 거야.

crude /krud/ (**cruder, crudest, crudes**) **1** ADJ A **crude** method or measurement is not exact or detailed, but may be useful or correct in a rough, general way. ❏ *Standard measurements of blood pressure are an important but crude way of assessing the risk of heart disease or strokes.* ● **crude|ly** ADV ❏ *The donors can be split – a little crudely – into two groups.* **2** ADJ If you describe an object that someone has made as **crude**, you mean that it has been made in a very simple way or from very simple parts. ❏ *...crude wooden boxes.* ● **crude|ly** ADV ❏ *...a crudely carved wooden form.* **3** ADJ If you describe someone as **crude**, you disapprove of them because they speak or behave in a rude, offensive, or unsophisticated way. [DISAPPROVAL] ❏ *Nev! Must you be quite so crude?* ● **crude|ly** ADV ❏ *He hated it when she spoke so crudely.* **4** ADJ **Crude** substances are in a natural or unrefined state, and have not yet been used in manufacturing processes. [ADJ n] ❏ *...6 million gallons of crude oil.* **5** N-MASS **Crude** is the same as **crude oil.** →see **oil**

1 형용사 대략적인 ❏ 일반적인 혈압 수치는 심장병이나 뇌졸중 발병 위험을 진단하는 데 있어서 대략적이기는 해도 중요한 사항이다. ● 대강 부사 ❏ 기증자는 대강 두 그룹으로 분류할 수 있다. **2** 형용사 투박한 ❏ 투박한 나무 상자들 ● 투박하게 부사 ❏ 투박하게 조각된 나무 형상 **3** 형용사 상스러운 [탐탁잖음] ❏ 네브! 너 그렇게 상스럽게 굴어야겠니? ● 상스럽게 부사 ❏ 그는 그녀가 그렇게 상스럽게 말하는 것을 몹시 싫어했다. **4** 형용사 가공하지 않은 ❏ 6백만 갤런의 원유 **5** 물질명사 원유

crude oil N-UNCOUNT **Crude oil** is oil in its natural state before it has been processed or refined. ❏ *A thousand tons of crude oil has spilled into the sea from an oil tanker.*

불가산명사 원유 ❏ 유조선에서 원유 수천 톤이 바다로 흘러나왔다.

cru|el /kruəl/ (**crueler, cruelest**) [BRIT **crueller, cruellest**] **1** ADJ Someone who is **cruel** deliberately causes pain or distress to people or animals. ❏ *Children can be so cruel.* ● **cru|el|ly** ADV [ADV with v] ❏ *Douglas was often cruelly tormented by jealous siblings.* **2** ADJ A situation or event that is **cruel** is very harsh and causes people distress. ❏ *...struggling to survive in a cruel world with which they cannot cope.* ● **cru|el|ly** ADV ❏ *His life has been cruelly shattered by an event not of his own making.*

[영국영어 crueller, cruellest] **1** 형용사 잔인한 ❏ 아이들은 무척 잔인해질 수도 있다. ● 잔인하게 부사 ❏ 더글러스는 시샘을 내는 형제들에게 종종 잔인한 괴롭힘을 당했다. **2** 형용사 가혹한 ❏ 그들이 어찌해 볼 길 없는 가혹한 세상에서 살아남으려 발버둥치는 ● 무참하게 부사 ❏ 그의 삶은 자신이 일으키지 않은 사건 때문에 무참하게 산산조각이 났다.

Thesaurus   cruel의 참조어

ADJ.	harsh, mean, nasty, unkind; (ant.) compassionate, gentle, kind **1** grim, severe **2**

cru|el|ty /kruəlti/ (**cruelties**) N-VAR **Cruelty** is behavior that deliberately causes pain or distress to people or animals. ❏ *Britain had laws against cruelty to animals but none to protect children.*

가산명사 또는 불가산명사 잔인한 짓, 학대 ❏ 영국에는 동물 학대 행위를 금하는 법은 있었지만 아동 보호에 관한 법은 없었다.

cruise ♦♢♢ /kruz/ (**cruises, cruising, cruised**) **1** N-COUNT A **cruise** is a vacation during which you travel on a ship or boat and visit a number of places. ❏ *He and his wife were planning to go on a world cruise.* **2** V-T/V-I If you **cruise** a sea, river, or canal, you travel around it or along it on a cruise. ❏ *She wants to cruise the canals of France in a barge.* **3** V-I If a car, ship, or aircraft **cruises** somewhere, it moves there at a steady comfortable speed. ❏ *A black and white police car cruised past.*

1 가산명사 유람선 여행 ❏ 그는 부인과 함께 유람선을 타고 세계 여행을 하려고 계획하고 있었다. **2** 타동사 자동사 유람선 여행하다 ❏ 그녀는 유람선을 타고 프랑스의 운하를 여행하고 싶어 한다. **3** 자동사 적당한 속도로 운행하다, 순찰하다 ❏ 경찰차가 순찰하며 지나갔다.

cruis|er /kruzər/ (**cruisers**) **1** N-COUNT A **cruiser** is a police car. [AM] ❏ *Police cruisers surrounded the bank throughout the day.* **2** N-COUNT A **cruiser** is a large fast warship. ❏ *Italy had lost three cruisers and two destroyers.* **3** N-COUNT A **cruiser** is a motorboat which has an area for people to live or sleep. ❏ *...a three hour journey in a small cruiser with indoor and outdoor seating.*

1 가산명사 경찰 순찰차 [미국영어] ❏ 경찰 순찰차가 하루 종일 그 은행을 에워쌌다. **2** 가산명사 순양함 ❏ 이탈리아는 순양함 세 척과 구축함 두 척을 잃었다. **3** 가산명사 유람선 ❏ 실내 및 갑판에 좌석이 마련된 작은 유람선을 타고 가는 세 시간의 여정

crumb /krʌm/ (**crumbs**) N-COUNT **Crumbs** are tiny pieces that fall from bread, coookies, or cake when you cut it or eat it. ❏ *I stood up, brushing crumbs from my trousers.*

가산명사 부스러기 ❏ 나는 일어서서 바지에 떨어진 부스러기를 털어냈다.

crum|ble /krʌmb°l/ (**crumbles, crumbling, crumbled**) **1** V-T/V-I If something **crumbles**, or if you **crumble** it, it breaks into a lot of small pieces. ❏ *Under the pressure, the flint crumbled into fragments.* **2** V-I If an old building or piece of land **is crumbling**, parts of it are breaking off. ❏ *The high and low-rise apartment blocks built in the 1960s are crumbling.* ● PHRASAL VERB **Crumble away** means the same as **crumble.** ❏ *Britain's coastline stretches 4000 kilometers and much of it is crumbling away.* **3** V-I If something such as a system, relationship, or hope **crumbles**, it comes to an end. ❏ *Their economy crumbled under the weight of United Nations sanctions.* ● PHRASAL VERB **Crumble away** means the same as **crumble.** ❏ *Opposition more or less crumbled away.*

1 타동사 자동사 부서지다; 부수다 ❏ 압력을 받아 부싯돌이 산산조각으로 부서졌다. **2** 자동사 허물어지다 ❏ 1960년대에 지어진 고층 및 저층 아파트가 조금씩 허물어져 가고 있다. ● 구동사 조금씩 허물어지다 ❏ 영국 해안선은 4,000킬로미터에 달하지만 대부분은 조금씩 허물어지고 있다. **3** 자동사 허물어지다 ❏ 그들의 경제가 국제 연합의 제재를 받아 허물어졌다. ● 구동사 허물어지다 ❏ 저항이 거의 허물어졌다.

crum|bly /krʌmbli/ (**crumblier, crumbliest**) ADJ Something that is **crumbly** is easily broken into a lot of little pieces. ❏ *...crumbly cheese.*

형용사 잘 부서지는 ❏ 잘 부서지는 치즈

crum|ple /krʌmp°l/ (**crumples, crumpling, crumpled**) V-T/V-I If you **crumple** something such as paper or cloth, or if it **crumples**, it is squashed and becomes full of untidy creases and folds. ❏ *She crumpled the paper in her hand.* ● PHRASAL VERB **Crumple up** means the same as **crumple.** ❏ *She crumpled up her coffee cup.* ● **crum|pled** ADJ ❏ *His uniform was crumpled, untidy, splashed with mud.*

타동사 자동사 구기다; 구겨지다 ❏ 그녀가 그 종이를 한 손으로 구겨 버렸다. ● 구동사 구기다; 구겨지다 ❏ 그녀는 커피가 든 종이컵을 찌그러뜨렸다. ● 구겨진 형용사 ❏ 그의 제복은 구겨지고 너저분한 데다 흙탕물도 튀어 있었다.

crunch /krʌntʃ/ (**crunches, crunching, crunched**) **1** V-T/V-I If you **crunch** something hard, such as a piece of candy, you crush it noisily between your teeth. ❏ *She sucked an ice cube into her mouth, and crunched it loudly.* **2** V-T/V-I If something **crunches** or if you **crunch** it, it makes a breaking or crushing noise, for example when you step on it. ❏ *A piece of china crunched under my foot.* ● N-COUNT; SOUND **Crunch** is also a noun. ❏ *She heard the crunch of tires on the gravel driveway.* **3** V-I If you **crunch** across a surface made of very small stones, you move across it causing it to make a crunching noise. ❏ *I crunched across the*

1 타동사 자동사 아삭아삭 씹어 먹다, 바삭바삭 씹어 먹다 ❏ 그녀는 얼음 한 조각을 입속으로 빨아들여 바삭바삭 소리를 내며 씹어 먹었다. **2** 타동사 자동사 바삭 하는 소리를 내다; 바삭 하는 소리가 나게 하다 ❏ 도자기가 내 발에 밟혀 바삭하고 부서지는 소리가 났다. ● 가산명사; 소리 바삭바삭 하는 소리, 저벅저벅 하는 소리 ❏ 그녀는 자갈 깔린 진입로 위로 차바퀴가 저그럭저그럭 굴러가는 소리를 들었다. **3** 자동사

gravel. ◼ N-SING You can refer to an important time or event, for example when an important decision has to be made, as **the crunch**. ❑ *He can rely on my support when the crunch comes.* ◼ V-T To **crunch** numbers means to do a lot of calculations using a calculator or computer. ❑ *I pored over the books with great enthusiasm, often crunching the numbers until 1:00 a.m.* ◼ N-COUNT A situation in which a business or economy has very little money can be referred to as a **crunch**. [BUSINESS] ❑ *The UN is facing a cash crunch.*

crunchy /krʌntʃi/ (**crunchier**, **crunchiest**) ADJ Food that is **crunchy** is pleasantly hard or crisp so that it makes a noise when you eat it. [APPROVAL] ❑ *...fresh, crunchy vegetables.*

cru|sade /kruseɪd/ (**crusades**, **crusading**, **crusaded**) ◼ N-COUNT A **crusade** is a long and determined attempt to achieve something for a cause that you feel strongly about. ❑ *He made it his crusade to teach children to love books.* ◼ V-I If you **crusade** for a particular cause, you make a long and determined effort to achieve something for it. ❑ *...a newspaper that has crusaded against the country's cocaine traffickers.*

cru|sad|er /kruseɪdər/ (**crusaders**) N-COUNT A **crusader for** a cause is someone who does a lot in support of it. ❑ *He has set himself up as a crusader for higher press and broadcasting standards.*

crush /krʌʃ/ (**crushes**, **crushing**, **crushed**) ◼ V-T To **crush** something means to press it very hard so that its shape is destroyed or so that it breaks into pieces. ❑ *Andrew crushed his empty can.* ❑ *...crushed ice.* ◼ V-T To **crush** a protest or movement, or a group of opponents, means to defeat it completely, usually by force. ❑ *The military operation was the first step in a plan to crush the uprising.* ● **crush|ing** N-UNCOUNT ❑ *...the violent crushing of anti-government demonstrations.* ◼ V-T If you **are crushed** by something, it upsets you a great deal. [usu passive] ❑ *Listen to criticism but don't be crushed by it.* ◼ V-T If you **are crushed** against someone or something, you are pushed or pressed against them. [usu passive] ❑ *We were at the front, crushed against the stage.* ◼ N-COUNT A **crush** is a crowd of people close together, in which it is difficult to move. ❑ *His thirteen-year-old son somehow got separated in the crush.* ◼ N-COUNT If you have a **crush on** someone, you are in love with them but do not have a relationship with them. [INFORMAL] ❑ *She had a crush on you, you know.*

crush|ing /krʌʃɪŋ/ ADJ A **crushing** defeat, burden, or disappointment is a very great or severe one. [EMPHASIS] [ADJ n] ❑ *...since their crushing defeat in the local elections.*

crust /krʌst/ (**crusts**) ◼ N-COUNT The **crust** on a loaf of bread is the outside part. ❑ *Cut the crusts off the bread and soak the bread in the milk.* ◼ N-COUNT A pie's **crust** is its cooked pastry. ❑ *As far as desserts go, the Key lime pie was bursting with flavor. Good crust, too.* ◼ N-COUNT A **crust** is a hard layer of something, especially on top of a softer or wetter substance. ❑ *As the water evaporates, a crust of salt is left on the surface of the soil.* ◼ N-COUNT The earth's **crust** is its outer layer. ❑ *Earthquakes leave scars in the earth's crust.* →see **continents, core, earthquake**

crusty /krʌsti/ (**crustier**, **crustiest**) ADJ **Crusty** bread has a hard, crisp outside. ❑ *...crusty French loaves.*

crutch /krʌtʃ/ (**crutches**) ◼ N-COUNT A **crutch** is a stick whose top fits around or under the user's arm, which someone with an injured foot or leg uses to support their weight when walking. ❑ *I can walk without the aid of crutches.* ◼ N-SING If you refer to someone or something as a **crutch**, you mean that they give you help or support. ❑ *He gave up the crutch of alcohol.* ◼ N-COUNT Your **crutch** is the same as your **crotch**. [mainly BRIT] ❑ *He kicked him in the crutch.*

crux /krʌks/ N-SING The **crux of** a problem or argument is the most important or difficult part of it which affects everything else. ❑ *He said the crux of the matter was economic policy.*

cry ◆◆◇ /kraɪ/ (**cries**, **crying**, **cried**) ◼ V-I When you **cry**, tears come from your eyes, usually because you are unhappy or hurt. ❑ *I hung up the phone and started to cry.* ❑ *He cried with anger and frustration.* ● N-SING **Cry** is also a noun. ❑ *A nurse patted me on the shoulder and said, "You have a good cry, dear."* ● **cry|ing** N-UNCOUNT ❑ *She had been unable to sleep for three days because of her 3-week-old son's crying.* ◼ V-T If you **cry** something, you shout it or say it loudly. ❑ *"Nancy Drew," she cried, "you're under arrest!"* ● PHRASAL VERB **Cry out** means the same as **cry**. ❑ *"You're wrong, quite wrong!" Henry cried out, suddenly excited.* ◼ N-COUNT A **cry** is a loud, high sound that you make when you feel a strong emotion such as fear, pain, or pleasure. ❑ *A cry of horror broke from me.* ◼ N-COUNT A **cry** is a shouted word or phrase, usually one that is intended to attract someone's attention. ❑ *Thousands of Ukrainians burst into cries of "bravo" on the steps of the parliament.* ◼ N-COUNT You can refer to a public protest about something or an appeal for something as a **cry** of some kind. [JOURNALISM] ❑ *There have been cries of outrage about this expenditure.* ◼ N-COUNT A bird's or animal's **cry** is the loud, high sound that it makes. ❑ *...the cry of a seagull.* ◼ →see also **crying** ◼ to **cry** your **eyes out** →see **eye**. **a shoulder to cry on** →see **shoulder**

Thesaurus   cry의 참조어

v.	sob, weep; (*ant.*) laugh ◼
	call, shout, yell ◼
	howl, moan, shriek ◼

Word Partnership   cry의 연어

v.	**begin to** cry, **start to** cry ◼
N.	cry **with anger** ◼◼◼
	cry **for help**, cry **with joy**, cry **of horror**, cry **of pain** ◼◼◼

저벅저벅 밟다 ❑ 나는 그 자갈길을 저벅저벅 밟고 갔다. ◼ 단수명사 중대한 시기 ❑ 중대한 시기가 오면 그는 내 지지를 기대해도 좋다. ◼ 타동사 대량으로 계산을 처리하다 ❑ 나는 종종 새벽 1시까지 데이터 처리를 해 보기도 하면서 대단한 열정으로 그 책들을 파고들었다. ◼ 가산명사 자금 부족 사태 [경제] ❑ 유엔이 자금 부족 사태에 당면하고 있다.

형용사 아삭아삭한, 바삭바삭한 [마음에 듦] ❑ 싱싱하고 아삭아삭한 채소

◼ 가산명사 (대의를 위한) 운동 ❑ 그는 어린이들이 책을 좋아하도록 가르치는 것을 자신의 지상 목표로 삼았다. ◼ 자동사 운동을 벌이다 ❑ 자국의 코카인 밀매업자 반대 운동을 벌여 온 신문사

가산명사 운동가 ❑ 그는 언론 및 방송의 수준 향상을 도모하는 운동가라고 자처해 왔다.

◼ 타동사 찌그러뜨리다, 으깨다 ❑ 앤드류가 자신의 빈 깡통을 찌그러뜨렸다. ❑ 으깬 얼음 ◼ 타동사 진압하다 ❑ 군사 작전은 폭동 진압 계획의 첫 번째 조치였다. ● 진압 불가산명사 ❑ 반정부 시위의 폭력 진압 ◼ 타동사 좌절하다 ❑ 비평에 귀를 기울이되 그로 인해 좌절하지는 마세요. ◼ 타동사 밀려나다, 밀치이다 ❑ 우리는 앞쪽에 있다가 무대 쪽으로 밀쳐졌다. ◼ 가산명사 북적대는 군중 ❑ 어쩌다가 열세 살 난 그의 아들이 북적대는 군중들 속에서 함께 갔던 사람들과 헤어지게 되었다. ◼ 가산명사 홀딱 반함 [비격식체] ❑ 알겠지만, 그녀가 너에게 홀딱 반했었어.

형용사 재기 불능의; 혹독한 [강조] ❑ 지역 선거에서 그들이 참패를 당한 이후

◼ 가산명사 빵 껍질 ❑ 빵의 껍질을 떼어 내고 우유에 흠뻑 적시세요. ◼ 가산명사 파이 껍질 ❑ 후식이라면, 키라임 파이가 진한 향기를 풍기는 데다 그 껍질도 맛있었다. ◼ 가산명사 딱딱한 껍질 ❑ 그 물이 증발하면서, 딱딱한 소금층이 대지 표면에 남는다. ◼ 가산명사 지각 ❑ 지진은 지각에 갈라진 흔적을 남긴다.

형용사 껍질이 딱딱한 ❑ 껍질이 딱딱한 프랑스 빵

◼ 가산명사 목발 ❑ 난 목발 없이도 걸을 수 있어요. ◼ 단수명사 의지할 대상 ❑ 그는 더 이상 술에 기대지 않았다. ◼ 가산명사 가랑이 [주로 영국영어] ❑ 그가 그 남자의 가랑이를 걷어찼다.

단수명사 핵심 ❑ 그가 이 문제의 핵심은 경제 정책이라고 말했다.

◼ 자동사 울부짖다 ❑ 난 전화를 끊고 울기 시작했다. ❑ 그는 분노와 좌절감에 흐느껴 울었다. ● 단수명사 흐느껴 움 ❑ 간호사가 내 어깨를 다독거리며 말했다. "애야, 실컷 울렴." ● 울음, 울음소리 불가산명사 ❑ 생후 13주 된 아들이 울어서 그녀는 삼 일 동안 잠을 잘 수 없었다. ◼ 타동사 고함치다, 외치다 ❑ "낸시 드류, 너를 체포한다!"라고 그녀가 고함쳤다. ● 구동사 고함치다, 외치다 ❑ "당신이 틀렸어, 완전히 틀렸어!"라고 헨리가 갑자기 흥분하며 외쳤다. ◼ 가산명사 외침, 고함, 비명 ❑ 공포의 비명이 내 안에서 터져 나왔다. ◼ 가산명사 외침, 함성 ❑ 수천 명의 우크라이나 인들이 의회 계단에서 "브라보"라며 함성을 터뜨렸다. ◼ 가산명사 항의 [언론] ❑ 이 지출에 대해서 격렬한 항의가 쏟아지고 있다. ◼ 가산명사 울음소리 ❑ 갈매기 울음소리

Word Web   cry

Have you ever seen someone **burst into tears** when something wonderful happened to them? We expect people to **cry** when they are **sad** or upset. But why do people sometimes **weep** when they are happy? Scientists have found there are three different types of **tears**. Basal tears lubricate the **eyes**. Reflex tears clear the eyes of dirt or smoke. The third type, emotional tears, contain high levels of manganese and prolactin. Decreasing the amount of these chemicals in the body helps us feel better. When people experience strong feelings, negative or positive, **shedding tears** may help restore emotional balance.

▶**cry out** PHRASAL VERB If you **cry out**, you call out loudly because you are frightened, unhappy, or in pain. ❏ *He was crying out in pain on the ground when the ambulance arrived.* →see also **cry 2**

구동사 울부짖다, 절규하다 ❏ 구급차가 도착했을 때 그는 땅바닥에서 아파서 울부짖고 있었다.

▶**cry out for** PHRASAL VERB If you say that something **cries out for** a particular thing or action, you mean that it needs that thing or action very much. ❏ *This is a disgraceful state of affairs and cries out for a thorough investigation.* →see Word Web: **cry**

구동사 반드시 ~을 필요로 하다 ❏ 이것은 불미스런 사안으로 반드시 철저한 조사가 필요하다.

cry|ing /kraɪɪŋ/ **1** PHRASE If you say that there is **a crying need for** something, you mean that there is a very great need for it. ❏ *There is a crying need for more magistrates from the ethnic minority communities.* **2** →see also **cry**

1 구 ~가 절실히 필요함 ❏ 소수 민족 공동체에서 치안 판사가 더 배출되는 것이 절실히 필요하다.

cryp|tic /krɪptɪk/ ADJ A **cryptic** remark or message contains a hidden meaning or is difficult to understand. ❏ *He has issued a short, cryptic statement denying the spying charges.* ● **cryp|ti|cal|ly** ADV [ADV with v] ❏ *"Not necessarily," she says cryptically.*

형용사 수수께끼 같은 ❏ 그가 첩보 혐의를 부인하며 수수께끼 같은 짧은 성명을 발표했다. ● 애매하게 부사 ❏ "꼭 그렇지는 않아요."라며 그녀는 애매하게 말한다.

crys|tal ♦◇◇ /krɪstᵊl/ (**crystals**) **1** N-COUNT A **crystal** is a small piece of a substance that has formed naturally in a regular symmetrical shape. ❏ *...salt crystals.* ❏ *...ice crystals.* **2** N-VAR **Crystal** is a transparent rock that is used to make jewelry and ornaments. ❏ *...a strand of crystal beads.* **3** N-UNCOUNT **Crystal** is a high quality glass, usually with patterns cut into its surface. ❏ *Some of the finest drinking glasses are made from lead crystal.* →see **sugar** →see Word Web: **crystal**

1 가산명사 결정체 ❏ 소금 결정체 ❏ 얼음 결정체 **2** 가산명사 또는 불가산명사 수정 ❏ 한 줄로 꿴 수정 구슬 **3** 불가산명사 크리스털 ❏ 일부 가장 좋은 유리잔은 레드 크리스털로 만들어진다.

crys|tal clear **1** ADJ Water that is **crystal clear** is absolutely clear and transparent like glass. ❏ *The cliffs, lapped by a crystal-clear sea, remind her of Capri.* **2** ADJ If you say that a message or statement is **crystal clear**, you are emphasizing that it is very easy to understand. [EMPHASIS] ❏ *The message is crystal clear – if you lose weight, you will have a happier, healthier, better life.*

1 형용사 수정같이 맑은 ❏ 수정같이 맑은 바다로 둘러싸인 그 절벽을 보면 그녀는 카프리 섬이 생각난다. **2** 형용사 아주 명료한 [강조] ❏ 그 취지는 아주 명료하다. 살을 빼면 더 행복하고 건강한, 보다 나은 삶을 살 수 있다.

crys|tal|lize /krɪstᵊlaɪz/ (**crystallizes, crystallizing, crystallized**) [BRIT also **crystallise**] **1** V-T/V-I If you **crystallize** an opinion or idea, or if it **crystallizes**, it becomes fixed and definite in someone's mind. ❏ *He has managed to crystallize the feelings of millions of ordinary Russians.* **2** V-T/V-I If a substance **crystallizes**, or something **crystallizes** it, it turns into crystals. ❏ *Don't stir or the sugar will crystallize.*

[영국영어 crystallise] **1** 타동사/자동사 형상화하다; 형상화되다 ❏ 그는 수백만 보통 러시아 사람들의 느낌을 형상화해 왔다. **2** 타동사/자동사 결정화가 되다; 결정체를 만들다 ❏ 휘젓지 마세요, 휘저으면 설탕이 엉기니까요.

cub /kʌb/ (**cubs**) N-COUNT A **cub** is a young wild animal such as a lion, wolf, or bear. ❏ *...three five-week-old lion cubs.*

가산명사 (야생동물의) 새끼 ❏ 생후 5주 된 사자 새끼 세 마리

cube /kyub/ (**cubes, cubing, cubed**) **1** N-COUNT A **cube** is a solid object with six square surfaces which are all the same size. ❏ *...cold water with ice cubes in it.* ❏ *...a box of sugar cubes.* **2** V-T When you **cube** food, you cut it into cube-shaped pieces. ❏ *Remove the seeds and stones and cube the flesh.* **3** N-COUNT **The cube of** a number is another number that is produced by multiplying the number by itself twice. For example, the cube of 2 is 8. →see **volume**

1 가산명사 입방체, 정육면체 ❏ 각얼음을 넣은 차가운 물 ❏ 각설탕 한 통 **2** 타동사 각둑썰기 하다 ❏ 씨를 빼내고 과육만 각둑썰기 하세요. **3** 가산명사 세제곱

cu|bic /kyubɪk/ ADJ **Cubic** is used in front of units of length to form units of volume such as "cubic meter" and "cubic foot." [ADJ n] ❏ *...3 billion cubic meters of soil.*

형용사 입방체의 ❏ 대지 30억 입방미터

Word Link   cle ≈ small : article, cubicle, particle

cu|bi|cle /kyubɪkᵊl/ (**cubicles**) N-COUNT A **cubicle** is a very small enclosed area, for example one where you can take a shower or change your clothes. ❏ *...a separate shower cubicle.* →see **office**

가산명사 칸막이 공간 ❏ 별도의 샤워 공간

cuckoo /kuku, kʊku/ (**cuckoos**) N-COUNT A **cuckoo** is a bird that has a call of two quick notes, and lays its eggs in other birds' nests.

가산명사 뻐꾸기

cu|cum|ber /kyukʌmbər/ (**cucumbers**) N-VAR A **cucumber** is a long thin vegetable with a hard green skin and wet transparent flesh. It is eaten raw in salads. ❏ *...a cheese and cucumber sandwich.*

가산명사 또는 불가산명사 오이 ❏ 치즈 오이 샌드위치

cud|dle /kʌdᵊl/ (**cuddles, cuddling, cuddled**) V-RECIP If you **cuddle** someone, you put your arms round them and hold them close as a way of showing your affection. ❏ *He cuddled the newborn girl.* ● N-COUNT **Cuddle** is also a noun. ❏ *It would have been nice to give him a cuddle and a kiss but there wasn't time.*

상호동사 껴안다 ❏ 그가 갓 태어난 여자 아기를 껴안았다. ● 가산명사 껴안음, 포옹 ❏ 그를 껴안고 입맞추어 주었으면 좋았을 테지만 시간이 없었어.

cud|dly /kʌdli/ (**cuddlier, cuddliest**) **1** ADJ A **cuddly** person or animal makes you want to cuddle them. [APPROVAL] ❏ *He is a small, cuddly man with spectacles.* **2** ADJ **Cuddly** toys are soft toys that look like animals. [ADJ n]

1 형용사 껴안아 주고 싶은 [마음에 듦] ❏ 그는 안경을 낀, 껴안아 주고 싶은 자그마한 남자야. **2** 형용사 (장난감이) 껴안기 좋은

cue ♦◇◇ /kyu/ (**cues, cueing, cued**) **1** N-COUNT In the theater or in a musical performance, a performer's **cue** is something another performer says or does that is a signal for them to begin speaking, playing, or doing something. ❏ *The actors not performing sit at the side of the stage in full view, waiting for their cues.* **2** V-T If one performer **cues** another, they say or do something which is a signal for the second performer to begin speaking, playing, or doing something. ❏ *He read the scene, with Seaton cueing him.* **3** N-COUNT If you say that

1 가산명사 (연기자에게 보내는 신호) 큐 ❏ 대기 중인 배우들은 무대가 전부 보이는 측면에 앉아서 큐를 받을 때까지 기다린다. **2** 타동사 큐를 보내다 ❏ 시튼이 큐를 주자 그는 그 장면을 낭독했다. **3** 가산명사 신호 ❏ 그것은 몇 달간 집중적인 거래가 이루어지게 될 것임을 보여주는 신호였다. **4** 가산명사 (남자)

Word Web   crystal

The outsides of **crystals** have smooth flat planes. These surfaces form because of the repeating patterns of atoms, molecules, or ions inside the crystal. Evaporation, temperature changes, and pressure can all help to form crystals. Crystals grow when sea water evaporates and leaves behind **salt**. When water freezes, **ice** crystals form. When magma cools, it becomes **rock** with a crystalline structure. Pressure can also create one of the hardest, most beautiful crystals—the **diamond**.

something that happens is a **cue for** an action, you mean that people start doing that action when it happens. ❑ *That was the cue for several months of intense bargaining.* ◢ N-COUNT A **cue** is a long, thin wooden stick that is used to hit the ball in games such as billiards, pool, and snooker.

cuff /kʌf/ (**cuffs**) ◼ N-COUNT The **cuffs** of a shirt or dress are the parts at the ends of the sleeves, which are thicker than the rest of the sleeve. ❑ *...a pale blue shirt with white collar and cuffs.* ◢ PHRASE An **off-the-cuff** remark is made without being prepared or thought about in advance. ❑ *I didn't mean any offence. It was a flippant, off-the-cuff remark.*

■ 가산명사 소맷부리, 소맷단 ❑ 깃과 소맷부리가 흰색인 담청색 셔츠 ◢ 구 즉흥적인 ❑ 난 악의는 없었어요. 그건 즉흥적으로 한 경솔한 발언이었어요.

cui|sine /kwɪzin/ (**cuisines**) N-VAR The **cuisine** of a country or district is the style of cooking that is characteristic of that place. ❑ *The cuisine of Japan is low in fat.*
→see **restaurant**

가산명사 또는 불가산명사 요리, 요리법 ❑ 일본 요리는 지방이 적다.

cul|i|nary /ˈkyulənɛri, kʌlə-, BRIT kʌlɪnəri/ ADJ **Culinary** means concerned with cooking. [FORMAL] [ADJ n] ❑ *She was keen to acquire more advanced culinary skills.*

형용사 조리의, 요리의 [격식체] ❑ 그녀는 더 고급 조리 기술을 간절히 배우고 싶어 했다.

cull /kʌl/ (**culls, culling, culled**) ◼ V-T If items or ideas **are culled from** a particular source or number of sources, they are taken and gathered together. ❑ *All this, needless to say, had been culled second-hand from radio reports.* ◢ V-T To **cull** animals means to kill the weaker animals in a group in order to reduce their numbers. ❑ *To save remaining herds and habitat, the national parks department is planning to cull 2000 elephants.* ● N-COUNT **Cull** is also a noun. ❑ *In the reserves of Zimbabwe and South Africa, annual culls are already routine.* ● **cull|ing** N-UNCOUNT ❑ *The culling of seal cubs has led to an outcry from environmental groups.*

■ 타동사 조금씩 따오다 ❑ 말할 것도 없이 이 모두는 라디오 보도문을 간접적으로 조금씩 따온 것들이었다. ◢ 타동사 솎아 내기를 하다, 선별 도태시키다 ❑ 남아 있는 동물들과 서식지를 보호하기 위해서 국립공원 담당 부처가 코끼리 2천 마리를 솎아 낼 계획이다. ● 가산명사 솎아내기, 선별 도태 ❑ 짐바브웨와 남아프리카 공화국의 특별 보호 구역에서는 매년 선별 도태를 하는 일이 이미 일상적인 일이다. ● 선별 도태시킴 불가산명사 ❑ 새끼 바다표범을 선별 도태시키는 일은 환경 보호 단체의 강력한 항의를 불러 왔다.

cul|mi|nate /kʌlmɪneɪt/ (**culminates, culminating, culminated**) V-I If you say that an activity, process, or series of events **culminates in** or **with** a particular event, you mean that event happens at the end of it. ❑ *They had an argument, which culminated in Tom getting drunk.*

자동사 ...로 결과를 낳다, ...로 최고조에 이르다 ❑ 그들이 말다툼을 했는데 결국 이로 인해 톰이 술에 취했다.

cul|mi|na|tion /kʌlmɪneɪʃ°n/ N-SING Something, especially something important, that is **the culmination of** an activity, process, or series of events happens at the end of it. ❑ *Their arrest was the culmination of an operation in which 120 other people were detained.*

단수명사 절정, 최고조 ❑ 그들을 검거함으로써 다른 사람들 120명을 구금했던 작전은 절정을 이루었다.

Word Link   culp ≈ blame, guilt : culpable, culprit, exculpate

cul|prit /kʌlprɪt/ (**culprits**) ◼ N-COUNT When you are talking about a crime or something wrong that has been done, you can refer to the person who did it as **the culprit**. ❑ *All the men were being deported even though the real culprits in the fight have not been identified.* ◢ N-COUNT When you are talking about a problem or bad situation, you can refer to its cause as **the culprit**. ❑ *About 10% of Japanese teenagers are overweight. Nutritionists say the main culprit is increasing reliance on Western fast food.*

■ 가산명사 범인 ❑ 그 싸움의 진범들이 확인되지 않았음에도 불구하고 그 모든 사람들이 추방당하고 있었다. ◢ 가산명사 원인 ❑ 일본 십대 청소년의 약 10퍼센트가 비만이다. 영양학자들은 그 주 원인이 서양식 패스트푸드 섭취량의 증가에 있다고 말한다.

cult /kʌlt/ (**cults**) ◼ N-COUNT A **cult** is a fairly small religious group, especially one which is considered strange. ❑ *The teenager may have been abducted by a religious cult.* ◢ ADJ **Cult** is used to describe things that are very popular or fashionable among a particular group of people. [ADJ n] ❑ *Since her death, she has become a cult figure.* ◤ N-SING Someone or something that is a **cult** has become very popular or fashionable among a particular group of people. ❑ *Ludlam was responsible for making Ridiculous Theater something of a cult.* ◥ N-COUNT The **cult of** something is a situation in which people regard that thing as very important or special. [DISAPPROVAL] ❑ *...the cult of youth that recently gripped publishing.*

■ 가산명사 소수의 사교(邪敎) 집단, 사이비 종교 집단 ❑ 그 십대 청소년은 사교 집단에 납치되었을 수도 있다. ◢ 형용사 (특정 집단의) 숭배를 받는, 컬트적인 ❑ 그녀는 죽은 후에 숭배의 대상이 되었다. ◤ 단수명사 숭배의 대상, 컬트 ❑ 러드럼은 '리디큘러스 씨어터'를 일종의 컬트로 만든 장본인이었다. ◥ 가산명사 숭배직 숭배 [탐탁찮음] ❑ 최근에 출판계를 사로잡은 젊음에 대한 숭배

cul|ti|vate /kʌltɪveɪt/ (**cultivates, cultivating, cultivated**) ◼ V-T If you **cultivate** land or crops, you prepare land and grow crops on it. ❑ *She also cultivated a small garden of her own.* ● **cul|ti|va|tion** /kʌltɪveɪʃ°n/ N-UNCOUNT ❑ *...the cultivation of fruits and vegetables.* ◢ V-T If you **cultivate** an attitude, image, or skill, you try hard to develop it and make it stronger or better. ❑ *He has written eight books and has cultivated the image of an elder statesman.* ● **cul|ti|va|tion** N-UNCOUNT ❑ *...the cultivation of a positive approach to life and health.* ◤ V-T If you **cultivate** someone or **cultivate** a friendship with them, you try hard to develop a friendship with them. ❑ *Howe carefully cultivated Daniel C. Roper, the Assistant Postmaster General.*
→see **farm, grain**

■ 타동사 경작하다 ❑ 그녀 역시 자신만의 작은 채소밭을 경작했다. ● 경작 불가산명사 ❑ 과일 및 채소 경작 ◢ 타동사 양성하다, 닦다 ❑ 그는 여덟 권의 저서를 썼고 원로 정치인의 상을 닦아 왔다. ● 연마 불가산명사 ❑ 건강과 삶에 대한 긍정적인 접근법의 연마 ◤ 타동사 친분을 쌓다 ❑ 호위는 우정 공사 부총재인 다니엘 시 로퍼와 조심스럽게 친분을 쌓아 갔다.

Thesaurus   cultivate의 참조어

v. farm, grow ◼
    develop ◢

cul|ti|vat|ed /kʌltɪveɪtɪd/ **1** ADJ If you describe someone as **cultivated**, you mean that they are well educated and have good manners. [FORMAL] ❑ *His mother was an elegant, cultivated woman.* **2** ADJ **Cultivated** plants have been developed for growing on farms or in gardens. [ADJ n] ❑ *...a mixture of wild and cultivated varieties.*

1 형용사 교양 있는 [격식체] ❑ 그의 어머니는 기품 있고 교양 있는 여인이었다. **2** 형용사 재배한 ❑ 야생종과 재배종의 혼합

cul|tur|al ♦♢♢ /kʌltʃərəl/ **1** ADJ **Cultural** means relating to a particular society and its ideas, customs, and art. ❑ *...a deep sense of personal honor which was part of his cultural heritage.* ● **cul|tur|al|ly** ADV ❑ *...an informed guide to culturally and historically significant sites.* **2** ADJ **Cultural** means involving or concerning the arts. [ADJ n] ❑ *...the sponsorship of sports and cultural events by tobacco companies.* ● **cul|tur|al|ly** ADV ❑ *...one of our better-governed, culturally active regional centers – Manchester or Birmingham, say.*

1 형용사 문화적인 ❑ 그의 문화적 전통의 일부였던 깊은 자부심 ● 문화적으로 부사 ❑ 문화적으로 또 역사적으로 의의 깊은 유적에 대해 정통한 안내서 **2** 형용사 문화의 ❑ 담배 회사가 스포츠 및 문화 행사를 후원함 ● 문화적으로 부사 ❑ 관리가 더 잘 되고 문화적으로 활발한 지역 중심지 중 하나, 말하자면 맨체스터나 버밍엄 같은.

cul|ture ♦♦♢ /kʌltʃər/ (**cultures**) **1** N-UNCOUNT **Culture** consists of activities such as the arts and philosophy, which are considered to be important for the development of civilization or of people's minds. ❑ *There is just not enough fun and frivolity in culture today.* ❑ *...aspects of popular culture.* **2** N-COUNT A **culture** is a particular society or civilization, especially considered in relation to its beliefs, way of life, or art. ❑ *...people from different cultures.* **3** N-COUNT The **culture** of a particular organization or group consists of the habits of the people in it and the way they generally behave. ❑ *But social workers say that this has created a culture of dependency, particularly in urban areas.* **4** N-COUNT In science, a **culture** is a group of bacteria or cells which are grown, usually in a laboratory as part of an experiment. [TECHNICAL] ❑ *...a culture of human cells.*
→see **myth**
→see Word Web: **culture**

1 불가산명사 문화 ❑ 요즘 문화에는 그저 재미와 가벼움이 충분하지 않을 뿐이다. ❑ 대중문화의 양상 **2** 가산명사 문화권 ❑ 다른 문화권의 사람들 **3** 가산명사 생활양식, 문화 ❑ 그러나 사회사업가들은 이것이, 특히 도시 지역에서, 의존적인 문화를 형성해 왔다고 말한다. **4** 가산명사 배양, 배양 세포 [과학 기술] ❑ 인간 세포의 배양

cul|tured /kʌltʃərd/ ADJ If you describe someone as **cultured**, you mean that they have good manners, are well educated, and know a lot about the arts. ❑ *He is a cultured man with a wide circle of friends.*

형용사 교양 있는 ❑ 그는 교제 범위가 넓은 교양 있는 남자이다.

-cum- /-kʌm-/ COMB in N-COUNT **-cum-** is put between two nouns to form a noun referring to something or someone that is partly one thing and partly another. ❑ *...a dining-room-cum-study.*

복합형-가산명사 겸용의 ❑ 식당 겸 서재

cum|ber|some /kʌmbərsəm/ **1** ADJ Something that is **cumbersome** is large and heavy and therefore difficult to carry, wear, or handle. ❑ *Although the machine looks cumbersome, it is actually easy to use.* **2** ADJ A **cumbersome** system or process is very complicated and inefficient. ❑ *...an old and cumbersome computer system.*

1 형용사 다루기 어려운 ❑ 그 기계가 다루기 어려울 것 같지만, 실은 사용하기 쉽다. **2** 형용사 주체스러운 ❑ 주체스러운 구식 컴퓨터

cu|mu|la|tive /kyuːmyələtɪv/ ADJ If a series of events have a **cumulative** effect, each event makes the effect greater. ❑ *It is simple pleasures, such as a walk on a sunny day, which have a cumulative effect on our mood.*

형용사 점증적인, 누적되는 ❑ 그것은 햇살 좋은 날에 산책하는 것처럼 소박한 즐거움이며 우리의 기분을 점점 더 좋아지게 한다.

cun|ning /kʌnɪŋ/ **1** ADJ Someone who is **cunning** has the ability to achieve things in a clever way, often by deceiving other people. ❑ *These disturbed kids can be cunning.* ● **cun|ning|ly** ADV ❑ *They were cunningly disguised in golf clothes.* **2** N-UNCOUNT **Cunning** is the ability to achieve things in a clever way, often by deceiving other people. ❑ *...one more example of the cunning of today's art thieves.*

1 형용사 교활한 ❑ 정서 장애가 있는 이 아이들은 교활할 수도 있다. ● 교활하게 부사 ❑ 그들은 교활하게 골프복장으로 변장했다. **2** 불가산명사 교활함, 간계함 ❑ 오늘날 예술품 절도의 교활함을 보여 주는 또 다른 실례

cup ♦♦♢ /kʌp/ (**cups, cupping, cupped**) **1** N-COUNT A **cup** is a small round container that you drink from. Cups usually have handles and are made from china or plastic. ❑ *...cups and saucers.* ● N-COUNT A **cup of** something is the amount of something contained in a cup. ❑ *Mix about four cups of white flour with a pinch of salt.* **2** N-COUNT Things, or parts of things, that are small, round, and hollow in shape can be referred to as **cups**. ❑ *...the brass cups of the small chandelier.* **3** N-COUNT A **cup** is a large metal cup with two handles that is given to the winner of a game or competition. ❑ *At five he presented a cup at a Windsor polo match.* **4** N-COUNT **Cup** is used in the names of some sports competitions in which the prize is a cup. ❑ *Sri Lanka's cricket team will play India in the final of the Asia Cup.* **5** V-T If you **cup** your **hands**, you make them into a curved shape like a cup. ❑ *He cupped his hands around his mouth and called out for Diane.* ❑ *David knelt, cupped his hands and splashed river water on to his face.* **6** V-T If you **cup** something in your hands, you make your hands into a curved dish-like shape and support it or hold it gently. ❑ *He cupped her chin in the palm of his hand.*

1 가산명사 컵, 잔 ❑ 컵과 받침 접시 ● 가산명사 한 컵 분량 ❑ 약 네 컵 분량의 밀가루에 소금을 약간 넣어 섞으세요. **2** 가산명사 컵 모양의 것 ❑ 작은 샹들리에에 달린 놋쇠 컵 모양들 **3** 가산명사 우승배, 우승컵 ❑ 그가 다섯 살 때 윈저 폴로 경기에서 우승배를 증정했다. **4** 가산명사 컵, 우승배 ❑ 스리랑카 크리켓 팀이 아시아컵 결승전에서 인도 팀과 겨룰 것이다. **5** 타동사 양손을 오므려 컵 모양으로 만들다 ❑ 그는 양손을 컵처럼 오므려 입가에 대고 다이앤을 소리쳐 불렀다. ❑ 데이비드는 무릎을 꿇고 양손을 컵 모양으로 오므려 강물을 떠서 얼굴에 끼얹었다. **6** 타동사 손을 잔 모양처럼 만들어 받치다 ❑ 그가 손바닥으로 턱을 괴었다.

cup|board /kʌbərd/ (**cupboards**) N-COUNT A **cupboard** is a piece of furniture that has one or two doors, usually contains shelves, and is used to store things. In British English, **cupboard** refers to all kinds of furniture like this. In American English, **closet** is usually used instead to refer to larger pieces of furniture. ❑ *The kitchen cupboard was stocked with tins of soup and food.*

가산명사 벽장, 찬장 ❑ 주방 찬장은 수프와 식품 통조림으로 채워져 있었다.

cur|able /kyʊərəbᵊl/ ADJ If a disease or illness is **curable**, it can be cured. ❑ *Most skin cancers are completely curable if detected in the early stages.*

형용사 치유 가능한 ❑ 대부분의 피부암은 초기에 발견하면 완전 치유가 가능하다.

cu|rate (**curates**, **curating**, **curated**)

The noun is pronounced /kyʊərɪt/. The verb is pronounced /kyʊreɪt/.

명사는 /kyʊərɪt/로 발음되고, 동사는 /kyʊreɪt/로 발음된다.

■ N-COUNT A **curate** is a clergyman in the Anglican Church who helps the priest. ■ V-T If an exhibition **is curated** by someone, they organize it. [usu passive] ❑ *The Hayward exhibition has been curated by the artist Bernard Luthi.*

■ 가산명사 성공회 부목사, 보좌 신부 ■ 타동사 관장되다 ❑ 헤이워드 전시회는 미술가인 버나드 루티가 관장했다.

cu|ra|tor /kyʊreɪtər, kyʊəreɪtər/ (**curators**) N-COUNT A **curator** is someone who is in charge of the objects or works of art in a museum or art gallery. ❑ *Peter Forey is curator of fossil fishes at the Natural History Museum.*

가산명사 큐레이터, (박물관이나 미술관의) 작품 관리자 ❑ 피터 포레이는 자연사 박물관의 물고기 화석 담당 관리자이다.

curb /kɜrb/ (**curbs**, **curbing**, **curbed**) ■ V-T If you **curb** something, you control it and keep it within limits. ❑ *...advertisements aimed at curbing the spread of Aids.* ● N-COUNT **Curb** is also a noun. ❑ *He called for much stricter curbs on immigration.* ■ V-T If you **curb** an emotion or your behaviour, you keep it under control. ❑ *He curbed his temper.* ■ N-COUNT The **curb** is the raised edge of a sidewalk which separates it from the road. [AM; BRIT **kerb**] ❑ *I pulled over to the curb.*

■ 타동사 억제하다 ❑ 에이즈 확산을 억제하기 위한 광고 ● 가산명사 억제 ❑ 그는 훨씬 더 엄격한 이민 억제책을 요구했다. ■ 타동사 (감정이나 행동을) 다스리다 ❑ 그는 자신의 성질을 다스렸다. ■ 가산명사 (인도나 차도 사이의) 연석 [미국영어; 영국영어 kerb] ❑ 나는 연석 쪽으로 차를 세웠다.

cure ◆◇◇ /kyʊər/ (**cures**, **curing**, **cured**) ■ V-T If doctors or medical treatments **cure** an illness or injury, they cause it to end or disappear. ❑ *An operation finally cured his shin injury.* ■ V-T If doctors or medical treatments **cure** a person, they make the person well again after an illness or injury. ❑ *MDT is an effective treatment and could cure all the leprosy sufferers worldwide.* ❑ *Almost overnight I was cured.* ■ N-COUNT A **cure for** an illness is a medicine or other treatment that cures the illness. ❑ *There is still no cure for a cold.* ■ V-T If someone or something **cures** a problem, they bring it to an end. ❑ *Private firms are willing to make large scale investments to help cure Russia's economic troubles.* ■ N-COUNT A **cure for** a problem is something that will bring it to an end. ❑ *The magic cure for inflation does not exist.* ■ V-T When food, tobacco, or animal skin **is cured**, it is dried, smoked, or salted so that it will last for a long time. [usu passive] ❑ *Legs of pork were cured and smoked over the fire.*

■ 타동사 (병이나 상처를) 치료하다 ❑ 수술을 받고 마침내 그의 정강이 부상이 나았다. ■ 타동사 (환자를) 치료하다 ❑ 엠디티는 효과적인 치료법이므로 전 세계의 모든 나병 환자를 치료할 수 있을 것이다. ❑ 나는 거의 하룻밤 사이에 치유되었다. ■ 가산명사 치료법 ❑ 아직도 감기 치료법은 없다. ■ 타동사 해결하다 ❑ 민간 기업들은 러시아 경제 문제 해결을 돕기 위해 기꺼이 대규모 투자를 할 용의가 있다. ■ 가산명사 해결책 ❑ 인플레이션에 대한 마법과 같은 해결책은 없다. ■ 타동사 보존 처리되다 ❑ 돼지다리고기는 보존 처리를 해서 불에 훈제를 했다.

cur|few /kɜrfyu/ (**curfews**) N-VAR A **curfew** is a law stating that people must stay inside their houses after a particular time at night, for example during a war. ❑ *The village was placed under curfew.*

가산명사 또는 불가산명사 야간 통행 금지령 ❑ 그 마을에는 야간 통행 금지령이 내려져 있었다.

cu|ri|os|ity /kyʊərɒsɪti/ (**curiosities**) ■ N-UNCOUNT **Curiosity** is a desire to know about something. ❑ *Ryle accepted more out of curiosity than anything else.* ❑ *...an enthusiasm and genuine curiosity about the past.* ■ N-COUNT A **curiosity** is something that is unusual, interesting, and fairly rare. ❑ *There is much to see in the way of castles, curiosities, and museums.*

■ 불가산명사 호기심 ❑ 라일은 무엇보다 호기심 때문에 더 많은 것을 받아들였다. ❑ 과거에 대한 열의와 진정한 호기심 ■ 가산명사 진기한 것 ❑ 성, 진기한 물건, 박물관에 관해서라면 볼거리가 많다.

cu|ri|ous ◆◇◇ /kyʊəriəs/ ■ ADJ If you are **curious about** something, you are interested in it and want to know more about it. ❑ *Steve was intensely curious about the world I came from.* ● **cu|ri|ous|ly** ADV [ADV after v] ❑ *The woman in the shop had looked at them curiously.* ■ ADJ If you describe something as **curious**, you mean that it is unusual or difficult to understand. ❑ *The pageant promises to be a curious mixture of the ancient and modern.* ● **cu|ri|ous|ly** ADV ❑ *Harry was curiously silent through all this.*

■ 형용사 호기심이 있는, 궁금해 하는 ❑ 스티브는 내가 있었던 세상에 대해 매우 궁금해 했다. ● 신기한 듯이, 호기심 어린 눈초리로 부사 ❑ 상점 안에 있던 그 여자가 그들을 호기심 어린 눈초리로 바라보았다. ■ 형용사 기이한 ❑ 그 야외극은 고대와 근대의 기이한 결합이 될 것이다. ● 이상하게도 부사 ❑ 이 모든 것이 진행되는 동안 해리는 이상하게도 아무 말이 없었다.

Word Partnership	*curious*의 연어
N.	curious **expression**, curious **gaze**, curious **glance**, curious **mixture of** *something* ■

curl /kɜrl/ (**curls**, **curling**, **curled**) ■ N-COUNT If you have **curls**, your hair is in the form of tight curves and spirals. ❑ *...the little girl with blonde curls.* ■ N-UNCOUNT If your hair has **curl**, it is full of curls. ❑ *Dry curly hair naturally for maximum curl and shine.* ■ V-T/V-I If your hair **curls** or if you **curl** it, it is full of curls. ❑ *She has hair that refuses to curl.* ❑ *Maria had curled her hair for the event.* ■ N-COUNT A **curl** of something is a thing or quantity of it that is curved or spiral in shape. ❑ *A thin curl of smoke rose from a rusty stove.* ■ V-T/V-I If your toes, fingers, or other parts of your body **curl**, or if you **curl** them, they form a curved or round shape. ❑ *His fingers curled gently round her wrist.* ❑ *Raise one foot, curl the toes and point the foot downwards.* ■ V-T/V-I If something **curls** somewhere, or if you **curl** it there, it moves there in a spiral or curve. ❑ *Smoke was curling up the chimney.* ■ V-T/V-I If a person or animal **curls into** a ball, they move into a position in which their body makes a rounded shape. ❑ *He wanted to curl into a tiny ball.* ● PHRASAL VERB **Curl up** means the same as **curl**. ❑ *In colder weather, your cat will curl up into a tight, heat-conserving ball.* ❑ *She curled up next to him.* ■ V-I When a leaf, a piece of paper, or another flat object **curls**, its edges bend towards the center. ❑ *The rose leaves have curled because of an attack by grubs.* ● PHRASAL VERB **Curl up** means the same as **curl**. ❑ *The corners of the rug were curling up.*

■ 가산명사 고수머리, 곱슬머리 ❑ 곱슬거리는 금발 머리의 어린 소녀 ■ 불가산명사 곱슬곱슬함 ❑ 곱슬머리는 최대한 곱슬곱슬하도록 자연스럽게 말린 후 돋보이게 하세요. ■ 타동사/자동사 곱슬곱슬하다; 곱슬곱슬하게 말다 ❑ 그녀의 머리카락은 좀처럼 곱슬곱슬해지지 않는다. ❑ 마리아는 그 행사를 위해 머리를 곱슬곱슬하게 말았다. ■ 가산명사 나선형 ❑ 연기가 가느다란 나선형을 그리면서 녹슨 난로 사이로 피어올랐다. ■ 타동사/자동사 오그라지다, 동글 말리다; 오그리다, 동글 말다 ❑ 그가 손가락으로 그녀 손목을 부드럽게 휘감았다. ❑ 한쪽 발을 들어서 발가락을 오그려 발이 아래쪽을 향하게 하세요. ■ 타동사/자동사 소용돌이치다; 소용돌이치게 하다 ❑ 연기가 굴뚝 위로 소용돌이치며 솟아오르고 있었다. ■ 타동사/자동사 웅크리다 ❑ 그는 몸을 조그맣게 웅크리고 싶어 했다. ● 구동사 웅크리다 ❑ 날씨가 더 추워지면 당신의 고양이는 몸을 단단히 웅크려 체온을 유지할 것이다. ❑ 그녀가 그의 옆에 몸을 웅크렸다. ■ 자동사 오그라들다, 동글 말리다 ❑ 땅벌레에게 시달려서 장미 꽃잎이 오그라들었다. ● 구동사 오그라들다, 동글 말리다 ❑ 양탄자 모서리가 말려 올라가고 있었다.

▶**curl up** →see **curl 7, 8**

curly /kɜrli/ (**curlier**, **curliest**) ■ ADJ **Curly** hair is full of curls. ❑ *I've got naturally curly hair.* ■ ADJ **Curly** is sometimes used to describe things that are curved or spiral in shape. ❑ *...cauliflowers with extra long curly leaves.*

■ 형용사 곱슬곱슬한 ❑ 난 태어날 때부터 머리카락이 곱슬곱슬했다. ■ 형용사 나선형의 ❑ 나선형의 긴 잎사귀가 더 붙은 꽃양배추

cur|ren|cy ◆◇◇ /kɜrənsi, BRIT kʌrənsi/ (**currencies**) N-VAR The money used in a particular country is referred to as its **currency**. ❑ *Tourism is the country's top earner of foreign currency.* ❑ *More people favor a single European currency than oppose it.* →see **money**

가산명사 또는 불가산명사 통화 ❑ 관광 산업은 그 나라에서 외화를 가장 많이 벌어들이는 분야이다. ❑ 유럽 내 단일 통화를 반대하는 사람보다 지지하는 사람들이 더 많다.

cur|rent ◆◆◆ /kɜrənt, BRIT kʌrənt/ (**currents**) **1** N-COUNT A **current** is a steady and continuous flowing movement of some of the water in a river, lake, or sea. ❑ *Under normal conditions, the ocean currents of the tropical Pacific travel from east to west.* **2** N-COUNT A **current** is a steady flowing movement of air. ❑ *I felt a current of cool air blowing in my face.* **3** N-COUNT An electric **current** is a flow of electricity through a wire or circuit. ❑ *A powerful electric current is passed through a piece of graphite.* **4** N-COUNT A particular **current** is a particular feeling, idea, or quality that exists within a group of people. ❑ *Each party represents a distinct current of thought.* **5** ADJ **Current** means happening, being used, or being done at the present time. ❑ *The current situation is very different to that in 1990.* ● **cur|rent|ly** ADV [ADV before v] ❑ *Twelve potential vaccines are currently being tested on human volunteers.* **6** ADJ Ideas and customs that are **current** are generally accepted and used by most people. ❑ *Current thinking suggests that toxins only have a small part to play in the build up of cellulite.* →see **erosion, ocean, tide**

1 가산명사 해류 ❑ 정상적인 조건이라면 열대 태평양의 해류는 동쪽에서 서쪽으로 흐른다. **2** 가산명사 기류 ❑ 시원한 기류가 내 얼굴 쪽으로 불어오는 것을 느꼈다. **3** 가산명사 전류 ❑ 강력한 전류가 흑연을 통해 흘려보낸다. **4** 가산명사 경향, 추세 ❑ 각 당은 확연히 다른 사조를 대표한다. **5** 형용사 현재의 ❑ 현재 상황은 1990년도의 상황과는 무척 다르다. ● 현재 부사 ❑ 가능성 있는 백신 열두 종이 현재 지원자들을 대상으로 시험 중이다. **6** 형용사 통례의 ❑ 통례적인 사고에 따르면 셀룰라이트 형성에 있어서 독소가 미치는 영향은 극히 일부이다.

cur|rent ac|count (**current accounts**) N-COUNT A **current account** is a personal bank account which you can take money out of at any time using your checkbook or cash card. [BRIT; AM **checking account**] ❑ *His current account was seriously overdrawn.*

가산명사 당좌 예금 [영국영어; 미국영어 checking account] ❑ 그의 당좌 예금은 심각할 정도로 초과 인출되었다.

cur|rent af|fairs N-PLURAL If you refer to **current affairs**, you are referring to political events and problems in society which are discussed in newspapers, and on television and radio. ❑ *I am ill-informed on current affairs.*

복수명사 시사 ❑ 나는 시사에 어둡다.

cur|ricu|lum /kərɪkyələm/ (**curriculums** or **curricula**) /kərɪkyələ/ **1** N-COUNT A **curriculum** is all the different courses of study that are taught in a school, college, or university. ❑ *There should be a broader curriculum in schools for post-16-year-old pupils.*

1 가산명사 교육 과정, 커리큘럼 ❑ 16세 이상의 학생들을 위해서는 학교 교육 과정이 더 폭넓게 마련되어야 한다.

> Outside of the required school classes in the **curriculum**, students may participate in a variety of **extracurricular** (non-compulsory) activities that develop their interests and skills. In North American high schools there are sports clubs and teams, newspapers, future scientists' clubs and drama or music groups to name a few. Students who participate in these groups use their experience as an advantage when they apply for university. Such activities are also found on college campuses.

> curriculum(교과 과정)에 있는 학교 필수 수업 외에 학생이 자신의 흥미와 기능을 개발하는 다양한 (필수가 아닌) extracurricular(과외) 활동에 참가할 수 있다. 북미 고등학교에는, 몇 가지만 예를 들면, 스포츠 클럽과 스포츠 팀, 신문, 미래 과학자 클럽, 연극 또는 음악 클럽이 있다. 이런 모임에 참가하는 학생들은 대학에 지원할 때 이 경험을 장점으로 활용할 수 있다. 이런 활동은 대학 캠퍼스에도 있다.

2 N-COUNT A particular **curriculum** is one particular course of study that is taught in a school, college, or university. ❑ *...the history curriculum.*

2 가산명사 교과 과정 ❑ 역사과 교과 과정

cur|ricu|lum vitae /kərɪkyələm vaɪtiː, BRIT -taɪ/ N-SING A **curriculum vitae** is the same as a **CV**. [mainly BRIT; AM usually **résumé**]

단수명사 이력서 [주로 영국영어; 미국영어 대개 résumé]

cur|ry /kɜri, BRIT kʌri/ (**curries, currying, curried**) **1** N-VAR **Curry** is a dish composed of meat and vegetables, or just vegetables, in a sauce containing hot spices. It is usually eaten with rice and is one of the main dishes of India. ❑ *...vegetable curry.* **2** PHRASE If one person tries to **curry favor with** another, they do things in order to try to gain their support or cooperation. ❑ *Politicians are eager to promote their "happy family" image to curry favor with voters.*

1 가산명사 또는 불가산명사 카레 ❑ 야채 카레 **2** 구 환심을 사다 ❑ 정치가들은 유권자들의 환심을 사기 위해 '단란한 가정'의 이미지를 열심히 홍보한다.

curse /kɜrs/ (**curses, cursing, cursed**) **1** V-I If you **curse**, you use very impolite or offensive language, usually because you are angry about something. [WRITTEN] ❑ *I cursed and hobbled to my feet.* **2** N-COUNT **Curse** is also a noun. ❑ *He shot her an angry look and a curse.* **2** V-T If you **curse** someone, you say insulting things to them because you are angry with them. ❑ *Grandma protested, but he cursed her and rudely pushed her aside.* **3** V-I If you **curse** something, you complain angrily about it, especially using very impolite language. ❑ *So we set off again, cursing the delay, towards the west.* **4** N-COUNT If you say that there is a **curse on** someone, you mean that there seems to be a supernatural power causing unpleasant things to happen to them. ❑ *Maybe there is a curse on my family.* **5** N-COUNT You can refer to something that causes a great deal of trouble or harm as a **curse**. ❑ *Apathy is the long-standing curse of British local democracy.*

1 자동사 욕을 하다 [문어체] ❑ 나는 욕을 하며 힘겹게 일어섰다. ● 가산명사 욕설 ❑ 그가 그녀를 화난 표정으로 쳐다보며 욕을 했다. **2** 타동사 악담을 퍼붓다 ❑ 할머니가 항변했지만, 그는 할머니에게 악담을 퍼붓고 무례하게 옆으로 밀쳤다. **3** 타동사 거칠게 항의하다 ❑ 그래서 우리는 지체된 것에 대해 거칠게 항의하며 서쪽을 향해 다시 출발했다. **4** 가산명사 저주 ❑ 아마도 우리 집안은 저주를 받은 것 같아. **5** 가산명사 재앙, 골칫거리 ❑ 무관심은 영국 지역 민주주의에 오랫동안 계속되어 온 골칫거리이다.

cur|sor /kɜrsər/ (**cursors**) N-COUNT On a computer screen, the **cursor** is a small shape that indicates where anything that is typed by the user will appear. [COMPUTING] ❑ *He moves the cursor, clicks the mouse.* →see **computer**

가산명사 (컴퓨터) 커서 [컴퓨터] ❑ 그는 커서를 옮기고 마우스를 클릭한다.

curt /kɜrt/ ADJ If you describe someone as **curt**, you mean that they speak or reply in a brief and rather rude way. ❑ *Her tone of voice was curt.* ● **curt|ly** ADV [ADV with v] ❑ *"I'm leaving," she said curtly.*

형용사 통명스러운 ❑ 그녀의 어조는 통명스러웠다. ● 통명스럽게 부사 ❑ "나 떠나."라고 그녀가 통명스럽게 말했다.

cur|tail /kɜrteɪl/ (**curtails, curtailing, curtailed**) V-T If you **curtail** something, you reduce or limit it. [FORMAL] ❑ *NATO plans to curtail the number of troops being sent to the region.*

타동사 축소하다 [격식체] ❑ 나토는 그 지역에 보낼 병력 규모를 축소할 계획이다.

cur|tain ◆◇◇ /kɜrtʰn/ (**curtains**) **1** N-COUNT **Curtains** are pieces of very thin material which you hang in front of windows in order to prevent people from seeing in. [AM; BRIT **net curtains**] **2** N-COUNT **Curtains** are large pieces of heavy material which you hang from the top of a window. [mainly BRIT; AM usually **drapes**] ❑ *Her bedroom curtains were drawn.* **3** N-SING In a theater, **the curtain** is the large piece of material that hangs in front of the stage until a performance begins. ❑ *The curtain rises toward the end of the Prelude.*

1 가산명사 발 [미국영어; 영국영어 net curtains] **2** 가산명사 커튼 [주로 영국영어; 미국영어 대개 drapes] ❑ 그녀 침실에 커튼이 드리워져 있었다. **3** 단수명사 막 ❑ 서곡이 끝날 무렵 막이 오른다.

curve /kɜrv/ (**curves, curving, curved**) **1** N-COUNT A **curve** is a smooth, gradually bending line, for example part of the edge of a circle. ❑ *...the curve of his lips.* **2** V-T/V-I If something **curves**, or if someone or something **curves** it, it has the shape of a curve. ❑ *Her spine curved.* ❑ *...a knife with a slightly curving blade.* **3** V-I If something **curves**, it moves in a curve, for example through the air. ❑ *The ball curved strangely in the air.* **4** N-COUNT You can refer to a change in something as a particular **curve**, especially when it is represented on a graph. ❑ *Youth crime overall is on a slow but steady downward curve.* →see also **learning curve**

1 가산명사 곡선 ❑ 그의 입술선 **2** 타동사/자동사 구부러지다, 휘다 ❑ 그녀의 척추는 휘었다. ❑ 약간 휜 칼 **3** 자동사 곡선을 그리다 ❑ 그 공은 이상한 곡선을 그리며 허공으로 날아갔다. **4** 가산명사 곡선 ❑ 청소년 범죄가 전체적으로 느리지만 꾸준히 하향 곡선을 그리고 있다.

curved /kɜrvd/ ADJ A **curved** object has the shape of a curve or has a smoothly bending surface. ❑ ...the curved lines of the chairs. →see **flight**

형용사 휘어진, 구부러진 ❑ 의자의 곡선

cush|ion /kʊʃⁿn/ (cushions, cushioning, cushioned) **1** N-COUNT A **cushion** is a fabric case filled with soft material, which you put on a seat to make it more comfortable. ❑ ...a velvet cushion. **2** N-COUNT A **cushion** is a soft pad or barrier, especially one that protects something. ❑ The company provides a styrofoam cushion to protect the tablets during shipping. **3** V-T Something that **cushions** an object when it hits something protects it by reducing the force of the impact. ❑ There is also a new steering wheel with an energy absorbing rim to cushion the driver's head in the worst impacts. **4** V-T To **cushion** the effect of something unpleasant means to reduce it. ❑ They said Western aid was needed to cushion the blows of vital reform. **5** N-COUNT Something that is a **cushion against** something unpleasant reduces its effect. ❑ Welfare provides a cushion against hardship.

1 가산명사 쿠션 ❑ 벨벳 쿠션 **2** 가산명사 (충격 흡수를 위한) 쿠션 ❑ 회사는 배로 운송되는 동안 그 알약들을 보호할 수 있도록 스티로폼 쿠션을 넣는다. **3** 타동사 충격을 완화하다 ❑ 최악의 충돌시 운전자의 머리에 가해지는 충격을 완화하기 위해 에너지 흡수 테두리가 달린 새로운 자동차 핸들도 있다. **4** 타동사 완화하다 ❑ 그들은 필수 불가결한 개혁이 가져올 충격을 줄이기 위해 서방 세계의 원조가 필요하다고 말했다. **5** 가산명사 완충제 ❑ 생활 보조비는 곤궁에 완충 역할을 한다.

cus|tard /kʌstərd/ (custards) **1** N-VAR **Custard** is a baked dessert made of milk, eggs, and sugar. [AM] ❑ ...a custard with a caramel sauce. **2** N-MASS **Custard** is a sweet yellow sauce made from milk and eggs or from milk and a powder. It is eaten with fruit and puddings. [mainly BRIT] ❑ ...bananas and custard. →see **dessert**

1 가산명사 또는 불가산명사 커스터드 [미국영어] ❑ 캐러멜 소스를 곁들인 커스터드 **2** 물질명사 커스터드 소스 [주로 영국영어] ❑ 커스터드 소스를 끼얹은 바나나

cus|to|dial /kʌstoʊdiəl/ **1** ADJ If a child's parents are divorced or separated, the **custodial** parent is the parent who has custody of the child. [LEGAL] [ADJ n] ❑ ...all the general expenses that come with being the custodial parent. **2** ADJ **Custodial** means relating to keeping people in prison. [mainly BRIT, FORMAL] [ADJ n] ❑ If he is caught again he will be given a custodial sentence.

1 형용사 양육권을 가진 [법률] ❑ 부모 중 양육권을 가진 사람이 감당해야 하는 제반 비용 **2** 형용사 징역의, 수감의 [주로 영국영어, 격식체] ❑ 그가 다시 체포된다면 징역형을 받을 것이다.

cus|to|dian /kʌstoʊdiən/ (custodians) N-COUNT The **custodian** of an official building, a companies' assets, or something else valuable is the person who is officially in charge of it. ❑ ...the custodian of the holy shrines in Mecca and Medina.

가산명사 관리인 ❑ 메카와 메디나에 있는 성지 관리인

cus|to|dy /kʌstədi/ **1** N-UNCOUNT **Custody** is the legal right to keep and take care of a child, especially the right given to a child's mother or father when they get divorced. ❑ I'm going to go to court to get custody of the children. ❑ Child custody is normally granted to the mother. **2** PHRASE Someone who is **in custody** or has been taken **into custody** has been arrested and is being kept in prison until they can be tried in a court. ❑ Three people appeared in court and two of them were remanded in custody. **3** N-UNCOUNT If someone is being held in a particular type of **custody**, they are being kept in a place that is similar to a prison. ❑ The youngster got nine months' youth custody.

1 불가산명사 양육권 ❑ 그 아이들에 대한 양육권을 얻기 위해 법원에 갈 겁니다. ❑ 자녀 양육권은 보통 어머니에게 주어진다. **2** 구 구치하는; 구치되는 ❑ 세 사람이 법정에 출두했고, 그들 중 두 사람은 법정 구속되었다. **3** 불가산명사 교정(矯正) 시설 ❑ 그 청소년은 9개월간 소년원 수감에 처해졌다.

cus|tom /kʌstəm/ (customs) **1** N-VAR A **custom** is an activity, a way of behaving, or an event which is usual or traditional in a particular society or in particular circumstances. ❑ The custom of lighting the Olympic flame goes back centuries. **2** N-SING If it is your **custom to** do something, you usually do it in particular circumstances. ❑ It was his custom to approach every problem cautiously. **3** N-UNCOUNT If a store has your **custom**, you regularly buy things there. [BRIT, FORMAL] ❑ You have the right to withhold your custom if you so wish. **4** →see also **customs** →see **culture**

1 가산명사 또는 불가산명사 관습, 전통 ❑ 올림픽 성화를 밝히는 전통의 기원은 수세기 전으로 거슬러 올라간다. **2** 단수명사 습관 ❑ 어떤 문제든 신중하게 접근하는 것은 그 남자의 습관이었다. **3** 불가산명사 단골 거래 [영국영어, 격식체] ❑ 네가 원한다면 단골 거래를 그만둘 권리가 있다.

cus|tom|ary /kʌstəmeri, BRIT kʌstəmri/ **1** ADJ **Customary** is used to describe things that people usually do in a particular society or in particular circumstances. [FORMAL] ❑ It is customary to offer a drink or a snack to guests. **2** ADJ **Customary** is used to describe something that a particular person usually does or has. [ADJ n] ❑ Yvonne took her customary seat behind her desk.

1 형용사 관습적인 [격식체] ❑ 손님에게 다과를 대접하는 것은 관습이다. **2** 형용사 습관적인 ❑ 이본은 그녀의 책상 뒤 항상 앉던 자리에 앉았다.

cus|tom|er ◆◆◇ /kʌstəmər/ (customers) N-COUNT A **customer** is someone who buys goods or services, especially from a store. ❑ ...a satisfied customer. ❑ ...the quality of customer service.

가산명사 고객 ❑ 만족한 고객 ❑ 고객 서비스의 질

When you buy goods from a particular shop or company, you are one of its **customers**. If you use the professional services of someone such as a lawyer or an accountant, you are one of their **clients**. Doctors and hospitals have **patients**, while hotels have **guests**. People who travel on public transportation are referred to as **passengers**.

특정한 상점이나 회사에서 상품을 사면, 그 상점이나 회사의 customer가 된다. 변호사나 회계사 같은 전문가의 서비스를 이용하면, 그들의 client가 된다. 의사와 병원은 patient를 받고, 호텔은 guest를 받는다. 대중 교통수단으로 이동하는 사람들은 passenger라고 일컫는다.

cus|tom|ize /kʌstəmaɪz/ (customizes, customizing, customized) [BRIT also **customise**] V-T If you **customize** something, you change its appearance or features to suit your tastes or needs. ❑ ...a control that allows photographers to customize the camera's basic settings.

[영국영어 customise] 타동사 취향이나 필요에 맞게 개조하다 ❑ 사진기 사용자의 취향과 필요에 맞게 기본 셋팅을 맞출 수 있게 만든 조절 장치

cus|toms /kʌstəmz/ **1** N-PROPER **Customs** is the official organization responsible for collecting taxes on goods coming into a country and preventing illegal goods from being brought in. ❑ What right do Customs have to search my car? **2** N-UNCOUNT **Customs** is the place where people arriving from a foreign country have to declare goods that they bring with them. ❑ He walked through customs. **3** ADJ **Customs** duties are taxes that people pay for importing and exporting goods. [ADJ n] ❑ Personal property which is to be re-exported at the end of your visit is not subject to customs duties. **4** →see also **custom**

1 고유명사 세관 ❑ 무슨 권리로 세관이 내 차를 수색하는 거지? **2** 불가산명사 통관 검사대 ❑ 그는 통관 검사대를 걸어 나갔다. **3** 형용사 관세의 ❑ 출국하실 때 다시 가지고 나가실 개인 소지품은 관세 부과 대상이 아닙니다.

cut ◆◆◆ /kʌt/ (cuts, cutting)

The form **cut** is used in the present tense and is the past tense and past participle.

cut은 동사의 현재, 과거, 과거 분사로 쓴다.

Picture Dictionary · cut

chop · peel · slice · dice · mince

grate · saw · chop down · tear off · rip up

1 V-T/V-I If you **cut** something, you use a knife or a similar tool to divide it into pieces, or to mark it or damage it. If you **cut** a shape or a hole in something, you make the shape or hole by using a knife or similar tool. ❑ *Mrs. Haines stood nearby, holding scissors to cut a ribbon.* ❑ *Cut the tomatoes in half vertically.* ❑ *The thieves cut a hole in the fence.* ● N-COUNT **Cut** is also a noun. ❑ *Carefully make a cut in the shell with a small serrated knife.* **2** V-T If you **cut yourself** or **cut** a part of your body, you accidentally injure yourself on a sharp object so that you bleed. ❑ *Johnson cut himself shaving.* ❑ *I started to cry because I cut my finger.* ● N-COUNT **Cut** is also a noun. ❑ *He had sustained a cut on his left eyebrow.* **3** V-T If you **cut** something such as grass, your hair, or your fingernails, you shorten them using scissors or another tool. ❑ *The most recent tenants hadn't even cut the grass.* ❑ *You've had your hair cut, it looks great.* ● N-SING **Cut** is also a noun. ❑ *Prices vary from salon to salon, starting at £17 for a cut and blow-dry.* **4** V-T The way that clothes **are cut** is the way they are designed and made. [usu passive] ❑ *...badly cut blue suits.* **5** V-I If you **cut across** or **through** a place, you go through it because it is the shortest route to another place. ❑ *Jesse cut across the parking lot and strolled through the main entrance.* →see also **short cut 6** V-T If you **cut** something, you reduce it. ❑ *The first priority is to cut costs.* ❑ *The UN force is to be cut by 90%.* ● N-COUNT **Cut** is also a noun. [with supp] ❑ *The economy needs an immediate 2 percent cut in interest rates.* **7** V-T If you **cut** a text, broadcast, or performance, you shorten it. If you **cut** a part of a text, broadcast, or performance, you do not publish, broadcast, or perform that part. ❑ *Branagh has cut the play judiciously.* ● N-COUNT **Cut** is also a noun. ❑ *It has been found necessary to make some cuts in the text.* **8** V-T To **cut** a supply of something means to stop providing it or stop it being provided. ❑ *Winds have knocked down power lines, cutting electricity to thousands of people.* ● N-COUNT **Cut** is also a noun. [with supp, usu N in n] ❑ *The strike had already led to cuts in electricity and water supplies in many areas.* **9** V-T If you **cut** a pack of playing cards, you divide it into two. ❑ *Place the cards face down on the table and cut them.* **10** CONVENTION When the director of a movie says "**cut**," they want the actors and the camera crew to stop filming. **11** V-T If you tell someone to **cut** something, you are telling them in an irritated way to stop it. [mainly AM, INFORMAL, FEELINGS] ❑ *"Cut the euphemisms, Daniel," Brenda snapped.* **12** N-COUNT A **cut** of meat is a piece or type of meat which is cut in a particular way from the animal, or from a particular part of it. ❑ *Use a cheap cut such as spare rib chops.* **13** N-SING Someone's **cut** of the profits or winnings from something, especially ones that have been obtained dishonestly, is their share. [INFORMAL] ❑ *The agency is expected to take a cut of the money awarded to its client.* **14** →see also **cutting 15** to cut something **to the bone** →see **bone**. to cut corners →see **corner**. to cut the mustard →see **mustard**
→see Picture Dictionary: cut

Thesaurus
cut의 참조어

N.	gash, incision, nick, slit, wound **1**-**3**
V.	carve, slice, trim **1**
	graze, nick, stab **2**
	mow, shave, trim **3**
	decrease, reduce, lower; (ant.) increase **6 7**

▶**cut across** PHRASAL VERB If an issue or problem **cuts across** the division between two or more groups of people, it affects or matters to people in all the groups. ❑ *The problem cuts across all socioeconomic lines and affects all age groups.*

▶**cut back** PHRASAL VERB If you **cut back** something such as expenditure or **cut back on** it, you reduce it. ❑ *Customers have cut back spending because of the economic slowdown.* ❑ *The Government has cut back on defence spending.* →see also **cutback**

1 타동사/자동사 자르다, 깎다, (구멍을) 내다 ❑ 헤인스 여사는 리본을 자르려고 가위를 들고 옆에 서 있었다. ❑ 토마토를 세로로 반 자르세요. ❑ 도둑들은 담장에 구멍을 냈다. ● 가산명사 자름, 깎음, (구멍을) 깸 ❑ 톱날이 있는 작은 칼로 조개에 조심스레 칼집을 내세요. **2** 타동사 베이다, 베다 ❑ 존슨은 면도하다 베였다. ❑ 나는 손가락이 베어서 울기 시작했다. ● 가산명사 벰, 베임, 베인 상처 ❑ 그는 왼쪽 눈썹에 자상을 입었다. **3** 타동사 (풀을) 베다, (머리, 손톱을) 깎다 ❑ 가장 최근의 소작인들은 풀도 베지 않았다. ❑ 머리 깎았구나. 보기 좋아. ● 단수명사 (풀을) 베기, (머리, 손톱을) 깎기 ❑ 머리 깎고 드라이하는 데 17파운드부터 미용실마다 가격이 다르다. **4** 타동사 감축하다, 절감하다 ❑ 형편없이 마름질 된 파란색 정장 **5** 자동사 가로질러 가다 ❑ 제시는 주차장을 가로질러 주 출입구로 어슬렁어슬렁 들어갔다. **6** 타동사 감축하다, 절감하다 ❑ 최우선 과제는 비용을 절감하는 것이다. ❑ 유엔군은 90퍼센트 감축될 것이다. ● 가산명사 감축, 절감 ❑ 경제 사정상 금리를 즉시 2퍼센트 낮출 필요가 있다. **7** 타동사 단축시키다; 부분 삭제하다 ❑ 브라나는 그 극을 적절히 삭제해서 단축시켰다. ● 가산명사 부분 삭제, 단축 ❑ 본문을 부분 삭제할 필요가 있는 것으로 밝혀졌다. **8** 타동사 (공급을) 중단하다 ❑ 바람 때문에 전선이 끊어져서, 수천 명에게 전력 공급이 중단되었다. ● 가산명사 (공급의) 중단 ❑ 그 파업 때문에 이미 많은 지역에 전기와 수도 공급이 끊긴 상태였다. **9** 타동사 (카드를) 둘로 나누다 ❑ 카드를 탁자 위에 뒤집어 놓고 둘로 나누세요. **10** 관용 표현 컷 (영화 촬영시) **11** 타동사 그만두다 [주로 미국영어, 비격식체, 감정 개입] ❑ "돌려서 말 하지 마, 다니엘." 하고 브렌다가 발끈해서 말했다. **12** 가산명사 (고기의) 조각, 부위 고기의 어느 부위의 한 조각 ❑ 여분의 갈빗살 같이 값싼 부위를 이용하세요. **13** 단수명사 몫 [비격식체] ❑ 그 대행사도 자신들의 고객이 받을 돈에서 한몫을 챙길 것으로 예상된다.

구동사 두루 영향을 미치다 ❑ 그 문제는 모든 사회 경제적인 문제와 연관이 있고 모든 연령대의 사람들에게 영향을 미친다.

구동사 줄이다, 삭감하다 ❑ 소비자들은 경기 침체 때문에 소비를 줄였다. ❑ 정부는 국방 예산을 삭감했다.

▶**cut down** ☐ PHRASAL VERB If you **cut down on** something or **cut down** something, you use or do less of it. ☐ *He cut down on coffee and cigarettes, and ate a balanced diet.* ☐ *Car owners were asked to cut down travel.* ☐ PHRASAL VERB If you **cut down** a tree, you cut through its trunk so that it falls to the ground. ☐ *A vandal with a chainsaw cut down a tree.*

▶**cut off** ☐ PHRASAL VERB If you **cut** something **off**, you remove it with a knife or a similar tool. ☐ *Mrs. Johnson cut off a generous piece of the meat.* ☐ *He threatened to cut my hair off.* ☐ PHRASAL VERB To **cut** someone or something **off** means to separate them from things that they are normally connected with. ☐ *One of the goals of the campaign is to cut off the elite Republican Guard from its supplies.* ● **cut off** ADJ *Without a car we still felt very cut off.* ☐ PHRASAL VERB To **cut off** a supply of something means to stop providing it or stop it being provided. ☐ *The rebels have cut off electricity from the capital.* ☐ PHRASAL VERB If you get **cut off** when you are on the telephone, the line is suddenly disconnected and you can no longer speak to the other person. ☐ *When you do get through, you've got to say your piece quickly before you get cut off.* ☐ →see also **cut-off**. to **cut off** your **nose to spite** your **face** →see **spite**

▶**cut out** ☐ PHRASAL VERB If you **cut** something **out**, you remove or separate it from what surrounds it using scissors or a knife. ☐ *I cut it out and pinned it to my studio wall.* ☐ PHRASAL VERB If you **cut out** a part of a text, you do not print, publish, or broadcast that part, because to include it would make the text too long or unacceptable. ☐ *I listened to the programme and found they'd cut out all the interesting stuff.* ☐ PHRASAL VERB To **cut out** something unnecessary or unwanted means to remove it completely from a situation. For example, if you **cut out** a particular type of food, you stop eating it, usually because it is bad for you. ☐ *I've simply cut egg yolks out entirely.* ☐ PHRASAL VERB If an object **cuts out** the light, it is between you and the light so that you are in the dark. ☐ *The curtains were half drawn to cut out the sunlight.* ☐ PHRASAL VERB If an engine **cuts out**, it suddenly stops working. ☐ *The helicopter crash landed when one of its two engines cut out.* ☐ →see also **cut out**

▶**cut up** PHRASAL VERB If you **cut** something **up**, you cut it into several pieces. ☐ *Halve the tomatoes, then cut them up coarsely.* →see also **cut up**

cut|back /kʌtbæk/ (**cutbacks**) also **cut-back** N-COUNT A **cutback** is a reduction that is made in something. ☐ *London Underground said it may have to axe 500 signaling jobs because of government cutbacks in its investment.*

cute /kyut/ (**cuter**, **cutest**) ☐ ADJ Something or someone that is **cute** is very pretty or attractive, or is intended to appear pretty or attractive. [INFORMAL] ☐ *Oh, look at that dog! He's so cute.* ☐ ADJ If you describe someone as **cute**, you think they are sexually attractive. [mainly AM, INFORMAL] ☐ *There was this girl, and I thought she was really cute.* ☐ ADJ If you describe someone as **cute**, you mean that they deal with things cleverly. [AM] ☐ *That's a cute trick.*

Thesaurus	*cute*의 참조어
ADJ.	adorable, charming, pretty; (*ant.*) homely, ugly ☐

cut|lery /kʌtləri/ N-UNCOUNT **Cutlery** consists of the knives, forks, and spoons that you eat your food with. [BRIT; AM **silverware**, **flatware**] ☐ *She arranged plates and cutlery on a small table.*

cut-off (**cut-offs**) also **cutoff** ☐ N-COUNT A **cut-off** or a **cut-off** point is the level or limit at which you decide that something should stop happening. ☐ *The cut-off date for registering is yet to be announced.* ☐ N-COUNT The **cut-off of** a supply or service is the complete stopping of the supply or service. ☐ *A total cut-off of supplies would cripple the country's economy.*

cut out ADJ If you are not **cut out for** a particular type of work, you do not have the qualities that are needed to be able to do it well. ☐ *I left medicine anyway. I wasn't really cut out for it.*

cut-price ADJ **Cut-price** goods or services are cheaper than usual. [BRIT; AM **cut-rate**] [ADJ n] ☐ *...a shop selling cut-price videos and CDs in Oxford Street.*

cut-rate ADJ **Cut-rate** goods or services are cheaper than usual. [ADJ n] ☐ *...cut-rate auto insurance.*

cut|ter /kʌtər/ (**cutters**) ☐ N-COUNT A **cutter** is a tool that you use for cutting through something. ☐ *...wire cutters.* ☐ N-COUNT A **cutter** is a person who cuts or reduces something. ☐ *...a glass cutter.*

cut-throat ADJ If you describe a situation as **cut-throat**, you mean that the people or companies involved all want success and do not care if they harm each other in getting it. [DISAPPROVAL] ☐ *...the cut-throat competition in personal computers.*

cut|ting ◆◇◇ /kʌtɪŋ/ (**cuttings**) ☐ N-COUNT A **cutting** from a plant is a part of the plant that you have cut off so that you can grow a new plant from it. ☐ *Take cuttings from it in July or August.* ☐ *Take cuttings from suitable garden tomatoes in late summer.* ☐ ADJ A **cutting** remark is unkind and likely to hurt someone's feelings. ☐ *People make cutting remarks to help themselves feel superior or powerful.* ☐ N-COUNT A **cutting** is a piece of writing which has been cut from a newspaper or magazine. [BRIT; AM **clipping**] ☐ *...a stack of old photographs and newspaper cuttings.*

cut|ting edge

The spelling **cutting-edge** is used for meaning ☐.

☐ N-SING If you are **at the cutting edge of** a particular field of activity, you are involved in its most important or most exciting developments. ☐ *This*

☐ 구동사 줄이다 ☐ 그는 커피와 담배를 줄이고, 균형 잡힌 식사를 했다. ☐ 자동차 소유자들은 운행을 줄이라는 요구를 받았다. ☐ 구동사 (나무를) 베다 ☐ 기계톱을 가진 공공 기물 훼손범이 기계톱을 가지고 나무를 한 그루 베어 버렸다.

☐ 구동사 잘라 내다, 잘라 버리다 ☐ 존슨 씨는 고기를 크게 한 덩이 잘라 냈다. ☐ 그는 내 머리카락을 잘라 버리겠다고 협박했다. ☐ 구동사 차단하다, 갈라놓다 ☐ 그 작전의 몇 가지 목표 중 하나는 엘리트 공화국 수비대의 보급품을 차단하는 것이다. ● 차단된, 고립된 형용사 ☐ 차가 없어서 우리는 여전히 몹시 고립감을 느꼈다. ☐ 구동사 (공급을) 차단하다, (공급을) 중단하다 ☐ 반군들은 수도의 전력 공급을 차단했다. ☐ 구동사 (전화가) 끊기다 ☐ 전화가 연결되면, 끊기기 전에 용건을 빨리 말씀하셔야 됩니다.

☐ 구동사 오려내다, 도려내다 ☐ 나는 그것을 오려 내서 핀으로 내 스튜디오 벽에 붙여 놓았다. ☐ 구동사 삭제하다 ☐ 나는 그 프로그램을 들었는데 재미있는 부분은 모두가 삭제된 것을 알 수 있었다. ☐ 구동사 골라내다, 들어내다 ☐ 나는 그냥 계란 노른자들은 다 골라냈다. ☐ 구동사 (빛을) 차단하다 ☐ 커튼은 햇빛을 차단하기 위해 반쯤 쳐져 있었다. ☐ 구동사 (엔진이) 갑자기 멈추다 ☐ 두 개의 엔진 중 하나가 갑자기 멈춰서 헬리콥터가 불시착했다.

구동사 조각조각 자르다, 썰다 ☐ 토마토를 반으로 잘라, 굵직굵직하게 써세요.

가산명사 삭감 ☐ 정부의 투자 삭감 때문에 500명의 신호 요원을 해고해야 할 것 같다고 런던 지하철이 발표했다.

☐ 형용사 귀여운, 깜찍한 [비격식체] ☐ 와, 저 개 좀 봐! 진짜 귀엽다. ☐ 형용사 섹시한 [주로 미국영어, 비격식체] ☐ 이 여자 애가 거기 있었고, 나는 그 애가 정말 섹시하다고 생각했다. ☐ 형용사 약삭빠른, 영리한 [미국영어] ☐ 그건 영리한 속임수야.

불가산명사 수저류 [영국영어; 미국영어 silverware, flatware] ☐ 그녀는 접시와 수저들을 작은 식탁 위에 차렸다.

☐ 가산명사 마감 ☐ 등록 마감일이 아직 발표되지 않았다. ☐ 가산명사 차단 ☐ 전면적인 공급 차단은 국가 경제를 무력하게 만들 것이다.

형용사 ~에 꼭 맞는, ~가 체질에 맞는 ☐ 어쨌든 난 의학계를 떠났어. 정말이지 내 체질이 아니었어.

형용사 할인 가격 [영국영어; 미국영어 cut-rate] ☐ 할인된 가격의 비디오와 시디를 파는 옥스퍼드 거리에 있는 가게

형용사 할인가의 ☐ 할인된 자동차 보험료

☐ 가산명사 절단기 ☐ 철사 절단기 ☐ 가산명사 자르는 사람, 삭감하는 사람 ☐ 풀을 베는 사람

형용사 살인적인, 필사적인 [탐탁찮음] ☐ 개인용 컴퓨터 부문의 살인적인 경쟁

☐ 가산명사 꺾꽂이 순 ☐ 7월이나 8월에 그것에서 꺾꽂이 순을 채취하세요. ☐ 늦여름에 적당한 정원용 토마토에서 꺾꽂이 순을 채취하세요. ☐ 형용사 감정을 상하게 하는 ☐ 사람들은 자신들이 우월하거나 힘이 있다고 느끼고 싶어서 남의 감정을 상하게 하는 발언을 한다. ☐ 가산명사 (신문이나 잡지에서) 잘라낸 것 [영국영어; 미국영어 clipping] ☐ 한 무더기의 오래된 사진들과 신문에서 오려 낸 부분들

철자 cutting-edge도 ☐ 의미로 쓴다.

☐ 단수명사 제일선 ☐ 이 조선소는 세계 조선 기술의 제일선에 있다. ☐ 형용사 최첨단의 ☐ 우리가 계획하고

a b c d e f g h i j k l m n o p q r s t u v w x y z

shipyard is at the cutting edge of world shipbuilding technology. ◨ ADJ **Cutting-edge** techniques or equipment are the most advanced that there are in a particular field. ❏ *What we are planning is cutting-edge technology never seen in Australia before.* →see **technology**

있는 것은 여태 호주에서 볼 수 없었던 최첨단 기술이다.

cut up ADJ If you are **cut up** about something that has happened, you are very unhappy because of it. [mainly BRIT, INFORMAL] [v-link ADJ] ❏ *Terry was very cut up about Jim's death.*

형용사 가슴이 에이는 [주로 영국영어, 비격식체] ❏ 짐의 죽음에 테리는 가슴이 에이도록 슬펐다.

CV /siː viː/ (**CVs**) N-COUNT Your **CV** is a brief written account of your personal details, your education, and the jobs you have had. You can send a CV when you are applying for a job. **CV** is an abbreviation for **curriculum vitae**. [mainly BRIT; AM usually **résumé**] ❏ *Send them a copy of your CV.*

가산명사 이력서 [주로 영국영어; 미국영어 대개 résumé] ❏ 그 사람들에게 네 이력서 한 장 보내.

cya|nide /saɪənaɪd/ N-UNCOUNT **Cyanide** is a highly poisonous substance. ❏ *His death has all the signs of cyanide poisoning.*

불가산명사 청산칼리, 시안화물 ❏ 그가 청산칼리 중독으로 죽은 흔적이 뚜렷하다.

cy|ber|café /saɪbərkæfeɪ/ (**cybercafés**) N-COUNT A **cybercafé** is a café where people can pay to use the Internet.

가산명사 인터넷 카페

cy|ber|sex /saɪbərsɛks/ N-UNCOUNT **Cybersex** involves using the Internet for sexual purposes, especially by exchanging sexual messages with another person. ❏ *It's a place where you can role-play and have cybersex.*

불가산명사 사이버 섹스 ❏ 그곳은 역할놀이나 사이버 섹스를 할 수 있는 곳이다.

cy|ber|space /saɪbərspeɪs/ N-UNCOUNT In computer technology, **cyberspace** refers to data banks and networks, considered as a place. [COMPUTING] ❏ *...a report circulating in cyberspace.*

불가산명사 가상공간 [컴퓨터] ❏ 가상공간에서 돌고 있는 보고서

Word Link	cycl ≈ circle : bicycle, cycle, cyclical

cy|cle ◆◇◇ /saɪkᵊl/ (**cycles, cycling, cycled**) ◨ N-COUNT A **cycle** is a series of events or processes that is repeated again and again, always in the same order. ❏ *...the life cycle of the plant.* ◩ N-COUNT A **cycle** is a single complete series of movements in an electrical, electronic, or mechanical process. ❏ *...10 cycles per second.* ▨ N-COUNT A **cycle** is a motorcycle. [AM] ❏ *The roar of the cycle could be heard as far away as the bridge at the Mason Road.* ◪ N-COUNT A **cycle** is a bicycle. ❏ *We supply the travel ticket for you and your cycle.* ◫ V-T/V-I If you **cycle**, you ride a bicycle. [mainly BRIT] ❏ *He cycled to Ingwold.* ❏ *Britain could save £4.6 billion a year in road transport costs if more people cycled.* ● **cy|cling** N-UNCOUNT ❏ *The quiet country roads are ideal for cycling.* →see **water**

◨ 가산명사 주기 ❏ 그 식물의 생활 주기 ◩ 가산명사 사이클 ❏ 초당 10사이클 ▨ 가산명사 오토바이 [미국영어] ❏ 오토바이가 부르릉거리는 소리가 메이슨 거리에 있는 다리까지 들릴 것이다. ◪ 가산명사 자전거 ❏ 귀하가 자전거를 가지고 여행하실 수 있는 표를 제공합니다. ◫ 타동사/자동사 자전거를 타다 [주로 영국영어] ❏ 그는 잉월드까지 자전거를 타고 갔다. ❏ 더 많은 사람들이 자전거를 탄다면 영국은 연간 도로 교통에 드는 비용 중 46억 파운드를 절약할 수 있을 것이다. ● 자전거 타기 불가산명사 ❏ 한적한 시골길은 자전거 타기에 안성맞춤이다.

cy|cli|cal /sɪklɪkᵊl, saɪk-/ ADJ A **cyclical** process is one in which a series of events happens again and again in the same order. ❏ *...the cyclical nature of the airline business.*

형용사 주기적인 ❏ 항공사 영업의 주기적인 측면

cy|clist /saɪklɪst/ (**cyclists**) N-COUNT A **cyclist** is someone who rides a bicycle, or is riding a bicycle. [mainly BRIT] ❏ *...better protection for pedestrians and cyclists.* →see **park**

가산명사 자전거 타는 사람 [주로 영국영어] ❏ 보행자와 자전거 이용자에 대한 더 나은 보호

cy|clone /saɪkloʊn/ (**cyclones**) N-COUNT A **cyclone** is a violent tropical storm in which the air goes around and around. ❏ *The race was called off as a cyclone struck.* →see **hurricane**

가산명사 사이클론 (열대성 저기압) ❏ 사이클론이 몰아쳐서 경주는 취소되었다.

cyl|in|der /sɪlɪndər/ (**cylinders**) ◨ N-COUNT A **cylinder** is an object with flat circular ends and long straight sides. ❏ *It was recorded on a wax cylinder.* ◩ N-COUNT A gas **cylinder** is a cylinder-shaped container in which gas is kept under pressure. ❏ *...oxygen cylinders.* ▨ N-COUNT In an engine, a **cylinder** is a cylinder-shaped part in which a piston moves backward and forward. ❏ *...a 2.5 litre, four-cylinder engine.* →see **engine, volume**

◨ 가산명사 원통 ❏ 그것은 밀랍 원통 위에 기록되어 있었다. ◩ 가산명사 가스통 ❏ 산소통 ▨ 가산명사 실린더, 기통 ❏ 2.5리터 4기통 엔진

cyn|ic /sɪnɪk/ (**cynics**) N-COUNT A **cynic** is someone who believes that people always act selfishly. ❏ *I have come to be very much of a cynic in these matters.*

가산명사 냉소적인 사람 ❏ 이 문제들에 대해 나는 대단히 냉소적이 되었다.

cyni|cal /sɪnɪkᵊl/ ◨ ADJ If you describe someone as **cynical**, you mean they believe that people always act selfishly. ❏ *...his cynical view of the world.* ● **cyni|cal|ly** ADV [ADV with v] ❏ *The fast-food industry cynically continues to target children.* ◩ ADJ If you are **cynical about** something, you do not believe that it can be successful or that the people involved are honest. ❏ *It's hard not to be cynical about reform.*

◨ 형용사 냉소적인 ❏ 그의 세상에 대한 냉소적인 시선 ● 냉소적으로; 아랑곳없다는 듯 부사 ❏ 패스트푸드 업계는 아랑곳없다는 듯 계속 어린이들을 대상으로 하고 있다. ◩ 형용사 냉소적인 ❏ 개혁에 대해 냉소적이지 않기란 어렵다.

cyni|cism /sɪnɪsɪzəm/ ◨ N-UNCOUNT **Cynicism** is the belief that people always act selfishly. ❏ *I found Ben's cynicism wearing at times.* ◩ N-UNCOUNT **Cynicism** about something is the belief that it cannot be successful or that the people involved are not honorable. ❏ *In an era of growing cynicism about politicians, Mr. Mandela is a model of dignity and integrity.*

◨ 불가산명사 냉소주의 ❏ 나는 때때로 벤의 냉소주의가 마모되어감을 알 수 있었다. ◩ 불가산명사 냉소주의 ❏ 정치인에 대한 냉소주의가 늘어 가는 시대에, 만델라는 위엄 있고 고결한 귀감이 되고 있다.

cyst /sɪst/ (**cysts**) N-COUNT A **cyst** is a growth containing liquid that appears inside your body or under your skin. ❏ *He had a minor operation to remove a cyst.*

가산명사 낭포(囊胞), 낭종(囊腫) ❏ 그는 낭종을 제거하기 위해서 간단한 수술을 받았다.

Dd

a
b
c
d
e
f
g
h
i
j
k
l
m
n
o
p
q
r
s
t
u
v
w
x
y
z

D, d /diː/ (**D's, d's**) N-VAR D is the fourth letter of the English alphabet.

dab /dæb/ (**dabs, dabbing, dabbed**) ■ V-T If you **dab** something, you touch it several times using quick, light movements. If you **dab** a substance onto a surface, you put it there using quick, light movements. ❑ *She arrived weeping, dabbing her eyes with a tissue.* ❑ *She dabbed iodine on the cuts on her forehead.* ■ N-COUNT A **dab of** something is a small amount of it that is put onto a surface. [INFORMAL] ❑ *...a dab of glue.*

dab|ble /dæbəl/ (**dabbles, dabbling, dabbled**) V-I If you **dabble in** something, you take part in it but not very seriously. ❑ *He dabbled in business.*

dad ◆◇◇ /dæd/ (**dads**) N-FAMILY Your **dad** is your father. [INFORMAL] ❑ *How do you feel, Dad?*

dad|dy /dædi/ (**daddies**) N-FAMILY Children often call their father **daddy**. [INFORMAL] ❑ *Look at me, Daddy!*

daf|fo|dil /dæfədɪl/ (**daffodils**) N-COUNT A **daffodil** is a yellow spring flower with a central part shaped like a tube and a long stem.

daft /dɑːft, dæft/ (**dafter, daftest**) ADJ If you describe a person or their behavior as **daft**, you think that they are stupid, impractical, or rather strange. [BRIT, INFORMAL] ❑ *He's not so daft as to listen to rumors.*

dag|ger /dægər/ (**daggers**) N-COUNT A **dagger** is a weapon like a knife with two sharp edges.

dai|ly ◆◇◇ /deɪli/ ■ ADV If something happens **daily**, it happens every day. [ADV after v] ❑ *Cathay Pacific flies daily non-stop to Hong Kong from Heathrow.* ● ADJ **Daily** is also an adjective. [ADJ n] ❑ *They held daily press briefings.* ■ ADJ **Daily** quantities or rates relate to a period of one day. [ADJ n] ❑ *...a diet containing adequate daily amounts of fresh fruit.* ■ PHRASE Your **daily life** is the things that you do every day as part of your normal life. ❑ *All of us in our daily life react favorably to people who take us and our views seriously.*

dain|ty /deɪnti/ (**daintier, daintiest**) ADJ If you describe a movement, person, or object as **dainty**, you mean that they are small, delicate, and pretty. ❑ *The girls were dainty and feminine.* ● **dain|ti|ly** ADV ❑ *She walked daintily down the steps.*

dairy /dɛəri/ (**dairies**) ■ N-COUNT A **dairy** is a store or company that sells milk and food made from milk, such as butter, cream, and cheese. ❑ *We used to have a bakery, and a dairy, and a wool-shop by the chapel.* ■ ADJ **Dairy** is used to refer to foods such as butter and cheese that are made from milk. [ADJ n] ❑ *...dairy produce.* ■ ADJ **Dairy** is used to refer to the use of cattle to produce milk rather than meat. [ADJ n] ❑ *...a small vegetable and dairy farm.*
→see Word Web: **dairy**

dai|sy /deɪzi/ (**daisies**) N-COUNT A **daisy** is a small wildflower with a yellow center and white petals. →see **plant**

dam /dæm/ (**dams**) N-COUNT A **dam** is a wall that is built across a river in order to stop the water flowing and to make a lake. ❑ *They went ahead with plans to build a dam on the Danube River.*
→see Word Web: **dam**

dam|age ◆◆◇ /dæmɪdʒ/ (**damages, damaging, damaged**) ■ V-T To **damage** an object means to break it, spoil it physically, or stop it from working properly. ❑ *He maliciously damaged a car with a baseball bat.* ■ V-T To **damage** something means to cause it to become less good, pleasant, or successful. ❑ *Jackson doesn't want to damage his reputation as a political personality.* ● **dam|ag|ing** ADJ ❑ *Is the recycling process in itself damaging to the environment?* ■ N-UNCOUNT **Damage** is physical harm that is caused to an object. ❑ *The blast had serious effects with quite extensive damage to the house.* ■ N-UNCOUNT **Damage** consists of the unpleasant

가산명사 또는 불가산명사 영어 알파벳의 네 번째 글자

■ 타동사/자동사 가볍게 문지르다, 가볍게 누르다 ❑ 그녀는 울면서 눈가를 티슈로 눌러 닦으며 도착했다. ❑ 그녀는 이마에 베인 상처에 요오드를 문질러 발랐다. ■ 가산명사 작은 양, 조금 [비격식체] ❑ 풀 조금

자동사 잠깐 손을 대다 ❑ 그는 사업에 잠깐 손을 댔었다.

친족명사 아빠 [비격식체] ❑ 아빠, 기분이 어때요?

친족명사 아빠 [비격식체] ❑ 아빠, 나 좀 보세요.

가산명사 수선화

형용사 얼간이의 [영국영어, 비격식체] ❑ 그는 소문에 귀 기울일 만큼 얼간이는 아니다.

가산명사 단검

■ 부사 매일의 ❑ 캐세이퍼시픽은 히드로 공항에서 홍콩까지 직항으로 매일 운항한다. ● 형용사 매일의 ❑ 그들은 매일 언론 브리핑을 했다. ■ 형용사 하루의 ❑ 하루 필요한 양의 신선한 과일이 적절히 들어간 식단 ■ 구 일상사 ❑ 우리는 일상사에서 우리와 우리의 견해를 진지하게 받아들이는 사람들에게 호의적으로 대한다.

형용사 예쁘장한, 깜찍한 ❑ 그 소녀들은 예쁘장하고 여성스러웠다. ● 깜찍하게 부사 ❑ 그녀는 깜찍하게 계단을 내려왔다.

■ 가산명사 유제품 판매점 ❑ 전에는 예배당 옆에 제과점, 유제품 판매점, 그리고 양모 판매점이 있었다. ■ 형용사 유제품의 ❑ 유제품 ■ 형용사 낙농의 ❑ 소규모의 채소 농장 겸 낙농원

가산명사 데이지; 들국화

가산명사 댐 ❑ 그들은 다뉴브 강에 댐을 건설하려는 계획을 추진했다.

■ 타동사 손상시키다, 해치다 ❑ 그는 악의를 가지고 야구 방망이로 자동차를 손상시켰다. ■ 타동사 흠을 내다 ❑ 잭슨은 정치 인사로서의 자신의 명성에 흠이 나게 하고 싶어 하지 않는다. ● 해로운 형용사 ❑ 재활용 공정 자체가 환경에 해로운 것은 아닌가? ■ 불가산명사 피해, 손실 ❑ 그 돌풍의 영향이 너무나 심해서 그 가옥은 엄청난 피해를 입었다. ■ 불가산명사 손상 ❑ 이러한 유형의 사건들은 그

Word Web   dairy

Gone are the days when the farmer **milked** one **cow** at a time. Today most dairy **farms** use machinery. The **milk** is taken from the cow by a vacuum-powered milking machine. Then it goes by pipeline directly to a refrigerated storage tank. From there it goes straight to the factory for **pasteurization** and packaging. The largest such dairy farm in the world is the Al Safi Dairy Farm in Saudi Arabia. It has 24,000 head of **cattle** and produces about 33 million gallons of milk a year.

Word Web — dam

The Egyptians built the world's first **dam** in about 2900 BC. It directed water into a **reservoir** near the capital city of Memphis*. Later they constructed another dam to prevent **flooding** just south of Cairo*. Today, dams are used with **irrigation** systems to prevent **droughts**. Modern **hydroelectric** dams also provide over 20% of the world's electricity. Brazil and Paraguay built the largest hydroelectric power station in the world—the Itaipu Dam. It took 18 years to build and cost 18 billion dollars! Hydroelectric power is non-polluting. However, the dams endanger some species of fish and sometimes destroy valuable forest lands.

Memphis: an ancient city in Egypt.
Cairo: the capital of Egypt.

effects that something has on a person, situation, or type of activity. ❑ *Incidents of this type cause irreparable damage to relations with the community.* **5** N-PLURAL If a court of law awards **damages** to someone, it orders money to be paid to them by a person who has damaged their reputation or property, or who has injured them. ❑ *He was vindicated in court and damages were awarded.*
→see **disaster**

공동체와의 관계에 돌이킬 수 없는 손상을 초래한다. **5** 복수명사 손해 배상금 ❑ 그는 재판에서 결백이 입증되었고 손해 배상금을 받게 되었다.

Thesaurus — damage의 참조어

V.	break, harm, hurt; (ant.) fix, repair **1**
	ruin, wreck **2**
N.	harm, loss **4**

Word Partnership — damage의 연어

N.	damage to *someone's* reputation **2**
	damage to *someone's* health, damage to the environment **4**
V.	damage caused by/to *something* **3** **4**
ADJ.	**extensive** damage, **permanent** damage **3** **4**

dam|age con|trol N-UNCOUNT **Damage control** is action that is taken to make the bad results of something as small as possible, when it is impossible to avoid bad results completely. [AM; BRIT **damage limitation**] ❑ *But Broomfield argues that the long-running case is now an exercise in damage control for the Los Angeles police.*

불가산명사 피해 최소화 대책 [미국영어; 영국영어 damage limitation] ❑ 그러나 브룸필드는 장기간 지속되는 그 사건이 로스앤젤레스 경찰에게는 일종의 피해 최소화 대책 훈련이 되고 있다고 주장한다.

dame /deɪm/ (**dames**) N-TITLE **Dame** is a title given to a woman as a special honor because of important service or work that she has done. [BRIT] ❑ *...Dame Judi Dench.*

경칭명사 영부인 작위를 받은 여자에 대한 존칭 [영국영어] ❑ 주디 덴치 영부인

damn /dæm/ (**damns, damning, damned**) **1** EXCLAM **Damn, damn it,** and **dammit** are used by some people to express anger or impatience. [INFORMAL, VULGAR, FEELINGS] ❑ *Don't be flippant, damn it! This is serious.* **2** ADJ **Damn** is used by some people to emphasize what they are saying. [INFORMAL, VULGAR, EMPHASIS] [ADJ n] ❑ *There's not a damn thing you can do about it now.* ● ADV **Damn** is also an adverb. [ADV adj/adv] ❑ *As it turned out, I was damn right.* **3** V-T If you say that a person or a news report **damns** something such as a policy or action, you mean that they are very critical of it. ❑ *...a sensational book in which she damns the ultra-right party.* **4** →see also **damned, damning** **5** PHRASE If you say that someone **does not give a damn** about something, you are emphasizing that they do not care about it at all. [INFORMAL, VULGAR, EMPHASIS] ❑ *I don't give a damn about the money, Nicole.*

1 감탄사 빌어먹을 [비격식체, 비속어, 감정 개입] ❑ 경솔하게 굴지 말란 말이야, 이 빌어먹을! 이건 심각한 일이라고. **2** 형용사 개뿔도 [비격식체, 비속어, 강조] ❑ 그것에 대해 네가 지금 할 수 있는 일이란 개뿔도 없단 말이야. ● 부사 정말 ❑ 판명난 대로, 나는 정말 옳았다. **3** 타동사 악평하다 ❑ 극우 정당에 대한 그녀의 악평으로 세상을 떠들썩하게 한 책 존칭 **5** 구 털끝만한 관심도 두지 않다 [비격식체, 비속어, 강조] ❑ 니콜, 나는 그 돈에 대해선 털끝만한 관심도 없어.

damned /dæmd/ **1** ADJ **Damned** is used by some people to emphasize what they are saying, especially when they are angry or frustrated. [INFORMAL, VULGAR, EMPHASIS] [ADJ n] ❑ *They're a damned nuisance most of the time.* ● ADV **Damned** is also an adverb. [ADV adj/adv] ❑ *We are making a damned good profit, I tell you that.* **2** PHRASE If someone says "**I'm damned if I'm going to do it**" or "**I'll be damned if I'll do it**," they are emphasizing that they do not intend to do something and think it is unreasonable for anyone to expect them to do it. [INFORMAL, VULGAR, EMPHASIS] ❑ *I was damned if I was going to ask for an explanation and beg to keep my job.*

1 형용사 넌더리가 나는, 지긋지긋한 [비격식체, 비속어, 강조] ❑ 그들은 항상 넌더리가 나도록 성가신 녀석들이다. ● 부사 굉장히 ❑ 우리는 굉장히 큰 이익을 남기고 있는데 내가 말해 줄게. **2** 구 손가락에 장을 지지다 [비격식체, 비속어, 강조] ❑ 내가 설명을 부탁하며 직장을 잃지 않도록 애걸복걸한다면 내 손에 장을 지질 일이다.

damn|ing /dæmɪŋ/ ADJ If you describe evidence or a report as **damning**, you mean that it suggests very strongly that someone is guilty of a crime or has made a serious mistake. ❑ *...a damning report into the government's handling of the salmonella affair.*

형용사 누구도 부인 못 할 ❑ 살모넬라 사건의 정부 대처에 대한 누구도 부인 못 할 보고서

damp /dæmp/ (**damper, dampest, damps, damping, damped**) **1** ADJ Something that is **damp** is slightly wet. ❑ *Her hair was still damp.* ❑ *...the damp, cold air.* **2** N-UNCOUNT **Damp** is moisture that is found on the inside walls of a house or in the air. ❑ *There was damp everywhere and the entire building was in need of rewiring.*
→see **weather**

1 형용사 축축한, 눅눅한 ❑ 그녀의 머리카락은 아직도 축축했다. ❑ 눅눅하고, 차가운 공기 **2** 불가산명사 습기 ❑ 사방에 습기가 차 있었고 건물 전체는 다시 배선 공사를 해야 했다.

▶**damp down** PHRASAL VERB To **damp down** something such as a strong emotion, an argument, or a crisis means to make it calmer or less intense. ❑ *His hand moved to his mouth as he tried to damp down the panic.*

구동사 가라앉히다 ❑ 그는 공포심을 가라앉히려 손을 입으로 가져갔다.

damp|en /dæmpən/ (**dampens, dampening, dampened**) V-T To **dampen** something such as someone's enthusiasm or excitement means to make it less

타동사 시들게 하다, 한풀 꺾이게 하다 ❑ 그 어떤 것도 꺼지지 않는 그의 열정을 시들게 할 수 없는 것 같다.

lively or intense. ❑ *Nothing seems to dampen his perpetual enthusiasm.* ● PHRASAL VERB To **dampen** something **down** means the same as to **dampen** it. ❑ *Although unemployment rose last month, this is unlikely to dampen down wage demands.*

damp|ness /dǽmpnɪs/ N-UNCOUNT **Dampness** is moisture in the air, or on the surface of something. ❑ *The tins had to be kept away from dampness, soot and cooking fumes.*

● 구동사 시들게 하다, 한풀 꺾이게 하다 ❑ 실업률이 지난달 상승했지만, 이로 인해 임금 인상 요구가 꺾어지는 않을 것이다.

불가산명사 습기 ❑ 통조림은 습기, 그을음, 그리고 조리시 발생하는 연기가 닿지 않는 곳에 보관해야 한다.

dance ♦♦◇ /dǽns/ (**dances, dancing, danced**) ◼ V-I When you **dance**, you move your body and feet in a way which follows a rhythm, usually in time to music. ❑ *Polly had never learned to dance.* ◼ N-COUNT A **dance** is a particular series of graceful movements of your body and feet, which you usually do in time to music. ❑ *Sometimes the people doing this dance hold brightly colored scarves.* ◼ V-RECIP When you **dance with** someone, the two of you take part in a dance together, as partners. You can also say that two people **dance**. ❑ *It's a terrible thing when nobody wants to dance with you.* ❑ *Shall we dance?* ● N-COUNT **Dance** is also a noun. ❑ *Come and have a dance with me.* ◼ N-COUNT A **dance** is a social event where people dance with each other. ❑ *At the school dance he sat and talked to her all evening.* ◼ N-UNCOUNT **Dance** is the activity of performing dances, as a public entertainment or an art form. ❑ *Their contribution to international dance, drama and music is inestimable.* ◼ V-T If you **dance** a particular kind of dance, you do it or perform it. ❑ *Then we put the music on, and we all danced the Charleston.* ◼ V-I If you **dance** somewhere, you move there lightly and quickly, usually because you are happy or excited. [LITERARY] ❑ *He danced off down the road.* ◼ V-I If you say that something **dances**, you mean that it moves about, or seems to move about, lightly and quickly. [LITERARY] ❑ *Patterns of light, reflected by the river, dance along the base of the cliffs.*

◼ 자동사 춤추다 ❑ 폴리는 결코 춤을 배운 적이 없었다. ◼ 가산명사 춤 ❑ 때때로 사람들은 밝은 색 스카프를 쥐고 이 춤을 춘다. ◼ 상호동사 춤을 추다 ❑ 아무도 너와 함께 춤을 추려 하지 않는다면 그것은 끔찍한 일이다. ❑ 우리 춤 출까요? ● 가산명사 춤 ❑ 저와 함께 춤을 춰요. ◼ 가산명사 무도회 ❑ 학교 무도회에서 그는 저녁 내내 앉아서 그녀와 이야기했다. ◼ 불가산명사 무용 ❑ 전세계적으로 무용, 연극, 음악에 그들이 끼친 공헌은 무한하다. ◼ 타동사 추다 ❑ 그런 후에 우리는 음악을 틀고, 모두 찰스턴 춤을 추었다. ◼ 자동사 (좋아서) 춤을 추다 [문예체] ❑ 그는 좋아서 춤을 추듯 길을 걸어 내려갔다. ◼ 자동사 (춤추듯) 흔들리다 [문예체] ❑ 강물에 비친 불빛 모양이 절벽의 밑 부분을 따라 춤추듯 흔들렸다.

dance floor (**dance floors**) also **dancefloor** N-COUNT In a restaurant or night club, the **dance floor** is the area where people can dance. ❑ *Everybody is on the dance floor with the men forming a circle around the women.*

danc|er /dǽnsər/ (**dancers**) ◼ N-COUNT A **dancer** is a person who earns money by dancing, or a person who is dancing. ❑ *His previous girlfriend was a dancer with the Royal Ballet.* ◼ N-COUNT If you say that someone is a good **dancer** or a bad **dancer**, you are saying how well or badly they can dance. ❑ *He was the best dancer in LA.*

danc|ing ♦◇◇ /dǽnsɪŋ/ N-UNCOUNT When people dance for enjoyment or to entertain others, you can refer to this activity as **dancing**. ❑ *All the schools have music and dancing as part of the curriculum.* ❑ *Let's go dancing tonight.*

dan|de|lion /dǽndɪlaɪən/ (**dandelions**) N-COUNT A **dandelion** is a wild plant which has yellow flowers with lots of thin petals. When the petals of each flower drop off, a fluffy white ball of seeds grows.

dan|druff /dǽndrəf/ N-UNCOUNT **Dandruff** is small white pieces of dead skin in someone's hair, or fallen from someone's hair. ❑ *He has very bad dandruff.*

dan|ger ♦♦◇ /déɪndʒər/ (**dangers**) ◼ N-UNCOUNT **Danger** is the possibility that someone may be harmed or killed. ❑ *My friends endured tremendous danger in order to help me.* ◼ N-COUNT A **danger** is something or someone that can hurt or harm you. ❑ *...the dangers of smoking.* ◼ N-SING If there is a **danger that** something unpleasant will happen, it is possible that it will happen. [also no det, N that, N of n/-ing] ❑ *There is a real danger that some people will no longer be able to afford insurance.* ❑ *There was no danger that any of these groups would be elected to power.* ◼ PHRASE If someone who has been seriously ill is **out of danger**, they are still ill, but they are not expected to die. ❑ *Last night the mother was out of danger and "comfortable" in hospital.* →see **hero**

가산명사 춤추는 무대 ❑ 모든 사람들이 춤추는 무대 위에 있는데 남자들이 여자들 주위로 원을 그리고 있다.

◼ 가산명사 무용수 ❑ 그의 전 여자 친구는 왕립 발레단의 무용수였다. ◼ 가산명사 춤추는 사람 ❑ 그는 엘에이에서 가장 춤을 잘 추는 사람이었다.

불가산명사 무용, 춤 ❑ 모든 학교에서 음악과 무용은 교육 과정의 일부이다. ❑ 우리 오늘밤 춤추러 가자.

가산명사 민들레

불가산명사 비듬 ❑ 그는 비듬이 매우 심하다.

◼ 불가산명사 위험 ❑ 내 친구들은 엄청난 위험을 감수하며 나를 도와주었다. ◼ 가산명사 위험 요소 ❑ 흡연으로 인한 위험 요소 ◼ 단수명사 위험 ❑ 일부 사람들이 더 이상 보험료를 낼 여력이 없을 거라는 현실적인 위험이 있다. ❑ 이 단체들에 속한 그 누구도 국가 요직에 선출될 위험은 없었다. ◼ 구 고비를 넘긴 ❑ 지난밤 어머니께서 고비는 넘기셨고 병원에서 안정을 찾으셨다.

dan|ger|ous ♦♦◇ /déɪndʒərəs, déɪndʒrəs/ ADJ If something is **dangerous**, it is able or likely to hurt or harm you. ❑ *It's a dangerous stretch of road.* ❑ *...dangerous drugs.* ● **dan|ger|ous|ly** ADV ❑ *He is dangerously ill.*

형용사 위험한 ❑ 도로가 위험하게 뻗어 있다. ❑ 위험한 약물 ● 위험하게, 위태롭게 부사 ❑ 그는 위독하다.

dan|gle /dǽŋg³l/ (**dangles, dangling, dangled**) ◼ V-T/V-I If something **dangles from** somewhere or if you **dangle** it somewhere, it hangs or swings loosely. ❑ *A gold bracelet dangled from his left wrist.* ◼ V-T If you say that someone **is dangling** something attractive **before** you, you mean they are offering it to you in order to try to influence you in some way. ❑ *Ever since, when they've dangled rich rewards before me, I've taken fright.*

◼ 타동사/자동사 매달리다, 달랑거리다; 매달다 ❑ 그의 왼쪽 손목에서 금팔찌가 달랑거렸다. ◼ 타동사 (유혹할 수 있는 것을) 내보이다, 제의하다 ❑ 그 이후로, 그들이 내게 충분한 대가를 내비치면 나는 공포에 사로잡혔다.

dare ♦◇◇ /déər/ (**dares, daring, dared**)

Dare sometimes behaves like an ordinary verb, for example "He dared to speak" and "He doesn't dare to speak" and sometimes like a modal, for example "He daren't speak."

dare는 'He dared to speak'나 'He doesn't dare to speak'에서처럼 일반 동사로 쓰이기도 하고, 'He daren't speak'에서처럼 조동사로 쓰이기도 한다.

1 V-T If you do not **dare to** do something, you do not have enough courage to do it, or you do not want to do it because you fear the consequences. If you **dare to** do something, you do something which requires a lot of courage. [oft with brd-neg] ❏ *Most people hate Harry but they don't dare to say so.* ● MODAL **Dare** is also a modal. ❏ *Dare she risk staying where she was?* ❏ *The yen is weakening. But Tokyo dare not raise its interest rates again.*

> You can leave out the word **to** after **dare**. ❏ *Nobody dared complain.* The form **dares** is never used in a question or in a negative statement. You use **dare** instead. ❏ *Dare she tell him?... He dare not enter.*

2 V-T If you **dare** someone **to** do something, you challenge them to prove that they are not frightened of doing it. ❏ *Over coffee, she lit a cigarette, her eyes daring him to comment.* **3** N-COUNT A **dare** is a challenge which one person gives to another to do something dangerous or frightening. ❏ *When found, the children said they'd run away for a dare.* **4** PHRASE If you say to someone **don't you dare** do something, you are telling them not to do it and letting them know that you are angry. [SPOKEN, FEELINGS] ❏ *Allen, don't you dare go anywhere else, you hear?* **5** PHRASE You say "**how dare you**" when you are very shocked and angry about something that someone has done. [SPOKEN, FEELINGS] ❏ *How dare you pick up the phone and listen in on my conversations!* **6** PHRASE You can use "**I dare say**" or "**I daresay**" before or after a statement to indicate that you believe it is probably true. ❏ *I dare say that the computer would provide a clear answer to that.*

daren't /dɛərnt/ **Daren't** is the usual spoken form of "dare not."

dar|ing /dɛərɪŋ/ **1** ADJ People who are **daring** are willing to do or say things which are new or which might shock or anger other people. ❏ *Bergit was probably more daring than I was.* **2** ADJ A **daring** person is willing to do things that might be dangerous. ❏ *His daring rescue saved the lives of the youngsters.* **3** N-UNCOUNT **Daring** is the courage to do things which might be dangerous or which might shock or anger other people. ❏ *His daring may have cost him his life.*

dark ♦♦◇ /dɑrk/ (**darker**, **darkest**) **1** ADJ When it is **dark**, there is not enough light to see properly, for example because it is night. ❏ *It was too dark inside to see much.* ❏ *People usually draw the curtains once it gets dark.* ● **dark|ness** N-UNCOUNT ❏ *The light went out, and the room was plunged into darkness.* ● **dark|ly** ADV [ADV -ed] ❏ *In a darkly lit, seedy dance hall, hundreds of men lounge around small tables.* **2** N-SING **The dark** is the lack of light in a place. ❏ *I've always been afraid of the dark.* **3** ADJ If you describe something as **dark**, you mean that it is black in color, or a shade that is close to black. ❏ *He wore a dark suit and carried a black attaché case.* ● **dark|ly** ADV ❏ *The freckles on Joanne's face suddenly stood out darkly against her pale skin.* **4** COMB in COLOR When you use **dark** to describe a color, you are referring to a shade of that color which is close to black, or seems to have some black in it. ❏ *She was wearing a dark blue dress.* **5** ADJ If someone has **dark** hair, eyes, or skin, they have brown or black hair, eyes, or skin. ❏ *He had dark, curly hair.* **6** ADJ A **dark** period of time is unpleasant or frightening. ❏ *Once again there's talk of very dark days ahead.* **7** ADJ A **dark** place or area is mysterious and not fully known about. [ADJ n] ❏ *The spacecraft is set to throw new light on to a dark corner of the solar system.* **8** ADJ **Dark** thoughts are sad, and show that you are expecting something unpleasant to happen. [LITERARY] ❏ *Troy's endless happy chatter kept me from thinking dark thoughts.* ● **dark|ly** ADV [ADV with v] ❏ *Her thoughts circled darkly round Bernard's strange behavior.* **9** ADJ If you describe something as **dark**, you mean that it is related to things that are serious or unpleasant, rather than light-hearted. ❏ *He smiled when he talked about their dark humor that never failed to astound him and that few adults understand.* ● **dark|ly** ADV [ADV adj] ❏ *The atmosphere after Wednesday's match was as darkly comic as the movie itself.* **10** PHRASE If you do something **after dark**, you do it when the sun has set and night has begun. ❏ *They avoid going out alone after dark.* **11** PHRASE If you do something **before dark**, you do it before the sun sets and night begins. ❏ *They'll be back well before dark.* **12** PHRASE If you are **in the dark about** something, you do not know anything about it. ❏ *The investigators admit that they are completely in the dark about the killing.*

Word Partnership   dark의 연어

N.	dark **clouds**, dark **suit** **3** **9**
V.	**get** dark **1** **8**
	afraid of the dark, **scared of** the dark **1** **5** **8**

dark|en /dɑrkən/ (**darkens**, **darkening**, **darkened**) **1** V-T/V-I If something **darkens** or if a person or thing **darkens** it, it becomes darker. ❏ *The sky darkened abruptly.* **2** V-T/V-I If someone's mood **darkens** or if something **darkens** their mood, they suddenly become rather unhappy. [LITERARY] ❏ *My sunny mood suddenly darkened.*

dark|room /dɑrkrum/ (**darkrooms**) N-COUNT A **darkroom** is a room which can be sealed off from natural light and is lit only by red light. It is used for developing photographs.

dar|ling /dɑrlɪŋ/ (**darlings**) **1** N-VOC You call someone **darling** if you love them or like them very much. [FEELINGS] ❏ *Thank you, darling.* **2** ADJ Some people use **darling** to describe someone or something that they love or like very much. [INFORMAL] [ADJ n] ❏ *To have a darling baby boy was the greatest gift I could imagine.* **3** N-COUNT If you describe someone as a **darling**, you are fond of them and think that they are nice. [INFORMAL] ❏ *He's such a darling.*

darn /dɑrn/ (**darns**, **darning**, **darned**) **1** V-T If you **darn** something knitted or made of cloth, you mend a hole in it by sewing stitches across the hole and then weaving stitches in and out of them. ❏ *Aunt Emilie darned old socks.* **2** ADJ

1 타동사 감히 -을 하다 ❏ 대부분의 사람들은 해리를 미워하지만 감히 그렇게 말하진 않는다. ● 법조동사 감히 -을 하다 ❏ 그녀가 감히 위험을 무릅쓰고 있던 곳에 계속 머무르려 할까? ❏ 엔화가 약세를 띠고 있다. 그러나 일본 정부는 감히 다시 환율을 올리려고 하지 못한다.

> dare 뒤에서는 to를 생략할 수 있다. ❏ 아무도 감히 불평하지 못했다. 의문문이나 부정문에서는 dares 형태를 절대 쓰지 않고 dare를 쓴다. ❏ 그녀가 그에게 말할 용기가 있을까요?... 그는 감히 들어가지 못한다.

2 타동사 (할 테면 해 보라고) 도전하다 ❏ 커피를 마시다가, 그녀는 그에게 뭐라고 할 테면 해 보라는 눈빛으로 담배에 불을 붙였다. **3** 가산명사 도전, 감행 ❏ 아이들은 발견되자 탈출을 감행해 보았다고 말했다. **4** 구 감히 -할 생각 마 [구어체, 감정 개입] ❏ 앨런, 감히 딴 데 갈 생각 마, 알아들어? **5** 구 감히 네가 [구어체, 감정 개입] ❏ 감히 네가 전화기를 들고 내 통화 내용을 엿듣다니! **6** 구 아마 -일 것이다 ❏ 아마 컴퓨터를 이용하면 그것에 대한 정확한 해답을 얻을 수 있을 거야.

감히 -하지 못하다

1 형용사 대담한 ❏ 버지트는 아마 나보다도 더 대담했을 것이다. **2** 형용사 용감한 ❏ 그의 용감한 구출작전으로 젊은 생명들이 목숨을 건졌다. **3** 불가산명사 용기 ❏ 그의 용기 있는 행동이 그의 목숨을 앗아갔을지도 모른다.

1 형용사 어두운 ❏ 내부가 너무 어두워 잘 볼 수 없었다. ❏ 날이 어두워지면 사람들은 대개 커튼을 친다. ● 어둡게 불가산명사 ❏ 전기가 나가자, 방안에 어두움이 엄습했다. ● 어둡게 부사 ❏ 어둡게 조명을 한 저급 댄스 홀에서, 남자들 수백 명이 작은 탁자 주위에서 빈둥거린다. **2** 단수명사 어둠 ❏ 나는 항상 어둠을 무서워했다. **3** 형용사 검정색의 ❏ 그는 검정색 계통의 정장을 입고 검은색 작은 서류 가방을 들고 있었다. ● 거무스름하게, 진하게 부사 ❏ 조앤느의 얼굴에 있는 주근깨가 그녀의 창백한 피부 때문에 갑자기 짙게 도드라져 보였다. **4** 복합형-색채어 검정색에 가까운 ❏ 그녀는 검정색에 가까운 푸른색 옷을 입고 있었다. **5** 형용사 나갈색의 ❏ 그는 다갈색의 곱슬머리를 하고 있었다. **6** 형용사 음울한 ❏ 다시 한 번 아주 음울한 날이 올 것이란 소문이 있다. **7** 형용사 알려지지 않은 ❏ 우주선이 태양계의 알려지지 않은 외딴 부분을 새롭게 밝히기 위해 준비되어 있다. **8** 형용사 불길한 [문예체] ❏ 트로이가 즐거운 잡담을 끊임없이 늘어놓는 우리는 불길한 생각을 할 수 없었다. ● 불길하게 부사 ❏ 그녀는 버나드의 이상한 행동에 관해 불길한 생각이 머리 속에 맴돌았다. **9** 형용사 우울한 ❏ 그는 항상 자신을 놀래게 하며, 어른들 대부분은 거의 이해할 수 없는 그들의 우울한 유머에 대해 이야기할 때 미소를 지었다. ● 우울하게 부사 ❏ 수요일 첫 상연 후의 분위기는 그 영화 자체만큼이나 우울하게 우스꽝스러웠다. **10** 구 해진 후에 ❏ 그들은 해진 후에 혼자 외출하는 것을 피한다. **11** 구 해지기 전에 ❏ 그들은 해지기 훨씬 전에 돌아올 것이다. **12** 구 아무것도 모르는 ❏ 수사관들은 자신들이 그 살인사건에 대해 아무것도 알지 못한다고 인정한다.

1 타동사/자동사 어두워지다; 어둡게 하다 ❏ 하늘이 갑자기 어두워졌다. **2** 타동사/자동사 (마음이) 어두워지다; (마음을) 어둡게 하다 [문예체] ❏ 명랑하던 내 마음이 갑자기 어두워졌다.

가산명사 암실

1 호격명사 당신, 여보 [감정 개입] ❏ 고마워요, 여보. **2** 형용사 사랑스러운 [비격식체] ❏ 사랑스러운 아들을 갖는 것이 내가 상상할 수 있는 가장 큰 선물이었다. **3** 가산명사 마음에 드는 사람 [비격식체] ❏ 그는 아주 맘에 드는 사람이야.

1 타동사 꿰매다 ❏ 에밀리에 숙모는 낡은 양말을 꿰매었다. **2** 형용사 빌어먹을, 제기랄 [비격식체, 강조] ❏ 그가 그 일에 대해 할 수 있는 일이란 빌어먹을

People sometimes use **darn** or **darned** to emphasize what they are saying, often when they are annoyed. [INFORMAL, EMPHASIS] [ADJ n] ❑ *There's not a darn thing he can do about it.* ● ADV Darn is also an adverb. [ADV adj/adv] ❑ *...the desire to be free to do just as we darn well please.* ❸ PHRASE You can say I'll be **darned** to show that you are very surprised about something. [AM, INFORMAL, FEELINGS] ❑ *"A talking pig!" he exclaimed. "Well, I'll be darned."*

dart /dɑrt/ (**darts, darting, darted**) ❶ V-I If a person or animal **darts** somewhere, they move there suddenly and quickly. [WRITTEN] ❑ *Ingrid darted across the deserted street.* ❷ V-T/V-I If you **dart** a look **at** someone or something, or if your eyes **dart to** them, you look at them very quickly. [LITERARY] ❑ *She darted a sly sideways glance at Bramwell.* ❸ N-COUNT A **dart** is a small, narrow object with a sharp point which can be thrown or shot. ❑ *Markov died after being struck by a poison dart.* ❹ N-UNCOUNT **Darts** is a game in which you throw darts at a round board which has numbers on it. ❑ *I started playing darts at 15.*

dash /dæʃ/ (**dashes, dashing, dashed**) ❶ V-I If you **dash** somewhere, you run or go there quickly and suddenly. ❑ *Suddenly she dashed down to the cellar.* ● N-SING Dash is also a noun. ❑ *...a 160-mile dash to the hospital.* ❷ V-I If you say that you have to **dash**, you mean that you are in a hurry and have to leave immediately. [INFORMAL] [no cont] ❑ *Oh, Tim! I'm sorry but I have to dash.* ❸ N-COUNT A **dash of** something is a small quantity of it which you add when you are preparing food or mixing a drink. ❑ *Pour over olive oil and a dash of balsamic vinegar to accentuate the sweetness.* ❹ N-COUNT A **dash of** a quality is a small amount of it that is found in something and often makes it more interesting or distinctive. ❑ *...a story with a dash of mystery thrown in.* ❺ V-T If you **dash** something **against** a wall or other surface, you throw or push it violently, often so hard that it breaks. [LITERARY] ❑ *She seized the doll and dashed it against the stone wall with tremendous force.* ❻ V-T If an event or person **dashes** someone's hopes or expectations, it destroys them by making it impossible that the thing that is hoped for or expected will ever happen. [LITERARY, JOURNALISM] ❑ *The Bank of England dashed hopes yesterday of a rush to economic recovery by warning that Britain's upturn will be slow.* ❼ N-COUNT A **dash** is a straight, horizontal line used in writing, for example to separate two main clauses whose meanings are closely connected. ❑ *...the dash between the birth date and death date.* ❽ N-COUNT The **dash** of a car is its **dashboard.** ❾ PHRASE If you **make a dash for** a place, you run there very quickly, for example to escape from someone or something. ❑ *I made a dash for the front door but he got there before me.*

▶dash off ❶ PHRASAL VERB If you **dash off to** a place, you go there very quickly. ❑ *He dashed off to lunch at the Hard Rock Cafe.* ❷ PHRASAL VERB If you **dash off** a piece of writing, you write or compose it very quickly, without thinking about it very much. ❑ *He dashed off a couple of novels.*

dash|board /dæʃbɔrd/ (**dashboards**) N-COUNT The **dashboard** in a car is the panel facing the driver's seat where most of the instruments and switches are. ❑ *The clock on the dashboard said it was five to two.*

dash|ing /dæʃɪŋ/ ADJ A **dashing** person or thing is very stylish and attractive. [OLD-FASHIONED] ❑ *He was the very model of the dashing RAF pilot.*

da|ta ♦♦◇ /deɪtə, dætə/ N-UNCOUNT; also N-PLURAL You can refer to information as **data**, especially when it is in the form of facts or statistics that you can analyze. In American English, **data** is usually a plural noun. In technical or formal British English, **data** is sometimes a plural noun, but at other times, it is an uncount noun. ❑ *The study was based on data from 2,100 women.* ❷ N-UNCOUNT **Data** is information that can be stored and used by a computer program. [COMPUTING] ❑ *This system uses powerful microchips to compress huge amounts of data on to a CD-ROM.* →see **forecast**

Thesaurus	*data*의 참조어
N.	facts, figures, information, results, statistics ❶

data bank (**data banks**) also databank N-COUNT A **data bank** is the same as a **database.**

data|base /deɪtəbeɪs, dætə-/ (**databases**) also data base N-COUNT A **database** is a collection of data that is stored in a computer and that can easily be used and added to. ❑ *They maintain a database of hotels that cater for businesswomen.*

da|ta pro|cess|ing N-UNCOUNT **Data processing** is the series of operations that are carried out on data, especially by computers, in order to present, interpret, or obtain information. ❑ *Taylor's company makes data-processing systems.*

date ♦♦◇ /deɪt/ (**dates, dating, dated**) ❶ N-COUNT A **date** is a specific time that can be named, for example a particular day or a particular year. ❑ *What's the date today?* ❷ V-T If you **date** something, you give or discover the date when it was made or when it began. ❑ *I think we can date the decline of Western Civilization quite precisely.* ❸ V-T When you **date** something such as a letter or a check, you write that day's date on it. ❑ *Once the decision is reached, he can date and sign the sheet.* ❹ PHRASE To **date** means up until the present time. ❑ *"Dottie" is by far his best novel to date.* ❺ V-I If something **dates**, it goes out of fashion and becomes unacceptable to modern tastes. ❑ *Blue and white is the classic color combination for bathrooms. It always looks smart and will never date.* ❻ N-COUNT A **date** is an appointment to meet someone or go out with them, especially someone with whom you are having, or may soon have, a romantic relationship. ❑ *I have a date with Bob.* ❼ N-COUNT If you have a date with someone with whom you are having, or may soon have, a romantic relationship, you can refer to that person as your **date.** ❑ *He lied to Essie, saying his date was one of the girls in the show.* ❽ V-RECIP If you **are dating** someone, you go out with them regularly because you are having, or may soon have, a romantic relationship with them. You can also say that two people **are dating.** ❑ *For a year I dated a woman who was a research assistant.* ❾ N-COUNT A **date** is a small, dark-brown, sticky fruit with a

---

아무것도 없다. ● 부사 정말로, 제기랄 ❑ 우리가 제기랄 자유롭게 원하는 대로 일을 하고 싶은 갈망 ❸ 구 깜짝 놀라다 [미국영어, 비격식체, 감정 개입] ❑ "말하는 돼지다!"라고 그가 소리쳤다. "원, 깜짝 놀랐네."

❶ 자동사 날쌔게 움직이다 [문어체] ❑ 잉그리드는 아무도 없는 거리를 날쌔게 건너갔다. ❷ 타동사/자동사 -에게 시선을 던지다 [문예체] ❑ 그녀는 곁눈으로 은밀히 브램웰을 힐끔 쳐다보았다. ❸ 가산명사 작은 화살 ❑ 마르코프는 독화살에 맞아 사망했다. ❹ 불가산명사 다트 던지기 ❑ 나는 열다섯 살 때부터 다트를 시작했다.

❶ 자동사 돌진하다 ❑ 갑자기 그녀가 지하실로 달려 내려갔다. ● 단수명사 돌진 ❑ 160마일의 속력으로 병원으로 돌진 ❷ 자동사 서둘러 떠나다 [비격식체] ❑ 아, 팀! 미안한데 내가 서둘러 가야 할 것 같아. ❸ 가산명사 소량, 약간 ❑ 단맛이 두드러지도록 올리브 오일과 발사믹 식초를 약간 붓는다. ❹ 가산명사 약간 ❑ 약간의 미스터리 요소가 첨가된 이야기 ❺ 타동사 내던지다 [문예체] ❑ 그녀가 그 인형을 쥐더니 무시무시하게 힘껏 돌벽에 내던졌다. ❻ 타동사 깨다, 날려버리다 [문예체, 언론] ❑ 잉글랜드 은행은 어제 영국의 경기 호전이 더딜 것이라고 경고하면서 상승 무드를 탈거라는 경제 회복에 대한 희망을 꺾었다. ❼ 가산명사 줄표, 생년월일과 사망일 사이의 줄표 ❽ 가산명사 계기판 ❾ 구 -을 향하여 단숨에 내달리다 ❑ 내가 앞문을 향하여 단숨에 내달렸으나 그가 먼저 도착했다.

❶ 구동사 급히 가다 ❑ 그는 하드락 카페에서 점심을 먹기 위해 급히 갔다. ❷ 구동사 급히 쓰다 ❑ 그는 소설 두세 편을 급히 써 내려갔다.

가산명사 계기판 ❑ 계기판의 시계가 2시 5분 전을 가리키고 있었다.

형용사 맵시 있는 [구식어] ❑ 그는 맵시 있는 영국 공군의 전형이었다.

❶ 불가산명사; 복수명사 자료 ❑ 그 연구는 2,100명의 여성으로부터 수집한 자료를 바탕으로 했다. ❷ 불가산명사 데이터 [컴퓨터] ❑ 이 시스템은 고성능 마이크로칩을 이용해서 시디롬에 어머어마한 양의 데이터를 압축시킨다.

가산명사 데이터 뱅크

가산명사 데이터베이스 ❑ 그들은 여성 기업인들을 주고객으로 하는 호텔에 대한 데이터베이스를 계속 관리하고 있다.

불가산명사 데이터 처리, 정보화 과정 ❑ 테일러의 회사는 데이터 처리 시스템을 만든다.

❶ 가산명사 날짜 ❑ 오늘 며칠이지? ❷ 타동사 날짜를 밝히다 ❑ 나는 우리가 '서양문명'의 몰락이 언제였는지를 꽤 정확히 밝힐 수 있다고 생각해. ❸ 타동사 날짜를 기입하다 ❑ 일단 결정이 나면, 그가 서류에 날짜를 기입하고 서명할 수 있다. ❹ 구 최근까지 ❑ '도티'는 지금까지 그가 쓴 소설 중에서 단연 최고이다. ❺ 자동사 뒤떨어지다, 낡다 ❑ 청색과 흰색은 욕실에 어울리는 고급스런 색채 조합이다. 항상 세련되어 보이고 결코 시대에 뒤떨어지지 않는다. ❻ 가산명사 데이트 ❑ 나는 밥과 데이트를 한다. ❼ 가산명사 데이트 상대자 ❑ 그는 에씨에게 그의 데이트 상대자가 그 쇼에서 나왔던 소녀들 중의 한 사람이라며 거짓말을 했다. ❽ 상호동사 데이트 중이다 ❑ 일 년 동안 나는 연구 보조원이었던 한 여자와 데이트를 했다. ❾ 가산명사 대추

A

stone inside. Dates grow on palm trees in hot countries. ⑩ →see also **dated, out of date**

B

	Word Partnership	*date*의 연어
N.	birth date, cut-off date, due date, expiration date ①	
V.	set a date ① ②	
	date and sign ⑦	

C

▶**date back** PHRASAL VERB If something **dates back to** a particular time, 구동사 (시대적으로) 거슬러 올라가다 ❑ 과거 it started or was made at that time. ❑ *The Royal Palace, which dates back to the 16th* 16세기에 지어진 그 왕궁은 전면적인 복원 공사 *century, is undergoing extensive restoration.* 중이다.

D

dat|ed /deɪtɪd/ ADJ **Dated** things seem old-fashioned, although they may once 형용사 시대에 뒤떨 ❑ 시대에 뒤떨 야회복을 입은 have been fashionable or modern. ❑ *...people in dated dinner-jackets.* 사람들

date of birth (**dates of birth**) N-COUNT Your **date of birth** is the exact date on 가산명사 생년월일 ❑ 출생 신고서에는 그의 which you were born, including the year. ❑ *The registration form showed his date of* 생년월일이 1979년 8월 2일이라고 나와 있었다. *birth as August 2, 1979.*

E

daub /dɔːb/ (**daubs, daubing, daubed**) V-T When you **daub** a substance such as 타동사 바르다, 칠하다 ❑ 마지막으로 그 남자가 mud or paint on something, you spread it on that thing in a rough or careless 분장사를 보았을 때 그녀는 제레미 폭스에게 가짜 피를 way. ❑ *The makeup woman had been daubing mock blood on Jeremy Fox when last he'd* 바르고 있었다. *seen her.*

F

daugh|ter ♦♦♦ /dɔːtər/ (**daughters**) N-COUNT Someone's **daughter** is their 가산명사 딸 ❑ 플로라와 그의 딸 캐서린 ❑ 대학교수의 female child. ❑ *...Flora and her daughter Catherine.* ❑ *...the daughter of a university* 딸 *professor.* →see **child**

G

daughter-in-law (**daughters-in-law**) N-COUNT Someone's **daughter-in-law** is 가산명사 며느리 the wife of their son.

H

daunt /dɔːnt/ (**daunts, daunting, daunted**) V-T If something **daunts** you, it 타동사 위압하다, 위축시키다 ❑ 나이가 그녀의 절반 makes you feel slightly afraid or worried about dealing with it. ❑ *...a grueling* 정도되는 여자라면 두려워했을 고달픈 여정 ● 위축된 *journey that would have daunted a woman half her age.* ● **daunt|ed** ADJ [v-link ADJ] 형용사 약간 위축되지 않고 그런 책을 선택하기는 ❑ *It is hard to pick up such a book and not to feel a bit daunted.* 어려운 일이다.

I

daunt|ing /dɔːntɪŋ/ ADJ Something that is **daunting** makes you feel slightly 형용사 힘에 부친 ❑ 그와 그의 아내 제인은 정원을 afraid or worried about dealing with it. ❑ *He and his wife Jane were faced with the* 예전처럼 화사하게 꾸며야 한다는 힘에 부친 일에 *daunting task of restoring the gardens to their former splendour.* 직면해 있었다.

J

dawn /dɔːn/ (**dawns, dawning, dawned**) ① N-VAR **Dawn** is the time of day when ① 가산명사 또는 불가산명사 새벽 ❑ 낸시는 새벽에 light first appears in the sky, just before the sun rises. ❑ *Nancy woke at dawn.* 잠이 깼다. ② 단수명사 여명 [문예체] ❑ 라디오 시대의 ② N-SING **The dawn of** a period of time or a situation is the beginning of it. 여명 ③ 자동사 서서히 시작하다 [문어체] ❑ 유럽 [LITERARY] ❑ *...the dawn of the radio age.* ③ V-I If something **is dawning**, it is 전역에 걸쳐 새로운 초고속 철도 시대가 서서히 beginning to develop or come into existence. [WRITTEN] ❑ *Throughout Europe a* 시작되고 있다. ● **dawn|ing** 단수명사 ❑ 우주 시대의 도래 *new railway age, that of the high-speed train, has dawned.* ● **dawn|ing** N-SING ❑ *...the dawning of the space age.*

K

L

M

▶**dawn on** or **dawn upon** PHRASAL VERB If a fact or idea **dawns on** you, you 구동사 분명해지다 ❑ 나는 여전히 재능이 있고 다시 realize it. ❑ *It gradually dawned on me that I still had talent and ought to run again.* 뛰어야 한다는 것을 차차 깨달아가고 있었다.

N

dawn raid (**dawn raids**) ① N-COUNT If police officers carry out a **dawn raid**, ① 가산명사 새벽 급습 ❑ 어제 새벽 급습을 통해 수천 they go to someone's house very early in the morning to search it or arrest 파운드 어치의 마약을 압수했다. ② 가산명사 개장 초 them. ❑ *Thousands of pounds worth of drugs were seized in dawn raids yesterday.* 특정주식의 대량매입 행위 [경제] ❑ 서던 ② N-COUNT If a person or company carries out a **dawn raid**, they try to buy a 회사는 월요일 개장 초에 스웹 주 11.2 퍼센트를 대량 large number of a company's shares at the start of a day's trading, especially 매입했다. because they want to buy the whole company. [BUSINESS] ❑ *Southern acquired* 11.2 per cent of Sweb in a dawn raid on Monday.

O

P

day ♦♦♦ /deɪ/ (**days**) ① N-COUNT A **day** is one of the seven twenty-four hour ① 가산명사 하루 ❑ 그리고 지난주에는 거의 매일 눈이 periods of time in a week. ❑ *And it has snowed almost every day for the past week.* 왔다. ② 가산명사 또는 불가산명사 낮, 낮 시간 ❑ 2천 ② N-VAR **Day** is the time when it is light, or the time when you are up and 7백만일의 근무 일수가 매년 직장 내 사고와 질병으로 doing things. ❑ *27 million working days are lost each year due to work accidents and* 허비된다. ❑ 그는 내가 일주일에 하루는 런던에 갈 수 *sickness.* ❑ *He arranged for me to go down to London one day a week.* ③ N-COUNT You 있도록 주선해 주었다. ③ 가산명사 당시, 시절 ❑ 그는 can refer to a particular period in history as a particular **day** or as particular 자기 삼촌이 살았던 당시의 우크라이나에 대해 **days**. ❑ *He began to talk about the Ukraine of his uncle's day.* ❑ *...his early days of* 이야기하기 시작했다. ❑ 투쟁과 뼈저린 빈곤으로 보낸 *struggle and deep poverty.* ④ PHRASE If something happens **day after day**, it 그의 어린 시절 ④ 구 매일매일 ❑ 그 신문사에서 나는 happens every day without stopping. ❑ *The newspaper job had me doing the same* 매일매일 똑같은 일을 했다. ⑤ 구 요즘 ⑤ 심지어 *thing day after day.* ⑤ PHRASE **In this day and age** means in modern times. 요즘에도 그 해목은 사고방식은 여전하다. ⑥ 구 ❑ *Even in this day and age the old attitudes persist.* ⑥ PHRASE If you say that 한때는 좋았다, 이젠 낡고 보잘것없다 ❑ 그녀가 입은 something **has seen better days**, you mean that it is old and in poor 트위드 재킷은 좋았다. ⑦ 구 일을 마치다, condition. ❑ *The tweed jacket she wore had seen better days.* ⑦ PHRASE If you **call it** 중도에 그만두다 ❑ 부채가 쌓이매 가다 보니, 일을 **a day**, you decide to stop what you are doing because you are tired of it or 작파하자는 결정이 불가피했다. ⑧ 구 ~을 아주 기쁘게 because it is not successful. ❑ *Faced with mounting debts, the decision to call it a day* 해 주다 [비격식체] ❑ 자, 빌, 카드를 보내 돔을 줘서 *was inevitable.* ⑧ PHRASE If something **makes** your **day**, it makes you feel very 기쁘게 해 주렴. ⑨ 구 언젠가 ❑ 나 역시 언젠가 happy. [INFORMAL] ❑ *Come on, Bill. Send Tom a card and make his day.* ⑨ PHRASE 런던에서 살기를 꿈꿨다. ❑ 언젠가 당신을 행복하게 해 **One day** or **some day** or **one of these days** means at some time in the future. 줄 여인을 찾게 되길 바랍니다. ⑩ 구 며칠 전에 ❑ 나 ❑ *I too dreamed of living in London one day.* ❑ *I hope some day you will find the woman* 며칠 전에 네 사무실로 전화했어. ⑪ 구 곤경을 *who will make you happy.* ⑩ PHRASE If you say that something happened **the** 모면하다 ❑ 그가 딸의 생일잔치 때 어떻게 곤경을 **other day**, you mean that it happened a few days ago. ❑ *I phoned your office the* 모면했는가에 대한 이 이야기 ⑫ 구 날마다 ❑ 당신이 *other day.* ⑪ PHRASE If someone or something **saves the day** in a situation 필요로 하는 것이 날마다 다를 수 있다. ⑬ 구 정확히 which seems likely to fail, they manage to make it successful. ❑ *...this story* ❑ 그 날은 그가 싱가포르에 도착한 지 정확히 일년이 *about how he saved the day at his daughter's birthday party.* ⑫ PHRASE If something 되는 1월 19일이었다. ⑭ 구 지금까지도 ❑ 지금까지도 happens **from day to day** or **day by day**, it happens each day. ❑ *Your needs can* 어린 줄루족 소년들은 싸움 연습을 한다. ⑮ 구 *differ from day to day.* ⑬ PHRASE If it is a month or a year **to the day** since a (힘들지만) 일상적인 일 ❑ 종군 기자들에게는, particular thing happened, it is exactly a month or a year since it happened. 저격수의 총알을 피하는 것은 아주 일상적인 일이다. ❑ *It was January 19, a year to the day since he had arrived in Singapore.* ⑭ PHRASE **To this day** means up until and including the present time. ❑ *To this day young Zulu boys practise fighting.* ⑮ PHRASE If you say that a task is **all in a day's work** for someone, you mean that they do not mind doing it although it may be difficult, because it is part of their job or because they often do it. ❑ *For war reporters, dodging snipers' bullets is all in a day's work.* ⑯ PHRASE your **day in court** →see **court**. **it is early days** →see **early**. **at the end of the day** →see **end**. **the good old days** →see **old** →see **year**

Q

R

S

T

U

V

W

X

Y

Z

day care N-UNCOUNT **Day care** is care that is provided during the day for people who cannot take care of themselves, such as small children, old people, or people who are ill. Day care is provided by paid workers. ❑ *...a day-care center for elderly people.*

불가산명사 주간 보호 시설 ❑ 고령자들을 위한 주간 보호 시설

day|dream /deɪdriːm/ (**daydreams**, **daydreaming**, **daydreamed**) ◼ V-I If you **daydream**, you think about pleasant things for a period of time, usually about things that you would like to happen. ❑ *Do you work hard for success rather than daydream about it?* ❑ *He daydreams of being a famous journalist.* ◻ N-COUNT A **daydream** is a series of pleasant thoughts, usually about things that you would like to happen. ❑ *He learnt to escape into daydreams of handsome men and beautiful women.*

◼ 자동사 공상에 잠기다, 백일몽을 꾸다 ❑ 성공에 대한 공상을 하기보다는 성공을 위해 열심히 노력합니까? ❑ 그는 저명한 기자가 되는 공상을 한다. ◻ 가산명사 공상, 백일몽 ❑ 그는 멋진 남성들과 아름다운 여성들에 대한 공상의 세계로 도피하는 법을 터득했다.

day|light /deɪlaɪt/ ◼ N-UNCOUNT **Daylight** is the natural light that there is during the day, before it gets dark. ❑ *Lack of daylight can make people feel depressed.* ◻ N-UNCOUNT **Daylight** is the time of day when it begins to get light. ❑ *Quinn returned shortly after daylight yesterday morning.*

◼ 불가산명사 새벽, 여명 ❑ 햇볕을 충분히 쬐지 못하면 사람이 우울해질 수 있다. ◻ 불가산명사 새벽 ❑ 퀸은 어제 아침 여명 후에 돌아왔다.

Clocks are set one hour fast in the spring and in the fall returned to the standard time so that residents have more convenient use of daylight hours. The saying "spring ahead, fall back" is used to remember which way to turn the clocks. This is not practiced uniformly across the United States. Some local areas have decided not to participate, often out of economic consideration for neighboring communities.

낮 시간을 좀 더 편리하게 이용하기 위해 봄에는 시계를 한 시간 빠르게 당겼다가, 가을에는 표준시간으로 되돌려 놓기도 한다. 어느 쪽으로 시계를 돌릴지 기억하기 위해 '봄에는 앞으로, 가을에는 뒤로'라는 말을 사용한다. 이 관행이 미국 전역에서 일률적으로 시행되지는 않는다. 인근 지역들의 경제적 사정을 고려하여 참여하지 않기로 결정한 지역들도 있다.

◼ PHRASE If you say that a crime is committed **in broad daylight**, you are expressing your surprise that it is done during the day when people can see it, rather than at night. [EMPHASIS] ❑ *A girl was attacked on a train in broad daylight.*

◼ 구 벌건 대낮에 [강조] ❑ 벌건 대낮에 한 소녀가 기차 안에서 공격을 받았다.

day nurse|ry (**day nurseries**) N-COUNT A **day nursery** is a place where children who are too young to go to school can be left all day while their parents are at work.

가산명사 탁아소

day off (**days off**) N-COUNT A **day off** is a day when you do not go to work, even though it is usually a working day. ❑ *It was Mrs. Dearden's day off, and Paul was on duty in her place.*

가산명사 휴일, 비번일 ❑ 그 날은 디어든 부인의 비번일이어서 폴이 그녀 대신 근무를 섰다.

day school (**day schools**) N-COUNT A **day school** is a school where the students go home every evening and do not live at the school. Compare **boarding school**.

가산명사 (기숙학교가 아닌) 일반 학교

day|time /deɪtaɪm/ ◼ N-SING The **daytime** is the part of a day between the time when it gets light and the time when it gets dark. [the N, also no det] ❑ *In the daytime he stayed up in his room, sleeping, or listening to music.* ◻ ADJ **Daytime** television and radio is broadcast during the morning and afternoon on weekdays. [ADJ n] ❑ *...ITV's new package of daytime programs.*

◼ 단수명사 낮 시간 ❑ 낮 시간에 그는 방에 머물러 있으면서 잠도 자고, 음악도 들었다. ◻ 형용사 주간의 ❑ '아이티브이'의 새로 편성된 주간 프로그램

day-to-day ADJ **Day-to-day** things or activities exist or happen every day as part of ordinary life. [ADJ n] ❑ *I am a vegetarian and use a lot of lentils in my day-to-day cooking.*

형용사 일상의 ❑ 나는 채식주의자이며 일상 요리시에 렌틸콩을 많이 사용한다.

day trad|er (**day traders**) N-COUNT On the stock market, **day traders** are traders who buy and sell particular securities on the same day. [BUSINESS] ❑ *Unlike the day traders, they tended to hold on to stocks for days and weeks, sometimes even months.*

가산명사 초단기 매매가 [경제] ❑ 초단기 매매가와는 달리, 그들은 수일 또는 수주 동안, 때로는 여러 달 동안 주식을 보유하는 경향이 있었다.

daze /deɪz/ N-SING If someone is **in a daze**, they are feeling confused and unable to think clearly, often because they have had a shock or surprise. ❑ *For 35 minutes I was walking around in a daze.*

단수명사 멍한 상태 ❑ 35분 동안 나는 멍한 상태로 이리저리 걷고 있었다.

dazed /deɪzd/ ADJ If someone is **dazed**, they are confused and unable to think clearly, often because of shock or a blow to the head. ❑ *At the end of the interview I was dazed and exhausted.*

형용사 멍한 상태의 ❑ 인터뷰를 마치자 나는 멍한 상태로 힘이 쭉 빠졌다.

daz|zle /dæzəl/ (**dazzles**, **dazzling**, **dazzled**) ◼ V-T If someone or something **dazzles** you, you are extremely impressed by their skill, qualities, or beauty. ❑ *George dazzled her with his knowledge of the world.* ◻ N-SING The **dazzle of** something is a quality it has, such as beauty or skill, which is impressive and attractive. ❑ *The dazzle of stardom and status attracts them.* ◼ V-T If a bright light **dazzles** you, it makes you unable to see properly for a short time. ❑ *The sun, glinting from the pool, dazzled me.*

◼ 타동사 현혹하다 ❑ 조지는 세상사에 대한 지식으로 그녀를 현혹했다. ◻ 단수명사 눈부심 ❑ 그들은 스타라는 위치와 지위가 갖는 눈부심에 이끌렸다. ◼ 타동사 눈부시게 하다 ❑ 해가 저수지에 반짝반짝 비쳐 나는 눈이 부셨다.

daz|zling /dæzlɪŋ/ ◼ ADJ Something that is **dazzling** is very impressive or beautiful. ❑ *He gave Alberg a dazzling smile.* ● **daz|zling|ly** ADV ❑ *The view was dazzlingly beautiful.* ◻ ADJ A **dazzling** light is very bright and makes you unable to see properly for a short time. ❑ *He shielded his eyes against the dazzling declining sun.* ● **daz|zling|ly** ADV [ADV adj] ❑ *The loading bay seemed dazzlingly bright.*

◼ 형용사 눈부신 ❑ 그가 앨버그에게 눈부신 미소를 지어 보였다. ● 화려찬란하게, 눈이 부시도록 부사 ❑ 그 광경은 눈이 부시도록 아름다웠다. ◻ 형용사 눈부신 ❑ 그는 지는 해가 눈부셔서 눈을 가렸다. ● 눈부시게 부사 ❑ 적재 구획은 눈부시게 밝아 보였다.

dead ♦♦◇ /ded/ ◼ ADJ A person, animal, or plant that is **dead** is no longer living. ❑ *"You're a widow?" — "Yes. My husband's been dead a year now."* ❑ *The group had shot dead another hostage.* ◻ N-PLURAL The **dead** are people who are dead. ❑ *The dead included six people attending a religious ceremony.*

◼ 형용사 죽은 ❑ "당신은 미망인이십니까?" "예, 제 남편은 일 년 전에 죽었습니다." ❑ 그 단체는 인질을 한 명 더 사살했다. ◻ 복수명사 죽은 사람들 ❑ 죽은 사람들 중에는 종교 의식에 참석 중이던 여섯 명의 사람들도 포함되어 있었다.

Do not confuse **dead** with **died**. **Died** is the past tense and past participle of the verb **die**, and thus indicates the action of dying. ❑ *She died in 1934... Two men have died since the rioting broke out.* You do not use **died** as an adjective. You use **dead** instead. ❑ *More than 2,200 dead birds have been found.*

dead와 died를 혼동하지 않도록 하라. died는 동사 die의 과거 및 과거 분사형이며, 따라서 죽는 행위를 나타낸다. ❑ 그녀는 1934년에 사망했다... 소요가 발생한 이래 남자 두 명이 죽었다. died는 형용사로 쓰지 않고 대신 dead를 쓴다. ❑ 2,200 마리 이상의 죽은 새가 발견되었다.

◻ ADJ If you describe a place or a period of time as **dead**, you do not like it because there is very little activity taking place in it. [DISAPPROVAL] ❑ *...some*

◻ 형용사 죽은 듯한 [탐탁잖음] ❑ 가장 활발한 게 파리인 죽어 있는 듯한 작은 마을 ◼ 형용사 쓸모없는,

a b c **d** e f g h i j k l m n o p q r s t u v w x y z

dead little town where the liveliest thing is the flies. ■ ADJ Something that is **dead** is no longer being used or is finished. ❏ The dead cigarette was still between his fingers. ■ ADJ If you say that an idea, plan, or subject is **dead**, you mean that people are no longer interested in it or willing to develop it any further. ❏ It's a dead issue, Baxter. ■ ADJ A telephone or piece of electrical equipment that is **dead** is no longer functioning, for example because it no longer has any electrical power. ❏ On another occasion I answered the phone and the line went dead. ■ ADJ **Dead** is used to mean "complete" or "absolute," especially before the words "center," "silence," and "stop." [EMPHASIS] [ADJ n] ❏ They hurried about in dead silence, with anxious faces. ■ ADV **Dead** means "precisely" or "exactly." [EMPHASIS] [ADV prep/adv/adj] ❏ Mars was visible, dead in the center of the telescope. ■ ADV **Dead** is sometimes used to mean "very." [BRIT, INFORMAL, SPOKEN, EMPHASIS] [ADV adj/adv/prep] ❏ I am dead against the legalisation of drugs. ■ CONVENTION If you reply "**Over my dead body**" when a plan or action has been suggested, you are emphasizing that you dislike it, and will do everything you can to prevent it. ❏ "Let's invite her to dinner." — "Over my dead body!" ■ PHRASE If you say that a person or animal **dropped dead** or **dropped down dead**, you mean that they died very suddenly and unexpectedly. ❏ He dropped dead on the quayside. ■ PHRASE If you say that you **feel dead** or **are half dead**, you mean that you feel very tired or ill and very weak. [INFORMAL, EMPHASIS] ❏ I thought you looked half dead at dinner, and who could blame you after that journey. ■ PHRASE If something happens **in the dead of night**, **at dead of night**, or **in the dead of winter**, it happens in the middle part of the night or the winter, when it is darkest or coldest. [LITERARY] ❏ We buried it in the garden at dead of night. ■ PHRASE If you say that you wouldn't **be seen dead** or **be caught dead** in particular clothes, places, or situations, you are expressing strong dislike or disapproval of them. [INFORMAL, EMPHASIS] ❏ I wouldn't be seen dead in a straw hat. ■ PHRASE To **stop dead** means to suddenly stop happening or moving. To **stop** someone or something **dead** means to cause them to suddenly stop happening or moving. ❏ We all stopped dead and looked at it. ■ to **stop dead in** your **tracks** →see track →see funeral

Thesaurus	dead의 참조어
ADJ.	deceased, lifeless; (ant.) alive, living ■

dead end (**dead ends**) ■ N-COUNT If a street is a **dead end**, there is no way out at one end of it. ❏ There was another alleyway which came to a dead end just behind the house. ■ N-COUNT A **dead end** job or course of action is one that you think is bad because it does not lead to further developments or progress. ❏ Waitressing was a dead-end job.

dead|line ♦♢♢ /dɛdlaɪn/ (**deadlines**) N-COUNT A **deadline** is a time or date before which a particular task must be finished or a particular thing must be done. ❏ We were not able to meet the deadline because of manufacturing delays.

dead|lock /dɛdlɒk/ (**deadlocks**) N-VAR If a dispute or series of negotiations reaches **deadlock**, neither side is willing to give in at all and no agreement can be made. ❏ They called for a compromise on all sides to break the deadlock in the world trade talks.

dead|ly /dɛdli/ (**deadlier, deadliest**) ■ ADJ If something is **deadly**, it is likely or able to cause someone's death, or has already caused someone's death. ❏ He was acquitted on charges of assault with a deadly weapon. ❏ ...a deadly disease currently affecting dolphins. ■ ADJ If you describe a person or their behavior as **deadly**, you mean that they will do or say anything to get what they want, without caring about other people. [DISAPPROVAL] ❏ The Duchess leveled a deadly look at Nikko. ■ ADV You can use **deadly** to emphasize that something has a particular quality, especially an unpleasant or undesirable quality. [EMPHASIS] [ADV adj] ❏ Broadcast news was accurate and reliable but deadly dull. ■ ADJ A **deadly** situation has unpleasant or dangerous consequences. ❏ ...the deadly combination of low expectations and low achievement.

deaf /dɛf/ (**deafer, deafest**) ■ ADJ Someone who is **deaf** is unable to hear anything or is unable to hear very well. ❏ She is now profoundly deaf. ● N-PLURAL The **deaf** are people who are deaf. ❏ Many regular TV programs are captioned for the deaf. ● **deaf|ness** N-UNCOUNT ❏ Because of her deafness she was hard to make conversation with. ■ to **fall on deaf ears** →see ear. to **turn a deaf ear** →see ear

deaf|en /dɛfən/ (**deafens, deafening, deafened**) ■ V-T If a noise **deafens** you, it is so loud that you cannot hear anything else at the same time. ❏ The noise of the typewriters deafened her. ■ V-T If you **are deafened by** something, you are made deaf by it, or are unable to hear for some time. [usu passive] ❏ He was deafened by the noise from the gun. ■ →see also deafening

deaf|en|ing /dɛfənɪŋ/ ■ ADJ A **deafening** noise is a very loud noise. ❏ ...the deafening roar of fighter jets taking off. ■ ADJ If you say there was a **deafening silence**, you are emphasizing that there was no reaction or response to something that was said or done. [EMPHASIS] ❏ What was truly despicable was the deafening silence maintained by the candidates concerning the riots.

---

deal

① QUANTIFIER USES
② VERB AND NOUN USES

---

① **deal** ♦♦♢ /dil/ QUANT If you say that you need or have **a great deal of** or a **good deal of** a particular thing, you are emphasizing that you need or have a lot of it. [EMPHASIS] [QUANT of n-uncount/def-n] ❏ ...a great deal of money. ● ADV **Deal** is also an adverb. ❏ As a relationship becomes more established, it also becomes a good deal

---

다 끝난 ❏ 그의 손가락 사이에 아직도 다 핀 담배가 끼워져 있었다. ■ 형용사 한물간 ❏ 그건 한물간 쟁점이야, 백스터. ■ 형용사 먹통이 된 ❏ 또 한 번은 내가 전화를 받았는데 전화선이 먹통이 되었다. ■ 형용사 완전한, 철저한 [강조] ❏ 그들은 근심 어린 얼굴로 전혀 아무런 말도 안 하고 서둘렀다. ■ 부사 정확하게 [강조] ❏ 화성이 정확히 망원경의 중앙에 잡혀 눈에 들어 왔다. ■ 부사 몹시, 죽어도 [영국영어, 비격식체, 구어체, 강조] ❏ 나는 마약 합법화를 죽어도 반대한다. ■ 관용 표현 내 살아생전에는 절대로 안돼, 나 죽고 나면 해 [비격식체, 강조] ❏ "그녀를 식사에 초대하자." "내 살아생전에는 절대 안 돼." ■ 구 갑자기 죽다 ❏ 그는 부둣가에서 갑자기 죽었다. ■ 구 다 죽어 가다 [비격식체, 강조] ❏ 네가 저녁 먹을 때 다 죽어 가는 것 같던데, 그런 여행을 한 뒤니 그럴 수 밖에. ■ 구 한밤중에; 한 겨울에 [문예체] ❏ 우리는 한밤중에 그것을 정원에 묻었다. ■ 구 죽기보다 싫어하다 [비격식체, 강조] ❏ 난 밀짚모자 쓰는 게 죽기보다 싫어. ■ 구 갑자기 멈추다; 갑자기 멈추게 하다 ❏ 우리 모두는 갑자기 멈추어 서서 그것을 바라보았다.

■ 가산명사 막다른 골목 ❏ 그 집 바로 뒤에 막다른 골목으로 이어지는 또 다른 좁은 길이 있었다. ■ 가산명사 장래성이 없는 ❏ 식당 종업원이란 직업은 장래성이 없었다.

가산명사 기한, 마감 시간 ❏ 우리는 생산 차질로 인해 기한을 맞출 수 없었다.

가산명사 또는 불가산명사 교착 상태 ❏ 그들은 국제 무역 회담의 교착 상태를 해결하고자 모든 당사자들에게 타협을 요구했다.

■ 형용사 치명적인 ❏ 그는 치명적인 무기를 사용한 폭행 혐의에 대해 무혐의로 풀려났다. ❏ 현재 돌고래에게 걸리는 치명적인 질병 ■ 형용사 지독하게 [탐탁잖음] ❏ 그 공작부인은 니코를 지독하게 쳐다 노려보았다. ■ 부사 몹시, 지독히도 [강조] ❏ 방송 뉴스는 정확하고 믿을 만하였으나 지독히도 재미없었다. ■ 형용사 최악의 ❏ 낮은 기대치와 낮은 성취라는 최악의 조합

■ 형용사 귀가 들리지 않는 ❏ 그녀는 이제 귀가 전혀 들리지 않는다. ● 복수명사 청각장애인 ❏ 일반 텔레비전 프로그램 중 다수가 청각장애인들을 위한 자막 방송을 한다. ● 귀가 안 들림 불가산명사 ❏ 그녀는 귀가 안 들려서 대화를 나누기가 어려웠다.

■ 타동사 귀가 멍하게 하다 ❏ 타자기들에서 나는 소음 때문에 그녀는 귀가 멍했다. ■ 타동사 귀가 멍해지다 ❏ 그는 총 소리에 귀가 멍했다.

■ 형용사 고막이 터질 것 같은, 귀를 멍하게 만드는 ❏ 이륙하는 전투 제트기에서 나는 고막이 터질 것 같은 굉음 ■ 형용사 철저한 (침묵) [강조] ❏ 참으로 비열한 것은 그 폭동에 관해 후보자들이 철저히 침묵을 지킨다는 점이었다.

수량사 많은 [강조] ❏ 많은 돈 ● 부사 상당히 ❏ 관계가 좀 더 정착될수록, 또한 그 관계는 상당히 더 복잡해진다. ● 대명사 많은 양 ❏ 그는 제프리 하드캐슬을 한번도 만난 적이 없었지만, 그에 대해

more complex. ● PRON **Deal** is also a pronoun. ❑ *Although he had never met Geoffrey Hardcastle, he knew a good deal about him.*

② **deal** ♦♦♦ /diːl/ (**deals, dealing, dealt**)→Please look at category 6 to see if the expression you are looking for is shown under another headword. 1 N-COUNT If you **make** a deal, **do** a deal, or **cut** a deal, you complete an agreement or an arrangement with someone, especially in business. [BUSINESS] ❑ *Japan will have to do a deal with America on rice imports.* ❑ *The two sides tried and failed to come to a deal.* 2 V-I If a person, company, or store **deals** in a particular type of goods, their business involves buying or selling those goods. [BUSINESS] ❑ *They deal in antiques.* 3 V-T If someone **deals** illegal drugs, they sell them. ❑ *I certainly don't deal drugs.* 4 N-COUNT If someone has had a **bad deal**, they have been unfortunate or have been treated unfairly. ❑ *The people of Liverpool have had a bad deal for many, many years.* 5 V-T If you **deal** playing cards, you give them out to the players in a game of cards. ❑ *The croupier dealt each player a card, face down.* ● PHRASAL VERB **Deal out** means the same as **deal**. ❑ *Dalton dealt out five cards to each player.* 6 →see also **dealings, wheel and deal**

	Word Partnership	deal의 연어
N.	business deal, peace deal ② 1	
	deal drugs ② 3	
V.	close a deal, seal a deal, strike a deal ② 1	
ADJ.	better deal, big deal ② 1	

▶**deal out** PHRASAL VERB If someone **deals out** a punishment or harmful action, they punish or harm someone. [WRITTEN] ❑ *...a failure by the governments of established states to deal out effective punishment to aggressors.* →see also **deal 5**

▶**deal with** 1 PHRASAL VERB When you **deal with** something or someone that needs attention, you give your attention to them, and often solve a problem or make a decision concerning them. ❑ *...the way that building societies deal with complaints.* 2 PHRASAL VERB If you **deal with** an unpleasant emotion or an emotionally difficult situation, you recognize it, and remain calm and in control of yourself in spite of it. ❑ *She saw a psychiatrist who used hypnotism to help her deal with her fear.* 3 PHRASAL VERB If a book, speech, or movie **deals with** a particular thing, it has that thing as its subject or is concerned with it. ❑ *...the parts of his book which deal with contemporary Paris.* 4 PHRASAL VERB If you **deal with** a particular person or organization, you have business relations with them. ❑ *When I worked in Florida I dealt with British people all the time.*

deal|er ♦♦◊ /diːlər/ (**dealers**) 1 N-COUNT A **dealer** is a person whose business involves buying and selling things. [BUSINESS] ❑ *...an antique dealer.* 2 N-COUNT A **dealer** is someone who buys and sells illegal drugs. ❑ *They will stay on the job for as long as it takes to clear every dealer from the street.*

deal|er|ship /diːlərʃɪp/ (**dealerships**) N-COUNT A **dealership** is a company that sells cars, usually for one car company. [BUSINESS] ❑ *...a car dealership.*

deal|ing room (**dealing rooms**) N-COUNT A **dealing room** is a place where shares, currencies, or commodities are bought and sold. [BUSINESS] ❑ *Make sure you have some Cable & Wireless shares was the message from London's dealing rooms last night.*

deal|ings /diːlɪŋz/ N-PLURAL Someone's **dealings with** a person or organization are the relations that they have with them or the business that they do with them. ❑ *He has learnt little in his dealings with the international community.*

dealt /delt/ **Dealt** is the past tense and past participle of **deal**.

dean /diːn/ (**deans**) 1 N-COUNT A **dean** is an important official at a university or college. ❑ *She is currently Dean of the faculty of International Studies at Sophia University.* 2 N-COUNT A **dean** is a priest who is the main administrator of a large church. ❑ *...Alan Webster, former Dean of St Paul's.*

dear ♦♦◊ /dɪər/ (**dearer, dearest**) 1 ADJ You use **dear** to describe someone or something that you feel affection for. [ADJ n] ❑ *Mrs. Cavendish is a dear friend of mine.* 2 ADJ If something is **dear to** you or **dear to** your **heart**, you care deeply about it. [v-link ADJ to n] ❑ *This is a subject very dear to the hearts of academics up and down the country.* 3 ADJ **Dear** is written at the beginning of a letter, followed by the name or title of the person you are writing to. [ADJ n] ❑ *Dear Peter, I have been thinking about you so much during the past few days.* 4 CONVENTION You begin formal letters with "**Dear Sir**" or "**Dear Madam**." In American English, you can also begin them with "Sir" or "Madam." [WRITTEN] ❑ *"Dear sir," she began.* 5 N-VOC You can call someone **dear** as a sign of affection. [FEELINGS] ❑ *You're a lot like me, dear.* 6 EXCLAM You can use **dear** in expressions such as "**oh dear**," "**dear me**," and "**dear, dear**" when you are sad, disappointed, or surprised about something. [FEELINGS] ❑ *"Oh dear, oh dear." McKinnon sighed. "You, too."* 7 ADJ If you say that something is **dear**, you mean that it costs a lot of money, usually more than you can afford or more than you think it should cost. [mainly BRIT, INFORMAL, DISAPPROVAL] ❑ *It's getting dearer now but it used to be pretty reasonable to buy.*

dear|est /dɪərɪst/ ADJ When you are writing to someone you are very fond of, you can use **dearest** at the beginning of the letter before the person's name or the word you are using to address them. [ADJ n] ❑ *Dearest Maria, Aren't I terrible, not coming back like I promised?*

dear|ly /dɪərli/ 1 ADV If you love someone **dearly**, you love them very much. [FORMAL, EMPHASIS] [ADV with v] ❑ *She loved her father dearly.* 2 ADV If you would **dearly** like to do or have something, you would very much like to do it or have it. [FORMAL, EMPHASIS] [ADV before v] ❑ *I would dearly love to marry.* 3 PHRASE If you **pay dearly for** doing something or if it **costs** you **dearly**, you suffer a lot as a result. [FORMAL] ❑ *He drank too much and is paying dearly for the pleasure.*

상당히 많이 알고 있었다.

1 가산명사 거래, 협약 [경제] ❑ 일본은 쌀 수입에 관해 미국과 협약을 해야만 할 것이다. ❑ 양측은 거래를 맺기 위해 노력했으나 실패했다. 2 자동사 취급하다, 거래하다 [경제] ❑ 그들은 골동품을 취급한다. 3 타동사 거래하다 ❑ 나는 단연코 마약 거래는 하지 않는다. 4 가산명사 부당한 대접 ❑ 리버풀 사람들은 정말 오랫동안 부당하게 대접받아 왔다. 5 타동사 (카드 패를) 돌리다 ❑ 카드 딜러가 선수들에게 카드를 뒤집어서 한 장씩 돌렸다. ● 구동사 (카드 패를) 돌리다 ❑ 달튼은 각 선수들에게 카드를 다섯 장씩 돌렸다.

구동사 가하다 [문어체] ❑ 기존 국가 정부들이 침략자들에 대해 효과적인 처벌을 가하지 못함

1 구동사 다루다, 처리하다 ❑ 주택 조합들이 불만을 처리하는 방식 2 구동사 대처하다 ❑ 그녀는 최면술을 이용해서 자신이 두려움에 대처하도록 도와준 정신과 의사를 만났다. 3 구동사 논하다, 다루다 ❑ 그의 저서에서 현대 파리에 대해 논하는 부분들 4 구동사 거래하다 ❑ 플로리다에서 근무할 때 나는 항상 영국인들과 거래했었다.

1 가산명사 -상, 판매인 [경제] ❑ 골동품상 2 가산명사 마약 거래자 ❑ 그들은 모든 마약 거래자가 길거리에서 사라질 때까지 그 일을 계속 할 것이다.

가산명사 대리점 [경제] ❑ 자동차 대리점

가산명사 거래소 [경제] ❑ 당신은 '케이블 앤 와이어리스 주식을 보유하고 계십니다'라는 메시지가 어젯밤 런던 거래소에서 온 메시지가 되도록 하십시오.

복수명사 거래 ❑ 그는 해외 기업들과의 거래에서 배운 게 거의 없다.

deal의 과거 및 과거 분사

1 가산명사 총장, 학장 ❑ 그녀는 현재 소피아 대학 국제학부의 학과장이다. 2 가산명사 사제장 ❑ 성 바오로 대성당의 전 사제장인 앨런 웹스터

1 형용사 친애하는, 소중한 ❑ 카벤디쉬 부인은 내 소중한 친구이다. 2 형용사 애착, 중요한, -에게 소중한 ❑ 이것은 전국의 모든 학자들에게 매우 중요한 주제이다. 3 형용사 친애하는 (편지의 서두) ❑ 피터에게, 지난 며칠 동안 너를 많이 생각했어. 4 관용 표현 안녕하세요 (공식적인 편지의 서두) [문어체] ❑ "안녕하세요."라고 그녀는 쓰기 시작했다. 5 호격명사 상대방에게 애정을 표현할 때 쓰는 호칭 [감정 개입] ❑ 얘야, 너는 나를 무척 닮았구나. 6 감탄사 이런 [감정 개입] ❑ "오 이런, 오 이럴 수가, 너마저."라고 맥키넌은 한숨을 지으며 말했다. 7 형용사 비싼 [주로 영국영어, 비격식체, 탐탁찮음] ❑ 요즘은 그 물건 값이 비싸지고 있지만 예전엔 가격이 꽤 괜찮았는데.

형용사 친애하는 ❑ 친애하는 마리아에게, 약속해 놓고도 돌아오지 않고. 나 너무 나쁜 애인 것 같지 않니?

1 부사 끔찍이 [격식체, 강조] ❑ 그녀는 아버지를 끔찍이 사랑했다. 2 부사 꼭 [격식체, 강조] ❑ 나는 결혼하고 싶어 죽겠다. 3 구 엄청난 대가를 치르다; 엄청난 대가를 치르게 하다 [격식체] ❑ 그는 술을 너무 많이 마셨고, 그 쾌락에 대해 지금 엄청난 대가를 치르고 있다.

a b c d e f g h i j k l m n o p q r s t u v w x y z

death ♦♦◇ /dεθ/ (deaths) **1** N-VAR **Death** is the permanent end of the life of a person or animal. □ 1.5 million people are in immediate danger of death from starvation. □ ...the thirtieth anniversary of Judy Garland's death. **2** N-SING **The death of** something is the permanent end of it. □ It meant the death of everything he had ever been or ever hoped to be. **3** PHRASE If you say that someone is **at death's door**, you mean they are very ill indeed and likely to die. [INFORMAL] □ He told his boss a tale about his mother being at death's door. **4** PHRASE If you say that you will **fight to the death** for something, you are emphasizing that you will do anything to achieve or protect it, even if you suffer as a consequence. [EMPHASIS] □ She'd have fought to the death for that child. **5** PHRASE If you say that something is a matter **of life and death**, you are emphasizing that it is extremely important, often because someone may die or suffer great harm if people do not act immediately. [EMPHASIS] □ Well, never mind, John, it's not a matter of life and death. **6** PHRASE If someone **is put to death**, they are executed. [FORMAL] □ Those put to death by firing squad included three generals. **7** PHRASE You use **to death** after an adjective or a verb to emphasize the action, state, or feeling mentioned. For example, if you are **frightened to death** or **bored to death**, you are extremely frightened or bored. [EMPHASIS] □ He scares teams to death with his pace and power.

1 가산명사 또는 불가산명사 죽음 □ 150만의 목숨이 아사 위기에 놓여 있다. □ 주디 갈랜드 서거 30주년 기념일 **2** 단수명사 종말, 끝장 □ 그것은 그가 누려 왔던 것, 그가 누리기 바랐던 모든 것들의 종말을 뜻했다. **3** 구 위독하여 [비격식체] □ 그는 사장에게 자기 어머니가 위독하시다고 말했다. **4** 구 사투를 벌이다 [강조] □ 그녀는 그 아이를 위해서라면 사투도 벌였을 것이다. **5** 구 생사가 걸린 [강조] □ 음, 걱정 마, 존. 이게 생사가 걸린 문제는 아니니까. **6** 구 처형되다 [격식체] □ 총살자들 중에는 세 명의 장성이 포함되어 있었다. **7** 구 죽을 지경의; 놀라 죽을 뻔한; 지겨워 죽겠는 [강조] □ 그는 속도와 힘으로 다른 팀들을 무섭게 위협했다.

death|ly /dεθli/ **1** ADV If you say that someone is **deathly** pale or **deathly** still, you are emphasizing that they are very pale or still, like a dead person. [LITERARY, EMPHASIS] [ADV adj] □ Bernadette turned deathly pale. **2** ADJ If you say that there is a **deathly** silence or a **deathly** hush, you are emphasizing that it is very quiet. [LITERARY, EMPHASIS] [ADJ n] □ A deathly silence hung over the square.

1 부사 사색이 된, 죽은 듯이 [문예체, 강조] □ 버나뎃의 얼굴이 사색이 되었다. **2** 형용사 쥐 죽은 듯이 [문예체, 강조] □ 광장은 쥐 죽은 듯이 조용했다.

death pen|al|ty N-SING The **death penalty** is the punishment of death used in some countries for people who have committed very serious crimes. □ If convicted for murder, both youngsters could face the death penalty.

단수명사 사형 □ 살인죄 유죄 판결이 난다면, 그 소년들은 둘 다 사형을 받게 될지도 모른다.

death rate (death rates) N-COUNT The **death rate** is the number of people per thousand who die in a particular area during a particular period of time. □ By the turn of the century, Pittsburgh had the highest death rate in the United States. →see **population**

가산명사 사망률 □ 세기가 바뀔 무렵에는 피츠버그의 사망률이 미국에서 가장 높았다.

death row /dεθ rou/ N-UNCOUNT If someone is **on death row**, they are in the part of a prison which contains the cells for criminals who have been sentenced to death. [AM] □ He has been on Death Row for 11 years.

불가산명사 사형수 감방 [미국영어] □ 그는 사형수 감방에서 11년 동안 복역하고 있다.

death sen|tence (death sentences) N-COUNT A **death sentence** is a punishment of death given by a judge to someone who has been found guilty of a serious crime such as murder. □ His original death sentence was commuted to life in prison.

가산명사 사형 선고 □ 그는 원래 사형에서 종신형으로 감형받았다.

death toll (death tolls) also **death-toll** N-COUNT The **death toll** of an accident, disaster, or war is the number of people who die in it. □ In Egypt, the death toll continues to rise from yesterday's major earthquake.

가산명사 사망자 수 □ 이집트에서 어제 일어난 대지진으로 사망자 수가 계속 증가하고 있다.

death trap (death traps) also **death-trap** N-COUNT If you say that a place or vehicle is a **death trap**, you mean it is in such bad condition that it might cause someone's death. [INFORMAL] □ Badly-built cars can be death traps.

가산명사 죽음의 덫 [비격식체] □ 잘못 만들어진 차는 죽음의 덫이 될 수도 있다.

de|ba|cle /dɪbɑ̱kəl, -bæ̱kəl, BRIT deɪbɑːkəl/ (debacles) [BRIT also **débâcle**] N-COUNT A **debacle** is an event or attempt that is a complete failure. □ People believed it was a privilege to die for your country, but after the debacle of the war they never felt the same again.

[영국영어 débâcle] 가산명사 대실패 □ 사람들은 자기 조국을 위해 죽는 것이 영광이라고 믿었다. 그러나 전쟁에서 참패한 후에는 다시는 그렇게 생각하지 않았다.

de|bat|able /dɪbeɪtəbəl/ ADJ If you say that something is **debatable**, you mean that it is not certain. □ It is debatable whether or not the shareholders were ever properly compensated.

형용사 논쟁의 여지가 있는 □ 주주들이 제대로 보상을 받았는지 안 받았는지는 논쟁의 여지가 있다.

de|bate ♦♦◇ /dɪbeɪt/ (debates, debating, debated) **1** N-VAR A **debate** is a discussion about a subject on which people have different views. □ An intense debate is going on within the Israeli government. □ There has been a lot of debate among scholars about this. **2** N-COUNT A **debate** is a formal discussion, for example in a parliament or institution, in which people express different opinions about a particular subject and then vote on it. □ There are expected to be some heated debates in parliament over the next few days. **3** V-RECIP If people **debate** a topic, they discuss it fairly formally, putting forward different views. You can also say that one person **debates** a topic **with** another person. □ The United Nations Security Council will debate the issue today. □ Scholars have debated whether or not Yagenta became a convert. **4** V-T If you **debate** whether to do something or what to do, you think or talk about possible courses of action before deciding exactly what you are going to do. □ Taggart debated whether to have yet another double vodka. →see **election**

1 가산명사 또는 불가산명사 논쟁, 토론 □ 이스라엘 정부 내에서 격렬한 논쟁이 진행 중이다. □ 이 사안에 관해서 학자들 간에 수많은 논쟁이 있어 왔다. **2** 가산명사 의사(議事), 토의 (의회나 기관에서 특정한 안건에 대해 서로 다른 의견을 표하고 표결하는 공식적인 회의) □ 이후 며칠 동안 의회에서 열띤 토의가 있을 것으로 예상된다. **3** 상호동사 논의하다, 논쟁하다 □ 그 문제는 오늘 유엔 안전 보장 이사회에서 논의될 것이다. □ 학자들은 야겐타가 개종했는지 안 했는지에 대해 논쟁해 왔다. **4** 타동사 따져 보다, 재다 □ 태거트는 보드카 더블을 한 잔 더 해야 하는지를 재어 보았다.

de|ben|ture /dɪbε̱ntʃər/ (debentures) N-COUNT A **debenture** is a type of savings bond which offers a fixed rate of interest over a long period. Debentures are usually issued by a company or a government agency. [BUSINESS]

가산명사 채권 [경제]

deb|it /dɛbɪt/ (debits, debiting, debited) ◼ v-т When your bank **debits** your account, money is taken from it and paid to someone else. ◻ *We will always confirm the revised amount to you in writing before debiting your account.* ◼ N-COUNT A **debit** is a record of the money taken from your bank account, for example when you write a check. ◻ *The total of debits must balance the total of credits.* ◼ →see also **direct debit**

◼ 타동사 출금되다 ◻ 귀하의 계좌에서 돈을 출금하기 전에 항상 변경된 금액을 문서로 확인해 드리겠습니다. ◼ 가산명사 출금 기록 ◻ 계좌의 총 출금 기록은 총 예금액 한도 이내라야 한다.

deb|it card (debit cards) N-COUNT A **debit card** is a bank card that you can use to pay for things. When you use it the money is taken out of your bank account immediately.

가산명사 직불 카드

de|bris /deɪbri, BRIT deɪbri/ N-UNCOUNT **Debris** is pieces from something that has been destroyed or pieces of trash or unwanted material that are spread around. ◻ *A number of people were killed by flying debris.*

불가산명사 파편 ◻ 튀어나온 파편에 맞아 수많은 사람들이 목숨을 잃었다.

debt ♦♦◇ /dɛt/ (debts) ◼ N-VAR A **debt** is a sum of money that you owe someone. ◻ *Three years later, he is still paying off his debts.* →see also **bad debt** ◼ N-UNCOUNT **Debt** is the state of owing money. ◻ *Fear of debt is discouraging some young people from going to university.* ● PHRASE If you are **in debt** or **get into debt**, you owe money. If you are **out of debt** or **get out of debt**, you succeed in paying all the money that you owe. ◻ *He was already deeply in debt through gambling losses.* ◼ N-COUNT You use **debt** in expressions such as **I owe you a debt** or **I am in your debt** when you are expressing gratitude for something that someone has done for you. [FORMAL, FEELINGS] ◻ *He was so good to me that I can never repay the debt I owe him.* ◻ *I owe a debt of thanks to Joyce Thompson, whose careful and able research was of great help.*

◼ 가산명사 또는 불가산명사 빚 ◻ 삼 년이 지났지만, 그는 아직도 부채를 변제 중이다. ◼ 불가산명사 빚지고 있는 상태 ◻ 젊은이들은 빚지는 것이 두려워서 대학 진학을 단념하기도 한다. ◼ 가산명사 (비유적 의미의) 빚; 신세 ● 구 빚을 지다; 빚을 갚다 ◻ 그는 도박으로 잃은 돈 때문에 이미 많은 빚을 지고 있었다. ◼ 가산명사 (비유적 의미의) 빚; 신세 많이 졌어 [격식체, 감정 개입] ◻ 그는 내게 너무 잘해 줘서 내가 결코 그 빚을 다 갚지 못할 것이다. ◻ 섬세하고 뛰어난 연구로 큰 도움을 준 조이스 톰슨에게 감사드리고 싶다.

debt bur|den (debt burdens) N-COUNT A **debt burden** is a large amount of money that one country or organization owes to another and which they find very difficult to repay. ◻ *The massive debt burden of the Third World has become a crucial issue for many leaders of poorer countries.*

가산명사 (정부나 기관의) 악성 부채 ◻ 제3 세계의 엄청난 악성 부채는 가난한 나라 지도자들에게 매우 중요한 문제가 되었다.

debt|or /dɛtər/ (debtors) N-COUNT A **debtor** is a country, organization, or person who owes money. ◻ *...important improvements in the situation of debtor countries.*

가산명사 채무국, 채무 기관, 채무자 ◻ 채무국들의 중요한 상황 호전

de|bug /dibʌg/ (debugs, debugging, debugged) v-т When someone **debugs** a computer program, they look for the faults in it and correct them so that it will run properly. [COMPUTING] ◻ *The production lines ground to a halt for hours while technicians tried to debug software.*

타동사 컴퓨터 프로그램의 오류를 수정하다 [컴퓨터] ◻ 기술자들이 소프트웨어의 오류를 수정하는 동안 생산 라인이 서서히 멈춰 섰다.

de|but ♦◇◇ /deɪbyu, BRIT deɪbyuː/ (debuts) N-COUNT The **debut** of a performer or sports player is their first public performance, appearance, or recording. ◻ *Dundee United's Dave Bowman makes his international debut.*

가산명사 데뷔 ◻ 던디 유나이트의 데이브 보우먼이 국제무대에 데뷔한다.

Dec. Dec. is a written abbreviation for **December**.

12월의 문어체 약어

dec|ade ♦♦◇ /dɛkeɪd/ (decades) N-COUNT A **decade** is a period of ten years, especially one that begins with a year ending in 0, for example 1980 to 1989. ◻ *...the last decade of the nineteenth century.*

가산명사 10년 ◻ 19세기 마지막 십년간 (즉, 1890년대)

deca|dent /dɛkədənt/ ADJ If you say that a person or society is **decadent**, you think that they have low moral standards and are interested mainly in pleasure. [DISAPPROVAL] ◻ *...the excesses and stresses of their decadent rock 'n' roll lifestyles.* ● **deca|dence** N-UNCOUNT ◻ *The empire had for years been falling into decadence.*

형용사 퇴폐적인 [탐탁찮음] ◻ 그들의 퇴폐적인 록앤롤 생활 스타일에 따른 향락과 스트레스 ● 퇴폐, 향락 불가산명사 ◻ 그 제국은 수년 동안 향락의 길로 들어서고 있었다.

de|caf|fein|at|ed /dikæfineɪtɪd, -kæfiə-/ ADJ **Decaffeinated** coffee has had most of the caffeine removed from it.

형용사 카페인을 제거한

de|capi|tate /dɪkæpɪteɪt/ (decapitates, decapitating, decapitated) v-т If someone **is decapitated**, their head is cut off. [FORMAL] ◻ *A worker was decapitated when a lift plummeted down the shaft on top of him.*

타동사 목이 잘려 나가다, 참수되다 [격식체] ◻ 승강기가 머리 위로 추락하는 바람에 승강기 통로에서 일하던 한 노동자의 목이 잘려 나갔다.

de|cath|lon /dɪkæθlɒn/ (decathlons) N-COUNT The **decathlon** is a competition in which athletes compete in 10 different sports events.

가산명사 10종 경기

de|cay /dɪkeɪ/ (decays, decaying, decayed) ◼ v-ɪ When something such as a dead body, a dead plant, or a tooth **decays**, it is gradually destroyed by a natural process. ◻ *The bodies buried in the fine ash slowly decayed.* ● N-UNCOUNT **Decay** is also a noun. ◻ *When not removed, plaque causes tooth decay and gum disease.* ● **de|cayed** ADJ ◻ *Even young children have teeth so decayed they need to be pulled.* ◼ v-ɪ If something such as a society, system, or institution **decays**, it gradually becomes weaker or its condition gets worse. ◻ *In practice, the agency system has decayed. Most "agents" now sell only to themselves or their immediate family.* ● N-UNCOUNT **Decay** is also a noun. ◻ *There are problems of urban decay and gang violence.* →see **teeth**

◼ 자동사 썩다, 부식하다 ◻ 고운 잿가루에 묻힌 시체는 서서히 썩어 갔다. ● 불가산명사 부패, 부식 ◻ 플라크는 제거하지 않으면 치아 부식과 치주 질환을 유발합니다. ● 썩은 형용사 ◻ 어린 아이들의 치아도 그렇게 썩으면 뽑아야 한다. ◼ 자동사 쇠퇴하다, 쇠락하다 ◻ 실제로, 대리점 시스템은 쇠퇴했다. 대부분의 대리점들이 이제 자사원이나 그 직계 가족을 대상으로만 영업을 하고 있다. ● 불가산명사 쇠퇴, 쇠락 ◻ 도시 쇠락과 집단 폭력의 문제가 있다.

de|ceased /dɪsist/

Deceased is both the singular and the plural form.

deceased은 단수형 및 복수형이다.

◼ N-COUNT **The deceased** is used to refer to a particular person or to particular people who have recently died. [LEGAL] ◻ *The Navy is notifying next of kin now that the identities of the deceased have been determined.* ◼ ADJ A **deceased** person is one who has recently died. [FORMAL] ◻ *...his recently deceased mother.* →see **funeral**

◼ 가산명사 고인, 최근에 사망한 사람 [법률] ◻ 해군은 최근 사망한 사람들의 신분이 확인되었다고 가족들에게 통보하고 있다. ◼ 형용사 최근에 사망한, 작고한 [격식체] ◻ 최근에 작고하신 그의 모친

de|ceit /dɪsit/ (deceits) N-VAR **Deceit** is behavior that is deliberately intended to make people believe something which is not true. ◻ *He was living a secret life of deceit and unfaithfulness.*

가산명사 또는 불가산명사 기만, 속임수 ◻ 그는 기만과 부정으로 얼룩진 은밀한 삶을 살고 있었다.

de|ceit|ful /dɪsitfəl/ ADJ If you say that someone is **deceitful**, you mean that they behave in a dishonest way by making other people believe something that is not true. ◻ *The ambassador called the report deceitful and misleading.*

형용사 기만적인 ◻ 대사는 그 보고서가 기만적이고 사람을 호도한다고 말했다.

a b c d e f g h i j k l m n o p q r s t u v w x y z

A

de|ceive /dɪsiːv/ (**deceives**, **deceiving**, **deceived**) **1** V-T If you **deceive** someone, you make them believe something that is not true, usually in order to get some advantage for yourself. ❑ He has deceived and disillusioned us all. **2** V-T If something **deceives** you, it gives you a wrong impression and makes you believe something that is not true. ❑ The alacrity with which he'd agreed did not deceive Joanna; she knew that he had no intention of abandoning his harebrained plan.

1 타동사 속이다 ❑ 그는 우리 모두를 속여 왔고, 우리에게 헛된 환상을 심어 주었다. **2** 타동사 -에 속다 ❑ 그가 선뜻 동의한 것에 조안나는 속지 않았다. 조안나는 그가 자신의 어리석은 계획을 포기할 의사가 없다는 것을 알고 있었다.

B

C

De|cem|ber ◆◆◆ /dɪsɛmbər/ (**Decembers**) N-VAR **December** is the twelfth and last month of the year in the Western calendar. ❑ ...a bright morning in mid-December.

가산명사 또는 불가산명사 12월 ❑ 12월 중순의 맑게 갠 아침

de|cen|cy /diːsᵊnsi/ **1** N-UNCOUNT **Decency** is the quality of following accepted moral standards. ❑ His sense of decency forced him to resign. **2** PHRASE If you say that someone **did not have the decency to** do something, you are criticizing them because there was a particular action which they did not do but which you believe they ought to have done. [DISAPPROVAL] ❑ Somebody should have had the decency to inform myself and John Prescott of what was planned.

1 불가산명사 체면, 품위 ❑ 그는 체면상 사임할 수밖에 없었다. **2** 구 염치가 있다 [탐탁찮음] ❑ 무슨 계획이 있었는지 나와 존 프레스콧에게는 알려 줄 정도로 염치 있는 사람 한 명 정도는 있었어야 하는 거 아냐?

D

E

de|cent /diːsᵊnt/ **1** ADJ **Decent** is used to describe something which is considered to be of an acceptable standard or quality. ❑ He didn't get a decent explanation. ● **de|cent|ly** ADV ❑ The allies say they will treat their prisoners decently. **2** ADJ **Decent** is used to describe something which is morally correct or acceptable. ❑ But, after a decent interval, trade relations began to return to normal. ● **de|cent|ly** ADV ❑ And can't you dress more decently – people will think you're a tramp. **3** ADJ **Decent** people are honest and behave in a way that most people approve of. ❑ The majority of people around here are decent people.

1 형용사 괜찮은, 쓸 만한 ❑ 그는 그럴듯한 설명을 듣지 못했다. ● 괜찮게, 걸맞게 부사 ❑ 연합군 측은 포로들에게 합당한 대우를 해 줄 것이라고 말한다. **2** 형용사 적절한 ❑ 그러나 적절한 기간 뒤에 무역 관계는 정상으로 돌아오기 시작했다. ● 점잖게 부사 ❑ 그리고 너, 옷 좀 더 점잖게 입을 수 없어? 사람들이 너 창녀인 줄 알겠다. **3** 형용사 점잖은 ❑ 이곳 사람들의 대다수는 점잖은 사람들이다.

F

G

H

Thesaurus	decent의 참조어	
ADJ.	acceptable, adequate, satisfactory; (ant.) unsatisfactory **1** honorable, respectable **2** **3**	

I

J

de|cen|tral|ize /diːsɛntrəlaɪz/ (**decentralizes**, **decentralizing**, **decentralized**) [BRIT also **decentralise**] V-T/V-I To **decentralize** government or a large organization means to move some departments away from the main administrative area, or to give more power to local departments. ❑ ...the need to decentralize and devolve power to regional governments. ● **de|cen|trali|za|tion** /diːsɛntrəlaɪzeɪʃᵊn/ N-UNCOUNT ❑ He seems set against the idea of increased decentralization and greater powers for regional authorities.

[영국영어 decentralise] 타동사/자동사 분산하다, 분권화하다 ❑ 분권화의 필요성과 지방 정부로의 권력 이양 ● 분산, 분권 불가산명사 ❑ 그는 분권 강화와 지방 정부 권력 증대라는 생각에 반대하고 있는 것처럼 보인다.

K

de|cep|tion /dɪsɛpʃᵊn/ (**deceptions**) N-VAR **Deception** is the act of deceiving someone or the state of being deceived by someone. ❑ He admitted conspiring to obtain property by deception.

가산명사 또는 불가산명사 기만 행위, 기만당함 ❑ 그는 남을 속여서 재산을 획득하려는 음모를 꾸미고 있었다는 것을 시인했다.

L

de|cep|tive /dɪsɛptɪv/ ADJ If something is **deceptive**, it encourages you to believe something which is not true. ❑ Johnston isn't tired of London yet, it seems, but appearances can be deceptive. ● **de|cep|tive|ly** ADV ❑ The storyline is deceptively simple.

형용사 기만적인, 믿을 수 없는 ❑ 존스턴은 아직 런던에 질리지 않은 것처럼 보이지만, 겉보기와 실제는 다를 수 있다. ● 믿기 어려울 정도로 부사 ❑ 그 줄거리는 믿기 어려울 정도로 간단했다.

M

deci|bel /dɛsɪbɛl/ (**decibels**) N-COUNT A **decibel** is a unit of measurement which is used to indicate how loud a sound is. ❑ Continuous exposure to sound above 80 decibels could be harmful.

가산명사 데시벨 ❑ 80데시벨 이상의 소음에 계속해서 노출되는 것은 해로울 수 있다.

N

de|cide ◆◆◆ /dɪsaɪd/ (**decides**, **deciding**, **decided**) **1** V-T/V-I If you **decide** to do something, you choose to do it, usually after you have thought carefully about the other possibilities. ❑ She decided to do a secretarial course. ❑ The jury decided that the cops had not used excessive force. ❑ Think about it very carefully before you decide. **2** V-T If a person or group of people **decides** something, they choose what something should be like or how a particular problem should be solved. ❑ She was still young, he said, and that would be taken into account when deciding her sentence. **3** V-T/V-I If an event or fact **decides** something, it makes it certain that a particular choice will be made or that there will be a particular result. ❑ The goal that decided the match came just before the interval. ❑ The results will decide if he will win a place at a good university. **4** V-T If you **decide** that something is true, you form that opinion about it after considering the facts. ❑ He decided Franklin must be suffering from a bad cold.

1 타동사/자동사 결정하다, 정하다 ❑ 그녀는 비서 양성 과정을 이수하기로 결정했다. ❑ 배심원들은 경찰들이 과도한 공권력을 사용하지 않았다고 평결했다. ❑ 결정하기 전에 신중하게 생각해 봐. **2** 타동사 결정하다 ❑ 그녀는 아직 어렸으므로, 겉보기에 대한 선고를 내릴 때 이 부분이 감안될 것이라고 말했다. **3** 타동사/자동사 결정짓다 ❑ 그 경기의 결정 골은 하프타임 직전에 터졌다. ❑ 그 결과에 그가 좋은 대학에 들어갈 수 있을지 여부가 달려 있다. **4** 타동사 결론짓다 ❑ 그는 프랭클린이 심한 감기로 고생하고 있을 거라고 결론지었다.

O

P

Q

R

Thesaurus	decide의 참조어	
V.	choose, elect, pick, select **1** **2**	

S

Word Partnership	decide의 연어	
V.	try to decide **1** **2** help (to) decide, let someone decide **1** **2** **3**	
ADJ.	unable to decide **1** **2** **4**	

T

U

▶**decide on** PHRASAL VERB If you **decide on** something or **decide upon** something, you choose it from two or more possibilities. ❑ After leaving university, Amy decided on a career in publishing.

구동사 정하다 ❑ 대학 졸업 후, 에이미는 출판으로 쪽으로 진로를 정했다.

V

de|cid|ed /dɪsaɪdɪd/ ADJ **Decided** means clear and definite. [ADJ n] ❑ They got involved in a long and exhausting struggle and were at a decided disadvantage in the afternoon.

형용사 명백한 ❑ 그들은 길고 소모적인 투쟁에 개입됐고 오후에는 명백히 불리한 입장에 처해 있었다.

W

de|cid|ed|ly /dɪsaɪdɪdli/ ADV **Decidedly** means to a great extent and in a way that is very obvious. [ADV group] ❑ He admits there will be moments when he's decidedly uncomfortable at what he sees on the screen.

부사 명백하게 ❑ 스크린에서 보는 장면이 명백히 불편하게 느껴지는 순간이 있을 것이라고 그는 인정했다.

X

Y

Word Link	dec ≈ ten : decade, decathlon, decimal	

deci|mal /dɛsɪmᵊl/ (**decimals**) **1** ADJ A **decimal** system involves counting in units of ten. [ADJ n] ❑ The mathematics of ancient Egypt were based on a decimal

1 형용사 십진법 ❑ 고대 이집트의 수학은 십진법에 기초를 두고 있었다. **2** 가산명사 소수 ❑ 소수나 분수

Z

system. **2** N-COUNT A **decimal** is a fraction that is written in the form of a dot followed by one or more numbers which represent tenths, hundredths, and so on: for example.5,.51,.517. ❑ ...*simple math concepts, such as decimals and fractions.*

decimal point (decimal points) N-COUNT A **decimal point** is the dot in front of a decimal fraction. ❑ *A waiter omitted the decimal point in the 13.09 euros bill.*

decimate /dɛsɪmeɪt/ (decimates, decimating, decimated) **1** V-T To **decimate** something such as a group of people or animals means to destroy a very large number of them. ❑ *The pollution could decimate the river's thriving population of kingfishers.* **2** V-T To **decimate** a system or organization means to reduce its size and effectiveness greatly. ❑ *...a recession which decimated the nation's manufacturing industry.*

decipher /dɪsaɪfər/ (deciphers, deciphering, deciphered) V-T If you **decipher** a piece of writing or a message, you work out what it says, even though it is very difficult to read or understand. ❑ *I'm still no closer to deciphering the code.*

decision ♦♦♦ /dɪsɪʒⁿn/ (decisions) **1** N-COUNT When you make a **decision**, you choose what should be done or which is the best of various possible actions. ❑ *I don't want to make the wrong decision and regret it later.* **2** N-UNCOUNT **Decision** is the act of deciding something or the need to decide something. ❑ *The growing pressures of the crisis may mean that the moment of decision can't be too long delayed.* **3** N-UNCOUNT **Decision** is the ability to decide quickly and definitely what to do. ❑ *He is very quick-thinking and very much a man of decision.*

Word Partnership	decision의 연어
V.	**arrive at a** decision, **make a** decision, **postpone a** decision, **reach a** decision **1**
ADJ.	**difficult** decision, **final** decision, **important** decision, **right** decision, **wise** decision, **wrong** decision **1**

decisive /dɪsaɪsɪv/ **1** ADJ If a fact, action, or event is **decisive**, it makes it certain that there will be a particular result. ❑ *...his decisive victory in the presidential elections.* ● **decisively** ADV ❑ *The plan was decisively rejected by Congress three weeks ago.* **2** ADJ If someone is **decisive**, they have or show an ability to make quick decisions in a difficult or complicated situation. ❑ *He should give way to a younger, more decisive leader.* ● **decisively** ADV ❑ *"I'll call for you at ten," she said decisively.* ● **decisiveness** N-UNCOUNT ❑ *His supporters admire his decisiveness.*

deck ♦♦◇ /dɛk/ (decks) **1** N-COUNT A **deck** on a vehicle such as a bus or ship is a lower or upper area of it. ❑ *...a luxury liner with five passenger decks.* **2** N-COUNT The **deck** of a ship is the top part of it that forms a floor in the open air which you can walk on. [also on N] ❑ *She stood on the deck and waved her hand to them as the steamer moved off.* **3** N-COUNT A tape **deck** or record **deck** is a piece of equipment on which you play tapes or records. ❑ *I stuck a tape in the deck.* **4** N-COUNT A **deck** of cards is a complete set of playing cards. [AM; BRIT usually **pack**] ❑ *Matt picked up the cards and shuffled the deck.* **5** N-COUNT A **deck** is a flat wooden area next to a house, where people can sit and relax or eat. ❑ *A natural timber deck leads into the main room of the home.*

declaration ♦♦◇ /dɛkləreɪʃⁿn/ (declarations) **1** N-COUNT A **declaration** is an official announcement or statement. ❑ *The opening speeches sounded more like declarations of war than offerings of peace.* **2** N-COUNT A **declaration** is a firm, emphatic statement which shows that you have no doubts about what you are saying. ❑ *...declarations of undying love.* **3** N-COUNT A **declaration** is a written statement about something which you have signed and which can be used as evidence in a court of law. ❑ *On the customs declaration, the sender labeled the freight as agricultural machinery.*

Word Link	clar ≈ clear : clarify, clarity, declare

declare ♦♦◇ /dɪklɛər/ (declares, declaring, declared) **1** V-T If you **declare** that something is true, you say that it is true in a firm, deliberate way. You can also **declare** an attitude or intention. [WRITTEN] ❑ *Speaking outside Ten Downing Street, Mrs. Thatcher declared that she would fight on.* ❑ *He declared his intention to become the best golfer in the world.* **2** V-T If you **declare** something, you state officially and formally that it exists or is the case. ❑ *The government is ready to declare a permanent ceasefire.* ❑ *His lawyers are confident that the judges will declare Mr. Stevens innocent.* **3** V-T If you **declare** goods that you have bought in another country or money that you have earned, you say how much you have bought or earned so that you can pay tax on it. ❑ *Declaring the wrong income by mistake will no longer lead to an automatic fine.* →see **war**

Word Link	clin ≈ leaning : decline, incline, recline

decline ♦♦◇ /dɪklaɪn/ (declines, declining, declined) **1** V-I If something **declines**, it becomes less in quantity, importance, or strength. ❑ *The number of staff has declined from 217,000 to 114,000.* ❑ *Hourly output by workers declined 1.3% in the first quarter.* **2** V-T/V-I If you **decline** something or **decline to** do something, you politely refuse to accept it or of do it. [FORMAL] ❑ *He declined their invitation.* ❑ *He offered the boys some coffee. They declined politely.* **3** N-VAR If there is a **decline** in something, it becomes less in quantity, importance, or quality. ❑ *Official figures show a sharp decline in the number of foreign tourists.* **4** PHRASE If something is **in decline** or **on the decline**, it is gradually decreasing in importance, quality, or power. ❑ *Thankfully the smoking of cigarettes is on the decline.* **5** PHRASE If something **goes** or **falls into decline**, it begins to gradually decrease in

---

같은 간단한 수학 개념들

가산명사 소수점 ❑ 웨이터가 13.09유로짜리 계산서에서 소수점을 빠뜨렸다.

1 타동사 대량 학살하다, 대량 살육하다 ❑ 그 강에 왕성히 번식하고 있는 물총새가 공해로 인해 떼죽음을 당할 수 있다. **2** 타동사 크게 위축시키다 ❑ 그 국가의 제조업을 크게 위축시킨 불경기

타동사 해독하다, 판독하다 ❑ 그 암호를 해독하려면 아직도 한참 멀었다.

1 가산명사 결정 ❑ 내가 결정을 잘못해서 나중에 후회하고 싶지 않다. **2** 불가산명사 결정 ❑ 위기의 압박감이 증가하는 것은 결정의 순간을 너무 오래 미룰 수 없다는 것을 뜻할 수 있다. **3** 불가산명사 결단력 ❑ 그는 생각하는 것이 굉장히 빠르고, 뛰어난 결단력을 가진 사람이다.

1 형용사 결정적인; 압도적인 ❑ 대선에서 그가 거둔 압도적인 승리 ● 결정적으로; 압도적으로 부사 ❑ 그 계획은 삼 주 전에 의회에서 압도적으로 거부됐다. **2** 형용사 단호한 있는 ❑ 그는 보다 젊고 결단력 있는 리더에게 양보해야 한다. ● 단호함 있게 부사 ❑ "내가 10시에 전화할게,"라고 그녀는 단호하게 말했다. ● 과단성 불가산명사 ❑ 그의 지지자들은 그의 과단성을 좋아한다.

1 가산명사 (버스나 배의) 층 ❑ 5층으로 된 호화 여객선 **2** 가산명사 갑판 ❑ 증기선이 움직이기 시작하자 그녀는 갑판에 서서 그들에게 손을 흔들어 보였다. **3** 가산명사 (카세트 테이프나 레코드) 플레이어 ❑ 나는 테이프를 플레이어에 넣었다. **4** 가산명사 (카드) 한 벌 [미국영어; 영국영어 대개 pack] ❑ 매트가 낱장들을 집어넣어 카드를 모두 함께 섞었다. **5** 가산명사 (나무된) 마루 ❑ 자연목으로 만들어진 마루는 집의 안방과 연결되어 있다.

1 가산명사 포고, 공표 ❑ 개회사는 평화를 제안한다기보다는 선전 포고문 같이 들렸다. **2** 가산명사 선언 ❑ 영원한 사랑의 서약 **3** 가산명사 신고식, 진술서 ❑ 발송인은 세관 신고서에 그 화물을 농기계라고 적었다.

1 타동사 표명하다 [문어체] ❑ 총리 관저 밖 연설에서, 대처 수상은 계속 싸워 나가겠다는 의지를 표명했다. ❑ 그는 세계 최고의 골프 선수가 되겠다는 결의를 표명했다. **2** 타동사 선언하다, 선고하다 ❑ 정부는 종전을 선언할 준비가 되어 있다. ❑ 스티븐스 씨의 변호사들은 판사가 그에게 무죄를 선고할 것이라고 자신한다. **3** 타동사 (과세 대상을) 신고하다 ❑ 실수로 잘못 소득 신고를 했다고 벌금이 자동적으로 붙는 일은 더 이상 없을 것이다.

1 자동사 줄다, 쇠퇴하다 ❑ 직원 수가 21만 7천 명에서 11만 4천 명으로 줄었다. ❑ 일사분기에 노동자 시간당 생산량이 1.3퍼센트 감소했다. **2** 타동사/자동사 (정중히) 거절하다, (정중히) 사양하다 [격식체] ❑ 그는 그들의 초대를 정중히 거절했다. ❑ 그 남자 아이들에게 커피를 권했으나, 그 애들은 정중히 사양했다. **3** 가산명사 또는 불가산명사 감소, 쇠퇴 ❑ 공식 통계를 보면 외국인 관광객 수가 급격히 감소했다는 것을 알 수 있다. **4** 구 감소하고 있는, 쇠퇴하고 있는 ❑ 고맙게도 담배 소비량이 감소하고 있다. **5** 구 쇠퇴 일로로, 감소하게 된 ❑ 도서관은

importance, quality, or power. ❑ *Libraries are an investment for the future and they should not be allowed to fall into decline.*

미래에 대한 투자이프로, 쇠퇴 일로로 접어들게 놔두어서는 안 된다.

Word Partnership   *decline*의 연어

ADJ.   **economic** decline, **gradual** decline, **rapid** decline, **steady** decline ❸

Word Link   *cod ≈ writing : code, decode, encode*

de|code /dikoud/ (decodes, decoding, decoded) ❶ V-T If you **decode** a message that has been written or spoken in a code, you change it into ordinary language. ❑ *All he had to do was decode it and pass it over.* ❷ V-T A device that **decodes** a broadcast signal changes it into a form that can be displayed on a television screen. ❑ *About 60,000 subscribers have special adapters to receive and decode the signals.*

❶ 타동사 해독하다 ❑ 그가 해야 할 일은 그것을 해독하고 넘기는 것뿐이었다. ❷ 타동사 변환하다 ❑ 6만 여 시청자들이 신호를 수신해서 변환하는 특별 장치를 두고 있다.

de|com|pose /dikəmpouz/ (decomposes, decomposing, decomposed) V-T/V-I When things such as dead plants or animals **decompose**, or when something **decomposes** them, they change chemically and begin to decay. ❑ *...a dead body found decomposing in a wood.* ❑ *The debris slowly decomposes into compost.*

타동사/자동사 썩어 없어지다, 분해되다; 분해시키다 ❑ 숲 속에서 썩어가고 있다가 발견된 사체 ❑ 찌꺼기들은 서서히 분해되어 퇴비가 된다.

de|cor /deɪkɔr, BRIT deɪkɔːʳ/ N-UNCOUNT The **decor** of a house or room is its style of furnishing and decoration. ❑ *The decor is simple – black lacquer panels on white walls.*

불가산명사 장식 ❑ 장식은 하얀 벽 위에 검게 옻칠한 패널로 붙인 것으로 간단했다.

deco|rate ♦◇◇ /dɛkəreɪt/ (decorates, decorating, decorated) ❶ V-T If you **decorate** something, you make it more attractive by adding things to it. ❑ *He decorated his room with pictures of all his favorite sports figures.* ❷ V-T/V-I If you **decorate** a room or the inside of a building, you put new paint or wallpaper on the walls and ceiling, and paint the woodwork. ❑ *When they came to decorate the rear bedroom, it was Jemma who had the final say.* ❑ *The boys are planning to decorate when they get the time.* ● deco|rat|ing N-UNCOUNT ❑ *I did a lot of the decorating myself.* ● deco|ra|tion N-UNCOUNT ❑ *From start to finish, the renovation process and decoration took four months.*

❶ 타동사 꾸미다 ❑ 그는 자기 방을, 좋아하는 스포츠 스타 사진으로 꾸몄다. ❷ 타동사/자동사 실내 장식을 하다 ❑ 그 사람들이 뒷방에 인테리어 작업을 하러 왔을 때, 최종 지시를 한 사람은 젬마였다. ❑ 소년들은 시간이 나면 실내 장식을 할 계획이다. ● 꾸미기 불가산명사 ❑ 많은 부분을 내가 직접 꾸몄다. ● 실내 장식 불가산명사 ❑ 개축과 실내 장식은 시작부터 끝까지 넉 달 걸렸다.

deco|ra|tion /dɛkəreɪʃⁿ/ (decorations) ❶ N-UNCOUNT The **decoration** of a room is its furniture, wallpaper, and ornaments. ❑ *The decoration and furnishings had to be practical enough for a family home.* ❷ N-VAR **Decorations** are features that are added to something in order to make it look more attractive. ❑ *The only wall decorations are candles and a single mirror.* ❸ N-COUNT **Decorations** are brightly colored objects such as pieces of paper and balloons, which you put up in a room on special occasions to make it look more attractive. ❑ *Colorful streamers and festive paper decorations had been hung from the ceiling.* ❹ →see also **decorate**

❶ 불가산명사 인테리어 ❑ 인테리어와 가구는 가족이 사는 집에 맞게 실용적이어야 한다. ❷ 가산명사 또는 불가산명사 장식 ❑ 촛불 몇 개와 거울 하나가 유일한 벽장식이다. ❸ 가산명사 장식물 ❑ 화려한 색의 리본과 축제 분위기가 나는 종이 장식들이 천장에 달려 늘어져 있었다.

deco|ra|tive /dɛkərətɪv, -əreɪtɪv/ ADJ Something that is **decorative** is intended to look pretty or attractive. ❑ *The curtains are for purely decorative purposes and do not open or close.*

형용사 장식용의 ❑ 그 커튼은 순전히 장식용이어서 여닫을 수가 없다.

deco|ra|tor /dɛkəreɪtər/ (decorators) ❶ N-COUNT A **decorator** is a person who is employed to design and decorate the inside of people's houses. [AM; BRIT **interior decorator**] ❑ *...Bloomberg's private palace, with its intricate interior design by decorator Jamie Drake.* ❷ N-COUNT A **decorator** is a person whose job is to paint houses or put wallpaper up. [BRIT] ❑ *He became a painter and decorator.*

❶ 가산명사 실내 장식가, 인테리어업자 [미국영어; 영국영어 interior decorator] ❑ 실내 장식가 제이미 드레이크가 다양한 정교한 실내 장식이 되어 있는 블룸버그의 개인 궁전 ❷ 가산명사 도배공 [영국영어] ❑ 그는 도색공 겸 실내 장식가가 되었다.

de|coy /dikɔɪ/ (decoys) N-COUNT If you refer to something or someone as a **decoy**, you mean that they are intended to attract people's attention and deceive them, for example by leading them into a trap or away from a particular place. ❑ *A plane was waiting at the airport with its engines running but this was just one of the decoys.*

가산명사 유인 책 ❑ 엔진 시동을 걸어 놓은 비행기가 공항에 대기 중이었으나, 이건 유인책 중 하나에 불과했다.

Word Link   *cresc, creas ≈ growing : crescent, decrease, increase*

de|crease (decreases, decreasing, decreased)

The verb is pronounced /dɪkris/. The noun is pronounced /dikris/.

동사는 /dɪkris/로 발음되고, 명사는 /dikris/로 발음된다.

❶ V-T/V-I When something **decreases** or when you **decrease** it, it becomes less in quantity, size, or intensity. ❑ *Population growth is decreasing by 1.4% each year.* ❑ *The number of independent firms decreased from 198 to 96.* ❑ *Since 1945 air forces have decreased in size.* ❷ N-COUNT A **decrease in** the quantity, size, or intensity of something is a reduction in it. ❑ *In Spain and Portugal there has been a decrease in the number of young people out of work.*

❶ 타동사/자동사 줄다, 감소하다; 줄이다 ❑ 인구 증가율은 매년 1.4퍼센트씩 감소하는다. ❑ 개인 기업의 수가 198개에서 96개로 감소했다. ❑ 1945년부터 공군의 규모는 축소되었다. ❷ 가산명사 감소, 축소 ❑ 스페인과 포르투갈에서는 청년 실업자 수가 감소했다.

Thesaurus   *decrease*의 참조어

v.   decline, diminish, go down; (ant.) increase ❶

---

de|cree /dɪkri/ (decrees, decreeing, decreed) ❶ N-COUNT A **decree** is an official order or decision, especially one made by the ruler of a country. [also by N] ❑ *In July he issued a decree ordering all unofficial armed groups in the country to disband.* ❷ V-T If someone in authority **decrees** that something must happen, they decide or state this officially. ❑ *The government decreed that all who wanted to live and work in Kenya must hold Kenyan passports.* ❸ N-COUNT A **decree** is a judgment made by a law court. [mainly AM] ❑ *...court decrees.*

❶ 가산명사 포고령 ❑ 7월에 그는 나라 안 모든 비공식 무장 세력의 무장 해제를 명하는 포고령을 내렸다. ❷ 타동사 포고령을 내리다 ❑ 정부는 케냐에서 살고 일하기 원하는 자는 모두 케냐 여권을 소지하고 있어야 한다는 포고령을 내렸다. ❸ 가산명사 판결 [주로 미국영어] ❑ 법정 판결

dedi|cate /dɛdɪkeɪt/ (dedicates, dedicating, dedicated) ❶ V-T If you say that someone **has dedicated** themselves **to** something, you approve of the fact that they have decided to give a lot of time and effort to it because they think that it is important. [APPROVAL] ❑ *For the next few years, she dedicated herself to her work.* ● dedi|cat|ed ADJ ❑ *He's quite dedicated to his students.* ● dedi|ca|tion

❶ 타동사 헌신하다; 전념하다 [마음에 듦] ❑ 그 이후 몇 년 동안, 그녀는 자기 일에 전념했다. ● 헌신 적인 형용사 ❑ 그 선생님은 학생들에게 참 헌신적이다. ● 헌신 불가산명사 ❑ 우리는 인류애와 정의와 평화를 위해 일해 온 그 분의 용기와 열정과 헌신에 경의를

N-UNCOUNT ❏ *We admire her courage, compassion, and dedication to the cause of humanity, justice, and peace.* ❷ V-T If someone **dedicates** something such as a book, play, or piece of music **to** you, they mention your name, for example in the front of a book or when a piece of music is performed, as a way of showing affection or respect for you. ❏ *She dedicated her first album to Woody Allen, who she says understands her obsession.*

표한다. ❷ 타동사 헌정하다 ❏ 그녀의 첫 음반을 자신의 집념을 이해해 줬다는 우디 앨런에게 헌정했다.

ded|i|cat|ed /dɛdɪkeɪtɪd/ ❶ ADJ You use **dedicated** to describe someone who enjoys a particular activity very much and spends a lot of time doing it. ❏ *Her great-grandfather had clearly been a dedicated and stoical traveller.* ❷ ADJ You use **dedicated** to describe something that is made, built, or designed for one particular purpose or thing. ❏ *Such areas should also be served by dedicated cycle routes.* ❏ *...the world's first museum dedicated to ecology.* ❸ →see also **dedicate**

❶ 형용사 전념하는 ❏ 그녀의 증조부는 분명히 여행에만 묵묵히 전념한 여행가였다. ❷ 형용사 전용의, 전문의 ❏ 그런 곳은 자전거 전용 도로로 이용되어야 한다. ❏ 세계 최초의 생태학 전문 박물관

de|duce /dɪdus, BRIT dɪdyuːs/ (**deduces, deducing, deduced**) V-T If you **deduce** something or **deduce** that something is true, you reach that conclusion because of other things that you know to be true. ❏ *Alison had got to work and cleverly deduced that I was the author of the letter.* ❏ *The date of the document can be deduced from references to the Civil War.*

타동사 추론하다 ❏ 앨리슨은 조사에 착수하기 시작했고 영리하게도 그 편지를 내가 썼다는 사실을 추론해 냈다. ❏ 그 문서의 작성 날짜는 남북 전쟁에 관한 다른 참고 문헌을 통해 추론할 수 있다.

de|duct /dɪdʌkt/ (**deducts, deducting, deducted**) V-T When you **deduct** an amount from a total, you subtract it from the total. ❏ *The company deducted this payment from his compensation.*

타동사 빼다, 공제하다 ❏ 회사는 그의 보상금에서 이 지불금을 공제했다.

de|duc|tion /dɪdʌkʃ°n/ (**deductions**) ❶ N-COUNT A **deduction** is a conclusion that you have reached about something because of other things that you know to be true. ❏ *It was a pretty astute deduction.* ❷ N-UNCOUNT **Deduction** is the process of reaching a conclusion about something because of other things that you know to be true. ❏ *Miss Allan beamed at him. "You are clever to guess. I'm sure I don't know how you did it." — "Deduction," James said.* ❸ N-COUNT A **deduction** is an amount that has been subtracted from a total. ❏ *...your gross income (before tax and National Insurance deductions).* →see **science**

❶ 가산명사 추론 ❏ 그것은 상당히 날카로운 추론이었다. ❷ 불가산명사 연역법 ❏ 앨런 양은 제임스에게 미소를 지어 보이며 "정말 머리가 좋으시네요. 어떻게 아셨는지 모르겠어요."라고 말했다. 제임스는 "연역법으로요."라고 대답했다. ❸ 가산명사 공제, 차감 ❏ 귀하의 (세금과 의료 보험료를 공제하기 전의) 총수입

deed /did/ (**deeds**) ❶ N-COUNT A **deed** is something that is done, especially something that is very good or very bad. [LITERARY] ❏ *The perpetrators of this evil deed must be brought to justice.* ❷ N-COUNT A **deed** is a document containing the terms of an agreement, especially an agreement concerning the ownership of land or a building. [LEGAL] ❏ *He asked if I had the deeds to his father's property.*

❶ 가산명사 업적, 행위 [문예체] ❏ 이런 사악한 짓을 한 인간들은 법의 심판을 받아야 한다. ❷ 가산명사 증서, 등기 서류 [법률] ❏ 그는 자기 아버지의 부동산 등기 서류를 내가 갖고 있는지 물었다.

deem /dim/ (**deems, deeming, deemed**) V-T If something **is deemed to** have a particular quality or **to** do a particular thing, it is considered to have that quality or do that thing. [FORMAL] ❏ *French and German were deemed essential.* ❏ *He says he would support the use of force if the UN deemed it necessary.*

타동사 여겨지다 [격식체] ❏ 불어와 독어는 필수로 여겨졌다. ❏ 국제 연합이 필요성을 인정한다면 군사력의 사용도 지지하겠다고 그는 말했다.

deep ◆◇◇ /dip/ (**deeper, deepest**) ❶ ADJ If something is **deep**, it extends a long way down from the ground or from the top surface of something. ❏ *The water is very deep and mysterious-looking.* ❏ *Den had dug a deep hole in the center of the garden.* ● ADV **Deep** is also an adverb. ❏ *Gingerly, she put her hand in deeper, to the bottom.* ● **deeply** ADV ❏ *There isn't time to dig deeply and put in manure or compost.* ❷ ADJ A **deep** container, such as a closet, extends or measures a long distance from front to back. ❏ *The wardrobe was very deep.* ❸ ADJ **Deep** in an area means a long way inside it. ❏ *Picking up his bag the giant strode off deep into the forest.* ❹ ADJ You use **deep** to emphasize the seriousness, strength, importance, or degree of something. [EMPHASIS] ❏ *I had a deep admiration for Sartre.* ❏ *He wants to express his deep sympathy to the family.* ● **deeply** ADV ❏ *He loved his brother deeply.* ❺ ADV If you experience or feel something **deep inside** you or **deep down**, you feel it very strongly even though you do not necessarily show it. ❏ *Deep down, she supported her husband's involvement in the organization.* ❻ ADJ If you are in a **deep** sleep, you are sleeping peacefully and it is difficult to wake you. [ADJ n] ❏ *Una soon fell into a deep sleep.* ● **deeply** ADV [ADV after v] ❏ *She slept deeply but woke early.* ❼ ADJ If you are **deep** in thought or **deep** in conversation, you are concentrating very hard on what you are thinking or saying and are not aware of the things that are happening around you. [v-link ADJ in n] ❏ *Before long, we were deep in conversation.* ❽ ADJ A **deep** breath or sigh uses or fills the whole of your lungs. [ADJ n] ❏ *Cal took a long, deep breath, struggling to control his own emotions.* ● **deeply** ADV [ADV after v] ❏ *She sighed deeply and covered her face with her hands.* ❾ COMB in COLOR You use **deep** to describe colors that are strong and fairly dark. ❏ *The sky was peach-colored in the east, deep blue and starry in the west.* ● ADJ **Deep** is also an adjective. ❏ *These Amish cushions in traditional deep colors are available in two sizes.* ❿ ADJ A **deep** sound is low in pitch. ❏ *His voice was deep and mellow.* ⓫ ADJ If you describe something such as a problem or a piece of writing as **deep**, you mean that it is important, serious, or complicated. ❏ *They're written as adventure stories. They're not intended to be deep.* ⓬ ADV If you are **deep in** debt, you have a lot of debts. [ADV in/into n] ❏ *He is so deep in debt and desperate for money that he's apparently willing to say anything.* ● **deeply** ADV [ADV in/into n] ❏ *Because of her medical and her legal bills, she is now penniless and deeply in debt.* ⓭ PHRASE If you say that something **goes deep** or **runs deep**, you mean that it is very serious or strong and is hard to change. ❏ *His anger and anguish clearly went deep.* ⓮ **in at the deep end** →see **end. in deep water** →see **water**

❶ 형용사 깊은 ❏ 물이 아주 깊고, 신비로워 보인다. ❏ 덴은 정원 한가운데에 구멍을 깊게 파두었다. ● 부사 깊게 ❏ 그녀는 아주 조심스럽게 손을 더 깊이, 바닥까지 넣었다. ● 깊이 부사 ❏ 깊게 파서 비료나 퇴비를 넣을 시간이 없다. ❷ 형용사 깊은 ❏ 옷장은 속이 깊숙했다. ❸ 부사 깊은 ❏ 거인은 자기 가방을 집어 들고는 깊은 숲 속으로 성큼성큼 가 버렸다. ❹ 형용사 깊은 [강조] ❏ 나는 사르트르를 깊이 존경했다. ❏ 그는 그의 가족에게 깊은 연민을 표하고 싶어 한다. ● 깊이 부사 ❏ 그는 자기 형을 깊이 사랑했다. ❺ 부사 가슴 깊이 ❏ 그녀는 자기 남편이 그 조직에서 활동하는 것을 가슴 깊이 지지했다. ❻ 형용사 (잠이) 깊은 ❏ 유나는 곧 깊이 잠들었다. ● 깊이 부사 ❏ 그녀는 숙면에 빠졌지만 일찍 일어났다. ❼ 형용사 -에 깊이 잠긴, -에 푹 빠진 ❏ 얼마 지나지 않아 우리는 대화에 푹 빠져 있었다. ❽ 형용사 (숨이나 한숨이) 깊은 ❏ 칼은 감정을 자제하려고 애쓰며 숨을 길고 깊게 들이쉬었다. ● 깊이 부사 ❏ 그녀는 한숨을 깊이 내쉬고는 두 손으로 얼굴을 감쌌다. ❾ 복합형·색채어 짙은 ❏ 동쪽 하늘은 복숭앗빛으로 물들었고, 서쪽 하늘은 진한 청색에 별이 빛나고 있었다. ● 형용사 짙은 ❏ 이 전통적인 짙은 색상의 아미시 쿠션은 두 가지 사이즈가 있습니다. ❿ 형용사 (소리가) 낮은 ❏ 그의 목소리는 낮고 부드러웠다. ⓫ 형용사 깊이가 있는, 심각한 ❏ 그것들은 모험 소설로 쓰인 것이지, 깊이가 있는 것은 아니다. ⓬ 부사 (빚이) 많은 ❏ 그는 많은 빚을 지고 있고 돈에 대해 필사적이어서 무슨 말이라도 할 것처럼 보인다. ● (빚을) 많이 진 부사 ❏ 의료비와 법정 비용 때문에 그녀는 지금 빈털터리에다 많은 빚을 지고 있다. ⓭ 구 깊어가다 ❏ 그의 분노와 고뇌가 확실히 깊어 갔다.

deep|en /dipən/ (**deepens, deepening, deepened**) ❶ V-T/V-I If a situation or emotion **deepens** or if something **deepens** it, it becomes stronger and more intense. ❏ *If this is not stopped, the financial crisis will deepen.* ❷ V-T If you **deepen** your knowledge or understanding of a subject, you learn more about it and become more interested in it. ❏ *The course is an exciting opportunity for anyone wishing to deepen their understanding of themselves and other people.* ❸ V-T/V-I When a sound **deepens** or **is deepened**, it becomes lower in tone. ❏ *The music room had been made to reflect and deepen sounds.* ❹ V-T If people **deepen** something, they increase its depth by digging out its lower surface. ❏ *A major project has now begun to deepen the main approach channel to a depth of between 12.5m and 13.0m.*

❶ 타동사/자동사 깊어지다; 깊어지게 하다 ❏ 이것을 멈출 수 없다면, 재정 위기는 심화될 것이다. ❷ 타동사 (지식이나 이해를) 넓히다 ❏ 이 강좌는 자기 자신과 타인에 대한 이해를 넓히고자 하는 사람 누구에게나 흥미로운 기회가 될 것이다. ❸ 타동사/자동사 (소리가) 깊어지다 ❏ 그 음악실은 소리를 반향시켜 깊은 소리를 만들어 내도록 만들어져 있었다. ❹ 타동사 깊게 파다 ❏ 주 접근 운하의 깊이를 12.5미터 내지 13.0미터로 만들려는 주요 프로젝트가 이제 시작되었다.

deep-seated ADJ A **deep-seated** problem, feeling, or belief is difficult to change because its causes have been there for a long time. ❏ *The country is still suffering from deep-seated economic problems.*

형용사 고질적인, 깊이 자리 잡은 ❏ 그 나라는 여전히 고질적인 경제 문제로 골머리를 썩이고 있다.

a b c d e f g h i j k l m n o p q r s t u v w x y z

deer /dɪər/

Deer is both the singular and the plural form.

N-COUNT A **deer** is a large wild animal that eats grass and leaves. A male deer usually has large, branching horns.

deer는 단수형 및 복수형이다.

가산명사 사슴

de|face /dɪfeɪs/ (**defaces, defacing, defaced**) V-T If someone **defaces** something such as a wall or a notice, they spoil it by writing or drawing things on it. ❑ *It's illegal to deface banknotes.*

타동사 낙서하다 ❑ 지폐에 낙서하는 것은 위법이다.

de|fault /dɪfɔlt/ (**defaults, defaulting, defaulted**)

Pronounced /dɪfɔlt/ for meaning ②.

② 의 의미일 때는 /dɪfɔlt/로 발음된다.

① V-I If a person, company, or country **defaults on** something that they have legally agreed to do, such as paying some money or doing a piece of work before a particular time, they fail to do it. [LEGAL] ❑ *The credit card business is down, and more borrowers are defaulting on loans.* ● N-UNCOUNT **Default** is also a noun. ❑ *The corporation may be charged with default on its contract with the government.* ② ADJ A **default** situation is what exists or happens unless someone or something changes it. [ADJ n] ❑ *The default setting on Windows Explorer will not show these files.* ③ N-UNCOUNT In computing, the **default** is a particular set of instructions which the computer always uses unless the person using the computer gives other instructions. [COMPUTING] ❑ *...default settings.* ④ PHRASE If something happens **by default**, it happens only because something else which might have prevented it or changed it has not happened. [FORMAL] ❑ *I would rather pay the individuals than let the money go to the State by default.*

① 자동사 불이행하다 [법률] ❑ 신용 카드 업계는 침체되어 있고, 많은 채무자들이 채무를 불이행하고 있다. ● 불가산명사 불이행 ❑ 그 회사는 정부와의 계약 불이행으로 고발당할지도 모른다. ② 형용사 기본 설정의 ❑ 윈도우 익스플로러에서는 이 파일들이 보이지 않게 초기 설정되어 있다. ③ 불가산명사 디폴트 값 [컴퓨터] ❑ 초기 설정 ④ 구 방치하여 [격식체] ❑ 나는 그 돈이 정부로 넘어가게 놔두기보다는 차라리 개인에게 지불하겠다.

de|feat ♦♦◇ /dɪfit/ (**defeats, defeating, defeated**) ① V-T If you **defeat** someone, you win a victory over them in a battle, game, or contest. ❑ *His guerrillas defeated the colonial army in 1954.* ② V-T If a proposal or motion in a debate **is defeated**, more people vote against it than for it. [usu passive] ❑ *In 1972 a proposal to knock down the 18th-century cloth market was defeated by just one vote.* ③ V-T If a task or a problem **defeats** you, it is so difficult that you cannot do it or solve it. ❑ *The book he most wanted to write was the one which nearly defeated him.* ④ V-T To **defeat** an action or plan means to cause it to fail. ❑ *The navy played a limited but significant role in defeating the rebellion.* ⑤ N-VAR **Defeat** is the experience of being beaten in a battle, game, or contest, or of failing to achieve what you wanted to. ❑ *The most important thing is not to admit defeat until you really have to.* ❑ *A 2-1 defeat by Sweden left them bottom of Group A.*

① 타동사 이기다, 물리치다 ❑ 그의 게릴라 부대는 1954년에 식민군대를 물리쳤다. ② 타동사 (투표에서) 기각되다, 거부되다 ❑ 18세기에 세워진 직물 시장을 헐어 버리자는 1972년에 있었던 제안은 한 표 차로 거부됐다. ③ 타동사 좌절시키다 ❑ 그가 가장 쓰고 싶었던 책은 쓰기가 어려워서 그를 거의 포기하게 만든 책이었다. ④ 타동사 제압하다, 저지하다 ❑ 반군을 제압하는 데 해군은 작지만 중요한 역할을 했다. ⑤ 가산명사 또는 불가산명사 패배, 실패 ❑ 가장 중요한 것은 마지막 순간까지 실패를 인정하지 않는 것이다. ❑ 스웨덴에 2대 1로 패함으로써 그 팀은 에이 조의 꼴찌가 되었다.

de|fect (**defects, defecting, defected**)

The noun is pronounced /difɛkt/. The verb is pronounced /dɪfɛkt/.

명사는 /difɛkt/로 발음되고, 동사는 /dɪfɛkt/로 발음된다.

① N-COUNT A **defect** is a fault or imperfection in a person or thing. ❑ *He was born with a hearing defect.* ❑ *A report has pointed out the defects of the present system.* ② V-I If you **defect**, you leave your country, political party, or other group, and join an opposing country, party, or group. ❑ *...a KGB officer who defected in 1963.* ● **de|fec|tion** /dɪfɛkʃn/ (**defections**) N-VAR ❑ *...the defection of at least sixteen Parliamentary deputies.*

① 가산명사 결함 ❑ 그는 청각 장애자로 태어났다. ❑ 한 보고서가 현 체제의 결함을 지적했다. ② 자동사 변절하다, 망명하다 ❑ 1963년에 망명한 케이지비 관리 ● 변절 가산명사 또는 불가산명사 ❑ 국회의원 최소 16명의 당적 이탈

de|fec|tive /dɪfɛktɪv/ ADJ If something is **defective**, there is something wrong with it and it does not work properly. ❑ *Retailers can return defective merchandise.*

형용사 결함이 있는 ❑ 소매상은 하자가 있는 상품을 반품할 수 있다.

de|fence /dɪfɛns/ →see **defense**

Word Link	fend ≈ striking : defend, fender, offend

de|fend ♦♦◇ /dɪfɛnd/ (**defends, defending, defended**) ① V-T If you **defend** someone or something, you take action in order to protect them. ❑ *His courage in defending religious and civil rights inspired many outside the church.* ② V-T If you **defend** someone or something when they have been criticized, you argue in support of them. ❑ *Clarence's move was unpopular, but Matt had to defend it, like he defended all of Clarence's decisions, right or wrong.* ③ V-T When a lawyer **defends** a person who has been accused of something, the lawyer argues on their behalf in a court of law that the charges are not true. ❑ *...a lawyer who defended political prisoners during the military regime.* ❑ *He has hired a lawyer to defend him against the allegation.* ④ V-T When a sports player plays in the tournament which they won the previous time it was held, you can say that they **are defending** their title. [JOURNALISM] ❑ *Torrence expects to defend her title successfully in the next Olympics.* →see **hero**

① 타동사 지키다, 방어하다 ❑ 종교적 권리와 시민권을 지켜 내기 위한 그의 용기는 많은 교회 외부 사람들을 고무시켰다. ② 타동사 옹호하다 ❑ 클라렌스의 행동은 인기가 없었지만, 매트는 옳든 그르든 간에 클라렌스의 모든 결정을 옹호했던 대로 그 행동을 옹호해야만 했다. ③ 타동사 변호하다 ❑ 군사 정권에서 정치범들을 변호한 변호사 ❑ 그는 그 주장에 맞서 자기를 변호하도록 변호사를 고용했다. ④ 타동사 (타이틀을) 방어하다 [언론] ❑ 토렌스는 다음 올림픽에서 자신의 타이틀을 훌륭하게 방어해 낼 수 있으리라고 예상한다.

Thesaurus	defend의 참조어

v.	protect; (ant.) attack ①
	back, support; (ant.) criticize ②

Word Link	ant ≈ one who does, has : defendant, deodorant, occupant

de|fend|ant /dɪfɛndənt/ (**defendants**) N-COUNT A **defendant** is a person who has been accused of breaking the law and is being tried in court. ❑ *The defendant pleaded guilty and was fined £500 and £200 costs.* →see **trial**

가산명사 피고 ❑ 피고는 유죄를 시인했고 500파운드의 벌금과 200파운드의 법정 소송 비용을 부과받았다.

de|fend|er /dɪfɛndər/ (**defenders**) ① N-COUNT If someone is a **defender of** a particular thing or person that has been criticized, they argue or act in support of that thing or person. ❑ *...the most ardent defenders of conventional family values.* ② N-COUNT A **defender** in a game such as soccer or hockey is a player whose main task is to try and stop the other side from scoring. ❑ *...Kit Symons, the Fulham defender.*

① 가산명사 옹호자 ❑ 전통적 가족의 가치에 대한 열렬한 옹호자 ② 가산명사 수비수 ❑ 풀햄의 수비수, 킷 사이먼스.

a

de|fense ♦♦◇ /dɪfɛns/ (defenses)

Defense in meaning 7 is pronounced /diːfɛns/. The spelling **defence** is used in British English.

1 N-UNCOUNT **Defense** is action that is taken to protect someone or something against attack. ❏ *The land was flat, giving no scope for defense.* 2 N-UNCOUNT **Defense** is the organization of a country's armies and weapons, and their use to protect the country or its interests. ❏ *Twenty-eight percent of the federal budget is spent on defense.* ❏ *...the French defense minister.* 3 N-PLURAL The **defenses** of a country or region are all its armed forces and weapons. ❏ *He emphasised the need to maintain Britain's defenses at a level sufficient to deal with the unexpected.* 4 N-COUNT A **defense** is something that people or animals can use or do to protect themselves. ❏ *Despite anything the science of medicine may have achieved, the immune system is our main defense against disease.* 5 N-COUNT A **defense** is something that you say or write which supports ideas or actions that have been criticized or questioned. [oft N of n, also in N] ❏ *Chomsky's defense of his approach goes further.* 6 N-SING The **defense** is the case that is presented by a lawyer in a trial for the person who has been accused of a crime. You can also refer to this person's lawyers as **the defense**. ❏ *The defense was that the records of the interviews were fabricated by the police.* 7 N-SING-COLL In games such as football or hockey, the **defense** is the group of players in a team who try to stop the opposing players scoring a goal or a point. [oft poss N, also in N] ❏ *Their defense, so strong last season, has now conceded 12 goals in six games.* 8 PHRASE If you come **to** someone's **defense**, you help them by doing or saying something to protect them. ❏ *He realized none of his schoolmates would come to his defense.*

de|fense|less /dɪfɛnslɪs/ [BRIT **defenceless**] ADJ If someone or something is **defenseless**, they are weak and unable to defend themselves properly. ❏ *...a savage attack on a defenseless young girl.*

de|fen|sive /dɪfɛnsɪv/ 1 ADJ You use **defensive** to describe things that are intended to protect someone or something. ❏ *The Government hastily organized defensive measures, deploying searchlights and anti-aircraft guns around the target cities.* 2 ADJ Someone who is **defensive** is behaving in a way that shows they feel unsure or threatened. ❏ *Like their children, parents are often defensive about their private lives.* ● **de|fen|sive|ly** ADV ❏ *"Oh, I know, I know," said Kate, defensively.* 3 PHRASE If someone is **on the defensive**, they are trying to protect themselves or their interests because they feel unsure or threatened. ❏ *The Government has been on the defensive over its record on law and order.* 4 ADJ In sports, **defensive** play is play that is intended to prevent your opponent from scoring goals or points against you. ❏ *I'd always played a defensive game, waiting for my opponent to make a mistake.* ● **de|fen|sive|ly** ADV [ADV after v] ❏ *Mexico did it not by playing defensively. They did it with exciting, flowing, attacking football.*

de|fer /dɪfɜr/ (defers, deferring, deferred) 1 V-T If you **defer** an event or action, you arrange for it to happen at a later date, rather than immediately or at the previously planned time. ❏ *Customers often defer payment for as long as possible.* 2 V-I If you **defer to** someone, you accept their opinion or do what they want you to do, even when you do not agree with it yourself, because you respect them or their authority. ❏ *Doctors are encouraged to defer to experts.*

def|er|ence /dɛfərəns/ N-UNCOUNT **Deference** is a polite and respectful attitude toward someone, especially because they have an important position. ❏ *The old sense of deference and restraint in royal reporting has vanished.*

de|fi|ance /dɪfaɪəns/ N-UNCOUNT **Defiance** is behavior or an attitude which shows that you are not willing to obey someone. [oft N of n] ❏ *...his courageous defiance of the government.*

de|fi|ant /dɪfaɪənt/ ADJ If you say that someone is **defiant**, you mean they show aggression or independence by refusing to obey someone. ❏ *The players are in defiant mood as they prepare for tomorrow's game.* ● **de|fi|ant|ly** ADV ❏ *They defiantly rejected any talk of a compromise.*

de|fi|cien|cy /dɪfɪʃnsi/ (deficiencies) 1 N-VAR **Deficiency in** something, especially something that your body needs, is not having enough of it. ❏ *They did blood tests on him for signs of vitamin deficiency.* 2 N-VAR A **deficiency** that someone or something has is a weakness or imperfection in them. [FORMAL] ❏ *The most serious deficiency in Nato's air defense is the lack of an identification system to distinguish friend from foe.*

de|fi|cient /dɪfɪʃnt/ ADJ If someone or something is **deficient in** a particular thing, they do not have the full amount of it that they need in order to function normally or work properly. [FORMAL] ❏ *...a diet deficient in vitamin B.*

def|i|cit ♦♦◇ /dɛfəsɪt/ (deficits) N-COUNT A **deficit** is the amount by which something is less than what is required or expected, especially the amount by which the total money received is less than the total money spent. ❏ *They're ready to cut the federal budget deficit for the next fiscal year.* ❏ *...a deficit of 3.275 billion francs.* ● PHRASE If an account or organization is **in deficit**, more money has been spent than has been received.

de|fine ♦◇◇ /dɪfaɪn/ (defines, defining, defined) V-T If you **define** something, you show, describe, or state clearly what it is and what its limits are, or what it is like. ❏ *I tried to define my own attitude: I found Rosie repulsive, but I didn't hate her.*

defi|nite /dɛfɪnɪt/ 1 ADJ If something such as a decision or an arrangement is **definite**, it is firm and clear, and unlikely to be changed. ❏ *It's too soon to give a definite answer.* ❏ *She made no definite plans for her future.* 2 ADJ **Definite** evidence or information is true, rather than being someone's opinion or guess. ❏ *We didn't have any definite proof.* 3 ADJ You use **definite** to emphasize the strength of your opinion or belief. [EMPHASIS] [ADJ n] ❏ *There has already been a definite*

7 의미의 defense는 /diːfɛns/로 발음된다. 영국영어에서는 철자 defence를 쓴다.

1 불가산명사 방어 ❏ 지형은 평평해서, 방어물이 될 여지가 전혀 없었다. 2 불가산명사 국방 ❏ 연방 예산의 28퍼센트가 국방비로 쓰이고 있다. ❏ 프랑스 국방 장관 3 복수명사 군대 ❏ 그는 영국 군대를 예기치 못한 일에 충분히 대처할 수 있는 수준으로 유지할 필요가 있다는 것을 강조했다. 4 가산명사 방어책 ❏ 의학의 발달이 많은 것을 가져 왔지만, 면역 체계는 아직도 질병에 대한 우리의 주요 방어 체계이다. 5 가산명사 반박 ❏ 자신의 접근법에 대한 촘스키의 논박은 더 나아간다. 6 단수명사 변호; 변호인 ❏ 경찰이 인터뷰 기록을 위조했다는 것이 변호 내용이었다. 7 단수명사 반 ❏ 저번 시즌에 그렇게 강했던 그 팀의 수비가 이번에는 여섯 경기에서 12골을 허용했다. 8 구 _의 편을 들다 ❏ 그 아이는 학교 친구 중 누구도 자기편을 들어주지 않을 거라는 걸 깨달았다.

[영국영어 defenceless] 형용사 무방비 상태의 ❏ 무방비 상태의 어린 소녀에게 가해진 무지막지한 공격

1 형용사 방어용의 ❏ 정부는 서치라이트와 대공포를 피격 예상 도시에 배치하면서 방어 체계를 서둘러 조직하였다. 2 형용사 방어적인 ❏ 부모도 아이들과 마찬가지로 자신들의 사생활에 대해 흔히 방어적이다. ● 방어적으로 부사 ❏ "응, 알아, 알아."라고 케이트가 방어적으로 말했다. 3 구 방어 태세를 취하는 ❏ 정부는 치안 기록에 대해 방어 태세를 취해 왔다. 4 형용사 방어적인 ❏ 나는 상대방이 실수하기를 기다리면서 항상 방어적으로 경기를 했었다. ● 방어적으로 부사 ❏ 멕시코 팀은 방어적으로 경기를 하지 않았다. 그들은 흥미진진하고 물 흐르는 듯하며 공격적인 축구를 했다.

1 타동사 연기하다 ❏ 소비자들은 흔히 지불을 최대한 연기하려고 한다. 2 자동사 _의 말을 따르다 ❏ 의사들은 전문가의 말을 따르기를 권장받고 있다.

불가산명사 경의 ❏ 왕의 근황 보고에 대해 가지고 있던 경의와 절제의 예전 개념이 사라졌다.

불가산명사 (권위에 대한) 반항, 저항 ❏ 그의 정부에 대한 용기 있는 저항

형용사 반항적인 ❏ 내일 경기를 준비하고 있는 선수들의 분위기는 반항적이다. ● 반항적으로 부사 ❏ 그들은 타협을 위한 대화를 반항적으로 거부했다.

1 가산명사 또는 불가산명사 결핍 ❏ 비타민 결핍의 징조가 있는지 보려고 그들은 그의 혈액 검사를 했다. 2 가산명사 또는 불가산명사 취약점 [격식체] ❏ 나토 항공 방어의 가장 심각한 취약점은 아군과 적군을 구별할 수 있는 식별 시스템이 부족하다는 것이다.

형용사 결핍된 [격식체] ❏ 비타민 B가 결핍된 식사

가산명사 결손, 적자 ❏ 그들은 내년 회계 연도에 연방 예산 적자를 줄일 준비가 되어 있다. ❏ 32억 7천 5백만 프랑의 적자 ● 구 적자 상태의

타동사 정의를 내리다, 규정하다 ❏ 나는 로시가 쌀쌀맞다고 느끼기는 했지만 그 애를 미워하지는 않기로 내 태도를 정리하려고 노력했다.

1 형용사 확정된, 명확한 ❏ 확답을 주기에는 너무 일러. ❏ 그녀는 자신의 미래에 대해 명확한 계획이 아무 것도 없었다. 2 형용사 확실한 ❏ 우리는 확실한 증거가 아무것도 없었다. 3 형용사 명백한 [강조] ❏ 이미 명백한 진전이 있었다. 4 형용사 확신에 찬 ❏ 메리는 이 점에 대해 아주 확신에 차 있다.

b
c
d
e
f
g
h
i
j
k
l
m
n
o
p
q
r
s
t
u
v
w
x
y
z

improvement. ◢ ADJ Someone who is **definite** behaves or talks in a firm, confident way. ❏ *Mary is very definite about this.*

Thesaurus *definite*의 참조어

ADJ. clear-cut, distinct, precise, specific; (ant.) ambiguous, vague ◢

---

def·i·nite ar·ti·cle (**definite articles**) N-COUNT The word "the" is sometimes called **the definite article.**

가산명사 정관사

def·i·nite·ly ◆◇◇ /dɛfɪnɪtli/ ◢ ADV You use **definitely** to emphasize that something is the case, or to emphasize the strength of your intention or opinion. [EMPHASIS] ❏ *I'm definitely going to get in touch with these people.* ◢ ADV If something has been **definitely** decided, the decision will not be changed. [ADV before v] ❏ *He told them that no venue had yet been definitely decided.*

◢ 부사 확실히 [강조] ❏ 제가 그 사람들과 확실히 접촉해 보도록 하겠습니다. ◢ 부사 확실히 ❏ 그는 개최 예정지가 아직 확정되지는 않았다고 그들에게 말했다.

def·i·ni·tion ◆◇◇ /dɛfɪnɪʃⁿ/ (**definitions**) ◢ N-COUNT A **definition** is a statement giving the meaning of a word or expression, especially in a dictionary. ❏ *There is no general agreement on a standard definition of intelligence.* ● PHRASE If you say that something has a particular quality **by definition**, you mean that it has this quality simply because of what it is. ◢ N-UNCOUNT **Definition** is the quality of being clear and distinct. ❏ *The first speakers at the conference criticized Prof. Johnson's new program for lack of definition.*

◢ 가산명사 뜻풀이, 정의 ❏ 지능의 표준적인 정의라고 일반적으로 합의된 것은 없다. ● 구 본질적으로 ◢ 불가산명사 명확성, 선명도 ❏ 회의 첫 번째 발언자는 존슨 교수의 새 프로그램이 명확성이 떨어진다고 비판했다.

de·fini·tive /dɪfɪnɪtɪv/ ◢ ADJ Something that is **definitive** provides a firm conclusion that cannot be questioned. ❏ *No one has come up with a definitive answer as to why this should be so.* ● **de·fini·tive·ly** ADV ❏ *The Constitution did not definitively rule out divorce.* ◢ ADJ A **definitive** book or performance is thought to be the best of its kind that has ever been done or that will ever be done. ❏ *His "An Orkney Tapestry" is still the definitive book on the islands.*

◢ 형용사 명확한 ❏ 왜 이게 이렇게 되어야 하는지에 대해 아무도 명확한 답을 내릴 수 없었다. ● 명확하게 부사 ❏ 헌법이 이혼을 명확히 불허하고 있지는 않았다. ◢ 형용사 결정판의, 최고의 ❏ 그가 쓴 책 '오크니 태피스트리'는 여전히 오크니 섬에 대한 최고의 책이다.

Word Link de ≈ from, down, away : de**flate**, de**scend**, de**tach**

---

de·flate /dɪfleɪt/ (**deflates, deflating, deflated**) ◢ V-T If you **deflate** someone or something, you take away their confidence or make them seem less important. ❏ *Britain's other hopes of medals were deflated earlier in the day.* ● **de·flat·ed** ADJ ❏ *When she refused I felt deflated.* ◢ V-T/V-I When something such as a tire or balloon **deflates**, or when you **deflate** it, all the air comes out of it. ❏ *When it returns to shore, the life-jacket will deflate.*

◢ 타동사 좌절감을 주다, 김을 빼다 ❏ 영국이 메달을 더 딸 수 있을 것이라는 기대는 그날 일찍 무너져 버렸다. ● 좌절한, 김이 빠진 형용사 ❏ 그녀가 거절하였을 때 나는 김이 빠졌다. ◢ 타동사/자동사 바람이 빠지다; 바람을 빼다 ❏ 해변으로 돌아오면 구명동의는 바람이 빠질 것이다.

de·fla·tion /dɪfleɪʃⁿ/ N-UNCOUNT **Deflation** is a reduction in economic activity that leads to lower levels of industrial output, employment, investment, trade, profits, and prices. [BUSINESS] ❏ *Deflation is beginning to take hold in the clothing industry.*

불가산명사 통화 수축, 디플레이션 [경제] ❏ 디플레이션이 의류 산업을 사로잡기 시작하고 있다.

de·fla·tion·ary /dɪfleɪʃəneri, BRIT diːfleɪʃnri/ ADJ A **deflationary** economic policy or measure is one that is intended to or likely to cause deflation. [BUSINESS] ❏ *...the government's refusal to implement deflationary measures.*

형용사 통화 긴축의, 디플레이션의 [경제] ❏ 정부의 통화 긴축 정책 실행 거부

de·flect /dɪflɛkt/ (**deflects, deflecting, deflected**) ◢ V-T If you **deflect** something such as criticism or attention, you act in a way that prevents it from being directed toward or affecting you. ❏ *Cage changed his name to deflect accusations of nepotism.* ◢ V-T To **deflect** someone **from** a course of action means to make them decide not to continue with it by putting pressure on them or by offering them something desirable. ❏ *The war did not deflect him from the path he had long ago taken.* ◢ V-T If you **deflect** something that is moving, you make it go in a slightly different direction, for example by hitting or blocking it. ❏ *My forearm deflected most of the first punch.*

◢ 타동사 (비난이나 관심을) 피하다 ❏ 케이지는 친인척을 등용한다는 비난을 피하기 위해 이름을 바꿨다. ◢ 타동사 그만두게 만들다 ❏ 전쟁이 그가 오래 전부터 걸어 왔던 길을 포기하게 하지는 못했다. ◢ 타동사 방향을 바꾸게 하다, 빗나가게 하다 ❏ 내 팔뚝이 첫 주먹의 대부분을 막아 냈다.

de·for·est /dɪfɔrɪst, BRIT diːfɒrɪst/ (**deforests, deforesting, deforested**) V-T If an area **is deforested**, all the trees there are cut down or destroyed. [usu passive] ❏ *...the 400,000 square kilometers of the Amazon basin that have already been deforested.* ● **de·for·es·ta·tion** /dɪfɔrɪsteɪʃⁿ, BRIT diːfɒrɪsteɪʃⁿn/ N-UNCOUNT ❏ *One percent of Brazil's total forest cover is being lost every year to deforestation.* →see **greenhouse effect**

타동사 벌채되다, 숲이 파괴되다 ❏ 이미 40만 평방킬로미터의 숲이 파괴된 아마존 강 유역 ● 벌채, 숲 파괴 불가산명사 ❏ 매년 브라질 전체 숲의 1퍼센트에 해당하는 면적의 숲이 파괴되고 있다.

de·form /dɪfɔrm/ (**deforms, deforming, deformed**) V-T/V-I If something **deforms** a person's body or something else, it causes it to have an unnatural shape. In technical English, you can also say that the second thing **deforms.** ❏ *Bad rheumatoid arthritis deforms limbs.* ● **de·formed** ADJ ❏ *He was born with a deformed right leg.*

타동사/자동사 기형이 되게 하다 ❏ 악성 류머티즘성 관절염은 사지를 보기 흉하게 만든다. ● 기형의 형용사 ❏ 그는 태어날 때부터 오른쪽 다리가 기형이었다.

de·form·ity /dɪfɔrmiti/ (**deformities**) ◢ N-COUNT A **deformity** is a part of someone's body which is not the normal shape because of injury or illness, or because they were born this way. ❏ *...facial deformities in babies.* ◢ N-UNCOUNT **Deformity** is the condition of having a deformity. ❏ *The object of these movements is to prevent stiffness or deformity of joints.*

◢ 가산명사 불구, 기형 ❏ 아기들의 얼굴 기형 ◢ 불가산명사 기형 ❏ 이 운동의 목적은 관절이 뻣뻣해지거나 뒤틀리는 것을 방지하는 것입니다.

de·fraud /dɪfrɔd/ (**defrauds, defrauding, defrauded**) V-T If someone **defrauds** you, they take something away from you or stop you from getting what belongs to you by means of tricks and lies. ❏ *He pleaded guilty to charges of conspiracy to defraud the government.*

타동사 편취하다 ❏ 정부로부터 돈을 사취하려고 공모한 혐의에 대해 그는 유죄를 인정했다.

deft /dɛft/ (**defter, deftest**) ADJ A **deft** action is skillful and often quick. [WRITTEN] ❏ *With a deft flick of his foot, Mr. Worth tripped one of the raiders up.* ● **deft·ly** ADV ❏ *One of the waiting servants deftly caught him as he fell.*

형용사 날렵한 [문어체] ❏ 워스 씨는 날렵한 발차기로 공격자 중 한 명을 넘어뜨렸다. ● 날렵하게 부사 ❏ 시종들 중 하나가 쓰러지는 그를 날렵하게 부축했다.

de·funct /dɪfʌŋkt/ ADJ If something is **defunct**, it no longer exists or has stopped functioning or operating. ❏ *...the leader of the now defunct Social Democratic Party.*

형용사 소멸한 ❏ 지금은 없는 사회 민주당의 총수

de·fuse /dɪfyuz/ (**defuses, defusing, defused**) ◢ V-T If you **defuse** a dangerous or tense situation, you calm it. ❏ *Police administrators credited the organization with helping defuse potentially violent situations.* ◢ V-T If someone **defuses** a bomb, they remove the fuse so that it cannot explode. ❏ *Police have defused a bomb found in a building in London.*

◢ 타동사 완화하다 ❏ 경찰청 관리들은 잠재적인 폭력 사태를 완화시킨 공로를 그 단체에게 돌렸다. ◢ 타동사 신관을 제거하다 ❏ 경찰이 런던의 한 건물에서 발견된 폭탄을 제거했다.

defy /dɪfaɪ/ (**defies, defying, defied**) **1** V-T If you **defy** someone or something that is trying to make you behave in a particular way, you refuse to obey them and behave in that way. ❑ *This was the first (and last) time that I dared to defy my mother.* **2** V-T If you **defy** someone **to** do something, you challenge them to do it when you think that they will be unable to do it or too frightened to do it. ❑ *I defy you to come up with one major accomplishment of the current Prime Minister.* **3** V-T If something **defies** description or understanding, it is so strange, extreme, or surprising that it is almost impossible to understand or explain. [no passive, no cont] ❑ *It's a devastating and barbaric act that defies all comprehension.*

de|gen|er|ate (**degenerates, degenerating, degenerated**)

> The verb is pronounced /dɪdʒenəreɪt/. The adjective is pronounced /dɪdʒenərɪt/.

1 V-I If you say that someone or something **degenerates**, you mean that they become worse in some way, for example weaker, lower in quality, or more dangerous. ❑ *Inactivity can make your joints stiff, and the bones may begin to degenerate.* ● **de|gen|era|tion** /dɪdʒenəreɪʃⁿn/ N-UNCOUNT ❑ *...various forms of physical and mental degeneration.* **2** ADJ If you describe a person or their behavior as **degenerate**, you disapprove of them because you think they have low standards of behavior or morality. [DISAPPROVAL] ❑ *...a group of degenerate computer hackers.*

deg|ra|da|tion /degrədeɪʃⁿn/ (**degradations**) **1** N-VAR You use **degradation** to refer to a situation, condition, or experience which you consider shameful and disgusting, especially one which involves poverty or immorality. [DISAPPROVAL] ❑ *They were sickened by the scenes of misery and degradation they found.* **2** N-UNCOUNT **Degradation** is the process of something becoming worse or weaker, or being made worse or weaker. ❑ *As in the past, to the degradation of democracy, the debate again turned into a screaming match.*

de|grade /dɪgreɪd/ (**degrades, degrading, degraded**) **1** V-T Something that **degrades** someone causes people to have less respect for them. ❑ *...the notion that pornography degrades women.* ● **de|grad|ing** ADJ ❑ *Mr. Porter was subjected to a degrading strip-search.* **2** V-T To **degrade** something means to cause it to get worse. [FORMAL] ❑ *...the ability to meet human needs indefinitely without degrading the environment.*

de|gree ♦♦◇ /dɪgriː/ (**degrees**) **1** N-COUNT You use **degree** to indicate the extent to which something happens or is the case, or the amount which something is felt. ❑ *These man-made barriers will ensure a very high degree of protection for several hundred years.* ❑ *Recent presidents have used television, as well as radio, with varying degrees of success.* ● PHRASE If something has **a degree of** a particular quality, it has a small but significant amount of that quality. **2** N-COUNT A **degree** is a unit of measurement that is used to measure temperatures. It is often written as °, for example 23°. ❑ *It's over 80 degrees outside.* **3** N-COUNT A **degree** is a unit of measurement that is used to measure angles, and also longitude and latitude. It is often written as °, for example 23°. ❑ *It was pointing outward at an angle of 45 degrees.* **4** N-COUNT A **degree** at a university or college is a course of study that you take there, or the qualification that you get when you have completed the course. ❑ *...an engineering degree.* **5** PHRASE You use expressions such as **to some degree**, **to a large degree**, or **to a certain degree** in order to indicate that something is partly true, but not entirely true. [VAGUENESS] ❑ *These statements are, to some degree, all correct.*
→see **graduation**

Word Partnership	*degree*의 연어
N.	degree **of** certainty, degree **of** difficulty **1**
	45/90 degree **angle 3**
	bachelor's/master's degree, **college** degree, degree **program 4**
ADJ.	**high** degree **1**
	honorary degree **4**

de|hy|drate /diːhaɪdreɪt/ (**dehydrates, dehydrating, dehydrated**) **1** V-T When something such as food **is dehydrated**, all the water is removed from it, often in order to preserve it. [usu passive] ❑ *Normally specimens have to be dehydrated.* **2** V-T/V-I If you **dehydrate** or if something **dehydrates** you, you lose too much water from your body so that you feel weak or ill. ❑ *People can dehydrate in weather like this.* ● **de|hy|dra|tion** /diːhaɪdreɪʃⁿn/ N-UNCOUNT ❑ *...a child who's got diarrhea and is suffering from dehydration.*

de|ity /diːɪti, BRIT deɪɪti/ (**deities**) N-COUNT A **deity** is a god or goddess. [FORMAL] ❑ *...a deity revered by thousands of Hindus and Buddhists.*
→see **religion**

de|lay ♦♦◇ /dɪleɪ/ (**delays, delaying, delayed**) **1** V-T/V-I If you **delay** doing something, you do not do it immediately or at the planned or expected time, but you leave it until later. ❑ *For sentimental reasons I wanted to delay my departure until June 1980.* ❑ *They had delayed having children, for the usual reason, to establish their careers.*

> If you **cancel** or **call off** an arrangement or an appointment, you stop it from happening. ❑ *His failing health forced him to cancel the meeting... The European Community has threatened to call off peace talks.* If you **postpone** or **put off** an arrangement or an appointment, you make another arrangement for it to happen at a later time. ❑ *Elections have been postponed until next year... The Senate put off a vote on the nomination for one week.* If you **delay** something that has been arranged, you make it happen later than planned. ❑ *Space agency managers*

1 타동사 반항하다 ❑ 어머니에게 감히 대들어 본 것은 이번이 처음이었다 (또한 마지막이기도 했다). **2** 타동사 감히 ~해 보라고 한다 ❑ 네가 현 수상이 이룬 큰 업적을 하나라도 떠올릴 수 있으면 말해 봐라. **3** 타동사 이해가 안 간다 ❑ 그것은 도저히 이해가 안 가는 파괴적이고도 야만적인 소행이다.

동사는 /dɪdʒenəreɪt /으로 발음되고, 형용사는 /dɪdʒenərɪt /으로 발음된다.

1 자동사 퇴락하다, 퇴화하다 ❑ 움직이지 않으면 관절이 뻣뻣해지고 뼈가 쇠퇴하기 시작할 수 있다. ● 퇴화 불가산명사 ❑ 다양한 형태의 신체적, 정신적 퇴화 **2** 형용사 타락한 [탐탁찮음] ❑ 타락한 컴퓨터 해커의 집단

1 가산명사 또는 불가산명사 타락 [탐탁찮음] ❑ 그들은 그들이 마주하게 된 그 끔찍하고 타락한 모습들에 넌더리를 냈다. **2** 불가산명사 퇴락 ❑ 과거에도 그랬듯, 그 토론회는 다시 민주주의 자체를 손괴할 정도로 고함이 난무하는 곳이 되고 말았다.

1 타동사 비하하다 ❑ 음란물이 여성을 비하한다는 견해 ● 비하하는 형용사 ❑ 포터 씨는 모멸감을 주는 알몸 수색을 당했다. **2** 타동사 타락시키다, 악화시키다 [격식체] ❑ 환경을 손상시키지 않고도 인간의 욕구를 무한정 채워 줄 수 있는 능력

1 가산명사 정도 ❑ 이 인공 방벽들 덕분에 앞으로 수백 년간은 안전을 걱정하지 않아도 될 것이다. ❑ 최근의 대통령들은 라디오만큼이나 텔레비전을 (즐겨) 이용해 왔는데, 얻은 성과는 각기 달랐다. ● 구 어느 정도의 **2** 가산명사 도 ❑ 바깥은 80도가 넘는다. **3** 가산명사 도 ❑ 그것은 45도 각도로 바깥쪽을 향하고 있었다. **4** 가산명사 학위 ❑ 공학 학위 **5** 구 어느 정도; 상당한 정도; 일정한 정도 [짐작투] ❑ 이 발언들이 어느 정도는 모두 참이다.

1 타동사 건조시키다 ❑ 대개 표본들은 건조시켜야만 한다. **2** 타동사/자동사 탈수되다; 탈수시키다 ❑ 이런 날씨에서는 사람들이 탈수증을 일으킬 수가 있다. ● 탈수 불가산명사 ❑ 설사와 탈수 증상을 보이는 아이

가산명사 신 [격식체] ❑ 수천 명의 힌두교도와 불교도들이 공경하는 신

1 타동사/자동사 미루다 ❑ 몇 가지 감정상의 이유로 나는 1980년 6월까지 출발을 미루고 싶었다. ❑ 그들은 직장에서 자리를 잡기 위해서라는 흔한 핑계를 대고 아이 가지는 것을 미룬 상태였다.

합의나 약속을 cancel 또는 call off하면, 그것이 일어나지 않도록 하는 것이다. ❑ 그는 건강이 나빠져서 회의를 취소해야 했다... 유럽 공동체가 평화 협상을 취소하겠다고 협박해 왔다. 어떤 조치나 약속을 연기(postpone 또는 put off)하면, 그것이 더 뒤의 어느 시기에 일어날 수 있도록 새로운 약속을 하는 것이다. ❑ 선거가 내년으로

*decided to delay the launch of the space shuttle. If something **delays** you or **holds** you **up**, you start or finish what you are doing later than you planned.* ❑ *He was delayed in traffic... Delivery of equipment had been held up by delays and disputes.*

연기되었다... 상원은 지명 투표를 일주일 동안 연기했다. 이미 약속된 것을 delay하면, 그것이 계획했던 것보다 나중에 일어나도록 하는 것이다. ❑ 우주항공 센터 관리자들이 우주선 발사를 연기하기로 결정했다. 무슨 일이 당신을 delay하거나 당신을 hold up하면, 일의 시작이나 마무리를 계획보다 늦게 하게 하는 것이다. ❑ 그 사람은 차가 막혀서 늦었다... 장비 배달이 일정 연기와 의견 충돌 때문에 지연되었다.

2 V-T To **delay** someone or something means to make them late or to slow them down. ❑ *Can you delay him in some way?* ❑ *Various set-backs and problems delayed production.* **3** V-I If you **delay**, you deliberately take longer than necessary to do something. ❑ *If he delayed any longer, the sun would be up.* **4** N-VAR If there is a **delay**, something does not happen until later than planned or expected. ❑ *They claimed that such a delay wouldn't hurt anyone.* **5** N-UNCOUNT **Delay** is a failure to do something immediately or in the required or usual time. ❑ *We'll send you a quote without delay.*

2 타동사 지연시키다 ❑ 그를 어떻게든 지연시킬 수 있어? ❑ 많은 차질과 장애가 생겨서 제작이 지연되었다. **3** 자동사 지체하다 ❑ 그가 더 지체했다가는 해가 떠오를 것이다. **4** 가산명사 또는 불가산명사 지연 ❑ 그렇게 한 번 지연되었다고 해서 누군가가 손해 보는 일 따위는 없을 거라고 그들은 주장했다. **5** 불가산명사 지체 ❑ 지체 없이 견적을 보내드리겠습니다.

Thesaurus	*delay*의 참조어
v.	hold up, postpone, stall; *(ant.)* hurry, rush **1**
n.	lag; *(ant.)* rush **4**

de|lay|er|ing /dɪleɪərɪŋ/ N-UNCOUNT **Delayering** is the process of simplifying the administrative structure of a large organization in order to make it more efficient. [BUSINESS] ❑ *...downsizing, delayering and other cost cutting measures.*

불가산명사 구조 조정 [경제] ❑ 기구축소, 구조 조정 등의 비용 절감 방안

del|egate ♦◇◇ (**delegates, delegating, delegated**)

The noun is pronounced /dɛlɪgɪt/. The verb is pronounced /dɛlɪgeɪt/.

명사는 /dɛlɪgɪt/로 발음되고, 동사는 /dɛlɪgeɪt/로 발음된다.

1 N-COUNT A **delegate** is a person who is chosen to vote or make decisions on behalf of a group of other people, especially at a conference or a meeting. ❑ *The Canadian delegate offered no reply.* **2** V-T/V-I If you **delegate**, or **delegate** duties, responsibilities, or power **to** someone, you give them those duties, those responsibilities, or that power so that they can act on your behalf. ❑ *He talks of traveling less, and delegating more authority to his deputies in Britain and Australia.* ● **del|ega|tion** N-UNCOUNT ❑ *A key factor in running a business is the delegation of responsibility.* **3** V-T If you **are delegated to** do something, you are given the duty of acting on someone else's behalf by making decisions, voting, or doing some particular work. [usu passive] ❑ *Officials have now been delegated to start work on a draft settlement.*

1 가산명사 대표; 대리인 ❑ 그 캐나다 대표는 어떤 답변도 내놓지 않았다. **2** 타동사/자동사 위임하다 ❑ 그는 스스로 돌아다니는 것을 줄이고 영국과 호주의 대리인들에게 더 많은 권한을 위임하겠노라고 말한다. ● 위임 불가산명사 ❑ 사업을 운영할 때 중요한 요소 중 하나가 책임의 위임이다. **3** 타동사 위임받다 ❑ 관리들은 현재 합의서 초안 작성을 시작하도록 위임받은 상태이다.

del|ega|tion ♦◇◇ /dɛlɪgeɪʃ°n/ (**delegations**) N-COUNT A **delegation** is a group of people who have been sent somewhere to have talks with other people on behalf of a larger group of people. ❑ *...the Chinese delegation to the UN talks in New York.* →see also **delegate**

가산명사 대표단 ❑ 뉴욕의 유엔 회담에 간 중국 대표단

de|lete /dɪliːt/ (**deletes, deleting, deleted**) V-T If you **delete** something that has been written down or stored in a computer, you cross it out or remove it. ❑ *He also deleted files from the computer system.*

타동사 삭제하다 ❑ 그는 그 컴퓨터 시스템에서 파일까지 삭제했다.

Thesaurus	*delete*의 참조어
v.	cut out, erase, remove

de|lib|er|ate ♦◇◇ (**deliberates, deliberating, deliberated**)

The adjective is pronounced /dɪlɪbərɪt/. The verb is pronounced /dɪlɪbəreɪt/.

형용사는 /dɪlɪbərɪt/으로 발음되고, 동사는 /dɪlɪbəreɪt/으로 발음된다.

1 ADJ If you do something that is **deliberate**, you planned or decided to do it beforehand, and so it happens on purpose rather than by chance. ❑ *Witnesses say the firing was deliberate and sustained.* ● **de|lib|er|ate|ly** ADV ❑ *It looks as if the blaze was started deliberately.* **2** ADJ If a movement or action is **deliberate**, it is done slowly and carefully. ❑ *...stepping with deliberate slowness up the steep paths.* ● **de|lib|er|ate|ly** ADV [ADV after v] ❑ *The Japanese have acted calmly and deliberately.* **3** V-I If you **deliberate**, you think about something carefully, especially before making a very important decision. ❑ *She deliberated over the decision for a good few years before she finally made up her mind.* →see **trial**

1 형용사 의도적인 ❑ 증언들의 말에 의하면, 발포는 의도적이고 지속적으로 이어졌다고 한다. ● 의도적으로 부사 ❑ 누군가가 고의적으로 불을 지른 것 같다. **2** 형용사 신중한 ❑ 가파른 길을 따라 신중하게 천천히 발걸음을 옮기며 ● 신중하게 부사 ❑ 일본인들은 침착하고도 신중하게 행동해 왔다. **3** 자동사 숙고하다 ❑ 최종적으로 마음을 정하기 전에 그녀는 꽤 여러 해 동안 그 결정에 대해 숙고를 거듭했다.

de|lib|era|tion /dɪlɪbəreɪʃ°n/ (**deliberations**) **1** N-UNCOUNT **Deliberation** is the long and careful consideration of a subject. ❑ *In this house nothing is there by chance: it is always the result of great deliberation.* **2** N-PLURAL **Deliberations** are formal discussions where an issue is considered carefully. ❑ *Their deliberations were rather inconclusive.*

1 불가산명사 숙고 ❑ 이 집에서는 무엇 하나 우연히 자리를 잡은 것이라고는 없다. 모든 것이 다 엄청난 고심의 결과이다. **2** 복수명사 심의 ❑ 그들의 심의는 그다지 명확한 결론을 이끌어 내지 못했다.

deli|ca|cy /dɛlɪkəsi/ (**delicacies**) **1** N-UNCOUNT **Delicacy** is the quality of being easy to break or harm, and refers especially to people or things that are attractive or graceful. ❑ *...the delicacy of a rose.* **2** N-UNCOUNT If you say that a situation or problem is **of** some **delicacy**, you mean that it is difficult to handle and needs careful and sensitive treatment. ❑ *There was a matter of some delicacy on which he would be grateful for her advice.* **3** N-UNCOUNT If someone handles a difficult situation **with delicacy**, they handle it very carefully, making sure that nobody is offended. ❑ *Both countries are behaving with rare delicacy.* **4** N-COUNT A **delicacy** is a rare or expensive food that is considered especially nice to eat. ❑ *Smoked salmon was considered an expensive delicacy.*

1 불가산명사 섬세함 ❑ 장미꽃의 섬세함 **2** 불가산명사 미묘함 ❑ 그가 그녀의 조언에 감사해할 만한 약간 미묘한 사안이 있었다. **3** 불가산명사 세심함 ❑ 두 나라 모두 보기 드물게 세심하게 행동하고 있다. **4** 가산명사 별미 ❑ 훈제 연어는 비싼 별미로 여겨졌다.

deli|cate /dɛlɪkɪt/ **1** ADJ Something that is **delicate** is small and beautifully shaped. ❑ *He had delicate hands.* ● **deli|cate|ly** ADV [ADV adj/-ed] ❑ *She was a shy, delicately pretty girl with enormous blue eyes.* **2** ADJ Something that is **delicate** has a color, taste, or smell which is pleasant and not strong or intense. ❑ *Young*

1 형용사 섬세한 ❑ 그는 섬세한 손을 가지고 있었다. ● 섬세하게 부사 ❑ 그녀는 커다란 푸른 눈과 우아한 아름다움을 지니고 있는 내성적인 소녀였다. **2** 형용사 은은한 ❑ 풋강낭콩은 조직이 연하고 맛은

haricot beans have a tender texture and a delicate, subtle flavor. ● **deli**|**cate**|**ly** ADV [ADV -ed/adj] ❑ ...a soup delicately flavored with nutmeg. ❸ ADJ If something is **delicate**, it is easy to harm, damage, or break, and needs to be handled or treated carefully. ❑ Although the coral looks hard, it is very delicate. ❹ ADJ Someone who is **delicate** is not healthy and strong, and becomes ill easily. ❑ She was physically delicate and psychologically unstable. ❺ ADJ You use **delicate** to describe a situation, problem, matter, or discussion that needs to be dealt with carefully and sensitively in order to avoid upsetting things or offending people. ❑ The European members are afraid of upsetting the delicate balance of political interests. ● **deli**|**cate**|**ly** ADV [ADV with v] ❑ Clearly, the situation remains delicately poised. ❻ ADJ A **delicate** task, movement, action, or product needs or shows great skill and attention to detail. ❑ ...a long and delicate operation carried out at a hospital in Florence. ❑ ...the delicately embroidered sheets.

deli|**ca**|**tes**|**sen** /dɪlɪkətɛsᵊn/ (**delicatessens**) N-COUNT A **delicatessen** is a store that sells cold cuts, cheeses, salads, and often a selection of imported foods.

de|**li**|**cious** /dɪlɪʃəs/ ADJ Food that is **delicious** has a very pleasant taste. ❑ There's always a wide selection of delicious meals to choose from. ● **de**|**li**|**cious**|**ly** ADV [ADV adj/-ed] ❑ This yoghurt has a deliciously creamy flavor.

de|**light** ♦◇◇ /dɪlaɪt/ (**delights, delighting, delighted**) ❶ N-UNCOUNT **Delight** is a feeling of very great pleasure. ❑ Throughout the house, the views are a constant source of surprise and delight. ❑ Andrew roared with delight when he heard Rachel's nickname for the baby. ❷ PHRASE If someone **takes delight** or **takes a delight in** something, they get a lot of pleasure from it. ❑ Haig took obvious delight in proving his critics wrong. ❸ N-COUNT You can refer to someone or something that gives you great pleasure or enjoyment as a **delight**. [APPROVAL] ❑ The aircraft was a delight to fly. ❹ V-T If something **delights** you, it gives you a lot of pleasure. ❑ She has created a style of music that has delighted audiences all over the world.

de|**light**|**ed** ♦◇◇ /dɪlaɪtɪd/ ❶ ADJ If you are **delighted**, you are extremely pleased and excited about something. ❑ I know Frank will be delighted to see you. ● **de**|**light**|**ed**|**ly** ADV [ADV with v] ❑ "There!" Jackson exclaimed delightedly. ❷ ADJ If someone invites or asks you to do something, you can say that you would be **delighted** to do it, as a way of showing that you are very willing to do it. [FEELINGS] [v-link ADJ, oft ADJ to-inf] ❑ "You must come to Tinsley's graduation party." — "I'd be delighted."

de|**light**|**ful** /dɪlaɪtfᵊl/ ADJ If you describe something or someone as **delightful**, you mean they are very pleasant. ❑ It was the most delightful garden I had ever seen. ● **de**|**light**|**ful**|**ly** ADV [ADV adj/-ed] ❑ This delightfully refreshing cologne can be splashed on liberally.

de|**lin**|**quen**|**cy** /dɪlɪŋkwənsi/ N-UNCOUNT **Delinquency** is criminal behavior, especially that of young people. ❑ He had no history of delinquency.

de|**lin**|**quent** /dɪlɪŋkwənt/ (**delinquents**) ADJ Someone, usually a young person, who is **delinquent** repeatedly commits minor crimes. ❑ ...remand homes for delinquent children. ● N-COUNT **Delinquent** is also a noun. ❑ ...a nine-year-old delinquent.

de|**lir**|**ious** /dɪlɪəriəs/ ❶ ADJ Someone who is **delirious** is unable to think or speak in a sensible and reasonable way, usually because they are very ill and have a fever. ❑ I was delirious and blacked out several times. ❷ ADJ Someone who is **delirious** is extremely excited and happy. ❑ His tax-cutting pledge brought a delirious crowd to their feet. ● **de**|**lir**|**ious**|**ly** ADV ❑ Dora returned from her honeymoon deliriously happy.

de|**list** /diːlɪst/ (**delists, delisting, delisted**) V-T/V-I If a company **delists** or if its shares **are delisted**, its shares are removed from the official list of shares that can be traded on the stock market. [BUSINESS] ❑ India's largest private industrial group asked the Bombay Stock Exchange to delist the shares of four of its companies.

de|**liv**|**er** ♦♦◇ /dɪlɪvər/ (**delivers, delivering, delivered**) ❶ V-T If you **deliver** something somewhere, you take it there. ❑ The Canadians plan to deliver more food to southern Somalia. ❷ V-T If you **deliver** something that you have promised to do, make, or produce, you do, make, or produce it. ❑ They have yet to show that they can really deliver working technologies. ❸ V-T If you **deliver** a lecture or speech, you give it in public. [FORMAL] ❑ The president will deliver a speech about schools. ❹ V-T When someone **delivers** a baby, they help the woman who is giving birth to the baby. ❑ Although we'd planned to have our baby at home, we never expected to deliver her ourselves! ❺ V-T If someone **delivers** a blow to someone else, they hit them. [WRITTEN] ❑ Those blows to the head could have been delivered by a woman.

Thesaurus
deliver의 참조어

v.   bring, give, hand over, transfer; (ant.) hold, keep, retain ❶

Word Partnership
deliver의 연어

N.   deliver **a letter**, deliver **mail**, deliver **a message**, deliver **news**,
deliver **a package** ❶
deliver **a service** ❷
deliver **a lecture**, deliver **a speech** ❸
deliver **a baby** ❹
deliver **a blow** ❺

de|**liv**|**ery** ♦◇◇ /dɪlɪvəri/ (**deliveries**) ❶ N-VAR **Delivery** or a **delivery** is the bringing of letters, parcels, or other goods to someone's house or to another place where they want them. ❑ Please allow 28 days for delivery. ❑ It is available at £108, including VAT and delivery. ❷ N-COUNT A **delivery** of something is the goods

---

은은하면서도 미묘하다. ● 은은하게 부사 ❑ 너트멕으로 은은한 맛을 낸 수프 한 그릇 ❸ 형용사 연약한 ❑ 산호는 단단해 보일지 몰라도 실은 굉장히 약하다. ❹ 형용사 허약한 ❑ 그녀는 몸이 허약한데다 심리적으로도 불안정한 상태였다. ❺ 형용사 미묘한 ❑ 유럽 회원들은 정치적 이해의 미묘한 균형을 깨뜨리는 것을 두려워한다. ● 미묘하게 부사 ❑ 미묘한 균형을 유지하고 있는 상태였다. ❻ 형용사 정교한 ❑ 플로렌스의 한 병원에서 행해졌던 오랜 시간에 걸쳐 실시한 정교한 수술 ● 정교하게 부사 ❑ 정교하게 수놓은 침대시트

가산명사 델리, 고급 조제 식품 가게

형용사 맛있는 ❑ 항상 골라 먹을 수 있게 맛있는 식사가 다양하게 준비되어 있다. ● 맛있게 부사 ❑ 이 요구르트는 맛 좋은 크림 맛이 난다.

❶ 불가산명사 기쁨 ❑ 집 곳곳에서 바깥으로 보이는 경치가 끝없는 경탄과 기쁨을 자아낸다. ❑ 레이첼이 아기에게 지어준 별명을 들었을 때 앤드류는 즐거움에 겨워 웃음을 터뜨렸다. ❷ 구 기뻐하고 있다 ❑ 헤이그가 자신을 비판하는 사람들이 틀렸음을 증명하는 데서 기쁨을 얻고 있는 게 분명했다. ❸ 가산명사 즐거움 [마음에 듦] ❑ 비행기는 타기에 너무 재미있었다. ❹ 타동사 즐겁게 하다 ❑ 그녀는 온 세계 청중을 즐겁게 하는 음악 스타일을 창조해 냈다.

❶ 형용사 기쁜 ❑ 프랭크가 너를 보면 분명히 매우 기뻐할 거야. ● 기쁨에 차서 부사 ❑ "거 봐!"라고 기쁨에 가득 차서 잭슨이 소리쳤다. ❷ 형용사 기쁜 [감정 개입] ❑ "틴슬리의 졸업 파티에 꼭 오셔야 해요." "기꺼이 가겠습니다."

형용사 매우 유쾌한 ❑ 그것은 내가 본 것 중 가장 보기 좋은 정원이었다. ● 유쾌하게 부사 ❑ 이 상쾌한 향수는 많이 뿌려도 무방하다.

불가산명사 (청소년) 비행 ❑ 청소년 시절에 그가 범죄를 저질렀다는 기록은 없다.

형용사 비행을 저지른 ❑ 비행 아동들을 위한 유치 가정 ● 가산명사 비행 청소년, 비행 아동 ❑ 아홉 살짜리 비행 아동

❶ 형용사 혼미한 ❑ 나는 정신이 혼미해져서 여러 번 의식을 잃었다. ❷ 형용사 몹시 흥분한 ❑ 그가 세금을 감하겠다고 약속하자 몹시 흥분한 관중이 자리를 박차고 일어났다. ● 몹시 흥분하여 부사 ❑ 도라는 좋아서 까무러칠 정도로 행복해하면서 신혼여행에서 돌아왔다.

타동사/자동사 상장 폐지하다; 상장 폐지당하다 [경제] ❑ 인도에서 가장 큰 민간 그룹이 자 회사 네 개에 대한 상장을 폐지해 달라고 뭄바이 증권 거래소에 요청했다.

❶ 타동사 배달하다, 전달하다 ❑ 캐나다 인들은 남부 소말리아에 더 많은 음식을 전달할 계획이다. ❷ 타동사 완수해 내다 ❑ 그들은 아직 실제로 도움이 될 만한 기술을 제대로 개발해 낼 수 있는지를 증명해 보여야만 한다. ❸ 타동사 (강연이나 연설을) 하다 [격식체] ❑ 대통령이 학교에 관한 연설을 할 것이다. ❹ 타동사 분만하다 ❑ 아기를 집에서 낳으려고 계획은 했었지만 우리 힘만으로 직접 분만하게 될 줄은 정말 몰랐다! ❺ 타동사 (타격을) 가하다 [문어체] ❑ 머리에 가해진 그 타격은 여성이 입힌 것일 수도 있다.

❶ 가산명사 또는 불가산명사 배송 ❑ 배송에 28일이 소요됩니다. ❑ 부가세와 배송료를 포함해서 가격은 108파운드입니다. ❷ 가산명사 배송물 ❑ 오늘 아침 신선한 달걀을 배송받았다. ❸ 형용사 배달의 ❑ 피자

a b c d e f g h i j k l m n o p q r s t u v w x y z

that are delivered. ❑ *I got a delivery of fresh eggs this morning.* ❸ ADJ A **delivery** person or service delivers things to a place. [ADJ n] ❑ *...a pizza delivery man.* ❹ N-UNCOUNT You talk about someone's **delivery** when you are referring to the way in which they give a speech or lecture. ❑ *His speeches were magnificently written but his delivery was hopeless.* ❺ N-VAR **Delivery** is the process of giving birth to a baby. ❑ *In the end, it was an easy delivery: a fine baby boy.*

배달부 ❹ 불가산명사 (연설이나 강연의) 방식 ❑ 그가 쓴 연설문 자체는 훌륭했지만 그가 연설하는 방식이 너무 형편없었다. ❺ 가산명사 또는 불가산명사 분만 ❑ 결국 순산을 해서 건강한 사내아이를 낳았다.

de|liv|ery charge (delivery charges) N-COUNT A **delivery charge** is the cost of transporting or delivering goods. [AM, FORMAL; BRIT usually **carriage**] ❑ *Again, buyers need to check if delivery charges are included in the price.*

가산명사 배송료 [미국영어, 격식체; 영국영어 대개 carriage] ❑ 다시, 구매자들은 다시 한 번 배송료가 가격에 포함되는지 여부를 확인해 봐야 한다.

del|ta /dɛltə/ (deltas) N-COUNT A **delta** is an area of low, flat land shaped like a triangle, where a river splits and spreads out into several branches before entering the sea. ❑ *...the Mississippi delta.* →see **river**

가산명사 삼각주 ❑ 미시시피 삼각주

de|lude /dɪlud/ (deludes, deluding, deluded) ❶ V-T If you **delude yourself**, you let yourself believe that something is true, even though it is not true. ❑ *The President was deluding himself if he thought he was safe from such action.* ❑ *We delude ourselves that we are in control.* ❷ V-T To **delude** someone **into** thinking something means to make them believe what is not true. ❑ *Television deludes you into thinking you have experienced reality, when you haven't.*

❶ 타동사 착각하다 ❑ 그러한 행위로 인해 피해를 받는 일은 없을 것이라고 생각했다면 그것은 대통령의 오산일 뿐이었다. ❑ 우리는 우리가 뭔가를 좌지우지할 수 있는 위치에 있다고 스스로를 기만하였다. ❷ 타동사 속이다 ❑ 텔레비전을 보면서 실상이 어떠한지 경험할 수 있다고 생각하기 쉽지만, 이는 사실이 아니다.

del|uge /dɛlyudʒ/ (deluges, deluging, deluged) ❶ N-COUNT A **deluge of** things is a large number of them which arrive or happen at the same time. ❑ *A deluge of manuscripts began to arrive in the post.* ❷ V-T If a place or person **is deluged with** things, a large number of them arrive or happen at the same time. [usu passive] ❑ *During 1933, Papen's office was deluged with complaints.*

❶ 가산명사 쇄도 ❑ 우편으로 원고가 쇄도하기 시작했다. ❷ 타동사 쇄도당하다 ❑ 1933년 내내 페펜의 사무실로 불평이 쇄도했다.

de|lu|sion /dɪluʒ°n/ (delusions) ❶ N-COUNT A **delusion** is a false idea. ❑ *I was under the delusion that he intended to marry me.* ❷ N-UNCOUNT **Delusion** is the state of believing things that are not true. ❑ *Insinuations about her mental state, about her capacity for delusion were being made.*

❶ 가산명사 착각 ❑ 나는 그가 나와 결혼하고 싶어 한다는 착각에 빠져 있었다. ❷ 불가산명사 망상 ❑ 그녀가 정신 질환을 앓고 있다는 등, 망상에 빠지는 경향이 있다는 등의 수군거림이 교묘하게 일고 있었다.

deluxe /dɪlʌks/ [BRIT also **de luxe**] ADJ **Deluxe** goods or services are better in quality and more expensive than ordinary ones. [ADJ n, n ADJ] ❑ *...a rare, highly prized deluxe wine.*

[영국영어 de luxe] 형용사 특급의 ❑ 귀하고 매우 높이 평가받는 특급 와인

delve /dɛlv/ (delves, delving, delved) V-I If you **delve into** something, you try to discover new information about it. ❑ *Tormented by her ignorance, Jenny delves into her mother's past.*

자동사 파고들다 ❑ 자신의 무지에 괴로워하며 제니는 어머니의 과거를 파고든다.

de|mand ♦♦♦ /dɪmænd/ (demands, demanding, demanded) ❶ V-T If you **demand** something such as information or action, you ask for it in a very forceful way. ❑ *Mr. Byers last night demanded an immediate explanation from the Education Secretary.* ❑ *Russia demanded that Unita send a delegation to the peace talks.* ❷ V-T If one thing **demands** another, the first needs the second in order to happen or be dealt with successfully. ❑ *He said the task of reconstruction would demand much patience, hard work, and sacrifice.* ❸ N-COUNT A **demand** is a firm request for something. ❑ *There have been demands for services from tenants up there.* ❹ N-UNCOUNT If you refer to **demand**, or to the **demand for** something, you are referring to how many people want to have it, do it, or buy it. ❑ *Another flight would be arranged on Saturday if sufficient demand arose.* ❺ N-PLURAL The **demands** of something or its **demands on** you are the things which it needs or the things which you have to do for it. ❑ *...the demands and challenges of a new job.* ❻ PHRASE If someone or something is **in demand** or **in great demand**, they are very popular and a lot of people want them. ❑ *He was much in demand as a lecturer in the U.S., as well as at universities all over Europe.* ❼ PHRASE If something is available or happens **on demand**, you can have it or it happens whenever you want it or ask for it. ❑ *...a national commitment to providing treatment on demand for drug abusers.*

❶ 타동사 요구하다 ❑ 어제 저녁 바이어스 씨는 교육부 장관에게 즉각적인 해명을 요구했다. ❑ 러시아 정부는 앙골라 완전 독립민족동맹에게 평화회담 대표단을 보내달라고 요구했다. ❷ 타동사 요구하다 ❑ 재건 사업에는 많은 인내와 고된 노동, 희생이 요구될 것이라고 그는 말했다. ❸ 가산명사 요구 ❑ 저 위쪽 동네에 사는 주민들이 서비스 개선을 요청해 오고 있다. ❹ 불가산명사 수요 ❑ 충분한 수요만 있다면 토요일에 추가로 항공편이 마련될 것이다. ❺ 복수명사 요구 사항 ❑ 새로운 일자리가 요구하는 책임과 과제 ❻ 구 인기가 있는 ❑ 그는 유럽 전역의 대학에서뿐만 아니라 미국에서도 인기 있는 강사였다. ❼ 구 요청받는 대로 ❑ 약물을 남용하는 이들에게 요청하면 무상 치료를 제공하겠다는 국가의 공약

Thesaurus   demand의 참조어

  v.   command, insist on, order; (ant.) give, grant, offer ❶
       necessitate, need, require; (ant.) give, supply ❷

de|mand|ing /dɪmændɪŋ/ ❶ ADJ A **demanding** job or task requires a lot of your time, energy, or attention. ❑ *He tried to return to work, but found he could no longer cope with his demanding job.* ❷ ADJ People who are **demanding** are not easily satisfied or pleased. ❑ *Ricky was a very demanding child.*

❶ 형용사 고된 ❑ 그는 복직하려고 시도는 했으나, 자신이 그 고된 일을 더 이상 감당할 수 없다는 사실을 깨달았다. ❷ 형용사 까다로운 ❑ 리키는 매우 까다로운 아이였다.

de|mean /dɪmin/ (demeans, demeaning, demeaned) V-T To **demean** someone or something means to make people have less respect for them. ❑ *Some groups say that pornography demeans women and incites rape.*

타동사 비하하다 ❑ 일부 단체들은 포르노가 여성을 비하하는데다 강간을 부추긴다고 주장한다.

de|mean|ing /dɪminɪŋ/ ADJ Something that is **demeaning** makes people have less respect for the person who is treated in that way, or who does that thing. ❑ *...making demeaning sexist comments.*

형용사 비하하는 ❑ 모멸적인 성차별주의적 발언을 하는

de|mean|or /dɪminər/ [BRIT **demeanour**] N-UNCOUNT Your **demeanor** is the way you behave, which gives people an impression of your character and feelings. [FORMAL] ❑ *...her calm and cheerful demeanor.*

[영국영어 demeanour] 불가산명사 행실, 품행 [격식체] ❑ 그녀의 침착하면서도 쾌활한 태도

de|men|tia /dɪmɛnʃə/ (dementias) N-VAR **Dementia** is a serious illness of the mind. [MEDICAL] ❑ *...a treatment for mental conditions such as dementia and Alzheimer's disease.*

가산명사 또는 불가산명사 치매 [의학] ❑ 치매나 알츠하이머병과 같은 정신 질환에 대한 치료

de|merge /dimɜrdʒ/ (demerges, demerging, demerged) V-T/V-I If a large company **is demerged** or **demerges**, it is broken down into several smaller companies. [BRIT, BUSINESS] ❑ *Have you ever wondered why so many companies merge and so few demerge?*

타동사/자동사 분할되다; 분할하다 [영국영어, 경제] ❑ 합병하는 회사는 그리 많은데 분할하는 회사는 어째서 그리 소수인지 궁금하게 여겨 보신 적이 있으세요?

de|merg|er /dimɜrdʒər/ (demergers) N-COUNT A **demerger** is the separation of a large company into several smaller companies. [BRIT, BUSINESS] ❑ *He soon emerged as chairman of Woolworths, overseeing the company's demerger from Kingfisher.*

가산명사 분할 [영국영어, 경제] ❑ 그는 곧 울워스의 회장이 되었고 회사와 킹피셔의 분할을 지휘했다.

a
b
c
d
e
f
g
h
i
j
k
l
m
n
o
p
q
r
s
t
u
v
w
x
y
z

Word Link *milit ≈ soldier : de*milit*arize,* milit*ary,* milit*ia*

de|mili|ta|rize /dɪmɪlɪtəraɪz/ (**demilitarizes, demilitarizing, demilitarized**) [BRIT also **demilitarise**] V-T To **demilitarize** an area means to ensure that all military forces are removed from it. ❑ *He said the UN had made remarkable progress in demilitarizing the region.*

de|mise /dɪmaɪz/ N-SING The **demise** of something or someone is their end or death. [FORMAL] ❑ *...the demise of the reform movement.*

demo /dɛmoʊ/ (**demos**) ◼ N-COUNT A **demo** is a CD or tape with a sample of someone's music recorded on it. [INFORMAL] ❑ *He listened to one of my demo tapes and said he was keen to work with me.* ◻ N-COUNT A **demo** is a **demonstration** by a group of people to show their opposition to something or their support for something. [BRIT, INFORMAL] ❑ *...an anti-racist demo.*

de|mo|bilize /dimoʊbɪlaɪz/ (**demobilizes, demobilizing, demobilized**) [BRIT also **demobilise**] V-T/V-I If a country or armed force **demobilizes** its troops, or if its troops **demobilize**, its troops are released from service and allowed to go home. ❑ *Dos Santos has demanded that UNITA sign a cease-fire and demobilize its troops.* ● **de|mo|bi|li|za|tion** /dimoʊbɪlɪzeɪʃ°n/ N-UNCOUNT ❑ *The government had previously been opposed to the demobilization of its 100,000 strong army.*

Word Link *cracy ≈ rule by : aristo*cracy*, demo*cracy*, bureau*cracy

Word Link *demo ≈ people : demo*cracy*, demo*graphic*, epi*demic

de|moc|ra|cy ◆◇◇ /dɪmɒkrəsi/ (**democracies**) ◼ N-UNCOUNT **Democracy** is a system of government in which people choose their rulers by voting for them in elections. ❑ *The spread of democracy in Eastern Europe appears to have had negative as well as positive consequences.* ◻ N-COUNT A **democracy** is a country in which the people choose their government by voting for it. ❑ *The new democracies face tough challenges.* →see **vote**

Word Link *crat ≈ power : aristo*crat*, bureau*crat*, demo*crat

demo|crat ◆◇◇ /dɛməkræt/ (**democrats**) ◼ N-COUNT A **Democrat** is a member or supporter of a particular political party which has the word "democrat" or "democratic" in its title, for example the Democratic Party in the United States. ❑ *...a senior Christian Democrat.* ◻ N-COUNT A **democrat** is a person who believes in the ideals of democracy, personal freedom, and equality. ❑ *This is the time for democrats and not dictators.*

demo|crat|ic ◆◇◇ /dɛməkrætɪk/ ◼ ADJ A **democratic** country, government, or political system is governed by representatives who are elected by the people. ❑ *Bolivia returned to democratic rule in 1982, after a series of military governments.* ● **demo|crati|cal|ly** /dɛməkrætɪkli/ ADV ❑ *That June, Yeltsin became Russia's first democratically elected President.* ◻ ADJ Something that is **democratic** is based on the idea that everyone should have equal rights and should be involved in making important decisions. ❑ *Education is the basis of a democratic society.* ● **demo|crati|cal|ly** ADV ❑ *This committee will enable decisions to be made democratically.*

de|mo|graph|ic /dɛmədɡræfɪk/ (**demographics**) ◼ N-PLURAL The **demographics** of a place or society are the statistics relating to the people who live there. ❑ *...the changing demographics of the United States.* ◻ N-SING In business, a **demographic** is a group of people in a society, especially people in a particular age group. [BUSINESS] ❑ *The station has won more listeners in the 25-39 demographic.*

de|mol|ish /dɪmɒlɪʃ/ (**demolishes, demolishing, demolished**) ◼ V-T To **demolish** something such as a building means to destroy it completely. ❑ *A storm moved directly over the island, demolishing buildings and flooding streets.* ◻ V-T If you **demolish** someone's ideas or arguments, you prove that they are completely wrong or unreasonable. ❑ *Our intention was quite the opposite – to demolish rumors that have surrounded him since he took office.*

demo|li|tion /dɛməlɪʃ°n/ (**demolitions**) N-VAR The **demolition** of a building is the act of deliberately destroying it, often in order to build something else in its place. ❑ *The project required the total demolition of the old bridge.*

de|mon /dimən/ (**demons**) ◼ N-COUNT A **demon** is an evil spirit. ❑ *...a woman possessed by demons.* ◻ N-COUNT If you approve of someone because they are very skilled at what they do or because they do it energetically, you can say that they do it like a **demon**. [APPROVAL] ❑ *She worked like a demon and expected everybody else to do the same.* ❑ *He is a demon organizer.*

de|mon|ic /dɪmɒnɪk/ ADJ **Demonic** means coming from or belonging to a demon or being like a demon. ❑ *...a demonic grin.*

dem|on|strate ◆◇◇ /dɛmənstreɪt/ (**demonstrates, demonstrating, demonstrated**) ◼ V-T To **demonstrate** a fact means to make it clear to people. ❑ *The study also demonstrated a direct link between obesity and mortality.* ❑ *They are anxious to demonstrate to the voters that they have practical policies.* ◻ V-T If you **demonstrate** a particular skill, quality, or feeling, you show by your actions that you have it. ❑ *Have they, for example, demonstrated a commitment to democracy?* ◼ V-I When people **demonstrate**, they march or gather somewhere to show their opposition to something or their support for something. ❑ *Some 30,000 angry farmers arrived in Brussels yesterday to demonstrate against possible cuts in subsidies.* ❑ *In the cities vast crowds have been demonstrating for change.* ◼ V-T If you **demonstrate** something, you show people how it works or how to

[영국영어 demilitarise] 타동사 비군사화하다 ❑ 그는 그 지역을 비군사화하는 데 유엔이 놀라운 진척을 이뤄냈노라고 말했다.

단수명사 종언; 사망 [격식체] ❑ 개혁 운동의 종언

◼ 가산명사 (시디나 테이프의) 데모 [비격식체] ❑ 그는 내 데모 테이프 하나를 들어 보고는 나와 같이 작업하고 싶다고 했다. ◻ 가산명사 시위 [영국영어, 비격식체] ❑ 반인종 차별주의자들의 시위

[영국영어 demobilise] 타동사/자동사 해산하다 ❑ 도스 산토스는 앙골라 완전 독립 민족 동맹에게 정전 협정에 서명하고 부대를 해산하도록 요구한 상태다. ● 해산 불가산명사 ❑ 그 정부는 건재한 십만 병력의 해산에 대해 이전까지는 반대하는 입장이었다.

◼ 불가산명사 민주주의 ❑ 동유럽에서 민주주의가 확산되면서 긍정적인 영향뿐만 아니라 부작용까지 함께 나타난 듯하다. ◻ 가산명사 민주주의 국가 ❑ 그 신생 민주주의 국가들은 몇 가지 난제에 직면해 있다.

◼ 가산명사 민주당원 ❑ 원로 기독민주당원 ◻ 가산명사 민주주의자 ❑ 지금은 독재자의 시대가 아니라 민주주의자들의 시대이다.

◼ 형용사 민주주의의 ❑ 볼리비아는 군사 정부 몇 개를 연속으로 겪은 후 1982년에야 민주통치로 돌아왔다. ● 민주적으로 부사 ❑ 그 해 6월, 옐친은 러시아에서 최초로 민주적으로 당선된 최초의 대통령이 되었다. ◻ 형용사 민주주의의 ❑ 교육이 민주주의 사회의 근간을 이룬다. ● 민주적으로 부사 ❑ 위원회는 결정이 민주적으로 이루어지도록 할 것이다.

◼ 복수명사 인구 통계 ❑ 변화하고 있는 미국의 인구 구성 ◻ 단수명사 특정 집단 [경제] ❑ 그 방송국은 25-39세 사이의 청취자를 더 많이 확보해 놓은 상태다.

◼ 타동사 부수다 ❑ 폭풍이 그 섬 전체를 직접 휩쓸고 지나가면서 건물들이 부서지고 모든 거리가 물에 잠겼다. ◻ 타동사 허물다, 불식시키다 ❑ 우리의 의도는 거의 정반대였다. 즉 그가 취임한 후 그를 둘러싼 소문들을 불식시키는 것이 우리의 의도였다.

가산명사 또는 불가산명사 철거 ❑ 프로젝트를 실행하려면 이전 다리를 완전히 철거할 필요가 있었다.

◼ 가산명사 악령 ❑ 악령이 들린 여자 ◻ 가산명사 귀신 [마음에 듦] ❑ 그녀는 신들린 듯 일했고 다른 사람들도 꼭 같이 하기를 바랐다. ❑ 그는 정리하는 데에는 귀신이나.

형용사 악마의 ❑ 악마와 같은 미소

◼ 타동사 증명하다 ❑ 그 연구를 통해서 비만이 사망률과 직접적으로 관계가 있다는 사실이 또한 밝혀졌다. ❑ 그들은 실제적으로 유용한 정책을 세우고 있다는 걸 유권자들에게 증명해 보이고 싶어 안달이다. ◻ 타동사 보여 주다 ❑ 가령 그들이 민주주의에 헌신하는 모습을 보여 준 적이 있나요? ◼ 자동사 시위하다 ❑ 3만 명의 분개한 농부들이 보조금의 삭감 가능성을 반대하는 시위를 하기 위해 브뤼셀에 도착했다. ❑ 도시에서는 많은 군중이 변화를 요구하며 시위를 벌이고 있는 중이다. ◼ 타동사 시범을 보이다 ❑ 비비시는 이제 막 새로운 디지털 라디오 송신

do it. ❑ *The BBC has just successfully demonstrated a new digital radio transmission system.*

시스템을 성공적으로 선보였다.

Thesaurus	*demonstrate*의 참조어

v. describe, illustrate, prove, show 🔲 🔳 🔳
    march, picket, protest 🔳

dem|on|stra|tion ♦◇◇ /dɛmənstreɪʃ°n/ (**demonstrations**) 🔳 N-COUNT A **demonstration** is a march or gathering which people take part in to show their opposition to something or their support for something. ❑ *Riot police used tear gas and truncheons this afternoon to break up a demonstration by students.* 🔳 N-COUNT A **demonstration** of something is a talk by someone who shows you how to do it or how it works. ❑ *...a cooking demonstration.* 🔳 N-COUNT A **demonstration** of a fact or situation is a clear proof of it. ❑ *It was an unprecedented demonstration of people power by the citizens of Moscow.* 🔳 N-COUNT A **demonstration** of a quality or feeling is an expression of it. ❑ *There's been no public demonstration of opposition to the President.*

🔳 가산명사 시위 ❑ 시위 경찰들은 학생들의 시위를 해산시키기 위해 오늘 오후에 최루탄과 경찰봉을 사용했다. 🔳 가산명사 시범 ❑ 조리 시범 🔳 가산명사 증명 ❑ 그것은 모스크바 시민들이 민중의 힘을 드러내 보인 전례 없는 본보기였다. 🔳 가산명사 표현 ❑ 대중이 대통령에 대한 반감을 드러낸 적은 없다.

de|mon|stra|tor ♦◇◇ /dɛmənstreɪtər/ (**demonstrators**) 🔳 N-COUNT **Demonstrators** are people who are marching or gathering somewhere to show their opposition to something or their support for something. ❑ *I saw the police using tear gas to try and break up a crowd of demonstrators.* 🔳 N-COUNT A **demonstrator** is a person who shows people how something works or how to do something. ❑ *...a demonstrator in a department store.*

🔳 가산명사 시위자 ❑ 나는 시위 군중을 해산시키기 위해 경찰들이 최루탄을 쓰는 것을 보았다. 🔳 가산명사 시범을 보이는 사람 ❑ 백화점에서 상품의 사용법을 시범해 보이는 사람

de|mor|al|ize /dɪmɒrəlaɪz, BRIT dɪmɒrəlaɪz/ (**demoralizes, demoralizing, demoralized**) [BRIT also **demoralise**] V-T If something **demoralizes** someone, it makes them lose so much confidence in what they are doing that they want to give up. ❑ *Clearly, one of the objectives is to demoralize the enemy troops in any way they can.* ● **de|mor|al|ized** ADJ ❑ *The Bismarck could now move only at a crawl and her crew were exhausted, hopeless and utterly demoralized.*

[영국영어 demoralise] 타동사 사기를 저하시키다 ❑ 분명히 목표 중의 하나는 어떻게든 그들이 적군의 사기를 저하시키는 것이다. ● 사기가 저하될 형용사 ❑ 비스마르크 호는 기어가는 듯한 속도로밖에 움직일 수 없었고 그 선원들은 기진맥진하여 모든 희망과 사기를 완전히 잃어버린 상태였다.

de|mor|al|iz|ing /dɪmɒrəlaɪzɪŋ, BRIT dɪmɒrəlaɪzɪŋ/ [BRIT also **demoralising**] ADJ If something is **demoralizing**, it makes you lose so much confidence in what you are doing that you want to give up. ❑ *Redundancy can be a demoralising prospect.*

[영국영어 demoralising] 형용사 기운 빠지게 하는 ❑ 정리 해고당할 수도 있다는 생각은 기운이 빠지게 만든다.

de|mote /dɪmoʊt/ (**demotes, demoting, demoted**) 🔳 V-T If someone **demotes** you, they give you a lower rank or a less important position than you already have, often as a punishment. ❑ *It's very difficult to demote somebody who has been standing in during maternity leave.* ● **de|mo|tion** /dɪmoʊʃ°n/ (**demotions**) N-VAR ❑ *He is seeking redress for what he alleges was an unfair demotion.* 🔳 V-T If a team in a sports league **is demoted**, that team has to compete in the next competition in a lower division, because it was one of the least successful teams in the higher division. [BRIT] [usu passive] ❑ *Swindon Town were demoted two divisions after the club admitted thirty-six breaches of the Football League's rules.* ● **de|mo|tion** N-VAR ❑ *The team now almost certainly faces demotion.*

🔳 타동사 강등시키다, 좌천시키다 ❑ 출산 휴가 도중 자리를 채워 준 사람을 좌천시키기란 매우 곤란한 일이다. ● 강등 가산명사 또는 불가산명사 ❑ 그는 그가 부당한 좌천이라고 주장하는 것에 대해서 보상을 요구하고 있다. 🔳 타동사 강등시키다 [영국영어] ❑ 스윈돈 타운 축구팀은 축구 연맹의 규칙을 36번 어긴 것을 시인한 뒤 2개 급(級) 아래로 강등당했다. ● 강등 가산명사 또는 불가산명사 ❑ 그 팀은 이제 강등당하게 될 게 거의 분명하다.

de|mu|tu|al|ize /dimyutʃuəlaɪz/ (**demutualizes, demutualizing, demutualized**) V-I If a savings and loan association or an insurance company **demutualizes**, it abandons its mutual status and becomes a different kind of company. [BUSINESS; BRIT also **demutualise**] ❑ *The group won the support of 97 percent of its members for plans to demutualize.* ● **de|mu|tu|al|iza|tion** /dimyutʃuəlaɪzeɪʃ°n/ N-UNCOUNT ❑ *The 503,000 policyholders who voted for demutualization should be represented.*

자동사 상호 회사에서 주식회사로 되다 [경제; 영국영어 demutualise] ❑ 그 그룹은 주식회사가 되고자 하는 계획에 대해 구성원 97퍼센트의 지지를 얻어 냈다. ● 상호 회사에서 주식회사로 되는 것 불가산명사 ❑ 주식회사가 되어야 한다고 투표한 503,000명의 보험 계약자의 의견은 충분히 대변되어야 한다.

den /dɛn/ (**dens**) 🔳 N-COUNT A **den** is the home of certain types of wild animals such as lions or foxes. 🔳 N-COUNT Your **den** is a quiet room in your house where you can go to study, work, or carry on a hobby without being disturbed. [AM] ❑ *The silver-haired retiree sits in his den surrounded by photos of sailing boats.* 🔳 N-COUNT A **den** is a secret place where people meet, usually for a dishonest purpose. ❑ *I could provide you with the addresses of at least three illegal drinking dens.* 🔳 N-COUNT If you describe a place as a **den of** a particular type of bad or illegal behavior, you mean that a lot of that type of behavior goes on there. ❑ *...the one-bedroomed apartment that was to become his den of savage debauchery.*

🔳 가산명사 굴 🔳 가산명사 (자기만의) 조용한 공간, 안식처 [미국영어] ❑ 백발이 성성한 퇴직자는 돛단배들 사진으로 둘러싸인 자신의 방에 앉아 있다. 🔳 가산명사 밀실 ❑ 밀주를 파는 곳의 주소를 내가 최소한 세 군데는 당신께 알려드릴 수 있습니다. 🔳 가산명사 소굴 ❑ 그의 막돼먹은 방탕한 행위의 소굴이 되게 된 침실 한 개짜리 그 아파트

de|ni|al /dɪnaɪəl/ (**denials**) 🔳 N-VAR A **denial** of something is a statement that it is not true, does not exist, or did not happen. ❑ *It seems clear that despite official denials, differences of opinion lay behind the Ambassador's decision to quit.* 🔳 N-UNCOUNT The **denial** of something to someone is the act of refusing to let them have it. [FORMAL] ❑ *...the denial of visas to international relief workers.* 🔳 N-UNCOUNT In psychology, **denial** is when a person cannot or will not accept an unpleasant truth. ❑ *With major life traumas, like losing a loved one, for instance, the mind's first reaction is denial.*

🔳 가산명사 또는 불가산명사 부인 ❑ 공식적으로 사실이 아니라고 부인했지만, 그 대사가 의견 차이를 견디지 못하고 물러난 게 거의 분명하다. 🔳 불가산명사 거부 [격식체] ❑ 국제 구호 노동자에게 비자 발급을 거부함 🔳 불가산명사 부정 ❑ 사랑하는 이를 잃게 되는 것과 같은 삶의 가장 큰 비극들에 대해 우리 마음이 최초로 보이는 반응은 바로 그것을 부정하려는 것이다.

den|im /dɛnɪm/ N-UNCOUNT **Denim** is a thick cotton cloth, usually blue, which is used to make clothes. Jeans are made from denim. ❑ *...a light blue denim jacket.*

불가산명사 데님 ❑ 연청색 데님 재킷

de|nomi|na|tion /dɪnɒmɪneɪʃ°n/ (**denominations**) 🔳 N-COUNT A particular **denomination** is a particular religious group which has slightly different beliefs from other groups within the same faith. ❑ *Acceptance of women preachers varies greatly from denomination to denomination.* 🔳 N-COUNT The **denomination** of a banknote or coin is its official value. ❑ *...a pile of bank notes, mostly in small denominations.*

🔳 가산명사 교파 ❑ 여성 설교자를 허용하느냐의 여부는 교파마다 크게 다르다. 🔳 가산명사 액면 금액 ❑ 대부분 액면가가 적은 화폐로만 이루어져 있는 지폐 한 뭉치

de|note /dɪnoʊt/ (**denotes, denoting, denoted**) 🔳 V-T If one thing **denotes** another, it is a sign or indication of it. [FORMAL] ❑ *Red eyes denote strain and fatigue.* 🔳 V-T What a symbol **denotes** is what it represents. [FORMAL] ❑ *In figure 24 "Dt" denotes quantity demanded in the current period and "St" denotes quantity supplied.*

🔳 타동사 의미하다 [격식체] ❑ 빨개진 눈은 긴장과 피로를 의미한다. 🔳 타동사 나타내다 [격식체] ❑ 도표 24에서 '디티'는 현시점의 수요 물량을 나타내고 '에스티'는 공급 물량을 나타냅니다.

Word Link	*nounce* ≈ reporting : an**nounce**, de**nounce**, pro**nounce**

de|nounce /dɪnaʊns/ (**denounces, denouncing, denounced**) 🔳 V-T If you **denounce** a person or an action, you criticize them severely and publicly

🔳 타동사 공개적으로 비난하다 ❑ 독일의 지도자들은 모두 그 기회를 빌어 그 공격을 비난했고 관용을

because you feel strongly that they are wrong or evil. □ *German leaders all took the opportunity to denounce the attacks and plead for tolerance.* ◼ V-T If you **denounce** someone who has broken a rule or law, you report them to the authorities. □ *They were at the mercy of informers who might at any moment denounce them.*

dense /dɛns/ (**denser, densest**) ◼ ADJ Something that is **dense** contains a lot of things or people in a small area. □ *Where Bucharest now stands, there once was a large, dense forest.* ● **densely** ADV □ *Java is a densely populated island.* ◼ ADJ **Dense** fog or smoke is difficult to see through because it is very heavy and dark. □ *A dense column of smoke rose several miles into the air.* ◼ ADJ In science, a **dense** substance is very heavy in relation to its volume. [TECHNICAL] □ *...a small dense star.*

density /dɛnsɪti/ (**densities**) N-VAR **Density** is the extent to which something is filled or covered with people or things. □ *The law which restricts the density of housing in the Balearics was changed recently.* ◼ N-VAR In science, the **density** of a substance or object is the relation of its mass or weight to its volume. [TECHNICAL] □ *Jupiter's moon Io, whose density is 3.5 grams per cubic centimetre, is all rock.*

dent /dɛnt/ (**dents, denting, dented**) ◼ V-T If you **dent** the surface of something, you make a hollow area in it by hitting or pressing it. □ *Its brass feet dented the carpet's thick pile.* ◼ N-COUNT A **dent** is a hollow in the surface of something which has been caused by hitting or pressing it. □ *I was convinced there was a dent in the hood which hadn't been there before.* ◼ V-T If something **dents** your ideas or your pride, it makes you realize that your ideas are wrong, or that you are not as good or successful as you thought. □ *This has not dented the City's enthusiasm for the company.*

Word Link   dent, dont ≈ tooth : den**tal**, den**tist**, **dent**ures

---

dental /dɛntᵊl/ ADJ **Dental** is used to describe things that relate to teeth or to the care and treatment of teeth. [ADJ n] □ *You can get free prescriptions and dental treatment while you are pregnant.*

dentist /dɛntɪst/ (**dentists**) N-COUNT A **dentist** is a person who is qualified to examine and treat people's teeth. □ *Visit your dentist twice a year for a check-up.* ● N-SING **The dentist** or the **dentist's** is used to refer to the surgery or clinic where a dentist works. □ *It's worse than being at the dentist's.* →see **teeth**

dentist's office (**dentist's offices**) N-COUNT A **dentist's office** is the room or house where a dentist works. [AM; BRIT **dentist's surgery**]

dentures /dɛntʃərz/

> The form **denture** is used as a modifier.

N-PLURAL **Dentures** are artificial teeth worn by people who no longer have all their own teeth. □ *People who wear dentures may sleep better if they leave them in overnight.* →see **teeth**

denunciation /dɪnʌnsieɪʃᵊn/ (**denunciations**) ◼ N-VAR **Denunciation of** someone or something is severe public criticism of them. □ *On September 24, he wrote a stinging denunciation of his critics.* ◼ N-VAR **Denunciation** is the act of reporting someone who has broken a rule or law to the authorities. □ *...memories of the denunciation of French Jews to the Nazis during the Second World War.*

Denver boot /dɛnvər bʊt/ (**Denver boots**) N-COUNT A **Denver boot** is a large metal device which is fitted to the wheel of an illegally parked car or other vehicle in order to prevent it from being driven away. The driver has to pay to have the device removed. [AM; BRIT **clamp, wheel clamp**] □ *I watched a couple of cops clap a Denver boot on a green Mercedes.*

deny /dɪnaɪ/ (**denies, denying, denied**) ◼ V-T When you **deny** something, you state that it is not true. □ *She denied both accusations.* □ *The government has denied that the authorities have uncovered a plot to assassinate the president.* ◼ V-T If you **deny** someone something that they need or want, you refuse to let them have it. □ *If he is unlucky, he may find that his ex-partner denies him access to his children.*

> Do not confuse **deny** and **refuse**. If you **deny** something, you say that it is not true. □ *The allegation was denied by government spokesmen.* If someone **denies** you something, they do not allow you to have it. □ *I never denied her anything.* If you **refuse** to do something, you deliberately do not do it, or you say firmly that you will not do it. □ *...people who refuse to change their opinions... He refused to condemn them.* You can **refuse** something that someone offers you. □ *The patient has the right to refuse treatment.* If someone does not allow you to have something you ask for, or to do something you have asked to do, you can say that they **refuse** you. □ *He can run to Dad for money if I refuse him.*

Word Partnership   deny의 연어

N.	deny **a charge**, **officials** deny ◼
	deny **access**, deny **entry**, deny **a request** ◼
V.	**confirm** or deny ◼

Word Link   ant ≈ one who does, has : defend**ant**, deodor**ant**, occup**ant**

---

deodorant /dioʊdərənt/ (**deodorants**) N-MASS **Deodorant** is a substance that you can use on your body to hide or prevent the smell of sweat.

depart /dɪpɑːrt/ (**departs, departing, departed**) ◼ V-T/V-I When something or someone **departs from** a place, they leave it and start a journey to another place. You can also say that someone or something **departs** a place. □ *Our tour*

베풀어 줄 것을 간청했다. ◼ 타동사 고발하다 □ 그들의 운명이 당장이라도 그들을 고발할지 모르는 밀고자들의 손에 달려 있었다.

◼ 형용사 밀집한 ▪ 부카레스트가 있는 현 위치에 한때 큰 밀림이 있었다. ● 밀집하게 부사 ▪ 자바는 인구 밀도가 높은 섬이다. ◼ 형용사 짙은 ▪ 자욱한 연기 기둥이 수 마일 상공으로 피어올랐다. ◼ 형용사 밀도가 높은 [과학 기술] ▪ 작지만 밀도가 높은 별

◼ 가산명사 또는 불가산명사 밀도 ▪ 발레아레스 제도의 주택 밀도를 제한하는 법이 최근에 변경되었다. ◼ 가산명사 또는 불가산명사 밀도 [과학 기술] ▪ 목성의 위성인 이오는 밀도가 입방 센티미터 당 3.5그램인데 전체가 바위로 구성되어 있다.

◼ 타동사 움푹 들어가게 하다 ▪ 그것의 황동 다리 때문에 카펫의 두툼한 섬유 표면에 움푹 패인 자국이 생겨 있었다. ◼ 가산명사 움푹 들어간 곳 ▪ 보닛에 전에 없었던 패인 자국이 생겼다고 나는 확신하고 있었다. ◼ 타동사 약화시키다 ▪ 이것 때문에 런던 금융가가 그 회사에 기울이고 있는 열의가 식지는 않았다.

형용사 치아의; 치과의 ▪ 임신한 동안에는 무료로 처방과 치과 치료를 받을 수 있다.

가산명사 치과 의사 ▪ 정기 검진을 위해 일년에 두 번 치과 의사를 방문해요. ● 단수명사 치과 ▪ 그것은 치과에 가는 것보다 더 안 좋다.

가산명사 치과 진료실 [미국영어; 영국영어 dentist's surgery]

> denture는 수식어구로 쓴다.

복수명사 틀니 ▪ 틀니를 끼는 사람들은 밤에도 그것을 끼고 자면 더 편안히 잘 수도 있다.

◼ 가산명사 또는 불가산명사 고발, 통렬한 비난, 탄핵 ▪ 9월 24일에 그는 자신의 비판자들을 통렬히 탄핵하는 글을 썼다. ◼ 가산명사 또는 불가산명사 고발 ▪ 2차 세계 대전 당시 프랑스의 유태인들을 나치에게 고발했던 일에 대한 기억

가산명사 (주차 위반 차량에 채우는) 바퀴 자물쇠 [미국영어; 영국영어 clamp, wheel clamp] ▪ 나는 경관 두 명이 녹색 메르세데스에 바퀴 자물쇠를 채우는 것을 지켜봤다.

◼ 타동사 부인하다 ▪ 그녀는 두 가지 혐의를 모두 부인했다. ▪ 정부는 대통령을 암살하려는 음모를 당국이 밝혀냈다는 사실을 부인했다. ◼ 타동사 거절하다 ▪ 그가 운이 없는 경우에는, 그가 아이들과 만나는 것을 전처가 허락하지 않을 수도 있다.

> deny와 refuse를 혼동하지 않도록 하시오. 무엇을 deny하면, 그것이 사실이 아니라고 말하는 것이다. ▪ 그 주장은 정부 대변인들에 의해 부인되었다. 누가 당신에게 무엇을 deny하면, 당신이 그것을 갖도록 허락하지 않는 것이다. ▪ 나는 결코 그녀에게 어떤 것도 거절하지 않았다. 무엇을 하는 것을 refuse하면, 의도적으로 그것을 하지 않거나 그것을 하지 않겠다고 확고하게 말하는 것이다. ▪ ...자기의 의견을 바꾸기를 거부하는 사람들... 그는 그들을 비난하기를 거부했다. 누가 당신에게 제공하는 것을 refuse할 수도 있다. ▪ 환자는 치료를 거부할 권리가 있다. 누가 당신이 요청하는 것을 갖도록 허락하지 않거나, 하겠다고 요청하는 것을 하도록 허락하지 않으면, 그 사람이 당신을 refuse한다고 말할 수 있다. ▪ 내가 그에게 거절하면 그는 아빠로부터 돈을 얻으려 달려갈 수 있다.

물질명사 탈취제

◼ 타동사/자동사 출발하다 ▪ 우리 관광단은 3월 31일에 히드로 공항을 출발해서 다음 4월 16일에 돌아온다. ▪ 아침에 맥도날드 씨가 시드니로 출발했다.

a b c d e f g h i j k l m n o p q r s t u v w x y z

A

departs from Heathrow Airport on 31 March and returns 16 April. ❑ In the morning Mr. McDonald departed for Sydney. ❷ V-I If you **depart from** a traditional, accepted, or agreed way of doing something, you do it in a different or unexpected way. ❑ Why is it in this country that we have departed from good educational sense?

가산명사 부서 ❑ 미국의 보건 및 교육, 복지 담당 부서 ❑ 그는 영업부로 자리를 옮겼다.

B

de|part|ment ♦♦♦ /dɪpɑ̱rtmənt/ (**departments**) N-COUNT A **department** is one of the sections in an organization such as a government, business, or university. A **department** is also one of the sections in a large store. ❑ ...the U.S. Department of Health, Education, and Welfare. ❑ He moved to the sales department.

C

de|part|men|tal /dɪ̱pɑrtme̱ntᵊl/ ADJ **Departmental** is used to describe the activities, responsibilities, or possessions of a department in a government, company, or other organization. [ADJ n] ❑ The Secretary of State for Education is right to seek a bigger departmental budget.

형용사 부서의 ❑ 교육부 장관이 교육부에 더 많은 예산을 책정해 달라고 요청한 것은 옳은 일이다.

D

de|part|ment store (**department stores**) N-COUNT A **department store** is a large store which sells many different kinds of goods. ❑ ...the dazzling window displays of world-famous department stores such as Macy's and Bloomingdales.

가산명사 백화점 ❑ 메이시즈나 블루밍데일즈 등과 같이 전 세계적으로 유명한 백화점들의 환상적인 상품 진열

E

de|par|ture ♦♢♢ /dɪpɑ̱rtʃər/ (**departures**) ❶ N-VAR **Departure** or a **departure** is the act of going away from somewhere. ❑ ...the President's departure for Helsinki. ❑ They hoped this would lead to the departure of all foreign forces from the country. ❷ N-COUNT If someone does something different or unusual, you can refer to their action as a **departure**. ❑ Taylor announced another departure from practice in that England will train at Wembley.

❶ 가산명사 또는 불가산명사 출발 ❑ 대통령이 헬싱키로 출발함 ❑ 그들은 이로 인해 모든 외국 병력이 국내에서 떠날 것이라고 기대했었다. ❷ 가산명사 이탈 ❑ 테일러는 다시 한 번 관행에서 벗어나 잉글랜드 팀이 웸블리에서 훈련하게 될 것이라고 밝혔다.

F

G

de|par|ture lounge (**departure lounges**) N-COUNT In an airport, the **departure lounge** is the place where passengers wait before they get onto their plane.

가산명사 (공항의) 출발 라운지

H

Word Link   pend ≈ hanging : de*pend*, *pend*ant, *pend*ing

I

de|pend ♦♦♦ /dɪpe̱nd/ (**depends, depending, depended**) ❶ V-I If you say that one thing **depends on** another, you mean that the first thing will be affected or determined by the second. ❑ The cooking time needed depends on the size of the potato. ❷ V-I If you **depend on** someone or something, you need them in order to be able to survive physically, financially, or emotionally. ❑ He depended on his writing for his income. ❸ V-I If you can **depend on** a person, organization, or law, you know that they will support you or help you when you need them. ❑ "You can depend on me," Cross assured him. ❹ V-I You use **depend** in expressions such as **it depends** to indicate that you cannot give a clear answer to a question because the answer will be affected or determined by other factors. ❑ "But how long can you stay in the house?" — "I don't know. It depends." ❺ PHRASE You use **depending on** when you are saying that something varies according to the circumstances described. ❑ I tend to have a different answer, depending on the family.

❶ 자동사 달려 있다 ❑ 조리 시간은 감자의 크기에 달려 있다. ❷ 자동사 의존하다 ❑ 그는 글을 써서 수입을 얻었다. ❸ 자동사 의지하다 ❑ "날 믿어도 돼."라고 크로스는 그를 안심시켰다. ❹ 자동사 상황에 따라 다르다 ❑ "그런데 그 집에 얼마나 오래 머물 수 있는데?" "잘 모르겠어. 상황에 따라 달라." ❺ 구 -에 따라 ❑ 나는 가족에 따라 다른 답변을 제공하곤 한다.

J

K

L

M

Word Partnership   depend의 연어

N.	depend **on circumstances**, **outcome will** depend, **survival will/may** depend, depend **on the weather** ❶
ADV.	depend **largely** ❶
PREP.	depend **on** *someone/something* ❶ ❷ ❸

N

O

de|pend|able /dɪpe̱ndəbᵊl/ ADJ If you say that someone or something is **dependable**, you approve of them because you feel that you can be sure that they will always act consistently or sensibly, or do what you need them to do. [APPROVAL] ❑ He was a good friend, a dependable companion.

형용사 믿을 수 있는 [마음에 듦] ❑ 그는 한 사람의 좋은 친구이자 믿을 수 있는 동료였다.

P

de|pend|ant /dɪpe̱ndənt/ →see **dependent**

Q

Word Link   ence ≈ state, condition : depend*ence*, excell*ence*, independ*ence*

R

de|pend|ence /dɪpe̱ndəns/ ❶ N-UNCOUNT Your **dependence on** something or someone is your need for them in order to succeed or be able to survive. ❑ ...the city's traditional dependence on tourism. ❷ N-UNCOUNT If you talk about drug **dependence** or alcohol **dependence**, you are referring to a situation where someone is addicted to drugs or is an alcoholic. ❑ French doctors tend to regard drug dependence as a form of deep-rooted psychological disorder. ❸ N-UNCOUNT You talk about the **dependence** of one thing **on** another when the first thing will be affected or determined by the second. ❑ ... the dependence of politicians on rich donors to fund their increasingly expensive campaigns.

❶ 불가산명사 의존 ❑ 그 도시가 전통적으로 관광 산업에 의존해 온 것 ❷ 불가산명사 의존 ❑ 프랑스 의사들은 약물에 대한 의존을 뿌리 깊은 정신 질환의 한 형태로 여기는 경향이 있다. ❸ 불가산명사 종속 ❑ 점점 늘어나는 선거 유세 비용을 지원해 줄 돈 많은 후원자들에 대한 정치인들의 의존

S

T

de|pend|en|cy /dɪpe̱ndənsi/ (**dependencies**) ❶ N-COUNT A **dependency** is a country which is controlled by another country. ❑ ...the tiny British dependency of Montserrat in the eastern Caribbean. ❷ N-UNCOUNT You talk about someone's **dependency** when they have a deep emotional, physical, or financial need for a particular person or thing, especially one that you consider excessive or undesirable. ❑ We saw his dependency on his mother and worried that he might not survive long if anything happened to her. ❸ N-VAR If you talk about alcohol **dependency** or chemical **dependency**, you are referring to a situation where someone is an alcoholic or is addicted to drugs. [mainly AM] ❑ In 1985, he began to show signs of alcohol and drug dependency.

❶ 가산명사 보호령 ❑ 카리브 해 동부에 있는 영국의 작은 보호령인 몬트세라트 ❷ 불가산명사 의존 ❑ 그가 어머니에게 얼마나 의존하는지를 보았기 때문에 우리는 그 어머니에게 무슨 일이라도 생긴다면 그가 오래 살지 못하지 않을까 걱정했다. ❸ 가산명사 또는 불가산명사 의존증 [주로 미국영어] ❑ 1985년에 그는 알코올과 약물 의존증 증상을 보이기 시작했다.

U

V

W

X

Word Link   ent ≈ one who does, has : depend*ent*, resid*ent*, superintend*ent*

Y

de|pend|ent /dɪpe̱ndənt/ (**dependents**) [BRIT also **dependant** for meaning ❸] ❶ ADJ To be **dependent** on something or someone means to need them in order to succeed or be able to survive. ❑ The local economy is overwhelmingly dependent on oil and gas extraction. ❷ ADJ If one thing is **dependent on** another, the first thing will be affected or determined by the second. [v-link ADJ on/upon n] ❑ ...companies whose earnings are largely dependent on the performance of the Chinese

[의미 ❸은 영국영어로 dependant] ❶ 형용사 의존하는 ❑ 그 지방 경제는 석유와 가스 생산에 지나치게 의존한다. ❷ 형용사 종속적인 ❑ 중국 경제의 성과에 따라 그 수입이 왔다 갔다 하는 회사들 ❸ 가산명사 피부양자 [격식체] ❑ 영국의 재향군인회는 퇴직 군인들과 그들의 피부양자들을

Z

(시작 부분 우상단)
❷ 자동사 이탈하다 ❑ 이 나라가 왜 교육에 대한 올바른 분별력을 버렸을까?

economy. ◼ N-COUNT Your **dependents** are the people you support financially, such as your children. [FORMAL] ❑ *The British Legion raises funds to help ex-service personnel and their dependents.*

돕기 위해 기금을 모은다.

Word Link   pict ≈ painting : de*pict*, *pict*ure, *pict*uresque

---

de|pict /dɪpɪkt/ (depicts, depicting, depicted) V-T To **depict** someone or something means to show or represent them in a work of art such as a drawing or painting. ❑ ...*a gallery of pictures depicting Nelson's most famous battles.*

타동사 묘사하다 ❑ 넬슨이 치른 가장 유명한 전투들을 묘사한 그림들의 전시관

Word Link   ple ≈ filling : com*ple*ment, com*ple*te, de*ple*te

---

de|plete /dɪplit/ (depletes, depleting, depleted) V-T To **deplete** a stock or amount of something means to reduce it. [FORMAL] ❑ ...*substances that deplete the ozone layer.* ● de|plet|ed ADJ ❑ ...*Lee's worn and depleted army.* ● de|ple|tion /dɪplɪʃⁿn/ N-UNCOUNT ❑ ...*the depletion of underground water supplies.*

타동사 고갈시키다 [격식체] ❑ 오존층을 고갈시키는 물질들 ● 고갈된 형용사 ❑ 리의 지치고 고갈된 군대 ● 고갈 불가산명사 ❑ 지하 수자원의 고갈

de|plor|able /dɪplɔrəbⁿl/ ADJ If you say that something is **deplorable**, you think that it is very bad and unacceptable. [FORMAL] ❑ *Many of them live under deplorable conditions.*

형용사 통탄할 [격식체] ❑ 그들 대부분은 비참한 조건 속에서 산다.

de|plore /dɪplɔr/ (deplores, deploring, deplored) V-T If you say that you **deplore** something, you think it is very wrong or immoral. [FORMAL] ❑ *He deplored the fact that the Foreign Secretary was driven into resignation.*

타동사 개탄하다 [격식체] ❑ 외무부 장관이 사임을 강요당했다는 사실에 그는 개탄했다.

de|ploy /dɪplɔɪ/ (deploys, deploying, deployed) V-T To **deploy** troops or military resources means to organize or position them so that they are ready to be used. ❑ *The president said he had no intention of deploying ground troops.* →see **army**

타동사 투입하다 ❑ 대통령은 지상군을 투입할 계획이 전혀 없다고 말했다.

de|ploy|ment /dɪplɔɪmənt/ (deployments) N-VAR The **deployment** of troops, resources, or equipment is the organization and positioning of them so that they are ready for quick action. ❑ ...*the deployment of troops into townships.*

가산명사 또는 불가산명사 투입 ❑ 병력의 마을 내 투입

de|port /dɪpɔrt/ (deports, deporting, deported) V-T If a government **deports** someone, usually someone who is not a citizen of that country, it sends them out of the country because they have committed a crime or because it believes they do not have the right to be there. ❑ ...*a government decision earlier this month to deport all illegal immigrants.* ● de|por|ta|tion /dipɔrteɪʃⁿn/ (deportations) N-VAR ❑ ...*thousands of Albanian migrants facing deportation.*

타동사 추방하다 ❑ 모든 불법 이민자를 추방한다고 정부가 이번 달 초에 내린 결정 ● 추방 가산명사 또는 불가산명사 ❑ 추방 조치에 직면한 수천 명의 알바니아 이주민

de|pose /dɪpoʊz/ (deposes, deposing, deposed) V-T If a ruler or political leader **is deposed**, they are forced to give up their position. [usu passive] ❑ *Mr. Ben Bella was deposed in a coup in 1965.*

타동사 면직당하다 ❑ 벤 벨라 씨는 1965년 쿠데타로 물러났다.

Word Link   pos ≈ placing : de*pos*it, pre*pos*ition, re*pos*itory

---

de|pos|it ♦◇◇ /dɪpɒzɪt/ (deposits, depositing, deposited) ◼ N-COUNT A **deposit** is a sum of money which is part of the full price of something, and which you pay when you agree to buy it. ❑ *The initial deposit required to open an account is a minimum 100 dollars.* ◼ N-COUNT A **deposit** is a sum of money which is in a bank account or savings account, especially a sum which will be left there for some time. ◼ N-COUNT A **deposit** is an amount of a substance that has been left somewhere as a result of a chemical or geological process. ❑ ...*underground deposits of gold and diamonds.* ◼ V-T To **deposit** someone or something somewhere means to put them or leave them there. ❑ *Just before the explosion someone was seen running from the scene after apparently depositing the packet.* ◼ V-T If you **deposit** something somewhere, you put it where it will be safe until it is needed again. ❑ *You are advised to deposit valuables in the hotel safe.* ◼ V-T If you **deposit** a sum of money, you pay it into a bank account or savings account. ❑ *The drawbacks here are that the customer has to deposit a minimum of £100 monthly.* →see **bank**

◼ 가산명사 보증금 ❑ 계좌를 만들기 위해 필요한 첫 예탁금은 최소 100달러이다. ◼ 가산명사 예금 ◼ 가산명사 광상 ❑ 금과 다이아몬드의 지하 광상 ◼ 타동사 두다 ❑ 폭발 직전에 그 꾸러미를 갖다 놓고 현장에서 도망치는 듯한 사람이 목격되었다. ◼ 타동사 맡기다 ❑ 귀중품은 호텔 금고에 맡기는 것이 좋습니다. ◼ 타동사 예금하다 ❑ 이 곳의 단점은 고객이 매달 최소한 100파운드는 예금해야 한다는 것이다.

de|pos|it ac|count (deposit accounts) N-COUNT A **deposit account** is a type of bank account where the money in it earns interest. [BRIT; AM **savings account**]

가산명사 예금 계좌 [영국영어; 미국영어 savings account]

depo|si|tion /dɛpəzɪʃⁿn/ (depositions) N-COUNT A **deposition** is a formal written statement, made for example by a witness to a crime, which can be used in a court of law if the witness cannot be present. ❑ *The material would be checked against the depositions from other witnesses.*

가산명사 진술 조서 ❑ 그 자료를 다른 증인들의 진술서와 대조해서 확인할 것이다.

de|pot /dɪpoʊ, BRIT depəʊ/ (depots) ◼ N-COUNT A **depot** is a bus station or train station. [AM] ❑ *She was reunited with her boyfriend in the bus depot of Ozark, Alabama.* ◼ N-COUNT A **depot** is a place where large amounts of raw materials, equipment, arms, or other supplies are kept until they are needed. ❑ ...*food depots.* ◼ N-COUNT A **depot** is a large building or open area where buses or train engines are kept when they are not being used. [mainly BRIT]

◼ 가산명사 정거장; 정류장 [미국영어] ❑ 그녀는 앨라배마 오자크의 버스 정류장에서 남자 친구와 재회했다. ◼ 가산명사 창고 ❑ 식품 창고 ◼ 가산명사 차고 [주로 영국영어]

de|pre|ci|ate /dɪpr:ʃieɪt/ (depreciates, depreciating, depreciated) V-T/V-I If something such as a currency **depreciates** or if something **depreciates** it, it loses some of its original value. ❑ *Inflation is rising rapidly; the yuan is depreciating.* ❑ *The demand for foreign currency depreciates the real value of local currencies.* ● de|pre|cia|tion /dɪpri:ʃieɪʃⁿn/ (depreciations) N-VAR ❑ ...*miscellaneous costs, including machinery depreciation and wages.*

타동사/자동사 평가 절하하다; 평가 절하되다 ❑ 물가가 급등하고 있다. 그래서 위안화가 평가 절하되고 있다. ❑ 외화에 대한 수요는 자국 화폐의 실질 가치를 떨어뜨린다. ● 절하 가산명사 또는 불가산명사 ❑ 기계 감가상각비와 임금까지 포함한 제반 비용

de|press /dɪpres/ (depresses, depressing, depressed) ◼ V-T If someone or something **depresses** you, they make you feel sad and disappointed. ❑ *I must admit the state of the country depresses me.* ◼ V-T If something **depresses** prices, wages, or figures, it causes them to become lower. ❑ *The stronger U.S. dollar depressed sales.*

◼ 타동사 우울하게 하다 ❑ 나라가 처한 상황이 나를 우울하게 한다는 것을 인정해야겠다. ◼ 타동사 떨어뜨리다 ❑ 강세인 미국 달러가 판매를 저하시켰다.

de|pressed /dɪprest/ ◼ ADJ If you are **depressed**, you are sad and feel that you cannot enjoy anything, because your situation is so difficult and unpleasant. ❑ *She's been very depressed and upset about this whole situation.* ◼ ADJ A **depressed** place or industry does not have enough business or employment to be successful. ❑ *Many states already have Enterprise Zones and legislation that encourage investment in depressed areas.*

◼ 형용사 우울한 ❑ 그녀는 이 상황 전체에 대해 크게 낙담하여 심란해 하고 있는 상태이다. ◼ 형용사 침체된 ❑ 많은 주들이 침체된 지역에 대한 투자를 장려하는 기업 지구와 법률을 이미 가지고 있다.

A

de|press|ing /dɪprɛsɪŋ/ ADJ Something that is **depressing** makes you feel sad and disappointed. ❑ *Yesterday's unemployment figures were as depressing as those of the previous 22 months.* ● **de|press|ing|ly** ADV ❑ *It all sounded depressingly familiar to Janet.*

형용사 우울하게 하는 ❑어제 발표된 실업 수치는 22개월 전에 발표되었던 실업 수치만큼이나 우울한 소식이었다. ● 우울하게 부사 ❑자넷에게 그 모든 것은 우울할 정도로 친숙하게 들렸다.

B

de|pres|sion ◆◇◇ /dɪprɛʃ⁰n/ (**depressions**) **1** N-VAR **Depression** is a mental state in which you are sad and feel that you cannot enjoy anything, because your situation is so difficult and unpleasant. ❑ *Mr. Thomas was suffering from depression.* **2** N-COUNT A **depression** is a time when there is very little economic activity, which causes a lot of unemployment and poverty. ❑ *He never forgot the hardships he witnessed during the Great Depression of the 1930s.* **3** N-COUNT A **depression** in a surface is an area which is lower than the parts surrounding it. ❑ *...an area pockmarked by rain-filled depressions.* **4** N-COUNT A **depression** is a mass of air that has a low pressure and that often causes rain. ❑ *To the northwest lies a depression with clouds and rain.*

C

1 가산명사 또는 불가산명사 우울증 ❑토머스 씨는 우울증에 시달리고 있었다. **2** 가산명사 불황 ❑1930년대의 대공황 때 목격한 고난을 그는 잊은 적이 없었다. **3** 가산명사 움푹 파인 곳 ❑빗물 웅덩이가 난잡하게 널려 있는 지역 **4** 가산명사 저기압 ❑북서쪽으로는 구름과 비를 동반한 저기압이 자리 잡고 있습니다.

D

dep|ri|va|tion /dɛprɪveɪʃ⁰n/ (**deprivations**) N-VAR If you suffer **deprivation**, you do not have or are prevented from having something that you want or need. ❑ *Millions more suffer from serious sleep deprivation caused by long work hours.*

가산명사 또는 불가산명사 결핍; 박탈 ❑또 수백만 명이나 되는 사람들은 장시간 근무로 인한 심각한 수면 결핍으로 고생한다.

E

de|prive /dɪpraɪv/ (**deprives, depriving, deprived**) V-T If you **deprive** someone **of** something that they want or need, you take it away from them, or you prevent them from having it. ❑ *They've been deprived of the fuel necessary to heat their homes.*

타동사 빼앗다, 박탈하다 ❑그들은 가정 난방에 필요한 연료를 박탈당해 왔다.

F

de|prived /dɪpraɪvd/ ADJ **Deprived** people or people from **deprived** areas do not have the things that people consider to be essential in life, for example acceptable living conditions or education. ❑ *...probably the most severely deprived children in the country.*

형용사 불우한, 혜택 받지 못한 ❑아마도 그 나라에서 가장 심하게 불우할 아이들

G

dept. (**depts.**) **Dept.** is used as a written abbreviation for **department**, usually in the name of a particular department. [BRIT **dept**] ❑ *...the Internal Affairs Dept.*

department의 약어 [영국영어 dept] ❑내무부

H

depth ◆◇◇ /dɛpθ/ (**depths**) **1** N-VAR The **depth** of something such as a river or hole is the distance downward from its top surface, or between its upper and lower surfaces. ❑ *The depth of a standard straight pelmet is usually about 32cm.* ❑ *The smaller lake ranges from five to fourteen feet in depth.* ❑ *The depth of the shaft is 520 yards.* **2** N-VAR The **depth** of something such as a closet or drawer is the distance between its front surface and its back. **3** N-VAR If an emotion is very strongly or intensely felt, you can talk about its **depth**. ❑ *I am well aware of the depth of feeling that exists in Londonderry.* **4** N-UNCOUNT The **depth** of a situation is its extent and seriousness. ❑ *The country's leadership had underestimated the depth of the crisis.* **5** N-UNCOUNT The **depth** of someone's knowledge is the great amount that they know. ❑ *We felt at home with her and were impressed with the depth of her knowledge.* **6** N-PLURAL The **depths** are places which are a long way below the surface of the sea or earth. [LITERARY] ❑ *Leaves, brown with long immersion, rose to the surface and vanished back into the depths.* **7** N-PLURAL If you talk about the **depths** of an area, you mean the parts of it which are very far from the edge. ❑ *...the depths of the countryside.* **8** N-PLURAL If you are **in the depths of** an unpleasant emotion, you feel that emotion very strongly. ❑ *I was in the depths of despair when the baby was terribly sick every day, and was losing weight.* **9** PHRASE If you deal with a subject **in depth**, you deal with it very thoroughly and consider all the aspects of it. ❑ *We will discuss these three areas in depth.* **10** PHRASE If you say that someone is **out of** their **depth**, you mean that they are in a situation that is much too difficult for them to be able to cope with it. ❑ *Mr. Gibson is clearly intellectually out of his depth.* **11** PHRASE If you are **out of** your **depth**, you are in water that is deeper than you are tall, with the result that you cannot stand up with your head above water. ❑ *Somehow I got out of my depth in the pool.*

I

J

K

L

M

1 가산명사 또는 불가산명사 깊이 ❑대개 일반적으로 주름 없는 커튼봉 덮개 장식의 세로 길이는 약 32센티미터이다. ❑더 작은 호수의 깊이는 5피트에서 14피트에 이른다. ❑그 수직갱의 깊이는 520야드이다. **2** 가산명사 또는 불가산명사 (서랍이나 선반 등의) 깊이 **3** 가산명사 또는 불가산명사 (감정의) 깊이, 강도 ❑런던데리에 퍼져 있는 감정의 강도에 대해 잘 알고 있다. **4** 불가산명사 심각성 ❑그 나라의 지도부는 위기의 심각성을 과소평가했었다. **5** 불가산명사 (학식의) 깊이 ❑우리는 그녀에게서 편안함을 느꼈고 그녀가 지닌 학식의 깊이에 깊은 감명을 받았다. **6** 복수명사 깊숙한 곳 [문예체] ❑오랫동안 침수되어 갈색이 된 잎사귀들이 수면으로 떠올랐다가 다시 깊은 곳으로 사라졌다. **7** 복수명사 깊숙이 들어간 곳, 오지 ❑시골의 오지 **8** 복수명사 (감정의) 깊은 골, 구렁텅이 ❑아기가 날마다 몹시 아팠을 때, 나는 절망의 구렁텅이에 빠져 몸무게가 줄고 있었다. **9** 구 깊이, 철저히 ❑우리는 이 세 가지 분야에 대해 철저히 논의할 것이다. **10** 구 역량이 미치지 못하는 ❑깁슨 씨는 확실히 지적 역량이 부족하다. **11** 구 키 높이보다 깊은 곳에 빠진 ❑어쩌다 보니 나는 저수지 속에서 키가 닿지 않는 깊은 곳에 빠졌다.

N

O

depu|ty ◆◆◇ /dɛpyəti/ (**deputies**) **1** N-COUNT A **deputy** is the second most important person in an organization such as a business or government department. Someone's **deputy** often acts on their behalf when they are not there. ❑ *...Jack Lang, France's minister for culture, and his deputy, Catherine Tasca.* **2** N-COUNT In some legislatures, the elected members are called **deputies**. ❑ *The president appealed to deputies to approve the plan quickly.*

P

1 가산명사 부-, 차관 ❑프랑스 문화부 장관 잭 랭과 차관 카트린느 타스카 **2** 가산명사 의원, 대의원 ❑대통령은 그 안을 빨리 승인해 달라고 의원들에게 호소했다.

Q

de|rail /dɪreɪl/ (**derails, derailing, derailed**) **1** V-T To **derail** something such as a plan or a series of negotiations means to prevent it from continuing as planned. [JOURNALISM] ❑ *The present wave of political killings is the work of people trying to derail peace talks.* **2** V-T/V-I If a train **is derailed** or if it **derails**, it comes off the track on which it is running. ❑ *At least six people were killed and about twenty injured when a train was derailed in an isolated mountain region.*

R

1 타동사 무산시키다 [언론] ❑현재의 과상적인 정치적 숙청은 평화 회담을 무산시키려는 사람들의 작품이다. **2** 타동사/자동사 탈선하다 ❑고립된 산간 지역에서 기차가 탈선하여 최소한 여섯 명이 숨지고 스무 명 가량이 부상당했다.

S

de|ranged /dɪreɪndʒd/ ADJ Someone who is **deranged** behaves in a wild and uncontrolled way, often as a result of mental illness. ❑ *Three years ago today a deranged man shot and killed 14 people in the main square.*

T

형용사 미친 ❑삼 년 전 오늘 어떤 미친 남자가 중앙 광장에서 총을 쏴서 14명을 죽였다.

de|regu|late /diregyəleɪt/ (**deregulates, deregulating, deregulated**) V-T To **deregulate** something means to remove controls and regulations from it. ❑ *...the need to deregulate the U.S. airline industry.*

U

타동사 (규제를) 철폐하다 ❑미국 항공 산업에 대한 규제를 철폐할 필요

de|regu|la|tion /diregyəleɪʃ⁰n/ N-UNCOUNT **Deregulation** is the removal of controls and restrictions in a particular area of business or trade. [BUSINESS] ❑ *Since deregulation, banks are permitted to set their own interest rates.*

V

불가산명사 규제 철폐 [경제] ❑규제 철폐 이후로, 은행들은 자체적으로 금리를 정할 수 있게 되었다.

der|elict /dɛrɪlɪkt/ ADJ A place or building that is **derelict** is empty and in a bad state of repair because it has not been used or lived in for a long time. ❑ *Her body was found dumped in a derelict warehouse less than a mile from her home.*

W

형용사 유기된, 버려진 ❑그녀의 시체는 집에서부터 1마일도 안 되는 안 쓰는 창고에 유기된 채로 발견되었다.

X

Word Link	rid, ris ≈ laughing : de**ride**, de**ris**ion, **rid**icule

de|ride /dɪraɪd/ (**derides, deriding, derided**) V-T If you **deride** someone or something, you say that they are stupid or have no value. [FORMAL] ❑ *Opposition MPs derided the Government's response to the crisis.*

Y

타동사 조롱하다, 비웃다 [격식체] ❑야당 의원들은 위기에 대한 정부의 대응을 조롱했다.

de|ri|sion /dɪrɪʒ⁰n/ N-UNCOUNT If you treat someone or something with **derision**, you express contempt for them. ❑ *He tried to calm them, but was greeted with shouts of derision.*

Z

불가산명사 조롱 ❑그는 그들을 진정시키려고 애썼지만, 돌아오는 것은 조롱하는 고함 소리였다.

de|ri|sive /dɪraɪsɪv/ ADJ A **derisive** noise, expression, or remark expresses contempt. ❏ *There was a short, derisive laugh.*

형용사 조롱하는 ❏ 짧고 조롱 섞인 웃음소리가 들렸다.

de|riva|tive /dɪrɪvətɪv/ (**derivatives**) N-COUNT A **derivative** is something which has been developed or obtained from something else. ❏ *...a poppy-seed derivative similar to heroin.*

가산명사 파생물 ❏ 헤로인과 유사한 양귀비씨 파생물

de|rive /dɪraɪv/ (**derives, deriving, derived**) ■ V-T If you **derive** something such as pleasure or benefit **from** a person or from something, you get it from them. [FORMAL] ❏ *Mr. Ying is one of those happy people who derive pleasure from helping others.* ■ V-T/V-I If you say that something such as a word or feeling **derives** or is **derived from** something else, you mean that it comes from that thing. ❏ *The name Anastasia is derived from a Greek word meaning "of the resurrection."*

■ 타동사 얻다, 이끌어 내다 [격식체] ❏ 잉 씨는 다른 사람을 돕는 일에서 기쁨을 얻는 행복한 사람들 중 하나이다. ■ 타동사/자동사 유래하다, 파생하다 ❏ 아나스타샤라는 이름은 '부활의'라는 뜻의 그리스어에서 유래한 것이다.

de|roga|tory /dɪrɒgətɔri, BRIT dɪrɒgətri/ ADJ If you make a **derogatory** remark or comment about someone or something, you express your low opinion of them. ❏ *He refused to withdraw derogatory remarks made about his boss.*

형용사 경멸적인 ❏ 그는 자신의 상사에 대해 했던 경멸적인 언사를 철회하기를 거부했다.

Word Link	de ≈ from, down, away : de**flate**, de**scend**, de**tach**

Word Link	scend ≈ climbing : a**scend**, conde**scend**, de**scend**

de|scend /dɪsɛnd/ (**descends, descending, descended**) ■ V-T/V-I If you **descend** or if you **descend** a staircase, you move downward from a higher to a lower level. [FORMAL] ❏ *Things are cooler and more damp as we descend to the cellar.* ■ V-I If a large group of people arrive to see you, especially if their visit is unexpected or causes you a lot of work, you can say that they **have descended on** you. ❏ *Some 3,000 city officials will descend on Capitol Hill on Tuesday to lobby for more money.* ■ V-I If you say that someone **descends** to behavior which you consider unacceptable, you are expressing your disapproval of the fact that they do it. [DISAPPROVAL] ❏ *We're not going to descend to such methods.* ■ V-I When you want to emphasize that the situation that someone is entering is very bad, you can say that they **are descending into** that situation. [EMPHASIS] ❏ *He was ultimately overthrown and the country descended into chaos.*

■ 타동사/자동사 내려가다 [격식체] ❏ 지하실로 내려가니 더 서늘하고 습기 차다. ■ 자동사 들이닥치다 ❏ 화요일에 3천 명 가량의 시 임원들이 돈을 더 달라고 로비를 하기 위해 국회에 들이닥칠 것이다. ■ 자동사 영락하다, 전락하다 [탐탁찮음] ❏ 우리는 야비하게 그런 방식을 쓰지는 않을 것이다. ■ 자동사 (나쁜 상황에) 빠져들다 [강조] ❏ 그는 마침내 타도되었고 나라는 혼란에 빠져들었다.

de|scend|ant /dɪsɛndənt/ (**descendants**) ■ N-COUNT Someone's **descendants** are the people in later generations who are related to them. ❏ *They are descendants of the original English and Scottish settlers.* ■ N-COUNT Something modern which developed from an older thing can be called a **descendant of** it. ❏ *His design was a descendant of a 1956 device.*

■ 가산명사 자손, 후예 ❏ 그들은 잉글랜드와 스코틀랜드 토착민들의 자손이다. ■ 가산명사 현대판 ❏ 그의 디자인은 1956년 고안된 장치의 현대판이었다.

de|scend|ed /dɪsɛndɪd/ ADJ A person who is **descended from** someone who lived a long time ago is directly related to them. [v-link ADJ from n] ❏ *She used to tell us that she was descended from some Scottish Lord but we thought she was bragging.*

형용사 -의 후손인 ❏ 그녀는 자신이 스코틀랜드 귀족의 후손이라고 우리에게 말하곤 했지만, 우리는 그녀가 허풍을 떨고 있다고 생각했다.

de|scent /dɪsɛnt/ (**descents**) ■ N-VAR A **descent** is a movement from a higher to a lower level or position. ❏ *Sixteen of the youngsters set off for help, but during the descent three collapsed in the cold and rain.* ■ N-COUNT A **descent** is a surface that slopes downward, for example the side of a steep hill. ❏ *On the descents, cyclists spin past cars, freewheeling downhill at tremendous speed.* ■ N-SING When you want to emphasize that a situation becomes very bad, you can talk about someone's or something's **descent** into that situation. [EMPHASIS] ❏ *...his swift descent from respected academic to struggling small businessman.* ■ N-UNCOUNT You use **descent** to talk about a person's family background, for example their nationality or social status. [FORMAL] ❏ *All the contributors were of African descent.*

■ 가산명사 또는 불가산명사 하강, 내려가기 ❏ 젊은이들 열 여섯 명이 돕기 위해 출발했지만, 하강 중에 세 명이 추위와 빗속에서 쓰러졌다. ■ 가산명사 내리받이, 내리막 경사 ❏ 내리받이에서 자전거 선수들은 자동차들을 지나쳐 질주하며, 굉장한 속도로 언덕을 활강해 내려갔다. ■ 단수명사 전락, 몰락 [강조] ❏ 존경받는 학자에서 이리둥바 하는 영세 사업가로의 급속한 그의 몰락 ■ 불가산명사 출신, 혈통 [격식체] ❏ 기부자들 모두가 아프리카 출신이었다.

de|scribe ♦♦♦ /dɪskraɪb/ (**describes, describing, described**) ■ V-T If you **describe** a person, object, event, or situation, you say what they are like or what happened. ❏ *We asked her to describe what kind of things she did in her spare time.* ❏ *She read a poem by Carver which describes their life together.* ■ V-T If a person **describes** someone or something **as** a particular thing, he or she believes that they are that thing and says so. ❏ *He described it as an extraordinarily tangled and complicated tale.* ❏ *Even his closest allies describe him as forceful, aggressive and determined.*

■ 타동사 묘사하다, 설명하다 ❏ 우리는 그녀에게 여가 시간에 무슨 일을 하는지 설명해 달라고 했다. ❏ 그녀는 그들이 함께 한 삶을 묘사한 카버의 시를 읽었다. ■ 타동사 (-라고) 평하다 ❏ 그는 그것을 엄청나게 그런 혼란스럽고 복잡한 이야기라고 평했다. ❏ 그의 가장 가까운 협력자들도 그를 가리켜 강압적이고 호전적이며 단호하다고 말한다.

> When you use **describe** with an indirect object, you must put **to** in front of the indirect object. ❏ *He later described to me what he had found... Could you describe the man to the police?* You do not say, for example, "He described me what he had found."

> describe를 간접 목적어와 함께 쓰면, 간접 목적어 앞에 to를 써야 한다. ❏ 그는 자기가 발견한 것을 나중에 내게 설명해 주었다... 그 남자의 인상착의를 경찰에게 말씀해 주시겠습니까? 예를 들어 "He described me what he had found."라고는 하지 않는다.

de|scrip|tion ♦♦◇ /dɪskrɪpʃən/ (**descriptions**) ■ N-VAR A **description** of someone or something is an account which explains what they are or what they look like. ❏ *Police have issued a description of the man who was aged between fifty and sixty.* ❏ *...a detailed description of the movements and battle plans of Italy's fleet.* ■ N-SING If something is **of** a particular **description**, it belongs to the general class of items that are mentioned. ❏ *Events of this description occurred daily.* ■ N-UNCOUNT You can say that something is **beyond description**, or that it **defies description**, to emphasize that it is very unusual, impressive, terrible, or extreme. [EMPHASIS] ❏ *His face is weary beyond description.*

■ 가산명사 또는 불가산명사 기술, 묘사 ❏ 경찰은 나이가 오십에서 육십 사이인 남자의 인상착의를 발표했다. ❏ 이탈리아 함대의 이동과 전투 계획에 대한 상세한 묘사 ■ 단수명사 종목; 종류 ❏ 이런 종류의 사건들이 날마다 일어났다. ■ 불가산명사 형언, 묘사 [강조] ❏ 그의 얼굴은 형언할 수 없을 정도로 피폐해 있다.

Thesaurus	description의 참조어
N.	account, characterization, summary ■
	category, class, kind, type ■

Word Partnership	description의 연어
ADJ.	**accurate** description, **brief** description, **detailed** description, **physical** description, **vague** description ■
V.	**fit a** description, **give a** description, **match a** description ■

a b c d e f g h i j k l m n o p q r s t u v w x y z

A
B
C
D
E
F
G
H
I
J
K
L
M
N
O
P
Q
R
S
T
U
V
W
X
Y
Z

de|scrip|tive /dɪskrɪptɪv/ ADJ Descriptive language or writing indicates what someone or something is like. ❏ The Group adopted the simpler, more descriptive title of Angina Support Group.

des|ecrate /dɛsɪkreɪt/ (**desecrates, desecrating, desecrated**) V-T If someone **desecrates** something which is considered to be holy or very special, they deliberately damage or insult it. ❏ She shouldn't have desecrated the picture of a religious leader. ● **des|ecra|tion** /dɛsɪkreɪʃⁿn/ N-UNCOUNT ❏ The whole area has been shocked by the desecration of the cemetery.

des|ert ♦♢♢ (**deserts, deserting, deserted**)

> The noun is pronounced /dɛzəʳt/. The verb is pronounced /dɪzɜːʳt/ and is hyphenated de|sert.

■ N-VAR A **desert** is a large area of land, usually in a hot region, where there is almost no water, rain, trees, or plants. ❏ ...the Sahara Desert. ❷ V-T If people or animals **desert** a place, they leave it and it becomes empty. ❏ Poor farmers are deserting their parched farm fields and coming here looking for jobs. ● **de|sert|ed** ADJ ❏ She led them into a deserted sidestreet. ❸ V-T If someone **deserts** you, they go away and leave you, and no longer help or support you. ❏ Mrs. Roding's husband deserted her years ago. ● **de|ser|tion** /dɪzɜːʳʃⁿn/ (**desertions**) N-VAR ❏ It was a long time since she'd referred to her father's desertion. ❹ V-T/V-I If you **desert** something that you support, use, or are involved with, you stop supporting it, using it, or being involved with it. ❏ The paper's new price rise, putting it up to 27p, will encourage readers to desert in even greater droves. ❏ He was pained to see many youngsters deserting kibbutz life. ● **de|ser|tion** N-VAR ❏ They blamed his proposal for much of the mass desertion by the Socialist electorate. ❺ V-T/V-I If someone **deserts**, or **deserts** a job, especially a job in the armed forces, they leave that job without permission. ❏ He was a second-lieutenant in the army until he deserted. ❏ He deserted from army intelligence last month.
→see Picture Dictionary: desert

de|sert|er /dɪzɜːʳtəʳ/ (**deserters**) N-COUNT A **deserter** is someone who leaves their job in the armed forces without permission. ❏ Peters had two deserters followed and shot.

de|serve ♦♢♢ /dɪzɜːʳv/ (**deserves, deserving, deserved**) V-T If you say that a person or thing **deserves** something, you mean that they should have it or receive it because of their actions or qualities. ❏ Government officials clearly deserve some of the blame as well. ❏ These people deserve to make more than the minimum wage.

Word Partnership   deserve의 연어

N.	deserve **a chance**, deserve **credit**, deserve **recognition**, deserve **respect**
V.	**don't** deserve, deserve **to know**
PRON.	deserve **anything**

형용사 기술적인, 설명적인 ❏ 그 단체는 '협심증 지원 단체'라는 보다 간단하고 설명적인 단체명을 채택했다.

타동사 (신성한 물건을) 훼손하다, 모독하다 ❏ 그녀는 종교 지도자의 사진을 훼손하지 말았어야 했다. ● 훼손, 신성 모독 불가산명사 ❏ 공동묘지 훼손 사건에 지역 전체가 충격을 받았다.

명사는 /dɛzəʳt/로 발음된다. 동사는 /dɪzɜːʳt/로 발음되고, de|sert로 분철된다.

■ 가산명사 또는 불가산명사 사막 ❏ 사하라 사막 ❷ 타동사 떠나다, 버리다 ❏ 가난한 농부들이 가뭄에 말라붙은 농토를 버리고 일자리를 찾아 여기로 오고 있다. ● 사람이 없는 형용사 ❏ 그녀는 그들을 사람이 없는 샛길로 이끌고 갔다. ❸ 타동사 (처자식 등을) 버리다 ❏ 로딩 여사의 남편은 수년 전 그녀를 버렸다. ● 버림; 불참 가산명사 또는 불가산명사 ❏ 그녀가 아버지로부터 버림받은 이야기를 한 이후 오랜 시간이 지난 뒤였다. ❹ 타동사/자동사 (신념 등을) 버리다 ❏ 27펜스까지 올라간 그 신문의 가격 상승은 독자들로 하여금 훨씬 더 큰 규모로 떨어져 나가도록 부채질할 것이다. ❏ 그는 많은 젊은이들이 키부츠 생활을 버리는 것을 보고 괴로워했다. ● 버림; 불참 가산명사 또는 불가산명사 ❏ 그들은 사회주의자 유권자들의 집단 불참을 그의 제안 탓으로 돌렸다. ❺ 타동사/자동사 탈영하다, 무단이탈하다 ❏ 그는 탈영할 때까지 육군 소위였다. ❏ 그는 지난 달 육군 정보부에서 무단이탈했다.

가산명사 탈영병 ❏ 피터스는 두 명의 탈영병을 추격해서 발포하도록 했다.

타동사 -을 받을 만하다, -할 만하다 ❏ 정부 관리들은 또한 확실히 그 비난의 일부를 받을 만도 하다. ❏ 이 사람들은 최저 임금보다 많은 돈을 받을 만한 사람들이다.

Picture Dictionary

desert
buzzard
cactus
palm tree
sand dune
oasis
lizard
scorpion
sand
snake

de|serv|ing /dɪzɜrvɪŋ/ ADJ If you describe a person, organization, or cause as **deserving**, you mean that you think they should be helped. ❑ *The money saved could be used for more deserving causes.*

형용사 가치 있는, 자격이 있는 ❑ 저축된 돈은 보다 가치 있는 일에 쓰일 수도 있을 것이다.

de|sign ♦♦♦ /dɪzaɪn/ (**designs, designing, designed**) **1** V-T When someone **designs** a garment, building, machine, or other object, they plan it and make a detailed drawing of it from which it can be built or made. ❑ *They wanted to design a machine that was both attractive and practical.* **2** V-T When someone **designs** a survey, policy, or system, they plan and prepare it, and decide on all the details of it. ❑ *We may be able to design a course to suit your particular needs.* **3** N-UNCOUNT **Design** is the process and art of planning and making detailed drawings of something. ❑ *He was a born mechanic with a flair for design.* **4** N-COUNT The **design** of something is the way in which it has been planned and made. ❑ *...a new design of clock.* **5** N-COUNT A **design** is a drawing which someone produces to show how they would like something to be built or made. ❑ *When Bernardello asked them to build him a home, they drew up the design in a week.* **6** N-COUNT A **design** is a pattern of lines, flowers, or shapes which is used to decorate something. ❑ *Many pictures have been based on simple geometric designs.* **7** V-T PASSIVE If something **is designed** for a particular purpose, it is intended for that purpose. ❑ *This project is designed to help landless people.* →see **architecture, quilt**

1 타동사 디자인하다, 설계하다 ❑ 그들은 매력적인 동시에 실용적인 기계를 설계하고 싶었다. **2** 타동사 계획하다, 꾸미다 ❑ 우리는 당신의 특정한 필요에 들어맞는 강좌를 꾸밀 수도 있습니다. **3** 불가산명사 디자인, 설계 ❑ 그는 디자인 재능을 갖춘 타고난 기술자였다. **4** 가산명사 설계 ❑ 새로운 시계 설계 **5** 가산명사 설계도 ❑ 버나델로가 집을 한 채 지어 달라고 의뢰하자, 그들은 일주일 만에 설계도를 그렸다. **6** 가산명사 무늬 ❑ 많은 그림들이 단순한 기하학적 무늬에 기초해 왔다. **7** 수동타동사 고안되다 ❑ 이 프로젝트는 토지가 없는 사람들을 돕기 위해 고안된 것이다.

des|ig|nate (**designates, designating, designated**)

동사는 /dɛzɪgneɪt/으로 발음되고, 형용사는 /dɛzɪgnɪt/으로 발음된다.

The verb is pronounced /dɛzɪgneɪt/. The adjective is pronounced /dɛzɪgnɪt/.

1 V-T When you **designate** someone or something **as** a particular thing, you formally give them that description or name. ❑ *...a man interviewed in one of our studies whom we shall designate as E.* ❑ *There are efforts under way to designate the bridge a historic landmark.* **2** V-T If something **is designated for** a particular purpose, it is set aside for that purpose. [usu passive] ❑ *Some of the rooms were designated as offices.* **3** V-T When you **designate** someone **as** something, you formally choose them to do that particular job. ❑ *Designate someone as the spokesperson.* **4** ADJ **Designate** is used to describe someone who has been chosen to do a particular job, but has not yet started doing it. [n ADJ] ❑ *Japan's Prime Minister-designate is completing his Cabinet today.*

1 타동사 지명하다, 지정하다 ❑ 우리가 조사를 하면서 면접한, 이라고 지명될 남자 및 그 다리를 사적으로 지정하려는 노력이 진행 중이다. **2** 타동사 지정되다 ❑ 몇몇 방들은 사무실로 지정되었다. **3** 타동사 지명하다, 임명하다 ❑ 누군가를 대변인으로 지명해라. **4** 형용사 지명된 ❑ 일본의 총리 지명자는 오늘 내각 구성을 완료할 예정이다.

de|sign|er ♦♦♢ /dɪzaɪnər/ (**designers**) **1** N-COUNT A **designer** is a person whose job is to design things by making drawings of them. ❑ *Carolyne is a fashion designer.* **2** ADJ **Designer** clothes or **designer** labels are expensive, fashionable clothes made by a famous designer, rather than being made in large quantities in a factory. [ADJ n] ❑ *He wears designer clothes and drives an antique car.* **3** ADJ You can use **designer** to describe things that are worn or bought because they are fashionable. [INFORMAL] [ADJ n] ❑ *Designer beers and trendy wines have replaced the good old British pint.*

1 가산명사 디자이너 ❑ 캐럴린은 패션 디자이너이다. **2** 형용사 유명 디자이너의 이름이 붙은 ❑ 그는 유명 디자이너 옷을 입고 고풍스러운 차를 몬다. **3** 형용사 최신 유행의 [비격식체] ❑ 정든 오랜 영국 맥주가 최신 유행하는 맥주와 와인에 의해 대체되어 왔다.

de|sign|er baby (**designer babies**) also **designer child** N-COUNT People sometimes refer to a baby that has developed from an embryo with certain desired characteristics as a **designer baby**. [MAINLY JOURNALISM] ❑ *A couple with a terminally ill child want to create a designer baby that could save the boy's life.*

가산명사 맞춤 아기 [주로 언론] ❑ 불치병에 걸린 아이를 가진 부부가 아이의 생명을 구할 수 있는 맞춤 아기를 생산하기를 원한다.

de|sir|able /dɪzaɪərəb(ə)l/ **1** ADJ Something that is **desirable** is worth having or doing because it is useful, necessary, or popular. ❑ *Prolonged negotiation was not desirable.* ● **de|sir|abil|ity** /dɪzaɪərəbɪlɪti/ N-UNCOUNT ❑ *...the desirability of democratic reform.* **2** ADJ Someone who is **desirable** is considered to be sexually attractive. ❑ *...the young women of his own age whom his classmates thought most desirable.* ● **de|sir|abil|ity** N-UNCOUNT ❑ *He had not at all overrated Veronica's desirability.*

1 형용사 바람직한 ❑ 질질 끄는 협상은 바람직하지 않았다. ● 바람직함 불가산명사 ❑ 민주적 개혁의 바람직함 **2** 형용사 매력 있는, 호감이 가는 ❑ 그의 급우들이 가장 매력을 느끼는 그 또래의 젊은 여성들 ● 매력 불가산명사 ❑ 그는 베로니카의 매력을 조금도 과대평가하지 않았다.

de|sire ♦♦♢ /dɪzaɪər/ (**desires, desiring, desired**) **1** N-COUNT A **desire** is a strong wish to do or have something. ❑ *I had a strong desire to help and care for people.* **2** V-T If you **desire** something, you want it. [FORMAL] [no cont] ❑ *She had remarried and desired a child with her new husband.* ● **de|sired** ADJ [ADJ n] ❑ *You may find that just threatening this course of action will produce the desired effect.* **3** N-UNCOUNT **Desire** for someone is a strong feeling of wanting to have sex with them. ❑ *Teenage sex, for instance, may come not out of genuine desire but from a need to get love.*

1 가산명사 욕구, 욕망 ❑ 사람들을 도와주고 돌보고 싶은 마음이 간절했다. **2** 타동사 원하다, 바라다 [격식체] ❑ 그녀는 재혼을 한 상태였고 새 남편과 아이를 갖길 원했다. ● 원하는, 바라는 형용사 ❑ 이러한 방침을 취하겠다고 위협하는 것만으로도 원하는 결과를 낳으리라는 것을 알 수 있을 것이다. **3** 불가산명사 욕구, 성욕 ❑ 예를 들어, 십대의 성관계는 진짜 정욕이 아니라 애정을 받고자 하는 욕구 때문에 이루어질 수도 있다.

Word Partnership		*desire*의 연어
ADJ.	**strong** desire **1 2**	
	sexual desire **3**	
V.	**have no** desire, **satisfy a** desire **1**	
	desire **to change 1 2**	
	express desire **1 3**	

desk ♦♦♢ /dɛsk/ (**desks**) **1** N-COUNT A **desk** is a table, often with drawers, which you sit at to write or work. **2** N-SING The place in a hotel, hospital, airport, or other building where you check in or where information is referred to as a particular **desk**. ❑ *I told the girl at the reception desk that I was terribly sorry, but I was half an hour late.* **3** N-SING A particular department of a broadcasting company, or of a newspaper or magazine company, can be referred to as a particular **desk**. ❑ *Let our news desk know as quickly as possible.* →see **office**

1 가산명사 책상 **2** 단수명사 (접수처, 안내처 등) 데스크 ❑ 나는 접수 데스크에 있는 여자에게, 정말 미안하지만 30분 늦었다고 말했다. **3** 단수명사 (언론사 등의) 국 ❑ 가능한 한 빨리 저희 보도국에 알려 주십시오.

desk clerk (**desk clerks**) N-COUNT A **desk clerk** is someone who works at the main desk in a hotel. [AM; BRIT **receptionist**]

가산명사 (호텔의) 접수계원 [미국영어; 영국영어 receptionist]

de|skill /diːskɪl/ (**deskills, deskilling, deskilled**) V-T If workers **are deskilled**, they no longer need special skills to do their work, especially because of modern methods of production. [oft passive] ❑ *Administrative staff may be deskilled through increased automation and efficiency.*

타동사 (자동화·분업화로) 일이 단순 작업화 되다 ❑ 늘어나는 자동화와 효율성 때문에 행정직이 하는 일이 단순 작업화될 수도 있다.

a b c d e f g h i j k l m n o p q r s t u v w x y z

A
B
C
D
E
F
G
H
I
J
K
L
M
N
O
P
Q
R
S
T
U
V
W
X
Y
Z

desk|top /dɛsktɒp/ (desktops) also **desk-top** ◧ ADJ **Desktop** computers are a convenient size for using on a desk or table, but are not designed to be portable. [ADJ n] ❑ *When launched, the Macintosh was the smallest desktop computer ever produced.* ◨ N-COUNT A **desktop** is a desktop computer. ❑ *We have stopped making desktops because no one is making money from them.* ◪ N-COUNT The **desktop** of a computer is the display of icons that you see on the screen when the computer is ready to use. ❑ *A dramatic full-sized lightning bolt will then fill your screen's desktop.*

❶ 형용사 탁상용의 ❑ 출시 당시, 매킨토시는 그때까지 생산된 가장 작은 탁상용 컴퓨터였다. ❷ 가산명사 탁상용 컴퓨터 ❑ 수익을 얻을 수가 없어서 탁상용 컴퓨터 생산을 중지했다. ❸ 가산명사 바탕화면 ❑ 그러고 나면 바탕화면 가득 인상적인 커다란 번개 모양이 뜰 것이다.

desk|top pub|lish|ing N-UNCOUNT **Desktop publishing** is the production of printed materials such as newspapers and magazines using a desktop computer and a laser printer, rather than using conventional printing methods. The abbreviation **DTP** is also used.

불가산명사 전자 출판

deso|late /dɛsəlɪt/ ◧ ADJ A **desolate** place is empty of people and lacking in comfort. ❑ *...a desolate landscape of flat green fields broken by marsh.* ◨ ADJ If someone is **desolate**, they feel very sad, alone, and without hope. [LITERARY] ❑ *He was desolate without her.*

❶ 형용사 황폐한, 황량한 ❑ 사이사이에 늪이 있는 평평한 초록 들판의 황량한 풍경 ❷ 형용사 우울한, 고독한 [문예체] ❑ 그는 그녀가 없어 고독했다.

deso|la|tion /dɛsəleɪʃ°n/ ◧ N-UNCOUNT **Desolation** is a feeling of great unhappiness and hopelessness. ❑ *Kozelek expresses his sense of desolation absolutely without self-pity.* ◨ N-UNCOUNT If you refer to **desolation** in a place, you mean that it is empty and frightening, for example because it has been destroyed by a violent force or army. [DISAPPROVAL] ❑ *We looked out upon a scene of desolation and ruin.*

❶ 불가산명사 절망감 ❑ 코즐렉은 전혀 자기 연민 없이 자신이 느끼는 절망감을 표현한다. ❷ 불가산명사 황폐함, 황량함 [탐탁잖음] ❑ 우리는 황량하게 폐허가 된 광경을 내다보았다.

des|pair /dɪspɛər/ (despairs, despairing, despaired) ◧ N-UNCOUNT **Despair** is the feeling that everything is wrong and that nothing will improve. ❑ *I looked at my wife in despair.* ◨ V-I If you **despair**, you feel that everything is wrong and that nothing will improve. ❑ *"Oh, I despair sometimes," he says in mock sorrow.* ◪ V-I If you **despair of** something, you feel that there is no hope that it will happen or improve. If you **despair of** someone, you feel that there is no hope that they will improve. ❑ *He wished to earn a living through writing but despaired of doing so.*

❶ 불가산명사 절망 ❑ 나는 절망에 빠져 아내를 바라보았다. ❷ 자동사 절망하다 ❑ "아, 나는 가끔 절망스럽다."라고 그가 슬픈 척하며 말한다. ❸ 자동사 단념하다 ❑ 그는 글을 써서 생계를 꾸리기 원했지만 단념하고 말았다.

des|patch /dɪspætʃ/ →see **dispatch**

des|per|ate ◆◇◇ /dɛspərɪt/ ◧ ADJ If you are **desperate**, you are in such a bad situation that you are willing to try anything to change it. ❑ *Troops are needed to help get food into Kosovo where people are in desperate need.* ● **des|per|ate|ly** ADV [ADV with v] ❑ *Thousands are desperately trying to leave their battered homes and villages.* ◨ ADJ If you are **desperate for** something or **desperate to** do something, you want or need it very much indeed. [v-link ADJ, usu ADJ to-inf, ADJ for n] ❑ *They'd been married nearly four years and June was desperate to start a family.* ● **des|per|ate|ly** ADV [ADV with v] ❑ *He was a boy who desperately needed affection.* ◪ ADJ A **desperate** situation is very difficult, serious, or dangerous. ❑ *India's United Nations ambassador said the situation is desperate.*

❶ 형용사 필사적인 ❑ 주민들이 몹시 굶주리고 있는 코소보로 식량을 들여가는 것을 돕기 위해 군대가 필요하다. ● 필사적으로 부사 ❑ 수천 명의 사람들이 부서진 집과 마을을 떠나려고 필사적으로 애쓰고 있다. ❷ 형용사 간절히 원하는 ❑ 그들은 결혼한 지 거의 사년이 되었었고 준은 아이를 갖기를 간절히 원했다. ● 간절히 부사 ❑ 그는 애정을 간절히 필요로 하는 아이였다. ❸ 형용사 절망적인 ❑ 인도 유엔 대사는 상황이 절망적이라고 말했다.

Word Partnership   desperate의 연어

V.	sound desperate ◧
	grow desperate ◧ ◪
N.	desperate **act**, desperate **attempt**, desperate **measures**, desperate **need**, desperate **struggle** ◧
	desperate **situation** ◪

---

des|pera|tion /dɛspəreɪʃ°n/ N-UNCOUNT **Desperation** is the feeling that you have when you are in such a bad situation that you will try anything to change it. ❑ *This feeling of desperation and helplessness was common to most of the refugees.*

불가산명사 절망; 필사적임 ❑ 이런 절망감과 무기력감은 대부분의 난민들에게서 흔히 볼 수 있는 것이었다.

des|pic|able /dɛspɪkəb°l, BRIT dɪspɪkəb°l/ ADJ If you say that a person or action is **despicable**, you are emphasizing that they are extremely nasty, cruel, or evil. [EMPHASIS] ❑ *The Minister, who visited the scene a few hours after the explosion, said it was a despicable crime.*

형용사 비열한, 야비한 [강조] ❑ 폭발 몇 시간 후에 현장을 방문한 장관은, 그 사건을 비열한 범죄라고 말했다.

des|pise /dɪspaɪz/ (despises, despising, despised) V-T If you **despise** something or someone, you dislike them and have a very low opinion of them. ❑ *I can never, ever forgive him. I despise him.*

타동사 경멸하다, 멸시하다 ❑ 나는 절대로 그를 용서할 수 없어. 나는 그를 경멸해.

de|spite ◆◆◇ /dɪspaɪt/ ◧ PREP You use **despite** to introduce a fact which makes the other part of the sentence surprising. [PREP n/-ing] ❑ *The National Health Service has visibly deteriorated, despite increased spending.* ◨ PREP You use **despite** to introduce an idea that appears to contradict your main statement, without suggesting that this idea is true or that you believe it. ❑ *She told friends she still stand by husband, despite reports that he sent another woman love notes.*

❶ 전치사 -에도 불구하고 ❑ 국민 보건 서비스는 지출이 늘어났음에도 불구하고 눈에 보이게 질이 저하되어 왔다. ❷ 전치사 -에도 불구하고 ❑ 남편이 다른 여자에게 연애편지를 보냈다는 보도에도 불구하고, 그녀는 남편 곁을 지키겠다고 친구들에게 말했다.

de|spond|ent /dɪspɒndənt/ ADJ If you are **despondent**, you are very unhappy because you have been experiencing difficulties that you think you will not be able to overcome. ❑ *John often felt despondent after dragging his portfolio around various agencies.*

형용사 낙담한 ❑ 존은 여러 소개소로 자신의 포트폴리오를 가져갔다가 자주 낙담하곤 했다.

des|sert /dɪzɜrt/ (desserts) N-MASS **Dessert** is something sweet, such as fruit or a pudding, that you eat at the end of a meal. ❑ *She had homemade ice cream for dessert.*
→see Picture Dictionary: **dessert**

물질명사 디저트 ❑ 그녀는 디저트로 집에서 만든 아이스크림을 먹었다.

Word Link   stab ≈ steady : destabilize, establish, instability

---

de|sta|bi|lize /disteɪbəlaɪz/ (destabilizes, destabilizing, destabilized) [BRIT also **destabilise**] V-T To **destabilize** something such as a country or government means to create a situation which reduces its power or influence. ❑ *Their sole aim is to destabilize the Indian government.*

[영국영어 destabilise] 타동사 불안정하게 하다, 동요시키다 ❑ 그들의 유일한 목표는 인도 정부를 동요시키는 것이다.

des|ti|na|tion /dɛstɪneɪʃ°n/ (destinations) N-COUNT The **destination** of someone or something is the place to which they are going or being sent. ❑ *Spain is still our most popular holiday destination.*

가산명사 목적지 ❑ 스페인은 여전히 가장 인기 좋은 휴가지이다.

Picture Dictionary   dessert

ice cream · cake · pie · cookies · sundae · cheesecake

custard · Jell-O™ · brownie · chocolate mousse · rice pudding · fruit salad

des|tined /dɛstɪnd/ **1** ADJ If something is **destined to** happen or if someone is **destined to** behave in a particular way, that thing seems certain to happen or be done. [v-link ADJ, ADJ to-inf, ADJ for n] ❑ *London seems destined to lose more than 2,000 hospital beds.* **2** ADJ If someone is **destined for** a particular place, or if goods are **destined for** a particular place, they are traveling toward that place or will be sent to that place. [v-link ADJ for n] ❑ *...products destined for Saudi Arabia.*

1 형용사 확실히 ~할 것 같은 ❑ 런던은 확실히 2천 개 이상의 병상을 잃게 될 것 같다. **2** 형용사 ~로 가는 ❑ 사우디아라비아로 가는 제품들

des|ti|ny /dɛstɪni/ (**destinies**) **1** N-COUNT A person's **destiny** is everything that happens to them during their life, including what will happen in the future, especially when it is considered to be controlled by someone or something else. ❑ *We are masters of our own destiny.* **2** N-UNCOUNT **Destiny** is the force which some people believe controls the things that happen to you in your life. ❑ *Is it destiny that brings people together, or is it accident?*

1 가산명사 운명 ❑ 우리는 자기 운명의 주인이다. **2** 불가산명사 운명, 운 ❑ 사람들을 맺어 주는 것은 운명일까, 우연일까?

des|ti|tute /dɛstɪtut, BRIT dɛstɪtyuːt/ ADJ Someone who is **destitute** has no money or possessions. [FORMAL] ❑ *...destitute children who live on the streets.*

형용사 극빈한 [격식체] ❑ 길거리에서 사는 극빈층 아동들

de|stroy ♦♦◊ /dɪstrɔɪ/ (**destroys, destroying, destroyed**) **1** V-T To **destroy** something means to cause so much damage to it that it is completely ruined or does not exist any more. ❑ *That's a sure recipe for destroying the economy and creating chaos.* **2** V-T To **destroy** someone means to ruin their life or to make their situation impossible to bear. ❑ *If I was younger or more naive, the criticism would have destroyed me.* **3** V-T If an animal is **destroyed**, it is killed, either because it is ill or because it is dangerous. [usu passive] ❑ *Lindsay was unhurt but the horse had to be destroyed.*

1 타동사 파괴하다, 부수다 ❑ 그것은 경제를 파괴하고 혼란을 일으키는 확실한 방법이다. **2** 타동사 파멸시키다 ❑ 내가 만약 더 어리거나 순진했다면, 그런 비난 때문에 파멸했을지도 모른다. **3** 타동사 도살하다 ❑ 린지는 다치지 않았지만 그 말은 도살해야 했다.

Thesaurus   destroy의 참조어

v.   annihilate, crush, demolish, eradicate, ruin, wipe out; (*ant.*) build, construct, create, repair **1**

de|struc|tion ♦◊◊ /dɪstrʌkʃ°n/ N-UNCOUNT **Destruction** is the act of destroying something, or the state of being destroyed. ❑ *...an international agreement aimed at halting the destruction of the ozone layer.*

불가산명사 파괴; 파멸 ❑ 오존층 파괴 방지를 목표로 한 국제 협약

Word Link   struct ≈ building : construct, destructive, instruct

de|struc|tive /dɪstrʌktɪv/ ADJ Something that is **destructive** causes or is capable of causing great damage, harm, or injury. ❑ *...the awesome destructive power of nuclear weapons.*

형용사 파괴적인 ❑ 핵무기의 가공할 파괴력

Word Link   de ≈ from, down, away : deflate, descend, detach

de|tach /dɪtætʃ/ (**detaches, detaching, detached**) **1** V-T/V-I If you **detach** one thing **from** another that it is fixed to, you remove it. If one thing **detaches from** another, it becomes separated from it. [FORMAL] ❑ *Detach the white part of the application form and keep it for reference only.* ❑ *Detach the currants from the stems by simply running a fork down the length of the stem.* **2** V-T If you **detach yourself from** something, you become less involved in it or less concerned about it than you used to be. ❑ *It helps them detach themselves from their problems and become more objective.*

1 타동사/자동사 떼다; 떨어지다 [격식체] ❑ 신청서의 흰색 부분을 떼어 내서 참고용으로 보관하세요. ❑ 간단하게 갈퀴로 줄기를 훑어 내려서 줄기에서 까치밥열매를 떼어 내세요. **2** 타동사 거리를 두다 ❑ 그것은 그들로 하여금 자신들의 문제와 거리를 두고 더 객관적이 될 수 있도록 돕는다.

de|tached /dɪtætʃt/ **1** ADJ Someone who is **detached** is not personally involved in something or has no emotional interest in it. ❑ *He tries to remain emotionally detached from the prisoners, but fails.* **2** ADJ A **detached** house is one that is not joined to any other house. ❑ *...a development of 38 detached houses by Liberty Homes.*

1 형용사 거리를 두는 ❑ 그는 죄수들로부터 감정적으로 거리를 두려고 노력하지만, 실패한다. **2** 형용사 단독 (주택) ❑ 리버티 홈즈에 의해 이루어지는 38채의 단독 주택 개발

de|tach|ment /dɪtætʃmənt/ N-UNCOUNT **Detachment** is the feeling that you have of not being personally involved in something or of having no emotional interest in it. ❑ *She did not care for the idea of socializing with her clients. It would detract from her professional detachment.*

불가산명사 초연함; 공평무사함 ❑ 그녀는 고객들과 교제하는 것을 좋아하지 않았다. 그런 일은 전문가로서의 공평무사함을 손상시킬 터였다.

de|tail ♦♦◊ /diteɪl/ (**details, detailing, detailed**)

The pronunciation /dɪteɪl/ is also used in American English.

미국 영어에서는 /dɪteɪl/이라는 발음도 사용된다.

A

B

C

D

E

F

G

H

I

J

K

L

M

N

O

P

Q

R

S

T

U

V

W

X

Y

Z

1 N-COUNT The **details of** something are its individual features or elements. ❑ *The details of the plan are still being worked out.* ❑ *No details of the discussions have been given.* **2** N-PLURAL **Details** about someone or something are facts or pieces of information about them. ❑ *See the bottom of this page for details of how to apply for this exciting offer.* **3** N-COUNT A **detail** is a minor point or aspect of something, as opposed to the central ones. ❑ *Only minor details now remain to be settled.* **4** N-UNCOUNT You can refer to the small features of something which are often not noticed as **detail**. ❑ *We like his attention to detail and his enthusiasm.* **5** V-T If you **detail** things, you list them or give information about them. ❑ *The report detailed the human rights abuses committed during the war.* **6** PHRASE If someone does not **go into details** about a subject, or does not **go into the detail**, they mention it without explaining it fully or properly. ❑ *He said he had been in various parts of Britain but did not go into details.* **7** PHRASE If you examine or discuss something **in detail**, you do it thoroughly and carefully. ❑ *We examine the wording in detail before deciding on the final text.*

1 가산명사 세목, 세부 사항 ❑ 그 계획의 세목은 아직 만들어지고 있는 중이다. ❑ 그 논의의 세부 사항은 전혀 알려지지 않았다. **2** 복수명사 상세 정보 ❑ 이 신나는 특가 제공을 신청하시는 방법에 대한 상세 정보는 이 페이지 아래쪽을 보세요. **3** 가산명사 지엽 ❑ 이제 지엽적인 부분들만이 해결이 안 된 채로 남아 있다. **4** 불가산명사 (놓치기 쉬운) 작은 부분 ❑ 우리는 그 사람의 작은 부분에 대한 관심과 열의가 마음에 든다. **5** 타동사 열거하다; 상술하다 ❑ 그 보고서에는 전쟁 중에 벌어진 인권 유린 사태가 열거되어 있었다. **6** 구 자세히 말하다 ❑ 그는 자신이 영국 각지에 가 보았다고 말했지만 상세히 얘기하지는 않았다. **7** 구 상세하게, 자세히 ❑ 우리는 최종 원고를 결정하기에 앞서 어휘 사용을 상세히 검토한다.

Thesaurus detail의 참조어

| N. | component, element, feature, point **1** **3** |
| V. | depict, describe, specify; (ant.) approximate, generalize **5** |

---

de|tailed ♦◇◇ /dɪteɪld, BRIT diːteɪld/ ADJ A **detailed** report or plan contains a lot of details. ❑ *Yesterday's letter contains a detailed account of the decisions.*

형용사 상세한 ❑ 어제의 서한에는 그 결정의 상세한 전말이 담겨 있다.

Word Partnership detailed의 연어

| N. | detailed **account**, detailed **analysis**, detailed **description**, detailed **instructions**, detailed **plan**, detailed **record** |

---

de|tain /dɪteɪn/ (detains, detaining, detained) **1** V-T When people such as the police **detain** someone, they keep them in a place under their control. [FORMAL] ❑ *The act allows police to detain a suspect for up to 48 hours.* **2** V-T To **detain** someone means to delay them, for example by talking to them. [FORMAL] ❑ *Millson stood up. "Thank you. We won't detain you any further, Mrs. Stebbing."*

1 타동사 구금하다, 억류하다 [격식체] ❑ 그 법령은 경찰이 용의자를 최대 48시간 동안 구금할 수 있도록 해 준다. **2** 타동사 붙들다, 붙잡다 [격식체] ❑ 밀슨이 일어섰다. "감사합니다. 더 이상 당신을 붙잡지 않겠습니다, 스테빙 여사."

de|tain|ee /dɪteɪniː/ (detainees) N-COUNT A **detainee** is someone who is held prisoner by a government because of his or her political views or activities. ❑ *Earlier this year, Amnesty International called for the release of more than 100 political detainees.*

가산명사 억류자, 구금자 ❑ 올해 초, 국제 사면 위원회는 100명이 넘는 정치적 억류자들의 석방을 요구했다.

de|tect /dɪtɛkt/ (detects, detecting, detected) **1** V-T To **detect** something means to find it or discover that it is present somewhere by using equipment or making an investigation. ❑ *...a sensitive piece of equipment used to detect radiation.* **2** V-T If you **detect** something, you notice it or sense it, even though it is not very obvious. ❑ *Arnold could detect a certain sadness in the old man's face.*

1 타동사 발견하다, 탐지하다 ❑ 방사능 탐지에 사용되는 민감한 장비 **2** 타동사 알아차리다, 감지하다 ❑ 아놀드는 그 늙은 남자의 얼굴에서 어떤 슬픔을 감지할 수 있었다.

de|tec|tion /dɪtɛkʃ°n/ N-UNCOUNT **Detection** is the act of noticing or sensing something. ❑ *...the early detection of breast cancer.*

불가산명사 발견, 탐지 ❑ 유방암의 조기 발견

de|tec|tive ♦◇◇ /dɪtɛktɪv/ (detectives) **1** N-COUNT A **detective** is someone whose job is to discover what has happened in a crime or other situation and to find the people involved. Some detectives work in the police force and others work privately. ❑ *Now detectives are appealing for witnesses who may have seen anything suspicious last night.* **2** ADJ A **detective** novel or story is one in which a detective tries to solve a crime. [ADJ n] ❑ *...Arthur Conan Doyle's classic detective novel.*

1 가산명사 탐정; 형사 ❑ 현재 형사들은 지난밤에 무엇이든 수상쩍은 일을 보았을지도 모르는 목격자들의 도움을 호소하고 있다. **2** 형용사 탐정의 ❑ 아서 코넌 도일의 명작 탐정 소설

de|tec|tor /dɪtɛktər/ (detectors) N-COUNT A **detector** is an instrument which is used to discover that something is present somewhere, or to measure how much of something there is. ❑ *...a metal detector.*

가산명사 탐지기; 검출기 ❑ 금속 탐지기

de|ten|tion /dɪtɛnʃ°n/ (detentions) **1** N-UNCOUNT **Detention** is when someone is arrested or put into prison, especially for political reasons. [also N in pl] ❑ *...the detention without trial of government critics.* **2** N-VAR **Detention** is a punishment for naughty schoolchildren, who are made to stay at school after the other children have gone home. ❑ *The teacher kept the boys in detention after school.*

1 불가산명사 구금, 유치 ❑ 정부 비판자들을 재판 없이 구금하는 것 **2** 가산명사 또는 불가산명사 (벌로) 방과 후 남게 하기 ❑ 선생님은 방과 후에 그 남자 애들을 학교에 남게 했다.

de|ter /dɪtɜr/ (deters, deterring, deterred) V-T To **deter** someone **from** doing something means to make them not want to do it or continue doing it. ❑ *Supporters of the death penalty argue that it would deter criminals from carrying guns.*

타동사 억제하다, 단념시키다 ❑ 사형 찬성론자들은 사형이 범죄자들의 총기 휴대를 억제할 것이라고 주장한다.

de|ter|gent /dɪtɜrdʒ°nt/ (detergents) N-MASS **Detergent** is a chemical substance, usually in the form of a powder or liquid, which is used for washing things such as clothes or dishes. ❑ *...a brand of detergent.* →see **soap**

물질명사 세제 ❑ 세제 상표

de|te|rio|rate /dɪtɪəriəreɪt/ (deteriorates, deteriorating, deteriorated) V-I If something **deteriorates**, it becomes worse in some way. ❑ *There are fears that the situation might deteriorate into full-scale war.* ● **de|te|rio|ra|tion** /dɪtɪəriəreɪʃ°n/ N-UNCOUNT ❑ *...concern about the rapid deterioration in relations between the two countries.*

자동사 악화되다, 나빠지다 ❑ 사태가 악화되어 전면전으로 갈지도 모른다는 우려가 있다. ● 악화 불가산명사 ❑ 양국 간 관계의 급속한 악화에 대한 염려

de|ter|mi|na|tion /dɪtɜrmɪneɪʃ°n/ N-UNCOUNT **Determination** is the quality that you show when you have decided to do something and you will not let anything stop you. ❑ *Everyone concerned acted with great courage and determination.* →see also **determine**

불가산명사 결의; 결단력 ❑ 관계된 모든 이들이 대단한 용기와 결의를 갖고 행동했다.

Word Partnership determination의 연어

| N. | **courage and** determination, **strength and** determination |
| ADJ. | **fierce** determination |

Word Link term, termin ≈ limit, end : de**termine**, **termin**al, **termin**ate

de|ter|mine ♦♦◇ /dɪtɜrmɪn/ (determines, determining, determined) **1** V-T If a particular factor **determines** the nature of a thing or event, it causes it to be of a particular kind. [FORMAL] ❑ *The size of the chicken pieces will determine the cooking time.* ● **de|ter|mi|na|tion** N-UNCOUNT ❑ *...the gene which is responsible for male sex determination.* **2** V-T To **determine** a fact means to discover it as a result of investigation. [FORMAL] ❑ *The investigation will determine what really happened.* ❑ *Experts say testing needs to be done on each contaminant to determine the long-term effects on humans.* **3** V-T If you **determine** something, you decide it or settle it. ❑ *The Baltic people have a right to determine their own future.* ● **de|ter|mi|na|tion** (determinations) N-COUNT ❑ *We must take into our own hands the determination of our future.* **4** V-T If you **determine** to do something, you make a firm decision to do it. [FORMAL] ❑ *He determined to rescue his two countrymen.*

❑ 타동사 결정된다, 조건 짓다 [격식체] ❑ 닭고기 조각의 크기에 따라 조리 시간이 결정된다. ● 결정 불가산명사 ❑ 성별을 남성으로 결정짓는 원인이 되는 유선자 ❑ 타동사 (조사 결과) 밝혀내다 [격식체] ❑ 조사를 통해 실제로 무슨 일이 일어났는지가 밝혀질 것이다. ❑ 전문가들은 인류에게 미치는 장기적인 영향을 밝혀낼 수 있도록 각각의 오염 물질에 대한 검사가 이루어져야 한다고 말한다. ❑ 타동사 결정하다 ❑ 발트 해 연안 주민들은 스스로의 미래를 결정할 권리가 있다. ● 결정 가산명사 ❑ 우리의 미래에 대한 결정은 우리 스스로 해 나가야 한다. ❑ 타동사 결심하다 [격식체] ❑ 그는 자기 동포 두 사람을 구출하기로 결심했다.

de|ter|mined ♦◇◇ /dɪtɜrmɪnd/ ADJ If you are **determined to** do something, you have made a firm decision to do it and will not let anything stop you. ❑ *His enemies are determined to ruin him.* ● **de|ter|mined|ly** ADV ❑ *She shook her head, determinedly.*

형용사 결심한; 결의가 굳은 ❑ 그의 적들은 그를 파멸시키려고 단단히 결심하고 있다. ● 단호히 부사 ❑ 그녀는 단호히 고개를 저었다.

de|ter|min|er /dɪtɜrmɪnər/ (determiners) N-COUNT In grammar, a **determiner** is a word which is used at the beginning of a noun group to indicate, for example, which thing you are referring to or whether you are referring to one thing or several. Common English determiners are "a," "the," "some," "this," and "each."

가산명사 한정사

de|ter|rence /dɪtɜrəns, BRIT dɪterəns/ N-UNCOUNT **Deterrence** is the prevention of something, especially war or crime, by having something such as weapons or punishment to use as a threat. ❑ *...policies of nuclear deterrence.*

불가산명사 제지, 억제 ❑ 핵억제 정책

de|ter|rent /dɪtɜrənt, BRIT dɪterənt/ (deterrents) **1** N-COUNT A **deterrent** is something that prevents people from doing something by making them afraid of what will happen to them if they do it. ❑ *They seriously believe that capital punishment is a deterrent.* **2** N-COUNT A **deterrent** is a weapon or set of weapons designed to prevent enemies from attacking by making them afraid to do so. ❑ *The idea of building a nuclear deterrent is completely off the political agenda.*

❑ 가산명사 단념시키는, 억제하는 ❑ 그들은 진심으로 사형이 억제 수단이라고 믿는다. ❑ 가산명사 (핵무기 등의) 억제력 ❑ 핵억제력을 보유한다는 생각은 정치적 의제를 완전히 벗어난 것이다.

de|test /dɪtɛst/ (detests, detesting, detested) V-T If you **detest** someone or something, you dislike them very much. ❑ *My mother detested him.*

타동사 몹시 싫어하다, 혐오하다 ❑ 우리 어머니는 그를 몹시 싫어했다.

deto|nate /dɛtəneɪt/ (detonates, detonating, detonated) V-T/V-I If someone **detonates** a device such as a bomb, or if it **detonates**, it explodes. ❑ *France is expected to detonate its first nuclear device in the next few days.*

타동사/자동사 폭발시키다; 폭발하다 ❑ 앞으로 며칠 안에 프랑스가 자국 최초의 핵폭탄을 터뜨릴 것으로 예상된다.

de|tour /ditʊər/ (detours) **1** N-COUNT If you make a **detour** on a journey, you go by a route which is not the shortest way, because you want to avoid something such as a traffic jam, or because there is something you want to do on the way. ❑ *He did not take the direct route to his home, but made a detour around the outskirts of the city.* **2** N-COUNT A **detour** is a special route for traffic to follow when the normal route is blocked, for example because it is being repaired. [AM; BRIT **diversion**] ❑ *A slight detour in the road is causing major headaches for businesses along El Camino Real.*

❑ 가산명사 우회 ❑ 그는 집으로 곧장 가는 길을 통하지 않고, 시 외곽을 따라 돌아갔다. ❑ 가산명사 우회로 [영국영어 diversion] ❑ 그 도로에 난 작은 우회로가 엘 카미노 리얼 일대 상가에 커다란 골칫거리를 안겨 주고 있다.

de|tract /dɪtrækt/ (detracts, detracting, detracted) V-T/V-I If one thing **detracts from** another, it makes it seem less good or impressive. ❑ *They feared that the publicity surrounding him would detract from their own election campaigns.*

타동사/자동사 (가치, 명성 등을) 떨어뜨리다, 손상시키다 ❑ 그들은 그를 둘러싼 세간의 관심 때문에 자기 선거 운동에 흠이 갈까 봐 두려워했다.

det|ri|ment /dɛtrɪmənt/ **1** PHRASE If something happens **to the detriment of** something or **to** a person's **detriment**, it causes harm or damage to them. [FORMAL] ❑ *These tests will give too much importance to written exams to the detriment of other skills.* **2** PHRASE If something happens **without detriment to** a person or thing, it does not harm or damage it. [FORMAL] ❑ *These difficulties have been overcome without detriment to performance.*

❑ 구 -을 손상시켜; -의 희생 아래 [격식체] ❑ 이 시험은 필기 평가에 지나치게 큰 비중을 두게 되어 다른 기능들을 희생시킬 것이다. ❑ 구 -을 손상시키지 않고; -에 손해 없이 [격식체] ❑ 작업에 손상을 입지 않은 채 이러한 어려움들을 극복해 냈다.

det|ri|men|tal /dɛtrɪmɛntᵊl/ ADJ Something that is **detrimental to** something else has a harmful or damaging effect on it. ❑ *Many foods are suspected of being detrimental to health because of the chemicals and additives they contain.*

형용사 유해한, 손해되는 ❑ 많은 식품들이 그 속에 함유된 화학 성분이나 첨가물 때문에 건강에 유해하다는 의심을 받는다.

de|value /divælyu/ (devalues, devaluing, devalued) **1** V-T To **devalue** something means to cause it to be thought less impressive or less deserving of respect. ❑ *They spread tales about her in an attempt to devalue her work.* **2** V-T To **devalue** the currency of a country means to reduce its value in relation to other currencies. ❑ *India has devalued the Rupee by about eleven per cent.* ● **de|valu|ation** /divælyueɪʃᵊn/ (devaluations) N-VAR ❑ *It will lead to devaluation of a number of European currencies.*

❑ 타동사 평가절하하다, 평가 절하하다 ❑ 그들은 그녀가 한 일을 깎아 내리려고 그녀에 대한 험담을 퍼뜨렸다. ❑ 타동사 평가 절하하다 ❑ 인도는 루피화를 11퍼센트 가량 평가 절하했다. ● 평가 절하 가산명사 또는 불가산명사 ❑ 그것을 통해 많은 유럽 국가 화폐의 평가 절하가 이루어질 것이다.

dev|as|tate /dɛvəsteɪt/ (devastates, devastating, devastated) V-T If something **devastates** an area or a place, it damages it very badly or destroys it totally. ❑ *A few days before, a fire had devastated large parts of Windsor Castle.*

타동사 유린하다, 폐허로 만들다 ❑ 며칠 앞서, 화재로 윈저 성의 많은 부분이 폐허가 되었었다.

dev|as|tat|ed /dɛvəsteɪtɪd/ ADJ If you are **devastated** by something, you are very shocked and upset by it. [V-link ADJ] ❑ *Teresa was devastated, her dreams shattered.*

형용사 망연자실한, 곤혹스러운 ❑ 테레사는 망연자실해 했고, 그녀의 꿈은 산산이 부서졌다.

dev|as|tat|ing /dɛvəsteɪtɪŋ/ **1** ADJ If you describe something as **devastating**, you are emphasizing that it is very harmful or damaging. [EMPHASIS] ❑ *Affairs do have a devastating effect on marriages.* **2** ADJ You can use **devastating** to emphasize that something is very shocking, upsetting, or terrible. [EMPHASIS] ❑ *The diagnosis was devastating. She had cancer.* **3** ADJ You can use **devastating** to emphasize that something or someone is very impressive. [EMPHASIS] ❑ *He returned to his best with a devastating display of galloping and jumping.*

❑ 형용사 폐허로 만드는, 파괴적인 [강조] ❑ 불륜은 결혼을 뿌리째 뒤흔드는 영향을 미친다. ❑ 형용사 충격적인 [강조] ❑ 진단 결과는 충격적이었다. 그녀는 암에 걸려 있었다. ❑ 형용사 굉장한, 매우 훌륭한 [강조] ❑ 그는 아주 뛰어난 전력 질주와 도약 실력을 과시하면서 자신의 최고 기량을 회복했다.

dev|as|ta|tion /dɛvəsteɪʃᵊn/ N-UNCOUNT **Devastation** is severe and widespread destruction or damage. ❑ *A huge bomb blast brought chaos and devastation to the center of Belfast yesterday.*

불가산명사 황폐화; 참화 ❑ 어제 폭탄에 의한 엄청난 폭발 사고로 벨파스트 중심부가 대혼란과 참화에 휩싸였다.

de|vel|op ♦♦♦ /dɪvɛləp/ (develops, developing, developed) **1** V-I When something **develops**, it grows or changes over a period of time and usually becomes more advanced, complete, or severe. ❑ *It's hard to say at this stage how*

❑ 자동사 발전하다, 발달하다 ❑ 시장이 어떻게 발전할지 지금 단계에서는 말하기 어렵다. ❑ 이러한 충돌이 공공연한 전투로 발전할 수도 있다. ● 발전된,

the market will develop. ❑ These clashes could develop into open warfare. ● de|vel|oped ADJ ❑ Their bodies were well-developed and super fit. ❷ V-I If a problem or difficulty **develops**, it begins to occur. ❑ A huge row has developed about the pollution emanating from a chemical plant. ❸ V-I If you say that a country **develops**, you mean that it changes from being a poor agricultural country to being a rich industrial country. ❑ All countries, it was predicted, would develop and develop fast. →see also **developed, developing** ❹ V-T/V-I If you **develop** a business or industry, or if it **develops**, it becomes bigger and more successful. [BUSINESS] ❑ An amateur hat-maker has won a scholarship to pursue her dreams of developing her own business. ● de|vel|oped ADJ ❑ Housing finance is less developed and less competitive in continental Europe. ❺ V-T To **develop** land or property means to make it more profitable, by building houses or factories or by improving the existing buildings. ❑ European entrepreneurs developed fashionable restaurants, bars, and discotheques in the area. ● de|vel|oped ADJ ❑ Developed land was to grow from 5.3% to 6.9%. ❻ V-T If you **develop** a habit, reputation, or belief, you start to have it and it then becomes stronger or more noticeable. ❑ Mr. Robinson has developed the reputation of a ruthless cost-cutter. ❼ V-T/V-I If you **develop** a skill, quality, or relationship, or if it **develops**, it becomes better or stronger. ❑ Now you have a good opportunity to develop a greater understanding of each other. ● de|vel|oped ADJ ❑ ...a highly developed instinct for self-preservation. ❽ V-T If a piece of equipment **develops** a fault, it starts to have the fault. ❑ The aircraft made an unscheduled landing at Gatwick after developing an electrical fault. ❾ V-T If someone **develops** a new product, they design it and produce it. ❑ He claims that several countries have developed nuclear weapons secretly. ❿ V-T/V-I If you **develop** an idea, theory, story, or theme, or if it **develops**, it gradually becomes more detailed, advanced, or complex. ❑ I would like to thank them for allowing me to develop their original idea. ⓫ V-T To **develop** photographs means to make negatives or prints from a photographic film. ❑ ...after developing one roll of film. →see **photography**

de|vel|oped /dɪvɛləpt/ ADJ If you talk about **developed** countries or the **developed** world, you mean the countries or the parts of the world that are wealthy and have many industries. ❑ This scarcity is inevitable in less developed countries.

de|vel|op|er /dɪvɛləpər/ (**developers**) ❶ N-COUNT A **developer** is a person or a company that buys land and builds houses, offices, stores, or factories on it, or buys existing buildings and makes them more modern. [BUSINESS] ❑ ...common land which would have a high commercial value if sold to developers. ❷ N-COUNT A **developer** is someone who develops something such as an idea, a design, or a product. ❑ John Bardeen was also co-developer of the theory of superconductivity.

de|vel|op|ing /dɪvɛləpɪŋ/ ADJ If you talk about **developing** countries or the **developing** world, you mean the countries or the parts of the world that are poor and have few industries. [ADJ n] ❑ In the developing world cigarette consumption is increasing.

de|vel|op|ment ♦♦♦ /dɪvɛləpmənt/ (**developments**) ❶ N-UNCOUNT **Development** is the gradual growth or formation of something. ❑ ...an ideal system for studying the development of the embryo. ❷ N-UNCOUNT **Development** is the growth of something such as a business or an industry. [BUSINESS] ❑ He firmly believes that education and a country's economic development are key factors to progress. ❸ N-VAR **Development** is the process or result of making a basic design gradually better and more advanced. ❑ It is spending $850m on research and development to get to the market place as soon as possible with faster microprocessors. ❹ N-UNCOUNT **Development** is the process of making an area of land or water more useful or profitable. ❑ The talks will focus on economic development of the region. ❺ N-COUNT A **development** is an event or incident which has recently happened and is likely to have an effect on the present situation. ❑ The police spokesman said: "We believe there has been a significant development in the case." ❻ N-COUNT A **development** is an area of houses or buildings which have been built by property developers. ❑ ...a 16-house development planned by Everlast Enterprises.

de|vel|op|ment bank (**development banks**) N-COUNT A **development bank** is a bank that provides money for projects in poor countries or areas. [BUSINESS] ❑ ...the Asian development bank.

de|vi|ant /diviənt/ ADJ **Deviant** behavior or thinking is different from what people normally consider to be acceptable. ❑ ...the social reactions to deviant and criminal behavior. ● de|vi|ance /diviəns/ N-UNCOUNT ❑ ...sexual deviance, including the abuse of children.

de|vi|ate /divieɪt/ (**deviates, deviating, deviated**) V-I To **deviate from** something means to start doing something different or not planned, especially in a way that causes problems for others. ❑ They stopped you as soon as you deviated from the script.

de|via|tion /divieɪʃⁿn/ (**deviations**) N-VAR **Deviation** means doing something that is different from what many people consider to be normal or acceptable. ❑ Deviation from the norm is not tolerated.

de|vice ♦♦♦ /dɪvaɪs/ (**devices**) N-COUNT A **device** is an object that has been invented for a particular purpose, for example for recording or measuring something. ❑ ...the electronic device that tells the starter when an athlete has moved from his blocks prematurely. →see **computer**

dev|il /dɛvⁿl/ (**devils**) ❶ N-PROPER In Judaism, Christianity, and Islam, **the Devil** is the most powerful evil spirit. ❷ N-COUNT A **devil** is an evil spirit. ❑ ...the idea of angels with wings and devils with horns and hoofs.

de|vi|ous /diviəs/ ADJ If you describe someone as **devious**, you do not like them because you think they are dishonest and like to keep things secret, often in a complicated way. [DISAPPROVAL] ❑ Newman was certainly devious, prepared to say one thing in print and something quite different in private.

발달된 형용사 ❑ 그들은 몸이 잘 발달했고 매우 건강했다. ❷ 자동사 발생하다 ❑ 화학 공장에서 유출되는 오염 물질을 둘러싸고 큰 다툼이 있어 왔다. ❸ 자동사 발전하다, 성장하다 ❑ 모든 국가들이 발전할 것이며, 빠른 속도로 성장하리라고 예측되었다. ❹ 타동사/자동사 발전시키다; 발전하다 [경제] ❑ 한 아마추어 제모 기술자가 이것을 자신의 사업으로 발전시키는 꿈을 펼칠 수 있도록 장학금을 받았다. ● 발전된 형용사 ❑ 주택 금융은 유럽 대륙에서는 발전이 덜 되었고 경쟁력이 떨어진다. ❺ 타동사 개발하다 ❑ 유럽 기업가들이 그 지역에 멋진 음식점과 술집, 디스코텍 등을 개발했다. ● 개발된 형용사 ❑ 개발된 땅이 5.3퍼센트에서 6.9퍼센트로 늘어날 예정이었다. ❻ 타동사 (습관을) 들이다; (평판을) 누리게 되다 ❑ 로빈슨 씨는 무자비한 비용 절감의 귀재라는 평판을 들어 왔다. ❼ 타동사/자동사 발전시키다; 발전하다 ❑ 이제 당신들은 서로에 대한 이해를 더욱 발전시킬 좋은 기회를 얻었다. ● 발전된, 발달된 형용사 ❑ 고도로 발달된 자기 보호 본능 ❽ 타동사 (결함 등을) 갖게 되다 ❑ 그 항공기는 전기적 결함이 발생한 이후 개트윅 공항에 불시착했다. ❾ 타동사 개발하다 ❑ 그는 몇몇 나라에서 비밀리에 핵무기를 개발해 왔다고 주장한다. ❿ 타동사/자동사 발전시키다; 발전하다 ❑ 원래의 안을 발전시킬 수 있도록 허락해 준 데 대해 그들에게 감사하고 싶다. ⓫ 타동사 현상하다 ❑ 필름 한 통을 현상한 후

형용사 선진의 ❑ 저개발국에서는 이러한 부족 현상이 불가피하다.

❶ 가산명사 택지 개발업자 [경제] ❑ 택지 개발업자에게 판다면 높은 상업적 가치를 갖게 될 수도 있을 공유지 ❷ 가산명사 개발자 ❑ 존 바딘은 초전도성 이론의 공동 개발자이기도 했다.

형용사 개발 도상의 ❑ 개발도상국들에서는 담배 소비가 증가하고 있다.

❶ 불가산명사 발육, 성장 ❑ 태아의 발육 연구를 위한 이상적인 시스템 ❷ 불가산명사 발전, 성장 [경제] ❑ 그는 교육과 국가 경제의 발전이 진보의 중요한 요소라고 확고하게 믿는다. ❸ 가산명사 또는 불가산명사 개발 ❑ 그 회사는 최대한 빠른 시일 내에 더 빠른 마이크로프로세서로 시장에 다가서기 위해 연구 개발에 8억 5천만 달러를 쓰고 있다. ❹ 불가산명사 개발 ❑ 회담의 초점은 그 지역의 경제 개발에 맞춰질 것이다. ❺ 가산명사 사태 진전, 추이 ❑ 경찰 대변인은 다음과 같이 말했다. "우리는 그 사건에 대해 중대한 진전이 있었다고 믿는다." ❻ 가산명사 조성지, 단지 ❑ 에버래스트 기업이 입안한 16 가구 단지

가산명사 개발은행 [경제] ❑ 아시아 개발은행

형용사 (표준에서) 벗어난, 일탈한 ❑ 일탈적이고 범죄적인 행동에 대한 사회의 반응 ● 이상, 일탈 불가산명사 ❑ 아동 학대를 포함한 성적 이상

자동사 벗어나다, 일탈하다 ❑ 네가 대본에서 벗어나자마자 그들이 너를 제지했다.

가산명사 또는 불가산명사 탈선, 일탈 ❑ 규범으로부터의 일탈은 용인되지 않는다.

가산명사 장치, 설비 ❑ 육상 선수가 발받침에서 일찍 발을 뗐을 때 출발 신호원에게 알려 주는 전자 장치

❶ 고유명사 사탄 ❷ 가산명사 악귀, 악마 ❑ 천사는 날개가 달려 있고 악마는 뿔과 발굽이 달려 있다는 생각

형용사 기만적인; 교활한 [탐탁잖음] ❑ 뉴먼은 확실히 기만적이고, 활자화된 말과 사적으로 하는 말이 완전히 딴판이었다.

de|vise /dɪvaɪz/ (devises, devising, devised) v-т If you **devise** a plan, system, or machine, you have the idea for it and design it. ❑ *We devised a scheme to help him.*

타동사 고안하다; 발명하다 ❑ 우리는 그를 돕기 위해 한 가지 계획을 고안했다.

Word Partnership   devise의 연어

N.   devise **new ways**, devise **a plan**, devise **a system**, devise **a strategy**

---

de|void /dɪvɔɪd/ ADJ If you say that someone or something is **devoid** of a quality or thing, you are emphasizing that they have none of it. [FORMAL, EMPHASIS] [v-link ADJ of n] ❑ *I have never looked on a face that was so devoid of feeling.*

형용사 ~이 결여된 [격식체, 강조] ❑ 나는 그처럼 감정이 결여된 얼굴을 본 적이 없다.

de|vo|lu|tion /diːvəluːʃⁿn, dɛv-/ N-UNCOUNT **Devolution** is the transfer of some authority or power from a central organization or government to smaller organizations or government departments. ❑ *...the devolution of power to the regions.*

불가산명사 권한 이양 ❑ 지방 분권

de|volve /dɪvɒlv/ (devolves, devolving, devolved) v-т/v-ı If you **devolve** power, authority, or responsibility **to** a less powerful person or group, or if it **devolves upon** them, it is transferred to them. ❑ *...the need to decentralize and devolve power to regional governments.* ❑ *The best companies are those that devolve responsibility as far as they can.*

타동사/자동사 (권한, 책임 등을) 이양하다; 이양되다 ❑ 권력을 분산시키고 지방 정부에 권한을 이양할 필요 ❑ 최고의 회사들은 책임을 최대한 널리 이양시키는 회사들이다.

de|vote /dɪvoʊt/ (devotes, devoting, devoted) **1** v-т If you **devote** yourself, your time, or your energy **to** something, you spend all or most of your time or energy on it. ❑ *He decided to devote the rest of his life to scientific investigation.* ❑ *Considerable resources have been devoted to proving him a liar.* **2** v-т If you **devote** a particular proportion of a piece of writing or a speech **to** a particular subject, you deal with the subject in that amount of space or time. ❑ *He devoted a major section of his massive report to an analysis of U.S. aircraft design.*

1 타동사 바치다, 쏟다 ❑ 그는 과학 연구에 여생을 바치기로 결심했다. ❑ 그가 거짓말쟁이임을 밝히는 데 상당한 자원을 쏟아 왔다. **2** 타동사 (지면이나 시간을) 할애하다 ❑ 그는 방대한 보고서의 대부분을 미국 항공기 설계 분석에 할애했다.

de|vot|ed /dɪvoʊtɪd/ **1** ADJ Someone who is **devoted to** a person loves that person very much. [ADJ n, v-link ADJ to n] ❑ *...a loving and devoted husband.* **2** ADJ If you are **devoted to** something, you care about it a lot and are very enthusiastic about it. [v-link ADJ to n, ADJ n] ❑ *I have personally been devoted to this cause for many years.* **3** ADJ Something that is **devoted to** a particular thing deals only with that thing or contains only that thing. [v-link ADJ to n] ❑ *...the original Jane Churchill shop, now devoted to a new range of accessories.*

1 형용사 열애하는, 아끼는 ❑ 애정이 깊고 아내를 열렬히 사랑하는 남편 **2** 형용사 몰두하는, 헌신적인 ❑ 나는 개인적으로 오랜 세월 동안 이 대의에 몰두해 왔다. **3** 형용사 ~만 전문으로 취급하는 ❑ 현재는 액세서리류 신제품만 전문으로 취급하는 제인 처칠 본점

de|vo|tion /dɪvoʊʃⁿn/ **1** N-UNCOUNT **Devotion** is great love, affection, or admiration for someone. ❑ *At first she was flattered by his devotion.* **2** N-UNCOUNT **Devotion** is commitment to a particular activity. ❑ *...devotion to the cause of the people and to socialism.*

1 불가산명사 헌신적인 애정, 열애 ❑ 처음에 그녀는 그의 헌신적인 애정에 기분이 좋았다. **2** 불가산명사 헌신, 전념 ❑ 국민 복지와 사회주의에의 헌신

de|vour /dɪvaʊər/ (devours, devouring, devoured) **1** v-т If a person or animal **devours** something, they eat it quickly and eagerly. ❑ *A medium-sized dog will devour at least one can of food plus biscuits per day.* **2** v-т If you **devour** a book or magazine, for example, you read it quickly and with great enthusiasm. ❑ *She began buying and devouring newspapers when she was only 12.*

1 타동사 게걸스럽게 먹다, 먹어 치우다 ❑ 중간 크기의 개 한 마리는 하루에 최소한 먹이 한 통에 비스킷까지 먹어 치운다. **2** 타동사 탐독하다 ❑ 그녀는 겨우 열두 살 때 신문을 사서 탐독하기 시작했다.

de|vout /dɪvaʊt/ **1** ADJ A **devout** person has deep religious beliefs. ❑ *She was a devout Christian.* ● N-PLURAL **The devout** are people who are devout. ❑ *...priests instructing the devout.* **2** ADJ If you describe someone as a **devout** supporter or a **devout** opponent of something, you mean that they support it enthusiastically or oppose it strongly. [ADJ n] ❑ *Devout Marxists believed fascism was the "last stand of the bourgeoisie."*

1 형용사 독실한, 경건한 ❑ 그녀는 독실한 기독교 신자였다. ● 복수명사 독실한 신자 ❑ 독실한 신자들을 교육하는 성직자들 **2** 형용사 열렬한 ❑ 열렬한 마르크스주의자들은 파시즘이 '부르주아 계급의 최후의 저항'이라고 믿었다.

dew /du, BRIT dyu/ N-UNCOUNT **Dew** is small drops of water that form on the ground and other surfaces outdoors during the night. ❑ *The dew gathered on the leaves.*

불가산명사 이슬 ❑ 나뭇잎에 이슬이 맺혔다.

dia|be|tes /daɪəbitɪs, -tiz, BRIT daɪəbiːtiːz/ N-UNCOUNT **Diabetes** is a medical condition in which someone has too much sugar in their blood. →see **sugar**

불가산명사 당뇨병

dia|bet|ic /daɪəbɛtɪk/ (diabetics) **1** N-COUNT A **diabetic** is a person who suffers from diabetes. ❑ *...an insulin-dependent diabetic.* ● ADJ **Diabetic** is also an adjective. ❑ *...diabetic patients.* **2** ADJ **Diabetic** means relating to diabetes. [ADJ n] ❑ *He found her in a diabetic coma.*

1 가산명사 당뇨병 환자 ❑ 인슐린에 의지하는 당뇨병 환자 ● 형용사 당뇨병 환자의 ❑ 당뇨병 환자 **2** 형용사 당뇨병의 ❑ 그는 그녀가 당뇨성 혼수에 빠져 있는 걸 발견했다.

Word Link   dia ≈ across, through : **diagnose, diagonal, dialog**

---

di|ag|nose /daɪəgnoʊs, BRIT daɪəgnoʊz/ (diagnoses, diagnosing, diagnosed) v-т If someone or something **is diagnosed as** having a particular illness or problem, their illness or problem is identified. If an illness or problem **is diagnosed**, it is identified. ❑ *The soldiers were diagnosed as having flu.* ❑ *Susan had a mental breakdown and was diagnosed with schizophrenia.* →see **diagnosis, illness**

타동사 진단받다 ❑ 그 병사들은 독감에 걸린 것으로 진단받았다. ❑ 수잔은 정신 이상을 겪고 정신 분열증 진단을 받았다.

di|ag|no|sis /daɪəgnoʊsɪs/ (diagnoses) N-VAR **Diagnosis** is the discovery and naming of what is wrong with someone who is ill or with something that is not working properly. ❑ *I need to have a second test to confirm the diagnosis.* →see Word Web: **diagnosis**

가산명사 또는 불가산명사 진단; 식별 ❑ 진단을 확인하기 위해 다시 한 번 검사를 할 필요가 있다.

Word Web   diagnosis

Many doctors recommend that their **patients** get a routine **physical examination** once a year—even if they're feeling perfectly well. This enables the **physician** to detect **symptoms** and **diagnose** possible **diseases** at an early stage. The doctor may begin by using a **tongue** depressor to look down the patient's throat for possible **infections**. Then he or she may use a stethoscope to listen to subtle sounds in the heart, lungs, and stomach. A **blood pressure** reading is always part of the exam and involves the use of a blood pressure cuff.

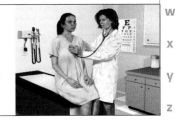

di|ag|nos|tic /daɪəgnɒstɪk/ ADJ **Diagnostic** equipment, methods, or systems are used for discovering what is wrong with people who are ill or with things that do not work properly. [ADJ n] ❑ ...X-rays and other diagnostic tools.

형용사 진단용의 ❑ 엑스선과 다른 진단 장비

Word Link
dia ≈ across, through : diagnose, diagonal, dialog

---

di|ag|o|nal /daɪægən³l, -ægn³l/ ADJ A **diagonal** line or movement goes in a sloping direction, for example, from one corner of a square across to the opposite corner. ❑ ...a pattern of diagonal lines. ● **di|ag|o|nal|ly** ADV ❑ Vaulting the stile, he headed diagonally across the paddock.

형용사 대각선의 ❑ 대각선 무늬 ● 대각선으로, 비스듬히 부사 ❑ 그는 층계를 뛰어넘어 방목장을 대각선으로 가로질러 갔다.

Word Link
gram ≈ writing : diagram, program, telegram

---

dia|gram /daɪəgræm/ (**diagrams**) N-COUNT A **diagram** is a simple drawing which consists mainly of lines and is used, for example, to explain how a machine works. ❑ ...a circuit diagram.

가산명사 도표 ❑ 회로도

Thesaurus   diagram의 참조어
N.   blueprint, chart, design, illustration, plan

---

dial /daɪəl/ (**dials, dialing, dialed**) [BRIT, sometimes AM **dialling, dialled**] **1** N-COUNT A **dial** is the part of a machine or instrument such as a clock or watch which shows you the time or a measurement that has been recorded. ❑ The luminous dial on the clock showed five minutes to seven. **2** N-COUNT A **dial** is a control on a device or piece of equipment which you can move in order to adjust the setting, for example to select or change the frequency on a radio or the temperature of a heater. ❑ He turned the dial on the radio. **3** V-T/V-I If you **dial** or if you **dial** a number, you turn the dial or press the buttons on a telephone in order to phone someone. ❑ He lifted the phone and dialed her number.

[영국영어, 미국영어 가끔 dialling, dialled] **1** 가산명사 눈금판 ❑ 시계의 발광 눈금판은 7시 5분 전을 가리켰다. **2** 가산명사 다이얼 ❑ 그는 라디오 다이얼을 돌렸다. **3** 타동사/자동사 (전화 번호를) 돌리다, (전화 번호를) 누르다 ❑ 그는 전화기를 들고 그녀의 번호를 눌렀다.

dia|lect /daɪəlɛkt/ (**dialects**) N-COUNT A **dialect** is a form of a language that is spoken in a particular area. [also in n] ❑ In Italy in the fifties, the number of Italians who spoke only local dialect was enormous. →see **English**

가산명사 방언 ❑ 50년대 이탈리아에는, 지방 방언만을 구사하는 이탈리아인이 엄청나게 많았다.

dial|ling code (**dialling codes**) N-COUNT A **dialling code** for a particular city or region is the series of numbers that you have to dial before a particular telephone number if you are making a call to that place from a different area. [mainly BRIT; AM **area code**] ❑ Australia's international dialling code is 0011, New Zealand's is 00.

가산명사 지역 번호; 국가 번호 [주로 영국영어; 미국영어 area code] ❑ 호주에서 국제 전화 통화시 호출번호는 0011이고 뉴질랜드에서 호출번호는 00이다.

dial|ling tone (**dialling tones**) N-COUNT The **dialling tone** is the same as the **dial tone**. [BRIT]

가산명사 발신음 [영국영어]

dia|log ♦◇◇ /daɪəlɒg, BRIT daɪəlɒg/ (**dialogs**) [BRIT, sometimes AM also **dialogue**] **1** N-VAR **Dialog** is communication or discussion between people or groups of people such as governments or political parties. ❑ People of all social standings should be given equal opportunities for dialog. **2** N-VAR A **dialog** is a conversation between two people in a book, film, or play. ❑ Although the dialog is sharp, the actors move rather too awkwardly around the stage.

[영국영어, 미국영어 가끔 dialogue] **1** 가산명사 또는 불가산명사 대화, 토론 ❑ 사회 각층의 사람들에게 동등한 발언 기회를 주어야 한다. **2** 가산명사 또는 불가산명사 대화 ❑ 대사는 완벽하지만 배우들의 무대 동작이 너무 굼뜬 감이 있다.

dia|log box (**dialog boxes**) N-COUNT A **dialog box** is a small area containing information or questions that appears on a computer screen when you are performing particular operations. [COMPUTING] ❑ You should now see a dialog box listing all of the print queues on your network.

가산명사 대화창 [컴퓨터] ❑ 이제 네트워크의 인쇄 대기열이 대화창에 나타날 것이다.

dial tone (**dial tones**) N-COUNT The **dial tone** is the noise which you hear when you pick up a telephone receiver and which means that you can dial the number you want. [AM; BRIT **dialling tone**] ❑ It was only as she tried for the second time that she realized that there was no dial tone.

가산명사 발신음 [미국영어; 영국영어 dialling tone] ❑ 수화기를 다시 들었을 때에야, 그녀는 발신음이 들리지 않는다는 것을 깨달았다.

di|am|eter /daɪæmɪtər/ (**diameters**) N-COUNT The **diameter** of a round object is the length of a straight line that can be drawn across it, passing through the middle of it. [also in n] ❑ ...a tube less than a fifth of the diameter of a human hair. →see **area, circle**

가산명사 지름, 직경 ❑ 사람 머리카락 굵기의 1/5도 안 되는 관

dia|mond /daɪmənd, daɪə-/ (**diamonds**) **1** N-VAR A **diamond** is a hard, bright, precious stone which is clear and colorless. Diamonds are used in jewelry and for cutting very hard substances. ❑ ...a pair of diamond earrings. **2** N-COUNT A **diamond** is a shape with four straight sides of equal length where the opposite angles are the same, but none of the angles is equal to 90°: ♦. ❑ ...forming his hands into the shape of a diamond. **3** N-UNCOUNT-COLL **Diamonds** is one of the four suits of cards in a pack of playing cards. Each card in the suit is marked with one or more red symbols in the shape of a diamond. ❑ He drew the seven of diamonds. ● N-COUNT A **diamond** is a playing card of this suit. ❑ ...win the ace of clubs and play a diamond. →see **crystal** →see Word Web: **diamond**

1 가산명사 또는 불가산명사 다이아몬드 ❑ 다이아몬드 귀걸이 한 쌍 **2** 가산명사 다이아몬드 모양, 마름모꼴 ❑ 그가 양손으로 다이아몬드 모양을 만들면서 **3** 불가산명사-집합 다이아몬드 패 ❑ 그는 다이아몬드 7을 뽑았다. ● 가산명사 다이아몬드 패 ❑ 클럽 에이스를 얻고 다이아몬드 패를 낸다.

dia|per /daɪpər, daɪə-/ (**diapers**) N-COUNT A **diaper** is a piece of soft towel or paper, which you fasten around a baby's bottom in order to contain its urine and feces. [AM; BRIT **nappy**] ❑ He never changed her diapers, never bathed her.

가산명사 기저귀 [미국영어; 영국영어 nappy] ❑ 그는 아이 기저귀를 갈아준 적도 목욕을 시킨 적도 없었다.

dia|phragm /daɪəfræm/ (**diaphragms**) **1** N-COUNT Your **diaphragm** is a muscle between your lungs and your stomach. It is used when you breathe. ❑ ...the skill of breathing from the diaphragm. **2** N-COUNT A **diaphragm** is a circular rubber contraceptive device that a woman places inside her vagina. →see **respiratory system**

1 가산명사 횡격막 ❑ 복식 호흡법 **2** 가산명사 피임 격막

di|ar|rhea /daɪəriə/ [BRIT **diarrhoea**] N-UNCOUNT If someone has **diarrhea**, a lot of liquid feces comes out of their body because they are ill. ❑ But the food itself was barely digestible, and many team members suffered from diarrhea or constipation.

[영국영어 diarrhoea] 불가산명사 설사 ❑ 하지만 음식 자체도 소화가 잘 안 되는 음식이었고 팀원 중 상당수가 설사나 변비로 고생했다.

Word Web   diamond

Diamonds are made of pure **carbon**. They are the hardest **mineral** to form and develop deep inside the earth. To create a diamond, the pressure must reach almost half a million pounds per square inch. The temperature must be at least 400°C*. Many of today's diamonds formed millions of years ago. They reach the surface of the earth through a process similar to a volcanic eruption. Then the diamonds are **mined**. A diamond is not beautiful until someone cuts it and exposes its many **facets**. **Jewelers** give the weight of a diamond in **carats**. One carat is about 200 milligrams.

400°C=*about 752°F.*

---

di|a|ry ◆◇◇ /da͟ɪəri/ (diaries) N-COUNT A **diary** is a book which has a separate space for each day of the year. You use a diary to write down things you plan to do, or to record what happens in your life day by day. ❑ *I had earlier read the entry from Harold Nicolson's diary for July 10, 1940.* →see **history** →see Word Web: **diary**

가산명사 일기 ❑ 나는 해롤드 니콜슨이 1940년 7월 10일에 쓴 일기를 전에 읽은 적이 있었다.

dice /da͟ɪs/ (dices, dicing, diced) **1** N-COUNT A **dice** is a small cube which has between one and six spots or numbers on its sides, and which is used in games to provide random numbers. In old-fashioned English, "dice" was used only as a plural form, and the singular was **die**, but now "dice" is used as both the singular and the plural form. ❑ *I throw both dice and get double 6.* **2** V-T If you **dice** food, you cut it into small cubes. ❑ *Dice the onion and boil in the water for about fifteen minutes.*

1 가산명사 주사위 ❑ 내가 던진 주사위 두 개 모두 6이 나왔다. **2** 타동사 깍두기 모양으로 썰다 ❑ 양파를 깍두기 모양으로 썰어서 15분간 물에서 익힌다.

Word Link   dict ≈ speaking : contra**dict**, **dict**ate, pre**dict**

dic|tate (dictates, dictating, dictated)

> The verb is pronounced /dɪkte͟ɪt, dɪkte͟ɪt/. The noun is pronounced /dɪkte͟ɪt/.

동사는 /dɪkte͟ɪt, dɪkte͟ɪt/으로 발음되고, 명사는 /dɪkte͟ɪt/으로 발음된다.

1 V-T If you **dictate** something, you say or read it aloud for someone else to write down. ❑ *Sheldon writes every day of the week, dictating his novels in the morning.* **2** V-T If someone **dictates to** someone else, they tell them what they should do or can do. ❑ *What right has one country to dictate the environmental standards of another?* ❑ *What gives them the right to dictate to us what we should eat?* **3** V-T If one thing **dictates** another, the first thing causes or influences the second thing. ❑ *The film's budget dictated a tough schedule.* ❑ *Of course, a number of factors will dictate how long an apple tree can survive.* **4** V-T You say that reason or common sense **dictates that** a particular thing is the case when you believe strongly that it is the case and that reason or common sense will cause other people to agree. ❑ *Common sense now dictates that it would be wise to sell a few shares.* **5** N-COUNT **Dictates** are principles or rules which you consider to be extremely important. ❑ *We have followed the dictates of our consciences and have done our duty.*

1 타동사 불러 주어 받아쓰게 하다 ❑ 셀던은 아침마다 자신의 소설을 받아쓰게 하면서 일주일에 하루도 쉬지 않고 글을 쓴다. **2** 타동사 명령하다, 지시하다 ❑ 한 국가가 다른 국가의 환경 기준에 대해 이래라 저래라 할 권리가 있는가? ❑ 도대체 무슨 권리로 그들이 우리에게 무엇을 먹어라 말하고 하는 거야? **3** 타동사 원인이 되다, 영향을 주다 ❑ 영화 예산 때문에 촬영 스케줄이 빡빡해졌다. ❑ 물론 다양한 요소들이 사과나무 수명에 영향을 줄 것이다. **4** 타동사 (이성이나 상식이) 지시하다 ❑ 이제 상식을 따른다면 지분을 조금 파는 편이 현명할 것이다. **5** 가산명사 명령, 법칙 ❑ 우리는 양심의 명령에 따라 맡은 바 임무를 다했다.

Word Partnership   dictate의 연어

> N.   **circumstances** dictate, **factors** dictate, **rules** dictate **3**

dic|ta|tion /dɪkte͟ɪʃən/ N-UNCOUNT **Dictation** is the speaking or reading aloud of words for someone else to write down. ❑ *...taking dictation from the dean of the Faculty.*

불가산명사 받아쓰기 ❑ 대학 학장님의 말을 받아 적으면서

dic|ta|tor /dɪkte͟ɪtər, BRIT dɪkte͟ɪtə'/ (dictators) N-COUNT A **dictator** is a ruler who has complete power in a country, especially power which is obtained by force and is used unfairly or cruelly. ❑ *...foreign dictators who contravene humanitarian conventions.*

가산명사 독재자 ❑ 인권 협약을 위반한 외국 독재자들

dic|ta|to|rial /dɪktətɔ͟ːriəl/ ADJ If you describe someone's behavior as **dictatorial**, you do not like the fact that they tell people what to do in a forceful and unfair way. [DISAPPROVAL] ❑ *...his dictatorial management style.*

형용사 독재적인 [탐탁찮음] ❑ 그의 독재적인 경영 스타일

dic|ta|tor|ship /dɪkte͟ɪtərʃɪp/ (dictatorships) **1** N-VAR **Dictatorship** is government by a dictator. ❑ *...a new era of democracy after a long period of military dictatorship in the country.* **2** N-COUNT A **dictatorship** is a country which is ruled by a dictator or by a very strict and harsh government. ❑ *Every country in the region was a military dictatorship.*

1 가산명사 또는 불가산명사 독재 정권 ❑ 오랫동안 군사 독재 정권의 지배를 받은 나라에 새로 열린 민주주의 시대 **2** 가산명사 독재 국가 ❑ 그 지역 내의 모든 국가가 군사 독재 국가였다.

dic|tion|ary /dɪ͟kʃəneri, BRIT dɪ͟kʃənri/ (dictionaries) N-COUNT A **dictionary** is a book in which the words and phrases of a language are listed alphabetically, together with their meanings or their translations in another language. ❑ *...a Welsh-English dictionary.*

가산명사 사전 ❑ 웨일즈 어-영어 사전

Word Web   diary

A **diary** is an informal daily written **record** of the events in someone's life. Most diaries are private **documents**. But sometimes an important diary is published. One such example is *The Diary of a Young Girl*. This is Anne Frank's World War II **chronicle** of her family's unsuccessful attempt to hide from the Nazis. They were eventually arrested, and later Anne died in a concentration camp. This **primary source** document offers us a personal view. It is full of rich details that are often missing from other historical **texts**. The book is now available in 60 different languages.

a b c d e f g h i j k l m n o p q r s t u v w x y z

A

did /dɪd/ **Did** is the past tense of **do**.

didn't ♦♦♦ /dɪdⁿt/ **Didn't** is the usual spoken form of "did not."

B

die ♦♦♦ /daɪ/ (**dies, dying, died**) **1** V-T/V-I When people, animals, and plants **die**, they stop living. [no passive] ❑ *A year later my dog died.* ❑ *Sadly, both he and my mother died of cancer.*

do의 과거형

did not의 축약형

1 타동사/자동사 죽다, 사망하다 ❑ 일 년 후에 우리 강아지가 죽었다. ❑ 안타깝게도 그와 우리 어머니 모두 암으로 사망했다.

C

Do not confuse **dead** with **died**. **Died** is the past tense and past participle of the verb **die**, and thus indicates the action of dying. ❑ *She died in 1934... Two men have died since the rioting broke out.* You do not use **died** as an adjective. You use **dead** instead. ❑ *More than 2,200 dead birds have been found.*

dead와 died를 혼동하지 않도록 하라. died는 동사 die의 과거 및 과거 분사형이며, 따라서 죽는 행위를 나타낸다. ❑ 그녀는 1934년에 사망했다... 소요가 발생한 이래 남자 두 명이 죽었다. died는 형용사로 쓰지 않고 대신 dead를 쓴다. ❑ 2,200 마리 이상의 죽은 새가 발견되었다.

D

2 V-I If a machine or device **dies**, it stops completely, especially after a period of working more and more slowly or inefficiently. [WRITTEN] ❑ *Then suddenly, the engine coughed, spluttered, and died.* **3** V-I You can say that you **are dying of** thirst, hunger, boredom, or curiosity to emphasize that you are very thirsty, hungry, bored, or curious. [INFORMAL, EMPHASIS] [only cont] ❑ *Order me a pot of tea, I'm dying of thirst.* **4** PHRASE You can say that you **are dying for** something or **are dying to** do something to emphasize that you very much want to have it or do it. [INFORMAL, EMPHASIS] [only cont] ❑ *I'm dying for a breath of fresh air.* **5** V-T/V-I You can use **die** in expressions such as "**I almost died**" or "**I'd die if anything happened**" where you are emphasizing your feelings about a situation, for example to say that it is very shocking, upsetting, embarrassing, or amusing. [INFORMAL, mainly SPOKEN, EMPHASIS] ❑ *I nearly died when I learned where I was ending up.* ❑ *I nearly died of shame.* **6** →see also **dying** **7** PHRASE If you say that habits or attitudes **die hard**, you mean that they take a very long time to disappear or change, so that it may not be possible to get rid of them completely. ❑ *Old habits die hard.*

E

F

G

2 자동사 멈추다 [문어체] ❑ 그리고 나서 갑자기 엔진이 덜컥대고 끽끽거리다 완전히 멈췄다. **3** 자동사 -해서 죽을 지경이다 [비격식체, 강조] ❑ 차 한 주전자 주문해 줘. 목말라 죽겠어. **4** 구 죽도록 -을 갖고 싶다; 죽도록 -하고 싶다 [비격식체, 강조] ❑ 신선한 공기를 마시고 싶어 죽겠다. **5** 타동사/자동사 상황에 대한 여러 가지 느낌을 강조할 때 사용 [비격식체, 주로 구어체, 강조] ❑ 내가 결국 어디로 갈지 알았을 때 난 거의 기절할 뻔했다. ❑ 창피해서 죽고 싶은 심정이었다. **7** 구 좀처럼 없어지지 않는다 ❑ 세 살 버릇 여든까지 간다.

H

Thesaurus   die의 참조어

I

V.   pass away; (*ant.*) live **1**
      break down, fail **2**

J

Word Partnership   die의 연어

K

V.   **deserve to die, going to die, live or die, sentenced to die, want to die, would rather** die **1**
N.   **right to die 1**

L

▶**die out 1** PHRASAL VERB If something **dies out**, it becomes less and less common and eventually disappears completely. ❑ *We used to believe that capitalism would soon die out.* **2** PHRASAL VERB If something such as a fire or wind **dies out**, it gradually stops burning or blowing. [AM] ❑ *Once the fire has died out, the salvage team will move in.*

M

1 구동사 점차 사라지다 ❑ 우리는 한때 자본주의가 곧 사라지리라고 믿었다. **2** 구동사 찾아지다, 잦아들다 [미국영어] ❑ 일단 불길이 잦아들면, 구조대가 투입될 것이다.

N

die·sel /diːzⁿl/ (**diesels**) **1** N-MASS **Diesel** or **diesel oil** is the heavy oil used in a diesel engine. **2** N-COUNT A **diesel** is a vehicle which has a diesel engine. ❑ *I keep hearing that diesels are better now than ever before.*

1 물질명사 디젤유 **2** 가산명사 디젤차 ❑ 요즘 디젤차가 전보다 좋아졌다는 소리가 많이 들린다.

die·sel en·gine (**diesel engines**) N-COUNT A **diesel engine** is an internal combustion engine in which oil is burned by very hot air. Diesel engines are used in buses and trucks, and in some trains and cars.

가산명사 디젤엔진

O

P

diet ♦♦◇ /daɪət/ (**diets, dieting, dieted**) **1** N-VAR Your **diet** is the type and range of food that you regularly eat. ❑ *It's never too late to improve your diet.* **2** N-COUNT If a doctor puts someone on a **diet**, he or she makes them eat a special type or range of foods in order to improve their health. ❑ *He was put on a diet of milky food.* **3** N-VAR If you are on a **diet**, you eat special kinds of food or less food than usual because you are trying to lose weight. ❑ *Have you been on a diet? You've lost a lot of weight.* **4** V-I If you **are dieting**, you eat special kinds of food or you eat less food than usual because you are trying to lose weight. ❑ *I've been dieting ever since the birth of my fourth child.* **5** ADJ **Diet** drinks or foods have been specially produced so that they do not contain many calories. [ADJ n] ❑ *...sugar-free diet drinks.* **6** N-COUNT If you are fed on a **diet** of something, especially something unpleasant or of poor quality, you receive or experience a very large amount of it. ❑ *The radio had fed him a diet of pop songs.* →see **vegetarian** →see Word Web: **diet**

Q

R

S

T

1 가산명사 또는 불가산명사 평상시 먹는 음식 ❑ 지금 식습관을 개선하긴 늦지 않다. **2** 가산명사 규정식, 식이 요법 ❑ 그는 유제품 중심의 식이 요법을 처방 받았다. **3** 가산명사 또는 불가산명사 다이어트 ❑ 다이어트 했어? 살이 많이 빠졌는데. **4** 자동사 다이어트 중이다 ❑ 나는 넷째 아이 출산 이후로 계속 다이어트 중이다. **5** 형용사 다이어트의, 저칼로리의 ❑ 무설탕 저칼로리 음료 **6** 가산명사 상당히 많은 양 ❑ 그는 라디오에서 팝송을 질리도록 들었다.

Word Partnership   diet의 연어

U

ADJ.   **balanced** diet, **healthy** diet, **proper** diet, **vegetarian** diet **1**
      strict diet **2 3**
N.   diet **and exercise 1 2 3**
      diet **soda 5**
PREP.   **on a** diet **2 3**

V

W

di·e·tary /daɪətɛri, BRIT daɪətri/ ADJ You can use **dietary** to describe anything that concerns a person's diet. ❑ *Dr. Susan Hankinson has studied the dietary habits of more than 50,000 women.*

형용사 음식의, 식이 요법의 ❑ 수잔 한킨슨 박사는 여성 5만 명 이상을 대상으로 식습관을 연구해 왔다.

X

dif·fer /dɪfər/ (**differs, differing, differed**) **1** V-RECIP If two or more things **differ**, they are unlike each other in some way. ❑ *The story he told police differed from the one he told his mother.* **2** V-RECIP If people **differ** about something, they do not agree with each other about it. ❑ *The two leaders had differed on the issue of sanctions.* ❑ *That is where we differ.* **3** to **agree to differ** →see **agree**

Y

1 상호동사 다르다 ❑ 그가 경찰에게 한 이야기와 어머니에게 한 이야기가 달랐다. **2** 상호동사 의견을 달리하다 ❑ 제재 문제에 관해 두 정상은 의견을 달리했다. ❑ 그 점에서 우리 의견이 다르다.

Z

dif·fer·ence ♦♦◇ /dɪfrəns, dɪfrəns/ (**differences**) **1** N-COUNT The **difference** between two things is the way in which they are unlike each other. ❑ *That is the fundamental difference between the two societies.* ❑ *...the vast difference in size.*

1 가산명사 다름, 차이 ❑ 그것이 바로 그 두 사회 간의 근본적인 차이다. ❑ 규모상의 엄청난 차이 **2** 단수명사 차, 차액 ❑ 차가 8532다. **3** 가산명사 의견 차 ❑ 두

Word Web　　diet

Recent U.S. government reports show that about 64% of American adults are **overweight** or **obese**. The number of people on **weight loss diets** is at an all-time high. And **fad** diets are everywhere. One diet advises people to eat mostly **protein**—meat, fish, and cheese—and very few **carbohydrates**. However, another diet recommends eating at least 40% carbohydrates. But when a weight-loss diet works, it's for one simple reason. When you burn more **calories** than you take in, you lose weight. Most doctors agree that a balanced diet with plenty of exercise is best.

② N-SING A **difference** between two quantities is the amount by which one quantity is less than the other. ❏ *The difference is 8532.* ❸ N-COUNT If people have their **differences** about something, they disagree about it. ❏ *The two communities are learning how to resolve their differences.* ❹ PHRASE If something **makes** a **difference** or **makes** a lot of **difference**, it affects you and helps you in what you are doing. If something **makes** no **difference**, it does not have any effect on what you are doing. ❏ *Where you live can make such a difference to the way you feel.* ❺ PHRASE If there is a **difference of opinion** between two or more people or groups, they disagree about something. ❏ *Was there a difference of opinion over what to do with the Nobel Prize money?*

공동체는 의견 차를 해소할 수 있는 방법을 배워 가고 있다. ❹ 구 영향을 주다, 효과가 있다; 효과가 없다 ❏ 한 사람이 사는 곳이 그 사람의 정서에 이와 같은 영향을 줄 수 있다. ❺ 구 의견 차 ❏ 노벨상 상금을 어떻게 할 것인지에 대해 의견 차이가 있었습니까?

Word Partnership　　difference의 연어

ADJ.	**big/major** difference ①
V.	**know the** difference, **notice a** difference, **tell the** difference ①
	pay the difference ②
	settle a difference ③
	make a difference ④
N.	difference **in age**, difference **in price** ②
	difference **of opinion** ⑤

dif|fer|ent ♦♦♦ /dɪfərənt, dɪfrənt/ ① ADJ If two people or things are **different**, they are not like each other in one or more ways. ❏ *London was different from most European capitals.* ❏ *If he'd attended music school, how might things have been different?* ● ADJ People sometimes say that one thing is **different than** another. This use is acceptable in American English, but is often considered incorrect in British English. [v-link *adj* than n/cl] ❏ *We're not really any different than they are.* ● In British English, people sometimes say that one thing is **different to** another. Some people consider this use to be incorrect. ❏ *My approach is totally different to his.* ● **dif|fer|ent|ly** ADV ❏ *Every individual learns differently.* ② ADJ You use **different** to indicate that you are talking about two or more separate and distinct things of the same kind. [ADJ n] ❏ *Different countries specialized in different products.* ③ ADJ You can describe something as **different** when it is unusual and not like others of the same kind. [v-link ADJ] ❏ *The result is interesting and different, but do not attempt the recipe if time is short.*

① 형용사 다른 ❏ 런던은 대부분의 유럽 수도와 달랐다. ❏ 그가 음악 학교에 다녔더라면, 상황이 얼마나 달랐을까? ● 형용사 -와 다른 ❏ 우리도 사실 그들과 많이 다르지 않다. ● [영국영어] -와 다른 ❏ 나의 접근 방식은 그와 완전히 다르다. ● 다르게 부사 ❏ 사람마다 각각 배우는 방식이 다르다. ② 형용사 서로 다른, 별개의 ❏ 나라마다 특화 상품이 다르다. ③ 형용사 색다른, 독특한 ❏ 그 결과 재미있고 색다른 음식이 완성됩니다. 하지만 시간이 부족할 경우 이 요리법을 사용하지 마세요.

Thesaurus　　different의 참조어

ADJ.	dissimilar ①
	distinct, odd, peculiar, unique ③

dif|fer|en|tial /dɪfərɛnʃl/ (**differentials**) ① N-COUNT In mathematics and economics, a **differential** is a difference between two values in a scale. ❏ *Germany and France pledged to maintain the differential between their two currencies.* ② N-COUNT A **differential** is a difference between things, especially rates of pay. [mainly BRIT] ❏ *During the Second World War, industrial wage differentials in Britain widened.*

① 가산명사 차이 ❏ 독일과 프랑스가 양국 통화 간의 환율 차이를 유지하겠다고 약속했다. ② 가산명사 임금 격차 [주로 영국영어] ❏ 2차 세계 대전 동안 영국 공업 부문의 임금 격차가 벌어졌다.

dif|fer|en|ti|ate /dɪfərɛnʃieɪt/ (**differentiates**, **differentiating**, **differentiated**) ① V-T/V-I If you **differentiate between** things or if you **differentiate** one thing **from** another, you recognize or show the difference between them. ❏ *A child may not differentiate between his imagination and the real world.* ② V-T A quality or feature that **differentiates** one thing **from** another makes the two things different. ❏ *...distinctive policies that differentiate them from the other parties.* ● **dif|fer|en|tia|tion** /dɪfərɛnʃieɪʃⁿn/ N-UNCOUNT ❏ *Their marketing director claims the differentiation between the two ranges will increase.*

① 타동사/자동사 구분하다 ❏ 어린아이는 상상과 현실을 구분하지 못할 수도 있다. ② 타동사 구분짓다, 차별하다 ❏ 다른 정당과 차별되는 이들만의 정책 ● 차별, 구별 불가산명사 ❏ 마케팅 담당은 두 제품군이 더욱더 차별화될 것이라고 힘주어 말한다.

dif|fi|cult ♦♦♦ /dɪfɪkʌlt, -kəlt/ ① ADJ Something that is **difficult** is not easy to do, understand, or deal with. ❏ *The lack of childcare provisions made it difficult for single mothers to get jobs.* ❏ *It was a very difficult decision to make.* ② ADJ Someone who is **difficult** behaves in an unreasonable and unhelpful way. ❏ *I had a feeling you were going to be difficult about this.*

① 형용사 어려운 ❏ 양육 시설이 부족해서 혼자 아이를 키우는 어머니가 직장을 구하기가 어려웠다. ❏ 그것은 정말 내리기 어려운 결정이었다. ② 형용사 까다로운 ❏ 이에 대해 네가 까다롭게 굴 것 같다는 생각이 들었어.

Thesaurus　　difficult의 참조어

ADJ.	challenging, demanding, hard, tough; (ant.) easy, simple, uncomplicated ①
	irritable, unreasonable; (ant.) cooperative ②

dif|fi|cul|ty ♦♦◇ /dɪfɪkʌlti, -kəlti/ (**difficulties**) ① N-COUNT A **difficulty** is a problem. ❏ *...the difficulty of getting accurate information.* ② N-UNCOUNT If you have **difficulty** doing something, you are not able to do it easily. ❏ *Do you have*

① 가산명사 어려움, 문제 ❏ 정확한 정보 획득의 어려움 ② 불가산명사 어려움 ❏ 아침에 일어나는 것이 어렵습니까? ③ 구 곤경에 처한, 곤란한 입장인 ❏ 사실

a
b
c
d
e
f
g
h
i
j
k
l
m
n
o
p
q
r
s
t
u
v
w
x
y
z

difficulty getting up? ③ PHRASE If you are **in difficulty** or **in difficulties**, you are having a lot of problems. ❑ *You have to admit that you are, in fact, in difficulties.*

당신이 지금 곤란한 상황에 처했음을 인정해야 합니다.

Thesaurus	*difficulty*의 참조어
N.	dilemma, problem, trouble ①

dif|fi|dent /dɪfɪdənt/ ADJ Someone who is **diffident** is rather shy and does not enjoy talking about themselves or being noticed by other people. ❑ *John was as bouncy and ebullient as Helen was diffident and reserved.* ● **dif|fi|dence** /dɪfɪdəns/ N-UNCOUNT ❑ *He tapped on the door, opened it and entered with a certain diffidence.*

형용사 수줍은, 숫기 없는 ❑ 헬렌은 수줍고 말없는 아이였고, 그와 정반대로 존은 명랑하고 쾌활했다. ● 수줍음 불가산명사 ❑ 그는 노크를 하고 문을 연 뒤에 약간은 수줍어하면서 들어왔다.

dif|fuse /dɪfyuz/ (**diffuses, diffusing, diffused**) ① V-T/V-I If something such as knowledge or information **is diffused**, or if it **diffuses** somewhere, it is made known over a wide area or to a lot of people. [WRITTEN] ❑ *Over time, however, the technology is diffused and adopted by other countries.* ❑ *...to diffuse new ideas obtained from elsewhere.* ● **dif|fu|sion** /dɪfyuʒ°n/ N-UNCOUNT ❑ *...the development and diffusion of ideas.* ② V-T To **diffuse** a feeling, especially an undesirable one, means to cause it to weaken and lose its power to affect people. ❑ *The arrival of letters from the Pope did nothing to diffuse the tension.* ③ V-T If something **diffuses** light, it causes the light to spread weakly in different directions. ❑ *Diffusing a light also reduces its power.* ④ V-I To **diffuse** or **be diffused** through something means to move and spread through it. ❑ *It allows nicotine to diffuse slowly and steadily into the bloodstream.* ● **dif|fu|sion** N-UNCOUNT ❑ *There are data on the rates of diffusion of molecules.*

① 타동사/자동사 퍼지다, 보급되다 [문어체] ❑ 하지만 시간이 흐르면서 다른 나라에서도 기술이 보급되고 사용된다. ❑ 다른 곳에서 배운 새로운 사상을 보급하다 ● 보급, 전파 불가산명사 ❑ 사상의 발전과 보급 ② 타동사 해소하다 ❑ 교황이 보낸 서신도 긴장 해소에 아무런 소용이 없었다. ③ 타동사 분산시키다 ❑ 빛을 분산시켜도 강도가 줄어든다. ④ 자동사 퍼지다, 확산되다 ❑ 이는 니코틴이 혈관 속으로 천천히 그리고 꾸준히 퍼지게 한다. ● 확산 불가산명사 ❑ 분자 확산 속도에 관한 자료가 있다.

dig ◆◇◇ /dɪg/ (**digs, digging, dug**) ① V-T/V-I If people or animals **dig**, they make a hole in the ground or in a pile of earth, stones, or trash. ❑ *They tried digging in a patch just below the cave.* ❑ *Dig a largish hole and bang the stake in first.* ② V-I If you **dig into** something such as a deep container, you put your hand in it to search for something. ❑ *He dug into his coat pocket for his keys.* ③ V-T/V-I If you **dig** one thing **into** another or if one thing **digs into** another, the first thing is pushed hard into the second, or presses hard into it. ❑ *She digs the serving spoon into the moussaka.* ④ V-I If you **dig into** a subject or a store of information, you study it very carefully in order to discover or check facts. ❑ *...as a special congressional enquiry digs deeper into the alleged financial misdeeds of his government.* ❑ *He has been digging into the local archives.* ⑤ V-T If you **dig yourself out of** a difficult or unpleasant situation, especially one which you caused yourself, you manage to get out of it. ❑ *He's taken these measures to try and dig himself out of a hole.* ⑥ N-COUNT If you have a **dig at** someone, you say something which is intended to make fun of them or upset them. ❑ *She couldn't resist a dig at Dave after his unfortunate performance.* ⑦ N-COUNT If you give someone a **dig** in a part of their body, you push them with your finger or your elbow, usually as a warning or as a joke. ❑ *Cassandra silenced him with a sharp dig in the small of the back.* ⑧ to dig one's **heels in**—see **heel**

① 타동사/자동사 파다 ❑ 그들은 동굴 바로 밑에 있는 작은 땅을 파 보았다. ❑ 먼저 큼직막한 구멍을 파서 말뚝을 박아라. ② 자동사 파헤치다, 뒤지다 ❑ 그는 열쇠를 찾기 위해 코트 주머니를 뒤적거렸다. ③ 타동사/자동사 찔러 넣다, 꽂다 ❑ 그녀가 무사카에 서빙스푼을 꽂는다. ④ 자동사 파고들다, 꼼꼼히 살피다 ❑ 의회 특별 조사 팀이 그의 행정부 재정 비리를 더욱 깊숙이 파고들면서 ❑ 그는 지방 공문서를 샅샅이 검토해 왔다. ⑤ 타동사 빠져나오다 ❑ 그는 곤경에서 빠져 나오기 위해 이 같은 조처를 취했다. ⑥ 가산명사 빈정대기 ❑ 데이브가 공연을 망치자 그녀는 약 올리고 싶어 참을 수가 없었다. ⑦ 가산명사 쿡 찌르기 ❑ 카산드라가 그에게 조용히 하라고 그의 허리를 쿡 찔렀다.

▶**dig out** ① PHRASAL VERB If you **dig** someone or something **out of** a place, you get them out by digging or by forcing them from the things surrounding them. ❑ *...digging minerals out of the Earth.* ② PHRASAL VERB If you **dig** something **out**, you find it after it has been stored, hidden, or forgotten for a long time. [INFORMAL] ❑ *Recently, I dug out Barstow's novel and read it again.*

① 구동사 파내다 ❑ 땅에서 광물을 채굴하는 ② 구동사 찾아내다 [비격식체] ❑ 나는 요전에 바스토우 소설을 찾아내서 다시 읽었다.

di|gest (**digests, digesting, digested**)

The verb is pronounced /daɪdʒɛst/. The noun is pronounced /daɪdʒɛst/.

동사는 /daɪdʒɛst/으로 발음되고, 명사는 /daɪdʒɛst/으로 발음된다.

① V-T/V-I When food **digests** or when you **digest** it, it passes through your body to your stomach. Your stomach removes the substances that your body needs and gets rid of the rest. ❑ *Do not undertake strenuous exercise for a few hours after a meal to allow food to digest.* ❑ *She couldn't digest food properly.* ② V-T If you **digest** information, you think about it carefully so that you understand it. ❑ *They learn well but seem to need time to digest information.* ③ V-T If you **digest** some unpleasant news, you think about it until you are able to accept it and know how to deal with it. ❑ *All this has upset me. I need time to digest it all.* ④ N-COUNT A **digest** is a collection of pieces of writing. They are published together in a shorter form than they were originally published. ❑ *...the Middle East Economic Digest.*

① 타동사/자동사 소화되다; 소화하다 ❑ 음식의 소화를 돕기 위해 식사 후 몇 시간 동안은 격렬한 운동을 삼가라. ❑ 그녀는 음식을 제대로 소화하지 못했다. ② 타동사 소화하니, 머하니 ❑ 그들이 잘 배우고 있긴 하지만 정보를 소화하기 위해서는 시간이 필요한 것 같다. ③ 타동사 곰곰이 생각하다 ❑ 이게 전부 무슨 말인지 모르겠어. 시간을 가지고 생각해 봐야겠어. ④ 가산명사 다이제스트 (원문을 요약한 글을 모아서 낸 출판물) ❑ 중동 경제 다이제스트

di|ges|tion /daɪdʒɛstʃən/ (**digestions**) ① N-UNCOUNT **Digestion** is the process of digesting food. ❑ *No liquids are served with meals because they interfere with digestion.* ② N-COUNT Your **digestion** is the system in your body which digests your food. ❑ *My digestion ain't so hot these days, either.*

① 불가산명사 소화 ❑ 소화에 방해가 되기 때문에 식사와 함께는 음료가 나오지 않는다. ② 가산명사 소화 기관 ❑ 요즘 나도 소화가 잘 안 돼.

di|ges|tive /daɪdʒɛstɪv/ ADJ You can describe things that are related to the digestion of food as **digestive**. [ADJ n] ❑ *...digestive juices that normally work on breaking down our food.*

형용사 소화의 ❑ 보통 음식 분해 작용을 하는 소화액

digi|cam /dɪdʒɪkæm/ (**digicams**) N-COUNT A **digicam** is the same as a **digital camera**. ❑ *Filmmaking was transformed by digital editing, digital f/x, and digicams.*

가산명사 디지털 카메라 ❑ 디지털 편집과 디지털 f/x, 디지털 카메라가 영화 제작의 새 장을 열었다.

dig|it /dɪdʒɪt/ (**digits**) N-COUNT A **digit** is a written symbol for any of the ten numbers from 0 to 9. ❑ *Her telephone number differs from mine by one digit.*

가산명사 아라비아 숫자 ❑ 나와 그녀는 숫자 하나만 빼고 전화번호가 같다.

digi|tal /dɪdʒɪt°l/ ① ADJ **Digital** systems record or transmit information in the form of thousands of very small signals. ❑ *The new digital technology would allow a rapid expansion in the number of TV channels.* ② ADJ **Digital** devices such as watches or clocks give information by displaying numbers rather than by having a pointer which moves round a dial. Compare **analog**. [ADJ n] ❑ *...a digital display.*—see **DVD, technology, television**

① 형용사 디지털 방식의 ❑ 새로운 디지털 기술로 텔레비전 채널 수가 급격히 증가할 것이다. ② 형용사 디지털 방식의 ❑ 디지털 화면

digi|tal cam|era (**digital cameras**) N-COUNT A **digital camera** is a camera that produces digital images that can be stored on a computer, displayed on a screen, and printed. ❑ *The speed with which digital cameras can take, process and transmit an image is phenomenal.*

가산명사 디지털 카메라 ❑ 디지털 카메라는 놀라운 속도로 사진을 찍고, 현상하고, 전송할 수 있다.

digital radio (digital radios) **1** N-UNCOUNT **Digital radio** is radio in which the signals are transmitted in digital form and decoded by the radio receiver. ❑ ...those with access to digital radio, satellite TV, or the Internet. **2** N-COUNT A **digital radio** is a radio that can receive digital signals. ❑ Manufacturers are working on a new generation of cheaper digital radios.

불가산명사 디지털 라디오 ❑ 디지털 라디오나 위성 텔레비전, 인터넷을 이용할 수 있는 사람들 **2** 가산명사 디지털 라디오 ❑ 생산자들이 더욱 저렴한 차세대 디지털 라디오를 개발 중이다.

digital television (digital televisions) **1** N-UNCOUNT **Digital television** is television in which the signals are transmitted in digital form and decoded by the television receiver. ❑ At present only 31 per cent of the population have access to digital television. **2** N-COUNT A **digital television** is a television that can receive digital signals. ❑ Other new technology products are also doing well, such as digital cameras and wide screen digital televisions.

1 불가산명사 디지털 텔레비전 ❑ 현재는 디지털 텔레비전 시청 인구가 31퍼센트밖에 되지 않는다. **2** 가산명사 디지털 텔레비전 ❑ 디지털 카메라나 와이드스크린 디지털 텔레비전 같은 다른 신기술 제품도 잘 팔리고 있다.

digital TV (digital TVs) **1** N-UNCOUNT **Digital TV** is the same as **digital television**. **2** N-COUNT A **digital TV** is the same as a **digital television**.

1 불가산명사 디지털 텔레비전 **2** 가산명사 디지털 텔레비전

dignified /dɪɡnɪfaɪd/ ADJ If you say that someone or something is **dignified**, you mean they are calm and impressive, and deserve respect. ❑ He seemed a very dignified and charming man.

형용사 위엄 있는, 기품 있는 ❑ 그는 매우 기품 있고 매력적인 남자처럼 보였다.

Word Link | **dign ≈ proper, worthy : dignity, dignitary, indignant**

---

dignitary /dɪɡnɪteri, BRIT dɪɡnɪtri/ (dignitaries) N-COUNT **Dignitaries** are people who are considered to be important because they have a high rank in government or in the Church. ❑ Wolsey was visited by dignitaries from all over Europe.

가산명사 고위 인사 ❑ 유럽 전역의 고위 인사들이 울시를 방문했다.

dignity /dɪɡnɪti/ **1** N-UNCOUNT If someone behaves or moves with **dignity**, they are calm, controlled, and admirable. ❑ ...her extraordinary dignity and composure. **2** N-UNCOUNT If you talk about the **dignity** of people or their lives or activities, you mean that they are valuable and worthy of respect. ❑ ...the sense of human dignity. **3** N-UNCOUNT Your **dignity** is the sense that you have of your own importance and value, and other people's respect for you. ❑ She still has her dignity.

1 불가산명사 위엄, 기품 ❑ 그녀의 특출난 기품과 침착함 **2** 불가산명사 존엄성 ❑ 인간의 존엄성 **3** 불가산명사 품위 ❑ 그녀는 여전히 품위를 유지하고 있다.

dike /daɪk/ (dikes) **1** N-COUNT A **dike** is a thick wall that is built to stop water flooding onto very low-lying land from a river or from the sea. **2** →see dyke 1

1 가산명사 제방, 둑

dilapidated /dɪlæpɪdeɪtɪd/ ADJ A building that is **dilapidated** is old and in a generally bad condition. ❑ ...an old dilapidated barn.

형용사 황폐한, 무너져 가는 ❑ 낡고 황폐한 헛간

dilate /daɪleɪt/ (dilates, dilating, dilated) V-T/V-I When things such as blood vessels or the pupils of your eyes **dilate** or when something **dilates** them, they become wider or bigger. ❑ At night, the pupils dilate to allow in more light. ● **dilated** ADJ ❑ His eyes seemed slightly dilated.

타동사/자동사 넓어지다, 커지다; 넓히다, 크게 하다 ❑ 밤에는 더 많은 빛을 받아들이기 위해 동공이 커진다. ● 넓은, 큰 형용사 ❑ 그의 눈이 좀 더 커진 것 같았다.

Word Link | **di ≈ two : dilemma, diverge, divide**

---

dilemma /dɪlemə, BRIT daɪlemə/ (dilemmas) N-COUNT A **dilemma** is a difficult situation in which you have to choose between two or more alternatives. ❑ He was faced with the dilemma of whether or not to return to his country.

가산명사 딜레마 ❑ 그는 고국으로 돌아갈 것인지 말 것인지를 두고 딜레마에 빠져 있었다.

diligent /dɪlɪdʒənt/ ADJ Someone who is **diligent** works hard in a careful and thorough way. ❑ Meyers is a diligent and prolific worker. ● **diligence** /dɪlɪdʒəns/ N-UNCOUNT ❑ The police are pursuing their inquiries with great diligence. ● **diligently** ADV [ADV with v] ❑ The two sides are now working diligently to resolve their differences.

형용사 근면한, 성실한 ❑ 마이어스는 근면하고 일도 많이 한다. ● 근면, 성실 불가산명사 ❑ 경찰이 아주 성실하게 조사하고 있다. ● 열심히, 부지런히 부사 ❑ 양측이 현재 의견 차를 좁히기 위해 열심히 노력하고 있다.

dilute /daɪlut/ (dilutes, diluting, diluted) **1** V-T/V-I If a liquid **is diluted** or **dilutes**, it is added to or mixes with water or another liquid, and becomes weaker. ❑ If you give your baby juice, dilute it well with cooled, boiled water. ❑ The liquid is then diluted. **2** ADJ A **dilute** liquid is very thin and weak, usually because it has had water added to it. ❑ ...a dilute solution of bleach. **3** V-T If someone or something **dilutes** a belief, quality, or value, they make it weaker and less effective. ❑ There was a clear intention to dilute black voting power.

1 타동사/자동사 희석하다; 희석되다 ❑ 갓난아이에게 주스를 줄 때는, 끓여서 식힌 물에 희석해서 주시오. ❑ 그러면 액체가 희석된다. **2** 형용사 희석한, 묽은 ❑ 희석한 표백제 **3** 타동사 희석시키다, 떨어뜨리다 ❑ 선거에서 흑인의 영향력을 희석시키려는 의도가 분명히 보였다.

dim /dɪm/ (dimmer, dimmest, dims, dimming, dimmed) **1** ADJ **Dim** light is not bright. ❑ She stood waiting, in the dim light. ● **dimly** ADV ❑ Two lamps burned dimly. **2** ADJ A **dim** place is rather dark because there is not much light in it. ❑ The room was dim and cool and quiet. **3** ADJ A **dim** figure or object is not very easy to see, either because it is in shadow or darkness, or because it is far away. ❑ Pete's torch picked out the dim figures of Bob and Chang. ● **dimly** ADV ❑ The shoreline could be dimly seen. **4** ADJ If you have a **dim** memory or understanding of something, it is difficult to remember or is unclear in your mind. ❑ It seems that the '60s era of social activism is all but a dim memory. ● **dimly** ADV ❑ Christina dimly recalled the procedure. **5** ADJ If the future of something is **dim**, you have no reason to feel hopeful or positive about it. ❑ The prospects for a peaceful solution are dim. **6** ADJ If you describe someone as **dim**, you think that they are stupid. [INFORMAL] ❑ Sometimes he thought George was a bit dim. **7** V-T/V-I If you **dim** a light or if it **dims**, it becomes less bright. ❑ Dim the lighting – it is unpleasant to lie with a bright light shining in your eyes. **8** V-T/V-I If your future, hopes, or emotions **dim** or if something **dims** them, they become less good or less strong. ❑ Their economic prospects have dimmed. **9** V-T/V-I If your memories **dim** or if something **dims** them, they become less clear in your mind. ❑ Their memory of what happened has dimmed.

1 형용사 희미한 ❑ 그녀가 희미한 불빛 아래서 기다리며 서 있었다. ● 희미하게 부사 ❑ 램프 두 개가 희미하게 타올랐다. **2** 형용사 어둑한 ❑ 방은 어둡고 서늘하며 조용했다. **3** 형용사 흐릿한 ❑ 피트가 불빛을 비추자 밥과 챙의 희미한 모습이 드러났다. ● 흐릿하게 부사 ❑ 흐릿하게나마 해안선이 보였다. **4** 형용사 어렴풋한 ❑ 사회 운동이 활발했던 60년대가 이제는 거의 흐릿한 기억이 되어 버린 것 같다. ● 어렴풋이 부사 ❑ 크리스티나가 그 과정을 어렴풋이 기억했다. **5** 형용사 어두운 ❑ 평화적 해결 방안에 대한 전망이 어둡다. **6** 형용사 멍청한 [비격식체] ❑ 그는 가끔씩 조지가 좀 멍청하다고 생각했다. **7** 타동사/자동사 어둡게 하다; 어두워지다 ❑ 불을 어둡게 하라. 환한 불빛을 받으면서 거짓말을 하면 기분이 찝찝하다. **8** 타동사/자동사 어두워지다, 사그라지다; 어둡게 하다, 사그라뜨리다 ❑ 경제 전망이 어두워졌다. **9** 타동사/자동사 흐릿해지다 ❑ 사건에 대한 그들의 기억이 흐릿해졌다.

dime /daɪm/ (dimes) N-COUNT A **dime** is an American coin worth ten cents. ❑ The penny meters are slowly being replaced by electronic ones that take nickels, dimes, and quarters.

가산명사 다임 (10센트 은화) ❑ 페니만 받는 주차 미터기가 니켈, 다임, 쿼터 등 다른 동전도 받는 전자식 주차 미터기로 서서히 교체되고 있다.

dimension /dɪmenʃn, daɪ-/ (dimensions) **1** N-COUNT A particular **dimension** of something is a particular aspect of it. ❑ There is a political dimension to the accusations. **2** N-PLURAL If you talk about the **dimensions** of a situation or problem, you are talking about its extent and size. ❑ The dimensions of the market collapse, in terms of turnover and price, were certainly not anticipated. **3** N-COUNT A **dimension** is a measurement such as length, width, or height. If you talk

1 가산명사 차원, 측면 ❑ 이 같은 비난에는 정치적인 측면이 있다. **2** 복수명사 규모 ❑ 매출과 가격 측면에서 그런 규모의 시장 붕괴는 확실히 예상하지 못했던 것이었다. **3** 가산명사 치수, 크기 ❑ 새 유전 지대의 규모를 측량하기 위해 시추 작업이 계속될 것이다.

about the **dimensions** of an object or place, you are referring to its size and proportions. ❑ *Drilling will continue on the site to assess the dimensions of the new oilfield.*

Word Partnership   dimension의 연어

ADJ.   **different** dimension, **important** dimension, **new** dimension, **spiritual** dimension ◼

Word Link   min = small, lessen : diminish, minus, minute

di|min|ish /dɪmɪnɪʃ/ (**diminishes, diminishing, diminished**) ◼ V-T/V-I When something **diminishes**, or when something **diminishes** it, it becomes reduced in size, importance, or intensity. ❑ *The threat of nuclear war has diminished.* ❑ *Federalism is intended to diminish the power of the central state.* ◗ V-T If you **diminish** someone or something, you talk about them or treat them in a way that makes them appear less important than they really are. ❑ *He never put her down or diminished her.*

◼ 타동사/자동사 줄다; 줄이다 ❑ 핵전쟁의 위험이 줄어들었다. ❑ 연방제의 목적은 중앙 정부 힘의 축소이다. ◗ 타동사 깎아내리다 ❑ 그는 결코 그녀를 무시하거나 깎아내리지 않았다

di|minu|tive /dɪmɪnyətɪv/ ADJ A **diminutive** person or object is very small. ❑ *Her eyes scanned the room until they came to rest on a diminutive figure standing at the entrance.*

형용사 자그마한 ❑ 방을 훑어보던 그녀의 두 눈이 입구에 서 있는 체구가 자그마한 사람에게 멈췄다.

din /dɪn/ N-SING A **din** is a very loud and unpleasant noise that lasts for some time. ❑ *They tried to make themselves heard over the din of the crowd.*

단수명사 소음 ❑ 그들은 시끌벅적한 군중 속에서 들리도록 이야기하려고 애를 썼다.

dine /daɪn/ (**dines, dining, dined**) V-I When you **dine**, you have dinner. [FORMAL] [no passive] ❑ *He dines alone most nights.*

자동사 식사하다 [격식체] ❑ 그는 보통 저녁을 혼자 먹는다.

din|er /daɪnər/ (**diners**) ◼ N-COUNT A **diner** is a small cheap restaurant that is open all day. [AM] ◗ N-COUNT The people who are having dinner in a restaurant can be referred to as **diners**. ❑ *They sat in a corner, away from other diners.*

◼ 가산명사 간이식당 [미국영어] ◗ 가산명사 식사하는 사람 ❑ 그들은 식사 중인 다른 사람들과 멀리 떨어진 구석에 앉았다.

din|ghy /dɪŋgi/ (**dinghies**) N-COUNT A **dinghy** is a small open boat that you sail or row. ❑ *...a rubber dinghy.*

가산명사 작은 보트 ❑ 고무보트

din|gy /dɪndʒi/ (**dingier, dingiest**) ◼ ADJ A **dingy** building or place is rather dark and depressing, and perhaps dirty. ❑ *Shaw took me to his rather dingy office.* ◗ ADJ **Dingy** clothes, curtains, or furnishings look dirty or dull. ❑ *...wallpaper with stripes of dingy yellow.*

◼ 형용사 음침한 ❑ 쇼가 다소 음침해 보이는 자신의 사무실로 나를 데려갔다. ◗ 형용사 거무죽죽한, 칙칙한 ❑ 칙칙한 노란색 줄무늬 벽지

din|ing room (**dining rooms**) also dining-room N-COUNT The **dining room** is the room in a house where people have their meals, or a room in a hotel where meals are served. →see house

가산명사 식당

din|ner ♦♦◇ /dɪnər/ (**dinners**) ◼ N-VAR **Dinner** is the main meal of the day, usually served in the early part of the evening. ❑ *She invited us to her house for dinner.* ❑ *Would you like to stay and have dinner?* ◗ N-VAR Any meal you eat in the middle of the day can be referred to as **dinner**. ❑ *There was a lot of men worked there 'cos they used to leave off at eleven thirty every day and come home for their dinner.* →see meal ◾ N-COUNT A **dinner** is a formal social event at which a meal is served. It is held in the evening. ❑ *...a series of official lunches and dinners.* →see meal

◼ 가산명사 또는 불가산명사 정찬, 만찬 ❑ 그녀가 저녁 식사 차 우리를 집으로 초대했다. ❑ 여기 있다가 식사하시겠어요? ◗ 가산명사 또는 불가산명사 식사 ❑ 매일 11시 반에 퇴근해서 집에서 식사를 하곤 했기 때문에 그곳에서 일하는 사람이 많았다. ◾ 가산명사 공식 만찬 ❑ 일련의 공식 오찬과 만찬

din|ner jack|et (**dinner jackets**) also dinner-jacket N-COUNT A **dinner jacket** is a jacket, usually black, worn by men for formal social events. [mainly BRIT; AM usually **tuxedo**]

가산명사 야회복 [주로 영국영어; 미국영어 대개 tuxedo]

di|no|saur /daɪnəsɔr/ (**dinosaurs**) ◼ N-COUNT **Dinosaurs** were large reptiles which lived in prehistoric times. ◗ N-COUNT If you refer to an organization as a **dinosaur**, you mean that it is large, inefficient, and out of date. [DISAPPROVAL] ❑ *...industrial dinosaurs.*

◼ 가산명사 공룡 ◗ 가산명사 크고 비효율적이며 시대에 뒤떨어진 기구 [탐탁찮음] ❑ 덩치만 크고 낡은 산업체

dip /dɪp/ (**dips, dipping, dipped**) ◼ V-T If you **dip** something **in** a liquid, you put it into the liquid for a short time, so that only part of it is covered, and take it out again. ❑ *Quickly dip the base in and out of cold water.* ● N-COUNT **Dip** is also a noun. ❑ *One dip into the bottle should do an entire nail.* ◗ V-T/V-I If you **dip** your hand **into** a container or **dip into** the container, you put your hand into it in order to take something out of it. ❑ *She dipped a hand into the jar of sweets and pulled one out.* ❑ *Watch your fingers as you dip into the pot.* ◾ V-I If something **dips**, it makes a downward movement, usually quite quickly. ❑ *Blake jumped in expertly; the boat dipped slightly under his weight.* ● N-COUNT **Dip** is also a noun. ❑ *I noticed little things, a dip of the head, a twitch in the shoulder.* ◖ V-I If an area of land, a road, or a path **dips**, it goes down quite suddenly to a lower level. ❑ *The road dipped and rose again as it neared the top of Parker Mountain.* ● N-COUNT **Dip** is also a noun. ❑ *Where the road makes a dip, soon after a small vineyard on the right, turn right.* ◗ V-I If the amount or level of something **dips**, it becomes smaller or lower, usually only for a short period of time. ❑ *Unemployment dipped to 6.9 per cent last month.* ● N-COUNT **Dip** is also a noun. ❑ *...the current dip in farm spending.* ◙ N-COUNT If you have or take a **dip**, you go for a quick swim in the sea, a river, or a swimming pool. ❑ *She flicked through a romantic paperback between occasional dips in the pool.* ◚ V-I If you **dip into** a book, you take a brief look at it without reading or studying it seriously. ❑ *...a chance to dip into a wide selection of books on Tibetan Buddhism.* ◛ V-I If you **dip into** a sum of money that you had intended to save, you use some of it to buy something or pay for something. ❑ *Just when she was ready to dip into her savings, Greg hastened to her rescue.*

◼ 타동사 살짝 담그다, 찍다 ❑ 아랫부분을 차가운 물에 재빨리 담갔다 꺼내라. ● 가산명사 담금, 찍기 ❑ 매니큐어 병에 한 번 담갔다가 빼면 손톱 하나를 다 발라야 한다. ◗ 타동사/자동사 손을 넣다 ❑ 그녀는 과자가 든 병 안에 손을 넣어 과자 하나를 꺼냈다. ❑ 용기 안으로 손을 넣을 때 손가락을 조심하시오. ◾ 자동사 내려가다, 가라앉다 ❑ 블레이크가 노련하게 뛰어들자 보트가 그의 무게에 눌려 약간 내려앉았다. ● 가산명사 내려감 ❑ 나는 고개가 살짝 내려가거나 어깨가 움찔하는 것처럼 사소한 것들을 잘 눈치 챘다. ◖ 자동사 움푹 들어가다 ❑ 파커마운틴 정상에 가까워지자 도로가 다시 올록볼록해졌다. ● 가산명사 움푹 들어감 ❑ 오른쪽에 작은 포도밭이 나온 직후에 길이 움푹 내려가는 곳에서 우회전하라. ◗ 자동사 일시 하락하다 ❑ 지난달 실업률이 6.9퍼센트로 떨어졌다. ● 가산명사 하락 ❑ 현재 농업 지출의 일시적 하락 ◙ 가산명사 짧은 수영 ❑ 그녀는 중간중간 풀장에서 잠깐 수영을 하면서 연애 소설 한 권을 훑어 읽었다. ◚ 자동사 대충 보다 ❑ 티베트 불교에 관한 다양한 책을 잠깐 볼 기회 ◛ 자동사 손을 대다 ❑ 그녀가 저축한 돈에 손을 대려고 하자, 때마침 그레그가 서둘러 그녀를 도왔다.

di|plo|ma /dɪploʊmə/ (**diplomas**) N-COUNT A **diploma** is a qualification which may be awarded to a student by a university or college, or by a high school in the United States. ❑ *...a new two-year course leading to a diploma in social work.* →see graduation

가산명사 졸업장 ❑ 졸업장이 나오는 신설 사회 복지 사업 2년 과정

di|plo|ma|cy /dɪploʊməsi/ ◼ N-UNCOUNT **Diplomacy** is the activity or profession of managing relations between the governments of different

◼ 불가산명사 외교 ❑ 유엔 안전 보장 이사회의 오늘 결의안은 미국 외교의 중대한 승리가 될 것이다.

countries. ❑ *Today's Security Council resolution will be a significant success for American diplomacy.* ❷ N-UNCOUNT **Diplomacy** is the skill of being careful to say or do things which will not offend people. ❑ *He stormed off in a fury, and it took all Minnelli's powers of diplomacy to get him to return.*

dip|lo|mat ◆◇◇ /dípləmæt/ (**diplomats**) N-COUNT A **diplomat** is a senior official who discusses affairs with another country on behalf of his or her own country, usually working as a member of an embassy. ❑ *...British diplomats in Baghdad.*

dip|lo|mat|ic ◆◇◇ /dípləmǽtɪk/ ❶ ADJ **Diplomatic** means relating to diplomacy and diplomats. ❑ *...before the two countries resume full diplomatic relations.* ● **dip|lo|mati|cal|ly** /dípləmǽtɪkli/ ADV ❑ *...a growing sense of doubt that the conflict can be resolved diplomatically.* ❷ ADJ Someone who is **diplomatic** is able to be careful to say or do things without offending people. ❑ *She is very direct. I tend to be more diplomatic, I suppose.* ● **dip|lo|mati|cal|ly** ADV [ADV with v] ❑ *"I really like their sound, although I'm not crazy about their lyrics," he says, diplomatically.*

Word Partnership	*diplomatic*의 연어
N.	diplomatic **activity**, diplomatic **mission**, diplomatic **relations**, diplomatic **skills**, diplomatic **solution**, diplomatic **ties** ❶

dip|lo|mat|ic corps

> Diplomatic corps is both the singular and the plural form.

N-COUNT-COLL The **diplomatic corps** is the group of all the diplomats who work in one city or country.

dire /dáɪər/ ❶ ADJ **Dire** is used to emphasize how serious or terrible a situation or event is. [EMPHASIS] ❑ *The government looked as if it would split apart, with dire consequences for domestic peace.* ❷ ADJ If you describe something as **dire**, you are emphasizing that it is of very low quality. [INFORMAL, EMPHASIS] ❑ *...a book of children's verse, which ranged from the barely tolerable to the utterly dire.*

di|rect ◆◆◇ /dɪrékt, daɪ-/ (**directs, directing, directed**) ❶ ADJ **Direct** means moving toward a place or object, without changing direction and without stopping, for example in a journey. ❑ *They'd come on a direct flight from Athens.* ● ADV **Direct** is also an adverb. [ADV after v] ❑ *You can fly direct to Amsterdam from most British airports.* ● **di|rect|ly** ADV [ADV after v] ❑ *The jumbo jet is due to fly the hostages directly back to London.* ❷ ADJ If something is in **direct** heat or light, it is strongly affected by the heat or light, because there is nothing between it and the source of heat or light to protect it. [ADJ n] ❑ *All medicines should be stored away from moisture, direct sunlight, and heat.* ❸ ADJ You use **direct** to describe an experience, activity, or system which only involves the people, actions, or things that are necessary to make it happen. ❑ *He has direct experience of the process of privatization.* ● ADV **Direct** is also an adverb. [ADV after v] ❑ *I can deal direct with your Inspector Kimble.* ● **di|rect|ly** ADV [ADV with v] ❑ *We cannot measure pain directly. It can only be estimated.* ❹ ADJ You use **direct** to emphasize the closeness of a connection between two things. [EMPHASIS] ❑ *They were unable to prove that the unfortunate lady had died as a direct result of his injection.* ❺ ADJ If you describe a person or their behavior as **direct**, you mean that they are honest and open, and say exactly what they mean. ❑ *He avoided giving a direct answer.* ● **di|rect|ly** ADV [ADV after v] ❑ *At your first meeting, explain simply and directly what you hope to achieve.* ● **di|rect|ness** N-UNCOUNT ❑ *Using "I" ensures clarity and directness, and it adds warmth to a piece of writing.* ❻ V-T If you **direct** something **at** a particular thing, you aim or point it at that thing. ❑ *I reached the cockpit and directed the extinguisher at the fire without effect.* ❼ V-T If your attention, emotions, or actions **are directed at** a particular person or thing, you are focusing them on that person or thing. ❑ *The learner's attention needs to be directed to the significant features.* ❽ V-T If a remark or look **is directed at** you, someone says something to you or looks at you. ❑ *She could hardly believe the question was directed toward her.* ❑ *The abuse was directed at the TV crews.* ❾ V-T If you **direct** someone somewhere, you tell them how to get there. ❑ *Could you direct them to Dr. Lamont's office, please?* ❿ V-T When someone **directs** a project or a group of people, they are responsible for organizing the people and activities that are involved. ❑ *Christopher will direct day-to-day operations.* ● **di|rec|tion** /dɪrékʃⁿn, daɪ-/ N-UNCOUNT ❑ *Organizations need clear direction, set priorities and performance standards, and clear controls.* ⓫ V-T/V-I When someone **directs** a movie, play, or television program, they are responsible for the way in which it is performed and for telling the actors and assistants what to do. ❑ *He directed various TV shows.* ⓬ →see also **direction, directly**

Thesaurus	*direct*의 참조어
ADJ.	nonstop, straight ❶
	personal ❸
	candid, frank, plain ❺

di|rect deb|it (**direct debits**) N-VAR If you pay a bill by **direct debit**, you give permission for the company who is owed money to transfer the correct amount from your bank account into theirs, usually every month. [mainly BRIT] ❑ *Switch to paying your mortgage by direct debit – you don't have to keep notifying the bank to alter your repayments.*

di|rect dis|course N-UNCOUNT In grammar, **direct discourse** is speech which is reported by using the exact words that the speaker used. [mainly AM; BRIT usually **direct speech**]

di|rec|tion ◆◆◇ /dɪrékʃⁿn, daɪ-/ (**directions**) ❶ N-VAR A **direction** is the general line that someone or something is moving or pointing in. ❑ *St Andrews was ten miles in the opposite direction.* ❑ *He got into Margie's car and swung out onto the road in*

❷ 불가산명사 외교적 수완 ❑ 미넬리가 온갖 외교적 수완을 동원해서 화가 잔뜩 나 뛰쳐나간 그를 돌아오게끔 했다.

가산명사 외교관 ❑ 바그다드 주재 영국 외교관

❶ 형용사 외교의 ❑ 양국이 국교 정상화를 재개하기 전에 ● 외교적인 수완으로 부사 ❑ 외교적 수단을 통한 분쟁 해결 가능성에 대해 커져 가는 의구심 ❷ 형용사 외교적 수완이 있는, 수완이 좋은 ❑ 그녀는 매우 직접적이다. 나는 그보다 외교적인 편이다. ● 수완 좋게 부사 ❑ "노래의 가사는 그저 그렇지만, 음악 자체는 정말 좋아해요."라고 그가 수완 좋게 말한다.

> diplomatic corps는 단수형 및 복수형이다.

가산명사-집합 외교단

❶ 형용사 끔찍한, 지독한 [강조] ❑ 정부가 분열되어 국내 평화에 끔찍한 결과를 초래할 것처럼 보였다. ❷ 형용사 형편없는 [비격식체, 강조] ❑ 그런대로 봐 줄만한 것부터 아주 형편없는 것까지 다양한 작품이 실린 아동 산문집

❶ 형용사 직행의, 직통의 ❑ 그들은 아테네에서 출발하는 직항기를 타고 올 것이다. ● 부사 직행으로, 곧장 ❑ 영국에 있는 대부분의 공항에서 암스테르담까지 직행으로 갈 수 있다. ● 직행으로, 곧장 부사 ❑ 초대형 여객기가 인질들을 싣고 영국으로 곧장 돌아올 것이다. ❷ 형용사 직접적인 ❑ 모든 약품은 습기, 직사광선, 열 등으로부터 안전한 곳에 보관해야 한다. ❸ 형용사 직접의 ❑ 그는 민영화 과정을 직접 경험했다. ● 부사 직접 ❑ 내가 당신네 킴블 경사를 직접 상대할 수 있다. ● 직접 부사 ❑ 고통을 직접 측정할 수는 없다. 단지 추측이 가능할 뿐이다. ❹ 형용사 직접적인 [강조] ❑ 그들은 그 불쌍한 부인의 직접적인 사인이 그가 놓은 주사 때문이라는 것을 증명할 수 없었다. ❺ 형용사 직접적인, 솔직한 ❑ 그는 솔직한 대답을 피했다. ● 직선적으로, 솔직하게 부사 ❑ 처음 면담에서, 당신이 성취하고자 하는 바를 간단하게 직선적으로 설명하라. ● 직선적임, 솔직함 불가산명사 ❑ '나'라는 단어의 사용은 명확성과 솔직성을 물론이고 글에 따뜻한 느낌도 더해 준다. ❻ 타동사 향하게 하다 ❑ 내가 조종석에 도착해 불길을 향해 소화기를 들이댔지만 소용이 없었다. ❼ 타동사 향하다, 집중되다 ❑ 학습자가 주요 사항에 집중할 수 있도록 할 필요가 있다. ❽ 타동사 향하다, 겨냥하다 ❑ 그녀는 그 질문이 자신을 향한 것이라는 사실이 믿기 어려웠다. ❑ 그것은 텔레비전 촬영진을 겨냥한 공격이었다. ❾ 타동사 길을 알려 주다 ❑ 그들에게 라몽 박사 사무실로 가는 길 좀 가르쳐 주시겠습니까? ❿ 타동사 지도하다, 감독하다 ❑ 크리스토퍼가 매일 진행되는 작업을 감독할 것이다. ● 지시 불가산명사 ❑ 조직에는 명확한 지시와 정립된 우선순위 및 성과 기준 그리고 분명한 통제 수단이 있어야 한다. ⓫ 타동사/자동사 감독하다 ❑ 그는 다양한 텔레비전 프로그램의 감독을 맡았다.

가산명사 또는 불가산명사 자동 이체 [주로 영국영어] ❑ 융자금 지불 방식을 자동 이체로 바꾸세요. 그러면 상환액 변경을 매번 은행에 알려야 하는 번거로움을 덜 수 있습니다.

불가산명사 직접 화법 [주로 미국영어; 영국영어 대개 direct speech]

❶ 가산명사 또는 불가산명사 방향 ❑ 세인트 앤드류스는 반대 방향으로 10마일 떨어진 곳에 있었다. ❑ 그는 마지막 차에 탄 후, 차를 돌려 래리의 가게

A
B

the direction of Larry's shop. **2** N-VAR A **direction** is the general way in which something develops or progresses. ❑ They threatened to lead a mass walk-out if the party did not sharply change direction. **3** N-PLURAL **Directions** are instructions that tell you what to do, how to do something, or how to get somewhere. ❑ I should know by now not to throw away the directions until we've finished cooking. **4** →see also **direct**

쪽으로 향하는 길로 들어섰다. **2** 가산명사 또는 불가산명사 방향 ❑ 당이 노선 변경을 분명히 하지 않으면, 집단 파업을 강행하겠다고 그들이 위협했다. **3** 복수명사 지시, 사용법 ❑ 이제는 요리를 마치기 전까지 조리법 설명서를 버리지 말아야겠어.

C
D

Word Partnership   direction의 연어

ADJ.	**opposite** direction, **right** direction, **wrong** direction **1**
	general direction **1** **2**
N.	**sense of** direction **1**
V.	**change** direction, **move in a** direction **1** **2**
	lack direction **2**

E

di|rec|tive /dɪrɛktɪv, daɪ-/ (**directives**) N-COUNT A **directive** is an official instruction that is given by someone in authority. ❑ Thanks to a new EU directive, insecticide labeling will be more specific.

가산명사 지령, 지침 ❑ 이유가 새 지침을 내놓음에 따라 살충제 라벨이 더욱 자세하게 표시될 것이다.

F

di|rect|ly /dɪrɛktli, daɪ-/ **1** ADV If something is **directly** above, below, or in front of something, it is in exactly that position. [ADV prep/adv] ❑ The second rainbow will be bigger than the first, and directly above it. **2** ADV If you do one action **directly after** another, you do the second action as soon as the first one is finished. [ADV prep/adv] ❑ Directly after the meeting, a senior cabinet minister spoke to the BBC. **3** →see also **direct**

1 부사 바로 ❑ 두 번째 무지개는 첫 번째 무지개 바로 위에 더 크게 생길 것이다. **2** 부사 직후에 ❑ 회담 직후에 고위 장관이 비비시와 인터뷰를 했다. **3** →참조 **direct**

G

di|rect mail N-UNCOUNT **Direct mail** is a method of marketing which involves companies sending advertising material directly to people who they think may be interested in their products. [BUSINESS] ❑ ...efforts to solicit new customers by direct mail and television advertising.

불가산명사 우편 광고 [경제] ❑ 우편 광고나 텔레비전 광고를 통해 신규 고객을 확보하려는 노력

H

di|rect mar|ket|ing N-UNCOUNT **Direct marketing** is the same as **direct mail**. [BUSINESS] ❑ The direct marketing industry has become adept at packaging special offers.

불가산명사 우편 광고 [경제] ❑ 우편 광고업이 기획 상품 개발에 능숙해졌다.

I

di|rect ob|ject (**direct objects**) N-COUNT In grammar, the **direct object** of a transitive verb is the noun group which refers to someone or something directly affected by or involved in the action performed by the subject. For example, in "I saw him yesterday," "him" is the direct object. Compare **indirect object**.

가산명사 직접 목적어

J

di|rec|tor ♦♦♦ /dɪrɛktər, daɪ-/ (**directors**) **1** N-COUNT The **director** of a play, movie, or television program is the person who decides how it will appear on stage or screen, and who tells the actors and technical staff what to do. ❑ "Cut!" the director yelled. "That was perfect." **2** N-COUNT In some organizations and public authorities, the person in charge is referred to as the **director**. ❑ ...the director of the intensive care unit at Guy's Hospital. **3** N-COUNT The **directors** of a company are its most senior managers, who meet regularly to make important decisions about how it will be run. [BUSINESS] ❑ He served on the board of directors of a local bank. **4** N-COUNT The **director** of an orchestra or choir is the person who is conducting it. [AM; BRIT **conductor**]

1 가산명사 감독 ❑ "컷!"하고 감독이 소리쳤다. "완벽했어." **2** 가산명사 책임자, 국장 ❑ 가이즈 병원 중환자실 책임자 **3** 가산명사 이사 [경제] ❑ 그는 지방 은행 이사로 재직하였다. **4** 가산명사 지휘자 [미국영어; 영국영어 conductor]

K
L
M

di|rec|to|rate /dɪrɛktərɪt, daɪ-/ (**directorates**) **1** N-COUNT A **directorate** is a board of directors in a company or organization. [BUSINESS] ❑ The European Central Bank would be managed by a directorate of around five professional bankers. **2** N-COUNT A **directorate** is a part of a government department which is responsible for one particular thing. ❑ ...the Health and Safety Directorate of the EU.

1 가산명사 이사회 [경제] ❑ 유럽 중앙 은행의 운영은 전문 금융가 5인 내외로 구성된 이사회가 맡을 것이다. **2** 가산명사 청 ❑ 이유 보건 안전청

N
O
P

di|rec|tor gen|er|al (**directors general**) N-COUNT The **director general** of a large organization is the person who is in charge of it. [BUSINESS]

가산명사 회상 [경제]

di|rec|tor|ship /dɪrɛktərʃɪp, daɪ-/ (**directorships**) N-COUNT A **directorship** is the job or position of a company director. [BUSINESS] ❑ Barry resigned his directorship in December 1973.

가산명사 이사직 [경제] ❑ 배리는 1973년 12월 이사직을 사임했다.

Q

di|rec|to|ry /dɪrɛktəri, daɪ-/ (**directories**) **1** N-COUNT A **directory** is a book which gives lists of facts, for example people's names, addresses, and telephone numbers, or the names and addresses of business companies, usually arranged in alphabetical order. ❑ ...a telephone directory. **2** N-COUNT A **directory** is an area of a computer disk which contains one or more files or other directories. [COMPUTING] ❑ This option lets you search your current directory for files by date, contents, and document summary. **3** N-COUNT On the World Wide Web, a **directory** is a list of the subjects that you can find information on. [COMPUTING] ❑ Yahoo is the oldest and best-known Web directory service.

1 가산명사 주소록 ❑ 전화번호부 **2** 가산명사 디렉터리 [컴퓨터] ❑ 이 옵션을 사용하면 현재 디렉터리에서 날짜, 내용, 문서 요약별로 파일을 찾을 수 있다. **3** 가산명사 웹 디렉터리, 웹사이트 주제별 분류 [컴퓨터] ❑ 야후는 가장 오래되고 가장 잘 알려진 웹 디렉터리 서비스이다.

R
S
T

di|rec|to|ry as|sis|tance N-UNCOUNT **Directory assistance** is a service which you can telephone to find out someone's telephone number. [AM; BRIT **directory enquiries**] ❑ He dialed directory assistance.

불가산명사 전화번호 안내 [미국영어; 영국영어 directory enquiries] ❑ 그는 전화번호 안내 서비스에 전화했다.

U

di|rect speech N-UNCOUNT In grammar, **direct speech** is speech which is reported by using the exact words that the speaker used. [mainly BRIT; AM usually **direct discourse**]

불가산명사 직접 화법 [주로 영국영어; 미국영어 대개 direct discourse]

V

di|rect tax (**direct taxes**) N-COUNT A **direct tax** is a tax which a person or organization pays directly to the government, for example income tax. [BUSINESS] ❑ ...Mr. Major's claim that what people have to pay in direct and indirect taxes had not gone up since 1979.

가산명사 직접세 [경제] ❑ 사람들이 지불해야 하는 직간접세가 1979년 이후 전혀 오르지 않았다고 메이저 수상은 주장한다.

W

dirt /dɜrt/ **1** N-UNCOUNT If there is **dirt** on something, there is dust, mud, or a stain on it. ❑ I started to scrub off the dirt. **2** N-UNCOUNT You can refer to the earth on the ground as **dirt**, especially when it is dusty. ❑ They all sit on the dirt in the dappled shade of a tree. **3** ADJ A **dirt** road or track is made from hard earth. A **dirt** floor is made from earth without any cement, stone, or wood laid on it. [ADJ n] ❑ I drove along the dirt road. **4** N-SING If you say that you have **the dirt on** someone, you mean that you have information that could harm their reputation or career. [INFORMAL] ❑ Steve was mad keen to get all the dirt he could on

1 불가산명사 먼지, 흙, 때 ❑ 나는 때를 문질러 없애기 시작했다. **2** 불가산명사 흙 ❑ 그들 모두 얼룩덜룩한 나무 그늘 밑의 땅바닥에 앉아 있다. **3** 형용사 흙으로 된 ❑ 나는 흙길을 따라 차를 몰았다. **4** 단수명사 험담거리, 먹칠할 내용 [비격식체] ❑ 스티브는 그 랑엔바흐 여인의 험담거리를 찾느라 여념이 없었다. **5** 구 업신여기다, 하찮게 생각하다 [탐탁찮음] ❑ 사람들이 나는 업신여겨도 된다고 생각한다니까!

X
Y
Z

the *Langenbach woman.* **5** PHRASE If you say that someone **treats** you **like dirt**, you are angry with them because you think that they treat you unfairly and with no respect. [DISAPPROVAL] ❑ *People think they can treat me like dirt!* →see **erosion**

dirty ♦◇◇ /dɜ̩rti/ (**dirtier, dirtiest, dirties, dirtying, dirtied**) **1** ADJ If something is **dirty**, it is marked or covered with stains, spots, or mud, and needs to be cleaned. ❑ *She still did not like the woman who had dirty fingernails.* **2** V-T To **dirty** something means to cause it to become dirty. ❑ *He was afraid the dog's hairs might dirty the seats.* **3** ADJ If you describe an action as **dirty**, you disapprove of it and consider it unfair, immoral, or dishonest. [DISAPPROVAL] ❑ *The gunman had been hired by a rival Mafia family to do the dirty deed.* ● ADV **Dirty** is also an adverb. [ADV after v] ❑ *Jim Browne is the kind of fellow who can fight dirty, but make you like it.* **4** ADJ If you describe something such as a joke, a book, or someone's language as **dirty**, you mean that it refers to sex in a way that some people find offensive. ❑ *He laughed at their dirty jokes and sang their raucous ballads.* ● ADV **Dirty** is also an adverb. [ADV after v] ❑ *I'm often asked whether the men talk dirty to me. The answer is no.* **5** PHRASE If someone gives you a **dirty look**, they look at you in a way which shows that they are angry with you. [INFORMAL] ❑ *Jack was being a real pain. Michael gave him a dirty look and walked out.* **6** PHRASE To **do** someone's **dirty work** means to do a task for them that is dishonest or unpleasant and which they do not want to do themselves. ❑ *As a member of an elite army hit squad, the army would send us out to do their dirty work for them.* **7** PHRASE If you say that an expression is **a dirty word** in a particular group of people, you mean it refers to an idea that they strongly dislike or disagree with. ❑ *Marketing became a dirty word at the company.*

Word Partnership   *dirty*의 연어

N.   dirty **diapers**, dirty **dishes**, dirty **laundry** **1**
     dirty *your* **hands** **2**
     dirty **joke** **4**
     dirty **look** **5**
     dirty **job** **6**
     dirty **word** **7**
V.   **get** dirty **1**
     talk dirty **4**

---

dis|abil|ity /dɪsəbɪlɪti/ (**disabilities**) **1** N-COUNT A **disability** is a permanent injury, illness, or physical or mental condition that tends to restrict the way that someone can live their life. ❑ *Facilities for people with disabilities are still insufficient.* **2** N-UNCOUNT **Disability** is the state of being disabled. ❑ *Disability can make extra demands on financial resources because the disabled need extra care.* →see Word Web: **disability**

dis|able /dɪseɪbᵊl/ (**disables, disabling, disabled**) **1** V-T If an injury or illness **disables** someone, it affects them so badly that it restricts the way that they can live their life. ❑ *She did all this tendon damage and it really disabled her.* **2** V-T If someone or something **disables** a system or mechanism, they stop it working, usually temporarily. ❑ *...if you need to disable a car alarm.*

dis|abled /dɪseɪbᵊld/ ADJ Someone who is **disabled** has an illness, injury, or condition that tends to restrict the way that they can live their life, especially by making it difficult for them to move about. ❑ *...an insight into the practical problems encountered by disabled people in the workplace.* ● N-PLURAL People who are disabled are sometimes referred to as **the disabled**. ❑ *There are toilet facilities for the disabled.*

In the United States there are many laws giving **disabled** people the same rights and benefits as other people. The adjectives **disabled, physically challenged** and **differently abled** are terms more in favor now than **handicapped**. The most sensitive ways of referring to people with a restricting physical condition are to call them **people with disabilities** or **people with special needs**.

dis|ad|van|tage /dɪsədvæntɪdʒ/ (**disadvantages**) **1** N-COUNT A **disadvantage** is a factor which makes someone or something less useful, acceptable, or successful than other people or things. ❑ *His two main rivals suffer the disadvantage of having been long-term political exiles.* **2** PHRASE If you are **at a disadvantage**, you have a problem or difficulty that many other people do not have, which makes it harder for you to be successful. ❑ *The children from poor*

Word Web   disability

Careful planning is making public places more **accessible** for people with **disabilities**. For hundreds of years **wheelchairs** have helped **paralyzed** people move around their homes. Today, **ramps** help these people cross the street, enter buildings, and get to work. Extra-wide doorways allow them to use public restrooms. **Blind** people are also more active and independent. **Seeing-Eye dogs, canes**, and beeping crosswalks all help them get around town safely. Some movie theaters rent headsets for the hearing-impaired. **Hearing dogs** help **deaf** people stay connected. And sign language allows people who are deaf or **dumb** to communicate.

---

1 형용사 더러운, 지저분한 ❑ 그녀는 손톱이 지저분한 그 여자를 여전히 탐탁하지 않게 생각했다. **2** 타동사 더럽히다 ❑ 그는 강아지 털 때문에 의자가 더러워질까 봐 걱정이었다. **3** 형용사 비열한 [탐탁찮음] ❑ 경쟁 마피아 조직이 저격수를 고용해 그 비열한 짓을 시켰던 것이다. ● 부사 비열하게 ❑ 비열하긴 해도 당신이 만족할 만큼 싸울 수 있는 친구가 바로 짐 브라운이다. **4** 형용사 지저분한, 외설적인 ❑ 그는 그들의 지저분한 농담을 들으며 웃고 요란한 노래도 따라 불렀다. ● 부사 지저분하게, 음란하게 ❑ 그 남자들이 나에게 지저분한 말을 하지 않느냐는 질문을 종종 받는데, 그렇지 않다. **5** 구 화난 인상 [비격식체] ❑ 잭이 정말 못 살게 굴었다. 마이클은 그를 한번 쏘아보고 나가 버렸다. **6** 구 더러운 일을 대신하다 ❑ 군대가 우리를 엘리트 타격 부대의 일원으로 자기네를 대신해서 더러운 일을 처리하도록 파견할 것이다. **7** 구 금기시하는 말 ❑ 마케팅이라는 단어가 회사 내에서 금기시되었다.

1 가산명사 장애 ❑ 장애인을 위한 시설이 아직도 부족하다. **2** 불가산명사 장애 ❑ 장애인들은 특별한 보살핌을 필요로 하기 때문에, 장애가 재정적인 부담을 가중시킬 수 있다.

1 타동사 불구로 만들다 ❑ 그녀는 이렇게 모든 힘줄이 손상되는 바람에 정말 불구가 되었다. **2** 타동사 정지시키다, 해제하다 ❑ 차량 경보기를 해제할 필요가 있으면

형용사 불구가 된 ❑ 장애인들이 직장에서 부딪치는 실제적인 문제에 대한 통찰력 ● 복수명사 장애인 ❑ 장애인 전용 화장실이 있다.

미국에는 장애가 있는 사람들에게 다른 사람과 똑같은 권리와 혜택을 주는 법률이 많다. 이들을 가리키는 형용사로는 disabled, physically challenged 또는 differently abled가 handicapped보다 더 선호된다. 신체적으로 불편한 사람들을 가장 신중하게 지칭하는 표현은 people with disabilities(장애인) 또는 people with special needs이다.

1 가산명사 불리 ❑ 그의 대표적인 라이벌 둘은 오랫동안 정치 망명 생활을 해서 불리한 편이 있다. **2** 구 불리한 입장에 있는 ❑ 가난한 집 출신 아이들은 분명히 불리한 입장에 있었다. **3** 구 불리하게 ❑ 자기들에게 불리하게 작용할 수 있는 선거를 막기 위한 야당의 시도

A

families were at a distinct disadvantage. **3** PHRASE If something is **to your disadvantage** or works **to your disadvantage**, it creates difficulties for you. ❑ *...an opposition attempt to prevent an election which would be to their disadvantage.*

B

dis|ad|van|taged /dɪsədvɑːntɪdʒd/ ADJ People who are **disadvantaged** or live in **disadvantaged** areas live in bad conditions and tend not to get a good education or have a reasonable standard of living. ❑ *...the educational problems of disadvantaged children.*

형용사 혜택 받지 못한, 불리한 조건의 ❑ 어려운 형편의 아이들이 안고 있는 교육 문제

C

dis|af|fect|ed /dɪsəfɛktɪd/ ADJ **Disaffected** people no longer fully support something such as an organization or political ideal which they previously supported. ❑ *He attracts disaffected voters.*

형용사 (마음이) 돌아선 ❑ 그가 돌아선 표심을 잡고 있다.

D

| Word Link | dis ≈ negative, not : *disagree, discomfort, disrespect* |

E

dis|agree /dɪsəgriː/ (**disagrees, disagreeing, disagreed**) **1** V-RECIP If you **disagree with** someone or **disagree with** what they say, you do not accept that what they say is true or correct. You can also say that two people **disagree**. ❑ *You must continue to see them no matter how much you may disagree with them.* ❑ *They can communicate even when they strongly disagree.* **2** V-I If you **disagree with** a particular action or proposal, you disapprove of it and believe that it is wrong. ❑ *I respect the president but I disagree with his decision.*

F

1 상호동사 의견이 다르다 ❑ 아무리 의견이 다르더라도 당신은 그들을 계속해서 만나야 한다. ❑ 강한 의견 대립이 있을 때에도 그들은 대화할 수 있다. **2** 자동사 반대하다 ❑ 나는 대통령을 존경하지만 그의 결정에는 반대이다.

G

dis|agree|ment /dɪsəgriːmənt/ (**disagreements**) **1** N-UNCOUNT **Disagreement** means objecting to something such as a proposal. ❑ *Britain and France have expressed some disagreement with the proposal.* **2** N-VAR When there is **disagreement** about something, people disagree or argue about what should be done. ❑ *The United States Congress and the President are still locked in disagreement over proposals to reduce the massive budget deficit.*

H

1 불가산명사 반대 ❑ 영국과 프랑스가 이번 제안에 대해 약간 반대 의사를 표명했다. **2** 가산명사 또는 불가산명사 의견 대립 ❑ 미국 의회와 대통령이 막대한 예산 적자 축소안을 두고 아직도 의견 대립을 보이고 있다.

I

dis|al|low /dɪsəlaʊ/ (**disallows, disallowing, disallowed**) V-T If something **is disallowed**, it is not allowed or accepted officially, because it has not been done correctly. ❑ *England scored again, but the whistle had gone and the goal was disallowed.*

타동사 인정되지 않다 ❑ 영국이 다시 득점을 했으나 이미 호루라기가 울린 뒤여서 골은 무효 처리되었다.

J

dis|ap|pear ♦◇◇ /dɪsəpɪər/ (**disappears, disappearing, disappeared**) **1** V-I If you say that someone or something **disappears**, you mean that you can no longer see them, usually because you or they have changed position. ❑ *The black car drove away from them and disappeared.* **2** V-I If someone or something **disappears**, they go away or are taken away somewhere where nobody can find them. ❑ *...a Japanese woman who disappeared thirteen years ago.* **3** V-I If something **disappears**, it stops existing or happening. ❑ *The immediate threat of the past has disappeared and the security situation in Europe has significantly improved.*

K

L

1 자동사 사라지다 ❑ 검은 차는 그들에게서 점점 멀어지더니 결국 시야에서 사라졌다. **2** 자동사 사라지다 ❑ 13년 전에 사라진 일본 여자 **3** 자동사 사라지다 ❑ 과거의 직접적인 위협은 사라졌고 유럽의 안보 상황은 상당히 개선되었다.

M

Word Partnership	*disappear*의 연어
V.	make *something/someone* disappear **1** **2** **3**
ADV.	disappear **forever** **2** **3**

N

dis|ap|pear|ance /dɪsəpɪərəns/ (**disappearances**) **1** N-VAR If you refer to someone's **disappearance**, you are referring to the fact that nobody knows where they have gone. ❑ *Her disappearance has baffled police.* **2** N-COUNT If you refer to the **disappearance** of an object, you are referring to the fact that it has been lost or stolen. ❑ *Police are investigating the disappearance from council offices of confidential files.* **3** N-UNCOUNT The **disappearance** of a type of thing, person, or animal is a process in which it becomes less common and finally no longer exists. ❑ *...the virtual disappearance of common dolphins from the western Mediterranean in recent years.*

O

P

1 가산명사 또는 불가산명사 실종 ❑ 그녀의 실종은 경찰을 당혹하게 만들었다. **2** 가산명사 사라짐, 분실 ❑ 경찰이 위원회 사무실에서 비밀문서가 사라진 사건을 수사하고 있다. **3** 불가산명사 별종 ❑ 근래에 서부 지중해에서 참돌고래가 거의 사라진 현상

Q

dis|ap|point /dɪsəpɔɪnt/ (**disappoints, disappointing, disappointed**) V-T If things or people **disappoint** you, they are not as good as you had hoped, or do not do what you hoped they would do. ❑ *She would do anything she could to please him, but she knew that she was fated to disappoint him.*

타동사 실망시키다 ❑ 그녀는 그를 만족시키기 위해 무엇이든 할 마음이 있었으나 결국은 그를 실망시키고 말 것이라는 것을 알고 있었다.

R

dis|ap|point|ed ♦◇◇ /dɪsəpɔɪntɪd/ **1** ADJ If you are **disappointed**, you are rather sad because something had not happened or because something is not as good as you had hoped. ❑ *Castle-hunters won't be disappointed with the Isle of Man.* ❑ *I was disappointed that John was not there.* **2** ADJ If you are **disappointed in** someone, you are rather sad because they have not behaved as well as you expected them to. [v-link ADJ in n] ❑ *You should have accepted that. I'm disappointed in you.*

S

T

1 형용사 실망한 ❑ 성을 찾고 있는 사람들이라면 맨 섬에서 실망하지는 않을 것이다. ❑ 존이 그곳에 없어서 나는 실망했다. **2** 형용사 -에게 실망한 ❑ 그것을 받아들여야지. 네게 실망했다.

U

dis|ap|point|ing /dɪsəpɔɪntɪŋ/ ADJ Something that is **disappointing** is not as good or as large as you hoped it would be. ❑ *The wine was excellent, but the meat was overdone and the vegetables disappointing.* ● **dis|ap|point|ing|ly** ADV ❑ *Progress is disappointingly slow.*

형용사 실망스러운 ❑ 와인은 훌륭했지만 고기는 지나치게 익혀졌고 야채는 실망스러웠다. ● 실망스럽게 부사 ❑ 진행이 실망스러울 정도로 느리다.

V

dis|ap|point|ment /dɪsəpɔɪntmənt/ (**disappointments**) **1** N-UNCOUNT **Disappointment** is the state of feeling disappointed. ❑ *Despite winning the title, their last campaign ended in great disappointment.* **2** N-COUNT Something or someone that is a **disappointment** is not as good as you had hoped. ❑ *For many, their long-awaited homecoming was a bitter disappointment.*

W

1 불가산명사 실망 ❑ 선수권을 차지했지만 그들의 마지막 경기는 크게 실망스럽게 끝났다. **2** 가산명사 실망거리 ❑ 많은 사람들에게 오랫동안 기다려 온 그들의 귀환은 매우 실망스러웠다.

X

dis|ap|prov|al /dɪsəpruːvəl/ N-UNCOUNT If you feel or show **disapproval** of something or someone, you feel or show that you do not approve of them. ❑ *His action had been greeted with almost universal disapproval.*

불가산명사 탐탁지 않음, 반대 ❑ 그의 행위는 거의 모든 사람들이 탐탁해 하지 않았다.

Y

dis|ap|prove /dɪsəpruːv/ (**disapproves, disapproving, disapproved**) V-I If you **disapprove of** something or someone, you feel or show that you do not like them or do not approve of them. ❑ *Most people disapprove of such violent tactics.*

자동사 탐탁지 않게 생각하다, 좋지 않게 생각하다 ❑ 대부분의 사람들은 그렇게 폭력적인 전략을 좋게 생각하지 않는다.

Z

dis|ap|prov|ing /dɪsəpruːvɪŋ/ ADJ A **disapproving** action or expression shows that you do not approve of something or someone. ❑ *Janet gave him a disapproving look.* ● **dis|ap|prov|ing|ly** ADV [ADV after v] ❑ *Antonio looked at him disapprovingly.*

형용사 탐탁해 하지 않는 ❑ 자넷은 그에게 탐탁지 않은 눈초리를 보냈다. ● 탐탁지 않다는 듯이 부사 ❑ 안토니오가 그를 탐탁지 않다는 듯이 쳐다봤다.

dis|arm /dɪsɑrm/ (disarms, disarming, disarmed) **1** V-T To **disarm** a person or group means to take away all their weapons. ❏ *We will agree to disarming troops and leaving their weapons at military positions.* **2** V-I If a country or group **disarms**, it gives up the use of weapons, especially nuclear weapons. ❏ *There has also been a suggestion that the forces in Lebanon should disarm.* **3** V-T If a person or their behavior **disarms** you, they cause you to feel less angry, hostile, or critical toward them. ❏ *His unease disarmed her.*

타동사 무장 해제시키다 ❏ 우리는 병력의 무장 해제와 무기를 군사 거점에 두는 것에 동의할 것이다. **2** 자동사 무기를 버리다, 무장 해제하다 ❏ 레바논에 있는 병력이 무장을 해제해야 한다는 제안도 있었다. **3** 타동사 (노여움, 반감 등을) 가시게 하다 ❏ 그의 불안 때문에 그녀가 풀어졌다.

dis|arma|ment /dɪsɑrməmənt/ N-UNCOUNT **Disarmament** is the act of reducing the number of weapons, especially nuclear weapons, that a country has. ❏ *The goal would be to increase political stability in the region and accelerate the pace of nuclear disarmament.*

불가산명사 군비 축소 ❏ 그 지역의 정치적 안정을 높이고 비핵화의 속도를 증가시키는 것이 목표이다.

dis|arm|ing /dɪsɑrmɪŋ/ ADJ If someone or something is **disarming**, they make you feel less angry or hostile. ❏ *Leonard approached with a disarming smile.* ● **dis|arm|ing|ly** ADV ❏ *He is, as ever, business-like, and disarmingly honest.*

형용사 (노여움, 반감 등을) 가시게 하는 ❏ 레너드는 경계심을 사라지게 하는 그런 미소를 띠고 다가왔다. ● (노여움, 반감 등을) 가시게 하도록 부사 ❏ 그는 예나 지금이나 사무적이며 상대방을 무장 해제시킬 정도로 솔직하다.

dis|ar|ray /dɪsəreɪ/ **1** N-UNCOUNT If people or things are **in disarray**, they are disorganized and confused. ❏ *The nation is in disarray following rioting led by the military.* **2** N-UNCOUNT If things or places are **in disarray**, they are in a very untidy state. ❏ *She was left lying on her side and her clothes were in disarray.*

1 불가산명사 혼란 ❏ 그 나라는 군대 주도의 폭동 이후 혼란에 빠진 상태이다. **2** 불가산명사 난잡 ❏ 그녀는 옆으로 눕혀진 채 버려져 있었으며 옷매무새는 흐트러져 있었다.

dis|as|ter ♦♢♢ /dɪzæstər/ (disasters) **1** N-COUNT A **disaster** is a very bad accident such as an earthquake or a plane crash, especially one in which a lot of people are killed. ❏ *It was the second air disaster in the region in less than two months.* **2** N-COUNT If you refer to something as a **disaster**, you are emphasizing that you think it is extremely bad or unacceptable. [EMPHASIS] ❏ *The whole production was just a disaster!* **3** N-UNCOUNT **Disaster** is something which has very bad consequences for you. ❏ *The government brought itself to the brink of fiscal disaster.* **4** PHRASE If you say that something is **a recipe for disaster**, you mean that it is very likely to have unpleasant consequences. ❏ *Lack of these virtues in any dog is a problem. In large dogs it is a recipe for disaster.* →see Word Web: **disaster**

1 가산명사 참사, 재난 ❏ 그것은 두 달이 못 되는 기간 동안 그 지역에서 발생한 두 번째 비행 참사였다. **2** 가산명사 실패작 [강조] ❏ 작품 전체가 엄청난 실패작이었어! **3** 불가산명사 재앙 ❏ 정부 자체가 재정적인 재앙을 맞이하는 지경에까지 이르게 되었다. **4** 구 재앙의 씨앗 ❏ 어떤 개든 이런 미덕을 갖추지 못하면 문제이다. 큰 개의 경우에는 그것이 재앙의 씨앗이 된다.

dis|as|trous /dɪzæstrəs/ **1** ADJ A **disastrous** event has extremely bad consequences and effects. ❏ *...the recent, disastrous earthquake.* ● **dis|as|trous|ly** ADV ❏ *The vegetable harvest is disastrously behind schedule.* **2** ADJ If you describe something as **disastrous**, you mean that it was very unsuccessful. ❏ *...after their disastrous performance in the general election of 1906.* ● **dis|as|trous|ly** ADV ❏ *...debts resulting from the company's disastrously timed venture into property development.*

1 형용사 대참사 ❏ 최근에 있었던 지진 참사 ● 참담한 정도로 부사 ❏ 야채 수확은 참담할 정도로 일정을 뒤처져 있다. **2** 형용사 참패한 ❏ 1906년 총선거에서 그들이 참패한 이후에 ● 참담하게 부사 ❏ 회사가 참담할 정도로 시기를 잘못 타고 부동산 개발에 뛰어들어 생긴 부채

dis|band /dɪsbænd/ (disbands, disbanding, disbanded) V-T/V-I If someone **disbands** a group of people, or if the group **disbands**, it stops operating as a single unit. ❏ *All the armed groups will be disbanded.*

타동사/자동사 해산하다 ❏ 모든 무장 단체들은 해산될 것이다.

dis|be|lief /dɪsbɪlif/ N-UNCOUNT **Disbelief** is not believing that something is true or real. ❏ *She looked at him in disbelief.*

불가산명사 불신 ❏ 그녀는 그를 믿을 수 없다는 듯이 쳐다봤다.

disc /dɪsk/ →see **disk** →see **DVD**

dis|card /dɪskɑrd/ (discards, discarding, discarded) V-T If you **discard** something, you get rid of it because you no longer want it or need it. ❏ *Read the manufacturer's guidelines before discarding the box.*

타동사 버리다 ❏ 상자를 버리기 전에 제조사의 설명서를 읽어라.

dis|cern /dɪsɜrn/ (discerns, discerning, discerned) **1** V-T If you can **discern** something, you are aware of it and know what it is. [FORMAL] ❏ *You need a long series of data to be able to discern such a trend.* **2** V-T If you can **discern** something, you can just see it, but not clearly. [FORMAL] ❏ *Below the bridge we could just discern a narrow, weedy ditch.*

1 타동사 인식하다, 파악하다 [격식체] ❏ 그런 추세를 파악하기 위해서는 상당한 기간 동안 축적된 자료가 필요하다. **2** 타동사 식별하다, 알아보다 [격식체] ❏ 다리 밑으로 좁고 잡초가 무성한 도랑이 겨우 보였다.

dis|cern|ible /dɪsɜrnəbəl/ ADJ If something is **discernible**, you can see it or recognize that it exists. [FORMAL] ❏ *Far away the outline of the island is just discernible.*

형용사 식별할 수 있는, 보이는 [격식체] ❏ 멀리 섬의 윤곽이 간신히 보인다.

dis|cern|ing /dɪsɜrnɪŋ/ ADJ If you describe someone as **discerning**, you mean that they are able to judge which things of a particular kind are good and which are bad. [APPROVAL] ❏ *...tailor-made holidays to suit the more discerning traveler.*

형용사 식견이 있는 [마음에 듦] ❏ 식견이 있는 여행자에게 보다 적합하도록 맞춘 휴가

dis|charge (discharges, discharging, discharged)

The verb is pronounced /dɪstʃɑrdʒ/. The noun is pronounced /dɪstʃɑrdʒ/.

동사는 /dɪstʃɑrdʒ/로 발음되고, 명사는 /dɪstʃɑrdʒ/로 발음된다.

1 V-T When someone **is discharged from** a hospital, prison, or one of the armed services, they are officially allowed to leave, or told that they must leave. ❏ *He has a broken nose but may be discharged today.* ● N-VAR **Discharge** is also a noun. ❏ *He was given a conditional discharge and ordered to pay Miss Smith £100 compensation.* **2** V-T If someone **discharges** their duties or responsibilities, they do everything that needs to be done in order to complete them. [FORMAL]

1 타동사 내보내다 ❏ 그는 코가 부러진 상태이지만 오늘 퇴원할지도 모른다. ● 가산명사 또는 불가산명사 내보냄 ❏ 그는 집행 유예로 석방되었으며 스미스 양에게 100파운드의 배상금을 지불하라는 명령을 받았다. **2** 타동사 수행하다 [격식체] ❏ 대학생으로서의 많은 의무를 수행한 그의 조용한

Word Web   disaster

We are learning more about nature's cycles. But natural **disasters** remain a big challenge. Some, such as **hurricanes** and **floods**, are predictable. However, we still can't avoid the **damage** they do. Each year **monsoons** strike southern Asia. Monsoons are a combination of **typhoons**, **tropical storms**, and heavy **rains**. In addition to the damage caused by flooding, **landslides** and mudslides add to the problem. In 2005 more than 90 million people were affected in China alone. Over 700 people died in that country and millions of acres of crops were destroyed. The **economic loss** totaled nearly 6 billion dollars.

❏ ...*the quiet competence with which he discharged his many college duties.* **3** V-T If something **is discharged** from inside a place, it comes out. [FORMAL] ❏ *The resulting salty water will be discharged at sea.* **4** N-COUNT When there is a **discharge** of a substance, the substance comes out from inside somewhere. [FORMAL] ❏ *They develop a fever and a watery discharge from their eyes.* →see **lightning**

능력 **3** 타동사 방출되다 [격식체] ❏ 결과물인 염수는 바다로 방류될 것이다. **4** 가산명사 방출 [격식체] ❏ 그것이 진행되면 열이 나고 눈에서 눈물이 흐른다.

dis|ci|ple /dɪsaɪp³l/ (**disciples**) N-COUNT If you are someone's **disciple**, you are influenced by their teachings and try to follow their example. ❏ ...*a major intellectual figure with disciples throughout Europe.*

가산명사 제자 ❏ 유럽 전역에 제자가 있는 주요 지식인

dis|ci|pli|nary /dɪsɪplɪneri, BRIT dɪsɪplɪnəri/ ADJ **Disciplinary** bodies or actions are concerned with making sure that people obey rules or regulations and that they are punished if they do not. [ADJ n] ❏ *He will now face a disciplinary hearing for having an affair.*

형용사 징계의 ❏ 그는 간통을 한 것에 대한 징계 심리를 받을 것이다.

dis|ci|pline ♦◇◇ /dɪsɪplɪn/ (**disciplines, disciplining, disciplined**) **1** N-UNCOUNT **Discipline** is the practice of making people obey rules or standards of behavior, and punishing them when they do not. ❏ *Order and discipline have been placed in the hands of headmasters and governing bodies.* **2** N-UNCOUNT **Discipline** is the quality of being able to behave and work in a controlled way which involves obeying particular rules or standards. ❏ *It was that image of calm, control, and discipline that appealed to millions of voters.* **3** N-VAR If you refer to an activity or situation as a **discipline**, you mean that, in order to be successful in it, you need to behave in a strictly controlled way and obey particular rules or standards. ❏ *The discipline of studying music can help children develop good work habits and improve self-esteem.* **4** V-T If someone **is disciplined** for something that they have done wrong, they are punished for it. ❏ *The workman was disciplined by his company but not dismissed.* **5** V-T If you **discipline yourself** to do something, you train yourself to behave and work in a strictly controlled and regular way. ❏ *Discipline yourself to check your messages once a day or every couple of days.* **6** N-COUNT A **discipline** is a particular area of study, especially a subject of study in a college or university. [FORMAL] ❏ *We're looking for people from a wide range of disciplines.*

1 불가산명사 훈육 ❏ 질서와 훈육의 책임은 교장과 이사회의 손에 주어져 있다. **2** 불가산명사 절제 ❏ 수백만 명의 유권자들의 호감을 산 것은 침착함, 통제력, 그리고 절제를 보여 준 그 이미지였다. **3** 가산명사 또는 불가산명사 훈련 ❏ 음악 공부로 훈련을 하면 아이들이 좋은 학습 습관을 기르고 자긍심을 키우는 데도 도움이 될 수 있다. **4** 타동사 징계하다 ❏ 그 근로자는 회사로부터 징계는 받았으나 해고당하지는 않았다. **5** 타동사 심신을 단련하다 ❏ 메시지를 하루에 혹은 이틀에 한 번만 확인하도록 스스로를 단련해라. **6** 가산명사 과목, 학문 분야 [격식체] ❏ 우리는 다양한 학문적 배경을 가진 사람들을 찾고 있다.

dis|ci|plined /dɪsɪplɪnd/ ADJ Someone who is **disciplined** behaves or works in a controlled way. ❏ *For me it meant being very disciplined about how I run my life.*

형용사 절제력이 있는 ❏ 내게 있어 그것은 내가 인생을 영위하는 데 있어 고도로 절제력을 발휘함을 의미했다.

disc jock|ey (**disc jockeys**) [AM also **disk jockey**] N-COUNT A **disc jockey** is someone who plays and introduces CDs on the radio or at a disco.

[미국영어 disk jockey] 가산명사 디스크 자키

dis|claim|er /dɪskleɪmər/ (**disclaimers**) N-COUNT A **disclaimer** is a statement in which a person says that they did not know about something or that they are not responsible for something. [FORMAL] ❏ *The company asserts in a disclaimer that it won't be held responsible for the accuracy of information.*

가산명사 부인 성명 [격식체] ❏ 그 회사는 부인 성명에서 정보의 정확성을 책임질 수 없다고 주장한다.

dis|close /dɪskloʊz/ (**discloses, disclosing, disclosed**) V-T If you **disclose** new or secret information, you tell people about it. ❏ *Neither side would disclose details of the transaction.*

타동사 공개하다, 밝히다 ❏ 어느 쪽도 거래의 세부 사항을 공개하려 하지 않았다.

dis|clo|sure /dɪskloʊʒər/ (**disclosures**) N-VAR **Disclosure** is the act of giving people new or secret information. ❏ ...*insufficient disclosure of negative information about the company.*

가산명사 또는 불가산명사 공개 ❏ 그 회사에 관한 부정적 정보의 불충분한 공개

dis|co /dɪskoʊ/ (**discos**) N-COUNT A **disco** is a place or event at which people dance to pop music. ❏ *Fridays and Saturdays are regular disco nights.*

가산명사 디스코 ❏ 금요일과 토요일 밤에는 정기적으로 디스코판이 벌어진다.

Word Link	dis ≈ negative, not : disagree, discomfort, disrespect

dis|com|fort /dɪskʌmfərt/ (**discomforts**) **1** N-UNCOUNT **Discomfort** is a painful feeling in part of your body when you have been hurt slightly or when you have been uncomfortable for a long time. ❏ *Steve had some discomfort, but no real pain.* **2** N-UNCOUNT **Discomfort** is a feeling of worry caused by shame or embarrassment. ❏ *She hears the discomfort in his voice.* **3** N-COUNT **Discomforts** are conditions which cause you to feel physically uncomfortable. ❏ ...*the discomforts of camping.*

1 불가산명사 불편 ❏ 스티브는 약간 불편했으나 사실 아프지는 않았다. **2** 불가산명사 불편 ❏ 그녀가 듣기에 그의 목소리에서 불편함이 느껴졌다. **3** 가산명사 불편한 요소 ❏ 캠핑의 불편함

dis|con|cert|ing /dɪskənsɜrtɪn/ ADJ If you say that something is **disconcerting**, you mean that it makes you feel anxious, confused, or embarrassed. ❏ *The reception desk is not at street level, which is a little disconcerting.* ● **dis|con|cert|ing|ly** ADV ❏ *She looks disconcertingly like a familiar aunt or grandmother.*

형용사 당황스러운, 혼란스러운 ❏ 안내 데스크가 1층에 있지 않아서 약간 혼란스럽다. ● 당황스럽게 부사 ❏ 그녀는 당황스러울 정도로 잘 아는 고모나 할머니 같은 인상을 풍긴다.

dis|con|nect /dɪskənekt/ (**disconnects, disconnecting, disconnected**) **1** V-T To **disconnect** a piece of equipment means to separate it from its source of power or to break a connection that it needs in order to work. ❏ *The device automatically disconnects the ignition when the engine is switched off.* **2** V-T If you **are disconnected** by a gas, electricity, water, or telephone company, they turn off the connection to your house, usually because you have not paid the bill. [usu passive] ❏ *You are likely to be given almost three months – until the time of your next bill – before you are disconnected.* **3** V-T If you **disconnect** something **from** something else, you separate the two things. ❏ *He disconnected the IV bottle from the overhead hook and carried it beside the moving cart.*

1 타동사 연결을 끊다 ❏ 그 장치는 엔진을 끌 때 자동적으로 점화 장치의 전원을 차단한다. **2** 타동사 차단당하다 ❏ 보통 가스, 전기, 수도, 전화 등은 서비스를 차단하기 전에 다음 청구서가 나올 때까지의 기간인 3개월을 준다. **3** 타동사 분리하다, 떼어 내다 ❏ 그가 정맥 주사병을 머리 위 갈고리에서 떼어 내어 밀차 옆에 달고 갔다.

dis|con|nect|ed /dɪskənektɪd/ ADJ **Disconnected** things are not linked in any way. ❏ ...*sequences of utterly disconnected events.*

형용사 연관이 없는 ❏ 전혀 연관이 없는 일련의 사건들

dis|con|tent /dɪskəntent/ N-UNCOUNT **Discontent** is the feeling that you have when you are not satisfied with your situation. ❏ *There are reports of widespread discontent in the capital.*

불가산명사 불만 ❏ 수도에 불만이 팽배하다는 보고들이 있다.

dis|con|tinue /dɪskəntɪnyu/ (**discontinues, discontinuing, discontinued**) **1** V-T If you **discontinue** something that you have been doing regularly, you stop doing it. [FORMAL] ❏ *Do not discontinue the treatment without consulting your doctor.* **2** V-T If a product **is discontinued**, the manufacturer stops making it. [usu passive] ❏ *The Leica M2 was discontinued in 1967.*

1 타동사 중단하다 [격식체] ❏ 의사와의 상의 없이 치료를 중단하지 말아라. **2** 타동사 중단되다 ❏ 라이카 M2 기종은 1967년에 생산이 중단되었다.

dis|count ♦◇◇ (**discounts**, **discounting**, **discounted**)

> Pronounced /dɪskaʊnt/ for meanings **1** and **2**, and /dɪskaʊnt/ for meaning **3**.

1 N-COUNT A **discount** is a reduction in the usual price of something. ❑ *They are often available at a discount.* ❑ *All full-time staff get a 20 percent discount.* **2** V-T If a store or company **discounts** an amount or percentage from something that they are selling, they take the amount or percentage off the usual price. ❑ *This has forced airlines to discount fares heavily in order to spur demand.* **3** V-T If you **discount** an idea, fact, or theory, you consider that it is not true, not important, or not relevant. ❑ *However, traders tended to discount the rumor.*

dis|cour|age /dɪskɜrɪdʒ, BRIT dɪskʌrɪdʒ/ (**discourages**, **discouraging**, **discouraged**) **1** V-T If someone or something **discourages** you, they cause you to lose your enthusiasm about your actions. ❑ *It may be difficult to do at first. Don't let this discourage you.* ● **dis|cour|aged** ADJ ❑ *She was determined not to be too discouraged.* ● **dis|cour|ag|ing** ADJ ❑ *Today's report is rather more discouraging for the economy.* **2** V-T To **discourage** an action or to **discourage** someone **from** doing it means to make them not want to do it. ❑ *...typhoons that discouraged shopping and leisure activities.*

dis|cour|age|ment /dɪskɜrɪdʒmənt, BRIT dɪskʌrɪdʒmənt/ N-UNCOUNT **Discouragement** is the act of trying to make someone not want to do something. ❑ *He persevered in the face of active discouragement from those around him.*

dis|course /dɪskɔrs/ **1** N-UNCOUNT **Discourse** is spoken or written communication between people, especially serious discussion of a particular subject. ❑ *...a tradition of political discourse.* **2** →see also **direct discourse, indirect discourse**

dis|cov|er ♦♦◇ /dɪskʌvər/ (**discovers**, **discovering**, **discovered**) **1** V-T If you **discover** something that you did not know about before, you become aware of it or learn of it. ❑ *She discovered that they'd escaped.* ❑ *It was difficult for the inspectors to discover which documents were important and which were not.* **2** V-T If a person or thing **is discovered**, someone finds them, either by accident or because they have been looking for them. ❑ *A few days later his badly beaten body was discovered on a roadside outside the city.* **3** V-T When someone **discovers** a new place, substance, scientific fact, or scientific technique, they are the first person to find it or become aware of it. ❑ *...the first European to discover America.* **4** V-T When an actor, musician, or other performer who is not well-known **is discovered**, someone recognizes that they have talent and helps them in their career. [usu passive] ❑ *The Beatles were discovered in the early 1960's.*

> You can use **discover**, **find**, or **find out** to talk about learning that something is the case. ❑ *He discovered the whole school knew about it... The young child finds that noise attracts attention... We found out that she was wrong.* **Discover** is a slightly more formal word than **find**, and is often used to talk about scientific research or formal investigations. For example, you can **discover** a cure for a particular disease. You can also use **discover** when you find something by accident. ❑ *This well-known flower was discovered in 1903.* If you cannot see something you are looking for, you say that you cannot **find** it. You do not use "discover" or 'find out' in this way. ❑ *I'm lost – I can't find the bridge.* You can say that someone **finds out** facts when this is easy to do, but you cannot "discover" or 'find' in this way. ❑ *I found out the train times.*

Thesaurus   discover의 참조어

v.   detect, find out, learn, uncover; (ant.) ignore, miss, overlook **1 3**

dis|cov|ery ♦◇◇ /dɪskʌvəri/ (**discoveries**) **1** N-VAR If someone makes a **discovery**, they become aware of something that they did not know about before. ❑ *I felt I'd made an incredible discovery.* **2** N-VAR If someone makes a **discovery**, they are the first person to find or become aware of a place, substance, or scientific fact that no one knew about before. ❑ *In that year, two momentous discoveries were made.* **3** N-VAR When the **discovery** of people or objects happens, someone finds them, either by accident or as a result of looking for them. ❑ *...the discovery and destruction by soldiers of millions of marijuana plants.*

dis|cred|it /dɪskrɛdɪt/ (**discredits**, **discrediting**, **discredited**) V-T To **discredit** someone or something means to cause them to lose people's respect or trust. ❑ *...a secret unit within the company that had been set up to discredit its major rival.* ● **dis|cred|it|ed** ADJ ❑ *The previous government is, by now, thoroughly discredited.*

dis|creet /dɪskrit/ **1** ADJ If you are **discreet**, you are polite and careful in what you do or say, because you want to avoid embarrassing or offending someone. ❑ *They were gossip and not always discreet.* ● **dis|creet|ly** ADV ❑ *I took the phone, and she went discreetly into the living room.* **2** ADJ If you are **discreet about** something you are doing, you do not tell other people about it, in order to avoid being embarrassed or to gain an advantage. ❑ *We were very discreet about the romance.* ● **dis|creet|ly** ADV ❑ *Everyone worked to make him welcome, and, more discreetly, to find out about him.* **3** ADJ If you describe something as **discreet**, you approve of it because it is small in size or degree, or not easily noticed. [APPROVAL] ❑ *She is wearing a noticeably stylish, feminine dress, plus discreet jewellery.* ● **dis|creet|ly** ADV [ADV -ed/adj] ❑ *...stately houses, discreetly hidden behind great avenues of sturdy trees.*

dis|crep|an|cy /dɪskrɛpənsi/ (**discrepancies**) N-VAR If there is a **discrepancy between** two things that ought to be the same, there is a noticeable difference between them. ❑ *...the discrepancy between press and radio reports.*

1, 2의 의미일 때는 /dɪskaʊnt/로, 3의 의미일 때 /dɪskaʊnt/로 발음된다.

1 가산명사 할인 ❑ 그것들은 대개 할인된 가격에 구할 수 있다. ❑ 모든 정규 직원은 20퍼센트의 할인을 받는다. **2** 타동사 할인하다 ❑ 이 때문에 항공사들은 수요를 촉진하기 위해 어쩔 수 없이 요금을 대폭 삭감했다. **3** 타동사 무시하다 ❑ 그러나 매매인들은 그 소문을 무시하려는 경향이 있었다.

1 타동사 낙담하게 만들다 ❑ 그것이 처음에는 하기 어려울 수도 있다. 그 때문에 좌절하지는 말아라. ● 낙담한 형용사 ❑ 지나치게 낙담하지 않겠다고 그녀는 다짐하고 있었다. ● 낙담하게 하는, 실망스러운 형용사 ❑ 오늘의 보도는 경제에 대해서 더욱 비관적이다. **2** 타동사 단념시키다, 만류하다 ❑ 쇼핑과 여가 활동을 단념시킨 태풍들

불가산명사 만류 ❑ 그는 주변 사람들의 적극적인 만류에도 불구하고 꿋꿋이 맞섰다.

1 불가산명사 담론, 담화 ❑ 정치적 담론의 전통

1 타동사 발견하다, 알아내다 ❑ 그들이 도망간 것을 그녀가 발견했다. ❑ 어떤 문서가 중요하고 어떤 것은 그렇지 않은지 알아내기가 어려웠다. **2** 타동사 발견되다 ❑ 며칠 후 심하게 구타를 당한 그의 시신이 도시 외곽 도로변에서 발견되었다. **3** 타동사 발견하다 ❑ 미국을 발견한 최초의 유럽인 **4** 타동사 주목을 받다 ❑ 비틀즈는 60년대 초에 주목을 받기 시작했다.

상황이 어떠하다는 것을 알게 되었음을 얘기할 때 discover, find, find out을 사용할 수 있다. ❑ 그는 학교 전체가 그것에 대해 알고 있음을 알게 되었다... 어린 아이는 시끄럽게 하면 주목받는다는 것을 안다... 우리는 그녀가 틀렸다는 것을 알아냈다. discover는 find보다 조금 더 격식을 갖춘 말이며, 흔히 과학 연구나 공식 조사에 관해 얘기할 때 쓴다. 예를 들면, 특정한 병의 치료법을 discover할 수 있다. 우연히 무엇을 찾아냈을 때에도 discover를 쓸 수 있다. ❑ 잘 알려진 이 꽃은 1903년에 발견되었다. 찾고 있는 어떤 것이 보이지 않으면, 그것을 find할 수 없다고 말한다. discover나 find out은 이런 식으로 쓰이지 않는다. ❑ 내가 길을 잃었어 – 다리가 안 보여. 어떤 사실을 알아내는 것이 쉬울 때는 누가 그 사실을 find out했다고 말할 수 있으며, 여기서 discover나 find를 쓰지는 않는다. ❑ 나는 기차 시간을 알아냈다.

1 가산명사 또는 불가산명사 발견 ❑ 나는 내가 놀라운 발견을 했다고 생각한다. **2** 가산명사 또는 불가산명사 발견 ❑ 그 해에 두 가지 중대한 발견이 이루어졌다. **3** 가산명사 또는 불가산명사 발견 ❑ 군인들이 수백만 그루의 대마를 발견하고 파괴함

타동사 실추시키다 ❑ 주요 경쟁사의 신뢰도를 떨어뜨리기 위해 회사 내에 설립된 비밀 부서 ● 실추된 형용사 ❑ 이전 정부는 이제 권위가 완전히 실추된 상태이다.

1 형용사 신중한 ❑ 그들은 남의 말을 잘했으면 말을 그다지 조심하지도 않았다. ● 신중하게 부사 ❑ 내가 전화를 받자 그녀가 사려 깊게 자리를 피해 거실로 들어갔다. **2** 형용사 조심을 삼가는 ❑ 우리는 연애를 남들이 모르도록 언행을 아주 조심했다. ● 조심스럽게 부사 ❑ 모든 사람들이 그를 환대하기 위해 노력하면서도 보다 깊은 조심은 그를 알아보기 위한 것이었다. **3** 형용사 작은, 그다지면 [마음에 들] ❑ 그녀는 눈에 띄게 멋지고 여성스러운 드레스를 입고 자그마한 보석들을 달고 있다. ● 살짝 부사 ❑ 듬직한 나무들이 늘어선 넓은 가로수길 뒤에 살짝 숨은 웅장한 집들

가산명사 또는 불가산명사 괴리 ❑ 언론과 라디오 보도 사이의 괴리

dis|cre|tion /dɪskrɛʃⁿn/ ■ N-UNCOUNT **Discretion** is the quality of behaving in a quiet and controlled way without drawing attention to yourself or giving away personal or private information. [FORMAL] ❑ *Larsson sometimes joined in the fun, but with more discretion.* ■ N-UNCOUNT If someone in a position of authority uses their **discretion** or has **the discretion** to do something in a particular situation, they have the freedom and authority to decide what to do. [FORMAL] ❑ *This committee may want to exercise its discretion to look into those charges.* ■ PHRASE If something happens **at** someone's **discretion**, it can happen only if they decide to do it or give their permission. [FORMAL] ❑ *We may vary the limit at our discretion and will notify you of any change.*

■ 불가산명사 신중함 [격식체] ❑ 라슨은 종종 놀이에 동참했으나 신중한 자세를 잃지는 않았다. ■ 불가산명사 재량권 [격식체] ❑ 이 위원회가 그러한 혐의를 조사할 수 있는 재량권을 발휘하고 싶어 하는지도 모른다. ■ 구 ~의 재량에 따라 [격식체] ❑ 한도는 저희의 재량에 따라 변경될 수도 있으므로 변경 시 통보해 드리겠습니다.

dis|cre|tion|ary /dɪskrɛʃəneri, BRIT dɪskrɛʃənri/ ADJ **Discretionary** things are not fixed by rules but are decided on by people in authority, who consider each individual case. ❑ *Magistrates were given wider discretionary powers.*

형용사 자유재량의 ❑ 치안 판사들에게 더 많은 재량권이 주어졌다.

dis|crimi|nate /dɪskrɪmɪneɪt/ (**discriminates, discriminating, discriminated**) ■ V-I If you can **discriminate between** two things, you can recognize that they are different. ❑ *He is incapable of discriminating between a good idea and a terrible one.* ■ V-I To **discriminate against** a group of people or **in favor of** a group of people means to unfairly treat them worse or better than other groups. ❑ *They believe the law discriminates against women.* ❑ *...legislation which would discriminate in favor of racial minorities.*

■ 자동사 식별하다, 분간하다 ❑ 그에겐 좋은 생각과 형편없는 생각을 분간할 수 있는 능력이 없다. ■ 자동사 차별하다 ❑ 그들은 그 법이 여성을 부당하게 차별한다고 생각한다. ❑ 소수 인종을 우대하게 될 법안

dis|crimi|na|tion /dɪskrɪmɪneɪʃⁿn/ ■ N-UNCOUNT **Discrimination** is the practice of treating one person or group of people less fairly or less well than other people or groups. ❑ *She is exempt from sex discrimination laws.* ■ N-UNCOUNT **Discrimination** is knowing what is good or of high quality. ❑ *They cooked without skill and ate without discrimination.* ■ N-UNCOUNT **Discrimination** is the ability to recognize and understand the differences between two things. ❑ *We will then have an objective measure of how color discrimination and visual acuity develop at the level of the brain.*

■ 불가산명사 차별 대우 ❑ 그녀는 성 차별법의 적용을 받지 않는다. ■ 불가산명사 분별력 ❑ 그들은 솜씨 없게 요리를 했고 가리지 않고 먹었다. ■ 불가산명사 식별력 ❑ 그러면 그때 어떻게 색깔 식별력과 시각적 예민함이 뇌에서 발달하게 되는지에 대한 객관적인 지표를 얻게 될 것이다.

dis|crimi|na|tory /dɪskrɪmɪnətɔri, BRIT dɪskrɪmɪnətri/ ADJ **Discriminatory** laws or practices are unfair because they treat one group of people worse than other groups. ❑ *These reforms will abolish racially discriminatory laws.*

형용사 차별적인 ❑ 이들 개혁으로 인종 차별적인 법들이 폐지될 것이다.

dis|cur|sive /dɪskɜrsɪv/ ADJ If a style of writing is **discursive**, it includes a lot of facts or opinions that are not necessarily relevant. [FORMAL] ❑ *...a livelier, more candid and more discursive treatment of the subject.*

형용사 두서없는, 방만한 [격식체] ❑ 그 주제에 대한 더 생기 있고 솔직하며 방만한 탐구

dis|cuss ◆◆◇ /dɪskʌs/ (**discusses, discussing, discussed**) ■ V-T If people **discuss** something, they talk about it, often in order to reach a decision. ❑ *I will be discussing the situation with colleagues tomorrow.* ■ V-T If you **discuss** something, you write or talk about it in detail. ❑ *I will discuss the role of diet in cancer prevention in Chapter 7.*

■ 타동사 논의하다 ❑ 나는 그 상황에 대해 내일 동료들과 의논할 것이다. ■ 타동사 자세히 다루다 ❑ 식습관이 암 예방에 어떤 역할을 하는지에 대해 7장에서 자세히 다룰 것이다.

Note that **discuss** is never used as an intransitive verb. You cannot say, for example, "They discussed," "I discussed with him," or "They discussed about politics." Instead, you can say that you **have a discussion** with someone about something. ❑ *I had a long discussion about all this with Stephen.* You can also add an object and say that you **discuss** something **with** someone. If the discussion is less formal, you can simply use the verb **talk**. ❑ *They come here and sit for hours talking about politics... We talked all night long.*

discuss는 자동사로는 결코 쓰이지 않는다는 점을 유의하라. 예를 들어, "They discussed," "I discussed with him," "They discussed about politics."라고 말할 수 없다. 대신 무엇에 대해 누구와 토의할 때는 have a discussion with someone about something이라고 할 수 있다. ❑ 나는 이 모든 것에 대해 스티븐과 긴 논의를 했다. 또한 목적어를 첨가하여 discuss something with someone이라고 할 수도 있다. 논의가 비격식적이면, 그냥 동사 talk을 쓸 수 있다. ❑ 그들은 여기에 와서 몇 시간이나 정치에 대해 얘기하며 앉아 있는다... 우리는 밤새도록 얘기했다.

Word Partnership discuss의 연어

V. meet to discuss, refuse to discuss ■
N. discuss options, discuss problems ■
discuss an issue, discuss a matter, discuss plans ■ ■

dis|cus|sion ◆◆◇ /dɪskʌʃⁿn/ (**discussions**) ■ N-VAR If there is **discussion** about something, people talk about it, often in order to reach a decision. ❑ *There was a lot of discussion about the wording of the report.* ❑ *Council members are due to have informal discussions later on today.* ● PHRASE If something is **under discussion**, it is still being talked about and a final decision has not yet been reached. ■ N-COUNT A **discussion of** a subject is a piece of writing or a lecture in which someone talks about it in detail. ❑ *For a discussion of biology and sexual politics, see chapter 4.* ■ ADJ A **discussion** document or paper is one that contains information and usually proposals for people to discuss. [ADJ n] ❑ *...a NASA discussion paper on long-duration ballooning.*

■ 가산명사 또는 불가산명사 논의 ❑ 보고서의 어휘 선택에 관해서 많은 논의가 있었다. ❑ 위원들은 오늘 나중에 비공식적인 논의를 할 계획이다. ● 구 논의 중인 ■ 가산명사 실술, 자세한 논의 ❑ 생물학과 성의 정치학에 대한 심도 높은 논의는 4장을 보시오. ■ 형용사 발제문, 논고 ❑ 열기구의 장기간 조정에 관한 나사의 발제문

Thesaurus discussion의 참조어

N. conference, conversation, debate, talk ■

---

dis|dain /dɪsdeɪn/ (**disdains, disdaining, disdained**) ■ N-UNCOUNT If you feel **disdain for** someone or something, you dislike them because you think that they are inferior or unimportant. ❑ *Janet looked at him with disdain.* ■ V-T If you **disdain** someone or something, you regard them with disdain. ❑ *Jackie disdained the servants that her millions could buy.*

■ 불가산명사 멸시 ❑ 재닛은 그를 멸시하는 눈초리로 쳐다봤다. ■ 타동사 멸시하다 ❑ 재키는 자신의 수백만에 달하는 재산으로 살 수 있는 하인들을 멸시했다.

dis|ease ◆◆◇ /dɪziz/ (**diseases**) N-VAR A **disease** is an illness which affects people, animals, or plants, for example one which is caused by bacteria or infection. ❑ *...the rapid spread of disease in the area.* →see **diagnosis, illness, medicine**

가산명사 또는 불가산명사 질병 ❑ 그 지역에서 질병의 빠른 확산

Word Partnership disease의 연어

V. cause disease, cure a disease, spread disease, treat a disease
ADJ. contagious disease, fatal disease, infectious disease, rare disease
N. death and disease, gum disease, heart disease,
symptoms of disease

dis|eased /dɪzizd/ ADJ Something that is **diseased** is affected by a disease. ❑ *The arteries are diseased and a transplant is the only hope.*

형용사 병에 걸린 ❑ 동맥에 병이 생겼으며 이식만이 유일한 희망이다.

dis|en|chant|ed /dɪsɪntʃæntɪd/ ADJ If you are **disenchanted with** something, you are disappointed with it and no longer believe that it is good or worthwhile. ❑ *I'm disenchanted with the state of British theater at the moment.*

형용사 환멸을 느끼는 ❑ 현재 영국 연극계의 현실에 대해 나는 환멸을 느낀다.

dis|en|chant|ment /dɪsɪntʃæntmənt/ N-UNCOUNT **Disenchantment** is the feeling of being disappointed with something, and no longer believing that it is good or worthwhile. ❑ *There's growing disenchantment with the Government.*

불가산명사 환멸 ❑ 정부에 대한 환멸이 점점 커지고 있다.

dis|en|fran|chise /dɪsɪnfræntʃaɪz/ (**disenfranchises, disenfranchising, disenfranchised**) V-T To **disenfranchise** a group of people means to take away their right to vote, or their right to vote for what they really want. ❑ *...fears of an organized attempt to disenfranchise supporters of Father Aristide.* →see **vote**

타동사 선거권을 박탈하다 ❑ 아리스티드 신부의 지지자로부터 선거권을 박탈하려는 조직적인 시도에 대한 두려움

dis|en|gage /dɪsɪngeɪdʒ/ (**disengages, disengaging, disengaged**) V-T/V-I If you **disengage** something, or if it **disengages**, it becomes separate from something which it has been attached to. ❑ *She disengaged the film advance mechanism on the camera.* ❑ *John gently disengaged himself from his sister's tearful embrace.*

타동사/자동사 분리하다; 분리되다 ❑ 그녀는 카메라의 필름 장전 장치를 분리했다. ❑ 존은 울먹이며 껴안는 누이에게서 몸을 살짝 빼냈다.

dis|fig|ure /dɪsfɪgyər, BRIT dɪsfɪgəʳ/ (**disfigures, disfiguring, disfigured**) V-T If someone is **disfigured**, their appearance is spoiled. [usu passive] ❑ *Many of the wounded had been badly disfigured.* ● **dis|fig|ured** ADJ ❑ *She tried not to look at the scarred, disfigured face.*

타동사 외관이 손상되다 ❑ 많은 부상자들이 심각한 외상을 입은 상태였다. ● 외관이 손상된, 형태가 망가진 형용사 ❑ 그녀는 흉터로 얼룩지고 일그러진 얼굴을 보지 않으려고 노력했다.

Word Link grac ≈ pleasing : dis*grace*, *grace*, *graceful*

---

dis|grace /dɪsgreɪs/ (**disgraces, disgracing, disgraced**) ◾ N-UNCOUNT If you say that someone is **in disgrace**, you are emphasizing that other people disapprove of them and do not respect them because of something that they have done. [EMPHASIS] ❑ *His vice president also had to resign in disgrace.* ◾ N-SING If you say that something is a **disgrace**, you are emphasizing that it is very bad or wrong, and that you find it completely unacceptable. [EMPHASIS] ❑ *The way the sales were handled was a complete disgrace.* ◾ N-SING You say that someone is a **disgrace to** someone else when you want to emphasize that their behavior causes the other person to feel ashamed. [EMPHASIS] ❑ *Republican leaders called him a disgrace to the party.* ◾ V-T If you say that someone **disgraces** someone else, you are emphasizing that their behavior causes the other person to feel ashamed. [EMPHASIS] ❑ *I have disgraced my family's name.*

◾ 불가산명사 불명예 [강조] ❑ 그의 부통령도 역시 불명예스럽게 사임해야 했다. ◾ 단수명사 망신거리, 수치스러운 것 [강조] ❑ 그 매매 방식은 완전한 망신거리였다. ◾ 단수명사 수치 [강조] ❑ 공화당 지도자들은 그를 당의 수치라고 불렀다. ◾ 타동사 치욕스럽게 만들다 [강조] ❑ 나는 우리 가문의 이름에 먹칠을 했다.

dis|graced /dɪsgreɪst/ ADJ You use **disgraced** to describe someone whose bad behavior has caused them to lose the approval and respect of the public or of people in authority. ❑ *...the disgraced leader of the coup.*

형용사 명예가 실추된, 망신을 당한 ❑ 명예가 실추된 쿠데타의 지도자

dis|grace|ful /dɪsgreɪsfəl/ ADJ If you say that something such as behavior or a situation is **disgraceful**, you disapprove of it strongly, and feel that the person or people responsible should be ashamed of it. [DISAPPROVAL] ❑ *It's disgraceful that they have detained him for so long.* ● **dis|grace|ful|ly** ADV ❑ *He felt that his brother had behaved disgracefully.*

형용사 수치스러운 [탐탁찮음] ❑ 그를 그렇게 오래 억류하다니 수치스러운 일이다. ● 수치스럽게 부사 ❑ 그는 형이 수치스럽게 행동했다고 생각했다.

dis|grun|tled /dɪsgrʌntʰld/ ADJ If you are **disgruntled**, you are angry and dissatisfied because things have not happened the way that you wanted them to happen. ❑ *Disgruntled employees recently called for his resignation.*

형용사 불만에 찬 ❑ 불만에 찬 직원들이 최근에 그의 사임을 요구했다.

dis|guise /dɪsgaɪz/ (**disguises, disguising, disguised**) ◾ N-VAR If you are **in disguise**, you are not wearing your usual clothes or you have altered your appearance in other ways, so that people will not recognize you. ❑ *You'll have to travel in disguise.* ◾ V-T If you **disguise yourself**, you put on clothes which make you look like someone else or alter your appearance in other ways, so that people will not recognize you. ❑ *She disguised herself as a man so she could fight on the battlefield.* ● **dis|guised** ADJ ❑ *The extremists entered the building disguised as medical workers.* ◾ V-T To **disguise** something means to hide it or make it appear different so that people will not know about it or will not recognize it. ❑ *He made no attempt to disguise his agitation.* ● **dis|guised** ADJ ❑ *The proposal is a thinly disguised effort to revive the price controls of the 1970s.*

◾ 가산명사 또는 불가산명사 변장 ❑ 변장을 하고 여행을 해야 할 것이다. ◾ 타동사 변장하다 ❑ 그녀는 전장에서 싸우기 위해 남장을 했다. ● 변장한 형용사 ❑ 극렬분자들이 의료 근로자로 변장을 하고 건물에 잠입했다. ◾ 타동사 감추다, 위장하다 ❑ 그는 조금도 자신의 불안을 감추려고 하지 않았다. ● 위장된 형용사 ❑ 그 제안은 1970년대의 가격 통제를 부활시키기 위한 얄팍한 위장술이다.

dis|gust /dɪsgʌst/ (**disgusts, disgusting, disgusted**) ◾ N-UNCOUNT **Disgust** is a feeling of very strong dislike or disapproval. ❑ *He spoke of his disgust at the incident.* ◾ V-T To **disgust** someone means to make them feel a strong sense of dislike and disapproval. ❑ *He disgusted many with his boorish behavior.*

◾ 불가산명사 혐오감 ❑ 그는 그 사건에 대한 자신의 혐오감을 이야기했다. ◾ 타동사 혐오감을 주다 ❑ 그는 상스러운 행동으로 많은 사람에게 혐오감을 주었다.

dis|gust|ed /dɪsgʌstɪd/ ADJ If you are **disgusted**, you feel a strong sense of dislike and disapproval at something. ❑ *I'm disgusted with the way that he was treated.* ● **dis|gust|ed|ly** ADV [ADV with v] ❑ *"It's a little late for that," Ritter said disgustedly.*

형용사 역겨워 하는, 혐오감을 느끼는 ❑ 그가 받은 처우에 대해 나는 역겨움을 느낀다. ● 혐오스럽다는 듯이 부사 ❑ "그러기에는 조금 늦은 것 같아."라고 리터가 혐오스럽다는 듯이 말했다.

dis|gust|ing /dɪsgʌstɪŋ/ ◾ ADJ If you say that something is **disgusting**, you are criticizing it because it is extremely unpleasant. ❑ *It tasted disgusting.* ◾ ADJ If you say that something is **disgusting**, you mean that you find it completely unacceptable. ❑ *It's disgusting that the taxpayer is subsidizing this project.*

◾ 형용사 역겨운 ❑ 그것은 맛이 정말 역겨웠어. ◾ 형용사 혐오스러운, 용납할 수 없는 ❑ 세납자가 이 프로젝트의 비용을 댄다는 것은 용납할 수 없는 일이다.

dish ◆◇◇ /dɪʃ/ (**dishes, dishing, dished**) ◾ N-COUNT A **dish** is a shallow container with a wide uncovered top. You eat and serve food from dishes and cook food in them. ❑ *...plastic bowls and dishes.* ◾ N-COUNT Food that is prepared in a particular style or combination can be referred to as a **dish**. ❑ *There are plenty of vegetarian dishes to choose from.* ◾ N-PLURAL All the objects that have been used to cook, serve, and eat a meal can be referred to as **the dishes**. ❑ *He'd cooked dinner and washed the dishes.* ◾ N-COUNT You can use **dish** to refer to anything that is round and hollow in shape with a wide uncovered top. ❑ *...a dish used to receive satellite broadcasts.* ◾ →see also **satellite dish** ◾ PHRASE If you **do the dishes**, you wash the dishes. ❑ *I hate doing the dishes.* →see **pottery** →see Picture Dictionary: **dish**

◾ 가산명사 접시 ❑ 플라스틱 사발과 접시들 ◾ 가산명사 요리 ❑ 고를 수 있는 채식 요리가 많이 있다. ◾ 복수명사 그릇 ❑ 그는 저녁 식사 준비를 다하고 설거지를 한 상태였다. ◾ 가산명사 접시 ❑ 위성 방송을 수신하는 접시 ◾ 구 설거지하다 ❑ 난 설거지하기 싫어.

a
b
c
d
e
f
g
h
i
j
k
l
m
n
o
p
q
r
s
t
u
v
w
x
y
z

Picture Dictionary — dish

salt & pepper shakers

sugar bowl

butter dish

mug

cup & saucer

dinner plate

salad plate

bread plate

bowl

platter

▶**dish out** 🔢 PHRASAL VERB If you **dish out** something, you distribute it among a number of people. [INFORMAL] ❑ *Doctors, not pharmacists, are responsible for dishing out drugs.* 🔢 PHRASAL VERB If someone **dishes out** criticism or punishment, they give it to someone. [INFORMAL] ❑ *Do you usually dish out criticism to someone who's doing you a favor?* 🔢 PHRASAL VERB If you **dish out** food, you serve it to people at the beginning of each course of a meal. [INFORMAL] ❑ *Here in the dining hall the cooks dish out sweet and sour pork.*

▶**dish up** PHRASAL VERB If you **dish up** food, you serve it. [INFORMAL] ❑ *They dished up a superb meal.*

dis|heart|ened /dɪshɑːrtªnd/ ADJ If you are **disheartened**, you feel disappointed about something and have less confidence or less hope about it than you did before. ❑ *He was disheartened by their hostile reaction.*

dis|heart|en|ing /dɪshɑːrtªnɪŋ/ ADJ If something is **disheartening**, it makes you feel disappointed and less confident or less hopeful. ❑ *The news was disheartening for investors.*

di|shev|eled /dɪʃɛvªld/ [BRIT, sometimes AM **dishevelled**] ADJ If you describe someone's hair, clothes, or appearance as **disheveled**, you mean that it is very untidy. ❑ *She arrived flushed and disheveled.*

dis|hon|est /dɪsɒnɪst/ ADJ If you say that a person or their behavior is **dishonest**, you mean that they are not truthful or honest and that you cannot trust them. ❑ *It would be dishonest to mislead people and not to present the data as fairly as possible.* ● **dis|hon|est|ly** ADV ❑ *The key issue was whether the four defendants acted dishonestly.*

dis|hon|es|ty /dɪsɒnɪsti/ N-UNCOUNT **Dishonesty** is dishonest behavior. ❑ *She accused the government of dishonesty and incompetence.*

dish|wash|er /dɪʃwɒʃər/ (**dishwashers**) N-COUNT A **dishwasher** is an electrically operated machine that washes and dries dishes, pans, and flatware.

dis|il|lu|sion /dɪsɪluːʒ³n/ (**disillusions, disillusioning, disillusioned**) 🔢 V-T If a person or thing **disillusions** you, they make you realize that something is not as good as you thought. ❑ *I'd hate to be the one to disillusion him.* 🔢 N-UNCOUNT **Disillusion** is the same as **disillusionment**. ❑ *There is disillusion with established political parties.*

dis|il|lu|sioned /dɪsɪluːʒ³nd/ ADJ If you are **disillusioned with** something, you are disappointed, because it is not as good as you had expected or thought. ❑ *I've become very disillusioned with politics.*

dis|il|lu|sion|ment /dɪsɪluːʒ³nmənt/ N-UNCOUNT **Disillusionment** is the disappointment that you feel when you discover that something is not as good as you had expected or thought. ❑ *There is evidence of a general sense of disillusionment with the government.*

dis|in|fect /dɪsɪnfɛkt/ (**disinfects, disinfecting, disinfected**) V-T If you **disinfect** something, you clean it using a substance that kills germs. ❑ *Chlorine is used to disinfect water.*

dis|in|fect|ant /dɪsɪnfɛktənt/ (**disinfectants**) N-MASS **Disinfectant** is a substance that kills germs. It is used, for example, for cleaning kitchens and bathrooms. ❑ *Effluent from the sedimentation tank is dosed with disinfectant to kill any harmful organisms.*

dis|in|fla|tion /dɪsɪnfleɪʃ³n/ N-UNCOUNT **Disinflation** is a reduction in the rate of inflation, especially as a result of government policies. ❑ *The 1990s was a period of disinflation, when companies lost much of their power to raise prices.*

dis|in|te|grate /dɪsɪntɪgreɪt/ (**disintegrates, disintegrating, disintegrated**) 🔢 V-I If something **disintegrates**, it becomes seriously weakened, and is divided or destroyed. ❑ *During October 1918 the Austro-Hungarian Empire began to disintegrate.* ● **dis|in|te|gra|tion** /dɪsɪntɪgreɪʃ³n/ N-UNCOUNT ❑ *...the violent disintegration of Yugoslavia.* 🔢 V-I If an object or substance **disintegrates**, it

🔢 구동사 배분하다, 나누어 주다 [비격식체] ❑ 약을 배분하는 책임은 약사가 아닌 의사에게 있다. 🔢 구동사 (비판, 처벌 등을) 하다 [비격식체] ❑ 너는 원래 네 부탁을 들어주는 사람한테 그렇게 비판을 함부로 하나? 🔢 구동사 (음식을) 나누어 주다 [비격식체] ❑ 이곳 대식당 홀에선 요리사들이 탕수육을 나눠 드릴 겁니다.

구동사 음식을 차리다 [비격식체] ❑ 그들은 훌륭한 식사를 차려 내놓았다.

형용사 낙담한 ❑ 그는 그들의 적대적인 반응에 낙담했다.

형용사 낙담시키는 ❑ 그 소식은 투자자들을 낙담시켰다.

[영국영어, 미국영어 가끔 dishevelled] 형용사 헝클어진, 흐트러진 ❑ 그녀는 얼굴이 상기되고 매우 머리가 흐트러진 채 나타났다.

형용사 부정직한 ❑ 사람들을 오도하고 자료를 가능한 한 공정하게 제시하지 않는 것은 부정직하다. ● 부정직하게 부사 ❑ 네 명의 피고가 부정직하게 행동했느냐가 주요 쟁점이다.

불가산명사 부정직 ❑ 그녀는 정부를 부정직하고 무능하다고 비난했다.

가산명사 식기 세척기

🔢 타동사 환상을 깨다, 환멸을 느끼게 하다 ❑ 그의 환상을 깨게 되는 것이 내가 아니었으면 좋겠다. 🔢 불가산명사 환멸 ❑ 기존 정당들에 대해 환멸을 느끼고들 있다.

형용사 환멸을 느낀 ❑ 나는 정치에 환멸을 느끼게 되었다.

불가산명사 환멸 ❑ 사람들이 정부에 대해 환멸을 느끼고 있다는 증거가 있다.

타동사 소독하다, 살균하다 ❑ 물을 소독하기 위해 염소를 사용한다.

물질명사 살균제, 소독제 ❑ 침전 탱크의 유출물에 있는 해로운 유기물을 없애기 위해 살균제를 처리한다.

불가산명사 디스인플레이션 ❑ 1990년대는 디스인플레이션의 시기여서 당시 기업들은 가격을 올릴 수 있는 권한의 상당 부분을 상실했다.

🔢 자동사 분열되다, 해체되다 ❑ 1918년 10월에 오스트리아-헝가리 제국이 해체되기 시작했다. ● 분열, 와해, 해체 불가산명사 ❑ 유고슬라비아의 격렬한 분열 🔢 자동사 해체되다 ❑ 시속 420마일에서 차 앞 유리가 산산조각이 났다. ● 해체 불가산명사 ❑ 그 보고서는

breaks into many small pieces or parts and is destroyed. ❑ *At 420 mph the windshield disintegrated.* ● **dis|in|te|gra|tion** N-UNCOUNT ❑ *The report describes the catastrophic disintegration of the aircraft after the explosion.*

dis|in|ter|est /dɪsɪntərɪst, -ɪntrɪst/ N-UNCOUNT If there is **disinterest in** something, people are not interested in it. ❑ *The fact Liberia has no oil seems to explain foreign disinterest in its internal affairs.*

dis|in|ter|est|ed /dɪsɪntərɛstɪd, -ɪntrɪstɪd/ **1** ADJ Someone who is **disinterested** is not involved in a particular situation or not likely to benefit from it and is therefore able to act in a fair and unselfish way. ❑ *The current sole superpower is far from being a disinterested observer.* **2** ADJ If you are **disinterested in** something, you are not interested in it. Some users of English believe that it is not correct to use **disinterested** with this meaning. ❑ *Lili had clearly regained her appetite but Doran was disinterested in food.*

dis|joint|ed /dɪsdʒɔɪntɪd/ ADJ **Disjointed** words, thoughts, or ideas are not presented in a smooth or logical way and are therefore difficult to understand. ❑ *Sally was used to hearing his complaints, usually in the form of disjointed, drunken ramblings.*

disk /dɪsk/ (**disks**)

> The spelling **disc** is usually used in British English for all meanings except meaning **3**.

1 N-COUNT A **disk** is a flat, circular shape or object. ❑ *Most shredding machines are based on a revolving disk fitted with replaceable blades.* **2** N-COUNT A **disk** is one of the thin, circular pieces of cartilage which separates the bones in your back. ❑ *I had slipped a disk and was frozen in a spasm of pain.* **3** N-COUNT In a computer, the **disk** is the part where information is stored. ❑ *The program takes up 2.5 megabytes of disk space and can be run on a standard personal computer.* →see also **disk drive, floppy disk, hard disk**

disk drive (**disk drives**) [BRIT also **disc drive**] N-COUNT The **disk drive** on a computer is the part that contains the disk or into which a disk can be inserted. The disk drive allows you to read information from the disk and store information on the disk.

disk|ette /dɪskɛt/ (**diskettes**) N-COUNT A **diskette** is the same as a **floppy disk**.

dis|like /dɪslaɪk/ (**dislikes, disliking, disliked**) **1** V-T If you **dislike** someone or something, you consider them to be unpleasant and do not like them. ❑ *Liver is a great favorite of his and we don't serve it often because so many people dislike it.* **2** N-UNCOUNT **Dislike** is the feeling that you do not like someone or something. ❑ *My dislike of thunder and even small earthquakes was due to Mother.* **3** N-COUNT Your **dislikes** are the things that you do not like. ❑ *Consider what your likes and dislikes are about your job.* **4** PHRASE If you **take a dislike to** someone or something, you decide that you do not like them. ❑ *He may suddenly take a dislike to foods that he's previously enjoyed.*

Thesaurus	*dislike*의 참조어
v.	disapprove of, object to **1**
N.	aversion to **2**

dis|lo|cate /dɪsloʊkeɪt, dɪsloʊkeɪt/ (**dislocates, dislocating, dislocated**) **1** V-T If you **dislocate** a bone or joint in your body, or in someone else's body, it moves out of its proper position in relation to other bones, usually in an accident. ❑ *Harrison dislocated a finger.* **2** V-T To **dislocate** something such as a system, process, or way of life means to disturb it greatly or prevent it from continuing as normal. ❑ *It would help to end illiteracy and disease, but it would also dislocate a traditional way of life.*

dis|lodge /dɪslɒdʒ/ (**dislodges, dislodging, dislodged**) **1** V-T To **dislodge** something means to remove it from where it was fixed or held. ❑ *Rainfall from a tropical storm dislodged the debris from the slopes of the volcano.* **2** V-T To **dislodge** a person from a position or job means to remove them from it. ❑ *He may challenge the Prime Minister even if he decides he cannot dislodge her this time.*

dis|loy|al /dɪslɔɪəl/ ADJ Someone who is **disloyal to** their friends, family, or country does not support them or does things that could harm them. ❑ *She was so disloyal to her deputy she made his position untenable.*

dis|loy|al|ty /dɪslɔɪəlti/ N-UNCOUNT **Disloyalty** is disloyal behavior. ❑ *Charges had already been made against certain officials suspected of disloyalty.*

dis|mal /dɪzmᵊl/ **1** ADJ Something that is **dismal** is bad in a sad or depressing way. ❑ *...Israel's dismal record in the Olympics.* **2** ADJ Something that is **dismal** is sad and depressing, especially in appearance. ❑ *The main part of the hospital is pretty dismal but the children's ward is really lively.*

dis|man|tle /dɪsmæntᵊl/ (**dismantles, dismantling, dismantled**) **1** V-T If you **dismantle** a machine or structure, you carefully separate it into its different parts. ❑ *He asked for immediate help from the United States to dismantle the warheads.* **2** V-T To **dismantle** an organization or system means to cause it to stop functioning by gradually reducing its power or purpose. ❑ *Public services of all kinds are being dismantled.*

dis|may /dɪsmeɪ/ (**dismays, dismaying, dismayed**) **1** N-UNCOUNT **Dismay** is a strong feeling of fear, worry, or sadness that is caused by something unpleasant and unexpected. [FORMAL] ❑ *Local councillors have reacted with dismay and indignation.* **2** V-T If you **are dismayed** by something, it makes you feel afraid, worried, or sad. [FORMAL] ❑ *The committee was dismayed by what it had been told.* ● **dis|mayed** ADJ ❑ *He was dismayed at the cynicism of the youngsters.*

폭발 후에 비행기가 끔찍하게 해체되는 과정을 묘사하고 있다.

불가산명사 무관심 ❑ 왜 외국들이 라이베리아의 국내 문제에 무관심한지는 그 나라에 석유가 없다는 사실로 설명할 수 있을 것 같다.

1 형용사 공평무사한, 사심 없는 ❑ 현재의 유일한 초강대국은 결코 공평무사한 관찰자가 아니다. **2** 형용사 무관심한 ❑ 릴리는 분명히 식욕을 되찾은 상태였으나 도란은 음식에 무관심했다.

형용사 횡설수설인, 조리가 없는 ❑ 대체로 술에 취한 채 횡설수설 투덜대는 그의 불평을 듣는 데 샐리는 익숙했다.

철자 disc는 대개 영국영어에서 **3**을 제외한 모든 의미에서 쓴다.

1 가산명사 원반 ❑ 대부분의 세절기는 교체 가능한 날이 장착된 회전 원반을 이용한다. **2** 가산명사 추간 연골, 디스크 ❑ 나는 등의 디스크가 어긋나서 갑자기 너무 아파 꼼짝할 수가 없었다. **3** 가산명사 디스크 ❑ 이 프로그램은 2.5메가바이트의 디스크 공간을 차지하며 일반 개인 컴퓨터에서 구동된다.

[영국영어 disc drive] 가산명사 디스크 드라이브

가산명사 디스켓

1 타동사 싫어하다 ❑ 간은 그가 굉장히 좋아하는 음식이지만 그것을 싫어하는 사람이 너무 많기 때문에 우리는 그것을 자주 차리지는 않는다. **2** 불가산명사 반감, 좋아하지 않음 ❑ 내가 천둥과 작은 지진 같은 것을 좋아하지 않는 것은 어머니 때문이었다. **3** 가산명사 싫어하는 것 ❑ 당신 직장에서 당신이 좋아하는 것과 싫어하는 것이 무엇인지 생각해 봐라. **4** 구 싫어하게 되다 ❑ 그가 이전에 좋아하던 음식들을 갑자기 싫어하게 될 수도 있다.

1 타동사 탈구시키다 ❑ 해리슨은 손가락을 삐었다. **2** 타동사 혼란스럽게 하다 ❑ 문맹과 질병을 없애는 데 도움이 되겠지만 또한 전통적인 삶의 방식을 혼란스럽게 만들기도 할 것이다.

1 타동사 분리시키다 ❑ 열대성 폭풍우가 화산 산비탈에 있던 화산 찌꺼기들을 쏟아 내렸다. **2** 타동사 몰아내다 ❑ 그가 이번에 수상을 몰아내지는 못할 것이라고 생각하더라도 그에게 도전은 할지도 모른다.

형용사 불충한, 불성실한 ❑ 그녀는 자신의 대리자에게 너무나도 무성의해서 그의 자리를 위태롭게 만들었다.

불가산명사 불충, 불성실 ❑ 불충의 혐의를 받는 몇몇 관료들에 대해 이미 고발이 이루어진 상태였다.

1 형용사 비참한 ❑ 올림픽에서 이스라엘이 거둔 비참한 성적 **2** 형용사 음울한, 음침한 ❑ 병원의 본관은 상당히 음울하지만 아동 병실은 정말로 생기가 넘친다.

1 타동사 분해하다 ❑ 그는 탄두를 분해하기 위해 미국의 즉각적인 도움을 요청했다. **2** 타동사 와해시키다 ❑ 온갖 종류의 공공 서비스가 와해되고 있다.

1 불가산명사 당혹감 [격식체] ❑ 지역 의원들은 당혹감과 분노를 드러내는 반응을 보여 왔다. **2** 타동사 당혹하게 하다 [격식체] ❑ 위원회는 전달된 소식을 듣고는 당혹해 했다. ● 당혹스러워 하는 형용사 ❑ 그는 청년들의 냉소주의에 당혹스러워했다.

A
B
C
D
E

Word Link   miss ≈ sending : dismiss, missile, missionary

dis|miss ◆◇◇ /dɪsmɪs/ (dismisses, dismissing, dismissed) **1** V-T If you **dismiss** something, you decide or say that it is not important enough for you to think about or consider. □ *Mr. Wakeham dismissed the reports as speculation.* **2** V-T If you **dismiss** something **from** your mind, you stop thinking about it. □ *I dismissed him from my mind.* **3** V-T When an employer **dismisses** an employee, the employer tells the employee that they are no longer needed to do the job that they have been doing. □ *...the power to dismiss civil servants who refuse to work.* **4** V-T If you **are dismissed** by someone in authority, they tell you that you can go away from them. □ *Two more witnesses were called, heard and dismissed.* **5** V-T When a judge **dismisses** a case against someone, he or she formally states that there is no need for a trial, usually because there is not enough evidence for the case to continue. □ *An American judge yesterday dismissed murder charges against Dr. Jack Kevorkian.*

1 타동사 무시하다 □ 웨이크햄 씨는 추정에 불과하다며 그 보고들을 무시했다. **2** 타동사 (생각을) 지우다 □ 나는 그를 내 머릿속에서 지웠다. **3** 타동사 해고하다 □ 일하기를 거부하는 공무원들을 해고할 권한 **4** 타동사 물러가도 좋다는 허락을 받다 □ 증인 두 명이 더 불려 나와 증언을 하고 물러갔다. **5** 타동사 각하하다 □ 어제 한 미국 판사가 잭 커보키언 박사에 대한 살인 혐의를 기각하였다.

F
G

Word Partnership   dismiss의 연어

ADJ.   **easy to** dismiss **1**
N.   dismiss **an idea**, dismiss **a possibility 1**
     dismiss **an employee 3**
     dismiss **a case**, dismiss **charges 5**

H
I

dis|mis|sal /dɪsmɪsˀl/ (dismissals) **1** N-VAR When an employee is dismissed from their job, you can refer to their **dismissal**. □ *...Mr. Low's dismissal from his post at the head of the commission.* **2** N-UNCOUNT **Dismissal of** something means deciding or saying that it is not important. □ *...bureaucratic indifference to people's rights and needs, and high-handed dismissal of public opinion.*

1 가산명사 또는 불가산명사 해고 □ 로우 씨의 위원회장 자리로부터의 면직 **2** 불가산명사 무시 □ 사람들의 권리와 필요에 대한 관료적 무관심과 고압적인 태도의 무시

dis|mis|sive /dɪsmɪsɪv/ ADJ If you are **dismissive** of someone or something, you say or show that you think they are not important or have no value. □ *Mr. Jones was dismissive of the report, saying it was riddled with inaccuracies.* ● **dis|mis|sive|ly** ADV □ *"Critical acclaim from people who don't know what they're talking about is meaningless," he claims dismissively.*

형용사 무시하는 □ 존스 씨는 그 보고서가 부정확한 정보 투성이라며 그것을 무시했다. ● 무시하듯이 부사 □ "무슨 소리인지도 모르고 떠드는 사람들로부터 받는 찬사는 무의미하다."라고 그는 무시하듯이 주장한다.

J
K

dis|obe|di|ence /dɪsəbidiəns/ N-UNCOUNT **Disobedience** is deliberately not doing what someone tells you to do, or what a rule or law says that you should do. □ *A single act of rebellion or disobedience was often enough to seal a woman's fate.*

불가산명사 불복종 □ 단 한 번의 반항 혹은 불복종만으로 흔히 한 여자의 인생이 결판나기도 했다.

dis|obey /dɪsəbeɪ/ (disobeys, disobeying, disobeyed) V-T/V-I When someone **disobeys** a person or an order, they deliberately do not do what they have been told to do. □ *...a naughty boy who often disobeyed his mother and father.*

타동사/자동사 불복종하다 □ 어머니와 아버지 말씀을 잘 듣지 않은 못된 남자애

L
M

dis|or|der /dɪsɔrdər/ (disorders) **1** N-VAR A **disorder** is a problem or illness which affects someone's mind or body. □ *...a rare nerve disorder that can cause paralysis of the arms.* **2** N-UNCOUNT **Disorder** is a state of being untidy, badly prepared, or badly organized. □ *The emergency room was in disorder.* **3** N-VAR **Disorder** is violence or rioting in public. □ *The government issued a decree calling on the authorities to uphold the law and stop public disorder.*

1 가산명사 또는 불가산명사 질환 □ 팔의 마비를 가져올 수도 있는 희귀한 신경 질환 **2** 불가산명사 혼란, 무질서 □ 응급실은 혼란스러웠다. **3** 가산명사 또는 불가산명사 소요 □ 정부는 당국자들에게 법을 수호하고 대중의 소요 사태를 진압하라는 명령을 발표했다.

N
O

dis|or|der|ly /dɪsɔrdərli/ **1** ADJ If you describe something as **disorderly**, you mean that it is messy, irregular, or disorganized. [FORMAL] □ *There were young men and women working away at tables all over the large and disorderly room.* **2** ADJ If you describe someone as **disorderly**, you mean that they are behaving in a noisy, rude, or violent way in public. You can also describe a place or event as **disorderly** if the people there behave in this way. [FORMAL] □ *He pleaded guilty to being disorderly on licensed premises.*

1 형용사 어수선한, 무질서한 [격식체] □ 크고 어수선한 그 방 안에서는 여러 남녀가 책상에 앉아 열심히 일을 하고 있었다. **2** 형용사 난폭한; 소란스러운 [격식체] □ 정규 주류 판매 업소에서 난폭하게 군 혐의에 대해 그는 유죄를 인정했다.

P
Q

dis|or|gani|za|tion /dɪsɔrgənɪzeɪʃˀn/ [BRIT also **disorganisation**] N-UNCOUNT If something is in a state of **disorganization**, it is disorganized. □ *The military, he says, is now in a state of disorganization.*

[영국영어 disorganisation] 불가산명사 혼란 □ 그는 군대가 지금 혼란 상태에 빠져 있다고 한다.

R
S

dis|or|gan|ized /dɪsɔrgənaɪzd/ [BRIT also **disorganised**] **1** ADJ Something that is **disorganized** is in a confused state or is badly planned or managed. □ *A report by the state prosecutor described the police action as confused and disorganized.* **2** ADJ Someone who is **disorganized** is very bad at organizing things in their life. □ *My boss is completely disorganized and leaves the most important items until very late.*

[영국영어 disorganised] **1** 형용사 혼란스러운, 체계가 없는 □ 주 검사의 보고서는 경찰의 그런 행위를 혼란스럽고 체계가 없는 것으로 기술했다. **2** 형용사 비조직적인 □ 나의 상관은 완전 비조직적이어서 가장 중요한 사안도 제때 처리를 하지 못한다.

T
U

dis|ori|ent /dɪsɔriɛnt/ (disorients, disorienting, disoriented) [BRIT also **disorientate**] V-T If something **disorients** you, you lose your sense of direction, or you generally feel lost and uncertain, for example because you are in an unfamiliar environment. □ *An overnight stay at a friend's house disorients me.* ● **dis|ori|ent|ed** ADJ □ *I feel dizzy and disoriented.* ● **dis|ori|en|ta|tion** /dɪsɔriɛnteɪʃˀn/ N-UNCOUNT □ *Morris was so stunned by this that he experienced a moment of total disorientation.*

[영국영어 disorientate] 타동사 갈피를 못 잡게 만들다, 방향 감각을 잃게 만들다 □ 친구 집에서 밤을 보내면 난 내가 어디 있는지 모르게 된다. ● 병병한, 어지러운 형용사 □ 어지럽고 정신이 병병하다. ● 병병함, 정신이 아득해짐 불가산명사 □ 모리스는 이것 때문에 너무 놀라서 순간 정신이 완전히 명해지는 것을 경험했다.

V

dis|ori|en|tate /dɪsɔriɛnteɪt/ (disorientates, disorientating, disorientated) →see **disorient**

W

dis|own /dɪsoʊn/ (disowns, disowning, disowned) V-T If you **disown** someone or something, you say or show that you no longer want to have any connection with them or any responsibility for them. □ *The man who murdered the girl is no son of mine.*

타동사 의절하다 □ 소녀를 살해한 남자는 절대로 내 아들이 아니다. 나는 그와의 인연을 끊는다.

X

dis|par|age /dɪspærɪdʒ/ (disparages, disparaging, disparaged) V-T If you **disparage** someone or something, you speak about them in a way which shows that you do not have a good opinion of them. [FORMAL] □ *...Larkin's tendency to disparage literature.*

타동사 얕보다 [격식체] □ 라킨의 문학을 얕보려는 경향

Y
Z

dis|par|ag|ing /dɪspærɪdʒɪŋ/ ADJ If you are **disparaging** about someone or something, or make **disparaging** comments about them, you say things which show that you do not have a good opinion of them. □ *He was critical of the people, disparaging of their crude manners.*

형용사 얕보는 □ 그는 그들에 대해 비판적이었고 그들의 거친 태도를 얕봤다.

Word Link *par ≈ equal : com*par*e, dis*par*ate, par*t

dis|par|ate /dɪspərɪt/ **1** ADJ **Disparate** things are clearly different from each other in quality or type. [FORMAL] ❑ *Scientists are trying to pull together disparate ideas in astronomy.* **2** ADJ A **disparate** thing is made up of very different elements. [FORMAL] ❑ *...a very disparate nation, with enormous regional differences.*

dis|par|ity /dɪspærɪti/ (**disparities**) N-VAR If there is a **disparity between** two or more things, there is a noticeable difference between them. [FORMAL] ❑ *...the economic disparities between East and West Berlin.*

dis|patch /dɪspætʃ/ (**dispatches, dispatching, dispatched**) [BRIT also **despatch**] **1** V-T If you **dispatch** someone to a place, you send them there for a particular reason. [FORMAL] ❑ *He had been continually dispatching scouts ahead.* ● N-UNCOUNT **Dispatch** is also a noun. ❑ *The dispatch of the task force is purely a contingency measure.* **2** V-T If you **dispatch** a message, letter, or parcel, you send it to a particular person or destination. [FORMAL] ❑ *The victory inspired him to dispatch a gleeful telegram to Roosevelt.* ● N-UNCOUNT **Dispatch** is also a noun. ❑ *We have 125 cases ready for dispatch.*

dis|pel /dɪspel/ (**dispels, dispelling, dispelled**) V-T To **dispel** an idea or feeling that people have means to stop them having it. ❑ *The President is attempting to dispel the notion that he has neglected the economy.*

dis|pen|sable /dɪspensəbᵊl/ ADJ If someone or something is **dispensable**, they are not really needed. ❑ *All those people in the middle are dispensable.*

dis|pense /dɪspens/ (**dispenses, dispensing, dispensed**) **1** V-T If someone **dispenses** something that they own or control, they give or provide it to a number of people. [FORMAL] ❑ *The Union had already dispensed £40,000 in grants.* **2** V-T If you obtain a product by getting it out of a machine, you can say that the machine **dispenses** the product. ❑ *For two weeks, the cash machine spewed out receipts apologizing for its inability to dispense money.* **3** V-T/V-I When a pharmacist **dispenses**, or **dispenses** medicine, he or she prepares it, and gives or sells it to the patient or customer. ❑ *Some shops gave wrong or inadequate advice when dispensing homeopathic medicines.*

▶**dispense with** PHRASAL VERB If you **dispense with** something, you stop using it or get rid of it completely, especially because you no longer need it. ❑ *Many households have dispensed with their old-fashioned vinyl turntable.*

dis|pens|er /dɪspensər/ (**dispensers**) N-COUNT A **dispenser** is a machine or container designed so that you can get an item or quantity of something from it in an easy and convenient way. ❑ *...cash dispensers.*

dis|perse /dɪspɜrs/ (**disperses, dispersing, dispersed**) **1** V-T/V-I When something **disperses** or when you **disperse** it, it spreads over a wide area. ❑ *The oil appeared to be dispersing.* **2** V-T/V-I When a group of people **disperses** or when someone **disperses** them, the group splits up and the people leave in different directions. ❑ *Police fired shots and used tear gas to disperse the demonstrators.*

dis|place /dɪspleɪs/ (**displaces, displacing, displaced**) **1** V-T If one thing **displaces** another, it forces the other thing out of its place, position, or role, and then occupies that place, position, or role itself. ❑ *These factories have displaced tourism as the country's largest source of foreign exchange.* **2** V-T If a person or group of people **is displaced**, they are forced to moved away from the area where they live. [usu passive] ❑ *In Europe alone thirty million people were displaced.*

dis|placed per|son (**displaced people**) N-COUNT A **displaced person** is someone who has been forced to leave the place where they live, especially because of a war. ❑ *There is an urgent need for food and shelter for these displaced people.*

dis|place|ment /dɪspleɪsmənt/ **1** N-UNCOUNT **Displacement** is the removal of something from its usual place or position by something which then occupies that place or position. [FORMAL] ❑ *No barrier prevents our gradual, purposeful displacement of tradition.* **2** N-UNCOUNT **Displacement** is the forcing of people away from the area or country where they live. ❑ *...the gradual displacement of the American Indian.*

dis|play ♦♦♢ /dɪspleɪ/ (**displays, displaying, displayed**) **1** V-T If you **display** something that you want people to see, you put it in a particular place, so that people can see it easily. ❑ *Among the protesters and war veterans proudly displaying their medals was Aubrey Rose.* ● N-UNCOUNT **Display** is also a noun. ❑ *Most of the other artists whose work is on display were his pupils or colleagues.* **2** V-T If you **display** something, you show it to people. ❑ *She displayed her wound to the twelve gentlemen of the jury.* **3** V-T If you **display** a characteristic, quality, or emotion, you behave in a way which shows that you have it. ❑ *It was unlike Gordon to display his feelings.* ● N-VAR **Display** is also a noun. ❑ *Normally, such an outward display of affection is reserved for his mother.* **4** V-T When a computer **displays** information, it shows it on a screen. ❑ *They started out by looking at the computer screens which display the images.* **5** N-COUNT A **display** is an arrangement of things that have been put in a particular place, so that people can see them easily. ❑ *...a display of your work.* **6** N-COUNT A **display** is a public performance or other event which is intended to entertain people. ❑ *...the fireworks display.* **7** N-COUNT The **display** on a computer screen is the information that is shown there. The screen itself can also be referred to as the **display**. ❑ *A hard copy of the screen display can also be obtained from a printer.*

dis|pleas|ure /dɪspleʒər/ N-UNCOUNT Someone's **displeasure** is a feeling of annoyance that they have about something that has happened. ❑ *The population has already begun to show its displeasure at the slow pace of change.*

1 형용사 상이한 [격식체] ❑ 과학자들은 천문학에서 상이한 개념들을 종합하려고 노력 중이다. **2** 형용사 이종의 [격식체] ❑ 지역 간의 차이가 엄청난, 이질적인 요소가 굉장히 많은 나라

가산명사 또는 불가산명사 차이, 상이 [격식체] ❑ 동베를린과 서베를린 사이의 경제적 불균형

[영국영어 despatch] **1** 타동사 파견하다 [격식체] ❑ 그는 정찰병을 꾸준히 내보내고 있었다. ● 불가산명사 파견 ❑ 기동 부대의 파견은 순전히 예비책이다. **2** 타동사 발송하다 [격식체] ❑ 승리로 기분이 고양된 그는 루즈벨트에게 득의에 찬 전보를 발송했다. ● 불가산명사 발송 ❑ 발송 준비된 상자가 125개가 있다.

타동사 일소하다 ❑ 대통령은 자신이 경제를 소홀히 했다는 생각을 일소하기 위해 노력하고 있다.

형용사 없어도 되는 ❑ 가운데 있는 그 사람들은 모두 없어도 된다.

1 타동사 분배하다 [격식체] ❑ 조합은 이미 40,000파운드를 보조금의 형태로 나누어 준 상태였다. **2** 타동사 (기계가 물건을) 뽑아 내다 ❑ 2주 동안 그 현금 인출기는 현금을 지급할 수 없음을 사과하는 영수증을 뱉어 냈다. **3** 타동사/자동사 조제해 주다 ❑ 어떤 약국들은 동종 요법 약품을 제조해 주면서 잘못되거나 부적절한 조언을 했다.

구동사 버리다, 없애다 ❑ 많은 가정들은 구식 레코드 턴테이블을 버렸다.

가산명사 자동 배급기 ❑ 현금 인출기

1 타동사/자동사 흩어지다; 분산시키다 ❑ 기름이 흘어지는 것처럼 보였다. **2** 타동사/자동사 해산하다; 해산시키다 ❑ 경찰은 시위자들을 해산시키기 위해 총을 쏘고 최루탄을 사용했다.

1 타동사 밀어 내다 ❑ 이 공장들이 관광을 밀어 내고 이 나라의 최대 외화 수입원이 되었다. **2** 타동사 (살던 곳에서) 밀려나다 ❑ 유럽에만 3천만 명이 살던 곳에서 밀려났다.

가산명사 난민 ❑ 이 난민들에겐 음식과 피난처가 절실히 필요하다.

1 불가산명사 대체 [격식체] ❑ 우리의 점진적이고 의도적인 전통의 대체를 어떠한 장벽도 막지 못한다. **2** 불가산명사 강제 이주 ❑ 미국 인디언의 점진적인 강제 이주

1 타동사 전시하다 ❑ 시위자들과 자신의 훈장을 자랑스럽게 과시하는 참전 용사들 사이에 오브리 로즈가 있었다. ● 불가산명사 전시 ❑ 작품을 전시 중인 다른 미술가들 대부분은 그의 제자이거나 동료였다. **2** 타동사 보여 주다 ❑ 그녀는 자신의 상처를 배심원인 열두 남자에게 보여 주었다. **3** 타동사 드러내다 ❑ 자신의 감정을 드러내는 것은 고든답지 못한 것이었다. ● 가산명사 또는 불가산명사 드러냄 ❑ 대개 그렇게 노골적인 애정 표현은 그가 어머니에게만 하는 것이다. **4** 타동사 (화면에 정보를) 보여 주다 ❑ 그들은 이미지를 보여 주는 컴퓨터 화면을 쳐다보면서 시작했다. **5** 가산명사 전시 ❑ 당신 작품 전시 **6** 가산명사 공연 ❑ 불꽃놀이 **7** 가산명사 화면 내용, 디스플레이 ❑ 화면 내용의 하드 카피를 프린터로 출력할 수도 있다.

불가산명사 불만, 불쾌 ❑ 주민들은 이미 더딘 변화 속도에 불만을 나타내기 시작했다.

A
B
C
D
E
F
G
H
I
J
K
L
M
N
O
P
Q
R
S
T
U
V
W
X
Y
Z

dis|pos|able /dɪspoʊzəbəl/ (disposables) **1** ADJ A **disposable** product is designed to be thrown away after it has been used. ❑ ...disposable diapers suitable for babies up to 8lb. ● N-COUNT Disposable products can be referred to as **disposables**. ❑ It's estimated that around 80 per cent of babies wear disposables. **2** ADJ Your **disposable** income is the amount of income you have left after you have paid taxes. [ADJ n] ❑ Gerald had little disposable income.

1 형용사 일회용의 ❑ 체중 8파운드 이하 유아에게 적합한 일회용 기저귀 ● 가산명사 일회용품 ❑ 약 80퍼센트의 아기들이 일회용 기저귀를 사용하는 것으로 추정된다. **2** 형용사 재량껏 쓸 수 있는 ❑ 제럴드에 대한 재량껏 쓸 수 있는 소득이 거의 없었다.

dis|pos|al /dɪspoʊzəl/ **1** PHRASE If you have something **at** your **disposal**, you are able to use it whenever you want, and for whatever purpose you want. If you say that you are **at** someone's **disposal**, you mean that you are willing to help them in any way you can. ❑ Do you have this information at your disposal? **2** N-UNCOUNT Disposal is the act of getting rid of something that is no longer wanted or needed. ❑ ...methods for the permanent disposal of radioactive wastes.

1 구 -의 재량에 맡겨진; -의 뜻에 따르는 ❑ 당신은 이 정보에 대한 재량권이 있습니까? **2** 불가산명사 처리 ❑ 방사능 폐기물의 영구적 처리 방식

dis|pose /dɪspoʊz/ (disposes, disposing, disposed)
▶ **dispose of** PHRASAL VERB If you **dispose of** something that you no longer want or need, you throw it away. ❑ ...the safest means of disposing of nuclear waste.

구동사 처분하다, 처리하다 ❑ 가장 안전한 핵폐기물 처리 방법

dis|posed /dɪspoʊzd/ **1** ADJ If you are **disposed to** do something, you are willing or eager to do it. [FORMAL] [v-link ADJ to-inf] ❑ We passed one or two dwellings, but were not disposed to stop. **2** ADJ You can use **disposed** when you are talking about someone's general attitude or opinion. For example, if you are well or favorably **disposed to** or **toward** someone or something, you like them or approve of them. [FORMAL] [adv ADJ, usu v-link ADJ, usu ADJ to/toward n] ❑ I saw that the publishers were well disposed toward my book.

1 형용사 -하고 싶어 하는 [격식체] ❑ 우리는 한두 집을 지나쳤지만, 멈추고 싶지 않았다. **2** 형용사 -쪽으로 마음이 기우는, -한 성질의 [격식체] ❑ 출판업자들이 내 책에 호의를 가지고 있다는 것을 알았다.

dis|po|si|tion /dɪspəzɪʃən/ (dispositions) N-COUNT Someone's **disposition** is the way that they tend to behave or feel. ❑ The rides are unsuitable for people of a nervous disposition.

가산명사 기질, 성향 ❑ 놀이 기구는 신경이 예민한 사람들에게는 부적합하다.

dis|pro|por|tion|ate /dɪsprəpɔrʃənɪt/ ADJ Something that is **disproportionate** is surprising or unreasonable in amount or size, compared with something else. ❑ A disproportionate amount of time was devoted to one topic. ● **dis|pro|por|tion|ate|ly** ADV ❑ There is a disproportionately high suicide rate among prisoners facing very long sentences.

형용사 균형이 맞지 않는; 지나친 ❑ 한 가지 주제에 너무 많은 시간이 할애되었다. ● 불균형하게 부사 ❑ 매우 긴 형량을 선고받은 죄수들 사이에 자살률이 불균형하게 높다.

dis|prove /dɪspruv/ (disproves, disproving, disproved, disproven) V-T To **disprove** an idea, belief, or theory means to show that it is not true. ❑ The statistics to prove or disprove his hypothesis will take years to collect. →see **science**

타동사 -의 그릇됨을 증명하다 ❑ 그의 가설이 옳거나 틀림을 증명할 통계를 수집하는 데는 수년이 걸릴 것이다.

Word Link put ≈ thinking : computer, dispute, reputation

dis|pute ♦♦◇ /dɪspyut/ (disputes, disputing, disputed) **1** N-VAR A **dispute** is an argument or disagreement between people or groups. ❑ They have won previous pay disputes with the government. **2** V-T If you **dispute** a fact, statement, or theory, you say that it is incorrect or untrue. ❑ He disputed the allegations. ❑ Nobody disputed that Davey was clever. **3** V-RECIP When people **dispute** something, they fight for control or ownership of it. You can also say that one group of people **dispute** something with another group. ❑ Russia and Ukraine have been disputing the ownership of the fleet. ❑ Fishermen from Bristol disputed fishing rights with the Danes. **4** PHRASE If two or more people or groups are **in dispute**, they are arguing or disagreeing about something. ❑ The two countries are in dispute over the boundaries of their coastal waters. **5** PHRASE If something is **in dispute**, people are questioning it or arguing about it. ❑ All those matters are in dispute and it is not for me to decide them.

1 가산명사 또는 불가산명사 논쟁, 쟁의 ❑ 그들은 이전에 정부와 벌였던 임금 쟁의에서 이겼다. **2** 타동사 반박하다 ❑ 그는 그 주장을 반박했다. ❑ 데이비가 똑똑하다는 걸 반박하는 사람은 아무도 없었다. **3** 상호동사 (-을 놓고) 다투다 ❑ 러시아와 우크라이나가 함대의 소유권을 놓고 다퉈 오고 있다. ❑ 브리스톨에서 온 어부들이 덴마크 어부들과 조업권을 놓고 다퉜다. **4** 구 논쟁하고 있는 ❑ 두 나라는 연해 수역 경계에 대해 논쟁을 벌이고 있다. **5** 구 논쟁 중의 ❑ 그 모든 문제들은 지금 논쟁되고 있는 중이며 내가 결정할 일이 아니다.

> Do not confuse **dispute** and **argument**. A **dispute** is a serious argument that can last for a long time. **Disputes** generally occur between organizations, political parties, or countries. ❑ ...a 10-year-old dispute over crude oil. An **argument** is a disagreement between people who may or may not know each other. ❑ She had an argument with her father about practicing the piano... Travis got in an argument with another motorist.

> dispute와 argument를 혼동하지 않도록 하라. dispute는 오랫동안 지속될 수도 있는 심각한 논쟁이다. dispute는 일반적으로 조직체, 정당, 국가 간에 발생한다. ❑ ...원유를 놓고 벌인 10년간의 분쟁. argument는 서로 알거나 또는 모를 수도 있는 사람들 사이의 언쟁이다. ❑ 그녀는 피아노 연습 문제를 두고 아버지와 언쟁을 했다... 트래비스는 다른 운전자와의 언쟁에 휘말렸다.

dis|quali|fy /dɪskwɒlɪfaɪ/ (disqualifies, disqualifying, disqualified) V-T When someone **is disqualified**, they are officially stopped from taking part in a particular event, activity, or competition, usually because they have done something wrong. ❑ He was convicted of corruption, and will be disqualified from office for seven years. ● **dis|quali|fi|ca|tion** /dɪskwɒlɪfɪkeɪʃən/ (disqualifications) N-VAR ❑ Livingston faces a four-year disqualification from athletics.

타동사 실격하다, 자격을 박탈당하다 ❑ 그는 부패 행위로 유죄 선고를 받았고, 칠 년간 공직 자격을 박탈당할 것이다. ● 실격 가산명사 또는 불가산명사 ❑ 리빙스턴은 사 년 동안 육상 경기 출전 자격을 박탈당했다.

dis|quiet /dɪskwaɪət/ N-UNCOUNT Disquiet is a feeling of worry or anxiety. [FORMAL] ❑ There is growing public disquiet about the cost of such policing.

불가산명사 불안, 동요 [격식체] ❑ 그와 같은 치안 유지 비용에 대해 국민들의 동요가 커지고 있다.

dis|re|gard /dɪsrɪgɑrd/ (disregards, disregarding, disregarded) V-T If you **disregard** something, you ignore it or do not take account of it. ❑ He disregarded the advice of his executives. ● N-UNCOUNT Disregard is also a noun. ❑ Whoever planted the bomb showed a total disregard for the safety of the public.

타동사 무시하다, 경시하다 ❑ 그는 간부들의 충고를 무시했다. ● 불가산명사 무시; 경시 ❑ 폭탄을 매설한 사람이 누구든, 그는 대중의 안전을 완전히 무시했다.

dis|re|pute /dɪsrɪpyut/ PHRASE If something **is brought into disrepute** or **falls into disrepute**, it loses its good reputation, because it is connected with activities that people do not approve of. ❑ It is a disgrace that such people should bring our profession into disrepute.

구 평판이 나빠지는 ❑ 그런 사람들이 우리 직업의 평판을 떨어뜨리다니 창피한 일이다.

Word Link dis ≈ negative, not : disagree, discomfort, disrespect

dis|re|spect /dɪsrɪspɛkt/ N-UNCOUNT If someone shows **disrespect**, they speak or behave in a way that shows lack of respect for a person, law, or custom. ❑ ...young people with attitudes and complete disrespect for authority.

불가산명사 무시, 불경 ❑ 권위를 완전히 무시하고 도전적인 태도를 가진 젊은이들

Word Link   rupt ≈ breaking : disrupt, erupt, interrupt

dis|rupt /dɪsrʌpt/ (disrupts, disrupting, disrupted) v-т If someone or something **disrupts** an event, system, or process, they cause difficulties that prevent it from continuing or operating in a normal way. ❏ *Anti-war protesters disrupted the debate.*

타동사 혼란시키다; 중단시키다 ❏ 반전 시위자들이 그 토론회를 중단시켰다.

dis|rup|tion /dɪsrʌpʃn/ (disruptions) N-VAR When there is **disruption** of an event, system, or process, it is prevented from continuing or operating in a normal way. ❏ *The strike is expected to cause delays and disruption to flights from Britain.*

가산명사 또는 불가산명사 혼란; 중단 ❏ 그 파업으로 인해 영국발 항공편이 지연되거나 운행 중단될 것으로 예상된다.

dis|rup|tive /dɪsrʌptɪv/ ADJ To be **disruptive** means to prevent something from continuing or operating in a normal way. ❏ *Alcohol can produce violent, disruptive behavior.*

형용사 파괴적인, 붕괴시키는 ❏ 알코올은 폭력적이고 파괴적인 행동을 불러일으킬 수도 있다.

Word Link   sat, satis ≈ enough : dissatisfaction, insatiable, satisfy

dis|sat|is|faction /dɪssætɪsfækʃn/ (dissatisfactions) N-VAR If you feel **dissatisfaction with** something, you are not contented or pleased with it. ❏ *She has already expressed her dissatisfaction with this aspect of the policy.*

가산명사 또는 불가산명사 불만 ❏ 그녀는 그 방침의 이런 측면에 대해 이미 불만을 표시했다.

dis|sat|is|fied /dɪssætɪsfaɪd/ ADJ If you are **dissatisfied with** something, you are not contented or pleased with it. ❏ *82% of voters are dissatisfied with the way their country is being governed.*

형용사 불만스러운 ❏ 유권자의 82퍼센트가 국가 통치 방식에 대해 불만을 가지고 있다.

Word Link   sect ≈ cutting : dissect, intersect, section

dis|sect /dɪsekt, daɪ-/ (dissects, dissecting, dissected) **1** v-т If someone **dissects** the body of a dead person or animal, they carefully cut it up in order to examine it scientifically. ❏ *We dissected a frog in biology class.* ● dis|sec|tion /dɪsekʃn, daɪ-/ (dissections) N-VAR ❏ *Researchers need a growing supply of corpses for dissection.* **2** v-т If someone **dissects** something such as a theory, a situation, or a piece of writing, they consider and talk about each detail of it. ❏ *People want to dissect his work and question his motives.* ● dis|sec|tion (dissections) N-VAR ❏ *...her calm, condescending dissection of my proposals.*

1 타동사 해부하다 ❏ 우리는 생물 시간에 개구리를 해부했다. ● 해부 가산명사 또는 불가산명사 ❏ 연구원들이 해부용 시체를 점점 더 많이 필요로 한다. **2** 타동사 자세히 조사하다, 해부하다 ❏ 사람들은 그의 작품을 자세히 뜯어보고 그의 동기에 의문을 제기하고 싶어 한다. ● 심사숙고; 정밀 검토, 해부 가산명사 또는 불가산명사 ❏ 내 제의에 대한 그녀의 차분하고 오만한 정밀 검토

dis|semi|nate /dɪsemɪneɪt/ (disseminates, disseminating, disseminated) v-т To **disseminate** information or knowledge means to distribute it so that it reaches many people or organizations. [FORMAL] ❏ *They disseminated anti-French propaganda.* ● dis|semi|na|tion /dɪsemɪneɪʃn/ N-UNCOUNT ❏ *He actively promoted the dissemination of scientific ideas about matters such as morality.*

타동사 유포하다, 보급시키다 [격식체] ❏ 그들은 반프랑스주의를 유포했다. ● 유포, 보급 불가산명사 ❏ 그는 도덕성 같은 문제에 대한 과학적 사고의 보급을 적극적으로 장려했다.

dis|sent /dɪsent/ (dissents, dissenting, dissented) **1** N-UNCOUNT **Dissent** is strong disagreement or dissatisfaction with a decision or opinion, especially one that is supported by most people or by people in authority. ❏ *He is the toughest military ruler yet and has responded harshly to any dissent.* **2** v-I If you **dissent**, you express disagreement with a decision or opinion, especially one that is supported by most people or by people in authority. [FORMAL] ❏ *Just one of the 10 members dissented.* ❏ *No one dissents from the decision to unify.*

1 불가산명사 반대, 이의 ❏ 그는 아직껏 가장 강압적인 군부 통치자이며, 어떤 반대에도 가혹하게 대응해 왔다. **2** 자동사 반대를 제기하다, 반대하다 [격식체] ❏ 10명의 회원들 중 한 명만이 이의를 제기했다. ❏ 통합 결정에 아무도 반대하지 않는다.

dis|sent|er /dɪsentər/ (dissenters) N-COUNT **Dissenters** are people who say that they do not agree with something that other people agree with or that is official policy. ❏ *The Party does not tolerate dissenters in its ranks.*

가산명사 반대자 ❏ 그 정당은 당원들 사이에서 반대자를 묵인하지 않는다.

dis|ser|ta|tion /dɪsərteɪʃn/ (dissertations) N-COUNT A **dissertation** is a long formal piece of writing on a particular subject, especially for the highest university degree. ❏ *He is currently writing a dissertation on the Somali civil war.*

가산명사 (학위) 논문 ❏ 그는 현재 소말리아 내전에 대한 논문을 집필하고 있다.

dis|si|dent /dɪsɪdənt/ (dissidents) **1** N-COUNT **Dissidents** are people who disagree with and criticize their government, especially because it is undemocratic. ❏ *...political dissidents.* **2** ADJ **Dissident** people disagree with or criticize their government or a powerful organization they belong to. [ADJ n] ❏ *...a dissident Russian novelist.*

1 가산명사 반대자, 반체제 인사 ❏ 정치적 반체제 인사 **2** 형용사 반체제적인 ❏ 러시아 반체제 작가

dis|simi|lar /dɪsɪmɪlər/ ADJ If one thing is **dissimilar to** another, or if two things are **dissimilar**, they are very different from each other. ❏ *His methods were not dissimilar to those used by Freud.* ❏ *It would be difficult to find two men who were more dissimilar.*

형용사 다른 ❏ 그의 방식은 프로이드가 사용한 방식과 다르지 않았다. ❏ 그 두 사람보다 더 서로 다른 두 사람을 찾기는 어려울 것이다.

dis|si|pate /dɪsɪpeɪt/ (dissipates, dissipating, dissipated) **1** v-т/v-I When something **dissipates** or when you **dissipate** it, it becomes less or becomes less strong until it disappears or goes away completely. [FORMAL] ❏ *The tension in the room had dissipated.* **2** v-т When someone **dissipates** money, time, or effort, they waste it in a foolish way. [FORMAL] ❏ *He needs someone who can keep him from dissipating his time and energy on too many different things.*

1 타동사/자동사 흩어져 사라지다; 흩뜨리다 [격식체] ❏ 그 방 안의 긴장은 사라졌다. **2** 타동사 낭비하다 [격식체] ❏ 그에게는 너무 많은 여러 가지 일들에 시간과 정력을 낭비하는 것을 막아 줄 누군가가 필요하다.

dis|so|ci|ate /dɪsoʊʃieɪt, -sieɪt/ (dissociates, dissociating, dissociated) **1** v-т If you **dissociate yourself from** something or someone, you say or show that you are not connected with them, usually in order to avoid trouble or blame. ❏ *It seems harder and harder for the president to dissociate himself from the scandals that surround Mr. Galdos.* **2** v-т If you **dissociate** one thing **from** another, you consider the two things as separate from each other, or you separate them. [FORMAL] ❏ *Almost the first lesson they learn is how to dissociate emotion from reason.*

1 타동사 ~와의 관계를 부인하다 ❏ 대통령이 갈도스 씨를 둘러싼 추문과의 연관성을 부인하기는 갈수록 어려워지는 것 같다. **2** 타동사 떼어서 생각하다; 분리하다 [격식체] ❏ 대체로 그들이 배우는 첫 번째 수업은 이성과 감정을 분리해서 생각하는 방법이다.

dis|so|lu|tion /dɪsəluʃn/ **1** N-UNCOUNT **Dissolution** is the act of breaking up officially an organization or institution, or of formally ending a parliament. [FORMAL] [also a N, oft N of n] ❏ *He stayed on until the dissolution of the firm in 1948.* **2** N-UNCOUNT **Dissolution** is the act of officially ending a formal agreement, for example a marriage or a business arrangement. [FORMAL] ❏ *...the statutory requirement for granting dissolution of a marriage.*

1 불가산명사 해산 [격식체] ❏ 그는 1948년에 회사가 해산될 때까지 남아 있었다. **2** 불가산명사 해체 [격식체] ❏ 법률상의 혼인 말소 승인 요구

dis|solve /dɪzɒlv/ (dissolves, dissolving, dissolved) **1** v-т/v-I If a substance **dissolves** in liquid or if you **dissolve** it, it becomes mixed with the liquid and

1 타동사/자동사 녹다; 녹이다 ❏ 설탕이 녹을 때까지 서서히 가열하세요. **2** 타동사 해산되다 ❏ 그 위원회는

disappears. ❑ *Heat gently until the sugar dissolves.* ② V-T When an organization or institution **is dissolved**, it is officially ended or broken up. ❑ *The committee has been dissolved.* ③ V-T When a parliament **is dissolved**, it is formally ended, so that elections for a new parliament can be held. ❑ *The present assembly will be dissolved on April 30th.* ④ V-T When a marriage or business arrangement **is dissolved**, it is officially ended. [usu passive] ❑ *The marriage was dissolved in 1976.* ⑤ V-T/V-I If something such as a problem or feeling **dissolves** or **is dissolved**, it becomes weaker and disappears. ❑ *His new-found optimism dissolved.*

이미 해산되었다. ③ 타동사 (의회가) 해산되다 ❑ 현재의 하원은 4월 30일에 해산될 것이다. ④ 타동사 말소되다 ❑ 그 혼인은 1976년에 말소되었다. ⑤ 타동사/자동사 점점 사라지다 ❑ 그가 새로 찾은 낙관적인 기분은 점점 사라져 갔다.

Word Link   suad, suas ≈ urging: *dissuade*, *persuade*, *persuasive*

---

dis|suade /dɪsweɪd/ (**dissuades**, **dissuading**, **dissuaded**) V-T If you **dissuade** someone **from** doing or believing something, you persuade them not to do or believe it. [FORMAL] ❑ *Doctors had tried to dissuade patients from smoking.* ❑ *She steadfastly maintained that her grandsons were innocent, and nothing could dissuade her from that belief.*

타동사 단념시키다 [격식체] ❑ 의사들은 환자들을 설득해서 담배를 끊게 하려고 노력했었다. ❑ 그녀는 손자들로 하여금 그와 같은 확신을 버리게 할 수 없었다.

dis|tance ♦♦◇ /dɪstəns/ (**distances**, **distancing**, **distanced**) ① N-VAR The **distance between** two points or places is the amount of space between them. ❑ *...the distance between the island and the nearby shore.* ② N-UNCOUNT When two things are very far apart, you talk about the **distance** between them. ❑ *The distance wouldn't be a problem.* ③ ADJ **Distance** learning or **distance** education involves studying at home and sending your work to a college or university, rather than attending the college or university in person. [ADJ n] ❑ *I'm doing a theology degree by distance learning.* ④ N-UNCOUNT When you want to emphasize that two people or things do not have a close relationship or are not the same, you can refer to the **distance between** them. [EMPHASIS] ❑ *There was a vast distance between psychological clues and concrete proof.* ⑤ N-SING If you can see something **in the distance**, you can see it, far away from you. [in/into the N] ❑ *We suddenly saw her in the distance.* ⑥ N-UNCOUNT **Distance** is coolness or unfriendliness in the way that someone behaves toward you. [FORMAL] ❑ *There were periods of sulking, of pronounced distance, of coldness.* ⑦ V-T If you **distance yourself from** a person or thing, or if something **distances** you **from** them, you feel less friendly or positive toward them, or become less involved with them. ❑ *The author distanced himself from some of the comments in his book.* ● **dis|tanced** ADJ [v-link ADJ, usu ADJ from n] ❑ *Clough felt he'd become too distanced from his fans.* ⑧ PHRASE If you are **at a distance** from something, or if you see it or remember it **from a distance**, you are a long way away from it in space or time. ❑ *The only way I can cope with my mother is at a distance.* ⑨ PHRASE If you **keep your distance** from someone or something or **keep** them **at a distance**, you do not become involved with them. ❑ *Jay had always tended to keep his girlfriends at a distance.*

① 가산명사 또는 불가산명사 거리, 간격 ❑ 섬과 인근 해안 사이의 거리 ② 불가산명사 먼 거리 ❑ 거리가 멀다고 문제가 되지는 않을 것이다. ③ 형용사 원격 (교육) ❑ 나는 원격 교육으로 신학 학위 과정을 밟고 있다. ④ 불가산명사 차이, 거리 [강조] ❑ 심리적 단서와 구체적 증거 사이에는 큰 차이가 있었다. ⑤ 단수명사 먼 곳에, 저 멀리 ❑ 갑자기 저 멀리 그녀가 보였다. ⑥ 불가산명사 거리감, 격의 [격식체] ❑ 서로 부루퉁하고 냉랭해서, 드러나게 서먹서먹했던 기간들이 있었다. ⑦ 타동사 거리를 두다; 멀어지게 하다 ❑ 그 저자는 자신의 저서 속 일부 견해들과는 거리를 두었다. ● 멀어진 형용사 ❑ 클러프는 자신이 팬들로부터 너무 멀어졌다고 느꼈다. ⑧ 구 멀리서 ❑ 내가 우리 어머니를 견딜 수 있는 유일한 방법은 멀리 떨어져 있는 것이다. ⑨ 구 거리를 유지하다 ❑ 제이는 항상 여자 친구들과 거리를 유지하는 경향이 있었다.

Word Partnership   *distance*의 연어

ADJ.	**safe** distance, **short** distance ①
PREP.	**within walking** distance ①
	distance **between** ①②④
	in the distance ⑤
	at a distance, **from a** distance ⑧

---

dis|tant /dɪstənt/ ① ADJ **Distant** means very far away. ❑ *The mountains rolled away to a distant horizon.* ② ADJ You use **distant** to describe a time or event that is very far away in the future or in the past. ❑ *There is little doubt, however, that things will improve in the not too distant future.* ③ ADJ A **distant** relative is one who you are not closely related to. ❑ *He's a distant relative of the mayor.* ● **dis|tant|ly** ADV ❑ *His father's distantly related to the Royal family.* ④ ADJ If you describe someone as **distant**, you mean that you find them cold and unfriendly. [v-link ADJ] ❑ *He found her cold, ice-like and distant.* ⑤ ADJ If you describe someone as **distant**, you mean that they are not concentrating on what they are doing because they are thinking about other things. ❑ *There was a distant look in her eyes from time to time, her thoughts elsewhere.*

① 형용사 (거리가) 먼 ❑ 그 산맥은 먼 지평선을 향해 굽이치며 뻗어 갔다. ② 형용사 (시간적으로) 먼 ❑ 하지만, 그리 멀지 않은 미래에 사정이 나아지리라는 것은 별로 의심할 여지가 없다. ③ 형용사 먼 (친척의) ❑ 그는 시장의 먼 친척이다. ● 먼 친척 관계로 부사 ❑ 그의 아버지는 왕가의 먼 친척이다. ④ 형용사 쌀쌀한, 냉담한 ❑ 그는 그녀가 얼음같이 차갑고 쌀쌀하다고 느꼈다. ⑤ 형용사 꿈꾸는 듯한 ❑ 이따금씩 그녀는 생각이 다른 데 가 있는 듯 꿈꾸는 듯한 눈을 했다.

Thesaurus   *distant*의 참조어

| ADJ. | faraway, remote; (ant.) close, near ① |
| | aloof, cool, unfriendly ④ |

---

dis|tant|ly /dɪstəntli/ ① ADV **Distantly** means very far away. [LITERARY] ❑ *Distantly, to her right, she could make out the town of Chiffa.* ② ADV If you are **distantly** aware of something or if you **distantly** remember it, you are aware of it or remember it, but not very strongly. ❑ *She became distantly aware that the light had grown strangely brighter and was flickering gently.* ③ →see also **distant**

① 부사 멀리 [문예체] ❑ 그녀는 멀리 오른편으로 쉬파슬을 알아볼 수 있었다. ② 부사 희미하게 ❑ 그녀는 불빛이 이상하게 밝아져서 조용히 깜박거리고 있음을 희미하게 알아차렸다.

dis|taste /dɪsteɪst/ N-UNCOUNT If you feel **distaste for** someone or something, you dislike them and consider them to be unpleasant, disgusting, or immoral. ❑ *He professed a violent distaste for everything related to commerce, production, and money.*

불가산명사 싫음, 혐오 ❑ 그는 상업, 생산, 돈 등과 관련된 모든 것을 극도로 싫어한다고 공언했다.

dis|taste|ful /dɪsteɪstfʊl/ ADJ If something is **distasteful to** you, you think it is unpleasant, disgusting, or immoral. ❑ *He found it distasteful to be offered a cold buffet and drinks before witnessing the execution.*

형용사 싫은, 혐오스러운 ❑ 그는 사형 집행을 지켜보기에 앞서 찬 음식과 마실 것을 제공받는 것이 혐오스럽다고 느꼈다.

dis|till /dɪstɪl/ (**distills**, **distilling**, **distilled**) [BRIT **distil**] ① V-T If a liquid such as whiskey or water **is distilled**, it is heated until it changes into steam or vapor and then cooled until it becomes liquid again. This is usually done in order to make it pure. ❑ *The whiskey had been distilled in 1926 and sat quietly maturing until 1987.* ● **dis|til|la|tion** /dɪstɪleɪʃ°n/ N-UNCOUNT ❑ *Any faults in the original cider stood*

[영국영어 distil] ① 타동사 증류되다 ❑ 그 위스키는 1926년에 증류되어 1987년까지 조용히 숙성되었다. ● 증류 불가산명사 ❑ 사과즙 원액에 있는 어떤 결함도 증류한 뒤에 뚜렷이 두드러졌다. ② 타동사 추출되다 ❑ 그 기름은 이 작은 나무의 열매로부터 추출된다.

out sharply after distillation. ◼ V-T If an oil or liquid **is distilled from** a plant, it is produced by a process which extracts the most essential part of the plant. To **distill** a plant means to produce an oil or liquid from it by this process. ❑ *The oil is distilled from the berries of this small tree.* ● **dis|til|la|tion** N-UNCOUNT ❑ *The distillation of rose petals to produce rosewater almost certainly originated in Ancient Persia.* ◼ V-T If a thought or idea **is distilled from** previous thoughts, ideas, or experiences, it comes from them. If it **is distilled into** something, it becomes part of that thing. ❑ *Reviews are distilled from articles previously published in the main column.* ❑ *Eventually passion was distilled into the natural beauty of a balmy night.* ● **dis|til|la|tion** N-SING ❑ *The material below is a distillation of his work.*

● 추출 불가산명사 ❑ 장미 꽃잎에서 장미 향수를 추출 생산하는 것은 거의 확실히 고대 페르시아에서부터 시작되었다. ◼ 타동사 ⌐로부터 나오다; ⌐로 스며들다 ❑ 평론은 이전에 주요 칼럼에 실렸던 글들에서 엄선된 것이다. ❑ 마침내 열정은 자연 그대로의 아름다움을 지닌 향기로운 밤 속으로 스며들었다. ● ⌐로부터 나온 것 단수명사 ❑ 아래 글은 그의 작품으로부터 나온 것이다.

dis|tinct /dɪstɪŋkt/ ◼ ADJ If something is **distinct from** something else of the same type, it is different or separate from it. ❑ *Engineering and technology are disciplines distinct from one another and from science.* ● **dis|tinct|ly** ADV [ADV adj] ❑ *...a banking industry with two distinctly different sectors.* ◼ ADJ If something is **distinct**, you can hear, see, or taste it clearly. ❑ *...to impart a distinct flavor with a minimum of cooking fat.* ● **dis|tinct|ly** ADV [ADV with v] ❑ *I distinctly heard the loudspeaker calling passengers for the Turin-Amsterdam flight.* ◼ ADJ If an idea, thought, or intention is **distinct**, it is clear and definite. ❑ *Now that Tony was no longer present, there was a distinct change in her attitude.* ● **dis|tinct|ly** ADV [ADV with v] ❑ *I distinctly remember wishing I had not got involved.* ◼ ADJ You can use **distinct** to emphasize that something is great enough in amount or degree to be noticeable or important. [EMPHASIS] [ADJ n] ❑ *Being 6ft 3in tall has some distinct disadvantages!* ● **dis|tinct|ly** ADV [ADV adj/-ed] ❑ *His government is looking distinctly shaky.* ◼ PHRASE If you say that you are talking about one thing **as distinct from** another, you are indicating exactly which thing you mean. ❑ *There's a lot of evidence that oily fish, as distinct from fatty meat, has a beneficial effect.*

◼ 형용사 다른 ❑ 공학과 공업 기술은 서로도 다르고 과학과도 다르다. ● 확연하게 부사 ❑ 확연히 다른 두 개의 영역을 지닌 은행업 ◼ 형용사 부명히 ❑ 최소한의 요리용 기름으로 뚜렷한 맛을 내는 것 무명의, 똑똑한 부사 ❑ 확성기를 통해 튜린-암스테르담 항공편 승객을 부르는 소리를 똑똑히 들었다. ◼ 형용사 명확한, 확실한 ❑ 이제 더 이상 토니가 없으니까, 그녀의 태도에 확실한 변화가 있었다. ● 확실히 부사 ❑ 나는 내가 말려들지 않았더라면 하고 바랐던 것을 확실히 기억한다. ◼ 형용사 확실한 [강조] ❑ 키가 6피트 3인치인 데는 확실히 어떤 불이익이 있다. ● 확실히 부사 ❑ 그의 정부는 확실히 위태위태해 보인다. ◼ 구 ⌐와는 달리 ❑ 기름기 많은 생선에는 지방이 많은 고기와는 달리 이로운 효과가 있다는 증거가 많이 있다.

dis|tinc|tion /dɪstɪŋkʃən/ (**distinctions**) ◼ N-COUNT A **distinction between** similar things is a difference. ❑ *There are obvious distinctions between the two wine-making areas.* ❑ *The distinction between craft and fine art is more controversial.* ● PHRASE If you **draw a distinction** or **make a distinction**, you say that two things are different. ◼ N-UNCOUNT **Distinction** is the quality of being very good or better than other things of the same type. [FORMAL] ❑ *Lewis emerges as a composer of distinction and sensitivity.* ◼ N-COUNT A **distinction** is a special award or honor that is given to someone because of their very high level of achievement. ❑ *The order was created in 1902 as a special distinction for eminent men and women.* ◼ N-SING If you say that someone or something has **the distinction of** being something, you are drawing attention to the fact that they have the special quality of being that thing. **Distinction** is normally used to refer to good qualities, but can sometimes also be used to refer to bad qualities. ❑ *He has the distinction of being regarded as the Federal Republic's greatest living writer.*

◼ 가산명사 차이 ❑ 두 곳의 와인 제조 지역 사이에는 명확한 차이가 있다. ❑ 공예와 미술의 차이에 대해서는 보다 논란의 여지가 많다. ● 구 차별을 두다 ◼ 불가산명사 탁월함, 우수함 [격식체] ❑ 루이스는 탁월함고 감수성이 뛰어난 작곡가로 인정을 받고 있다. ◼ 가산명사 포상, 상벌, 영예 ❑ 그 훈장은 훌륭한 사람들에게 주는 포상으로 1902년에 만들어졌다. ◼ 단수명사 특기할 점 ❑ 그에 관해 특기할 점은 연방 공화국 최고의 현존 작가로 여겨지고 있다는 것이다.

dis|tinc|tive /dɪstɪŋktɪv/ ADJ Something that is **distinctive** has a special quality or feature which makes it easily recognizable and different from other things of the same type. ❑ *...the distinctive odor of chlorine.* ● **dis|tinc|tive|ly** ADV [ADV adj/-ed] ❑ *...the distinctively fragrant taste of elderflowers.*

형용사 독특한 ❑ 염소의 독특한 냄새 ● 독특하게 부사 ❑ 딱총나무 꽃의 독특하게 향기로운 맛

dis|tin|guish /dɪstɪŋgwɪʃ/ (**distinguishes, distinguishing, distinguished**) ◼ V-T/V-I If you can **distinguish** one thing **from** another or **distinguish between** two things, you can see or understand how they are different. ❑ *Could he distinguish right from wrong?* ❑ *Research suggests that babies learn to see by distinguishing between areas of light and dark.* ◼ V-T A feature or quality that **distinguishes** one thing **from** another causes the two things to be regarded as different, because only the first thing has the feature or quality. ❑ *There is something about music that distinguishes it from all other art forms.* ◼ V-T If you can **distinguish** something, you can see, hear, or taste it although it is very difficult to detect. [FORMAL] ❑ *There were cries, calls. He could distinguish voices.* ◼ V-T If you **distinguish yourself**, you do something that makes you famous or important. ❑ *Over the next few years he distinguished himself as a leading constitutional scholar.*

◼ 타동사/자동사 구별하다, 분별하다 ❑ 그가 옳고 그른 것을 구별할 수 있었을까? ❑ 연구에 의하면 아기들은 밝은 영역과 어두운 영역을 구별하는 것을 통해 보는 법을 익힌다고 한다. ◼ 타동사 ⌐의 차이를 나타내다 ❑ 음악에는 여타의 예술 형식들과는 다른 뭔가가 있다. ◼ 타동사 식별하다 [격식체] ❑ 사람들이 울부짖고 외쳐댔다. 그는 목소리를 식별할 수 있었다. ◼ 타동사 두각을 나타내다 ❑ 이후 몇 년 동안에 걸쳐 그는 뛰어난 헌법 학자로 두각을 나타냈다.

dis|tin|guished /dɪstɪŋgwɪʃt/ ◼ ADJ If you describe a person or their work as **distinguished**, you mean that they have been very successful in their career and have a good reputation. ❑ *...a distinguished academic family.* ◼ ADJ If you describe someone as **distinguished**, you mean that they look very noble and respectable. ❑ *His suit was immaculately cut and he looked very distinguished.*

◼ 형용사 저명한 ❑ 저명한 학자 가족 ◼ 형용사 당당한, 훌륭한 ❑ 그의 의복은 재단이 흠잡을 데 없었고 그는 매우 당당해 보였다.

dis|tort /dɪstɔrt/ (**distorts, distorting, distorted**) ◼ V-T If you **distort** a statement, fact, or idea, you report or represent it in an untrue way. ❑ *The media distorts reality; categorizes people as all good or all bad.* ● **dis|tort|ed** ADJ ❑ *These figures give a distorted view of the significance for the local economy.* ◼ V-T/V-I If something you can see or hear **is distorted** or **distorts**, its appearance or sound is changed so that it seems unclear. ❑ *A painter may exaggerate or distort shapes and forms.* ● **dis|tort|ed** ADJ ❑ *Sound was becoming more and more distorted through the use of hearing aids.*

◼ 타동사 왜곡하다 ❑ 언론 매체는 사실을 왜곡하고, 사람을 선하기만 한 사람과 악하기만 한 사람으로 가른다. ● 왜곡된 형용사 ❑ 이런 수치들은 지역 경제의 중요성에 대한 왜곡된 견해를 보여 준다. ◼ 타동사/자동사 뒤틀다; 뒤틀리다 ❑ 화가는 형상과 모양을 과장하거나 뒤틀 수도 있다. ● 뒤틀린, 왜곡된 형용사 ❑ 보청기 사용 때문에 소리가 갈수록 더 왜곡되어 들렸다.

dis|tor|tion /dɪstɔrʃən/ (**distortions**) ◼ N-VAR **Distortion** is the changing of something into something that is not true or not acceptable. [DISAPPROVAL] ❑ *I think it would be a gross distortion of reality to say that they were motivated by self-interest.* ◼ N-VAR **Distortion** is the changing of the appearance or sound of something in a way that makes it seem strange or unclear. ❑ *He demonstrated how audio signals could be transmitted along cables without distortion.*

◼ 가산명사 또는 불가산명사 왜곡 [탐탁찮음] ❑ 그들이 사리사욕을 위해 행동했다고 말하는 것은 사실에 대한 심대한 왜곡이라고 생각한다. ◼ 가산명사 또는 불가산명사 왜곡 ❑ 그는 어떻게 음성 신호가 왜곡되지 않고 케이블을 따라 전달될 수 있는지 시범을 보였다.

dis|tract /dɪstrækt/ (**distracts, distracting, distracted**) V-T If something **distracts** you or your attention **from** something, it takes your attention away from it. ❑ *Tom admits that playing video games sometimes distracts him from his homework.* ❑ *Don't let yourself be distracted by fashionable theories.*

타동사 (정신을) 산만하게 만들다 ❑ 탐은 전자오락 때문에 정신이 팔려서 때때로 숙제를 못 한다는 것을 인정한다. ❑ 유행하는 이론들에 미혹되지 마라.

dis|tract|ed /dɪstræktɪd/ ADJ If you are **distracted**, you are not concentrating on something because you are worried or are thinking about something else. ❑ *She had seemed curiously distracted.* ● **dis|tract|ed|ly** ADV [ADV with v] ❑ *He looked up distractedly. "Be with you in a second."*

형용사 심란한, 산란한 ❑ 그녀는 이상하게 마음이 심란해 보였다. ● 심란하여, 마음이 어수선하여 부사 ❑ 그는 심란한 듯 올려다보며 말했다. "곧 갈게."

A
B
C
D
E
F
G
H
I
J
K
L
M
N
O
P
Q
R
S
T
U
V
W
X
Y
Z

dis|tract|ing /dɪstr**æ**ktɪŋ/ ADJ If you say that something is **distracting**, you mean that it makes it difficult for you to concentrate properly on what you are doing. ❑ *I find it slightly distracting to have someone watching me while I work.*

형용사 심란하게 만드는, 정신을 산만하게 만드는 ❑ 나는 내가 일할 때 누군가가 지켜보면 정신이 좀 산란스러워진다.

dis|trac|tion /dɪstr**æ**kʃ°n/ (**distractions**) N-VAR A **distraction** is something that turns your attention away from something you want to concentrate on. ❑ *Total concentration is required with no distractions.*

가산명사 또는 불가산명사 정신을 산만하게 하는 것 ❑ 일체 정신을 산만하게 하는 것 없이 완전히 집중해야 한다.

dis|traught /dɪstr**ɔ**t/ ADJ If someone is **distraught**, they are so upset and worried that they cannot think clearly. ❑ *Mr. Barker's distraught parents were last night being comforted by relatives.*

형용사 제 정신이 아닌, 반쯤 정신이 나간 ❑ 지난밤 반쯤 정신이 나간 바커 씨 부모를 친척들이 위로하고 있었다.

dis|tress /dɪstr**e**s/ (**distresses, distressing, distressed**) **1** N-UNCOUNT **Distress** is a state of extreme sorrow, suffering, or pain. ❑ *Jealousy causes distress and painful emotions.* **2** N-UNCOUNT **Distress** is the state of being in extreme danger and needing urgent help. ❑ *He expressed concern that the ship might be in distress.* **3** V-T If someone or something **distresses** you, they cause you to be upset or worried. ❑ *The idea of Toni being in danger distresses him enormously.*

1 불가산명사 고뇌, 비탄 ❑ 질투는 비탄과 괴로운 감정들을 불러일으킨다. **2** 불가산명사 재난; 조난 ❑ 그는 배가 조난당했을지도 모른다고 염려했다. **3** 타동사 괴롭히다, 고민케 하다 ❑ 토니가 위험에 처했다는 생각이 그를 몹시 괴롭혔다.

dis|tressed /dɪstr**e**st/ ADJ If someone is **distressed**, they are upset or worried. ❑ *I feel very alone and distressed about my problem.*

형용사 괴로워하는 ❑ 나는 대단히 고독하고 내가 가진 문제 때문에 괴롭다.

dis|tress|ing /dɪstr**e**sɪŋ/ ADJ If something is **distressing**, it upsets you or worries you. ❑ *It is very distressing to see your baby attached to tubes and monitors.* ● **dis|tress|ing|ly** ADV ❑ *A distressingly large number of firms have been breaking the rules.*

형용사 괴로운 ❑ 아기 몸에 갖가지 호스와 모니터가 연결되어 있는 것을 보는 일은 매우 괴로운 일이다. ● 괴로울 정도로 부사 ❑ 괴로울 만큼 많은 회사들이 규정을 어겨 왔다.

<table>
<tr><td>**Word Link**</td><td>tribute ≈ giving: at**tribute**, con**tribute**, dis**tribute**</td></tr>
</table>

dis|trib|ute /dɪstr**ɪ**bjut/ (**distributes, distributing, distributed**) **1** V-T If you **distribute** things, you hand them or deliver them to a number of people. ❑ *Students shouted slogans and distributed leaflets.* **2** V-T When a company **distributes** goods, it supplies them to the stores or businesses that sell them. [BUSINESS] ❑ *We didn't understand how difficult it was to distribute a national paper.* **3** V-T To **distribute** a substance **over** something means to scatter it over it. [FORMAL] ❑ *Distribute the topping evenly over the fruit.*

1 타동사 배포하다, 분배하다 ❑ 학생들이 구호를 외치며 전단을 배포했다. **2** 타동사 배급하다, 보급하다 [경제] ❑ 우리는 전국지를 배급하는 일이 얼마나 어려운지 이해하지 못했다. **3** 타동사 뿌리다, 살포하다 [격식체] ❑ 토핑을 과일 위에 골고루 뿌리세요.

dis|tri|bu|tion ♦♦◇ /dɪstrɪbj**u**ʃ°n/ (**distributions**) **1** N-UNCOUNT The **distribution** of things involves giving or delivering them to a number of people or places. ❑ *...the council which controls the distribution of foreign aid.* **2** N-VAR The **distribution** of something is how much of it there is in each place or at each time, or how much of it each person has. ❑ *Mr. Roh's economic planners sought to achieve a more equitable distribution of wealth.*

1 불가산명사 배급, 배부 ❑ 외국 원조 물자의 배급을 관리하는 위원회 **2** 가산명사 또는 불가산명사 분배 ❑ 노 대통령 정부의 경제 기획자들은 보다 공평한 부의 분배를 달성하고자 했다.

dis|tribu|tor /dɪstr**ɪ**bjətər/ (**distributors**) N-COUNT A **distributor** is a company that supplies goods to stores or other businesses. [BUSINESS] ❑ *...Spain's largest distributor of petroleum products.*

가산명사 배급사 [경제] ❑ 스페인 최대 석유 제품 배급사

dis|tribu|tor|ship /dɪstr**ɪ**bjətərʃɪp/ (**distributorships**) N-COUNT A **distributorship** is a company that supplies goods to stores or other businesses, or the right to supply goods to stores and businesses. [BUSINESS] ❑ *...the general manager of an automobile distributorship.*

가산명사 배급사; 배급권 [경제] ❑ 자동차 배급사 책임자

dis|trict ♦♦◇ /dɪstr**ɪ**kt/ (**districts**) N-COUNT A **district** is a particular area of a town or country. ❑ *I drove around the business district.*

가산명사 지역, 지구 ❑ 나는 차를 몰고 상업 지구를 돌아다녔다.

dis|trust /dɪstr**ʌ**st/ (**distrusts, distrusting, distrusted**) **1** V-T If you **distrust** someone or something, you think they are not honest, reliable, or safe. ❑ *I don't have any particular reason to distrust them.* **2** N-UNCOUNT **Distrust** is the feeling of doubt that you have toward someone or something you distrust. [also a N, oft N of n] ❑ *What he saw there left him with a profound distrust of all political authority.*

1 타동사 불신하다, 의심하다 ❑ 그들을 불신할 특별한 이유가 있다. **2** 불가산명사 불신; 의심 ❑ 그곳에서 본 것 때문에 그는 모든 정치적 권위에 대해 깊은 불신을 품게 되었다.

dis|turb /dɪst**ɜ**rb/ (**disturbs, disturbing, disturbed**) **1** V-T If you **disturb** someone, you interrupt what they are doing and upset them. ❑ *Did you sleep well? I didn't want to disturb you. You looked so peaceful.* **2** V-T If something **disturbs** you, it makes you feel upset or worried. ❑ *I dream about him, dreams so vivid that they disturb me for days.* **3** V-T If something **is disturbed**, its position or shape is changed. ❑ *He'd placed his notes in the brown envelope. They hadn't been disturbed.* **4** V-T If something **disturbs** a situation or atmosphere, it spoils it or causes trouble. ❑ *What could possibly disturb such tranquility?*

1 타동사 방해하다 ❑ 잘 잤니? 방해하고 싶지 않았어. 네가 아주 평온해 보였거든. **2** 타동사 ~의 마음을 어지럽히다 ❑ 나는 그의 꿈을 꾼다. 그 꿈들이 너무 생생해서 며칠 동안이나 내 마음을 어지럽힌다. **3** 타동사 이지럽히다, 흐트러뜨리다 ❑ 그는 갈색 봉투 속에 영수증들을 넣어 놓았었다. 그래서 영수증들은 흐트러지지 않고 그대로 있었다. **4** 타동사 어지럽히다 ❑ 무엇이 그와 같은 평온함을 어지럽힐 수 있겠는가?

<table>
<tr><td colspan="2">**Word Partnership**</td><td>disturb의 연어</td></tr>
<tr><td>V.</td><td colspan="2">**do not** disturb **1**
be sorry to disturb **1 2 4**
be careful not to disturb **1 3**</td></tr>
<tr><td>N.</td><td colspan="2">disturb **the neighbors 1**
disturb **the peace 4**</td></tr>
</table>

dis|turb|ance /dɪst**ɜ**rbəns/ (**disturbances**) **1** N-COUNT A **disturbance** is an incident in which people behave violently in public. ❑ *During the disturbance which followed, three Englishmen were hurt.* **2** N-UNCOUNT **Disturbance** means upsetting or disorganizing something which was previously in a calm and well-ordered state. ❑ *Successful breeding requires quiet, peaceful conditions with as little disturbance as possible.* **3** N-VAR You can use **disturbance** to refer to a medical or psychological problem, when someone's body or mind is not working in the normal way. ❑ *Poor educational performance is related to emotional disturbance.*

1 가산명사 소동 ❑ 이어진 소동에서 영국인 세 명이 다쳤다. **2** 불가산명사 어지럽게 만듦, 어수선하게 함 ❑ 부화가 성공적으로 이루어지려면, 가능한 한 어수선하지 않고 조용하고 평온한 환경이 필요하다. **3** 가산명사 또는 불가산명사 장애 ❑ 낮은 학업 성취도는 정서적 장애와 결부된다.

dis|turbed /dɪst**ɜ**rbd/ **1** ADJ A **disturbed** person is very upset emotionally, and often needs special care or treatment. ❑ *...working with severely emotionally disturbed children.* **2** ADJ You can say that someone is **disturbed** when they are

1 형용사 정서 장애의 ❑ 정서 장애가 심한 아이들을 대상으로 일하면서 **2** 형용사 우려하는, 동요한 ❑ 의사들은 환자들 중 30퍼센트 미만이 여자라는 것을

very worried or anxious. □ *Doctors were disturbed that less than 30 percent of the patients were women.* ▪ ADJ If you describe a situation or period of time as **disturbed**, you mean that it is unhappy and full of problems. □ *...women from disturbed backgrounds.*

dis|turb|ing /dɪstɜrbɪŋ/ ADJ Something that is **disturbing** makes you feel worried or upset. □ *There was something about him she found disturbing.*
● dis|turb|ing|ly ADV □ *The Government has itself recognized the disturbingly high frequency of racial attacks.*

dis|used /dɪsyuzd/ ADJ A **disused** place or building is empty and is no longer used. □ *...a disused airfield near Maidenhead.*

ditch /dɪtʃ/ (ditches, ditching, ditched) ▪ N-COUNT A **ditch** is a long narrow channel cut into the ground at the side of a road or field. □ *Both vehicles ended up in a ditch.* ▪ V-T If you **ditch** something that you have or are responsible for, you abandon it or get rid of it, because you no longer want it. [INFORMAL] □ *I decided to ditch the sofa bed.* ▪ V-T If someone **ditches** someone, they end a relationship with that person. [INFORMAL] □ *I can't bring myself to ditch him and start again.* ▪ V-T/V-I If a pilot **ditches** an aircraft or if it **ditches**, the pilot makes an emergency landing. □ *One American pilot was forced to ditch his jet in the Gulf.* ▪ →see also **last-ditch**

dith|er /dɪðər/ (dithers, dithering, dithered) V-I When someone **dithers**, they hesitate because they are unable to make a quick decision about something. □ *We have been living together for five years, and we're still dithering over whether to marry.*

dit|to /dɪtoʊ/ In informal English, you can use **ditto** to represent a word or phrase that you have just used in order to avoid repeating it. In written lists, **ditto** can be represented by ditto marks - the symbol " - underneath the word that you want to repeat. □ *Lister's dead. Ditto three Miami drug dealers and a lady.*

dive /daɪv/ (dives, diving, dived)

> American English sometimes uses the form **dove**, pronounced /doʊv/, for the past tense.

▪ V-I If you **dive into** some water, you jump in head first with your arms held straight above your head. □ *He tried to escape by diving into a river.* □ *She was standing by a pool, about to dive in.* ● N-COUNT **Dive** is also a noun. □ *Pat had earlier made a dive of 80 feet from the Chasm Bridge.* ▪ V-I If you **dive**, you go under the surface of the sea or a lake, using special breathing equipment. □ *Bezanik is diving to collect marine organisms.* ● N-COUNT **Dive** is also a noun. □ *This sighting occurred during my dive to a sunken wreck off Sardinia.* ▪ V-I When birds and animals **dive**, they go quickly downward, head first, through the air or through water. □ *...a pelican which had just dived for a fish.* ▪ V-I If you **dive** in a particular direction or into a particular place, you jump or move there quickly. □ *They dived into a taxi.* ● N-COUNT **Dive** is also a noun. □ *He made a sudden dive for Uncle Jim's legs to try to trip him up.* ▪ V-I If shares, profits, or figures **dive**, their value falls suddenly and by a large amount. [JOURNALISM] □ *If we cut interest rates, the pound would dive.* □ *Profits have dived from $7.7m to $7.1m.* ● N-COUNT **Dive** is also a noun. □ *Stock prices took a dive.* ▪ N-COUNT If you describe a bar or club as a **dive**, you mean that it is dirty and dark, and not very respectable. [INFORMAL, DISAPPROVAL] □ *We've played in all the little pubs and dives around Liverpool.*

div|er /daɪvər/ (divers) N-COUNT A **diver** is a person who swims under water using special breathing equipment. □ *Police divers have recovered the body of a sixteen year old boy.* →see **scuba diving**

Word Link	di ≈ two : dilemma, diverge, divide

Word Link	verg, vert ≈ turning : converge, diverge, subvert

di|verge /daɪvɜrdʒ, BRIT daɪvɜː'dʒ/ (diverges, diverging, diverged) ▪ V-RECIP If one thing **diverges from** another similar thing, the first thing becomes different from the second or develops differently from it. You can also say that two things **diverge**. □ *His interests increasingly diverged from those of his colleagues.* ▪ V-RECIP If one opinion or idea **diverges from** another, they contradict each other or are different. You can also say that two opinions or ideas **diverge**. [no cont] □ *The view of the Estonian government does not diverge that far from Lipmaa's thinking.*

di|ver|gence /daɪvɜrdʒəns, BRIT daɪvɜː'dʒəns/ (divergences) N-VAR A **divergence** is a difference between two or more things, attitudes, or opinions. [FORMAL] □ *There's a substantial divergence of opinion within the party.*

di|ver|gent /daɪvɜrdʒənt, BRIT daɪvɜː'dʒənt/ ADJ **Divergent** things are different from each other. [FORMAL] □ *Two people who have divergent views on this question are George Watt and Bob Marr.*

di|verse /daɪvɜrs, BRIT daɪvɜː'rs/ ▪ ADJ If a group or range of things is **diverse**, it is made up of a wide variety of things. □ *...shops selling a diverse range of gifts.* ▪ ADJ **Diverse** people or things are very different from each other. □ *Albert Jones' new style will inevitably put him in touch with a much more diverse and perhaps younger audience.*

Word Link	ify ≈ making : clarify, diversify, intensify

di|ver|si|fy /daɪvɜrsɪfaɪ, BRIT daɪvɜː'sɪfaɪ/ (diversifies, diversifying, diversified) V-T/V-I When an organization or person **diversifies** into other things, or

우려했다. ▪ 형용사 불우한 □ 불우한 환경 출신의 여자들

형용사 불안하게 하는 □ 그에게는 그녀를 불안하게 하는 뭔가가 있었다. ● 불안할 정도로 부사 □ 인종 간 공격 사건이 불안할 정도로 잦음을 정부 스스로도 인정해 왔다.

형용사 쓰이지 않는, 퇴락한 □ 메이든헤드 부근의 쓰이지 않는 비행장

▪ 가산명사 도랑 □ 두 대의 차량 모두 결국 도랑에 빠졌다. ▪ 타동사 버리다, 폐기하다 [비격식체] □ 나는 침대 겸용 소파를 버리기로 결심했다. ▪ 타동사 차다, 관계를 끊다 [비격식체] □ 그를 차 버리고 다시 시작할 마음이 생기지 않는다. ▪ 타동사/자동사 불시착시키다; 불시착하다 □ 한 미국인 비행사가 제트기를 멕시코 만에 불시착시켜야 했다.

자동사 망설이다 □ 우리는 오 년 동안 함께 살아 왔지만, 아직까지 결혼할지 말지를 두고 망설이고 있다.

상동 □ 리스터가 죽었다. 마이애미의 마약상 세 명과 여자 한 명도 죽었다.

미국영어에서 가끔 과거 시제로 dove를 쓰며 /doʊv/로 발음된다.

▪ 자동사 (물속에) 뛰어들다, 잠수하다 □ 그는 강물로 뛰어들어 탈출하려고 했다. □ 그녀는 풀장 옆에 서서 막 뛰어들 참이었다. ● 가산명사 잠수, 다이빙 □ 패트는 앞서 캐즘 다리에서 80피트짜리 다이빙을 했었다. ▪ 자동사 잠수하다 □ 베자니크는 해양 생물을 수집하기 위해 잠수를 하고 있다. ● 가산명사 잠수 □ 나는 사르디니아 앞바다에 가라앉은 난파선 잔해를 향해 잠수하던 중 이와 같은 것을 목격했다. ▪ 자동사 급강하하다 □ 물고기를 노리고 막 급강하했던 펠리컨 ▪ 자동사 쏙 들어가다; 급히 달려들다 □ 그들은 급히 택시를 집어탔다. ● 가산명사 불쑥 달려듦 □ 그가 갑자기 짐 아저씨에게 달려들어 다리를 걸어 넘어뜨리려 했다. ▪ 자동사 급격히 떨어지다, 폭락하다 [언론] □ 우리가 금리를 내리면, 파운드화가 급락할 것이다. □ 수익이 770만 달러에서 710만 달러로 폭락했다. ● 가산명사 폭락 □ 주가가 폭락했다. ▪ 가산명사 싸구려 술집 [비격식체, 탐탁잖음] □ 우리는 리버풀 일대의 온갖 싸구려 술집과 바에서 연주를 해 왔다.

가산명사 잠수부 □ 경찰 잠수부들이 열여섯 살짜리 소년의 시체를 찾아냈다.

▪ 상호동사 달라지다, 갈라지다 □ 그와 동료들의 관심사는 점점 달라져 갔다. ▪ 상호동사 갈리다, 다르다 □ 에스토니아 정부의 견해는 리프마의 생각과 그리 크게 다르지 않다.

가산명사 또는 불가산명사 차이, 상이 [격식체] □ 당내에 커다란 의견 차이가 존재한다.

형용사 서로 다른 [격식체] □ 이 문제에 대해 서로 다른 견해를 가진 두 사람은 조지 와트와 보브 마르이다.

▪ 형용사 다양한, 가지각색의 □ 다양한 종류의 선물을 파는 상점들 ▪ 형용사 서로 다른, 다양한 □ 앨버트 존스는 새로운 스타일을 통해 필연적으로 훨씬 더 다양하고 아마도 더 젊은 관객들과 만나게 될 것이다.

타동사/자동사 다각화하다, 다양화하다 □ 신상품으로 사업을 다각화했을 때에서야 그 회사의 문제가

diversifies their range of something, they increase the variety of things that they do or make. ❑ *The company's troubles started only when it diversified into new products.* ❑ *As demand has increased, so manufacturers have been encouraged to diversify and improve quality.* ● di|ver|si|fi|ca|tion /dɪvɜrsɪfɪkeɪʃ³n, BRIT daɪvɜːˌsɪfɪkeɪʃ³n/ (**diversifications**) N-VAR *The seminar was to discuss diversification of agriculture.*

시작되었다. ❑ 수요가 증가하면 그만큼 생산자들은 사업 다각화와 품질 개선을 하고자 하는 마음을 품게 된다. ● 다각화, 다양화 가산명사 또는 불가산명사 ❑ 그 세미나에서는 농경의 다각화에 대해 논의할 예정이었다.

di|ver|sion /dɪvɜrʒ³n, BRIT daɪvɜːˌʃ³n/ (**diversions**) **1** N-COUNT A **diversion** is an action or event that attracts your attention away from what you are doing or concentrating on. ❑ *...armed robbers who escaped after throwing smoke bombs to create a diversion.* **2** N-COUNT A **diversion** is a special route arranged for traffic to follow when the normal route cannot be used. [BRIT; AM **detour**] ❑ *They turned back because of traffic diversions.* **3** N-UNCOUNT The **diversion of** something involves changing its course or destination. ❑ *...the illegal diversion of profits from secret arms sales.*

1 가산명사 주의를 딴 데로 돌리게 하는 것 ❑ 주의를 딴 데로 돌리기 위해 연막탄을 던진 뒤 탈출한 무장 강도들 **2** 가산명사 우회로 [영국영어; 미국영어 detour] ❑ 그들은 교통 우회로 때문에 되돌아왔다. **3** 불가산명사 전환; 유용 ❑ 비밀 무기 판매 수익금의 불법 유용

di|ver|sion|ary /dɪvɜrʒəneri, BRIT daɪvɜːˌʃənri/ ADJ A **diversionary** activity is one intended to attract people's attention away from something which you do not want them to think about, know about, or deal with. ❑ *It's thought the fires were started by the prisoners as a diversionary tactic.*

형용사 주의를 딴 데로 쏠리게 하는 ❑ 그 화재는 죄수들이 사람들의 주의를 딴 데로 돌리기 위한 방책으로 저지른 것으로 생각된다.

di|ver|sity /dɪvɜrsɪti, BRIT daɪvɜːˌsɪti/ (**diversities**) **1** N-VAR The **diversity** of something is the fact that it contains many very different elements. ❑ *...the cultural diversity of British society.* **2** N-SING A **diversity** of things is a range of things which are very different from each other. ❑ *Forslan's object is to gather as great a diversity of genetic material as possible.* →see **zoo**

1 가산명사 또는 불가산명사 다양성 ❑ 영국 사회의 문화적 다양성 **2** 단수명사 다양함 ❑ 포슬란의 목표는 가능한 한 다양한 유전학적 자료를 모으는 것이다.

di|vert /dɪvɜrt, daɪ-, BRIT daɪvɜːˌt/ (**diverts, diverting, diverted**) **1** V-T/V-I To **divert** vehicles or travelers means to make them follow a different route or go to a different destination than they originally intended. You can also say that someone or something **diverts from** a particular route or **to** a particular place. ❑ *...Rainham Marshes, east London, where a new bypass will divert traffic from the A13.* ❑ *We diverted a plane to rescue 100 passengers.* **2** V-T To **divert** money or resources means to cause them to be used for a different purpose. ❑ *The government is trying to divert more public funds from west to east.* **3** V-T To **divert** a phone call means to send it to a different number or place from the one that was dialed by the person making the call. ❑ *He instructed switchboard staff to divert all Laura's calls to him.* **4** V-T If you say that someone **diverts** your attention from something important or serious, you disapprove of them behaving or talking in a way that stops you thinking about it. [DISAPPROVAL] ❑ *They want to divert the attention of the people from the real issues.*

1 타동사/자동사 (딴 데로) 돌리다 ❑ 새로운 우회도로가 에이13번 도로로부터 교통량이 돌려질 런던 동부의 레인햄 마쉬스 ❑ 우리는 100명의 승객을 구조하기 위해 비행기의 기수를 돌렸다. **2** 타동사 (자금을) 돌리다, 전용하다 ❑ 정부는 더 많은 공적 자금을 서부에서 동부로 돌리려 하고 있다. **3** 타동사 (전화를) 돌리다 ❑ 그는 로라에게로 걸려 오는 모든 전화를 자신에게 돌리라고 교환원에게 지시했다. **4** 타동사 (주의, 관심을) 돌리다 [탐탁찮음] ❑ 그들은 사람들의 주의를 진짜 문제로부터 딴 데로 돌리고 싶어 한다.

Word Link di ≈ two : dilemma, diverge, divide

di|vide ♦♦◇ /dɪvaɪd/ (**divides, dividing, divided**) **1** V-T/V-I When people or things **are divided** or **divide into** smaller groups or parts, they become separated into smaller parts. ❑ *The physical benefits of exercise can be divided into three factors.* ❑ *Divide the pastry in half and roll out each piece.* **2** V-T If you **divide** something **among** people or things, you separate it into several parts or quantities which you distribute to the people or things. ❑ *Divide the sauce among 4 bowls.* **3** V-T If you **divide** a larger number **by** a smaller number or **divide** a smaller number **into** a larger number, you calculate how many times the smaller number can fit exactly into the larger number. ❑ *Measure the floor area of the greenhouse and divide it by six.* **4** V-T If a border or line **divides** two areas or **divides** an area into two, it keeps the two areas separate from each other. ❑ *...remote border areas dividing Tamil and Muslim settlements.* **5** V-T/V-I If people **divide** over something or if something **divides** them, it causes strong disagreement between them. ❑ *She has done more to divide the Conservatives than anyone else.* **6** N-COUNT A **divide** is a significant distinction between two groups, often one that causes conflict. ❑ *...a deliberate attempt to create a Hindu-Muslim divide in India.*

1 타동사/자동사 나뉘다, 쪼개지다 ❑ 운동이 신체에 주는 유익함은 세 가지 요소로 나뉠 수 있다. ❑ 가루반죽을 반으로 나눠서 각각 밀어 편다. **2** 타동사 분배하다, 나눠 주다 ❑ 소스를 4개의 그릇에 나눠 담는다. **3** 타동사 나누다 ❑ 온실의 면적을 측정해서 6으로 나눈다. **4** 타동사 가르다, 구획하다 ❑ 타밀과 이슬람 거주지를 가르는 먼 접경 지역 **5** 타동사/자동사 (의견이) 갈리다; 분열시키다 ❑ 그녀는 보수당원들을 분열시키는 데 어느 누구보다 큰 요인이 되었다. **6** 가산명사 분열 ❑ 인도 내 힌두교와 이슬람교 간의 분열을 조장하려는 계획적인 시도

Thesaurus divide의 참조어

V.	categorize, group, segregate, separate, split **1**
	part, separate, split; (ant.) unite **2** **4**

Word Partnership divide의 연어

PREP.	divide **into** **1** **3**
	divide **among** **2**
	divide **between**, divide **by** **3**
N.	divide **in half** **3**

▶ **divide up** **1** PHRASAL VERB If you **divide** something **up**, you separate it into smaller or more useful groups. ❑ *The idea is to divide up the country into four sectors.* **2** PHRASAL VERB If you **divide** something **up**, you share it out among a number of people or groups in approximately equal parts. ❑ *The aim was to divide up the business, give everyone an equal stake in its future.*

1 구동사 분할하다 ❑ 그 안은 나라를 네 개의 영역으로 분할하는 것이다. **2** 구동사 분할하다 ❑ 그 목적은 사업을 네 개로 분할하여 장차 모두에게 동일한 지분을 주는 것이었다.

di|vid|ed high|way (**divided highways**) N-COUNT A **divided highway** is a road which has two lanes of traffic traveling in each direction with a strip of grass or concrete down the middle to separate the traffic. [AM; BRIT **dual carriageway**]

가산명사 중앙 분리대가 있는 고속도로 [미국영어; 영국영어 dual carriageway]

divi|dend ♦♦◇ /dɪvɪdɛnd/ (**dividends**) **1** N-COUNT A **dividend** is the part of a company's profits which is paid to people who have shares in the company. [BUSINESS] ❑ *The first quarter dividend has been increased by nearly 4 per cent.* **2** PHRASE If something **pays dividends**, it brings advantages at a later date. ❑ *Steps taken now to maximize your health will pay dividends later on.* →see **company**

1 가산명사 배당금 [경제] ❑ 일사분기 배당금이 4퍼센트 가까이 증가했다. **2** 구 나중에 도움이 되다 ❑ 건강을 극대화하기 위해 지금 조치를 취해 놓으면 나중에 도움이 될 것입니다.

di|vine /dɪvaɪn/ ADJ You use **divine** to describe something that is provided by or relates to a god or goddess. ❑ He suggested that the civil war had been a divine punishment. ● **di|vine|ly** ADV ❑ The law was divinely ordained. →see **religion**

형용사 신의 ❑ 그는 그 내전이 신이 내린 천벌이었다고 넌지시 말했다. ● 신에 의하여 부사 ❑ 그 율법은 신께서 정하신 것이었다.

div|ing /daɪvɪŋ/ **1** N-UNCOUNT **Diving** is the activity of working or looking around underwater, using special breathing equipment. ❑ …equipment and accessories for diving. **2** N-UNCOUNT **Diving** is the sport or activity in which you jump into water head first with your arms held straight above your head, usually from a diving board. ❑ Weight is crucial in diving because the aim is to cause the smallest splash possible.

1 불가산명사 잠수 ❑ 잠수용 장비와 용품들 **2** 불가산명사 다이빙 ❑ 다이빙에서는 최소한 물을 적게 튀기는 것이 목표이기 때문에 몸무게가 대단히 중요하다.

di|vi|sion ♦♦◇ /dɪvɪʒ°n/ (**divisions**) **1** N-UNCOUNT The **division of** a large unit **into** two or more distinct parts is the act of separating it into these parts. ❑ …the unification of Germany, after its division into two states at the end of World War Two. **2** N-UNCOUNT The **division of** something among people or things is its separation into parts which are distributed among the people or things. ❑ The current division of labor between workers and management will alter. **3** N-UNCOUNT **Division** is the arithmetical process of dividing one number into another number. ❑ I taught my daughter how to do division at the age of six **4** N-VAR A **division** is a significant distinction or argument between two groups, which causes the two groups to be considered as very different and separate. ❑ The division between the prosperous west and the impoverished east remains. **5** N-COUNT In a large organization, a **division** is a group of departments whose work is done in the same place or is connected with similar tasks. ❑ …the bank's Latin American division. **6** N-COUNT A **division** is a group of military units which fight as a single unit. ❑ Several armored divisions are being moved from Germany. **7** N-COUNT In some sports, such as soccer, baseball, and basketball, a **division** is one of the groups of teams which make up a league. The teams in each division are considered to be approximately the same standard, and they all play against each other during the season. ❑ Villa had just been relegated from the First Division. →see **mathematics**

1 불가산명사 분할 ❑ 제2차 세계 대전 말미에 두 개의 나라로 분할된 이후 이뤄진 독일의 통일 **2** 불가산명사 분배 ❑ 노동자와 경영자 간의 지금과 같은 분배 형태는 바뀔 것이다. **3** 불가산명사 나눗셈 ❑ 나는 내 딸이 여섯 살 때 나눗셈 하는 법을 가르쳤다. **4** 가산명사 또는 불가산명사 분화, 분열 ❑ 번창하고 있는 서부와 가난해진 동부 사이의 분화는 여전하다. **5** 가산명사 (회사나 관청의) 부 ❑ 그 은행의 라틴 아메리카 사업부 **6** 가산명사 사단 ❑ 몇 개 기갑 사단이 독일로부터 이동되고 있다. **7** 가산명사 (프로 스포츠 리그의) 지구, 지역, 지부 ❑ 빌라는 이제 막 1부 리그 팀에서 밀려난 상태였다.

<table>
<tr><td colspan="2">**Word Partnership**   division의 연어</td></tr>
<tr><td>N.</td><td>division **of labor** **2**
multiplication and division **3**
division **head** **5**
infantry division **6**</td></tr>
</table>

di|vi|sive /dɪvaɪsɪv/ ADJ Something that is **divisive** causes unfriendliness and argument between people. ❑ Abortion has always been a divisive issue.

형용사 분열을 초래하는 ❑ 낙태는 언제나 의견 대립을 일으켜 온 문제이다.

di|vorce ♦◇◇ /dɪvɔrs/ (**divorces, divorcing, divorced**) **1** N-VAR A **divorce** is the formal ending of a marriage by law. ❑ Numerous marriages now end in divorce. **2** V-RECIP If a man and a woman **divorce** or if one of them **divorces** the other, their marriage is legally ended. ❑ He and Lillian had got divorced. ❑ I am absolutely furious that he divorced me to marry her. **3** N-SING A **divorce of** one thing **from** another, or a divorce **between** two things is a separation between them which is permanent or is likely to be permanent. ❑ …this divorce of Christian culture from the roots of faith. **4** V-T If you say that one thing cannot **be divorced from** another, you mean that the two things cannot be considered as different and separate things. ❑ Good management in the police cannot be divorced from accountability. ❑ Democracy cannot be divorced from social and economic progress.

1 가산명사 또는 불가산명사 이혼 ❑ 오늘날 많은 결혼이 이혼으로 끝난다. **2** 상호동사 이혼하다 ❑ 그와 릴리언은 이혼했다. ❑ 그가 그녀와 결혼하기 위해 나와 이혼했다는 데 무척 화가 치민다. **3** 단수명사 분리 ❑ 이처럼 기독교 문화가 신앙의 뿌리로부터 분리된 것 **4** 타동사 불가분의 관계에 있다 ❑ 경찰에게 훌륭한 행정과 책임은 불가분의 관계에 있다. ❑ 민주주의는 사회적·경제적 진보와 분리해서 생각할 수 없다.

<table>
<tr><td colspan="2">**Word Partnership**   divorce의 연어</td></tr>
<tr><td>N.</td><td>divorce **court,** divorce **lawyer,** divorce **papers,** divorce **rate,** divorce **settlement** **1**</td></tr>
<tr><td>V.</td><td>**file for** divorce, **get a** divorce, **want a** divorce **1**</td></tr>
</table>

di|vorced /dɪvɔrst/ **1** ADJ Someone who **is divorced** from their former husband or wife has separated from them and is no longer legally married to them. ❑ He is divorced, with a young son. **2** ADJ If you say that one thing **is divorced from** another, you mean that one thing is very different and separate from each other. [v-link ADJ from n] ❑ …speculative theories divorced from political reality.

1 형용사 이혼한 ❑ 그는 어린 아들을 두고 있는 이혼남이다. **2** 형용사 동떨어진 있는, 거리가 먼다 ❑ 정치적 현실과는 동떨어진 공론

di|vor|cee /dɪvɔrseɪ, -si/ (**divorcees**) N-COUNT A **divorcee** is a person, especially a woman, who is divorced. ❑ In 1939 he married Clare Hollway, a divorcee 13 years his senior.

가산명사 이혼한 사람 (특히 여자) ❑ 1939년에 그는 자기보다 열세 살 많은 이혼녀인 클레어 홀웨이와 결혼했다.

di|vulge /dɪvʌldʒ, BRIT daɪvʌldʒ/ (**divulges, divulging, divulged**) V-T If you **divulge** a piece of secret or private information, you tell it to someone. [FORMAL] ❑ Officials refuse to divulge details of the negotiations.

타동사 누설하다, 밝히다 [격식체] ❑ 간부들은 협상의 세부 내용을 밝히기를 거부한다.

DIY /diː aɪ waɪ/ N-UNCOUNT **DIY** is the activity of making or repairing things yourself, especially in your home. **DIY** is an abbreviation for **do-it-yourself**. [mainly BRIT] ❑ He's useless at DIY. He won't even put up a shelf.

불가산명사 디 아이 와이 (집 수리 등을 손수 하는 일) [주로 영국영어] ❑ 그는 디 아이 와이에는 도움이 안 된다. 심지어 선반 하나도 못 단다.

diz|zy /dɪzi/ (**dizzier, dizziest, dizzies, dizzying, dizzied**) **1** ADJ If you feel **dizzy**, you feel that you are losing your balance and are about to fall. ❑ Her head still hurt, and she felt slightly dizzy and disoriented. ● **diz|zi|ness** N-UNCOUNT ❑ His complaint causes dizziness and nausea. **2** ADJ You can use **dizzy** to describe a woman who is careless and forgets things, but is easy to like. ❑ She is famed for playing dizzy blondes. **3** PHRASE If you say that someone has reached **the dizzy heights of** something, you are emphasizing that they have reached a very high level by achieving it. [HUMOROUS, EMPHASIS] ❑ I escalated to the dizzy heights of director's secretary.

1 형용사 현기증 나는 ❑ 그녀는 여전히 머리가 아팠고 약간 현기증도 나고 정신이 멍했다. ● 현기증 불가산명사 ❑ 그의 불평 때문에 현기증이 나고 메스껍다. **2** 형용사 경박한, 덜렁대는 ❑ 그녀는 경박한 금발 미녀 역할로 매우 유명하다. **3** 구 라는 대단한 자리 [해학체, 강조] ❑ 나는 이사 비서라는 대단한 자리까지 올라갔다.

DJ /ˌdiː ˈdʒeɪ/ (DJs) also **D.J.**, **dj** ◼ N-COUNT A **DJ** is the same as a **disc jockey**. ◼ N-COUNT A **DJ** is the same as a **dinner jacket**. [BRIT]

DNA /ˌdiː ɛn ˈeɪ/ N-UNCOUNT **DNA** is an acid in the chromosomes in the center of the cells of living things. DNA determines the particular structure and functions of every cell and is responsible for characteristics being passed on from parents to their children. **DNA** is an abbreviation for "deoxyribonucleic acid." ❑ *A routine DNA sample was taken.* →see **clone**

◼ 가산명사 디스크자키 ◼ 가산명사 야회복 [영국영어]

불가산명사 디엔에이 (디옥시리보핵산) ; deoxyribonucleic acid의 약자 ❑ 의례적인 디엔에이 샘플이 채취되었다.

---

do
① AUXILIARY VERB USES
② OTHER VERB USES
③ NOUN USES

---

① **do** ♦♦♦ /də, STRONG duː/ (**does, doing, did, done**)

> Do is used as an auxiliary with the simple present tense. Did is used as an auxiliary with the simple past tense. In spoken English, negative forms of **do** are often shortened, for example **do not** is shortened to **don't** and **did not** is shortened to **didn't**.

◼ AUX **Do** is used to form the negative of main verbs, by putting "not" after "do" and before the main verb in its infinitive form, that is the form without "to." ❑ *They don't want to work.* ❑ *I did not know Jamie had a knife.* ◼ AUX **Do** is used to form questions, by putting the subject after "do" and before the main verb in its infinitive form, that is the form without "to." ❑ *Do you like music?* ❑ *What did he say?* ◼ AUX **Do** is used in question tags. ❑ *You know about Andy, don't you?* ◼ AUX You use **do** when you are confirming or contradicting a statement containing "do," or giving a negative or positive answer to a question. ❑ *"Did he think there was anything suspicious going on?" — "Yes, he did."* ◼ V-T/V-I **Do** can be used to refer back to another verb group when you are comparing or contrasting two things, or saying that they are the same. ❑ *I make more money than he does.* ❑ *I had fantasies, as do all mothers, about how life would be when my girls were grown.* ◼ V-T You use **do** after "so" and "nor" to say that the same statement is true for two people or groups. ❑ *You know that's true, and so do I.*

do는 단순 현재시제 보조 동사로 쓰인다. did는 단순 과거시제 보조 동사로 쓰인다. 구어체 영어에서 부정 형태 do not은 don't로, did not은 didn't로 종종 축약된다.

◼ 준조동사 not을 동반하여 부정문을 만들 때 쓰는 조동사 ❑ 그들은 일하기를 원치 않는다. ❑ 제이미가 칼을 가지고 있다는 걸 몰랐다. ◼ 준조동사 의문문을 만들 때 쓰는 조동사 ❑ 음악 좋아하세요? ❑ 그가 뭐라고 말했어? ◼ 준조동사 부가 의문문을 만들 때 쓴다. ❑ 너 앤디에 대해서 알지? ◼ 준조동사 do 조동사를 사용한 의문문에 대한 대답에 쓴다. ❑ "그 사람은 뭔가 의심스러운 일이 일어나고 있다고 생각했나요?" "네, 그랬습니다." ◼ 타동사/자동사 앞에서 나온 동사구를 대신하는 대동사 ❑ 나는 그 사람보다 돈을 더 많이 번다. ❑ 모든 어머니들이 그러하듯이, 나는 내 딸들이 자라났을 때의 삶은 어떨까를 상상해 보곤 한다. ◼ 타동사 so나 nor 뒤에 쓰여 '도 마찬가지다'는 뜻을 만든다. ❑ 너는 그것이 사실이라는 걸 알고, 나도 마찬가지이다.

② **do** ♦♦♦ /duː/ (**does, doing, did, done**)

> Do is used in a large number of expressions which are explained under other words in the dictionary. For example, the expression "easier said than done" is explained at "easy."

◼ V-T When you **do** something, you take some action or perform an activity or task. **Do** is often used instead of a more specific verb, to talk about a common action involving a particular thing. For example you can say "do your teeth" instead of "brush your teeth." ❑ *I was trying to do some work.* ❑ *After lunch Elizabeth and I did the washing up.* ◼ V-T **Do** can be used to stand for any verb group, or to refer back to another verb group, including one that was in a previous sentence. ❑ *What are you doing?* ◼ V-T You can use **do** in a clause at the beginning of a sentence after words like "what" and "all," to give special emphasis to the information that comes at the end of the sentence. [EMPHASIS] ❑ *All she does is complain.* ◼ V-T When you **do** a particular thing **with** something, you use it in that particular way. ❑ *I was allowed to do whatever I wanted with my life.* ◼ V-T If you **do** something **about** a problem, you take action to try to solve it. ❑ *They refuse to do anything about the real cause of crime: poverty.* ◼ V-T If an action or event **does** a particular thing, such as harm or good, it has that result or effect. ❑ *A few bombs can do a lot of damage.* ◼ V-T If you ask someone what they **do**, you want to know what their job or profession is. ❑ *"What does your father do?" — "Well, he's a civil servant."* ◼ V-T If you **are doing** something, you are busy or active in some way, or have planned an activity for some time in the future. ❑ *Are you doing anything tomorrow night?* ◼ V-I If you say that someone or something **does** well or badly, you are talking about how successful or unsuccessful they are. ❑ *Connie did well at school and graduated with honours.* ◼ V-T You can use **do** when referring to the speed or rate that something or someone achieves or is able to achieve. ❑ *They were doing 70 miles an hour.* ◼ V-T If you **do** a subject, author, or book, you study them at school or college. [SPOKEN] ❑ *She planned to do math at night school.* ◼ V-T If someone **does** drugs, they take illegal drugs. ❑ *I don't do drugs.* ◼ V-T/V-I If you say that something **will do** or **will do** you, you mean that there is enough of it or that it is of good enough quality to meet your requirements or to satisfy you. ❑ *Anything to create a scene and attract attention will do.* ◼ PHRASE If you say that you **could do with** something, you mean that you need it or would benefit from it. ❑ *I could do with a cup of tea.* ◼ PHRASE You can ask someone **what** they **did with** something as another way of asking them where they put it. ❑ *What did you do with that notebook?* ◼ PHRASE If you ask **what** someone or something **is doing** in a particular place, you are asking why they are there. ❑ *"Dr. Campbell," he said, clearly surprised. "What are you doing here?"* ◼ PHRASE If you say that one thing **has** something **to do with** or is something **to do with** another thing, you mean that the two things are connected or that the first thing is about the second thing. ❑ *Mr. Butterfield denies having anything to do with the episode.*

이 사전에서 do가 포함된 많은 표현들이 다른 표제어에서 설명된다. 예를 들어, 'easier said than done'은 'easy'에서 설명된다.

◼ 타동사 하다 ❑ 나는 일을 좀 하려고 노력하는 중이었다. ◼ 타동사 하다 ❑ 너 뭐하는 거야? ◼ 타동사 'all S+do'나 'what S+do'의 형태로 뒷부분에 오는 내용을 강조하는 용법으로 쓴다. [강조] ❑ 그녀가 하는 일이라곤 불평하는 것뿐이었다. ◼ 타동사 -를 어떻게 쓰다 ❑ 나는 내 삶을 내가 원하는 대로 살도록 허락받았다. ◼ 타동사 조치를 취하다 ❑ 그들은 범죄의 진짜 원인인 가난에 대해서는 어떤 조치를 취하려 들지 않는다. ◼ 타동사 (이익, 손해 따위를) 주다 ❑ 몇 개의 폭탄이 큰 피해를 입힐 수 있다. ◼ 타동사 (직업으로서) -을 하다 ❑ "아버지는 뭘 하시죠?" "저, 공무원이세요." ◼ 타동사 하고 있다; 할 일이 있다 ❑ 너 내일 밤에 뭐 할 일 있나? ◼ 자동사 성적, 실적 등이 좋거나 나쁘다를 표현하다 ❑ 코니는 학교 성적이 좋았고 우등으로 졸업했다. ◼ 타동사 (-의 속도로) 나아가다 ❑ 그들은 시속 70마일의 속도로 달리고 있었다. ◼ 타동사 공부하다 [구어체] ❑ 그녀는 야간 학교에서 수학을 공부할 계획을 했다. ◼ 타동사 (마약을) 하다 ❑ 나는 마약을 하지 않는다. ◼ 타동사/자동사 충분하다, 족하다 ❑ 무엇이든 소동을 일으켜서 주의를 끌 만한 것이면 된다. ◼ 구 -했으면 좋겠다 ❑ 차 한 잔 했으면 좋겠다. ◼ 구 -는 어떻게 했니?, -를 어디다 뒀니? ❑ 그 공책 어떻게 했니? ◼ 구 - (에서) 뭐해? ❑ "캠벨 박사님," 그는 분명히 놀라서 말했다. "여기서 뭐 하시는 겁니까?" ◼ 구 -와 관계가 있다 ❑ 버터필드 씨는 그 일과 관계가 있음을 부인했다.

▶**do away with** ◼ PHRASAL VERB To **do away with** something means to remove it completely or put an end to it. ❑ *The long-range goal must be to do away with nuclear weapons altogether.* ◼ PHRASAL VERB If one person **does away with** another, the first murders the second. If you **do away with yourself**, you kill yourself. [INFORMAL] ❑ *...a woman whose husband had made several attempts to do away with her.*

◼ 구동사 -을 없애다, -을 폐지하다 ❑ 장기적 목표는 핵무기의 완전 폐기가 돼야 한다. ◼ 구동사 -을 죽이다 [비격식체] ❑ 남편의 몇 차례에 걸친 살해 기도의 표적이 되었었던 여인

▶**do up** ◼ PHRASAL VERB If you **do** something **up**, you fasten it. ❑ *Mari did up the buttons.* ◼ PHRASAL VERB If you **do up** an old building, you decorate and repair

◼ 구동사 (단추, 지퍼 따위를) 채우다 ❑ 마리는 단추를 채웠다. ◼ 구동사 수리하다, 손보다 [영국영어]

it so that it is in a better condition. [BRIT] □ *Nicholas has bought a barn in Provence and is spending August doing it up.* ▣ PHRASAL VERB If you say that a person or room **is done up** in a particular way, you mean they are dressed or decorated in that way, often a way that is rather ridiculous or extreme. □ ...*Beatrice, usually done up like the fairy on the Christmas tree.*

▶**do without** ▣ PHRASAL VERB If you **do without** something you need, want, or usually have, you are able to survive, continue, or succeed although you do not have it. □ *We can't do without the help of your organization.* ▣ PHRASAL VERB If you say that you could **do without** something, you mean that you would prefer not to have it or it is of no benefit to you. [INFORMAL] □ *He could do without her rhetorical questions at five o'clock in the morning.*

③ **do** /duː/ (**dos**) ▣ N-COUNT A **do** is a party, dinner party, or other social event. [mainly BRIT, INFORMAL] □ *A friend of his is having a do in Stoke.* ▣ PHRASE If someone tells you the **dos and don'ts** of a particular situation, they advise you what you should and should not do in that situation. □ *Please advise me on the most suitable color print film and some dos and don'ts.*

dock /dɒk/ (**docks, docking, docked**) ▣ N-COUNT A **dock** is an enclosed area in a harbor where ships go to be loaded, unloaded, and repaired. [also in/into N] □ *She headed for the docks, thinking that Ricardo might be hiding in one of the boats.* ▣ V-T/V-I When a ship **docks** or **is docked**, it is brought into a dock. □ *The vessel docked at Liverpool in April 1811.* ▣ V-RECIP When one spacecraft **docks** or **is docked with** another, the two crafts join together in space. □ *The space shuttle Atlantis is scheduled to dock with Russia's Mir space station.* ▣ N-COUNT A **dock** is a platform for loading vehicles or trains. [AM] □ *The truck left the loading dock with hoses still attached.* ▣ N-COUNT A **dock** is a small structure at the edge of water where boats can tie up, especially one that is privately owned. [AM] □ *He had a house there and a dock and a little aluminum boat.* ▣ N-SING In a law court, the **dock** is where the person accused of a crime stands or sits. □ *What about the odd chance that you do put an innocent man in the dock?* ▣ V-T If you **dock** someone's wages or money, you take some of the money away. If you **dock** someone points in a contest, you take away some of the points that they have. □ *He threatens to dock her fee.*

doc|tor ♦♦◇ /dɒktər/ (**doctors, doctoring, doctored**) ▣ N-COUNT; N-TITLE; N-VOC A **doctor** is someone who is qualified in medicine and treats people who are sick or injured. □ *Do not discontinue the treatment without consulting your doctor.* ▣ N-COUNT; N-TITLE; N-VOC A **dentist** or **veterinarian** can also be called **doctor**. [AM] ▣ N-COUNT The **doctor's** is used to refer to the office where a doctor works. □ *I have an appointment at the doctor's.* ▣ N-COUNT; N-TITLE A **doctor** is someone who has been awarded the highest academic or honorary degree by a university. □ *He is a doctor of philosophy.* ▣ V-T If someone **doctors** something, they change it in order to deceive people. □ *They doctored the prints, deepening the lines to make her look as awful as possible.*

doc|tor|ate /dɒktərət/ (**doctorates**) N-COUNT A **doctorate** is the highest degree awarded by a university. □ *Professor Lanphier obtained his doctorate in Social Psychology from the University of Michigan.*

doc|tor's of|fice (**doctor's offices**) N-COUNT A **doctor's office** is the room or house where a doctor works. [AM; BRIT **doctor's surgery**] □ *Some people made it as far as a doctor's office, only to pass out and die within minutes.*

doc|tri|nal /dɒktrɪnᵊl, BRIT dɒktraɪnᵊl/ ADJ **Doctrinal** means relating to doctrines. [FORMAL] □ *Doctrinal differences were vigorously debated among religious leaders.*

doc|trine /dɒktrɪn/ (**doctrines**) N-VAR A **doctrine** is a set of principles or beliefs, especially religious ones. □ ...*the Marxist doctrine of perpetual revolution.*

doc|u|ment ♦♦◇ (**documents, documenting, documented**)

The noun is pronounced /dɒkyəmənt/. The verb is pronounced /dɒkyəmɛnt/.

▣ N-COUNT A **document** is one or more official pieces of paper with writing on them. □ ...*a policy document for the Labour Party conference.* ▣ N-COUNT A **document** is a piece of text or graphics, for example a letter, that is stored as a file on a computer and that you can access in order to read it or change it. [COMPUTING] □ *When you are finished typing, remember to save your document.* ▣ V-T If you **document** something, you make a detailed record of it in writing or on film or tape. □ *He wrote a book documenting his prison experiences.* →see **copy, diary, history, printing**

docu|men|tary /dɒkyəmɛntəri, -tri/ (**documentaries**) ▣ N-COUNT A **documentary** is a television or radio program, or a movie, which shows real events or provides information about a particular subject. □ ...*a TV documentary on homelessness.* ▣ ADJ **Documentary** evidence consists of things that are written down. [ADJ n] □ *The government says it has documentary evidence that the two countries were planning military action.*

docu|men|ta|tion /dɒkyəmɛnteɪʃᵊn/ N-UNCOUNT **Documentation** consists of documents which provide proof or evidence of something, or are a record of something. □ *Passengers must carry proper documentation.*

docu|soap /dɒkyəsoʊp/ (**docusoaps**) N-COUNT A **docusoap** is a television program that shows the daily lives of people who work in a place such as a hospital or an airport, and is broadcast at a regular time each week or day. □ ...*the new docusoap about undergraduates at St Hilda's, Oxford's last single-sex college.*

dodge /dɒdʒ/ (**dodges, dodging, dodged**) ▣ V-I If you **dodge**, you move suddenly, often to avoid being hit, caught, or seen. □ *He dodged among the seething crowds of men.* ▣ V-T If you **dodge** something, you avoid it by quickly moving aside or out of reach so that it cannot hit or reach you. □ *He desperately dodged a speeding car trying to run him down.* ▣ V-T If you **dodge** something, you

□ 니콜라스는 프로방스에 헛간을 하나 사서 그것을 손보며 8월 한 달을 보내고 있다. ▣ 구동사 (어떤 식으로) 차려입다, 치장되다 □ 평소 크리스마스트리에 걸린 요정처럼 차려입는 베아트리체

▣ 구동사 -없이 해 나가다 □ 우리는 귀 단체의 도움 없이는 헤쳐 나갈 수 없습니다. ▣ 구동사 없는 편이 낫다, 필요 없다 [비격식체] □ 새벽 5시에 그녀로부터 받는 수사적인 질문 따위는 그에게는 없는 편이 나았다.

▣ 가산명사 파티 [주로 영국영어, 비격식체] □ 그의 친구 하나가 스토크에서 파티를 연다. ▣ 구 주의 사항 □ 가장 적당한 칼라 프린트 필름과 주의 사항에 대한 조언 부탁합니다.

▣ 가산명사 선창, 부두 □ 그녀는 부두로 향했다. 리카르도가 정박하고 있는 배들 중 하나에 숨어있을지도 모른다는 생각에서였다. ▣ 타동사/자동사 부두에 넣다 □ 함선은 1811년 4월 리버풀에 닿았다. ▣ 상호동사 도킹하다 □ 우주 왕복선 아틀란티스 호가 러시아 우주 정거장 미르와 도킹할 예정이다. ▣ 가산명사 독, 적화장 [미국영어] □ 트럭이 호스를 매단 채 적화장에서 떠났다. ▣ 가산명사 나루 [미국영어] □ 그는 그곳에 집 한 채와 나루 그리고 작은 알루미늄 보트가 있었다. ▣ 단수명사 피고석 □ 어쩌다 무고한 사람을 피고석에 앉히게 되면 어떡하지? ▣ 타동사 감봉하다, 감점하다 □ 그는 감봉하겠다며 그녀를 협박한다.

▣ 가산명사; 경칭명사; 호격명사 의사 □ 치료를 중단할 때는 반드시 주치의와 상의하라. ▣ 가산명사; 경칭명사; 호격명사 치과 의사; 수의사 [미국영어] ▣ 가산명사 의원, 진료실 □ 진료 예약이 있어. ▣ 가산명사; 경칭명사 박사 □ 그는 박사 학위 소지자이다. ▣ 타동사 변조하다 □ 그들은 주름을 깊게 만들어 그녀가 최대한 끔찍하게 보이도록 사진을 변조했다.

가산명사 박사 학위 □ 랑피에르 교수는 미시간 대학에서 사회 심리학 박사 학위를 취득하였다.

가산명사 의원, 진료실 [미국영어; 영국영어 doctor's surgery] □ 어떤 사람들은 겨우 진료실까지 와서 기절해 몇 분 내에 사망해 버렸다.

형용사 교리상의, 원칙상의 [격식체] □ 종교 지도자들이 교리상의 차이점을 맹렬히 논의했다.

가산명사 또는 불가산명사 교리, 주의 □ 항구적 혁명을 표방하는 마르크스주의

명사는 /dɒkyəmənt/로 발음되고, 동사는 /dɒkyəmɛnt/로 발음됨.

▣ 가산명사 문서, 서류 □ 노동당 대회 정책 문서 ▣ 가산명사 컴퓨터 문서 [컴퓨터] □ 타이핑을 끝내면, 반드시 작성한 문서를 저장하라. ▣ 타동사 기록하다 □ 그는 감옥에서 겪은 일들을 기록한 책을 썼다.

▣ 가산명사 다큐멘터리 □ 노숙 문제를 다룬 티브이(TV) 다큐멘터리 ▣ 형용사 증거 서류 □ 정부는 그 두 국가의 군사적 행동 계획 사실을 뒷받침하는 증거 서류를 가지고 있다고 말한다.

불가산명사 증거 서류, 증거 자료 □ 승객은 필요한 서류를 소지해야 한다.

가산명사 다큐멘터리 드라마 □ 옥스퍼드의 마지막 여학교인 세인트힐다 고등학교 재학생들의 이야기를 담은 새 다큐멘터리 드라마

▣ 자동사 재빨리 피하다 □ 그는 성난 남자들 사이로 피해 나아갔다. ▣ 타동사 재빨리 피하다, 재빨리 비키다 □ 그는 자신을 치려고 달려오는 차를 필사적으로 피했다. ▣ 타동사 회피하다, 기피하다 □ 그는 꾀병을 부려 병역을 기피했다며 자랑한다.

deliberately avoid thinking about it or dealing with it, often by being deceitful. ❑ *He boasts of dodging military service by feigning illness.* ● N-COUNT **Dodge** is also a noun. ❑ *This was not just a tax dodge.*

● 가산명사 회피, 기피 ❑ 이는 단순한 탈세가 아니었다.

dodgy /dɒdʒi/ (**dodgier**, **dodgiest**) **1** ADJ If you describe someone or something as **dodgy**, you disapprove of them because they seem rather dishonest and unreliable. [BRIT, INFORMAL, DISAPPROVAL] ❑ *He was a bit of a dodgy character.* **2** ADJ If you say that something is **dodgy**, you mean that it seems rather risky, dangerous, or unreliable. [BRIT, INFORMAL] ❑ *Predicting voting trends from economic forecasts is a dodgy business.*

1 형용사 믿을 수 없는 [영국영어, 비격식체, 탐탁찮음] ❑ 그는 그다지 믿을 만한 사람이 아니었다. **2** 형용사 위험한 [영국영어, 비격식체] ❑ 경제 전망을 통해 유권자 동향을 예측하는 일은 위험하다.

does /dəz, STRONG dʌz/ **Does** is the third person singular in the present tense of **do**.

do의 3인칭 단수 현재시제

doesn't ♦♦♦ /dʌzªnt/ **Doesn't** is the usual spoken form of "does not."

does not의 축약형

dog ♦♦◇ /dɒg, BRIT dɒg/ (**dogs, dogging, dogged**) **1** N-COUNT A **dog** is a very common four-legged animal that is often kept by people as a pet or to guard or hunt. There are many different breeds of dog. ❑ *The British are renowned as a nation of dog lovers.* **2** N-COUNT People use **dog** to refer to something that they consider unsatisfactory or of poor quality. [AM, INFORMAL, DISAPPROVAL] ❑ *It's a real dog.* **3** V-T If problems or injuries **dog** you, they are with you all the time. ❑ *His career has been dogged by bad luck.* **4** →see also **dogged 5** PHRASE You describe something as a **dog's breakfast** or **dog's dinner** in order to express your disapproval of it, for example because it is very messy, badly organized, or badly done. [BRIT, INFORMAL, DISAPPROVAL] ❑ *The whole place was a bit of a dog's dinner, really.* **6** PHRASE You use **dog eat dog** to express your disapproval of a situation where everyone wants to succeed and is willing to harm other people in order to do so. [DISAPPROVAL] ❑ *It is very much dog eat dog out there.* **7** PHRASE If you say that something **is going to the dogs**, you mean that it is becoming weaker and worse in quality. [INFORMAL, DISAPPROVAL] ❑ *They sit in impotent opposition while the country goes to the dogs.* →see **pet**

1 가산명사 개 ❑ 영국인은 개를 사랑하는 국민으로 유명하다. **2** 가산명사 마음에 들지 않거나 질이 떨어지는 물건 [미국영어, 비격식체, 탐탁찮음] ❑ 이거 정말 형편없는다. **3** 타동사 항상 따라다니다 ❑ 그의 이력에는 항상 불운이 따라다녔다. **5** 구 개판, 엉망진창 [영국영어, 비격식체, 탐탁찮음] ❑ 그 일대가 정말이지 개판이다. **6** 구 인정사정없는, 먹고 먹히는 [탐탁찮음] ❑ 거기서는 먹고 먹히는 경쟁이 치열하다. **7** 구 황폐해지다, 파멸하다 [비격식체, 탐탁찮음] ❑ 나라가 망해 가는 동안에도 그들은 무력한 야당의 자리를 지키고 있다.

dog|ged /dɒgɪd, BRIT dɒgɪd/ ADJ If you describe someone's actions as **dogged**, you mean that they are determined to continue with something even if it becomes difficult or dangerous. [ADJ n] ❑ *They have, through sheer dogged determination, slowly gained respect for their efforts.* ● **dog|ged|ly** ADV ❑ *She would fight doggedly for her rights as the children's mother.* ● **dog|ged|ness** N-UNCOUNT ❑ *Most of my accomplishments came as the result of sheer doggedness rather than talent.*

형용사 끈질긴, 불굴의 ❑ 그들은 불굴의 의지를 가지고 노력한 결과 조금씩 인정을 받기 시작했다. ● 끈질기게 부사 ❑ 그녀는 아이들 어머니로서의 권리를 인정받기 위해 끝까지 싸울 것이다. ● 끈기 불가산명사 ❑ 내가 거둔 성과의 대부분은 타고난 재능이 아니라 순전히 끈기로 이룬 것이다.

dog|house /dɒghaʊs, BRIT dɒghaʊs/ (**doghouses**) also **dog-house 1** N-COUNT A **doghouse** is a small building made especially for a dog to sleep in. [AM; BRIT **kennel**] **2** PHRASE If you are **in the doghouse**, people are annoyed or angry with you. [INFORMAL] ❑ *Her husband was in the doghouse for leaving her to cope on her own.*

1 가산명사 개집 [미국영어; 영국영어 kennel] **2** 구 미움을 사다 [비격식체] ❑ 그녀의 남편은 그녀를 혼자 내버려 두어서 미움을 샀다.

dog|ma /dɒgmə, BRIT dɒgmə/ (**dogmas**) N-VAR If you refer to a belief or a system of beliefs as a **dogma**, you disapprove of it because people are expected to accept that it is true, without questioning it. [DISAPPROVAL] ❑ *Their political dogma has blinded them to the real needs of the country.*

가산명사 또는 불가산명사 독단 [탐탁찮음] ❑ 그들은 정치적 독단 때문에 나라가 진정 필요로 하는 것을 보지 못했다.

dog|mat|ic /dɒgmætɪk, BRIT dɒgmætɪk/ ADJ If you say that someone is **dogmatic**, you are critical of them because they are convinced that they are right, and refuse to consider that other opinions might also be justified. [DISAPPROVAL] ❑ *Many writers at this time held rigidly dogmatic views.* ● **dog|mati|cal|ly** /dɒgmætɪkli, BRIT dɒgmætɪkli/ ADV [ADV with v] ❑ *Bennett had wanted this list of books to be dogmatically imposed on the nation's universities.*

형용사 독단적인 [탐탁찮음] ❑ 그 당시 많은 작가들이 융통성 없이 독단적인 견해를 고수했다. ● 독단적으로 부사 ❑ 베넷은 이 도서 목록을 국내 대학에 일방적으로 적용하고 싶어 했었다.

dog|ma|tism /dɒgmətɪzəm, BRIT dɒgmətɪzəm/ N-UNCOUNT If you refer to an opinion as **dogmatism**, you are criticizing it for being strongly stated without considering all the relevant facts or other people's opinions. [DISAPPROVAL] ❑ *We cannot allow dogmatism to stand in the way of progress.*

불가산명사 독단주의 [탐탁찮음] ❑ 우리는 독단주의가 진보의 길을 막게 놔둘 수 없다.

do-it-yourself N-UNCOUNT **Do-it-yourself** is the same as DIY.

불가산명사 손수 만들기

dol|drums /dɒuldrəmz/ PHRASE If an activity or situation is **in the doldrums**, it is very quiet and nothing new or exciting is happening. ❑ *The economy is in the doldrums.*

구 침체 상태 ❑ 경제가 침체 상태에 있다.

dole /dɒul/ **1** N-UNCOUNT **The dole** or **dole** is money that is given regularly by the government to people who are unemployed. [mainly BRIT; AM usually **welfare**] [also the N] ❑ *If you collect the dole you are counted as unemployed.* **2** PHRASE Someone who is **on the dole** is registered as unemployed and receives money from the government. [mainly BRIT; AM usually **on welfare**] ❑ *It's not easy living on the dole.*

1 불가산명사 실업 수당 [주로 영국영어; 미국영어 대개 welfare] ❑ 실업 수당을 받으면 실업자로 집계된다. **2** 구 실업 수당을 받는 [주로 영국영어; 미국영어 대개 on welfare] ❑ 실업 수당으로 먹고 살기가 쉽지 않다.

dole queue (**dole queues**) N-COUNT When people talk about **the dole queue**, they are talking about the state of being unemployed, especially when saying how many people are unemployed. [BRIT; AM usually **unemployment line**] ❑ *Another 29,100 people have joined the dole queue.*

가산명사 실업자 수 [영국영어; 미국영어 대개 unemployment line] ❑ 실업자가 29,100명 늘어났다.

doll /dɒl/ (**dolls**) N-COUNT A **doll** is a child's toy which looks like a small person or baby.

가산명사 인형

dol|lar ♦♦♦ /dɒlər/ (**dollars**) N-COUNT The **dollar** is the unit of money used in the U.S., Canada, Australia, and some other countries. It is represented by the symbol $. A dollar is divided into one hundred smaller units called cents. ❑ *She gets paid seven dollars an hour.* ● N-SING **The dollar** is also used to refer to the American currency system. ❑ *In early trading in Tokyo, the dollar fell sharply against the yen.*

가산명사 달러 ❑ 그녀는 시간당 7달러를 받는다. ● 단수명사 미국 달러 ❑ 도쿄 외환 시장 개장 초반에 엔화 대비 달러화 가치가 급락했다.

dol|phin /dɒlfɪn/ (**dolphins**) N-COUNT A **dolphin** is a mammal which lives in the sea and looks like a large fish with a pointed mouth. →see **whale**

가산명사 돌고래

Word Link   *dom, domin ≈ rule, master : dominate, domain, predominant*

---

do|main /dɒumeɪn/ (**domains**) **1** N-COUNT A **domain** is a particular field of thought, activity, or interest, especially one over which someone has control,

1 가산명사 영역, 분야 [격식체] ❑ 예술 분야의 위대한 실험자들 **2** 가산명사 도메인 [컴퓨터] ❑ 한 인터넷

influence, or rights. [FORMAL] ❑ ...*the great experimenters in the domain of art.* ◻2 N-COUNT On the Internet, a **domain** is a set of addresses that shows, for example, the category or geographical area that an Internet address belongs to. [COMPUTING] ❑ *An Internet society spokeswoman said .org domain users will not experience any disruptions during the transition.*

업체 대변인은 이전 과정 동안 '.org' 도메인 사용자에게 어떤 차질도 없을 것이라고 밝혔다.

do|main name (domain names) N-COUNT A **domain name** is the name of a person's or organization's website on the Internet, for example "cobuild.collins.co.uk." [COMPUTING] ❑ *Users need to find out if a domain name is already registered or is still available.*

가산명사 도메인 네임 [컴퓨터] ❑ 사용자들은 도메인 네임이 이미 등록된 것인지 사용할 수 있는 것인지 확인해 봐야 한다.

dome /doʊm/ (domes) ◻1 N-COUNT A **dome** is a round roof. ❑ ...*the dome of St Paul's cathedral.* ◻2 N-COUNT A **dome** is any object that has a similar shape to a dome. ❑ ...*the dome of the hill.*

◻1 가산명사 돔 ❑ 성 베드로 성당의 돔 ◻2 가산명사 돔 모양, 반구형 ❑ 둥근 언덕

do|mes|tic ◆◆◇ /dəmɛstɪk/ ◻1 ADJ **Domestic** political activities, events, and situations happen or exist within one particular country. ❑ ...*over 100 domestic flights a day to 15 UK destinations.* →see also **gross domestic product** ◻2 ADJ **Domestic** duties and activities are concerned with the running of a home and family. [ADJ n] ❑ ...*a plan for sharing domestic chores.* ◻3 ADJ **Domestic** items and services are intended to be used in people's homes rather than in factories or offices. [ADJ n] ❑ ...*domestic appliances.* ◻4 ADJ A **domestic** situation or atmosphere is one which involves a family and their home. ❑ *It was a scene of such domestic bliss.* ◻5 ADJ A **domestic** animal is one that is not wild and is kept either on a farm to produce food or in someone's home as a pet. ❑ ...*a domestic cat.*

◻1 형용사 국내의 ❑ 매일 영국 15개 지역으로 운항하는 100대 이상의 국내 항공기 ◻2 형용사 가사의 ❑ 가사 분담 계획 ◻3 형용사 가정의 ❑ 가전제품 ◻4 형용사 집안의, 가족의 ❑ 그것은 지극히 행복한 가족의 모습을 보여 주는 장면이었다. ◻5 형용사 가축의, 애완동물의 ❑ 애완용 고양이

dom|i|nance /dɒmɪnəns/ N-UNCOUNT The **dominance** of a particular person or thing is the fact that they are more powerful, successful, or important than other people or things. ❑ *The latest fighting appears to be an attempt by each group to establish dominance over the other.*

불가산명사 우위, 우세 ❑ 가장 최근에 있었던 싸움은 각 단체가 서로 우위를 차지하려는 시도로 보인다.

Thesaurus	dominance의 참조어
N.	authority, control, power, supremacy, upper hand

dom|i|nant /dɒmɪnənt/ ADJ Someone or something that is **dominant** is more powerful, successful, influential, or noticeable than other people or things. ❑ ...*a change which would maintain his party's dominant position in Scotland.*

형용사 우세한, 두드러진 ❑ 그의 당이 스코틀랜드에서 우위를 유지할 수 있도록 한 변화

Word Link	dom, domin ≈ rule, master : *dominate, domain, predominant*

dom|i|nate ◆◆◇ /dɒmɪneɪt/ (dominates, dominating, dominated) ◻1 V-T To **dominate** a situation means to be the most powerful or important person or thing in it. ❑ *The book is expected to dominate the best-seller lists.* ❑ ...*countries where life is dominated by war.* ● dom|i|na|tion /dɒmɪneɪʃᵊn/ N-UNCOUNT ❑ ...*the domination of the market by a small number of organizations.* ◻2 V-T If one country or person **dominates** another, they have power over them. ❑ *He denied that his country wants to dominate Europe.* ❑ *Women are no longer dominated by the men in their relationships.* ● dom|i|na|tion N-UNCOUNT ❑ *They had five centuries of domination by the Romans.* ◻3 V-T If a building, mountain, or other object **dominates** an area, it is so large or impressive that you cannot avoid seeing it. ❑ *It's one of the biggest buildings in this area, and it really dominates this whole place.*

◻1 타동사 지배하다 ❑ 이 책은 각종 베스트셀러 1위를 석권할 것으로 예상된다. ❑ 전쟁이 삶을 지배하는 국가들 ● 지배 불가산명사 ❑ 소수 기관의 시장 지배 ◻2 타동사 지배하다, 통치하다 ❑ 그는 자국이 유럽을 지배하려 한다는 사실을 부인했다. ❑ 남녀 관계에서 여성이 더 이상 남성의 지배를 받지 않는다. ● 지배, 통치 불가산명사 ❑ 그들은 5세기 동안 로마인의 지배를 받았다. ◻3 타동사 우뚝 솟다 ❑ 이는 이 지역에서 가장 큰 건물 중 하나이며, 사실 지역 전체에서 가장 눈에 띈다.

dom|i|nat|ing /dɒmɪneɪtɪŋ/ ADJ A **dominating** person has a very strong personality and influences the people around them. ❑ *She certainly was a dominating figure, a leader who gave her name to a political philosophy.*

형용사 유력한, 지배적인 ❑ 그녀는 자신의 이름을 내건 정치 철학이 있을 만큼 확실히 유력한 인물이었다.

do|min|ion /dəmɪnyən/ (dominions) N-COUNT A **dominion** is an area of land that is controlled by a ruler. ❑ *The Republic is a dominion of the Brazilian people.*

가산명사 영토 ❑ 그 공화국은 브라질 국민의 영토이다.

domi|no /dɒmɪnoʊ/ (dominoes) ◻1 N-COUNT **Dominoes** are small rectangular blocks marked with two groups of spots on one side. They are used for playing various games. ◻2 N-UNCOUNT **Dominoes** is a game in which players put dominoes onto a table in turn. ❑ *I used to play dominoes there.*

◻1 가산명사 도미노 ◻2 불가산명사 도미노 놀이 ❑ 나는 거기서 도미노를 하곤 했다.

domi|no ef|fect N-SING If one event causes another similar event, which in turn causes another event, and so on, you can refer to this as a **domino effect**. ❑ *The timetable for trains is so tight that if one is a bit late, the domino effect is enormous.*

단수명사 도미노 효과 ❑ 기차 시간표가 워낙 빡빡하기 때문에, 한 대가 조금이라도 늦으면 도미노 효과가 어마어마하게 나타난다.

Word Link	don ≈ giving : *donate, donor, pardon*

do|nate /doʊneɪt/ (donates, donating, donated) ◻1 V-T If you **donate** something **to** a charity or other organization, you give it to them. ❑ *He frequently donates large sums to charity.* ● do|na|tion /doʊneɪʃᵊn/ N-UNCOUNT ❑ ...*the donation of his collection to the art gallery.* ◻2 V-T If you **donate** your blood or a part of your body, you allow doctors to use it to help someone who is ill. ❑ ...*people who are willing to donate their organs for use after death.* ● do|na|tion N-UNCOUNT ❑ ...*measures aimed at encouraging organ donation.* →see **donor**

◻1 타동사 기부하다, 기증하다 ❑ 그는 자선 단체에 거액을 자주 기부한다. ● 기부, 기증 불가산명사 ❑ 그가 미술관에 기증한 수집품 ◻2 타동사 헌혈하다, 장기를 기증하다 ❑ 사망 후 장기를 기증할 의향이 있는 사람들 ● 헌혈, 장기 기증 불가산명사 ❑ 장기 기증 장려 대책

do|na|tion /doʊneɪʃᵊn/ (donations) N-COUNT A **donation** is something which someone gives to a charity or other organization. ❑ *Employees make regular donations to charity.* →see also **donate**

가산명사 기부금, 기증물 ❑ 직원들이 자선 단체에 정기적으로 기부하고 있다.

Word Partnership	donation의 연어
V.	**accept** a donation, **make** a donation, **receive** a donation
ADJ.	**charitable** donation, **generous** donation

done ◆◇◇ /dʌn/ ◻1 **Done** is the past participle of **do**. ◻2 ADJ A task or activity that is **done** has been completed successfully. [v-link ADJ] ❑ *When her deal is done,*

◻1 do의 과거 분사 ◻2 형용사 끝난, 완료된 ❑ 계약이 끝나자 고객은 구매한 물건을 들고 모습을 드러낸다.

a
b
c
d
e
f
g
h
i
j
k
l
m
n
o
p
q
r
s
t
u
v
w
x
y
z

the client emerges with her purchase. **3** ADJ When something that you are cooking is **done**, it has been cooked long enough and is ready. [v-link ADJ] ❑ _As soon as the cake is done, remove it from the oven._ **4** CONVENTION You say "**Done**" when you are accepting a deal, arrangement, or bet that someone has offered to make with you. [SPOKEN, FORMULAE] ❑ _"You lead and we'll look for it." — "Done."_

3 형용사 잘 익은, 완성된 ❑ 케이크가 다 구워지면 바로 오븐에서 꺼내라. **4** 관용 표현 (계약 등에 동의하며) 좋아요 [구어체, 의례적인 표현] ❑ "네가 앞장 서, 우리가 찾아보게." "좋아."

don|key /dɒŋki/ (**donkeys**) N-COUNT A **donkey** is an animal which is like a horse but which is smaller and has longer ears.

가산명사 당나귀

Word Link don ≈ giving : _don_ate, _don_or, par_don_

do|nor /dounər/ (**donors**) **1** N-COUNT A **donor** is someone who gives a part of their body or some of their blood to be used by doctors to help a person who is ill. ❑ _Doctors removed the healthy kidney from the donor._ **2** ADJ **Donor** organs or parts are organs or parts of the body which people allow doctors to use to help people who are ill. [ADJ n] ❑ _...the severe shortage of donor organs._ **3** N-COUNT A **donor** is a person or organization who gives something, especially money, to a charity, organization, or country that needs it. ❑ _Donor countries are becoming more choosy about which countries they are prepared to help._
→see Word Web: donor

1 가산명사 기증자 ❑ 의사들이 기증자의 몸에서 건강한 신장을 떼어냈다. **2** 형용사 기증한 ❑ 심각한 기증 장기 부족 **3** 가산명사 기부자, 기부 기관 ❑ 공여국들은 원조 대상국을 점점 더 까다롭게 선택하고 있다.

don't /dount/ **Don't** is the usual spoken form of "do not."

do not의 축약형

do|nut /dounʌt, -nət/ (**donuts**) →see doughnut

doo|dle /duːd°l/ (**doodles, doodling, doodled**) **1** N-COUNT A **doodle** is a pattern or picture that you draw when you are bored or thinking about something else. ❑ _Dillworthy was staring into space, with a scrawl of doodles on the pad in front of him._ **2** V-I When someone **doodles**, they draw doodles. ❑ _He looked across at Jackson, doodling on his notebook._

1 가산명사 낙서 ❑ 딜워디는 앞에 놓인 종이에 낙서를 하면서 허공을 응시하고 있었다. **2** 자동사 낙서하다 ❑ 그는 공책에 낙서를 하면서 잭슨을 바라보았다.

doom /duːm/ (**dooms, dooming, doomed**) **1** N-UNCOUNT **Doom** is a terrible future state or event which you cannot prevent. ❑ _...his warnings of impending doom._ **2** N-UNCOUNT If you have a sense or feeling of **doom**, you feel that things are going very badly and are likely to get even worse. ❑ _Why are people so full of gloom and doom?_ **3** V-T If a fact or event **dooms** someone or something **to** a particular fate, it makes certain that they are going to suffer in some way. ❑ _That argument was the turning point for their marriage, and the one which doomed it to failure._

1 불가산명사 운명, 재난 ❑ 그가 경고한 임박한 재난 **2** 불가산명사 불길한 예감 ❑ 왜 사람들이 이렇게 잔뜩 우울하고 불길해 보이지? **3** 타동사 운명짓다, 파탄이 나다 ❑ 그때의 말다툼을 전환점으로 그들의 결혼 생활은 파탄이 났다.

doomed /duːmd/ **1** ADJ If something **is doomed to** happen, or if you **are doomed to** a particular state, something unpleasant is certain to happen, and you can do nothing to prevent it. [v-link ADJ, ADJ to n, ADJ to-inf] ❑ _Their plans seemed doomed to failure._ **2** ADJ Someone or something that is **doomed** is certain to fail or be destroyed. ❑ _I used to pour time and energy into projects that were doomed from the start._

1 형용사 -할 운명이다 ❑ 그들의 계획은 실패할 수밖에 없어 보였다. **2** 형용사 가망이 없는, 불운한 ❑ 나는 시작부터 가망이 없는 프로젝트에 시간과 노력을 쏟아 붓곤 했다.

door ♦♦♦ /dɔːr/ (**doors**) **1** N-COUNT A **door** is a piece of wood, glass, or metal, which is moved to open and close the entrance to a building, room, closet, or vehicle. ❑ _I was knocking at the front door there was no answer._ **2** N-COUNT A **door** is the space in a wall when a door is open. ❑ _She looked through the door of the kitchen. Her daughter was at the stove._ **3** N-PLURAL **Doors** is used in expressions such as **a few doors down** or **three doors up** to refer to a place that is a particular number of buildings away from where you are. [INFORMAL] [amount N down/up] ❑ _Mrs. Cade's house was only a few doors down from her daughter's apartment._ **4** →see also **next door** **5** PHRASE When you **answer the door**, you go and open the door because a visitor has knocked on it or rung the bell. ❑ _Carol answered the door as soon as I knocked._ **6** PHRASE If you say that someone gets or does something **by the back door** or **through the back door**, you are criticizing them for doing it secretly and unofficially. [DISAPPROVAL] ❑ _The government would not allow anyone to sneak in by the back door and seize power by force._ **7** PHRASE If people have talks and discussions **behind closed doors**, they have them in private because they want them to be kept secret. ❑ _...decisions taken in secret behind closed doors._ **8** PHRASE If someone goes **from door to door** or goes **door to door**, they go along a street calling at each house in turn, for example selling something. ❑ _They are going from door to door collecting money from civilians._ **9** PHRASE If you talk about a distance or journey **from door to door** or **door to door**, you are talking about the distance from the place where the journey starts to the place where it finishes. ❑ _...tickets covering the whole journey from door to door._ **10** PHRASE If you say that something helps someone to get their **foot in the door** or their **toe in the door**, you mean that it gives them an opportunity to start doing something new, usually in an area that is difficult to succeed in. ❑ _The bondholding may help the firm get its foot in the door to win the business._ **11** PHRASE If someone **shuts the door in** your **face** or **slams the door in** your **face**, they refuse to talk to you or give you any information. ❑ _Did you say anything to him or just shut the door in his face?_ **12** PHRASE If you **lay** something **at** someone's **door**, you blame them for an unpleasant event or situation. ❑ _The_

1 가산명사 문 ❑ 내가 앞문을 계속 두드렸지만 대답이 없었다. **2** 가산명사 문 ❑ 그녀는 부엌문을 들여다봤다. 딸이 스토브에서 뭔가를 하고 있었다. **3** 복수명사 집; 몇 집 아래; 세 집 위쪽에 [비격식체] ❑ 케이드 부인의 집은 딸의 아파트에서 몇 집 아래 가까운 곳에 있었다. **5** 구 (노크나 벨소리를 듣고) 문을 열다 ❑ 내가 노크를 하자마자 캐롤이 문을 열었다. **6** 구 몰래, 뒷문으로 [탐탁찮음] ❑ 정부는 그 누구도 비공식적인 통로로 몰래 들어와 강압적으로 권력을 차지하게 놔두지 않을 것이다. **7** 구 밀실에서 ❑ 밀실에서 비밀리에 내린 결정 **8** 구 집집마다, 가가호호 ❑ 그들은 집집마다 방문하며 민간인으로부터 돈을 모으고 있다. **9** 구 출발지에서 도착지까지 ❑ 출발지에서 도착지까지 전 거리를 여행할 수 있는 티켓 **10** 구 발을 들여놓음 ❑ 회사가 채권을 소유하면 사업을 따낼 수 있는 기회를 잡기가 수월해질지도 모른다. **11** 구 - 앞에서 입을 다물다 ❑ 그에게 무슨 이야기라도 했나요, 아니면 그냥 입을 다물었나요? **12** 구 -의 탓으로 돌리다 ❑ 비난의 화살은 보통 정부에게 돌아간다. **13** 구 옥외에서, 바깥에서 ❑ 바깥에서 일하기 딱 좋게 날씨가 화창했다. **14** 구 현관까지 배웅하다 ❑ 그는 정중하게 그녀를 현관까지 배웅하면서 문을 열어주었다. **15** 구 쫓아내다 ❑ 그들이 그를 용서하고 잊어줄까, 아니면 쫓아내버릴까?

Word Web donor

Many people **give donations**. They like to **help** others. They **donate money**, clothes, food, or their time. Some people even give parts of themselves. Doctors performed the first successful human **organ transplants** in the 1950s. Today this type of operation is a relatively routine procedure. The problem now is finding enough **donors** to meet the needs of potential **recipients**. Organs such as the **kidney** and the **liver** often come from a living donor. **Hearts, lungs,** and other vital organs come from deceased donors. Of course our health care system relies on **blood** donors. They help save lives every day.

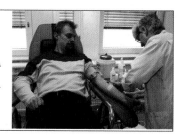

blame is generally laid at the door of the government. **IB PHRASE** When you are **out of doors**, you are not inside a building, but in the open air. ❏ *The weather was fine enough for working out of doors.* **IA PHRASE** If you **see** someone **to the door**, you go to the door with a visitor when they leave. ❏ *Politely he saw her to the door and opened it for her.* **IB PHRASE** If someone **shows** you **the door**, they ask you to leave because they are angry with you. ❏ *Would they forgive and forget – or show him the door?* **IB at death's door** →see **death**

door|man /dɔːrmæn, -mən/ (**doormen**) N-COUNT A **doorman** is a man who stands at the door of a club, prevents unwanted people from coming in, and makes people leave if they cause trouble.

가산명사 현관 안내인

door|step /dɔːrstɛp/ (**doorsteps**) **1** N-COUNT A **doorstep** is a step in front of a door on the outside of a building. ❏ *...a youth who was sitting on a doorstep, drinking.* **2** PHRASE If a place is **on** your **doorstep**, it is very near to where you live. If something happens **on** your **doorstep**, it happens very close to where you live. ❏ *It is too easy to lose sight of what is happening on our own doorstep.*

1 가산명사 현관 앞 계단 ❏ 현관 앞 계단에 앉아서 술을 마시던 젊은이 **2** 구 바로 코앞에서 ❏ 바로 코앞에서 일어나는 일들을 그냥 지나치기가 쉽다.

door|way /dɔːrweɪ/ (**doorways**) **1** N-COUNT A **doorway** is a space in a wall where a door opens and closes. ❏ *Hannah looked up to see David and another man standing in the doorway.* **2** N-COUNT A **doorway** is a covered space just outside the door of a building. ❏ *...homeless people sleeping in shop doorways.*

1 가산명사 문간, 출입구 ❏ 한나가 고개를 들자 데이비드와 다른 남자 하나가 문간에 서 있는 모습이 보였다. **2** 가산명사 입구, 문 앞 ❏ 가게 입구에서 잠을 자는 노숙자들

dope /doʊp/ (**dopes, doping, doped**) **1** N-UNCOUNT **Dope** is a drug, usually an illegal drug such as marijuana or cocaine. [INFORMAL] ❏ *A man asked them if they wanted to buy some dope.* **2** V-T If someone **dopes** a person or animal or **dopes** their food, they put drugs into their food or force them to take drugs. ❏ *Anyone could have got in and doped the wine.* ❏ *I'd been doped with Somnolin.* **3** N-COUNT If someone calls a person a **dope**, they think that the person is stupid. [INFORMAL, DISAPPROVAL] ❏ *I'm more comfortable with them. I don't feel I'm such a dope.*

1 불가산명사 마약 [비격식체] ❏ 한 남자가 그들에게 마약을 사겠느냐고 물었다. **2** 타동사 마약을 먹이다, 약을 타다 ❏ 누군가 들어와서 와인에 약을 탔을 수도 있었다. ❏ 누군가 내게 수면제를 먹였었다. **3** 가산명사 멍청이 [비격식체, 탐탁잖음] ❏ 그들과 함께 있을 때 더 편안해. 내가 멍청이이라는 생각도 안 들고.

dor|mant /dɔːrmənt/ ADJ Something that is **dormant** is not active, growing, or being used at the present time but is capable of becoming active later on. ❏ *...when the long dormant volcano of Mount St Helens erupted in 1980.* →see **plant**

형용사 휴지 상태의, 잠복 상태의 ❏ 오랫동안 휴화산이던 세인트 헬렌스 화산이 1980년 폭발했을 때

dor|mi|tory /dɔːrmɪtɔːri, BRIT dɔːˈmɪtri/ (**dormitories**) **1** N-COUNT A **dormitory** is a building in a college or university where students live. [AM; BRIT **hall of residence**] ❏ *She lived in a college dormitory.*

1 가산명사 기숙사 [미국영어; 영국영어 hall of residence] ❏ 그녀는 대학 기숙사에서 살았다.

A college **dormitory** usually provides both a place to sleep and meals, called **room and board**. Some students choose to live in privately rented accommodation outside the college, which is owned by a **landlord**. A landlord only provides the room(s) and the renter must supply his or her own food.

대학 dormitory(기숙사)는 대개 숙박 장소와 식사를 제공해서 room and board라고 불린다. 일부 학생들은 대학 밖에서 개인적으로 임대한 숙소에 사는데 이는 landlord(집주인)가 따로 있다. 집주인은 방만 제공하고 먹는 것은 세입자가 스스로 해결해야 한다.

2 N-COUNT A **dormitory** is a large bedroom where several people sleep, for example in a boarding school. ❏ *...the boys' dormitory.* **3** ADJ If you refer to a place as a **dormitory** suburb or town, you mean that most of the people who live there travel to work in another, larger town a short distance away. [mainly BRIT] [ADJ n] ❏ *It had become almost a dormitory suburb of the city.*

2 가산명사 공동 숙소 ❏ 남학생 숙소 **3** 형용사 인근 도시로 통근하는 사람들이 사는 곳의 [주로 영국영어] ❏ 이 지역은 도시 통근자들의 거주지처럼 되어 있었다.

DOS /dɒs/ N-UNCOUNT **DOS** is the part of a computer operating system that controls and manages files and programs stored on disk. **DOS** is an abbreviation for "disk operating system." [COMPUTING, TRADEMARK] ❏ *Where do I find the instructions to load DOS programs from Windows 98?*

불가산명사 도스 [컴퓨터, 상표] ❏ 윈도우98에서 도스 프로그램 실행하는 방법을 어디서 찾으면 됩니까?

dos|age /doʊsɪdʒ/ (**dosages**) N-COUNT A **dosage** is the amount of a medicine or drug that someone takes or should take. ❏ *He was put on a high dosage of vitamin C.*

가산명사 복용량 ❏ 그는 비타민 시를 많이 먹으라는 처방을 받았다.

dose /doʊs/ (**doses, dosing, dosed**) **1** N-COUNT A **dose of** medicine or a drug is a measured amount of it which is intended to be taken at one time. ❏ *One dose of penicillin can wipe out the infection.* **2** V-T If you **dose** a person or animal **with** medicine, you give them an amount of it. ❏ *The doctor fixed the rib, dosed him heavily with drugs, and said he would probably get better.* ● PHRASAL VERB **Dose up** means the same as dose. ❏ *I dosed him up with Valium.*

1 가산명사 1회 복용량 ❏ 페니실린 한방이면 감염을 치료할 수 있다. **2** 타동사 약을 먹이다, 복용시키다 ❏ 의사가 갈비뼈를 맞추고 약을 엄청 먹인 후에 그가 괜찮아질 것 같다고 말했다. ● 구동사 약을 먹이다, 복용시키다 ❏ 나는 그에게 발륨을 먹였다.

dosh /dɒʃ/ N-UNCOUNT **Dosh** is money. [BRIT, INFORMAL] ❏ *...a chap who'd made lots of dosh.*

불가산명사 돈 [영국영어, 비격식체] ❏ 떼돈을 번 친구

dos|si|er /dɒsieɪ/ (**dossiers**) N-COUNT A **dossier** is a collection of papers containing information on a particular event, or on a person such as a criminal or a spy. ❏ *The company is compiling a dossier of evidence to back its allegations.*

가산명사 서류 일체 ❏ 회사가 주장을 뒷받침해 줄 증거 서류 일체를 모아 정리하고 있다.

dot /dɒt/ (**dots, dotting, dotted**) **1** N-COUNT A **dot** is a very small round mark, for example one that is used as the top part of the letter "i," as a period, or as a decimal point. ❏ *...a system of painting using small dots of color.* **2** V-T When things **dot** a place or an area, they are scattered or spread all over it. ❏ *Small coastal towns dot the landscape.* **3** →see also **dotted** **4** PHRASE If you arrive somewhere or do something **on the dot**, you arrive there or do it at exactly the time that you were supposed to. ❏ *They appeared on the dot of 9.50 pm as always.*

1 가산명사 점; 소수점 ❏ 색색의 작은 점을 사용해 그리는 기법 **2** 타동사 점점이 흩어져 있다 ❏ 작은 해안 마을에 점점이 흩어져 있다. **4** 구 정각에 ❏ 그들은 항상 그렇듯 9시 50분 정각에 나타났다.

dot-com (**dot-coms**) N-COUNT A **dot-com** is a company that does all or most of its business on the Internet. ❏ *In 1999, dot-coms spent more than $1 billion on TV spots.*

가산명사 닷컴 기업 ❏ 1999년 닷컴 기업이 텔레비전 코너에 10억 달러 이상을 사용했다.

dote /doʊt/ (**dotes, doting, doted**) V-I If you say that someone **dotes on** a person or a thing, you mean that they love or care about them very much and ignore any faults they may have. ❏ *He dotes on his nine-year-old son.*

자동사 애지중지하다 ❏ 그는 9살 난 아들을 애지중지한다.

dot|ing /doʊtɪŋ/ ADJ If you say that someone is, for example, a **doting** mother, husband, or friend, you mean that they show a lot of love for someone. ❏ *His doting parents bought him his first racing bike at 13.*

형용사 애지중지하는, 맹목적으로 사랑하는 ❏ 그를 애지중지하는 부모님은 그가 13살 때 첫 경주용 자전거를 사주었다.

dot|ted /dɒtɪd/ **1** ADJ A **dotted line** is a line which is made of a row of dots. ❏ *Cut along the dotted line.* ● PHRASE If you **sign on the dotted line**, you formally agree to something by signing an official document. **2** ADJ If a place or object is **dotted with** things, it has many of those things scattered over its surface. [v-link ADJ with n] ❏ *The maps were dotted with the names of small towns.* **3** ADJ If

1 형용사 점선의 ❏ 점선을 따라 자르시오. ● 구 서명하다 ❏ 지도에는 작은 마을의 이름이 여기저기 써 있는 ❏ 지도에는 작은 마을의 이름이 여기저기 써 있었다. **3** 형용사 주변에 흩어져 있는 ❏ 많은 조각품들이 집 주변 여기저기에 놓여져 있다.

things are **dotted around** a place, they can be found in many different parts of that place. [v-link ADJ prep] ❑ *Many pieces of sculpture are dotted around the house.* 4 →see also **dot**

dou|ble ♦♦◇ /dʌbəl/ (**doubles, doubling, doubled**) 1 ADJ You use **double** to indicate that something includes or is made of two things of the same kind. [ADJ n] ❑ *...a pair of double doors into the room from the new entrance hall.* 2 ADJ You use **double** before a singular noun to refer to two things of the same type that occur together, or that are connected in some way. [ADJ n] ❑ *...an extremely nasty double murder.* 3 PREDET If something is **double the** amount or size of another thing, it is twice as large. [PREDET the n] ❑ *The offer was to start a new research laboratory at double the salary he was getting.* ● PRON **Double** is also a pronoun. ❑ *On average doctors write just over seven prescriptions each year per patient; in Germany it is double.* 4 ADJ You use **double** to describe something which is twice the normal size or can hold twice the normal quantity of something. ❑ *...a double helping of ice cream.* 5 ADJ A **double** room is a room intended for two people, usually a couple, to stay or live in. ❑ *...bed and breakfast for £180 for two people in a double room.* ● N-COUNT **Double** is also a noun. ❑ *The Great Western Hotel is ideal, costing around £60 a night for a double.* 6 ADJ A **double** bed is a bed that is wide enough for two people to sleep in. [ADJ n] ❑ *One bedroom had a double bed and the other had single beds for the boys.* 7 ADJ You use **double** to describe a drink that is twice the normal measure. [ADJ n] ❑ *He was drinking his double whiskey too fast and scowling.* ● N-COUNT **Double** is also a noun. ❑ *"Give me a whiskey," Debilly said to Francis. "Make it a double."* 8 ADJ **Double** is used when you are spelling a word or telling someone a number to show that a letter or digit is repeated. [mainly BRIT] [ADJ n] ❑ *Call four two double two double two if you'd like to speak to our financial adviser.* 9 V-T/V-I When something **doubles** or when you **double** it, it becomes twice as great in number, amount, or size. ❑ *The number of managers must double to 100 within 3 years.* 10 N-COUNT If you refer to someone as a person's **double**, you mean that they look exactly like them. ❑ *Your mother sees you as her double.* 11 V-I If a person or thing **doubles as** someone or something else, they have a second job or purpose as well as their main one. ❑ *Lots of homes in town double as businesses.* ● PHRASAL VERB **Double up** means the same as **double**. ❑ *The lids of the casserole dishes are designed to double up as baking dishes.* 12 N-UNCOUNT In tennis or badminton, when people play **doubles**, two teams consisting of two players on each team play against each other on the same court. ❑ *In the doubles, the British pair beat Hungary's Renata Csay and Kornelia Szanda.* 13 PHRASE If you are **bent double**, the top half of your body is bent downward so that your head is close to your knees. ❑ *I was bent double in agony.* 14 PHRASE If you are **seeing double**, there is something wrong with your eyes, and you can see two images instead of one. ❑ *For 35 minutes I was walking around in a daze. I was dizzy, seeing double.* 15 in **double figures** →see **figure**
→see **hotel, tennis**

▶**double up** 1 PHRASAL VERB If something **doubles** you **up**, or if you **double up**, you bend your body quickly or violently, for example because you are laughing a lot or because you are feeling a lot of pain. ❑ *...a savage blow which doubled him up.* ● PHRASAL VERB **Double over** means the same as **double up**. ❑ *Everyone was doubled over in laughter.* 2 →see also **double 11**

dou|ble bass /dʌbəl beɪs/ (**double basses**) also **double-bass** N-VAR A **double bass** is the largest instrument in the violin family. →see **orchestra**

double-check (**double-checks, double-checking, double-checked**) V-T/V-I If you **double-check** something, you examine or test it a second time to make sure that it is completely correct or safe. ❑ *Check and double-check spelling and punctuation.* ❑ *Double-check that the ladder is secure.*

double-decker (**double-deckers**) N-COUNT A **double-decker** or a **double-decker bus** is a bus that has two levels, so that passengers can sit upstairs or downstairs. [mainly BRIT]

double-edged 1 ADJ If you say that a comment is **double-edged**, you mean that it has two meanings, so that you are not sure whether the person who said it is being critical or is giving praise. ❑ *Even his praise is double-edged.* 2 ADJ If you say that something is **double-edged**, you mean that its positive effects are balanced by its negative effects, or that its negative effects are greater. ❑ *But tourism is double-edged, for although it's boosting the country's economy, the Reef could be damaged.* **a double-edged sword** →see **sword**

double-glaze (**double-glazes, double-glazing, double-glazed**) V-T If someone **double-glazes** a house or its windows, they fit windows that have two layers of glass which keeps the inside of the house warmer and quieter. [mainly BRIT] ❑ *The company is now offering to double-glaze the windows for £3,900.* ● **double-glazed** ADJ ❑ *Make sure double-glazed windows can be opened easily in an emergency.*

double-glazing N-UNCOUNT If someone has **double-glazing** in their house, their windows are fitted with two layers of glass. People put in double-glazing in order to keep buildings warmer or to keep out noise. [mainly BRIT]

dou|bly /dʌbli/ 1 ADV You use **doubly** to indicate that there are two aspects or features that are having an influence on a particular situation. ❑ *Employees choosing to move with a relocating company benefit doubly from employer-related housing assistance and lower house prices.* 2 ADV You use **doubly** to emphasize that something exists or happens to a greater degree than usual. [EMPHASIS] [ADV adj/adv] ❑ *In pregnancy a high fiber diet is doubly important.*

doubt ♦♦◇ /daʊt/ (**doubts, doubting, doubted**) 1 N-VAR If you have **doubt** or **doubts** about something, you feel uncertain about it and do not know whether it is true or possible. If you say you have **no doubt about** it, you mean that you are certain it is true. ❑ *There can be little doubt that he will offend again.* 2 V-T If you **doubt** whether something is true or possible, you believe that it is probably not true or possible. ❑ *Others doubted whether that would happen.* ❑ *He doubted if he would learn*

---

1 형용사 이중의 ❑ 새로운 현관 복도에서 방으로 통하는 문 2 형용사 똑같은 ❑ 너무나도 끔찍한 똑같은 살인 사건 두 건 3 전치 한정사 두 배의 ❑ 그는 당시 받고 있던 연봉 두 배에 새 연구소에서 일하라는 제안을 받았다. 4 대명사 두 배 ❑ 의사가 환자 한 명당 일년에 내리는 처방은 평균 일곱 번을 조금 넘는다. 독일의 경우는 그 두 배이다. 4 형용사 두 배의, 곱빼기의 ❑ 아이스크림 2인분 5 형용사 2인용의, 더블 룸의 2인용 실 2인 투숙시 숙식 제공으로 180파운드 ● 가산명사 2인용 방, 더블 룸 ❑ 그레이트 웨스턴 호텔이 더블룸 1박 이용에 60파운드 정도로, 이상적이다. 6 형용사 2인용의 ❑ 침실 하나에는 2인용 침대가 있고 나머지 하나에는 아이들을 위한 1인용 침대들이 있다. 7 형용사 다른 역할도 하다; 부업으로 하다 ❑ 그는 더블 위스키를 너무 빨리 마시면서 얼굴을 찡그리고 있었다. ● 가산명사 더블 ❑ "위스키 한 잔 주세요."라고 데빌리가 프랜시스에게 말했다. "더블로 주세요." 8 형용사 두 개의 [주로 영국영어] ❑ 재정 상담원과 연결을 원하시면 422222번으로 전화하세요. 9 타동사/자동사 두 배로 하다 ❑ 3년 내에 지배인 수를 100명으로 두 배 늘려야 한다. 10 가산명사 똑같이 닮은 사람 ❑ 네 어머니는 네가 자기와 똑 닮았다고 생각하셔. 11 자동사 다른 역할도 하다; 부업으로 하다 ❑ 마을의 상당수의 집이 사업도 한다. ● 구동사 다른 역할도 하다; 부업으로 하다 ❑ 캐서롤 냄비 뚜껑은 구이판으로도 사용할 수 있도록 만들어졌다. 12 불가산명사 복식 경기 ❑ 복식 경기에서 영국이 헝가리의 레나타 차이와 코르넬리아 잔다 조를 꺾었다. 13 구 몸을 구부리다 ❑ 나는 아파서 몸을 웅크렸다. 14 구 둘로 보이다 ❑ 나는 35분 동안 명한 상태에서 정처 없이 걷고 있었다. 어지러웠고, 사물이 둘로 보였다.

1 구동사 몸을 구부리다 ❑ 그가 고꾸라지도록 세게 걷어 참 ● 구동사 몸을 구부리다 ❑ 모든 사람이 포복절도했다.

가산명사 또는 불가산명사 더블베이스

타동사/자동사 재확인하다 ❑ 스펠링과 구두점을 확인하고 또 확인하라. ❑ 사다리가 안전한지 다시 한 번 확인하라.

가산명사 이층 버스 [주로 영국영어]

1 형용사 두 가지로 해석될 수 있는 ❑ 그의 칭찬조차 두 가지로 해석될 수 있다. 2 형용사 상반된 효과를 가져오는 ❑ 하지만 관광은 나라 경제를 살리는 동시에 산호초를 파괴할 수 있다는 점에서 상반된 측면을 지니고 있다.

타동사 이중 유리를 끼우다 [주로 영국영어] ❑ 요즘 회사에서 3900파운드에 이중 유리를 끼워 주고 있다. ● 이중 유리의 형용사 ❑ 비상시에는 반드시 이중 유리가 쉽게 열릴 수 있게 하라.

불가산명사 이중 유리 [주로 영국영어]

1 부사 이중으로 ❑ 회사가 이전할 때 함께 이사하는 직원들은 회사에서 제공하는 주택 마련 보조금과 저렴한 주택가격으로 두 가지 혜택을 보게 된다. 2 부사 두 배로 [강조] ❑ 임신시에는 섬유질 함량이 높은 음식 섭취가 두 배로 중요하다.

1 가산명사 또는 불가산명사 의심, 회의 ❑ 이는 광고의 취지에 대한 의문이 생기게 한다. ❑ 거의 의심할 여지없이 그는 재범을 저지를 것이다. 2 타동사 미심쩍게 생각하다 ❑ 다른 사람들은 그 일이 실제로 일어날지 미심쩍게 생각했다. ❑ 그는 마리에게서 뭔가 새로운 것을 배우리라고 생각하지 않았다. 3 타동사 의심하다 ❑ 아무도 그의 능력을

anything new from Marie. ❸ V-T If you **doubt** something, you believe that it might not be true or genuine. ❑ *No one doubted his ability.* ❹ V-T If you **doubt** someone or **doubt** their word, you think that they may not be telling the truth. ❑ *No one directly involved with the case doubted him.* ❺ PHRASE You say that something is **beyond doubt** or **beyond reasonable doubt** when you are certain that it is true and it cannot be contradicted or disproved. [EMPHASIS] ❑ *A referendum showed beyond doubt that voters wanted independence.* ❻ PHRASE If you are **in doubt** about something, you feel unsure or uncertain about it. ❑ *He is in no doubt as to what is needed.* ❼ CONVENTION You say **I doubt it** as a response to a question or statement about something that you think is untrue or unlikely. ❑ *"Somebody would have seen her." — "I doubt it, not on Monday."* ❽ PHRASE If you say that something is **in doubt** or **open to doubt**, you consider it to be uncertain or unreliable. ❑ *The outcome was still in doubt.* ❾ PHRASE You use **no doubt** to emphasize that something seems certain or very likely to you. [EMPHASIS] ❑ *The contract for this will no doubt be widely advertised.* ❿ PHRASE You use **no doubt** to indicate that you accept the truth of a particular point, but that you do not think it is important or contradicts the rest of what you are saying. ❑ *No doubt many will regard these as harsh words, but regrettably they are true.* ⓫ PHRASE If you say that something is true **without doubt** or **without a doubt**, you are emphasizing that it is definitely true. [EMPHASIS] ❑ *Without doubt this has become the most important relationship I've developed while at college.* ⓬ **the benefit of the doubt** →see **benefit**. **a shadow of a doubt** →see **shadow**

doubt|ful /daʊtfəl/ ❶ ADJ If it is **doubtful that** something will happen, it seems unlikely to happen or you are uncertain whether it will happen. ❑ *For a time it seemed doubtful that he would move at all.* ❷ ADJ If you are **doubtful about** something, you feel unsure or uncertain about it. ❑ *I was still very doubtful about the chances for success.* ● **doubt|ful|ly** ADV [ADV after v] ❑ *Keeton shook his head doubtfully.* ❸ ADJ If you say that something is **of doubtful** quality or value, you mean that it is of low quality or value. [DISAPPROVAL] ❑ *...selling something that is overpriced or of doubtful quality.* ❹ ADJ If a sports player is **doubtful for** a match or event, he or she seems unlikely to play, usually because of injury. [JOURNALISM] ❑ *Forsyth is doubtful for tonight's game with a badly bruised leg.*

> Do not confuse **doubtful**, **dubious**, and **suspicious**. If you feel **doubtful** about something, you are unsure about it or about whether it will happen or be successful. ❑ *Do you feel insecure and doubtful about your ability?... It was doubtful he would ever see her again.* If you are **dubious** about something, you are not sure whether it is the right thing to do. ❑ *Alison sounded very dubious... The men in charge were a bit dubious about taking women on.* If you describe something as **dubious**, you think it is not completely honest, safe, or reliable. ❑ *...his dubious abilities as a teacher.* If you are **suspicious** of a person, you do not trust them and think they might be involved in something dishonest or illegal. ❑ *I am suspicious of his intentions... Miss Lenaut had grown suspicious.* If you describe something as **suspicious**, it suggests behavior that is dishonest, illegal, or dangerous. ❑ *He listened for any suspicious sounds.*

doubt|less /daʊtlɪs/ ADV If you say that something is **doubtless** the case, you mean that you think it is probably or almost certainly the case. [ADV with cl/group] ❑ *He will doubtless try and persuade his colleagues to change their minds.*

dough /doʊ/ (**doughs**)

> In meaning ❷, **dough** is used in informal American English, and is considered old-fashioned in informal British English.

❶ N-MASS **Dough** is a fairly firm mixture of flour, water, and sometimes also fat and sugar. It can be cooked to make bread or pastry. ❑ *Roll out the dough into one large circle.* ❷ N-UNCOUNT You can refer to money as **dough**. ❑ *He worked hard for his dough.*

dough|nut /doʊnʌt, -nət/ (**doughnuts**) [AM also **donut**] N-COUNT A **doughnut** is a bread-like cake made from sweet dough that has been cooked in hot fat.

dour /dʊər, daʊər/ ADJ If you describe someone as **dour**, you mean that they are very serious and unfriendly. ❑ *...a dour, taciturn man.*

의심하지 않았다. ❹ 타동사 의심하다 ❑ 사건과 직접적으로 관련된 사람 중 누구도 그를 의심하지 않았다. ❺ 구 의심할 여지없이 [강조] ❑ 국민 투표 결과 의심의 여지없이 유권자들이 독립을 원한다는 사실이 드러났다. ❻ 구 의심하여, 미심쩍어 ❑ 그는 무엇이 필요한지 확신하고 있다. ❼ 관용 표현 아닐 것 같다 ❑ "누군가 그녀를 봤을지도 몰라." "아닐걸, 월요일엔 아닐 거야." ❽ 구 불확실한 ❑ 결과는 아직 불확실했다. ❾ 구 분명히 [강조] ❑ 이번 계약은 분명히 널리 알려질 것이다. ❿ 구 물론 ❑ 이 말이 물론 많은 사람들에게 잔인하게 들리겠지만, 안타깝게도 사실은 사실이다. ⓫ 구 의심할 바 없이 [강조] ❑ 의심할 바 없이 이는 내가 대학 시절에 형성한 가장 중요한 관계가 되었다.

❶ 형용사 의심스러운 ❑ 그가 조금이라도 움직일지 의심스러워 보일 때도 있었다. ❷ 형용사 확신이 없는, 자신이 없는 ❑ 나는 아직 성공 가능성에 대해 정말 자신이 없었다. ● 반신반의하며 부사 ❑ 키튼이 잘 모르겠다는 듯이 고개를 저었다. ❸ 형용사 질 좋지 못이 떨어지는, 의심스러운 [탐탁찮음] ❑ 지나치게 비싸거나 품질이 의심스러운 물건 판매 ❹ 형용사 출전이 어려울 것 같은 [언론] ❑ 심한 다리 타박상으로 포사이드의 오늘밤 경기 출전이 불투명하다.

> doubtful, dubious, suspicious를 혼동하지 않도록 하라. 무엇에 대해 doubtful한 생각이 들면, 그것에 대해 확신이 없거나 그것이 일어날지 또는 성공할지에 대해 확신하지 못하는 것이다. ❑ 너는 네 능력에 대해 불안하고 확신이 없니?... 그가 과연 그녀를 다시 보게 될지는 분명치 않았다. 무엇에 대해 dubious하면, 그것을 하는 것이 올바른 일인지 아닌지 확신이 없는 것이다. ❑ 앨리슨은 반신반의하는 것 같아 보였다... 책임을 맡고 있는 남자들은 여자들을 고용하는 것에 조금 반신반의했다. 무엇을 dubious하다고 표현하면, 그것이 완전히 정직하거나, 안전하거나, 믿을 만하지 않다고 생각하는 것이다. ❑ ... 교사로서 의심스러운 그의 능력. 어떤 사람에 대해 suspicious하면, 그 사람을 믿지 않고 또 그 사람이 정직하지 못하거나 불법적인 일에 연루되어 있을지도 모른다고 생각하는 것이다. ❑ 나는 그의 의도가 의심스럽다... 르노 양은 의심을 품게 되었다. 무엇을 suspicious하다고 표현하면, 그것이 정직하지 못하거나, 불법이거나, 위험한 행동임을 의미한다. ❑ 그는 조금이라도 의심스러운 소리가 나지 않는지 주의를 기울였다.

부사 분명히, 의심할 여지없이 ❑ 그는 분명히 동료들을 설득해서 그들의 마음을 돌리려 할 것이다.

> ❷ 의미로 dough은 비격식체 미국영어에서 쓰며, 비격식체 영국영어에서는 구식이어다.

❶ 물질명사 반죽 ❑ 반죽을 크고 둥글게 밀어라. ❷ 불가산명사 돈 ❑ 그는 돈을 벌기 위해 열심히 일했다.

[미국영어 donut] 가산명사 도넛

형용사 뚱한 ❑ 뚱하고 무뚝뚝한 남자

douse /daʊs/ (**douses, dousing, doused**) also **dowse** 🞂 V-T If you **douse** a fire, you stop it from burning by pouring a lot of water over it. ❑ *The pumps were started and the crew began to douse the fire with water.* 🞂 V-T If you **douse** someone or something **with** a liquid, you throw a lot of that liquid over them. ❑ *They hurled abuse at their victim as they doused him with petrol.*

dove (**doves**)

Pronounced /dʌv/ for meanings 🞂 and 🞂, and /doʊv/ for meaning 🞂.

🞂 N-COUNT A **dove** is a bird that looks like a pigeon but is smaller and lighter in color. Doves are often used as a symbol of peace. 🞂 N-COUNT In politics, you can refer to people who support the use of peaceful methods to solve difficult situations as **doves**. Compare **hawk**. ❑ *A clear split over tactics appears to be emerging between doves and hawks in the party.* 🞂 In American English, **dove** is sometimes used as the past tense of **dive**.

---
down
---

① PREPOSITION AND ADVERB USES
② ADJECTIVE USES
③ VERB USES
④ NOUN USES

① **down** ♦♦♦ /daʊn/

Down is often used with verbs of movement, such as "fall" and "pull," and also in phrasal verbs such as "bring down" and "calm down."

→Please look at category 🞂 to see if the expression you are looking for is shown under another headword. 🞂 PREP To go **down** something such as a slope or a pipe means to go toward the ground or to a lower level. ❑ *We're going down a mountain.* ❑ *A man came down the stairs to meet them.* ● ADV **Down** is also an adverb. [ADV after v] ❑ *She went down to the kitchen again.* 🞂 PREP If you are a particular distance **down** something, you are that distance below the top or surface of it. [amount PREP n] ❑ *He managed to cling on to a ledge 4oft down the rock face.* ● ADV **Down** is also an adverb. [amount ADV] ❑ *For the last 18 months miners have cut a face to develop a new shaft 400 meters down.* 🞂 ADV You use **down** to say that you are looking or facing in a direction that is toward the ground or toward a lower level. [ADV after v] ❑ *She was still looking down at her papers.* 🞂 ADV If you put something **down**, you put it onto a surface. [ADV after v] ❑ *Danny put down his glass.* 🞂 PREP If you go or look **down** something such as a road or river, you go or look along it. If you are **down** a road or river, you are somewhere along it. ❑ *They set off at a jog up one street and down another.* 🞂 ADV If an amount of something goes **down**, it decreases. If an amount of something is **down**, it has decreased and is at a lower level than it was. ❑ *Interest rates came down today.* ❑ *Inflation will be down to three percent.* 🞂 PHRASE **Down to** a particular detail means including everything, even that detail. **Down to** a particular person means including everyone, even that person. ❑ *When he designed St Catherine's College, in Oxford, he was responsible for everything, right down to the silverware.* 🞂 PHRASE If you are **down** to a certain amount of something, you have only that amount left. ❑ *The poor man's down to his last £3.* 🞂 PHRASE If a situation is **down** to a particular person or thing, it has been caused by that person or thing. [mainly BRIT] ❑ *Any mistakes are entirely down to us.* 🞂 PHRASE If someone or something is **down for** a particular thing, it has been arranged that they will do that thing, or that thing will happen. ❑ *Mark had told me that he was down for an interview.* 🞂 PHRASE If you pay money **down** on something, you pay part of the money you owe for it. [mainly AM] ❑ *He had a simple, conventional deal and paid 20 percent down at settlement.* →see also **put down** 🞂 PHRASE If people shout "**down with**" something or someone, they are saying that they dislike them and want to get rid of them. [SPOKEN, DISAPPROVAL] ❑ *Demonstrators chanted "down with the rebels."* 🞂 **up and down** →see **up**

② **down** /daʊn/ 🞂 ADJ If you are feeling **down**, you are feeling unhappy or depressed. [INFORMAL] [v-link ADJ] ❑ *The old man sounded really down.* 🞂 ADJ If something is **down** on paper, it has been written on the paper. [v-link ADJ, usu ADJ on n] ❑ *That date wasn't down on our news sheet.* 🞂 ADJ If a piece of equipment, especially a computer system, is **down**, it is temporarily not working because of a fault. Compare **up**. [v-link ADJ] ❑ *The computer's down again.*

③ **down** /daʊn/ (**downs, downing, downed**) 🞂 V-T If you say that someone **downs** food or a drink, you mean that they eat or drink it. ❑ *We downed bottles of local wine.* 🞂 V-T If something or someone is **downed**, they fall to the ground because they have been hurt or damaged in some way. [JOURNALISM] ❑ *A couple of jet fighters were downed during the five-week rebellion.*

④ **down** /daʊn/ 🞂 N-UNCOUNT **Down** consists of the small, soft feathers on young birds. **Down** is used to make bed-covers and pillows. ❑ *... goose down.* 🞂 N-UNCOUNT **Down** is very fine hair. ❑ *The whole plant is covered with fine down.*

down-and-out (**down-and-outs**) ADJ If you describe someone as **down-and-out**, you mean that they have no job and nowhere to live, and they have no real hope of improving their situation. ❑ *...a short story about a down-and-out advertising copywriter.* ● N-COUNT **Down-and-out** is also a noun. [BRIT] ❑ *...some poor down-and-out in need of a meal.*

down·fall /daʊnfɔl/ (**downfalls**) 🞂 N-COUNT The **downfall** of a successful or powerful person or institution is their loss of success or power. ❑ *His lack of experience had led to his downfall.* 🞂 N-COUNT The thing that was a person's **downfall** caused them to fail or lose power. ❑ *His honesty had been his downfall.*

🞂 타동사 물을 뿌리다 ● 펌프에서 물이 나오자 대원들이 물을 뿌려 불을 끄기 시작했다. 🞂 타동사 뿌리다 ❑ 그들은 그에게 휘발유를 뿌리며 욕설을 퍼부었다.

🞂, 🞂의 의미일 때는 /dʌv/로, 🞂의 의미일 때 /doʊv/로 발음된다.

🞂 가산명사 비둘기 🞂 가산명사 온건파 ❑ 당내에서 온건파와 강경파 사이에 전술을 두고 분명한 대립이 일고 있는 것으로 보인다. 🞂 dive의 과거형

down은 종종 'fall', 'pull'과 같은 이동 동사와 함께 쓰이며 'bring down', 'calm down'과 같은 구동사에도 쓰인다.

🞂 전치사 ~의 아래로 ❑ 우리는 산을 내려가고 있다. ❑ 한 남자가 그들을 만나기 위해 계단 아래로 내려왔다. ● 부사 아래로 ❑ 그녀가 부엌으로 다시 내려왔다. 🞂 전치사 ~의 아래쪽으로 ❑ 그는 암벽 정상 아래 40피트 지점에서 간신히 레지에 매달렸다. ● 부사 아래로 ❑ 지난 18개월 동안 광부들이 400미터 깊이의 갱을 새로 만들기 위해 채굴 작업을 벌였다. 🞂 부사 아래로, 밑으로 ❑ 그녀는 여전히 종이를 내려다보고 있었다. 🞂 부사 내려놓아 ❑ 대니가 잔을 내려놓았다. 🞂 전치사 ~을 따라 ❑ 그들은 길을 따라 오르락내리락하면서 조깅을 시작했다. 🞂 부사 내려가 ❑ 오늘 금리가 내려갔다. ❑ 인플레이션이 3퍼센트로 떨어질 것이다. 🞂 구 ~까지 ❑ 그가 옥스퍼드 성 캐서린 대학 설계를 맡았을 때, 숟가락 하나까지 모든 것이 그의 책임 하에 있었다. 🞂 구 ~밖에 남지 않은 ❑ 이 가난한 남자는 이제 돈이 3파운드 밖에 남지 않았다. 🞂 구 ~의 책임인 [주로 영국영어] ❑ 어떤 실수가 일어나도 전적으로 우리의 책임이다. 🞂 구 ~하기로 되어 있는 ❑ 마크는 자기가 인터뷰하기로 되어 있다고 나에게 말했다. 🞂 구 계약금으로 [주로 미국영어] ❑ 그는 간단하고 관례적인 계약을 하고 계약금으로 20퍼센트를 지불했다. 🞂 구 ~을 타도하라 [구어체, 탐탁잖음] ❑ 시위자들이 '반군 타도'를 외쳤다.

🞂 형용사 풀이 죽은, 의기소침한 [비격식체] ❑ 그 노인은 목소리에 힘이 너무 없었다. 🞂 형용사 ~에 쓰여 있는 ❑ 우리 뉴스레터에는 그 날짜가 안 쓰여 있었다. 🞂 형용사 고장 난 ❑ 컴퓨터가 또 고장 났다.

🞂 타동사 먹다, 마시다 ❑ 우리는 지방산 와인 두 병을 마셨다. 🞂 타동사 격추되다, 쓰러지다 [언론] ❑ 폭동 5주 동안 제트 전투기 두 대가 격추되었다.

🞂 불가산명사 (어린 새의) 깃털 ❑ 오리털 🞂 불가산명사 솜털 ❑ 그 식물에는 전체적으로 고운 솜털이 덮여 있었다.

형용사 빈털터리의, 희망이 없는 ❑ 빈털터리 광고 카피라이터에 관한 단편 소설 ● 가산명사 부랑자, 빈털터리 [영국영어] ❑ 한 끼 식사가 필요한 가난한 부랑자

🞂 가산명사 몰락 ❑ 그는 경험 부족으로 몰락했다. 🞂 가산명사 몰락의 원인 ❑ 그의 정직이 몰락을 자초했다.

down|grade /daʊngreɪd/ (**downgrades, downgrading, downgraded**) **1** V-T If something **is downgraded**, it is given less importance than it used to have or than you think it should have. [usu passive] ❏ *The boy's condition has been downgraded from critical to serious.* **2** V-T If someone **is downgraded**, their job or status is changed so that they become less important or receive less money. ❏ *There was no criticism of her work until after she was downgraded.*

1 타동사 하향 조정되다 ❏ 아이의 상태는 위독한 상태에서 중태로 위험도가 하향 조정되었다. **2** 타동사 강등되다, 좌천되다 ❏ 좌천되기 전까지는 그녀가 한 일에 대한 비판이 전혀 없었다.

down|hill /daʊnhɪl/ **1** ADV If something or someone is moving **downhill** or is **downhill**, they are moving down a slope or are located toward the bottom of a hill. ❏ *He headed downhill toward the river.* ● ADJ **Downhill** is also an adjective. [ADJ n] ❏ *...downhill ski runs.* **2** ADV If you say that something **is going downhill**, you mean that it is becoming worse or less successful. ❏ *Since I started to work longer hours things have gone steadily downhill.* **3** ADJ If you say that a task or situation is **downhill** after a particular stage or time, you mean that it is easy to deal with after that stage or time. [v-link ADJ] ❏ *Well, I guess it's all downhill from here.*

1 부사 내리막길로 ❏ 그들은 언덕을 내려가 강으로 향했다. ● 형용사 내리막의 ❏ 스키 활강 ❏ 부사 악화 일로로, 내리막길로 ❏ 내가 장시간 근무하기 시작한 이후로 상황이 계속 나빠졌다. **3** 형용사 수월한 ❏ 뭐, 여기서부터는 전부 수월할 것 같아.

Down|ing Street /daʊnɪŋ striːt/ N-PROPER **Downing Street** is the street in London in which the Prime Minister and the Chancellor of the Exchequer live. You can also use **Downing Street** to refer to the Prime Minister and his or her officials. ❏ *The Prime Minister arrived back at Downing Street from Paris this morning.*

고유명사 다우닝 가 (영국 수상과 재무장관의 관저가 있는 거리), 영국 정부 ❏ 수상이 오늘 아침 파리에서 돌아와 다우닝 가에 도착했다.

down|load /daʊnloʊd/ (**downloads, downloading, downloaded**) V-T To **download** data means to transfer it to or from a computer along a line such as a telephone line, a radio link, or a computer network. ❏ *Users can download their material to a desktop PC back in the office.*

타동사 다운로드 하다 ❏ 사용자는 자료를 사무실 데스크톱 피시에 다운로드 할 수 있다.

down|market /daʊnmɑːrkɪt/ also **down-market** ADJ If you describe a product or service as **downmarket**, you think that they are cheap and are not very good in quality. ❏ *It is a downmarket eating house, seating about 60.* ● ADV **Downmarket** is also an adverb. [ADV after v] ❏ *Why is the company going downmarket and developing smaller machines?*

형용사 저가의 ❏ 이곳은 60여 석을 갖춘 저가 식당이다. ● 부사 저가에 ❏ 회사가 저가 시장으로 선회하면서 더 작은 기계를 개발하는 이유는 무엇일까?

down pay|ment (**down payments**) also **downpayment** N-COUNT If you make a **down payment on** something, you pay only a percentage of the total cost when you buy it. You then finish paying for it later, usually by paying a certain amount every month. ❏ *Celeste asked for the money as a down payment on an old farmhouse.*

가산명사 계약금, 첫 할부금 ❏ 셀레스테는 그 돈을 낡은 농가 매매 계약금으로 요구했다.

down|pour /daʊnpɔːr/ (**downpours**) N-COUNT A **downpour** is a sudden and unexpected heavy fall of rain. ❏ *...sheltering from a sudden downpour of rain.*

가산명사 폭우 ❏ 갑자기 내리는 폭우를 피하면서

down|right /daʊnraɪt/ ADV You use **downright** to emphasize unpleasant or bad qualities or behavior. [EMPHASIS] [ADV adj] ❏ *...ideas that would have been downright dangerous if put into practice.* ● ADJ **Downright** is also an adjective. [ADJ n] ❏ *...downright bad manners.*

부사 아주, 완전히 [강조] ❏ 실행으로 옮겼으면 아주 위험했을 뻔한 아이디어 ● 형용사 철저한, 순전한 ❏ 정말 형편없는 태도

down|shift /daʊnʃɪft/ (**downshifts, downshifting, downshifted**) V-I If someone **downshifts**, they leave a job that is well-paid but stressful for a less demanding job and a more enjoyable way of life. [BRIT] ❏ *Lynda now sees many of her clients downshifting in search of a new way of living.* ● **down|shift|ing** N-UNCOUNT ❏ *The latest lifestyle trend in the media and retail industries of America is downshifting.* ● **down|shift|er** (**downshifters**) N-COUNT ❏ *Downshifters are being tempted to leave the sophisticated city and go simple.*

자동사 쉽고 편한 일로 바꾸다 [영국영어] ❏ 요즘 린다의 고객 중에 새로운 생활 방식을 추구하며 쉽고 편한 일로 바꾸는 사람들이 많다. ● 쉽고 편한 일로 전업 불가산명사 ❏ 미국 언론과 소매업에 나타나는 최신 라이프스타일은 쉽고 편한 일로의 전업이다. ● 쉽고 편한 일로 전업한 사람 가산명사 ❏ 쉽고 편한 일로 전업한 사람들은 복잡한 도시를 떠나 간소한 생활 방식을 추구하고 싶어 한다.

down|side /daʊnsaɪd/ N-SING The **downside of** a situation is the aspect of it which is less positive, pleasant, or useful than its other aspects. ❏ *The downside of this approach is a lack of clear leadership.*

단수명사 단점 ❏ 이 같은 접근 방식의 단점은 지도부가 뚜렷하지 않다는 것이다.

down|size /daʊnsaɪz/ (**downsizes, downsizing, downsized**) V-T To **downsize** something such as a business or industry means to make it smaller. [BUSINESS] ❏ *American manufacturing organizations have been downsizing their factories.* ❏ *...today's downsized economy.* ● **down|siz|ing** N-UNCOUNT ❏ *...a trend toward downsizing in the personal computer market.*

타동사 구조 조정하다, 감원하다 [경제] ❏ 미국 제조업체들이 공장 구조 조정을 단행해 왔다. ❏ 현재 군살을 뺀 경제 ● 감원, 구조조정 불가산명사 ❏ 개인용 컴퓨터 시장의 구조 조정 바람

down|stairs /daʊnstɛərz/ **1** ADV If you go **downstairs** in a building, you go down a staircase toward the ground floor. [ADV after v] ❏ *Denise went downstairs and made some tea.* **2** ADV If something or someone is **downstairs** in a building, they are on the ground floor or on a lower floor than you. ❏ *The telephone was downstairs in the entrance hall.* **3** ADJ **Downstairs** means situated on the ground floor of a building or on a lower floor than you are. [ADJ n] ❏ *She repainted the downstairs rooms and closed off the second floor.* **4** N-SING The **downstairs** of a building is its lower floor or floors. ❏ *The downstairs of the two little houses had been entirely refashioned.*

1 부사 아래층으로 ❏ 데니스가 아래층으로 내려가 차를 끓였다. **2** 부사 아래층에 ❏ 전화는 아래층 현관 복도에 있었다. **3** 형용사 아래층에 있는 ❏ 그는 아래층 방에 새로 페인트를 칠하고 2층을 막아 놓았다. **4** 단수명사 아래층 ❏ 작은 집 두 채 아래층은 전면 개조된 것이었다.

down|stream /daʊnstriːm/ ADV Something that is moving **downstream** is moving toward the mouth of a river, from a point further up the river. Something that is **downstream** is further toward the mouth of a river than where you are. ❏ *We had drifted downstream.* ● ADJ **Downstream** is also an adjective. [ADJ n] ❏ *Breaking the dam could submerge downstream cities such as Wuhan.*

부사 하류로 ❏ 우리는 강 하류로 떠내려갔다. ● 형용사 하류의 ❏ 댐을 부수면 우한과 같은 하류 도시를 침수시킬 수 있다.

down|swing /daʊnswɪŋ/ (**downswings**) N-COUNT A **downswing** is a sudden downward movement in something such as an economy, that had previously been improving. ❏ *Industry may disappear if the manufacturing economy remains on a downswing.*

가산명사 하락 ❏ 제조업 경기가 계속 하락세를 타면 제조업이 사라질지도 모른다.

down|time /daʊntaɪm/ **1** N-UNCOUNT In industry, **downtime** is the time during which machinery or equipment is not operating. ❏ *On the production line, downtime has been reduced from 55% to 26%.* **2** N-UNCOUNT In computing, **downtime** is time when a computer is not working. ❏ *Downtime due to worm removal from networks cost close to $450 million.* **3** N-UNCOUNT **Downtime** is time when people are not working. [mainly AM] ❏ *Downtime in Hollywood can cost a lot of money.*

1 불가산명사 휴지 시간 ❏ 생산 라인의 휴지 시간이 55퍼센트에서 26퍼센트로 줄어들었다. **2** 불가산명사 시스템 중단 시간 ❏ 네트워크 웜바이러스 제거 작업으로 시스템 운영이 중단되면서 4억 5천만 달러에 가까운 손실을 보았다. **3** 불가산명사 작업 중단 [주로 미국영어] ❏ 할리우드 영화 제작이 멈추면 손실이 엄청날 것이다.

down-to-earth ADJ If you say that someone is **down-to-earth**, you approve of the fact that they concern themselves with practical things and actions, rather than with abstract theories. [APPROVAL] ❏ *Gloria is probably the most down-to-earth person I've ever met.*

형용사 현실적인 [마음에 듦] ❏ 글로리아는 내가 만난 사람 중 아마 가장 현실적인 사람일 것이다.

down|town /dauntaun/ ADJ **Downtown** places are in or toward the center of a large town or city, where the stores and places of business are. [mainly AM] [ADJ n] ❑ ...*an office in downtown Chicago.* ● ADV **Downtown** is also an adverb. ❑ *By day he worked downtown for American Standard.* ● N-UNCOUNT **Downtown** is also a noun. [oft the N] ❑ ...*in a large vacant area of the downtown.*

형용사 도심의 [주로 미국영어] ❑ 시카고 도심에 위치한 사무실 ● 부사 도심에서 ❑ 그는 낮 동안 시내 중심가에서 아메리칸 스탠더드 직원으로 일했다. ● 불가산명사 도심 ❑ 도심의 크고 텅 빈 지역에서

down|trend /dauntrend/ N-SING A **downtrend** is a general downward movement in something such as a company's profits or the economy. ❑ *The increase slowed to 0.4 percent, possibly indicating the start of a downtrend.*

단수명사 (경기의) 하향추세 ❑ 경기 상승률이 0.4 퍼센트로까지 저하되었으니 아마도 경기가 하향 추세를 타기 시작한 것 같았다.

down|turn /dauntɜrn/ (**downturns**) N-COUNT If there is a **downturn** in the economy or in a company or industry, it becomes worse or less successful than it had been. ❑ *They predicted a severe economic downturn.*

가산명사 경기 하향 ❑ 그들은 심각한 경기 하향을 예견했다.

down|ward /daunwərd/

> In British English and sometimes in American English, the form **downwards** is used for the adverb.

영국영어와 가끔 미국영어에서 부사로 **downwards**를 쓴다.

1 ADJ A **downward** movement or look is directed toward a lower place or a lower level. [ADJ n] ❑ ...*a firm downward movement of the hands.* **2** ADJ If you refer to a **downward** trend, you mean that something is decreasing or that a situation is getting worse. [ADJ n] ❑ *The downward trend in home ownership is likely to continue.* **3** ADV If you move or look **downward**, you move or look toward the ground or a lower level. ❑ *Benedict pointed downward again with his stick.* **4** ADV If an amount or rate moves **downward**, it decreases. [ADV after v] ❑ *Inflation is moving firmly downward.* **5** ADV If you want to emphasize that a statement applies to everyone in an organization, you can say that it applies from its leader **downward**. [EMPHASIS] [from n ADV] ❑ ...*from the Prime Minister downward.*

1 형용사 아래쪽의 ❑ 두 손을 단호히 아래로 내림 **2** 형용사 하향의 ❑ 주택 소유에 대한 하향 추세는 계속될 것 같다. **3** 부사 아래로 ❑ 베네딕트가 그의 지팡이로 다시 아래쪽을 가리켰다. **4** 부사 감소하여 ❑ 물가 상승률이 확실하게 감소하고 있다. **5** 부사 부하 직원들까지 [강조] ❑ 수상에서부터 부하 직원들까지 모두

dowse /daus/ (**dowses, dowsing, dowsed**) →see **douse**

doze /douz/ (**dozes, dozing, dozed**) V-I When you **doze**, you sleep lightly or for a short period, especially during the daytime. ❑ *For a while she dozed fitfully.* →see **sleep**

자동사 졸다, 잠깐 자다 ❑ 그녀는 잠시 동안 꼬박꼬박 졸았다.

▸ **doze off** PHRASAL VERB If you **doze off**, you fall into a light sleep, especially during the daytime. ❑ *I closed my eyes for a minute and must have dozed off.*

구동사 졸다 ❑ 나는 잠간 눈을 감았었는데 그 때 분명히 졸았던 것 같다.

doz|en ♦♦◇ /dʌzən/ (**dozens**)

> The plural form is **dozen** after a number, or after a word or expression referring to a number, such as "several" or "a few."

숫자 또는 'several', 'a few'와 같이 수를 지칭하는 단어나 표현 뒤에서 복수형은 dozen이다.

1 NUM If you have a **dozen** things, you have twelve of them. ❑ *You will be able to take ten dozen bottles free of duty through customs.* **2** NUM You can refer to a group of approximately twelve things or people as **a dozen**. You can refer to a group of approximately six things or people as **half a dozen**. ❑ *In half a dozen words, he had explained the bond that linked them.* **3** QUANT If you refer to **dozens of** things or people, you are emphasizing that there are very many of them. [EMPHASIS] [QUANT of pl-n] ❑ ...*a storm which destroyed dozens of homes and buildings.* ● PRON You can also use **dozens** as a pronoun. ❑ *Just as revealing are Mr. Johnson's portraits, of which there are dozens.*

1 수사 열두 개 ❑ 세관을 통과할 때 120병은 무관세로 들여올 수 있을 것이다. **2** 수사 어림은; 대여섯 ❑ 그는 그들을 서로 연결해 주는 그 관계에 대해서 대여섯 마디로 설명했었다. **3** 수량사 수십의 [강조] ❑ 수십 채의 주택과 건물을 파괴시킨 폭풍 ● 대명사 수십 개 ❑ 밝혀진 대로 존슨 씨의 초상화는 수십 점이 있다.

Dr. ♦♦◇ (**Drs.**) **Dr.** is a written abbreviation for **Doctor**. [BRIT Dr] ❑ ...*Dr. John Hardy of St. Mary's Medical School in London.*

박사 [영국영어 Dr] ❑ 런던 소재 세인트 매리 메디칼 스쿨의 존 하디 박사

drab /dræb/ (**drabber, drabbest**) ADJ If you describe something as **drab**, you think that it is dull and boring to look at or experience. ❑ ...*his drab little office.* ● **drab|ness** N-UNCOUNT ❑ ...*the dusty drabness of nearby villages.*

형용사 칙칙한 ❑ 칙칙한 그의 작은 사무실 ● 칙칙함 불가산명사 ❑ 칙칙한 황토빛 인근 마을들

dra|co|nian /dreɪkoʊniən, drə-/ ADJ **Draconian** laws or measures are extremely harsh and severe. [FORMAL] ❑ ...*indications that there would be no draconian measures to lower U.S. healthcare costs.*

형용사 엄격한, 가혹한 [격식체] ❑ 미국의 건강 보험료를 낮추는 가혹한 조치는 없을 것이라는 암시

draft ♦♦◇ /dræft/ (**drafts, drafting, drafted**) **1** N-COUNT A **draft** is an early version of a letter, book, or speech. ❑ *I rewrote his rough draft, which was published under my name.* ❑ *I faxed a first draft of this article to him.* **2** V-T When you **draft** a letter, book, or speech, you write the first version of it. ❑ *He drafted a letter to the editors.* **3** V-T If you **are drafted**, you are ordered to serve in the armed forces, usually for a limited period of time. [mainly AM] [usu passive] ❑ *During the Second World War, he was drafted into the U.S. Army.* **4** V-T If people **are drafted into** a place, they are moved there to do a particular job. ❑ *Extra police have been drafted into the town after the violence.* **5** N-SING The **draft** is the practice of ordering people to serve in the armed forces, usually for a limited period of time. [mainly AM] ❑ ...*his effort to avoid the draft.* **6** N-COUNT A **draft** is a written order for payment of money by a bank, especially from one bank to another. ❑ *The money was payable by a draft drawn by the home.* **7** N-COUNT A **draft** is a current of air that comes into a place in an undesirable way. [AM; BRIT **draught**] ❑ *Block drafts around doors and windows.*

1 가산명사 초안 ❑ 나는 그가 쓴 개략적인 초안 원고를 다시 썼는데, 그것은 내 이름으로 출간되었다. ❑ 나는 이 기사의 초고를 그에게 팩스로 보냈다. **2** 타동사 초고를 쓰다 ❑ 그는 편집자들에게 보낼 편지 초안을 썼다. **3** 타동사 징집되다 [주로 미국영어] ❑ 2차 세계 대전 때, 그는 미군에 징집되었다. **4** 타동사 파견되다 ❑ 그 폭동 이후에 경찰이 추가로 그 마을에 파견되었다. **5** 단수명사 징집 [주로 미국영어] ❑ 군대 징집을 피해 보려는 그의 노력 **6** 가산명사 환어음 ❑ 그 집에서 발행한 환어음으로 그 돈을 지불할 수 있었다. **7** 가산명사 외풍 [미국영어; 영국영어 draught] ❑ 문과 창문 사이로 들어오는 외풍을 막아라.

Word Partnership	*draft*의 연어
ADJ.	**final** draft, **rough** draft **1**
V.	**revise** a draft, **write** a draft **1**
	dodge the draft **5**
	feel a draft **7**
N.	draft a **letter**, draft a **speech 2**
	bank draft **6**

drag ♦♦◇ /dræg/ (**drags, dragging, dragged**) **1** V-T If you **drag** something, you pull it along the ground, often with difficulty. ❑ *He got up and dragged his chair toward the table.* **2** V-T To **drag** a computer image means to use the mouse to

1 타동사 질질 끌다 ❑ 그는 일어나서 식탁 쪽으로 의자를 질질 끌어당겼다. **2** 타동사 (컴퓨터) 드래그 [컴퓨터] ❑ 마우스로 그 그림을 드래그해서 새로운

move the position of the image on the screen, or to change its size or shape. [COMPUTING] ❏ *Use your mouse to drag the pictures to their new size.* ❸ V-T If someone **drags** you somewhere, they pull you there, or force you to go there by physically threatening you. ❏ *The vigilantes dragged the men out of the vehicles.* ❹ V-T If someone **drags** you somewhere you do not want to go, they make you go there. ❏ *When you can drag him away from his work, he can also be a devoted father.* ❺ V-T If you say that you **drag yourself** somewhere, you are emphasizing that you have to make a very great effort to go there. [EMPHASIS] ❏ *I find it really hard to drag myself out and exercise regularly.* ❻ V-T If you **drag** your foot or your leg behind you, you walk with great difficulty because your foot or leg is injured in some way. ❏ *He was barely able to drag his poisoned leg behind him.* ❼ V-T If the police **drag** a river or lake, they pull nets or hooks across the bottom of it in order to look for something. ❏ *Yesterday police frogmen dragged a small pond on the Common.* ❽ V-I If a period of time or an event **drags**, it is very boring and seems to last a long time. ❏ *The minutes dragged past.* ❾ N-SING If something is **a drag on** the development or progress of something, it slows it down or makes it more difficult. ❏ *The satellite acts as a drag on the shuttle.* ❿ N-SING If you say that something is **a drag**, you mean that it is unpleasant or very dull. [INFORMAL, DISAPPROVAL] ❏ *As far as shopping for clothes goes, it's a drag.* ⓫ N-COUNT If you take **a drag** on a cigarette or pipe that you are smoking, you take in air through it. [INFORMAL] ❏ *He took a drag on his cigarette, and exhaled the smoke.* ⓬ N-UNCOUNT **Drag** is the wearing of women's clothes by a male entertainer. ❏ *Entertainment is laid on too, in the form of drag on Wednesdays and strippers on Sundays.* ● PHRASE If a man is **in drag**, he is wearing women's clothes. ⓭ PHRASE If you **drag** your **feet** or **drag** your **heels**, you delay doing something or do it very slowly because you do not want to do it. ❏ *The government, he claimed, was dragging its feet, and this was definitely threatening moves toward peace.*
→see **flight**

▶**drag out** ❶ PHRASAL VERB If you **drag** something **out**, you make it last for longer than is necessary. ❏ *...a company that was willing and able to drag out the proceedings for years.* ❷ PHRASAL VERB If you **drag** something **out of** a person, you persuade them to tell you something that they do not want to tell you. ❏ *The families soon discovered that every piece of information had to be dragged out of the authorities.*

drag|on /drǽgən/ (**dragons**) N-COUNT In stories and legends, a **dragon** is an animal like a big lizard. It has wings and claws, and breathes out fire. →see **fantasy**

dragon|fly /drǽgənflaɪ/ (**dragonflies**) N-COUNT **Dragonflies** are brightly-colored insects with long, thin bodies and two sets of wings. Dragonflies are often found near slow-moving water.

drain ♦◇◇ /dreɪn/ (**drains, draining, drained**) ❶ V-T/V-I If you **drain** a liquid from a place or object, you remove the liquid by causing it to flow somewhere else. If a liquid **drains** somewhere, it flows there. ❏ *Miners built the tunnel to drain water out of the mines.* ❏ *Now the focus is on draining the water.* ❷ V-T/V-I If you **drain** a place or object, you dry it by causing water to flow out of it. If a place or object **drains**, water flows out of it until it is dry. ❏ *The authorities have mobilized vast numbers of people to drain flooded land and build or repair dykes.* ❸ V-T/V-I If you **drain** food or if food **drains**, you remove the liquid that it has been in, especially after it has been cooked or soaked in water. ❏ *Drain the pasta well, arrange on four plates, and pour over the sauce.* ❹ N-COUNT A **drain** is a pipe that carries water or sewage away from a place, or an opening in a surface that leads to the pipe. ❏ *Tony built his own house and laid his own drains.* ❺ V-I If the color or the blood **drains** or **is drained from** someone's face, they become very pale. You can also say that someone's face **drains** or **is drained of** color. [LITERARY] ❏ *Harry felt the color drain from his face.* ❻ V-T If something **drains** you, it leaves you feeling physically and emotionally exhausted. ❏ *My emotional turmoil had drained me.* ● **drained** ADJ ❏ *I began to suffer from headaches, which left me feeling completely drained.* ● **drain|ing** ADJ ❏ *This work is physically exhausting and emotionally draining.* ❼ N-SING If you say that something is **a drain on** an organization's finances or resources, you mean that it costs the organization a large amount of money, and you do not think that it is worth it. ❏ *...an ultra-modern printing plant, which has been a big drain on resources.* ❽ V-T If you say that a country's or a company's resources or finances **are drained**, you mean that they are used or spent completely. ❏ *The state's finances have been drained by drought and civil disorder.* ❾ PHRASE If you say that something **is going down the drain**, you mean that it is being destroyed or wasted. [INFORMAL] ❏ *They were aware that their public image was rapidly going down the drain.* →see **plumbing**

drain|age /dreɪnɪdʒ/ N-UNCOUNT **Drainage** is the system or process by which water or other liquids are drained from a place. ❏ *Line the pots with pebbles to ensure good drainage.* →see **farm**

dra|ma ♦◇◇ /drɑmə, drǽmə/ (**dramas**) ❶ N-COUNT A **drama** is a serious play for the theater, television, or radio. ❏ *He acted in radio dramas.* ❷ N-UNCOUNT You use **drama** to refer to plays in general or to work that is connected with plays and the theater, such as acting or producing. ❏ *He knew nothing of Greek drama.* ❸ N-VAR You can refer to a real situation which is exciting or distressing as **drama**. ❏ *There was none of the drama and relief of a hostage release.*

dra|mat|ic ♦♦◇ /drəmǽtɪk/ ❶ ADJ A **dramatic** change or event happens suddenly and is very noticeable and surprising. ❏ *A fifth year of drought is expected to have dramatic effects on the California economy.* ● **dra|mati|cal|ly** /drəmǽtɪkli/ ADV ❏ *At speeds above 50mph, serious injuries dramatically increase.* ❷ ADJ A **dramatic** action, event, or situation is exciting and impressive. ❏ *He witnessed many dramatic escapes as people jumped from as high as the fourth floor.* ● **dra|mati|cal|ly** ADV ❏ *He tipped his head to one side and sighed dramatically.* ❸ ADJ

크기로 만들어라. ❸ 타동사 끌고 가다 ❏ 그 자경 단원들은 그 남자들을 차 밖으로 끌어냈다. ❹ 타동사 끌어내다 ❏ 당신이 그를 직장에서 끌어낼 수만 있다면, 그 사람도 역시 헌신적인 아버지가 될 수 있다. ❺ 타동사 무진 애를 쓰다 [강조] ❏ 나는 무진 애를 써서 정기적으로 운동을 하는 것이 정말 어렵다는 것을 알고 있다. ❻ 타동사 질질 끌다 ❏ 그는 독이 퍼진 다리를 거의 질질 끌 수도 없었다. ❼ 타동사 (못 밑바닥을) 훑다 ❏ 경찰 잠수부가 어제 커먼에 있는 작은 연못 밑바닥을 훑었다. ❽ 자동사 (지루하게) 질질 끌다 ❏ 그 시간이 지루하게 흘렀다. ❾ 단수명사 장애물 ❏ 인공위성이 우주 왕복선의 장애물이 되고 있다. ❿ 단수명사 지겨운 것 [비격식체, 탐탁찮음] ❏ 적어도 옷 사러 다니는 것은 지겨운 일이다. ⓫ 가산명사 (담배를) 깊이 빨아들이다 [비격식체] ❏ 그는 담배를 깊이 빨아들이며 연기를 내뿜었다. ⓬ 불가산명사 여장(女裝) ❏ 또한 여흥으로서, 수요일에는 여장이, 일요일은 스트립퍼가 배치되어 있다. ● 구 여장을 한 ⓭ 구 지연시키다, 질질 끌다 ❏ 정부가 결정을 질질 끄는 것은 분명 평화를 위협하는 조치라고 그는 주장했다.

❶ 구동사 (필요 이상으로) 오래 끌다 ❏ 그 소송 절차를 수년 간 의도적으로 오래 끌고 갈 수 있었던 회사 ❷ 구동사 (말을) 끌어내다 ❏ 그 가구들은 모든 정보를 당국으로부터 끌어내야 한다는 사실을 곧 깨달았다.

가산명사 용

가산명사 잠자리

❶ 타동사/자동사 (물을) 빼다; (물이) 빠지다 ❏ 광부들은 광산에 있는 물을 밖으로 빠져 나가게 하기 위해서 굴을 팠다. ❏ 이제 중요한 건 그 물을 밖으로 빼내는 일이다. ❷ 타동사/자동사 (물을) 다 빼내다; (물이) 다 빠지다 ❏ 관계 당국은 엄청난 사람들을 동원해서 침수 지역의 물을 다 빼내고 둑을 쌓거나 복구했다. ❸ 타동사/자동사 물기를 빼다; 물기가 빠지다 ❏ 파스타의 물기를 잘 빼서 네 개의 접시에 나눠 담은 후 위에 소스를 부어라. ❹ 가산명사 배수관 ❏ 토니는 자기 집을 직접 짓고 배수관도 직접 설치했다. ❺ 자동사 (얼굴의 핏기 등이) 가시다 [문예체] ❏ 해리는 자신의 얼굴에 핏기가 가시는 것을 느꼈다. ❻ 타동사 (육체적, 정신적으로) 지치게 만들다 ❏ 심리적 동요로 나는 완전히 지친 상태였다. ● 지친 형용사 ❏ 나는 두통을 앓기 시작해서, 완전히 진이 빠진 느낌이 들었다. ● 지치게 하는 형용사 ❏ 이 일은 육체적으로 피곤하고 정신적으로 지치게 한다. ❼ 단수명사 (자금의) 고갈(의) 근원 ❏ 자원을 크게 고갈시켜 온 원인이 된 초현대적 인쇄 공장 ❽ 타동사 고갈되다 ❏ 주 새정이 가뭄과 시민 소요로 고갈되어 왔다. ● 구 망쳐지는, 실추되는 [비격식체] ❏ 그들은 자신들의 대외 이미지가 빠르게 실추되고 있다는 것을 의식하고 있었다.

불가산명사 배수 장치 ❏ 배수가 잘 되도록 화분 바닥에 자갈을 깔아라.

❶ 가산명사 드라마 ❏ 그는 라디오 드라마에 출연했다. ❷ 불가산명사 희곡 ❏ 그는 그리스 희곡에 대해서는 전혀 아는 게 없었다. ❸ 가산명사 또는 불가산명사 극적인 상황 ❏ 인질 석방에 대해서는 극적인 상황이나 안도감 같은 것은 전혀 없었다.

❶ 형용사 엄청난, 극적인 ❏ 5년째 계속되는 가뭄 때문에 캘리포니아 경제가 엄청난 영향을 받을 것으로 예상된다. ● 극적으로, 엄청나게 부사 ❏ 시속 50마일 이상의 속도가 되면 심한 부상이 발생할 가능성이 엄청나게 증가한다. ❷ 형용사 극적인, 인상적인 ❏ 사람들이 4층이나 되는 높이에서 뛰어내릴 때 그는 많은 극적인 탈출 장면을 목격했다. ● 과장되게, ❸

You use **dramatic** to describe things connected with or relating to the theater, drama, or plays. [ADJ n] ❑ ...a dramatic arts major in college.

연극하듯 부사 ❑ 그가 머리를 한쪽으로 기울이더니 과장되게 한숨을 쉬었다. **3** 형용사 연극의 ❑ 대학의 극예술 전공자

drama|tist /drǽmətɪst/ (**dramatists**) N-COUNT A **dramatist** is someone who writes plays.

가산명사 극작가

drama|tize /drǽmətaɪz/ (**dramatizes, dramatizing, dramatized**) [BRIT also **dramatise**] **1** V-T If a book or story **is dramatized**, it is written or presented as a play, movie, or television drama. [usu passive] ❑ ...an incident later dramatized in the movie "The Right Stuff". ● **drama|ti|za|tion** /drǽmətɪzéɪʃn/ (**dramatizations**) N-COUNT ❑ ...a dramatization of D H Lawrence's novel, "Lady Chatterley's Lover." **2** V-T If you say that someone **dramatizes** a situation or event, you mean that they try to make it seem more serious, more important, or more exciting than it really is. [DISAPPROVAL] ❑ They have a tendency to show off, to dramatize almost every situation.

[영국영어 dramatise] **1** 타동사 각색되다 ❑ 나중에 영화 '더 라이트 스터프'로 각색된 한 사건 ● 각색 가산명사 ❑ 디 에이치 로렌스의 소설 '채털리 부인의 사랑'을 각색한 작품 **2** 타동사 극적으로 보이게 만들다 [탐탁잖음] ❑ 그들은 거의 모든 상황을 극적으로 만들려 과장하려는 경향이 있다.

drank /drǽŋk/ **Drank** is the past tense of **drink**.

drink의 과거

drape /dreɪp/ (**drapes, draping, draped**) **1** V-T If you **drape** a piece of cloth somewhere, you place it there so that it hangs down in a casual and graceful way. ❑ Natasha took the coat and draped it over her shoulders. **2** V-T If someone or something **is draped in** a piece of cloth, they are loosely covered by it. ❑ The coffin had been draped in a Union Jack. **3** N-COUNT **Drapes** are pieces of heavy fabric that you hang from the top of a window and can close to keep the light out or stop people from looking in. [AM; BRIT **curtains**] ❑ He pulled the drapes shut, locked the door behind him.

1 타동사 걸치다, 늘어뜨리다 ❑ 나타샤는 코트를 집어서 어깨에 걸쳤다. **2** 타동사 걸쳐놓다, 덮이다 ❑ 그 관에는 영국 국기가 덮여 있었다. **3** 가산명사 두꺼운 커튼, 휘장 [미국영어; 영국영어 curtains] ❑ 그는 커튼을 끌어당겨 닫고, 등 뒤로 문도 잠갔다.

dras|tic /drǽstɪk/ **1** ADJ If you have to take **drastic** action in order to solve a problem, you have to do something extreme and basic to solve it. ❑ Drastic measures are needed to clean up the profession. **2** ADJ A **drastic** change is a very great change. ❑ Foreign food aid has led to a drastic reduction in the numbers of people dying of starvation. ● **dras|ti|cal|ly** ADV [ADV with v] ❑ As a result, services have been drastically reduced.

1 형용사 과감한 ❑ 동업자들의 부패를 청산하기 위해서는 과감한 조치가 필요하다. **2** 형용사 엄청난 ❑ 외국의 식량 원조 덕분에 굶주림으로 죽어 가는 사람들이 엄청나게 감소했다. ● 엄청나게 부사 ❑ 결과적으로 서비스가 엄청나게 줄어들었다.

draughts /drǽfts/ N-UNCOUNT **Draughts** is a game for two people, played with 24 round pieces on a board. [BRIT; AM **checkers**] ❑ He was in the study playing draughts by the fire with Albert.

불가산명사 드래프트 (체스의 일종) [영국영어; 미국영어 checkers] ❑ 그는 서재 안 난로가에 앨버트와 드래프트를 하고 있었다.

draw ♦♦♦ /drɔː/ (**draws, drawing, drew, drawn**) **1** V-T/V-I When you **draw**, or when you **draw** something, you use a pencil or pen to produce a picture, pattern, or diagram. ❑ She would sit there drawing with the pencil stub. ● **draw|ing** N-UNCOUNT ❑ I like dancing, singing, and drawing. **2** V-I When a vehicle **draws** somewhere, it moves there smoothly and steadily. ❑ Claire had seen the taxi drawing away. **3** V-I If you **draw** somewhere, you move there slowly. [WRITTEN] ❑ She drew away and did not smile. **4** V-T If you **draw** something or someone in a particular direction, you move them in that direction, usually by pulling them gently. [WRITTEN] ❑ He drew his chair nearer the fire. ❑ He put his arm around Caroline's shoulders and drew her close to him. **5** V-T When you **draw** a curtain or blind, you pull it across a window, either to cover or to uncover it. ❑ After drawing the curtains, she lit a candle. **6** V-T If someone **draws** a gun, knife, or other weapon, they pull it out of its container and threaten you with it. ❑ He drew his dagger and turned to face his pursuers. **7** V-T If you **draw** a deep breath, you breathe in deeply once. ❑ He paused, drawing a deep breath. **8** V-I If you **draw on** a cigarette, you breathe the smoke from it into your mouth or lungs. ❑ He drew on an American cigarette. **9** V-T To **draw** something such as water or energy **from** a particular source means to take it from that source. ❑ Villagers still have to draw their water from wells. **10** V-T If something that hits you or presses part of your body **draws** blood, it cuts your skin so that it bleeds. ❑ Any practice that draws blood could increase the risk of getting the virus. **11** V-T If you **draw** money out of a bank account, you get it from the account so that you can use it. ❑ She was drawing out cash from a cash machine. **12** V-T To **draw** something means to choose it or to be given it, as part of a competition, game, or lottery. ❑ We delved through a sackful of letters to draw the winning name. ● N-COUNT **Draw** is also a noun. ❑ ...the draw for the quarter-finals of the UEFA Cup. **13** V-T To **draw** something **from** a particular thing or place means to take or get it from that thing or place. ❑ I draw strength from the millions of women who have faced this challenge successfully. **14** V-T If you **draw** a particular conclusion, you decide that that conclusion is true. ❑ He draws two conclusions from this. **15** V-T If you **draw** a comparison, parallel, or distinction, you compare or contrast two different ideas, systems, or other things. ❑ ...literary critics drawing comparisons between George Sand and George Eliot. **16** V-T If you **draw** someone's attention to something, you make them aware of it or make them think about it. ❑ He was waving his arms to draw their attention. **17** V-T If someone or something **draws** a particular reaction, people react to it in that way. ❑ Such a policy would inevitably draw fierce resistance from farmers. **18** V-T If something such as a movie or an event **draws** a lot of people, it is so interesting or entertaining that a lot of people go to it. ❑ The game is currently drawing huge crowds. **19** V-T If someone or something **draws** you, it attracts you very strongly. ❑ In no sense did he draw and enthrall her as Alex had done. **20** V-T If someone will not **be drawn** or refuses to **be drawn**, they will not reply to questions in the way that you want them to, or will not reveal information or their opinion. [mainly BRIT] [with brd-neg, usu passive] ❑ The ambassador would not be drawn on questions of a political nature. **21** V-RECIP In a game or competition, if one person or team **draws** with another one, or if two people or teams **draw**, they have the same number of points or goals at the end of the game. [mainly BRIT] ❑ Holland and the Republic of Ireland drew one-one. ❑ We drew with Ireland in the first game. ● N-COUNT **Draw** is also a noun. [AM usually **tie**] ❑ We were happy to come away with a draw against Sweden. **22** →see also **drawing** **23** PHRASE When an event or period of time **draws to a close** or **draws to an end**, it finishes. ❑ Another celebration had drawn to its close. **24** PHRASE If an event or period of time **is drawing closer** or **is drawing nearer**, it is

1 타동사/자동사 그리다 ❑ 그녀는 몽당연필로 그림을 그리면서 저기에 앉아 있곤 했다. ● (연필이나 펜으로) 그림 그리기 불가산명사 ❑ 나는 춤추기, 노래하기, 그림 그리기를 좋아한다. **2** 자동사 (차가) 슬슬 움직이다 ❑ 클레어는 그 택시가 슬슬 빠져 나가는 것을 봤다. **3** 자동사 슬슬 가다 [문어체] ❑ 그녀는 슬슬 나가면서 웃지도 않았다. **4** 타동사 (부드럽게) 끌어당기다 [문어체] ❑ 그는 의자를 난로 더 가까이로 끌어당겼다. ❑ 그는 캐롤라인의 어깨로 팔을 감싸며 그녀를 부드럽게 가까이 끌어당겼다. **5** 타동사 (커튼이나 블라인드를) 치다; (커튼이나 블라인드를) 드리우다 ❑ 커튼을 친 후에 그녀는 촛불을 켰다. **6** 타동사 (총이나 무기를) 뽑아 들다 ❑ 그는 단검을 뽑아 들고 쫓아오는 사람을 향해 돌아섰다. **7** 타동사 들이쉬다 ❑ 그는 숨을 깊이 들이쉬며 잠깐 멈췄다. **8** 자동사 (담배 연기를) 빨아들이다 ❑ 그는 미국산 담배를 빨아들였다. **9** 타동사 끌어내다 ❑ 마을 사람들은 아직도 우물에서 물을 길어서 써야 한다. **10** 타동사 (피를) 흘리게 하다 ❑ 피를 흘리게 되는 수술이라면 어떤 것도 바이러스 감염의 위험을 증가시킬 수 있을 것이다. **11** 타동사 인출하다 ❑ 그녀는 현금 인출기에서 현금을 인출하고 있었다. **12** 타동사 제비뽑다, 추첨하다 ❑ 우리는 당첨자의 이름을 뽑기 위해서 쪽지더 한 부대 속에 손을 집어넣었다. ● 가산명사 추첨 ❑ 유럽축구연맹 컵 4강전을 위한 조 추첨 **13** 타동사 얻어내다 ❑ 나는 이 도전적인 일에 훌륭하게 맞섰던 수백만 여성들에게서 힘을 얻었다. **14** 타동사 끌어내다 ❑ 그는 이것으로부터 두 가지 결론을 끌어낸다. **15** 타동사 비교하다; 대조하다 ❑ 조지 샌드와 조지 엘리어트를 비교하는 문학 비평가들 **16** 타동사 (관심을) 끌다 ❑ 그가 그들의 관심을 끌려고 두 팔을 흔들고 있었다. **17** 타동사 불러일으키다 ❑ 그런 정책은 불가피하게 농부들의 거센 저항을 불러 일으킬 것이다. **18** 타동사 (사람들을) 끌어 모으다 ❑ 그 경기는 요즘 엄청난 군중들을 끌어 모으고 있다. **19** 타동사 끌다 ❑ 그는 알렉스가 그랬던 것처럼 그녀의 마음을 끌어 매혹시키는 일을 전혀 하지 못했다. **20** 타동사 말하다 [주로 영국영어] ❑ 그 대사는 정치적 성격의 문제에 대해서는 의견을 말하려 하지 않을 것이다. **21** 상호동사 비기다 [주로 영국영어] ❑ 네덜란드와 아일랜드는 일 대 일로 비겼다. ● 우리는 첫 번째 경기에서 아일랜드와 비겼다. ● 가산명사 동점 [미국영어 대개 tie] ❑ 우리는 스웨덴과 동점으로 끝나서 기분 좋았다. **22** 구 끝나다 ❑ 또 한번의 축하 의식이 끝이 났었다. **24** 구 다가오다 ❑ 그리고 동시에 내년 봄 선거가 다가오고 있다.

approaching. ❏ *And all the time next spring's elections are drawing closer.* 25 to **draw the line** →see **line**. to **draw lots** →see **lot** →see **animation**

Thesaurus   *draw*의 참조어

v.	illustrate, sketch, trace 1
	bring out 6
	inhale 7 8
	extract, take 9
	conclude, decide, make a decision, settle on 14

▶**draw in** PHRASAL VERB If you **draw** someone **in** or **draw** them **into** something you are involved with, you cause them to become involved with it. ❏ *It won't be easy for you to draw him in.*

구동사 끌어들이다 ❏ 네가 그 사람을 끌어들이기는 쉽지 않을걸.

▶**draw on** PHRASAL VERB If you **draw on** or **draw upon** something such as your skill or experience, you make use of it in order to do something. ❏ *He drew on his experience as a yachtsman to make a documentary program.*

구동사 활용하다 ❏ 그는 다큐멘터리 프로그램을 만들기 위해서 요트 조종사로서의 자신의 경험을 활용했다.

▶**draw up** PHRASAL VERB If you **draw up** a document, list, or plan, you prepare it and write it out. ❏ *They agreed to establish a working party to draw up a formal agreement.*

구동사 (문서를) 작성하다 ❏ 그들은 정식 합의서를 작성하기 위해서 실무 위원회를 발족시키는 것에 동의했다.

▶**draw upon** →see **draw on**

draw|back /drɔ́bæk/ (drawbacks) N-COUNT A **drawback** is an aspect of something or someone that makes them less acceptable than they would otherwise be. ❏ *He felt the apartment's only drawback was that it was too small.*

가산명사 단점 ❏ 그 사람 생각에 그 아파트의 유일한 단점은 공간이 너무 좁다는 것이었다.

draw|er /drɔ́r/ (drawers) N-COUNT A **drawer** is part of a desk, chest, or other piece of furniture that is shaped like a box and is designed for putting things in. You pull it toward you to open it. ❏ *He opened a drawer in his writing-table and brought out a sheet of notepaper.*

가산명사 서랍 ❏ 그는 책상 서랍을 열고 메모지 한 장을 꺼내 왔다.

draw|ing /drɔ́ɪŋ/ (drawings) N-COUNT A **drawing** is a picture made with a pencil or pen. ❏ *She did a drawing of me.* →see also **draw** →see Word Web: **drawing**

가산명사 (연필이나 펜으로 그린) 그림 ❏ 그녀가 펜으로 내 그림을 그렸다.

draw|ing pin (drawing pins) also **drawing-pin** N-COUNT A **drawing pin** is a short pin with a broad, flat top which is used for fastening papers or pictures to a board, wall, or other surface. [BRIT; AM **thumbtack**]

가산명사 압정 [영국영어; 미국영어 thumbtack]

draw|ing room (drawing rooms) N-COUNT A **drawing room** is a room, especially a large one in a large house, where people sit and relax, or entertain guests. [OLD-FASHIONED]

가산명사 응접실 [구식어]

drawl /drɔ́l/ (drawls, drawling, drawled) V-T/V-I If someone **drawls**, they speak slowly and not very clearly, with long vowel sounds. ❏ *"I guess you guys don't mind if I smoke?" he drawled.* ● N-COUNT **Drawl** is also a noun. ❏ *Jack's southern drawl had become more pronounced as they'd traveled southward.*

타동사/자동사 느릿느릿 말하다 ❏ "담배 피워도 되겠지?"라고 그가 느릿느릿 말했다. ● 가산명사 느린 발음 ❏ 그들이 남부 지방으로 여행할수록 잭은 남부 지방의 느린 말투를 더 많이 썼다.

drawn /drɔ́n/ 1 **Drawn** is the past participle of **draw**. 2 ADJ If someone or their face looks **drawn**, their face is thin and they look very tired, ill, worried, or unhappy. ❏ *She looked drawn and tired when she turned toward me.*

1 draw의 과거 분사 2 형용사 초췌한 ❏ 그녀가 우리 쪽을 돌아보았을 때, 그녀는 초췌하고 피곤해 보였다.

drawn-out ADJ You can describe something as **drawn-out** when it lasts or takes longer than you would like it to. ❏ *The road to peace will be long and drawn-out.*

형용사 오래 걸리는 ❏ 평화를 향한 길은 멀고도 오래 걸릴 것이다.

dread /drɛ́d/ (dreads, dreading, dreaded) 1 V-T If you **dread** something which may happen, you feel very anxious and unhappy about it because you think it will be unpleasant or upsetting. ❏ *I'm dreading Christmas this year.* ❏ *I dreaded coming back, to be honest.* 2 N-UNCOUNT **Dread** is a feeling of great anxiety and fear about something that may happen. ❏ *She thought with dread of the cold winters to come.* 3 →see also **dreaded** 4 PHRASE If you say that you **dread to think** what might happen, you mean that you are anxious about it because it is likely to be very unpleasant. ❏ *I dread to think what will happen in the case of a major emergency.*

1 타동사 걱정하다, 두려워하다 ❏ 나는 이번 크리스마스가 걱정이다. ❏ 솔직히 말하면, 나는 돌아오는 것이 두려웠다. 2 불가산명사 걱정 ❏ 그녀는 다가올 추운 겨울을 걱정했다. 4 구 생각만 해도 걱정이다 ❏ 나는 정말 위급한 상태에 일어날 일들이 생각만 해도 걱정이다.

dread|ed /drɛ́dɪd/ 1 ADJ **Dreaded** means terrible and greatly feared. [ADJ n] ❏ *No one knew how to treat this dreaded disease.* 2 ADJ You can use **the dreaded** to describe something that you, or a particular group of people, find annoying, inconvenient, or undesirable. [INFORMAL, FEELINGS] [ADJ n] ❏ *She's a victim of the dreaded hay fever.*

1 형용사 무시무시한 ❏ 이 무시무시한 질병을 어떻게 치료해야 할 지 아무도 몰랐다. 2 형용사 지긋지긋한 [비격식체, 감정 개입] ❏ 그녀는 그 지긋지긋한 건초열 때문에 고생하고 있다.

Word Web   drawing

The first thing **art** students must learn is how to **draw**. They often carry sketchbooks and soft **graphite pencils** around with them. You'll see them sitting and **sketching** everyday objects and **scenes**. Many famous **works of art** began as simple **pen** and **ink drawings**. For example, Leonardo da Vinci* did several **sketches** before he started painting "The Last Supper"*. Other sketching materials include **charcoal sticks** and pastels. They allow greater shading. However, they require fixative to prevent **smudging**.

Leonardo da Vinci (1452-1519): an Italian artist.
"The Last Supper": a famous painting.

A
B
C
D
E
F
G
H
I
J
K
L
M
N
O
P
Q
R
S
T
U
V
W
X
Y
Z

Word Link

ful ≈ filled with : beauti*ful*, care*ful*, dread*ful*

dread|ful /drɛdfəl/ **1** ADJ If you say that something is **dreadful**, you mean that it is very bad or unpleasant, or very poor in quality. ❑ *They told us the dreadful news.* ● **dread|fully** ADV [ADV with v] ❑ *You behaved dreadfully.* **2** ADJ **Dreadful** is used to emphasize the degree or extent of something bad. [EMPHASIS] [ADJ n] ❑ *We've made a dreadful mistake.* ● **dread|fully** ADV ❑ *He looks dreadfully ill.*

dream ♦♦◇ /drim/ (dreams, dreaming, dreamed, dreamt)

> The forms **dreamed** and **dreamt** can both be used for the past tense and past participle.

1 N-COUNT A **dream** is an imaginary series of events that you experience in your mind while you are asleep. ❑ *He had a dream about Claire.* **2** V-T/V-I When you **dream**, you experience imaginary events in your mind while you are asleep. ❑ *Ivor dreamed that he was on a bus.* **3** N-COUNT You can refer to a situation or event as a **dream** if you often think about it because you would like it to happen. ❑ *He had finally accomplished his dream of becoming a pilot.* **4** V-I If you often think about something that you would very much like to happen or have, you can say that you **dream** of it. ❑ *As a schoolgirl, she had dreamed of becoming an actress.* ❑ *For most of us, a brand new designer kitchen is something we can only dream about.* **5** ADJ You can use **dream** to describe something that you think is ideal or perfect, especially if it is something that you thought you would never be able to have or experience. [ADJ n] ❑ *...a dream holiday to Jamaica.* **6** N-SING If you describe something as a particular person's **dream**, you think that it would be ideal for that person and that he or she would like it very much. ❑ *Greece is said to be a botanist's dream.* **7** N-COUNT You can refer to a situation or event that does not seem real as a **dream**, especially if it is very strange or unpleasant. ❑ *When the right woman comes along, this bad dream will be over.* **8** V-I If you say that you **would not dream of** doing something, you are emphasizing that you would never do it because you think it is wrong or is not possible or suitable for you. [EMPHASIS] [with neg] ❑ *I wouldn't dream of making fun of you.* **9** V-T If you say that you **never dreamed that** something would happen, you are emphasizing that you did not think that it would happen because it seemed very unlikely. [EMPHASIS] [with brd-neg] ❑ *I never dreamed that I would be able to afford a home here.* **10** PHRASE If you say that someone does something **like a dream**, you think that they do it very well. If you say that something happens **like a dream**, you mean that it happens successfully without any problems. ❑ *She cooked like a dream.* **11** PHRASE If you describe someone or something as the person or thing **of** your **dreams**, you mean that you consider them to be ideal or perfect. ❑ *This could be the man of my dreams.* **12** PHRASE If you say that you could not imagine a particular thing **in** your **wildest dreams**, you are emphasizing that you think it is extremely strange or unlikely. [EMPHASIS] ❑ *Never in my wildest dreams could I imagine there would be this kind of money in the game.* **13** PHRASE If you describe something as being **beyond** your **wildest dreams**, you are emphasizing that it is better than you could have imagined or hoped for. [EMPHASIS] ❑ *She had already achieved success beyond her wildest dreams.*
→see Word Web: **dream**

Thesaurus

dream의 참조어

N.   nightmare, vision **1**
      ambition, aspiration, design, hope, wish **3**
V.   hope, long for, wish **4**

Word Partnership

dream의 연어

V.   **have a** dream **1**
      fulfill a dream, **pursue a** dream, **realize a** dream **3**
N.   dream **interpretation 1**
      dream **home,** dream **vacation 5**

1 형용사 끔찍한 ❑ 그들이 우리에게 그 끔찍한 소식을 전했다. ● 지독하게, 끔찍스럽게 부사 ❑ 너는 지독하게 굴었어. **2** 형용사 무시무시한, 엄청난 [강조] ❑ 우리가 엄청난 실수를 저질렀다. ● 몹시, 엄청나게 부사 ❑ 그는 몹시 아파 보인다.

> dreamed와 dreamt 모두 과거 및 과거 분사로 쓸 수 있다.

1 가산명사 꿈 ❑ 그는 클레어 꿈을 꿨다. **2** 타동사/자동사 꿈꾸다 ❑ 이보르는 버스에 타고 있는 꿈을 꿨다. **3** 가산명사 소망, 꿈 ❑ 그는 마침내 비행사가 되는 꿈을 이룬 참이었다. **4** 자동사 (소망이 이뤄지기를) 꿈꾸다 ❑ 학창시절에 그녀는 배우가 되기를 꿈꿨다. ❑ 대부분 사람들에게, 고가의 최신형 부엌은 단지 꿈으로만 꿀 수 있는 그런 것이다. **5** 형용사 꿈같은 ❑ 자메이카로의 꿈 같은 휴가 **6** 단수명사 이상 ❑ 그리스는 식물학자들의 이상으로 일컬어진다. **7** 가산명사 꿈 (같은 일) ❑ 바로 그 여자가 나타나면, 이 나쁜 꿈은 끝날 거야. **8** 자동사 꿈꾸다 [강조] ❑ 내가 너를 놀리는 것은 꿈도 못 꿀 일이야. **9** 타동사 꿈꾸다 [강조] ❑ 내가 여기에 가정을 꾸리리라고는 꿈에도 생각 못 했다. **10** 구 아주 잘하는 ❑ 그녀는 요리를 아주 잘했다. **11** 구 이상적인 ❑ 이 사람이 내 이상형일 수 있다. **12** 구 꿈에서도 [강조] ❑ 그 게임으로 이만한 돈을 따게 되리라고는 정말 꿈에서도 생각 못 할 일이다. **13** 구 상상했던 것보다 나은 [강조] ❑ 그녀는 이미 그녀가 상상했던 것 보다 훨씬 더 큰 성공을 거두었었다.

Word Web

dream

Dreams appear to happen most frequently during REM **sleep.** During these periods, the eyes move around quickly, the heart rate goes up, and respiration becomes more rapid. Seventy percent to 90 percent of people awakened during REM sleep report dreams. Only 10 percent to 15 percent of people **roused** during non-REM sleep remember dreaming. One of the most common dreams reported is of the person flying. Some people look for meaning in their dreams. They try to **interpret** the sights, sounds, and sensations of the dream. Some psychoanalysts say dreams show us the **unconscious** mind. Some later researchers argue that dreams are just random electrical impulses in the brain.

▶**dream up** PHRASAL VERB If you **dream up** a plan or idea, you work it out or create it in your mind. ❑ *I dreamed up a plan to solve both problems at once.*

구동사 고안하다 ❑ 나는 그 두 가지 문제를 한번에 해결할 수 있는 방안을 고안했다.

dream|er /dr**i**:mər/ (**dreamers**) N-COUNT If you describe someone as a **dreamer**, you mean that they spend a lot of time thinking about and planning for things that they would like to happen but which are improbable or impractical. ❑ *Far from being a dreamer, she's a level-headed pragmatist.*

가산명사 몽상가 ❑ 그녀는 몽상가와는 거리가 먼 냉철한 실용주의자이다.

dreamy /dr**i**:mi/ (**dreamier, dreamiest**) **1** ADJ If you say that someone has a **dreamy** expression, you mean that they are not paying attention to things around them and look as if they are thinking about something pleasant. ❑ *His face assumed a sort of dreamy expression.* **2** ADJ If you describe something as **dreamy**, you mean that you like it and that it seems gentle and soft, like something in a dream. [APPROVAL] ❑ *...dreamy shots of beautiful sunsets.*

1 형용사 꿈꾸는 듯한 ❑ 그는 다소 꿈꾸는 듯한 표정을 짓고 있었다. **2** 형용사 꿈이 같은 [마음에 듦] ❑ 아름다운 석양을 담은 꿈만 같은

dreary /dr**i**əri/ (**drearier, dreariest**) ADJ If you describe something as **dreary**, you mean that it is dull and depressing. ❑ *...a dreary little town in the Midwest.*

형용사 황량한 ❑ 미드웨스트에 있는 황량한 작은 마을

dredge /dr**ɛ**dʒ/ (**dredges, dredging, dredged**) V-T When people **dredge** a harbor, river, or other area of water, they remove mud and unwanted material from the bottom with a special machine in order to make it deeper or to look for something. ❑ *Police have spent weeks dredging the lake but have not found his body.*

타동사 물 밑바닥을 훑다 ❑ 경찰은 수주일 동안 그 호수 밑바닥을 훑어보았지만 그의 시체는 찾지는 못했다.

▶**dredge up** **1** PHRASAL VERB If someone **dredges up** a piece of information they learned a long time ago, or if they **dredge up** a distant memory, they manage to remember it. ❑ *...an American trying to dredge up some French or German learned in high school.* **2** PHRASAL VERB If someone **dredges up** a damaging or upsetting fact about your past, they remind you of it or tell other people about it. ❑ *She dredges up a minor misdemeanour: "You didn't give me money for the school trip."*

1 구동사 기억을 떠올리다 ❑ 고등학교 때 배웠던 불어나 독일어를 기억해 내려고 애쓰는 한 미국인 **2** 구동사 (과거사를) 들추다 ❑ 그녀는 "너 그 때 수학 여행비 안 냈었지?"라고 말하면서, 사소한 내 잘못을 들추어낸다.

drench /dr**ɛ**ntʃ/ (**drenches, drenching, drenched**) V-T To **drench** something or someone means to make them completely wet. ❑ *They turned fire hoses on the people and drenched them.* ❑ *...the idea of spending two whole days hanging on to a raft and getting drenched by icy water.*

타동사 흠뻑 적시다 ❑ 그들은 소방용 호스를 돌려 그 사람들을 물에 흠뻑 젖게 했다. ❑ 이틀 내내 뗏목에 매달려 차가운 얼음물에 흠뻑 젖는다는 생각

dress ◆◇◇ /dr**ɛ**s/ (**dresses, dressing, dressed**) **1** N-COUNT A **dress** is a piece of clothing worn by a woman or girl. It covers her body and part of her legs. ❑ *She was wearing a black dress.* **2** N-UNCOUNT You can refer to clothes worn by men or women as **dress**. ❑ *He's usually elegant in his dress.* **3** V-T/V-I When you **dress** or **dress yourself**, you put on clothes. ❑ *He told Sarah to wait while he dressed.* **4** V-T If you **dress** someone, for example a child, you put clothes on them. ❑ *She bathed her and dressed her in clean clothes.* →see **wear** **5** V-I If someone **dresses** in a particular way, they wear clothes of a particular style or color. ❑ *He dresses in a way that lets everyone know he's got authority.* **6** V-I If you **dress for** something, you put on special clothes for it. ❑ *We don't dress for dinner here.* **7** V-T When someone **dresses** a wound, they clean it and cover it. ❑ *The poor child never cried or protested when I was dressing her wounds.* **8** →see also **dressing, dressed**

1 가산명사 드레스, 원피스 ❑ 그녀는 검정 드레스를 입고 있었다. **2** 불가산명사 의복 ❑ 그는 평소 품위 있게 옷을 입는다. **3** 타동사/자동사 옷을 입다 ❑ 그는 사라에게 옷 입을 동안 기다리라고 말했다. **4** 타동사 옷을 입히다 ❑ 그녀는 아이를 목욕시킨 후 깨끗한 옷을 입혔다. **5** 자동사 옷 입다 ❑ 그는 그의 권위가 살아나도록 옷을 입는다. **6** 자동사 (특별한 모임을 위한) 정장하다 ❑ 이 곳에서는 만찬용 정장을 입지 않는다. **7** 타동사 붕대를 감다 ❑ 내가 상처를 붕대로 감쌀 때도 그 불쌍한 아이는 전혀 울지도 저항하지도 않았다.

Word Partnership	dress의 연어
V.	**put on** a dress, **wear a** dress **1**
ADJ.	**casual** dress, **formal** dress, **traditional** dress **2**
ADV.	dress **well 5**

▶**dress down** PHRASAL VERB If you **dress down**, you wear clothes that are less formal than usual. ❑ *She dresses down in dark glasses and baggy clothes to avoid hordes of admirers.*

구동사 허름한 옷을 입다 ❑ 그녀는 팬들을 피하기 위해서 검은 안경을 쓰고 헐렁한 옷을 입는다.

▶**dress up** **1** PHRASAL VERB If you **dress up** or **dress** yourself **up**, you put on different clothes, in order to make yourself look more formal than usual or to disguise yourself. ❑ *You do not need to dress up for dinner.* ❑ *I just love the fun of dressing up in another era's clothing.* **2** PHRASAL VERB If you **dress** someone **up**, you give them special clothes to wear, in order to make them look more formal or to disguise them. ❑ *Mother loved to dress me up.* **3** PHRASAL VERB If you **dress** something **up**, you try to make it seem more attractive, acceptable, or interesting than it really is. ❑ *Politicians are happier to dress up their ruthless ambition as a necessary pursuit of the public good.*

1 구동사 옷을 차려 입다 ❑ 만찬을 위해 옷을 차려입을 필요는 없다. ❑ 나는 다른 시대의 옷을 차려입어 보는 것을 정말 좋아한다. **2** 구동사 옷을 차려입히다 ❑ 어머니는 나에게 옷을 차려입히는 것을 좋아하셨다. **3** 구동사 치장하다 ❑ 정치인들은 무자비한 자신들의 야망을 공공의 이익을 위해 반드시 추구해야 할 것이라고 치장하는 것에 더 즐거워한다.

dressed ◆◇◇ /dr**ɛ**st/ **1** ADJ If you are **dressed**, you are wearing clothes rather than being naked or wearing your nightclothes. If you **get dressed**, you put on your clothes. ❑ *He was fully dressed, including shoes.* →see **wear** **2** ADJ If you are **dressed** in a particular way, you are wearing clothes of a particular color or kind. [v-link ADJ in/as n, adv ADJ] ❑ *...a tall thin woman dressed in black.* →see also **well-dressed**

1 형용사 옷을 입고 있는 ❑ 그는 구두까지 포함해서 옷을 다 갖춰 입고 있었다. **2** 형용사 옷을 입은 ❑ 검은 옷을 입은 키가 크고 마른 여성

dress|er /dr**ɛ**sər/ (**dressers**) **1** N-COUNT A **dresser** is a chest of drawers, sometimes with a mirror on the top. [AM] **2** N-COUNT A **dresser** is a piece of furniture which has cabinets or drawers in the lower part and shelves in the top part. It is usually used for storing china. [mainly BRIT] **3** N-COUNT You can use **dresser** to refer to the kind of clothes that a person wears. For example, if you say that someone is a **casual dresser**, you mean that they wear casual clothes. ❑ *She had always been an elegant dresser and had on one of her linen frocks.*

1 가산명사 화장대 [미국영어] **2** 가산명사 찬장 [주로 영국영어] **3** 가산명사 옷차림이 ~한 사람 ❑ 그녀는 항상 옷차림이 우아했고 당시 마침 드레스를 입고 있었다.

dress|ing /dr**ɛ**sɪŋ/ (**dressings**) **1** N-MASS A salad **dressing** is a mixture of oil, vinegar, and herbs or flavorings, which you pour over salad. ❑ *Mix the ingredients for the dressing in a bowl.* **2** N-COUNT A **dressing** is a covering that is put on a wound to protect it while it heals. ❑ *Miss Finkelstein will put a dressing on your thumb.*

1 물질명사 샐러드 드레싱 ❑ 드레싱 재료를 그릇에 넣고 섞어라. **2** 가산명사 붕대 ❑ 핀켈스타인 양이 네 손가락에 붕대를 감아 줄 것이다.

dress|ing gown (**dressing gowns**) also **dressing-gown** N-COUNT A **dressing gown** is a long, loose garment which you wear over your nightclothes when you are not in bed. ❑ *What was he doing in his dressing gown at this time of day?*

가산명사 (잠옷 위에 덧입는) 가운 ❑ 이런 대낮에 그 남자는 잠옷 가운을 입고 뭐하고 있었던 거니?

a b c d e f g h i j k l m n o p q r s t u v w x y z

dress re|hears|al (dress rehearsals) **■** N-COUNT The **dress rehearsal** of a play, opera, or show is the final rehearsal before it is performed, in which the performers wear their costumes and the lights and scenery are all used as they will be in the performance. ❏ *We went to all the dress rehearsals together.* **■** N-COUNT You can describe an event as a **dress rehearsal** for a later, more important event when it indicates how the later event will be. ❏ *These elections, you could almost say, are a dress rehearsal for the real elections.*

■ 가산명사 (무대 의상을 입고 하는) 총연습 ❏ 우리는 모두 총연습을 했다. **■** 가산명사 전초전 ❏ 당신이 이미 알겠지만, 이번 선거는 실제 선거의 전초전이다.

drew /dru/ **Drew** is the past tense of **draw**.

draw의 과거

drib|ble /drɪbⁿl/ (dribbles, dribbling, dribbled) **■** V-T/V-I If a liquid **dribbles** somewhere, or if you **dribble** it, it drops down slowly or flows in a thin stream. ❏ *Sweat dribbled down Hart's face.* **■** V-T/V-I When players **dribble** the ball in a game such as basketball or soccer, they keep kicking or tapping it quickly in order to keep it moving. ❏ *He dribbled the ball toward Ferris.* ❏ *He dribbled past four defenders.* **■** V-I If a person **dribbles**, saliva drops slowly from their mouth. ❏ *...to protect cot sheets when the baby dribbles.*

■ 타동사/자동사 (물이) 똑똑 흐르다; (물이) 똑똑 떨어지다 ❏ 하트의 얼굴에서 땀이 뚝뚝 떨어졌다. **■** 타동사/자동사 드리블하다 ❏ 그는 페리스 쪽으로 공을 드리블해 갔다. ❏ 그는 공을 드리블해서 수비수 네 명을 제쳤다. **■** 자동사 침을 흘리다 ❏ 아기가 침을 흘릴 때 침대보를 안 젖게 하려고

dried /draɪd/ ADJ **Dried** food or milk has had all the water removed from it so that it will last for a long time. [ADJ N] ❏ *...an infusion which may be prepared from the fresh plant or the dried herb.* →see also **dry**

형용사 건조된 ❏ 날 채소와 건조된 약초를 우려낸 물

dri|er /draɪər/ →see **dry** →see **dryer**

drift ◆◇◇ /drɪft/ (drifts, drifting, drifted) **■** V-I When something **drifts** somewhere, it is carried there by the movement of wind or water. ❏ *We proceeded to drift on up the river.* **■** V-I If someone or something **drifts into** a situation, they get into that situation in a way that is not planned or controlled. ❏ *We need to offer young people drifting into crime an alternative set of values.* **■** V-I If you say that someone **drifts** around, you mean that they travel from place to place without a plan or settled way of life. [DISAPPROVAL] ❏ *You've been drifting from job to job without any real commitment.* **■** N-COUNT A **drift** is a movement away from somewhere or something, or a movement toward somewhere or something different. ❏ *...the drift toward the cities.* **■** V-I To **drift** somewhere means to move there slowly or gradually. ❏ *As rural factories shed labour, people drift toward the cities.* **■** V-I If sounds **drift** somewhere, they can be heard but they are not very loud. ❏ *Cool summer dance sounds are drifting from the stereo indoors.* **■** V-I If snow **drifts**, it builds up into piles as a result of the movement of the wind. ❏ *The snow, except where it drifted, was only calf-deep.* **■** N-COUNT A **drift** is a mass of snow that has built up into a pile as a result of the movement of wind. ❏ *A nine-year-old boy was trapped in a snow drift.* **■** N-SING The **drift of** an argument or speech is the general point that is being made in it. ❏ *Grace was beginning to get his drift.*
→see **continents**

■ 자동사 표류하다 ❏ 우리는 강 상류에서 계속 표류해 나아갔다. **■** 자동사 -한 상황으로 빠져들다 ❏ 우리는 범죄에 빠져드는 젊은이들에게 가치 있는 다른 삶이 있음을 알려줄 필요가 있다. **■** 자동사 (정처 없이) 떠돌다 [탕탕줄음] ❏ 당신은 어느 한 군데 몰두하지 못하고 이 직장 저 직장 떠돌아다니고 있다. **■** 가산명사 이동 **■** 자동사 천천히 이동하다 ❏ 지방에 있는 공장들이 노동자들을 해고함에 따라, 사람들이 도시로 이동하고 있다. **■** 자동사 들려오다 ❏ 실내 스테레오에서 멋진 여름 무곡이 들려온다. **■** 자동사 (바람에 날려) 쌓이다 ❏ 바람에 날려 쌓인 곳 말고는 눈이 겨우 종아리 정도 깊이만큼 쌓였다. **■** 가산명사 눈더미 ❏ 아홉 살 난 소년이 쌓인 눈더미에 갇혔다. **■** 단수명사 취지 ❏ 그레이스는 그 사람이 말하는 취지를 파악하기 시작했다.

▶**drift off** PHRASAL VERB If you **drift off** to sleep, you gradually fall asleep. ❏ *It was only when he finally drifted off to sleep that the headaches eased.*

구동사 서서히 -에 떨어지다 ❏ 그가 마침내 잠에 떨어지고 나서야 두통이 잠잠해졌다.

drill /drɪl/ (drills, drilling, drilled) **■** N-COUNT A **drill** is a tool or machine that you use for making holes. ❏ *...a dentist's drill.* **■** V-T/V-I When you **drill into** something or **drill** a hole in something, you make a hole in it using a drill. ❏ *He drilled into the wall of Lili's bedroom.* **■** V-I When people **drill for** oil or water, they search for it by drilling deep holes in the ground or in the bottom of the sea. ❏ *There have been proposals to drill for more oil.* **■** N-VAR A **drill** is repeated training for a group of people, especially soldiers, so that they can do something quickly and efficiently. ❏ *The Marines carried out landing exercises in a drill that includes 18 ships and 90 aircraft.* **■** N-COUNT A **drill** is a routine exercise or activity, in which people practice what they should do in dangerous situations. ❏ *...a fire drill.* →see **oil**

■ 가산명사 드릴 ❏ 치과 의사가 쓰는 드릴 **■** 타동사/자동사 드릴로 구멍을 뚫다 ❏ 그는 드릴로 릴리의 침실 벽에 구멍을 뚫었다. **■** 자동사 시추하다 ❏ 더 많은 석유를 얻을 수 있도록 시추를 해야 한다는 안들이 제기되어 왔다. **■** 가산명사 또는 불가산명사 군사 훈련 ❏ 해병대는 18척의 함대와 90대의 항공기가 동원된 군사 훈련에서 상륙 훈련을 했다. **■** 가산명사 훈련 ❏ 소방 훈련

drink ◆◆◇ /drɪŋk/ (drinks, drinking, drank, drunk) **■** V-T/V-I When you **drink** a liquid, you take it into your mouth and swallow it. ❏ *He drank his cup of tea.* **■** V-I To **drink** means to drink alcohol. ❏ *By his own admission, he was smoking and drinking too much.* ● **drink|ing** N-UNCOUNT ❏ *She had left him because of his drinking.* **■** N-COUNT A **drink** is an amount of a liquid which you drink. ❏ *I'll get you a drink of water.* **■** N-COUNT A **drink** is an alcoholic drink. ❏ *She felt like a drink after a hard day.* **■** N-UNCOUNT **Drink** is alcohol, such as beer, wine, or whiskey. ❏ *Too much drink is bad for your health.*

■ 타동사/자동사 마시다 ❏ 그는 차 한잔을 마셨다. **■** 자동사 술을 마시다 ❏ 본인이 인정하는 바에 의하면, 그는 지나치게 흡연과 음주를 하고 있었다. ● 음주 불가산명사 ❏ 그녀는 그의 음주 때문에 그를 떠났다. **■** 가산명사 한 잔, 한 모금 ❏ 물 한 잔 갖다 줄게. **■** 가산명사 술 한 잔 ❏ 그녀는 힘든 하루를 보내고 나니 술 한 잔이 생각났다. **■** 불가산명사 술 ❏ 지나친 음주는 건강에 해롭다.

Thesaurus	drink의 참조어
v.	gulp, sip **■**
N.	beer, liquor, spirits, wine **■**

▶**drink to** PHRASAL VERB When people **drink to** someone or something, they wish them success, good luck, or good health before having an alcoholic drink. ❏ *Let's drink to his memory, eh?*

구동사 건배하다 ❏ 그 사람을 기억하며 건배하자.

drink-driver (drink-drivers) N-COUNT also **drink driver** A **drink-driver** is someone who drives after drinking more than the amount of alcohol that is legally allowed. [BRIT; AM **drunk driver**] ❏ *Drink-drivers cause ten deaths a week.*

가산명사 음주 운전자 [영국영어; 미국영어 **drunk driver**] ❏ 음주 운전자로 인해 일 주일에 10건의 사망 사고가 난다.

drink|er /drɪŋkər/ (drinkers) **■** N-COUNT If someone is a tea **drinker** or a beer **drinker**, for example, they regularly drink tea or beer. ❏ *Sherry drinkers far outnumber wine drinkers or whiskey drinkers.* **■** N-COUNT If you describe someone as a **drinker**, you mean that they drink alcohol, especially in large quantities. ❏ *I'm not a heavy drinker.*

■ 가산명사 -을 즐겨 마시는 사람 ❏ 셰리주를 즐겨 마시는 사람이 와인이나 위스키 애주가보다 수적으로 훨씬 많다. **■** 가산명사 음주가 ❏ 나는 폭주가는 아니다.

drip /drɪp/ (drips, dripping, dripped) **■** V-T/V-I When liquid **drips** somewhere, or you **drip** it somewhere, it falls in individual drops. ❏ *Sit your child forward and let the blood drip into a tissue or on to the floor.* ❏ *Amid the trees the sea mist was dripping and moisture formed on Tom's glasses.* **■** V-I When something **drips**, drops of liquid fall from it. ❏ *A tap in the kitchen was dripping.* ❏ *Lou was dripping with perspiration.* **■** N-COUNT A **drip** is a small individual drop of a liquid. ❏ *Drips*

■ 타동사/자동사 똑똑 떨어지다; 똑똑 떨어뜨리다 ❏ 아이가 몸을 앞으로 숙이도록 앉힌 다음 피가 휴지나 바닥으로 떨어지게 해라. ❏ 나무 사이로 바다 안개가 방울져 떨어지며 톰의 안경에는 물기가 맺혔다. **■** 자동사 물방울을 떨어뜨리다 ❏ 부엌 수도꼭지에서 물방울이 떨어지고 있었다. ❏ 로우는 땀을 뚝뚝 흘리고

of water rolled down the trousers of his uniform. 4 N-COUNT A **drip** is a piece of medical equipment by which a liquid is slowly passed through a tube into a patient's blood. ❑ *I had a bad attack of pneumonia and spent two days in hospital on a drip.* 5 V-I If you say that something **is dripping with** a particular thing, you mean that it contains a lot of that thing. [LITERARY] [usu cont] ❑ *They were dazed by window displays dripping with diamonds and furs.*

있었다. 3 가산명사 물방울 ❑ 물방울들이 그의 유니폼 바지를 타고 흘러내렸다. 4 가산명사 링거 주사 ❑ 나는 심한 폐렴에 걸려서 이틀 동안 병원에서 링거 주사를 맞으며 지냈다. 5 자동사 -이 넘쳐나다 [문예체] ❑ 그들은 쇼윈도에 넘쳐 나게 진열되어 있는 다이아몬드와 모피에 눈이 부셨다.

drive ♦♦♦ /draɪv/ (**drives, driving, drove, driven**) 1 V-T/V-I When you **drive** somewhere, you operate a car or other vehicle and control its movement and direction. ❑ *I drove into town and went to a restaurant for dinner.* ❑ *She never learned to drive.* ● **driv|ing** N-UNCOUNT ❑ *...a qualified driving instructor.* 2 V-T If you **drive** someone somewhere, you take them there in a car or other vehicle. ❑ *His daughter Carly drove him to the train station.* 3 N-COUNT A **drive** is a trip in a car or other vehicle. ❑ *I thought we might go for a drive on Sunday.* 4 N-COUNT A **drive** is a wide piece of hard ground, or sometimes a private road, that leads from the road to a person's house. ❑ *The boys followed Eleanor up the drive to the house.* 5 V-T If something **drives** a machine, it supplies the power that makes it work. ❑ *The current flows into electric motors that drive the wheels.* 6 N-COUNT You use **drive** to refer to the mechanical part of a computer which reads the data on disks and tapes, or writes data onto them. ❑ *The firm specialized in supplying pieces of equipment, such as terminals, tape drives, or printers.* →see also **disk drive** 7 V-T If you **drive** something such as a nail **into** something else, you push it in or hammer it in using a lot of effort. ❑ *I had to use our sledgehammer to drive the pegs into the side of the path.* 8 V-I If the wind, rain, or snow **drives** in a particular direction, it moves with great force in that direction. ❑ *Rain drove against the window.* ● **driv|ing** ADJ [ADJ n] ❑ *He crashed into a tree in driving rain.* 9 V-T If you **drive** people or animals somewhere, you make them go to or from that place. ❑ *The last offensive drove thousands of people into Thailand.* 10 V-T To **drive** someone **into** a particular state or situation means to force them into that state or situation. ❑ *The recession and hospital bills drove them into bankruptcy.* 11 V-T The desire or feeling that **drives** a person **to** do something, especially something extreme, is the desire or feeling that causes them to do it. ❑ *More than once, depression drove him to attempt suicide.* ❑ *Jealousy drives people to murder.* 12 N-UNCOUNT If you say that someone has **drive**, you mean they have energy and determination. ❑ *John will be best remembered for his drive and enthusiasm.* 13 N-COUNT A **drive** is a very strong need or desire in human beings that makes them act in particular ways. ❑ *...compelling, dynamic sex drives.* 14 N-SING A **drive** is a special effort made by a group of people for a particular purpose. ❑ *The ANC is about to launch a nationwide recruitment drive.* 15 N-IN-NAMES **Drive** is used in the names of some streets. ❑ *...23 Queen's Drive, Malvern, Worcestershire.* 16 →see also **driving** →see **car**

1 타동사/자동사 운전하다 ❑ 나는 저녁 식사를 하러 시내로 차를 몰아 한 식당으로 갔다. ❑ 그녀는 운전하는 법을 한 번도 배우지 않았다. ● 운전 불가산명사 ❑ 자격 있는 운전 강사 2 타동사 차로 데려다 주다 ❑ 그의 딸 칼리가 차로 그를 기차역까지 데려다 주었다. 3 가산명사 드라이브 ❑ 난 우리가 일요일에 드라이브를 할 수도 있을 거라고 생각했다. 4 가산명사 (도로에서 집 차고까지의) 진입로 ❑ 그 소년들은 진입로에서 집까지 엘리노를 따라갔다. 5 타동사 가동시키다, 움직이게 하다 ❑ 전류가 바퀴를 움직이게 하는 전기 모터 쪽으로 흐른다. 6 가산명사 (컴퓨터) 드라이브 ❑ 그 회사는 단말기나 테이프 드라이브, 혹은 프린터와 같은 컴퓨터 장비를 공급하는 전문 업체였다. 7 타동사 (망치로) 박다 ❑ 나는 길 한쪽에 말뚝을 박기 위해서 큰 망치를 사용해야만 했다. 8 자동사 강하게 몰아치다 ❑ 비가 창문을 때리며 몰아쳤다. ● (비나 바람이) 몰아치는 형용사 ❑ 그는 몰아치는 빗속에서 나무를 들이받았다. 9 타동사 몰고 가다 ❑ 마지막 공격 때문에 수천 명의 사람들이 태국으로 가야 했다. 10 타동사 -한 상태로 만들다 ❑ 불경기와 병원 치료비 때문에 그들은 파산하게 되었다. 11 타동사 -하도록 내몰다 ❑ 그는 여러 번 우울증 때문에 자살을 시도했었다. ❑ 질투는 사람들이 살인을 하도록 내몬다. 12 불가산명사 추진력 ❑ 존은 추진력과 열정 때문에 가장 많이 기억될 것이다. 13 가산명사 충동 ❑ 강하고 역동적인 성적 충동 14 단수명사 조직적인 운동 ❑ 에이엔 씨는 전국적으로 회원 모집 운동을 시작하려고 한다. 15 이름명사 드라이브 (거리 이름) ❑ 우스터셔 주의 맬번 퀸즈 드라이브 23번지

▸**drive away** PHRASAL VERB To **drive** people **away** means to make them want to go away or stay away. ❑ *Patrick's boorish rudeness soon drove Monica's friends away.*

구동사 -를 쫓아버리다 ❑ 패트릭이 거칠고 무례하게 굴어서 모니카의 친구들이 곧 가버렸다.

drive-by ADJ A **drive-by** shooting or a **drive-by** murder involves shooting someone from a moving car. [ADJ n] ❑ *He was killed by three shots to the head in a drive-by shooting.*

형용사 (폭력단들이) 차를 타고 가며 ❑ 그는 폭력단들이 차를 타고 가면서 쏜 총알 세 발을 머리에 맞고 사망했다.

drive-in (**drive-ins**) N-COUNT A **drive-in** is a restaurant, movie theater, or other commercial place which is specially designed so that customers can use the services provided while staying in their cars. ❑ *...a small neat town, uncluttered by stores, gas stations, or fast food drive-ins.*

가산명사 자동차 전용 ❑ 상점, 주유소, 자동차 전용, 패스트푸드 점들이 잘 정리되어 늘어서 있는 작고 깨끗한 마을

driv|en /drɪvᵊn/ **Driven** is the past participle of **drive**.

drive의 과거 분사

driv|er ♦♦◊ /draɪvər/ (**drivers**) 1 N-COUNT The **driver** of a vehicle is the person who is driving it. ❑ *The driver got out of his van.* 2 N-COUNT A **driver** is a computer program that controls a device such as a printer. [COMPUTING] ❑ *Printer driver software includes standard features such as print layout and fit-to-page printing.*

1 가산명사 운전자 ❑ 그 운전자가 자신의 트럭에서 내렸다. 2 가산명사 드라이버 (컴퓨터 프로그램) [컴퓨터] ❑ 프린터 드라이버 소프트웨어는 인쇄 양식과 페이지 조절 기능과 같은 표준 사양이 들어 있다.

driv|er's li|cense (**driver's licenses**) N-COUNT A **driver's license** is a card showing that you are qualified to drive because you have passed a driving test. [AM; BRIT **driving licence**]

가산명사 운전면허증 [미국영어; 영국영어 driving licence]

drive-through (**drive-throughs**) ADJ A **drive-through** store, bank, or restaurant is one where you can be served without leaving your car. [ADJ n] ❑ *...a drive-through burger bar.* ● N-COUNT **Drive-through** is also a noun. ❑ *I got some dinner at a drive-through and headed home.*

형용사 자동차를 탄 채로 이용 가능한 ❑ 자동차를 탄 채로 이용 가능한 햄버거 가게 ● 가산명사 드라이브스루 (자동차를 탄 채로 이용하는 식당, 은행 등) ❑ 나는 드라이브스루 식당에서 저녁을 사서 집으로 향했다.

drive|way /draɪvweɪ/ (**driveways**) N-COUNT A **driveway** is a piece of hard ground that leads from the road to the front of a house, garage, or other building. ❑ *I was running down the driveway to the car and I lost my balance.*

가산명사 진입로 ❑ 나는 집에서 차 있는 데까지 진입로를 달려가다가 몸의 중심을 잃었다.

driv|ing /draɪvɪŋ/ ADJ The **driving** force or idea behind something that happens or is done is the main thing that has a strong effect on it and makes it happen or be done in a particular way. [ADJ n] ❑ *Consumer spending was the driving force behind the economic growth in the summer.* →see also **drive**

형용사 원동력이 되는 ❑ 소비자 지출이 여름철 경제 성장을 가능하게 한 원동력이었다.

driv|ing li|cence (**driving licences**) N-COUNT A **driving licence** is a card showing that you are qualified to drive because you have passed a driving test. [BRIT; AM **driver's license**]

가산명사 운전면허증 [영국영어; 미국영어 driver's license]

driz|zle /drɪzᵊl/ (**drizzles, drizzling, drizzled**) 1 N-UNCOUNT **Drizzle** is light rain falling in fine drops. [also *a* N] ❑ *The drizzle had now stopped and the sun was breaking through.* 2 V-I If it **is drizzling**, it is raining very lightly. ❑ *Clouds had come down and it was starting to drizzle.* →see **precipitation**

1 불가산명사 보슬비, 이슬비 ❑ 보슬비가 이제 멈추고 태양이 구름 사이를 헤치고 나오고 있었다. 2 자동사 보슬비가 내리다 ❑ 구름이 짙어지더니 비가 부슬부슬 내리기 시작했다.

drone /droʊn/ (**drones, droning, droned**) 1 V-I If something **drones**, it makes a low, continuous, dull noise. ❑ *Above him an invisible plane droned through the night sky.* ● N-SING **Drone** is also a noun. ❑ *...the constant drone of the motorways.* 2 V-I If you say that someone **drones**, you mean that they keep talking about something in a boring way. [DISAPPROVAL] ❑ *Chambers' voice droned, maddening as an insect around his head.* ● N-SING **Drone** is also a noun. ❑ *The minister's voice was a*

1 자동사 윙윙거리다 ❑ 그의 머리 위에 보이지 않는 비행기 한 대가 밤하늘을 가르며 윙윙거렸다. ● 단수명사 윙윙거리는 소리 ❑ 고속도로에서 끊임없이 웅웅거리는 소리 2 자동사 웅웅거리듯 말하다 [탐탁찮음] ❑ 의원들의 말소리가 마치 벌레소리처럼 미치도록 그의 머리 주변에서

A

relentless **drone**. ● PHRASAL VERB **Drone on** means the same as **drone**. ❑ *Aunt Maimie's voice droned on.*

● 단수명사 웅웅거리는 말투 ❑ 그 목사의 목소리가 끝이 없이 웅웅거렸다. ● 구동사 따분하게 웅웅거리다 ❑ 메이미 이모는 계속해서 뭐라고 웅웅거렸다.

B

drool /dru̱l/ (**drools, drooling, drooled**) **1** V-I To **drool over** someone or something means to look at them with great pleasure, perhaps in an exaggerated or ridiculous way. [DISAPPROVAL] ❑ *Fashion editors drooled over every item.* **2** V-I If a person or animal **drools**, saliva drops slowly from their mouth. ❑ *My dog Jacques is drooling on my shoulder.*

1 자동사 (좋아서) 침을 흘리다 [탐탁찮음] ❑ 패션지 편집자들이 모든 품목에 침을 흘렸다. **2** 자동사 침을 흘리다 ❑ 내 개 자크가 내 어깨 위에서 침을 계속 흘리고 있다.

C

droop /dru̱p/ (**droops, drooping, drooped**) V-I If something **droops**, it hangs or leans downward with no strength or firmness. ❑ *Crook's eyelids drooped and he yawned.* ● N-SING **Droop** is also a noun. ❑ *...the droop of his shoulders.*

자동사 축 처지다 ❑ 크룩이 눈꺼풀이 처지며 하품을 했다. ● 단수명사 축 처짐 ❑ 그의 어깨가 축 처짐

D

drop ♦♦◇ /dro̱p/ (**drops, dropping, dropped**) **1** V-T/V-I If a level or amount **drops** or if someone or something **drops** it, it quickly becomes less. ❑ *Temperatures can drop to freezing at night.* ❑ *His blood pressure had dropped severely.* ● N-COUNT **Drop** is also a noun. ❑ *He was prepared to take a drop in wages.* **2** V-T If you **drop** something, you accidentally let it fall. ❑ *I dropped my glasses and broke them.* **3** V-I If something **drops onto** something else, it falls onto that thing. If something **drops from** somewhere, it falls from that place. ❑ *He felt hot tears dropping onto his fingers.* **4** V-T/V-I If you **drop** something somewhere or if it **drops** there, you deliberately let it fall there. ❑ *Drop the noodles into the water.* ❑ *Bombs drop around us and the floor shudders.* ● **dropping** N-UNCOUNT [usu N of n] ❑ *...the dropping of the first atomic bomb.* **5** V-T/V-I If a person or a part of their body **drops** to a lower position, or if they **drop** a part of their body to a lower position, they move to that position, often in a tired and lifeless way. ❑ *Nancy dropped into a nearby chair.* ❑ *She let her head drop.* **6** V-I To **drop** is used in expressions such as **to be about to drop** and **to dance until you drop** to emphasize that you are exhausted and can no longer continue doing something. [EMPHASIS] [no cont] ❑ *She looked about to drop.* **7** V-T/V-I If your voice **drops** or if you **drop** your voice, you speak more quietly. ❑ *Her voice will drop to a dismissive whisper.* **8** V-T If you **drop** someone or something somewhere, you take them somewhere and leave them there, usually in a car or other vehicle. ❑ *He dropped me outside the hotel.* ● PHRASAL VERB **Drop off** means the same as **drop**. ❑ *Just drop me off at the airport.* **9** V-T If you **drop** an idea, course of action, or habit, you do not continue with it. ❑ *He was told to drop the idea.* ● **dropping** N-UNCOUNT ❑ *This was one of the factors that led to President Suharto's dropping of his previous objections.* **10** V-T If someone **is dropped** by a sports team or organization, they are no longer included in that team or employed by that organization. [usu passive] ❑ *The country's captain was dropped from the tour party to England.* **11** V-I If you **drop** to a lower position in a sports competition, you move to that position. ❑ *Britain has dropped from second to third place in the league.* **12** N-COUNT A **drop of** a liquid is a very small amount of it shaped like a little ball. In informal English, you can also use **drop** when you are referring to a very small amount of something such as a drink. ❑ *...a drop of blue ink.* **13** N-PLURAL **Drops** are a kind of medicine which you put drop by drop into your ears, eyes, or nose. ❑ *And he had to have these drops in his eyes as well.* **14** N-COUNT You use **drop** to talk about vertical distances. For example, a thirty-foot **drop** is a distance of thirty feet between the top of a cliff or wall and the bottom of it. ❑ *There was a sheer drop just outside my window.*

1 타동사/자동사 떨어지다 ❑ 밤에는 온도가 영하로 떨어질 수도 있다. ❑ 그의 혈압이 상당히 떨어졌었다. ● 가산명사 삭감 ❑ 그는 임금 삭감을 각오하고 있었다. **2** 타동사 떨어뜨리다 ❑ 내가 안경을 떨어뜨려서 깨져버렸다. **3** 자동사 떨어지다 ❑ 그는 뜨거운 눈물이 손가락 위로 떨어지는 것을 느꼈다. **4** 타동사/자동사 떨어뜨리다, -에 넣다; 떨어지다 ❑ 국수를 물속에 넣어라. ❑ 폭탄이 우리 주위로 떨어져서 바닥이 흔들렸다. ● 투하 불가산명사 최초의 핵폭탄 투하 **5** 타동사/자동사 푹 쓰러지다; 폴싹 내려놓다 ❑ 낸시는 옆에 있는 의자에 푹 쓰러졌다. ❑ 그녀가 머리가 푹 수그러졌다. **6** 자동사 쓰러지다 [강조] ❑ 그녀는 금방이라도 쓰러질 것 같았다. **7** 타동사/자동사 (목소리를) 낮추다 ❑ 그녀가 무시하듯 목소리를 낮출 것이다. **8** 타동사 (차에서) 내려 주다 ❑ 그는 나를 호텔 밖에다 내려 주었다. ● 구동사 (차에서) 내려주다 ❑ 저를 그냥 공항에 내려 주세요. **9** 타동사 (생각, 습관 등을) 중단하다 ❑ 그는 그 계획을 중단하라고 들었다. ● 취하 불가산명사 ❑ 이것이 수하르토 대통령이 그가 이전에 행사했던 거부권을 취하하도록 만든 요인들 중 하나였다. **10** 타동사 탈락되다 ❑ 그 나라의 팀장은 영국행 여행단에서 탈락되었다. **11** 자동사 떨어지다 ❑ 영국팀은 그 리그 전에서 2위에서 3위로 떨어졌다. **12** 가산명사 방울 ❑ 파란 잉크 한 방울 **13** 복수명사 (눈, 귀, 코에 떨어뜨리는) 물약 ❑ 그리고 그는 눈에도 이 안약을 넣어야 했다. **14** 가산명사 급경사 ❑ 내 창문 바로 바깥쪽으로 급경사가 나 있었다.

Do not confuse **drop** and **fall**. Although things can **drop** or **fall** by accident, note that **fall** is not followed by an object, so you cannot say that someone "falls" something. However, you can say that they **drop** something, or that something **drops**. ❑ *Leaves were falling to the ground... He dropped his cigar... Plate after plate dropped from his fingers.* You say that a person **drops** when they jump straight down from something, for example, when someone jumps from a plane using a parachute. If someone **falls**, it is usually because of an accident. ❑ *He stumbled and fell.* **Drop** and **fall** are also nouns. A **drop** is the height of something when you imagine falling off it. ❑ *Sixteen hundred feet is a considerable drop.* A **fall** is what happens when someone has an accident. ❑ *I had been badly bruised by the fall.*

drop과 fall을 혼동하지 않도록 하라. 사물이 우연히 drop 또는 fall 할 수는 있지만, fall은 뒤에 목적어가 오지 않는다는 점을 유의하라. 그러니, 누군가가 무엇을 drop하거나, 무엇이 drop한다고 말할 수 있다. ❑ 나뭇잎이 땅으로 떨어지고 있었다... 그가 피우던 여송연을 떨어뜨렸다... 접시들이 연이어 그의 손 끝에서 떨어졌다. 누가 어디에서 바로 뛰어내린다면, 예를 들어 낙하산으로 비행기에서 뛰어내리면, 그 사람이 drop한다고 말한다. 누가 fall하면, 대개 사고 때문이다. ❑ 그는 비틀거리다가 넘어졌다. drop과 fall은 명사이기도 하다. drop은 무엇으로부터 떨어지는 것을 상상할 때 그 높이를 말한다. ❑ 1,600 피트는 상당한 낙차이다. fall은 사고가 났을 때 발생하는 것이다. ❑ 나는 그 추락으로 심한 타박상을 입었다.

15 PHRASE If you **drop a hint**, you give a hint or say something in a casual way. ❑ *If I drop a few hints he might give me a cutting.* **16** PHRASE If you want someone to **drop the subject**, **drop it**, or **let it drop**, you want them to stop talking about something, often because you are annoyed that they keep talking about it. ❑ *Mary Ann wished he would just drop it.* **17** to **drop dead** →see **dead**. **at the drop of a hat** →see **hat**. **a drop in the ocean** →see **ocean**

15 구 힌트를 주다 ❑ 내가 힌트 몇 가지를 주면 그가 내게 할인을 해 줄지도 모른다. **16** 구 그만 말하다, 그만하다 ❑ 메리 앤은 그가 그만 좀 했으면 하고 바랐다.

Word Partnership	drop의 연어	
N.	drop **in sales** **1**	
	drop **a ball** **2**	
	drop **a bomb** **4**	
	drop **of blood, tear** drop, drop **of water** **12**	
	drop **a hint** **15**	
ADJ.	**sudden** drop **1**	
	steep drop **14**	

▶**drop by** PHRASAL VERB If you **drop by**, you visit someone informally. ❑ *She and Danny will drop by later.*

구동사 잠깐 들르다 ❑ 그녀와 대니는 나중에 잠깐 들를 것이다.

▶**drop in** PHRASAL VERB If you **drop in on** someone, you visit them informally, usually without having arranged it. ❑ *Why not drop in for a chat?*

▶**drop off** ◼ →see **drop** 8 ◻ PHRASAL VERB If you **drop off** to sleep, you go to sleep. [INFORMAL] ❑ *I must have dropped off to sleep.* ◼ PHRASAL VERB If the level of something **drops off**, it becomes less. ❑ *Sales to the British forces are expected to drop off.*

▶**drop out** PHRASAL VERB If someone **drops out of** college or a race, for example, they leave it without finishing what they started. ❑ *He'd dropped out of high school at the age of 16.* →see also **dropout**

Word Link	*let* ≈ *little : book*let*, *drop*let*, *in*let*

drop|let /drɒplɪt/ (**droplets**) N-COUNT A **droplet** is a very small drop of liquid. ❑ *Droplets of sweat were welling up on his forehead.* →see **precipitation**

drop|out /drɒpaʊt/ (**dropouts**) also **drop-out** ◼ N-COUNT If you describe someone as a **dropout**, you disapprove of the fact that they have rejected the accepted ways of society, for example by not having a regular job. [DISAPPROVAL] ❑ *...long-haired, dope-smoking dropouts.* ◻ N-COUNT A **dropout** is someone who has left school or college before they have finished their studies. ❑ *...high-school dropouts.* ◼ ADJ If you refer to the **dropout** rate, you are referring to the number of people who leave a school or college early, or leave a course or other activity before they have finished it. [ADJ n] ❑ *The dropout rate among students is currently one in three.*

drought /draʊt/ (**droughts**) N-VAR A **drought** is a long period of time during which no rain falls. ❑ *...a country where drought and famines have killed up to two million people during the last eighteen years.* →see **dam**

drove /droʊv/ **Drove** is the past tense of **drive**.

drown /draʊn/ (**drowns, drowning, drowned**) ◼ V-T/V-I When someone **drowns** or **is drowned**, they die because they have gone or been pushed under water and cannot breathe. ❑ *A child can drown in only a few inches of water.* ❑ *Last night a boy was drowned in the river.* ◻ V-T/V-I If you say that a person or thing **is drowning** in something, you are emphasizing that they have a very large amount of it, or are completely covered in it. [EMPHASIS] ❑ *...people who gradually find themselves drowning in debt.* ◼ V-T If something **drowns** a sound, it is so loud that you cannot hear that sound properly. ❑ *Clapping drowned the speaker's words for a moment.* ● PHRASAL VERB **Drown out** means the same as **drown**. ❑ *Their cheers drowned out the protests of demonstrators.* ◼ PHRASE If you say that someone **is drowning** their **sorrows**, you mean that they are drinking alcohol in order to forget something sad or upsetting that has happened to them. ❑ *His girlfriend dumped him so he went off to the pub to drown his sorrows.*

drowsy /draʊzi/ (**drowsier, drowsiest**) ADJ If you feel **drowsy**, you feel sleepy and cannot think clearly. ❑ *He felt pleasantly drowsy and had to fight off the urge to sleep.* ● **drowsi|ness** N-UNCOUNT ❑ *Big meals during the day cause drowsiness.*

drug ♦♦◇ /drʌg/ (**drugs, drugging, drugged**) ◼ N-COUNT A **drug** is a chemical which is given to people in order to treat or prevent an illness or disease. ❑ *The drug will be useful to hundreds of thousands of infected people.* ◻ N-COUNT **Drugs** are substances that some people take because of their pleasant effects, but which are usually illegal. ❑ *His mother was on drugs, on cocaine.* ❑ *She was sure Leo was taking drugs.* ◼ V-T If you **drug** a person or animal, you give them a chemical substance in order to make them sleepy or unconscious. ❑ *She was drugged and robbed.* ◼ V-T If food or drink **is drugged**, a chemical substance is added to it in order to make someone sleepy or unconscious when they eat or drink it. ❑ *I wonder now if that drink had been drugged.*

Word Partnership	*drug*의 연어
ADJ.	**dangerous** drug, **experimental** drug, **generic** drug ◼
	illegal drug ◻
N.	drug **abuse**, **effect of a** drug ◼ ◻
	drug **dealer**, drug **money**, drug **overdose**, drug **problem**, drug **test**, drug **use** ◻

drug ad|dict (**drug addicts**) N-COUNT A **drug addict** is someone who is addicted to illegal drugs.

drug|gist /drʌgɪst/ (**druggists**) ◼ N-COUNT A **druggist** is someone who is qualified to sell medicines and drugs ordered by a doctor. [AM; BRIT usually **chemist**] ❑ *Find out if your drugs are depressants. If you're not sure, ask your druggist.* ◻ N-COUNT A **druggist** or a **druggist's** is a store where medicines and drugs ordered by a doctor are sold. [AM; BRIT usually **chemist**] [oft the N]

drug|store /drʌgstɔr/ (**drugstores**) N-COUNT In the United States, a **drugstore** is a store where drugs and medicines are sold or given out, and where you can buy cosmetics, some household goods, and also drinks and snacks.

> In American English, the usual way of referring to a store where medicines are sold is a **drugstore**. ❑ *She went into a drugstore and bought some aspirin.* **Pharmacy** refers specifically to a part of the drugstore where you get prescription medicines. Pharmacies are often located in stores that mainly sell other merchandise, such as food supermarkets and discount centers. In Britain, the nearest equivalent of a drugstore is a **chemist's**.

구동사 잠깐 들르다 ❑ 수다 좀 떨게 잠깐 들르지 그러니?

◻ 구동사 (잠이) 들다 [비격식체] ❑ 내가 분명히 잠이 들었을 거야. ◼ 구동사 떨어지다 ❑ 영국군에 대한 매출액이 떨어질 것으로 예상된다.

구동사 중퇴하다, 중도 탈락하다 ❑ 그는 열여섯 살 때 고등학교를 중퇴했었다.

가산명사 작은 물방울 ❑ 그의 이마에 작은 땀방울들이 맺히고 있었다.

◼ 가산명사 낙오자 [탐탁찮음] ❑ 장발에, 마리화나를 피우는 낙오자들 ◻ 가산명사 중퇴자 ❑ 고등학교 중퇴자들 ◼ 형용사 중퇴한 ❑ 학생들의 중퇴 비율은 현재 3명 중 1명꼴이다.

가산명사 또는 불가산명사 가뭄 ❑ 지난 십팔 년간 가뭄과 기근으로 이백만 명에 이르는 사람들이 죽어간 나라

drive의 과거

◼ 타동사/자동사 익사하다; 익사시키다 ❑ 어린이는 그리 깊지 않은 물속에서도 익사할 수 있다. ❑ 어젯밤 한 소년이 그 강에서 익사했습니다. ◻ 타동사/자동사 -에 빠져 있다 [강조] ❑ 자신이 빚더미에 빠져 있음을 차츰 깨닫는 사람들 ◼ 타동사 (소리를) 압도하다 ❑ 박수 소리에 연사의 말이 잠깐 동안 들리지 않았다. ● 구동사 (소리를) 압도하다 ❑ 그들이 환호하는 소리에 시위자들의 항변이 들리지 않았다. ◼ 구 슬픔을 술로 달래다 ❑ 여자 친구가 자신을 차버리자 그는 주점에 가서 슬픔을 술로 달랬다.

형용사 졸리는 ❑ 그는 기분 좋게 졸렸지만, 자고 싶은 충동을 물리쳐야만 했다. ● 졸음 불가산명사 ❑ 낮에 식사를 많이 하면 졸음이 온다.

◼ 가산명사 약 ❑ 그 약은 수십만 명의 감염자들에게 유용할 것이다. ◻ 가산명사 마약 ❑ 그의 어머니는 마약과 코카인에 중독되어 있었다. ❑ 그녀는 레오가 마약을 복용하고 있다고 확신했다. ◼ 타동사 약을 먹이다 ❑ 그녀에게 약을 먹인 뒤 강도짓을 했다. ◼ 타동사 약을 타다 ❑ 이제야 그 음료에 약을 탔던 건 아닐까 하는 생각이 든다.

가산명사 약물 중독자

◼ 가산명사 약사 [미국영어; 영국영어 대개 chemist] ❑ 네 약에 진정 작용이 있는지 알아봐. 모르겠거든, 약사에게 물어봐. ◻ 가산명사 약국 [미국영어; 영국영어 대개 chemist]

가산명사 약국 (미국에서 약 외에 생활 잡화 등을 파는 곳)

> 미국 영어에서는 약을 파는 상점을 흔히 drugstore라고 한다. ❑ 그녀는 약국에 들어가서 아스피린을 좀 샀다. pharmacy는 약국에서 특별히 처방약을 사는 곳을 지칭한다. pharmacy는 흔히 식료품 슈퍼마켓이나 할인점과 같이 주로 다른 상품을 파는 상점 안에 있다. 영국에서 drugstore와 가장 비슷한 것은 chemist's이다.

a b c d e f g h i j k l m n o p q r s t u v w x y z

drum ♦♢♢ /drʌm/ (**drums, drumming, drummed**) **1** N-COUNT A **drum** is a musical instrument consisting of a skin stretched tightly over a round frame. You play a drum by beating it with sticks or with your hands. ❑ ...a worker who died while beating a drum during a demonstration. **2** N-COUNT A **drum** is a large cylindrical container which is used to store fuel or other substances. ❑ ...an oil drum. **3** V-T/V-I If something **drums on** a surface, or if you **drum** something **on** a surface, it hits it regularly, making a continuous beating sound. ❑ He drummed his fingers on the leather top of his desk. →see Word Web: **drum**

▶**drum into** PHRASAL VERB If you **drum** something **into** someone, you keep saying it to them until they understand it or remember it. ❑ Standard examples were drummed into students' heads.

▶**drum up** PHRASAL VERB If you **drum up** support or business, you try to get it. ❑ It is to be hoped that he is merely drumming up business.

drum|mer /drʌmər/ (**drummers**) N-COUNT A **drummer** is a person who plays a drum or drums in a band or group. ❑ He was a drummer in a rock band. →see **drum**

drunk /drʌŋk/ (**drunks**) **1** ADJ Someone who is **drunk** has drunk so much alcohol that they cannot speak clearly or behave sensibly. ❑ I got drunk and had to be carried home. **2** N-COUNT A **drunk** is someone who is drunk or frequently gets drunk. ❑ A drunk lay in the alley. **3** **Drunk** is the past participle of **drink**.

drunk driv|er (**drunk drivers**) N-COUNT A **drunk driver** is someone who drives after drinking more than the amount of alcohol that is legally allowed. [mainly AM; BRIT usually **drink-driver**] ❑ ...a car accident caused by a drunk driver.

drunk|en /drʌŋkən/ **1** ADJ **Drunken** is used to describe events and situations that involve people who are drunk. [ADJ n] ❑ The pain roused him from his drunken stupor. **2** ADJ A **drunken** person is drunk or is frequently drunk. [ADJ n] ❑ Groups of drunken hooligans smashed shop windows and threw stones. ● **drunk|en|ly** ADV [ADV with v] ❑ One night Bob stormed drunkenly into her house and smashed some chairs. ● **drunk|en|ness** N-UNCOUNT ❑ He was arrested for drunkenness.

dry ♦♦♢ /draɪ/ (**drier** or **dryer, driest, dries, drying, dried**) **1** ADJ If something is **dry**, there is no water or moisture on it or in it. ❑ Clean the metal with a soft dry cloth. ❑ Pat it dry with a soft towel. ● **dry|ness** N-UNCOUNT ❑ ...the parched dryness of the air. **2** V-T/V-I When something **dries** or when you **dry** it, it becomes dry. ❑ Leave your hair to dry naturally whenever possible. **3** V-T When you **dry** the dishes after a meal, you wipe the water off the plates, cups, knives, pans, and other things when they have been washed, using a cloth. ❑ Mrs. Madrigal picked up a towel and began drying dishes next to her daughter. ● PHRASAL VERB **Dry up** means the same as **dry**. [BRIT] ❑ He got up and stood beside Julie, drying up the dishes while she washed. **4** ADJ If you say that your skin or hair is **dry**, you mean that it is less oily than, or not as soft as, normal. ❑ Nothing looks worse than dry, cracked lips. ● **dry|ness** N-UNCOUNT ❑ Dryness of the skin can also be caused by living in centrally heated homes and offices. **5** ADJ If the weather or a period of time is **dry**, there is no rain or there is much less rain than average. ❑ Exceptionally dry weather over the past year had cut agricultural production. **6** ADJ A **dry** place or climate is one that gets very little rainfall. ❑ It was one of the driest and dustiest places in Africa. ● **dry|ness** N-UNCOUNT ❑ He was advised to spend time in the warmth and dryness of Italy. **7** N-SING In **the dry** means in a place or at a time that is not damp, wet, or rainy. [mainly BRIT] ❑ Such cars, however, do grip the road well, even in the dry. **8** ADJ If a river, lake, or well is **dry**, it is empty of water, usually because of hot weather and lack of rain. ❑ The aquifer which had once fed the wells was pronounced dry. **9** ADJ If an oil well is **dry**, it is no longer producing any oil. ❑ To harvest oil and gas profitably from the North Sea, I must focus on the exploitation of small reserves as the big wells run dry. **10** ADJ If your mouth or throat is **dry**, it has little or no saliva in it, and so feels very unpleasant, perhaps because you are tense or ill. ❑ His mouth was still dry, he would certainly be glad of a drink. ● **dry|ness** N-UNCOUNT ❑ Symptoms included frequent dryness in the mouth. **11** ADJ If someone has **dry** eyes, there are no tears in their eyes; often used with negatives or in contexts where you are expressing surprise that they are not crying. ❑ There were few dry eyes in the house when I finished. **12** ADJ **Dry** humor is very amusing, but in a subtle and clever way. [APPROVAL] ❑ Though the pressure Fulton is under must be considerable, he has retained his dry humor. ● **dry|ness** N-UNCOUNT ❑ It has a wry dryness you won't recognize. **13** ADJ If you describe something such as a book, play, or activity as **dry**, you mean that it is dull and uninteresting. [DISAPPROVAL] ❑ My eyelids were drooping over the dry, academic phrases. **14** ADJ **Dry** sherry or wine does not have a sweet taste. ❑ ...a glass of chilled, dry white wine. **15 high and dry** →see **high**. **home and dry** →see **home** →see **weather**

Korean column:

1 가산명사 북, 드럼 ❑ 시위 중에 북을 치다 실신해 사망한 어떤 근로자 **2** 가산명사 드럼통 ❑ 석유 드럼통 **3** 타동사/자동사 둥둥 소리를 내다; 둥둥 치다 ❑ 그가 손가락으로 책상 윗부분의 가죽 면을 톡톡 두드렸다.

구동사 반복하여 주입시키다 ❑ 모범 예제는 반복해서 학생들에게 주입되었다.

구동사 홍보하다 ❑ 그는 단지 사업을 홍보하려 할 것이라고 생각된다.

가산명사 드러머 ❑ 그는 록 밴드의 드러머였다.

1 형용사 술에 취한 ❑ 내가 술에 취해서 누군가가 나를 집으로 데려다 줘야만 했다. **2** 가산명사 술 취한 사람 ❑ 술 취한 사람 하나가 골목에 누워 있었다. **3** drink의 과거

가산명사 음주 운전자 [주로 미국영어; 영국영어 대개 drink-driver] ❑ 음주 운전자가 일으킨 자동차 사고

1 형용사 취중의 ❑ 통증 때문에 그가 취중 혼수상태에서 깨어났다. **2** 형용사 술에 취한 ❑ 술 취한 광적인 축구팬들이 상점 진열창을 부수고 돌을 던졌다. ● 술김에, 술에 취해 부사 ❑ 어느 날 밤 봅은 술김에 그녀의 집에 난입해서 의자 몇 개를 때려부쉈다. ● 취기, 술에 취함 불가산명사 ❑ 그는 음주로 체포되었다.

1 형용사 물기 없는, 마른 ❑ 그 금속 제품은 물기 없는 부드러운 천으로 닦으세요. ❑ 그건 부드러운 타월로 가볍게 두드려서 말리세요. ● 건조한 상태 불가산명사 ❑ 아주 건조한 대기 **2** 타동사/자동사 마르다; 말리다 ❑ 가능하면 머리카락이 저절로 마르도록 두어라. **3** 타동사 물기를 닦아내다 ❑ 마드리갈 부인은 행주를 집어 들어 딸 옆에 놓인 식기의 물기를 닦아내기 시작했다. ● 구동사 물기를 닦아내다 ❑ 그가 일어나 줄리 옆에 서서 그녀가 설거지하는 동안 식기의 물기를 닦아냈다. **4** 형용사 건조한 ❑ 건조하고 갈라진 입술보다 더 보기 안 좋은 것은 없다. ● 건조한 상태 불가산명사 ❑ 건조한 피부 역시 중앙난방 방식의 주택과 사무실이 그 원인이 될 수 있다. **5** 형용사 (날씨가) 가문 ❑ 지난해 유난히 가물었던 날씨 때문에 농작물 생산량이 감소했습니다. **6** 형용사 건조한 ❑ 그 곳은 아프리카에서 가장 건조하고 가장 먼지가 많은 지역 중 하나였다. ● 건조한 기후 불가산명사 ❑ 그는 온난하고 건조한 이탈리아에서 좀 지내라는 권유를 받았다. **7** 단수명사 건조한 지역; 건조기 [주로 영국영어] ❑ 그러나, 그런 승용차는 심지어 건조한 지역에서도 도로에서 미끄러지지 않고 잘 달린다. **8** 형용사 바라붙은 ❑ 한때 그 우물의 젖줄이던 대수층이 말라붙었다고 발표되었다. **9** 형용사 고갈된 ❑ 북해에서 석유와 휘발유를 이윤이 남을 만큼 채취하려면, 큰 유정들이 고갈되어 가므로 작은 규모의 매장지들을 집중적으로 개발해야 한다. **10** 형용사 (입이나 목이) 마르는 ❑ 그는 여전히 입 안이 말라 있어서 음료수 한 모금에도 틀림없이 좋아했을 것이다. ● 마름 불가산명사 ❑ 입 안이 자주 마르는 증상도 있었다. **11** 형용사 눈물을 흘리지 않는 ❑ 내가 말을 끝마쳤을 때 그 집 안에는 눈물을 흘리지 않는 사람이 거의 없었다. **12** 형용사 천연덕스러운 [마음에 듦] ❑ 풀턴은 받고 있는 압박감이 틀림없이 상당할 것임에도 불구하고, 천연덕스러운 유머를 잃지 않고 있다. ● 천연덕스러움 불가산명사 ❑ 거기에는 당신은 알아채지 못할 묘한 천연덕스러움이 있습니다. **13** 형용사 지루한, 재미없는 [탐탁찮음] ❑ 그 지루하고 학구적인 문구들을 보자니 눈꺼풀이 감겼다. **14** 형용사 단맛이 없는 ❑ 단맛이 없는 차가운 백포도주 한 잔

The "talking **drum**" has been common in central Africa for centuries. People use it to communicate between villages up to five miles apart. **Drummers** can **beat** a wide variety of sounds and **rhythms** on these **percussion instruments**. The languages in this part of the world are tonal. This means that different parts of a sentence are spoken at higher or lower pitches. The **tone** and the **beat** of the drum duplicate the sounds of the language very closely. This allows listeners to interpret a **drummer's** playing almost as if it were spoken language.

▶**dry out** 🔢 PHRASAL VERB If something **dries out** or **is dried out**, it loses all the moisture that was in it and becomes hard. ❏ *If the soil is allowed to dry out the tree could die.* 🔢 PHRASAL VERB If someone **dries out** or **is dried out**, they are cured of addiction to alcohol. [INFORMAL] ❏ *He checked into Cedars Sinai Hospital to dry out.*

▶**dry up** 🔢 PHRASAL VERB If something **dries up** or if something **dries it up**, it loses all its moisture and becomes completely dry and shriveled or hard. ❏ *As the day goes on, the pollen dries up and becomes hard.* 🔢 PHRASAL VERB If a river, lake, or well **dries up**, it becomes empty of water, usually because of hot weather and a lack of rain. ❏ *Reservoirs are drying up and farmers have begun to leave their land in search of water.* 🔢 PHRASAL VERB If a supply of something **dries up**, it stops. ❏ *The main source of income and employment, tourism, is expected to dry up completely this summer.* 🔢 PHRASAL VERB If you **dry up** when you are speaking, you stop in the middle of what you were saying, because you cannot think what to say next. ❏ *When he turned around and saw her, his conversation dried up.* 🔢 →see **dry** 3

dry-clean (**dry-cleans, dry-cleaning, dry-cleaned**) V-T When things such as clothes **are dry-cleaned**, they are cleaned with a liquid chemical rather than with water. [usu passive] ❏ *Natural-filled duvets must be dry-cleaned by a professional.* →see Word Web: **dry cleaning**

dry|er /draɪər/ (**dryers**) also **drier** N-COUNT A **dryer** is a machine for drying things. There are different kinds of dryers, for example ones designed for drying clothes, crops, or people's hair or hands. ❏ *...hot air electric hand dryers.* →see also **dry, tumble dryer**

dry run (**dry runs**) N-COUNT If you have a **dry run**, you practice something to make sure that you are ready to do it properly. ❏ *The competition is planned as a dry run for the World Cup finals.*

DTP /di ti pi/ **DTP** is an abbreviation for **desktop publishing**.

dual /duəl, BRIT dyuːəl/ ADJ **Dual** means having two parts, functions, or aspects. [ADJ n] ❏ *...his dual role as head of the party and head of state.*

dub /dʌb/ (**dubs, dubbing, dubbed**) 🔢 V-T If someone or something **is dubbed** a particular thing, they are given that description or name. [JOURNALISM] ❏ *...the man whom the Labour opposition dubbed as the "no change Prime Minister."* 🔢 V-T If a movie or soundtrack in a foreign language **is dubbed**, a new soundtrack is added with actors giving a translation. [usu passive] ❏ *It was dubbed into Spanish for Mexican audiences.*

du|bi|ous /dubiəs, BRIT dyuːbiəs/ 🔢 ADJ If you describe something as **dubious**, you mean that you do not consider it to be completely honest, safe, or reliable. ❏ *This claim seems to us to be rather dubious.* ● **du|bi|ous|ly** ADV ❏ *Carter was dubiously convicted of shooting three white men in a bar.* 🔢 ADJ If you are **dubious about** something, you are not completely sure about it and have not yet made up your mind about it. [v-link ADJ, oft ADJ about n] ❏ *My parents were a bit dubious about it all at first but we soon convinced them.* ● **du|bi|ous|ly** ADV ❏ *He eyed Coyne dubiously.*

Do not confuse **dubious**, **doubtful**, and **suspicious**. If you are **dubious** about something, you are not sure whether it is the right thing to do. ❏ *Alison sounded very dubious... The men in charge were a bit dubious about taking women on.* If you describe something as **dubious**, you think it is not completely honest, safe, or reliable. ❏ *...his dubious abilities as a teacher.* If you feel **doubtful** about something, you are unsure about it or about whether it will happen or be successful. ❏ *Do you feel insecure and doubtful about your ability?... It was doubtful he would ever see her again.* If you are **suspicious** of a person, you do not trust them and think they might be involved in something dishonest or illegal. ❏ *I am suspicious of his intentions... Miss Lenaut had grown suspicious.* If you describe something as **suspicious**, it suggests behavior that is dishonest, illegal, or dangerous. ❏ *He listened for any suspicious sounds.*

---

duch|ess /dʌtʃɪs/ (**duchesses**) N-COUNT A **duchess** is a woman who has the same rank as a duke, or who is a duke's wife or widow. ❏ *...the Duchess of Kent.*

🔢 구동사 바싹 마르다; 바싹 말리다 ❏ 땅이 바싹 마르게 내버려 둔다면 그 나무가 죽을 수도 있다. 🔢 구동사 알코올 중독에서 벗어나다; 알코올 중독에서 벗어나게 하다 [비격식체] ❏ 그는 알코올 중독을 치료하기 위해 세다스 시나이 병원에 입원했다.

🔢 구동사 바싹 말라붙다; 바싹 말라붙게 하다 ❏ 날이 갈수록, 꽃가루가 바싹 말라붙어서 딱딱해진다. 🔢 구동사 (강이나 호수가) 바닥을 드러내다 ❏ 저수지가 바닥을 드러내고 있어서 농부들은 물을 찾아 자신들의 땅을 떠나기 시작했다. 🔢 구동사 정지되다 ❏ 주된 수입원이자 일자리를 많이 제공하는 관광업이 이번 여름에는 완전히 정지될 것으로 예상된다. 🔢 구동사 말문이 막히다 ❏ 뒤돌아서서 그녀를 보자, 그는 말문이 막혔다.

타동사 드라이클리닝하다 ❏ 천연 깃털 이불은 전문가가 드라이클리닝해야 한다.

가산명사 건조기, 드라이어 ❏ 온풍이 나오는 전기 손 건조기

가산명사 예행연습 ❏ 그 경기는 월드컵 결승전의 예행연습으로 계획된 것이다.

DTP는 전자 출판의 약어

형용사 둘의, 이중의 ❏ 당수와 국가 수반으로서의 그의 두 가지 역할

🔢 타동사 별칭을 붙이다 [언론] ❏ 야당인 노동당에서 '불변의 수상'이라고 별칭을 지어준 사람 🔢 타동사 더빙되다, 번역 녹음되다 ❏ 그것은 멕시코인 관객들을 위해 스페인어로 더빙되었다.

🔢 형용사 수상한, 의심스러운 ❏ 우리가 보기에 이 주장은 좀 수상하다. ● 수상하게, 미심쩍게 부사 ❏ 카터는 미심쩍게도 술집에서 백인 3명을 총으로 쏘았다는 죄로 유죄 선고를 받았다. 🔢 형용사 반신반의하는, 미심쩍어하는 ❏ 우리 부모님께서는 처음엔 그 모든 것에 대해 약간 반신반의하셨지만 우리가 곧 그 분들을 설득했다. ● 미심쩍은 듯 부사 ❏ 그는 코인을 미심쩍은 듯 쳐다보았다.

---

dubious, doubtful, suspicious를 혼동하지 않도록 하라. 무엇에 대해 dubious하면, 그것을 하는 것이 올바른 일인지 아닌지 확신이 없는 것이다. ❏ 앨리슨은 반신반의하는 것 같아 보였다... 책임을 맡고 있는 남자들은 여자들을 고용하는 것에 조금 반신반의했다. 무엇을 dubious하다고 표현하면, 그것이 완전히 정직하거나, 안전하거나, 믿을 만하지 않다고 생각하는 것이다. ❏ ... 교사로서 의심스러운 그의 능력. 무엇에 대해 doubtful한 생각이 들면, 그것에 대해 확신이 없거나 그것이 일어날지에 대해 확신이 없는 것이다. ❏ 너는 네 능력에 대해 불안하고 확신이 없니?... 그가 과연 그녀를 다시 보게 될지는 분명치 않았다. 어떤 사람에 대해 suspicious하면, 그 사람을 믿지 않고 또 그 사람이 정직하지 못하거나 불법적인 일에 연루되어 있을지도 모른다고 생각하는 것이다. ❏ 나는 그의 의도가 의심스럽다... 르노 양은 의심을 품게 되었다. 무엇을 suspicious하다고 표현하면, 그것이 정직하지 못하거나, 불법이거나, 위험한 행동임을 의미한다. ❏ 그는 조금이라도 의심스러운 소리가 나지 않는지 주의를 기울였다.

가산명사 공작 부인 ❏ 켄트 공작 부인

Dry cleaning is not actually dry at all. It **cleans clothes** with liquid **chemicals** instead of water. The first dry cleaning **solvent** was **kerosene**. A Frenchman named Jolly discovered dry cleaning by accident in 1855. He had spilled kerosene from a lamp on a tablecloth. He noticed the **stains** came out when the kerosene **washed** over them. Soon Jolly opened the first dry cleaning **service**. Since then, cleaners have also used **gasoline** and other dangerous chemicals. Recently, a company developed a safer dry cleaning system using **carbon dioxide**. The washer is pressurized which turns the CO_2 gas into a liquid.

duck /dʌk/ (ducks, ducking, ducked) **1** N-VAR A **duck** is a very common water bird with short legs, a short neck, and a large flat beak. ❏ *Chickens and ducks scratch around the outbuildings.* ● N-UNCOUNT **Duck** is the flesh of this bird when it is eaten as food. ❏ *...honey roasted duck.* **2** V-T/V-I If you **duck**, you move your head or the top half of your body quickly downward to avoid something that might hit you, or to avoid being seen. ❏ *He ducked in time to save his head from a blow from the poker.* **3** V-T If you **duck** your head to hide his admiration. **3** V-T If you **duck** something such as a blow, you avoid it by moving your head or body quickly downward. ❏ *Hans deftly ducked their blows.* **4** V-T You say that someone **ducks** a duty or responsibility when you disapprove of the fact that they have. [INFORMAL, DISAPPROVAL] ❏ *The Opposition reckons the Health Secretary has ducked all the difficult decisions.* **5** PHRASE You say that criticism is **like water off a duck's back** or **water off a duck's back** to emphasize that it is not having any effect on the person being criticized. [EMPHASIS] ❏ *All the criticism is water off a duck's back to me.* **6** PHRASE If you **take to** something **like a duck to water**, you discover that you are naturally good at it or that you find it very easy to do. ❏ *Some mothers take to breastfeeding like a duck to water, while others find they need some help to get started.*

▶ **duck out** PHRASAL VERB If you **duck out of** something that you are supposed to do, you avoid doing it. [INFORMAL] ❏ *George ducked out of his forced marriage to a cousin.*

duct /dʌkt/ (ducts) N-COUNT A **duct** is a pipe, tube, or channel which carries a liquid or gas. ❏ *...a big air duct in the ceiling.*

dud /dʌd/ (duds) ADJ **Dud** means not working properly or not successful. [INFORMAL] [ADJ n] ❏ *He replaced a dud valve.* ● N-COUNT **Dud** is also a noun. ❏ *The mine was a dud.*

dude /dud, BRIT dyu:d/ (dudes) N-COUNT A **dude** is a man. In very informal situations, **dude** is sometimes used as a greeting or form of address to a man. [AM, INFORMAL] ❏ *My doctor is a real cool dude.*

due ♦♦◇ /du, BRIT dyu:/ (dues) **1** PHRASE If an event is **due to** something, it happens or exists as a direct result of that thing. ❏ *The country's economic problems are largely due to the weakness of the recovery.* **2** PHRASE You can say **due to** to introduce the reason for something happening. Some speakers of English believe that it is not correct to use **due to** in this way. ❏ *Due to the large volume of letters he receives Dave regrets he is unable to answer queries personally.* **3** ADJ If something is **due** at a particular time, it is expected to happen, be done, or arrive at that time. ❏ *The results are due at the end of the month.* ❏ *Mr. Carter is due in London on Monday.* **4** ADJ **Due** attention or consideration is the proper, reasonable, or deserved amount of it under the circumstances. [ADJ n] ❏ *After due consideration it was decided to send him away to live with foster parents.* **5** ADJ Something that is **due**, or that is **due to** someone, is owed to them, either as a debt or because they have a right to it. [v-link ADJ, oft ADJ to n] ❏ *I was sent a check and advised that no further pension was due.* **6** ADJ If someone is **due for** something, that thing is planned to happen or be given to them now, or very soon, often after they have been waiting for it for a long time. [v-link ADJ for n] ❏ *Although not due for release until 2001, he was let out of his low-security prison to spend a weekend with his wife.* **7** PHRASE If you say that something will happen or take place **in due course**, you mean that you cannot make it happen any quicker and it will happen when the time is right for it. ❏ *In due course the baby was born.* **8** PHRASE You can say "**to give** him his **due**," or "**giving** him his **due**" when you are admitting that there are some good things about someone, even though there are things that you do not like about them. ❏ *To give Linda her due, she had tried to encourage John in his school work.* **9** PHRASE You can say "**with due respect**" when you are about to disagree politely with someone. [POLITENESS] ❏ *With all due respect I submit to you that you're asking the wrong question.*

duel /duəl, BRIT dyu:əl/ (duels) N-COUNT A **duel** is a formal fight between two people in which they use guns or swords in order to settle a quarrel. ❏ *He killed a man in one duel and was himself wounded in another.*

duet /duet, BRIT dyu:et/ (duets) N-COUNT A **duet** is a piece of music sung or played by two people. ❏ *Tonight she sings a duet with first husband Maurice Gibb.*

dug /dʌg/ **Dug** is the past tense and past participle of **dig.** →see **tunnel**

duke /duk, BRIT dyu:k/ (dukes) N-COUNT A **duke** is a man with a very high social rank in the nobility. ❏ *...the Queen and the Duke of Edinburgh.*

dull /dʌl/ (duller, dullest, dulls, dulling, dulled) **1** ADJ If you describe someone or something as **dull**, you mean they are not interesting or exciting. [DISAPPROVAL] ❏ *I felt she found me boring and dull.* ● **dull|ness** N-UNCOUNT ❏ *They enjoy anything that breaks the dullness of their routine life.* **2** ADJ Someone or something that is **dull** is not very lively or energetic. ❏ *The body's natural rhythms mean we all feel dull and sleepy between 1 and 3pm.* ● **dul|ly** ADV [ADV after v] ❏ *His giant face had a rough growth of stubble, his eyes looked dully ahead.* ● **dull|ness** N-UNCOUNT ❏ *Did you notice any unusual depression or dullness of mind?* **3** ADJ A **dull** color or light is not bright. ❏ *The stamp was a dark, dull blue color with a heavy black postmark.* ● **dul|ly** ADV [ADV with v] ❏ *The street lamps gleamed dully through the night's mist.* **4** ADJ You say the weather is **dull** when it is very cloudy. ❏ *It's always dull and raining.* **5** ADJ **Dull** sounds are not very clear or loud. ❏ *The coffin closed with a dull thud.* ● **dul|ly** ADV [ADV after v] ❏ *He heard his heart thump dully but more quickly.* **6** ADJ **Dull** feelings are weak and not intense. [ADJ n] ❏ *The pain, usually a dull ache, gets worse with exercise.* ● **dul|ly** ADV ❏ *His arm throbbed dully.* **7** V-T/V-I If something **dulls** or if it **is dulled**, it becomes less intense, bright, or lively. ❏ *Her eyes dulled and she gazed blankly.*

Thesaurus	*dull*의 참조어
ADJ.	dingy, drab, plain **3**

---

1 가산명사 또는 불가산명사 오리 오리 ❏ 닭과 오리가 헛간 주변을 파헤친다. ● 불가산명사 오리 고기 ❏ 꿀을 발라 구운 오리 고기 **2** 타동사/자동사 (몸을) 휙 숙이다 ❏ 그가 제 때에 머리를 휙 숙여 부지깽이에 의한 일격을 피했다. **3** 타동사 휙 숙여 홈모의 감정을 감추었다. **3** 타동사 몸을 낮춰 피하다 ❏ 한스는 교묘하게 그들의 주먹을 피했다. **4** 타동사 회피하다 [비격식체, 탐탁잖음] ❏ 야당은 보건 장관이 어려운 결정을 모두 회피해 왔다고 생각한다. **5** 구 전혀 영향을 끼치지 못하는 (강조) ❏ 그 모든 비난이 내게는 전혀 영향을 끼치지 못한다. **6** 구 별 힘들이지 않고 하다 ❏ 어떤 엄마들은 별 힘들이지 않고 모유 수유를 하는가 하면, 어떤 이들은 처음 시작할 때 도움을 필요로 한다.

구동사 피하다 [비격식체] ❏ 조지는 사촌과의 강요된 결혼을 피했다.

가산명사 도관, 수송관 ❏ 천장의 큰 환기 도관

형용사 망가진 [비격식체] ❏ 그가 망가진 밸브를 교체했다. ● 가산명사 쓸모없는 것 ❏ 그 광산은 쓸모없었다.

가산명사 친구, 사람 [미국영어, 비격식체] ❏ 내 주치의는 정말 멋진 친구야.

1 구 ~ 때문인 ❏ 그 나라의 경제 문제는 주로 경기 회복력이 약해서 생긴 것이다. **2** 구 ~ 때문에 ❏ 데이브는 받는 편지가 너무나 많아서 일일이 질의에 답할 수 없는 것을 안타까워한다. **3** 형용사 (시기가) 예정인 ❏ 결과가 이달 말에 나올 예정이다. ❏ 카터 씨는 월요일에 런던에 도착할 예정이다. **4** 형용사 적절한, 충분한 ❏ 충분히 심사숙고한 후에 그를 양부모에게 보내서 함께 살게 하기로 결정이 났다. **5** 형용사 마땅히 지급되어야 할 ❏ 나는 수표와 함께 더 이상 받을 연금이 없다는 통지를 받았다. **6** 형용사 ~이 예정된 ❏ 2001년 이전에도, 그는 경비가 삼엄하지 않은 교도소에서 나가 주말을 부인과 보내도록 허락받았다. **7** 구 때가 되어 ❏ 때가 되자 아기가 태어났다. **8** 구 인정해 주다 ❏ 린다를 인정할 건 인정해 준다면, 그녀는 존이 학교 공부에 자신을 갖도록 노력했었다. **9** 구 외람됩니다만 [공손체] ❏ 외람됩니다만 저는 당신이 잘못된 질문을 하시고 있다고 말씀드리고 싶군요.

가산명사 결투 ❏ 그는 어떤 결투에서 한 남자를 죽였고 또 다른 결투에서는 자신이 부상당했다.

가산명사 듀엣 곡, 이중창 곡 ❏ 오늘 밤에 그녀는 첫 남편인 모리스 깁과 듀엣 곡을 부른다.

dig의 과거 및 과거 분사

가산명사 공작 ❏ 여왕 폐하와 에든버러 공작

1 형용사 재미없는 [탐탁잖음] ❏ 그녀가 나를 지루하고 재미없다고 생각하는 것 같았다. ● 단조로움 불가산명사 ❏ 그들은 일상적인 삶의 단조로움을 깨뜨리는 일이라면 무엇이나 즐긴다. **2** 형용사 기운 없는, 나른한 ❏ 정상적인 신체 리듬이라면 오후 1시부터 3시 사이에 우리는 모두 기운이 없고 졸리게 된다. ● 나른하게 부사 ❏ 나른하게 부사 ❏ 그는 얼굴에는 짧은 수염이 거칠게 자랐고 두 눈은 나른하게 앞쪽을 보고 있었다. ● 나른함, 무기력함 불가산명사 ❏ 혹시 평소와 달리 우울하거나 무기력한 마음이 드나요? **3** 형용사 흐릿한, 우중충한 ❏ 그 우표는 거무스름하고 흐릿한 푸른색이었고 진한 검정색 소인이 찍혀 있었다. ● 흐릿하게 부사 ❏ 가로등이 밤안개 사이로 희미하게 빛났다. **4** 형용사 (날씨가) 잔뜩 흐린 ❏ 항상 날이 흐리고 비가 내린다. **5** 형용사 둔탁한 ❏ 관이 둔탁한 소리를 내며 닫혔다. ● 둔탁하게 부사 ❏ 그는 자신의 심장이 둔탁하지만 더 빠르게 뛰는 소리를 들었다. **6** 형용사 약한 ❏ 평소에는 약하게 쑤시던 것이 운동을 하니 더 아프다. ● 약하게 부사 ❏ 그의 팔이 약간 욱신거렸다. **7** 타동사/자동사 흐려지다; 흐려지게 하다 ❏ 그녀는 두 눈빛이 흐려지더니 멍하니 바라보았다.

duly /dˈuːli, BRIT dyuːli/ **1** ADV If you say that something **duly** happened or was done, you mean that it was expected to happen or was requested, and it did happen or it was done. [ADV before v] □ *Westcott appealed to Waite for an apology, which he duly received.* **2** ADV If something is **duly** done, it is done in the correct way. [FORMAL] [ADV before v] □ *He is a duly elected president of the country and we're going to be giving him all the support we can.*

dumb /dˈʌm/ (**dumber, dumbest, dumbs, dumbing, dumbed**) **1** ADJ Someone who is **dumb** is completely unable to speak. □ *...a young deaf and dumb man.* **2** ADJ If someone is **dumb** on a particular occasion, they cannot speak because they are angry, shocked, or surprised. [LITERARY] [v-link ADJ] □ *We were all struck dumb for a minute.* **3** ADJ If you call a person **dumb**, you mean that they are stupid or foolish. [INFORMAL, DISAPPROVAL] □ *The questions were set up to make her look dumb.* **4** ADJ If you say that something is **dumb**, you think that it is silly and annoying. [AM, INFORMAL, DISAPPROVAL] □ *I came up with this dumb idea.*

▶**dumb down** PHRASAL VERB If you **dumb down** something, you make it easier for people to understand, especially when this spoils it. □ *This sounded like a case for dumbing down the magazine, which no one favored.*

dum|my /dˈʌmi/ (**dummies**) **1** N-COUNT A **dummy** is a model of a person, often used to display clothes. □ *...the bottom half of a shop-window dummy.* **2** N-COUNT You can use **dummy** to refer to things that are not real, but have been made to look or behave as if they are real. □ *Dummy patrol cars will be set up beside motorways to frighten speeding motorists.* **3** N-COUNT A baby's **dummy** is a rubber or plastic object that you give the baby to suck so that he or she feels comforted. [BRIT; AM usually **pacifier**]

dump ♦◇◇ /dˈʌmp/ (**dumps, dumping, dumped**) **1** V-T If you **dump** something somewhere, you put it or unload it there quickly and carelessly. [INFORMAL] □ *We dumped our bags at the nearby Grand Hotel and hurried toward the market.* **2** V-T If something **is dumped** somewhere, it is put or left there because it is no longer wanted or needed. [INFORMAL] □ *The getaway car was dumped near the freeway.* ● **dump|ing** N-UNCOUNT □ *German law forbids the dumping of hazardous waste on German soil.* **3** N-COUNT A **dump** is a place where garbage and waste material are left, for example on open ground outside a town. □ *...companies that bring their rubbish straight to the dump.* **4** N-COUNT If you say that a place is a **dump**, you think it is ugly and unpleasant to live in or visit. [INFORMAL, DISAPPROVAL] □ *"What a dump!" Christabel said, standing in the doorway of the youth hostel.* **5** V-T To **dump** something such as an idea, policy, or practice means to stop supporting or using it. [INFORMAL] □ *Ministers believed it was vital to dump the poll tax before the election.* **6** V-T If a firm or company **dumps** goods, it sells large quantities of them at prices far below their real value, usually in another country, in order to gain a bigger market share or to keep prices high in the home market. [BUSINESS] □ *It produces more than it needs, then dumps its surplus onto the world market.* **7** V-T If you **dump** someone, you end your relationship with them. [INFORMAL] □ *My heart sank because I thought he was going to dump me for another girl.* **8** V-T To **dump** computer data or memory means to copy it from one storage system onto another, such as from disk to magnetic tape. [COMPUTING] □ *All the data is then dumped into the main computer.* **9** N-COUNT A **dump** is a list of the data that is stored in a computer's memory at a particular time. **Dumps** are often used by computer programmers to find out what is causing a problem with a program. [COMPUTING] □ *...print it out and it'll do a screen dump of what's there.*

Dump|ster /dˈʌmpstər/ (**Dumpsters**) N-COUNT A **Dumpster** is a large metal container for holding trash. [AM, TRADEMARK; BRIT usually **skip**]

dune /dˈuːn, BRIT dyuːn/ (**dunes**) N-COUNT A **dune** is a hill of sand near the sea or in a desert. □ *Large dunes make access to the beach difficult in places.* →see **beach, desert**

dung /dˈʌŋ/ N-UNCOUNT **Dung** is feces from animals, especially from large animals such as cattle and horses. □ *Workers at Sydney's harborside Taronga zoo are refusing to collect animal dung in a protest over wages.*

dun|ga|rees /dˌʌŋɡəriːz/ **1** N-PLURAL **Dungarees** are the same as **jeans**. [AM] [also *a pair of* N] **2** N-PLURAL **Dungarees** are a one-piece garment consisting of pants, a piece of cloth which covers your chest, and straps which go over your shoulders. [AM **overalls**] [also *a pair of* N] □ *At the door is the plumber, a big burly fellow in dungarees.*

dun|geon /dˈʌndʒən/ (**dungeons**) N-COUNT A **dungeon** is a dark underground prison in a castle.

dun|no /dənˈoʊ/ **Dunno** is sometimes used in written English to represent an informal way of saying "don't know." □ *"How on earth did she get it?" —"I dunno."*

duo /dˈuːoʊ, BRIT dyuːoʊ/ (**duos**) **1** N-COUNT A **duo** is two musicians, singers, or other performers who perform together as a pair. □ *...a famous dancing and singing duo.* **2** N-COUNT You can refer to two people together as a **duo**, especially when they have something in common. [MAINLY JOURNALISM] □ *...Britain's former golden Olympic duo of Linford Christie and Sally Gunnell.*

duopoly /dˌuːˈɒpəli/ /dˌjuːpəli/ (**duopolies**) **1** N-VAR If two companies or people have a **duopoly on** something such as an industry, they share complete control over it and it is impossible for others to become involved in it. [BUSINESS] □ *...they are no longer part of a duopoly on overseas routes.* **2** N-COUNT A **duopoly** is a group of two companies which are the only ones which provide a particular product or service, and which therefore have complete control over an industry. [BUSINESS] □ *Their smaller rival is battling to end their duopoly.*

1 부사 당연히 □ 웨스트코트는 웨이트에게 사과를 요구했는데 그것은 그가 당연히 받아야 하는 것이었다. **2** 부사 정당하게 [격식체] □ 그는 정당하게 선출된 이 나라의 대통령이므로 우리가 할 수 있는 한 최대로 그를 지지해 주고자 한다.

1 형용사 언어 장애를 가진, 벙어리의 □ 농아인 젊은 남자 **2** 형용사 빈정하여 말문이 막힌 [문예체] □ 우리는 모두 깜짝 놀라 잠깐 동안 말문이 막혔다. **3** 형용사 멍청한 [비격식체, 탐탁잖음] □ 그녀를 멍청하게 보이도록 질문을 만들어 놓았다. **4** 형용사 어이없는 [미국영어, 비격식체, 탐탁잖음] □ 내가 이 어이없는 생각을 했어.

구동사 쉽게 고치다 □ 이것은 그 잡지를 사람들이 이해하기 쉽게 바꾸자는 주장처럼 들렸는데, 이를 아무도 좋아하지 않았다.

1 가산명사 마네킹 □ 가게 진열창에 두는 마네킹의 하반신 **2** 가산명사 진짜처럼 만든 가짜, 모형 □ 과속 운전자들을 겁주기 위해 가짜 순찰차가 고속도로 옆에 설치될 것이다. **3** 가산명사 (아기를 위한) 고무 젖꼭지 [영국영어; 미국영어 대개 pacifier]

1 타동사 털썩 내리다, 던지듯 내려놓다 [비격식체] □ 우리는 가까운 그랜드 호텔에 가방을 던져 놓고 시장으로 서둘러 갔다. **2** 타동사 버려지다 [비격식체] □ 도주 차량은 고속도로 근처에 버려져 있었다. ● 버리기 불가산명사 □ 독일에서는 유해 폐기물을 자국 땅에 버리는 것을 법으로 금한다. **3** 가산명사 쓰레기 하치장 □ 자사의 쓰레기를 쓰레기 하치장에 바로 버리는 업체들 **4** 가산명사 지저분한 곳, (비유적) 쓰레기장 [비격식체, 탐탁잖음] □ "완전 쓰레기장이구먼!"라고 크리스타벨이 유스 호스텔 입구에 선 채로 말했다. **5** 타동사 안 쓰다, 페기하다 [비격식체] □ 각료들은 선거 전에 인두세를 없애는 것이 필수적이라고 믿었다. **6** 타동사 덤핑으로 팔다, 투매하다 [경제] □ 그곳은 필요량보다 많이 생산하고서는 그 잉여분을 세계 시장에 덤핑으로 판다. **7** 타동사 (사귀던 사람을) 차버리다 [비격식체] □ 그가 딴 여자 때문에 나를 차버릴 것이라는 생각에 나는 가슴이 무너져 내렸다. **8** 타동사 (컴퓨터에서 자료를) 옮기다 [컴퓨터] □ 그러면 모든 자료가 메인 컴퓨터로 옮겨집니다. **9** 가산명사 컴퓨터 기억 장치에 담긴 프로그램 및 자료의 목록으로 더버깅에 사용되기도 한 [컴퓨터] □ 그것을 출력하면 그 안에 담긴 내용에 대해 스크린 덤프를 수행하게 된다.

가산명사 대형 쓰레기 컨테이너 [미국영어, 상표; 영국영어 대개 skip]

가산명사 모래 언덕 □ 여기저기 쌓인 모래 언덕 때문에 해변에 가까이 가기가 어렵다. →참조 beach, desert

불가산명사 배설물 □ 시드니 항구에 면해 있는 타롱가 동물원의 직원들이 임금 인상 시위로써 동물들의 배설물 수거를 거부하고 있다.

1 복수명사 청바지 [미국영어] **2** 복수명사 멜빵 작업복 [미국영어 overalls] □ 문가에 배관공이 서 있는데, 멜빵 작업복을 입은 크고 건장한 남자이다.

가산명사 지하 감옥

몰라 ('don't know'의 구어적 표현) □ "대체 그녀가 그걸 어떻게 얻었대?"—"몰라."

1 가산명사 듀엣, 2인조 □ 유명한 2인조 댄싱 가수 **2** 가산명사 콤비 [주로 언론] □ 전 영국 올림픽 금메달 수상자 콤비인 린포드 크리스티와 샐리 거넬

1 가산명사 또는 불가산명사 양대 주도권 [경제] □ 그들은 더 이상 해외 판로에 있어서 양대 주도권을 쥐고 있지 않다. **2** 가산명사 복점(複占) [경제] □ 규모가 더 작은 경쟁 업체가 그들의 복점을 종식시키려 애쓰고 있다.

a
b
c
d
e
f
g
h
i
j
k
l
m
n
o
p
q
r
s
t
u
v
w
x
y
z

dupe /dup, BRIT dyuːp/ (**dupes, duping, duped**) **1** V-T If a person **dupes** you, they trick you into doing something or into believing something which is not true. ❑ ...a plot to dupe stamp collectors into buying fake rarities. **2** N-COUNT A **dupe** is someone who is tricked by someone else. ❑ He was accused of being a dupe of the communists.

duplicate (**duplicates, duplicating, duplicated**)

The verb is pronounced /duplikeit/. The noun and adjective are pronounced /duplikit/.

1 V-T If you **duplicate** something that has already been done, you repeat or copy it. ❑ His task will be to duplicate his success overseas here at home. ● N-COUNT **Duplicate** is also a noun. ❑ He was organising a duplicate of Operation Gladio to be activated if the left gained power. **2** V-T To **duplicate** something which has been written, drawn, or recorded onto tape means to make exact copies of it. ❑ ...a business which duplicates video tapes for the movie makers. ● N-COUNT **Duplicate** is also a noun. [also in N] ❑ I'm on my way to Switzerland, but I've lost my card. I've got to get a duplicate. **3** ADJ **Duplicate** is used to describe things that have been made as an exact copy of other things, usually in order to serve the same purpose. [ADJ n] ❑ He let himself in with a duplicate key.

duplication /duplikeiʃⁿn, BRIT dyuːplikeiʃⁿn/ N-UNCOUNT If you say that there has been **duplication** of something, you mean that someone has done a task unnecessarily because it has already been done before. ❑ There could be a serious loss of efficiency through unnecessary duplication of resources.

durable /dʊərəbⁿl, BRIT dyʊərəbⁿl/ ADJ Something that is **durable** is strong and lasts a long time without breaking or becoming weaker. ❑ Fine bone china is eminently practical, since it is strong and durable. ● **durability** /dʊərəbɪliti, BRIT dyʊərəbɪliti/ N-UNCOUNT ❑ Airlines recommend hard-sided cases for durability.

durable goods also **durables** N-PLURAL **Durable goods** or **durables** are goods such as televisions or cars which are expected to last a long time, and are bought infrequently. [mainly AM; BRIT usually **consumer durables**] ❑ ...a 2.6% rise in orders for durable goods in January.

duration /dʊəreiʃⁿn, BRIT dyʊəreiʃⁿn/ **1** N-UNCOUNT The **duration of** an event or state is the time during which it happens or exists. ❑ He was given the task of protecting her for the duration of the trial. **2** PHRASE If you say that something will happen **for the duration**, you mean that it will happen for as long as a particular situation continues. ❑ His wounds knocked him out of combat for the duration.

during ♦♦♦ /dʊəriŋ, BRIT dyʊəriŋ/ **1** PREP If something happens **during** a period of time or an event, it happens continuously, or happens several times between the beginning and end of that period or event. ❑ Sandstorms are common during the Saudi Arabian winter. **2** PREP If something develops **during** a period of time, it develops gradually from the beginning to the end of that period. ❑ Wages have fallen by more than twenty percent during the past two months. **3** PREP An event that happens **during** a period of time happens at some point or moment in that period. ❑ During his visit, the Pope will also bless the new hospital.

You do not use **during** to say how long something lasts. You use **for**. You do not say, for example, "I went to Florida during two weeks." You say "**I went to Florida for two weeks.**"

dusk /dʌsk/ N-UNCOUNT **Dusk** is the time just before night when the daylight has almost gone but when it is not completely dark. ❑ We arrived home at dusk.

dust ♦◇◇ /dʌst/ (**dusts, dusting, dusted**) **1** N-UNCOUNT **Dust** is very small dry particles of earth or sand. ❑ Tanks raise huge trails of dust when they move. **2** N-UNCOUNT **Dust** is the very small pieces of dirt which you find inside buildings, for example on furniture, floors, or lights. ❑ I could see a thick layer of dust on the stairs. **3** N-UNCOUNT **Dust** is a fine powder which consists of very small particles of a substance such as gold, wood, or coal. ❑ The air is so black with diesel fumes and coal dust, I can barely see. **4** V-T/V-I When you **dust** something such as furniture, you remove dust from it, usually using a cloth. ❑ I vacuumed and dusted and polished the living room. **5** V-T/V-I If you **dust** something **with** a fine substance such as powder or if you **dust** a fine substance **onto** something, you cover it lightly with that substance. ❑ Lightly dust the fish with flour. **6** PHRASE If you say that something **has bitten the dust**, you are emphasizing that it no longer exists or that it has failed. [HUMOROUS, INFORMAL, EMPHASIS] ❑ In the last 30 years many cherished values have bitten the dust. **7** PHRASE If you say that something will happen when **the dust settles**, you mean that a situation will be clearer after it has calmed down. If you let **the dust settle** before doing something, you let a situation calm down before you try to do anything else. [INFORMAL] ❑ Once the dust had settled Beck defended his decision. **8** PHRASE If you say that something **is gathering dust**, you mean that it has been left somewhere and nobody is using it or doing anything with it. ❑ Many of the machines are gathering dust in basements.

dustbin /dʌstbin/ (**dustbins**) N-COUNT A **dustbin** is a large container with a lid which people put their trash in and which is usually kept outside their house. [BRIT; AM usually **garbage can**]

dusty /dʌsti/ (**dustier, dustiest**) **1** ADJ If places, roads, or other things outside are **dusty**, they are covered with tiny bits of earth or sand, usually because it has not rained for a long time. ❑ They started strolling down the dusty road in the moonlight. **2** ADJ If a room, house, or object is **dusty**, it is covered with very small pieces of dirt. ❑ ...a dusty attic.

---

1 타동사 속이다 ❑ 우표 수집가들을 속여서 위조된 희귀 우표를 사게 하려는 수작 **2** 가산명사 속아 넘어간 사람 ❑ 그는 공산주의자들에게 속아 넘어갔다고 비난 받았다.

동사는 /duplikeit /으로 발음되고, 명사와 형용사는 /duplikit /으로 발음된다.

1 타동사 재현하다, 반복하다 ❑ 그의 과제는 해외에서 자신이 이룬 성공을 고국에서도 재현하는 일일 것이다. ● 가산명사 재현, 반복 ❑ 그는 좌익이 권력을 얻게 되면 글라디오 작전을 재현하려고 준비하고 있었다. **2** 타동사 복사하다 ❑ 영화 제작사에 비디오테이프를 복사해 주는 업체 ● 가산명사 복제품, 사본 ❑ 나는 스위스로 가는 길인데 카드를 잃어버려서 사본을 만들어야 한다. **3** 형용사 복제한, 복사한 ❑ 그가 복제한 열쇠로 문을 열고 들어왔다.

불가산명사 중복 ❑ 자원을 불필요하게 중복 사용함으로써 효율성이 심각하게 떨어질 수 있다.

형용사 내구성 있는 ❑ 품질 좋은 본차이나는 튼튼하고 내구성이 있어 놀랍도록 실용적이다. ● 내구성 불가산명사 ❑ 항공사들은 하드케이스 가방의 내구성이 좋다고 추천한다.

복수명사 내구 소비재 [주로 미국영어; 영국영어 대개 consumer durables] ❑ 1월 내구 소비재 주문량의 2.6퍼센트 상승

1 불가산명사 지속 기간 ❑ 그는 공판 기간 동안 그녀를 보호하라는 임무를 받았다. **2** 구 그 기간 내내 ❑ 그는 부상을 입어서 전투 기간 내내 전투에 참가하지 못했다.

1 전치사 – 동안 ❑ 사우디아라비아에서는 모래 폭풍이 동절기 동안 흔히 발생한다. **2** 전치사 – 사이에 ❑ 임금이 지난 두 달 사이에 20퍼센트 이상이나 떨어졌다. **3** 전치사 – 중에 ❑ 교황이 방문 기간 중에, 새로 건립된 그 병원에 축사도 할 것이다.

무엇이 얼마 동안 지속되는지를 말할 때는 during을 쓰지 않고 for를 쓴다. 예를 들어, "I went to Florida during two weeks."라고 하지 않고 "I went to Florida for two weeks."라고 한다.

불가산명사 해질녘 ❑ 우리는 해질녘에 집에 도착했다.

1 불가산명사 흙먼지 ❑ 탱크는 이동하면서 지나가는 자리에 엄청난 흙먼지를 일으킨다. **2** 불가산명사 먼지 ❑ 계단에 먼지가 두껍게 내려앉은 것을 볼 수 있었다. **3** 불가산명사 가루, 입자 ❑ 대기가 디젤 가스와 석탄 가루 때문에 너무 침침해서, 앞을 거의 볼 수 없다. **4** 타동사/자동사 먼지를 닦아내다 ❑ 나는 거실에 진공청소기를 돌리고 먼지를 닦아내고 윤을 냈다. **5** 타동사/자동사 뿌리다 ❑ 생선에 밀가루를 살짝 뿌리세요. **6** 구 사라지다 [해학체, 비격식체, 강조] ❑ 소중히 여겼던 가치들이 지난 30년 동안 많이 사라졌다. **7** 구 사태가 진정되다 [비격식체] ❑ 일단 사태가 진정되자 벡이 자신의 결정을 옹호했다. **8** 구 먼지가 쌓이다 ❑ 많은 기계들이 지하실에서 먼지가 쌓이고 있다.

가산명사 쓰레기통 [영국영어; 미국영어 대개 garbage can]

1 형용사 먼지투성이의 ❑ 그들은 달빛 아래 먼지가 날리는 길을 따라 한가로이 거닐기 시작했다. **2** 형용사 먼지가 쌓인 ❑ 먼지 쌓인 다락방

du|ti|ful /dˈutɪfəl, BRIT dyuˈːtɪfʊl/ ADJ If you say that someone is **dutiful**, you mean that they do everything that they are expected to do. ❑ *The days of the dutiful wife, who sacrifices her career for her husband, are over.* ● **du|ti|ful|ly** ADV [ADV with v] ❑ *The inspector dutifully recorded the date in a large red book.*

duty ◆◇◇ /dˈuti, BRIT dyuˈːti/ (**duties**) 1 N-UNCOUNT **Duty** is work that you have to do for your job. ❑ *Staff must report for duty at their normal place of work.* 2 N-PLURAL Your **duties** are tasks which you have to do because they are part of your job. ❑ *I carried out my duties conscientiously.* 3 N-SING If you say that something is your **duty**, you believe that you ought to do it because it is your responsibility. ❑ *I consider it my duty to write to you and thank you.* 4 N-VAR **Duties** are taxes which you pay to the government on goods that you buy. ❑ *Import duties still average 30%.* 5 PHRASE If someone such as a police officer or a nurse is **off duty**, they are not working. If someone is **on duty**, they are working. ❑ *I'm off duty.*

형용사 순종적인, 의무를 다하는 ❑ 남편을 위해 자신의 직업을 희생하는 순종적인 아내의 시대는 끝났다. ● 성실하게 부사 ❑ 검사관이 붉은 표지의 커다란 명부에 성실하게 날짜를 기록했다.

1 불가산명사 근무, 임무 ❑ 직원은 그들의 정규 근무지에 출근해야만 한다. 2 복수명사 직무 ❑ 나는 양심적으로 내 직무를 수행했다. 3 단수명사 의무 ❑ 나는 너에게 편지를 쓰고 감사를 표하는 것이 내 의무라고 생각한다. 4 가산명사 또는 불가산명사 세금, 관세 ❑ 수입 관세가 아직도 평균 30퍼센트이다. 5 구 비번인; 근무 중인 ❑ 나는 비번이야.

Thesaurus   duty의 참조어

N.	assignment, responsibility, task 1 2
	obligation 3

Word Partnership   duty의 연어

N.	**guard** duty, **jury** duty, **sense of** duty 3
ADJ.	**civic** duty, **military** duty, **patriotic** duty 3
PREP.	**off** duty, **on** duty 5

Word Link   *free ≈ without : care*free, duty-*free*, tax-*free*

duty-free ADJ **Duty-free** goods are sold at airports or on planes or ships at a cheaper price than usual because you do not have to pay import tax on them. ❑ *...duty-free cigarettes.*

형용사 면세의 ❑ 면세 담배

duty-free shop (**duty-free shops**) N-COUNT A **duty-free shop** is a shop, for example at an airport, where you can buy goods at a cheaper price than usual, because no tax is paid on them.

가산명사 면세점

du|vet /dˈuveɪ, BRIT duˈːveɪ/ (**duvets**) N-COUNT A **duvet** is a large cover filled with feathers or similar material which you put over yourself in bed instead of a sheet and blankets. [mainly BRIT; AM usually **comforter**]

가산명사 (속에 깃털이나 솜을 채운) 이불 [주로 영국영어; 미국영어 대개 comforter]

DVD /dˌi vi dˈi/ (**DVDs**) N-COUNT A **DVD** is a disk on which a movie or music is recorded. DVD disks are similar to compact disks but hold a lot more information. **DVD** is an abbreviation for "digital video disk" or "digital versatile disk." ❑ *...a DVD player.* →see **laser** →see Word Web: **DVD**

가산명사 디브이디 ❑ 디브이디 플레이어

DVT /dˌi vi tˈi/ (**DVTs**) N-VAR **DVT** is a serious medical condition caused by blood clots in the legs moving up to the lungs. **DVT** is an abbreviation for "deep vein thrombosis." [MEDICAL]

가산명사 또는 불가산명사 심부정맥 혈전증 [의학]

dwarf /dwˈɔrf/ (**dwarves, dwarfs, dwarfing, dwarfed**)

The spellings **dwarves** or **dwarfs** are used for the plural form of the noun.

철자 dwarves와 dwarfs는 명사의 복수형으로도 쓴다.

1 V-T If one person or thing **is dwarfed** by another, the second is so much bigger than the first that it makes them look very small. ❑ *His figure is dwarfed by the huge red McDonald's sign.* 2 ADJ **Dwarf** is used to describe varieties or species of plants and animals which are much smaller than the usual size for their kind. [ADJ n] ❑ *...dwarf shrubs.* 3 N-COUNT In children's stories, a **dwarf** is an imaginary creature that is like a small man. Dwarfs often have magical powers.

1 타동사 작아 보이다 ❑ 거대한 빨간 색 맥도날드 간판 때문에 그의 모습이 작아 보인다. 2 형용사 난쟁이의, 키 작은 ❑ 키 작은 관목 3 가산명사 난쟁이

dwell /dwˈɛl/ (**dwells, dwelling, dwelt** or **dwelled**) 1 V-I If you **dwell on** something, especially something unpleasant, you think, speak, or write about it a lot or for quite a long time. ❑ *"I'd rather not dwell on the past," he told me.* 2 →see also **dwelling**

1 자동사 연연하다 ❑ "지난 일에 연연하고 싶지 않아."라고 그가 내게 말했다.

dwell|er /dwˈɛlər/ (**dwellers**) N-COUNT A city **dweller** or slum **dweller**, for example, is a person who lives in the kind of place or house indicated. ❑ *The number of city dwellers is growing.*

가산명사 거주자 ❑ 도시 거주자의 수가 증가하고 있다.

dwell|ing /dwˈɛlɪŋ/ (**dwellings**) N-COUNT A **dwelling** or a **dwelling place** is a place where someone lives. [FORMAL] ❑ *Some 3,500 new dwellings are planned for the area.*

가산명사 거주지 [격식체] ❑ 대략 3,500채의 신 거주지가 그 지역에 마련될 계획이다.

Word Web   DVD

DVDs aren't just for **movies** anymore. New DVDs (**digital video discs**) provide even better sound quality than audio **CDs** (**compact discs**). Since the 1980s, CDs have provided high fidelity sound reproduction. Both CDs and DVDs **sample** the **music**, but DVDs are able to store more information and they have more samples per second. The information is also more accurate. Many people think that when you **play** a DVD, it sounds more like live music.

a b c d e f g h i j k l m n o p q r s t u v w x y z

dwelt /dwɛlt/ Dwelt is the past tense and past participle of **dwell**.

dwin|dle /dwɪndəl/ (dwindles, dwindling, dwindled) V-I If something **dwindles**, it becomes smaller, weaker, or less in number. ❑ *The factory's workforce has dwindled from over 4,000 to a few hundred.*

dye /daɪ/ (dyes, dyeing, dyed) ■ V-T If you **dye** something such as hair or cloth, you change its color by soaking it in a special liquid. ❑ *The women prepared, spun and dyed the wool.* ■ N-MASS **Dye** is a substance made from plants or chemicals which is mixed into a liquid and used to change the color of something such as cloth or hair. ❑ *...bottles of hair dye.* →see **hair**

dy|ing /daɪɪŋ/ ■ **Dying** is the present participle of **die**. ■ ADJ A **dying** person or animal is very ill and likely to die soon. [ADJ n] ❑ *...a dying man.* ● N-PLURAL The **dying** are people who are dying. ❑ *By the time our officers arrived, the dead and the dying were everywhere.* ■ ADJ You use **dying** to describe something which happens at the time when someone dies, or is connected with that time. [ADJ n] ❑ *It'll stay in my mind till my dying day.* ■ ADJ The **dying** days or **dying** minutes of a state of affairs or an activity are its last days or minutes. [ADJ n] ❑ *The islands were seized by the Soviet army in the dying days of the second world war.* ■ ADJ A **dying** tradition or industry is becoming less important and is likely to disappear completely. [ADJ n] ❑ *Shipbuilding is a dying business.*

dyke /daɪk/ (dykes) ■ N-COUNT A **dyke** is a lesbian. [INFORMAL, OFFENSIVE] ■ →see **dike 1**

Word Link   *dyn ≈ power : dynamic, dynamite, dynamo*

---

dy|nam|ic /daɪnæmɪk/ (dynamics) ■ ADJ If you describe someone as **dynamic**, you approve of them because they are full of energy or full of new and exciting ideas. [APPROVAL] ❑ *He seemed a dynamic and energetic leader.* ● **dy|nami|cal|ly** /daɪnæmɪkli/ ADV ❑ *He's one of the most dynamically imaginative jazz pianists still functioning.* ■ ADJ If you describe something as **dynamic**, you approve of it because it is very active and energetic. [APPROVAL] ❑ *South Asia continues to be the most dynamic economic region in the world.* ■ ADJ A **dynamic** process is one that constantly changes and progresses. ❑ *...a dynamic, evolving worldwide epidemic.* ● **dy|nami|cal|ly** ADV ❑ *Germany has a dynamically growing market at home.* ■ N-COUNT The **dynamic** of a system or process is the force that causes it to change or progress. ❑ *The dynamics of the market demands constant change and adjustment.* ■ N-PLURAL The **dynamics** of a situation or group of people are the opposing forces within it that cause it to change. ❑ *What is needed is insight into the dynamics of the social system.*

dy|na|mism /daɪnəmɪzəm/ ■ N-UNCOUNT If you say that someone or something has **dynamism**, you are expressing approval of the fact that they are full of energy or full of new and exciting ideas. [APPROVAL] ❑ *...a situation that calls for dynamism and new thinking.* ■ N-UNCOUNT If you refer to the **dynamism** of a situation or system, you are referring to the fact that it is changing in an exciting and dramatic way. [APPROVAL] ❑ *Such changes are also indicators of economic dynamism and demographic expansion.*

dy|na|mite /daɪnəmaɪt/ ■ N-UNCOUNT **Dynamite** is a type of explosive that contains nitroglycerin. ❑ *Fifty yards of track was blown up with dynamite.* ■ N-UNCOUNT If you describe a piece of information as **dynamite**, you think that people will react strongly to it. [INFORMAL] ❑ *The book is dynamite, and if she publishes it, there will be no hiding place for her.* ■ N-UNCOUNT If you describe someone or something as **dynamite**, you think that they are exciting. [INFORMAL, APPROVAL] ❑ *The first kiss is dynamite.*

dy|na|mo /daɪnəmoʊ/ (dynamos) N-COUNT A **dynamo** is a device that uses the movement of a machine or vehicle to produce electricity. ❑ *...a bicycle with a dynamo.*

dyn|as|ty /daɪnəsti, BRIT dɪnəsti/ (dynasties) ■ N-COUNT A **dynasty** is a series of rulers of a country who all belong to the same family. ❑ *The Seljuk dynasty of Syria was founded in 1094.* ■ N-COUNT A **dynasty** is a period of time during which a country is ruled by members of the same family. ❑ *...carvings dating back to the Ming dynasty.* ■ N-COUNT A **dynasty** is a family which has members from two or more generations who are important in a particular field of activity, for example in business or politics. ❑ *This is a family-owned company – the current president is the fourth in this dynasty.*

dys|lexia /dɪslɛksiə/ N-UNCOUNT If someone suffers from **dyslexia**, they have difficulty with reading because of a slight disorder of their brain. [TECHNICAL]

---

dwell의 과거 및 과거 분사

자동사 그 공장의 총 근로자 수가 4천 명 이상에서 몇 백 명으로 줄어들었다.

■ 타동사 염색하다 ❑ 여자들이 양모를 준비해서, 실을 잣고 그것을 염색했다. ■ 물질명사 염료 ❑ 머리 염색약 여러 병

■ die의 현재 분사 ■ 형용사 죽어 가는 ❑ 죽어 가는 남자 ● 복수명사 죽어 가는 사람들 ❑ 이 지역 경관들이 도착했을 때, 여기저기에 죽은 사람들과 죽어 가는 사람들이 있었다. ■ 형용사 죽는 ❑ 내가 죽는 날까지 그걸 잊지 못할 거야. ■ 형용사 마지막의 ❑ 그 섬들은 2차 세계 대전이 끝날 무렵에 구 소련군에게 장악당했다. ■ 형용사 사라져 가는 ❑ 조선업은 사양 사업이다.

■ 가산명사 여자 동성애자, 레즈비언 [비격식체, 모욕어]

■ 형용사 역동적인 [마음에 듦] ❑ 그는 역동적이고 원기 왕성한 지도자인 듯했다. ● 정열적으로 부사 ❑ 그는 아직도 가장 정열적으로 활동하는 상상력이 풍부한 재즈 피아니스트 중 한 명이다. ■ 형용사 역동적인 [마음에 듦] ❑ 남아시아는 여전히 세계에서 가장 역동적인 경제 지역이다. ■ 형용사 계속 진행되는 ❑ 전 세계적으로 퍼져 나가며 계속 진행되는 전염병 ● 역동적으로 부사 ❑ 독일에는 자국 내에서 역동적으로 성장하는 시장이 있다. ■ 가산명사 원동력 ❑ 시장의 원동력은 지속적인 변화와 조정을 요구한다. ■ 복수명사 역학 ❑ 필요한 것은 사회 체제의 역학에 대한 통찰력이다.

■ 불가산명사 패기 [마음에 듦] ❑ 패기와 새로운 사고를 요구하는 상황 ■ 불가산명사 역동성 [마음에 듦] ❑ 그러한 변화 역시 경제적 역동성과 인구 팽창을 보여 주는 지표이다.

■ 불가산명사 다이너마이트 ❑ 다이너마이트로 오십 야드에 걸친 선로가 폭파되었다. ■ 불가산명사 스캔들이 될 만한 것 [비격식체] ❑ 그 책은 스캔들이 될 만한 것으로, 그녀가 그것을 출판한다면 그녀로서는 숨을 곳이 없을 것이다. ■ 불가산명사 끝내 주는 것 [비격식체, 마음에 듦] ❑ 첫 키스는 끝내 준다.

가산명사 발전기 ❑ 발전기가 달린 자전거

■ 가산명사 왕조 ❑ 시리아의 셀주크 왕조는 1094년에 세워졌다. ■ 가산명사 왕조 시대 ❑ 중국 명 왕조 시대에 만들어진 조각품 ■ 가산명사 명가 ❑ 이 기업은 가족 소유이며, 현재 사장은 이 명가 출신 중 네 번째이다.

불가산명사 난독증 [전문 용어]

Ee

E, e /iː/ (E's, e's) N-VAR **E** is the fifth letter of the English alphabet.

가산명사 또는 불가산명사 영어 알파벳의 다섯 번째 글자

each ♦♦♦ /iːtʃ/ **1** DET If you refer to **each** thing or **each** person in a group, you are referring to every member of the group and considering them as individuals. ❏ *Each book is beautifully illustrated.* ❏ *Each year, hundreds of animals are killed in this way.* ● PRON **Each** is also a pronoun. ❏ *...two bedrooms, each with three beds.* ● PRON-EMPH **Each** is also an emphasizing pronoun. ❏ *We each have different needs and interests.* ● ADV **Each** is also an adverb. [amount ADV] ❏ *The children were given one each, handed to them or placed on their plates.* ● QUANT **Each** is also a quantifier. [QUANT of def-pl-n] ❏ *He handed each of them a page of photos.* ❏ *Each of these exercises takes one or two minutes to do.* **2** QUANT If you refer to **each one** of the members of a group, you are emphasizing that something applies to every one of them. [EMPHASIS] [QUANT of def-pl-n] ❏ *He picked up forty of these publications and read each one of them.* **3** PHRASE You can refer to **each and every** member of a group to emphasize that you mean all the members of that group. [EMPHASIS] ❏ *My goal was that each and every person responsible for Yankel's murder be brought to justice.* **4** PRON-RECIP You use **each other** when you are saying that each member of a group does something to the others or has a particular connection with the others. [V PRON, prep PRON] ❏ *We looked at each other in silence, each equally shocked.* ❏ *Both sides are willing to make allowances for each other's political sensitivities.*

> You use **each** to refer to every person or thing in a group when you are thinking about them as individuals. You use **every** to refer to all the members of a group that has more than two members. ❏ *He listened to every news bulletin...an equal chance for every child.* Note that **each** can be used to refer to both members of a pair. ❏ *Each apartment has two bedrooms... We each carried a suitcase.* Note that **each** and **every** are only used with singular nouns.

1 한정사 각각의, 각자의 ❏ 각각의 책은 삽화로 아름답게 꾸며져 있다. ❏ 매년, 수백 마리의 동물이 이런 식으로 도살된다. ● 대명사 각각, 각자 ❏ 각각 세 개의 침대가 구비된 침실 두 개 ● 강조대명사 제각각 ❏ 우리는 제 각각의 요구와 관심사가 다르다. ● 부사 각각, 각기 ❏ 아이들 각자에게 하나씩 건네주거나 접시에 놓아 주었다. ● 수량사 각각, 각자 ❏ 그는 그들 각자에게 사진 한 장씩을 건넸다. ❏ 이 연습 문제들은 각각을 푸는 데 일 분 정도 걸린다. **2** 수량사 하나하나, 각각 [강조] ❏ 그는 이 간행물들 중 사십 개를 골라 그것들을 하나하나 다 읽었다. **3** 구 하나도 빠짐없이 [강조] ❏ 내 목표는 얀켈의 살인에 책임이 있는 사람들을 한 명도 빠짐없이 법의 심판을 받게 하는 것이었다. **4** 상호대명사 서로 ❏ 우리는 둘 다 똑같이 충격을 받아서, 아무 말도 없이 서로를 쳐다보았다. ❏ 양측 다 기꺼이 서로에게 정치적으로 민감한 사안은 감안할 용의가 있다.

> each는 한 집단의 모든 사람이나 사물을 개별적으로 생각할 때 그 각 개체를 가리킨다. every는 세 명 이상인 집단의 모든 구성원을 가리킨다. ❏ 그는 모든 뉴스 속보를 들었다....모든 아이들에게 공평한 기회. each는 한 쌍의 두 구성원을 모두 지칭할 수도 있음을 유의하라. ❏ 각 아파트에는 침실이 각각 두 개가 있다... 우리는 각자 여행 가방을 하나씩 갖고 있었다. each와 every는 단수 명사만 함께 쓰임을 유의하라.

eager ♦♢♢ /iːgər/ **1** ADJ If you are **eager to** do or have something, you want to do or have it very much. ❏ *Robert was eager to talk about life in the Army.* ❏ *When my own son was five years old, I became eager for another baby.* ● **eager|ness** N-UNCOUNT ❏ *...an eagerness to learn.* **2** ADJ If you look or sound **eager**, you look or sound as if you expect something interesting or enjoyable to happen. ❏ *Arty sneered at the crowd of eager faces around him.* ● **eager|ly** ADV ❏ *"So what do you think will happen?" he asked eagerly.* ● **eager|ness** N-UNCOUNT ❏ *It was the voice of a woman speaking with breathless eagerness.*

1 형용사 간절히 바라는 ❏ 로버트는 군대 생활에 대해 간절히 이야기하고 싶어 했다. ❏ 우리 아들이 다섯 살이 되었을 때, 나는 아이를 하나 더 간절히 바라게 되었다. ● 열망 불가산명사 ❏ 배우고자 하는 열망 **2** 형용사 열망어린 ❏ 알티는 자기 주변 군중들의 열망어린 표정을 비웃었다. ● 간절히 부사 ❏ "그럼 무슨 일이 일어날 것 같은가요?"라고 그가 간절히 물었다. ● 간절함 불가산명사 ❏ 그것은 숨 막힐 듯 간절한 여인의 목소리였다.

eagle /iːgl/ (eagles) N-COUNT An **eagle** is a large bird that lives by eating small animals.

가산명사 독수리

ear ♦♢♢ /ɪər/ (ears) **1** N-COUNT Your **ears** are the two parts of your body, one on each side of your head, with which you hear sounds. ❏ *He whispered something in her ear.* **2** N-SING If you have an **ear** for music or language, you are able to hear its sounds accurately and to interpret them or reproduce them well. ❏ *Moby certainly has a fine ear for a tune.* **3** N-COUNT **Ear** is often used to refer to people's willingness to listen to what someone is saying. ❏ *What would cause the masses to give him a far more sympathetic ear?* **4** N-COUNT The **ears** of a cereal plant such as wheat or barley are the parts at the top of the stem, which contain the seeds or grains. ❏ *American farmers use machines to pick the ears of corn from the plants.* **5** PHRASE If a request **falls on deaf ears** or if the person to whom the request is made **turns a deaf ear to** it, they take no notice of it. ❏ *I hope that our appeals will not fall on deaf ears.* **6** PHRASE If you **play by ear** or **play** a piece of music **by ear**, you play music by relying on your memory rather than by reading printed music. ❏ *Neil sat at the piano and began playing, by ear, the music he'd heard his older sister practicing.* **7** music to your ears →see music
→see face
→see Word Web: ear

1 가산명사 귀 ❏ 그는 그녀의 귀에 대고 무슨 말을 속삭였다. **2** 단수명사 음감 ❏ 모비는 정말 음감이 예민하다. **3** 가산명사 경청 ❏ 어떻게 하면 군중이 그의 말에 훨씬 더 호의적으로 귀를 기울이겠는가? **4** 가산명사 이삭, 곡식 열매 ❏ 미국의 농부들은 옥수수에서 옥수수 알갱이를 따는 데 기계를 사용한다. **5** 구 묵살되다, 묵살하다 ❏ 우리의 호소가 묵살되지 않기를 바란다. **6** 구 귀로 본 기억을 살려 연주하다 ❏ 닐은 피아노 앞에 앉아서 누나가 연습할 때 들은 적이 있는 곡을 연주하기 시작했다.

ear|ache /ɪəreɪk/ (earaches) N-VAR **Earache** is a pain in the inside part of your ear. ❏ *As a lad, Jim Joel often suffered from earache.*

가산명사 또는 불가산명사 귓병 ❏ 소년 시절에 짐 조엘은 자주 귓병을 앓았다.

ear|drum /ɪərdrʌm/ (eardrums) also **ear drum** N-COUNT Your **eardrums** are the thin pieces of tightly stretched skin inside each ear, which vibrate when sound waves reach them. ❏ *Ahmad Zabadne, 24, from North London, suffered a perforated eardrum in the blast.* →see ear

가산명사 고막 ❏ 런던 북부 출신인 24세의 아마드 자바드네는 그 폭파 사고로 고막이 파열되었다.

earl /ɜːrl/ (earls) N-COUNT An **earl** is a British nobleman. ❏ *...the first Earl of Birkenhead.*

가산명사 백작 ❏ 버컨헤드 백작 1세

Word Web   ear

The **ear** collects **sound waves** and sends them to the brain. First the **external ear** picks up sound waves. Then these sound **vibrations** travel along the **ear canal** and strike the **eardrum**. The eardrum pushes against a series of tiny bones. These bones carry the vibrations into the **inner ear**. There they are picked up by the hair cells in the **cochlea**. At that point, the vibrations turn into electronic impulses. The cochlea is connected to the hearing **nerve**. It sends the electronic impulses to the brain.

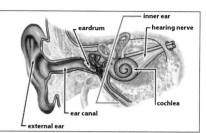

ear|li|er ♦♦◇ /ɜ́rliər/ **1** Earlier is the comparative of **early**. **2** ADV **Earlier** is used to refer to a point or period in time before the present or before the time you are talking about. ❑ *As mentioned earlier, the University supplements this information with an interview.* ❑ *...political reforms announced by the President earlier this year.* ● ADJ **Earlier** is also an adjective. [ADJ n] ❑ *Earlier reports of gunshots have not been substantiated.*

1 early의 비교급 **2** 부사 이전에, 앞서 ❑ 앞서 언급했듯이, 그 대학은 이 자료에 면접을 추가합니다. ❑ 올해 초에 대통령이 발표한 정치 개혁 ● 형용사 지난번 ❑ 총격에 관한 지난번 보도는 확인되지 않았다.

ear|li|est /ɜ́rliɪst/ **1** Earliest is the superlative of **early**. **2** PHRASE **At the earliest** means not before the date or time mentioned. ❑ *The first official results are not expected until Tuesday at the earliest.*

1 early의 최상급 **2** 구 빨라도 ❑ 최초의 공식 결과는 빨라도 화요일은 되어야 나올 것이다.

ear|lobe /ɪ́ərloʊb/ (**earlobes**) also **ear lobe** N-COUNT Your **earlobes** are the soft parts at the bottom of your ears. ❑ *...the holes in her earlobes.* →see **face**

가산명사 귓불 ❑ 그녀의 귓불에 난 구멍

ear|ly ♦♦♦ /ɜ́rli/ (**earlier, earliest**) **1** ADV **Early** means before the usual time that a particular event or activity happens. [ADV after v] ❑ *I knew I had to get up early.* ● ADJ **Early** is also an adjective. [ADJ n] ❑ *I decided that I was going to take early retirement.* **2** ADJ **Early** means near the beginning of a day, week, year, or other period of time. [ADJ n] ❑ *...in the 1970s and the early 1980s.* ❑ *She was in her early teens.* ● ADV **Early** is also an adverb. ❑ *We'll hope to see you some time early next week.* **3** ADV **Early** means before the time that was arranged or expected. [ADV after v] ❑ *She arrived early to secure a place at the front.* ● ADJ **Early** is also an adjective. ❑ *I'm always early.* **4** ADJ **Early** means near the beginning of a period in history, or in the history of something such as the world, a society, or an activity. [ADJ n] ❑ *...the early stages of pregnancy.* ❑ *...Fassbinder's early movies.* **5** ADJ **Early** means near the beginning of something such as a piece of work or a process. [ADJ n] ❑ *...the book's early chapters.* ● ADV **Early** is also an adverb. ❑ *...an incident which occurred much earlier in the game.* **6** ADJ **Early** refers to plants which flower or crop before or at the beginning of the main season. [ADJ n] ❑ *...these early cabbages and cauliflowers.* ● ADV **Early** is also an adverb. ❑ *This early flowering gladiolus is not very hardy.* **7** ADJ **Early** reports or indications of something are the first reports or indications about it. [FORMAL] [ADJ n] ❑ *The early indications look encouraging.* **8** PHRASE You can use **as early as** to emphasize that a particular time or period is surprisingly early. [EMPHASIS] ❑ *Inflation could fall back into single figures as early as this month.* **9** PHRASE If you say about something that might be true that **it is early days**, you mean that it is too soon for you to be completely sure about it. [mainly BRIT, INFORMAL] ❑ *It is early days but we think it is a major breakthrough.*

1 부사 일찍 ❑ 나는 일찍 일어나야 한다는 것을 알고 있었다. **●** 형용사 이른, 조기의 ❑ 나는 조기 퇴직을 결심했다. **2** 형용사 초기 ❑ 1970년대와 1980년대 초에 ❑ 그녀는 십대 초반이었다. **●** 부사 초기에 ❑ 우리는 다음 주 초에 당신을 만나고 싶습니다. **3** 부사 일찍 ❑ 그녀는 앞 자리를 잡으려고 일찍 도착했다. **●** 형용사 이른 ❑ 나는 항상 일찍 온다. **4** 형용사 초기의 ❑ 임신 초기 ❑ 패스빈더의 초기 영화들 **5** 형용사 전반의, 앞쪽의 ❑ 그 책의 전반부 ● 부사 초반에 ❑ 경기의 아주 초반에 일어난 사건 **6** 형용사 조생종의, 철이른 ❑ 이 철 이른 양배추와 콜리플라워 ● 부사 제철보다 빨리 ❑ 제철보다 빨리 피는 이 글라디올러스는 내한성이 적다. **7** 형용사 초기의 [격식체] ❑ 초기의 조짐은 좋아 보인다. **8** 구 빠르게도, 벌써 [강조] ❑ 인플레가 빠르면 이번 달에 한 자리 수로 떨어질 수도 있다. **9** 구 시기상조이다, 좀 이른 감이 있다 [주로 영국영어, 비격식체] ❑ 좀 이른 감이 있긴 하지만 우리는 이것이 중대한 성과라고 생각한다.

ear|ly bird (**early birds**) **1** N-COUNT An **early bird** is someone who does something or goes somewhere very early, especially very early in the morning. ❑ *We've always been early birds, getting up at 5.30 or 6 a.m.* **2** ADJ An **early bird** deal or offer is one that is available at a reduced price, but which you must buy earlier than you would normally do. [ADJ n] ❑ *Early bird discounts are usually available at the beginning of the season.*

1 가산명사 아침 일찍 일어나는 사람 ❑ 우리는 항상 아침 일찍 5시 30분이나 6시에 일어난다. **2** 형용사 조기할인의 ❑ 조기 구입 할인은 보통 계절의 초반에 이용 가능하다.

ear|mark /ɪ́ərmɑrk/ (**earmarks, earmarking, earmarked**) **1** V-T If resources such as money **are earmarked for** a particular purpose, they are reserved for that purpose. ❑ *...the extra money being earmarked for the new projects.* ❑ *China has earmarked more than $20bn for oil exploration.* **2** V-T If something **has been earmarked for** closure or disposal, for example, people have decided that it will be closed or got rid of. [usu passive] ❑ *Their support meant that he was not forced to sell the business which was earmarked for disposal last year.*

1 타동사 따로 배정하다, 지정하다 ❑ 새 프로젝트를 위해 따로 배정된 가외 자금 ❑ 중국은 석유 탐사를 위해 200억 달러 이상을 배정했다. **2** 타동사 _으로 지정되다 ❑ 그들의 후원으로 그는 작년에 매각 처분이 내려진 사업장을 팔지 않아도 되었다.

earn ♦♦◇ /ɜ́rn/ (**earns, earning, earned**) **1** V-T If you **earn** money, you receive money in return for work that you do. ❑ *What a lovely way to earn a living.* **2** V-T If something **earns** money, it produces money as profit or interest. ❑ *...a bank account which earns little or no interest.* **3** V-T If you **earn** something such as praise, you get it because you deserve it. ❑ *Companies must earn a reputation for honesty.*

1 타동사 벌다 ❑ 생활비를 버는 정말 멋진 방법이군요. **2** 타동사 수익을 내다 ❑ 이자가 거의 없는 은행 계좌 **3** 타동사 얻다, 획득하다 ❑ 기업은 정직하다는 평판을 얻어야만 한다.

Thesaurus   earn의 참조어

v.   bring in, make, take in **1**

earn|er /ɜ́rnər/ (**earners**) N-COUNT An **earner** is someone or something that earns money or produces profit. ❑ *...a typical wage earner.*

가산명사 수입자, 수익원 ❑ 전형적인 임금 생활자

ear|nest /ɜ́rnɪst/ **1** PHRASE If something is done or happens **in earnest**, it happens to a much greater extent and more seriously than before. ❑ *Campaigning will begin in earnest tomorrow.* **2** ADJ **Earnest** people are very serious and sincere in what they say or do, because they think that their actions and beliefs are important. ❑ *Ella was a pious, earnest woman.*

1 구 본격적으로 ❑ 선거 유세는 내일부터 본격적으로 시작될 것이다. **2** 형용사 진지한 ❑ 엘라는 신앙심이 깊고 진지한 여자였다.

ear|nest|ly /ɜ́rnɪstli/ **1** ADV If you say something **earnestly**, you say it very seriously, often because you believe that it is important or you are trying to persuade someone else to believe it. [ADV with v] ❑ *"Did you?" she asked earnestly.* **2** ADV If you do something **earnestly**, you do it in a thorough and serious way, intending to succeed. ❑ *She always listened earnestly as if this might help her to understand.*

1 부사 진지하게 ❑ "그랬어?"라고 그녀가 진지하게 물었다. **2** 부사 진지하게 ❑ 마치 자신이 이해하는 데 도움이 되기라도 하는 듯, 그녀는 항상 진지하게 귀를 기울였다.

Word Web — earth

The **earth** is made of material left over when the **sun** formed. In the beginning, about 4 billion years ago, the earth was liquid **rock**. During its first million years, it cooled into solid rock. **Life**, in the form of bacteria, began in the **oceans** about 3.5 billion years ago. During the next billion years, the **continents** formed. At the same time, the level of **oxygen** in the **atmosphere** increased. **Life forms evolved**, and some of them began to use oxygen. **Evolution** allowed **plants** and **animals** to move from the oceans onto the **land**.

earn|ings ♦◇◇ /ɜ́rnɪŋz/ N-PLURAL Your **earnings** are the sums of money that you earn by working. ❑ *Average weekly earnings rose by 1.5% in July.*

복수명사 소득, 수입 ❑ 6월에는 평균 주간 소득이 1.5퍼센트 증가했다.

ear|phone /ɪ́ərfoʊn/ (**earphones**) N-COUNT **Earphones** are a small piece of equipment which you wear over or inside your ears so that you can listen to a radio or cassette recorder without anyone else hearing.

가산명사 이어폰, 수신기

ear|ring /ɪ́ərɪŋ/ (**earrings**) N-COUNT **Earrings** are pieces of jewelry which you attach to your ears. ❑ *...a pair of diamond earrings.* →see **jewelry**

가산명사 귀걸이 ❑ 다이아몬드 귀걸이 한 쌍

ear|shot /ɪ́ərʃɒt/ PHRASE If you are **within earshot** of someone or something, you are close enough to be able to hear them. If you are **out of earshot**, you are too far away to hear them. ❑ *It is within earshot of a main road.*

구 부르면 들리는 곳에, 불러도 들리지 않는 곳에 ❑ 그것은 큰길에서 부르면 들리는 곳에 있다.

earth ♦♦◇ /ɜ́rθ/ ❶ N-PROPER **Earth** or **the Earth** is the planet on which we live. People usually say **Earth** when they are referring to the planet as part of the universe, and **the Earth** when they are talking about the planet as the place where we live. ❑ *The space shuttle Atlantis returned safely to earth today.* ❷ N-SING **The earth** is the land surface on which we live and move about. ❑ *The earth shook and swayed and the walls of neighboring houses fell around them.* ❸ N-UNCOUNT **Earth** is the substance on the land surface of the earth, for example clay or sand, in which plants grow. ❑ *The road winds for miles through parched earth, scrub, and cactus.* ❹ N-SING The **earth** in an electric plug or piece of electrical equipment is the wire through which electricity can pass into the ground, which makes the equipment safe if something goes wrong with it. [BRIT; AM **ground**] ❑ *The earth wire was not connected.* ❺ →see also **down-to-earth** ❻ PHRASE **On earth** is used for emphasis in questions that begin with words such as "how," "why," "what," or "where." It is often used to suggest that there is no obvious or easy answer to the question being asked. [EMPHASIS] ❑ *How on earth did that happen?* ❼ PHRASE **On earth** is used for emphasis after some negative noun groups, for example "no reason." [EMPHASIS] ❑ *There was no reason on earth why she couldn't have moved in with us.* ❽ PHRASE If you come **down to earth** or **back to earth**, you have to face the reality of everyday life after a period of great excitement. ❑ *When he came down to earth after his win he admitted: "It was an amazing feeling."* →see **core, eclipse, erosion** →see Word Web: **earth**

❶ 고유명사 지구 ❑ 우주 왕복선 아틀란티스호가 오늘 무사히 지구로 돌아왔다. ❷ 단수명사 땅 ❑ 땅이 진동하고 흔들렸으며 이웃집들의 담장이 무너졌다. ❸ 불가산명사 토양 ❑ 그 길은 메마른 토양과 관목, 그리고 선인장 사이로 수 마일에 걸쳐 구불구불하게 나 있다. ❹ 단수명사 접지 [영국영어; 미국영어 ground] ❑ 접지선이 연결되어 있지 않았다. ❻ 구 세상에, 도대체 [강조] ❑ 도대체 어떻게 그런 일이 일어났니? ❼ 구 전혀, 조금도 [강조] ❑ 그녀가 우리 집에 들어와 함께 살지 못할 이유가 조금도 없었다. ❽ 구 (꿈에서 깨어나) 현실로 돌아오다, 정신을 차리다 ❑ 승리한 이후 정신을 차리고서 그는 그것이 기막힌 느낌이었다고 인정했다.

earth|ly /ɜ́rθli/ ❶ ADJ **Earthly** means happening in the material world of our life on earth and not in any spiritual life or life after death. [ADJ n] ❑ *...the need to confront evil during the earthly life.* ❷ ADJ **Earthly** is used for emphasis in phrases such as **no earthly reason**. If you say that there is **no earthly reason why** something should happen, you are emphasizing that there is no reason at all why it should happen. [EMPHASIS] [ADJ n] ❑ *There is no earthly reason why they should ever change.*

❶ 형용사 현세의, 이승의 ❑ 현세의 삶을 사는 동안 악에 맞설 필요 ❷ 형용사 전혀 [강조] ❑ 그들이 변해야 할 이유가 전혀 없다.

earth|quake /ɜ́rθkweɪk/ (**earthquakes**) N-COUNT An **earthquake** is a shaking of the ground caused by movement of the earth's crust. ❑ *...the San Francisco earthquake of 1906.* →see Word Web: **earthquake**

가산명사 지진 ❑ 1906년도의 샌프란시스코 지진

earthy /ɜ́rθi/ (**earthier, earthiest**) ❶ ADJ If you describe someone as **earthy**, you mean that they are open and direct, and talk about subjects which other people avoid or feel ashamed about. [APPROVAL] ❑ *...his extremely earthy humor.* ❷ ADJ If you describe something as **earthy**, you mean it looks, smells, or feels like earth. ❑ *I'm attracted to warm, earthy colors.*

❶ 형용사 솔직한, 현실적인 [마음에 듦] ❑ 그의 극도로 솔직한 유머 ❷ 형용사 흙 같은, 황토의 ❑ 나는 따스한 황토색에 마음이 끌린다.

Word Web — earthquake

Earthquakes occur when two tectonic **plates** meet and start to slide past each other. This meeting point is called the focus. It may be located anywhere from a few hundred meters to a few hundred kilometers below the surface. The resulting pressure causes a split in the earth's **crust** called a **fault**. Vibrations travel out from the focus in all directions. These **seismic waves** cause little damage until they reach the surface. The epicenter, directly above the focus, receives the greatest damage. Seismologists use seismographs to measure the amount of ground movement during an earthquake.

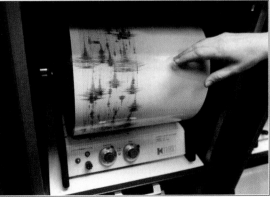

A seismograph recording a major earthquake.

A

ear|wig /ˈɪərwɪɡ/ (**earwigs**) N-COUNT An **earwig** is a small, thin, brown insect that has a pair of claws at the back end of its body.

가산명사 집게벌레

ease ◇◇◇ /iːz/ (**eases**, **easing**, **eased**) **1** PHRASE If you do something **with ease**, you do it easily, without difficulty or effort. ☐ *Anne was intelligent and capable of passing her exams with ease.* **2** N-UNCOUNT If you talk about the **ease** of a particular activity, you are referring to the way that it has been made easier to do, or to the fact that it is already easy to do. ☐ *For ease of reference, only the relevant extracts of the regulations are included.* **3** N-UNCOUNT **Ease** is the state of being very comfortable and able to live as you want, without any worries or problems. ☐ *She lived a life of ease.* **4** V-T/V-I If something unpleasant **eases** or if you **ease** it, it is reduced in degree, speed, or intensity. ☐ *Tensions had eased.* ☐ *I gave him some brandy to ease the pain.* **5** V-T/V-I If you **ease** your **way** somewhere or **ease** somewhere, you move there slowly, carefully, and gently. If you **ease** something somewhere, you move it there slowly, carefully, and gently. ☐ *I eased my way toward the door.* ☐ *He eased his foot off the accelerator.* **6** PHRASE If you are **at ease**, you are feeling confident and relaxed, and are able to talk to people without feeling nervous or anxious. If you put someone **at** their **ease**, you make them feel at ease. ☐ *It is essential to feel at ease with your therapist.* **7** PHRASE If you are **ill at ease**, you feel rather uncomfortable, anxious, or worried. ☐ *He appeared embarrassed and ill at ease with the sustained applause that greeted him.*

1 구 쉽게 ☐ 앤은 총명해서 시험에 쉽게 합격할 수 있었다. **2** 불가산명사 용이함, 편리함 ☐ 참고하기 쉽도록, 법규의 관련 부분만 발췌해 놓았다. **3** 불가산명사 안락 ☐ 그녀는 안락한 생활을 했다. **4** 타동사/자동사 완화되다, 완화시키다 ☐ 긴장이 완화되어 있었다. ☐ 통증을 완화시키기 위해 나는 그에게 브랜디를 좀 주었다. **5** 타동사/자동사 천천히 조심해서 움직이다 ☐ 나는 천천히 문으로 다가갔다. ☐ 그는 천천히 가속기에서 발을 떼었다. **6** 구 편안한 ☐ 치료사와 함께 있을 때는 마음을 편히 하는 것이 중요하다. **7** 구 안절부절 못하는 ☐ 그는 자신을 환영하는 지속적인 박수갈채에 당황해서 어쩔 줄 모르는 것 같았다.

▶**ease up** **1** PHRASAL VERB If something **eases up**, it is reduced in degree, speed, or intensity. ☐ *The rain had eased up.* **2** PHRASAL VERB If you **ease up**, you start to make less effort. ☐ *He told supporters not to ease up even though he's leading in the presidential race.*

1 구동사 완화되다 ☐ 빗줄기가 약해져 있었다. **2** 구동사 느슨해지다 ☐ 그는 비록 자기가 대선에서 앞서긴 하지만 지지자들에게 긴장을 늦추지 말라고 말했다.

eas|el /ˈiːzəl/ (**easels**) N-COUNT An **easel** is a wooden frame that supports a picture which an artist is painting or drawing. →see **painting**

가산명사 이젤, 화가(畵架)

eas|i|ly ◇◇◇ /ˈiːzɪli/ **1** ADV You use **easily** to emphasize that something is very likely to happen, or is very likely to be true. [EMPHASIS] ☐ *It could easily be another year before the economy starts to show some improvement.* **2** ADV You use **easily** to say that something happens more quickly or more often than is usual or normal. [ADV after v] ☐ *He had always cried very easily.* **3** →see also **easy**

1 부사 아마도 [강조] ☐ 내년이 되어야 아마도 경제가 회복 기미를 보이기 시작할 것이다. **2** 부사 쉽게, 잘 ☐ 그는 항상 아주 잘 울었다.

east ◇◇◇ /iːst/ also **East** **1** N-UNCOUNT **The east** is the direction where the sun rises. [also the N] ☐ *...the vast swamps which lie to the east of the River Nile.* **2** N-SING **The east** of a place, country, or region is the part which is in the east. ☐ *...a village in the east of the country.* **3** ADV If you go **east**, you travel toward the east. [ADV after v] ☐ *To drive, go east on Route 9.* **4** ADV Something that is **east** of a place is positioned to the east of it. ☐ *...just east of the center of town.* **5** ADJ The **east** edge, corner, or part of a place or country is the part which is toward the east. [ADJ n] ☐ *...a low line of hills running along the east coast.* **6** ADJ **East** is used in the names of some countries, states, and regions in the east of a larger area. [ADJ n] ☐ *He had been on safari in East Africa with his son.* **7** ADJ An **east** wind is a wind that blows from the east. ☐ *...a bitter east wind.* **8** N-SING **The East** is used to refer to the southern and eastern part of Asia, including India, China, and Japan. ☐ *Every so often, a new martial art arrives from the East.* **9** →see also **Middle East, Far East**

1 불가산명사 동쪽 ☐ 나일 강 동쪽에 위치한 거대한 늪 **2** 단수명사 동부 ☐ 지방의 동부에 있는 마을 **3** 부사 동쪽으로 ☐ 운전해서 가려면, 9번 도로로 를 동쪽으로 가시오. **4** 부사 -의 동쪽 ☐ 시내 중심가의 바로 동쪽 **5** 형용사 동쪽의 ☐ 동부 해안을 따라 이어지는 낮은 구릉 **6** 형용사 동 ☐ 그는 아들과 함께 동아프리카에서 수렵 탐험을 했다. **7** 형용사 동쪽에서 부는 ☐ 매서운 동풍 **8** 단수명사 동양 ☐ 가끔 동양에서 새로운 무술이 전해져 온다.

East|er /ˈiːstər/ (**Easters**) N-VAR **Easter** is a Christian festival when Jesus Christ's return to life is celebrated. It is celebrated on a Sunday in March or April. [oft N n] ☐ *"Happy Easter," he yelled.*

가산명사 또는 불가산명사 부활절 ☐ "즐거운 부활절이 되세요."라고 그가 외쳤다.

east|er|ly /ˈiːstərli/ **1** ADJ An **easterly** point, area, or direction is to the east or toward the east. ☐ *He progressed slowly along the coast in an easterly direction.* **2** ADJ An **easterly** wind is a wind that blows from the east. ☐ *...the cold easterly winds from Scandinavia.*

1 형용사 동쪽 방향의 ☐ 그는 해안을 따라 동쪽 방향으로 천천히 나아갔다. **2** 형용사 동쪽에서 부는 ☐ 스칸디나비아에서 불어오는 차가운 동풍

east|ern ◇◇◇ /ˈiːstərn/ **1** ADJ **Eastern** means in or from the east of a region, state, or country. [ADJ n] ☐ *...Eastern Europe.* **2** ADJ **Eastern** means coming from or associated with the people or countries of the East, such as India, China, or Japan. [ADJ n] ☐ *In many Eastern countries massage was and is a part of everyday life.*

1 형용사 동부의 ☐ 동부 유럽 **2** 형용사 동양의, 동방의 ☐ 동양의 많은 나라에서는 마사지가 일상생활의 일부였고 지금도 그렇다.

east|ward /ˈiːstwərd/

The form **eastwards** is also used.

ADV **Eastward** or **eastwards** means toward the east. [ADV after v] ☐ *A powerful snow storm is moving eastward.* ● ADJ **Eastward** is also an adjective. ☐ *...the eastward expansion of the City of London.*

eastwards도 쓴다.

부사 동쪽으로 ☐ 강력한 눈보라가 동쪽으로 움직이고 있다. ● 형용사 동쪽으로의 ☐ 런던 시의 동쪽으로의 팽창

easy ◇◇◇ /ˈiːzi/ (**easier**, **easiest**) **1** ADJ If a job or action is **easy**, you can do it without difficulty or effort, because it is not complicated and does not cause you problems. ☐ *The shower is easy to install.* ☐ *This is not an easy task.* ● **easily** ADV ☐ *Dress your child in layers of clothes you can remove easily.* **2** ADJ If you describe an action or activity as **easy**, you mean that it is done in a confident, relaxed way. If someone is **easy about** something, they feel relaxed and confident about it. ☐ *He was an easy person to talk to.* ● **easily** ADV [ADV with v] ☐ *They talked amiably and easily about a range of topics.* **3** ADJ If you say that someone has an **easy** life, you mean that they live comfortably without any problems or worries. ☐ *She has not had an easy life.* **4** ADJ If you say that something is **easy** or too **easy**, you are criticizing someone because they have done the most obvious or least difficult thing, and have not considered the situation carefully enough. [DISAPPROVAL] [v-link ADJ, v-link ADJ to-inf, ADJ to-inf] ☐ *That's easy for you to say.* **5** PHRASE If you tell someone to **go easy on** something, you are telling them to use only a small amount of it. [INFORMAL] ☐ *Go easy on the alcohol.* **6** PHRASE If you tell someone to **go easy on**, or **be easy on**, a particular person, you are telling them not to punish or treat that person very severely. [INFORMAL] ☐ *"Go easy on him," Sam repeated, opening the door.* **7** PHRASE If someone tells you to **take it easy** or **take things easy**, they mean

1 형용사 쉬운 ☐ 샤워 장치는 설치하기 쉽다. ☐ 이것은 쉬운 일이 아니다. ● 쉽게 부사 ☐ 아이에게는 쉽게 벗을 수 있는 옷을 겹쳐 입혀라. **2** 형용사 편안한 ☐ 그는 이야기하기 편한 사람이었다. ● 편하게 부사 ☐ 그들은 여러 주제에 대해 다정하고 편하게 이야기했다. **3** 형용사 안락한 ☐ 그녀의 삶은 안락하지 못했다. **4** 형용사 쉬운 [탐탁찮음] ☐ 당신이 그런 말을 하기는 쉽다. **5** 구 적당히 -하다 [비격식체] ☐ 술을 적당히 마셔라. **6** 구 관대하게 대하다 [비격식체] ☐ "그에게 관대하게 대해라."라고 문을 열면서 샘이 재차 말했다. **7** 구 천천히 하다, 서두르지 않다 [비격식체] ☐ 한, 두 주 정도 서두르지 않고 있는 것이 최선이다.

B C D E F G H I J K L M N O P Q R S T U V W X Y Z

that you should relax and not do very much at all. [INFORMAL] ❑ *It is best to take things easy for a week or two.* ◳ →see also **easily**

Thesaurus　　　　*easy*의 참조어

ADJ.　　basic, elementary, simple, uncomplicated; *(ant.)* complicated, difficult, hard ◳

---

easy|going /íːzigóʊɪŋ/ [BRIT **easy-going**] ADJ If you describe someone as **easygoing**, you mean that they are not easily annoyed, worried, or upset, and you think this is a good quality. [APPROVAL] ❑ *He was easygoing and good-natured.*

[영국영어 easy-going] 형용사 대범한, 느긋한 [마음에 듦] ❑ 그는 느긋하고 성격 좋은 사람이었다.

eat ♦♦◇ /íːt/ (**eats, eating, ate, eaten**) ◳ V-T/V-I When you **eat** something, you put it into your mouth, chew it, and swallow it. ❑ *She was eating a sandwich.* ◳ V-I If you **eat** sensibly or healthily, you eat food that is good for you. ❑ *...a campaign to persuade people to eat more healthily.* ◳ V-I If you **eat**, you have a meal. ❑ *Let's go out to eat.* ◳ V-T If something **is eating** you, it is annoying or worrying you. [INFORMAL] [only cont] ❑ *"What the hell's eating you?" he demanded.* ◳ **dog eat dog** →see **dog.** to **eat humble pie** →see **humble** →see **food**

◳ 타동사/자동사 먹다 ❑ 그녀는 샌드위치를 먹고 있었다. ◳ 자동사 (건강하게) 먹다 ❑ 사람들이 건강에 더 좋은 식습관을 갖도록 권유하는 운동 ◳ 자동사 밥을 먹다 ❑ 우리 식사하러 나가자. ◳ 타동사 걱정시키다 [비격식체] ❑ "대체 무슨 걱정을 하고 있니?"라고 그가 물었다.

Thesaurus　　　　*eat*의 참조어

V.　　chew, consume, munch, nibble, taste ◳
　　　dine, feast ◳
　　　bother, trouble, worry ◳

Word Partnership　　　　*eat*의 연어

ADV.　　eat **too much** ◳
　　　eat **properly**, eat **well** ◳
　　　eat **alone**, eat **together** ◳
V.　　want *something* to eat ◳
　　　eat **and drink**, eat **and sleep** ◳ ◳

▶**eat away** PHRASAL VERB If one thing **eats away** another or **eats away at** another, it gradually destroys or uses it up. ❑ *Water pours through the roof, encouraging rot to eat away the interior of the house.*

구동사 침식하다, 부식하다 ❑ 지붕에서 물이 쏟아져 들어와 집 내부를 썩게 만들었다.

▶**eat into** ◳ PHRASAL VERB If something **eats into** your time or your resources, it uses them, when they should be used for other things. ❑ *Responsibilities at home and work eat into his time.* ◳ PHRASAL VERB If a substance such as acid or rust **eats into** something, it destroys or damages its surface. ❑ *Ulcers occur when the stomach's natural acids eat into the lining of the stomach.*

◳ 구동사 침식하다 ❑ 가정과 직장에서의 책무가 그의 시간을 침식한다. ◳ 구동사 손상시키다 ❑ 궤양은 위산이 위장의 내벽을 손상시켜 발생한다.

eat|er /íːtər/ (**eaters**) N-COUNT You use **eater** to refer to someone who eats in a particular way or who eats particular kinds of food. ❑ *I've never been a fussy eater.*

가산명사 먹는 사람 ❑ 나는 식성이 까다로웠던 적이 없다.

eaves /íːvz/ N-PLURAL The **eaves** of a house are the lower edges of its roof. ❑ *There were icicles hanging from the eaves.*

복수명사 처마 ❑ 처마에 고드름이 매달려 있었다.

eaves|drop /íːvzdrɒp/ (**eavesdrops, eavesdropping, eavesdropped**) V-I If you **eavesdrop on** someone, you listen secretly to what they are saying. ❑ *The government illegally eavesdropped on his telephone conversations.*

자동사 엿듣다, 도청하다 ❑ 정부가 불법적으로 그의 전화 통화들을 도청했다.

ebb /éb/ (**ebbs, ebbing, ebbed**) ◳ V-I When the tide or the sea **ebbs**, its level gradually falls. ❑ *When the tide ebbs, you can paddle out for a mile and barely get your ankles wet.* ◳ N-COUNT The **ebb** or the **ebb** tide is one of the regular periods, usually two per day, when the sea gradually falls to a lower level as the tide moves away from the land. ❑ *...the spring ebb tide.* ◳ V-I If someone's life, support, or feeling **ebbs**, it becomes weaker and gradually disappears. [FORMAL] ❑ *Were there occasions when enthusiasm ebbed?* ● PHRASAL VERB **Ebb away** means the same as **ebb.** ❑ *His little girl's life ebbed away.* ◳ PHRASE If someone or something is **at a low ebb** or **at their lowest ebb**, they are not being very successful or profitable. ❑ *...a time when everyone is tired and at a low ebb.* →see **ocean, tide**

◳ 자동사 바닷물이 빠지다 ❑ 바닷물이 빠지면, 1마일 정도 걸어 들어가도 발목까지 물이 올라오지 않을 정도이다. ◳ 가산명사 썰물 ❑ 봄철의 썰물 ◳ 자동사 사그라들다 [격식체] ❑ 열정이 사그라드는 경우가 있었는가? ● 구동사 사그라들다 ❑ 그의 어린 딸의 생명이 사그라져 갔다. ◳ 구 저조한 ❑ 모두가 지치고 저조한 상태에 있을 때

Word Link　　　*e ≈ electronic* : *e-book, e-commerce, e-mail*

---

e-book (**e-books**) N-COUNT An **e-book** is a book which is produced for reading on a computer screen. **E-book** is an abbreviation for "electronic book." ❑ *In addition to the classics, the new e-books will include a host of Rough Guide titles.*

가산명사 전자 도서 ❑ 새로 나오는 전자 도서는 고전 작품들 외에도 다수의 러프 가이드 시리즈 책들을 포함할 것이다.

ebul|lient /ɪbʌliənt, -bʊl-/ ADJ If you describe someone as **ebullient**, you mean that they are lively and full of enthusiasm or excitement about something. [FORMAL] ❑ *...the ebullient Russian President.* ● **ebul|lience** /ɪbʌliəns, -bʊl-/ N-UNCOUNT ❑ *His natural ebullience began to return.*

형용사 열정이 넘치는 [격식체] ❑ 열정이 넘치는 러시아 대통령 ● 열정 불가산명사 ❑ 그의 타고난 열정이 되돌아오기 시작했다.

e-business (**e-businesses**) ◳ N-COUNT An **e-business** is a business which uses the Internet to sell goods or services, especially one which does not also have stores or offices that people can visit or phone. [BUSINESS] ❑ *JSL Trading, an e-business in Vancouver.* ◳ N-UNCOUNT **E-business** is the buying, selling, and ordering of goods and services using the Internet. [BUSINESS] ❑ *...proven e-business solutions.*

◳ 가산명사 인터넷 사업 [경제] ❑ 밴쿠버 소재의 인터넷 사업체인 제이 에스 엘 무역 ◳ 불가산명사 인터넷 거래 [경제] ❑ 검증된 인터넷 거래 솔루션

Word Link　　　*ec ≈ away, from, out* : *eccentric, eclectic, ecstatic*

---

ec|cen|tric /ɪkséntrɪk/ (**eccentrics**) ADJ If you say that someone is **eccentric**, you mean that they behave in a strange way, and have habits or opinions that are different from those of most people. ❑ *He is an eccentric character who likes wearing a*

형용사 별난 ❑ 그는 베레모와 색안경을 쓰기 좋아하는 별난 사람이다. ● 가산명사 기인, 별난 사람 ❑ 첫 인상을 보면 듀크를 기인이라 치부하기 쉬울 것이다.

a b c d e f g h i j k l m n o p q r s t u v w x y z

Word Web   echo

We can learn a lot from studying **echoes**. Geologists use **sound reflection** to predict how earthquake waves will travel through the earth. They also use echolocation to find underground oil reservoirs. Oceanographers use sonar to expolore the ocean. Marine mammals, bats, and humans also use sonar for navigation. Architects study building materials and surfaces to understand how they absorb or **reflect** sound **waves**. They may use hard reflective surfaces to help create a noisy, exciting atmosphere in a restaurant. They may suggest soft drapes and carpeting to create a quiet, calm library.

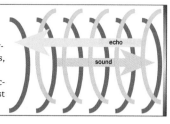

beret and dark glasses. ● N-COUNT An **eccentric** is an eccentric person. ❑ On first impressions it would be easy to dismiss Duke as an eccentric.

ec|cen|tri|ci|ty /ɛksɛntrɪsɪti/ (eccentricities) **1** N-UNCOUNT **Eccentricity** is unusual behavior that other people consider strange. ❑ She is unusual to the point of eccentricity. **2** N-COUNT **Eccentricities** are ways of behaving that people think are strange, or habits or opinions that are different from those of most people. ❑ We all have our eccentricities.

1 불가산명사 기벽 ❑ 그녀는 기벽이 있다고 할 정도로 특이하다. **2** 가산명사 특이한 행동 방식 ❑ 우리 모두 자기만의 특이한 행동 방식이 있다.

ec|cle|si|as|ti|cal /ɪkliziæstɪkəl/ ADJ **Ecclesiastical** means belonging to or connected with the Christian Church. ❑ My ambition was to travel upward in the ecclesiastical hierarchy.

형용사 교회에 관한, 성직의 ❑ 나의 야망은 높은 성직자 자리에 올라 출세하는 것이었다.

eche|lon /ɛʃəlɒn/ (echelons) N-COUNT An **echelon** in an organization or society is a level or rank in it. [FORMAL] ❑ ...the lower echelons of society.

가산명사 계층, 계급 [격식체] ❑ 사회의 하층민

echo ♦◇◇ /ɛkoʊ/ (echoes, echoing, echoed) **1** N-COUNT An **echo** is a sound which is caused by a noise being reflected off a surface such as a wall. ❑ He listened and heard nothing but the echoes of his own voice dying in the cave. **2** V-I If a sound **echoes**, it is reflected off a surface and can be heard again after the original sound has stopped. ❑ His feet echoed on the bare board floor. **3** V-I In a place that **echoes**, a sound is reflected off a surface, and is repeated after the original sound has stopped. ❑ The room echoed. ❑ The corridor echoed with the barking of a dozen dogs. **4** V-T If you **echo** someone's words, you repeat them or express agreement with their attitude or opinion. ❑ Their views often echo each other. **5** N-COUNT A detail or feature which reminds you of something else can be referred to as an **echo**. ❑ The accident has echoes of past disasters. **6** V-T If one thing **echoes** another, the first is a copy of a particular detail or feature of the other. ❑ Pinks and beiges were chosen to echo the colors of the ceiling. **7** V-I If something **echoes**, it continues to be discussed and remains important or influential in a particular situation or among a particular group of people. ❑ The old fable continues to echo down the centuries.
→see **sound**
→see Word Web: **echo**

1 가산명사 메아리, 반향 ❑ 그는 귀를 기울여 보았으나 동굴 속으로 사라져 가는 자기 목소리의 메아리만 들렸다. **2** 자동사 메아리치다, 소리가 울리다 ❑ 맨 마루 바닥 위를 걷는 그의 발자국 소리가 울렸다. **3** 자동사 울려 퍼지다 ❑ 그 방에서는 소리가 울렸다. ❑ 복도에는 열 두 마리의 개들이 짖는 소리가 울려 퍼졌다. **4** 타동사 그대로 받아 말하다, 그대로 반영하다 ❑ 그들의 견해는 종종 서로의 의견을 그대로 반영한다. **5** 가산명사 흔적, 자취 ❑ 그 사고는 과거의 재난과 비슷한 점이 있다. **6** 타동사 그대로 흉내내다 ❑ 천장의 색과 맞추기 위해 분홍색과 베이지색을 골랐다. **7** 자동사 회자되다 ❑ 그 옛 우화는 수세기에 걸쳐 계속 회자된다.

Word Link   ec ≈ away, from, out : eccentric, eclectic, ecstatic

ec|lec|tic /ɪklɛktɪk/ ADJ An **eclectic** collection of objects, ideas, or beliefs is wide-ranging and comes from many different sources. [FORMAL] ❑ ...an eclectic collection of paintings, drawings, and prints.

형용사 폭넓은 [격식체] ❑ 회화, 도화, 판화 등 폭넓은 소장품

eclipse /ɪklɪps/ (eclipses, eclipsing, eclipsed) **1** N-COUNT An **eclipse of** the sun is an occasion when the moon is between the earth and the sun, so that for a short time you cannot see part or all of the sun. An **eclipse of** the moon is an occasion when the earth is between the sun and the moon, so that for a short time you cannot see part or all of the moon. ❑ ...an eclipse of the sun. ❑ ...the solar eclipse on May 21st. **2** V-T If one thing **is eclipsed by** a second thing that is bigger, newer, or more important than it, the first is no longer noticed because the second thing gets all the attention. ❑ Records have been eclipsed by new technology such as the compact disks.
→see Word Web: **eclipse**

1 가산명사 일식, 월식 ❑ 일식 ❑ 5월 21일의 일식 **2** 타동사 가리다, 무색해지다 ❑ 레코드 음반은 콤팩트디스크 같은 새로운 기술 때문에 빛을 잃었다.

eco-friendly /ɛkoʊ frɛndli, ik-/ ADJ **Eco-friendly** products or services are less harmful to the environment than other similar products or services. ❑ ...eco-friendly soap powder.

형용사 친환경적인 ❑ 친환경적 세제

eco|logi|cal /ɛkəlɒdʒɪkəl, ik-/ **1** ADJ **Ecological** means involved with or concerning ecology. [ADJ n] ❑ Large dams have harmed Siberia's delicate ecological balance. ● eco|logi|cal|ly /ɛkəlɒdʒɪkli, ik-/ ADV ❑ It is economical to run and ecologically sound. **2** ADJ **Ecological** groups, movements, and people are concerned with preserving the environment and natural resources, so that they can be used in a sensible way, rather than being wasted. [ADJ n] ❑ Ecological groups say that nothing is being done to tackle the problem.

1 형용사 생태상의 ❑ 큰 댐들이 시베리아의 섬세한 생태 균형에 해를 끼쳐 왔다. ● 생태적으로 부사 ❑ 그것은 운영하기에 경제적이고 생태적으로도 안전하다. **2** 형용사 생태 보호의 ❑ 생태 보호 단체들은 그 문제를 해결하기 위해 어떤 조치도 실행되고 있지 않다고 말한다.

Word Web   eclipse

When the **earth** passes between the **sun** and the **moon**, we see a **lunar eclipse**. When the moon passes between the sun and the earth, we see a solar eclipse. A total eclipse of the sun happens when the moon covers it completely. In the past, people were frightened of eclipses. Leaders of some civilizations understood eclipses. They pretended to control the sun in order to gain the respect of their people. On July 22, 2009, a total eclipse of the sun will be visible in North America.

ecolo|gist /ɪkɒlədʒɪst/ (**ecologists**) N-COUNT An **ecologist** is a person who studies ecology. ❑ *Ecologists argue that the benefits of treating sewage with disinfectants are doubtful.*

ecol|ogy /ɪkɒlədʒi/ (**ecologies**) ◼ N-UNCOUNT **Ecology** is the study of the relationships between plants, animals, people, and their environment, and the balances between these relationships. ❑ *...a professor in ecology.* ◼ N-VAR When you talk about the **ecology** of a place, you are referring to the pattern and balance of relationships between plants, animals, people, and the environment in that place. ❑ *...the ecology of the rocky Negev desert in Israel.*

가산명사 생태학자 ❑ 생태학자들은 살균제로 하수를 처리하는 것이 이득이 되는지 의심스럽다고 주장한다.

◼ 불가산명사 생태학 ❑ 생태학 교수 ◼ 가산명사 또는 불가산명사 생태, 생태 환경 ❑ 이스라엘의 바위투성이인 네게브 사막의 생태 환경

Word Link   e ≈ electronic : e-book, e-commerce, e-mail

---

e-commerce N-UNCOUNT **E-commerce** is the same as **e-business**. [BUSINESS] ❑ *...the anticipated explosion of e-commerce.*

불가산명사 전자 상거래 [경제] ❑ 예기된 전자 상거래의 폭주

eco|nom|ic ♦♦♦ /ɛkənɒmɪk, iːk-/ ◼ ADJ **Economic** means concerned with the organization of the money, industry, and trade of a country, region, or society. ❑ *...Poland's radical economic reforms.* ● **eco|nomi|cal|ly** /ɛkənɒmɪkli, iːk-/ ADV ❑ *...an economically depressed area.* ◼ ADJ If something is **economic**, it produces a profit. ❑ *Critics say that the new system may be more economic but will lead to a decline in program quality.*

◼ 형용사 경제의 ❑ 폴란드의 급진적인 경제 개혁 ● 경제적으로 부사 ❑ 경제적으로 침체된 지역 ◼ 형용사 실리적인 ❑ 비판적 입장에 있는 사람들은 새 체계가 더 실리적일지는 모르나 프로그램의 질적 저하를 가져올 수 있다고 말한다.

eco|nomi|cal /ɛkənɒmɪkᵊl, iːk-/ ◼ ADJ Something that is **economical** does not require a lot of money to operate. For example a car that only uses a small amount of gasoline is **economical**. ❑ *...plans to trade in their car for something smaller and more economical.* ● **eco|nomi|cal|ly** ADV [ADV after v] ❑ *Services could be operated more efficiently and economically.* ◼ ADJ Someone who is **economical** spends money sensibly and does not want to waste it on things that are unnecessary. A way of life that is **economical** does not need a lot of money. ❑ *...ideas for economical housekeeping.* ◼ ADJ **Economical** means using the minimum amount of time, effort, or language that is necessary. ❑ *His gestures were economical, his words generally mild.*

◼ 형용사 경제적인 ❑ 자기들의 헌 차를 주고 더 작고 경제적인 새 차로 바꾸려는 계획 ● 경제적으로 부사 ❑ 서비스를 더 효율적이고 경제적으로 운영할 수 있을 것이다. ◼ 형용사 절약하는, 알뜰한 ❑ 알뜰하게 가계를 꾸리기 위한 발상 ◼ 형용사 경제적인, 간결한 ❑ 그의 몸짓은 간결하였고, 그의 말은 대체로 부드러웠다.

Thesaurus   economical의 참조어

ADJ.	cost-effective, inexpensive ◼
	careful, frugal, practical ◼

Word Link   ics ≈ system, knowledge : economics, electronics, physics

---

eco|nom|ics ♦♦◇ /ɛkənɒmɪks, iːk-/ N-UNCOUNT **Economics** is the study of the way in which money, industry, and trade are organized in a society. ❑ *He gained a first class Honours degree in economics.*
→see Word Web: **economics**

불가산명사 경제학 ❑ 그는 최우수 성적으로 경제학 학위를 획득했다.

econo|mies of scale N-PLURAL **Economies of scale** are the financial advantages that a company gains when it produces large quantities of products. [BUSINESS] ❑ *Car firms are desperate to achieve economies of scale.*

복수명사 규모의 경제 [경제] ❑ 자동차 회사들은 규모의 경제를 성취하고자 필사적이다.

econo|mist ♦◇◇ /ɪkɒnəmɪst/ (**economists**) N-COUNT An **economist** is a person who studies, teaches, or writes about economics.

가산명사 경제학자

econo|mize /ɪkɒnəmaɪz/ (**economizes**, **economizing**, **economized**) [BRIT also **economise**] V-I If you **economize**, you save money by spending it very carefully. ❑ *We're going to have to economize from now on.*

[영국영어 economise] 자동사 절약하다 ❑ 우리는 지금부터 절약해야만 할 거야.

econ|o|my ♦♦♦ /ɪkɒnəmi/ (**economies**) ◼ N-COUNT An **economy** is the system according to which the money, industry, and trade of a country or region are organized. ❑ *Zimbabwe boasts Africa's most industrialized economy.* ◼ N-COUNT A country's **economy** is the wealth that it gets from business and industry. ❑ *The Japanese economy grew at an annual rate of more than 10 percent.* ◼ N-UNCOUNT **Economy** is the use of the minimum amount of money, time, or other resources needed to achieve something, so that nothing is wasted. ❑ *...improvements in the fuel economy of cars.* ◼ N-COUNT If you make **economies**, you try to save money by not spending money on unnecessary things. ❑ *They will make economies by hiring fewer part-time workers.* ◼ ADJ **Economy** services such as travel are cheap and have no luxuries or extras. [ADJ n] ❑ *...the limitations that come with economy travel.* →see **economy class** ◼ ADJ **Economy** is used to describe large packs of goods which are cheaper than normal sized packs. [ADJ n] ❑ *...an economy pack containing 150 assorted screws.* ◼ PHRASE If you describe an attempt to save money as **a false economy**, you mean that you have not saved any money as you will have to spend a lot more later. ❑ *A cheap bed can be a false economy, so spend as much as you can afford.*

◼ 가산명사 경제 ❑ 짐바브웨는 아프리카에서 가장 산업화된 경제를 자랑한다. ◼ 가산명사 경제 ❑ 일본 경제는 연간 10퍼센트 이상의 비율로 성장했다. ◼ 불가산명사 절약, 절감 ❑ 자동차 연료 절감상의 개선 ◼ 가산명사 절약 ❑ 그들은 더 적은 수의 비상근 근로자를 고용하여 절약할 것이다. ◼ 형용사 일반석의 ❑ 일반석 여행에 수반되는 제약 ◼ 형용사 경제적인, 값싸고 큰 ❑ 150가지 종류의 나사를 갖춰 놓은 경제적인 세트 ◼ 구 값싼 비지떡 ❑ 가격이 싼 침대는 값싼 게 비지떡처럼 될 수 있으니 여유가 되는 대로 돈을 많이 들여라.

Word Web   economics

The study of **economics** explores how a society distributes its **wealth**. This subject is divided into two main areas: macroeconomics and microeconomics. Macroeconomics looks at how a society as a whole handles money, **capital**, and **commodities**. Microeconomics focuses on individuals and businesses. A key microeconomic principle is the law of supply and demand. This theory says that prices of **goods** and **services** are based on a balance between two factors. The first is how much of something is available (supply). The second is how much people are willing to pay for it (demand).

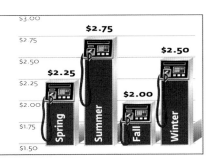

a b c d e f g h i j k l m n o p q r s t u v w x y z

eco|nomy class ADJ On an airplane, an **economy class** ticket or seat is the cheapest available. [ADJ n] ❑ *The price includes two economy class airfares from Brisbane to Los Angeles.*

형용사 일반석 ❑ 그 가격에는 브리즈번에서 로스앤젤레스까지 가는 두 장의 일반석 항공료가 포함된다.

eco|sys|tem /ˈɛkoʊsɪstəm, ik-, BRIT iːˈkoʊsɪstəm/ (**ecosystems**) N-COUNT An **ecosystem** is all the plants and animals that live in a particular area together with the complex relationship that exists between them and their environment. [TECHNICAL] ❑ *...the forest ecosystem.*

가산명사 생태계 [과학 기술] ❑ 산림 생태계

eco|tour|ism /ˈɛkoʊtʊərɪzəm, ik-/ [BRIT **eco-tourism**] N-UNCOUNT **Ecotourism** is the business of providing vacations and related services which are not harmful to the environment of the area. ● **eco|tour|ist** /ˈɛkoʊtʊərɪst, ik-/ (**ecotourists**) N-COUNT [BUSINESS] ❑ *an environmentally sensitive project to cater to ecotourists.*

[영국영어 eco-tourism] 불가산명사 친환경 관광 여행, ● 친환경 관광객 가산명사 [경제] ❑ 친환경 여행자의 요구에 맞추어 환경을 세심하게 고려한 계획

ec|sta|sy /ˈɛkstəsi/ (**ecstasies**) ◪ N-VAR **Ecstasy** is a feeling of very great happiness. ❑ *...a state of almost religious ecstasy.* ◪ N-UNCOUNT **Ecstasy** is an illegal drug which makes people feel happy and energetic. ❑ *The teenager died after taking ecstasy on her birthday.*

◪ 가산명사 또는 불가산명사 무아경, 황홀경 ❑ 거의 종교적 무아경의 상태 ◪ 불가산명사 환각제 ❑ 십대 소녀가 생일에 환각제를 먹고 사망했다.

Word Link   ec ≈ away, from, out : *eccentric*, *eclectic*, *ecstatic*

---

ec|stat|ic /ɛkˈstætɪk/ ◪ ADJ If you are **ecstatic**, you feel very happy and full of excitement. ❑ *His wife gave birth to their first child, and he was ecstatic about it.* ● **ec|stati|cal|ly** /ɛkˈstætɪkli/ ADV ❑ *We are both ecstatically happy.* ◪ ADJ You can use **ecstatic** to describe reactions that are very enthusiastic and excited. For example, if someone receives an **ecstatic** reception or an **ecstatic** welcome, they are greeted with great enthusiasm and excitement. [ADJ n] ❑ *They gave an ecstatic reception to the speech.*

◪ 형용사 희열에 넘친 ❑ 그의 부인이 그들의 첫아이를 출산했고 그는 그 때문에 희열에 넘쳤다. ● 희열에 넘칠 정도로 부사 ❑ 우리는 둘 다 희열에 넘칠 정도로 행복하다. ◪ 형용사 열렬한 ❑ 그들은 그 연설에 열렬한 환영을 보냈다.

ec|ze|ma /ˈɛksəmə, ˈɛgzə-, ɪgˈzi-, BRIT ˈɛksmə/ N-UNCOUNT **Eczema** is a skin disease which makes your skin itch and become sore, rough, and broken.

불가산명사 습진

edge ♦♦◇ /ɛdʒ/ (**edges, edging, edged**) ◪ N-COUNT The **edge** of something is the place or line where it stops, or the part of it that is farthest from the middle. ❑ *We were on a hill, right on the edge of town.* ❑ *She was standing at the water's edge.* ◪ N-COUNT The **edge** of something sharp such as a knife or an ax is its sharp or narrow side. ❑ *...the sharp edge of the sword.* ◪ V-I If someone or something **edges** somewhere, they move very slowly in that direction. ❑ *He edged closer to the telephone, ready to grab it.* ◪ N-SING **The edge of** something, especially something bad, is the point at which it may start to happen. ❑ *They have driven the rhino to the edge of extinction.* ◪ N-SING If someone or something has an **edge**, they have an advantage that makes them stronger or more likely to be successful than another thing or person. ❑ *The three days France have to prepare could give them the edge over England.* ◪ N-SING If you say that someone or something has an **edge**, you mean that they have a powerful quality. ❑ *Featuring new bands gives the show an edge.* ◪ N-SING If someone's voice has an **edge** to it, it has a sharp, bitter, or emotional quality. ❑ *But underneath the humor is an edge of bitterness.* ◪ →see also **cutting edge, leading edge** ◪ PHRASE If you or your nerves are **on edge**, you are tense, nervous, and unable to relax. ❑ *My nerves were constantly on edge.* ◪ PHRASE If something **takes the edge off** a situation, usually an unpleasant one, it weakens its effect or intensity. ❑ *A spell of poor health took the edge off her performance.*

◪ 가산명사 끝, 가장자리 ❑ 우리는 바로 시 외곽의 언덕 위에 있었다. ❑ 그녀는 물가에 서 있었다. ◪ 가산명사 날 ❑ 칼의 예리한 날 ◪ 자동사 아주 조금씩 다가가다 ❑ 그는 전화를 움켜잡을 준비를 하고 전화 가까이로 아주 조금씩 다가갔다 ◪ 단수명사 경계; 위기 ❑ 그들은 무소를 멸종의 위기까지 몰고 갔다. ◪ 단수명사 우세, 유리 ❑ 프랑스는 3일간의 여유 있는 준비 기간 때문에 영국보다 유리할 수 있다. ◪ 단수명사 기세; 특성 ❑ 새로운 악단을 출연시키면 쇼에 활기를 주게 된다. ◪ 단수명사 날카로움, 신랄함 ❑ 그러나 그 유머 속에는 신랄함이 들어 있다. ◪ 구 예민하여, 불안하여 ❑ 나는 항상 신경이 예민했다. ◪ 구 기세를 꺾다 ❑ 한동안 좋지 않았던 건강 때문에 그녀의 공연에 힘이 없었다.

Thesaurus   edge의 참조어

N.   border, boundary, rim; *(ant.)* center, middle ◪
      advantage; *(ant.)* disadvantage ◪

▶**edge out** PHRASAL VERB If someone **edges out** someone else, they just manage to beat them or get in front of them in a game, race, or contest. ❑ *In the second race, Germany and France edged out the British team by less than a second.*

구동사 근소한 차로 앞서다 ❑ 두 번째 경주에서 독일과 프랑스는 영국 팀을 1초 미만의 차로 앞섰다.

edged /ɛdʒd/ ADJ If something is **edged with** a particular thing, that thing forms a border around it. [v-link ADJ with/in n] ❑ *...a large lawn edged with flowers and shrubs.* ● COMB in ADJ **Edged** is also a combining form. ❑ *...clutching a lace-edged handkerchief.*

형용사 -로 테를 두른 ❑ 가장자리에 꽃과 관목이 심어져 있는 넓은 잔디밭 ● 복합형-형용사 - 테가 달린 ❑ 레이스 테가 달린 손수건을 움켜쥐며

edgy /ˈɛdʒi/ (**edgier, edgiest**) ADJ If someone is **edgy**, they are nervous and anxious, and seem likely to lose control of themselves. [INFORMAL] ❑ *She was nervous and edgy, still chain-smoking.*

형용사 초조한, 불안한 [비격식체] ❑ 그녀는 여전히 줄담배를 피우면서 불안 초조해 했다.

ed|ible /ˈɛdɪbəl/ ADJ If something is **edible**, it is safe to eat and not poisonous. ❑ *...edible fungi.*

형용사 식용의 ❑ 식용 버섯

edict /ˈidɪkt/ (**edicts**) N-COUNT An **edict** is a command or instruction given by someone in authority. [FORMAL] ❑ *He issued an edict that none of his writings be destroyed.*

가산명사 칙령, 엄명 [격식체] ❑ 그는 자기 글을 하나도 파기하지 말라는 엄명을 내렸다.

edi|fice /ˈɛdɪfɪs/ (**edifices**) N-COUNT An **edifice** is a large and impressive building. [FORMAL] ❑ *The taxi-driver reeled off a list of historic edifices they must not fail to visit.*

가산명사 대건축물 [격식체] ❑ 택시 기사는 그들이 꼭 구경해야 할 역사적 대건축물들을 줄줄 읊었다.

edit ♦◇◇ /ˈɛdɪt/ (**edits, editing, edited**) ◪ V-T If you **edit** a text such as an article or a book, you correct and adapt it so that it is suitable for publishing. ❑ *The majority of contracts give the publisher the right to edit a book after it's done.* ◪ V-T If you **edit** a book or a series of books, you collect several pieces of writing by different authors and prepare them for publishing. ❑ *This collection of essays is edited by Ellen Knight.* ❑ *She has edited the media studies quarterly, Screen.* ◪ V-T If you **edit** a movie or a television or radio program, you choose some of what has been filmed or recorded and arrange it in a particular order. ❑ *He taught me to edit and splice film.* ◪ V-T Someone who **edits** a newspaper, magazine, or journal is in charge of it. ❑ *I used to edit the college paper in the old days.*

◪ 타동사 편집하다, 수정하다 ❑ 대다수 계약에서 출판사가 책이 완성된 후 편집할 권리를 갖게 된다. ◪ 타동사 편집하다 ❑ 이 수필집은 엘런 나이트가 편집했다. ❑ 그녀는 언론 방송학 계간지인 '스크린'을 편집했다. ◪ 타동사 편집하다 ❑ 그는 내게 필름을 자르고 편집하는 것을 가르쳐 주었다. ◪ 타동사 편집하다 ❑ 나는 옛날에 대학 신문을 편집했다.

edi|tion ♦♦◇ /ɪdɪʃᵊn/ (editions) **1** N-COUNT An **edition** is a particular version of a book, magazine, or newspaper that is printed at one time. ❑ *A paperback edition is now available at bookshops.* **2** N-COUNT An **edition** is the total number of copies of a particular book or newspaper that are printed at one time. ❑ *The second edition was published only in America.* **3** N-COUNT An **edition** is a single television or radio program that is one of a series about a particular subject. ❑ *They appeared on an edition of BBC2's Arena.*

1 가산명사 판 ❑ 지금 서점에 종이 표지 보급판이 나와 있다. **2** 가산명사 판 ❑ 재판은 미국에서만 출판되었다. **3** 가산명사 부, 시리즈 중 한 편 ❑ 그들은 비비시2의 '아레나' 편에 출연했다.

Word Partnership   edition의 연어

N.	**collector's** edition, **paperback** edition **1**
ADJ.	**limited** edition, **special** edition **1 2**
	new edition **1 2 3**
---

edi|tor ♦♦◇ /ɛdɪtər/ (editors) **1** N-COUNT An **editor** is the person who is in charge of a newspaper or magazine and who decides what will be published in each edition of it. ❑ *...Rosie Boycott, the former editor of the Daily Express.* **2** N-COUNT An **editor** is a journalist who is responsible for a particular section of a newspaper or magazine. ❑ *Cookery Editor Moyra Fraser takes you behind the scenes.* **3** N-COUNT An **editor** is a person who checks and corrects texts before they are published. ❑ *Your role as editor is important, for you can look at a piece of writing objectively.* **4** N-COUNT An **editor** is a radio or television journalist who reports on a particular type of news. ❑ *...our economics editor, Dominic Harrod.* **5** N-COUNT An **editor** is a person who prepares a movie, or a radio or television program, by selecting some of what has been filmed or recorded and putting it in a particular order. ❑ *A few years earlier, she had worked at 20th Century Fox as a film editor.* **6** N-COUNT An **editor** is a person who collects pieces of writing by different authors and prepares them for publication in a book or a series of books. ❑ *Michael Rosen is the editor of the anthology.* **7** N-COUNT An **editor** is a computer program that enables you to change and correct stored data. [COMPUTING] ❑ *To edit it, you need to run the built-in Windows Registry editor.*

1 가산명사 편집장 ❑ 데일리 익스프레스의 전 편집장 로지 보이콧 **2** 가산명사 편집인 ❑ 요리 편집인 모이라 프레이저가 당신을 무대 뒤로 안내합니다. **3** 가산명사 편집자 ❑ 편집자로서 너의 역할은 중요하다. 왜냐하면 너는 글을 객관적으로 볼 수 있기 때문이다. **4** 가산명사 전문 부장 ❑ 경제 전문 부장 도미니크 해로드 **5** 가산명사 (영화 등의) 편집인 ❑ 그보다 몇 년 전, 그녀는 20세기 폭스 사에서 영화 편집인으로 일했었다. **6** 가산명사 편자, 엮은이 ❑ 마이클 로우즌이 그 명문선집의 편자이다. **7** 가산명사 편집 프로그램 [컴퓨터] ❑ 그것을 편집하려면 내장된 윈도우 등록 편집 프로그램을 실행해야 한다.

edi|to|rial ♦◇◇ /ɛdɪtɔ́riᵊl/ (editorials) **1** ADJ **Editorial** means involved in preparing a newspaper, magazine, or book for publication. [ADJ n] ❑ *I went to the editorial board meetings when I had the time.* **2** ADJ **Editorial** means involving the attitudes, opinions, and contents of something such as a newspaper, magazine, or television program. [ADJ n] ❑ *We are not about to change our editorial policy.* **3** N-COUNT An **editorial** is an article in a newspaper which gives the opinion of the editor or owner on a topic or item of news. ❑ *In an editorial, The Independent suggests the victory could turn nasty.* →see **newspaper**

1 형용사 편집의 ❑ 나는 시간이 날 때면 편집 이사회에 참석했다. **2** 형용사 사설의, 논설의 ❑ 우리의 사설 방침을 바로 바꾸지는 않을 것이다. **3** 가산명사 사설 ❑ 인디펜던트 지 사설에서는 그 승리가 변질될 수도 있다고 했다.

edu|cate /ɛdʒʊkeɪt/ (educates, educating, educated) **1** V-T When someone, especially a child, **is educated**, he or she is taught at a school or college. [usu passive] ❑ *He was educated at Yale and Stanford.* **2** V-T To **educate** people means to teach them better ways of doing something or a better way of living. ❑ *...World AIDS Day, an event designed to educate people about AIDS and raise money for the fight against it.*

1 타동사 교육을 받다 ❑ 그는 예일과 스탠퍼드에서 교육을 받았다. **2** 타동사 교육하다 ❑ 에이즈에 대해 교육하고 에이즈 퇴치를 위한 기금을 모으기 위해 계획된 행사인 세계 에이즈의 날

Note that you do not use **educate** or **education** to talk about the way parents look after their children and teach them about good behavior and life in general. Instead, you should use the verb **bring up** or the noun **upbringing**. ❑ *His parents brought him up to be polite and courteous.*

부모가 자식을 돌보며 일반적인 생활과 바른 행실에 대해 가르치는 방식에 대해 말할 때는 educate나 education을 쓰지 않는다는 점을 유의하라. 그 대신, 동사 bring up 또는 명사 upbringing을 써야 한다. ❑ 그의 부모는 그를 공손하고 예의가 바르도록 키웠다.

Thesaurus   educate의 참조어

V.	coach, instruct, teach, train **1 2**
---

edu|cat|ed /ɛdʒʊkeɪtɪd/ ADJ Someone who is **educated** has a high standard of learning. ❑ *The general secretary of the TUC is an educated, amiable, and decent man.*

형용사 교양 있는, 교육 받은 ❑ 노동조합 회의의 총무는 교양 있고 상냥하며 의젓한 사람이다.

Word Link   ation ≈ state of : educ**ation**, elev**ation**, preserv**ation**
---

edu|ca|tion ♦♦◇ /ɛdʒʊkeɪʃᵊn/ (educations) **1** N-VAR **Education** involves teaching people various subjects, usually at a school or college, or being taught. ❑ *They're cutting funds for education.* **2** N-UNCOUNT **Education** of a particular kind involves teaching the public about a particular issue. ❑ *...better health education.* **3** →see also **further education, higher education** →see **educate**

1 가산명사 또는 불가산명사 (학교) 교육 ❑ 그들은 학교 교육 기금을 삭감할 것이다. **2** 불가산명사 교육 ❑ 더 좋은 건강 교육

edu|ca|tion|al ♦◇◇ /ɛdʒʊkeɪʃᵊnᵊl/ **1** ADJ **Educational** matters or institutions are concerned with or relate to education. ❑ *...the British educational system.* **2** ADJ An **educational** experience teaches you something. ❑ *The staff should make sure the kids have an enjoyable and educational day.*

1 형용사 교육의 ❑ 영국의 교육 제도 **2** 형용사 교육적인 ❑ 직원들은 반드시 아이들이 즐겁고 교육적인 하루를 보낼 수 있도록 해야 한다.

eel /il/ (eels) N-COUNT An **eel** is a long, thin fish that looks like a snake. ● N-UNCOUNT **Eel** is the flesh of this fish which is eaten as food. ❑ *...smoked eel.*

가산명사 또는 불가산명사 뱀장어 ● 불가산명사 식용 뱀장어 ❑ 훈제 뱀장어

ee|rie /ɪəri/ (eerier, eeriest) ADJ If you describe something as **eerie**, you mean that it seems strange and frightening, and makes you feel nervous. ❑ *I walked down the eerie dark path.* ● **eeri|ly** /ɪərɪli/ ADV ❑ *Monrovia after the fighting is eerily quiet.*

형용사 으스스한, 기분 나쁜 ❑ 나는 으스스하고 캄캄한 길을 걸어 내려왔다. ● 으스스한 정도로 부사 ❑ 전투가 끝난 후의 먼로비아는 으스스할 정도로 조용하다.

ef|fect ♦♦♦ /ɪfɛkt/ (effects, effecting, effected) **1** N-VAR The **effect of** one thing **on** another is the change that the first thing causes in the second thing. ❑ *Parents worry about the effect of music on their adolescent's behavior.* **2** N-COUNT An **effect** is an impression that someone creates deliberately, for example in a place or in a piece of writing. ❑ *The whole effect is cool, light, and airy.* **3** N-PLURAL A person's **effects** are the things that they have with them at a particular time, for example when they are arrested or admitted to a hospital, or the things that they owned when they died. [FORMAL] ❑ *His daughters were collecting*

1 가산명사 또는 불가산명사 영향; 결과 ❑ 부모들은 청소년 자녀의 행동에 미치는 음악의 영향에 대해서 걱정한다. **2** 가산명사 효과 ❑ 전반적인 효과는 시원하고 밝고 활기차다. **3** 복수명사 소지품; 유품 [격식체] ❑ 그의 딸들은 그의 유품을 모으고 **4** 복수명사 특수 효과 ❑ 고질라는 굉장한 특수 효과로 파괴하는 장면에서는 매우 재미있다. **5** 타동사 달성하다; ~을 초래하다 [격식체] ❑ 진정한 정치적

his effects. **4** N-PLURAL The **effects** in a movie are the specially created sounds and scenery. □ *Godzilla is a whole lot of fun, in a destructive kind of way, with great effects.* **5** V-T If you **effect** something that you are trying to achieve, you succeed in causing it to happen. [FORMAL] □ *Prospects for effecting real political change seemed to have taken a major step backward.* **6** →see also **greenhouse effect, side-effect, special effect**

> Note that the verb **affect** is connected with the noun **effect**. You can say that something **affects** you. □ *Noise affects different people in different ways.* You can also say that something has an **effect** on you □ *...the effect that noise has on people in factories.*

7 PHRASE If you say that someone is doing something **for effect**, you mean that they are doing it in order to impress people and to draw attention to themselves. □ *The Cockney accent was put on for effect.* **8** PHRASE You add **in effect** to a statement or opinion that is not precisely accurate, but which you feel is a reasonable description or summary of a particular situation. [VAGUENESS] □ *That deal would create, in effect, the world's biggest airline.* **9** PHRASE If you **put, bring,** or **carry** a plan or idea **into effect**, you cause it to happen in practice. □ *These and other such measures ought to have been put into effect in 1985.* **10** PHRASE If a law or policy **takes effect** or **comes into effect** at a particular time, it officially begins to apply or be valid from that time. If it **remains in effect**, it still applies or is still valid. □ *...the ban on new logging permits which will take effect from July.* **11** PHRASE You can say that something **takes effect** when it starts to produce the results that are intended. □ *The second injection should only have been given once the first drug had taken effect.* **12** PHRASE You use **effect** in expressions such as **to good effect** and **to no effect** in order to indicate how successful or impressive an action is. □ *Mr. Morris feels the museum is using advertising to good effect.* **13** PHRASE You use **to this effect, to that effect,** or **to the effect that** to indicate that you have given or are giving a summary of something that was said or written, and not the actual words used. □ *I understand that a circular to this effect will be issued in the next few weeks.* **14** PHRASE If you say that something will happen **with immediate effect** or **with effect from** a particular time, you mean that it will begin to apply or be valid immediately or from the stated time. [BRIT, mainly FORMAL] □ *The price of the Saturday edition is going up with effect from 3 November.*

Word Partnership   *effect*의 연어

ADJ.	**adverse** effect, **negative/positive** effect **1**
	immediate effect, **lasting** effect **1** **2**
V.	**have an** effect **1**
	produce an effect **2**
	take effect **11**
N.	effect **a change** **5**

ef|fec|tive ♦♦◇ /ɪfɛktɪv/ **1** ADJ Something that is **effective** works well and produces the results that were intended. □ *The project looks at how we could be more effective in encouraging students to enter teacher training.* □ *Simple antibiotics are effective against this organism.* ● **ef|fec|tive|ly** ADV □ *...the team roles which you believe to be necessary for the team to function effectively.* ● **ef|fec|tive|ness** N-UNCOUNT □ *...the effectiveness of computers as an educational tool.* **2** ADJ **Effective** means having a particular role or result in practice, though not officially or in theory. [ADJ n] □ *They have had effective control of the area since the security forces left.* **3** ADJ When something such as a law or an agreement becomes **effective**, it begins officially to apply or be valid. [v-link ADJ] □ *The new rules will become effective in the next few days.*

Word Partnership   *effective*의 연어

N.	effective **means**, effective **method**, effective **treatment**, effective **use** **1**
ADV.	**highly** effective **1**
	effective **immediately** **3**

ef|fec|tive|ly /ɪfɛktɪvli/ ADV You use **effectively** with a statement or opinion to indicate that it is not accurate in every detail, but that you feel it is a reasonable description or summary of a particular situation. □ *The region was effectively independent.*

ef|fi|ca|cy /ɛfɪkəsi/ N-UNCOUNT If you talk about the **efficacy** of something, you are talking about its effectiveness and its ability to do what it is supposed to. [FORMAL] □ *Recent medical studies confirm the efficacy of a healthier lifestyle.*

ef|fi|cien|cy /ɪfɪʃnsi/ N-UNCOUNT **Efficiency** is the quality of being able to do a task successfully, without wasting time or energy. □ *There are many ways to increase agricultural efficiency in the poorer areas of the world.*

ef|fi|cient ♦♦◇ /ɪfɪʃnt/ ADJ If something or someone is **efficient**, they are able to do tasks successfully, without wasting time or energy. □ *With today's more efficient contraception women can plan their families and careers.* ● **ef|fi|cient|ly** ADV □ *I work very efficiently and am decisive, and accurate in my judgement.*

Word Partnership   *efficient*의 연어

N.	**energy** efficient, **fuel** efficient, efficient **method**, efficient **system**, efficient **use of** *something*
ADV.	**highly** efficient

변화를 일으킬 가능성은 크게 한발 뒤로 물러난 것 같았다.

> 동사 affect는 명사 effect와 연관되어 있음을 유의하라. 어떤 것이 당신을 affect한다고 말할 수 있다. □ 소음은 사람에 따라 다른 방식으로 영향을 미친다. 어떤 것이 당신에게 영향을 주는 것을 something has an effect on you라고 할 수도 있다. □ ...공장에서 소음이 사람들에게 미치는 영향

7 구 효과를 노리고 □ 효과를 노리고 일부러 런던 토박이 어투를 썼다. **8** 구 사실상 [짐작투] □ 그 거래는 사실상 세계 최대 항공사를 만들어 낼 것이다. **9** 구 실행하다 □ 이러저러한 조치들은 1985년에 실행되었어야 했다. **10** 구 실시되다 □ 7월부터 실시되는 새로운 벌목 허가 금지령 **11** 구 효력을 내다 □ 일단 첫 번째 약이 효력을 낼 때 두 번째 주사를 놓았어야 했다. **12** 구 효과적으로 □ 모리스 씨는 박물관이 광고를 효과적으로 이용하고 있다고 생각한다. **13** 구 이러한/그러한 취지로 □ 나는 이러한 취지로 광고 전단이 다음 몇 주 동안 배포될 것이라고 알고 있다. **14** 구 (즉각) 적용되는 [영국영어, 주로 격식체] □ 토요일 판의 가격 상승은 11월 3일 자부터 적용된다.

1 형용사 효과적인 □ 그 계획은 학생에게 교사 연수에 들어가도록 격려하는 데 있어서 어떻게 우리가 더욱 효과적일 수 있는지를 살펴본다. □ 보통의 항생제는 이 생물에 효과적이다. ● 효과적으로 부사 □ 팀이 효과적으로 기능하는 데 필요하다고 당신이 믿는 팀의 역할 ● 효과적임, 효율성 불가산명사 □ 교육 도구로서의 컴퓨터의 효율성 **2** 형용사 사실상의 □ 보안군이 떠난 이후로 사실상 그들이 이 지역을 관리하고 있다. **3** 형용사 발효되는 □ 새로운 법률들이 며칠 후에 발효될 것이다.

부사 사실상 □ 그 지역은 사실상 독립 지역이었다.

불가산명사 실효성; 효험 [격식체] □ 최근의 의학 연구는 더 건강한 삶의 방식의 실효성을 입증한다.

불가산명사 능률 □ 세상 빈곤 지역에서 농업의 능률을 증가시킬 수 있는 많은 방법이 있다.

형용사 효율적인 □ 오늘날 더욱 효율적인 피임법으로 여성들은 가정과 직장 생활을 계획할 수 있게 되었다. ● 효율적으로 부사 □ 나는 매우 효율적으로 일하고, 결단성 있고, 판단력도 정확하다.

ef|fort ♦♦♦ /ɛfərt/ (efforts) **1** N-VAR If you make an **effort to** do something, you try very hard to do it. ❑ *He made no effort to hide his disappointment.* ❑ *Finding a cure requires considerable time and effort.* **2** N-VAR If you say that someone did something **with effort** or **with an effort**, you mean it was difficult for them to do. [WRITTEN] [usu *with* N, also *a* N] ❑ *She took a deep breath and sat up slowly and with great effort.* **3** N-COUNT An **effort** is a particular series of activities that is organized by a group of people in order to achieve something. ❑ *...a famine relief effort in Angola.* **4** N-SING If you say that something is **an effort**, you mean that an unusual amount of physical or mental energy is needed to do it. ❑ *Even carrying the camcorder while hiking in the forest was an effort.* **5** PHRASE If you **make the effort to** do something, you do it, even though you need extra energy to do it or you do not really want to. ❑ *I don't get lonely now because I make the effort to see people.*

Thesaurus	*effort*의 참조어
N.	attempt **1**
	labor, work **4**

---

1 가산명사 또는 불가산명사 노력 ❑ 그는 실망을 감추려고 노력하지도 않았다. ❑ 치료법을 발견하는 것은 상당한 시간과 노력을 요구한다. **2** 가산명사 또는 불가산명사 수고 [문어체] ❑ 그녀는 크게 숨을 쉬고 천천히 그리고 몹시 힘들게 일어나 앉았다. **3** 가산명사 작업 ❑ 앙골라의 기근 구조 작업 **4** 단수명사 분투 ❑ 숲에서 하이킹할 때는 캠코더를 가지고 다니는 것만도 힘든 일이었다. **5** 구 노력을 기울이다 ❑ 나는 사람들을 만나려고 노력하고 있기 때문에 이제 외롭지 않게 되었다.

ef|fort|less /ɛfərtlɪs/ **1** ADJ Something that is **effortless** is done easily and well. ❑ *...effortless and elegant Italian cooking.* ● **ef|fort|less|ly** ADV ❑ *Her son Peter adapted effortlessly to his new surroundings.* **2** ADJ You use **effortless** to describe a quality that someone has naturally and does not have to learn. ❑ *She liked him above all for his effortless charm.*

1 형용사 쉬운 ❑ 쉽고 고상한 이탈리아 요리 ● 쉽게 부사 ❑ 그녀의 아들 피터는 쉽게 새로운 환경에 적응했다. **2** 형용사 천부적인, 타고난 ❑ 그녀는 무엇보다도 그의 타고난 매력 때문에 그를 좋아했다.

e-fit /ifɪt/ (e-fits) also E-fit N-COUNT An **e-fit** is a computer-generated picture of someone who is suspected of a crime. ❑ *Police have released an E-fit picture of the suspected gunman.*

가산명사 컴퓨터 합성 용의자 사진 ❑ 경찰은 컴퓨터로 합성한 살인 용의자의 사진을 배포했다.

EFL /i ɛf ɛl/ N-UNCOUNT **EFL** is the teaching of English to people whose first language is not English. **EFL** is an abbreviation for "English as a Foreign Language." [oft N N] ❑ *...an EFL teacher.*

불가산명사 외국어로서 영어 교육 ❑ 외국어로서 영어를 가르치는 영어 교사

e.g. /i dʒi/ **e.g.** is an abbreviation that means "for example." It is used before a noun, or to introduce another sentence. ❑ *We need helpers of all types, engineers, scientists (e.g., geologists), and teachers.*

예를 들어 ❑ 우리는 기술자, 과학자(예를 들어, 지질학자)와 교사 등 모든 종류의 조력자가 필요합니다.

egg ♦♦◇ /ɛg/ (eggs, egging, egged) **1** N-COUNT An **egg** is an oval object that is produced by a female bird and which contains a baby bird. Other animals such as reptiles and fish also lay eggs. ❑ *...a baby bird hatching from its egg.* **2** N-VAR In Western countries, **eggs** often means hen's eggs, eaten as food. ❑ *Break the eggs into a shallow bowl and beat them lightly.* **3** N-COUNT **Egg** is used to refer to an object in the shape of a hen's egg. ❑ *...a chocolate egg.* **4** N-COUNT An **egg** is a cell that is produced in the bodies of female animals and humans. If it is fertilized by a sperm, a baby develops from it. ❑ *It only takes one sperm to fertilize an egg.* **5** PHRASE If someone puts **all** their **eggs in one basket**, they put all their effort or resources into doing one thing so that, if it fails, they have no alternatives left. ❑ *The key word here is diversify; don't put all your eggs in one basket.* **6** PHRASE If someone has **egg on** their **face** or has **egg all over** their **face**, they have been made to look foolish. ❑ *If they take this game lightly they could end up with egg on their faces.* →see bird

1 가산명사 알 ❑ 알에서 부화하고 있는 새끼 새 **2** 가산명사 또는 불가산명사 계란 ❑ 계란을 얕은 그릇에 깨서 넣고 저으세요. **3** 가산명사 달걀 모양 ❑ 달걀 모양의 초콜릿 **4** 가산명사 난자 ❑ 난자와 수정하는 것은 단 하나의 정자이다. **5** 구 한곳에만 총력을 모으다 ❑ 여기서 핵심 단어는 분산입니다. 한곳에 모두 쏟아붓지 마세요. **6** 구 계란 세례를 받다 ❑ 이 게임을 가볍게 한다면, 그들은 얼굴에 계란 세례를 받게 될 것이다.

▶**egg on** PHRASAL VERB If you **egg** a person **on**, you encourage them to do something, especially something dangerous or foolish. ❑ *He was lifting up handfuls of leaves and throwing them at her. She was laughing and egging him on.*

구동사 부추기다 ❑ 그는 낙엽을 한 움큼씩 집어 들고 그녀에게 던지고 있었다. 그녀는 깔깔대며 그를 부추겨댔다.

egg|plant /ɛgplænt/ (eggplants) N-VAR An **eggplant** is a vegetable with a smooth, dark purple skin. [AM; BRIT **aubergine**]

가산명사 또는 불가산명사 가지 [미국영어; 영국영어 aubergine]

ego /igoʊ, ɛgoʊ/ (egos) N-VAR Someone's **ego** is their sense of their own worth. For example, if someone has a large **ego**, they think they are very important and valuable. ❑ *He had a massive ego, never would he admit he was wrong.*

가산명사 또는 불가산명사 자아 ❑ 그는 엄청난 자아를 가지고 있었고, 절대로 자기가 틀렸다고 인정하지 않으려 했다.

Word Partnership	*ego*의 연어
ADJ.	**big** ego
V.	**boost** *someone's* ego

---

eh /eɪ/ CONVENTION **Eh** is used in writing to represent a noise that people make as a response in conversation, for example to express agreement or to ask for something to be explained or repeated. ❑ *Let's talk all about it outside, eh?*

관용 표현 음, 어 ❑ 밖에서 그것에 대해 모두 얘기해 보자, 응?

eight ♦♦♦ /eɪt/ (eights) NUM **Eight** is the number 8. ❑ *So far eight workers have been killed.*

수사 8, 여덟 ❑ 지금까지 여덟 명의 인부들이 목숨을 잃었다.

| **Word Link** | *teen ≈ plus ten, from 13-19 :* eighteen, seventeen, teenager |

---

eight|een ♦♦♦ /eɪtin/ (eighteens) NUM **Eighteen** is the number 18. ❑ *He was employed by them for eighteen years.*

수사 열여덟 ❑ 그는 그들에게 18년 동안 고용되었다.

eight|eenth ♦♦◇ /eɪtinθ/ ORD The **eighteenth** item in a series is the one that you count as number eighteen. ❑ *The siege is now in its eighteenth day.*

서수 열여덟 번째 ❑ 지금은 포위 공격한 지 18일째이다.

eighth ♦♦◇ /eɪtθ/ (eighths) **1** ORD The **eighth** item in a series is the one that you count as number eight. ❑ *...the eighth prime minister of India.* **2** FRACTION An **eighth** is one of eight equal parts of something. ❑ *The Kuban produces an eighth of Russia's grain, meat and milk.*

1 서수 여덟 번째 ❑ 인도의 여덟 번째 수상 **2** 분수 8분의 1 ❑ 쿠반은 러시아의 곡물, 고기, 그리고 우유의 8분의 1을 생산한다.

eight|ieth ♦♦◇ /eɪtiəθ/ ORD The **eightieth** item in a series is the one that you count as number eighty. ❑ *Mr. Stevens recently celebrated his eightieth birthday.*

서수 80번째 ❑ 스티븐스 씨는 최근에 팔순 생일을 지냈다.

eighty ♦♦♦ /eɪti/ (eighties) **1** NUM **Eighty** is the number 80. ❑ *Eighty horses trotted up.* **2** N-PLURAL When you talk about the **eighties**, you are referring to numbers between 80 and 89. For example, if you are **in** your **eighties**, you are

1 수사 여든 ❑ 말 여든 마리가 달려 올라갔다. **2** 복수명사 80대의 ❑ 그는 80대 후반이었고 그 나라에서 가장 존경 받는 정계의 원로가 되었다.

aged between 80 and 89. If the temperature is **in the eighties**, the temperature is between 80 and 89 degrees. ❑ *He was in his late eighties and had become the country's most respected elder statesman.* ◗ N-PLURAL **The eighties** is the decade between 1980 and 1989. ❑ *He ran a property development business in the eighties.*

᠍ 복수명사 80년대 ❑ 그는 80년대에 토지 개발 사업체를 경영했다.

either ♦♦♦ /iðər, aɪðər/ ◗ You use **either** in front of the first of two or more alternatives, when you are stating the only possibilities or choices that there are. The other alternatives are introduced by "or." ❑ *Sightseeing is best done either by tour bus or by bicycles.* ❑ *The former President was demanding that he should be either put on trial or set free.* ◗ CONJ You use **either** in a negative statement in front of the first of two alternatives to indicate that the negative statement refers to both the alternatives. ❑ *There had been no indication of either breathlessness or any loss of mental faculties right until his death.* ◗ PRON You can use **either** to refer to one of two things, people, or situations, when you want to say that they are both possible and it does not matter which one is chosen or considered. ❑ *There were glasses of iced champagne and cigars. Unfortunately not many of either were consumed.* ● QUANT **Either** is also a quantifier. [QUANT of def-pl-n] ❑ *Do either of you smoke or drink heavily?* ● DET **Either** is also a determiner. ❑ *...a special Indian drug police that would have the authority to pursue suspects into either country.* ◗ PRON You use **either** in a negative statement to refer to each of two things, people, or situations to indicate that the negative statement includes both of them. [with brd-neg] ❑ *She warned me that I'd never marry or have children. — "I don't want either."* ● QUANT **Either** is also a quantifier. ❑ *There are no simple answers to either of those questions.* ● DET **Either** is also a determiner. ❑ *He sometimes couldn't remember either man's name.* ◗ ADV You use **either** by itself in negative statements to indicate that there is a similarity or connection with a person or thing that you have just mentioned. [ADV after v, with brd-neg] ❑ *He did not even say anything to her, and she did not speak to him either.* ◗ ADV When one negative statement follows another, you can use **either** at the end of the second one to indicate that you are adding an extra piece of information, and to emphasize that both are equally important. [ADV after v] ❑ *Don't agree, but don't argue either.* ◗ DET You can use **either** to introduce a noun that refers to each of two things when you are talking about both of them. ❑ *The basketball nets hung down from the ceiling at either end of the gymnasium.*

◗ 접속사 어느 한쪽의 ❑ 관광은 버스나 자전거로 하는 것이 최고이다. ❑ 전 대통령은 재판에 회부하거나 아니면 석방해 줄 것을 요구하고 있었다. ◗ 접속사 (부정문에서) ―거나 ❑ 그가 죽기 바로 직전까지 호흡 곤란이나 정신 기능에 어떠한 손상의 흔적이 전혀 없었었다. ◗ 대명사 둘 중 하나 ❑ 차게 한 샴페인과 시가가 있었다. 불행하게도 둘 중 어느 것도 많이 소비되지 않았다. ● 수량사 (둘 중) 어느 한 쪽 ❑ 두 분 중 어느 한 분이라도 흡연이나 음주를 많이 합니까? ● 한정사 어느 ❑ 어느 나라든 권한을 갖고 용의자를 추적할 수 있는 인도의 특수 마약 경찰 ◗ 대명사 (부정문에서) 둘 중 어떤 쪽 ❑ 그녀는 내가 절대로 결혼을 못 하거나 아이를 낳지 못할 것이라고 경고했다. "나는 둘 중 어떤 것도 원하지 않는다." ● 수량사 어느 쪽 ❑ 그 질문의 어떤 것이든지 간단한 답은 없다. ● 한정사 어느 ❑ 그는 가끔 어느 남자의 이름도 기억할 수가 없었다. ◗ 부사 (부정문에서) 또한 ❑ 그는 그녀에게 어떤 말도 하지 않았고, 그녀 또한 그에게 말하지 않았다. ◗ 부사 또한 ❑ 동의하지도 말고, 싸우지도 마. ◗ 한정사 (둘 중) 각각의 ❑ 농구 골대는 체육관 양쪽 끝 각 천장에 매달려 있었다.

Word Link   e ≈ away, out : *e*ject, *e*migrate, *e*mit

eject /ɪdʒɛkt/ (**ejects, ejecting, ejected**) ◗ V-T If you **eject** someone **from** a place, you force them to leave. ❑ *Officials used guard dogs to eject the protesters.* ● **ejec|tion** /ɪdʒɛkʃən/ (**ejections**) N-VAR ❑ *...the ejection and manhandling of hecklers at the meeting.* ◗ V-T To **eject** something means to remove it or push it out forcefully. ❑ *He aimed his rifle, fired a single shot, then ejected the spent cartridge.* ◗ V-I When a pilot **ejects from** an aircraft, he or she leaves the aircraft quickly using an ejector seat, usually because the plane is about to crash. ❑ *The pilot ejected from the plane and escaped injury.*

◗ 타동사 쫓아내다 ❑ 직원들은 순찰견을 이용해서 항의자들을 쫓아냈다. ● 불가산명사 또는 가산명사 축출 ❑ 회의에서 야유하는 사람들을 거칠게 다루어 내보냄 ◗ 타동사 빼내다 ❑ 그는 총을 겨누고, 한 발을 발사했고, 그리고 다 쓴 탄창을 빼냈다. ◗ 자동사 뛰어나오다 ❑ 파일럿은 비행기에서 빠져나와서 부상을 면했다.

Word Link   labor ≈ working : col*labor*ate, e*labor*ate, *labor*atory

elabo|rate (**elaborates, elaborating, elaborated**)

> The adjective is pronounced /ɪlæbərɪt/. The verb is pronounced /ɪlæbəreɪt/.

형용사는 /ɪlæbərɪt /으로 발음되고, 동사는 /ɪlæbəreɪt /으로 발음된다.

◗ ADJ You use **elaborate** to describe something that is very complex because it has a lot of different parts. ❑ *...an elaborate research project.* ◗ ADJ **Elaborate** plans, systems, and procedures are complicated because they have been planned in very great detail, sometimes too much detail. ❑ *...elaborate efforts at the highest level to conceal the problem.* ● **elabo|rate|ly** ADV ❑ *It was clearly an elaborately planned operation.* ◗ ADJ **Elaborate** clothing or material is made with a lot of detailed artistic designs. ❑ *He is known for his elaborate costumes.* ◗ V-T If you **elaborate** a plan or theory, you develop it by making it more complicated and more effective. ❑ *His task was to elaborate policies which would make a market economy compatible with a clean environment.* ● **elabo|ra|tion** /ɪlæbəreɪʃən/ N-UNCOUNT ❑ *...the elaboration of specific policies and mechanisms.* ◗ V-I If you **elaborate on** something that has been said, you say more about it, or give more details. ❑ *A spokesman declined to elaborate on a statement released late yesterday.*

◗ 형용사 복잡한 ❑ 복잡한 연구 계획서 ◗ 형용사 정교한 ❑ 문제를 감추기 위한 최고 수준의 정교한 노력 ● 정교하게 부사 ❑ 명백히 그것은 정교하게 계획된 작전이었다. ◗ 형용사 공들인 ❑ 그는 공들여 옷을 짓는 것으로 잘 알려져 있다. ◗ 타동사 고심하여 만들다 ❑ 깨끗한 환경과 공존하는 시장 경제를 만드는 정책을 공들여 짜는 것이 그의 업무였다. ● 상술 불가산명사 ❑ 세부 정책과 과정에 대한 상술 ◗ 자동사 상술하다 ❑ 대변인은 어제 늦게 발표된 성명서에 대해 상술하는 것을 거절했다.

Word Link   lapse ≈ falling : col*lapse*, e*lapse*, *lapse*

elapse /ɪlæps/ (**elapses, elapsing, elapsed**) V-I When time **elapses**, it passes. [FORMAL] ❑ *Forty-eight hours have elapsed since his arrest.*

자동사 경과하다 [격식체] ❑ 그가 체포된 후로 48시간이 경과되었다.

elas|tic /ɪlæstɪk/ (**elastics**) ◗ N-UNCOUNT **Elastic** is a rubber material that stretches when you pull it and returns to its original size and shape when you let it go. Elastic is often used in clothes to make them fit tightly, for example around the waist. ❑ *...a piece of elastic.* ◗ ADJ Something that is **elastic** is able to stretch easily and then return to its original size and shape. ❑ *Beat it until the dough is slightly elastic.*

◗ 불가산명사 고무줄 ❑ 고무줄은 당기면 늘어났다가 놓으면 원래 크기와 모양으로 돌아가는 고무 소재다. ◗ 형용사 탄력성 있는 ❑ 약간 탄력이 생길 때까지 반죽을 치대세요.

elas|tic band (**elastic bands**) N-COUNT An **elastic band** is a thin circle of very stretchy rubber that you can put around things in order to hold them together. [mainly BRIT; AM **rubber band**]

가산명사 고무 밴드 [주로 영국영어; 미국영어 rubber band]

elas|tic|ity /ɪlæstɪsɪti, ɪlæst-/ N-UNCOUNT The **elasticity** of a material or substance is its ability to return to its original shape, size, and condition after it has been stretched. ❑ *Daily facial exercises help her to retain the skin's elasticity.*

불가산명사 탄력 ❑ 매일 하는 얼굴 운동은 그녀의 피부의 탄력을 유지하게 해 준다.

elat|ed /ɪleɪtɪd/ ADJ If you are **elated**, you are extremely happy and excited because of something that has happened. ❑ *I was elated that my recent second bypass had been successful.*

형용사 의기양양한, 매우 행복한 ❑ 최근의 두 번째 혈관 수술이 성공해서 나는 매우 행복했다.

ela|tion /ɪleɪʃ°n/ N-UNCOUNT **Elation** is a feeling of great happiness and excitement about something that has happened. ❑ *His supporters have reacted to the news with elation.* →see **emotion**

불가산명사 의기양양 ❑ 그의 후원자들은 그 소식에 의기양양해 했다.

el|bow /ɛlboʊ/ (elbows, elbowing, elbowed) **1** N-COUNT Your **elbow** is the part of your arm where the upper and lower halves of the arm are joined. ❑ *He slipped and fell, badly bruising an elbow.* **2** V-T If you **elbow** people **aside** or **elbow** your **way** somewhere, you push people with your elbows in order to move somewhere. ❑ *They also claim that the security team elbowed aside a steward.* ❑ *Mr. Smith elbowed me in the face.* **3** V-T If someone or something **elbows** their **way** somewhere, or **elbows** other people or things **out of the way**, they achieve success by being aggressive and determined. ❑ *Non-state firms gradually elbow aside the inefficient state-owned ones.* **4** to **rub elbows with** →see **rub** →see **body**

1 가산명사 팔꿈치 ❑ 그는 미끄러져서 넘어졌고, 심하게 팔꿈치에 멍이 들었다. **2** 타동사 팔꿈치로 밀치다 ❑ 그들은 또한 경비 팀이 진행 요원을 팔꿈치로 밀쳤다고 주장한다. ❑ 스미스 씨가 팔꿈치로 내 얼굴을 밀었다. **3** 타동사 공격적으로 성취하다 ❑ 주에서 소유하지 않은 회사들이 점점 주가 소유한 비효율적인 회사들을 물리치고 성공하게 되었다.

el|der /ɛldər/ (elders) **1** ADJ The **elder of** two people is the one who was born first. [ADJ n, the ADJ, the ADJ of n] ❑ *...his elder brother.* **2** N-COUNT A person's **elder** is someone who is older than them, especially someone quite a lot older. [FORMAL] ❑ *The young have no respect for their elders.* **3** N-COUNT In some societies, an **elder** is one of the respected older people who have influence and authority. ❑ *...a meeting of political figures and tribal elders.*

1 형용사 손위의 ❑ 그의 형 **2** 가산명사 연장자, 손윗사람 [격식체] ❑ 젊은이들은 연장자에 대한 존경심이 없다. **3** 가산명사 원로 ❑ 정치적 인물들과 부족의 원로들의 모임

> The adjective **elder** means "older" when it is followed by brother, sister, son, daughter, or other terms for relatives that are in your generation or younger. You use **older** to talk about the age of other people or things. **Elder** cannot be followed by "than" but **older** can be. ❑ *I've got a sister who is older than me.* Do not confuse **elder** and **elderly**. If you describe someone as **elderly**, you mean that they are old, but this is a slightly more polite word than **old**. The **elderly** are elderly people.

> 형용사 elder는 뒤에 형제, 자매, 아들, 딸, 혹은 자신과 동세대이거나 손아래 세대의 친척을 일컫는 다른 말이 나오면 older를 뜻한다. older는 다른 사람들의 나이나 사물의 햇수에 대해 말할 때 쓴다. elder는 뒤에 than이 올 수 없지만, older는 가능하다. ❑ 내게는 나보다 나이가 많은 여형제가 있다. elder와 elderly를 혼동하지 않도록 하라. 어떤 사람을 elderly라고 하면, 그 사람이 나이가 들었다는 뜻이고 old 보다는 조금 더 공손한 말이다. the elderly는 '나이 든 사람들'을 말한다.

el|der|ly ◆◇◇ /ɛldərli/ ADJ You use **elderly** as a polite way of saying that someone is old. [POLITENESS] ❑ *There was an elderly couple on the terrace.* ● N-PLURAL The **elderly** are people who are old. ❑ *The elderly are a formidable force in any election.* →see **elder** →see **age**

형용사 나이가 지긋한 [공손체] ❑ 테라스에 나이가 지긋한 커플이 있었다. ● 복수명사 노인들 ❑ 어떠한 선거에서도 노인들이 힘이 강력하다.

eld|est /ɛldɪst/ ADJ The **eldest** person in a group is the one who was born before all the others. ❑ *The eldest child was a daughter called Fiona.* ❑ *David was the eldest of three boys.*

형용사 가장 나이가 많은 ❑ 가장 나이가 많은 자녀는 피오나라는 이름을 가진 딸이었다. ❑ 데이비드는 세 명의 소년 중에서 가장 나이가 많았다.

elect ◆◇◇ /ɪlɛkt/ (elects, electing, elected) **1** V-T When people **elect** someone, they choose that person to represent them, by voting for them. ❑ *The people of the Philippines have voted to elect a new president.* ❑ *Manchester College elected him Principal in 1956.* **2** V-T If you **elect to** do something, you choose to do it. [FORMAL] ❑ *Those electing to smoke will be seated at the rear.* **3** ADJ **Elect** is added after words such as "president" or "governor" to indicate that a person has been elected to the post but has not officially started to carry out the duties involved. [FORMAL] [n ADJ] ❑ *...the date when the president-elect takes office.* →see **election**

1 타동사 선출하다 ❑ 필리핀 사람들은 대통령을 선출하는 투표를 하였다. ❑ 맨체스터 대학은 1956년에 그를 학장으로 선출했다. **2** 타동사 선택하다 [격식체] ❑ 흡연하고자 하는 사람들은 뒷자리에 좌석이 배정될 것이다. **3** 형용사 당선된 [격식체] ❑ 대통령 당선자가 취임하는 날짜

elec|tion ◆◆◆ /ɪlɛkʃ°n/ (elections) **1** N-VAR An **election** is a process in which people vote to choose a person or group of people to hold an official position. ❑ *...Poland's first fully free elections for more than fifty years.* ❑ *During his election campaign he promised to put the economy back on its feet.* **2** N-UNCOUNT The **election** of a particular person or group of people is their success in winning an election. [usu with poss] ❑ *...the election of the Labour government in 1964.* ❑ *...Vaclav Havel's election as president of Czechoslovakia.* →see Word Web: **election**

1 가산명사 또는 불가산명사 선거 ❑ 오십 년 이상 동안에 폴란드에서 처음으로 실시된 완전 자유선거 ❑ 선거 운동 동안 그는 경제를 회복시키겠다고 약속했다. **2** 불가산명사 선출, 당선 ❑ 1964년 선거에서의 노동당 정부의 입각 ❑ 바츨라프 하벨의 체코슬로바키아 대통령 선출

Word Partnership	election의 연어
N.	election **campaign**, election **day**, election **official**, election **results** **1**
V.	**hold an** election, **lose an** election, **vote in an** election, **win an** election **1**

elec|tor /ɪlɛktər/ (electors) N-COUNT An **elector** is a person who has the right to vote in an election. ❑ *He called on electors to vote for his reform program.*

가산명사 선거인, 유권자 ❑ 그는 유권자들에게 자신의 개혁 프로그램에 찬성해 달라고 부탁했다.

elec|tor|al ◆◇◇ /ɪlɛktərəl/ ADJ **Electoral** is used to describe things that are connected with elections. [ADJ n] ❑ *The Mongolian Democratic Party is campaigning for electoral reform.* ● **elec|tor|al|ly** ADV ❑ *He believed that the policies were both wrong and electorally disastrous.*

형용사 선거의 ❑ 몽고의 민주당은 선거 개혁 캠페인을 벌이고 있다. ● 선거로 부사 ❑ 그는 정책들이 잘못되기도 했고 선거에도 피해가 클 것이라고 믿었다.

elec|tor|ate /ɪlɛktərɪt/ (electorates) N-COUNT-COLL The **electorate** of a country or area is all the people in it who have the right to vote in an election. ❑ *He has the backing of almost a quarter of the electorate.*

가산명사-집합 유권자 ❑ 그는 유권자의 거의 4분의 1의 지지를 얻고 있다.

Word Web	election

Presidential candidates spend millions of dollars on their **campaigns**. They give **speeches**, appear on TV, and **debate** each other. On election day, **voters cast** their **votes** at local **polling places**. **Citizens** living outside of the US mail in **absentee ballots**. But voters don't directly **elect** their **president**. States send representatives to the electoral college. There, representatives from all but two states must cast all their votes for one candidate—even if 49% of the people wanted the other candidate. Four times a candidate has **won** the popular vote and lost the election. This happened when George W. Bush won in 2000.

electric ◆◇◇ /ɪlɛktrɪk/ **1** ADJ An **electric** device or machine works by means of electricity, rather than using some other source of power. ❑ ...her electric guitar. **2** ADJ An **electric** current, voltage, or charge is one that is produced by electricity. [ADJ n] ❑ It involves the insertion of a very fine needle into each hair follicle, through which a small electric current is passed. **3** ADJ **Electric** plugs, sockets, or power lines are designed to carry electricity. [ADJ n] ❑ More people are deciding that electric power lines could present a health risk. **4** ADJ **Electric** is used to refer to the supply of electricity. [INFORMAL] [ADJ n] ❑ An average electric bill might go up $2 or $3 per month. **5** ADJ If you describe the atmosphere of a place or event as **electric**, you mean that people are in a state of great excitement. ❑ The mood in the hall was electrical.

1 형용사 전기로 움직이는 ❑ 그녀의 전기 기타 **2** 형용사 전기의 ❑ 거기에는 각각의 모낭 속으로 매우 가느다란 바늘을 투입하는 것이 포함되는데, 그 바늘을 통해서 작은 전류가 통과한다. **3** 형용사 전기가 통하는 ❑ 이 많은 사람들이 송전선이 건강에 위험할 수도 있다고 판단하고 있다. **4** 형용사 전기 공급의 [비격식체] ❑ 평균 전기세가 월 2달러 또는 3달러 오를지도 모른다. **5** 형용사 들뜬 ❑ 홀의 분위기는 들떠 있었다.

electrical /ɪlɛktrɪkᵊl/ **1** ADJ **Electrical** goods, equipment, or appliances work by means of electricity. ❑ ...shipments of electrical equipment. ● **electrically** /ɪlɛktrɪkli/ ADV [ADV -ed] ❑ ...electrically-powered vehicles. **2** ADJ **Electrical** systems or parts supply or use electricity. ❑ ...lighting and other electrical systems on the new runway. **3** ADJ **Electrical** energy is energy in the form of electricity. ❑ ...brief pulses of electrical energy. ● **electrically** ADV ❑ ...electrically charged particles. **4** ADJ **Electrical** industries, engineers, or workers are involved in the production and supply of electricity or electrical goods. [ADJ n] ❑ ...company representatives from the electrical industry. →see **electricity, energy**

1 형용사 전기의 ❑ 전기 장비의 선적 ● 전기로 부사 ❑ 전기 동력 자동차 **2** 형용사 전기의 ❑ 새로운 활주로의 조명과 다른 전기 장치들 **3** 형용사 전기의 ❑ 전기 에너지의 짧은 파동 ● 전기로 부사 ❑ 전기로 충전된 입자들 **4** 형용사 전기와 관련된 ❑ 전기 산업의 기업 대표들

electric chair (electric chairs) N-COUNT The **electric chair** is a method of killing criminals, used especially in the United States, in which a person is strapped to a special chair and killed by a powerful electric current. ❑ Murderer Walter Kemmler was the first man to die in the electric chair.

가산명사 전기의자 ❑ 살인자 월터 켐러는 최초로 전기의자에서 처형된 사람이었다.

Word Link   electr ≈ electric : electron, electricity, electrician

electrician /ɪlɛktrɪʃᵊn, ilɛk-/ (electricians) N-COUNT An **electrician** is a person whose job is to install and repair electrical equipment.

가산명사 전기 기사

electricity ◆◇◇ /ɪlɛktrɪsiti, ilɛk-/ N-UNCOUNT **Electricity** is a form of energy that can be carried by wires and is used for heating and lighting, and to provide power for machines. ❑ We moved into a cabin with electricity but no running water. →see **energy, light bulb** →see Word Web: **electricity**

불가산명사 전기 ❑ 우리는 전기는 들어오나 수돗물은 나오지 않는 오두막집으로 이사했다.

electric shock (electric shocks) N-COUNT If you get an **electric shock**, you get a sudden painful feeling when you touch something which is connected to a supply of electricity.

가산명사 전기 쇼크, 감전

electrification /ɪlɛktrɪfɪkeɪʃᵊn/ N-UNCOUNT The **electrification** of a house, town, or area is the connecting of that place with a supply of electricity. ❑ ...rural electrification.

불가산명사 전력 공급 ❑ 시골의 전력 공급

electrify /ɪlɛktrɪfaɪ/ (electrifies, electrifying, electrified) **1** V-T If people **are electrified by** an event or experience, it makes them feel very excited and surprised. [usu passive] ❑ The world was electrified by his courage and resistance. ● **electrifying** ADJ ❑ He gave an electrifying performance. **2** V-T When a rail system or rail line is **electrified**, electric cables are put over the tracks, or electric rails are put beside them, so that the trains can be powered by electricity. [usu passive] ❑ The west-coast line was electrified as long ago as 1974.

1 타동사 깜짝 놀라게 하다 ❑ 세계는 그의 용기와 저항에 몹시 놀랐다. ● 전율을 느끼게 하는 형용사 ❑ 그는 전율을 느끼게 하는 연기를 했다. **2** 타동사 전기를 통하게 하다 ❑ 서해안선은 1974년까지 전기가 통하게 연결되어 있었다.

electrocute /ɪlɛktrəkyut/ (electrocutes, electrocuting, electrocuted) **1** V-T If someone is **electrocuted**, they are accidentally killed or badly injured when they touch something connected to a source of electricity. ❑ Three people were electrocuted by falling power-lines. **2** V-T If a criminal is **electrocuted**, he or she is executed using electricity. [usu passive] ❑ He was electrocuted for a murder committed when he was 17. ● **electrocution** /ɪlɛktrəkyuʃᵊn/ (electrocutions) N-VAR ❑ The court pronounced him guilty and sentenced him to death by electrocution.

1 타동사 감전시키다 ❑ 송전선이 떨어져서 세 명이 감전당했다. **2** 타동사 전기의자로 처형하다 ❑ 그는 17세일 때 저지른 살인죄로 전기의자로 처형되었다. ● 전기의자 사형 가산명사 또는 불가산명사 ❑ 법원은 그의 유죄를 인정하고 전기의자 사형을 선고했다.

electrode /ɪlɛktroʊd/ (electrodes) N-COUNT An **electrode** is a small piece of metal or other substance that is used to take an electric current to or from a source of power, a piece of equipment, or a living body. ❑ Two electrodes which measure changes in the body's surface moisture are attached to the palms of your hands.

가산명사 전극 ❑ 신체의 표면 수분의 변화를 측정하는 두 개의 전극이 당신의 손바닥에 부착되어 있다.

electron /ɪlɛktrɒn/ (electrons) N-COUNT An **electron** is a tiny particle of matter that is smaller than an atom and has a negative electrical charge. [TECHNICAL] ❑ Most things are balanced - with equal numbers of electrons and protons. →see **television**

가산명사 전자 [과학 기술] ❑ 대부분의 물질은 같은 전자 수와 양성자 수로 균형을 이루고 있다.

electronic ◆◇◇ /ɪlɛktrɒnɪk, i-/ **1** ADJ An **electronic** device has transistors or silicon chips which control and change the electric current passing through the device. [ADJ n] ❑ ...expensive electronic equipment. **2** ADJ An **electronic** process or activity involves the use of electronic devices. ❑ ...electronic music. ● **electronically** ADV [ADV with v] ❑ Data is transmitted electronically.

1 형용사 전자의 ❑ 값비싼 전자 장비 **2** 형용사 전자의 ❑ 전자 음악 ● 전자 공학적으로 부사 ❑ 데이터는 전자 공학적으로 전송된다.

Word Web   electricity

Demand for **electrical** power in the U.S. will likely rise by 35 percent over the next 20 years. **Power companies** are moving quickly to meet this need. At the heart of every **power station** are electrical **generators**. Traditionally, they ran on hydroelectric power or **fossil fuel**. However, today new sources of **energy** are available. On **wind farms**, wind **turbines** use the power of moving air to run generators. Seaside tidal power stations make use of rising and falling tides to turn turbines. And in sunny climates, photovoltaic cells produce electrical power from the sun's rays.

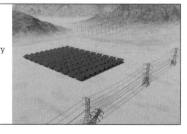

elec|tron|ic book (**electronic books**) N-COUNT An **electronic book** is the same as an **e-book**. [COMPUTING]

가산명사 전자책 [컴퓨터]

elec|tron|ic mail N-SING **Electronic mail** is the same as **e-mail**.

단수명사 전자 우편

elec|tron|ic pub|lish|ing N-UNCOUNT **Electronic publishing** is the publishing of documents in a form that can be read on a computer, for example as a CD-ROM.

불가산명사 전자 출판

Word Link

ics ≈ system, knowledge : economics, electronics, physics

---

elec|tron|ics /ɪlɛktrɒnɪks, i-/ N-UNCOUNT **Electronics** is the technology of using transistors and silicon chips, especially in devices such as radios, televisions, and computers. ❑ ...Europe's three main electronics companies.

불가산명사 전자 공학 ❑ 유럽의 주요한 세 개 전자 회사

el|egant ◆◇◇ /ɛlɪgənt/ ■ ADJ If you describe a person or thing as **elegant**, you mean that they are pleasing and graceful in appearance or style. ❑ Patricia looked beautiful and elegant as always. ● **el|egance** N-UNCOUNT ❑ The furniture managed to combine practicality with elegance. ● **el|egant|ly** ADV ❑ ...a tall, elegantly dressed man with a mustache. ② ADJ If you describe a piece of writing, an idea, or a plan as **elegant**, you mean that it is simple, clear, and clever. ❑ The document impressed me with its elegant simplicity. ● **el|egant|ly** ADV ❑ ...an elegantly simple idea.

■ 형용사 우아한 ❑ 퍼트리셔는 늘 그랬듯이 아름답고 우아했다. ● 고상, 우아 불가산명사 ❑ 그 가구는 그런대로 실용성과 우아함을 결합시켰다. ● 우아하게 부사 ❑ 우아하게 차려입고 콧수염을 기른 키 큰 남자 ② 형용사 명쾌한 ❑ 그 문서는 명쾌한 간결성으로 나에게 강한 인상을 남겼다. ● 명쾌하게 부사 ❑ 명쾌하게 간단한 견해

Thesaurus

elegant의 참조어

ADJ.   chic, exquisite, luxurious, stylish ■

---

el|ement ◆◇◇ /ɛlɪmənt/ (**elements**) ■ N-COUNT The different **elements** of something are the different parts it contains. ❑ The exchange of prisoners of war was one of the key elements of the UN's peace plan. ② N-COUNT A particular **element** of a situation, activity, or process is an important quality or feature that it has or needs. ❑ Fitness has now become an important element in our lives. ③ N-COUNT When you talk about **elements** within a society or organization, you are referring to groups of people who have similar aims, beliefs, or habits. ❑ The government must weed out criminal elements from within the security forces. ④ N-COUNT If something has an **element** of a particular quality or emotion, it has a certain amount of this quality or emotion. ❑ These reports clearly contain elements of propaganda. ⑤ N-COUNT An **element** is a substance such as gold, oxygen, or carbon that consists of only one type of atom. ⑥ N-COUNT The **element** in an electric fire or water heater is the metal part which changes the electric current into heat. ⑦ N-PLURAL You can refer to the weather, especially wind and rain, as **the elements**. ❑ The area where most refugees are waiting is exposed to the elements. ⑧ PHRASE If you say that someone is **in their element**, you mean that they are in a situation they enjoy. ❑ My stepmother was in her element, organizing everything.
→see Word Web: **element**

■ 가산명사 요소 ❑ 전쟁 포로 교환은 유엔 평화 계획의 중요한 요소 중 하나였다. ② 가산명사 요소 ❑ 건강은 이제 우리의 삶에서 중요한 요소가 되었다. ③ 가산명사 집단 ❑ 정부는 공안 부대 내부에서 범죄 집단을 뿌리 뽑아야 한다. ④ 가산명사 요소 ❑ 이 보고서들은 명백하게 정치적 선전의 요소들을 포함하고 있다. ⑤ 가산명사 원소 ⑥ 가산명사 전류 ⑦ 복수명사 풍우, 비바람 ❑ 대부분의 난민들이 기다리고 있는 지역은 비바람에 노출되어 있다. ⑧ 구 물 만난 고기 같은 ❑ 나의 새엄마는 물 만난 고기같이 모든 것을 정리해 나갔다.

el|emen|ta|ry /ɛlɪmɛntəri, -tri/ ADJ Something that is **elementary** is very simple and basic. ❑ Literacy now includes elementary computer skills.

형용사 기본의 ❑ 요즘은 읽고 쓰는 능력이라고 하면 기본적인 컴퓨터 기술을 포함한다.

el|emen|ta|ry school (**elementary schools**) N-VAR An **elementary school** is a school where children are taught for the first six or sometimes seven years of their education. [mainly AM] ❑ The move from elementary school to middle school or junior high can be difficult.

가산명사 또는 불가산명사 초등학교 [주로 미국영어] ❑ 초등학교에서 중학교로 올라가는 것이 어려울 수 있다.

el|ephant /ɛlɪfənt/ (**elephants**) N-COUNT An **elephant** is a very large animal with a long, flexible nose called a trunk, which it uses to pick up things. Elephants live in India and Africa.

가산명사 코끼리

el|evate /ɛlɪveɪt/ (**elevates, elevating, elevated**) ■ V-T When someone or something is elevated to a more important rank or status, you can say that they **are elevated to** it. [FORMAL] [usu passive] ❑ He was elevated to the post of prime minister. ● **el|eva|tion** /ɛlɪveɪʃⁿn/ N-UNCOUNT ❑ The Prime Minister is known to favor the elevation of more women to the Cabinet. ② V-T If you **elevate** something **to** a higher status, you consider it to be better or more important than it really is. ❑ Don't elevate your superiors to superstar status. ③ V-T To **elevate** something means to increase it in amount or intensity. [FORMAL] ❑ Emotional stress can elevate blood pressure. ④ V-T If you **elevate** something, you raise it above a horizontal level. [FORMAL] ❑ Jack elevated the gun at the sky.

■ 타동사 승진시키다, 등용하다 [격식체] ❑ 그는 수상의 자리에 등용되었다. ● 등용 불가산명사 ❑ 수상은 더 많은 여성을 내각에 등용하고자 하는 것으로 알려져 있다. ② 타동사 승격시키다 ❑ 너보다 나은 사람들을 슈퍼스타 지위로 승격시키지 말아라. ③ 타동사 증가시키다 [격식체] ❑ 감정적인 스트레스는 혈압을 높일 수 있다. ④ 타동사 들어올리다 [격식체] ❑ 잭은 하늘을 향해 총을 들어올렸다.

Word Web   element

Elements—like copper, sodium, and oxygen—are made from only one type of **atom**. Each element has its own unique **properties**. For instance, oxygen is a gas at room temperature and copper is a solid. Often elements come

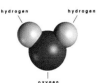
hydrogen   hydrogen

oxygen

together with other types of elements to make **compounds**. When the atoms in a compound bind together, they form a **molecule**. One of the best known molecules is H_2O. It is made up of two hydrogen atoms and one oxygen atom. This molecule is also known as water. The periodic table is a complete listing of all the elements.

The Periodic Table of Elements

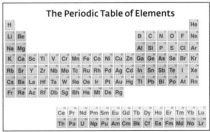

a b c d e f g h i j k l m n o p q r s t u v w x y z

Word Link ation ≈ state of : *education*, *elevation*, *preservation*

ele|va|tion /ˌɛlɪveɪʃən/ (elevations) **1** N-COUNT The **elevation** of a place is its height above sea level. ❑ *We're probably at an elevation of about 13,000 feet above sea level.* **2** N-COUNT An **elevation** is a piece of ground that is higher than the area around it. ❑ *...the monument at the head of Elgin St. - on an elevation, which could be seen from the new Knox Church.*

1 가산명사 해발 ❑ 우리는 아마도 대략 해발 13,000피트 정도에 있다. **2** 가산명사 고지대 ❑ 녹스 교회에서 보이는 고지대인 엘긴 가 들머리에 있는 기념비

ele|va|tor /ˈɛlɪveɪtər/ (elevators) N-COUNT An **elevator** is a device that carries people up and down inside buildings. [AM; BRIT **lift**] ❑ *We took the elevator to the fourteenth floor.*

가산명사 엘리베이터 [미국영어; 영국영어 lift] ❑ 우리는 14층까지 엘리베이터를 타고 올라갔다.

elev|en ♦♦♦ /ɪlɛvᵊn/ (elevens) NUM **Eleven** is the number 11. ❑ *...the Princess and her eleven friends.*

수사 11 ❑ 공주와 그녀의 열한 명의 친구들

elev|enth ♦♦◇ /ɪlɛvᵊnθ/ ORD The **eleventh** item in a series is the one that you count as number eleven. ❑ *We were working on the eleventh floor.*

서수 열한 번째의 ❑ 우리는 11층에서 일하고 있었다.

elic|it /ɪlɪsɪt/ (elicits, eliciting, elicited) **1** V-T If you **elicit** a response or a reaction, you do or say something which makes other people respond or react. ❑ *Mr. Norris said he was hopeful that his request would elicit a positive response.* **2** V-T If you **elicit** a piece of information, you get it by asking the right questions. [FORMAL] ❑ *They promised to make enquiries for us, but several phone calls elicited no further information.*

1 타동사 이끌어 내다 ❑ 노리스 씨는 그의 요구가 긍정적인 반응을 이끌어 내기를 바란다고 말했다. **2** 타동사 유도해 내다 [격식체] ❑ 그들은 우리를 대신해서 문의를 하기로 약속했지만 몇 차례 전화로 추가 정보를 알아내지 못했다.

eli|gible /ˈɛlɪdʒɪbᵊl/ **1** ADJ Someone who is **eligible to** do something is qualified or able to do it, for example because they are old enough. ❑ *Almost half the population are eligible to vote in today's election.* ● **eli|gi|bil|ity** /ˌɛlɪdʒəbɪlɪti/ N-UNCOUNT ❑ *The rules covering eligibility for benefits changed in the 1980s.* **2** ADJ An **eligible** man or woman is not yet married and is thought by many people to be a suitable partner. ❑ *He's the most eligible bachelor in Japan.*

1 형용사 적격의, 적령기의 ❑ 오늘 선거에서는 인구의 거의 절반에게 투표권이 있다. ● 적격성 불가산명사 ❑ 보조금의 적격성을 다루는 규정은 1980년대에 바뀌었다. **2** 형용사 결혼 상대로 적합한 ❑ 그는 일본에서 결혼 상대로 가장 적합한 총각이다.

elimi|nate ♦◇◇ /ɪlɪmɪneɪt/ (eliminates, eliminating, eliminated) **1** V-T To **eliminate** something, especially something that you do not want or need, means to remove it completely. [FORMAL] ❑ *The Sex Discrimination Act has not eliminated discrimination in employment.* ● **elimi|na|tion** /ɪˌlɪmɪneɪʃən/ N-UNCOUNT ❑ *...the prohibition and elimination of chemical weapons.* **2** V-T PASSIVE When a person or team **is eliminated from** a competition, they are defeated and so take no further part in the competition. ❑ *I was eliminated from the 400 meters in the semi-finals.* **3** V-T If someone says that they **have eliminated** an enemy, they mean that they have killed them. By using the word "eliminate," they are trying to make the action sound more positive than if they used the word "kill." ❑ *He declared war on the government and urged right-wingers to eliminate their opponents.*

1 타동사 제거하다 [격식체] ❑ 성 차별법은 고용에 있어서의 차별을 없애지 못했다. ● 제거 불가산명사 ❑ 화학 무기의 금지와 제거 **2** 수동 타동사 실격시키다 ❑ 나는 400미터 준결승에서 실격되었다. **3** 타동사 제거하다 ❑ 그는 정부에 전쟁을 선포했고 우익 사람들에게 반대자들을 제거하라고 촉구했다.

Thesaurus *eliminate*의 참조어

v. dispose of, erase, expel, remove; (ant.) choose, include **1**
    defeat, exclude, knock out **2**

elite /ɪlit, eɪ-/ (elites) **1** N-COUNT You can refer to the most powerful, rich, or talented people within a particular group, place, or society as the **elite**. ❑ *...a government comprised mainly of the elite.* **2** ADJ **Elite** people or organizations are considered to be the best of their kind. [ADJ n] ❑ *...the elite troops of the President's bodyguard.*

1 가산명사 엘리트 ❑ 주로 엘리트로 구성된 정부 **2** 형용사 정예의 ❑ 대통령 경호원의 정예 부대

elit|ism /ɪlitɪzəm, eɪ-/ N-UNCOUNT **Elitism** is the quality or practice of being elitist. ❑ *It became difficult to promote conventional ideas of excellence without being instantly accused of elitism.*

불가산명사 엘리트주의 ❑ 엘리트주의라는 비난을 즉각 받지 않고 우수성에 대한 전통적인 생각을 촉진시키기가 어렵게 되었다.

elit|ist /ɪlitɪst, eɪ-/ (elitists) **1** ADJ **Elitist** systems, practices, or ideas favor the most powerful, rich, or talented people within a group, place, or society. [DISAPPROVAL] ❑ *The legal profession is starting to be less elitist and more representative.* **2** N-COUNT An **elitist** is someone who has elitist ideas or is part of an elite. [DISAPPROVAL] ❑ *He was an elitist who had no time for the masses and an unquenchable ego.*

1 형용사 엘리트주의의 [탐탁잖음] ❑ 법률 관련 직업에서는 엘리트주의가 줄고 좀 더 대표성을 중시하기 시작하고 있다. **2** 가산명사 엘리트주의자 [탐탁잖음] ❑ 그는 대중을 위해서는 시간을 낼 줄 모르는, 만족을 모르는 자아를 지닌 엘리트주의자였다.

elm /ɛlm/ (elms) N-VAR An **elm** is a tree that has broad leaves which it loses in winter. ● N-UNCOUNT **Elm** is the wood of this tree. ❑ *It was a good table too, sturdily constructed of elm.*

가산명사 또는 불가산명사 느릅나무 ● 불가산명사 느릅나무 목재 ❑ 그것은 또한 좋은 탁자였는데, 느릅나무 목재로 튼튼하게 만들어져 있었다.

elo|quent /ˈɛləkwənt/ **1** ADJ Speech or writing that is **eloquent** is well expressed and effective in persuading people. ❑ *I heard him make a very eloquent speech at that dinner.* ● **elo|quence** N-UNCOUNT ❑ *...the eloquence of his prose.* ● **elo|quent|ly** ADV ❑ *Jan speaks eloquently about her art.* **2** ADJ A person who is **eloquent** is good at speaking and able to persuade people. [APPROVAL] ❑ *He was eloquent about his love of books.* ● **elo|quence** N-UNCOUNT ❑ *I wish I'd had the eloquence of Helmut Schmidt.*

1 형용사 설득력이 있는 ❑ 나는 그가 그 저녁 식사 자리에서 매우 설득력 있는 연설을 하는 것을 들었다. ● 웅변; 설득력 불가산명사 ❑ 그의 산문의 설득력 ● 웅변적으로, 설득력 있게 부사 ❑ 잔은 자신의 예술에 대해서 웅변적으로 말한다. **2** 형용사 웅변의 ❑ 그는 책에 대한 자신의 사랑을 웅변적으로 말했다. ● 웅변술 불가산명사 ❑ 나에게 헬무트 슈미트의 웅변술이 있었으면 좋을 텐데.

else ♦♦♦ /ɛls/ **1** ADJ You use **else** after words such as "anywhere," "someone," and "what," to refer in a vague way to another person, place, or thing. [pron-indef/quest ADJ] ❑ *If I can't make a living at painting, at least I can teach someone else to paint.* ❑ *We had nothing else to do on those long trips.* ● ADV **Else** is also an adverb. [adv ADV] ❑ *I never wanted to live anywhere else.* **2** ADJ You use **else** after words such as "everyone," "everything," and "everywhere" to refer in a vague way to all the other people, things, or places except the one you are talking about. [pron-indef ADJ] ❑ *As I try to be truthful, I expect everyone else to be truthful.* ● ADV **Else** is also an adverb. [adv ADV] ❑ *London seems so much dirtier than everywhere else.* **3** PHRASE You use **or else** after stating a logical conclusion, to indicate that what you are about to say is evidence for that conclusion. ❑ *Evidently no lessons have been learnt or else the government would not have handled the problem so sloppily.* **4** PHRASE You use **or else** to introduce a statement that indicates the unpleasant results that

1 형용사 다른, 그 외 ❑ 내가 그림으로 생계를 꾸려 갈 수 없다면, 적어도 다른 누군가에게 그림 그리는 것을 가르칠 수는 있겠지. ❑ 우리는 그 긴 여행길에서 다른 할 일이 없었다. ● 부사 그 밖에 ❑ 나는 그 밖의 다른 곳에서는 살고 싶지 않았다. **2** 형용사 다른 ❑ 제가 진실하도록 노력하듯이, 저는 다른 모든 사람이 진실하기를 바랍니다. ● 부사 다른 ❑ 런던은 다른 어떤 곳보다 훨씬 더러워 보인다. **3** 구 _이 아니면 ❑ 명백히 어떤 교훈도 배우지 못했던 것이다. 그게 아니었다면 정부가 그토록 엉성하게 그 문제를 처리하지 않았을 것이다. **4** 구 그렇지 않으면 ❑ 이번에 우리는 정말 성공해야만 한다. 그렇지 않으면 사람들이 우리를 우습게보기 시작할 것이다. **5** 구 아니면 _이거나

will occur if someone does or does not do something. ❑ *This time we really need to succeed or else people will start giving us funny looks.* **5** PHRASE You use **or else** to introduce the second of two possibilities when you do not know which one is true. ❑ *You are either a total genius or else you must be absolutely raving mad.* **6** PHRASE **Above all else** is used to emphasize that a particular thing is more important than other things. [EMPHASIS] ❑ *Above all else I hate the cold.* **7** PHRASE You can say "**if nothing else**" to indicate that what you are mentioning is, in your opinion, the only good thing in a particular situation. ❑ *If nothing else, you'll really enjoy meeting them.* **8** PHRASE You say "**or else**" after a command to warn someone that if they do not obey, you will be angry and may harm or punish them. [SPOKEN] ❑ *Behave, or else!*

너는 절대적인 천재이거나 아니면 완전히 미치광이 짓을 하고 있는 것이 틀림없다. **6** 구 다른 무엇보다도 [강조] ❑ 다른 무엇보다도 나는 추위를 싫어한다. **7** 구 다른 수가 없으니 ❑ 다른 수가 없으니, 너는 그들을 만나서 정말로 즐길 수 있을 거야. **8** 구 안 그러면 [구어체] ❑ 제대로 행동해, 안 그랬단 봐!

else|where ◆◇◇ /ɛlswɛər/ ADV **Elsewhere** means in other places or to another place. ❑ *Almost 80 percent of the state's residents were born elsewhere.* ❑ *They were living rather well, in comparison with people elsewhere in the world.*

부사 다른 곳에 ❑ 그 주의 거주자 중 거의 80퍼센트가 다른 곳에서 태어난 사람이었다. ❑ 그들은 세계의 다른 곳 사람들과 비교하여 꽤 잘 살고 있었다.

ELT /i ɛl ti/ N-UNCOUNT **ELT** is the teaching of English to people whose first language is not English. **ELT** is an abbreviation for "English Language Teaching." [mainly BRIT]

불가산명사 영어 교육 [주로 영국영어]

elude /ɪlud/ (**eludes, eluding, eluded**) **1** V-T If something that you want **eludes** you, you fail to obtain it. [no passive] ❑ *Sleep eluded her.* **2** V-T If you **elude** someone or something, you avoid them or escape from them. ❑ *He eluded the police for 13 years.* **3** V-T If a fact or idea **eludes** you, you do not succeed in understanding it, realizing it, or remembering it. [no passive] ❑ *The appropriate word eluded him.*

1 타동사 빠져나가다 ❑ 그녀는 잠을 못 잤다. **2** 타동사 피하다 ❑ 그는 13년 동안 경찰을 피했다. **3** 타동사 빗나가다 ❑ 그는 적절한 단어를 못 찾았다.

elu|sive /ɪlusɪv/ ADJ Something or someone that is **elusive** is difficult to find, describe, remember, or achieve. ❑ *In London late-night taxis are elusive and far from cheap.*

형용사 잘도 빠져나가는, 잘 잡히지 않는 ❑ 런던에서 밤늦은 시각에는 택시가 잡히지도 않고 요금도 절대로 싸지 않다.

Word Link	*e ≈ electronic : e-book, e-commerce, e-mail*

e-mail (**e-mails, e-mailing, e-mailed**) also **E-mail, email** **1** N-VAR **E-mail** is a system of sending written messages electronically from one computer to another. **E-mail** is an abbreviation of **electronic mail**. ❑ *You can contact us by e-mail.* ❑ *Do you want to send an E-mail?* **2** V-T If you **e-mail** someone, you send them an e-mail. ❑ *Jamie e-mailed me to say he couldn't come.* →see **Internet**

1 가산명사 또는 불가산명사 전자 우편, 이메일 ❑ 저희에게 이메일로 연락하시면 됩니다. ❑ 이메일을 보내시겠어요? **2** 타동사 이메일을 보내다 ❑ 제이미는 못 올 거라는 이메일을 나에게 보냈다.

ema|nate /ɛməneɪt/ (**emanates, emanating, emanated**) **1** V-T/V-I If a quality **emanates** from you, or if you **emanate** a quality, you give people a strong sense that you have that quality. [FORMAL] ❑ *Intelligence and cunning emanated from him.* **2** V-I If something **emanates from** somewhere, it comes from there. [FORMAL] ❑ *The heady aroma of wood fires emanated from the stove.*

1 타동사/자동사 (특성을) 풍기다 [격식체] ❑ 그에게서는 지성과 노련함이 풍겼다. **2** 자동사 (향기 등이) 나다, 발산되다 [격식체] ❑ 장작불의 짙은 향이 난로에서 뿜어져 나왔다.

eman|ci|pate /ɪmænsɪpeɪt/ (**emancipates, emancipating, emancipated**) V-T If people **are emancipated**, they are freed from unpleasant or unfair social, political, or legal restrictions. [FORMAL] ❑ *Catholics were emancipated in 1792.* ❑ *That war preserved the Union and emancipated the slaves.* ● **eman|ci|pa|tion** /ɪmænsɪpeɪʃ⁰n/ N-UNCOUNT [oft N of n] ❑ *...the emancipation of women.*

타동사 해방시키다 [격식체] ❑ 가톨릭교도는 1792년에 해방되었다. ❑ 그 전쟁으로 연방이 유지되고 노예가 해방되었다. ● 해방 불가산명사 ❑ 여성 해방

em|bank|ment /ɪmbæŋkmənt/ (**embankments**) N-COUNT An **embankment** is a thick wall of earth that is built to carry a road or railroad track over an area of low ground, or to prevent water from a river or the sea from flooding the area. ❑ *They climbed a steep embankment.* ❑ *...a railway embankment.*

가산명사 제방, 둑 ❑ 그들은 가파른 제방을 기어올랐다. ❑ 철둑

em|bar|go /ɪmbɑrgoʊ/ (**embargoes, embargoing, embargoed**) **1** N-COUNT If one country or group of countries imposes an **embargo** against another, it forbids trade with that country. ❑ *The United Nations imposed an arms embargo against the country.* **2** V-T If goods of a particular kind **are embargoed**, people are not allowed to import them from a particular country or export them to a particular country. ❑ *The fruit was embargoed.* ❑ *They embargoed oil shipments to the U.S.*

1 가산명사 통상 금지 ❑ 국제 연합은 그 나라에 무기 통상 금지 처분을 내렸다. **2** 타동사 (통상을) 금지하다 ❑ 그 과일은 수출입이 금지되었다. ❑ 그들은 미국으로의 석유 선적을 금지했다.

em|bark /ɪmbɑrk/ (**embarks, embarking, embarked**) **1** V-I If you **embark on** something new, difficult, or exciting, you start doing it. ❑ *He's embarking on a new career as a writer.* **2** V-I When someone **embarks on** a ship, they go on board before the start of a journey. ❑ *They embarked on a ship bound for Europe.*

1 자동사 착수하다 ❑ 그는 작가로 새 활동을 시작하고 있다. **2** 자동사 승선하다 ❑ 그들은 유럽행 배에 승선했다.

em|bar|rass /ɪmbærəs/ (**embarrasses, embarrassing, embarrassed**) **1** V-T If something or someone **embarrasses** you, they make you feel shy or ashamed. ❑ *His clumsiness embarrassed him.* **2** V-T If something **embarrasses** a public figure such as a politician or an organization such as a political party, it causes problems for them. ❑ *The Republicans are trying to embarrass the president by thwarting his economic program.*

1 타동사 무끄럽게 하다, 무안하게 하다 ❑ 그가 서툴러서 무안해 했다. **2** 타동사 난처하게 하다 ❑ 공화당은 대통령의 경제 정책을 좌절시켜 그를 난처하게 만들려고 한다.

em|bar|rassed /ɪmbærəst/ ADJ A person who is **embarrassed** feels shy, ashamed, or guilty about something. ❑ *He looked a bit embarrassed.*

형용사 무안해 하는 ❑ 그는 좀 무안한 것 같았다.

em|bar|rass|ing /ɪmbærəsɪŋ/ **1** ADJ Something that is **embarrassing** makes you feel shy or ashamed. ❑ *That was an embarrassing situation for me.* ● **em|bar|rass|ing|ly** ADV ❑ *The lyrics of the song are embarrassingly banal.* **2** ADJ Something that is **embarrassing to** a public figure such as a politician or an organization such as a political party causes problems for them. ❑ *He has put the government in an embarrassing position.*

1 형용사 무안게 하는, 당혹게 하는 ❑ 그 상황은 내게 당혹스러웠다. ● 무안할 정도로 부사 ❑ 그 노래의 가사는 무안하리 만큼 진부했다. **2** 형용사 난감한 ❑ 그가 정부를 난감한 상황에 빠뜨렸다.

em|bar|rass|ment /ɪmbærəsmənt/ (**embarrassments**) **1** N-VAR **Embarrassment** is the feeling you have when you are embarrassed. ❑ *I think I would have died of embarrassment.* ❑ *We apologize for any embarrassment this may have caused.* **2** N-COUNT An **embarrassment** is an action, event, or situation which causes problems for a politician, political party, government, or other public group. ❑ *The poverty figures were undoubtedly an embarrassment to the president.* **3** N-SING If you refer to a person as **an embarrassment**, you mean that you disapprove of them but cannot avoid your connection with them.

1 가산명사 또는 불가산명사 무안함, 당혹감 ❑ 난 창피해서 죽을 뻔했어. ❑ 저희는 이 일 때문에 발생했을지 모르는 불편에 대해 사과드립니다. **2** 가산명사 난제, 곤란거리 ❑ 빈곤 수치는 대통령에게 있어 분명히 난제였다. **3** 단수명사 골칫거리 [탐탁잖음] ❑ 더글러스가 너와 결혼한 그날부터 너는 우리의 골칫거리였다.

A

[DISAPPROVAL] *You have been an embarrassment to us from the day Douglas married you.*

B

em|bas|sy ♦◇◇ /ɛmbəsi/ (**embassies**) N-COUNT An **embassy** is a group of government officials, headed by an ambassador, who represent their government in a foreign country. The building in which they work is also called an **embassy**. ❏ *The American Embassy has already complained.*

가산명사 대사관 직원; 대사관 ❏ 미국 대사관 측이 이미 불만을 표시했다.

C

Word Link	**em** ≈ making, putting : em**bed**, em**bellish**, em**power**

D

em|bed /ɪmbɛd/ (**embeds, embedding, embedded**) ◼ V-T If an object **embeds itself** in a substance or thing, it becomes fixed there firmly and deeply. ❏ *One of the bullets passed through Andrea's chest before embedding itself in a wall.* ● **em|bed|ded** ADJ ❏ *The fossils at Dinosaur Cove are embedded in hard sandstones.* ◼ V-T If something such as an attitude or feeling **is embedded in** a society or system, or in someone's personality, it becomes a permanent and noticeable feature of it. [usu passive] ❏ *This agreement will be embedded in a state treaty to be signed soon.* ● **em|bed|ded** ADJ ❏ *I think that hatred of the other is deeply embedded in our society.*

◼ 타동사 ~에 박히다 ❏ 총탄 하나가 안드레아의 가슴을 관통하고서 벽에 박혔다. ● 박혀 있는; 내포된 형용사 ❏ 다이너소 코브 만에 있는 화석은 단단한 사암 속에 박혀 있다. ◼ 타동사 깊숙이 박히다, 내포되다 ❏ 이 동의안은 곧 서명될 국가 간 조약에 삽입될 것이다. ● 뿌리박힌 형용사 ❏ 상대에 대한 증오가 우리 사회에 깊게 뿌리박혀 있다고 생각한다.

E

F

em|bel|lish /ɪmbɛlɪʃ/ (**embellishes, embellishing, embellished**) ◼ V-T If something **is embellished with** decorative features or patterns, it has those features or patterns on it and they make it look more attractive. ❏ *The stern was embellished with carvings in red and blue.* ❏ *Ivy leaves embellish the front of the dresser.* ◼ V-T If you **embellish** a story, you make it more interesting by adding details which may be untrue. ❏ *I launched into the parable, embellishing the story with invented dialogue and extra details.*

◼ 타동사 ~로 장식되다 ❏ 선미는 붉은색과 푸른색의 조각으로 장식되어 있었다. ❏ 담쟁이덩굴 잎이 화장대의 앞면을 장식하고 있다. ◼ 타동사 윤색하다 ❏ 나는 대화를 꾸며 내고 세부 내용을 덧붙여 이야기를 윤색하면서 우화를 들려주기 시작했다.

G

H

em|bez|zle /ɪmbɛzᵊl/ (**embezzles, embezzling, embezzled**) V-T If someone **embezzles** money that their organization or company has placed in their care, they take it and use it illegally for their own purposes. ❏ *One former director embezzled $34 million in company funds.*

타동사 횡령하다 ❏ 전직 이사 한 명이 회사 자금에서 3,400만 달러를 횡령했다.

I

em|bez|zle|ment /ɪmbɛzᵊlmənt/ N-UNCOUNT **Embezzlement** is the crime of embezzling money. ❏ *He was later charged with embezzlement.*

불가산명사 횡령, 착복 ❏ 그는 후에 횡령 혐의로 기소되었다.

J

em|blem /ɛmbləm/ (**emblems**) ◼ N-COUNT An **emblem** is a design representing a country or organization. ❏ *...the emblem of the Soviet Union.* ◼ N-COUNT An **emblem** is something that represents a quality or idea. ❏ *The eagle was an emblem of strength and courage.*

◼ 가산명사 상징, 표상 ❏ 소련 연방의 표상 ◼ 가산명사 상징 ❏ 독수리는 힘과 용기의 상징이었다.

K

em|bodi|ment /ɪmbɒdimənt/ N-SING If you say that someone or something is **the embodiment of** a quality or idea, you mean that that is their most noticeable characteristic or the basis of all they do. [FORMAL] ❏ *A baby is the embodiment of vulnerability.*

단수명사 구현, 화신 [격식체] ❏ 아기는 연약함의 화신이다.

L

M

em|body /ɪmbɒdi/ (**embodies, embodying, embodied**) ◼ V-T To **embody** an idea or quality means to be a symbol or expression of that idea or quality. ❏ *Jack Kennedy embodied all the hopes of the 1960s.* ❏ *For twenty-nine years, Checkpoint Charlie embodied the Cold War.* ◼ V-T If something **is embodied in** a particular thing, the second thing contains or consists of the first. ❏ *The proposal has been embodied in a draft resolution.* ❏ *UK employment law embodies arbitration and conciliation mechanisms for settling industrial disputes.*

◼ 타동사 구현하다, 상징하다 ❏ 잭 케네디는 1960년대의 모든 희망을 상징했다. ❏ 29년 동안 체크 포인트 찰리 검문소가 냉전을 상징했다. ◼ 타동사 ~에 포함되어 있다 ❏ 그 제안은 결의안 초안에 포함되어 있다. ❏ 영국 고용법은 산업 분쟁 해결을 위한 중재와 조정 절차를 포함하고 있다.

N

O

em|brace /ɪmbreɪs/ (**embraces, embracing, embraced**) ◼ V-RECIP If you **embrace** someone, you put your arms around them and hold them tightly, usually in order to show your love or affection for them. You can also say that two people **embrace**. ❏ *Penelope came forward and embraced her sister.* ❏ *At first people were sort of crying for joy and embracing each other.* ● N-COUNT **Embrace** is also a noun. ❏ *...a young couple locked in an embrace.* ◼ V-T If you **embrace** a change, political system, or idea, you accept it and start supporting it or believing in it. [FORMAL] ❏ *He embraces the new information age.* ● N-SING **Embrace** is also a noun. ❏ *The marriage signaled James's embrace of the Catholic faith.* ◼ V-T If something **embraces** a group of people, things, or ideas, it includes them in a larger group or category. [FORMAL] ❏ *...a theory that would embrace the whole field of human endeavor.*

◼ 상호동사 포옹하다, 껴안다 ❏ 페넬로페는 앞으로 나와 언니를 포옹했다. ❏ 처음에 사람들은 다소 기쁨의 눈물을 흘리며 서로를 끌어안았다. ● 가산명사 포옹 ❏ 포옹한 젊은 한 쌍 ◼ 타동사 포용하다 ❏ 그는 새 정보화 시대를 포용한다. ● 단수명사 포용 ❏ 그 결혼은 제임스가 가톨릭 신앙을 포용한다는 신호였다. ◼ 타동사 포함하다, 아우르다 [격식체] ❏ 인간 노고가 담기는 모든 분야를 아우르는 이론

P

Q

R

S

em|broi|der /ɪmbrɔɪdər/ (**embroiders, embroidering, embroidered**) ◼ V-T/V-I If something such as clothing or cloth **is embroidered with** a design, the design is stitched into it. ❏ *The collar was embroidered with very small red strawberries.* ❏ *I have a pillow with my name embroidered on it.* ◼ V-T/V-I If you **embroider** a story or account of something, or if you **embroider on** it, you try to make it more interesting by adding details which may be untrue. ❏ *He told some lies and sometimes just embroidered the truth.*

◼ 타동사/자동사 수놓다 ❏ 옷깃에는 아주 작고 빨간 딸기무늬 자수가 놓여 있다. ❏ 나는 내 이름을 수놓은 베개를 가지고 있다. ◼ 타동사/자동사 윤색하다 ❏ 그는 거짓말을 좀 했고 때로는 진실을 윤색하기만 하기도 했다.

T

U

em|broi|dery /ɪmbrɔɪdəri/ (**embroideries**) ◼ N-VAR **Embroidery** consists of designs stitched into cloth. ❏ *The shorts had blue embroidery over the pockets.* ◼ N-UNCOUNT **Embroidery** is the activity of stitching designs onto cloth. ❏ *She learned sewing, knitting, and embroidery.* →see **quilt**

◼ 가산명사 또는 불가산명사 자수 ❏ 그 반바지는 주머니에 파란색 자수가 있었다. ◼ 불가산명사 자수 놓기 ❏ 그녀는 바느질과 뜨개질, 그리고 자수 놓기를 배웠다.

V

em|broiled /ɪmbrɔɪld/ ADJ If you become **embroiled in** a fight or argument, you become deeply involved in it. [v-link ADJ, usu ADJ in n] ❏ *The Government insisted that troops would not become embroiled in battles in Bosnia.*

형용사 ~에 휘말린 ❏ 정부는 군대가 보스니아 전투에 휘말려서는 안 된다고 주장했다.

W

X

em|bryo /ɛmbrioʊ/ (**embryos**) ◼ N-COUNT An **embryo** is an unborn animal or human being in the very early stages of development. ❏ *The embryo lives in the amniotic cavity.* ◼ ADJ An **embryo** idea, system, or organization is in the very early stages of development, but is expected to grow stronger. [ADJ n] ❏ *They are an embryo party of government.*

◼ 가산명사 태아 ❏ 태아는 양막 공간에 산다. ◼ 형용사 초기의, 미발달 단계의 ❏ 그들은 초기 단계의 정부 여당이다.

Y

Z

em|bry|on|ic /ɛmbriɒnɪk/ ADJ An **embryonic** process, idea, organization, or organism is one at a very early stage in its development. [FORMAL] ❏ *...Romania's embryonic democracy.* ❏ *...the embryonic European central bank.*

형용사 초기의, 미발달 단계의 [격식체] ❏ 이제 막 시작된 루마니아의 민주주의 ❏ 발달 초기의 유럽 중앙은행

em|er|ald /ɛmərəld, ɛmrəld/ (emeralds) 1 N-COUNT An **emerald** is a precious stone which is clear and bright green. 2 COLOR Something that is **emerald** is bright green in color. ❑ ...an emerald valley.

1 가산명사 에메랄드, 취옥 2 색채어 밝은 초록색 ❑ 에메랄드빛 계곡

Word Link merg ≈ sinking : emerge, merge, submerge

---

emerge ♦♦◇ /ɪmɜrdʒ/ (emerges, emerging, emerged) 1 V-I To **emerge** means to come out from an enclosed or dark space such as a room or a vehicle, or from a position where you could not be seen. ❑ Richard was waiting outside the door as she emerged. ❑ The postman emerged from his van soaked to the skin. 2 V-I If you **emerge from** a difficult or bad experience, you come to the end of it. ❑ There is growing evidence that the economy is at last emerging from recession. 3 V-I If a fact or result **emerges** from a period of thought, discussion, or investigation, it becomes known as a result of it. ❑ ...the growing corruption that has emerged in the past few years. ❑ It soon emerged that neither the July nor August mortgage repayment had been collected. 4 V-I If someone or something **emerges as** a particular thing, they become recognized as that thing. [JOURNALISM] ❑ Vietnam has emerged as the world's third-biggest rice exporter. 5 V-I When something such as an organization or an industry **emerges**, it comes into existence. [JOURNALISM] ❑ ...the new republic that emerged in October 1917.

1 자동사 ~에서 나오다, 나타나다 ❑ 그녀가 나왔을 때 리처드는 문 밖에서 기다리고 있었다. ❑ 우편집배원이 흠뻑 젖은 채로 그의 소형 트럭에서 나왔다. 2 자동사 ~에서 벗어나다, 빠져 나오다 ❑ 경제가 마침내 불경기에서 벗어나고 있다는 증거가 분명해지고 있다. 3 자동사 밝혀지다, 드러나다 ❑ 지난 몇 해 동안 밝혀진 계속 늘어가는 부패 ❑ 주택 담보 대출금이 7월에도 8월에도 상환되지 않았다는 것이 곧 드러났다. 4 자동사 드러나다, 판명되다 [언론] ❑ 베트남은 세계 3위 쌀 수출국으로 등장했다. 5 자동사 등장하다 [언론] ❑ 1917년에 등장한 신생 공화국

Thesaurus   emerge의 참조어

v.   appear, come out; (ant.) disappear 1

---

emer|gence /ɪmɜrdʒəns/ N-UNCOUNT The **emergence of** something is the process or event of its coming into existence. ❑ ...the emergence of new democracies in East and Central Europe.

불가산명사 출현, 등장 ❑ 동유럽과 중유럽에서의 신생 민주국가들의 출현

emer|gen|cy ♦♦◇ /ɪmɜrdʒənsi/ (emergencies) 1 N-COUNT An **emergency** is an unexpected and difficult or dangerous situation, especially an accident, which happens suddenly and which requires quick action to deal with it. ❑ He deals with emergencies promptly. 2 ADJ An **emergency** action is one that is done or arranged quickly and not in the normal way, because an emergency has occurred. [ADJ n] ❑ The Prime Minister has called an emergency meeting of parliament. 3 ADJ **Emergency** equipment or supplies are those intended for use in an emergency. [ADJ n] ❑ The plane is carrying emergency supplies for refugees. →see hospital

1 가산명사 비상사태 ❑ 그는 비상사태를 신속히 처리한다. 2 형용사 긴급한, 비상시의 ❑ 수상은 의회 긴급회의를 소집했다. 3 형용사 비상의, 응급의 ❑ 그 비행기는 난민을 위한 비상 보급품을 싣고 있다.

Word Partnership   emergency의 연어

ADJ.   major emergency, medical emergency, minor emergency 1
N.   state of emergency 1
       emergency care, emergency surgery 2
       emergency supplies, emergency vehicle 3

---

emer|gen|cy brake (emergency brakes) N-COUNT In a vehicle, the **emergency brake** is a brake which the driver operates with his or her hand, and uses, for example, in emergencies or when parking. [mainly AM; BRIT **handbrake**] ❑ He stopped just as his truck tilted down the steep incline, put on the emergency brake, and stepped out.

가산명사 비상 브레이크 [주로 미국영어; 영국영어 handbrake] ❑ 그는 자기 트럭이 가파른 비탈 아래로 기우뚱하는 바로 그 순간에 멈춰서, 비상 브레이크를 걸고 빠져나왔다.

emer|gen|cy room (emergency rooms) N-COUNT The **emergency room** is the room or department in a hospital where people who have severe injuries or sudden illnesses are taken for emergency treatment. The abbreviation **ER** is often used. [mainly AM; BRIT usually **casualty, A & E**] ❑ She began hyperventilating and was rushed to the emergency room.

가산명사 응급실 [주로 미국영어; 영국영어 대개 casualty, A & E] ❑ 그녀는 숨을 헐떡이기 시작했고 서둘러 응급실로 보내졌다.

emer|gen|cy ser|vices N-PLURAL The **emergency services** are the public organizations whose job is to take quick action to deal with emergencies when they occur, especially the fire department, the police, and the ambulance service. ❑ ...members of the emergency services.

복수명사 (앰뷸런스 등) 비상 구호대 ❑ 비상 구호대원

Word Link migr ≈ moving, changing : emigrant, immigrant, migrant

---

emi|grant /ɛmɪgrənt/ (emigrants) N-COUNT An **emigrant** is a person who has left their own country to live in another country. Compare **immigrant**. ❑ ...Irish emigrants to America.

가산명사 이민자, 이주자 ❑ 미국행 아일랜드 이민자들

Word Link e ≈ away, out : eject, emigrate, emit

---

emi|grate /ɛmɪgreɪt/ (emigrates, emigrating, emigrated) V-I If you **emigrate**, you leave your own country to live in another country. ❑ He emigrated to Belgium. ● emi|gra|tion /ɛmɪgreɪʃən/ N-UNCOUNT ❑ ...the huge emigration of workers to the West.

자동사 이민 가다, 이주하다 ❑ 그는 벨기에로 이주했다. ● 이민, 이주 불가산명사 ❑ 서부로의 노동자 대 이주

emi|nence /ɛmɪnəns/ N-UNCOUNT **Eminence** is the quality of being very well-known and highly respected. ❑ Many of the pilots were to achieve eminence in the aeronautical world.

불가산명사 지명, 명성 ❑ 많은 조종사들이 항공계에서 명성을 얻게 되었다.

emi|nent /ɛmɪnənt/ ADJ An **eminent** person is well-known and respected, especially because they are good at their profession. ❑ ...an eminent scientist.

형용사 저명한, 탁월한 ❑ 저명한 과학자

emi|nent|ly /ɛmɪnəntli/ ADV You use **eminently** in front of an adjective describing a positive quality in order to emphasize the quality expressed by that adjective. [EMPHASIS] [ADV adj/-ed] ❑ His books on diplomatic history were eminently readable.

부사 대단히, 매우 [강조] ❑ 외교사에 관한 그의 책들은 대단히 읽을 만했다.

emis|sion /ɪmɪʃən/ (emissions) N-VAR An **emission** of something such as gas or radiation is the release of it into the atmosphere. [FORMAL] ❑ The emission of gases such as carbon dioxide should be stabilized at their present level. →see pollution

가산명사 또는 불가산명사 방출, 발산 [격식체] ❑ 이산화탄소와 같은 기체의 방출은 현재 수준에서 안정되어야 한다.

a
b
c
d
e
f
g
h
i
j
k
l
m
n
o
p
q
r
s
t
u
v
w
x
y
z

A
B
C
D
E
F
G
H
I
J
K
L
M
N
O
P
Q
R
S
T
U
V
W
X
Y
Z

Word Link
e ≈ away, out : *e*ject, *e*migrate, *e*mit

emit /ɪmɪt/ (**emits, emitting, emitted**) **1** V-T If something **emits** heat, light, gas, or a smell, it produces it and sends it out by means of a physical or chemical process. [FORMAL] ❑ *The new device emits a powerful circular column of light.* [FORMAL] **2** V-T To **emit** a sound or noise means to produce it. [FORMAL] ❑ *Polly blinked and emitted a long, low whistle.*

1 타동사 (열 등을) 내뿜다, 방출하다 [격식체] ❑ 새 장치는 나선식 원주 모양의 강한 빛을 내뿜는다. **2** 타동사 (소리를) 내다 [격식체] ❑ 폴리는 눈을 깜박이며 길고 낮은 휘파람 소리를 냈다.

emo|ti|con /ɪmoʊtɪkɒn/ (**emoticons**) N-COUNT An **emoticon** is a symbol used in e-mail to show how someone is feeling. :-) is an emoticon showing happiness. [COMPUTING] →see **writing**

가산명사 이모티콘 [컴퓨터]

emo|tion ♦♢♢ /ɪmoʊʃⁿn/ (**emotions**) **1** N-VAR An **emotion** is a feeling such as happiness, love, fear, anger, or hatred, which can be caused by the situation that you are in or the people you are with. ❑ *Happiness was an emotion that Reynolds was having to relearn.* **2** N-UNCOUNT **Emotion** is the part of a person's character that consists of their feelings, as opposed to their thoughts. ❑ *...the split between reason and emotion.* →see Word Web: **emotion**

1 가산명사 또는 불가산명사 감정, 정서 ❑ 행복은 레이놀즈가 다시 배워야 하는 감정이었다. **2** 불가산명사 감성 ❑ 이성과 감성의 분리

emo|tion|al ♦♢♢ /ɪmoʊʃⁿnᵊl/ **1** ADJ **Emotional** means concerned with emotions and feelings. ❑ *I needed this man's love, and the emotional support he was giving me.* ● **emo|tion|al|ly** ADV [ADV adj/-ed] ❑ *Are you saying that you're becoming emotionally involved with me?* **2** ADJ An **emotional** situation or issue is one that causes people to have strong feelings. ❑ *It's a very emotional issue. How can you advocate selling the ivory from elephants?* ● **emo|tion|al|ly** ADV [ADV adj/-ed] ❑ *In an emotionally charged speech, he said he was resigning.* **3** ADJ If someone is or becomes **emotional**, they show their feelings very openly, especially because they are upset. ❑ *He is a very emotional man.*

1 형용사 감정의 ❑ 나는 이 남자의 사랑과 그가 내게 주는 정서적 뒷받침이 필요했다. ● 감정적으로 부사 ❑ 당신이 제게 특별한 감정을 가지게 되었다고 말하는 건가요? **2** 형용사 감정적인 ❑ 그것은 아주 감정적인 문제야. 넌 어떻게 코끼리의 상아를 파는 것을 옹호할 수 있니? ● 감정이 격해서 부사 ❑ 격한 감정을 담은 연설에서 그는 사퇴하겠다고 말했다. **3** 형용사 감정적인 ❑ 그는 매우 감정적인 사람이다.

emo|tive /ɪmoʊtɪv/ ADJ An **emotive** situation or issue is likely to make people feel strong emotions. ❑ *Embryo research is an emotive issue.*

형용사 민감한 ❑ 배아 연구는 민감한 사안이다.

Word Link
path ≈ feeling : *a*pathy, *em*pathy, *sym*pathy

em|pa|thy /ɛmpəθi/ N-UNCOUNT **Empathy** is the ability to share another person's feelings and emotions as if they were your own. ❑ *Having begun my life in a children's home, I have great empathy with the little ones.*

불가산명사 공감 ❑ 고아원에서 자랐기 때문에 나는 어린 아이들의 마음을 아주 잘 안다.

em|per|or /ɛmpərər/ (**emperors**) N-COUNT; N-TITLE An **emperor** is a man who rules an empire or is the head of state in an empire. ❑ *...the emperor of Japan.* →see **empire**

가산명사; 경칭명사 황제 ❑ 일본 천황

em|pha|sis ♦♢♢ /ɛmfəsɪs/ (**emphases**) /ɛmfəsiz/ **1** N-VAR **Emphasis** is special or extra importance that is given to an activity or to a part or aspect of something. ❑ *Too much emphasis is placed on research.* **2** N-VAR **Emphasis** is extra force that you put on a syllable, word, or phrase when you are speaking in order to make it seem more important. ❑ *The emphasis is on the first syllable of the last word.*

1 가산명사 또는 불가산명사 중요성, 강조 ❑ 연구가 지나치게 강조되어 있다. **2** 가산명사 또는 불가산명사 강세 ❑ 마지막 단어의 첫째 음절에 강세가 있다.

em|pha|size ♦♢♢ /ɛmfəsaɪz/ (**emphasizes, emphasizing, emphasized**) [BRIT also **emphasise**] V-T To **emphasize** something means to indicate that it is particularly important or true, or to draw special attention to it. ❑ *But it's also been emphasized that no major policy changes can be expected to come out of the meeting.*

[영국영어 emphasise] 타동사 강조하다 ❑ 그러나 그 회의에서 큰 정책 변화가 나올 것이라고 기대할 수 없다는 것 또한 강조되었다.

em|phat|ic /ɪmfætɪk/ **1** ADJ An **emphatic** response or statement is one made in a forceful way, because the speaker feels very strongly about what they are saying. ❑ *His response was immediate and emphatic.* **2** ADJ If you are **emphatic about** something, you use forceful language which shows that you feel very strongly about what you are saying. [v-link ADJ, oft ADJ that, ADJ about n] ❑ *The rebels are emphatic that this is not a surrender.* **3** ADJ An **emphatic** win or victory is one in which the winner has won by a large amount or distance. ❑ *Yesterday's emphatic victory was their fifth in succession.*

1 형용사 단호한 ❑ 그의 대답은 즉각적이고 단호했다. **2** 형용사 단호한 ❑ 반군들은 단호하게 이것은 항복이 아니라고 한다. **3** 형용사 현저한, 분명한 ❑ 어제 그들의 압도적인 승리는 5연승째였다.

em|phati|cal|ly /ɪmfætɪkli/ **1** ADV If you say something **emphatically**, you say it in a forceful way which shows that you feel very strongly about what you are saying. [ADV with v] ❑ *"No fast food," she said emphatically.* **2** ADV You use **emphatically** to emphasize the statement you are making. [EMPHASIS] [ADV with cl/group] ❑ *Making people feel foolish is emphatically not my strategy.*

1 부사 단호히 ❑ "즉석식품은 안 돼."라고 그녀는 단호히 말했다. **2** 부사 전혀, 결코 [강조] ❑ 사람들에게 무안을 주려는 것은 결코 내 계획이 아니다.

em|pire ♦♢♢ /ɛmpaɪər/ (**empires**) **1** N-COUNT An **empire** is a number of individual nations that are all controlled by the government or ruler of one particular country. ❑ *...the Roman Empire.* **2** N-COUNT You can refer to a group of companies controlled by one person as an **empire**. ❑ *...the big Mondadori publishing empire.* →see **history** →see Word Web: **empire**

1 가산명사 제국 ❑ 로마 제국 **2** 가산명사 (거대 기업) 왕국 ❑ 거대한 몬다도리 출판 왕국

Word Web
emotion

Scientists believe that animals experience **emotions** such as happiness and sadness just like humans do. Research shows animals also feel **anger**, **fear**, **love**, and **hate**. Biochemical changes in mammals' brains trigger these emotions. When an elephant gives birth, a **hormone** floods her bloodstream. This causes feelings of **adoration** for her baby. The same thing happens to human mothers. When a dog chews on a bone, levels of a chemical increase in its brain. This produces feelings of **joy**. The same chemical produces **elation** in humans. Scientists aren't sure whether animals experience **shame**. However, they do know that animals experience **stress**.

Word Web   empire

An **empire** is formed when a strong nation-state **conquers** other states and creates a larger **political union**. An early example is the Roman Empire which began in 31 BC. The Roman **emperor** Augustus Caesar* ruled a vast area from the Mediterranean Sea* to Western Europe. Later, the British Empire flourished from about 1600 to 1900 AD. Queen Victoria's* empire spread across oceans and continents. One of her many titles was **Empress** of India. Both of these empires spread their political influence as well as their language and culture over large areas.

British Empire (1900 AD)
Roman Empire (117 AD)
British and Roman Empires

Augustus Caesar: the first emperor of Rome.
Mediterranean Sea: between Europe and Africa.
Queen Victoria (1819-1901): queen of the United Kingdom.

em|piri|cal /ɪmpɪrɪkᵊl/ ADJ **Empirical** evidence or study relies on practical experience rather than theories. ❑ *There is no empirical evidence to support his thesis.* ● **em|piri|cal|ly** ADV ❑ *They approached this part of their task empirically.*

형용사 경험적인 ❑ 그의 이론을 뒷받침할 경험적 증거가 없다. ● 경험적으로 부사 ❑ 그들은 자신들 임무의 이 부분을 경험적으로 접근했다.

em|ploy ◆◇◇ /ɪmplɔɪ/ (**employs, employing, employed**) ◼ V-T If a person or company **employs** you, they pay you to work for them. ❑ *The company employs 18 staff.* ❑ *More than 3,000 local workers are employed in the tourism industry.* ◼ V-T If you **employ** certain methods, materials, or expressions, you use them. ❑ *The tactics the police are now to employ are definitely uncompromising.* ◼ V-T If your time **is employed in** doing something, you are using the time you have to do that thing. [usu passive] ❑ *Your time could be usefully employed in attending to professional matters.*

◼ 타동사 고용하다 ❑ 그 회사는 18명의 직원을 고용하고 있다. ❑ 지역 근로자 3,000명 이상이 관광 산업에 종사하고 있다. ◼ 타동사 사용하다 ❑ 경찰이 지금 사용하려는 전술은 확실히 단호하다. ◼ 타동사 (시간이) -에 쓰이다 ❑ 전문적인 문제에 전념함으로써 당신의 시간을 유용하게 사용할 수 있다.

em|ploy|ee ◆◆◇ /ɪmplɔɪiː/ (**employees**) N-COUNT An **employee** is a person who is paid to work for an organization or for another person. ❑ *He is an employee of Fuji Bank.* →see **factory**

가산명사 피고용인, 직원 ❑ 그는 후지은행의 직원이다.

em|ploy|er ◆◆◇ /ɪmplɔɪər/ (**employers**) N-COUNT Your **employer** is the person or organization that you work for. ❑ *He had been sent to Rome by his employer.*

가산명사 고용주 ❑ 그는 그의 고용주에 의해 로마로 보내졌었다.

em|ploy|ment ◆◇◇ /ɪmplɔɪmənt/ ◼ N-UNCOUNT **Employment** is the fact of having a paid job. ❑ *She was unable to find employment.* ◼ N-UNCOUNT **Employment** is the fact of employing someone. ❑ *...the employment of children under nine.* ◼ N-UNCOUNT **Employment** is the work that is available in a country or area. ❑ *...economic policies designed to secure full employment.*

◼ 불가산명사 일자리 ❑ 그녀는 일자리를 찾을 수 없었다. ◼ 불가산명사 고용 ❑ 9세 미만의 어린이 고용 ◼ 불가산명사 일자리 ❑ 완전 고용을 확보하기 위해 고안된 경제 정책

em|ploy|ment agen|cy (**employment agencies**) N-COUNT An **employment agency** is a company whose business is to help people to find work and help employers to find the workers they need. [BUSINESS]

가산명사 직업소개소 [경제]

Word Link   em ≈ making, putting : em**bed**, em**bellish**, em**power**

em|power /ɪmpaʊər/ (**empowers, empowering, empowered**) ◼ V-T If someone **is empowered to** do something, they have the authority or power to do it. [FORMAL] ❑ *The army is now empowered to operate on a shoot-to-kill basis.* ◼ V-T To **empower** someone means to give them the means to achieve something, for example to become stronger or more successful. ❑ *You must delegate effectively and empower people to carry out their roles with your full support.*

◼ 타동사 _할 권한을 부여받다 [격식체] ❑ 군대는 이제 즉각 사살 체계로의 작전 수행권이 부여되어 있다. ◼ 타동사 힘을 주다, 권한을 부여하다 ❑ 당신은 사람들이 당신의 전폭적인 지원 하에 각자의 역할을 수행할 수 있도록 효율적으로 임무를 부여하고 힘을 실어 주어야 한다.

em|pow|er|ment /ɪmpaʊərmənt/ N-UNCOUNT The **empowerment of** a person or group of people is the process of giving them power and status in a particular situation. ❑ *This government believes very strongly in the empowerment of women.*

불가산명사 권한 부여, 권리 강화 ❑ 이 정부는 여성의 권리를 강화시키는 데 강한 신념을 가지고 있다.

em|press /ɛmprɪs/ (**empresses**) N-COUNT; N-TITLE An **empress** is a woman who rules an empire or who is the wife of an emperor. ❑ *...Catherine II, Empress of Russia.* →see **empire**

가산명사; 경칭명사 황후 ❑ 러시아 황후 캐서린 2세

emp|ti|ness /ɛmptɪnɪs/ ◼ N-UNCOUNT A feeling of **emptiness** is an unhappy or frightening feeling that nothing is worthwhile, especially when you are very tired or have just experienced something upsetting. ❑ *The result later in life may be feelings of emptiness and depression.* ◼ N-UNCOUNT The **emptiness** of a place is the fact that there is nothing in it. ❑ *...the emptiness of the desert.*

◼ 불가산명사 공허감 ❑ 노년에 올 결과는 공허감과 우울한 느낌일 것이다. ◼ 불가산명사 공허, 텅 빔 ❑ 사막의 공허

emp|ty ◆◇◇ /ɛmpti/ (**emptier, emptiest, empties, emptying, emptied**) ◼ ADJ An **empty** place, vehicle, or container is one that has no people or things in it. ❑ *The room was bare and empty.* ❑ *...empty cans of lager.* ◼ ADJ An **empty** gesture, threat, or relationship has no real value or meaning. ❑ *His father had threatened disinheritance, but both men had known it was an empty threat.* ◼ ADJ If you describe a person's life or a period of time as **empty**, you mean that nothing interesting or valuable happens in it. ❑ *My life was very hectic but empty before I met him.* ◼ ADJ If you **feel empty**, you feel unhappy and have no energy, usually because you are very tired or have just experienced something upsetting. ❑ *I feel so empty, my life just doesn't seem worth living any more.* ◼ V-T If you **empty** a container, or **empty** something out of it, you remove its contents, especially by tipping it up. ❑ *I emptied the ashtray.* ❑ *Empty the noodles and liquid into a serving bowl.* ◼ V-T/V-I If someone **empties** a room or place, or if it **empties**, everyone that is in it goes away. ❑ *The stadium emptied at the end of the first day of athletics.* ◼ V-I A river or canal that **empties into** a lake, river, or sea flows into it. ❑ *The South Esk*

◼ 형용사 빈 ❑ 그 방은 세간이 없이 텅 비어 있었다. ❑ 라거 맥주 빈 캔들 ◼ 형용사 하찮은, 무의미한 ❑ 그의 아버지는 상속권을 박탈하겠다고 위협했으나 둘 다 그것이 무의미한 협박이라는 것을 알고 있었다. ◼ 형용사 실없는, 무의미한 ❑ 그를 만나기 전에 내 삶은 분주했지만 무의미했다. ◼ 형용사 공허한 ❑ 나는 너무 공허한 느낌이 들고, 그저 내 삶이 더 이상 살 가치가 없는 것 같다. ◼ 타동사 비우다 ❑ 나는 재떨이를 비웠다. ❑ 면과 국물을 차려 낼 그릇에 옮겨 담아라. ◼ 타동사/자동사 비우다, 비워지다 ❑ 경기장은 첫날의 육상 경기가 끝나고 비어 있었다. ◼ 자동사 -에 흘러들다 ❑ 사우스 에스크 강은 몬트로즈 유역으로 흘러 들어가는 작고 맑은 강이다. ◼ 가산명사 빈 병, 빈 통 ❑ 우리는 빈 병을 자루에 넣을 것이다.

a
b
c
d
e
f
g
h
i
j
k
l
m
n
o
p
q
r
s
t
u
v
w
x
y
z

is a small, clear river which empties into the Montrose basin. ◻ N-COUNT **Empties** are bottles or containers which no longer have anything in them. ◻ *We'll take the empties down in the sack.*

Thesaurus   *empty*의 참조어

ADJ.	vacant; *(ant.)* full 🔳
	meaningless, without substance 🔳 🔳
V.	drain, pour out 🔳 🔳
	evacuate, go out, leave 🔳

Word Partnership   *empty*의 연어

N.	empty **bottle**, empty **box**, empty **building**, empty **room**, empty **seat**, empty **space**, empty **stomach** 🔳
	empty **promise**, empty **threat** 🔳
	empty **the trash** 🔳
V.	**feel** empty 🔳

empty-handed ADJ If you come away from somewhere **empty-handed**, you have failed to get what you wanted. [ADJ after v] ◻ *Delegates from the warring sides held a new round of peace talks but went away empty-handed.*

형용사 빈손의 ◻ 서로 전쟁 중인 양측 대표단은 새로 한 차례 평화 회담을 열었으나 빈손으로 돌아갔다.

emu|late /ɛmyʊleɪt/ (**emulates**, **emulating**, **emulated**) V-T If you **emulate** something or someone, you imitate them because you admire them a great deal. [FORMAL] ◻ *Sons are traditionally expected to emulate their fathers.*

타동사 모방하다, 본받다 [격식체] ◻ 전통적으로 아들은 아버지를 본받도록 기대된다.

Word Link   en ≈ making, putting : enable, enact, encode

en|able ♦◇◇ /ɪneɪbᵊl/ (**enables**, **enabling**, **enabled**) 🔳 V-T If someone or something **enables** you **to** do a particular thing, they give you the opportunity to do it. ◻ *The new test should enable doctors to detect the disease early.* 🔳 V-T To **enable** something to happen means to make it possible for it to happen. ◻ *The hot sun enables the grapes to reach optimum ripeness.* 🔳 V-T To **enable** someone **to** do something means to give them permission or the right to do it. ◻ *...the republic's legislation which enables young people to do a form of alternative service.*

🔳 타동사 -할 수 있게 하다 ◻ 새 검사법으로 의사가 그 병을 조기에 발견할 수 있다. 🔳 타동사 가능하게 하다 ◻ 뜨거운 태양은 포도가 아주 잘 익게 해 준다. 🔳 타동사 -할 권리나 자격을 주다 ◻ 젊은이가 대체 복무 형식을 취할 수 있도록 하는 공화국의 법률

Thesaurus   *enable*의 참조어

V.	allow, approve, authorize, facilitate, permit; *(ant.)* block, disallow, forbid, prevent 🔳 🔳 🔳

en|act /ɪnækt/ (**enacts**, **enacting**, **enacted**) 🔳 V-T When a government or authority **enacts** a proposal, they make it into a law. [TECHNICAL] ◻ *The authorities have failed so far to enact a law allowing unrestricted emigration.* 🔳 V-T If people **enact** a story or play, they perform it by acting. ◻ *She often enacted the stories told to her by her father.* 🔳 V-T If a particular event or situation **is enacted**, it happens; used especially to talk about something that has happened before. [JOURNALISM] [usu passive] ◻ *It was a scene which was enacted month after month for eight years.*

🔳 타동사 (법률을) 제정하다 [과학 기술] ◻ 당국이 자유로운 국외 이주를 허락하는 법률 제정에 아직까지 성공하지 못했다. 🔳 타동사 (연극을) 상연하다 ◻ 그녀는 아버지가 들려 준 이야기를 종종 연극으로 상연해 보였다. 🔳 타동사 (사건이) 다시 일어나다 [언론] ◻ 그것은 8년 동안 매달 일어났던 장면이었다.

en|act|ment /ɪnæktmənt/ (**enactments**) N-VAR The **enactment of** a law is the process in a legislature or other law-making body by which the law is agreed upon and made official. [TECHNICAL] ◻ *We support the call for the enactment of a Bill of Rights.*

가산명사 또는 불가산명사 (법의) 제정 [과학 기술] ◻ 우리는 인권 법안 제정 요구를 지지한다.

enam|el /ɪnæmᵊl/ (**enamels**) 🔳 N-MASS **Enamel** is a substance like glass which can be heated and put onto metal, glass, or pottery in order to decorate or protect it. ◻ *...a white enamel saucepan on the oil stove.* 🔳 N-MASS **Enamel** is a hard, shiny paint that is used especially for painting metal and wood. ◻ *...enamel polymer paints.* 🔳 N-UNCOUNT **Enamel** is the hard white substance that forms the outer part of a tooth.

🔳 물질명사 에나멜, 유약 ◻ 석유 스토브 위의 흰색 법랑 냄비 🔳 물질명사 에나멜 도료, 광택제 ◻ 중합 광택 도료 🔳 불가산명사 (치아의) 법랑질

en|am|ored /ɪnæmərd/ [BRIT **enamoured**] ADJ If you are **enamored of** something, you like or admire it a lot. If you are not **enamored of** something, you dislike or disapprove of it. [LITERARY] ◻ *I became totally enamored of the wildflowers there.*

[영국영어 enamoured] 형용사 -에 반하다 [문예체] ◻ 나는 저기의 들꽃에 완전히 매혹되었다.

en|cap|su|late /ɪnkæpsəleɪt, -syu-/ (**encapsulates**, **encapsulating**, **encapsulated**) V-T To **encapsulate** particular facts or ideas means to represent all their most important aspects in a very small space or in a single object or event. ◻ *A Wall Street Journal editorial encapsulated the views of many conservatives.*

타동사 압축하다, 요약하다 ◻ 월 스트리트 저널의 한 사설이 많은 보수적인 사람들의 견해를 압축했다.

Word Link   cas ≈ box, hold : case, encase, suitcase

en|case /ɪnkeɪs/ (**encases**, **encasing**, **encased**) V-T If a person or an object **is encased** in something, they are completely covered or surrounded by it. ◻ *When nuclear fuel is manufactured it is encased in metal cans.* ◻ *These weapons also had a heavy brass guard which encased almost the whole hand.*

타동사 -에 싸여 있다, -에 넣어지다 ◻ 핵연료가 생산되면 금속 용기에 넣는다. ◻ 이 무기들에는 손을 거의 완전히 덮는 육중한 놋쇠 보호대도 있었다.

en|chant /ɪntʃænt/ (**enchants**, **enchanting**, **enchanted**) 🔳 V-T If you **are enchanted by** someone or something, they cause you to have feelings of great delight or pleasure. ◻ *Dena was enchanted by the house.* 🔳 V-T In fairy tales and legends, to **enchant** someone or something means to put a magic spell on them. ◻ *King Arthur hid his treasures here and Merlin enchanted the cave so that nobody should ever find them.*

🔳 타동사 -에 매혹되다, -에 매료되다 ◻ 데나는 그 집에 매료되었다. 🔳 타동사 요술을 걸다, 호리다 ◻ 아서 왕이 그의 보물을 여기에 감추었고 멀린이 동굴에 요술을 걸어 아무도 보물을 찾지 못하게 만들었다.

en|chant|ing /ɪntʃǽntɪŋ/ ADJ If you describe someone or something as **enchanting**, you mean that they are very attractive or charming. ❏ *She's an absolutely enchanting child.*

형용사 매혹적인 ❏ 그 여자 애는 아주 매혹적인 아이다.

en|cir|cle /ɪnsɜ́rkᵊl/ (**encircles, encircling, encircled**) V-T To **encircle** something or someone means to surround or enclose them, or to go around them. ❏ *A forty-foot-high concrete wall encircles the jail.*

타동사 에워싸다 ❏ 40피트 높이의 콘크리트 벽이 감옥을 에워싸고 있다.

en|clave /ɛ́nkleɪv, ɒn-/ (**enclaves**) N-COUNT An **enclave** is an area within a country or a city where people live who have a different nationality or culture from the people living in the surrounding country or city. ❏ *Nagorno-Karabakh is an Armenian enclave inside Azerbaijan.*

가산명사 다국인 또는 다문화 집단의 거주 지역 ❏ 나고르노카라바크는 아제르바이잔 내에 있는 아르메니아 사람들의 거주 지역이다.

en|close /ɪnklóʊz/ (**encloses, enclosing, enclosed**) **1** V-T If a place or object **is enclosed** by something, the place or object is inside that thing or completely surrounded by it. ❏ *The rules state that samples must be enclosed in two watertight containers.* ❏ *Enclose the flower in a small muslin bag.* **2** V-T If you **enclose** something with a letter, you put it in the same envelope as the letter. ❏ *I have enclosed a check for $100.*

1 타동사 에워싸여 있다, 담겨 있다 ❏ 규정에 의하면 샘플은 두 개의 방수 용기에 담아야 한다. ❏ 꽃을 작은 모슬린 가방에 넣으시오. **2** 타동사 동봉하다 ❏ 10달러 수표를 동봉했습니다.

en|clo|sure /ɪnklóʊʒər/ (**enclosures**) N-COUNT An **enclosure** is an area of land that is surrounded by a wall or fence and that is used for a particular purpose. ❏ *This enclosure was so vast that the outermost wall could hardly be seen.*

가산명사 울로 둘러싼 땅 ❏ 울로 둘러싼 이 땅은 너무도 광대하여 가장 먼 곳의 담이 거의 보이지 않았다.

Word Link	cod ≈ writing : code, decode, encode

Word Link	en ≈ making, putting : enable, enact, encode

en|code /ɪnkóʊd/ (**encodes, encoding, encoded**) V-T If you **encode** a message or some information, you put it into a code or express it in a different form or system of language. ❏ *The two parties encode confidential data in a form that is not directly readable by the other party.*

타동사 (정보 등을) 암호로 바꾸다, 기호로 바꾸다 ❏ 그 두 당사자는 기밀 자료를 다른 상대방이 직접 읽을 수 없는 형태로 암호화한다.

en|com|pass /ɪnkʌ́mpəs/ (**encompasses, encompassing, encompassed**) **1** V-T If something **encompasses** particular things, it includes them. ❏ *His repertoire encompassed everything from Bach to Schoenberg.* **2** V-T To **encompass** a place means to completely surround or cover it. ❏ *The map shows the rest of the western region, encompassing nine states.*

1 타동사 포함하다 ❏ 그의 레퍼토리는 바흐에서 쇤베르크까지 모든 것을 포함했다. **2** 타동사 포함하다, 에워싸다 ❏ 이 지도는 9주를 포함하는 나머지 서부 지역을 보여 준다.

en|core /ɒ́ŋkɔr, -kɔr/ (**encores**) N-COUNT An **encore** is a short extra performance at the end of a longer one, which an entertainer gives because the audience asks for it. ❏ *Lang's final encore last night was "Barefoot."*

가산명사 앙코르, 재청 ❏ 어젯밤 랑의 마지막 앙코르 곡은 '베어풋'이었다.

en|coun|ter ♦◇◇ /ɪnkáʊntər/ (**encounters, encountering, encountered**) **1** V-T If you **encounter** problems or difficulties, you experience them. ❏ *Every day of our lives we encounter major and minor stresses of one kind or another.* **2** V-T If you **encounter** someone, you meet them, usually unexpectedly. [FORMAL] ❏ *Did you encounter anyone in the building?* **3** N-COUNT An **encounter with** someone is a meeting with them, particularly one that is unexpected or significant. ❏ *The author tells of a remarkable encounter with a group of South Vietnamese soldiers.* **4** N-COUNT An **encounter** is a particular type of experience. ❏ *...a sexual encounter.*

1 타동사 (어려움 등에) 부닥치다 ❏ 매일매일의 삶에서 우리는 이런저런 종류의 크고 작은 정신적 압박을 받는다. **2** 타동사 우연히 마주치다 [격식체] ❏ 건물에서 혹시 누구와 마주쳤니? **3** 가산명사 -와 마주침 ❏ 작가는 한 무리의 남베트남 군인들과의 놀랄 만한 조우에 대하여 말하고 있다. **4** 가산명사 경험 ❏ 성적 경험

Thesaurus	encounter의 참조어
v.	bump into, come across, meet, run into; (ant.) avoid, miss **2**

en|cour|age ♦♦◇ /ɪnkɜ́rɪdʒ, BRIT ɪnkʌ́rɪdʒ/ (**encourages, encouraging, encouraged**) **1** V-T If you **encourage** someone, you give them confidence, for example by letting them know that what they are doing is good and telling them that they should continue to do it. ❏ *When things aren't going well, he encourages me, telling me not to give up.* **2** V-T If someone **is encouraged by** something that happens, it gives them hope or confidence. [usu passive] ❏ *Investors were encouraged by the news.* ● **en|cour|aged** ADJ [v-link ADJ, oft ADJ that] ❏ *We were very encouraged, after over 17,000 pictures were submitted.* **3** V-T If you **encourage** someone **to** do something, you try to persuade them to do it, for example by telling them that it would be a pleasant thing to do, or by trying to make it easier for them to do it. You can also **encourage** an activity. ❏ *Herbie Hancock was encouraged by his family to learn music at a young age.* **4** V-T If something **encourages** a particular activity or state, it causes it to happen or increase. ❏ *...a natural substance that encourages cell growth.*

1 타동사 용기를 북돋우다, 격려하다 ❏ 일이 잘 풀리지 않을 때면 그는 나에게 포기하지 말라고 말하면서 격려한다. **2** 타동사 기운이 나다 ❏ 투자자들은 그 소식에 기운이 났다. ● 기운이 나는 형용사 ❏ 17,000장 이상의 사진이 제출되고 나서 우리는 아주 기운이 솟았다. **3** 타동사 격려하여 -하도록 하다, 장려하다 ❏ 허비 핸콕은 어렸을 적에 그의 가족의 격려를 받아 음악을 배우게 되었다. **4** 타동사 촉진하다 ❏ 세포의 성장을 촉진하는 자연 물질

en|cour|age|ment /ɪnkɜ́rɪdʒmənt, BRIT ɪnkʌ́rɪdʒmənt/ (**encouragements**) N-VAR **Encouragement** is the activity of encouraging someone, or something that is said or done in order to encourage them. ❏ *I also had friends who gave me a great deal of encouragement.*

가산명사 또는 불가산명사 격려, 장려 ❏ 나에게는 또한 많은 격려를 보내 준 친구들이 있었다.

en|cour|ag|ing /ɪnkɜ́rɪdʒɪŋ, BRIT ɪnkʌ́rɪdʒɪŋ/ ADJ Something that is **encouraging** gives people hope or confidence. ❏ *There are encouraging signs of an artistic revival.* ❏ *The results have been encouraging.* ● **en|cour|ag|ing|ly** ADV ❏ *The people at the next table watched me eat and smiled encouragingly.*

형용사 고무적인, 자신감을 주는 ❏ 예술적 부흥의 고무적인 기미가 보인다. ❏ 그 결과는 고무적이었다. ● 격려하듯이 부사 ❏ 옆 테이블 사람들이 내가 먹는 것을 지켜보고 격려하듯이 미소를 시었다.

en|croach /ɪnkróʊtʃ/ (**encroaches, encroaching, encroached**) **1** V-I If one thing **encroaches on** another, the first one spreads or becomes stronger, and slowly begins to restrict the power, range, or effectiveness of the second thing. [FORMAL, DISAPPROVAL] ❏ *The new institutions do not encroach on political power.* **2** V-I If something **encroaches on** a place, it spreads and takes over more and more of that place. [FORMAL] ❏ *The rhododendrons encroached ever more on the twisting drive.*

1 자동사 -을 침해하다 [격식체, 탐탁잖음] ❏ 새 제도는 정치권력을 침해하지 않는다. **2** 자동사 -을 잠식하다 [격식체] ❏ 철쭉이 대문에서 현관까지의 꼬불꼬불한 차도를 더 잠식했다.

A

en|croach|ment /ɪnkroʊtʃmənt/ (**encroachments**) N-VAR You can describe the action or process of encroaching on something as **encroachment**. [FORMAL, DISAPPROVAL] ❑ *It's a sign of the encroachment of commercialism in medicine.*

가산명사 또는 불가산명사 침해 [격식체, 탐탁잖음] ❑ 그것은 의학분야에 상업주의가 침해했다는 징조이다.

B

en|cy|clo|pedia /ɪnsaɪkləpiːdiə/ (**encyclopedias**)

The spelling **encyclopaedia** is also used, mainly in British English.

철자 encyclopaedia도 특히 영국영어에서 쓴다.

C

N-COUNT An **encyclopedia** is a book or set of books in which facts about many different subjects or about one particular subject are arranged for reference, usually in alphabetical order.

가산명사 백과사전

D

end ♦♦♦ /ɛnd/ (**ends, ending, ended**) **1** N-SING The **end of** something such as a period of time, an event, a book, or a movie is the last part of it or the final point in it. ❑ *The report is expected by the end of the year.* ❑ *The £5 banknote was first issued at the end of the 18th century.* **2** V-T/V-I When a situation, process, or activity **ends**, or when something or someone **ends** it, it reaches its final point and stops. ❑ *The meeting quickly ended and Steve and I left the room.* ● **ending** N-SING ❑ *The ending of a marriage by death is different in many ways from an ending occasioned by divorce.* **3** N-COUNT An **end to** something or the **end of** it is the act or result of stopping it so that it does not continue any longer. ❑ *The French government today called for an end to the violence.* ❑ *I was worried she would walk out or bring the interview to an end.* **4** V-T/V-I If you say that someone or something **ends** a period of time in a particular way, you are indicating what the final situation was like. You can also say that a period of time **ends** in a particular way. ❑ *The markets ended the week on a quiet note.* **5** V-I If a period of time **ends**, it reaches its final point. ❑ *Monthly reports on program trading usually come out about three weeks after each month ends.* **6** V-T/V-I If something such as a book, speech, or performance **ends with** a particular thing or the writer or performer **ends** it **with** that thing, its final part consists of the thing mentioned. ❑ *His statement ended with the words: "Pray for me."* ❑ *The book ends on a lengthy description of Hawaii.* **7** V-I If a situation or event **ends** in a particular way, it has that particular result. ❑ *The incident could have ended in tragedy.* ❑ *Our conversations ended with him saying he would try to be more understanding.* **8** N-COUNT The two **ends** of something long and narrow are the two points or parts of it that are farthest away from each other. ❑ *The company is planning to place surveillance equipment at both ends of the tunnel.* **9** N-COUNT The **end** of a long, narrow object such as a finger or a pencil is the tip or smallest edge of it, usually the part that is furthest away from you. ❑ *He tapped the ends of his fingers together.* **10** V-I If an object **ends with** or in a particular thing, it has that thing on its tip or point, or as its last part. ❑ *It has three pairs of legs, each ending in a large claw.* **11** V-I A journey, road, or river that **ends** at a particular place stops there and goes no further. ❑ *The road ended at a T-junction.* **12** N-COUNT **End** is used to refer to either of the two extreme points of a scale, or of something that you are considering as a scale. ❑ *At the other end of the social scale was the grocer, the village's only merchant.* **13** N-COUNT The **other end** is one of two places that are connected because people are communicating with each other by telephone or writing, or are traveling from one place to the other. ❑ *When he answered the phone, Ferguson was at the other end.* **14** N-COUNT If you refer to a particular **end** of a project or piece of work, you mean a part or aspect of it, for example a part of it that is done by a particular person or in a particular place. [SPOKEN] ❑ *You take care of your end, kid, I'll take care of mine.* **15** N-COUNT An **end** is the purpose for which something is done or toward which you are working. ❑ *The police force is being manipulated for political ends.* **16** V-I If you say that something **ends** at a particular point, you mean that it is applied or exists up to that point, and no further. ❑ *Helen is also 25 and from Birmingham, but the similarity ends there.* **17** V-I If you **end by** doing something or **end** in a particular state, you do that thing or get into that state even though you did not originally intend to. ❑ *They ended by making themselves miserable.* **18** PHRASE If someone **ends it all**, they kill themselves. ❑ *He grew suicidal, thinking up ways to end it all.* **19** PHRASE If something is **at an end**, it has finished and will not continue. ❑ *The recession is definitely at an end.* **20** PHRASE If something **comes to an end**, it stops. ❑ *The cold war came to an end.* **21** PHRASE You say "**at the end of the day**" when you are talking about what happens after a long series of events or what appears to be the case after you have considered the relevant facts. [INFORMAL] ❑ *At the end of the day it's up to the Germans to decide.* **22** PHRASE If you **are thrown in at the deep end**, you are put in a completely new situation without any help or preparation. If you **jump in at the deep end**, you go into a completely new situation without any help or preparation. [mainly BRIT] ❑ *It's a superb job. You get thrown in at the deep end and it's all down to you.* **23** PHRASE You say "**in the end**" when you are saying what is the final result of a series of events, or what is your final conclusion after considering all the relevant facts. ❑ *I toyed with the idea of calling the police, but in the end I didn't.* **24** PHRASE If you find it difficult to **make ends meet**, you can only just manage financially because you hardly have enough money for the things you need. ❑ *With Betty's salary they barely made ends meet.* **25** PHRASE **No end** means a lot. [INFORMAL] ❑ *Teachers inform me that Tracey's behavior has improved no end.* **26** PHRASE When something happens for hours, days, weeks, or years **on end**, it happens continuously and without stopping for the amount of time that is mentioned. ❑ *He is a wonderful companion and we can talk for hours on end.* **27** PHRASE Something that is **on end** is upright, instead of in its normal or natural position, for example lying down, flat, or on its longest side. ❑ *Wet books should be placed on end with their pages kept apart.* **28** PHRASE To **put an end to** something means to cause it to stop. ❑ *Only a political solution could put an end to the violence.* **29** PHRASE If a process or person has reached the **end of the road**, they are unable to progress any further. ❑ *Given the results of the vote, is this the end of the road for the hardliners in Congress?* **30** PHRASE If you say that something bad is **not the end of the world**, you are trying to stop yourself or someone else being so upset by it, by suggesting that it is not the worst thing that could happen. ❑ *Obviously I'd be disappointed if we don't make it, but it wouldn't be the end of the world.*

1 단수명사 끝, 말; 마지막, 결말 ❑ 그 보고서는 연말까지 나올 것으로 예상되고 있다. ❑ 5파운드짜리 지폐는 18세기 말에 처음 발행되었다. **2** 타동사/자동사 끝나다; 끝내다 ❑ 회의가 신속히 끝났고 스티브와 나는 방을 떠났다. ● 종결 단수명사 ❑ 사망에 의한 결혼의 종결은 이혼에 의한 종결과는 여러 가지 점에서 다르다. **3** 가산명사 종식, 종결 ❑ 오늘 프랑스 정부는 그 폭력 사태의 종결을 요구했다. ❑ 나는 그녀가 갑자기 자리를 뜨거나 면접을 끝내지 않을까 걱정했다. **4** 타동사/자동사 -로 끝내다; -로 끝나다 ❑ 금융 시장은 조용한 분위기로 한 주를 마감했다. **5** 자동사 끝나다 ❑ 프로그램 거래 관련 월간 보고서는 대개 월말이 지나고 3주 후에 나온다. **6** 타동사/자동사 결말을 내다; 결말이 나다 ❑ 그는 "나를 위해 기도해 주세요."라는 말로 진술을 마쳤다. ❑ 그 책은 하와이에 대한 장황한 서술로 끝을 맺는다. **7** 자동사 -으로 끝나다 ❑ 그 사건은 비극으로 끝날 수도 있었다. ❑ 우리의 대화는 자기가 더 이해심을 가지도록 노력하겠다는 그의 말로 끝났다. **8** 가산명사 양 끝 ❑ 그 회사는 터널의 양 끝에 감시 장비를 설치할 계획이다. **9** 가산명사 끄트머리, 말단 ❑ 그는 자기 손가락 끝 부분 끼리를 가볍게 두드렸다. **10** 자동사 -의 끝을 형성하다 ❑ 그것은 세 쌍의 다리가 있는데 그 끝에는 각각 큰 갈고리 발톱이 달렸다. **11** 자동사 -에서 끝나다 ❑ 그 길은 티자 길과 마나면서 끝났다. **12** 가산명사 한쪽 끝 ❑ 사회 계급의 다른 한쪽 끝에는 마을의 유일한 상인인 식료품 장수가 있었다. **13** 가산명사 다른 한쪽 끝 ❑ 그가 전화를 받았을 때 전화를 건 상대편은 퍼거슨이었다. **14** 가산명사 부분, 면 [구어체] ❑ 꼬마야, 너는 네가 맡은 부분을 처리해. 나는 내 부분을 맡을게. **15** 가산명사 목적 ❑ 경찰이 정치적 목적을 위해 조종되고 있다. **16** 자동사 -에서 끝나다 ❑ 헬렌 또한 25세이고 버밍엄 출신이지만 유사점은 거기까지이다. **17** 자동사 결국 -로 끝나다 ❑ 그들은 결국 스스로를 비참하게 만들면서 끝났다. **18** 구 자살하다 ❑ 그는 자살이 하고 싶어져서 자살할 방법을 궁리해 냈다. **19** 구 끝난 ❑ 불경기는 확실히 끝났다. **20** 구 끝나다 ❑ 냉전이 끝났다. **21** 구 최종 결론은, 결국 [비격식체] ❑ 결국 결정은 독일인들에게 달려 있다. **22** 구 마침내, 결국 ❑ 나는 그냥 경찰을 부를까 하는 생각도 했지만 결국 그러지 않았다. **23** 구 수지를 겨우 맞추다 ❑ 베티의 봉급으로는 그들이 수지를 맞추기가 어려웠다. **24** 구 많이 [비격식체] ❑ 트레이시의 태도가 많이 좋아졌다고 선생님들이 내게 알려준다. **25** 구 계속하여 ❑ 그는 좋은 벗이며 우리는 몇 시간이고 계속 이야기를 나눌 수 있다. **26** 구 곧추서서 ❑ 젖은 책은 먼끼리 붙지 않게 해서 곧추세워 놓아야 한다. **27** 구 -을 끝내다 ❑ 정치적 해결만이 그 폭력을 끝낼 수 있었다. **28** 구 막다른 끝 ❑ 표결의 결과를 보면, 이제 의회의 강경파들은 궁지에 몰린 것입니까? **29** 구 세상의 종말은 아님, 모든 것이 끝난 것은 아님 ❑ 우리가 세상에 성공하지 못하면 분명히 나는 실망하겠지만 그게 세상의 종말은 아닐 것이다.

31 the end of your **tether** →see **tether**. to make your **hair stand on end** →see **hair**. to be on the **receiving end** →see **receive**. to get the **wrong end of the stick** →see **stick**

Thesaurus   *end*의 참조어

N.   close, conclusion, finale, finish, stop; (*ant.*) beginning **1** **3**
V.   conclude, finish, wrap up; (*ant.*) begin, start **2**

▶**end up** **1** PHRASAL VERB If someone or something **ends up** somewhere, they eventually arrive there, usually by accident. ❑ *She fled with her children, moving from neighbor to neighbor and ending up in a friend's cellar.* **2** PHRASAL VERB If you **end up** doing something or **end up** in a particular state, you do that thing or get into that state even though you did not originally intend to. ❑ *If you don't know what you want, you might end up getting something you don't want.* ❑ *Every time they went dancing they ended up in a bad mood.*

en|dan|ger /ɪndeɪndʒər/ (**endangers, endangering, endangered**) V-T To **endanger** something or someone means to put them in a situation where they might be harmed or destroyed completely. ❑ *The debate could endanger the proposed Mideast peace talks.*

en|dear /ɪndɪər/ (**endears, endearing, endeared**) V-T If something **endears** you to someone or if you **endear** yourself to them, you become popular with them and well liked by them. ❑ *Their taste for gambling has endeared them to Las Vegas casino owners.*

en|dear|ing /ɪndɪərɪŋ/ ADJ If you describe someone's behavior as **endearing**, you mean that it causes you to feel very fond of them. [v-link ADJ] ❑ *She has such an endearing personality.*

en|deav|or /ɪndevər/ (**endeavors, endeavoring, endeavored**) [BRIT **endeavour**] **1** V-T If you **endeavor to** do something, you try very hard to do it. [FORMAL] ❑ *They are endeavoring to protect labor union rights.* **2** N-VAR An **endeavor** is an attempt to do something, especially something new or original. [FORMAL] ❑ *His first endeavors in the field were wedding films.*

en|dem|ic /ɛndemɪk/ ADJ If you say that a condition or problem is **endemic**, you mean that it is very common and strong, and cannot be dealt with easily. [WRITTEN] ❑ *Discrimination against Catholics is endemic in Northern Ireland's institutions.*

end|ing /ɛndɪŋ/ (**endings**) **1** N-COUNT You can refer to the last part of a book, story, play, or movie as the **ending**, especially when you are considering the way that the story ends. ❑ *The film has a Hollywood happy ending.* **2** N-COUNT The **ending** of a word is the last part of it. ❑ *...common word endings, like "ing" in walking.* **3** →see also **end**

end|less /ɛndlɪs/ ADJ If you say that something is **endless**, you mean that it is very large or lasts for a very long time, and it seems as if it will never stop. ❑ *The war was endless.* ● **end|less|ly** ADV ❑ *They talk about it endlessly.*

en|dorse /ɪndɔrs/ (**endorses, endorsing, endorsed**) **1** V-T If you **endorse** someone or something, you say publicly that you support or approve of them. ❑ *I can endorse their opinion wholeheartedly.* **2** V-T If you **endorse** a product or company, you appear in advertisements for it. ❑ *The twins endorsed a line of household cleaning products.*

en|dorse|ment /ɪndɔrsmənt/ (**endorsements**) **1** N-COUNT An **endorsement** is a statement or action which shows that you support or approve of something or someone. ❑ *This is a powerful endorsement for his softer style of government.* **2** N-COUNT An **endorsement for** a product or company involves appearing in advertisements for it or showing support for it. ❑ *His commercial endorsements for everything from Castrol to Coca-Cola will take his earnings to more than $10m a year.*

en|dow /ɪndaʊ/ (**endows, endowing, endowed**) **1** V-T You say that someone is **endowed with** a particular desirable ability, characteristic, or possession when they have it by chance or by birth. [usu passive] ❑ *You are endowed with wealth, good health, and a lively intellect.* **2** V-T If you **endow** something **with** a particular feature or quality, you provide it with that feature or quality. ❑ *Herbs have been used for centuries to endow a whole range of foods with subtle flavors.* **3** V-T If someone **endows** an institution, scholarship, or project, they provide a large amount of money which will produce the income needed to pay for it. ❑ *The ambassador has endowed a $1 million public-service fellowships program.*

en|dow|ment /ɪndaʊmənt/ (**endowments**) **1** N-COUNT An **endowment** is a gift of money that is made to an institution or community in order to provide it with an annual income. ❑ *...the National Endowment for the Arts.* **2** N-COUNT In finance, an **endowment** policy or mortgage is an insurance policy or mortgage which you pay toward each month and which should then provide you with enough money to pay for your house at the end of a fixed period. [BRIT] ❑ *...homeowners with endowment mortgages.*

end prod|uct (**end products**) N-COUNT The **end product of** something is the thing that is produced or achieved by means of it. [oft N of n] ❑ *It is the end product of exhaustive research and development.*

end re|sult (**end results**) N-COUNT The **end result of** an activity or a process is the final result that it produces. ❑ *The end result is very good and very successful.*

en|dur|ance /ɪndʊrəns, BRIT ɪndyʊərəns/ N-UNCOUNT **Endurance** is the ability to continue with an unpleasant or difficult situation, experience, or activity over a long period of time. ❑ *The exercise obviously will improve strength and endurance.*

1 구동사 결국 ~에 도달하다 ❑ 그녀는 아이들을 데리고 피신했는데, 이 집 저 집으로 옮겨 다니다가 마지막에는 한 친구의 지하실에까지 이르렀다. **2** 구동사 결국 ~으로 되다, ~에서 마치다 ❑ 네가 무엇을 원하는지 모르면, 결국 원하지 않는 것을 갖게 될 수 있다. ❑ 그들은 춤추러 갈 때마다 마지막에는 기분이 좋지 않게 끝났다.

타동사 위험에 빠뜨리다 ❑ 그 토론은 제안된 중동 평화 회담을 위험에 빠뜨릴 수 있다.

타동사 ~에게 사랑받게 하다 ❑ 도박 취미 때문에 그들은 라스베가스 카지노 소유자들로부터 사랑을 받게 되었다.

형용사 사랑스러운 ❑ 그녀는 정말 성격이 사랑스럽다.

[영국영어 endeavour] **1** 타동사 ~하려고 애쓰다 [격식체] ❑ 그들은 노동조합의 권리를 보호하려고 애쓰고 있다. **2** 가산명사 또는 불가산명사 시도 [격식체] ❑ 그 방면에서의 그의 첫 시도는 결혼식 영화였다.

형용사 고질적인 [문어체] ❑ 북아일랜드의 제도에는 가톨릭 신자에 대한 차별이 고착되어 있다.

1 가산명사 결말 ❑ 그 영화는 할리우드 방식의 행복한 결말로 끝난다. **2** 가산명사 어미, 끝 부분 ❑ walking의 'ing'와 같이 단어의 흔한 어미

형용사 끝이 없는 ❑ 전쟁은 끝이 없었다. ● 끝없이 부사 ❑ 그들은 그것에 대해 끝없이 이야기한다.

1 타동사 승인하다 ❑ 나는 진심으로 그들의 의견을 지지할 수 있다. **2** 타동사 광고에 출연하다 ❑ 그 쌍둥이들은 가정용 청소 용품 광고에 출연했다.

1 가산명사 승인, 지지 ❑ 이것은 유연한 양식의 정부에 대한 그의 강력한 지지이다. **2** 가산명사 광고 출연 ❑ 캐스트롤부터 코카콜라까지 이르는 모든 상업 광고 출연으로 그는 일년에 천만 파운드를 벌게 될 것이다.

1 타동사 (소질 등을) 부여받다 ❑ 당신은 부와 건강, 그리고 날카로운 지성을 부여받았다. **2** 타동사 부여하다 ❑ 허브는 수 세기 동안 모든 종류의 음식에 미묘한 향을 내는 데 사용되어 왔다. **3** 타동사 (기부금을) 기부하다 ❑ 그 대사는 100만 달러를 공익사업 장학 프로그램에 기부하였다.

1 가산명사 기증, 기부 ❑ 국가 예술 기금 **2** 가산명사 양로 보험 증권 [영국영어] ❑ 양로 보험 저당에 들어 있는 집주인들

가산명사 최종 산출물 ❑ 그것은 철저한 조사와 개발의 최종 산출물이다.

가산명사 최종 결과 ❑ 최종 결과는 매우 훌륭하고 매우 성공적이다.

불가산명사 인내력 ❑ 이 운동은 명백하게 체력과 인내력을 향상시킬 것이다.

a
b
c
d
e
f
g
h
i
j
k
l
m
n
o
p
q
r
s
t
u
v
w
x
y
z

en|dure /ɪndʊər, BRIT ɪndyʊəʳ/ (**endures, enduring, endured**) ◻ V-T If you **endure** a painful or difficult situation, you experience it and do not avoid it or give up, usually because you cannot. ◻ *The company endured heavy financial losses.* ◻ V-I If something **endures**, it continues to exist without any loss in quality or importance. ◻ *Somehow the language endures and continues to survive.* ● **en|dur|ing** ADJ ◻ *This chance meeting was the start of an enduring friendship.*

1 타동사 견디다 ◻ 그 기업은 심한 재정적 손실을 겪었다. 2 자동사 지속되다 ◻ 어떻게든 그 언어는 지속되어 계속 존재한다. ● 지속하는 형용사 ◻ 이 우연한 만남은 지속적인 우정의 시발점이었다.

end user (**end users**) N-COUNT The **end user** of a piece of computer equipment is the user that it has been designed for, rather than the person who installs or maintains it. [COMPUTING] ◻ *You have to be able to describe things in a form that the end user can understand.*

가산명사 최종 사용자 [컴퓨터] ◻ 당신은 물건을 최종 사용자가 이해할 수 있는 형태로 묘사할 수 있어야 합니다.

en|emy ♦♢♢ /ɛnəmi/ (**enemies**) ◻ N-COUNT If someone is your **enemy**, they hate you or want to harm you. ◻ *Imagine loving your enemy and doing good to those who hated you.* 2 N-COUNT If someone is your **enemy**, they are opposed to you and to what you think or do. ◻ *The Government's political enemies were quick to pick up on this series of disasters.* 3 N-SING-COLL The **enemy** is an army or other force that is opposed to you in a war, or a country with which your country is at war. [the N, N n] ◻ *The enemy were pursued for two miles.* 4 N-COUNT If one thing is the **enemy of** another thing, the second thing cannot happen or succeed because of the first thing. [FORMAL] ◻ *Reform, as we know, is the enemy of revolution.*

1 가산명사 적 ◻ 적을 사랑하는 것과 당신을 싫어했던 사람들에게 친절을 베푸는 것을 상상해 보시오. 2 가산명사 적 ◻ 정부의 정적들이 이 일련의 재난을 재빠르게 포착해 내었다. 3 단수명사-집합 적군 ◻ 적군은 2마일 정도 추격당했다. 4 가산명사 적 [격식체] ◻ 우리가 알고 있듯이 개혁은 변혁의 적이다.

→see calories, electricity, food
→see Word Web: energy

Word Partnership   enemy의 연어

V.	**make an** enemy 1
	defeat an enemy 3
N.	enemy **attack**, enemy **position**, enemy **territory**, enemy **troops** 3

en|er|get|ic /ɛnərdʒɛtɪk/ ◻ ADJ If you are **energetic** in what you do, you have a lot of enthusiasm and determination. ◻ *Blackwell is 59, strong looking, enormously energetic and accomplished.* ● **en|er|geti|cal|ly** /ɛnərdʒɛtɪkli/ ADV [ADV with v] ◻ *He had worked energetically all day on his new book.* 2 ADJ An **energetic** person is very active and does not feel at all tired. An **energetic** activity involves a lot of physical movement and power. ◻ *Ten-year-olds are incredibly energetic.* ● **en|er|geti|cal|ly** ADV [ADV with v] ◻ *David chewed energetically on the gristled steak.*

1 형용사 원기 왕성한 ◻ 블랙웰은 59세로 건강해 보이고, 원기 왕성하며 성공한 사람이다. ● 원기 왕성하게, 열정적으로 부사 ◻ 그는 하루 종일 원기 왕성하게 새 책 집필 작업을 했었다. 2 형용사 활동적인 ◻ 열살 된 아이들은 엄청 활동적이다. ● 활동적으로 부사 ◻ 데이비드는 연골이 있는 스테이크를 열심히 씹었다.

en|er|gy ♦♢♢ /ɛnərdʒi/ (**energies**) ◻ N-UNCOUNT **Energy** is the ability and strength to do active physical things and the feeling that you are full of physical power and life. ◻ *He was saving his energy for next week's race in Belgium.* 2 N-UNCOUNT **Energy** is determination and enthusiasm about doing things. [APPROVAL] ◻ *You have drive and energy for those things you are interested in.* 3 N-COUNT Your **energies** are your efforts and attention, which you can direct toward a particular aim. ◻ *She had started to devote her energies to teaching rather than performing.* 4 N-UNCOUNT **Energy** is the power from sources such as electricity and coal that makes machines work or provides heat. ◻ *...those who favor nuclear energy.*

1 불가산명사 정력, 기력 ◻ 그는 벨기에에서 열리는 다음 주의 경주를 대비하여 기력을 아껴 두고 있었다. 2 불가산명사 열정 [마음에 듦] ◻ 당신은 관심 있는 것에 대해 활력과 열정을 가지고 있군요. 3 가산명사 노력, 힘 ◻ 그녀는 연주하는 것보다 가르치는 데 힘을 집중하기 시작했었다. 4 불가산명사 에너지 ◻ 원자력 에너지를 선호하는 사람들

Word Partnership   energy의 연어

ADJ.	**physical** energy, **sexual** energy 1
	full of energy 1 2
	atomic energy, **nuclear** energy, **solar** energy 4
V.	**focus** energy 1 2
	conserve/save energy 4

en|force /ɪnfɔrs/ (**enforces, enforcing, enforced**) ◻ V-T If people in authority **enforce** a law or a rule, they make sure that it is obeyed, usually by punishing people who do not obey it. ◻ *Until now, the government has only enforced the ban with regard to American ships.* 2 V-T To **enforce** something means to force or cause it to be done or to happen. ◻ *They struggled to limit the cost by enforcing a low-tech specification.*

1 타동사 (법률 등을) 시행하다 ◻ 지금까지, 정부는 미국의 선박들에 관한 금지 조치만 시행했다. 2 타동사 적용하다 ◻ 그들은 저차원 기술 항목들만 적용해서 비용을 제한하려고 안간힘을 썼다.

en|force|ment /ɪnfɔrsmənt/ N-UNCOUNT If someone carries out the **enforcement** of an act or rule, they enforce it. ◻ *The doctors want stricter enforcement of existing laws, such as those banning sales of cigarettes to children.*

불가산명사 시행 ◻ 의사들은 아동들에 대한 담배 판매를 금지하는 것과 같은 현행법의 더욱 엄격한 시행을 원한다.

en|gage ♦♢♢ /ɪngeɪdʒ/ (**engages, engaging, engaged**) ◻ V-I If you **engage in** an activity, you do it or are actively involved with it. [FORMAL] ◻ *I have never engaged in the drug trade.* 2 V-T If something **engages** you or your attention or interest, it keeps you interested in it and thinking about it. ◻ *They never learned*

1 자동사 -에 관여하다 [격식체] ◻ 나는 절대로 마약 거래에 관여한 적이 없다. 2 타동사 -의 마음을 끌다 ◻ 그들은 다른 사람들의 관심을 끄는 기술을 결코 배우지 못했다. 3 타동사 대화하다 ◻ 그들은 그들

Word Web   energy

Wood was the primary **energy** source for American settlers. Then, as industry developed, factories began to use **coal**. Coal was also used to **generate** most of the **electrical power** in the early 1900s. However, widespread automobile use soon made **petroleum** the most important **fuel**. **Natural gas** remains popular for home heating and industrial use. Hydroelectric power isn't a major source of energy in the U.S. It requires too much land and water to produce. Some companies built **nuclear** power plants to make **electricity** in the 1970s. Today **solar** panels convert sunlight and giant wind farms convert wind into electricity.

skills to *engage the attention of the others.* **3** V-T If you **engage** someone **in** conversation, you have a conversation with them. ❑ *They tried to engage him in conversation.* **4** V-I If you **engage with** something or **with** a group of people, you get involved with that thing or group and feel that you are connected with it or have real contact with it. ❑ *She found it hard to engage with office life.* ● **engagement** N-UNCOUNT ❑ *And she, too, suffers from a lack of critical engagement with the literary texts.* **5** V-T If you **engage** someone to do a particular job, you appoint them to do it. [FORMAL] ❑ *We engaged the services of a recognized engineer.* **6** →see also **engaged, engaging**

대화에 끌어들이려고 했다. **4** 자동사 종사하다 ❑ 그녀는 사무실 업무에 종사하는 것이 힘든 일이라고 생각했다. ● 제약 불가산명사 ❑ 그리고 그녀 또한 문학 작품에 대해 비판적인 교감을 못 얻고 있다. **5** 타동사 고용하다 [격식체] ❑ 우리는 공인된 기술자에게서 서비스를 받았다.

engaged /ɪnɡeɪdʒd/ **1** ADJ Someone who is **engaged in** or **engaged on** a particular activity is doing that thing. [v-link ADJ in/on n] ❑ *...the various projects he was engaged on.* **2** ADJ When two people are **engaged**, they have agreed to marry each other. ❑ *We got engaged on my eighteenth birthday.* **3** ADJ If a telephone or a telephone line is **engaged**, it is already being used by someone else so that you are unable to speak to the person you are phoning. [BRIT; AM **busy**] [v-link ADJ] ❑ *The line is engaged.* **4** ADJ If a public toilet is **engaged**, it is already being used by someone else. [mainly BRIT; AM usually **occupied**] [v-link ADJ] ❑ *By now Ben has realized the urgency of his needs, but the boys' toilet is engaged when we get there.*

1 형용사 종사하는 [격식체] ❑ 그가 종사했던 여러 가지 사업들 **2** 형용사 약혼한 ❑ 우리는 내 열여덟 번째 생일날 약혼했다. **3** 형용사 통화 중인 [영국영어; 미국영어 busy] ❑ 통화 중입니다. **4** 형용사 (화장실이) 사용 중인 [주로 영국영어; 미국영어 대개 occupied] ❑ 이때쯤 벤은 소변이 매우 급하다는 것을 깨달았지만, 남자 화장실은 우리가 도착했을 때 이미 사용 중이다.

engagement /ɪnɡeɪdʒmənt/ (**engagements**) **1** N-COUNT An **engagement** is an arrangement that you have made to do something at a particular time. [FORMAL] ❑ *He had an engagement at a restaurant at eight.* **2** N-COUNT An **engagement** is an agreement that two people have made with each other to get married. ❑ *I've broken off my engagement to Arthur.* **3** N-COUNT You can refer to the period of time during which two people are engaged as their **engagement**. ❑ *We spoke every night during our engagement.* **4** N-VAR A military **engagement** is an armed conflict between two enemies. ❑ *The constitution prohibits them from military engagement on foreign soil.* **5** →see also **engage**

1 가산명사 약속 [격식체] ❑ 그는 8시에 한 음식점에서 약속이 있었다. **2** 가산명사 약혼 ❑ 나는 아서와의 약혼을 깼다. **3** 가산명사 약혼 기간 ❑ 우리는 약혼 기간 동안에 밤마다 이야기했다. **4** 가산명사 또는 불가산명사 교전 ❑ 헌법은 그들이 외국 땅에서 군사적 교전을 하는 것을 금한다.

engaging /ɪnɡeɪdʒɪŋ/ ADJ An **engaging** person or thing is pleasant, interesting, and entertaining. ❑ *...one of her most engaging and least known novels.*

형용사 마음을 끄는 ❑ 사람의 마음을 가장 끌지만 가장 덜 알려진 그녀의 소설들 중 하나

engender /ɪndʒendər/ (**engenders, engendering, engendered**) V-T If someone or something **engenders** a particular feeling, atmosphere, or situation, they cause it to occur. [FORMAL] ❑ *It helps engender a sense of common humanity.*

타동사 발생시키다 [격식체] ❑ 그것은 공통적인 인간애가 발생하게 도와준다.

engine ♦♢♢ /endʒɪn/ (**engines**) **1** N-COUNT The **engine** of a car or other vehicle is the part that produces the power which makes the vehicle move. ❑ *He got into the driving seat and started the engine.* **2** N-COUNT An **engine** is also the large vehicle that pulls a train. ❑ *In 1941, the train would have been pulled by a steam engine.* →see **car, flight**
→see Word Web: **engine**

1 가산명사 엔진 ❑ 그는 운전석으로 가서 시동을 걸었다. **2** 가산명사 기관차 ❑ 1941년, 기차는 증기 기관차가 끌기도 했다.

engineer ♦♢♢ /endʒɪnɪər/ (**engineers, engineering, engineered**) **1** N-COUNT An **engineer** is a person who uses scientific knowledge to design, construct, and maintain engines and machines or structures such as roads, railroads, and bridges. **2** N-COUNT An **engineer** is a person who repairs mechanical or electrical devices. ❑ *They send a service engineer to fix the disk drive.* **3** N-COUNT An **engineer** is a person who is responsible for maintaining the engine of a ship while it is at sea. **4** V-T When a vehicle, bridge, or building **is engineered**, it is planned and constructed using scientific methods. [usu passive] ❑ *Many of Kuwait's spacious freeways were engineered by W S Atkins.* **5** V-T If you **engineer** an event or situation, you arrange for it to happen, in a clever or indirect way. ❑ *Some people believe that his murder was engineered by Stalin.*

1 가산명사 기사 **2** 가산명사 기술자 ❑ 그들은 디스크 드라이브를 고치기 위해 서비스 기술자를 보낸다. **3** 가산명사 기관사 **4** 타동사 설계되다, 건조되다 ❑ 쿠웨이트의 넓은 고속도로 중 많은 것이 더블유. 에스. 앳킨스에 의해서 설계되고 건설되었다. **5** 타동사 (사건 등을) 계획하다 ❑ 일부 사람들은 그의 살인이 스탈린에 의해 계획된 것이라고 생각한다.

Thesaurus   engineer의 참조어

V.   arrange, concoct, create, devise, originate, plan, set up **5**

---

engineering ♦♢♢ /endʒɪnɪərɪŋ/ N-UNCOUNT **Engineering** is the work involved in designing and constructing engines and machinery, or structures such as roads and bridges. **Engineering** is also the subject studied by people who want to do this work. ❑ *...graduates with degrees in engineering.* →see also **genetic engineering**

불가산명사 공학 ❑ 공학 학위를 받은 졸업생들

Word Web   engine

In the **internal combustion engine** found in most cars, there are four, six, or eight **cylinders**. To produce an engine stroke, the intake valve opens and a small amount of **fuel** enters the **combustion** chamber of the cylinder. A spark plug ignites the fuel and air mixture, causing it to explode. This **combustion** moves the **cylinder head**, which causes the crankshaft to turn. Next, the **exhaust valve** opens and the burned gases are drawn out. As the cylinder head returns to its original position, it compresses the new gas and air mixture and the process repeats itself.

camshaft, rocker arm, intake valve, spark plug, exhaust valve, fuel, cylinder head, combustion chamber, piston, cylinder, crankshaft

internal combustion engine

A

English ◆◆◇ /ˈɪŋglɪʃ/ **1** ADJ **English** means belonging or relating to England, or to its people or language. It is also often used to mean belonging or relating to Great Britain, although many people object to this. ❑ ...the English way of life. ● N-PLURAL The **English** are English people. ❑ The English are obsessed with doing up houses. **2** N-UNCOUNT **English** is the language spoken by people who live in Great Britain and Ireland, the United States, Canada, Australia, and many other countries.
→see Word Web: **English**

1 형용사 영국의, 잉글랜드의 ❑ 영국식 삶 ● 복수명사 영국 사람들 ❑ 영국 사람들은 집을 꾸미는 생각에 사로잡혀 있다. **2** 불가산명사 영어

B

C

en|graved /ɪnˈgreɪvd/ ADJ If you say that something is **engraved on** your mind or memory or **on** your heart, you are emphasizing that you will never forget it, because it has made a very strong impression on you. [EMPHASIS] [v-link ADJ in/on/upon n] ❑ Her image is engraved upon my heart.

형용사 아로새겨진 [강조] ❑ 그녀의 모습은 내 마음에 아로새겨져 있다.

D

en|grossed /ɪnˈgroʊst/ ADJ If you are **engrossed in** something, it holds your attention completely. ❑ Tony didn't notice because he was too engrossed in his work.

형용사 몰두한 ❑ 토니는 너무 자기 일에 몰두해 있었기 때문에 알아차리지 못했다.

E

en|gulf /ɪnˈgʌlf/ (**engulfs, engulfing, engulfed**) **1** V-T If one thing **engulfs** another, it completely covers or hides it, often in a sudden and unexpected way. ❑ A seven-year-old boy was found dead after a landslide engulfed an apartment block. **2** V-T If a feeling or emotion **engulfs** you, you are strongly affected by it. ❑ ...the pain that engulfed him.

1 타동사 집어삼키다, 휩쓸어 버리다 ❑ 산사태가 아파트 한 동을 집어삼킨 후에 일곱 살 된 소년이 사체로 발견되었다. **2** 타동사 휩싸다 ❑ 그를 휩싼 고통

F

G

en|hance ◆◇◇ /ɪnˈhæns/ (**enhances, enhancing, enhanced**) V-T To **enhance** something means to improve its value, quality, or attractiveness. ❑ They'll be keen to enhance their reputation abroad.

타동사 높이다, (매력 등을) 고양시키다 ❑ 그들은 해외에서 명성을 높이는 데 열중할 것이다.

H

Thesaurus	enhance의 참조어

v.   boost, complement, improve; (ant.) decrease, diminish

I

en|hance|ment /ɪnˈhænsmənt/ (**enhancements**) N-VAR The **enhancement of** something is the improvement of it in relation to its value, quality, or attractiveness. [FORMAL] ❑ Music is merely an enhancement to the power of her words.

가산명사 또는 불가산명사 증진, 고양 [격식체] ❑ 음악은 단순히 그녀가 하는 말의 힘을 증진시켜 주는 것일 뿐이다.

J

enig|ma /ɪˈnɪgmə/ (**enigmas**) N-COUNT If you describe something or someone as an **enigma**, you mean they are mysterious or difficult to understand. [usu sing] ❑ Iran remains an enigma for the outside world.

가산명사 수수께끼 ❑ 이란은 외부 세계에 수수께끼로 남아 있다.

K

en|ig|mat|ic /ˌenɪgˈmætɪk/ ADJ Someone or something that is **enigmatic** is mysterious and difficult to understand. ❑ She starred in one of Welles's most enigmatic films. ● **en|ig|mati|cal|ly** ADV ❑ "Corbiere didn't deserve this," she said enigmatically.

형용사 수수께끼 같은, 이해하기 어려운 ❑ 그녀는 웰레스의 가장 난해한 영화 중 하나에 주연을 맡았다. ● 수수께끼같이, 불가사의하게 부사 ❑ "코비에르는 이것을 받을 만하지 않았어,"라고 그녀가 불가사의하게 말했다.

L

Word Link	joy ≈ being glad : enjoy, joyful, joyous

M

en|joy ◆◆◇ /ɪnˈdʒɔɪ/ (**enjoys, enjoying, enjoyed**) **1** V-T If you **enjoy** something, you find pleasure and satisfaction in doing it or experiencing it. ❑ Ross had always enjoyed the company of women. ❑ He was a guy who enjoyed life to the full. **2** V-T If you **enjoy yourself**, you do something that you like doing or you take pleasure in the situation that you are in. ❑ I must say I am really enjoying myself at the moment. **3** V-T If you **enjoy** something such as a right, benefit, or privilege, you have it. [FORMAL] ❑ The average German will enjoy 40 days' paid holiday this year.

1 타동사 즐기다 ❑ 로스는 항상 여자들과 함께 있는 것을 즐겼다. ❑ 그는 인생을 최대로 즐겼던 남자였다. **2** 타동사 즐거워하다 ❑ 나는 정말이 순간이 즐겁다. **3** 타동사 누리다 [격식체] ❑ 올해 평균 독일인은 40일 동안의 유급 휴가를 누릴 것이다.

N

O

Word Partnership	enjoy의 연어

N.   enjoy *someone's* company, enjoy **life**, enjoy **a meal** **1**
       enjoy **privileges**, enjoy **success** **3**

P

Q

en|joy|able /ɪnˈdʒɔɪəbəl/ ADJ Something that is **enjoyable** gives you pleasure. ❑ It was much more enjoyable than I had expected.

형용사 즐거운 ❑ 그것은 내가 기대했던 것보다 훨씬 더 즐거웠다.

R

en|joy|ment /ɪnˈdʒɔɪmənt/ N-UNCOUNT **Enjoyment** is the feeling of pleasure and satisfaction that you have when you do or experience something that you like. ❑ I apologize if your enjoyment of the movie was spoiled.

불가산명사 즐거움 ❑ 즐겁게 영화 보시는 것을 제가 망쳤다면 사과드립니다.

S

en|large /ɪnˈlɑrdʒ/ (**enlarges, enlarging, enlarged**) **1** V-T/V-I When you **enlarge** something or when it **enlarges**, it becomes bigger. ❑ ...the plan to enlarge Ewood Park into a 30,000 all-seater stadium. **2** V-I If you **enlarge on** something that has been mentioned, you give more details about it. [FORMAL] ❑ He didn't enlarge on the form that the interim government and assembly would take. →see **photography**

1 타동사/자동사 넓히다, 확대하다; 넓어지다, 확대되다 ❑ 이우드 공원을 3만석의 경기장으로 넓히는 계획 **2** 자동사 -에 대해 상술하다 [격식체] ❑ 그는 임시 정부와 의회가 취할 형태에 대해서는 상술하지 않았다.

T

en|large|ment /ɪnˈlɑrdʒmənt/ (**enlargements**) **1** N-UNCOUNT The **enlargement of** something is the process or result of making it bigger. ❑ There is insufficient space for enlargement of the buildings. **2** N-COUNT An **enlargement** is a

1 불가산명사 확장, 증대 ❑ 건물들의 확장을 위한 공간이 부족하다. **2** 가산명사 확대 ❑ 재현상과 확대를 주문하는 것은 이전 어느 때보다 더 쉽다.

U

V

Word Web	English

W

The **English language** has more **words** than any other language. Early English grew out of a Germanic language. Much of its **grammar** and basic **vocabulary** came from that language. But in 1066, England was conquered by the Normans. Norman French became the language of the rulers. Therefore many French and **Latin** words came into the English language. The playwright Shakespeare* **coined** over 1,600 new words in his plays. English has become an international language with many regional **dialects**.

X

Y

William Shakespeare (1564-1616): an English playwright and poet.

Z

photograph that has been made bigger. ❏ *Ordering reprints and enlargements is easier than ever.*

Word Link

light ≈ shining: day*light*, en*lighten*, *light*

en|light|en /ɪnlaɪtᵊn/ (enlightens, enlightening, enlightened) v-t To **enlighten** someone means to give them more knowledge and greater understanding about something. [FORMAL] [no cont] ❏ *A few dedicated doctors have fought for years to enlighten the profession.* ● **en|light|en|ing** ADJ *A representative from Shaldon Wildlife Trust gave an enlightening talk on the work done at the animal park.*

타동사 계몽하다 [격식체] ❏ 그 직업을 알리기 위해서 소수의 헌신적인 의사들이 여러 해 동안 싸워왔다. ● 계몽적인 형용사 ❏ '샬돈 와일드라이프 트러스트'에서 온 대표가 동물 공원에서 있었던 일에 대하여 계몽적인 연설을 했다.

en|light|ened /ɪnlaɪtᵊnd/ ADJ If you describe someone or their attitudes as **enlightened**, you mean that they have sensible, modern attitudes and ways of dealing with things. [APPROVAL] ❏ *...an enlightened policy.*

형용사 진보한 [마음에 듦] ❏ 진보한 정책

en|list /ɪnlɪst/ (enlists, enlisting, enlisted) ◼ v-t/v-i If someone **enlists** or **is enlisted**, they join the army, navy, marines, or air force. ❏ *Michael Hughes of Lackawanna, Pennsylvania, enlisted in the 82nd Airborne 20 years ago.* ❏ *He enlisted as a private in the Mexican War.* ◻ v-t If you **enlist** the help of someone, you persuade them to help or support you in doing something. ❏ *I had to cut down a tree and enlist the help of seven neighbors to get it out of the garden!*

◼ 타동사/자동사 입대하다, 입대시키다 ❏ 펜실베이니아 주 랙카와나 출신의 마이클 휴즈 20년 전에 제82공수 부대에 입대했다. ❏ 그는 멕시코 전쟁 때 이등병으로 입대했다. ◻ 타동사 손을 빌다, 도움을 얻다 ❏ 나는 정원에서 나무 한 그루를 베어 그것을 정원 밖으로 들어내기 위해 이웃 사람 7명의 도움을 받아야했다.

en|liv|en /ɪnlaɪvᵊn/ (enlivens, enlivening, enlivened) v-t To **enliven** events, situations, or people means to make them more lively or cheerful. ❏ *Even the most boring meeting was enlivened by Dan's presence.*

타동사 활기차게 하다 ❏ 가장 지루한 회의조차도 댄이 있으면 활기가 찼다.

en masse /ɒn mæs/ ADV If a group of people do something **en masse**, they do it all together and at the same time. ❏ *The people marched en masse.*

부사 무리지어 ❏ 사람들은 무리지어 행진했다.

en|mity /ɛnmɪti/ (enmities) N-VAR **Enmity** is a feeling of hatred toward someone that lasts for a long time. ❏ *I think there is an historic enmity between them.*

가산명사 또는 불가산명사 원한 ❏ 나는 그들 사이에 어떤 해묵은 원한이 있다고 생각한다.

enor|mity /ɪnɔrmɪti/ ◼ N-UNCOUNT If you refer to **the enormity of** something that you consider to be a problem or difficulty, you are referring to its very great size, extent, or seriousness. ❏ *I was numbed by the enormity of the responsibility.* ◻ N-UNCOUNT If you refer to **the enormity of** an event, you are emphasizing that it is terrible and frightening. [EMPHASIS] ❏ *It makes no sense to belittle the enormity of the disaster which has occurred.*

◼ 불가산명사 막중함 ❏ 나는 그 책임의 막중함에 정신이 멍했다. ◻ 불가산명사 어마어마함, 엄청남 [강조] ❏ 이미 발생한 재난의 엄청남을 축소해 봐야 아무런 의미가 없다.

enor|mous ◆◇◇ /ɪnɔrməs/ ◼ ADJ Something that is **enormous** is extremely large in size or amount. ❏ *The main bedroom is enormous.* ◻ ADJ You can use **enormous** to emphasize the great degree or extent of something. [EMPHASIS] ❏ *It was an enormous disappointment.* ● **enor|mous|ly** ADV ❏ *This book was enormously influential.*

◼ 형용사 거대한 ❏ 중앙 침실은 거대하다. ◻ 형용사 엄청난 [강조] ❏ 그것은 엄청난 실망감이었다. ● 엄청나게 부사 ❏ 이 책은 엄청난 영향력이 있었다.

Thesaurus

enormous의 참조어

ADJ.	colossal, gigantic, huge, immense, massive, tremendous; (ant.) minute, tiny ◼ ◻

enough ◆◆◆ /ɪnʌf/ ◼ DET **Enough** means as much as you need or as much as is necessary. ❏ *They had enough cash for a one-way ticket.* ● ADV **Enough** is also an adverb. ❏ *I was old enough to work and earn money.* ❏ *Do you believe that sentences for criminals are tough enough at present?* ● PRON **Enough** is also a pronoun. ❏ *Although the UK says efforts are being made, they are not doing enough.* ● QUANT **Enough** is also a quantifier. [QUANT of def-n] ❏ *All parents worry about whether their child is getting enough of the right foods.* ● ADJ **Enough** is also an adjective. [n ADJ] ❏ *It was downright panic – the frozen expressions on the faces of the actors was proof enough of that.* ◻ PRON If you say that something is **enough**, you mean that you do not want it to continue any longer or get any worse. ❏ *I met him only the once, and that was enough.* ❏ *I think I have said enough.* ● QUANT **Enough** is also a quantifier. [QUANT of def-n] ❏ *Ann had enough of this.* ● DET **Enough** is also a determiner. ❏ *Would you shut up, please! I'm having enough trouble with these children!* ● ADV **Enough** is also an adverb. [adj ADV] ❏ *I'm serious, things are difficult enough as they are.* ◼ ADV You can use **enough** to say that something is the case to a moderate or fairly large degree. [adj/adv ADV] ❏ *Winter is a common enough German surname.* ◼ ADV You use **enough** in expressions such as **strangely enough** and **interestingly enough** to indicate that you think a fact is strange or interesting. [adv ADV with cl] ❏ *Strangely enough, the last thing he thought of was his beloved Tanya.* ◼ PHRASE If you say that you **have had enough**, you mean that you are unhappy with a situation and you want it to stop. ❏ *I had had enough of the people for one night.* ◼ **fair enough** →see **fair**. **sure enough** →see **sure**

◼ 한정사 충분한 ❏ 그들은 편도 승차권을 살만큼 충분한 현금이 있었다. ● 부사 충분히 ❏ 나는 충분히 일을 해서 돈을 벌 수 있는 나이였다. ❏ 현재 범죄자에게 가해지는 형이 충분히 가혹하다고 생각합니까? ● 대명사 충분한 양 ❏ 비록 영국이 노력한다고 하지만, 그 노력은 충분한 것이 아니다. ● 수량사 충분히 ❏ 모든 부모가 그들의 자녀가 몸에 좋은 음식을 충분히 섭취하는지를 걱정한다. ● 형용사 충분한 ❏ 그것은 공포 그 자체였다. 얼어붙은 배우들의 얼굴 표정에서 그것은 충분히 입증되었다. ◻ 대명사 충분함 ❏ 나는 그를 단지 그 때 한 번 만났는데, 그것으로 충분했다. ● 수량사 충분한 양 ❏ 앤은 이것에 대해 충분히 들었다. ● 한정사 충분한 ❏ 제발 조용히 좀 해! 나는 이 아이들로도 충분히 애를 먹고 있다고! ● 부사 충분히 ❏ 나는 심각하고, 문제는 있는 그대로 충분히 복잡하다. ◼ 부사 상당히 ❏ 빈터는 상당히 흔한 독일 성이다. ◼ 부사 참으로 ❏ 참으로 이상하게도, 그가 마지막으로 생각한 것이 사랑하는 타냐였다. ◼ 구 겪을 만큼 겪다 ❏ 나는 하룻밤 동안 대할 다른 사람들은 이미 대할 만큼 대했었다.

Thesaurus

enough의 참조어

ADJ.	adequate, complete, satisfactory, sufficient; (ant.) deficient, inadequate, insufficient ◼

en|quire /ɪnkwaɪər/ →see **inquire**

en|quiry /ɪnkwaɪəri/ →see **inquiry**

en|rage /ɪnreɪdʒ/ (enrages, enraging, enraged) v-t If you **are enraged** by something, it makes you extremely angry. ❏ *Craig Tibbles, a tree surgeon, was enraged by news of plans to demolish the pub.*

타동사 격노하게 만들다 ❏ 나무 의사인 크레이그 티블즈는 술집을 폐쇄하려는 계획에 대한 소식에 격노하였다.

en|rich /ɪnrɪtʃ/ (enriches, enriching, enriched) ◼ v-t To **enrich** something means to improve its quality, usually by adding something to it. ❏ *It is important to enrich the soil prior to planting.* ◻ v-t To **enrich** someone means to increase the amount of money that they have. ❏ *He will drain, rather than enrich, the country.*

◼ 타동사 비옥하게 하다 ❏ 씨 뿌리기 전에 토양을 비옥하게 하는 것이 중요하다. ◻ 타동사 부유하게 만들다 ❏ 그는 나라를 부유하게 만들기보다는 고갈시킬 것이다.

en|rich|ment /ɪnrɪtʃmənt/ N-UNCOUNT **Enrichment** is the act of enriching someone or something or the state of being enriched. □ ...the enrichment of society.

불가산명사 부유하게 하기 □ 사회를 부유하게 하기 [영국영어 enrol] 타동사/자동사 등록하다, 등록시키다

en|roll /ɪnroʊl/ (**enrolls, enrolling, enrolled**) [BRIT **enrol**] V-T/V-I If you **enroll** or **are enrolled** at an institution or on a course, you officially join it and pay a fee for it. □ Cherny was enrolled at the University in 1945. □ I thought I'd enroll you with an art group at the school.

□ 체르니는 1945년에 그 대학에 등록했다. □ 나는 너를 학교의 예술 동아리에 등록시키려고 생각했다.

en|roll|ment /ɪnroʊlmənt/ [BRIT **enrolment**] N-UNCOUNT **Enrollment** is the act of enrolling at an institution or on a course. □ A fee is charged for each year of study and is payable at enrollment.

[영국영어 enrolment] 불가산명사 등록 □ 등록금은 매년 부가되며 등록시에 지불하면 된다.

en route /ɒn rut/ →see **route**

en|sem|ble /ɒnsɒmbəl/ (**ensembles**) N-COUNT An **ensemble** is a group of musicians, actors, or dancers who regularly perform together. □ ...an ensemble of young musicians.

가산명사 (연주자 등의) 앙상블 □ 젊은 음악가들의 앙상블

en|sue /ɪnsu, BRIT ɪnsjuː/ (**ensues, ensuing, ensued**) V-I If something **ensues**, it happens immediately after another event, usually as a result of it. [no cont] □ If the Europeans did not reduce subsidies, a trade war would ensue.

자동사 뒤따르다 □ 유럽인들이 보조금을 줄이지 않으면, 무역 전쟁이 뒤따를 것이다.

en|su|ing /ɪnsuɪŋ, ɪnsjuːɪŋ/ ■ ADJ **Ensuing** events happen immediately after other events. [ADJ n] □ The ensuing argument had been bitter. ■ ADJ **Ensuing** months or years follow the time you are talking about. [det ADJ] □ The two companies grew tenfold in the ensuing ten years.

■ 형용사 뒤따른 □ 뒤따른 언쟁이 더욱 격렬했었다. ■ 형용사 그 다음의 □ 두 회사는 그 다음 10년 동안에 열 배로 성장했다.

en suite /ɒn swit/ ADJ An **en suite** bathroom is next to a bedroom and can only be reached by a door in the bedroom. An **en suite** bedroom has an en suite bathroom. [BRIT; AM **private bathroom**] [ADJ n]

형용사 (화장실이) 방에 딸린 [영국영어; 미국영어 private bathroom]

en|sure ♦♦◇ /ɪnʃʊər/ (**ensures, ensuring, ensured**) V-T To **ensure** something, or to **ensure that** something happens, means to make certain that it happens. [FORMAL] □ We must ensure that all patients have access to high quality care.

타동사 보장하다 [격식체] □ 우리는 환자 모두가 높은 수준의 의료 서비스를 받을 수 있도록 보장해 주어야 한다.

en|tail /ɪnteɪl/ (**entails, entailing, entailed**) V-T If one thing **entails** another, it involves it or causes it. [FORMAL] □ Such a decision would entail a huge political risk in the midst of the presidential campaign.

타동사 수반하다 [격식체] □ 그러한 결정은 대선 운동 한창때에 매우 큰 정치적 위험을 수반할 것이다.

en|tan|gle /ɪntæŋgəl/ (**entangles, entangling, entangled**) ■ V-T If one thing **entangles itself with** another, the two things become caught together very tightly. □ The blade of the oar had entangled itself with the strap of her bag. ■ V-T If something **entangles** you **in** problems or difficulties, it causes you to become involved in problems or difficulties from which it is hard to escape. □ Bureaucracy can entangle ventures for months.

■ 타동사 얽히게 하다 □ 노대가 그녀의 가방 끈과 얽혀 있었다. ■ 타동사 (곤란에) 말려들게 하다 □ 관료제는 몇 달 동안 벤처 기업들을 곤란하게 할 수 있다.

en|tan|gled /ɪntæŋgəld/ ■ ADJ If something is **entangled in** something such as a rope, wire, or net, it is caught in it very firmly. □ Divers battled for hours to try to free a whale that became entangled in crab nets. ■ ADJ If you become **entangled in** problems or difficulties, you become involved in problems or difficulties from which it is hard to escape. [v-link ADJ, oft ADJ in/with n] □ This case was bound to get entangled in international politics.

■ 형용사 뒤얽힌 □ 잠수부들은 게를 잡는 그물에 걸린 고래를 풀어주기 위해서 몇 시간 동안 애를 썼다. ■ 형용사 휘말린 □ 이번 사건은 틀림없이 국제 정치에 휘말리게 될 것이었다.

en|tan|gle|ment /ɪntæŋgəlmənt/ (**entanglements**) ■ N-COUNT An **entanglement** is a complicated or difficult relationship or situation. □ ...a military and political entanglement the Government probably doesn't want. ■ N-VAR If things become entangled, you can refer to this as **entanglement**. □ Many dolphins are accidentally killed through entanglement with fishing equipment.

■ 가산명사 얽힘, 연루 □ 아마도 정부가 원치 않는 군사적, 정치적 연루 ■ 가산명사 또는 불가산명사 걸림 □ 많은 돌고래들이 어쩌다가 낚시 장비에 걸려서 죽는다.

en|ter ♦♦◇ /ɛntər/ (**enters, entering, entered**) ■ V-T/V-I When you **enter** a place such as a room or building, you go into it or come into it. [FORMAL] □ He entered the room briskly and stood near the door. ■ V-T If you **enter** an organization or institution, you start to work there or become a member of it. □ He entered the BBC as a general trainee. ■ V-T If something new **enters** your mind, you suddenly think about it. □ Dreadful doubts began to enter my mind. ■ V-T If it does not **enter** your head **to** do, think or say something, you do not think of doing that thing although you should have done. [with brd-neg] □ It never enters his mind that anyone is better than him. ■ V-T If someone or something **enters** a particular situation or period of time, they start to be in it or part of it. □ The war has entered its second month. □ A million young people enter the labour market each year. ■ V-T/V-I If you **enter** a competition, race, or examination, you officially state that you will compete or take part in it. □ I run so well I'm planning to enter some races. □ As a boy soprano he entered for many competitions, winning several gold medals. ■ V-T If you **enter** someone **for** a race or competition, you officially state that they will compete or take part in it. □ His wife Marie secretly entered him for the Championship. ■ V-T If you **enter** something in a notebook, register, or financial account, you write it down. □ Each week she meticulously entered in her notebooks all sums received. ■ V-T To **enter** information **into** a computer or database means to record it there, for example by typing it on a keyboard. □ When a baby is born, they enter that baby's name into the computer.

■ 타동사/자동사 -에 들어가다 [격식체] □ 그는 기운차게 방으로 들어가서 문 근처에 섰다. ■ 타동사 가입하다, 입사하다 □ 나는 일반 수습사원으로 비비시 방송국에 입사했다. ■ 타동사 갑자기 생각나다 □ 갑자기 무시무시한 의심이 들기 시작했다. ■ 타동사 생각이 들다 □ 그에게는 그 사람도 자신보다 더 낫다는 생각이 절대 들지 않는다. ■ 자동사 접어들다, 들어가다 □ 전쟁은 2개월째로 접어들었다. □ 백만 명의 젊은이들이 매년 노동 시장에 들어간다. ■ 타동사/자동사 참가하다 □ 나는 달리기를 아주 잘 하기 때문에 몇몇의 경주에 참가할 계획이다. □ 소년 소프라노로서 그는 많은 대회에 나가서 몇 차례 금메달을 땄다. ■ 타동사 참가시키다, 등록시키다 □ 그의 부인 마리는 비밀리에 그를 선수권 대회에 등록시켰다. ■ 타동사 기재하다, 기입하다 □ 매주 그녀는 받는 모든 총액을 자기 공책에 꼼꼼히 기입했다. ■ 타동사 입력하다 □ 아이가 태어났을 때, 그들은 아이의 이름을 그 컴퓨터에 입력한다.

Thesaurus	enter의 참조어
v.	come in; (ant.) exit, leave ■
	join; (ant.) leave ■ ■

▶**enter into** PHRASAL VERB-RECIP If you **enter into** something such as an agreement, discussion, or relationship, you become involved in it. You can also say that two people **enter into** something. [FORMAL] □ I have not entered into any financial agreements with them. □ There has been some talk recently that the United States and Canada may enter into an agreement that would allow easier access to jobs across the border.

상호 구동사 (관계를) 맺다, -에 들어가다 [격식체] □ 나는 그들과 어떠한 금전적 합의도 맺은 적이 없다. □ 미국과 캐나다가 국경을 넘어 더욱 쉽게 일자리를 구할 수 있게 하는 합의를 맺을 수도 있다는 이야기가 최근에 있었다.

en|ter|prise ♦♦◇ /ɛntərpraɪz/ (**enterprises**) ■ N-COUNT An **enterprise** is a company or business, often a small one. [BUSINESS] □ There are plenty of small industrial enterprises. ■ N-COUNT An **enterprise** is something new, difficult, or important that you do or try to do. □ Horse breeding is indeed a risky enterprise.

■ 가산명사 기업체 [경제] □ 규모가 작은 산업체들이 많이 있다. ■ 가산명사 사업 □ 말 사육은 정말로 위험 부담이 큰 사업이다. ■ 불가산명사 기업 경영 [경제] □ 그는 여전히 지역 기업 경영을 촉진시키는 일을

3 N-UNCOUNT **Enterprise** is the activity of managing companies and businesses and starting new ones. [BUSINESS] ❑ *He is still involved in voluntary work promoting local enterprise.* **4** N-UNCOUNT **Enterprise** is the ability to think of new and effective things to do, together with an eagerness to do them. [APPROVAL] ❑ *...the spirit of enterprise worthy of a free and industrious people.*

자발적으로 하고 있다. **4** 불가산명사 진취력 [마음에 듦] ❑ 자유롭고 근면한 사람들에게 걸맞은 진취적인 정신

en|ter|pris|ing /ɛntərpraɪzɪŋ/ ADJ An **enterprising** person is willing to try out new, unusual ways of doing or achieving something. ❑ *Some enterprising members found ways of reducing their expenses or raising their incomes.*

형용사 모험적인, 진취적인 ❑ 몇몇 모험적인 회원들은 그들의 비용을 줄이거나 수입을 늘릴 방법을 찾았다.

en|ter|tain ♦◇◇ /ɛntərteɪn/ (entertains, entertaining, entertained) **1** V-T/V-I If a performer, performance, or activity **entertains** you, it amuses you, interests you, or gives you pleasure. ❑ *They were entertained by top singers, dancers and celebrities.* ● en|ter|tain|ing ADJ ❑ *To generate new money the sport needs to be more entertaining.* **2** V-T/V-I If you **entertain** people, you provide food and drink for them, for example when you have invited them to your house. ❑ *I don't like to entertain guests anymore.* ● en|ter|tain|ing N-UNCOUNT ❑ *...a cosy area for entertaining and relaxing.* **3** V-T If you **entertain** an idea or suggestion, you allow yourself to consider it as possible or as worth thinking about seriously. [FORMAL] ❑ *I feel how foolish I am to entertain doubts.*

1 타동사/자동사 접대하다, 즐겁게 하다 ❑ 그들은 최고 인기 가수들과 무용가들, 그리고 유명 연예인들의 접대를 받았다. ● 즐겁게 해 주는 형용사 ❑ 새로운 자본을 창출하기 위해서는 그 스포츠가 더 재미있어져야 한다. **2** 타동사/자동사 대접하다, 환대하다 ❑ 나는 더 이상 손님 접대를 하고 싶지 않다. ● 접대 불가산명사 ❑ 접대와 휴식을 위한 편안한 영역 **3** 타동사 마음에 품다 [격식체] ❑ 나는 의심을 품는 내가 얼마나 어리석은가 하는 생각이 든다.

en|ter|tain|er /ɛntərteɪnər/ (entertainers) N-COUNT An **entertainer** is a person whose job is to entertain audiences, for example by telling jokes, singing, or dancing. ❑ *Some have called him the greatest entertainer of the twentieth century.*

가산명사 예능인, 연예인 ❑ 어떤 사람들은 그를 20세기의 가장 훌륭한 연예인이라 부른다.

en|ter|tain|ment ♦◇◇ /ɛntərteɪnmənt/ N-VAR **Entertainment** consists of performances of plays and movies, and activities such as reading and watching television, that give people pleasure. ❑ *...the world of entertainment and international stardom.* →see **radio**

가산명사 또는 불가산명사 연예 ❑ 연예계와 국제적인 스타들의 세계

en|thrall /ɪnθrɔl/ (enthralls, enthralling, enthralled) [BRIT enthral, enthrals] V-T If you **are enthralled by** something, you enjoy it and give it your complete attention and interest. ❑ *The passengers were enthralled by the scenery.*

[영국영어 enthral, enthrals] 타동사 온 마음을 사로잡다 ❑ 승객들은 풍경에 마음을 다 빼앗겼다.

en|thuse /ɪnθuz, BRIT ɪnθyuːz/ (enthuses, enthusing, enthused) **1** V-I If you **enthuse about** something, you talk about it in a way that shows how excited you are about it. ❑ *Elizabeth David enthuses about the taste, fragrance and character of Provencal cuisine.* **2** V-T If you **are enthused by** something, it makes you feel excited and enthusiastic. ❑ *I was immediately enthused.*

1 자동사 열변을 토하다 ❑ 엘리자베스 데이비드는 프로방스 음식의 맛과 향, 그리고 특성에 대해서 열변을 토한다. **2** 타동사 열광하게 만들다 ❑ 나는 바로 열광했다.

en|thu|si|asm ♦◇◇ /ɪnθuziæzəm, BRIT ɪnθyuːziæzəm/ (enthusiasms) **1** N-VAR **Enthusiasm** is great eagerness to be involved in a particular activity which you like and enjoy or which you think is important. ❑ *Their skill, enthusiasm, and running has got them in the team.* **2** N-COUNT An **enthusiasm** is an activity or subject that interests you very much and that you spend a lot of time on. ❑ *Draw him out about his current enthusiasms and future plans.*

1 가산명사 또는 불가산명사 열정 ❑ 그들의 기술, 열정, 그리고 달리기가 그들이 팀으로 뭉치게 했다. **2** 가산명사 열정 ❑ 그에게 자신이 현재 열정을 갖고 있는 분야나 미래 계획에 대해서 말하게 하십시오.

Thesaurus	enthusiasm의 참조어	
N.	energy, excitement, passion, zest; *(ant.)* apathy, indifference **1**	

en|thu|si|ast /ɪnθuziæst, BRIT ɪnθyuːziæst/ (enthusiasts) N-COUNT An **enthusiast** is a person who is very interested in a particular activity or subject and who spends a lot of time on it. ❑ *He is a great sports enthusiast.*

가산명사 열광자 ❑ 그는 열광적인 스포츠 팬이다.

en|thu|si|as|tic /ɪnθuziæstɪk, BRIT ɪnθyuːziæstɪk/ ADJ If you are **enthusiastic about** something, you show how much you like or enjoy it by the way that you behave and talk. ❑ *Tom was very enthusiastic about the place.* ● en|thu|si|as|ti|cal|ly /ɪnθuziæstɪkli, BRIT ɪnθyuːziæstɪli/ ADV ❑ *The announcement was greeted enthusiastically.*

형용사 열광적인 ❑ 탐은 그 장소에 매우 열광했다. ● 열광적으로 부사 ❑ 그 발표는 열광적으로 받아들여졌다.

en|tice /ɪntaɪs/ (entices, enticing, enticed) V-T To **entice** someone **to** go somewhere or **to** do something means to try to persuade them to go to that place or to do that thing. ❑ *They'll entice thousands of doctors to move from the cities to the rural areas by paying them better salaries.* ❑ *Retailers have tried almost everything, from cheap credit to free flights, to entice shoppers through their doors.*

타동사 유혹하다 ❑ 그들은 더 많은 급여를 지급함으로써 수천 명의 의사들을 도시에서 시골 지역으로 이동하도록 유혹할 것이다. ❑ 소매상들은 쇼핑객을 자기들 가게로 유인하기 위해 저리 신용 판매부터 무료 비행기표에 이르기까지 거의 모든 것을 시도해 보았다.

en|tic|ing /ɪntaɪsɪŋ/ ADJ Something that is **enticing** is extremely attractive and makes you want to get it or to become involved with it. ❑ *A prospective premium of about 30 percent on their initial investment is enticing.*

형용사 매혹적인 ❑ 초기 투자의 30퍼센트 정도를 예상하는 권리금은 매우 매혹적이다.

en|tire ♦◇◇ /ɪntaɪər/ ADJ You use **entire** when you want to emphasize that you are referring to the whole of something, for example, the whole of a place, time, or population. [EMPHASIS] [det ADJ] ❑ *He had spent his entire life in China as a doctor.* ❑ *There are only 60 swimming pools in the entire country.*

형용사 전체의 [강조] ❑ 그는 의사로서 중국에서 일생을 보냈다. ❑ 나라 전체에 수영장이 60개밖에 없다.

Thesaurus	entire의 참조어	
ADJ.	absolute, complete, total, whole; *(ant.)* incomplete, limited, partial	

en|tire|ly ♦◇◇ /ɪntaɪərli/ **1** ADV **Entirely** means completely and not just partly. ❑ *...an entirely new approach.* ❑ *Their price depended almost entirely on their scarcity.* **2** ADV **Entirely** is also used to emphasize what you are saying. [EMPHASIS] ❑ *I agree entirely.*

1 부사 완전히 ❑ 완전히 새로운 접근 방법 ❑ 그것들의 가격은 거의 전적으로 그것의 희귀성에 달려 있다. **2** 부사 전적으로 [강조] ❑ 나는 전적으로 동의한다.

en|tire|ty /ɪntaɪərti, -taɪrɪti/ PHRASE If something is used or affected **in** its **entirety**, the whole of it is used or affected. ❑ *The peace plan has not been accepted in its entirety by all parties.*

구 전체 ❑ 그 평화 계획안이 모든 정당에 의해서 그 전부가 받아들여진 것은 아니다.

en|ti|tle ♦◇◇ /ɪntaɪtᵊl/ (entitles, entitling, entitled) **1** V-T If you **are entitled to** something, you have the right to have it or do it. ❑ *If the warranty is limited, the terms may entitle you to a replacement or refund.* ❑ *They are entitled to first class travel.* **2** V-T If the title of something such as a book, movie, or painting is, for example, "Sunrise," you can say that it **is entitled** "Sunrise." [usu passive] ❑ *...a performance entitled "United States".*

1 타동사 (자격이나 권한을) 부여하다 ❑ 보증이 제한된다면, 계약 조건에 의해서 교환이나 환불을 받을 수 있습니다. ❑ 그들은 1등석 여행을 하게 되어 있다. **2** 타동사 제목을 부여하다 ❑ '미국'이라는 제목이 붙은 공연

en|ti|tle|ment /ɪntaɪt³lmənt/ (entitlements) N-VAR An **entitlement to** something is the right to have it or do it. [FORMAL] ❑ They lose their entitlement to welfare when they start work.

가산명사 또는 불가산명사 자격 [격식체] ❑ 그들은 일을 시작하면 실업 수당을 받을 자격을 잃는다.

en|ti|ty /ɛntɪti/ (entities) N-COUNT An **entity** is something that exists separately from other things and has a clear identity of its own. [FORMAL] ❑ ...the earth as a living entity.

가산명사 실체, 존재 [격식체] ❑ 살아 있는 실재로서의 지구

en|tou|rage /ɒntʊraːʒ/ (entourages) N-COUNT A famous or important person's **entourage** is the group of assistants, servants, or other people who travel with them. ❑ Rachel was quickly whisked away by her entourage.

가산명사 수행원들 ❑ 수행원들이 레이첼을 눈 깜짝할 사이에 데려가 버렸다.

---

entrance

① NOUN USES
② VERB USE

---

① **en|trance** ♦♢♢ /ɛntrəns/ (entrances) **1** N-COUNT The **entrance to** a place is the way into it, for example a door or gate. ❑ Beside the entrance to the church, turn right. ❑ He was driven out of a side entrance with his hand covering his face. **2** N-COUNT You can refer to someone's arrival in a place as their **entrance**, especially when you think that they are trying to be noticed and admired. ❑ If she had noticed her father's entrance, she gave no indication. **3** N-COUNT When a performer makes his or her **entrance** onto the stage, he or she comes onto the stage. ❑ When he made his entrance on stage there was uproar. **4** N-UNCOUNT If you gain **entrance to** a particular place, you manage to get in there. [FORMAL] ❑ Hewitt had gained entrance to the Hall by pretending to be a heating engineer. **5** N-UNCOUNT If you gain **entrance to** a particular profession, society, or institution, you are accepted as a member of it. ❑ Entrance to universities and senior secondary schools was restricted. **6** N-SING If you make an **entrance into** a particular activity or system, you succeed in becoming involved in it. ❑ The acquisition helped BCCI make its initial entrance into the U.S. market.

1 가산명사 출입구 ❑ 교회 입구 옆에서 우회전 하세요. ❑ 그는 손으로 얼굴을 감싼 채 옆문으로 쫓겨났다. **2** 가산명사 등장 ❑ 설령 그녀가 아버지의 등장을 알고 있었어도, 그녀는 전혀 티를 내지 않았다. **3** 가산명사 (배우의) 등장 ❑ 그가 무대에 등장하자 매우 소란스러워졌다. **4** 불가산명사 들어감 [격식체] ❑ 헤위트는 난방 장치 기술자인 척하여 홀로 들어갈 수 있었다. **5** 불가산명사 입학, 입회 ❑ 대학과 중등학교에 입학하는 것은 제한되어 있었다. **6** 단수명사 진출 ❑ 그 인수로 인해 비시시아이는 미국 시장에 처음으로 진출할 수 있었다.

	Thesaurus	entrance의 참조어
N.	doorway, entry; (ant.) exit① **1**	
	appearance, approach, debut ① **2 3**	

② **en|trance** /ɪntrɑːns/ (entrances, entrancing, entranced) V-T If something or someone **entrances** you, they cause you to feel delight and wonder, often so that all your attention is taken up and you cannot think about anything else. ❑ As soon as I met Dick, he entranced me because he has a lovely voice. ● **en|tranced** ADJ [v-link ADJ, ADJ after v, ADJ n] ❑ He is entranced by the kindness of her smile.

타동사 황홀하게 하다, 도취시키다 ❑ 내가 딕을 만나자마자, 그는 사랑스러운 목소리로 나를 도취시켰다. ● 도취된 형용사 ❑ 그는 그녀의 친절한 미소에 도취되어 있다.

en|trance hall (entrance halls) N-COUNT The **entrance hall** of a large house, hotel, or other large building, is the area just inside the main door.

가산명사 현관 홀

en|trant /ɛntrənt/ (entrants) **1** N-COUNT An **entrant** is a person who has recently become a member of an institution such as a university. ❑ ...a young school entrant. **2** N-COUNT An **entrant** is a person who is taking part in a competition. ❑ All items entered for the competition must be the entrant's own work.

1 가산명사 신입생, 신입 회원 ❑ 어린 신입생 **2** 가산명사 (대회) 참가자 ❑ 대회에 출품되는 모든 품목들은 참가자가 직접 만든 것이어야 한다.

en|trench /ɪntrɛntʃ/ (entrenches, entrenching, entrenched) V-T If something such as power, a custom, or an idea is **entrenched**, it is firmly established, so that it would be difficult to change it. ❑ ...a series of measures designed to entrench democracy and the rule of law. ● **en|trenched** ADJ ❑ The recession remains deeply entrenched.

타동사 확고히 하다, 고착시키다 ❑ 민주주의를 확고히 하기 위한 일련의 조치들과 그와 관련된 법률 규칙 ● 고착된 형용사 ❑ 불경기가 여전히 고착이 심하다.

Word Link	eur ≈ one who does : amateur, chauffeur, entrepreneur

en|tre|pre|neur /ɒntrəprənɜːr, -nʊər/ (entrepreneurs) N-COUNT An **entrepreneur** is a person who sets up businesses and business deals. [BUSINESS]

가산명사 기업가 [경제]

en|tre|pre|neur|ial /ɒntrəprənɜːriəl, -nʊər-/ ADJ **Entrepreneurial** means having the qualities that are needed to succeed as an entrepreneur. [BUSINESS] ❑ ...her prodigious entrepreneurial flair.

형용사 기업가의 [경제] ❑ 그녀의 비상한 기업가로서의 수완

en|trust /ɪntrʌst/ (entrusts, entrusting, entrusted) V-T If you **entrust** something important **to** someone or **entrust** them with it, you make them responsible for looking after it or dealing with it. ❑ He entrusted his cash to a friend and business partner for investment in a series of projects. ❑ They can be entrusted to solve major national problems.

타동사 맡기다, 위탁하다 ❑ 그는 연속되는 프로젝트에 투자하기 위해서 사업 파트너인 친구에게 그의 현금을 맡겼다. ❑ 그들은 주요한 국가 문제를 해결하는 일에 위임될 수 있다.

en|try ♦♦♢ /ɛntri/ (entries) **1** N-UNCOUNT If you gain **entry to** a particular place, you are able to go in. ❑ Bill was among the first to gain entry to Buckingham Palace when it opened to the public recently. ❑ Entry to the museum is free. ● PHRASE **No Entry** is used on signs to indicate that you are not allowed to go into a particular area or go through a particular door or gate. **2** N-COUNT You can refer to someone's arrival in a place as their **entry**, especially when you think that they are trying to be noticed and admired. ❑ He made his triumphal entry into Mexico City. **3** N-UNCOUNT Someone's **entry into** a particular society or group is their joining of it. ❑ He described Britain's entry into the European Exchange Rate Mechanism as an historic move. **4** N-COUNT An **entry** in a diary, account book, computer file, or reference book is a short piece of writing in it. ❑ Violet's diary entry for April 20, 1917 records Brigit admitting to the affair. **5** N-COUNT An **entry for** a competition is a piece of work, for example a story or drawing, or the answers to a set of questions, which you complete in order to take part in the competition. ❑ The closing date for entries is December 31st. **6** N-SING Journalists sometimes use **entry** to refer to the total number of people taking part in an event or competition. For example, if a competition has an **entry of** twenty people, twenty people take part in it. ❑ Our competition has attracted a huge entry. **7** N-UNCOUNT **Entry** in a competition is the act of taking part in it. ❑ Entry to

1 불가산명사 입장 ❑ 버킹엄 궁전이 최근 일반인들에게 공개됐을 때, 빌은 맨 처음으로 거기에 입장하는 사람들 사이에 있었다. ❑ 박물관 입장은 무료이다. ● 구 입장 불가, 출입 불가 **2** 가산명사 등장 ❑ 그는 멕시코 시티로 개선하듯이 등장했다. **3** 불가산명사 가입 ❑ 그는 영국의 유럽 환율 기구 가입을 역사적인 움직임으로 묘사하였다. **4** 가산명사 기입 사항 ❑ 바이올렛의 1917년 4월 20일자 일기 내용은 브릿이 불륜을 인정했음을 적고 있다. **5** 가산명사 출전 등록 ❑ 출전 등록 마감일은 12월 31일이다. **6** 단수명사 참가자 수 ❑ 우리 시합이 엄청난 참가자를 끌어 모았다. **7** 불가산명사 참가 ❑ 이 대회 참가는 초청으로만 이뤄진다. **8** 가산명사 들어가는 길 ❑ 펠리칸 포인트 단지로 들어가는 길을 나타내는 높이 솟은 아치형 대리석 탑

this competition is by invitation only. ◼ N-COUNT The **entry to** a place is the way into it, for example a door or gate. ❑ ...the towering marble archway that marked the entry to the Pelican Point development.

entry-level ◼ ADJ **Entry-level** is used to describe basic low-cost versions of products such as cars or computers that are suitable for people who have no previous experience or knowledge of them. [BUSINESS] ❑ Several companies are offering new, entry-level models in hopes of attracting more buyers. ◼ ADJ **Entry-level** jobs are suitable for people who do not have previous experience or qualifications in a particular area of work. [BUSINESS] ❑ Many entry-level jobs were filled by school leavers.

◼ 형용사 초보자용의 [경제] ❑ 여러 회사가 더 많은 구매자를 끌기 위해서 새로운 초보자용 모델을 선보이고 있다. ◼ 형용사 초보자적인 [경제] ❑ 많은 초보급 일자리가 의무 교육을 막 마친 사람들로 채워져 있었다.

en|vel|op /ɪnvɛ̱ləp/ (envelops, enveloping, enveloped) V-T If one thing **envelops** another, it covers or surrounds it completely. ❑ That lovely, rich fragrant smell of the forest enveloped us.

타동사 에워싸다 ❑ 그렇게 사랑스럽고 향기로운 숲의 진한 향기가 우리를 에워쌌다.

en|ve|lope /ɛ̱nvəloʊp, ɒ̱n-/ (envelopes) ◼ N-COUNT An **envelope** is the rectangular paper cover in which you send a letter to someone through the mail. ◼ PHRASE If someone **pushes the envelope**, they do something to a greater degree or in a more extreme way than it has ever been done before. ❑ There's a valuable place for fashion and design that pushes the envelope a bit. →see **office**

◼ 가산명사 편지 봉투 ◼ 구 능력을 증가시키다 ❑ 능력을 향상시키고 패션과 디자인하기에 좋은 장소가 있다.

en|vi|able /ɛ̱nviəbᵊl/ ADJ You describe something such as a quality as **enviable** when someone else has it and you wish that you had it too. ❑ Japan, unlike other big economies, is in the enviable position of having a budget surplus.

형용사 부러운 ❑ 다른 경제 대국들과는 달리 일본은 예산이 남는 부러운 위치에 있다.

en|vi|ous /ɛ̱nviəs/ ADJ If you are **envious of** someone, you want something that they have. ❑ I don't think I'm envious of your success. ❑ Do I sound envious? I pity them, actually. ● en|vi|ous|ly ADV [ADV with v] ❑ "You haven't changed," I am often enviously told.

형용사 부러워하는 ❑ 나는 너의 성공이 부러운 것 같지 않다. ❑ 내가 부러워하는 것 같아? 사실 나는 그들이 불쌍해. ● 부러운 듯이 부사 ❑ "전혀 안 변했군요."라는 부러워하는 듯한 말을 나는 자주 듣는다.

en|vi|ron|ment ◆◆◇ /ɪnva̱ɪrənmənt, -va̱ɪərn-/ (environments) ◼ N-VAR Someone's **environment** is all the circumstances, people, things, and events around them that influence their life. ❑ Pupils in our schools are taught in a safe, secure environment. ❑ The moral characters of men are formed not by heredity but by environment. ◼ N-COUNT Your **environment** consists of the particular natural surroundings in which you live or exist, considered in relation to their physical characteristics or weather conditions. ❑ ...the maintenance of a safe environment for marine mammals. ◼ N-SING The **environment** is the natural world of land, sea, air, plants, and animals. ❑ ...persuading people to respect the environment. →see **pollution**

◼ 가산명사 또는 불가산명사 환경 ❑ 우리 학교 학생들은 안전한 환경에서 배운다. ❑ 사람의 도덕적 성격은 유전에 의해서가 아니라 환경에 의해서 형성된다. ◼ 가산명사 환경 ❑ 해양 동물을 위한 안전한 환경의 유지 ◼ 단수명사 자연 환경 ❑ 사람들에게 자연 환경 존중을 설득하는 것

Word Partnership   environment의 연어

ADJ.	**hostile** environment, **safe** environment, **supportive** environment, **unhealthy** environment ◼
	natural environment ◼
V.	**damage the** environment, **protect the** environment ◼

---

en|vi|ron|men|tal ◆◆◇ /ɪnva̱ɪrənmentᵊl, -va̱ɪərn-/ ◼ ADJ **Environmental** means concerned with the protection of the natural world of land, sea, air, plants, and animals. [ADJ n] ❑ Environmental groups plan to stage public protests during the conference. ● en|vi|ron|men|tal|ly ADV [ADV adj] ❑ ...the high price of environmentally friendly goods. ◼ ADJ **Environmental** means relating to or caused by the surroundings in which someone lives or something exists. [ADJ n] ❑ It protects against environmental hazards such as wind and sun.

◼ 형용사 자연 환경의 ❑ 환경 보호 단체들이 그 회의가 진행되는 중에 대중 시위를 계획하고 있다. ● 환경적으로 부사 ❑ 환경 친화적인 상품의 높은 가격 ◼ 형용사 주위 환경의 ❑ 그것은 바람과 태양과 같은 주위 환경의 위험으로부터 보호해 준다.

en|vi|ron|men|tal|ist /ɪnva̱ɪrənmentᵊlɪst, -va̱ɪərn-/ (environmentalists) N-COUNT An **environmentalist** is a person who is concerned with protecting and preserving the natural environment, for example by preventing pollution.

가산명사 환경 보호주의자

en|vis|age /ɪnvɪ̱zɪdʒ/ (envisages, envisaging, envisaged) V-T If you **envisage** something, you imagine that it is true, real, or likely to happen. ❑ He envisages the possibility of establishing direct diplomatic relations in the future. ❑ He had never envisaged spending the whole of his working life in that particular job.

타동사 (마음속으로) 그려 보다, 상상하다 ❑ 그는 앞으로 직접적인 외교 관계를 확립하는 가능성을 그려 본다. ❑ 그는 그 특정한 일에 자신이 일을 하는 모든 세월을 보내게 되리라고는 상상도 하지 못했었다.

en|vi|sion /ɪnvɪ̱ʒ³n/ (envisions, envisioning, envisioned) V-T If you **envision** something, you envisage it. [AM, also BRIT, LITERARY] ❑ In the future we envision a federation of companies.

타동사 상상하다 [미국, 영국영어, 문예체] ❑ 장차 회사들이 연합하는 것을 마음속으로 그려 본다.

en|voy /ɛ̱nvɔɪ, ɒ̱n-/ (envoys) ◼ N-COUNT An **envoy** is someone who is sent as a representative from one government or political group to another. ❑ ...Lord Levy, Tony Blair's personal envoy to the Middle East. ◼ N-COUNT An **envoy** is a diplomat in an embassy who is immediately below the ambassador in rank.

◼ 가산명사 외교 사절 ❑ 토니 블레어가 중동으로 보낸 개인 특사 레비 경 ◼ 가산명사 공사

en|vy /ɛ̱nvi/ (envies, envying, envied) ◼ N-UNCOUNT **Envy** is the feeling you have when you wish you could have the same thing or quality that someone else has. ❑ Gradually he began to acknowledge his feelings of envy toward his mother. ◼ V-T If you **envy** someone, you wish that you had the same things or qualities that they have. ❑ I don't envy the young ones who've become TV superstars and know no other world. ◼ N-SING If a thing or quality is **the envy of** someone, they wish very much that they could have or achieve it. ❑ Britain is now the envy of the world's record companies.

◼ 불가산명사 부러움 ❑ 차츰 그는 자신이 어머니에 대해 부러움을 느낀다는 것을 인정하기 시작했다. ◼ 타동사 부러워하다 ❑ 텔레비전 슈퍼스타가 되어 다른 것은 아무것도 모르는 아이들이 나는 부럽지 않다. ◼ 단수명사 선망의 대상 ❑ 영국은 이제 전 세계 레코드 회사들의 선망의 대상이다.

en|zyme /ɛ̱nzaɪm/ (enzymes) N-COUNT An **enzyme** is a chemical substance that is found in living creatures which produces changes in other substances without being changed itself. [TECHNICAL]

가산명사 효소 [과학 기술]

epic /ɛ̱pɪk/ (epics) ◼ N-COUNT An **epic** is a long book, poem, or movie, whose story extends over a long period of time or tells of great events. ❑ ...the Middle High German epic, "Nibelungenlied," written about 1200. ● ADJ **Epic** is also an adjective. ❑ ...epic narrative poems. ◼ ADJ Something that is **epic** is very large and impressive. ❑ ...Columbus's epic voyage of discovery. →see **hero**

◼ 가산명사 서사시, 서사시적 작품 ❑ 1200년경에 쓰인 중세 고지 독일어 서사시 '니벨룽겐의 노래' ● 형용사 서사시적인 ❑ 서사적 이야기체의 시들 ◼ 형용사 웅장한, 대규모의 ❑ 콜럼버스의 장대한 발견의 항해

A

B

C

D

E

F

G

H

I

J

K

L

M

N

O

P

Q

R

S

T

U

V

W

X

Y

Z

Word Link *demo ≈ people* : demo**cracy**, demo**graphic**, epi**dem**ic

epi|dem|ic /ɛpɪdɛ̱mɪk/ (**epidemics**) **1** N-COUNT If there is an **epidemic of** a particular disease somewhere, it affects a very large number of people there and spreads quickly to other areas. ❑ *A flu epidemic is sweeping through Moscow.* **2** N-COUNT If an activity that you disapprove of is increasing or spreading rapidly, you can refer to this as an **epidemic of** that activity. [DISAPPROVAL] ❑ *...an epidemic of serial killings.* →see **illness**

epi|lep|sy /ɛ̱pɪlɛpsi/ N-UNCOUNT **Epilepsy** is a brain condition which causes a person to suddenly lose consciousness and sometimes to have fits. ❑ *Gemma suffers from epilepsy.*

epi|lep|tic /ɛpɪlɛ̱ptɪk/ (**epileptics**) **1** ADJ Someone who is **epileptic** suffers from epilepsy. ❑ *He was epileptic and refused to take medication for his condition.* ● N-COUNT An **epileptic** is someone who is epileptic. ❑ *His wife is an epileptic.* **2** ADJ An **epileptic** fit is caused by epilepsy. [ADJ n] ❑ *He suffered an epileptic fit.*

epi|sode /ɛ̱pɪsoʊd/ (**episodes**) **1** N-COUNT You can refer to an event or a short period of time as an **episode** if you want to suggest that it is important or unusual, or has some particular quality. ❑ *This episode is bound to be a deep embarrassment for Washington.* **2** N-COUNT An **episode** of something such as a series on radio or television or a story in a magazine is one of the separate parts in which it is broadcast or published. ❑ *The final episode will be shown next Sunday.* →see **animation**

epit|ome /ɪpɪ̱təmi/ N-SING If you say that a person or thing is **the epitome of** something, you are emphasizing that they are the best possible example of a particular type of person or thing. [FORMAL, EMPHASIS] ❑ *Maureen was the epitome of sophistication.*

epit|omize /ɪpɪ̱təmaɪz/ (**epitomizes, epitomizing, epitomized**) [BRIT also **epitomise**] V-T If you say that something or someone **epitomizes** a particular thing, you mean that they are a perfect example of it. ❑ *Lyonnais cooking is epitomized by the so-called "bouchons."*

epoch /ɛ̱pək, BRIT i̱ːpɒk/ (**epochs**) N-COUNT If you refer to a long period of time as an **epoch**, you mean that important events or great changes took place during it. ❑ *The birth of Christ was the beginning of a major epoch of world history.*

equal ♦◇◇ /i̱ːkwəl/ (**equals, equaling, equaled**) [BRIT, sometimes AM **equalling, equalled**] **1** ADJ If two things are **equal** or if one thing is **equal to** another, they are the same in size, number, standard, or value. ❑ *Investors can borrow an amount equal to the property's purchase price.* ❑ *...in a population having equal numbers of men and women.* **2** ADJ If different groups of people have **equal** rights or are given **equal** treatment, they have the same rights or are treated the same as each other, however different they are. ❑ *We will be justly demanding equal rights at work.* ❑ *...the commitment to equal opportunities.* **3** ADJ If you say that people are **equal**, you mean that they have or should have the same rights and opportunities as each other. [v-link ADJ] ❑ *We are equal in every way.* **4** N-COUNT Someone who is your **equal** has the same ability, status, or rights as you have. ❑ *She was one of the boys, their equal.* **5** ADJ If someone is **equal to** a particular job or situation, they have the necessary ability, strength, or courage to deal successfully with it. [v-link ADJ to n] ❑ *She was determined that she would be equal to any test the corporation put to them.* **6** V-LINK If something **equals** a particular number or amount, it is the same as that amount or the equivalent of that amount. ❑ *9 percent interest less 7 percent inflation equals 2 percent.* **7** V-T To **equal** something or someone means to be as good or as great as them. ❑ *The victory equaled the team's best in history.* **8** PHRASE If you say **other things being equal** or **all things being equal** when talking about a possible situation, you mean if nothing unexpected happens or if there are no other factors which affect the situation. ❑ *It appears reasonable to assume that, other things being equal, most hostel tenants would prefer single to shared rooms.*

equal|ity /ɪkwɒ̱lɪti/ N-UNCOUNT **Equality** is the same status, rights, and responsibilities for all the members of a society, group, or family. ❑ *...equality of the sexes.*

equal|ize /i̱ːkwəlaɪz/ (**equalizes, equalizing, equalized**) [BRIT also **equalise**] **1** V-T To **equalize** a situation means to give everyone the same rights or opportunities, for example in education, wealth, or social status. ❑ *Such measures are needed to equalize wage rates between countries.* ● **equali|za|tion** /i̱ːkwəlɪzeɪ̱ʃən/ N-UNCOUNT ❑ *...the equalization of parenting responsibilities between men and women.* **2** V-I In sports such as soccer, if a player **equalizes**, he or she scores a goal that makes the scores of the two teams equal. [BRIT] ❑ *Keegan equalized with only 16 minutes remaining.*

equal|ly ♦◇◇ /i̱ːkwəli/ **1** ADV **Equally** means in sections, amounts, or spaces that are the same size as each other. ❑ *Try to get into the habit of eating at least three small meals a day, at equally spaced intervals.* **2** ADV **Equally** means to the same degree or extent. ❑ *All these techniques are equally effective.* **3** ADV **Equally** is used to introduce another comment on the same topic, which balances or contrasts with the previous comment. [ADV with cl] ❑ *Subscribers should be allowed call-blocking services, but equally, they should be able to choose whether to accept calls from blocked numbers.*

equal op|por|tu|nity em|ploy|er (**equal opportunity employers**) N-COUNT An **equal opportunity employer** is an employer who gives people the same opportunities for employment, pay, and promotion, without discrimination against anyone. [BUSINESS] ❑ *The police force is committed to being an equal opportunity employer.*

1 가산명사 유행병 ❑ 유행성 독감이 모스크바 전역을 휩쓸고 있다. **2** 가산명사 창궐 [탐탁찮음] ❑ 연쇄 살인의 창궐

불가산명사 간질 ❑ 제마는 간질을 앓고 있다.

1 형용사 간질병의 ❑ 그는 간질을 앓고 있었지만 자기 증세에 대한 약물 치료를 거부했다. ● 가산명사 간질 환자 ❑ 그의 아내는 간질 환자이다. **2** 형용사 간질병의 ❑ 그는 간질 발작을 일으켰다.

1 가산명사 일화, 사건 ❑ 이 사건은 필시 워싱턴에 상당히 난처한 일이 될 것이다. **2** 가산명사 (텔레비전 등의) 1회분 이야기 ❑ 마지막 회는 다음 일요일에 방영될 것이다.

단수명사 전형 [격식체, 강조] ❑ 모린은 세련됨의 전형이었다.

[영국영어 epitomise] 타동사 -의 전형이다 ❑ 리오네의 요리는 이른바 '부숑'이라고 불리는 것으로 대표된다.

가산명사 신기원 ❑ 예수의 탄생은 세계 역사의 주요한 신기원의 시작이었다.

[영국영어, 미국영어 가끔 equalling, equalled] **1** 형용사 동등한, 같은 ❑ 투자자는 부동산의 구매 가격과 동일한 액수를 빌릴 수 있다. ❑ 남녀의 수가 동일한 인구에서 **2** 형용사 동등한 ❑ 우리는 정당하게 직장에서 동등한 권리를 요구할 것이다. ❑ 기회 균등에 대한 헌신 **3** 형용사 평등한 ❑ 우리는 모든 면에서 평등하다. **4** 가산명사 동등한 사람 ❑ 그녀는 소년들과 동등한 일원이었다. **5** 형용사 적합한, 자질을 갖춘 ❑ 그녀는 그 기업이 부과하는 어떤 시험에라도 통과할 수 있는 자질을 갖추겠다고 결심했다. **6** 연결동사 같다, (수학) 값이 -가 되다 ❑ 9퍼센트의 이자에서 7퍼센트의 인플레를 빼면 2퍼센트이다. **7** 타동사 필적하다, 맞먹다 ❑ 그 승리는 팀 사상 최고의 승리나 다름없었다. **8** 구 다른 조건이 같다면 ❑ 다른 조건이 같다면 대부분의 호텔 투숙객들은 방을 같이 쓰기보다는 독방을 선호할 것이라고 추정하는 것은 타당할 것 같다.

불가산명사 평등 ❑ 양성 간의 평등

[영국영어 equalise] **1** 타동사 평등하게 하다, 균등하게 하다 ❑ 그러한 조치는 국가간 임금 수준을 평준화하기 위해 필요하다. ● 동등화, 균등화 불가산명사 ❑ 남녀 간 육아 책임의 균등화 **2** 자동사 (경기에서) 동점을 만들다 [영국영어] ❑ 키건이 16분밖에 안 남았을 때 동점 골을 넣었다.

1 부사 똑같이, 균등하게 ❑ 간격을 균등하게 유지하면서 하루에 적어도 세 끼의 소식을 하는 습관을 들여 보아라. **2** 부사 똑같이 ❑ 이 모든 기술들은 똑같이 효과적이다. **3** 부사 그와 마찬가지로 ❑ 가입자들은 수신 거부 서비스를 받을 수 있어야 한다. 그러나 마찬가지로 수신 거부로 등록된 번호로부터 걸려온 전화를 받을 지 여부를 선택할 수도 있어야 한다.

가산명사 기회 균등 실행 고용주 [경제] ❑ 경찰은 기회 균등을 보장하는 직장이 되려고 열심히 노력하고 있다.

equal sign (**equal signs**) N-COUNT An **equal sign** is the sign =, which is used in arithmetic to indicate that two numbers or sets of numbers are equal.

가산명사 이퀄 기호, 등호

equate /ɪkweɪt/ (**equates, equating, equated**) V-T/V-I If you **equate** one thing **with** another, or if you say that one thing **equates with** another, you believe that they are strongly connected. ❑ I'm always wary of men wearing suits, as I equate this with power and authority. ❑ The author doesn't equate liberalism and conservatism. ● **equa|tion** N-UNCOUNT ❑ The equation of gangsterism with business in general in Coppola's movie was intended to be subversive.

타동사/자동사 동등하게 간주하다, 동일시하다 ❑ 나는 항상 정장을 입은 남자를 경계한다. 왜냐하면 나는 그것을 권력과 권위를 나타내는 것으로 여기기 때문이다. ❑ 그 작가는 자유주의와 보수주의를 동일시하지 않는다. ● 동일시 불가산명사 ❑ 코폴라 영화에서 폭력 조직과 일반적인 사업을 동일시하는 것은 기존 시각을 파괴하려고 의도된 것이다.

equa|tion /ɪkweɪʒəⁿn/ (**equations**) ◼ N-COUNT An **equation** is a mathematical statement saying that two amounts or values are the same, for example 6x4=12x2. ◢ N-COUNT An **equation** is a situation in which two or more parts have to be considered together so that the whole situation can be understood or explained. ❑ The equation is simple: research breeds new products. ❑ The party fears the equation between higher spending and higher taxes.

◼ 가산명사 방정식 ◢ 가산명사 상관관계 ❑ 상관관계는 간단하다. 연구는 새로운 제품을 낳는다. ❑ 그 정당은 높은 소비와 높은 세금 사이의 상관관계를 걱정한다.

equa|tor /ɪkweɪtər/ N-SING The **equator** is an imaginary line around the middle of the earth at an equal distance from the North Pole and the South Pole.

단수명사 적도

eques|trian /ɪkwɛstriən/ ADJ **Equestrian** means connected with the activity of riding horses. ❑ ...his equestrian skills.

형용사 승마의 ❑ 그의 승마 기술

equi|lib|rium /iːkwɪlɪbriəm/ (**equilibria**) ◼ N-VAR **Equilibrium** is a balance between several different influences or aspects of a situation. [FORMAL] ❑ Stocks seesawed ever lower until prices found some new level of equilibrium. ◢ N-UNCOUNT Someone's **equilibrium** is their normal calm state of mind. ❑ I paused in the hall to take three deep breaths to restore my equilibrium.

◼ 가산명사 또는 불가산명사 평형, 균형 [격식체] ❑ 주가는 새로운 수준의 평형을 찾을 때까지 아주 낮게 오르내렸다. ◢ 불가산명사 안정, 평정 ❑ 나는 평정을 찾으려고 복도에 멈춰 서서 심호흡을 세 번 했다.

equip /ɪkwɪp/ (**equips, equipping, equipped**) ◼ V-T If you **equip** a person or thing with something, you give them the tools or equipment that are needed. ❑ They become obsessed with trying to equip their vehicles with gadgets to deal with every possible contingency. ❑ Owners of restaurants would have to equip them to admit disabled people. ◢ V-T If something **equips** you **for** a particular task or experience, it gives you the skills and attitudes you need for it, especially by educating you in a particular way. ❑ Relative poverty, however, did not prevent Martin from equipping himself with an excellent education.

◼ 타동사 장착하다, 갖추다 ❑ 그들은 차량에 모든 가능한 우발 사건에 대비한 장치를 장착하는 데 집착하게 되었다. ❑ 식당 소유주는 장애인이 들어갈 수 있도록 식당의 설비를 갖추어야 할 것이다. ◢ 타동사 갖추게 하다 ❑ 그러나 상대적 빈곤 때문에 마틴이 스스로 훌륭한 교육을 못 받게 된 것은 아니었다.

Thesaurus   equip의 참조어
---
v.   prepare, provide with, stock, supply ◼ ◢
---

equip|ment ♦♦◇ /ɪkwɪpmənt/ N-UNCOUNT **Equipment** consists of the things which are used for a particular purpose, for example a hobby or job. ❑ ...computers, electronic equipment, and machine tools.

불가산명사 장비 ❑ 컴퓨터와 전자 장비, 그리고 공구

Thesaurus   equipment의 참조어

N.   accessories, facilities, gear, machinery, supplies, tools, utensils
---

equi|table /ɛkwɪtəbᵊl/ ADJ Something that is **equitable** is fair and reasonable in a way that gives equal treatment to everyone. ❑ He has urged them to come to an equitable compromise that gives Hughes his proper due.

형용사 공평한 ❑ 그는 공평하게 타협을 하여 휴에게 적절한 몫을 나누어 주도록 그들을 독려했다.

equi|ties /ɛkwɪtiz/ N-PLURAL **Equities** are shares in a company that are owned by people who have a right to vote at the company's meetings and to receive part of the company's profits after the holders of preference shares have been paid. [BUSINESS] ❑ Investors have poured money into U.S. equities. →see also **preference shares**

복수명사 보통주 [경제] ❑ 투자자들은 미국 주식에 돈을 쏟아 부었다.

equi|ty ♦◇◇ /ɛkwɪti/ N-UNCOUNT In finance, your **equity** is the sum of your assets, for example the value of your house, once your debts have been subtracted from it. [BUSINESS] ❑ To capture his equity, Murphy must either sell or refinance. →see also **negative equity**

불가산명사 (채무를 뺀) 순자산 총액 [경제] ❑ 자기의 자산 총액을 회복하기 위해 머피는 주식을 매각해야만 한다.

equiva|lent ♦◇◇ /ɪkwɪvələnt/ (**equivalents**) ◼ N-SING If one amount or value is **the equivalent of** another, they are the same. ❑ Mr. Li's pay is the equivalent of about $80 a month. ● ADJ **Equivalent** is also an adjective. ❑ They will react with hostility to the price rises and calls for equivalent wage increases are bound to be heard. ◢ N-COUNT The **equivalent** of someone or something is a person or thing that has the same function in a different place, time, or system. ❑ ...the Red Cross emblem, and its equivalent in Muslim countries, the Red Crescent. ● ADJ **Equivalent** is also an adjective. ❑ ...a decrease of 10% in property investment compared with the equivalent period in 1991. ◢ N-SING You can use **equivalent** to emphasize the great or severe effect of something. [EMPHASIS] ❑ His party has just suffered the equivalent of a near-fatal heart attack.

◼ 단수명사 동등한 것, 등가물 ❑ 리 씨의 임금은 한 달에 약 80달러 상당액이다. ● 형용사 동등한, 등가의 ❑ 그들은 물가 상승에 적대적으로 반응할 것이고 반드시 그에 맞먹는 임금 인상을 요구해 올 것이다. ◢ 가산명사 등가물, 맞먹는 것 ❑ 적십자 상징 표시와 회교 국가에서 이에 해당하는 상징인 적신월 ● 형용사 맞먹는, 해당하는 ❑ 1991년의 해당 기간과 비교할 때 부동산 투자의 10퍼센트 감소 ◢ 단수명사 상당하는 것 [강조] ❑ 그의 당은 막 거의 치명적인 심장마비에 맞먹는 사태를 겪었다.

Thesaurus   equivalent의 참조어

N.   counterpart, match, parallel, peer, substitute ◢
ADJ.   equal, similar; (ant.) different, dissimilar ◢
---

er /ɜr/ Er is used in writing to represent the sound that people make when they hesitate, especially while they decide what to say next. ❑ People that are addicted to drugs get help from the government one way or another.

저어, 에에 (말이 막힌 때) ❑ 약물에 중독된 사람은, 에에, 정부로부터 이런 저런 방법으로 도움을 얻는다.

ER /i ɑr/ (**ERs**) N-COUNT The **ER** is the part of a hospital where people who have severe injuries or sudden illnesses are taken for emergency treatment. **ER** is an abbreviation for **emergency room**. [AM; BRIT **casualty, A & E**] ❑ ...people who come to the ER thinking they're having heart attacks.

가산명사 응급실 [미국영어; 영국영어 casualty, A & E] ❑ 심장마비를 일으켰다고 생각하고 응급실로 오는 사람들

era ♦◇◇ /ɪ́ərə/ (**eras**) N-COUNT You can refer to a period of history or a long period of time as an **era** when you want to draw attention to a particular feature or quality that it has. ❑ *...the nuclear era.* ❑ *...the Reagan-Bush era.*

가산명사 시대 ❑ 핵 시대 ❑ 레이건-부시 시대

eradicate /ɪrǽdɪkeɪt/ (**eradicates, eradicating, eradicated**) V-T To **eradicate** something means to get rid of it completely. [FORMAL] ❑ *They are already battling to eradicate illnesses such as malaria and tetanus.* ● **eradication** /ɪrǽdɪkeɪʃ°n/ N-UNCOUNT ❑ *He is seen as having made a significant contribution toward the eradication of corruption.*

타동사 근절하다, 박멸하다 [격식체] ❑ 그들은 이미 말라리아와 파상풍 같은 질병을 박멸하려고 분투 중이다. ● 근절, 박멸 불가산명사 ❑ 그는 부패 근절을 위해 상당한 기여를 해온 것으로 보인다.

erase /ɪreɪs, BRIT ɪreɪz/ (**erases, erasing, erased**) **1** V-T If you **erase** a thought or feeling, you destroy it completely so that you can no longer remember something or no longer feel a particular emotion. ❑ *They are desperate to erase the memory of that last defeat in Cardiff.* **2** V-T If you **erase** sound which has been recorded on a tape or information which has been stored in a computer, you completely remove or destroy it. ❑ *He was found by the girls in the studio tearfully erasing all the tapes he'd slaved over.* **3** V-T If you **erase** something such as writing or a mark, you remove it, usually by rubbing it with a cloth. ❑ *It was unfortunate that she had erased the message.*

1 타동사 지워 버리다, 잊어버리다 ❑ 그들은 지난번 카디프에서의 패배의 기억을 잊으려고 안간힘을 쓰고 있다. **2** 타동사 (녹음 또는 정보를) 지우다 ❑ 그가 스튜디오에서 자신이 애써 녹음한 테이프들을 눈물을 머금고 지우고 있는 것을 그 여자들이 보았다. **3** 타동사 지우다, 삭제하다 ❑ 그녀가 그 메시지를 삭제해 버린 것은 유감스런 일이었다.

eraser /ɪreɪsər, BRIT ɪreɪzər/ (**erasers**) N-COUNT An **eraser** is an object, usually a piece of rubber or plastic, which is used for removing something that has been written using a pencil or a pen. [AM, also BRIT, FORMAL]

가산명사 지우개 [미국, 영국영어, 격식체]

erect /ɪrɛkt/ (**erects, erecting, erected**) **1** V-T If people **erect** something such as a building, bridge, or barrier, they build it or create it. [FORMAL] ❑ *Opposition demonstrators have erected barricades in roads leading to the parliament building.* ❑ *The building was erected in 1900 – 1901 for the Glasgow Parish Council.* **2** V-T If you **erect** a system, a theory, or an institution, you create it. ❑ *Japanese proprietors are erecting a complex infrastructure of political influence throughout America.* **3** ADJ People or things that are **erect** are straight and upright. ❑ *Stand reasonably erect, your arms hanging naturally.*

1 타동사 세우다, 건립하다 [격식체] ❑ 반대 시위자들이 국회의사당으로 통하는 길에 바리케이드를 세워 놓았다. ❑ 그 건물은 1900 – 1901년 사이에 글라스고 지방 의회를 위해 건립되었다. **2** 타동사 수립하다, 세우다 ❑ 일본인 사업자들이 미국 전역에 정치적 영향력을 행사할 복잡한 하부 조직을 구축하고 있다. **3** 형용사 직립의, 똑바로 선 ❑ 팔은 자연스럽게 내리고 무리 없이 똑바로 서라.

erection /ɪrɛkʃ°n/ (**erections**) **1** N-COUNT If a man has an **erection**, his penis is stiff, swollen, and sticking up because he is sexually aroused. ❑ *The drug gave them erections.* **2** N-UNCOUNT The **erection of** something is the act of building it or placing it in an upright position. ❑ *...the erection of temporary fencing to protect hedges under repair.*

1 가산명사 발기 ❑ 그 약이 그들의 발기를 유발시켰다. **2** 불가산명사 건설 ❑ 복구 중인 생나무 울타리를 보호하기 위한 임시 담장 건설

erode /ɪroʊd/ (**erodes, eroding, eroded**) **1** V-T/V-I If rock or soil **erodes** or is **eroded** by the weather, sea, or wind, it cracks and breaks so that it is gradually destroyed. ❑ *By 1980, Miami beach had all but totally eroded.* **2** V-T/V-I If someone's authority, right, or confidence **erodes** or is **eroded**, it is gradually destroyed or removed. [FORMAL] ❑ *His critics say his fumbling of the issue of reform has eroded his authority.* **3** V-T/V-I If the value of something **erodes** or is **eroded** by something such as inflation or age, its value decreases. ❑ *Competition in the financial marketplace has eroded profits.* →see **beach**

1 타동사/자동사 (땅이) 침식되다 ❑ 1980년에 이르러 마이애미 해변은 거의 완전히 침식되었다. **2** 타동사/자동사 (권위가) 손상되다, 손상시키다 [격식체] ❑ 그를 비판하는 사람들은 그가 개혁 문제를 뭉기적거리는 바람에 그의 권위가 손상되었다고 말한다. **3** 타동사/자동사 (가치가) 손상되다; (가치를) 손상시키다 ❑ 금융 시장에서의 경쟁이 이윤을 잠식해 왔다.

erosion /ɪroʊʒ°n/ **1** N-UNCOUNT **Erosion** is the gradual destruction and removal of rock or soil in a particular area by rivers, the sea, or the weather. ❑ *...erosion of the river valleys.* **2** N-UNCOUNT The **erosion of** a person's authority, rights, or confidence is the gradual destruction or removal of them. ❑ *...the erosion of confidence in world financial markets.* **3** N-UNCOUNT The **erosion of** support, values, or money is a gradual decrease in its level or standard. ❑ *...the erosion of moral standards.* →see **beach**
→see Word Web: erosion

1 불가산명사 침식 ❑ 강이 흐르는 계곡의 침식 **2** 불가산명사 손상 ❑ 세계 금융 시장에서 신뢰성의 손상 **3** 불가산명사 퇴조 ❑ 도덕 수준의 퇴조

Word Link | otic ≈ affecting, causing : erotic, neurotic, patriotic

erotic /ɪrɒtɪk/ ADJ If you describe something as **erotic**, you mean that it involves sexual feelings or arouses sexual desire. ❑ *It might sound like some kind of wild fantasy, but it wasn't an erotic experience at all.*

형용사 색정적인, 성욕을 자극하는 ❑ 어쩌면 일종의 광란의 환상처럼 들릴 수도 있겠지만 그것은 전혀 색정적인 경험이 아니었다.

err /ɜr, ɛr/ (**errs, erring, erred**) **1** V-I If you **err**, you make a mistake. [FORMAL, OLD-FASHIONED] ❑ *It criticizes the main contractor for seriously erring in its original estimates.* **2** PHRASE If you **err on the side of** caution, for example, you decide to act in a cautious way, rather than take risks. ❑ *They may be wise to err on the side of caution.*

1 자동사 실수하다 [격식체, 구식어] ❑ 그것은 주 계약자가 최초의 견적에서 크게 실수한 것을 비난하고 있다. **2** 구 -에 치우치다 ❑ 그들이 조심스럽게 행동하는 것이 현명한 일일 것이다.

errand /ɛrənd/ (**errands**) **1** N-COUNT An **errand** is a short trip that you make in order to do a job for someone, for example when you go to a store to buy something for them. ❑ *She went off on some errand.* **2** PHRASE If you **run an errand for** someone, you do or get something for them, usually by making a short trip somewhere. ❑ *Run an errand for me, will you? Go find Roger for me.*

1 가산명사 심부름 ❑ 그녀는 심부름을 떠났다. **2** 구 심부름 가다 ❑ 내 심부름 좀 해 줄래? 로저 좀 찾아줘.

erratic /ɪrǽtɪk/ ADJ Something that is **erratic** does not follow a regular pattern, but happens at unexpected times or moves along in an irregular way. ❑ *Argentina's erratic inflation rate threatens to upset the plans.* ● **erratically** /ɪrǽtɪkli/ ADV ❑ *Police stopped him for driving erratically.*

형용사 변덕스러운 ❑ 아르헨티나의 변덕이 심한 인플레 때문에 그 계획을 망칠 우려가 있다. ● 제멋대로 부사 ❑ 경찰이 난폭 운전을 한다고 그를 저지했다.

Word Web | erosion

There are two main causes of **soil erosion**—water and wind. **Rainfall**, especially heavy **thunderstorms**, breaks down **dirt**. Small particles of **earth**, **sand**, and **silt** are then carried away by the water. The runoff may form **gullies** on hillsides. Heavy rain sometimes even causes a large, flat soil surface to wash away all at once. This is called sheet erosion. When the soil contains too much water, mudslides occur. Strong **currents** of **air** cause wind erosion. There are two major ways to prevent this damage. Permanent **vegetation** anchors the soil and windbreaks reduce the force of the wind.

er|ro|ne|ous /ɪrouniəs/ ADJ Beliefs, opinions, or methods that are **erroneous** are incorrect or only partly correct. □ *Some people have the erroneous notion that one can contract AIDS by giving blood.* ● er|ro|ne|ous|ly ADV [ADV with v] □ *It had been widely and erroneously reported that Armstrong had refused to give evidence.*

er|ror ♦◇◇ /ɛrər/ (errors) **1** N-VAR An **error** is something you have done which is considered to be incorrect or wrong, or which should not have been done. □ *NASA discovered a mathematical error in its calculations.* **2** PHRASE If you do something **in error** or if it happens **in error**, you do it or it happens because you have made a mistake, especially in your judgment. □ *The plane was shot down in error by a NATO missile.* **3** PHRASE If someone sees **the error of** their **ways**, they realize or admit that they have made a mistake or behaved badly. □ *I wanted an opportunity to talk some sense into him and try to make him see the error of his ways.*

Word Partnership	error의 연어
ADJ.	clerical error, common error, fatal error, human error **1**
V.	commit an error, correct an error, make an error **1**

Word Link	rupt ≈ breaking : disrupt, erupt, interrupt

erupt /ɪrʌpt/ (erupts, erupting, erupted) **1** V-I When a volcano **erupts**, it throws out a lot of hot, melted rock called lava, as well as ash and steam. □ *The volcano erupted in 1980, devastating a large area of Washington state.* ● erup|tion /ɪrʌpʃ°n/ (eruptions) N-VAR □ *...the volcanic eruption of Tambora in 1815.* **2** V-I If violence or fighting **erupts**, it suddenly begins or gets worse in an unexpected, violent way. [JOURNALISM] □ *Heavy fighting erupted there today after a two-day cease-fire.* ● erup|tion N-COUNT □ *...this sudden eruption of violence.* **3** V-I When people in a place suddenly become angry or violent, you can say that they **erupt** or that the place **erupts**. [JOURNALISM] □ *In Los Angeles, the neighborhood known as Watts erupted into riots.* **4** V-I You say that someone **erupts** when they suddenly have a change in mood, usually becoming quite noisy. □ *Then, without warning, she erupts into laughter.* ● erup|tion N-COUNT □ *...an eruption of despair.* →see **volcano**

Word Link	scal, scala ≈ ladder, stairs : escalate, escalator, scale

es|ca|late /ɛskəleɪt/ (escalates, escalating, escalated) V-T/V-I If a bad situation **escalates** or if someone or something **escalates** it, it becomes greater in size, seriousness, or intensity. [JOURNALISM] □ *Both unions and management fear the dispute could escalate.* □ *The protests escalated into five days of rioting.* ● es|ca|la|tion /ɛskəleɪʃ°n/ (escalations) N-VAR □ *The threat of nuclear escalation remains.*

es|ca|la|tor /ɛskəleɪtər/ (escalators) N-COUNT An **escalator** is a moving staircase on which people can go from one level of a building to another. □ *Take the escalator to the third floor.*

es|cape ♦♦◇ /ɪskeɪp/ (escapes, escaping, escaped) **1** V-I If you **escape from** a place, you succeed in getting away from it. [no passive] □ *A prisoner has escaped from a jail in northern England.* □ *They are reported to have escaped to the other side of the border.* **2** N-COUNT Someone's **escape** is the act of escaping from a particular place or situation. □ *The man made his escape.* **3** V-T/V-I You can say that you **escape** when you survive something such as an accident. □ *The two officers were extremely lucky to escape serious injury.* □ *The man's girlfriend managed to escape unhurt.* ● **Escape** is also a noun. □ *I hear you had a very narrow escape on the bridge.* **4** N-COUNT If something is an **escape**, it is a way of avoiding difficulties or responsibilities. □ *But for me television is an escape.* **5** ADJ You can use **escape** to describe things which allow you to avoid difficulties or problems. For example, an **escape route** is an activity or opportunity that lets you improve your situation. An **escape clause** is part of an agreement that allows you to avoid having to do something that you do not want to do. [ADJ n] □ *We all need the occasional escape route from the boring, routine aspects of our lives.* **6** V-T If something **escapes** you or **escapes** your attention, you do not know about it, do not remember it, or do not notice it. □ *It was an actor whose name escapes me for the moment.* **7** V-I When gas, liquid, or heat **escapes**, it comes out from a pipe, container, or place. □ *Leave a vent open to let some moist air escape.* **8** →see also **fire escape**

Thesaurus	escape의 참조어
V.	break out, flee, run away **1**
N.	breakout, flight, getaway **2**

Word Partnership	escape의 연어
N.	chance to escape, escape from prison **1**
	escape route **5**
V.	try to escape **1**
	manage to escape **1** **3**
	make an escape **2**

es|cap|ism /ɪskeɪpɪzəm/ N-UNCOUNT If you describe an activity or type of entertainment as **escapism**, you mean that it makes people think about pleasant things instead of the uninteresting or unpleasant aspects of their life. □ *Horoscopes are merely harmless escapism from an ever-bleaker world.*

형용사 잘못된, 그릇된 □ 어떤 사람들은 헌혈을 통해 에이즈에 감염될 수 있다는 그릇된 생각을 가지고 있다. ● 그릇되게, 사실과 다르게 부사 □ 암스트롱이 증거 제시를 거부했다고 널리 잘못 보도되었었다.

1 가산명사 또는 불가산명사 잘못, 과실 □ 나사는 그것의 계산에서 수학적 오류를 발견했다. **2** 구 실수로 □ 그 비행기는 나토군 미사일에 의해 실수로 격추되었다. **3** 구 실수를 인정하다, 실책을 인식하다 □ 나는 그가 분별력을 가질 수 있게 이야기를 해 주고 자신의 잘못을 깨닫게 해 줄 수 있었으면 했다.

1 자동사 분출하다, 폭발하다 □ 1980년에 그 화산이 폭발해서, 워싱턴 주의 광대한 지역을 쑥밭으로 만들었다. ● 분출, 폭발 가산명사 또는 불가산명사 □ 1815년의 탐보라 화산 폭발 **2** 자동사 갑자기 터지다 [언론] □ 이틀간의 휴전 끝에 오늘 거기에서 갑자기 격렬한 전투가 벌어졌다. ● 발발, 폭발 가산명사 □ 갑작스런 폭력 사태의 발발 **3** 자동사 터지다, 발발하다 [언론] □ 로스앤젤레스의 와츠라는 인근 지역에서 폭동이 터졌다. **4** 자동사 갑자기 ~하다 □ 그때 갑자기 그녀가 웃음을 터뜨린다. ● 분출 가산명사 □ 절망감의 분출

타동사/자동사 점차 확대되다, 차츰 확대시키다 [언론] □ 노사 모두 분규가 확산될 것을 우려한다. □ 항의 시위는 5일 간에 걸친 폭동으로 확대되었다. ● 확산, 확대 가산명사 또는 불가산명사 □ 핵 확산 위험은 여전히 존재한다.

가산명사 에스컬레이터 □ 에스컬레이터를 타고 3층으로 가세요.

1 자동사 탈출하다, 도주하다 □ 죄수 한 명이 영국 북부의 한 감옥에서 탈출했다. □ 그들이 국경 반대편으로 도주했다고 보도되었다. **2** 가산명사 도주, 탈출 □ 그 남자는 도주했다. **3** 타동사/자동사 피하다, 모면하다 □ 그 두 명의 장교는 아주 운 좋게 중상을 모면했다. □ 그 남자의 애인은 용케 무사히 빠져나갔다. ● 가산명사 모면, 피함 □ 나는 당신이 다리 위에서 구사일생으로 살아남았다고 들었다. **4** 가산명사 도피구 □ 그러나 내게 텔레비전은 도피 수단이다. **5** 형용사 탈출구, 면책 조항 □ 우리 모두는 때때로 우리 삶의 지루한 일상으로부터 벗어날 탈출구가 필요하다 **6** 타동사 잊혀지다, 벗어나다 □ 그게 어떤 배우였는데 그 이름이 지금 생각이 안 나네. **7** 자동사 (가스 등이) 새다, 유출되다 □ 습한 공기가 좀 빠져나가도록 배출구를 열어 두어라.

불가산명사 현실 도피 □ 별점은 단지 너무나도 황폐한 세계로부터의 무해한 현실 도피일 따름이다.

es|cap|ist /ɪskeɪpɪst/ ADJ **Escapist** ideas, activities, or types of entertainment make people think about pleasant or unlikely things instead of the uninteresting or unpleasant aspects of their life. ❑ ...*a little escapist fantasy.*

형용사 현실 도피적인 ❑ 약간 현실 도피적인 환상

es|cort (escorts, escorting, escorted)

The noun is pronounced /ɛskɔrt/. The verb is pronounced /ɪskɔrt/.

명사는 /ɛskɔrt/으로 발음되고, 동사는 /ɪskɔrt/으로 발음된다.

◼ N-COUNT An **escort** is a person who travels with someone in order to protect or guard them. ❑ *He arrived with a police escort shortly before half past nine.* ● PHRASE If someone is taken somewhere **under escort**, they are accompanied by guards, either because they have been arrested or because they need to be protected. ◨ N-COUNT An **escort** is a person who accompanies another person of the opposite sex to a social event. Sometimes people are paid to be escorts. ❑ *My sister needed an escort for a company dinner.* ◩ V-T If you **escort** someone somewhere, you accompany them there, usually in order to make sure that they leave a place or get to their destination. ❑ *I escorted him to the door.*

◼ 가산명사 호송자 ❑ 그는 호송 경찰과 9시 30분 조금 전에 도착했다. ● 구 호위 하에 ◨ 가산명사 (사교 모임의) 동반자, 파트너 ❑ 내 여동생은 회사 회식에 함께 갈 파트너가 필요했다. ◩ 타동사 바래다주다 ❑ 나는 그를 문까지 바래다주었다.

ESL /i ɛs ɛl/ **ESL** is taught to people whose native language is not English but who live in a society in which English is the main language or one of the main languages. **ESL** is an abbreviation for "English as a second language."

제2언어로서 영어

eso|ter|ic /ɛsəterɪk, BRIT iːsoʊterɪk/ ADJ If you describe something as **esoteric**, you mean it is known, understood, or appreciated by only a small number of people. [FORMAL] ❑ ...*esoteric knowledge.*

형용사 비전(秘傳)의, 소수에게만 전해지는 [격식체] ❑ 비밀리에 전해 내려오는 지식

es|pe|cial|ly ♦♦◇ /ɪspeʃⁱli/ ◼ ADV You use **especially** to emphasize that what you are saying applies to one person, thing, or area more than to any others. [EMPHASIS] [ADV with cl/group] ❑ *Millions of wild flowers color the valleys, especially in April and May.* ◨ ADV You use **especially** to emphasize a characteristic or quality. [EMPHASIS] [ADV adj/adv] ❑ *Babies lose heat much faster than adults, and are especially vulnerable to the cold in their first month.*

◼ 부사 특히 [강조] ❑ 무수한 야생화가 특히 사월과 오월에 계곡을 물들인다. ◨ 부사 특히, 유달리 [강조] ❑ 아기는 어른보다 열을 더 빨리 손실하며 생후 한 달 동안 추위에 특히 더 약하다.

Thesaurus	*especially*의 참조어
ADV.	exclusively, only, solely ◼
	particularly ◨

es|pio|nage /ɛspiənɑʒ/ N-UNCOUNT **Espionage** is the activity of finding out the political, military, or industrial secrets of your enemies or rivals by using spies. [FORMAL] ❑ *The authorities have arrested several people suspected of espionage.*

불가산명사 첩보 활동 [격식체] ❑ 당국은 첩보 활동이 의심되는 몇 사람을 체포했다.

es|pouse /ɪspaʊz/ (espouses, espousing, espoused) V-T If you **espouse** a particular policy, cause, or belief, you become very interested in it and give your support to it. [FORMAL] ❑ *She ran away with him to Mexico and espoused the revolutionary cause.*

타동사 신봉하다, 지지하다 [격식체] ❑ 그녀는 그와 함께 멕시코로 달아나서 혁명의 대의를 지지했다.

es|say /ɛseɪ/ (essays) ◼ N-COUNT An **essay** is a short piece of writing on one particular subject written by a student. ❑ *We asked Jason to write an essay about his hometown.* ◨ N-COUNT An **essay** is a short piece of writing on one particular subject that is written by a writer for publication. ❑ ...*Thomas Malthus's essay on population.*

◼ 가산명사 작문; 에세이 ❑ 우리는 제이슨에게 그의 고향에 대해 작문을 하라고 했다. ◨ 가산명사 소론 ❑ 토머스 맬더스의 인구론

es|sence /ɛsⁿs/ (essences) ◼ N-UNCOUNT The **essence of** something is its basic and most important characteristic which gives it its individual identity. ❑ *The essence of consultation is to listen to, and take account of, the views of those consulted.* ● PHRASE You use **in essence** to emphasize that you are talking about the most important or central aspect of an idea, situation, or event. [FORMAL, EMPHASIS] ❑ *Though off-puttingly complicated in detail, local taxes are in essence simple.* ● PHRASE If you say that something **is of the essence**, you mean that it is absolutely necessary in order for a particular action to be successful. [FORMAL] ❑ *Speed was of the essence in a project of this type.* ◨ N-MASS **Essence** is a very concentrated liquid that is used for flavoring food or for its smell. ❑ ...*a few drops of vanilla essence.*

◼ 불가산명사 본질, 정수 ❑ 상담의 본질은 상담을 받는 사람의 견해를 듣고 고려하는 것이다. ● 구 본질적으로 [격식체, 강조] ❑ 지방세는 세부적으로는 귀찮을 정도로 복잡하지만 본질적으로는 단순하다. ● 구 없어서는 안 될, 가장 중요한 [격식체] ❑ 이런 유형의 사업에서는 속도가 가장 중요하다. ◨ 물질명사 농축액, 에센스 ❑ 바닐라 농축액 몇 방울

es|sen|tial ♦♦◇ /ɪsenʃⁱl/ (essentials) ◼ ADJ Something that is **essential** is extremely important or absolutely necessary to a particular subject, situation, or activity. ❑ *It was absolutely essential to separate crops from the areas that animals used as pasture.* ❑ *As they must also sprint over short distances, speed is essential.* ◨ N-COUNT The **essentials** are the things that are absolutely necessary for the situation you are in or for the task you are doing. ❑ *The apartment contained the basic essentials for bachelor life.* ◩ ADJ The **essential** aspects of something are its most basic or important aspects. ❑ *Most authorities agree that play is an essential part of a child's development.* ◪ N-PLURAL The **essentials** are the most important principles, ideas, or facts of a particular subject. ❑ ...*the essentials of everyday life, such as eating and exercise.*

◼ 형용사 필수적인, 매우 중요한 ❑ 농작물을 동물 방목 지역과 분리하는 것이 매우 중요하다. ❑ 그들이 또한 단거리를 전력 질주해야 하기 때문에 속도가 매우 중요하다. ◨ 가산명사 필수 요소 ❑ 그 아파트에는 독신 생활에 필수적인 것들이 구비되어 있었다. ◩ 형용사 본질적인, 매우 중요한 ❑ 놀이가 아동 발달에 매우 중요한 부분이라는 것에 대부분의 권위자들이 동의한다. ◪ 복수명사 본질적 요소 ❑ 먹고 운동하는 것과 같은 일상생활의 본질적 요소

Word Partnership	*essential*의 연어
N.	essential **personnel**, essential **services** ◼
	essential **information**, essential **ingredients** ◼ ◩
	essential **element**, essential **function**, essential **nutrients** ◩

es|sen|tial|ly ♦◇◇ /ɪsenʃⁱli/ ◼ ADV You use **essentially** to emphasize a quality that someone or something has, and to say that it is their most important or basic quality. [FORMAL, EMPHASIS] [ADV with cl/group] ❑ *It's been believed for centuries that great writers, composers, and scientists are essentially quite different from ordinary people.* ◨ ADV You use **essentially** to indicate that what you are saying is mainly true, although some parts of it are wrong or more complicated than has been stated. [FORMAL, VAGUENESS] ❑ *His analysis of urban use of agricultural land has been proved essentially correct.*

◼ 부사 본질적으로, 본래 [격식체, 강조] ❑ 위대한 작가, 작곡가, 과학자는 보통사람과는 본질적으로 다르다고 수세기 동안 여겨져 왔다. ◨ 부사 기본적으로 [격식체, 짐작투] ❑ 도시의 농지 사용에 대한 그의 분석이 기본적으로는 옳은 것으로 판명되었다.

Word Link   stab ≈ steady : *de*stabilize, *e*stablish, *in*stability

es|tab|lish ♦♦◇ /ɪstǽblɪʃ/ (**establishes**, **establishing**, **established**) ◼ v-T If someone **establishes** something such as an organization, a type of activity, or a set of rules, they create it or introduce it in such a way that it is likely to last for a long time. ❑ *The UN has established detailed criteria for who should be allowed to vote.* ◻ v-RECIP If you **establish** contact with someone, you start to have contact with them. You can also say that two people, groups, or countries **establish** contact. [FORMAL] ❑ *We had already established contact with the museum.* ◼ v-T If you **establish that** something is true, you discover facts that show that it is definitely true. [FORMAL] ❑ *Medical tests established that she was not their own child.* ❑ *It will be essential to establish how the money is being spent.* ● **es|tab|lished** ADJ ❑ *That link is an established medical fact.* ◼ v-T If you **establish yourself**, your reputation, or a good quality that you have, you succeed in doing something, and achieve respect or a secure position as a result of this. ❑ *This is going to be the show where up-and-coming comedians will establish themselves.* ❑ *He has established himself as a pivotal figure in U.S. politics.*

Word Partnership   *establish*의 연어

N.   establish **control**, establish **independence**, establish **rules** ◼
      establish **contact**, establish **relations** ◻
      establish **credibility**, establish *someone's* **identity**, establish **a reputation** ◼

es|tab|lished /ɪstǽblɪʃt/ ADJ If you use **established** to describe something such as an organization, you mean that it is officially recognized or generally approved of because it has existed for a long time. ❑ *Their religious adherence is not to the established church.*

es|tab|lish|ment ♦◇◇ /ɪstǽblɪʃmənt/ (**establishments**) ◼ N-SING The **establishment of** an organization or system is the act of creating it or beginning it. [FORMAL] ❑ *The establishment of the regional government in 1980 did not end terrorism.* ◻ N-COUNT An **establishment** is a store, business, or organization occupying a particular building or place. [FORMAL] ❑ *...a scientific research establishment.* ◼ N-SING You refer to the people who have power and influence in the running of a country, society, or organization as **the establishment**. ❑ *Shopkeepers would once have been pillars of the Tory establishment.*

es|tate ♦♦◇ /ɪstéɪt/ (**estates**) ◼ N-COUNT An **estate** is a large area of land in the country which is owned by a person, family, or organization. ❑ *...a shooting party on Lord Wyville's estate in Yorkshire.* ◻ N-COUNT Someone's **estate** is all the money and property that they leave behind them when they die. [LEGAL] ❑ *His estate was valued at $150,000.* ◼ N-COUNT People sometimes use **estate** to refer to a housing estate or an industrial estate. [BRIT] ❑ *He used to live on the estate.* ◼ →see also **housing estate, industrial estate, real estate**

es|tate agen|cy (**estate agencies**) N-COUNT An **estate agency** is a company that sells houses and land for people. [BRIT; AM **real estate agency**]

es|tate agent (**estate agents**) N-COUNT An **estate agent** is someone who works for a company that sells houses and land for people. [BRIT; AM **Realtor, real estate agent**]

es|teem /ɪstím/ ◼ N-UNCOUNT **Esteem** is the admiration and respect that you feel toward another person. [FORMAL] ❑ *He is held in high esteem by colleagues in the construction industry.* ◻ →see also **self-esteem**

es|thet|ic /ɛsθétɪk, BRIT iːsθétɪk/ →see **aesthetic**

es|ti|mate ♦♦◇ (**estimates**, **estimating**, **estimated**)

The verb is pronounced /ɛstɪmeɪt/. The noun is pronounced /ɛstɪmɪt/.

◼ v-T If you **estimate** a quantity or value, you make an approximate judgment or calculation of it. ❑ *Try to estimate how many steps it will take to get to a close object.* ❑ *I estimated that total cost for treatment will go from $9,000 to $12,500.* ● **es|ti|mat|ed** ADJ [*a* ADJ *amount*] ❑ *There are an estimated 90,000 gangsters in the country.* ◻ N-COUNT An **estimate** is an approximate calculation of a quantity or value. ❑ *...the official estimate of the election result.* ◼ N-COUNT An **estimate** is a judgment about a person or situation which you make based on the available evidence. ❑ *I hadn't been far wrong in my estimate of his grandson's capabilities.* ◼ N-COUNT An **estimate** from someone you employ to do a job for you, such as a builder or a plumber, is a written statement of how much the job is likely to cost. ❑ *Quotes and estimates can be prepared by computer on the spot.*

Thesaurus   *estimate*의 참조어

V.   appraise, guess, judge; (*ant.*) calculate ◼
N.   appraisal, valuation ◻
      guess ◼

Word Partnership   *estimate*의 연어

ADJ.   **best** estimate, **conservative** estimate, **rough** estimate ◻
        original estimate ◻ ◼
        make an estimate ◻ ◼

◼ 타동사 실립하다; 세정하다 ❑ 유엔은 투표권을 갖게 될 사람에 대한 세부 기준을 마련했다. ◻ 상호동사 실립시키다 [격식체] ❑ 우리는 이미 박물관과 접촉한 상태였다. ◼ 타동사 확증하다 [격식체] ❑ 의학 테스트에 의해 그녀가 그들의 자녀가 아니라는 것이 확증되었다. ❑ 그 돈이 어떻게 쓰이고 있는지 확인하는 것이 매우 중요할 것이다. ● 확증된 형용사 ❑ 그러한 연관성은 확증된 의학적 사실이다. ◼ 타동사 확고히 자리 잡다 ❑ 이것은 유망한 코미디언들이 입지를 굳히는 쇼 프로그램이 될 것이다. ❑ 그는 미국 정치에서 중추적 인물로 자리 잡았다.

형용사 확립된, 기존의 ❑ 그들은 종교적으로 기존의 교회에 의존하지 않는다.

◼ 단수명사 설립 [격식체] ❑ 1980년 지방정부가 설립되었지만 테러를 종식시키지는 못했다. ◻ 가산명사 (회사 등의) 시설 [격식체] ❑ 과학 연구 시설 ◼ 단수명사 권력층 ❑ 가게 상인들이 한때는 토리당 권력층의 중심 세력이었을 것이다.

◼ 가산명사 소유지 ❑ 요크셔 소재 와이빌 경 소유지에서의 사냥 모임 ◻ 가산명사 유산 [법률] ❑ 그의 유산은 15만 달러로 평가되었다. ◼ 가산명사 (주택, 공업) 단지 [영국영어] ❑ 그는 한때 주택 단지에 살았었다.

가산명사 부동산 중개소 [영국영어; 미국영어 real estate agency]

가산명사 부동산 중개업자 [영국영어; 미국영어 Realtor, real estate agent]

◼ 불가산명사 존중, 존경 [격식체] ❑ 그는 건설 산업에서 동료들에 의해 대단히 존경받는다.

동사는 / ɛstɪmeɪt /로 발음되고, 명사는 /ɛstɪmɪt /으로 발음된다.

◼ 타동사 추정하다, 어림잡다 ❑ 가까운 물건에 도달하는 데 몇 걸음이나 가야 하겠는지 어림잡아 보아라. ❑ 치료비 총액이 9,000달러에서 12,500달러 정도일 것으로 어림잡는다. ● 추정된, 추산된 형용사 ❑ 이 나라에는 9만 명 정도로 추산되는 폭력 단원이 있다. ◻ 가산명사 추정 ❑ 선거 결과에 대한 공식 추정 ◼ 가산명사 (인물, 상황 등의) 평가 ❑ 그의 손자의 능력에 대한 나의 평가가 아주 틀린 것은 아니었다. ◼ 가산명사 견적 ❑ 견적은 즉석에서 컴퓨터로 뽑을 수 있다.

es|ti|ma|tion /ɛstɪmeɪʃ°n/ (estimations) **1** N-SING Your **estimation** of a person or situation is the opinion or impression that you have formed about them. [FORMAL] ❑ *He has gone down considerably in my estimation.* **2** N-COUNT An **estimation** is an approximate calculation of a quantity or value. ❑ *...estimations of pre-tax profits of $12.25 million.*

1 단수명사 (인물, 상황 등의) 평가 [격식체] ❑ 그에 대한 내 평가가 상당히 낮아졌다. **2** 가산명사 추정 ❑ 세전 이익 추정액 1,225만 파운드

es|tranged /ɪstreɪndʒd/ **1** ADJ An **estranged** wife or husband is no longer living with their husband or wife. [FORMAL] ❑ *...his estranged wife.* **2** ADJ If you are **estranged from** your family or friends, you have quarreled with them and are not communicating with them. [FORMAL] ❑ *Joanna, 30, spent most of her twenties virtually estranged from her father.* **3** ADJ If you describe someone as **estranged from** something such as society or their profession, you mean that they no longer seem involved in it. [FORMAL] [v-link ADJ, usu ADJ from n] ❑ *Arran became increasingly estranged from the mainstream of Hollywood.*

1 형용사 별거 중인 [격식체] ❑ 별거 중인 그의 부인 **2** 형용사 소원한 [격식체] ❑ 서른인 조안나는 10대의 대부분을 아버지와 남남이나 다름없이 보냈다. **3** 형용사 -와 멀어진 [격식체] ❑ 애런은 할리우드의 주류계층과 점점 멀어지게 되었다.

es|tu|ary /ɛstʃʊɛri, BRIT ɛstʃʊri/ (estuaries) N-COUNT; N-IN-NAMES An **estuary** is the wide part of a river where it joins the sea. ❑ *...naval manoeuvres in the Clyde estuary.*

가산명사; 이름명사 강어귀 ❑ 클라이드 강어귀에서의 해군 기동 연습

e|tailer /iteɪlər/ (etailers) also **e-tailer** N-COUNT An **etailer** is a person or company that sells products on the Internet. [COMPUTING] ❑ *This company is the biggest wine e-tailer in the UK.*

가산명사 인터넷 상거래인, 인터넷 상거래 회사 [컴퓨터] ❑ 이 회사는 영국에서 가장 큰 인터넷 상거래 와인 회사이다.

e|tailing /iteɪlɪŋ/ N-UNCOUNT **Etailing** is the business of selling products on the Internet. [COMPUTING] ❑ *Electronic retailing has predictably become known as etailing.*

불가산명사 이테일링, 인터넷 상거래 [컴퓨터] ❑ 전자 소매 거래는 예상대로 이테일링으로 알려지게 되었다.

et al. /ɛt æl, ɑl/ **et al.** is used after a name or a list of names to indicate that other people are also involved. It is used especially when referring to books or articles which were written by more than two people. ❑ *...Blough et al.*

- 외 ❑ 블라우 외

etc. ◆◇◇ /ɛt sɛtərə, sɛtrə/ **etc.** is used at the end of a list to indicate that you have mentioned only some of the items involved and have not given a full list. **etc.** is a written abbreviation for "etcetera." [BRIT also etc] ❑ *She knew all about my schoolwork, my hospital work, etc.*

기타, - 등등 [영국영어 etc] ❑ 그녀는 나의 학업, 병원 일 등등 모든 것을 알고 있었다.

etch /ɛtʃ/ (etches, etching, etched) V-T If a line or pattern **is etched into** a surface, it is cut into the surface by means of acid or a sharp tool. You can also say that a surface **is etched with** a line or pattern. ❑ *Crosses were etched into the walls.* ❑ *Windows are etched with the vehicle identification number.*

타동사 에칭 기법으로 새겨지다, 새겨지다 ❑ 벽에는 십자가들이 새겨져 있었다. ❑ 유리창에는 차량 인식 번호가 새겨져 있다.

etch|ing /ɛtʃɪŋ/ (etchings) N-COUNT An **etching** is a picture printed from a metal plate that has had a design cut into it with acid.

가산명사 부식 동판화, 에칭

eter|nal /ɪtɜrn°l/ **1** ADJ Something that is **eternal** lasts forever. ❑ *...the quest for eternal youth.* ● **eter|nal|ly** ADV ❑ *She is eternally grateful to her family for their support.* **2** ADJ If you describe something as **eternal**, you mean that it seems to last forever, often because you think it is boring or annoying. ❑ *In the background was that eternal hum.*

1 형용사 영원한 ❑ 영원한 젊음에 대한 추구 ● 영원히 부사 ❑ 그녀는 가족들의 성원에 끝없이 고마워하고 있다. **2** 형용사 끊임없는 ❑ 배경에서는 끊임없이 그 웅성거림이 들려왔다.

eter|nity /ɪtɜrnɪti/ **1** N-UNCOUNT **Eternity** is time without an end or a state of existence outside time, especially the state which some people believe they will pass into after they have died. ❑ *I have always found the thought of eternity terrifying.* **2** N-SING If you say that a situation lasted for **an eternity**, you mean that it seemed to last an extremely long time, usually because it was boring or unpleasant. ❑ *The war continued for an eternity.*

1 불가산명사 영원; 영원의 세계, 내세 ❑ 나는 영생에 대해 생각을 하면 항상 겁이 났다. **2** 단수명사 오랜 시간, 영원 ❑ 전쟁은 끝없이 계속되었다.

ethe|real /ɪθɪəriəl/ ADJ Someone or something that is **ethereal** has a delicate beauty. [FORMAL] ❑ *She's the prettiest, most ethereal romantic heroine in the movies.*

형용사 (자태가) 빼어난 [격식체] ❑ 그녀는 영화에서 가장 예쁘고, 빼어난 아름다움을 지닌 로맨스의 여주인공이다.

eth|ic /ɛθɪk/ (ethics) **1** N-PLURAL **Ethics** are moral beliefs and rules about right and wrong. ❑ *Refugee workers said such action was a violation of medical ethics.* **2** N-PLURAL Someone's **ethics** are the moral principles about right and wrong behavior which they believe in. ❑ *He told the police that he had thought honestly about the ethics of what he was doing.* **3** N-UNCOUNT **Ethics** is the study of questions about what is morally right and wrong. ❑ *...the teaching of ethics and moral philosophy.* **4** N-SING An **ethic** of a particular kind is an idea or moral belief that influences the behavior, attitudes, and philosophy of a group of people. ❑ *...the ethic of public service.*

1 복수명사 윤리 ❑ 난민 근로자들이 그런 행동은 의학 윤리에 위배된다고 말했다. **2** 복수명사 도덕, 도덕성 ❑ 그는 자신이 하고 있는 일의 도덕성에 대해 진지하게 고려해 보았다고 경찰에게 말했다. **3** 불가산명사 윤리학 ❑ 윤리학과 도덕 철학의 가르침 **4** 단수명사 윤리 ❑ 대민 서비스의 윤리

ethi|cal /ɛθɪk°l/ **1** ADJ **Ethical** means relating to beliefs about right and wrong. ❑ *...the medical, nursing and ethical issues surrounding terminally-ill people.* ● **ethi|cal|ly** /ɛθɪkli/ ADV ❑ *Attorneys are ethically and legally bound to absolute confidentiality.* **2** ADJ If you describe something as **ethical**, you mean that it is morally right or morally acceptable. ❑ *...ethical investment schemes.* ● **ethi|cal|ly** ADV [ADV after v] ❑ *Mayors want local companies to behave ethically.*

1 형용사 윤리적인 ❑ 말기 환자를 둘러싼 의료와 간호, 그리고 윤리상의 문제들 ● 윤리적으로 부사 ❑ 변호사는 윤리적으로 또 법적으로 철저하게 비밀을 지켜야 한다. **2** 형용사 도덕적인 ❑ 도덕적인 투자 계획 ● 도덕적으로 부사 ❑ 시장은 지역 회사들이 도덕적으로 행동하기를 원한다.

eth|nic ◆◇◇ /ɛθnɪk/ **1** ADJ **Ethnic** means connected with or relating to different racial or cultural groups of people. ❑ *...a survey of Britain's ethnic minorities.* ● **eth|ni|cal|ly** /ɛθnɪkli/ ADV ❑ *...a predominantly young, ethnically mixed audience.* **2** ADJ You can use **ethnic** to describe people who belong to a particular racial or cultural group but who, usually, do not live in the country where most members of that group live. [ADJ n] ❑ *There are still several million ethnic Germans in Russia.* ● **eth|ni|cal|ly** ADV [ADV adj] ❑ *...a large ethnically Albanian population.* **3** ADJ **Ethnic** clothing, music, or food is characteristic of the traditions of a particular ethnic group, and different from what is usually found in modern Western culture. ❑ *...a magnificent range of ethnic fabrics.*

1 형용사 인종의, 민족의 ❑ 영국의 소수 인종에 대한 조사 ● 인종적으로 부사 ❑ 대다수가 젊고, 다양한 인종이 섞여 있는 청중 **2** 형용사 소수 민족의 ❑ 러시아에는 아직 수백만 명의 독일계 소수 민족이 있다. ● 소수 민족적으로 부사 ❑ 많은 알바니아 소수 민족 사람들 **3** 형용사 민족 특유의 ❑ 대단히 다양하고 멋진 민족 전통 직물들

eth|nic cleans|ing N-UNCOUNT **Ethnic cleansing** is the process of using violent methods to force certain groups of people out of a particular area or country. [DISAPPROVAL] ❑ *In late May, government forces began the "ethnic cleansing" of the area around the town.*

불가산명사 인종 청소, 인종 말살 [탐탁잖음] ❑ 오월 말에 정부군이 시 주변 지역의 '인종 청소'를 시작했다.

ethos /iθɒs/ N-SING An **ethos** is the set of ideas and attitudes that is associated with a particular group of people or a particular type of activity. [FORMAL] ❑ *The whole ethos of the hotel is effortless service.*

단수명사 기풍, 정신 [격식체] ❑ 그 호텔의 전반적인 정신은 용이한 서비스이다.

etiquette /ɛtɪkɛt/ N-UNCOUNT **Etiquette** is a set of customs and rules for polite behavior, especially among a particular class of people or in a particular profession. ❏ *This was such a great breach of etiquette, he hardly knew what to do.*

불가산명사 에의범절, 에티켓 ❏ 이것이 너무도 예의에 어긋나는 일이어서 그는 어쩔 줄을 몰랐다.

EU /i yu/ N-PROPER **The EU** is an organization of European countries which have joint policies on matters such as trade, agriculture, and finance. **EU** is an abbreviation for **European Union**. ❏ *...the ten new EU members.*

고유명사 유럽연합, 'European Union'의 약자 ❏ 유럽 연합에 새로 가입한 10개 회원국

euphemism /yufəmɪzəm/ (**euphemisms**) N-COUNT A **euphemism** is a polite word or expression that is used to refer to things which people may find upsetting or embarrassing to talk about, for example sex, the human body, or death. ❏ *The term "early retirement" is nearly always a euphemism for layoffs nowadays.*

가산명사 완곡 어구, 완곡어법 ❏ 요즘에 '조기 퇴직'이라는 용어는 거의 항상 정리 해고를 완곡하게 표현하는 말이다.

euphemistic /yufəmɪstɪk/ ADJ **Euphemistic** language uses polite, pleasant, or neutral words and expressions to refer to things which people may find unpleasant, upsetting, or embarrassing to talk about, for example sex, the human body, or death. ❏ *...a euphemistic way of saying that someone has been lying.* ● **euphemistically** /yufəmɪstɪkli/ ADV [ADV with v] ❏ *...political prisons, called euphemistically "re-education camps."*

형용사 완곡한 ❏ 누가 거짓말을 해왔다는 것을 완곡하게 말하는 방식 ● 완곡하게 부사 ❏ 완곡하게 말해 '재교육 캠프'라고 하는 정치범 수용소

euphoria /yufɔriə/ N-UNCOUNT **Euphoria** is a feeling of intense happiness and excitement. ❏ *There was euphoria after the elections.*

불가산명사 행복감, 도취감 ❏ 선거 후 도취감이 있었다.

euphoric /yufɔrɪk/, BRIT yu:fɒrɪk/ ADJ If you are **euphoric**, you feel intense happiness and excitement. ❏ *The war had received euphoric support from the public.*

형용사 열광적인, 도취된 ❏ 그 전쟁은 대중들부터 열광적인 지지를 받았었다.

euro /yʊəroʊ/ (**euros**) N-COUNT The **euro** is a unit of currency that is used by the member countries of the European Union which have accepted European monetary union. ❏ *Millions of words have been written about the introduction of the euro.*

가산명사 유로 (유럽연합의 화폐 단위) ❏ 유로화 도입에 대하여는 무수히 많은 글들이 쓰였다.

Euroland /yʊəroʊlænd/ N-PROPER **Euroland** is used by journalists to refer to the countries in the European Union which have formed a monetary union using the euro as their common currency. [JOURNALISM] ❏ *Euroland is now irrevocably on the map.*

고유명사 유로랜드 (유로화를 사용하는 국가들) [언론] ❏ 유로랜드는 이제 지도상에서 지울 수 없는 뚜렷한 존재이다.

European ◆◇◇ /yʊərəpiən/ (**Europeans**) **1** ADJ **European** means belonging or relating to, or coming from Europe. ❏ *...in some other European countries.* **2** N-COUNT A **European** is a person who comes from Europe. ❏ *Three-quarters of working-age Americans work, compared with roughly 60% of Europeans.*

1 형용사 유럽의 ❏ 다른 일부 유럽 국가들에서 **2** 가산명사 유럽사람 ❏ 유럽인은 근로 연령 인구의 60퍼센트가 일을 하는데 비해, 미국인은 4분의 3이 일을 한다.

European Union N-PROPER **The European Union** is an organization of European countries which have joint policies on matters such as trade, agriculture, and finance.

고유명사 유럽 연합

euthanasia /yuθəneɪʒə/, BRIT yu:θəneɪzɪə/ N-UNCOUNT **Euthanasia** is the practice of killing someone who is very ill and will never get better in order to end their suffering, usually done at their request or with their consent. ❏ *...those in favor of voluntary euthanasia.*

불가산명사 안락사 ❏ 자유 의지에 의한 안락사에 찬성하는 사람들

Word Link vac ≈ empty : evacuate, vacant, vacate

evacuate /ɪvækyueɪt/ (**evacuates, evacuating, evacuated**) **1** V-T To **evacuate** someone means to send them to a place of safety, away from a dangerous building, town, or area. ❏ *They were planning to evacuate the seventy American officials still in the country.* ● **evacuation** /ɪvækyueɪʃⁿn/ (**evacuations**) N-VAR ❏ *...the evacuation of the sick and wounded.* ❏ *An evacuation of the city's four-million inhabitants is planned for later this week.* **2** V-T/V-I If people **evacuate** a place, they move out of it for a period of time, especially because it is dangerous. ❏ *The fire is threatening about sixty homes, and residents have evacuated the area.* ● **evacuation** (**evacuations**) N-VAR ❏ *...the mass evacuation of the Bosnian town of Srebrenica.*

1 타동사 대피시키다 ❏ 그들은 아직 그 나라에 있는 70명의 미국 관리들을 대피시킬 계획을 세우고 있었다. ● 대피 가산명사 또는 불가산명사 ❏ 병자와 부상자의 대피 ❏ 그 도시 4백만 주민의 소개가 금주 후반에 계획되어 있다. **2** 타동사/자동사 비우다, 대피하다 ❏ 불은 약 60가구 정도를 위협하고 있으며, 주민들은 그 지역에서 대피했다. ● 대피 가산명사 또는 불가산명사 ❏ 보스니아 도시 스레브레니카의 집단 대피

evacuee /ɪvækyui/ (**evacuees**) N-COUNT An **evacuee** is someone who has been sent away from a dangerous place to somewhere safe, especially during a war.

가산명사 소개된 주민, 피난민

evade /ɪveɪd/ (**evades, evading, evaded**) **1** V-T If you **evade** something, you find a way of not doing something that you really ought to do. ❏ *By his own admission, he evaded taxes as a Florida real-estate speculator.* **2** V-T If you **evade** a question or a topic, you avoid talking about it or dealing with it. ❏ *Too many companies, she says, are evading the issue.* **3** V-T If you **evade** someone or something, you move so that you can avoid meeting them or avoid being touched or hit. ❏ *She turned and gazed at the river, evading his eyes.*

1 타동사 회피하다 ❏ 그 자신의 고백에 따르면, 그는 플로리다의 부동산 투기업자로서 탈세를 했다. **2** 타동사 모면하다, 회피하다 ❏ 너무도 많은 회사들이 그 문제를 회피하고 있다고 그녀는 말한다. **3** 타동사 피하다 ❏ 그녀는 그의 눈길을 피해 돌아서서 강을 바라보았다.

evaluate /ɪvælyueɪt/ (**evaluates, evaluating, evaluated**) V-T If you **evaluate** something or someone, you consider them in order to make a judgment about them, for example about how good or bad they are. ❏ *The market situation is difficult to evaluate.* ● **evaluation** /ɪvælyueɪʃⁿn/ (**evaluations**) N-VAR ❏ *...the opinions and evaluations of college supervisors.*

타동사 평가하다 ❏ 시장 상황을 평가하기가 어렵다. ● 평가 가산명사 또는 불가산명사 ❏ 대학 지도 교수들의 의견과 평가

evaporate /ɪvæpəreɪt/ (**evaporates, evaporating, evaporated**) **1** V-T/V-I When a liquid **evaporates**, or **is evaporated**, it changes from a liquid state to a gas, because its temperature has increased. ❏ *Moisture is drawn to the surface of the fabric so that it evaporates.* ❏ *The water is evaporated by the sun.* ● **evaporation** /ɪvæpəreɪʃⁿn/ N-UNCOUNT ❏ *The soothing, cooling effect is caused by the evaporation of the sweat on the skin.* **2** V-I If a feeling, plan, or activity **evaporates**, it gradually becomes weaker and eventually disappears completely. ❏ *My anger evaporated and I wanted to cry.* →see **matter sweat**, **water**

1 타동사/자동사 증발하다, 증발되다 ❏ 수분이 증발하도록 수분을 직물의 표면으로 끌어낸다. ❏ 물은 태양에 의해 증발된다. ● 증발 불가산명사 ❏ 피부의 땀 증발은 진정 및 냉각 효과를 준다. **2** 자동사 사그라지다, 증발하다 ❏ 분노가 사그라지고 나는 울고 싶어졌다.

evasion /ɪveɪʒⁿn/ (**evasions**) **1** N-VAR **Evasion** means deliberately avoiding something that you are supposed to do or deal with. ❏ *He was arrested for tax evasion.* **2** N-VAR If you accuse someone of **evasion** when they have been asked a question, you mean that they are deliberately avoiding giving a clear direct answer. ❏ *We want straight answers. No evasions.*

1 가산명사 또는 불가산명사 회피 ❏ 그는 탈세로 체포되었다. **2** 가산명사 또는 불가산명사 얼버무림, 둘러댐 ❏ 우리는 솔직한 대답을 원합니다. 얼버무리지 마십시오.

eva|sive /ɪveɪsɪv/ **1** ADJ If you describe someone as **evasive**, you mean that they deliberately avoid giving clear direct answers to questions. ❑ *He was evasive about the circumstances of his first meeting with Stanley Dean.* ● **eva|sive|ly** ADV [ADV with v] ❑ *"Until I can speak to your husband I can't come to any conclusion about that," Millson said evasively.* **2** PHRASE If you **take evasive action**, you deliberately move away from someone or something in order to avoid meeting them or being hit by them. ❑ *At least four high-flying warplanes had to take evasive action.*

eve /iːv/ (**eves**) N-COUNT The **eve of** a particular event or occasion is the day before it, or the period of time just before it. [JOURNALISM] ❑ *...on the eve of his 27th birthday.* →see also **Christmas Eve**

---
even
---

① DISCOURSE USES
② ADJECTIVE USES
③ PHRASAL VERB USES

---

① **even** ♦♦♦ /iːvᵊn/ **1** ADV You use **even** to suggest that what comes just after or just before it in the sentence is rather surprising. ❑ *He kept calling me for years, even after he got married.* ❑ *Even dark-skinned women should use sunscreens.* **2** ADV You use **even** with comparative adjectives and adverbs to emphasize a quality that someone or something has. [EMPHASIS] [ADV compar] ❑ *It was on television that he made an even stronger impact as an interviewer.* **3** PHRASE You use **even if** or **even though** to indicate that a particular fact does not make the rest of your statement untrue. ❑ *Cynthia is not ashamed of what she does, even if she ends up doing something wrong.* **4** PHRASE You use **even so** to introduce a surprising fact which relates to what you have just said. [SPOKEN] ❑ *The bus was only half full. Even so, a young man asked Nina if the seat next to her was taken.* **5** PHRASE You use **even then** to say that something is the case in spite of what has just been stated or whatever the circumstances may be. ❑ *Peace could come only gradually, in carefully measured steps. Even then, it sounds almost impossible to achieve.*

② **even** /iːvᵊn/ →**Please look at category** ⑧ **to see if the expression you are looking for is shown under another headword.** **1** ADJ An **even** measurement or rate stays at about the same level. ❑ *How important is it to have an even temperature when you're working?* ● **even|ly** ADV ❑ *He looked at Ellen, breathing evenly in her sleep.* **2** ADJ An **even** surface is smooth and flat. ❑ *The tables are fitted with a glass top to provide an even surface.* **3** ADJ If there is an **even** distribution or division of something, each person, group, or area involved has an equal amount. ❑ *Divide the dough into 12 even pieces and shape each piece into a ball.* ● **even|ly** ADV ❑ *The meat is divided evenly and boiled in a stew.* **4** ADJ An **even** contest or competition is equally balanced between the two sides who are taking part. ❑ *It was an even game.* ● **even|ly** ADV [ADV -ed] ❑ *They must choose between two evenly matched candidates for governor.* **5** ADJ An **even** number can be divided exactly by the number two. **6** ADJ If there is an **even** chance that something will happen, it is no more likely that it will happen than it will not happen. [ADJ n] ❑ *They have a more than even chance of winning the next election.* **7** PHRASE When a company or a person running a business **breaks even**, they make neither a profit nor a loss. [BUSINESS] ❑ *The airline hopes to break even next year and return to profit the following year.* **8** to **be on an even keel** →see **keel**

③ **even** /iːvᵊn/ (**evens, evening, evened**)
▶**even out** PHRASAL VERB If something **evens out**, or if you **even** it **out**, the differences between the different parts of it are reduced. ❑ *Relative rates of house price inflation have evened out across the country.*

eve|ning ♦♦◇ /iːvnɪŋ/ (**evenings**) N-VAR The **evening** is the part of each day between the end of the afternoon and the time when you go to bed. ❑ *All he did that evening was sit around the flat.* ❑ *Supper is from 5:00 to 6:00 in the evening.*

eve|ning class (**evening classes**) N-COUNT An **evening class** is a course for adults that is taught in the evening rather than during the day. ❑ *Jackie has been learning flamenco dancing at an evening class for three years.*

event ♦♦♦ /ɪvent/ (**events**) **1** N-COUNT An **event** is something that happens, especially when it is unusual or important. You can use **events** to describe all the things that are happening in a particular situation. ❑ *...the events of Black Wednesday.* **2** N-COUNT An **event** is a planned and organized occasion, for example a social gathering or a sports match. ❑ *...major sporting events.* **3** N-COUNT An **event** is one of the races or competitions that are part of an organized occasion such as a sports match. ❑ *The main events start at 1 p.m.* **4** PHRASE You use **in the event of**, **in the event that**, and **in that event** when you are talking about a possible future situation, especially when you are planning what to do if it occurs. ❑ *The bank has agreed to give an immediate refund in the unlikely event of an error being made.* **5** PHRASE You say "**in any event**" after you have been discussing a situation, in order to indicate that what you are saying is true or possible, in spite of anything that has happened or may happen. ❑ *In any event, the bowling alley restaurant proved quite acceptable.* **6** PHRASE You say **in the event** after you have been discussing what could have happened in a particular situation, in order to indicate that you are now describing what actually did happen. [BRIT] ❑ *"Don't underestimate us," Norman Willis warned last year. There was, in the event, little danger of that.* →see **history**

Thesaurus	event의 참조어
N.	happening, occasion, occurrence **1**
	competition, contest, game, tournament **3**

---

1 형용사 회피하는, 둘러대는 ❑ 그는 스탠리 딘과 처음 만났을 당시 상황에 대해서는 말을 회피하고 있었다. ● 회피하며 부사 ❑ "내가 당신 남편에게 말할 수 있을 때까지는 그것에 대해 어떤 결론도 내릴 수 없어요."라고 밀슨이 회피조로 말했다. **2** 구 회피하다 ❑ 적어도 네 대의 전투기가 피신 조치를 취해야 했다.

가산명사 전날, 직전 [언론] ❑ 그의 스물일곱 번째 생일 전날에

1 부사 조차도, 심지어 ❑ 그는 여러 해 동안, 심지어 결혼을 한 후에도 나에게 계속 전화를 걸었다. ❑ 피부가 검은 여성들조차도 자외선 차단 로션을 사용해야 한다. **2** 부사 훨씬 [강조] ❑ 그가 회견 기자로 훨씬 더 강한 영향을 미치는 것은 바로 텔레비전에서였다. **3** 구 비록 ~한다 해도 ❑ 신시아는 설령 결국 잘못된 일을 한 것으로 결론이 나게 될지라도 지금 하는 일이 부끄럽지 않다. **4** 구 그렇기는 하나, 그래도 [구어체] ❑ 그 버스는 단지 반 정도만 차 있었다. 그래도 젊은 남자는 니나에게 옆자리에 앉아도 되는지를 물어보았다. **5** 구 그 경우에도 ❑ 평화는 단지 조금씩 그리고 아주 조심스럽고 신중하게 다가온다. 그 경우에도, 성취하기는 거의 불가능한 듯하다.

1 형용사 일정한, 한결같은 ❑ 일하고 있을 동안 일정 온도를 유지하는 것이 얼마나 중요한가? ● 고르게 부사 ❑ 그는 엘렌을 바라보았다. 그녀는 고른 숨을 쉬며 잠이 들어 있었다. **2** 형용사 평평한, 반반한 ❑ 그 탁자들은 표면이 반반하도록 유리 덮개를 끼워 놓았다. **3** 형용사 고른, 균등한 ❑ 반죽을 균등하게 12조각으로 나누어 각 조각을 동그랗게 만드세요. ● 균등하게 부사 ❑ 고기를 똑같이 나누어 스튜에 넣고 끓인다. **4** 형용사 막상막하의 ❑ 그 게임은 막상막하였다. ● 대등하게 부사 ❑ 그들은 두 명의 대등한 주지사 후보들 중에서 선택해야 한다. **5** 형용사 짝수의 **6** 형용사 (가능성이) 반반인 ❑ 그들이 다음 선거에서 승리할 가능성이 절반 이상이다. **7** 구 본전이다, 손해도 이익도 없다 [경제] ❑ 그 항공사는 내년에 본전을 하고 그 다음해에 다시 이윤을 창출하게 되기를 희망한다.

구동사 균일하게 하다 ❑ 집값 폭등의 상대적 비율이 전국적으로 균일해졌다.

가산명사 또는 불가산명사 저녁 ❑ 그날 저녁에 그가 한 일은 아파트에 앉아 있는 것뿐이다. ❑ 저녁 식사는 저녁 5시에서 6시까지이다.

가산명사 야간 수업 ❑ 잭키는 3년 동안 저녁 시간에 플라멩코 춤을 배워왔다.

1 가산명사 사건 ❑ 검은 수요일의 사건들 **2** 가산명사 행사 ❑ 주요 스포츠 행사들 **3** 가산명사 경기, 대회 ❑ 주요 경기는 오후 1시에 시작한다. **4** 구 ~하는 경우에는 ❑ 있을 수 없는 일이지만 만일 실수가 있을 경우에는 은행이 즉각 환불해주기로 동의했다. **5** 구 어쨌든 ❑ 어쨌든 볼링 레인이 깔린 식당은 상당히 환영받을 만한 것으로 입증되었다. **6** 구 그 경우에는, 긴급시로는 [영국영어] ❑ "우리를 과소평가하지 마시오."라고 노먼 윌리스가 지난해 경고했다. 그 경우에는 그런 위험이 거의 없었다.

even|tful /ɪvɛntfəl/ ADJ If you describe an event or a period of time as **eventful**, you mean that a lot of interesting, exciting, or important things have happened during it. ❏ *Her eventful life included holding senior positions in the Colonial Service.*

형용사 다채로운 ❏ 그녀의 다채로운 인생에는 콜로니얼 서비스에서 고위직을 지낸 것도 포함되어 있었다.

even|tual /ɪvɛntʃuəl/ ADJ You use **eventual** to indicate that something happens or is the case at the end of a process or period of time. [ADJ n] ❏ *There are many who believe that civil war will be the eventual outcome of the racial tension in the country.*

형용사 종국의 ❏ 그 나라에서 인종 간 긴장 때문에 종내에는 내란이 일어날 것이라고 믿는 사람들이 많다.

even|tu|al|ity /ɪvɛntʃuælɪti/ (**eventualities**) N-COUNT An **eventuality** is a possible future event or result, especially one that is unpleasant or surprising. [FORMAL] ❏ *Every eventuality is covered, from running out of gas to needing water.*

가산명사 궁극적으로 가능한 사태 [격식체] ❏ 석유 고갈부터 식수 부족까지 궁극적으로 가능한 모든 사태가 다뤄진다.

even|tu|al|ly ◆◇◇ /ɪvɛntʃuəli/ 🔟 ADV **Eventually** means in the end, especially after a lot of delays, problems, or arguments. ❏ *Eventually, the army caught up with him in Latvia.* 🔂 ADV **Eventually** means at the end of a situation or process or as the final result of it. ❏ *Eventually your child will leave home to lead her own life as a fully independent adult.*

🔟 부사 마침내 ❏ 마침내 군대가 라트비아에서 그를 따라잡았다. 🔂 부사 결국에는 ❏ 결국 당신의 아이는 집을 떠나 완전히 독립된 성인으로 자기 자신의 삶을 살아갈 것이다.

> Do not confuse **eventually** and **finally**. When something happens after a lot of delays or complications, you can say that it **eventually** happens. ❏ *Eventually they got to the hospital... I found Victoria Avenue eventually.* You can also use **eventually** to talk about what happens at the end of a series of events, often as a result of them. ❏ *Eventually, they were forced to return to Chicago.* You say that something **finally** happens after you have been waiting for it or expecting it for a long time. ❏ *Finally I went to bed... The heat of the sun finally became too much for me.* You can also use **finally** to show that something happens last in a series of events. ❏ *The sky turned red, then purple, and finally black.*

> eventually와 finally를 혼동하지 않도록 하라. 어떤 일이 많은 지연과 복잡한 문제들 뒤에 일어나면, 그 일이 마침내(eventually) 일어났다고 말할 수 있다. ❏ 마침내 그들은 병원에 도착했다... 나는 마침내 빅토리아 애비뉴를 찾았다. 또한 eventually는 일련의 사건 마지막에 흔히 그 사건들의 결과로 발생하는 것을 얘기할 때에도 쓸 수 있다. ❏ 결국, 그들은 시카고로 돌아가지 않을 수 없었다. 어떤 일이 오랫동안 기다려왔거나 기대해 온 뒤에 일어나는 경우에는, finally를 써서 그 일이 마침내 일어난다고 말한다. ❏ 드디어 나는 잠자리에 들었다... 태양의 열기가 드디어 내게 너무 심하게 되었다. 어떤 일이 일련의 사건들에서 마지막으로 일어남을 나타낼 때는 finally를 쓸 수 있다. ❏ 하늘이 붉게, 다음엔 자줏빛으로, 마지막으로 검게 변했다.

ever ◆◆◆ /ɛvər/

> **Ever** is an adverb which you use to add emphasis in negative sentences, commands, questions, and conditional structures.

🔟 ADV **Ever** means at any time. It is used in questions and negative statements. ❏ *I'm not sure I'll ever trust people again.* ❏ *Neither of us had ever skied.* 🔂 ADV You use **ever** in expressions such as **did you ever** and **have you ever** to express surprise or shock at something you have just seen, heard, or experienced, especially when you expect people to agree with you. [EMPHASIS] [in questions, ADV before v] ❏ *Have you ever seen anything like it?* 🔳 ADV You use **ever** after comparatives and superlatives to emphasize the degree to which something is true or when you are comparing a present situation with the past or the future. [EMPHASIS] ❏ *She's got a great voice and is singing better than ever.* ❏ *Japan is wealthier and more powerful than ever before.*

> ever는 부사로서 부정문, 명령문, 의문문, 조건문에서 강조를 위해 쓴다.

🔟 부사 (의문문, 부정문에서) 언제 ❏ 내가 사람들을 과연 다시 믿게 될지 확신이 들지 않는다. ❏ 우리들 중 누구도 스키를 타본 적이 없었다. 🔂 부사 일찍이 [강조] ❏ 일찍이 이와 같은 거 본 적이 있어? 🔳 부사 그 어느 때 [강조] ❏ 그녀는 목소리가 아주 좋고 노래를 그 어느 때보다 더 잘 부르고 있다. ❏ 일본은 과거 어느 때보다 더 부유하고 강력하다.

> Do not confuse **ever** and **always**. You use **ever**, for example in negative sentences, questions, and with superlatives, to talk about any time at all when referring to the past, present, or future. ❏ *No one ever came... Will I ever see France?...the nicest thing anyone's ever said to me.* If something **always** happens, it happens regularly or on every occasion. ❏ *I would always ask for the radio to be turned down... He's always been an active person.* If something is **always** the case, it is true at all times. ❏ *No matter what she did, she would always be forgiven.*

> ever와 always를 혼동하지 않도록 하라. ever는 예를 들면 부정문과 의문문에서, 또는 최상급과 함께 과거, 현재, 미래의 어떤 시간을 말할 때에나 쓴다. ❏ 아무도 오지 않았다... 내가 과연 프랑스를 보게 될까?...누가 지금까지 내게 한 말 중에서 가장 좋은 말. 어떤 일이 '항상(always)' 일어난다는 것은 그 일이 규칙적으로 또는 매번 일어남을 나타낸다. ❏ 나는 매번 라디오 소리를 줄여 달라고 부탁하곤 했다... 그는 언제나 활동적인 사람이었다. 어떤 것이 always the case라면, 그것이 언제나 사실이라는 뜻이다. ❏ 그녀는 무슨 짓을 해도 항상 용서받았다.

🔄 ADV You use **ever** to say that something happens more all the time. [ADV adj/adv] ❏ *They grew ever further apart.* 🔵 ADV You can use **ever** for emphasis after "never." [INFORMAL, EMPHASIS] [ADV before v] ❏ *I can never, ever, forgive myself.* 🔶 ADV You use **ever** in questions beginning with words such as "why," "when," and "who" when you want to emphasize your surprise or shock. [EMPHASIS] [quest ADV] ❏ *Why ever didn't you tell me?* 🔷 PHRASE If something has been the case **ever since** a particular time, it has been the case all the time from then until now. ❏ *He's been there ever since you left!* ● ADV **Ever** is also an adverb. ❏ *I simply gave in to him, and I've regretted it ever since.* 🔸 →see also **forever** 🔹 PHRASE You use the expression **all** someone **ever does** when you want to emphasize that they do the same thing all the time, and this annoys you. [EMPHASIS] ❏ *All she ever does is complain.* 🔟 PHRASE You say **as ever** in order to indicate that something or someone's behaviour is not unusual because it is like that all the time or very often. ❏ *As ever, the meals are primarily fish-based.* 🔟 **hardly ever** →see **hardly**

🔄 부사 훨씬 ❏ 그들은 훨씬 더 멀리 떨어지게 되었다. 🔵 부사 결코, 절대로 [비격식체, 강조] ❏ 나는 내 자신을 절대로, 절대로 용서할 수 없다. 🔶 부사 어째서, 도대체 [강조] ❏ 도대체 왜 나에게 말 안 했어? 🔷 구 그 후 줄곧 ❏ 그는 당신이 떠난 후로 내내 그곳에 있었다고! ● 부사 ~후, 쭉 ❏ 내가 간단히 그에게 굴복했는데 그 후로 그것을 쭉 후회해 왔다. 🔹 구 항상 하는 것 [강조] ❏ 그녀가 하는 거라곤 불평뿐이다. 🔟 구 변함없이, 어느 때와 다름없이 ❏ 어느 때와 마찬가지로, 식사는 주로 생선 중심이다.

Word Partnership	ever의 연어
ADV.	ever **again** 🔟
	better than ever, ever **more**, **more than** ever 🔳
	never ever 🔵
	hardly ever 🔟
V.	ever **forget**, ever **known**, ever **made**, ever **seen** 🔟
	have you ever 🔂
ADJ.	**best** ever 🔳

a b c d e f g h i j k l m n o p q r s t u v w x y z

ever- /ɛvər-/ COMB in ADJ You use **ever** in adjectives such as **ever-increasing** and **ever-present**, to show that something exists or continues all the time. ❑ ...the ever-increasing traffic on our roads.

복합형용사 계속 ❑ 도로에 계속 증가하는 교통량

ever|green /ɛvərgriːn/ (**evergreens**) N-COUNT An **evergreen** is a tree or bush which has green leaves all the year round. ❑ Holly, like ivy and mistletoe, is an evergreen. • ADJ **Evergreen** is also an adjective. ❑ Plant evergreen shrubs around the end of the month.

가산명사 상록수 ❑ 담쟁이덩굴과 겨우살이와 같이 호랑가시나무는 상록수이다. • 형용사 상록의 ❑ 월말쯤에 상록수 관목을 심으세요.

every ♦♦♦ /ɛvri/ **1** DET You use **every** to indicate that you are referring to all the members of a group or all the parts of something and not only some of them. ❑ Every room has a window facing the ocean. ❑ Record every expenditure you make. • ADJ **Every** is also an adjective. [poss ADJ n] ❑ His every utterance will be scrutinized. **2** DET You use **every** in order to say how often something happens or to indicate that something happens at regular intervals. ❑ We were made to attend meetings every day. ❑ A burglary occurs every three minutes in London. **3** DET You use **every** in front of a number when you are saying what proportion of people or things something happens to or applies to. ❑ Two out of every three Britons already own a video recorder. **4** DET You can use **every** before some nouns, for example "sign", "effort", "reason," and "intention" in order to emphasize what you are saying. [EMPHASIS] ❑ The Congressional Budget Office says the federal deficit shows every sign of getting larger. ❑ I think that there is every chance that you will succeed. **5** ADJ If you say that someone's **every** whim, wish, or desire will be satisfied, you are emphasizing that everything they want will happen or be provided. [EMPHASIS] [poss ADJ n] ❑ Dozens of servants had catered to his every whim.

1 한정사 모든, 개개의 ❑ 모든 방에 바다 쪽으로 창문이 있다. ❑ 지출 비용을 모두 기록하시오. • 형용사 모든 ❑ 그의 모든 발언은 정말 조사를 받을 것이다. **2** 한정사 매, -마다 ❑ 우리는 매일 회의에 참석해야 했다. ❑ 런던에서는 빈집털이 범죄가 3분마다 한 건씩 일어난다. **3** 한정사 -마다, 매 ❑ 영국인 세 명 중 두 명은 이미 비디오 레코더를 가지고 있다. **4** 한정사 모든 [강조] ❑ 의회 예산처는 연방의 적자가 점점 커지고 있다는 모든 징조가 보인다고 말한다. ❑ 나는 내가 성공할 기회가 분명히 있다고 생각한다. **5** 형용사 어떠한 [강조] ❑ 수십 명의 하인들이 그의 어떠한 변덕에도 비위를 맞춰 주었었다.

> You use **every** to refer to all the members of a group that has more than two members. ❑ He listened to every news bulletin...an equal chance for every child. You use **each** to refer to every person or thing in a group when you are thinking about them as individuals. Note that **each** can be used to refer to both members of a pair. ❑ Each apartment has two bedrooms... We each carried a suitcase. Note that **each** and **every** are only used with singular nouns.

> every는 두 명 이상의 구성원이 있는 집단의 모든 구성원을 가리킬 때 쓴다. ❑ 그는 모든 뉴스 속보에 귀를 기울였다....모든 아이들에게 동등한 기회. each는 한 집단의 모든 구성원이나 구성체를 각각 개별적인 개체로 생각하여 언급할 때에 쓴다. each는 한 쌍의 두 구성원 또는 구성체를 언급할 때에도 쓰인다는 점을 유의하라. ❑ 각 아파트에는 침실이 두 개씩 있다... 우리는 각자 여행 가방을 하나씩 들고 있었다. each와 every는 단수 명사하고만 쓰인다는 점에 유의하라.

6 PHRASE You use **every** in the expressions **every now and then**, **every now and again**, **every once in a while**, and **every so often** in order to indicate that something happens occasionally. ❑ Stir the batter every now and then to keep it from separating. **7** PHRASE If something happens **every other day** or **every second day**, for example, it happens one day, then does not happen the next day, then happens the day after that, and so on. You can also say that something happens **every third week**, **every fourth year**, and so on. ❑ I went home every other week. **8** **every bit as** good as →see bit

6 구 때때로 ❑ 반죽이 분리되지 않도록 가끔 저어 주세요. **7** 구 걸러서; 3주마다; 4년에 한번씩 ❑ 나는 2주마다 집에 갔다.

every|body ♦♦◇ /ɛvribɒdi, -bʌdi/ **Everybody** means the same as **everyone**.

모두

every|day /ɛvrideɪ/ ADJ You use **everyday** to describe something which happens or is used every day, or forms a regular and basic part of your life, so it is not especially interesting or unusual. ❑ In the course of my everyday life, I had very little contact with teenagers.

형용사 매일 ❑ 일상 생활에서 나는 십대들과 거의 접촉을 하지 않았다.

every|one ♦♦◇ /ɛvriwʌn/

> The form **everybody** is also used.

> everybody도 쓴다.

1 PRON-INDEF You use **everyone** or **everybody** to refer to all the people in a particular group. ❑ Everyone in the street was shocked when they heard the news. ❑ Not everyone thinks that the government is being particularly generous. **2** PRON-INDEF You use **everyone** or **everybody** to refer to all people. ❑ Everyone wrestles with self-doubt and feels like a failure at times. ❑ Everyone needs some free time for rest and relaxation.

1 부정(不定)대명사 모두 ❑ 거리에 있는 모든 사람들이 그 소식을 듣고 충격을 받았다. ❑ 모든 사람이 정부가 특별히 관대하다고 생각하지는 않는다. **2** 부정(不定)대명사 모든 사람 ❑ 모든 사람이 자기 불신과 싸우며 때때로 실패자처럼 느끼곤 한다. ❑ 모든 사람이 휴식과 긴장을 풀기 위한 자유 시간이 필요하다.

> Do not confuse **everyone** with **every one**. **Everyone** always refers to people. In the phrase **every one**, "one" is a pronoun that can refer to any person or thing, depending on the context. It is often followed by the word **of**. ❑ We've saved seeds from every one of our plants... Every one of them phoned me. In these examples, **every one** is a more emphatic way of saying **all**.

> everyone과 every one을 혼동하지 않도록 하라. everyone은 항상 사람을 가리킨다. 구 every one에서 one은 문맥에 따라 어떤 사람이나 사물도 가리킬 수 있는 대명사이며, 흔히 그 뒤에는 단어 of가 온다. ❑ 우리는 우리 화초 하나하나에서 씨앗을 모았다... 그들 사람 한 사람 모두가 내게 전화를 했다. 이들 예문에서 every one은 all의 의미를 더 강조해서 나타내는 말이다.

every|thing ♦♦♦ /ɛvriθɪŋ/ **1** PRON-INDEF You use **everything** to refer to all the objects, actions, activities, or facts in a particular situation. ❑ He'd gone to Seattle long after everything else in his life had changed. **2** PRON-INDEF You use **everything** to refer to all possible or likely actions, activities, or situations. ❑ "This should have been decided long before now." — "We can't think of everything." ❑ Noel and I do everything together. **3** PRON-INDEF You use **everything** to refer to a whole situation or to life in general. ❑ She says everything is going smoothly. ❑ Is everything all right? **4** PRON-INDEF If you say that someone or something is **everything**, you mean you consider them to be the most important thing in your life, or the most important thing that there is. ❑ I love him. He is everything to me. **5** PRON-INDEF If you say that someone or something has **everything**, you mean they have all the things or qualities that most people consider to be desirable. ❑ This man had everything. He had the house, the sailboat, and a full life with friends and family.

1 부정(不定)대명사 모든 것 ❑ 그는 자기 인생의 다른 모든 것이 변한 지 한참 후에 시애틀에 갔다. **2** 부정(不定)대명사 모든 것 ❑ "이것은 지금보다 오래 전에 이미 결정되었어야 한다." "우리가 모든 것을 다 생각할 수는 없다." 노엘과 나는 모든 것을 함께 한다. **3** 부정(不定)대명사 모든 것, 모두 ❑ 그녀는 모든 것이 순조롭게 진행되고 있다고 말한다. ❑ 모든 일이 다 잘 되고 있어요? **4** 부정(不定)대명사 전부 ❑ 나는 그를 사랑해. 그는 나의 전부야. **5** 부정(不定)대명사 모든 것 ❑ 그 남자는 모든 것을 갖고 있었다. 그에게는 집과 요트, 그리고 친구들과 가족과 함께 하는 다채로운 생활이 있었다.

every|where ♦◇◇ /ɛvriwɛər/ **1** ADV You use **everywhere** to refer to a whole area or to all the places in a particular area. ❑ Working people everywhere object to paying taxes. ❑ We went everywhere together. **2** ADV You use **everywhere** to refer to all the places that someone goes to. ❑ Bradley is still accustomed to traveling everywhere in style. **3** ADV You use **everywhere** to emphasize that you are talking about a large number of places, or all possible places. [EMPHASIS] ❑ I saw her

1 부사 어디에나 ❑ 어디에서든 일하는 사람들은 세금 납부에 반대한다. ❑ 우리는 어디든지 함께 갔다. **2** 부사 어디에나 ❑ 브래들리는 여전히 멋진 곳에만 어디든 여행하곤 한다. **3** 부사 곳곳에 [강조] ❑ 나는 그녀의 사진을 곳곳에서 보았다. **4** 부사 도처에 ❑ 도처에 담쟁이가 있었다.

A B C D E F G H I J K L M N O P Q R S T U V W X Y Z

picture everywhere. ◳ ADV If you say that someone or something is **everywhere**, you mean that they are present in a place in very large numbers. ❑ *There were cartons of cigarettes everywhere.*

evict /ɪvɪkt/ (evicts, evicting, evicted) V-T If someone **is evicted from** the place where they are living, they are forced to leave it, usually because they have broken a law or contract. ❑ *They were evicted from their apartment after their mother became addicted to drugs.* ❑ *In the first week, the city police evicted ten families.*

타동사 퇴거시키다 ❑ 어머니가 마약에 중독 된 후에 그들은 아파트에서 쫓겨났다. ❑ 첫째 주에 시 경찰들이 열 집을 퇴거시켰다.

evic|tion /ɪvɪkʃən/ (evictions) N-VAR **Eviction** is the act or process of officially forcing someone to leave a house or piece of land. ❑ *He was facing eviction, along with his wife and family.*

가산명사 또는 불가산명사 강제 퇴거, 쫓아냄 ❑ 그는 부인과 가족들과 함께 쫓겨날 위기에 처해 있었다.

evi|dence ♦♦◇ /ɛvɪdəns/ ◳ N-UNCOUNT **Evidence** is anything that you see, experience, read, or are told that causes you to believe that something is true or has really happened. ❑ *Ganley said he'd seen no evidence of widespread fraud.* ◳ N-UNCOUNT **Evidence** is the information which is used in a court of law to try to prove something. Evidence is obtained from documents, objects, or witnesses. [LEGAL] ❑ *The evidence against him was purely circumstantial.* ◳ PHRASE If you **give evidence** in a court of law or an official inquiry, you officially say what you know about people or events, or describe an occasion at which you were present. ❑ *The forensic scientists who carried out the original tests will be called to give evidence.* ◳ PHRASE If someone or something **is in evidence**, they are present and can be clearly seen. ❑ *Few soldiers were in evidence.* →see **trial**

◳ 불가산명사 증거 ❑ 갠리는 사기가 팽배해 있다는 어떤 증거도 본 적이 없다고 말했다. ◳ 불가산명사 증거 [법률] ❑ 그에게 불리한 증거는 순전히 정황적인 것이었다. ◳ 구 증언하다 ❑ 본래의 테스트를 실행했던 법의학자가 증언을 하도록 소환될 것이다. ◳ 구 눈에 띄다 ❑ 병사들은 거의 눈에 띄지 않았다.

Word Partnership	*evidence*의 연어
V.	**find** evidence, **gather** evidence, **present** evidence, **produce** evidence, evidence **to support** *something* ◳ ◳
ADJ.	**new** evidence, **physical** evidence, **scientific** evidence ◳ ◳

evi|dent /ɛvɪdənt/ ◳ ADJ If something is **evident**, you notice it easily and clearly. ❑ *His footprints were clearly evident in the heavy dust.* ❑ *The threat of inflation is already evident in bond prices.* ◳ ADJ You use **evident** to show that you are certain about a situation or fact and your interpretation of it. [EMPHASIS] ❑ *It was evident that she had once been a beauty.* ◳ →see also **self-evident**

◳ 형용사 뚜렷한 ❑ 두터운 먼지 속에 그의 발자국이 뚜렷이 보였다. ❑ 인플레이션의 위험이 이미 채권 가격에서 뚜렷이 나타난다. ◳ 형용사 분명한 [강조] ❑ 그녀는 한 때 미인이었음이 분명했다.

evi|dent|ly /ɛvɪdəntli, -dɛnt-/ ◳ ADV You use **evidently** to say that something is obviously true, for example because you have seen evidence of it yourself. ❑ *The man wore a bathrobe and had evidently just come from the bathroom.* ◳ ADV You use **evidently** to show that you think something is true or have been told something is true, but that you are not sure, because you do not have enough information or proof. ❑ *From childhood, he was evidently at once rebellious and precocious.* ◳ ADV You can use **evidently** to introduce a statement or opinion and to emphasize that you feel that it is true or correct. [FORMAL, EMPHASIS] [ADV with cl] ❑ *Quite evidently, it has nothing to do with social background.*

◳ 부사 명백하게, 분명하게 ❑ 그 남자는 목욕 가운을 입고 있었는데 막 욕실에서 나온 것이 분명했다. ◳ 부사 분명히 ❑ 어린 시절부터 분명히 그는 반항적이면서도 조숙했다. ◳ 부사 분명히 [격식체, 강조] ❑ 꽤 분명히 그것은 사회적 배경과 관계가 없다.

evil ♦◇◇ /iv°l/ (evils) ◳ N-UNCOUNT **Evil** is a powerful force that some people believe to exist, and which causes wicked and bad things to happen. ❑ *There's always a conflict between good and evil in his plays.* ◳ N-UNCOUNT **Evil** is used to refer to all the wicked and bad things that happen in the world. ❑ *He could not, after all, stop all the evil in the world.* ◳ N-COUNT If you refer to an **evil**, you mean a very unpleasant or harmful situation or activity. ❑ *Higher taxes may be a necessary evil.* ◳ ADJ If you describe someone as **evil**, you mean that they are very wicked by nature and take pleasure in doing things that harm other people. ❑ *...the country's most evil terrorists.* ◳ ADJ If you describe something as **evil**, you mean that you think it causes a great deal of harm to people and is morally bad. ❑ *After 1760 few Americans refrained from condemning slavery as evil.* ◳ ADJ If you describe something as **evil**, you mean that you think it is influenced by the devil. ❑ *I think this is an evil spirit at work.* ◳ PHRASE If you have two choices, but think that they are both bad, you can describe the one which is less bad as **the lesser of two evils**, or **the lesser evil**. ❑ *People voted for him as the lesser of two evils.*

◳ 불가산명사 악 ❑ 그의 희곡 작품 속에는 항상 선과 악의 대립이 있다. ◳ 불가산명사 사악한 것 ❑ 결국 그가 세상의 모든 악을 막을 수는 없는 일이었다. ◳ 가산명사 악 ❑ 더 높은 세금은 필요악일 것이다. ◳ 형용사 사악한 ❑ 그 나라에서 가장 사악한 테러리스트들 ◳ 형용사 해로운 ❑ 1760년 이후에 노예 제도가 나쁘다고 비난하지 않는 미국인은 거의 없었다. ◳ 형용사 악마 같은 ❑ 나는 이것을 악령이 하는 짓이라고 생각한다. ◳ 구 두 해악 중에서 덜한 쪽 ❑ 사람들은 둘 다 나쁘지만 그래도 그 중 덜 나쁘다고 그에게 투표를 했다.

evoc|a|tive /ɪvɒkətɪv/ ADJ If you describe something as **evocative**, you mean that it is good or interesting because it produces pleasant memories, ideas, emotions, and responses in people. [FORMAL] ❑ *Her story is sharply evocative of Italian provincial life.*

형용사 불러일으키는, 환기시키는 [격식체] ❑ 그녀의 이야기는 이탈리아의 시골 생활을 생생하게 환기시킨다.

evoke /ɪvoʊk/ (evokes, evoking, evoked) V-T To **evoke** a particular memory, idea, emotion, or response means to cause it to occur. [FORMAL] ❑ *...the scene evoking memories of those old movies.*

타동사 불러일으키다, 환기시키다 [격식체] ❑ 옛날 영화에 대한 추억을 불러일으키는 장면

evo|lu|tion /iːvəluʃᵊn, ɛv-/ (evolutions) ◳ N-UNCOUNT **Evolution** is a process of gradual change that takes place over many generations, during which species of animals, plants, or insects slowly change some of their physical characteristics. ❑ *...the evolution of plants and animals.* ◳ N-VAR **Evolution** is a process of gradual development in a particular situation or thing over a period of time. [FORMAL] ❑ *...a crucial period in the evolution of modern physics.* →see **earth**

◳ 불가산명사 진화 ❑ 동식물의 진화 ◳ 가산명사 또는 불가산명사 (점진적인) 발전 [격식체] ❑ 현대 물리학의 발전에 있어서 중요한 시기

evo|lu|tion|ary /iːvəluʃᵊneri, BRIT iːvəluːʃᵊnri/ ADJ **Evolutionary** means relating to a process of gradual change and development. ❑ *...an evolutionary process.*

형용사 진화하는 ❑ 진화 과정

evolve /ɪvɒlv/ (evolves, evolving, evolved) ◳ V-I When animals or plants **evolve**, they gradually change and develop into different forms. ❑ *The bright plumage of many male birds was thought to have evolved to attract females.* ❑ *Maize evolved from a wild grass in Mexico.* ◳ V-T/V-I If something **evolves** or you **evolve** it, it gradually develops over a period of time into something different and usually more advanced. ❑ *...a tiny airline which eventually evolved into Pakistan International Airlines.* ❑ *Popular music evolved from folk songs.* →see **earth**

◳ 자동사 진화하다 ❑ 많은 수컷 새들의 선명한 깃털은 암컷들을 유혹하기 위해 진화한 것으로 여겨진다. ❑ 옥수수는 멕시코의 야생풀에서 진화했다. ◳ 타동사/자동사 발전하다, 발전시키다 ❑ 마침내 파키스탄 국제 항공사로 발전한 아주 작은 항공사 ❑ 팝송은 포크 음악에서 발전했다.

ewe /yu/ (ewes) N-COUNT A **ewe** is an adult female sheep.

가산명사 암양

ex|ac|er|bate /ɪgzæsərbeɪt/ (exacerbates, exacerbating, exacerbated) V-T If something **exacerbates** a problem or bad situation, it makes it worse. [FORMAL]

타동사 악화시키다 [격식체] ❑ 장기적으로 지속되던 빈곤이 인종 간 불화로 더 악화되어 왔다. ●악화

a
b
c
d
e
f
g
h
i
j
k
l
m
n
o
p
q
r
s
t
u
v
w
x
y
z

❏ *Longstanding poverty has been exacerbated by racial divisions.* ● **ex|ac|er|ba|tion** /ɪgzæsərbeɪʃᵊn/ N-UNCOUNT ❏ *...the exacerbation of global problems.*

불가산명사 ❏ 지구상 문제들의 악화

ex|act ♦♦◇ /ɪgzækt/ (**exacts, exacting, exacted**) **1** ADJ **Exact** means correct in every detail. For example, an **exact** copy is the same in every detail as the thing it is copied from. ❏ *I don't remember the exact words.* ❏ *The exact number of protest calls has not been revealed.* ● **ex|act|ly** ADV ❏ *Try to locate exactly where the smells are entering the room.* ❏ *Both drugs will be exactly the same.* **2** ADJ You use **exact** before a noun to emphasize that you are referring to that particular thing and no other, especially something that has a particular significance. [EMPHASIS] [ADJ n] ❏ *I hadn't really thought about it until this exact moment.* ● **ex|act|ly** ADV [ADV n/wh] ❏ *These are exactly the people who do not vote.* **3** V-T When someone **exacts** something, they demand and obtain it from another person, especially because they are in a superior or more powerful position. [FORMAL] ❏ *Already he has exacted a written apology from the chairman of the commission.* **4** V-T If someone **exacts** revenge **on** a person, they have their revenge on them. ❏ *She uses the media to help her exact a terrible revenge.* **5** V-T If something **exacts** a high price, it has a bad effect on a person or situation. ❏ *The sheer physical effort had exacted a heavy price.* **6** →see also **exactly** **7** PHRASE You say **to be exact** to indicate that you are slightly correcting or giving more detailed information about what you have been saying. ❏ *A small number – five, to be exact – have been bad.*

1 형용사 정확한 ❏ 정확한 말은 기억하지 못하겠다. ❏ 항의 전화의 정확한 횟수는 밝혀지지 않았다. ● 정확히 부사 ❏ 그 냄새가 정확히 어디서 방으로 들어오는지를 알아내도록 하시오. ❏ 두 가지 약은 정확히 똑같을 것이다. **2** 형용사 바로 [강조] ❏ 나는 바로 이 순간까지 그것에 대해서 정말로 생각해 본 적이 없었다. ● 정확히 말해서, 틀림없이 부사 ❏ 이들이 바로 투표하지 않는 사람들이다. **3** 타동사 강요하다 [격식체] ❏ 이미 그가 위원회 회장으로부터의 사과문을 요구했다. **4** 타동사 복수를 가하다 ❏ 그녀는 가혹하게 복수를 하기 위해 대중 매체를 이용한다. **5** 타동사 요구하다, 필요로 하다 ❏ 완전히 육체적인 노력은 높은 대가를 요구했다. **7** 구 엄밀히 말해서 ❏ 작은 숫자, 정확히 말해서 다섯은 좋지 않았다.

Thesaurus   *exact*의 참조어

ADJ. accurate, clear, precise, true; (*ant.*) inaccurate, wrong **1**

Word Partnership   *exact*의 연어

N. exact **change**, exact **duplicate**, exact **number**, exact **opposite**,
exact **replica**, exact **science**, exact **words** **1**
exact **cause**, exact **location**, exact **moment** **2**
exact **revenge** **4**

---

ex|act|ing /ɪgzæktɪŋ/ ADJ You use **exacting** to describe something or someone that demands hard work and a great deal of care. ❏ *The Duke was not well enough to carry out such an exacting task.*

형용사 노력을 요하는, 매우 힘든 ❏ 그 공작은 그렇게 힘든 일을 수행할 정도로 건강하지 않았다.

ex|act|ly ♦♦◇ /ɪgzæktli/ **1** ADV You use **exactly** before an amount, number, or position to emphasize that it is no more, no less, or no different from what you are stating. [EMPHASIS] ❏ *Each corner had a guard tower, each of which was exactly ten meters in height.* **2** ADV If you say **Exactly**, you are agreeing with someone or emphasizing the truth of what they say. If you say **Not exactly**, you are telling them politely that they are wrong in part of what they are saying. [ADV as reply] ❏ *Eve nodded, almost approvingly. "Exactly."* **3** ADV You use **not exactly** to indicate that a meaning or situation is slightly different from what people think or expect. [VAGUENESS] ❏ *He's not exactly homeless, he just hangs out in this park.* **4** ADV You can use **not exactly** to show that you mean the opposite of what you are saying. [EMPHASIS] ❏ *This was not exactly what I wanted to hear.* **5** ADV You use **exactly** with a question to show that you disapprove of what the person you are talking to is doing or saying. [DISAPPROVAL] [ADV with quest] ❏ *What exactly do you mean?* **6** →see also **exact**

1 부사 정확히 [강조] ❏ 각 코너에는 높이가 정확히 10미터인 감시탑이 있었다. **2** 부사 그렇습니다, 바로 말씀대로입니다 ❏ 이브는 거의 승인하듯이 고개를 끄덕이며 말했다. "그렇습니다." **3** 부사 완전히 ~는 아니다 [짐작투] ❏ 그가 완전히 거지는 아니다. 그냥 이 공원에서 살 뿐이다. **4** 부사 결코 ~가 아니다 [강조] ❏ 이것은 결코 내가 듣고 싶어하던 말이 아니었다. **5** 부사 정확하게 [탐탁찮음] ❏ 당신이 의미하는 바가 정확히 뭡니까?

ex|ag|ger|ate /ɪgzædʒəreɪt/ (**exaggerates, exaggerating, exaggerated**) **1** V-T/V-I If you **exaggerate**, you indicate that something is, for example, worse or more important than it really is. ❏ *He thinks I'm exaggerating.* ● **ex|ag|ge|ra|tion** /ɪgzædʒəreɪʃᵊn/ (**exaggerations**) N-VAR ❏ *Like many stories about him, it smacks of exaggeration.* **2** V-T If something **exaggerates** a situation, quality, or feature, it makes the situation, quality, or feature appear greater, more obvious, or more important than it really is. ❏ *These figures exaggerate the loss of competitiveness.*

1 타동사/자동사 과장하다 ❏ 그는 내가 과장하고 있는 것으로 생각한다. ● 과장 가산명사 또는 불가산명사 ❏ 그에 대한 많은 이야기처럼, 그것에는 과장의 기미가 있다. **2** 타동사 과장되게 보여 주다 ❏ 이러한 수치들은 경쟁력 상실을 과장되게 보여 준다.

ex|ag|ger|at|ed /ɪgzædʒəreɪtɪd/ ADJ Something that is **exaggerated** is or seems larger, better, worse, or more important than it actually needs to be. ❏ *Western fears, he insists, are greatly exaggerated.*

형용사 과장된 ❏ 서방에 대한 공포는 크게 과장된 것이라고 그는 주장한다.

ex|alt|ed /ɪgzɔltɪd/ ADJ Someone or something that is at an **exalted** level is at a very high level, especially with regard to rank or importance. [FORMAL] ❏ *You must decide how to make the best use of your exalted position.*

형용사 높은, 고귀한 [격식체] ❏ 당신은 당신의 높은 지위를 어떻게 가장 잘 이용할 것인지를 결정해야 합니다.

exam /ɪgzæm/ (**exams**) **1** N-COUNT An **exam** is a formal test that you take to show your knowledge or ability in a particular subject, or to obtain a qualification. ❏ *I don't want to take any more exams.* **2** N-COUNT If you have a medical **exam**, a doctor looks at your body, feels it, or does simple tests in order to check how healthy you are. [mainly AM] ❏ *These medical exams have shown I am in perfect physical condition.*

1 가산명사 시험 ❏ 나는 더 이상 시험을 보고 싶지 않아. **2** 가산명사 검사, 진찰 [주로 미국영어] ❏ 이러한 병원 진찰들은 내가 아주 건강하다는 것을 보여 주었다.

ex|ami|na|tion ♦◇◇ /ɪgzæmɪneɪʃᵊn/ (**examinations**) **1** N-COUNT An **examination** is a formal test that you take to show your knowledge or ability in a particular subject, or to obtain a qualification. [FORMAL] ❏ *...university examination results.* →see also **examine** **2** N-COUNT If you have a medical **examination**, a doctor looks at your body, feels it, or does simple tests in order to check how healthy you are. ❏ *You must see your doctor for a thorough examination.* →see **diagnosis**

1 가산명사 시험 [격식체] ❏ 대학 시험 결과 **2** 가산명사 검사, 진찰 ❏ 의사한테 가서 꼭 정밀 검사를 받아 보셔야 합니다.

ex|am|ine ♦♦◇ /ɪgzæmɪn/ (**examines, examining, examined**) **1** V-T If you **examine** something, you look at it carefully. ❏ *He examined her passport and stamped it.* ● **ex|ami|na|tion** /ɪgzæmɪneɪʃᵊn/ (**examinations**) N-VAR ❏ *The Navy is to carry out an examination of the wreck tomorrow.* **2** V-T If a doctor **examines** you, he or she looks at your body, feels it, or does simple tests in order to check how healthy you are. ❏ *Another doctor examined her and could still find nothing wrong.* ● **ex|ami|na|tion** N-VAR ❏ *He was later discharged after an examination at Westminster Hospital.* **3** V-T If an idea, proposal, or plan **is examined**, it is

1 타동사 조사하다, 검사하다 ❏ 그가 그녀의 여권을 검사하고 도장을 찍어 주었다. ● 조사 가산명사 또는 불가산명사 ❏ 해군이 내일 난파선에 대한 조사를 수행하기로 되어 있다. **2** 타동사 진찰하다, 검사하다 ❏ 다른 의사가 그녀를 진찰했지만 여전히 잘못된 곳을 발견할 수가 없었다. ● 검사, 진찰 가산명사 또는 불가산명사 ❏ 그는 나중에 웨스트민스터 병원에서 검사를 받은 후에 퇴원하였다. **3** 타동사

considered very carefully. ❑ *The plans will be examined by EU environment ministers.* ● ex|am|i|na|tion N-VAR ❑ *The government said it was studying the implications, which "required very careful examination and consideration."* ◢ V-T If you **are examined**, you are given a formal test in order to show your knowledge of a subject. [usu passive] ❑ *...learning to cope with the pressures of being judged and examined by our teachers.*

Thesaurus	*examine*의 참조어
v.	analyze, go over, inspect, investigate, research, scrutinize ◼ ◼

ex|am|in|er /ɪgzæmɪnər/ (examiners) N-COUNT An **examiner** is a person who sets or marks an examination. ❑ *He was also an examiner and teacher at several other educational organizations.* **external examiner** →see external

ex|am|ple ◆◆◆ /ɪgzæmpᵊl/ (examples) ◼ N-COUNT An **example of** something is a particular situation, object, or person which shows that what is being claimed is true. ❑ *The doctors gave numerous examples of patients being expelled from hospital.* ◪ N-COUNT An **example of** a particular class of objects or styles is something that has many of the typical features of such a class or style, and that you consider clearly represents it. ❑ *Symphonies 103 and 104 stand as perfect examples of early symphonic construction.* ◼ PHRASE You use **for example** to introduce and emphasize something which shows that something is true. ❑ *Take, for example, the simple sentence: "The man climbed up the hill."* ◪ N-COUNT If you refer to a person or their behavior as an **example to** other people, you mean that he or she behaves in a good or correct way that other people should copy. [APPROVAL] ❑ *He is a model professional and an example to the younger lads.* ◼ PHRASE If you **follow** someone's **example**, you behave in the same way as they did in the past, or in a similar way, especially because you admire them. ❑ *Following the example set by her father, she has fulfilled her role and done her duty.* ◼ PHRASE To **make an example of** someone who has done something wrong means to punish them severely as a warning to other people not to do the same thing. ❑ *Let us at least see our courts make an example of these despicable criminals.* ◼ PHRASE If you **set an example**, you encourage or inspire people by your behavior to behave or act in a similar way. ❑ *An officer's job was to set an example.*

Thesaurus	*example*의 참조어
N.	model, representation, sample ◼ ◪
	ideal, role model, standard ◪

Word Partnership	*example*의 연어
ADJ.	**classic** example, **obvious** example, **perfect** example,
	typical example ◼ ◪
	good example ◼ ◪ ◪
V.	**give an** example ◼ ◪
	follow an example ◼

ex|as|per|ate /ɪgzæspəreɪt/ (exasperates, exasperating, exasperated) V-T If someone or something **exasperates** you, they annoy you and make you feel frustrated or upset. ❑ *The sheer futility of it all exasperates her.* ● ex|as|pe|ra|tion /ɪgzæspəreɪʃᵊn/ N-UNCOUNT ❑ *Mahoney clenched his fist in exasperation.*

ex|as|per|at|ed /ɪgzæspəreɪtɪd/ ADJ If you describe a person as **exasperated**, you mean that they are frustrated or angry because of something that is happening or something that another person is doing. ❑ *The president was clearly exasperated by the whole saga.*

Word Link	*cav ≈ hollow : cave, cavity, excavate*

ex|ca|vate /ɛkskəveɪt/ (excavates, excavating, excavated) ◼ V-T When archaeologists or other people **excavate** a piece of land, they remove earth carefully from it and look for things such as pots, bones, or buildings which are buried there, in order to discover information about the past. ❑ *A new Danish expedition is again excavating the site in annual summer digs.* ● ex|ca|va|tion /ɛkskəveɪʃᵊn/ (excavations) N-VAR ❑ *She worked on the excavation of a Norse archaeological site.* ◪ V-T To **excavate** means to dig a hole in the ground, for example in order to build there. ❑ *A contractor was hired to drain the reservoir and to excavate soil from one area for replacement with clay.* ● ex|ca|va|tion N-VAR ❑ *...the excavation of canals.*

Word Link	*ex ≈ away, from, out : exceed, exit, explode*

ex|ceed /ɪksid/ (exceeds, exceeding, exceeded) ◼ V-T If something **exceeds** a particular amount or number, it is greater or larger than that amount or number. [FORMAL] ❑ *Its research budget exceeds $700 million a year.* ◪ V-T If you **exceed** a limit or rule, you go beyond it, even though you are not supposed to or it is against the law. [FORMAL] ❑ *He accepts he was exceeding the speed limit.*

ex|ceed|ing|ly /ɪksidɪŋli/ ADV **Exceedingly** means very or very much. [OLD-FASHIONED] ❑ *We had an exceedingly good lunch.*

ex|cel /ɪksɛl/ (excels, excelling, excelled) V-I If someone **excels in** something or **excels at** it, they are very good at doing it. ❑ *Mary was a better rider than either of them and she excelled at outdoor sports.* ❑ *Academically he began to excel.*

검토되다 ❑ 그 계획은 이유(EU) 환경부 장관들에 의해서 검토될 것이다. ● 검토 가산명사 또는 불가산명사 ❑ 정부는 '매우 조심스런 검토와 고려가 요구되는'이라는 표현이 갖는 함의를 연구하고 있다고 말했다. ◢ 타동사 시험을 보다 ❑ 선생님들이 평가하고 시험을 부과하는 데서 받게 되는 압박감에 대처하는 법을 배우는 것

가산명사 시험관 ❑ 그는 또한 다른 여러 교육 기관의 시험관이자 교사였다.

◼ 가산명사 예 ❑ 의사들은 병원에서 추방되는 환자들의 수많은 예를 보여 주었다. ◪ 가산명사 표본 ❑ 교향곡 103번과 104번은 초기 교향곡 구성의 완벽한 표본을 보여 준다. ◼ 구 예를 들어 ❑ 예를 들어, "그 남자가 언덕을 올라갔다."라는 간단한 문장을 봅시다. ◪ 가산명사 모범 [마음에 듦] ❑ 그는 본보기가 되는 전문가이자 젊은이들에게 좋은 모범이다. ◼ 구 ~의 본을 뜨다 ❑ 아버지의 본을 따라서 그녀는 자기 역할을 충실히 이행했고 자신의 의무를 다했다. ◼ 구 ~을 본보기로 징계하다 ❑ 적어도 법정이 이러한 비열한 범죄자들을 본보기로 징계하는 것을 보게 해 주세요. ◼ 구 모범을 보이다 ❑ 경관의 일은 모범을 보이는 것이었다.

타동사 성나게 하다 ❑ 그 모든 것의 부질없음이 그녀를 화나게 한다. ● 격분 불가산명사 ❑ 마호니는 격분하여 주먹을 꽉 쥐었다.

형용사 화가 난 ❑ 대통령은 그 모든 이야기들에 분명히 화가 난 것 같았다.

◼ 타동사 발굴하다 ❑ 새로운 덴마크 탐험대가 연례 하계 발굴 지역에 있는 그 지점을 다시 발굴하고 있다. ● 발굴 가산명사 또는 불가산명사 ❑ 그녀는 노르웨이 고고학적 유적을 발굴하는 작업을 했다. ◪ 타동사 파내다 ❑ 저수지 물을 빼내고, 한 지역에서 흙을 파내고 진흙으로 대체하기 위해 하청업자가 고용되었다. ● 파기, 굴착 가산명사 또는 불가산명사 ❑ 운하 굴착

◼ 타동사 넘다 [격식체] ❑ 그것의 연구 예산은 일년에 7억이 넘는다. ◪ 타동사 초과하다 [격식체] ❑ 그는 제한 속도를 초과했다는 것을 인정한다.

부사 매우 [구식어] ❑ 우리는 매우 맛있는 점심을 먹었다.

자동사 뛰어나다 ❑ 메리는 그들 둘 중 누구보다도 말을 잘 탔으며 야외 스포츠에도 뛰어났다. ❑ 학술적으로 그는 탁월한 면을 보이기 시작했다.

A

Word Link   ence ≈ state, condition : depend**ence**, excell**ence**, independ**ence**

ex|cel|lence /ˈɛksələns/ N-UNCOUNT If someone or something has the quality of **excellence**, they are extremely good in some way. ❑ ...*the top U.S. award for excellence in journalism and the arts.*

불가산명사 우수 ❑ 언론과 예술 분야의 우수성에 대해 주는 미국 최고의 상

C

ex|cel|lent ♦♦◇ /ˈɛksələnt/ ◻ ADJ Something that is **excellent** is very good indeed. ❑ *The recording quality is excellent.* ● **ex|cel|lent|ly** ADV ❑ *They're both playing excellently.* ◻ EXCLAM Some people say "**Excellent!**" to show that they approve of something. [FEELINGS] ❑ *"Excellent!" he shouted, yelping happily in the rain. "Now we see how this boat really performs!"*

◻ 형용사 우수한 ❑ 녹음의 질이 우수하다. ● 우수하게 부사 ❑ 그 둘 모두 우수한 연기를 하고 있다. ◻ 감탄사 좋다 [감정 개입] ❑ "좋았어!"라고 그가 비를 바라보며 행복하게 소리처 말했다. "자, 이제 우리는 이 보트가 정말로 어떻게 움직이는지 보는 거야!"

D

ex|cept ♦♦◇ /ɪkˈsɛpt/ ◻ PREP You use **except** to introduce the only thing or person that a statement does not apply to, or a fact that prevents a statement from being completely true. ❑ *I wouldn't have accepted anything except a job in Europe.* ● CONJ **Except** is also a conjunction. ❑ *Freddie would tell me nothing about what he was writing, except that it was to be a Christmas play.* ◻ PHRASE You use **except for** to introduce the only thing or person that prevents a statement from being completely true. ❑ *He hadn't eaten a thing except for one forkful of salad.*

◻ 전치사 제외하고 ❑ 나는 유럽에서 일하는 거 말고는 어떤 것도 받아들이지 않았을 것이다. ● 접속사 -라는 것을 제외하고 ❑ 프레디는 자기가 쓰는 것이 크리스마스 연극이라는 것 말고는 나에게 아무것도 말하려 하지 않았다. ◻ 구 -을 빼고 ❑ 그는 샐러드 한 포크 말고는 아무것도 먹지 않았다.

E

Do not confuse **except**, **except for**, **besides**, and **unless**. You use **except** to introduce the only things, situations, people, or ideas that a statement does not apply to. ❑ *All of his body relaxed except his right hand... Traveling was impossible, except in the cool of the morning.* You use **except for** before something that prevents a statement from being completely true. ❑ *The classrooms were silent, except for the scratching of pens on paper... I had absolutely no friends except for Tom.* You use **besides** to introduce extra things in addition to the ones you are mentioning already. ❑ *Fruit will give you, besides enjoyment, a source of vitamins.* However, note that if you talk about "the only thing" or "the only person" **besides** a particular person or thing, **besides** means the same as "apart from." ❑ *He was the only person besides Gertrude who talked to Guy.* **Unless** is used to introduce the only situation in which something will take place or be true. ❑ *In the 1940s, unless she wore gloves a woman was not properly dressed... You must not give compliments unless you mean them.*

except, except for, besides, unless를 혼동하지 않도록 하라. except는 진술이 적용되지 않는 유일한 사물, 상황, 사람, 생각을 말할 때 쓴다. ❑ 그는 오른손을 제외한 몸 전체가 긴장이 풀렸다... 아침에 서늘한 때를 제외하면 여행은 불가능했다. except for는 진술이 완벽한 진실이 되지 못하게 하는 것 앞에 쓴다. ❑ 교실은 고요했고 종이 위에 펜 긁히는 소리만 들렸다... 나는 톰을 빼면 친구가 한 명도 없었다. besides는 이미 언급한 것에 더하여 추가로 다른 것을 소개할 때 쓴다. ❑ 과일은 즐거움뿐만 아니라 비타민도 제공한다. 그러나 특정한 사람이나 물건 이외(besides)의 the only thing 또는 the only person이라고 하면, 이 때 besides는 apart from과 같은 뜻이다. ❑ 그는 거트루드를 제외하고는 가이에게 말을 건 유일한 사람이었다. unless는 어떤 일이 발생하거나 사실이 될 수 있는 유일한 상황을 언급할 때 쓴다. ❑ 1940년대에는 여자가 장갑을 끼지 않으면 복장을 갖추어 입지 않은 것이었다... 진심이 아니면 칭찬을 해서는 안 된다.

F

G

H

I

J

K

L

ex|cept|ed /ɪkˈsɛptɪd/ ADV You use **excepted** after you have mentioned a person or thing to show that you do not include them in the statement you are making. [FORMAL] [n ADV] ❑ *Jeremy excepted, the men seemed personable.*

부사 예외로 [격식체] ❑ 제레미는 예외로 하고, 남자들은 매력적인 것 같았다.

M

ex|cept|ing /ɪkˈsɛptɪŋ/ PREP You use **excepting** to introduce the only thing that prevents a statement from being completely true. [FORMAL] ❑ *The source of meat for much of this region (excepting Japan) has traditionally been the pig.*

전치사 -을 제외하고 [격식체] ❑ 일본을 제외하고 이 지역 대부분의 육류는 전통적으로 돼지고기였다.

ex|cep|tion ♦◇◇ /ɪkˈsɛpʃ⁰n/ (**exceptions**) ◻ N-COUNT An **exception** is a particular thing, person, or situation that is not included in a general statement, judgment, or rule. ❑ *Few guitarists can sing as well as they can play; Eddie, however, is an exception.* ❑ *The law makes no exceptions.* ◻ PHRASE If you make a general statement, and then say that something or someone is **no exception**, you are emphasizing that they are included in that statement. [EMPHASIS] ❑ *Marketing is applied to everything these days, and books are no exception.* ◻ PHRASE If you **take exception to** something, you feel offended or annoyed by it, usually with the result that you complain about it. ❑ *He also took exception to having been spied on.* ◻ PHRASE You use **with the exception of** to introduce a thing or person that is not included in a general statement that you are making. ❑ *Yesterday was a day off for everybody, with the exception of Lawrence.* ◻ PHRASE You use **without exception** to emphasize that the statement you are making is true in all cases. [EMPHASIS] ❑ *The vehicles are without exception old, rusty, and dented.*

◻ 가산명사 제외, 예외 ❑ 연주하는 것만큼 노래를 잘 부르는 기타리스트는 거의 없다. 그러나 에디는 예외이다. ❑ 그 법에는 예외가 없다. ◻ 구 예외가 아닌 [강조] ❑ 오늘날에는 마케팅이 모든 것에 적용이 되는데, 책도 예외가 아니다. ◻ 구 -에 화를 내다 ❑ 그는 또한 몰래 감시당한 것에 화를 냈다. ◻ 구 -외에는, -을 제외하고는 ❑ 어제는 로렌스를 제외하고 모두가 쉬는 날이었다. ◻ 구 예외 없이 [강조] ❑ 그 자동차들은 예외 없이 낡고, 녹슬고, 움푹 찍혀 있다.

N

O

P

Q

R

ex|cep|tion|al /ɪkˈsɛpʃən⁰l/ ◻ ADJ You use **exceptional** to describe someone or something that has a particular quality, usually a good quality, to an unusually high degree. [APPROVAL] ❑ ...*children with exceptional ability.* ● **ex|cep|tion|al|ly** ADV [ADV adj/adv] ❑ *He's an exceptionally talented dancer and needs to practice several hours every day.* ◻ ADJ **Exceptional** situations and incidents are unusual and only likely to happen very infrequently. [FORMAL] ❑ *School governors have the discretion to allow parents to withdraw pupils in exceptional circumstances.* ● **ex|cep|tion|al|ly** ADV [ADV with cl] ❑ *Exceptionally, in times of emergency, we may send a team of experts.*

◻ 형용사 비범한 [마음에 듦] ❑ 비범한 능력을 가지고 있는 아이들 ● 매우 부사 ❑ 그는 매우 재능이 있는 무용수로 매일 여러 시간의 연습을 필요로 한다. ◻ 형용사 예외적인 [격식체] ❑ 학교장 이사는 예외적인 상황에서 부모가 학생을 자퇴하게 하도록 하는 결정권을 가지고 있다. ● 예외적으로 부사 ❑ 예외적으로, 긴급 상황 때는 우리가 전문가 팀을 보낼 수도 있다.

S

T

ex|cerpt ♦◇◇ /ˈɛksɜrpt/ (**excerpts**) N-COUNT An **excerpt** is a short piece of writing or music which is taken from a larger piece. ❑ ...*an excerpt from Tchaikovsky's Nutcracker.*

가산명사 발췌문 ❑ 차이코프스키의 호두까기 인형에서 따온 발췌문

U

ex|cess ♦◇◇ (**excesses**)

V

The noun is pronounced /ɪkˈsɛs/ or /ˈɛksɛs/. The adjective is pronounced /ˈɛksɛs/.

명사는 /ɪksɛs/ 또는 /ɛksɛs/로, 형용사는 /ɛksɛs/로 발음된다.

◻ N-VAR An **excess of** something is a larger amount than is needed, allowed, or usual. ❑ *An excess of houseplants in a small apartment can be oppressive.* ◻ ADJ **Excess** is used to describe amounts that are greater than what is needed, allowed, or usual. [ADJ n] ❑ *After cooking the fish, pour off any excess fat.* ◻ ADJ **Excess** is used to refer to additional amounts of money that need to be paid for services and activities that were not originally planned or taken into account. [FORMAL] [ADJ n] ❑ *Make sure that you don't have to pay expensive excess charges.* ◻ PHRASE **In excess of** means more than a particular amount. [FORMAL] ❑ *The value of the company is well in excess of $2 billion.* ◻ PHRASE If you do something **to excess**, you do it too much. [DISAPPROVAL] ❑ *I was reasonably fit, played a lot of tennis, and didn't smoke or drink to excess.*

◻ 가산명사 또는 불가산명사 과다 ❑ 작은 아파트에 과다하게 화분이 있으면 답답할 수 있다. ◻ 형용사 과다한 양 ❑ 생선을 요리한 후에, 기름이 너무 많으면 부어버리세요. ◻ 형용사 초과액 [격식체] ❑ 비싼 초과 요금을 내지 않도록 확인하시오. ◻ 구 -을 초과하여 [격식체] ❑ 그 회사의 가치는 20억 달러를 훨씬 넘는다. ◻ 구 지나치게 [탐탁찮음] ❑ 나는 꽤 튼튼했고, 테니스를 많이 쳤고, 그리고 지나치게 담배를 피우나 술을 마시지도 않았다.

W

X

Y

Z

ex|ces|sive /ɪksɛsɪv/ ADJ If you describe the amount or level of something as **excessive**, you disapprove of it because it is more or higher than is necessary or reasonable. [DISAPPROVAL] ❑ *The government says that local authority spending is excessive.* ● **ex|ces|sive|ly** ADV ❑ *Managers are also accused of paying themselves excessively high salaries.*

형용사 지나친, 과도한 [탐탁찮음] ❑ 정부는 지방 당국의 지출이 과도하다고 말했다. ● 과도하게 부사 ❑ 경영자들은 또한 자신들의 봉급을 과도하게 지불한다는 혐의도 받고 있다.

ex|change ♦♦◇ /ɪkstʃeɪndʒ/ (**exchanges, exchanging, exchanged**) **1** V-RECIP If two or more people **exchange** things of a particular kind, they give them to each other at the same time. ❑ *We exchanged addresses and Christmas cards.* ❑ *The two men exchanged glances.* ● N-COUNT **Exchange** is also a noun. ❑ *He ruled out any exchange of prisoners with the militants.* **2** V-T If you **exchange** something, you replace it with a different thing, especially something that is better or more satisfactory. ❑ *...the chance to sell back or exchange goods.* **3** N-COUNT An **exchange** is a brief conversation, usually an angry one. [FORMAL] ❑ *There've been some bitter exchanges between the two groups.* **4** N-COUNT An **exchange of** fire, for example, is an incident in which people use guns or missiles against each other. ❑ *There was an exchange of fire during which the gunman was wounded.* **5** N-COUNT An **exchange** is an arrangement in which people from two different countries visit each other's country, to strengthen links between them. ❑ *...a series of sporting and cultural exchanges with Seoul.* **6** →see also **foreign exchange, stock exchange 7** PHRASE If you do or give something **in exchange for** something else, you do it or give it in order to get that thing. ❑ *It is illegal for public officials to solicit gifts or money in exchange for favors.*

1 상호동사 주고받다, 교환하다 ❑ 우리는 주소와 크리스마스카드를 주고받았다. ❑ 그 두 남자가 서로 눈짓을 했다. ● 가산명사 교환 ❑ 그는 포로와 반군의 어떤 교환 가능성도 배제했다. **2** 타동사 교환하다 ❑ 상품을 다시 팔거나 교환할 기회 **3** 가산명사 입씨름, 언쟁 [격식체] ❑ 그 두 그룹 사이에 심한 언쟁이 있어 왔다. **4** 가산명사 총격전 ❑ 총격전이 벌어져 무장 범인이 다치는 일이 있었다. **5** 가산명사 교류 ❑ 서울과의 일련의 스포츠와 문화 교류 **7** 구 - 대신에, -와 교환하여 ❑ 공무원이 호의를 베풀고 선물이나 돈을 요구하는 것은 불법이다.

Word Partnership   exchange의 연어

N.	exchange **gifts**, exchange **greetings 1**
	currency exchange **2**
	exchange **student 5**
ADJ.	**brief** exchange **3**
	cultural exchange **5**

ex|change rate ♦◇◇ (**exchange rates**) N-COUNT The **exchange rate** of a country's unit of currency is the amount of another country's currency that you get in exchange for it. ❑ *...a high exchange rate for the pound.*

가산명사 환율 ❑ 파운드의 높은 환율

Ex|cheq|uer /ɪkstʃɛkər/ N-PROPER The **Exchequer** is the department in the British government which is responsible for receiving, issuing, and accounting for money belonging to the state. ❑ *...revenue to the Exchequer from North Sea oil.*

고유명사 재무부 ❑ 북해 석유에서 들어오는 재무부의 세입

ex|cise /ɛksaɪz/ (**excises**) N-VAR **Excise** is a tax that the government of a country puts on particular goods, such as cigarettes and alcoholic drinks, which are produced for sale in its own country. ❑ *...this year's rise in excise duties.*

가산명사 또는 불가산명사 소비세, 물품세 ❑ 금년의 소비세 증가

ex|cit|able /ɪksaɪtəbˀl/ ADJ If you describe someone as **excitable**, you mean that they behave in a rather nervous way and become excited very easily. ❑ *Mary sat beside Elaine, who today seemed excitable.*

형용사 흥분을 잘 하는, 화를 잘 내는 ❑ 메리는 일레인 옆에 앉았는데, 요즘 일레인은 화를 잘 내는 것 같았다.

ex|cite /ɪksaɪt/ (**excites, exciting, excited**) **1** V-T If something **excites** you, it makes you feel very happy, eager, or enthusiastic. ❑ *I only take on work that excites me, even if it means turning down lots of money.* **2** V-T If something **excites** a particular feeling, emotion, or reaction in someone, it causes them to experience it. ❑ *Daniel's early exposure to motor racing did not excite his interest.*

1 타동사 흥미를 불러일으키다 ❑ 나는 비록 돈을 많이 못 벌어도, 나에게 흥미로운 일만 맡는다. **2** 타동사 불러일으키다 ❑ 대니얼이 일찍 자동차 경주를 접했던 것이 그의 흥미를 불러일으키지는 않았다.

ex|cit|ed /ɪksaɪtɪd/ **1** ADJ If you are **excited**, you are so happy that you cannot relax, especially because you are thinking about something pleasant that is going to happen to you. ❑ *I'm very excited about the possibility of playing for England's first team.* ● **ex|cit|ed|ly** ADV [ADV with v] ❑ *"You're coming?" he said excitedly. "That's fantastic! That's incredible!"* **2** ADJ If you are **excited**, you are very worried or angry about something, and so you are very alert and cannot relax. ❑ *I don't think there's any reason to get excited about inflation.* ● **ex|cit|ed|ly** ADV [ADV with v] ❑ *Larry rose excitedly to the edge of his seat, shook a fist at us and spat.*

1 형용사 흥분한, 신이 난 ❑ 나는 잉글랜드의 최고 팀에서 뛸 가능성에 매우 흥분해 있다. ● 흥분하여, 신이 나서 부사 ❑ "너 오는 거야?"라고 그가 흥분하여 말했다. "멋져! 믿을 수가 없어!" **2** 형용사 흥분한 ❑ 나는 인플레이션에 대해 흥분할 이유가 없다고 생각한다. ● 흥분해서 부사 ❑ 래리는 흥분해서 의자를 박차고 일어나더니 우리를 향해서 주먹을 흔들고는 침을 뱉었다.

ex|cite|ment /ɪksaɪtmənt/ (**excitements**) N-VAR You use **excitement** to refer to the state of being excited, or to something that excites you. ❑ *Everyone is in a state of great excitement.*

가산명사 또는 불가산명사 흥분, 흥분거리 ❑ 모두가 매우 흥분한 상태이다.

ex|cit|ing ♦◇◇ /ɪksaɪtɪŋ/ ADJ If something is **exciting**, it makes you feel very happy or enthusiastic. ❑ *The race itself is very exciting.*

형용사 신나는, 마음 설레게 하는 ❑ 그 경주 자체가 매우 신나는 일이다.

Word Link   claim, clam ≈ shouting : ac*claim*, *clam*or, ex*claim*

ex|claim /ɪkskleɪm/ (**exclaims, exclaiming, exclaimed**) V-T Writers sometimes use **exclaim** to show that someone is speaking suddenly, loudly, or emphatically, often because they are excited, shocked, or angry. ❑ *"He went back to the lab," Iris exclaimed impatiently.*

타동사 외치다 ❑ "그가 실험실로 다시 돌아갔어요."라고 아이리스가 참지 못하고 소리쳤다.

ex|cla|ma|tion /ɛkskləmeɪʃˀn/ (**exclamations**) N-COUNT An **exclamation** is a sound, word, or sentence that is spoken suddenly, loudly, or emphatically and that expresses excitement, admiration, shock, or anger. ❑ *Sue gave an exclamation as we got a clear sight of the house.*

가산명사 외침 ❑ 수는 그 집이 분명하게 보이게 되었을 때 소리를 질렀다.

ex|cla|ma|tion point (**exclamation points**) or **exclamation mark** N-COUNT An **exclamation point** is the sign ! which is used in writing to show that a word, phrase, or sentence is an exclamation.

가산명사 느낌표

ex|clude /ɪksklud/ (**excludes, excluding, excluded**) **1** V-T If you **exclude** someone **from** a place or activity, you prevent them from entering it or taking part in it. ❑ *Many of the youngsters feel excluded.* **2** V-T If you **exclude** something that has some connection with what you are doing, you deliberately do not use it or consider it. ❑ *In some schools, Christmas carols are being modified to exclude any reference to Christ.* **3** V-T To **exclude** a possibility means to decide or prove that it is wrong and not worth considering. [usu with brd-neg] ❑ *I cannot*

1 타동사 제외하다, 배제하다 ❑ 많은 젊은이들은 배제되었다는 느낌을 갖는다. **2** 타동사 배제하다 ❑ 어떤 학교에서는, 크리스마스 캐럴을 예수와의 관련성을 배제하도록 수정하고 있다. **3** 타동사 배제하다 ❑ 나는 어떤 형태의 압력이 목에 가해졌다는 가능성을 전적으로 배제할 수 없다. **4** 타동사 차단하다 ❑ 이것은 태양의 직사광선을 차단하기 위한

entirely exclude _the possibility that some form of pressure was applied to the neck._ ◳ V-T To **exclude** something such as the sun's rays or harmful germs means to prevent them physically from reaching or entering a particular place. ❑ _This was intended to exclude the direct rays of the sun._

ex|clud|ing /ɪkskluːdɪŋ/ PREP You use **excluding** before mentioning a person or thing to show that you are not including them in your statement. ❑ _Excluding water, half of the body's weight is protein._

전치사 -을 제외하고 ❑ 물을 제외하고, 몸무게의 절반은 단백질이다.

ex|clu|sion /ɪkskluːʒ³n/ (**exclusions**) ◳ N-VAR The **exclusion of** something is the act of deliberately not using, allowing, or considering it. ❑ _It calls for the exclusion of all commercial lending institutions from the college loan program._ ◲ N-UNCOUNT **Exclusion** is the act of preventing someone from entering a place or taking part in an activity. ❑ _...women's exclusion from political power._ ◳ PHRASE If you do one thing **to the exclusion of** something else, you only do the first thing and do not do the second thing at all. ❑ _Diane had dedicated her life to caring for him to the exclusion of all else._

◳ 가산명사 또는 불가산명사 제외, 배제 ❑ 그것은 학자금 대출 프로그램에서 모든 상업적 대부 기관의 배제를 요구한다. ◲ 불가산명사 배제 ❑ 정치권력에서 여성 배제 ◳ 구 -을 제외하고, -을 제외할 만큼 ❑ 다이앤은 다른 모든 것을 제외하고 그를 돌보는 데 자기 삶을 바쳤다.

ex|clu|sive /ɪkskluːsɪv/ (**exclusives**) ◳ ADJ If you describe something as **exclusive**, you mean that it is limited to people who have a lot of money or who belong to a high social class, and is therefore not available to everyone. ❑ _He is already a member of Britain's most exclusive club._ ◲ ADJ Something that is **exclusive** is used or owned by only one person or group, and not shared with anyone else. ❑ _Our group will have exclusive use of a 60-foot boat._ ◳ ADJ If a newspaper, magazine, or broadcasting organization describes one of its reports as **exclusive**, they mean that it is a special report which does not appear in any other publication or on any other channel. ❑ _He told the magazine in an exclusive interview: "All my problems stem from drink."_ ● N-COUNT An **exclusive** is an exclusive article or report. ❑ _Some papers thought they had an exclusive._ ◳ ADJ If a company states that its prices, goods, or services are **exclusive of** something, that thing is not included in the stated price, although it usually still has to be paid for. ❑ _All charges for service are exclusive of value added tax._ ◳ PHRASE If two things are **mutually exclusive**, they are separate and very different from each other, so that it is impossible for them to exist or happen together. ❑ _They both have learnt that ambition and successful fatherhood can be mutually exclusive._

◳ 형용사 상류의, 고급의 ❑ 그는 이미 영국 최상류 클럽의 회원이다. ◲ 형용사 독점적인 ❑ 우리 팀은 60피트 보트의 독점 사용권을 전용할 것이다. ◳ 형용사 독점의 ❑ 그는 그 잡지의 독점 인터뷰에서 "내 모든 문제는 음주에서 비롯되었다."라고 말했다. ● 가산명사 독점 기사, 특종 ❑ 몇몇 신문들은 특종을 실었다고 생각했다. ◳ 형용사 -을 제외하고, 계산에 넣지 않고 ❑ 모든 서비스 요금에는 부가가치세가 포함되어 있지 않습니다. ◳ 구 서로 배타적인, 양립할 수 없는 ❑ 그들 둘 다 야망과 성공적인 아버지 역할은 서로 배타적일 수 있다는 것을 배웠다.

ex|clu|sive|ly /ɪkskluːsɪvli/ ADV **Exclusively** is used to refer to situations or activities that involve only the thing or things mentioned, and nothing else. ❑ _...an exclusively male domain._

부사 독점적으로, 배타적으로 ❑ 남성 전용 영역

ex|crete /ɪkskriːt/ (**excretes, excreting, excreted**) V-T When a person or animal **excretes** waste matter from their body, they get rid of it in feces, urine, or sweat. [FORMAL] ❑ _Your open pores excrete sweat and dirt._

타동사 배설하다, 배출하다 [격식체] ❑ 열린 땀구멍으로 땀과 오물이 배출된다.

ex|cru|ci|at|ing /ɪkskruːʃieɪtɪŋ/ ADJ If you describe something as **excruciating**, you are emphasizing that it is extremely painful, either physically or emotionally. [EMPHASIS] ❑ _I was in excruciating pain and one leg wouldn't move._

형용사 몹시 괴로운 [강조] ❑ 나는 극도의 통증을 느꼈고, 한쪽 다리가 움직이지 않았다.

ex|cur|sion /ɪkskɜːrʒ³n, BRIT ɪkskɜːʃ³n/ (**excursions**) ◳ N-COUNT You can refer to a short trip as an **excursion**, especially if it is taken for pleasure or enjoyment. ❑ _In Bermuda, Sam's father took him on an excursion to a coral barrier._ ◲ N-COUNT An **excursion** is a trip or visit to an interesting place, especially one that is arranged or recommended by a travel agency or tourist organization. ❑ _Another pleasant excursion is Malaga, 18 miles away._

◳ 가산명사 소풍, 유람 ❑ 버뮤다에서 샘의 아버지는 그에게 산호초 유람을 시켜 주었다. ◲ 가산명사 관광 ❑ 또 하나의 즐거운 관광지는 말라가인데 18마일 떨어져 있다.

ex|cuse ◆◇◇ (**excuses, excusing, excused**)

The noun is pronounced /ɪkskyuːs/. The verb is pronounced /ɪkskyuːz/.

명사는 /ɪkskyuːs/로 발음되고, 동사는 /ɪkskyuːz/로 발음된다.

◳ N-COUNT An **excuse** is a reason which you give in order to explain why something has been done or has not been done, or in order to avoid doing something. ❑ _It is easy to find excuses for his indecisiveness._ ❑ _If you stop making excuses and do it you'll wonder what took you so long._ ● PHRASE If you say that there is **no excuse** for something, you are emphasizing that it should not happen, or expressing disapproval that it has happened. [DISAPPROVAL] ❑ _There's no excuse for behavior like that._ ◲ V-T To **excuse** someone or **excuse** their behavior means to provide reasons for their actions, especially when other people disapprove of these actions. ❑ _He excused himself by saying he was "forced to rob to maintain my wife and cat."_ ◳ V-T If you **excuse** someone **for** something wrong that they have done, you forgive them for it. ❑ _Many people might have excused them for shirking some of their responsibilities._ ◳ V-T If someone **is excused from** a duty or responsibility, they are told that they do not have to carry it out. [usu passive] ❑ _She is usually excused from her duties during the school holidays._ ◳ V-T If you **excuse yourself**, you use a phrase such as "Excuse me" as a polite way of saying that you are about to leave. ❑ _He excused himself and went up to his room._ ◳ CONVENTION You say "**Excuse me**" when you want to politely get someone's attention, especially when you are about to ask them a question. [FORMULAE] ❑ _Excuse me, but are you Mr. Honig?_ ◳ CONVENTION You use "**Excuse me**" to apologize to someone when you have disturbed or interrupted them. [FORMULAE] ❑ _Excuse me interrupting, but there's a thing I feel I've got to say._ ◳ CONVENTION You use "**Excuse me**" or a phrase such as "**If you'll excuse me**" as a polite way of indicating that you are about to leave or that you are about to stop talking to someone. [POLITENESS] ❑ _"Excuse me," she said to Jarvis, and left the room._ ◳ CONVENTION You use "**Excuse me, but**" to indicate that you are about to disagree with someone. ❑ _Excuse me, but I want to know what all this has to do with us._ ◳ PHRASE You say "**Excuse me**" to apologize when you have bumped into someone, or when you need to move past someone in a crowd. [FORMULAE] ❑ _Saying excuse me, pardon me, Seaton pushed his way into the crowded living room._ ◳ CONVENTION You say "**Excuse me**" to apologize when you have done something slightly embarrassing or impolite, such as burping, hiccuping, or sneezing. [FORMULAE] ◳ CONVENTION You say "**Excuse me?**" to show that you want someone to repeat what they have just said. [AM, FORMULAE]

◳ 가산명사 핑계, 변명 ❑ 그의 우유부단함에 대한 핑계는 쉽게 찾을 수 있다. ❑ 변명은 그만하고 그것을 실제로 해 보면 그 동안 왜 그렇게 오래 걸렸는지 의아할 것이다. ● 구 변명의 여지가 없음 [탐탁찮음] ❑ 그런 식의 행동에는 변명의 여지가 없다. ◲ 타동사 변명하다 ❑ 그는 "아내와 고양이를 부양하기 위해 어쩔 수 없이 강도짓을 했다."라고 변명했다. ◳ 타동사 용서하다 ❑ 많은 사람들이 그들이 책임을 회피한 것을 용서했을지도 모른다. ◳ 타동사 면제되다 ❑ 그녀는 방학 동안 대개 자기의 의무를 면제받는다. ◳ 타동사 (자리를 뜰 때) 실례하다, 양해를 구하다 ❑ 그는 실례한다고 말하고 자기 방으로 올라갔다. ◳ 관용 표현 실례합니다 (주의를 끌 때) [의례적인 표현] ❑ 실례합니다만 혹시 호니그 씨인가요? ◳ 관용 표현 죄송합니다 [의례적인 표현] ❑ 방해해서 죄송합니다만, 꼭 드려야 할 말이 있는 것 같습니다. ◳ 관용 표현 실례합니다 (자리를 뜰 때) [공손체] ❑ "실례합니다"라고 그녀는 자비스에게 말하고 방을 나갔다. ◳ 관용 표현 실례합니다만 (상대방의 말을 반박할 때) ❑ 실례지만 이 모든 것이 우리와 무슨 관계가 있다는 건지 알고 싶습니다. ◳ 구 실례합니다 (다른 사람 옆을 지나갈 때) [의례적인 표현] ❑ 실례합니다, 죄송합니다고 말하면서 시튼은 사람이 가득 찬 거실로 들어갔다. ◳ 관용 표현 실례합니다 (재채기 등을 할 때) [의례적인 표현] ◳ 관용 표현 뭐라고 하셨습니까? [미국영어, 의례적인 표현] [영국영어 대개 pardon, sorry] ❑ "뭐라고 하셨나요?"라고 케이트는 자기가 제대로 들었는지 확실치 않아 말했다.

[BRIT usually **pardon**, **sorry**] ❏ *"Excuse me?" Kate said, not sure she'd heard correctly.*

Thesaurus   *excuse*의 참조어

N.   apology, explanation, reason 🔳

V.   forgive, pardon, spare; (ant.) accuse, blame, punish 🔳

---

ex-directory ADJ If a person or their telephone number is **ex-directory**, the number is not listed in the telephone directory, and the telephone company will not give it to people who ask for it. [BRIT; AM **unlisted**] ❏ *His telephone number is ex-directory.*

exec /ɪgzɛk/ (execs) N-COUNT Exec is an abbreviation for **executive**. [INFORMAL]

ex|e|cute ♦◇◇ /ɛksɪkyut/ (executes, executing, executed) 🔳 V-T To **execute** someone means to kill them as a punishment for a serious crime. ❏ *He said nobody had been executed as a direct result of the events.* ❏ *One group claimed to have executed the American hostage.* ● **ex|e|cu|tion** /ɛksɪkyuʃⁿn/ (executions) N-VAR ❏ *Execution by lethal injection is scheduled for July 30th.* 🔳 V-T If you **execute** a plan, you carry it out. [FORMAL] ❏ *We are going to execute our campaign plan to the letter.* ● **ex|e|cu|tion** N-UNCOUNT ❏ *U.S. forces are fully prepared for the execution of any action once the order is given by the president.* 🔳 V-T If you **execute** a difficult action or movement, you successfully perform it. ❏ *The landing was skilfully executed.*

ex|ecu|tive ♦♦◇ /ɪgzɛkyətɪv/ (executives) 🔳 N-COUNT An **executive** is someone who is employed by a business at a senior level. Executives decide what the business should do, and ensure that it is done. ❏ *...an advertising executive.* 🔳 ADJ The **executive** sections and tasks of an organization are concerned with the making of decisions and with ensuring that decisions are carried out. [ADJ n] ❏ *A successful job search needs to be as well organized as any other executive task.* 🔳 ADJ **Executive** goods are expensive goods designed or intended for executives and other people at a similar social or economic level. [ADJ n] ❏ *...an executive briefcase.* 🔳 N-SING The **executive** committee or board of an organization is a committee within that organization which has the authority to make decisions and ensures that these decisions are carried out. [the N, N n] ❏ *He sits on the executive committee that manages Lloyds.* 🔳 N-SING The **executive** is the part of the government of a country that is concerned with carrying out decisions or orders, as opposed to the part that makes laws or the part that deals with criminals. [the N, N n] ❏ *The government, the executive, and the judiciary are supposed to be separate.*

ex|em|pla|ry /ɪgzɛmpləri/ ADJ If you describe someone or something as **exemplary**, you think they are extremely good. ❏ *Underpinning this success has been an exemplary record of innovation.*

ex|em|pli|fy /ɪgzɛmplɪfaɪ/ (exemplifies, exemplifying, exemplified) V-T If a person or thing **exemplifies** something such as a situation, quality, or class of things, they are a typical example of it. [FORMAL] ❏ *The room's style exemplifies Conran's ideal of "beauty and practicality."*

ex|empt /ɪgzɛmpt/ (exempts, exempting, exempted) 🔳 ADJ If someone or something is **exempt from** a particular rule, duty, or obligation, they do not have to follow it or do it. ❏ *Men in college were exempt from military service.* 🔳 V-T To **exempt** a person or thing **from** a particular rule, duty, or obligation means to state officially that they are not bound or affected by it. ❏ *South Carolina claimed the power to exempt its citizens from the obligation to obey federal law.* ● **ex|emp|tion** /ɪgzɛmpʃⁿn/ (exemptions) N-VAR [oft N from n] ❏ *...the exemption of employer-provided health insurance from taxation.*

ex|er|cise ♦♦◇ /ɛksərsaɪz/ (exercises, exercising, exercised) 🔳 V-T If you **exercise** something such as your authority, your rights, or a good quality, you use it or put it into effect. [FORMAL] ❏ *They are merely exercising their right to free speech.* ● N-SING Exercise is also a noun. ❏ *Social structures are maintained through the exercise of political and economic power.* 🔳 V-I When you **exercise**, you move your body energetically in order to get fit and to remain healthy. ❏ *She exercises two or three times a week.* ● N-UNCOUNT Exercise is also a noun. ❏ *Lack of exercise can lead to feelings of depression and exhaustion.* 🔳 V-T If a movement or activity **exercises** a part of your body, it keeps it strong, healthy, or in good condition. ❏ *They call rowing the perfect sport. It exercises every major muscle group.* 🔳 N-COUNT **Exercises** are a series of movements or actions which you do in order to get fit, remain healthy, or practice for a particular physical activity. ❏ *I do special neck and shoulder exercises.* 🔳 N-COUNT **Exercises** are military activities and operations which are not part of a real war, but which allow the armed forces to practice for a real war. [usu pl, also on N] ❏ *General Powell predicted that in the future it might even be possible to stage joint military exercises.* 🔳 N-COUNT An **exercise** is a short activity or piece of work that you do, for example in school, which is designed to help you learn a particular skill. ❏ *Try working through the opening exercises in this chapter.* →see **muscle**

Thesaurus   *exercise*의 참조어

V.   practice, use 🔳
     work out 🔳

---

ex|ert /ɪgzɜrt/ (exerts, exerting, exerted) 🔳 V-T If someone or something **exerts** influence, authority, or pressure, they use it in a strong or determined way, especially in order to produce a particular effect. [FORMAL] ❏ *He exerted considerable influence on the thinking of the scientific community on these issues.* 🔳 V-T If you **exert yourself**, you make a great physical or mental effort, or work hard to do something. ❏ *Do not exert yourself unnecessarily.* ● **ex|er|tion** (exertions)

형용사 전화번호부에 실리지 않은, 미수록의 [영국영어; 미국영어 unlisted] ❏ 그의 전화번호는 전화번호부에 없다.

가산명사 기업의 간부 [비격식체]

🔳 타동사 사형시키다, 처형하다 ❏ 그는 그 사건들의 직접적인 결과로 처형된 사람은 아무도 없었다고 말했다. ❏ 한 단체가 미국인 인질을 처형했다고 주장했다. ● 사형 집행 가산명사 또는 불가산명사 ❏ 독극물 주사에 의한 사형 집행이 7월 30일로 예정되어 있다. 🔳 타동사 실행하다 [격식체] ❏ 우리는 캠페인 계획을 엄밀히 실행할 것이다. ● 실행, 수행 불가산명사 ❏ 미군은 대통령의 명령이 떨어지는 즉시 어떤 군사 행동도 수행할 만반의 준비가 되어 있다. 🔳 타동사 완수하다 ❏ 착륙이 능숙하게 이루어졌다.

🔳 가산명사 기업의 간부, 이사 ❏ 홍보이사 🔳 형용사 행정상의, 관리적인 ❏ 구직에 성공하기 위해서는 다른 모든 행정적인 일과 마찬가지로 계획을 잘 세울 필요가 있다. 🔳 형용사 간부의, 고급의 ❏ 간부용 고급 서류 가방 🔳 단수명사 집행부의, 이사회의 ❏ 그는 로이드사를 운영하는 이사회의 일원이다. 🔳 단수명사 행정부 ❏ 정부, 행정부, 사법부는 분리되어야 한다.

형용사 훌륭한 ❏ 훌륭한 기록적 혁신이 이 성공의 토대를 이루고 있다.

타동사 예시하다, ~의 표본이 되다 [격식체] ❏ 이 방의 스타일은 콘란이 이상으로 삼는 '미와 실용성'의 표본이 된다.

🔳 형용사 면제된 ❏ 대학에 재학 중인 남자는 군복무에서 면제되었다. 🔳 타동사 면제하다 ❏ 사우스 캐롤라이나 주는 주민들이 연방법을 따라야 하는 의무를 면제시킬 수 있는 권한을 요구했다. ● 면제 가산명사 또는 불가산명사 ❏ 고용주 부담 건강 보험의 세금 면제

🔳 타동사 (권력 등을) 행사하다 [격식체] ❏ 그들은 단지 언론의 자유에 대한 권리를 행사하고 있을 뿐이다. ● 단수명사 (권력 등의) 행사 ❏ 사회 구조는 정치력과 경제력의 행사를 통해 유지된다. 🔳 자동사 운동하다 ❏ 그녀는 일주일에 두세 번 운동한다. ● 단수명사 운동 ❏ 운동 부족은 우울과 피로감을 유발시킬 수 있다. 🔳 타동사 운동시키다 ❏ 노 젓기는 완벽한 운동이라고 한다. 그것은 모든 주요 근육을 단련시킨다. 🔳 가산명사 운동 ❏ 나는 목과 어깨에 특별한 운동을 한다. 🔳 가산명사 군사 훈련 ❏ 파월 장군은 장차는 합동 군사 훈련을 하는 것도 가능할 수 있으리라 예측했다. 🔳 가산명사 연습 문제 ❏ 이 장의 시작 부분 연습 문제를 해 보도록 해라.

🔳 타동사 (영향력 등을) 행사하다 [격식체] ❏ 그는 이들 문제에 대한 과학계의 사고에 상당한 영향력을 행사했다. 🔳 타동사 노력하다, 애쓰다 ❏ 쓸데없이 애쓰지 말아라. ● 진력, 격심한 활동 불가산명사 ❏ 그는 격심한 육체적 활동이 사람을 원기 왕성하게 만든다는 것을 분명히 알게 되었다.

A

N-UNCOUNT [also N in pl] ❑ *He clearly found the physical exertion exhilarating.* →see **motion**

B

ex|hale /ɛksheɪl/ (**exhales, exhaling, exhaled**) V-I When you **exhale**, you breathe out the air that is in your lungs. [FORMAL] ❑ *Hold your breath for a moment and exhale.* →see **respiratory**

자동사 (숨을) 내쉬다 [격식체] ❑ 잠시 숨을 참았다가 내쉬어라.

ex|haust ♦♢♢ /ɪgzɔːst/ (**exhausts, exhausting, exhausted**) ■ V-T If something **exhausts** you, it makes you so tired, either physically or mentally, that you have no energy left. ❑ *Don't exhaust him.* ● **ex|haust|ed** ADJ ❑ *She was too exhausted and distressed to talk about the tragedy.* ● **ex|haust|ing** ADJ ❑ *It was an exhausting schedule she had set herself.* ■ V-T If you **exhaust** something such as money or food, you use or finish it all. ❑ *We have exhausted all our material resources.* ■ V-T If you **have exhausted** a subject or topic, you have talked about it so much that there is nothing more to say about it. ❑ *She and Chantal must have exhausted the subject of babies and clothes.* ■ N-COUNT The **exhaust** or the **exhaust pipe** is the pipe which carries the gas out of the engine of a vehicle. [mainly BRIT] ❑ *The woman driver asked for a new exhaust to be fitted.* ■ N-UNCOUNT **Exhaust** is the gas or steam that is produced when the engine of a vehicle is running. [also N in pl] ❑ *...the exhaust from a car engine.* ❑ *The city's streets are filthy and choked with exhaust fumes.* →see **engine, pollution**

■ 타동사 기진맥진하게 하다 ❑ 그를 기진맥진하게 만들지 말아라. ● 지칠 대로 지친, 기진맥진한 형용사 ❑ 그녀는 너무 지치고 괴로운 나머지 참사에 대해 말을 할 수 없었다. ● 지치게 하는, 소모적인 형용사 ❑ 그녀가 자신에게 부과한 것은 녹초로 만드는 스케줄이었다. ■ 타동사 다 써버리다, 고갈시키다 ❑ 우리는 우리의 천연자원을 고갈시켜 왔다. ■ 타동사 속속들이 말하다 ❑ 그녀와 찬탈은 아이와 옷에 대해 온갖 얘기를 다 나누었음에 틀림없었다. ■ 가산명사 배기관 [주로 영국영어] ❑ 여성 운전자는 새 배기관을 달아 달라고 부탁했다. ■ 불가산명사 배기가스 ❑ 자동차 엔진에서 나오는 배기가스 ❑ 도시의 거리는 더럽고 배기가스 연기로 숨이 막힌다.

C

D

E

F

ex|haus|tion /ɪgzɔːstʃən/ N-UNCOUNT **Exhaustion** is the state of being so tired that you have no energy left. ❑ *Staff say he is suffering from exhaustion.*

불가산명사 피로, 기진맥진 ❑ 직원들에 의하면 그가 기진맥진해 버렸다고 한다.

G

ex|haus|tive /ɪgzɔːstɪv/ ADJ If you describe a study, search, or list as **exhaustive**, you mean that it is very thorough and complete. ❑ *This is by no means an exhaustive list but it gives an indication of the many projects taking place.* ● **ex|haus|tive|ly** ADV ❑ *Martin said these costs were scrutinized exhaustively by independent accountants.*

형용사 완벽한, 철저히 망라된 ❑ 이것은 결코 완벽하지 못 되지만 현재 진행되고 있는 많은 프로젝트가 어떤 건지는 보여 준다. ● 철저하게 부사 ❑ 마틴은 이 비용은 독립 회계사가 철저히 검토한 것이라고 말했다.

H

ex|hib|it /ɪgzɪbɪt/ (**exhibits, exhibiting, exhibited**) ■ V-T If someone or something shows a particular quality, feeling, or type of behavior, you can say that they **exhibit** it. [FORMAL] ❑ *He has exhibited symptoms of anxiety and overwhelming worry.* ■ V-T When a painting, sculpture, or object of interest **is exhibited**, it is put in a public place such as a museum or art gallery so that people can come to look at it. You can also say that animals **are exhibited** in a zoo. [usu passive] ❑ *His work was exhibited in the best galleries in America, Europe, and Asia.* ● **ex|hi|bi|tion** N-UNCOUNT ❑ *Five large pieces of the wall are currently on exhibition.* ■ V-I When artists **exhibit**, they show their work in public. ❑ *By 1936 she was exhibiting at the Royal Academy.* ■ N-COUNT An **exhibit** is a painting, sculpture, or object of interest that is displayed to the public in a museum or art gallery. ❑ *Shona showed me around the exhibits.* ■ N-COUNT An **exhibit** is a public display of paintings, sculpture, or objects of interest, for example in a museum or art gallery. [AM; BRIT **exhibition**] ❑ *...an exhibit at the Metropolitan Museum of Art.* ■ N-COUNT An **exhibit** is an object that a lawyer shows in court as evidence in a legal case. ❑ *One of the most spectacular exhibits in the case to prosecute I.T. Botham was the broken bed.*

■ 타동사 나타내다, 보이다 [격식체] ❑ 그는 걱정과 지나친 근심의 징후를 보여 왔다. ■ 타동사 전시되다 ❑ 그의 작품은 미국, 유럽, 아시아의 최고 화랑들에서 전시되었다. ● 전시 불가산명사 ❑ 그 벽의 커다란 조각 다섯 개가 현재 전시 중이다. ■ 자동사 전시회를 열다 ❑ 1936년이 되자 그녀는 왕립 학술원에서 전시회를 열게 되었다. ■ 가산명사 전시품 ❑ 쇼나는 나를 데리고 다니며 전시품들을 보여 주었다. ■ 가산명사 전시회 [미국영어; 영국영어 exhibition] ❑ 메트로폴리탄 미술관에서의 전시회 ■ 가산명사 증거물 ❑ 아이 티 보담의 기소 사건에서 가장 눈길을 끄는 증거물 한 가지는 부서진 침대였다.

I

J

K

L

M

ex|hi|bi|tion ♦♦♢ /ɛksɪbɪʃən/ (**exhibitions**) ■ N-COUNT An **exhibition** is a public event at which pictures, sculptures, or other objects of interest are displayed, for example at a museum or art gallery. ❑ *...an exhibition of expressionist art.* ■ N-SING An **exhibition of** a particular skillful activity is a display or example of it that people notice or admire. ❑ *He responded in champion's style by treating the fans to an exhibition of power and speed.* ■ →see also **exhibit**

■ 가산명사 전시회, 전람회 ❑ 표현주의 미술 전시회 ■ 단수명사 과시 ❑ 그는 챔피언답게 팬들에게 그의 힘과 속도를 과시했다.

N

ex|hi|bi|tion game (**exhibition games**) N-COUNT In sport, an **exhibition game** is a match which is not part of a competition, and is played for entertainment or practice, often without any serious effort to win. [AM; BRIT **friendly**]

가산명사 시범 경기 [미국영어; 영국영어 friendly]

O

P

ex|hibi|tor /ɪgzɪbɪtər/ (**exhibitors**) N-COUNT An **exhibitor** is a person whose work is being shown in an exhibition. ❑ *Schedules will be sent out to all exhibitors.*

가산명사 출품자 ❑ 모든 출품자들에게 일정표를 보낼 것이다.

Q

ex|hil|arat|ing /ɪgzɪləreɪtɪŋ/ ADJ If you describe an experience or feeling as **exhilarating**, you mean that it makes you feel very happy and excited. ❑ *It was exhilarating to be on the road again and his spirits rose.*

형용사 아주 상쾌한, 생기를 돋우는 ❑ 다시 여행길에 오르자 그는 아주 상쾌했고 신이 났다.

R

ex|hila|ra|tion /ɪgzɪləreɪʃən/ N-UNCOUNT **Exhilaration** is a strong feeling of excitement and happiness. ❑ *The exhilaration of winning such a famous event has stayed with him.*

불가산명사 유쾌한 기분, 날을 듯한 기쁨 ❑ 그렇게 유명한 대회에서 승리한 기쁨은 그에게 계속 남아 있다.

S

ex|ile ♦♦♢ /ɛksaɪl, ɛgz-/ (**exiles, exiling, exiled**) ■ N-UNCOUNT If someone is living **in exile**, they are living in a foreign country because they cannot live in their own country, usually for political reasons. ❑ *He is now living in exile in Egypt.* ❑ *He returned from exile earlier this year.* ■ V-T If someone **is exiled**, they are living in a foreign country because they cannot live in their own country, usually for political reasons. ❑ *His second wife, Hilary, had been widowed, then exiled from South Africa.* ❑ *They threatened to exile her in southern Spain.* ■ N-COUNT An **exile** is someone who has been exiled. ❑ *He is also an exile, a native of Palestine who has long given up the idea of going home.* ■ V-T If you say that someone **has been exiled from** a particular place or situation, you mean that they have been sent away from it or removed from it against their will. [usu passive] ❑ *He has been exiled from the first team and forced to play in third team matches.* ● N-UNCOUNT **Exile** is also a noun. ❑ *Rovers lost 4-1 and began their long exile from the First Division.*

■ 불가산명사 망명 ❑ 그는 지금 이집트에서 망명 생활을 하고 있다. ❑ 그는 올해 초 망명에서 돌아왔다. ■ 타동사 추방되다 ❑ 그의 두 번째 아내인 힐러리는 과부가 되고 나서, 남아프리카로부터 추방되었다. ❑ 그들은 그녀를 스페인 남부로 추방하겠다고 위협했다. ■ 가산명사 망명자 ❑ 그 또한 망명자이고, 고향으로 돌아갈 생각은 예전에 포기한 팔레스타인 사람이다. ■ 타동사 -에서 쫓겨나다 ❑ 그는 일진 팀에서 쫓겨나 삼진 팀 경기에서 뛰어야 했다. ● 불가산명사 추방 ❑ 로버즈 팀이 4대1로 지고 일부 리그로부터의 장기 추방 길에 접어들었다.

T

U

V

W

X

Word Partnership		exile의 연어
V.	**force into** exile, **go into** exile, **live in** exile, **return from** exile, **send into** exile ■	
ADJ.	**self-imposed** exile ■	
	political exile ■ ■	

Y

ex|ist ♦♦♢ /ɪgzɪst/ (**exists, existing, existed**) ■ V-I If something **exists**, it is present in the world as a real thing. [no cont] ❑ *He thought that if he couldn't see something, it didn't exist.* ❑ *Research opportunities exist in a wide range of pure and applied areas of entomology.* ■ V-I To **exist** means to live, especially under

■ 자동사 존재하다 ❑ 그는 만일 어떤 것을 볼 수 없다면, 그것은 존재하지 않는다고 생각했다. ❑ 순수 및 응용 곤충학의 광범위한 분야에 대해 연구 기회가 있다. ■ 자동사 생존하다, 살아가다 ❑ 나는 간신히

Z

difficult conditions or with very little food or money. ❑ *I was barely existing.* ❑ *Some people exist on melons or coconuts for weeks at a time.*

살아가고 있었다. ❑ 어떤 사람들은 한번에 몇 주씩 멜론과 코코넛만 먹고 산다.

ex|ist|ence ♦◇◇ /ɪgzɪstəns/ (**existences**) ◼ N-UNCOUNT The **existence** of something is the fact that it is present in the world as a real thing. ❑ *...the existence of other galaxies.* ❑ *Public worries about accidents are threatening the very existence of the nuclear power industry.* ◻ N-COUNT You can refer to someone's way of life as an **existence**, especially when they live under difficult conditions. ❑ *You may be stuck with a miserable existence for the rest of your life.*

◼ 불가산명사 실재, 존재 ❑ 다른 은하계의 존재 ❑ 사고에 대한 일반 국민의 걱정 때문에 원자력 산업 존재 자체가 위협을 받고 있다. ◻ 가산명사 생존 ❑ 당신은 어쩌면 여생 동안 비참하게 생존해 나가야 할지도 모른다.

<table>
<tr><td colspan="2">**Word Partnership**   *existence*의 연어</td></tr>
<tr><td>V.</td><td>**come into** existence, **deny the** existence ◼</td></tr>
<tr><td>ADJ.</td><td>**daily** existence, **everyday** existence ◼ ◻</td></tr>
</table>

ex|ist|ing ♦◇◇ /ɪgzɪstɪŋ/ ADJ **Existing** is used to describe something which is now present, available, or in operation, especially when you are contrasting it with something which is planned for the future. [ADJ n] ❑ *...the need to improve existing products and develop new lines.* ❑ *Existing timbers are replaced or renewed.*

형용사 기존의, 현존하는 ❑ 기존의 상품들을 개선하고 새로운 종류를 개발할 필요 ❑ 기존의 목재는 새것으로 대치하거나 보수했다.

Word Link   *ex ≈ away, from, out : ex**ceed**, ex**it**, ex**plode***

exit /ɛgzɪt, ɛksɪt/ (**exits, exiting, exited**) ◼ N-COUNT The **exit** is the door through which you can leave a public building. ❑ *He picked up the case and walked toward the exit.* ◻ N-COUNT An **exit** on a highway is a place where traffic can leave it. ❑ *Take the A422 exit at Old Stratford.* ◼ N-COUNT If you refer to someone's **exit**, you are referring to the way that they left a room or building, or the fact that they left it. [FORMAL] ❑ *I made a hasty exit and managed to open the gate.* ◼ N-COUNT If you refer to someone's **exit**, you are referring to the way that they left a situation or activity, or the fact that they left it. [FORMAL] ❑ *...after England's exit from the European Championship.* ◼ V-T/V-I If you **exit** from a room or building, you leave it. [FORMAL] ❑ *She exits into the tropical storm.* ❑ *As I exited the final display, I entered a hexagonal room.* ◼ V-T If you **exit** a computer program or system, you stop running it. [COMPUTING] ❑ *I can open other applications without having to exit WordPerfect.* ● N-SING **Exit** is also a noun. ❑ *Press Exit to return to your document.*

◼ 가산명사 출구 ❑ 그는 상자를 집어 들고 출구 쪽으로 걸어갔다. ◻ 가산명사 (고속도로의) 진출로 ❑ 올드 스트래퍼드에서 에이 422 도로의 진출로로 나오시오. ◼ 가산명사 퇴장, 나감 [격식체] ❑ 나는 서둘러 나와 간신히 문을 열었다. ◼ 가산명사 탈락, 퇴진 [격식체] ❑ 유럽 챔피언쉽에서 영국이 탈락한 이후 ◼ 타동사/자동사 나가다 [격식체] ❑ 그녀는 열대 폭풍 속으로 나간다. ❑ 나는 마지막 전시실을 나와서 육각형 모양의 방으로 들어갔다. ◼ 타동사 (컴퓨터 프로그램을) 닫다 [컴퓨터] ❑ 나는 워드퍼펙트를 닫지 않은 채 다른 응용 프로그램을 열 수 있다. ● 단수명사 (컴퓨터의) '되돌아가기' 표시 ❑ 사용하던 문서로 돌아가려면 '되돌아가기'를 누르시오.

exit visa (**exit visas**) N-COUNT An **exit visa** is an official stamp in someone's passport, or an official document, which allows them to leave the country that they are visiting or living in.

가산명사 출국 사증

exo|dus /ɛksədəs/ N-SING If there is an **exodus** of people **from** a place, a lot of people leave that place at the same time. ❑ *The medical system is facing collapse because of an exodus of doctors.*

단수명사 대규모 탈출, 출국 ❑ 의사들의 대규모 출국으로 의료체계가 와해에 직면해 있다.

ex|or|bi|tant /ɪgzɔrbɪtənt/ ADJ If you describe something such as a price or fee as **exorbitant**, you are emphasizing that it is much greater than it should be. [EMPHASIS] ❑ *Exorbitant housing prices have created an acute shortage of affordable housing for the poor.*

형용사 과도한, 터무니없는 [강조] ❑ 주택 시세가 터무니없이 높아서 가난한 사람들이 얻을 수 있는 집이 극도로 부족하게 되었다.

ex|ot|ic /ɪgzɒtɪk/ ADJ Something that is **exotic** is unusual and interesting, usually because it comes from or is related to a distant country. ❑ *...brilliantly colored, exotic flowers.* ● **ex|oti|cal|ly** ADV ❑ *...exotically beautiful scenery.*

형용사 이국적인 ❑ 화려한 색채의 이국적인 꽃들 ● 이국적으로 부사 ❑ 아름다운 이국적인 풍경

ex|pand ♦◇◇ /ɪkspænd/ (**expands, expanding, expanded**) ◼ V-T/V-I If something **expands** or is **expanded**, it becomes larger. ❑ *Engineers noticed that the pipes were not expanding as expected.* ❑ *We have to expand the size of the image.* ◻ V-T/V-I If something such as a business, organization, or service **expands**, or if you **expand** it, it becomes bigger and includes more people, goods, or activities. [BUSINESS] ❑ *The popular ceramics industry expanded toward the middle of the 19th century.*

◼ 타동사/자동사 팽창하다, 늘어나다 ❑ 기술자들은 도관이 예상대로 늘어나지 않는다는 것을 알았다. ❑ 우리는 영상의 크기를 늘려야 한다. ◻ 타동사/자동사 확장되다, 팽창하다 [경제] ❑ 대중적인 도자기 산업은 19세기 중반 무렵에 팽창했다.

▶**expand on** or **expand upon** PHRASAL VERB If you **expand on** or **expand upon** something, you give more information or details about it when you write or talk about it. ❑ *The president used today's speech to expand on remarks he made last month.*

구동사 자세히 말하다, 부연하다 ❑ 회장은 오늘 연설에서 지난달에 했던 말에 대해 부연설명을 했다.

ex|panse /ɪkspæns/ (**expanses**) N-COUNT An **expanse of** something, usually sea, sky, or land, is a very large amount of it. ❑ *...a vast expanse of grassland.*

가산명사 무량광대 ❑ 광대하게 펼쳐진 초원

ex|pan|sion ♦◇◇ /ɪkspænʃⁿn/ (**expansions**) N-VAR **Expansion** is the process of becoming greater in size, number, or amount. ❑ *...the rapid expansion of private health insurance.*

가산명사 또는 불가산명사 확장, 확대 ❑ 민간 건강 보험의 빠른 확대

ex|pan|sive /ɪkspænsɪv/ ADJ If you are **expansive**, you talk a lot, or are friendly or generous, because you are feeling happy and relaxed. ❑ *He was becoming more expansive as he relaxed.*

형용사 개방적인, 포용력 있는 ❑ 그는 마음이 느긋해지자 더 너그러워졌다.

ex|pat|ri|ate /ɛkspeɪtriət, -pæt-/ (**expatriates**) N-COUNT An **expatriate** is someone who is living in a country which is not their own. ❑ *...British expatriates in Spain.* ● ADJ **Expatriate** is also an adjective. [ADJ n] ❑ *The French military is preparing to evacuate women and children of expatriate families.*

가산명사 국외 거주자 ❑ 스페인에 사는 영국인들 ● 형용사 국외에 거주하는 ❑ 프랑스 군대는 국외 거주 가족의 여자와 어린이들을 소개시킬 준비를 하고 있다.

ex|pect ♦♦♦ /ɪkspɛkt/ (**expects, expecting, expected**) ◼ V-T If you **expect** something **to** happen, you believe that it will happen. ❑ *...a workman who expects to lose his job in the next few weeks.* ❑ *The talks are expected to continue until tomorrow.* ◻ V-T If you **are expecting** something or someone, you believe that they will be delivered to you or come to you soon, often because this has been arranged earlier. [usu cont] ❑ *I wasn't expecting a visitor.* ◼ V-T If you **expect** something, or **expect** a person **to** do something, you believe that it is your right to have that thing, or the person's duty to do it for you. ❑ *He wasn't expecting our hospitality.* ❑ *I do expect to have some time to myself in the evenings.* ◼ V-T If you tell someone not to **expect** something, you mean that the thing is unlikely to happen as they have planned or imagined, and they should not hope that it will. [with brd-neg] ❑ *Don't expect an instant cure.* ❑ *You cannot expect*

◼ 타동사 예상하다 ❑ 앞으로 몇 주 내에 실직할 것을 예상하고 있는 노동자 ❑ 회담은 내일까지 계속될 것으로 예상된다. ◻ 타동사 기대하고 있다 ❑ 손님이 방문하리라고 기대하지 않고 있었다. ◼ 타동사 (당연한 일로) 기대하다 ❑ 그는 우리의 환대를 기대하지 않고 있었다. ❑ 저녁에는 내 자신만을 위한 시간을 좀 갖기를 기대한다. ◼ 타동사 기대하다 ❑ 금방 나으리라고는 기대하지 마세요. ❑ 당신과 함께 일할 모든 사람들을 다 좋아하게 될 것이라고 기대해선 안 됩니다. ◼ 타동사/자동사 임신 중이다 ❑ 그녀는 또 한 명의 아이를 임신 중이었다. ◼ 구 그러리라고 생각하다 [구어체] ❑ 무슨 일이 뒤따를지는 네가

A

to like all the people you will work with. ⑤ V-T/V-I If you say that a woman **is expecting** a baby, or that she **is expecting**, you mean that she is pregnant. [only cont] ❑ *She was expecting another baby.* ⑥ PHRASE You say "**I expect**" to suggest that a statement is probably correct, or a natural consequence of the present situation, although you have no definite knowledge. [SPOKEN] ❑ *I expect you can guess what follows.* ❑ *I expect you're tired.*

추측할 수 있으리라고 생각한다. ❑ 네가 지쳤으리라고 생각한다.

B

Do not confuse **expect**, **wait for**, and **look forward to**. When you are **expecting** someone or something, you think that the person or thing is going to arrive or that the thing is going to happen. ❑ *I sent a postcard so they were expecting me... We are expecting rain.* When you **wait for** someone or something, you stay in the same place until the person arrives or the thing happens. ❑ *Whisky was served while we waited for him... We got off the plane and waited for our luggage.* When you **look forward to** something that is going to happen, you feel happy because you think you will enjoy it. ❑ *I'll bet you're looking forward to your holidays... I always looked forward to seeing her.*

C

D

expect, wait for, look forward to를 혼동하지 않도록 하라. 누구를 또는 그것을 expect하면, 그 사람 또는 그것이 도착하거나 그것이 일어날 것이라고 생각한다. ❑ 내가 엽서를 보내서 그들이 나를 기다리고 있었다... 우리는 비가 오리라고 생각하고 있다. 누구를 또는 무엇을 wait for하면 그 사람이 도착하거나 그것이 일어날 때까지 같은 장소에 머무르는 것이다. ❑ 우리가 그를 기다리는 동안 위스키가 제공되었다... 우리는 비행기에서 내려 짐을 기다렸다. 일어날 무엇을 look forward to하면, 그것이 즐거울 것이라고 생각해서 기분이 좋음을 나타낸다. ❑ 너는 틀림없이 휴가를 고대하고 있을 거야... 나는 항상 그녀를 보게 되기를 고대했다.

E

F

ex|pec|tan|cy /ɪkspɛktənsi/ N-UNCOUNT **Expectancy** is the feeling or hope that something exciting, interesting, or good is about to happen. ❑ *The supporters had a tremendous air of expectancy.*

불가산명사 기대, 대망 ❑ 지지자들이 엄청 기대를 하는 분위기였다.

G

ex|pec|tant /ɪkspɛktənt/ ① ADJ If someone is **expectant**, they are excited because they think something interesting is about to happen. ❑ *An expectant crowd gathered.* ● **ex|pect|ant|ly** ADV [ADV after v] ❑ *The others waited, looking at him expectantly.* ② ADJ An **expectant** mother or father is someone whose baby is going to be born soon. [ADJ n] ❑ *...a magazine for expectant mothers.*

H

① 형용사 기대에 찬 ❑ 기대에 찬 군중이 모여들었다. ● 기대에 차서 부사 ❑ 다른 사람들은 그를 기대에 차서 바라보며 기다렸다. ② 형용사 곧 부모가 되는 ❑ 임산부를 위한 잡지

I

ex|pec|ta|tion ♦◇◇ /ɛkspɛkteɪʃⁿn/ (**expectations**) ① N-UNCOUNT Your **expectations** are your strong hopes or beliefs that something will happen or that you will get something that you want. [also n in pl] ❑ *Students' expectations were as varied as their expertise.* ② N-COUNT A person's **expectations** are strong beliefs which they have about the proper way someone should behave or something should happen. ❑ *Stephen Chase had determined to live up to the expectations of the Company.*

J

① 불가산명사 기대 ❑ 학생들의 기대는 그들의 전문 기술과 마찬가지로 다양했다. ② 가산명사 기대 ❑ 스티븐 체이스는 회사의 기대에 부응하여 살기로 결심했다.

K

L

Word Partnership   expectation의 연어

N.	expectation **of privacy**, **sense of** expectation ①
ADJ.	**reasonable** expectation, **realistic** expectation ① ②

M

ex|pedi|en|cy /ɪkspidiənsi/ N-UNCOUNT **Expediency** means doing what is convenient rather than what is morally right. [FORMAL] ❑ *This was a matter less of morals than of expediency.*

불가산명사 편의 [격식체] ❑ 이것은 도덕보다는 편의상의 문제였다.

N

ex|pedi|ent /ɪkspidiənt/ (**expedients**) ① N-COUNT An **expedient** is an action that achieves a particular purpose, but may not be morally right. ❑ *Surgical waiting lists were reduced by the simple expedient of striking off all patients awaiting varicose vein operations.* ② ADJ If it is **expedient to** do something, it is useful or convenient to do it, even though it may not be morally right. ❑ *Governments frequently ignore human rights abuses in other countries if it is politically expedient to do so.*

O

① 가산명사 방법, 편법 ❑ 정맥류 수술 대기 환자 모두를 빼는 편법을 써서 수술 대기자 명단을 줄였다. ② 형용사 편리한, 정략적인 ❑ 세계 국가들의 정부가 정치적 편의에 따라 다른 나라의 인권 탄압을 모른 척하는 경우가 자주 있다.

P

ex|pedi|tion /ɛkspɪdɪʃⁿn/ (**expeditions**) ① N-COUNT An **expedition** is an organized journey that is made for a particular purpose such as exploration. ❑ *...Byrd's 1928 expedition to Antarctica.* ② N-COUNT You can refer to a group of people who are going on an expedition as an **expedition**. ❑ *Forty-three members of the expedition were killed.* ③ N-COUNT An **expedition** is a short journey or trip that you make for pleasure. ❑ *...a fishing expedition.*

Q

① 가산명사 원정, 탐험 ❑ 버드의 1928년 남극 원정 ② 가산명사 원정대, 탐험대 ❑ 원정대의 대원 43명이 죽었다. ③ 가산명사 짧은 여행 ❑ 낚시 여행

R

Word Link   pel ≈ driving, forcing : compel, expel, propel

S

ex|pel /ɪkspɛl/ (**expels, expelling, expelled**) ① V-T If someone **is expelled from** a school or organization, they are officially told to leave because they have behaved badly. [usu passive] ❑ *More than five-thousand secondary school students have been expelled for cheating.* ② V-T If people **are expelled from** a place, they are made to leave it, often by force. ❑ *An American academic was expelled from the country yesterday.* ③ V-T To **expel** something means to force it out from a container or from your body. ❑ *As the lungs exhale this waste, gas is expelled into the atmosphere.*

T

① 타동사 제명되다 ❑ 5천 명 이상의 중등학교 학생들이 부정행위로 퇴학당했다. ② 타동사 쫓겨나다, 추방되다 ❑ 한 미국인 교수가 어제 그 나라로부터 추방되었다. ③ 타동사 방출하다 ❑ 폐가 이 폐기물을 발산하면서 가스가 대기로 방출된다!

U

ex|pend /ɪkspɛnd/ (**expends, expending, expended**) V-T To **expend** something, especially energy, time, or money, means to use it or spend it. [FORMAL] ❑ *Children expend a lot of energy and may need more high-energy food than adults.*

V

타동사 (시간 등을) 소비하다 [격식체] ❑ 어린이는 에너지를 많이 소모해서 고열량 식품을 어른보다 더 필요로 할 수도 있다.

ex|pen|di|ture /ɪkspɛndɪtʃər/ (**expenditures**) N-VAR **Expenditure** is the spending of money on something, or the money that is spent on something. [FORMAL] ❑ *Policies of tax reduction must lead to reduced public expenditure.*

W

가산명사 또는 불가산명사 소비, 지출 [격식체] ❑ 세금 감면 정책은 결국은 반드시 공적 경비 지출 축소로 이어진다.

ex|pense ♦◇◇ /ɪkspɛns/ (**expenses**) ① N-VAR **Expense** is the money that something costs you or that you need to spend in order to do something. ❑ *He's bought a specially big TV at vast expense so that everyone can see properly.* ② N-PLURAL **Expenses** are amounts of money that you spend while doing something in the course of your work, which will be paid back to you afterward. [BUSINESS] ❑ *As a member of the International Olympic Committee her fares and hotel expenses were paid by the IOC.* ③ PHRASE If you do something **at** someone's **expense**, they provide the money for it. ❑ *Should architects continue to be trained for five years at public expense?* ④ PHRASE If someone laughs or makes a joke **at** your **expense**, they do it to make you seem foolish. ❑ *I think he's having*

X

Y

① 가산명사 또는 불가산명사 비용 ❑ 그는 모든 사람들이 잘 볼 수 있도록 거액의 비용을 들여 특별히 큰 텔레비전을 샀다. ② 복수명사 소요 경비 [경제] ❑ 국제 올림픽 위원회 회원인 그녀의 교통비와 호텔비는 올림픽 위원회에서 지불되었다. ③ 구 -의 비용으로 ❑ 건축사들을 공공 비용을 들여 5년 동안 계속 양성해야만 하는가? ④ 구 -을 희생시켜 ❑ 나는 그가 우리를 놀림감으로 만들어 재미있어 한다고 생각한다. ⑤ 구 -을 희생시켜 ❑ 이 연구에 따르면 여자는 남자를 희생시켜 뚜렷한 이득을 보아온 것으로

Z

fun at our expense. **5** PHRASE If you achieve something **at the expense of** someone, you do it in a way which might cause them some harm or disadvantage. ❑ *According to this study, women have made notable gains at the expense of men.* **6** PHRASE If you say that someone does something **at the expense of** another thing, you are expressing concern at the fact that they are not doing the second thing, because the first thing uses all their resources. [DISAPPROVAL] ❑ *The orchestra has more discipline now, but at the expense of spirit.* **7** PHRASE If you **go to the expense of** doing something, you do something which costs a lot of money. If you **go to** great **expense to** do something, you spend a lot of money in order to achieve it. ❑ *Why go to the expense of buying an electric saw?*

나타난다. **6** 구 -을 희생시켜 [탐탁잖음]
❑ 오케스트라는 이제 기강이 잡혔지만 활기를 잃었다.
7 구 -하는 데 많은 돈을 쓰다 ❑ 왜 많은 돈을 들여
전기톱을 삽니까?

Word Partnership	expense의 연어
ADJ.	**additional** expense, **extra** expense, **medical** expense **1**
N.	**business** expense **1**

ex|pense ac|count (**expense accounts**) N-COUNT An **expense account** is an arrangement between an employer and an employee which allows the employee to spend the company's money on things relating to their job, for example traveling or dealing with clients. [BUSINESS] ❑ *He put Elizabeth's motel bill and airfare on his expense account.*

가산명사 소요 경비 계정 [경제] ❑ 그는 엘리자베스의
모텔비 계산서와 항공료를 자기의 소요 경비 계정에
넣었다.

ex|pen|sive ♦♦◇ /ɪkspɛnsɪv/ ADJ If something is **expensive**, it costs a lot of money. ❑ *Wine's so expensive in this country.* ● **ex|pen|sive|ly** ADV ❑ *She was expensively dressed, with fine furs and jewels.*

형용사 값비싼 ❑ 포도주는 이 나라에서 아주 비싸다.
● 비싸게, 사치스럽게 부사 ❑ 그녀는 고급 모피와
보석으로 값비싸게 치장하고 있었다.

Thesaurus	expensive의 참조어
ADJ.	costly, pricey, upscale; (ant.) cheap, economical, inexpensive

ex|pe|ri|ence ♦♦♦ /ɪkspɪəriəns/ (**experiences, experiencing, experienced**) **1** N-UNCOUNT **Experience** is knowledge or skill in a particular job or activity, which you have gained because you have done that job or activity for a long time. ❑ *He has also had managerial experience on every level.* **2** N-UNCOUNT **Experience** is used to refer to the past events, knowledge, and feelings that make up someone's life or character. ❑ *I should not be in any danger here, but experience has taught me caution.* **3** N-COUNT An **experience** is something that you do or that happens to you, especially something important that affects you. ❑ *His only experience of gardening so far proved immensely satisfying.* **4** V-T If you **experience** a particular situation, you are in that situation or it happens to you. ❑ *We had never experienced this kind of holiday before and had no idea what to expect.* **5** V-T If you **experience** a feeling, you feel it or are affected by it. ❑ *Widows seem to experience more distress than do widowers.* ● N-SING **Experience** is also a noun. ❑ *...the experience of pain.*

1 불가산명사 경험 ❑ 그는 모든 직급에서 관리 경험
또한 가지고 있다. **2** 불가산명사 경험 ❑ 여기서는
위험할 리가 없지만 나는 경험을 통해 조심해야 한다는
것을 안다. **3** 가산명사 경험, 체험 ❑ 그가 지금까지 해
본 유일한 원예 체험은 대단히 만족스러웠다.
4 타동사 경험하다 ❑ 우리는 전에 이런 종류의 휴가를
경험해 본 적이 없어서 무엇을 기대해야 할지를
몰랐다. **5** 타동사 -을 겪다 ❑ 과부가 홀아비보다 더
많이 비통해 하는 것 같다. ● 단수명사 겪음, 느낌
❑ 고통을 겪음

Thesaurus	experience의 참조어
N.	know-how, knowledge, wisdom; (ant.) inexperience **1**

Word Partnership	experience의 연어
ADJ.	**professional** experience **1**
	valuable experience **1** **2** **3**
	past experience **2** **3**
	learning experience, **religious** experience, **traumatic** experience **3**
N.	**work** experience **1**
	life experience **2** **3**
	experience **a loss** **4**
	experience **symptoms** **5**

ex|pe|ri|enced /ɪkspɪəriənst/ ADJ If you describe someone as **experienced**, you mean that they have been doing a particular job or activity for a long time, and therefore know a lot about it or are very skillful at it. ❑ *...lawyers who are experienced in these matters.*

형용사 경험이 있는 ❑ 이런 문제들에 경험이 있는
변호사들

ex|peri|ment ♦◇◇ (**experiments, experimenting, experimented**)

The noun is pronounced /ɪkspɛrɪmənt/. The verb is pronounced /ɪkspɛrɪmɛnt/.

명사는 /ɪkspɛrɪmənt/로 발음되고, 동사는
/ɪkspɛrɪmɛnt/로 발음된다.

1 N-VAR An **experiment** is a scientific test which is done in order to discover what happens to something in particular conditions. ❑ *The astronauts are conducting a series of experiments to learn more about how the body adapts to weightlessness.* **2** V-I If you **experiment with** something or **experiment on** it, you do a scientific test on it in order to discover what happens to it in particular conditions. ❑ *In 1857 Mendel started experimenting with peas in his monastery garden.* ❑ *The scientists have experimented on the tiny neck arteries of rats.* ● **ex|peri|men|ta|tion** /ɪkspɛrɪmɛnteɪʃn/ N-UNCOUNT ❑ *...the ethical aspects of animal experimentation.* **3** N-VAR An **experiment** is the trying out of a new idea or method in order to see what it is like and what effects it has. ❑ *As an experiment, we bought Ted a watch.* **4** V-I To **experiment** means to try out a new idea or method to see what it is like and what effects it has. ❑ *...if you like cooking and have the time to experiment.* ● **ex|peri|men|ta|tion** N-UNCOUNT ❑ *Decentralization and experimentation must be encouraged.* →see **laboratory, science** →see Word Web: **experiment**

1 가산명사 또는 불가산명사 실험 ❑ 우주 비행사들은
신체가 무중력 상태에 어떻게 적응하는지 더 알아보기
위해 일련의 실험을 하고 있다. **2** 자동사 -으로
실험하다 ❑ 1857년에 멘델은 그의 수도원 정원에서
완두콩으로 실험을 시작했다. ❑ 과학자들은 쥐의
가느다란 경부 동맥으로 실험을 했다. ● 실험
불가산명사 ❑ 동물 실험에 대한 윤리적 측면
3 가산명사 또는 불가산명사 실제로 해봄 ❑ 시험 삼아
우리는 테드에게 시계를 사주었다. **4** 자동사 실험해
보다 ❑ 당신이 요리하기를 좋아하고 시험해 볼 시간이
있으면 ● 실험 불가산명사 ❑ 분산화와 실험이
장려되어야 한다.

Word Web — experiment

Scientists learn much of what they know through controlled **experiments**. The **scientific method** provides a dependable way to understand natural phenomena. The first step in any experiment is **observation**. During this stage researchers examine the situation and ask a question about it. They may also read what others have discovered about it. Next, they state a **hypothesis**. Then they use the hypothesis to design an experiment and **predict** what will happen. Next comes the **testing** phase. Often researchers do several experiments using different **variables**. If all of the **evidence** supports the hypothesis, it becomes a new **theory**.

Word Partnership — experiment의 연어

V.	**conduct an** experiment ∎
	perform an experiment, **try an** experiment ∎ ∎
ADJ.	**scientific** experiment ∎
	simple experiment ∎ ∎

ex|peri|men|tal /ɪksperɪment³l/ ∎ ADJ Something that is **experimental** is new or uses new ideas or methods, and might be modified later if it is unsuccessful. ❑ *...an experimental air conditioning system.* ∎ ADJ **Experimental** means using, used in, or resulting from scientific experiments. [ADJ n] ❑ *...the main techniques of experimental science.* ● **ex|peri|men|tal|ly** ADV [ADV with v] ❑ *...an ecology laboratory, where communities of species can be studied experimentally under controlled conditions.* ∎ ADJ An **experimental** action is done in order to see what it is like, or what effects it has. ❑ *The British Sports Minister is reported to be ready to argue for an experimental lifting of the ban.* ● **ex|peri|men|tal|ly** ADV [ADV with v] ❑ *This system is being tried out experimentally at many universities.*

ex|pert ◆◇◇ /ɛkspɜrt/ (**experts**) ∎ N-COUNT An **expert** is a person who is very skilled at doing something or who knows a lot about a particular subject. ❑ *...a yoga expert.* ∎ ADJ Someone who is **expert at** doing something is very skilled at it. ❑ *The Japanese are expert at lowering manufacturing costs.* ● **ex|pert|ly** ADV [ADV with v] ❑ *Shopkeepers expertly rolled spices up in bay leaves.* ∎ ADJ If you say that someone has **expert** hands or an **expert** eye, you mean that they are very skillful or experienced in using their hands or eyes for a particular purpose. [ADJ n] ❑ *When the horse suffered a back injury Harvey cured it with his own expert hands.* ∎ ADJ **Expert** advice or help is given by someone who has studied a subject thoroughly or who is very skilled at a particular job. [ADJ n] ❑ *We'll need an expert opinion.*

Word Partnership — expert의 연어

ADJ.	**leading** expert ∎
N.	expert **advice**, expert **opinion** ∎

ex|per|tise /ɛkspɜrtiz/ N-UNCOUNT **Expertise** is special skill or knowledge that is acquired by training, study, or practice. ❑ *The problem is that most local authorities lack the expertise to deal sensibly in this market.*

ex|pi|ra|tion date (**expiration dates**) N-COUNT The **expiration date** on a food container is the date by which the food should be sold or eaten before it starts to decay. [AM; BRIT **sell-by date**] ❑ *But soda past its expiration date goes flat and loses much of its taste.*

ex|pire /ɪkspaɪər/ (**expires, expiring, expired**) V-I When something such as a contract, deadline, or visa **expires**, it comes to an end or is no longer valid. ❑ *He had lived illegally in the United States for five years after his visitor's visa expired.*

ex|plain ◆◇◇ /ɪkspleɪn/ (**explains, explaining, explained**) ∎ V-T/V-I If you **explain** something, you give details about it or describe it so that it can be understood. ❑ *Not every judge, however, has the ability to explain the law in simple terms.* ❑ *Don't sign anything until your solicitor has explained the contract to you.* ❑ *Professor Griffiths explained how the drug appears to work.* ∎ V-T/V-I If you **explain** something that has happened, you give people reasons for it, especially in an attempt to justify it. ❑ *"Let me explain, sir." — "Don't tell me about it. I don't want to know."* ❑ *Before she ran away, she left a note explaining her actions.* ❑ *Explain why you didn't telephone.*

Thesaurus — explain의 참조어

V.	describe, tell ∎
	account for, justify ∎

▶**explain away** PHRASAL VERB If someone **explains away** a mistake or a bad situation they are responsible for, they try to indicate that it is unimportant or that it is not really their fault. ❑ *He evaded her questions about the war and tried to explain away the atrocities.*

ex|pla|na|tion ◆◇◇ /ɛkspləneɪʃ³n/ (**explanations**) ∎ N-COUNT If you give an **explanation** of something that has happened, you give people reasons for it, especially in an attempt to justify it. [also of/in N] ❑ *She told the court she would give a full explanation of the prosecution's decision on Monday.* ∎ N-COUNT If you say there is an **explanation for** something, you mean that there is a reason for it. ❑ *The deputy airport manager said there was no apparent explanation for the crash.*

∎ 형용사 시험적인 ❑ 시험용 공기 조절 장치 ∎ 형용사 실험적인 ❑ 실험 과학의 주요 기술 ● 실험적으로 부사 ❑ 여러 종의 군집을 통제된 상황에서 실험 연구할 수 있는 생태 실험실 ∎ 형용사 시험적인 ❑ 영국 스포츠부 장관이 그 금지 조치의 시험적 해제에 찬성할 태세가 되어 있다고 보도되었다. ● 시험적으로 부사 ❑ 이 제도는 많은 대학에서 시험적으로 사용되고 있다.

∎ 가산명사 전문가 ❑ 요가 전문가 ∎ 형용사 숙련된, 능숙한 ❑ 일본 사람은 제조비용을 내리는 데 능숙하다. ● 능숙하게 부사 ❑ 상점 점원들은 월계수 잎으로 향신료를 싸서 능숙하게 말았다. ∎ 형용사 노련한, 숙련된 ❑ 말이 허리 부상을 입었을 때 하비는 노련한 손으로 직접 그 부상을 치료했다. ∎ 형용사 전문가에 의한, 전문적인 ❑ 우리에게는 전문가의 의견이 필요할 것이다.

불가산명사 전문직 기술, 전문적 지식 ❑ 문제는 대부분의 지방 당국이 이 시장에서 분별 있게 거래할 수 있는 전문적 지식을 결여하고 있는 점이다.

가산명사 유통 기한 [미국영어; 영국영어 sell-by date] ❑ 유통 기한이 지난 소다수는 김이 빠지고 맛도 상당 부분 잃게 된다.

자동사 만기가 되다 ❑ 그는 방문 비자가 만료된 후 5년 동안 미국에서 불법으로 살았다.

∎ 타동사/자동사 설명하다 ❑ 그러나 모든 판사가 다 법을 쉬운 말로 설명할 능력이 있는 것은 아니다. ❑ 변호사가 계약 내용을 설명해 줄 때까지는 어떤 것도 서명하지 말아라. ❑ 그리피스 교수는 그 약이 어떻게 작용하는 것처럼 보이는지 설명했다. ∎ 타동사/자동사 해명하다 ❑ "선생님, 제가 말씀드리겠습니다." "얘기할 것 없다. 알고 싶지 않아." ❑ 그녀는 달아나기 전에 자기의 행동을 해명하는 쪽지를 남겼다. ❑ 왜 전화하지 않았는지 해명해 봐.

구동사 얼버무리고 넘어가다 ❑ 그는 전쟁에 대한 그녀의 질문을 회피하고 잔혹 행위들에 대해 대충 얼버무리려고 했다.

∎ 가산명사 해명 ❑ 그녀는 기소자 측의 결정에 대한 충분한 해명은 월요일에 하겠다고 법정에서 말했다. ∎ 가산명사 (설명이 되는) 이유 ❑ 공항 관리 부소장은 비행기 추락에 대한 분명한 이유가 없다고 말했다. ∎ 가산명사 설명 ❑ 그는 자기의 언급과 그 말을 하게 된 상황에 대해 아주 명확하게 설명을 했다.

3 N-COUNT If you give an **explanation of** something, you give details about it or describe it so that it can be understood. ❑ *He has given a very clear explanation of his remarks and the context in which they were made.*

Word Partnership	*explanation의 연어*
ADJ.	**only** explanation, **possible** explanation **1 2**
	brief explanation, **detailed** explanation,
	logical explanation **1 2 3**
V.	**give an** explanation, **offer an** explanation,
	provide an explanation **1 2 3**

ex|plana|tory /ɪksplǽnətɔri, BRIT ɪksplǽnətəri/ ADJ **Explanatory** statements or theories are intended to make people understand something by describing it or giving the reasons for it. [FORMAL] ❑ *These statements are accompanied by a series of explanatory notes.*

형용사 설명적인, 해설의 [격식체] ❑ 이런 진술에는 일련의 해설적 주석이 따른다.

ex|plic|it /ɪksplɪsɪt/ **1** ADJ Something that is **explicit** is expressed or shown clearly and openly, without any attempt to hide anything. ❑ *Sexually explicit scenes in films and books were taboo under the old regime.* ● ex|plic|it|ly ADV ❑ *The play was the first commercially successful work dealing explicitly with homosexuality.* **2** ADJ If you are **explicit about** something, you speak about it very openly and clearly. [V-link ADJ, oft ADJ about n] ❑ *He was explicit about his intention to overhaul the party's internal voting system.* ● ex|plic|it|ly ADV [ADV with v] ❑ *She has been talking very explicitly about AIDS to these groups.*

1 형용사 명백한, 숨김없는 ❑ 영화와 책 속의 노골적인 성적 장면은 구체제하에서는 금기였다. ● 명백히, 공공연히 부사 ❑ 그 연극은 동성애를 공공연히 다루어 상업적 성공을 거둔 최초의 작품이었다. **2** 형용사 분명한, 노골적인 ❑ 그는 당대 투표 제도를 일신하려는 의도를 분명해 했다. ● 분명하게, 터놓고 부사 ❑ 그녀는 이 그룹들에게 에이즈에 대해 아주 터놓고 말해 왔다.

Word Link	*ex ≈ away, from, out : exceed, exit, explode*

ex|plode ◆◇◇ /ɪksploʊd/ (**explodes, exploding, exploded**) **1** V-T/V-I If an object such as a bomb **explodes** or if someone or something **explodes** it, it bursts loudly and with great force, often causing damage or injury. ❑ *They were clearing up when the second bomb exploded.* **2** V-T/V-I If someone **explodes**, they express strong feelings suddenly and violently. ❑ *Do you fear that you'll burst into tears or explode with anger in front of her?* ❑ *"What happened!" I exploded.* **3** V-I If something **explodes**, it increases suddenly and rapidly in number or intensity. ❑ *The population explodes to 40,000 during the tourist season.* **4** V-T If someone **explodes** a theory or myth, they prove that it is wrong or impossible. ❑ *Electricity privatization has exploded the myth of cheap nuclear power.*

1 타동사/자동사 폭발하다; 폭발시키다 ❑ 그들이 정리를 하고 있는데 두 번째 폭탄이 터졌다. **2** 타동사/자동사 (감정이) 폭발하다 ❑ 그녀 앞에서 갑자기 울음을 터뜨리거나 격분할까 봐 걱정이니? ❑ "어떻게 된 거야!"라고 나는 격분했다 **3** 자동사 (규격히) 증가하다 ❑ 관광 여행 시즌 동안에는 거주민 수가 4만 명으로 급격히 증가한다. **4** 타동사 (학설 등을) 타파하다 ❑ 전력의 민영화는 원자력이 저렴하다는 통념을 깨버렸다.

Thesaurus	*explode의 참조어*
V.	blow up, erupt, go off **1**
	discredit, disprove **4**

Word Partnership	*explode의 연어*
N.	**bombs** explode, **missiles** explode **1**
	populations explode **3**
ADJ.	**ready to** explode **1 2**
PREP.	**about to** explode **1 2 3**

ex|ploit ◆◇◇ (**exploits, exploiting, exploited**)

The verb is pronounced /ɪksplɔɪt/. The noun is pronounced /ɛksplɔɪt/.	동사는 /ɪksplɔɪt /으로 발음되고, 명사는 /ɛksplɔɪt /으로 발음된다.

1 V-T If you say that someone **is exploiting** you, you think that they are treating you unfairly by using your work or ideas and giving you very little in return. ❑ *Critics claim he exploited black musicians for personal gain.* ● ex|ploi|ta|tion /ɛksplɔɪteɪʃⁿn/ N-UNCOUNT ❑ *Extra payments should be made to protect the interests of the staff and prevent exploitation.* **2** V-T If you say that someone **is exploiting** a situation, you disapprove of them because they are using it to gain an advantage for themselves, rather than trying to help other people or do what is right. [DISAPPROVAL] ❑ *The government and its opponents compete to exploit the troubles to their advantage.* ● ex|ploi|ta|tion N-SING ❑ *...the exploitation of the famine by local politicians.* **3** V-T If you **exploit** something, you use it well, and achieve something or gain an advantage from it. ❑ *You'll need a good aerial to exploit the radio's performance.* **4** V-T To **exploit** resources or raw materials means to develop them and use them for industry or commercial activities. ❑ *I think we're being very short-sighted in not exploiting our own coal.* ● ex|ploi|ta|tion N-UNCOUNT ❑ *...the planned exploitation of its potential oil and natural gas reserves.* **5** N-COUNT If you refer to someone's **exploits**, you mean the brave, interesting, or amusing things that they have done. ❑ *His wartime exploits were later made into a film and a television series.*

1 타동사 착취하다 ❑ 비판가들은 그가 사적 이익을 위해 흑인 음악가들을 착취했다고 주장한다. ● 착취 불가산명사 ❑ 직원의 이익을 보호하고 착취를 막기 위해서는 별도의 지불금을 내야 한다. **2** 타동사 악용하다, 이용하다 [탐탁찮음] ❑ 정부와 야당이 경쟁적으로 그 문제를 자기들에게 유리하게 이용하려 하고 있다. ● 악용 단수명사 ❑ 지역 정치인들의 기근 악용 **3** 타동사 이용하다, 활용하다 ❑ 라디오의 성능을 잘 활용하기 위해서는 좋은 안테나가 필요할 것이다. **4** 타동사 (자원을) 개발하다 ❑ 나는 우리가 우리의 석탄을 개발하지 않는 것은 매우 근시안적이라고 생각한다. ● 개발 불가산명사 ❑ 계획된 석유와 천연가스 잠재 자원 개발 **5** 가산명사 공훈, 공적 ❑ 그의 전쟁시 공훈은 나중에 영화와 텔레비전 연속물로 제작되었다.

ex|plora|tory /ɪksplɔrətɔri, BRIT ɪksplɒrətri/ ADJ **Exploratory** actions are done in order to discover something or to learn the truth about something. ❑ *Exploratory surgery revealed her liver cancer.*

형용사 답사의; 예비적인 ❑ 예비 수술로 그녀의 간암이 밝혀졌다.

ex|plore ◆◇◇ /ɪksplɔr/ (**explores, exploring, explored**) **1** V-T/V-I If you **explore** a place, you travel around it to find out what it is like. ❑ *I just wanted to explore Paris, read Sartre, listen to Sidney Bechet.* ❑ *After exploring the old part of town there is a guided tour of the cathedral.* ● ex|plo|ra|tion /ɛksplɔreɪʃⁿn/ (**explorations**) N-VAR ❑ *We devote several days to the exploration of the magnificent Maya sites of Copan.* **2** V-T If you **explore** an idea or suggestion, you think about it or comment on it in detail, in order to assess it carefully. ❑ *The film is eloquent as it explores the relationship between artist and instrument.* ● ex|plo|ra|tion N-VAR ❑ *I looked forward to the exploration of their theories.* **3** V-I If people **explore** an area **for** a substance

1 타동사 또는 자동사 답사하다, 답사하다 ❑ 나는 그저 파리를 답사하고, 사르트르를 읽고, 시드니 베쳇을 듣고 싶었다. ❑ 구시가지를 답사하시고 나면 안내원이 딸린 대성당 관람이 있습니다. ● 답사 가산명사 또는 불가산명사 ❑ 우리는 코판의 웅대한 마야 유적을 답사하면서 며칠을 보냈다. **2** 타동사 탐구하다 ❑ 그 영화는 예술가와 도구와의 관계를 면밀히 탐구하는 점에서 설득력이 있다. ● 탐구 가산명사 또는 불가산명사 ❑ 저는 그들의 이론에 대한

A

such as oil or minerals, they study the area and do tests on the land to see whether they can find it. □ *Central to the operation is a mile-deep well, dug originally to explore for oil.* ● ex|plo|ra|tion N-UNCOUNT □ *Oryx is a Dallas-based oil and gas exploration and production concern.* ◳ V-T If you **explore** something with your hands or fingers, you touch it to find out what it feels like. □ *He explored the wound with his finger, trying to establish its extent.*

B

탐구를 기대합니다. ◳ 자동사 탐사하다 □ 이 공사의 핵심에 원래 석유를 탐사하기 위해 파놓은 1마일 깊이의 유정이 있다. ● 탐사 불가산명사 □ 오릭스는 댈러스에 소재한 석유와 가스의 탐사 및 생산 회사이다. ◳ 타동사 (손으로) 만져 보다, 탐색하다 □ 그는 상처의 정도를 확인하려고 손가락으로 만져 보았다.

C

ex|plor|er /ɪksplɔ̱rər/ (explorers) N-COUNT An **explorer** is someone who travels to places about which very little is known, in order to discover what is there. □ *...the travels of Columbus, Magellan, and many other explorers.*

가산명사 탐험가 □ 콜럼버스, 마젤란, 그리고 많은 다른 탐험가들의 여행

D

ex|plo|sion ♦♦◇ /ɪksplo̱ʊʒ³n/ (explosions) ◳ N-COUNT An **explosion** is a sudden, violent burst of energy, for example one caused by a bomb. □ *After the second explosion, all of London's main train and subway stations were shut down.* ◳ N-VAR **Explosion** is the act of deliberately causing a bomb or similar device to explode. □ *Bomb disposal experts blew up the bag in a controlled explosion.* ◳ N-COUNT An **explosion** is a large rapid increase in the number or amount of something. □ *The study also forecast an explosion in the diet soft-drink market.* ◳ N-COUNT An **explosion** is a sudden violent expression of someone's feelings, especially anger. □ *Every time they met, Myra anticipated an explosion.* ◳ N-COUNT An **explosion** is a sudden and serious political protest or violence. □ *...the explosion of protest and violence sparked off by the killing of seven workers.*

E

◳ 가산명사 폭발 □ 두 번째 폭발 후 런던의 모든 주요 철도와 지하철역이 폐쇄되었다. ◳ 가산명사 또는 불가산명사 폭파 □ 폭탄 제거 전문가들이 통제된 폭발로 그 가방을 폭파했다. ◳ 가산명사 폭발적 증가 □ 그 연구는 다이어트용 탄산음료 시장의 폭발적 증가 또한 예상했다. ◳ 가산명사 (분노의) 폭발 □ 그들이 만날 때마다 미라는 분노가 폭발할 것을 예상했다. ◳ 가산명사 (항의 등의) 폭발 □ 7명의 근로자의 사망이 기폭제가 되어 폭발한 항의와 폭력 사태

F

ex|plo|sive /ɪksplo̱ʊsɪv/ (explosives) ◳ N-VAR An **explosive** is a substance or device that can cause an explosion. □ *...one-hundred-and-fifty pounds of Semtex explosive.* ◳ ADJ Something that is **explosive** is capable of causing an explosion. □ *The explosive device was timed to go off at the rush hour.* ◳ ADJ An **explosive** growth is a sudden, rapid increase in the size or quantity of something. □ *The explosive growth in casinos is one of the most conspicuous signs of Westernization.* ◳ ADJ An **explosive** situation is likely to have difficult, serious, or dangerous effects. □ *He appeared to be treating the potentially explosive situation with some sensitivity.* ◳ ADJ If you describe someone as **explosive**, you mean that they tend to express sudden violent anger. □ *He's inherited his father's explosive temper.* →see **tunnel**

G

H

I

J

◳ 가산명사 또는 불가산명사 폭발물 □ 150파운드 무게의 셈텍스 폭발물 ◳ 형용사 폭발의 □ 그 폭발 장치는 출퇴근 혼잡 시간에 터지도록 맞춰져 있었다. ◳ 형용사 폭발적인 □ 카지노의 폭발적인 증가는 가장 눈에 띄는 서구화의 징표 중 하나이다. ◳ 형용사 심각한 □ 그는 어쩌면 심각해질 수도 있는 상황을 세심하게 다루고 있는 것 같았다. ◳ 형용사 격한 □ 그는 아버지의 격한 성질을 물려받았다.

K

ex|po /e̱kspoʊ/ (expos) also Expo N-COUNT An **expo** is a large event where goods, especially industrial goods, are displayed. □ *...the 1995 Queensland Computer Expo.*

가산명사 박람회, 엑스포 □ 1995년 퀸즐랜드 컴퓨터 박람회

ex|po|nent /ɪkspo̱ʊnənt/ (exponents) ◳ N-COUNT An **exponent of** an idea, theory, or plan is a person who supports and explains it, and who tries to persuade other people that it is a good idea. [FORMAL] □ *...a leading exponent of test-tube baby techniques.* ◳ N-COUNT An **exponent of** a particular skill or activity is a person who is good at it. □ *...the great exponent of expressionist dance, Kurt Jooss.*

L

◳ 가산명사 주창자 [격식체] □ 시험관 아기 기술의 주된 주창자 ◳ 가산명사 대표적 인물 □ 표현주의 무용의 위대한 대표적 인물인 커트 주스

M

Word Link
port ≈ carrying : export, import, portable

ex|port ♦♦◇ (exports, exporting, exported)

N

The verb is pronounced /ɪkspɔ̱rt/. The noun is pronounced /e̱kspɔrt/.

동사는 /ɪkspɔ̱rt/로 발음되고, 명사는 /e̱kspɔrt/로 발음된다.

O

◳ V-T/V-I To **export** products or raw materials means to sell them to another country. □ *The nation also exports beef.* □ *They expect the antibiotic products to be exported to Southeast Asia and Africa.* ● N-UNCOUNT **Export** is also a noun. [also N in pl] □ *...the production and export of cheap casual wear.* □ *A lot of our land is used to grow crops for export.* ◳ N-COUNT **Exports** are goods which are sold to another country and sent there. □ *Ghana's main export is cocoa.* ◳ V-T To **export** something means to introduce it into another country or make it happen there. □ *It has exported inflation at times.* ◳ V-T In computing, if you **export** files or information from one type of software into another type, you change their format so that they can be used in the new software. □ *Files can be exported in ASCII or PCX formats.*

P

Q

◳ 타동사/자동사 수출하다 □ 그 나라는 쇠고기도 수출한다. □ 그들은 항생제 제품이 동남아시아와 아프리카에 수출되리라 예상한다. ● 불가산명사 수출 □ 값싼 평상복의 생산과 수출 □ 우리 토지의 많은 부분이 수출용 곡식을 재배한다. 데 사용된다. ◳ 가산명사 수출품 □ 가나의 주요 수출품은 코코아이다. ◳ 타동사 야기하다 □ 그것은 때때로 인플레이션을 야기했다. ◳ 타동사 변환시키다 □ 파일들은 ASCII 또는 PCX 형식으로 변환될 수 있다.

R

ex|port|able /ɪkspɔ̱rtəb³l/ ADJ **Exportable** products are suitable for being exported. □ *They are reliant on a very limited number of exportable products.*

형용사 수출용의 □ 그들은 극히 제한된 수의 수출 가능 제품에 의존하고 있다.

ex|port|er /e̱kspɔrtər, ɪkspɔ̱rtər/ (exporters) N-COUNT An **exporter** is a country, firm, or person that sells and sends goods to another country. □ *France is the world's second-biggest exporter of agricultural products.*

가산명사 수출하는 사람, 수출국, 수출 회사 □ 프랑스는 세계에서 두 번째로 큰 농산물 수출국이다.

S

ex|pose ♦◇◇ /ɪkspo̱ʊz/ (exposes, exposing, exposed) ◳ V-T To **expose** something that is usually hidden means to uncover it so that it can be seen. □ *Lowered sea levels exposed the shallow continental shelf beneath the Bering Sea.* ◳ V-T To **expose** a person or situation means to reveal that they are bad or immoral in some way. □ *The Budget does expose the lies ministers were telling a year ago.* ◳ V-T If someone **is exposed to** something dangerous or unpleasant, they are put in a situation in which it might affect them. □ *They had not been exposed to most diseases common to urban populations.* □ *A wise mother never exposes her children to the slightest possibility of danger.* ◳ V-T If someone **is exposed to** an idea or feeling, usually a new one, they are given experience of it, or introduced to it. □ *...local people who've not been exposed to glimpses of Western life before.*

T

U

V

◳ 타동사 드러내어 보이다 □ 해수면이 낮아지면서 베링 해의 얕은 대륙붕이 드러났다. ◳ 타동사 폭로하다, 드러내다 □ 예산은 일년 전에 장관들이 했던 거짓말을 그대로 드러내 준다. ◳ 타동사 노출되다 □ 그들은 도시인들에게 흔한 대부분의 질병들에 노출되지 않았었다. □ 현명한 어머니는 아이들을 최소한의 위험의 가능성이 있는 상황에도 노출시키지 않는다. ◳ 타동사 경험하다, 접하다 □ 이전에 서구의 삶을 한 번도 눈으로 접해 본 적이 없는 시골 사람들

W

ex|po|sure ♦◇◇ /ɪkspo̱ʊʒər/ (exposures) ◳ N-UNCOUNT **Exposure to** something dangerous means being in a situation where it might affect you. □ *Exposure to lead is known to damage the brains of young children.* ◳ N-UNCOUNT **Exposure** is the harmful effect on your body caused by very cold weather. □ *He was suffering from exposure and shock but his condition was said to be stable.* ◳ N-UNCOUNT The **exposure** of a well-known person is the revealing of the fact that they are bad or immoral in some way. □ *...the exposure of Anthony Blunt as a former Soviet spy.* ◳ N-UNCOUNT **Exposure** is publicity that a person, company, or product receives. □ *All the candidates had been getting an enormous amount of exposure on television and in the press.* ◳ N-COUNT In photography, an **exposure** is a single photograph. [TECHNICAL] □ *Larger drawings tend to require two or three exposures to cover them.*

X

Y

Z

◳ 불가산명사 노출 □ 납에 대한 노출은 어린 아이들의 두뇌에 손상을 입히는 것으로 알려져 있다. ◳ 불가산명사 (극심한 추위에 의한) 신체적 악영향 □ 그는 추위로 인한 신체적 영향과 충격을 겪었으나 그의 상태는 안정되었다고 하였다. ◳ 불가산명사 폭로 □ 앤터니 블런트가 이전에 소련 스파이였다는 사실의 폭로 ◳ 불가산명사 (텔레비전 등) 출연, 노출 □ 모든 후보들은 텔레비전과 신문에서 매우 많이 다뤄지고 있다. ◳ 가산명사 필름의 한 컷 [과학 기술] □ 더 큰 그림을 찍으려면 두세 컷의 필름이 필요할 것이다.

ex|pound /ɪkspaʊnd/ (expounds, expounding, expounded) v-т If you **expound** an idea or opinion, you give a clear and detailed explanation of it. [FORMAL] ❑ *Schmidt continued to expound his views on economics and politics.* ● PHRASAL VERB **Expound on** means the same as **expound**. ❑ *Lawrence expounded on the military aspects of guerrilla warfare.*

타동사 상세히 설명하다 [격식체] ❑ 슈미트는 정치와 경제에 대한 자기 견해를 계속해서 상세히 말했다. ● 구동사 상세히 설명하다 ❑ 로렌스는 게릴라전의 군사적 측면을 상세히 설명했다.

ex|press ♦♦◇ /ɪkspres/ (expresses, expressing, expressed) **1** v-т When you **express** an idea or feeling, or **express yourself**, you show what you think or feel. ❑ *He expressed grave concern at American attitudes.* **2** v-т If an idea or feeling **expresses itself** in some way, it can be clearly seen in someone's actions or in its effects on a situation. ❑ *The anxiety of the separation often expresses itself as anger toward the child for getting lost.* **3** ADJ An **express** command or order is one that is clearly and deliberately stated. [FORMAL] [ADJ n] ❑ *The ship was sunk on express orders from the Prime Minister.* ● ex|press|ly ADV [ADV before v] ❑ *He has expressly forbidden her to go out on her own.* **4** ADJ If you refer to an **express** intention or purpose, you are emphasizing that it is a deliberate and specific one that you have before you do something. [EMPHASIS] [ADJ n] ❑ *I had obtained my first camera for the express purpose of taking railway photographs.* ● ex|press|ly ADV ❑ *...projects expressly designed to support cattle farmers.* **5** ADJ **Express** is used to describe special services which are provided by companies or organizations such as the U.S. Postal Service, in which things are sent or done faster than usual for a higher price. [ADJ n] ❑ *A special express service is available by fax.* ● ADV **Express** is also an adverb. ❑ *Send it express.* **6** N-COUNT An **express** or an **express** train is a fast train which stops at very few stations. ❑ *Punctually at 7.45, the express to Kuala Lumpur left Singapore station.*

1 타동사 표현하다 ❑ 그는 미국인의 태도에 대해서 깊은 우려를 표명했다. **2** 타동사 드러나다 ❑ 헤어짐으로 인한 불안은 종종 미아가 되었던 아이에 대한 화풀이의 형태로 나타나게 된다. **3** 형용사 분명한, 명확한 [격식체] ❑ 수상의 명확한 지시에 따라 그 배는 격침되었다. ● 분명히 부사 ❑ 그는 그녀 혼자서는 밖으로 나가지 말라고 분명히 말해 왔다. **4** 형용사 특별한 [강조] ❑ 나는 철도 사진을 찍으려는 분명한 목표를 가지고 처음으로 카메라를 마련했다. ● 특별히 부사 ❑ 가축 농가를 지원하기 위해 특별히 고안된 계획들 **5** 형용사 속달 ❑ 특급 속달 서비스를 팩스로 이용가능하다. ● 부사 속달로 ❑ 그것을 속달로 보내시오. **6** 가산명사 급행 ❑ 정확하게 7시 45분에 쿠알라룸푸르 행 급행열차는 싱가포르 역을 떠났다.

Word Partnership   express의 연어

N.   express **appreciation**, express *your* **emotions**, express **gratitude**, express **sympathy**, **words** to express *something* **1**
     express **purpose** **4**
     express **mail**, express **service** **5**

ex|pres|sion ♦◇◇ /ɪkspreʃn/ (expressions) **1** N-VAR The **expression** of ideas or feelings is the showing of them through words, actions, or artistic activities. ❑ *Laughter is one of the most infectious expressions of emotion.* ❑ *...the rights of the individual to freedom of expression.* **2** N-VAR Your **expression** is the way that your face looks at a particular moment. It shows what you are thinking or feeling. ❑ *Levin sat there, an expression of sadness on his face.* **3** N-UNCOUNT **Expression** is the showing of feeling when you are acting, singing, or playing a musical instrument. ❑ *I don't sing perfectly in tune, but I think I put more expression into my lyrics than a lot of other singers do.* **4** N-COUNT An **expression** is a word or phrase. ❑ *She spoke in a quiet voice but used remarkably coarse expressions.*

1 가산명사 또는 불가산명사 표현 ❑ 웃음은 가장 전염성이 강한 감정 표현 중의 하나이다. ❑ 표현의 자유에 대한 개인의 권리를 **2** 가산명사 또는 불가산명사 표정 ❑ 레빈은 얼굴에 슬픈 표정을 지은 채 거기에 앉아 있었다. **3** 불가산명사 감정 표출 ❑ 나는 음정을 완벽하게 지키지는 못하지만 많은 다른 가수들보다도 가사에 더 많은 감정 이입을 한다고 생각한다. **4** 가산명사 말, 표현 ❑ 그녀는 조용한 목소리로 말했으나 놀라울 정도로 거친 표현들을 사용했다.

ex|pres|sive /ɪkspresɪv/ ADJ If you describe a person or their behavior as **expressive**, you mean that their behavior clearly indicates their feelings or intentions. ❑ *You can train people to be more expressive.* ❑ *...the present fashion for intuitive, expressive painting.* ● ex|pres|sive|ly ADV [ADV with v] ❑ *He moved his hands expressively.*

형용사 표현의, 표정의 ❑ 사람들이 감정 표현을 보다 잘하도록 훈련시킬 수 있다. ❑ 직관적이고 표현적인 그림을 선호하는 현재의 유행 ● 의미 있는 듯이 부사 ❑ 그는 손을 무슨 뜻을 전하려는 듯이 움직였다.

ex|pul|sion /ɪkspʌlʃn/ (expulsions) **1** N-VAR **Expulsion** is when someone is forced to leave a school, university, or organization. ❑ *Her hatred of authority led to her expulsion from high school.* **2** N-VAR **Expulsion** is when someone is forced to leave a place. [FORMAL] ❑ *...the expulsion of Yemeni workers.*

1 가산명사 또는 불가산명사 퇴학, 퇴출 ❑ 권위에 대한 증오 때문에 그녀는 고등학교에서 퇴학당했다. **2** 가산명사 또는 불가산명사 축출 [격식체] ❑ 예멘 노동자들의 축출

ex|qui|site /ɪkskwɪzɪt, ɛkskwɪzɪt/ ADJ Something that is **exquisite** is extremely beautiful or pleasant, in a delicate way. ❑ *The Indians brought in exquisite beadwork to sell.* ● ex|qui|site|ly ADV ❑ *...exquisitely crafted dolls' houses.*

형용사 아주 아름다운, 정교한 ❑ 인디언들은 정교한 구슬 장식품을 가져와 팔았다. ● 정교하게, 아름답게 부사 ❑ 정교하게 만들어진 인형의 집들

ext. N-VAR **Ext.** is the written abbreviation for **extension** when it is used to refer to a particular telephone number. [N num] ❑ *For a full festival program call 01629 580000 ext 6591.*

가산명사 또는 불가산명사 내선 ❑ 축제 전체 프로그램에 대해서는 01629 580000 (내선 6591)으로 전화하세요.

ex|tend ♦♦◇ /ɪkstend/ (extends, extending, extended) **1** v-ı If you say that something, usually something large, **extends for** a particular distance or **extends from** one place **to** another, you are indicating its size or position. ❑ *The caves extend for some 18 kilometers.* ❑ *The main stem will extend to around 12ft, if left to develop naturally.* **2** v-ı If an object **extends** from a surface or place, it sticks out from it. ❑ *Billing's legs extended from the bushes and Anthony tripped over them as he retraced his steps.* **3** v-ı If an event or activity **extends over** a period of time, it continues for that time. ❑ *...a playing career in first-class cricket that extended from 1894 to 1920.* **4** v-ı If something **extends to** a group of people, things, or activities, it includes or affects them. ❑ *The service also extends to wrapping and delivering gifts.* ❑ *The talks will extend to the church, human rights groups, and other social organizations.* **5** v-т If you **extend** something, you make it longer or bigger. ❑ *This year they have introduced three new products to extend their range.* ❑ *The building was extended in 1500.* **6** v-ı If a piece of equipment or furniture **extends**, its length can be increased. ❑ *... a table which extends to accommodate extra guests.* **7** v-т If you **extend** something, you make it last longer than before or end at a later date. ❑ *They have extended the deadline by twenty-four hours.* **8** v-т If you **extend** something **to** other people or things, you make it include or affect more people or things. ❑ *It might be possible to extend the technique to other crop plants.* **9** v-т If someone **extends** their hand, they stretch out their arm and hand to shake hands with someone. ❑ *The man extended his hand: "I'm Chuck."*

1 자동사 뻗어 있다; (거리나 크기가) ...에서 ...까지 미치다 ❑ 동굴들은 18킬로미터 정도 뻗어 있다. ❑ 자연적으로 성장하게 두면 큰 줄기는 12피트 정도까지 자랄 것이다. **2** 자동사 -로부터 뻗어 나오다 ❑ 빌링의 다리가 덤불 밖으로 삐져나와 있었는데 앤터니가 되돌아 가다가 다리에 걸려 넘어졌다. **3** 자동사 -동안 계속되다 ❑ 1894년부터 1920년까지 1급 크리켓에서 활동한 경기 경력 **4** 자동사 포함하다, 아우르다 ❑ 선물 포장 및 배달을 해 주는 서비스 또한 제공한다. ❑ 그 강연은 교회, 인권 단체들, 그리고 다른 사회단체들까지 아우를 것이다. **5** 타동사 확장하다, 증축하다 ❑ 올해 그들은 사업영역을 확장하기 위해 세 개의 신제품을 팔기 시작하였다. ❑ 그 건물은 1500년에 증축되었다. **6** 자동사 늘어나다 ❑ 추가 손님을 대접할 수 있도록 더 넓게 펼 수 있는 식탁 **7** 타동사 연장하다 ❑ 그들은 마감 시간을 24시간 연장했다. **8** 타동사 -로 확대하다 ❑ 그 기술을 다른 작물로 확대하는 것이 가능할 수도 있다. **9** 타동사 뻗다 ❑ 그 남자는 손을 내밀며 말했다. "저는 척입니다."

ex|ten|sion /ɪkstenʃn/ (extensions) **1** N-COUNT An **extension** is a new room or building which is added to an existing building or group of buildings. ❑ *We are thinking of having an extension built, as we now require an extra bedroom.* **2** N-COUNT An **extension** is a new section of a road or rail line that is added to an existing road or line. ❑ *...the Jubilee Line extension.* **3** N-COUNT An **extension** is an extra period of time for which something lasts or is valid, usually as a

1 가산명사 증축, 증설 ❑ 이제 침실이 더 필요해서, 증축을 생각하는 중이다. **2** 가산명사 연장선 ❑ 주빌리 라인 연장 노선 **3** 가산명사 연장 ❑ 그는 처음에 6개월짜리 비자로 영국에 입국했다가, 6개월을 연장받았다. **4** 가산명사 연장, 발전 ❑ 많은 필리핀 사람들은 그 군 기지들을 미국 식민지 통치의 연장으로

result of official permission. ❑ *He first entered Britain on a six-month visa, and was given a further extension of six months.* ◳ N-COUNT Something that is an **extension** of something else is a development of it that includes or affects more people, things, or activities. ❑ *Many Filipinos see the bases as an extension of American colonial rule.* ◳ N-COUNT An **extension** is a telephone line that is connected to the switchboard of a company or institution, and that has its own number. The written abbreviation **ext.** is also used. [also N num] ❑ *She can get me on extension 308.* ◳ N-COUNT An **extension** is a part which is connected to a piece of equipment in order to make it reach something further away. ❑ *...30-foot extension cord.*

ex|ten|sive ◆◇◇ /ɪkstɛnsɪv/ ◳ ADJ Something that is **extensive** covers or includes a large physical area. ❑ *...an extensive tour of Latin America.* ● ex|ten|sive|ly ADV [ADV after v] ❑ *Mark, however, needs to travel extensively with his varied business interests.* ◳ ADJ Something that is **extensive** covers a wide range of details, ideas, or items. ❑ *Developments in South Africa receive extensive coverage in The Sunday Telegraph.* ● ex|ten|sive|ly ADV ❑ *All these issues have been extensively researched in recent years.* ◳ ADJ If something is **extensive**, it is very great. ❑ *The security forces have extensive powers of search and arrest.* ● ex|ten|sive|ly ADV ❑ *Hydrogen is used extensively in industry for the production of ammonia.*

ex|tent ◆◇◇ /ɪkstɛnt/ ◳ N-SING If you are talking about how great, important, or serious a difficulty or situation is, you can refer to the **extent** of it. ❑ *The government itself has little information on the extent of industrial pollution.* ◳ N-SING **The extent of** something is its length, area, or size. ❑ *Industry representatives made it clear that their commitment was only to maintain the extent of forests, not their biodiversity.* ◳ PHRASE You use expressions such as **to a large extent, to some extent,** or **to a certain extent** in order to indicate that something is partly true, but not entirely true. [VAGUENESS] ❑ *It was and, to a large extent, still is a good show.* ❑ *To some extent this was the truth.* ◳ PHRASE You use expressions such as **to what extent, to that extent,** or **to the extent that** when you are discussing how true a statement is, or in what ways it is true. [VAGUENESS] ❑ *It's still not clear to what extent this criticism is originating from within the ruling party.* ◳ PHRASE You use expressions such as **to the extent of, to the extent that,** or **to such an extent that** in order to emphasize that a situation has reached a difficult, dangerous, or surprising stage. [EMPHASIS] ❑ *Ford kept his suspicions to himself, even to the extent of going to jail for a murder he obviously didn't commit.*

Word Partnership   extent의 연어

N.	extent **of the damage** ◳
V.	**determine** the extent, **know the** extent ◳
ADJ.	**lesser** extent ◳
	full extent ◳ ◳
	a certain extent ◳

Word Link   exter ≈ outside of : exterior, exterminate, external

ex|te|ri|or /ɪkstɪəriər/ (**exteriors**) ◳ N-COUNT The **exterior** of something is its outside surface. ❑ *The exterior of the building was a masterpiece of architecture, elegant and graceful.* ◳ N-COUNT You can refer to someone's usual appearance or behavior as their **exterior**, especially when it is very different from their real character. ❑ *According to Mandy, Pat's tough exterior hides a shy and sensitive soul.* ◳ ADJ You use **exterior** to refer to the outside parts of something or things that are outside something. [ADJ n] ❑ *The exterior walls were made of pre-formed concrete.*

Thesaurus   exterior의 참조어

N.	coating, cover, outside, shell, skin ◳
ADJ.	external, outer, outermost, surface ◳

ex|ter|mi|nate /ɪkstɜrmɪneɪt/ (**exterminates, exterminating, exterminated**) V-T To **exterminate** a group of people or animals means to kill all of them. ❑ *A huge effort was made to exterminate the rats.* ● ex|ter|mi|na|tion /ɪkstɜrmɪneɪʃ⁰n/ N-UNCOUNT ❑ *...the extermination of hundreds of thousands of their brethren.*

ex|ter|nal /ɪkstɜrn⁰l/ ◳ ADJ **External** is used to indicate that something is on the outside of a surface or body, or that it exists, happens, or comes from outside. ❑ *...a much reduced heat loss through external walls.* ● ex|ter|nal|ly ADV ❑ *Vitamins can be applied externally to the skin.* ◳ ADJ **External** means involving or intended for foreign countries. [ADJ n] ❑ *...the commissioner for external affairs.* ❑ *...Jamaica's external debt.* ● ex|ter|nal|ly ADV ❑ *...protecting the value of the mark both internally and externally.* ◳ ADJ **External** means happening or existing in the world in general and affecting you in some way. [ADJ n] ❑ *Such events occur only when the external conditions are favorable.* ◳ ADJ **External** experts, for example **external examiners**, come into an organization from outside in order to do a particular job fairly and impartially, or to check that a particular job was done properly. [mainly BRIT] [ADJ n] ❑ *He was an external examiner for several universities.* →see **ear**

ex|tinct /ɪkstɪŋkt/ ◳ ADJ A species of animal or plant that is **extinct** no longer has any living members, either in the world or in a particular place. ❑ *It is 250 years since the wolf became extinct in Britain.* ◳ ADJ If a particular kind of worker, way of life, or type of activity is **extinct**, it no longer exists, because of changes in society. ❑ *Herbalism had become an all but extinct skill in the Western world.* ◳ ADJ An **extinct** volcano is one that does not erupt or is not expected to erupt anymore. ❑ *Its tallest volcano, long extinct, is Olympus Mons.*

여긴다. ❺ 가산명사 내선 ❑ 그녀는 내선 308번으로 나에게 연락할 수 있다. ❻ 가산명사 연장 코드 ❑ 30피트 길이의 연장 코드

❶ 형용사 광대한, 대규모의 ❑ 라틴 아메리카의 전 지역 순방 ● 광범위하게 부사 ❑ 그러나 마크는 다양한 사업적 흥미를 가지고 광범위하게 여행하는 것이 필요하다. ❷ 형용사 광범위한, 포괄적인 ❑ 남아프리카 공화국에서 전개되는 일들이 선데이 텔레그래프 지에서 광범위하게 보도되고 있다. ● 광범위하게 부사 ❑ 이러한 모든 논점들은 최근 몇 년 동안 광범위하게 연구되었다. ❸ 형용사 큰, 거대한 ❑ 치안 유지군은 수색과 체포하는 데 막강한 힘을 가지고 있다. ● 막대하게, 거대하게 부사 ❑ 수소는 암모니아를 생산하는 산업에서 막대하게 사용된다.

❶ 단수명사 -의 정도 ❑ 정부조차도 산업 오염의 정도에 대한 정보를 거의 갖고 있지 못한다. ❷ 단수명사 길이; 넓이; 크기 ❑ 그들의 의무는 숲의 생물학적 다양성을 유지하는 것이 아니라 숲의 크기를 유지하는 것일 뿐이라는 것을 업계 대표들은 분명히 했다. ❸ 구 대부분의; 어느 정도까지는, 다소 [짐작투] ❑ 그것은 훌륭한 쇼였고, 대체로는 여전히 그러하다. ❑ 어느 정도까지는 이것이 사실이었다. ❹ 구 어느 정도로; 그 정도로 [짐작투] ❑ 이러한 비판이 어느 정도로 집권 정당 내부로부터 나오는 것인지는 여전히 분명하지 않다. ❺ 구 - 정도까지 [강조] ❑ 포드는 심지어 그가 분명히 저지르지 않은 살인 때문에 교도소에 가야 할 지경에 이르렀어도 속에 품은 의심을 발설하지 않았다.

❶ 가산명사 외부, 외형 ❑ 그 건물의 외형은 건축의 최고 걸작으로 고상하고 우아했다. ❷ 가산명사 외모, 외견 ❑ 맨디에 의하면 팻의 남성적인 외모 밑에는 수줍고 예민한 성격이 숨어 있다. ❸ 형용사 외부의 ❑ 외벽은 미리 만들어진 콘크리트로 되어 있다.

타동사 박멸하다, 근절하다 ❑ 쥐를 근절하는 데 업청난 노력을 기울였다. ● 근절, 박멸, 몰살 불가산명사 ❑ 수십만 동포들의 몰살

❶ 형용사 외부의 ❑ 훨씬 줄어든 외벽을 통한 열 손실 ● 외부적으로, 외부에서 부사 ❑ 비타민을 외용적으로 피부에 직접 바를 수도 있다. ❷ 형용사 대외적인, 국제적인 ❑ 외무 위원 ❑ 자메이카의 외채 ● 대외적으로 부사 ❑ 대내외적으로 상표의 가치를 보호하는 것 ❸ 형용사 외부의 ❑ 그러한 일들은 외부 조건들이 양호할 때만 일어난다. ❹ 형용사 외부의 [주로 영국영어] ❑ 그는 여러 대학의 논문 외부 심사 위원이었다.

❶ 형용사 멸종된 ❑ 늑대가 영국에서 멸종된 지 250년이다. ❷ 형용사 사멸한, 사라진 ❑ 약초 연구는 서구에서 거의 사라진 기술이 되어 있었다. ❸ 형용사 활동을 그친 ❑ 그곳의 가장 큰 화산은 오래전에 활동을 멈춘 올림포스 몬스이다.

ex|tinc|tion /ɪkstɪŋkʃ^ən/ N-UNCOUNT The **extinction** of a species of animal or plant is the death of all its remaining living members. ❑ *An operation is beginning to try to save a species of crocodile from extinction.* ❷ N-UNCOUNT If someone refers to the **extinction** of a way of life or type of activity, they mean that the way of life or activity stops existing. ❑ *The loggers say their jobs are faced with extinction because of declining timber sales.*

ex|tin|guish /ɪkstɪŋgwɪʃ/ (extinguishes, extinguishing, extinguished) ❶ V-T If you **extinguish** a fire or a light, you stop it from burning or shining. [FORMAL] ❑ *It took about 50 minutes to extinguish the fire.* ❷ V-T If something **extinguishes** a feeling or idea, it destroys it. ❑ *The message extinguished her hopes of Richard's return.*

ex|tol /ɪkstoʊl/ (extols, extolling, extolled) V-T If you **extol** something or someone, you praise them enthusiastically. ❑ *Now experts are extolling the virtues of the humble potato.*

ex|tor|tion|ate /ɪkstɔrʃ^ənɪt/ ADJ If you describe something such as a price as **extortionate**, you are emphasizing that it is much greater than it should be. [EMPHASIS] ❑ *...a specially prepared menu on which basic dishes are charged at extortionate prices.*

ex|tra ♦♦◇ /ɛkstrə/ (extras) ❶ ADJ You use **extra** to describe an amount, person, or thing that is added to others of the same kind, or that can be added to others of the same kind. [ADJ n] ❑ *Police warned motorists to allow extra time to get to work.* ❑ *There's an extra blanket in the bottom drawer of the cupboard.* ❷ ADJ If something is **extra**, you have to pay more money for it in addition to what you are already paying for something. [v-link ADJ] ❑ *For foreign orders postage is extra.* ● PRON **Extra** is also a pronoun. ❑ *She won't pay any extra.* ● ADV **Extra** is also an adverb. ❑ *You may be charged 10% extra for this service.* ❸ N-COUNT **Extras** are additional amounts of money that are added to the price that you have to pay for something. ❑ *There are no hidden extras.* ❹ N-COUNT **Extras** are things which are not necessary in a situation, activity, or object, but which make it more comfortable, useful, or enjoyable. ❑ *Optional extras include cooking tuition at a top restaurant.* ❺ N-COUNT The **extras** in a movie are the people who play unimportant parts, for example as members of a crowd. ❑ *In 1944, Kendall entered films as an extra.* ❻ ADV You can use **extra** in front of adjectives and adverbs to emphasize the quality that they are describing. [INFORMAL, EMPHASIS] [ADV adj/adv] ❑ *I'd have to be extra careful.*

Word Link   extra ≈ outside of : ex**tra**ct, ex**tra**dite, ex**tra**ordinary

---

ex|tract (extracts, extracting, extracted)

The verb is pronounced /ɪkstrækt/. The noun is pronounced /ɛkstrækt/.

❶ V-T To **extract** a substance means to obtain it from something else, for example by using industrial or chemical processes. ❑ *...the traditional method of pick and shovel to extract coal.* ❑ *Citric acid can be extracted from the juice of oranges, lemons, limes, or grapefruit.* ● ex|trac|tion N-UNCOUNT ❑ *Petroleum engineers plan and manage the extraction of oil.* ❷ V-T If you **extract** something **from** a place, you take it out or pull it out. ❑ *He extracted a small notebook from his hip pocket.* ❸ V-T When a dentist **extracts** a tooth, they remove it from the patient's mouth. ❑ *A dentist may decide to extract the tooth to prevent recurrent trouble.* ● ex|trac|tion (extractions) N-VAR ❑ *In those days, dentistry was basic. Extractions were carried out without anaesthetic.* ❹ V-T If you say that someone **extracts** something, you disapprove of them because they take it for themselves to gain an advantage. [DISAPPROVAL] ❑ *He sought to extract the maximum political advantage from the cut in interest rates.* ❺ V-T If you **extract** information or a response **from** someone, you get it from them with difficulty, because they are unwilling to say or do what you want. ❑ *He made the mistake of trying to extract further information from our director.* ❻ V-T If you **extract** a particular piece of information, you obtain it from a larger amount or source of information. ❑ *I've simply extracted a few figures.* ❑ *Britain's trade figures can no longer be extracted from export-and-import documentation at ports.* ❼ V-T PASSIVE If part of a book or text is **extracted from** a particular book, it is printed or published. [JOURNALISM] ❑ *This material has been extracted from "Collins Good Wood Handbook".* ❽ N-COUNT An **extract from** a book or piece of writing is a small part of it that is printed or published separately. ❑ *Read this extract from an information booklet about the work of an airline cabin crew.* ❾ N-MASS An **extract** is a substance that has been obtained from something else, for example by means of a chemical or industrial process. ❑ *Blend in the lemon extract, lemon peel, and walnuts.* →see **industry, mineral**

ex|tra|dite /ɛkstrədaɪt/ (extradites, extraditing, extradited) V-T If someone is **extradited**, they are officially sent back to their own or another country to be tried for a crime that they have been accused of. [FORMAL] ❑ *The authorities refused to extradite him.* ● ex|tra|di|tion /ɛkstrədɪʃ^ən/ (extraditions) N-VAR ❑ *A New York court turned down the British government's request for his extradition.*

ex|traor|di|nary ♦♦◇ /ɪkstrɔrd^əneri, BRIT ɪkstrɔː^rdənri/ ❶ ADJ If you describe something or someone as **extraordinary**, you mean that they have some extremely good or special quality. [APPROVAL] ❑ *We've made extraordinary progress as a society in that regard.* ❑ *The task requires extraordinary patience and endurance.* ● ex|traor|di|nar|i|ly /ɪkstrɔrdənerɪli, BRIT ɪkstrɔː^rdənrɪli/ ADV [ADV adj] ❑ *She's extraordinarily disciplined.* ❷ ADJ If you describe something as **extraordinary**, you mean that it is very unusual or surprising. [EMPHASIS] ❑ *What an extraordinary thing to happen!* ● ex|traor|di|nar|i|ly ADV ❑ *Apart from the hair, he looked extraordinarily unchanged.* ❸ ADJ An **extraordinary** meeting is arranged specially to deal with a particular situation or problem, rather than happening regularly. [FORMAL] [ADJ n] ❑ *...at an extraordinary meeting of the sport's ruling body.*

❶ 불가산명사 절멸, 멸종 ❑ 한 악어 종을 멸종으로부터 구하려는 작업이 시작되고 있다. ❷ 불가산명사 사멸 ❑ 목재 판매 감소 때문에 벌목꾼들은 자신들이 직업이 사라질 위기에 처해 있다고 말한다.

❶ 타동사 끄다, 진화하다 [격식체] ❑ 그 화재를 진화하는 데 약 50분 걸렸다. ❷ 타동사 소멸시키다 ❑ 그 서신으로 리처드가 돌아오기를 바라는 그녀의 희망은 사라졌다.

타동사 격찬하다 ❑ 현재 전문가들은 소박한 감자의 가치를 격찬하고 있다.

형용사 터무니없는, 과대한 [강조] ❑ 기본 요리에 대해 터무니없는 가격을 제시한 특별히 준비된 메뉴판

❶ 형용사 여분의 ❑ 경찰은 운전자들에게 출근 시간이 좀 더 길어질 수 있음을 경고했다. ❑ 벽장 아래 서랍에 여분의 담요가 있다. ❷ 형용사 추가 요금의 ❑ 해외 주문은 추가 우편 요금이다. ● 대명사 추가 요금 ❑ 그녀는 어떠한 추가 요금도 내지 않을 것이다. ● 부사 추가로 ❑ 이 서비스에 10퍼센트의 추가 요금이 부과될 것입니다. ❸ 가산명사 추가 요금 ❑ 감춰진 추가 요금은 없다. ❹ 가산명사 부대 품목 ❑ 선택할 수 있는 부대 품목에는 최고의 레스토랑에서 하는 요리 강습이 포함된다. ❺ 가산명사 단역 배우, 엑스트라 ❑ 1944년에 켄달은 단역 배우로 영화에 출연하기 시작했다. ❻ 부사 특별히, 더욱 [비격식체, 강조] ❑ 나는 각별히 주의해야 할 것이다.

동사는 /ɪkstrækt/으로 발음되고, 명사는 /ɛkstrækt/으로 발음된다.

❶ 타동사 추출하다 ❑ 곡괭이와 삽을 이용해서 석탄을 캐는 전통적인 방법 ❑ 구연산은 오렌지, 레몬, 라임, 또는 자몽의 주스에서 추출할 수 있다. ● 추출 불가산명사 ❑ 석유 기술자는 석유의 추출을 계획하고 관리한다. ❷ 타동사 꺼내다 ❑ 그는 뒷주머니에서 작은 수첩을 꺼냈다. ❸ 타동사 뽑다 ❑ 치과 의사가 문제의 재발을 막기 위해 이를 뽑기로 결정할지도 모른다. ● 뽑아냄 가산명사 또는 불가산명사 ❑ 그 당시 치과 기술은 초보적이었다. 마취도 하지 않고 이를 뽑았다. ❹ 타동사 끄집어내다, (이득을) 챙기다 [탐탁찮음] ❑ 그는 금리 인하에서 최대의 정치적인 이득을 챙기려고 했다. ❺ 타동사 (힘겹게) 얻다, 도출하다 ❑ 그는 우리 감독으로부터 더 많은 정보를 얻어내려고 하는 실수를 범했다. ❻ 타동사 뽑아내다, 뽑아 얻다 ❑ 나는 단지 몇 명의 수치들을 뽑아냈을 뿐이다. ❑ 더 이상 항구의 수출입 선적 서류에서 영국의 무역 수치를 얻을 수 없다. ❼ 수동태동사 발췌되다 [언론] ❑ 이 자료는 '콜린스 굿 우드 핸드북'에서 발췌한 것이다. ❽ 가산명사 발췌문 ❑ 항공기 객실 승무원의 업무에 대한 한 안내서에서 발췌한 이 부분을 읽어보시오. ❾ 물질명사 추출물 ❑ 레몬 추출물에 레몬 껍질과 호두를 잘 섞으시오.

타동사 인도되다, 소환되다 [격식체] ❑ 당국은 그를 인도하기를 거부했다. ● 소환, 인도 가산명사 또는 불가산명사 ❑ 뉴욕 법정은 그를 인도해 달라는 영국 정부의 요청을 거절했다.

❶ 형용사 훌륭한, 특별한 [마음에 듦] ❑ 그런 측면에서 본다면 한 사회로서 우리는 대단한 진보를 이루었다. ❑ 그 일은 대단한 인내와 참을성을 요구한다. ● 대단하게, 특별하게 부사 ❑ 그녀는 교육을 아주 잘 받은 사람이다. ❷ 형용사 터무니없는, 놀라운 [강조] ❑ 정말 놀라운 일이 일어났군! ● 놀랍게 부사 ❑ 머리만 빼고는, 놀랍게도 그는 전혀 변한 것이 없어 보였다. ❸ 형용사 특별한 [격식체] ❑ 그 스포츠 지도부의 특별 회의에서

ex|trapo|late /ɪkstræpəˈleɪt/ (**extrapolates, extrapolating, extrapolated**) V-T/V-I
If you **extrapolate from** known facts, you use them as a basis for general statements about a situation or about what is likely to happen in the future. [FORMAL] ❑ *Extrapolating from his American findings, he reckons about 80% of these deaths might be attributed to smoking.* ● **ex|trapo|la|tion** /ɪkstræpəleɪʃ°n/ (**extrapolations**) N-VAR ❑ *His estimate of half a million HIV positive cases was based on an extrapolation of the known incidence of the virus.*

타동사/자동사 ... 로부터 추정하다 [격식체] ❑ 그가 산출한 미국의 결과로부터 추정해 보아, 그는 이러한 사망의 80퍼센트 정도가 흡연으로 인한 것이라고 생각한다. ● 추정 가산명사 또는 불가산명사 ❑ HIV 양성 반응자가 50만 정도라는 그의 추정 수치는 그 질병의 알려진 발생 건수를 외삽해서 얻은 것이었다.

ex|trava|gance /ɪkstrævəgəns/ (**extravagances**) **1** N-UNCOUNT **Extravagance** is the spending of more money than is reasonable or than you can afford. ❑ *When the company went under, tales of his extravagance surged through the industry.* **2** N-COUNT An **extravagance** is something that you spend money on but cannot really afford. ❑ *Why waste money on such extravagances?*

1 불가산명사 낭비 ❑ 그 회사가 파산했을 때, 그의 낭비에 대한 소문이 업계에 파다하게 퍼졌다. **2** 가산명사 사치품 ❑ 그러한 사치품에 왜 돈을 낭비하는가?

ex|trava|gant /ɪkstrævəgənt/ **1** ADJ Someone who is **extravagant** spends more money than they can afford or uses more of something than is reasonable. ❑ *We are not extravagant; restaurant meals are a luxury and designer clothes are out.* ● **ex|trava|gant|ly** ADV [ADV with v] ❑ *The day before they left Jeff had shopped extravagantly for presents for the whole family.* **2** ADJ Something that is **extravagant** costs more money than you can afford or uses more of something than is reasonable. ❑ *Her Aunt Sallie gave her an uncharacteristically extravagant gift.* ❑ *Baking a whole cheese in pastry may seem extravagant.* ● **ex|trava|gant|ly** ADV [ADV adj/-ed] ❑ *By supercar standards, though, it is not extravagantly priced for a beautifully engineered machine.* **3** ADJ **Extravagant** behavior is extreme behavior that is often done for a particular effect. ❑ *He was extravagant in his admiration of Hellas.* ● **ex|trava|gant|ly** ADV ❑ *She had on occasions praised him extravagantly.* **4** ADJ **Extravagant** claims or ideas are unrealistic or impractical. [DISAPPROVAL] ❑ *Don't be afraid to consider apparently extravagant ideas.*

1 형용사 돈을 함부로 쓰는, 낭비벽이 있는 ❑ 우리는 낭비하지 않습니다. 레스토랑 식사는 사치이고 디자이너의 옷은 입지 않습니다. ● 흥청망청, 엄청나게 부사 ❑ 그들이 떠나기 전 날 제프는 가족 전체에게 줄 선물을 산다고 엄청나게 쇼핑을 했다. **2** 형용사 과분한, 지나친 ❑ 샐리 고모는 평소와는 달리 과분한 선물을 그녀에게 주었다. ❑ 페이스추리에 치즈를 다 넣어 굽는 것은 지나쳐 보일 수 있다. ● 터무니없이 비싸게 부사 ❑ 그러나 슈퍼 카 기준으로 보면 그것은 정교하게 제작된 자동차로 터무니없이 비싼 것은 아니다. **3** 형용사 지나친, 과도한 ❑ 그는 헬라스를 지나치게 흠모했다. ● 지나치게 부사 ❑ 그녀는 이따금 그를 지나치게 칭찬했다. **4** 형용사 얼토당토않은, 터무니없는 [탐탁잖음] ❑ 터무니없어 보이는 생각을 품는 것을 두려워하지 말아라.

ex|trava|gan|za /ɪkstrævəgænzə/ (**extravaganzas**) N-COUNT An **extravaganza** is a very elaborate and expensive show or performance. ❑ *...a magnificent firework extravaganza.*

가산명사 호화 쇼 ❑ 웅장하고 화려한 불꽃놀이

ex|treme ♦♢♢ /ɪkstriːm/ (**extremes**) **1** ADJ **Extreme** means very great in degree or intensity. ❑ *The girls were afraid of snakes and picked their way along with extreme caution.* ❑ *...people living in extreme poverty.* **2** ADJ You use **extreme** to describe situations and behavior which are much more severe or unusual than you would expect, especially when you disapprove of them because of this. [DISAPPROVAL] ❑ *The extreme case was Poland, where 29 parties won seats.* ❑ *It is hard to imagine Lineker capable of anything so extreme.* **3** ADJ You use **extreme** to describe opinions, beliefs, or political movements which you disapprove of because they are very different from those that most people would accept as reasonable or normal. [DISAPPROVAL] ❑ *This extreme view hasn't captured popular opinion.* **4** N-COUNT You can use **extremes** to refer to situations or types of behavior that have opposite qualities to each other, especially when each situation or type of behavior has such a quality to the greatest degree possible. ❑ *...a "middle way" between the extremes of success and failure, wealth and poverty.* **5** ADJ The **extreme** end or edge of something is its farthest end or edge. [ADJ n] ❑ *...the room at the extreme end of the corridor.* **6** PHRASE If a person **goes to extremes** or **takes** something **to extremes**, they do or say something in a way that people consider to be unacceptable, unreasonable, or foolish. ❑ *The police went to the extremes of installing the most advanced safety devices in the man's house.*

1 형용사 극도의 ❑ 소녀들은 뱀을 무서워해서 매우 조심하며 갈 길을 나아갔다. ❑ 극도로 가난한 삶을 사는 사람들 **2** 형용사 극단적인 [탐탁잖음] ❑ 극단적인 경우는 폴란드로 의석을 차지한 정당이 29개였다. ❑ 라이너커가 그렇게 극단적인 일을 할 수 있을 거라고는 상상도 하기 힘들다. **3** 형용사 과격한 [탐탁잖음] ❑ 이 과격한 견해는 여론을 포착하지 못했다. **4** 가산명사 양극단 ❑ 성공과 실패, 그리고 부와 가난이라는 양극단 사이의 '중도' **5** 형용사 맨 끝의 ❑ 복도 맨 끝에 있는 방 **6** 구 극단으로 치닫다, 극단으로 몰다 ❑ 경찰은 그 남자의 집에 가장 최신의 안전장치를 설치하는 극단의 방법을 썼다.

Word Partnership   extreme의 연어

N.	extreme **caution**, extreme **difficulty** **1**
	extreme **case** **2**
	extreme **left**, extreme **right**, extreme **views** **3**

---

ex|treme|ly ♦♢♢ /ɪkstriːmli/ ADV You use **extremely** in front of adjectives and adverbs to emphasize that the specified quality is present to a very great degree. [EMPHASIS] [ADV adj/adv] ❑ *My mobile phone is extremely useful.* ❑ *Three of them are working extremely well.*

부사 대단히, 극도로 [강조] ❑ 내 핸드폰은 대단히 유용하다. ❑ 그들 중 세 명이 일을 대단히 잘 하고 있다.

Thesaurus   extremely의 참조어

ADV.	exceedingly, greatly, highly, very; (ant.) mildly

---

ex|trem|ism /ɪkstriːmɪzəm/ N-UNCOUNT **Extremism** is the behavior or beliefs of extremists. ❑ *Greater demands were being placed on the police by growing violence and left and right-wing extremism.*

불가산명사 극단론 ❑ 폭력, 그리고 좌익과 우익 극단론의 증가로 경찰에게 더 많은 부담이 가고 있었다.

ex|trem|ist /ɪkstriːmɪst/ (**extremists**) **1** N-COUNT If you describe someone as an **extremist**, you disapprove of them because they try to bring about political change by using violent or extreme methods. [DISAPPROVAL] ❑ *He said the country needed a strong intelligence service to counter espionage, terrorism, and foreign extremists.* ❑ *A previously unknown extremist group has said it carried out Friday's bomb attack.* **2** ADJ If you say that someone has **extremist** views, you disapprove of them because they believe in bringing about change by using violent or extreme methods. [DISAPPROVAL] ❑ *...his determination to purge the party of extremist views.*

1 가산명사 극단주의자 [탐탁잖음] ❑ 그는 국가에 첩보, 테러, 그리고 외국 극단주의자에 맞설 강력한 정보 부서가 필요하다고 말했다. ❑ 이전에는 알려지지 않았던 한 극단주의 단체가 금요일의 폭탄 공격을 자행했다고 말했다. **2** 형용사 극단론의, 과격론의 [탐탁잖음] ❑ 당에서 극단론의 견해를 제거하려는 그의 결의

extro|vert /ɛkstrəvɜːrt/ (**extroverts**) ADJ Someone who is **extrovert** is very active, lively, and friendly. [mainly BRIT] ❑ *His footballing skills and extrovert personality won the hearts of the public.* ● N-COUNT An **extrovert** is someone who is extrovert. [AM usually **extroverted**] ❑ *He was a showman, an extrovert who reveled in controversy.*

형용사 외향적인 [주로 영국영어] ❑ 그의 축구 기술과 외향적인 성격은 대중의 사랑을 얻었다. ● 가산명사 외향적인 사람 [미국영어 대개 extroverted] ❑ 논쟁을 즐기고 외향적인 그는 타고난 끼를 가진 사람이었다.

extro|vert|ed /ɛkstrəvɜːrtɪd/ ADJ Someone who is **extroverted** is very active, lively, and friendly. [mainly AM; BRIT usually **extrovert**] ❑ *Some young people*

형용사 외향적인 [주로 미국영어; 영국영어 대개 extrovert] ❑ 어렸을 적에는 무난하고 외향적인

who were easy-going and extroverted as children become self-conscious in early adolescence.

exu|ber|ance /ɪgzubərəns, BRIT ɪgzyu:bərəns/ N-UNCOUNT **Exuberance** is behavior which is energetic, excited, and cheerful. ❑ *Her burst of exuberance and her brightness overwhelmed me.*

exu|ber|ant /ɪgzubərənt, BRIT ɪgzyu:bərənt/ ADJ If you are **exuberant**, you are full of energy, excitement, and cheerfulness. ❑ *So the exuberant young girl with dark hair and blue eyes decided to become a screen actress.* ● **exu|ber|ant|ly** ADV ❑ *They both laughed exuberantly.*

ex|ude /ɪgzud, ɪksud, BRIT ɪgzyu:d/ (**exudes, exuding, exuded**) **1** V-T If someone **exudes** a quality or feeling, or if it **exudes**, they show that they have it to a great extent. [FORMAL] ❑ *The guerrillas exude confidence. Every town, they say, is under their control.* ❑ *She exudes an air of relaxed calm.* **2** V-T/V-I If something **exudes** a liquid or smell or if a liquid or smell **exudes from** it, the liquid or smell comes out of it slowly and steadily. [FORMAL] ❑ *Nearby was a factory which exuded a pungent smell.*

eye ♦♦♦ /aɪ/ (**eyes, eyeing** or **eying, eyed**) **1** N-COUNT Your **eyes** are the parts of your body with which you see. ❑ *I opened my eyes and looked.* ❑ *...a tall, thin white-haired lady with piercing dark brown eyes.*

> **Eye contact** is an important aspect of North American culture. If someone does not look at the person with whom he or she is speaking, the speaker is thought to be rude or even dishonest. An honest person is praised for **looking you straight in the eye**. Take care not to look for too long, or you'll be guilty of **staring**, which is considered bad manners.

2 V-T If you **eye** someone or something in a particular way, you look at them carefully in that way. ❑ *Sally eyed Claire with interest.* ❑ *We eyed each other thoughtfully.* **3** N-COUNT You use **eye** when you are talking about a person's ability to judge things or about the way in which they are considering or dealing with things. ❑ *William was a man of discernment, with an eye for quality.* ❑ *He first learned to fish under the watchful eye of his grandmother.* **4** N-COUNT An **eye** is a small metal loop which a hook fits into, as a fastening on a piece of clothing. ❑ *There were lots of hooks and eyes in Victorian costumes!* **5** N-COUNT The **eye** of a needle is the small hole at one end which the thread passes through. ❑ *The only difficult part was threading the cotton through the eye of the needle!* **6** N-SING **The eye** of a storm, tornado, or hurricane is the center of it. ❑ *The eye of the hurricane hit Florida just south of Miami.* **7** →see also **black eye 8** PHRASE If you say that something happens **before** your **eyes**, **in front of** your **eyes**, or **under** your **eyes**, you are emphasizing that it happens where you can see it clearly and often implying that it is surprising or unpleasant. [EMPHASIS] ❑ *A lot of them died in front of our eyes.* **9** PHRASE If you **cast** your **eye** or **run** your **eye** over something, you look at it or read it quickly. ❑ *I would be grateful if he could cast an expert eye over it and tell me what he thought of it.* **10** PHRASE If something **catches** your **eye**, you suddenly notice it. ❑ *As she turned back, a movement across the lawn caught her eye.* →see also **eye-catching 11** PHRASE If you **catch** someone's **eye**, you do something to attract their attention, so that you can speak to them. ❑ *I tried to catch Chrissie's eye to find out what she was playing at.* **12** PHRASE If you **close** your **eyes to** something bad or if you **shut** your **eyes to** it, you ignore it. ❑ *Most governments must simply be shutting their eyes to the problem.* **13** PHRASE If you **cry** your **eyes out**, you cry very hard. [INFORMAL] ❑ *He didn't mean to be cruel but I cried my eyes out.* **14** PHRASE If there is something **as far as the eye can see**, there is a lot of it and you cannot see anything else beyond it. ❑ *There are pine trees as far as the eye can see.* **15** PHRASE If you say that someone **has an eye for** something, you mean that they are good at noticing it or making judgments about it. ❑ *Susan has a keen eye for detail, so each dress is beautifully finished off.* **16** PHRASE You use expressions such as **in** his **eyes** or **to** her **eyes** to indicate that you are reporting someone's opinion and that other people might think differently. ❑ *The other serious problem in the eyes of the new government is communalism.* **17** PHRASE If you **keep** your **eyes open** or **keep an eye out** for someone or something, you watch for them carefully. [INFORMAL] ❑ *I ask the mounted patrol to keep their eyes open.* **18** PHRASE If you **keep an eye on** something or someone, you watch them carefully, for example to make sure that they are satisfactory or safe, or not causing trouble. ❑ *I went for a run there, keeping an eye on the children the whole time.* **19** PHRASE If you say that **all eyes are on** something or that the **eyes of the world are on** something, you mean that everyone is paying careful attention to it and what will happen. [JOURNALISM] ❑ *All eyes will be on tomorrow's vote.* **20** PHRASE If someone **has** their **eye on** you, they are watching you carefully to see what you do. ❑ *As the boat plodded into British waters and up the English Channel, Customs had their eye on her.* **21** PHRASE If you **have** your **eye on** something, you want to have it. [INFORMAL] ❑ *If you're saving up for a new outfit you've had your eye on, cheap dinners for a month might let you buy it.* **22** PHRASE If you say that you did something **with** your **eyes open** or **with** your **eyes wide open**, you mean that you knew about the problems and difficulties that you were likely to have. ❑ *We want all our members to undertake this trip responsibly, with their eyes open.* **23** PHRASE If something **opens** your **eyes**, it makes you aware that something is different from the way that you thought it was. ❑ *Watching your child explore the world about her can open your eyes to delights long forgotten.* **24** PHRASE If you **see eye to eye with** someone, you agree with them and have the same opinions and views. ❑ *Yuriko saw eye to eye with Yul on almost every aspect of the production.* **25** PHRASE When you **take** your **eyes off** the thing you have been watching or looking at, you stop looking at it. ❑ *She took her eyes off the road to glance at me.* **26** PHRASE If you say that you are **up to** your **eyes in** something, you are emphasizing that you have a lot of it to deal with, and often that you are

---

성격이었다가 사춘기 초기에 자의식이 강한 성격으로 바뀌는 청소년들도 있다.

불가산명사 활력 ❑ 그녀의 활력과 명랑함이 나를 압도했다.

형용사 위기 왕성한, 화려이 넘치는 ❑ 그렇게 검은 머리에 푸른 눈을 가진 활력이 넘치는 그 젊은 처녀는 영화배우가 되기로 결심했다. ● 활발하게 부사 ❑ 그 둘 모두 활발하게 웃었다.

1 타동사 발산시키다, 표출되다 [격식체] ❑ 그 게릴라들은 자신감을 표출한다. 모든 도시가 그들 통제 하에 있다고 그들은 말한다. ❑ 그녀에게선 평온한 분위기가 뿜어 나온다. **2** 타동사/자동사 흘러나오게 하다, 스며 나오다 [격식체] ❑ 근처에 심한 악취를 내뿜는 공장이 있었다.

1 가산명사 눈 ❑ 나는 눈을 뜨고 보았다. ❑ 성긴 흰머리에 날카로운 짙은 갈색 눈을 지닌 키가 크고 몸이 마른 부인

> eye contact(마주 바라보기)은 북미 문화의 중요한 부분이다. 대화 중에 상대방을 바라보지 않으면 무례하거나 심지어 정직하지 않다고 여긴다. 상대방의 눈을 똑바로 쳐다보면 (looking you straight in the eye) 정직한 사람으로 좋게 여겨진다. 그러나 너무 오래 계속 쳐다 보지 않도록 주의해야 한다. 그랬다간 무례하게 빤히 쳐다본다(staring)는 비난을 받을 수도 있다.

2 타동사 바라보다 ❑ 샐리는 클레어를 흥미롭게 바라보았다. ❑ 우리는 골똘히 생각하며 서로를 바라보았다. **3** 가산명사 관찰력, 안목 ❑ 윌리엄은 좋은 것을 알아보는 통찰력 있는 사람이었다. ❑ 그는 할머니의 주시 하에 낚시를 처음 배웠다. **4** 가산명사 고리, 닷고리 ❑ 빅토리아 시대의 의상에는 고리와 닷고리가 참 많았다. **5** 가산명사 바늘구멍, 바늘귀 ❑ 유일하게 힘든 부분은 바늘귀에 무명실을 꿰는 것이었다! **6** 단수명사 중심, 눈 ❑ 허리케인의 눈은 마이애미 바로 남쪽 플로리다를 강타했다. **7** →보라 **black eye 8** 구 바로 눈앞에서, 드러내 놓고 [강조] ❑ 그들 중 많은 사람이 우리 눈앞에서 죽었다. **9** 구 -을 대강 훑어 보다 ❑ 그가 그것을 전문가의 눈으로 한번 훑어보고 어떻게 생각하는지 나에게 말해 준다면 정말 고마울 것이다. **10** 구 눈에 띄다 ❑ 그녀가 뒤돌아보았을 때, 뭔가가 잔디밭을 가로질러 가는 것이 눈에 띄었다. **11** 구 눈길을 끌다 ❑ 나는 그녀가 어떤 꿍꿍이속인지 알아내려고 크리시의 시선을 잡아보려 했다. **12** 구 외면하다 ❑ 대부분의 정부들이 그저 그 문제를 외면하고 있음이 틀림없다. **13** 구 눈이 퉁퉁 붓도록 울다 [비격식체] ❑ 그는 잔혹하게 하려고 한 것은 아니었지만 나는 눈이 퉁퉁 붓도록 울었다. **14** 구 눈에 보이는 것은 온통, 같이 안 보일 정도로 ❑ 눈에 보이는 것은 온통 소나무들이었다. **15** 구 -에 대한 안목이 있다 ❑ 수잔은 세부적인 것에도 안목이 있어서 각각의 드레스는 마무리 손질이 아주 잘 되어 있다. **16** 구 -의 눈에는 ❑ 새 정부의 눈으로 볼 때도 한 가지 심각한 문제는 지방 자치주의이다. **17** 구 두 눈 부릅뜨고 지켜보다 [비격식체] ❑ 나는 기마 순찰자에게 두 눈 부릅뜨고 잘 살펴보라고 당부했다. **18** 구 방심하지 않고 지켜보다, -에서 눈을 떼지 않다 ❑ 나는 그곳에 달리기하러 가면서, 내내 아이들에게서 눈을 떼지 않았다. **19** 구 -에 이목이 집중되다 [언론] ❑ 내일 선거에 모든 이목이 집중될 것이다. **20** 구 주의 깊게 살펴보다 ❑ 배가 영국 수역 안으로 들어와 영국 해협을 따라 올라오자 세관 직원들은 배를 주시했다. **21** 구 눈독을 들이다 [비격식체] ❑ 눈독을 들이고 있는 새 옷을 사기 위해 돈을 모으고 있다면, 한 달 동안 싼 저녁으로 때우면 그것을 살 수 있을지도 모른다. **22** 구 다 알고서, 잘 분별하여 ❑ 우리는 구성원 모두가 눈을 크게 뜨고 이 여행을 책임감 있게 다녀오기를 바란다. **23** 구 (새로운 사실을) 깨닫다 ❑ 아이가 주변 세상을 탐구하는 것을 지켜보면 오랫동안 잊고 있던 기쁨을 깨닫게 될 수도 있다. **24** 구 -와 견해가 완전히 일치하다 ❑ 유리코는 생산의 거의 모든 측면에서 율과 견해가 완전히 일치했다. **25** 구 -에서 눈을 떼다 ❑ 그녀가 길에서 눈길을 거둬 나를 쳐다보았다. **26** 구 (할 일이) 목에까지 차 있는 [비격식체, 강조] ❑ 나는 할 일이 목에까지 차 있다.

a b c d e f g h i j k l m n o p q r s t u v w x y z

Word Web   eye

Light enters the **eye** through the cornea. The cornea bends the light and directs it through the **pupil**. The colored **iris** opens and closes the **lens**. This helps focus the **image** clearly on the **retina**. Nerve cells in the retina change the light into electrical signals. The **optic nerve** then carries these signals to the brain. In a **nearsighted** person the light rays focus in front of the lens. The image comes onto focus in back of the lens in a **farsighted** person. An irregularity in the cornea can cause astigmatism. Glasses or **contact lenses** can correct all three problems.

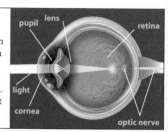

very busy. [INFORMAL, EMPHASIS] ❏ *I am up to my eyes in work.* ☒ to **turn a blind eye** →see **blind**. to **feast** your **eyes** →see **feast**. in your **mind's eye** →see **mind** →see **cry, face, hurricane** →see Word Web: **eye**

eye|ball /aɪbɔl/ (**eyeballs**) ■ N-COUNT Your **eyeballs** are your whole eyes, rather than just the part which can be seen between your eyelids. ☑ PHRASE You use **up to the eyeballs** to emphasize that someone is in an undesirable state to a very great degree. [INFORMAL, EMPHASIS] ❏ *He is out of a job and up to his eyeballs in debt.*

■ 가산명사 안구 ☑ 구 극도의 곤경에 처한 [비격식체, 강조] ❏ 그는 일자리도 잃고 엄청난 빚에 시달리는 상태이다.

eye|brow /aɪbraʊ/ (**eyebrows**) ■ N-COUNT Your **eyebrows** are the lines of hair which grow above your eyes. ☑ PHRASE If something causes you to **raise an eyebrow** or to **raise** your **eyebrows**, it causes you to feel surprised or disapproving. ❏ *An intriguing item on the news pages caused me to raise an eyebrow over my morning coffee.* ❏ *He raised his eyebrows over some of the suggestions.* →see **face**

■ 가산명사 눈썹 ☑ 구 (불만 등으로) 눈썹을 치켜 올리다 ❏ 아침 커피를 마시다가 뉴스 면에 나온 야릇한 기사를 보고 나는 눈썹을 치켜 올렸다. ❏ 그 제안 중 몇 개에 대해 그는 놀라서 눈썹을 치켜 올렸다.

eye-catching ADJ Something that is **eye-catching** is very noticeable. ❏ *...a series of eye-catching ads.*

형용사 눈길을 끄는 ❏ 눈길을 끄는 일련의 광고

eye|glasses /aɪglæsɪz/ N-PLURAL **Eyeglasses** are two lenses in a frame that some people wear in front of their eyes in order to help them see better. [AM; BRIT usually **glasses**] ❏ *...the 140 million Americans who wear eyeglasses or contact lenses.*

복수명사 안경 [미국영어; 영국영어 대개 glasses] ❏ 안경을 쓰거나 콘택트 렌즈를 하는 1억 4천만 미국인들

eye|lash /aɪlæʃ/ (**eyelashes**) N-COUNT Your **eyelashes** are the hairs which grow on the edges of your eyelids. →see **face**

가산명사 속눈썹

eye|lid /aɪlɪd/ (**eyelids**) N-COUNT Your **eyelids** are the two pieces of skin which cover your eyes when they are closed. →see **face**

가산명사 눈꺼풀

eye-opener (**eye-openers**) N-COUNT If you describe something as an **eye-opener**, you mean that it surprises you and that you learn something new from it. [INFORMAL] ❏ *Writing these scripts has been quite an eye-opener to me. It proves that one can do anything if the need is urgent.*

가산명사 눈이 휘둥그래지게 하는 것, 놀랄 만한 일 [비격식체] ❏ 이 대본을 쓰는 것은 나에게 꽤나 놀랄 만한 일이었다. 그것은 누구나 긴급하면 어떤 것도 할 수 있다는 것을 보여 준다.

eye|sight /aɪsaɪt/ N-UNCOUNT Your **eyesight** is your ability to see. ❏ *He suffered from poor eyesight and could no longer read properly.*

불가산명사 시력 ❏ 그는 시력이 안 좋아 고생했고 더 이상 제대로 글을 읽을 수가 없었다.

eye|sore /aɪsɔr/ (**eyesores**) N-COUNT You describe a building or place as an **eyesore** when it is extremely ugly and you dislike it or disapprove of it. [DISAPPROVAL] [usu sing] ❏ *Poverty leads to slums, which are an eyesore and a health hazard.*

가산명사 눈에 거슬리는 것 [탐탁잖음] ❏ 가난은 결국 빈민가를 만들고, 이러한 빈민가는 눈에 거슬리고 보건상 위험하다.

eye|witness /aɪwɪtnɪs/ (**eyewitnesses**) N-COUNT An **eyewitness** is a person who was present at an event and can therefore describe it, for example in a law court. ❏ *Eyewitnesses say the police then opened fire on the crowd.*

가산명사 목격자 ❏ 목격자들에 의하면 경찰이 그 때에 군중에게 발포를 했다고 한다.

e-zine /izin/ (**e-zines**) N-COUNT An **e-zine** is a website which contains the kind of articles, pictures, and advertisements that you would find in a magazine.

가산명사 인터넷 잡지

Ff

F, f /ɛf/ (**F's, f's**) N-VAR F is the sixth letter of the English alphabet.

fa|ble /feɪbʰl/ (**fables**) ◧ N-VAR A **fable** is a story which teaches a moral lesson. Fables sometimes have animals as the main characters. ❑ *...the fable of the tortoise and the hare.* ◨ N-VAR You can describe a statement or explanation that is untrue but that many people believe as **fable**. ❑ *Is reincarnation fact or fable?*

fab|ric ◆◇◇ /fæbrɪk/ (**fabrics**) ◧ N-MASS **Fabric** is cloth or other material produced by weaving together cotton, nylon, wool, silk, or other threads. Fabrics are used for making things such as clothes, curtains, and sheets. ❑ *...small squares of red cotton fabric.* ◨ N-SING The **fabric** of a society or system is its basic structure, with all the customs and beliefs that make it work successfully. ❑ *The fabric of society has been deeply damaged by the previous regime.* →see **quilt**

fab|ri|cate /fæbrɪkeɪt/ (**fabricates, fabricating, fabricated**) V-T If someone **fabricates** information, they invent it in order to deceive people. ❑ *All four claim that officers fabricated evidence against them.* ● **fab|ri|ca|tion** /fæbrɪkeɪʃʰn/ (**fabrications**) N-VAR ❑ *She described the interview with her in an Italian magazine as a "complete fabrication."*

fabu|lous /fæbyələs/ ADJ If you describe something as **fabulous**, you are emphasizing that you like it a lot or think that it is very good. [INFORMAL, EMPHASIS] ❑ *This is a fabulous album. It's fresh, varied, fun.*

fa|cade /fəsɑd/ (**facades**) also façade ◧ N-COUNT The **facade** of a building, especially a large one, is its front wall or the wall that faces the street. ❑ *...the repairs to the building's facade.* ◨ N-SING A **facade** is an outward appearance which is deliberately false and gives you a wrong impression about someone or something. ❑ *They hid the troubles plaguing their marriage behind a facade of family togetherness.*

---

face

① NOUN USES
② VERB AND PHRASAL VERB USES

---

① **face** ◆◆◆ /feɪs/ (**faces**) →Please look at category ⑱ to see if the expression you are looking for is shown under another headword. ◧ N-COUNT Your **face** is the front part of your head from your chin to the top of your forehead, where your mouth, eyes, nose, and other features are. ❑ *He rolled down his window and stuck his face out.* ❑ *He was going red in the face and breathing with difficulty.* ❑ *She had a beautiful face.* ◨ N-COUNT If your **face** is happy, sad, or serious, for example, the expression on your face shows that you are happy, sad, or serious. ❑ *He was walking around with a sad face.* ③ N-COUNT The **face** of a cliff, mountain, or building is a vertical surface or side of it. ❑ *Harrer was one of the first to climb the north face of the Eiger.* ④ N-COUNT The **face** of a clock or watch is the surface with the numbers or hands on it, which shows the time. ❑ *It was too dark to see the face of my watch.* ⑤ N-SING If you say that **the face of** an area, institution, or field of activity is changing, you mean its appearance or nature is changing. ❑ *...the changing face of the British countryside.* ⑥ N-SING If you refer to something as **the** particular **face of** an activity, belief, or system, you mean that it is one particular aspect of it, in contrast to other aspects. ❑ *Brothels, he insists, are the acceptable face of prostitution.* ⑦ N-UNCOUNT If you lose **face**, you do something which makes you appear weak and makes people respect or admire you less. If you do something in order to save **face**, you do it in order to avoid appearing weak and losing people's respect or admiration. ❑ *England doesn't want a war but it doesn't want to lose face.* ❑ *To cancel the airport would mean a loss of face for the present governor.* ⑧ →see also **face value** ⑨ PHRASE If someone or something is **face down**, their face or front points downward. If they are **face up**, their face or front points upward. ❑ *All the time Stephen was lying face down and unconscious in the bath tub.* ⑩ PHRASE If you come **face to face** with someone, you meet them and can talk to them or look at them directly. ❑ *We were strolling into the town when we came face to face with Jacques Dubois.* ⑪ PHRASE If you come **face to face with** a difficulty or reality, you cannot avoid it and have to deal with it. ❑ *Eventually, he came face to face with discrimination again.* ⑫ PHRASE If an action or belief **flies in the face of** accepted ideas or rules, it seems to completely oppose or contradict them. ❑ *...scientific principles that seem to fly in the face of common sense.* ⑬ PHRASE If you take a particular action or attitude **in the face of** a problem or difficulty, you respond to that problem or difficulty in that way. ❑ *The Prime Minister has called for national unity in the face of the violent anti-government protests.* ⑭ PHRASE If you **make a face**, you show a feeling such as dislike or disgust by putting an exaggerated expression on your face, for example by sticking out your tongue. In British English, you can also say **pull**

가산명사 또는 불가산명사 영어 알파벳의 여섯 번째 글자

◧ 가산명사 또는 불가산명사 우화 ❑ 토끼와 거북이 이야기 ◨ 가산명사 또는 불가산명사 속설, 근거 없는 통념 ❑ 환생은 사실인가, 속설인가?

◧ 물질명사 직물, 천 ❑ 사각의 작고 빨간 면직물 조각 ◨ 단수명사 구조, 체제 ❑ 사회 구조가 전 정권에 의해 심하게 파괴되었다.

타동사 꾸며 내다, 조작하다 ❑ 네 사람 모두 경찰관들이 자신들에게 불리한 증거를 꾸며 냈다고 주장한다. ● 조작 가산명사 또는 불가산명사 ❑ 그녀는 한 이탈리아 잡지에 실린 자기의 인터뷰 기사를 '완전한 조작'이라고 일컬었다.

형용사 굉장한 [비격식체, 강조] ❑ 이것은 굉장한 앨범이야. 신선하고 다양하고 재미있어.

◧ 산명사 (건물의) 정면 ❑ 건물 정면 수리 ◨ 단수명사 겉보기, 허울 ❑ 그들은 부부 관계를 둘러싼 불화를 가족의 단란함이라는 허울 뒤로 감추었다.

◧ 가산명사 얼굴 ❑ 그가 차창을 내리고 얼굴을 밖으로 내밀었다. ❑ 그가 얼굴이 붉어지면서 간신히 숨을 쉬었다. ❑ 그녀는 얼굴이 아름다웠다. ◨ 가산명사 인색, 표정 ❑ 그가 슬픈 얼굴을 한 채 이리저리 걷고 있었다. ③ 가산명사 벽 ❑ 하러는 아이거 봉 북쪽 벽을 최초로 오른 사람 중 한 명이었다. ④ 가산명사 (시계 등의) 문자반 ❑ 너무 어두워서 나는 손목시계의 시간을 알아볼 수 없었다. ⑤ 단수명사 형세 ❑ 변해 가는 영국 시골의 형세 ⑥ 단수명사 일면 ❑ 그녀는 사창가는 매춘이 용인된다는 일면을 보여 주는 것이라고 주장한다. ⑦ 불가산명사 체면, 위신 ❑ 잉글랜드는 전쟁을 원하지 않지만 위신을 잃기도 원하지 않는다. ❑ 공항 계획을 취소하게 되면 현 주지사가 체면을 잃을 것이다. ⑨ 구 얼굴[정면]을 아래/위로 하고, 엎어져/바로 ❑ 그 시간 내내 스테판은 욕조 안에서 엎어진 채 의식이 없었다. ⑩ 구 마주 보고 ❑ 우리는 그 도시를 향해 한가로이 거닐다가 자크 뒤보아와 마주쳤다. ⑪ 구 직면하여 ❑ 결국 그는 다시 한 번 차별 대우에 직면했다. ⑫ 구 정면으로 반(反)하다 ❑ 상식에 정면으로 반하는 듯한 과학적 원리 ⑬ 구 —에 맞서 ❑ 수상이 격렬한 반정부 시위에 맞서 범국민적인 화합을 요구해 왔다. ⑭ 구 얼굴을 찌푸리다 ❑ 그녀가 문을 열고 곰팡내를 맡으며 얼굴을 찌푸렸다. ⑮ 구 언뜻 보기에는 ❑ 언뜻 보기에는 맞는 것 같지만 총계가 맞지 않는다. ⑯ 구 나타나다, 모습을 드러내다 ❑ 그녀가 매사추세츠 주에 다시 모습을 드러내며 자신의 체포 영장이 발부된 것을 알게 될 것이다. ⑰ 구 정색한 얼굴, 웃음을 참는 얼굴 ❑ 톰이 무엇을 떠올렸는지 나는 상상할 수 없지만, 그는 가까스로 웃음을 참았다. ⑱ 구 면전에 대고, 노골적으로 ❑ 그녀의 경쟁자가 면전에 대고 그녀를 거짓말쟁이라고 불렀다.

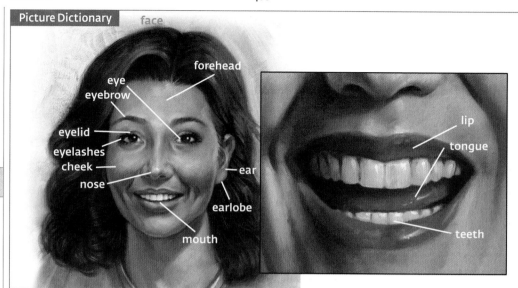

Picture Dictionary: face

forehead
eye
eyebrow
eyelid
eyelashes
cheek
nose
ear
earlobe
mouth
lip
tongue
teeth

a face. ❑ *Opening the door, she made a face at the musty smell.* 15 PHRASE You say **on the face of it** when you are describing how something seems when it is first considered, in order to suggest that people's opinion may change when they know or think more about the subject. ❑ *On the face of it that seems to make sense. But the figures don't add up.* 16 PHRASE If you **show** your **face** somewhere, you go there and see people, although you are not welcome, are rather unwilling to go, or have not been there for some time. ❑ *If she shows her face again back in Massachusetts she'll find a warrant for her arrest waiting.* 17 PHRASE If you manage to keep **a straight face**, you manage to look serious, although you want to laugh. ❑ *What went through Tom's mind I can't imagine, but he did manage to keep a straight face.* 18 PHRASE If you say something **to** someone's **face**, you say it openly in their presence. ❑ *Her opponent called her a liar to her face.* 19 **to shut the door in** someone's **face** →see door. **to have egg on** your **face** →see egg →see Picture Dictionary: face

② **face** ♦♦♦ /feɪs/ (**faces, facing, faced**) →Please look at category 8 to see if the expression you are looking for is shown under another headword. 1 V-T/V-I If someone or something **faces** a particular thing, person, or direction, they are positioned opposite them or are looking in that direction. ❑ *They stood facing each other.* 2 V-T If you **face** someone or something, you turn so that you are looking at them. ❑ *She stood up from the table and faced him.* 3 V-T If you have to **face** a person or group, you have to stand or sit in front of them and talk to them, although it may be difficult and unpleasant. ❑ *Christie looked relaxed and calm as he faced the press.* 4 V-T If you **face** or **are faced** with something difficult or unpleasant, or if it **faces** you, it is going to affect you and you have to deal with it. ❑ *Williams faces life in prison if convicted of attempted murder.* ❑ *The immense difficulties facing European businessmen in Russia were only too evident.* 5 V-T If you **face** the truth or **face** the facts, you accept that something is true. If you **face** someone with the truth or with the facts, you try to make them accept that something is true. ❑ *Although your heart is breaking, you must face the truth that a relationship has ended.* ❑ *He accused the Government of refusing to face facts about the economy.* ● PHRASAL VERB **Face up to** means the same as **face**. ❑ *I have grown up now and I have to face up to my responsibilities.* 6 V-T If you **cannot face** something, you do not feel able to do it because it seems so difficult or unpleasant. [with neg] ❑ *I couldn't face the prospect of spending a Saturday night there, so I decided to press on.* ❑ *My children want me with them for Christmas Day, but I can't face it.* 7 PHRASE You use the expression "**let's face it**" when you are stating a fact or making a comment about something which you think the person you are talking to may find unpleasant or be unwilling to admit. ❑ *She was always attracted to younger men. But, let's face it, who is not?* 8 **face the music** →see music

▶**face up to** →see face 5

face|less /feɪslɪs/ ADJ If you describe someone or something as **faceless**, you dislike them because they are uninteresting and have no character. [DISAPPROVAL] ❑ *Ordinary people are at the mercy of faceless bureaucrats.*

face|lift /feɪslɪft/ (**facelifts**) also **face lift** 1 N-COUNT If you give a place or thing a **facelift**, you do something to make it look better or more attractive. ❑ *Nothing gives a room a faster facelift than a coat of paint.* 2 N-COUNT A **facelift** is an operation in which a surgeon tightens the skin on someone's face in order to make them look younger. ❑ *I had a facelift in 1995, which went wrong.*

fac|et /fæsɪt/ (**facets**) 1 N-COUNT A **facet** of something is a single part or aspect of it. ❑ *The caste system shapes nearly every facet of Indian life.* 2 N-COUNT The **facets** of a diamond or other precious stone are the flat surfaces that have been cut on its outside. →see diamond

face value 1 N-SING The **face value** of things such as coins, paper money, investment documents, or tickets is the amount of money that they are worth, and that is written on them. ❑ *Tickets were selling at twice their face value.*

1 타동사/자동사 –을 향하다, –와 마주 보다 ❑ 그들은 마주 보고 서 있었다. 2 타동사 –을 향해 얼굴을 돌리다 ❑ 그녀가 탁자에서 일어나 그를 향해 돌아섰다. 3 타동사 대면하다 ❑ 기자단과 대면했을 때 크리스티는 편안하고 차분해 보였다. 4 타동사 직면하다; (문제 등이) 다가오다 ❑ 살인 미수로 유죄 판결을 받으면 윌리엄즈는 종신형에 처하게 된다. ❑ 러시아에서 활동하는 유럽 인 사업가들이 직면한 막대한 어려움은 너무나 명백했다. 5 타동사 직시하다, 받아들이다; 직시하게 하다, 받아들이게 하다 ❑ 가슴이 아프겠지만, 너는 관계가 끝나 버렸다는 사실을 받아들여야 해. ❑ 정부가 경제 현실을 직시하려고 하지 않는다고 그는 비난했다. ● 구동사 감수하다 ❑ 이제 성인이 되었으니 내 책임은 내가 감수해야 한다. 6 타동사 감당하다, 견디다 ❑ 거기서 토요일 밤을 지낸다는 생각을 견딜 수 없어서, 나는 서둘러 떠나기로 마음을 굳혔다. ❑ 우리 아이들은 내가 크리스마스를 함께 보내기를 바라지만, 난 그걸 감당할 수 없다. 7 구 있는 그대로 보자, 현실을 직시하자 ❑ 그녀는 항상 연하의 남자에게 호감을 느꼈다. 그런데, 현실을 직시하면, 누구는 안 그럴까?

형용사 익명의 [탐탁잖음] ❑ 보통 사람들은 익명의 관료들에 의해 좌지우지된다.

1 가산명사 새 단장 ❑ 방을 새로 치장하는 데는 페인트칠만한 것이 없다. 2 가산명사 안면 주름 제거 수술 ❑ 내가 1995년에 안면 주름 제거 수술을 받았는데 잘 안 됐다.

1 가산명사 단면 ❑ 카스트 제도가 인도인의 삶의 거의 모든 면을 결정한다. 2 가산명사 깎은 면, 작은 면

1 단수명사 액면가 ❑ 표를 액면가의 두 배로 팔고 있었다. 2 구 액면 그대로 ❑ 여러 관련 집단의 공식 성명을 꼭 액면 그대로 받아들일 필요는 없다.

2 PHRASE If you take something **at face value**, you accept it and believe it without thinking about it very much, even though it might untrue. ❑ *Public statements from the various groups involved should not necessarily be taken at face value.*

fa|cial /feɪʃ*l/ ADJ **Facial** means appearing on or being part of your face. [ADJ n] ❑ *Cross didn't answer; his facial expression didn't change.*

fa|cili|tate /fəsɪlɪteɪt/ (**facilitates, facilitating, facilitated**) V-T To **facilitate** an action or process, especially one that you would like to happen, means to make it easier or more likely to happen. ❑ *The new airport will facilitate the development of tourism.*

fa|cili|ta|tor /fəsɪlɪteɪtər/ (**facilitators**) N-COUNT A **facilitator** is a person or organization that helps another person or organization to do or to achieve a particular thing. [FORMAL] ❑ *The conference is chaired by a highly skilled facilitator who has been fully trained.*

fa|cil|ity ♦♦◇ /fəsɪlɪti/ (**facilities**) **1** N-COUNT **Facilities** are buildings, pieces of equipment, or services that are provided for a particular purpose. ❑ *What recreational facilities are now available?* **2** N-COUNT A **facility** is something such as an additional service provided by an organization or an extra feature on a machine which is useful but not essential. ❑ *One of the new models has the facility to reproduce speech as well as text.*

fact ♦♦♦ /fækt/ (**facts**) **1** PHRASE You use **the fact that** after some verbs or prepositions, especially in expressions such as **in view of the fact that, apart from the fact that,** and **despite the fact that,** to link the verb or preposition with a clause. ❑ *His chances do not seem good in view of the fact that the Chief Prosecutor has already voiced his public disapproval.* ❑ *Despite the fact that the disease is so prevalent, treatment is still far from satisfactory.* **2** PHRASE You use **the fact that** instead of a simple that-clause either for emphasis or because the clause is the subject of your sentence. ❑ *My family now accepts the fact that I don't eat sugar or bread.* **3** PHRASE You use **in fact, in actual fact,** or **in point of fact** to indicate that you are giving more detailed information about what you have just said. ❑ *We've had a pretty bad time while you were away. In fact, we very nearly split up this time.* ❑ *He apologized as soon as he realized what he had done. In actual fact he wrote a nice little note to me.* **4** PHRASE You use **in fact, in actual fact,** or **in point of fact** to introduce or draw attention to a comment that modifies, contradicts, or contrasts with a previous statement. ❑ *That sounds rather simple, but in fact it's very difficult.* ❑ *They complained that they had been trapped inside the police station, but in fact most were seen escaping over the adjacent roofs to safety in nearby buildings.* **5** N-VAR When you refer to something as a **fact** or as **fact,** you mean that you think it is true or correct. ❑ *...a statement of verifiable historical fact.* **6** N-COUNT **Facts** are pieces of information that can be discovered. ❑ *There is so much information you can almost effortlessly find the facts for yourself.* ❑ *His opponent swamped him with facts and figures.* **7** PHRASE You use **as a matter of fact** to introduce a statement that gives more details about what has just been said, or an explanation of it, or something that contrasts with it. ❑ *The local people saw all the suffering to which these deportees were subjected. And, as a matter of fact, the local people helped the victims of these deportations.* **8** PHRASE If you say that you know something **for a fact,** you are emphasizing that you are completely certain that it is true. [EMPHASIS] ❑ *I know for a fact that baby corn is very expensive in Europe.* **9** PHRASE You use **the fact is** or **the fact of the matter is** to introduce and draw attention to a summary or statement of the most important point about what you have been saying. ❑ *The fact is blindness hadn't stopped the children from doing many of the things that sighted children enjoy.* →see **history**

Word Partnership　　*fact*의 연어

ADJ.	**hard** fact, **historical** fact, **important** fact, **obvious** fact, **random** fact, **simple** fact **5**
N.	fact **and fiction 5**
	as a matter of fact **7**
V.	**accept a** fact, **check the** facts, **face a** fact **5 6**
	know for a fact **8**

---

fac|tion ♦◇◇ /fækʃ°n/ (**factions**) N-COUNT A **faction** is an organized group of people within a larger group, which opposes some of the ideas of the larger group and fights for its own ideas. ❑ *A peace agreement will be signed by the leaders of the country's warring factions.*

fac|tion|al /fækʃ°nəl/ ADJ **Factional** arguments or disputes involve two or more small groups from within a larger group. ❑ *...factional disputes between the various groups that make up the leadership.*

Word Link　　*fact, fic ≈ making : artifact, artificial, factor*

---

fac|tor ♦♦◇ /fæktər/ (**factors, factoring, factored**) **1** N-COUNT A **factor** is one of the things that affects an event, decision, or situation. ❑ *Physical activity is an important factor in maintaining fitness.* **2** N-COUNT If an amount increases by a **factor of** two, for example, or by a **factor of** eight, then it becomes two times bigger or eight times bigger. ❑ *The cost of butter quadrupled and bread prices increased by a factor of five.* **3** N-SING You can use **factor** to refer to a particular level on a scale of measurement. ❑ *A suncream with a protection factor of 8 allows you to stay in the sun without burning.*

Word Partnership　　*factor*의 연어

ADJ.	**crucial** factor, **important** factor, **key** factor **1**
N.	**risk** factor **1 3**

형용사 얼굴의 ❑ 크로스는 대꾸하지 않았고, 그의 얼굴 표정은 변하지 않았다.

타동사 촉진하다 ❑ 새로 여는 공항이 관광 산업 발전을 촉진할 것이다.

가산명사 조력자, 용이하게 하는 사람 [격식체] ❑ 충분히 훈련된 매우 노련한 진행자가 그 회의의 의장직을 맡았다.

1 가산명사 시설, 설비 ❑ 어떤 휴양 시설을 지금 이용할 수 있습니까? **2** 가산명사 편의, 부가 서비스 ❑ 새로 출시된 모델 중 하나에는 글자뿐 아니라 소리도 재생하는 부가 기능이 있다.

1 구 몇몇 동사나 전치사 뒤에 쓰여서 뒤에 따라오는 결과 연결하는 기능을 함 ❑ 수석 검사가 이미 동의하지 않는다는 견해를 공식적으로 표명했음을 볼 때 그의 운이 좋을 것 같지 않다. ❑ 그 병이 만연함에도 불구하고, 치료는 여전히 만족할 수 없는 수준이다. **2** 구 that 절 내용을 강조하기 위해 쓰임 ❑ 내가 설탕이나 빵을 먹지 않는다는 사실을 우리 가족이 지금은 받아들인다. **3** 구 사실 ❑ 네가 없는 동안 우리는 꽤 사이가 안 좋았어. 사실, 이번엔 하마터면 헤어질 뻔했다니까. ❑ 자신이 무슨 일을 했는지 깨닫는 즉시 그가 사과했다. 사실 그는 상냥하고 짧은 편지를 나에게 써 주었다. **4** 구 사실은 ❑ 그게 꽤 간단한 것처럼 들리지만 사실은 아주 어려워. ❑ 경찰서 안에 잡혀 있었다고 그들이 불평했지만 실제로는 대부분이 인접한 지붕을 타고 근처 건물로 대피하는 것이 목격되었다. **5** 가산명사 또는 불가산명사 사실 ❑ 역사적 사실을 입증할 만한 진술 **6** 가산명사 진상 ❑ 너 스스로 거의 힘들이지 않고 진상을 파악할 수 있는 정보가 무척 많다. ❑ 그의 경쟁자는 정확한 정보로 그를 궁지에 빠트렸다. **7** 구 실제로 ❑ 추방당한 이 사람들이 겪은 모든 고통을 그 지역 주민들이 목격했고, 실제로, 그들은 이 추방으로 인한 피해자들을 도왔다. **8** 구 확실히 [강조] ❑ 내가 확실히 아는 데 유럽에서는 베이비콘이 비싸다구. **9** 구 실은 ~이다 ❑ 실은 눈이 안 보인다고 해서 정상 아동들이 즐기는 여러 가지 일을 시각 장애 아동들이 하지 못했던 것은 아니었다.

가산명사 당파, 파벌 ❑ 그 나라의 적대 파벌의 지도자들이 평화 협정에 서명할 것이다.

형용사 당파적인, 파벌의 ❑ 지도부를 구성하는 여러 집단 간의 당파 분쟁

1 가산명사 요인 ❑ 신체 활동은 건강 유지에 있어 중요한 요인이다. **2** 가산명사 배, 배수 ❑ 버터 값은 네 배가 되고 빵 값은 다섯 배 뛰었다. **3** 단수명사 지수 ❑ 차단 지수 8인 자외선 차단 크림을 바르면 햇볕에 피부를 그을리지 않고도 양지에 머무를 수 있다.

a b c d e f g h i j k l m n o p q r s t u v w x y z

▶**factor in** or **factor into** PHRASAL VERB If you **factor** a particular cost or element **into** a calculation you are making, or if you **factor** it **in**, you include it. [mainly AM] ❑ *You'd better consider this and factor this into your decision making.*

구동사 –을 계산에 넣다 [주로 미국영어] ❑ 네 의사를 결정할 때 이것을 고려하고 계산에 넣어라.

fac|to|ry ♦♦◇ /fˈæktəri, -tri/ (**factories**) N-COUNT A **factory** is a large building where machines are used to make large quantities of goods. ❑ *He owned furniture factories in New York State.* →see **mass production** →see Word Web: **factory**

가산명사 공장 ❑ 그는 뉴욕 주에 가구 공장을 가지고 있었다.

fact sheet (**fact sheets**) N-COUNT A **fact sheet** is a short, printed document with information about a particular subject, especially a summary of information that has been given on a radio or television programme. ❑ *The institute's free fact sheet, Driving Abroad, is available from 020 8994 4403.*

가산명사 요약판 자료 책자 ❑ 그 기관에서 발간한 무료 정보지인 드라이빙 어브로드를 받기 원하시면 020 8994 4403으로 전화 주세요.

fac|tual /fˈæktʃuəl/ ADJ Something that is **factual** is concerned with facts or contains facts, rather than giving theories or personal interpretations. ❑ *The editorial contained several factual errors.*

형용사 사실에 입각한, 실제의 ❑ 그 사설에는 몇 가지 사실적 오류가 있었다.

fac|ul|ty /fˈækəlti/ (**faculties**) ■ N-COUNT Your **faculties** are your physical and mental abilities. ❑ *He was drunk and not in control of his faculties.* ② N-VAR A **faculty** is all the teaching staff of a university or college, or of one department. [AM] ❑ *The faculty agreed on a change in the requirements.* ❑ *How can faculty improve their teaching so as to encourage creativity?* ③ N-VAR A **faculty** is a group of related departments in some universities, or the people who work in them. [BRIT] ❑ *...the Faculty of Social and Political Sciences.*

■ 가산명사 (신체적, 정신적) 자질 ❑ 그는 술에 취해서 자신을 추스르지 못했다. ② 가산명사 또는 불가산명사 교수진 [미국영어] ❑ 교수진이 필요조건들의 개정에 대해 합의를 보았다. ❑ 독창성을 북돋우기 위해 교수진이 자신들의 교수법을 어떻게 개선할 수 있을까? ③ 가산명사 또는 불가산명사 학부; 교직원 [영국영어] ❑ 정치 사회학부

fad /fˈæd/ (**fads**) N-COUNT You use **fad** to refer to an activity or topic of interest that is very popular for a short time, but which people become bored with very quickly. ❑ *Hamnett does not believe environmental concern is a passing fad.* →see **diet**

가산명사 일시적 유행 ❑ 햄넷은 환경에 대한 관심이 잠깐 동안의 대유행이라고 생각하지 않는다.

fade ♦◇◇ /fˈeɪd/ (**fades, fading, faded**) ■ V-T/V-I When a colored object **fades** or when the light **fades** it, it gradually becomes paler. ❑ *All color fades – especially under the impact of direct sunlight.* ❑ *No matter how soft the light is, it still plays havoc, fading carpets and curtains in every room.* ● **fad|ed** ADJ ❑ *...a girl in a faded dress.* ② V-I When light **fades**, it slowly becomes less bright. When a sound **fades**, it slowly becomes less loud. ❑ *Seaton lay on his bed and gazed at the ceiling as the light faded.* ③ V-I If memories, feelings, or possibilities **fade**, they slowly become less intense or less strong. ❑ *Sympathy for the rebels, the government claims, is beginning to fade.* ❑ *Prospects for peace had already started to fade.*

■ 타동사/자동사 바래다 ❑ 모든 색깔은 바래기 마련이고, 특히 직접 내리쬐는 햇볕 아래서 더욱 바랜다. ❑ 아무리 부드럽다고 해도, 빛은 여전히 모든 방의 카펫과 커튼을 바래게 하는 피해를 준다. ● 빛깔이 바랜 형용사 ❑ 빛깔이 바랜 옷을 입은 소녀 ② 자동사 (빛이) 희미해지다; (소리가) 약해지다 ❑ 날이 어둑해질 때 시튼이 침대에 누워 천장을 응시했다. ③ 자동사 수그러들다, 잦아들다 ❑ 반란군에 대한 호감이 수그러들기 시작했다고 정부는 주장한다. ❑ 평화에 대한 기대가 벌써 잦아들기 시작했다.

Word Partnership   *fade*의 연어

N.	**colors** fade, **images** fade ■
	memories fade ③
v.	**begin to** fade ■ ② ③

---

fae|ces /fˈiːsiz/ →see **feces**

Fahr|en|heit /fˈærənhaɪt/ ADJ **Fahrenheit** is a scale for measuring temperature, in which water freezes at 32 degrees and boils at 212 degrees. It is represented by the symbol °F. [n/num ADJ] ❑ *By mid-morning, the temperature was already above 100 degrees Fahrenheit.* ● N-UNCOUNT **Fahrenheit** is also a noun. ❑ *He was asked for the boiling point of water in Fahrenheit.* →see **temperature, climate**

형용사 화씨의 ❑ 아침나절이 되자 온도가 벌써 화씨 100도를 넘어섰다. ● 불가산명사 화씨 온도계 ❑ 그는 물의 끓는점이 화씨 온도로 얼마인지 질문을 받았다.

fail ♦♦♦ /fˈeɪl/ (**fails, failing, failed**) ■ V-T/V-I If you **fail** to do something that you were trying to do, you are unable to do it or do not succeed in doing it. ❑ *The Workers' Party failed to win a single governorship.* ❑ *He failed in his attempt to take control of the company.* ② V-T/V-I If an activity, attempt, or plan **fails**, it is not successful. ❑ *We tried to develop plans for them to get along, which all failed miserably.* ❑ *He was afraid the revolution they had started would fail.* ③ V-T If someone or something **fails** to do a particular thing that they should have done, they do not do it. [FORMAL] ❑ *Some schools fail to set any homework.* ❑ *He failed to file tax returns for 1982.* ④ V-I If something **fails**, it stops working properly, or does not do what it is supposed to do. ❑ *The lights mysteriously failed, and we stumbled around in complete darkness.* ⑤ V-T/V-I If a business, organization, or system **fails**, it becomes unable to continue in operation or in existence. [BUSINESS] ❑ *So far this year, 104 banks have failed.* ❑ *...a failed hotel business.* ⑥ V-I If something such as your health or a physical quality **is failing**, it is becoming gradually weaker or less effective. ❑ *He was 58, and his health was failing rapidly.* ❑ *Here in the hills, the light failed more quickly.* ⑦ V-T If someone **fails** you, they do not do what you had expected or trusted them to do. ❑ *We waited twenty-one years, don't fail us now.* ⑧ V-T If someone **fails** a test, examination, or course, they perform badly in it and do not reach the standard that is required. ❑ *I lived in fear of failing my end-of-term exams.* ● N-COUNT **Fail** is also a noun. ❑ *It's the difference between a pass and a fail.* ⑨ V-T If someone **fails** you in a test, examination, or course, they judge that you have not reached a high enough standard in it. ❑ *...the two men who had failed him during his first year of law school.* ⑩ PHRASE You say **if all else fails** to

■ 타동사/자동사 –하지 못하다 ❑ 근로자당은 장직원 한 석도 확보하지 못했다. ❑ 그가 회사를 장악하려 시도했으나 이루지 못했다. ② 타동사/자동사 실패로 끝나다 ❑ 그들이 함께 잘 지낼 수 있도록 계획을 세우려 노력해 보았지만 모든 계획이 대실패로 끝났다. ❑ 그들이 일으킨 혁명이 실패로 끝날 수 있다고 그는 걱정했다. ③ 타동사 –하지 않다 [격식체] ❑ 일부 학교는 숙제를 전혀 내주지 않는다. ❑ 그가 1982년 세금 신고서를 제출하지 못했다. ④ 자동사 작동하지 않다 ❑ 이상하게도 불이 안 켜졌고, 칠흑 같은 어둠 속에서 우리는 넘어질 듯 비틀거리며 걸었다. ⑤ 타동사/자동사 파산하다 [경제] ❑ 올해 들어 지금까지 은행 104개가 파산했다. ❑ 파산한 호텔 사업 ⑥ 자동사 쇠약해지다 ❑ 그가 58세 때 급속히 몸이 쇠약해지고 있었다. ❑ 여기 언덕 위에서는 햇빛이 더 빨리 어두워졌다. ⑦ 타동사 실망시키다 ❑ 21년을 기다렸으니 이제는 우리 기대를 저버리지 말아라. ⑧ 타동사 낙제하다 ❑ 나는 기말 시험에서 낙제할까 걱정하며 살았다. ● 가산명사 낙제 ❑ 그것이 합격과 낙제 간의 차이점이다. ⑨ 타동사 낙제점을 주다 ❑ 그가 법과 대학 1학년이었을 때 그에게 낙제점을 준 두 사람 ⑩ 구 더 이상 해 볼 도리가 없다면 ❑ 더 이상 해 볼 도리가 없다면 나는 트럭이나 계속 몰 생각이다.

Word Web   factory

Life in a 19th-century **factory** was extremely difficult. **Employees** often **worked** twelve hours a day, six days a week. **Wages** were low and **child labor** was common. Many **workers** were not allowed to take **breaks**. Some even had to eat while continuing to work. As early as 1832, doctors started warning about the dangers of **air pollution**. The 20th century brought some big changes. Workers began to join **unions**. During World War I, **government regulations** set standards for **minimum wages** and improved **working conditions**. In addition, automation took over some of the most difficult and dangerous jobs.

suggest what could be done in a certain situation if all the other things you have tried are unsuccessful. ❑ *If all else fails, I could always drive a truck.* **11** PHRASE You use **without fail** to emphasize that something always happens. [EMPHASIS] ❑ *He attended every meeting without fail.* **12** PHRASE You use **without fail** to emphasize an order or a promise. [EMPHASIS] ❑ *On the 30th you must without fail hand in some money for Alex.*

fail|ing /ˈfeɪlɪŋ/ (**failings**) **1** N-COUNT The **failings** of someone or something are their faults or unsatisfactory features. ❑ *Like many in Russia, she blamed the country's failings on futile attempts to catch up with the West.* **2** PHRASE You say **failing that** to introduce an alternative, in case what you have just said is not possible. ❑ *Find someone who will let you talk things through, or failing that, write down your thoughts.*

fail|ure ♦♦◇ /ˈfeɪljər/ (**failures**) **1** N-UNCOUNT **Failure** is a lack of success in doing or achieving something, especially in relation to a particular activity. ❑ *This policy is doomed to failure.* ❑ *Three attempts on the British 200-metre record also ended in failure.* **2** N-COUNT If something is **a failure**, it is not a success. ❑ *The marriage was a failure and they both wanted to be free of it.* **3** N-COUNT If you say that someone is **a failure**, you mean that they have not succeeded in a particular activity, or that they are unsuccessful at everything they do. ❑ *Elgar received many honors and much acclaim and yet he often considered himself a failure.* **4** N-UNCOUNT Your **failure to** do a particular thing is the fact that you do not do it, even though you were expected to do it. ❑ *They see their failure to produce an heir as a curse from God.* **5** N-VAR If there is a **failure** of something, for example a machine or part of the body, it goes wrong and stops working or developing properly. ❑ *There were also several accidents mainly caused by engine failures on take-off.* **6** N-VAR If there is a **failure** of a business or bank, it is no longer able to continue operating. [BUSINESS] ❑ *Business failures rose 16% last month.*

Word Partnership	*failure*의 연어
V.	failure **to communicate** **1**
ADJ.	**afraid** of failure, **doomed to** failure **1**
	complete failure **1** **2** **3**
	dismal failure **2** **3**
N.	**feelings of** failure, **risk of** failure, **success or** failure **1**
	engine failure, **heart** failure, **kidney** failure, **liver** failure **5**
	business failure **6**

faint /feɪnt/ (**fainter, faintest, faints, fainting, fainted**) **1** ADJ A **faint** sound, color, mark, feeling, or quality has very little strength or intensity. ❑ *He became aware of the soft, faint sounds of water dripping.* ❑ *There was still the faint hope deep within him that he might never need to know.* ● **faint|ly** ADV ❑ *He was already asleep in the bed, which smelled faintly of mildew.* **2** ADJ A **faint** attempt at something is one that is made without proper effort and with little enthusiasm. [ADJ n] ❑ *Caroline made a faint attempt at a laugh.* ❑ *A faint smile crossed the Monsignor's face and faded quickly.* ● **faint|ly** ADV [ADV after v] ❑ *John smiled faintly and shook his head.* **3** V-I If you **faint**, you lose consciousness for a short time, especially because you are hungry, or because of pain, heat, or shock. ❑ *She suddenly fell forward on to the table and fainted.* ● N-COUNT **Faint** is also a noun. ❑ *She slumped to the ground in a faint.* **4** ADJ Someone who is **faint** feels weak and unsteady as if they are about to lose consciousness. [v-link ADJ] ❑ *Other signs of angina are nausea, sweating, feeling faint and shortness of breath.*

faint|est /ˈfeɪntɪst/ ADJ You can use **faintest** for emphasis in negative statements. For example, if you say that someone hasn't the **faintest** idea what to do, you are emphasizing that they do not know what to do. [EMPHASIS] [ADJ n, with neg] ❑ *I haven't the faintest idea how to care for a snake.*

fair ♦♦◇ /feər/ (**fairer, fairest, fairs**) **1** ADJ Something or someone that is **fair** is reasonable, right, and just. ❑ *It didn't seem fair to leave out her father.* ❑ *Do you feel they're paying their fair share?* ❑ *I wanted them to get a fair deal.* ● **fairly** ADV ❑ *...demonstrating concern for employees and solving their problems quickly and fairly.* **2** ADJ A **fair** amount, degree, size, or distance is quite a large amount, degree, size, or distance. [ADJ n] ❑ *My neighbors across the street travel a fair amount.* **3** ADJ A **fair** guess or idea about something is one that is likely to be correct. [ADJ n] ❑ *It's a fair guess to say that the damage will be extensive.* **4** ADJ If you describe someone or something as **fair**, you mean that they are average in standard or quality, neither very good nor very bad. ❑ *Reimar had a fair command of English.* **5** ADJ Someone who is **fair**, or who has **fair** hair, has light-colored hair. ❑ *Both children were very like Robina, but were much fairer than she was.* ● COMB in ADJ **Fair** is also a combining form. ❑ *...a tall, fair-haired Englishman.* **6** ADJ **Fair** skin is very pale and usually burns easily. ❑ *It's important to protect my fair skin from the sun.* ● COMB in ADJ **Fair** is also a combining form. ❑ *Fair-skinned people who spend a great deal of time in the sun have the greatest risk of skin cancer.* **7** ADJ When the weather is **fair**, it is quite sunny and not raining. [FORMAL] ❑ *Weather conditions were fair.* **8** N-COUNT A county, state, or country **fair** is an event where there are, for example, displays of goods and animals, rides, amusements, games, and competitions. ❑ *Every fall I go to the county fair.* **9** N-COUNT A **fair** is an event at which people display and sell goods, especially goods of a particular type. ❑ *...an antiques fair.* →see also **trade fair** **10** PHRASE You use **fair enough** when you want to say that a statement, decision, or action seems reasonable to a certain extent, but that perhaps there is more to be said or done. [mainly SPOKEN] ❑ *If you don't like it, fair enough, but that's hardly a justification to attack the whole thing.* **11** PHRASE If you say that someone won a competition **fair and square**, you mean that they won

11 구 어김없이, 반드시 [강조] ❑ 그는 모든 회의에 반드시 참석했다. **12** 구 반드시 [강조] ❑ 30일에 너는 반드시 알렉스를 대신해서 돈을 좀 건네주어야 해.

1 가산명사 결점, 취약함 ❑ 러시아에 있는 많은 사람들처럼, 그녀도 이 나라의 취약함이 서방 세계를 따라잡으려는 헛된 시도 때문이라고 비난했다. **2** 구 그게 안 되면 ❑ 일의 자초지종을 들어 줄 수 있는 사람을 찾아보고, 그게 안 되면, 네 생각을 적어라.

1 불가산명사 실패 ❑ 이 정책은 결국 실패하게 되어 있다. ❑ 200미터 영국 최고 기록에 도전한 세 건의 시도는 역시 실패로 끝났다. **2** 가산명사 실패작 ❑ 결혼은 실패였고 그 둘 모두 실패한 결혼으로부터 자유로워지기를 원했다. **3** 가산명사 실패자 ❑ 엘가는 훈장과 갈채를 많이 받았지만 종종 자신이 실패자라고 생각했다. **4** 불가산명사 불이행 ❑ 그들은 자신들이 후계자를 낳지 못하는 것을 신의 저주로 여긴다. **5** 가산명사 또는 불가산명사 고장 ❑ 이륙 단계의 엔진 고장이 주요 원인이 된 사고가 몇 건 더 있었다. **6** 가산명사 또는 불가산명사 도산, 파산 [경제] ❑ 기업 도산이 지난달에 16퍼센트가 상승했다.

1 형용사 희미한, 어렴풋한 ❑ 그가 물방울이 떨어지는 부드럽고 약한 소리를 알아차리게 되었다. ❑ 그의 마음 깊은 곳에는 그녀는 결코 알 필요가 없을 수도 있다는 실낱같은 희망이 여전히 있었다. ● 약간 부사 ❑ 그가 벌써 침대에서 잠들었는데, 거기서 곰팡내가 약간 났다. **2** 형용사 마음 내키지 않는 ❑ 캐롤라인이 내키지 않는 웃음을 지으려 했다. ❑ 마음에 없는 미소가 주교님의 얼굴에 번지더니 이내 자취를 감추었다. ● 희미하게 부사 ❑ 존이 희미하게 미소 지으며 고개를 흔들었다. **3** 자동사 기절하다, 정신을 잃다 ❑ 그녀가 갑자기 식탁 위로 쓰러져 정신을 잃었다. ● 가산명사 기절 ❑ 그녀가 기절하여 땅바닥에 폭 쓰러졌다. **4** 형용사 어질어질한 ❑ 후두염의 다른 증세로는 메스꺼움, 발한, 현기증, 숨가쁨을 들 수 있다.

형용사 일말의 [강조] ❑ 나는 뱀을 돌보는 방법에 대해 최소한의 인식도 갖고 있지 않다.

1 형용사 올바른, 적정한 ❑ 그녀의 아버지를 방치하는 것은 옳지 않은 일인 듯했다. ❑ 네 생각에는 그들이 적정한 몫을 지불하고 있는 것 같니? ❑ 나는 그들이 마땅한 대우를 받기를 원했다. ● 공평하게 부사 ❑ 근로자에 대한 관심을 드러내고 그들의 문제를 신속하고 공평하게 해결하려는 것. **2** 형용사 상당한, 상당히 많은 ❑ 길 건너 사는 우리 이웃 사람들은 여행을 상당히 많이 한다. **3** 형용사 이치에 맞는 ❑ 손실의 규모가 엄청날 것이라고 말하는 것이 사리에 맞는 추측이다. **4** 형용사 적당한, 보통의 ❑ 레이마르의 영어 구사력은 보통 수준이었다. **5** 형용사 금발 ❑ 두 아이 모두 로비나와 무척 닮았지만, 그녀보다 더욱 더 밝은 금발이었다. ● 복합형-형용사 복합어를 이룸 ❑ 키가 큰 금발의 잉글랜드 인 **6** 형용사 살결이 흰 ❑ 내 흰 살결이 햇볕에 안 타는 것이 중요하다. ● 복합형-형용사 복합어를 이룸 ❑ 살결이 흰 사람들이 햇볕에서 오랜 시간을 보내면 피부암에 걸릴 위험이 더 높아진다. **7** 형용사 (날씨가) 갠 [격식체] ❑ 날씨가 개었다. **8** 가산명사 장터, 정기 장 ❑ 매년 가을이면 나는 시골 정기 장에 간다. **9** 가산명사 바람회 ❑ 골동품 박람회 **10** 구 그건 좋아 [주로 구어체] ❑ 그게 네 맘에 안 든다면, 그건 좋아, 하지만 전체를 공격하는 것은 정당하지 못해. **11** 구 정정당당하게 ❑ 변명할 거리가 없다. 우리는 정정당당하게 싸워서 졌다.

honestly and without cheating. ❑ *There are no excuses. We were beaten fair and square.*

Word Partnership　　*fair*의 연어

ADJ.	fair **and balanced** ▮
N.	fair **chance**, fare **deal**, fair **fight**, fair **game**, fair **play**, fair **price**, fair **share**, fair **trade**, fair **treatment**, fair **trial** ▮
	fair **amount** ▯
	fair **hair** ▤
	fair **skin** ▥
	craft fair, **science** fair ▨

fair|ground /fɛərɡraʊnd/ (**fairgrounds**) N-COUNT A **fairground** is an area of land where a fair is held.

가산명사 행사장, 장터

fair|ly ♦◇◇ /fɛərli/ ▮ ADV **Fairly** means to quite a large degree. For example, if you say that something is **fairly** old, you mean that it is old but not very old. [ADV adj/adv] ❑ *We did fairly well but only fairly well.* ▯ ADV You use **fairly** instead of "very" to add emphasis to an adjective or adverb without making it sound too forceful. [VAGUENESS] [ADV adj/adv] ❑ *Were you always fairly bright at school?* ❑ *You've got to be fairly single-minded about it.* ▯ →see also **fair**

▮ 부사 꽤 ❑ 우리가 꽤 잘하기는 했지만, 그렇게 썩 잘한 것은 아니다. ▯ 부사 상당히 [짐작투] ❑ 넌 학교에서 줄곧 상당히 똑똑한 편이었니? ❑ 넌 그것에 상당히 푹 빠졌구나.

fair|ness /fɛərnɪs/ N-UNCOUNT **Fairness** is the quality of being reasonable, right, and just. ❑ *...concern about the fairness of the election campaign.*

불가산명사 공명성 ❑ 선거 운동의 공명성에 대한 우려

fair trade N-UNCOUNT **Fair trade** is the practice of buying goods directly from producers in developing countries at a fair price. ❑ *...fair trade coffee.*

불가산명사 공정 무역 ❑ 공정 무역에 따른 커피

fairy /fɛəri/ (**fairies**) N-COUNT A **fairy** is an imaginary creature with magical powers. Fairies are often represented as small people with wings. →see **fantasy**

가산명사 요정

fairy tale (**fairy tales**) also **fairytale** N-COUNT A **fairy tale** is a story for children involving magical events and imaginary creatures. ❑ *She was like a princess in a fairy tale.*

가산명사 동화 ❑ 그녀는 동화 속에 나오는 공주 같았다.

faith ♦◇◇ /feɪθ/ (**faiths**) ▮ N-UNCOUNT If you have **faith in** someone or something, you feel confident about their ability or goodness. ❑ *People have lost faith in the British Parliament.* ▯ N-COUNT A **faith** is a particular religion, for example Christianity, Buddhism, or Islam. [also no det, usu adj N] ❑ *England shifted officially from a Catholic to a Protestant faith in the 16th century.* ▯ N-UNCOUNT **Faith** is strong religious belief in a particular God. ❑ *Umberto Eco's loss of his own religious faith is reflected in his novels.* ▰ PHRASE If you do something **in good faith**, you seriously believe that what you are doing is right, honest, or legal, even though this may not be the case. ❑ *This report was published in good faith but we regret any confusion which may have been caused.*

▮ 불가산명사 믿음 ❑ 국민들은 영국 의회를 더 이상 믿지 않게 되었다. ▯ 가산명사 종교 ❑ 잉글랜드는 16세기에 국교를 가톨릭에서 개신교로 바꿨다. ▯ 불가산명사 신앙 ❑ 움베르토 에코의 소설을 읽어 보면 그가 신앙심을 잃었다는 것을 알 수 있다. ▰ 구 확고한 신념에서 ❑ 이 보고서는 확고한 신념을 바탕으로 작성된 것이지만, 이로 인해 조금이라도 혼란이 야기되었다면 저희는 이에 유감을 표하는 바입니다.

Word Partnership　　*faith*의 연어

V.	**have** faith, **lose** faith ▮ ▯
	practice *your* faith ▯
ADJ.	**blind** faith, **little** faith ▮ ▯
	religious faith ▯ ▯
N.	faith **in God** ▯

faith|ful /feɪθfəl/ ▮ ADJ Someone who is **faithful to** a person, organization, idea, or activity remains firm in their belief in them or support for them. ❑ *She had been faithful to her promise to guard this secret.* ● N-PLURAL The **faithful** are people who are faithful to someone or something. ❑ *He spends his time making speeches at factories or gatherings of the Party faithful.* ● **faith|ful|ly** ADV [ADV with v] ❑ *He has since 1965 faithfully followed and supported every twist and turn of government policy.* ▯ ADJ Someone who is **faithful to** their husband, wife, or lover does not have a sexual relationship with anyone else. ❑ *I'm very faithful when I love someone.* ▯ ADJ A **faithful** account, translation, or copy of something represents or reproduces the original accurately. ❑ *Colin Welland's screenplay is faithful to the novel.* ● **faith|ful|ly** ADV [ADV with v] ❑ *When I adapt something I translate from one meaning to another as faithfully as I can.*

▮ 형용사 충성스런, 충실한 ❑ 그녀는 이 비밀을 지키겠다는 약속을 충실히 지켜왔다. ● 복수명사 신봉자 ❑ 그는 공장이나 열성 당원이 모인 데서 연설을 하는 데 시간을 보낸다. ● 충실히 부사 ❑ 그는 1965년부터 죽 끓듯이 변하는 모든 정부 정책을 충실히 따라왔고 지지해 왔다. ▯ 형용사 외도하지 않는, 한눈팔지 않는 ❑ 나는 누군가를 사랑하면, 절대로 한눈을 팔지 않아. ▯ 형용사 충실한 ❑ 콜린 웰랜드의 시나리오는 원작 소설을 충실히 따랐다. ● 충실하게 부사 ❑ 나는 번안할 때 뜻 하나하나를 최대한 충실하게 번역한다.

faith|ful|ly /feɪθfəli/ CONVENTION When you start a formal or business letter with "Dear Sir" or "Dear Madam," you write **Yours faithfully** before your signature at the end. →see also **faithful** [BRIT; AM **Sincerely yours**]

관용 표현 올림, 배상 [영국영어; 미국영어 sincerely yours]

fake /feɪk/ (**fakes, faking, faked**) ▮ ADJ A **fake** fur or a **fake** painting, for example, is a fur or painting that has been made to look valuable or genuine, usually in order to deceive people. ❑ *The bank manager is said to have issued fake certificates.* ● N-COUNT A **fake** is something that is fake. ❑ *The gallery is filled with famous works of art, and every one of them is a fake.* ▯ V-T If someone **fakes** something, they try to make it look valuable or genuine, although in fact it is not. ❑ *It's safer to fake a tan with makeup rather than subject your complexion to the harsh rays of the sun.* ❑ *...faked evidence.* ▯ N-COUNT Someone who is a **fake** is not what they claim to be, for example because they do not have the qualifications that they claim to have. ❑ *I think Jack is a good man. He isn't a fake.* ▰ V-T If you **fake** a feeling, emotion, or reaction, you pretend that you are experiencing it when you are not. ❑ *Jon faked nonchalance.*

▮ 형용사 위조의, 가짜의 ❑ 그 은행 지점장이 위조 증명서를 발급했다고 한다. ● 가산명사 가짜, 모조품 ❑ 그 미술관은 유명 예술 작품으로 가득 차 있는데, 그 하나하나가 다 모조품이다. ▯ 타동사 꾸며대다, 날조하다 ❑ 강렬한 태양 광선에 피부를 노출시키는 것보다 화장으로 약간 볕에 그을린 듯 보이게 꾸미는 것이 더 안전하다. ❑ 날조된 증거 ▯ 가산명사 사기꾼 ❑ 나는 잭이 좋은 사람이라고 봐. 그는 사기꾼이 아니야. ▰ 타동사 ‑ 척하다 ❑ 존은 냉정한 척했다.

Thesaurus　　*fake*의 참조어

ADJ.	artificial, counterfeit, imitation; (*ant.*) authentic, genuine ▮
V.	falsify, pretend ▰

fall ♦♦♦ /fɔl/ (**falls, falling, fell, fallen**) ▮ V-I If someone or something **falls**, they

▮ 자동사 떨어지다 ❑ 찰스 황태자가 또 말에서

move quickly downward onto or toward the ground, by accident or because of a natural force. ❑ *Prince Charles has again fallen from his horse.* ❑ *Bombs fell in the town.* ● N-COUNT **Fall** is also a noun. ❑ *The helmets are designed to withstand impacts equivalent to a fall from a bicycle.* **2** V-I If a person or structure that is standing somewhere **falls**, they move from their upright position, so that they are then lying on the ground. ❑ *The woman gripped the shoulders of her man to stop herself from falling.* ❑ *He lost his balance and fell backwards.* ● N-COUNT **Fall** is also a noun. ❑ *She broke her right leg in a bad fall.* ● PHRASAL VERB **Fall down** means the same as **fall.** ❑ *I hit him so hard he fell down.* ● **fallen** ADJ [ADJ n] ❑ *A number of roads have been blocked by fallen trees.*

Note that you can use **fall down** to talk about people and objects, but for things like prices you should use the verb **fall** by itself. ❑ *Suddenly she just fell down beside me... Share prices fell sharply during the day.* Do not confuse **fall** and **drop**. Although things can **drop** or **fall** by accident, note that **fall** is not followed by an object, so you cannot say that someone "falls" something. However, you can say that they **drop** something, or that something **drops**. ❑ *Leaves were falling to the ground... He dropped his cigar... Plate after plate dropped from his fingers.* You say that a person **drops** when they jump straight down from something, for example, when someone jumps from a plane using a parachute. If someone **falls** it is usually because of an accident. ❑ *He stumbled and fell.* **Drop** and **fall** are also nouns. A **drop** is the height of something when you imagine falling off it. ❑ *Sixteen hundred feet is a considerable drop.* A **fall** is what happens when someone has an accident. ❑ *I had been badly bruised by the fall.*

---

3 V-I When rain or snow **falls**, it comes down from the sky. ❑ *Winds reached up to 100mph in some places with an inch of rain falling within 15 minutes.* ● N-COUNT **Fall** is also a noun. ❑ *One night there was a heavy fall of snow.* →see also **rainfall** **4** V-I If you **fall** somewhere, you allow yourself to drop there in a hurried or disorganized way, often because you are very tired. ❑ *Totally exhausted, he tore his clothes off and fell into bed.* **5** V-I If something **falls**, it decreases in amount, value, or strength. ❑ *Output will fall by 6%.* ❑ *The rate of convictions has fallen.* ● N-COUNT **Fall** is also a noun. ❑ *There was a sharp fall in the value of the pound.* **6** If a powerful or successful person **falls**, they suddenly lose their power or position. ❑ *Regimes fall, revolutions come and go, but places never really change.* ● N-SING **Fall** is also a noun. ❑ *Following the fall of the military dictator in March, the country has had a civilian government.* **7** V-I If a place **falls** in a war or election, an enemy army or a different political party takes control of it. ❑ *Croatian army troops retreated from northern Bosnia and the area fell to the Serbs.* ● N-SING **Fall** is also a noun. ❑ *...the fall of Rome.* **8** V-LINK You can use **fall** to show that someone or something passes into another state. For example, if someone **falls ill**, they become ill, and if something **falls into disrepair**, it is then in a state of disrepair. ❑ *It is almost impossible to visit Florida without falling in love with the state.* ❑ *Almost without exception these women fall victim to exploitation.* **9** V-I If you say that something or someone **falls into** a particular group or category, you mean that they belong in that group or category. ❑ *The problems generally fall into two categories.* **10** V-I If a celebration or other special event **falls on** a particular day or date, it happens to be on that day or date. ❑ *...the oddly named Quasimodo Sunday which falls on the first Sunday after Easter.* **11** V-I When light or shadow **falls** on something, it covers it. ❑ *Nancy, out of the corner of her eye, saw the shadow that suddenly fell across the doorway.* **12** V-I If you say that someone's eyes **fell on** something, you mean they suddenly noticed it. [WRITTEN] ❑ *As he laid the flowers on the table, his eye fell upon a note in Grace's handwriting.* **13** V-I When night or darkness **falls**, night begins and it becomes dark. ❑ *As darkness fell outside, they sat down to eat at long tables.* **14** N-PLURAL; N-IN-NAMES You can refer to a **waterfall** as **the falls**. ❑ *The falls have always been an insurmountable obstacle for salmon and sea trout.* **15** N-VAR **Fall** is the season between summer and winter when the weather becomes cooler. [AM; BRIT **autumn**] ❑ *He was elected judge in the fall of 1991.* **16** →see also **fallen** **17** PHRASE To **fall to pieces**, or in British English to **fall to bits**, means the same as to **fall apart.** ❑ *At that point the radio handset fell to pieces.* **18** to **fall on** your **feet** →see **foot.** to **fall foul of** →see **foul.** to **fall flat** →see **flat.** to **fall into place** →see **place.** to **fall short** →see **short**

Thesaurus · *fall*의 참조어

v.	plunge, topple over **1** **2**
	come down **3**
	decline, decrease, drop, plunge; (ant.) increase, rise **5**

▶**fall apart** **1** PHRASAL VERB If something **falls apart**, it breaks into pieces because it is old or badly made. ❑ *The work was never finished and bit by bit the building fell apart.* **2** PHRASAL VERB If an organization or system **falls apart**, it becomes disorganized or unable to work effectively, or breaks up into its different parts. ❑ *Europe's monetary system is falling apart.* **3** PHRASAL VERB If you say that someone **is falling apart**, you mean that they are becoming emotionally disturbed and are unable to think calmly or to deal with the difficult or unpleasant situation that they are in. [INFORMAL] ❑ *I was falling apart. I wasn't getting any sleep.*

떨어졌다. ❑ 폭탄이 도시로 떨어졌다. ● 가산명사 추락, 낙하 ❑ 이 안전모는 자전거에서 떨어지는 정도의 충격도 견뎌낼 수 있도록 만들어졌다. **2** 자동사 넘어지다, 쓰러지다, 무너지다 ❑ 그 여자는 넘어지지 않으려고 남자의 어깨를 꽉 잡았다. ❑ 그는 균형을 잃고 뒤로 쓰러졌다. ● 가산명사 쓰러짐, 넘어짐, 무너짐 ❑ 그녀는 심하게 넘어져서 오른쪽 다리가 부러졌다. ● 구동사 넘어지다, 쓰러지다, 무너지다 ❑ 그는 나한테 한 대 세게 맞고 쓰러졌다. ● 쓰러진 형용사 ❑ 수많은 도로들이 쓰러진 나무로 막혀 있다.

---

fall down은 사람과 사물에 대해 말할 때 쓸 수 있지만, 가격과 같은 것에 대해서는 동사 fall만 써야 한다는 점을 유의하라. ❑ 갑자기 그녀가 내 옆에서 그냥 쓰러졌다... 주가가 하루 동안 급락했다. drop과 fall을 혼동하지 않도록 하라. 사물이 우연히 drop 또는 fall할 수는 있지만, fall은 뒤에 목적어가 오지 않는다는 점을 유의하라. 그러니, 누군가가 무엇을 '떨어뜨린다'를 someone falls something으로 나타낼 수는 없다. 그러나, 누가 무엇을 drop하거나, 무엇이 drop한다고는 말할 수 있다. ❑ 나뭇잎이 땅으로 떨어지고 있었다... 그가 피우던 여송연을 떨어뜨렸다... 접시들이 연이어 그의 손 끝에서 떨어졌다. 누가 어디에서 바로 뛰어내린다면, 예를 들어 낙하산으로 비행기에서 뛰어내리면, 그 사람이 drop한다고 말한다. 누가 fall하면, 대개 사고 때문이다. ❑ 그는 비틀거리다가 넘어졌다. drop과 fall은 명사이기도 하다. drop은 무엇으로부터 떨어지는 것을 상상할 때 높이를 말한다. ❑ 1,600 피트는 상당한 낙차이다. fall은 사고가 났을 때 발생하는 것이다. ❑ 나는 그 추락으로 심한 타박상을 입었다.

---

3 자동사 (비, 눈이) 내리다 ❑ 몇몇 지역에서는 풍속이 시속 100마일에 달했고 15분간 1인치의 비가 내렸다. ● 가산명사 강우, 강설 ❑ 언젠가는 밤에 폭설이 내렸다. **4** 자동사 푹 쓰러지다 ❑ 그는 완전히 기진맥진해서 옷을 벗어던지고는 침대에 푹 쓰러졌다. **5** 자동사 줄다, 감소하다 ❑ 생산량이 6퍼센트 감소할 것이다. ❑ 유죄 판결율이 줄었다. ● 가산명사 하락, 감소 ❑ 파운드화 가치가 급격히 하락했다. **6** 실권하다, 몰락하다 ❑ 정권들이 몰락하고, 혁명의 물결이 오고 가도, 장소는 절대 바뀌지 않는다. ● 단수명사 실권, 몰락, 몰락 ❑ 3월에 군부 독재 정권이 붕괴하고, 그 나라에는 문민 정권이 들어섰다. **7** 자동사 수중으로 들어가다, 함락되다 ❑ 크로아티아군은 북부 보스니아에서 물러났고, 그 지역은 세르비아 수중으로 들어갔다. ● 단수명사 함락 ❑ 로마의 함락 **8** 연결동사 ~해지다, (~한 상태에) 빠지다 ❑ 누구든 플로리다에 가 보면 그 주를 사랑하지 않을 수 없게 된다. ❑ 이런 여자들은 거의 예외 없이 착취의 대상으로 전락한다. **9** 자동사 분류되다 ❑ 이러한 문제들은 보통 두 가지 범주로 분류된다. **10** 자동사 (날짜가) ~이다 ❑ 부활절 다음의 첫 번째 일요일인 괴이한 이름의 콰시모도 일요일 **11** 자동사 비취지다, 드리워지다 ❑ 갑자기 그림자가 현관에 드리워지는 것이 낸시의 눈 한 켠에 들어왔다. **12** 자동사 눈길이 머물다 [문어체] ❑ 그가 꽃을 탁자 위에 놓는 순간, 그레이스가 쓴 메모가 눈에 들어왔다. **13** 자동사 (어둠이) 내리다 ❑ 밖에 어둠이 내리자, 그들은 식사를 하려고 길다란 식탁에 앉았다. **14** 복수명사; 이름명사 폭포 ❑ 연어나 송어에게 폭포는 언제나 감당해 내기 힘든 장애물이다. **15** 가산명사 또는 불가산명사 가을 [미국영어; 영국영어 autumn] ❑ 그는 1991년 가을에 판사로 선출되었다. **17** 구 산산조각이 나다 ❑ 그 순간 무선 수신기가 산산조각이 났다.

---

1 구동사 부서지나 ❑ ...그 일은 좀처럼 끝나지 않았고, 건물은 조금씩 조금씩 무너졌다. **2** 구동사 와해되다, 붕괴되다 ❑ 유럽의 통화 제도가 붕괴되고 있다. **3** 구동사 신경이 쇠약해지다 [비격식체] ❑ 나는 신경이 쇠약해졌다. 잠도 오지 않았다.

---

a b c d e f g h i j k l m n o p q r s t u v w x y z

A

▶**fall back on** PHRASAL VERB If you **fall back on** something, you do it or use it after other things have failed. ❑ *When necessary, instinct is the most reliable resource you can fall back on.*

구동사 의지하다 ❑ 본능은 필요할 때 가장 의지할 만한 방편이 되기도 한다.

▶**fall behind 1** PHRASAL VERB If you **fall behind**, you do not make progress or move forward as fast as other people. ❑ *Boris is falling behind all the top players.* **2** PHRASAL VERB If you **fall behind** with something or let it **fall behind**, you do not do it or produce it when you should, according to an agreement or schedule. ❑ *He faces losing his home after falling behind with the payments.* ❑ *Thousands of people could die because the relief effort has fallen so far behind.*

1 구동사 뒤처지다 ❑ 보리스는 최상위 선수권에서 밀려나고 있다. **2** 구동사 지연하다, 지연시키다, 연체하다 ❑ 지불 날짜를 지키지 못해서, 그는 집을 잃게 될 처지에 놓였다. ❑ 구호 활동이 너무나 지연되어서 수천 명의 사람이 목숨을 잃을 수도 있다.

▶**fall for 1** PHRASAL VERB If you **fall for** someone, you are strongly attracted to them and start loving them. ❑ *He was fantastically handsome – I just fell for him right away.* **2** PHRASAL VERB If you **fall for** a lie or trick, you believe it or are deceived by it. ❑ *It was just a line to get you out here, and you fell for it!*

1 구동사 반하다 ❑ 그가 환상적일 정도로 잘 생겨서 나는 그냥 당장 반해 버렸다. **2** 구동사 속다 ❑ 그건 그냥 널 여기서 내보내기 위한 술책이었어. 넌 거기에 속아 넘어간 거고!

▶**fall off 1** PHRASAL VERB If something **falls off**, it separates from the thing to which it was attached and moves towards the ground. ❑ *When your exhaust falls off, you have to replace it.* **2** PHRASAL VERB If the degree, amount, or size of something **falls off**, it decreases. ❑ *Unemployment is rising again and retail buying has fallen off.*

1 구동사 떨어지다 ❑ 배기관이 떨어지면, 갈아야 한다. **2** 구동사 감소하다 ❑ 실업은 다시 증가하고 있고 소비자 구매는 감소했다.

▶**fall out 1** PHRASAL VERB If something such as a person's hair or a tooth **falls out**, it comes out. ❑ *Her hair started falling out as a result of radiation treatment.* **2** PHRASAL VERB-RECIP If you **fall out** with someone, you have an argument and stop being friendly with them. You can also say that two people **fall out**. ❑ *She fell out with her husband.* **3** →see also **fallout**

1 구동사 빠지다 ❑ 방사선 치료의 결과로 그 여자의 머리카락이 빠지기 시작했다. **2** 상호 구동사 사이가 틀어지다 ❑ 그녀는 남편과 사이가 틀어졌다.

▶**fall over** PHRASAL VERB If a person or object that is standing **falls over**, they accidentally move from their upright position so that they are then lying on the ground or on the surface supporting them. ❑ *If he drinks more than two glasses of wine he falls over.*

구동사 쓰러지다 ❑ 그는 포도주 두 잔 이상만 마시면 그냥 쓰러진다.

▶**fall through** PHRASAL VERB If an arrangement, plan, or deal **falls through**, it fails to happen. ❑ *They wanted to turn the estate into a private golf course and offered £20 million, but the deal fell through.*

구동사 무산되다 ❑ 그들은 그 땅에 사설 골프장을 만들려고 2천만 파운드를 제시했으나, 그 거래는 무산됐다.

▶**fall to** PHRASAL VERB If a responsibility, duty, or opportunity **falls to** someone, it becomes their responsibility, duty, or opportunity. ❑ *He's been very unlucky that no chances have fallen to him.*

구동사 (책임, 의무, 기회가) 주어지다 ❑ 그는 여태껏 아무런 기회도 갖지 못할 정도로 정말 운이 없었다.

fal|la|cy /fǽləsi/ (**fallacies**) N-VAR A **fallacy** is an idea which many people believe to be true, but which is in fact false because it is based on incorrect information or reasoning. ❑ *It's a fallacy that the affluent give relatively more to charity than the less prosperous.*

가산명사 또는 불가산명사 잘못된 생각 ❑ 부유한 사람들이 그렇지 못한 사람들보다 상대적으로 더 많은 기부를 한다는 것은 잘못된 생각이다.

fall|en /fɔ́lən/ **Fallen** is the past participle of **fall**.

fall의 과거 분사

fall|out /fɔ́laʊt/ **1** N-UNCOUNT **Fallout** is the radiation that affects a particular place or area after a nuclear explosion has taken place. ❑ *They were exposed to radioactive fallout during nuclear weapons tests.* **2** N-UNCOUNT If you refer to the **fallout from** something that has happened, you mean the unpleasant consequences that follow it. ❑ *Grundy lost his job in the fallout from the incident.*

1 불가산명사 낙진 ❑ 그들은 핵무기 실험 동안 방사선 낙진에 노출되었다. **2** 불가산명사 여파 ❑ 그룬디는 그 사건의 여파로 직장을 잃었다.

false ◆◇◇ /fɔ́ls/ **1** ADJ If something is **false**, it is incorrect, untrue, or mistaken. ❑ *It was quite clear that the President was being given false information by those around him.* ❑ *You do not know whether what you're told is true or false.* • **false|ly** ADV [ADV with v] ❑ *...a man who is falsely accused of a crime.* **2** ADJ You use **false** to describe objects which are artificial but which are intended to look like the real thing or to be used instead of the real thing. ❑ *...a set of false teeth.* **3** ADJ If you describe a person or their behavior as **false**, you are criticizing them for being insincere or for hiding their real feelings. [DISAPPROVAL] ❑ *"Thank you," she said with false enthusiasm.* • **false|ly** ADV ❑ *"This food is divine," they murmur, falsely.*

1 형용사 거짓된, 허위의 ❑ 대통령은 명백히 그의 측근들로부터 허위 정보를 받고 있었다. ❑ 너는 네가 들은 것이 진실인지 거짓인지 모르고 있어. • 잘못 부사 ❑ 잘못 기소된 남자 **2** 형용사 인조의 ❑ 의치 한 세트 **3** 형용사 가식적인 [탐탁찮음] ❑ "감사합니다." 그녀는 가식적인 열정을 섞어 말했다. • 가식적으로 부사 ❑ "이 음식은 하나님이 주신 것입니다."라고 그들은 가식적으로 중얼거린다.

false alarm (**false alarms**) N-COUNT When you think something dangerous is about to happen, but then discover that you were mistaken, you can say that it was a **false alarm**. ❑ *...a bomb threat that turned out to be a false alarm.*

가산명사 허위 경보 ❑ 폭파 위협은 공갈로 드러났다.

false start (**false starts**) **1** N-COUNT A **false start** is an attempt to start something, such as a speech, project, or plan, which fails because you were not properly prepared or ready to begin. ❑ *Any economic reform, he said, faced false starts and mistakes.* **2** N-COUNT If there is a **false start** at the beginning of a race, one of the competitors moves before the person who starts the race has given the signal. ❑ *He powered away after two false starts to win comfortably.*

1 가산명사 잘못된 시작 ❑ 모든 경제 개혁이 잘못된 시작과 오류에 직면했다고 그는 말했다. **2** 가산명사 부정 출발 ❑ 그는 여유 있게 이기려고 두 번의 부정 출발을 범한 후 힘있게 뛰어나갔다.

fal|si|fy /fɔ́lsɪfaɪ/ (**falsifies, falsifying, falsified**) V-T If someone **falsifies** something, they change it or add untrue details to it in order to deceive people. ❑ *The charges against him include fraud, bribery, and falsifying business records.*

타동사 위조하다, 왜곡하다 ❑ 그의 혐의에는 사기, 뇌물 공여, 사업 기록 위조가 포함된다.

fal|ter /fɔ́ltər/ (**falters, faltering, faltered**) **1** V-I If something **falters**, it loses power or strength in an uneven way, or no longer makes much progress. ❑ *Normal life is at a standstill, and the economy is faltering.* **2** V-I If you **falter**, you lose your confidence and stop doing something or start making mistakes. ❑ *I have not faltered in my quest for a new future.*

1 자동사 주춤거리다 ❑ 일상생활은 답보 상태에 있고, 경제는 주춤거리고 있다. **2** 자동사 머뭇거리다 ❑ 나는 새로운 미래를 위한 탐색에서 머뭇거려 본 적이 없다.

fame /feɪm/ N-UNCOUNT If you achieve **fame**, you become very well-known. ❑ *At the height of his fame, his every word was valued.* ❑ *The film earned him international fame.*

불가산명사 명예, 명성 ❑ 그의 명성이 최고조에 이르렀을 때, 그의 말 한마디 한마디가 가치를 지녔다. ❑ 그 영화로 그는 국제적인 명성을 얻었다.

Word Partnership	*fame*의 연어
V.	**bring** fame, **gain** fame, **rise to** fame
N.	**claim to** fame, fame **and fortune**
ADJ.	**international** fame

famed /feɪmd/ ADJ If people, places, or things are **famed for** a particular thing, they are very well known for it. ❑ *The city is famed for its outdoor restaurants.*

형용사 ~로 유명한 ❑ 그 도시는 노천 식당들로 유명하다.

fa|mil|iar ♦○○ /fəmɪ́lyər/ **1** ADJ If someone or something is **familiar** to you, you recognize them or know them well. ❑ *He talked of other cultures as if they were more familiar to him than his own.* ❑ *They are already familiar faces on our TV screens.* ● **fa|mil|iar|ity** /fəmɪliǽrɪti/ N-UNCOUNT ❑ *Tony was unnerved by the uncanny familiarity of her face.* **2** ADJ If you are **familiar with** something, you know or understand it well. [v-link ADJ with n] ❑ *Most people are familiar with this figure from Wagner's opera.* ● **fa|mil|iar|ity** N-UNCOUNT ❑ *The enemy would always have the advantage of familiarity with the rugged terrain.* **3** ADJ If someone you do not know well behaves in a **familiar** way towards you, they treat you very informally in a way that you might find offensive. [DISAPPROVAL] ❑ *The driver of that taxi-cab seemed to me familiar to the point of impertinence.* ● **fa|mil|iar|ity** N-UNCOUNT ❑ *She needed to control her surprise at the easy familiarity with which her host greeted the head waiter.* ● **fa|mil|iar|ly** ADV ❑ *"Gerald, isn't it?" I began familiarly.*

Thesaurus
familiar의 참조어

ADJ.	accustomed to, recognizable **1**
	aware of, informed about **2**

Word Partnership
familiar의 연어

N.	familiar **face 1**
V.	look familiar, **seem** familiar, **sound** familiar **1**
	become familiar **2**
PREP.	familiar **with** *someone/something* **2**

---

fa|mil|iar|ize /fəmɪ́lyəraɪz/ (**familiarizes, familiarizing, familiarized**) [BRIT also **familiarise**] V-T If you **familiarize** yourself **with** something, or if someone **familiarizes** you **with** it, you learn about it and start to understand it. ❑ *The goal of the experiment was to familiarize the people with the new laws.*

fam|ily ♦♦♦ /fǽmɪli, fǽmli/ (**families**) **1** N-COUNT-COLL A **family** is a group of people who are related to each other, especially parents and their children. ❑ *There's room in there for a family of five.* ❑ *Does he have any family?* **2** N-COUNT-COLL When people talk about a **family**, they sometimes mean children. ❑ *They decided to start a family.* **3** N-COUNT-COLL When people talk about their **family**, they sometimes mean their ancestors. ❑ *Her family came to Los Angeles at the turn of the century.* **4** ADJ You can use **family** to describe things that belong to a particular family. [ADJ n] ❑ *He returned to the family home.* **5** ADJ You can use **family** to describe things that are designed to be used or enjoyed by both parents and children. [ADJ n] ❑ *It had been designed as a family house.* **6** N-COUNT A **family** of animals or plants is a group of related species. ❑ *...foods in the cabbage family, such as Brussels sprouts.*
→see Picture Dictionary: **family**

1 형용사 잘 알고 있는, 잘 알려진 ❑ 그는 다른 문화들을 자기 문화보다 더 잘 알고 있는 듯이 얘기했다. ❑ 그 사람들은 텔레비전 화면을 통해 이미 잘 알려진 얼굴들이다. ● 친숙함 불가산명사 ❑ 토니는 이상하리만큼 친숙한 그녀의 얼굴에 깜짝 놀랐다. **2** 형용사 익숙한 사람들 대부분이 바그너 오페라에 나오는 이 인물에 익숙하다. ● 익숙함 불가산명사 ❑ 적군은 험한 지형에 익숙하다는 이점을 항상 잘 활용할 것이다. **3** 형용사 막 대하는 [탐탁찮음] ❑ 그 택시 기사는 무례하다 싶을 정도로 나를 막 대했다. ● 막 대함 불가산명사 ❑ 그녀는 주인이 수석 웨이터에게 막 대하면서 인사하는 것에 놀란 가슴을 진정시킬 필요가 있었다. ● 막 대하며 부사 ❑ "제럴드, 너지?"라고 나는 친숙하게 말을 시작했다.

[영국영어 familiarise] 타동사 배우다, 알리다 ❑ 그 실험의 목적은 사람들에게 새 법을 알리는 것이었다.

1 가산명사-집합 가족 ❑ 거기에는 5인 가족용 방이 있습니다. ❑ 그는 가족이 있어요? **2** 가산명사-집합 자식, 아이들 ❑ 그들은 아이를 가지기로 결정했다. **3** 가산명사-집합 선조, 집안 ❑ 그녀의 집안은 금세기 초에 로스앤젤레스로 왔다. **4** 형용사 가족의 ❑ 그는 자기 집으로 돌아갔다. **5** 형용사 가정용의 ❑ 그 건물은 가정집으로 설계되었다. **6** 가산명사 과 ❑ 방울양배추같이 양배추과에 속하는 식품

Picture Dictionary　family

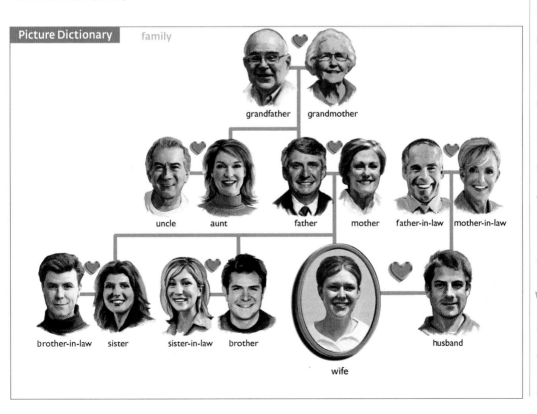

grandfather　grandmother

uncle　aunt　father　mother　father-in-law　mother-in-law

brother-in-law　sister　sister-in-law　brother　husband

wife

a b c d e f g h i j k l m n o p q r s t u v w x y z

fam|i|ly plan|ning N-UNCOUNT **Family planning** is the practice of using contraception to control the number of children you have. ❑ *...a family planning clinic.*

불가산명사 가족계획 ❑ 가족계획 클리닉

fam|ine /fæmɪn/ (famines) N-VAR **Famine** is a situation in which large numbers of people have little or no food, and many of them die. ❑ *Thousands of refugees are trapped by war, drought and famine.*

가산명사 또는 불가산명사 기근 ❑ 수천 명의 난민들이 전쟁과 가뭄과 기근에 시달리고 있다.

fa|mous ◆◇◇ /feɪməs/ ADJ Someone or something that is **famous** is very well known. ❑ *...England's most famous landscape artist, John Constable.*

형용사 유명한 ❑ 잉글랜드의 가장 저명한 풍경화가 존 컨스터블

A **famous** person or thing is known to more people than a **well-known** one. A **notorious** person or thing is famous because they are connected with something bad or undesirable. **Infamous** is not the opposite of **famous**. It has a similar meaning to **notorious**, but is a stronger word. Someone or something that is **notable** is important or interesting.

famous한 사람이나 사물은 well-known한 사람이나 사물보다 더 많은 사람들에게 알려져 있다. notorious한 사람이나 사물은 나쁘거나 바람직하지 않은 것과 연관되어 있기 때문에 유명하다. infamous는 '유명하다(famous)'의 반대말이 아니라, '악명 높다(notorious)'와 비슷한 뜻이며 더 강한 말이다. notable한 사람이나 사물은 중요하거나 흥미로움을 나타낸다.

Thesaurus *famous*의 참조어

ADJ. celebrated, prominent, renowned; *(ant.)* anonymous, obscure, unknown

fa|mous|ly /feɪməsli/ ADV You use **famously** to refer to a fact that is well known, usually because it is remarkable or extreme. ❑ *Authors are famously ignorant about the realities of publishing.*

부사 유명하게 ❑ 작가들은 출판계 현실에 무지하기로 유명하다.

fan ◆◇◇ /fæn/ (fans, fanning, fanned) **1** N-COUNT If you are a **fan** of someone or something, especially a famous person or a sport, you like them very much and are very interested in them. ❑ *If you're a Billy Crystal fan, you'll love this movie.* ❑ *I am a great fan of rave music.* **2** N-COUNT A **fan** is a flat object that you hold in your hand and wave in order to move the air and make yourself feel cooler. ❑ *...hundreds of dancing girls waving peacock fans.* **3** V-T If you **fan** yourself or your face when you are hot, you wave a fan or other flat object in order to make yourself feel cooler. ❑ *She would have to wait in the truck, fanning herself with a piece of cardboard.* **4** N-COUNT A **fan** is a piece of electrical or mechanical equipment with blades that go around and around. It keeps a room or machine cool or gets rid of unpleasant smells. ❑ *He cools himself in front of an electric fan.*
→see concert

1 가산명사 팬 ❑ 빌리 크리스탈의 팬이라면, 이 영화를 좋아할 거야. ❑ 나는 레이브 음악의 열성 팬이다. **2** 가산명사 부채 ❑ 공작 깃털로 만든 부채를 흔들며 춤추는 수백 명의 여자들 **3** 타동사 부채질하다 ❑ 그녀는 아마 트럭 안에서 판지로 부채질하면서 기다려야 할 거야. **4** 가산명사 선풍기, 환풍기 ❑ 그는 선풍기 앞에서 더위를 식힌다.

▶**fan out** PHRASAL VERB If a group of people or things **fan out**, they move forward away from a particular point in different directions. ❑ *The main body of British, American, and French troops had fanned out to the west.*

구동사 흩어지다 ❑ 영국군, 미국군, 프랑스군 주력 부대는 서쪽으로 흩어졌다.

fa|nat|ic /fənætɪk/ (fanatics) **1** N-COUNT If you describe someone as a **fanatic**, you disapprove of them because you consider their behavior or opinions to be very extreme, for example in the way they support particular religious or political ideas. [DISAPPROVAL] ❑ *I am not a religious fanatic but I am a Christian.* **2** N-COUNT If you say that someone is a **fanatic**, you mean that they are very enthusiastic about a particular activity, sport, or way of life. ❑ *Both Rod and Phil are football fanatics.* **3** ADJ **Fanatic** means the same as **fanatical**.

1 가산명사 광신도 [탐탁찮음] ❑ 나는 광신도가 아니라 기독교인이다. **2** 가산명사 열성 팬 ❑ 로드와 필은 둘 다 축구 열성 팬이다. **3** 형용사 광적인

fa|nati|cal /fənætɪkəl/ ADJ If you describe someone as **fanatical**, you disapprove of them because you consider their behavior or opinions to be very extreme. [DISAPPROVAL] ❑ *As a boy he was a fanatical patriot.*

형용사 광적인 [탐탁찮음] ❑ 그는 젊었을 때 광적인 애국자였다.

fan|ci|ful /fænsɪfəl/ ADJ If you describe an idea as **fanciful**, you disapprove of it because you think it comes from someone's imagination, and is therefore unrealistic or unlikely to be true. [DISAPPROVAL] ❑ *...fanciful ideas about Martian life.*

형용사 허무맹랑한 [탐탁찮음] ❑ 화성 생명체에 대한 허무맹랑한 생각들

━━━━━ **fancy** ━━━━━
① WANTING, LIKING, OR THINKING
② ELABORATE OR EXPENSIVE

① **fan|cy** ◆◇◇ /fænsi/ (fancies, fancying, fancied) **1** V-T If you **fancy** something, you want to have it or to do it. [mainly BRIT, INFORMAL] ❑ *What do you fancy doing, anyway?* ❑ *I just fancied a drink.* **2** V-T If you **fancy** someone, you feel attracted to them, especially in a sexual way. [INFORMAL] ❑ *The boys would tease you to death if they didn't fancy you.* **3** V-T If you **fancy yourself as** a particular kind of person or fancy **yourself** doing a particular thing, you like the idea of being that kind of person or doing that thing. ❑ *So you fancy yourself as the boss someday?* **4** V-T If you say that someone **fancies themselves as** a particular kind of person, you mean that they think, often wrongly, that they have the good qualities which that kind of person has. ❑ *She fancies herself a bohemian.* **5** V-T If you say that you **fancy** a particular competitor or team in a competition, you think they will win. [BRIT] ❑ *I fancy England to win through.* **6** EXCLAM You say "**fancy**" or "**fancy that**" when you want to express surprise or disapproval. [FEELINGS] ❑ *"Fancy that!" smiled Conti.* **7** PHRASE If you **take a fancy to** someone or something, you start liking them, usually for no understandable reason. ❑ *Sylvia took quite a fancy to him.* **8** PHRASE If something **takes** your **fancy** or **tickles** your **fancy**, you like it a lot when you see it or think of it. ❑ *She makes most of her own clothes, copying any fashion which takes her fancy.*

1 타동사 -고 싶다 [주로 영국영어, 비격식체] ❑ 그런데 넌 뭐하고 싶어? ❑ 그냥 한 잔 마시고 싶었어. **2** 타동사 매력을 느끼다 [비격식체] ❑ 네가 걔네들 맘에 안 들면, 널 죽도록 괴롭힐 거야. **3** 타동사 상상하다 ❑ 그래서 너는 네가 나중에 사장이 되어 있는 걸 상상해 본다고? **4** 타동사 -라고 착각하다 ❑ 그녀는 자기가 보헤미안의 기질을 지녔다고 착각하고 있다. **5** 타동사 -일 것 같다고 생각하다 [영국영어] ❑ 나는 잉글랜드 팀이 계속 이길 것 같은 생각이 든다. **6** 감탄사 저것 좀 봐 [감정 개입] ❑ "저것 좀 봐!" 콘티가 웃으며 말했다. **7** 구 끌리기 시작하다, 매료되다 ❑ 실비아는 그에게 상당히 마음이 끌리기 시작했다. **8** 구 맘에 쏙 들다 ❑ 그녀는 자기 옷의 대부분을 맘에 쏙 드는 옷들을 본떠 직접 만든다.

② **fan|cy** /fænsi/ (fancier, fanciest) **1** ADJ If you describe something as **fancy**, you mean that it is special, unusual, or elaborate, for example because it has a lot of decoration. ❑ *The magazine was packaged in a fancy plastic case with attractive graphics.* **2** ADJ If you describe something as **fancy**, you mean that it is very expensive or of very high quality, and you often dislike it because of this. [INFORMAL] ❑ *My parents sent me to a fancy private school.*

1 형용사 최고급의 ❑ 그 잡지는 멋진 그림이 그려져 있는 최고급 플라스틱 케이스에 포장돼 있었다. **2** 형용사 최고의 [비격식체] ❑ 부모님은 나를 최고급 사립학교에 보내셨다.

Thesaurus *fancy*의 참조어

ADJ. elegant, lavish; *(ant.)* plain, simple ② **2**

fan|fare /fˈænfeər/ (**fanfares**) N-COUNT A **fanfare** is a short, loud tune played on trumpets or other similar instruments to announce a special event. ❑ *The ceremony opened with a fanfare of trumpets.*

가산명사 팡파르 ❑ 트럼펫 팡파르로 의식은 시작되었다.

fang /fˈæŋ/ (**fangs**) N-COUNT **Fangs** are the two long, sharp, upper teeth that some animals have. ❑ *The cobra sank its venomous fangs into his hand.*

가산명사 송곳니 ❑ 코브라는 독니로 그의 손을 물었다.

fan|ta|size /fˈæntəsaɪz/ (**fantasizes, fantasizing, fantasized**) [BRIT also **fantasise**] V-T/V-I If you **fantasize** about an event or situation that you would like to happen, you give yourself pleasure by imagining that it is happening, although it is untrue or unlikely to happen. ❑ *I fantasised about writing music.*

[영국영어 fantasise] 타동사/자동사 공상하다 ❑ 나는 작곡가가 되는 것을 공상해 본다.

fan|tas|tic /fˈæntˈæstɪk/ ❑ ADJ If you say that something is **fantastic**, you are emphasizing that you think it is very good or that you like it a lot. [INFORMAL, EMPHASIS] ❑ *I have a fantastic social life.* ❑ ADJ A **fantastic** amount or quantity is an extremely large one. [ADJ n] ❑ *...fantastic amounts of money.* ● **fan|tas|ti|cal|ly** /fˈæntˈæstɪkli/ ADV [ADV adj/adv] ❑ *...a fantastically expensive restaurant.*

❑ 형용사 아주 멋진 [비격식체, 강조] ❑ 나는 아주 멋진 사회생활을 하고 있다. ❑ 형용사 상당히 많은 ❑ 상당히 많은 금액 ● 상당히 부사 ❑ 상당히 비싼 레스토랑

fan|ta|sy ◆◇◇ /fˈæntəsi/ (**fantasies**) also **phantasy** ❑ N-COUNT A **fantasy** is a pleasant situation or event that you think about and that you want to happen, but that is unlikely to happen. ❑ *...fantasies of romance and true love.* ❑ N-VAR You can refer to a story or situation that someone creates from their imagination and that is not based on reality as **fantasy**. ❑ *The film is more of an ironic fantasy than a horror story.* ❑ N-UNCOUNT **Fantasy** is the activity of imagining things. ❑ *...a world of imagination, passion, fantasy, reflection.*
→see Word Web: **fantasy**

❑ 가산명사 환상 ❑ 연애와 진실한 사랑에 대한 환상 ❑ 가산명사 또는 불가산명사 공상 소설 ❑ 그 영화는 공포물이라기보다는 역설적인 공상 소설에 더 가깝다. ❑ 불가산명사 공상 ❑ 상상과 열정, 공상과 사색의 세계

FAO You use **FAO** when addressing a letter or parcel to a particular person. **FAO** is a written abbreviation for "for the attention of." ❑ *Send the coupon with your deposit to House Beautiful Weekend, FAO Heidi Ross.*

(편지나 소포에서) ~ 앞 ❑ 너의 예치금과 쿠폰을 '하우스 뷰티플 위켄드'의 하이디 로스 앞으로 보내라.

FAQ /fˈæk/ (**FAQs**) N-PLURAL **FAQ** is used especially on websites to refer to questions about computers and the Internet. **FAQ** is an abbreviation for "frequently asked questions."

복수명사 자주 하는 질문

far ◆◆◆ /fˈɑr/

> Far has two comparatives, **farther** and **further**, and two superlatives, **farthest** and **furthest**. Farther and farthest are used mainly in sense ❑, and are dealt with here. **Further** and **furthest** are dealt with in separate entries.

> far는 비교급으로 farther와 further가 있으며, 최상급으로 farthest와 furthest가 있다. farther와 farthest는 주로 의미 ❑로 쓰이며 여기서 다룬다. further와 furthest는 다른 표제어에서 다룬다.

❑ ADV If one place, thing, or person is **far** away from another, there is a great distance between them. ❑ *I know a nice little Italian restaurant not far from here.* ❑ *Both of my sisters moved even farther away from home.* ❑ ADV If you ask **how far** a place is, you are asking what distance it is from you or from another place. If you ask **how far** someone went, you are asking what distance they traveled, or what place they reached. ❑ *How far is Pawtucket from Providence?* ❑ *How far is it to Malcy?* ❑ *She followed the tracks as far as the road.* ❑ ADJ When there are two things of the same kind in a place, **the far** one is the one that is a greater distance from you. [ADJ n] ❑ *He had wandered to the far end of the room.* ❑ ADJ You can use **far** to refer to the part of an area or object that is the greatest distance from the center in a particular direction. For example, **the far** north **of** a country is the part of it that is the greatest distance to the north. [ADJ n] ❑ *I've spent a lot of time walking around Britain from the far north of Scotland down to Cornwall.* ❑ ADV A time or event that is **far** away in the future or the past is a long time from the present or from a particular point in time. ❑ *...hidden conflicts whose roots lie far back in time.* ❑ *I can't see any farther than the next six months.* ❑ ADV You can use **far** to talk about the extent or degree to which something happens or is true. ❑ *How far did the film tell the truth about Barnes Wallis?* ❑ ADV You can talk about how **far** someone or something gets to describe the progress that they make. ❑ *Discussions never progressed very far.* ❑ *Think of how far we have come in a little time.* ❑ ADV You can talk about how **far** a person or action goes to describe the degree to which someone's behavior or actions are extreme. [ADV with v] ❑ *It's still not clear how far the Russian parliament will go to implement its own plans.* ❑ *Competition can be healthy, but if it is pushed too far it can result in bullying.* ❑ ADV You can use **far** to mean "very much" when you are comparing two things and emphasizing the difference between them. For example, you can say that something is **far better** or **far worse** than something else to indicate that it is very much better or worse. You can also say that something is, for example,

❑ 부사 먼 ❑ 여기서 멀지 않은 곳에 아담하고 괜찮은 이태리 레스토랑 하나를 알고 있다. ❑ 내 여동생 둘 다 집에서 훨씬 더 먼 곳으로 이사 갔다. ❑ 부사 (거리가) 떨어져 있는 ❑ 프로비던스에서 포투켓까지 거리가 얼마나 되지? ❑ 말씨까지 거리가 얼마나 되지? ❑ 그녀는 길이 끝나는 데까지 발자국을 따라갔다. ❑ 형용사 맨 끝 쪽의 ❑ 그는 그 방 맨 끝 쪽까지 돌아다녔었다. ❑ 형용사 가장 구석진 ❑ 나는 스코틀랜드 북쪽 구석에서부터 콘월에 이르기까지 영국 전역을 오랫동안 도보로 여행했다. ❑ 부사 (시간상으로) 먼 ❑ 그 원인이 생긴 지 아주 오래된 숨겨진 갈등 ❑ 나는 향후 6개월 이후는 내다볼 수가 없다. ❑ 부사 ~ 정도까지 ❑ 그 영화가 어느 정도까지 바네스 월리스에 대해 진실을 보여 줬다? ❑ 부사 많이, 대단히 ❑ 토론은 큰 진전을 보이지 않았다. ❑ 우리가 짧은 시간 내에 얼마나 많이 발전해 왔나 생각해 보라. ❑ 부사 ~한 정도까지 ❑ 러시아 의회가 계획을 어느 정도까지 실행에 옮길지는 아직 확실치 않다. ❑ 경쟁하는 것은 건전할 수 있지만, 너무 정도가 심하면 약자 괴롭히기가 될 수도 있다. ❑ 부사 훨씬 [강조] ❑ 신선한 야채를 많이 먹는 여성은 불안감이나 우울증을 겪을 가능성이 훨씬 적다. ❑ 경찰은 그 반응이 기대했던 것보다는 훨씬 더 좋았다고 말한다. ❑ 형용사 극단적인 ❑ 현재 극우파가 극좌파보다 훨씬 더 위협적인 존재이다. ❑ 부사 ~하는 한 [집작컨] ❑ 내가 아는 한, 그것은 단지 2년 정도 지속됐을 뿐이다.

Word Web　　fantasy

All **fictional** writing involves the use of **imaginary** situations and characters. However, **fantasy** goes a few steps further. This **genre** leaves **reality** behind and moves into the area of **imagination**. It involves creating new creatures, **myths**, and **legends**. A **novelist** usually incorporates **realistic** people and settings. But a fantasy writer is free to create a whole different world where earthly laws no longer apply. Contemporary movies have found a rich source of stories in the genre. Today you can see a wide variety of films about **fairies**, **wizards**, and **dragons**.

far too big to indicate that it is very much too big. [EMPHASIS] ❑ *Women who eat plenty of fresh vegetables are far less likely to suffer anxiety or depression.* ❑ *The police say the response has been far better than expected.* 🔟 ADJ You can describe people with extreme left-wing or right-wing political views as the **far** left or the **far** right. [ADJ n] ❑ *The far right is now a greater threat than the extreme left.* 🔢 ADV You can use **far** in expressions like "**as far as I know**" and "**so far as I remember**" to indicate that you are not absolutely sure of the statement you are about to make or have just made, and you may be wrong. [VAGUENESS] [as/so ADV as] ❑ *It only lasted a couple of years, as far as I know.*

> **Far** is used in negative sentences and questions about distance, but not usually in affirmative sentences. ❑ *We stood by a stream not far from our house.* If you want to state the distance of a particular place from where you are, you can say that it is that distance **away**. ❑ *...Omaha, which is over 300 miles away.* If a place is very distant, you can say that it is **a long way away**, or that it is **a long way from** another place. ❑ *It is a long way from Atlanta... Anna was still a long way away.*

🔢 PHRASE You use the expression **by far** when you are comparing something or someone with others of the same kind, in order to emphasize how great the difference is between them. For example, you can say that something is **by far the best** or **the best by far** to indicate that it is definitely the best. [EMPHASIS] ❑ *By far the most important issue for them is unemployment.* 🔢 PHRASE If you say that something is **far from** a particular thing or **far from** being the case, you are emphasizing that it is not that particular thing or not at all the case, especially when people expect or assume that it is. [EMPHASIS] ❑ *It was obvious that much of what they recorded was far from the truth.* ❑ *Far from being relaxed, we both felt so uncomfortable we hardly spoke.* 🔢 PHRASE You can use the expression "**far from it**" to emphasize a negative statement that you have just made. [EMPHASIS] ❑ *Being dyslexic does not mean that one is unintelligent. Far from it.* 🔢 PHRASE If you say that someone **will go far**, you mean that they will be very successful in their career. ❑ *I was very impressed with the talent of Michael Ball. He will go far.* 🔢 PHRASE Someone or something that is **far gone** is in such a bad state or condition that not much can be done to help or improve them. ❑ *In his last few days the pain seemed to have stopped, but by then he was so far gone that it was no longer any comfort.* 🔢 PHRASE You can use the expression "**as far as I can see**" when you are about to state your opinion of a situation, or have just stated it, to indicate that it is your personal opinion. ❑ *That's the problem as far as I can see.* 🔢 PHRASE If you say that something only goes **so far** or can only go **so far**, you mean that its extent, effect, or influence is limited. ❑ *Their loyalty only went so far.* 🔢 PHRASE If you tell or ask someone what has happened **so far**, you are telling or asking them what has happened up until the present point in a situation or story, and often implying that something different might happen later. ❑ *It's been quiet so far.* ❑ *So far, they have met with no success.* 🔢 PHRASE You can say "**so far so good**" to express satisfaction with the way that a situation or activity is progressing, developing, or happening. [FEELINGS] ❑ *Of course, it's a case of so far, so good, but it's only one step.* 🔢 **near and far →see near**

far|away /fɑ̱rəweɪ/ also **far-away** ADJ A **faraway** place is a long distance from you or from a particular place. [ADJ n] ❑ *They have just returned from faraway places with wonderful stories to tell.*

farce /fɑ̱rs/ (**farces**) 🔢 N-COUNT A **farce** is a humorous play in which the characters become involved in complicated and unlikely situations. ❑ *...the West End farce, Run For Your Wife.* 🔢 N-UNCOUNT **Farce** is the style of acting and writing that is typical of farces. ❑ *The plot often borders on farce.* 🔢 N-SING If you describe a situation or event as a **farce**, you mean that it is so disorganized or ridiculous that you cannot take it seriously. [DISAPPROVAL] [also no det] ❑ *The elections have been reduced to a farce.*

far|ci|cal /fɑ̱rsɪkəl/ ADJ If you describe a situation or event as **farcical**, you mean that it is so silly or extreme that you are unable to take it seriously. [DISAPPROVAL] ❑ *...a farcical nine months' jail sentence imposed yesterday on a killer.*

fare ♦♦♢ /fe̱ər/ (**fares, faring, fared**) 🔢 N-COUNT A **fare** is the money that you pay for a trip that you make, for example, in a bus, train, or taxi. ❑ *He could barely afford the railway fare.* 🔢 V-I If you say that someone or something **fares** well or badly, you are referring to the degree of success they achieve in a particular situation or activity. ❑ *It is unlikely that the marine industry will fare any better in September.*

Far East N-PROPER **The Far East** is used to refer to all the countries of Eastern Asia, including China, Japan, North and South Korea, and Indochina.

fare|well /fe̱ərwe̱l/ (**farewells**) CONVENTION **Farewell** means the same as goodbye. [LITERARY, OLD-FASHIONED] ● N-COUNT **Farewell** is also a noun. ❑ *They said their farewells there at the cafe.*

far-fetched ADJ If you describe a story or idea as **far-fetched**, you are criticizing it because you think it is unlikely to be true or practical. [DISAPPROVAL] ❑ *The storyline was too far-fetched and none of the actors were particularly good.*

farm ♦♦♢ /fɑ̱rm/ (**farms, farming, farmed**) 🔢 N-COUNT A **farm** is an area of land, together with the buildings on it, that is used for growing crops or raising animals, usually in order to sell them. ❑ *Farms in France are much smaller than those in the United States or even Britain.* 🔢 V-T/V-I If you **farm** an area of land, you grow crops or keep animals on it. ❑ *They farmed some of the best land in Scotland.* 🔢 N-COUNT A mink **farm** or a fish **farm**, for example, is a place where a particular kind of animal or fish is bred and kept in large quantities in order to be sold. ❑ *...trout fresh from a local trout farm.* →see **dairy** →see Word Web: **farm**

far는 거리를 얘기할 때 대개 긍정문에서는 쓰지 않고 부정문과 의문문에 쓴다. ❑ 우리는 우리 집에서 멀지 않은 시냇가에 서 있었다. 현재 있는 곳에서부터 특정한 장소까지의 거리를 말하고 싶으면, 거기가 그 거리만큼 away하다고 말할 수 있다. ❑ ...오마하, 300마일 이상 떨어진 곳. 장소가 아주 먼 경우에는, 거기가 a long way away하다고 말하거나 '어떤 장소에서부터 멀리 떨어져(a long way from another place)있다고' 말할 수 있다. ❑ 거기는 애틀랜타에서 멀다... 안나는 아직 멀리 떨어져 있었다.

🔢 구 단연코 [강조] ❑ 그들에게 단연코 가장 중요한 문제는 실업 문제이다. 🔢 구 -와는 거리가 먼, ...이기는커녕 [강조] ❑ 그들이 녹음한 내용의 많은 부분이 분명히 사실과 거리가 멀었다. ❑ 긴장을 풀기는커녕, 우리 두 사람 모두 너무나 불편해서 서로 말도 거의 못했다. 🔢 구 전혀 그렇지 않다 [강조] ❑ 난독증이 있다는 것이 그 사람의 지능이 낮다는 의미는 아니다. 전혀 그렇지 않다. 🔢 구 대성공하다 ❑ 나는 마이클 볼의 재능에 아주 감탄했다. 그는 대성공할 것이다. 🔢 구 더 이상 손쓸 수 없는 상태가 되어 ❑ 마지막 며칠간은 그의 통증이 멈췄던 것처럼 보였지만, 그때쯤에는 더 이상 손쓸 수 없는 상태에까지 이르러 그건 이미 편안한 상태가 아니었다. 🔢 구 내 생각으로는 ❑ 내 생각으로는 그것이 문제점이다. 🔢 구 그 정도까지 ❑ 그들의 충성심은 단지 그 정도까지였다. 🔢 구 현재까지는 ❑ 현재까지는 조용하다. ❑ 현재까지는, 그들이 별 성과 없이 만나 왔다. 🔢 구 지금까지는 잘 되고 있다 [감정 개입] ❑ 물론 이것이 지금까지는 잘 되고 있는 상황이지만, 아직 첫 단계일 뿐이다.

형용사 먼 ❑ 그들은 놀라운 이야깃거리들을 가지고 먼 곳에서 방금 돌아왔다.

🔢 가산명사 소극, 익살극 ❑ 웨스트 엔드 소극인 '런 포 유어 와이프' 🔢 불가산명사 소극 ❑ 그 글의 구성은 흔히 소극과 매우 비슷하다. 🔢 단수명사 코미디 같은 일, 우스꽝스러운 일 [탐탁잖음] ❑ 선거가 코미디같이 되고 말았다.

형용사 터무니없는 [탐탁잖음] ❑ 어제 살인자에게 내려진 터무니없는 징역 9개월의 선고

🔢 가산명사 요금 ❑ 그는 기차 요금도 내기 어려운 형편이었다. 🔢 자동사 (일이) 되어 가다 ❑ 해양 산업이 9월에도 더 좋아질 기미가 보이지 않는다.

고유명사 극동 지역

관용 표현 안녕 [문예체, 구식어] ● 가산명사 작별 인사 ❑ 그들은 거기 카페에서 서로 작별 인사를 했다.

형용사 터무니없는 [탐탁잖음] ❑ 그 이야기의 사건 전개가 너무나 터무니없었고, 배우들도 하나같이 별 볼일 없었다.

🔢 가산명사 농장 ❑ 프랑스에 있는 농장은 미국이나 심지어 영국보다도 규모가 훨씬 작다. 🔢 타동사/자동사 경작하다, 축산을 하다 ❑ 그들은 스코틀랜드에서 가장 좋은 축에 드는 토지를 경작했다. 🔢 가산명사 양식장, 사육장 ❑ 지역 송어 양식장에서 막 잡아 온 송어

Word Web   farm

Gone are the days of simply planting a **crop** and **harvesting** it. Today's **farmer** relies on engineering and technology to make a living. Careful **irrigation** and **drainage** control the amount of water **plants** receive. **Insecticides** and fungicides protect plants from insect damage. **Fertilizers** guarantee maximum growth. Another high-tech **agricultural** approach promises to increase the world's **food** supply. Employing hydroponic methods, farmers use **chemical** solutions to **cultivate** plants. This has several advantages. **Soil** can contain **pests** and diseases not present in water alone. Growing plants hydroponically also requires less water and less labor than conventional growing methods.

farm|er ♦♦◇ /fɑrmər/ (**farmers**) N-COUNT A **farmer** is a person who owns or manages a farm. →see **farm**

가산명사 농장주, 농부

farm|house /fɑrmhaʊs/ (**farmhouses**) also farm house N-COUNT A **farmhouse** is the main house on a farm, usually where the farmer lives.

가산명사 농가

farm|ing /fɑrmɪŋ/ N-UNCOUNT **Farming** is the activity of growing crops or keeping animals on a farm. ❑ ...a career in farming.

불가산명사 농업, 동물 사육 ❑ 농장일

farm|land /fɑrmlænd/ (**farmlands**) N-UNCOUNT **Farmland** is land which is farmed, or which is suitable for farming. [also N in pl] ❑ It is surrounded by 62 acres of farmland.

불가산명사 농지 ❑ 그곳은 62에이커의 농지로 둘러싸여 있다.

farm|yard /fɑrmyɑrd/ (**farmyards**) N-COUNT On a farm, the **farmyard** is an area of land near the farmhouse which is enclosed by walls or buildings. ❑ ...farmyard animals including chickens, geese, and rabbits.

가산명사 농가 마당 ❑ 닭, 거위, 토끼를 포함하여 농가 마당에서 기르는 동물들

far off (**further off**, **furthest off**) ◾ ADJ If you describe a moment in time as **far off**, you mean that it is a long time from the present, either in the past or the future. ❑ In those far off days it never entered anyone's mind that she could be Prime Minister. ◾ ADJ If you describe something as **far off**, you mean that it is a long distance from you or from a particular place. ❑ ...stars in far-off galaxies. ● ADV **Far off** is also an adverb. [ADV after v] ❑ The band was playing far off in their blue and yellow uniforms.

◾ 형용사 (시간상으로) 아주 먼 ❑ 아주 먼 옛날 그 당시에는, 그녀가 수상이 될 수 있을 것이라는 생각은 누구도 하지 못했다. ◾ 형용사 (거리가) 아주 멀리 떨어진 ❑ 아주 멀리 떨어진 은하계의 별들 ● 부사 멀리 떨어져서 ❑ 그 밴드는 파랗고 노란 유니폼을 입고서 멀리 떨어져서 연주하고 있었다.

far-reaching ADJ If you describe actions, events, or changes as **far-reaching**, you mean that they have a very great influence and affect a great number of things. ❑ The economy is in danger of collapse unless far-reaching reforms are implemented.

형용사 대대적인 ❑ 대대적인 개혁이 이행되지 않으면 경제가 붕괴될 위험에 처해 있다.

far|sighted /fɑrsaɪtɪd/ also far-sighted ADJ If you describe someone as **farsighted**, you admire them because they understand what is likely to happen in the future, and therefore make wise decisions and plans. [APPROVAL] ❑ Haven't farsighted economists been telling us for some time now that in the future we will work less, not more? →see **eye**

형용사 긴 안목을 가진 [마음에 듦] ❑ 긴 안목을 가진 경제학자들이 미래에는 우리가 일을 더 하는 것이 아니라 덜 하게 되리라고 오래전부터 말하지 않았나요?

far|ther /fɑrðər/ **Farther** is a comparative form of **far**.

더 먼

far|thest /fɑrðɪst/ **Farthest** is a superlative form of **far**.

가장 먼

fas|ci|nate /fæsɪneɪt/ (**fascinates**, **fascinating**, **fascinated**) V-T If something **fascinates** you, it interests and delights you so much that your thoughts tend to concentrate on it. ❑ Politics fascinated Franklin's father.

타동사 매혹시키다 ❑ 정치학은 프랭클린의 아버지를 매혹시켰다.

fas|ci|nat|ed /fæsɪneɪtɪd/ ADJ If you are **fascinated by** something, you find it very interesting and attractive, and your thoughts tend to concentrate on it. ❑ I sat on the stairs and watched, fascinated.

형용사 매혹된 ❑ 나는 계단에 앉아서 지켜보았다. 매혹된 채로.

fas|ci|nat|ing /fæsɪneɪtɪŋ/ ADJ If you describe something as **fascinating**, you find it very interesting and attractive, and your thoughts tend to concentrate on it. ❑ Madagascar is the most fascinating place I have ever been to.

형용사 매혹적인 ❑ 마다가스카르는 내가 가 보았던 곳 중에서 가장 매혹적인 곳이다.

fas|ci|na|tion /fæsɪneɪʃⁿn/ N-UNCOUNT **Fascination** is the state of being greatly interested in or delighted by something. ❑ I've had a lifelong fascination with the sea and with small boats.

불가산명사 마음이 홀림, 매혹 ❑ 나는 바다와 작은 배들에 평생 홀려 있다.

fas|cism /fæʃɪzəm/ N-UNCOUNT **Fascism** is a set of right-wing political beliefs that includes strong control of society and the economy by the state, a powerful role for the armed forces, and the stopping of political opposition. ❑ ...the rise of fascism in the 1930s.

불가산명사 파시즘 ❑ 1930년대 파시즘의 발흥

fas|cist /fæʃɪst/ (**fascists**) ADJ You use **fascist** to describe organizations, ideas, or systems which follow the principles of fascism. ❑ ...an upsurge of support for extreme rightist, nationalist, and fascist organisations. ● N-COUNT A **fascist** is someone who has fascist views. ❑ ...a reluctant supporter of Mussolini's Fascists.

형용사 파시즘의 극우파, 국수주의자, 파시즘 조직에 대한 지지 급증 ● 가산명사 파시스트 ❑ 무솔리니의 파시스트 당원들 중 소극적인 지지자

fash|ion ♦♦◇ /fæʃⁿn/ (**fashions**) ◾ N-UNCOUNT **Fashion** is the area of activity that involves styles of clothing and appearance. ❑ There are 20 full-color pages of fashion for men. ◾ N-COUNT A **fashion** is a style of clothing or a way of behaving that is popular at a particular time. ❑ In the early seventies I wore false eyelashes, as was the fashion. ❑ Queen Mary started the fashion for blue and white china in England. ◾ N-SING If you do something **in** a particular **fashion** or **after** a particular **fashion**, you do it in that way. ❑ There is another drug called DHE that works in a similar fashion. ◾ →see also **old-fashioned** ◾ PHRASE If something is **in fashion**, it is popular and approved of at a particular time. If it is **out of fashion**, it is not popular or approved of. ❑ That sort of house is back in fashion.

◾ 불가산명사 패션 ❑ 남성복 패션이 20페이지에 걸쳐 총천연색으로 소개되어 있다. ◾ 가산명사 유행 ❑ 70년대 초반, 나는 그 당시 유행대로 가짜 속눈썹을 붙였었다. ❑ 메리 여왕이 청백색 도자기 그릇을 영국에 처음 유행시켰다. ◾ 단수명사 -하는 식, -하는 방법 ❑ 비슷한 효과가 있는 또 다른 약으로 디에이치이라고 불리는 것이 있다. ◾ 구 유행하는; 유행하지 않는 ❑ 그런 종류의 주택이 다시 유행하고 있다.

fash|ion|able /fæʃənəbⁿl/ ADJ Something or someone that is **fashionable** is popular or approved of at a particular time. ❑ It became fashionable to eat certain kinds of fish. ● **fash|ion|ably** ADV ❑ ...women who are perfectly made up and fashionably dressed.

형용사 유행하는 ❑ 특정 종류의 생선을 먹는 것이 유행이 되었다. ● 유행에 맞게 부사 ❑ 화장을 완벽하게 하고 유행에 맞춰서 옷을 입은 여자들

fast ♦♦◇ /fæst/ (**faster**, **fastest**, **fasts**, **fasting**, **fasted**) ◾ ADJ **Fast** means

◾ 형용사 빠르게 달리는, 빠른 ❑ 전조등을 번쩍이고

A

happening, moving, or doing something at great speed. You also use **fast** in questions or statements about speed. ❑ ...*fast cars with flashing lights and sirens.* ❑ *The only question is how fast the process will be.* ● ADV **Fast** is also an adverb. [ADV with v] ❑ *They work terrifically fast.* ❑ *It would be nice to go faster and break the world record.* ❑ *How fast would the disease develop?* 2 ADV You use **fast** to say that something happens without any delay. [ADV after v] ❑ *When you've got a crisis like this you need professional help – fast!* ● ADJ **Fast** is also an adjective. [ADJ n] ❑ *That would be an astonishingly fast action on the part of the Congress.* 3 ADJ If a watch or clock is **fast**, it is showing a time that is later than the real time. [v-link ADJ] ❑ *That clock's an hour fast.* 4 ADV If you hold something **fast**, you hold it tightly and firmly. If something is stuck **fast**, it is stuck very firmly and cannot move. [ADV after v] ❑ *She climbed the staircase cautiously, holding fast to the rail.* 5 ADV If you hold **fast** to a principle or idea, or if you stand **fast**, you do not change your mind about it, even though people are trying to persuade you to. [ADV after v] ❑ *We can only try to hold fast to the age-old values of honesty, decency, and concern for others.* 6 ADJ If colors or dyes are **fast**, they do not come out of the fabrics they are used on when they get wet. ❑ *The fabric was ironed to make the colors fast.* 7 V-I If you **fast**, you eat no food for a period of time, usually for either religious or medical reasons, or as a protest. ❑ *I fasted for a day and half and asked God to help me.* ● N-COUNT **Fast** is also a noun. ❑ *The fast is broken at sunset, traditionally with dates and water.* ● **fast|ing** N-UNCOUNT ❑ ...*the Muslim holy month of fasting and prayer.* 8 PHRASE Someone who is **fast asleep** is completely asleep. ❑ *When he went upstairs five minutes later, she was fast asleep.* 9 to **make a fast buck** →see buck

---

Thesaurus   *fast*의 참조어

ADJ.	hasty, quick, rapid, speedy, swift; (ant.) leisurely, slow 1
ADV.	soon; (ant.) leisurely 2

---

fas|ten /fɑːsᵊn, fæs-/ (fastens, fastening, fastened) 1 V-T/V-I When you **fasten** something, you close it by means of buttons or a strap, or some other device. If something **fastens** with buttons or straps, you can close it in this way. ❑ *She got quickly into her Mini and fastened the seat-belt.* ❑ *Her long fair hair was fastened at the nape of her neck by an elastic band.* 2 V-T If you **fasten** one thing **to** another, you attach the first thing to the second, for example with a piece of string or tape. ❑ *There were no instructions on how to fasten the carrying strap to the box.* 3 →see also **fastening**

fas|ten|ing /fæsənɪŋ/ (fastenings) N-COUNT A **fastening** is something such as a clasp or zipper that you use to fasten something and keep it shut. ❑ *The sundress has a neat back zipper fastening.*

fast food N-UNCOUNT **Fast food** is hot food, such as hamburgers and French fries, that you obtain from particular types of restaurants, and which is served quickly after you order it. ❑ *James works as assistant chef at a fast food restaurant.* →see **meal**

fast for|ward (fast forwards, fast forwarding, fast forwarded) also **fast-forward** V-T/V-I When you **fast forward** the tape in a video or tape recorder or when you **fast forward**, you make the tape go forward. Compare **rewind**. ❑ *Just fast forward the video.* ❑ *He fast-forwarded the tape past the explosion.*

fas|tid|i|ous /fæstɪdiəs, fə-/ ADJ If you say that someone is **fastidious**, you mean that they pay great attention to detail because they like everything to be very neat, accurate, and in good order. ❑ ...*her fastidious attention to historical detail.*

fast lane (fast lanes) 1 N-COUNT On a highway, **the fast lane** is the part of the road where the vehicles that are traveling fastest go. [mainly BRIT] ❑ *His G-registration Volvo veered from the fast lane to the slow lane at 70mph.* 2 N-SING If someone is living **in the fast lane**, they have a very busy, exciting life, although they sometimes seem to take a lot of risks. ❑ ..*a tale of life in the fast lane.*

fast track (fast tracks, fast tracking, fast tracked) also **fast-track** 1 N-SING The **fast track** to a particular goal, especially in politics or in your career, is the quickest route to achieving it. ❑ *Many Croats and Slovenes saw independence as the fast track to democracy.* 2 V-T To **fast track** something means to make it happen or progress faster or earlier than normal. ❑ *A Federal Court case had been fast tracked to Wednesday.*

fat ♦♦◇ /fæt/ (fatter, fattest, fats) 1 ADJ If you say that a person or animal is **fat**, you mean that they have a lot of flesh on their body and that they weigh too much. You usually use **fat** when you think that this is a bad thing. [DISAPPROVAL] ❑ *I could eat what I liked without getting fat.*

> If you describe someone as **fat**, you are speaking in a very direct way, and this may be considered rude. If you want to say more politely that someone is rather fat, it is better to describe them as **plump**, or more informally, as **chubby**. **Overweight** and **obese** are used to describe someone who may have health problems because of their size or weight. **Obese** is also a medical term used to describe someone who is extremely fat or overweight. In general you should avoid using any of these words in the presence of the person you are describing.

2 N-UNCOUNT **Fat** is the extra flesh that animals and humans have under their skin, which is used to store energy and to help keep them warm. ❑ *Because you're not burning calories, everything you eat turns to fat.* 3 N-MASS **Fat** is a solid or liquid substance obtained from animals or vegetables, which is used in cooking. ❑ *When you use oil or fat for cooking, use as little as possible.* 4 N-MASS **Fat**

경적을 울리면서 빠르게 달려가는 자동차들 ❑ 유일한 문제점은 그 진행 과정이 얼마나 빠를까 하는 것이다. ● 부사 빨리 ❑ 그들은 일을 굉장히 빨리 한다. ❑ 더 빨라져서 세계 기록을 깨면 좋을 텐데. ❑ 그 병이 얼마나 빨리 진행될까요? 2 부사 즉시 ❑ 당신이 이런 위기를 겪게 되면 즉시 전문가의 도움이 필요합니다. ● 형용사 빠른 ❑ 그것은 의회로서는 놀랄 만큼 빠른 조치가 될 것이다. 3 형용사 (시계가) 빠른 ❑ 그 시계는 한 시간이 빠르다. 4 부사 단단히 ❑ 그녀는 난간을 단단히 잡고서, 조심스럽게 계단을 올라갔다. 5 부사 확고히 ❑ 우리는 정직, 품위, 배려와 같은 오래된 가치를 확고히 고수하려고 노력할 뿐이다. 6 형용사 (옷감의) 염료가 빠지지 않는 ❑ 그 섬유는 염료가 빠지지 않도록 열처리되어 있다. 7 자동사 단식하다 ❑ 나는 하루 반을 단식하면서 신의 도움을 간구했다. ● 가산명사 단식 ❑ 전통적으로 해가 질 무렵, 대추야자 열매와 물로 단식을 끝낸다. ● 단식하기 불가산명사 ❑ 단식과 기도를 하는 무슬림의 성월 9 구 깊이 잠든 ❑ 그가 5분 후에 올라갔을 때, 그녀는 깊이 잠들어 있었다.

1 타동사/자동사 매다, 묶다, (단추를) 잠그다 ❑ 그녀는 재빨리 자신의 미니카에 올라타서 안전벨트를 맸다. ❑ 그녀는 긴 금발을 목 뒤로 하여 고무줄로 묶고 있었다. 2 타동사 부착하다 ❑ 그 상자에 운반용 끈을 어떻게 부착하는지에 대한 설명이 전혀 없었다.

가산명사 (옷을 채우는) 지퍼나 단추 ❑ 그 여름 원피스는 등 쪽에 지퍼가 깔끔하게 달려 있다.

불가산명사 패스트푸드, 즉석식품 ❑ 제임스는 패스트푸드 식당에서 보조 요리사로 일한다.

타동사/자동사 (녹음 테이프나 비디오 테이프를) 앞으로 감다 ❑ 그 비디오 테이프를 앞으로 감기만 해라. ❑ 그는 테이프를 앞으로 감아서 그 폭발 장면을 그냥 지나가게 했다.

형용사 세심한 ❑ 세부적인 역사적 사실에 대해 기울이는 그녀의 세심한 주의

1 가산명사 추월 차선 [주로 영국영어] ❑ 그의 G등록 번호판 볼보 차가 추월 차선에서 시속 70마일의 속도로 갑자기 차선을 바꿨다. 2 단수명사 (사람이) 잘나가는 때; (일이) 잘 되어 가는 때 ❑ 잘나가던 때에 관한 이야기

1 단수명사 빠른 길 ❑ 많은 크로아티아 인들과 슬로베니아 인들은 그들의 독립이 민주주의를 향한 가장 빠른 길이라고 생각했다. 2 타동사 (평상시보다) 더 빨리 진행시키다 ❑ 한 연방 법원 사건이 평상시보다 빠르게 수요일에 처리됐다.

1 형용사 살찐 [탐탁찮음] ❑ 나는 살찌지 않으면서도 좋아하는 음식을 먹을 수 있었다.

어떤 사람을 fat으로 묘사하면, 아주 직접적으로 말하는 것이며 무례하게 생각될 수도 있다. 누가 다소 뚱뚱하다는 것을 더 예의를 차려 말하고 싶으면, plump이라고 하거나 격식을 덜 갖추어 chubby라고 하는 것이 더 낫다. overweight와 obese는 몸집이나 체중으로 인해 건강에 문제가 있을지도 모르는 사람을 말할 때 쓴다. obese는 또 아주 뚱뚱하거나 과체중인 사람을 말할 때 쓰는 의학 용어이기도 하다. 일반적으로 언급하고 있는 사람의 면전에서 이런 말을 사용하는 것은 피해야 한다.

2 불가산명사 지방 ❑ 너는 열량을 소모하지 않기 때문에 먹는 것이 모두 지방으로 변한다. 3 물질명사 지방, 기름 ❑ 요리에 기름이나 지방을 쓸 때는 가능한 한 적게 쓰도록 해라. 4 물질명사 지방 ❑ 음식에 함유된 지방 섭취를 줄이는 쉬운 방법은 붉은색 고기를

is a substance contained in foods such as meat, cheese, and butter which forms an energy store in your body. ❑ *An easy way to cut the amount of fat in your diet is to avoid eating red meats.* ◳ ADJ A **fat** object, especially a book, is very thick or wide. ❑ *...'Europe in Figures,' a fat book published on September 22nd.* ◳ ADJ A **fat** profit or fee is a large one. [INFORMAL] [ADJ n] ❑ *They are set to make a big fat profit.* ◳ PHRASE If you say that there is **fat chance** of something happening, you mean that you do not believe that it will happen. [INFORMAL, mainly SPOKEN, FEELINGS] ❑ *"Would your car be easy to steal?" — "Fat chance. I've got a device that shuts down the gas and ignition."* →see **calories**

먹지 않는 것이다. ◳ 형용사 두꺼운 ❑ 9월 22일에 출판된 두꺼운 책인 '유럽 인 피겨즈' ◳ 형용사 (수입이) 짭짤한 [비격식체] ❑ 그들은 수입이 짭짤할 것이다. ◳ 구 그럴 리 없음, 가망 없음 [비격식체, 주로 구어체, 감정 개입] ❑ "네 차를 쉽게 훔칠 수 있을까?" "꿈 깨지지. 연료와 시동 장치를 잠가 두는 장치를 해 두었는 걸."

fa|tal /feɪtᵊl/ ◳ ADJ A **fatal** action has very undesirable effects. ❑ *It would clearly be fatal for Europe to quarrel seriously with America.* ❑ *He made the fatal mistake of compromising early.* ● **fa|tal|ly** ADV [ADV with v] ❑ *Failure now could fatally damage his chances in the future.* ◳ ADJ A **fatal** accident or illness causes someone's death. ❑ *...the fatal stabbing of a police sergeant.* ● **fa|tal|ly** ADV ❑ *The dead soldier is reported to have been fatally wounded in the chest.*

◳ 형용사 치명적인 ❑ 미국과 심하게 싸우는 것은 분명 유럽에게는 치명적일 것이다. ❑ 그는 일찍 협상을 하는 치명적인 실수를 했다. ● 치명적으로 부사 ❑ 지금의 실패는 그의 장래성에 치명적인 손상을 입힐 수 있을 것이다. ◳ 형용사 죽음을 초래하는, 치명적인 ❑ 한 경사를 칼로 찔러 죽게 한 ● 치명적으로 부사 ❑ 그 사망한 군인은 흉부에 치명상을 입은 것으로 보도되었다.

fa|tal|ity /fətælɪti/ (**fatalities**) N-COUNT A **fatality** is a death caused by an accident or by violence. [FORMAL] ❑ *Drunk driving fatalities in this country have declined more than 10 percent over the past 10 years.*

가산명사 (사고로 인한) 사망 [격식체] ❑ 이 나라의 음주 운전으로 인한 사망률은 지난 10년 동안 10퍼센트 이상 줄었다.

fat cat (**fat cats**) N-COUNT If you refer to a businessman or politician as a **fat cat**, you are indicating that you disapprove of the way they use their wealth and power. [INFORMAL, BUSINESS, DISAPPROVAL] ❑ *...the fat cats who run the bank.*

가산명사 거물 [비격식체, 경제, 탐탁찮음] ❑ 그 은행을 경영하는 거물들

fate ♦◇◇ /feɪt/ (**fates**) ◳ N-UNCOUNT **Fate** is a power that some people believe controls and decides everything that happens, in a way that cannot be prevented or changed. You can also refer to the **fates**. [also n in pl] ❑ *I see no use quarrelling with fate.* ❑ *...the fickleness of fate.* ◳ N-COUNT A person's or thing's **fate** is what happens to them. ❑ *The Russian Parliament will hold a special session later this month to decide his fate.* ❑ *He seems for a moment to be again holding the fate of the country in his hands.*

◳ 불가산명사 운명 ❑ 나는 운명에 대항해 봐야 소용없다고 생각한다. ❑ 운명의 변덕스러움 ◳ 가산명사 운명 ❑ 러시아 의회는 그의 운명을 결정하기 위해 이달 말에 특별 회의를 개최할 것이다. ❑ 그가 잠시나마 다시 한 번 그 나라의 운명을 손에 쥐는 듯해 보인다.

fate|ful /feɪtfᵊl/ ADJ If an action or a time when something happened is described as **fateful**, it is considered to have an important, and often very bad, effect on future events. ❑ *It was a fateful decision, one which was to break the Government.*

형용사 중대한, 치명적인 ❑ 그것은 후에 정부를 붕괴시키게 된 중대한 결정이었다.

fa|ther ♦♦♦ /fɑðər/ (**fathers, fathering, fathered**) ◳ N-FAMILY Your **father** is your male parent. You can also call someone your **father** if he brings you up as if he was this man. ❑ *His father was a painter.* ❑ *He would be a good father to my children.*

◳ 친족명사 아버지 ❑ 그의 아버지는 화가였다. ❑ 그는 내 아이들에게 좋은 아버지가 되어 줄 것이다.

Father's Day is a special day on which children give cards and presents to their fathers as a sign of their love for them. Grown-up children often try to visit, and perhaps take their father out for the day or for a special meal. "Father's Day" is the third Sunday in June.

Father's Day(아버지의 날)는 자녀들이 아버지에게 사랑의 표시로 카드와 선물을 드리는 특별한 날이다. 장성한 자녀들은 흔히 이날 가급적이면 아버지를 방문하여 함께 하루 동안 외출을 하거나 특별한 외식을 하기도 한다. '아버지의 날'은 6월 세 번째 일요일이다.

◳ V-T When a man **fathers** a child, he makes a woman pregnant and their child is born. ❑ *She claims Mark fathered her child.* ◳ N-COUNT The man who invented or started something is sometimes referred to as the **father of** that thing. ❑ *...Max Dupain, regarded as the father of modern photography.* →see **family**

◳ 타동사 -의 아버지가 되다 ❑ 그녀는 마크가 자기 아이의 아버지라고 주장한다. ◳ 가산명사 창시자 ❑ 현대 사진학의 창시자로 여겨지는 막스 두팽

father|hood /fɑðərhʊd/ N-UNCOUNT **Fatherhood** is the state of being a father. ❑ *...the joys of fatherhood.*

불가산명사 아버지임 ❑ 아버지로서 느끼는 환희

father-in-law (**fathers-in-law**) N-COUNT Someone's **father-in-law** is the father of their husband or wife. →see **family**

가산명사 시아버지; 장인

fath|om /fæðəm/ (**fathoms, fathoming, fathomed**) ◳ N-COUNT A **fathom** is a measurement of 6 feet or 1.8 meters, used when referring to the depth of water. ❑ *We sailed into the bay and dropped anchor in five fathoms of water.* ◳ V-T If you cannot **fathom** something, you are unable to understand it, although you think carefully about it. [no cont, oft with brd-neg] ❑ *I really couldn't fathom what Steiner was talking about.* ● PHRASAL VERB **Fathom out** means the same as **fathom**. ❑ *We're trying to fathom out what's going on.*

◳ 가산명사 패덤 (1.8미터), 수심 측정 단위 ❑ 우리는 배를 타고 그 만으로 들어가서 수심 9미터 아래로 닻을 내렸다. ◳ 타동사 헤아리다, 가늠하다 ❑ 나는 스타이너가 무슨 말을 하고 있는지 정말이지 가늠할 수가 없었다. ● 구동사 헤아리다, 가늠하다 ❑ 우리는 무슨 일이 일어나고 있는지 가늠하려고 노력하는 중이다.

fa|tigue /fətiɡ/ (**fatigues**) ◳ N-UNCOUNT **Fatigue** is a feeling of extreme physical or mental tiredness. ❑ *She continued to have severe stomach cramps, aches, fatigue, and depression.* ◳ N-UNCOUNT You can say that people are suffering from a particular kind of **fatigue** when they have been doing something for a long time and feel they can no longer continue to do it. ❑ *...compassion fatigue caused by endless TV and celebrity appeals.* ◳ N-PLURAL **Fatigues** are clothes that soldiers wear when they are fighting or when they are doing routine jobs. ❑ *He never expected to return home wearing U.S. combat fatigues.* ◳ N-UNCOUNT **Fatigue** in metal or wood is a weakness in it that is caused by repeated stress. Fatigue can cause the metal or wood to break. ❑ *The problem turned out to be metal fatigue in the fuselage.*

◳ 불가산명사 피로 ❑ 그녀는 지속적으로 심한 복통, 근육통, 피로, 우울증을 느꼈다. ◳ 불가산명사 피로감 ❑ 텔레비전과 명사들의 계속적인 호소로 인해 생긴 동정 피로감 ◳ 복수명사 군복 ❑ 그는 미군 전투복 차림으로 집에 돌아가리라고는 전혀 예상하지 못했다. ◳ 불가산명사 (금속이나 목재의) 약화 ❑ 그 문제는 비행기 동체의 금속 약화 때문으로 밝혀졌다.

A

fat|ten /fǽtᵊn/ (**fattens, fattening, fattened**) v-t If you say that someone **is fattening** something such as a business or its profits, you mean that they are increasing the value of the business or its profits, in a way that you disapprove of. [BUSINESS, DISAPPROVAL] ❏ *They have kept the price of sugar artificially high and so fattened the company's profits.* ● PHRASAL VERB **Fatten up** means the same as **fatten.** ❏ *The Government is making the taxpayer pay to fatten up a public sector business for private sale.*

타동사 배를 불리다, 제 잇속을 챙기다 [경제, 탐탁잖음] ❏ 그들은 설탕 값을 인위적으로 올려서 회사 잇속만 챙겼다. ● 구동사 배를 불리다 ❏ 정부가 납세자에게 물건을 살 때 세금을 내게 해서 결국 민간 판매를 하는 공기업의 배만 불려 주고 있다.

B

C

fat|ten|ing /fǽtᵊnɪŋ/ ADJ Food that is **fattening** is considered to make people fat easily. ❏ *Some foods are more fattening than others.*

형용사 살찌는, 살이 찌게 하는 ❏ 어떤 음식은 다른 음식보다 살이 더 찐다.

fat|ty /fǽti/ (**fattier, fattiest**) ❶ ADJ **Fatty** food contains a lot of fat. ❏ *Don't eat fatty food or chocolates.* ❷ ADJ **Fatty** acids or **fatty** tissues, for example, contain or consist of fat. [ADJ n] ❏ *...fatty acids.*

❶ 형용사 기름진 ❏ 기름진 음식이나 초콜릿을 먹지 말아라. ❷ 형용사 지방을 함유한, 지방의 ❏ 지방산

D

fau|cet /fɔ́sɪt/ (**faucets**) N-COUNT A **faucet** is a device that controls the flow of a liquid or gas from a pipe or container. Sinks and baths have faucets attached to them. [mainly AM; BRIT usually **tap**] ❏ *She turned off the faucet and dried her hands.*

가산명사 꼭지 [주로 미국영어; 영국영어 대개 tap] ❏ 그녀는 수도꼭지를 잠그고 손의 물기를 닦았다.

E

F

fault ♦♢♢ /fɔ́lt/ (**faults, faulting, faulted**) ❶ N-SING If a bad or undesirable situation is your **fault**, you caused it or are responsible for it. ❏ *There was no escaping the fact: it was all his fault.* ❷ N-COUNT A **fault** is a mistake in what someone is doing or in what they have done. ❏ *It is a big fault to think that you can learn how to manage people in business school.* ❸ N-COUNT A **fault** in someone or something is a weakness in them or something that is not perfect. ❏ *His manners had always made her blind to his faults.* ❹ V-T If you **cannot fault** someone, you cannot find any reason for criticizing them or the things that they are doing. [with brd-neg] ❏ *You can't fault them for lack of invention.* ❺ N-COUNT A **fault** is a large crack in the surface of the earth. ❏ *...the San Andreas Fault.* ❻ N-COUNT A **fault** in tennis is a service that is wrong according to the rules. ❏ *He caught the ball on his first toss and then served a fault.* ❼ PHRASE If someone or something **is at fault**, they are to blame or are responsible for a particular situation that has gone wrong. ❏ *He could never accept that he had been at fault.* ❽ PHRASE If you **find fault with** something or someone, you look for mistakes and complain about them. ❏ *I was disappointed whenever the cook found fault with my work.* →see **earthquake**

❶ 단수명사 책임, 닷 ❏ 피할 수 없는 사실은, 그것이 모두 그의 책임이라는 것이었다. ❷ 가산명사 실수 ❏ 경영 대학에서 사람을 다루는 법을 배울 수 있다고 생각하면 큰 실수다. ❸ 가산명사 결점, 결함 ❏ 항상 그의 매너로 인해 그녀가 그의 결점을 알아차리지 못했다. ❹ 타동사 -을 비난하다 ❏ 발명의 재능이 없다고 해서 그들을 비난할 수는 없다. ❺ 가산명사 단층 ❏ '샌앤드레이어스 단층' ❻ 가산명사 (테니스의) 폴트, 서브 실패 ❏ 그가 첫 토스에 볼을 잡고는 폴트를 냈다. ❼ 구 -에 대해 책임이 있어 ❏ 그는 자신에게 책임이 있다는 것을 절대 받아들일 수 없었다. ❽ 구 -을 탓하다 ❏ 요리사가 내 솜씨를 탓할 때마다 나는 실망했다.

G

H

I

J

K

Thesaurus   fault의 참조어

N. blunder, error, mistake, wrongdoing ❷
    defect, flaw, imperfection, weakness; (ant.) strength ❸

L

Word Partnership   fault의 연어

V.   **find** fault ❷
PREP. **at** fault ❼

M

N

fault|less /fɔ́ltlɪs/ ADJ Something that is **faultless** is perfect and has no mistakes at all. ❏ *...Mary Thomson's faultless and impressive performance on the show.*

형용사 흠 잡을 데 없는, 완전무결한 ❏ 메리 톰슨이 그 공연에서 보여 준 완벽하고 인상적인 연기

O

faulty /fɔ́lti/ ❶ ADJ A **faulty** piece of equipment has something wrong with it and is not working properly. ❏ *The money will be used to repair faulty equipment.* ❷ ADJ If you describe someone's argument or reasoning as **faulty**, you mean that it is wrong or contains mistakes, usually because they have not been thinking in a logical way. ❏ *Their interpretation was faulty – they had misinterpreted things.*

❶ 형용사 결함이 있는 ❏ 그 돈은 결함이 있는 장비를 수리하는 데 쓰일 것이다. ❷ 형용사 부적절한 ❏ 그들의 해석은 부적절했다. 즉, 그들이 사태를 잘못 해석했다.

P

fau|na /fɔ́nə/ (**faunas**) N-COUNT-COLL Animals, especially the animals in a particular area, can be referred to as **fauna**. [TECHNICAL] ❏ *...the flora and fauna of the African jungle.*

가산명사-집합 (특정 지역의) 동물군 [과학 기술] ❏ 아프리카 밀림 지대의 동식물

Q

R

fa|vor ♦♦♢ /féɪvər/ (**favors, favoring, favored**) [BRIT **favour**] ❶ N-UNCOUNT If you regard something or someone with **favor**, you like or support them. ❏ *It remains to be seen if the show will find favor with an audience.* ❏ *No one would look with favor on the continuing military rule.* ❷ N-COUNT If you **do** someone **a favor**, you do something for them even though you do not have to. ❏ *I've come to ask you to do me a favor.* ❸ V-T If you **favor** something, you prefer it to the other choices available. ❏ *The French say they favor a transition to democracy.* ❹ V-T If you **favor** someone, you treat them better or in a kinder way than you treat other people. ❏ *The company has no rules about favoring U.S. citizens during layoffs.* ❺ PHRASE If you are **in favor of** something, you support it and think that it is a good thing. ❏ *I wouldn't be in favor of income tax cuts.* ❏ *Yet this is a Government which proclaims that it is all in favor of openness.* ❻ PHRASE If someone makes a judgment **in your favor**, they say that you are right about something. ❏ *If the commission rules in Mr. Welch's favor the case will go to the European Court of Human Rights.* ❼ PHRASE If something is **in your favor**, it helps you or gives you an advantage. ❏ *The protection that farmers have enjoyed amounts to a bias in favor of the countryside.* ❽ PHRASE If one thing is rejected **in favor of** another, the second thing is done or chosen instead of the first. ❏ *The policy was rejected in favor of a more cautious approach.* ❾ PHRASE If someone or something is **in favor**, people like or support them. If they are **out of favor**, people no longer like or support them. ❏ *Governments and party leaders can only hope to remain in favor with the public for so long.*

[영국영어 favour] ❶ 불가산명사 지지 ❏ 그 공연이 관객의 애호를 받을지는 두고 볼 일이다. ❏ 아무도 계속되는 군부 통치에 지지를 보내지 않을 것이다. ❷ 가산명사 부탁, 청 ❏ 너에게 부탁할 것이 있어서 왔어. ❸ 타동사 선호하다 ❏ 프랑스 사람들은 자신들이 민주주의로의 이행을 선호한다고 말한다. ❹ 타동사 편애하다 ❏ 그 회사는 휴업기간 동안에 미국 시민을 우대하는 규정이 없다. ❺ 구 -을 지지하여, -을 찬성하여 ❏ 나라면 소득세 삭감을 지지하지 않을 것이다. ❏ 그러나 전적으로 개방을 지지한다고 선언한 것이 바로 이 정부이다. ❻ 구 -의 의견에 따라 ❏ 만약 위원회가 웰치 씨의 의견에 따라 판결을 내린다면 그 사건은 유럽 인권 재판소에서 시비를 가리게 될 것이다. ❼ 구 -에게 유리하게 ❏ 농부들이 누려온 보호 정책은 결과적으로 시골에 유리하도록 하는 편파 정책인 셈이 된다. ❽ 구 -을 위하여 ❏ 좀 더 신중한 접근을 위하여 그 정책은 거부되었다. ❾ 구 인기 있는 – 인기 없는 ❏ 각국 정부와 당 지도자들은 그저 오랫동안 대중의 인기를 얻을 수 있기만 바랄 뿐이다.

S

T

U

V

W

Word Partnership   favor의 연어

PREP. **with** favor ❶
      out of favor ❾
      in *someone's* favor ❻ ❼
V.   **ask for a** favor, **do** *someone* **a** favor, **need a** favor, **return a** favor ❷
ADJ. **big** favor ❷

X

Y

Z

fa|vor|able /feɪvərəbʰl/ [BRIT **favourable**] **1** ADJ If your opinion or your reaction is **favorable** to something, you agree with it and approve of it. [ADJ n, v-link ADJ to n] ❑ *His recently completed chapel for Fitzwilliam is attracting favorable comment.* **2** ADJ **Favorable** conditions make something more likely to succeed or seem more attractive. ❑ *It's believed the conditions in which the elections are being held are too favorable to the government.* **3** ADJ If you make a **favorable** comparison between two things, you say that the first is better than or as good as the second. ❑ *The film bears favorable technical comparison with Hollywood productions costing 10 times as much.*

fa|vor|ite ♦♦◇ /feɪvərɪt, feɪvrɪt/ (**favorites**) [BRIT **favourite**] **1** ADJ Your **favorite** thing or person of a particular type is the one you like most. [ADJ n] ❑ *He celebrated by opening a bottle of his favorite champagne.* ● N-COUNT **Favorite** is also a noun. ❑ *The Liverpool Metropole is my favorite. I love those huge, anonymous hotels.* ● PHRASE If you refer to something as an **old favorite**, you mean that it has been in existence for a long time and everyone knows it or likes it. ❑ *This recipe is an adaptation of an old favorite.* **2** N-COUNT The **favorite** in a race or contest is the competitor that is expected to win. In a team game, the team that is expected to win is referred to as the **favorites**. ❑ *The Belgian Cup has been won by the favorites F.C. Liege.*

fa|vor|it|ism /feɪvərɪtɪzəm, feɪvrɪt-/ [BRIT **favouritism**] N-UNCOUNT If you accuse someone of **favoritism**, you disapprove of them because they unfairly help or favor one person or group much more than another. [DISAPPROVAL] ❑ *Maria loved both the children. There was never a hint of favoritism.*

fawn /fɔn/ (**fawns**) **1** COLOR **Fawn** is a pale yellowish-brown color. ❑ *Tania was standing there in her light fawn coat.* **2** N-COUNT A **fawn** is a very young deer. ❑ *The fawn ran to the top of the ridge.*

fax /fæks/ (**faxes, faxing, faxed**) **1** N-COUNT A **fax** or a **fax machine** is a piece of equipment used to copy documents by sending information electronically along a telephone line, and to receive copies that are sent in this way. [also by n] ❑ *...a modern reception desk with telephone and fax.* **2** V-T If you **fax** a document to someone, you send it from one fax machine to another. ❑ *I faxed a copy of the agreement to each of the investors.* ❑ *Did you fax him a reply?* **3** N-COUNT You can refer to a copy of a document that is transmitted by a fax machine as a **fax**. ❑ *I sent him a long fax, saying I didn't need a maid.*

fear ♦♦♦ /fɪər/ (**fears, fearing, feared**) **1** N-VAR **Fear** is the unpleasant feeling you have when you think that you are in danger. ❑ *I was sitting on the floor shivering with fear because a bullet had been fired through a window.* **2** V-T If you **fear** someone or something, you are frightened because you think that they will harm you. ❑ *It seems to me that if people fear you they respect you.* **3** N-VAR A **fear** is a thought that something unpleasant might happen or might have happened. ❑ *These youngsters are motivated not by a desire to achieve, but by fear of failure.* ❑ *Then one day his worst fears were confirmed.* **4** V-T If you **fear** something unpleasant or undesirable, you are worried that it might happen or might have happened. ❑ *She had feared she was going down with pneumonia or bronchitis.* **5** N-VAR If you say that there is a **fear that** something unpleasant or undesirable will happen, you mean that you think it is possible or likely. ❑ *There is a fear that the freeze on bank accounts could prove a lasting deterrent to investors.* **6** V-I If you **fear for** someone or something, you are very worried because you think that they might be in danger. ❑ *Carla fears for her son.* **7** N-VAR If you have **fears for** someone or something, you are very worried because you think that they might be in danger. ❑ *He also spoke of his fears for the future of his country's culture.* **8** PHRASE If you are **in fear of** doing or experiencing something unpleasant or undesirable, you are very worried that you might have to do it or experience it. ❑ *The elderly live in fear of assault and murder.* **9** PHRASE If you take a particular course of action **for fear of** something, you take the action in order to prevent that thing happening. ❑ *She was afraid to say anything to them for fear of hurting their feelings.* →see **emotion**

Thesaurus　　　*fear*의 참조어

N.　　alarm, apprehension, dread, panic, terror **1**
　　　concern, worry **3**

Word Partnership　　　*fear*의 연어

ADJ.　　**constant** fear **1**
　　　irrational fear **1**-**4**
　　　worst fear **3**
V.　　**face** *your* fear, **hide** *your* fear, **live in** fear, **overcome** *your* fear **1** **3**
N.　　fear **of failure**, fear **of the unknown** **4**
　　　nothing to fear **2**
　　　fear **the worst** **3**
　　　fear **change** **4**

---

fear|ful /fɪərfəl/ **1** ADJ If you are **fearful of** something, you are afraid of it. [FORMAL] ❑ *Bankers were fearful of a world banking crisis.* **2** ADJ You use **fearful** to emphasize how serious or bad a situation is. [FORMAL, EMPHASIS] [ADJ n] ❑ *The region is in a fearful recession.*

fear|less /fɪərlɪs/ ADJ If you say that someone is **fearless**, you mean that they are not afraid at all, and you admire them for this. [APPROVAL] ❑ *...his fearless campaigning for racial justice.*

[영국영어 favourable] **1** 형용사 호의적인 ❑ 그가 피츠윌리엄을 위해 최근에 완공한 예배당은 호평을 받고 있다. **2** 형용사 유리한 ❑ 선거가 실시되는 현재의 조건이 정부 측에 너무나 유리하다고 사람들은 믿고 있다. **3** 형용사 더 좋은 ❑ 그 영화는 10배나 더 많은 비용을 들이는 할리우드 영화와 비교해 볼 때 기술적으로 더 뛰어나다.

[영국영어 favourite] **1** 형용사 가장 좋아하는 ❑ 그는 자신이 가장 좋아하는 샴페인을 따서 축하했다. ● 가산명사 가장 좋아하는 것 ❑ 리버풀 메트로폴은 내가 가장 좋아하는 곳이다. 나는 그렇게 거대하고 이름 없는 호텔들을 좋아한다. ● 구 오랫동안 사랑을 받아 온 것 ❑ 이 조리법은 오랫동안 애호된 조리법에 변화를 준 것이다. **2** 가산명사 우승 후보 ❑ 벨기에 컵은 우승 후보인 에프 시 리쥐에게 돌아갔다.

[영국영어 favouritism] 불가산명사 편애 [탐탁찮음] ❑ 마리아는 두 아이 모두를 사랑했다. 편애의 기미라고는 전혀 없었다.

1 색채어 엷은 황갈색 ❑ 타니아가 밝고 엷은 황갈색 코트를 입고 거기에 서 있었다. **2** 가산명사 (한 살 미만의) 새끼 사슴 ❑ 새끼 사슴이 산마루 꼭대기로 뛰어갔다.

1 가산명사 팩스, 팩시밀리 ❑ 전화와 팩스가 놓여 있는 현대식 접수창구 **2** 타동사 팩시밀리로 보내다 ❑ 내가 각 투자자에게 협정서 사본을 팩스로 보냈어요. ❑ 그 사람에게 회답을 팩스로 보냈니? **3** 가산명사 팩스 ❑ 난 그에게 내겐 하녀가 필요 없다는 장문의 팩스를 보냈어요.

1 가산명사 또는 불가산명사 두려움 ❑ 창문을 꿰뚫고 총알이 발사되어서 나는 방바닥에 앉은 채 두려움에 와들와들 떨고 있었다. **2** 타동사 두려워하다 ❑ 내가 보기에는 사람들이 너를 두려워한다면 너를 존경하는 것이다. **3** 가산명사 또는 불가산명사 불안, 염려 ❑ 이 젊은이들은 성취욕 때문이 아니라, 실패에 대한 불안 때문에 하고자 하는 의욕을 느낀다. ❑ 그러던 어느 날 그가 염려했던 최악의 상황이 현실로 나타났다. **4** 타동사 걱정하다 ❑ 그녀는 자신이 폐렴이나 기관지염에 걸리지 않을까 걱정했다. **5** 가산명사 또는 불가산명사 우려 ❑ 은행 구좌를 동결하면 투자자들의 투자 심리를 지속적으로 억제할 우려가 있다. **6** 자동사 -에 대해 노심초사하다 ❑ 칼라는 아들에 대해 노심초사를 한다. **7** 가산명사 또는 불가산명사 -에 대한 염려 ❑ 그 역시 자국 문화의 장래에 대한 염려를 언급했다. **8** 구 -을 두려워하여 ❑ 나이가 지긋한 사람들은 폭행과 살인을 당할까 봐 두려워한다. **9** 구 -할까 두려워, -을 하지 않도록 ❑ 그녀는 그들의 감정을 다칠까 두려워 그들에게 어떤 말도 하기가 두려웠다.

1 형용사 우려하는, 두려워하는 [격식체] ❑ 은행가들은 세계적인 금융 위기를 우려했다. **2** 형용사 지독한 [격식체, 강조] ❑ 그 지역이 지독한 불경기에 처해 있다.

형용사 대담무쌍한 [마음에 듦] ❑ 인종 간 정의를 위한 그의 대담무쌍한 캠페인

Word Link	some ≈ causing: awesome, fearsome, troublesome

fear|some /fɪərsəm/ ADJ **Fearsome** is used to describe things that are frightening, for example because of their large size or extreme nature. ❑ He had developed a fearsome reputation for intimidating people.

형용사 무시무시한 ❑ 그는 사람들을 위협하는 것으로 무시무시한 평판을 얻었다.

fea|sible /fizəbəl/ ADJ If something is **feasible**, it can be done, made, or achieved. ❑ She questioned whether it was feasible to stimulate investment in these regions. ● **fea|sibil|ity** /fizəbɪlɪti/ N-UNCOUNT ❑ The committee will study the feasibility of setting up a national computer network.

형용사 실현 가능한 ❑ 그녀는 이 지역에서 투자를 고무시키는 것이 실현 가능한가에 의문을 가졌다. ● 실현 가능성 불가산명사 ❑ 위원회는 전국적인 컴퓨터 네트워크 구성의 실현 가능성을 조사할 것이다.

feast /fist/ (feasts, feasting, feasted) **1** N-COUNT A **feast** is a large and special meal. ❑ Lunch was a feast of meat and vegetables, cheese, yoghurt and fruit, with unlimited wine. ❑ The fruit was often served at wedding feasts. **2** V-I If you **feast on** a particular food, you eat a large amount of it with great enjoyment. ❑ They feasted well into the afternoon on mutton and corn stew. **3** V-I If you **feast**, you take part in a feast. ❑ Only a few feet away, their captors feasted in the castle's banqueting hall. ● **feast|ing** N-UNCOUNT ❑ The feasting, drinking, dancing and revelry continued for several days. **4** N-COUNT A **feast** is a day or time of the year when a special religious celebration takes place. ❑ The Jewish feast of Passover began last night. **5** PHRASE If you **feast** your **eyes on** something, you look at it for a long time with great attention because you find it very attractive. ❑ She stood feasting her eyes on the view.

1 가산명사 성찬; 잔치 ❑ 점심은 고기와 야채, 치즈, 요구르트와 과일, 그리고 무제한의 포도주가 나오는 성찬이었다. **2** 자동사 (음식을) 마음껏 즐기다 ❑ 그들은 오후까지 양고기와 콘 스튜를 먹으며 맘껏 즐겼다. **3** 자동사 잔치에 참석하다 ❑ 겨우 몇 피트 떨어진 곳에서, 그들을 포획한 자들이 성의 연회장에서 열리는 잔치에 참석했다. ● 잔치를 벌임 불가산명사 ❑ 잔치를 벌이고 술을 마시고 춤을 추고 흥청대는 게 며칠간 계속되었다. **4** 가산명사 축제 ❑ 유대인의 축제인 유월절이 어젯밤에 시작되었다. **5** 구 -을 보며 즐기다 ❑ 그녀가 선 채로 경치를 보며 즐기고 있었다.

feat /fit/ (feats) N-COUNT If you refer to an action, or the result of an action, as a **feat**, you admire it because it is an impressive and difficult achievement. [APPROVAL] ❑ A racing car is an extraordinary feat of engineering.

가산명사 위업, 공훈 [마음에 듦] ❑ 경주용 자동차는 공학의 놀랄 만한 위업이다.

feath|er /fɛðər/ (feathers) **1** N-COUNT A bird's **feathers** are the soft covering on its body. Each **feather** consists of a lot of smooth hairs on each side of a thin stiff center. ❑ ...a hat that she had made herself from black ostrich feathers. →see also **feathered 2** to ruffle someone's **feathers** →see **ruffle** →see **bird**

1 가산명사 깃털 ❑ 검정색 타조 깃털로 그녀가 직접 만든 모자

feath|ered /fɛðərd/ ADJ If you describe something as **feathered**, you mean that it has feathers on it. ❑ Her mother was the proud lady in the feathered hat.

형용사 깃을 단, 깃털로 장식된 ❑ 그녀의 어머니는 깃털로 장식된 모자를 쓴 그 꼿꼿한 부인이었다.

fea|ture ♦♢♢ /fitʃər/ (features, featuring, featured) **1** N-COUNT A **feature of** something is an interesting or important part or characteristic of it. ❑ Patriotic songs have long been a feature of Kuwaiti life. ❑ The spacious gardens are a special feature of this property. **2** N-PLURAL Your **features** are your eyes, nose, mouth, and other parts of your face. ❑ His features seemed to change. **3** V-T When something such as a movie or exhibition **features** a particular person or thing, they are an important part of it. ❑ It's a great movie and it features a Spanish actor who is going to be a world star within a year. ❑ The hour-long program will be updated each week and feature highlights from recent games. **4** V-I If someone or something **features in** something such as a show, exhibition, or magazine, they are an important part of it. ❑ Jon featured in one of the show's most thrilling episodes. **5** N-COUNT A **feature** is a special article in a newspaper or magazine, or a special program on radio or television. ❑ We are delighted to see the Sunday Times running a long feature on breast cancer. **6** N-COUNT A **feature** or a **feature** film or movie is a full-length film about a fictional situation, as opposed to a short film or a documentary. ❑ ...the first feature-length cartoon, Snow White and the Seven Dwarfs. **7** N-COUNT A geographical **feature** is something noticeable in a particular area of country, for example a hill, river, or valley. ❑ ...one of England's oddest geographical features - an eight-mile bank of pebbles shelving abruptly into the sea.

1 가산명사 특징 ❑ 애국적인 노래가 오랫동안 쿠웨이트 사람들의 삶의 특징이 되어 왔다. ❑ 넓은 정원이 이 집의 두드러진 특징이다. **2** 복수명사 얼굴 생김새 ❑ 그의 얼굴이 변한 것 같았다. **3** 타동사 -을 주연시키다; -을 특집으로 다루다 ❑ 그것은 훌륭한 영화이고 일 년 안에 세계적인 스타가 될 스페인 배우가 주연한다. ❑ 한 시간에 걸친 그 프로그램은 매주 새롭게 갱신될 것이고 최근 경기의 하이라이트를 특집으로 다룰 것이다. **4** 자동사 주연하다; 중요한 역할을 하다 ❑ 존이 그 시리즈물의 가장 재미있는 에피소드 중 하나에 주연했다. **5** 가산명사 특집 기사; 특별 프로그램 ❑ 우리는 선데이 타임스가 유방암에 대한 긴 특집 기사를 싣는 걸 보니 몹시 기쁘다. **6** 가산명사 장편 영화 ❑ 첫 장편 만화 영화인 '백설 공주와 일곱 난쟁이' **7** 가산명사 지세 ❑ 잉글랜드의 지세 중 가장 기묘한 형세 중 하나인, 8마일에 걸쳐 완만하게 비탈을 이루다 갑자기 바다와 맞닿는 조약돌 더미

Word Partnership	feature의 연어
ADJ.	**key** feature **1**
	special feature **1 5**
	best feature, **striking** feature **1 2**
	facial feature **2**
	animated feature, **double** feature, **full-length** feature **6**

Feb. **Feb.** is a written abbreviation for **February**.

2월

Feb|ru|ary ♦♦♢ /fɛbyueri, febru-, BRIT febyuəri/ (Februaries) N-VAR **February** is the second month of the year in the Western calendar. ❑ He joined the Army in February 1943. ❑ His exhibition opens on 5 February.

가산명사 또는 불가산명사 2월 ❑ 그가 1943년 2월에 육군에 입대했다. ❑ 그의 전시회가 2월 5일에 열린다.

fe|ces /fisiz/ BRIT **faeces** N-UNCOUNT **Feces** is the solid waste substance that people and animals get rid of from their body by passing it through the anus. [FORMAL] ❑ ...grass contaminated by feces from infected dogs.

[영국영어 faeces] 불가산명사 배설물 [격식체] ❑ 감염된 개들의 배설물에 의해 오염된 잔디

fed /fɛd/ **Fed** is the past tense and past participle of **feed**. See also **fed up**.

feed의 과거, 과거 분사

fed|er|al ♦♦♢ /fɛdərəl/ (federals) **1** ADJ A **federal** country or system of government is one in which the different states or provinces of the country have important powers to make their own laws and decisions. [ADJ n] ❑ Five of the six provinces are to become autonomous regions in a new federal system of government. **2** ADJ Some people use **federal** to describe a system of government which they disapprove of, in which the different states or provinces are controlled by a strong central government. [DISAPPROVAL] [ADJ n] ❑ He does not believe in a federal Europe with centralizing powers. **3** ADJ **Federal** also means belonging or relating to the national government of a federal country rather than to one of the states within it. [ADJ n] ❑ The federal government controls just 6% of the education budget. ● **fed|er|al|ly** ADV [ADV -ed] ❑ ...residents of public housing and federally subsidized apartments.

1 형용사 연합의 ❑ 새로운 연합 정부 체제에서는 여섯 지방 중 다섯 지방이 자치 지역이 된다. **2** 형용사 연맹의 [탐탁찮음] ❑ 그는 중앙 집권력을 가진 유럽 연맹을 믿지 않는다. **3** 형용사 연방의 ❑ 연방 정부는 교육 예산의 6퍼센트만을 관리한다. ● 연방 정부에 의해 부사 ❑ 임대 주택과 연방 정부가 보조금을 지급하는 아파트의 거주자들

fed|er|al|ist /fɛdərəlɪst/ (federalists) ADJ Someone or something that is **federalist** believes in, supports, or follows a federal system of government. ❑ ...the federalist idea of Europe. ● N-COUNT **Federalist** is also a noun. ❑ Many Quebeckers are federalists.

형용사 연방주의의; 연방주의자의 ❑ 유럽의 연방주의 개념 ● 가산명사 연방주의자 ❑ 많은 퀘백 사람들이 연방주의자이다.

fed|era|tion ♦◇◇ /fˈedəreɪʃ°n/ (**federations**) ◼1 N-COUNT A **federation** is a federal country. ❑ ...the Russian Federation. ◼2 N-COUNT A **federation** is a group of societies or other organizations which have joined together, usually because they share a common interest. ❑ ...the British Athletic Federation.

fed up ADJ If you are **fed up**, you are unhappy, bored, or tired of something, especially something that you have been experiencing for a long time. [INFORMAL] [v-link ADJ, oft ADJ with/of n/-ing] ❑ I am fed up with reading how women should dress to please men. ❑ He had become fed up with city life.

fee ♦◇◇ /fˈiː/ (**fees**) ◼1 N-COUNT A **fee** is a sum of money that you pay to be allowed to do something. ❑ He paid his license fee, and walked out with a brand-new driver's license. ◼2 N-COUNT A **fee** is the amount of money that a person or organization is paid for a particular job or service that they provide. ❑ Lawyers' fees can be substantial.

fee|ble /fˈiːb°l/ (**feebler, feeblest**) ◼1 ADJ If you describe someone or something as **feeble**, you mean that they are weak. ❑ He told them he was old and feeble and was not able to walk so far. ● **fee|bly** ADV [ADV with v] ❑ His left hand moved feebly at his side. ◼2 ADJ If you describe something that someone says as **feeble**, you mean that it is not very good or convincing. ❑ This is a particularly feeble argument. ● **fee|bly** ADV [ADV with v] ❑ I said "Sorry," very feebly, feeling rather embarrassed.

feed ♦◇◇ /fˈiːd/ (**feeds, feeding, fed**) ◼1 V-T If you **feed** a person or animal, you give them food to eat and sometimes actually put it in their mouths. ❑ We brought along pieces of old bread and fed the birds. ● N-COUNT **Feed** is also a noun. [mainly BRIT] ❑ She's had a good feed. ● **feed|ing** N-UNCOUNT ❑ The feeding of dairy cows has undergone a revolution. ◼2 V-T To **feed** a family or a community means to supply food for them. ❑ Feeding a hungry family can be expensive. ◼3 V-I When an animal **feeds**, it eats or drinks something. ❑ After a few days the caterpillars stopped feeding. ◼4 V-T/V-I When a baby **feeds**, or when you **feed** it, it drinks breast milk or milk from a bottle. ❑ When a baby is thirsty, it feeds more often. ◼5 N-MASS Animal **feed** is food given to animals, especially farm animals. [usu n N] ❑ The grain just rotted and all they could use it for was animal feed. ◼6 V-T To **feed** something to a place, means to supply it to that place in a steady flow. ❑ ...blood vessels that feed blood to the brain. ◼7 V-T If you **feed** something **into** a container or piece of equipment, you put it into it. ❑ He took the compact disc from her, then fed it into the player. ◼8 V-T If you **feed** a plant, you add substances to it to make it grow well. ❑ Feed plants to encourage steady growth. ◼9 V-I If one thing **feeds** on another, it becomes stronger as a result of the other thing's existence. ❑ The drinking and the guilt fed on each other. ◼10 V-T To **feed** information **into** a computer means to gradually put it into it. ❑ An automatic weather station feeds information on wind direction to the computer. ◼ to **bite the hand that feeds you** →see **bite**. **mouths to feed** →see **mouth**

Word Partnership	feed의 연어
N.	feed **the baby**, feed **the cat**, feed **the children**, feed **your** family, feed **the hungry** ◼1

feed|back /fˈiːdbæk/ ◼1 N-UNCOUNT If you get **feedback on** your work or progress, someone tells you how well or badly you are doing, and how you could improve. If you get good feedback you have worked or performed well. ❑ Continue to ask for feedback on your work. ◼2 N-UNCOUNT **Feedback** is the unpleasant high-pitched sound produced by a piece of electrical equipment when part of the signal that comes out goes back into it. ❑ ...when the microphone screeched with feedback.

feel ♦♦♦ /fˈiːl/ (**feels, feeling, felt**) ◼1 V-LINK If you **feel** a particular emotion or physical sensation, you experience it. ❑ I am feeling very depressed. ❑ Suddenly I felt a sharp pain in my shoulder. ❑ I felt as if all my strength had gone. ❑ I felt like I was being kicked in the teeth every day. ◼2 V-LINK If you talk about how an experience or event **feels**, you talk about the emotions and sensations connected with it. [no cont] ❑ It feels good to have finished a piece of work. ❑ The speed at which everything moved felt strange. ❑ Within five minutes of arriving back from vacation, it feels as if I've never been away. ◼3 V-LINK If you talk about how an object **feels**, you talk about the physical quality that you notice when you touch or hold it. For example, if something feels soft, you notice that it is soft when you touch it. [no cont] ❑ The metal felt smooth and cold. ❑ The ten-foot oars felt heavy and awkward. ● N-SING **Feel** is also a noun. ❑ He remembered the feel of her skin. ◼4 V-LINK If you talk about how the weather **feels**, you describe the weather, especially the temperature or whether or not you think it is going to rain or snow. [no cont] ❑ It felt wintry cold that day. ◼5 V-T/V-I If you **feel** an object, you touch it deliberately with your hand, so that you learn what it is like, for example what shape it is or whether it is rough or smooth. ❑ The doctor felt his head. ❑ Feel how soft the skin is in the small of the back. ◼6 V-T If you can **feel** something, you are aware of it because it is touching you. [no cont] ❑ Through several layers of clothes I could feel his muscles. ◼7 V-T If you **feel** something happening, you become aware of it because of the effect it has on your body. ❑ She felt something being pressed into her hands. ❑ He felt something move beside him. ◼8 V-T If you **feel yourself** doing something or being in a particular state, you are aware that something is happening to you which you are unable to control. ❑ I felt myself blush. ❑ If at any point you feel yourself becoming tense, make a conscious effort to relax. ◼9 V-T If you **feel** the presence of someone or something, you become aware of them, even though you cannot see or hear them. [no cont] ❑ He felt her eyes on him. ❑ I could feel that a man was watching me very intensely. ◼10 V-T/V-I If you **feel** that something is the case, you have a strong idea in your mind that it is the case. [no cont] ❑ I feel that not enough is being done to protect the local animal life. ❑ I will feel certain that it will all turn out well. ◼11 V-T/V-I If you **feel** that you should do something, you think that you should do it. [no cont] ❑ I feel I should resign. ❑ You need not feel obliged to

◼1 가산명사 연방 국가 ❑ 러시아 연방 ◼2 가산명사 연맹 ❑ 영국 체육 연맹

형용사 진력이 난, 싫증이 난 [비격식체] ❑ 나는 남자의 마음에 들도록 여자가 어떻게 옷을 입어야 하는지에 관해 읽는 것에 진력이 난다. ❑ 그는 도시 생활에 싫증이 났었다.

◼1 가산명사 요금 ❑ 그는 면허료를 내고, 새 운전면허증을 가지고 걸어 나갔다. ◼2 가산명사 수임료, 수수료 ❑ 변호사비가 상당할 지도 모른다.

◼1 형용사 약한 ❑ 그가 자신은 나이 들고 약해서 그렇게 멀리까지 걸어갈 수 없다고 그들에게 말했다. ● 힘없이 부사 ❑ 그의 왼손이 그의 옆구리에서 힘없이 움직였다. ◼2 형용사 설득력 없는 ❑ 이것은 특히 설득력 없는 주장이다. ● 가냘프게 부사 ❑ 나는 좀 당황해서 아주 가냘픈 목소리로 "미안해요."라고 말했다.

◼1 타동사 먹을 것을 주다, (음식을) 먹이다 ❑ 우리는 오래된 빵 몇 조각을 가지고 와서 새에게 먹이로 주었다. ● 가산명사 식사 [주로 영국영어] ❑ 그녀는 맛있는 음식을 배불리 먹었다. ● 사육 불가산명사 ❑ 젖소 사육은 대변혁을 겪었다. ◼2 타동사 부양하다 ❑ 굶주린 가족을 부양하는 데는 돈이 많이 들 수 있다. ◼3 자동사 (동물이) 먹다 ❑ 며칠 후에 애벌레가 먹이 먹는 것을 그만두었다. ◼4 타동사/자동사 (아기가) 젖을 먹다; (아기에게) 젖을 먹이다 ❑ 아기가 목이 마르면 더 자주 젖을 먹는다. ◼5 물질명사 사료 ❑ 곡물이 아주 못쓰게 되어서 쓸 데라곤 가축 사료뿐이었다. ◼6 타동사 (연료 등을) 공급하다 ❑ 뇌에 피를 보내는 혈관 ◼7 타동사 ...에 넣다 ❑ 그가 그녀에게서 시디를 받아서 그것을 플레이어에 넣었다. ◼8 타동사 (식물에) 영양을 공급하다 ❑ 식물에 영양을 주어서 꾸준히 성장하도록 하십시오. ◼9 자동사 ~을 먹고 자라다 ❑ 음주와 죄책감이 서로를 부추기는 격이었다. ◼10 타동사 입력하다 ❑ 자동 제어 기상 관측소가 풍향 정보를 컴퓨터에 입력한다.

◼1 불가산명사 평가, 피드백 ❑ 계속해서 네 작품에 대한 평가를 부탁해라. ◼2 불가산명사 (전자 신호의 반향에 의한) 날카로운 쇳소리 ❑ 마이크가 반향으로 날카로운 쇳소리를 냈을 때

◼1 연결동사 느끼다 ❑ 나는 지금 아주 우울해. ❑ 갑자기 나는 어깨에 심한 통증을 느꼈다. ❑ 내 모든 힘이 사라진 것처럼 느껴졌다. ❑ 매일 죽도록 걸어왔던 기분이었다. ◼2 연결동사 ~한 기분이 들다 ❑ 작품 하나를 마치고 나면 기분이 좋다. ❑ 모든 사물이 움직이는 속도가 느낌이 이상했다. ❑ 휴가에서 돌아온 지 5분도 안 되어, 마치 내가 전혀 어디 간 적이 없었던 듯한 기분이다. ◼3 연결동사 (만져 보면) ~한 느낌이 들다 ❑ 그 금속은 촉감이 매끄럽고 차가웠다. ❑ 10피트짜리 노는 들어 보니 무겁고 다루기 불편했다. ● 단수명사 촉감, 감촉 ❑ 그는 그녀 살결의 감촉을 기억했다. ◼4 연결동사 (날씨가) ~한 느낌이 들다 ❑ 그 날은 겨울처럼 춥게 느껴졌다. ◼5 타동사/자동사 ~을 만져 보다 ❑ 의사가 그의 이마에 손을 대어 보았다. ❑ 등허리 아랫부분의 살결이 얼마나 보드라운지 만져 봐. ◼6 타동사 ~이 느껴지다 ❑ 겹겹이 옷을 입었지만 그의 근육의 감촉이 느껴졌다. ◼7 타동사 감지하다 ❑ 그녀는 무언가가 두 손 안으로 밀려들어오는 것을 감지했다. ❑ 그는 곁에서 무언가가 움직이는 것을 감지했다. ◼8 타동사 느낌이 들다 ❑ 나는 얼굴이 붉어지는 것을 느꼈다. ❑ 언제라도 네가 긴장감이 들거든, 마음을 편히 가지려고 의식적으로 노력해라. ◼9 타동사 느끼다 ❑ 그는 그녀의 두 눈이 그를 지켜보고 있음을 느꼈다. ❑ 나는 한 남자기 나를 매우 유심히 지켜보고 있는 것을 느낄 수 있었다. ◼10 타동사/자동사 ...라고 생각하다 ❑ 나는 지역 동물을 보호하기 위한 조치가 충분하지 않다고 생각한다. ❑ 모든 일이 잘 될 거라고 나는 확신한다. ◼11 타동사/자동사 ...라고 생각하다 ❑ 나는 내가 사임해야 한다고 생각한다. ❑ 네가 꼭 기부해야 한다고 생각할 필요는 없다. ◼12 타동사/자동사 (어떤) 생각을 하다 ❑ 우리는 당신이 인공 유산에 대해 어떻게

contribute. **12** V-T/V-I If you talk about how you **feel about** something, you talk about your opinion, attitude, or reaction to it. [no cont] ❑ *We'd like to know what you feel about abortion.* ❑ *She feels guilty about spending less time lately with her two kids.* **13** V-I If you **feel like** doing something or having something, you want to do it or have it because you are in the right mood for it and think you would enjoy it. ❑ *Neither of them felt like going back to sleep.* **14** →see also **feeling, felt. feel free** →see **free**

Thesaurus　　*feel*의 참조어

V-LINK.　　experience, perceive, sense **1**

▶**feel for** **1** PHRASAL VERB If you **feel for** something, for example in the dark, you try to find it by moving your hand around until you touch it. ❑ *I felt for my wallet and papers in my inside pocket.* **2** PHRASAL VERB If you **feel for** someone, you have sympathy for them. ❑ *She cried on the phone and things like that and I really felt for her.*

feel|good /fiːlɡʊd/ **1** ADJ A **feelgood** movie is a movie which presents people and life in a way that makes the people who watch it feel happy and optimistic. [ADJ n] ❑ *This could be the feelgood movie of the autumn.* **2** PHRASE When journalists refer to **the feelgood factor**, they mean that people are feeling hopeful and optimistic about the future. ❑ *There were obvious signs of the feelgood factor in the last survey taken in the wake of the election result.*

feel|ing ♦♦◇ /fiːlɪŋ/ (**feelings**) **1** N-COUNT A **feeling** is an emotion, such as anger or happiness. ❑ *It gave me a feeling of satisfaction.* ❑ *He was unable to contain his own destructive feelings.* **2** N-PLURAL Your **feelings** about something are the things that you think and feel about it, or your attitude toward it. ❑ *She has strong feelings about the alleged growth in violence against female officers.* ❑ *I think that sums up the feelings of most discerning and intelligent Indians.* **3** N-PLURAL When you refer to someone's **feelings**, you are talking about the things that might embarrass, offend, or upset them. For example, if you hurt someone's **feelings**, you upset them by something that you say or do. ❑ *He was afraid of hurting my feelings.* **4** N-UNCOUNT **Feeling** is a way of thinking and reacting to things which is emotional and not planned rather than logical and practical. ❑ *He was prompted to a rare outburst of feeling.* **5** N-UNCOUNT **Feeling** for someone is love, affection, sympathy, or concern for them. ❑ *Thomas never lost his feeling for Harriet.* **6** N-COUNT If you have a **feeling** of hunger, tiredness, or other physical sensation, you experience it. ❑ *I also had a strange feeling in my neck.* ❑ *Focus on the feeling of relaxation.* **7** N-UNCOUNT **Feeling** in part of your body is the ability to experience the sense of touch in this part of the body. ❑ *After the accident he had no feeling in his legs.* **8** N-COUNT If you have a **feeling that** something is the case or **that** something is going to happen, you think that is probably the case or that it is probably going to happen. ❑ *I have a feeling that everything will come right for us one day.* **9** N-UNCOUNT **Feeling** is used to refer to a general opinion that a group of people has about something. ❑ *There is still some feeling in the art world that the market for such works may be declining.* **10** N-SING If you have a **feeling** of being in a particular situation, you feel that you are in that situation. ❑ *I had the terrible feeling of being left behind to bring up the baby while he had fun.* **11** N-SING If something such as a place or book creates a particular kind of **feeling**, it creates a particular kind of atmosphere. ❑ *That's what we tried to portray in the book, this feeling of opulence and grandeur.* **12** →see also **feel 13** PHRASE **Bad feeling** or **ill feeling** is bitterness or anger which exists between people, for example after they have had an argument. ❑ *There's been some bad feeling between the two families.* **14** PHRASE **Hard feelings** are feelings of anger or bitterness towards someone who you have had an argument with or who has upset you. If you say "**no hard feelings,**" you are making an agreement with someone not to be angry or bitter about something. ❑ *I don't want any hard feelings between our companies.*

Word Partnership　　*feeling*의 연어

N.　　**good** feeling, feeling **of inadequacy**, feeling **of satisfaction** **1**
　　　strong feeling **1 2 3 5 7**
　　　depth of feeling **1 5**
　　　strange feeling **1 6 7 8**
　　　bad feeling **1 9**
V.　　**get a** feeling **1 4 6**
　　　express a feeling **1 5**
　　　have a feeling **1 8 10**

---

feet /fiːt/ **Feet** is the plural of **foot**.

feign /feɪn/ (**feigns, feigning, feigned**) V-T If someone **feigns** a particular feeling, attitude, or physical condition, they try to make other people think that they have it or are experiencing it, although this is not true. [FORMAL] ❑ *One morning, I didn't want to go to school, and decided to feign illness.*

fell /fel/ (**fells, felling, felled**) **1** **Fell** is the past tense of **fall**. **2** V-T If trees **are felled**, they are cut down. [usu passive] ❑ *Badly infected trees should be felled and burned.* **3** **in one fell swoop** →see **swoop**

fel|low ♦♦◇ /feloʊ/ (**fellows**) **1** ADJ You use **fellow** to describe people who are in the same situation as you, or people you feel you have something in common with. [ADJ n] ❑ *She discovered to her pleasure, a talent for making her fellow guests laugh.* **2** N-COUNT A **fellow** is a man or boy. [INFORMAL, OLD-FASHIONED] ❑ *By all accounts, Rodger would appear to be a fine fellow.* **3** N-PLURAL Your **fellows** are the people who you work with, do things with, or who are like you in some way. [FORMAL] [poss N] ❑ *He stood out in terms of competence from all his fellows.*

생각하는지 알고 싶습니다. ❑ 그녀는 요즈음 두 자녀와 함께 보내는 시간이 줄어들어서 마음이 꺼림칙하다. **13** 자동사 -하고 싶은 생각이 들다 ❑ 그들 둘 다 다시 잠들고 싶은 생각이 없었다.

1 구동사 -을 더듬어 찾다 ❑ 나는 안쪽 주머니에서 지갑과 서류를 더듬어 찾았다. **2** 구동사 -을 안쓰러워하다 ❑ 그녀는 수화기에 대고 울부짖고 하는 그런 식이었는데 나는 그런 그녀가 정말 안쓰러웠다.

1 형용사 기분을 좋게 하는 ❑ 이 영화는 가을철에 보면 기분이 좋아질 거야. **2** 구 낙관 ❑ 선거 결과가 나온 후 실시된 지난번 여론 조사에는 사람들의 낙관을 보여주는 증후들이 분명히 있었다.

1 가산명사 감정 ❑ 그것을 통해 나는 만족감을 느꼈다. ❑ 그는 자신의 파괴적인 욕구를 억누를 수 없었다. **2** 복수명사 느낌, 감정 ❑ 그녀는 여성 경찰관을 대상으로 한 폭력이 증가하고 있는 듯한 현실에 대해 유감이 많다. ❑ 나는 그것이 가장 명민하고 지적인 인디언들의 감정을 요약한 것이라고 생각한다. **3** 복수명사 기분 ❑ 그는 내 기분을 상하게 할까 봐 염려했다. **4** 불가산명사 감정 ❑ 그가 자극을 받아 좀처럼 드러내지 않는 감정을 표출했다. **5** 불가산명사 마음 ❑ 토머스는 결코 해리엇에 대한 마음을 잃지 않았다. **6** 가산명사 느낌 ❑ 나 역시 목이 이상한 느낌이 든다. ❑ 편안한 느낌을 갖도록 집중하세요. **7** 불가산명사 감각 ❑ 사고 후 그는 다리에 감각을 느끼지 못했다. **8** 가산명사 느낌, 예감 ❑ 언젠가는 모든 게 잘 될 거라는 느낌이 든다. **9** 불가산명사 분위기 ❑ 예술계에서는 아직도 그러한 작품에 대한 시장이 감소하고 있다는 분위기가 있다. **10** 단수명사 느낌, 인상 ❑ 나는 그가 즐겁게 보내는 동안 홀로 남아 아기를 키워야 한다는 끔찍한 느낌이 들었다. **11** 단수명사 느낌 ❑ 그것이 바로 우리가 이 책에서 묘사하려고 했던 풍부하고 웅대한 느낌일 것이다. **12** 구 안 좋은 감정 ❑ 두 가문 간에는 약간 안 좋은 감정이 있어 왔다. **14** 구 악감정 ❑ 나는 우리 회사들 간에 어떠한 악감정도 원하지 않는다.

foot의 복수형

타동사 -한 척하다, -을 가장하다 [격식체] ❑ 어느 날 아침, 난 학교에 가기 싫었고, 그래서 아픈 척하기로 마음먹었다.

1 fall의 과거 **2** 타동사 베이다 ❑ 심하게 상한 나무는 베어서 태워야 한다.

1 형용사 동지, 동료 ❑ 그녀는 기쁘게도 동료 손님들을 웃게 하는 재능이 있다는 것을 발견했다. **2** 가산명사 사나이, 녀석 [비격식체, 구식어] ❑ 사람들 말을 들어 보면, 로저는 보기에 멋진 사나이일 것이다. **3** 복수명사 동료 [격식체] ❑ 그는 모든 동료들보다 능력 면에서 돋보였다. **4** 가산명사 특별 회원 ❑ 런던 동물 학회 특별 회원

4 N-COUNT A **fellow of** an academic or professional association is someone who is a specially elected member of it, usually because of their work or achievements or as a mark of honor. ❑ ...the fellows of the Zoological Society of London.

fel|low|ship /fɛloʊʃɪp/ (**fellowships**) **1** N-COUNT A **fellowship** is a group of people that join together for a common purpose or interest. ❑ ...the National Schizophrenia Fellowship. **2** N-COUNT A **fellowship** at a university is a post which involves research work. ❑ He was offered a research fellowship at Clare College. **3** N-UNCOUNT **Fellowship** is a feeling of friendship that people have when they are talking or doing something together and sharing their experiences. ❑ ...a sense of community and fellowship.

felo|ny /fɛləni/ (**felonies**) N-COUNT In countries where the legal system distinguishes between very serious crimes and less serious ones, a **felony** is a very serious crime such as armed robbery. [LEGAL] ❑ He pleaded guilty to six felonies.

felt /fɛlt/ **1** **Felt** is the past tense and past participle of **feel**. **2** N-UNCOUNT **Felt** is a thick cloth made from wool or other fibers packed tightly together. ❑ ...traditional Tibetan boots made of colorfully embroidered felt.

felt-tip (**felt-tips**) N-COUNT A **felt-tip** or a **felt-tip pen** is a pen which has a piece of fiber at the end that the ink comes through.

Word Link	*fem, femin* ≈ *woman* : *female, feminine, feminist*

fe|male ♦♦◇ /fiːmeɪl/ (**females**) **1** ADJ Someone who is **female** is a woman or a girl. ❑ ...a sixteen-piece dance band with a female singer. **2** N-COUNT Women and girls are sometimes referred to as **females** when they are being considered as a type. ❑ Hay fever affects males more than females. **3** ADJ **Female** matters and things relate to, belong to, or affect women rather than men. [ADJ n] ❑ ...female infertility. **4** N-COUNT You can refer to any creature that can lay eggs or produce babies from its body as a **female**. ❑ Each female will lay just one egg in April or May. ● ADJ **Female** is also an adjective. ❑ ...the scent given off by the female aphid to attract the male.

fem|i|nine /fɛmɪnɪn/ **1** ADJ **Feminine** qualities and things relate to or are considered typical of women, in contrast to men. ❑ ...male leaders worrying about their women abandoning traditional feminine roles. **2** ADJ Someone or something that is **feminine** has qualities that are considered typical of women, especially being pretty or gentle. [APPROVAL] ❑ I've always been attracted to very feminine women who are not overpowering, the delicate English-rose type. **3** ADJ In some languages, a **feminine** noun, pronoun, or adjective has a different form from a masculine or neuter one, or behaves in a different way.

fem|i|nin|ity /fɛmɪnɪniti/ **1** N-UNCOUNT A woman's **femininity** is the fact that she is a woman. ❑ ...the drudgery behind the ideology of motherhood and femininity. **2** N-UNCOUNT **Femininity** means the qualities that are considered to be typical of women. ❑ I wonder if there isn't a streak of femininity in him, a kind of sweetness.

fem|i|nism /fɛmɪnɪzəm/ N-UNCOUNT **Feminism** is the belief and aim that women should have the same rights, power, and opportunities as men. ❑ ...Barbara Johnson, that champion of radical feminism.

fem|i|nist /fɛmɪnɪst/ (**feminists**) **1** N-COUNT A **feminist** is a person who believes in and supports feminism. ❑ Only 16 percent of young women in a 1990 survey considered themselves feminists. **2** ADJ **Feminist** groups, ideas, and activities are involved in feminism. [ADJ n] ❑ ...the concerns addressed by the feminist movement.

fence ♦◇◇ /fɛns/ (**fences, fencing, fenced**) **1** N-COUNT A **fence** is a barrier between two areas of land, made of wood or wire supported by posts. ❑ Villagers say the fence would restrict public access to the hills. **2** V-T If you **fence** an area of land, you surround it with a fence. ❑ The first task was to fence the wood to exclude sheep. **3** N-COUNT A **fence** in show jumping or horse racing is an obstacle or barrier that horses have to jump over. ❑ Nine horses fell at the first fence in the Martell Grand National this year. **4** PHRASE If you **sit on the fence**, you avoid supporting a particular side in a discussion or argument. ❑ They are sitting on the fence and refusing to commit themselves.

fenc|ing /fɛnsɪŋ/ **1** N-UNCOUNT **Fencing** is a sport in which two competitors fight each other using very thin swords. The ends of the swords are covered and the competitors wear protective clothes, so that they do not hurt each other. ❑ ...the English amateur fencing champion. **2** N-UNCOUNT Materials such as wood or wire that are used to make fences are called **fencing**. ❑ ...old wooden fencing.

fend /fɛnd/ (**fends, fending, fended**) V-I If you have to **fend for** yourself, you have to look after yourself without relying on help from anyone else. ❑ The woman and her young baby had been thrown out and left to fend for themselves.

▶**fend off** **1** PHRASAL VERB If you **fend off** unwanted questions, problems, or people, you stop them from affecting you or defend yourself from them, but often only for a short time and without dealing with them completely. ❑ He looked relaxed and determined as he fended off questions from the world's Press. **2** PHRASAL VERB If you **fend off** someone who is attacking you, you use your arms or something such as a stick to defend yourself from their blows. ❑ He raised his hand to fend off the blow.

Word Link	*fend* ≈ *striking* : *defend, fender, offend*

fend|er /fɛndər/ (**fenders**) N-COUNT The **fenders** of a car are the parts of the body over the wheels. [AM; BRIT **wing**] ❑ Tod sat on the front fender, his legs dangling toward the ground.

---

1 가산명사 협회, 단체 ❑ 전국 정신 분열증 협회 **2** 가산명사 특별 연구원직 ❑ 그는 클레어 칼리지에서 특별 연구원직을 제안 받았다. **3** 불가산명사 유대감 ❑ 공동체 정신과 유대감

가산명사 중죄 [법률] ❑ 그는 여섯 건의 중죄에 대해 자신의 유죄를 인정했다.

1 feel의 과거, 과거 분사 **2** 불가산명사 펠트 ❑ 화려하게 수놓은 펠트로 제작된 티베트 전통 장화

가산명사 펠트 펜

1 형용사 여자의 ❑ 여성 가수 한 명이 포함된 16인조 댄스밴드 **2** 가산명사 여성 ❑ 여성보다 남성이 건초열에 더 많이 걸린다. **3** 형용사 여성의 ❑ 여성 불임 **4** 가산명사 암컷 ❑ 모든 암컷은 4월과 5월 중에 단 한 개의 알만 낳을 것이다. ● 형용사 암컷의 ❑ 수컷을 유혹하려고 암컷 진딧물이 내뿜는 냄새

1 형용사 여성의, 여성다운 ❑ 전통적인 여성의 역할을 버리는 자신들의 여인들을 우려하는 남성 지도자들 **2** 형용사 상냥한, 부드러운 [마음에 듦] ❑ 난 항상 매우 상냥한 여자에게 이끌리는데, 기가 센 여자가 아닌, 섬세한 잉글랜드 장미 같은 타입 말이야. **3** 형용사 (문법에서) 여성의

1 불가산명사 여성성 ❑ 모성과 여성성이라는 이데올로기 뒤에 감춰진 고역 **2** 불가산명사 여성다움 ❑ 나는 그에게 일말의 여성다움 즉, 일종의 부드러움이 있지 않을까 싶다.

불가산명사 여성 신장주의, 페미니즘 ❑ 급진적 여권 신장주의의 선봉자인 바바라 존슨

1 가산명사 여권주의자, 페미니스트 ❑ 1990년에 실시한 한 조사에 의하면 젊은 여성 중 단지 16퍼센트만이 자신을 여권주의자라고 생각했다. **2** 형용사 여권 신장의, 페미니스트의 ❑ 여권 신장 운동에 의해 제기되는 관심사

1 가산명사 울타리 ❑ 마을 사람들은 울타리가 있으면 일반인들이 그 언덕에 접근하는 것이 제한될 것이라고 한다. **2** 타동사 울타리를 치다 ❑ 첫 번째 임무는 양들이 못 들어오게 나무로 울타리를 치는 것이었다. **3** 가산명사 장애물 ❑ 올해 '마텔 그랜드 내셔널' 대회에서 아홉 마리의 말이 첫 번째 장애물에서 넘어졌다. **4** 구 중립적인 태도를 취하다 ❑ 그들은 중립적인 태도를 취하며 어느 한쪽에 동의하기를 거부하고 있다.

1 불가산명사 펜싱 ❑ 영국 아마추어 펜싱 챔피언 **2** 불가산명사 울타리 ❑ 오래된 나무 울타리

자동사 자활하다 ❑ 그 여자와 그녀의 어린 아기는 내쳐져 자기들 힘으로 살아가야 했다.

1 구동사 받아넘기다 ❑ 해외 언론 기자들의 질문을 받아넘길 때 그는 느긋하고 단호해 보였다. **2** 구동사 방어하다, 막다 ❑ 그는 손을 올려서 가해지는 타격을 막았다.

가산명사 펜더, 흙받이 [미국영어; 영국영어 wing] ❑ 토드는 앞쪽 펜더에 앉아 다리를 아래로 내리고 흔들거렸다.

a b c d e f g h i j k l m n o p q r s t u v w x y z

fer|ment (ferments, fermenting, fermented)

The noun is pronounced /fɜrmɛnt/. The verb is pronounced /fərmɛnt/.

명사는 /fɜrmɛnt/으로 발음되고, 동사는 /fərmɛnt/으로 발음된다.

1 N-UNCOUNT **Ferment** is excitement and trouble caused by change or uncertainty. □ *The whole country has been in a state of political ferment for some months.* **2** V-T/V-I If a food, drink, or other natural substance **ferments**, or if it **is fermented**, a chemical change takes place in it so that alcohol is produced. This process forms part of the production of alcoholic drinks such as wine and beer. □ *The dried grapes are allowed to ferment until there is no sugar left and the wine is dry.* ● **fer|men|ta|tion** /fɜrmɛnteɪʃⁿn/ N-UNCOUNT □ *Yeast is essential for the fermentation that produces alcohol.* →see **fungus**

1 불가산명사 대소동, 동요 □ 나라 전체가 몇 달 동안 정치적으로 큰 소동에 휩싸여 있다. **2** 타동사/자동사 발효하다, 발효되다 □ 말린 포도는 당분이 없어지고 포도주가 단맛이 없어질 때까지 발효되도록 놓아둔다. ● 발효 불가산명사 □ 이스트는 알코올을 생산하는 발효 작용에 필수적이다.

fern /fɜrn/ (ferns) N-VAR A **fern** is a plant that has long stems with feathery leaves and no flowers. There are many types of fern.

가산명사 또는 불가산명사 양치식물

fe|ro|cious /fərouʃəs/ **1** ADJ A **ferocious** animal, person, or action is very fierce and violent. □ *By its very nature a lion is ferocious.* **2** ADJ A **ferocious** war, argument, or other form of conflict involves a great deal of anger, bitterness, and determination. □ *Fighting has been ferocious.*

1 형용사 사나운, 흉포한 □ 사자는 본성이 사납다. **2** 형용사 맹렬한 □ 맹렬한 싸움이 계속되고 있다.

fe|roc|ity /fərɒsɪti/ N-UNCOUNT The **ferocity** of something is its fierce or violent nature. □ *The armed forces seem to have been taken by surprise by the ferocity of the attack.*

불가산명사 사나움, 흉포함 □ 군대가 그 공격의 흉포함에 놀라고 있는 것 같다.

fer|ry /fɛri/ (ferries, ferrying, ferried) **1** N-COUNT A **ferry** is a boat that transports passengers and sometimes also vehicles, usually across rivers or short stretches of sea. [also by N] □ *They had recrossed the River Gambia by ferry.* **2** V-T If a vehicle **ferries** people or goods, it transports them, usually by means of regular trips between the same two places. □ *Every day, a plane arrives to ferry guests to and from Bird Island Lodge.* □ *It was still dark when five coaches started to ferry the miners the 140 miles from the Silverhill colliery.* →see **ship**

1 가산명사 나룻배, 연락선 □ 그들은 나룻배로 감비아 강을 다시 건넜다. **2** 타동사 (나룻배 등으로) 실어 나르다 □ 매일 비행기가 손님들을 실어 나르기 위해 '버드 아일랜드 랏지'를 왕래한다. □ 다섯 칸의 객차가 실버힐 탄갱으로부터 140마일 되는 곳으로 광부들을 실어 나르기 시작했을 때에는 아직 날이 어두웠다.

fer|tile /fɜrtⁿl, BRIT fɜːrtaɪl/ **1** ADJ Land or soil that is **fertile** is able to support the growth of a large number of strong healthy plants. □ *...fertile soil.* ● **fer|til|ity** /fɜrtɪlɪti/ N-UNCOUNT □ *He was able to bring large sterile acreages back to fertility.* **2** ADJ A **fertile** mind or imagination is able to produce a lot of good, original ideas. □ *...a product of Flynn's fertile imagination.* **3** ADJ A situation or environment that is **fertile** in relation to a particular activity or feeling encourages the activity or feeling. [ADJ n] □ *...a fertile breeding ground for this kind of violent racism.* **4** ADJ A person or animal that is **fertile** is able to reproduce and have babies or young. □ *The operation cannot be reversed to make her fertile again.* ● **fer|til|ity** N-UNCOUNT □ *Doctors will tell you that pregnancy is the only sure test for fertility.*

1 형용사 비옥한 □ 비옥한 토양 ● 비옥함 불가산명사 □ 그가 대규모 불모지대를 다시 비옥하게 만들 수 있었다. **2** 형용사 창의력이 풍부한 □ 플린의 풍부한 상상이 낳은 산물 **3** 형용사 조장하는 □ 이러한 인종주의적 폭력을 조장하는 온상 **4** 형용사 출산할 수 있는, 번식력이 있는 □ 그녀가 그 수술을 받는다고 다시 출산할 수 있는 것은 아니다. ● 출산력, 번식력 불가산명사 □ 의사들은 임신을 해 봐야만 아이를 가질 수 있는지를 확실히 알 수 있을 것이라고 내게 말해 줄 것이다.

fer|ti|lize /fɜrtⁿlaɪz/ (fertilizes, fertilizing, fertilized) [BRIT also fertilise] **1** V-T When an egg from the ovary of a woman or female animal **is fertilized**, a sperm from the male joins with the egg, causing a baby or young animal to begin forming. A female plant **is fertilized** when its reproductive parts come into contact with pollen from the male plant. □ *Certain varieties cannot be fertilized with their own pollen.* □ *...the normal sperm levels needed to fertilize the female egg.* ● **fer|ti|li|za|tion** /fɜrtⁿlɪzeɪʃⁿn/ N-UNCOUNT □ *The average length of time from fertilization until birth is about 266 days.* **2** V-T To **fertilize** land means to improve its quality in order to make plants grow well on it, by spreading solid animal waste or a chemical mixture on it. □ *The faeces contain nitrogen and it is that which fertilizes the desert soil.*

[영국영어 fertilise] **1** 타동사 수정시키다, 수분시키다 □ 어떤 변종들은 자가 수분할 수 없다. ● 난자를 수정시키기 위해 필요한 정상 정자 수 ● 수정, 수태 불가산명사 □ 수정 후 출산까지의 평균 기간은 약 266일이다. **2** 타동사 비옥하게 하다, 거름을 주다 □ 배설물은 질소를 함유하고 있기 때문에 불모지를 비옥하게 한다.

fer|ti|liz|er /fɜrtⁿlaɪzər/ (fertilizers) [BRIT also fertiliser] N-MASS **Fertilizer** is a substance such as solid animal waste or a chemical mixture that you spread on the ground in order to make plants grow more successfully. □ *...farming without any purchased chemical, fertilizer, or pesticide.* →see **farm**, **pollution**

[영국영어 fertiliser] 물질명사 비료 □ 시중에서 파는 어떠한 화학 물질, 비료 또는 살충제도 쓰지 않고 짓는 농사

fer|vent /fɜrvⁿnt/ ADJ A **fervent** person has or shows strong feelings about something, and is very sincere and enthusiastic about it. □ *...a fervent admirer of Morisot's work.* ● **fer|vent|ly** ADV □ *Their claims will be fervently denied.*

형용사 열렬한 □ 모리조의 작품을 열렬히 추앙하는 사람 ● 강력히, 열렬히 부사 □ 그들의 주장은 강력히 거부될 것이다.

fer|vor /fɜrvər/ [BRIT fervour] N-UNCOUNT **Fervor** for something is a very strong feeling for or belief in it. [FORMAL] □ *They were concerned only with their own religious fervor.*

[영국영어 fervour] 불가산명사 열성, 열정 [격식체] □ 그들은 자신들의 종교적 열성에만 관심을 가졌다.

fes|ter /fɛstər/ (festers, festering, festered) **1** V-I If you say that a situation, problem, or feeling **is festering**, you disapprove of the fact that it is being allowed to grow more unpleasant or full of anger, because it is not being properly recognized or dealt with. [DISAPPROVAL] □ *Resentments are starting to fester.* **2** V-I If a wound **festers**, it becomes infected, making it worse. □ *The wound is festering, and gangrene has set in.*

1 자동사 심해지다, 악화되다 [탐탁잖음] □ 분노가 심해지기 시작하고 있다. **2** 자동사 곪다 □ 상처가 곪고 있으며 괴저가 생겼다.

fes|ti|val ♦♦◇ /fɛstɪvⁿl/ (festivals) **1** N-COUNT A **festival** is an organized series of events such as musical concerts or drama productions. □ *Numerous Umbrian towns hold their own summer festivals of music, theater, and dance.* **2** N-COUNT A **festival** is a day or time of the year when people do not go to work or school and celebrate some special event, often a religious event. □ *Shavuot is a two-day festival for Orthodox Jews and a one-day festival for Reform and Israeli Jews.*

1 가산명사 축제, 잔치 □ 수많은 움브리아 마을이 음악, 연극, 춤으로 자체 하계 축제를 연다. **2** 가산명사 축제일, 축제 □ 오순절이 정통 유대교인들에게는 이틀간의 축일이고 개혁파와 이스라엘 유대교도들에게는 하루 동안의 축일이다.

fes|tive /fɛstɪv/ **1** ADJ Something that is **festive** is special, colorful, or exciting, especially because of a holiday or celebration. □ *The town has a festive holiday atmosphere.* **2** ADJ **Festive** means relating to a holiday or celebration, especially Christmas. [ADJ n] □ *With Christmas just around the corner, starting your festive cooking now will give cakes and puddings time to mature.*

1 형용사 축제의, 흥겨운 □ 그 마을은 축제 분위기이다. **2** 형용사 축제의, 축일의 □ 크리스마스가 곧 다가오므로, 잔치 요리를 지금 시작하면 케이크와 푸딩을 완성할 시간이 충분할 것이다.

Thesaurus   *festive*의 참조어

ADJ.   happy, joyous, merry; (ant.) gloomy, somber **1**

fes|tiv|ity /fɛstɪvɪti/ (**festivities**) ■ N-UNCOUNT **Festivity** is the celebration of something in a happy way. ❑ *There was a general air of festivity and abandon.* ② N-COUNT **Festivities** are events that are organized in order to celebrate something. ❑ *The festivities included a huge display of fireworks.*

fetch /fɛtʃ/ (**fetches, fetching, fetched**) ■ V-T If you **fetch** something or someone, you go and get them from the place where they are. ❑ *Sylvia fetched a towel from the bathroom.* ❑ *Fetch me a glass of water.* ② V-T If something **fetches** a particular sum of money, it is sold for that amount. ❑ *The painting is expected to fetch between two and three million pounds.* ③ →see also **far-fetched**

fete /feɪt, fɛt/ (**fetes, feting, feted**) [AM, sometimes BRIT **fête**] ■ N-COUNT A **fete** is a fancy party or celebration. [AM] ❑ *The pop star flew 100 friends in from London and Paris for a two-day fete.* ② N-COUNT A **fete** is an event that is usually held outdoors and includes competitions, entertainments, and the selling of used and home-made goods. [mainly BRIT] ❑ *...the school fete.* ③ V-T If someone **is feted**, they are celebrated, welcomed, or admired by the public. [usu passive] ❑ *Anouska Hempel, the British dress designer, was feted in New York this week at a spectacular dinner.*

fe|tus /fiːtəs/ (**fetuses**) N-COUNT A **fetus** is an animal or human being in its later stages of development before it is born. [BRIT usually **foetus**] ❑ *Pregnant women who are heavy drinkers risk damaging the unborn fetus.*

feud /fjuːd/ (**feuds, feuding, feuded**) ■ N-COUNT A **feud** is a quarrel in which two people or groups remain angry with each other for a long time, although they are not always fighting or arguing. ❑ *...a long and bitter feud between the state government and the villagers.* ② V-RECIP If one person or group **feuds with** another, they have a quarrel that lasts a long time. You can also say that two people or groups **feud**. ❑ *He feuded with his ex-wife.*

feu|dal /fjuːdəl/ ADJ **Feudal** means relating to the system or the time of feudalism. [ADJ n] ❑ *...the emperor and his feudal barons.*

feu|dal|ism /fjuːdəlɪzəm/ N-UNCOUNT **Feudalism** was a system in which people were given land and protection by people of higher rank, and worked and fought for them in return. ❑ *As feudalism decayed in the West it gave rise to a mercantile class.*

fe|ver /fiːvər/ (**fevers**) N-VAR If you have a **fever** when you are ill, your body temperature is higher than usual. ❑ *My Uncle Jim had a high fever.* →see also **hay fever** →see **illness**

fe|ver|ish /fiːvərɪʃ/ ■ ADJ **Feverish** activity is done extremely quickly, often in a state of nervousness or excitement because you want to finish it as soon as possible. ❑ *Hours of feverish activity lay ahead. The tents had to be erected, the stalls set up.* ② ADJ If you are **feverish**, you are suffering from a fever. ❑ *A feverish child refuses to eat and asks only for cold drinks.* ● **fe|ver|ish|ly** ADV ❑ *He slept feverishly all afternoon and into the night.*

few ♦♦♦ /fjuː/ (**fewer, fewest**) ■ DET You use **a few** to indicate that you are talking about a small number of people or things. You can also say **a very few**. ❑ *I gave a dinner party for a few close friends.* ❑ *Here are a few more ideas to consider.* ● PRON **Few** is also a pronoun. ❑ *Doctors work an average of 90 hours a week, while a few are on call for up to 120 hours.* ● QUANT **Few** is also a quantifier. [QUANT of def-pl-n] ❑ *There are many ways eggs can be prepared; here are a few of them.* ② ADJ You use **few** after adjectives and determiners to indicate that you are talking about a small number of things or people. [adj/det ADJ n] ❑ *The past few weeks of her life had been the most pleasant she could remember.* ❑ *...in the last few chapters.* ③ DET You use **few** to indicate that you are talking about a small number of people or things. You can use "so", "too", and "very" in front of **few**. ❑ *She had few friends, and was generally not functioning up to her potential.* ❑ *Few members planned to vote for him.* ● PRON **Few** is also a pronoun. ❑ *The trouble is that few want to buy, despite the knockdown prices on offer.* ● QUANT **Few** is also a quantifier. [QUANT of def-pl-n] ❑ *Few of the beach houses still had lights on.* ● ADJ **Few** is also an adjective. ❑ *...spending her few waking hours in front of the TV.* ④ N-SING **The few** means a small set of people considered as separate from the majority, especially because they share a particular opportunity or quality that the others do not have. ❑ *This should not be an experience for the few.*

Few and **a few** are both used in front of the plural of count nouns, but they do not have the same meaning. For example, if you say **I have a few friends**, this is a positive statement and you are saying that you have some friends. However, if you say **I have few friends**, this is a negative statement and you are saying that you have almost no friends. You use **fewer** to talk about things that can be counted. ❑ *...fewer potatoes.* When you are talking about amounts that cannot be counted, you should use **less**. ❑ *...less meat.*

---

⑤ PHRASE You use **as few as** before a number to suggest that it is surprisingly small. [EMPHASIS] ❑ *One study showed that even as few as ten cigarettes a day can damage fertility.* ⑥ PHRASE Things that are **few and far between** are very rare or do not happen very often. [EMPHASIS] ❑ *Successful women politicians are few and far between.* ⑦ PHRASE You use **no fewer than** to emphasize that a number is surprisingly large. [EMPHASIS] ❑ *No fewer than thirteen foreign ministers attended the session.*

fi|an|cé /fiɒnseɪ, BRIT fiɒnseɪ/ (**fiancé**) N-COUNT A woman's **fiancé** is the man to whom she is engaged to be married.

fi|an|cée /fiɒnseɪ, BRIT fiɒnseɪ/ (**fiancées**) N-COUNT A man's **fiancée** is the woman to whom he is engaged to be married.

fi|as|co /fiæskoʊ/ (**fiascos**) N-COUNT If you describe an event or attempt to do something as a **fiasco**, you are emphasizing that it fails completely. [EMPHASIS] ❑ *The blame for the Charleston fiasco did not lie with him.*

■ 불가산명사 축제, 축하 ② 전반적으로 축제와 자유분방한 분위기였다. ② 가산명사 축하 행사 ❑ 축하 행사에는 장대한 불꽃놀이도 있었다.

■ 타동사 가지고 오다, 데리고 오다 ❑ 실비아는 욕실에서 타월 한 장을 가지고 왔다. ❑ 내게 물 한 잔 갖다 줘. ② 타동사 -에 팔리다 ❑ 그 그림은 이백만에서 삼백만 파운드 사이에 팔릴 것으로 예상된다. ③

[미국영어, 가끔 영국영어 fête] ■ 가산명사 축연, 향연 [미국영어] ❑ 그 대중 스타는 이틀간의 향연을 위해 런던과 파리에서 100명의 친구를 비행기로 불러들였다. ② 가산명사 축제, 잔치 [주로 영국영어] ❑ 교내 축제 ③ 타동사 성대하게 축하받다 ❑ 영국 의상 디자이너 아노스카 헴펠은 이번 주 뉴욕에서 호화로운 만찬으로 성대하게 축하를 받았다.

가산명사 태아 [영국영어 대개 foetus] ❑ 술을 많이 마시는 임산부는 태아에게 손상을 입힐 위험이 있다.

■ 가산명사 반목, 불화 ❑ 주정부와 마을 주민들 간에 오랫동안 지속되어 온 극심한 반목 ② 상호동사 -와 반목하다, 서로 다투다 ❑ 그는 전처와 불화를 겪었다.

형용사 봉건 제도의 ❑ 황제와 그의 봉건 귀족들

불가산명사 봉건주의 ❑ 서양에서는 봉건주의가 쇠퇴하자 상인 계층이 생겨났다.

가산명사 또는 불가산명사 열 ❑ 짐 삼촌이 고열이 있었다.

■ 형용사 후닥닥하는; 열띤 ❑ 몇 시간 동안 후닥닥 해치워야 할 일들이 있었다. 텐트를 세우고, 칸막이도 설치해야 했다. ② 형용사 열이 있는 ❑ 열이 있는 아이는 음식은 먹기 싫어하고 찬 음료수만을 달라고 한다. ● 지독하게, 열심히 부사 ❑ 그는 오후 내내 뿐만 아니라 밤까지 지독하게 잠을 잤다.

■ 한정사 몇몇의, 다소의 ❑ 나는 가까운 친구 몇몇을 위해 만찬 파티를 열었다. ❑ 고려해야 할 생각들이 몇 가지 더 있다. ● 대명사 소수 ❑ 의사들은 주당 평균 90시간을 근무하며, 일부는 120시간까지 호출에 대기하기도 한다. ● 수량사 몇 가지의 ❑ 계란을 요리하는 방법에는 여러 가지가 있는데 여기 몇 가지 방법이 있다. ② 형용사 몇몇의 ❑ 지난 몇 주 동안은 그녀가 기억하는 한 생애에서 가장 즐거운 시간이었다. ❑ 마지막 몇 장에서 ③ 한정사 몇 안 되는, 소수의 ❑ 그녀는 친구도 거의 없었고 대체로 자기 잠재 능력을 충분히 발휘하지 못하고 있었다. ❑ 소수의 회원들만 그에게 투표하기로 계획했다. ● 대명사 소수 ❑ 문제는 최저 가격을 내놓아도 살 사람이 거의 없다는 것이다. ● 수량사 몇몇 ❑ 해안가 주택 중에 아직 불을 켜 놓은 집은 몇 안 되었다. ● 형용사 몇몇의 ❑ 그녀가 깨어 있는 얼마 안 되는 시간을 텔레비전 앞에서 보내며 ④ 단수명사 소수의 사람들 ❑ 이것이 소수만을 위한 경험이 되어서는 안 된다.

---

few와 a few는 둘 다 복수 가산명사 앞에 쓰이지만 뜻이 다르다. 예를 들어 "I have a few friends."라고 하면, 이것은 긍정적인 진술로 당신에게 친구가 몇 명 있다는 것을 뜻한다. 그러나 "I have few friends."라고 하면, 이것은 부정적인 진술로 당신에게 친구가 거의 없다는 뜻이다. 셀 수 있는 사물에 대해 말할 때는 fewer를 쓴다. ❑ 더 적은 수의 감자. 셀 수 없는 사물의 양을 말할 때는 less를 써야 한다. ❑ 더 적은 양의 고기

---

⑤ 구 -만큼 적은 수의 [강조] ❑ 한 연구에 의하면 심지어 1일 열 개피라는 적은 수의 담배도 생식력에 피해를 줄 수 있다. ⑥ 구 극히 드문 [강조] ❑ 성공한 여성 정치인은 극히 드물다. ⑦ 구 -이나 되는, -만큼이나 [강조] ❑ 13명이나 되는 각국 장관들이 회의에 참석했다.

가산명사 약혼자

가산명사 약혼녀

가산명사 대실패 [강조] ❑ 찰스턴 대실패에 대한 책임은 그에게 있지 않았다.

fi|ber /ˈfaɪbər/ (fibers) [BRIT fibre] **1** N-COUNT A **fiber** is a thin thread of a natural or artificial substance, especially one that is used to make cloth or rope. ❑ *If you look at the paper under a microscope you will see the fibers.* **2** N-VAR A particular **fiber** is a type of cloth or other material that is made from or consists of threads. ❑ *The ball is made of rattan – a natural fiber.* **3** N-UNCOUNT **Fiber** consists of the parts of plants or seeds that your body cannot digest. Fibre is useful because it makes food pass quickly through your body. ❑ *Most vegetables contain fiber.* **4** N-COUNT A **fiber** is a thin piece of flesh like a thread which connects nerve cells in your body or which muscles are made of. ❑ *...the nerve fibers.* →see **paper, rope, vegetable**

[영국영어 fibre] **1** 가산명사 섬유소, 섬유질 ❑ 현미경으로 종이를 관찰하면 섬유소를 볼 수 있다. **2** 가산명사 또는 불가산명사 섬유 ❑ 이 공은 천연 섬유인 등나무 줄기로 만들었다. **3** 불가산명사 섬유질 ❑ 대부분의 채소는 섬유질을 함유하고 있다. **4** 가산명사 (신경 또는 근 등의) 섬유 ❑ 신경 섬유

fi|ber op|tics

The spelling **fibre optics** is also used in British English. The form **fiber optic** is used as a modifier.

철자 fibre optics도 영국영어에서 쓴다. fiber optic은 수식어구로 쓴다.

1 N-UNCOUNT **Fiber optics** is the use of long thin threads of glass to carry information in the form of light. ❑ *Thanks to fiber optics, it is now possible to illuminate many of the body's remotest organs and darkest orifices.* **2** ADJ **Fiber optic** means relating to or involved in fiber optics. [ADJ n] ❑ *...fiber optic cables.* →see **laser**

1 불가산명사 광섬유 ❑ 광섬유 덕택으로 인해, 이제는 신체 깊숙이 위치한 장기와 어두운 구멍들도 비춰 볼 수 있다. **2** 형용사 광섬유의 ❑ 광섬유 케이블

fick|le /ˈfɪkəl/ **1** ADJ If you describe someone as **fickle**, you disapprove of them because they keep changing their mind about what they like or want. [DISAPPROVAL] ❑ *The group has been notoriously fickle in the past.* **2** ADJ If you say that something is **fickle**, you mean that it often changes and is unreliable. ❑ *Orta's weather can be fickle.*

1 형용사 변덕스러운 [탐탁잖음] ❑ 그 단체는 과거에 변덕스러웠다고 악평이 나 있다. **2** 형용사 변하기 쉬운, 변덕스러운 ❑ 오르타의 날씨는 쉽게 변할 수 있다.

fic|tion /ˈfɪkʃən/ (fictions) **1** N-UNCOUNT **Fiction** refers to books and stories about imaginary people and events, rather than books about real people or events. ❑ *Immigrant tales have always been popular themes in fiction.* →see also **science fiction** **2** N-UNCOUNT A statement or account that is **fiction** is not true. ❑ *The truth or fiction of this story has never been truly determined.* **3** N-COUNT If something is a **fiction**, it is not true, although people sometimes pretend that it is true. ❑ *Total recycling is a fiction.* →see **library**

1 불가산명사 소설 ❑ 이주자에 관한 이야기는 언제나 인기 있는 소설 주제이다. **2** 불가산명사 허구 ❑ 이 이야기가 사실인지 허구인지는 확정된 적이 없다. **3** 가산명사 가상 ❑ 완전 재활용이란 가상일 뿐이다.

fic|tion|al /ˈfɪkʃənəl/ ADJ **Fictional** characters or events occur only in stories, plays, or movies and never actually existed or happened. ❑ *It is drama featuring fictional characters.* →see **fantasy**

형용사 허구적인 ❑ 그것은 허구적인 인물들이 등장하는 연극이다.

fic|ti|tious /fɪkˈtɪʃəs/ **1** ADJ **Fictitious** is used to describe something that is false or does not exist, although some people claim that it is true or exists. ❑ *We're interested in the source of these fictitious rumors.* **2** ADJ A **fictitious** character, thing, or event occurs in a story, play, or film but never really existed or happened. ❑ *The persons and events portrayed in this production are fictitious.*

1 형용사 허위의 ❑ 우리는 이러한 허위 소문의 출처에 관심이 있다. **2** 형용사 허구의 ❑ 이 작품에 묘사되는 인물들과 사건들은 허구이다.

fid|dle /ˈfɪdəl/ (fiddles, fiddling, fiddled) **1** V-I If you **fiddle with** an object, you keep moving it or touching it with your fingers. ❑ *Harriet fiddled with a pen on the desk.* **2** V-I If you **fiddle with** something, you change it in minor ways. ❑ *She told Whistler that his portrait of her was finished and to stop fiddling with it.* **3** V-I If you **fiddle with** a machine, you adjust it. ❑ *He turned on the radio and fiddled with the knob until he got a talk show.* **4** V-T If someone **fiddles** financial documents, they alter them dishonestly so that they get money for themselves. [BRIT, INFORMAL] ❑ *He's been fiddling the books.* **5** N-VAR Some people call violins **fiddles**, especially when they are used to play folk music. ❑ *Hardy as a young man played the fiddle at local dances.*

1 자동사 만지작거리다 ❑ 해리엇은 책상 위의 펜을 만지작거렸다. **2** 자동사 손질하다 ❑ 그녀는 위슬러에게 그가 그린 자기의 초상화는 그만하면 됐으니, 손질을 끝내라고 전했다. **3** 자동사 조정하다 ❑ 그는 라디오를 켠후 토크쇼가 나올 때까지 다이얼을 조정하였다. **4** 타동사 조작하다 [영국영어, 비격식체] ❑ 그는 장부를 조작해 왔다. **5** 가산명사 또는 불가산명사 바이올린 ❑ 하디는 젊을 때 지역 무도회에서 바이올린을 연주하였다.

fid|dly /ˈfɪdli/ (fiddlier, fiddliest) ADJ Something that is **fiddly** is difficult to do or use because it involves small or complicated objects. [BRIT] ❑ *Fish can be fiddly to cook.*

형용사 까다로운 [영국영어] ❑ 생선은 요리하기 까다로울 수 있다.

fi|del|ity /fɪˈdɛlɪti/ **1** N-UNCOUNT **Fidelity** is loyalty to a person, organization, or set of beliefs. [FORMAL] ❑ *I had to promise fidelity to the Queen.* **2** N-UNCOUNT **Fidelity** is being loyal to your husband, wife, or partner by not having a sexual relationship with anyone else. ❑ *British women expect fidelity from their men.*

1 불가산명사 충성 [격식체] ❑ 나는 여왕에게 충성을 맹세해야만 했다. **2** 불가산명사 정절 ❑ 영국 여자들은 남편이 정절을 지켜 주기를 기대한다.

fidg|et /ˈfɪdʒɪt/ (fidgets, fidgeting, fidgeted) **1** V-I If you **fidget**, you keep moving your hands or feet slightly or changing your position slightly, for example because you are nervous, bored, or excited. ❑ *Brenda fidgeted in her seat.* ● PHRASAL VERB **Fidget around** and **fidget about** mean the same as **fidget**. ❑ *There were two new arrivals, fidgeting around, waiting to ask questions.* **2** V-I If you **fidget with** something, you keep moving it or touching it with your fingers with small movements, for example because you are nervous or bored. ❑ *He fidgeted with his tie.*

1 자동사 안절부절못하다 ❑ 브렌다는 자리에서 안절부절못하고 있었다. ● 구동사 안절부절못하다 ❑ 새로 온 두 사람은 안절부절못하며 질문을 하려고 기다렸다. **2** 자동사 만지작거리다 ❑ 그는 넥타이를 만지작거렸다.

field /ˈfild/ (fields, fielding, fielded) **1** N-COUNT A **field** is an area of grass, for example in a park or on a farm. A **field** is also an area of land on which a crop is grown. ❑ *...a field of wheat.* **2** N-COUNT A sports **field** is an area of grass where sports are played. ❑ *...a football field.* ❑ *He was the fastest thing I ever saw on a baseball field.* **3** N-COUNT A **field** is an area of land or sea bed under which large amounts of a particular mineral have been found. ❑ *...an extensive natural gas field in Alaska.* **4** N-COUNT A magnetic, gravitational, or electric **field** is the area in which that particular force is strong enough to have an effect. ❑ *Some people are worried that electromagnetic fields from electric power lines could increase the risk of cancer.* **5** N-COUNT A particular **field** is a particular subject of study or type of activity. ❑ *Each of the authors of the tapes is an expert in his field.* **6** N-COUNT A **field** is an area of a computer's memory or a program where data can be entered, edited, or stored. [COMPUTING] ❑ *Go to a site like Yahoo! Finance and enter "AOL" in the Get Quotes field.* **7** N-COUNT Your **field** of vision or your visual **field** is the area that you can see without turning your head. ❑ *Our field of vision is surprisingly wide.* **8** N-COUNT-COLL The **field** is a way of referring to all the competitors taking part in a particular race or sports contest. ❑ *Going into the fourth lap, the two most broadly experienced riders led the field.* **9** ADJ You use **field** to describe work or study that is done in a real, natural environment rather than in a theoretical way or in controlled conditions. [ADJ n] ❑ *I also conducted a field*

1 가산명사 들판, 논밭 ❑ 밀밭 **2** 가산명사 경기장 ❑ 축구장 ❑ 그는 야구장에서 내가 본 사람 중 가장 빨랐다. **3** 가산명사 매장 지대 ❑ 알래스카의 광대한 천연 가스 매장 지대 **4** 가산명사 자기장, 중력장, 전기장 ❑ 몇몇 사람들은 전력선에서 나오는 전기 자기장이 암을 유발할 수 있다고 우려하고 있다. **5** 가산명사 분야 ❑ 그 테이프의 각 저자들은 자기 분야의 전문가들이다. **6** 가산명사 난(欄) [컴퓨터] ❑ '야후' 같은 사이트로 가세요. 금융 항목으로 가서 '시세 알아보기'란에서 '에이오엘'을 치세요. **7** 가산명사 시야 ❑ 우리 시야는 놀랄 만치 넓다. **8** 가산명사-집합 (경기) 참가자, 선수들 ❑ 네 바퀴째를 돌면서, 가장 경험이 풍부한 기수 두 사람이 앞서 나갔다. **9** 형용사 현장의 ❑ 나는 남녀관계에 대한 남자 아이들의 태도를 주제로 한 현장 연구도 실시했다. **10** 자동사 (크리켓, 야구에서) 수비하다 ❑ 우리가 수비를 하고 있을 때, 주심을 좀을 지켜보고 있었다. **11** 타동사 (질문을) 조리 있게 잘 받아치다 [언론] ❑ 그가 질문을 조리 있게 잘 받아치는 장면이 나중에 텔레비전에 방영되었다. **12** 타동사

study among the boys about their attitude to relationships. ⑩ V-I In a game of baseball, cricket, or rounders, the team that **is fielding** is trying to catch the ball, while the other team is trying to hit it. [usu cont] ❏ *When we are fielding, the umpires keep looking at the ball.* ⑪ V-T If you say that someone **fields** a question, you mean that they answer it or deal with it, usually successfully. [JOURNALISM] ❏ *He was later shown on television, fielding questions.* ⑫ V-T If a sports team **fields** a particular number or type of players, the players are chosen to play for the team on a particular occasion. ❏ *We're going to field an exciting and younger team.* ⑬ V-T If a candidate in an election is representing a political party, you can say that the party **is fielding** that candidate. [JOURNALISM] ❏ *There are signs that the new party aims to field candidates in elections scheduled for February next year.* ⑭ →see also **minefield, playing field**

(팀을) 구성하다 ❏ 우리는 활기차고 더 젊은 팀을 구성할 것이다. ⑬ 타동사 공천하다 [언론] ❏ 새 정당이 내년 2월로 예정된 선거에 후보를 공천하려고 한다는 징표가 있다.

Word Partnership	field의 연어
ADJ.	**open** field ①
	magnetic field ④
V.	**work in a** field ① ⑤
N.	**ball** field, field **hockey, track and** field ②
	oil field ③
	expert in a field, field **trip** ⑤
	field **of vision** ⑦
	field **questions** ⑪

field|er /fíldər/ (**fielders**) N-COUNT A **fielder** is a player in baseball, cricket, or rounders who is fielding or one who has a particular skill at fielding. ❏ *He hit 10 home runs in the Coast League and he's a real good fielder.*

가산명사 수비수 ❏ 그 선수는 코스트 리그에서 홈런 10개를 쳤고, 정말 훌륭한 수비수이기도 하다.

field hock|ey N-UNCOUNT **Field hockey** is an outdoor game played on a grass field between two teams of 11 players who use long curved sticks to hit a small ball and try to score goals. [AM; BRIT **hockey**] [oft N n]

불가산명사 하키 [미국영어; 영국영어 hockey]

fierce ♦♢♢ /fɪərs/ (**fiercer, fiercest**) ① ADJ A **fierce** animal or person is very aggressive or angry. ❏ *They look like the teeth of some fierce animal.* ● **fierce|ly** ADV ❏ *"I don't know," she said fiercely.* ② ADJ **Fierce** feelings or actions are very intense or enthusiastic, or involve great activity. ❏ *Competition has been fierce to win a stake in Skoda.* ❏ *The town was captured after a fierce battle with rebels at the weekend.* ● **fierce|ly** ADV ❏ *He has always been ambitious and fiercely competitive.*

① 형용사 사나운 ❏ 그것들은 맹수의 이빨 같아 보인다. ● 사납게 부사 ❏ "몰라." 그녀는 사납게 쏘아붙였다. ② 형용사 격렬한, 치열한 ❏ 스코다 상금을 타기 위한 경쟁이 치열했다. ❏ 그 도시는 주말 동안 반군과의 격렬한 전투 끝에 함락되었다. ● 격렬하게 부사 ❏ 그는 항상 야심이 많고, 몹시 경쟁적이어 왔다.

fiery /faɪəri/ (**fieriest**) ① ADJ If you describe something as **fiery**, you mean that it is burning strongly or contains fire. [LITERARY] ❏ *A helicopter crashed in a fiery explosion in Vallejo.* ② ADJ You can use **fiery** for emphasis when you are referring to bright colors such as red or orange. [LITERARY, EMPHASIS] ❏ *The sky turned from fiery orange to lemon yellow.*

① 형용사 작열하는 [문예체] ❏ 발레조에서 헬리콥터 한 대가 강한 폭발과 함께 추락했다. ② 형용사 (색깔이) 불타는 듯한 [문예체, 강조] ❏ 하늘이 불타는 듯한 오렌지색에서 레몬색으로 변했다.

fif|teen ♦♦♢ /fɪftíːn/ (**fifteens**) NUM **Fifteen** is the number 15. ❏ *In India, there are fifteen official languages.*

수사 15 ❏ 인도는 공용어가 15개이다.

fif|teenth ♦♦♢ /fɪftíːnθ/ ORD The **fifteenth** item in a series is the one that you count as number fifteen. ❏ *...the invention of the printing press in the fifteenth century.*

서수 열다섯 번째 ❏ 15세기의 인쇄술 발명

fifth ♦♦♢ /fɪfθ/ (**fifths**) ① ORD The **fifth** item in a series is the one that you count as number five. ❏ *Joe has recently returned from his fifth trip to Australia.* ② FRACTION A **fifth** is one of five equal parts of something. ❏ *India spends over a fifth of its budget on defence.*

① 서수 다섯 번째 ❏ 조우는 최근에 다섯 번째 호주 여행에서 돌아왔다. ② 분수 5분의 1 ❏ 인도는 국가 예산의 5분의 1을 국방비로 지출한다.

fif|ti|eth ♦♦♢ /fɪftiəθ/ ORD The **fiftieth** item in a series is the one that you count as number fifty. ❏ *He retired in 1970, on his fiftieth birthday.*

서수 오십 번째 ❏ 그는 1970년, 자신의 쉰 살 생일에 은퇴했다.

fif|ty ♦♦♦ /fɪfti/ (**fifties**) ① NUM **Fifty** is the number 50. ② N-PLURAL When you talk about the **fifties**, you are referring to numbers between 50 and 59. For example, if you are **in your fifties**, you are aged between 50 and 59. If the temperature is **in the fifties**, the temperature is between 50 and 59 degrees. ❏ *I probably look as if I'm in my fifties rather than my seventies.* ③ N-PLURAL The **fifties** is the decade between 1950 and 1959. ❏ *He began performing in the early fifties, singing and playing guitar.*

① 수사 50 ② 복수명사 오십 대 ❏ 나는 아마 칠십 대로보다는 오십 대로 보일 것이다. ③ 복수명사 1950년대 ❏ 그는 50년대 초반에 노래와 기타 연주 공연을 시작했다.

fifty-fifty ADV If something such as money or property is divided or shared **fifty-fifty** between two people, each person gets half of it. [INFORMAL] [ADV after v] ❏ *The proceeds of the sale are split fifty-fifty.* ● ADJ **Fifty-fifty** is also an adjective. ❏ *The new firm was owned on a fifty-fifty basis by the two parent companies.*

부사 오십 대 오십 [비격식체] ❏ 판매 수익금은 오십 대 오십으로 나눈다. ● 형용사 오십 대 오십의 ❏ 새 회사의 지분은 두 모회사가 오십 대 오십으로 갖고 있었다.

fig /fɪg/ (**figs**) ① N-COUNT A **fig** is a soft sweet fruit that grows in hot countries. It is full of tiny seeds and is often eaten dried. ② N-COUNT A **fig** or a **fig tree** is a tree on which figs grow.

① 가산명사 무화과 열매 ② 가산명사 무화과나무

fig. In books and magazines, **fig.** is used as an abbreviation for **figure** in order to tell the reader which picture or diagram is being referred to. ❏ *Draw the basic outlines in black felt-tip pen (see fig. 4).*

도표 ❏ 검은색 펠트펜으로 기본 윤곽선을 그리시오. (도표 4 참조)

fight ♦♦♦ /faɪt/ (**fights, fighting, fought**) ① V-T/V-I If you **fight** something unpleasant, you try in a determined way to prevent it or stop it from happening. ❏ *More units to fight forest fires are planned.* ❏ *I've spent a lifetime fighting against racism and prejudice.* ● N-COUNT **Fight** is also a noun. ❏ *...the fight against drug addiction.* ② V-I If you **fight** for something, you try in a determined way to get it or achieve it. ❏ *Lee had to fight hard for his place on the expedition.* ❏ *I told him how we had fought to hold on to the company.* ● N-COUNT **Fight** is also a noun. ❏ *I too am committing myself to continue the fight for justice.* ③ V-RECIP If an army or group **fights** a battle with another army or group, they oppose each other with weapons. You can also say that two armies or groups **fight** a battle. ❏ *In the latest incident at the weekend police fought a gun battle with a gang which used hand grenades against them.* ④ V-T/V-I If a person or army **fights** in a battle or a

① 타동사/자동사 싸우다 ❏ 산불을 진화하기 위해 더 많은 부대가 계획되고 있다. ❏ 나는 인종주의와 편견에 맞서 싸우는 데에 평생을 바쳤다. ● 가산명사 싸움 ❏ 약물 중독과의 전쟁 ② 자동사 분투하다 ❏ 리는 그 탐험대에서 자기 자리를 지키기 위해 몹시 분투해야 했다. ❏ 나는 우리가 회사를 지켜 내기 위해 어떻게 분투해 왔는지 그에게 알려 줬다. ● 가산명사 분투, 투쟁 ❏ 저도 자유를 위한 투쟁을 계속하기로 맹세합니다. ③ 상호동사 접전하다 ❏ 주말에 있었던 최근 사건에서 경찰은 수류탄까지 사용했던 갱들과 총격전을 벌였다. ④ 타동사/자동사 참전하다 ❏ 그는 그 전쟁에 참전했다가, 미군에게 포로로 잡혔다.

war, they take part in it. ❑ *He fought in the war and was taken prisoner by the Americans.* ❑ *If I were a young man I would sooner go to prison than fight for this country.* ● **fight|ing** N-UNCOUNT ❑ *More than nine hundred people have died in the fighting.* **5** V-RECIP If one person **fights** with another, or **fights** them, the two people hit or kick each other because they want to hurt each other. You can also say that two people **fight**. ❑ *As a child she fought with her younger sister.* ❑ *I did fight him, I punched him but it was like hitting a wall.* ● N-COUNT **Fight** is also a noun. [oft N with n] ❑ *He had had a fight with Smith and bloodied his nose.* **6** V-RECIP If one person **fights** with another, or **fights** them, they have an angry disagreement or quarrel. You can also say that two people **fight**. [INFORMAL] ❑ *She was always arguing with him and fighting with him.* ❑ *Gwendolen started fighting her teachers.* ● N-COUNT **Fight** is also a noun. ❑ *We think maybe he took off because he had a big fight with his dad the night before.* **7** V-T If you **fight** your way to a place, you move toward it with great difficulty, for example because there are a lot of people or obstacles in your way. ❑ *I fought my way into a carriage just before the doors closed.* **8** N-COUNT A **fight** is a boxing match. ❑ *The referee stopped the fight.* **9** V-T/V-I To **fight** means to take part in a boxing match. ❑ *In a few hours' time one of the world's most famous boxers will be fighting in Britain for the first time.* ❑ *I'd like to fight him because he's undefeated and I want to be the first man to beat him.* **10** V-T If you **fight** an election, you are a candidate in the election and try to win it. ❑ *The former party treasurer helped raise almost £40 million to fight the election campaign.* **11** N-COUNT You can use **fight** to refer to a contest such as an election or a sports match. [JOURNALISM] ❑ *He repeated his intention to fight for the presidency in the multi-party elections planned next year.* **12** V-T If you **fight** a case or a court action, you make a legal case against someone in a way determined every, or you put forward a defense when a legal case is made against you. ❑ *Watkins sued the Army and fought his case in various courts for 10 years.* **13** N-UNCOUNT **Fight** is the desire or ability to keep fighting. ❑ *I thought that we had a lot of fight in us.* **14** V-T/V-I If you **fight** an emotion or desire, you try very hard not to feel it, show it, or act on it, but do not always succeed. ❑ *I desperately fought the urge to giggle.* ❑ *He fought with the urge to smoke one of the cigars he'd given up awhile ago.* **15** PHRASE Someone who **is fighting for** their **life** is making a great effort to stay alive, either when they are being physically attacked or when they are very ill. ❑ *He is still fighting for his life in the hospital.* →see **army**

Thesaurus   *fight*의 참조어

v.	scuffle, squabble, tussle **5**
	argue, bicker, quarrel **6**
N.	argument, disagreement, squabble **6**

Word Partnership   *fight*의 연어

N.	fight **crime**, fight **fire** **1**
	fight **a battle/ war**, fight **an enemy** **3**
v.	**stay and** fight **1 2 3**
	join a fight **1 2 4-6**
	lose a fight, **win a** fight **1 2 4-6 8 11**
	break up a fight, **have a** fight, **pick a** fight, **start a** fight **5 6**

▶**fight back** **1** PHRASAL VERB If you **fight back** against someone or something that is attacking or harming you, you resist them actively or attack them. ❑ *We should take some comfort from the ability of the judicial system to fight back against corruption.* **2** PHRASAL VERB If you **fight back** an emotion or a desire, you try very hard not to feel it, show it, or act on it. ❑ *She fought back the tears.*

▶**fight off** **1** PHRASAL VERB If you **fight off** something, for example an illness or an unpleasant feeling, you succeed in getting rid of it and in not letting it overcome you. ❑ *Unfortunately these drugs are quite toxic and hinder the body's ability to fight off infection.* **2** PHRASAL VERB If you **fight off** someone who has attacked you, you fight with them, and succeed in making them go away or stop attacking you. ❑ *She fought off three armed robbers.*

fight|er ◆◇◇ /faɪtər/ (**fighters**) **1** N-COUNT A **fighter** or a **fighter plane** is a fast military aircraft that is used for destroying other aircraft. ❑ *...a fighter pilot.* **2** N-COUNT If you describe someone as a **fighter**, you approve of them because they continue trying to achieve things in spite of great difficulties or opposition. [APPROVAL] ❑ *From the start it was clear this tiny girl was a real fighter.* **3** N-COUNT A **fighter** is a person who physically fights another person, especially a professional boxer. ❑ *He was a real street fighter who'd do anything to win.* **4** →see also **fire fighter**

fig|ura|tive /fɪɡyərətɪv, BRIT fɪɡərətɪv/ **1** ADJ If you use a word or expression in a **figurative** sense, you use it with a more abstract or imaginative meaning than its ordinary literal one. ❑ *...an event that will change your route – in both the literal and figurative sense.* ● **fig|ura|tive|ly** ADV ❑ *Europe, with Germany literally and figuratively at its center, is still at the start of a remarkable transformation.* **2** ADJ **Figurative** art is a style of art in which people and things are shown in a realistic way. ❑ *His career spanned some 50 years and encompassed both abstract and figurative painting.*

fig|ure ◆◆◆ /fɪɡyər, BRIT fɪɡər/ (**figures, figuring, figured**) **1** N-COUNT A **figure** is a particular amount expressed as a number, especially a statistic. ❑ *It would be very nice if we had a true figure of how many people in this country haven't got a job.* ❑ *It will not be long before the inflation figure starts to fall.* **2** N-COUNT A **figure** is any of the ten written symbols from 0 to 9 that are used to represent a number. ❑ *...the glowing red figures on the radio alarm clock which read 4.22 a.m.* **3** N-PLURAL An amount or number that is in single **figures** is between zero and nine. An

---

❑ 내가 아직도 젊다면, 이 나라를 위해 참전하느니 차라리 감옥에 가겠다. ● 전투 불가산명사 ❑ 그 전투에서 구백 명 이상이 목숨을 잃었다. **5** 상동사 싸우다 ❑ 그녀는 어렸을 때 여동생과 싸웠다. ❑ 나는 그와 사실 싸웠다. 내가 주먹으로 쳤지만 그는 꿈쩍도 하지 않았다. ● 가산명사 싸움 ❑ 그는 스미스와 싸웠고 코피를 흘렸다. **6** 상동사 다투다, 싸우다 [비격식체] ❑ 그녀는 항상 그와 다투고 싸웠다. ❑ 궨돌렌은 선생님과 싸우기 시작했다. ● 가산명사 말싸움 ❑ 우리는 아마 그가 전날 밤에 아버지와 한바탕 크게 다퉜기 때문에 떠났을 거라고 본다. **7** 타동사 (힘들게) 나아가다 ❑ 나는 문이 닫히기 바로 직전에 객차 안으로 비집고 들어갔다. **8** 가산명사 권투 시합 ❑ 심판이 시합을 중단시켰다. **9** 타동사/자동사 권투 경기에 출전하다 ❑ 몇 시간 후면 영국에서 처음으로 세계 유명 권투선수 중 하나가 경기를 갖는다. ❑ 나는 무패의 전적을 가지고 있는 그 사람을 때려눕힌 첫 선수가 되고 싶기 때문에 나는 그와 시합을 갖고 싶다. **10** 타동사 출마하다 ❑ 당의 전 재정 위원장은 선거 운동 자금 4천만 파운드 조성에 기여했다. **11** 가산명사 경쟁, 선거, 경기 [언론] ❑ 그는 내년에 실시될 예정인 다당제 선거에서 대통령 출마 의지를 재확인했다. **12** 타동사 법정 싸움을 하다 ❑ 왓킨스는 육군을 고소했고, 10년 동안 여러 법정에서 싸웠다. **13** 불가산명사 투지, 투쟁력 ❑ 나는 우리의 투지가 대단하다고 생각했다. **14** 타동사/자동사 꾹 참다 ❑ 나는 웃음이 터져 나오려는 것을 필사적으로 참았다. ❑ 그는 얼마 전에 끊었던 여송연 한 대가 생각나는 것을 꾹 참았다. **15** 구 사투를 벌이다 ❑ 그는 아직도 병원에서 사투를 벌이고 있다.

1 구동사 반격하다 ❑ 부정부패에 맞서 싸우는 사법 제도의 능력에서 어느 정도 위안을 얻어야 한다. **2** 구동사 참으려고 안간힘을 쓰다 ❑ 그녀는 눈물을 참으려고 안간힘을 썼다.

1 구동사 이겨 내다 ❑ 불행히도 이 약들은 상당히 독하고 인체 면역력을 저하시킵니다. **2** 구동사 물리치다, 격퇴하다 ❑ 그녀는 무장 강도 세 명을 물리쳤다.

1 가산명사 전투기 ❑ 전투기 조종사 **2** 가산명사 투사 [마음에 듦] ❑ 시작부터 이 조그마한 소녀는 명백히 진정한 투사였다. **3** 가산명사 싸움꾼 ❑ 그는 이기기 위해서라면 어떤 짓이라도 하는 진짜 길거리 싸움꾼이었다.

1 형용사 비유적인 ❑ 자구적인 의미에서도 또 비유적인 의미에서도 당신의 행로를 바꿔 놓게 될 사건 ● 비유적으로 부사 ❑ 유럽은 여전히, 글자 그대로도 또 비유적으로도 유럽의 중심인 독일과 함께, 주목할 만한 변화의 시작 단계에 있다. **2** 형용사 조형 (미술) ❑ 50년이 넘는 그의 작품 세계는 추상화와 구상화를 망라한다.

1 가산명사 (통계) 수치 ❑ 이 나라 사람들이 얼마나 많이 직장이 없는지에 대한 정확한 통계 수치가 있다면 정말 좋을 텐데. ❑ 오래지 않아 인플레이션 수치가 떨어지기 시작할 것이다. **2** 가산명사 숫자 ❑ 오전 4시 22분을 가리키는 라디오 자명종의 적열등 숫자 **3** 복수명사 자릿수 ❑ 보통 한 자릿수였던 인플레이션이 12퍼센트 이상에 이르고 있다.

amount or number that is in double **figures** is between ten and ninety-nine. You can also say, for example, that an amount or number is in three **figures** when it is between one hundred and nine hundred and ninety-nine. ❑ *Inflation, which has usually been in single figures, is running at more than 12%.* ◆ N-COUNT You refer to someone that you can see as a **figure** when you cannot see them clearly or when you are describing them. ❑ *Alistair saw the dim figure of Rose in the chair.* ◆ N-COUNT In art, a **figure** is a person in a drawing or a painting, or a statue of a person. ❑ *...a life-size bronze figure of a brooding, hooded woman.* ◆ N-COUNT Your **figure** is the shape of your body. ❑ *Take pride in your health and your figure.* ◆ N-COUNT Someone who is referred to as a **figure** of a particular kind is a person who is well-known and important in some way. ❑ *The movement is supported by key figures in the three main political parties.* ◆ N-COUNT If you say that someone is, for example, a mother **figure** or a hero **figure**, you mean that other people regard them as the type of person stated or suggested. ❑ *Daniel Boone, the great hero figure of the frontier.* ◆ N-COUNT In books and magazines, the diagrams which help to show or explain information are referred to as **figures**. [also N num] ❑ *If you look at a world map (see Figure 1) you can identify the major wine-producing regions.* ◆ N-COUNT In geometry, a **figure** is a shape, especially a regular shape. [TECHNICAL] ❑ *Draw a pentagon, a regular five-sided figure.* ◆ V-T If you **figure** that something is the case, you think or guess that it is the case. [INFORMAL] ❑ *She figured that both she and Ned had learned a lot from the experience.* ◆ V-I If you say **That figures** or **It figures**, you mean that the fact referred to is not surprising. [INFORMAL] ❑ *When I finished, he said, "Yeah. That figures."* ◆ V-I If a person or thing **figures in** something, they appear in or are included in it. [no passive] ❑ *Human rights violations figured prominently in the report.*

▶**figure out** PHRASAL VERB If you **figure out** a solution to a problem or the reason for something, you succeed in solving it or understanding it. [INFORMAL] ❑ *It took them about one month to figure out how to start the equipment.* ❑ *They're trying to figure out the politics of this whole situation.*

figure|head /fɪɡərhɛd, BRIT fɪɡəʳhed/ (**figureheads**) ◆ N-COUNT If someone is the **figurehead** of an organization or movement, they are recognized as being its leader, although they have little real power. ❑ *The President will be little more than a figurehead.* ◆ N-COUNT A **figurehead** is a large wooden model of a person that was put just under the pointed front of a sailing ship in former times.

file ◆◆◇ /faɪl/ (**files, filing, filed**) ◆ N-COUNT A **file** is a box or a folded piece of heavy paper or plastic in which letters or documents are kept. ❑ *...a file of insurance papers.* ◆ N-COUNT A **file** is a collection of information about a particular person or thing. ❑ *We already have files on people's tax details, mortgages and poll tax.* ◆ V-T If you **file** a document, you put it in the correct place. ❑ *They are all filed alphabetically under author.* ◆ N-COUNT In computing, a **file** is a set of related data that has its own name. ❑ *Be sure to save the revised version of the file under a new filename.* ◆ V-T/V-I If you **file** a formal or legal accusation, complaint, or request, you make it officially. ❑ *I filed for divorce on the grounds of adultery a few months later.* ◆ V-T When someone **files** a report or a news story, they send or give it to their employer. ❑ *He had to rush back to the office and file a housing story before the secretaries went home.* ◆ N-COUNT A **file** is a hand tool which is used for rubbing hard objects to make them smooth, shape them, or cut through them. ◆ V-T If you **file** an object, you smooth it, shape it, or cut it with a file. ❑ *Manicurists are skilled at shaping and filing nails.* ◆ →see also **rank and file** ◆ PHRASE A group of people who are walking or standing **in single file** or **single file** are in a line, one behind the other. ❑ *We were walking in single file to the lake.*

fil|ing cabi|net (**filing cabinets**) N-COUNT A **filing cabinet** is a piece of office furniture, usually made of metal, which has drawers in which files are kept. →see **office**

fill ◆◆◇ /fɪl/ (**fills, filling, filled**) ◆ V-T/V-I If you **fill** a container or area, or if it **fills**, an amount of something enters it that is enough to make it full. ❑ *She went to the bathroom, filled a glass with water, returned to the bed.* ❑ *The boy's eyes filled with tears.* ● PHRASAL VERB **Fill up** means the same as **fill**. ❑ *Warehouses at the frontier between the two countries fill up with sacks of rice and flour.* ◆ V-T If something **fills** a space, it is so big or there are such large quantities of it, that there is very little room left. ❑ *He cast his eyes at the rows of cabinets that filled the enormous work area.* ● PHRASAL VERB **Fill up** means the same as **fill**. ❑ *...the complicated machines that fill up today's laboratories.* ● **filled** ADJ [v-link ADJ with n] ❑ *...four museum buildings filled with historical objects.* ◆ V-T If you **fill** a crack or hole, you put a substance into it in order to make the surface smooth again. ❑ *Fill small holes with wood filler in a matching color.* ● PHRASAL VERB **Fill in** means the same as **fill**. ❑ *Start by filling in any cracks and gaps between window and door frames and the wall.* ◆ V-T If a sound, smell, or light **fills** a space, or the air, it is very strong or noticeable. ❑ *In the parking lot of the school, the siren fills the air.* ◆ V-T If something **fills** you **with** an emotion, or if an emotion **fills** you, you experience this emotion strongly. ❑ *I admired my father, and his work filled me with awe and curiosity.* ◆ V-T If you **fill** a period of time with a particular activity, you spend the time in this way. ❑ *If she wants a routine to fill her day, let her do community work.* ● PHRASAL VERB **Fill up** means the same as **fill**. ❑ *On Thursday night she went to her yoga class, glad to have something to fill up the evening.* ◆ V-T If something **fills** a need or a gap, it puts an end to this need or gap by existing or being active. ❑ *She brought him a sense of fun, of gaiety that filled a gap in his life.* ◆ V-T If something **fills** a role, position, or function, they have that role or position, or perform that function, often successfully. ❑ *Dena was filling the role of diplomat's wife with the skill she had learned over the years.* ◆ V-T If a company or organization **fills** a job vacancy, they choose someone to do the job. If someone **fills** a job vacancy, they accept a job that they have been offered. ❑ *A vacancy has arisen which I intend to fill.* ◆ V-T When a dentist **fills** someone's tooth, he or she puts a filling in it. ❑ *Dentists fill teeth and repair broken ones.*

◆ 가산명사 유곽, 모습 ❑ 알리스테어는 의자에 앉아 있는 로즈의 희미한 모습을 보았다. ◆ 가산명사 초상, 상(像) ❑ 머리에 수건을 쓰고 곰곰이 생각하고 있는 여인의 청동 등신상 ◆ 가산명사 몸매 ❑ 여러분의 건강과 몸매에 자신감을 가지세요. ◆ 가산명사 핵심 인물 ❑ 그 운동은 주요 3당의 핵심 인사들이 지지하고 있다. ◆ 가산명사 모범상, 영웅상 ❑ 다니엘 분, 전선의 위대한 영웅상 ◆ 가산명사 도표 ❑ 세계 지도(도표 1 참조)를 보시면 포도주 주요 생산지를 찾으실 수 있을 겁니다. ◆ 가산명사 도형 [과학 기술] ❑ 일반 5면체의 정오각형을 그리시오. ◆ 타동사 생각하다 [비격식체] ❑ 그녀는 자기와 네드 둘 다 이번 경험으로 많이 배웠다고 생각했다. ◆ 자동사 거 봐 [비격식체] ❑ 내가 다 끝마쳤을 때, 그가 "그래, 거 봐!"라고 말했다. ◆ 자동사 나오다 ❑ 그 보고서에는 인권 침해 사례들이 뚜렷이 드러나 있다.

구동사 알아내다, 풀어내다 [비격식체] ❑ 그 사람들이 그 장비를 어떻게 작동시키는지를 알아내는 데 거의 한 달이 걸렸다. ❑ 그들은 이 상황을 타개할 해법을 찾아내려고 애쓰고 있다.

◆ 가산명사 대표 ❑ 대통령은 명목상 대표에 지나지 않을 것이다. ◆ 가산명사 항해 선수상(船首像)

◆ 가산명사 파일 ❑ 보험 서류 파일 ◆ 가산명사 자료철 ❑ 우리는 납세 세부 내역, 저당 여부, 인두세에 대한 자료철을 이미 갖고 있습니다. ◆ 타동사 철하다 ❑ 그것들은 모두 저자명 알파벳순으로 철해져 있다. ◆ 가산명사 (컴퓨터) 파일 ❑ 개정된 파일 내용을 새 파일 이름으로 저장하는 것을 잊지 마세요. ◆ 타동사/자동사 제출하다 ❑ 나는 몇 달 후에 간통을 이유로 이혼 청구서를 제출하였다. ◆ 타동사 제출하다 ❑ 그는 사무실로 다시 뛰어 들어가 비서가 퇴근하기 전에 주택 관련 기사를 제출해야만 했다. ◆ 가산명사 줄 ◆ 타동사 줄질하다 ❑ 손톱 미용사들은 손톱 모양을 만들고 다듬는 것에 능숙하다. ◆ 구 일렬로, 일렬 ❑ 우리는 호수까지 일렬로 걷고 있었다.

가산명사 (서류 정리) 캐비닛

◆ 타동사/자동사 채우다, 차다 ❑ 그녀는 화장실로 가서 잔에 물을 채우고 침대로 돌아왔다. ❑ 소년의 눈에 눈물이 가득 고였다. ● 구동사 채우다, 차다 ❑ 두 나라의 국경에 있는 창고는 쌀자루와 밀가루 자루로 가득 찬다. ◆ 타동사 메우다, 공간을 다 차지하다 ❑ 그는 넓은 작업장을 꽉 메운 죽 늘어서 있는 캐비닛들을 훑어보았다. ● 구동사 메우다, 공간을 다 차지하다 ❑ 오늘날의 연구실 공간을 다 차지하고 있는 복잡한 기계들 ● 역사적 유물들로 가득 채워진 박물관 건물 네 동 ◆ 타동사 메우다 ❑ 작은 구멍들을 색깔이 맞는 나무 조각들로 메워라. ● 구동사 메우다 ❑ 창틀, 문틀과의 깨진 곳이랑 틈을 메우는 것으로 시작해라. ◆ 타동사 (소리, 냄새, 불빛 등이 공간을) 채우다 ❑ 학교의 주차 구역에는 사이렌 소리가 요란했다. ◆ 타동사 충만하다 ❑ 나는 아버지를 존경했고 아버지의 일은 나에게 경외감과 호기심을 가득 심어 주었다. ◆ 타동사 충만하다 ❑ 그녀는 하루하루를 보낼 일을 찾는다면, 사회봉사를 시키세요. ● 구동사 시간을 보내다, 시간을 메우다 ❑ 목요일 밤에 그녀는 요가 수업에 갔는데, 밤에 뭔가를 하면서 시간을 보낼 수 있다는 것을 기뻐했다. ◆ 타동사 메워 주다, 채워 주다 ❑ 그녀는 그에게 삶의 공백을 메워 줄 재미와 즐거움을 안겨 주었다. ◆ 타동사 충만하다 ❑ 데나는 수년간 익힌 노련함으로 외교관 부인의 역할을 잘 수행해 내고 있었다. ◆ 타동사 충원하다 ❑ 내가 노리고 있던 직장에 빈자리가 생겼다. ◆ 타동사 (치아를) 메우다 ❑ 치과의사는 치아를 메우고 부러진 이를 고친다. ◆ 타동사 (명령, 처방을) 따르다, 처방에 따라 조제하다 [주로 미국영어] ❑ 처방전이 유효하다면

A

⑪ V-T If you **fill** an order or a prescription, you provide the things that are asked for. [mainly AM] ❏ *A pharmacist can fill any prescription if, in his or her judgment, the prescription is valid.* **⑫** to **fill the bill** →see **bill**

약사는 각자의 판단에 따라 무슨 약이든지 그 처방대로 조제할 수 있다.

B

Thesaurus	fill의 참조어
v.	inflate, load, pour into, put into; *(ant.)* empty, pour out **①**
	crowd, take up **②**
	block, close, plug, seal **③**

C

D

▶**fill in** **①** PHRASAL VERB If you **fill in** a form or other document requesting information, you write information in the spaces on it. [mainly BRIT; AM usually **fill out**] ❏ *Fill in the coupon and send it first class to the address shown.* **②** PHRASAL VERB If you **fill in** a shape, you cover the area inside the lines with color or shapes so that none of the background is showing. ❏ *With a lip pencil, outline lips and fill them in.* **③** PHRASAL VERB If you **fill** someone **in**, you give them more details about something that you know about. [INFORMAL] ❏ *He filled her in on Wilbur Kantor's visit.* **④** PHRASAL VERB If you **fill in** for someone, you do the work or task that they normally do because they are unable to do it. ❏ *Vice-presidents' wives would fill in for first ladies.* **⑤** →see also **fill 3**

① 구동사 작성하다 [주로 영국영어; 미국영어 대개 fill out] ❏ 이 교환권을 작성하신 후 1급 우편으로 표시된 주소로 보내 주세요. **②** 구동사 채워 넣다 ❏ 립펜슬로 윤곽선을 그리고 그 안을 채워 넣으세요. **③** 구동사 상세한 정보를 주다 [비격식체] ❏ 그는 그녀에게 윌버 칸터의 방문에 대한 상세 정보를 줬다. **④** 구동사 (빈자리를) 채우다 ❏ 부통령 부인이 영부인의 빈 자리를 채울 것이다.

E

F

G

▶**fill out** PHRASAL VERB If you **fill out** a form or other document requesting information, you write information in the spaces on it. [mainly AM; BRIT usually **fill in**] ❏ *Fill out the application carefully, and keep copies of it.*

구동사 작성하다 [주로 미국영어; 영국영어 대개 fill in] ❏ 이 원서를 주의해서 작성하시고, 사본을 보관하고 계세요.

H

▶**fill up** **①** PHRASAL VERB If you **fill up** or **fill** yourself **up** with food, you eat so much that you do not feel hungry. ❏ *Fill up on potatoes, bread and pasta, which are high in carbohydrate and low in fat.* **②** PHRASAL VERB A type of food that **fills** you **up** makes you feel that you have eaten a lot, even though you have only eaten a small amount. ❏ *Potatoes fill us up without overloading us with calories.* **③** →see also **fill 1, 2, 6**

① 구동사 (배를) 채우다 ❏ 탄수화물은 풍부하고 저지방인 감자, 빵, 파스타로 배를 채우시오. **②** 구동사 포만감을 주다 ❏ 감자는 칼로리는 적으면서 포만감을 준다.

I

fil|let /fɪleɪ, BRIT fɪlɪt/ (**fillets**, **filleting**, **filleted**) **①** N-VAR **Fillet** is a strip of meat, especially beef, that has no bones in it. ❏ *...fillet of beef with shallots.* ❏ *...chicken breast fillets.* **②** N-COUNT A **fillet** of fish is the side of a fish with the bones removed. ❏ *...anchovy fillets.* **③** V-T When you **fillet** fish or meat, you prepare it by taking the bones out. ❏ *Don't be afraid to ask your fishmonger to fillet flat fish.*

① 가산명사 또는 불가산명사 (뼈를 발라 얇게 뜬) 살코기, 필레 ❏ 설롯을 곁들인 쇠고기 살코기 요리 ❏ 닭가슴살 필레 **②** 가산명사 (뼈를 발라 포를 뜬) 생선살, 필레 ❏ 뼈를 발라낸 멸치 **③** 타동사 뼈를 바르다 ❏ 걱정하지 말고 생선 장수에게 납작한 생선의 뼈를 발라 달라고 부탁해라.

J

K

fill|ing /fɪlɪŋ/ (**fillings**) **①** N-COUNT A **filling** is a small amount of metal or plastic that a dentist puts in a hole in a tooth to prevent further decay. ❏ *The longer your child can go without needing a filling, the better.* **②** N-MASS The **filling** in something such as a cake, pie, or sandwich is a substance or mixture that is put inside it. ❏ *Spread some of the filling over each cold pancake and then either roll or fold.* **③** N-MASS The **filling** in a piece of soft furniture or in a cushion is the soft substance inside it. ❏ *...second-hand sofas with old-style foam fillings.* **④** ADJ Food that is **filling** makes you feel full when you have eaten it. ❏ *Although it is tasty, crab is very filling.* →see **teeth**

① 가산명사 (치과에서 쓰는) 충전재 ❏ 당신의 아이가 충전재가 필요 없이 지낼 수 있으면 있을수록 더 좋다. **②** 물질명사 (케이크나 파이 등의) 소 ❏ 식은 팬케이크 위에 소를 좀 펴 넣은 다음, 둥글게 말거나 접는다. **③** 물질명사 (쿠션이나 소파의) 속 ❏ 구식의 고무 재질로 속을 넣은 중고 소파들 **④** 형용사 포만감을 주는 ❏ 게는 맛있기는 하지만 먹고 나면 포만감이 너무 많이 든다.

L

M

N

film ◆◆◇ /fɪlm/ (**films**, **filming**, **filmed**) **①** N-COUNT A **film** consists of moving pictures that have been recorded so that they can be shown in a theater or on television. A film tells a story, or shows a real situation. ❏ *Everything about the film was good. Good acting, good story, good fun.* **②** V-T/V-I If you **film** something, you use a camera to take moving pictures which can be shown on a screen or on television. ❏ *He had filmed her life story.* **③** N-UNCOUNT **Film** of something is moving pictures of a real event that are shown on television or on a screen. ❏ *They have seen news film of families queuing in Russia to buy a loaf of bread.* **④** N-VAR A **film** is the narrow roll of plastic that is used in a camera to take photographs. ❏ *The photographers had already shot a dozen rolls of film.* **⑤** N-UNCOUNT The making of films, considered as a form of art or a business, can be referred to as **film** or **films**. [also N in pl] ❏ *Film is a business with limited opportunities for actresses.* **⑥** N-COUNT A **film of** powder, liquid, or oil is a very thin layer of it. ❏ *The sea is coated with a film of raw sewage.* **⑦** N-UNCOUNT Plastic **film** is a very thin sheet of plastic used to wrap and cover things. [BRIT; AM **plastic wrap, Saran wrap**] ❏ *Cover with plastic film and refrigerate for 24 hours.* →see **photography**

O

P

Q

R

① 가산명사 영화 ❏ 그 영화는 모든 것이 다 좋았다. 연기도 훌륭하고 내용도 좋고 재미도 상당히 있고, **②** 타동사/자동사 영화를 찍다 ❏ 그는 그녀의 일생을 영화로 찍었다. **③** 불가산명사 영상 ❏ 그들은 러시아에서 빵 한 덩어리를 사기 위해 줄을 서 있는 가족들의 뉴스를 영상으로 본 적이 있다. **④** 가산명사 또는 불가산명사 필름 ❏ 그 사진사들은 이미 필름 열두 통을 다 찍은 상태이다. **⑤** 불가산명사 영화 산업 ❏ 영화 산업이 여배우들에게는 기회를 좀처럼 잡기

S

Word Partnership	film의 연어
v.	direct a film, edit film **①**
	watch a film **① ③**
	develop film **④**
N.	film clip, film critic, film director, film festival, film producer **①**
	film studio **⑤**
	roll of film **④**

T

U

힘든 사업이다. **⑥** 가산명사 (얇은) 막 ❏ 그 바다는 정화 처리 되지 않은 오페수가 막처럼 덮여 있다. **⑦** 불가산명사 랩 [영국영어; 미국영어 plastic wrap, saran wrap] ❏ 비닐 랩으로 덮어서 24시간 동안 냉장고에 보관해라.

V

film|ing /fɪlmɪŋ/ N-UNCOUNT **Filming** is the activity of making a film including the acting, directing, and camera shots. ❏ *Filming was due to start next month.*

불가산명사 영화 제작 ❏ 영화 제작이 다음 달에 시작될 예정이었다.

W

fil|ter /fɪltər/ (**filters**, **filtering**, **filtered**) **①** V-T To **filter** a substance means to pass it through a device which is designed to remove certain particles contained in it. ❏ *The best prevention for cholera is to boil or filter water, and eat only well-cooked food.* **②** N-COUNT A **filter** is a device through which a substance is passed when it is being filtered. ❏ *...a paper coffee filter.* **③** N-COUNT A **filter** is a device through which sound or light is passed and which blocks or reduces particular sound or light frequencies. ❏ *You might use a yellow filter to improve the clarity of a hazy horizon.* **④** V-I If light or sound **filters into** a place, it comes in weakly or slowly, either through a partly covered opening, or from a long distance away. ❏ *Light filtered into my kitchen through the soft, green shade of the honey locust tree.* **⑤** V-I When news or information **filters** through to people, it

X

Y

Z

① 타동사 거르다 ❏ 최상의 콜레라 예방법은 물을 끓이거나 정수하라, 음식을 잘 익혀 먹는 것이다. **②** 가산명사 여과기 ❏ 커피 여과지 **③** 가산명사 여과 장치, 필터 ❏ 흐릿한 수평선을 잘 보이게 하기 위해서는 노란색 필터를 사용할 수 있다. **④** 자동사 새어들다 ❏ 햇빛이 쥐엄나무의 부드럽고 푸른 그늘 사이로 부엌으로 새어들어 왔다. **⑤** 자동사 (소식이나 정보가) 전해지다 ❏ 여러 달이 지난 후에야 그 결과가 그 정치가들에게 전해지기 시작했다. ❏ 공격 소식이 빠르게 그 대학으로 전해졌다.

gradually reaches them. ❑ *It took months before the findings began to filter through to the politicians.* ❑ *News of the attack quickly filtered through the college.*

filth /fɪlθ/ **1** N-UNCOUNT **Filth** is a disgusting amount of dirt. ❑ *Thousands of tons of filth and sewage pour into the Ganges every day.* **2** N-UNCOUNT People refer to words or pictures, usually ones relating to sex, as **filth** when they think they are very disgusting and rude. [DISAPPROVAL] ❑ *The dialogue was all filth and innuendo.*

1 불가산명사 오물 ❑ 매일 수천 톤의 오물과 하수가 갠지스 강으로 쏟아져 들어간다. **2** 불가산명사 음담패설, 음란물 [탐탁찮음] ❑ 그 대화는 온통 음담패설과 성적인 농담뿐이었다.

filthy /fɪlθi/ (filthier, filthiest) **1** ADJ Something that is **filthy** is very dirty indeed. ❑ *He never washed, and always wore a filthy old jacket.* **2** ADJ If you describe something as **filthy**, you mean that you think it is morally very unpleasant and disgusting, sometimes in a sexual way. [DISAPPROVAL] ❑ *Apparently, well known actors were at these filthy parties.*

1 형용사 더러운 ❑ 그는 씻지도 않고 늘 더러운 낡은 재킷만 입었다. **2** 형용사 음탕한 [탐탁찮음] ❑ 듣기로는, 유명한 배우들이 이런 음탕한 파티 석상에 있었대.

fin /fɪn/ (fins) **1** N-COUNT A fish's **fins** are the flat objects which stick out of its body and help it to swim and keep its balance. **2** N-COUNT A **fin** on something such as an airplane, rocket, or bomb is a flat part which sticks out and which is intended to help control its movement.

1 가산명사 지느러미 **2** 가산명사 (비행기의) 수직 안정판

Word Link   fin ≈ end : **final, finale, finish**

---

final ♦♦♦ /faɪnəl/ (finals) **1** ADJ In a series of events, things, or people, the **final** one is the last one. [det ADJ] ❑ *Astronauts will make a final attempt today to rescue a communications satellite from its useless orbit.* ❑ *This is the fifth and probably final day of testimony before the Senate Judiciary Committee.* **2** ADJ **Final** means happening at the end of an event or series of events. [ADJ n] ❑ *You must have been on stage until the final curtain.* **3** ADJ If a decision or someone's authority is **final**, it cannot be changed or questioned. ❑ *The judges' decision is final.* **4** N-COUNT The **final** is the last game or contest in a series and decides who is the winner. ❑ *...the Scottish Cup Final.* →see also **quarter-final, semifinal** **5** N-PLURAL The **finals** of a sports tournament consist of a smaller tournament that includes only players or teams that have won earlier games. The finals decide the winner of the whole tournament. ❑ *Poland know they have a chance of qualifying for the World Cup Finals.*

1 형용사 마지막의 ❑ 오늘 우주 비행사들은 위성 통신을 쓸모없는 궤도에서 회수하려는 마지막 시도를 할 것이다. ❑ 이번이 다섯 번째로 아마도 상원 법사 위원회에 회부되기 전에 증언하는 마지막 날이 될 것이다. **2** 형용사 마지막의 ❑ 너는 분명히 마지막 막이 내려올 때까지 무대에 있었을 것이다. **3** 형용사 최종적인 ❑ 그 판사들의 판결은 최종적인 것이다. **4** 가산명사 결승전 ❑ 스코틀랜드컵 결승전 **5** 복수명사 결승전 ❑ 폴란드는 자신들이 월드컵 결승전에 나갈 가능성이 있다는 걸 알고 있다.

Thesaurus   final의 참조어

ADJ.   first, last, ultimate **1**
         absolute, decisive, definite, settled **3**

---

finale /fɪnɑːli, -næli/ (finales) N-COUNT The **finale** of a show, piece of music, or series of shows is the last part of it or the last one of them, especially when this is exciting or impressive. ❑ *... the finale of Shostakovich's Fifth Symphony.*

가산명사 (음악이나 연극의) 대단원, 피날레 ❑ 쇼스타코비치 심포니 5악장의 대단원

finalist /faɪnəlɪst/ (finalists) N-COUNT A **finalist** is someone who reaches the last stages of a competition or tournament by doing well or winning in its earlier stages. ❑ *The twelve finalists will be listed in the Sunday Times.*

가산명사 결승전 진출자 ❑ 12명의 결승전 진출자 이름이 '선데이 타임스'에 실릴 것이다.

Word Link   ize ≈ making : **finalize, minimize, normalize**

---

finalize /faɪnəlaɪz/ (finalizes, finalizing, finalized) [BRIT also **finalise**] V-T If you **finalize** something such as a plan or an agreement, you complete the arrangements for it, especially by discussing it with other people. ❑ *Negotiators from the three countries finalized the agreement in August.* ❑ *We are saying nothing until all the details have been finalized.*

[영국영어 finalise] 타동사 종결짓다 ❑ 3개국 협상 담당자들이 8월에 그 협의서를 종결지었다. ❑ 모든 세부 사항이 종결될 때까지 우리는 아무 말도 하지 않을 것이다.

finally ♦♦◇ /faɪnəli/ **1** ADV You use **finally** to suggest that something happens after a long period of time, usually later than you wanted or expected it to happen. ❑ *The food finally arrived at the end of last week and distribution began.* **2** ADV You use **finally** to indicate that something is last in a series of actions or events. [ADV with cl/group] ❑ *The action slips from comedy to melodrama and finally to tragedy.*

1 부사 드디어 ❑ 그 식량이 지난 주말에 드디어 도착해서 분배가 시작되었다. **2** 부사 마지막으로 ❑ 그 극은 희극에서 멜로드라마로, 마지막에는 비극으로 조금씩 바뀐다.

Do not confuse **finally** and **eventually**. You say that something **finally** happens after you have been waiting for it or expecting it for a long time. ❑ *Finally I went to bed... The heat of the sun finally became too much for me.* You can also use **finally** to show that something happens last in a series of events. ❑ *The sky turned red, then purple, and finally black.* When something happens after a lot of delays or complications, you can say that it **eventually** happens. ❑ *Eventually they got to the hospital... I found Victoria Avenue eventually.* You can also use **eventually** to talk about what happens at the end of a series of events, often as a result of them. ❑ *Eventually, they were forced to return to Chicago.*

finally와 eventually를 혼동하지 않도록 하라. 어떤 일이 오랫동안 기다려왔거나 기대하던 일이 마침내 일어나는 경우에는, finally를 써서 그 일이 마침내 일어난다고 말한다. ❑ 드디어 나는 잠자리에 들었다... 태양의 열기가 드디어 내게 너무 심하게 되었다. 어떤 일이 일련의 사건들에서 마지막으로 일어남을 나타낼 때는 finally를 쓸 수 있다. ❑ 하늘이 붉게, 다음엔 자줏빛으로, 마지막으로 검게 변했다. 어떤 일이 많은 지연과 복잡한 문제 뒤에 일어나면, 그 일이 마침내(eventually) 일어났다고 말할 수 있다. ❑ 마침내 그들은 병원에 도착했다... 나는 마침내 빅토리아 애비뉴를 찾았다. 또한 eventually는 일련의 사건 마지막에 흔히 그 사건들의 결과로 발생하는 것을 얘기할 때에도 쓸 수 있다. ❑ 결국, 그들은 시카고로 돌아가지 않을 수 없었다.

finance ♦♦◇ /faɪnæns, fɪnæns/ (finances, financing, financed) **1** V-T When someone **finances** something such as a project or a purchase, they provide the money that is needed to pay for them. ❑ *The fund has been used largely to finance the construction of federal prisons.* ● N-UNCOUNT **Finance** is also a noun. ❑ *A United States delegation is in Japan seeking finance for a major scientific project.* **2** N-UNCOUNT **Finance** is the commercial or government activity of managing money, debt, credit, and investment. [also N in pl] ❑ *...a major player in the world of high finance.* ❑ *The report recommends an overhaul of public finances.* **3** N-UNCOUNT You can refer to the amount of money that you have and how well it is organized as your **finances**. [also N in pl, oft with poss] ❑ *Be prepared for unexpected news concerning your finances.*

1 타동사 자금을 공급하다 ❑ 그 기금은 연방 교도소 건립용 자금 공급에 주로 사용되어 왔다. ● 불가산명사 자금 ❑ 한 미국 대표단이 일본에서 주요 과학 프로젝트를 위한 자금 확보를 위해 노력하고 있다. **2** 불가산명사 금융, 재정 ❑ 고급 금융계의 선두 주자 ❑ 그 보고서는 공공 재정 쇄신을 권고하고 있다. **3** 불가산명사 자금 사정 ❑ 당신의 자금 사정과 관련하여 예상치 못한 소식에 대비해라.

A

fi|nance com|pa|ny (**finance companies**) N-COUNT A **finance company** is a business which lends money to people and charges them interest while they pay it back. [BUSINESS]

가산명사 (할부) 금융 회사 [경제]

B

fi|nan|cial ◆◆◇ /faɪnænʃl, fɪn-/ ADJ **Financial** means relating to or involving money. □ *The company is in financial difficulties.* ● **fi|nan|cial|ly** ADV □ *She would like to be more financially independent.*

형용사 재정적인 □ 그 회사는 재정적인 어려움을 겪고 있다. ● 재정적으로 부사 □ 그녀는 재정적으로 좀 더 독립하기를 원한다.

C

fi|nan|cial year (**financial years**) N-COUNT A **financial year** is a period of twelve months, used by government, business, and other organizations in order to calculate their budgets, profits, and losses. [BRIT, BUSINESS; AM **fiscal year**] □ *...33,000 possible job losses in the coming financial year.*

가산명사 회계 연도 [영국영어, 경제; 미국영어 fiscal year] □ 다음 회계 연도에 3만 3천 명 정도의 실업자가 생길 가능성

D

fi|nan|ci|er /fɪnænsɪər, faɪn-/ (**financiers**) N-COUNT A **financier** is a person, company, or government that provides money for projects or businesses. [BUSINESS] □ *Archangel and Eastern Scotland Investments are IBS's main financiers.*

가산명사 자금원 [경제] □ 아케인젤과 이스턴 스코틀랜드 투자 회사가 아이비에스의 주된 자금원이다.

E

find ◆◆◆ /faɪnd/ (**finds, finding, found**) **1** V-T If you **find** someone or something, you see them or learn where they are. □ *The police also found a pistol.* □ *They have spent ages looking at the map and can't find a trace of anywhere called Darrowby.* **2** V-T If you **find** something that you need or want, you succeed in achieving or obtaining it. □ *Many people here cannot find work.* □ *He has to apply for a permit and we have to find him a job.* **3** V-T PASSIVE If something **is found** in a particular place or thing, it exists in that place. □ *Two thousand of France's 4,200 species of flowering plants are found in the park.* **4** V-T If you **find** someone or something in a particular situation, they are in that situation when you see them or come into contact with them. □ *They found her walking alone and depressed on the beach.* □ *She returned to her east London home to find her back door forced open.* **5** V-T If you **find yourself** doing something, you are doing it without deciding or intending to do it. □ *It's not the first time that you've found yourself in this situation.* □ *I found myself having more fun than I had had in years.* **6** V-T If you **find** that something is the case, you become aware of it or realize that it is the case. □ *The two biologists found, to their surprise, that both groups of birds survived equally well.* □ *At my age I would find it hard to get another job.* **7** V-T When a court or jury decides that a person on trial is guilty or innocent, you say that the person **has been found** guilty or not guilty. □ *She was found guilty of manslaughter and put on probation for two years.* **8** V-T You can use **find** to express your reaction to someone or something. □ *I find most of the young men of my own age so boring.* □ *I find it ludicrous that nothing has been done to protect passengers from fire.* **9** V-T If you **find** a feeling such as pleasure or comfort **in** a particular thing or activity, you experience the feeling mentioned as a result of this thing or activity. □ *How could anyone find pleasure in hunting and killing this beautiful creature?* **10** V-T If you **find** the time or money **to** do something, you succeed in making or obtaining enough time or money to do it. □ *I was just finding more time to write music.* **11** N-COUNT If you describe someone or something that has been discovered as a **find**, you mean that they are valuable, interesting, good, or useful. □ *Another of his lucky finds was a pair of candle-holders.* **12** →see also **finding, found**

가산명사 (할부) 금융 회사 [경제]

1 타동사 찾다 □ 경찰은 권총도 찾았다. □ 그들은 아주 오랫동안 지도를 들여다보면서 다로비라는 곳의 흔적도 찾지 못했다. **2** 타동사 얻다, 찾다 □ 여기 있는 많은 사람들이 일자리를 얻지 못한다. □ 그는 허가증을 신청해야 하고 우리는 그에게 일자리를 찾아 주어야 한다. **3** 수동 타동사 있다, 존재하다 □ 그 공원에는 4천2백 종의 프랑스산 꽃나무 중 2천 종이 있다. **4** 타동사 알다, 알게 되다 □ 그녀가 풀이 죽어서 해변가를 혼자 걷고 있다는 것을 그들은 알았다. □ 그녀가 런던 동부에 있는 자기 집에 돌아와 보니 집 뒷문에 침입 흔적이 있었다. **5** 타동사 ~한 상태에 있다, ~한 기분이다 □ 네가 이런 상황에 처했던 것이 이번이 처음이 아니잖아. □ 나는 지난 몇 년간 그 어느 때보다 즐거운 시간을 보내고 있었다. **6** 타동사 ~임을 깨닫다 □ 그 두 생물학자는 놀랍게도 두 그룹의 새가 똑같이 잘 살아가고 있다는 것을 깨달았다. □ 지금 내 나이에 다른 직업을 얻기란 어려울 것이다. **7** 타동사 판결을 받다 □ 그녀는 과실 치사로 유죄 판결을 받고 2년의 집행 유예를 선고받았다. **8** 타동사 ~라고 생각한다 □ 나는 내 나이 또래의 젊은이들은 대부분 너무나 재미없다고 생각한다. **9** 타동사 느끼다, 찾다 □ 승객들을 화재로부터 보호하기 위한 조치가 아무 것도 취해지지 않은 것은 말이 안 된다고 생각한다. □ 어떻게 이처럼 아름다운 생명체를 사냥하고 죽이는 것에서 쾌감을 찾을 수가 있을까? **10** 타동사 (시간이나 돈을) 마련하다 □ 나는 단지 곡을 쓸 수 있는 시간이 더 났다. **11** 가산명사 (가치있는) 발견 □ 그가 운 좋게 또 하나 발견한 것은 촛대 한 쌍이었다.

You can use **find**, **find out**, or **discover** to talk about learning that something is the case. □ *The young child finds that noise attracts attention... He discovered the whole school knew about it... We found out that she was wrong.* **Discover** is a slightly more formal word than **find**, and is often used to talk about scientific research or formal investigations. For example, you can **discover** a cure for a particular disease. You can also use **discover** when you find something by accident. □ *This well-known flower was discovered in 1903.* Note that if you cannot see something you are looking for, you say that you cannot **find** it. You do not use "discover" or 'find out' in this way. □ *I'm lost – I can't find the bridge.* You can also say that someone **finds out** facts when this is easy to do, but you cannot use "discover" or 'find' in this way. □ *I found out the train times.*

상황이 어떠하다는 것을 알게 되었음을 얘기할 때 find, find out, discover를 사용할 수 있다. □ 어린 아이는 시끄럽게 하면 주목받는다는 것을 안다... 그는 학교 전체가 그것에 대해 알고 있음을 알게 되었다... 우리는 그녀가 틀렸다는 것을 알아냈다. discover는 find보다 조금 더 격식을 갖춘 말이며, 흔히 과학 연구나 공식 조사에 관해 얘기할 때 쓴다. 예를 들면, 특정한 병의 치료법을 discover할 수 있다. 우연히 무엇을 찾아냈을 때에도 discover를 쓸 수 있다. 잘 알려진 이 꽃이 1903년에 발견되었다. 찾고 있는 어떤 것이 보이지 않으면, 그것을 find할 수 없다고 말한다. discover나 find out은 이런 식으로 쓰이지 않는다. □ 내가 길을 잃었어 – 다리가 안 보여. 어떤 사실을 알아내는 것이 쉬울 때는 누가 그 사실을 find out했다고 말할 수 있으며, 여기서 discover나 find를 쓰지는 않는다. □ 나는 기차 시간을 알아냈다.

13 PHRASE If you **find** your **way** somewhere, you successfully get there by choosing the right way to go. □ *He was an expert at finding his way, even in strange surroundings.* **14** PHRASE If something **finds its way** somewhere, it comes to that place, especially by chance. □ *It is one of the very few Michelangelos that have found their way out of Italy.* **15** to **find fault with** →see **fault**. to **find** one's **feet** →see **foot**

13 구 (길을) 찾아 가다 □ 그는 심지어 낯선 곳에서도 길 찾는 데는 명수였다. **14** 구 ~에 이르다 □ 그것은 이태리 밖으로 나온 몇 안 되는 미켈란젤로 작품 중의 하나이다.

▶**find out** **1** PHRASAL VERB If you **find** something **out**, you learn something that you did not already know, especially by making a deliberate effort to do so. □ *It makes you want to watch the next episode to find out what's going to happen.* □ *I was relieved to find out that my problems were due to a genuine disorder.* **2** PHRASAL VERB If you **find** someone **out**, you discover that they have been doing something dishonest. □ *Her face was so grave, I wondered for a moment if she'd found me out.*

1 구동사 알아내다 □ 그것을 보면 그 다음에 무슨 일이 일어나는지 알아내고 싶어서 다음 회를 보고 싶어진다. □ 나는 내 문제가 진짜 병 때문이라는 걸 알고는 안도감을 느꼈다. **2** 구동사 (비행을) 알아채다 □ 그녀의 얼굴이 너무나 심각해서 나는 순간 그녀가 혹시 내 비행을 알아챈 건 아닐까 하고 생각했다.

find|ing /faɪndɪŋ/ (**findings**) **1** N-COUNT Someone's **findings** are the information they get or the conclusions they come to as the result of an investigation or some research. □ *One of the main findings of the survey was the confusion about the facilities already in place.* **2** N-COUNT The **findings** of a court are the decisions that it reaches after a trial or an investigation. □ *The government hopes the court will announce its findings before the end of the month.* →see **laboratory, science**

1 가산명사 (연구나 실험) 결과 □ 그 설문 조사에서 얻은 주요 결론 중 하나는 이미 설치된 시설들이 혼란을 낳고 있다는 것이었다. **2** 가산명사 (법원의) 평결 □ 정부는 법원이 이 달 말 전에 그 평결을 발표하기를 바란다.

---

fine

① ADJECTIVE USES
② PUNISHMENT

---

① **fine** ◆◆◇ /faɪn/ (**finer, finest**) **1** ADJ You use **fine** to describe something that

1 형용사 아주 좋은 □ 시골 풍경을 볼 수 있는 전망이

you admire and think is very good. ❑ *There is a fine view of the countryside.* ❑ *This is a fine book.* ● **fine|ly** ADV [ADV -ed] ❑ *They are finely engineered boats.* ❷ ADJ If you say that you are **fine**, you mean that you are in good health or reasonably happy. [v-link ADJ] ❑ *Lina is fine and sends you her love and best wishes.* ❸ ADJ If you say that something is **fine**, you mean that it is satisfactory or acceptable. ❑ *The skiing is fine.* ❑ *Everything was going to be just fine.* ● ADV Fine is also an adverb. ❑ *All the instruments are working fine.* ❹ CONVENTION You say **"fine"** or **"that's fine"** to show that you do not object to an arrangement, action, or situation that has been suggested. [FORMULAE] ❑ *If competition is the best way to achieve it, then, fine.* ❺ ADJ Something that is **fine** is very delicate, narrow, or small. ❑ *The heat scorched the fine hairs on her arms.* ● **fine|ly** ADV [ADV with v] ❑ *Chop the ingredients finely and mix them together.* ❻ ADJ **Fine** objects or clothing are of good quality, delicate, and expensive. ❑ *We waited in our fine clothes.* ❼ ADJ A **fine** detail or distinction is very delicate, small, or exact. ❑ *The market likes the broad outline but is reserving judgment on the fine detail.* ● **fine|ly** ADV ❑ *They had to take the finely balanced decision to let the visit proceed.* ❽ ADJ A **fine** person is someone you consider good, moral, and worth admiring. [APPROVAL] ❑ *He was an excellent journalist and a very fine man.* ❾ ADJ When the weather is **fine**, the sun is shining and it is not raining. ❑ *He might be doing a spot of gardening if the weather is fine.*

② **fine** ◆◇◇ /faɪn/ (**fines, fining, fined**) ❶ N-COUNT A **fine** is a punishment in which a person is ordered to pay a sum of money because they have done something illegal or broken a rule. ❷ V-T If someone **is fined**, they are punished by being ordered to pay a sum of money because they have done something illegal or broken a rule. ❑ *She was fined 300 and banned from driving for one month.*

Word Partnership	*fine*의 연어
N.	fine **example**, fine **time** ① ❶
	fine **grain**, fine **hair**, fine **line**, fine **powder** ① ❺
	fine **clothes**, fine **wine** ① ❻
V.	look fine, seem fine ① ❶ ❸
	do fine, feel fine ① ❷
	charge **a** fine, impose **a** fine, pay **a** fine, receive **a** fine ② ❶

fine art (**fine arts**) ❶ N-UNCOUNT Painting and sculpture, in which objects are produced that are beautiful rather than useful, can be referred to as **fine art** or as the **fine arts**. [also N in pl] ❑ *He deals in antiques and fine art.* ❷ PHRASE If you **have got** something **down to a fine art**, you are able to do it in a very skillful or efficient way because you have had a lot of experience of doing it. ❑ *They've got fruit retailing down to a fine art. You can be sure that your pears will ripen in a day.*

fine print N-UNCOUNT In a contract or agreement, the **fine print** is the same as the **small print**.

fi|nesse /fɪnɛs/ N-UNCOUNT If you do something with **finesse**, you do it with great skill and style. ❑ *...handling momentous diplomatic challenges with tact and finesse.*

fine-tune (**fine-tunes, fine-tuning, fine-tuned**) V-T If you **fine-tune** something, you make very small and precise changes to it in order to make it as successful or effective as it possibly can be. ❑ *We do not try to fine-tune the economy on the basis of short-term predictions.*

fin|ger ◆◆◇ /fɪŋgər/ (**fingers, fingering, fingered**) ❶ N-COUNT Your **fingers** are the long thin parts at the end of each hand, sometimes also including the thumb. ❑ *She suddenly held up a small, bony finger and pointed across the room.* ❑ *She ran her fingers through her hair.* ❷ N-COUNT The **fingers** of a glove are the parts that a person's fingers fit into. ❑ *He bit the fingers of his right glove and pulled it off.* ❸ N-COUNT A **finger of** something such as smoke or land is an amount of it that is shaped rather like a finger. ❑ *...a thin finger of land that separates Pakistan from the former Soviet Union.* ❹ V-T If you **finger** something, you touch or feel it with your fingers. ❑ *He fingered the few coins in his pocket.* ❺ PHRASE If you **cross your fingers**, you put one finger on top of another and hope for good luck. If you say that someone **is keeping their fingers crossed**, you mean they are hoping for good luck. ❑ *He crossed his fingers, asking for luck for the first time in his life.* ❻ PHRASE If you say that someone did not **lay a finger on** a particular person or thing, you are emphasizing that they did not touch or harm them at all. [EMPHASIS] ❑ *I must make it clear I never laid a finger on her.* ❼ PHRASE If you say that a person does not **lift a finger** or **raise a finger** to do something, especially to help someone, you are critical of them because they do nothing. [DISAPPROVAL] ❑ *She never lifted a finger around the house.* ❽ PHRASE If you **point the finger at** someone or **point an accusing finger at** someone, you blame them or accuse them of doing wrong. ❑ *He said he wasn't pointing an accusing finger at anyone in the government or the army.* ❾ PHRASE If you **put** your **finger on** something, for example a reason or problem, you see and identify exactly what it is. ❑ *Midge couldn't quite put her finger on the reason.* ❿ to **have green fingers** →see **green**
→see **hand**

Word Partnership	*finger*의 연어
V.	poke **a** finger, run **a** finger ❶
	point **a** finger ❽

fin|ger|nail /fɪŋgərneɪl/ (**fingernails**) N-COUNT Your **fingernails** are the thin hard areas at the end of each of your fingers. →see **hand**

아주 좋다. ❑ 이것은 아주 좋은 책이다. ● 정밀하게 부사 ❑ 그것들은 정밀하게 설계된 배들이다. ❷ 형용사 잘 지내는, 건강한 ❑ 리나는 잘 지내고 있고 네게 안부 전한다. ❸ 형용사 만족스러운 ● 스키는 탈 만해. ❑ 모든 것이 매우 만족스러울 것이었다. ● 부사 잘 ❑ 모든 장비가 잘 작동하고 있다. ❹ 관용 표현 (제안에 대해) 좋다 [의례적인 표현] ❑ 그것을 얻는 데 경쟁이 최선책이라면, 그럼 좋다. ❺ 형용사 가는, 고운, 미세한 ❑ 그 열기에 그녀 팔에 난 고운 털이 그슬렸다. ❻ 형용사 고급의, 질 좋은 ❑ 우리는 고급 옷을 입고 기다렸다. ❼ 형용사 자세한, 세세한 ❑ 시장이 전반적인 개요는 좋아하지만 자세한 세부 사항에 대해서는 판단을 유보하고 있다. ● 자세하게, 세세하게 부사 ❑ 그들은 방문이 진행되도록 세심하게 균형 잡힌 결정을 내려야만 했다. ❽ 형용사 훌륭한, 인정 있는 [마음에 듦] ❑ 그는 뛰어난 저널리스트이고 매우 훌륭한 사람이었다. ❾ 형용사 (날씨가) 맑은 ❑ 날씨가 맑으면 그는 정원 가꾸기를 조금 할 것 같다.

❶ 가산명사 벌금 ❷ 타동사 벌금을 물다 ❑ 그녀는 벌금 300파운드를 물고 한 달간 운전 정지를 당했다.

❶ 불가산명사 미술품 ❑ 그는 골동품과 미술품을 취급한다. ❷ 구 능숙하게 하다 ❑ 그들이 과일 파는 솜씨는 예술이다. 당신이 산 배가 하루만 지나면 다 익겠구나 하는 확신을 갖게 할 정도니까.

불가산명사 (문서에 작은 글씨로 된) 세목

불가산명사 수완, 능숙함 ❑ 중요한 외교적인 난제를 재치와 수완 있게 다루는

타동사 세세히 조정하다 ❑ 우리는 경제를 단기 예측에 근거하여 세세히 조정하려고 하지는 않는다.

❶ 가산명사 손가락 ❑ 그녀가 갑자기 뼈가 앙상한 작은 손가락을 들어 방 건너편을 가리켰다. ❑ 그녀는 머리카락을 손가락으로 쓸어 내렸다. ❷ 가산명사 (장갑의) 손가락 부분 ❑ 그는 손가락 부분을 물어 당겨 오른쪽 장갑을 벗었다. ❸ 가산명사 손가락 모양의 것 ❑ 파키스탄과 구소련 연방 지역을 가르는 가는 손가락 모양의 땅 ❹ 타동사 만지다 ❑ 그는 주머니에 있는 동전 몇 개를 만져 보았다. ❺ 구 (행운을 비는 의미로) 손가락을 꼬다 ❑ 그는 평생 처음 행운을 비는 마음으로 손가락을 꼬아 보았다. ❻ 구 ~에 손을 대다 [강조] ❑ 나는 그녀에게 손끝 하나 대지 않았다는 것을 확실히 해야겠다. ❼ 구 (~를 돕기 위해) 손가락 하나 까딱 안하다 [탐탁잖음] ❑ 그녀는 집안에서 손끝 하나 까딱하지 않았다. ❽ 구 (~를 지목해서) 비난하다 ❑ 그는 정부나 군부에서 어느 한 사람을 꼭 집어 비난하지는 않을 것이라고 말했다. ❾ 구 (이유나 문제점을) 정확히 알다 ❑ 미쩌는 그 이유를 정확하게 알 수 없었다.

가산명사 손톱

finger|print /fɪŋgərprɪnt/ (**fingerprints, fingerprinting, fingerprinted**) **1** N-COUNT **Fingerprints** are marks made by a person's fingers which show the lines on the skin. Everyone's fingerprints are different, so they can be used to identify criminals. ❏ *The detective discovered no fewer than 35 fingerprints.* ❏ *...his fingerprint on the murder weapon.* ● PHRASE If the police **take** someone's **fingerprints**, they make that person press their fingers onto a pad covered with ink, and then onto paper, so that they know what that person's fingerprints look like. **2** V-T If someone **is fingerprinted**, the police take their fingerprints. [usu passive] ❏ *He took her to jail, where she was fingerprinted and booked.*

finger|tip /fɪŋgərtɪp/ (**fingertips**) also **finger-tip 1** N-COUNT Your **fingertips** are the ends of your fingers. ❏ *The fat and flour are rubbed together with the fingertips as for pastry.* **2** PHRASE If you say that something is **at your fingertips**, you approve of the fact that you can reach it easily or that it is easily available to you. [APPROVAL] ❏ *I had the information at my fingertips and hadn't used it.*

■ 가산명사 지문 ❏ 그 탐정은 35개나 되는 지문을 발견했다. ❏ 그 살인에 사용된 무기에 묻은 그의 지문 ● 구 지문을 채취하다 **2** 타동사 지문을 채취당하다 ❏ 그는 그녀를 교도소로 데리고 가서 지문을 채취하고 이름을 적었다.

■ 가산명사 손끝 ❏ 패스트리를 만들 때처럼 기름과 밀가루 섞은 것을 손끝으로 비댄다. **2** 구 쉽게 찾을 수 있는, 쉽게 사용할 수 있는 [마음에 듦] ❏ 나는 그 정보를 쉽게 사용할 수 있었지만 한 번도 써 보지 않았어.

---

fin|ish ♦♦◇ /fɪnɪʃ/ (**finishes, finishing, finished**) **1** V-T When you **finish** doing or dealing with something, you do or deal with the last part of it, so that there is no more for you to do or deal with. ❏ *As soon as he'd finished eating, he excused himself.* ❏ *Mr. Gould was given a standing ovation and loud cheers when he finished his speech.* ● PHRASAL VERB **Finish up** means the same as **finish**. [AM] ❏ *We waited a few minutes outside his office while he finished up his meeting.* **2** V-T When you **finish** something that you are making or producing, you reach the end of making or producing it, so that it is complete. ❏ *The consultants have been working to finish a report this week.* ● PHRASAL VERB **Finish off** and, in American English, **finish up** mean the same as **finish**. ❏ *Now she is busy finishing off a biography of Queen Caroline.* **3** V-T/V-I When something such as a course, show, or sale finishes, for example, in a race or competition, it ends. ❏ *The teaching day finishes at around 4pm.* **4** V-T/V-I You say that someone or something **finishes** a period of time or an event in a particular way to indicate what the final situation was like. You can also say that a period of time or an event **finishes** in a particular way. ❏ *The two of them finished by kissing each other goodbye.* ❏ *The evening finished with the welcoming of three new members.* **5** V-I If someone **finishes** second, for example, in a race or competition, they are in second place at the end of the race or competition. ❏ *He finished second in the championship four years in a row.* **6** V-I To **finish** means to reach the end of saying something. ❏ *Her eyes flashed, but he held up a hand. "Let me finish."* **7** N-SING The **finish** of something is the end of it or the last part of it. [the N, with poss] ❏ *I intend to continue it and see the job through to the finish.* **8** N-COUNT The **finish** of a race is the end of it. ❏ *Win a trip to see the finish of the Tour de France!* **9** N-COUNT If the surface of something that has been made has a particular kind of **finish**, it has the appearance or texture mentioned. ❏ *The finish and workmanship of the woodwork was excellent.* **10**→see also **finished 11** PHRASE If you add **the finishing touches** to something, you add or do the last things that are necessary to complete it. ❏ *Right up until the last minute, workers were still putting the finishing touches on the pavilions.*

■ 타동사 끝내다 ❏ 그는 식사를 끝내자마자 자리를 떴다. ❏ 고울드 씨가 연설을 끝내자 모두 기립하여 우레와 같은 박수를 보냈다. ● 구동사 끝내다 [미국영어] ❏ 그가 회의를 끝낼 동안 우리는 사무실 밖에서 몇 분 동안 기다렸다. **2** 타동사 마무리하다 ❏ 그 자문 위원들은 이번 주에 보고서를 마무리하기 위해 작업을 하고 있었다. ● 구동사 마무리하다 ❏ 그녀는 지금 캐롤라인 여왕의 전기문을 마무리하느라 바쁘다. **3** 타동사/자동사 끝나다 ❏ 수업이 오후 4시경에 끝난다. **4** 타동사/자동사 (하는 것으로) 끝나다 ❏ 그 둘이 작별 키스를 하는 것으로 끝이 났다. ❏ 그날 밤은 세 명의 신입 회원을 환영하면서 끝났다. **5** 자동사 (결승점에) 닿다 ❏ 그는 4년 연속 그 선수권 대회에서 2등을 했다. **6** 자동사 (말을) 마무리 짓다 ❏ 그녀가 눈을 번득였지만, 그가 손을 들고서 "제 말을 끝까지 들어보세요."라고 말했다. **7** 단수명사 마지막 ❏ 나는 그 일을 지속적으로 해서 마지막까지 지켜볼 작정이다. **8** 가산명사 마지막, 끝 ❏ 여행 공모에 당첨되면 '뚜르 드 프랑스' 여행 상품의 마지막 지역까지 경험할 수 있습니다. **9** 가산명사 마무리 ❏ 그 목제품의 마무리와 세공이 뛰어났다. **11** 구 마무리 손질 ❏ 마지막 순간까지 여전히 일꾼들은 그 전시관에 마무리 손질을 하고 있었다.

▶**finish off** PHRASAL VERB If you **finish off** something that you have been eating or drinking, you eat or drink the last part of it with the result that there is none left. ❏ *Kelly finished off his coffee.* **2** PHRASAL VERB If someone **finishes off** a person or thing that is already badly injured or damaged, they kill or destroy them. ❏ *They meant to finish her off, swiftly and without mercy.* **3**→see finish 2

■ 구동사 마저 먹다, 마저 마시다 ❏ 켈리는 커피를 마저 마셨다. **2** 구동사 없애 버리다 ❏ 그들은 그녀를 가차 없이 신속하게 없애 버리려 했다.

▶**finish up** PHRASAL VERB If you **finish up** in a particular place or situation, you are in that place or situation after doing or experiencing several things. ❏ *They had met by chance at university and finished up getting married.* **2** PHRASAL VERB If you **finish up** something that you have been eating or drinking, you eat or drink the last part of it. ❏ *Finish up your drinks now, please.* **3**→see also finish 1, 2

■ 구동사 마침내 하다 ❏ 그들은 대학에서 우연히 만나 마침내 결혼까지 했다. **2** 구동사 마저 마시다, 마저 먹다 ❏ 음료수를 지금 마저 마셔요.

▶**finish with** PHRASAL VERB If you **finish with** someone or something, you stop dealing with them, being involved with them, or being interested in them. ❏ *My boyfriend was threatening to finish with me.*

구동사 절교하다, 끝을 내다 ❏ 내 남자 친구가 나와 절교하겠다고 위협했다.

fin|ished /fɪnɪʃt/ **1** ADJ Someone who is **finished with** something is no longer doing it or dealing with it or is no longer interested in it. [v-link ADJ with n] ❏ *One suspects he will be finished with boxing.* **2** ADJ Something that is **finished** no longer exists or is no longer happening. [v-link ADJ n] ❏ *I go back on the dole when the shooting season's finished.* **3** ADJ Someone or something that is **finished** is no longer important, powerful, or effective. [v-link ADJ n] ❏ *Her power over me is finished.*

■ 형용사 더 이상 하지 않는 ❏ 사람들은 그가 더 이상 권투를 하지 않을 것이라고 생각한다. **2** 형용사 끝난 ❏ 사냥철이 끝나면 나는 다시 실업 수당을 받게 된다. **3** 형용사 끝장난 ❏ 그녀는 이제 더 이상 내게 힘이 없다.

fi|nite /faɪnaɪt/ ADJ Something that is **finite** has a definite fixed size or extent. [FORMAL] ❏ *...a finite set of elements.* ❏ *Only a finite number of situations can arise.*

형용사 한정된 [격식체] ❏ 한정된 요소들 ❏ 한정된 몇 가지 상황들만이 발생할 수 있다.

fir /fɜːr/ (**firs**) N-VAR A **fir** or a **fir tree** is a tall evergreen tree that has thin needle-like leaves.

가산명사 또는 불가산명사 전나무

---

fire

① BURNING, HEAT, OR ENTHUSIASM
② SHOOTING OR ATTACKING
③ DISMISSAL

---

① **fire** ♦♦♦ /faɪər/ (**fires, firing, fired**) →Please look at category ⑪ to see if the expression you are looking for is shown under another headword. ■ N-UNCOUNT **Fire** is the hot, bright flames produced by things that are burning. ❑ *They saw a big flash and a huge ball of fire reaching hundreds of feet into the sky.* ② N-VAR A **fire** or **fire** is an occurrence of uncontrolled burning which destroys buildings, forests, or other things. ❑ *87 people died in a fire at the Happy Land Social Club.* ❑ *A forest fire is sweeping across portions of north Maine this evening.* ③ N-COUNT A **fire** is a burning pile of wood, coal, or other fuel that you make, for example to use for heat, light, or cooking. ❑ *There was a fire in the grate.* ④ N-COUNT A **fire** is a device that uses electricity or gas to give out heat and warm a room. [mainly BRIT; AM usually **heater**] ❑ *The gas fire was still alight.* ⑤ V-T When a pot or clay object **is fired**, it is heated at a high temperature in a special oven, as part of the process of making it. ❑ *After the pot is dipped in this mixture, it is fired.* ⑥ V-I When the engine of a motor vehicle **fires**, an electrical spark is produced which causes the fuel to burn and the engine to work. ❑ *The engine fired and we moved off.* ⑦ V-T If you **fire** someone **with** enthusiasm, you make them feel very enthusiastic. If you **fire** someone's imagination, you make them feel interested and excited. ❑ *...the potential to fire the imagination of an entire generation.* ❑ *It was Allen who fired this rivalry with real passion.* ⑧ PHRASE If an object or substance **catches fire**, it starts burning. ❑ *My home catches fire and everything is destroyed.* ⑨ PHRASE If something is **on fire**, it is burning and being damaged or destroyed by an uncontrolled fire. ❑ *The captain radioed that the ship was on fire.* ⑩ PHRASE If you **set fire to** something or if you **set** it **on fire**, you start it burning in order to damage or destroy it. ❑ *They set fire to vehicles outside that building.* ⑪ to **have irons on the fire** →see **iron**. **like a house on fire** →see **house**. **there's no smoke without fire** →see **smoke**
→see **pottery**
→see Word Web: **fire**

■ 불가산명사 불 ❑ 그들은 강한 섬광과 거대한 불덩이가 수백 피트 하늘 높이 치솟는 것을 보았다. ② 가산명사 또는 불가산명사 화재, 불 ❑ 87명이 '해피 랜드 소셜 클럽' 화재로 죽었다. ❑ 오늘 저녁 산불이 메인 주 북쪽 지역을 삼키고 있다. ③ 가산명사 (난방·요리용) 불 ❑ 벽난로에서는 불이 타고 있었다. ④ 가산명사 난방기 [주로 영국영어; 미국영어 대개 heater] ❑ 가스 난방기가 아직도 켜져 있었다. ⑤ 타동사 (가마 속에서) 불에 구워지다 ❑ 그 옹기를 이 혼합액에 잠깐 담갔다가 가마에서 굽는다. ⑥ 자동사 시동이 걸리다 ❑ 엔진에 시동이 걸려 우리는 떠났다. ⑦ 타동사 흥미를 느끼도록 만들다, 불을 붙이다 ❑ 모든 세대의 상상력에 불을 붙일 수 있는 가능성 ❑ 진정한 열정으로 이 경쟁에 불을 붙였던 사람이 바로 알렌이었다. ⑧ 구 불이 나다 ❑ 우리 집에 불이 나서 모든 것이 다 타고 있다. ⑨ 구 불이 나서 ❑ 선장이 배에 불이 났다고 무선 연락을 했다. ⑩ 구 ～에 불을 지르다 ❑ 그들이 그 건물 밖에 세워 둔 차량에 불을 질렀다.

② **fire** ♦♦♦ /faɪər/ (**fires, firing, fired**) →Please look at category ⑪ to see if the expression you are looking for is shown under another headword. ■ V-T/V-I If someone **fires** a gun or a bullet, or if they **fire**, a bullet is sent from a gun that they are using. ❑ *Seven people were wounded when soldiers fired rubber bullets to disperse crowds.* ● **firing** N-UNCOUNT ❑ *The firing continued even while the protestors were fleeing.* ② N-UNCOUNT You can use **fire** to refer to the shots fired from a gun or guns. ❑ *His car was raked with fire from automatic weapons.* ③ V-T If you **fire** an arrow, you send it from a bow. ❑ *He fired an arrow into a clearing in the forest.* ④ V-T If you **fire** questions at someone, you ask them a lot of questions very quickly, one after another. ❑ *They were bombarded by more than 100 representatives firing questions on pollution.* ⑤ PHRASE If someone **holds** their **fire** or **holds fire**, they stop shooting or they wait before they start shooting. ❑ *Devereux ordered his men to hold their fire until the ships got closer.* ⑥ PHRASE If you are in the **line of fire**, you are in a position where someone is aiming their gun at you. If you move into their **line of fire**, you move into a position between them and the thing they were aiming at. ❑ *He cheerfully blows away any bad guy stupid enough to get in his line of fire.* ⑦ PHRASE If you **open fire on** someone, you start shooting at them. ❑ *Then without warning, the troops opened fire on the crowd.* ⑧ PHRASE If you **return fire** or you **return** someone's **fire**, you shoot back at someone who has shot at you. ❑ *The soldiers returned fire after being attacked.* ⑨ PHRASE If you come **under fire** or are **under fire**, someone starts shooting at you. ❑ *The Belgians fell back as the infantry came under fire.* ⑩ PHRASE If you come **under fire from** someone or are **under fire**, they criticize you strongly. ❑ *The president's plan first came under fire from critics who said he hadn't included enough spending cuts.* ⑪ to **fire from the hip** →see **hip**

■ 타동사/자동사 발포하다 ❑ 군중을 해산시키려고 군인들이 고무탄을 발포했을 때 일곱 사람이 부상당했다. ● 발포 불가산명사 ❑ 시위자들이 도망치는 와중에도 발포는 계속되었다. ② 불가산명사 발포 ❑ 그의 차에 대고 자동화기로 연달아 마구 발포했다. ③ 타동사 (화살을) 쏘다 ❑ 그가 숲 속 개간지로 화살을 쏘았다. ④ 타동사 (질문을) 퍼붓다 ❑ 그들은 100명이 넘는 대표자들이 오염에 관해 퍼붓는 질문 공세를 받았다. ⑤ 구 발포를 멈추다; 발포할 때를 기다리다 ❑ 데브로가 병사들에게 선박들이 더 가까이 올 때까지 발포하지 말고 기다리도록 지시했다. ⑥ 구 사정거리 ❑ 그는 어리석게도 자신의 사정거리 안에 들어오는 악당은 누구라도 기꺼이 사살한다. ⑦ 구 사격을 개시하다 ❑ 그리고서 아무런 경고도 없이 군대가 군중을 향해 사격을 개시했다. ⑧ 구 응사하다 ❑ 군인들이 공격받은 후 응사했다. ⑨ 구 포화를 받다, 피격당하다 ❑ 벨기에 인들은 보병대가 포화를 받자 후퇴했다. ⑩ 구 맹비난을 받고 ❑ 처음에는 대통령의 계획이 비평가들로부터 지출 삭감이 충분하지 않다며 심한 비난을 받았다.

③ **fire** /faɪər/ (**fires, firing, fired**) V-T If an employer **fires** you, they dismiss you from your job. ❑ *If he hadn't been so good at the rest of his job, I probably would have fired him.* ● **firing** N-COUNT ❑ *There was yet another round of firings.*

타동사 해고하다 ❑ 그가 나머지 직무에 능숙하지 않았다면 난 아마 그를 해고했을 거야. ● 발포 가산명사 ❑ 한 차례 더 발포가 있었다.

fire alarm (**fire alarms**) N-COUNT A **fire alarm** is a device that makes a noise, for example with a bell, to warn people when there is a fire. ❑ *The smoke sets off the fire alarm.*

가산명사 화재경보기 ❑ 연기를 감지하면 화재경보기가 울린다.

fire|arm /faɪərɑːrm/ (**firearms**) N-COUNT **Firearms** are guns. [FORMAL] ❑ *He was also charged with illegal possession of firearms.* →see **war**

가산명사 총기 [격식체] ❑ 그는 불법 총기 소지 혐의도 함께 받고 있었다.

Word Web · fire

A single **match**, a **campfire**, or even a bolt of lightning can **spark** a **wildfire**. Wildfires race across grasslands and **burn down** forests. Huge **firestorms** can **burn** out of control for days. They cause death and destruction. However, some ecosystems depend on fire. Once the fire passes, the **smoke** clears, the **smoldering embers** cool, and the **ash** settles. Then the cycle of life begins again. Humans have learned to use fire. The **heat** cooks our food. People build fires in **fireplaces** and **wood** stoves. The **flames** warm our hands. And before electricity, the **glow** of **candlelight** lit our homes.

fire bri|gade (**fire brigades**) N-COUNT-COLL The **fire brigade** is an organization which has the job of putting out fires; used especially to refer to the people who actually fight the fires. [mainly BRIT] ❏ *Get everyone out and call the fire brigade.*

가산명사-집합 소방대 [주로 영국영어] ❏ 모든 사람을 내보내고 소방대를 불러라.

fire de|part|ment (**fire departments**) N-COUNT-COLL The **fire department** is an organization which has the job of putting out fires. [AM; BRIT **fire service**] [usu the N]

가산명사-집합 소방서 [미국영어; 영국영어 fire service]

fire en|gine (**fire engines**) N-COUNT A **fire engine** is a large vehicle which carries fire fighters and equipment for putting out fires.

가산명사 소방차

fire es|cape (**fire escapes**) also **fire-escape** N-COUNT A **fire escape** is a metal staircase on the outside of a building, which can be used to escape from the building if there is a fire.

가산명사 (화재 대비용) 비상계단

fire ex|tin|guish|er (**fire extinguishers**) also **fire-extinguisher** N-COUNT A **fire extinguisher** is a metal cylinder which contains water or chemicals at high pressure which can put out fires.

가산명사 소화기

fire fight|er (**fire fighters**) also **fire-fighter** N-COUNT **Fire fighters** are people whose job is to put out fires.

가산명사 소방관

fire|man /faɪərmən/ (**firemen**) N-COUNT A **fireman** is a person, usually a man, whose job is to put out fires.

가산명사 소방관

fire|place /faɪərpleɪs/ (**fireplaces**) N-COUNT In a room, the **fireplace** is the place where a fire can be lit and the area on the wall and floor surrounding this place. ❏ *In the evenings, we gathered around the fireplace and talked in hushed whispers.* →see **fire**

가산명사 벽난로 ❏ 저녁이면 벽난로 주위에 모여서 소곤소곤 얘기를 나누었다.

fire|power /faɪərpaʊər/ N-UNCOUNT The **firepower** of an army, ship, tank, or aircraft is the amount of ammunition it can fire. ❏ *The U.S. also had superior firepower.*

불가산명사 (군대·무기의) 화력 ❏ 미국 역시 우세한 화력을 지니고 있었다.

fire truck (**fire trucks**) N-COUNT A **fire truck** is a large vehicle which carries firefighters and equipment for putting out fires. [AM, AUSTRALIAN; BRIT usually **fire engine**]

가산명사 소방차 [미국영어, 호주영어; 영국영어 대개 fire engine]

fire|wall /faɪərwɔl/ (**firewalls**) N-COUNT A **firewall** is a computer system or program that automatically prevents an unauthorized person from gaining access to a computer when it is connected to a network such as the Internet. [COMPUTING] ❏ *New technology should provide a secure firewall against hackers.* →see **Internet**

가산명사 (컴퓨터) 접속 보안 장치 [컴퓨터] ❏ 신기술이 해커의 침입 우려가 없는 보안 장치를 제공해야 한다.

fire|wood /faɪərwʊd/ N-UNCOUNT **Firewood** is wood that has been cut into pieces so that it can be burned on a fire. ❏ *Young Geoffrey made money by chopping and selling firewood.*

불가산명사 장작 ❏ 어린 제프리는 장작을 패서 내다 파는 것으로 돈을 벌었다.

fire|work /faɪərwɜrk/ (**fireworks**) N-COUNT **Fireworks** are small objects that are lit to entertain people on special occasions. They contain chemicals and burn brightly or attractively, often with a loud noise, when you light them. ❏ *Berlin people drank champagne, set off fireworks, and tooted their car horns.* →see Word Web: **fireworks**

가산명사 폭죽 ❏ 베를린 사람들은 샴페인을 마시고 폭죽을 쏘아 올리고 자동차 경적을 울려 댔다.

firm ♦♦♦ /fɜrm/ (**firms, firmer, firmest**) ◗ N-COUNT A **firm** is an organization which sells or produces something or which provides a service which people pay for. ❏ *The firm's employees were expecting large bonuses.* ◗ ADJ If something is **firm**, it does not change much in shape when it is pressed but is not completely hard. ❏ *Fruit should be firm and in excellent condition.* ◗ ADJ If something is **firm**, it does not shake or move when you put weight or pressure on it, because it is strongly made or securely fastened. ❏ *If you have to climb up, use a firm platform or a sturdy ladder.* ● **firm|ly** ADV ❏ *The front door is locked and all the windows are firmly shut.* ◗ ADJ If someone's grip is **firm** or if they perform a physical action in a **firm** way, they do it with quite a lot of force or pressure but also in a controlled way. ❏ *The quick handshake was firm and cool.* ● **firm|ly** ADV [ADV after v] ❏ *She held me firmly by the elbow and led me to my aisle seat.* ◗ ADJ If you describe someone as **firm**, you mean they behave in a way that shows that they are not going to change their mind, or that they are the person who is in control. ❏ *She had to be firm with him. "I don't want to see you again."* ● **firm|ly** ADV [ADV with v] ❏ *"A good night's sleep is what you want," he said firmly.* ◗ ADJ A **firm** decision or opinion is definite and unlikely to change. ❏ *He made a firm decision to leave Fort Multry by boat.* ● **firm|ly** ADV ❏ *Political values and opinions are firmly held, and can be slow to change.* ◗ ADJ **Firm** evidence or information is based on facts and so is likely to be true. [ADJ n] ❏ *This man may have killed others but unfortunately we have no firm evidence.* ◗ ADJ You use **firm** to describe control or a basis or position when it is strong and unlikely to be ended or removed. ❏ *Although the Yakutians are a minority, they have firm control of the territory.* ● **firm|ly** ADV ❏ *This tradition is also firmly rooted in the past.* ◗ PHRASE If someone **stands**

◗ 가산명사 회사 ❏ 그 회사 직원들은 두둑한 보너스를 바라고 있었다. ◗ 형용사 단단한 ❏ 과일이 단단하고 보존 상태가 최상이어야 한다. ◗ 형용사 단단한 ❏ 높은 곳에 올라가야 한다면 탄탄한 발판이나 튼튼한 사다리를 이용해라. ● 굳게 부사 ❏ 정문은 잠기고 창문은 모두 굳게 닫혀 있다. ◗ 형용사 단호한 ❏ 짧은 악수는 단호하고 냉담했다. ● 꼭 부사 ❏ 그녀가 나의 팔꿈치를 꼭 붙들고 통로 쪽 좌석으로 이끌었다. ◗ 형용사 단호한 ❏ 그녀는 그에게 단호해야 했다. "다시는 만나고 싶지 않아요." ● 단호히 부사 ❏ "하룻밤 잘 자는 것이 바로 네게 필요한 것이야."라고 그가 단호히 말했다. ◗ 형용사 확고한 ❏ 그는 배를 타고 '포트 멀트리'를 떠나기로 확고한 결정을 내렸다. ● 확고하게 부사 ❏ 정치적 가치관과 견해가 확고해서, 좀처럼 변하지 않을 수 있다. ◗ 형용사 확실한 ❏ 이 남자가 다른 사람들을 죽였을 수도 있지만 불행히도 우리에게는 확실한 증거가 없다. ◗ 형용사 굳건한 ❏ 야쿠시아 인이 소수 민족이기는 하지만, 그들의 영토를 굳건하게 지배하고 있다. ● 단단히 부사 ❏ 이 전통 역시 과거에 단단히 뿌리박고 있다. ◗ 구 단호한 태도를 취하다 ❏ 평의회가 연속되는 시위에 대해 단호한 태도를 취하고 있다.

Word Web | fireworks

Fireworks originated in China over a thousand years ago. Historians believe that the discovery was made by **alchemists** who were looking for the elixir of life. They heated **sulfur, potassium nitrate, charcoal**, and **arsenic** together and the mixture **exploded**. It produced an extremely hot, bright fire. Later they mixed these **chemicals** in a hollow bamboo tube and threw it in the fire. Thus the **firecracker** was born. Marco Polo brought firecrackers to Europe from the Orient in 1292. Soon the Italians began experimenting with ways of producing elaborate, colorful fireworks displays. This launched the era of modern **pyrotechnics**.

firm, they refuse to change their mind about something. ❑ *The council is standing firm against the barrage of protest.*

Thesaurus	*firm*의 참조어
N.	business, company, enterprise, organization ■
ADJ.	dense, hard, sturdy ②

first ♦♦♦ /fɜrst/ ■ ORD The **first** thing, person, event, or period of time is the one that happens or comes before all the others of the same kind. ❑ *She lost 16 pounds in the first month of her diet.* ● PRON **First** is also a pronoun. ❑ *The second paragraph startled me even more than the first.* ② ADV If you do something **first**, you do it before anyone else does, or before you do anything else. ❑ *I do not remember who spoke first, but we all expressed the same opinion.* ❑ *First, tell me what you think of my products.* ③ ORD When something happens or is done for the **first** time, it has never happened or been done before. ❑ *This is the first time she has experienced disappointment.* ● ADV **First** is also an adverb. [ADV with v] ❑ *Anne and Steve got engaged two years after they had first started going out.* ④ N-SING An event that is described as a **first** has never happened before and is important or exciting. ❑ *It is a first for New York. An outdoor exhibition of Fernando Botero's sculpture on Park Avenue.* ⑤ PRON The **first** you hear of something or the **first** you know about it is the time when you first become aware of it. [the PRON that] ❑ *We heard it on the TV last night – that was the first we heard of it.* ⑥ ADV You use **first** when you are talking about what happens in the early part of an event or experience, in contrast to what happens later. [ADV before v] ❑ *When he first came home he wouldn't say anything about what he'd been doing.* ● ORD **First** is also an ordinal. ❑ *She told him that her first reaction was disgust.* ⑦ ADV In order to emphasize your determination not to do a particular thing, you can say that rather than do it, you would do something else **first**. [EMPHASIS] [ADV after v] ❑ *Marry that fat son of a fat cattle dealer? She would die first!* ⑧ ORD The **first** thing, person, or place in a line is the one that is nearest to you or nearest to the front. ❑ *Before him, in the first row, sat the President.* ⑨ ORD You use **first** to refer to the best or most important thing or person of a particular kind. ❑ *The first duty of any government must be to protect the interests of the taxpayers.* ⑩ ORD **First** is used in the title of the job or position of someone who has a higher rank than anyone else with the same basic job title. ❑ *...the First Lord of the Admiralty.* ⑪ PHRASE You use **first of all** to introduce the first of a number of things that you want to say. ❑ *The cut in the interest rates has not had very much impact in California for two reasons. First of all, banks are still afraid to loan.* ⑫ PHRASE You use **at first** when you are talking about what happens in the early stages of an event or experience, or just after something else has happened, in contrast to what happens later. ❑ *At first, he seemed surprised by my questions.* ⑬ PHRASE If you say that someone or something **comes first** for a particular person, you mean they treat or consider that person or thing as more important than anything else. ❑ *There's no time for boyfriends, my career comes first.* ⑭ PHRASE If you learn or experience something **at first hand**, you experience it yourself or learn it directly rather than being told about it by other people. ❑ *He arrived in Natal to see at first hand the effects of the recent heavy fighting.* ⑮ PHRASE If you say that you **do not know the first thing about** something, you are emphasizing that you know absolutely nothing about it. [EMPHASIS] ❑ *You don't know the first thing about farming.* ⑯ PHRASE If you **put** someone or something **first**, you treat or consider them as more important than anything else. ❑ *Somebody has to think for the child and put him first.* ⑰ **first and foremost** →see **foremost**

first aid N-UNCOUNT **First aid** is simple medical treatment given as soon as possible to a person who is injured or who suddenly becomes ill. ❑ *There are many emergencies which need prompt first aid treatment.*

first-class also **first class** ■ ADJ If you describe something or someone as **first-class**, you mean that they are extremely good and of the highest quality. ❑ *The food was first-class.* ② ADJ You use **first-class** to describe something that is in the group that is considered to be of the highest standard. [ADJ n] ❑ *He officially announced his retirement from first-class cricket yesterday.* ③ ADJ **First-class** accommodations on a train, airplane, or ship are the best and most expensive type of accommodations. [ADJ n] ❑ *He won himself two first-class tickets to fly to Dublin.* ● ADV **First-class** is also an adverb. [ADV after v] ❑ *She had never flown first class before.* ● N-UNCOUNT **First-class** is the first-class accommodations on a train, airplane, or ship. ❑ *He paid for and was assigned a cabin in first class.* ④ ADJ In the United States, **first-class** postage is the type of postage that is used for sending letters and postcards. In Britain, **first-class** postage is the quicker and more expensive type of postage. [ADJ n] ❑ *Two first-class stamps, please.* ● ADV **First-class** is also an adverb. [mainly BRIT] [ADV after v] ❑ *It took six days to arrive despite being posted first-class.*

first floor (**first floors**) ■ N-COUNT The **first floor** of a building is the one at ground level. [AM; BRIT **ground floor**] ② N-COUNT The **first floor** of a building is the floor immediately above the one at ground level. [BRIT; AM **second floor**]

first hand also **first-hand, firsthand** ■ ADJ **First hand** information or experience is gained or learned directly, rather than from other people or from books. [ADJ n] ❑ *School trips give children firsthand experience not available in the classroom.* ● ADV **First-hand** is also an adverb. [ADV after v] ❑ *We've been through Germany and seen first-hand what's happening there.* ② **at first hand** →see **first**

first|ly /fɜrstli/ ADV You use **firstly** in speech or writing when you want to give a reason, make a point, or mention an item that will be followed by others connected with it. [ADV with cl/group] ❑ *The programme will be now seven years behind schedule as a result, firstly of increased costs, then of technical problems.*

First Min|is|ter (**First Ministers**) N-COUNT In the Scottish Assembly and the Northern Ireland Assembly, the **First Minister** is the leader of the ruling party.

■ 서수 첫 번째의, 처음의 ❑ 그녀는 다이어트를 시작한 첫 번째 달에 16 파운드를 뺐다. ❑ 처음 내리는 눈송이가 몇 개 ● 대명사 첫 번째 것 ❑ 두 번째 단락은 첫 번 것보다도 훨씬 더 놀라웠다. ② 부사 맨 먼저, 우선 ❑ 누가 맨 먼저 말했는지 기억나지 않지만 우리는 전부 같은 의견을 표명했다. ❑ 우선 내 작품을 어떻게 생각하는지 말해 줘. ③ 서수 처음의 ❑ 그녀가 실망감을 겪은 것은 이번이 처음이다. ● 부사 처음으로 ❑ 앤과 스티브는 처음으로 데이트한 지 2년 만에 약혼했다. ④ 단수명사 처음 ❑ 뉴욕에서 처음 있는 일로서, '파크 애비뉴에서 페르난도 보테로 조각품 야외 전시회가 열린다. ⑤ 대명사 처음 ❑ 우리는 어젯밤에 텔레비전에서 그 소식을 들었는데, 그것이 처음으로 듣는 것이었다. ⑥ 부사 처음에는 ❑ 그가 처음 집에 왔을 때에는 자신이 무엇을 하고 지냈는지 전혀 얘기하려 하지 않았다. ● 서수 첫째의 ❑ 그녀가 자신의 첫 반응은 메스꺼움이다고 그에게 말했다. ⑦ 부사 차라리 [강조] ❑ 뚱뚱한 소 장수의 그 뚱뚱한 아들과 결혼을 하라구? 그녀는 차라리 죽겠다고 할 걸! ⑧ 서수 첫 번째의 ❑ 그 사람의 앞쪽 첫 번째 줄에 대통령이 앉았다. ⑨ 서수 가장 중요한, 맨 첫 ❑ 어느 정부이든 가장 중요한 임무는 납세자들의 이익을 보호하는 것이어야만 한다. ⑩ 서수 수석의 ❑ 해군 본부 위원회 수석 위원 ⑪ 구 무엇보다도 ❑ 금리 삭감이 캘리포니아에서 별다른 영향을 미치지 못한 데는 두 가지 이유가 있다. 무엇보다도, 은행이 여전히 대출해 주기를 꺼린다. ⑫ 구 처음에는 ❑ 처음에는 그가 내 질문을 받고 놀라는 듯 보였다. ⑬ 구 최우선이다 ❑ 남자 친구 사귈 시간은 없어, 내 일이 최우선이야. ⑭ 구 직접 ❑ 그는 최근의 격렬한 교전 결과를 직접 보기 위해 나탈에 도착했다. ⑮ 구 ~에 대해 아무것도 모르다 [강조] ❑ 넌 농사에 대해 아무것도 모르는구나. ⑯ 구 가장 중시하다 ❑ 누군가는 그 아이만을 생각하고 가장 중시해야 한다.

불가산명사 응급 처치 ❑ 신속한 응급 처치를 해야 할 긴박한 경우가 많이 있다.

■ 형용사 최고급의 ❑ 그 음식은 최고급이었다. ② 형용사 우수한, 일급의 ❑ 그가 어제 일급 크리켓에서 은퇴한다고 공식적으로 발표했다. ③ 형용사 일등석의 ❑ 그가 더블린 행 비행기 일등석 티켓 두 장을 땄다. ● 부사 일등석으로 ❑ 그녀는 전에 비행기 일등석에 타 본 적이 없었다. ● 불가산명사 일등석 ❑ 그는 돈을 지불하고 일등칸을 할당받았다. ④ 형용사 (영국 우편) 빠른 배달의, (미국 우편) 1종의 ❑ 1종 우편 우표 두 장 주세요. ● 부사 1종 우편으로 [주로 영국영어] ❑ 1종 우편으로 부쳤는데도 엿새나 걸려서 도착했다.

■ 가산명사 1층 [미국영어; 영국영어 ground floor] ② 가산명사 (영국에서) 2층 [영국영어; 미국영어 second floor]

■ 형용사 직접 얻은 ❑ 수학여행을 통해 어린이들은 교실에서 얻을 수 없는 직접 체험을 한다. ● 부사 직접 ❑ 우리는 독일을 거쳐 왔고 거기서 일어나는 일을 직접 목격했다.

부사 첫째로 ❑ 결과적으로 그 프로그램이 현재 예정보다 칠 년 늦어질 것인데, 첫째로는 경비 증가와, 그 다음으로는 기술적 문제에 원인이 있다.

가산명사 (스코틀랜드 의회와 북아일랜드 의회의) 여당 대표

first name (**first names**) N-COUNT Your **first name** is the first of the names that were given to you when you were born. You can also refer to all of your names except your surname as your **first names**. ❑ *Her first name was Mary. I don't know what her surname was.*

가산명사 이름 ❑ 그녀의 이름은 메리였어. 그녀의 성은 잘 모르겠어.

first-rate also **first rate** ADJ If you say that something or someone is **first-rate**, you mean that they are extremely good and of the highest quality. [APPROVAL] ❑ *People who used his service knew they were dealing with a first-rate professional.*

형용사 일류의 [마음에 듦] ❑ 그의 서비스를 받는 사람들은 자신이 일류 전문가와 거래하고 있다는 것을 알았다.

First Secretary (**First Secretaries**) N-COUNT The First Secretary of the Welsh Assembly is the leader of the ruling party.

가산명사 (웨일스 의회의) 여당 대표

fis|cal ◆◇◇ /fɪskəl/ ADJ Fiscal is used to describe something that relates to government money or public money, especially taxes. [ADJ n] ❑ *...in 1987, when the government tightened fiscal policy.*

형용사 국고의, 회계의 ❑ 정부가 재정 긴축 정책을 폈던 해인 1987년에

fis|cal year (**fiscal years**) N-COUNT The **fiscal year** is the same as the **financial year**. [BUSINESS] ❑ *...the budget for the coming fiscal year.*

가산명사 회계 연도 [경제] ❑ 차기 회계 연도 예산

fish ◆◆◇ /fɪʃ/ (**fishes, fishing, fished**)

The form **fish** is usually used for the plural, but **fishes** can also be used.

fish를 대개 복수로 쓰지만 fishes도 쓸 수 있다.

1 N-COUNT A **fish** is a creature that lives in water and has a tail and fins. There are many different kinds of fish. ❑ *An expert angler was casting his line and catching a fish every time.* **2** N-UNCOUNT **Fish** is the flesh of a fish eaten as food. ❑ *Does dry white wine go best with fish?* **3** V-I If you **fish**, you try to catch fish, either for food or as a form of sport or recreation. ❑ *Brian remembers learning to fish in the River Cam.* **4** V-I If you say that someone is **fishing for** information or praise, you disapprove of the fact that they are trying to get it from someone in an indirect way. [DISAPPROVAL] ❑ *He didn't want to create the impression that he was fishing for information.* **5** →see also **fishing**
→see **pet, shark**

1 가산명사 물고기 ❑ 노련한 낚시꾼이 낚싯줄을 던지고 그때마다 물고기를 낚아 올리고 있었다. **2** 불가산명사 생선 ❑ 달지 않은 백포도주가 생선과 가장 잘 어울릴까요? **3** 자동사 낚시하다 ❑ 브라이언은 캠 강에서 낚시질을 배웠다고 기억한다. **4** 자동사 (정보나 찬사를) 캐내려고 하다 [탐탁찮음] ❑ 그는 자신이 정보를 캐내려 한다는 인상을 주고 싶지 않았다.

fisher|man /fɪʃərmən/ (**fishermen**) N-COUNT A **fisherman** is a person who catches fish as a job or for sport. ❑ *The Algarve is a paradise for fishermen whether river anglers or deep-sea fishermen.*

가산명사 어부 ❑ 알가르베는 강 낚시꾼이건 원양 어업을 하는 어부이건 간에 상관없이 어부들의 천국이다.

fish|ery /fɪʃəri/ (**fisheries**) **1** N-COUNT **Fisheries** are areas of the sea where fish are caught in large quantities for commercial purposes. ❑ *...the fisheries off Newfoundland.* **2** N-COUNT A **fishery** is a place where fish are bred and reared.

1 가산명사 어장 ❑ 뉴펀들랜드 어장 **2** 가산명사 양어장, 양식장

fish|ing ◆◇◇ /fɪʃɪŋ/ N-UNCOUNT **Fishing** is the sport, hobby, or business of catching fish. ❑ *Despite the poor weather the fishing has been pretty good.*

불가산명사 낚시 ❑ 날씨가 좋지 않았음에도 불구하고 낚시는 제법 잘 됐다.

fist /fɪst/ (**fists**) N-COUNT Your hand is referred to as your **fist** when you have bent your fingers in toward the palm in order to hit someone, to make an angry gesture, or to hold something. ❑ *Angry protestors with clenched fists shouted their defiance.*

가산명사 주먹 ❑ 주먹을 꼭 쥔 성난 시위자들이 소리치며 저항했다.

---

fit

① BEING RIGHT OR GOING IN THE RIGHT PLACE
② HEALTHY
③ UNCONTROLLABLE MOVEMENTS OR EMOTIONS

---

① **fit** ◆◆◇ /fɪt/ (**fits, fitting, fitted**)

In American English the form **fit** is used in the present tense and sometimes also as the past tense and past participle of the verb.

미국영어에서는 fit을 현재 시제로 쓰는데 가끔 과거 및 과거 분사로도 쓴다.

→Please look at category **13** to see if the expression you are looking for is shown under another headword. **1** V-T/V-I If something **fits**, it is the right size and shape to go onto a person's body or onto a particular object. ❑ *The sash, kimono, and other garments were made to fit a child.* ❑ *She has to go to the men's department to find trousers that fit at the waist.* **2** N-SING If something is a good **fit**, it fits well. ❑ *Eventually he was happy that the sills and doors were a reasonably good fit.*

1 타동사/자동사 -에 맞다 ❑ 허리띠, 기모노, 그리고 다른 의류 품목이 아이에게 맞게 만들어졌다. ❑ 그녀는 허리에 맞는 바지를 찾으려고 남성복 매장에 가야만 했다. **2** 단수명사 들어맞음, 적합함 ❑ 마침내 그가 문과 문턱이 상당히 잘 들어맞는다며 만족스러워했다.

You do not use the verb **fit** to say that something seems attractive on a person or in a place. The verb you need is **suit**. ❑ *It is really feminine and pretty and it certainly suits you.* You use the verb **fit** to say that clothes are the right size for you. ❑ *The size 12 gown was gorgeous and fitted perfectly... The gloves didn't fit.* You cannot usually say that one color, pattern, or object **suits** another. The verb you need is **match**. ❑ *She wears a straw hat with a yellow ribbon to match her yellow cheesecloth dress... His clothes don't quite match.*

어떤 것이 사람이나 장소에 잘 어울린다고 말할 때는 fit이 아니라 suit을 쓴다. ❑ 그건 정말 여성스럽고 예뻐. 그리고 네게 정말 잘 어울려. fit은 사람에게 옷의 사이즈가 맞을 때 쓴다. ❑ 사이즈 12짜리 드레스는 정말 멋지고 아주 잘 맞았다... 그 장갑은 안 맞았다. 어떤 색이나, 패턴, 물건이 다른 것과 어울린다고 할 때는 suit이 아니라 match를 쓴다. ❑ 그녀는 자신의 노란 무명 원피스와 어울리도록 노란 리본이 달린 밀짚모자를 쓰고 있다... 그의 옷은 서로 어울리지가 않는다.

3 V-T If you **are fitted for** a particular piece of clothing, you try it on so that the person who is making it can see where it needs to be altered. [usu passive] ❑ *She was being fitted for her wedding dress.* **4** V-I If something **fits** somewhere, it can be put there or is designed to be put there. ❑ *...a pocket computer which is small enough to fit into your pocket.* ❑ *He folded his long legs to fit under the table.* **5** V-T If you **fit** something into a particular space or place, you put it there. ❑ *...she fitted her key in the lock.* ❑ *Who could cut the millions of stone blocks and fit them together?* **6** V-T If you **fit** something somewhere, you attach it there, or put it there carefully and securely. ❑ *Fit hinge bolts to give extra support to the door lock.* ❑ *Peter had built the overhead ladders, and the next day he fitted them to the wall.* **7** V-T/V-I If something **fits** something else or **fits** into it, it goes together well with that thing or is able to be part of it. ❑ *My daughter doesn't fit the current feminine ideal.* ❑ *Fostering is a full-time job and you should carefully consider how it will fit into your career.* **8** V-T You can say that something **fits** a particular person or thing when it is appropriate or suitable for them or it. ❑ *The punishment must always fit the crime.* **9** ADJ If something is **fit** for a particular purpose, it is

3 타동사 (맞춤복의 치수가 맞나 보기 위해) 입혀 보다, 가봉을 하다 ❑ 그녀는 자신의 웨딩드레스를 가봉을 하고 있었다. **4** 자동사 -에 쏙 들어가다 ❑ 주머니에 쏙 들어갈 정도로 작은 휴대용 컴퓨터 ❑ 그는 식탁 밑으로 다리가 쏙 들어가도록 긴 다리를 포개고 앉았다. **5** 타동사 -에 끼워 맞추다 ❑ 그녀가 자물쇠에 키를 끼워 맞추었다. ❑ 누가 수만 개의 돌 블록을 쪼개어 함께 끼워 맞출 수가 있겠니? **6** 타동사 -을 달다 ❑ 경첩 걸쇠를 달아서 문 자물쇠가 힘을 더 받도록 해라. ❑ 피터가 구름사다리를 만들어 다음 날 벽에 붙였다. **7** 타동사/자동사 -에 쏙 어울리다 ❑ 그녀의 딸은 현대 여성상에 쏙 어울리지는 않는다. ❑ 양육은 내내 매달려야 하는 일이니 그 일이 직업상의 일과 어떻게 어울리게 할지를 심사 숙고해야 한다. **8** 타동사 알맞다 ❑ 형벌은 언제나 죄질에 알맞게 내려져야 한다. **9** 형용사 적합한 ❑ 우리가 가진

suitable for that purpose. ❑ *Of the seven bicycles we had, only two were fit for the road.* 🔟 ADJ If someone is **fit** to do something, they have the appropriate qualities or skills that will allow them to do it. ❑ *You're not fit to be a mother! In a word, this government isn't fit to rule.* ● **fit|ness** N-UNCOUNT ❑ *There is a debate about his fitness for the highest office.* 🔢 V-T If something **fits** someone for a particular task or role, it makes them good enough or suitable for it. [FORMAL] ❑ *...a man whose past experience fits him for the top job in education.* 🔢 PHRASE If you say that someone **sees fit to** do something, you mean that they are entitled to do it, but that you disapprove of their decision to do it. [FORMAL, DISAPPROVAL] ❑ *He's not a friend, you say, yet you saw fit to lend him money.* 🔢 →see also **fitted, fitting. fit the bill** →see **bill. to fit like a glove** →see **glove. not in a fit state** →see **state**

▶**fit in** 🔢 PHRASAL VERB If you manage to **fit** a person or task **in**, you manage to find time to deal with them. ❑ *We work long hours both outside and inside the home and we rush around trying to fit everything in.* 🔢 PHRASAL VERB If you **fit in** as part of a group, you seem to belong there because you are similar to the other people in it. ❑ *She was great with the children and fitted in beautifully.* 🔢 PHRASAL VERB If you say that someone or something **fits in**, you understand how they form part of a particular situation or system. [BRIT also **fit up**] ❑ *He knew where I fitted in and what he had to do to get the best out of me.*

▶**fit out** PHRASAL VERB If you **fit** someone or something **out**, or you **fit** them **up**, you provide them with equipment and other things that they need. ❑ *We helped to fit him out for a trip to the Baltic.* ❑ *I suggest we fit you up with an office suite.*

② **fit** ♦♢♢ /fɪt/ (**fitter, fittest**) ADJ Someone who is **fit** is healthy and physically strong. ❑ *An averagely fit person can master easy ski runs within a few days.* ● **fit|ness** N-UNCOUNT ❑ *Squash was once thought to offer all-round fitness.*

③ **fit** /fɪt/ (**fits**) 🔢 N-COUNT If someone has a **fit** they suddenly lose consciousness and their body makes uncontrollable movements. ❑ *About two in every five epileptic fits occur during sleep.* 🔢 N-COUNT If you have a **fit of** coughing or laughter, you suddenly start coughing or laughing in an uncontrollable way. ❑ *Halfway down the cigarette she had a fit of coughing.* 🔢 N-COUNT If you do something in a **fit of** anger or panic, you are very angry or afraid when you do it. ❑ *Pattie shot Tom in a fit of jealous rage.*

fit|ted /fɪtɪd/ 🔢 ADJ A **fitted** piece of clothing is designed so that it is the same size and shape as your body rather than being loose. ❑ *...baggy trousers with fitted jackets.* 🔢 ADJ A **fitted** piece of furniture, for example a cabinet, is designed to fill a particular space and is fixed in place. ❑ *I've re-carpeted our bedroom and added fitted wardrobes.* 🔢 ADJ A **fitted** carpet is cut to the same shape as a room so that it covers the floor completely. [ADJ n] ❑ *...fitted carpets, central heating, and double glazing.* 🔢 ADJ A **fitted** sheet has the corners sewn so that they fit over the corners of the mattress and do not have to be folded. [ADJ n]

fit|ting /fɪtɪŋ/ (**fittings**) 🔢 N-COUNT A **fitting** is one of the smaller parts on the outside of a piece of equipment or furniture, for example a handle or a faucet. ❑ *...brass light fittings.* ❑ *...industrial fittings for kitchen and bathroom.* 🔢 N-PLURAL **Fittings** are things such as ovens or heaters, that are fitted inside a building, but can be removed if necessary. ❑ *...a detailed list of what fixtures and fittings are included in the purchase price.* 🔢 ADJ Something that is **fitting** is right or suitable. ❑ *A solitary man, it was perhaps fitting that he should have died alone.* ● **fit|ting|ly** ADV ❑ *...the four-storeyed, and fittingly named, High House.* 🔢 N-COUNT If someone has a **fitting**, they try on a piece of clothing that is being made for them to see if it fits. ❑ *She lunched and shopped and went for fittings for clothes she didn't need.*

five ♦♦♦ /faɪv/ (**fives**) NUM **Five** is the number 5. ❑ *Eric Edward Bullus was born in Peterborough, the second of five children.*

fiv|er /faɪvər/ (**fivers**) 🔢 N-COUNT A **fiver** is a five dollar bill. [AM, INFORMAL] 🔢 N-COUNT A **fiver** is a five pound note. [BRIT, INFORMAL]

fix ♦♦♢ /fɪks/ (**fixes, fixing, fixed**) 🔢 V-T If something **is fixed** somewhere, it is attached there firmly or securely. ❑ *It is fixed on the wall.* ❑ *Most blinds can be fixed directly to the top of the window-frame.* 🔢 V-T If you **fix** something, for example a date, price, or policy, you decide and say exactly what it will be. ❑ *He's going to fix a time when I can see him.* ❑ *The date of the election was fixed.* 🔢 V-T If you **fix** something for someone, you arrange for it to happen or you organize it for them. ❑ *I've fixed it for you to see Bonnie Lachlan.* ❑ *It's fixed. He's going to meet us at the airport.* ❑ *He vanished after you fixed him with a job.* 🔢 V-T If you **fix** something which is damaged or which does not work properly, you repair it. ❑ *He cannot fix the electricity.* 🔢 V-T If you **fix** a problem or a bad situation, you deal with it and make it satisfactory. ❑ *It's not too late to fix the problem, although time is clearly getting short.* 🔢 N-COUNT You can refer to a solution to a problem as a **fix**. [INFORMAL] ❑ *Many of these changes could just be a temporary fix.* →see also **quick fix** 🔢 V-T/V-I If you **fix** your eyes **on** someone or something or if your eyes **fix on** them, you look at them with complete attention. ❑ *She fixes her steel-blue eyes on an unsuspecting local official.* ❑ *Her soft brown eyes fixed on Kelly.* 🔢 V-T If someone or something **is fixed in** your mind, you remember them well, for example because they are very important, interesting, or unusual. ❑ *Leonard was now fixed in his mind.* 🔢 V-T If someone **fixes** a gun, camera, or radar on something, they point it at that thing. ❑ *The U.S. crew fixed its radar on the Turkish ship.* 🔟 N-SING If you get a **fix on** someone or something, you have a clear idea or understanding of them. [INFORMAL] ❑ *It's hard to get a steady fix on what's going on.* 🔢 V-T If you **fix** some food or a drink for someone, you make it or prepare it for them. ❑ *Sarah fixed some food for us.* ❑ *Let me fix you a drink.* 🔢 V-T If you **fix** your hair, clothes, or makeup, you arrange or adjust them so you look neat and tidy, showing you have taken care with your appearance. [INFORMAL] [no passive] ❑ *"I've got to fix my hair," I said and retreated to my bedroom.* 🔢 V-T If someone **fixes** a race, election, contest, or other event, they make unfair or

자전거 일곱 대 중에서 단지 두 대만 그 길에 적합했다. 🔟 형용사 자격이 있는 ❑ 넌 엄마가 될 자격이 없어! ❑ 한 마디로, 이 정부는 통치할 자격이 없다. ● 적합한 불가산명사 ❑ 최고 직책이 그에게 적합한가에 대한 논란이 있다. 🔢 타동사 -에게 자격을 갖춰 주다 [격식체] ❑ 과거 경력으로 볼 때 교육 관련 최고직에 맞는 자격을 갖춘 남자 🔢 구 -하려다 [격식체, 탐탁잖음] ❑ 네 말은, 그가 친구는 아니지만, 그에게 돈을 빌려 줄 만은 했다는 것이군.

🔢 구동사 시간을 내다 ❑ 우리는 집 안팎에서 오랜 시간 일하고 모든 일에 시간을 내려고 서둘러 다닌다. 🔢 구동사 -과 어울리다 ❑ 그녀는 아이들과 있을 때 멋졌고 아주 잘 어울렸다. 🔢 구동사 -에 적합하다 [영국영어 fit up] ❑ 그는 내가 어디에 적합한지, 그리고 내 능력을 최대한 발휘하도록 하려면 그가 무엇을 해야 하는지를 알았다.

구동사 (필요한 물건을) 마련해 주다 ❑ 우리는 그가 발트 해로 여행 가는 데 필요한 물건을 마련해 주는 걸 도왔다. ❑ 우리가 당신들에게 사무용 가구를 갖추어 주면 어떻겠습니까.

형용사 건강한 ❑ 평균적으로 건강한 사람이라면 쉬운 스키 활강은 며칠 안에 숙달할 수 있다. ● 체력 불가산명사 ❑ 한때는 스쿼시를 하면 전반적인 체력을 기를 수 있다고 여겨졌다.

🔢 가산명사 발작 ❑ 간질 발작 다섯 번 중 두 번쯤은 수면 중에 발생한다. 🔢 가산명사 (웃음이나 기침 따위의) 한바탕 ❑ 담배를 반쯤 피웠을 때 그녀가 한바탕 기침을 했다. 🔢 가산명사 (감정의) 복받침 ❑ 패티가 질투심으로 화가 나서 톰을 총으로 쐈다.

🔢 형용사 몸에 꼭 맞는 ❑ 헐렁헐렁한 바지와 몸에 꼭 맞는 재킷 🔢 형용사 붙박이의 ❑ 나는 우리 침실 카펫을 다시 깔고 붙박이 옷장을 달았다. 🔢 형용사 꼭 들어맞는 ❑ 꼭 들어맞는 카펫, 중앙난방 장치, 그리고 이중 유리창 🔢 형용사 (매트에 씌울 수 있게) 모서리가 꿰매진

🔢 가산명사 (기구나 가구의) 부속품, 기구 ❑ 놋쇠 조명용 기구 ❑ 주방과 욕실용 공산품 기구 🔢 복수명사 부속 기구류 ❑ 어떤 붙박이 설비와 부속 기구류가 구매 가격에 포함되었는지 보여 주는 상세한 목록 🔢 형용사 적절한 ❑ 고독한 남자, 그는 홀로 세상을 떠났어야 했다는 게 아마도 적절했을 것이다. ● 적절히, 꼭 어울리게 부사 ❑ 4층에, 이름까지 꼭 어울리는 '하이 하우스' 🔢 가산명사 입어 보기 ❑ 그녀는 점심 후에 쇼핑을 하며 필요치 않은 옷들을 입어 보았다.

수사 5, 다섯 ❑ 에릭 에드워드 불루스는 피터보로에서 다섯 자녀 중 둘째로 태어났다.

🔢 가산명사 5달러짜리 지폐 [미국영어, 비격식체] 🔢 가산명사 5파운드짜리 지폐 [영국영어, 비격식체]

🔢 타동사 고정되다 ❑ 그것은 벽에 고정되어 있다. ❑ 블라인드는 대부분 창틀 꼭대기에 바로 고정시킬 수 있다. 🔢 타동사 정하다 ❑ 내가 언제 그를 만날 수 있는지는 그가 정할 것이다. ❑ 선거일이 정해졌다. 🔢 타동사 -을 주선해 주다, -을 준비해 주다 ❑ 내가 보니 라클란을 만날 수 있도록 내가 주선해 두었다. ❑ 그 일은 준비가 되어 있어. 그가 공항에 우리를 마중하러 공항에 나올 거야. ❑ 내가 그에게 일자리를 주선해 준 후에 그가 사라졌다. 🔢 타동사 고치다 ❑ 그는 전기를 못 고친다. 🔢 타동사 처리하다 ❑ 시간이 분명히 촉박하긴 하지만 그 문제를 처리할 수 있을 만큼 늦은 건 아니다. 🔢 가산명사 해결책 [비격식체] ❑ 그러한 변화의 대부분은 일시적인 해결책이 될 뿐이다. 🔢 타동사/자동사 -을 집중해서 보다; 시선이 -에 집중되다 ❑ 그녀는 아무것도 모르고 있는 지역 관리를 강철빛 눈으로 뚫어지게 바라본다. ❑ 그녀의 연갈색 눈이 켈리에게 박혀 있었다. 🔢 타동사 (마음에) 새겨지다 ❑ 레너드는 이제 그의 마음속에 새겨져 있었다. 🔢 타동사 겨누다, 고정시키다 ❑ 미국 승무원이 그 터키 선박에 레이더를 고정했다. 🔟 단수명사 파악 [비격식체] ❑ 진행 상황을 계속 파악하고 있기가 쉽지는 않다. 🔢 타동사 (음식을) 준비하다, (음식을) 만들다 ❑ 사라는 우리를 위해 음식을 차려 주었다. ❑ 내가 술 한 잔 만들어 줄게. 🔢 타동사 매만지다 [비격식체] ❑ "머리 좀 매만져야겠어."라고 말한 후 나는 침실로 다시 들어갔다. 🔢 타동사 조작하다, 미리 짜고 하다 [탐탁잖음] ❑ 그들은 상대편 선수들에게 뇌물을 주어

illegal arrangements or use deception to affect the result. [DISAPPROVAL] ❏ *They offered opposing players bribes to fix a decisive league match against Valenciennes.* ● N-COUNT **Fix** is also a noun. ❏ *It's all a fix, a deal they've made.* ᴵ⁴ V-T If you accuse someone of **fixing** prices, you accuse them of making unfair arrangements to charge a particular price for something, rather than allowing market forces to decide it. [BUSINESS, DISAPPROVAL] ❏ *...a suspected cartel that had fixed the price of steel for the construction market.* ᴵ⁵ →see also **fixed**

발렌시엔 팀과의 매우 중요한 리그전을 조작하려고 했다. ● 가산명사 조작 ❏ 그것은 완전 조작, 그들이 꾸민 짓거리야. ᴵ⁴ 타동사 (가격을) 정하다, 담합하다 [경제, 탐탁찮음] ❏ 건설 시장의 철강 가격을 담합했다는 의혹을 받고 있던 기업 연합

Thesaurus　　fix의 참조어

v.　fasten, nail, secure ❶
　　agree on, decide, establish, work out ❷
　　arrange, plan ❸
　　adjust, correct, repair, restore ❹

▸**fix up** ❶ PHRASAL VERB If you **fix** something **up**, you arrange it. ❏ *I fixed up an appointment to see her.* ❷ PHRASAL VERB If you **fix** something **up**, you do work that is necessary in order to make it more suitable or attractive. ❏ *I've fixed up Matthew's old room.* ❸ PHRASAL VERB If you **fix** someone **up with** something they need, you provide it for them. ❏ *We'll fix him up with a tie.*

❶ 구동사 정하다 ❏ 나는 그녀를 만나기로 약속을 정했다. ❷ 구동사 정리하다 ❏ 나는 매튜의 옛날 방을 정리했다. ❸ 구동사 마련해 주다 ❏ 우리가 그에게 넥타이를 마련해 줄 것이다.

fixed ♦◇◇ /fɪkst/ ❶ ADJ You use **fixed** to describe something which stays the same and does not or cannot vary. ❏ *They issue a fixed number of shares that trade publicly.* ❏ *Many restaurants offer fixed-price menus.* ❷ ADJ If you say that someone has **fixed** ideas or opinions, you mean that they do not often change their ideas and opinions, although perhaps they should. ❏ *...people who have fixed ideas about things.* ❸ ADJ If someone has a **fixed** smile on their face, they are smiling even though they do not feel happy or pleased. ❏ *I had to go through the rest of the evening with a fixed smile on my face.* ❹ PHRASE Someone who is of **no fixed address**, or in British English **no fixed abode**, does not have a permanent place to live. [FORMAL] ❏ *They are not able to get a job interview because they have no fixed address.* ❺ →see also **fix** →see **interest rate**

❶ 형용사 고정된 ❏ 그들은 공식적으로 거래되는 주식을 고정된 수로 발행한다. ❏ 많은 레스토랑이 고정 가격 메뉴를 선보인다. ❷ 형용사 변치 않는 ❏ 세상사에 대해 변치 않는 생각을 가진 사람들 ❸ 형용사 억지로 하는 ❏ 나는 그날 저녁 남은 시간 동안 줄곧 억지웃음을 지어야 했다. ❹ 구 주거 부정의 [격식체] ❏ 그들은 주거 부정의 이유로 구직 면접을 볼 수 없다.

Word Link　　fix ≈ fastening : fixture, prefix, suffix

---

fix|ture /fɪkstʃər/ (**fixtures**) ❶ N-COUNT **Fixtures** are pieces of furniture or equipment, for example baths and sinks, which are fixed inside a house or other building and which stay there if you move. ❏ *...a detailed list of what fixtures and fittings are included in the purchase price.* ❷ N-COUNT A **fixture** is a sports event which takes place on a particular date. [BRIT] ❏ *City won this fixture 3-0 last season.*

❶ 가산명사 붙박이 설비 ❏ 어떤 붙박이 설비와 부속 기구류가 구매 가격에 포함되었는지를 보여 주는 상세한 목록 ❷ 가산명사 (날짜가 정해진) 스포츠 경기 [영국영어] ❏ 맨체스터 시티가 지난 시즌에 이 경기를 3대 0으로 승리했다.

fizz /fɪz/ (**fizzes, fizzing, fizzed**) V-I If a drink **fizzes**, it produces a lot of little bubbles of gas and makes a sound like a long "s." ❏ *After a while their mother was back, holding a tray of glasses that fizzed.* ● N-UNCOUNT **Fizz** is also a noun. ❏ *I wonder if there's any fizz left in the lemonade.*

자동사 쉿 하며 거품을 내다 ❏ 잠시 후에 그들의 어머니가 탄산음료 잔이 놓인 쟁반을 든 채 돌아오셨다. ● 불가산명사 (음료 따위의) 거품 ❏ 나는 이 레모네이드에 거품이 남아 있는지 궁금하다.

fizzy /fɪzi/ (**fizzier, fizziest**) ADJ **Fizzy** drinks are drinks that contain small bubbles of carbon dioxide. They make a sound like a long "s" when you pour them. [mainly BRIT; AM usually **carbonated**] ❏ *...fizzy water.*

형용사 거품이 이는 [주로 영국영어; 미국영어 대개 carbonated] ❏ 거품이 이는 탄산수

flag ♦◇◇ /flæg/ (**flags, flagging, flagged**) ❶ N-COUNT A **flag** is a piece of cloth which can be attached to a pole and which is used as a sign, signal, or symbol of something, especially of a particular country. ❏ *The Marines climbed to the roof of the embassy building to raise the American flag.* ❷ N-COUNT Journalists sometimes refer to the **flag** of a particular country or organization as a way of referring to the country or organization itself and its power. ❏ *Joining John Whitaker will be his brother Michael also riding under the British flag.* ❸ V-I If you **flag** or if your spirits **flag**, you begin to lose enthusiasm or energy. ❏ *His enthusiasm was in no way flagging.*
→see Word Web: **flag**

❶ 가산명사 기 ❏ 해병대는 대사관 건물 지붕으로 올라가서 성조기를 게양했다. ❷ 가산명사 기 ❏ 존 휘태커와 함께 그의 형제인 마이클도 영국 국기를 달고 달릴 것이다. ❸ 자동사 시들해지다 ❏ 그의 열정은 결코 시들해지지 않았다.

fla|grant /fleɪɡrənt/ ADJ You can use **flagrant** to describe an action, situation, or someone's behavior that you find extremely bad or shocking in a very obvious way. [DISAPPROVAL] [ADJ n] ❏ *The judge called the decision "a flagrant violation of international law."*

형용사 극악무도한 [탐탁찮음] ❏ 그 판사는 그 판결을 '극악무도한 국제법 위반'이라고 일컬었다.

flag|ship /flæɡʃɪp/ (**flagships**) ❶ N-COUNT A **flagship** is the most important ship in a fleet of ships, especially the one on which the commander of the fleet is sailing. ❏ *...the Royal Navy's flagship, HMS Ark Royal.* ❷ N-COUNT The **flagship** of a group of things that are owned or produced by a particular organization is the most important one. ❏ *The hospital is the government's flagship, leading the health service reforms...*

❶ 가산명사 기함 ❏ 영국 해군 기함인 '에이치엠에스 아크 로열' ❷ 가산명사 기함, 거점, 가장 중요한 것 ❏ 그 병원이 보건 개혁을 이끄는 정부의 기함이었다.

flail /fleɪl/ (**flails, flailing, flailed**) V-T/V-I If your arms or legs **flail** or if you **flail** them about, they wave about in an energetic but uncontrolled way. ❏ *His arms were flailing in all directions.* ● PHRASAL VERB **Flail around** means the same as **flail**. ❏ *He started flailing around and hitting Vincent in the chest.*

타동사/자동사 마구 흔들리다; 마구 흔들다 ❏ 그의 팔이 이리저리 마구 흔들리고 있었다. ● 구동사 마구 흔들리다; 마구 흔들다 ❏ 그는 마구 몸을 흔들어대며 빈센트의 가슴을 치기 시작했다.

Word Web　　flag

Flags are **symbols**. Some flags **symbolize** countries. At the Olympics, each group of athletes proudly carries their country's standard. The Olympics even has its own flag. It **flies** at all Olympic games. Flags can also send messages. Most people understand that a white flag means "we **surrender**." Before radios, people used semaphore to communicate between ships. They used different colored flags. They hoisted them in special positions to spell out words. Flags can also signal danger. When people carry long pieces of wood on their cars, they use a red flag to warn other drivers.

flair /flɛər/ ◼ N-SING If you have **a flair for** a particular thing, you have a natural ability to do it well. □ ...a friend who has a flair for languages. ◼ N-UNCOUNT If you have **flair**, you do things in an original, interesting, and stylish way. [APPROVAL] □ Their work has all the usual punch, panache, and flair you'd expect.

flak /flæk/ N-UNCOUNT If you get a lot of **flak** from someone, they criticize you severely. If you take **flak**, you get the blame for something. [INFORMAL] □ The President is getting a lot of flak for that.

flake /fleɪk/ (flakes, flaking, flaked) ◼ N-COUNT A **flake** is a small thin piece of something, especially one that has broken off a larger piece. □ ...flakes of paint. □ Large flakes of snow began swiftly to fall. ◼ V-I If something such as paint **flakes**, small thin pieces of it come off. □ They can see how its colors have faded and where paint has flaked. ● PHRASAL VERB **Flake off** means the same as **flake**. □ The surface corrosion was worst where the paint had flaked off.

flam|boy|ant /flæmbɔɪənt/ ADJ If you say that someone or something is **flamboyant**, you mean that they are very noticeable, stylish, and exciting. □ Freddie Mercury was a flamboyant star of the British hard rock scene. ● **flam|boy|ance** N-UNCOUNT □ Campese was his usual mixture of flamboyance and flair.

Word Link   flam ≈ burning : flame, flammable, inflame

flame /fleɪm/ (flames, flaming, flamed) ◼ N-VAR A **flame** is a hot bright stream of burning gas that comes from something that is burning. □ The heat from the flames was so intense that roads melted. ◼ N-COUNT A **flame** is an e-mail message which severely criticizes or attacks someone. [INFORMAL, COMPUTING] □ The best way to respond to a flame is to ignore it. ● V-T **Flame** is also a verb. □ Ever been flamed? →see also **flaming** ◼ PHRASE If something **bursts into flames** or **bursts into flame**, it suddenly starts burning strongly. □ She managed to scramble out of the vehicle as it burst into flames. ◼ PHRASE Something that is **in flames** is on fire. □ I woke to a city in flames. →see **fire**

flam|ing /fleɪmɪŋ/ ADJ **Flaming** is used to describe something that is burning and producing a lot of flames. □ The plane, which was full of fuel, scattered flaming fragments over a large area.

flam|mable /flæməbəl/ ADJ **Flammable** chemicals, gases, cloth, or other things catch fire and burn easily. □ ...flammable liquids such as petrol or paraffin.

flank /flæŋk/ (flanks, flanking, flanked) ◼ N-COUNT An animal's **flank** is its side, between the ribs and the hip. □ He put his hand on the dog's flank. ◼ N-COUNT A **flank** of an army or navy force is one side of it when it is organized for battle. □ The assault element, led by Captain Ramirez, opened up from their right flank. ◼ N-COUNT The side of anything large can be referred to as its **flank**. □ They continued along the flank of the mountain. ◼ V-T If something **is flanked by** things, it has them on both sides of it, or sometimes on one side of it. □ The altar was flanked by two Christmas trees.

flan|nel /flænəl/ (flannels) ◼ N-UNCOUNT **Flannel** is a soft cloth, usually made of cotton or wool, that is used for making clothes. [oft N n] □ He wore a faded red flannel shirt. ◼ N-COUNT A **flannel** is a small cloth that you use for washing yourself. [BRIT; AM **washcloth**]

flap /flæp/ (flaps, flapping, flapped) ◼ V-T/V-I If something such as a piece of cloth or paper **flaps** or if you **flap** it, it moves quickly up and down or from side to side. □ Grey sheets flapped on the clothes line. ◼ V-T/V-I If a bird or insect **flaps** its wings or if its wings **flap**, the wings move quickly up and down. □ The bird flapped its wings furiously. ◼ V-T If you **flap** your arms, you move them quickly up and down as if they were the wings of a bird. □ ...a kid running and flapping her arms. ◼ N-COUNT A **flap** of cloth or skin, for example, is a flat piece of it that can move freely up and down or from side to side because it is held or attached by only one edge. □ He drew back the tent flap and strode out into the blizzard. ◼ N-COUNT A **flap** on the wing of an aircraft is an area along the edge of the wing that can be raised or lowered to control the movement of the aircraft. □ ...the sudden slowing as the flaps were lowered.

flare /flɛər/ (flares, flaring, flared) ◼ N-COUNT A **flare** is a small device that produces a bright flame. Flares are used as signals, for example on ships. □ ...a ship which had fired a distress flare. ◼ V-I If a fire **flares**, the flames suddenly become larger. □ Camp fires flared like beacons in the dark. ● PHRASAL VERB **Flare up** means the same as **flare**. □ Don't spill too much fat on the barbecue as it could flare up. ◼ V-I If something such as trouble, violence, or conflict **flares**, it starts or becomes more violent. □ Even as the President appealed for calm, trouble flared in several American cities. ● PHRASAL VERB **Flare up** means the same as **flare**. □ Dozens of people were injured as fighting flared up. ◼ V-I If people's tempers **flare**, they get angry. □ Tempers flared and harsh words were exchanged.

flare-up (flare-ups) N-COUNT If there is a **flare-up** of violence or an illness, it suddenly starts or gets worse. □ There's been a flare-up of violence in South Africa.

flash ◆◇◇ /flæʃ/ (flashes, flashing, flashed) ◼ N-COUNT A **flash** is a sudden burst of light or of something shiny or bright. □ A sudden flash of lightning lit everything up for a second. □ The wire snapped at the wall plug with a blue flash and the light fused. ◼ V-T/V-I If a light **flashes** or if you **flash** a light, it shines with a sudden bright light, especially as quick, regular flashes of light. □ Lightning flashed among the distant dark clouds. □ He lost his temper after a driver flashed his headlights as he overtook. ◼ V-I If something **flashes** past or by, it moves past you so fast that you cannot see it properly. □ It was a busy road, cars flashed by every few minutes. ◼ V-I If something **flashes** through or into your mind, you suddenly think about it. □ A ludicrous thought flashed through Harry's mind. ◼ V-T If you **flash** something such as an identification card, you show it to people quickly and

◼ 단수명사 천부적 재능 ◼ 언어에 대해 천부적인 재능이 있는 친구 ◼ 불가산명사 세련됨 [마음에 듦] □ 그들의 작품에는 네가 기대하는 일상적인 활력, 당당한 태도, 그리고 세련됨이 모두 담겨 있다.

불가산명사 혹평 [비격식체] □ 대통령이 그 일에 대해 혹평을 많이 받고 있다.

◼ 가산명사 얇은 조각 ◼ 페인트 조각 ◼ 커다란 눈송이들이 펑펑 쏟아지기 시작했다. ◼ 자동사 조각조각 떨어져 나가다 □ 그들은 그 색깔이 얼마나 바래고 페인트가 어디에서 조각조각 떨어져 나갔는지 볼 수 있다. ● 구동사 벗겨져 떨어지다 □ 페인트가 벗겨져 떨어져 나간 부분의 표면 부식은 최악의 상황이었다.

형용사 화려한, 휘황한 □ 프레디 머큐리는 영국 하드락 계의 눈부신 스타였다. ● 화려함 불가산명사 □ 캄페세는 늘 그렇듯 그의 화려함과 천부적 재능을 혼합해 놓은 것이었다.

◼ 가산명사 또는 불가산명사 화염 □ 화염의 열기가 매우 강렬하여 도로가 녹았다. ◼ 가산명사 (전자우편에서) 무례한 표현, 플레임 [비격식체, 컴퓨터] □ 플레임에 대응하는 최선의 방법은 무시하는 것이다. ● 자동사 타오르다; (얼굴이 빨갛게) 달아오르다 □ 얼굴이 빨갛게 달아올라 본 적이 있는가? ◼ 구 화 타오르다, 화염에 휩싸이다 □ 그녀는 차가 화염에 휩싸일 때 가까스로 기어 나왔다. ◼ 구 화염에 휩싸여 □ 내가 잠에서 깨어 보니 도시가 화염에 휩싸여 있었다.

형용사 불타는 □ 연료가 가득 찬 그 비행기는 불길에 휩싸인 채 산산조각 나서 광범위한 지역에 걸쳐 흩어졌다.

형용사 가연성의 □ 휘발유 또는 파라핀과 같은 가연성 액체

◼ 가산명사 옆구리 □ 그는 손을 그 개의 옆구리에 갖다 댔다. ◼ 가산명사 (군대 대형의) 측면 □ 라미레즈 장군이 이끄는 돌격 부대가 대형 우측 측면에서 총격을 개시했다. ◼ 가산명사 측면, 옆구리 □ 그들은 산 옆구리를 끼고 계속 갔다. ◼ 자동사 -의 측면에 두다 □ 그 제단 양 측면엔 크리스마스트리가 한 그루씩 서 있었다.

◼ 불가산명사 플란넬 □ 그는 빛바랜 붉은색 플란넬 셔츠를 입고 있었다. ◼ 가산명사 목욕용 수건 [영국영어; 미국영어 washcloth]

◼ 타동사/자동사 펄럭이다; 펄럭이게 하다 □ 빨랫줄에는 회색 시트가 펄럭이고 있었다. ◼ 타동사/자동사 퍼덕거리다, 퍼덕이다 □ 그 새가 날개를 맹렬히 퍼덕거렸다. ◼ 타동사 날갯짓 하듯 움직이다 □ 두 팔을 날개처럼 퍼덕거리며 뛰어다니는 소녀 ◼ 가산명사 (천이나 피부의) 늘어진 부분, 낮게 같은 부분 □ 그는 텐트 덮개를 젖히고 눈보라 속으로 성큼성큼 나아갔다. ◼ 가산명사 보조익 □ 보조익을 낮출 때의 갑작스런 속도 저하

◼ 가산명사 조명탄 □ 조난 신호용 조명탄을 발사했던 선박 ◼ 자동사 확 타오르다 □ 캠프파이어는 어둠 속의 횃불처럼 확 타올랐다. ● 구동사 확 타오르다 □ 확 타오를 수 있으니 바비큐 판 위에 기름을 너무 많이 붓지 말아라. ◼ 자동사 격렬해지다 □ 심지어 대통령이 자제를 호소했을 때에도, 분쟁은 미국 내 여러 도시에서 격렬해졌다. ● 구동사 격렬해지다 □ 싸움이 격렬해짐에 따라 수십 명의 사람들이 부상을 입었다. ◼ 자동사 격분하다 □ 서로 격분을 해서 험한 말이 오고 갔다.

가산명사 (사건, 질병 등의) 돌발, 악화 □ 남아프리카에서 폭력 사태가 돌발했다.

◼ 가산명사 섬광, 번쩍 하는 불빛 □ 갑자기 번득이는 번개에 잠시 모든 게 환해졌다. □ 벽에 설치된 플러그의 전선에서 푸른 물빛과 함께 찰싹 하고 소리가 나더니 전기가 나갔다. ◼ 타동사/자동사 번쩍 빛나다; 번쩍 비추다 □ 저 멀리 먹구름 속에서 번개가 번쩍였다. □ 그가 앞차를 추월하자 그 차의 운전자가 전조등을 번쩍 비추었고 이에 그가 성질이 났다. ◼ 자동사 쌩 지나가다 □ 그 도로는 몇 분 간격으로 차가 쌩쌩 지나가는 혼잡한 도로였다. ◼ 자동사 문득 떠오르다 □ 해리의 마음속에 문득 터무니없는 생각이 떠올랐다. ◼ 타동사 휙 보여 주다 [비격식체] □ 할름은

then put it away again. [INFORMAL] □ *Halim flashed his official card, and managed to get hold of a soldier to guard the Land Rover.* **6** V-T/V-I If a picture or message **flashes up on** a screen, or if you **flash** it **onto** a screen, it is displayed there briefly or suddenly, and often repeatedly. □ *The figures flash up on the scoreboard.* □ *The words "Good Luck" were flashing on the screen.* **7** V-T If you **flash** a look or a smile at someone, you suddenly look at them or smile at them. [WRITTEN] □ *I flashed a look at Sue.* **8** N-UNCOUNT **Flash** is the use of special bulbs to give more light when taking a photograph. □ *He was one of the first people to use high speed flash in bird photography.* **9** N-COUNT A **flash** is the same as a **flashlight**. [AM, INFORMAL] □ *Stopping to rest, Pete shut off the flash.* **10** PHRASE If you say that something happens **in a flash**, you mean that it happens suddenly and lasts only a very short time. □ *The answer had come to him in a flash.* **11** PHRASE If you say that someone reacts to something **quick as a flash**, you mean that they react to it extremely quickly. □ *Quick as a flash, the man said, "I have to, don't I?"*

flash|back /ˈflæʃbæk/ (**flashbacks**) **1** N-COUNT In a movie, novel, or play, a **flashback** is a scene that returns to events in the past. □ *There is even a flashback to the murder itself.* **2** N-COUNT If you have a **flashback** to a past experience, you have a sudden and very clear memory of it. □ *He has recurring flashbacks to the night his friends died.*

flash|light /ˈflæʃlaɪt/ (**flashlights**) N-COUNT A **flashlight** is a small electric light which gets its power from batteries and which you can carry in your hand. [mainly AM; BRIT **torch**] [also *by* N] □ *Len studied it a moment in the beam of his flashlight.*

flashy /ˈflæʃi/ (**flashier, flashiest**) ADJ If you describe a person or thing as **flashy**, you mean they are smart and noticeable, but in a rather vulgar way. [INFORMAL, DISAPPROVAL] □ *He was much less flashy than his brother.*

flask /flæsk/ (**flasks**) **1** N-COUNT A **flask** is a bottle which you use for carrying drinks around with you. □ *He took out a metal flask from a canvas bag.* ● N-COUNT A **flask** of liquid is the flask and the liquid which it contains. □ *There's some sandwiches here and a flask of coffee.* **2** N-COUNT A **flask** is a bottle or other container which is used in science laboratories and industry for holding liquids. □ *Flasks for the transport of spent fuel are extremely strong containers made of steel or steel and lead.*

flat ♦♦♦◇ /flæt/ (**flats, flatter, flattest**) **1** N-COUNT A **flat** is a set of rooms for living in, usually on one floor and part of a larger building. A flat usually includes a kitchen and bathroom. [BRIT; AM **apartment**] [also N num] □ *Sara lives with her husband and children in a flat in central London.* □ *It started a fire in a block of flats.* **2** ADJ Something that is **flat** is level, smooth, or even, rather than sloping, curved, or uneven. □ *Tiles can be fixed to any surface as long as it's flat, firm and dry.* □ *...windows which a thief can reach from a drainpipe or flat roof.* **3** ADJ **Flat** means horizontal and not upright. [ADJ N, v-link ADJ, ADJ after v] □ *Two men near him threw themselves flat.* **4** ADJ A **flat** object is not very tall or deep in relation to its length and width. □ *Ellen is walking down the drive with a square flat box balanced on one hand. It's a health food pizza, she declares.* **5** ADJ **Flat** land is level, with no high hills or other raised parts. [ADJ N, v-link ADJ, ADJ after v] □ *To the north lie the flat and fertile farmlands of the Solway plain.* **6** N-COUNT A low flat area of uncultivated land, especially an area where the ground is soft and wet, can be referred to as **flats** or a **flat**. □ *The salt marshes and mud flats attract large numbers of waterfowl.* **7** N-COUNT You can refer to one of the broad flat surfaces of an object as **the flat** of that object. □ *He slammed the counter with the flat of his hand.* **8** ADJ **Flat** shoes have no heels or very low heels. □ *People wear slacks, sweaters, flat shoes, and all manner of casual attire for travel.* ● N-PLURAL **Flats** are flat shoes. [AM] □ *His mother looked ten years younger in jeans and flats like a teenager.* **9** ADJ A **flat** tire, ball, or balloon does not have enough air in it. □ *One vehicle with a flat tyre can bring the M8 to a standstill.* **10** N-COUNT A **flat** is a tire that does not have enough air in it. □ *Then, after I finally got back on the highway, I developed a flat.* **11** ADJ A drink that is **flat** has lost its fizz. □ *Could this really stop the champagne from going flat?* **12** ADJ A **flat** battery has lost some or all of its electrical charge. [mainly BRIT; AM **dead**] □ *His car alarm had been going off for two days and, as a result, the battery was flat.* **13** ADJ If you have **flat** feet, the arches of your feet are too low. □ *The condition of flat feet runs in families.* **14** ADJ A **flat** denial or refusal is definite and firm, and is unlikely to be changed. [ADJ N] □ *The Foreign Ministry has issued a flat denial of any involvement.* ● **flat|ly** ADV □ *He flatly refused to discuss it.* **15** ADJ If you say that something happened, for example, in ten seconds **flat** or ten minutes **flat**, you are emphasizing that it happened surprisingly quickly and only took ten seconds or ten minutes. [EMPHASIS] [num n ADJ] □ *You're sitting behind an engine that'll move you from 0 to 60mph in six seconds flat.* **16** ADJ A **flat** rate, price, or percentage is one that is fixed and which applies in every situation. [ADJ N] □ *Fees are charged at a flat rate, rather than on a percentage basis.* **17** ADJ If trade or business is **flat**, it is slow and inactive, rather than busy and improving or increasing. □ *During the first eight months of this year, sales of big pickups were up 14% while car sales stayed flat.* **18** ADJ If you describe something as **flat**, you mean that it is dull and not exciting or interesting. □ *The past few days have seemed comparatively flat and empty.* **19** ADJ **Flat** is used after a letter representing a musical note to show that the note should be played or sung half a tone lower than the note which otherwise matches that letter. **Flat** is often represented by the symbol ♭ after the letter. [n ADJ] □ *...Schubert's B flat Piano Trio (Opus 99).* **20** ADV If someone sings **flat** or if a musical instrument is flat, their singing or the instrument is slightly lower in pitch than it should be. [ADV after v] □ *Her vocal range was, to say the least of it, limited, and she had a distressing tendency to sing flat.* ● ADJ **Flat** is also an adjective. □ *He had been fired because his singing was flat.* **21** PHRASE If you **fall flat** on your face, you fall over. □ *A man walked in off the street and fell flat on his face, unconscious.* **22** PHRASE If an event or attempt **falls flat** or **falls flat on** its **face**, it is unsuccessful. □ *Liz meant it as a joke but it fell flat.* **23** PHRASE If you do something **flat out**, you do it as fast or as hard as you can. □ *Everyone is working flat out to try to trap those responsible.* **24** PHRASE You use **flat**

그의 공무원증을 살짝 보여 주며 랜드 로버를 지키고 있는 군인과 가까스로 이야기를 할 수 있었다. **⑥** 타동사/자동사 반짝거리며 나타나다; 반짝반짝 보여 주다 □ 접수판에 숫자가 반짝거리며 나타난다. **⑦** 타동사 확 보니, 언뜻 웃다 [문어체] □ 나는 수를 확 쳐다보았다. **⑧** 불가산명사 플래시 □ 그는 초고속 플래시를 처음으로 조류 촬영에 사용한 사람들 중 한 명이었다. **⑨** 가산명사 손전등 [미국영어, 비격식체] □ 쉬려고 멈춰 서서, 피트는 손전등을 껐다. **⑩** 구 순식간에 □ 순식간에 그는 해답을 떠올렸다. **⑪** 구 번개처럼, 아주 빨리 □ 그는 "내가 해야죠, 그렇죠?"라고 재빨리 말했다.

① 가산명사 플래시백 □ 심지어는 살인 장면 자체에 대한 플래시백도 있다. **②** 가산명사 생생하게 떠올림 □ 그는 친구들이 죽은 그날 밤이 계속해서 생생하게 떠오른다.

가산명사 손전등 [주로 미국영어; 영국영어 torch] □ 렌은 손전등을 비추며 잠시 그것을 살펴보았다.

형용사 번지르르한 [비격식체, 탐탁잖음] □ 그는 동생보다는 훨씬 덜 번지르르했다.

① 가산명사 휴대용 병, 플라스크 □ 그는 천으로 된 가방에서 금속 플라스크를 꺼냈다. ● 가산명사 플라스크에 가득한 양 □ 여기 샌드위치 몇 조각과 커피 한 병이 있다. **②** 가산명사 플라스크 □ 다 쓴 연료를 운반하는 플라스크는 강철 또는 강철과 납 합금으로 만든 매우 튼튼한 용기이다.

① 가산명사 플랫, 아파트, 다세대 주택 [영국영어; 미국영어 apartment] □ 사라는 남편과 아이들과 함께 런던 중심가의 한 플랫에 산다. □ 한 다세대 주택 구역에서 그것으로 인해 화재가 발생했다. **②** 형용사 편평한, 평탄한 □ 타일은 편평하고, 단단하고 건조한 곳이라면 어떤 표면에도 붙일 수 있다. □ 배수관이나 편평한 지붕을 통해 도둑이 손을 뻗칠 수 있는 창문 **③** 형용사 수평의 □ 그 사람의 근처에 있던 두 남자가 몸을 납작하게 엎드렸다. **④** 형용사 편평한 모양의, 납작한 □ 엘렌이 사각형의 납작한 상자를 한 손에 기울이지 않게 들고 진입로를 걸어간다. "몸에 좋은 피자예요."라고 그녀는 말한다. **⑤** 형용사 평평한 □ 북쪽으로 평평하고 비옥한 농작지인 솔웨이 평야가 펼쳐져 있다. **⑥** 가산명사 평지 □ 소금기가 함유된 습지와 진흙 개펄은 수많은 물새들을 불러들이고 있다. **⑦** 가산명사 평면, 편평한 부분 □ 그는 손의 편평한 부분으로 계산대를 세차게 쳤다. **⑧** 형용사 납작한 □ 사람들은 여행을 할 때 느슨한 바지에, 스웨터, 굽이 낮은 신발에, 온갖 형태의 편안한 복장을 한다. ● 복수명사 굽이 낮은 신발 [미국영어] □ 그의 어머니는 십대처럼 청바지 차림에 굽이 낮은 구두를 신으니 십 년은 젊어 보였다. **⑨** 형용사 바람이 빠진 □ 타이어가 바람이 빠진 대만 있어도 엠 8 도로가 정체될 수 있다. **⑩** 가산명사 바람이 빠진 타이어 □ 그런 뒤 마침내 고속도로에 다시 올라섰는데 타이어에 바람이 빠진 거다. **⑪** 형용사 김이 빠진 □ 이걸 쓰면 샴페인에서 김이 정말 안 빠질까? **⑫** 형용사 (전지, 배터리가) 방전된 [주로 영국영어; 미국영어 dead] □ 그의 자동차 경보기가 이틀 동안 울렸었고 그로 인해 배터리가 방전되었다. **⑬** 형용사 평발인 □ 평발은 유전이다. **⑭** 형용사 단호한 □ 외무 장관은 어떠한 개입도 없다고 단호히 부정했다. ● 단호히 부사 □ 그는 그 문제에 대한 논의를 단호히 거절했다. **⑮** 형용사 정확한 [강조] □ 당신이 앉은 자리 뒤에는 정확히 6초 만에 60마일을 이동시켜 줄 수 있는 엔진이 있다. **⑯** 형용사 균일한, 변동 없는 □ 요금은 백분율제가 아니라 균일제로 부과된다. **⑰** 형용사 침체된 □ 올해 초반 8개월 동안, 자동차 판매가 침체된 와중에도 준중형 트럭 판매는 14퍼센트가 증가했다. **⑱** 형용사 지루한, 단조로운 □ 지난 며칠 동안은 비교적 지루하고 공허한 것 같았다. **⑲** 형용사 플랫인 □ 슈베르트의 비 플랫 피아노 트리오(작품 제99번) **⑳** 부사 반음 낮게 □ 그녀의 가창 영역은 아무리 좋게 보아도 그리 넓지 않았고, 그녀는 괴롭게도 노래를 반음 낮게 부르는 경향이 있었다. ● 형용사 반음 낮은 □ 그는 음정이 낮게 노래를 불렀기 때문에 해고되었었다. **㉑** 구 쓰러지다 □ 한 남자가 길을 벗어나 걷다가 푹 엎어지더니 의식을 잃었다. **㉒** 구 완전히 실패하다 □ 그건 리즈가 농담으로 한 말이었지만 완전히 실패했다. **㉓** 구 전력을 다해서 □ 모두가 책임 있는 사람들을 잡으려 전력을 다해 일하고 있다. **㉔** 구 순전한 [주로 미국영어, 비격식체, 강조] □ 그 주장은 순전히 거짓이다.

out to emphasize that something is completely the case. [mainly AM, INFORMAL, EMPHASIS] ❑ *That allegation is a flat-out lie.*

Thesaurus *flat*의 참조어

ADJ. even, horizontal, level, smooth; *(ant.)* uneven ②

flat|mate /flǽtmeɪt/ (flatmates) also flat-mate N-COUNT Someone's **flatmate** is a person who shares a flat with them. [BRIT; AM **roommate**]

flat|ten /flǽtⁿn/ (flattens, flattening, flattened) ① V-T/V-I If you **flatten** something or if it **flattens**, it becomes flat or flatter. ❑ *He carefully flattened the wrappers and put them between the leaves of his book.* ❑ *The dog's ears flattened slightly as Cook spoke his name.* ● PHRASAL VERB **Flatten out** means the same as **flatten**. ❑ *The hills flattened out just south of the mountain.* ② V-T To **flatten** something such as a building, town, or plant means to destroy it by knocking it down or crushing it. ❑ *...explosives capable of flattening a five-storey building.* ❑ *...bombing raids flattened much of the area.* ③ V-T If you **flatten yourself against** something, you press yourself flat against it, for example to avoid getting in the way or being seen. ❑ *He flattened himself against a brick wall as I passed.* ④ V-T If you **flatten** someone, you make them fall over by hitting them violently. ❑ *"I've never seen a woman flatten someone like that," said a crew member. "She knocked him out cold."*

flat|ter /flǽtər/ (flatters, flattering, flattered) ① V-T If someone **flatters** you, they praise you in an exaggerated way that is not sincere, because they want to please you or to persuade you to do something. [DISAPPROVAL] ❑ *I knew she was just flattering me.* ② V-T If you **flatter yourself** that something is the case, you believe that it is true, although others may disagree. If someone says to you "**you're flattering yourself**" or "**don't flatter yourself**," they mean that they disagree with your good opinion of yourself. ❑ *I flatter myself that this campaign will put an end to the war.* ③ →see also **flat, flattered, flattering**

flat|tered /flǽtərd/ ADJ If you are **flattered** by something that has happened, you are pleased about it because it makes you feel important or special. [V-link ADJ, oft ADJ by n, ADJ that/to-inf] ❑ *She was flattered by Roberto's long letter.*

flat|ter|ing /flǽtərɪŋ/ ① ADJ If something is **flattering**, it makes you appear more attractive. ❑ *It wasn't a very flattering photograph.* ② ADJ If someone's remarks are **flattering**, they praise you and say nice things about you. ❑ *Most of his colleagues had positive, even flattering things to say.*

flat|ware /flǽtwɛər/ N-UNCOUNT You can refer to the knives, forks, and spoons that you eat your food with as **flatware**. [AM; BRIT **cutlery**] ❑ *An assortment of pots, pans, plates, cups, and flatware is provided.*

flaunt /flɔnt/ (flaunts, flaunting, flaunted) V-T If you say that someone **flaunts** their possessions, abilities, or qualities, you mean that they display them in a very obvious way in, especially in order to try to obtain other people's admiration. [DISAPPROVAL] ❑ *They drove around in Rolls-Royces, openly flaunting their wealth.*

fla|vor ◆◇◇ /fléɪvər/ (flavors, flavoring, flavored) [BRIT **flavour**] ① N-VAR The **flavor** of a food or drink is its taste. ❑ *I always add some paprika for extra flavor.* ② N-COUNT If something is orange **flavor** or beef **flavor**, it is made to taste of orange or beef. ❑ *It has an orange flavor and smooth texture.* ③ V-T If you **flavor** food or drink, you add something to it to give it a particular taste. ❑ *Lime preserved in salt is a north African speciality which is used to flavor chicken dishes.*

-flavored /-fléɪvərd/ [BRIT **-flavoured**] COMB in ADJ **-flavored** is used after nouns such as strawberry and chocolate to indicate that a food or drink is flavored with strawberry or chocolate. ❑ *...strawberry-flavored sweets.*

fla|vor|ing /fléɪvərɪŋ/ (flavorings) [BRIT **flavouring**] N-VAR **Flavorings** are substances that are added to food or drink to give it a particular taste. ❑ *...lemon flavoring.*

flaw /flɔ/ (flaws) ① N-COUNT A **flaw** in something such as a theory or argument is a mistake in it, which causes it to be less effective or valid. ❑ *There were, however, a number of crucial flaws in his monetary theory.* ② N-COUNT A **flaw in** someone's character is an undesirable quality that they have. ❑ *The only flaw in his character seems to be a short temper.* ③ N-COUNT A **flaw in** something such as a pattern or material is a fault in it that should not be there. ❑ *It's like having a flaw in a piece of material - the longer you leave it, the weaker it gets.*

flawed /flɔd/ ADJ Something that is **flawed** has a mark, fault, or mistake in it. ❑ *These tests were so seriously flawed as to render the results meaningless.*

flaw|less /flɔlɪs/ ADJ If you say that something or someone is **flawless**, you mean that they are extremely good and that there are no faults or problems with them. ❑ *Discovery's takeoff this morning from Cape Canaveral was flawless.* ● **flaw|less|ly** ADV ❑ *Each stage of the battle was carried off flawlessly.*

flea /fli/ (fleas) N-COUNT A **flea** is a very small jumping insect that has no wings and feeds on the blood of humans or animals.

fleck /flɛk/ (flecks) N-COUNT **Flecks** are small marks on a surface, or objects that look like small marks. ❑ *He went to the men's room to wash flecks of blood from his shirt.*

fled /flɛd/ **Fled** is the past tense and past participle of **flee**.

fledg|ling /flɛdʒlɪŋ/ (fledglings) ① N-COUNT A **fledgling** is a young bird that has its feathers and is learning to fly. ❑ *...when fledglings are almost ready to leave the nests.* ② ADJ You use **fledgling** to describe a person, organization, or system that is new or without experience. [ADJ n] ❑ *...Russia's fledgling democracy.*

flee ◆◇◇ /fli/ (flees, fleeing, fled) V-T/V-I If you **flee from** something or someone, or **flee** a person or thing, you escape from them. [WRITTEN] [no passive] ❑ *He slammed*

가산명사 룸메이트 [영국영어; 미국영어 roommate]

① 타동사/자동사 펴다; 펴지다 ❑ 그는 포장지를 조심스럽게 편 후 책갈피 사이에 넣었다. ❑ 쿡이 이름을 부르자 그 개는 귀를 약간 늡혔다. ● 구동사 펴다; 펴지다 ❑ 그 언덕은 산 남쪽에서 평평해졌다. ② 타동사 납작하게 만들다, 없애 버리다 ❑ 5층짜리 건물을 날려 버릴 수 있는 폭약 ❑ 그 지방 대부분을 초토화시킨 폭격 ③ 타동사 몸을 바짝 붙이다 ❑ 그는 내가 지나갈 때 벽돌벽 쪽으로 몸을 바짝 붙였다. ④ 타동사 매려눕히다 ❑ "난 여자가 사람을 그렇게 때려눕히는 걸 처음 봤어. 그 남자를 초주검을 만들어 놨어."라고 한 선원이 말했다.

① 타동사 아부하다, 좋게 말해 주다 [탐탁찮음] ❑ 난 그녀가 그냥 아부를 하고 있다는 거 알고 있었어. ② 타동사 자신하다; 넌 자만하고 있어; 자만하지 마 ❑ 나는 누가 뭐래도 이 반전 운동이 전쟁을 끝낼 것이라고 자신한다.

형용사 우쭐해진, 으쓱한 ❑ 로베르토의 긴 편지를 받고 그녀는 우쭐해졌다.

① 형용사 돋보이게 하는 ❑ 이건 그렇게 잘 나온 사진은 아니야. ② 형용사 으쓱하게 만드는, 우쭐하게 하는 ❑ 그의 동료들 대부분은 그에게 긍정적으로 말했고, 심지어 으쓱하게 하는 말을 하기도 했다.

불가산명사 수저류 [미국영어; 영국영어 cutlery] ❑ 주전자, 프라이 팬, 접시, 컵, 그리고 수저류로 구성된 식기 세트가 제공된다.

타동사 과시하다 [탐탁찮음] ❑ 그들은 부를 과시하며 롤스로이스를 몰고 다녔다.

[영국영어 flavour] ① 가산명사 또는 불가산명사 맛 ❑ 나는 맛을 더 내기 위해 파프리카를 항상 넣는다. ② 가산명사 맛 (의 향) ❑ 그것은 오렌지 맛의 향이 들어 있고, 조직이 부드럽다. ③ 타동사 향료를 넣다 ❑ 소금에 절인 라임은 닭요리에 향료로 쓰이는 북아프리카 특산품이다.

[영국영어 -flavoured] 복합형-형용사 – 맛 ❑ 딸기 맛 사탕

[영국영어 flavouring] 가산명사 또는 불가산명사 향료 ❑ 레몬향

① 가산명사 결함 ❑ 그러나 그의 통화 이론에는 결정적인 결함이 몇 가지 있었다. ② 가산명사 결점 ❑ 그의 성격에서 유일한 결점은 성질이 급하다는 것이다. ③ 가산명사 흠 ❑ 그건 물건에 흠이 있는 것과 같아. 오래 두면 둘수록 더 약해져.

형용사 흠이 있는 ❑ 그 테스트들은 너무나 심각한 결함들이 있어서 그 결과는 무의미해졌다.

형용사 완전무결한, 순조로운 ❑ 디스커버리호는 오늘 아침 케이프 캐너버럴에서 순조롭게 발사됐다. ● 완전무결하게, 순조롭게 부사 ❑ 전투의 모든 단계들이 순조롭게 이행되었다.

가산명사 벼룩

가산명사 점, 얼룩 ❑ 그는 셔츠에 묻은 핏방울들을 씻으러 화장실로 갔다.

flee의 과거, 과거 분사

① 가산명사 (겨우 날 수 있는) 어린 새 ❑ 날 수 있는 어린 새가 둥지를 떠날 준비가 거의 다 되었을 때 ② 형용사 초보의, 걸음마 단계의 ❑ 걸음마 단계에 있는 러시아의 민주주의

타동사/자동사 도망가다, 달아나다 [문어체] ❑ 그는 등 뒤로 침실 문을 쾅 닫고는 도망갔다. ❑ 내무부 장관은

the bedroom door behind him and fled. ❑ *The Home Secretary wants to protect the rights of refugees fleeing persecution or torture.*

박해와 고문을 피해 온 난민들의 권리를 보호하기를 원한다.

fleece /fliːs/ (**fleeces, fleecing, fleeced**) ■ N-COUNT A sheep's **fleece** is the coat of wool that covers it. ❑ *...a special protein which triggers the animal to shed its fleece.* ■ N-COUNT A **fleece** is the wool that is cut off one sheep in a single piece. ❑ *Wool can be spun from fleeces.* ■ V-T If you **fleece** someone, you get a lot of money from them by tricking them or charging them too much. [INFORMAL] ❑ *She claims he fleeced her out of thousands of pounds.* ■ N-VAR **Fleece** is a soft warm artificial fabric. A **fleece** is also a jacket or other garment made from this fabric. ❑ *...white leather slippers with fleece lining.*

■ 가산명사 양털, 털 ❑ 그 동물의 털갈이를 유발하는 특수한 단백질 ② 가산명사 양모 ❑ 털실은 양모에서 자아낼 수 있다. ③ 타동사 등쳐먹다 [비격식체] ❑ 그녀는 그가 자기 돈 수천 파운드를 등쳐먹었다고 주장했다. ④ 가산명사 또는 불가산명사 인조 양모 ❑ 안에 인조 양모를 댄 가죽 슬리퍼

fleet ♦◇◇ /fliːt/ (**fleets**) ■ N-COUNT A **fleet** is a group of ships organized to do something together, for example to fight battles or to catch fish. ❑ *A fleet sailed for New South Wales to establish the first European settlement in Australia.* ■ N-COUNT A **fleet** of vehicles is a group of them, especially when they all belong to a particular organization or business, or when they are all going somewhere together. ❑ *With its own fleet of trucks, the company delivers most orders overnight.*

■ 가산명사 함대, 선단 ❑ 호주에 유럽인의 첫 개척지를 건설할 선단이 뉴 사우스 웨일스로 갔다. ② 가산명사 차대(車隊), (한 회사 소유의) 차량들 ❑ 그 회사는 거의 모든 주문품을 자회사 소유의 트럭들로 밤 사이에 배달한다.

fleet|ing /fliːtɪŋ/ ADJ **Fleeting** is used to describe something which lasts only for a very short time. ❑ *The girls caught only a fleeting glimpse of the driver.* ● **fleet|ing|ly** ADV ❑ *A smile passed fleetingly across his face.*

형용사 순식간에 지나가는 ❑ 그 여자 애들은 그 운전자를 아주 잠깐 흘깃 봤을 뿐이다. ● 잠깐, 순식간에 부사 ❑ 그의 얼굴에 미소가 잠깐 스쳐 지나갔다.

flesh /flɛʃ/ (**fleshes, fleshing, fleshed**) ■ N-UNCOUNT **Flesh** is the soft part of a person's or animal's body between the bones and the skin. ❑ *...the pale pink flesh of trout and salmon.* ② N-UNCOUNT You can use **flesh** to refer to human skin and the human body, especially when you are considering it in a sexual way. ❑ *...the warmth of her flesh.* ③ N-UNCOUNT The **flesh** of a fruit or vegetable is the soft inside part of it. ❑ *Cut the flesh from the olives and discard the stones.* ④ PHRASE You use **flesh and blood** to emphasize that someone has human feelings or weaknesses, often when contrasting them with machines. ❑ *I'm only flesh and blood, like anyone else.* ⑤ PHRASE If you say that someone is your **own flesh and blood**, you are emphasizing that they are a member of your family. [EMPHASIS] ❑ *The kid, after all, was his own flesh and blood. He deserved a second chance.* ⑥ PHRASE If something **makes** your **flesh creep** or **makes** your **flesh crawl**, it makes you feel disgusted, shocked or frightened. ❑ *It makes my flesh creep to think of it.* ⑦ PHRASE If you meet or see someone **in the flesh**, you actually meet or see them, rather than, for example, seeing them in a movie or on television. ❑ *The first thing viewers usually say when they see me in the flesh is "You're smaller than you look on TV."*

■ 불가산명사 살 ❑ 송어와 연어의 연분홍 어육 ② 불가산명사 몸 ❑ 그녀의 따뜻한 몸 ③ 불가산명사 과육 ❑ 올리브 과육을 잘라 내고 씨는 버려라. ④ 구 (기계가 아닌) 인간 [강조] ❑ 나도 다른 사람처럼 기계가 아닌 인간일 뿐이다. ⑤ 구 혈육 [강조] ❑ 어쨌거나 그 아이는 그의 혈육이었다. 그 아이에게는 다른 기회가 주어져야 했다. ⑥ 구 온몸이 오싹하게 만들다, 소름이 끼치게 하다 ❑ 그건 생각만 해도 소름이 끼쳐. ⑦ 구 실제로 (만나다) ❑ 시청자들이 나를 실제로 봤을 때 보통 가장 먼저 하는 말은 "텔레비전에서 보는 것보다 아담하시네요."이다.

▶**flesh out** PHRASAL VERB If you **flesh out** something such as a story or plan, you add details and more information to it. ❑ *Permission for a warehouse development has already been granted and the developers are merely fleshing out the details.*

구동사 살을 붙이다 ❑ 창고 건설 허가는 이미 나왔고 건설업자는 단지 세부적인 살만 붙이고 있다.

flew /fluː/ **Flew** is the past tense of **fly**.

fly의 과거

Word Link	flex ≈ *bending* : *flex, flexible, reflex*

flex /flɛks/ (**flexes, flexing, flexed**) ■ N-VAR A **flex** is an electric cable containing two or more wires that is connected to an electrical appliance. [mainly BRIT; AM **cord**] ❑ *A naked bulb dangled on a flex.* ② V-T If you **flex** your muscles or parts of your body, you bend, move, or stretch them for a short time in order to exercise them. ❑ *He slowly flexed his muscles and tried to stand.* ③ to **flex** your **muscles** →see **muscle**

■ 가산명사 또는 불가산명사 전선 [주로 영국영어; 미국영어 cord] ❑ 전구 하나가 전선에 달랑 매달려 있었다. ② 타동사 펴다; 구부리다 ❑ 그는 근육을 천천히 펴며 일어서려고 애썼다.

Word Link	ible ≈ *able to be* : *audible, flexible, possible*

flex|ible ♦◇◇ /flɛksɪbəl/ ■ ADJ A **flexible** object or material can be bent easily without breaking. ❑ *...brushes with long, flexible bristles.* ● **flexi|bil|ity** /flɛksɪbɪlɪti/ N-UNCOUNT ❑ *The flexibility of the lens decreases with age; it is therefore common for our sight to worsen as we get older.* ② ADJ Something or someone that is **flexible** is able to change easily and adapt to different conditions and circumstances as they occur. [APPROVAL] ❑ *...flexible working hours.* ● **flexi|bil|ity** N-UNCOUNT ❑ *The flexibility of distance learning would be particularly suited to busy managers.*

■ 형용사 유연한 ❑ 길고 유연한 털이 달린 붓 ● 유연성 불가산명사 ❑ 나이를 먹으면 수정체의 탄성이 떨어진다. 그래서 나이를 먹을수록 시력이 나빠지는 것이 보통이다. ② 형용사 유연한, 융통성 있는, 탄력적인 [마음에 듦] ❑ 탄력적 근무 시간 ● 유연성, 융통성, 탄력성 불가산명사 ❑ 원격 학습의 탄력성이 바쁜 관리자들에겐 안성맞춤일 것이다.

flex|time /flɛkstaɪm/ [BRIT, sometimes AM **flexitime**] N-UNCOUNT **Flextime** is a system that allows employees to vary the time that they start or finish work, provided that an agreed total number of hours are spent at work. [BUSINESS] ❑ *I have recently introduced flextime for all my staff.*

[영국영어, 미국영어 가끔 flexitime] 불가산명사 선택적 근로 시간제 [경제] ❑ 최근 나는 전 직원에게 선택적 근로 시간제를 도입했다.

flick /flɪk/ (**flicks, flicking, flicked**) ■ V-T/V-I If something **flicks** in a particular direction, or if someone **flicks** it, it moves with a short, sudden movement. ❑ *His tongue flicked across his lips.* ❑ *He flicked his cigarette out of the window.* ● N-COUNT **Flick** is also a noun. ❑ *...a flick of a paintbrush.* ② V-T If you **flick** something away, or off something else, you remove it with a quick movement of your hand or finger. ❑ *Shirley flicked a speck of fluff from the sleeve of her black suit.* ③ V-T If you **flick** something such as a whip or a towel, or **flick** something with it, you hold one end of it and move your hand quickly up and then forward, so that the other end moves. ❑ *She sighed and flicked a dishcloth at the counter.* ● N-COUNT **Flick** is also a noun. ❑ *...a flick of the whip.* ④ V-T If you **flick** a switch, or **flick** an electrical appliance on or off, you press the switch sharply so that it moves into a different position and turns on or off the equipment. ❑ *Sam was flicking a flashlight on and off.* ⑤ V-I If you **flick through** a book or magazine, you turn its pages quickly, for example to get a general idea of its contents or to look for a particular item. If you **flick through** television channels, you continually change channels very quickly, for example using a remote control. ❑ *She was flicking through some magazines on a table.* ● N-SING **Flick** is also a noun. ❑ *I thought I'd have a quick flick through some recent issues.*

■ 타동사/자동사 휙 움직이다 ❑ 그는 혀를 휙 내밀어 입술을 핥았다. ❑ 그는 담배꽁초를 창밖으로 휙 튀겨 버렸다. ● 가산명사 휙 움직임, 휙 튀기기 ❑ 화필을 휙 움직임 ② 타동사 휙 털다 ❑ 설리는 검정색 정장 소매에 묻은 보푸라기를 휙 털어 버렸다. ③ 타동사 휙 내리치다 ❑ 그녀는 한숨을 쉬고는, 행주로 카운터를 휙 내리쳤다. ● 가산명사 휙 내리치기 ❑ 채찍을 한 번 휙 내리침 ④ 타동사 휙 끄다; 휙 켜다 ❑ 샘은 손전등의 스위치를 휙 켰다 껐다 하고 있었다. ⑤ 자동사 휙 넘기다 ❑ 그녀는 탁자 위의 잡지들을 몇 권 휙휙 넘기고 있었다. ● 단수명사 휙 넘기기 ❑ 최신호들을 한 번 휙 넘겨봐야 할 것 같다.

flick|er /flíkər/ (flickers, flickering, flickered) v-I If a light or flame **flickers**, it shines unsteadily. ❑ *Fluorescent lights flickered, and then the room was brilliantly, blindingly bright.* ● N-COUNT **Flicker** is also a noun. ❑ *Looking through the cabin window I saw the flicker of flames.*

자동사 깜박거리다, (불빛이) 춤추다 ❑ 형광등이 깜박거리더니, 방이 눈부시게 환해졌다. ● 가산명사 깜박임 ❑ 선실 창밖으로 불꽃이 춤추는 것이 보였다.

flight ♦♦◇ /flaít/ (flights) **1** N-COUNT A **flight** is a journey made by flying, usually in an airplane. ❑ *The flight will take four hours.* **2** N-COUNT You can refer to an airplane carrying passengers on a particular journey as a particular **flight**. [also N num] ❑ *BA flight 286 was two hours late.* **3** N-UNCOUNT **Flight** is the action of flying, or the ability to fly. ❑ *Supersonic flight could become a routine form of travel in the 21st century.* **4** N-UNCOUNT **Flight** is the act of running away from a dangerous or unpleasant situation or place. ❑ *The family was often in flight, hiding out in friends' houses.* **5** N-COUNT A **flight** of steps or stairs is a set of steps or stairs that lead from one level to another without changing direction. ❑ *We walked in silence up a flight of stairs and down a long corridor.* →see **fly**
→see Word Web: **flight**

1 가산명사 비행 ❑ 비행 시간은 네 시간 걸릴 것이다. **2** 가산명사 항공편 ❑ 영국 항공 286편은 두 시간 지연됐다. **3** 불가산명사 비행, 비행력 ❑ 초음속 비행이 21세기에는 일상적인 여행 형태가 될 수도 있다. **4** 불가산명사 탈출, 피신 ❑ 그 가족은 종종 달아나서 친구들 집에 숨어 지냈다. **5** 가산명사 (연이은) 계단 ❑ 우리는 계단을 조용히 걸어 올라가 긴 복도를 따라갔다.

flight at|tend|ant (flight attendants) N-COUNT On an airplane, the **flight attendants** are the people whose job is to take care of the passengers and serve their meals.

가산명사 항공기 승무원

flim|sy /flímzi/ (flimsier, flimsiest) **1** ADJ A **flimsy** object is weak because it is made of a weak material, or is badly made. ❑ *...a flimsy wooden door.* **2** ADJ **Flimsy** cloth or clothing is thin and does not give much protection. ❑ *...a very flimsy pink chiffon nightgown.* **3** ADJ If you describe something such as evidence or an excuse as **flimsy**, you mean that it is not very good or convincing. ❑ *The charges were based on very flimsy evidence.*

1 형용사 부실한 ❑ 부실한 나무문 **2** 형용사 얇은 ❑ 아주 얇은 분홍색 시폰 나이트가운 **3** 형용사 빈약한 (증거), 궁색한 (변명) ❑ 그 혐의는 빈약한 증거에 근거를 두고 있었다.

flinch /flíntʃ/ (flinches, flinching, flinched) **1** v-I If you **flinch**, you make a small sudden movement, especially when something surprises you or hurts you. [usu neg] ❑ *Leo stared back at him without flinching.* **2** v-I If you **flinch** from something unpleasant, you are unwilling to do it or think about it, or you avoid doing it. ❑ *The world community should not flinch in the face of this challenge.*

1 자동사 움찔하다 ❑ 리오는 눈 하나 꿈쩍하지 않고 그를 되노려보았다. **2** 자동사 주춤하다 ❑ 세계는 이 도전 앞에서 주춤거려서는 안 된다.

fling /flíŋ/ (flings, flinging, flung) **1** v-T If you **fling** something somewhere, you throw it there using a lot of force. ❑ *The woman flung the cup at him.* **2** v-T If you **fling yourself** somewhere, you move or jump there suddenly and with a lot of force. ❑ *He flung himself to the floor.* **3** v-T If you **fling** a part of your body in a particular direction, especially your arms or head, you move it there suddenly. ❑ *She flung her arms around my neck and kissed me.* **4** v-T If you **fling** someone to the ground, you push them very roughly so that they fall over. ❑ *The youth got him by the front of his shirt and flung him to the ground.* **5** v-T If you **fling** something into a particular place or position, you put it there in a quick or angry way. ❑ *Peter flung his shoes into the corner.* **6** v-T If you **fling yourself into** a particular activity, you do it with a lot of enthusiasm and energy. ❑ *She flung herself into her career.* **7** N-COUNT If two people have a **fling**, they have a brief sexual relationship. [INFORMAL] ❑ *She claims she had a brief fling with him 30 years ago.* **8** **Fling** can be used instead of "throw" in many expressions that usually contain "throw."

1 타동사 내던지다 ❑ 그 여자는 그에게 컵을 내던졌다. **2** 타동사 몸을 던지다 ❑ 그는 바닥에 몸을 던졌다. **3** 타동사 휙 움직이다 ❑ 그녀가 갑자기 내 목을 얼싸안고는 키스를 했다. **4** 타동사 내동댕이치다 ❑ 그 청년은 그의 멱살을 잡고 땅바닥에 내동댕이쳤다. **5** 타동사 내팽개치다 ❑ 피터는 구두를 구석으로 내팽개쳤다. **6** 타동사 (온몸을) 던지다 ❑ 그녀는 자기 일에 온몸을 던졌다. **7** 가산명사 육체관계 [비격식체] ❑ 그녀는 자기가 그와 30년 전에 잠깐 육체관계가 있었다고 주장한다. **8** 던지다

flip /flíp/ (flips, flipping, flipped) **1** v-T If you **flip** a device on or off, or if you **flip** a switch, you turn it on or off by pressing the switch quickly. ❑ *He didn't flip on the headlights until he was two blocks away.* ❑ *Then he walked out, flipping the lights off.* **2** v-T/v-I If you **flip** through the pages of a book, for example, you quickly turn over the pages in order to find a particular one or to get an idea of the contents. ❑ *He was flipping through a magazine in the living room.* **3** v-T/v-I If something **flips** over, or if you **flip** it over or into a different position, it moves or is moved into a different position. ❑ *The plane then flipped over and burst into flames.* **4** v-T If you **flip** something, especially a coin, you use your thumb to make it turn over and over, as it goes through the air. ❑ *I pulled a coin from my pocket and flipped it.*

1 타동사 (똑 치서) 켜다, 끄다 ❑ 그는 두 블록 떨어질 때까지 전조등을 켜지 않았다. ❑ 그리고 나서 그는 불을 끄고 걸어 나갔다. **2** 타동사/자동사 휙휙 넘기다 ❑ 그는 거실에서 잡지를 휙휙 넘겨보고 있었다. **3** 타동사/자동사 (위치를 휙) 옮기다, (제대로 휙) 바꾸다 ❑ 그러다가 비행기가 휙 뒤집어지더니 불길에 휩싸였다. **4** 타동사 공중으로 통기다 ❑ 나는 호주머니에서 동전 하나를 꺼내 공중으로 통겼다.

flip|chart /flíptʃɑrt/ (flipcharts) N-COUNT A **flipchart** is a stand with large sheets of paper which is used when presenting information at a meeting. ❑ *There are three conference rooms each of which is equipped with a screen, flipchart, and audio visual equipment.*

가산명사 괘도 ❑ 스크린과 괘도, 시청각 기자재가 구비된 회의실 세 곳이 있다.

flirt /flɜ́rt/ (flirts, flirting, flirted) **1** v-RECIP If you **flirt with** someone, you behave as if you are sexually attracted to them, in a playful or not very serious way. ❑ *Dad's flirting with all the ladies, or they're all flirting with him, as usual.* ● **flir|ta|tion** /flɜrteíʃⁿn/ (flirtations) N-VAR [oft N with n] ❑ *She was aware of his attempts at flirtation.* **2** N-COUNT Someone who is a **flirt** likes to flirt a lot. ❑ *I've always been a real flirt, I had a different boyfriend every week.* **3** v-I If you **flirt with** the idea of something, you consider it but do not do anything about it. ❑ *My mother used to flirt with Anarchism.* ● **flir|ta|tion** N-VAR ❑ *...the party's brief flirtation with economic liberalism.*

1 상호동사 추근거리다 ❑ 아빠는 모든 여자들한테 추근거렸고, 모든 여자들도 늘 그렇듯이 아빠에게 추근거렸다. ● 추근거림 가산명사 또는 불가산명사 ❑ 그녀는 그가 추근거리려 하는 것을 알고 있었다. **2** 가산명사 바람둥이 ❑ 난 정말 바람둥이여서, 매주 다른 남자 친구를 만났다. **3** 자동사 (실행은 않고) 생각만 하다 ❑ 우리 어머니는 생각뿐이 무정부주의자셨다. ● 생각만 함 가산명사 또는 불가산명사 ❑ 그 정당이 잠깐 생각만 해 본 경제적 자유주의

flit /flít/ (flits, flitting, flitted) **1** v-I If you **flit** around or **flit** between one place and another, you go to lots of places without staying for very long in any of them. ❑ *Laura flits about New York hailing taxis at every opportunity.* **2** v-I If someone

1 자동사 (이리저리) 돌아다니다 ❑ 로라는 기회가 있을 때마다 택시를 잡아서 뉴욕 시내를 돌아다녔다. **2** 자동사 이랬다저랬다 하다 ❑ 그는 주제를 너무나도

Word Web   flight

In order for an airplane to **fly**, it must overcome the force of **gravity** and also move forward through the air. The **propellers** or **jet engines** provide the **thrust** that helps the plane move ahead. This force is opposed by the **drag** on the wings as they encounter **air resistance**. The upper part of the wing is **curved**, which reduces the **air pressure** over it. This airflow over the wing provides the lift that allows the plane to rise from the ground.

a b c d e f g h i j k l m n o p q r s t u v w x y z

A

flits from one thing or situation to another, they move or turn their attention from one to the other very quickly. ❑ *He's prone to flit between subjects with amazing ease.* ▣ V-I If something such as a bird or a bat **flits** about, it flies quickly from one place to another. ❑ *...the parrot that flits from tree to tree.*

쉽게 바꾸는 경향이 있다. ❸ 자동사 (이리저리) 날아다니다 ❑이 나무 저 나무 날아다니는 앵무새

B

float ♦♦◇ /floʊt/ (**floats, floating, floated**) ▣ V-T/V-I If something or someone is **floating** in a liquid, they are in the liquid, on or just below the surface, and are being supported by it. You can also **float** something on a liquid. ❑ *They noticed fifty and twenty dollar bills floating in the water.* ❑ *It's minus three and small icebergs are floating by.* ▣ V-I Something that **floats** lies on or just below the surface of a liquid when it is put in it and does not sink. ❑ *They will also float if you drop them in the water.* ▣ N-COUNT A **float** is a light object that is used to help someone or something float. ❑ *Armbands, swim rings, and floats will provide confidence in the water.* ▣ N-COUNT A **float** is a small object attached to a fishing line which floats on the water and moves when a fish has been caught. ▣ V-I Something that **floats** in or through the air hangs in it or moves slowly and gently through it. ❑ *The white cloud of smoke floated away.* ▣ V-T If you **float** a project, plan, or idea, you suggest it for others to think about. ❑ *The French had floated the idea of placing the diplomatic work in the hands of the UN.* ▣ V-T If a company director **floats** their company, they start to sell shares in it to the public. [BUSINESS] ❑ *He floated his firm on the stock market.* ▣ V-T/V-I If a government **floats** its country's currency or allows it to **float**, it allows the currency's value to change freely in relation to other currencies. [BUSINESS] ❑ *On January 15th Brazil was forced to float its currency.* ▣ N-COUNT A **float** is a truck on which displays and people in special costumes are carried in a parade. ❑ *...a procession of makeshift floats bearing loudspeakers and banners.*

▣ 타동사/자동사 뜨다; 띄우다 ❑그들은 물 위에 50달러와 20달러짜리 지폐들이 떠 있는 것을 발견했다. ❑현재 기온은 영하 3도이고, 작은 빙산들이 떠간다. ▣ 자동사 뜨다 ❑그것들도 물에 집어넣으면 뜰 거야. ▣ 가산명사 부기 ❑팔 튜브, 일반 튜브, 그 외 물에 뜨는 부기들은 물속에서 자신감을 갖게 해 줄 것이다. ▣ 가산명사 찌 ❹ 자동사 떠가다, 떠다니다 ❑하얀 구름 같은 연기가 멀리 떠갔다. ▣ 타동사 (생각을) 내놓다 ❑프랑스 인들은 그 외교 사안을 유엔의 손에 넘기자는 생각을 내놓았었다. ▣ 타동사 상장하다 [경제] ❑그는 자신의 회사를 주식 시장에 상장하였다. ▣ 타동사/자동사 변동 환율제를 시행하다 [경제] ❑1월 15일에 브라질은 변동 환율제를 시행해야만 했다. ▣ 가산명사 (축제 때의) 이동식 무대차 ❑확성기와 현수막을 단 임시 이동식 무대차들의 행렬

C
D
E
F
G

flock /flɒk/ (**flocks, flocking, flocked**) ▣ N-COUNT-COLL A **flock of** birds, sheep, or goats is a group of them. ❑ *They kept a small flock of sheep.* ▣ N-COUNT-COLL You can refer to a group of people or things as a **flock of** them to emphasize that there are a lot of them. [EMPHASIS] ❑ *These cases all attracted flocks of famous writers.* ▣ V-T/V-I If people **flock to** a particular place or event, a very large number of them go there, usually because it is pleasant or interesting. ❑ *The public have flocked to the show.* ❑ *The criticisms will not stop people flocking to see the film.*

▣ 가산명사-집합 떼 ❑그들은 양을 몇 마리 키웠다. ▣ 가산명사-집합 아주 많음 [강조] ❑이 사건들은 수많은 인기 작가의 관심을 끌었다. ▣ 타동사/자동사 몰려가다 ❑사람들이 그 쇼를 보러 몰려갔다. ❑그러한 비평이 사람들이 그 영화를 보러 몰려가는 것을 막지는 못할 것이다.

H
I
J

flog /flɒg/ (**flogs, flogging, flogged**) ▣ V-T If someone **is flogged**, they are hit very hard with a whip or stick as a punishment. ❑ *In these places people starved, were flogged, were clubbed to death.* ● **flog|ging** (**floggings**) ▣ V-T If someone tries to **flog** something, they try to sell it. [BRIT, INFORMAL] ❑ *They are trying to flog their house.*

▣ 타동사 매 맞다 ❑이곳들에서는 사람들이 굶주리고, 채찍질 당하고, 죽을 때까지 몽둥이로 맞았다. ● 매질, 태형 가산명사-집합 또는 불가산명사 ❑그는 재판장으로 끌려가서 태형과 종신형을 언도받는다. ▣ 타동사 팔다 [영국영어, 비격식체] ❑그들은 집을 팔려고 노력하고 있다.

K
L

flood ♦◇◇ /flʌd/ (**floods, flooding, flooded**) ▣ N-VAR If there is a **flood**, a large amount of water covers an area which is usually dry, for example when a river flows over its banks or a pipe bursts. ❑ *More than 70 people were killed in the floods, caused when a dam burst.* ❑ *This is the type of flood dreaded by cavers.* ▣ V-T/V-I If something such as a river or a burst pipe **floods** an area that is usually dry or if the area **floods**, it becomes covered with water. ❑ *The kitchen flooded.* ▣ V-T/V-I If a river **floods**, it overflows, especially after very heavy rain. ❑ *...the relentless rain that caused twenty rivers to flood.* ▣ N-COUNT If you say that a **flood of** people or things arrive somewhere, you are emphasizing that a very large number of them arrive there. [EMPHASIS] ❑ *The administration is trying to stem the flood of refugees out of Haiti and into Florida.* ▣ V-I If you say that people or things **flood** into a place, you are emphasizing that they arrive there in large numbers. [EMPHASIS] ❑ *Large numbers of immigrants flooded into the area.* ❑ *Enquiries flooded in from all over the world.* ▣ V-T If you **flood** a place **with** a particular type of thing, or if a particular type of thing **floods** a place, the place becomes full of so many of them that it cannot hold or deal with any more. ❑ *Manufacturers are destroying American jobs by flooding the market with cheap imports.* →see **disaster**, **storm**

▣ 가산명사 또는 불가산명사 홍수 ❑댐 붕괴로 일어난 홍수로 70명 이상이 목숨을 잃었다. ❑이것은 동굴 탐험가들이 두려워하는 유형의 홍수이다. ▣ 타동사/자동사 물바다로 만들다; 물바다가 되다 ❑부엌이 물바다가 되었다. ▣ 타동사/자동사 범람하다 ❑20군데의 강을 범람시킨 무지하게 내린 비 ▣ 가산명사 (사람, 물건의) 홍수 [강조] ❑정부는 아이티에서 플로리다로 물밀듯이 밀려오는 난민들을 저지하려고 노력 중이다. ▣ 자동사 물밀듯이 밀려오다, 쏟아지다 [강조] ❑수많은 이민자들이 그 지방으로 물밀듯이 밀려왔다. ❑전 세계에서 질문이 쏟아졌다. ▣ 타동사 넘치게 하다; 넘치다 ❑생산자들이 시장에 싸구려 수입품들을 넘치게 함으로써 미국의 일자리를 없애고 있다.

M
N
O
P
Q

flood|ing /flʌdɪŋ/ N-UNCOUNT If **flooding** occurs, an area of land that is usually dry is covered with water after heavy rain or after a river or lake flows over its banks. ❑ *The flooding, caused by three days of torrential rain, is the worst in sixty-five years.* →see **dam**

불가산명사 홍수 ❑3일 동안의 호우로 야기된 이 홍수는 65년 만의 최악의 홍수이다.

R

flood|light /flʌdlaɪt/ (**floodlights, floodlighting, floodlit**) ▣ N-COUNT **Floodlights** are very powerful lamps that are used outside to light public buildings, sports grounds, and other places at night. ❑ *PSG were leading 1-0 on aggregate when the floodlights failed.* ▣ V-T If a building or place **is floodlit**, it is lit by floodlights. ❑ *In the evening the facade is floodlit.*

▣ 가산명사 투광 조명, (경기장의) 조명탑 ❑피에스지는 경기장 조명탑이 나갔을 때, 통산 1대 0으로 앞서고 있었다. ▣ 타동사 투광 조명을 밝히다, (경기장을) 밝히다 ❑저녁이면 그 건물의 전면을 투광 조명으로 밝힌다.

S
T

floor ♦♦◇ /flɔːr/ (**floors, flooring, floored**) ▣ N-COUNT The **floor** of a room is the part of it that you walk on. ❑ *Jack's sitting on the floor watching TV.* ▣ N-COUNT A **floor** of a building is all the rooms that are on a particular level. ❑ *The café was on the top floor of the hospital.*

▣ 가산명사 바닥 ❑잭은 바닥에 앉아서 텔레비전을 보고 있었다. ▣ 가산명사 층 ❑카페는 병원의 맨 꼭대기 층에 있었다.

U
V

In North America, the **floor** at street level is the first floor and the next floor up is the second floor. In Britain, the **floor** at street level is the ground floor and the first floor is one floor up.

북미에서는 도로와 같은 높이인 1층이 first floor이고, 2층은 second floor이다. 영국에서는 도로와 같은 높이의 1층을 ground floor라 하고, 한 층 위의 2층을 first floor라 한다.

W

▣ N-COUNT The ocean **floor** is the ground at the bottom of an ocean. The valley **floor** is the ground at the bottom of a valley. ❑ *They spend hours feeding on the ocean floor.* ▣ N-COUNT The place where official debates and discussions are held, especially between members of parliament, is referred to as the **floor**. ❑ *The issues were debated on the floor of the House.* ▣ N-SING-COLL In a debate or discussion, **the floor** is the people who are listening to the arguments being put forward but who are not among the main speakers. ❑ *The president is taking questions from the floor.* ▣ V-T If you **are floored** by something, you are unable to respond to it because you are so surprised by it. [usu passive] ❑ *He was floored by the announcement.* ▣ →see also **flooring, dance floor, first floor, ground floor, shop floor** ▣ PHRASE If you **take to the floor**, you start dancing at a dance or

▣ 가산명사 (바다나 계곡 등의) 밑바닥 ❑그것들은 해저에서 먹이를 먹으며 몇 시간을 보낸다. ▣ 가산명사 회의장 ❑그 안건들은 의회에서 논의되었다. ▣ 단수명사-집합 (토론 프로의) 방청자 ❑대통령은 방청객들로부터 질문을 받고 있다. ▣ 타동사 할 말을 잃다 ❑그는 그 발표에 할 말을 잃었다. ▣ 구 춤추다 ❑신랑 신부와 양가 부모님이 춤을 추기 시작하였다. ▣ 구 (시합이나 토론에서) 완전히 제압하다 [비격식체] ❑그는 총리를 완전히 제압할 수 있었다.

X
Y
Z

disco. ❏ *The happy couple and their respective parents took to the floor.* ◳ PHRASE If you **wipe the floor with** someone, you defeat them completely in a competition or discussion. [INFORMAL] ❏ *He could wipe the floor with the Prime Minister.*

	Word Partnership *floor*의 연어
V.	**fall on the** floor; **sit on the** floor; **sweep the** floor ◳
N.	floor **to ceiling,** floor **space** ◳
	floor **plan** ◳
	forest floor, **ocean** floor ◳

---

floor|board /flɔrbɔrd/ (**floorboards**) N-COUNT **Floorboards** are the long pieces of wood that a wooden floor is made up of.

가산명사 마루장

floor|ing /flɔrɪŋ/ (**floorings**) N-MASS **Flooring** is a material that is used to make the floor of a room. ❏ *Quarry tiles are a popular kitchen flooring.*

물질명사 바닥재 ❏ 석재 타일은 흔히 쓰이는 부엌용 바닥재이다.

flop /flɒp/ (**flops, flopping, flopped**) ◳ V-I If you **flop** into a chair, for example, you sit down suddenly and heavily because you are so tired. ❏ *Bunbury flopped down upon the bed and rested his tired feet.* ◳ V-I If something **flops** onto something else, it falls there heavily or untidily. ❏ *The briefcase flopped onto the desk.* ◳ N-COUNT If something is a **flop**, it is completely unsuccessful. [INFORMAL] ❏ *It is the public who decide whether a film is a hit or a flop.* ◳ V-I If something **flops**, it is completely unsuccessful. [INFORMAL] ❏ *The film flopped badly at the box office.*

◳ 자동사 털썩 주저앉다 ❏ 번버리는 침대에 털썩 주저앉아서 두 발의 피로를 풀었다. ◳ 자동사 널브러지다 ❏ 그 서류 가방이 책상 위에 널브러져 있었다. ◳ 가산명사 실패작, 실패작 [비격식체] ❏ 영화가 히트작이냐 실패작이냐를 결정하는 사람은 대중들이다. ◳ 자동사 완전히 실패하다 [비격식체] ❏ 그 영화는 흥행에 완전히 실패했다.

flop|py /flɒpi/ ADJ Something that is **floppy** is loose rather than stiff, and tends to hang downward. ❏ *...the girl with the floppy hat and glasses.*

형용사 헐렁한 ❏ 헐렁한 모자와 안경을 쓰고 있는 그 소녀

flop|py disk (**floppy disks**) [BRIT also **floppy disc**] N-COUNT A **floppy disk** is a small magnetic disk that is used for storing computer data and programs. Floppy disks are used especially with personal computers.

[영국영어 floppy disc] 가산명사 플로피 디스크

flo|ra /flɔrə/ N-UNCOUNT-COLL You can refer to plants as **flora**, especially the plants growing in a particular area. [FORMAL] ❏ *...the variety of food crops and flora which now exists in Dominica.*

불가산명사-집합 (특정 지역에만 자라는) 식물군 [격식체] ❏ 지금 도미니카에서 자라는 농작물과 식물들

flo|ral /flɔrəl/ ◳ ADJ A **floral** fabric or design has flowers on it. ❏ *...a bright yellow floral fabric.* ◳ ADJ You can use **floral** to describe something that contains flowers or is made of flowers. [ADJ n] ❏ *...eye-catching floral arrangements.*

◳ 형용사 꽃무늬의 ❏ 밝은 노란색 꽃무늬가 있는 천 ◳ 형용사 꽃의 ❏ 눈을 사로잡을 만큼 잘 된 꽃꽂이

flo|rist /flɔrist, BRIT flɒrist/ (**florists**) ◳ N-COUNT A **florist** is a storekeeper who arranges and sells flowers and sells houseplants. ◳ N-COUNT A **florist** or a **florist's** is a store where flowers and houseplants are sold. ❏ *He bought her some roses at the florist's in the arcade near the theater.*

◳ 가산명사 꽃장수 ◳ 가산명사 꽃집 ❏ 그는 극장 근처 아케이드에 있는 꽃집에서 그녀에게 장미를 몇 송이 사 주었다.

flo|ta|tion /floʊteɪ∫n/ (**flotations**) N-VAR The **flotation** of a company is the selling of shares in it to the public. [BUSINESS] ❏ *Prudential's flotation will be the third largest this year, behind Kraft Foods and Agere Systems.*

가산명사 또는 불가산명사 회사채 발행 [경제] ❏ 올해 프루덴셜 사의 회사채 발행 규모는 크래프트 푸드 사와 아거시스템 사에 이어 세 번째로 가장 클 것이다.

floun|der /flaʊndər/ (**flounders, floundering, floundered**) ◳ V-I If something **is floundering**, it has many problems and may soon fail completely. ❏ *What a pity that his career was left to flounder.* ◳ V-I If you say that someone **is floundering**, you are criticizing them for not making decisions or for not knowing what to say or do. [DISAPPROVAL] ❏ *Right now, you've got a president who's floundering, trying to find some way to get his campaign jump-started.* ◳ V-I If you **flounder** in water or mud, you move in an uncontrolled way, trying not to sink. ❏ *Three men were floundering about in the water.*

◳ 자동사 힘들어지다 ❏ 그의 일이 갈수록 힘들어져 어쩌나. ◳ 자동사 허우적대다 [탑탁찮음] ❏ 지금 당신들은 허우적대며 선거 운동을 촉진시킬 수 있는 방안을 모색하고 있는 대통령을 모시고 있다. ◳ 자동사 허우적대다 ❏ 세 사람이 물 속에서 마구 허우적거리고 있었다.

flour /flaʊər/ (**flours**) N-MASS **Flour** is a white or brown powder that is made by grinding grain. It is used to make bread, cakes, and pastry. →see **grain**

물질명사 곡물 가루, 밀가루

flour|ish /flɜrɪʃ, BRIT flʌrɪʃ/ (**flourishes, flourishing, flourished**) ◳ V-I If something **flourishes**, it is successful, active, or common, and developing quickly and strongly. ❏ *Business flourished and within six months they were earning 18,000 roubles a day.* ● **flour|ish|ing** ADJ ❏ *London quickly became a flourishing port.* ◳ V-I If a plant or animal **flourishes**, it grows well or is healthy because the conditions are right for it. ❏ *The plant flourishes particularly well in slightly harsher climes.* ● **flour|ish|ing** ADJ ❏ *Britain has the largest and most flourishing fox population in Europe.* ◳ V-T If you **flourish** an object, you wave it about in a way that makes people notice it. ❏ *He flourished the glass to emphasize the point.* ● N-COUNT **Flourish** is also a noun. ❏ *He took his peaked cap from under his arm with a flourish and pulled it low over his eyes.*

◳ 자동사 번창하다 ❏ 그들은 사업이 번창해서 육 개월 만에 하루에 18,000루블을 벌고 있었다. ● 번창하는 형용사 ❏ 런던은 급성장하는 항구 도시가 되었다. ◳ 자동사 잘 자라다 ❏ 그 식물은 다소 척박한 땅에서 특히 잘 자란다. ● 잘 자라는, 번성하는 형용사 ❏ 영국은 유럽에서 가장 많은 수의 여우가 가장 잘 서식하는 곳이다. ◳ 타동사 흔들어 대다 ❏ 그는 그 위치를 알려 주려고 컵을 흔들어 댔다. ● 가산명사 야단스러운 몸짓 ❏ 그는 야단스럽게 챙 모자를 겨드랑이에서 꺼내서는 눈 바로 위까지 눌러썼다.

flout /flaʊt/ (**flouts, flouting, flouted**) V-T If you **flout** something such as a law, an order, or an accepted way of behaving, you deliberately do not obey it or follow it. ❏ *...illegal campers who persist in flouting the law.*

타동사 (고의적으로) 어기다 ❏ 법을 계속 어기면서 불법적으로 텐트 생활을 하는 사람들

flow ♦♦♦ /floʊ/ (**flows, flowing, flowed**) ◳ V-I If a liquid, gas, or electrical current **flows** somewhere, it moves there steadily and continuously. ❏ *A stream flowed gently down into the valley.* ❏ *The current flows into electric motors that drive the wheels.* ● N-VAR **Flow** is also a noun. ❏ *It works only in the veins, where the blood flow is slower.* ◳ V-I If a number of people or things **flow** from one place to another, they move there steadily in large groups, usually without stopping. ❏ *Large numbers of refugees continue to flow from the troubled region into the no-man's land.* ● N-VAR **Flow** is also a noun. ❏ *She watched the frantic flow of cars and buses along the street.* ◳ V-I If information or money **flows** somewhere, it moves freely between people or organizations. ❏ *A lot of this information flowed through other police departments.* ● N-VAR **Flow** is also a noun. ❏ *...the opportunity to control the flow of information.* →see also **cash flow** ◳ PHRASE If you say that an activity, or the person who is performing the activity, is **in full flow**, you mean that the activity has started and is being carried out with a great deal of energy and enthusiasm. ❏ *Lunch at Harry's Bar was in full flow when Irene made a splendid entrance.* →see **ocean, traffic**

◳ 자동사 흐르다 ❏ 시냇물이 잔잔히 계곡으로 흘러들어갔다. ❏ 바퀴를 돌리는 전기 모터 속으로 전류가 흐른다. ● 가산명사 또는 불가산명사 흐름 ❏ 그것은 혈류 속도가 느린 정맥에서만 효력이 있다. ◳ 자동사 (대규모로) 이동하다 ❏ 많은 피난민들이 분쟁 지역에서 비분쟁 지역으로 끊임없이 이동하고 있다. ● 가산명사 또는 불가산명사 이동, 물결 ❏ 그녀는 도로 위를 정신없이 달려가는 자동차와 버스의 흐름을 지켜보았다. ◳ 자동사 (정보가) 유포되다; (화폐가) 유통되다 ❏ 이 많은 정보들이 다른 경찰서로 유포되었다. ● 가산명사 또는 불가산명사 유포, 정보 유포를 통제할 기회 ◳ 구 한창 진행 중인 ❏ 아이린이 멋지게 등장했을 때, 해리스 바에서는 점심 식사가 한창이었다.

flow chart (**flow charts**) N-COUNT A **flow chart** or a **flow diagram** is a diagram which represents the sequence of actions in a particular process or activity. ❏ *This flow chart, shown below, summarizes the overall costing process.*

가산명사 플로 차트 ❏ 아래에 제시된 이 플로 차트에는 전반적인 비용 처리 과정이 요약되어 있다.

a b c d e f g h i j k l m n o p q r s t u v w x y z

flow|er ♦♦ /fláʊər/ (**flowers, flowering, flowered**) **1** N-COUNT A **flower** is the part of a plant which is often brightly colored, grows at the end of a stem, and only survives for a short time. □ *Each individual flower is tiny.* **2** N-COUNT A **flower** is a stem of a plant that has one or more flowers on it and has been picked, usually with others, for example to give as a present or to put in a vase. □ *...a bunch of flowers sent by a new admirer.* **3** N-COUNT **Flowers** are small plants that are grown for their flowers as opposed to trees, shrubs, and vegetables. □ *...a lawned area surrounded by screening plants and flowers.* **4** V-I When a plant or tree **flowers**, its flowers appear and open. □ *Several of these rhododendrons will flower this year for the first time.* **5** V-I When something **flowers**, for example a political movement or a relationship, it gets stronger and more successful. □ *Their relationship flowered.*
→see Word Web: **flower**

1 가산명사 꽃, 꽃송이 □ 꽃송이가 하나하나는 아주 작다. **2** 가산명사 꽃 □ 한 새로운 추종자가 보낸 꽃다발 **3** 가산명사 화초 □ 나무와 화초가 병풍처럼 둘러싸고 있는 잔디밭 **4** 자동사 꽃이 피다 □ 이 진달래들 중 몇 그루는 올해 처음으로 꽃이 필 것이다. **5** 자동사 (비유적으로) 꽃을 피우다 □ 그들의 관계가 꽃을 피웠다.

Word Partnership   *flower*의 연어

ADJ.	**dried** flower, **fresh** flower **1 2**
V.	**pick** a flower **2**
N.	flower **arrangement**, flower **garden**, flower **shop**, flower **show 2 3**

---

flow|er|ing /fláʊərɪŋ/ **1** N-UNCOUNT The **flowering of** something such as an idea or artistic style is the development of its popularity and success. □ *He may be happy with the flowering of new thinking, but he has yet to contribute much to it himself.* **2** ADJ **Flowering** shrubs, trees, or plants are those which produce noticeable flowers. [ADJ n] □ *...a late summer flowering plant like an aster.* →see **fruit**

1 불가산명사 개화 □ 그는 새로운 사상의 개화에 행복해할지 모르지만, 아직도 그 자신이 그것에 대해 상당한 노력을 해야 한다. **2** 형용사 꽃을 피우는 □ 과꽃과 같이 늦여름에 꽃을 피우는 식물

flown /floʊn/ **Flown** is the past participle of **fly**.

fly의 과거 분사

flu /flu/ N-UNCOUNT **Flu** is an illness which is similar to a bad cold but more serious. It often makes you feel very weak and makes your muscles hurt. [also the N] □ *I got flu.*

불가산명사 독감 □ 독감에 걸렸어.

fluc|tu|ate /flʌktʃueɪt/ (**fluctuates, fluctuating, fluctuated**) V-I If something **fluctuates**, it changes a lot in an irregular way. □ *Body temperature can fluctuate if you are ill.* ● **fluc|tua|tion** /flʌktʃueɪʃⁿn/ (**fluctuations**) N-VAR □ *Don't worry about tiny fluctuations in your weight.*

자동사 변화가 심하다, 변동하다 □ 아플 때는 체온 변화가 심할 수 있다. ● 변동, 요동 가산명사 또는 불가산명사 □ 작은 체중 변화를 걱정하지 마라.

flu|ent /fluənt/ **1** ADJ Someone who is **fluent in** a particular language can speak the language easily and correctly. You can also say that someone speaks **fluent** French, Chinese, or some other language. □ *She studied eight foreign languages but is fluent in only six of them.* ● **flu|en|cy** N-UNCOUNT □ *To work as a translator, you need fluency in at least one foreign language.* ● **flu|ent|ly** ADV □ *He spoke three languages fluently.* **2** ADJ If your speech, reading, or writing is **fluent**, you speak, read, or write easily, smoothly, and clearly with no mistakes. □ *He had emerged from being a hesitant and unsure candidate into a fluent debater.* ● **flu|en|cy** N-UNCOUNT □ *His son was praised for speeches of remarkable fluency.* ● **flu|ent|ly** ADV [ADV with v] □ *Alex didn't read fluently till he was nearly seven.*

1 형용사 유창한 □ 그녀는 여덟 개의 외국어를 공부했지만, 지금은 그 중 여섯 개 외국어에만 유창하다. ● 유창성 불가산명사 □ 번역가로서 일하려면, 적어도 한 가지 외국어라도 유창하게 할 필요가 있다. ● 유창하게 부사 □ 그는 세 개 언어를 유창하게 했다. **2** 형용사 유창한 □ 그는 머뭇거리고 자신감 없는 후보자에서 유창한 토론자로 변신했었다. ● 유창함 불가산명사 □ 그의 아들은 놀랄 만큼 유창한 연설로 찬사를 받았다. ● 유창하게 부사 □ 알렉스는 일곱 살이 다 되도록 글을 유창하게 읽지 못했다.

fluff /flʌf/ N-UNCOUNT **Fluff** consists of soft threads or fibers in the form of small, light balls or lumps. For example, you can refer to the fur of a small animal as **fluff**. □ *...the nestbox which contained two chicks: just small gray balls of fluff.*

불가산명사 보푸라기, 솜털 □ 그냥 아주 작은 회색 솜털 뭉치 같아 보이는 병아리 두 마리가 들어 있는 둥지 상자

fluffy /flʌfi/ (**fluffier, fluffiest**) **1** ADJ If you describe something such as a towel or a toy animal as **fluffy**, you mean that it is very soft. □ *...fluffy white towels.* **2** ADJ A cake or other food that is **fluffy** is very light because it has a lot of air in it. □ *Cream together the margarine and sugar with a wooden spoon until light and fluffy.*

1 형용사 보송보송한 □ 보송보송한 하얀색 타월 **2** 형용사 부풀어 오른 □ 마가린과 설탕을 가볍게 부풀어 오를 때까지 나무 숟가락으로 섞어라.

flu|id /fluɪd/ (**fluids**) **1** N-MASS A **fluid** is a liquid. [FORMAL] □ *The blood vessels may leak fluid, which distorts vision.* □ *Make sure that you drink plenty of fluids.* **2** ADJ **Fluid** movements or lines or designs are smooth and graceful. □ *His painting became less illustrational and more fluid.*

1 물질명사 액체 [격식체] □ 혈관에서 혈액이 흐를 수도 있는데, 그렇게 되면 시야가 일그러져 보이게 된다. □ 반드시 음료수를 많이 마셔라. **2** 형용사 부드러운, 유연한 □ 그의 그림은 덜 묘사적인 반면 더 부드러워졌다.

fluke /fluk/ (**flukes**) N-COUNT If you say that something good is a **fluke**, you mean that it happened accidentally rather than by being planned or arranged. [INFORMAL] [usu sing, also by N] □ *The discovery was something of a fluke.*

가산명사 요행 [비격식체] □ 그 발견은 일종의 요행이었다.

flung /flʌŋ/ **Flung** is the past tense and past participle of **fling**.

fling의 과거, 과거 분사

flunk /flʌŋk/ (**flunks, flunking, flunked**) V-T If you **flunk** an exam or a course, you fail to reach the required standard. [mainly AM, INFORMAL] □ *Your son is upset because he flunked a history exam.*

타동사 낙제하다 [주로 미국영어, 비격식체] □ 당신 아들이 역사 과목에 낙제점을 받아서 맘 상해 있어요.

fluo|res|cent /flʊresⁿnt/ **1** ADJ A **fluorescent** surface, substance, or color has a very bright appearance when light is directed onto it, as if it is actually shining itself. □ *...a piece of fluorescent tape.* **2** ADJ A **fluorescent** light shines with a very hard, bright light and is usually in the form of a long strip. □ *Fluorescent lights flickered, and then the room was brilliantly, blindingly bright.* →see **light bulb**

1 형용사 형광색의 □ 형광색 테이프 조각 **2** 형용사 형광등의 □ 형광등이 몇 번 깜박거리더니, 방이 너무나 환하게 밝아졌다.

Word Web   flower

People love **flowers** because they are **colorful** and they smell good. But the **color** and **scent** of flowers are also important in **reproduction**. Sometimes the wind helps pollinate a plant. However, most plants must attract **insects**, hummingbirds, or **bats** to guarantee fertilization. If this doesn't happen, no **seeds** form. As one of these creatures lands on a flower, **grains** of pollen stick to its body. It carries these to another flower. Different colors attract different insects and animals. Yellow and blue flowers seem to draw **bees** and **butterflies**. Red flowers attract hummingbirds. At night, **bats** seek out white flowers.

fluo|ride /ˈflʊəraɪd/ N-UNCOUNT **Fluoride** is a mixture of chemicals that is sometimes added to drinking water and toothpaste because it is considered to be good for people's teeth. →see **teeth**

불가산명사 불소 화합물

flur|ry /ˈflɜri, BRIT ˈflʌri/ (**flurries**) **1** N-COUNT A **flurry** of something such as activity or excitement is a short intense period of it. ❑ ...*a flurry of diplomatic activity aimed at ending the war.* **2** N-COUNT A **flurry** of something such as snow is a small amount of it that suddenly appears for a short time and moves in a quick, swirling way. ❑ *The Alps expect heavy cloud over the weekend with light snow flurries and strong winds.*

1 가산명사 한 차례의 동요, 작은 소란 ❑ 종전을 위한 한차례 분주한 외교 활동 **2** 가산명사 눈 보라, 비바람 ❑ 알프스 산에는 주말에 강풍과 가벼운 눈보라를 동반한 짙은 구름이 낄 것으로 예상된다.

flush /flʌʃ/ (**flushes, flushing, flushed**) **1** V-I If you **flush**, your face gets red because you are hot or ill, or because you are feeling a strong emotion such as embarrassment or anger. ❑ *Do you sweat a lot or flush a lot?* ● N-COUNT **Flush** is also a noun. ❑ *There was a slight flush on his cheeks.* ● **flushed** ADJ ❑ *Her face was flushed with anger.* **2** V-T/V-I When someone **flushes** a toilet after using it, they fill the toilet bowl with water in order to clean it, usually by pressing a handle or pulling a chain. You can also say that a toilet **flushes**. ❑ *She flushed the toilet and went back in the bedroom.* ● N-COUNT **Flush** is also a noun. ❑ *He heard the flush of a toilet.* **3** V-T If you **flush** something **down** the toilet, you get rid of it by putting it into the toilet bowl and flushing the toilet. ❑ *He was found trying to flush banknotes down the toilet.* **4** V-T If you **flush** a part of your body, you clean it or make it healthier by using a large amount of liquid to get rid of dirt or harmful substances. ❑ *Flush the eye with clean cold water for at least 15 minutes.* ● PHRASAL VERB **Flush out** means the same as **flush**. ❑ *...an "alternative" therapy that gently flushes out the colon to remove toxins.* **5** V-T If you **flush** dirt or a harmful substance **out** of a place, you get rid of it by using a large amount of liquid. ❑ *That won't flush out all the sewage, but it should unclog some stinking drains.* **6** V-T If you **flush** people or animals **out** of a place where they are hiding, you find or capture them by forcing them to come out of that place. ❑ *They flushed them out of their hiding places.* →see **plumbing**

1 자동사 (얼굴이) 달아오르다 ❑ 땀을 많이 흘리나요, 아니면 얼굴이 많이 달아오르나요? ● 가산명사 홍조 ❑ 그는 양 볼에 약간 홍조를 띠고 있었다. ● 얼굴이 붉어진 형용사 ❑ 그녀가 화가 나서 얼굴이 붉어졌다. **2** 타동사/자동사 (변기의) 물을 내리다 ❑ 그녀는 변기의 물을 내리고 침실로 돌아갔다. ● 가산명사 (변기의) 물 내리기 ❑ 그는 변기 물 내리는 소리를 들었다. **3** 타동사 변기 속에 넣고 씻어 내리다 ❑ 그가 변기에 지폐를 버리고 물을 내리려고 하다가 발각되었다. **4** 타동사 씻어 내리다, 헹구다 ❑ 적어도 15분간 깨끗한 냉수로 눈을 씻어라. ● 구동사 씻어 내리다, 헹구다 ❑ 결장의 독소를 부드럽게 씻어 내는 대체 요법 **5** 타동사 씻어 내다 ❑ 그것이 모든 오물을 씻어 내지는 못해도, 악취 나는 막힌 하수구를 뚫기는 할 것이다. **6** 타동사 (숨은 곳에서) 몰아내다 ❑ 그들은 그 사람들을 은신처에서 몰아내었다.

Word Partnership	flush의 연어
N.	*someone's* **face** flushes, flush **of embarrassment** **1**
	flush **a toilet** **2**
ADJ.	**slight** flush **1**

flushed /flʌʃt/ ADJ If you say that someone is **flushed with** success or pride you mean that they are very excited by their success or pride. [v-link ADJ with n] ❑ *Grace was flushed with the success of the venture.*

형용사 의기양양한 ❑ 그레이스는 그 벤처 사업의 성공으로 의기양양했다.

flus|ter /ˈflʌstər/ (**flusters, flustering, flustered**) V-T If you **fluster** someone, you make them feel nervous and confused by rushing them and preventing them from concentrating on what they are doing. ❑ *The General refused to be flustered.* ● **flus|tered** ADJ ❑ *She was so flustered that she forgot her reply.*

타동사 당황하게 하다, 정신 못 차리게 하다 ❑ 그 사령관은 좀처럼 당황하지 않았다. ● 정신 못 차리는 형용사 ❑ 그녀는 너무나 정신이 없어서 대답할 말을 잊어버렸다.

flute /fluːt/ (**flutes**) N-VAR A **flute** is a musical instrument of the woodwind family. You play it by blowing over a hole near one end while holding it sideways to your mouth. →see **orchestra**

가산명사 또는 불가산명사 플루트

flut|ter /ˈflʌtər/ (**flutters, fluttering, fluttered**) **1** V-T/V-I If something thin or light **flutters**, or if you **flutter** it, it moves up and down or from side to side with a lot of quick, light movements. ❑ *Her chiffon skirt was fluttering in the night breeze.* ❑ *...a butterfly fluttering its wings.* ● N-COUNT **Flutter** is also a noun. ❑ *...a flutter of white cloth.* **2** V-I If something light such as a small bird or a piece of paper **flutters** somewhere, it moves through the air with small quick movements. ❑ *The paper fluttered to the floor.*

1 타동사/자동사 나풀거리다; 퍼덕거리다 ❑ 그녀의 시폰 치마가 부드러운 밤바람에 나풀거렸다. ❑ 날개를 퍼덕이는 나비 한 마리 ● 가산명사 펄럭임, 나풀거림 ❑ 흰 천의 펄럭임 **2** 자동사 팔랑거리다 ❑ 그 종이가 팔랑거리며 바닥으로 떨어졌다.

flux /flʌks/ N-UNCOUNT If something is in **a state of flux**, it is constantly changing. ❑ *Education remains in a state of flux which will take some time to settle down.*

불가산명사 끊임없는 변화 ❑ 교육은 계속 끊임없이 변하고 있어서 정착되려면 어느 정도 시간이 필요할 것이다.

fly ♦♦♦ /flaɪ/ (**flies, flying, flew, flown**) **1** N-COUNT A **fly** is a small insect with two wings. There are many kinds of flies, and the most common are black in color. ❑ *Flies buzzed at the animals' swishing tails.* **2** V-I When something such as a bird, insect, or aircraft **flies**, it moves through the air. ❑ *The planes flew through the clouds.* **3** V-I If you **fly** somewhere, you travel there in an aircraft. ❑ *He flew to Los Angeles.* ❑ *He flew back to London.* **4** V-T/V-I When someone **flies** an aircraft, they control its movement in the air. ❑ *Parker had successfully flown both aircraft.* ❑ *He flew a small plane to Cuba.* ● **fly|ing** N-UNCOUNT ❑ *...a flying instructor.* **5** V-T To **fly** someone or something somewhere means to take or send them there in an aircraft. ❑ *It may be possible to fly the women and children out on Thursday.* **6** V-I If something such as your hair **is flying** about, it is moving about freely and loosely in the air. ❑ *His long, uncovered hair flew back in the wind.* **7** V-T/V-I If you **fly** a flag or if it **is flying**, you display it at the top of a pole. ❑ *They flew the flag of the African National Congress.* **8** V-I If you say that someone or something **flies** in a particular direction, you are emphasizing that they move there with a lot of speed or force. [EMPHASIS] ❑ *She flew to their bedsides when they were ill.* **9** N-COUNT The front opening on a pair of pants is referred to as the **fly**, or in British English the **flies**. It usually consists of a zipper or row of buttons behind a band of cloth. ❑ *I'm the kind of person who checks to see if my fly is undone.* **10** →see also **flying** **11** PHRASE If you say that someone wouldn't **hurt a fly** or wouldn't **harm a fly**, you are emphasizing that they are very kind and gentle. [EMPHASIS] ❑ *Ray wouldn't hurt a fly.* **12** PHRASE If you **let fly**, you attack someone, either physically by hitting them, or with words by insulting them. ❑ *A simmering dispute ended with her letting fly with a stream of obscenities.* **13** PHRASE If you **send** someone or something **flying** or if they **go flying**, they move through the air and fall down with a lot of force. ❑ *The blow sent the young man flying.* →see also **fly-on-the-wall** **14** to **fly in the face of** →see **face**. to **fly off the handle**

1 가산명사 파리 ❑ 그 동물들이 휘두르는 꼬리 쪽에서 파리가 윙윙거리며 날아다녔다. **2** 자동사 날다 ❑ 그 비행기들이 구름을 뚫고 날아갔다. **3** 자동사 비행기를 타고 가다 ❑ 그는 비행기를 타고 로스앤젤레스로 갔다. ❑ 그는 비행기 편으로 런던으로 돌아갔다. **4** 타동사/자동사 (항공기를) 조종하다 ❑ 파커는 성공적으로 두 항공기를 조종했다. ❑ 그는 경비행기를 조종해서 쿠바로 갔다. ● 비행 불가산명사 ❑ 비행 교관 **5** 타동사 비행기로 나르다 ❑ 목요일에 여자들과 아이들을 비행기에 태워 내보내는 것이 가능할지도 모른다. **6** 자동사 흩날리다 ❑ 아무것도 쓰지 않은 그의 긴 머리카락이 바람결에 흩날렸다. **7** 타동사/자동사 (깃발을) 내걸다; (깃발이) 내걸리다 ❑ 그들은 아프리카 국회 깃발을 내걸었다. **8** 자동사 쏜살같이 가다 [강조] ❑ 그들이 아팠을 때 그녀는 쏜살같이 그들의 침상으로 달려갔다. **9** 가산명사 (바지의) 앞 지퍼 ❑ 나는 혹시 바지 앞 지퍼를 안 채운 건 아닌가 꼭 확인하는 그런 사람이다. **10** 구 파리 한 마리도 못 죽이다 [강조] ❑ 레이는 파리 한 마리도 못 죽일 사람이다. **12** 구 공격하다 ❑ 언쟁이 서서히 격해져서 마지막에는 그녀는 쉴새없이 외설적인 욕설로 공격했다. **13** 구 나가떨어지게 만들다; 나가떨어지다 ❑ 그 젊은이는 그 한 방에 나가떨어졌다.

Word Web   fly

About 500 years ago, Leonardo da Vinci* designed some simple flying machines. His sketches look a lot like modern **parachutes** and **helicopters**. About 300 years later, the Montgolfier Brothers amazed the king of France with hot-air **balloon** flights. Soon inventors in many countries began experimenting with blimps, hang gliders, and human-powered **aircraft**. Most inventors tried to imitate the **flight** of birds. Then in 1903, the Wright brothers invented the first true **airplane**. Their gasoline-powered **craft** carried one **passenger**. The trip lasted 59 seconds. And amazingly, 70 years later **jumbo jets** carrying 400 passengers became an everyday occurrence.

Leonardo da Vinci (1452-1519): an Italian artist.

→see **handle**. a **fly in the ointment** →see **ointment**. **pigs might fly** →see **pig**. **sparks fly** →see **spark**. **time flies** →see **time**
→see **flag**, **flight**
→see Word Web: **fly**

▶**fly into** PHRASAL VERB If you **fly into** a bad temper or a panic, you suddenly become very angry or anxious and show this in your behavior. ❑ *Losing a game would cause him to fly into a rage.*

구동사 갑자기 ~하다 ❑ 경기에 지면 그는 갑자기 격분하곤 했다.

fly-drive ADJ On a **fly-drive** vacation, you travel part of the way to your destination by airplane, and collect a rental car at the airport so that you can drive the rest of the way. [ADJ n] ❑ *...a fly-drive break in New Zealand.*

형용사 비행기를 타고 목적지로 가서 렌터카로 여행하는 ❑ 비행기를 타고 뉴질랜드로 가서 그곳을 렌터카로 여행하는 휴가

fly|er /flaɪr/ (**flyers**) also **flier** ◼ N-COUNT A **flyer** is a pilot of an aircraft. ❑ *The American flyers sprinted for their planes and got into the cockpit.* ◾ N-COUNT You can refer to someone who travels by airplane as a **flyer**. ❑ *...regular business flyers.* ◼ N-COUNT A **flyer** is a small printed notice which is used to advertise a particular company, service, or event. ❑ *...although thousands of flyers advertising the tour were handed out during the Reading festival.* →see **advertising**

◼ 가산명사 항공기 조종사 ❑ 그 미국인 조종사들은 그들의 비행기를 향해 질주해서 조종석으로 들어갔다. ◾ 가산명사 비행기 승객 ❑ 정기적으로 사업차 비행기를 타는 승객들 ◼ 가산명사 광고 전단 ❑ 비록 레딩 축제 기간 동안 수천 장의 그 여행 광고 전단이 뿌려졌지만

fly|ing /flaɪɪŋ/ ◼ ADJ A **flying** animal has wings and is able to fly. [ADJ n] ❑ *...species of flying insects.* ◾ PHRASE If someone or something **gets off to a flying start**, or **makes a flying start**, they start very well, for example in a race or a new job. ❑ *Advertising revenue in the new financial year has got off to a flying start.*

◼ 형용사 날아다니는 ❑ 날아다니는 곤충류 ◾ 구 출발이 아주 좋다 ❑ 새로운 회계 연도의 첫 광고 수익이 아주 좋다.

fly-on-the-wall ADJ A **fly-on-the-wall** documentary is made by filming people as they do the things they normally do, rather than by interviewing them or asking them to talk directly to the camera. [ADJ n] ❑ *...a fly-on-the-wall documentary about the Queen's life.*

형용사 자연스러운 모습을 담은 ❑ 여왕의 자연스러운 일상생활을 담은 기록 영화

fly|over /flaɪoʊvər/ (**flyovers**) N-COUNT A **flyover** is a structure which carries one road over the top of another road. [BRIT; AM **overpass**]

가산명사 고가 도로 [영국영어; 미국영어 overpass]

foal /foʊl/ (**foals, foaling, foaled**) ◼ N-COUNT A **foal** is a very young horse. ◾ V-I When a female horse **foals**, it gives birth. ❑ *The mare is due to foal today.*

◼ 가산명사 망아지 ◾ 자동사 (말이) 새끼를 낳다 ❑ 그 암말이 오늘 새끼를 낳을 예정이다.

foam /foʊm/ (**foams**) ◼ N-UNCOUNT **Foam** consists of a mass of small bubbles that are formed when air and a liquid are mixed together. ❑ *The water curved round the rocks in great bursts of foam.* ◾ N-MASS **Foam** is used to refer to various kinds of manufactured products which have a soft, light texture like a thick liquid. ❑ *...shaving foam.* ◼ N-MASS **Foam** or **foam rubber** is soft rubber full of small holes which is used, for example, to make mattresses and cushions. ❑ *...modern three-piece suites filled with foam rubber.*

◼ 불가산명사 물거품 ❑ 물이 수많은 물거품을 일으키며 바위를 돌아 흘렀다. ◾ 물질명사 거품제 ❑ 면도용 거품제 ◼ 물질명사 스펀지 고무 ❑ 스펀지 고무 속을 채운 3개 한 조로 된 현대식 소파

fo|cal point /foʊkᵊl pɔɪnt/ (**focal points**) N-COUNT The **focal point** of something is the thing that people concentrate on or pay most attention to. ❑ *...the focal point for the town's many visitors – the Royal Shakespeare Theatre.*

가산명사 관심의 초점 ❑ 그 도시를 방문하는 사람들의 관심의 초점인 로열 셰익스피어 극장

fo|cus ♦♦◇ /foʊkəs/ (**foci**) /foʊsaɪ/ (**focusing, focused**)

The spellings **focusses, focussing, focussed** are also used, especially in British English. The plural of the noun can be either **foci** or **focuses**.

철자 focusses, focussing, focussed도 특히 영국영어에서 쓴다. 명사의 복수형으로 foci 또는 focuses를 쓸 수 있다.

◼ V-T/V-I If you **focus on** a particular topic or if your attention **is focused on** it, you concentrate on it and think about it, discuss it, or deal with it, rather than dealing with other topics. ❑ *The research effort has focused on tracing the effects of growing levels of five compounds.* ❑ *Today he was able to focus his message exclusively on the economy.* ◾ N-COUNT The **focus** of something is the main topic or main thing that it is concerned with. ❑ *The UN's role in promoting peace is increasingly the focus of international attention.* ❑ *The new system is the focus of controversy.* ◼ N-COUNT Your **focus** on something is the special attention that you pay it. ❑ *He said his sudden focus on foreign policy was not motivated by presidential politics.* ◢ N-UNCOUNT If you say that something has a **focus**, you mean that you can see a purpose in it. ❑ *Somehow, though, their latest LP has a focus that the others have lacked.* ◣ V-T/V-I If you **focus** your eyes or if your eyes **focus**, your eyes adjust so that you can clearly see the thing that you want to look at. If you **focus** a camera, telescope, or other instrument, you adjust it so that you can see clearly through it. ❑ *Kelly couldn't focus his eyes well enough to tell if the figure was male or female.* ❑ *His eyes slowly began to focus on what looked like a small dark ball.* ◥ N-UNCOUNT You use **focus** to refer to the fact of adjusting your eyes or a camera, telescope, or other instrument, and to the degree to which you can see clearly. ❑ *His focus switched to the little white ball.* ◧ V-T If you **focus** rays of light on a particular point, you pass them through a lens or reflect them from a mirror so that they meet at that point. ❑ *Magnetic coils focus the electron beams into fine spots.* ◨ PHRASE If an image or a camera, telescope, or other instrument is **in focus**, the edges of what you see are clear and sharp. ❑ *Pictures should be in focus, with realistic colors, and well composed groups.* ◩ PHRASE If something is **in focus**, it is being discussed or its purpose and nature are clear. ❑ *This aggression is the real issue the world should be concerned about. We want to keep*

◼ 타동사/자동사 집중하다 ❑ 그 연구 활동은 다섯 가지 성분의 농도가 증가함에 따라 나타나는 효과를 규명하는 데 집중되었다. ❑ 그는 오늘 그가 전달하려는 내용을 오로지 경제에만 집중시킬 수 있었다. ◾ 가산명사 초점, 중심 ❑ 평화 증진을 위한 유엔의 역할이 점점 국제적인 관심의 초점이 되고 있다. ❑ 그 새로운 시스템이 논란의 중심이다. ◼ 가산명사 관심 ❑ 그가 갑자기 외교 정책에 관심을 두는 것이 대통령의 정책 때문은 아니라고 말했다. ◢ 불가산명사 핵심 ❑ 그래도 아무튼, 그들이 최근에 개발한 엘피는 다른 것에는 없는 핵심이 있다. ◣ 타동사/자동사 초점을 맞추다; 초점이 맞다 ❑ 켈리는 그 사람이 남자인지 여자인지 분간할 수 있을 정도로는 두 눈의 초점을 맞출 수 없었다. ❑ 그의 두 눈은 흑점처럼 보이는 것에 서서히 두 눈의 초점을 맞추기 시작했다. ◥ 불가산명사 초점 맞추기 ❑ 그는 작은 흰 공 쪽으로 초점을 맞췄다. ◧ 타동사 초점을 맞추다 ❑ 자석 코일에 의해 전자 빔이 미세한 지점에 초점을 맞춘다. ◨ 구 초점이 맞는 ❑ 사진은 사실적인 색상과 잘 맞는 구도와 함께 초점도 맞아야 한다. ◩ 구 초점이 되고 있는 ❑ 이 침략 행위는 온 세계가 우려해야 할 진정한 사안이다. 우리는 이 문제가 지속적으로 논의되기를 바란다. ◪ 구 초점이 맞지 않는 ❑ 사진 중에 일부는 배경은 선명한데 인물의 초점이 맞지 않는다.

that in focus. 🔟 PHRASE If an image or a camera, telescope, or other instrument is **out of focus**, the edges of what you see are unclear. ❑ *In some of the pictures the subjects are out of focus while the background is sharp.* →see **photography**

Word Partnership　*focus의 연어*

N.	focus **attention** 🔟
	focus *your* eyes, focus **a** camera 🔢
V.	**shift** *your* focus 🔢 🔢 🔢
	come into focus 🔢

fo|cus group (focus groups) N-COUNT A **focus group** is a specially selected group of people who are intended to represent the general public. Focus groups have discussions in which their opinions are recorded as a form of market research. ❑ *The market research company BMRB conducted 12 focus groups for the project in London, Cardiff, Liverpool, and Glasgow.*

가산명사 선발 그룹, 포커스 그룹 ❑ 시장 조사 회사인 비엠알비는 런던, 카디프, 리버풀, 글라스고우에서 실시한 프로젝트에서 12개의 포커스 그룹을 관리했다.

fod|der /fɒdər/ 🔟 N-UNCOUNT **Fodder** is food that is given to cows, horses, and other animals. ❑ *...fodder for horses.* 🔢 N-UNCOUNT If you say that something is **fodder** for a particular purpose, you mean that it is useful for that purpose and perhaps nothing else. [DISAPPROVAL] ❑ *The press conference simply provided more fodder for another attack on his character.*

🔟 불가산명사 사료 ❑ 말 사료 🔢 불가산명사 빌미, 꽹개 [탐탁찮음] ❑ 그 기자 회견은 그의 인격에 대한 또 다른 공격의 빌미만 제공했을 뿐이다.

foe /foʊ/ (foes) N-COUNT Someone's **foe** is their enemy. [WRITTEN] ❑ *But he soon discovers that his old foe may be leading him into a trap.*

가산명사 원수, 적 [문어체] ❑ 그러나 그는 곧 그의 오랜 원수가 자신을 함정으로 몰고 가고 있는지도 모른다는 것을 깨닫는다.

foe|tus /fiːtəs/ →see **fetus**

fog /fɒg/ (fogs) 🔟 N-VAR When there is **fog**, there are tiny drops of water in the air which form a thick cloud and make it difficult to see things. ❑ *The crash happened in thick fog.* 🔢 N-SING A **fog** is an unpleasant cloud of something such as smoke inside a building or room. ❑ *...a fog of stale cigarette smoke.*

🔟 가산명사 또는 불가산명사 안개 ❑ 그 교통사고는 짙은 안개 속에서 발생했다. 🔢 단수명사 (자욱한) 연기 ❑ 자욱하게 떠 있는 탁한 담배 연기

fog|gy /fɒgi/ (foggier, foggiest) 🔟 ADJ When it is **foggy**, there is fog. ❑ *It's quite foggy now.* 🔢 PHRASE If you say that you **haven't the foggiest** or you **haven't the foggiest idea**, you are emphasizing that you do not know something. [INFORMAL, EMPHASIS] ❑ *I did not have the foggiest idea what he meant.*

🔟 형용사 안개가 낀 ❑ 지금 안개가 자욱해. 🔢 구 오리무중이다, 전혀 모르다 [비격식체, 강조] ❑ 난 그가 무슨 뜻으로 말하는 건지 전혀 몰랐다.

foil /fɔɪl/ (foils, foiling, foiled) 🔟 N-UNCOUNT **Foil** consists of sheets of metal as thin as paper. It is used to wrap food in. ❑ *Pour cider around the meat and cover with foil.* 🔢 V-T If you **foil** someone's plan or attempt to do something, for example to commit a crime, you succeed in stopping them from doing what they want. [JOURNALISM] ❑ *A brave police chief foiled an armed robbery on a jeweler's by grabbing the raiders' shotgun.*

🔟 불가산명사 포일, 은박지 ❑ 고기 둘레에 사과주를 붓고 호일로 싸라. 🔢 타동사 저지하다 [언론] ❑ 용감한 경찰서장이 귀금속상에 든 침입자의 엽총을 낚아채서 무장 강도 사건을 저지했다.

fold ♦◇◇ /foʊld/ (folds, folding, folded) 🔟 V-T If you **fold** something such as a piece of paper or cloth, you bend it so that one part covers another part, often pressing the edge so that it stays in place. ❑ *He folded the paper carefully.* ❑ *Fold the omelet in half.* 🔢 N-COUNT A **fold** in a piece of paper or cloth is a bend that you make in it when you put one part of it over another part and press the edge. ❑ *Make another fold and turn the ends together.* 🔢 N-COUNT The **folds** in a piece of cloth are the curved shapes which are formed when it is not hanging or lying flat. ❑ *The priest fumbled in the folds of his gown.* 🔢 V-T/V-I If a piece of furniture or equipment **folds** or if you can **fold** it, you can make it smaller by bending or closing parts of it. ❑ *The back of the bench folds forward to make a table.* ❑ *This portable seat folds flat for easy storage.* ● PHRASAL VERB **Fold up** means the same as **fold**. ❑ *When not in use it folds up out of the way.* 🔢 V-T If you **fold** your arms or hands, you bring them together and cross or link them, for example over your chest. ❑ *Meer folded his arms over his chest and turned his head away.* 🔢 V-I If a business or organization **folds**, it is unsuccessful and has to close. [mainly BRIT, BUSINESS] ❑ *But as other shops fold, the march of the superstores continues.*

🔟 타동사 접다 ❑ 그가 조심스럽게 그 종이를 접었다. ❑ 오믈렛을 반으로 접으세요. 🔢 가산명사 주름 ❑ 주름을 하나 더 만들어서 양쪽 끝을 함께 접어라. 🔢 가산명사 구김살 ❑ 사제가 가운에 구김이 간 곳을 만지작거렸다. 🔢 타동사/자동사 접히다; 접다 그 벤치의 등 부분을 들어올려 접으면 탁자가 된다. ❑ 이 휴대용 의자는 납작하게 접을 수 있으므로 보관이 편리하다. ● 구동사 접히다; 접다 사용하지 않을 때는 그것을 접어서 치울 수가 있다. 🔢 타동사 (팔짱이나 깍지를) 끼다 ❑ 미르가 팔짱을 끼고 고개를 돌렸다. 🔢 자동사 (사업 등이) 망하다 [주로 영국영어, 경제] ❑ 하지만 다른 가게들이 망하는 동안 대형 슈퍼마켓의 행진은 계속된다.

Word Partnership　*fold의 연어*

N.	fold **clothes**, fold **paper** 🔟
	fold *your* **arms/hands** 🔢

▶**fold up** PHRASAL VERB If you **fold** something **up**, you make it into a smaller, neater shape by folding it, usually several times. ❑ *She folded it up, and tucked it into her purse.* →see also **fold 4**

구동사 반듯하게 접다 ❑ 그녀가 그것을 반듯하게 접어 지갑에 챙겨 넣었다.

fold|er /foʊldər/ (folders) 🔟 N-COUNT A **folder** is a thin piece of cardboard in which you can keep loose papers. 🔢 N-COUNT A **folder** is a group of files that are stored together on a computer. →see **office**

🔟 가산명사 종이 끼우개, 서류철 🔢 가산명사 (컴퓨터 운영 프로그램에서의) 폴더

fo|li|age /foʊliɪdʒ/ N-UNCOUNT The leaves of a plant are referred to as its **foliage**. ❑ *...shrubs with grey or silver foliage.*

불가산명사 잎 ❑ 회색 또는 은빛 잎의 관목

folk ♦◇◇ /foʊk/ (folks)

Folk can also be used as the plural form for meaning 🔟.

folk은 🔟 의미의 복수형으로도 쓸 수 있다.

🔟 N-PLURAL You can refer to people as **folk** or **folks**. ❑ *Country folk can tell you that there are certain places which animals avoid.* ❑ *These are the folks from the local TV station.* 🔢 N-PLURAL You can refer to your close family, especially your mother and father, as your **folks**. [INFORMAL] ❑ *I've been avoiding my folks lately.* 🔢 N-VOC You can use **folks** as a term of address when you are talking to several people. [INFORMAL] ❑ *"It's a question of money, folks," I announced.* 🔢 ADJ **Folk** art and customs are traditional or typical of a particular community or nation. [ADJ n] ❑ *...South American folk art.* 🔢 ADJ **Folk** music is music which is traditional or typical of a particular community or nation. [ADJ n] ❑ *...Irish folk music.* ● N-UNCOUNT **Folk** is also a noun. ❑ *...a variety of music including classical, jazz, and folk.*

🔟 복수명사 사람들 ❑ 시골 사람들은 동물들이 가기 꺼리는 어떤 장소가 있다는 것을 너에게 알려줄 수 있다. ❑ 이 사람들은 지역 텔레비전 방송국에서 나온 사람들이다. 🔢 복수명사 가족, 부모 [비격식체] ❑ 요즈음 나는 부모님들을 피하고 있다. 🔢 호격명사 여러분 [비격식체] ❑ "그것은 돈에 관한 문제입니다, 여러분."이라고 내가 알렸다. 🔢 형용사 민속의 ❑ 남미 민속 예술 🔢 형용사 민속의 ❑ 아일랜드 민요 ● 불가산명사 민요 ❑ 클래식, 재즈, 민요를 포함하는 다양한 음악

a b c d e f g h i j k l m n o p q r s t u v w x y z

folk|lore /foʊklɔr/ N-UNCOUNT **Folklore** is the traditional stories, customs, and habits of a particular community or nation. ◻ *In Chinese folklore the bat is an emblem of good fortune.* ◻ 불가산명사 민속 ◻ 중국 민속에서 박쥐는 행운의 상징이다.

fol|low ♦♦♦ /fɒloʊ/ (**follows, following, followed**) **1** V-T/V-I If you **follow** someone who is going somewhere, you move along behind them because you want to go to the same place. ◻ *We followed him up the steps into a large hall.* ◻ *Please follow me, madam.* **2** V-T If you **follow** someone who is going somewhere, you move along behind them without their knowledge, in order to catch them or find out where they are going. ◻ *She realized that the Mercedes was following her.* **3** V-T If you **follow** someone to a place where they have recently gone and where they are now, you go to join them there. ◻ *He followed Janice to New York, where she was preparing an exhibition.* **4** V-T/V-I An event, activity, or period of time that **follows** a particular thing happens or comes after that thing, at a later time. ◻ *...the rioting and looting that followed the verdict.* ◻ *Other problems may follow.* **5** V-T If you **follow** one thing **with** another, you do or say the second thing after you have done or said the first thing. ◻ *Her first major role was in Martin Scorsese's "Goodfellas" and she followed this with a part in Spike Lee's "Jungle Fever".* ● PHRASAL VERB **Follow up** means the same as **follow.** ◻ *The book proved such a success that the authors followed it up with "The Messianic Legacy".* **6** V-T/V-I If it **follows** that a particular thing is the case, that thing is a logical result of something else being true or being the case. ◻ *Just because a bird does not breed one year, it does not follow that it will fail the next.* ◻ *If the explanation is right, two things follow.* **7** V-T/V-I If you refer to the words that **follow** or **followed,** you are referring to the words that come next or came next in a piece of writing or speech. ◻ *What follows is an eye-witness account.* ◻ *There followed a list of places where Hans intended to visit.* **8** V-T If you **follow** a path, route, or set of signs, you go somewhere using the path, route, or signs to direct you. ◻ *If they followed the road, they would be certain to reach a village.* ◻ *All we had to do was follow the map.* **9** V-T If something such as a path or river **follows** a particular route or line, it goes along that route or line. ◻ *Our route follows the Pacific coast through densely populated neighborhoods.* **10** V-T If you **follow** something with your eyes, or if your eyes **follow** it, you watch it as it moves or you look along its route or course. ◻ *Ann's eyes followed a police car as it drove slowly past.* **11** V-T Something that **follows** a particular course of development happens or develops in that way. ◻ *His release turned out to follow the pattern set by that of the other six hostages.* **12** V-T If you **follow** advice, an instruction, or a recipe, you act or do something in the way that it indicates. ◻ *Take care to follow the instructions carefully.* **13** V-T/V-I If you **follow** what someone else has done, you do it too because you think it is a good thing or because you want to copy them. ◻ *His admiration for the athlete did not extend to the point where he would follow his example in taking drugs.* **14** V-T If you **follow** someone in what you do, you do the same thing or job as they did previously. ◻ *He followed his father and became a surgeon.* **15** V-T/V-I If you are able to **follow** something such as an explanation or the story of a movie, you understand it as it continues and develops. ◻ *Can you follow the plot so far?* **16** V-T If you **follow** something, you take an interest in it and keep informed about what happens. ◻ *...the millions of people who follow football because they genuinely love it.* **17** V-T If you **follow** a particular religion or political belief, you have that religion or belief. ◻ *"Do you follow any particular religion?" — "Yes, we're all Hindus."* **18** →see also **following** **19** PHRASE You use **as follows** in writing or speech to introduce something such as a list, description, or explanation. ◻ *The winners are as follows: E. Walker; R. Foster; R. Gates; A. Mackintosh.* **20** PHRASE You use **followed by** to say what comes after something else in a list or ordered set of things. ◻ *Potatoes are still the most popular food, followed by white bread.* **21** to **follow in** someone's **footsteps** →see footstep. to **follow** your **nose** →see nose. to **follow suit** →see suit

1 타동사/자동사 따라가다, 따라오다 ◻ 우리는 그를 따라 큰 홀로 이어지는 계단을 올라갔다. ◻ 저를 따라 오세요, 부인. **2** 타동사 뒤쫓다 ◻ 그녀는 그 메르세데스 벤츠 승용차가 자신을 뒤쫓고 있다는 사실을 깨달았다. **3** 타동사 동행하다 ◻ 그는 재니스와 뉴욕까지 동행했는데, 거기서 그녀가 전시회를 준비하고 있는 중이었다. **4** 타동사/자동사 뒤따르다, 뒤를 잇다 ◻ 평결이 있은 뒤 일어난 폭동과 약탈 행위 ◻ 다른 문제들이 뒤따라 일어날지도 모른다. **5** 타동사 뒤이어 하다 ◻ 그녀가 처음으로 주요 배역을 맡은 영화는 마틴 스콜세지의 '굿펠라스'였고 이에 뒤이어 스파이크 리의 '정글 피버'에서 한 역할을 맡았다. ● 구동사 뒤따르다, 뒤를 잇다 ◻ 작가들이 그 후속으로 '메시아의 유산'을 낼 정도로 그 책은 대단한 성공을 거두었다. **6** 타동사/자동사 당연히 _이 되다 ◻ 단지 새가 한 해 알을 부화시키지 않는다는 이유로 다음 해에도 부화시키지 못할 것이라고는 할 수 없다. ◻ 그 설명이 옳다면 두 가지가 당연해진다. **7** 타동사/자동사 이어지다 ◻ 이어지는 내용은 목격자의 진술이다. ◻ 한스가 방문하고자 했던 장소의 목록이 이어졌다. **8** 타동사 _을 따라서 나아가다 ◻ 그들이 그 길을 따라서 간다면 자신들이 어떤 마을에 도달하리라고 확신할 수 있을 텐데. ◻ 우리가 해야 할 일이라고는 그 지도를 따라서 가는 것뿐이었다. **9** 타동사 (길이나 강 따위가) _을 따라서 가다 ◻ 우리의 노정은 인구 밀도가 높은 인근 지역들을 통과하며 태평양 연안을 따라서 간다. **10** 타동사 (움직임이나 진로 따위를) 주시하다 ◻ 앤은 두 눈으로 경찰차가 천천히 지나가는 것을 주시했다. **11** 타동사 따르다 ◻ 그의 석방은 다른 인질 여섯 명의 석방에 의해 정해진 패턴을 따랐던 것으로 밝혀졌다. **12** 타동사 신중하게 _의 설명서를 따르도록 주의하세요. **13** 타동사/자동사 본받다, 따라 하다 ◻ 그 운동선수에 대한 동경 때문에 그가 그 선수의 약물 복용을 따라 하는 정도까지 가지는 않았다. **14** 타동사 (_의 전례를) 따르다 ◻ 그는 아버지를 따라 외과 의사가 되었다. **15** 타동사/자동사 이해하다 ◻ 지금까지의 줄거리를 이해할 수 있겠어요? **16** 타동사 (계속) 지켜보다 ◻ 진정으로 축구를 사랑해서 축구를 지켜보는 수백만의 사람들 **17** 타동사 신봉하다, 믿다 ◻ "여러분은 어떤 특정 종교를 믿습니까?" "네, 우리는 모두 힌두교 신자입니다." **19** 구 다음과 같다 ◻ 수상자는 다음과 같습니다. 이 워커, 알 포스터, 알 게이츠, 에이 매킨토시. **20** 구 다음으로 ◻ 감자는 여전히 가장 대중적인 식품이고 흰 빵이 그 다음이다.

▶**follow through** PHRASAL VERB If you **follow through** an action, plan, or idea or **follow through** with it, you continue doing or thinking about it until you have done everything possible. ◻ *The leadership has been unwilling to follow through the implications of these ideas.* ◻ *I was trained to be an actress but I didn't follow it through.* ◻ 구동사 끝까지 해 내다 ◻ 지도부가 이러한 생각들이 갖는 함축적인 의미를 계속 고려하는 것을 탐탁치 않아 했다. ◻ 나는 연기자가 되는 교육을 받았지만 그것을 끝까지 하지는 않았다.

▶**follow up** PHRASAL VERB If you **follow up** something that has been said, suggested, or discovered, you try to find out more about it or take action about it. ◻ *State security police are following up several leads.* →see also **follow 5, follow-up** ◻ 구동사 계속 추적하다; 후속 조치를 취하다 ◻ 비밀경찰이 몇몇 단서를 계속 추적하고 있다.

fol|low|er /fɒloʊər/ (**followers**) N-COUNT A **follower** of a particular person, group, or belief is someone who supports or admires that person, group, or belief. ◻ *...followers of the Zulu Inkatha movement.* ◻ 가산명사 신봉자, 추종자 ◻ 줄루 잉카타 운동의 신봉자들

fol|low|ing ♦♦♦ /fɒloʊɪŋ/ (**followings**) **1** PREP **Following** a particular event means after that event. ◻ *In the centuries following Christ's death, Christians genuinely believed the world was about to end.* **2** ADJ The **following** day, week, or year **1** 전치사 _의 뒤에 ◻ 예수 그리스도의 죽음 뒤 몇 세기 동안 기독교인들은 세계가 곧 종말을 맞을 것이라고 진심으로 믿었다. **2** 형용사 다음에 오는 ◻ 그 다음날

is the day, week, or year after the one you have just mentioned. [det ADJ] ❑ *The following day the picture appeared on the front pages of every newspaper in the world.* ❑ *We went to dinner the following Monday evening.* ◼ ADJ You use **following** to refer to something that you are about to mention. [det ADJ] ❑ *Write down the following information: name of product, type, date purchased and price.* ● PRON **The following** refers to the thing or things that you are about to mention. [the PRON] ❑ *The following is a paraphrase of what was said.* ◼ N-COUNT A person or organization that has a **following** has a group of people who support or admire their beliefs or actions. ❑ *Australian rugby league enjoys a huge following in New Zealand.*

그 사진이 전 세계 모든 신문의 일 면에 실렸다. ❑ 우리는 그 다음 월요일 저녁에 저녁 식사를 하러 갔다. ◼ 형용사 다음의 ❑ 다음의 정보를 기록하시오: 상품명, 유형, 구매 날짜 및 구매 가격 ● 대명사 다음 (의 내용) ❑ 다음은 앞에 말씀드린 내용을 풀어 쓴 것입니다. ◼ 가산명사 신봉자들, 추종자들 ❑ 뉴질랜드에는 호주 럭비 리그 추종자들이 엄청나게 많다.

follow-up (**follow-ups**) N-VAR A **follow-up** is something that is done to continue or add to something done previously. ❑ *They are recording a follow-up to their successful 1989 album.*

가산명사 또는 불가산명사 후속 조치, 후속 작업 ❑ 그들은 자신들의 히트작인 1989년 앨범의 후속 앨범을 녹음하고 있다.

folly /fɒli/ (**follies**) N-VAR If you say that a particular action or way of behaving is **folly** or a **folly**, you mean that it is foolish. ❑ *It's sheer folly to build nuclear power stations in a country that has dozens of earthquakes every year.*

가산명사 또는 불가산명사 어리석은 짓 ❑ 매년 수십 건의 지진이 발생하는 나라에 원자력 발전소를 세운다는 것은 정말이지 어리석은 짓이다.

fond /fɒnd/ (**fonder, fondest**) ◼ ADJ If you are **fond of** someone, you feel affection for them. [v-link ADJ of n] ❑ *I am very fond of Michael.* ● **fond|ness** N-UNCOUNT ❑ *...a great fondness for children.* ◼ ADJ You use **fond** to describe people or their behavior when they show affection. [ADJ n] ❑ *...a fond father.* ● **fond|ly** ADV [ADV after v] ❑ *Liz saw their eyes meet fondly across the table.* ◼ ADJ If you are **fond of** something, you like it or you like doing it very much. [v-link ADJ of n/-ing] ❑ *He was fond of marmalade.* ● **fond|ness** N-UNCOUNT ❑ *I've always had a fondness for jewels.* ◼ ADJ If you have **fond** memories of someone or something, you remember them with pleasure. [ADJ n] ❑ *I have very fond memories of living in our village.* ● **fond|ly** ADV [ADV with v] ❑ *My dad took us there when I was about four and I remembered it fondly.* ◼ ADJ You use **fond** to describe hopes, wishes, or beliefs which you think are foolish because they seem unlikely to be fulfilled. [ADJ n] ❑ *My fond hope is that we will be ready by Christmastime.* ● **fond|ly** ADV [ADV with v] ❑ *I fondly imagined that surgery meant a few stitches and an overnight stay in the hospital.*

◼ 형용사 좋아하는 ❑ 나는 마이클을 무척 좋아해. ● 애정, 좋아함 불가산명사 ❑ 아이들을 무척 좋아함 ◼ 형용사 다정한 ❑ 다정한 아버지 ● 다정하게 부사 ❑ 리즈는 식탁을 사이에 두고 그들이 다정한 눈빛을 주고받는 것을 보았다. ◼ 형용사 ~을 무척 좋아하는 ❑ 그는 마멀레이드를 무척 좋아했다. ● 애호 불가산명사 ❑ 나는 항상 보석을 좋아했다. ◼ 형용사 기분 좋은 ❑ 나는 우리 마을에서의 삶에 대해 아주 기분 좋은 기억들이 있다. ◼ 형용사 터무니없는, 황당한 ❑ 내 터무니없는 바람은 크리스마스 시즌까지 우리가 준비를 마치는 것이다. ● 황당하게도 부사 ❑ 나는 어리석게도 수술이란 게 몇 바늘 꿰매고 병원에서 하룻밤만 지내면 되는 것이라고 생각했다.

font /fɒnt/ (**fonts**) N-COUNT In printing, a **font** is a set of characters of the same style and size. ❑ *...the immense variety of fonts available in Microsoft Word and Publisher.*

가산명사 글자체 ❑ '마이크로소프트 워드' 및 '마이크로소프트 퍼블리셔'에서 제공되는 엄청나게 다양한 글자체

food ♦♦♦ /fuːd/ (**foods**) ◼ N-MASS **Food** is what people and animals eat. ❑ *Enjoy your food.* ❑ *...frozen foods.* →see also **fast food, junk food** ◼ PHRASE If you give someone **food for thought**, you make them think carefully about something. ❑ *Lord Fraser's speech offers much food for thought.* →see **can, farm, rice, sugar, vegetarian** →see Word Web: **food**

◼ 물질명사 음식, 식품 ❑ 즐겁게 음식을 먹어라. ❑ 냉동식품 ◼ 구 생각할 거리 ❑ 프레이저 경의 연설은 생각할 거리를 많이 제공한다.

food|stuff /fuːdstʌf/ (**foodstuffs**) N-VAR **Foodstuffs** are substances which people eat. ❑ *...basic foodstuffs such as sugar, cooking oil, and cheese.*

가산명사 또는 불가산명사 식료품 ❑ 설탕, 요리용 기름, 치즈와 같은 기초 식료품

fool ♦◇◇ /fuːl/ (**fools, fooling, fooled**) ◼ N-COUNT If you call someone a **fool**, you are indicating that you think they are not at all sensible and show a lack of good judgment. [DISAPPROVAL] ❑ *"You fool!" she shouted.* ◼ ADJ **Fool** is used to describe an action or person that is not at all sensible and shows a lack of good judgment. [mainly AM, INFORMAL, DISAPPROVAL] [ADJ n] ❑ *What a damn fool thing to do!* ◼ V-T If someone **fools** you, they deceive or trick you. ❑ *Art dealers fool a lot of people.* ❑ *Don't be fooled by his appearance.* ◼ V-I If you say that a person **is fooling with** something or someone, you mean that the way they are behaving is likely to cause problems. ❑ *What are you doing fooling with such a staggering sum of money?* ◼ PHRASE If you **make a fool of** someone, you make them seem silly by telling people about something stupid that they have done, or by tricking them. ❑ *Your brother is making a fool of you.* ◼ PHRASE If you **make a fool of** yourself, you behave in a way that makes other people think that you are silly or lacking in good judgment. ❑ *He was drinking and making a fool of himself.* ◼ PHRASE If you **play the fool** or **act the fool**, you behave in a playful, childish, and foolish way, usually in order to make other people laugh. ❑ *They used to play the fool together, calling each other silly names and giggling.*

◼ 가산명사 바보 [탐탁찮음] ❑ "넌 바보야!"라고 그녀가 외쳤다. ◼ 형용사 바보짓; 바보 [주로 미국영어, 비격식체, 탐탁찮음] ❑ 그 따위 일을 하다니 얼마나 한심한 바보짓이냐! ◼ 타동사 속이다 ❑ 미술품 거래인들은 사람들을 많이 속인다. ❑ 그의 겉모습에 속지 말아라. ◼ 자동사 황당한 짓을 하다 ❑ 너 그렇게 엄청난 돈으로 무슨 엉뚱한 짓을 하고 있는 거니? ◼ 구 ~을 웃음거리로 만들다 ❑ 네 형이 너를 웃음거리로 만들고 있어. ◼ 구 웃음거리가 되다 ❑ 그가 술을 마시고는 웃음거리가 되고 있었다. ◼ 구 우스꽝스러운 짓을 해서 사람들을 웃기다 ❑ 그들은 서로를 웃기는 별명으로 부르고 킬킬거리면서, 함께 우스꽝스러운 짓을 해서 사람들을 웃기곤 했다.

▶**fool around** PHRASAL VERB If you **fool around**, you behave in a silly, dangerous, or irresponsible way. ❑ *They were fooling around on an Army firing range.*

구동사 함부로 장난치다 ❑ 그들은 육군 사격 연습장에서 함부로 장난치고 있었다.

fool|ish /fuːlɪʃ/ ◼ ADJ If someone's behavior or action is **foolish**, it is not sensible and shows a lack of good judgment. ❑ *It would be foolish to raise hopes unnecessarily.* ● **fool|ish|ly** ADV ❑ *He admitted that he had acted foolishly.* ● **fool|ish|ness** N-UNCOUNT ❑ *They don't accept any foolishness when it comes to spending money.* ◼ ADJ If you look or feel **foolish**, you look or feel so silly or ridiculous that people are likely to laugh at you. ❑ *I just stood there feeling foolish and watching him.* ● **fool|ish|ly** ADV [ADV after v] ❑ *He saw me standing there, grinning foolishly at him.*

◼ 형용사 어리석은 ❑ 쓸데없이 희망을 부추기는 것은 어리석은 것일 것이다. ● 바보같이 부사 ❑ 그는 자신이 바보같이 행동했다고 인정했다. ● 어리석음 불가산명사 ❑ 그들은 돈을 쓰는 일에 관해서라면 어떤 어리석음도 용납하지 않는다. ◼ 형용사 바보 같은 ❑ 나는 그저 거기 서서 바보가 된 것 같은 기분으로 그를 지켜보고 있었다. ● 바보같이 부사 ❑ 그는 내가 거기 서서 자기를 보고 바보같이 히죽거리고 있는 것을 보았다.

| **Word Web** | food |

The food chain begins with sunlight. Green **plants** absorb and store **energy** from the sun through photosynthesis. This energy is passed on to an herbivore (such as a mouse) that **eats** these plants. The mouse is then eaten by a **carnivore** (such as a snake). The snake may be eaten by a **top predator** (such as a hawk). When the hawk dies, its body is broken down by bacteria. Soon its **nutrients** become food for plants and the cycle begins again.

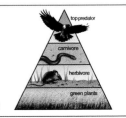

Food chain

a
b
c
d
e
f
g
h
i
j
k
l
m
n
o
p
q
r
s
t
u
v
w
x
y
z

fool|proof /fúlpruf/ ADJ Something such as a plan or a machine that is **foolproof** is so well designed, easy to understand, or easy to use that it cannot go wrong or be used wrongly. ❑ *The system is not 100 per cent foolproof.*

foot ◆◆◆ /fút/ (**feet**) **1** N-COUNT Your **feet** are the parts of your body that are at the ends of your legs, and that you stand on. ❑ *She stamped her foot again.* ❑ *...a foot injury.* **2** N-SING **The foot of** something is the part that is farthest from its top. ❑ *David called to the children from the foot of the stairs.* ❑ *...the foot of Highgate Hill.* **3** N-SING **The foot of** a bed is the end nearest to the feet of the person lying in it. ❑ *Friends stood at the foot of the bed, looking at her with serious faces.* **4** N-COUNT A **foot** is a unit for measuring length, height, or depth, and is equal to 12 inches or 30.48 centimeters. When you are giving measurements, the form "foot" is often used as the plural instead of the plural form "feet." ❑ *This beautiful and curiously shaped lake lies at around fifteen thousand feet.* ❑ *He occupies a cell 10 foot long, 6 foot wide and 10 foot high.* **5** ADJ A **foot** brake or **foot** pump is operated by your foot rather than by your hand. [ADJ n] ❑ *I tried to reach the foot brakes but I couldn't.* **6** ADJ A **foot** patrol or **foot** soldiers walk rather than traveling in vehicles or on horseback. [ADJ n] ❑ *Paratroopers and foot-soldiers entered the building on the government's behalf.* **7** →see also **footing** **8** PHRASE If you get **cold feet about** something, you become nervous or frightened about it because you think it will fail. ❑ *The Government is getting cold feet about the reforms.* **9** PHRASE If you say that someone **is finding** their **feet** in a new situation, you mean that they are starting to feel confident and to deal with things successfully. ❑ *I don't know anyone in England but I am sure I will manage when I find my feet.* **10** PHRASE If you say that someone has their **feet on the ground**, you approve of the fact that they have a sensible and practical attitude towards life, and do not have unrealistic ideas. [APPROVAL] ❑ *In that respect he needs to keep his feet on the ground and not get carried away.* **11** PHRASE If you go somewhere **on foot**, you walk, rather than using any form of transport. ❑ *We rowed ashore, then explored the island on foot for the rest of the day.* **12** PHRASE If you are **on** your **feet**, you are standing up. ❑ *Everyone was on their feet applauding wildly.* **13** PHRASE If you say that someone or something is **on** their **feet** again after an illness or difficult period, you mean that they have recovered and are back to normal. ❑ *You need someone to take the pressure off and help you get back on your feet.* **14** PHRASE If you say that someone always **falls** or **lands on** their **feet**, you mean that they are always successful or lucky, although they do not seem to achieve this by their own efforts. ❑ *He has good looks and charm, and always falls on his feet.* **15** PHRASE If someone **puts** their **foot down**, they use their authority in order to stop something happening. ❑ *He had planned to go skiing on his own in March but his wife had decided to put her foot down.* **16** PHRASE If someone **puts** their **foot down** when they are driving, they drive as fast as they can. ❑ *I asked the driver to put his foot down for Nagchukka.* **17** PHRASE If someone **puts** their **foot in it** or **puts** their **foot in** their **mouth**, they accidentally do or say something which embarrasses or offends people. [INFORMAL] ❑ *Our chairman has really put his foot in it, poor man, though he doesn't know it.* **18** PHRASE If you **put** your **feet up**, you relax or have a rest, especially by sitting or lying with your feet supported off the ground. ❑ *After supper he'd put his feet up and read. It was a pleasant prospect.* **19** PHRASE If you never **put a foot wrong**, you never make any mistakes. ❑ *When he's around, we never put a foot wrong.* **20** PHRASE If you say that someone **sets foot** in a place, you mean that they enter it or reach it, and you are emphasizing the significance of their action. If you say that someone **never sets foot** in a place, you are emphasizing that they never go there. [EMPHASIS] ❑ *...the day the first man set foot on the moon.* **21** PHRASE If someone has to **stand on** their **own two feet**, they have to be independent and manage their lives without help from other people. ❑ *My father didn't mind whom I married, so long as I could stand on my own two*

형용사 아주 쉬운, 확실한 ❑ 그 시스템은 100퍼센트 확실하지가 않다.

1 가산명사 발 ❑ 그녀가 다시 발을 굴렀다. ❑ 발 부상 **2** 단수명사 최하부, 밑치 ❑ 데이비드가 계단 밑에서 아이들에게 소리쳤다. ❑ 하이게이트 힐 기슭 **3** 단수명사 (침대의) 밑치 ❑ 친구들이 침대 밑치에 서서 심각한 얼굴로 그녀를 바라보았다. **4** 가산명사 피트 (길이를 재는 단위) ❑ 이 아름답고 기묘한 모양의 호수는 그 넓이가 대략 15,000피트에 달한다. ❑ 그가 길이 10피트, 폭 6피트, 높이 10피트의 독방을 차지하고 있다. **5** 형용사 발로 조작하는 ❑ 나는 브레이크를 밟으려고 했지만 그럴 수가 없었다. **6** 형용사 도보로 이동하는 ❑ 낙하산병과 보병이 정부를 대표해서 그 건물로 들어갔다. **8** 구 겁먹은 ❑ 정부가 개혁에 대해 겁을 먹고 있다. **9** 구 (새로운 환경에서) 자리를 잡다 ❑ 난 잉글랜드에 아는 사람이 아무도 없지만 일단 자리를 잡고 나면 잘 해 나갈 수 있을 거라고 확신한다. **10** 구 현실감을 잃지 않다 [마음에 듦] ❑ 그런 점에서 그는 현실감을 잃지 않고 도를 지나치지 않아야 할 필요가 있다. **11** 구 걸어서 ❑ 우리는 물가로 배를 저어 갔고 그리고는 그날 남은 시간 동안 그 섬을 걸어서 답사했다. **12** 구 일어서서 ❑ 모두 일어서서 열광적으로 박수갈채를 보내고 있었다. **13** 구 회복하여 ❑ 당신은 그 부담을 덜어 주고 다시 회복할 수 있도록 도와줄 누군가가 필요합니다. **14** 구 운이 좋다 ❑ 그는 잘 생겼고 매력적이고, 거기다 항상 운이 좋다. **15** 구 완강히 반대하다, 강경하게 나가다 ❑ 그가 혼자서 3월에 스키를 타러 가려 했었지만 그의 부인이 완강히 반대했다. **16** 구 전속력을 내다 ❑ 내가 운전기사에게 전속력으로 나그추카로 가 달라고 부탁했다. **17** 구 난처한 실수를 하다 [비격식체] ❑ 우리 회장님이 곤란한 실수를 하셨는데, 참 안 됐어, 자신은 그걸 모른다니까. **18** 구 편히 쉬다 ❑ 저녁 식사 후에 그는 편히 쉬면서 책을 읽을 것이었다. 그것은 즐거운 기대였다. **19** 구 실수하다 ❑ 그가 근처에 있을 때면 우리는 절대 실수하지 않는다. **20** 구 자기 발로 서다, 자립하다 ❑ 인간이 최초로 달에 발을 내딛던 날 **21** 구 자기 발로 서다, 자립하다 ❑ 아버지는 내가 자립할 수 있고 남편에게 의존하지 않기만 한다면 내가 누구와 결혼하든 반대하지 않으셨다. **22** 구 일어선 ❑ 물론은 일어서서 자신의 상관을 따라 스위처룸에 나갔다. ❑ 대표단이 환호하며 일어서 있었다. **23** 구 첫발을 잘못 내딛다 ❑ 그들은 자기들이 선거를 요구했고 꽤 오랫동안 그것을 준비했는데도 불구하고 첫발을 잘못 내디뎠다.

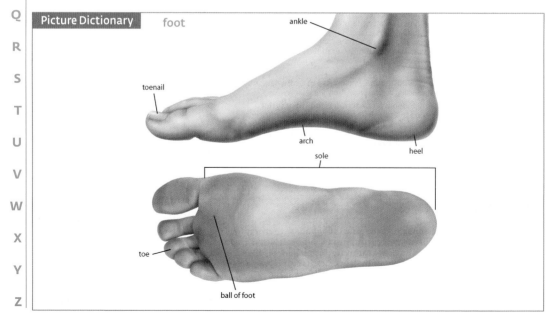

Picture Dictionary   foot

ankle

toenail

arch

heel

sole

toe

ball of foot

feet and wasn't dependent on my husband. **22** PHRASE If you get or rise **to** your **feet**, you stand up. ❏ *Malone got to his feet and followed his superior out of the suite.* ❏ *The delegates cheered and rose to their feet.* **23** PHRASE If someone **gets off on the wrong foot** in a new situation, they make a bad start by doing something in completely the wrong way. ❏ *Even though they called the election and had been preparing for it for some time, they got off on the wrong foot.* **24 foot in the door** →see door. **drag** your **feet** →see drag. **to vote with** your **feet** →see vote
→see body
→see Picture Dictionary: **foot**

foot|age /f**ʊ**tɪdʒ/ N-UNCOUNT **Footage** of a particular event is a film of it or the part of a film which shows this event. ❏ *They are planning to show exclusive footage from this summer's festivals.*

불가산명사 장면 ❏ 그들은 이번 여름 페스티벌의 특종 장면을 보여 주려고 계획 중이다.

foot-and-mouth disease N-UNCOUNT **Foot-and-mouth disease** or **foot-and-mouth** is a serious and highly infectious disease that affects cattle, sheep, pigs, and goats.

불가산명사 구제역

foot|ball ◆◇◇ /f**ʊ**tbɔl/ (**footballs**) **1** N-UNCOUNT **Football** is a game played by two teams of eleven players using an oval ball. Players carry the ball in their hands or throw it to each other as they try to score goals that are called touchdowns. [AM; BRIT **American football**] ❏ *Two blocks beyond our school was a field where boys played football.* **2** N-COUNT A **football** is a ball that is used for playing football. ❏ *...a heavy leather football.* **3** N-UNCOUNT **Football** is a game played by two teams of eleven players using a round ball. Players kick the ball to each other and try to score goals by kicking the ball into a large net. [BRIT; AM **soccer**] ❏ *Several boys were still playing football on the waste ground.* ❏ *...Arsenal Football Club.*
→see Picture Dictionary: **football**

1 불가산명사 미식축구 [미국영어; 영국영어 American football] ❏ 우리 학교에서 두 블록을 더 가면 소년들이 축구를 하는 들판이 있었다. **2** 가산명사 축구공 **3** 불가산명사 축구 [영국영어; 미국영어 soccer] ❏ 소년 몇 명이 버려진 공터에서 아직도 축구를 하고 있었다. ❏ 아스날 축구 팀

foot|ball|er /f**ʊ**tbɔlər/ (**footballers**) N-COUNT A **footballer** is a person who plays football (soccer), especially as a profession. [BRIT; AM **soccer player**]

가산명사 축구 선수 [영국영어; 미국영어 soccer player]

foot|er /f**ʊ**tər/ (**footers**) N-COUNT A **footer** is text such as a name or page number that can be automatically displayed at the bottom of each page of a printed document. Compare **header**. [COMPUTING] ❏ *Page Mode shows headers, footers, footnotes and page numbers.* →see also **header**

가산명사 꼬리말 [컴퓨터] ❏ 페이지 모드에서 머리말, 꼬리말, 각주, 쪽 번호를 볼 수 있다.

foot|hills /f**ʊ**thɪlz/ N-PLURAL The **foothills** of a mountain or a range of mountains are the lower hills or mountains around its base. ❏ *Pasadena lies in the foothills of the San Gabriel mountains.*

복수명사 (산기슭의) 작은 언덕 ❏ 파사데나는 산 가브리엘 산기슭의 작은 언덕에 위치해 있다.

foot|hold /f**ʊ**thoʊld/ (**footholds**) **1** N-COUNT A **foothold** is a strong or favorable position from which further advances or progress may be made. ❏ *If British business is to have a successful future, companies must establish a firm foothold in Europe.* **2** N-COUNT A **foothold** is a place such as a small hole or area of rock where you can safely put your foot when climbing. ❏ *He lowered his legs until he felt he had a solid foothold on the rockface beneath him.*

1 가산명사 거점, 발판 ❏ 영국 경기가 성공적인 앞날을 맞고자 한다면, 회사들이 유럽에서 탄탄한 거점을 수립해야만 한다. **2** 가산명사 발판 ❏ 그는 밑에 발을 디딜 수 있는 견고한 암벽이 있다고 느껴질 때까지 다리를 내려보았다.

foot|ing /f**ʊ**tɪŋ/ **1** N-UNCOUNT If something is put **on** a particular **footing**, it is defined, established, or changed in a particular way, often so that it is able to develop or exist successfully. ❏ *The new law will put official corruption on the same legal footing as treason.* **2** N-UNCOUNT If you are **on** a particular kind of **footing** with someone, you have that kind of relationship with them. ❏ *They decided to put their relationship on a more formal footing.* **3** N-UNCOUNT You refer to your **footing** when you are referring to your position and how securely your feet are placed on the ground. For example, if you lose your **footing**, your feet slip and you fall. ❏ *He was cautious of his footing, wary of the edge.*

1 불가산명사 기반 ❏ 신규 법안은 공직자들의 부패를 법적으로 반역죄와 동일한 기반 위에 둘 것이다. **2** 불가산명사 입지 ❏ 그들은 좀 더 공식적인 입지에서 관계를 갖기로 결정했다. **3** 불가산명사 발 디딤 ❏ 그는 가장자리를 밟지 않도록 조심스럽게 발을 디뎠다.

foot|note /f**ʊ**tnoʊt/ (**footnotes**) **1** N-COUNT A **footnote** is a note at the bottom of a page in a book which provides more detailed information about something that is mentioned on that page. **2** N-COUNT If you refer to what you are saying as a **footnote**, you mean that you are adding some information that is related to what has just been mentioned. ❏ *As a footnote, I should add that there was one point on which his bravado was more than justified.* **3** N-COUNT If you describe an event as a **footnote**, you mean that it is fairly unimportant although it will probably be remembered. ❏ *I'm afraid that his name will now become a footnote in history.*

1 가산명사 각주 **2** 가산명사 보충 설명 ❏ 보충 설명을 하자면 그의 허세가 정당한 것 이상이라고 보는 한 가지 이유가 있었다는 것을 덧붙이고 싶다. **3** 가산명사 부수적인 것 ❏ 유감이지만 그의 이름이 이제 역사에서 부수적인 것이 될 것이라고 생각한다.

foot|path /f**ʊ**tpæθ/ (**footpaths**) N-COUNT A **footpath** is a path for people to walk on, especially in the countryside.

가산명사 (시골의) 좁은 길

foot|print /f**ʊ**tprɪnt/ (**footprints**) N-COUNT A **footprint** is a mark in the shape of a foot that a person or animal makes in or on a surface. ❏ *His footprints were clearly evident in the heavy dust.* →see fossil

가산명사 발자국 ❏ 두텁게 쌓인 먼지 위에 그의 발자국이 선명하게 보였다.

foot|step /f**ʊ**tstɛp/ (**footsteps**) **1** N-COUNT A **footstep** is the sound or mark that is made by someone walking each time their foot touches the ground. ❏ *I*

1 가산명사 발소리, 발자국 ❏ 나는 밖에서 발소리가 나는 것을 들었다. **2** 구 선례를 따르다 ❏ 우리

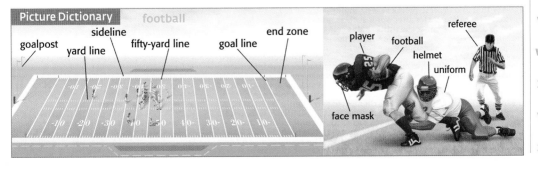

Picture Dictionary   football

goalpost   yard line   sideline   fifty-yard line   goal line   end zone

player   football   referee
helmet
uniform
face mask

A

heard footsteps outside. **2** PHRASE If you **follow in** someone's **footsteps**, you do the same things as they did earlier. ▢ My father is extremely proud that I followed in his footsteps and became a doctor.

B

foot|wear /fʊtweər/ N-UNCOUNT **Footwear** refers to things that people wear on their feet, for example shoes and boots. ▢ Some football players get paid millions for endorsing footwear.

for ♦♦♦ /fər, STRONG fɔr/

C

In addition to the uses shown below, **for** is used after some verbs, nouns, and adjectives in order to introduce extra information, and in phrasal verbs such as "account for" and "make up for." It is also used with some verbs that have two objects in order to introduce the second object.

D

E

1 PREP If something is **for** someone, they are intended to have it or benefit from it. ▢ Isn't that enough for you? ▢ ...a table for two. ▢ He wanted all the running of the business for himself. **2** PREP If you work or do a job **for** someone, you are employed by them. ▢ I knew he worked for a security firm. ▢ Have you had any experience writing for radio? **3** PREP If you speak or act **for** a particular group or organization, you represent them. ▢ She appears nightly on the television news, speaking for the State Department. **4** PREP If someone does something **for** you, they do it so that you do not have to do it. ▢ If your pharmacy doesn't stock the product you want, have them order it for you. ▢ I hold a shop door open for an old person. **5** PREP If you feel a particular emotion **for** someone, you feel it on their behalf. [adj/n PREP] ▢ This is the best thing you've ever done – I am so happy for you! **6** PREP If you feel a particular emotion **for** someone or something, they are the object of that emotion, and you feel it when you think about them. [adj/n PREP] ▢ John, I'm sorry for Steve, but I think you've made the right decisions. **7** PREP You use **for** after words such as "time," "space," "money," or "energy" when you say how much there is or whether there is enough of it in order to be able to do or use a particular thing. ▢ Many new trains have space for wheelchair users. ▢ ...a huge room with plenty of room for books. **8** PREP If something is **for** sale, hire, or use, it is available to be sold, hired, or used. ▢ ...fishmongers displaying freshwater fish for sale. ▢ ...a room for rent. **9** PREP You use **for** when you state or explain the purpose of an object, action, or activity. [PREP n/-ing] ▢ ...drug users who use unsterile equipment for injections of drugs. ▢ The knife for cutting sausage was sitting in the sink. **10** PREP You use **for** after nouns expressing reason or cause. [n PREP n/-ing] ▢ He's soon to make a speech in parliament explaining his reasons for going. ▢ The county hospital could find no physical cause for Sumner's problems. **11** PREP **For** is used in conditional sentences, in expressions such as "**if not for**" and "**were it not for**," to introduce the only thing which prevents the main part of the sentence from being true. ▢ If not for John, Brian wouldn't have learned the truth. ▢ The earth would be a frozen ball if it were not for the radiant heat of the sun. **12** PREP You use **for** to say how long something lasts or continues. [PREP amount] ▢ The toaster remained on for more than an hour. ▢ They talked for a bit. **13** PREP You use **for** to say how far something extends. [PREP amount] ▢ We drove on for a few miles. **14** PREP If something is bought, sold, or done **for** a particular amount of money, that amount of money is its price. [PREP amount] ▢ We got the bus back to Tange for 30 cents. ▢ The Martins sold their house for about 1.4 million pounds. **15** PREP If something is planned **for** a particular time, it is planned to happen then. ▢ ...the Welsh Boat Show, planned for July 30 – August 1. ▢ Marks & Spencer will be unveiling its latest fashions for autumn and winter. **16** PREP If you do something **for** a particular occasion, you do it on that occasion or to celebrate that occasion. ▢ He asked his daughter what she would like for her birthday. **17** PREP If you leave **for** a particular place or if you take a bus, train, plane, or boat **for** a place, you are going there. ▢ They would be leaving for Rio early the next morning. **18** PREP You use **for** when you make a statement about something in order to say how it affects or relates to someone, or what their attitude to it is. ▢ What matters for most scientists is money and facilities. ▢ For her, books were as necessary to life as bread. **19** PREP After some adjective, noun, and verb phrases, you use **for** to introduce the subject of the action indicated by the following infinitive verb. [PREP n to-inf] ▢ It might be possible for a single woman to be accepted as a foster parent. ▢ I had made arrangements for my affairs to be dealt with by one of my children. **20** PREP You use **for** when you say that an aspect of something or someone is surprising in relation to other aspects of them. ▢ He was tall for an eight-year-old. **21** PREP If you say that you are **for** a particular activity, you mean that this is what you want or intend to do. [v-link PREP n/-ing] ▢ Right, who's for a toasted sandwich then? **22** PREP If you say that something is **not for** you, you mean that you do not enjoy it or that it is not suitable for you. [INFORMAL] [with neg] ▢ Wendy decided the sport was not for her. **23** PREP If it is **for** you to do something, it is your responsibility or right to do it. [PREP n to-inf] ▢ I wish you would come back to Washington with us, but that's for you to decide. **24** PREP If you are **for** something, you agree with it or support it. [v-link PREP n/-ing] ▢ Are you for or against public transport? **25** PREP You use **for** after words such as "argue," "case," "evidence," or "vote" in order to introduce the thing that is being supported or proved. [n/v PREP n] ▢ Another union has voted for industrial action in support of a pay claim. ▢ The case for nuclear power is impressive. ● ADV **For** is also an adverb. [ADV after v] ▢ 833 delegates voted for, and only 432 against. **26** PREP **For** is the preposition that is used after some nouns, adjectives, or verbs in order to introduce more information or to indicate what a quality, thing, or action relates to. [n/adj/v PREP n/-ing] ▢ Reduced-calorie cheese is a great substitute for cream cheese. ▢ Car park owners should be legally responsible for protecting vehicles. **27** PREP To be named **for** someone means to be given the same name as them. [AM; BRIT **after**] ▢ The Brady Bill is named for former White House Press Secretary James Brady. **28** PREP You use **for** with "every" when you are stating a ratio, to introduce one of the things in the ratio. ▢ For every farm job that is lost, two or three other jobs in the area are put at risk. **29** PREP You can use **for** in expressions such as **pound for pound** or **mile for mile** when you are making comparisons between the values or qualities of

아버지는 내가 당신의 선례를 따라 의사가 된 것을 매우 자랑스러워하신다.

불가산명사 신발류 ▢ 일부 축구 선수들은 신발 선전의 대가로 수백만 달러를 받는다.

for는 아래 용법 외에도 추가 정보를 나타내기 위해 일부의 동사, 명사, 형용사 뒤에 쓴다. 또한 'account for', 'make up for'와 같은 구동사에도 쓰인다. for는 목적어를 두 개 갖는 동사에서 두 번째 목적어를 도입하기 위해서도 쓰인다.

1 전치사 -를 위한 ▢ 그것이 너에게는 충분치 않니? ▢ 2인용 식탁 ▢ 그는 사업 운영의 전반적인 사안을 스스로 하기 원했다. **2** 전치사 -를 위해 ▢ 나는 그가 경비 회사에서 일하고 있다는 것을 알고 있었다. ▢ 라디오용 대본을 써 본 경험이 있습니까? **3** 전치사 -을 대표하여 ▢ 그녀는 국무부를 대표하기 위해 매일 밤 텔레비전 뉴스에 출연한다. **4** 전치사 -을 대신하여 ▢ 약국에 네가 바라는 상품이 없으면 네 대신 주문해 달라고 해라. ▢ 나는 나이 드신 분들 대신 상점의 문을 연 채 잡아 준다. **5** 전치사 -을 대신해서 ▢ 이것은 네가 지금까지 해온 일 중 가장 멋져. 내가 아주 기뻐. **6** 전치사 -에 대해서 ▢ 존, 스티브에게 유감이지만, 나는 생각에 자네가 올바른 결정을 한 것 같네. **7** 전치사 -을 위한 ▢ 새로 제작된 많은 기차에는 휠체어 사용자들을 위한 공간이 마련되어 있다. ▢ 서적을 위한 넉넉한 공간을 갖춘 커다란 방 **8** 전치사 -을 목적으로 한 ▢ 판매용 민물고기를 진열한 생선 가게들 ▢ 셋방 **9** 전치사 -을 위해, -을 위한 ▢ 마약 주입을 위해 불결한 기구를 쓰는 마약 사용자들 ▢ 소시지를 자르는 칼이 싱크대에 놓여 있었다. **10** 전치사 -에 대한 ▢ 그는 가는 것에 대한 이유를 설명하기 위해 곧 의회 연설을 할 것이다. ▢ 그 군 병원은 숨너 씨의 질병에 대한 신체적 원인을 밝혀 낼 수 없었다. **11** 전치사 (조건절에서) -이 없다면 ▢ 존이 없다면, 브라이언은 진실을 알 수 없었을 텐데. ▢ 태양의 복사열이 없다면 지구는 꽁꽁 얼어 붙을 텐데. **12** 전치사 -동안 ▢ 토스터가 한 시간이 넘게 켜져 있었다. ▢ 그들은 잠시 동안 대화를 나누었다. **13** 전치사 -만큼의 거리를 ▢ 우리는 몇 마일을 계속 운전해 나아갔다. **14** 전치사 -의 값으로 ▢ 우리는 30센트를 주고 탄게로 돌아오는 버스를 탔다. ▢ 마틴 씨 부부는 약 140만 파운드에 자신들의 집을 팔았다. **15** 전치사 (특정한 때를) 위한 ▢ 7월 30일에서 8월 1일까지로 계획된 웨일스 보트 쇼 ▢ 마크 앤 스펜서사는 가을과 겨울철 최신 패션을 선보일 것이다. **16** 전치사 (특별한) -날에 ▢ 그는 딸에게 생일에 갖고 싶은 것이 무엇인지를 물어 보았다. **17** 전치사 -을 향해 ▢ 그들은 다음 날 아침 일찍 리오를 향해 떠날 것이었다. **18** 전치사 -에 있어서 ▢ 과학자 대부분에게 중요한 것은 자금과 설비이다. ▢ 그녀에게 있어서 책은 빵처럼 삶에 꼭 필요한 것이었다. **19** 전치사 -가, -의 ▢ 독신 여성이 양부모로서 인정될 가능성도 있을지 모른다. ▢ 나는 내 일들을 내 아이들 중 한 명이 처리하도록 마련해 두었었다. **20** 전치사 -에 비해 ▢ 그는 여덟 살치고는 키가 컸다. **21** 전치사 -을 원하는 ▢ 맞아, 그러면 토스트 샌드위치는 누구 거지? **22** 전치사 -을 위한 [비격식체] ▢ 웬디는 그 스포츠가 자신에게 맞지 않는다고 결론 내렸다. **23** 전치사 -가 해야 할 ▢ 나는 네가 우리와 함께 워싱턴으로 돌아오기를 바라지만, 그건 네가 결정할 일이다. **24** 전치사 -에 찬성하는 ▢ 대중교통에 찬성하십니까? 반대하십니까? **25** 전치사 -을 지지하는, -을 뒷받침하는 ▢ 다른 조합은 임금 인상을 지지하는 행위에 찬성표를 던졌다. ▢ 원자력을 찬성하는 이번 판례는 인상적이다. ● 부사 -을 지지하여 ▢ 833명의 대표가 찬성표를 던졌고, 단지 432명만이 반대했다. **26** 전치사 -에 대해 ▢ 칼로리 함량을 낮춘 치즈는 크림치즈 대용으로는 일품이다. ▢ 주차장 소유주는 차량 보호에 대해 법적 책임을 져야 한다. **27** 전치사 -의 이름을 따서 [미국영어; 영국영어 after] ▢ 브래디 법안은 전 백악관 공보 비서인 제임스 브래디의 이름을 딴 것다. **28** 전치사 -에 대하여 ▢ 농업 관련 직종이 하나씩 없어질 때마다, 이 분야의 둘 내지 세 개의 다른 직종이 위태로워진다. **29** 전치사 어느 모로 봐도 ▢ 남극, 어디를 봐도 지구상에서 가장 생명체가 적은 지역 중 한 곳 ▢ 햇볕에서 나는 것을 전문 용어로는 홍반이라 한다. **30** 전치사 -에 관해서는 ▢ 윌리엄 제임스 시디스의 생애에 관해서는 에이미 월리스의 '프로디지'를 보시오. **31** 구 -을 전적으로 찬성하는 ▢ 그는 선수들이 경기를 뛰는 동안 벌 수 있을 만큼 버는 것에 대해 전적으로 찬성한다. **32** 구 처음으로,

F **G** **H** **I** **J** **K** **L** **M** **N** **O** **P** **Q** **R** **S** **T** **U** **V** **W** **X** **Y** **Z**

different things. [n PREP n] □ ...the Antarctic, mile for mile one of the planet's most lifeless areas. ㉚ PREP If a word or expression has the same meaning as another word or expression, you can say that the first one is another word or expression **for** the second one. □ The technical term for sunburn is erythema. ㉛ PREP You use **for** in a piece of writing when you mention information which will be found somewhere else. □ For further information on the life of William James Sidis, see Amy Wallace, "The Prodigy". ㉜ PHRASE If you say that you are **all for** doing something, you agree or strongly believe that it should be done, but you are also often suggesting that other people disagree with you or that there are practical difficulties. □ He is all for players earning what they can while they are in the game. ㉝ PHRASE You use expressions such as **for the first time** and **for the last time** when you are talking about how often something has happened before. □ He was married for the second time, this time to a Belgian. ㉞ **as for** →see **as**. **but for** →see **but**. **for all** →see **all**

마지막으로. □ 그는 두 번째로 결혼을 했는데, 이번에는 벨기에 사람이었다.

for|age /fɔrɪdʒ, BRIT fɒrɪdʒ/ (**forages, foraging, foraged**) ❶ V-I If someone **forages for** something, they search for it in a busy way. □ They were forced to forage for clothing and fuel. ❷ V-I When animals **forage**, they search for food. □ We disturbed a wild boar that had been foraging by the roadside.

❶ 자동사 _을 찾아다니다 □ 그들은 옷가지와 땔감을 찾아다녀야만 했다. ❷ 자동사 먹이를 찾아다니다 □ 우리는 길가에서 먹이를 찾아다니던 멧돼지 한 마리를 성가시게 했다.

for|ay /fɔreɪ, BRIT fɒreɪ/ (**forays**) ❶ N-COUNT If you make a **foray into** a new or unfamiliar type of activity, you start to become involved in it. □ Emporio Armani, the Italian fashion house, has made a discreet foray into furnishings. ❷ N-COUNT You can refer to a short trip that you make as a **foray** if it seems to involve excitement or risk, for example because it is to an unfamiliar place or because you are looking for a particular thing. □ Most guests make at least one foray into the town. ❸ N-COUNT If a group of soldiers make a **foray into** enemy territory, they make a quick attack there, and then return to their own territory. □ These base camps were used by the PKK guerrillas to make forays into Turkey.

❶ 가산명사 진출 □ 이탈리아 패션가인 엠포리오 알마니가 가구업계로 조심스런 진출을 했다. ❷ 가산명사 (짧지만 짜릿한) 여행 □ 대부분의 손님들은 이 도시로 적어도 한 번씩은 여행을 한다. ❸ 가산명사 급습 □ 이 베이스캠프는 피케이케이 게릴라들이 터키를 급습하기 위해 사용하였다.

for|bid /fɔrbɪd, fər-/ (**forbids, forbidding, forbade, forbidden**) ❶ V-T If you **forbid** someone **to** do something, or if you **forbid** an activity, you order that it must not be done. □ They'll forbid you to marry. □ She was shut away and forbidden to read. ❷ V-T If something **forbids** a particular course of action or state of affairs, it makes it impossible for the course of action or state of affairs to happen. □ His own pride forbids him to ask Arthur's help.

❶ 타동사 금하다 □ 그들이 너의 결혼을 금할 것이다. □ 그녀는 격리되었고 책을 읽는 것을 금지 당했다. ❷ 타동사 가로막다 □ 그는 자존심 때문에 아서에게 도움을 청하지 않는다.

for|bid|den /fɔrbɪdᵊn, fər-/ ❶ ADJ If something is **forbidden**, you are not allowed to do it or have it. □ Smoking was forbidden everywhere. ❷ ADJ A **forbidden** place is one that you are not allowed to visit or enter. □ This was a forbidden area for foreigners. ❸ ADJ **Forbidden** is used to describe things that people strongly disapprove of or feel guilty about, and that are not often mentioned or talked about. □ The war was a forbidden subject. □ Men fantasize as a substitute for acting out forbidden desires.

❶ 형용사 금지된 □ 흡연은 어디서나 금지되어 있었다. ❷ 형용사 금단의 □ 이곳은 외국인들에게는 금단의 영역이었다. ❸ 형용사 금기된, 터부시된 □ 그 전쟁은 금기된 주제였다. □ 남자들은 금기된 욕구를 실행하는 대안책으로 공상에 잠기곤 한다.

force ♦♦♦ /fɔrs/ (**forces, forcing, forced**) ❶ V-T If someone **forces** you **to** do something, they make you do it even though you do not want to, for example by threatening you. □ He was charged with abducting a taxi driver and forcing him to drive a bomb to Downing Street. □ They were grabbed by three men who appeared to force them into a car. ❷ V-T If a situation or event **forces** you to do something, it makes it necessary for you to do something that you would not otherwise have done. □ A back injury forced her to withdraw from Wimbledon. □ He turned right, down a dirt road that forced him into four-wheel drive. ❸ V-T If someone **forces** something **on** or **upon** you, they make you accept or use it when you would prefer not to. □ To force this agreement on the nation is wrong. ❹ V-T If you **force** something into a particular position, you use a lot of strength to make it move there. □ They were forcing her head under the icy waters, drowning her. ❺ V-T If someone **forces** a lock, a door, or a window, they break the lock or fastening in order to get into a building without using a key. □ That evening police forced the door of the flat and arrested Mr. Roberts. ❻ N-UNCOUNT If someone uses **force** to do something, or if it is done by **force**, strong and violent physical action is taken in order to achieve it. □ The government decided against using force to break-up the demonstrations. ❼ N-UNCOUNT **Force** is the power or strength which something has. □ The force of the explosion shattered the windows of several buildings. ❽ N-COUNT If you refer to someone or something as a **force** in a particular type of activity, you mean that they have a strong influence on it. □ For years the army was the most powerful political force in the country. □ The band is still an innovative force in music. ❾ N-UNCOUNT The **force** of something is the powerful effect or quality that it has. □ He changed our world through the force of his ideas. ❿ N-COUNT You can use **forces** to refer to processes and events that do not appear to be caused by human beings, and are therefore difficult to understand or control. □ ...the protection of mankind against the forces of nature: epidemics, predators, floods, hurricanes. □ The principle of market forces was applied to some of the country's most revered institutions. ⓫ N-VAR In physics, a **force** is the pulling or pushing effect that something has on something else. □ ...the earth's gravitational force. ⓬ N-UNCOUNT **Force** is used before a number to indicate a wind of a particular speed or strength, especially a very strong wind. □ The airlift was conducted in force ten winds. ⓭ N-COUNT **Forces** are groups of soldiers or military vehicles that are organized for a particular purpose. □ ...the deployment of American forces in the region. ⓮ N-PLURAL **The forces** means the army, the navy, or the air force, or all three. □ The more senior you become in the forces, the more likely you are to end up in a desk job. ⓯ N-SING **The force** is sometimes used to mean the police force. □ It was hard for a police officer to make friends outside the force. ⓰ →see also **air force, armed forces, labor force, workforce** ⓱ PHRASE If you do something **from force of habit**, you do it because you have always done it in the past, rather than because you have thought carefully about it. □ He looked around from force of habit, but nobody paid any attention to him. ⓲ PHRASE A law, rule, or system that is **in force** exists or is being used. □ Although the new tax is already in force, you have until November to lodge an appeal. ⓳ PHRASE When people do something **in force**, they do it in large numbers. □ Voters turned out in force for their first taste of multi-party elections. ⓴ PHRASE If you **join forces with** someone, you work together in

❶ 타동사 강요하다 □ 그는 택시 기사를 유괴해 다우닝 가로 폭탄을 싣고 가도록 강요한 죄로 기소되었다. □ 그들은 세 남자에게 잡혔는데 그 남자들이 그들을 강제로 차에 태운 것 같았다. ❷ 타동사 _하게 만들다 □ 허리 부상으로 인해 그녀는 윔블던 대회에서 은퇴해야만 했다. □ 그가 오른쪽으로 돌자, 사륜 구동을 해야만 하는 흙길로 들어서게 되었다. ❸ 타동사 강요하다 □ 국민에게 이 합의를 강요하는 것은 옳지 못하다. ❹ 타동사 강제로 _하다 □ 그들은 그녀를 익사시키기 위해 얼음처럼 차가운 물속에 그녀의 머리를 강제로 밀어 넣고 있었다. ❺ 타동사 강제로 열다 □ 그날 저녁 경찰은 아파트 문을 강제로 열고 로버트 씨를 체포했다. ❻ 불가산명사 무력, 강압 □ 정부는 시위 해산을 위해 무력을 사용하지 않기로 결정했다. ❼ 불가산명사 힘 □ 그 폭발로 인해 몇몇 건물의 유리창이 산산조각 났다. ❽ 가산명사 세력 □ 여러 해 동안 군대는 이 나라에서 가장 영향력 있는 정치 세력이었다. □ 그 밴드는 여전히 음악계의 혁신적인 세력이다. ❾ 불가산명사 영향력 □ 그는 영향력 있는 그의 사상으로 우리들의 세상을 바꾸었다. ❿ 가산명사 불가항력, 힘 □ 자연의 불가항력으로부터 인류를 보호하는 것: 전염병, 육식 동물, 홍수, 허리케인 등 자연의 불가항력으로부터 인류를 보호한다 □ 시장의 힘이라는 원리는 그 나라의 가장 존중되던 조직들에도 적용되었다. ⓫ 가산명사 또는 불가산명사 힘 □ 지구의 중력 ⓬ 불가산명사 풍력 □ 공수는 대기의 풍력이 10인 가운데 행해졌다. ⓭ 가산명사 군사력 □ 그 지역에 미군 병력을 배치함 ⓮ 복수명사 군대 □ 군대에서는 상급자가 되어 갈수록 결국에는 사무직을 맡게 될 가능성이 커진다. ⓯ 단수명사 경찰 □ 경찰관이 경찰 외부에서 친구를 사귀기는 어려웠다. ⓰ 구 습관(의 힘), 타성 □ 그는 습관적으로 주위를 둘러보았으나, 아무도 그에게 관심을 보이지 않았다. ⓲ 구 시행 중인 □ 신설 조세가 이미 시행되고 있지만, 11월까지는 항소할 수 있다. ⓳ 구 대대적으로 □ 유권자들이 여러 정당이 참가한 선거에서 대거 처음의 투표를 했다. ⓴ 구 협력하다 □ 두 단체는 협력해서 유권자들이 그 산업 분야에 대한 세제 혜택을 친성하도록 설득했다. ⓴ 구 밀치고 나아가다 □ 그 광부들은 곤봉으로 무장한 채 경찰 저지선을 밀치고 나아갔다.

order to achieve a common aim or purpose. ❏ *Both groups joined forces to persuade voters to approve a tax break for the industry.* ◨ PHRASE If you **force** your **way through** or **into** somewhere, you have to push or break things that are in your way in order to get there. ❏ *The miners were armed with clubs as they forced their way through a police cordon.* →see **motion**

Thesaurus
*force*의 참조어

V.	coerce, make ◨ ◨
	push, thrust ◨
	break in, break open ◨
N.	energy, pressure, strength ◨

Word Partnership
*force*의 연어

V.	force **to resign** ◨ ◨
	force **a smile** ◨
N.	**use of** force ◨
	force **of gravity** ◨
ADJ.	**excessive** force, **necessary** force ◨
	driving force, **powerful** force ◨
	enemy forces, **military** forces ◨

---

forced /fɔrst/ ◨ ADJ A **forced** action is something that you do because someone else makes you do it. [ADJ n] ❏ *A system of forced labour was used on the cocoa plantations.* ◨ ADJ A **forced** action is something that you do because circumstances make it necessary. [ADJ n] ❏ *He made a forced landing on a highway.* ◨ If you describe something as **forced**, you mean it does not happen naturally and easily. ❏ *...a forced smile.*

force|ful /fɔrsfəl/ ◨ ADJ If you describe someone as **forceful**, you approve of them because they express their opinions and wishes in a strong, emphatic, and confident way. [APPROVAL] ❏ *He was a man of forceful character, with considerable insight and diplomatic skills.* ● **force|ful|ly** ADV [ADV with v] ❏ *Mrs. Dambar was talking very rapidly and somewhat forcefully.* ◨ ADJ Something that is **forceful** has a very powerful effect and causes you to think or feel something very strongly. ❏ *It made a very forceful impression on me.* ● **force|ful|ly** ADV [ADV with v] ❏ *Daytime television tended to remind her too forcefully of her own situation.* ◨ ADJ A **forceful** point or argument in a discussion is one that is good, valid, and convincing. ❏ *...although you may need to be armed with some forceful arguments to persuade a partner into seeing things your way.*

for|cible /fɔrsɪbəl/ ADJ **Forcible** action involves physical force or violence. ❏ *Reports are coming in of the forcible resettlement of villagers from the countryside into towns.*

fore /fɔr/ ◨ PHRASE If someone or something comes **to the fore** in a particular situation or group, they become important or popular. ❏ *A number of low-budget independent films brought new directors and actors to the fore.* ◨ ADJ **Fore** is used to refer to parts at the front of an animal, ship, or aircraft. [ADJ n] ❏ *There had been no direct damage in the fore part of the ship.*

fore|arm /fɔrɑrm/ (**forearms**) N-COUNT Your **forearm** is the part of your arm between your elbow and your wrist. ❏ *...the tattoo on his forearm.*

Word Link
*fore ≈ before : fore*cast, *fore*name, *fore*sight

---

fore|cast ◆◇◇ /fɔrkæst/ (**forecasts, forecasting, forecasted**)

> The forms **forecast** and **forecasted** can both be used for the past tense and past participle.

◨ N-COUNT A **forecast** is a statement of what is expected to happen in the future, especially in relation to a particular event or situation. ❏ *...a forecast of a 2.25 percent growth in the economy.* ❏ *He delivered his election forecast.* ◨ V-T If you **forecast** future events, you say what you think is going to happen in the future. ❏ *They forecast a humiliating defeat for the Prime Minister.* ◨ →see also **weather forecast**
→see Word Web: **forecast**

fore|close /fɔrklouz/ (**forecloses, foreclosing, foreclosed**) V-I If the person or organization that lent someone money **forecloses**, they take possession of a property that was bought with the borrowed money, for example because regular repayments have not been made. [BUSINESS] ❏ *The bank foreclosed on the mortgage for his previous home.*

Word Web
forecast

Meteorologists depend on good information. They make **observations**. They gather **data** about barometric **pressure**, **temperature**, and **humidity**. They track **storms** with **radar** and **satellites**. They track cold **fronts** and warm fronts. They put all of this information into their computers and **model** possible weather patterns. Today scientists are trying to make better **weather forecasts**. They are installing thousands of small, inexpensive **radar** units on rooftops and cell phone towers. They will gather information near the Earth's surface and high in the sky. This will give meteorologists more information to help them **predict** tomorrow's weather.

◨ 형용사 강요된 ❏ 코코아 재배 농장에서는 강제 노동 제도가 행해졌다. ◨ 형용사 비상시의 ❏ 그는 고속도로에 비상 착륙을 했다. ◨ 형용사 억지의 ❏ 억지웃음

◨ 형용사 힘찬 [마음에 듦] ❏ 그는 힘찬 성격에 사려 깊은 통찰력과 외교적 수완을 갖춘 사람이었다. ● 힘차게 부사 ❏ 댐버 부인은 매우 빨리, 다소 힘 있게 말을 하고 있었다. ◨ 형용사 강한 ❏ 나는 그것에 매우 강한 인상을 받았다. ● 강력하게 부사 ❏ 낮 시간 텔레비전 방송을 보면 그녀는 자신의 처한 상황을 강력하게 떠올리곤 했다. ◨ 형용사 설득력 있는 ❏ 네가 설득력 있는 주장으로 동업자를 너와 같은 생각을 하게끔 설득할 필요가 있을지 몰라도

형용사 강제적인, 무력을 쓰는 ❏ 시골 주민들을 도시로 강제 이주시켰다는 보고서가 들어오고 있다.

◨ 구 세상의 주목을 받게 된 ❏ 많은 지예산 독립 영화를 통해 신진 감독들과 배우들이 세상의 주목을 끌었다. ◨ 형용사 앞부분의 ❏ 선박 앞부분에 직접적인 손상은 없었다.

가산명사 팔뚝 ❏ 그의 팔뚝에 새겨진 문신

forecast와 forecasted 모두 과거 및 과거 분사로 쓸 수 있다.

◨ 가산명사 예상, 예보 ❏ 경제가 2.25퍼센트 성장하리라는 예상 ❏ 그는 그의 선거 예측을 발표했다. ◨ 타동사 예상하다, 예보하다 ❏ 그들은 총리가 굴욕적인 패배를 할 것이라고 예상했다.

자동사 압류하다 [경제] ❏ 은행은 담보 대출을 해 준 그의 이전 집을 압류했다.

fore|clo|sure /fɔrkloʊʒər/ (**foreclosures**) N-VAR **Foreclosure** is when someone who has lent money to a person or organization so that they can buy property takes possession of the property because the money has not been repaid. [BUSINESS] ❑ *If homeowners can't keep up the payments, they face foreclosure.*

가산명사 또는 불가산명사 압류 [경제] ❑ 집주인이 돈을 계속 지불할 수 없다면, 압류를 당하게 될 것이다.

fore|court /fɔrkɔrt/ (**forecourts**) N-COUNT The **forecourt** of a large building or gas station is the open area at the front of it. [mainly BRIT] ❑ *I locked the bike in the forecourt of the Kirey Hotel.* →see **tennis**

가산명사 앞뜰 [주로 영국영어] ❑ 나는 키리 호텔의 앞뜰에 그 자전거를 자물쇠로 채워 두었다.

fore|finger /fɔrfɪŋgər/ (**forefingers**) N-COUNT Your **forefinger** is the finger that is next to your thumb. ❑ *He took the pen between his thumb and forefinger.*

가산명사 집게손가락 ❑ 그는 엄지와 집게손가락으로 펜을 잡았다.

fore|front /fɔrfrʌnt/ ➊ N-SING If you are at the **forefront** of a campaign or other activity, you have a leading and influential position in it. ❑ *They have been at the forefront of the campaign for political change.* ➋ N-SING If something is at the **forefront** of people's minds or attention, they think about it a lot because it is particularly important to them. ❑ *The pension issue was not at the forefront of his mind in the spring of 1985.*

➊ 단수명사 선두 ❑ 그들은 정치 개혁 운동의 선두주자로서 활동해 오고 있다. ➋ 단수명사 주요 관심사 ❑ 1985년 봄에는 연금 문제가 그의 주요 관심사가 아니었다.

fore|go /fɔrgoʊ/ (**foregoes, foregoing, forewent, foregone**) also **forgo** V-T If you **forego** something, you decide to do without it, although you would like to. [FORMAL] ❑ *Keen skiers are happy to forego a summer holiday to go skiing.*

타동사 ~없이 지내다 [격식체] ❑ 스키 광들은 스키를 타기 위해서는 여름휴가 없이 지내도 기쁘기만 하다.

fore|gone /fɔrgɒn/ ➊ **Foregone** is the past participle of **forego**. ➋ PHRASE If you say that a particular result is a **foregone conclusion**, you mean you are certain that it will happen. ❑ *Most voters believe the result is a foregone conclusion.*

➊ forego의 과거 분사 ➋ 구 확실한 결과, 뻔한 결과 ❑ 대부분의 유권자들은 그 결과가 뻔하다고 믿는다.

Word Link ground ≈ bottom : back*ground*, fore*ground*, *ground*work

fore|ground /fɔrgraʊnd/ (**foregrounds**) ➊ N-VAR The **foreground** of a picture or scene you are looking at is the part or area of it that appears nearest to you. ❑ *He is the bowler-hatted figure in the foreground of Orpen's famous painting.* ➋ N-SING If something or someone is in the **foreground**, or comes to the **foreground**, they receive a lot of attention. ❑ *This is another worry that has come to the foreground in recent years.*

➊ 가산명사 또는 불가산명사 전경 ❑ 그가 오르펜의 유명한 그림의 전경에 나오는 중산모자를 쓴 사람이다. ➋ 단수명사 많은 주목을 받는 위치 ❑ 이것은 최근 몇 년 들어 많은 주목을 받아 온 또 다른 걱정거리이다.

fore|head /fɔrhɛd, fɔrɪd/ (**foreheads**) N-COUNT Your **forehead** is the area at the front of your head between your eyebrows and your hair. ❑ *...the lines on her forehead.* →see **face**

가산명사 이마 ❑ 그녀의 이마선

for|eign ♦♦♦ /fɔrɪn, BRIT fɒrɪn/ ➊ ADJ Something or someone that is **foreign** comes from or relates to a country that is not your own. ❑ *She was on her first foreign holiday without her parents.* ❑ *...a foreign language.* ➋ ADJ In politics and journalism, **foreign** is used to describe people, jobs, and activities relating to countries that are not the country of the person or government concerned. [ADJ n] ❑ *...the German foreign minister.* ❑ *I am the foreign correspondent in Washington of La Tribuna newspaper of Honduras.* ➌ ADJ A **foreign** object is something that has got into something else, usually by accident, and should not be there. [FORMAL] ❑ *The patient's immune system would reject the transplanted organ as a foreign object.*

➊ 형용사 외국의, 해외의 ❑ 그녀는 부모님의 동행 없는 첫 해외 휴가 중이었다. ❑ 외국어 ➋ 형용사 대외의, 해외의 ❑ 독일 외무 장관 ❑ 나는 온두라스의 '라 트리부나' 신문의 워싱턴 주재 특파원이다. ➌ 형용사 이질의 [격식체] ❑ 그 환자의 면역 체계가 이식된 장기를 이질적인 것으로 여겨 거부 반응을 일으킬 것이다.

Thesaurus foreign의 참조어

ADJ. alien, exotic, strange; (*ant.*) domestic, native ➊ ➌

for|eign|er ♦♢♢ /fɔrɪnər, BRIT fɒrɪnər/ (**foreigners**) N-COUNT A **foreigner** is someone who belongs to a country that is not your own. ❑ *They are discouraged from becoming close friends with foreigners.* →see **stranger**

가산명사 외국인 ❑ 그들은 외국인과 친한 친구가 되는 데 지장을 받는다.

for|eign ex|change (**foreign exchanges**) ➊ N-PLURAL **Foreign exchanges** are the institutions or systems involved with changing one currency into another. ❑ *On the foreign exchanges, the U.S. dollar is up point forty-five.* ➋ N-UNCOUNT **Foreign exchange** is used to refer to foreign currency that is obtained through the foreign exchange system. ❑ *...an important source of foreign exchange.*

➊ 복수명사 외환 시장 ❑ 외환 시장에서, 미국 달러가 45포인트 올랐다. ➋ 불가산명사 외환, 외화 ❑ 중요한 외화 수입원

For|eign Of|fice (**Foreign Offices**) N-COUNT The **Foreign Office** is the government department, especially in Britain, which has responsibility for the government's dealings and relations with foreign governments. ❑ *...a Foreign Office spokesman.*

가산명사 (영국) 외무부 ❑ 외무부 대변인

Word Link man ≈ human being : fore*man*, hu*man*e, wo*man*

fore|man /fɔrmən/ (**foremen**) ➊ N-COUNT A **foreman** is a person, especially a man, in charge of a group of workers. ❑ *He still visited the dairy daily, but left most of the business details to his manager and foreman.* ➋ N-COUNT The **foreman** of a jury is the person who is chosen as their leader. ❑ *There was applause from the public gallery as the foreman of the jury announced the verdict.*

➊ 가산명사 십장, (인부들의) 감독 ❑ 그는 여전히 치즈 공장을 매일 방문했지만, 대부분의 세부 업무를 그의 공장장과 감독에게 위임했다. ➋ 가산명사 배심원장 ❑ 배심원장이 평결을 낭독할 때 방청석에서 박수 소리가 났다.

fore|most /fɔrmoʊst/ ➊ ADJ The **foremost** thing or person in a group is the most important or best. ❑ *He was one of the world's foremost scholars of ancient Indian culture.* ➋ PHRASE You use **first and foremost** to emphasize the most important quality of something or someone. [EMPHASIS] ❑ *It is first and foremost a trade agreement.*

➊ 형용사 으뜸가는 ❑ 그는 고대인도 문화에 대해 세계적으로 으뜸가는 학자들 중 한 사람이었다. ➋ 구 단연코 [강조] ❑ 그것은 단연코 무역 협정이다.

Word Link fore ≈ before : fore*cast*, fore*name*, fore*sight*

fore|name /fɔrneɪm/ (**forenames**) N-COUNT Your **forename** is your first name. Your **forenames** are your names other than your surname. [FORMAL] ❑ *...the unusual spelling of his forename.*

가산명사 (성에 대하여) 이름 [격식체] ❑ 철자가 특이한 그의 이름

fo|ren|sic /fərɛnsɪk/ (**forensics**) ➊ ADJ **Forensic** is used to describe the work of scientists who examine evidence in order to help the police solve crimes. [ADJ

➊ 형용사 법의학의 ❑ 그들은 법의학적 증거만으로 유죄 판결을 받았다. ❑ 법의학 전문가들은 단서를 찾기

Word Web   forest

Four hundred years ago, newly arrived colonists in North America encountered endless **forests**. This abundant supply of **wood** helped them get started. They used **timber** to build homes and make furniture. They burned wood for cooking and heating. They cut down the **woods** to create farmland. By the late 1800s, most of the old growth forests on the East Coast had disappeared. The **lumbering** industry has also destroyed millions of trees. Reforestation has replaced some of them. However, logging companies usually plant single species forests. Some people say these are not really forests at all—just **tree** farms.

n] ❏ *They were convicted on forensic evidence alone.* ❏ *Forensic experts searched the area for clues.* ❷ N-UNCOUNT **Forensics** is the use of scientific techniques to solve crimes. ❏ *...the newest advances in forensics.*

위해 그 지역을 자세히 조사했다. ❷ 불가산명사 법의학 ❏ 법의학의 최신 발달

fore|run|ner /fɔ́ːrʌnər/ (**forerunners**) N-COUNT If you describe a person or thing as the **forerunner of** someone or something similar, you mean they existed before them and either influenced their development or were a sign of what was going to happen. ❏ *...a machine which, in some respects, was the forerunner of the modern helicopter.*

가산명사 전신, 선구자 ❏ 어떤 면에서 보면 현대 헬리콥터의 전신이 되는 기계

fore|see /fɔːrsíː/ (**foresees, foreseeing, foresaw, foreseen**) V-T If you **foresee** something, you expect and believe that it will happen. ❏ *He did not foresee any problems.*

타동사 예견하다 ❏ 그는 어떤 문제점도 예견하지 않았다.

fore|see|able /fɔːrsíːəbᵊl/ ❶ ADJ If a future event is **foreseeable**, you know that it will happen or that it can happen, because it is a natural or obvious consequence of something else that you know. ❏ *It seems to me that this crime was foreseeable and this death preventable.* ❷ PHRASE If you say that something will happen **for the foreseeable future**, you think that it will continue to happen for a long time. ❏ *Profit and dividend growth looks like being above average for the foreseeable future.*

❶ 형용사 예견할 수 있는 ❏ 내가 보기엔 이번 범죄는 예견할 수 있었고 이 죽음도 예방할 수 있었던 것으로 보인다. ❷ 구 당분간은 ❏ 당분간은 수익과 배당금 증가가 평균을 웃돌 것으로 보인다.

Word Link   fore ≈ before : *forecast*, *forename*, *foresight*

fore|sight /fɔ́ːrsaɪt/ N-UNCOUNT Someone's **foresight** is their ability to see what is likely to happen in the future and to take appropriate action. [APPROVAL] ❏ *They had the foresight to invest in new technology.*

불가산명사 선견지명 [마음에 듦] ❏ 그들은 신기술에 투자하는 선견지명이 있었다.

for|est ♦◇◇ /fɔ́ːrɪst, BRIT fɒ́rɪst/ (**forests**) N-VAR A **forest** is a large area where trees grow close together. ❏ *Parts of the forest are still dense and inaccessible.* →see Word Web: **forest**

가산명사 또는 불가산명사 숲 ❏ 그 숲의 여러 곳은 아직도 울창해서 접근이 불가능하다.

fore|stall /fɔːrstɔ́ːl/ (**forestalls, forestalling, forestalled**) V-T If you **forestall** someone, you realize what they are likely to do and prevent them from doing it. ❏ *Large numbers of police were in the square to forestall any demonstrations.*

타동사 미연에 방지하다 ❏ 집회를 원천 봉쇄하려고 나온 경찰들이 광장에 쫙 깔려 있었다.

for|est|ry /fɔ́ːrɪstri, BRIT fɒ́rɪstri/ N-UNCOUNT **Forestry** is the science or skill of growing and taking care of trees in forests, especially in order to obtain wood. ❏ *...his great interest in forestry.* →see **industry**

불가산명사 산림학 ❏ 산림학에 대해 그가 갖고 있는 지대한 관심

for|ev|er /fərévər, far-/ ❶ ADV If you say that something will happen or continue **forever**, you mean that it will always happen or continue. [ADV with v] ❏ *I think that we will live together forever.* ❷ ADV If something has gone or changed **forever**, it has gone or changed completely and permanently. [ADV after v] ❏ *The old social order was gone forever.* ❸ ADV If you say that something takes **forever** or lasts **forever**, you are emphasizing that it takes or lasts a very long time, or that it seems to. [INFORMAL, EMPHASIS] [ADV after v] ❏ *The drive seemed to take forever.*

❶ 부사 영원히 ❏ 나는 우리가 영원히 함께 살 수 있을 거라고 생각해. ❷ 부사 영원히 ❏ 구 사회 질서는 영원히 사라졌다. ❸ 부사 영원히 [비격식체, 강조] ❏ 그 주행이 영원히 계속 될 것만 같았다.

fore|went /fɔːrwént/ **Forewent** is the past tense of **forego**.

forego의 과거

fore|word /fɔ́ːrwɜːrd/ (**forewords**) N-COUNT The **foreword** to a book is an introduction by the author or by someone else. ❏ *The Queen has written the foreword to a book of curry recipes.*

가산명사 서문 ❏ 한 카레 요리책에 여왕이 서문을 썼다.

forex /fɔ́ːreks/ N-UNCOUNT **Forex** is an abbreviation for **foreign exchange**. ❏ *...the forex market.*

불가산명사 외환 ❏ 외환 시장

for|feit /fɔ́ːrfɪt/ (**forfeits, forfeiting, forfeited**) ❶ V-T If you **forfeit** something, you lose it or are forced to give it up because you have broken a rule or done something wrong. ❏ *He was ordered to forfeit more than £1.5m.* ❷ V-T If you **forfeit** something, you give it up willingly, especially so that you can achieve something else. ❏ *Do you think that they would forfeit profit in the name of safety?* ❸ N-COUNT A **forfeit** is something that you have to give up because you have done something wrong. ❏ *That is the forfeit he must pay.*

❶ 타동사 몰수당하다 ❏ 그는 150만 파운드가 넘는 몰수 명령을 받았다. ❷ 타동사 포기하다 ❏ 당신은 그 사람들이 안전 때문에 이익을 포기할 것 같소? ❸ 가산명사 벌금 ❏ 그것은 그가 내야 하는 벌금이다.

for|gave /fərgéɪv/ **Forgave** is the past tense of **forgive**.

forgive의 과거

forge /fɔːrdʒ/ (**forges, forging, forged**) ❶ V-RECIP If one person or institution **forges** an agreement or relationship with another, they create it with a lot of hard work, hoping that it will be strong or lasting. ❏ *The Prime Minister is determined to forge a good relationship with America's new leader.* ❏ *They agreed to forge closer economic ties.* ❷ V-T If someone **forges** something such as a banknote, a document, or a painting, they copy it or make it so that it looks genuine, in order to deceive people. ❏ *He admitted seven charges including forging passports.* ● **forg|er** (**forgers**) N-COUNT ❏ *They used forged documents to leave the country.* ❏ *...the most prolific art forger in the country.*

❶ 상호동사 (협정, 관계등) 맺다 ❏ 수상은 미국의 새 지도자와 호의적인 관계를 맺기로 했다. ❏ 그들은 좀 더 긴밀한 경제적 유대 관계를 맺기로 합의했다. ❷ 타동사 위조하다 ❏ 그는 여권 위조를 포함한 일곱 개의 기소 내용을 시인했다. ❏ 그들은 그 나라를 빠져나가려고 위조된 서류를 이용했다. ● 위조범 가산명사 ❏ 그 나라에서 위조 예술품을 가장 많이 만드는 사람

Word Partnership   *forge*의 연어

N.   forge **a bond**, forge **a friendship**, forge **links**, forge **a relationship**, forge **ties** ❶
       forge **documents**, forge **an identity**, forge **a signature** ❷

▶**forge ahead** PHRASAL VERB If you **forge ahead** with something, you continue with it and make a lot of progress with it. ❑ *He again pledged to forge ahead with his plans for reform.*

구동사 계속 추진하다 ❑ 그는 개혁을 위한 자신의 계획을 계속 추진하겠다고 다시 한 번 서약했다.

for|gery /fɔ́rdʒəri/ (**forgeries**) ◼ N-UNCOUNT **Forgery** is the crime of forging money, documents, or paintings. ❑ *He was found guilty of forgery.* ◼ N-COUNT You can refer to a forged document, banknote, or painting as a **forgery**. ❑ *The letter was a forgery.*

◼ 불가산명사 위조죄 ❑ 그는 위조죄 유죄로 판명 났다. ◼ 가산명사 위조품 ❑ 그 편지는 위조된 것이었다.

for|get ♦♦◇ /fərɡét/ (**forgets, forgetting, forgot, forgotten**) ◼ V-T If you **forget** something or **forget** how to do something, you cannot think of it or think how to do it, although you knew it or knew how to do it in the past. ❑ *She forgot where she left the car and it took us two days to find it.* ◼ V-T/V-I If you **forget** something or **forget** to do it, you fail to think about it or fail to remember to do it, for example because you are thinking about other things. ❑ *She never forgets her daddy's birthday.* ❑ *She forgot to lock her door one day and two men got in.* ◼ V-T If you **forget** something that you had intended to bring with you, you do not bring it because you did not think about it at the right time. ❑ *Once when we were going to Paris, I forgot my passport.*

◼ 타동사 잊다 ❑ 그녀는 자기의 차를 어디다 두었는지 잊어버렸고, 우리는 이를 걸려서 그 차를 찾았다. ◼ 타동사/자동사 깜빡하다 ❑ 그녀는 자기 아버지의 생신을 잊은 적이 없다. ❑ 하루는 그녀가 문을 잠그는 것을 깜빡해서 두 남자가 들어왔다. ◼ 타동사 잊고 안 가져가다 ❑ 한번은 우리가 파리에 가려던 참이었는데, 내가 여권을 잊고 안 가져갔다.

> Note that you cannot use the verb **forget** to say that you have put something somewhere and left it there. Instead you use the verb **leave**. ❑ *I left my bag on the bus.*

> 무엇을 어딘가에 놓고 왔다고 할 때는 동사 forget이 아니라 동사 leave를 쓴다는 점을 유의하라. ❑ 나는 가방을 버스에 두고 내렸다.

◼ V-T/V-I If you **forget** something or someone, you deliberately put them out of your mind and do not think about them any more. ❑ *I hope you will forget the bad experience you had today.* ❑ *I found it very easy to forget about Sumner.* ◼ CONVENTION You say "**Forget it**" in reply to someone as a way of telling them not to worry or bother about something, or as an emphatic way of saying no to a suggestion. [SPOKEN, FORMULAE] ❑ *"Sorry, Liz. I think I was a bit rude to you." — "Forget it, but don't do it again!"* ◼ PHRASE You say **not forgetting** a particular thing or person when you want to include them in something that you have already talked about. ❑ *The first thing is to support as many shows as one can, not forgetting the small local ones.*

◼ 타동사/자동사 잊다 ❑ 네가 오늘 겪은 끔찍한 경험들을 잊기를 바래. ❑ 섬너를 잊는 것은 생각보다 아주 쉬웠다. ◼ 관용 표현 괜찮아 [구어체, 의례적인 표현] ❑ "리즈, 미안해. 내가 너한테 좀 심했던 것 같아." "괜찮아, 하지만 다시는 그러지 마." ◼ 구 ―까지 포함해서 ❑ 첫째는 지방의 작은 것까지도 포함하는 가능한 한 많은 쇼를 지원하는 것이다.

Thesaurus 　　　*forget*의 참조어

v. 　　　neglect, omit, overlook ◼

Word Partnership 　　　*forget*의 연어

ADV. 　　　**never** forget, **soon** forget ◼
　　　almost forget ◼ ◼ ◼
ADJ. 　　　**easy/hard to** forget ◼-◼

for|get|ful /fərɡétfəl/ ADJ Someone who is **forgetful** often forgets things. ❑ *My mother has become very forgetful and confused recently.*

형용사 건망증이 심한 ❑ 우리 어머니는 최근에 건망증이 심해지셨고, 자주 헷갈려하신다.

for|give /fərɡív/ (**forgives, forgiving, forgave, forgiven**) ◼ V-T/V-I If you **forgive** someone who has done something bad or wrong, you stop being angry with them and no longer want to punish them. ❑ *Hopefully Jane will understand and forgive you, if she really loves you.* ❑ *Irene forgave Terry for stealing her money.* ❑ *He could forgive Petal anything if the children were safe.* ◼ V-T PASSIVE If you say that someone could **be forgiven for** doing something, you mean that they were wrong or mistaken, but not seriously, because many people would have done the same thing in those circumstances. ❑ *Looking at the figures, you could be forgiven for thinking the recession is already over.* ◼ V-T **Forgive** is used in polite expressions and apologies like "**forgive me**" and "**forgive my ignorance**" when you are saying or doing something that might seem rude, silly, or complicated. [POLITENESS] ❑ *Forgive me, I don't mean to insult you.* ❑ *I do hope you'll forgive me but I've got to leave.*

◼ 타동사/자동사 용서하다 ❑ 아마 제인이 널 정말 사랑한다면 이해하고 용서해 줄 거야. ❑ 아이린은 테리가 돈을 훔쳐간 것을 용서해 주었다. ❑ 아이들만 무사하다면 그가 페탈을 모두 용서해 줄 수도 있다. ◼ 수동 타동사 ―하는 것도 무리가 아니다, ―해도 나무랄 수 없다 ❑ 이 수치를 보면 누구나 다 자네처럼 불경기가 다 끝났다고 오판할 거야. ◼ 타동사 죄송합니다; 제 무지를 용서해 주십시오 [공손체] ❑ 죄송합니다. 선생님을 욕보이려고 하는 게 아니라. ❑ 죄송하지만, 이만 가 봐야겠는데요.

for|give|ness /fərɡívnɪs/ N-UNCOUNT If you ask for **forgiveness**, you ask to be forgiven for something wrong that you have done. ❑ *...a spirit of forgiveness and national reconciliation.*

불가산명사 용서 ❑ 용서하는 마음과 국민 화합

for|giv|ing /fərɡívɪŋ/ ADJ Someone who is **forgiving** is willing to forgive. ❑ *Voters can be remarkably forgiving of presidents who fail to keep their campaign promises.*

형용사 관대한 ❑ 유권자들은 선거 공약을 지키지 못한 대통령에 대해 상당히 관대하다.

for|go /fɔrɡóu/ →see **forego**

for|got /fərɡɒ́t/ **Forgot** is the past tense of **forget**.

forget의 과거

for|got|ten /fərɡɒ́tᵊn/ **Forgotten** is the past participle of **forget**. →see **memory**

forget의 과거 분사

fork /fɔrk/ (**forks, forking, forked**) ◼ N-COUNT A **fork** is a tool used for eating food which has a row of three or four long metal points at the end. ❑ *...knives and forks.* ◼ V-T If you **fork** food **into** your mouth or **onto** a plate, you put it there using a fork. ❑ *He forked an egg onto a piece of bread and folded it into a sandwich.* ◼ N-COUNT A garden **fork** is a tool used for breaking up soil which has a row of three or four long metal points at the end. ◼ N-COUNT A **fork** in a road, path, or river is a point at which it divides into two parts and forms a "Y" shape. ❑ *We arrived at a fork in the road.* ❑ *The road divides; you should take the right fork.* ◼ V-I If a road, path, or river **forks**, it forms a fork. [no cont] ❑ *Beyond the village the road forked.*
→see **silverware**

◼ 가산명사 포크 ❑ 칼과 포크 ◼ 타동사 포크로 먹다; 포크로 담다 ❑ 그는 포크로 달걀 하나를 집어서 빵 위에 놓은 후 접어서 샌드위치를 만들었다. ◼ 가산명사 쇠스랑 ◼ 가산명사 갈림길 ❑ 우리는 갈림길에 다다랐다. ❑ 길이 갈리면 너는 오른쪽 갈림길로 가야 한다. ◼ 자동사 (길, 강이) 갈라지다 ❑ 그 마을 뒤로 길이 갈라진다.

▶**fork out** PHRASAL VERB If you **fork out for** something, you spend a lot of money on it. [INFORMAL] ❑ *Visitors to Windsor Castle also had to fork out for a guidebook.*

구동사 많은 돈을 쓰다 [비격식체] ❑ 윈저 성 방문자들은 안내 책자를 사는 데에도 많은 돈을 들여야 했다.

for|lorn /fərlɔ́rn/ ◼ ADJ If someone is **forlorn**, they feel alone and unhappy. [LITERARY] [ADJ n, v-link ADJ, ADJ after v] ❑ *One of the demonstrators, a young woman, sat forlorn on the pavement.* ◼ ADJ A **forlorn** hope or attempt is one that you think

◼ 형용사 처량한 [문예체] ❑ 시위 참가자 중 한 젊은 여자가 보도 위에 처량하게 앉아 있었다. ◼ 형용사 가망 없는 ❑ 농부들은 도시에서 더 나은 삶을 살 수

a
b
c
d
e
f
g
h
j
k
l
m
n
o
p
q
r
s
t
u
v
w
x
y
z

A

has no chance of success. ❑ *Peasants have left the land in the forlorn hope of finding a better life in cities.*

form ♦♦♦ /fɔːm/ (forms, forming, formed) **1** N-COUNT A **form of** something is a type or kind of it. ❑ *He contracted a rare form of cancer.* ❑ *I am against hunting in any form.* **2** N-COUNT When something can exist or happen in several possible ways, you can use **form** to refer to one particular way in which it exists or happens. ❑ *They received a benefit in the form of a tax reduction.* **3** V-T/V-I When a particular shape **forms** or **is formed**, people or things move or are arranged so that this shape is made. ❑ *A queue forms outside Peter's study.* ❑ *They formed a circle and sang "Auld Lang Syne".* **4** N-COUNT The **form** of something is its shape. ❑ ...*the form of the body.* **5** N-COUNT You can refer to something that you can see as a **form** if you cannot see it clearly, or if its outline is the clearest or most striking aspect of it. ❑ *His form lay still under the blankets.* **6** V-T If something is arranged or changed so that it becomes similar to a thing with a particular structure or function, you can say that it **forms** that thing. ❑ *These panels folded up to form a screen some five feet tall.* **7** V-T If something consists of particular things, people, or features, you can say that they **form** that thing. ❑ ...*the articles that formed the basis of Randolph's book.* **8** V-T If you **form** an organization, group, or company, you start it. ❑ *They tried to form a study group on human rights.* **9** V-T/V-I When something natural **forms** or **is formed**, it begins to exist and develop. ❑ *The stars must have formed 10 to 15 billion years ago.* **10** V-T/V-I If you **form** a relationship, a habit, or an idea, or if it **forms**, it begins to exist and develop. ❑ *She had formed the habit of giving herself freely to men.* ❑ *An idea formed in his mind.* **11** V-T If you say that something **forms** a person's character or personality, you mean that it has a strong influence on them and causes them to develop in a particular way. ❑ *Anger at injustice formed his character.* **12** N-UNCOUNT In sports, **form** refers to the ability or success of a person or animal over a period of time. ❑ *His form this season has been brilliant.* **13** N-COUNT A **form** is a paper with questions on it and spaces marked where you should write the answers. Forms usually ask you to give details about yourself, for example when you are applying for a job or joining an organization. ❑ *You will be asked to fill in a form with details of your birth and occupation.* **14** →see also **sixth form** **15** PHRASE If you say that someone is **on form**, you think that they are performing their usual activity very well. [BRIT] ❑ *Robert Redford is back on form in his new movie "Sneakers".*

Thesaurus	form의 참조어
N.	class, description, kind **1**
	body, figure, frame, shape **4**
	application, document, sheet **13**
V.	construct, create, develop, establish, influence **7**-**11**

formal ♦♦◇ /fɔːməl/ (formals) **1** ADJ **Formal** speech or behavior is very correct and serious rather than relaxed and friendly, and is used especially in official situations. ❑ *He wrote a very formal letter of apology to Douglas.* ● **formally** ADV [ADV with v] ❑ *He took her back to Vincent Square in a taxi, saying goodnight formally on the doorstep.* ● **formality** N-UNCOUNT ❑ *Lillith's formality and seriousness amused him.* **2** ADJ A **formal** action, statement, or request is an official one. [ADJ n] ❑ *UN officials said a formal request was passed to American authorities.* ❑ *No formal announcement had been made.* ● **formally** ADV [ADV with v] ❑ *Diplomats haven't formally agreed to Anderson's plan.* **3** ADJ **Formal** occasions are special occasions at which people wear elegant clothes and behave according to a set of accepted rules. ❑ *One evening the company arranged a formal dinner after the play.* ● N-COUNT **Formal** is also a noun. ❑ ...*a wide array of events, including school formals and speech nights, weddings, and balls.* **4** ADJ **Formal** clothes are very elegant clothes that are suitable for formal occasions. [ADJ n] ❑ *They wore ordinary ties instead of the more formal high collar and cravat.* ● **formally** ADV ❑ *It was really too warm for her to dress so formally.* **5** ADJ **Formal** education or training is given officially, usually in a school, college, or university. [ADJ n] ❑ *Wendy didn't have any formal dance training.* ● **formally** ADV [ADV -ed] ❑ *Usually only formally-trained artists from established schools are chosen.* **6** →see also **formality**

formality /fɔːmælɪti/ (formalities) **1** N-COUNT If you say that an action or procedure is just a **formality**, you mean that it is done only because it is normally done, and that it will not have any real effect on the situation. ❑ *Some contracts are a mere formality.* **2** N-COUNT **Formalities** are formal actions or procedures that are carried out as part of a particular activity or event. ❑ *They are whisked through the immigration and customs formalities in a matter of minutes.* **3** →see also **formal**

formalize /fɔːməlaɪz/ (formalizes, formalizing, formalized) [BRIT also **formalise**] V-T If you **formalize** a plan, idea, arrangement, or system, you make it formal and official. ❑ *A recent treaty signed by Russia, Canada, and Japan formalized an agreement to work together to stop the pirates.*

format /fɔːmæt/ (formats, formatting, formatted) **1** N-COUNT The **format** of something is the way or order in which it is arranged and presented. ❑ *I had met with him to explain the format of the programme and what we had in mind.* **2** N-COUNT The **format** of a piece of computer software or a musical recording is the type of equipment on which it is designed to be used or played. For example, possible formats for a musical recording are CD and cassette. ❑ *His latest album is available on all formats.* **3** V-T To **format** a computer disk means to run a program so that the disk can be written on. [COMPUTING] ❑ ...*a menu that includes the choice to format a disk.* **4** V-T To **format** a piece of computer text or graphics means to arrange the way in which it appears when it is printed or is displayed on a screen. [COMPUTING] ❑ *When text is saved from a Web page, it is often very badly formatted with many short lines.*

있다는 가망 없는 희망으로 그 땅을 떠났다.

1 가산명사 형식 ❑ 그는 흔치 않은 암에 걸렸다. ❑ 나는 어떠한 형태든 사냥에는 반대다. **2** 가산명사 형태 ❑ 그들은 세금 감면의 형태로 혜택을 받았다. **3** 타동사/자동사 (모양이) 만들어지다; (모양을) 만들다 ❑ 피터의 서재 밖에 긴 줄이 늘어섰다. ❑ 그들은 원을 그리고 '올드 랭 사인'을 불렀다. **4** 가산명사 형태 ❑ 체형 **5** 가산명사 윤곽 ❑ 담요 아래에 그가 누웠던 자국이 아직도 남아 있었다. **6** 타동사 이루다 ❑ 접혀 올라간 이 판자들은 약 1.5미터 높이의 스크린을 이루고 있었다. **7** 타동사 이루다, 형성하다 ❑ 랜돌프가 쓴 책의 기초를 이룬 글들 **8** 타동사 만들다, 조직하다 ❑ 그들은 인권을 연구하는 모임을 만들려고 노력했다. **9** 타동사/자동사 형성되다; 형성하다 ❑ 그 별들은 틀림없이 100억 년 전에서 150억 년 전 사이에 형성되었을 것이다. **10** 타동사/자동사 (아이디어가) 생기다 ❑ 그녀는 남자들에게 몸을 헤프게 허락하는 버릇이 생겼었다. ❑ 그의 머릿속에 아이디어 하나가 떠올랐다. **11** 타동사 (성격을) 형성하다 ❑ 그는 불의를 보면 못 참는다. **12** 불가산명사 (스포츠에서) 성적 ❑ 그의 올 시즌 성적은 대단했다. **13** 가산명사 양식 ❑ 귀하의 생년월일과 직업에 대한 세부 내용을 양식에 써 넣으셔야 될 겁니다. **15** 구 예전의 [영국영어] ❑ 로버트 레드포드는 그의 새 영화 '스니커즈'에서 예전의 실력을 유감없이 발휘했다.

1 형용사 정중한 ❑ 그는 더글라스에게 정중히 사과하는 편지를 썼다. ● 정중히 부사 ❑ 그는 그녀를 빈센트 광장까지 택시로 바래다 준 후, 현관 계단에서 정중히 작별 인사를 했다. ● 정중함 불가산명사 ❑ 그는 릴리스의 정중하고 심각한 모습이 우스웠다. **2** 형용사 공식적인 ❑ 국제 연합 관리는 미국 정부 당국에 공식 요청을 했다고 전했다. ❑ 아무런 공식 성명도 없었다. ● 공식적으로 부사 ❑ 외교관들은 앤더슨의 계획에 공식적으로 동의하지는 않았다. **3** 형용사 공식적인 ❑ 어느 하루 저녁에는 그 회사가 공연 후에 공식 만찬을 마련했다. ● 가산명사 공식 행사 ❑ 학교 공식 행사와 야간 강연, 결혼식과 댄스 파티를 포함한 다양한 행사들 **4** 형용사 격식을 갖춘 ❑ 그들은 격식을 갖춰 폭넓은 깃 속에 정식 넥타이를 매는 대신 보통 넥타이를 맸다. ● 격식을 갖춰 부사 ❑ 그녀가 그렇게 격식을 갖춰 옷을 입기에는 날씨가 정말이지 너무 따뜻했다. **5** 형용사 정규 (교육, 훈련) ❑ 웬디는 정식으로 춤을 배워 본 적이 없었다. ● 정식으로 부사 ❑ 보통 공인된 학교에서 정규 교육을 받은 예술가들만 선발된다.

1 가산명사 형식적인 것 ❑ 어떤 계약들은 순전히 형식적이다. **2** 가산명사 공식 절차 ❑ 그들은 출입국 절차와 통관 절차를 수 분만에 휙 끝낸다.

[영국영어 formalise] 타동사 공식화하다 ❑ 최근 러시아와 캐나다, 일본이 서명한 조약은 저작권 침해 행위 방지를 위해 협력하기로 한다는 합의를 공식화한 것이었다.

1 가산명사 체재 ❑ 나는 그 프로그램의 체재와 우리의 생각에 대해 설명하려고 그를 만났었다. **2** 가산명사 형태 ❑ 그의 최신 앨범은 다양한 형태로 시중에 나와 있다. **3** 타동사 포맷하다 [컴퓨터] ❑ 디스크를 포맷하는 것도 선택할 수 있는 메뉴 **4** 타동사 체재를 구성하다, [컴퓨터] ❑ 웹페이지에서 텍스트를 저장할 때, 포맷이 자주 잘못되어 끊긴 줄이 잔뜩 들어가는 경우가 많다.

for|ma|tion /fɔrmeɪʃⁿn/ (formations) **1** N-UNCOUNT The **formation** of something is the starting or creation of it. ❑ *Time is running out for the formation of a new government.* **2** N-UNCOUNT The **formation** of an idea, habit, relationship, or character is the process of developing and establishing it. ❑ *My profession had an important influence in the formation of my character and temperament.* **3** N-COUNT If people or things are **in formation**, they are arranged in a particular pattern as they move. ❑ *He was flying in formation with seven other jets.* **4** N-COUNT A rock or cloud **formation** is rock or cloud of a particular shape or structure. ❑ *...a vast rock formation shaped like a pillar.*

for|ma|tive /fɔrmətɪv/ ADJ A **formative** period of time or experience is one that has an important and lasting influence on a person's character and attitudes. ❑ *She was born in Barbados but spent her formative years growing up in east London.*

for|mer ♦♦♦ /fɔrmər/ **1** ADJ **Former** is used to describe someone who used to have a particular job, position, or role, but no longer has it. [ADJ n] ❑ *The unemployed executives include former sales managers, directors and accountants.* ❑ *...former President Richard Nixon.* **2** ADJ **Former** is used to refer to countries which no longer exist or whose boundaries have changed. [ADJ n] ❑ *...the former Soviet Union.* **3** ADJ **Former** is used to describe something which used to belong to someone or which used to be a particular thing. [ADJ n] ❑ *...the former home of Sir Christopher Wren.* **4** PRON When two people, things, or groups have just been mentioned, you can refer to the first of them as **the former**. [the PRON] ❑ *Given the choice between a pure white T-shirt and a more expensive cream one, most people can be forgiven for choosing the former.*

> **The latter** should only be used to refer to the second of two items which have already been mentioned: ❑ *Given the choice between working for someone else and being on call day and night for the family business, she'd prefer the latter.* The last of three or more items can be referred to as **the last-named**. Compare this with **the former** which is used to talk about the first of two things already mentioned.

Thesaurus	*former*의 참조어
ADJ.	past, previous; (*ant.*) future, next **1 3** prior **3**

for|mer|ly /fɔrmərli/ ADV If something happened or was true **formerly**, it happened or was true in the past. ❑ *He had formerly been in the Navy.*

for|mi|dable /fɔrmɪdəbⁿl, fɔrmɪd-/ ADJ If you describe something or someone as **formidable**, you mean that you feel slightly frightened by them because they are very great or impressive. ❑ *We have a formidable task ahead of us.*

for|mu|la ♦♦♦ /fɔrmyələ/ (formulae) /fɔrmyəli/ or formulas **1** N-COUNT A **formula** is a plan that is invented in order to deal with a particular problem. ❑ *...a peace formula.* **2** N-SING A **formula for** a particular situation, usually a good one, is a course of action or a combination of actions that is certain or likely to result in that situation. ❑ *After he was officially pronounced the world's oldest man, he offered this simple formula for a long and happy life.* **3** N-COUNT A **formula** is a group of letters, numbers, or other symbols which represents a scientific or mathematical rule. ❑ *He developed a mathematical formula describing the distances of the planets from the Sun.* **4** N-COUNT In science, the **formula** for a substance is a list of the amounts of various substances which make up that substance, or an indication of the atoms that it is composed of. ❑ *Glucose and fructose have the same chemical formula but have very different properties.*

for|mu|late /fɔrmyəleɪt/ (formulates, formulating, formulated) **1** V-T If you **formulate** something such as a plan or proposal, you invent it, thinking about the details carefully. ❑ *Little by little, he formulated his plan for escape.* **2** V-T If you **formulate** a thought, opinion, or idea, you express it or describe it using particular words. ❑ *I was impressed by the way he could formulate his ideas.*

for|mu|la|tion /fɔrmyəleɪʃⁿn/ (formulations) **1** N-VAR The **formulation** of something such as a medicine or a beauty product is the way in which different ingredients are combined to make it. You can also say that the finished product is a **formulation**. ❑ *You can buy a formulation containing royal jelly, pollen and vitamin C.* **2** N-UNCOUNT The **formulation** of something such as a policy or plan is the process of creating or inventing it. ❑ *...the process of policy formulation and implementation.* **3** N-VAR A **formulation** is the way in which you express your thoughts and ideas. ❑ *This is a far weaker formulation than is in the draft resolution which is being proposed.*

for|sake /fərseɪk/ (forsakes, forsaking, forsook) /fɔrsʊk/ (forsaken) **1** V-T If you **forsake** someone, you leave them when you should stay, or you stop helping them or looking after them. [LITERARY, DISAPPROVAL] ❑ *I still love him and I would never forsake him.* **2** V-T If you **forsake** something, you stop doing it, using it, or having it. [LITERARY] ❑ *He doubted their claim to have forsaken military solutions to the civil war.*

fort /fɔrt/ (forts) **1** N-COUNT; N-IN-NAMES A **fort** is a strong building or a place with a wall or fence around it where soldiers can stay and be safe from the enemy. **2** PHRASE If you **hold the fort** for someone, or, in American English, if you **hold down the fort**, you take care of things for them while they are somewhere else or are busy doing something else. ❑ *His business partner is holding the fort while he is away.*

forth ♦♦♦ /fɔrθ/

> In addition to the uses shown below, **forth** is also used in the phrasal verbs "put forth" and "set forth."

1 ADV When someone goes **forth** from a place, they leave it. [LITERARY] [ADV after v] ❑ *Go forth into the desert.* **2** ADV If one thing brings **forth** another, the

---

1 불가산명사 형성 ❑ 새 정부 수립을 위한 시간이 얼마 남지 않았다. **2** 불가산명사 발달 ❑ 내가 이러한 성격과 기질을 갖게 된 데는 내 직업의 영향이 크다. **3** 가산명사 대형을 이룸, 편대를 이룸 ❑ 그는 다른 일곱 대의 제트기와 편대를 이뤄 비행하고 있었다. **4** 가산명사 모양 ❑ 기둥 모양을 하고 있는 거대한 바위

형용사 인격이 형성되는 (시기) ❑ 그녀는 바베이도스에서 태어났지만, 인격이 형성되는 시기를 런던 동부에서 보냈다

1 형용사 전직의 ❑ 실업 상태에 있는 간부들에는 전직 영업 과장, 부장, 회계사들이 있다. ❑ 리처드 닉슨 전 대통령 **2** 형용사 구 ❑ 구소련 **3** 형용사 이전의 ❑ 크리스토퍼 렌 경의 이전 집 **4** 대명사 전자 ❑ 순백색 티셔츠와 더 비싼 크림색 셔츠 둘 중 하나를 고르라고 할 때, 대부분의 사람들이 전자를 고르는 것은 나무랄 수 없다.

the latter는 이미 언급된 두 가지 중의 두 번째 것을 지칭할 때만 써야 한다. ❑ 남 밑에서 일하는 것과 밤낮으로 대기하며 집안에서 하는 사업에 종사하는 것 중에서 고르라고 한다면, 그녀는 후자를 택할 것이다. 세 개 또는 그 이상의 항목에서 마지막 것은 the last-named로 가리킬 수 있다. 이와 같은 내용을 이미 언급된 두 개 중 첫 번째 것을 말할 때 쓰는 the former와 비교해 보라.

부사 이전에 ❑ 그는 전에 해군에 복무했었다.

형용사 만만찮은 ❑ 우리는 만만찮은 과제를 앞에 두고 있다.

1 가산명사 해결책 ❑ 평화 구현책 **2** 단수명사 비결, 처방 ❑ 그는 자신이 세계에서 가장 나이가 많은 사람이라고 공표된 후, 장수와 행복한 삶을 위한 간단한 이 비결을 알려 줬다. **3** 가산명사 공식 ❑ 그는 행성들과 태양 간의 거리를 측정하는 수학 공식을 정리해 냈다. **4** 가산명사 화학 분자식 ❑ 포도당과 과당은 화학 분자식이 같지만 아주 다른 특질을 지니고 있다.

1 타동사 구상해 내다 ❑ 조금씩 조금씩, 그는 탈출 계획을 구상해 냈다. **2** 타동사 체계적으로 기술하다 ❑ 그가 자신의 생각을 체계적으로 기술하는 방식이 감동적이었다.

1 가산명사 또는 불가산명사 복합 제제 ❑ 로열 젤리, 꽃가루, 비타민 시가 들어간 복합 제제를 살 수 있다. **2** 불가산명사 (정책, 계획 등의) 수립 ❑ 정책 수립과 집행 과정 **3** 가산명사 또는 불가산명사 체계적인 기술 ❑ 이것은 현재 제기되고 있는 결의안 초안에 있는 것보다 기술상의 체계성이 훨씬 약하다.

1 타동사 저버리다 [문예체, 탐탁잖음] ❑ 나는 그를 여전히 사랑하고 있고, 절대로 저버리지 않을 거야. **2** 타동사 그만두다 [문예체] ❑ 그는 내전에 대한 군사적 해결을 포기했다는 그들의 주장을 의심했다.

1 가산명사; 이름명사 성 **2** 구 잠깐 남의 일을 보아 주다 ❑ 그가 자리를 비운 동안 그의 동업자가 일을 봐 주고 있다.

forth는 아래 용법 외에도 'put forth', 'set forth'와 같은 구동사에 쓰인다.

1 부사 앞으로 [문예체] ❑ 사막으로 나아가라. **2** 부사 이끌어 내어 [문예체] ❑ 나는 심사숙고했지만 아무런

---

a b c d e f g h i j k l m n o p q r s t u v w x y z

first thing produces the second. [LITERARY] [ADV after v] ❑ *My reflections brought forth no conclusion.* ❸ ADV When someone or something is brought **forth**, they are brought to a place or moved into a position where people can see them. [LITERARY] [ADV after v] ❑ *Pilate ordered Jesus to be brought forth.* ❹ **back and forth** →see **back**. **to hold forth** →see **hold**

결론도 내지 못했다. ❸ 부사 앞으로 [문예체] ❑ 빌라도는 예수를 앞으로 데리고 나오라고 명령하였다.

forth|com|ing /fɔrθkʌmɪŋ/ ❶ ADJ A **forthcoming** event is planned to happen soon. [ADJ n] ❑ *...his opponents in the forthcoming elections.* ❷ ADJ If something that you want, need, or expect is **forthcoming**, it is given to you or it happens. [FORMAL] [v-link ADJ] ❑ *They promised that the money would be forthcoming.* ❑ *One source suggested no major shift in policy will be forthcoming at the committee hearings.* ❸ ADJ If you say that someone is **forthcoming**, you mean that they willingly give information when you ask them. ❑ *William, sadly, was not very forthcoming about any other names he might have, where he lived, or what his phone number was.*

❶ 형용사 다가오는 ❑ 다가오는 선거에서 그의 상대 후보가 될 사람들 ❷ 형용사 곧 마련될, 곧 찾아올 [격식체] ❑ 그들은 그 돈을 곧 마련해 주겠다고 약속했다. ❑ 정책의 중요 변화는 없을 것이라고 청문회에서 한 관계자가 말했다. ❸ 형용사 협조적인 ❑ 애석하게도 윌리엄은 그가 알고 있는 다른 사람들의 이름, 자신의 주소, 자신의 전화번호 등을 말하는 데 비협조적이었다.

forth|right /fɔrθraɪt/ ADJ If you describe someone as **forthright**, you admire them because they show clearly and strongly what they think and feel. [APPROVAL] ❑ *...a deeply religious man with forthright opinions.*

형용사 확고한 [마음에 듦] ❑ 신앙이 독실하고 견해가 확고한 남자

for|ti|eth ✦◇◇ /fɔrtiəθ/ ORD The **fortieth** item in a series is the one that you count as number forty. ❑ *It was the fortieth anniversary of the death of the composer.*

서수 40번째의 ❑ 그 작곡가의 서거 40주년 기념일이었다.

for|ti|fy /fɔrtɪfaɪ/ (**fortifies, fortifying, fortified**) ❶ V-T To **fortify** a place means to make it stronger and more difficult to attack, often by building a wall or ditch round it. ❑ *...British soldiers working to fortify an airbase in Bahrain.* ❷ V-T If food or drink **is fortified**, another substance is added to it to make it healthier or stronger. [usu passive] ❑ *Choose margarine or butter fortified with vitamin D.* ❑ *All sherry is made from wine fortified with brandy.*

❶ 타동사 강화하다 ❑ 바레인의 공군 기지 강화 작업을 하고 있는 영국 군인들 ❷ 타동사 강화되다 ❑ 마가린이나 비타민 디가 강화된 버터를 골라라. ❑ 모든 셰리주는 브랜디를 첨가한 포도주로 만든다.

fort|night /fɔrtnaɪt/ (**fortnights**) N-COUNT A **fortnight** is a period of two weeks. [mainly BRIT] ❑ *I hope to be back in a fortnight.*

가산명사 2주일 [주로 영국영어] ❑ 2주일 이내에 돌아오길 바래.

fort|night|ly /fɔrtnaɪtli/ ADJ A **fortnightly** event or publication happens or appears once every two weeks. [BRIT] [ADJ n] ❑ *...a new fortnightly magazine.* ● ADV **Fortnightly** is also an adverb. [AM **biweekly**] [ADV after v] ❑ *...Overseas Jobs Express, published fortnightly.*

형용사 격주로 시행되는 [영국영어] ❑ 새로 발간되는 격주간 잡지 ● 부사 격주로 [미국영어 biweekly] ❑ 격주로 발행되는 '해외 직업 특보'

for|tress /fɔrtrɪs/ (**fortresses**) N-COUNT A **fortress** is a castle or other large strong building, or a well-protected place, which is intended to be difficult for enemies to enter. ❑ *...a 13th-century fortress.*

가산명사 요새 ❑ 13세기 요새

for|tu|nate /fɔrtʃənɪt/ ADJ If you say that someone or something is **fortunate**, you mean that they are lucky. ❑ *He was extremely fortunate to survive.* ❑ *She is in the fortunate position of having plenty of choice.*

형용사 운이 좋은 ❑ 그는 정말 운 좋게 살아남았다. ❑ 그녀는 여러 가지 선택권이 있는 운 좋은 위치에 있다.

for|tu|nate|ly /fɔrtʃənɪtli/ ADV **Fortunately** is used to introduce or indicate a statement about an event or situation that is good. ❑ *Fortunately, the weather that winter was reasonably mild.*

부사 다행히 ❑ 다행히도, 그 겨울의 날씨는 상당히 따뜻했다.

for|tune ✦◇◇ /fɔrtʃən/ (**fortunes**) ❶ N-COUNT You can refer to a large sum of money as **a fortune** or **a small fortune** to emphasize how large it is. [EMPHASIS] ❑ *He made a small fortune in the London property boom.* ❷ N-COUNT Someone who has a **fortune** has a very large amount of money. ❑ *He made his fortune in car sales.* ❸ N-UNCOUNT **Fortune** or good **fortune** is good luck. Ill **fortune** is bad luck. ❑ *Government ministers are starting to wonder how long their good fortune can last.* ❹ N-PLURAL If you talk about someone's **fortunes** or the **fortunes** of something, you are talking about the extent to which they are doing well or being successful. ❑ *The company had to do something to reverse its sliding fortunes.* ❺ PHRASE When someone **tells** your **fortune**, they tell you what they think will happen to you in the future, which they say is shown, for example, by the lines on your hand. ❑ *I was just going to have my fortune told by a gypsy.*

❶ 가산명사 거금 [강조] ❑ 그는 런던 부동산 붐 때 약간의 거금을 벌었다. ❷ 가산명사 거금 ❑ 그는 자동차 판매로 거금을 벌었다. ❸ 불가산명사 운 ❑ 정부 각료들은 자신들에게 언제까지 운이 따를 수 있을는지에 대해 회의가 들기 시작했다. ❹ 복수명사 운 ❑ 그 회사는 쇠하는 사운을 되살리기 위해 무슨 조치를 취해야 했다. ❺ 구 점치다 ❑ 나는 한 집시에게서 점을 보려고 하던 참이었다.

for|ty ✦✦✦ /fɔrti/ (**forties**) ❶ NUM **Forty** is the number 40. ❷ N-PLURAL When you talk about the **forties**, you are referring to numbers between 40 and 49. For example, if you are **in** your **forties**, you are aged between 40 and 49. If the temperature is **in the forties**, the temperature is between 40 and 49 degrees. ❑ *He was a big man in his forties, smartly dressed in a suit and tie.* ❸ N-PLURAL The **forties** is the decade between 1940 and 1949. ❑ *Steel cans were introduced sometime during the forties.*

❶ 수사 숫자 40 ❷ 복수명사 40대 ❑ 그는 말쑥하게 정장에 넥타이를 맨 40대의 체구가 큰 남자였다. ❸ 복수명사 1940년대 ❑ 1940년대의 언제쯤에 양철 깡통이 처음으로 도입되었다.

fo|rum /fɔrəm/ (**forums**) N-COUNT A **forum** is a place, situation, or group in which people exchange ideas and discuss issues, especially important public issues. ❑ *Members of the council agreed that it still had an important role as a forum for discussion.*

가산명사 토론장, 토론회 ❑ 지방 의회 의원들은 그곳이 여전히 토론의 장으로서 중요한 역할을 하고 있다는 데 의견을 같이했다.

Word Link **ward ≈ in the direction of :** back**ward**, for**ward**, in**ward**

---

for|ward ✦◇◇ /fɔrwərd/ (**forwards, forwarding, forwarded**) ❶ ADV If you move or look **forward**, you move or look in a direction that is in front of you. In British English, you can also move or look **forwards**. [ADV after v] ❑ *He came forward with his hand out. "Mr. and Mrs. Selby?" he enquired.* ❑ *She fell forwards on to her face.* ❷ ADV **Forward** means in a position near the front of something such as a building or a vehicle. ❑ *The best seats are in the aisle and as far forward as possible.* ● ADJ **Forward** is also an adjective. [ADJ n] ❑ *Reinforcements were needed to allow more troops to move to forward positions.* ❸ ADV If you say that someone looks **forward**, you approve of them because they think about what will happen in the future and plan for it. In British English, you can also say that someone looks **forwards**. [APPROVAL] ❑ *Now the leadership wants to look forward, and to outline a strategy for the rest of the century.* ❑ *People should forget and look forwards.* ● ADJ **Forward** is also an adjective. [ADJ n] ❑ *The university system requires more forward planning.* ❹ ADV If you move a clock or watch **forward**, you change the time shown on it so that it shows a later time, for example when the time changes to daylight saving time or British summer time. [ADV after v] ❑ *When we put the clocks forward in March we go into British Summer Time.* ❺ ADV When you are referring to a particular time, if you say that something was true **from** that

❶ 부사 앞으로 ❑ 그는 손을 내밀면서, "셀비 부부이신가요?" 하며 앞으로 다가왔다. ❑ 그녀는 코를 박고 앞으로 넘어졌다. ❷ 부사 앞쪽 자리에 ❑ 가장 좋은 자리는 복도 쪽 자리 중에 가능한 한 가장 앞쪽이다. ● 형용사 전방의 ❑ 더 많은 군대를 전방으로 이동시키려면 증원 부대가 필요했다. ❸ 부사 앞을 내다보아, 장래를 내다보아 [마음에 듦] ❑ 그 지도부는 이제 장래를 생각하고 남은 21세기를 위한 전략의 전반적인 윤곽을 그리기 시작한다. ❑ 사람들은 과거는 잊고 앞을 내다봐야 한다. ● 형용사 앞을 내다보는 ❑ 대학 체계는 좀 더 앞을 내다보는 계획이 필요하다. ❹ 부사 (시계바늘을 실시로) 시간을 앞당겨 ❑ 영국은 3월이 되면 시간을 앞당겨 서머 타임제가 시작된다. ❺ 부사 계속 ❑ 벨라스케스의 작품은 그 후로 계속 주로 왕가의 초상화로 한정되었다. ❻ 부사 진척되는, 진전되는 ❑ 멕시코, 캐나다, 미국의 경기를 부양시킴으로써, 우리 모두가 우려하는 사안들을 진척시킬 수 있을 것이다. ❑ 그들은 그저

time **forward**, you mean that it became true at that time, and continued to be true afterward. [from n ADV] ❑ *Velazquez's work from that time forward was confined largely to portraits of the royal family.* ◼ ADV You use **forward** to indicate that something progresses or improves. In British English, you can also use **forwards**. ❑ *And by boosting economic prosperity in Mexico, Canada, and the United States, it will help us move forward on issues that concern all of us.* ❑ *They just couldn't see any way forward.* ◼ ADV If something or someone is put **forward**, or comes **forward**, they are suggested or offered as suitable for a particular purpose. [ADV after v] ❑ *Over the years several similar theories have been put forward.* ❑ *Investigations have ground to a standstill because no witnesses have come forward.* ◼ V-T If a letter or message **is forwarded to** someone, it is sent to the place where they are, after having been sent to a different place earlier. ❑ *When he's out on the road, office calls are forwarded to the cellular phone in his truck.* ◼ N-COUNT In basketball, soccer, or hockey, a **forward** is a player whose usual position is in the opponents' half of the field, and whose usual job is to attack or score goals. ❑ *The 4-3-3 system allowed midfield players to be forwards or defenders.* ◼ **backward and forward** →see **backward**

fos|sil /fɒsᵊl/ (fossils) N-COUNT A **fossil** is the hard remains of a prehistoric animal or plant that are found inside a rock. →see Word Web: **fossil**

fos|sil fuel (fossil fuels) also **fossil-fuel** N-MASS **Fossil fuel** is fuel such as coal or oil that is formed from the decayed remains of plants or animals. ❑ *Burning fossil fuels uses oxygen and produces carbon dioxide.* →see **electricity**, **greenhouse effect**

fos|ter /fɒstər, BRIT fɒstəʳ/ (fosters, fostering, fostered) ◼ ADJ **Foster** parents are people who officially take a child into their family for a period of time, without becoming the child's legal parents. The child is referred to as their **foster** child. [ADJ n] ❑ *Little Jack was placed with foster parents.* ◼ V-T If you **foster** a child, you take it into your family for a period of time, without becoming its legal parent. ❑ *She has since gone on to find happiness by fostering more than 100 children.* ◼ V-T To **foster** something such as an activity or idea means to help it to develop. ❑ *He said that developed countries had a responsibility to foster global economic growth to help new democracies.*

fought /fɔt/ **Fought** is the past tense and past participle of **fight**.

foul /faʊl/ (fouler, foulest, fouls, fouling, fouled) ◼ ADJ If you describe something as **foul**, you mean it is dirty and smells or tastes unpleasant. ❑ *...foul polluted water.* ◼ ADJ **Foul** language is offensive and contains swear words or rude words. ❑ *He was sent off for using foul language in a match last Sunday.* ◼ ADJ If someone has a **foul** temper or is in a **foul** mood, they become angry or violent very suddenly and easily. ❑ *Collins was in a foul mood even before the interviews began.* ◼ ADJ **Foul** weather is unpleasant, windy, and stormy. ❑ *No amount of foul weather, whether hail, wind, rain, or snow, seems to deter them.* ◼ V-T If an animal **fouls** a place, it drops feces onto the ground. ❑ *It is an offence to let your dog foul a footpath.* ◼ V-T In a game or sport, if a player **fouls** another player, they touch them or block them in a way which is not allowed according to the rules. ❑ *Nowitzki fouled Mitchell early in the third quarter.* ◼ N-COUNT A **foul** is an act in a game or sport that is not allowed according to the rules. ❑ *Ballack got his second yellow card for a foul on Lee Chun-Soo.* ● **Foul** is also an adjective. [ADJ n] ❑ *...a foul tackle.* ◼ PHRASE If you **fall foul of** someone or **run foul of** them, you do something which gets you into trouble with them. [mainly BRIT; AM usually **run foul of**] ❑ *He had fallen foul of the FBI.*

found ◆◇◇ /faʊnd/ (founds, founding, founded) ◼ **Found** is the past tense and past participle of **find**. ◼ V-T When an institution, company, or organization **is founded** by someone or by a group of people, they get it started, often by providing the necessary money. ❑ *The Independent Labour Party was founded in Bradford on January 13, 1893.* ❑ *He founded the Center for Journalism Studies at University College Cardiff.* ● **foun|da|tion** /faʊndeɪʃⁿn/ N-SING [with poss] ❑ *...the 150th anniversary of the foundation of Kew Gardens.* ● **found|ing** N-SING ❑ *I have been a member of The Sunday Times Wine Club since its founding in 1973.* ◼ V-T When a town, important building, or other place **is founded** by someone or by a group of people, they cause it to be built. [usu passive] ❑ *The town was founded in 1610.* ◼ →see also **founded**, **founding**

Word Link	found ≈ base : found**ation**, found**ed**, found**er**

foun|da|tion ◆◇◇ /faʊndeɪʃⁿn/ (foundations) ◼ N-COUNT The **foundation** of something such as a belief or way of life is the things on which it is based. ❑ *Best friends are the foundation of my life.* ❑ *The issue strikes at the very foundation of our community.* ◼ N-PLURAL The **foundations** of a building or other structure are the layer of bricks or concrete below the ground that it is built on. ◼ N-COUNT A **foundation** is an organization which provides money for a special purpose such as research or charity. ❑ *...the National Foundation for Educational Research.* ◼ N-UNCOUNT If a story, idea, or argument has **no foundation**, there are no facts to prove that it is true. ❑ *The allegations were without foundation.* ◼ N-MASS **Foundation** is a skin-colored cream that you put on your face before putting on the rest of your makeup. ❑ *Use foundation and/or face powder afterwards for an even skin tone.* ◼ →see also **found** →see **makeup**

Word Partnership	*foundation*의 연어
ADJ.	**firm** foundation, **solid** foundation ◼
	charitable foundation ◼
V.	**build a** foundation, **lay a** foundation ◼ ◼
	establish a foundation ◼ ◼
	apply foundation ◼

상황을 진전시킬 수 있는 어떤 방법도 전혀 알 수 없었다. ◼ 부사 제시되어, 추천되어 ❑ 비슷한 몇 가지 이론들이 여러 해에 걸쳐 제시되고 있다. ❑ 목격자가 아무도 나서지 않았기 때문에 수사 진행이 점점 지연되다가 결국 중단되었다. ◼ 타동사 (편지나 전화 등이) 연결되다 ❑ 그가 외부에 나가 있을 때는, 회사 전화가 그의 트럭에 있는 휴대폰으로 연결된다. ◼ 가산명사 (구기 종목의) 공격수 ❑ 축구의 4-3-3 구조에서는 미드필더가 공격수나 수비수의 역할을 한다.

가산명사 화석

물질명사 화석 연료 ❑ 화석 연료가 탈 때는 산소가 없어지고 이산화탄소가 발생한다.

◼ 형용사 (일정 기간 동안) 맡아 기르는, 양 ❑ 어린 잭은 양부모님과 같이 살았다. ◼ 타동사 (아이를 잠깐) 맡아 키우다 ❑ 그 후 지금까지 그녀는 100명이 넘는 아이들을 맡아 키우는 것에서 행복을 느끼고 있다. ◼ 타동사 촉진시키다 ❑ 선진국들은 세계 경제 성장을 촉진시켜 신생 민주주의 국가를 도울 책임이 있다고 그는 말했다.

fight의 과거, 과거 분사

◼ 형용사 더러운 ❑ 오염된 더러운 물 ◼ 형용사 욕설의 ❑ 그는 지난 일요일 경기에서 욕설을 한 것으로 인해 퇴장 당했다. ◼ 형용사 다혈질의, 쉽게 흥분하는 ❑ 콜린스는 인터뷰가 시작되기도 전에 벌써 흥분한 상태였다. ◼ 형용사 (날씨가) 사나운 ❑ 우박이 내리든, 바람이 불고 눈, 비가 오든, 어떤 사나운 날씨도 그들을 말릴 수는 없는 것 같다. ◼ 타동사 배설하다 ❑ 당신의 개가 보도 위에 배설을 하도록 내버려 두는 것은 사람들의 기분을 상하게 하는 일이다. ◼ 타동사 반칙하다 ❑ 노비츠키가 3쿼터 초반에 미첼에게 반칙을 했다. ◼ 가산명사 반칙 ❑ 발락이 이천수에게 반칙을 해서 두 번째 경고를 받았다. ● 형용사 반칙의 ❑ 반칙 태클 ◼ 구 ~와 사이가 좋지 않다 [주로 영국영어; 미국영어 대개 run foul of] ❑ 그는 에프비아이와 사이가 좋지 않았다.

◼ find의 과거, 과거 분사 ◼ 타동사 창립하다, 세우다 ❑ 독립 노동당은 1893년 1월 13일, 브래드퍼드에서 창당되었다. ❑ 그는 카디프 대학교에 언론 연구 센터를 세웠다. ● 설립 단수명사 ❑ 큐 가든스 설립 150주년 기념일 ● 창립 단수명사 ❑ 나는 1973년 선데이 타임스 와인 클럽이 창립되었던 그 해 이후로 계속 회원으로 있다. ◼ 타동사 세워지다 ❑ 그 마을은 1610년에 세워졌다.

◼ 가산명사 기반 ❑ 좋은 친구는 내 인생의 기반이다. ❑ 그 사건은 우리 사회의 기반 자체를 흔들고 있다. ◼ 복수명사 갚도, 토대 ◼ 가산명사 재단 ❑ 국립 교육 연구 재단 ◼ 불가산명사 근거 ❑ 그 주장들은 근거가 없었다. ◼ 물질명사 파운데이션 ❑ 피부 톤을 고르게 하려면 나중에 파운데이션과 화장분을 바르거나 그 중 하나를 발라라.

a b c d e f g h i j k l m n o p q r s t u v w x y z

Word Web   fossil

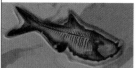

There are two types of animal **fossils**—body fossils and **trace** fossils. Body fossils help us understand how the animal looked when it was alive. Trace fossils, such as **tracks** and **footprints**, show us how the animal moved. Since we don't find tracks of dinosaurs' tails, we know they lifted them up as they walked. Footprints tell us about the weight of the dinosaur and how fast it moved. Scientists use two methods to calculate the date of a fossil. They sometimes count the number of **rock** layers covering it. They also use carbon dating.

found|ed /faʊndɪd/ ADJ If something is **founded on** a particular thing, it is based on it. [v-link ADJ on n] ❑ *The criticisms are founded on facts as well as on convictions.* →see also **found**

형용사 -에 근거하여 ❑ 그 비난은 확신뿐만 아니라 사실에도 근거를 두고 있다.

found|er ♦◇◇ /faʊndər/ (founders, foundering, foundered) **1** N-COUNT The **founder** of an institution, organization, or building is the person who got it started or caused it to be built, often by providing the necessary money. ❑ *He was one of the founders of the university's medical faculty.* **2** V-I If something such as a plan or project **founders**, it fails because of a particular point, difficulty, or problem. ❑ *The talks have foundered, largely because of the reluctance of some members of the government to do a deal with criminals.*

1 가산명사 창설자, 설립자 ❑ 그는 그 대학 의학부를 창설한 사람들 중 한 명이다. **2** 자동사 (계획 등이) 실패하다 ❑ 그 회담이 결렬된 주 원인은 범죄자 문제 처리에 대한 정부측 일부 구성원들의 미온적 태도 때문이었다.

found|ing /faʊndɪŋ/ ADJ **Founding** means relating to the starting of a particular institution or organization. [ADJ n] ❑ *The committee held its founding congress in the capital, Riga.* →see also **found**

형용사 기초를 세우는 ❑ 그 위원회는 수도인 리가에 제헌 의회를 세웠다.

foun|tain /faʊntɪn/ (fountains) **1** N-COUNT A **fountain** is an ornamental feature in a pool or lake which consists of a long narrow stream of water that is forced up into the air by a pump. ❑ *...the fountains of Trafalgar Square.* **2** N-COUNT A **fountain of** a liquid is an amount of it which is sent up into the air and falls back. [LITERARY] ❑ *The volcano spewed a fountain of molten rock 650 feet in the air.*

1 가산명사 분수 ❑ 트라팔가 광장의 분수 **2** 가산명사 분수 (비유적) [문예체] ❑ 그 화산은 650피트 상공으로 분수 같은 용암을 분출했다.

four ♦♦♦ /fɔr/ (fours) **1** NUM **Four** is the number 4. ❑ *Judith is married with four children.* **2** PHRASE If you are **on all fours**, your knees, feet, and hands are on the ground. ❑ *She crawled on all fours over to the window.*

1 수사 4 ❑ 주디스는 아이가 넷인 기혼자이다. **2** 구 네 발로 기어 ❑ 그녀는 창문까지 네 발로 기어갔다.

four|some /fɔrsəm/ (foursomes) N-COUNT-COLL A **foursome** is a group of four people or things. ❑ *The London-based foursome are set to release their fourth single this month.*

가산명사-집합 4인조 그룹, 4개 한 조 ❑ 런던에서 활동 중인 그 4인조 그룹은 이 달에 네 번째 싱글 앨범을 낼 예정이다.

four|teen ♦♦◇ /fɔrtin/ (fourteens) NUM **Fourteen** is the number 14. ❑ *I'm fourteen years old.*

수사 14 ❑ 나는 열네 살이다.

four|teenth ♦◇◇ /fɔrtinθ/ ORD The **fourteenth** item in a series is the one that you count as number fourteen. ❑ *The Festival, now in its fourteenth year, has become a major international jazz event.*

서수 열네 번째의 ❑ 올해 14년째인 그 페스티벌이 이제는 국제적인 주요 재즈 행사로 자리 잡았다.

fourth ♦♦◇ /fɔrθ/ (fourths) **1** ORD The **fourth** item in a series is the one that you count as number four. ❑ *Last year's winner Greg Lemond of the United States is in fourth place.* **2** FRACTION A **fourth** is one of four equal parts of something. [AM; BRIT **quarter**] ❑ *Three-fourths of the public say they favor a national referendum on the issue.*

1 서수 네 번째의 ❑ 지난해 승자였던 미국 출신 그레그 레몬드가 4위이다. **2** 분수 4분의 1 [미국영어; 영국영어 quarter] ❑ 국민의 4분의 3이 그 사안에 대해 국민 투표를 실시하는 것에 찬성한다고 말한다.

four-wheel drive (four-wheel drives) N-COUNT A **four-wheel drive** is a vehicle in which all four wheels receive power from the engine to help with steering. This makes the vehicle easier to drive on rough roads or surfaces such as sand or snow.

가산명사 4륜 구동차

fowl /faʊl/ (fowls)

Fowl can also be used as the plural form.

fowl도 복수형으로 쓸 수 있다.

N-COUNT A **fowl** is a bird, especially one that can be eaten as food, such as a duck or a chicken. ❑ *Carve the fowl into 8 pieces.*

가산명사 가금, 식용 조류 ❑ 그 닭을 8조각으로 나눠라.

fox /fɒks/ (foxes) N-COUNT A **fox** is a wild animal which looks like a dog and has reddish-brown fur, a pointed face and ears, and a thick tail. Foxes eat smaller animals.

가산명사 여우

foy|er /fɔɪər, fɔɪeɪ, fwaɪeɪ/ (foyers) N-COUNT The **foyer** is the large area where people meet or wait just inside the main doors of a building such as a theater or hotel. ❑ *I went and waited in the foyer.*

가산명사 로비, (극장이나 호텔 등의) 현관 ❑ 나는 들어가서 로비에서 기다렸다.

Word Link   fract, frag ≈ breaking : fraction, fracture, fragile

frac|tion /frækʃn/ (fractions) **1** N-COUNT A **fraction of** something is a tiny amount or proportion of it. ❑ *She hesitated for a fraction of a second before responding.* ❑ *Here's how to eat like the stars, at a fraction of the cost.* **2** N-COUNT A **fraction** is a number that can be expressed as a proportion of two whole numbers. For example, ½ and ⅓ are both fractions. ❑ *The students had a grasp of decimals, percentages, and fractions.*

1 가산명사 부분, 일부 ❑ 그녀는 대답하기 전에 아주 잠깐 동안 머뭇거렸다. ❑ 이것이 아주 적은 비용으로 스타들처럼 먹는 방법이다. **2** 가산명사 분수 ❑ 그 학생들은 십진법, 백분율, 분수에 대해 이해했다.

frac|ture /fræktʃər/ (fractures, fracturing, fractured) **1** N-COUNT A **fracture** is a slight crack or break in something, especially a bone. ❑ *At least one-third of all women over ninety have sustained a hip fracture.* **2** V-T/V-I If something such as a bone **is fractured** or **fractures**, it gets a slight crack or break in it. ❑ *You've fractured a rib, maybe more than one.* ❑ *One strut had fractured and been crudely repaired in several places.* **3** V-T/V-I If something such as an organization or society **is fractured** or **fractures**, it splits into several parts or stops existing. [FORMAL] ❑ *His policy risks fracturing the coalition.*

1 가산명사 골절 ❑ 아흔 살 이상 여성들 중 적어도 삼분의 일은 고관절 골절을 당한 적이 있다. **2** 타동사/자동사 부러지다, 금이 가다 ❑ 갈비뼈가 부러졌는데, 아마도 한 대 이상 부러진 것 같다. ❑ 버팀대 하나가 부러져서 여러 군데 조악하게 수리가 되어 있었다. **3** 타동사/자동사 와해시키다; 와해되다 [격식체] ❑ 그의 정책이 그 연합을 와해시킬 위험에 처해 있다.

Word Link	fract, frag ≈ breaking : fraction, fracture, fragile

fragile /frædʒ³l, BRIT frædʒaɪl/ ■ ADJ If you describe a situation as **fragile**, you mean that it is weak or uncertain, and unlikely to be able to resist strong pressure or attack. [JOURNALISM] ❑ *The fragile economies of several southern African nations could be irreparably damaged.* ● **fra|gil|ity** /frədʒɪlɪti/ N-UNCOUNT ❑ *By mid-1988 there were clear indications of the extreme fragility of the Right-wing coalition.* ■ ADJ Something that is **fragile** is easily broken or damaged. ❑ *He leaned back in his fragile chair.* ● **fra|gil|ity** N-UNCOUNT ❑ *Older drivers are more likely to be seriously injured because of the fragility of their bones.*

■ 형용사 취약한 [언론] ❑ 몇몇 남아프리카 국가들의 취약한 경제가 돌이킬 수 없을 정도로 손상될 수도 있다. ● 약해짐 불가산명사 ❑ 1988년 중반, 우익 연합이 극도로 약해질 조짐이 분명했다. ■ 형용사 잘 부서지는 ❑ 그는 부서질 것 같은 의자에 앉아 몸을 뒤로 기댔다. ● 부서짐 불가산명사 ❑ 나이든 운전자는 쉽게 골절이 되기 때문에 심하게 다칠 가능성이 더 많다.

Thesaurus	*fragile*의 참조어
ADJ.	unstable, weak; (ant.) stable, strong ■
	delicate; (ant.) sturdy ■

frag|ment (fragments, fragmenting, fragmented)

The noun is pronounced /frægmənt/. The verb is pronounced /frægmɛnt/.

명사는 /frægmənt/로 발음되고, 동사는 /frægmɛnt/로 발음된다.

■ N-COUNT A **fragment of** something is a small piece or part of it. ❑ *The only reminder of the shooting is a few fragments of metal in my shoulder.* ❑ *She read everything, digesting every fragment of news.* ■ V-T/V-I If something **fragments** or **is fragmented**, it breaks or separates into small pieces or parts. ❑ *The clouds fragmented and out came the sun.* ● **frag|men|ta|tion** /frægmɛnteɪʃⁿn/ N-UNCOUNT ❑ *...the extraordinary fragmentation of styles on the music scene.*

■ 가산명사 조각, 파편, 부분 ❑ 그 총격의 흔적은 내 어깨에 남아 있는 몇 개의 금속 파편뿐이다. ❑ 그녀는 의미를 잘 새기며 뉴스의 모든 부분들을 다 읽었다. ■ 타동사/자동사 (산산이) 부서지다; (산산이) 부수다 ❑ 구름이 흩어지며 그 사이로 태양이 나왔다. ● 분파, 분열 불가산명사 ❑ 음악계에 등장한 여러 가지 색다른 스타일의 분파

fra|grance /freɪgrəns/ (fragrances) ■ N-VAR A **fragrance** is a pleasant or sweet smell. ❑ *...a shrubby plant with a strong characteristic fragrance.* ■ N-MASS **Fragrance** is a pleasant-smelling liquid which people put on their bodies to make themselves smell nice. ❑ *The advertisement is for a male fragrance.*

■ 가산명사 또는 불가산명사 향기 ❑ 아주 강한 독특한 향을 가진 관목 ■ 물질명사 향수 ❑ 그것은 남성용 향수에 대한 광고이다.

fra|grant /freɪgrənt/ ADJ Something that is **fragrant** has a pleasant, sweet smell. ❑ *...fragrant oils and perfumes.*

형용사 향기로운 ❑ 향기로운 오일과 향수들

frail /freɪl/ (frailer, frailest) ■ ADJ Someone who is **frail** is not very strong or healthy. ❑ *She lay in bed looking particularly frail.* ■ ADJ Something that is **frail** is easily broken or damaged. ❑ *The frail craft rocked as he clambered in.*

■ 형용사 허약한 ❑ 그녀는 침대에 누워 있었는데 아주 허약해 보였다. ■ 형용사 깨지기 쉬운 ❑ 그가 기어오르자, 깨지기 쉬운 그 공예품이 심하게 흔들렸다.

frail|ty /freɪlti, freɪəl-/ (frailties) ■ N-VAR If you refer to the **frailties** or **frailty** of people, you are referring to their weaknesses. ❑ *...the frailties of human nature.* ■ N-UNCOUNT **Frailty** is the condition of having poor health. ❑ *She died after a long period of increasing frailty.*

■ 가산명사 또는 불가산명사 약점 ❑ 인간 본성의 약점 ■ 불가산명사 허약한 상태 ❑ 그녀는 오랜 기간 건강이 안 좋다가 결국 사망했다.

frame ♦◇◇ /freɪm/ (frames, framing, framed) ■ N-COUNT The **frame** of a picture or mirror is the wood, metal, or plastic that is fitted around it, especially when it is displayed or hung on a wall. ❑ *Estelle kept a photograph of her mother in a silver frame on the kitchen mantelpiece.* ■ N-COUNT The **frame** of an object such as a building, chair, or window is the arrangement of wooden, metal, or plastic bars between which other material is fitted, and which give the object its strength and shape. ❑ *He supplied housebuilders with modern timber frames.* ❑ *With difficulty he released the mattress from the metal frame, and groped beneath it.* ■ N-COUNT The **frames** of a pair of glasses are all the metal or plastic parts of it, but not the lenses. ❑ *He was wearing new spectacles with gold wire frames.* ■ N-COUNT You can refer to someone's body as their **frame**, especially when you are describing the general shape of their body. ❑ *Their belts are pulled tight against their bony frames.* ■ N-COUNT A **frame** of movie film is one of the many separate photographs that it consists of. ❑ *Standard 8mm projects at 16 frames per second.* ■ V-T When a picture or photograph **is framed**, it is put in a frame. [usu passive] ❑ *The picture is now ready to be mounted and framed.* ■ V-T If an object **is framed** by a particular thing, it is surrounded by that thing in a way that makes the object more striking or attractive to look at. [usu passive] ❑ *The swimming pool is framed by tropical gardens.* ■ V-T If someone **frames** an innocent person, they make other people think that that person is guilty of a crime, by lying or inventing evidence. [INFORMAL] ❑ *I need to find out who tried to frame me.* →see **painting**

■ 가산명사 틀 ❑ 에스텔은 자신의 어머니 사진을 은빛 사진틀에 넣어 부엌 벽난로 선반 위에 놓아두었다. ■ 가산명사 골조, 뼈대 ❑ 그는 주택 건설업자들에게 현대적 감각의 목재 골조를 공급했다. ❑ 그는 가까스로 매트리스를 금속 뼈대에서 빼낸 후, 그 아래를 손으로 더듬어 보았다. ■ 가산명사 안경테 ❑ 그는 안경테가 금으로 된 새 안경을 쓰고 있었다. ■ 가산명사 체격 ❑ 그들은 마른 체격에 벨트를 바짝 졸라매고 있다. ■ 가산명사 (영화 필름의) 한 장, 프레임 ❑ 표준 8미리는 1초에 16프레임을 영사한다. ■ 타동사 (그림이나 사진을) 액자에 끼우다 ❑ 이제 그 그림을 안을 받쳐서 액자에 끼우기만 하면 된다. ■ 타동사 둘러싸이다 ❑ 그 수영장은 열대 정원으로 둘러싸여 있다. ■ 타동사 죄를 뒤집어씌우다 [비격식체] ❑ 나는 누가 내게 죄를 뒤집어씌우려고 했는지 알아내야 한다.

frame of mind (frames of mind) N-COUNT Your **frame of mind** is the mood that you are in, which causes you to have a particular attitude to something. ❑ *Lewis was not in the right frame of mind to continue.*

가산명사 기분 ❑ 루이스는 계속 할 기분이 아니었다.

frame|work /freɪmwɜrk/ (frameworks) ■ N-COUNT A **framework** is a particular set of rules, ideas, or beliefs which you use in order to deal with problems or to decide what to do. ❑ *... within the framework of federal regulations.* ■ N-COUNT A **framework** is a structure that forms a support or frame for something. ❑ *...wooden shelves on a steel framework.*

■ 가산명사 틀, 구조 ❑ 연방 규정 틀 안에서 ■ 가산명사 구조물 ❑ 강철 구조물 위에 올려진 나무 선반

fran|chise /fræntʃaɪz/ (franchises, franchising, franchised) ■ N-COUNT A **franchise** is an authority that is given by an organization to someone, allowing them to sell its goods or services or to take part in an activity which the organization controls. [BUSINESS] ❑ *...fast-food franchises.* ❑ *...the franchise to build and operate the tunnel.* ■ V-T If a company **franchises** its business, it sells franchises to other companies, allowing them to sell its goods or services. [BUSINESS] ❑ *She has recently franchised her business.* ■ N-UNCOUNT **Franchise** is the right to vote in an election. [also the N] ❑ *...the introduction of universal franchise.*

■ 가산명사 체인점 영업권, 프랜차이즈, 독점권 [경제] ❑ 패스트푸드 프랜차이즈 ❑ 그 터널 건설 및 운영 독점권 ■ 타동사 종관권을 허가하다 [경제] ❑ 그녀는 최근에 자신의 회사의 종관권을 허가했다. ■ 불가산명사 선거권 ❑ 보통 선거권의 도입

fran|chi|see /fræntʃaɪzi/ (franchisees) N-COUNT A **franchisee** is a person or group of people who buy a particular franchise. [BUSINESS] ❑ *...National Restaurants, a New York franchisee for Pizza Hut.*

가산명사 총판, 가맹점 [경제] ❑ 피자헛 뉴욕 총판인 내셔널 레스토랑

fran|chi|ser /fræntʃaɪzər/ (**franchisers**) N-COUNT A **franchiser** is an organization which sells franchises. [BUSINESS] ❑ *Coca-Cola, Pepsi, and Cadbury use franchisers to manufacture, bottle, and distribute their products within geographical areas.*

frank /fræŋk/ (**franker, frankest**) ADJ If someone is **frank**, they state or express things in an open and honest way. ❑ *"It is clear that my client has been less than frank with me," said his lawyer.* ● **frank|ly** ADV [ADV with v] ❑ *You can talk frankly to me.* ● **frank|ness** N-UNCOUNT ❑ *The reaction to his frankness was hostile.*

frank|ly /fræŋkli/ ADV You use **frankly** when you are expressing an opinion or feeling to emphasize that you mean what you are saying, especially when the person you are speaking to may not like it. [EMPHASIS] ❑ *"You don't give a damn about my feelings, do you?" — "Quite frankly, I don't."* ❑ *Frankly, Thomas, this question of your loan is beginning to worry me.* →see also **frank**

fran|tic /fræntɪk/ ❑ ADJ If you are **frantic**, you are behaving in a wild and uncontrolled way because you are frightened or worried. ❑ *A bird had been locked in and was by now quite frantic.* ● **fran|ti|cal|ly** /fræntɪkli/ ADV [ADV with v] ❑ *She clutched frantically at Emily's arm.* ❑ ADJ If an activity is **frantic**, things are done quickly and in an energetic but disorganized way, because there is very little time. ❑ *A busy night in the restaurant can be frantic in the kitchen.* ● **fran|ti|cal|ly** ADV [ADV with v] ❑ *We have been frantically trying to save her life.*

fra|ter|nity /frətɜrnɪti/ (**fraternities**) ❑ N-UNCOUNT **Fraternity** refers to friendship and support between people who feel they are closely linked to each other. [FORMAL] ❑ *Bob needs the fraternity of others who share his mission.* ❑ N-COUNT You can refer to people who have the same profession or the same interests as a particular **fraternity**. ❑ *...the spread of stolen guns among the criminal fraternity.* ❑ N-COUNT In the United States, a **fraternity** is a society of male university or college students. ❑ *He must have been the most popular guy at the most popular fraternity in college.*

fraud ♦◇◇ /frɔd/ (**frauds**) ❑ N-VAR **Fraud** is the crime of gaining money or financial benefits by a trick or by lying. ❑ *He was jailed for two years for fraud and deception.* ❑ N-COUNT A **fraud** is something or someone that deceives people in a way that is illegal or dishonest. ❑ *He believes many "psychics" are frauds who rely on perception and subtle deception.*

fraudu|lent /frɔdʒələnt/ ADJ A **fraudulent** activity is deliberately deceitful, dishonest, or untrue. ❑ *...fraudulent claims about being a nurse.* ● **fraudu|lent|ly** ADV [ADV with v] ❑ *All 5,000 of the homes were fraudulently obtained.*

fraught /frɔt/ ❑ ADJ If a situation or action is **fraught with** problems or risks, it is filled with them. [v-link ADJ with n] ❑ *The earliest operations employing this technique were fraught with dangers.* ❑ ADJ If you say that a situation or action is **fraught**, you mean that it is worrying or difficult. ❑ *It has been a somewhat fraught day.*

fray /freɪ/ (**frays, fraying, frayed**) ❑ V-T/V-I If something such as cloth or rope **frays**, or if something **frays** it, its threads or fibers start to come apart from each other and spoil its appearance. ❑ *The fabric is very fine or frays easily.* ❑ *The stitching had begun to fray at the edges.* ❑ V-T/V-I If your nerves or your temper **fray**, or if something **frays** them, you become nervous or easily annoyed because of mental strain and anxiety. ❑ *Tempers began to fray as the two teams failed to score.*

freak /frik/ (**freaks**) ❑ ADJ A **freak** event or action is one that is a very unusual or extreme example of its type. [ADJ n] ❑ *Weir broke his leg in a freak accident playing golf.* ❑ N-COUNT If you describe someone as a particular kind of **freak**, you are emphasizing that they are very enthusiastic about a thing or activity, and often seem to think about nothing else. [INFORMAL] ❑ *Oat bran became the darling of health freaks last year.* ❑ N-COUNT People are sometimes referred to as **freaks** when their behavior or attitude is very different from that of the majority of people. [DISAPPROVAL] ❑ *Not so long ago, transsexuals were regarded as freaks.*

freck|le /frɛkəl/ (**freckles**) N-COUNT **Freckles** are small light brown spots on someone's skin, especially on their face. ❑ *He had short ginger-colored hair and freckles.*

free ♦♦♦ /fri/ (**freer, freest, frees, freeing, freed**) ❑ ADJ If something is **free**, you can have it or use it without paying for it. ❑ *The seminars are free, with lunch provided.* **free of charge** →see **charge** ❑ ADJ Someone or something that is **free** is not restricted, controlled, or limited, for example by rules, customs, or other people. ❑ *The government will be free to pursue its economic policies.* ❑ *The elections were free and fair.* ● **free|ly** ADV [ADV with v] ❑ *They cast their votes freely and without coercion on election day.* ❑ V-T If you **free** someone of something that is unpleasant or restricting, you remove it from them. ❑ *It will free us of a whole lot of debt.* ❑ ADJ Someone who is **free** is no longer a prisoner or a slave. [ADJ n, v-link ADJ, ADJ after v] ❑ *He walked from the court house a free man.* ❑ V-T To **free** a prisoner or a slave means to let them go or release them from prison. ❑ *Israel is set to free more Lebanese prisoners.* ❑ ADJ If someone or something is **free of** or **free from** an unpleasant thing, they do not have it or they are not affected by it. [v-link ADJ of/from n] ❑ *...a future far more free of fear.* ❑ *She retains her slim figure and is free of wrinkles.* ❑ ADJ A sum of money or type of **free** of tax or duty is one that you do not have to pay tax on. [v-link ADJ of n] ❑ *This benefit is free of tax under current UK legislation.* →see also **duty-free, interest-free, tax-free** ❑ V-T To **free** someone or something means to make them available for a task or function that they were previously not available for. ❑ *Toolbelts free both hands and lessen the risk of dropping hammers.* ❑ *His deal with Disney will run out shortly, freeing him to pursue his own project.* ● PHRASAL VERB **Free up** means the same as **free**. ❑ *It can handle even the most complex graphic jobs, freeing up your computer for other tasks.* ❑ ADJ If you have a **free** period of time or are **free** at a particular time, you are not working or occupied then. ❑ *She spent her free time shopping.*

가산명사 환불업자, 프랜차이저 [경제] ❑ 코카콜라, 펩시, 캐드버리사는 제품을 만들고 병으로 포장해서 지역 내에 공급하는 데 프랜차이저를 이용한다.

형용사 솔직한 ❑ "내 의뢰인이 나에게 솔직하지 않은 것은 분명하다." 라고 그의 변호인이 말했다. ● 솔직하게 부사 ❑ 내게는 솔직하게 말해도 돼. ● 솔직함 불가산명사 ❑ 그가 보여 준 솔직함에 대한 반응은 냉담했다.

부사 솔직하게 [강조] ❑ "넌 내 기분 따위는 전혀 개의치 않는구나, 그렇지?" " 아주 솔직히 말하자면, 그래." ❑ 솔직히 말하면, 토머스, 자네 대출 문제가 슬슬 걱정되기 시작하는걸.

❶ 형용사 미친 듯한 ❑ 새 한 마리가 갇혀 있었는데, 지금쯤이면 거의 미쳐버렸을 것이다. ● 미친 듯이 부사 ❑ 그녀가 미친 듯이 에밀리의 팔을 움켜잡았다. ❷ 형용사 정신없는 ❑ 손님이 많은 밤이면 그 식당 주방에서는 정신이 없을 것이다. ● 정신없이, 미친 듯이 부사 ❑ 우리는 미친 듯이 그녀의 목숨을 구하려고 애써 왔다.

❶ 불가산명사 동지애 [격식체] ❑ 봅은 자신과 임무를 함께 할 사람들의 동지애를 원하고 있다. ❷ 가산명사 (같은 직업이나 관심을 가진) 부류 ❑ 범죄 집단 사이에서 퍼지고 있는 장물 총기 ❸ 가산명사 (미국 대학의) 남학생 사교 클럽 ❑ 그는 대학의 가장 인기 있는 사교 클럽에서 가장 인기 있는 남학생이었음에 틀림없다.

❶ 가산명사 또는 불가산명사 사기죄 ❑ 그는 사기죄로 2년간 복역했다. ❷ 가산명사 사기꾼 ❑ 그는 많은 심령술사들이 직관과 치밀한 속임수에 의지하는 사기꾼이라고 믿고 있다.

형용사 사기의 ❑ 간호사라는 사기성 주장 ● 사기로 부사 ❑ 5천 가구 모두를 사기로 손에 넣었다.

❶ 형용사 -를 내포한, -로 가득 찬 ❑ 이 기술을 이용한 초기의 수술은 위험을 내포하고 있었다. ❷ 형용사 걱정되는 ❑ 좀 걱정되는 하루였다.

❶ 타동사/자동사 (천이) 해지다; (올이) 풀리다 ❑ 그 천은 올이 매우 가늘어서 쉽게 헤진다. ❑ 가장자리부터 솔기가 풀리기 시작하고 있었다. ❷ 타동사/자동사 (신경이) 날카로워지다; (신경을) 날카롭게 하다 ❑ 그 두 팀원들은 득점을 하지 못하자 신경이 날카로워지기 시작했다.

❶ 형용사 기이한, 별나 ❑ 위어는 골프를 치다가 기이한 사고로 다리가 부러졌다. ❷ 가산명사 -광, 열광자 [비격식체] ❑ 귀리 기울은 건강이라면 사족을 못 쓰는 사람들에게 작년에 엄청난 사랑을 받았다. ❸ 가산명사 괴짜, 괴물 [탐탁찮음] ❑ 얼마 전까지만 해도 성전환자들은 괴물처럼 취급당했다.

가산명사 주근깨 ❑ 그는 연한 갈색 머리에 주근깨가 있었다.

❶ 형용사 무료의 ❑ 그 세미나는 무료입장에 점심까지 제공된다. ❷ 형용사 자유로운; 자주적인 ❑ 그 정부는 경제 정책을 자유롭게 추진할 것이다. ● 자유롭게 부사 ❑ 그들은 선거날에 어떤 강제성도 없이 자유롭게 투표했다. ❸ 타동사 자유롭게 해 주다, 면하게 하다 ❑ 이것으로 우리는 모든 빚을 면하게 될 것이다. ❹ 형용사 죄수가 아닌, 자유인의 ❑ 그는 자유인이 되어 법원을 걸어 나왔다. ❺ 타동사 석방시키다 ❑ 이스라엘은 레바논 죄수들을 더 석방시킬 예정이다. ❻ 형용사 -이 없는 ❑ 훨씬 더 공포감이 없는 미래 ❑ 그녀는 날씬한 몸매를 유지하며 주름도 없다. ❼ 형용사 -이 면제되는 ❑ 현행 영국법상 이 보조금은 세금이 면제된다. ❽ 타동사 -을 자유롭게 하다, -을 자유롭게 사용하다 ❑ 공구를 꽂을 수 있는 벨트가 있어서 양 손을 자유롭게 쓸 수 있고 망치를 떨어뜨릴 위험도 줄어든다. ❑ 디즈니와의 계약이 곧 끝나면 그는 자신의 프로젝트를 자유롭게 추진할 수 있을 것이다. ● 구동사 자유롭게 하다 ❑ 그것을 이용하면 아주 복잡한 그래픽 작업도 할 수 있어, 컴퓨터는 다른 일을 하는 데 자유롭게 사용할 수 있다. ❾ 형용사 여가의, 여가 시간을 쇼핑하면서 보냈다. ❿ 형용사 비어 있는 ❑ 그 기차엔 빈 좌석이 딱 한 자리 있었다. ⓫ 형용사 (속박이나

A B C D E F G H I J K L M N O P Q R S T U V W X Y Z

❏ *I used to write during my free periods at school.* ⑨ ADJ If something such as a table or seat is **free**, it is not being used or occupied by anyone, or is not reserved for anyone to use. ❏ *There was only one seat free on the train.* ⑩ ADJ If you get something **free** or if it gets **free**, it is no longer trapped by anything or attached to anything. [v n ADJ, v-link ADJ, oft ADJ of n] ❏ *He pulled his arm free, and strode for the door.* ⑫ V-T If you **free** someone or something, you remove them from the place in which they have been trapped or become fixed. ❏ *It took firemen two hours to cut through the drive belt to free him.* ⑬ ADJ When someone is using one hand or arm to hold or move something, their other hand or arm is referred to as their **free** one. [ADJ n] ❏ *He snatched up the receiver and his free hand groped for the switch on the bedside lamp.* ⑭ PHRASE You say "**feel free**" when you want to give someone permission to do something, in a very willing way. [INFORMAL, FORMULAE] ❏ *If you have any questions at all, please feel free to ask me.* ⑮ PHRASE If you do something or get something **for free**, you do it without being paid or get it without having to pay for it. [INFORMAL] ❏ *I wasn't expecting you to do it for free.* ⑯ to **give** someone **a free hand** →see **hand**

Thesaurus *free의 참조어*

ADJ.	complimentary ①
	independent, unrestricted ②
	available, vacant; (ant.) occupied ⑩
V.	emancipate, let go, liberate; (ant.) capture ⑫

▶**free up** ① →see **free 8** ② PHRASAL VERB To **free up** a market, economy, or system means to make it operate with fewer restrictions and controls. [BUSINESS] ❏ *...policies for freeing up markets and extending competition.*

Word Link *dom ≈ state of being : bore*dom, *free*dom, *wis*dom

free|dom ♦♦◇ /fríːdəm/ (**freedoms**) ① N-UNCOUNT **Freedom** is the state of being allowed to do what you want to do. **Freedoms** are instances of this. [also N in pl] ❏ *...freedom of speech.* ❏ *The United Nations Secretary-General has spoken of the need for individual freedoms and human rights.* ② N-UNCOUNT When prisoners or slaves are set free or escape, they gain their **freedom**. ❏ *...the agreement worked out by the UN, under which all hostages and detainees would gain their freedom.* ③ N-UNCOUNT **Freedom from** something you do not want means not being affected by it. ❏ *...all the freedom from pain that medicine could provide.*

Word Partnership *freedom의 연어*

ADJ.	**artistic** freedom, **political** freedom, **religious** freedom ①
N.	freedom **of choice, feeling/sense of** freedom, freedom **of the press**, freedom **of speech** ①
	struggle for freedom ① ②

free en|ter|prise N-UNCOUNT **Free enterprise** is an economic system in which businesses compete for profit without much government control. [BUSINESS] ❏ *...a believer in democracy and free enterprise.*

free|lance /fríːlɑːns/ ADJ Someone who does **freelance** work or who is, for example, a **freelance** journalist or photographer is not employed by one organization, but is paid for each piece of work they do by the organization they do it for. [BUSINESS] ❏ *Michael Cross is a freelance journalist.* ● ADV **Freelance** is also an adverb. [ADV after v] ❏ *He is now working freelance from his home in Hampshire.*

free|ly /fríːli/ ① ADV **Freely** means many times or in large quantities. ❏ *We have referred freely to his ideas.* ❏ *George was spending very freely.* ② ADV If you can talk **freely**, you can talk without needing to be careful about what you say. [ADV after v] ❏ *She wondered whether he had someone to whom he could talk freely.* ③ ADV If someone gives or does something **freely**, they give or do it willingly, without being ordered or forced to do it. [ADV with v] ❏ *Danny shared his knowledge freely with anyone interested.* ④ ADV If something or someone moves **freely**, they move easily and smoothly, without any obstacles or resistance. [ADV after v] ❏ *The clay court was slippery and he was unable to move freely.* ⑤ →see also **free**

free mar|ket (**free markets**) N-COUNT A **free market** is an economic system in which business organizations decide things such as prices and wages, and are not controlled by the government. [BUSINESS] ❏ *...the creation of a free market.*

free-marketeer (**free-marketeers**) N-COUNT A **free-marketeer** is someone, especially a politician, who is in favor of letting market forces control the economy. [BUSINESS] ❏ *Free marketeers would argue that governments do not need to intervene in the currency and interest rate process unduly.*

free port (**free ports**) N-COUNT A **free port** is a port or airport where goods can be brought in from foreign countries without payment of duty if they are going to be exported again. [BUSINESS]

freer /fríːər/ **Freer** is the comparative of **free**.

free-range ADJ **Free-range** means relating to a system of keeping animals in which they can move and feed freely on an area of open ground. ❏ *...free-range eggs.*

freest /fríːst/ **Freest** is the superlative of **free**.

free|ware /fríːweər/ N-UNCOUNT **Freeware** is computer software that you can use without payment. [COMPUTING] ❏ *Is there a freeware program that I can use to produce my own clip art?*

구속에서) 풀려난, 매이지 않은 ❏ 그는 팔을 빼고 문 쪽으로 성큼성큼 걸어갔다. ⑫ 타동사 풀어 주다 ❏ 소방관들이 드라이브 벨트를 잘라서 그 사람을 풀어 주는 데 2시간이 걸렸다. ⑬ 형용사 사용하지 않은 (손) ❏ 그는 한 손으로는 수화기를 움켜쥐고, 나머지 한 손으로는 침대 옆 램프를 켜려고 더듬거렸다. ⑭ 구 자유롭게 –하다 [비격식체, 의례적인 표현] ❏ 어떤 질문이라도 있다면, 자유롭게 물어보세요. ⑮ 구 공짜로 [비격식체] ❏ 나는 당신이 그것을 공짜로 하리라고는 예상하지 않고 있었다.

② 구동사 (규제를 완화해서) 자유롭게 하다 [경제] ❏ 시장을 자유롭게 하고 경쟁을 강화시키는 정책들

① 불가산명사 자유 ❏ 언론의 자유 ❏ 유엔 사무총장이 개인의 자유와 인권의 필요성을 역설했다. ② 불가산명사 자유 ❏ 모든 인질과 억류자들이 자유의 몸이 될 수 있도록 유엔이 노력하여 성취해 낸 협정 ③ 불가산명사 –로부터의 해방 ❏ 약에 의한 고통으로부터의 해방

불가산명사 자유 기업 제도 [경제] ❏ 민주주의와 자유 기업 제도의 신봉자

형용사 자유 계약의, 프리랜스의 [경제] ❏ 마이클 크로스는 프리랜스 언론인이다. ● 부사 자유 계약으로, 프리랜스로 ❏ 그는 현재 햄프셔의 집에서 프리랜스로 일하고 있다.

① 부사 자주; 아낌없이 ❏ 우리는 그의 사상을 자주 언급한다. ❏ 조지는 매우 아낌없이 돈을 쓰고 있었다. ② 부사 마음 터놓고 ❏ 그녀는 그가 마음 터놓고 이야기할 수 있는 사람이 있는지 알고 싶었다. ③ 부사 기꺼이 ❏ 대니는 관심을 가진 사람이라면 누구와도 기꺼이 자신의 지식을 공유했다. ④ 부사 자유롭게 ❏ 흙으로 된 테니스 코트가 미끄러워서 그는 자유롭게 움직일 수 없었다.

가산명사 자유 시장 [경제] ❏ 자유 시장 창출

가산명사 자유 시장 지지자 [경제] ❏ 자유 시장 지지자들은 정부가 통화 및 금리 변화에 과도하게 개입할 필요가 없다고 주장할 것이다.

가산명사 자유항 [경제]

free의 비교급 형용사 방목의, (닭을) 놓아먹인 ❏ 놓아먹인 닭의 계란

free의 최상급

불가산명사 무상 소프트웨어 [컴퓨터] ❏ 제 클립아트를 만드는 데 쓸 수 있는 무상 소프트웨어 프로그램이 있습니까?

free|way /fríweɪ/ (**freeways**) N-COUNT A **freeway** is a major road that has been specially built for fast travel over long distances. Freeways have several lanes and special places where traffic gets on and leaves. [AM; BRIT usually **motorway**] ❑ *The speed limit on the freeway is 55mph.*

가산명사 고속도로 [미국영어; 영국영어 대개 motorway] ❑ 그 고속도로에서의 제한 속도는 시속 55마일이다.

free will ■ N-UNCOUNT If you believe in **free will**, you believe that people have a choice in what they do and that their actions have not been decided in advance by God or by any other power. ❑ *...the free will of the individual.* ② PHRASE If you do something of **your own free will**, you do it by choice and not because you are forced to do it. ❑ *Would Bethany return of her own free will, as she had promised, or would she have to be fetched?*

■ 불가산명사 자유 의지 ❑ 개인의 자유 의지 ② 구 자유 의지로, 자진하여 ❑ 베타니는 약속대로 자진하여 돌아올까, 아니면 누가 그녀를 데리러 가야 할까?

freeze ♦♢♢ /fríz/ (**freezes, freezing, froze, frozen**) ■ V-T/V-I If a liquid or a substance containing a liquid **freezes**, or if something **freezes** it, it becomes solid because of low temperatures. ❑ *If the temperature drops below 0°C, water freezes.* ❑ *The ground froze solid.* ② V-T/V-I If you **freeze** something such as food, you preserve it by storing it at a temperature below freezing point. You can also talk about how well food **freezes**. ❑ *You can freeze the soup at this stage.* ③ V-I When **it freezes** outside, the temperature falls below freezing point. ❑ *What if it rained and then froze all through those months?* ● N-COUNT **Freeze** is also a noun. ❑ *The trees were damaged by a freeze in December.* ④ V-I If you **freeze**, you feel extremely cold. ❑ *The windows didn't fit at the bottom so for a while we froze even in the middle of summer.* ⑤ V-I If someone who is moving **freezes**, they suddenly stop and become completely still and quiet. [WRITTEN] ❑ *She froze when the beam of the flashlight struck her.* ⑥ V-T If the government or a company **freeze** things such as prices or wages, they state officially that they will not allow them to increase for a fixed period of time. [BUSINESS] ❑ *They want the government to freeze prices.* ● N-COUNT **Freeze** is also a noun. ❑ *A wage freeze was imposed on all staff earlier this month.* ⑦ V-T If someone in authority **freezes** something such as a bank account, fund, or property, they obtain a legal order which states that it cannot be used or sold for a particular period of time. [BUSINESS] ❑ *The governor's action freezes 300,000 accounts.* ● N-COUNT **Freeze** is also a noun. [with supp] ❑ *...a freeze on private savings.* ⑧ →see also **freezing, frozen** →see **water**

■ 타동사/자동사 얼다; 얼리다 ❑ 기온이 섭씨 0도 아래로 떨어지면 물은 언다. ❑ 땅이 꽁꽁 얼었다. ② 타동사/자동사 냉동 보관하다; 냉동 보관되다 ❑ 수프는 이 단계에서 냉동 보관할 수 있습니다. ③ 자동사 기온이 영하이다 ❑ 만약 비가 내린 후에 그 수개월 내내 기온이 영하였다면 어땠을까? ● 가산명사 혹한 ❑ 나무들이 12월의 혹한으로 해를 입었다. ④ 자동사 몹시 춥다를 뜻하는 ❑ 창문이 바닥과 잘 들어맞지 않아서 한여름이었는데도 한동안 우리는 얼어 죽을 것 같았다. ⑤ 자동사 멈칫하고 꼼짝하지 않다 [문어체] ❑ 그녀는 손전등 빛이 자신을 비추었을 때 멈춰서 꼼짝하지 않았다. ⑥ 타동사 동결시키다 [경제] ❑ 그들은 정부가 물가를 동결시키기를 원한다. ● 가산명사 동결 ❑ 임금 동결이 이번 달 직원 모두에게 적용되었다. ⑦ 타동사 거래를 정지하다, 동결시키다 [경제] ❑ 주지사의 결정에 따라 3십만 개의 구좌에 대해 거래를 정지한다. ● 가산명사 거래 정지, 동결 ❑ 개인 저축에 대한 거래 정지

freez|er /frízər/ (**freezers**) N-COUNT A **freezer** is a large container like a fridge in which the temperature is kept below freezing point so that you can store food inside it for long periods. →see **refrigerator**

가산명사 냉동고

freez|ing /frízɪŋ/ ■ ADJ If you say that something is **freezing** or **freezing cold**, you are emphasizing that it is very cold. [EMPHASIS] ❑ *The movie theater was freezing.*

■ 형용사 얼어 붙을 듯 추운 [강조] ❑ 그 영화관은 얼어 붙을 듯이 추웠다.

> If you want to emphasize how cold the weather is, you can say that it is **freezing**, especially in winter when there is ice or frost. In summer, if the temperature is below average, you can say that it is **cool**. In general, **cold** suggests a lower temperature than **cool**, and **cool** things may be pleasant or refreshing. ❑ *A cool breeze swept off the sea; it was pleasant out there.* If it is very **cool** or too **cool**, you can also say that it is **chilly**.

> 특히 얼음이 얼거나 서리가 내리는 겨울에 날씨가 추운 것을 강조하고 싶으면, 날씨가 freezing하다고 할 수 있다. 여름에 기온이 평균 이하면, 날씨가 cool하다고 할 수 있다. 일반적으로 cold는 cool보다 낮은 기온을 의미하고, cool한 것은 쾌적하거나 상쾌할 수 있다. 시원한 미풍이 바다에서 불어 왔다; 거기에 나가 있으니 쾌적했다. 날씨가 아주 cool하거나 너무 cool하면, 날씨가 chilly하다고도 말할 수 있다.

② ADJ If you say that you are **freezing** or **freezing cold**, you emphasizing that you feel very cold. [EMPHASIS] [v-link ADJ] ❑ *"You must be freezing," she said.* ③ N-UNCOUNT **Freezing** means the same as **freezing point**. ❑ *It's 15 degrees below freezing.* ④ →see also **freeze**

② 형용사 추위 죽겠는 [강조] ❑ "너 추위 죽겠는 모양이구나."라고 그녀가 말했다. ③ 불가산명사 빙점 ❑ 영하 15도이다.

freez|ing point (**freezing points**) also **freezing-point** ■ N-UNCOUNT **Freezing point** is 0° Celsius, the temperature at which water freezes. Freezing point is often used when talking about the weather. ❑ *The temperature remained below freezing point throughout the day.* ② N-COUNT The **freezing point** of a particular substance is the temperature at which it freezes. ❑ *It was the seventeenth century before Newton determined the freezing point of water.*

■ 불가산명사 섭씨 0도 ❑ 기온이 종일 영하에 머물렀다. ② 가산명사 어는 점, 빙점 ❑ 그것은 뉴턴이 물의 어는 점을 확인하기 전인 17세기였다.

freight /freɪt/ ■ N-UNCOUNT **Freight** is the movement of goods by trucks, trains, ships, or airplanes. ❑ *France derives 16 percent of revenue from air freight.* ② N-UNCOUNT **Freight** is goods that are transported by trucks, trains, ships, or airplanes. ❑ *...26 tons of freight.* →see **train**

■ 불가산명사 화물 운송 ❑ 프랑스는 항공 화물 운송에서 세입의 16퍼센트를 얻는다. ② 불가산명사 운송 화물 ❑ 26톤에 이르는 운송 화물

freight car (**freight cars**) N-COUNT On a train, a **freight car** is a large container in which goods are transported. [mainly AM]

가산명사 화물차 [주로 미국영어]

freight|er /freɪtər/ (**freighters**) N-COUNT A **freighter** is a large ship or airplane that is designed for carrying freight.

가산명사 화물선, 화물 수송기

French fries /frɛntʃ fraɪz/ N-PLURAL **French fries** are long, thin pieces of potato fried in oil or fat.

복수명사 (얇게 썰어서 튀긴) 감자튀김

frenetic /frɪnétɪk/ ADJ If you describe an activity as **frenetic**, you mean that it is fast and energetic, but rather uncontrolled. ❑ *...the frenetic pace of life in New York.*

형용사 정신없이 돌아가는 ❑ 정신없이 돌아가는 뉴욕 생활

fren|zied /frénzid/ ADJ **Frenzied** activities or actions are wild, excited, and uncontrolled. ❑ *...the frenzied activity of the general election.*

형용사 광적인 ❑ 총선거의 광적인 활기

frenzy /frénzi/ (**frenzies**) N-VAR **Frenzy** or a **frenzy** is great excitement or wild behavior that often results from losing control of your feelings. ❑ *"Get out!" she ordered in a frenzy.*

가산명사 또는 불가산명사 열광; 광분, 히스테리 ❑ "나가!"라고 그녀가 광분해서 명령했다.

fre|quen|cy /fríkwənsi/ (**frequencies**) ■ N-UNCOUNT The **frequency** of an event is the number of times it happens during a particular period. ❑ *The frequency of Kara's phone calls increased rapidly.* ② N-VAR In physics, the **frequency** of a sound wave or a radio wave is the number of times it vibrates within a specified period of time. ❑ *You can't hear waves of such a high frequency.* ❑ *...a frequency of 24 kilohertz.* →see **sound, wave**

■ 불가산명사 횟수, 빈도 ❑ 카라가 전화하는 횟수가 급속히 증가했다. ② 가산명사 또는 불가산명사 주파수 ❑ 그러한 고주파의 파동은 들을 수 없다. ❑ 24킬로헤르츠의 주파수

fre|quent ♦♦◇ ADJ If something is **frequent**, it happens often. ❑ *Bordeaux is on the main Paris-Madrid line so there are frequent trains.* ● **fre|quent|ly** ADV ❑ *Iron and folic acid supplements are frequently given to pregnant women.*

형용사 자주 일어나는 ❑ 보르도는 파리와 마드리드를 잇는 본선에 위치하므로 기차가 자주 다닌다. ● 자주 부사 ❑ 임산부들은 자주 철분과 엽산 보충제를 제공받는다.

Thesaurus	*frequent*의 참조어
ADJ.	common, everyday, habitual; (ant.) occasional, rare

fresh ♦♦◇ /frɛʃ/ (**fresher, freshest**) **1** ADJ A **fresh** thing or amount replaces or is added to a previous thing or amount. [ADJ n] ❑ *He asked Strathclyde police, which carried out the original investigation, to make fresh inquiries.* **2** ADJ Something that is **fresh** has been done, made, or experienced recently. ❑ *There were no fresh car tracks or footprints in the snow.* ❑ *A puppy stepped in the fresh cement.* **3** ADJ **Fresh** food has been picked or produced recently, and has not been preserved, for example by being frozen or put in a can. ❑ *...locally caught fresh fish.* **4** ADJ If you describe something as **fresh**, you like it because it is new and exciting. ❑ *These designers are full of fresh ideas.* **5** ADJ If you describe something as **fresh**, you mean that it is pleasant, bright, and clean in appearance. ❑ *Gingham fabrics always look fresh and pretty.* **6** ADJ If something smells, tastes, or feels **fresh**, it is clean or cool. ❑ *The air was fresh and for a moment she felt revived.* **7** ADJ If you feel **fresh**, you feel full of energy and enthusiasm. ❑ *It's vital we are as fresh as possible for those matches.* **8** ADJ **Fresh** paint is not yet dry. [AM; BRIT **wet**] ❑ *There was fresh paint on the walls.* **9** ADJ If you are **fresh from** a particular place or experience, you have just come from that place or you have just had that experience. You can also say that someone is **fresh out of** a place. [v-link ADJ *from/out of* n] ❑ *I returned to the office, fresh from Heathrow.* →see **vegetable**

fresh air N-UNCOUNT You can describe the air outside as **fresh air**, especially when you mean that it is good for you because it does not contain dirt or dangerous substances. [also *the* N] ❑ *"Let's take the baby outside," I suggested. "We all need some fresh air."*

fresh|ly /frɛʃli/ ADV If something is **freshly** made or done, it has been recently made or done. [ADV -ed] ❑ *...freshly baked bread.*

fresh|water /frɛʃwɔtər/ ADJ A **freshwater** lake contains water that is not salty, usually in contrast to the sea. **Freshwater** creatures live in water that is not salty. [ADJ n] ❑ *...Lake Balaton, the largest freshwater lake in Europe.* →see **wetland**

fret /frɛt/ (**frets, fretting, fretted**) V-T/V-I If you **fret** about something, you worry about it. ❑ *I was working all hours and constantly fretting about everyone else's problems.* ❑ *But congressional staffers fret that the project will eventually cost billions more.*

Fri. Fri. is a written abbreviation for **Friday.**

fric|tion /frɪkʃən/ **1** N-UNCOUNT If there is **friction** between people, there is disagreement and argument between them. [also N in pl] ❑ *Sara sensed that there had been friction between her children.* **2** N-UNCOUNT **Friction** is the force that makes it difficult for things to move freely when they are touching each other. ❑ *The pistons are graphite-coated to reduce friction.*

Fri|day ♦♦♦ /fraɪdeɪ, -di/ (**Fridays**) N-VAR **Friday** is the day after Thursday and before Saturday. ❑ *Mr. Cook is intending to go to the Middle East on Friday.* ❑ *...Friday 6 November.*

fridge /frɪdʒ/ (**fridges**) N-COUNT A **fridge** is a large metal container which is kept cool, usually by electricity, so that food that is put in it stays fresh. [BRIT, also AM, INFORMAL; AM usually **refrigerator**]

friend ♦♦♦ /frɛnd/ (**friends**) **1** N-COUNT A **friend** is someone who you know well and like, but who is not related to you. ❑ *I had a long talk about this with my best friend.* ❑ *She never was a close friend of mine.* **2** N-PLURAL If you are **friends with** someone, you are their friend and they are yours. ❑ *I still wanted to be friends with Alison.* ❑ *We remained good friends.* **3** N-PLURAL; N-IN-NAMES The **friends of** a country, cause, organization, or a famous politician are the people and organizations who help and support them. ❑ *...the friends of Israel.* **4** N-COUNT If one country refers to another as a **friend**, they mean that the other country is not an enemy of theirs. ❑ *The president said that Japan is now a friend and international partner.* **5** PHRASE If you **make friends with** someone, you begin a friendship with them. You can also say that two people **make friends**. ❑ *He has made friends with the kids on the street.* ❑ *Dennis made friends easily.*

Word Partnership		*friend*의 연어
ADJ.	**best** friend, **close** friend, **dear** friend, **faithful** friend, **former** friend, **good** friend, **loyal** friend, **mutual** friend, **old** friend, **personal** friend **1**	
V.	**tell** a friend **1**	
	make a friend **1 5**	
N.	**childhood** friend, friend **of the family**, friend **or relative** **1**	
	friend **or foe** **1 2**	

friend|ly ♦◇◇ /frɛndli/ (**friendlier, friendliest, friendlies**) **1** ADJ If someone is **friendly**, they behave in a pleasant, kind way, and like to be with other people. ❑ *Godfrey had been friendly to me.* ❑ *...a man with a pleasant, friendly face.* ● **friend|li|ness** N-UNCOUNT ❑ *She also loves the friendliness of the people.* **2** ADJ If you are **friendly with** someone, you like each other and enjoy spending time together. [v-link ADJ, usu ADJ *with* n] ❑ *I'm friendly with his mother.* **3** ADJ You can describe another country or their government as **friendly** when they have good relations with your own country rather than being an enemy. ❑ *...a worsening in relations between the two previously friendly countries.* **4** N-COUNT In

1 형용사 새로운, 추가의 ❑ 그가 초기 수사를 진행했던 스트래스클라이드 경찰에게 추가 조사를 요청했다. **2** 형용사 새로 발생한, 갓 만든 ❑ 눈 위에 새로 생긴 자동차 바퀴 자국이나 발자국은 없었다. ❑ 강아지 한 마리가 갓 바른 시멘트에 발을 디뎠다. **3** 형용사 신선한, 갓 수확한 ❑ 근처에서 갓 잡은 물고기 **4** 형용사 참신한 ❑ 이 디자이너들은 참신한 아이디어로 가득하다. **5** 형용사 산뜻한 ❑ 깅엄 직물은 항상 산뜻하고 예뻐 보인다. **6** 형용사 상쾌한 ❑ 공기는 상쾌했고 그녀는 잠깐 동안 기운이 솟는 듯한 기분이 들었다. **7** 형용사 기운 넘치는 ❑ 그 경기들을 위해서는 우리가 최대한 기운이 넘치는 것이 중요하다. **8** 형용사 (페인트가) 채 마르지 않은 [미국영어; 영국영어 wet] ❑ 벽에 페인트가 채 마르지 않았었다. **9** 형용사 ~에서 방금 나온 ❑ 나는 히드로 공항에서 방금 사무실로 돌아왔다.

불가산명사 신선한 공기 ❑ "아기를 밖으로 데리고 나가자. 우리 모두 신선한 공기가 필요해."라고 내가 제안했다.

부사 갓 ❑ 갓 구운 빵

형용사 담수의 ❑ 유럽에서 가장 큰 담수호인 발라톤 호수

타동사/자동사 걱정하다 ❑ 나는 내내 일하고 있었고 끊임없이 다른 사람들의 문제에 대해 걱정하고 있었다. ❑ 하지만 의회 직원들은 그 계획에 결국 수십억이 더 들 것이라고 걱정한다.

금

1 불가산명사 불화, 마찰 ❑ 사라는 아이들 사이에 불화가 있었다는 것을 알아챘다. **2** 불가산명사 마찰 ❑ 피스톤에 흑연을 덧입혀서 마찰을 줄인다.

가산명사 또는 불가산명사 금요일 ❑ 쿡 씨는 금요일에 중동에 갈 작정이다. ❑ 11월 6일 금요일

가산명사 냉장고 [영국, 미국영어, 비격식체; 미국영어 대개 refrigerator]

1 가산명사 친구 ❑ 나는 이것에 대해서 내 가장 친한 친구와 오랫동안 대화를 나눴다. ❑ 그녀는 절대 내 친한 친구가 아니었다. **2** 복수명사 친구 ❑ 나는 여전히 앨리슨과 친구로 지내고 싶었다. ❑ 우리는 여전히 좋은 친구였다. **3** 복수명사; 이름명사 지지자 ❑ 이스라엘의 지지자 **4** 가산명사 우방 ❑ 대통령이 일본은 이제 우방이자 국제 사회에서의 파트너라고 말했다. **5** 구 친구가 되다 ❑ 그는 거리에서 그 아이들과 친구가 되었다. ❑ 데니스는 쉽게 친구를 사귀었다.

1 형용사 호의적인, 상냥한 ❑ 고드프리는 내게 호의적으로 대해 왔었다. ❑ 상냥하고 호의적인 표정을 한 남자 ● 호의, 상냥함 불가산명사 ❑ 그녀 역시 그 사람들의 상냥함을 좋아한다. **2** 형용사 친한 ❑ 나는 그의 어머니와 친하다. **3** 형용사 우호적인 ❑ 이전에 우호적이었던 두 국가의 관계 악화 **4** 가산명사 친선 경기 [영국영어] ❑ 아틀레틱 빌바오가 레알 소시에다드와 친선 경기를 하기로 동의했다. ● 형용사 친선의 [미국영어 exhibition game] ❑ 수요일에

A

sports, a **friendly** is a match which is not part of a competition, and is played for entertainment or practice, often without any serious effort to win. [BRIT] ❑ *Athletic Bilbao agreed to play a friendly at Real Sociedad.* ● ADJ **Friendly** is also an adjective. [AM **exhibition game**] [ADJ n] ❑ *Austria beat Hungary 3-nil in a friendly match at Salzburg on Wednesday.*

잘츠부르크에서 열린 친선 경기에서 오스트리아가 헝가리에 3대 0으로 이겼다.

B

Do not confuse **friendly** and **sympathetic**. A person who is **friendly** or has a **friendly** attitude is kind and pleasant and behaves the way a friend would. ❑ *...a friendly woman who offered me cakes and tea....a pleasant, friendly smile.* If you have a problem and someone is **sympathetic** or shows a **sympathetic** attitude, they show that they care and would like to help you. ❑ *My boyfriend was very sympathetic.* Note that people sometimes refer to characters in a play or novel who are easy to like as **sympathetic**. ❑ *There were no sympathetic characters in my book.* You usually say that real people are "nice" or "likable."

friendly와 sympathetic을 혼동하지 않도록 하라. friendly하거나 friendly한 태도를 지닌 사람은 친절하거나 상냥하고 친구처럼 행동한다. ❑ ...내게 케이크와 차를 권했던 친절한 여자...상냥하고 친근한 미소. 당신에게 고민이 있는데 누군가가 sympathetic하거나 sympathetic한 태도를 보이면, 그들이 당신에 대해 염려하고 도와주고 싶어 하는 것이다. ❑ 내 남자친구는 몹시 가여워했다. 때때로 연극이나 소설 속에 나오는 호감이 가는 등장인물을 sympathetic하다고 표현하기도 한다. ❑ 내 책에는 호감이 가는 인물이 하나도 없었다. 실제 사람들에 대해서는 대개 nice나 likable을 쓴다.

Word Partnership   friendly의 연어

N.	friendly **face**, friendly **neighbors**, friendly **service**, friendly **voice** 🄰
	friendly **relationship** 🄰 🄲
	friendly **game**, friendly **match** 🄳
V.	**become** friendly 🄱

F

-friendly /-frɛndli/ 🄰 COMB in ADJ **-friendly** combines with nouns to form adjectives which describe things that are not harmful to the specified part of the natural world. ❑ *Palm oil is environment-friendly.* 🄱 COMB in ADJ **-friendly** combines with nouns to form adjectives which describe things which are intended for or suitable for the specified person, especially things that are easy for them to understand, appreciate, or use. ❑ *...customer-friendly banking facilities.* →see also **user-friendly**

🄰 복합형-형용사 -에 친화적인, -에 해롭지 않은 ❑ 야자유는 환경 친화적이다. 🄱 복합형-형용사 -의 편의를 위한 ❑ 고객 편의를 위한 은행 시설

Word Link   ship ≈ condition or state : censor**ship**, citizen**ship**, friend**ship**

J

friend|ship ♦◇◇ /frɛndʃɪp/ (**friendships**) 🄰 N-VAR A **friendship** is a relationship between two or more friends. ❑ *Giving advice when it's not called for is the quickest way to end a good friendship.* ❑ *She struck up a close friendship with Desiree during the week of rehearsals.* 🄱 N-UNCOUNT You use **friendship** to refer in a general way to the state of being friends, or the feelings that friends have for each other. ❑ *...a hobby which led to a whole new world of friendship and adventure.* 🄲 N-VAR **Friendship** is a relationship between two countries in which they help and support each other. ❑ *The President set the targets for the future to promote friendship with East Europe.*

🄰 가산명사 또는 불가산명사 친구 사이 ❑ 바라지도 않는 조언은 좋은 친구 사이에 종지부를 찍는 가장 빠른 길이다. ❑ 그녀는 한 주간의 리허설 기간 동안 데지레와 가까운 친구 사이가 되었다. 🄱 불가산명사 우정 ❑ 우정과 모험이라는 전혀 새로운 세계로 이끌어 준 취미 🄲 가산명사 또는 불가산명사 우호 ❑ 대통령이 동유럽과의 우호 증진을 위해 향후 목표를 설정했다.

M

frig|ate /frɪgət/ (**frigates**) N-COUNT A **frigate** is a fairly small ship owned by the navy that can move at fast speeds. Frigates are often used to protect other ships.

가산명사 소형 구축함

fright /fraɪt/ (**frights**) 🄰 N-UNCOUNT **Fright** is a sudden feeling of fear, especially the fear that you feel when something unpleasant surprises you. ❑ *The steam pipes rattled suddenly, and Franklin uttered a shriek and jumped with fright.* ❑ *The birds smashed into the top of their cages in fright.* 🄱 N-COUNT A **fright** is an experience which makes you suddenly afraid. ❑ *The snake picked up its head and stuck out its tongue which gave everyone a fright.*

🄰 불가산명사 공포감 ❑ 증기관이 갑자기 덜컹거리며 움직이자, 프랭클린은 날카로운 비명을 내지르며 공포감에 소스라쳤다. ❑ 새들이 공포심에 휩싸여 퍼더거리다 새장 꼭대기에 몸을 세게 부딪쳤다. 🄱 가산명사 경악 ❑ 뱀이 머리를 세우고 혀를 날름거려서 모든 사람들이 경악했다.

P

fright|en /fraɪtᵊn/ (**frightens**, **frightening**, **frightened**) 🄰 V-T If something or someone **frightens** you, they cause you to suddenly feel afraid, anxious, or nervous. ❑ *He knew that Soli was trying to frighten him, so he smiled to hide his fear.* 🄱 PHRASE If something **frightens the life out of** you, **frightens the wits out of** you, or **frightens** you **out of your wits**, it causes you to feel suddenly afraid or gives you a very unpleasant shock. [EMPHASIS] ❑ *Fairground rides are intended to frighten the life out of you.*

🄰 타동사 겁주다 ❑ 그는 솔리가 자신을 겁주려고 한다는 것을 알았고, 그래서 미소를 지어 자신의 무서움을 감추었다. 🄱 구 -의 간담을 서늘하게 하다 [강조] ❑ 박람회장의 탈것들은 사람들의 간담을 서늘하게 하도록 만들어진 것이다.

▸**frighten away** or **frighten off** 🄰 PHRASAL VERB If you **frighten away** a person or animal or **frighten** them **off**, you make them afraid so that they run away or stay some distance away from you. ❑ *The fishermen said the company's seismic survey was frightening away fish.* 🄱 PHRASAL VERB To **frighten** someone **away** or **frighten** them **off** means to make them nervous so that they decide not to become involved with a particular person or activity. ❑ *Repossessions have frightened buyers off.*

🄰 구동사 위협하여 쫓아버리다 ❑ 어민들은 그 회사의 지진 측량이 물고기를 위협하여 쫓아버리고 있다고 말했다. 🄱 구동사 겁주어 -와 멀어지게 하다 ❑ 소유권 환수로 구매자들이 놀라 발을 빼고 있다.

S

▸**frighten off** →see **frighten away**

fright|ened /fraɪtᵊnd/ ADJ If you are **frightened**, you are anxious or afraid, often because of something that has just happened or that you think may happen. ❑ *She was frightened of flying.*

형용사 -에 겁을 먹은 ❑ 그녀는 비행기를 탈 생각에 겁을 먹고 있었다.

fright|en|ing /fraɪtᵊnɪŋ/ ADJ If something is **frightening**, it makes you feel afraid, anxious, or nervous. ❑ *It was a very frightening experience and they were very courageous.* ● **fright|en|ing|ly** ADV ❑ *The country is frighteningly close to possessing nuclear weapons.*

형용사 무서운, 겁나는 ❑ 그건 정말이지 무서운 경험이었는데 그들은 아주 용감했다. ● 무서울 정도로 부사 ❑ 그 나라는 무서울 정도로 핵무기 보유에 근접해 있다.

W

fright|ful /fraɪtfəl/ 🄰 ADJ **Frightful** means very bad or unpleasant. [OLD-FASHIONED] ❑ *My father was unable to talk about the war, it was so frightful.* 🄱 ADJ **Frightful** is used to emphasize the extent or degree of something, usually something bad. [INFORMAL, OLD-FASHIONED, EMPHASIS] [ADJ n] ❑ *He got himself into a frightful muddle.*

🄰 형용사 소름끼치는 [구식어] ❑ 내 아버지는 그 전쟁에 관해 아무 말도 할 수 없었다. 그것은 너무도 소름끼치는 일이었다. 🄱 형용사 지독한 [비격식체, 구식어, 강조] ❑ 그는 스스로 지독한 혼란 속으로 들어갔다.

frill /frɪl/ (**frills**) 🄰 N-COUNT A **frill** is a long narrow strip of cloth or paper with many folds in it, which is attached to something as a decoration. ❑ *...net curtains with frills.* 🄱 N-COUNT If you describe something as having **no frills**, you mean that it has no extra features, but is acceptable or good if you want something simple. [APPROVAL] ❑ *This booklet restricts itself to facts without frills.*

🄰 가산명사 주름 장식 ❑ 주름 장식이 달린 그물 모양의 커튼 🄱 가산명사 꾸밈, 불필요한 것 [마음에 듦] ❑ 이 소책자는 꼭 필요한 사실만 다룬다.

fringe /frɪndʒ/ (**fringes**) 🄰 N-COUNT A **fringe** is hair which is cut so that it hangs over your forehead. [BRIT; AM **bangs**] ❑ *She has dark hair; a long fringe flops over her face.* 🄱 N-COUNT A **fringe** is a decoration attached to clothes, or other

🄰 가산명사 이마에 드리운 앞머리 [영국영어; 미국영어 bangs] ❑ 그녀의 머리카락은 새까만데, 이마 위로 길게 드리운 앞머리가 찰랑거린다. 🄱 가산명사

objects such as curtains, consisting of a row of hanging strips or threads. ❑ *The jacket had leather fringes.* **3** N-COUNT To be **on the fringe** or **the fringes of** a place means to be on the outside edge of it, or to be in one of the parts that are farthest from its center. ❑ *...black townships located on the fringes of the city.* **4** N-COUNT The **fringe** or **the fringes of** an activity or organization are its less important, least typical, or most extreme parts, rather than its main and central part. ❑ *The party remained on the fringe of the political scene until last year.* **5** ADJ **Fringe** groups or events are less important or popular than other related groups or events. [ADJ n] ❑ *The monarchists are a small fringe group who quarrel fiercely among themselves.*

fringe ben|efit (**fringe benefits**) N-COUNT **Fringe benefits** are extra things that some people get from their job in addition to their salary, for example a car. [BUSINESS] ❑ *...insecure, badly paid jobs without any of the fringe benefits - such as healthcare.*

fringed /frɪndʒd/ **1** ADJ **Fringed** clothes, curtains, or lampshades are decorated with fringes. [ADJ n] ❑ *Emma wore a fringed scarf round her neck.* **2** ADJ If a place or object **is fringed with** something, that thing forms a border around it or is situated along its edges. [v-link ADJ with n] ❑ *Her eyes were large and brown and fringed with incredibly long lashes.*

friv|olous /frɪvələs/ **1** ADJ If you describe someone as **frivolous**, you mean they behave in a silly or light-hearted way, rather than being serious and sensible. ❑ *I just decided I was a bit too frivolous to be a doctor.* **2** ADJ If you describe an activity as **frivolous**, you disapprove of it because it is not useful and wastes time or money. [DISAPPROVAL] ❑ *The group says it wants politicians to stop wasting public money on what it believes are frivolous projects.*

fro /froʊ/ **to and fro** →see **to**

frog /frɒg, BRIT frɒg/ (**frogs**) N-COUNT A **frog** is a small creature with smooth skin, big eyes, and long back legs which it uses for jumping. Frogs usually live near water.

frol|ic /frɒlɪk/ (**frolics, frolicking, frolicked**) V-I When people or animals **frolic**, they play or move in a lively, happy way. ❑ *Tourists sunbathe and frolic in the ocean.*

from ♦♦♦ /frəm, STRONG fræm, BRIT frɒm/

In addition to the uses shown below, **from** is used in phrasal verbs such as "date from" and "grow away from."

1 PREP If something comes **from** a particular person or thing, or if you get something **from** them, they give it to you or they are the source of it. ❑ *He appealed for information from anyone who saw the attackers.* ❑ *...an anniversary present from his wife.*

When you are talking about the person who has written you a letter or sent a message to you, you say that the letter or message is **from** that person. ❑ *He received a message from Vito Corleone.* When you are talking about an author, a composer, or a painter, you say the work is **by** that person or is written or painted **by** him or her. ❑ *...three books by Michael Moorcock....a collection of piano pieces by Mozart.*

2 PREP Someone who comes **from** a particular place lives in that place or originally lived there. Something that comes **from** a particular place was made in that place. ❑ *...an art dealer from Zurich.* ❑ *Katy Jones is nineteen and comes from Birmingham.* **3** PREP A person **from** a particular organization works for that organization. ❑ *...a representative from the Israeli embassy.* **4** PREP If someone or something moves or is moved **from** a place, they leave it or are removed, so that they are no longer there. ❑ *The guests watched as she fled from the room.* **5** PREP If you take one thing or person **from** another, you move that thing or person so that they are no longer with the other or attached to the other. ❑ *In many bone transplants, bone can be taken from other parts of the patient's body.* **6** PREP If you take something **from** an amount, you reduce the amount by that much. ❑ *The $103 is deducted from Mrs. Adams' salary every month.* **7** PREP **From** is used in expressions such as **away from** or **absent from** to say that someone or something is not present in a place where they are usually found. ❑ *Her husband worked away from home a lot.* **8** PREP If you return **from** a place or an activity, you return after being in that place or doing that activity. ❑ *My son Colin has just returned from Amsterdam.* **9** PREP If you are back **from** a place or activity, you have left it and have returned to your former place. ❑ *Our economics correspondent, James Morgan, is just back from Germany.* **10** PREP If you see or hear something **from** a particular place, you are in that place when you see it or hear it. [PREP n, PREP prep, PREP adv] ❑ *Visitors see the painting from behind a plate glass window.* **11** PREP If something hangs or sticks out **from** an object, it is attached to it or held by it. [v PREP n] ❑ *Hanging from his right wrist is a heavy gold bracelet.* ❑ *...large fans hanging from ceilings.* **12** PREP You can use **from** when giving distances. For example, if a place is fifty miles **from** another place, the distance between the two places is fifty miles. [amount PREP n] ❑ *...a small park only a few hundred yards from Zurich's main shopping center.* ❑ *How far is it from here?* **13** PREP If a road or railway line goes **from** one place to another, you can travel along it between the two places. ❑ *...the road from St Petersburg to Tallinn.* **14** PREP **From** is used, especially in the expression **made from**, to say what substance has been used to make something. [v PREP n] ❑ *...bread made from white flour.* **15** PREP You can use **from** when you are talking about the beginning of a period of time. ❑ *She studied painting from 1926 and also worked as a commercial artist.* ❑ *Breakfast is available to fishermen from 6 a.m.* **16** PREP You say **from** one thing **to** another when you are stating the range of things that are possible, or when saying that the range of things includes everything in a certain category. [PREP n/-ing] ❑ *There are 94 countries represented in Barcelona, from Algeria to Zimbabwe.* **17** PREP If something changes **from** one thing **to** another, it stops

술 장식 ❑그 재킷에는 가죽 술 장식이 달려 있었다. **3** 가산명사 -의 가장자리, -의 변두리 ❑그 도시의 변두리에 위치한 흑인들의 거주 구역 **4** 가산명사 주변부 ❑그 당은 작년까지는 정치계의 주변부에 머물러 있었다. **5** 형용사 비주류의 ❑군주제주의자들은 자기들끼리 맹렬하게 말다툼하는 소규모 비주류 집단에 지나지 않는다.

가산명사 부가 급부 [경제] ❑의료 보험과 같은 부가 급부가 없고 불안정한 저임금 일자리들

1 형용사 술 장식이 달린 ❑엄마는 목에 술 장식이 달린 스카프를 두르고 있었다. **2** 형용사 -의 가장자리를 두른 ❑그녀의 두 눈은 크고 갈색이었는데 눈가로 놀라울 정도로 긴 속눈썹이 나 있었다.

1 형용사 경솔한 ❑나는 그저 내가 너무 경솔해서 의사가 될 수 없다고 결정했다. **2** 형용사 하찮은 [탐탁찮음] ❑그 단체는 그들이 생각하기에는 하찮은 계획들에 정치가들이 공적 자금을 그만 낭비하기를 바란다고 말한다.

가산명사 개구리

자동사 장난치며 놀다 ❑관광객들이 일광욕을 하고 바다에 들어가 장난치며 논다.

from은 아래 용법 이외에도 'date from', 'grow away from'과 같은 구동사에 쓰인다.

1 전치사 -에게서 ❑그는 공격한 사람을 목격한 사람이면 누구든 정보를 알려 달라고 호소했다. ❑그가 부인에게서 받은 기념일 선물

당신에게 편지나 전갈을 보낸 사람에 대해 말할 때는, 그 편지나 전갈이 그 사람으로부터(from)왔다고 말한다. ❑그는 비토 콜리오네로부터 전갈을 받았다. 작가나 작곡가, 화가에 대해 말할 때는, 그 작품이 그 사람에 의해(by) 쓰여졌거나 그려졌다고 말한다. ❑ ...마이클 무어콕의 책 3권....모차르트의 피아노 곡 모음집

2 전치사 -출신의; -에서 생산된 ❑취리히 출신의 미술상 ❑케이티 존스는 열아홉 살이고 버밍엄 출신이다. **3** 전치사 -소속의 ❑이스라엘 대사관 소속 대표 **4** 전치사 -에서, -로부터 (나와서) ❑투숙객들은 그녀가 방에서 달아나는 것을 지켜보았다. **5** 전치사 -에서, -로부터 (떼어 내어) ❑뼈 이식 수술에서는 많은 경우에 환자 본인의 신체 다른 부분에서 뼈를 떼어 낼 수 있다. **6** 전치사 -에서 (덜어내어) ❑103달러가 아담스 여사의 급여에서 매달 공제된다. **7** 전치사 -에서 떨어져서; -에서 부재중인 ❑그녀의 남편은 자주 집을 떠나 있어 일했다. **8** 전치사 -에서 ❑내 아들 콜린이 암스테르담에서 막 돌아왔다. **9** 전치사 -에서 ❑우리의 경제 통신원인 제임스 모르간이 독일에서 방금 돌아왔다. **10** 전치사 -에서 ❑판유리가 끼워진 창문 뒤쪽에서부터 그 그림을 본다. **11** 전치사 -에서, -에 ❑그의 오른쪽 손목에서 흔들리고 있는 것은 묵직한 금팔찌이다. ❑천장에 매달린 큰 선풍기들 **12** 전치사 -에서 ❑취리히의 주요 쇼핑센터에서 겨우 몇 백 야드 떨어진 작은 공원 ❑여기서 거리가 얼마나 되지요? **13** 전치사 -부터, -에서 ❑상트페테르부르크부터 탈린까지 이어지는 도로 **14** 전치사 -로, -을 재료로 하여 ❑흰 밀가루로 만든 빵 **15** 전치사 -부터 ❑그녀는 1926년부터 그림을 공부했고 상업 미술가로서도 일했다. ❑어민들에게는 오전 6시부터 아침 식사가 제공된다. **16** 전치사 -부터 (...까지) ❑바르셀로나에는 알제리부터 짐바브웨까지 94개국의 대표가 있다. **17** 전치사 -에서 (...으로) ❑그의 얼굴 표정이 동정에서 놀람으로 바뀌었다. ❑실업률이 7.5에서 7.2퍼센트로 떨어졌다. **18** 전치사 -에서 ❑그 문제는 단지 의견 차이에서 나온 것이었다. ❑그들은 정말로 다른 사람들에게 돈을 쓰는 것에서 즐거움을 얻는다. **19** 전치사 -을 통해 ❑그녀는 그가 자기에게 곧 진실을 말할 거라는 것을 경험을 통해 알고 있었다. ❑그는 그녀의 얼굴 표정을 보고 그녀가 할 말이 있다는 것을 감지했다. **20** 전치사 -로부터 ❑그러한 법이 해롭거나 위험한 치료법으로부터 소비자를 보호할 수 있다.

being the first thing and becomes the second thing. ❏ *The expression on his face changed from sympathy to surprise.* ❏ *Unemployment has fallen from 7.5 to 7.2%.* **18** PREP You use **from** after some verbs and nouns when mentioning the cause of something. [PREP n/-ing] ❏ *The problem really resulted from a difference of opinion.* ❏ *They really do get pleasure from spending money on other people.* **19** PREP You use **from** when you are giving the reason for an opinion. ❏ *She knew from experience that Dave was about to tell her the truth.* ❏ *He sensed from the expression on her face that she had something to say.* **20** PREP **From** is used after verbs with meanings such as "protect," "free," "keep," and "prevent" to introduce the action that does not happen, or that someone does not want to happen. ❏ *Such laws could protect the consumer from harmful or dangerous remedies.*

front ♦♦♦ /frʌnt/ (fronts) **1** N-COUNT The **front of** something is the part of it that faces you, or that faces forward, or that you normally see or use. ❏ *One man sat in an armchair, and the other sat on the front of the desk.* ❏ *Stand at the front of the line.* **2** N-COUNT The **front of** a building is the side or part of it that faces the street. ❏ *Attached to the front of the house, there was a large veranda.* **3** N-SING A person's or animal's **front** is the part of their body between their head and their legs that is on the opposite side to their back. ❏ *When baby is lying on his front, hold something so that he has to raise his head to see it.* **4** ADJ **Front** is used to refer to the side or part of something that is toward the front or nearest to the front. [ADJ n] ❏ *I went out there on the front porch.* ❏ *She was only six and still missing her front teeth.* **5** ADJ The **front** page of a newspaper is the outside of the first page, where the main news stories are printed. [ADJ n] ❏ *The Guardian's front page carries a photograph of the two foreign ministers.* →see also **front-page** **6** N-COUNT In a war, the **front** is a line where two opposing armies are facing each other. ❏ *Sonja's husband is fighting at the front.* →see also **front line** **7** N-COUNT If you say that something is happening on a particular **front**, you mean that it is happening with regard to a particular situation or field of activity. ❏ *...research across a wide academic front.* **8** N-COUNT If someone puts on a particular kind of **front**, they pretend to have a particular quality. ❏ *Michael kept up a brave front both to the world and in his home.* **9** N-COUNT An organization or activity that is **a front for** one that is illegal or secret is used to hide it. ❏ *...a firm later identified by the police as a front for crime syndicates.* **10** N-COUNT In relation to the weather, a **front** is a line where a mass of cold air meets a mass of warm air. ❏ *The snow signaled the arrival of a front, and a high-pressure area seemed to be settling in.* **11** PHRASE If a person or thing is **in front**, they are ahead of others in a moving group, or further forward than someone or something else. ❏ *Officers will crack down on lunatic motorists who speed or drive too close to the car in front.* **12** PHRASE Someone who is **in front** in a competition or contest at a particular point is winning at that point. ❏ *Richard Dunwoody is in front in the jockeys' title race.* **13** PHRASE If someone or something is **in front of** a particular thing, they are facing it, ahead of it, or close to the front part of it. ❏ *She sat down in front of her dressing-table mirror to look at herself.* ❏ *Something darted out in front of my car, and my car hit it.* **14** PHRASE If you do or say something **in front of** someone else, you do or say it when they are present. ❏ *They never argued in front of their children.* →see **forecast**

> **Word Partnership**   front의 연어
>
> N.   front **of the line 1**
> front **door**, front **end**, front **porch**, front **room**, front **tire**, front **wheel**, front **window 2 4**
> front **paws**, front **teeth 4**

front|al /frʌntᵊl/ ADJ **Frontal** means relating to or involving the front of something, for example the front of an army, a vehicle, or the brain. [FORMAL] ❏ *Military leaders are not expecting a frontal assault by the rebels.*

front desk N-SING The **front desk** in a hotel is the desk or office that books rooms for people and answers their questions. [mainly AM; BRIT **reception**] [the N, oft N n, also at N] ❏ *Call the hotel's front desk and cancel your early morning wake-up call.* →see **hotel**

fron|tier /frʌntɪər, frɒn-/ (frontiers) **1** N-COUNT A **frontier** is a border between two countries. [BRIT; AM usually **border**] ❏ *It wasn't difficult then to cross the frontier.* **2** N-COUNT When you are talking about the western part of America before the twentieth century, you use **frontier** to refer to the area beyond the part settled by Europeans. ❏ *...a far-flung outpost on the frontier.* **3** N-COUNT The **frontiers** of something, especially knowledge, are the limits to which it extends. ❏ *...pushing back the frontiers of science.*

front line (front lines) also **front-line 1** N-COUNT The **front line** is the place where two opposing armies are facing each other and where fighting is going on. ❏ *...a massive concentration of soldiers on the front line.* **2** PHRASE Someone who is **in the front line** has to play a very important part in defending or achieving something. ❏ *Information officers are in the front line of putting across government policies.*

front-page ADJ A **front-page** article or picture appears on the front page of a newspaper because it is very important or interesting. [ADJ n] ❏ *...a front-page article in last week's paper.*

front-runner (front-runners) N-COUNT In a competition or contest, the **front-runner** is the person who seems most likely to win it. ❏ *Neither of the front-runners in the presidential election is a mainstream politician.*

frost /frɒst, BRIT frɒst/ (frosts) N-VAR When there is **frost** or a **frost**, the temperature outside falls below freezing point and the ground becomes covered in ice crystals. ❏ *There is frost in the ground and snow is forecast.*

1 가산명사 앞면, 앞 ❏ 한 남자가 안락의자에 앉아 있었고, 다른 남자는 책상 앞에 앉아 있었다. ❏ 그 줄의 맨 앞에 서라. **2** 가산명사 정면 ❏ 그 집 정면엔 큰 베란다가 달려 있었다. **3** 단수명사 앞 몸의 앞부분 ❏ 아이가 엎드려 있을 때는 고개를 들고 쳐다볼 수 있도록 뭘 들고 보여 주어라. **4** 형용사 앞쪽 ❏ 나는 앞쪽 현관의 그곳으로 나갔다. ❏ 그 애는 겨우 여섯 살이었고 아직 앞니가 빠져 있었다. **5** 형용사 맨 앞의 ❏ 가디언 지의 제일 면에는 두 외무 장관의 사진이 실려 있다. **6** 가산명사 전선 ❏ 소냐의 남편은 전선에서 싸우고 있다. **7** 가산명사 분야 ❏ 광범위한 학문 분야에 걸친 연구 **8** 가산명사 태도, 외양 ❏ 마이클은 대외적으로 용감한 태도를 유지했다. **9** 가산명사 위장 단체 ❏ 경찰에 의해 나중에 범죄 조직의 위장 단체로 밝혀진 한 회사 **10** 가산명사 (기상의) 전선 ❏ 그 눈이 전선이 다가오고 고기압 영역이 자리를 잡는 듯했다. **11** 구 전방에 있는, 앞서 가는 ❏ 경찰관들이 속도를 내거나 앞서 가는 차와 너무 가깝게 차를 모는 난폭한 자동차 운전자들을 대상으로 강력한 단속을 펼칠 것이다. **12** 구 선두에 ❏ 리처드 던우디는 기수 선수권 경주에서 선두에 있다. **13** 구 ~의 앞에 ❏ 그녀는 화장대 거울 앞에 앉아 거울에 비친 자신의 모습을 바라보았다. ❏ 무언가가 내 차 앞으로 돌진하더니, 내 차에 치였다. **14** 구 ~의 면전에서 ❏ 그들은 자녀들 앞에서는 절대 다투지 않았다.

형용사 정면의 [격식체] ❏ 군 지도자들은 반군의 정면 공격을 예상하지 않고 있다.

단수명사 프런트 [주로 미국영어; 영국영어 reception] ❏ 호텔 프런트에 전화를 해서 이른 아침 기상 전화를 취소해라.

1 가산명사 국경 [영국영어; 미국영어 대개 border] ❏ 당시 그 국경을 넘는 건 어려운 일이 아니었다. **2** 가산명사 (미국 개척 시대의 미개척지와 개척지의) 변경 ❏ 변경의 오지에 있던 식민지 **3** 가산명사 한계 ❏ 과학의 한계를 밀어젖히며

1 가산명사 최전방 ❏ 병력의 대대적인 최전방 집중 배치 **2** 구 최전선에서 ❏ 정보 장교들은 정부 정책들을 전달하는 최전선에 서 있다.

형용사 신문 1면에 실을 만한 ❏ 지난주 신문에 실렸던 제1면 기사

가산명사 선두 주자 ❏ 대통령 선거전의 선두 주자 두 사람 다 주류 정치인이 아니다.

가산명사 또는 불가산명사 서리 ❏ 땅에 서리가 내렸고 눈이 온다는 예보가 있다.

frost|ing /frɔstɪŋ, BRIT frɒstɪŋ/ N-UNCOUNT **Frosting** is a sweet substance made from powdered sugar that is used to cover and decorate cakes. [AM; BRIT usually **icing**] ❑ ...a huge pastry with green frosting on it.

frosty /frɔsti, BRIT frɒsti/ (**frostier, frostiest**) ◼ ADJ If the weather is **frosty**, the temperature is below freezing. ❑ ...sharp, frosty nights. ◼ ADJ You describe the ground or an object as **frosty** when it is covered with frost. ❑ The street was deserted except for a cat lifting its paws off the frosty stones.

froth /frɔθ, BRIT frɒθ/ (**froths, frothing, frothed**) ◼ N-UNCOUNT **Froth** is a mass of small bubbles on the surface of a liquid. ❑ ...the froth of bubbles on the top of a glass of beer. ◼ V-I If a liquid **froths**, small bubbles appear on its surface. ❑ The sea froths over my feet.

frown /fraʊn/ (**frowns, frowning, frowned**) V-I When someone **frowns**, their eyebrows become drawn together, because they are annoyed, worried, or puzzled, or because they are concentrating. ❑ Nancy shook her head, frowning. ❑ He frowned at her anxiously. ● N-COUNT **Frown** is also a noun. ❑ There was a deep frown on the boy's face.

▶**frown upon** or **frown on** PHRASAL VERB If something **is frowned upon** or **is frowned on** people disapprove of it. ❑ This practice is frowned upon as being wasteful.

froze /froʊz/ **Froze** is the past tense of **freeze**.

fro|zen /froʊz²n/ ◼ **Frozen** is the past participle of **freeze**. ◼ ADJ If the ground is **frozen** it has become very hard because the weather is very cold. ❑ It was bitterly cold now and the ground was frozen hard. ◼ ADJ **Frozen** food has been preserved by being kept at a very low temperature. ❑ Frozen fish is a very healthy convenience food. ◼ ADJ If you say that you are **frozen**, or a part of your body is **frozen**, you are emphasizing that you feel very cold. [EMPHASIS] ❑ He put one hand up to his frozen face. ❑ I'm frozen to the bone out here. ● PHRASE **Frozen stiff** means the same as **frozen**.

fru|gal /fruːɡ²l/ ◼ ADJ People who are **frugal** or who live **frugal** lives do not eat much or spend much money on themselves. ❑ She lives a frugal life. ● **fru|gal|ity** N-UNCOUNT ❑ We must practise the strictest frugality and economy. ◼ ADJ A **frugal** meal is small and not expensive. ❑ The diet was frugal: cheese and water, rice and beans.

fruit ♦♦◇ /fruːt/ (**fruits, fruiting, fruited**)

> The plural form is usually **fruit**, but can also be **fruits**.

◼ N-VAR **Fruit** or a **fruit** is something which grows on a tree or bush and which contains seeds or a stone covered by a substance that you can eat. ❑ Fresh fruit and vegetables provide fiber and vitamins. ❑ ...bananas and other tropical fruits. ◼ V-I If a plant **fruits**, it produces fruit. ❑ The scientists will study the variety of trees and observe which are fruiting. ◼ N-COUNT The **fruits** or the **fruit of** someone's work or activity are the good things that result from it. ❑ The team have really worked hard and Mansell is enjoying the fruits of that labor. ◼ →see also **kiwi fruit** ◼ PHRASE If the effort that you put into something or a particular way of doing something **bears fruit**, it is successful and produces good results. ❑ Eleanor's work among the women will, I trust, bear fruit. →see **dessert, grain** →see Word Web: **fruit**

fruit|ful /fruːtfəl/ ADJ Something that is **fruitful** produces good and useful results. ❑ We had a long, happy, fruitful relationship.

frui|tion /fruɪʃ²n/ N-UNCOUNT If something comes **to fruition**, it starts to succeed and produce the results that were intended or hoped for. [FORMAL] ❑ These plans take time to come to fruition.

fruit|less /fruːtlɪs/ ADJ **Fruitless** actions, events, or efforts do not achieve anything at all. ❑ It was a fruitless search.

fruity /fruːti/ (**fruitier, fruitiest**) ◼ ADJ Something that is **fruity** smells or tastes of fruit. ❑ This shampoo smells fruity and leaves the hair beautifully silky. ◼ ADJ A **fruity** voice or laugh is pleasantly rich and deep. ❑ Jerrold laughed again, a solid, fruity laugh.

frus|trate ♦◇◇ /frʌstreɪt, BRIT frʌstreɪt/ (**frustrates, frustrating, frustrated**) ◼ V-T If something **frustrates** you, it upsets or angers you because you are unable to do anything about the problems it creates. ❑ These questions frustrated me. ● **frus|trat|ed** ADJ ❑ Roberta felt frustrated and angry. ● **frus|tra|tion** /frʌstreɪʃ²n/ (**frustrations**) N-VAR ❑ The results show the level of frustration among hospital doctors. ◼ V-T If someone or something **frustrates** a plan or attempt to do something, they prevent it from succeeding. ❑ The government has deliberately frustrated his efforts to gain work permits for his foreign staff.

frus|trat|ing /frʌstreɪtɪŋ/ ADJ Something that is **frustrating** annoys you or makes you angry because you cannot do anything about the problems it causes. ❑ The current situation is very frustrating for us.

불가산명사 당의(糖衣) [미국영어; 영국영어 대개 **icing**] ❑ 초록색 당의가 얹힌 커다란 패스트리

◼ 형용사 매우 추운 ❑ 살을 에는 듯이 매우 추운 밤 ◼ 형용사 서리로 덮인 ❑ 서리 앉은 돌멩이들이 발이 시려 피하는 고양이 한 마리 외에는 거리가 텅 비어 있었다.

◼ 불가산명사 거품 ❑ 맥주잔 위에 이는 거품 ◼ 자동사 거품을 내다 ❑ 내 발 위로 바다가 거품을 일으키며 밀려온다.

자동사 눈살을 찌푸리다, 얼굴을 찌푸리다 ❑ 낸시는 고개를 흔들며 눈살을 찌푸렸다. ❑ 그는 그녀를 향해 걱정스러운 듯 눈살을 찌푸렸다. ● 가산명사 얼굴을 찡그림 ❑ 그 소년은 심하게 얼굴을 찡그렸다.

구동사 불만을 사다, 찬성을 못 받다 ❑ 이 연습이 헛된 것이라는 불만 섞인 소리가 있다.

freeze의 과거

◼ freeze의 과거 분사 ◼ 형용사 얼어 붙은 ❑ 이제 날이 몹시 추웠고 땅은 꽁꽁 얼어 붙어 있었다. ◼ 형용사 냉동된 ❑ 냉동 생선은 매우 위생적이고 편리한 식품이다. ◼ 형용사 꽁꽁 언 [강조] ❑ 그는 자신의 꽁꽁 언 얼굴에 손을 갖다 댔다. ❑ 여기 나와 있으니 뼛속까지 얼어 붙는 것 같다. ● 구 꽁꽁 언

◼ 형용사 검소한 ❑ 그녀는 검소하게 산다. ● 검소함 불가산명사 ❑ 우리는 가장 엄격하게 검소함과 절약을 실천해야 한다. ◼ 형용사 소박한 ❑ 그 음식은 소박했다. 치즈, 물, 밥과 콩이었다.

복수형은 대개 fruit이지만 fruits도 쓸 수 있다.

◼ 가산명사 또는 불가산명사 과일 ❑ 신선한 과일과 채소는 섬유질과 비타민을 제공한다. ❑ 바나나와 다른 열대 과일들 ◼ 자동사 열매를 맺다 ❑ 과학자들은 다양한 나무를 연구해서 그 중 어느 것이 열매를 맺는지 관찰할 것이다. ◼ 가산명사 성과 ❑ 그 팀은 정말로 열심히 일했고 만셀은 그 노력의 성과를 만끽하고 있다. ◼ 구 결실을 맺다 ❑ 그 여자들 가운데 엘리노의 작품은, 내가 믿건대, 결실을 맺을 거야.

형용사 유익한, 생산적인 ❑ 우리는 오랫동안 행복하고 유익한 관계를 유지했다.

불가산명사 결실 맺기, 실현 [격식체] ❑ 이 계획들은 실현되기까지 시간이 좀 걸린다.

형용사 소득이 없는 ❑ 그것은 소득이 없는 조사였다.

◼ 형용사 과일향이 나는, 과일 맛이 나는 ❑ 이 샴푸를 사용하면 머리에서 과일향이 나고 머리를 아주 보드랍게 해 준다. ◼ 형용사 감미로운 (소리) ❑ 제롤드가 다시 웃었는데 윤기 나고 감미로운 웃음소리였다.

◼ 타동사 좌절시키다 ❑ 이 문제들 때문에 나는 좌절감을 느꼈다. ● 좌절한 형용사 ❑ 로베르타는 좌절하고 분노했다. ● 좌절 가산명사 또는 불가산명사 ❑ 그 결과는 병원 의사들의 좌절감이 어느 정도인지 보여 준다. ◼ 타동사 방해하다, 좌절시키다 ❑ 정부가 외국인 직원에 대한 노동 허가증을 받으려는 그의 노력을 의도적으로 방해하고 있다.

형용사 좌절감을 주는 ❑ 현 상황은 우리에게 대단히 좌절감을 준다.

Word Web   fruit

Fruit only appear on **flowering plants**. They are fleshy and **sweet** and contain **seeds** or a **stone** or pit. The fruit serves the plant in two ways. First, it protects seeds from damage. Secondly, it helps make sure seeds are carried to new places. After an animal eats a seed, it passes through its body unharmed. When the animal leaves droppings in a new location, the seed may start a new plant there. Fruits contain a **sugar** called fructose—an important source of energy for animals and humans. But not all fruits are sweet. **Lemons**, for example, are **sour**.

a
b
c
d
e
f
g
h
i
j
k
l
m
n
o
p
q
r
s
t
u
v
w
x
y
z

fry ◆◇◇ /fraɪ/ (**fries, frying, fried**) ◼ V-T When you **fry** food, you cook it in a pan that contains hot fat or oil. ◻ *Fry the breadcrumbs until golden brown.* ◻ N-PLURAL **Fries** are the same as **French fries.** →see **cook**

◼ 타동사 튀기다 ◻ 노릇노릇해질 때까지 빵 부스러기를 튀겨라. ◻ 복수명사 감자튀김

fry|ing pan (**frying pans**) N-COUNT A **frying pan** is a flat metal pan with a long handle, in which you fry food. →see **pan**

가산명사 프라이팬

ft ft is a written abbreviation for **feet** or **foot.** ◻ *Flying at 1,000 ft, he heard a peculiar noise from the rotors.*

피트 ◻ 1,000피트 상공에 이르자, 그는 회전 날개에서 이상한 소음이 나는 걸 들었다.

fuck /fʌk/ (**fucks, fucking, fucked**)

> **Fuck** is a vulgar and offensive word which you should avoid using.

fuck은 쓰지 말아야 할 비속어, 모욕어이다.

EXCLAM **Fuck** is used to express anger or annoyance.

감탄사 제기랄

▶**fuck off** [VULGAR, FEELINGS] PHRASAL VERB Telling someone to **fuck off** is an insulting way of telling them to go away. [VULGAR] [usu imper, v P]

[비속어, 감정 개입] 구동사 꺼져 버려 [비속어]

fuck|ing /fʌkɪŋ/ ADJ **Fucking** is used by some people to emphasize a word or phrase, especially when they are feeling angry or annoyed. [VULGAR, EMPHASIS] [ADJ n; ADV: ADV adj]

형용사 지긋지긋한 [비속어, 강조]

fudge /fʌdʒ/ (**fudges, fudging, fudged**) ◼ N-UNCOUNT **Fudge** is a soft brown sweet that is made from butter, cream, and sugar. ◻ V-T If you **fudge** something, you avoid making a clear and definite decision, distinction, or statement about it. ◻ *Both have fudged their calculations and avoided specifics.*

◼ 불가산명사 퍼지 (버터, 크림, 설탕으로 만든 단것) ◻ 타동사 얼버무리다 ◻ 양측 모두 자신들의 추정을 얼버무리고 세부적인 내용은 피하고 있다.

fuel ◆◆◇ /fyuəl/ (**fuels, fueling, fueled**) [BRIT, sometimes AM **fuelling, fuelled**] ◼ N-MASS **Fuel** is a substance such as coal, oil, or gasoline that is burned to provide heat or power. ◻ *They ran out of fuel.* ◻ V-T To **fuel** a situation means to make it become worse or more intense. ◻ *The result will inevitably fuel speculation about the Prime Minister's future.* →see **car, energy, oil**

[영국영어, 미국영어 가끔 fuelling, fuelled] ◼ 물질명사 연료 ◻ 그들은 연료가 바닥났다. ◻ 타동사 부채질하다 ◻ 그 결과는 어쩔 수 없이 총리의 미래에 대한 억측들을 부채질할 것이다.

> **Word Partnership** fuel의 연어
>
> N. **cost of** fuel, fuel **oil**, fuel **pump**, fuel **shortage**, fuel **supply**, fuel **tank** ◼
>
> ADJ. **unleaded** fuel ◼

fu|gi|tive /fyudʒɪtɪv/ (**fugitives**) N-COUNT A **fugitive** is someone who is running away or hiding, usually in order to avoid being caught by the police. ◻ *The rebel leader was a fugitive from justice.*

가산명사 도망자 ◻ 반군 지도자는 도피 중인 범죄자였다.

ful|fill ◆◇◇ /fʊlfɪl/ (**fulfills, fulfilling, fulfilled**) [BRIT usually **fulfil**] ◼ V-T If you **fulfill** something such as a promise, dream, or hope, you do what you said or hoped you would do. ◻ *President Kaunda fulfilled his promise of announcing a date for the referendum.* ◻ V-T To **fulfill** a task, role, or requirement means to do or be what is required, necessary, or expected. ◻ *Without them you will not be able to fulfill the tasks you have before you.* ◻ V-T If something **fulfills** you, or if you **fulfill yourself**, you feel happy and satisfied with what you are doing or with what you have achieved. ◻ *The war was the biggest thing in her life and nothing after that quite fulfilled her.* ● **ful|filled** ADJ ◻ *She has courageously continued to lead a fulfilled life.* ● **ful|fil|ling** ADJ ◻ *...a fulfilling career.*

[영국영어 대개 fulfil] ◼ 타동사 이행하다 ◻ 카운다 대통령은 국민 투표 일자를 발표하겠다는 약속을 이행했다. ◻ 타동사 달성하다 ◻ 그들 없이는 당신 앞에 놓인 직무를 달성할 수 없을 것이다. ◻ 타동사 만족시키다; 만족하다 ◻ 그 전쟁은 그녀의 생애 중 가장 큰 사건이었고 그 후 어떤 것도 그녀를 만족시키지 못했다. ● 만족스러운, 충족된 형용사 ◻ 그녀는 용감하게 충족된 삶을 계속 살아오고 있다. ● 만족감을 주는 형용사 ◻ 만족감을 주는 직업

> **Word Partnership** fulfill의 연어
>
> N. fulfill *your* destiny, fulfill a dream, fulfill a promise, fulfill a role ◼
> fulfill obligations ◻

ful|fill|ment /fʊlfɪlmənt/ [BRIT usually **fulfilment**] ◼ N-UNCOUNT **Fulfillment** is a feeling of satisfaction that you get from doing or achieving something, especially something useful. ◻ *...professional fulfillment.* ◻ N-UNCOUNT The **fulfillment of** a promise, threat, request, hope, or duty is the event or act of it happening or being made to happen. ◻ *Visiting Angkor was the fulfillment of a childhood dream.*

[영국영어 대개 fulfilment] ◼ 불가산명사 성취감 ◻ 직업상의 성취감 ◻ 불가산명사 실현 ◻ 앙코르를 가 보는 것은 어린 시절의 꿈을 실현하는 것이었다.

full ◆◆◆ /fʊl/ (**fuller, fullest**) ◼ ADJ If something is **full**, it contains as much of a substance or as many objects as it can. ◻ *Once the container is full, it stays shut until you turn it clockwise.* ◻ ADJ If a place or thing **is full of** things or people, it contains a large number of them. [v-link ADJ of n] ◻ *The case was full of clothes.* ◻ *The streets are still full of debris from two nights of rioting.* ◻ ADJ If someone or something **is full of** a particular feeling or quality, they have a lot of it. [v-link ADJ of n] ◻ *I feel full of confidence and so open to possibilities.* ◻ *Mom's face was full of pain.* ◻ ADJ You say that a place or vehicle is **full** when there is no space left in it for any more people or things. ◻ *The parking lot was full when I left about 10:45.* ◻ *They stay here a few hours before being sent to refugee camps, which are now almost full.* ◻ ADJ If your hands or arms are **full**, you are carrying or holding as much as you can carry. [v-link ADJ] ◻ *Sylvia entered, her arms full of packages.* ◻ ADJ If you feel **full**, you have eaten or drunk so much that you do not want anything else. [v-link ADJ] ◻ *It's healthy to eat when I'm hungry and to stop when I'm full.* ● **full|ness** N-UNCOUNT ◻ *High fiber diets give the feeling of fullness.* ◻ ADJ You use **full** before a noun to indicate that you are referring to all the details, things, or people that it can possibly include. [ADJ n] ◻ *May I have your full name?* ◻ ADJ **Full** is used to describe a sound, light, or physical force which is being produced with the greatest possible power or intensity. [ADJ n] ◻ *From his study came the sound of Mahler, playing at full volume.* ◻ *Officials say the operation will be carried out in full daylight.* ◻ ADJ You use **full** to emphasize the completeness, intensity, or extent of something. [EMPHASIS] [ADJ n] ◻ *We should conserve oil and gas by making full use of other energy sources.* ◻ *The lane leading to the farm was in full view of the house windows.* ◻ ADJ A **full** statement or report contains a lot of information and detail. ◻ *Mr. Primakov gave a full account of his meeting with the President.* ◻ ADJ If you say that

◼ 형용사 가득 찬 ◻ 그 용기가 일단 가득 차면, 시계 방향으로 돌려야 열수 있다. ◻ 형용사 ~으로 가득 차 있는 ◻ 그 상자에는 옷이 가득 들어 있었다. ◻ 그 거리는 이틀 밤의 폭동으로 인해 아직도 이곳저곳 파편 투성이다. ◻ 형용사 ~이 넘치는 ◻ 나는 자신감이 넘치는 기분이고 그래서 모든 가능성을 열어 두었다. ◻ 어머니의 얼굴에 고통이 가득했다. ◻ 형용사 만원인 ◻ 10시 45분쯤 내가 떠날 때 그 주차장은 만원이었다. ◻ 그들은 현재 거의 만원 상태에 이른 피난민 수용소로 보내지기 전에 여기서 몇 시간 동안 머무른다. ◻ 형용사 꽉 찬, 가득 안은 ◻ 실비아가 들어왔는데, 양팔로 꾸러미를 가득 안고 있었다. ◻ 형용사 배부른 ◻ 배고플 때 식사를 하고 배부르면 그만 먹는 것이 건강에 좋다. ● 포만감 불가산명사 ◻ 고섬유질 식품은 포만감을 준다. ◻ 형용사 모든, 정식의 ◻ 당신의 지원이 받아들여지면 모든 세부 내용을 모두 드릴 겁니다. ◻ 정식 이름이 어떻게 되시죠? ◻ 형용사 최대의, 한껏의 ◻ 그의 서재에서 최대 음량으로 틀어 놓은 말러의 곡이 흘러나왔다. ◻ 관리들은 그 작전이 한낮에 수행될 것이라고 말한다. ◻ 형용사 충분한, 완전한 [강조] ◻ 우리는 대체 에너지원을 충분히 이용함으로써 석유와 가스를 절약해야 한다. ◻ 그 농장으로 가는 차로는 그 집의 창문에서 완전히 보였다. ◻ 형용사 자세한 ◻ 프리마코프 씨는 대통령과의 회동에 대해서 자세히 설명을 했다. ◻ 형용사 충실한 [마음에 듦]

someone has or leads a **full** life, you approve of the fact that they are always busy and do a lot of different things. [APPROVAL] ❑ *You will be successful in whatever you do and you will have a very full and interesting life.* 12 ADV You use **full** to emphasize the force or directness with which someone or something is hit or looked at. [EMPHASIS] [ADV prep] ❑ *She kissed him full on the mouth.* 13 ADJ You use **full** to refer to something which gives you all the rights, status, or importance for a particular position or activity, rather than just some of them. [ADJ n] ❑ *How did the meeting go, did you get your full membership?* 14 ADJ A **full** flavor is strong and rich. [ADJ n] ❑ *Italian plum tomatoes have a full flavor, and are best for cooking.* 15 ADJ If you describe a part of someone's body as **full**, you mean that it is rounded and rather large. ❑ *The Juno Collection specializes in large sizes for ladies with a fuller figure.* 16 ADJ A **full** skirt or sleeve is wide and has been made from a lot of fabric. ❑ *My wedding dress has a very full skirt so I need to wear a good quality net petticoat.* ● **full|ness** N-UNCOUNT ❑ *The coat has raglan sleeves, and is cut to give fullness at the back.* 17 ADJ When there is a **full** moon, the moon appears as a bright, complete circle. ❑ *...those nights when the moon is full.* 18 PHRASE You say that something has been done or described **in full** when everything that was necessary has been done or described. ❑ *The medical experts have yet to report in full.* 19 PHRASE If you say that a person **knows full well** that something is true, especially something unpleasant, you are emphasizing that they are definitely aware of it, although they may behave as if they are not. [EMPHASIS] ❑ *He knew full well he'd be ashamed of himself later.* 20 PHRASE Something that is done or experienced **to the full** is done to as great an extent as is possible. ❑ *She probably has a good mind, which should be used to the full.* 21 **full blast** →see **blast**. to **have** your **hands full** →see **hand**. **in full swing** →see **swing**

Thesaurus   *full*의 참조어

ADJ.   loaded, packed full of, packed with 2 4 5
        bursting *with* 2 4

---

full-blown ADJ **Full-blown** means having all the characteristics of a particular type of thing or person. [ADJ n] ❑ *Before becoming a full-blown director, he worked as the film editor on Citizen Kane.*

full board also **full-board** N-UNCOUNT If the price at a hotel includes **full board**, it includes all your meals. [mainly BRIT] ❑ *Prices, from ?99, include full board, flights and all taxes.*

full-length 1 ADJ A **full-length** book, record, or movie is the normal length, rather than being shorter than normal. [ADJ n] ❑ *...his first full-length recording in well over a decade.* 2 ADJ A **full-length** coat or skirt is long enough to reach the lower part of a person's leg, almost to the ankles. A full-length sleeve reaches a person's wrist. [ADJ n] 3 ADJ **Full-length** curtains or other furnishings reach to the floor. [ADJ n] 4 ADJ A **full-length** mirror or painting shows the whole of a person. [ADJ n] 5 ADJ Someone who is lying **full-length**, is lying down flat and stretched out. [ADV after v] ❑ *She stretched herself out full-length.*

full-scale 1 ADJ **Full-scale** means as complete, intense, or great in extent as possible. [ADJ n] ❑ *...the possibility of a full-scale nuclear war.* 2 ADJ A **full-scale** drawing or model is the same size as the thing that it represents. [ADJ n] ❑ *...working, full-scale prototypes.*

full-size or **full-sized** ADJ A **full-size** or **full-sized** model or picture is the same size as the thing or person that it represents. [ADJ n] ❑ *I made a full-size cardboard model.*

full stop (**full stops**) N-COUNT A **full stop** is the punctuation mark. which you use at the end of a sentence when it is not a question or exclamation. [BRIT; AM **period**]

full-time also **full time** 1 ADJ **Full-time** work or study involves working or studying for the whole of each normal working week rather than for part of it. ❑ *...a full-time job.* ● ADV **Full-time** is also an adverb. [ADV after v] ❑ *Deirdre works full-time.* 2 N-UNCOUNT In games such as soccer, **full-time** is the end of a match. [BRIT] ❑ *The score at full-time was Arsenal 1, Sampdoria 1.*

full up also **full-up** 1 ADJ Something that is **full up** has no space left for any more people or things. [v-link ADJ] ❑ *The prisons are all full up.* 2 ADJ If you are **full up** you have eaten or drunk so much that you do not want to eat or drink anything else. [INFORMAL] [v-link ADJ] ❑ *He found that he was so full-up from all the liquid in his diet that he hardly had room for his evening meal.*

ful|ly ◆◇◇ /fʊli/ 1 ADV **Fully** means to the greatest degree or extent possible. ❑ *She was fully aware of my thoughts.* 2 ADV You use **fully** to say that a process is completely finished. [ADV with v] ❑ *He had still not fully recovered.* 3 ADV If you describe, answer, or deal with something **fully**, you leave out nothing that should be mentioned or dealt with. [ADV with v] ❑ *Fiers promised to testify fully and truthfully.*

Word Partnership   *fully*의 연어

ADJ.   fully **adjustable**, fully **aware**, fully **clothed**, fully **functional**, fully
        operational, fully **prepared** 1
V.   fully **agree**, fully **expect**, fully **extend**, fully **understand** 1
        fully **decide**, fully **develop**, fully **heal**, fully **realize**, fully **recover** 2
        fully **explain** 3

---

fully-fledged ADJ **Fully-fledged** means complete or fully developed. [ADJ n] ❑ *Hungary is to have a fully-fledged Stock Exchange from today.*

❑ 너는 무엇을 하든지 성공할 것이고 매우 충실하고 흥미롭게 살 거야. 12 부사 힘껏 [강조] ❑ 그녀는 그의 입에 힘껏 키스했다. 13 형용사 정식의 ❑ 모임은 어땠어? 정회원이 되었니? 14 형용사 풍부한 ❑ 이탈리아 플럼 토마토는 향이 풍부하고 요리에 안성맞춤이다. 15 형용사 통통한 ❑ 주노 컬렉션은 통통한 몸매를 지닌 여성들을 위해 치수가 큰 옷을 전문으로 한다. 16 형용사 품이 넉넉한 ❑ 내 웨딩드레스의 치맛자락은 품이 아주 넉넉해서 고급 망사 페티코트를 입어야 한다. ● 넉넉함 불가산명사 ❑ 그 코트는 래글런형 소매가 달려 있고, 넉넉함을 주기 위해 뒤쪽이 트여 있다. 17 형용사 보름날의 ❑ 만월이 되는 기간의 그 밤들. 18 구 상세히 ❑ 의료 전문가들은 아직도 상세한 보고를 하지 않고 있다. 19 구 충분히 알고 있다 [강조] ❑ 그는 후에 자기 자신을 부끄러워 할 것이라는 것을 충분히 알고 있었다. 20 구 최대한 ❑ 그녀는 아마도 마음씨가 고울 것이니, 최대한 이를 이용하는 게 좋겠다.

형용사 본격적인 ❑ 본격적으로 감독이 되기 전에, 그는 '시민 케인'에서 영화 편집을 맡았다.

불가산명사 세 끼 식사가 딸린 숙박 [주로 영국영어] ❑ 99파운드부터 시작하는 금액에는 세 끼 식사가 딸린 숙박, 항공료, 일체의 세금이 포함된다.

1 형용사 전체의, 생략 없는 ❑ 십 년이 족히 넘는 기간 동안 처음으로 그가 전곡을 녹음함 2 형용사 발목까지 내려오는 (외투나 치마); 손목까지 내려오는 (소매) 3 형용사 바닥까지 내려오는 (커튼) 4 형용사 전신의 5 부사 팔다리를 쭉 뻗고 ❑ 그녀는 팔다리를 쭉 뻗었다.

1 형용사 전면적인 ❑ 전면적인 핵전쟁의 가능성 2 형용사 실물 크기의 ❑ 작동하고 있는 실물 크기의 시제품

형용사 실제 크기의 ❑ 나는 판지로 실제 크기의 모형을 만들었다.

가산명사 마침표 [영국영어; 미국영어 **period**]

1 형용사 상근직의 ❑ 상근직 ● 부사 상근 ❑ 데이드레는 상근 직원으로 일한다. 2 불가산명사 경기 종료 [영국영어] ❑ 경기 종료 시 점수는 아스날 1점, 삼프도리아 1점이었다.

1 형용사 꽉꽉 찬 ❑ 그 교도소들은 전부 꽉꽉 찼다. 2 형용사 배부른, 독까지 찬 [비격식체] ❑ 그는 음식에 나온 음료로 배가 불러서 저녁 식사를 거의 할 수 없다는 것을 알게 되었다.

1 부사 완전히 ❑ 그녀는 내 생각을 완전히 알고 있었다. 2 부사 완전히 ❑ 그는 아직도 완전히 회복되지 못했었다. 3 부사 완전히 ❑ 피어스는 완전히 그리고 충실히 증언하기로 약속했다.

형용사 다 자란, 완전히 갖춰진 ❑ 헝가리는 오늘부터 완전히 갖춰진 주식 시장을 갖게 될 것이다.

A

fum|ble /fʌmbᵊl/ (**fumbles, fumbling, fumbled**) **1** V-I If you **fumble for** something or **fumble with** something, you try and reach for it or hold it in a clumsy way. □ *She crept from the bed and fumbled for her dressing gown.* **2** V-T/V-I When you are trying to say something, if you **fumble for** the right words, you speak in a clumsy and unclear way. □ *I fumbled for something to say.*

B

1 자동사 더듬어 찾다 □ 그녀는 침대에서 기어 나와 실내복을 더듬어 찾았다. **2** 타동사/자동사 말을 더듬다 □ 나는 더듬거리며 무슨 말인가 하려고 했다.

fume /fyum/ (**fumes, fuming, fumed**) **1** N-PLURAL **Fumes** are the unpleasant and often unhealthy smoke and gases that are produced by fires or by things such as chemicals, fuel, or cooking. □ *...car exhaust fumes.* **2** V-T/V-I If you **fume** over something, you express annoyance and anger about it. □ *He was still fuming over the remark.*

C

1 복수명사 가스, 연기 **2** 자동차 배기가스 **2** 타동사/자동사 성을 내다 □ 그는 여전히 그 말에 대해 성을 내고 있었다.

fun ♦♦◇ /fʌn/ **1** N-UNCOUNT You refer to an activity or situation as **fun** if you think it is pleasant and enjoyable and it causes you to feel happy. □ *This year promises to be terrifically good fun.* □ *It could be fun to watch them.* **2** N-UNCOUNT If you say that someone is **fun**, you mean that you enjoy being with them because they say and do interesting or amusing things. [APPROVAL] □ *Liz was wonderful fun to be with.* **3** ADJ If you describe something as a **fun** thing, you mean that you think it is enjoyable. If you describe someone as a **fun** person, you mean that you enjoy being with them. [INFORMAL] [ADJ n] □ *It was a fun evening.* **4** PHRASE If you do something **for fun** or **for the fun of it**, you do it in order to enjoy yourself rather than because it is important or necessary. □ *We used to drive too fast, just for fun.* **5** PHRASE If you do something **in fun**, you do it as a joke or for amusement, without intending to cause any harm. □ *Don't say such things, even in fun.* **6** PHRASE If you **make fun of** someone or something or **poke fun at** them, you laugh at them, tease them, or make jokes about them in a way that causes them to seem ridiculous. □ *Don't make fun of me.*

D

E

F

1 불가산명사 재미 □ 올해에는 무척 재미있을 거야. □ 그들을 지켜보는 것은 재미있을 거야. **2** 불가산명사 재미있는 사람 [마음에 듦] □ 리즈와 같이 있으면 아주 재미있었다. **3** 형용사 즐거운 [비격식체] □ 즐거운 저녁이었어. **4** 구 재미로 □ 우리는 재미 삼아 차를 지나치게 빨리 몰곤 했다. **5** 구 장난으로 □ 그런 말 하지 마라. 설령 장난이라 해도. **6** 구 놀리다 □ 날 놀리지 마.

G

H

Thesaurus   *fun*의 참조어

N.	amusement, enjoyment, play; (ant.) misery **1**
ADJ.	amusing, enjoyable, happy, pleasant; (ant.) boring **3**

Word Partnership   *fun*의 연어

V.	have fun, join the fun, ought to/should be fun, fun to watch **1 3**
N.	*your* idea of fun, fun part, sense of fun, fun stuff, fun time **1**

I

J

K

---

func|tion ♦♦◇ /fʌŋkʃᵊn/ (**functions, functioning, functioned**) **1** N-COUNT The **function** of something or someone is the useful thing that they do or are intended to do. □ *The main function of the merchant banks is to raise capital for industry.* **2** V-I If a machine or system **is functioning**, it is working or operating. □ *The authorities say the prison is now functioning normally.* **3** V-I If someone or something **functions as** a particular thing, they do the work or fulfill the purpose of that thing. □ *On weekdays, one third of the room functions as workspace.* **4** N-COUNT A **function** is a large formal dinner or party. □ *...a private function hosted by one of his students.*

L

M

N

1 가산명사 기능 □ 상업 은행의 주요 기능은 산업 자본을 모으는 것이다. **2** 자동사 작동되다, 운영되다 □ 정부 관계자는 이제 그 교도소가 정상적으로 운영되고 있다고 한다. **3** 자동사 운용되다, 이용되다 □ 주중에는 그 방의 3분의 1이 작업장으로 이용된다. **4** 가산명사 공식 만찬, 공식 연회 □ 그의 학생 중 한 명이 사적으로 주최한 만찬

Thesaurus   *function*의 참조어

N.	action, duty, job, responsibility **1**
	celebration, gathering, occasion **4**
V.	operate, perform, work **3**

O

P

---

func|tion|al /fʌŋkʃᵊnᵊl/ **1** ADJ **Functional** things are useful rather than decorative. □ *...modern, functional furniture.* **2** ADJ **Functional** equipment works or operates in the way that it is supposed to. □ *We have fully functional smoke alarms on all staircases.*

Q

R

1 형용사 기능적인 □ 현대적이고 기능적인 가구 **2** 형용사 정상 작동되는 □ 정상 작동되는 화재경보기가 모든 계단에 설치되어 있습니다.

func|tion key (**function keys**) N-COUNT **Function keys** are the keys along the top of a computer keyboard, usually numbered from F1 to F12. Each key is designed to make a particular thing happen when you press it. [COMPUTING] □ *Just hit the F5 function key to send and receive your e-mails.*

S

가산명사 기능키 [컴퓨터] □ 이메일을 보내거나 받으려면 에프(F)5 기능키를 치기만 하세요.

fund ♦♦♦ /fʌnd/ (**funds, funding, funded**) **1** N-PLURAL **Funds** are amounts of money that are available to be spent, especially money that is given to an organization or person for a particular purpose. □ *The concert will raise funds for research into AIDS.* →see also **fund-raising 2** N-COUNT A **fund** is an amount of money that is collected or saved for a particular purpose. □ *...a scholarship fund for undergraduate engineering students.* →see also **trust fund 3** V-T When a person or organization **funds** something, they provide money for it. □ *The Bush Foundation has funded a variety of faculty development programs.* □ *The airport is being privately funded by a construction group.*

T

U

V

1 복수명사 기금 □ 그 콘서트로 에이즈 연구 기금을 조성할 것이다. **2** 가산명사 기금 □ 공과 대학 학부생을 위한 장학 기금 **3** 타동사 자금을 제공하다 □ 부시 재단은 다양한 교원 연수 개발 프로그램에 자금을 제공해 왔다. □ 한 건설 그룹이 사적으로 그 공항에 자금을 제공하고 있다.

fun|da|men|tal ♦♦◇ /fʌndəmɛntᵊl/ **1** ADJ You use **fundamental** to describe things, activities, and principles that are very important or essential. They affect the basic nature of other things or are the most important element upon which other things depend. □ *Our constitution embodies all the fundamental principles of democracy.* □ *A fundamental human right is being withheld from these people.* **2** ADJ You use **fundamental** to describe something which exists at a deep and basic level, and is therefore likely to continue. □ *But on this question, the two leaders have very fundamental differences.* **3** ADJ If one thing **is fundamental to** another, it is absolutely necessary to it, and the second thing cannot exist, succeed, or be imagined without it. [v-link ADJ to n] □ *He believes better relations with China are fundamental to the well-being of the area.* **4** ADJ You can use **fundamental** to show that you are referring to what you consider to be the most important aspect of a situation, and that you are not concerned with

W

X

Y

Z

1 형용사 기본적인 □ 우리의 헌법은 민주주의의 모든 기본 원칙을 구현하고 있다. □ 그 사람들은 기본 인권을 유린당하고 있다. **2** 형용사 근본적인 □ 그러나 이 사안에 관해서는 두 지도자가 근본적으로 견해를 달리하고 있다. **3** 형용사 -에 필수 불가결한 □ 그는 그 지역의 번영을 위해서는 중국과의 우호적인 관계가 필수 불가결하다고 믿고 있다. **4** 형용사 근본적인 □ 그들이 현실과 허구를 구별할 능력이 없다는 것이 가장 근본적인 문제점이다.

Word Web — funeral

Many modern **funeral** practices may have their roots in ancient beliefs. Today's **wake** resembles the early custom of providing plentiful food for the departed. In some cultures the food was meant to pacify the spirits. In others, it was for the **deceased** to eat in the afterlife. In some societies **mourners** waited by the **dead** in hopes that the person would return to life. People brought flowers to please the spirit of the dead person. **Ceremonial** candles resemble the fires lit to protect the living from dangerous spirits. Wearing special clothing was also supposed to confuse the spirits.

less important details. [ADJ n] ❏ *The fundamental problem lies in their inability to distinguish between reality and invention.*

Thesaurus — fundamental의 참조어

ADJ.   basic, essential, necessary, original, primary 1 2 3

fun|da|men|tal|ism /fʌndəmentᵊlɪzəm/ N-UNCOUNT **Fundamentalism** is the belief in the original form of a religion or theory, without accepting any later ideas. ❏ *Religious fundamentalism was spreading in the region.* ● **fun|da|men|tal|ist** (**fundamentalists**) N-COUNT ❏ *...fundamentalist Christians.*

불가산명사 근본주의 ❏ 종교적 근본주의가 그 지역에 번지고 있었다. ● 근본주의자 가산명사 ❏ 기독교 근본주의자들

fun|da|men|tal|ly /fʌndəmentᵊli/ 1 ADV You use **fundamentally** for emphasis when you are stating an opinion, or when you are making an important or general statement about something. [EMPHASIS] [ADV with cl/group] ❏ *Fundamentally, women like him for his sensitivity and charming vulnerability.* 2 ADV You use **fundamentally** to indicate that something affects or relates to the deep, basic nature of something. [ADV with v] ❏ *He disagreed fundamentally with the President's judgment.* ❏ *Environmentalists say the treaty is fundamentally flawed.*

1 부사 기본적으로 [강조] ❏ 기본적으로 여자들은 그의 감수성과 매력적인 유약함 때문에 그를 좋아한다. 2 부사 근본적으로 ❏ 그는 대통령의 판단에 근본적으로 반대했다. ❏ 환경 운동가들은 그 조약에 근본적인 결함이 있다고 주장하고 있다.

fun|da|men|tals /fʌndəmentᵊlz/ N-PLURAL The **fundamentals** of something are its simplest, most important elements, ideas, or principles, in contrast to more complicated or detailed ones. ❏ *They agree on fundamentals, like the need for further political reform.*

복수명사 기본, 기본적인 것 ❏ 그들은 추가 정치 개혁의 필요 같은 기본적인 사안에 합의했다.

fund|ing ◆◇◇ /fʌndɪŋ/ N-UNCOUNT **Funding** is money which a government or organization provides for a particular purpose. ❏ *They hope for government funding for the scheme.*

불가산명사 기금 ❏ 그들은 그 계획에 정부가 기금을 지원해 주길 바라고 있다.

fund|rais|er /fʌndreɪzər/ (**fundraisers**) also **fund-raiser** 1 N-COUNT A **fundraiser** is an event which is intended to raise money for a particular purpose, for example, for a charity. ❏ *Organize a fundraiser for your church.* 2 N-COUNT A **fundraiser** is someone who works to raise money for a particular purpose, for example, for a charity. ❏ *Sir Anthony was a keen fundraiser for the Liberal Democrats.*

1 가산명사 기금 모금 행사 ❏ 여러분들의 교회를 위한 기금 모금 행사를 조직하세요. 2 가산명사 기금 조달자 ❏ 앤소니 경은 자유 민주당의 열성적인 기금 조달자였다.

fund-raising also **fundraising** N-UNCOUNT **Fund-raising** is the activity of collecting money to support a charity or political campaign or organization. ❏ *Encourage her to get involved in fund-raising for charity.*

불가산명사 기금 모금 ❏ 자선 사업을 위한 기금 모금에 그녀가 참여하도록 독려하세요.

fu|ner|al /fyunərəl/ (**funerals**) N-COUNT A **funeral** is the ceremony that is held when the body of someone who has died is buried or cremated. ❏ *His funeral will be on Thursday at Blackburn Cathedral.*
→see Word Web: **funeral**

가산명사 장례식 ❏ 그의 장례식은 목요일 블랙번 대성당에서 있을 것이다.

fun|gus /fʌŋgəs/ (**fungi**) N-MASS A **fungus** is a plant that has no flowers, leaves, or green coloring, such as a mushroom or a toadstool. Other types of fungus such as mold are extremely small and look like a fine powder.
→see Word Web: **fungus**

물질명사 균류(菌類)

funky /fʌŋki/ (**funkier, funkiest**) ADJ **Funky** jazz, blues, or pop music has a very strong, repeated bass part. ❏ *It's a funky sort of rhythm.*

형용사 펑키한 ❏ 이건 약간 펑키한 리듬이다.

fun|nel /fʌnᵊl/ (**funnels, funneling, funneled**) [BRIT, sometimes AM **funnelling, funnelled**] 1 N-COUNT A **funnel** is an object with a wide, circular top and a narrow short tube at the bottom. Funnels are used to pour liquids into containers which have a small opening, for example bottles. ❏ *Rain falls through the funnel into the jar below.* 2 N-COUNT A **funnel** is a metal chimney on a ship or railroad engine powered by steam. ❏ *...a merchantman with three masts and two funnels.* 3 N-COUNT You can describe as a **funnel** something that is narrow, or narrow at one end, through which a substance flows and is directed. ❏ *Along the road, funnels of dark grey smoke rose from Serb villages.* 4 V-T/V-I If something **funnels** somewhere or **is funneled**, it is directed through a

[영국영어, 미국영어 가끔 funnelling] 1 가산명사 깔때기 ❏ 빗물은 깔때기를 통해 밑에 있는 물병으로 들어간다. 2 가산명사 (증기 기관의) 굴뚝 ❏ 세 개의 돛대와 두 개의 굴뚝이 있는 상선 3 가산명사 줄기, 가닥 ❏ 그 길을 따라 세르비아 마을들에서 진회색 연기가 몇 가닥 피어올랐다. 4 타동사/자동사 (좁은 곳을) 지나가다; (좁은 곳을) 지나가게 하다 ❏ 북쪽에서 불어온 바람은 평원을 지나 골짜기 아래로 불었다. 5 타동사 (돈, 물건을) 보내다, (정보를) 흘리다 ❏ 그는 신용카드 정보를 은밀히 위조범들에게 흘렸다.

Word Web — fungus

Some fungi are destructive. For example, **mold** and mildew destroy crops, ruin clothing, cause diseases, and can even lead to death. But many fungi are useful. For instance, a single-cell fungus called **yeast** makes bread rise. Another form of yeast helps wine **ferment**. It turns the sugar in grape juice into alcohol. And **mushrooms** are a part of the diet of people all over the world. Cheese makers use a specific fungus to produce the creamy white skin on Brie. A different **microorganism** gives blue cheese its characteristic color. Truffles, the most expensive fungi, cost more than $100 an ounce.

narrow space. ❑ *The winds came from the north, across the plains, funneling down the valley.* ⑤ V-T If you **funnel** money, goods, or information from one place or group to another, you cause it to be sent there as it becomes available. ❑ *He secretly funneled credit-card information to counterfeiters.*

fun|ni|ly /fʌnɪli/ PHRASE You use **funnily enough** to indicate that, although something is surprising, it is true or really happened. ❑ *Funnily enough I can remember what I had for lunch on July 5th, 1906, but I've forgotten what I had for breakfast today.*

구 정말 우습게도 ❑ 정말 우스운 것은, 1906년 7월 5일에 내가 점심으로 뭘 먹었는지는 기억이 나는데, 오늘 아침 뭘 먹었는지는 전혀 기억이 안 난다는 거야.

fun|ny ♦♦♢ /fʌni/ (**funnier, funniest**) ① ADJ Someone or something that is **funny** is amusing and likely to make you smile or laugh. ❑ *I'll tell you a funny story.* ② ADJ If you describe something as **funny**, you think it is strange, surprising, or puzzling. ❑ *Children get some very funny ideas sometimes!* ❑ *There's something funny about him.* ③ ADJ If you feel **funny**, you feel slightly ill. [INFORMAL] ❑ *My head had begun to ache and my stomach felt funny.*

① 형용사 우스운 ❑ 내가 우스운 얘기 하나 해 줄게. ② 형용사 재미있는 ❑ 아이들은 때때로 아주 재미있는 생각을 해 내기도 한다. ❑ 그는 좀 재미있는 데가 있어. ③ 형용사 약간 아픈 [비격식체] ❑ 머리가 지끈거리기 시작했고, 배도 약간 아팠어요.

Thesaurus
funny의 참조어

| ADJ. | amusing, comical; (ant.) serious ① |
| | bizarre, odd, peculiar ② |

fur /fɜr/ (**furs**) ① N-MASS **Fur** is the thick and usually soft hair that grows on the bodies of many mammals. ❑ *This creature's fur is short, dense and silky.* ② N-VAR **Fur** is the fur-covered skin of an animal that is used to make clothing or small carpets. ❑ *She had on a black coat with a fur collar.* ❑ *...the trading of furs from Canada.* ③ N-COUNT A **fur** is a coat made from real or artificial fur, or a piece of fur worn around your neck. ❑ *There were women in furs and men in comfortable overcoats.* ④ N-MASS **Fur** is an artificial fabric that looks like fur and is used, for example, to make clothing, soft toys, and seat covers.

① 물질명사 털 (포유동물의) ❑ 이 동물의 털은 짧고 촘촘하며 부드럽다. ② 가산명사 또는 불가산명사 모피 ❑ 그녀는 모피 깃이 달린 검은색 외투를 입고 있었다. ❑ 캐나다산 모피 매매 ③ 가산명사 모피 코트, 모피 목도리 ❑ 모피 코트를 입은 여자들과 편한 외투를 입은 남자들이 있었다. ④ 물질명사 인조 모피

fu|ri|ous /fyʊəriəs/ ① ADJ Someone who is **furious** is extremely angry. ❑ *He is furious at the way his wife has been treated.* ● **fu|ri|ous|ly** ADV ❑ *He stormed out of the apartment, slamming the door furiously behind him.*

① 형용사 격노한 ❑ 그는 자기 부인이 그렇게 취급당하는 데 격노하고 있다. ● 격노하여 부사 ❑ 그는 아주 화가 나서 문을 꽝 닫으며 아파트를 뛰쳐나갔다.

Angry is normally used to talk about someone's mood or feelings on a particular occasion. If someone is often angry, you can describe them as **bad-tempered**. ❑ *She's a bad-tempered young lady.* If someone is very angry, you can describe them as **furious**. ❑ *Senior police officers are furious at the blunder.* If they are less angry, you can describe them as **annoyed** or **irritated**. ❑ *The Premier looked annoyed but calm....a man irritated by the barking of his neighbor's dog.* Typically, someone is **irritated** by something because it happens constantly or continually. If someone is often irritated, you can describe them as **irritable**.

angry는 보통 특정한 경우에 어떤 사람의 기분이나 감정을 얘기할 때 쓴다. 누가 자주 화를 내면, 그 사람은 bad-tempered라고 할 수 있다. ❑ 그녀는 성질이 나쁜 젊은 여자다. 누가 아주 화가 났으면, furious하다고 표현할 수 있다. ❑ 고참 경찰들이 그 중대한 실수에 격노했다. angry보다 덜 한 경우에는 annoyed나 irritated를 써서 표현할 수 있다. ❑ 수상은 불쾌해 하는 것 같았으나 침착했다....이웃집 개 짖는 소리에 짜증이 난 남자. 대체로 누가 무엇에 의해 irritated되는 것은 그것이 끊임없이 계속 일어나기 때문이다. 누가 자주 짜증을 내면, 그 사람을 irritable(짜증을 잘 내는)하다고 표현할 수 있다.

② ADJ **Furious** is also used to describe something that is done with great energy, effort, speed, or violence. ❑ *A furious gunbattle ensued.* ● **fu|ri|ous|ly** ADV ❑ *Officials worked furiously to repair the center court.*

② 형용사 격렬한, 열정적인 ❑ 격렬한 총격전이 뒤를 이었다. ● 격렬하게, 열정적으로 부사 ❑ 관계자들은 중앙 코트를 수리하기 위해 열심히 일했다.

fur|long /fɜrlɒŋ, BRIT fɜːlɒŋ/ (**furlongs**) N-COUNT A **furlong** is a unit of length that is equal to 220 yards or 201.2 meters. ❑ *If the race was over 10 furlongs today Hawk Wing would be a certainty.*

가산명사 펄롱 (201.2미터에 해당하는 길이) ❑ 오늘 경주가 2킬로미터가 넘는다면 호크 윙이 틀림없이 우승을 차지할 거야.

fur|lough /fɜrloʊ/ (**furloughs, furloughing, furloughed**) ① N-VAR If workers are given **furlough**, they are told to stay away from work for a certain period because there is not enough for them to do. [AM] ❑ *This could mean a massive furlough of government workers.* ② V-T If people who work for a particular organization **are furloughed**, they are given a furlough. [AM; BRIT **leave**] ❑ *We regret to inform you that you are being furloughed indefinitely.*

① 가산명사 또는 불가산명사 일시 해고 [미국영어] ❑ 이건 정부 공무원의 대량 일시 해고를 뜻할 수도 있다. ② 타동사 일시 해고되다 [미국영어; 영국영어 leave] ❑ 알려 드리기 유감스럽지만 귀하는 추후 연락이 있을 때까지 일시 해고되었습니다.

fur|nace /fɜrnɪs/ (**furnaces**) N-COUNT A **furnace** is a container or enclosed space in which a very hot fire is made, for example to melt metal, burn rubbish, or produce steam.

가산명사 노(爐), 용광로, 소각로

fur|nish /fɜrnɪʃ/ (**furnishes, furnishing, furnished**) ① V-T If you **furnish** a room or building, you put furniture and furnishings into it. ❑ *Many proprietors try to furnish their hotels with antiques.* ② V-T If you **furnish** someone with something, you provide or supply it. [FORMAL] ❑ *They'll be able to furnish you with the rest of the details.*

① 타동사 가구를 들여놓다 ❑ 많은 호텔 경영자들은 자신들의 호텔을 고풍스런 가구로 치장하려고 노력한다. ② 타동사 [격식체] 제공하다 ❑ 그 사람들이 나머지 세부적인 내용을 제공해 줄 수 있을 것이다.

fur|nish|ings /fɜrnɪʃɪŋz/ N-PLURAL The **furnishings** of a room or house are the furniture, curtains, carpets, and decorations such as pictures. ❑ *To enable rental increases, you have to have luxurious furnishings.*

복수명사 세간 ❑ 세가 잘 나가게 하려면 호화스런 실내 장식을 해야 한다.

fur|ni|ture ♦♢♢ /fɜrnɪtʃər/ N-UNCOUNT **Furniture** consists of large objects such as tables, chairs, or beds that are used in a room for sitting or lying on or for putting things on or in. ❑ *Each piece of furniture in their home suited the style of the house.*

불가산명사 가구 ❑ 그들의 집에 있는 가구 하나하나가 그 집의 스타일과 어울렸다.

Note that **furniture** is only ever used as an uncount noun. You cannot say "a furniture" or "furnitures." If you want to refer in general terms to something such as a table, a chair, or a bed, you can say **a piece of furniture** or **an item of furniture**.

furniture는 불가산 명사로만 쓰임을 유의하라. a furniture나 furnitures라고 할 수 없다. 의자, 침대와 같은 것을 통칭해서 가리키려면 a piece of furniture 또는 an item of furniture라고 한다.

fu|ror /fyʊərɔr, -ər/ [BRIT **furore**] N-SING A **furor** is a very angry or excited reaction by people to something. ❑ *...an international furor over the plan.*

[영국영어 furore] 단수명사 격노, 격앙 ❑ 그 계획에 대한 국제적인 분노

fur|row /fɜroʊ, BRIT fʌroʊ/ (**furrows**) ① N-COUNT A **furrow** is a long, thin line in the earth which a farmer makes in order to plant seeds or to allow water to flow along. ❑ *...furrows of roses and corn.* ② N-COUNT A **furrow** is a deep, fairly

① 가산명사 고랑 ❑ 장미와 옥수수를 섞어 놓은 고랑 ② 가산명사 깊고 넓게 패인 자국, 고랑 ❑ 나는 쟁기로 넓은 고랑을 파고 있는 암갈색의 비옥한 들을 보았다.

wide line in the surface of something. ❑ *I saw a dark brown fertile field in which a plough was cutting large furrows.* ⬛ N-COUNT A **furrow** is a deep fold or line in the skin of someone's face. ❑ *He was his old self again, except for the deep furrows that marked the corners of his mouth.*

fur|ry /f3ri/ ⬛ ADJ A **furry** animal is covered with thick, soft hair. ❑ *People like having small furry animals to stroke, but pets can be expensive to feed.* ⬛ ADJ If you describe something as **furry**, you mean that it has a soft rough texture like fur. ❑ *The leaves are soft, round and rather furry.*

❸ 가산명사 깊은 주름살 ❑ 입가의 깊은 주름살을 펴면 그는 다시 예전의 모습 그대로였다.

⬛ 형용사 부드러운 털이 있는 ❑ 사람들은 쓰다듬을 수 있는, 부드러운 털이 난 작은 동물을 갖기를 좋아하지만, 애완동물은 기르는 데 많은 비용이 들 수도 있다. ⬛ 형용사 모피같이 부드러운 ❑ 그 잎들은 부드럽고 둥글며 털같이 부드러운 느낌이 난다.

fur|ther ♦♦♦ /f3rðər/ (furthers, furthering, furthered)

Further is a comparative form of **far**. It is also a verb.

⬛ ADV **Further** means to a greater extent or degree. [ADV with v] ❑ *Inflation is below 5% and set to fall further.* ❑ *The rebellion is expected to further damage the country's image.* ⬛ ADV If you go or get **further** with something, or take something **further**, you make some progress. [ADV with v] ❑ *They lacked the scientific personnel to develop the technical apparatus much further.* ⬛ ADV If someone goes **further** in a discussion, they make a more extreme statement or deal with a point more thoroughly. [ADV after v] ❑ *To have a better comparison, we need to go further and address such issues as repairs and insurance.* ⬛ ADJ A **further** thing, number of things, or amount of something is an additional thing, number of things, or amount. [ADJ n, pron-indef ADJ] ❑ *Further evidence of slowing economic growth is likely to emerge this week.* ⬛ ADV **Further** means a greater distance than before or than something else. [ADV adv/prep] ❑ *Now we live further away from the city center.* ❑ *He came to a halt at a crossroads fifty yards further on.* ⬛ ADV **Further** is used in expressions such as "**further back**" and "**further ahead**" to refer to a point in time that is earlier or later than the time you are talking about. [ADV adv/prep] ❑ *Looking still further ahead, by the end of the next century world population is expected to be about ten billion.* ⬛ V-T If you **further** something, you help it to progress, to be successful, or to be achieved. ❑ *Education needn't only be about furthering your career.* ⬛ PHRASE **Further to** is used in letters in expressions such as "**further to your letter**" or "**further to our conversation**," in order to indicate what you are referring to in the letter. [BRIT, FORMAL] ❑ *Further to your letter, I agree that there are some presentational problems, politically speaking.*

further는 far의 비교급 형태이며 동사이기도 하다.

⬛ 부사 더욱 ❑ 인플레이션은 5퍼센트 이하이고, 더욱 떨어지게 될 것이다. ❑ 반군이 그 나라의 이미지를 더욱 손상시킬 것으로 예상된다. ⬛ 부사 더 이상 ❑ 그들은 그 기술 조직을 더 이상 발전시키기에는 과학 인력이 부족했다. ⬛ 부사 더 나아가 ❑ 더 바람직한 비교를 하기 위해서는 더 나아가, 수리나 보험 같은 문제도 다뤄야 한다. ⬛ 형용사 추가의 ❑ 경제 성장이 둔화되고 있다는 추가 증거가 이번 주에 드러날 것 같다. ⬛ 부사 더 멀리 ❑ 지금 우리는 시내에서 더 멀리 떨어진 곳에 살고 있다. ❑ 그는 50야드 더 떨어진 교차로에 와서야 멈췄다. ⬛ 부사 더 옛날로 되돌아보면; 먼 훗날을 생각해 보면 ❑ 훨씬 더 먼 훗날을 생각해 보면, 다음 세기 말경에는 전 세계 인구가 100억에 이를 것으로 예상된다. ⬛ 타동사 발전시키다, 촉진하다 ❑ 교육이 꼭 출세만을 위한 것일 필요는 없다. ⬛ 구 -와 관련해서 [영국영어, 격식체] ❑ 귀하의 편지와 관련해서, 정치적으로 말씀드리자면, 발표상에 몇 가지 문제가 있다는 것에 저도 동의합니다.

fur|ther edu|ca|tion N-UNCOUNT **Further education** is the education of people who have left school but who are not at a university or a college of education. [mainly BRIT; AM **continuing education**] ❑ *She is now in further education with new career possibilities ahead of her.*

불가산명사 성인 교육 [주로 영국영어; 미국영어 continuing education] ❑ 그녀는 지금 새로운 진로를 개척할 수 있으리라는 가능성을 갖고 성인 교육을 받고 있다.

fur|ther|more /f3rðərmɔr/ ADV **Furthermore** is used to introduce a piece of information or opinion that adds to or supports the previous one. [FORMAL] [ADV with cl] ❑ *Furthermore, they claim that any such interference is completely ineffective.*

부사 더욱이 [격식체] ❑ 더욱이 그들은 그러한 간섭이 완전히 비효과적이라고 주장하고 있다.

fur|thest /f3rðɪst/

Furthest is a superlative form of **far**.

⬛ ADV **Furthest** means to a greater extent or degree than ever before or than anything or anyone else. [ADV with v] ❑ *The south of England, where prices have fallen furthest, will remain the weakest market.* ⬛ ADV **Furthest** means at a greater distance from a particular point than anyone or anything else, or for a greater distance than anyone or anything else. ❑ *The risk of thunder is greatest in those areas furthest from the coast.* ● ADJ **Furthest** is also an adjective. [ADJ n] ❑ *...the furthest point from earth that any controlled spacecraft has ever been.*

furthest는 far의 최상급 형태이다.

⬛ 부사 가장 많이 ❑ 물가가 가장 많이 떨어진 남부 잉글랜드는 가장 취약한 시장으로 남을 것이다. ⬛ 부사 가장 멀리 ❑ 해안에서 가장 멀리 떨어진 곳이 벼락의 위험이 가장 크다. ● 형용사 가장 멀리 떨어진 ❑ 지금까지 통제되는 우주선이 도달해 본 지점 중 지구에서 가장 멀리 떨어진 곳

fur|tive /f3rtIv/ ADJ If you describe someone's behavior as **furtive**, you disapprove of them behaving as if they want to keep something secret or hidden. [DISAPPROVAL] ❑ *With a furtive glance over her shoulder, she unlocked the door and entered the house.*

형용사 남의 이목을 꺼리는 [탐탁잖음] ❑ 그녀는 남의 이목이 신경 쓰이는 듯 고개를 뒤로 돌려 획 한번 살펴보고는 문을 따고 집으로 들어갔다.

fury /fyuəri/ N-UNCOUNT **Fury** is violent or very strong anger. ❑ *She screamed, her face distorted with fury and pain.*

불가산명사 격분, 격노 ❑ 그녀는 비명을 질렀는데, 격분하고 고통스러워 얼굴이 일그러져 있었다.

fuse /fyuz/ (fuses, fusing, fused) ⬛ N-COUNT A **fuse** is a safety device in an electric plug or circuit. It contains a piece of wire which melts when there is a fault so that the flow of electricity stops. ❑ *The fuse blew as he pressed the button to start the motor.* ⬛ V-T/V-I When an electric device **fuses** or when you **fuse** it, it stops working because of a fault. [BRIT] ❑ *The wire snapped at the wall plug and the light fused.* ⬛ N-COUNT A **fuse** is a device on a bomb or firework which delays the explosion so that people can move a safe distance away. ❑ *A bomb was deactivated at the last moment, after the fuse had been lit.* ⬛ V-RECIP When things **fuse** or **are fused**, they join together physically or chemically, usually to become one thing. You can also say that one thing **fuses** with another. ❑ *The skull bones fuse between the ages of fifteen and twenty-five.* ❑ *Conception occurs when a single sperm fuses with an egg.* ❑ *Manufactured glass is made by fusing various types of sand.*

⬛ 가산명사 퓨즈 ❑ 그가 모터를 돌리기 위해 단추를 누르자 퓨즈가 나가 버렸다. ⬛ 타동사/자동사 (전기 기구의 퓨즈가) 나가다 [영국영어] ❑ 벽 플러그에 있는 전선에서 툭 끊어지는 소리가 나더니 전기가 나갔다. ⬛ 가산명사 도화선 ❑ 도화선에 불을 붙은 폭탄은 마지막 순간에 제거되었다. ⬛ 상호동사 융합되다; 융합시키다 ❑ 두개골은 열다섯에서 스물다섯 살 사이에 붙는다. ❑ 수정은 단 하나의 정자가 난자와 융합될 때 일어난다. ❑ 대량 생산되는 유리는 여러 종류의 모래를 융합시켜 만든다.

fu|se|lage /fyusɪlɑʒ, -lɪdʒ, -zɪ-/ (fuselages) N-COUNT The **fuselage** is the main body of an airplane, missile, or rocket. It is usually cylindrical in shape. ❑ *The force of the impact ripped apart the plane's fuselage.*

가산명사 (비행기 등의) 동체 ❑ 그 충격의 힘으로 비행기 동체가 산산조각 나 버렸다.

fu|sion /fyuʒ³n/ (fusions) ⬛ N-COUNT A **fusion of** different qualities, ideas, or things is something new that is created by joining them together. ❑ *His previous fusions of jazz, pop and African melodies have proved highly successful.* ⬛ N-VAR The **fusion** of two or more things involves joining them together to form one thing. ❑ *His final reform was the fusion of regular and reserve forces.* ⬛ N-UNCOUNT In physics, **fusion** is the process in which atomic particles combine and produce a large amount of nuclear energy. ❑ *...research into nuclear fusion.*

⬛ 가산명사 퓨전, 결합 ❑ 그가 전에 시도했던 재즈, 팝, 아프리카 음악의 결합은 상당히 성공적이었던 것으로 판명났다. ⬛ 가산명사 또는 불가산명사 통합 ❑ 그의 최종 개혁은 정규군과 예비군의 통합이었다. ⬛ 불가산명사 (핵) 융합 ❑ 핵융합 연구

fuss /fʌs/ (fusses, fussing, fussed) ⬛ N-SING **Fuss** is anxious or excited behavior which serves no useful purpose. [also no det] ❑ *I don't know what all the fuss is about.* ⬛ V-I If you **fuss**, you worry or behave in a nervous, anxious way about

⬛ 단수명사 야단법석, 부산 ❑ 난 왜 이렇게 야단법석들을 떠는지 통 모르겠다. ⬛ 자동사 부산을 떨다, 야단법석을 떨다 ❑ 캐롤은 나에게 마실 것을

unimportant matters or rush around doing unnecessary things. ❑ *Carol fussed about getting me a drink.* ❑ *My wife was fussing over the food and clothing we were going to take.* ❑ *"Stop fussing," he snapped.* ◳ V-I If you **fuss over** someone, you pay them a lot of attention and do things to make them happy or comfortable. ❑ *Auntie Hilda and Uncle Jack couldn't fuss over them enough.* ◱ PHRASE If you **make a fuss** or **kick up a fuss** about something, you become angry or excited about it and complain. [INFORMAL] ❑ *I don't know why everybody makes such a fuss about a few mosquitoes.*

fussy /fʌsi/ (**fussier, fussiest**) ADJ Someone who is **fussy** is very concerned with unimportant details and is difficult to please. [DISAPPROVAL] ❑ *She is not fussy about her food.*

fu|tile /fyutʲl, BRIT fyuːtaɪl/ ADJ If you say that something is **futile**, you mean there is no point in doing it, usually because it has no chance of succeeding. ❑ *He brought his arm up in a futile attempt to ward off the blow.*

fu|til|ity /fyutɪlɪti/ N-UNCOUNT **Futility** is a total lack of purpose or usefulness. ❑ *Brown's article tells of the tragedy and futility of war.*

fu|ture ♦♦♢ /fyutʃər/ (**futures**) ◳ N-SING **The future** is the period of time that will come after the present, or the things that will happen then. ❑ *The spokesman said no decision on the proposal was likely in the immediate future.* ❑ *He was making plans for the future.* ◰ ADJ **Future** things will happen or exist after the present time. [ADJ n] ❑ *She said if the world did not act conclusively now, it would only bequeath the problem to future generations.* ❑ *...the future King and Queen.* ◳ N-COUNT Someone's **future**, or **the future of** something, is what will happen to them or what they will do after the present time. ❑ *His future as prime minister depends on the outcome of the elections.* ❑ *...a proposed national conference on the country's political future.* ◱ N-PLURAL When people trade in **futures**, they buy stocks and shares, commodities such as coffee or oil, or foreign currency at a price that is agreed at the time of purchase for items which are delivered some time in the future. [BUSINESS] ❑ *This report could spur some buying in corn futures when the market opens today.* ◵ PHRASE You use **in the future** when saying what will happen from now on, which will be different from what has previously happened. The form **in future** is used in British English. ❑ *I asked her to be more careful in the future.*

Word Partnership	*future*의 연어
ADJ.	**bright** future, **distant** future, **immediate** future, **near** future, **uncertain** future ◳
V.	**discuss the** future, **have a** future, **plan for the** future, **predict/see the** future ◳
N.	future **date**, future **events**, future **generations**, future **plans**, for future **reference** ◰

fu|tur|is|tic /fyutʃərɪstɪk/ ◳ ADJ Something that is **futuristic** looks or seems very modern and unusual, like something from the future. ❑ *The theater is a futuristic steel and glass structure.* ◰ ADJ A **futuristic** movie or book tells a story that is set in the future, when things are different. [ADJ n] ❑ *...the futuristic hit film, "Terminator 2".*

fuzzy /fʌzi/ (**fuzzier, fuzziest**) ◳ ADJ **Fuzzy** hair sticks up in a soft, curly mass. ❑ *He had fuzzy black hair and bright black eyes.* ◰ ADJ If something is **fuzzy**, it has a covering that feels soft and like fur. ❑ *...fuzzy material.* ◳ ADJ A **fuzzy** picture, image, or sound is unclear and hard to see or hear. ❑ *A couple of fuzzy pictures have been published.* ◱ ADJ If you or your thoughts are **fuzzy**, you are confused and cannot think clearly. ❑ *He had little patience for fuzzy ideas.*

대접하려고 부산을 떨었다. ❑ 아내는 우리가 가지고 갈 음식과 옷 때문에 부산을 떨었다. ❑ "부산떨지 마." 그가 불쑥 화를 내며 말했다. ◳ 자동사 끔찍이 위하다 ❑ 힐다 아주머니와 잭 아저씨는 더할 수 없이 서로를 끔찍이 위한다. ◱ 구 야단법석을 떨다 [비격식체] ❑ 나는 왜 모든 사람들이 모기 몇 마리 때문에 저렇게 야단법석을 떠는지 모르겠다.

형용사 까탈 부리는 [탐탁잖음] ❑ 그녀는 음식 갖고 까탈 부리지 않는다.

형용사 부질없는 ❑ 그는 강타를 막아 보려고 팔을 들어올리는 부질없는 시도를 했다.

불가산명사 부질없음 ❑ 브라운의 기사는 전쟁의 비극과 부질없음을 말해 준다.

◳ 단수명사 미래 ❑ 그 제안에 대해 무슨 결정이 조만간 나오지는 않을 것이라고 대변인은 말했다. ❑ 그는 미래를 위한 계획을 짜고 있었다. ◰ 형용사 미래의 ❑ 지금 세계가 단호하게 행동하지 않는다면, 그 문제를 미래 세대에게 물려주는 것밖에 되지 않을 것이라고 그녀는 말했다. ❑ 미래의 왕과 왕비 ◳ 가산명사 장래, 미래 ❑ 총리로서의 그의 장래는 선거 결과에 달려 있다. ❑ 국가의 정치적 미래에 관해 제안된 전국 회의 ◱ 복수명사 선물(先物) [경제] ❑ 이 보고서 때문에 오늘 시장이 열리면 옥수수 선물 거래에 박차가 가해질 수도 있다. ◵ 구 앞으로는 ❑ 나는 그녀에게 앞으로는 좀 더 주의하라고 했다.

◳ 형용사 초현대적인 ❑ 그 극장은 초현대적 감각의 강철과 유리 구조물이다. ◰ 형용사 미래를 배경으로 하는 ❑ 미래를 배경으로 한 히트 영화 '터미네이터 2'

◳ 형용사 곱슬곱슬한 ❑ 그는 검은 곱슬머리에 눈동자가 밝은 검은색이었다. ◰ 형용사 보드로 덮인 ❑ 보풀로 덮인 물질 ◳ 형용사 희미한 ❑ 희미한 그림 두어 장이 인쇄되었다. ◱ 형용사 애매한 ❑ 그는 애매한 생각을 잘 참아 내지 못했다.

Gg

G, g /dʒiː/ (**G's, g's**) N-VAR **G** is the seventh letter of the English alphabet.

가산명사 또는 불가산명사 영어 알파벳의 일곱 번째 글자

gad|get /gædʒɪt/ (**gadgets**) N-COUNT A **gadget** is a small machine or device which does something useful. You sometimes refer to something as a **gadget** when you are suggesting that it is complicated and unnecessary. ❏ ...sales of kitchen gadgets including toasters, kettles and percolators.
→see **technology**

가산명사 작은 기계, 복잡한 장치 ❏ 토스터, 주전자, 그리고 커피 추출기를 포함한 부엌용품 매출액

Gael|ic ❶ N-UNCOUNT **Gaelic** is a language spoken by people in parts of Scotland and Ireland. ❏ We weren't allowed to speak Gaelic at school. ● ADJ **Gaelic** is also an adjective. ❏ ...the Gaelic language. ❷ ADJ **Gaelic** means coming from or relating to Scotland and Ireland, especially the parts where Gaelic is spoken. ❏ ...an evening of Gaelic music and drama.

❶ 불가산명사 게일어 ❏ 우리는 학교에서 게일어를 쓸 수 없었다. ● 형용사 게일어의 ❏ 게일어 ❷ 형용사 게일족의 ❏ 게일 음악과 연극의 밤

gag /gæg/ (**gags, gagging, gagged**) ❶ N-COUNT A **gag** is something such as a piece of cloth that is tied around or put inside someone's mouth in order to stop them from speaking. ❏ His captors had put a gag of thick leather in his mouth. ❷ V-T If someone **gags** you, they tie a piece of cloth around your mouth in order to stop you from speaking or shouting. ❏ I gagged him with a towel. ❸ V-T If a person **is gagged** by someone in authority, they are prevented from expressing their opinion or from publishing certain information. [DISAPPROVAL] ❏ Judges must not be gagged. ❹ V-I If you **gag**, you cannot swallow and nearly vomit. ❏ I knelt by the toilet and gagged. ❺ N-COUNT A **gag** is a joke. [INFORMAL] ❏ ...a gag about policemen giving evidence in court.

❶ 가산명사 재갈 ❏ 그를 납치한 사람들은 그의 입에 두꺼운 가죽재갈을 물렸다. ❷ 타동사 재갈을 물리다 ❏ 나는 수건으로 그에게 재갈을 물렸다. ❸ 타동사 할 말을 못하게 하다 [탐탁찮음] ❏ 판사들의 입을 막아서는 안 된다. ❹ 자동사 토하려고 하다, 구역질이 나다 ❏ 나는 변기에 앉아 구역질을 했다. ❺ 가산명사 농담 [비격식체] ❏ 법정에서 증언하는 경찰관에 대한 농담

gain ♦♦◊ /geɪn/ (**gains, gaining, gained**) ❶ V-T If a person or place **gains** something such as an ability or quality, they gradually get more of it. ❏ Students can gain valuable experience by working on the campus radio or magazine. ❷ V-T/V-I If you **gain from** something such as an event or situation, you get some advantage or benefit from it. ❏ The company didn't disclose how much it expects to gain from the two deals. ❏ There is absolutely nothing to be gained by feeling bitter. ❸ V-T To **gain** something such as weight or speed means to have an increase in that particular thing. ❏ Some people do gain weight after they stop smoking. ❏ The BMW started coming forward, passing the other cars and gaining speed as it approached. ● N-VAR **Gain** is also a noun. [usu with supp] ❏ News on new home sales is brighter, showing a gain of nearly 8% in June. ❹ V-T If you **gain** something, you obtain it, especially after a lot of hard work or effort. ❏ To gain a promotion, you might have to work overtime. ❺ PHRASE If something such as an idea or an ideal **gains ground**, it gradually becomes more widely known or more popular. ❏ There are strong signs that his views are gaining ground.

❶ 타동사 얻다 ❏ 학생들은 교내 라디오 방송이나 잡지 관련 일을 하면서 값진 경험을 얻을 수 있다. ❷ 타동사/자동사 이득을 보다 ❏ 그 회사는 두 건의 거래에서 이익을 얼마나 얻으리라 예상하는지 밝히지 않았다. ❏ 속상해 한다고 득이 될 것이 하나도 없다. ❸ 타동사 (무게, 속도 등이) 늘다 ❏ 어떤 사람들은 담배를 끊고 나서 정말로 몸무게가 는다. ❏ 그 비엠더블유 차가 다른 차들을 추월하고, 가까이 다가서면서 속도를 높이더니, 앞으로 나서기 시작했다. ● 가산명사 또는 불가산명사 수익; 신장 ❏ 새 주택의 매출 소식은 더 긍정적이어서 6월에 거의 8퍼센트 신장을 보였다. ❹ 타동사 획득하다 ❏ 승진을 하려면 초과 근무를 해야 할지도 모른다. ❺ 구 점차 우세해지다, 점점 유명해지다 ❏ 그의 견해가 점점 더 설득력을 얻고 있다는 징후가 뚜렷하다.

	Thesaurus gain의 참조어
v.	acquire, collect, obtain; (ant.) lose ❶
	grow, enlarge, increase ❸

gait /geɪt/ (**gaits**) N-COUNT A particular kind of **gait** is a particular way of walking. [WRITTEN] ❏ ...a tubby little man in his fifties, with sparse hair and a rolling gait.

가산명사 걸음걸이 [문어체] ❏ 숱이 성긴 머리를 하고 흔들흔들 걸어가는 50대의 땅딸막한 남자

gala /geɪlə, BRIT gɑːlə/ (**galas**) N-COUNT A **gala** is a special public celebration, entertainment, performance, or festival. ❏ ...a gala evening at the Royal Opera House.

가산명사 특별 공연, 축제 ❏ 왕립 오페라 극장의 특별 공연의 밤

gal|axy /gæləksi/ (**galaxies**) also **Galaxy** ❶ N-COUNT A **galaxy** is an extremely large group of stars and planets that extends over many billions of light years. ❏ Astronomers have discovered a distant galaxy. ❷ N-PROPER **The Galaxy** is the extremely large group of stars and planets to which the Earth and the solar system belong. ❏ The Galaxy consists of 100 billion stars. →see **star**
→see Word Web: **galaxy**

❶ 가산명사 은하, 은하수 ❏ 천문학자들은 멀리 떨어진 은하를 발견했다. ❷ 고유명사 은하계 ❏ 은하계는 천억 개의 별들로 이루어져 있다.

gale /geɪl/ (**gales**) ❶ N-COUNT A **gale** is a very strong wind. ❏ ...forecasts of fierce gales over the next few days. ❷ N-COUNT You can refer to the loud noise made by a lot of people all laughing at the same time as a **gale of** laughter or **gales of** laughter. [WRITTEN] ❏ This was greeted with gales of laughter from the audience. →see **wind**

❶ 가산명사 강풍, 질풍 ❏ 앞으로 며칠간 사나운 강풍이 불 것이라는 기상 예보 ❷ 가산명사 폭소, 박장대소 [문어체] ❏ 이것을 보고 청중들은 폭소를 터뜨렸다.

gall /gɔːl/ (**galls, galling, galled**) ❶ N-UNCOUNT If you say that someone has **the gall to** do something, you are criticizing them for behaving in a rude or disrespectful way. [DISAPPROVAL] ❏ I daresay he thought he was above the law. I can't get over the gall of the fellow. ❷ V-T If someone's action **galls** you, it makes you feel very angry or annoyed, often because it is unfair to you and you cannot do anything about it. ❏ It must have galled him that Nick thwarted each of these measures.

❶ 불가산명사 뻔뻔스러움, 철면피 [탐탁찮음] ❏ 그는 자신이 법을 초월한다고 생각하나 봐. 나는 그가 그렇게 뻔뻔한 데 정말 놀랐어. ❷ 타동사 화나게 하다 ❏ 닉이 이 대책들을 모두 망쳐 버려서 그가 화가 난 게 틀림없었다.

Word Web galaxy

The word **galaxy** with a small g refers to an extremely large group of **stars** and **planets**. It measures billions of **light years** across. There are about 100 billion galaxies in the **universe**. **Astronomers** classify galaxies into four different types. Irregular galaxies have no particular shape. Elliptical galaxies look like flattened spheres. Spiral galaxies have long curving arms. A barred spiral galaxy has straight lines of stars extending from its nucleus. Galaxy with a capital G refers to our own **solar system**. The name of this galaxy is the Milky Way. It is about 100,000 light years wide.

gal|lant /gǽlənt/

Pronounced /gəlǽnt/ or /gǽlənt/ for meaning 2.

1 ADJ If someone is **gallant**, they behave bravely and honorably in a dangerous or difficult situation. [OLD-FASHIONED] ❏ *The gallant soldiers lost their lives so that peace might reign again.* ● **gal|lant|ly** ADV [ADV with v] ❏ *The town responded gallantly to the War.* **2** ADJ If a man is **gallant**, he is kind, polite, and considerate toward women. [OLD-FASHIONED] ❏ *Douglas was a complex man, thoughtful, gallant, and generous.* ● **gal|lant|ly** ADV [ADV with v] ❏ *He gallantly kissed Marie's hand as we prepared to leave.*

gall blad|der (gall bladders) N-COUNT Your **gall bladder** is the organ in your body which contains bile and is next to your liver.

gal|lery ♦♢♢ /gǽləri/ (galleries) **1** N-COUNT; N-IN-NAMES A **gallery** is a place that has permanent exhibitions of works of art in it. ❏ *...an art gallery.* **2** N-COUNT A **gallery** is a privately owned building or room where people can look at and buy works of art. ❏ *The painting is in the gallery upstairs.* **3** N-COUNT A **gallery** is an area high above the ground at the back or at the sides of a large room or hall. ❏ *A crowd already filled the gallery.* **4** N-COUNT The **gallery** in a theater or concert hall is an area high above the ground that usually contains the cheapest seats. ❏ *They had been forced to find cheap tickets in the gallery.* ● PHRASE If you **play to the gallery**, you do something in public in a way which you hope will impress people. ❏ *...but I must tell you that in my opinion you're both now playing to the gallery.*
→see Word Web: gallery

gal|ley /gǽli/ (galleys) **1** N-COUNT On a ship or aircraft, the **galley** is the kitchen. ❏ *I awoke to the smell of sizzling bacon in the galley.* **2** N-COUNT In former times, a **galley** was a ship with sails and a lot of oars, which was often rowed by slaves or prisoners. ❏ *...his months pulling the oar on the galleys.*

gal|lon /gǽlən/ (gallons) N-COUNT A **gallon** is a unit of measurement for liquids that is equal to eight pints. In America, it is equal to 3.785 liters. In Britain, it is equal to 4.564 liters. ❏ *...80 million gallons of water a day.*

gal|lop /gǽləp/ (gallops, galloping, galloped) **1** V-T/V-I When a horse **gallops**, it runs very fast so that all four legs are off the ground at the same time. If you **gallop** a horse, you make it gallop. ❏ *The horses galloped away.* **2** V-I If you **gallop**, you ride a horse that is galloping. ❏ *Major Winston galloped into the distance.* **3** N-SING A **gallop** is a ride on a horse that is galloping. ❏ *I was forced to attempt a gallop.* **4** V-I If something such as a process **gallops**, it develops very quickly and is often difficult to control. ❏ *China's economy galloped ahead.* **5** V-I If you **gallop**, you run somewhere very quickly. [mainly BRIT] ❏ *They are galloping around the garden playing football.* **6** PHRASE If you do something **at a gallop**, you do it very quickly. ❏ *I read the book at a gallop.*

ga|lore /gəlɔ́r/ ADJ You use **galore** to emphasize that something you like exists in very large quantities. [INFORMAL, WRITTEN, EMPHASIS] [n ADJ] ❏ *You'll be able to win prizes galore.*

gal|va|nize /gǽlvənaɪz/ (galvanizes, galvanizing, galvanized) [BRIT also **galvanise**] V-T To **galvanize** someone means to cause them to take action, for example by making them feel very excited, afraid, or angry. ❏ *The aid appeal has galvanised the German business community.*

gam|ble /gǽmbᵊl/ (gambles, gambling, gambled) **1** N-COUNT A **gamble** is a risky action or decision that you take in the hope of gaining money, success, or an advantage over other people. ❏ *Yesterday, he named his cabinet and took a big gamble in the process.* **2** V-T/V-I If you **gamble on** something, you take a risky action or decision in the hope of gaining money, success, or an advantage over other people. ❏ *Few firms will be willing to gamble on new products.* ❏ *They are not*

2의 의미일 때는 /gəlǽnt/ 또는 /gǽlənt/으로 발음된다.

1 형용사 용감한 [구식어] ❏ 용감한 군인들이 평화를 되찾기 위해 목숨을 잃었다. ● 용감하게 부사 ❏ 그 도시 사람들은 용감하게 전쟁과 맞섰다. **2** 형용사 여성에게 자상한 [구식어] ❏ 더글러스는 사려 깊으면서도 관대하고 동시에 여성에게는 자상한 복잡다단한 인물이었다. ● (여성에게) 정중하게 부사 ❏ 우리가 떠날 채비를 하자 그가 마리의 손에 정중하게 입을 맞추었다.

가산명사 담낭

1 가산명사; 이름명사 미술관 ❏ 미술관 **2** 가산명사 화랑 ❏ 그 그림은 위층 화랑에 있다. **3** 가산명사 극장의 맨 위층, 극장의 발코니 ❏ 한 무리의 관중이 이미 발코니를 가득 메우고 있었다. **4** 가산명사 맨 위층 관람석 ❏ 그들은 맨 위층 관람석의 값이 싼 입장권을 구해야만 했다. ● 구 대중에 영합하다 ❏ 하지만 제가 보기에는 두 분 모두 지금 대중에 영합하고 있다고 말씀드려야 할 것 같습니다.

1 가산명사 (배, 항공기의) 주방 ❏ 나는 주방의 지글거리는 베이컨 냄새에 잠이 깼다. **2** 가산명사 갤리선 ❏ 그가 갤리선에서 노를 저으며 보낸 여러 달

가산명사 갤런 ❏ 하루에 8천만 갤런의 물

1 타동사/자동사 말이 전속력으로 달리다; 밝은 전속력으로 달리게 하다 ❏ 말들이 전속력으로 달려 나갔다. **2** 자동사 말을 타고 전속력으로 달리다 ❏ 윈스턴 소령은 말을 타고 멀리 질주해 갔다. **3** 단수명사 전속력으로 말 타기 ❏ 나는 말을 타고 질주해야만 했다. **4** 자동사 빠르게 진행되다 ❏ 중국 경제는 빠르게 성장해 나갔다. **5** 자동사 질주하다 [주로 영국영어] ❏ 그들은 정원에서 축구를 하며 뛰어다니는 중이다. **6** 구 단숨에 ❏ 나는 그 책을 아주 단숨에 읽었다.

형용사 많은, 다량의 [비격식체, 문어체, 강조] ❏ 당신은 많은 상을 탈 수 있을 겁니다.

[영국영어 galvanise] 타동사 자극하다 ❏ 그 원조 요청은 독일 재계를 자극시켰다.

1 가산명사 도박, 실패를 건 모험 ❏ 어제 그는 내각을 임명했는데 그 과정에서 큰 모험을 했다. **2** 타동사/자동사 운을 걸다 ❏ 신제품에 기꺼이 모험을 할 회사는 거의 없을 것이다. ❏ 그들이 이 문제를 놓고 자신들의 경력을 걸 준비는 되어 있지 않다. **3** 타동사/자동사 도박을 하다 ❏ 대부분의 사람들은

Word Web gallery

The Uffizi **Gallery** in Florence, Italy, is a world-famous art **museum**. It contains many magnificent **paintings** and **sculptures**. These include **works of art** by da Vinci, Botticelli, and Michelangelo. The building was constructed in the 1550s to house government offices. The Medici family, who ruled the area at that time, were great art **collectors**. Gradually they began to convert parts of the building into art galleries. In 1737, the Medici family gave their art collection to the people of Italy.

prepared to gamble their careers on this matter. ▣ V-T/V-I If you **gamble** an amount of money, you bet it in a game such as cards or on the result of a race or competition. People who **gamble** usually do it frequently. ❑ *Most people visit Las Vegas to gamble their hard-earned money.* ❑ *John gambled heavily on the horses.* →see **lottery**

애써서 번 돈으로 도박을 하려고 라스베거스를 찾는다. ❑ 존은 그 말들에 많은 돈을 걸었다.

gam|bler /gǽmblər/ (**gamblers**) ▣ N-COUNT A **gambler** is someone who gambles regularly, for example in card games or horse racing. ❑ *There was a fellow in that casino tonight who's a very heavy gambler.* ▣ N-COUNT If you describe someone as a **gambler**, you mean that they are ready to take risks in order to gain advantages or success. ❑ *He had never been afraid of failure: he was a gambler, ready to go off somewhere else and start all over again.*

▣ 가산명사 도박꾼, 노름꾼 ❑ 오늘밤 그 카지노에는 골수 도박꾼인 사람이 하나 와 있었다. ▣ 가산명사 모험가 ❑ 그는 실패를 두려워해 본 적이 없었다. 그는 어딘가 다른 곳에 가서 처음부터 다시 시작할 준비가 되어 있는 모험가였다.

gam|bling /gǽmblɪŋ/ N-UNCOUNT **Gambling** is the act or activity of betting money, for example in card games or on horse racing. ❑ *Gambling is a form of entertainment.*

불가산명사 도박 ❑ 도박은 일종의 여흥이다.

game ♦♦♢ /geɪm/ (**games**) ▣ N-COUNT A **game** is an activity or sport usually involving skill, knowledge, or chance, in which you follow fixed rules and try to win against an opponent or to solve a puzzle. ❑ *...the wonderful game of football.* ❑ *...a playful game of hide-and-seek.* ▣ N-COUNT A **game** is one particular occasion on which a game is played. ❑ *It was the first game of the season.* ❑ *He regularly watched our games from the stands.* ▣ N-COUNT A **game** is a part of a match, for example in tennis or bridge, consisting of a fixed number of points. ❑ *She won six games to love in the second set.* ▣ N-PLURAL **Games** are an organized event in which competitions in several sports take place. ❑ *...the 1996 Olympic Games at Atlanta.* ▣ N-COUNT You can use **game** to describe a way of behaving in which a person uses a particular plan, usually in order to gain an advantage for himself or herself. ❑ *Until now, the Americans have been playing a very delicate political game.* ▣ N-UNCOUNT Wild animals or birds that are hunted for sport and sometimes cooked and eaten are referred to as **game**. ❑ *As men who shot game for food, they were natural marksmen.* ▣ ADJ If you are **game for** something, you are willing to do something new, unusual, or risky. [v-link ADJ, oft ADJ to-inf, ADJ for n] ❑ *He said he's game for a similar challenge next year.* ▣ PHRASE If someone or something **gives the game away**, they reveal a secret or reveal their feelings, and this puts them at a disadvantage. ❑ *The faces of the two conspirators gave the game away!* ▣ PHRASE If you are **new to** a particular **game**, you have not done a particular activity or been in a particular situation before. ❑ *Don't forget that she's new to this game and will take a while to complete the task.* ▣ PHRASE If you beat someone **at their own game**, you use the same methods that they have used, but more successfully, so that you gain an advantage over them. ❑ *He must anticipate the maneuvers of the other lawyers and beat them at their own game.* ▣ PHRASE If you say that someone is **playing games** or **playing silly games**, you mean that they are not treating a situation seriously and you are annoyed with them. [DISAPPROVAL] ❑ *This seemed to annoy Professor Steiner. "Don't play games with me," he thundered.* →see **chess**

▣ 가산명사 게임, 경기 ❑ 멋진 축구 경기 ❑ 재미있는 숨바꼭질 놀이 ▣ 가산명사 시합, 경기 ❑ 그것은 그 시즌의 첫 시합이었다. ❑ 그는 정기적으로 스탠드에서 우리 시합을 관전했다. ▣ 가산명사 게임 ❑ 그녀는 두 번째 세트에서 게임 점수 6대 0으로 이겼다. ▣ 복수명사 대회 ❑ 1996년의 애틀랜타 올림픽 대회 ▣ 가산명사 책략적 게임, 게임 ❑ 지금까지 미국 사람들은 아주 미묘한 정치적 게임을 해 왔다. ▣ 불가산명사 사냥감 ❑ 식량을 얻고자 사냥감을 잡는 그들은 타고난 명사수들이었다. ▣ 형용사 ∼할 용의가 있는 ❑ 그는 내년에도 비슷한 도전을 할 용의가 있다고 말했다. ▣ 구 속내를 보이다, 의도를 드러내다 ❑ 두 공모자의 얼굴에 그들의 속내가 드러나 버렸지! ▣ 구 어떤 일에 생소한 ❑ 그녀는 이 일에 익숙하지 않아서 그 일을 완수하려면 시간이 꽤 걸릴 거라는 사실을 잊지 말아라. ▣ 구 상대가 잘 쓰는 방법으로 ∼을 하는 ❑ 그는 다른 변호사들의 책략을 예측한 다음 그들이 잘 쓰는 수법을 써서 이겨야 한다. ▣ 구 무책임하게 행동하다, 아무렇게나 하다 [탐탁찮음] ❑ 이 일이 스타이너 교수를 화나게 한 듯 했다. "나한테 장난하지 마."라고 그는 고함을 질렀다.

game show (**game shows**) N-COUNT **Game shows** are television programs on which people play games in order to win prizes. ❑ *Being a good game-show host means getting to know your contestants.*

가산명사 게임 쇼 프로그램 ❑ 훌륭한 게임 쇼 진행자가 되려면 참가자들을 잘 알아야 한다.

gam|ing /geɪmɪŋ/ N-UNCOUNT **Gaming** means the same as **gambling**. ❑ *...offences connected with vice, gaming and drugs.*

불가산명사 도박 ❑ 비행, 도박, 마약과 관련된 범죄

gang ♦♢♢ /gæŋ/ (**gangs, ganging, ganged**) ▣ N-COUNT A **gang** is a group of people, especially young people, who go around together and often deliberately cause trouble. ❑ *During the fight with a rival gang he lashed out with his flick knife.* ❑ *Gang members were behind a lot of the violence.* ▣ N-COUNT A **gang** is a group of criminals who work together to commit crimes. ❑ *Police were hunting for a gang who had allegedly stolen fifty-five cars.* ❑ *...an underworld gang.* ▣ N-SING **The gang** is a group of friends who frequently meet. [INFORMAL] ❑ *Come on over, we've got lots of the old gang here.* ▣ N-COUNT A **gang** is a group of workers who do physical work together. ❑ *...a gang of labourers.*

▣ 가산명사 비행 청소년 집단 ❑ 경쟁 관계에 있는 폭력단과의 싸움에서 그는 잭크 나이프를 휘둘렀다. ❑ 수많은 폭력 사건의 배후에 비행 청소년들이 있었다. ▣ 가산명사 범죄 조직, 폭력단, 갱단 ❑ 경찰은 55대의 차를 훔친 혐의가 있는 범죄 조직을 쫓고 있었다. ▣ 단수명사 친구들, 패거리 [비격식체] ❑ 이리로 와 봐, 여기 오랜 친구들이 많이 있다. ▣ 가산명사 무리 ❑ 한 무리의 노동자들

Thesaurus	*gang*의 참조어
N.	crowd, group, pack ▣
	mob, ring ▣

▶ **gang up** PHRASAL VERB If people **gang up on** someone, they unite against them for a particular reason, for example in a fight or argument. [INFORMAL] ❑ *Harrison complained that his colleagues ganged up on him.* ❑ *All the other parties ganged up to keep them out of power.*

구동사 단체로 행동하다, 집단적으로 공격하다 [비격식체] ❑ 해리슨은 동료들이 집단적으로 자신을 공격한다고 불평했다. ❑ 다른 당들이 모두 단합하여 그들을 실각시키려 했다.

gan|grene /gǽŋgriːn/ N-UNCOUNT **Gangrene** is the decay that can occur in a part of a person's body if the blood stops flowing to it, for example as a result of illness or injury. ❑ *Once gangrene has developed the tissue is dead and the only hope is to contain the damage.*

불가산명사 괴저 ❑ 일단 괴저가 생기면 조직이 괴사하게 되고 유일한 희망은 상처의 확산을 막는 것뿐이다.

gang|ster /gǽŋstər/ (**gangsters**) N-COUNT A **gangster** is a member of an organized group of violent criminals. ❑ *...a gangster movie.*

가산명사 조직 폭력배 ❑ 갱 영화

gang|way /gǽŋweɪ/ (**gangways**) N-COUNT **The gangway** is the passage between rows of seats, for example in a theater or aircraft, for people to walk along. [BRIT] ❑ *A man in the gangway suddenly stood up to reach for something in the overhead locker.*

가산명사 (좌석 사이의) 통로 [영국영어] ❑ 통로 쪽에 있던 남자가 갑자기 벌떡 일어나더니 무언가를 꺼내려고 머리 위 락커로 손을 뻗었다.

gaol /dʒeɪl/ (**gaols, gaoling, gaoled**) →see **jail**

gap ♦♦♢ /gæp/ (**gaps**) ▣ N-COUNT A **gap** is a space between two things or a hole in the middle of something solid. ❑ *He pulled the thick curtains together, leaving just a narrow gap.* ▣ N-COUNT A **gap** is a period of time when you are not busy or when you stop doing something that you normally do. ❑ *There followed a gap of four years, during which William joined the Army.* ▣ N-COUNT If there is something missing from a situation that prevents it being complete or

▣ 가산명사 간격, 틈 ❑ 그는 두꺼운 커튼을 잡아당겨 약간의 좁은 틈만 남겨 놓고 닫았다. ▣ 가산명사 공백 기간 ❑ 4년의 공백이 생겼고, 그동안 윌리엄은 군에 입대했다. ▣ 가산명사 부족, 공백 ❑ 그 성명은 앞으로 10년 동안 예상되는 퇴직 여파로 생길 공백을 메워 줄 젊은 과학자들을 충원하기 위해 더욱 노력할 것을

A

satisfactory, you can say that there is a **gap**. ❑ *The manifesto calls for a greater effort to recruit young scientists to fill the gap left by a wave of retirements expected over the next decade.* ◪ N-COUNT A **gap between** two groups of people, things, or sets of ideas is a big difference between them. ❑ *...the gap between rich and poor.* ❑ *America's trade gap widened.*

촉구하고 있다. ◪ 가산명사 격차, 간극 ❑ 빈부 간의 격차 ❑ 미국의 무역 수지 적자가 늘어났다.

B

Word Partnership	gap의 연어	
ADJ.	narrow gap ◫ ◪	
V.	bridge a gap ◫ ◪ ◰	
	fill a gap, leave a gap, widen a gap ◫ ◪ ◰ ◪	
PREP.	gap between *something* ◫ ◪	

C

D

E

gape /geɪp/ (**gapes, gaping, gaped**) ◫ V-I If you **gape**, you look at someone or something in surprise, usually with an open mouth. ❑ *His secretary stopped taking notes to gape at me.* ❑ *He was not the type to wander round gaping at everything like a tourist.* ◪ V-I If you say that something such as a hole or a wound **gapes**, you are emphasizing that it is big or wide. [EMPHASIS] ❑ *The front door was missing. A hole gaped in the roof.* ● **gap|ing** ADJ ❑ *The aircraft took off with a gaping hole in its fuselage.*

◫ 자동사 놀라서 입을 딱 벌리고 바라보다 ❑ 그의 비서는 메모를 하다 말고 나를 보고 놀라서 입이 딱 벌어졌다. ❑ 그는 여기저기 돌아보고 다니며 만사에 입을 딱 벌리고 감탄이나 하는 관광객과 같은 부류의 사람은 아니었다. ◪ 자동사 (틈이) 벌어지다 [강조] ❑ 현관문이 없어졌다. 지붕에는 구멍이 뻥 뚫려 있었다. ● 뻥 뚫린 형용사 ❑ 그 비행기는 동체에 구멍이 뻥 뚫린 채 이륙했다.

F

G

gap year N-SING A **gap year** is a period of time during which a student takes a break from studying after they have finished school and before they enter a college or university. [BRIT] ❑ *I went around the world in my gap year.*

단수명사 휴학년 (대학 가기 전에 쉬는 기간) [영국영어] ❑ 나는 휴학년 동안 세계 일주를 했다.

gar|age /ɡærɑːʒ, BRIT ɡærɑːʒ, -rɪdʒ/ (**garages**) ◫ N-COUNT A **garage** is a building in which you keep a car. A garage is often built next to or as part of a house. ❑ *They have turned the garage into a study.* ◪ N-COUNT; N-IN-NAMES A **garage** is a place where you can get your car repaired. In Britain, you can also buy fuel for your car, or buy cars. ❑ *Nancy took her car to a local garage for a check-up.*

◫ 가산명사 차고 ❑ 그들은 차고를 개조해 서재로 만들었다. ◪ 가산명사; 이름명사 자동차 정비소 ❑ 낸시는 차를 점검받기 위해 인근 정비소에 가져갔다.

H

I

gar|bage /ɡɑrbɪdʒ/ ◫ N-UNCOUNT **Garbage** is waste material, especially waste from a kitchen. [mainly AM] ❑ *This morning a bomb in a garbage bag exploded and injured 15 people.* ◪ N-UNCOUNT If someone says that an idea or opinion is **garbage**, they are emphasizing that they believe it is untrue or unimportant. [INFORMAL, DISAPPROVAL] ❑ *I personally think this is complete garbage.* →see pollution

◫ 불가산명사 쓰레기 [주로 미국영어] ❑ 오늘 아침 쓰레기봉투에 든 폭탄이 터져 15명이 부상을 입었다. ◪ 불가산명사 쓰레기, 가치가 없는 생각 [비격식체, 탐탁찮음] ❑ 나는 개인적으로 이것은 완전히 쓰레기라고 생각한다.

J

K

In American English, the words **garbage** and **trash** are most commonly used to refer to waste material that is thrown away. ❑ *...the smell of rotting garbage... She threw the bottle into the trash.* In British English, **rubbish** is the usual word. **Garbage** and **trash** are sometimes used in British English, but only informally and metaphorically. ❑ *I don't have to listen to this garbage... The book was trash.*

미국 영어에서는 버리는 물건을 가리킬 때 garbage와 trash가 가장 흔히 사용된다. ❑ ...쓰레기 썩는 냄새... 그녀는 그 병을 쓰레기 속에 던져 넣었다. 영국 영어에서는 rubbish가 흔히 쓰인다. garbage와 trash가 때때로 영국 영어에서 쓰이기도 하지만, 비격식체나 은유적으로만 쓴다. ❑ 난 이런 쓰레기 같은 이야기를 들을 필요가 없다... 그 책은 허섭스레기였다.

L

M

Thesaurus	garbage의 참조어	
N.	junk, litter, rubbish, trash ◫	
	nonsense ◪	

N

O

gar|bage can (**garbage cans**) N-COUNT A **garbage can** is a container that you put waste material into. [AM; BRIT **dustbin**] ❑ *A bomb planted in a garbage can exploded early today.*

가산명사 쓰레기통 [미국영어; 영국영어 dustbin] ❑ 오늘 아침에 쓰레기통에 장착된 폭탄이 폭발했다.

P

gar|bage dump (**garbage dumps**) N-COUNT A **garbage dump** is a place where waste material is left. [AM; BRIT **rubbish tip**]

가산명사 쓰레기 처리장 [미국영어; 영국영어 rubbish tip]

Q

gar|bage truck (**garbage trucks**) N-COUNT A **garbage truck** is a large truck which collects the garbage from outside people's houses. [AM; BRIT **dustcart**]

가산명사 쓰레기 수거차 [미국영어; 영국영어 dustcart]

gar|bled /ɡɑrbᵊld/ ADJ A **garbled** message or report contains confused or wrong details, often because it is spoken by someone who is nervous or in a hurry. ❑ *The Coastguard was forced to decipher garbled messages in a few minutes.*

형용사 와전된, 왜곡된 ❑ 해안 경비대는 수 분 안에 교란된 메시지를 해독해야 한다.

R

gar|den ◆◆◇ /ɡɑrdᵊn/ (**gardens, gardening, gardened**) ◫ N-COUNT In British English, a **garden** is a piece of land next to a house, with flowers, vegetables, other plants, and often grass. In American English, the usual word is **yard**, and a **garden** refers only to land which is used for growing flowers and vegetables. ❑ *...the most beautiful garden on Earth.* ◪ V-I If you **garden**, you do work in your garden such as weeding or planting. ❑ *Jim gardened at the homes of friends on weekends.* ● **gar|den|ing** N-UNCOUNT ❑ *I have taken up gardening again.* ◰ N-PLURAL **Gardens** are places like a park that have areas of plants, trees, and grass, and that people can visit and walk around. ❑ *The Gardens are open from 10.30 a.m. until 5 p.m.* ◪ N-IN-NAMES **Gardens** is sometimes used as part of the name of a street. ❑ *He lives at 9, Acacia Gardens.* →see park

◫ 가산명사 정원 ❑ 지상에서 가장 아름다운 정원 ◪ 자동사 정원을 가꾸다 ❑ 짐은 주말이면 친구들 집에서 정원을 가꿨다. ● 원예 불가산명사 ❑ 나는 원예를 다시 시작했다. ◰ 복수명사 공원 ❑ 공원은 오전 10시 30분부터 오후 5시까지 개방된다. ◪ 이름명사 일부 거리의 이름에 붙는 이름 ❑ 그는 아카시아 가든스 9번지에 산다.

S

T

gar|den|er /ɡɑrdənər/ (**gardeners**) ◫ N-COUNT A **gardener** is a person who is paid to work in someone else's garden. ❑ *She employed a gardener.* ◪ N-COUNT A **gardener** is someone who enjoys working in their own garden growing flowers or vegetables. ❑ *The majority of sweet peas are still bred by enthusiastic amateur gardeners.*

◫ 가산명사 정원사 ❑ 그녀는 정원사를 고용했다. ◪ 가산명사 원예가 ❑ 대다수의 스위트피는 여전히 열정적인 아마추어 원예가들에 의해 재배된다.

U

V

gar|den|ing leave N-UNCOUNT If someone who leaves their job is given **gardening leave**, they continue to receive their salary and in return they agree not to work for anyone else for a period of time. [BRIT, BUSINESS] ❑ *The settlement means that the three executives can return from gardening leave and start their new jobs.*

불가산명사 조건부 유급 휴직 [영국영어, 경제] ❑ 타협안은 3명의 이사가 조건부 유급 휴직에서 돌아와 새로 맡은 일을 시작한다는 것이었다.

W

X

gar|gle /ɡɑrɡᵊl/ (**gargles, gargling, gargled**) V-I If you **gargle**, you wash your mouth and throat by filling your mouth with a liquid, tipping your head back and using your throat to blow bubbles through the liquid, and finally spitting it out. ❑ *Try gargling with salt water as soon as a cough begins.*

자동사 양치하다 ❑ 기침이 나면 바로 소금물로 양치해 보세요.

Y

Z

gar|ish /ˈɡɛərɪʃ/ ADJ You describe something as **garish** when you dislike it because it is very bright in an unattractive, showy way. [DISAPPROVAL] ❑ *They climbed the garish purple-carpeted stairs.*

형용사 지나치게 화려한, 요란한 [탐탁찮음] ❑ 그들은 요란한 보랏빛 카펫이 깔린 계단을 올라갔다.

gar|land /ˈɡɑːrlənd/ (**garlands**) N-COUNT A **garland** is a circular decoration made from flowers and leaves. People sometimes wear garlands of flowers on their heads or around their necks. ❑ *They wore blue silk dresses with cream sashes and garlands of summer flowers in their hair.*

가산명사 화환 ❑ 그들은 크림색 띠가 달린 푸른색 비단 드레스를 입고 여름 꽃으로 장식된 화환을 머리에 쓰고 있었다.

gar|lic /ˈɡɑːrlɪk/ N-UNCOUNT **Garlic** is the small, white, round bulb of a plant that is related to the onion plant. Garlic has a very strong smell and taste and is used in cooking. ❑ *...a clove of garlic.* →see **spice**

불가산명사 마늘 ❑ 마늘 한 쪽

gar|ment /ˈɡɑːrmənt/ (**garments**) N-COUNT A **garment** is a piece of clothing; used especially in contexts where you are talking about the manufacture or sale of clothes. ❑ *Many of the garments have the customers' name tags sewn into the linings.* →see **clothes**

가산명사 의복, 옷 ❑ 많은 옷의 안감에 고객의 이름표가 붙어 있다.

gar|ner /ˈɡɑːrnər/ (**garners, garnering, garnered**) V-T If someone **has garnered** something useful or valuable, they have gained it or collected it. [FORMAL] ❑ *Durham had garnered three times as many votes as Carey.* ❑ *He has garnered extensive support for his proposals.*

타동사 획득하다, 얻다 [격식체] ❑ 더럼은 캐리보다 세 배나 많은 표를 얻어냈다. ❑ 그는 자신의 계획안에 대해 폭넓은 지지를 얻었다.

gar|nish /ˈɡɑːrnɪʃ/ (**garnishes, garnishing, garnished**) ◼ N-VAR A **garnish** is a small amount of salad, herbs, or other food that is used to decorate cooked or prepared food. ❑ *...a garnish of chopped raw onion, tomato and fresh coriander.* ◻ V-T If you **garnish** cooked or prepared food, you decorate it with a garnish. ❑ *She had finished the vegetables and was garnishing the roast.*

◼ 가산명사 또는 불가산명사 고명 ❑ 잘게 썬 생양파와 토마토 그리고 신선한 고수열매로 만든 고명 ◻ 타동사 요리에 고명을 얹다 ❑ 그녀는 야채 손질을 마치고 나서 오븐에 구운 고기에 고명을 얹고 있었다.

gar|ri|son /ˈɡærɪsən/ (**garrisons, garrisoning, garrisoned**) ◼ N-COUNT-COLL A **garrison** is a group of soldiers whose task is to guard the town or building where they live. ❑ *...a five-hundred man French army garrison.* ◻ N-COUNT A **garrison** is the buildings which the soldiers live in. ❑ *The approaches to the garrison have been heavily mined.* ◾ V-T To **garrison** a place means to put soldiers there in order to protect it. You can also say that soldiers **are garrisoned** in a place. ❑ *British troops still garrisoned the country.* ❑ *No other soldiers were garrisoned there.*

◼ 가산명사-집합 수비대 ❑ 5백 명의 프랑스 육군 수비대 ◻ 가산명사 주둔지 ❑ 주둔지까지의 접근로에는 지뢰가 빽빽하게 매설되어 있다. ◾ 타동사 ~에 주둔시키다; ~에 주둔하다 ❑ 영국군이 여전히 그 나라에 주둔하였다. ❑ 다른 어떤 병사도 거기에 주둔하지 않았다.

gas ◆◇◇ /ɡæs/ (**gases, gasses, gassing, gassed**)

> The form **gases** is the plural of the noun. The form **gasses** is the third person singular of the verb.

gases은 명사의 복수이다. gasses은 동사의 3인칭 단수이다.

◼ N-UNCOUNT **Gas** is a substance like air that is neither liquid nor solid and burns easily. It is used as a fuel for cooking and heating. ❑ *Coal is actually cheaper than gas.* ◻ N-VAR A **gas** is any substance that is neither liquid nor solid, for example oxygen or hydrogen. ❑ *Helium is a very light gas.* ◾ N-MASS **Gas** is a poisonous gas that can be used as a weapon. ❑ *The problem was that the exhaust gases contain many toxins.* ◿ N-UNCOUNT **Gas** is the fuel which is used to drive motor vehicles. [AM; BRIT **petrol**] ❑ *...a tank of gas.* ⬓ V-T To **gas** a person or animal means to kill them by making them breathe poisonous gas. ❑ *Her husband ran a pipe from her car exhaust to the bedroom in an attempt to gas her.* ⬢ →see also **gas mask, greenhouse gas, tear gas** →see **energy, greenhouse effect, matter, solar system**

◼ 불가산명사 가스 ❑ 실은 석탄이 가스보다 값이 싸다. ◻ 가산명사 또는 불가산명사 기체 ❑ 헬륨은 매우 가벼운 기체이다. ◾ 물질명사 독가스 ❑ 문제는 배기가스가 많은 독소를 포함하고 있다는 것이었다. ◿ 불가산명사 휘발유 [미국영어; 영국영어 petrol] ❑ 휘발유 한 통 ⬓ 타동사 독가스로 죽이다 ❑ 그녀의 남편은 그녀를 독가스로 죽이려고 그녀의 자동차 배기관으로부터 파이프를 침실로 끌어들였다.

gash /ɡæʃ/ (**gashes, gashing, gashed**) ◼ N-COUNT A **gash** is a long, deep cut in your skin or in the surface of something. ❑ *There was an inch-long gash just above his right eye.* ◻ V-T If you **gash** something, you accidentally make a long and deep cut in it. ❑ *He gashed his leg while felling trees.*

◼ 가산명사 깊은 상처 ❑ 그의 오른쪽 눈 바로 위에 1인치 길이의 깊은 상처가 있었다. ◻ 타동사 ~에 깊은 상처를 입히다 ❑ 그는 나무를 베다가 다리에 깊은 상처를 입었다.

gas mask (**gas masks**) N-COUNT A **gas mask** is a device that you wear over your face in order to protect yourself from poisonous gases.

가산명사 방독면

gaso|line /ˈɡæsəliːn/ N-UNCOUNT **Gasoline** is the fuel which is used to drive motor vehicles. [AM; BRIT **petrol**] →see **dry cleaning, oil**

불가산명사 가솔린, 휘발유 [미국영어; 영국영어 petrol]

gasp /ɡæsp/ (**gasps, gasping, gasped**) ◼ N-COUNT A **gasp** is a short quick breath of air that you take in through your mouth, especially when you are surprised, shocked, or in pain. ❑ *An audible gasp went round the court as the jury announced the verdict.* ◻ V-I When you **gasp**, you take a short quick breath through your mouth, especially when you are surprised, shocked, or in pain. ❑ *She gasped for air and drew in a lungful of water.* ◾ PHRASE You describe something as **the last gasp** to emphasize that it is the final part of something or happens at the last possible moment. [EMPHASIS] ❑ *...the last gasp of a dying system of censorship.*

◼ 가산명사 헉 하는 소리, 숨이 막히는 듯한 소리 ❑ 배심원이 평결을 발표하자 법정에는 헉 하는 소리가 여기저기서 들려왔다. ◻ 자동사 (숨을) 헐떡거리다 ❑ 그녀는 숨을 쉬려고 헐떡거리다가 폐에 물을 가득 들이켰다. ◾ 구 최후, 마지막 [강조] ❑ 사라져 가는 검열 제도의 최후

gas sta|tion (**gas stations**) N-COUNT A **gas station** is a place where you can buy fuel for your car. [AM; BRIT **petrol station**]

가산명사 주유소 [미국영어; 영국영어 petrol station]

gas|tric /ˈɡæstrɪk/ ADJ You use **gastric** to describe processes, pain, or illnesses that occur in someone's stomach. [MEDICAL] [ADJ n] ❑ *He suffered from diabetes and gastric ulcers.*

형용사 위의 [의학] ❑ 그는 당뇨와 위궤양을 앓았다.

gate ◆◇◇ /ɡeɪt/ (**gates**) ◼ N-COUNT A **gate** is a structure like a door which is used at the entrance to a field, a garden, or the grounds of a building. ❑ *He opened the gate and started walking up to the house.* ◻ N-COUNT In an airport, a **gate** is a place where passengers leave the airport and get on their airplane. ❑ *Passengers with hand luggage can go straight to the departure gate to check in there.*

◼ 가산명사 출입문 ❑ 그는 대문을 열고 그 집 쪽으로 걸어 올라가기 시작했다. ◻ 가산명사 탑승구 ❑ 수하물을 소지한 승객은 곧바로 탑승구로 가서 그곳에서 탑승 수속을 할 수 있다.

gate|crash /ˈɡeɪtkræʃ/ (**gatecrashes, gatecrashing, gatecrashed**) V-T If someone **gatecrashes** a party or other social event, they go to it, even though they have not been invited. ❑ *Scores of people tried desperately to gatecrash the party.* ● **gate|crash|er** (**gatecrashers**) N-COUNT Panic set in as gatecrashers tried to force their way through the narrow doors and corridors.

타동사 초대받지 않고 들어가다 ❑ 수십 명의 사람들이 초대받지 않은 그 파티에 입장하려고 필사적으로 애를 썼다. ● 불청객 가산명사 ❑ 불청객들이 좁은 문과 복도로 떠밀고 들어오려고 시도하자 사람들이 겁을 집어먹기 시작했다.

gate|way /ˈɡeɪtweɪ/ (**gateways**) ◼ N-COUNT A **gateway** is an entrance where there is a gate. ❑ *He walked across the park and through a gateway.* ◻ N-COUNT A **gateway to** somewhere is a place which you go through because it leads you to a much larger place. ❑ *Lyons is the gateway to the Alps for motorists driving out*

◼ 가산명사 대문 ❑ 그는 걸어서 공원을 지나고 대문을 통과했다. ◻ 가산명사 ~로 가는 통로 ❑ 영국에서 출발하는 자동차 여행자에게 리용은 알프스로 가는 통로이다. ◾ 가산명사 ~에 이르는 길 ❑ 명성이 있는

A

from Britain. ◼ N-COUNT If something is a **gateway to** a job, career, or other activity, it gives you the opportunity to make progress or get further success in that activity. ❑ *The prestigious title offered a gateway to success in the highly competitive world of modelling.* ◼ N-COUNT In computing, a **gateway** connects different computer networks so that information can be passed between them. [COMPUTING] ❑ *The network has a gateway into the hospital mainframe.* →see **Internet**

직함이 경쟁이 치열한 패션모델의 세계에서 성공하도록 이끌어 주었다. ◼ 가산명사 (컴퓨터) 게이트웨이 [컴퓨터] ❑ 그 네트워크에는 병원의 메인프레임에 연결되는 게이트웨이가 있다.

B

C

gath|er ◆◆◇ /gǽðər/ (**gathers, gathering, gathered**) ◼ V-T/V-I If people **gather** somewhere or if someone **gathers** people somewhere, they come together in a group. ❑ *In the evenings, we gathered around the fireplace and talked.* ◼ V-T If you **gather** things, you collect them together so that you can use them. ❑ *I suggest we gather enough firewood to last the night.* ● PHRASAL VERB **Gather up** means the same as **gather**. ❑ *When Sutcliffe had gathered up his papers, he went out.* ◼ V-T If you **gather** information or evidence, you collect it, especially over a period of time and after a lot of hard work. ❑ *...a private detective using a hidden tape recorder to gather information.* ◼ V-T If something **gathers** speed, momentum, or force, it gradually becomes faster or more powerful. ❑ *Demands for his dismissal have gathered momentum in recent weeks.* ◼ V-T When you **gather** something such as your strength, courage, or thoughts, you make an effort to prepare yourself to do something. ❑ *You must gather your strength for the journey.* ● PHRASAL VERB **Gather up** means the same as **gather**. ❑ *She was gathering up her courage to approach him when he called to her.* ◼ V-T You use **gather** in expressions such as "**I gather**" and "**as far as I can gather**" to introduce information that you have found out, especially when you have found it out in an indirect way. ❑ *I gather his report is highly critical of the trial judge.* ❑ *"He speaks English," she said to Graham. "I gathered that."* ◼ to **gather dust** →see **dust**

◼ 타동사/자동사 ~에 모이다 ❑ 저녁이면 우리는 벽난로 주위에 모여 이야기를 나누었다. ◼ 타동사 모으다 ❑ 나는 우리가 밤새 쓰기에 충분한 땔감을 모으자고 제안하고 싶다. ● 구동사 모으다 ❑ 섯크리프는 자기 서류를 다 챙기고 나서 밖으로 나갔다. ◼ 타동사 수집하다 ❑ 정보를 수집하려고 몰래 녹음기를 사용하는 사설탐정 ◼ 타동사 (속도를) 더하다 ❑ 최근 몇 주 사이에 그의 면직을 요구하는 목소리가 탄력을 받고 있다. ◼ 타동사 (힘을 끌어) 모으다 ❑ 너는 그 여정을 위해 있는 힘을 다 내야 한다. ● 구동사 모으다 ❑ 그녀는 그가 자신을 불렀을 때 그에게 다가가기 위해 있는 용기를 끌어 모으고 있었다. ◼ 타동사 추측하다; 내가 추측하는 바로는 ❑ 그의 보고서가 예심 판사에 대해 매우 비판적인 것으로 추측된다. ❑ "그는 영어를 해."라고 그녀가 그레이엄에게 말했다. "나도 그럴 거라고 생각했어."

D

E

F

G

H

Thesaurus   *gather*의 참조어

v.   accumulate, collect, group; (*ant.*) scatter ◼ ◼

▶**gather up** →see **gather** 2, 5

J

gath|er|ing /gǽðərɪŋ/ (**gatherings**) ◼ N-COUNT A **gathering** is a group of people meeting together for a particular purpose. ❑ *...the twenty-second annual gathering of the South Pacific Forum.* ◼ ADJ If there is **gathering** darkness, the light is gradually decreasing, usually because it is nearly night. ❑ *The lighthouse beam was quite distinct in the gathering dusk.* →see also **gather**

◼ 가산명사 모임 ❑ 제22회 남태평양 포럼 연례 모임 ◼ 형용사 점점 더해 가는 ❑ 점점 짙어가는 어스름 속에서 등대의 불빛이 아주 선명했다.

K

L

gaudy /gɔ́di/ (**gaudier, gaudiest**) ADJ If something is **gaudy**, it is very brightly-colored and showy. [DISAPPROVAL] ❑ *...her gaudy orange-and-purple floral hat.*

형용사 눈부신, 화려한 [탐탁잖음] ❑ 그녀의 오렌지 빛과 자줏빛이 섞인 화려한 꽃무늬 모자

M

gauge /geɪdʒ/ (**gauges, gauging, gauged**) ◼ V-T If you **gauge** the speed or strength of something, or if you gauge an amount, you measure or calculate it, often by using a device of some kind. ❑ *He gauged the wind at over thirty knots.* ◼ N-COUNT A **gauge** is a device that measures the amount or quantity of something and shows the amount measured. [oft n N] ❑ *...temperature gauges.* ◼ V-T If you **gauge** people's actions, feelings, or intentions in a particular situation, you carefully consider and judge them. ❑ *His mood can be gauged by his reaction to the most trivial of incidents.* ◼ N-SING A **gauge of** someone's feelings or a situation is a fact or event that can be used to judge them. ❑ *The index is the government's chief gauge of future economic activity.*

◼ 타동사 측정하다 ❑ 그는 바람이 30노트 이상이라고 측정했다. ◼ 가산명사 측정계기 ❑ 온도계 ◼ 타동사 파악하다 ❑ 아주 하찮은 일에 대해 그가 어떻게 반응하는지를 보고 그의 기분을 파악할 수 있다. ◼ 단수명사 척도 ❑ 그 지수는 정부가 미래의 경제 활동을 측정하는 주요 척도이다.

N

O

gaunt /gɔnt/ ◼ ADJ If someone looks **gaunt**, they look very thin, usually because they have been very ill or worried. ❑ *Looking gaunt and tired, he denied there was anything to worry about.* ◼ ADJ If you describe a building as **gaunt**, you mean it is very plain and unattractive. [LITERARY] [ADJ n] ❑ *Above on the hillside was a large, gaunt, gray house.*

◼ 형용사 수척한, 핼쑥한 ❑ 수척하고 피곤해 보였지만 그는 걱정거리가 있음을 부인했다. ◼ 형용사 볼품없는 [문예체] ❑ 산허리 위에 크고 볼품없는 회색 집이 서 있었다.

P

Q

gaunt|let /gɔ́ntlɪt/ (**gauntlets**) ◼ N-COUNT **Gauntlets** are long, thick, protective gloves. ❑ *The smart biker also wears boots, gauntlets, and protective clothing.* ◼ PHRASE If you **pick up the gauntlet** or **take up the gauntlet**, you accept the challenge that someone has made. ❑ *She picked up the gauntlet in her incisive Keynote Address to the Conference.* ◼ PHRASE If you **run the gauntlet**, you go through an unpleasant experience in which a lot of people criticize or attack you. ❑ *The trucks tried to drive to the British base, running the gauntlet of marauding bands of gunmen.* ◼ PHRASE If you **throw down the gauntlet** to someone, you say or do something that challenges them to argue or compete with you. ❑ *Luxury car firm Jaguar has thrown down the gauntlet to competitors by giving the best guarantee on the market.*

◼ 가산명사 (보호용) 장갑 ❑ 현명한 폭주족은 부츠, 보호 장갑, 보호복을 착용한다. ◼ 구 도전에 응하다 ❑ 그녀는 그 학술 대회에서 신랄한 기조연설을 통해 응수했다. ◼ 구 혹평을 받다; 혹심한 공격을 받다 ❑ 트럭들은 무장 습격대의 공격을 뚫고 영국 기지로 가고자 했다. ◼ 구 도전장을 던지다 ❑ 고급 자동차 회사인 재규어는 업계 최고의 보증을 내세우며 경쟁사들에 도전장을 던졌다.

R

S

T

gave /geɪv/ **Gave** is the past tense of **give**.

give의 과거

U

gay ◆◆◇ /geɪ/ (**gays**) ADJ A **gay** person is homosexual. ❑ *The quality of life for gay men has improved over the last two decades.* ● N-PLURAL **Gays** are homosexual people, especially homosexual men. ❑ *More importantly, gays have proved themselves to be style leaders.* ● **gay|ness** N-UNCOUNT ❑ *...Mike's admission of his gayness.*

형용사 동성애의 ❑ 지난 20년에 걸쳐 남성 동성애자의 삶의 질이 향상되었다. ● 복수명사 (특히 남성) 동성애자 ❑ 좀더 주목할 만한 사실은, 동성애자들이 유행의 선도자로 입증되었다는 것이다. ● 불가산명사 동성애임 ❑ 자기가 동성애자라는 마이크의 고백

V

W

gaze /geɪz/ (**gazes, gazing, gazed**) ◼ V-I If you **gaze at** someone or something, you look steadily at them for a long time, for example because you find them attractive or interesting, or because you are thinking about something else. ❑ *...gazing at herself in the mirror. Sitting in his wicker chair, he gazed reflectively at the fire.* ◼ N-COUNT You can talk about someone's **gaze** as a way of describing how they are looking at something, especially when they are looking steadily at it. [WRITTEN] ❑ *The Monsignor turned his gaze from the flames to meet the Colonel's.* ❑ *She felt increasingly uncomfortable under the woman's steady gaze.* ◼ PHRASE If someone or something is **in the public gaze**, they are receiving a lot of attention from the general public. ❑ *You won't find a couple more in the public gaze than Michael and Lizzie.*

◼ 자동사 뚫어지게 보다, 응시하다 ❑ 거울 속의 그녀 자신을 응시하고 있는 ❑ 그는 고리버들 의자에 앉아 생각에 잠긴 채 불꽃을 응시했다. ◼ 가산명사 응시, 눈길, 시선 [문어체] ❑ 신부님은 불길을 바라보던 눈길을 돌려 대령의 눈을 마주보았다. ❑ 그녀는 그 여자가 빤히 쳐다보는 눈길에 점점 불편해졌다. ◼ 구 대중의 시선을 받고 있는 ❑ 마이클과 리지보다 대중의 시선을 많이 받고 있는 한 쌍은 없을 것이다.

X

Y

Z

The verbs **gaze** and **stare** are both used to talk about looking at something for a long time. If you **gaze at** something, it is often because you think it is marvelous or impressive. ❏ *A fresh-faced little girl gazes in wonder at the bright fairground lights.* If you **stare at** something or someone, it is often because you think they are strange or shocking. ❏ *Various families came out and stared at us.*

동사 gaze와 stare는 둘 다 어떤 것을 오랫동안 쳐다보는 것을 말할 때 쓴다. 무엇을 gaze at 하는 것은 흔히 그것이 멋지거나 인상적이라고 생각하기 때문이다. ❏ 맑은 얼굴의 어린 소녀가 환한 풍물장터의 불빛을 신기한 듯 바라본다. 사람이나 사물을 stare at 하는 것은 흔히 그것이 이상하거나 충격적이라고 여기기 때문인 경우가 많다. ❏ 여러 가족들이 나와서 우리를 빤히 쳐다보았다.

ga|zette /gəzɛt/ (**gazettes**) **1** N-IN-NAMES **Gazette** is often used in the names of newspapers. [N N] ❏ *...the Arkansas Gazette.* **2** N-COUNT In Britain, a **gazette** is an official publication in which information such as honors, public appointments, and important decisions are announced. ❏ *...an advertisement in the official gazette of the province.*

1 이름명사 신문의 명칭 ❏ 아칸소 신문 **2** 가산명사 (영국의) 관보, 공보 ❏ 그 지방의 공식 관보에 난 광고

GB /dʒi bi/ N-PROPER **GB** is an abbreviation for **Great Britain**.

고유명사 '영국(Great Britain)'의 약자

GCSE /dʒi si ɛs i/ (**GCSEs**) N-VAR **GCSEs** are British educational qualifications which schoolchildren take when they are fifteen or sixteen years old. **GCSE** is an abbreviation for "General Certificate of Secondary Education." ❏ *She quit school as soon as she had taken her GCSEs.*

가산명사 또는 불가산명사 (영국의) 중등 교육 자격시험 ❏ 그녀는 중등 교육 자격시험을 보자마자 학교를 그만두었다.

GDP /dʒi di pi/ (**GDPs**) N-VAR In economics, a country's **GDP** is the total value of goods and services produced within a country in a year, not including its income from investments in other countries. **GDP** is an abbreviation for "gross domestic product." Compare **GNP**. ❏ *In the final quarter of 2001, GDP rose by just 0.2% on the previous quarter.*

가산명사 또는 불가산명사 국내 총생산 ❏ 2001년 4분기에 국내 총생산은 지난 분기보다 0.2퍼센트 상승했다.

gear ♦♢♢ /gɪər/ (**gears, gearing, geared**) **1** N-COUNT The **gears** on a machine or vehicle are a device for changing the rate at which energy is changed into motion. ❏ *On hills, he must use low gears.* ❏ *The car was in fourth gear.* **2** N-UNCOUNT The **gear** involved in a particular activity is the equipment or special clothing that you use. ❏ *About 100 officers in riot gear were needed to break up the fight.* ❏ *...fishing gear.* **3** N-UNCOUNT **Gear** means clothing. [INFORMAL] ❏ *I used to wear trendy gear but it just looked ridiculous.* **4** V-T PASSIVE If someone or something **is geared to** or **towards** a particular purpose, they are organized or designed in order to achieve that purpose. ❏ *Colleges are not always geared to the needs of mature students.* ❏ *My training was geared towards winning gold in Munich.*

1 가산명사 변속기 ❏ 언덕에서 그는 저속 기어를 사용해야 한다. ❏ 자동차는 4단 기어에 놓여 있었다. **2** 불가산명사 기구, 장비 ❏ 그 폭력 사태를 해결하는 데 폭동 진압용 장비를 갖춘 경관 100명의 경관이 필요했다. ❏ 낚시 장비 **3** 불가산명사 의상 [비격식체] ❏ 나는 유행하는 의상을 입곤 했으나 우스꽝스러워 보이기만 했다. **4** 수동 타동사 -에 맞추어지다 ❏ 대학이 늦깎이 학생들의 필요에 항상 맞추어져 있지는 않다. ❏ 내 훈련은 뮌헨에서 금메달을 따는데 맞추어져 있다.

Word Partnership	gear의 연어
V.	put *something* in gear, shift gear **1**
	change gear **1** **4**
ADJ.	protective gear **2**

▶**gear up** PHRASAL VERB If someone **is gearing up for** a particular activity, they are preparing to do it. If they **are geared up to** do a particular activity, they are prepared to do it. ❏ *...another indication that the Government is gearing up for an election.*

구동사 -할 준비를 하다; -할 준비가 되어 있다 ❏ 정부가 선거를 준비하고 있다는 또 다른 징후

gear lev|er (**gear levers**) or **gear stick** N-COUNT In a vehicle, the **gear lever** or the **gear stick** is the same as the **gearshift**. [BRIT]

가산명사 변속 레버 [영국영어]

gear|shift /gɪərʃɪft/ (**gearshifts**) also **gear shift** N-COUNT In a vehicle, the **gearshift** is the lever that you use to change gear in a car or other vehicle. [mainly AM; BRIT usually **gear lever, gear stick**]

가산명사 변속 레버 [주로 미국영어; 영국영어 대개 gear lever, gear stick]

gee /dʒi/ EXCLAM People sometimes say **gee** to emphasize a reaction or remark. [AM, INFORMAL, EMPHASIS] ❏ *Gee, it's hot.*

감탄사 아이고, 저런 [미국영어, 비격식체, 강조] ❏ 아이고 더워라.

geese /gis/ **Geese** is the plural of **goose**.

goose의 복수

gel /dʒɛl/ (**gels, gelling, gelled**)

The spelling **jell** is usually used in American English and is sometimes used in British English for meanings **1** and **2**.

철자 jell은 대개 미국영어에서 쓰며, 가끔 영국영어에서 **1**과 **2** 의미로 쓴다.

1 V-RECIP If people **gel with** each other, or if two groups of people **gel**, they work well together because their skills and personalities fit together well. ❏ *They have gelled very well with the rest of the side.* ❏ *Their partnership gelled and scriptwriting for television followed.* **2** V-I If a vague shape, thought, or creation **gels**, it becomes clearer or more definite. ❏ *Even if her interpretation has not yet gelled into a satisfying whole, she displays real musicianship.* **3** N-MASS **Gel** is a thick jelly-like substance, especially one used to keep your hair in a particular style.

1 상호동사 손발이 맞다 ❏ 그들은 그 편의 나머지 사람들과 손발이 아주 잘 맞는다. ❏ 그들은 손발이 잘 맞아서 텔레비전용 대본을 집필하게 되었다. **2** 자동사 구체화되다 ❏ 곡 해석이 아직 전체적으로 만족스럽게 드러나지는 않았지만 그녀는 진정한 연주가의 자질을 보여 준다. **3** 물질명사 젤

gem /dʒɛm/ (**gems**) **1** N-COUNT A **gem** is a jewel or stone that is used in jewelry. ❏ *The mask is formed of a gold-platinum alloy inset with emeralds and other gems.* **2** N-COUNT If you describe something or someone as a **gem**, you mean that they are especially pleasing, good, or helpful. [INFORMAL] ❏ *...a gem of a hotel, Castel Clara.*

1 가산명사 보석 ❏ 그 가면은 금과 백금의 합금으로 만들어졌고 에메랄드와 다른 보석들이 박혀 있었다. **2** 가산명사 보석 같은 것, 보석처럼 소중한 사람 [비격식체] ❏ 보석 같은 호텔인 카스텔 클라라

gen|der /dʒɛndər/ (**genders**) **1** N-VAR A person's **gender** is the fact that they are male or female. ❏ *Women are sometimes denied opportunities solely because of their gender.* **2** N-COUNT You can refer to all male people or all female people as a particular **gender**. ❏ *While her observations may be true about some men, they could hardly apply to the entire gender.* **3** N-VAR In grammar, the **gender** of a noun, pronoun, or adjective is whether it is masculine, feminine, or neuter. A word's gender can affect its form and behavior. In English, only personal pronouns such as "she," reflexive pronouns such as "itself," and possessive determiners such as "his" have gender. ❏ *In both Welsh and Irish the word for "moon" is of feminine gender.*

1 가산명사 또는 불가산명사 성별 ❏ 여성은 때로 단지 여성이라는 이유만으로 기회를 박탈당한다. **2** 가산명사 성 ❏ 어떤 남자들에 대해서는 그 여자의 소견이 들어맞을 수도 있겠으나 그렇다고 남성 전체에 적용될 수는 없을 것이다. **3** 가산명사 또는 불가산명사 성 (문법) ❏ 웨일스 말과 아일랜드 말 모두에서 '달'이라는 단어는 여성성을 띤다.

gene ♦♢♢ /dʒin/ (**genes**) N-COUNT A **gene** is the part of a cell in a living thing which controls its physical characteristics, growth, and development. ❏ *The gene for asthma has been identified.*

→see Word Web: gene

가산명사 유전자 ❏ 천식 유전자가 규명되었다.

A
B
C
D

Word Web   gene

Gregor Mendel* studied the **inheritance** of **traits** in plants. He discovered how plants pass on their physical **characteristics** from **generation** to generation. He **bred** and cross-bred seven varieties of pea plants. He showed that each new plant was not just a general blend of its parents. Each characteristic (for example, flower color) is inherited separately. Some characteristics are **dominant** and some are recessive. When dominant and recessive **genes** combine, there is predictable pattern of inheritance. Today we know that genes form long strings called **DNA**.

Gregor Mendel (1822-1884): a scientist.

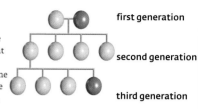

first generation

second generation

third generation

E

ge|neal|ogy /dʒiːniˈælədʒi/ N-UNCOUNT **Genealogy** is the study of the history of families, especially through studying historical documents to discover the relationships between particular people and their families. ● **ge|nea|logi|cal** /dʒiːniəˈlɒdʒɪkəl/ ADJ [ADJ n] ❑ *He had engaged in genealogical research on his family shortly before the War.*

F

불가산명사 계보학 ● 계보의, 족보의 형용사 ❑ 그는 전쟁 직전에 자기 가문의 족보에 대한 연구를 했었다.

G

gen|era /ˈdʒenərə/ **Genera** is the plural of **genus**.

genus의 복수

gen|er|al ♦♦♦ /ˈdʒenrəl/ (**generals**) **1** N-COUNT; N-TITLE; N-VOC A **general** is a high-ranking officer in the armed forces, usually in the army. ❑ *The General's visit to Sarajevo is part of preparations for the deployment of extra troops.* **2** ADJ If you talk about the **general** situation somewhere or talk about something in **general** terms, you are describing the situation as a whole rather than considering its details or exceptions. [ADJ n] ❑ *The figures represent a general decline in employment.* ❑ *...the general deterioration of English society.* ● PHRASE If you describe something **in general terms**, you describe it without giving details. **3** ADJ You use **general** to describe several items or activities when there are too many of them or when they are not important enough to mention separately. [ADJ n] ❑ *£2,500 for software is soon swallowed up in general costs.* **4** ADJ You use **general** to describe something that involves or affects most people, or most people in a particular group. [ADJ n] ❑ *The project should raise general awareness about bullying.* **5** ADJ If you describe something as **general**, you mean that it is not restricted to any one thing or area. [ADJ n] ❑ *...a general ache radiating from the back of the neck.* ❑ *...a general sense of well-being.* **6** ADJ **General** is used to describe a person's job, usually as part of their title, to indicate that they have complete responsibility for the administration of an organization or business. [BUSINESS] [ADJ n] ❑ *He joined Sanders Roe, moving on later to become General Manager.* **7** →see also **generally** **8** PHRASE You use **in general** to indicate that you are talking about something as a whole, rather than about part of it. ❑ *I think we need to improve our educational system in general.* **9** PHRASE You say **in general** to indicate that you are referring to most people or things in a particular group. ❑ *People in general will support us.*

H
I
J
K
L
M
N

1 가산명사; 경칭명사; 호격명사 장군 ❑ 그 장군의 사라예보 방문은 추가 병력 배치 준비의 일환이다. **2** 형용사 전반적인 ❑ 그 수치는 전반적인 고용 감소를 나타낸다. ❑ 영국 사회의 전반적인 퇴보 ● 구 전반적으로 **3** 형용사 잡음의 ❑ 소프트웨어 몫으로 두 2,500파운드가 곧 잡비로 낭비된다. **4** 형용사 세상 일반의 ❑ 그 연구 과제는 약자를 괴롭히는 폭력에 대한 일반 사람들의 인식을 높일 것이다. **5** 형용사 전반적인, 일부에 국한되지 않은 ❑ 목 뒤에서부터 퍼져 나오는 전신 통증 ❑ 전반적으로 건강하고 행복하다는 느낌 **6** 형용사 총괄의, 총 [경제] ❑ 그는 샌더스 로우에 입사해서 나중에는 총지배인에게까지 이르렀다. **8** 구 전반적으로 ❑ 나는 우리의 교육 제도를 전반적으로 개선할 필요가 있다고 생각한다. **9** 구 대개의, 일반적인 ❑ 대부분의 사람들이 우리를 지지할 것이다.

O

gen|er|al elec|tion ♦♦◇ (**general elections**) **1** N-COUNT In the United States, a **general election** is a local, state, or national election where the candidates have been selected by a primary election. Compare **primary**. ❑ *Street raised $10 million during his primary and general election in 1999.* **2** N-COUNT In Britain, a **general election** is an election where everyone votes for people to represent them in Parliament. ❑ *Spain holds a general election next year.*

1 가산명사 총선거 ❑ 스트리트는 1999년 예비 선거 및 총선거 기간 동안 1,000만 달러를 모았다. **2** 가산명사 총선거 ❑ 스페인에서는 내년에 총선거가 있다.

P

gen|er|ali|za|tion /ˌdʒenrəlaɪˈzeɪʃən/ (**generalizations**) [BRIT also **generalisation**] N-VAR A **generalization** is a statement that seems to be true in most situations or for most people, but that may not be completely true in all cases. ❑ *He is making sweeping generalizations to get his point across.*

Q

[영국영어 generalisation] 가산명사 또는 불가산명사 일반화 ❑ 그는 자신의 요점을 전달하기 위해 포괄적인 일반화를 하고 있다.

gen|er|al|ize /ˈdʒenrəlaɪz/ (**generalizes, generalizing, generalized**) [BRIT also **generalise**] **1** V-I If you **generalize**, you say something that seems to be true in most situations or for most people, but that may not be completely true in all cases. ❑ *Critics love to generalize, to formulate trends into which all new work must be fitted, however contradictory.* **2** V-T If you **generalize** something such as an idea, you apply it more widely than in its original context, as if it was true in many other situations. ❑ *A child first labels the household pet cat as a "cat" and then generalizes this label to other animals that look like it.*

R
S

[영국영어 generalise] **1** 자동사 일반화하여 말하다 ❑ 비평가들은 일반화하기를 좋아해서 아무리 모순되더라도 모든 새 작품들을 함께 묶는 사조를 만들어 낸다. **2** 타동사 일반화시키다 ❑ 아이는 집에서 기르는 애완 고양이를 먼저 '고양이'라고 부르고 그 다음엔 고양이와 유사하게 보이는 다른 동물에 그 호칭을 일반화시킨다.

T

gen|er|al|ized /ˈdʒenrəlaɪzd/ [BRIT also **generalised**] **1** ADJ **Generalized** means involving many different things, rather than one or two specific things. ❑ *...a generalized discussion about admirable singers.* **2** ADJ You use **generalized** to describe medical conditions or problems which affect the whole of someone's body, or the whole of a part of their body. [MEDICAL] ❑ *She experienced an increase in generalized aches and pains.*

U

[영국영어 generalised] **1** 형용사 일반적인 ❑ 훌륭한 가수들에 대한 일반적인 토론 **2** 형용사 총체적인, 전신의 [의학] ❑ 그녀는 전신의 통증과 고통이 심해지는 것을 느꼈다.

V

gen|er|al knowl|edge N-UNCOUNT **General knowledge** is knowledge about many different things, as opposed to detailed knowledge about one particular subject. ❑ *...a general knowledge quiz show.*

불가산명사 일반 상식 ❑ 일반 상식을 묻는 퀴즈 쇼

W

gen|er|al|ly ♦♦◇ /ˈdʒenrəli/ **1** ADV You use **generally** to give a summary of a situation, activity, or idea without referring to the particular details of it. ❑ *University teachers generally have admitted a lack of enthusiasm about their subjects.* **2** ADV You use **generally** to say that something happens or is used on most occasions but not on every occasion. ❑ *As women we generally say and feel too much about these things.* ❑ *In the diet, it is generally true that the darker the fruit the higher its iron content.*

X
Y

1 부사 일반적으로 ❑ 일반적으로 대학 강사들은 자신들이 맡고 있는 과목에 대한 열정이 부족하다는 점을 인정했다. **2** 부사 보통, 대개 ❑ 여성으로서 우리는 보통 이러한 것들에 대해 너무 많이 말하고 느낀다. ❑ 음식에서, 과일 색깔이 어두울수록 철 성분이 더 높다는 것은 대체로 사실이다.

Thesaurus   generally의 참조어

ADV.   mainly, usually **2**

Z

gen|er|al prac|ti|tion|er (general practitioners) N-COUNT A **general practitioner** is the same as a **GP**. [FORMAL]

가산명사 일반 의사, 비전문의 [격식체]

gen|er|al pub|lic N-SING-COLL You can refer to the people in a society as **the general public**, especially when you are contrasting people in general with a small group. ☐ *These charities depend on the compassionate feelings and generosity of the general public.*

단수명사-집합 일반 대중 ☐ 이러한 자선 사업은 일반 대중의 동정심과 관대함에 의존한다.

gen|er|al strike (general strikes) N-COUNT A **general strike** is a situation where most or all of the workers in a country are on strike and are refusing to work.

가산명사 총파업

gen|er|ate ♦◇◇ /dʒɛnəreɪt/ (generates, generating, generated) **1** V-T To **generate** something means to cause it to begin and develop. ☐ *The Employment Minister said the reforms would generate new jobs.* **2** V-T To **generate** a form of energy or power means to produce it. ☐ *The company, New England Electric, burns coal to generate power.* →see **energy**

1 타동사 발생시키다, 일으키다 ☐ 노동부 장관은 이번 개혁이 새로운 일자리를 창출할 것이라고 말했다. **2** 타동사 발생시키다 ☐ '뉴잉글랜드 일렉트릭'이라는 회사는 석탄을 연소시켜 전기를 발전한다.

gen|era|tion ♦◇◇ /dʒɛnəreɪʃⁿn/ (generations) **1** N-COUNT A **generation** is all the people in a group or country who are of a similar age, especially when they are considered as having the same experiences or attitudes. ☐ *...the younger generation of Party members.* **2** N-COUNT A **generation** is the period of time, usually considered to be about thirty years, that it takes for children to grow up and become adults and have children of their own. ☐ *Within a generation flight has become the method used by many travellers.* **3** N-COUNT You can use **generation** to refer to a stage of development in the design and manufacture of machines or equipment. [N of n] ☐ *...a new generation of IBM/Apple computers.* **4** ADJ **Generation** is used to indicate how long members of your family have had a particular nationality. For example, second generation means that you were born in the country you live in, but your parents were not. [ord ADJ n] ☐ *...second generation Asians in Britain.*

1 가산명사 세대 ☐ 당원 중 젊은 세대들 **2** 가산명사 세대 ☐ 한 세대 사이에 비행기는 많은 여행자들이 사용하는 수단이 되었다. **3** 가산명사 시대 ☐ 아이비엠/애플 컴퓨터의 새로운 시대 **4** 형용사 세대의 ☐ 아시아계 영국인 2세대

gen|era|tor /dʒɛnəreɪtər/ (generators) **1** N-COUNT A **generator** is a machine which produces electricity. ☐ *The house is far from mains water or electricity and relies on its own generators.* **2** N-COUNT A **generator of** something is a person, organization, product, or situation which produces it or causes it to happen. ☐ *The company has been a very good cash generator.* →see **electricity**

1 가산명사 발전기 ☐ 그 집은 수도와 전기 본선에서 멀리 떨어져 있어 자체 발전기에 의존한다. **2** 가산명사 ~을 발생시키는 사람, ~을 발생시키는 물건 ☐ 그 회사는 아주 훌륭한 현금 제조기였다.

ge|ner|ic /dʒɪnɛrɪk/ (generics) **1** ADJ You use **generic** to describe something that refers or relates to a whole class of similar things. ☐ *Parmesan is a generic term used to describe a family of hard Italian cheeses.* **2** ADJ A **generic** drug or other product is one that does not have a trademark and is known by a general name, rather than the manufacturer's name. ☐ *They encourage doctors to prescribe cheaper generic drugs instead of more expensive brand names.* ● N-COUNT **Generic** is also a noun. ☐ *The program saved $11 million in 1988 by substituting generics for brand-name drugs.*

1 형용사 총칭적인, 포괄적인 ☐ 파르메산은 딱딱한 이탈리아 치즈 종류를 나타내는 데 쓰이는 총칭이다. **2** 형용사 (상품, 약 등) 일반명의 ☐ 그들은 의사들에게 상표 있는 비싼 약 대신 일반명의 싼 약으로 처방하라고 한다. ● 가산명사 상표 없는 것 ☐ 그 프로그램은 상표 있는 약 대신 일반명의 약을 사용하여 1988년에 1,100만 달러를 절약했다.

gen|er|os|ity /dʒɛnərɒsiti/ N-UNCOUNT If you refer to someone's **generosity**, you mean that they are generous, especially in doing or giving more than is usual or expected. ☐ *There are stories about his generosity, the massive amounts of money he gave to charities.*

불가산명사 관대함, 관용 ☐ 자선 단체에 엄청난 돈을 기부하는 등의 그의 후한 마음씨에 관한 이야기들이 있다.

gen|er|ous ♦◇◇ /dʒɛnərəs/ **1** ADJ A **generous** person gives more of something, especially money, than is usual or expected. ☐ *German banks are more generous in their lending.* ● **gen|er|ous|ly** ADV [ADV with v] ☐ *We would like to thank all the judges who gave so generously of their time.* **2** ADJ A **generous** person is friendly, helpful, and willing to see the good qualities in someone or something. ☐ *He was always generous in sharing his enormous knowledge.* ● **gen|er|ous|ly** ADV [ADV with v] ☐ *The students generously gave them instruction in social responsibility.* **3** ADJ A **generous** amount of something is much larger than is usual or necessary. ☐ *He should be able to keep his room tidy with the generous amount of storage space.* ● **gen|er|ous|ly** ADV ☐ *Season the steaks generously with salt and pepper.*

1 형용사 관대한, 후한 ☐ 독일 은행들은 대출을 해 주는 데 더 관대하다. ● 관대하게 부사 ☐ 친절하게 시간을 내 주신 모든 판사님들께 감사를 드리고 싶습니다. **2** 형용사 사람 좋은, 너그러운 ☐ 그는 항상 너그러이 자신의 해박한 지식을 나누어 주었다. ● 너그럽게 부사 ☐ 그 학생들은 너그러이 그들에게 사회적 책임에 대해서 가르쳐 주었다. **3** 형용사 넉넉한, 많은 ☐ 이렇게 넉넉한 저장 공간이면 그가 충분히 자기 방을 깨끗이 쓸 수 있을 것이다. ● 넉넉하게 부사 ☐ 스테이크에 소금과 후추를 넉넉히 넣어 양념을 하세요.

Thesaurus generous의 참조어

ADJ. charitable, kind; (ant.) mean, selfish, stingy **1 2**
abundant; (ant.) meager **3**

---

ge|net|ic /dʒɪnɛtɪk/ ADJ You use **genetic** to describe something that is concerned with genetics or with genes. ☐ *Cystic fibrosis is the most common fatal genetic disease in the United States.* ● **ge|neti|cal|ly** /dʒɪnɛtɪkli/ ADV ☐ *Some people are genetically predisposed to diabetes.*

형용사 유전의 ☐ 미국 내에서 낭포성 섬유증은 가장 흔하면서도 치명적인 유전병이다. ● 유전적으로 부사 ☐ 유전적으로 당뇨병에 걸리기 쉬운 사람들이 있다.

ge|neti|cal|ly modi|fied ADJ **Genetically modified** plants and animals have had one or more genes changed, for example so that they resist pests and diseases better. **Genetically modified** food contains ingredients made from genetically modified plants or animals. The abbreviation **GM** is often used. ☐ *Top supermarkets are to ban many genetically modified foods.*

형용사 유전자 변형의, 유전자 조작의 ☐ 최고급 슈퍼마켓에서는 여러 유전자 변형 식품을 금지할 예정이다.

ge|net|ic en|gi|neer|ing N-UNCOUNT **Genetic engineering** is the science or activity of changing the genetic structure of an animal, plant, or other organism in order to make it stronger or more suitable for a particular purpose. ☐ *Scientists have used genetic engineering to protect tomatoes against the effects of freezing.* →see **clone**

불가산명사 유전 공학 ☐ 과학자들은 결빙으로부터 토마토를 보호하기 위해 유전 공학을 이용해 왔다.

ge|net|ics /dʒɪnɛtɪks/ N-UNCOUNT **Genetics** is the study of heredity and how qualities and characteristics are passed on from one generation to another by means of genes. ☐ *Genetics is also bringing about dramatic changes in our understanding of cancer.*

불가산명사 유전학 ☐ 유전학은 또한 암에 대한 우리의 이해를 극적으로 변화시키고 있다.

gen|ial /dʒinyəl/ ADJ Someone who is **genial** is kind and friendly. [APPROVAL] ☐ *Bob was always genial and welcoming.* ● **gen|ial|ly** ADV ☐ *"If you don't mind," Mrs. Dambar said genially.* ● **ge|ni|al|ity** /dʒiniæliti/ N-UNCOUNT ☐ *He soon recovered his habitual geniality.*

형용사 온화한, 다정한 [마음에 듦] ☐ 밥은 항상 온화했고 환영해 주었다. ● 온화하게, 다정하게 부사 ☐ "괜찮으시다면,"이라고 댐버 부인은 온화하게 말했다. ● 온화함, 상냥함 불가산명사 ☐ 그는 곧 예전과 같은 상냥함을 되찾았다.

Word Web — genre

Each of the arts includes a variety of types called **genre**. The four basic types of **literature** are **fiction**, nonfiction, **poetry**, and **drama**. In painting, some of the special areas are **realism**, expressionism, and Cubism. In music, they include **classical**, **jazz**, and popular forms. Each genre contains several subdivisions. For example, popular music takes in country and western, **rap music**, and **rock**. Modern movie-making has produced a wide variety of genres. These include **horror films**, **comedies**, **action movies**, film noir, and **westerns**. Some artists don't like working within just one genre.

genital /dʒenɪtᵊl/ (**genitals**) **1** N-PLURAL Someone's **genitals** are their external sexual organs. ❑ *Without thinking, Neil cupped his hands over his genitals.* **2** ADJ **Genital** means relating to a person's external sexual organs. [ADJ n] ❑ *Wear loose clothing in the genital area.*

■ 복수명사 생식기 ❑ 생각할 것도 없이 닐은 자기 사타구니 부위를 두 손으로 감쌌다. ❷ 형용사 생식기의 ❑ 사타구니 부분이 헐렁한 옷을 입으세요.

genius /dʒiːnyəs/ (**geniuses**) **1** N-UNCOUNT **Genius** is very great ability or skill in a particular subject or activity. ❑ *This is the mark of her real genius as a designer.* ❑ *The man had genius and had made his mark in the aviation world.* **2** N-COUNT A **genius** is a highly talented, creative, or intelligent person. ❑ *Chaplin was not just a genius, he was among the most influential figures in film history.*

■ 불가산명사 천재성 ❑ 이것은 그녀가 디자이너로서 천재성을 지니고 있다는 증거이다. ❑ 그 남자는 천부적인 재능을 가지고 있었고, 항공 업계에서 두각을 드러냈다. ❷ 가산명사 천재 ❑ 채플린은 천재였을 뿐만 아니라, 영화 역사상 가장 영향력 있는 인물 중 한 사람이었다.

Word Link — cide ≈ killing : geno**cide**, homi**cide**, pesti**cide**

genocide /dʒenəsaɪd/ N-UNCOUNT **Genocide** is the deliberate murder of a whole community or race. ❑ *They have alleged that acts of genocide and torture were carried out.*

불가산명사 대량 학살 ❑ 그들은 대량 학살 및 고문 행위가 자행되었다고 주장하였다.

genre /ʒɒnrə/ (**genres**) N-COUNT A **genre** is a particular type of literature, painting, music, film, or other art form which people consider as a class because it has special characteristics. [FORMAL] ❑ *...his love of films and novels in the horror genre.* →see **fantasy** →see Word Web: genre

가산명사 장르 [격식체] ❑ 공포 장르의 영화와 소설에 대한 그의 사랑

gent /dʒent/ (**gents**) **1** N-COUNT **Gent** is an informal and old-fashioned word for **gentleman**. ❑ *Mr Blake was a gent. He knew how to behave.* **2** N-SING-COLL People sometimes refer to a public toilet for men as **the gents**. [BRIT, INFORMAL] ❑ *There are fewer loos in the Ladies than the Gents.* **3** N-VOC **Gents** is used when addressing men in an informal, humorous way, especially in the expression "ladies and gents." [HUMOROUS, INFORMAL] ❑ *Don't be left standing, ladies and gents, while a bargain slips past your eyes.*

■ 가산명사 신사 ❑ 블레이크 씨는 신사였다. 그는 예절 바르게 행동할 줄 알았다. ❷ 단수명사-집합 남자 화장실 [영국영어, 비격식체] ❑ 남자 화장실보다 여자 화장실에 변기의 수가 적다. ❸ 호격명사 신사분들 [해학체, 비격식체] ❑ 여러분, 망설이지 마십시오, 그러는 사이 여러분은 절호의 기회를 놓치게 됩니다.

genteel /dʒentiːl/ **1** ADJ A **genteel** person is respectable and well-mannered, and comes or seems to come from a high social class. ❑ *It was a place to which genteel families came in search of health and quiet.* **2** ADJ A **genteel** place or area is quiet and traditional, but may also be old-fashioned and dull. ❑ *...the genteel towns of Winchester and Chichester.*

■ 형용사 품위 있는, 상류층의 ❑ 그곳은 상류층 집안 사람들이 한적함과 건강을 위해 찾아오는 장소였다. ❷ 형용사 한적하고 고풍스러운 ❑ 윈체스터와 치체스터에 있는 한적하고 고풍스러운 소도시들

gentle ♦◇◇ /dʒentᵊl/ (**gentler**, **gentlest**) **1** ADJ Someone who is **gentle** is kind, mild, and calm. ❑ *My son was a quiet and gentle man who liked sports and enjoyed life.* ● **gently** ADV [ADV with v] ❑ *She smiled gently at him.* ● **gentleness** N-UNCOUNT ❑ *...the gentleness with which she treated her pregnant mother.* **2** ADJ **Gentle** actions or movements are performed in a calm and controlled manner, with little force. ❑ *...a gentle game of tennis.* ● **gently** ADV ❑ *Patrick took her gently by the arm and led her to a chair.* **3** ADJ A **gentle** slope or curve is not steep or severe. ❑ *...gentle, rolling meadows.* ● **gently** ADV ❑ *With its gently rolling hills it looks like Tuscany.* **4** ADJ A **gentle** heat is a fairly low heat. ❑ *Cook for 30 minutes over a gentle heat.* ● **gently** ADV [ADV with v] ❑ *Add the onion and cook gently for about 5 minutes.*

■ 형용사 친절한, 온화한 ❑ 나의 아들은 스포츠를 좋아하고 인생을 즐기는 조용하고 온화한 사람이었다. ● 온화하게 부사 ❑ 그녀는 그를 향해 온화한 미소를 지었다. ● 온화함 불가산명사 ❑ 임신한 어머니를 돌보는 그녀의 온화함 ❷ 형용사 평온한, 차분한 ❑ 차분한 테니스 경기 ● 차분히, 부드럽게 부사 ❑ 패트릭은 그녀의 팔을 부드럽게 잡고 의자로 데리고 갔다. ❸ 형용사 완만한 ❑ 완만하면서도 기복이 있는 초원 ● 완만하게 부사 ❑ 완만하게 기복이 있는 언덕 때문에 그곳은 마치 투스카니 지방처럼 보인다. ❹ 형용사 약한, 낮은 ❑ 약한 불에서 30분 동안 조리하세요. ● 낮은 온도로 부사 ❑ 양파를 넣고 5분 동안 약한 불로 조리하세요.

gentleman ♦◇◇ /dʒentᵊlmən/ (**gentlemen**) **1** N-COUNT A **gentleman** is a man who comes from a family of high social standing. ❑ *...this wonderful portrait of English gentleman Joseph Greenaway.* **2** N-COUNT If you say that a man is a **gentleman**, you mean he is polite and educated, and can be trusted. ❑ *He was always such a gentleman.* **3** N-COUNT; N-VOC You can address men as **gentlemen**, or refer politely to them as **gentlemen**. [POLITENESS] ❑ *It seems this gentleman was waiting for the doctor.*

■ 가산명사 신사, 양반 ❑ 영국 신사 요셉 그린웨이의 멋진 초상화 ❷ 가산명사 신사 ❑ 그는 언제나 정말 신사였다. ❸ 가산명사; 호격명사 남자분들 [공손체] ❑ 이 남자분께서 의사를 기다리고 있었던 것 같습니다.

genuine ♦◇◇ /dʒenyuɪn/ **1** ADJ **Genuine** is used to describe people and things that are exactly what they appear to be, and are not false or an imitation. ❑ *There was a risk of genuine refugees being returned to Vietnam.* ❑ *...genuine leather.* **2** ADJ **Genuine** refers to things such as emotions that are real and not pretended. ❑ *If this offer is genuine I will gladly accept it.* ● **genuinely** ADV ❑ *He was genuinely surprised.* **3** ADJ If you describe a person as **genuine**, you approve of them because they are honest, truthful, and sincere in the way they live and in their relationships with other people. [APPROVAL] ❑ *She is very caring and very genuine.*

■ 형용사 진짜의 ❑ 진짜 망명자들이 베트남으로 송환될 위험이 있었다. ❑ 진짜 가죽 ❷ 형용사 정말인, 가식이 없는 ❑ 이 제안이 진짜라면 저는 기꺼이 받아들이겠습니다. ● 진정으로, 정말로 부사 ❑ 그는 정말 놀랐다. ❸ 형용사 신실한, 진실한 [마음에 듦] ❑ 그녀는 매우 상냥하고 신실하다.

Thesaurus — genuine의 참조어

ADJ. actual, original, real, true; *(ant.)* bogus, fake **1** **2**
honest, open, sincere, true, valid; *(ant.)* dishonest, insincere **3**

genus /dʒiːnəs, BRIT dʒenəs/ (**genera** /dʒenərə/) N-COUNT A **genus** is a class of similar things, especially a group of animals or plants that includes several closely related species. [TECHNICAL] ❑ *...a genus of plants called Sinningia.*

가산명사 종류, 속(屬) [과학 기술] ❑ 신닝기아라고 불리는 식물의 한 종류

geo|graph|i|cal /dʒiəgræfɪkªl/

The form **geographic** /dʒiəgræfɪk/ is also used.

ADJ **Geographical** or **geographic** means concerned with or relating to geography. ❑ *Its geographical location stimulated overseas mercantile enterprise.* ● **geo|graph|i|cal|ly** /dʒiəgræfɪkli/ ADV ❑ *It is geographically more diverse than any other continent.*

geographic /dʒiəgræfɪk/도 쓴다.

형용사 지리학의, 지리적인 ❑그곳의 지리적 위치가 해외 상업 활동에 활기를 띠게 하였다. ● 지리학적으로 부사 ❑그 곳이 어느 다른 대륙보다도 지형적으로 다양하다.

Word Link　　　*geo ≈ earth : geography, geological, geology*

geo|ra|phy /dʒiɒgrəfi/ ■ N-UNCOUNT **Geography** is the study of the countries of the world and of such things as the land, seas, climate, towns, and population. ■ N-UNCOUNT The **geography** of a place is the way that features such as rivers, mountains, towns, or streets are arranged within it. ❑ *...policemen who knew the local geography.*

■ 불가산명사 지리학 ■ 불가산명사 지리, 지형 ❑지역 지리를 잘 아는 경찰들

geo|logi|cal /dʒiəlɒdʒɪkªl/ ADJ **Geological** means relating to geology. ❑ *With geological maps, books, and atlases you can find out all the proven sites of precious minerals.*

형용사 지질학의 ❑지질학 지도, 서적, 그리고 지도책을 이용하면 값비싼 광석이 있다고 검증된 모든 곳을 찾을 수 있을 것이다.

geo|ol|ogy /dʒiɒlədʒi/ ■ N-UNCOUNT **Geology** is the study of the Earth's structure, surface, and origins. ❑ *He was visiting professor of geology at the University of Jordan.* ● **geo|ol|o|gist** (**geologists**) N-COUNT ❑ *Geologists have studied the way that heat flows from the earth.* ■ N-UNCOUNT The **geology** of an area is the structure of its land, together with the types of rocks and minerals that exist within it. ❑ *...an expert on the geology of southeast Asia.*

■ 불가산명사 지질학 ❑그는 요르단 대학의 지질학과 초빙 교수였다. ●지질학자 가산명사 ❑지질학자들은 열이 지구로부터 유출되는 방법을 연구해 왔다. ■ 불가산명사 지질 ❑동남아시아 지역의 지질에 대한 전문가

geo|met|ric /dʒiəmɛtrɪk/

The form **geometrical** /dʒiəmɛtrɪkªl/ is also used.

■ ADJ **Geometric** or **geometrical** patterns or shapes consist of regular shapes or lines. ❑ *Geometric designs were popular wall decorations in the 14th century.* ■ ADJ **Geometric** or **geometrical** means relating to or involving the principles of geometry. ❑ *Euclid was trying to convey his idea of a geometrical point.*

geometrical /dʒiəmɛtrɪkªl/도 쓴다.

■ 형용사 기하학의 ❑14세기에는 벽장식으로 기하학적인 도안이 유행하였다. ■ 형용사 기하학 원리의 ❑유클리드는 기하학적 원리에 대한 자신의 생각을 전하려 하고 있었다.

geo|ome|try /dʒiɒmɪtri/ ■ N-UNCOUNT **Geometry** is the branch of mathematics concerned with the properties and relationships of lines, angles, curves, and shapes. ❑ *...the very ordered way in which mathematics and geometry describe nature.* ■ N-UNCOUNT The **geometry** of an object is its shape or the relationship of its parts to each other. ❑ *They have tinkered with the geometry of the car's nose.* →see **mathematics**

■ 불가산명사 기하학 ❑수학과 기하학이 자연을 기술하는 매우 질서 정연한 방식 ■ 불가산명사 형상; 결합 구조 ❑그들은 차의 앞부분의 모양을 만지작거렸다.

Geor|gian /dʒɔːdʒªn/ ADJ **Georgian** means belonging to or connected with Britain in the eighteenth and early nineteenth centuries, during the reigns of King George I to King George IV. ❑ *...the restoration of his Georgian house.*

형용사 조지 왕조 시대의, 조지 왕조풍의 ❑그의 조지 왕조풍 집의 복원

geri|at|ric /dʒɛriætrɪk/ (**geriatrics**) ■ ADJ **Geriatric** is used to describe things relating to the illnesses and medical care of old people. [MEDICAL] [ADJ n] ❑ *There is a question mark over the future of geriatric care.* ■ N-COUNT If you describe someone as a **geriatric**, you are implying that they are old and that their mental or physical condition is poor. This use could cause offense. [DISAPPROVAL] ❑ *He will complain about having to spend time with such a boring bunch of geriatrics.*

■ 형용사 노인병의 [의학] ❑노인 의료의 미래에 대해 의문점이 존재한다. ■ 가산명사 노인, 노인병 환자 [탐탁찮음] ❑따분한 노인 일당과 함께 시간을 보내야 한다는 것에 대해 그가 불평을 할 것이다.

germ /dʒɜːrm/ (**germs**) ■ N-COUNT A **germ** is a very small organism that causes disease. ❑ *Chlorine is widely used to kill germs.* ■ N-SING The **germ of** something such as an idea is something which developed or might develop into that thing. ❑ *This was the germ of a book.* →see **medicine**, **spice**

■ 가산명사 병균, 세균 ❑염소는 세균을 죽이는 데 널리 쓰인다. ■ 단수명사 근원, 기원 ❑이것이 책의 기원이었다.

ger|mi|nate /dʒɜːrmɪneɪt/ (**germinates, germinating, germinated**) ■ V-T/V-I If a seed **germinates** or if it **is germinated**, it starts to grow. ❑ *Some seed varieties germinate fast, so check every day or so.* ● **ger|mi|na|tion** /dʒɜːrmɪneɪ ªn/ N-UNCOUNT [usu with supp] ❑ *The poor germination of your seed could be because the soil was too cold.* ■ V-I If an idea, plan, or feeling **germinates**, it comes into existence and begins to develop. ❑ *He wrote to Eliot about a "big book" that was germinating in his mind.* →see **tree**

■ 타동사/자동사 싹트게 하다; 싹트다 ❑빨리 싹트는 종류의 씨앗도 있으니 거의 매일 체크하세요. ●발아 불가산명사 ❑씨의 싹이 잘 트지 않는 것은 토양이 너무 냉했기 때문일 수도 있다. ■ 자동사 (사상, 감정 등이) 싹트다 ❑그는 엘리엇에게 자신의 마음속에 싹트고 있는 '대단한 책'에 관한 생각을 써 보냈다.

ger|und /dʒɛrʌnd/ (**gerunds**) N-COUNT A **gerund** is a noun formed from a verb which refers to an action, process, or state. In English, gerunds end in "-ing," for example "running" and "thinking."

가산명사 동명사

ges|ture /dʒɛstʃər/ (**gestures, gesturing, gestured**) ■ N-COUNT A **gesture** is a movement that you make with a part of your body, especially your hands, to express emotion or information. ❑ *Sarah made a menacing gesture with her fist.* ■ N-COUNT A **gesture** is something that you say or do in order to express your attitude or intentions, often something that you know will not have much effect. ❑ *He questioned the government's commitment to peace and called on it to make a gesture of goodwill.* ■ V-I If you **gesture**, you use movements of your hands or head in order to tell someone something or draw their attention to something. ❑ *I gestured towards the boathouse, and he looked inside.*

■ 가산명사 몸짓, 손짓 ❑사라가 주먹으로 위협적인 자세를 취했다. ■ 가산명사 자세, 태도 ❑그는 정부의 평화 약속에 대해서 의문을 제기하는 한편, 호의적인 자세를 보이도록 요구했다. ■ 자동사 손짓이나 몸짓을 하다 ❑나는 보트 창고 쪽으로 손짓을 했고, 그는 안쪽을 살펴보았다.

get

① CHANGING, CAUSING, MOVING, OR REACHING
② OBTAINING, RECEIVING, OR CATCHING
③ PHRASES AND PHRASAL VERBS

① **get** ♦♦♦ /gɛt/ (**gets, getting, got, gotten** or **got**)

In most of its uses **get** is a fairly informal word. **Gotten** is an American form of the past participle. **Got** is the British form of the past participle, sometimes used in American English.

대부분의 용법에 있어서 get은 상당히 비격식체 단어이다. gotten은 미국영어 과거 분사이다. got은 영국영어 과거 분사인데 가끔 미국영어에서도 쓴다.

■ V-LINK You use **get** with adjectives to mean "become." For example, if someone **gets cold**, they become cold, and if they **get angry**, they become

■ 연결동사 ~로 되다 ❑그 소년들은 점점 지루함을 느꼈다. ❑여기서부터는 계속, 좋아지기만 할 것이다.

angry. □ *The boys were getting bored. □ From here on, it can only get better.* ◻2 V-LINK **Get** is used with expressions referring to states or situations. For example, to **get into trouble** means to start being in trouble. □ *Half the pleasure of an evening out is getting ready.* □ *Perhaps I shouldn't say that – I might get into trouble.* ◻3 V-T To **get** someone or something into a particular state or situation means to cause them to be in it. □ *I don't know if I can get it clean. □ Brian will get them out of trouble.* ◻4 V-T If you **get** someone to do something, you cause them to do it by asking, persuading, or telling them to do it. □ *...a long campaign to get US politicians to take the AIDS epidemic more seriously.* ◻5 V-T If you **get** something done, you cause it to be done. □ *I might benefit from getting my teeth fixed.* ◻6 V-I To **get** somewhere means to move there. □ *I got off the bed and opened the door. □ How can I get past her without her seeing me?* ◻7 V-I When you **get** to a place, you arrive there. □ *Generally I get to work at 9.30 a.m.* ◻8 V-T To **get** something or someone into a place or position means to cause them to move there. □ *Mack got his wallet out. □ Go and get your coat on.* ◻9 AUX **Get** is often used in place of "be" as an auxiliary verb to form passives. □ *A pane of glass got broken.* ◻10 V-T If you **get** to do something, you eventually or gradually reach a stage at which you do it. □ *No one could figure out how he got to be so wealthy.* ◻11 V-T If you **get to** do something, you manage to do it or have the opportunity to do it. □ *How do these people get to be the bosses of major companies? □ Do you get to see him often?* ◻12 V-T You can use **get** in expressions like **get moving**, **get going**, and **get working** when you want to tell people to begin moving, going, or working quickly. □ *I aim to be off the lake before dawn, so let's get moving.* ◻13 V-I If you **get to** a particular stage in your life or in something you are doing, you reach that stage. □ *We haven't got to the stage of a full-scale military conflict. □ It got to the point where I was so ill I was waiting to die.* ◻14 V-T/V-I You can use **get** to talk about the progress that you are making. For example, if you say that you **are getting somewhere**, you mean that you are making progress, and if you say that something **won't get you anywhere**, you mean it will not help you to progress at all. □ *Radical factions say the talks are getting nowhere and they want to withdraw.* ◻15 V-LINK When **it gets to** a particular time, it is that time. If **it is getting toward** a particular time, it is approaching that time. □ *It got to after 1 a.m. and I was exhausted. □ It was getting towards evening when we got back.* ◻16 V-I If something that has continued for some time **gets to** you, it starts causing you to suffer. □ *That's the first time I lost my cool in 20 years in this job. This whole thing's getting to me.*

② **get** ♦♦♦ /gɛt/ (**gets, getting, got, gotten** or **got**) ◻1 V-T If you **get** something that you want or need, you obtain it. □ *I got a job at the sawmill.* ◻2 V-T If you **get** something, you receive it or are given it. □ *I'm getting a bike for my birthday. □ He gets a lot of letters from women.* ◻3 V-T If you **get** someone or something, you go and bring them to a particular place. □ *I came down this morning to get the newspaper. □ Go and get me a large brandy.* ◻4 V-T If you **get** a particular result, you obtain it from some action that you take, or from a calculation or experiment. □ *What do you get if you multiply six by nine?* ◻5 V-T If you **get** a particular price **for** something that you sell, you obtain that amount of money by selling it. □ *He can't get a good price for his crops.* ◻6 V-T If you **get** the time or opportunity to do something, you have the time or opportunity to do it. □ *You get time to think in prison.* ◻7 V-T If you **get** an idea, impression, or feeling, you begin to have that idea, impression, or feeling as you learn or understand more about something. □ *I get the feeling that you're an honest man.* ◻8 V-T If you **get** a feeling or benefit from an activity or experience, the activity or experience gives you that feeling or benefit. □ *Charles got a shock when he saw him. □ She gets enormous pleasure out of working freelance.* ◻9 V-T If you **get** a look, view, or glimpse of something, you manage to see it. □ *Young men climbed on buses and fences to get a better view.* ◻10 V-T If you **get** a joke or **get** the point of something that is said, you understand it. □ *Did you get that joke, Ann? I'll explain later.* ◻11 V-T If you **get** an illness or disease, you become ill with it. □ *When I was five I got measles.* ◻12 V-T When you **get** a train, bus, plane, or boat, you leave a place on a particular train, bus, plane, or boat. □ *It'll be two pounds to get the bus.* ◻13 →see also **got**

Thesaurus	get의 참조어
V-LINK.	become① ◻1
V.	bring, collect, pick up ② ◻3
	know, sense ② ◻7 ◻8

③ **get** ♦♦♦ /gɛt/ (**gets, getting, got, gotten** or **got**) ◻1 PHRASE You can say that something is, for example, **as good as you can get** to mean that it is as good as it is possible for that thing to be. □ *Consort has a population of 714 and is about as rural and isolated as you can get. □ ...the diet that is as near to perfect as you can get.* ◻2 PHRASE If you say **you can't get away from** something or **there is no getting away from** something, you are emphasizing that it is true, even though people might prefer it not to be true. [INFORMAL, EMPHASIS] □ *There is no getting away from the fact that he is on the left of the party.* ◻3 PHRASE If you **get away from it all**, you have a holiday in a place that is very different from where you normally live and work. □ *...the ravishing island of Ischia, where rich Italians get away from it all.* ◻4 CONVENTION **Get** is used in rude expressions like **get stuffed** and **get lost** to express contempt, disagreement, or refusal to do something. [VULGAR, FEELINGS] ◻5 PHRASE You can use **you get** instead of "there is" or "there are" to say that something exists, happens, or can be experienced. [SPOKEN] □ *That's where you get some differences of opinion.*

▶ **get about** PHRASAL VERB If you **get about**, you go to different places and visit different people. [mainly BRIT] □ *So you're getting about a bit again? Not shutting yourself away?*

▶ **get across** PHRASAL VERB When an idea **gets across** or when you **get** it **across**, you succeed in making other people understand it. □ *Officers felt their point of view was not getting across to ministers.*

◻2 연결동사 (상태로) 되다; 곤란해지다 □ 저녁 외출에서 얻는 즐거움의 절반이 준비하는 과정에서 나온다. □ 내가 그것을 말하지 않는 것이 낫겠다. 잘못했다간 내가 곤란해질 수도 있을 것 같다. ◻3 타동사 - 되게 하다 □ 제가 그것을 깨끗하게 할 수 있을지 모르겠습니다. □ 브라이언은 그들을 곤경에서 벗어나게 해줄 것이다. ◻4 타동사 - 시키다 □ 미국 정치인들이 에이즈를 더 심각하게 인식하도록 하는 장기간 캠페인 ◻5 타동사 - 되게 하다; -당하다 □ 이를 고쳐서 내가 덕을 볼 수도 있다. ◻6 자동사 움직이다 □ 나는 침대에서 나와 문을 열었다. □ 어떻게 하면 그녀 눈에 띄지 않고 지나갈 수 있지? ◻7 자동사 -에 이르다 / 가다 □ 나는 보통 9시 30분에 출근한다. ◻8 타동사 ...을 -에 이르게 하다 □ 맥은 지갑을 꺼냈다. ◻9 준조동사 수동태에서 'be' 동사 대신 사용 □ 유리창 하나가 깨졌다. ◻10 타동사 결국 -에 이르다 □ 어떻게 그가 그렇게 부자가 되었는지는 아무도 알아낼 수 없었다. ◻11 타동사 그럭저럭 - 할 수 있다, -하게 되다 □ 어떻게 이런 사람들이 주요 회사의 사장이 될 수 있을까? □ 그를 자주 보게 됩니까? ◻12 타동사 -하기 시작하다 □ 새벽이 되기 전에 호수를 벗어날 생각이니까 빨리 움직이기 시작하자. ◻13 자동사 -에 도달하다 □ 우리가 전면적인 군사 충돌 단계로는 접어들지 않았다. □ 나는 너무 아파서 죽음을 기다리는 지경에까지 이르렀다. ◻14 타동사/자동사 진척되다 □ 급진파들은 회담이 전혀 진척되는 바가 없으니 철수하고 싶다고 말했다. ◻15 연결동사 (시간이) 가까워지다 □ 가까워지고 있다 □ 우리가 돌아왔을 때는 이미 저녁이 다 되어 갔다. ◻16 자동사 -을 괴롭히다 □ 이 일을 해온 20년 동안 내가 냉정을 잃었던 것은 그 때가 처음이다. 이 모든 것이 나를 괴롭히기 시작한다.

◻1 타동사 얻다, 획득하다 □ 나는 제재소에 일자리를 얻었다. ◻2 타동사 받다 □ 나는 생일 선물로 자전거를 받을 것이다. □ 그는 여성들로부터 수많은 편지를 받는다. ◻3 타동사 가져가다, 데리고 가다; 가져오다, 데려오다 □ 오늘 아침에 나는 신문을 가지러 내려왔다. □ 가서 큰 잔으로 브랜디 한 잔을 가져와라. ◻4 타동사 (결과를) 얻다 □ 6에 9를 곱하면 얼마입니까? ◻5 타동사 벌다 □ 그는 자기 작품에 대해 좋은 값을 받지 못한다. ◻6 타동사 (시간이나 기회가) 있다 □ 감옥에서는 생각할 시간이 있다. ◻7 타동사 (생각, 감정 등을) 갖기 시작하다 □ 나는 당신이 정직한 사람이라는 느낌이 들기 시작한다. ◻8 타동사 갖다 □ 찰스는 그를 보고 충격을 받았다. □ 그녀는 프리랜서로 일하는 것에서 큰 즐거움을 얻는다. ◻9 타동사 보게 되다 □ 젊은이들은 더 잘 보기 위해 버스와 담장 위로 올라왔다. ◻10 타동사 이해하다 □ 그 농담이 무슨 말인지 알겠어, 앤? 내가 나중에 설명해 줄게. ◻11 타동사 병에 걸리다 □ 다섯 살 때 나는 홍역을 앓았다. ◻12 타동사 (버스 등을) 타다 □ 그 버스를 타려면 2파운드 내야 한다.

◻1 구 최대한 -한 □ 콘소트의 인구는 714명이고 아주 촌스럽고 외진 곳이다. □ 가능한 한 완벽에 가까운 식이 요법 ◻2 구 피할 수 없는 사실이다 [비격식체, 강조] □ 그가 그 정당에서 좌파 계열인 것은 피할 수 없는 사실이다. ◻3 구 모든 일상에서 벗어나다 □ 부유한 이탈리아 사람들이 일상에서 벗어나 휴일을 보내는 곳인 환상적인 섬 이스키아 ◻4 관용 표현 혐오감, 경멸 등을 나타내는 표현에 사용: 꺼져, 말도 안 돼, 냉큼 꺼져 버려 [비속어, 감정 개입] ◻5 구 -이 있다, -이 존재한다 [구어체] □ 바로 그 부분에서 의견들이 좀 다르다.

구동사 여기저기 돌아다니다 [주로 영국영어] □ 그래서 다시 나다니고 있니? 어디서 은둔 생활 하는 것은 아니고?

구동사 이해되다; 납득시키다 □ 공무원들은 자신의 견해가 장관을 납득시키지 못하고 있다고 생각하였다.

▶**get along** PHRASAL VERB-RECIP If you **get along with** someone, you have a friendly relationship with them. You can also say that two people **get along**. ❑ *It's impossible to get along with him.*

▶**get around** ◰ PHRASAL VERB To **get around** a problem or difficulty means to overcome it. ❑ *None of these countries has found a way to get around the problem of the polarization of wealth.* ◱ PHRASAL VERB If you **get around** a rule or law, you find a way of doing something that the rule or law is intended to prevent, without actually breaking it. ❑ *Although tobacco ads are prohibited, companies get around the ban by sponsoring music shows.* ◲ PHRASAL VERB If news **gets around**, it becomes well known as a result of being told to lots of people. ❑ *They threw him out because word got around that he was taking drugs.* ◳ PHRASAL VERB If you **get around** someone, you persuade them to allow you to do or have something by pleasing them or flattering them. ❑ *Max could always get round her.* ◴ PHRASAL VERB If you **get around**, you visit a lot of different places as part of your way of life. ❑ *He claimed to be a journalist, and he got around.* ◵ PHRASAL VERB The way that someone **gets around** is the way that they walk or go from one place to another. [BRIT also **get round to**] ❑ *It is difficult for Gail to get around since she broke her leg.*

▶**get around to** PHRASAL VERB When you **get around to** doing something that you have delayed doing or have been too busy to do, you finally do it. ❑ *I said I would write to you, but as usual I never got around to it.*

▶**get at** ◰ PHRASAL VERB To **get at** something means to succeed in reaching it. ❑ *A goat was standing up against a tree on its hind legs, trying to get at the leaves.* ◱ PHRASAL VERB If you **get at** the truth about something, you succeed in discovering it. ❑ *We want to get at the truth. Who killed him? And why?* ◲ PHRASAL VERB If you ask someone what they **are getting at**, you are asking them to explain what they mean, usually because you think that they are being unpleasant or are suggesting something that is untrue. ❑ *"What are you getting at now?" demanded Rick.*

▶**get away** ◰ PHRASAL VERB If you **get away**, you succeed in leaving a place or a person's company. ❑ *She'd gladly have gone anywhere to get away from the cottage.* ◱ PHRASAL VERB If you **get away**, you go away for a period of time in order to have a vacation. ❑ *He is too busy to get away.* ◲ PHRASAL VERB When someone or something **gets away**, or when you **get** them **away**, they escape. ❑ *Dr Dunn was apparently trying to get away when he was shot.*

▶**get away with** PHRASAL VERB If you **get away with** doing something wrong or risky, you do not suffer any punishment or other bad consequences because of it. ❑ *The criminals know how to play the system and get away with it.*

▶**get back** ◰ PHRASAL VERB If someone or something **gets back to** a state they were in before, they are then in that state again. ❑ *Then life started to get back to normal.* ◱ PHRASAL VERB If you **get back to** a subject that you were talking about before, you start talking about it again. ❑ *It wasn't until we had sat down to eat that we got back to the subject of Tom Halliday.* ◲ PHRASAL VERB If you **get** something **back** after you have lost it or after it has been taken from you, you then have it again. ❑ *You have 14 days in which you can cancel the contract and get your money back.*

▶**get back to** PHRASAL VERB If you **get back to** an activity, you start doing it again after you have stopped doing it. ❑ *I think I ought to get back to work.*

▶**get by** PHRASAL VERB If you can **get by** with what you have, you can manage to live or do things in a satisfactory way. ❑ *I'm a survivor. I'll get by.*

▶**get down** ◰ PHRASAL VERB If something **gets** you **down**, it makes you unhappy. ❑ *At times when my work gets me down, I like to fantasize about being a farmer.* ◱ PHRASAL VERB If you **get down**, you lower your body until you are sitting, kneeling, or lying on the ground. ❑ *"Get down!" she yelled. "Somebody's shooting!"*

▶**get down to** PHRASAL VERB If you **get down to** something, especially something that requires a lot of attention, you begin doing it. ❑ *With the election out of the way, the government can get down to business.*

▶**get in** ◰ PHRASAL VERB If a political party or a politician **gets in**, they are elected. ❑ *If the Conservatives got in they might decide to change it.* ◱ PHRASAL VERB If you **get** something **in**, you manage to do it at a time when you are very busy doing other things. ❑ *I plan to get a few lessons in.* ◲ PHRASAL VERB When a train, bus, or plane **gets in**, it arrives. ❑ *We would have come straight here, except our flight got in too late.*

▶**get into** ◰ PHRASAL VERB If you **get into** a particular kind of work or activity, you manage to become involved in it. ❑ *He was eager to get into politics.* ◱ PHRASAL VERB If you **get into** a school, college, or university, you are accepted there as a student. ❑ *I was working hard to get into Cambridge.*

▶**get off** ◰ PHRASAL VERB If someone who has broken a law or rule **gets off**, they are not punished, or are given only a very small punishment. ❑ *He is likely to get off with a small fine.* ◱ PHRASAL VERB If you tell someone to **get off** a piece of land or a property, you are telling them to leave, because they have no right to be there and you do not want them there. ❑ *I told you. Get off the farm.* ◲ PHRASAL VERB You can tell someone to **get off** when they are touching something and you do not want them to. ❑ *I kept telling him to get off.*

▶**get on** ◰ PHRASAL VERB If you **get on with** something, you continue doing it or start doing it. ❑ *Jane got on with her work.* ◱ PHRASAL VERB If you **get on with** someone, you like them and have a friendly relationship with them. [mainly BRIT] ❑ *The host fears the guests won't get on.* ◲ PHRASAL VERB If you say how someone **is getting on**, you are saying how much success they are having with what they are trying to do. [mainly BRIT] ❑ *Livy's getting on very well in Russian. She learns very quickly.* ◳ PHRASAL VERB If you try to **get on**, you try to be successful in your career. [mainly BRIT] ❑ *Politics is seen as a man's world. It is very difficult for women to get on.*

상호 구동사 -와 친하게 지내다 ❑ 그와 친하게 지내는 것은 불가능하다.

◰ 구동사 극복하다 ❑ 이들 국가들 모두 부의 양극화 문제를 극복할 방법을 아직 찾아내지 못했다. ◱ 구동사 교묘히 피하다 ❑ 담배 광고는 금지되어 있지만, 음악 공연을 후원하는 것으로 회사들이 교묘히 법망을 피한다. ◲ 구동사 퍼지다 ❑ 그가 마약을 하고 있다는 말이 돌았기 때문에 그들은 그를 내쫓았다. ◳ 구동사 구워삶다 ❑ 맥스는 항상 그녀를 구워삶을 수 있었다. ◴ 구동사 여기저기 돌아다니다 ❑ 그는 기자라고 주장했고, 여기저기 돌아다녔다. ◵ 구동사 여기저기 돌아다니다 [영국영어 get round to] ❑ 게일은 다리가 부러져서 여기저기 돌아다니기가 어렵다.

구동사 -할 여유를 찾다 ❑ 당신에게 편지를 쓸 거라고 말은 했지만, 늘 그렇듯이 저는 그럴 여유가 전혀 없었습니다.

◰ 구동사 -에 다가가다 ❑ 염소 한 마리가 뒷다리를 나무에 기대고 서서, 나뭇잎을 잡으려고 애쓰고 있었다. ◱ 구동사 밝히다 ❑ 우리는 사실을 밝히기를 원합니다. 누가 그를 죽였습니까? 그리고 왜 그랬습니까? ◲ 구동사 뜻하다 ❑ "지금 무슨 말을 하는 거지?"라고 릭은 다그쳤다.

◰ 구동사 가 버리다, 도망치다 ❑ 그녀는 그 오두막에서 벗어날 수 있다면 어디로든 기꺼이 가려고 했었다. ◱ 구동사 휴가를 떠나다 ❑ 그는 너무 바빠서 휴가를 떠날 수도 없다. ◲ 구동사 달아나다, 피신시키다 ❑ 총을 맞았을 때 던 박사는 달아나려고 했던 것 같다.

구동사 (곤경에서) 용케 헤어나다, 잘 해내다 ❑ 범죄자들은 제도를 악용하면서도 걸리지 않는 법을 안다.

◰ 구동사 -한 상태로 돌아오다 ❑ 그리고 나서 생활은 평소와 같은 상태로 돌아오기 시작했다. ◱ 구동사 되돌아오다 ❑ 우리는 식사를 하려고 앉고 나서야 탐 할리데이에 대한 주제로 다시 되돌아갔다. ◲ 구동사 되찾다 ❑ 계약 후 14일 안에 계약을 취소하고 환불받을 수 있습니다.

구동사 다시 시작하다 ❑ 나는 일을 다시 시작해야 할 것 같다.

구동사 그럭저럭 살아가다 ❑ 나는 역경에 굴하지 않는 사람이거든. 어떻게 해서든 살아갈 거야.

◰ 구동사 -을 우울하게 하다 ❑ 일 때문에 우울해질 때마다 나는 농부가 되는 공상에 잠기는 것을 좋아한다. ◱ 구동사 몸을 낮추다, 구부리다 ❑ "숙여!"라고 그녀가 소리치며 말했다. "누군가가 총을 쏘고 있어!"

구동사 -을 시작하다 ❑ 선거가 끝난 지금 정부는 이제 제대로 일을 시작할 수 있다.

◰ 구동사 당선되다 ❑ 보수당이 당선된다면 그들이 그것을 바꾸려 할지도 모른다. ◱ 구동사 (스케줄에) 넣다, 바쁜 가운데 그럭저럭 해내다 ❑ 바쁜 중에서도 수업을 몇 개 들을 계획이다. ◲ 구동사 도착하다 ❑ 비행기만 늦게 도착하지 않았다면 우리가 이곳에 바로 올 수 있었을 텐데.

◰ 구동사 -으로 들어가다, -의 회원이 되다 ❑ 그는 몹시 정치에 뛰어들고 싶어 했다. ◱ 구동사 입학하다, 들어가다 ❑ 나는 케임브리지 대학에 들어가기 위해서 열심히 공부하고 있다.

◰ 구동사 벌을 면하다, 벌을 가볍게 받다 ❑ 그는 적은 벌금만 내고 가볍게 끝날 것 같다. ◱ 구동사 -을 떠나다 ❑ 내가 너에게 말했지. 농장에서 떠나라고. ◲ 구동사 손을 떼다 ❑ 나는 그에게 손을 떼라고 계속 말했다.

◰ 구동사 -을 계속하다; -을 하기 시작하다 ❑ 제인은 일을 계속했다. ◱ 구동사 -와 잘 지내다 [주로 영국영어] ❑ 주인은 손님들이 서로 잘 지내지 못할 것 같아 걱정한다. ◲ 구동사 -을 진척시키다 [주로 영국영어] ❑ 리비는 러시아어 공부를 매우 잘 해내고 있다. 그녀는 매우 빠르게 배운다. ◳ 구동사 성공하다 [주로 영국영어] ❑ 정치는 남성의 세계로 간주된다. 그곳에서 여성이 성공하기는 매우 어렵다.

A

▶**get on to** ■ PHRASAL VERB If you **get on to** a topic when you are speaking, you start talking about it. ❏ *We got on to the subject of relationships.* ■ PHRASAL VERB If you **get on to** someone, you contact them in order to ask them to do something or to give them some information. [mainly BRIT] ❏ *I got on to him and explained some of the things I had been thinking of.*

■ 구동사 -을 말하기 시작하다 ❏ 우리는 인간관계를 주제로 이야기하기 시작했다. ■ 구동사 접촉하다, 연락하다 [주로 영국영어] ❏ 나는 그에게 연락해서 내가 생각하고 있던 것 몇 가지를 설명했다.

B

▶**get out** ■ PHRASAL VERB If you **get out**, you leave a place because you want to escape from it, or because you are made to leave it. ❏ *They probably wanted to get out of the country.* ■ PHRASAL VERB If you **get out**, you go to places and meet people, usually in order to have a more enjoyable life. ❏ *Get out and enjoy yourself, make new friends.* ■ PHRASAL VERB If you **get out of** an organization or a commitment, you withdraw from it. ❏ *I wanted to get out of the group, but they wouldn't let me.* ■ PHRASAL VERB If news or information **gets out**, it becomes known. ❏ *If word got out now, a scandal could be disastrous.*

■ 구동사 벗어나다, 떠나다 ❏ 그들은 아마도 그 나라를 떠나고 싶어 했을 것이다. ■ 구동사 외출하다 ❏ 나가서 즐기면서 새로운 친구를 사귀어라. ■ 구동사 -에서 나오다 ❏ 나는 그 단체에서 나오기를 원했으나, 그들이 나를 놓아주지 않았다. ■ 구동사 알려지다 ❏ 지금 말이 새어 나간다면, 스캔들은 재앙이 될 수도 있다.

C

D

▶**get out of** PHRASAL VERB If you **get out of** doing something that you do not want to do, you succeed in avoiding doing it. ❏ *It's amazing what people will do to get out of paying taxes.*

구동사 -을 모면하다 ❏ 세금을 안 내기 위해 사람들이 하려고 하는 짓들을 보면 정말 놀라울 따름이다.

E

▶**get over** ■ PHRASAL VERB If you **get over** an unpleasant or unhappy experience or an illness, you recover from it. ❏ *It took me a very long time to get over the shock of her death.* ■ PHRASAL VERB If you **get over** a problem or difficulty, you overcome it. ❏ *How would they get over that problem, he wondered?*

■ 구동사 -에서 회복하다 ❏ 그녀가 죽었다는 충격에서 벗어나는 데 나는 매우 오랜 시간이 필요했다. ■ 구동사 극복하다 ❏ 그는 그들이 그 문제를 어떻게 극복할지 궁금했다.

F

▶**get round** →see **get around**

▶**get round to** →see **get around to**

G

▶**get through** ■ PHRASAL VERB If you **get through** a task or an amount of work, especially when it is difficult, you complete it. ❏ *I think you can get through the first two chapters.* ■ PHRASAL VERB If you **get through** a difficult or unpleasant period of time, you manage to live through it. ❏ *It is hard to see how people will get through the winter.* ■ PHRASAL VERB If you **get through to** someone, you succeed in making them understand something that you are trying to tell them. ❏ *An old friend might well be able to get through to her and help her.* ■ PHRASAL VERB If you **get through to** someone, you succeed in contacting them on the telephone. ❏ *Look, I can't get through to this number.* ■ PHRASAL VERB If a law or proposal **gets through**, it is officially approved by something such as a parliament or committee. ❏ *Such a radical proposal would never get through parliament.* ■ PHRASAL VERB If you **get through** a large amount of something, you use it. [mainly BRIT] ❏ *We've got through a lot of tyres.* ■ PHRASAL VERB If you **get through** an examination or **get through**, you pass it. [mainly BRIT] ❏ *Did you have to get through an entrance examination?*

■ 구동사 -을 완수하다 ❏ 네가 처음 두 단원 정도는 끝낼 수 있다고 생각해. ■ 구동사 -를 그럭저럭 보내다, -를 견디어 내다 ❏ 사람들이 겨울을 과연 어떻게 견디어 낼 수 있을지 모르겠다. ■ 구동사 이해시키다 ❏ 오랜 친구라면 그녀를 잘 납득시키고 도움을 줄 수 있을지도 모른다. ■ 구동사 -에 전화 연락을 하다 ❏ 보세요, 이 전화번호로는 연락이 안 됩니다. ■ 구동사 통과되다 ❏ 그런 과격한 제안이 의회에서 통과될 리는 없다. ■ 구동사 탕진하다, 사용하다 [주로 영국영어] ❏ 우리는 많은 타이어를 사용했다. ■ 구동사 합격하다, 통과하다 [주로 영국영어] ❏ 입학시험에 합격해야 했습니까?

H

I

J

K

L

▶**get together** ■ PHRASAL VERB When people **get together**, they meet in order to discuss something or to spend time together. →see also **get-together** ❏ *...so a whole range of people from all backgrounds can get together and enjoy themselves.* ■ PHRASAL VERB If you **get** something **together**, you organize it. ❏ *Paul and I were getting a band together, and we needed a new record deal.* ■ PHRASAL VERB If you **get** an amount of money **together**, you succeed in getting all the money that you need in order to pay for something. ❏ *Now you've finally got enough money together to put down a deposit on your dream home.*

■ 구동사 모이다 ❏ 그래서 다양한 배경을 가진 사람들이 함께 모여서 즐거운 시간을 보낼 수 있다. ■ 구동사 -을 잘 정리하다, -을 조직하다 ❏ 폴과 나는 밴드를 결성하고 있었고, 새 음반 제작 계약이 필요했다. ■ 구동사 모으다 ❏ 이제 마침내 당신이 꿈꾸던 집에 대한 계약금을 지불하기 위한 돈을 다 모았군요.

M

N

▶**get up** ■ PHRASAL VERB When someone who is sitting or lying down **gets up**, they rise to a standing position. ❏ *I got up and walked over to where he was.* ■ PHRASAL VERB When you **get up**, you get out of bed. ❏ *They have to get up early in the morning.*

■ 구동사 일어서다 ❏ 나는 일어서서 그가 있는 곳으로 걸어갔다. ■ 구동사 일어나다 ❏ 그들은 아침에 일찍 일어나야 한다.

O

P

▶**get up to** PHRASAL VERB If you say that someone **gets up to** something, you mean that they do it and you do not approve of it. [BRIT, mainly SPOKEN, DISAPPROVAL] ❏ *They get up to all sorts behind your back.*

구동사 (나쁜 짓을) 하다 [영국영어, 주로 구어체, 탐탁잖음] ❏ 그들은 당신 모르게 온갖 짓을 한다.

Q

get|away /gɛtəweɪ/ (**getaways**) also **get-away** ■ N-COUNT If someone makes a **getaway**, they leave a place quickly, especially after committing a crime or when trying to avoid someone. ❏ *They made their getaway along a pavement on a stolen motorcycle.* ■ N-COUNT A **getaway** is a short holiday somewhere. [INFORMAL] ❏ *Weekend tours are ideal for families who want a short getaway.*

■ 가산명사 도망, 도주 ❏ 그들은 훔친 오토바이를 타고 보도 위로 도주했다. ■ 가산명사 단기 휴가, 짧은 휴가 [비격식체] ❏ 주말여행은 짧은 휴가를 원하는 가족들에게 이상적이다.

R

get|ting /gɛtɪŋ/ **Getting** is the present participle of **get**.

get의 현재 분사

S

get-together (**get-togethers**) N-COUNT A **get-together** is an informal meeting or party, usually arranged for a particular purpose. ❏ *...a get-together I had at my home.*

가산명사 모임, 파티 ❏ 나의 집에서 가졌던 작은 모임

T

ghast|ly /gɑːstli/ ADJ If you describe someone or something as **ghastly**, you mean that you find them very unpleasant or shocking. [INFORMAL] ❏ *...a mother accompanied by her ghastly unruly child.* ❏ *It was the worst week of my life. It was ghastly.*

형용사 끔찍한, 지긋지긋한 [비격식체] ❏ 엄청나게 제멋대로인 아이와 함께 온 애 엄마 ❏ 내 생애 최악의 한 주였다. 정말 지긋지긋했다.

U

ghet|to /gɛtoʊ/ (**ghettos** or **ghettoes**) N-COUNT A **ghetto** is a part of a city in which many poor people or many people of a particular race, religion, or nationality live separately from everyone else. ❏ *...the black ghettos of New York and Los Angeles.*

가산명사 빈민가, 고립된 지역 ❏ 뉴욕과 로스앤젤레스의 흑인 빈민가

V

ghost /goʊst/ (**ghosts**) ■ N-COUNT A **ghost** is the spirit of a dead person that someone believes they can see or feel. ❏ *...the ghost of Marie Antoinette.* ■ N-COUNT The **ghost** of something, especially of something bad that has happened, is the memory of it. ❏ *...the ghost of anti-Americanism.*

■ 가산명사 유령, 혼령 ❏ 마리 앙투아네트의 유령 ■ 가산명사 (비유적) 망령 ❏ 반미주의의 망령

W

ghost|ly /goʊstli/ ■ ADJ Something that is **ghostly** seems unreal or unnatural and may be frightening because of this. ❏ *...Sonia's ghostly laughter.* ■ ADJ A **ghostly** presence is the ghost or spirit of a dead person. [ADJ n] ❏ *...the ghostly presences which haunt these islands.*

■ 형용사 유령 같은 ❏ 소니아의 유령 같은 웃음소리 ■ 형용사 유령의 ❏ 이 섬들에 나타나는 유령들

X

GI /dʒiː aɪ/ (**GIs**) N-COUNT A **GI** is a soldier in the United States armed forces, especially the army. ❏ *...the GIs who came to Europe to fight the Nazis.*

가산명사 (미국 육군의) 병사 ❏ 나치와 싸우기 위해 유럽에 왔던 미군 병사들

Y

gi|ant ♦◇◇ /dʒaɪənt/ (**giants**) ■ ADJ Something that is described as **giant** is much larger or more important than most others of its kind. [ADJ n] ❏ *...Italy's giant car maker, Fiat.* ❏ *...a giant oak table.* ■ N-COUNT **Giant** is often used to refer to any large, successful business organization or country. [JOURNALISM]

■ 형용사 거대한 ❏ 이탈리아의 거대 자동차 회사인 피아트 ❏ 거대한 오크재의 탁자 ■ 가산명사 거대 기업 [언론] ❏ 일본의 거대 전자 회사인 소니 ■ 가산명사 거인 ❏ 거인들에 대한 북유럽의 전설

Z

□ ...*Japanese electronics giant Sony.* ☑ N-COUNT A **giant** is an imaginary person who is very big and strong, especially one mentioned in old stories. □ ...*a Nordic saga of giants.*

☑ 그는 현기증이 나고
어지러웠다. ☑ 형용사 ―에 들뜬 □ 앤터니는 자기
만족감에 들떠 있었다.

> **Thesaurus**　　giant의 참조어
>
> | ADJ. | colossal, enormous, gigantic, huge, immense, mammoth; (*ant.*) miniature ☑ |
> | --- | --- |

gibe /dʒaɪb/ →see **jibe**

gid|dy /ɡɪdi/ (**giddier, giddiest**) ☑ ADJ If you feel **giddy**, you feel unsteady and think that you are about to fall over, usually because you are not well. □ *He felt giddy and light-headed.* ☑ ADJ If you feel **giddy with** delight or excitement, you feel so happy or excited that you find it hard to think or act normally. □ *Anthony was giddy with self-satisfaction.*

☑ 형용사 현기증이 나는 □ 그는 현기증이 나고 어지러웠다. ☑ 형용사 ―에 들뜬 □ 앤터니는 자기 만족감에 들떠 있었다.

gift ◆◇◇ /ɡɪft/ (**gifts**) ☑ N-COUNT A **gift** is something that you give someone as a present. □ ...*a gift of $50.00.* □ *They believed the unborn child was a gift from God.* ☑ N-COUNT If someone has a **gift for** doing something, they have a natural

☑ 가산명사 선물 □ 50달러 선물 □ 그들은 뱃속의 아이가 하느님의 선물이라고 믿었다. ☑ 가산명사 천부적인 재능, 자질 □ 젊었을 때 그는 자기가 가르치는 데 재능이 있다는 것을 알았다.

> **Thesaurus**　　gift의 참조어
>
> | N. | present ☑ |
> | --- | --- |
> | | ability, talent ☑ |

ability for doing it. □ *As a youth he discovered a gift for teaching.*

gift|ed /ɡɪftɪd/ ☑ ADJ Someone who is **gifted** has a natural ability to do something well. □ ...*one of the most gifted players in the world.* ☑ ADJ A **gifted** child is much more intelligent or talented than average. □ ...*a state program for gifted children.*

☑ 형용사 타고난 재능이 있는 □ 세계에서 가장 재능 있는 연주가들 중 한 명 ☑ 형용사 뛰어난 재능이 있는 □ 영재들을 위한 정부 프로그램

gig /ɡɪɡ/ (**gigs**) N-COUNT A **gig** is a live performance by someone such as a musician or a comedian. [INFORMAL] □ *The two bands join forces for a gig at the Sheffield Arena on November 28.*

가산명사 라이브 공연 [비격식체] □ 두 악단이 11월 28일에 셰필드 아레나에서 열리는 라이브 공연을 위해 합세한다.

gi|ga|byte /ɡɪɡəbaɪt/ (**gigabytes**) N-COUNT In computing, a **gigabyte** is one thousand and twenty-four megabytes.

가산명사 기가바이트

gi|gan|tic /dʒaɪɡæntɪk/ ADJ If you describe something as **gigantic**, you are emphasizing that it is extremely large in size, amount, or degree. [EMPHASIS] □ *In Red Rock Valley the road is bordered by gigantic rocks.*

형용사 거대한, 엄청난 [강조] □ 레드락 계곡의 도로는 거대한 바위들이 경계를 이루고 있다.

gig|gle /ɡɪɡ°l/ (**giggles, giggling, giggled**) ☑ V-T/V-I If someone **giggles**, they laugh in a childlike way, because they are amused, nervous, or embarrassed. □ *Both girls began to giggle.* □ *"I beg your pardon?" she giggled.* ● N-COUNT **Giggle** is also a noun. □ *She gave a little giggle.* ☑ N-PLURAL If you say that someone has **the giggles**, you mean they cannot stop giggling. □ *I was so nervous I got the giggles.* ☑ N-SING If you say that something is **a giggle**, you mean it is fun or is amusing. [mainly BRIT, INFORMAL] □ *I might buy one for a friend's birthday as a giggle.* →see **laugh**

☑ 타동사/자동사 킬킬거리고 웃다 □ 두 소녀 모두 킬킬대며 웃기 시작했다. □ "뭐라고 하셨어요?"하며 그녀는 킬킬댔다. ● 가산명사 킬킬 웃음 □ 그녀는 조금 킬킬 웃었다. ☑ 복수명사 킬킬거림 □ 나는 너무 신경과민이 되어 계속 킬킬거렸다. ☑ 단수명사 장난, 재미 [주로 영국영어, 비격식체] □ 내가 친구 생일에 주려고 장난삼아 하나 살 수도 있겠다.

gilt /ɡɪlt/ (**gilts**) ☑ ADJ A **gilt** object is covered with a thin layer of gold or gold paint. □ ...*marble columns and gilt spires.* ☑ N-COUNT **Gilts** are gilt-edged stocks or securities. [BRIT, BUSINESS] □ *Gilts offer an attractive fixed rate of return in the current climate.*

☑ 형용사 도금한 □ 대리석 기둥과 금박 입힌 첨탑들 ☑ 가산명사 금테 증권, 우량 증권 [영국영어, 경제] □ 현 상황에서 우량 증권에는 매력적인 고정 수익률이 있다.

gilt-edged ADJ **Gilt-edged** stocks or securities are issued by the government for people to invest in for a fixed period of time at a fixed rate of interest. [BRIT, BUSINESS] [ADJ n] □ *So a proportion of the fund will be kept in Government gilt-edged stocks and other fixed-interest investments.*

형용사 금테를 두른, 우량의 [영국영어, 경제] □ 그러므로 기금의 일부는 우량 국공채와 고정 이율을 주는 다른 투자 대상에 묶어 둘 것이다.

gim|mick /ɡɪmɪk/ (**gimmicks**) N-COUNT A **gimmick** is an unusual and unnecessary feature or action whose purpose is to attract attention or publicity. [DISAPPROVAL] □ *It is just a public relations gimmick.*

가산명사 (주의를 끌기 위한) 수법, 장치 [탐탁찮음] □ 이것은 단지 홍보 장치일 뿐이다.

gin /dʒɪn/ (**gins**) N-MASS **Gin** is a strong colorless alcoholic drink made from grain and juniper berries. ● N-COUNT A **gin** is a glass of gin. □ ...*another gin and tonic.*

물질명사 진 (酒類) ● 가산명사 진 한잔 □ 진토닉 한 잔 더

gin|ger /dʒɪndʒər/ ☑ N-UNCOUNT **Ginger** is the root of a plant that is used to flavor food. It has a sweet spicy flavor and is often sold in powdered form. ☑ COLOR **Ginger** is used to describe things that are orangey-brown in color. □ *She was a mature lady with dyed ginger hair.*

☑ 불가산명사 생강 ☑ 색채어 생강빛, 황갈색 □ 그녀는 생강빛 염색머리를 한 원숙한 여인이었다.

gin|ger|ly /dʒɪndʒərli/ ADV If you do something **gingerly**, you do it in a careful manner, usually because you expect it to be dangerous, unpleasant, or painful. [WRITTEN] [ADV with v] □ *She was touching the dressing gingerly with both hands.*

부사 아주 조심스럽게, 신중하게 [문어체] □ 그녀는 붕대를 두 손으로 조심스럽게 만지고 있었다.

gip|sy /dʒɪpsi/ →see **gypsy**

gi|raffe /dʒɪræf/ (**giraffes**) N-COUNT A **giraffe** is a large African animal with a very long neck, long legs, and dark patches on its body.

가산명사 기린

girl ◆◆◇ /ɡɜrl/ (**girls**) ☑ N-COUNT A **girl** is a female child. □ ...*an eleven year old girl.* ☑ N-COUNT You can refer to someone's daughter as a **girl**. □ *We had a little girl.* ☑ N-COUNT Young women are often referred to as **girls**. This use could cause offense. □ ...*a pretty twenty-year-old girl.* ☑ N-COUNT Some people refer to a man's girlfriend as his **girl**. [INFORMAL] □ *I've been with my girl for nine years.*

☑ 가산명사 소녀, 여자애 □ 열한 살짜리 소녀 ☑ 가산명사 딸 □ 우리에게는 어린 딸이 있었다. ☑ 가산명사 아가씨, 처녀 □ 어여쁜 20세 처녀 ☑ 가산명사 여자 친구, 애인 [비격식체] □ 나는 내 여자 친구와 9년 동안 사귀었다.

girl|friend /ɡɜrlfrɛnd/ (**girlfriends**) ☑ N-COUNT Someone's **girlfriend** is a girl or woman with whom they are having a romantic or sexual relationship. □ *He had been going out with his girlfriend for seven months.*

☑ 가산명사 애인 □ 그는 자기 애인과 7개월 동안 만나고 있었다.

> A **girlfriend** is the female person in a romantic relationship. Women can also describe their female friends as their **girlfriends**, but men do not usually use this word to talk about anyone except the woman they are in a romantic relationship with.

> girlfriend는 연애하는 사이에서 여성을 가리킨다. 여자는 자기 여자 친구들을 가리켜 girlfriends라고도 한다. 그러나 남자는 자기와 연애 중인 여자를 제외한 다른 여자를 지칭할 때에는 대개 이 말을 사용하지 않는다.

a b c d e f g h i j k l m n o p q r s t u v w x y z

A

2 N-COUNT A **girlfriend** is a female friend. ❏ *I met a girlfriend for lunch.*

2 가산명사 여자 친구 ❏ 나는 점심 때 여자 친구를 만났다.

girth /gɜrθ/ (**girths**) N-VAR The **girth** of an object, for example a person's or an animal's body, is its width or thickness, considered as the measurement around its circumference. [FORMAL] ❏ *A girl he knew had upset him by commenting on his increasing girth.*

가산명사 또는 불가산명사 몸통 둘레 [격식체] ❏ 그가 아는 어떤 여자가 점점 불어나는 그의 몸통 둘레에 대해 언급해서 그를 화나게 했다.

gist /dʒɪst/ N-SING The **gist of** a speech, conversation, or piece of writing is its general meaning. ❏ *He related the gist of his conversation to Smith.*

단수명사 요지, 골자 ❏ 그는 스미스에게 자기 대화의 골자를 말했다.

B

C

D

───────────── **give** ─────────────

① USED WITH NOUNS DESCRIBING ACTIONS
② TRANSFERRING
③ OTHER USES, PHRASES, AND PHRASAL VERBS

E

① **give** ♦♦♦ /gɪv/ (**gives, giving, gave, given**) 1 V-T You can use **give** with nouns that refer to physical actions. The whole expression refers to the performing of the action. For example, **She gave a smile** means almost the same as "She smiled." [no cont] ❏ *She stretched her arms out and gave a great yawn.* ❏ *He gave her a fond smile.* 2 V-T You use **give** to say that a person does something for another person. For example, if you **give** someone a lift, you take them somewhere in your car. ❏ *I gave her a lift back out to her house.* ❏ *He was given mouth-to-mouth resuscitation.* 3 V-T You use **give** with nouns that refer to information, opinions, or greetings to indicate that something is communicated. For example, if you **give** someone some news, you tell it to them. ❏ *He gave no details.* ❏ *Would you like to give me your name?* 4 V-T You use **give** to say how long you think something will last or how much you think something will be. ❏ *A BBC poll gave the Labour Party a 12 per cent lead.* 5 PHRASE People use **give** in expressions such as **I don't give a damn** to show that they do not care about something. [INFORMAL, FEELINGS] [no cont, no passive, with brd-neg] ❏ *They don't give a damn about the country.* 6 V-T If someone or something **gives** you a particular idea or impression, it causes you to have that idea or impression. ❏ *They gave me the impression that they were doing exactly what they wanted in life.* 7 V-T If someone or something **gives** you a particular physical or emotional feeling, it makes you experience it. ❏ *He gave me a shock.* 8 V-T If you **give** a performance or speech, you perform or speak in public. ❏ *Kotto gives a stupendous performance.* 9 V-T If you **give** something thought or attention, you think about it, concentrate on it, or deal with it. ❏ *I've been giving it some thought.* 10 V-T If you **give** a party or other social event, you organize it. ❏ *That evening, I gave a dinner party for a few close friends.*
→see **donor**

1 타동사 (행동을) 하다 ❏ 그녀는 팔을 쭉 뻗고 크게 하품을 했다. ❏ 그는 그녀에게 다정한 미소를 지었다. 2 타동사 -을 해 주다 ❏ 나는 그녀를 집까지 차를 태워 주었다. ❏ 그는 구강 대 구강 인공호흡을 받았다. 3 타동사 (정보 등을) 주다 ❏ 그는 세부 사항을 알려주지 않았다. ❏ 이름을 말해 주시겠어요? 4 타동사 (생각 등을) 제시하다 ❏ 비비시 여론 조사는 노동당이 12퍼센트 앞선 것으로 나타났다. 5 타동사 주다; 전혀 관심이 없다 [비격식체, 감정 개입] ❏ 그들은 나라에 대해 전혀 관심이 없다. 6 타동사 (인상 등을) 주다 ❏ 그들은 내게 자기들이 평생 하고 싶었던 일을 하고 있다는 인상을 주었다. 7 타동사 (감정 등을) 주다 ❏ 그는 내게 충격을 주었다. 8 타동사 (연설 등을) 하다 ❏ 코토는 굉장한 공연을 했다. 9 타동사 (관심을) 기울이다 ❏ 난 그것을 조금 생각해 보고 있다. 10 타동사 (파티 등을) 개최하다, 열다 ❏ 그날 저녁, 나는 몇몇 친한 친구들을 위해 만찬회를 열었다.

F

G

H

I

J

K

L

② **give** ♦♦♦ /gɪv/ (**gives, giving, gave, given**) 1 V-T If you **give** someone something that you own or have bought, you provide them with it, so that they have it or can use it. ❏ *They gave us T-shirts and stickers.* ❏ *He gave money to the World Health Organisation to help defeat smallpox.* 2 V-T If you **give** someone something that you are holding or that is near you, you pass it to them, so that they are then holding it. ❏ *Give me that pencil.* 3 V-T To **give** someone or something a particular power or right means to allow them to have it. ❏ *...a citizen's charter giving rights to gays.*

1 타동사 (물건 등을) 주다 ❏ 그들은 우리에게 티셔츠와 스티커를 주었다. ❏ 그는 천연두 박멸을 도우려고 세계 보건 기구에 돈을 기부했다. 2 타동사 건네주다 ❏ 저 연필 좀 줘. 3 타동사 부여하다 ❏ 동성애자들에게 권리를 부여하는 시민헌장

M

N

③ **give** ♦♦♦ /gɪv/ (**gives, giving, gave, given**) →Please look at category 7 to see if the expression you are looking for is shown under another headword. 1 V-I If something **gives**, it collapses or breaks under pressure. ❏ *My knees gave under me.* 2 V-T PASSIVE You say that you **are given to** understand or believe that something is the case when you do not want to say how you found out about it, or who told you. [FORMAL, VAGUENESS] ❏ *We were given to understand that he was ill.* 3 →see also **given** 4 PHRASE You use **give me** to say that you would rather have one thing than another, especially when you have just mentioned the thing that you do not want. ❏ *I've never had anything barbecued and I don't want it. Give me a good roast dinner any day.* 5 PHRASE If you say that something requires **give and take**, you mean that people must compromise or co-operate for it to be successful. ❏ *...a happy relationship where there's a lot of give and take.* 6 PHRASE **Give or take** is used to indicate that an amount is approximate. For example, if you say that something is fifty years old, **give or take** a few years, you mean that it is approximately fifty years old. ❏ *They grow to a height of 12 in. – give or take a couple of inches.* 7 PHRASE to **give the game away** →see **game**. to **give notice** →see **notice**. to **give rise to** →see **rise**. to **give way** →see **way**

1 자동사 무너지다 ❏ 다리에 힘이 쑥 빠졌다. 2 수동태 타동사 -라고 듣다 [격식체, 짐작투] ❏ 우리는 그가 아프다고 알고 있으리라고 들었다. 4 구 -을 선호하다 ❏ 난 바비큐 요리는 전혀 먹어 본 적이 없고, 먹고 싶지도 않아. 언제든 맛있는 구이 요리로 저녁을 해 줘. 5 구 주고받음, 양보와 협조 ❏ 주고받는 것이 많은 행복한 관계 6 구 (수량이) 다소의 차이가 있더라도 ❏ 그들은 대략 2-3인치 정도 차이는 있더라도 12인치 높이로 자란다.

O

P

Q

R

S

▶**give away** 1 PHRASAL VERB If you **give away** something that you own, you give it to someone, rather than selling it, often because you no longer want it. ❏ *He was giving his collection away for nothing.* 2 PHRASAL VERB If someone **gives away** an advantage, they accidentally cause their opponent or enemy to have that advantage. ❏ *Military advantages should not be given away.* 3 PHRASAL VERB If you **give away** information that should be kept secret, you reveal it to other people. ❏ *She would give nothing away.* 4 PHRASAL VERB To **give** someone or something **away** means to show their true nature or identity, which is not obvious. ❏ *Although they are pretending hard to be young, grey hair and cellulite give them away.*

1 구동사 (거저) 주다 ❏ 그는 자기 소장품을 거저 나누어 주고 있었다. 2 구동사 (기회를) 놓치다 ❏ 군사적 이점을 놓쳐서는 안 된다. 3 구동사 누설하다, 폭로하다 ❏ 그녀는 어떤 것도 누설하려 하지 않았다. 4 구동사 정체를 드러내다 ❏ 비록 그들이 젊어 보이려고 애쓰지만, 백발과 울퉁불퉁한 피하 지방이 그들의 본 모습을 드러낸다.

T

U

V

▶**give back** PHRASAL VERB If you **give** something **back**, you return it to the person who gave it to you. ❏ *I gave the textbook back to him.* ❏ *You gave me back the projector.*

구동사 돌려주다 ❏ 나는 그에게 교재를 돌려주었다. ❏ 넌 내게 영사기를 돌려주었다.

W

▶**give in** 1 PHRASAL VERB If you **give in**, you admit that you are defeated or that you cannot do something. ❏ *My 10-year-old is nagging me to get her a mobile phone. Should I give in?* 2 PHRASAL VERB If you **give in**, you agree to do something that you do not want to do. ❏ *I pressed my parents until they finally gave in and registered me for skating classes.*

1 구동사 굴복하다 ❏ 열 살짜리 내 딸이 핸드폰을 사 달라고 나를 성가시게 한다. 내가 굴복해야 하는가? 2 구동사 굴복하다, 양보하다 ❏ 내가 부모님을 졸라 부모님은 마침내 항복하고 나를 스케이트 강습에 등록시켜 주셨다.

X

Y

▶**give off** or **give out** PHRASAL VERB If something **gives off** or **gives out** a gas, heat, or a smell, it produces it and sends it out into the air. ❏ *...natural gas, which gives off less carbon dioxide than coal.*

구동사 (가스 등을) 방출하다, 내뿜다 ❏ 석탄보다 이산화탄소 방출량이 적은 천연가스

Z

Word Web   glacier

Two-thirds of all fresh **water** is **frozen**. The largest **glaciers** in the world are the **polar** ice caps of Antarctica and Greenland. They cover more than six million square miles. Their average depth is almost one mile. If all the glaciers **melted**, the average **sea level** would rise by over 250 feet. Glaciologists have noted that the Antarctic is about 1°C* warmer than it was 50 years ago. Some of them are worried. Continued warming might cause floating **ice** shelves there to begin to disintegrate. This, in turn, could cause disastrous coastal flooding in low-lying areas around the world.

1° Celsius = 33.8° Fahrenheit

▶**give out** ◼ PHRASAL VERB If you **give out** a number of things, you distribute them among a group of people. ❑ *There were people at the entrance giving out leaflets.* ◪ PHRASAL VERB If you **give out** information, you make it known to people. ❑ *He wouldn't give out any information.* ◉ →see **give off**

▶**give over to** or **give up to** PHRASAL VERB If something is **given over** or **given up to** a particular use, it is used entirely for that purpose. ❑ *Much of the garden was given over to vegetables.*

▶**give up** ◼ PHRASAL VERB If you **give up** something, you stop doing it or having it. ❑ *Coastguards had given up all hope of finding the two divers alive.* ◪ PHRASAL VERB If you **give up**, you decide that you cannot do something and stop trying to do it. ❑ *After a fruitless morning sitting at his desk he had given up.* ◉ PHRASAL VERB If you **give up** your job, you resign from it. ❑ *She gave up her job to join her husband's campaign.* ◖ PHRASAL VERB If you **give up** something that you have or that you are entitled to, you allow someone else to have it. ❑ *One of the men with him gave up his place on the bench.* ◗ PHRASAL VERB If you **give yourself up**, you let the police or other people know where you are, after you have been hiding from them. ❑ *A 28-year-old man later gave himself up and will appear in court today.*

▶**give up on** PHRASAL VERB If you **give up on** something or someone, you decide that you will never succeed in doing what you want to with them, and you stop trying to. ❑ *He urged them not to give up on peace efforts.*

▶**give up to** →see **give over to**

give|away /ɡɪvəweɪ/ (**giveaways**) also **give-away** N-COUNT A **giveaway** is something that a company or organization gives to someone, usually in order to encourage people to buy a particular product. ❑ *Next week "TODAY" is celebrating with a great giveaway of FREE garden seeds.*

giv|en ◆◇◇ /ɡɪvⁿn/ ◼ **Given** is the past participle of **give**. ◪ ADJ If you talk about, for example, any **given** position or a **given** time, you mean the particular position or time that you are discussing. [det ADJ] ❑ *In chess there are typically about 36 legal moves from any given board position.* ◉ PREP **Given** is used when indicating a possible situation in which someone has the opportunity or ability to do something. For example, **given the chance** means "if I had the chance." ❑ *Write down the sort of thing you would like to do, given the opportunity.* ◖ PHRASE If you say **given that** something is the case, you mean taking that fact into account. ❑ *Usually, I am sensible with money, as I have to be, given that I don't earn that much.* ◗ PREP If you say **given** something, you mean taking that into account. ❑ *Given the uncertainty over Leigh's future I was left with little other choice.*

gla|cial /ɡleɪʃ⁰l/ ADJ **Glacial** means relating to or produced by glaciers or ice. [TECHNICAL] ❑ *...a true glacial landscape with U-shaped valleys.* →see **lake**

glaci|er /ɡleɪʃər, BRIT ɡlæsiəʳ/ (**glaciers**) N-COUNT A **glacier** is an extremely large mass of ice which moves very slowly, often down a mountain valley. →see **climate**
→see Word Web: **glacier**

glad ◆◇◇ /ɡlæd/ ◼ ADJ If you are **glad** about something, you are happy and pleased about it. [v-link ADJ, oft ADJ that, ADJ to-inf, ADJ of/about n] ❑ *The people seem genuinely glad to see you.* ❑ *I'd be glad if the books were a little longer so I could do some ironing.* ● **glad|ly** ADV [ADV with v] ❑ *Mallarmé gladly accepted the invitation.* ◪ ADJ If you say that you will be **glad to** do something, usually for someone else, you mean that you are willing and eager to do it. [FEELINGS] [v-link ADJ to-inf] ❑ *I'll be glad to show you everything.* ● **glad|ly** ADV [ADV with v] ❑ *The counselors will gladly baby-sit during their free time.*

glam|or /ɡlæmər/ [BRIT also **glamour**] N-UNCOUNT **Glamor** is the quality of being more attractive, exciting, or interesting than ordinary people or things. ❑ *...the glamor of show biz.*

glam|or|ous /ɡlæmərəs/ ADJ If you describe someone or something as **glamorous**, you mean that they are more attractive, exciting, or interesting than ordinary people or things. ❑ *...some of the world's most beautiful and glamorous women.*

glance ◆◇◇ /ɡlæns/ (**glances, glancing, glanced**) ◼ V-I If you **glance at** something or someone, you look at them very quickly and then look away again immediately. ❑ *He glanced at his watch.* ◪ V-I If you **glance through** or **at** a newspaper, report, or book, you spend a short time looking at it without reading it very carefully. ❑ *I picked up the phone book and glanced through it.* ◉ N-COUNT A **glance** is a quick look at someone or something. ❑ *Trevor and I exchanged a glance.* ◖ PHRASE If you see something **at a glance**, you see or recognize it immediately, and without having to look or think carefully. ❑ *One*

a
b
c
d
e
f
g
h
i
j
k
l
m
n
o
p
q
r
s
t
u
v
w
x
y
z

◼ 구동사 나눠 주다 ❑ 입구에 전단을 나누어 주는 사람들이 있었다. ◪ 구동사 알리다, 공표하다 ❑ 그는 어떤 정보도 알려 주려고 하지 않았다.

구동사 _에 바쳐지다, _에 충당하다 ❑ 정원의 많은 부분이 야채 심는 데 사용되었다.

◼ 구동사 단념하다, 버리다 ❑ 해안 경비대는 두 명의 잠수부가 생존해 있을 것이라는 희망을 모두 버렸었다. ◪ 구동사 포기하다 ❑ 오전 내내 소득 없이 책상에 앉아 있은 후에 그는 포기했다. ◉ 구동사 사임하다 ❑ 그녀는 남편의 선거 운동에 동참하기 위해 사직했다. ◖ 구동사 양보하다 ❑ 그와 같이 있던 사람 하나가 벤치의 자리를 양보했다. ◗ 구동사 항복하다, 자수하다 ❑ 28세 되는 남자가 나중에 자수했고 오늘 법정에 출두할 것이다.

구동사 포기하다, 단념하다 ❑ 그는 그들에게 평화를 위한 노력을 포기하지 말라고 촉구했다.

가산명사 사은품 ❑ 다음 주에 '투데이'는 원예용 꽃씨를 무료로 나누어 드리는 큰 사은 행사를 엽니다.

◼ give의 과거 분사 ◪ 형용사 주어진, 정해진 ❑ 체스에는 체스 판 위의 어떤 위치든 어느 정해진 위치로부터 적정하게 움직일 수 있는 방법이 일반적으로 36가지 정도가 있다. ◉ 전치사 _이 주어지면 ❑ 기회가 주어질 경우 당신이 하고 싶은 일을 적으세요. ◖ 구 _라는 것을 감안하면 ❑ 대체로 나는 분별 있게 돈을 쓴다. 내가 그렇게 많이 벌지 못한다는 것을 감안하면 그래야 하고요. ◗ 전치사 _을 감안하면 ❑ 리의 장래가 불투명한 것을 고려하면 내겐 다른 선택의 여지가 거의 없었다.

형용사 빙하의 [과학 기술] ❑ 유(U) 자형의 계곡을 한 전형적인 빙하 지형

가산명사 빙하

◼ 형용사 기쁜 ❑ 그 사람들은 당신을 만난 것을 진심으로 기뻐하는 것 같다. ❑ 내가 다림질을 좀 할 수 있게 이 책들이 좀 더 오래 간다면 좋겠다. ● 기꺼이 부사 ❑ 말라르메는 기꺼이 그 초대를 받아들였다. ◪ 형용사 기꺼이 _하는 [감정 개입] ❑ 당신에게 기꺼이 모두 보여 드리겠습니다. ● 기꺼이 부사 ❑ 상담사들은 여유 시간에 기꺼이 아이를 봐줄 것이다.

[영국영어 glamour] 불가산명사 매력, 화려함 ❑ 쇼 비즈니스의 매력

형용사 매력적인, 멋진 ❑ 세계에서 가장 아름답고 매력적인 여성들 중 몇 명

◼ 자동사 흘끗 보다, 얼핏 보다 ❑ 그가 시계를 흘끗 보았다. ◪ 자동사 대충 훑어보다 ❑ 나는 전화번호부를 집어 들고 대충 훑어보았다. ◉ 가산명사 일별, 흘끗 봄 ❑ 트레버와 나는 서로 흘깃 쳐다보았다. ◖ 구 첫눈에, 대번에 ❑ 사람들은 그녀가 인정 많은 사람이라는 것을 대번에 알아볼 수 있었다. ◗ 구 얼핏 보기에는 ❑ 얼핏 보기에는 유기농업이 농부들에게 훨씬 비용이 많이 드는 것처럼 보인다.

could tell at a glance that she was a compassionate person. **5** PHRASE If you say that something is true or seems to be true **at first glance**, you mean that it seems to be true when you first see it or think about it, but that your first impression may be wrong. ❑ *At first glance, organic farming looks much more expensive for the farmer.*

Word Partnership	*glance의 연어*	
PREP.	glance **at** *someone/something*, glance **over**, glance **over** *someone's* **shoulder** **1**	
	glance **through** **2**	
V.	**exchange a** glance **3**	
ADJ.	**quick** glance **3**	

gland /glænd/ (**glands**) N-COUNT A **gland** is an organ in the body which produces chemical substances for the body to use or get rid of. [usu supp N] ❑ *...the hormones secreted by our endocrine glands.* →see **sweat**

가산명사 분비선 ❑ 내분비선에서 분비되는 호르몬

glare /glɛər/ (**glares, glaring, glared**) **1** V-I If you **glare at** someone, you look at them with an angry expression on your face. ❑ *The old woman glared at him.* ❑ *Jacob glared and muttered something.* **2** N-COUNT A **glare** is an angry, hard, and unfriendly look. ❑ *His glasses magnified his irritable glare.* **3** V-I If the sun or a light **glares**, it shines with a very bright light which is difficult to look at. ❑ *The sunlight glared.* **4** N-UNCOUNT **Glare** is very bright light that is difficult to look at. ❑ *...the glare of a car's headlights.* **5** N-SING If someone is in **the glare of** publicity or public attention, they are constantly being watched and talked about by a lot of people. ❑ *Norma is said to dislike the glare of publicity.*

1 자동사 노려보다 ❑ 노파는 그를 노려보았다. ❑ 제이콥이 노려보며 무슨 말을 중얼거렸다. **2** 가산명사 노려봄 ❑ 안경 때문에 화나서 노려보는 그의 눈이 더 크게 보였다. **3** 자동사 눈부시게 빛나다 ❑ 햇빛이 눈부시게 빛났다. **4** 불가산명사 눈부신 빛 ❑ 자동차 전조등의 눈부신 빛 **5** 단수명사 관심의 초점 ❑ 노마는 세간의 관심을 받는 것을 싫어한다고들 한다.

Word Partnership	*glare의 연어*	
PREP.	glare **at** *someone* **1**	
N.	glare **of light** **3** **4**	
	glare **of publicity** **5**	
ADJ.	**irritable** glare **2**	
	full glare **4** **5**	

glaring /glɛərɪŋ/ ADJ If you describe something bad as **glaring**, you are emphasizing that it is very obvious and easily seen or noticed. [EMPHASIS] ❑ *I never saw such a glaring example of misrepresentation.* ● **glaringly** ADV ❑ *It was glaringly obvious.* →see also **glare**

형용사 빤히 보이는, 역력한 [강조] ❑ 나는 그렇게 드러나게 오도한 경우는 본 적이 없다. ● 빤히 보이게 부사 ❑ 그것은 너무도 명백했다.

glass ♦♦◇ /glɑs, glæs/ (**glasses**) **1** N-UNCOUNT **Glass** is a hard transparent substance that is used to make things such as windows and bottles. ❑ *...a pane of glass.* **2** N-COUNT A **glass** is a container made from glass, which you can drink from and which does not have a handle. ❑ *Grossman raised the glass to his lips.* ● N-COUNT The contents of a glass can be referred to as a **glass of** something. ❑ *...a glass of milk.* **3** N-UNCOUNT **Glass** is used to mean objects made of glass, for example drinking containers and bowls. ❑ *There's a glittering array of glass to choose from at markets.* **4** N-PLURAL **Glasses** are two lenses in a frame that some people wear in front of their eyes in order to help them see better. ❑ *He took off his glasses.* →see **light bulb**

1 불가산명사 유리 ❑ 창유리 한 장 **2** 가산명사 유리컵, 유리잔 ❑ 그로스만은 잔을 입술로 가져갔다. ● 가산명사 ‐ 한 컵, ‐ 한 잔 ❑ 우유 한 컵 **3** 불가산명사 유리 제품 ❑ 시장에는 반짝반짝 빛나는 유리 제품이 다양하게 선택할 수 있도록 나와 있다. **4** 복수명사 안경 ❑ 그는 안경을 벗었다.

glass ceiling (**glass ceilings**) N-COUNT When people refer to a **glass ceiling**, they are talking about the attitudes and traditions in a society that prevent women from rising to the top jobs. [JOURNALISM] ❑ *In her current role she broke through the glass ceiling as the first woman to reach senior management level in the company.*

가산명사 (여성의 승진을 막는) 장벽, 유리 천장 [언론] ❑ 현재 직무에서 그녀는 여성 승진을 막는 보이지 않는 장벽을 극복하고 회사의 이사급 경영진에 오른 최초의 여성이 되었다.

glaze /gleɪz/ (**glazes, glazing, glazed**) **1** N-COUNT A **glaze** is a thin layer of liquid which is put on a piece of pottery and becomes hard and shiny when the pottery is heated in a very hot oven. ❑ *...hand-painted French tiles with decorative glazes.* **2** N-COUNT A **glaze** is a thin layer of beaten egg, milk, or other liquid that you spread onto food in order to make the surface shine and look attractive. ❑ *Brush the glaze over the top and sides of the hot cake.* **3** V-T When you **glaze** food such as bread or pastry, you spread a layer of beaten egg, milk, or other liquid onto it before you cook it in order to make its surface shine and look attractive. ❑ *Glaze the pie with beaten egg.*

1 가산명사 유약칠 ❑ 장식용 유약을 사용하여 손으로 직접 칠한 프랑스제 타일 **2** 가산명사 (음식의) 글레이즈 ❑ 글레이즈를 뜨거운 케이크의 윗면과 옆면에 붓으로 바른다. **3** 타동사 글레이즈를 바르다 ❑ 잘 저은 계란을 파이에 바르세요.

▶ **glaze over** PHRASAL VERB If your eyes **glaze over**, they become dull and lose all expression, usually because you are bored or are thinking about something else. ❑ *...movie actors whose eyes glaze over as soon as the subject wavers from themselves.* →see **pottery**

구동사 (눈이) 흐릿해지다, 초점을 잃다 ❑ 대화 주제가 자신들에게서 벗어나자마자 눈의 초점이 흐려지는 영화배우들

glazed /gleɪzd/ **1** ADJ If you describe someone's eyes as **glazed**, you mean that their expression is dull or dreamy, usually because they are tired or are having difficulty concentrating on something. ❑ *Doctors with glazed eyes sat chain-smoking in front of a television set.* **2** ADJ **Glazed** pottery is covered with a thin layer of a hard shiny substance. ❑ *...a large glazed pot.* **3** ADJ A **glazed** window or door has glass in it. ❑ *...the new office, with glazed windows to the corridor.*

1 형용사 (눈이) 흐리멍덩한, 초점을 잃은 ❑ 흐리멍덩한 눈빛의 의사들이 줄담배를 피우며 텔레비전 앞에 앉아 있었다. **2** 형용사 유약을 칠한 ❑ 유약을 바른 큰 도기 **3** 형용사 유리를 끼운 ❑ 복도 쪽으로 유리창이 나 있는 새 사무실

gleam /glim/ (**gleams, gleaming, gleamed**) **1** V-I If an object or a surface **gleams**, it reflects light because it is shiny and clean. ❑ *His black hair gleamed in the sun.* **2** N-COUNT A **gleam of** something is a faint sign of it. ❑ *There was a gleam of hope for a peaceful settlement.*

1 자동사 빛을 반사하다 ❑ 그의 검은 머리가 햇빛에 반짝거렸다. **2** 가산명사 희미한 빛, 어슴푸레한 빛 ❑ 평화적 해결에 한 줄기 희망이 보였다.

glean /glin/ (**gleans, gleaning, gleaned**) V-T If you **glean** something such as information or knowledge, you learn or collect it slowly and patiently, and perhaps indirectly. ❑ *At present we're gleaning information from all sources.*

타동사 (정보 등을) 수집하다 ❑ 현재 우리는 모든 출처로부터 조금씩 정보를 수집하고 있다.

glee /gli/ N-UNCOUNT **Glee** is a feeling of happiness and excitement, often caused by someone else's misfortune. ❑ *His victory was greeted with glee by his fellow American golfers.*

불가산명사 환희; 고소해함 ❑ 그의 승리를 미국인 동료 골프 선수들은 환호로 맞이했다.

glee|ful /ɡliːfʊl/ ADJ Someone who is **gleeful** is happy and excited, often because of someone else's bad luck. [WRITTEN] ❑ *He took an almost gleeful delight in showing how wrong they can be.* ● **glee|ful|ly** ADV [ADV with v] ❑ *I spent the rest of their visit gleefully boring them with tedious details.*

형용사 신나 하는, 고소해하는 [문어체] ❑ 그들이 얼마나 틀렸는지를 보여 주면서 그는 거의 신이 나 했다. ● 신이 나서, 고소해하며 부사 ❑ 나는 지루한 세부 설명으로 그들 방문의 나머지 시간을 따분하게 만들며 고소해했다.

glib /ɡlɪb/ ADJ If you describe what someone says as **glib**, you disapprove of it because it implies that something is simple or easy, or that there are no problems involved, when this is not the case. [DISAPPROVAL] ❑ *...the glib talk of "past misery."* ● **glib|ly** ADV [ADV with v] ❑ *We talk glibly of equality of opportunity.*

형용사 입빠른, 그럴 듯한 [탐탁찮음] ❑ '과거의 불행이라는 입에 발린 말 ● 입빠르게, 그럴 듯하게 부사 ❑ 우리는 기회 균등에 대해 입에 발린 말을 한다.

glide /ɡlaɪd/ (**glides**, **gliding**, **glided**) **1** V-I If you **glide** somewhere, you move silently and in a smooth and effortless way. ❑ *Waiters glide between tightly packed tables bearing trays of pasta.* **2** V-I When birds or airplanes **glide**, they float on air currents. ❑ *Our only companion is the wandering albatross, which glides effortlessly and gracefully behind the yacht.*

1 자동사 미끄러지듯 움직이다 ❑ 웨이터들이 파스타 쟁반을 들고 빽빽한 테이블 사이를 미끄러지듯 움직인다. **2** 자동사 활공하다, 활공하다 ❑ 우리의 유일한 벗은 부유하는 신천옹인데, 요트 뒤에서 힘들이지 않고 우아하게 활공하고 있다.

glid|er /ɡlaɪdər/ (**gliders**) N-COUNT A **glider** is an aircraft without an engine, which flies by floating on air currents.

가산명사 글라이더

glim|mer /ɡlɪmər/ (**glimmers**, **glimmering**, **glimmered**) **1** V-I If something **glimmers**, it produces or reflects a faint, gentle, often unsteady light. ❑ *The moon glimmered faintly through the mists.* **2** N-COUNT A **glimmer** is a faint, gentle, often unsteady light. ❑ *In the east there is the slightest glimmer of light.* **3** N-COUNT A **glimmer of** something is a faint sign of it. ❑ *Despite an occasional glimmer of hope, this campaign has not produced any results.*

1 자동사 희미하게 빛나다, 가물거리다 ❑ 달이 안개 사이로 희미하게 빛났다. **2** 가산명사 희미한 빛 ❑ 동쪽으로 아주 희미한 불빛이 가물거린다. **3** 가산명사 ...의 기미 ❑ 간간이 희망의 빛이 비칠 때가 있지만 이 캠페인은 아무런 성과가 없다.

glimpse /ɡlɪmps/ (**glimpses**, **glimpsing**, **glimpsed**) **1** N-COUNT If you get a **glimpse** of someone or something, you see them very briefly and not very well. ❑ *Some of the fans had waited 24 hours outside the Hyde Park Hotel to catch a glimpse of their heroine.* **2** V-T If you **glimpse** someone or something, you see them very briefly and not very well. ❑ *She glimpsed a group of people standing on the bank of a river.* **3** N-COUNT A **glimpse of** something is a brief experience of it or an idea about it that helps you understand or appreciate it better. ❑ *As university campuses become increasingly multi-ethnic, they offer a glimpse of the conflicts society will face tomorrow.*

1 가산명사 일견, 일별 ❑ 일부 팬들은 자기들의 여주인공을 한번이라도 보려고 하이드파크 호텔 밖에서 24시간 동안 기다렸다. **2** 타동사 일별 보다, 얼핏 보다 ❑ 그녀는 강둑에 서 있는 한 무리의 사람을 힐끗 보았다. **3** 가산명사 일견 ❑ 대학 캠퍼스가 점점 다인종화 됨에 따라, 이를 통해 미래의 사회가 직면할 갈등의 일면을 볼 수 있다.

glint /ɡlɪnt/ (**glints**, **glinting**, **glinted**) **1** V-I If something **glints**, it produces or reflects a quick flash of light. [WRITTEN] ❑ *The sea glinted in the sun.* ❑ *Sunlight glinted on his spectacles.* **2** N-COUNT A **glint** is a quick flash of light. [WRITTEN] [usu N of n] ❑ *...glints of sunlight.*

1 자동사 반짝이다 [문어체] ❑ 바다가 햇빛에 반짝였다. ❑ 햇빛이 그의 안경 위에 반짝였다. **2** 가산명사 반짝임 [문어체] ❑ 햇빛의 반짝임

glis|ten /ɡlɪsən/ (**glistens**, **glistening**, **glistened**) V-I If something **glistens**, it shines, usually because it is wet or oily. ❑ *The calm sea glistened in the sunlight.* ❑ *Darcy's face was white and glistening with sweat.*

자동사 반짝거리다 ❑ 고요한 바다가 햇빛에 반짝거렸다. ❑ 다시의 얼굴은 하얗고 땀으로 번들거렸다.

glit|ter /ɡlɪtər/ (**glitters**, **glittering**, **glittered**) **1** V-I If something **glitters**, light comes from or is reflected off different parts of it. ❑ *The bay glittered in the sunshine.* **2** N-UNCOUNT **Glitter** consists of tiny shining pieces of metal. It is glued to things for decoration. ❑ *Cut out a piece of sandpaper and sprinkle it with glitter.* **3** N-UNCOUNT You can use **glitter** to refer to superficial attractiveness or to the excitement connected with something. ❑ *She was blinded by the glitter and the glamour of her own life.*

1 자동사 반짝반짝 빛나다 ❑ 만은 햇빛에 반짝반짝 빛났다. **2** 불가산명사 작은 장식물, 반짝이 ❑ 사포 한 조각을 잘라서 그 위에 반짝이를 뿌리시오. **3** 불가산명사 광휘 ❑ 그녀는 자신의 삶이 지닌 광채와 화려함에 눈이 멀어 있었다.

gloat /ɡloʊt/ (**gloats**, **gloating**, **gloated**) V-I If someone **is gloating**, they are showing pleasure at their own success or at other people's failure in an arrogant and unpleasant way. [DISAPPROVAL] ❑ *Anti-abortionists are gloating over the court's decision.*

자동사 흡족해하다 [탐탁찮음] ❑ 낙태 반대론자들은 법원의 결정에 흡족해하고 있다.

Word Link   glob ≈ sphere : *global*, *globe*, *globalize*

---

glob|al ◆◇◇ /ɡloʊbəl/ **1** ADJ You can use **global** to describe something that happens in all parts of the world or affects all parts of the world. ❑ *...a global ban on nuclear testing.* ● **glob|al|ly** ADV ❑ *...a globally familiar trade name.* **2** ADJ A **global** view or vision of a situation is one in which all the different aspects of it are considered. ❑ *...a global vision of contemporary societies.*

1 형용사 전 세계적인 ❑ 전 세계적인 핵실험 금지 ● 전 세계적으로 부사 ❑ 전 세계적으로 알려진 상품명 **2** 형용사 전체적인, 포괄적인 ❑ 현대 사회를 보는 포괄적인 시각

glob|al|ize /ɡloʊbəlaɪz/ (**globalizes**, **globalizing**, **globalized**) [BRIT also **globalise**] V-T/V-I When industry **globalizes** or **is globalized**, companies from one country link with companies from another country in order to do business with them. [BUSINESS] ❑ *One way to lower costs will be to forge alliances with foreign companies or to expand internationally through appropriate takeovers – in short, to "globalize."* ● **glob|al|iza|tion** /ɡloʊbəlaɪzeɪʃən/ N-UNCOUNT ❑ *Trends toward the globalization of industry have dramatically affected food production in California.*

[영국영어 globalise] 타동사/자동사 세계화하다 [경제] ❑ 비용을 낮추는 한 가지 방법은 외국 회사와 제휴하거나 적절한 인수를 통해 국제적으로 확장하는 것, 즉 세계화하는 것이다. ● 세계화 불가산명사 ❑ 산업의 세계화 경향이 캘리포니아의 식량 생산에 엄청난 타격을 주었다.

glob|al vil|lage N-SING People sometimes refer to the world as a **global village** when they want to emphasize that all the different parts of the world form one community linked together by electronic communications, especially the Internet. ❑ *Now that we are all part of the global village, everyone becomes a neighbor.*

단수명사 지구촌 마을 ❑ 이제는 우리 모두 지구촌 마을의 일부이기 때문에 모두가 이웃이 된다.

glob|al warm|ing N-UNCOUNT **Global warming** is the gradual rise in the earth's temperature caused by high levels of carbon dioxide and other gases in the atmosphere. ❑ *The threat of global warming will eventually force the US to slow down its energy consumption.* →see **greenhouse effect**

불가산명사 지구 온난화 ❑ 지구 온난화의 위협으로 결국 미국은 에너지 소비를 줄일 수밖에 없을 것이다.

globe /ɡloʊb/ (**globes**) **1** N-SING You can refer to the world as **the globe** when you are emphasizing how big it is or that something happens in many different parts of it. ❑ *...bottles of beer from every corner of the globe.* ❑ *70% of our globe's surface is water.* **2** N-COUNT A **globe** is a ball-shaped object with a map of the world on it. It is usually fixed on a stand. ❑ *Three large globes stand on the floor.* **3** N-COUNT Any ball-shaped object can be referred to as a **globe**. ❑ *The overhead light was covered now with a white globe.*

1 단수명사 지구, 세계 ❑ 전 세계 방방곡곡에서 온 맥주 ❑ 지구 표면의 70퍼센트는 물이다. **2** 기산명사 지구의 ❑ 세 개의 커다란 지구의가 바닥에 세워져 있다. **3** 가산명사 구체 ❑ 머리 위의 전등이 이제는 하얀 공모양의 갓으로 덧씌워져 있었다.

gloom /ɡluːm/ **1** N-SING **The gloom** is a state of near darkness. ❑ *...the gloom of a foggy November morning.* **2** N-UNCOUNT **Gloom** is a feeling of sadness and lack of hope. ❑ *...the deepening gloom over the economy.*

1 단수명사 어두침침함 ❑ 안개가 자욱한 11월 아침의 어두침침함 **2** 불가산명사 우울함, 침울함 ❑ 경제에 대해 점점 깊어지가는 침울함

gloomy /ˈgluːmi/ (**gloomier, gloomiest**) **1** ADJ If a place is **gloomy**, it is almost dark so that you cannot see very well. ❑ Inside it's gloomy after all that sunshine. **2** ADJ If people are **gloomy**, they are unhappy and have no hope. ❑ Miller is gloomy about the fate of the serious playwright in America. ● **gloomily** ADV [ADV with v] ❑ He tells me gloomily that he has been called up for army service. **3** ADJ If a situation is **gloomy**, it does not give you much hope of success or happiness. ❑ ...a gloomy picture of an economy sliding into recession. ❑ Officials say the outlook for next year is gloomy. →see **weather**

1 형용사 어두침침한 ❑ 그렇게 햇빛이 나는데도 불구하고 내부는 어두침침하다. **2** 형용사 우울한, 암울해하는 ❑ 밀러는 미국에서 진지한 극작가의 운명을 암울하다고 본다. ● 침울하게 부사 ❑ 그는 징집되었다고 나에게 침울하게 말한다. **3** 형용사 암울한 ❑ 침체 속으로 빠져드는 경제의 암울한 모습 ❑ 정부 관리에 의하면 내년 전망이 암울하다고 한다.

glo|ri|fied /ˈglɔːrɪfaɪd/ ADJ You use **glorified** to indicate that something is less important or impressive than its name suggests. [ADJ n] ❑ Sometimes they tell me I'm just a glorified waitress.

형용사 미화된, 꾸며진 ❑ 때로로 그들은 내가 미화된 여종업원일 뿐이라고 내게 말한다.

glo|ri|fy /ˈglɔːrɪfaɪ/ (**glorifies, glorifying, glorified**) V-T To **glorify** something means to praise it or make it seem good or special, usually when it is not. ❑ This magazine in no way glorifies gangs. ● **glo|ri|fi|ca|tion** /ˌglɔːrɪfɪˈkeɪʃ°n/ N-UNCOUNT ❑ ...the glorification of violence.

타동사 미화하다, 꾸미다 ❑ 이 잡지는 결코 폭력배를 미화하지 않는다. ● 미화 불가산명사 ❑ 폭력의 미화

glo|ri|ous /ˈglɔːriəs/ **1** ADJ Something that is **glorious** is very beautiful and impressive. ❑ ...a glorious rainbow in the air. ❑ She had missed the glorious blooms of the Mediterranean spring. ● **glo|ri|ous|ly** ADV ❑ A tree, gloriously lit by autumn, pressed against the windowpane. **2** ADJ If you describe something as **glorious**, you are emphasizing that it is wonderful and it makes you feel very happy. [EMPHASIS] ❑ The win revived glorious memories of his championship-winning days. ● **glo|ri|ous|ly** ADV ❑ ...her gloriously happy love life. **3** ADJ A **glorious** career, victory, or occasion involves great fame or success. ❑ Harrison had a glorious career spanning more than six decades. ● **glo|ri|ous|ly** ADV ❑ But the mission was successful, gloriously successful.

1 형용사 찬란한, 미려한 ❑ 하늘의 찬란한 무지개 ❑ 그녀는 지중해 봄의 찬란한 개화를 놓쳤다. ● 찬란하게 부사 ❑ 가을빛으로 찬란하게 물든 나무 한 그루가 창유리에 닿아 있었다. **2** 형용사 찬란한, 멋진 [강조] ❑ 그 승리는 그가 선수권을 차지하던 시절의 멋진 기억을 되살려 주었다. ● 찬란하게 부사 ❑ 그녀의 찬란하게 행복한 애정 생활 **3** 형용사 영예로운 ❑ 해리슨은 60년 이상에 달하는 영예로운 경력을 지니고 있었다. ● 영예롭게 부사 ❑ 그러나 임무는 성공, 영예롭게 성공이었다.

glo|ry /ˈglɔːri/ (**glories**) **1** N-UNCOUNT **Glory** is the fame and admiration that you gain by doing something impressive. ❑ Walsham had his moment of glory when he won a 20km race. **2** N-PLURAL A person's **glories** are the occasions when they have done something people greatly admire which makes them famous. ❑ The album sees them re-living past glories but not really breaking any new ground.

1 불가산명사 영예, 영광 ❑ 왈샴에게는 20킬로 경주에서 우승했던 그 때가 영광의 순간이었다. **2** 복수명사 영광의 날들 ❑ 이 음반에서 그들은 과거의 영광을 재현하지만 실제로 새로운 영역을 개척하지는 않고 있다.

Word Partnership   glory의 연어

N.   **blaze** of glory, glory **days**, **hope and** glory, **moment of** glory **1**
V.   **bask in the** glory **1**

---

gloss /ˈglɒs/ (**glosses, glossing, glossed**) **1** N-SING A **gloss** is a bright shine on the surface of something. ❑ Sheets of rain were falling and produced a black gloss on the asphalt. **2** N-UNCOUNT **Gloss** is an appearance of attractiveness or good quality which sometimes hides less attractive features or poor quality. ❑ Television commercials might seem more professional but beware of mistaking the gloss for the content. **3** N-SING If you put **a gloss on** a bad situation, you try to make it seem more attractive or acceptable by giving people a false explanation or interpretation of it. ❑ He used his diary to put a fine gloss on the horrors the regime perpetrated. **4** N-MASS **Gloss** is the same as **gloss paint**. **5** V-T If you **gloss** a difficult word or idea, you provide an explanation of it. ❑ Older editors glossed "drynke" as "love-potion."

1 단수명사 광택 ❑ 호우가 내리면서 아스팔트가 검은 빛으로 번들거렸다. **2** 불가산명사 겉치레 ❑ 텔레비전 광고가 더 전문적으로 보일 수 있으나 번드르한 겉모양을 속내용물로 오인하지 마십시오. **3** 단수명사 그럴 듯한 포장 ❑ 그는 자신의 일기를 그 정권이 저지른 만행을 미화하는 포장으로 이용했다. **4** 물질명사 유광 페인트 **5** 타동사 주석을 달다 ❑ 예전 편집인들이 'drynke'에 '사랑의 묘약'이라고 주석을 달았다.

▶ **gloss over** PHRASAL VERB If you **gloss over** a problem, a mistake, or an embarrassing moment, you try and make it seem unimportant by ignoring it or by dealing with it very quickly. ❑ Some foreign governments appear happy to gloss over continued human rights abuses.

구동사 그럴 듯하게 얼버무리다 ❑ 몇몇 외국 정부는 계속된 인권 침해를 그럴듯하게 얼버무려 버리는 것에 만족하는 것 같다.

glos|sa|ry /ˈglɒsəri/ (**glossaries**) N-COUNT A **glossary** of special, unusual, or technical words or expressions is an alphabetical list of them giving their meanings, for example at the back of a book on a particular subject. ❑ A glossary of terms is included for the reader's convenience.

가산명사 용어 해설 목록 ❑ 독자의 편의를 위해 용어 해설 목록이 포함되어 있다.

gloss paint N-UNCOUNT **Gloss paint** is paint that forms a shiny surface when it dries. ❑ ...a fresh coat of white gloss paint.

불가산명사 유광 페인트 ❑ 갓 칠한 흰색 유광 페인트

glossy /ˈglɒsi/ (**glossier, glossiest**) **1** ADJ **Glossy** means smooth and shiny. ❑ ...glossy black hair. **2** ADJ You can describe something as **glossy** if you think that it has been designed to look attractive but has little practical value or may have hidden faults. ❑ ...a glossy new office. **3** ADJ **Glossy** magazines, leaflets, books, and photographs are produced on expensive, shiny paper. [ADJ n] ❑ ...a glossy magazine called "Women Today".

1 형용사 윤이 나는 ❑ 윤이 나는 검은 머리 **2** 형용사 겉만 번지르한 ❑ 겉만 번지르한 새 사무실 **3** 형용사 값비싼 유광지로 만든 ❑ '오늘의 여성'이라는 값비싼 유광지로 만든 잡지

glove /ˈglʌv/ (**gloves**) **1** N-COUNT **Gloves** are pieces of clothing which cover your hands and wrists and have individual sections for each finger. You wear gloves to keep your hands warm or dry or to protect them. ❑ He stuck his gloves in his pocket. **2** PHRASE If you say that something **fits like a glove**, you are emphasizing that it fits exactly. [EMPHASIS] ❑ I gave one of the bikinis to my sister Sara and it fitted like a glove.

1 가산명사 장갑 ❑ 그는 장갑을 주머니에 찔러 넣었다. **2** 구 꼭 맞다 [강조] ❑ 나는 비키니 수영복 한 벌을 내 동생 사라에게 주었는데 꼭 맞았다.

glow /ˈgloʊ/ (**glows, glowing, glowed**) **1** N-COUNT A **glow** is a dull, steady light, for example the light produced by a fire when there are no flames. ❑ The cigarette's red glow danced about in the darkness. **2** N-SING A **glow** is a pink color on a person's face, usually because they are healthy or have been exercising. ❑ The moisturiser gave my face a healthy glow that lasted all day. **3** N-SING If you feel a **glow** of satisfaction or achievement, you have a strong feeling of pleasure because of something that you have done or that has happened. ❑ Exercise will give you a glow of satisfaction at having achieved something. **4** V-I If something **glows**, it produces a dull, steady light. ❑ The night lantern glowed softly in the darkness. **5** V-I If someone's skin **glows**, it looks pink because they are healthy or excited, or have been doing physical exercise. ❑ Her freckled skin glowed with health again. **6** V-I If someone **glows with** an emotion such as pride or pleasure, the expression on their face shows how they feel. ❑ The expectant mothers that

1 가산명사 백열광, 불꽃이 없이 타는 빛 ❑ 빨간 담뱃불이 어둠 속에서 이리저리 춤을 추었다. **2** 단수명사 홍조 ❑ 보습제가 내 얼굴을 하루 종일 건강한 홍조빛을 만들어 주었다. **3** 단수명사 만족감 ❑ 운동을 하면 무엇인가를 성취했다는 만족감을 갖게 될 것이다. **4** 자동사 백열광을 내다, 빛나다 ❑ 밤에 등불이 어둠 속에서 은은히 빛났다. **5** 자동사 홍조를 띠다 ❑ 주근깨가 있는 그녀의 피부가 다시 건강한 홍조를 띠었다. **6** 자동사 (기쁨 등이) 넘치다 ❑ 에이미가 만난 임산부들은 정말 자부심에 넘쳐 있었다.

Amy had encountered positively **glowed** with pride. **7** →see also **glowing**
→see **fire, light bulb**

N.	beam, glimmer, light **1**
	blush, flush, radiance **2**
V.	gleam, radiate, shine **4 6**

glow|er /ɡlaʊr/ (**glowers, glowering, glowered**) V-I If you **glower at** someone or something, you look at them angrily. ❑ *He glowered at me but said nothing.*

glow|ing /ɡloʊɪŋ/ ADJ A **glowing** description or opinion about someone or something praises them highly or supports them strongly. ❑ *The media has been speaking in glowing terms of the relationship between the two countries.* →see also **glow**

glu|cose /ɡluːkoʊs/ N-UNCOUNT **Glucose** is a type of sugar that gives you energy.

glue /ɡluː/ (**glues, glueing** or **gluing**) (**glued**) **1** N-MASS **Glue** is a sticky substance used for joining things together, often for repairing broken things. ❑ *...a tube of glue.* **2** V-T If you **glue** one object to another, you stick them together using glue. ❑ *Glue the fabric around the window.* ❑ *The material is cut and glued in place.* **3** V-T PASSIVE If you say that someone **is glued to** something, you mean that they are giving it all their attention. ❑ *They are all glued to the Olympic Games.*

glum /ɡlʌm/ (**glummer, glummest**) ADJ Someone who is **glum** is sad and quiet because they are disappointed or unhappy about something. ❑ *She was very glum and was obviously missing her children.* ● **glum|ly** ADV [ADV with v] ❑ *When Eleanor returned, I was still sitting glumly on the settee.*

glut /ɡlʌt/ (**gluts, glutting, glutted**) **1** N-COUNT If there is a **glut of** something, there is so much of it that it cannot all be sold or used. [usu sing, usu with supp] ❑ *There's a glut of agricultural products in Western Europe.* **2** V-T If a market **is glutted with** something, there is a glut of that thing. [BUSINESS] ❑ *The region is glutted with hospitals.*

gm

The plural can be **gm** or **gms**.

gm is a written abbreviation for **gram**. ❑ *...450 gm (1 lb) mixed soft summer fruits.*

GM /dʒiː ɛm/ **1** ADJ **GM** crops have had one or more genes changed, for example in order to make them resist pests better. **GM** food contains ingredients made from GM crops. **GM** is an abbreviation for **genetically modified**. ❑ *Many of us may be eating food containing GM ingredients without realising it.* **2** ADJ In Britain, **GM** schools receive money directly from the government rather than from a local authority. **GM** is an abbreviation for **grant-maintained**. ❑ *GM schools receive better funding than other state schools.*

GMO /dʒiː ɛm oʊ/ (**GMOs**) N-COUNT A **GMO** is an animal, plant, or other organism whose genetic structure has been changed by genetic engineering. **GMO** is an abbreviation for "genetically modified organism." ❑ *...the presence of GMOs in many processed foods.*

GMT /dʒiː ɛm tiː/ **GMT** is the standard time in Great Britain which is used to calculate the time in the rest of the world. **GMT** is an abbreviation for "Greenwich Mean Time." ❑ *New Mexico is seven hours behind GMT.*

gnaw /nɔː/ (**gnaws, gnawing, gnawed**) **1** V-T/V-I If people or animals **gnaw** something or **gnaw at** it, they bite it repeatedly. ❑ *Woodlice attack living plants and gnaw at the stems.* **2** V-I If a feeling or thought **gnaws at** you, it causes you to keep worrying. [WRITTEN] ❑ *...the nagging disquiet that had gnawed at him for days.*

GNP /dʒiː ɛn piː/ (**GNPs**) N-VAR In economics, a country's **GNP** is the total value of all the goods produced and services provided by that country in one year. **GNP** is an abbreviation for "gross national product." Compare **GDP**. ❑ *By 1973 the government deficit equalled thirty per cent of GNP.*

GNVQ /dʒiː ɛn viː kjuː/ (**GNVQs**) N-COUNT In Britain, **GNVQs** are qualifications in practical subjects such as business, design, and information technology. **GNVQ** is an abbreviation for "general national vocational qualification." ❑ *We have a 90 per cent pass rate for GNVQs.*

go

① MOVING OR LEAVING
② LINK VERB USES
③ OTHER VERB USES, NOUN USES, AND PHRASES
④ PHRASAL VERBS

① **go** ♦♦♦ /ɡoʊ/ (**goes, going, went, gone**)

In most cases the past participle of **go** is **gone**, but occasionally you use "been": see **been**.

1 V-T/V-I When you **go** somewhere, you move or travel there. ❑ *We went to Rome.* ❑ *I went home at the weekend.* ❑ *It took us an hour to go three miles.* **2** V-I When you **go**, you leave the place where you are. ❑ *Let's go.* **3** V-T/V-I You use **go** to say that someone leaves the place where they are and does an activity, often a leisure activity. ❑ *We went swimming very early.* ❑ *They've just gone shopping.* **4** V-T/V-I When you **go to** do something, you move to a place in order to do it and you do it. You can also **go and** do something, and in American English, you can **go** do something. However, you always say that someone **went** and did something. ❑ *His second son, Paddy, had gone to live in Canada.* ❑ *I must go and see this film.* **5** V-I If you **go to** school, work, or church, you attend it regularly as part of your normal life. ❑ *She will have to go to school.* **6** V-I When you say where

자동사 노려보다, 쏘아보다 ❑ 그는 나를 노려보았으나 아무 말도 하지 않았다.

형용사 열렬한 찬사의 ❑ 언론이 두 나라 사이의 관계에 대해 열렬한 찬사를 보내왔다.

불가산명사 포도당

1 물질명사 접착제 ❑ 튜브형 접착제 한 개 **2** 타동사 접착제로 붙이다, 바르다 ❑ 창문 주위에 천을 접착제로 붙이시오. ❑ 재료를 절단하여 제자리에 접착제로 붙였다. **3** 수동 타동사 -에 열중하다 ❑ 그들은 모두 올림픽 대회에 열중하고 있다.

형용사 시무룩한 ❑ 그녀는 아주 시무룩한 게 분명히 자식들을 그리워하고 있었다. ● 시무룩하게 부사 ❑ 엘리너가 돌아왔을 때, 나는 긴 의자에 여전히 시무룩하게 앉아 있었다.

1 가산명사 공급 과잉 ❑ 서유럽에는 농산물이 공급 과잉이다. **2** 타동사 공급 과잉이다 [경제] ❑ 그 지역은 병원이 필요 이상으로 많다.

복수는 gm 또는 gms이다.

그램 ❑ 여러 가지 부드러운 여름 과일 450그램(1파운드)

1 형용사 유전자 변형의 ❑ 많은 사람들이 모르고 유전자가 변형된 재료를 함유한 음식을 먹고 있을지 모른다. **2** 형용사 (영국) 국가 보조금을 받는, 국립의 ❑ 국립 학교가 다른 주립 학교보다 보조금을 더 잘 받는다.

가산명사 유전자 변형 물질 ❑ 많은 가공 식품 속에 포함된 유전자 변형 물질

그리니치 표준시 ❑ 뉴멕시코는 그리니치 표준시보다 7시간 늦다.

1 타동사/자동사 갉다, 갉아먹다 ❑ 쥐며느리는 살아 있는 식물을 공격하여 줄기를 갉아먹는다. **2** 자동사 괴롭히다 [문어체] ❑ 며칠 동안 그를 괴롭혔던 지속적인 불안

가산명사 또는 불가산명사 국민 총생산 ❑ 1973년까지 정부 적자가 국민 총생산의 30퍼센트와 맞먹었다.

가산명사 (영국의) 국가 직업 자격시험 ❑ 우리는 국가 직업 자격시험에 90퍼센트의 합격률을 갖고 있다.

go의 과거 분사는 대부분의 경우 gone이지만 가끔 'been'을 쓰는 경우도 있다. 항목 been을 참조.

1 타동사/자동사 가다 ❑ 우리는 로마에 갔다. ❑ 나는 주말에 집에 갔다. ❑ 우리는 3마일 가는 데 한 시간 걸렸다. **2** 자동사 떠나다 ❑ 우리 갑시다. **3** 타동사/자동사 -하러 가다 ❑ 우리는 아주 일찍 수영하러 갔다. ❑ 아마도 그냥 쇼핑하러 간 것일게. **4** 타동사/자동사 -하러 가다 ❑ 그의 둘째 아들 패디는 캐나다에 살러 갔다. ❑ 나는 이 영화를 보러 가야 해. **5** 자동사 다니다 ❑ 그녀는 학교에 다녀야 할 거야. **6** 자동사 (길 등이) 이르다 ❑ 브레어스타운에서 밀브룩빌리지에 이르는 산악 도로가 있다. **7** 자동사 전진하다, 나아가다 ❑ 수상은 더 나아가 모든 정책

a road or path **goes**, you are saying where it begins or ends, or what places it is in. ❑ *There's a mountain road that goes from Blairstown to Millbrook Village.* **7** V-I You can use **go** with words like "further" and "beyond" to show the degree or extent of something. ❑ *The Prime Minister went further by agreeing that all policy announcements should be made first in the House.* **8** V-I If you say that a period of time **goes** quickly or slowly, you mean that it seems to pass quickly or slowly. ❑ *The weeks go so quickly!* **9** V-I If you say where money **goes**, you are saying what it is spent on. ❑ *Most of my money goes on bills.* **10** V-I If you say that something **goes to** someone, you mean that it is given to them. ❑ *A lot of credit must go to the chairman and his father.* **11** V-I If someone **goes** on television or radio, they take part in a television or radio program. ❑ *The Turkish president has gone on television to defend stringent new security measures.* **12** V-I If something **goes**, someone gets rid of it. ❑ *The Institute of Export now fears that 100,000 jobs will go.* **13** V-I If someone **goes**, they leave their job, usually because they are forced to. ❑ *He had made a humiliating tactical error and he had to go.* **14** V-I If something **goes into** something else, it is put in it as one of the parts or elements that form it. ❑ *…the really interesting ingredients that go into the dishes that we all love to eat.* **15** V-I If something **goes** in a particular place, it belongs there or should be put there, because that is where you normally keep it. ❑ *The shoes go on the shoe shelf.* **16** V-I If you say that one number **goes into** another number a particular number of times, you are dividing the second number by the first. ❑ *Six goes into thirty five times.* **17** V-I If one of a person's senses, such as their sight or hearing, **is going**, it is getting weak and they may soon lose it completely. [INFORMAL] ❑ *His eyes are going; he says he has glaucoma.* **18** V-I If something such as a light bulb or a part of an engine **is going**, it is no longer working properly and will need to be replaced. ❑ *I thought it looked as though the battery was going.*

② **go** ♦♦♦ /goʊ/ (**goes, going, went, gone**) V-LINK You can use **go** to say that a person or thing changes to another state or condition. For example, if someone **goes crazy**, they become crazy, and if something **goes green**, it changes color and becomes green. ❑ *I'm going bald.* ❑ *You'd better serve it to them before it goes cold.*

③ **go** ♦♦♦ /goʊ/ (**goes, going, went, gone**) **1** V-I You use **go** to talk about the way something happens. For example, if an event or situation **goes well**, it is successful. ❑ *She says everything is going smoothly.* **2** V-I If a machine or device is **going**, it is working. ❑ *What about my copier? Can you get it going again?* **3** V-I If a bell **goes**, it makes a noise, usually as a signal for you to do something. ❑ *The bell went for the break.* **4** V-RECIP If something **goes with** something else, or if two things **go together**, they look or taste good together. ❑ *I was searching for a pair of grey gloves to go with my new gown.* ❑ *I can see that some colors go together and some don't.* **5** V-T/V-I You use **go** to introduce something you are quoting. For example, you say **the story goes** or **the argument goes** just before you quote all or part of it. ❑ *The story goes that she went home with him that night.* ❑ *The story goes like this.* **6** V-T You use **go** when indicating that something makes or produces a sound. For example, if you say that something **goes "bang,"** you mean it produces the sound "bang." ❑ *She stopped in front of a painting of a dog and she started going "woof woof."* **7** V-T You can use **go** instead of "say" when you are quoting what someone has said or what you think they will say. [INFORMAL] ❑ *He goes to me: "Oh, what do you want?"* **8** N-COUNT A **go** is an attempt at doing something. ❑ *I always wanted to have a go at football.* ❑ *She won on her first go.* **9** N-COUNT If it is your **go** in a game, it is your turn to do something, for example to play a card or move a piece. [poss N] ❑ *Now whose go is it?* **10** →see also **going, gone** **11** PHRASE If you do something **as you go along**, you do it while you are doing another thing, without preparing it beforehand. ❑ *Learning how to become a parent takes time. It's a skill you learn as you go along.* **12** PHRASE If someone **has a go at** you, they criticize you, often in a way that you feel is unfair. [mainly BRIT, INFORMAL] ❑ *Some people had a go at us for it, which made us more angry.* **13** CONVENTION If someone says **"Where do we go from here?"** they are asking what should be done next, usually because a problem has not been solved in a satisfactory way. **14** PHRASE If you say that someone **is making a go of** something such as a business or relationship, you mean that they are having some success with it. ❑ *I knew we could make a go of it and be happy.* **15** PHRASE If you say that someone is always **on the go**, you mean that they are always busy and active. [INFORMAL] ❑ *I got a new job this year where I am on the go all the time.* **16** PHRASE If you **have** something **on the go**, you have started it and are busy doing it. ❑ *Do you like to have many projects on the go at any one time?* **17** PHRASE If you say that there are a particular number of things **to go**, you mean that they still remain to be dealt with. ❑ *I still had another five operations to go.* **18** PHRASE If you say that there is a certain amount of time **to go**, you mean that there is that amount of time left before something happens or ends. ❑ *There is a week to go until the elections.* **19** PHRASE If you are in a café or restaurant and ask for an item of food **to go**, you mean that you want to take it away with you and not eat it there. [mainly AM; BRIT **to take away**] ❑ *Large fries to go.*

④ **go** ♦♦♦ /goʊ/ (**goes, going, went, gone**)

▶**go about 1** PHRASAL VERB The way you **go about** a task or problem is the way you approach it and deal with it. ❑ *I want him back, but I just don't know how to go about it.* **2** PHRASAL VERB When you **are going about** your normal activities, you are doing them. ❑ *We were simply going about our business when we were pounced upon by these police officers.*

▶**go after** PHRASAL VERB If you **go after** something, you try to get it, catch it, or hit it. ❑ *We're not going after civilian targets.*

▶**go against 1** PHRASAL VERB If a person or their behavior **goes against** your wishes, beliefs, or expectations, their behavior is the opposite of what you want, believe in, or expect. ❑ *Changes are being made here which go against my principles and I cannot agree with them.* **2** PHRASAL VERB If a decision, vote, or result **goes against** you, you do not get the decision, vote, or result that you wanted. ❑ *The prime minister will resign if the vote goes against him.*

발표는 의회에서 먼저 해야 한다는 데 동의하였다. **8** 자동사 (시간이) 지나가다 ❑ 몇 주가 너무도 빨리 지나가는군! **9** 자동사 (돈이) 쓰이다 ❑ 내 돈의 대부분은 각종 공과금을 내는 데 쓰인다. **10** 자동사 -에게 주어지다 ❑ 회장과 그의 부친의 공로가 크게 인정되어야 한다. **11** 자동사 출연하다 ❑ 터키 대통령은 엄격한 새 안보 조치를 옹호하기 위해 텔레비전에 출연했다. **12** 자동사 없어지다 ❑ 수출 협회는 이제 10만 개의 일자리가 없어질 것이라고 우려한다. **13** 자동사 (직장을) 그만두다 ❑ 그는 면목 없는 전술적 실수를 저질러 직장을 그만두어야 했다. **14** 자동사 -의 일부가 되다 ❑ 우리 모두가 먹기 좋아하는 요리에 들어가는 정말 흥미로운 재료들 **15** 자동사 속하다, 놓이다 ❑ 신발은 신발장에 둔다. **16** 자동사 들어가다 ❑ 30에는 6이 5번 들어간다. **17** 자동사 (시력, 청력이) 약해지다, 가다 [비격식체] ❑ 그의 시력이 약해지고 있다. 그는 녹내장이 있다고 한다. **18** 자동사 (전구 등의) 수명이 다하다 ❑ 나는 배터리가 수명이 다해 가는 것 같다고 생각했다.

연결동사 (상태로) 되다 ❑ 나는 대머리가 되어가고 있다. ❑ 음식이 식기 전에 그들에게 대접하는 것이 좋겠다.

1 자동사 (일이) 진행되다 ❑ 모든 일이 원활히 진행되고 있다고 그녀는 말한다. **2** 자동사 (기계 등이) 움직이다, 조화를 이루다 ❑ 내 복사기는 어떻게 된 거지? 다시 작동하게 해 줄 수 있어? **3** 자동사 (종이) 울리다 ❑ 휴식 시간을 알리는 종이 울렸다. **4** 상호동사 -와 어울리다, 조화를 이루다 ❑ 나는 새 이브닝드레스에 잘 어울리는 회색 장갑을 찾고 있었다. ❑ 몇 가지 색은 서로 잘 어울리고 몇 가지는 그렇지 않다는 걸 알 수 있다. **5** 타동사/자동사 -이라고 말하고 있다, -이라고 되어 있다, 이야기에 -라고 되어 있다; 주장은 -와 같다 ❑ 그 이야기에 따르면 그녀는 그날 밤 그와 함께 집으로 갔다고 한다. ❑ 이 이야기는 다음과 같이 시작한다. **6** 타동사 (소리가) 나다; '쿵' 소리가 나다 ❑ 그녀는 강아지 그림 앞에 멈춰 서서 '으르렁 으르렁'하는 소리를 내기 시작했다. **7** 타동사 -라고 말하다 [비격식체] ❑ "어, 당신이 원하는 것은 무엇입니까?"라고 그가 나에게 말한다. **8** 가산명사 시도 ❑ 나는 축구를 한 번 해 보는 것이 소원이었다. ❑ 그녀는 첫 번째 시도에서 이겼다. **9** 가산명사 차례, 기회 ❑ 이제 누구 차례지? **11** 구 자연스럽게 터득하다 ❑ 부모가 되는 법을 배우는 데에는 시간이 걸린다. 그것은 지나면서 자연스럽게 터득하게 되는 기술이다. **12** 구 -에게 아단치다, -을 비난하다 [주로 영국영어, 비격식체] ❑ 어떤 사람들은 그것 때문에 우리를 비난했고, 그것이 우리를 더욱 화나게 만들었다. **13** 관용 표현 앞으로 어떻게 하면 좋지?, 무슨 묘안 없어? **14** 구 (사업 등을) 잘 해 나가다, 성공시키다 ❑ 나는 우리가 그것을 성공시켜 행복해질 줄 알았다. **15** 구 끊임없이 활동하여, 바쁘고 활동적인 [비격식체] ❑ 나는 올 해 끊임없이 바쁘게 일하는 새로운 일자리를 얻었다. **16** 구 -로 바쁘다 ❑ 당신은 한 번에 여러 가지 프로젝트로 바쁘게 일하는 것을 좋아합니까? **17** 구 앞으로 해야 할 ❑ 나는 아직도 앞으로 수술을 다섯 번 더 해야 한다. **18** 구 (시간이) 남은 ❑ 선거까지 일주일 남아 있다. **19** 구 (식당에서) 가져가기 위한 [주로 미국영어; 영국영어 to take away] ❑ 감자튀김 큰 것 하나 포장해 주세요.

1 구동사 처리하다 ❑ 그가 돌아왔으면 좋겠지만, 나는 그저 어떻게 처리해야 할지 모르겠다. **2** 구동사 (일을) 하는 중이다 ❑ 이 경찰관들이 갑자기 들이닥쳤을 때 우리는 그저 우리 일을 하고 있었을 뿐이었다.

구동사 -을 구하다, -을 얻으려 하다, -을 목표로 삼다 ❑ 우리는 민간인을 목표로 하고 있지 않다.

1 구동사 -에 반대하다 ❑ 여기에서 나의 원칙에 위배되는 변화들이 일어나고 있고, 나는 그러한 변화를 인정할 수 없다. **2** 구동사 -에게 불리하게 끝나다 ❑ 수상은 선거에서 패하면 사임할 것이다.

▶**go ahead** ◆ PHRASAL VERB If someone **goes ahead with** something, they begin to do it or make it, especially after planning, promising, or asking permission to do it. ❑ *The district board will vote today on whether to go ahead with the plan.* ◆ PHRASAL VERB If a process or an organized event **goes ahead**, it takes place or is carried out. ❑ *The event will go ahead as planned in Sheffield next summer.*

▶**go along with** ◆ PHRASAL VERB If you **go along with** a rule, decision, or policy, you accept it and obey it. ❑ *Whatever the majority decided I was prepared to go along with.* ◆ PHRASAL VERB If you **go along with** a person or an idea, you agree with them. [BRIT also **go round**] ❑ *"I don't think a government has properly done it for about the past twenty-five years." — "I'd go along with that."*

▶**go around** ◆ PHRASAL VERB If you **go around to** someone's house, you go to visit them at their house. ❑ *I asked them to go around to the house to see if they were there.* ◆ PHRASAL VERB If you **go around** in a particular way, you behave or dress in that way, often as part of your normal life. ❑ *I had got in the habit of going around with bare feet.* ◆ PHRASAL VERB If a piece of news or a joke **is going around**, it is being told by many people in the same period of time. ❑ *There's a nasty sort of rumor going around about it.* ◆ PHRASAL VERB If there is enough of something **to go around**, there is enough of it to be shared among a group of people, or to do all the things for which it is needed. ❑ *Eventually we will not have enough water to go around.*

▶**go away** ◆ PHRASAL VERB If you **go away**, you leave a place or a person's company. ❑ *I think we need to go away and think about this.* ◆ PHRASAL VERB If you **go away**, you leave a place and spend a period of time somewhere else, especially as a vacation. ❑ *Why don't you and I go away this weekend?*

▶**go back on** PHRASAL VERB If you **go back on** a promise or agreement, you do not do what you promised or agreed to do. ❑ *The budget crisis has forced the President to go back on his word.*

▶**go back to** ◆ PHRASAL VERB If you **go back to** a task or activity, you start doing it again after you have stopped doing it for a period of time. ❑ *I now look forward to going back to work as soon as possible.* ◆ PHRASAL VERB If you **go back to** a particular point in a lecture, discussion, or book, you start to discuss it. ❑ *Let me just go back to the point I was making.*

▶**go before** ◆ PHRASAL VERB Something that **has gone before** has happened or been discussed at an earlier time. ❑ *This is a rejection of most of what has gone before.* ◆ PHRASAL VERB To **go before** a judge, tribunal, or court of law means to be present there as part of an official or legal process. ❑ *The case went before Mr Justice Henry on December 23 and was adjourned.*

▶**go by** ◆ PHRASAL VERB If you say that time **goes by**, you mean that it passes. ❑ *My grandmother was becoming more and more sad and frail as the years went by.* ◆ PHRASAL VERB If you **go by** something, you use it as a basis for a judgment or action. ❑ *If they prove that I was wrong, then I'll go by what they say.*

▶**go down** ◆ PHRASAL VERB If a price, level, or amount **goes down**, it becomes lower or less than it was. ❑ *Income from sales tax went down.* ❑ *Crime has gone down 70 percent.* ◆ PHRASAL VERB If you **go down on** your knees or **on** all fours, you lower your body until it is supported by your knees, or by your hands and knees. ❑ *I went down on my knees and prayed for guidance.* ◆ PHRASAL VERB If you say that a remark, idea, or type of behavior **goes down** in a particular way, you mean that it gets a particular kind of reaction from a person or group of people. ❑ *Solicitors advised their clients that a tidy look went down well with the magistrates.* ◆ PHRASAL VERB When the sun **goes down**, it goes below the horizon. ❑ *...the glow left in the sky after the sun has gone down.* ◆ PHRASAL VERB If a ship **goes down**, it sinks. If a plane **goes down**, it crashes out of the sky. ❑ *Their aircraft went down during a training exercise.* ◆ PHRASAL VERB If a computer **goes down**, it stops functioning temporarily. ❑ *The main computers went down for 30 minutes.*

▶**go down with** PHRASAL VERB If you **go down with** an illness or a disease, you catch it. [INFORMAL] ❑ *Three members of the band went down with flu.*

▶**go for** ◆ PHRASAL VERB If you **go for** a particular thing or way of doing something, you choose it. ❑ *People tried to persuade him to go for a more gradual reform program.* ◆ PHRASAL VERB If you **go for** someone, you attack them. ❑ *Pantieri went for him, gripping him by the throat.* ◆ PHRASAL VERB If you say that a statement you have made about one person or thing also **goes for** another person or thing, you mean that the statement is also true of this other person or thing. ❑ *It is illegal to dishonour bookings; that goes for restaurants as well as customers.* ◆ PHRASAL VERB If something **goes for** a particular price, it is sold for that amount. ❑ *Some old machines go for as much as 35,000 pounds.*

▶**go in** PHRASAL VERB If the sun **goes in**, a cloud comes in front of it and it can no longer be seen. ❑ *The sun went in, and the breeze became cold.*

▶**go in for** PHRASAL VERB If you **go in for** a particular activity, you decide to do it as a hobby or interest. ❑ *They go in for tennis and bowls.*

▶**go into** ◆ PHRASAL VERB If you **go into** something, you describe or examine it fully or in detail. ❑ *It was a private conversation and I don't want to go into details about what was said.* ◆ PHRASAL VERB If you **go into** something, you decide to do it as your job or career. ❑ *Mr Pok has now gone into the tourism business.* ◆ PHRASAL VERB If an amount of time, effort, or money **goes into** something, it is spent or used to do it, get it, or make it. ❑ *Is there a lot of effort and money going into this sort of research?*

▶**go off** ◆ PHRASAL VERB If you **go off** someone or something, you stop liking them. [BRIT, INFORMAL] ❑ *"Why have they gone off him now?" — "It could be something he said."* ◆ PHRASAL VERB If an explosive device or a gun **goes off**, it explodes or fires. ❑ *A few minutes later the bomb went off, destroying the vehicle.* ◆ PHRASAL VERB If an alarm bell **goes off**, it makes a sudden loud noise. ❑ *Then the fire alarm went off. I just grabbed my clothes and ran out.* ◆ PHRASAL VERB If an electrical device

❶ 구동사 ~을 진행시키다 ❑ 자치구 의회는 오늘 그 계획을 진행할지 여부를 두고 투표를 할 것이다. ❷ 구동사 진행되다 ❑ 그 행사는 내년 여름 셰필드에서 계획대로 진행될 것이다.

❶ 구동사 ~에 따른다 ❑ 다수가 어떤 결정을 내리든 나는 그것을 따를 준비가 되어 있었다. ❷ 구동사 ~에 동의하다 [영국영어 go round] ❑ "지난 25년 정도 동안 정부가 그것을 제대로 해 왔다고 생각하지 않아요." "저도 그것에 동의합니다."

❶ 구동사 ~에 들르다 ❑ 나는 그들에게 그 집에 가서 그들이 그곳에 있는지 알아보라고 부탁했다. ❷ 구동사 행동하다; 복장을 하다 ❑ 나는 맨발로 다니는 버릇이 있었다. ❸ 구동사 퍼지고 있다 ❑ 그것에 관해서 뭔가 나쁜 소문이 퍼지고 있다. ❹ 구동사 골고루 돌아가다 ❑ 결국엔 우리에게 돌아올 식수가 충분하지 않을 것이다.

❶ 구동사 떠나다, 가버리다 ❑ 나는 우리가 이곳에서 벗어나서 이것에 대해 생각할 필요가 있다고 생각한다. ❷ 구동사 (휴가 등을) 떠나다 ❑ 이번 주말에 같이 휴가를 떠나는 게 어때?

구동사 ~을 취소하다, 철회하다 ❑ 예산 위기로 인해 대통령은 그가 한 말을 취소해야 했다.

❶ 구동사 (하던 일로) 다시 돌아가다 ❑ 현재 나는 가능한 한 빨리 일로 다시 돌아가기 바라고 있다. ❷ 구동사 되돌아가다 ❑ 제가 말하고자 하는 요점으로 다시 돌아가겠습니다.

❶ 구동사 앞서 일어나다 ❑ 이것은 지금까지 이루어진 것의 대부분을 부정하는 것이다. ❷ 구동사 ~의 앞에 출두하다 ❑ 그 사건은 12월 23일에 헨리 판사가 맡았고 휴정되었다.

❶ 구동사 (시간이) 경과하다 ❑ 시간이 지날수록 할머니는 점점 애처롭고 여위어갔다. ❷ 구동사 ~을 따르다, ~에 의거하다 ❑ 내가 틀렸다는 것을 그들이 입증한다면, 나는 그들이 말하는 것에 따르겠다.

❶ 구동사 내려가다, 하락하다 ❑ 판매 세금에서 오는 수입이 줄어들었다. ❑ 범죄가 70퍼센트 감소했다. ❷ 구동사 자세를 낮추다; 무릎을 꿇다, 엎드리다 ❑ 나는 무릎을 꿇고 나를 인도해 주기를 기도하였다. ❸ 구동사 ~하게 받아들여지다 ❑ 소송 대리인은 단정한 모습이 판사한테 좋은 인상을 준다고 그들의 의뢰인들에게 일러 주었다. ❹ 구동사 (해가) 지다 ❑ 해가 진 후 하늘에 남아 있는 저녁놀 ❺ 구동사 침몰하다; 추락하다 ❑ 그들이 탄 비행기는 훈련 중에 추락했다. ❻ 구동사 멈다, 꺼지다 ❑ 중앙 컴퓨터가 30분 동안 꺼져 있었다.

구동사 (병에) 걸리다 [비격식체] ❑ 밴드 멤버 중 3명이 독감에 걸렸다.

❶ 구동사 ~을 선택하다 ❑ 사람들은 그가 좀 더 점진적인 개혁 프로그램을 선택하도록 설득하였다. ❷ 구동사 ~에게 덤벼들다 ❑ 판티에리가 그에게 덤벼들어 그의 멱살을 잡았다. ❸ 구동사 ~에 적용되다 ❑ 예약된 사항을 어기는 것은 불법이다. 이는 고객뿐만 아니라 음식점에도 해당한다. ❹ 구동사 ~의 값에 팔리다 ❑ 어떤 오래된 기계들은 35,000파운드나 되는 값에 팔린다.

구동사 (구름 사이로) 들어가다 ❑ 해가 구름 사이로 들어갔고, 바람이 쌀쌀해졌다.

구동사 ~을 취미로 삼다 ❑ 그들은 취미로 테니스와 볼링을 한다.

❶ 구동사 ~을 기술하다; ~을 조사하다 ❑ 그것은 사적인 대화였으므로 상세한 대화 내용을 기술하고 싶지는 않다. ❷ 구동사 (직업에) 종사하게 되다 ❑ 포크 씨는 이제 관광업계에 종사하게 되었다. ❸ 구동사 (노력 등이) 들어가다 ❑ 이런 종류의 연구에는 노력과 비용이 많이 들어갑니까?

❶ 구동사 ~에 흥미를 잃다, ~이 싫어지다 [영국영어, 비격식체] ❑ "어쩌다 지금은 그들이 그를 싫어하게 되었지요?" "아마 그가 말한 무슨 말 때문이겠지요." ❷ 구동사 폭발하다 ❑ 몇 분 후에 폭탄이 터져 자동차가 파괴되었다. ❸ 구동사 (경보가) 울리다 ❑ 화재 경보가 울렸을 때, 나는 바로 옷을 집어 들고

A

goes off, it stops operating. □ *As the water came in the windows, all the lights went off.* **5** PHRASAL VERB Food or drink that **has gone off** has gone bad. [BRIT] □ *Don't eat that! It's mouldy. It's gone off!*

박으로 달려 나갔다. **4** 구동사 작동이 멈추다, (전기가) 나가다 □ 물이 창문으로 들어오면서 모든 조명이 다 나갔다. **5** 구동사 상하다 [영국영어] □ 저것을 먹지 마! 곰팡이가 피어 있어. 상했어!

B

▶**go off with** **1** PHRASAL VERB If someone **goes off with** another person, they leave their husband, wife, or lover and have a relationship with that person. □ *I suppose Carolyn went off with some man she'd fallen in love with.* **2** PHRASAL VERB If someone **goes off with** something that belongs to another person, they leave and take it with them. □ *He's gone off with my passport.*

1 구동사 -와 함께 떠나가 □ 나는 캐롤린이 사랑에 빠진 어떤 남자와 함께 떠났다고 생각한다. **2** 구동사 -를 가지고 도망치다 □ 그가 내 여권을 가지고 도망쳤다.

C

D

▶**go on** **1** PHRASAL VERB If you **go on** doing something, or **go on** with an activity, you continue to do it. □ *Unemployment is likely to go on rising this year.* □ *I'm all right here. Go on with your work.* **2** PHRASAL VERB If something **is going on**, it is happening. □ *While this conversation was going on, I was listening with earnest attention.* **3** PHRASAL VERB If a process or institution **goes on**, it continues to happen or exist. □ *The population failed to understand the necessity for the war to go on.* **4** PHRASAL VERB If you say that a period of time **goes on**, you mean that it passes. □ *Renewable energy will become progressively more important as time goes on.* **5** PHRASAL VERB If you **go on to** do something, you do it after you have done something else. □ *Alliss retired from golf in 1969 and went on to become a successful broadcaster.* **6** PHRASAL VERB If you **go on to** a place, you go to it from the place that you have reached. □ *He goes on to Holland tomorrow.* **7** PHRASAL VERB If you **go on**, you continue saying something or talking about something. □ *Meer cleared his throat several times before he went on.* **8** PHRASAL VERB If you **go on about** something, or in British English **go on at** someone, you continue talking about the same thing, often in an annoying way. [INFORMAL] □ *She's always going on at me to have a baby.* **9** PHRASAL VERB You say "**Go on**" to someone to persuade or encourage them to do something. [INFORMAL] [only imper] □ *Go on, it's fun.* **10** PHRASAL VERB If you talk about the information you have **to go on**, you mean the information you have available to base an opinion or judgment on. □ *But you have to go on the facts.* **11** PHRASAL VERB If an electrical device **goes on**, it begins operating. □ *A light went on at seven every evening.*

1 구동사 -을 계속하다, 계속해서 -하다 □ 올해 실업은 계속 증가할 것 같다. □ 나는 괜찮아. 가서 너의 일이나 계속해. **2** 구동사 진행되다 □ 이 대화가 계속 진행되고 있는 동안 나는 열중해서 듣고 있었다. **3** 구동사 계속되다 □ 모든 주민들은 전쟁이 계속되어야 할 필요성을 이해하지 못했다. **4** 구동사 (시간이) 지나가다, 경과되다 □ 재생 가능한 에너지는 시간이 지날수록 점차 더욱 중요하게 될 것이다. **5** 구동사 넘어가다 □ 앨리스는 1969년 골프를 은퇴하고 성공적인 방송인이 되었다. **6** 구동사 -로 나아가다 □ 그는 내일 네덜란드로 간다. **7** 구동사 계속 말하다 □ 미르는 그가 계속 말하기 전에 여러 번 헛기침을 했다. **8** 구동사 -에 대해 끊임없이 지껄이다, -에 대해 떠들어 대다 [비격식체] □ 그녀는 항상 나보고 애를 가지라고 끊임없이 귀찮게 한다. **9** 구동사 계속해라 [비격식체] □ 계속해 봐, 재미있어. **10** 구동사 -를 근거로 하다 □ 그러나 너는 사실을 근거로 해야 한다. **11** 구동사 작동되다 □ 매일 저녁 7시에 전등이 들어왔다.

E

F

G

H

I

J

▶**go out** **1** PHRASAL VERB If you **go out**, you leave your home in order to do something enjoyable, for example to go to a party, a bar, or the movies. □ *I'm going out tonight.* **2** PHRASAL VERB-RECIP If you **go out with** someone, the two of you spend time together socially, and have a romantic or sexual relationship. □ *I once went out with a French man.* **3** PHRASAL VERB If you **go out to** do something, you make a deliberate effort to do it. □ *You do not go out to injure opponents.* **4** PHRASAL VERB If a light **goes out**, it stops shining. □ *The bedroom light went out after a moment.* **5** PHRASAL VERB If something that is burning **goes out**, it stops burning. □ *The fire seemed to be going out.* **6** PHRASAL VERB If a message **goes out**, it is announced, published, or sent out to people. □ *Word went out that a column of tanks was on its way.* **7** PHRASAL VERB When a television or radio program **goes out**, it is broadcast. [BRIT] □ *The series goes out at 10.30 p.m., Fridays, on Channel 4.* **8** PHRASAL VERB When the tide **goes out**, the water in the sea gradually moves back to a lower level. □ *The tide was going out.* **9** PHRASE You can say "**My heart goes out to him**" or "**My sympathy goes out to her**" to express the strong sympathy you have for someone in a difficult or unpleasant situation. [FEELINGS] □ *My heart goes out to Mrs Adams and her fatherless children.*

1 구동사 외출하다 □ 오늘 밤 나는 외출할 것이다. **2** 상호 구동사 (이성과) 사귀다 □ 이전에 나는 프랑스 남자와 사귀었다. **3** 구동사 일부러 -을 하다 □ 상대편을 일부러 다치게 해서는 안 된다. **4** 구동사 (전등이) 꺼지다 □ 잠시 후에 침실 조명이 꺼졌다. **5** 구동사 (불이) 꺼지다, 진화되다 □ 화재는 진화된 것 같았다. **6** 구동사 공개되다, 출판되다 □ 탱크 행렬이 접근하고 있다는 말이 전해졌다. **7** 구동사 방송되다 [영국영어] □ 그 시리즈는 채널 4에서 금요일 밤 10시 30분에 방송된다. **8** 구동사 (썰물이) 빠지다 □ 썰물이 빠져 나가고 있었다. **9** 구 (마음이) 쏠리다 [감정 개입] □ 나의 마음은 아담스 부인과 아버지 없는 아이들에게 쏠렸다.

K

L

M

N

O

▶**go over** PHRASAL VERB If you **go over** a document, incident, or problem, you examine, discuss, or think about it very carefully. □ *I won't know how successful it is until an accountant has gone over the books.*

구동사 -을 세밀히 조사하다 □ 회계사가 그 장부들을 세밀히 다 조사할 때까지는 내가 그 일이 얼마나 성공적인지 알 수 없을 것이다.

P

▶**go round** →see **go around**

▶**go through** **1** PHRASAL VERB If you **go through** an experience or a period of time, especially an unpleasant or difficult one, you experience it. □ *He was going through a very difficult time.* **2** PHRASAL VERB If you **go through** a lot of things such as papers or clothes, you look at them, usually in order to sort them into groups or to search for a particular item. □ *It was evident that someone had gone through my possessions.* **3** PHRASAL VERB If you **go through** a list, story, or plan, you read or check it from beginning to end. □ *Going through his list of customers is a massive job.* **4** PHRASAL VERB If a law, agreement, or official decision **goes through**, it is approved by a parliament or committee. □ *The bill might have gone through if the economy was growing.*

1 구동사 겪다, 경험하다 □ 그는 아주 힘든 시기를 겪고 있었다. **2** 구동사 -을 살피다, -을 뒤지다 □ 누군가가 나의 물건들을 뒤진 게 분명했다. **3** 구동사 철저히 읽다, 살펴보다 □ 그가 고객 명단을 살펴보는 것은 엄청난 일이다. **4** 구동사 (법안이) 통과하다 □ 경제가 성장하고 있었다면 그 법안은 통과됐을지도 모른다.

Q

R

S

▶**go through with** PHRASAL VERB If you **go through with** an action you have decided on, you do it, even though it may be very unpleasant or difficult for you. □ *Richard pleaded for Belinda to reconsider and not to go through with the divorce.*

구동사 완수하다 □ 리처드는 벨린다에게 다시 생각해 보자고, 이혼을 하지 말자고 간청했다.

T

U

▶**go under** PHRASAL VERB If a business or project **goes under**, it becomes unable to continue in operation or in existence. [BUSINESS] □ *If one firm goes under it could provoke a cascade of bankruptcies.*

구동사 실패하다, 파산하다 [경제] □ 한 회사가 파산한다면, 연쇄 부도 사태를 일으킬지도 모른다.

V

▶**go up** **1** PHRASAL VERB If a price, amount, or level **goes up**, it becomes higher or greater than it was. □ *Interest rates went up.* □ *The cost has gone up to $1.95 a minute.* **2** PHRASAL VERB When a building, wall, or other structure **goes up**, it is built or fixed in place. □ *He noticed a new building going up near Whitaker Park.* **3** PHRASAL VERB If something **goes up**, it explodes or starts to burn, usually suddenly and with great intensity. □ *The hotel went up in flames.* **4** PHRASAL VERB If a shout or cheer **goes up**, it is made by a lot of people together. □ *A cheer went up from the other passengers.*

1 구동사 올라가다, 오르다 □ 금리가 올랐다. □ 가격이 1분에 1.95달러까지 올라갔다. **2** 구동사 (건물이) 들어서다, 세워지다 □ 그는 휘타커 공원 근처에 새 빌딩이 세워지고 있다는 것을 알았다. **3** 구동사 폭발하다 □ 화염에 휩싸이다 □ 그 호텔은 불길에 휩싸였다. **4** 구동사 터져 나오다 □ 다른 승객들로부터 환호가 터져 나왔다.

W

X

▶**go with** **1** PHRASAL VERB If one thing **goes with** another thing, the two things officially belong together, so that if you get one, you also get the other. □ *...the lucrative $250,000 salary that goes with the job.* **2** PHRASAL VERB If one thing **goes with** another thing, it is usually found or experienced together with the other thing. □ *For many women, the status which goes with being a wife is important.*

1 구동사 -에 속하다 □ 그 일자리에 대한 250,000달러라는 거액 연봉 **2** 구동사 -에 동반되다 □ 많은 여성에게 있어서, 아내가 되는 것에 동반되는 신분적 지위 또한 중요하다.

Y

Z

▶**go without** PHRASAL VERB If you **go without** something that you need or usually have or do, you do not get it or do it. ❑ *I have known what it is like to go without food for days.*

구동사 ~이 없이 지내다 ❑ 며칠 동안 먹을 것 없이 지내는 것이 어떤 것인지 나는 안다.

goad /goʊd/ (**goads, goading, goaded**) V-T If you **goad** someone, you deliberately make them feel angry or irritated, often causing them to react by doing something. ❑ *Charles was always goading me.* ● N-COUNT **Goad** is also a noun. ❑ *Her presence was just one more goad to Joanna's unravelling nerves.*

타동사 자극하다, 못살게 굴다 ❑ 찰스는 항상 나를 못살게 굴었다. ● 가산명사 자극 ❑ 그녀의 존재는 조안나의 복잡한 신경을 더욱 자극할 따름이었다.

go-ahead 🇠 N-SING If you give someone or something **the go-ahead**, you give them permission to start doing something. ❑ *The Greek government today gave the go-ahead for five major road schemes.* 🇡 ADJ A **go-ahead** person or organization tries hard to succeed, often by using new methods. [ADJ n] ❑ *Fairview Estate is one of the oldest and the most go-ahead wine producers in South Africa.*

🇠 단수명사 승인, 인가 ❑ 그리스 정부는 오늘 다섯 개의 주요 도로 계획안을 승인하였다. 🇡 형용사 진취적인 ❑ 페어뷰 에스테이트는 남아프리카에서 가장 오래되고 가장 진취적인 와인 제조사 중 한 곳이다.

goal ♦♦◇ /goʊl/ (**goals**) 🇠 N-COUNT In games such as soccer or hockey, the **goal** is the space into which the players try to get the ball in order to score a point for their team. ❑ *The Spaniards put all their strokes past Mason in the England goal to emerge 5-4 winners.* 🇡 N-COUNT In games such as soccer or hockey, a **goal** is when a player gets the ball into the goal, or the point that is scored by doing this. ❑ *They scored five goals in the first half of the match.* 🇢 N-COUNT Something that is your **goal** is something that you hope to achieve, especially when much time and effort will be needed. ❑ *It's a matter of setting your own goals and following them.* →see **soccer**

🇠 가산명사 골 ❑ 스페인 팀은 메이슨을 제치고 잉글랜드 골 쪽으로 모든 공격을 퍼부어서 5대 4로 이겼다. 🇡 가산명사 득점 ❑ 그들은 전반전에서 다섯 골을 득점하였다. 🇢 가산명사 목표, 목적 ❑ 목표를 세우고 그 목표에 따라 하느냐에 달려 있다.

Word Partnership	*goal*의 연어
V.	shoot at a goal 🇠
	score a goal 🇡
	accomplish a goal, share a goal 🇢
ADJ.	winning goal 🇡
	main goal 🇢

goalie /goʊli/ (**goalies**) N-COUNT A **goalie** is the same as a **goalkeeper**. [INFORMAL]

가산명사 골키퍼 [비격식체]

goal|keeper /goʊlkipər/ (**goalkeepers**) N-COUNT A **goalkeeper** is the player on a sports team whose job is to guard the goal.

가산명사 골키퍼

goal|less /goʊllɪs/ ADJ In soccer, a **goalless** draw is a game which ends without any goals having been scored. ❑ *The fixture ended in a goalless draw.*

형용사 무득점의 ❑ 그 경기는 무득점 무승부로 끝났다.

goal|post /goʊlpoʊst/ (**goalposts**) also **goal post** 🇠 N-COUNT A **goalpost** is one of the two upright wooden posts that are connected by a crossbar and form the goal in games such as soccer and rugby. 🇡 PHRASE If you accuse someone of **moving the goalposts**, you mean that they have changed the rules in a situation or an activity, in order to gain an advantage for themselves and to make things difficult for other people. [DISAPPROVAL] ❑ *They seem to move the goal posts every time I meet the conditions which are required.* →see **football**

🇠 가산명사 골대 🇡 구 (몰래) 규칙을 바꾸다 [탐탁찮음] ❑ 내가 요구되는 조건에 합당하게 될 때마다 그들이 조건을 바꾸는 것 같다.

goat /goʊt/ (**goats**) N-COUNT A **goat** is a farm animal or a wild animal that is about the size of a sheep. Goats have horns, and hairs on their chin which resemble a beard.

가산명사 염소

gob|ble /gɒbəl/ (**gobbles, gobbling, gobbled**) V-T If you **gobble** food, you eat it quickly and greedily. ❑ *Pete gobbled all the beef stew.* ● PHRASAL VERB **Gobble down** and **gobble up** mean the same as **gobble**. ❑ *There were dangerous beasts in the river that might gobble you up.*

타동사 ~을 급하게 먹다, 게걸스럽게 먹다 ❑ 피트는 비프스튜를 게걸스럽게 다 먹었다. ● 구동사 ~을 통째로 삼키다; ~을 급하게 먹다 ❑ 너를 통째로 삼켜 버릴지도 모르는 위험한 짐승이 강에 있었다.

go-between (**go-betweens**) N-COUNT A **go-between** is a person who takes messages between people who are unable or unwilling to meet each other. ❑ *He will act as a go-between to try and work out an agenda.*

가산명사 중개자, 중매인 ❑ 그는 계획안을 실험해 보고 실행하는 중개자 역할을 할 것이다.

god ♦♦◇ /gɒd/ (**gods**) 🇠 N-PROPER The name **God** is given to the spirit or being who is worshipped as the creator and ruler of the world, especially by Jews, Christians, and Muslims. ❑ *He believes in God.* 🇡 CONVENTION People sometimes use **God** in exclamations to emphasize something that they are saying, or to express surprise, fear, or excitement. This use could cause offense. [EMPHASIS] ❑ *Oh my God, he's shot somebody.* ❑ *Good God, it's Mr Harper!* 🇢 N-COUNT In many religions, a **god** is one of the spirits or beings that are believed to have power over a particular part of the world or nature. ❑ *...Zeus, king of the gods.* 🇣 N-COUNT Someone who is admired very much by a person or group of people, and who influences them a lot, can be referred to as a **god**. ❑ *To his followers he was a god.* 🇤 PHRASE You can say **God knows**, **God only knows**, or **God alone knows** to emphasize that you do not know something. [EMPHASIS] ❑ *God alone knows what she thinks.* 🇥 PHRASE If someone says **God knows** in reply to a question, they mean that they do not know the answer. [EMPHASIS] ❑ *"Where is he now?" — "God knows."* 🇦 PHRASE If someone uses such expressions as **what in God's name**, **why in God's name**, or **how in God's name**, they are emphasizing how angry, annoyed, or surprised they are. [INFORMAL, EMPHASIS] ❑ *What in God's name do you expect me to do?* 🇧 PHRASE If someone **plays God**, they act as if they have unlimited power and can do anything they want. [DISAPPROVAL] ❑ *You have no right to play God in my life!* 🇨 PHRASE You can use **God** in expressions such as **I hope to God**, or **I wish to God**, or **I swear to God**, in order to emphasize what you are saying. [EMPHASIS] ❑ *I hope to God they are paying you well.* 🇩 PHRASE If you say **God willing**, you are saying that something will happen if all goes well. ❑ *God willing, there will be a breakthrough.* 🇪 **honest to God** →see **honest**. **for God's sake** →see **sake**. **thank God** →see **thank** →see **religion**

🇠 고유명사 하느님, 창조주 ❑ 그는 신을 믿는다. 🇡 관용 표현 맙소사, 아닷났다 [강조] ❑ 오, 이럴 수가. 그가 사람을 쐈어요.. ❑ 어머나, 하퍼 씨군요. 🇢 가산명사 신 ❑ 모든 신들 중 최고신인 제우스 🇣 가산명사 신, 우상 ❑ 그를 따르는 사람들에게 그는 신이었다. 🇤 구 ~은 아무도 모른다 [강조] ❑ 그녀가 무엇을 생각하는지는 아무도 모른다. 🇥 구 모르다 [강조] ❑ "지금 그는 어디에 있지?" "모르죠." 🇦 구 도대체 [비격식체, 강조] ❑ 도대체 당신은 내가 어떻게 하길 기대하는 겁니까? 🇧 구 (신처럼) 전능한 것처럼 행세하다 [탐탁찮음] ❑ 당신이 내 삶을 좌지우지할 권리는 없어! 🇨 구 진심으로 [강조] ❑ 나는 정말로 당신이 보수를 잘 받고 있기를 바랍니다. 🇩 구 만사가 잘되면 ❑ 잘되면, 난국을 돌파할 수 있을 것이다.

god|dess /gɒdɪs/ (**goddesses**) N-COUNT In many religions, a **goddess** is a female spirit or being that is believed to have power over a particular part of the world or nature. ❑ *...Diana, the goddess of war.* →see **religion**

가산명사 여신 ❑ 전쟁의 여신인 다이애나

a b c d e f g h i j k l m n o p q r s t u v w x y z

going ♦♦♦ /ɡoʊɪŋ/ **1** PHRASE If you say that something **is going to** happen, you mean that it will happen in the future, usually quite soon. ❑ I think it's going to be successful. ❑ You're going to enjoy this. **2** PHRASE You say that you **are going to** do something to express your intention or determination to do it. ❑ I'm going to go to bed. ❑ He announced that he's going to resign. **3** N-UNCOUNT You use **the going** to talk about how easy or difficult it is to do something. You can also say that something is, for example, **hard going** or **tough going**. ❑ He has her support to fall back on when the going gets tough. **4** ADJ The **going** rate or the **going** salary is the usual amount of money that you expect to pay or receive for something. [ADJ n] ❑ That's about half the going price on world oil markets. **5** →see also **go 6** PHRASE If someone or something **has** a lot **going for** them, they have a lot of advantages. ❑ This area has a lot going for it. **7** PHRASE When you **get going**, you start doing something or start a journey, especially after a delay. ❑ Now what about that shopping list? I've got to get going. **8** PHRASE If you say that someone should do something **while the going is good**, you are advising them to do it while things are going well and they still have the opportunity, because you think it will become much more difficult to do. ❑ People are leaving in their thousands while the going is good. **9** PHRASE If you **keep going**, you continue doing things or doing a particular thing. ❑ I like to keep going. I hate to sit still. **10** PHRASE If you say that something is enough **to be going on with**, you mean that it is enough for your needs at the moment, although you will need something better at some time in the future. [mainly BRIT] ❑ It was a good enough description for Mattie to be going on with. **11** **going concern** →see **concern**

goings-on N-PLURAL If you describe events or activities as **goings-on**, you mean that they are strange, interesting, amusing, or dishonest. ❑ The Swiss girl had found out about the goings-on in the factory.

gold ♦♦◇ /ɡoʊld/ (**golds**) **1** N-UNCOUNT **Gold** is a valuable, yellow-colored metal that is used for making jewelry and ornaments, and as an international currency. ❑ ...a sapphire set in gold. ❑ The price of gold was going up. **2** N-UNCOUNT **Gold** is jewelry and other things that are made of gold. ❑ We handed over all our gold and money. **3** COLOR Something that is **gold** is a bright yellow color, and is often shiny. ❑ I'd been wearing Michel's black and gold shirt. **4** N-VAR A **gold** is the same as a **gold medal**. [INFORMAL] ❑ His ambition was to win gold at the Atlanta Games in 1996. **5** PHRASE If you say that a child is being **as good as gold**, you are emphasizing that they are behaving very well and are not causing you any problems. [EMPHASIS] ❑ The boys were as good as gold on our walk. **6** PHRASE If you say that someone has **a heart of gold**, you are emphasizing that they are very good and kind to other people. [EMPHASIS] ❑ They are all good boys with hearts of gold. They would never steal. →see **metal**, **mineral**, **money**

gold card (**gold cards**) N-COUNT A **gold card** is a special type of credit card that gives you extra benefits such as a higher spending limit.

gold|en ♦◇◇ /ɡoʊldən/ **1** ADJ Something that is **golden** is bright yellow in color. ❑ She combed and arranged her golden hair. **2** ADJ **Golden** things are made of gold. ❑ ...a gold chain with a golden locket. **3** ADJ If you describe something as **golden**, you mean it is wonderful because it is likely to be successful and rewarding, or because it is the best of its kind. [ADJ n] ❑ He says there's a golden opportunity for peace which must be seized. **4** PHRASE If you refer to a man as a **golden boy** or a woman as a **golden girl**, you mean that they are especially popular and successful. ❑ When the movie came out the critics went wild, hailing Tarantino as the golden boy of the 1990s.

gold|en goal (**golden goals**) N-COUNT In some soccer matches, a **golden goal** is the first goal scored in extra time, which wins the match for the team that scores it. [BRIT] ❑ Trezeguet joined the Turin club after scoring France's golden goal in the final of Euro 2000.

gold|en hand|shake (**golden handshakes**) N-COUNT A **golden handshake** is a large sum of money that a company gives to an employee when he or she leaves, as a reward for long service or good work. [BUSINESS] ❑ And if Mr Pell, 49, is axed following a takeover he would be in line to collect a golden handshake of £1 million.

gold|en para|chute (**golden parachutes**) N-COUNT A **golden parachute** is an agreement to pay a large amount of money to a senior executive of a company if they are forced to leave. [BUSINESS] ❑ Golden parachutes entitle them to a full year's salary if they get booted out of the company.

gold|en rule (**golden rules**) N-COUNT A **golden rule** is a principle you should remember because it will help you to be successful. ❑ Hanson's golden rule is to add value to whatever business he buys.

gold|fish /ɡoʊldfɪʃ/

Goldfish is both the singular and the plural form.

N-COUNT **Goldfish** are small gold or orange fish which are often kept as pets.

gold med|al (**gold medals**) N-COUNT A **gold medal** is a medal made of gold which is awarded as first prize in a contest or competition. ❑ ...her ambition to win a gold medal at the Winter Olympics.

gold|mine /ɡoʊldmaɪn/ N-SING If you describe something such as a business or idea as a **goldmine**, you mean that it produces large profits. ❑ The book is a goldmine.

golf ♦◇◇ /ɡɒlf/ N-UNCOUNT **Golf** is a game in which you use long sticks called clubs to hit a small, hard ball into holes that are spread out over a large area of grassy land. ❑ "Do you play golf?" he asked me suddenly.

golf club (**golf clubs**) **1** N-COUNT A **golf club** is a long, thin, metal stick with a piece of wood or metal at one end that you use to hit the ball in golf. **2** N-COUNT A **golf club** is a social organization which provides a golf course and a building to meet in for its members.

---

1 구 -할 것이다 ❑ 나는 그것이 성공할 것이라고 생각한다. ❑ 당신은 이것을 좋아할 겁니다. **2** 구 -할 것이다 ❑ 나는 자러 갈 것이다. ❑ 그는 사임할 것이라고 발표했다. **3** 불가산명사 상태, 상황; 어려운 상태, 힘든 상태 ❑ 그에게는 상황이 힘들 때면 기댈 수 있는 그녀의 후원이 있다. **4** 형용사 현행의 ❑ 그것은 국제 석유 시장에서 현 시세의 약 반값이다. **6** 구 이점이 많다 ❑ 이 지역은 그것에 이점이 많다. **7** 구 (다시) 시작하다; 출발하다 ❑ 이젠 쇼핑 목록에 뭐가 문제야? 난 곧 출발해야 해. **8** 구 상황이 아직 좋을 때, 때가 늦기 전에 ❑ 상황이 아직 좋을 때 사람들이 몇 천 명씩 떠나고 있다. **9** 구 계속 하다 ❑ 나는 일을 계속하는 것을 좋아한다. 멍하니 앉아 있는 것을 싫어한다. **10** 구 현재로서는 만족스러운 [주로 영국영어] ❑ 그것은 일단 마티에가 만족할 만큼 괜찮은 설명이었다.

복수명사 행실, 짓; 일 ❑ 그 스위스 소녀가 공장에서 벌어지는 일들을 알아냈다.

1 불가산명사 금 ❑ 금에 박은 사파이어 세트 ❑ 금값이 올라가고 있었다. **2** 불가산명사 금제품 ❑ 우리는 가지고 있는 금붙이와 돈을 모두 넘겨줬다. **3** 색채어 금빛, 황금색 ❑ 나는 마이클의 검은색과 금빛이 섞인 셔츠를 입고 있었다. **4** 가산명사 또는 불가산명사 금메달 [비격식체] ❑ 그의 목표는 1996년 애틀랜타 경기에서 금메달을 따는 것이었다. **5** 구 아주 얌전한, 아주 예절 바른 [강조] ❑ 우리가 산책할 때 그 소년들은 매우 얌전했다. **6** 구 아주 착한 [강조] ❑ 그들은 모두 아주 착한 마음씨를 지닌 소년들이다. 그들은 결코 도둑질을 하지 않을 것이다.

가산명사 (신용 카드의) 골드 카드

1 형용사 금빛의, 황금색의 ❑ 그녀는 자신의 금발 머리를 빗질하며 가지런히 정돈하였다. **2** 형용사 금으로 된, 금의 ❑ 금으로 된 로켓이 달려 있는 금 목걸이 **3** 형용사 훌륭한, 최고의 ❑ 평화를 위한 놓칠 수 없는 절호의 기회가 있다고 그는 말한다. **4** 구 최고, 아주 인기 있는 사람 ❑ 그 영화가 개봉했을 때 비평가들은 몹시 흥분해서 타란티노를 1990년대의 가장 인기 있는 감독이라고 추켜세웠다.

가산명사 연장전의 우승 결정 골 [영국영어] ❑ 트레제게는 유로 2000 결승에서 연장전의 우승 결정 골을 넣은 뒤 튀린 팀으로 들어갔다.

가산명사 특별 퇴직금 [경제] ❑ 그리고 만일 49세인 펠씨가 회사의 매각 이후에 해고된다면, 그는 백만 파운드의 특별 퇴직금을 받을 가망이 있게 된다.

가산명사 조기 퇴직 특별 우대 조치 [경제] ❑ 그들이 회사에서 해고되면, 이들에게는 특별 우대 조치로 일년 치의 봉급을 지급한다.

가산명사 황금률 ❑ 핸슨이 지키는 황금률은, 그가 인수하는 모든 사업에 가치를 부여하도록 하는 것이다.

goldfish는 단수형 및 복수형이다.

가산명사 금붕어

가산명사 금메달 ❑ 동계 올림픽에서 금메달을 따고자 하는 그녀의 야망

단수명사 금광, 보고 ❑ 책은 지식의 보고이다.

불가산명사 골프 ❑ "골프 치십니까?"라고 그가 갑자기 나에게 물었다.

1 가산명사 골프채 **2** 가산명사 골프 클럽

golf course (**golf courses**) also **golf-course** N-COUNT A **golf course** is a large area of grass which is specially designed for people to play golf on.

golf|er /ɡɒlfər/ (**golfers**) N-COUNT A **golfer** is a person who plays golf for pleasure or as a profession. ❑ ...*one of the world's top golfers.*

golf|ing /ɡɒlfɪŋ/ ■ ADJ **Golfing** is used to describe things that involve the playing of golf or that are used while playing golf. [ADJ n] ❑ *He was wearing a cream silk shirt and a tartan golfing cap.* ■ N-UNCOUNT **Golfing** is the activity of playing golf. ❑ *You can play tennis or go golfing.*

gone ◆◇◇ /ɡɒn/ ■ **Gone** is the past participle of **go**. ■ ADJ When someone is **gone**, they have left the place where you are and are no longer there. When something is **gone**, it is no longer present or no longer exists. [v-link ADJ] ❑ *While he was gone she had tea with the Colonel.* ❑ *He's already been gone four hours!* ■ PREP If you say it is **gone** a particular time, you mean it is later than that time. [BRIT, INFORMAL] ❑ *It was just gone 7 o'clock this evening when I finished.*

gong /ɡɒŋ/ (**gongs**) N-COUNT A **gong** is a large, flat, circular piece of metal that you hit with a hammer to make a sound like a loud bell. Gongs are sometimes used as musical instruments, or to give a signal that it is time to do something. ❑ *On the stroke of seven, a gong summons guests into the dining-room.*

gon|na /ɡɒnə/ **Gonna** is used in written English to represent the words "going to" when they are pronounced informally. ❑ *Then what am I gonna do?*

good ◆◆◆ /ɡʊd/ (**better, best**) ■ ADJ **Good** means pleasant or enjoyable. ❑ *We had a really good time together.* ❑ *I know they would have a better life here.* ■ ADJ **Good** means of a high quality, standard, or level. ❑ *Exercise is just as important to health as good food.* ❑ *His parents wanted Raymond to have the best possible education.* ■ ADJ If you are **good at** something, you are skillful and successful at doing it. ❑ *He was very good at his work.* ❑ *I'm not very good at singing.* ■ ADJ If you describe a piece of news, an action, or an effect as **good**, you mean that it is likely to result in benefit or success. ❑ *On balance biotechnology should be good news for developing countries.* ❑ *I think the response was good.* ■ ADJ A **good** idea, reason, method, or decision is a sensible or valid one. ❑ *They thought it was a good idea to make some offenders do community service.* ❑ *There is good reason to doubt this.* ■ ADJ If you say that **it is good that** something should happen or **good to** do something, you mean it is desirable, acceptable, or right. ❑ *I think it's good that some people are going.* ■ ADJ A **good** estimate or indication of something is an accurate one. ❑ *We have a fairly good idea of what's going on.* ❑ *This is a much better indication of what a school is really like.* ■ ADJ If you get a **good** deal or a **good** price when you buy or sell something, you receive a lot in exchange for what you give. ❑ *Whether such properties are a good deal will depend on individual situations.* ■ ADJ If something is **good for** a person or organization, it benefits them. [v-link ADJ for] ❑ *Rain water was once considered to be good for the complexion.* ■ N-SING If something is done for **the good** of a person or organization, it is done in order to benefit them. [with poss] ❑ *Furlaud urged him to resign for the good of the country.* ❑ *Victims want to see justice done not just for themselves, but for the greater good of society.* ■ N-UNCOUNT If someone or something is **no good** or is **not any good**, they are not satisfactory or are of a low standard. [with brd-neg] ❑ *If the weather's no good then I won't take any pictures.* ■ N-UNCOUNT If you say that doing something is **no good** or does **not** do **any good**, you mean that doing it is not of any use or will not bring any success. ❑ *It's no good worrying about it now.* ❑ *We gave them water and kept them warm, but it didn't do any good.* ■ N-UNCOUNT **Good** is what is considered to be right according to moral standards or religious beliefs. ❑ *Good and evil may co-exist within one family.* ■ ADJ Someone who is **good** is morally correct in their attitudes and behavior. ❑ *The president is a good man.* ■ ADJ Someone, especially a child, who is **good** obeys rules and instructions and behaves in a socially correct way. ❑ *The children were very good.* ❑ *I'm going to be a good boy now.* ■ ADJ Someone who is **good** is kind and thoughtful. ❑ *You are good to me.* ❑ *Her good intentions were thwarted almost immediately.* ■ ADJ Someone who is in a **good** mood is cheerful and pleasant to be with. ❑ *People were in a pretty good mood.* ❑ *He exudes natural charm and good humor.* ■ ADJ If people are **good** friends, they get along well together and are very close. [ADJ n] ❑ *She and Gavin are good friends.* ■ ADJ You use **good** to emphasize the great extent or degree of something. [EMPHASIS] [a ADJ n] ❑ *We waited a good fifteen minutes.* ■ CONVENTION You say "**Good**" or "**Very good**" to express pleasure, satisfaction, or agreement with something that has been said or done, especially when you are in a position of authority. ❑ *"Are you all right?" — "I'm fine." — "Good. So am I."* ❑ *Oh good, Tom's just come in.* ■ →see also **best, better, goods** ■ PHRASE **As good as** can be used to mean "almost." ❑ *His career is as good as over.* ■ PHRASE If you say that something will **do** someone **good**, you mean that it will benefit them or improve them. ❑ *The outing will do me good.* ❑ *It's probably done you good to get away for a few hours.* ■ PHRASE If something changes or disappears **for good**, it never changes back or comes back as it was before. ❑ *The days of big-time racing at Herne Hill had gone for good.* ■ PHRASE If you say **it's a good thing**, or in British English **it's a good job**, **that** something is the case, you mean that it is fortunate. ❑ *It's a good thing you aren't married.* ■ PHRASE If someone **makes good** a threat or promise or **makes good on** it, they do what they have threatened or promised to do. [mainly AM] ❑ *He was confident the allies would make good on their pledges.* ■ PHRASE If you say that something or someone is **as good as new**, you mean that they are in a very good condition or state, especially after they have been damaged or ill. ❑ *I only ever use that on special occasions so it's as good as new.* ■ PHRASE You use **good old** before the name of a person, place, or thing when you are referring to them in an affectionate way. [FEELINGS] ❑ *Good old Harry. Reliable to the end.* **good deal** →see **deal. in good faith** →see **faith. so far so good** →see **far. good as gold** →see **gold. good gracious** →see **gracious. good grief** →see **grief. good heavens** →see **heaven. good job** →see **job. good lord** →see **lord. the good old days** →see **old. in good shape** →see **shape.** **to stand**

가산명사 골프장, 골프 코스

가산명사 골프 선수, 골프 치는 사람 ❑ 세계 최고 골프 선수 중 한 명

■ 형용사 골프의 ❑ 그는 크림색 실크 셔츠를 입고 체크무늬 모직 골프 모자를 쓰고 있었다. ■ 불가산명사 골프 치기 ❑ 테니스를 칠 수도 있고 골프를 칠 수도 있다.

■ go의 과거 분사 ■ 형용사 가버린, 가고 없는 ❑ 그가 없는 동안 그녀는 대령과 차를 마셨다. ❑ 그가 자리를 비운 지 벌써 4시간째야. ■ 전치사 (시각이) 지난 [영국영어, 비격식체] ❑ 오늘 저녁 내가 일을 끝마쳤을 때는 저녁 7시가 막 지나 있었다.

가산명사 (신호용) 징, 꽹 ❑ 시계가 7시를 가리키면 징이 울려 손님들을 식당으로 부른다.

-할 것이다 ❑ 그러면 나는 어떻게 해야 하지?

■ 형용사 좋은, 즐거운 ❑ 우리는 함께 정말로 즐거운 시간을 보냈다. ❑ 나는 그들이 이곳에서 더 나은 삶을 살리라는 것을 안다. ■ 형용사 훌륭한 ❑ 운동은 좋은 음식만큼이나 몸에 중요하다. ❑ 그의 부모님은 레이몬드가 가능한 최고의 교육을 받기를 원하셨다. ■ 형용사 -에 능숙한 ❑ 그는 자기 일에 매우 능숙했다. ❑ 나는 노래를 잘 부르지 못한다. ■ 형용사 (효과가) 좋은, 유익한 ❑ 결국 생물 공학은 개발도상국에 희소식이 될 것이다. ❑ 나는 그 반응이 효과가 있었다고 생각한다. ■ 형용사 타당한, 적절한 ❑ 몇몇 범죄자들에게 지역 봉사 활동을 시키는 것은 적절한 방법이라고 그들은 생각했다. ❑ 이것을 의심할 타당한 이유가 있다. ■ 형용사 -해서 다행이다 ❑ 가는 사람들이 몇 명이 있어서 다행이라고 나는 생각한다. ■ 형용사 정확한 ❑ 우리는 무슨 일이 일어나고 있는지 꽤나 정확히 알고 있다. ❑ 이것은 실제 학교생활이 어떤지를 훨씬 더 정확히 보여 주는 증거이다. ■ 형용사 유죽한, 충분한 ❑ 그런 부동산이 좋은 거래인지의 여부는 각 상황마다 다를 것이다. ■ 형용사 -에 이익이 되는 ❑ 한때 빗물이 얼굴에 좋다고 여겨진 적이 있었다. ■ 단수명사 이익 ❑ 펄로드는 그에게 국익을 위해서 사임하라고 촉구하였다. ❑ 희생자들은 자신들을 위해서 뿐만 아니라 더 크게 사회를 위해서 정의가 구현되는 것을 보기를 원한다. ■ 불가산명사 불만족스러움 ❑ 날씨가 좋지 않으면 나는 사진을 한 장도 찍지 않을 것이다. ■ 불가산명사 쓸모없음, 소용없음 ❑ 지금 그것을 걱정해도 소용없다. ❑ 나는 그들에게 물을 주고 몸을 녹이도록 해 주었으나, 그것은 아무 소용이 없었다. ■ 불가산명사 선 ❑ 선과 악은 한 집안에서도 공존할 수 있다. ■ 형용사 (도덕적으로) 선한, 좋은 ❑ 대통령은 좋은 사람이다. ■ 형용사 온순한, 행실이 바른 ❑ 그 아이들은 매우 행실이 좋았다. ❑ 이젠 얌전한 아이가 될게요. ■ 형용사 친절한 ❑ 당신은 저에게 친절하십니다. ❑ 그녀의 사려 깊은 친절은 거의 즉시 거절당했다. ■ 형용사 유쾌한, 즐거운 ❑ 사람들은 매우 즐거워했다. ❑ 그는 자연스러운 매력과 유쾌한 재치가 넘친다. ■ 형용사 친한 ❑ 그녀와 가빈은 친한 친구 사이이다. ■ 형용사 -씨이나 [강조] ❑ 우리는 15분씩이나 기다렸다. ■ 관용 표현 좋아, 잘됐어 ❑ "잘 지내시죠?" "잘 지내요." "잘 됐군요. 저도요." ❑ 아, 됐어요. 탐이 막 들어왔어요. ■ 구 거의 ❑ 그의 경력은 사실상 끝이다. ■ 구 -에게 도움이 되다 ❑ 잠깐 여행을 하는 게 나에게 도움이 될 것이다. ❑ 몇 시간 동안이라도 자리를 떴던 것이 당신에게 도움이 된 것 같다. ■ 구 영원히 ❑ 헤른 힐에서 최고의 경주가 열리던 시대는 영원히 끝나 버렸다. ■ 구 -이어서 다행이다 ❑ 당신이 결혼하지 않아서 다행이다. ■ 구 (약속을) 지키다 [주로 미국영어] ❑ 동맹군이 약속을 지킬 것이라고 그는 확신했다. ■ 구 마치 새 것 같은 ❑ 나는 그 물건을 특별한 경우에만 사용하기 때문에 마치 새 것 같습니다. ■ 구 그리운 [감정 개입] ❑ 끝까지 믿을 수 있었던, 그리운 해리.

A

someone **in good stead** →see **stead**. **in good time** →see **time**. **too good to be true** →see **true**

B

Thesaurus
*good*의 참조어

ADJ.   agreeable, enjoyable, nice, pleasant; (*ant.*) unpleasant **1**
able, capable, skilled; (*ant.*) unqualified, unskilled **3**

C

good after|noon CONVENTION You say "**Good afternoon**" when you are greeting someone in the afternoon. [FORMAL, FORMULAE]

관용 표현 (오후 인사) 안녕하십니까 [격식체, 의례적인 표현]

D

good|bye /gʊdbaɪ/ (**goodbyes**) also **good-bye 1** CONVENTION You say "**Goodbye**" to someone when you or they are leaving, or at the end of a telephone conversation. [FORMULAE] **2** N-COUNT When you say your **goodbyes**, you say something such as "Goodbye" when you leave. □ *He said his goodbyes knowing that a long time would pass before he would see his child again.* □ *Perry and I exchanged goodbyes.* **3** PHRASE If you **say goodbye** or **wave goodbye to** something that you want or usually have, you accept that you are not going to have it. □ *He has probably said goodbye to his last chance of Olympic gold.* **4** to **kiss** something **goodbye** →see **kiss**

1 관용 표현 안녕히 계십시오, 안녕 [의례적인 표현] **2** 가산명사 작별 인사 □ 그는 아이를 오랫동안 못 볼 것을 알았기 때문에 작별 인사를 했다. □ 페리와 나는 작별 인사를 주고받았다. **3** 구 작별을 고하다 □ 그는 올림픽 금메달을 딸 수 있는 마지막 기회에 작별을 고한 것 같다.

E

F

good eve|ning CONVENTION You say "**Good evening**" when you are greeting someone in the evening. [FORMAL, FORMULAE]

관용 표현 (저녁인사) 안녕하세요 [격식체, 의례적인 표현]

G

good-looking (**better-looking**, **best-looking**) ADJ Someone who is **good-looking** has an attractive face. □ *Cassandra noticed him because he was good-looking.*

형용사 잘 생긴 □ 그가 잘 생겼기 때문에 카산드라가 그를 주목했다.

When you are describing someone's appearance, you generally use **pretty** and **beautiful** to describe women, girls, and babies. **Beautiful** is a much stronger word than **pretty**. The equivalent word for a man is **handsome**. **Good-looking** and **attractive** can be used to describe people of either sex. **Pretty** can also be used to modify adjectives and adverbs but is less strong than **very**. In this sense, **pretty** is informal.

사람의 외모를 묘사할 때, 여성, 소녀, 아기에 대해서는 대개 pretty와 beautiful을 쓴다. beautiful은 pretty보다 더 강한 말이다. 이에 상응하는 말로 남성에게 쓸 수 있는 것이 handsome이다. good-looking과 attractive는 남녀 모두에게 쓸 수 있다. pretty는 형용사와 부사를 수식하기 위해서도 쓸 수 있으나 very 보다는 강도가 약하다. 이런 의미로 쓰인 pretty는 비격식체이다.

H

I

J

good morn|ing CONVENTION You say "**Good morning**" when you are greeting someone in the morning. [FORMAL, FORMULAE]

관용 표현 (아침인사) 안녕하세요, 좋은 아침입니다 [격식체, 의례적인 표현]

K

good-natured ADJ A **good-natured** person or animal is naturally friendly and does not get angry easily. □ *Bates looks like a good-natured lad.*

형용사 착한, 온후한 □ 베이츠는 착한 젊은이인 것 같다.

good|ness /gʊdnəs/ **1** EXCLAM People sometimes say "**goodness**" or "**my goodness**" to express surprise. [FEELINGS] □ *Goodness, I wonder if he knows.* **for goodness sake** →see **sake**. **thank goodness** →see **thank 2** N-UNCOUNT **Goodness** is the quality of being kind, helpful, and honest. □ *He retains a faith in human goodness.*

1 감탄사 저런!, 어머나! [감정 개입] □ 저런! 그가 아는지 모르겠네. **2** 불가산명사 선량함 □ 그는 인간이 선하다는 믿음을 간직하고 있다.

L

M

good|night /gʊdnaɪt/ also **good night 1** CONVENTION You say "**Goodnight**" to someone late in the evening before one of you goes home or goes to sleep. [FORMULAE] **2** PHRASE If you **say goodnight to** someone or **kiss** them **goodnight**, you say something such as "Goodnight" to them or kiss them before one of you goes home or goes to sleep. □ *Eleanor went upstairs to say goodnight to the children.* □ *Both men rose to their feet and kissed her goodnight.*

1 관용 표현 안녕히 가세요, 안녕히 계세요, 잘 자요 [의례적인 표현] **2** 구 ~에게 잘 가라고 인사하다, ~에게 잘 자라고 키스하다 □ 엘레너는 아이들에게 잘 자라고 말하려고 이층으로 올라갔다. □ 두 남자는 모두 일어섰고 그녀에게 잘 자라고 키스했다.

N

O

goods ♦♦◇ /gʊdz/ **1** N-PLURAL **Goods** are things that are made to be sold. □ *Money can be exchanged for goods or services.* **2** N-PLURAL Your **goods** are the things that you own and that can be moved. □ *All his worldly goods were packed into a neat checked carrier bag.* →see **economics**

1 복수명사 상품 □ 돈은 재화나 용역과 교환될 수 있다. **2** 복수명사 동산, 소유물 □ 그의 모든 재물이 산뜻한 체크무늬 쇼핑백에 담겨졌다.

P

Word Partnership
*goods*의 연어

V.   **buy** goods, **sell** goods, **transport** goods **1**
N.   **consumer** goods, **delivery of** goods, **exchange of** goods, **variety of** goods **1**
ADJ.   **sporting** goods, **stolen** goods **1**

Q

R

S

good|will /gʊdwɪl/ **1** N-UNCOUNT **Goodwill** is a friendly or helpful attitude toward other people, countries, or organizations. □ *I invited them to dinner, a gesture of goodwill.* **2** N-UNCOUNT The **goodwill** of a business is something such as its good reputation, which increases the value of the business. [BUSINESS] □ *We do not want to lose the goodwill built up over 175 years.*

1 불가산명사 호의, 친선 □ 나는 그들을 호의의 표시로 저녁 식사에 초대했다. **2** 불가산명사 명성, 신용 [경제] □ 우리는 175년에 걸쳐 쌓아온 명성을 잃고 싶지 않다.

T

goose /gus/ (**geese**) **1** N-COUNT A **goose** is a large bird that has a long neck and webbed feet. Geese are often farmed for their meat. **2** N-UNCOUNT **Goose** is the meat from a goose that has been cooked. □ *...roast goose.*

1 가산명사 거위 **2** 불가산명사 거위 고기 □ 구운 거위 고기

U

gore /gɔr/ (**gores**, **goring**, **gored**) **1** V-T If someone **is gored** by an animal, they are badly wounded by its horns or tusks. [usu passive] □ *Carruthers had been gored by a rhinoceros.* **2** N-UNCOUNT **Gore** is blood from a wound that has become thick. □ *There were pools of blood and gore on the pavement.*

1 타동사 ~의 뿔에 받히다 □ 카러더스는 코뿔소에게 받혔었다. **2** 불가산명사 엉긴 피, 피막지 □ 도로 위에는 여러 군데 피가 고여 있기도 하고 말라붙어 있기도 했다.

V

W

gorge /gɔrdʒ/ (**gorges**, **gorging**, **gorged**) **1** N-COUNT A **gorge** is a deep, narrow valley with very steep sides, usually where a river passes through mountains or an area of hard rock. □ *...the deep gorge between these hills.* **2** V-T/V-I If you **gorge on** something or **gorge yourself on** it, you eat lots of it in a very greedy way. □ *I could spend each day gorging on chocolate.* →see **river**

1 가산명사 협곡 □ 이 구릉들 사이의 깊은 협곡 **2** 타동사/자동사 게걸스럽게 많이 먹다 □ 나는 매일 초콜릿으로 포식하며 지낼 수 있었다.

X

gor|geous /gɔrdʒəs/ **1** ADJ If you say that something is **gorgeous**, you mean that it gives you a lot of pleasure or is very attractive. [INFORMAL] □ *...gorgeous mountain scenery.* □ *It's a gorgeous day.* **2** ADJ If you describe someone as **gorgeous**, you mean that you find them very sexually attractive. [INFORMAL] □ *The cosmetics industry uses gorgeous women to sell its skincare products.*

1 형용사 찬란한, 화려한; 멋진, 근사한 [비격식체] □ 산의 멋진 풍경 □ 정말 날씨 좋다. **2** 형용사 매력적인, 매혹적인 [비격식체] □ 화장품 산업은 피부 보호 제품을 팔기 위해 매력적인 여인들을 이용한다.

Y

Z

go|ril|la /gərɪlə/ (**gorillas**) N-COUNT A **gorilla** is a very large ape. It has long arms, black fur, and a black face. →see **primate**

가산명사 고릴라

gory /gɔːri/ (**gorier, goriest**) ADJ **Gory** situations involve people being injured or dying in a horrible way. ❑ ...the gory details of Mayan human sacrifices.

형용사 유혈의, 잔학한 ❑ 마야 족의 인간 제물에 대한 잔학한 세부 내용

gosh /gɒʃ/ EXCLAM Some people say "**Gosh**" when they are surprised. [OLD-FASHIONED] ❑ Gosh, there's a lot of noise.

감탄사 아이쿠! [구식어] ❑ 아이쿠! 소음이 심하군.

go-slow (**go-slows**) N-COUNT A **go-slow** is a protest by workers in which they deliberately work slowly in order to cause problems for their employers. [BRIT; AM **slowdown**] ❑ The spectre of a strike or go-slow did not bear thinking about, said Dr. Harbison.

가산명사 태업 [영국영어; 미국영어 slowdown] ❑ 파업 또는 태업의 망령에 대해서는 생각할 가치가 없다고 하비슨 박사가 말했다.

gos|pel /gɒspᵊl/ (**gospels**) ◻ N-COUNT; N-IN-NAMES In the New Testament of the Bible, the **Gospels** are the four books which describe the life and teachings of Jesus Christ. ❑ ...the parable in St Matthew's Gospel. ◻ N-SING In the Christian religion, **the gospel** refers to the message and teachings of Jesus Christ, as explained in the New Testament. ❑ I didn't shirk my duties. I visited the sick and I preached the gospel. ◻ N-UNCOUNT **Gospel** or **gospel music** is a style of religious music that uses strong rhythms and vocal harmony. It is especially popular among black Christians in the southern United States. ❑ I had to go to church, so I grew up singing gospel. ◻ N-UNCOUNT If you take something **as gospel**, or it is **the gospel truth**, you believe that it is completely true. ❑ He wouldn't say this if it weren't the gospel truth.

◻ 가산명사; 이름명사 복음서 ❑ 마태복음의 우화 ◻ 단수명사 복음 ❑ 나는 내 의무를 회피하지 않았다. 나는 병자를 방문하고 복음을 전했다. ◻ 불가산명사 복음 성가, 영가적 음악 ❑ 나는 교회에 다녀야 했다. 그래서 나는 찬송가를 부르며 자랐다. ◻ 불가산명사 절대적인 사실 ❑ 그게 절대적인 사실이 아니면 그는 말하지 않을 것이다.

gos|sip /gɒsɪp/ (**gossips, gossiping, gossiped**) ◻ N-UNCOUNT **Gossip** is informal conversation, often about other people's private affairs. [also a N] ❑ He spent the first hour talking gossip. ❑ There has been much gossip about the possible reasons for his absence. ◻ V-RECIP If you **gossip with** someone, you talk informally, especially about other people or local events. You can also say that two people **gossip**. ❑ We spoke, debated, gossiped into the night. ❑ Eva gossiped with Sarah. ◻ N-COUNT If you describe someone as a **gossip**, you mean that they enjoy talking informally to people about the private affairs of others. [DISAPPROVAL] ❑ He was a vicious gossip.

◻ 불가산명사 험담, 뒷말; 수다 ❑ 그는 첫 한 시간을 남 이야기를 하며 보냈다. ❑ 그의 불참에 관한 있음직한 이유에 대해 뒷말이 많았다. ◻ 상호동사 남 이야기를 지껄이다, 수다를 떨다 ❑ 우리는 밤이 깊도록 얘기하고, 토론하고, 잡담을 했다. ❑ 에바는 사라와 수다를 떨었다. ◻ 가산명사 수다쟁이, 험담꾼 [탐탁찮음] ❑ 그는 심술궂은 험담꾼이었다.

got ◆◆◆ /gɒt/ ◻ In American English, **got** is the past tense and sometimes the past participle of **get**. In British English, **got** is the past tense and the past participle of **get**. ◻ PHRASE You use **have got** to say that someone has a particular thing, or to mention a quality or characteristic that someone or something has. In informal American English, people sometimes just use "got." [SPOKEN] ❑ I've got a coat just like this. ❑ Have you got any ideas? ◻ PHRASE You use **have got to** when you are saying that something is necessary or must happen in the way stated. In informal American English, the "have" is sometimes omitted. [SPOKEN] ❑ I'm not happy with the situation, but I've just got to accept it. ❑ There has got to be a degree of flexibility. ◻ PHRASE People sometimes use **have got to** in order to emphasize that they are certain that something is true, because of the facts or circumstances involved. In informal American English, the "have" is sometimes omitted. [SPOKEN, EMPHASIS] ❑ "You've got to be joking!" he wisely replied.

◻ get의 과거 및 과거 분사 ◻ 구 가지고 있다 [구어체] ❑ 나는 이것과 꼭 같은 외투가 있어요. ❑ 좋은 생각이 있습니까? ◻ 구 -해야 한다 [구어체] ❑ 나는 그 상황이 만족스럽지는 않지만 받아들여야만 한다. ❑ 어느 정도 융통성이 있어야 한다. ◻ 구 -임에 틀림없다 [구어체, 강조] ❑ "농담하고 있는 게 틀림없지!"라고 그가 현명하게 대답했다.

Goth|ic /gɒθɪk/ ◻ ADJ **Gothic** architecture and religious art was produced in the Middle Ages. Its features include tall pillars, high curved ceilings, and pointed arches. ❑ ...a vast, lofty Gothic cathedral. ❑ ...Gothic stained glass windows. ◻ ADJ In **Gothic** stories, strange, mysterious adventures happen in dark and lonely places such as graveyards and old castles. ❑ This novel is not science fiction, nor is it Gothic horror.

◻ 형용사 고딕 양식의 ❑ 거대하고, 우뚝 솟은 고딕 양식의 대성당 ❑ 고딕 양식의 착색 유리창 ◻ 형용사 고딕풍의, 괴기적인 ❑ 이 소설은 공상 과학물도 아니고 괴기 공포물도 아니다.

got|ta /gɒtə/ **Gotta** is used in written English to represent the words "got to" when they are pronounced informally, with the meaning "have to" or "must." ❑ Prices are high and our kids gotta eat.

-해야 한다 ❑ 물가는 비싸고 우리 아이들은 먹어야 한다.

got|ten /gɒtᵊn/ **Gotten** is the past participle of **get** in American English.

get의 과거 분사

gouge /gaʊdʒ/ (**gouges, gouging, gouged**) V-T If you **gouge** something, you make a hole or a long cut in it, usually with a pointed object. ❑ He gouged her cheek with a screwdriver.

타동사 구멍을 뚫다, 상처를 내다 ❑ 그는 스크루 드라이버로 그녀의 볼에 깊은 상처를 냈다.

▶**gouge out** PHRASAL VERB To **gouge out** a piece or part of something means to cut, dig, or force it from the surrounding surface. You can use **gouge out** a hole in the ground. ❑ He has accused her of threatening to gouge his eyes out.

구동사 둥글게 잘라내다, 둥글게 파내다 ❑ 그는 자기의 눈을 파 버릴 거라며 위협했다고 그녀를 고발했다.

gour|met /gʊərmeɪ/ (**gourmets**) ◻ ADJ **Gourmet** food is nicer or more unusual or sophisticated than ordinary food, and is often more expensive. [ADJ n] ❑ Flavored coffee is sold at gourmet food stores and coffee shops. ❑ The couple share a love of gourmet cooking. ◻ N-COUNT A **gourmet** is someone who enjoys good food, and who knows a lot about food and wine. ❑ ...and the seafood is a gourmet's delight.

◻ 형용사 고급의 ❑ 특별히 향이 좋은 커피는 고급 식품 상점과 커피 가게에서 판다. ❑ 그들 부부는 둘 다 고급 요리하는 것을 좋아한다. ◻ 가산명사 미식가 ❑ 그리고 해물은 미식가의 낙이다.

gov|ern ◆◇◇ /gʌvərn/ (**governs, governing, governed**) ◻ V-T To **govern** a place such as a country, or its people, means to be officially in charge of the place, and to have responsibility for making laws, managing the economy, and controlling public services. ❑ They go to the polls on Friday to choose the people they want to govern their country. ◻ V-T If a situation or activity **is governed by** a particular factor, rule, or force, it is controlled by that factor, rule, or force. ❑ Marine insurance is governed by a strict series of rules and regulations.

◻ 타동사 통치하다, 다스리다 ❑ 그들은 금요일에 자기네 나라를 통치할 자기들이 원하는 사람들을 선택하는 투표를 한다. ◻ 타동사 좌우되다, 결정되다 ❑ 해상 보험은 일련의 엄격한 규칙과 규정에 따른다.

Thesaurus	govern의 참조어
v.	administer, command, control, direct, guide, head, lead, manage, reign, rule ◻

gov|ern|ment ◆◆◆ /gʌvərnmənt/ (**governments**) ◻ N-COUNT-COLL The **government** of a country is the group of people who are responsible for governing it. ❑ The Government has insisted that confidence is needed before the economy can improve. ❑ ...democratic governments in countries like Britain and the U.S.

◻ 가산명사-집합 정부 ❑ 정부는 경제가 호전되기까지는 신뢰가 필요하다고 주장해 왔다. ◻ 영국, 미국과 같은 나라의 민주 정부 ◻ 불가산명사 정치, 통치 ❑ 처음 4년간의 통치는 완전히 파탄이었다.

A

2 N-UNCOUNT **Government** consists of the activities, methods, and principles involved in governing a country or other political unit. ❏ *The first four years of government were completely disastrous.*
→see **factory**

B

In the United States, the head of the government is the **President**, who appoints the members of his **administration**. Policies are debated and approved by **Congress**, which consists of the **House of Representatives** and the **Senate**. Members of the House of Representatives are known as **congressmen** and **congresswomen**, and members of the **Senate** are called **senators**. In Britain, the head of the government is the **Prime Minister**. The Prime Minister appoints the other **ministers**, who are responsible for particular areas of policy. The Prime Minister and other senior ministers together form the **Cabinet**. The policies of the government are debated and approved by **Parliament**, which consists of the **House of Commons** and the **House of Lords**. There are about 650 elected **Members of Parliament** (or **MPs**) in the House of Commons.

미국 행정부의 수반은 대통령(President)이고 그는 국무위원들을 임명한다. 정책은 국회(Congress)에서 논의하고 승인하는데, Congress는 하원(House of Representatives)과 상원(Senate)으로 구성된다. 하원의원들은 congressmen과 congresswomen이라 하고, 상원의원들은 senators라고 한다. 영국에서는 행정부의 수반이 수상(Prime Minister)이다. 수상은 특정한 정책분야를 책임지는 다른 각료(ministers)를 임명한다. 수상과 다른 고위각료들이 내각(Cabinet)을 구성한다. 정부정책은 의회(Parliament)에서 논의하고 승인하는데, 의회는 하원(House of Commons)과 상원(House of Lords)으로 이루어진다. 하원에는 선거를 통해 선출된 650 명의 국회의원(Members of Parliament or MPs) 이 있다.

F

G

gov|ern|men|tal /ˌgʌvərnˈmentᵊl/ ADJ **Governmental** means relating to a particular government, or to the practice of governing a country. [ADJ n] ❏ *...a governmental agency for providing financial aid to developing countries.*

형용사 정부의, 통치의 ❏ 개발 도상 국가에 재정 원조를 제공하는 정부 기관

gov|er|nor ♦♦♢ /ˈgʌvərnər/ (**governors**) **1** N-COUNT; N-TITLE In some systems of government, a **governor** is a person who is in charge of the political administration of a state, colony, or region. ❏ *He was governor of the province in the late 1970s.* **2** N-COUNT A **governor** is a member of a committee which controls an organization such as a school or a hospital. ❏ *Governors are using the increased powers given to them to act against incompetent headteachers.* **3** N-COUNT In some British institutions, the **governor** is the most senior official, who is in charge of the institution. ❏ *The incident was reported to the prison governor.*

1 가산명사; 경칭명사 지사, 총독 ❏ 그는 1970년대 후반에 그 도의 지사였다. **2** 가산명사 운영 위원 ❏ 운영 위원들은 자기들에게 주어진 강화된 힘을 무능한 교장들에게 불리하게 작용하도록 이용하고 있다. **3** 가산명사 소장 ❏ 그 사건은 교도소장에게 보고되었다.

H

I

gown /ɡaʊn/ (**gowns**) **1** N-COUNT A **gown** is a dress, usually a long dress, which women wear on formal occasions. ❏ *The new ball gown was a great success.* **2** N-COUNT A **gown** is a loose black garment worn on formal occasions by people such as lawyers and academics. ❏ *...an old headmaster in a flowing black gown.*

1 가산명사 여성용 예복, 드레스 ❏ 새 무도회 드레스는 대성공이었다. **2** 가산명사 법복; 학위복 ❏ 멋지게 드리워진 검은 학위복을 입은 연로한 교장

J

K

GP /ˌdʒiː ˈpiː/ (**GPs**) N-COUNT A **GP** is a doctor who does not specialize in any particular area of medicine, but who has a medical practice in which he or she treats all types of illness. **GP** is an abbreviation for **general practitioner**. ❏ *Her husband called their local GP.*

가산명사 일반 의사 ❏ 그녀의 남편은 지역 일반 의사를 불렀다.

L

grab ♦♢♢ /ɡræb/ (**grabs, grabbing, grabbed**) **1** V-T If you **grab** something, you take it or pick it up suddenly and roughly. ❏ *I managed to grab her hand.* **2** V-I If you **grab** at something, you try to grab it. ❏ *He was clumsily trying to grab at Alfred's arms.* ● N-COUNT **Grab** is also a noun. [usu sing, N for/at n] ❏ *I made a grab for the knife.* **3** V-T If you **grab** someone who is walking past, you succeed in getting their attention. [INFORMAL] ❏ *Grab that waiter, Mary Ann.* **4** V-T If you **grab** someone's attention, you do something in order to make them notice you. ❏ *I jumped on the wall to grab the attention of the crowd.* **5** V-T If you **grab** something such as food, drink, or sleep, you manage to get some quickly. [INFORMAL] ❏ *Grab a beer.* **6** to **grab hold of** →see **hold** **7** PHRASE If something is **up for grabs**, it is available to anyone who is interested. [INFORMAL] ❏ *The famous Ritz hotel is up for grabs for £100m.*

1 타동사 잡아채다, 움켜잡다 ❏ 나는 용케 그녀의 손을 움켜잡았다. **2** 자동사 잡으려고 하다 ❏ 그는 어설프게 알프레드의 팔을 붙잡으려고 하고 있었다. ● 가산명사 움켜잡기 ❏ 나는 칼을 움켜잡으려고 했다. **3** 타동사 ─를 불러 세우다 [비격식체] ❏ 저 웨이터를 불러 세워, 메리 앤. **4** 타동사 (주의를) 끌다 ❏ 나는 군중의 주의를 끌기 위해 벽 위로 뛰어올라 갔다. **5** 타동사 잡히나 잠을 간단히 취하다 [비격식체] ❏ 얼른 맥주 한 잔 마셔. **7** 구 손에 넣을 수 있는 [비격식체] ❏ 유명한 릿쯔 호텔을 1억 파운드에 손에 넣을 수 있다.

P

Q

Thesaurus	*grab*의 참조어
v.	capture, catch, seize, snap up; (ant.) release **1**

R

Word Link	grac ≈ pleasing : dis**grac**e, **grac**e, **grac**eful

grace /ɡreɪs/ (**graces, gracing, graced**) **1** N-UNCOUNT If someone moves with **grace**, they move in a smooth, controlled, and attractive way. ❏ *He moved with the grace of a trained boxer.* **2** N-PLURAL The **graces** are the ways of behaving and doing things which are considered polite and well-mannered. ❏ *She didn't fit in and she had few social graces.* **3** V-T If you say that something **graces** a place or a person, you mean that it makes them more attractive. [FORMAL] ❏ *He went to the beautiful old Welsh dresser that graced this homely room.* **4** N-UNCOUNT In Christianity and some other religions, **grace** is the kindness that God shows to people because He loves them. ❏ *It was only by the grace of God that no one died.* **5** N-VAR When someone says **grace** before or after a meal, they say a prayer in which they thank God for the food and ask Him to bless it. ❏ *Leo, will you say grace?*

1 불가산명사 우아함, 기품 ❏ 그는 단련된 권투 선수처럼 우아하게 움직였다. **2** 복수명사 세련미 ❏ 그녀는 잘 맞지 않았고 사교적 세련미가 거의 없었다. **3** 타동사 아름답게 꾸미다 [격식체] ❏ 그는 이 아담한 방을 아름답게 꾸며주는 멋지고 오래된 웨일스 서랍장으로 갔다. **4** 불가산명사 은총 ❏ 아무도 죽지 않은 것은 오직 신의 은총 때문이었다. **5** 가산명사 또는 불가산명사 (식사 시) 감사기도 ❏ 리오야, 기도드리겠니?

S

T

U

Word Partnership	*grace*의 연어
N.	grace **of a dancer** **1**
	grace **of God** **4**
ADJ.	**social** graces **2**
V.	**fall from** grace **4**

W

grace|ful /ˈɡreɪsfʊl/ **1** ADJ Someone or something that is **graceful** moves in a smooth and controlled way which is attractive to watch. ❏ *His movements were so graceful they seemed effortless.* ● **grace|ful|ly** ADV [ADV with v] ❏ *She stepped gracefully onto the stage.* **2** ADJ Something that is **graceful** is attractive because it has a pleasing shape or style. ❏ *His handwriting, from earliest young manhood, was flowing and graceful.* ● **grace|ful|ly** ADV [ADV adj/-ed] ❏ *She loved the gracefully high ceiling, with its white-painted cornice.*

1 형용사 우아한 ❏ 그의 움직임은 너무도 우아하여 전혀 힘들지 않아 보였다. ● 우아하게 부사 ❏ 그녀는 우아하게 무대로 올라갔다. **2** 형용사 우아한, 품위 있는 ❏ 그의 필체는 일찍이 성년이 될 무렵부터 유려하고 우아했다. ● 우아하게, 품위 있게 부사 ❏ 그녀는 흰색으로 칠한, 돌림띠 장식된 우아하게 높은 천장을 좋아했다.

X

Y

Z

gra|cious /ˈɡreɪʃəs/ **1** ADJ If you describe someone, especially someone you think is superior to you, as **gracious**, you mean that they are very well-mannered and pleasant. [FORMAL] ❑ *She is a lovely and gracious woman.* **2** ADJ If you describe the behavior of someone in a position of authority as **gracious**, you mean that they behave in a polite and considerate way. [FORMAL] ❑ *She closed with a gracious speech of thanks.* ● **gra|cious|ly** ADV [ADV with v] ❑ *Hospitality at the Presidential guest house was graciously declined.* **3** ADJ You use **gracious** to describe the comfortable way of life of wealthy people. ❑ *He drove through the gracious suburbs with the swimming pools and tennis courts.* **4** EXCLAM Some people say **good gracious** or **goodness gracious** in order to express surprise or annoyance. [FEELINGS] ❑ *Good gracious, look at that specimen, will you?*

grade ♦♢♢ /ɡreɪd/ (**grades**, **grading**, **graded**) **1** V-T If something **is graded**, its quality is judged, and it is often given a number or a name that indicates how good or bad it is. ❑ *Dust masks are graded according to the protection they offer.* ❑ *South Point College does not grade the students' work.* **2** N-COUNT The **grade** of a product is its quality, especially when this has been officially judged. [with supp, oft adj N, n num] ❑ *...a good grade of plywood.* ● COMB in ADJ **Grade** is also a combining form. ❑ *...weapons-grade plutonium.* **3** N-COUNT Your **grade** in an examination or piece of written work is the mark you get, usually in the form of a letter or number, that indicates your level of achievement. ❑ *What grade are you hoping to get?* **4** N-COUNT Your **grade** in a company or organization is your level of importance or your rank. ❑ *Staff turnover is particularly high among junior grades.* **5** N-COUNT In the United States, a **grade** is a group of classes in which all the children are of a similar age. When you are six years old you go into the first grade and you leave school after the twelfth grade. ❑ *Mr. White teaches first grade in south Georgia.* **6** N-COUNT A **grade** is a slope. [AM; BRIT **gradient**] ❑ *She drove up a steep grade and then began the long descent into the desert.* **7** N-COUNT Someone's **grade** is their military rank. [AM] ❑ *I was a naval officer, lieutenant junior grade.* **8** PHRASE If someone **makes the grade**, they succeed, especially by reaching a particular standard. ❑ *She had a strong desire to be a dancer but failed to make the grade.*

grade cross|ing (**grade crossings**) N-COUNT A **grade crossing** is a place where a railroad track crosses a road at the same level. [AM; BRIT **level crossing**]

grade school (**grade schools**) N-VAR In the United States, a **grade school** is the same as an **elementary school**. ❑ *I was just in grade school at the time, but I remember it perfectly.*

gra|di|ent /ˈɡreɪdiənt/ (**gradients**) N-COUNT A **gradient** is a slope, or the degree to which the ground slopes. [BRIT; AM usually **grade**] ❑ *The courses are long and punishing, with steep gradients.*

grad|ual /ˈɡrædʒuəl/ ADJ A **gradual** change or process occurs in small stages over a long period of time, rather than suddenly. ❑ *Losing weight is a slow, gradual process.*

grad|ual|ly ♦♢♢ /ˈɡrædʒuəli/ ADV If something changes or is done **gradually**, it changes or is done in small stages over a long period of time, rather than suddenly. [ADV with v] ❑ *Electricity lines to 30,000 homes were gradually being restored yesterday.*

gradu|ate ♦♢♢ (**graduates**, **graduating**, **graduated**)

The noun is pronounced /ˈɡrædʒuɪt/. The verb is pronounced /ˈɡrædʒueɪt/.

1 N-COUNT In the United States, a **graduate** is a student who has successfully completed a course at a high school, college, or university. ❑ *The top one-third of all high school graduates are entitled to a education at the California State University.* **2** N-COUNT In Britain, a **graduate** is a person who has successfully completed a degree at a university or college and has received a certificate that shows this. ❑ *In 1973, the first Open University graduates received their degrees.* **3** V-I In the United States, when a student **graduates**, they complete their studies successfully and leave their school or university. ❑ *When the boys graduated from high school, Ann moved to a small town in Vermont.* **4** V-I In Britain, when a student **graduates** from a university, they have successfully completed a degree course. ❑ *She graduated in English and Drama from Manchester University.* **5** V-I If you **graduate from** one thing **to** another, you go from a less important job or position to a more important one. ❑ *Bruce graduated to chef at the Bear Hotel.* →see **graduation**

gradu|ate school (**graduate schools**) N-VAR In the United States, a **graduate school** is a department in a university or college where graduate students are taught. ❑ *She was in graduate school, studying for a master's degree in social work.*

gradu|ate stu|dent (**graduate students**) N-COUNT In the United States, a **graduate student** is a student with a first degree from a university who is studying or doing research at a more advanced level. [AM; BRIT **postgraduate**]

gradu|a|tion /ˌɡrædʒuˈeɪʃən/ (**graduations**) **1** N-UNCOUNT **Graduation** is the successful completion of a course of study at a university, college, or school, for which you receive a degree or diploma. ❑ *They asked what his plans were after graduation.* **2** N-COUNT A **graduation** is a special ceremony at a university, college, or school, at which degrees and diplomas are given to students who have successfully completed their studies. ❑ *...the graduation ceremony at Yale.* →see Word Web: **graduation**

graf|fi|ti /ɡrəˈfiːti/ N-UNCOUNT-COLL **Graffiti** is words or pictures that are written or drawn in public places, for example on walls or posters. ❑ *Buildings old and new are thickly covered with graffiti.*

graft /ɡræft, BRIT ɡrɑːft/ (**grafts**, **grafting**, **grafted**) **1** N-COUNT A **graft** is a piece of healthy skin or bone, or a healthy organ, which is attached to a damaged part of your body by a medical operation in order to replace it. ❑ *I am having a skin graft on my arm soon.* **2** V-T If a piece of healthy skin or bone or a healthy

---

1 형용사 상냥한, 친절한 [격식체] ❑ 그녀는 아름답고 상냥한 여인이다. **2** 형용사 점잖은, 예의를 갖춘 [격식체] ❑ 그녀는 공손한 감사의 말로 끝맺었다. ● 점잖게, 예의를 갖춘 부사 ❑ 대통령 영빈관에서의 접대는 공손하게 거절되었다. **3** 형용사 품격 있는 ❑ 그는 수영장과 테니스장을 갖춘 품격 있는 교외 주택 지구를 차로 지나갔다. **4** 감탄사 이런, 아뿔싸! [감정 개입] ❑ 이런, 저 견본 좀 봐 줄래?

1 타동사 등급이 매겨지다 ❑ 방진 마스크는 보호 정도에 따라 등급이 매겨진다. ❑ 사우스포인트 대학은 학생의 학업에 성적을 매기지 않는다. **2** 가산명사 등급, 품질 ❑ 좋은 등급의 합판 ● 복합형용사 -급 ❑ 무기급 플루토늄 **3** 가산명사 성적 ❑ 어떤 성적을 받기를 기대하고 있니? **4** 가산명사 직위 ❑ 직원 이직률은 하급 직위에서 특히 높다. **5** 가산명사 학년 ❑ 화이트 씨는 남부 조지아에서 1학년을 가르친다. **6** 가산명사 경사, 비탈 [미국영어; 영국영어 gradient] ❑ 그녀는 차를 몰고 가파른 경사를 오른 다음 사막으로 이어지는 긴 내리막길을 내려가기 시작했다. **7** 가산명사 계급 [미국영어] ❑ 나는 해군 장교 중위였다. **8** 구 성공하다 ❑ 그녀는 무용가가 되려는 강렬한 욕망이 있었으나 그 수준에 미치지 못했다.

가산명사 수평 건널목 [미국영어; 영국영어 level crossing]

가산명사 또는 불가산명사 (미국의) 초등학교 ❑ 나는 당시 막 초등학교에 들어갔으나 그것을 완벽하게 기억하고 있다.

가산명사 비탈, 비탈의 경사도 [영국영어; 미국영어 대개 grade] ❑ 코스들은 길고 급경사가 져있어 대단히 힘들다.

형용사 점진적인, 단계적인 ❑ 체중을 줄이는 것은 느리고 점진적인 과정이다.

부사 점진적으로, 단계적으로 ❑ 3만 가구에 대한 전선이 어제 단계적으로 복구되고 있었다.

명사는 /ˈɡrædʒuɪt/으로 발음되고, 동사는 /ˈɡrædʒueɪt/으로 발음된다.

1 가산명사 (미국의 고등학교, 대학) 졸업생 ❑ 모든 고등학교 졸업생 중 상위 3분의 1은 캘리포니아 주립 대학교에서 교육받을 자격이 있다. **2** 가산명사 (영국의 대학) 졸업생, 학사 ❑ 1973년에 개방 대학교의 첫 졸업생들이 학위를 받았다. **3** 자동사 (미국에서) 졸업하다 ❑ 아이들이 고등학교를 졸업하자 앤은 버몬트의 작은 읍으로 이사를 갔다. **4** 자동사 (영국에서 대학을) 졸업하다 ❑ 그녀는 영어와 희곡 전공으로 맨체스터 대학교를 졸업했다. **5** 자동사 승진하다 ❑ 브루스는 베어 호텔에서 주방장으로 승진했다.

가산명사 또는 불가산명사 (미국의) 대학원 ❑ 그녀는 대학원 재학 중이었는데 사회사업 석사 학위를 위해 공부하고 있었다.

가산명사 대학원생 [미국영어; 영국영어 postgraduate]

1 불가산명사 졸업 ❑ 그들은 졸업 후 그의 계획이 무엇인지 물었다. **2** 가산명사 졸업식 ❑ 예일 대학의 졸업식

불가산명사-집합 그라피티 (건물벽의 낙서나 그림) ❑ 오래된 건물이나 새 건물 모두가 그라피티로 잔뜩 뒤덮여 있다.

1 가산명사 (장기 등의) 이식용 조직 ❑ 나는 곧 팔에 피부 이식을 한다. **2** 타동사 -에 이식하다 ❑ 피부의 표피를 화상 자리에 이식해야 한다. **3** 타동사 -을 접목하다 ❑ 배나무를 모과 대목에 접목한다.

A B C D E F **G** H I J K L M N O P Q R S T U V W X Y Z

Word Web — graduation

High school and **college graduations** are important rites of passage. This **ceremony** tells the world that the **student** is an accomplished scholar. In college, **graduates** receive different types of **diplomas** depending on their subject and level of study. After four years of study, students earn a Bachelor of Arts or Bachelor of Science **degree**. A Master of Arts or Master of Science usually takes one or two more years. The PhD, or doctor of philosophy degree, may require several additional years. In addition, a PhD student must write a **thesis** and defend it in front of a group of **professors**.

organ **is grafted onto** a damaged part of your body, it is attached to that part of your body by a medical operation. [usu passive] ❑ *The top layer of skin has to be grafted onto the burns.* **3** V-T If a part of one plant or tree **is grafted** onto another plant or tree, they are joined together so that they will become one plant or tree, often in order to produce a new variety. ❑ *Pear trees are grafted on quince rootstocks.* **4** N-UNCOUNT **Graft** means hard work. [BRIT, INFORMAL] ❑ *His career has been one of hard graft.*

grain ◆◇◇ /ɡreɪn/ (grains) **1** N-COUNT A grain of wheat, rice, or other cereal crop is a seed from it. ❑ *...a grain of wheat.* **2** N-MASS **Grain** is a cereal crop, especially wheat or corn, that has been harvested and is used for food or in trade. ❑ *...a bag of grain.* **3** N-COUNT A **grain** of something such as sand or salt is a tiny hard piece of it. ❑ *...a grain of sand.* **4** N-SING A **grain of** a quality is a very small amount of it. [N of n] ❑ *There's more than a grain of truth in that.* **5** N-SING The **grain** of a piece of wood is the direction of its fibers. You can also refer to the pattern of lines on the surface of the wood as **the grain**. ❑ *Brush the paint generously over the wood in the direction of the grain.* **6** PHRASE If you say that an idea or action **goes against the grain**, you mean that it is very difficult for you to accept it or do it, because it conflicts with your previous ideas, beliefs, or principles. ❑ *Privatisation goes against the grain of their principle of opposition to private ownership of industry.* →see **flower**, **rice**
→see Word Web: **grain**

gram /ɡræm/ (grams) [BRIT also **gramme**] N-COUNT A **gram** is a unit of weight. One thousand grams are equal to one kilogram. ❑ *A soccer ball weighs about 400 grams.*

gram|mar /ˈɡræmər/ (grammars) **1** N-UNCOUNT **Grammar** is the ways that words can be put together in order to make sentences. ❑ *He doesn't have mastery of the basic rules of grammar.* **2** N-UNCOUNT Someone's **grammar** is the way in which they obey or do not obey the rules of grammar when they write or speak. ❑ *His vocabulary was sound and his grammar excellent.* →see **English**

gram|mar school (grammar schools) **1** N-VAR; N-IN-NAMES A **grammar school** is the same as an **elementary school**. [AM] ❑ *Jennifer hadn't been home to watch television in the afternoon since grammar school.* **2** N-VAR; N-IN-NAMES A **grammar school** is a school in Britain for children aged between eleven and eighteen who have a high academic ability. ❑ *He is in the third year at Leeds Grammar School.*

gram|mati|cal /ɡrəˈmætɪkᵊl/ **1** ADJ **Grammatical** is used to indicate that something relates to grammar. [ADJ n] ❑ *Should the teacher present grammatical rules to students?* **2** ADJ If someone's language is **grammatical**, it is considered correct because it obeys the rules of grammar. ❑ *...a new test to determine whether students can write grammatical English.*

gramme /ɡræm/ →see **gram**

gran /ɡræn/ (grans) N-FAMILY Some people refer to or address their grandmother as **gran**. [BRIT, INFORMAL] ❑ *My gran's given us some apple jam.*

grand ◆◆◇ /ɡrænd/ (grander, grandest, grands)

The form **grand** is used as the plural for meaning **6**.

1 ADJ If you describe a building or a piece of scenery as **grand**, you mean that its size or appearance is very impressive. ❑ *This grand building in the center of town used to be the hub of the capital's social life.* **2** ADJ **Grand** plans or actions are intended to achieve important results. ❑ *The grand design of Europe's monetary union is already agreed.* **3** ADJ People who are **grand** think they are important or socially superior. [DISAPPROVAL] ❑ *He is grander and even richer than the Prince of Wales.* **4** ADJ A **grand** total is one that is the final amount or the final result of a calculation. [ADJ n] ❑ *It came to a grand total of £220,329.* **5** ADJ **Grand** is often used in the names of buildings such as hotels, especially when they are very large. [ADJ n] ❑ *They stayed at The Grand Hotel, Budapest.* **6** N-COUNT A **grand** is a

4 불가산명사 힘든 노력 [영국영어, 비격식체] ❑ 그의 직장 생활은 몹시 힘들었다.

1 구동사 ~에 들르다 ❑ 나는 그들에게 그 집에 가서 그들이 그곳에 있는지 알아보라고 부탁했다. **2** 구동사 행동하다; 복장을 하다 ❑ 나는 맨발로 다니는 버릇이 있었다. **3** 구동사 퍼지고 있다 ❑ 그것에 관해서 뭔가 나쁜 소문이 퍼지고 있다. **4** 구동사 골고루 돌아가다 ❑ 결국엔 우리에게 돌아올 식수가 충분하지 않을 것이다.

[영국영어 gramme] 가산명사 그램 ❑ 축구공은 무게가 약 400그램 정도이다.

1 불가산명사 문법 ❑ 그는 문법의 기본 규칙을 다 터득하지 못했다. **2** 불가산명사 어법 ❑ 그의 어휘는 충분했고, 그의 어법은 우수했다.

1 가산명사 또는 불가산명사; 이름명사 초등학교 [미국영어] ❑ 제니퍼는 초등학교 이후 오후에 텔레비전을 보려고 집에 있은 적이 없었다. **2** 가산명사 또는 불가산명사; 이름명사 그래머 스쿨 (영국의 중등 학교) ❑ 그는 리즈 그래머 스쿨의 3학년이다.

1 형용사 문법의 ❑ 교사가 학생들에게 문법 규칙을 가르쳐야 합니까? **2** 형용사 문법적인 ❑ 학생들이 문법에 맞는 영어를 쓸 수 있는지를 파악하기 위한 새로운 평가

친족명사 할머니 [영국영어, 비격식체] ❑ 우리 할머니께서 우리에게 사과잼을 조금 주셨다.

grand은 **6** 의미의 복수로 쓴다.

1 형용사 웅장한 ❑ 시내 한 가운데에 있는 이 웅장한 건물은 한때 수도의 사교 활동의 중심지였다. **2** 형용사 원대한 ❑ 유럽의 화폐를 통일하려는 원대한 계획은 이미 합의되었다. **3** 형용사 저명한 [탐탁찮음] ❑ 그는 영국 황태자보다도 더 저명하고 심지어 더 부자이다. **4** 형용사 총 ❑ 총액이 22만 329파운드가 되었다. **5** 형용사 대, 그랜드 ❑ 그들은 부다페스트의 그랜드 호텔에 묵었다. **6** 가산명사 천 달러; 천 파운드 [비격식체] ❑ 그들은 옛날 희곡들의 각색물 값으로 이제 당신에게 만 달러를 지불할 것이다.

Word Web — grain

People first began **cultivating grain** about 10,000 years ago in Asia. Working in groups made growing and **harvesting** the **crop** easier. This probably led Stone Age people to form the first communities. Today grain is still the principal food source for humans and domestic animals. Half of all the farmland in the world is used to produce grain. The most popular are **wheat, rice, corn,** and **oats.** An individual kernel of grain is actually a dry, one-seeded **fruit.** It combines the walls of the seed and the flesh of the fruit. Grain is often **ground** into **flour** or meal.

thousand dollars or a thousand pounds. [INFORMAL] ❏ *They're paying you ten grand now for those adaptations of old plays.*

gran|dad /grǽndæd/ (**grandads**) also **granddad** N-FAMILY Your **grandad** is your grandfather. [INFORMAL] ❏ *My grandad is 85.*

친족명사 할아버지 [비격식체] ❏ 우리 할아버지는 여든다섯 살이시다.

grand|child /grǽntʃaɪld/ (**grandchildren**) N-COUNT Someone's **grandchild** is the child of their son or daughter. ❏ *Mary loves her grandchildren.*

가산명사 손주 ❏ 메리는 손주들을 귀여워한다.

grand|dad /grǽndæd/ →see **grandad**

grand|daughter /grǽndɔtər/ (**granddaughters**) N-COUNT Someone's **granddaughter** is the daughter of their son or daughter. ❏ *...a drawing of my granddaughter Amelia.*

가산명사 손녀 ❏ 내 손녀 어멜리아가 그린 그림

gran|deur /grǽndʒər/ **1** N-UNCOUNT If something such as a building or a piece of scenery has **grandeur**, it is impressive because of its size, its beauty, or its power. ❏ *Venezuela is the ideal starting point to explore the grandeur and natural beauty of South America.* **2** N-UNCOUNT Someone's **grandeur** is the great importance and social status that they have, or think they have. ❏ *He is wholly concerned with his own grandeur.*

1 불가산명사 장대함, 웅장함 ❏ 남아메리카의 웅장함과 자연미를 답사하려면 베네수엘라가 이상적인 출발점이다. **2** 불가산명사 위세, 위엄 ❏ 그는 오로지 자기 자신의 위세에만 관심이 있다.

grand|father /grǽnfɑðər/ (**grandfathers**) N-FAMILY Your **grandfather** is the father of your father or mother. ❏ *His grandfather was a professor.* →see **family**

친족명사 할아버지 ❏ 그의 할아버지는 교수였다.

gran|di|ose /grǽndioʊs/ ADJ If you describe something as **grandiose**, you mean it is bigger or more elaborate than necessary. [DISAPPROVAL] ❏ *The sad truth is that not one of Tim's grandiose plans has even begun.*

형용사 거창한; 장엄한 [탐탁찮음] ❏ 슬픈 사실은 팀의 거창한 계획 중 아무것도 아직 시작도 하지 못했다는 것이다.

grand jury (**grand juries**) N-COUNT A **grand jury** is a jury, usually in the United States, which considers a criminal case in order to decide if someone should be tried in a court of law. ❏ *They have already given evidence before a grand jury in Washington.*

가산명사 대배심, 기소 배심 ❏ 그들은 워싱턴의 기소 배심에 이미 증거를 제시했다.

grand|ma /grǽnmɑ/ (**grandmas**) N-FAMILY Your **grandma** is your grandmother. [INFORMAL] ❏ *Grandma was from Scotland.*

친족명사 할머니 [비격식체] ❏ 할머니는 스코틀랜드 출신이다.

grand|mother /grǽnmʌðər/ (**grandmothers**) N-FAMILY Your **grandmother** is the mother of your father or mother. ❏ *My grandmothers are both widows.* →see **family**

친족명사 할머니 ❏ 친할머니와 외할머니 모두 미망인이시다.

grand|pa /grǽnpɑ/ (**grandpas**) N-FAMILY Your **grandpa** is your grandfather. [INFORMAL] ❏ *Grandpa was not yet back from the war.*

친족명사 할아버지 [비격식체] ❏ 우리 할아버지는 아직 전쟁에서 돌아오시지 않고 계셨다.

grand|parent /grǽnpɛrənt, -pær-/ (**grandparents**) N-COUNT Your **grandparents** are the parents of your father or mother. ❏ *Tammy was raised by her grandparents.*

가산명사 조부모 ❏ 태미는 조부모 밑에서 컸다.

grand|son /grǽnsʌn/ (**grandsons**) N-COUNT Someone's **grandson** is the son of their son or daughter. ❏ *My grandson's birthday was on Tuesday.*

가산명사 손자 ❏ 내 손자의 생일이 화요일이었다.

grand|stand /grǽndstænd/ (**grandstands**) N-COUNT A **grandstand** is a covered stand with rows of seats for people to sit on at sporting events.

가산명사 특별 관람석

gran|ite /grǽnɪt/ (**granites**) N-MASS **Granite** is a very hard rock used in building.

물질명사 화강암

gran|ny /grǽni/ (**grannies**) also **grannie** N-FAMILY Some people refer to their grandmother as **granny**. [INFORMAL] ❏ *...my old granny.*

친족명사 할머니 [비격식체] ❏ 연로하신 우리 할머니

grant ♦♢◇ /grǽnt, BRIT grɑːnt/ (**grants, granting, granted**) **1** N-COUNT A **grant** is an amount of money that a government or other institution gives to an individual or to an organization for a particular purpose such as education or home improvements. ❏ *They'd got a special grant to encourage research.* **2** V-T If someone in authority **grants** you something, or if something **is granted to** you, you are allowed to have it. [FORMAL] ❏ *France has agreed to grant him political asylum.* ❏ *It was a Labour government which granted independence to India and Pakistan.* **3** V-T If you **grant that** something is true, you accept that it is true, even though your opinion about it does not change. ❏ *The magistrates granted that the charity was justified in bringing the action.* **4** PHRASE If you say that someone **takes** you **for granted**, you are complaining that they benefit from your help, efforts, or presence without showing that they are grateful. ❏ *What right has the family to take me for granted, Martin?* **5** PHRASE If you **take** something **for granted**, you believe that it is true or accept it as normal without thinking about it. ❏ *I was amazed that virtually all the things I took for granted up north just didn't happen in London.* **6** PHRASE If you **take it for granted that** something is the case, you believe that it is true or you accept it as normal without thinking about it. ❏ *He seemed to take it for granted that he should speak as a representative.*

1 가산명사 장학금, 보조금 ❏ 그들은 연구 장려를 위한 특별 보조금을 받았다. **2** 타동사 승인하다; 승인되다 [격식체] ❏ 프랑스가 그에게 정치적 망명을 승인하기로 했다. ❏ 인도와 파키스탄에 독립을 승인한 것은 노동당 정부였다. **3** 타동사 인정하다 ❏ 예심 판사들은 그 자선 단체가 소송을 제기한 것이 정당하다고 인정했다. **4** 구 -을 당연시하다 ❏ 마틴, 무슨 권리로 가족이 내 도움을 당연하게 여기지? **5** 구 -을 당연하게 생각하다 ❏ 내가 북부에서 당연하게 여겼던 거의 모든 일들이 런던에서는 일어나지 않는다는 데 놀랐다. **6** 구 -을 당연한 일로 생각하다 ❏ 그는 자기가 대표로 연설해야 하는 것을 당연한 일로 생각하는 것 같았다.

Word Partnership	grant의 연어
N.	grant **amnesty**, grant **equal rights**, grant **independence**, grant **membership**, grant **money**, grant **permission**, grant **a wish** **2**
V.	**refuse** to grant **2**

grant-maintained ADJ In Britain, a **grant-maintained school** is one which receives money directly from the national government rather than from a local authority. The abbreviation **GM** is also used.

형용사 (영국의) 공립학교

grape /greɪp/ (**grapes**) **1** N-COUNT **Grapes** are small green or purple fruit which grow in bunches. Grapes can be eaten raw, used for making wine, or dried. ❏ *...a bunch of grapes.* **2** PHRASE If you describe someone's attitude as **sour grapes**, you mean that they say something is worthless or undesirable because they want it themselves but cannot have it. ❏ *These accusations have been going on for some time now, but it is just sour grapes.*

1 가산명사 포도 ❏ 포도 한 송이 **2** 구 오기, 신 포도 ❏ 이런 비난은 이제 한동안 계속되어 왔지만 그건 단지 오기에 불과하다.

grape|fruit /greɪpfruːt/

The plural can be either **grapefruit** or **grapefruits**.

복수는 grapefruit 또는 grapefruits이다.

N-VAR A **grapefruit** is a large, round, yellow fruit, similar to an orange, that has a sharp, slightly bitter taste.

가산명사 또는 불가산명사 그레이프프루트, 자몽

Word Web   graph

There are three main elements in a line or **bar graph**:
- a **vertical axis** (the y-axis)
- a **horizontal axis** (the x-axis)
- at least one line or set of bars.

To understand a **graph**, do the following:
1. Read the **title** of the graph.
2. Read the **labels** and the **range** of numbers along the side (the **scale** or vertical axis).
3. Read the information along the bottom (horizontal axis) of the graph.
4. Determine what **units** the graph uses. This information can be found on the axis or in the **key**.
5. Look for patterns, groups, and differences.

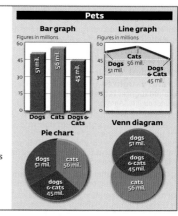

grape|vine /ˈɡreɪpvaɪn/ N-SING If you hear or learn something **on** or **through the grapevine**, you hear it or learn it in casual conversation with other people. ❑ *I had heard through the grapevine that he was quite critical of what we were doing.*

단수명사 소문, 풍문 ❑ 우리가 하고 있는 일에 대해 그가 상당히 비판적이라는 것을 소문을 통해서 들었다.

Word Link   graph ≈ writing : auto*graph*, bio*graphy*, *graph*

graph /ɡræf, BRIT ɡrɑːf/ (**graphs**) N-COUNT A **graph** is a mathematical diagram which shows the relationship between two or more sets of numbers or measurements. ❑ *...a graph showing that breast cancer deaths rose about 20 per cent from 1960 to 1985.*
→see Word Web: **graph**

가산명사 도표, 그래프 ❑ 유방암 사망률이 1960년부터 1985년까지 약 20퍼센트 증가했음을 보여 주는 도표

graph|ic /ˈɡræfɪk/ (**graphics**) ■ ADJ If you say that a description or account of something unpleasant is **graphic**, you are emphasizing that it is clear and detailed. [EMPHASIS] ❑ *The descriptions of sexual abuse are graphic.* ● **graph|ical|ly** /ˈɡræfɪkli/ ADV [ADV with v] ❑ *Here, graphically displayed, was confirmation of the entire story.* ■ ADJ **Graphic** means concerned with drawing or pictures, especially in publishing, industry, or computing. [ADJ n] ❑ *...fine and graphic arts.* ■ N-UNCOUNT **Graphics** is the activity of drawing or making pictures, especially in publishing, industry, or computing. ❑ *...a computer manufacturer which specialises in graphics.* ■ N-COUNT **Graphics** are drawings and pictures that are composed using simple lines and sometimes strong colors. ❑ *The Agriculture Department today released a new graphic to replace the old symbol.*

■ 형용사 생생한, 자세한 [강조] ❑ 성적 학대에 대한 서술이 생생하다. ● 생생하게, 자세하게 부사 ❑ 여기에 전체 이야기에 대한 확실한 증거가 생생하게 드러나 있다. ■ 형용사 도안의, 그래픽의 ❑ 회화 및 시각 예술 작품 ■ 불가산명사 도안, 그래픽 ❑ 그래픽을 전문으로 하는 컴퓨터 생산업체 ■ 가산명사 도안, 그래픽 아트 작품 ❑ 농무부는 오늘 구 심벌을 대체할 새 도안을 공개했다.

graph|ic de|sign N-UNCOUNT **Graphic design** is the art of designing advertisements, magazines, and books by combining pictures and words. ❑ *...the graphic design department.*

불가산명사 그래픽 디자인 ❑ 그래픽 디자인부

graph|ite /ˈɡræfaɪt/ N-UNCOUNT **Graphite** is a soft black substance that is a form of carbon. It is used in pencils and electrical equipment. →see **drawing**

불가산명사 흑연

graph pa|per N-UNCOUNT **Graph paper** is paper that has small squares printed on it so that you can use it for drawing graphs.

불가산명사 모눈종이

grap|ple /ˈɡræpəl/ (**grapples, grappling, grappled**) ■ V-I If you **grapple with** a problem or difficulty, you try hard to solve it. ❑ *The economy is just one of several critical problems the country is grappling with.* ■ V-RECIP If you **grapple with** someone, you take hold of them and struggle with them, as part of a fight. You can also say that two people **grapple**. ❑ *He was grappling with an alligator in a lagoon.*

■ 자동사 붙들고 애쓰다, 씨름하다 ❑ 경제는 그 나라가 해결을 위해 씨름하고 있는 몇 가지 중대한 문제 중 하나에 불과하다. ■ 상호동사 맞붙어 싸우다, 격투하다 ❑ 그는 늪에서 악어와 사투를 벌이고 있었다.

grasp /ɡræsp, BRIT ɡrɑːsp/ (**grasps, grasping, grasped**) ■ V-T/V-I If you **grasp** something, you take it in your hand and hold it very firmly. ❑ *He grasped both my hands.* ■ N-SING A **grasp** is a very firm hold or grip. ❑ *His hand was taken in a warm, firm grasp.* ■ N-SING If you say that something is **in** someone's **grasp**, you disapprove of the fact that they possess or control it. If something slips **from** your **grasp**, you lose it or lose control of it. ❑ *The people in your grasp are not guests, they are hostages.* ❑ *She allowed victory to slip from her grasp.* ■ V-T If you **grasp** something that is complicated or difficult to understand, you understand it. ❑ *The Government has not yet grasped the seriousness of the crisis.* ■ N-SING A **grasp of** something is an understanding of it. ❑ *They have a good grasp of foreign languages.* ■ PHRASE If you say that something is **within** someone's **grasp**, you mean that it is very likely that they will achieve it. ❑ *Peace is now within our grasp.*

■ 타동사/자동사 붙잡다, 움켜잡다 ❑ 그는 내 두 손을 꽉 잡았다. ■ 단수명사 꽉 잡기 ❑ 그의 손을 따뜻하게 꽉 잡아주었다. ■ 단수명사 손아귀; 장악, 통제 ❑ 당신의 통제 하에 있는 사람들은 손님이 아니라 인질이다. ❑ 그녀는 승리를 놓쳐 버렸다. ■ 타동사 파악하다 ❑ 정부는 아직 위기의 심각성을 파악하지 못하고 있다. ■ 단수명사 이해, 파악 ❑ 그들은 외국어를 잘 한다. ■ 구 손에 잡힐 듯한, 실사 가능한 ❑ 평화는 이제 우리 손에 잡힐 듯하다.

grass ♦♢♢ /ɡræs, BRIT ɡrɑːs/ (**grasses, grassing, grassed**) ■ N-MASS **Grass** is a very common plant consisting of large numbers of thin, spiky, green leaves that cover the surface of the ground. ❑ *Small things stirred in the grass around the tent.* ■ V-I If you say that one person **grasses on** another, the first person tells the police or other authorities about something criminal or wrong which the second person has done. [BRIT, INFORMAL, DISAPPROVAL] ❑ *His wife wants him to grass on the members of his own gang.* ● PHRASAL VERB **Grass up** means the same as **grass**. ❑ *How many of them are going to grass up their own kids to the police?* ■ N-COUNT A **grass** is someone who tells the police or other authorities about criminal activities that they know about. [BRIT, INFORMAL, DISAPPROVAL] ❑ *I am worried that the label of being a grass will remain with me through the rest of my career.* ■ PHRASE If you say **the grass is greener** somewhere else, you mean that other people's situations always seem better or more attractive than your own, but may not really be so. ❑ *He was very happy with us but wanted to see if the grass was greener elsewhere.*

■ 물질명사 잔디, 풀숲 ❑ 텐트 주위의 풀숲에서 작은 물체들이 움직였다. ■ 자동사 밀고하다 [영국영어, 비격식체, 탐탁찮음] ❑ 부인은 남편이 자신이 속한 폭력 단체 단원들을 경찰에 밀고하기를 원한다. ● 구동사 -를 밀고하다 ❑ 그들 중 몇 명이나 자기 아이들을 경찰에 밀고하겠는가? ■ 가산명사 밀고자 [영국영어, 비격식체, 탐탁찮음] ❑ 나는 밀고자라는 꼬리표가 내 남은 사회생활 내내 나에게 붙어 다닐까 우려된다. ■ 구 남의 떡이 커 보이다 ❑ 그는 우리와 함께 일하는 데 아주 만족했으나 혹시 더 나은 곳이 있는지 알고 싶어했다.

grass|hopper /ɡræshɒpər, BRIT ɡrɑːs-/ (**grasshoppers**) N-COUNT A **grasshopper** is an insect with long back legs that jumps high into the air and makes a high, vibrating sound.

가산명사 메뚜기

grass|roots /ɡræsruːts, BRIT ɡrɑːs-/ N-PLURAL The **grassroots** of an organization or movement are the ordinary people who form the main part of it, rather than its leaders. ❏ *You have to join the party at grassroots level from what I understand.*

복수명사 민초, 일반 대중 ❏ 내가 알고 있는 바로는 당신은 평당원 수준에서 입당해야 한다.

grassy /ɡræsi/, BRIT ɡrɑːsi/ (**grassier, grassiest**) ADJ A **grassy** area of land is covered in grass. ❏ *The buildings are half-hidden behind grassy banks.*

형용사 풀이 무성한 ❏ 건물들은 풀이 무성한 둑 뒤쯤 가려져 있다.

grate /ɡreɪt/ (**grates, grating, grated**) ◼ N-COUNT A **grate** is a framework of metal bars in a fireplace, which holds the coal or wood. ❏ *A wood fire burned in the grate.* ◻ V-T If you **grate** food such as cheese or carrots, you rub it over a metal tool called a grater so that the food is cut into very small pieces. ❏ *Grate the cheese into a mixing bowl.* ◼ V-I When something **grates**, it rubs against something else making a harsh, unpleasant sound. ❏ *His chair grated as he got to his feet.* ◼ V-I If something such as someone's behavior **grates on** you or **grates**, it makes you feel annoyed. ❏ *His manner always grated on me.*

◼ 가산명사 (벽난로의) 쇠살대 ❏ 쇠살대 안에서 장작불이 탔다. ◻ 타동사 (강판에 음식을) 갈다 ❏ 치즈를 갈아서 반죽 그릇에 넣으시오. ◼ 자동사 삐걱거리다 ❏ 그가 일어나자 의자가 삐걱거렸다. ◼ 자동사 (신경에) 거슬리다 ❏ 그의 태도가 항상 내 신경에 거슬렸다.

grate|ful /ɡreɪtfəl/ ADJ If you are **grateful for** something that someone has given you or done for you, you have warm, friendly feelings towards them and wish to thank them. ❏ *She was grateful to him for being so good to her.* ● **grate|ful|ly** ADV [ADV with v] ❏ *"That's kind of you, Sally," Claire said gratefully.*

형용사 고맙게 여기는, 감사하는 ❏ 그녀는 자기에게 잘 해 준 데 대해서 그에게 고마워했다. ● 감사하여 부사 ❏ "고마워, 샐리"라고 클레어가 감사하며 말했다.

Thesaurus   *grateful의 참조어*

ADJ.   appreciative, thankful; (ant.) ungrateful

---

grat|er /ɡreɪtər/ (**graters**) N-COUNT A **grater** is a kitchen tool which has a rough surface that you use for cutting food into very small pieces.

가산명사 강판

Word Link   *grat ≈ pleasing : con*gratulate, *grat*ify, *grat*itude

---

grati|fy /ɡrætɪfaɪ/ (**gratifies, gratifying, gratified**) ◼ V-T If you **are gratified** by something, it gives you pleasure or satisfaction. [FORMAL] ❏ *Mr. Dambar was gratified by his response.* ● **grati|fy|ing** ADJ ❏ *We took a chance and we've won. It's very gratifying.* ● **grati|fi|ca|tion** N-UNCOUNT ❏ *He is waiting for them to recognise him and eventually they do, much to his gratification.* ◻ V-T If you **gratify** your own or another person's desire, you do what is necessary to please yourself or them. [FORMAL] ❏ *We gratified our friend's curiosity.* ● **grati|fi|ca|tion** N-UNCOUNT ❏ *...sexual gratification.*

◼ 타동사 만족해하다 [격식체] ❏ 댐바 씨는 그의 대답에 만족했다. ● 유쾌한, 만족스러운 형용사 ❏ 우리는 위험을 무릅썼고, 그리고 이겼다. 아주 유쾌했다. ● 만족 불가산명사 ❏ 그는 그들이 자기를 알아보기를 기다리고 있고 마침내 만족스럽게도 그들이 알아본다. ◻ 타동사 만족시키다 [격식체] ❏ 우리는 우리 친구의 호기심을 만족시켜 주었다. ● 만족, 희열 불가산명사 ❏ 성적 만족

gra|tis /ɡrætɪs/ ADV If something is done or provided **gratis**, it does not have to be paid for. [ADV after v] ❏ *David gives the first consultation gratis.* ● ADJ **Gratis** is also an adjective. ❏ *What I did for you was free, gratis, and an adjective.*

부사 무료로 ❏ 데이비드는 첫 상담을 무료로 해 준다. ● 무료의 형용사 ❏ 너를 위해 내가 해 준 것은 공짜야, 무료지, 알겠어?

grati|tude /ɡrætɪtud, BRIT ɡrætɪtjuːd/ N-UNCOUNT **Gratitude** is the state of feeling grateful. ❏ *I wish to express my gratitude to Kathy Davis for her immense practical help.*

불가산명사 감사, 사의 ❏ 저는 캐시 데이비스의 막대한 실제적 도움에 대해 그분께 사의를 표하고 싶습니다.

gra|tui|tous /ɡrətuɪtəs, BRIT ɡrətjuːɪtəs/ ADJ If you describe something as **gratuitous**, you mean that it is unnecessary, and often harmful or upsetting. ❏ *There's too much crime and gratuitous violence on TV.* ● **gra|tui|tous|ly** ADV ❏ *They wanted me to change the title to something less gratuitously offensive.*

형용사 불필요한 ❏ 텔레비전에 너무 많은 범죄와 불필요한 폭력이 방영된다. ● 불필요하게, 쓸데없이 부사 ❏ 그들은 내가 쓸데없이 거슬리는 점이 좀 덜한 제목으로 바꾸기를 원했다.

gra|tu|ity /ɡrətuɪti, BRIT ɡrətjuːɪti/ (**gratuities**) N-COUNT A **gratuity** is a gift of money to someone who has done something for you. [FORMAL] ❏ *The porter expects a gratuity.*

가산명사 사례금, 팁 [격식체] ❏ 짐꾼은 팁을 기대한다.

grave ♦◇◇ (**graves, graver, gravest**)

Pronounced /ɡreɪv/, except for meaning ◼, when it is pronounced /ɡrɑːv/.

◼의 의미일 때는 /ɡrɑːv/로 발음되고, 그 외에는 /ɡreɪv/로 발음된다.

◼ N-COUNT A **grave** is a place where a dead person is buried. ❏ *They used to visit her grave twice a year.* ◻ ADJ A **grave** event or situation is very serious, important, and worrying. ❏ *He said that the situation in his country is very grave.* ● **grave|ly** ADV ❏ *They had gravely impaired the credibility of the government.* ◼ ADJ A **grave** person is quiet and serious in their appearance or behavior. ❏ *Anxiously, she examined his unusually grave face.* ● **grave|ly** ADV ❏ *"I think I've covered that business more than adequately," he said gravely.* ◼ ADJ In some languages such as French, a **grave** accent is a symbol that is placed over a vowel in a word to show how the vowel is pronounced. For example, the word "mère" has a grave accent over the first "e." [ADJ n] ◼ PHRASE If you say that someone who is dead would **turn** or **turn over in** their **grave at** something that is happening now, you mean that they would be very shocked or upset by it, if they were alive. ❏ *Darwin must be turning in his grave at the thought of what is being perpetrated in his name.*

◼ 가산명사 무덤, 묘 ❏ 그들은 일년에 두 번 그녀의 묘를 찾곤 했다. ◻ 형용사 중대한, 심각한 ❏ 그는 자기 나라의 상황이 매우 심각하다고 말했다. ● 심각하게 부사 ❏ 그들은 정부의 신용을 심각하게 손상시켰다. ◼ 형용사 근엄한, 심각한 ❏ 걱정스럽게 그녀는 평소와 달리 심각한 그의 얼굴을 유심히 보았다. ● 엄숙하게 부사 ❏ "나는 그 일에 대해서는 충분하고도 남을 만큼 논의했다고 생각한다."라고 그는 엄숙하게 말했다. ◼ 형용사 저 악센트의 ◼ 구 (고인이 무덤 속에서) 탄식하다 ❏ 지금 자기 이름으로 행해지는 일들을 보면 다윈이 무덤 속에서 탄식할 것임에 틀림없다.

grav|el /ɡrævᵊl/ N-UNCOUNT **Gravel** consists of very small stones. It is often used to make paths. ❏ *...a gravel path leading to the front door.*

불가산명사 자갈 ❏ 현관까지 이어진 자갈길

grave|yard /ɡreɪvyɑrd/ (**graveyards**) N-COUNT A **graveyard** is an area of land, sometimes near a church, where dead people are buried. ❏ *They made their way to a graveyard to pay their traditional respects to the dead.*

가산명사 묘지 ❏ 그들은 망자에게 전통적인 예를 드리기 위해 묘지에 갔다.

gravi|tate /ɡrævɪteɪt/ (**gravitates, gravitating, gravitated**) V-I If you **gravitate toward** a particular place, thing, or activity, you are attracted by it and go to it or get involved in it. ❏ *Traditionally young Asians in Britain have gravitated toward medicine, law and engineering.*

자동사 -에 끌리다 ❏ 전통적으로 영국에 있는 아시아 젊은이들은 의학, 법학, 공학 분야에 관심을 가져왔다.

gravi|ta|tion|al /ɡrævɪteɪʃənᵊl/ ADJ **Gravitational** means relating to or resulting from the force of gravity. [TECHNICAL] [ADJ n] ❏ *If a spacecraft travels faster than 11 km a second, it escapes the earth's gravitational pull.* →see **tide**

형용사 중력의 [과학 기술] ❏ 우주선이 초속 11킬로 이상으로 비행하면 지구의 인력을 벗어날 수 있다.

grav|ity /ɡrævɪti/ ◼ N-UNCOUNT **Gravity** is the force which causes things to drop to the ground. ❏ *Arrows would continue to fly forward forever in a straight line were it not for gravity, which brings them down to earth.* ◻ N-UNCOUNT The **gravity of**

◼ 불가산명사 중력 ❏ 화살은 땅으로 끌어내리는 중력이 없다면 영원히 직선으로 계속 날아갈 것이다. ◻ 불가산명사 중대함 ❏ 대통령은 폭력으로 권력을

a
b
c
d
e
f
g
h
i
j
k
l
m
n
o
p
q
r
s
t
u
v
w
x
y
z

a situation or event is its extreme importance or seriousness. ❑ *The president said those who grab power through violence deserve punishment which matches the gravity of their crime.* ❸ N-UNCOUNT The **gravity** of someone's behavior or speech is the extremely serious way in which they behave or speak. ❑ *There was an appealing gravity to everything she said.* →see **flight**, **moon**

잡는 사람들은 당연히 죄의 중대함에 합당한 벌을 받아야 한다고 말했다. ❸ 불가산명사 진지함 ❑ 그녀가 말한 모든 것에는 마음에 와 닿는 진지함이 있었다.

gra|vy /ɡreɪvi/ (**gravies**) N-MASS **Gravy** is a sauce made from the juices that come from meat when it cooks.

물질명사 육즙 소스, 그레이비

gray ◆◇◇ /ɡreɪ/ (**grayer**, **grayest**) [BRIT **grey**] ❶ COLOR **Gray** is the color of ashes or of clouds on a rainy day. ❑ *...a gray suit.* ❷ ADJ If the weather is **gray**, there are many clouds in the sky and the light is dull. ❑ *It was a gray, wet April Sunday.* ❸ ADJ If you describe a situation as **gray**, you mean that it is dull, unpleasant, or difficult. ❑ *Brazilians look gloomily forward to a New Year that even the president admits will be gray and cheerless.* ❹ ADJ If you describe someone or something as **gray**, you think that they are boring and unattractive, and very similar to other things or other people. [DISAPPROVAL] ❑ *Mils is one of those little gray men you find in every company.*

[영국영어 grey] ❶ 색채어 회색 ❑ 회색 정장 한 벌 ❷ 형용사 흐린, 우중충한 ❑ 우중충하고 비 내리는 4월의 일요일이었다. ❸ 형용사 음울한 ❑ 브라질 사람들은 심지어 대통령까지도 음울하고 쓸쓸한 것이리라고 말한 새해를 침울하게 기다리고 있다. ❹ 형용사 따분한, 눈에 띄지 않는 [탐탁찮음] ❑ 밀스는 어떤 회사에서나 볼 수 있는 작고 눈에 띄지 않는 그런 남자이다.

Word Partnership   gray의 연어

N.	gray **eyes**, gray **hair**, **shades of** gray, gray **sky**, gray **suit** ❶
V.	**go** gray, **turn** gray ❶

gray area (**gray areas**) [BRIT **grey area**] N-COUNT If you refer to something as a **gray area**, you mean that it is unclear, for example because nobody is sure how to deal with it or who is responsible for it, or it falls between two separate categories of things. ❑ *At the moment, the law on compensation is very much a gray area.*

[영국영어 grey area] 가산명사 애매한 부분, 애매한 상황 ❑ 현재 보상에 관한 법이 아주 애매한 부분이다.

gray mar|ket (**gray markets**) [BRIT **grey market**] ❶ N-SING **Gray market** goods are bought unofficially and then sold to customers at lower prices than usual. [BUSINESS] ❑ *Gray-market perfumes and toiletries are now commonly sold by mail.* ❷ N-SING **Gray market** shares are sold to investors before they have been officially issued. [BUSINESS] ❑ *An unofficial gray market in the shares has been operating for about two weeks.*

[영국영어 grey market] ❶ 단수명사 회색시장 (암시장에 가까운 시장) [경제] ❑ 회색시장의 향수와 화장품이 이제 흔히 우편 판매된다. ❷ 단수명사 (주식시장의) 회색시장 [경제] ❑ 비공식 주식 회색시장이 약 2주 동안 열리고 있다.

graze /ɡreɪz/ (**grazes**, **grazing**, **grazed**) ❶ V-T/V-I When animals **graze** or **are grazed**, they eat the grass or other plants that are growing in a particular place. You can also say that a field **is grazed** by animals. ❑ *Five cows graze serenely around a massive oak.* ❑ *Several horses grazed the meadowland.* ❷ V-T If you **graze** a part of your body, you injure your skin by scraping against something. ❑ *I had grazed my knees a little.* ❸ N-COUNT A **graze** is a small wound caused by scraping against something. ❑ *Although cuts and grazes are not usually very serious, they can be quite painful.* ❹ V-T If something **grazes** another thing, it touches that thing lightly as it passes by. ❑ *A bullet had grazed his arm.*

❶ 타동사/자동사 (풀을) 뜯어먹다; 방목되다 ❑ 젖소 다섯 마리가 커다란 떡갈나무 주위에서 평화롭게 풀을 뜯고 있다. ❑ 말 몇 마리가 목초지에 방목되어 있었다. ❷ 타동사 찰과상을 입다, (피부가) 쓸리다 ❑ 나는 무릎에 가벼운 찰과상을 입었다. ❸ 가산명사 찰과상 ❑ 베인 상처와 찰과상은 대체로 그리 심각한 것이 아니지만 많이 아플 수는 있다. ❹ 타동사 스치다 ❑ 총알이 그의 팔을 스쳤다.

GRE /dʒi ɑr i/ N-PROPER The **GRE** is the examination which you have to take to be admitted to graduate schools in the United States. **GRE** is an abbreviation for "Graduate Record Examination."

고유명사 지알이 (미국 대학원 진학을 위한 시험)

grease /ɡris/ (**greases**, **greasing**, **greased**) ❶ N-UNCOUNT **Grease** is a thick, oily substance which is put on the moving parts of cars and other machines in order to make them work smoothly. ❑ *...grease-stained hands.* ❷ V-T If you **grease** a part of a car, machine, or device, you put grease on it in order to make it work smoothly. ❑ *I greased front and rear hubs and adjusted the brakes.* ❸ N-UNCOUNT **Grease** is an oily substance that is produced by your skin. ❑ *His hair is thick with grease.* ❹ N-UNCOUNT **Grease** is animal fat that is produced by cooking meat. You can use **grease** for cooking. ❑ *He could smell the bacon grease.* ❺ V-T If you **grease** a dish, you put a small amount of fat or oil around the inside of it in order to prevent food sticking to it during cooking. ❑ *Grease two sturdy baking sheets and heat the oven to 400 degrees.*

❶ 불가산명사 그리스, 윤활유 ❑ 그리스로 더러워진 손 ❷ 타동사 -에 그리스를 치다 ❑ 나는 앞바퀴와 뒷바퀴 허브에 그리스를 치고 브레이크를 조정했다. ❸ 불가산명사 기름기, 지방분 ❑ 그의 머리는 기름기가 많다. ❹ 불가산명사 고기기름 ❑ 그는 베이컨 기름 냄새를 맡을 수 있었다. ❺ 타동사 -에 기름을 두르다 ❑ 단단한 구이판 두 개에 기름을 두르고 오븐을 400도로 가열하시오.

greasy /ɡrisi, -zi/ (**greasier**, **greasiest**) ADJ Something that is **greasy** has grease on it or in it. ❑ *He propped his elbows upon a greasy counter.*

형용사 기름기 있는 ❑ 그는 기름기 있는 카운터 위에 대고 팔꿈치를 괴었다.

great ◆◆◆ /ɡreɪt/ (**greater**, **greatest**, **greats**) ❶ ADJ You use **great** to describe something that is very large. **Great** is more formal than **big**. [ADJ n] ❑ *The room had a great bay window.* ❷ ADJ **Great** means large in amount or degree. ❑ *Benjamin Britten did not live to a great age.* ❸ ADJ You use **great** to describe something that is important, famous, or exciting. ❑ *...the great cultural achievements of the past.* ● **great|ness** N-UNCOUNT ❑ *A nation must take certain risks to achieve greatness.* ❹ ADJ You can describe someone who is successful and famous for their actions, knowledge, or skill as **great**. ❑ *Wes Hall was once one of the West Indies' great cricketers.* ● **great|ness** N-UNCOUNT ❑ *Abraham Lincoln achieved greatness.* ❺ N-PLURAL The **greats** in a particular subject or field of activity are the people who have been most successful or famous in it. [JOURNALISM] ❑ *...all the greats of Hollywood.* ❻ ADJ If you describe someone or something as **great**, you approve of them or admire them. [INFORMAL, APPROVAL] ❑ *Arturo has this great place in Cazadero.* ❑ *They're a great bunch of guys.* ❼ ADJ If you **feel great**, you feel very healthy, energetic, and enthusiastic. [feel ADJ] ❑ *I feel just great.* ❽ ADJ You use **great** in order to emphasize the size or degree of a characteristic or quality. [EMPHASIS] ❑ *...a great big Italian wedding.* ❾ EXCLAM You say **great** in order to emphasize that you are pleased or enthusiastic about something. [FEELINGS] ❑ *Oh great! That'll be good for Fergus.*

❶ 형용사 큰, 대- ❑ 그 방은 큰 퇴창이 있었다. ❷ 형용사 많은, 상당한 ❑ 벤자민 브리튼은 장수하지 않았다. ❸ 형용사 위대한, 저명한, 굉장한 ❑ 과거의 위대한 문화적 위업 ● 위대한, 위대한 업적 불가산명사 ❑ 국가가 위대한 업적을 이루기 위해서는 어느 정도 위험을 감수해야 한다. ❹ 형용사 탁월한, 위대한 ❑ 웨스 홀은 한때 서인도 제도의 탁월한 크리켓 선수 중 한 명이었다. ● 위대한 불가산명사 ❑ 에이브러햄 링컨은 위대해졌다. ❺ 복수명사 명사들, 위인들 [언론] ❑ 할리우드의 모든 명사들 ❻ 형용사 대단한 [비격식체, 마음에 듦] ❑ 아르투로는 이 대단한 집을 카자데로에 가지고 있다. ❑ 그들은 대단한 녀석들이다. ❼ 형용사 아주 기분이 좋은 ❑ 나는 아주 기분이 좋다. ❽ 형용사 대단한, 굉장한 [강조] ❑ 아주 성대한 이태리식 결혼 ❾ 감탄사 좋아! [감정 개입] ❑ 아, 좋아! 퍼거스에게 괜찮을 것 같아.

Great, **big**, and **large** are all used to talk about size. In general, **great** is more formal than **large**, and **large** is more formal than **big**. You normally use **great** to emphasize the importance of someone or something. ❑ *...the great English architect, Inigo Jones.* However, you can also use **great** to suggest that something is impressive because of its size. ❑ *The great bird of prey was a dark smudge against the sun.* **Big** and **large** are normally used to describe objects, but you can also use **big** to suggest that something is important or

great, big, large는 모두 크기를 말할 때 쓴다. 일반적으로 large가 big보다, great이 large보다 더 격식체이다. 사람이나 사물의 중요성을 강조할 때는 보통 great을 쓴다. great은 대개 사물이 그 크기 때문에 인상적임을 시사할 때도 쓸 수 있다. ❑ 그 거대한 맹금은 햇빛을 배경으로 하나의 흐릿한 검은

impressive. ❑ *...his influence over the big advertisers.* You can use **large** or **great**, but not **big**, to describe amounts. ❑ *...a large amount of blood on the floor....the coming of tourists in great numbers.* Both **great** and **big** can be used to emphasize the intensity of something, although **great** is more formal. ❑ *It gives me great pleasure to welcome you... Most of them act like big fools.*

점처럼 보였다. big과 large는 보통 사물을 묘사할 때 쓰지만, big은 무엇이 중요하거나 인상적임을 시사할 때에도 쓴다. ❑ ...주요 광고주들에 대한 그의 영향력. great나 large 때는 잴나 great은 쓸 수 있지만 big은 못 쓴다. ❑ ...바닥 위의 많은 양의 피.... 수많은 여행객의 방문. great와 big은 어떤 것의 강도를 강조를 쓸 수 있는데 great이 더 격식체이다. ❑ 이렇게 환영 인사를 드리게 되어 정말 기쁩니다... 그들 대부분은 엄청난 바보처럼 행동한다.

Thesaurus　　　great의 참조어

ADJ.　　enormous, immense, vast; *(ant.)* small **1 2**
　　　　distinguished, famous, important, remarkable, successful **3 4**

---

great|ly /ɡreɪtli/ ADV You use **greatly** to emphasize the degree or extent of something. [FORMAL, EMPHASIS] ❑ *People would benefit greatly from a pollution-free vehicle.*

부사 크게, 매우 [격식체, 강조] ❑ 사람들은 무공해 자동차로 큰 혜택을 볼 것이다.

greed /ɡriːd/ N-UNCOUNT **Greed** is the desire to have more of something, such as food or money, than is necessary or fair. ❑ *...an insatiable greed for personal power.*

불가산명사 탐욕 ❑ 개인 권력에 대한 끝없는 탐욕

greed|y /ɡriːdi/ (**greedier**, **greediest**) ADJ If you describe someone as **greedy**, you mean that they want to have more of something such as food or money than is necessary or fair. ❑ *He attacked greedy bosses for awarding themselves big raises.* ● **greed|ily** ADV [ADV with v] ❑ *Livy ate the pasties greedily and with huge enjoyment.*

형용사 탐욕스러운, 게걸스러운 ❑ 그는 탐욕스러운 사장들이 자기들의 수당을 크게 올린 것에 대해 비난했다. ● 게걸스럽게, 탐욕스럽게 부사 ❑ 라이비는 고기 파이를 게걸스럽고 아주 즐거워하며 먹었다.

green ♦♦♦ /ɡriːn/ (**greens**, **greener**, **greenest**) **1** COLOR **Green** is the color of grass or leaves. ❑ *Yellow and green together make a pale green.* **2** ADJ A place that is **green** is covered with grass, plants, and trees and not with houses or factories. ❑ *Cairo has only thirteen square centimeters of green space for each inhabitant.* ● **green|ness** N-UNCOUNT ❑ *...the lush greenness of the river valleys.* **3** ADJ **Green** issues and political movements relate to or are concerned with the protection of the environment. [ADJ n] ❑ *The power of the Green movement in Germany has made that country a leader in the drive to recycle more waste materials.* **4** ADJ If you say that someone or something is **green**, you mean that they harm the environment as little as possible. ❑ *...trying to persuade governments to adopt greener policies.* ● **green|ness** N-UNCOUNT ❑ *A Swiss company offers to help environmental investors by sending teams round factories to ascertain their greenness.* **5** N-COUNT **Greens** are members of green political movements. ❑ *The Greens see themselves as a radical alternative to the two major British political parties.* **6** N-COUNT A **green** is a smooth, flat area of grass around a hole on a golf course. ❑ *...the 18th green.* **7** N-COUNT A **green** is an area of land covered with grass, especially in a town or in the middle of a village. ❑ *...the village green.* **8** N-IN-NAMES **Green** is used in the names of places that contain or used to contain an area of grass. [n N] ❑ *...Bethnal Green.* **9** ADJ If you say that someone is **green**, you mean that they have had very little experience of life or a particular job. ❑ *He was a young lad, very green, very immature.* **10** PHRASE If someone has **a green thumb**, they are very good at gardening and their plants grow well. [AM; BRIT **green fingers**] ❑ *She has an unbelievably green thumb, she can grow anything.* **11** to **give** someone **the green light** →see **light** →see **rainbow**

1 색채어 초록빛, 녹색 ❑ 노란색과 초록색을 섞으면 연녹색이 된다. **2** 형용사 녹지의 ❑ 카이로에는 주민 1인당 13평방 센티미터의 녹지 공간밖에 없다. ● 녹음 불가산명사 ❑ 강가 계곡의 무성한 녹음 **3** 형용사 환경 보호의 ❑ 독일은 자국의 강력한 환경 보호 운동에 힘입어 더 많은 폐기물의 재활용 추진 노력에 있어 선도자가 되었다. **4** 형용사 환경 친화적인 ❑ 더 친환경적인 정책을 채택하도록 정부를 설득하려는 ● 환경 친화, 친환경 불가산명사 ❑ 한 스위스 회사가 공장의 환경 친화도를 확인하도록 여러 공장에 팀을 보냄으로써 친환경적 투자자들을 돕겠다고 제안한다. **5** 가산명사 녹색당원 ❑ 녹색당원들은 스스로를 영국의 두 주요 정당에 대한 급진파라고 여긴다. **6** 가산명사 퍼팅 그린 (홀 주변의 잔디) ❑ 18번째 퍼팅 그린 **7** 가산명사 녹지 ❑ 마을 녹지 **8** 이름명사 녹지대 ❑ 베스날 녹지대 **9** 형용사 애송이의, 풋내기의 ❑ 그는 풋내기이자 아주 미숙한 젊은 청년이었다. **10** 구 원예의 재능 [미국영어; 영국영어 green fingers] ❑ 그녀는 원예에 믿기지 어려운 재능이 있으며 무엇이든 기를 수 있다.

green belt (**green belts**) N-VAR A **green belt** is an area of land with fields or parks around a town or city, where people are not allowed to build houses or factories by law. ❑ *What is the point of a green belt if it is going to be built on regardless?*

가산명사 또는 불가산명사 (도시 주변의) 녹지대, 그린벨트 ❑ 아무 상관없이 그린벨트에 건물을 세운다면 그린벨트가 무슨 의미가 있습니까?

green card (**green cards**) N-COUNT A **green card** is a document showing that someone who is not a citizen of the United States has permission to live and work there. ❑ *Nicollette married Harry so she could get a green card.*

가산명사 (미국의) 영주권 ❑ 니콜레트는 해리와 결혼해서 영주권을 받을 수 있었다.

An alien resident may apply to stay in the US through the help of his employer or family. The **green card** identifies a legal resident and permits the cardholder to apply for citizenship after 5 years (in the case of singles) or 3 years (if they are married to an American).

외국인 체류자도 고용주나 가족의 도움으로 미국 거주를 신청할 수 있다. green card(외국인 거주 허가증)는 합법적 체류자임을 밝혀주며, 이 허가증 소지자는 독신자의 경우는 5년 후, 미국인과 결혼한 경우에는 3년 후에 시민권을 신청할 수 있다.

---

green|ery /ɡriːnəri/ N-UNCOUNT Plants that make a place look attractive are referred to as **greenery**. ❑ *They have ordered a bit of greenery to brighten up the new wing at Guy's Hospital.*

불가산명사 관상식물 ❑ 그들은 가이스 병원의 새 부속 건물을 화사하게 만들기 위해 관상식물을 좀 주문했다.

green|field /ɡriːnfiːld/ ADJ **Greenfield** is used to refer to land that has not been built on before. [ADJ n] ❑ *The Government has ruled out the building of a new airport on a greenfield site.*

형용사 (미개발) 전원 지역의 ❑ 정부는 전원 지역에 새 공항을 건설하려던 계획을 백지화했다.

green|house /ɡriːnhaʊs/ (**greenhouses**) **1** N-COUNT A **greenhouse** is a glass building in which you grow plants that need to be protected from bad weather. **2** ADJ **Greenhouse** means relating to or causing the greenhouse effect. [ADJ n] ❑ *...controls on greenhouse emissions.*

1 가산명사 온실 **2** 형용사 온실 효과를 일으키는 ❑ 온실 효과를 일으키는 배출 가스에 대한 규제

green|house ef|fect N-SING The **greenhouse effect** is the problem caused by increased quantities of gases such as carbon dioxide in the air. These gases trap the heat from the sun, and cause a gradual rise in the temperature of the Earth's atmosphere. ❑ *...gases that contribute to the greenhouse effect.* →see **Word Web: greenhouse efffect**

단수명사 온실 효과 ❑ 지구 대기의 온실 효과를 일으키는 가스들

green|house gas (**greenhouse gases**) N-VAR **Greenhouse gases** are the gases which are responsible for causing the greenhouse effect. The main greenhouse gas is carbon dioxide.

가산명사 또는 불가산명사 이산화탄소

green|mail /ɡriːnmeɪl/ N-UNCOUNT **Greenmail** is when a company buys enough shares in another company to threaten a takeover and makes a profit if the other company buys back its shares at a higher price. [mainly AM, BUSINESS] ❑ *Family control would prevent any hostile takeover or greenmail attempt.*

불가산명사 주식의 매점 [주로 미국영어, 경제] ❑ 친족 지배는 어떠한 적대적 경영권 인수나 주식 매점 시도도 방지할 것이다.

greet /ɡriːt/ (**greets**, **greeting**, **greeted**) **1** V-T When you **greet** someone, you say "Hello" or shake hands with them. ❑ *She liked to be home to greet Steve when he came in from school.* **2** V-T If something is **greeted** in a particular way, people react to it in that way. [usu passive] ❑ *The European Court's decision has been greeted with dismay by fishermen.*

1 타동사 인사하다 ❑ 그녀는 스티브가 학교에서 돌아올 때 그를 맞이하기 위해 집에 있기를 좋아했다. **2** 타동사 받아들여지다 ❑ 유럽 재판소의 결정을 어부들은 실망스럽게 받아들였다.

Word Web — greenhouse effect

Over the past 100 years, the global average **temperature** has risen dramatically. Researchers believe that this **global warming** comes from added **carbon dioxide** and other **gases** in the **atmosphere**. With **water vapor**, they form a shield that holds in heat. It acts a little like the glass in a greenhouse. Scientists call this the **greenhouse effect**. Some natural causes of this warming may include increased **solar radiation** and tiny changes in the earth's orbit. However, human activities, such as **deforestation**, and the use of **fossil fuels** seem to play a much more important role.

Sun

Some heat gets out.

Solar radiation comes in.

Some heat can't get out.

Heat is absorbed by greenhouse gases.

---

greet|ing /gríːtɪŋ/ (**greetings**) N-VAR A **greeting** is something friendly that you say or do when you meet someone. ❑ *His greeting was familiar and friendly.* ❑ *They exchanged greetings.*

가산명사 또는 불가산명사 인사 ❑ 그의 인사는 친근하고 다정했다. ❑ 그들은 인사를 나누었다.

gre|nade /grɪneɪd/ (**grenades**) N-COUNT A **grenade** or a **hand grenade** is a small bomb that can be thrown by hand. ❑ *A hand grenade was thrown at an army patrol.*

가산명사 수류탄 ❑ 수류탄 한 발이 군 순찰대에 던져졌다.

grew /gruː/ **Grew** is the past tense of **grow**.

grow의 과거

grey /greɪ/ →see **gray**

grey|hound /gréɪhaʊnd/ (**greyhounds**) N-COUNT A **greyhound** is a dog with a thin body and long thin legs, which can run very fast. Greyhounds sometimes run in races and people bet on them. ❑ *...his love of greyhound racing.*

가산명사 그레이하운드 ❑ 그의 그레이하운드 경주 애호

grid /grɪd/ (**grids**) ■ N-COUNT A **grid** is something which is in a pattern of straight lines that cross over each other, forming squares. On maps the grid is used to help you find a particular thing or place. ❑ *...a grid of ironwork.* ❑ *...a grid of narrow streets.* ■ N-COUNT A **grid** is a network of wires and cables by which sources of power, such as electricity, are distributed throughout a country or area. ❑ *...breakdowns in communications and electric power grids.* ■ N-COUNT **The grid** or **the starting grid** is the starting line on a car-racing track. ❑ *The Ferrari driver was starting second on the grid.*

■ 가산명사 격자 모양 ❑ 석쇠 ❑ 격자 모양으로 얽힌 좁은 길들 ❷ 가산명사 송전선망 ❑ 통신과 전기 송전선망의 고장 ❸ 가산명사 (자동차 경주장의) 출발선 ❑ 페라리 레이서가 출발선에서 두 번째로 출발하고 있었다.

grid|lock /grɪdlɒk/ ■ N-UNCOUNT **Gridlock** is the situation that exists when all the roads in a particular place are so full of vehicles that none of them can move. ❑ *The streets are wedged solid with the chaos of poorly regulated parking and near-constant traffic gridlock.* ■ N-UNCOUNT You can use **gridlock** to refer to a situation in an argument or dispute when neither side is prepared to give in, so no agreement can be reached. ❑ *He agreed that these policies will lead to gridlock in the future.* →see **traffic**

■ 불가산명사 교통 정체, 교통마비 상태 ❑ 어설픈 주차 통제와 거의 항상 일어나는 교통 정체가 빚어낸 대혼란으로 도로가 꽉 막혔다. ❷ 불가산명사 (의견의) 대립 상황, 교착 상태 ❑ 그는 이런 정책들이 장차 극단적 대립 상황으로 이어질 것이라는 데 동의했다.

grief /griːf/ (**griefs**) ■ N-VAR **Grief** is a feeling of extreme sadness. ❑ *...a huge outpouring of national grief for the victims of the shootings.* ■ PHRASE If something **comes to grief**, it fails. If someone **comes to grief**, they fail in something they are doing, and may be hurt. ❑ *So many marriages have come to grief over lack of money.* ■ EXCLAM Some people say "**Good grief**" when they are surprised or shocked. [FEELINGS] ❑ *"He's been arrested for theft and burglary." — "Good grief!"*

■ 가산명사 또는 불가산명사 큰 슬픔, 비탄 ❑ 총기 난사 사건의 희생자들에 대해 대규모로 표출되는 국민의 애도 ❷ 구 실패하다 ❑ 너무도 많은 결혼이 돈이 없어 파경을 맞는다. ❸ 감탄사 아이고!, 저런! [감정 개입] ❑ "그는 절도와 강도죄로 체포됐어." "저런!"

griev|ance /gríːvəns/ (**grievances**) N-VAR If you have a **grievance** about something that has happened or been done, you believe that it was unfair. ❑ *They had a legitimate grievance.* ❑ *The main grievance of the drivers is the imposition of higher fees for driving licences.*

가산명사 또는 불가산명사 불만, 불평 ❑ 그들의 불만은 정당했다. ❑ 운전자들의 주요 불만은 운전 면허증에 대한 높은 수수료 부과다.

grieve /griːv/ (**grieves, grieving, grieved**) V-I If you **grieve over** something, especially someone's death, you feel very sad about it. ❑ *He's grieving over his dead wife and son.* ❑ *I didn't have any time to grieve.*

자동사 몹시 슬퍼하다, 애통해하다 ❑ 그는 죽은 아내와 아들에 대해 마음아파하고 있다. ❑ 나는 슬퍼할 시간이 전혀 없었다.

griev|ous /gríːvəs/ ■ ADJ If you describe something such as a loss as **grievous**, you mean that it is extremely serious or worrying in its effects. ❑ *Mr. Morris said the victims had suffered from a very grievous mistake.* ● **griev|ous|ly** ADV [ADV with v] ❑ *Birds, sea-life and the coastline all suffered grievously.* ■ ADJ A **grievous** injury to your body is one that causes you great pain and suffering. ❑ *He survived in spite of suffering grievous injuries.* ● **griev|ous|ly** ADV ❑ *Nelson Piquet, three times world champion, was grievously injured.*

■ 형용사 심각한, 중대한 ❑ 모리스 씨는 피해자들이 아주 중대한 과실 때문에 고통을 받았다고 말했다. ● 심하게 부사 ❑ 조류, 해양 생물, 그리고 해안선 모두가 심각한 영향을 받았다. ❷ 형용사 (부상이) 심한 ❑ 그는 심한 부상을 입었음에도 불구하고 살아남았다. ● 심하게 부사 ❑ 세 번이나 세계 챔피언을 차지했던 넬슨 피켓이 심하게 부상했다.

grill /grɪl/ (**grills, grilling, grilled**) ■ N-COUNT A **grill** is a part of a stove which produces strong direct heat to cook food that has been placed underneath it. [BRIT; AM **broiler**] ❑ *Place the omelette under a gentle grill until the top is set.* ■ N-COUNT A **grill** is a flat frame of metal bars on which food can be cooked over a fire. ❑ *Jarod forced scrap wood through the vents in the grill to stoke the fire.* ■ V-T When you **grill** food, or when it **grills**, you cook it on metal bars above a fire or barbecue. ❑ *Grill the steaks over a wood or charcoal fire that is quite hot.* ■ V-T/V-I When you **grill** food, or when it **grills**, you cook it in a stove using very strong heat directly above it. [BRIT; AM **broil**] ❑ *Grill the meat for 20 minutes each side.* ❑ *Apart from peppers and aubergines, many other vegetables grill well.* ● V-T N-UNCOUNT ❑ *The breast can be cut into portions for grilling.* →see **cook** ■ V-T If you **grill** someone **about** something, you ask them a lot of questions for a long period of time. [INFORMAL] ❑ *Grill your travel agent about the facilities for families with children.* ● **grill|ing** (**grillings**) N-COUNT ❑ *They gave him a grilling about the implications of a united Europe.* ■ N-COUNT A **grill** is a restaurant that serves grilled food. ❑ *...patrons of the Savoy Grill.*

■ 가산명사 그릴 [영국영어; 미국영어 broiler] ❑ 오믈렛을 약한 불로 맞춘 그릴 아래에 놓고 윗부분이 익을 때까지 두세요. ❷ 가산명사 석쇠 ❑ 자로드는 불길을 돋우려고 나무토막을 그릴의 통풍구 속으로 밀어 넣었다. ❸ 타동사 (음식을) 굽다; (음식이) 구워지다 ❑ 스테이크를 아주 뜨거운 장작불이나 숯불 위에 구우시오. ❹ 타동사/자동사 (음식을) 굽다; (음식이) 구워지다 [영국영어; 미국영어 broil] ❑ 고기를 양면을 각각 20분씩 직화로 구우시오. ❑ 피망과 가지를 제외하고, 다른 야채들은 불에 잘 구워진다. ● 타동사 불가산명사 ❑ 가슴살은 그릴에 굽기 위해 1인분씩 잘라도 된다. ❺ 타동사 마구 질문을 퍼붓다 [비격식체] ❑ 아이가 딸린 가족을 위한 시설에 대해 여행사 직원에게 얼마든지 물어보세요. ● 많은 질문 가산명사 ❑ 그들은 그에게 유럽 통합의 여파에 대해 수없이 질문을 해 댔다. ❻ 가산명사 그릴 음식 전문 식당 ❑ 사보이 그릴의 단골손님들

grille /grɪl/ (**grilles**) also **grill** N-COUNT A **grille** is a framework of metal bars or wire which is placed in front of a window or a piece of machinery, in order to protect it or to protect people. ❑ *The single window was protected by a rusted iron grille.*

가산명사 방범창; 쇠창살 ❑ 단 하나의 창문에는 녹슨 방범창이 달려 있었다.

grim /grɪm/ (**grimmer, grimmest**) **1** ADJ A situation or piece of information that is **grim** is unpleasant, depressing, and difficult to accept. ❑ *They painted a grim picture of growing crime.* ❑ *There was further grim economic news yesterday.* **2** ADJ A place that is **grim** is unattractive and depressing in appearance. ❑ *The city might be grim at first, but there is a vibrancy and excitement.*

1 형용사 암울한 ❑ 그들은 증가하는 범죄에 대한 암울한 그림을 그렸다. ❑ 암울한 경제에 대한 추가 뉴스가 어제 보도되었다. **2** 형용사 음침한, 칙칙음은 ❑ 그 도시가 처음에는 음침해 보일 수도 있지만 활기와 신나는 구석이 있다.

gri|mace /grɪməs, grɪmeɪs/ (**grimaces, grimacing, grimaced**) V-I If you **grimace**, you twist your face in an ugly way because you are annoyed, disgusted, or in pain. [WRITTEN] ❑ *She started to sit up, grimaced, and sank back weakly against the pillow.* ● N-COUNT **Grimace** is also a noun. ❑ *He took another drink of his coffee. "Awful," he said with a grimace.*

자동사 얼굴을 찌푸리다 [문어체] ❑ 그녀는 일어나 앉으려다가 얼굴을 찌푸리며 베개 위로 다시 쓰러졌다. ● 가산명사 얼굴을 찌푸림 ❑ 그는 커피를 한 모금 더 마셨다. 얼굴을 찌푸리며 "형편없군."이라고 말했다.

grime /graɪm/ N-UNCOUNT **Grime** is dirt which has collected on the surface of something. ❑ *Kelly got the grime off his hands before rejoining her in the kitchen.*

불가산명사 먼지 ❑ 켈리는 손에서 먼지를 털고서 부엌에 가서 그녀와 다시 합류했다.

grimy /graɪmi/ (**grimier, grimiest**) ADJ Something that is **grimy** is very dirty. ❑ *...a grimy industrial city.*

형용사 더러운 ❑ 지저분한 산업 도시

grin /grɪn/ (**grins, grinning, grinned**) **1** V-I When you **grin**, you smile broadly. ❑ *He grins, delighted at the memory.* ❑ *Sarah tried several times to catch Philip's eye, but he just grinned at her.* **2** N-COUNT A **grin** is a broad smile. ❑ *...a big grin on her face.* **3** PHRASE If you **grin and bear it**, you accept a difficult or unpleasant situation without complaining because you know there is nothing you can do to make things better. ❑ *They cannot stand the sight of each other, but they will just have to grin and bear it.*

1 자동사 활짝 웃다, 씩 웃다 ❑ 그는 회상하며 즐거워하며 활짝 웃는다. ❑ 사라는 필립과 눈을 마주치려고 여러 번 애를 썼으나 그는 그녀에게 씩 웃기만 했다. **2** 가산명사 활짝 웃음 ❑ 그녀의 활짝 웃음 띤 얼굴 **3** 구 쓴웃음 지으며 참다 ❑ 그들은 서로 얼굴도 마주치지 않으려 하지만 그저 쓴웃음 지으며 참아야 할 것이다.

grind /graɪnd/ (**grinds, grinding, ground**) **1** V-T If you **grind** a substance such as corn, you crush it between two hard surfaces or with a machine until it becomes a fine powder. ❑ *Store the peppercorns in an airtight container and grind the pepper as you need it.* ● PHRASAL VERB **Grind up** means the same as **grind**. ❑ *He makes his own paint, grinding up the pigment with a little oil.* **2** V-T If you **grind** something **into** a surface, you press and rub it hard into the surface using small circular or sideways movements. ❑ *"Well," I said, grinding my cigarette nervously into the granite step.* ● PHRASE If you **grind** your **teeth**, you rub your upper and lower teeth together as though you are chewing something. **3** V-T If you **grind** something, you make it smooth or sharp by rubbing it against a hard surface. ❑ *It was beyond my ability to grind a blade this broad.* **4** V-I If a vehicle **grinds** somewhere, it moves there very slowly and noisily. ❑ *Tanks had crossed the border at five fifteen and were grinding south.* **5** N-SING The **grind of** a machine is the harsh, scraping noise that it makes, usually because it is old or is working too hard. ❑ *The grind of heavy machines could get on their nerves.* **6** N-SING If you refer to routine tasks or activities as **the grind**, you mean they are boring and take up a lot of time and effort. [INFORMAL, DISAPPROVAL] ❑ *The daily grind of government is done by Her Majesty's Civil Service.* **7** PHRASE If a country's economy or something such as a process **grinds to a halt**, it gradually becomes slower or less active until it stops. ❑ *The peace process has ground to a halt while Israel struggles to form a new government.* **8** PHRASE If a vehicle **grinds to a halt**, it stops slowly and noisily. ❑ *The tanks ground to a halt after a hundred yards because the fuel had been siphoned out.*

1 타동사 가루로 빻다, 갈다 ❑ 통후추를 밀폐된 용기에 저장하고 필요할 때 후추를 갈아 쓰시오. ● 구동사 가루로 빻다, 갈다 ❑ 그는 안료에 기름을 조금 넣고 빻아서 물감을 직접 만든다. **2** 타동사 비비다 ❑ 나는 화강암 계단에 초조하게 담배를 비벼 끄면서 "글쎄."라고 말했다. ● 구 이를 갈다 **3** 타동사 갈다, 연마하다 ❑ 이렇게 폭이 넓은 칼날을 가는 것은 내 능력 밖의 일이었다. **4** 자동사 삐거덕거리며 움직이다 ❑ 탱크들이 5시 15분에 국경을 넘어 삐거덕거리며 남쪽으로 움직이고 있었다. **5** 단수명사 삐거덕거리는 소리 ❑ 중장비의 삐거덕거리는 소리가 그들의 신경에 거슬릴 수 있다. **6** 단수명사 고역, 고되고 단조로운 일 [비격식체, 탐탁잖음] ❑ 정부의 일상적인 고된 업무는 영국 공무원이 한다. **7** 구 서서히 멈추다 ❑ 이스라엘이 새 정부를 구성하려고 애쓰는 동안 평화 협상이 서서히 중단되었다. **8** 구 삐거덕거리며 멈추다 ❑ 탱크들은 100야드를 간 다음 연료가 바닥이 나서 삐거덕거리며 멈춰 섰다.

▶**grind down** PHRASAL VERB If you say that someone **grinds** you **down**, you mean that they treat you very harshly and cruelly, reducing your confidence or your will to resist them. ❑ *"You see," said Hughes, "there's people who want to humiliate you and grind you down."*

구동사 짓누르다, 억누르다 ❑ "자, 보시오. 당신에게 창피를 주고 짓누르기를 원하는 사람들이 있어요."라고 휴스가 말했다.

▶**grind up** →see **grind 1**

grind|er /graɪndər/ (**grinders**) **1** N-COUNT In a kitchen, a **grinder** is a device for crushing food such as coffee or meat into small pieces or into a powder. ❑ *...an electric coffee grinder.* **2** N-COUNT A **grinder** is a machine or tool for sharpening, smoothing, or polishing the surface of something. ❑ *The grinder is used for making precision tooling.*

1 가산명사 분쇄기 ❑ 전기 커피 분쇄기 **2** 가산명사 연삭기, 그라인더 ❑ 연삭기는 정밀 공구 세공에 사용된다.

grip ◆◇◇ /grɪp/ (**grips, gripping, gripped**) **1** V-T If you **grip** something, you take hold of it with your hand and continue to hold it firmly. ❑ *She gripped the rope.* **2** N-COUNT A **grip** is a firm, strong hold on something. ❑ *His strong hand eased the bag from her grip.* **3** N-SING Someone's **grip on** something is the power and control they have over it. ❑ *The president maintains an iron grip on his country.* **4** V-T If something **grips** you, it affects you very strongly. ❑ *The entire community has been gripped by fear.* **5** V-T If you **are gripped by** something such as a story or a series of events, your attention is concentrated on it and held by it. [usu passive] ❑ *The nation is gripped by the dramatic story.* ● **grip|ping** ADJ ❑ *The film turned out to be a gripping thriller.* **6** N-UNCOUNT If things such as shoes or car tires have **grip**, they do not slip. ❑ *...a new way of reinforcing rubber which gives car tyres better grip.* **7** PHRASE If you **come to grips with** a problem or, in British English, you **get to grips with** it, you consider it seriously, and start taking action to deal with it. ❑ *The government's first task is to come to grips with the economy.* **8** PHRASE If you **get a grip** on yourself, you make an effort to control or improve your behavior or work. ❑ *A bit of me was very frightened and I consciously had to get a grip on myself.* **9** PHRASE If a person, group, or place is **in the grip of** something, they are being severely affected by it. ❑ *Britain is still in the grip of recession.* **10** PHRASE If you **lose** your **grip**, you become less efficient and less confident, and less able to deal with things. ❑ *He wondered if perhaps he was getting old and losing his grip.* **11** PHRASE If you say that someone has a **grip on reality**, you mean they recognize the true situation and do not have mistaken ideas about it. ❑ *Shakur loses his fragile grip on reality and starts blasting away at friends and foe alike.*

1 타동사 꽉 잡다 ❑ 그녀는 밧줄을 꽉 잡았다. **2** 가산명사 움켜잡기 ❑ 그는 힘센 손으로 그녀가 손으로 꽉 잡고 있는 가방을 빼앗았다. **3** 단수명사 지배력, 장악 ❑ 그 대통령은 자기 나라에 대해 강철 같은 지배력을 유지한다. **4** 타동사 강한 영향을 끼치다, (마음을) 사로잡다 ❑ 전 지역 사회가 공포에 사로잡혀 있다. **5** 타동사 몰두하다, (마음이) 사로잡히다 ❑ 전국이 그 극적인 이야기에 몰두하고 있다. ● 흥미진진한 형용사 ❑ 그 영화는 흥미진진한 공포물로 드러났다. **6** 불가산명사 밀착력 ❑ 자동차 타이어의 밀착력을 향상시키는 새로운 고무 강화법 **7** 구 본격적으로 다루다 ❑ 정부의 첫 과제는 경제 문제를 본격적으로 처리하는 것이다. **8** 구 자제하다 ❑ 나는 한편으로 깜짝 놀라서 애써 마음을 진정시켰다. **9** 구 -에 붙잡혀, -에 사로잡혀 ❑ 영국은 아직 불경기에서 벗어나지 못하고 있다. **10** 구 자신감을 잃다, 장악력을 잃다 ❑ 그는 자기가 나이가 들고 자신감을 잃어가고 있지 않나 생각했다. **11** 구 현실 인식 ❑ 샤쿠르는 가뜩이나 박약한 현실 인식이 흐려져서 친구와 적을 똑같이 비난하기 시작한다.

a
b
c
d
e
f
g
h
i
j
k
l
m
n
o
p
q
r
s
t
u
v
w
x
y
z

gripe /graɪp/ (gripes, griping, griped) **1** V-I If you say that someone **is griping**, you mean they are annoying you because they keep on complaining about something. [INFORMAL, DISAPPROVAL] □ *Why are football players griping when the average salary is half a million dollars?* ● **griping** N-UNCOUNT □ *Still, the griping went on.* **2** N-COUNT A **gripe** is a complaint about something. [INFORMAL] □ *My only gripe is that one main course and one dessert were unavailable.*

grisly /grɪzli/ (grislier, grisliest) ADJ Something that is **grisly** is extremely unpleasant, and usually involves death and violence. □ *He was insane when he carried out the grisly murders.*

grit /grɪt/ (grits, gritting, gritted) **1** N-UNCOUNT **Grit** is very small pieces of stone. It is often put on roads in winter to make them less slippery. □ *He felt tiny bits of grit and sand peppering his knees.* **2** N-UNCOUNT If someone has **grit**, they have the determination and courage to continue doing something even though it is very difficult. □ *If they gave gold medals for grit, Karen would be right up there on the winners' podium.* **3** V-T If you **grit** your **teeth**, you press your upper and lower teeth tightly together, usually because you are angry about something. □ *Gritting my teeth, I did my best to stifle one or two remarks.* **4** PHRASE If you **grit** your **teeth**, you make up your mind to carry on even if the situation is very difficult. □ *There is going to be hardship, but we have to grit our teeth and get on with it.*

gritty /grɪti/ (grittier, grittiest) **1** ADJ Something that is **gritty** contains grit, is covered with grit, or has a texture like that of grit. □ *The sheets fell on the gritty floor, and she just let them lie.* **2** ADJ Someone who is **gritty** is brave and determined. □ *We have to prove how gritty we are.* **3** ADJ A **gritty** description of a tough or unpleasant situation shows it in a very realistic way. □ *...gritty social comment.*

groan /groʊn/ (groans, groaning, groaned) **1** V-I If you **groan**, you make a long, low sound because you are in pain, or because you are upset or unhappy about something. □ *Slowly, he opened his eyes. As he did so, he began to groan with pain.* □ *They glanced at the man on the floor, who began to groan.* ● N-COUNT **Groan** is also a noun. □ *She heard him let out a pitiful, muffled groan.* **2** V-T If you **groan** something, you say it in a low, unhappy voice. □ *"My leg – I think it's broken," Eric groaned.* **3** V-I If you **groan about** something, you complain about it. □ *His parents were beginning to groan about the price of college tuition.* ● N-COUNT **Groan** is also a noun. □ *Listen sympathetically to your child's moans and groans about what she can't do.* **4** V-I If wood or something made of wood **groans**, it makes a loud sound when it moves. □ *The timbers groan and creak and the floorboards shift.* **5** V-I If you say that something such as a table **groans under** the weight of food, you are emphasizing that there is a lot of food on it. [EMPHASIS] □ *The bar counter groans under the weight of huge plates of the freshest fish.* **6** V-I If you say that someone or something is **groaning under** the weight of something, you think there is too much of that thing. [DISAPPROVAL] [usu cont] □ *Consumers were groaning under the weight of high interest rates.*

grocer /groʊsər/ (grocers) **1** N-COUNT A **grocer** is a storekeeper who sells foods such as flour, sugar, and canned foods. **2** N-COUNT A **grocer** or a **grocer's** is the same as a **grocery**. [mainly BRIT] □ *Trade slumped further when the grocer's closed.*

grocery /groʊsəri, groʊsri/ (groceries) **1** N-COUNT A **grocery** or a **grocery store** is a small store that sells foods such as flour, sugar, and canned goods. [mainly AM] □ *They run a small grocery store.* **2** N-PLURAL **Groceries** are foods you buy at a grocery or at a supermarket. □ *...a small bag of groceries.*

groin /grɔɪn/ (groins) N-COUNT Your **groin** is the front part of your body between your legs. □ *I underwent an operation on my groin once.*

groom /grum/ (grooms, grooming, groomed) **1** N-COUNT A **groom** is the same as a **bridegroom**. □ *...the bride and groom.* **2** N-COUNT A **groom** is someone whose job is to look after the horses in a stable and to keep them clean. **3** V-T If you **groom** an animal, you clean its fur, usually by brushing it. □ *The horses were exercised and groomed with special care.* **4** V-T If you **are groomed for** a special job, someone prepares you for it by teaching you the skills you will need. [usu passive] □ *George was already being groomed for the top job.*

groomed /grumd/ ADJ You use **groomed** in expressions such as **well groomed** and **badly groomed** to say how neat and clean a person is. □ *...a very well groomed man.*

grooming /grumɪŋ/ N-UNCOUNT **Grooming** refers to the things that people do to keep themselves clean and make their face, hair, and skin look nice. □ *...a growing concern for personal grooming.*

groove /gruv/ (grooves) N-COUNT A **groove** is a deep line cut into a surface. □ *Prior to assembly, grooves were made in the shelf, base and sides to accommodate the back panel.*

grope /groʊp/ (gropes, groping, groped) **1** V-I If you **grope for** something that you cannot see, you try to find it by moving your hands around in order to feel it. □ *With his left hand he groped for the knob, turned it, and pulled the door open.* **2** V-T If you **grope** your **way** to a place, you move there, holding your hands in front of you and feeling the way because you cannot see anything. □ *I didn't turn on the light, but groped my way across the room.* **3** V-I If you **grope for** something, for example the solution to a problem, you try to think of it, when you have no real idea what it could be. □ *He groped for solutions to the problems facing the country.*

gross ♦◇◇ /groʊs/ (grosser, grossest, grosses, grossing, grossed)

The plural of the number is **gross**.

1 ADJ You use **gross** to describe something unacceptable or unpleasant to a very great amount, degree, or intensity. [ADJ n] □ *The company was guilty of gross*

negligence. ● **gross|ly** ADV [ADV -ed/adj] ❑ *Funding of education had been grossly inadequate for years.* **2** ADJ If you say that someone's speech or behavior is **gross**, you think it is very coarse, vulgar or unacceptable. [DISAPPROVAL] ❑ *He abused the Admiral in the grossest terms.* **3** ADJ If you describe something as **gross**, you think it is very unpleasant. [INFORMAL, DISAPPROVAL] ❑ *They had a commercial on the other night for Drug Free America that was so gross I thought Daddy was going to faint.* **4** ADJ If you describe someone as **gross**, you mean that they are extremely fat and unattractive. [DISAPPROVAL] [v-link ADJ] ❑ *I only resist things like chocolate if I feel really gross.* **5** ADJ **Gross** means the total amount of something, especially money, before any has been taken away. [ADJ n] ❑ *...a fixed rate account guaranteeing 10.4% gross interest or 7.8% net until October.* ● ADV **Gross** is also an adverb. [ADV after v] ❑ *Interest is paid gross, rather than having tax deducted.* **6** ADJ **Gross** means the total amount of something, after all the relevant amounts have been added together. [ADJ n] ❑ *National Savings gross sales in June totalled £709 million.* **7** V-T If a person or a business **grosses** a particular amount of money, they earn that amount of money before tax has been taken away. [BUSINESS] ❑ *The company grossed $16.8 million last year.* **8** NUM A **gross** is a group of 144 things. ❑ *In all honesty he could not have justified ordering more than twelve gross of the disks.*

Word Partnership	*gross의 연어*
N.	**act of gross injustice**, gross **mismanagement**, gross **negligence** **1**
	gross **income** **5**
V.	**feel gross** **3**

gross do|mes|tic prod|uct (**gross domestic products**) N-VAR A country's **gross domestic product** is the total value of all the goods it has produced and the services it has provided in a particular year, not including its income from investments in other countries. [BUSINESS]

gross na|tion|al prod|uct (**gross national products**) N-VAR A country's **gross national product** is the total value of all the goods it has produced and the services it has provided in a particular year, including its income from investments in other countries. [BUSINESS]

gro|tesque /ɡroʊtesk/ (**grotesques**) **1** ADJ You say that something is **grotesque** when it is unnatural, unpleasant, and exaggerated that it upsets or shocks you. ❑ *...the grotesque disparities between the wealthy few and nearly everyone else.* ● **gro|tesque|ly** ADV ❑ *He called it the most grotesquely tragic experience that he's ever had.* **2** ADJ If someone or something is **grotesque**, they are very ugly. ❑ *They tried to avoid looking at his grotesque face and his crippled body.* ● **gro|tesque|ly** ADV [ADV adj/-ed] ❑ *...grotesquely deformed beggars.* **3** N-COUNT A **grotesque** is a person who is very ugly in a strange or unnatural way, especially one in a novel or painting. ❑ *Grass's novels are peopled with outlandish characters: grotesques, clowns, scarecrows, dwarfs.*

grot|ty /ɡrɒti/ (**grottier, grottiest**) ADJ If you describe something as **grotty**, you mean that it is unpleasant or of poor quality and you dislike it strongly. [BRIT, INFORMAL, DISAPPROVAL] ❑ *...a grotty little flat in Camden.*

ground ♦♦♦ /ɡraʊnd/ (**grounds, grounding, grounded**) **1** N-SING The **ground** is the surface of the earth. [the N] ❑ *Forty or fifty women were sitting cross-legged on the ground.* ❑ *We slid down the roof and dropped to the ground.* ● PHRASE Something that is **below ground** is under the earth's surface or under a building. Something that is **above ground** is on top of the earth's surface. **2** N-SING If you say that something takes place **on the ground**, you mean it takes place on the surface of the earth and not in the air. ❑ *Coordinating airline traffic on the ground is as complicated as managing the traffic in the air.* **3** N-SING The **ground** is the soil and rock on the earth's surface. ❑ *The ground had eroded.* **4** N-UNCOUNT You can refer to land as **ground**, especially when it has very few buildings on it or when it is considered to be special in some way. ❑ *...a stretch of waste ground.* **5** N-COUNT You can use **ground** to refer to an area of land, sea, or air which is used for a particular activity. ❑ *The best fishing grounds are around the islands.* **6** N-PLURAL The **grounds** of a large or important building are the garden or area of land which surrounds it. ❑ *...the palace grounds.* **7** N-VAR You can use **ground** to refer to a place or situation in which particular methods or ideas can develop and be successful. ❑ *The company has maintained its reputation as the developing ground for new techniques.* **8** N-UNCOUNT You can use **ground** in expressions such as **on shaky ground** and **the same ground** to refer to a particular subject, area of experience, or basis for an argument. ❑ *Sensing she was on shaky ground, Marie changed the subject.* ❑ *The French are on solid ground when they argue that competitiveness is no reason for devaluation.* **9** N-UNCOUNT **Ground** is used in expressions such as **gain ground**, **lose ground**, and **give ground** in order to indicate that someone gets or loses an advantage. [JOURNALISM] ❑ *There are signs that the party is gaining ground in the latest polls.* **10** N-VAR If something is **grounds for** a feeling or action, it is a reason for it. If you do something **on the grounds of** a particular thing, that thing is the reason for your action. ❑ *In the interview he gave some grounds for optimism.* ❑ *The court overturned that decision on the grounds that the Prosecution had withheld crucial evidence.* **11** V-T If an argument, belief, or opinion **is grounded** in something, that thing is used to justify it. ❑ *Her argument was grounded in fact.* **12** V-T If an aircraft or its passengers **are grounded**, they are made to stay on the ground and are not allowed to take off. ❑ *The civil aviation minister ordered all the planes to be grounded.* **13** V-T/V-I If a ship or boat **is grounded** or if it **grounds**, it touches the bottom of the sea, lake, or river it is on, and is unable to move off. ❑ *Residents have been told to stay away from the region where the ship was grounded.* ❑ *The boat finally grounded on a soft, underwater bank.* **14** N-COUNT The **ground** in an electric plug or piece of electrical equipment is the wire through which electricity passes into the ground and which makes the equipment safe. [AM;

지원이 몇 년 동안 엄청나게 부족했다. **2** 형용사 천한, 추잡한 [탐탁잖음] ❑ 그는 해군 제도를 최대한 추잡한 말로 욕했다. **3** 형용사 역겨운 [비격식체, 탐탁잖음] ❑ 그들은 요전날 밤에 '마약이 없는 미국' 광고를 보았는데 너무 역겨워서 내 생각엔 아빠가 기절할 것 같았다. **4** 형용사 뚱뚱한 [탐탁잖음] ❑ 내가 정말 뚱뚱하다고 느껴지면 초콜릿 같은 것은 그냥 참고 안 먹는다. **5** 형용사 (공제하기 전의) 총액의 ❑ 10월까지 10.4퍼센트 공제 전 총 이자율 7.8퍼센트 순 이자를 보장하는 고정 이율 예금 ● 부사 총액으로 ❑ 이자는 세금을 공제하지 않고 공제 전의 총 이자로 지급된다. **6** 형용사 총계의, 모두 합친 ❑ 국민 저축의 6월 총 판매고는 7억 9백만 파운드에 달했다. ❑ 그 회사는 작년에 … 의 세전 총수익을 올린다 [경제] ❑ 그 회사는 작년에 1,680만 달러의 세전 수익을 올렸다. **8** 수사 그로스 (144개) ❑ 솔직히 말해서 그가 디스크를 12그로스 이상 주문하는 것은 정당화될 수 없었을 것이다.

가산명사 또는 불가산명사 국내 총생산 [경제]

가산명사 또는 불가산명사 국민 총생산 [경제]

1 형용사 기괴한, 괴상한 ❑ 부유한 극소수와 거의 모든 다른 사람들 간의 기괴한 불균형 ● 기괴하게 부사 ❑ 그는 그것을 자기가 겪었던 가장 기이하고 비극적인 경험이라고 불렀다. **2** 형용사 흉측한 ❑ 그들은 그의 흉측한 얼굴과 불구인 신체를 보지 않으려고 애썼다. ● 흉측하게 부사 ❑ 흉측하게 불구가 된 거지들 **3** 가산명사 흉측하게 생긴 사람 ❑ 그라스의 소설에는 흉측하게 생긴 사람, 어릿광대, 허수아비, 난쟁이 등 기이한 등장인물들이 많다.

형용사 볼품없는, 꾀죄죄한 [영국영어, 비격식체, 탐탁잖음] ❑ 캠든에 있는 꾀죄죄한 작은 아파트

1 단수명사 지면, 땅바닥 ❑ 사오십 명의 여자들이 땅바닥에 책상다리로 앉아 있었다. ❑ 우리는 지붕 아래로 미끄러져 땅에 떨어졌다. ● 구 지하의; 지상의 **2** 단수명사 지상에서 ❑ 지상에서 항공 교통을 조정하는 것은 공중에서 항공 교통을 처리하는 것만큼 복잡하다. **3** 단수명사 지면 ❑ 지반이 침식되어 있었다. **4** 불가산명사 땅, 용지 ❑ 불모지 지역 **5** 가산명사 장소 ❑ 최고의 낚시 장소는 섬 주변이다. **6** 복수명사 (건물 주위의) 뜰, 구내 ❑ 궁전 뜰 **7** 가산명사 또는 불가산명사 기반, 장 ❑ 그 회사는 새 기술을 위한 개발의 장으로서 그 명성을 유지해 왔다. **8** 불가산명사 논거, 근거; 논거가 불안정한, 동일한 근거 ❑ 자기의 논거가 불안정함을 알아차리고 마리는 주제를 바꾸었다. ❑ 경쟁이 평가 절하의 이유는 되지 못한다고 주장하는 프랑스의 논거는 확고하다. **9** 불가산명사 우세해지다; 세력을 잃다, 후퇴하다 [언론] ❑ 최근 여론 조사에서 그 당이 우세해지고 있다는 징후가 있다. **10** 가산명사 또는 불가산명사 ~한 이유; ~라는 이유로 ❑ 인터뷰에서 그는 낙관할 만한 몇 가지 이유를 밝혔다. ❑ 검찰이 결정적인 증거를 숨겼다는 이유로 법원은 그 판결을 번복했다. **11** 타동사 ~에 근거하다 ❑ 그녀의 주장은 사실에 입각한 것이었다. **12** 타동사 이륙을 금지하다 ❑ 민간 항공청장은 모든 비행기의 이륙 금지를 명령했다. **13** 타동사/자동사 좌초되다, 좌초하다 ❑ 주민들은 배가 좌초된 지역 가까이에 머물라는 말을 들었다. ❑ 작은 배가 마침내 부드러운 수중 모래톱에 좌초하였다. **14** 가산명사 접지, 어스 [미국영어; 영국영어 earth] ❑ 절연 접지 [형용사 간, 분쇄한 [주로 미국영어; 영국영어 minced] ❑ 소시지는 굵게 간 돼지고기로 만들어진다. **16** grind의 과거 및 과거 분사 ❑ 구 신기원을 이루다, 새로운 지평을 열다 [마음에 듦] ❑ 겔혼은 스페인 내전에 관한 첫 보고서를 제출하면서 새로운 지평을 연 것인지도 모른다. **19** 구 전소하다, 폭삭 타 버리다 [강조] ❑ 그 시는 프랑스 혁명 이후 완전히 전소하였다. **20** 구 합의점 ❑ 참석자들이 농업 문제에 대해서 합의점을 찾지 못하는 것 같다. **21** 구 (은신처에) 숨다 [영국영어] ❑ 동베이루트 시민들은 지하실과 대피소에 숨었다.

BRIT **earth**] [usu sing] ❏ *...an insulated ground.* **15** ADJ **Ground** meat has been cut into very small pieces in a machine. [mainly AM; BRIT usually **minced**] ❏ *...The sausages are made of coarsely ground pork.* **16 Ground** is the past tense and past participle of **grind**. **17** →see also **grounding 18** PHRASE If you **break new ground**, you do something completely different or you do something in a completely different way. [APPROVAL] ❏ *Gellhorn may have broken new ground when she filed her first report on the Spanish Civil War.* **19** PHRASE If you say that a town or building **is burned to the ground** or **is razed to the ground**, you are emphasizing that it has been completely destroyed by fire. [EMPHASIS] ❏ *The town was razed to the ground after the French Revolution.* **20** PHRASE If two people or groups find **common ground**, they agree about something, especially when they do not agree about other things. ❏ *The participants seem unable to find common ground on the issue of agriculture.* **21** PHRASE If you **go to ground**, you hide somewhere where you cannot easily be found. [BRIT] ❏ *Citizens of East Beirut went to ground in basements and shelters.* **22** PHRASE The **middle ground** between two groups, ideas, or plans involves things which do not belong to either of these groups, ideas, or plans but have elements of each, often in a less extreme form. ❏ *The sooner we find a middle ground between freedom of speech and protection of the young, the better for everyone.* **23** PHRASE If something such as a project gets **off the ground**, it begins or starts functioning. ❏ *We help small companies to get off the ground.* **24** PHRASE If you **prepare the ground for** a future event, course of action, or development, you make it easier for it to happen. ❏ *...a political initiative which would prepare the ground for war.* **25** PHRASE If you **shift** your **ground** or **change** your **ground**, you change the basis on which you are arguing. ❏ *Calendar considered this, then shifted his ground slightly in line with a new thought.* **26** PHRASE If you **stand** your **ground** or **hold** your **ground**, you do not run away from a situation, but face it bravely. ❏ *She had to force herself to stand her ground when she heard someone approaching.* →see **grain**

ground floor (ground floors) N-COUNT The **ground floor** of a building is the floor that is level or almost level with the ground outside. [BRIT; AM **first floor**] ❏ *She showed him around the ground floor of the empty house.* →see **floor**

가산명사 1층 [영국영어; 미국영어 first floor] ❏ 그녀는 그에게 빈 집의 1층을 두루 보여 주었다.

ground|ing /ɡraʊndɪŋ/ N-SING If you have a **grounding in** a subject, you know the basic facts or principles of that subject, especially as a result of a particular course of training or instruction. ❏ *The degree provides a thorough grounding in both mathematics and statistics.*

단수명사 기초 지식 ❏ 그 학위 과정은 수학과 통계학의 단단한 기초 지식을 마련해 준다.

ground|less /ɡraʊndlɪs/ ADJ If you say that a fear, accusation, or story is **groundless**, you mean that it is not based on evidence and is unlikely to be true or valid. ❏ *Fears that the world was about to run out of fuel proved groundless.*

형용사 사실무근의, 근거가 없는 ❏ 전 세계의 연료가 곧 고갈될 것이라는 우려는 근거가 없는 것으로 드러났다.

Word Partnership	groundless의 연어
N.	**charges are** groundless
V.	**call** *something* groundless, **dismiss** *something* **as** groundless, **prove** groundless

ground rule (ground rules) N-COUNT The **ground rules for** something are the basic principles on which future action will be based. ❏ *The panel says the ground rules for the current talks should be maintained.*

가산명사 기본 원칙 ❏ 위원단은 현재 회담의 기본 원칙이 유지되어야 한다고 말한다.

Word Link	ground ≈ bottom : back**ground**, fore**ground**, **ground**work

ground|work /ɡraʊndwɜrk/ N-SING The **groundwork for** something is the early work on it which forms the basis for further work. ❏ *Yesterday's meeting was to lay the groundwork for the task ahead.*

단수명사 기초, 기초 작업 ❏ 어제 회의는 향후 과제에 대한 토대를 마련하기 위한 것이었다.

group ♦♦♦ /ɡruːp/ (groups, grouping, grouped) **1** N-COUNT-COLL A **group of** people or things is a number of people or things which are together in one place at one time. ❏ *The trouble involved a small group of football supporters.* **2** N-COUNT A **group** is a set of people who have the same interests or aims, and who organize themselves to work or act together. ❏ *Members of an environmental group are staging a protest inside a chemical plant.* **3** N-COUNT A **group** is a set of people, organizations, or things which are considered together because they have something in common. ❏ *She is among the most promising players in her age group.* **4** N-COUNT A **group** is a number of separate commercial or industrial firms which all have the same owner. [BUSINESS] ❏ *The group made a pre-tax profit of £1.05 million.* **5** N-COUNT A **group** is a number of musicians who perform together, especially ones who play popular music. ❏ *At school he played bass in a pop group called The Urge.* **6** V-T/V-I If a number of things or people **are grouped together** or **group together**, they are put together in one place or within one organization or system. ❏ *Plants are grouped into botanical "families" that have certain characteristics in common.* ❏ *The G-7 organization groups together the world's seven leading industrialized nations.* **7** →see also **grouping**, **pressure group**

1 가산명사-집합 집단, 그룹 ❏ 그 문제에 일단의 축구 팬들이 관련되어 있었다. **2** 가산명사 모임 ❏ 한 환경 모임 회원들이 화학 공장 안에서 시위를 하고 있다. **3** 가산명사 집단 ❏ 그녀는 자기 나이 또래에서 가장 유망한 선수 중 한 사람이다. **4** 가산명사 (회사의) 그룹 [경제] ❏ 그 그룹은 105만 파운드의 세전 이익을 냈다. **5** 가산명사 (대중음악) 그룹 ❏ 학교 다닐 때 그는 '디 어지'라고 불리는 팝 그룹에서 베이스를 맡았다. **6** 타동사/자동사 분류되다, 무리를 짓다 ❏ 식물은 식물학상 일정한 특성을 서로 공유하는 '과'로 분류된다. ❏ 지7 조직은 전세계의 선진 산업 국가 7개국을 한데 묶고 있다.

Thesaurus	group의 참조어
N.	collection, crowd, gang, organization, society **1**
V.	arrange, categorize, class, order, rank, sort **6**

group|ing /ɡruːpɪŋ/ (groupings) N-COUNT A **grouping** is a set of people or things that have something in common. ❏ *There were two main political groupings pressing for independence.*

가산명사 집단 ❏ 독립을 요구하는 두 개의 주요 정치 집단이 있었다.

22 구 중용, 중도 ❏ 우리가 언론의 자유와 청소년 보호 사이의 중간 지점을 빨리 찾을수록 모든 사람들에게 더 낫다. 23 구 착수하여 ❏ 우리는 중소기업이 사업에 착수하는 것을 돕는다. 24 구 -의 기반을 조성하다 ❏ 전쟁의 기반을 조성할 정치적 주도권 25 구 주장을 바꾸다, 입장을 바꾸다 ❏ 캘린더는 이것을 고려한 다음 새로운 생각과 일치하게 자기의 주장을 조금 바꾸었다. 26 구 물러서지 않다, 입장을 고수하다 ❏ 그녀는 누군가가 다가오는 소리를 들었을 때 달아나지 않고 용감히 맞서기 위해 마음을 단단히 먹어야 했다.

grov|el /grɒvᵊl/ (grovels, groveling, groveled) [BRIT grovelling, grovelled] **1** V-I If you say that someone **grovels**, you think they are behaving too respectfully towards another person, for example because they are frightened or because they want something. [DISAPPROVAL] □ *I don't grovel to anybody.* □ *Speakers have been shouted down, classes disrupted, teachers made to grovel.* **2** V-I If you **grovel**, you crawl on the ground, for example in order to find something. □ *We groveled around the club on our knees.*

grow ♦♦♦ /groʊ/ (grows, growing, grew, grown) **1** V-I When people, animals, and plants **grow**, they increase in size and change physically over a period of time. □ *We stop growing at maturity.* **2** V-I If a plant or tree **grows** in a particular place, it is alive there. □ *The station had roses growing at each end of the platform.* **3** V-T If you **grow** a particular type of plant, you put seeds or young plants in the ground and look after them as they develop. □ *Lettuce was grown by the Ancient Romans.* **4** V-I When someone's hair **grows**, it gradually becomes longer. Your nails also **grow**. □ *Then the hair began to grow again and I felt terrific.* **5** V-T If someone **grows** their hair, or **grows** a beard or mustache, they stop cutting their hair or shaving so that their hair becomes longer. You can also **grow** your nails. □ *I'd better start growing my hair.* **6** V-I If someone **grows** mentally, they change and develop in character or attitude. □ *They began to grow as persons.* **7** V-LINK You use **grow** to say that someone or something gradually changes until they have a new quality, feeling, or attitude. □ *I grew a little afraid of the guy next door.* □ *He's growing old.* **8** V-I If an amount, feeling, or problem **grows**, it becomes greater or more intense. □ *The number of unemployed people in Poland has grown by more than a quarter in the last month.* □ *Opposition grew and the government agreed to negotiate.* **9** V-I If one thing **grows into** another, it develops or changes until it becomes that thing. □ *The boys grew into men.* **10** V-I If something such as an idea or a plan **grows out of** something else, it develops from it. □ *The idea for this book grew out of conversations with Philippa Brewster.* **11** V-I If the economy or a business **grows**, it increases in wealth, size, or importance. [BUSINESS] □ *The economy continues to grow.* **12** V-T If someone **grows** a business, they take actions that will cause it to increase in wealth, size, or importance. [BUSINESS] □ *To grow the business, he needs to develop management expertise and innovation across his team.* **13** →see also **grown**

Thesaurus   grow의 참조어

V.   develop, mature **1** **6**-**8**
        germinate, spring up, thrive **2**
        cultivate, plant, produce **3**
        heighten, intensify **7**

Word Partnership   grow의 연어

V.   **continue to** grow **1**-**8** **11**
        try to grow **3** **5** **12**
        grow **bored**, grow **silent** **7**
N.   grow **food** **3**

▶**grow apart** PHRASAL VERB-RECIP If people who have a close relationship **grow apart**, they gradually start to have different interests and opinions from each other, and their relationship starts to fail. □ *He and his wife grew apart.*

▶**grow into** PHRASAL VERB When a child **grows into** an item of clothing, they become taller or bigger so that it fits them properly. □ *It's a bit big, but she'll soon grow into it.*

▶**grow on** PHRASAL VERB If someone or something **grows on** you, you start to like them more and more. □ *Slowly and strangely, the place began to grow on me.*

▶**grow out of** **1** PHRASAL VERB If you **grow out of** a type of behavior or an interest, you stop behaving in that way or having that interest, as you develop or change. □ *Most children who stammer grow out of it.* **2** PHRASAL VERB When a child **grows out of** an item of clothing, they become so tall or big that it no longer fits them properly. □ *You've grown out of your shoes again.*

▶**grow up** **1** PHRASAL VERB When someone **grows up**, they gradually change from being a child into being an adult. □ *She grew up in Tokyo.* →see also **grown-up** **2** PHRASAL VERB If you tell someone to **grow up**, you are telling them to stop behaving in a silly or childish way. [INFORMAL, DISAPPROVAL] □ *It's time you grew up.* **3** PHRASAL VERB If something **grows up**, it starts to exist and then becomes larger or more important. □ *A variety of heavy industries grew up alongside the port.* →see **bring up**

grow|er /groʊər/ (growers) N-COUNT A **grower** is a person who grows large quantities of a particular plant or crop in order to sell them. □ *England's apple growers are fighting an uphill battle against foreign competition.*

growl /graʊl/ (growls, growling, growled) **1** V-I When a dog or other animal **growls**, it makes a low noise in its throat, usually because it is angry. □ *The dog was biting, growling and wagging its tail.* ● N-COUNT **Growl** is also a noun. □ *The bear exposes its teeth in a muffled growl.* **2** V-T If someone **growls** something, they say something in a low, rough, and angry voice. [WRITTEN] □ *His fury was so great he could hardly speak. He growled some unintelligible words at Pete.* ● N-COUNT **Growl** is also a noun. □ *...with an angry growl of contempt for her own weakness.*

[영영영어 grovelling, grovelled] **1** 자동사 굽실거리다 [탐탁찮음] □ 나는 누구에게도 굽실거리지 않아. □ 자기 의사를 발언하는 사람들은 호통을 듣고 침묵하게 되었고 수업은 중단되었고 교사들은 굽실거리게 되었다. **2** 자동사 기다 □ 우리는 무릎을 꿇고 클럽을 이리저리 기어 다녔다.

1 자동사 성장하다, 생장하다 □ 우리는 다 자라면 성장을 멈춘다. **2** 자동사 (초목이) 자라다 □ 그 역에는 승강장 양 끝에 장미가 자라고 있었다. **3** 타동사 기르다, 재배하다 □ 고대 로마인들이 양상추를 재배했다. **4** 자동사 (머리가) 길다, 자라다 □ 그 후에 머리가 다시 자라기 시작했고 나는 기분이 엄청 좋았다. **5** 타동사 (머리 등을) 기르다 □ 내 머리를 기르기 시작하는 편이 낫겠다. **6** 자동사 성숙하다 □ 그들은 인간적으로 성숙하기 시작했다. **7** 연결동사 ~하게 되다 □ 나는 옆집 남자를 조금 무서워하게 되었다. □ 그는 나이가 들어 있다. **8** 자동사 커지다, 증대하다 □ 폴란드의 실업자 수가 지난 달에 4분의 1 이상 늘었다. □ 반대가 커져서 정부가 협상에 응했다. **9** 자동사 (성장하여 ~이) 되다 □ 소년들이 성장하여 성인이 되었다. **10** 자동사 ~에서 생기다 □ 이 책에 대한 착상은 필립과 브루스터와의 대화에서 나왔다. **11** 자동사 (사업 등이) 성장하다 [경제] □ 경제가 계속 성장한다. **12** 타동사 (사업을) 성장시키다 [경제] □ 사업을 성장시키려면 그는 팀 전반에 걸쳐 경영 전문 지식 개발과 경영 혁신을 이룰 필요가 있다.

상호 구동사 소원해지다 □ 그와 그의 부인은 소원해졌다.

구동사 자라서 옷이 몸에 맞다 □ 그건 조금 크지만 그녀가 자라면 곧 몸에 맞게 될 것이다.

구동사 ~이 점점 좋아지다 □ 서서히 그리고 이상하게도 나는 그곳이 좋아지기 시작했다.

1 구동사 (자라면서) 탈피하다 □ 말을 더듬는 아이들 대부분이 자라면서 괜찮아진다. **2** 구동사 자라서 옷이 몸에 맞지 않다 □ 네가 커서 신발이 또 작아졌구나.

1 구동사 성장하다, 어른이 되다 □ 그녀는 도쿄에서 자랐다. **2** 구동사 철이 들다 [비격식체, 탐탁찮음] □ 이제는 철이 좀 들어야지. **3** 구동사 발달하다 □ 갖가지 중공업이 항만을 따라 발달했다.

가산명사 재배자, 생산자 □ 영국의 사과 생산자들은 외국 경쟁에 대항하여 힘든 전쟁을 치르고 있다.

1 자동사 으르렁거리다 □ 그 개가 물고 으르렁거리고 꼬리를 흔들고 있었다. ● 가산명사 으르렁거리는 소리 □ 곰이 이빨을 드러내며 속으로 으르렁거렸다. **2** 타동사 으르렁거리듯 말하다 [문어체] □ 그는 너무도 격분해서 거의 말을 할 수 없었다. 그는 으르렁거리듯 알아들을 수 없는 말을 피트에게 중얼거렸다. ● 가산명사 으르렁거리는 소리 □ 그녀 자신의 나약함에 대해 성이 나서 경멸조로 으르렁거리며

a b c d e f g h i j k l m n o p q r s t u v w x y z

grown /groʊn/ ADJ A **grown** man or woman is one who is fully developed and mature, both physically and mentally. [ADJ n] ❑ *Few women can understand a grown man's love of sport.*

형용사 성숙한 ❑ 성인 남자가 스포츠를 좋아하는 것을 이해하는 여자는 거의 없다.

grown-up (grown-ups)

The spelling **grownup** is also used. The syllable **up** is not stressed when it is a noun.

철자 grownup도 쓴다. 음절 up은 명사일 때 강세가 없다.

◼ N-COUNT A **grown-up** is an adult; used by or to children. ❑ *Jan was almost a grown-up.* ◼ ADJ Someone who is **grown-up** is physically and mentally mature and no longer depends on their parents or another adult. ❑ *I seem to have everything anyone could want – a good husband, a lovely home, grown-up children who're doing well.* ◼ ADJ If you say that someone is **grown-up**, you mean that they behave in an adult way, often when they are in fact still a child. ❑ *She's very grown-up.* ◼ ADJ **Grown-up** things seem suitable for or typical of adults. [INFORMAL] ❑ *Her songs tackle grown-up subjects.*

◼ 가산명사 성인 ❑ 잰은 거의 성인이었다. ◼ 형용사 성숙한 ❑ 나는 좋은 남편, 멋진 집, 잘하고 있는 성숙한 아이들 등 사람들이 원하는 모든 것을 다 가진 것 같다. ◼ 형용사 어른스러운 ❑ 그녀는 아주 어른스럽다. ◼ 형용사 성인용의 [비격식체] ❑ 그녀의 노래들은 성인용 주제를 다룬다.

growth ♦♦◇ /groʊθ/ (**growths**) ◼ N-UNCOUNT The **growth of** something such as an industry, organization, or idea is its development in size, wealth, or importance. ❑ *...the growth of nationalism.* ❑ *...Japan's enormous economic growth.* ◼ N-UNCOUNT The **growth** in something is the increase in it. [also a N, oft supp N, N in n, N of amount] ❑ *A steady growth in the popularity of two smaller parties may upset the polls.* ❑ *The area has seen a rapid population growth.* ◼ ADJ A **growth** industry, area, or market is one which is increasing in size or activity. [BUSINESS] [ADJ n] ❑ *Computers and electronics are growth industries and need skilled technicians.* ◼ N-UNCOUNT Someone's **growth** is the development and progress of their character. ❑ *...the child's emotional and intellectual growth.* ◼ N-UNCOUNT **Growth** in a person, animal, or plant is the process of increasing in physical size and development. ❑ *...hormones which control fertility and body growth.* ◼ N-VAR You can use **growth** to refer to plants which have recently developed or which developed at the same time. ❑ *This helps to ripen new growth and makes it flower profusely.* ◼ N-COUNT A **growth** is a lump that grows inside or on a person, animal, or plant, and that is caused by a disease. ❑ *This type of surgery could even be used to extract cancerous growths.*

◼ 불가산명사 성장, 발달 ❑ 민족주의의 발달 ❑ 일본의 엄청난 경제 성장 ◼ 불가산명사 증대, 증가 ❑ 두 소수 정당의 꾸준한 인기 증가가 투표 결과를 뒤엎을 수도 있다. ❑ 그 지역에 급속한 인구 증가가 있었다. ◼ 형용사 성장 중인 [경제] ❑ 컴퓨터와 전자는 성장 중인 산업이며 숙련된 기술자가 필요하다. ◼ 불가산명사 성장, 발달 ❑ 그 아이의 정서적, 지적 성장 ◼ 불가산명사 성장, 생장 ❑ 생식 능력과 신체 성장을 조절하는 호르몬 ◼ 가산명사 또는 불가산명사 (생장한) 초목 ❑ 이것은 새로 생장한 초목이 무럭이는 데 도움을 주고 꽃이 많이 피게 한다. ◼ 가산명사 종양 ❑ 이런 종류의 수술은 심지어 암 종양을 적출하는 데도 사용될 수 있다.

grub /grʌb/ (**grubs, grubbing, grubbed**) ◼ N-COUNT A **grub** is a young insect which has just come out of an egg and looks like a short fat worm. ◼ N-UNCOUNT **Grub** is food. [INFORMAL] ❑ *Get yourself some grub and come and sit down.* ◼ V-I If you **grub** around, you search for something. ❑ *I simply cannot face grubbing through all this paper.*

◼ 가산명사 굼벵이, 구더기 ◼ 불가산명사 음식 [비격식체] ❑ 네가 먹을 것을 들고 와서 앉아라. ◼ 자동사 찾다 ❑ 난 이 종이들을 뒤진다는 것이 정말로 엄두가 나지 않는다.

grub|by /grʌbi/ (**grubbier, grubbiest**) ◼ ADJ A **grubby** person or object is rather dirty. ❑ *His white coat was grubby and stained.* ◼ ADJ If you call an activity or someone's behavior **grubby**, you mean that it is not completely honest or respectable. [DISAPPROVAL] ❑ *...the grubby business of politics.*

◼ 형용사 더러운 ❑ 그의 흰색 외투는 더럽고 얼룩이 져 있었다. ◼ 형용사 비열한, 더러운 [탐탁찮음] ❑ 정치라는 더러운 일

grudge /grʌdʒ/ (**grudges**) N-COUNT If you have or bear a **grudge against** someone, you have unfriendly feelings towards them because of something they did in the past. ❑ *He appears to have a grudge against certain players.*

가산명사 반감 ❑ 그는 어떤 선수들에 대해서는 반감을 가지고 있는 듯하다.

grudg|ing /grʌdʒɪŋ/ ADJ A **grudging** feeling or action is felt or done very unwillingly. ❑ *He even earned his opponents' grudging respect.* ● **grudg|ing|ly** ADV [ADV with v] ❑ *The film studio grudgingly agreed to allow him to continue working.*

형용사 마지못해 하는, 내키지 않는 ❑ 그는 심지어 자기의 적들로부터 내키지 않는 존경도 받았다. ● 마지못해 부사 ❑ 그 영화 스튜디오는 그가 계속 일하도록 하는 것에 마지못해 동의했다.

gru|el|ing /gruələ ʊ ̃ŋ/ [BRIT **gruelling**] ADJ A **grueling** activity is extremely difficult and tiring to do. ❑ *He had complained of exhaustion after his grueling schedule over the past week.*

[영국영어 gruelling] 형용사 녹초로 만드는, 격렬한 ❑ 그는 지난 한 주 녹초로 만드는 스케줄을 마친 다음 극도로 피로해졌다고 불평했었다.

grue|some /grusəm/ ADJ Something that is **gruesome** is extremely unpleasant and shocking. ❑ *There has been a series of gruesome murders in the capital.*

형용사 섬뜩한, 소름끼치는 ❑ 수도에서 섬뜩한 연쇄 살인이 났었다.

grum|ble /grʌmbʲl/ (**grumbles, grumbling, grumbled**) ◼ V-T/V-I If someone **grumbles**, they complain about something in a bad-tempered way. ❑ *I shouldn't grumble about Mom – she's lovely really.* ❑ *Taft grumbled that the law so favored the criminal that trials seemed like a game of chance.* ● N-COUNT **Grumble** is also a noun. ❑ *My only grumble is that there isn't a non-smoking section and it can spoil your enjoyment if the people on nearby tables light up.* ◼ V-I If something **grumbles**, it makes a low continuous sound. [LITERARY] ❑ *It was quiet now, the thunder had grumbled away to the west.* ● N-SING **Grumble** is also a noun. [usu N of n] ❑ *One could often hear, far to the east, the grumble of guns.*

◼ 타동사/자동사 투덜거리다, 불평하다 ❑ 나는 엄마에 대해 불평해선 안 돼. 엄마는 정말 멋져. ❑ 태프트는 법이 범인에게 너무 유리해서 재판이 마치 운에 맡기고 하는 승부처럼 보였다고 불평했다. ● 가산명사 투덜댐, 불평 ❑ 내 유일한 불만은 금연 구역이 없어 근처 테이블 사람들이 담뱃불을 붙이면 흥을 깨 버릴 수 있다는 것이다. ◼ 자동사 우르릉거리다 [문예체] ❑ 이제 조용해졌다. 우르릉거리는 천둥소리가 서쪽으로 물러가 버렸다. ● 단수명사 우르릉거리는 소리 ❑ 멀리 동쪽에서 우르릉거리는 총탄 소리가 자주 들린다.

grumpy /grʌmpi/ (**grumpier, grumpiest**) ADJ If you say that someone is **grumpy**, you mean that they are bad-tempered and miserable. ❑ *Some folk think I'm a grumpy old man.* ● **grump|i|ly** ADV [ADV with v] ❑ *"I know, I know," said Ken, grumpily, without looking up.*

형용사 까다로운, 심술궂은 ❑ 어떤 사람들은 내가 까다로운 노인이라고 생각한다. ● 심술궂게 부사 ❑ 켄은 쳐다보지도 않고 "알아, 알아."라고 심술궂게 말했다.

grunt /grʌnt/ (**grunts, grunting, grunted**) ◼ V-T/V-I If you **grunt**, you make a low sound, especially because you are annoyed or not interested in something. ❑ *The driver grunted, convinced that Michael was crazy.* ❑ *"Rubbish," I grunted.* ● N-COUNT **Grunt** is also a noun. [oft N of n] ❑ *Their replies were no more than grunts of acknowledgement.* ◼ V-I When an animal **grunts**, it makes a low rough noise. ❑ *...the sound of a pig grunting.*

◼ 타동사/자동사 툴툴거리다 ❑ 마이클이 제정신이 아니라고 확신하고 운전기사가 툴툴거렸다. ❑ "쓸데없어."라고 나는 툴툴거렸다. ● 가산명사 툴툴 소리 ❑ 그들의 대답은 툴툴거리며 알았다고 한 게 다였다. ◼ 자동사 꿀꿀거리다 ❑ 돼지가 꿀꿀거리는 소리

GSM /dʒiː ɛs ɛm/ N-UNCOUNT **GSM** is a digital mobile telephone system, used across Europe and in other parts of the world. **GSM** is an abbreviation for "global system for mobile communication." ❑ *Their latest financial performance was a direct result of consistent growth in GSM mobile subscribers.*

불가산명사 범유럽 디지털 통신 방식 ❑ 그들의 최근 금융 실적은 지에스엠 이동 통신 가입자의 꾸준한 증가에 의한 직접적 결과였다.

guar|an|tee ♦♦◇ /gærənti/ (**guarantees, guaranteeing, guaranteed**) ◼ V-T If one thing **guarantees** another, the first is certain to cause the second thing

◼ 타동사 보증하다 ❑ 잉여 자원만으로는 성장을 보증하지 못한다. ◼ 가산명사 보증 ❑ 어떤 회사가

to happen. ❑ *Surplus resources alone do not guarantee growth.* ◻2◻ N-COUNT
Something that is a **guarantee of** something else makes it certain that it will
happen or that it is true. ❑ *A famous old name on a firm is not necessarily a guarantee
of quality.* ◻3◻ V-T If you **guarantee** something, you promise that it will
definitely happen, or that you will do or provide it for someone. ❑ *Most states
guarantee the right to free and adequate education.* ❑ *We guarantee that you will find a
community with which to socialise.* ● N-COUNT **Guarantee** is also a noun. ❑ *The
Editor can give no guarantee that they will fulfil their obligations.* ◻4◻ N-COUNT A
guarantee is a written promise by a company to replace or repair a product
free of charge if it has any faults within a particular time. [also *under* N]
❑ *Whatever a guarantee says, when something goes wrong, you can still claim your rights
from the shop.* ◻5◻ V-T If a company **guarantees** its product or work, they provide
a guarantee for it. ❑ *Some builders guarantee their work.* ❑ *All Dreamland's electric
blankets are guaranteed for three years.* ◻6◻ N-COUNT A **guarantee** is money or
something valuable which you give to someone to show that you will do
what you have promised. ❑ *Males between 18 and 20 had to leave a deposit as a
guarantee of returning to do their military service.*

guar|an|tor /gǽrəntɔr/ (guarantors) N-COUNT A **guarantor** is a person who
gives a guarantee or who is bound by one. [LEGAL] ❑ *Someone thinking about acting
as a guarantor should be clear what their obligations will be.*

guard ♦♦◇ /gɑrd/ (guards, guarding, guarded) ◻1◻ V-T If you **guard** a place,
person, or object, you stand near them in order to watch and protect them.
❑ *Gunmen guarded homes near the cemetery with shotguns.* ◻2◻ V-T If you **guard**
someone, you watch them and keep them in a particular place to stop them
from escaping. ❑ *Marines with rifles guarded them.* ◻3◻ N-COUNT A **guard** is
someone such as a soldier, police officer, or prison officer who is guarding a
particular place or person. ❑ *The prisoners overpowered their guards and locked them
in a cell.* ◻4◻ N-SING-COLL A **guard** is a specially organized group of people, such
as soldiers or police officers, who protect or watch someone or something.
❑ *We have a security guard around the whole area.* ◻5◻ N-COUNT On a train, a **guard** is
a person whose job is to travel on the train in order to help passengers, check
tickets, and make sure that the train travels safely and on time. [BRIT; AM
conductor] ◻6◻ V-T If you **guard** some information or advantage that you have,
you try to protect it or keep it for yourself. ❑ *He closely guarded her identity.*
◻7◻ N-COUNT A **guard** is a protective device which covers a part of someone's
body or a dangerous part of a piece of equipment. [usu with supp] ❑ *...the chin
guard of my helmet.* ◻8◻ →see also **guarded, bodyguard, Coast Guard, lifeguard**
◻9◻ PHRASE If someone **catches** you **off guard**, they surprise you by doing
something you do not expect. If something **catches** you **off guard**, it
surprises you by happening when you are not expecting it. ❑ *Charm the
audience and catch them off guard.* ◻10◻ PHRASE If you **lower** your **guard**, **let** your
guard down or **drop** your **guard**, you relax when you should be careful and
alert, often with unpleasant consequences. ❑ *The ANC could not afford to lower
its guard until everything had been carried out.* ❑ *You can't let your guard down.*
◻11◻ PHRASE If you **mount guard** or if you **mount a guard**, you organize people to
watch or protect a person or place. ❑ *They've even mounted guard outside the main
hotel in the capital.* ◻12◻ PHRASE If you are **on** your **guard** or **on guard**, you are
being very careful because you think a situation might become difficult or
dangerous. ❑ *The police have questioned him thoroughly, and he'll be on his guard.*
◻13◻ PHRASE If someone is **on guard**, they are on duty and responsible for
guarding a particular place or person. ❑ *Police were on guard at Barnet town hall.*
◻14◻ PHRASE If you **stand guard**, you stand near a particular person or place
because you are responsible for watching or protecting them. ❑ *One young
policeman stood guard outside the locked embassy gates.* ◻15◻ PHRASE If someone is
under guard, they are being guarded. ❑ *Three men were arrested and one was under
guard in hospital.*

Word Partnership	guard의 연어
N.	guard a door/house/prisoner ◻1◻ ◻2◻
	prison guard, security guard ◻3◻ ◻4◻
V.	catch *someone* off guard ◻9◻
	let your guard down ◻10◻
	be on guard, stand guard ◻12◻-◻14◻

▸guard against PHRASAL VERB If you **guard against** something, you are careful
to prevent it from happening, or to avoid being affected by it. ❑ *The armed forces
were on high alert to guard against any retaliation.*

guard|ed /gɑrdɪd/ ADJ If you describe someone as **guarded**, you mean that they
are careful not to show their feelings or give away information. ❑ *The boy gave
him a guarded look.*

guard|ian /gɑrdiən/ (guardians) ◻1◻ N-COUNT A **guardian** is someone who has
been legally appointed to look after the affairs of another person, for example
a child or someone who is mentally ill. ❑ *Destiny's legal guardian was her
grandmother.* ◻2◻ N-COUNT The **guardian of** something is someone who defends
and protects it. ❑ *The National Party is lifting its profile as socially conservative
guardian of traditional values.*

guer|ril|la ♦◇◇ /gərílə/ (guerrillas) also guerilla N-COUNT A **guerrilla** is someone
who fights as part of an unofficial army, usually against an official army or
police force. ❑ *The guerrillas threatened to kill their hostages.*

guess ♦♦◇ /gɛs/ (guesses, guessing, guessed) ◻1◻ V-T/V-I If you **guess**
something, you give an answer or provide an opinion which may not be true
because you do not have definite knowledge about the matter concerned.
❑ *The suit was faultless: Wood guessed that he was a very successful publisher or a banker.*

붙여진 유명하고도 친숙한 이름이 반드시 질을
보증하지는 않는다. ◻3◻ 타동사 보증하다, 확언하다
❑ 대부분의 국가는 무상 및 적절한 교육을 받을 권리를
보증한다. ❑ 우리는 당신이 사람들과 어울릴 수 있는
모임을 꼭 찾을 거라고 보장합니다. ● 가산명사 보증
❑ 편집장은 그들이 자기들의 의무를 이행할 것이라고
보장할 수 없다. ◻4◻ 가산명사 보증서 ❑ 보증서에
뭐라고 쓰여 있든지 간에 무엇인가 고장이 나면
상점에서 당신의 권리를 주장할 수 있다. ◻5◻ 타동사
보증하다 ❑ 어떤 건축업자들은 자기들의 공사에
보증을 한다. ❑ 드림랜드의 모든 전기담요는 3년간
보증이 된다. ◻6◻ 가산명사 담보 ❑ 18세에서 20세
사이의 남자는 군복무를 하러 돌아온다는 담보로서
공탁금을 맡겨야만 했다.

가산명사 보증인 [법률] ❑ 보증인이 될 것을 생각하고
있는 사람들은 자기의 의무가 무엇인지 잘 납득하고
있어야 한다.

◻1◻ 타동사 지키다, 수호하다 ❑ 무장 경비원들이
산탄총을 들고 묘지 근처의 집들을 지켰다. ◻2◻ 타동사
감시하다 ❑ 소총을 지닌 해병대원들이 그들을
감시했다. ◻3◻ 가산명사 보호, 감수 ❑ 죄수들이
간수들을 제압하고 그들을 감방에 가두었다.
◻4◻ 단수명사-집합 호위대, 경비대 ❑ 우리는 이 지역
전체에 경비대를 배치했다. ◻5◻ 가산명사 (열차의) 차장
[영국영어; 미국영어 conductor] ◻6◻ 타동사 유출을 막다
❑ 그는 그녀의 신분 노출을 철저히 차단했다.
◻7◻ 가산명사 보호대 ❑ 내 헬멧의 턱 보호대 ◻8◻ 구 -의
허를 찌르다 ❑ 관객을 매료시키고 그들의 허를 찔러라.
◻10◻ 구 방심하다 ❑ 아프리카 민족회의는 모든 일이
수행될 때까지 방심할 수 없었다. ❑ 방심해서는 안 돼.
◻11◻ 구 경비를 세우다 ❑ 그들은 수도에 있는 주요 호텔
외부에 경비도 세웠다. ◻12◻ 구 경계하여, 조심하여
❑ 경찰이 그를 철저하게 심문해 왔기 때문에 그는
조심할 것이다. ◻13◻ 구 경비 중 ❑ 경찰이 바넷 시청을
경비 중이었다. ◻14◻ 구 보초 서다 ❑ 젊은 경찰 한 명이
잠긴 대사관 문 밖에서 보초를 섰다. ◻15◻ 구 감시를 받는
중 ❑ 남자 세 명이 체포되었고 한 명은 병원에서
감시를 받는 중이었다.

구동사 예방 조치하다, 대비하다 ❑ 군대는 보복에
대비해 빈틈없는 경계 중이었다.

형용사 조심성 있는, 신중한 ❑ 그 소년은 그에게
조심스런 눈길을 보냈다.

◻1◻ 가산명사 보호자, 후견인 ❑ 데스티니의 법적
보호자는 할머니였다. ◻2◻ 가산명사 수호자 ❑ 국민당은
사회적으로 전통적 가치를 고수하는 보수파
수호자로서의 태도를 고양시키고 있다.

가산명사 게릴라, 비정규병 ❑ 게릴라들이 인질들을
죽인다고 협박했다.

◻1◻ 타동사/자동사 추측하다, 짐작하다, 추정하다 ❑ 그
신사복은 흠잡을 데 없었다. 우드는 그가 크게 성공한
출판업자나 은행가라고 짐작했다. ❑ 그들이 어떤
정신적 고통을 겪고 있는지 단지 추측만 할 수 있을

a b c d e f g h i j k l m n o p q r s t u v w x y z

❑ *You can only guess at what mental suffering they endure.* ❑ *Guess what I did for the whole of the first week.* **2** V-T If you **guess that** something is the case, you correctly form the opinion that it is the case, although you do not have definite knowledge about it. ❑ *By now you will have guessed that I'm back in Ireland.* ❑ *He should have guessed what would happen.* **3** N-COUNT A **guess** is an attempt to give an answer or provide an opinion which may not be true because you do not have definite knowledge about the matter concerned. ❑ *My guess is that the chance that these vaccines will work is zero.* ❑ *He'd taken her pulse and made a guess at her blood pressure.* **4** PHRASE If you say that something is **anyone's guess** or **anybody's guess**, you mean that no-one can be certain about what is really true. [INFORMAL] ❑ *Just when this will happen is anyone's guess.* **5** PHRASE You say **at a guess** to indicate that what you are saying is only an estimate or what you believe to be true, rather than being a definite fact. [VAGUENESS] ❑ *At a guess he's been dead for two days.* **6** PHRASE You say **I guess** to show that you are slightly uncertain or reluctant about what you are saying. [mainly AM, INFORMAL, VAGUENESS] ❑ *I guess he's right.* ❑ *"I think you're being paranoid." — "Yeah. I guess so."* **7** PHRASE If someone **keeps** you **guessing**, they do not tell you what you want to know. ❑ *The author's intention is to keep everyone guessing until the bitter end.* **8** CONVENTION You say **guess what** to draw attention to something exciting, surprising, or interesting that you are about to say. [INFORMAL] ❑ *Guess what, I just got my first part in a movie.*

뿐이다. ❑ 첫 주 내내 내가 무엇을 했는지 추측해 보아라. **2** 타동사 추측하다, 짐작하다 ❑ 지금쯤 넌 내가 아일랜드에 돌아왔을 거라고 추측할 것이다. ❑ 그는 어떤 일이 일어날지 짐작했어야만 했다. **3** 가산명사 추측, 짐작, 추정 ❑ 내 추측에는 이 백신들이 효과가 있을 가능성이 전혀 없다. ❑ 그는 그녀의 맥박을 재고 나서 혈압을 추정했다. **4** 구 짐작에 지나지 않는 것 [비격식체] ❑ 정확히 언제 이 일이 일어날지는 짐작만 할 수 있을 뿐이다. **5** 구 추측으로, 짐작으로 [짐작투] ❑ 추측하건대 그는 죽은 지 이틀이 되었다. **6** 구 ~라고 생각하다, ~인 것 같다 [주로 미국영어, 비격식체, 짐작투] ❑ 그가 옳다고 생각한다. ❑ "내 생각엔 네가 피해망상인 것 같아." "맞아. 나도 그런 것 같아." **7** 구 (마음을) 졸이게 하다 ❑ 작가의 의도는 막판까지 모든 이의 마음을 졸이게 하는 것이다. **8** 관용 표현 이거 알아, 있잖아 [비격식체] ❑ 이거 알아. 내가 막 영화의 첫 배역을 맡았어.

Thesaurus *guess*의 참조어

V.	estimate, predict, suspect **1**
N.	assumption, prediction, theory **3**

Word Partnership *guess*의 연어

N.	guess **a secret** **1**
V.	**make a** guess **3**
ADJ.	**educated** guess, **good** guess, **wild** guess **3**

guess|ti|mate /gɛstɪmət/ (**guesstimates**) N-COUNT A **guesstimate** is an approximate calculation which is based mainly or entirely on guessing. [INFORMAL] ❑ *The 30 percent figure may be no more than a guesstimate.*

가산명사 어림짐작으로 한 추측 [비격식체] ❑ 30퍼센트라는 숫자는 단지 어림짐작으로 한 추측일 것이다.

guest ♦♦◇ /gɛst/ (**guests**) **1** N-COUNT A **guest** is someone who is visiting you or is at an event because you have invited them. ❑ *She was a guest at the wedding.* **2** N-COUNT A **guest** is someone who visits a place or organization or appears on a radio or television show because they have been invited to do so. ❑ *...a frequent chat show guest.* ❑ *Dr. Gerald Jeffers is the guest speaker.* **3** N-COUNT A **guest** is someone who is staying in a hotel. ❑ *I was the only hotel guest.* →see **client** **4** CONVENTION If you say **be my guest** to someone, you are giving them permission to do something. ❑ *If anybody wants to work on this, be my guest.* →see **hotel**

1 가산명사 손님, 내빈 ❑ 그녀는 결혼식의 손님이었다. **2** 가산명사 초청 손님, 특별 출연자 ❑ 토크 쇼의 단골 특별 출연자 ❑ 제럴드 제퍼스 박사가 초청 연사이다. **3** 가산명사 숙박객 ❑ 내가 호텔의 유일한 숙박객이었다. **4** 관용 표현 좋으실 대로 하세요 ❑ 이 일에 참여하고 싶은 사람은 누구나 환영입니다.

Word Partnership *guest*의 연어

ADJ.	**unwelcome** guest **1**
V.	**be** ***someone's*** guest, **entertain a** guest **1** **2**
	accommodate a guest **1** **2** **3**
N.	guest **appearance**, guest **list**, guest **speaker** **1** **2**
	hotel guest **3**

guest house (**guest houses**) also **guesthouse** **1** N-COUNT A **guest house** is a small hotel. **2** N-COUNT A **guest house** is a small house in the grounds of a large house, where visitors can stay. [AM]

1 가산명사 숙박업소, 작은 호텔 **2** 가산명사 손님용 숙소 [미국영어]

guid|ance /gaɪdᵊns/ N-UNCOUNT **Guidance** is help and advice. ❑ *...an opportunity for young people to improve their performance under the guidance of professional coaches.*

불가산명사 안내, 지도 ❑ 전문 코치들의 지도 하에 젊은이들이 실력을 향상시킬 수 있는 기회

guide ♦♦◇ /gaɪd/ (**guides, guiding, guided**) **1** N-COUNT; N-IN-NAMES A **guide** is a book that gives you information or instructions to help you do or understand something. ❑ *Our 10-page guide will help you to change your life for the better.* **2** N-COUNT; N-IN-NAMES A **guide** is a book that gives tourists information about a town, area, or country. ❑ *The Rough Guide to Paris lists accommodation for as little as £25 a night.* **3** N-COUNT A **guide** is someone who shows tourists around places such as museums or cities. ❑ *We've arranged a walking tour of the city with your guide.* **4** V-T If you **guide** someone around a city, museum, or building, you show it to them and explain points of interest. ❑ *...a young Egyptologist who guided us through tombs and temples with enthusiasm.* **5** N-COUNT A **guide** is someone who shows people the way to a place in a difficult or dangerous region. ❑ *The mountain people say that, with guides, the journey can be done in fourteen days.* **6** N-COUNT A **guide** is something that can be used to help you plan your actions or to form an opinion about something. ❑ *As a rough guide, a horse needs 2.5 percent of his body weight in food every day.* **7** V-T If you **guide** someone somewhere, you go there with them in order to show them the way. ❑ *He took the bewildered Elliott by the arm and guided him out.* **8** V-T If you **guide** a vehicle somewhere, you control it carefully to make sure that it goes in the right direction. ❑ *Captain Shelton guided his plane down the runway and took off.* **9** V-T If something **guides** you somewhere, it gives you the information you need in order to go in the right direction. ❑ *They sailed across the Baltic and North Seas with only a compass to guide them.* **10** V-T If something or someone **guides** you, they influence your actions or decisions. ❑ *He should have let his instinct guide him.* ❑ *Development has been guided by a concern for the ecology of the area.* **11** V-T If you **guide** someone through something that is difficult to understand or to

1 가산명사; 이름명사 안내서 ❑ 우리의 10쪽짜리 안내서는 당신의 삶을 한층 더 좋게 변화시키는 데 도움이 될 것이다. **2** 가산명사; 이름명사 여행 안내서 ❑ 파리에 관한 러프 여행 안내서에는 하룻밤에 25파운드밖에 안 하는 숙박 시설이 나와 있다. **3** 가산명사 관광 안내원 ❑ 시내 도보 관광을 안내원과 함께 할 수 있도록 준비했다. **4** 타동사 안내하다 ❑ 우리들에게 열의를 가지고 무덤들과 사원들을 안내해 준 젊은 이집트학 학자 **5** 가산명사 오지 안내원 ❑ 산지 주민들에 의하면 안내원과 함께 가면 여행을 2주 만에 마칠 수 있다고 한다. **6** 가산명사 지침 ❑ 개괄적으로 알려주면, 말 한 마리는 매일 자기 몸의 2.5퍼센트 무게의 음식을 필요로 한다. **7** 타동사 인도하다 ❑ 그는 당황한 엘리엇의 팔을 잡고 밖으로 데리고 나왔다. **8** 타동사 방향을 조정하다 ❑ 쉘튼 대위는 자기 비행기를 조정해서 활주로로 끌고 가서 이륙했다. **9** 타동사 인도하다 ❑ 그들은 자기들을 인도하는 것은 나침반만 있는 가운데 발틱 해와 북해를 횡단하였다. **10** 타동사 좌우하다 ❑ 그는 자기 본능대로 했어야만 했다. ❑ 개발은 그 지역의 생태계에 대한 고려에 따라서 좌우되어 왔다. **11** 타동사 지도하다, 가르치다 ❑ 사업가들에게 미로처럼 복잡한 정부와 유럽 연합 보조금에 대해 알려 주는 무료 전화 서비스가 글래스고에 마련되었다.

A B C D E F G H I J K L M N O P Q R S T U V W X Y Z

achieve, you help them to understand it or to achieve success in it. ❑ *A free helpline to guide businessmen through the maze of government and EU grants has been set up in Glasgow.*

Thesaurus　　　*guide*의 참조어

N.　directory, handbook **1** **2**
V.　accompany, direct, instruct, lead, navigate; *(ant.)* follow **4** **7**

---

guide|book /gaɪdbʊk/ (**guidebooks**) also **guide book** N-COUNT A **guidebook** is a book that gives tourists information about a town, area, or country.

guide|line /gaɪdlaɪn/ (**guidelines**) **1** N-COUNT If an organization issues **guidelines on** something, it issues official advice about how to do it. ❑ *The government should issue clear guidelines on the content of religious education.* **2** N-COUNT A **guideline** is something that can be used to help you plan your actions or to form an opinion about something. ❑ *A written IQ test is merely a guideline.*

guild /gɪld/ (**guilds**) N-COUNT A **guild** is an organization of people who do the same job. ❑ *...the Writers' Guild of America.*

guilt /gɪlt/ **1** N-UNCOUNT **Guilt** is an unhappy feeling that you have because you have done something wrong or think that you have done something wrong. ❑ *Her emotions had ranged from anger to guilt in the space of a few seconds.* **2** N-UNCOUNT **Guilt** is the fact that you have done something wrong or illegal. ❑ *The trial is concerned only with the determination of guilt according to criminal law.*

Word Partnership　　　*guilt*의 연어

N.　**burden** of guilt, **feelings of** guilt, **sense of** guilt **1**
V.　**admit** guilt **2**

---

guilty ♦◇◇ /gɪlti/ (**guiltier**, **guiltiest**) **1** ADJ If you feel **guilty**, you feel unhappy because you think that you have done something wrong or have failed to do something which you should have done. ❑ *I feel so guilty, leaving all this to you.* ● **guilt|ly** ADV [ADV with v] ❑ *He glanced guiltily over his shoulder.* **2** ADJ **Guilty** is used of an action or fact that you feel guilty about. [ADJ n] ❑ *Many may be keeping it a guilty secret.* **guilty conscience** →see **conscience** **3** ADJ If someone is **guilty of** a crime or offense, they have committed that crime or offense. ❑ *They were found guilty of murder.* **4** ADJ If someone is **guilty of** doing something wrong, they have done that thing. ❑ *He claimed Mr. Brooke had been guilty of a "gross error of judgment."* →see **trial**

Word Partnership　　　*guilty*의 연어

V.　**feel** guilty, **look** guilty **1**
　　find someone guilty, **plead (not)** guilty,
　　prove someone guilty **3** **4**
N.　guilty **conscience**, guilty **secret** **2**
　　guilty **party**, guilty **plea**, guilty **verdict** **3** **4**
PREP.　guilty **of** something **3** **4**

---

guinea pig /gɪni pɪg/ (**guinea pigs**) also **guinea-pig** **1** N-COUNT If someone is used as a **guinea pig** in an experiment, something is tested on them that has not been tested on people before. ❑ *Dr. Roger Altounyan used himself as a human guinea pig to perfect a treatment which has since saved the lives of countless people.* **2** N-COUNT A **guinea pig** is a small furry animal without a tail. Guinea pigs are often kept as pets.

guise /gaɪz/ (**guises**) N-COUNT You use **guise** to refer to the outward appearance or form of someone or something, which is often temporary or different from their real nature. ❑ *He turned up at a fancy dress Easter dance in the guise of a white rabbit.*

gui|tar ♦◇◇ /gɪtɑr/ (**guitars**) N-VAR A **guitar** is a musical instrument with six strings and a long neck. You play the guitar by plucking or strumming the strings.

gui|tar|ist /gɪtɑrɪst/ (**guitarists**) N-COUNT A **guitarist** is someone who plays the guitar.

gulf /gʌlf/ (**gulfs**) **1** N-COUNT A **gulf** is an important or significant difference between two people, things, or groups. ❑ *Within society, there is a growing gulf between rich and poor.* **2** N-COUNT A **gulf** is a large area of sea which extends a long way into the surrounding land. ❑ *Hurricane Andrew was last night heading into the Gulf of Mexico.*

gul|lible /gʌlɪbᵊl/ ADJ If you describe someone as **gullible**, you mean they are easily tricked because they are too trusting. ❑ *What point is there in admitting that the stories fed to the gullible public were false?* ● **gul|li|bil|ity** /gʌləbɪlɪti/ N-UNCOUNT ❑ *Was she taking part of the blame for her own gullibility?*

gul|ly /gʌli/ (**gullies**) also **gulley** N-COUNT A **gully** is a long narrow valley with steep sides. ❑ *The bodies of the three climbers were located at the bottom of a steep gully.* →see **erosion**

gulp /gʌlp/ (**gulps**, **gulping**, **gulped**) **1** V-T If you **gulp** something, you eat or drink it very quickly by swallowing large quantities of it at once. ❑ *She quickly gulped her tea.* **2** V-I If you **gulp**, you swallow air, often making a noise in your throat as you do so, because you are nervous or excited. [WRITTEN] ❑ *I gulped, and then proceeded to tell her the whole story.* **3** V-T If you **gulp** air, you breathe in a

가산명사 여행 안내서

1 가산명사 지침 ❑ 정부는 종교 교육의 내용에 대해 분명한 지침을 발표해야 한다. **2** 가산명사 지표 ❑ 지능 지수 필기 검사는 단지 하나의 지표일 뿐이다.

가산명사 동업 조합 ❑ 미국 작가 조합

1 불가산명사 죄의식 ❑ 그녀의 감정은 몇 초 사이에 분노에서 죄의식으로 변했다. **2** 불가산명사 죄를 범함, 죄 ❑ 재판은 형법에 따라 죄에 대한 판결만 소관한다.

1 형용사 죄책감을 느끼는 ❑ 나는 이 모든 것을 너에게 맡기면서 너무도 죄책감을 느낀다. ● 죄책감을 느끼며 부사 ❑ 그는 죄진 것처럼 어깨너머로 힐끗 보았다. **2** 형용사 떳떳하지 못한 ❑ 많은 사람들이 그것을 떳떳하지 못한 비밀로 간직하고 있을지 모른다. **3** 형용사 유죄의 ❑ 그들은 살인죄로 판결받았다. **4** 형용사 과실이 있는 ❑ 그는 브룩 씨가 '심각한 오판'을 한 과실이 있다고 주장받았다.

1 가산명사 실험 대상 ❑ 로저 알투난 박사는 이후 수많은 사람들의 목숨을 구해낸 치료법을 완성하기 위해 자신을 인간 실험 대상으로 삼았다. **2** 가산명사 모르모트

가산명사 외관, 겉모양, 가장 ❑ 그는 흰 토끼로 가장하고 부활절 가장 무도회에 나타났다.

가산명사 또는 불가산명사 기타

가산명사 기타 연주가

1 가산명사 큰 간격, 큰 차이 ❑ 사회 내부에서 점점 빈부의 격차가 커지고 있다. **2** 가산명사 만 ❑ 허리케인 앤드루가 어젯밤 멕시코 만으로 향하고 있었다.

형용사 잘 속는 ❑ 잘 속는 대중에게 했던 이야기들이 거짓이었다고 인정하는 것이 무슨 소용이 있는가? ● 잘 속음 불가산명사 ❑ 그녀가 본인이 쉽게 속은 데 대해 일부 책임을 지고 있었는가?

가산명사 협곡 ❑ 등반자 세 명의 시신이 가파른 협곡의 밑바닥에 놓여 있었다.

1 타동사 꿀꺽꿀꺽 먹다, 꿀꺽꿀꺽 마시다 ❑ 그녀는 급히 차를 꿀꺽꿀꺽 마셨다. **2** 자동사 침을 꿀꺽 삼키다 [문어체] ❑ 나는 침을 꿀꺽 삼킨 다음 그녀에게 전부 다 이야기해 주었다. **3** 타동사 (숨을) 들이쉬다 ❑ 그녀는 폐로 공기를 크게 들이마셨다. **4** 가산명사

large amount of air quickly through your mouth. ❑ *She gulped air into her lungs.* ❹ N-COUNT A **gulp** of air, food, or drink, is a large amount of it that you swallow at once. ❑ *I took in a large gulp of air.*

한입 가득 들어가는 양 ❑ 나는 입안 가득 공기를 들이마셨다.

gum /gʌm/ (**gums, gumming, gummed**) ❶ N-MASS **Gum** is a substance, usually tasting of mint, which you chew for a long time but do not swallow. ❑ *I do not chew gum in public.* ❷ N-COUNT Your **gums** are the areas of firm, pink flesh inside your mouth, which your teeth grow out of. ❑ *The toothbrush gently removes plaque without damaging the gums or causing bleeding.* ❸ N-MASS **Gum** is a type of glue that is used to stick two pieces of paper together. [mainly BRIT] ❑ *He was holding up a pound note that had been torn in half and stuck together with gum.* ❹ ADJ If two things are **gummed together**, they are stuck together. [BRIT] ❑ *It is a mild infection in which a baby's eyelashes can become gummed together.* →see **teeth**

❶ 물질명사 껌 ❑ 나는 남들이 있는 데서 껌을 씹지 않는다. ❷ 가산명사 잇몸 ❑ 그 칫솔은 잇몸을 손상시키거나 피가 나게 하지 않고 부드럽게 플라크를 제거한다. ❸ 물질명사 고무풀 [주로 영국영어] ❑ 그는 두 조각으로 찢어져서 고무풀로 붙인 파운드화 지폐 한 장을 들고 있었다. ❹ 형용사 붙은 [영국영어] ❑ 그것은 아기의 속눈썹이 붙게 되는 경미한 감염이다.

gun ♦♦♢ /gʌn/ (**guns, gunning, gunned**) ❶ N-COUNT A **gun** is a weapon from which bullets or other things are fired. ❑ *He fled, pointing the gun at officers as they chased him.* ❑ *The inner-city has guns and crime and drugs and deprivation.* ❷ N-COUNT A **gun** or a **starting gun** is an object like a gun that is used to make a noise to signal the start of a race. ❑ *The starting gun blasted and they were off.* ❸ V-T To **gun** an engine or a vehicle means to make it start or go faster by pressing on the accelerator pedal. [mainly AM] ❑ *He gunned his engine and drove off.* ❹ →see also **shotgun** ❺ PHRASE If you come out with **guns blazing** or with **all guns blazing**, you put all your effort and energy into trying to achieve something. ❑ *The company came out with guns blazing.* ❻ PHRASE If you **jump the gun**, you do something before everyone else or before the proper or right time. [INFORMAL] ❑ *It wasn't due to be released until September 10, but some booksellers have jumped the gun and decided to sell it early.* ❼ PHRASE If you **stick to** your **guns**, you continue to have your own opinion about something even though other people are trying to tell you that you are wrong. [INFORMAL] ❑ *He should have stuck to his guns and refused to meet her.*

❶ 가산명사 총 ❑ 경찰이 그를 추격하자 그는 그들에게 총을 겨누었고 ❑ 도심에는 총기와 범죄와 마약과 빈곤이 있다. ❷ 가산명사 출발 신호용 총 ❑ 출발 신호용 총이 울렸고 그들은 출발했다. ❸ 타동사 가속시키다 [주로 미국영어] ❑ 그는 엔진을 가속시켜 떠나 버렸다. ❺ 구 전력을 총동원하여 ❑ 그 회사는 전력을 총동원했다. ❻ 구 스타트를 먼저 하다, 조급하게 굴다 [비격식체] ❑ 그것은 9월 10일까지는 시판하지 않기로 되어 있었는데 일부 서적상들이 조급하게 굴며 일찍 시판하기로 했다. ❼ 구 입장을 고수하다, 굴복하지 않다 [비격식체] ❑ 그는 자기 입장을 고수하고 그녀를 만나지 말았어야 했다.

> ### Word Partnership   gun의 연어
>
> v.   **aim** a gun, **carry** a gun, **fire** a gun, **load** a gun, **own** a gun, **shoot** a gun, **use** a gun ❶
>
> n.   **toy** gun ❶
>   gun **an engine** ❸

▶**gun down** PHRASAL VERB If someone **is gunned down**, they are shot and severely injured or killed. [JOURNALISM] ❑ *He had been gunned down and killed at point-blank range.*

구동사 총을 맞고 쓰러지다 [언론] ❑ 그는 아주 가까운 거리에서 총을 맞아 쓰러져 죽었다.

gun|fire /gʌnfaɪr/ N-UNCOUNT **Gunfire** is the repeated shooting of guns. ❑ *The sound of gunfire and explosions grew closer.*

불가산명사 포화 ❑ 포화와 폭발 소리가 점점 가까워졌다.

gun|man /gʌnmən/ (**gunmen**) N-COUNT A **gunman** is a man who uses a gun to commit a crime such as murder or robbery. [JOURNALISM] ❑ *Two policemen were killed when gunmen opened fire on their patrol vehicle.*

가산명사 총기 휴대자, 무장 괴한 [언론] ❑ 무장 괴한들이 순찰차에 총격을 가해 경찰 두 명이 사망했다.

gun|point /gʌnpɔɪnt/ PHRASE If you are held **at gunpoint**, someone is threatening to shoot and kill you if you do not obey them. ❑ *She and her two daughters were held at gunpoint by a gang who burst into their home.*

구 총으로 위협받고 ❑ 그녀와 두 딸은 집으로 난입한 폭력단에게 총으로 위협을 받았다.

gun|shot /gʌnʃɒt/ (**gunshots**) ❶ N-UNCOUNT **Gunshot** is used to refer to bullets that are fired from a gun. ❑ *They had died of gunshot wounds.* ❷ N-COUNT A **gunshot** is the firing of a gun or the sound of a gun being fired. ❑ *They heard thousands of gunshots.*

❶ 불가산명사 총탄 ❑ 그들은 총상으로 죽었다. ❷ 가산명사 발포, 발포 소리 ❑ 그들은 수천 발의 발포 소리를 들었다.

gur|gle /gɜrg̍°l/ (**gurgles, gurgling, gurgled**) ❶ V-I If water **is gurgling**, it is making the sound that it makes when it flows quickly and unevenly through a narrow space. ❑ *...a narrow stone-edged channel along which water gurgles unseen.* ● N-COUNT **Gurgle** is also a noun. ❑ *We could hear the swish and gurgle of water against the hull.* ❷ V-I If someone, especially a baby, **is gurgling**, they are making a sound in their throat similar to the gurgling of water. ❑ *Henry gurgles happily in his baby chair.* ● N-COUNT **Gurgle** is also a noun. ❑ *There was a gurgle of laughter on the other end of the line.*

❶ 자동사 쿨렁쿨렁 하는 소리를 내다 ● 시야에는 보이지 않는 물이 쿨렁쿨렁 하며 흐르고 가장자리에 돌이 둘러진 좁은 수로 ● 가산명사 쿨렁쿨렁 하는 소리 ❑ 우리는 물이 선체에 부딪쳐 철썩철썩 하고 쿨렁쿨렁 하는 소리를 들을 수 있었다. ❷ 자동사 옹알거리다, 가르랑거리다 ❑ 헨리가 자기 아기 의자에 앉아 행복하게 옹알거린다. ● 가산명사 가르랑거리는 소리 ❑ 그 줄 다른 쪽 끝에서 가르랑거리는 웃음소리가 났다.

gur|ney /gɜrni/ (**gurneys**) N-COUNT A **gurney** is a bed on wheels that is used in hospitals for moving sick or injured people. [AM; BRIT **trolley**] ❑ *A man on a gurney was being handled by an orderly.*

가산명사 (바퀴 달린) 이동식 침대 [미국영어; 영국영어 trolley] ❑ 이동식 침대 위의 남자는 환자 이동 담당이 돌보고 있었다.

guru /guru/ (**gurus**) ❶ N-COUNT A **guru** is a person who some people regard as an expert or leader. ❑ *Fashion gurus create crazy ideas such as squeezing oversized bodies into tight trousers.* ❷ N-COUNT; N-TITLE A **guru** is a religious and spiritual leader and teacher, especially in Hinduism.

❶ 가산명사 지도자, 전문가 ❑ 패션 전문가들은 꽉 끼는 바지에 거대한 몸을 억지로 쑤셔 넣는 것과 같이 정신 나간 발상을 강요한다. ❷ 가산명사, 경칭명사 힌두교 지도자

gush /gʌʃ/ (**gushes, gushing, gushed**) ❶ V-T/V-I When liquid **gushes** out of something, or when something **gushes** a liquid, the liquid flows out very quickly and in large quantities. ❑ *Piping-hot water gushed out.* ❷ N-SING A **gush** of liquid is a sudden, rapid flow of liquid, or a quantity of it that suddenly flows out. [usu N of n] ❑ *I heard a gush of water.* ❸ V-T/V-I If someone **gushes**, they express their admiration or pleasure in an exaggerated way. ❑ *"Oh, it was brilliant," he gushes.* ● **gush|ing** ADJ ❑ *He delivered a gushing speech.*

❶ 타동사/자동사 세차게 흘러나오다, 분출하다 ❑ 펄펄 끓는 물이 세차게 흘러나왔다. ❷ 단수명사 솟아 나옴, 분출 ❑ 나는 물이 분출하는 소리를 들었다. ❸ 타동사/자동사 과장하여 떠벌리다 ❑ "아, 그것 멋졌어."라고 그는 과장하여 떠벌린다. ● 과장해서 표현하는 형용사 ❑ 그는 표현이 과장된 연설을 했다.

gust /gʌst/ (**gusts, gusting, gusted**) ❶ N-COUNT A **gust** is a short, strong, sudden rush of wind. ❑ *A gust of wind drove down the valley.* ❷ V-I When the wind **gusts**, it blows with short, strong, sudden rushes. ❑ *The wind gusted again.* ❸ N-COUNT If you feel a **gust of** emotion, you feel the emotion suddenly and intensely. [N of n] ❑ *...a small gust of pleasure.*

❶ 가산명사 돌풍 ❑ 한바탕 돌풍이 계곡 아래로 세차게 몰아쳤다. ❷ 자동사 (강풍이) 불다 ❑ 바람이 다시 강하게 불었다. ❸ 가산명사 (감정의) 폭발 ❑ 즐거움의 작은 폭발

gut /gʌt/ (**guts, gutting, gutted**) ❶ N-PLURAL A person's or animal's **guts** are all the organs inside them. ❑ *By the time they finish, the crewmen are standing ankle-deep in fish guts.* ❷ V-T When someone **guts** a dead animal or fish, they prepare it for cooking by removing all the organs from inside it. ❑ *It is not always*

❶ 복수명사 내장 ❑ 일을 마칠 무렵이면 선원들은 발목까지 차는 생선 내장 속에 있게 된다. ❷ 타동사 내장을 빼내다 ❑ 요리하기 전에 항상 생선의 내장을 빼낼 필요는 없다. ❸ 단수명사 창자 ❑ 독소가

necessary to gut the fish prior to freezing. **3** N-SING **The gut** is the tube inside the body of a person or animal through which food passes while it is being digested. [the/poss N] ❑ *Toxins can leak from the gut into the bloodstream.* **4** N-UNCOUNT **Guts** is the will and courage to do something which is difficult or unpleasant, or which might have unpleasant results. [INFORMAL] ❑ *The new Chancellor has the guts to push through unpopular tax increases.* **5** ADJ A **gut** feeling is based on instinct or emotion rather than reason. ❑ *Let's have your gut reaction to the facts as we know them.* **6** N-COUNT You can refer to someone's stomach as their **gut**, especially when it is very large and sticks out. [INFORMAL] ❑ *His gut sagged out over his belt.* **7** V-T To **gut** a building means to destroy the inside of it so that only its outside walls remain. ❑ *Over the weekend, a firebomb gutted a building where 60 people lived.* **8** N-UNCOUNT **Gut** is string made from part of the stomach of an animal. Traditionally, it is used to make the strings of sports rackets or musical instruments such as violins. ❑ *Connolly's violin strings are made of gut rather than steel.* **9** PHRASE If you **hate** someone's **guts**, you dislike them very much indeed. [INFORMAL, EMPHASIS] ❑ *We hate each other's guts.* **10** PHRASE If you say that you **are working** your **guts out** or, in British English, **slogging** your **guts out**, you are emphasizing that you are working as hard as you can. [INFORMAL, EMPHASIS] ❑ *Most have worked their guts out and made sacrifices.*

gut|ter /gʌtər/ (**gutters**) **1** N-COUNT **The gutter** is the edge of a road next to the pavement, where rainwater collects and flows away. ❑ *It is supposed to be washed down the gutter and into the city's vast sewerage system.* **2** N-COUNT A **gutter** is a plastic or metal channel fixed to the lower edge of the roof of a building, which rainwater drains into. ❑ *Did you fix the gutter?* **3** N-SING If someone is **in the gutter**, they are very poor and live in a very bad way. ❑ *Instead of ending up in jail or in the gutter he was remarkably successful.*

guy ◆◇◇ /gaɪ/ (**guys**) **1** N-COUNT A **guy** is a man. [INFORMAL] ❑ *I was working with a guy from Manchester.* **2** N-VOC; N-PLURAL Americans sometimes address a group of people, whether they are male or female, as **guys** or **you guys**. [INFORMAL] [you N] ❑ *Hi, guys. How are you doing?*

gym /dʒɪm/ (**gyms**) **1** N-COUNT A **gym** is a club, building, or large room, usually containing special equipment, where people go to do physical exercise and get fit. ❑ *While the lads are golfing, I work out in the gym.* **2** N-UNCOUNT **Gym** is the activity of doing physical exercises in a gym, especially at school. ❑ *...gym classes.*

gym|na|sium /dʒɪmneɪziəm/ (**gymnasiums** or **gymnasia** /dʒɪmneɪziə/) N-COUNT A **gymnasium** is the same as a **gym**. [FORMAL]

gym|nast /dʒɪmnæst/ (**gymnasts**) N-COUNT A **gymnast** is someone who is trained in gymnastics.

gym|nas|tics /dʒɪmnæstɪks/

The form **gymnastic** is used as a modifier.

N-UNCOUNT **Gymnastics** consists of physical exercises that develop your strength, coordination, and ease of movement. ❑ *...the British Amateur Gymnastics Association.*

gy|ne|col|ogy /gaɪnɪkɒlədʒi/ [BRIT **gynaecology**] N-UNCOUNT **Gynecology** is the branch of medical science which deals with women's diseases and medical conditions. ● **gy|ne|colo|gist** (**gynecologists**) N-COUNT ❑ *Gynecologists at Aberdeen Maternity Hospital have successfully used the drug on 60 women.* ● **gy|ne|co|logi|cal** /gaɪnɪkələdʒɪkəl/ ADJ [ADJ n] ❑ *Breast examination is a part of a routine gynecological examination.*

gyp|sy /dʒɪpsi/ (**gypsies**) also **gipsy** N-COUNT A **gypsy** is a member of a race of people who travel from place to place, usually in caravans, rather than living in one place. ❑ *I'm proud of being brought up by gypsies.* ● ADJ **Gypsy** is also an adjective. ❑ *...the largest gypsy community of any country.*

창자에서 혈관으로 새어 나갈 수 있다. **4** 불가산명사 용기, 배짱 [비격식체] ❑ 새 재무 장관은 대중의 지지를 받지 않는 세금 인상을 밀고 나갈 배짱이 있다. **5** 형용사 본능적인 ❑ 우리가 아는 그대로의 사실에 대해 본능적으로 반응해 봐. **6** 가산명사 (불룩 나온) 배 [비격식체] ❑ 그의 배가 허리띠 위로 불룩 튀어 나와 있었다. **7** 타동사 내부를 파괴하다 ❑ 주말에 소이탄 한 발에 60명이 살고 있던 건물 내부가 파괴되었다. **8** 불가산명사 (라켓, 현악기 등의) 거트, 장선 ❑ 코놀리의 바이올린 줄은 강철이 아니라 거트로 만들어진다. **9** 구 죽도록 싫어하다 [비격식체, 강조] ❑ 우리는 서로 꼴도 보기 싫어한다. **10** 구 뼈 빠지게 열심히 일하다 [비격식체, 강조] ❑ 대부분 사람들은 뼈 빠지게 일하고 희생도 했다.

1 가산명사 (길가의) 배수구 ❑ 그것은 배수구를 따라 씻겨 내려가서 시의 거대한 하수 설비 체계로 들어가게 되어 있다. **2** 가산명사 낙수홈통 ❑ 낙수홈통을 고쳤어요? **3** 단수명사 빈민굴 ❑ 감옥이나 빈민굴에서 살게 되는 대신 그는 눈부시게 성공했다.

1 가산명사 사내, 남자 [비격식체] ❑ 나는 맨체스터에서 온 남자와 일을 하고 있었다. **2** 호격명사; 복수명사 친구들, 여러분 [비격식체] ❑ 안녕, 여러분. 어떻게 지내요?

1 가산명사 체육관 ❑ 남자들이 골프를 치고 있는 동안 나는 체육관에서 운동을 한다. **2** 불가산명사 체육 ❑ 체육 수업

가산명사 체육관 [격식체]

가산명사 체조 선수

gymnastic은 수식어구로 쓴다.

불가산명사 체조 ❑ 영국 아마추어 체조 협회

[영국영어 gynaecology] 불가산명사 부인과 의학 ● 부인과 의사 가산명사 ❑ 애버딘 산과 병원의 부인과 의사들이 그 약을 60명의 여성에게 성공적으로 사용했다. ● 부인과 의학의 형용사 ❑ 유방 검사는 일상적인 부인과 검사의 일부이다.

가산명사 집시 ❑ 나는 집시에게서 자란 것을 자랑스럽게 여긴다. ● 형용사 집시의 ❑ 세계 각국에서 가장 큰 집시 사회

a b c d e f g h i j k l m n o p q r s t u v w x y z

Hh

H, h /eɪtʃ/ (H's, h's /eɪtʃɪz/) N-VAR H is the eighth letter of the English alphabet.

hab|it ♦◇◇ /hǽbɪt/ (**habits**) **1** N-VAR A **habit** is something that you do often or regularly. ❑ He has an endearing habit of licking his lips when he's nervous. ❑ Many people add salt to their food out of habit, without even tasting it first. **2** N-COUNT A **habit** is an action which is considered bad that someone does repeatedly and finds it difficult to stop doing. ❑ A good way to break the habit of eating too quickly is to put your knife and fork down after each mouthful. **3** N-COUNT A drug **habit** is an addiction to a drug such as heroin or cocaine. ❑ She became a prostitute in order to pay for her cocaine habit. **4** PHRASE If you say that someone is **a creature of habit**, you mean that they usually do the same thing at the same time each day, rather than doing new and different things. ❑ Jesse is a creature of habit and always eats breakfast. **5** PHRASE If you are **in the habit of** doing something, you do it regularly or often. If you **get into the habit of** doing something, you begin to do it regularly or often. ❑ They were in the habit of giving two or three dinner parties a month. **6** PHRASE If you **make a habit of** doing something, you do it regularly or often. ❑ You can phone me at work as long as you don't make a habit of it.

	Word Partnership	habit의 연어
V.	develop/form a habit, a habit of doing *something*, do *something* out of habit **1** **2**	
	break a habit, kick a habit, give up a habit, smoking habit **2**	
N.	force of habit **1**	
	cocaine habit, drug habit **3**	
ADJ.	bad/nasty habit **2**	

habi|tat /hǽbɪtæt/ (**habitats**) N-VAR The **habitat** of an animal or plant is the natural environment in which it normally lives or grows. ❑ In its natural habitat, the hibiscus will grow up to 25ft.

ha|bit|u|al /həbɪ́tʃuəl/ **1** ADJ A **habitual** action, state, or way of behaving is one that someone usually does or has, especially one that is considered to be typical or characteristic of them. ❑ If bad posture becomes habitual, you risk long-term effects. ● **ha|bit|u|al|ly** ADV ❑ His mother had a patient who habitually flew into rages. **2** ADJ You use **habitual** to describe someone who usually or often does a particular thing. [ADJ n] ❑ Three out of four of them would become habitual criminals if actually sent to jail.

hack /hǽk/ (**hacks, hacking, hacked**) **1** V-T/V-I If you **hack** something or **hack** at it, you cut it with strong, rough strokes using a sharp tool such as an ax or a knife. ❑ An armed gang barged onto the train and began hacking and shooting anyone in sight. ❑ Matthew desperately hacked through the leather. **2** V-T/V-I If you **hack at** or **hack** something which is too large, too long, or too expensive, you reduce its size, length, or cost by cutting out or getting rid of large parts of it. ❑ He hacked away at the story, throwing out much of the flashback material and eliminating one character entirely. **3** N-COUNT If you refer to a professional writer, such as a journalist, as a **hack**, you disapprove of them because they write for money without worrying very much about the quality of their writing. [DISAPPROVAL] ❑ ...tabloid hacks, always eager to find victims in order to sell newspapers. **4** N-COUNT If you refer to a politician as a **hack**, you disapprove of them because they are too loyal to their party and perhaps do not deserve the position they have. [DISAPPROVAL] ❑ Far too many party hacks from the old days still hold influential jobs. **5** V-I If someone **hacks into** a computer system, they break into the system, especially in order to get secret information. ❑ The saboteurs had demanded money in return for revealing how they hacked into the systems. ● **hack|ing** N-UNCOUNT ❑ ...the common and often illegal art of computer hacking. **6** PHRASE If you say that someone **can't hack it** or **couldn't hack it**, you mean that they do not or did not have the qualities needed to do a task or cope with a situation. [INFORMAL] ❑ You have to be strong and confident and never give the slightest impression that you can't hack it.

hack|er /hǽkər/ (**hackers**) N-COUNT A computer **hacker** is someone who tries to break into computer systems, especially in order to get secret information. ❑ ...a hacker who steals credit card numbers. →see **Internet**

had

The auxiliary verb is pronounced /həd, STRONG hæd/. For the main verb, and for the meanings **2** to **5**, the pronunciation is /hæd/.

가산명사 또는 불가산명사 영어 알파벳의 여덟 번째 글자

1 가산명사 또는 불가산명사 습관, 버릇 ❑ 그는 초조할 때 자신의 입술을 핥는 귀여운 버릇이 있다. ❑ 많은 사람들이 음식을 처음 맛보기도 전에 습관적으로 소금을 친다. **2** 가산명사 버릇 ❑ 너무 빨리 먹는 버릇을 없애는 좋은 방법은 한 입 먹을 때마다 먹고 난 뒤 나이프와 포크를 내려놓는 것이다. **3** 가산명사 중독 ❑ 그녀는 코카인 중독 때문에 드는 돈을 대기 위해서 창녀가 되었다. **4** 구 습관이 강한 사람 ❑ 제시는 습관이 확고해서 아침을 항상 먹는다. **5** 구 -을 자주 하는, -하는 습관이 있는; -하는 버릇이 된 ❑ 그들은 한 달에 두어 번씩 저녁 파티를 열곤 했다. **6** 구 -을 자주 하다 ❑ 자주 하지만 않으면, 회사로 전화해도 괜찮다.

가산명사 또는 불가산명사 서식지 ❑ 천연 서식지에서 히비스커스는 25피트까지 자랄 것이다.

1 형용사 습관적인 ❑ 나쁜 자세가 습관이 되면 장기적으로 부작용이 생길 위험이 있다. ● 습관적으로 부사 ❑ 그의 어머니에게는 습관적으로 벌컥 화를 내는 환자가 있었다. **2** 형용사 상습적인 ❑ 실제로 감옥에 보내진다면, 그들 넷 중 세 명은 상습적인 범죄자가 될 것이다.

1 타동사/자동사 난도질하다, 마구 자르다 ❑ 무장한 일당이 기차에 난입하여 보이는 대로 아무에게나 난도질하고 총을 쏘기 시작했다. ❑ 매튜는 필사적으로 가죽을 칼로 베어 줄였다 **2** 타동사/자동사 베어 줄이다 ❑ 그는 많은 부분의 플래시백 장면을 삭제하고 등장인물 한 명을 완전히 제거하여 그 이야기를 대폭 줄였다. **3** 가산명사 돈벌이 문필가, 글을 팔아먹는 사람 [탐탁찮음] ❑ 신문을 팔아먹기 위해 항상 희생자를 찾으려 드는 타블로이드판 글쟁이들 **4** 가산명사 해바라기 정치인 [탐탁찮음] ❑ 오래 전부터 지나치게 많은 정당의 해바라기 정치인들이 여전히 영향력 있는 자리에 있다. **5** 자동사 (컴퓨터) 침입하다, 해킹하다 ❑ 파괴 공작원들은 어떻게 그들이 시스템을 해킹했는지를 밝혀 주는 답례로 돈을 요구했었다. ● 해킹 불가산명사 ❑ 흔하지만 대개는 불법인 컴퓨터 해킹 기술 **6** 구 잘 해낼 수 없다; 잘 해낼 수 없었다 [비격식체] ❑ 강해지고 자신감을 가져야 하며, 잘할 수 없다는 인상을 약간이라도 주어서는 안 된다.

가산명사 (컴퓨터) 불법 침입자, 해커 ❑ 신용 카드 번호를 훔치는 해커

조동사일 때는 /həd, 강형은 hæd /로 발음되고, 일반 동사일 때와 **2**에서 **5**까지의 의미일 때는 /hæd/ 로 발음된다.

Word Web   hair

At any given moment, only about 90 percent of the **hair** on your **scalp** is alive. The other 10 percent is dead and getting ready to **fall out**. Each hair grows about a centimeter a month for two to six years. Then it falls out and the cycle starts all over again. It's normal to lose about 100 hairs a day from your scalp. To keep hair healthy, eat a healthy diet and use a good **shampoo** and conditioner. Gently **brush** and **comb** your hair. Avoid strong **dyes**. Using the "cool" setting on your hairdryer also helps.

1 **Had** is the past tense and past participle of **have**. **2** AUX **Had** is sometimes used instead of "if" to begin a clause which refers to a situation that might have happened but did not. For example, the clause "had he been elected" means the same as "if he had been elected." ❏ *Had he succeeded, he would have acquired a monopoly.* **3** PHRASE If you **have been had**, someone has tricked you, for example by selling you something at too high a price. [INFORMAL] ❏ *If your customer thinks he's been had, you have to make him happy.* **4** PHRASE If you say that someone **has had it**, you mean they are in very serious trouble or have no hope of succeeding. [INFORMAL] ❏ *Unless she loses some weight, she's had it.* **5** PHRASE If you say that you **have had it**, you mean that you are very tired of something or very annoyed about it, and do not want to continue doing it or it to continue happening. [INFORMAL] ❏ *I've had it. Let's call it a day.*

had|dock /ˈhædək/

Haddock is both the singular and the plural form.

N-VAR **haddock** are a type of edible sea fish that are found in the North Atlantic. ❏ *...fishing boats which normally catch a mix of cod, haddock and whiting.*

hadn't /ˈhædᵊnt/ **Hadn't** is the usual spoken form of 'had not.'

haemo|philia /ˌhiːməˈfɪliə/ →see **hemophilia**

haemo|phili|ac /ˌhiːməˈfɪliæk/ →see **hemophiliac**

haem|or|rhage →see **hemorrhage**

hag|gle /ˈhægᵊl/ (**haggles**, **haggling**, **haggled**) V-RECIP If you **haggle**, you argue about something before reaching an agreement, especially about the cost of something that you are buying. ❏ *Ella showed her the best places to go for a good buy, and taught her how to haggle with used furniture dealers.* ❏ *Of course he'll still haggle over the price.* ● **hag|gling** N-UNCOUNT ❏ *After months of haggling, they recovered only three-quarters of what they had lent.*

hail /heɪl/ (**hails**, **hailing**, **hailed**) **1** V-T If a person, event, or achievement **is hailed as** important or successful, they are praised publicly. [usu passive] ❏ *Faulkner has been hailed as the greatest American novelist of his generation.* **2** N-UNCOUNT **Hail** consists of small balls of ice that fall like rain from the sky. ❏ *...a sharp short-lived storm with heavy hail.* **3** V-I When **it hails**, hail falls like rain from the sky. ❏ *It started to hail, huge great stones.* **4** N-SING A **hail of** things, usually small objects, is a large number of them that hit you at the same time and with great force. ❏ *The victim was hit by a hail of bullets.* **5** V-I Someone who **hails from** a particular place was born there or lives there. [FORMAL] ❏ *I hail from Brighton.* **6** V-T If you **hail** a taxi, you wave at it in order to stop it because you want the driver to take you somewhere. ❏ *I hurried away to hail a taxi.* →see **storm**

hair ♦♦◇ /heər/ (**hairs**) **1** N-VAR Your **hair** is the fine threads that grow in a mass on your head. ❏ *I wash my hair every night.* ❏ *I get some grey hairs but I pull them out.* **2** N-VAR **Hair** is the short, fine threads that grow on different parts of your body. ❏ *The majority of men have hair on their chest.* **3** N-VAR **Hair** is the threads that cover the body of an animal such as a dog, or make up a horse's mane and tail. ❏ *I am allergic to cat hair.* **4** PHRASE If you **let your hair down**, you relax completely and enjoy yourself. ❏ *...the world-famous Oktoberfest, a time when everyone in Munich really lets their hair down.* **5** PHRASE Something that **makes your hair stand on end** shocks or frightens you very much. ❏ *This was the kind of smile that made your hair stand on end.* **6** PHRASE If you say that someone has **not a hair out of place**, you are emphasizing that they are extremely neat and well-dressed. [EMPHASIS] ❏ *She had a lot of makeup on and not a hair out of place.* **7** PHRASE If you say that someone **is splitting hairs**, you mean that they are making unnecessary distinctions between things when the differences between them are so small they are not important. ❏ *Don't split hairs. You know what I'm getting at.* →see Word Web: **hair**

Word Partnership   hair의 연어

V.	**bleach your** hair, **brush/comb your** hair, **color your** hair, **cut your** hair, **do your** hair, **dry your** hair, **fix your** hair, **lose your** hair, **pull** *someone's* hair, **wash your** hair **1**
N.	**lock of** hair **1**
ADJ.	**black/blonde/brown/gray** hair, **curly/straight/wavy** hair **1 2**

hair|cut /ˈheərkʌt/ (**haircuts**) **1** N-COUNT If you get a **haircut**, someone cuts your hair for you. ❏ *Your hair is all right; it's just that you need a haircut.* **2** N-COUNT A **haircut** is the style in which your hair has been cut. ❏ *Who's that guy with the funny haircut?*

---

1 have의 과거 및 과거 분사 **2** 준조동사 -했다면 ❏ 그가 성공했다면 독점권을 획득했을 것이다. **3** 구 바가지를 썼다 [비격식체] ❏ 고객이 바가지를 썼다고 생각한다면, 고객을 만족시켜야 한다. **4** 구 볼장 다 보다 [비격식체] ❏ 체중을 좀 줄이지 않으면, 그녀는 볼장 다 본 거다. **5** 구 지긋지긋하다 [비격식체] ❏ 지긋지긋하다. 이제 마감하자.

haddock은 단수형 및 복수형이다.

가산명사 또는 불가산명사 해덕 ❏ 평소대로 대구, 해덕, 그리고 민어를 같이 잡는 어선들

had not을 줄인 형태로 보통 구어체에 씀

상호동사 (거래에서) 승강이하다, 값을 끈질기게 깎다 ❏ 엘라는 그녀에게 싸게 살 수 있는 가장 괜찮은 곳을 알려 주었고, 중고 가구 판매자와 흥정하는 방법을 가르쳐 주었다. ❏ 물론 그는 여전히 가격을 가지고 흥정을 할 것이다. ● (값을 깎으려는) 옥신각신, 입씨름 불가산명사 ❏ 몇 개월 동안 옥신각신한 후에 그들은 이전에 빌려 준 것의 4분의 3 정도만 되돌려 받았다.

1 타동사 칭송받다, 인정받다 ❏ 포크너는 그의 세대의 가장 위대한 미국 소설가라고 칭송받아 왔다. **2** 불가산명사 우박 ❏ 많은 우박을 동반한 강력하고 일시적인 폭풍우 **3** 자동사 우박이 쏟아지다 ❏ 굉장히 큰 우박이 쏟아지기 시작했다. **4** 단수명사 - 세례 ❏ 희생자는 총탄 세례를 받았다. **5** 자동사 - 출신이다 [격식체] ❏ 나는 브라이튼 출신이다. **6** 타동사 -을 불러 세우다 ❏ 나는 서둘러 나가서 택시를 잡았다.

1 가산명사 또는 불가산명사 머리카락, 머리 ❏ 나는 매일 밤 머리를 감는다. ❏ 나는 흰머리가 몇 가닥 있지만 뽑아 버린다. **2** 가산명사 또는 불가산명사 털, 체모 ❏ 대다수의 남자들은 가슴에 털이 있다. **3** 가산명사 또는 불가산명사 (동물의) 털 ❏ 나는 고양이 털에 알레르기가 있다. **4** 구 느긋하게 즐기다 ❏ 뮌헨에 있는 모든 사람들이 느긋하게 즐기는 시간으로 세계적으로 유명한 옥토버페스트 **5** 구 머리끝이 쭈뼛해지게 하다 ❏ 이것은 머리끝이 쭈뼛하게 하는 그런 종류의 웃음이었다. **6** 구 머리카락 한 올 흐트러짐 없이 [강조] ❏ 그녀는 화장을 많이 했고 머리카락 한 올 흐트러진 데가 없었다. **7** 구 (사소한 일을) 꼬치꼬치 따지다, 세밀하게 구별하다 ❏ 꼬치꼬치 따지지 마. 내가 무얼 말하고 있는지 너는 알고 있어.

1 가산명사 이발, 머리 컷 ❏ 너의 머리 스타일은 괜찮다. 그냥 이발만 하면 된다. **2** 가산명사 머리 스타일 ❏ 우스꽝스러운 머리 스타일을 한 저 남자는 누구지?

A B C D E F G H I J K L M N O P Q R S T U V W X Y Z

hair|dresser /ˈheərdresər/ (**hairdressers**) ■ N-COUNT A **hairdresser** is a person who cuts, colors, and arranges people's hair. ■ N-COUNT A **hairdresser** or a **hairdresser's** is a shop where a hairdresser works. ❑ *I work in this new hairdresser's.*
　■ 가산명사 미용사, 이발사　■ 가산명사 미용실, 이발소 ❑ 나는 이곳 새로운 미용실에서 일한다.

hair|dressing /ˈheərdresɪŋ/ N-UNCOUNT **Hairdressing** is the job or activity of cutting, coloring, and arranging people's hair. ❑ *...personal services such as hairdressing and dry cleaning.*
　불가산명사 이발, 미용 ❑ 미용과 드라이클리닝과 같은 개인적인 서비스

hair|style /ˈheərstaɪl/ (**hairstyles**) N-COUNT Your **hairstyle** is the style in which your hair has been cut or arranged. ❑ *I think her new short hairstyle looks simply great.*
　가산명사 머리 모양, 헤어스타일 ❑ 나는 그녀의 새로운 짧은 헤어스타일이 정말로 멋져 보인다고 생각한다.

hairy /ˈheəri/ (**hairier, hairiest**) ■ ADJ Someone or something that is **hairy** is covered with hairs. ❑ *He was wearing shorts which showed his long, muscular, hairy legs.* ■ ADJ If you describe a situation as **hairy**, you mean that it is exciting, worrying, and rather frightening. [INFORMAL] ❑ *His driving was a bit hairy.*
　■ 형용사 털이 많은 ❑ 그는 자신의 근육질과 털이 덥수룩한 긴 다리가 보이는 짧은 바지를 입고 있었다. ■ 형용사 섬뜩한, 위험한 [비격식체] ❑ 그는 꽤나 위험하게 운전을 했다.

half ♦♦♦ /hæf, BRIT hɑːf/ (**halves**) /hævz, BRIT hɑːvz/ ■ FRACTION **Half** of an amount or object is one of two equal parts that together make up the whole number, amount, or object. ❑ *She wore a diamond ring worth half a million dollars.* ❑ *More than half of all households report incomes above £35,000.* ● PREDET **Half** is also a predeterminer. ❑ *We just sat and talked for half an hour or so.* ❑ *They had only received half the money promised.* ● ADJ **Half** is also an adjective. [ADJ n] ❑ *...a half measure of fresh lemon juice.* ■ ADV You use **half** to say that something is only partly the case or happens to only a limited extent. ❑ *His eyes were half closed.* ❑ *His refrigerator frequently looked half empty.* ■ N-COUNT In games such as football, soccer, rugby, and basketball, games are divided into two equal periods of time which are called **halves**. ❑ *The only goal was scored by Jakobsen early in the second half.* ■ ADV You use **half** to say that someone has parents of different nationalities. For example, if you are **half** German, one of your parents is German but the other is not. [ADV adj] ❑ *She was half Italian and half English.* ■ PHRASE You use **half past** to refer to a time that is thirty minutes after a particular hour. ❑ *"What time were you planning lunch?" — "Half past twelve, if that's convenient."* ■ ADV You can use **half** before an adjective describing an extreme quality, as a way of emphasizing and exaggerating something. [INFORMAL, EMPHASIS] [ADV adj] ❑ *He felt half dead with tiredness.* ● PREDET **Half** can also be used in this way with a noun referring to a long period of time or a large quantity. ❑ *I thought about you half the night.* ■ ADV **Half** is sometimes used in negative statements, with a positive meaning, to emphasize a particular fact or quality. For example, if you say "**he isn't half lucky**," you mean that he is very lucky. [BRIT, INFORMAL, EMPHASIS] ❑ *You don't half sound confident.* ❑ *My kick wasn't half a bad effort for an old man.* ■ ADV You use **not half** to emphasize a negative quality that someone has. [EMPHASIS] ❑ *You're not half the man you think you are.* ■ PHRASE If two people **go halves**, they divide the cost of something equally between them. ❑ *He's constantly on the phone to his girlfriend. We have to go halves on the phone bill which drives me mad.*
　■ 분수 절반, 2분의 1 ❑ 그녀는 50만 달러 상당의 다이아몬드 반지를 끼고 있었다. ❑ 절반 이상의 가구가 35,000파운드 이상의 수입을 신고한다. ● 전치 한정사 절반의 ❑ 우리는 그냥 앉아서 30분 정도 이야기를 나누었다. ❑ 그들은 약속한 돈의 절반만 받았다. ● 형용사 절반의 ❑ 신선한 레몬주스 절반의 양 ■ 부사 부분적인, 불완전한 ❑ 그의 눈이 반쯤 감겼다. ❑ 그의 냉장고는 자주 반쯤 비어 있는 것처럼 보였다. ■ 가산명사 시합의 전후반전 ❑ 유일한 골을 야콥슨이 후반전 초에 터뜨렸다. ■ 부사 절반의 ❑ 그녀는 이탈리아 인과 영국인 사이의 혼혈이었다. ■ 구 30분 (지나서) ❑ "몇 시에 점심 먹을 생각이야?" "괜찮다면, 12시 반에." ■ 부사 거의 [비격식체, 강조] ❑ 그는 피로해서 거의 죽을 지경이었다. ● 전치 한정사 거의 ❑ 나는 거의 밤새 너를 생각했다. ■ 부사 (부정문에서) 매우; 그는 매우 운이 좋다 [영국영어, 비격식체, 강조] ❑ 당신은 매우 자신 있어 보인다. ❑ 나의 킥은 늙은 남자치고는 못친 것이 아니었다. ■ 부사 조금도 ~ 아닌 [강조] ❑ 너는 네가 생각하는 것만큼 그렇게 대단한 남자가 결코 아니다. ■ 구 절반씩 부담하다 ❑ 그는 끊임없이 여자 친구와 전화 통화를 한다. 나를 화나게 하는 것은 그 전화 요금을 우리가 반반씩 내야 한다는 것이다.

half board N-UNCOUNT If you stay at a hotel and have **half board**, your breakfast and evening meal are included in the price of your stay at the hotel, but not your lunch. [mainly BRIT] ❑ *A week's half-board with flights and car hire costs £849–£1,345.*
　불가산명사 조식과 석식이 포함된 숙박 시설 [주로 영국영어] ❑ 항공료와 자동차 사용료 및 일주일분의 조식과 석식이 포함된 숙박 시설의 가격은 849파운드부터 1,345파운드까지 나온다.

half-brother (**half-brothers**) N-COUNT Someone's **half-brother** is a boy or man who has either the same mother or the same father as they have.
　가산명사 이복형제, 의붓형제

half-day (**half-days**) also **half day** N-COUNT A **half-day** is a day when you work only in the morning or in the afternoon, but not all day. ❑ *"If I could have just what I wanted," Sharon mused, "I'd work half days. It would give me a chance to be mother as well as researcher."*
　가산명사 한나절, 반나 ❑ "내가 하고 싶은 대로 할 수만 있다면, 한나절씩만 일할 텐데. 그러면 나에게 연구자뿐만 아니라 어머니가 될 수 있는 기회도 생길 텐데."라고 샤론은 생각했다.

half-hearted ADJ If someone does something in a **half-hearted** way, they do it without any real effort, interest, or enthusiasm. ❑ *...a half-hearted apology.* ● **half-heartedly** ADV [ADV with v] ❑ *I can't do anything half-heartedly. I have to do everything 100 per cent.*
　형용사 별로 내키지 않는, 건성으로 하는 ❑ 내키지 않는 사과 ● 별로 내키지 않아서, 건성으로 부사 ❑ 나는 어떤 것도 건성으로 할 수 없다. 나는 모든 것을 100퍼센트로 해야 한다.

half-price ■ ADJ If something is **half-price**, it costs only half what it usually costs. [v-link ADJ, ADJ n, ADJ after v] ❑ *Main courses are half price from 12:30 p.m. to 2 p.m.* ❑ *Mind you, a half-price suit still cost $400.* ■ N-UNCOUNT If something is sold **at** or **for half-price**, it is sold for only half of what it usually costs. ❑ *By yesterday she was selling off stock at half price.*
　■ 형용사 반액의, 반값의 ❑ 12시 30분부터 2시까지는 메인 요리가 반값이다. ❑ 잊지 마, 반값인 정장이라도 여전히 400달러나 해. ■ 불가산명사 반값에 ❑ 어제까지 그녀는 재고 상품을 반값에 팔았다.

half-sister (**half-sisters**) N-COUNT Someone's **half-sister** is a girl or woman who has either the same mother or the same father as they have.
　가산명사 이복 자매, 의붓자매

half-time N-UNCOUNT **Half-time** is the short period of time between the two parts of a sports event such as a football, rugby, or basketball game, when the players take a short rest. ❑ *The game started in brilliant sunshine but during half-time fog closed in.*
　불가산명사 중간 휴식, 하프타임 ❑ 경기가 시작할 때는 햇볕이 쨍쨍했으나 하프타임 때 안개가 몰려왔다.

half|way /ˈhæfweɪ, BRIT hɑːfweɪ/ also **half-way** ■ ADV **Halfway** means in the middle of a place or between two points, at an equal distance from each of them. ❑ *Half-way across the car-park, he noticed she was walking with her eyes closed.* ■ ADV **Halfway** means in the middle of a period of time or of an event. [ADV prep/adv] ❑ *By then, it was October and we were more than halfway through our tour.* ● ADJ **Halfway** is also an adjective. [ADJ n] ❑ *Yeovil held a 12-point advantage at the halfway point.* ■ PHRASE If you **meet** someone **halfway**, you accept some of the points they are making so that you can come to an agreement with them. ❑ *The Democrats are willing to meet the president halfway.* ■ ADV **Halfway** means fairly or reasonably. [INFORMAL] [ADV adj] ❑ *You need hard currency to get anything halfway decent.*
　■ 부사 중간 지점에 ❑ 주차장의 중간 지점에서 그녀가 눈을 감은 채 걷고 있는 것을 그가 발견했다. ■ 부사 중간에 ❑ 그쯤 되자 10월이었고 우리의 여정은 중간 이상 지나 있었다. ● 형용사 중간의 ❑ 요빌은 중반에 12점 리드를 유지하고 있었다. ■ 구 타협하다 ❑ 민주당원들은 기꺼이 대통령과 타협할 것이다. ■ 부사 어느 정도, 꽤나 [비격식체] ❑ 어느 정도 쓸 만한 것을 얻으려면 현찰이 필요하다.

half-yearly ■ ADJ **Half-yearly** means happening in the middle of a calendar year or a financial year. [BRIT; AM **semiannual**] [ADJ n] ❑ *...the Central Bank's half-yearly report on the state of the economy.* ■ ADJ A company's **half-yearly** profits are the profits that it makes in six months. [BRIT; AM **semiannual**] [ADJ n] ❑ *The company announced a half-yearly profit of just £2 million.*
　■ 형용사 반년마다의 [영국영어; 미국영어 semiannual] ❑ 경제 상황에 대한 중앙은행의 반년간 보고서 ■ 형용사 반년 동안의 [영국영어; 미국영어 semiannual] ❑ 그 회사는 반년 동안의 수익이 겨우 2백만 파운드라고 발표했다.

hall ♦◇◇ /hɔl/ (**halls**) **1** N-COUNT The **hall** in a house or an apartment is the area just inside the front door, into which some of the other rooms open. ❑ *The lights were on in the hall and in the bedroom.* **2** N-COUNT A **hall** in a building is a long passage with doors to rooms on both sides of it. [mainly AM; BRIT **hallway**] ❑ *There are 10 rooms along each hall.* **3** N-COUNT A **hall** is a large room or building which is used for public events such as concerts, exhibitions, and meetings. ❑ *We picked up our conference materials and filed into the lecture hall.* →see also **town hall 4** N-COUNT If students live **in a hall** in American English, or **in hall** in British English, they live in a university or college building called a **residence hall** or **hall of residence**. [also prep N] ❑ *There are times when living in hall is a great option. Like when the hall is 10 minutes walk from college, for example.* **5** N-IN-NAMES **Hall** is sometimes used as part of the name of a large house in the country. [mainly BRIT] ❑ *He died at Holly Hall, his wife's family home.* →see **house**

Word Partnership	*hall*의 연어
PREP.	**across the** hall, **down the** hall, **in the** hall **1 2**
N.	**concert** hall, **lecture** hall, **meeting** hall, **pool** hall **3**

hall|mark /hɔlmɑrk/ (**hallmarks**) **1** N-COUNT The **hallmark** of something or someone is their most typical quality or feature. ❑ *It's a technique that has become the hallmark of Amber Films.* **2** N-COUNT A **hallmark** is an official mark put on things made of gold, silver, or platinum that indicates the quality of the metal, where the object was made, and who made it. ❑ *Early pieces of Scottish silver carry the hallmarks of individual silversmiths working in rural areas of the country.*

hal|lo /hæloʊ/ →see **hello**

hall of resi|dence (**halls of residence**) N-COUNT **Halls of residence** are buildings with rooms or flats, usually built by universities or colleges, in which students live during the term. [mainly BRIT; AM usually **dormitory, residence hall**]

hal|lowed /hæloʊd/ **1** ADJ **Hallowed** is used to describe something that is respected and admired, usually because it is old, important, or has a good reputation. [ADJ n] ❑ *They protested that there was no place for a school of commerce in their hallowed halls of learning.* **2** ADJ **Hallowed** is used to describe something that is considered to be holy. [ADJ n] ❑ *...hallowed ground.*

Hal|low|een /hæloʊwin/ also **Hallowe'en** N-UNCOUNT **Halloween** is the night of the 31st of October and is traditionally said to be the time when ghosts and witches can be seen. On Halloween, children often dress up in costumes and go from door to door asking their neighbors for candy. ❑ *He had insisted that she come up to Lawford for the Halloween party.*

In olden times people believed that **Halloween** (October 31) was the night when the spirits of the dead returned to earth. Nowadays it provides a chance for children to dress up as witches and ghosts and knock on their neighbours' doors, asking "trick or treat?" If sweets or money do not appear (the "treat"), the children will threaten to play a "trick" on you.

hal|lu|ci|nate /həlusɪneɪt/ (**hallucinates, hallucinating, hallucinated**) V-I If you **hallucinate**, you see things that are not really there, either because you are ill or because you have taken a drug. ❑ *Hunger made him hallucinate.*

hal|lu|ci|na|tion /həlusɪneɪʃ°n/ (**hallucinations**) N-VAR A **hallucination** is the experience of seeing something that is not really there because you are ill or have taken a drug. ❑ *The drug induces hallucinations at high doses.*

hall|way /hɔlweɪ/ (**hallways**) **1** N-COUNT A **hallway** in a building is a long passage with doors into rooms on both sides of it. ❑ *They took the elevator up to the third floor and walked along the quiet hallway.* **2** N-COUNT A **hallway** in a house or an apartment is the area just inside the front door, into which some of the other rooms open. ❑ *...the coats hanging in the hallway.*

halo /heɪloʊ/ (**haloes** or **halos**) N-COUNT A **halo** is a circle of light that is shown in pictures around the head of a holy figure such as a saint or angel.

halt ♦◇◇ /hɔlt/ (**halts, halting, halted**) **1** V-T/V-I When a person or a vehicle **halts** or when something **halts** them, they stop moving in the direction they were going and stand still. ❑ *They halted at a short distance from the house.* **2** V-T/V-I When something such as growth, development, or activity **halts** or when you **halt** it, it stops completely. ❑ *Striking workers halted production at the auto plant yesterday.* **3** PHRASE If someone **calls a halt to** something such as an activity, they decide not to continue with it or to end it immediately. ❑ *The Russian government had called a halt to the construction of a new project in the Rostov region.* **4** PHRASE If someone or something comes **to a halt**, they stop moving. ❑ *The elevator creaked to a halt at the ground floor.* **5** PHRASE If something such as growth, development, or activity **comes** or **grinds to a halt** or **is brought to a halt**, it stops completely. ❑ *Her political career came to a halt in December 1988.*

Word Partnership	*halt*의 연어
V.	**call a** halt **to** *something* **4**
	bring *something* **to a** halt, **come/grind/screech to a** halt **5**

halve /hæv, BRIT hɑːv/ (**halves, halving, halved**) **1** V-T/V-I When you **halve** something or when it **halves**, it is reduced to half its previous size or amount. ❑ *Dr. Lee believes that men who exercise can halve their risk of cancer of the colon.* **2** V-T If you **halve** something, you divide it into two equal parts. ❑ *Halve the pineapple and scoop out the inside.* **3** **Halves** is the plural of **half**.

1 가산명사 현관 ❑ 현관과 침실에 불이 켜져 있었다. **2** 가산명사 복도, 통로 [주로 미국영어; 영국영어 hallway] ❑ 각 복도마다 10개의 방이 있다. **3** 가산명사 회관, 홀 ❑ 우리는 회의 자료들을 집어 들고 강연장 안으로 줄지어 들어갔다. **4** 가산명사 기숙사 ❑ 기숙사에 사는 것이 좋은 선택일 때가 있다. 예를 들어, 기숙사가 학교에서 걸어서 10분 거리에 위치에 있다면 말이다. **5** 이름명사 대저택 [주로 영국영어] ❑ 그는 처갓집인 홀리홀에서 죽었다.

1 가산명사 가장 전형적인 특징 ❑ 그것은 앰버 필름의 가장 전형적인 특징이 된 기술이다. **2** 가산명사 (금은의 순도) 검증 각인 ❑ 스코틀랜드의 옛날 은제품에는 그 나라의 시골 지방에서 일하던 개인 은세공의 검증 각인이 있다.

가산명사 기숙사 [주로 영국영어; 미국영어 대개 dormitory, residence hall]

1 형용사 거룩한, 성스러운 ❑ 거룩한 배움의 전당에 통상 전공 학교를 위한 자리는 없다고 그들은 항의했다. **2** 형용사 신성한 ❑ 성지(聖地)

불가산명사 할로윈(만성절의 전야인 10월 31일 밤) ❑ 그는 그녀에게 할로윈 파티를 하러 러포드로 오라고 고집했었다.

옛날 사람들은 Halloween(핼로윈: 10월 31일) 날 밤에 죽은 영혼들이 땅에 내려온다고 믿었다. 요즘에는 이 날이 되면 아이들이 마녀나 유령의 분장을 하고 이웃집을 돌아다니며, 'trick or treat? (장난칠까요 사탕 줄래요)'라고 묻는다. 만일 돈이나 사탕으로 대접(treat)하지 않으면, 장난(trick)을 치겠다고 위협하는 것이다.

자동사 환각에 빠지다 ❑ 배고픔 때문에 그는 환각 상태에 빠졌다.

가산명사 또는 불가산명사 환각 ❑ 마약은 많은 양을 투여할 경우 환각을 일으킨다.

1 가산명사 복도 ❑ 그들은 엘리베이터를 타고 3층으로 올라가서 조용한 복도를 따라 걸었다. **2** 가산명사 현관 ❑ 현관에 걸려 있는 코트

가산명사 원광, 후광

1 타동사/자동사 서다, 정지하다 ❑ 그들은 집에서 가까운 거리에 멈춰 섰다. **2** 타동사/자동사 멈추다; 중단하다 ❑ 파업 중인 근로자들은 어제 자동차 공장의 생산을 중단했다. **3** 구 –의 정지를 명하다, –의 중단을 결정하다 ❑ 러시아 정부는 로스토프 지역의 새로운 프로젝트 건설의 중단을 결정하였다. **4** 구 멈춰서 ❑ 엘리베이터가 끼꺽거리더니 1층에서 멈춰 버렸다. **5** 구 완전히 멈추다 ❑ 그녀의 정치 인생은 1988년 12월에 완전히 끝났다.

1 타동사/자동사 반으로 줄이다 ❑ 이 박사는 운동을 하는 사람들은 결장암의 위험을 반으로 줄일 수 있다고 생각한다. **2** 타동사 반으로 나누다 ❑ 파인애플을 반으로 나눠서 안을 도려내라. **3** half의 복수형

ham 620

ham /hæm/ (hams) N-VAR **Ham** is meat from the top of the back leg of a pig, specially treated so that it can be kept for a long period of time. ❏ ...ham sandwiches.

가산명사 또는 불가산명사 햄 ❏ 햄 샌드위치

ham|burg|er /hæmbɜrgər/ (hamburgers) N-COUNT A **hamburger** is ground meat which has been shaped into a flat circle. Hamburgers are fried or grilled and then eaten, often in a bread roll.

가산명사 햄버거

ham|mer /hæmər/ (hammers, hammering, hammered) ◤ N-COUNT A **hammer** is a tool that consists of a heavy piece of metal at the end of a handle. It is used, for example, to hit nails into a piece of wood or a wall, or to break things into pieces. ❏ He used a hammer and chisel to chip away at the wall. ❷ V-T If you **hammer** an object such as a nail, you hit it with a hammer. ❏ To avoid damaging the tree, hammer a wooden peg into the hole. ❸ V-I If you **hammer on** a surface, you hit it several times in order to make a noise, or to emphasize something you are saying when you are angry. ❏ We had to hammer and shout before they would open up. ❏ A crowd of reporters was hammering on the door. ❹ V-T/V-I If you **hammer** something such as an idea **into** people or you **hammer at** it, you keep repeating it so that it will have an effect on people. ❏ He hammered it into me that I had not suddenly become a rotten goalkeeper. ❺ V-T If you say that someone **hammers** another person, you mean that they attack, criticize, or punish the other person severely. ❏ The report hammers the private motorist. ❻ V-T In sports, if you say that one player or team **hammered** another, you mean that the first player or team defeated the second completely and easily. ❏ He hammered the young left-hander in four straight sets. ❼ N-COUNT In track and field, a **hammer** is a heavy weight on a wire, which the athlete throws as far as possible. ● N-SING The **hammer** also refers to the sport of throwing the hammer. ❏ Events like the hammer and the discus are not traditional crowd-pullers in the West. ❽ PHRASE If you say that someone **was going at** something **hammer and tongs**, you mean that they were doing it with great enthusiasm or energy. ❏ He loved gardening. He went at it hammer and tongs as soon as he got back from work.

◤ 가산명사 망치 ❏ 그는 망치와 끌을 이용해서 벽을 조금씩 깎아냈다. ❷ 타동사 망치로 치다 ❏ 나무에 피해 주지 않도록 구멍에 나무로 된 못을 박아라. ❸ 자동사 -을 강타하다 ❏ 우리가 문을 쾅쾅 두드리고 소리를 지르고 난 뒤에야 그들이 문을 열었다. ❏ 기자들 한 떼가 문을 쾅쾅 두드리고 있었다. ❹ 타동사/자동사 (강제로) 주입하다 ❏ 그는 내가 갑자기 썩어빠진 골키퍼가 되지는 않았다고 계속 주입시켰다. ❺ 타동사 질타하다 ❏ 그 보도는 개인 자가용 운전자를 질타하고 있다. ❻ 타동사 압승하다 ❏ 그는 젊은 왼손잡이 선수에게 4세트 연속 일방적인 압승을 거두었다. ❼ 가산명사 (육상 경기용) 해머 ● 단수명사 (육상 경기용) 해머 던지기 ❏ 서양에서 해머나 원반던지기 같은 경기는 전통적으로 인기있는 종목이 아니다. ❽ 구 맹렬히 ❏ 그는 정원 가꾸기를 좋아했다. 그는 퇴근하자마자 열심히 정원을 가꾸었다.

▸**hammer out** PHRASAL VERB If people **hammer out** an agreement or treaty, they succeed in producing it after a long or difficult discussion. ❏ I think we can hammer out a solution.

구동사 -을 고심하여 도출하다 ❏ 우리가 고심하면 해결책을 낼 수 있다고 생각한다.

ham|per /hæmpər/ (hampers, hampering, hampered) ◤ V-T If someone or something **hampers** you, they make it difficult for you to do what you are trying to do. ❏ The bad weather hampered rescue operations. ❷ N-COUNT A **hamper** is a basket containing food of various kinds that is given to people as a present. ❏ ...a luxury food hamper. ❸ N-COUNT A **hamper** is a large basket with a lid, used especially for carrying food in. ❏ ...a picnic hamper.

◤ 타동사 훼방하다, 방해하다 ❏ 나쁜 날씨가 구조 작업을 방해했다. ❷ 가산명사 선물 바구니 ❏ 호화로운 음식 선물 바구니 ❸ 가산명사 음식 바구니 ❏ 소풍 바구니

ham|ster /hæmstər/ (hamsters) N-COUNT A **hamster** is a small furry animal which is similar to a mouse, and which is often kept as a pet.

가산명사 햄스터

ham|string /hæmstrɪŋ/ (hamstrings) N-COUNT A **hamstring** is a length of tissue or tendon behind your knee which joins the muscles of your thigh to the bones of your lower leg. ❏ Webster has not played since suffering a hamstring injury in the opening game.

가산명사 무릎 뒤의 건(腱), 대퇴이두근 ❏ 웹스터는 개막전에서 대퇴이두근 부상을 당한 후로 뛰지 못하고 있다.

---

hand

① NOUN USES AND PHRASES
② VERB USES

---

① **hand** ♦♦♦ /hænd/ (hands) →Please look at category ⑩ to see if the expression you are looking for is shown under another headword. ◤ N-COUNT Your **hands** are the parts of your body at the end of your arms. Each hand has four fingers and a thumb. ❏ I put my hand into my pocket and pulled out the letter. ❷ N-SING The **hand** of someone or something is their influence in an event or situation. ❏ The hand of the military authorities can be seen in the entire electoral process. ❸ N-PLURAL If you say that something is **in** a particular person's **hands**, you mean that they are taking care of it, own it, or are responsible for it. ❏ I feel that possibly the majority of these dogs are in the wrong hands. ❏ We're in safe hands. ❹ N-SING If you ask someone for **a hand** with something, you are asking them to help you in what you are doing. ❏ Come and give me a hand in the garden. ❺ N-SING If someone asks an audience to give someone **a hand**, they are asking the audience to clap loudly, usually before or after that person performs. ❏ Let's give 'em a big hand. ❻ N-COUNT In a game of cards, your **hand** is the set of cards that you are holding in your hand at a particular time or the cards that are dealt to you at the beginning of the game. ❏ He carefully inspected his hand. ❼ N-COUNT The **hands** of a clock or watch are the thin pieces of metal or plastic that indicate what time it is. ❏ The hands of the clock on the wall moved with a slight click. Half past ten. ❽ PHRASE If something is **at hand**, **near at hand**, or **close at hand**, it is very near in place or time. ❏ Having the right equipment at hand will be enormously helpful. ❾ PHRASE If someone experiences a particular kind of treatment, especially unpleasant treatment, **at the hands of** a person or organization, they receive it from them. ❏ The civilian population were suffering greatly at the hands of the security forces. ⑩ PHRASE If you do something **by hand**, you do it using your hands rather than a machine. ❏ Each pleat was stitched in place by hand. ⑪ PHRASE When something **changes hands**, its ownership changes, usually because it is sold to someone else. ❏ The firm has changed hands many times over the years. ⑫ PHRASE If you **have** your **hands full** with something, you are very busy because of it. ❏ She had her hands full with new arrivals. ⑬ PHRASE If someone gives you **a free hand**, they give you the freedom to use your own judgment and to do exactly as you wish. ❏ He gave Stephanie a free hand in the decoration. ⑭ PHRASE If you **get** your **hands on** something or **lay** your **hands on** something, you manage to find it or obtain it, usually after some difficulty. [INFORMAL] ❏ Patty began reading everything she could get her hands on. ⑮ PHRASE If two people are **hand in hand**, they are holding each other's nearest hand,

◤ 가산명사 손 ❏ 나는 손을 호주머니에 넣어 편지를 꺼냈다. ❷ 단수명사 영향력 ❏ 군 당국의 영향력은 선거의 전 과정에서 찾아볼 수 있다. ❸ 복수명사 책임하 ❏ 아마도 여기 이 개들의 대다수가 주인을 잘못 만났다고 나는 생각한다. ❏ 우리는 안전하다. ❹ 단수명사 도움 ❏ 정원으로 와서 나 좀 도와줘. ❺ 단수명사 박수 ❏ 그들에게 큰 박수를 쳐 줍시다. ❻ 가산명사 패 ❏ 그는 자신의 패를 유심히 보았다. ❼ 가산명사 시계 바늘 ❏ 벽에 걸린 시계 바늘이 살짝 찰칵 하면서 움직였다. 10시 30분이었다. ❽ 구 가까이에 ❏ 가까운 곳에 적절한 장비를 가지고 있는 것은 매우 도움이 될 것이다. ❾ 구 -의 손을 통해 ❏ 민간인들은 공안 부대의 손에 심한 고통을 당하고 있었다. ⑩ 구 손으로 ❏ 모든 주름이 손으로 꿰매어져 있었다. ⑪ 구 주인이 바뀌다, 남의 손에 넘어가다 ❏ 그 회사는 그 세월 동안 여러 번 사주(社主)가 바뀌었다. ⑫ 구 바빴다 ❏ 그녀는 새로 사람들을 맞느라 매우 바빴다. ⑬ 구 자유재량 ❏ 그는 스테파니에게 꾸미고 싶은 대로 하라고 재량권을 주었다. ⑭ 구 -을 손에 넣다 [비격식체] ❏ 패티는 손에 잡히는 대로 뭐든 읽기 시작했다. ⑮ 구 손을 잡고 ❏ 나는 그들이 손을 잡고 그 길로 내려가는 것을 보았다. ⑯ 구 밀접하게 관련되다 ❏ 우리에게 연구하는 것과 가르치는 것은 밀접한 관련이 있다. ⑰ 구 인정하다, 관여하다 ❏ 그는 자신의 석방에 일조한 모든 이들에게 감사했다. ⑱ 구 손을 잡다 ❏ 그녀는 벤치에 앉아 손잡고 앉아있는 젊은 커플에게 다가갔다. ⑲ 구 치뤄야 할 (경기) [영국영어] ❏ 웨일스는 같은 그룹에 속해 있는 루마니아에 3점 뒤처져 있으나 남은 경기가 하나 더 있다. ⑳ 구 여분의, 남은 [영국영어] ❏ 휴즈는 15초 남기고 끝냈다. ㉑ 구 진행 중에 있는 ❏ 진행 중인 사업이 일종의 최고조에 가까워지고 있었다. ㉒ 구 올림픽 조직 관계자들은 상황이 순조롭게 통제되고 있다고 말한다. ㉓ 구 도와주다, 손을 빌려 주다 ❏ 기꺼이 손을 빌려 주겠어요. ㉔ 구 하루살이 생활을 하다, 근근이 먹고

usually while they are walking or sitting together. People often do this to show their affection for each other. ❑ *I saw them making their way, hand in hand, down the path.* 15 PHRASE If two things **go hand in hand**, they are closely connected and cannot be considered separately from each other. ❑ *For us, research and teaching go hand in hand.* 16 PHRASE If you **have a hand in** something such as an event or activity, you are involved in it. ❑ *He thanked all who had a hand in his release.* 17 PHRASE If two people **are holding hands**, they are holding each other's nearest hand, usually while they are walking or sitting together. People often do this to show their affection for each other. ❑ *She approached a young couple holding hands on a bench.* 18 PHRASE In a competition, if someone has games or matches **in hand**, they have more games or matches left to play than their opponent and therefore have the possibility of scoring more points. [BRIT] ❑ *Wales are three points behind Romania in the group but have a game in hand.* 19 PHRASE If you have time or money **in hand**, you have more time or money than you need. [BRIT] ❑ *Hughes finished with 15 seconds in hand.* 20 PHRASE The job or problem **in hand** is the job or problem that you are dealing with at the moment. ❑ *The business in hand was approaching some kind of climax.* 21 PHRASE If a situation is **in hand**, it is under control. ❑ *The Olympic organisers say that matters are well in hand.* 22 PHRASE If you **lend** someone **a hand**, you help them. ❑ *I'd be glad to lend a hand.* 23 PHRASE If someone **lives hand to mouth** or **lives from hand to mouth**, they have hardly enough food or money to live on. ❑ *I have a wife and two children and we live from hand to mouth on what I earn.* →see also **hand-to-mouth** 24 PHRASE If you tell someone to **keep their hands off** something or to **take their hands off** it, you are telling them in a rather aggressive way not to touch it or interfere with it. ❑ *Keep your hands off my milk.* 25 PHRASE If you do not know something **off hand**, you do not know it without having to ask someone else or look it up in a book. [SPOKEN] ❑ *I can't think of any off hand.* 26 PHRASE If you have a problem or responsibility **on your hands**, you have to deal with it. If it is **off your hands**, you no longer have to deal with it. ❑ *They now have yet another drug problem on their hands.* 27 PHRASE If someone or something is **on hand**, they are near and able to be used if they are needed. ❑ *There are experts on hand to give you all the help and advice you need.* 28 PHRASE You use **on the one hand** to introduce the first of two contrasting points, facts, or ways of looking at something. It is always followed later by **on the other hand** or "on the other." ❑ *On the one hand, if the body doesn't have enough cholesterol, we would not be able to survive. On the other hand, if the body has too much cholesterol, the excess begins to line the arteries.* 29 PHRASE You use **on the other hand** to introduce the second of two contrasting points, facts, or ways of looking at something. ❑ *Well, all right, hospitals lose money. But, on the other hand, if people are healthy, don't think of it as losing money; think of it as saving lives.*

> Do not confuse **on the other hand** with **on the contrary**. **On the other hand** is used to state a different, often contrasting aspect of the situation you are considering. **On the contrary** is used to contradict someone, to say that they are wrong. ❑ *He had no wish to hurt her. On the contrary, he thought of her with warmth and affection.*

30 PHRASE If a person or a situation gets **out of hand**, you are no longer able to control them. ❑ *His drinking had got out of hand.* 31 PHRASE If you dismiss or reject something **out of hand**, you do so immediately and do not consider believing or accepting it. ❑ *I initially dismissed the idea out of hand.* 32 PHRASE If you **take** something or someone **in hand**, you take control or responsibility over them, especially in order to improve them. ❑ *I hope that Parliament will soon take it in hand.* 33 PHRASE If you say that your **hands are tied**, you mean that something is preventing you from acting in the way that you want to. ❑ *Politicians are always saying that they want to help us but their hands are tied.* 34 PHRASE If you have something **to hand** or **near to hand**, you have it with you or near you, ready to use when needed. [BRIT] ❑ *You may want to keep this brochure safe, so you have it to hand whenever you may need it.* 35 PHRASE If you **try** your **hand at** an activity, you attempt to do it, usually for the first time. ❑ *After he left school, he tried his hand at a variety of jobs – bricklayer, cinema usher, coal man.* 36 PHRASE If you **turn** your **hand to** something such as a practical activity, you learn about it and do it for the first time. ❑ *...a person who can turn his hand to anything.* 37 PHRASE If you **wash** your **hands of** someone or something, you refuse to be involved with them any more or to take responsibility for them. ❑ *He seems to have washed his hands of the job.* 38 PHRASE If you **win hands down**, you win very easily. ❑ *We have been beaten in some games which we should have won hands down.* 39 with one's **bare hands** →see **bare**. to **shake** someone's **hand** →see **shake**. to **shake hands** →see **shake** →see **body** →see Picture Dictionary: **hand**

② **hand** ◆◇◇ /hænd/ (**hands, handing, handed**) V-T If you **hand** something **to** someone, you pass it to them. ❑ *He handed me a little rectangle of white paper.*

▶**hand down** PHRASAL VERB If you **hand down** something such as knowledge, a possession, or a skill, you give or leave it to people who belong to a younger generation. ❑ *The idea of handing down his knowledge from generation to generation is important to McLean.*

▶**hand in** 1 PHRASAL VERB If you **hand in** something such as homework or something that you have found, you give it to a teacher, police officer, or other person in authority. ❑ *I'm supposed to have handed in a first draft of my dissertation.* 2 PHRASAL VERB If you **hand in** your notice or resignation, you tell your employer, in speech or in writing, that you no longer wish to work for them. ❑ *I handed my notice in on Saturday.*

▶**hand on** PHRASAL VERB If you **hand** something **on**, you give it or transfer it to another person, often someone who replaces you. ❑ *The government is criticized for not handing on information about missing funds.*

살다 ❑ 나는 아내와 두 아이가 있는데 내가 번 돈으로 근근이 먹고 산다. ◨구 ~을 손대지 않다, ~에 간섭하지 않다 ❑ 내 우유에 손대지 마. ◨구 준비 없이, 즉석에서 [구어체] ❑ 나는 아무런 준비 없이는 어떤 것도 생각할 수 없다. ◨구 ~의 책임으로, ~의 손에 있는; ~의 손을 떠나, ~의 책임이 끝나 ❑ 그들은 이제 또 하나의 마약 문제를 더 다루어야 한다. ◨구 이용 가능한 ❑ 모든 필요한 조언이나 도움을 줄 수 있는 전문가들이 있다. ◨구 한편으로는; 다른 한편으로는 ❑ 한편으로는, 만일 몸에 충분한 콜레스테롤이 없다면 우리는 살아갈 수가 없을 것이다. 다른 한편으로는 몸에 콜레스테롤이 너무 많다면 과도한 콜레스테롤이 동맥 벽에 달라붙기 시작할 것이다. ◨구 한편 ❑ 그래, 좋다. 병원들은 돈을 못 벌고 있다. 하지만 한편 사람들이 건강하다면 돈을 못 번다고 생각하지 말아라. 생명을 구하는 것으로 여겨라.

> on the other hand와 on the contrary를 혼동하지 않도록 하라. on the other hand는 고려하고 있는 상황의 다른, 흔히 대조되는 측면을 말할 때 쓴다. on the contrary는 누군가에게 반박하며 그가 틀렸다고 말할 때 쓴다. ❑ 그는 그녀에게 상처를 주고 싶은 생각은 전혀 없었다. 오히려, 그는 다정하고 애정 어린 마음으로 그녀를 생각했다.

◨구 통제가 안 되는 ❑ 그의 음주는 더 이상 통제가 안 되었다. ◨구 즉시 ❑ 나는 처음에 바로 그 생각을 버렸다. ◨구 통제하다 ❑ 나는 곧 국회가 그것을 통제하기를 바란다. ◨구 손이 묶이다, 활동하지 못하게 되다 ❑ 정치인들은 자신들이 우리를 돕고 싶으나 손이 묶여 있다고 항상 말해 왔다. ◨구 손닿는 곳에, 가까이에 [영국영어] ❑ 이 안내서를 필요할 때마다 볼 수 있게 안전하게 보관하는 것이 좋을 것이다. ◨구 시도하다, 손을 대보다 ❑ 그는 학교를 떠난 후에 벽돌공, 영화관 안내원, 광부 등의 여러 가지 일을 시도했다. ◨구 착수하다 ❑ 어떤 일이든 착수할 수 있는 사람 ◨구 손을 씻다, ~와 관계를 끊다 ❑ 그는 그 일에서 손을 뗀 것처럼 보인다. ◨구 쉽게 이기다 ❑ 우리는 쉽게 이길 수 있었던 몇 경기에서 졌다.

타동사 넘겨주다, 건네주다 ❑ 그가 작은 사각형의 하얀 종이 한 장을 건네주었다.

구동사 후세에 전하다 ❑ 대대로 자신의 지식을 전하려는 생각은 맥린에게 중요하다.

1 구동사 제출하다 ❑ 나는 학위 논문 초고를 제출하기로 되어 있었다. 2 구동사 제출하다 ❑ 토요일에 나는 사직서를 제출했다.

구동사 전수하다, 인계하다 ❑ 정부는 사라진 자금에 대한 정보를 인도하지 않은 것에 대해 비판을 받고 있다.

A B C D E F G H I J K L M N O P Q R S T U V W X Y Z

Picture Dictionary — hand

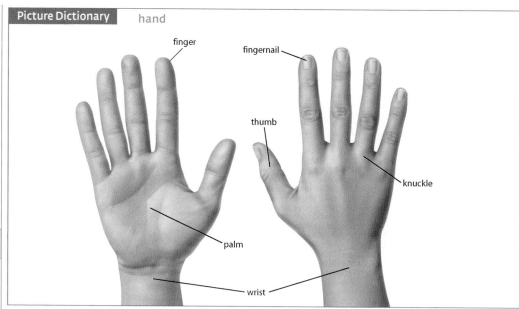

finger — fingernail — thumb — knuckle — palm — wrist

▶hand out ❶ PHRASAL VERB If you **hand** things **out** to people, you give one or more to each person in a group. ❑ *One of my jobs was to hand out the prizes.* ❷ PHRASAL VERB When people in authority **hand out** something such as advice or permission to do something, they give it. ❑ *I listened to a lot of people handing out a lot of advice.* ❸ →see also **handout**

▶hand over ❶ PHRASAL VERB If you **hand** something **over** to someone, you pass it to them. ❑ *He also handed over a letter of apology from the Prime Minister.* ❷ PHRASAL VERB If you **hand over to** someone or **hand** something **over** to them, you give them the responsibility for dealing with a particular situation or problem. ❑ *The present leaders have to decide whether to hand over to a younger generation.*

hand|bag /hǽndbæg/ (handbags) N-COUNT A **handbag** is a small bag which a woman uses to carry things such as her money and keys in when she goes out.

hand|book /hǽndbʊk/ (handbooks) N-COUNT A **handbook** is a book that gives you advice and instructions about a particular subject, tool, or machine. ❑ *If you have not kept a pet parrot before, it would be wise to purchase a handbook on the subject.*

hand|cuff /hǽndkʌf/ (handcuffs, handcuffing, handcuffed) ❶ N-PLURAL **Handcuffs** are two metal rings which are joined together and can be locked round someone's wrists, usually by the police during an arrest. [also *a pair of* N] ❑ *He was led away to jail in handcuffs.* ❷ V-T If you **handcuff** someone, you put handcuffs around their wrists. ❑ *They tried to handcuff him but, despite his injuries, he fought his way free.*

hand|ful /hǽndfʊl/ (handfuls) ❶ N-SING A **handful of** people or things is a small number of them. ❑ *He surveyed the handful of customers at the bar.* ❷ N-COUNT A **handful** of something is the amount of it that you can hold in your hand. ❑ *She scooped up a handful of sand and let it trickle through her fingers.* ❸ N-SING If you say that someone, especially a child, is a **handful**, you mean that they are difficult to control. [INFORMAL] ❑ *Zara can be a handful sometimes.*

hand-held (hand-helds) also handheld ADJ A **hand-held** device such as a camera or a computer is small and light enough to be used while you are holding it. ❑ *...a hand-held electric mixer.* ● N-COUNT **Hand-held** is also a noun. ❑ *Users will be able to use their hand-helds to look up timetables on the net, search for a local hotel, and check their bank accounts.*

handi|cap /hǽndikæp/ (handicaps, handicapping, handicapped) ❶ N-COUNT A **handicap** is a physical or mental disability. ❑ *He lost his leg when he was ten, but learnt to overcome his handicap.* ❷ N-COUNT A **handicap** is an event or situation that places you at a disadvantage and makes it harder for you to do something. ❑ *Being a foreigner was not a handicap.* ❸ V-T If an event or a situation **handicaps** someone or something, it places them at a disadvantage. ❑ *Greater levels of stress may seriously handicap some students.* ❹ N-COUNT In golf, a **handicap** is an advantage given to someone who is not a good player, in order to make the players more equal. As you improve, your handicap gets lower. ❑ *I see your handicap is down from 16 to 12.* ❺ N-COUNT In horse racing, a **handicap** is a race in which some competitors are given a disadvantage of extra weight in an attempt to give everyone an equal chance of winning. ❑ *...the Melbourne Cup, a two-mile handicap.*

handi|capped /hǽndikæpt/ ADJ Someone who is **handicapped** has a physical or mental disability that prevents them from living a totally normal life. ❑ *I'm going to work two days a week teaching handicapped kids to fish.* ● N-PLURAL You can refer to people who are handicapped as **the handicapped**. ❑ *...measures to prevent discrimination against the handicapped.*

❶ 구동사 나누어 주다 ❑ 내가 하는 일 중 하나가 상을 나누어 주는 것이었다. ❷ 구동사 주다 ❑ 나는 많은 사람들의 조언을 들었다.

❶ 구동사 -을 전달하다 ❑ 그는 수상의 사과 편지도 전달하였다. ❷ 구동사 -을 넘기다 ❑ 현 지도자들은 더 젊은 세대에게 자리를 넘겨줄 지 여부를 결정해야 한다.

가산명사 핸드백

가산명사 편람, 안내서 ❑ 이전에 애완 앵무새를 키운 경험이 없다면 그 주제에 관한 안내 책자를 사는 것이 좋을 것이다.

❶ 복수명사 수갑 ❑ 그는 수갑을 차고 감옥으로 끌려갔다. ❷ 타동사 수갑을 채우다 ❑ 그들은 그에게 수갑을 채우려 했으나, 부상을 입었는데도 그는 싸워 달아났다.

❶ 단수명사 소량, 소수 ❑ 그는 술집에 있는 소수의 손님들을 조사했다. ❷ 가산명사 한 줌, 한 움큼 ❑ 그녀는 모래 한 줌을 떠서 손가락 사이로 흘러 떨어지게 했다. ❸ 단수명사 다루기 힘든 사람 [비격식체] ❑ 때때로 자라를 다루기 힘들 때가 있다.

형용사 손에 들고 사용하는, 한 손에 들어오는 ❑ 한 손에 들어오는 소형 전기 믹서 ● 가산명사 소형 기기, 초소형 컴퓨터 ❑ 사용자들은 초소형 컴퓨터를 이용하여 인터넷에 나와 있는 시간표를 조회해 보거나 그 지역의 호텔을 찾고 예금 계좌를 확인할 수 있을 것이다.

❶ 가산명사 장애 ❑ 그는 열 살 때 한쪽 다리를 잃었으나 장애를 극복하는 것을 배웠다. ❷ 가산명사 불리한 조건, 핸디캡 ❑ 외국인이라는 점은 불리한 조건이 아니었다. ❸ 타동사 불리한 입장에 두다 ❑ 높은 수준의 스트레스는 일부 학생들에게 아주 불리하게 작용할 수도 있다. ❹ 가산명사 (골프 선수의) 핸디캡 ❑ 나는 너의 핸디캡이 16에서 12로 떨어진 것을 안다. ❺ 가산명사 핸디캡이 붙는 경우 ❑ 2마일의 핸디캡이 붙는 멜버른 컵 경주

형용사 장애가 있는 ❑ 나는 일주일에 이틀씩 장애아들에게 낚시를 가르치러 가고 있다. ● 복수명사 장애자 ❑ 장애자 차별 금지 조치들

hand|ker|chief /hǽŋkərtʃɪf/ (**handkerchiefs**) N-COUNT A **handkerchief** is a small square piece of fabric which you use for blowing your nose.

가산명사 손수건

han|dle ◆◇ /hǽndʳl/ (**handles, handling, handled**) **1** N-COUNT A **handle** is a small round object or a lever that is attached to a door and is used for opening and closing it. □ *I turned the handle and found the door was open.* **2** N-COUNT A **handle** is the part of an object such as a tool, bag, or cup that you hold in order to be able to pick up and use the object. □ *...a broom handle.* **3** V-T If you say that someone can **handle** a problem or situation, you mean that they have the ability to deal with it successfully. □ *To tell the truth, I don't know if I can handle the job.* **4** V-T If you talk about the way that someone **handles** a problem or situation, you mention whether or not they are successful in achieving the result they want. □ *I think I would handle a meeting with Mr. Siegel very badly.* ● **han|dling** N-UNCOUNT □ *The family has criticized the military's handling of Robert's death.* **5** V-T If you **handle** a particular area of work, you have responsibility for it. □ *She handled travel arrangements for the press corps during the presidential campaign.* **6** V-T When you **handle** something, you hold it or move it with your hands. □ *Wear rubber gloves when handling cat litter.* **7** PHRASE If you **fly off the handle**, you suddenly and completely lose your temper. [INFORMAL] □ *He flew off the handle at the slightest thing.* →see **silverware**

1 가산명사 손잡이 □ 나는 손잡이를 돌리다가 문이 열려 있다는 것을 알게 되었다. **2** 가산명사 손잡이 **3** 타동사 처리하다 **4** 사실을 말하자면, 나는 이 일을 잘 해낼 수 있을지 모르겠다. **4** 타동사 다루다, 처리하다 □ 나는 시겔 씨와의 면담을 매우 형편없이 처리할 것 같다. ● 취급, 처리 불가산명사 □ 가족들은 로버트의 죽음에 대한 군의 처리를 비판하였다. **5** 타동사 -을 맡다 □ 그녀는 대통령 캠페인 기간 동안 출입 기자단 이동 일을 맡았다. **6** 타동사 -을 손으로 쥐다 □ 고양이 배설물을 처리할 때 고무장갑을 껴라. **7** 구 화내다, 자제심을 잃다 [비격식체] □ 그는 아주 사소한 일에 화를 냈다.

	Word Partnership handle의 연어
N.	handle a **job/problem/situation**, handle **pressure/responsibility** **3 4**
	ability to handle *something* **3-5**
ADJ.	**difficult/easy/hard to** handle **3 4**

han|dler /hǽndlər/ (**handlers**) **1** N-COUNT A **handler** is someone whose job is to be in charge of and control an animal. □ *Fifty officers, including frogmen and dog handlers, are searching for her.* **2** N-COUNT A **handler** is someone whose job is to deal with a particular type of object. □ *...baggage handlers at Gatwick airport.*

1 가산명사 조련사 □ 잠수부와 개 조련사를 포함한 50명의 경찰들이 그녀를 찾고 있다. **2** 가산명사 -을 다루는 사람 □ 개트윅 공항의 화물 담당자들

hand lug|gage N-UNCOUNT When you travel by air, your **hand luggage** is the luggage you have with you in the plane, rather than the luggage that is carried in the hold. □ *...a ban on all knives in hand luggage.*

불가산명사 수하물 □ 수하물에 칼 소지 금지

hand|made /hǽndméɪd/ also **hand-made** ADJ **Handmade** objects have been made by someone using their hands or using tools rather than by machines. □ *As they're handmade, each one varies slightly.*

형용사 수제의, 손으로 만든 □ 그것들은 손으로 만들었기 때문에 각각 조금씩 다르다.

hand|out /hǽndaʊt/ (**handouts**) **1** N-COUNT A **handout** is a gift of money, clothing, or food, which is given free to poor people. □ *Each family is being given a cash handout of six thousand rupees.* **2** N-COUNT If you call money that is given to someone a **handout**, you disapprove of it because you believe that the person who receives it has done nothing to earn or deserve it. [DISAPPROVAL] □ *...the tendency of politicians to use money on vote-buying handouts rather than on investment in the future.* **3** N-COUNT A **handout** is a document which contains news or information about something and which is given, for example, to journalists or members of the public. □ *Official handouts describe the Emperor as "particularly noted as a scholar."*

1 가산명사 (가난한 사람들에게) 거저 주는 것 □ 한 가구당 6천 루피의 보조금을 현금으로 받고 있다. **2** 가산명사 불로 소득, 빗자금 [탐탁찮음] □ 미래를 위한 투자보다는 표를 매수하는 빗자금으로 돈을 사용하는 정치인들의 성향 **3** 가산명사 유인물, 인쇄물 □ 공식 유인물은 황제를 '뛰어난 학자'로 묘사한다.

hand|set /hǽndset/ (**handsets**) **1** N-COUNT The **handset** of a telephone is the part that you hold next to your face in order to speak and listen. □ *With a Freestyle cordless phone you can use the handset anywhere within 100 meters of the base unit.* **2** N-COUNT You can refer to a device such as the remote control of a television or stereo as a **handset**. □ *Most VCRs can be programmed using a remote control handset.*

1 가산명사 수화기 □ 프리스타일 무선 전화기를 쓰면 본체로부터 100미터 내의 어디에서든지 수화기를 사용할 수 있다. **2** 가산명사 (리모컨과 같은) 핸드세트 □ 대부분의 브이시알은 리모컨 핸드세트를 사용하여 작동할 수 있다.

hands-free ADJ A **hands-free** telephone or other device can be used without being held in your hand. [ADJ n] □ *...legislation to ban both handheld and hands-free mobile phones in moving vehicles.*

형용사 핸즈프리의 □ 운전 중 휴대 전화와 핸즈프리 폰의 사용을 금지하는 법령

hand|shake /hǽndʃeɪk/ (**handshakes**) N-COUNT If you give someone a **handshake**, you take their right hand with your own right hand and hold it firmly or move it up and down, as a sign of greeting or to show that you have agreed about something such as a business deal. □ *He has a strong handshake.* →see also **golden handshake**

가산명사 악수 □ 그는 악수를 세게 한다.

hand|some /hǽnsəm/ **1** ADJ A **handsome** man has an attractive face with regular features. □ *...a tall, dark, handsome sheep farmer.*

1 형용사 잘생긴 □ 피부가 검고, 키 크고 잘 생긴 목양업자

When you are describing someone's appearance, you generally use **pretty** and **beautiful** to describe women, girls, and babies. **Beautiful** is a much stronger word than **pretty**. The equivalent word for a man is **handsome**. **Good-looking** and **attractive** can be used to describe people of either sex. **Pretty** can also be used to modify adjectives and adverbs but is less strong than **very**. In this sense, **pretty** is informal.

사람의 외모를 묘사할 때, 여성, 소녀, 아기에 대해서는 대개 pretty와 beautiful을 쓴다. beautiful은 pretty보다 훨씬 더 강한 말이다. 이에 상응하는 말로 남성에게 쓸 수 있는 것이 handsome이다. good-looking과 attractive는 남녀 모두에 대해 쓸 수 있다. pretty는 형용사와 부사를 수식하기 위해서도 쓸 수 있으나 very 보다는 강도가 약하다. 이런 의미에서의 pretty는 비격식체이다.

2 ADJ A **handsome** sum of money is a large or generous amount. [FORMAL] [ADJ n] □ *They will make a handsome profit on the property.*

2 형용사 상당한 [격식체] □ 그들은 부동산에서 상당한 이윤을 낼 것이다.

hands-on ADJ **Hands-on** experience or work involves actually doing a particular thing, rather than just talking about it or getting someone else to do it. □ *This hands-on management approach often stretches his workday from 6 a.m. to 11 p.m.*

형용사 실제로 참가하는, 실제의 □ 이 실제 경영 접근방식으로 그의 일하는 시간이 종종 오전 6시부터 오후 11시까지로 늘어난다.

hand-to-mouth ADJ A **hand-to-mouth** existence is a way of life in which you have hardly enough food or money to live on. □ *Unloved and uncared-for, they live a meaningless hand-to-mouth existence.* ● ADV **Hand-to-mouth** is also an adverb. [ADV after v] □ *I just can't live hand-to-mouth, it's too frightening.*

형용사 하루살이의, 하루 벌어 하루 먹는 □ 사랑받지 못하고 돌봐주는 사람도 없이 그들은 무의미한 하루살이의 삶을 살고 있다. ● 부사 하루살이로 □ 나는 하루살이로는 정말 살 수 없다. 그것은 너무 끔찍하다.

hand|writing /hǽndraɪtɪŋ/ N-UNCOUNT Your **handwriting** is your style of writing with a pen or pencil. □ *The address was in Anna's handwriting.*

불가산명사 필적, 서체 □ 주소는 안나가 직접 쓴 것이었다.

hand|written /hǽndrɪtᵊn/ ADJ A piece of writing that is **handwritten** is one that someone has written using a pen or pencil rather than by typing it. ❑ ...a handwritten note.

형용사 손으로 쓴, 육필의 ❑ 손으로 쓴 메모

handy /hǽndi/ (**handier, handiest**) ■ ADJ Something that is **handy** is useful. ❑ The book gives handy hints on looking after indoor plants. ■ PHRASE If something **comes in handy**, it is useful in a particular situation. ❑ The $20 check came in very handy. ■ ADJ A thing or place that is **handy** is nearby and therefore easy to get or reach. ❑ It would be good to have a pencil and paper handy.

■ 형용사 쓸모 있는 ❑ 그 책은 실내 식물들을 보살피는 데 유용한 사항들을 알려 준다. ■ 구 편리하다, 도움이 되다 ❑ 20달러짜리 수표는 매우 편리했다. ■ 형용사 곁에 있는, 바로 쓸 수 있는 ❑ 연필과 종이를 손쉬운 곳에 두면 좋을 것이다.

hang ♦♦◇ /hǽŋ/ (**hangs, hanging, hung, hanged**)

> The form **hung** is used as the past tense and past participle. The form **hanged** is used as the past tense for meaning ■.

hung은 과거 및 과거 분사로 쓴다. hanged는 ■ 의미의 과거 시제로 쓴다.

■ V-T/V-I If something **hangs** in a high place or position, or if you **hang** it there, it is attached there so it does not touch the ground. ❑ Notices painted on sheets hang at every entrance. ❑ ...small hanging lanterns. ● PHRASAL VERB **Hang up** means the same as hang. ❑ I found his jacket, which was hanging up in the hallway. ■ V-I If a piece of clothing or fabric **hangs** in a particular way or position, that is how it is worn or arranged. ❑ ...a ragged fur coat that hung down to her calves. ■ V-I If something **hangs** loose or **hangs** open, it is partly fixed in position, but is not firmly held, supported, or controlled, often in such a way that it moves freely. ❑ ...her long golden hair which hung loose about her shoulders. ■ V-T If something such as a wall **is hung with** pictures or other objects, they are attached to it. [usu passive] ❑ The walls were hung with huge modern paintings. ■ V-T/V-I If someone **is hanged** or if they **hang**, they are killed, usually as a punishment, by having a rope tied around their neck and the support taken away from under their feet. ❑ The five were expected to be hanged at 7 a.m. on Tuesday. ❑ He hanged himself two hours after arriving at a mental hospital. ■ V-I If something such as someone's breath or smoke **hangs** in the air, it remains there without appearing to move or change position. ❑ His breath was hanging in the air before him. ■ V-I If a possibility **hangs over** you, it worries you and makes your life unpleasant or difficult because you think it might happen. ❑ A constant threat of unemployment hangs over thousands of university researchers. ■ →see also **hung** ■ PHRASE If you **get the hang of** something such as a skill or activity, you begin to understand or realize how to do it. [INFORMAL] ❑ It's a bit tricky at first till you get the hang of it. ■ PHRASE If you tell someone to **hang in there** or to **hang on in there**, you are encouraging them to keep trying to do something and not to give up even though it might be difficult. [INFORMAL] ❑ Hang in there and you never know what is achievable.

■ 타동사/자동사 매달리다; 매달다 ❑ 모든 입구마다 종이에 쓴 공지가 걸려 있다. ❑ 목에 걸 수 있는 작은 랜턴 ● 구동사 매달다, 걸다 ❑ 나는 현관에 걸려 있는 그의 재킷을 발견했다. ■ 자동사 늘어지다, 드리워지다 ❑ 그녀의 종아리까지 늘어져 있는 너덜너덜한 털 코트 ■ 자동사 늘어지다, 축 처지다 ❑ 어깨 정도까지 늘어뜨린 그녀의 긴 금발 머리 ■ 타동사 붙어 있다, 걸려 있다 ❑ 벽들에는 큰 현대식 그림이 걸려 있었다. ■ 타동사/자동사 교수형을 당하다 ❑ 그 다섯 명은 화요일 아침 7시에 교수형을 당할 예정이었다. ❑ 그는 정신 병원에 도착한 지 2시간 만에 목매달아 자살했다. ■ 자동사 한곳에 정체하다, 감돌다 ❑ 그의 숨결은 그 주변의 허공에 감돌고 있었다. ■ 자동사 걱정을 끼치다 ❑ 계속되는 실업의 위협이 수천 명의 대학 연구자들에게 걱정을 끼치고 있다. ■ 구 감을 잡기 시작하다 [비격식체] ❑ 감을 잡기 시작할 때까지 처음에는 조금 까다롭다. ■ 구 (끝까지) 버티다, 견디다 [비격식체] ❑ 어려움을 견디어 내면 뭐는 이루어 낼 수 있을 것이다.

▶**hang back** ■ PHRASAL VERB If you **hang back**, you move or stay slightly behind a person or group, usually because you are nervous about something. ❑ I saw him step forward momentarily but then hang back, nervously massaging his hands. ■ PHRASAL VERB If a person or organization **hangs back**, they do not do something immediately. ❑ They will then hang back on closing the deal.

■ 구동사 주춤거리다 ❑ 나는 그가 잠시 앞으로 발을 내딛다가 뒤로 물러나서 손을 초조하게 문지르며 주춤거리는 것을 보았다. ■ 구동사 망설이다 ❑ 그리고 나서 그들은 그 거래를 마무리 짓기를 망설일 것이다.

▶**hang on** ■ PHRASAL VERB If you ask someone to **hang on**, you ask them to wait or stop what they are doing or saying for a moment. [INFORMAL] ❑ Can you hang on for a minute? ■ PHRASAL VERB If you **hang on**, you manage to survive, achieve success, or avoid failure in spite of great difficulties or opposition. ❑ Manchester United hung on to take the Cup. ■ PHRASAL VERB If you **hang on to** or **hang onto** something that gives you an advantage, you succeed in keeping it for yourself, and prevent it from being taken away or given to someone else. ❑ The British driver was unable to hang on to his lead. ■ PHRASAL VERB If you **hang on to** or **hang onto** something, you hold it very tightly, for example to stop it from falling or to support yourself. ❑ She was conscious of a second man hanging on to the rail. ❑ ...a flight stewardess who helped save the life of a pilot by hanging onto his legs. ■ PHRASAL VERB If you **hang on to** or **hang onto** something, you keep it for a longer time than you would normally expect. [INFORMAL] ❑ You could, alternatively, hang onto it in the hope that it will be worth millions in 10 years time. ■ PHRASAL VERB If one thing **hangs on** another, it depends on it in order to be successful. ❑ Much hangs on the success of the collaboration between the Group of Seven governments and Brazil.

■ 구동사 기다리다 [비격식체] ❑ 잠시 동안 기다려 줄래? ■ 구동사 계속해 나가다, 해내다 ❑ 맨체스터 유나이티드는 결국 우승컵을 차지했다. ■ 구동사 보유하다, 보전하다 ❑ 그 영국인 운전자는 선두를 유지할 수 없었다. ■ 구동사 매달리다 ❑ 그녀는 난간에 남자가 한 명 더 매달려 있다는 사실을 인지하고 있었다. ❑ 파일럿의 다리를 잡아 그의 생명을 구하는 데 일조한 여승무원 ■ 구동사 붙잡고 늘어지다 [비격식체] ❑ 그 대신에, 그것이 10년 후에는 몇 백만의 가치가 있을 것이라는 희망을 갖고 그것을 잡고 늘어질 수 있다. ■ 구동사 -에 의존하다, -에 달려 있다 ❑ 많은 것이 7개국 정부의 모임과 브라질 사이의 공조의 성공 여부에 달려 있다.

▶**hang out** ■ PHRASAL VERB If you **hang out** clothes that you have washed, you hang them on a clothes line to dry. ❑ I was worried I wouldn't be able to hang my washing out. ■ PHRASAL VERB If you **hang out** in a particular place or area, you go and stay there for no particular reason, or spend a lot of time there. [mainly AM, INFORMAL] ❑ I often used to hang out in supermarkets.

■ 구동사 내다 말리다, 내다 넌다 ❑ 나는 세탁물을 밖에서 말릴 수 없을까 봐 걱정했다. ■ 구동사 어정거리다 [주로 미국영어, 비격식체] ❑ 나는 자주 슈퍼마켓에서 어정거리곤 했다.

▶**hang up** ■ →see hang 1 ■ PHRASAL VERB If you **hang up** or you **hang up** the phone, you end a phone call. If you **hang up on** someone you are speaking to on the phone, you end the phone call suddenly and unexpectedly. ❑ Mom hung up the phone. ❑ Don't hang up!

■ 구동사 전화를 끊다 ❑ 어머니는 전화를 끊었다. ❑ 전화 끊지 마!

Word Partnership	hang의 연어
N.	hang *up* clothes ■
ADV.	hang *something* upside down ■

hang|ar /hǽŋər/ (**hangars**) N-COUNT A **hangar** is a large building in which aircraft are kept.

가산명사 항공기의 격납고(格納庫)

hang|er /hǽŋər/ (**hangers**) N-COUNT A **hanger** is the same as a **coat hanger**.

가산명사 옷걸이

hang|over /hǽŋoʊvər/ (**hangovers**) ■ N-COUNT If someone wakes up with a **hangover**, they feel sick and have a headache because they have drunk a lot of alcohol the night before. ❑ It was a great night and I had a massive hangover. ■ N-COUNT Something that is a **hangover from** the past is an idea or way of behaving which people used to have in the past but which people no longer generally have. ❑ As a hangover from rationing, they mixed butter and margarine.

■ 가산명사 숙취 ❑ 정말 대단한 밤이었으나 나는 심한 숙취로 고생했다. ■ 가산명사 유물 ❑ 배급 제도 하에서 하던 대로 그들은 버터와 마가린을 섞었다.

hap|haz|ard /hǽphæzərd/ ADJ If you describe something as **haphazard**, you are critical of it because it is not at all organized or is not arranged according to a plan. [DISAPPROVAL] ❑ *The investigation does seem haphazard.* ● **hap|haz|ard|ly** ADV ❑ *She looked at the books jammed haphazardly in the shelves.*

hap|less /hǽpləs/ ADJ A **hapless** person is unlucky. [FORMAL] [ADJ n] ❑ *...his hapless victim.*

hap|pen ♦♦♦ /hǽpən/ (**happens, happening, happened**) ◼ V-I Something that **happens** occurs or is done without being planned. ❑ *We cannot say for sure what will happen.* ◼ V-I If something **happens**, it occurs as a result of a situation or course of action. ❑ *She wondered what would happen if her parents found her.* ◼ V-I When something, especially something unpleasant, **happens to** you, it takes place and affects you. ❑ *If we had been spotted at that point, I don't know what would have happened to us.* ◼ V-T If you **happen to** do something, you do it by chance. If **it happens that** something is the case, it occurs by chance. ❑ *We happened to discover we had a friend in common.* ◼ PHRASE You use **as it happens** in order to introduce a statement, especially one that is rather surprising. ❑ *She called Amy to see if she had any idea of her son's whereabouts. As it happened, Amy had.*

hap|pen|ing /hǽpənɪŋ/ (**happenings**) N-COUNT **Happenings** are things that happen, often in a way that is unexpected or hard to explain. ❑ *The Budapest office plans to hire freelance reporters to cover the latest happenings.*

hap|pi|ly /hǽpɪli/ ADV You can add **happily** to a statement to indicate that you are glad that something happened. [ADV with cl] ❑ *Happily, his neck injuries were not serious.* →see also **happy**

hap|py ♦♦◇ /hǽpi/ (**happier, happiest**) ◼ ADJ Someone who is **happy** has feelings of pleasure, usually because something nice has happened or because they feel satisfied with their life. ❑ *Marina was a confident, happy child.* ● **hap|pi|ly** ADV ❑ *Albert leaned back happily and lit a cigarette.* ● **hap|pi|ness** N-UNCOUNT ❑ *I think mostly she was looking for happiness.* ◼ ADJ A **happy** time, place, or relationship is full of happy feelings and pleasant experiences, or has an atmosphere in which people feel happy. ❑ *Except for her illnesses, she had had a particularly happy childhood.* ❑ *It had always been a happy place.* ◼ ADJ If you are **happy about** a situation or arrangement, you are satisfied with it, for example because you think that something is being done in the right way. [v-link ADJ, ADJ about/with n/-ing, ADJ that, ADJ to-inf] ❑ *If you are not happy about a repair, go back and complain.* ❑ *He's happy that I deal with it myself.* ◼ ADJ If you say you are **happy to** do something, you mean that you are very willing to do it. [v-link ADJ, usu ADJ to-inf] ❑ *I'll be happy to answer any questions if there are any.* ● **hap|pi|ly** ADV [ADV with v] ❑ *If I've caused any offence over something I have written, I will happily apologise.* ◼ ADJ **Happy** is used in greetings and other conventional expressions to say that you hope someone will enjoy a special occasion. [ADJ n] ❑ *Happy Birthday!*

ha|rangue /hərǽŋ/ (**harangues, haranguing, harangued**) V-T If someone **harangues** you, they try to persuade you to accept their opinions or ideas in a forceful way. ❑ *An argument ensued, with various band members joining in and haranguing Simpson and his girlfriend for over two hours.*

har|ass /hərǽs, hǽrəs/ (**harasses, harassing, harassed**) V-T If someone **harasses** you, they trouble or annoy you, for example by attacking you repeatedly or by causing you as many problems as they can. ❑ *A woman reporter complained one of them sexually harassed her in the locker room.*

har|assed /hərǽst, hǽrəst/ ADJ If you are **harassed**, you are anxious and tense because you have too much to do or too many problems to cope with. ❑ *This morning, looking harassed and drawn, Lewis tendered his resignation.*

har|ass|ment /hərǽsmənt, hǽrəs-/ N-UNCOUNT **Harassment** is behavior which is intended to trouble or annoy someone, for example repeated attacks on them or attempts to cause them problems. ❑ *Another survey found that 51 per cent of women had experienced some form of sexual harassment in their working lives.*

har|bor ♦◇◇ /hɑ́rbər/ (**harbors, harboring, harbored**) [BRIT **harbour**] ◼ N-COUNT; N-IN-NAMES A **harbor** is an area of the sea at the coast which is partly enclosed by land or strong walls, so that boats can be left there safely. ❑ *She led us to a room with a balcony overlooking the harbor.* ◼ V-T If you **harbor** an emotion, thought, or secret, you have it in your mind over a long period of time. ❑ *He might have been murdered by a former client or someone harboring a grudge.* ◼ V-T If a person or country **harbors** someone who is wanted by the police, they let them stay in their house or country and offer them protection. ❑ *Accusations of harboring suspects were raised against the former Hungarian leadership.*

hard ♦♦♦ /hɑ́rd/ (**harder, hardest**) ◼ ADJ Something that is **hard** is very firm and stiff to touch and is not easily bent, cut, or broken. ❑ *He shuffled his feet on the hard wooden floor.* ● **hard|ness** N-UNCOUNT ❑ *He felt the hardness of the iron*

형용사 무계획적인, 되는 대로인 [탐탁잖음] ❑ 조사가 엉망으로 되어 가는 것 같다. ● 무계획적으로, 마구잡이로 부사 ❑ 그녀는 선반에 아무렇게나 쌓여 있는 책들을 보았다.

형용사 불운한 [격식체] ❑ 운이 없는 그의 희생자

◼ 자동사 일어나다 ❑ 무슨 일이 일어날지 확실하게 말할 수 없다. ◼ 자동사 일어나다, 생기다 ❑ 부모님이 그녀를 찾아낸다면 무슨 일이 일어날지 그녀는 궁금했다. ◼ 자동사 닥쳐오다, -에게 일어나다 ❑ 만일 우리가 그 지점에서 발견되었다면 우리에게 무슨 일이 일어났을지 모르겠다. ◼ 타동사 우연히 -을 하나 ❑ 우리는 서로 알고 있는 친구가 있다는 것을 우연히 알게 되었다. ◼ 구 때마침, 공교롭게도 ❑ 그녀는 에이미에게 전화를 걸어 그녀의 아들이 있는 곳을 알고 있는지 물었다. 때마침, 에이미는 알고 있었다.

가산명사 사건 ❑ 부다페스트 지부에서는 최근에 일어난 사건들을 취재하기 위해서 프리랜서 리포터를 고용할 계획이다.

부사 다행히 ❑ 다행히, 그의 목 부상은 심하지 않았다.

◼ 형용사 행복한 ❑ 마리나는 자신감 넘치고 행복한 아이였다. ● 행복하게 부사 ❑ 앨버트는 행복하게 몸을 기대고 담배에 불을 붙였다. ● 행복 불가산명사 ❑ 나는 그녀가 주로 행복을 찾고 있었다고 생각한다. ◼ 형용사 행복한, 즐거운 ❑ 아픈 것을 제외하면 그녀는 특별히 행복한 유년기를 보냈었다. ❑ 그곳은 항상 즐거운 곳이었다. ◼ 형용사 -에 만족한 ❑ 만일 수선한 것에 만족하지 않으면, 가서 따져라. ❑ 내가 그것을 다룬다는 것에 만족한다. ◼ 형용사 기꺼이 -하는 ❑ 질문이 있다면 기꺼이 대답하겠습니다. ● 기쁘게, 기꺼이 부사 ❑ 혹시라도 제가 쓴 글이 불쾌하셨다면 기꺼이 사과드리겠습니다. ◼ 형용사 (인사말로) 축하합니다 ❑ 생일 축하합니다!

타동사 열변을 토하다 ❑ 여러 밴드 멤버들이 참견하여 2시간이 넘도록 심슨과 그의 여자 친구를 향해 열변을 토하면서 논쟁은 계속 되었다.

타동사 괴롭히다 ❑ 그들 중 한 명이 탈의실에서 자기를 성추행했다고 여자 리포터가 항의했다.

형용사 괴로운, 시달리는 ❑ 오늘 아침, 수척하고 일에 시달려 보이는 루이스가 사표를 제출했다.

불가산명사 괴롭히기, 희롱 ❑ 다른 여론 조사에서는 여성의 51퍼센트가 직장에서 어떤 형태로든지 성희롱 당한 경험이 있다고 나왔다.

[영국영어 harbour] ◼ 가산명사; 이름명사 항구 ❑ 그녀는 항구가 멀리 바라보이는 발코니가 있는 방으로 우리를 안내했다. ◼ 타동사 품다 ❑ 그는 원한을 품은 이전 의뢰인이나 누군가에 의해서 살해되었을지도 모른다. ◼ 타동사 숨기다, 은신처를 제공하다 ❑ 전 헝가리 지도부가 용의자들에게 은신처를 제공했다는 혐의가 제기되었다.

◼ 형용사 단단한, 딱딱한 ❑ 그는 딱딱한 나무 바닥 위를 발을 질질 끌며 걸어갔다. ● 단단함, 딱딱함 불가산명사 ❑ 자신의 등뼈를 짓누르는 듯한 철제

A

railing press against his spine. ② ADJ Something that is **hard** is very difficult to do or deal with. □ *It's hard to tell what effect this latest move will have.* □ *That's a very hard question.* ③ ADV If you work **hard** doing something, you are very active or work intensely, with a lot of effort. [ADV after v] □ *I'll work hard. I don't want to let him down.* ● ADJ **Hard** is also an adjective. [ADJ n] □ *I admired him as a true scientist and hard worker.* ④ ADJ **Hard** work involves a lot of activity and effort. □ *Coping with three babies is very hard work.* □ *...a hard day's work.* ⑤ ADV If you look, listen, or think **hard**, you do it carefully and with a great deal of attention. [ADV after v] □ *He looked at me hard.* ● ADJ **Hard** is also an adjective. □ *It might be worth taking a long hard look at your frustrations and resentments.* ⑥ ADV If you strike or take hold of something **hard**, you strike or take hold of it with a lot of force. [ADV after v] □ *I kicked a trash can very hard and broke my toe.* ● ADJ **Hard** is also an adjective. [ADJ n] □ *He gave her a hard push which toppled her backwards into an armchair.* ⑦ ADV You can use **hard** to indicate that something happens intensely and for a long time. [ADV after v] □ *I've never seen Terry laugh so hard.* ⑧ ADJ If a person or their expression is **hard**, they show no kindness or sympathy. □ *His father was a hard man.* ⑨ ADJ If you are **hard** on someone, you treat them severely or unkindly. [v-link ADJ on n] □ *Don't be so hard on him.* ● ADV **Hard** is also an adverb. [ADV after v] □ *He said the security forces would continue to crack down hard on the protestors.* ⑩ ADJ If you say that something is **hard** on a person or thing, you mean it affects them in a way that is likely to cause them damage or suffering. [v-link ADJ on n] □ *The grey light was hard on the eyes.* ⑪ ADJ If you have a **hard** life or a **hard** period of time, your life or that period is difficult and unpleasant for you. □ *It had been a hard life for her.* ● **hard**|**ness** N-UNCOUNT □ *In America, people don't normally admit to the hardness of life.* ⑫ ADJ **Hard** evidence or facts are definitely true and do not need to be questioned. [ADJ n] □ *He wanted more hard evidence.* ⑬ ADJ **Hard** drugs are very strong illegal drugs such as heroin or cocaine. [ADJ n] □ *He then graduated from soft drugs to hard ones.* ⑭ PHRASE If you say that something is **hard going**, you mean it is difficult and requires a lot of effort. □ *The talks had been hard going at the start.* ⑮ PHRASE To be **hard hit by** something means to be affected very severely by it. □ *California's been particularly hard hit by the recession.* ⑯ PHRASE If someone **plays hard to get**, they pretend not to be interested in another person or in what someone is trying to persuade them to do. □ *I wanted her and she was playing hard to get.*

Thesaurus   hard의 참조어

ADJ.   firm, solid, tough; *(ant.)* gentle, soft ①
        complicated, difficult, simple, tough; *(ant.)* easy ②

hard|**back** /hɑrdbæk/ (**hardbacks**) N-COUNT A **hardback** is a book which has a stiff hard cover. Compare **paperback**. [also in n] □ *"The Secret History" was published in hardback last October.*

hard cash N-UNCOUNT **Hard cash** is money in the form of bills and coins as opposed to a check or a credit card. □ *There is no confusion about what the real dividend is since the payment comes in hard cash.*

hard copy (**hard copies**) N-VAR A **hard copy** of a document is a printed version of it, rather than a version that is stored on a computer. □ *...eight pages of hard copy.*

hard cur|**ren**|**cy** (**hard currencies**) N-VAR A **hard currency** is one which is unlikely to lose its value and so is considered to be a good one to have or to invest in. □ *The government is running short of hard currency to pay for imports.*

hard disk (**hard disks**) N-COUNT A computer's **hard disk** is a stiff magnetic disk on which data and programs can be stored. [BRIT also **hard disc**]

hard|**en** /hɑrdᵊn/ (**hardens, hardening, hardened**) ① V-T/V-I When something **hardens** or when you **harden** it, it becomes stiff or firm. □ *Mold the mixture into shape while hot, before it hardens.* ② V-T/V-I When an attitude or opinion **hardens** or **is hardened**, it becomes harsher, stronger, or fixed. □ *Their action can only serve to harden the attitude of landowners.* ● **hard**|**en**|**ing** N-SING □ *...a hardening of the government's attitude towards rebellious parts of the army.* ③ V-T/V-I When events **harden** people or when people **harden**, they become less easily affected emotionally and less sympathetic and gentle than they were before. □ *Her years of drunken bickering hardened my heart.* ④ V-I If you say that someone's face or eyes **harden**, you mean that they suddenly look serious or angry. □ *His smile died and the look in his face hardened.*

hard|**line** /hɑrdlaɪn/ also **hard-line** ADJ If you describe someone's policy or attitude as **hardline**, you mean that it is strict or extreme, and they refuse to change it. □ *The United States has taken a lot of criticism for its hard-line stance.*

hard|**ly** ◆◇◇ /hɑrdli/ ① ADV You use **hardly** to modify a statement when you want to emphasize that it is only a small amount or detail which makes it true, and that therefore it is best to consider the opposite statement as being true. [EMPHASIS] □ *I hardly know you.* □ *Nick, on the sofa, hardly slept.* ② ADV You use **hardly** in expressions such as **hardly ever**, **hardly any**, and **hardly anyone** to mean almost never, almost none, or almost no one. [ADV ever/any] □ *We ate chips every night, but hardly ever had fish.* □ *Most of the others were so young they had hardly any experience.* ③ ADV You use **hardly** before a negative statement in order to emphasize that something is usually true or usually happens. [EMPHASIS] [ADV n] □ *Hardly a day goes by without a visit from someone.* ④ ADV When you say you can **hardly** do something, you are emphasizing that it is very difficult for you to do it. [EMPHASIS] [can/could ADV inf] □ *My garden was covered with so many butterflies that I could hardly see the flowers.* ⑤ ADV You use **hardly** to mean "not" when you want to suggest that you are expecting your listener or reader to agree with your comment. □ *We have not seen the letter, so we can hardly comment on it.* ⑥ CONVENTION You use "**hardly**" to mean "no," especially when you want to express surprise or annoyance at a statement that you disagree with.
[SPOKEN] □ *"They all thought you were marvelous!" — "Well, hardly."*

난간의 단단함이 그에게 느껴졌다. ② 형용사 어려운 □ 이러한 최근의 움직임이 어떤 영향을 끼칠지는 알기 어렵다. □ 그건 매우 어려운 질문이다. ③ 부사 열심히 □ 나는 열심히 일할 것이다. 그를 실망시키고 싶지 않다. ● 형용사 근면한 □ 나는 그를 진정한 과학자이자 열심히 일하는 사람으로 존경했다. ④ 형용사 고된 □ 아이 셋을 계속 돌보기란 매우 고된 일이다. □ 고된 하루의 일 ⑤ 부사 주의 깊게, 뚫어지라 □ 그는 나를 뚫어져라 바라보았다. ● 형용사 주의 깊은 □ 자신의 좌절과 분개를 오랫동안 주의를 기울여 들여다 볼 가치가 있을 것이다. ⑥ 부사 세게, 심하게 □ 나는 쓰레기통을 발로 힘껏 차다가 발가락이 부러졌다. ● 형용사 강력한 □ 그가 그녀를 힘껏 밀어 안락의자 위로 주저앉게 만들었다. ⑦ 부사 심하게, 많이 □ 나는 테리가 그렇게 많이 웃는 것을 본 적이 없다. ⑧ 형용사 엄격한 □ 그의 아버지는 엄격한 분이었다. ⑨ 형용사 가혹한, 심한 □ 그에게 너무 심하게 하지 말아라. ● 부사 가혹하게, 심하게 □ 공안 부대가 시위자들을 계속 가혹하게 탄압할 것이라고 그는 말했다. ⑩ 형용사 나쁜 영향을 주는 □ 침침한 불빛은 눈에 나쁜 영향을 주었다. ⑪ 형용사 힘든, 고된 □ 그것은 그녀에게 고된 삶이었다. ● 고됨, 힘듦 불가산명사 □ 미국에서는 사람들이 보통 생활의 고됨을 인정하지 않는다. ⑫ 형용사 엄연한, 부정할 수 없는 □ 그는 더 확실한 증거를 원했다. ⑬ 형용사 불법의, (마약이) 강력한 □ 그리고 나서 그는 약한 마약을 졸업하고 중독성이 강한 마약에 손을 대기 시작하였다. ⑭ 구 어렵고 힘든, 좀처럼 진전이 없는 □ 회담은 시작부터 힘들게 진행되었다. ⑮ 구 심한 타격을 받은 □ 캘리포니아가 불경기에 특히 심한 타격을 받았다. ⑯ 구 일부러 관심이 없는 체하다 □ 나는 그녀를 원했으나 그녀는 일부러 관심이 없는 체하고 있었다.

가산명사 따뜻한 표지로 제본한 책, 하드커버 □ '비사(秘史)'는 지난 10월 하드커버로 출판되었다.

불가산명사 현금 □ 지불은 현금으로 하므로 실제 배당금이 얼마인지에 대한 혼동은 없다.

가산명사 또는 불가산명사 종이에 인쇄된 문서 □ 8페이지의 인쇄 문서

가산명사 또는 불가산명사 경화(硬貨), (금, 달러와) 교환 가능 통화 □ 정부가 수입 비용을 지불할 교환 가능 통화가 부족하다.

가산명사 하드 디스크 [영국영어 hard disc]

① 타동사/자동사 굳어지다; 굳히다 □ 굳어지기 전 뜨거울 때 혼합물의 모양을 만들어라. ② 타동사/자동사 굳어지다, 강경해지다 □ 그들의 행동은 지주의 태도를 강경하게 만들 뿐이다. ● 강경화 단수명사 □ 군의 반역 세력에 대한 정부의 강경책 ③ 타동사/자동사 무감각하게 만들다 □ 수 년 동안 그녀가 술에 취해서 해온 술주정이 나의 마음을 무감각하게 만들었다. ④ 자동사 (표정이) 굳어지다 □ 미소가 사라지고 그의 얼굴 표정이 굳어졌다.

형용사 강경 노선 □ 미국은 강경 노선 태도에 대하여 비판을 많이 받아 왔다.

① 부사 거의 ~ 아닌 [강조] □ 나는 당신을 잘 모른다. □ 소파에서 닉은 거의 잠을 못 잤다. ② 부사 거의 전혀 ~하지 않는 □ 우리는 매일 밤 감자칩을 먹었지만 생선은 거의 한 번도 먹지 못했다. □ 다른 사람들은 대부분이 너무 어려서 거의 아무런 경험이 없었다. ③ 부사 거의 없는 [강조] □ 하루도 사람이 방문하지 않는 날은 거의 없다. ④ 부사 하기 힘든, 거의 ~하기 어려운 [강조] □ 정원에 나비가 너무 많아서 꽃을 보기 힘들 정도였다. ⑤ 부사 ~할 수 없는 □ 우리는 그 편지를 본 적이 없기 때문에 그것에 대한 의견을 말할 수 없다. ⑥ 관용 표현 아니다 [구어체] □ "그들 모두가 당신이 아주 멋지다고 생각했어요." "글쎄요, 별로 그렇지 않은데요."

hard-pressed also **hard pressed** ■ ADJ If someone is **hard-pressed**, they are under a great deal of strain and worry, usually because they do not have enough money. [JOURNALISM] ❏ *The region's hard-pressed consumers are spending less on luxuries.* ■ ADJ If you will be **hard-pressed to** do something, you will have great difficulty doing it. [v-link ADJ to-inf] ❏ *This year the airline will be hard-pressed to make a profit.*

hard sell N-SING A **hard sell** is a method of selling in which the salesperson puts a lot of pressure on someone to make them buy something. ❏ *...a double-glazing firm whose hard-sell techniques were exposed by a consumer program.*

hard|ship /hɑrdʃɪp/ (**hardships**) N-VAR **Hardship** is a situation in which your life is difficult or unpleasant, often because you do not have enough money. ❏ *Many people are suffering economic hardship.*

hard|ware /hɑrdwɛr/ ■ N-UNCOUNT In computer systems, **hardware** refers to the machines themselves as opposed to the programs which tell the machines what to do. Compare **software**. ❏ *To be totally secure, you need a piece of hardware that costs about $200.* ■ N-UNCOUNT Military **hardware** is the machinery and equipment that is used by the armed forces, such as tanks, aircraft, and missiles. ❏ *...the billions which are spent on military hardware.* ■ N-UNCOUNT **Hardware** refers to tools and equipment that are used in the home and garden, for example saucepans, screwdrivers, and lawnmowers. ❏ *...a shop from which an uncle had sold hardware and timber.*

har|dy /hɑrdi/ (**hardier, hardiest**) ADJ Plants that are **hardy** are able to survive cold weather. ❏ *The silver-leaved varieties of cyclamen are not quite as hardy.*

hare /hɛər/ (**hares, haring, hared**) ■ N-VAR A **hare** is an animal like a rabbit but larger with long ears, long legs, and a small tail. ■ V-I If you **hare off** somewhere, you go there very quickly. [BRIT, INFORMAL] ❏ *...an over-protective mother who keeps haring off to ring the babysitter.*

hark /hɑrk/ (**harks, harking, harked**)
►**hark back to** PHRASAL VERB If you say that one thing **harks back to** another thing, you mean it is similar to it or takes it as a model. ❏ *...pitched roofs, which hark back to the Victorian era.*

harm ◆◇◇ /hɑrm/ (**harms, harming, harmed**) ■ V-T To **harm** a person or animal means to cause them physical injury, usually on purpose. ❏ *The hijackers seemed anxious not to harm anyone.* ■ N-UNCOUNT **Harm** is physical injury to a person or an animal which is usually caused on purpose. ❏ *All dogs are capable of doing harm to human beings.* ■ V-T To **harm** a thing, or sometimes a person, means to damage them or make them less effective or successful than they were. ❏ *...a warning that the product may harm the environment.* ■ N-UNCOUNT **Harm** is the damage to something which is caused by a particular course of action. ❏ *The abuse of your powers does harm to all other officers who do their job properly.* ■ PHRASE If you say that someone or something **will come to no harm** or that **no harm will come to** them, you mean that they will not be hurt or damaged in any way. ❏ *There is always a lifeguard to ensure that no one comes to any harm.* ■ PHRASE If you say **it does no harm** to do something or **there is no harm** in doing something, you mean that it might be worth doing, and you will not be blamed for doing it. ❏ *They are not always willing to take on untrained workers, but there's no harm in asking.* ■ PHRASE If you say that there is **no harm done**, you are telling someone not to worry about something that has happened because it has not caused any serious injury or damage. ❏ *There, now, you're all right. No harm done.* ■ PHRASE If someone or something is **out of harm's way**, they are in a safe place away from danger or from the possibility of being damaged. ❏ *For parents, it is an easy way of keeping their children entertained, or simply out of harm's way.*

<table>
<tr><td colspan="2">**Thesaurus**   *harm의 참조어*</td></tr>
<tr><td>V.</td><td>abuse, damage, hurt, injure, ruin, wreck; (ant.) benefit ■ ■</td></tr>
<tr><td>N.</td><td>abuse, damage, hurt, injury, ruin, violence ■ ■</td></tr>
</table>

<table>
<tr><td colspan="2">**Word Partnership**   *harm의 연어*</td></tr>
<tr><td>V.</td><td>**cause** harm ■ ■
not mean any harm ■</td></tr>
<tr><td>N.</td><td>harm **the environment** ■</td></tr>
<tr><td>ADJ.</td><td>**bodily** harm ■</td></tr>
<tr><td>ADV.</td><td>**more** harm **than good** ■</td></tr>
</table>

harm|ful /hɑrmfʊl/ ADJ Something that is **harmful** has a bad effect on something else, especially on a person's health. ❏ *...the harmful effects of smoking.*

harm|less /hɑrmlɪs/ ■ ADJ Something that is **harmless** does not have any bad effects, especially on people's health. ❏ *This experiment was harmless to the animals.* ■ ADJ If you describe someone or something as **harmless**, you mean that they are not important and therefore unlikely to annoy other people or cause trouble. ❏ *He seemed harmless enough.*

har|mon|ic /hɑrmɒnɪk/ ADJ **Harmonic** means composed, played, or sung using two or more notes which sound right and pleasing together. ❏ *I had been looking for ways to combine harmonic and rhythmic structures.*

har|mo|ni|ous /hɑrmoʊniəs/ ADJ A **harmonious** relationship, agreement, or discussion is friendly and peaceful. ❏ *Their harmonious relationship resulted in part from their similar goals.* ● **har|mo|ni|ous|ly** ADV [ADV after v] ❏ *To live together harmoniously as men and women is an achievement.*

har|mo|nize /hɑrmənaɪz/ (**harmonizes, harmonizing, harmonized**) [BRIT also **harmonise**] ■ V-RECIP If two or more things **harmonize with** each other, they

---

■ 형용사 (돈에) 쪼들리는 [언론] ❏ 돈에 쪼들리는 그 지역의 소비자들이 사치품을 덜 소비하고 있다. ■ 형용사 어려움이 있는 ❏ 올해 그 항공사는 이윤을 내기 어려울 것이다.

단수명사 강매, 끈질긴 판매 ❏ 소비자 프로그램을 통해 강매 기술이 드러난 이중창 회사

가산명사 또는 불가산명사 곤란, 역경 ❏ 많은 사람들이 경제적 곤란을 겪고 있다.

■ 불가산명사 하드웨어 ❏ 완벽한 보안을 위해서는 200달러 정도 드는 하드웨어 하나가 필요하다. ■ 불가산명사 무기, 병기 ❏ 군사 무기에 지출한 수십억 ■ 불가산명사 철물 ❏ 삼촌이 철물과 목재를 팔았던 가게

형용사 내한성의, 추위에 강한 ❏ 시클라멘의 은빛 잎 종류들은 그다지 추위에 강하지 않다.

■ 가산명사 또는 불가산명사 토끼 ■ 자동사 빨리 달리다 [영국영어, 비격식체] ❏ 애를 봐 주는 사람에게 계속 전화를 하러 뛰어다니는 과잉 보호형 엄마

구동사 과거의 -와 유사한 ❏ 과거 빅토리아 시대의 양식과 비슷한 경사진 지붕

■ 타동사 해치다 ❏ 납치범들은 아무도 해치지 않으려고 애쓰는 것 같았다. ■ 불가산명사 상해, 손상 ❏ 모든 개는 인간에게 해를 입힐 수 있다. ■ 타동사 해를 끼치다 ❏ 그 제품이 환경에 해를 끼칠 수 있다는 경고 ■ 불가산명사 손해 ❏ 당신의 권력 남용은 각자의 일을 제대로 하고 있는 다른 모든 공무원들에게 해를 입힌다. ■ 구 해를 입지 않다; 해가 되지 않다 ❏ 아무도 다치지 않도록 안전하게 지키는 감시 구조원이 항시 있다. ■ 구 무방하다, 나쁠 건 없다 ❏ 항상 훈련되지 않은 직원을 고용하려고 하는 것은 아니지만, 물어봐서 나쁠 건 없다. ■ 구 큰 부상 없음 ❏ 자, 이제는 괜찮습니다. 다치신 데 없습니다. ■ 구 안전한 장소에 ❏ 부모들의 입장에서는, 이는 아이들을 즐겁게 해줄 수도 있고, 혹은 그냥 안전한 곳에 있도록 하는 손쉬운 방법이다.

형용사 해로운 ❏ 흡연의 해로운 영향

■ 형용사 해롭지 않은, 무해한 ❏ 이 실험은 그 동물들에게 해롭지 않았다. ■ 형용사 (다른 사람에게) 무해한, 말썽을 부리지 않을 것 같은 ❏ 그는 전혀 문제를 일으킬 것 같지 않아 보였다.

형용사 화성의 ❏ 나는 화성 체계와 리듬 체계를 결합하는 방법을 찾고 있었다.

형용사 화목한, 사이좋은 ❏ 그들이 서로 사이좋게 지낼 수 있었던 것은 부분적으로 비슷한 목표를 가지고 있었기 때문이었다. ● 화목하게 부사 ❏ 남성과 여성으로 모두 함께 화목하게 사는 것 자체가 하나의 위업이다.

[영국영어 harmonise] ■ 상호동사 -와 조화를 이루다, -와 잘 어울리다 ❏ 그녀의 옷은 모두 서로 얼마나 잘

A

fit in well with each other. ❑ *How well all her garments harmonized with each other.* **2** V-T When governments or organizations **harmonize** laws, systems, or regulations, they agree in a friendly way to make them the same or similar. ❑ *How far will members have progressed towards harmonizing their economies?*

어울리는지. **2** 타동사 ~에 조화시키다 ❑ 구성원들이 얼마나 더 경제와 조화를 이루는 쪽으로 나아갈 것인가?

B

har|mo|ny /hɑ́rməni/ (harmonies) **1** N-UNCOUNT If people are living **in harmony with** each other, they are living together peacefully rather than fighting or arguing. ❑ *...the notion that man should dominate nature rather than live in harmony with it.* **2** N-VAR **Harmony** is the pleasant combination of different notes of music played at the same time. ❑ *...singing in harmony.* **3** N-UNCOUNT The **harmony** of something is the way in which its parts are combined into a pleasant arrangement. ❑ *...the ordered harmony of the universe.*

1 불가산명사 조화 ❑ 자연과 조화를 이루어 살기보다는 인간이 자연을 지배해야 한다는 생각 **2** 가산명사 또는 불가산명사 화음, 화성 ❑ 화음을 넣어 노래 부르기 **3** 불가산명사 조화, 화합 ❑ 우주의 질서 잡힌 조화

C

har|ness /hɑ́rnɪs/ (harnesses, harnessing, harnessed) **1** V-T If you **harness** something such as an emotion or natural source of energy, you bring it under your control and use it. ❑ *Turkey plans to harness the waters of the Tigris and Euphrates rivers for big hydro-electric power projects.* **2** N-COUNT A **harness** is a set of straps which fit under a person's arms and fasten around their body in order to keep a piece of equipment in place or to prevent the person moving from a place. **3** N-COUNT A **harness** is a set of leather straps and metal links fastened round a horse's head or body so that the horse can have a carriage, cart, or plow fastened to it. **4** V-T If a horse or other animal **is harnessed**, a harness is put on it, especially so that it can pull a carriage, cart, or plow. [usu passive] ❑ *On Sunday the horses were harnessed to a heavy wagon for a day-long ride over the Border.*

D

E

F

1 타동사 다스려 활용하다 ❑ 터키는 티그리스와 유프라테스 강의 물을 이용하여 대형 수력 발전소를 세울 계획이다. **2** 가산명사 무구(武具), 갑옷 **3** 가산명사 마구(馬具) **4** 타동사 마구를 달다 ❑ 일요일에 국경을 넘나들는 당일 여행을 위해서 말들을 대형 마차에 연결하였다.

G

H

harp /hɑ́rp/ (harps, harping, harped) N-VAR A **harp** is a large musical instrument consisting of a row of strings stretched from the top to the bottom of a frame. You play the harp by plucking the strings with your fingers.

가산명사 또는 불가산명사 하프

▶**harp on** PHRASAL VERB If you say that someone **harps on** a subject, or **harps on about** it, you mean that they keep on talking about it in a way that other people find annoying. ❑ *Jones harps on this theme more than on any other.*

구동사 같은 말을 되풀이하여 말하다 ❑ 존스는 다른 어떤 것보다 이 주제에 대해서 되풀이하여 말한다.

I

har|row|ing /hǽroʊɪŋ/ ADJ A **harrowing** experience is extremely upsetting or disturbing. ❑ *You've had a harrowing time this past month.*

형용사 비참한, 괴로운 ❑ 지난 한 달 동안 당신은 괴로운 시간을 보냈다.

J

harsh /hɑ́rʃ/ (harsher, harshest) **1** ADJ **Harsh** climates or conditions are very difficult for people, animals, and plants to live in. ❑ *...the harsh desert environment.* ● **harsh|ness** N-UNCOUNT ❑ *...the harshness of their living conditions.* **2** ADJ **Harsh** actions or speech are unkind and show no understanding or sympathy. ❑ *He said many harsh and unkind things about his opponents.* ● **harsh|ly** ADV [ADV with v] ❑ *She's been told that her husband is being harshly treated in prison.* ● **harsh|ness** N-UNCOUNT ❑ *...treating him with great harshness.* **3** ADJ Something that is **harsh** is so hard, bright, or rough that it seems unpleasant or harmful. ❑ *Tropical colors may look rather harsh in our dull northern light.* ● **harsh|ness** N-UNCOUNT ❑ *...as the wine ages, losing its bitter harshness.* **4** ADJ **Harsh** voices and sounds are ones that are rough and unpleasant to listen to. ❑ *It's a pity she has such a loud harsh voice.* ● **harsh|ly** ADV [ADV with v] ❑ *Chris laughed harshly.* ● **harsh|ness** N-UNCOUNT ❑ *Then in a tone of abrupt harshness, he added, "Open these trunks!"* **5** ADJ If you talk about **harsh** realities or facts, or the **harsh** truth, you are emphasizing that they are true or real, although they are unpleasant and people try to avoid thinking about them. [EMPHASIS] ❑ *The harsh truth is that luck plays a big part in who will live or die.*

K

L

M

N

O

1 형용사 혹독한 ❑ 혹독한 사막 환경 ● 혹독함 불가산명사 ❑ 그들의 혹독한 생활환경 **2** 형용사 가혹한, 무자비한 ❑ 그는 상대방에 대해서 무자비하고 냉정한 말들을 많이 했다. ● 혹독하게, 가혹하게 부사 ❑ 그녀는 감옥에서 가혹한 대우를 받고 있다는 이야기를 들었다. ● 혹독함, 가혹함 불가산명사 ❑ 매우 가혹하게 그를 다룸 **3** 형용사 거슬리는 ❑ 열대 지방의 색깔들은 우리의 흐릿한 북부 지방 빛에서 보면 다소 거슬리게 보일 수도 있다. ● 불쾌함, 거슬림 불가산명사 ❑ 포도주는 해가 갈수록 불쾌한 신맛이 없어진다. **4** 형용사 거친 ❑ 그녀의 목소리가 그렇게 거칠고 커서 안됐다. ● 거칠게 부사 ❑ 크리스가 거칠게 웃었다. ● 거침 불가산명사 ❑ 그 때 갑작스럽게 거친 목소리로 그가 "이 트렁크들을 여시오!"라고 덧붙였다. **5** 형용사 가혹한 [강조] ❑ 가혹한 사실은, 생사(生死)를 결정하는 데 운이 큰 역할을 한다는 것이다.

P

har|vest /hɑ́rvɪst/ (harvests, harvesting, harvested) **1** N-SING The **harvest** is the gathering of a crop. ❑ *There was about 300 million tons of grain in the fields at the start of the harvest.* **2** N-COUNT A **harvest** is the crop that is gathered in. ❑ *Millions of people are threatened with starvation as a result of drought and poor harvests.* **3** V-T When you **harvest** a crop, you gather it in. ❑ *Rice farmers here still plant and harvest their crops by hand.* →see **farm**, **grain**

Q

1 단수명사 수확, 추수 ❑ 추수가 시작될 무렵 들판에는 3억 톤의 곡식이 있었다. **2** 가산명사 수확량 ❑ 몇 백만 명의 사람들이 가뭄과 형편없는 수확의 결과로 기아의 위협을 받고 있다. **3** 타동사 수확하다, 추수하다 ❑ 여기서 쌀을 재배하는 농부들은 여전히 손으로 모내기와 추수를 한다.

R

has

The auxiliary verb is pronounced /həz, STRONG hæz/. The main verb is usually pronounced /hǽz/.

조동사는 /həz, 강형은 hæz/로 발음되고, 일반 동사는 대개 /hǽz/로 발음된다.

Has is the third person singular of the present tense of **have**.

have의 3인칭 단수 현재

S

has-been (has-beens) N-COUNT If you describe someone as a **has-been**, you are indicating in an unkind way that they were important or respected in the past, but they are not now. [DISAPPROVAL] ❑ *...the so-called experts and various has-beens who foist opinions on us.*

가산명사 한물간 사람 [탐탁잖음] ❑ 우리에게 자기들 의견을 강요한 소위 전문가와 여러 한물간 사람들

T

hash /hǽʃ/ PHRASE If you **make a hash of** a job or task, you do it very badly. [INFORMAL] ❑ *The Government made a total hash of things and squandered a small fortune.*

구 ~을 망쳐 놓다 [비격식체] ❑ 정부는 일을 완전히 망쳤고, 적지 않은 돈을 낭비했다.

U

hasn't /hǽz³nt/ **Hasn't** is the usual spoken form of 'has not.'

has not의 구어체

has|sle /hǽs³l/ (hassles, hassling, hassled) **1** N-VAR A **hassle** is a situation that is difficult and involves problems, effort, or arguments with people. [INFORMAL] ❑ *I don't think it's worth the money or the hassle.* **2** V-T If someone **hassles** you, they cause problems for you, often by repeatedly telling you or asking you to do something, in an annoying way. [INFORMAL] ❑ *Then my husband started hassling me.*

V

1 가산명사 또는 불가산명사 야단, 난리 [비격식체] ❑ 그런 일에 돈이나 야단을 피울 가치가 없다고 생각한다. **2** 타동사 괴롭히다, 들볶다 [비격식체] ❑ 그러자 남편이 나를 들볶기 시작했다.

W

haste /héɪst/ **1** N-UNCOUNT **Haste** is the quality of doing something quickly, sometimes too quickly so that you are careless and make mistakes. ❑ *In their haste to escape the rising water, they dropped some expensive equipment.* **2** PHRASE If you do something **in haste**, you do it quickly and hurriedly, and sometimes carelessly. ❑ *Don't act in haste or be hot-headed.*

X

1 불가산명사 신속함, 성급함 ❑ 불어나는 물을 급히 피하느라 그들은 몇몇 값비싼 장비를 빠뜨렸다. **2** 구 급히, 서둘러 ❑ 서두르거나 성급하게 굴지 말아라.

Y

has|ten /héɪs³n/ (hastens, hastening, hastened) **1** V-T If you **hasten** an event or process, often an unpleasant one, you make it happen faster or sooner. ❑ *But if he does this, he may hasten the collapse of his own country.* **2** V-T If you **hasten to** do something, you are quick to do it. ❑ *She more than anyone had hastened to sign the contract.*

Z

1 타동사 재촉하다 ❑ 그러나 그가 이것을 한다면 자기 나라의 붕괴를 재촉하게 될지도 모른다. **2** 타동사 서두르다 ❑ 그녀는 다른 누구보다도 서둘러서 그 계약에 서명했었다.

hasty /heɪsti/ (**hastier, hastiest**) **1** ADJ A **hasty** movement, action, or statement is sudden, and often done in reaction to something that has just happened. ❑ *One company is giving its employees airplane tickets in the event they need to make a hasty escape.* ● **hastily** /heɪstɪli/ ADV [ADV with v] ❑ *"It may be satisfying, but it's not fun." — "No, I'm sure it's not," said Virginia hastily. "I didn't mean that."* **2** ADJ If you describe a person or their behavior as **hasty**, you mean that they are acting too quickly, without thinking carefully, for example because they are angry. [DISAPPROVAL] ❑ *A number of the United States' allies had urged him not to take a hasty decision.* ● **hastily** ADV [ADV with v] ❑ *I decided that nothing should be done hastily, that things had to be sorted out carefully.*

hat ♦♢♢ /hæt/ (**hats**) **1** N-COUNT A **hat** is a head covering, often with a brim round it, which is usually worn out of doors to give protection from the weather. ❑ *...a plump woman in a red hat.* **2** N-COUNT If you say that someone is wearing a particular **hat**, you mean that they are performing a particular role at that time. If you say that they wear several **hats**, you mean that they have several roles or jobs. ❑ *Now I'll take off my "friend hat" and put on my "therapist hat."* **3** PHRASE If you say that you are ready to do something **at the drop of a hat**, you mean that you are willing to do it immediately, without hesitating. ❑ *India is one part of the world I would go to at the drop of a hat.* **4** PHRASE If you tell someone to **keep** a piece of information **under** their **hat**, you are asking them not to tell anyone else about it. ❑ *Look, if I tell you something, will you promise to keep it under your hat?* **5** PHRASE If you say that you **take** your **hat off to** someone, you mean that you admire them for something that they have done. [APPROVAL] ❑ *I take my hat off to Mr. Clarke for taking this action.* **6** PHRASE To **pull** something **out of the hat** means to do something unexpected which helps you to succeed, often when you are failing. ❑ *Southampton had somehow managed to pull another Cup victory out of the hat.* **7** PHRASE In competitions, if you say that the winners will be drawn or picked **out of the hat**, you mean that they will be chosen randomly, so everyone has an equal chance of winning. ❑ *The first 10 correct entries drawn out of the hat will win a pair of tickets, worth £20 each.*

hatch /hætʃ/ (**hatches, hatching, hatched**) **1** V-T/V-I When a baby bird, insect, or other animal **hatches**, or when it **is hatched**, it comes out of its egg by breaking the shell. ❑ *The young disappeared soon after they were hatched.* **2** V-T/V-I When an egg **hatches** or when a bird, insect, or other animal **hatches** an egg, the egg breaks open and a baby comes out. ❑ *The eggs hatch after a week or ten days.* **3** V-T If you **hatch** a plot or a scheme, you think of it and work it out. ❑ *He has accused opposition parties of hatching a plot to assassinate the Pope.* **4** N-COUNT A **hatch** is an opening in the deck of a ship, through which people or cargo can go. You can also refer to the door of this opening as a **hatch**. ❑ *He stuck his head up through the hatch.*

hatch|et /hætʃɪt/ (**hatchets**) **1** N-COUNT A **hatchet** is a small ax that you can hold in one hand. **2** PHRASE If two people **bury the hatchet**, they become friendly again after a quarrel or disagreement. ❑ *It is time to bury the hatchet and forget about what has happened in the past.*

hate ♦♢♢ /heɪt/ (**hates, hating, hated**) **1** V-T If you **hate** someone or something, you have an extremely strong feeling of dislike for them. ❑ *Most people hate him, but they don't dare to say so, because he still rules the country.* ● N-UNCOUNT **Hate** is also a noun. ❑ *I was 17 and filled with a lot of hate.* **2** V-T If you say that you **hate** something such as a particular activity, you mean that you find it very unpleasant. [no cont] ❑ *Ted hated parties, even gatherings of people he liked individually.* ❑ *He hates to be interrupted during training.* ❑ *He hated coming home to the empty house.* **3** V-T You can use **hate** in expressions such as "**I hate to trouble you**" or "**I hate to bother you**" when you are apologizing to someone for interrupting them or asking them to do something. [POLITENESS] [no cont] ❑ *I hate to rush you but I have another appointment later on.* **4** V-T You can use **hate** in expressions such as "**I hate to say it**" or "**I hate to tell you**" when you want to express regret about what you are about to say, because you think it is unpleasant or should not be the case. [FEELINGS] [no cont] ❑ *I hate to tell you this, but tomorrow's your last day.* **5** To **hate** someone's **guts** →see **gut** **6** V-T You can use **hate** in expressions such as "**I hate to see**" or "**I hate to think**" when you are emphasizing that you find a situation or an idea unpleasant. [EMPHASIS] [no cont] ❑ *I just hate to see you doing this to yourself.* **7** V-T You can use **hate** in expressions such as "**I'd hate to think**" when you hope that something is not true or that something will not happen. [no cont] ❑ *I'd hate to think my job would not be secure if I left it temporarily.* →see **emotion**

Word Partnership	hate의 연어
N.	hate **the thought of** *something* **2**
V.	hate **to admit** *something* **4**
	hate **to see** *something* **6**
	hate **to think** *something* **6** **7**

ha|tred /heɪtrɪd/ (**hatreds**) N-UNCOUNT **Hatred** is an extremely strong feeling of dislike for someone or something. ❑ *Her hatred of them would never lead her to murder.*

hat-trick (**hat-tricks**) N-COUNT A **hat-trick** is a series of three achievements, especially in a sports event, for example three goals scored by the same person in a soccer game. ❑ *I scored a hat-trick against Arsenal.*

haul /hɔl/ (**hauls, hauling, hauled**) **1** V-T If you **haul** something which is heavy or difficult to move, you move it using a lot of effort. ❑ *A crane had to be used to haul the car out of the stream.* **2** V-T If someone **is hauled before** a court or someone in authority, they are made to appear before them because they are accused of having done something wrong. [usu passive] ❑ *He was hauled before the managing director and fired.* ● PHRASAL VERB **Haul up** means the same as **haul**.

1 형용사 급한 ❑ 한 회사는 긴급히 탈출해야 하는 경우에는 사원들에게 비행기표를 지급할 것이다. ● 서둘러서 부사 ❑ "만족스러울지는 몰라도 재미있지는 않아." "맞아, 재미있지는 않아."라고 버지니아는 서둘러서 말했다. "재미있게 하려던 게 아니니까." **2** 형용사 성급한 [탐탁찮음] ❑ 미국의 많은 동맹국들이 그에게 성급한 결정을 내리지 말라고 촉구했었다. ● 성급하게 부사 ❑ 나는 어떤 것도 성급하게 하지 않고 주의를 기울여 처리하기로 결심했다.

1 가산명사 모자 ❑ 빨간 모자를 쓴 통통한 여자 **2** 가산명사 임무, 직업 ❑ 나는 이제부터는 '친구'로서가 아니라 '치료사'로서 대할 것이다. **3** 구 즉시 ❑ 인도는 내가 주저하지 않고 바로 가고픈 세계의 한 부분이다. **4** 구 비밀로 하다 ❑ 봐, 네게 말해 줄 게 있는데, 비밀로 하겠다고 약속할 수 있겠? **5** 구 정찬하다, 경의를 표하다 [마음에 듦] ❑ 나는 이러한 조치를 취한 클라크 씨에게 경의를 표합니다. **6** 구 (기대하지 않은 일을) 해내다 ❑ 사우스햄턴 팀이 예상 밖으로 또 한 번 우승컵을 차지해 냈었다. **7** 구 무작위로 뽑다 ❑ 정답을 맞춘 사람 중 무작위로 10명을 뽑아 한 장에 20파운드 하는 티켓 두 장을 수여할 것이다.

1 타동사/자동사 부화하다 ❑ 새끼들은 부화하자마자 바로 사라졌다. **2** 타동사/자동사 부화하다 ❑ 그 알들은 일주일이나 열흘 후에 부화한다. **3** 타동사 꾸미다 ❑ 그는 야당들이 교황을 암살할 음모를 꾸미고 있다는 혐의를 제기했다. **4** 가산명사 해치, 승강구 ❑ 그는 승강구 밖으로 머리를 내밀었다.

1 가산명사 작은도끼 **2** 구 화해하다 ❑ 이제 화해하고 과거에 있었던 일은 잊어버릴 때이다.

1 타동사 매우 싫어하다, 증오하다 ❑ 사람들 대부분이 그를 증오하고 있으나 그가 여전히 그 나라를 통치하고 있기 때문에 그들이 감히 그가 싫다고 말하지 못한다. ● 불가산명사 증오 ❑ 나는 17세였고 증오로 가득 차 있었다. **2** 타동사 혐오하다, 싫어하다 ❑ 테드는 개인적으로 좋아하는 사람들의 모임이라 하더라도 파티를 혐오했다. ❑ 그는 훈련 중에 방해받는 것을 싫어한다. ❑ 그는 아무도 없는 빈 집에 들어가는 것을 싫어했다. **3** 타동사 죄송합니다만 [공손체] ❑ 서둘러서 죄송하지만 제가 나중에 다른 약속이 있습니다. **4** 타동사 말하고 싶지 않다 [감정 개입] ❑ 이런 말 하고 싶지 않지만, 내일이 마지막 날이군요. **6** 타동사 보고 싶지 않다; 생각하고 싶지 않다 [강조] ❑ 나는 그저 네가 네 자신에게 그런 짓을 하는 것을 보고 싶지 않다. **7** 타동사 생각하고 싶지도 않다 ❑ 내가 잠시 떠난다고 내 직장이 보장되지 않을 거라고는 생각하고 싶지도 않다.

불가산명사 증오 ❑ 그들에 대한 그녀의 증오가 그녀를 살인으로 끌고 가지는 않을 것이다.

가산명사 해트 트릭 (한 사람이 한 시합에서 3점을 넣기) ❑ 나는 아스날 전에서 해트 트릭을 기록했다.

1 타동사 운반하다, 끌어당기다 ❑ 차를 개울에서 끌어내는 데 크레인이 동원되어야만 했다. **2** 타동사 소환하다 ❑ 그는 상무이사 앞에 불려 가서 해고당했다. ● 구동사 소환하다 ❑ 그는 이사회에 소환되었다. **3** 가산명사 획득물, 압수품 ❑ 밀매된 마약의 규모를 보면 헤로인을 대상으로 한 국제적인 무역이 여전히

A

□ *He was hauled up before the Board of Trustees.* **B** N-COUNT A **haul** is a quantity of things that are stolen, or a quantity of stolen or illegal goods found by police or customs. □ *The size of the drugs haul shows that the international trade in heroin is still flourishing.* **4** PHRASE If you say that a task or a journey is a **long haul**, you mean that it takes a long time and a lot of effort. □ *Revitalising the Romanian economy will be a long haul.* →see also **long-haul**

번창하고 있다는 것을 알 수 있다. **4** 구 오랜 시간 (의 노력) □ 로마의 경제가 다시 활기를 찾는 데는 오랜 시간이 걸릴 것이다.

B

haul|age /hɔ́lɪdʒ/ N-UNCOUNT **Haulage** is the business of transporting goods by road. [mainly BRIT] □ *The haulage company was a carrier of machine parts to Turkey.*

불가산명사 운송 [주로 영국영어] □ 그 운송 회사는 터키에 기계 부품 나르는 일을 했다.

C

haul|er /hɔ́lər/ (**haulers**) N-COUNT A **hauler** is a company or a person that transports goods by road. [AM; BRIT **haulier**]

가산명사 운송 회사, 운송하는 사람 [미국영어; 영국영어 haulier]

haul|ier /hɔ́liər/ (**hauliers**) N-COUNT A **haulier** is the same as a **hauler**.

가산명사 운송 회사, 운송하는 사람

D

E

haunt /hɔ́nt/ (**haunts, haunting, haunted**) **1** V-T If something unpleasant **haunts** you, you keep thinking or worrying about it over a long period of time. □ *He would always be haunted by that scene in Well Park.* **2** V-T Something that **haunts** a person or organization regularly causes them problems over a long period of time. □ *The stigma of being a bankrupt is likely to haunt him for the rest of his life.* **3** N-COUNT A place that is the **haunt** of a particular person is one which they often visit because they enjoy going there. □ *The Channel Islands are a favorite summer haunt for UK and French yachtsmen alike.* **4** V-T A ghost or spirit that **haunts** a place or a person regularly appears in the place, or is seen by the person and frightens them. □ *His ghost is said to haunt some of the rooms, banging a toy drum.*

1 타동사 뇌리를 떠나지 않다 □ 웰 파크에서의 그 광경이 항상 그의 뇌리를 떠나지 않을 것이다. **2** 타동사 계속 괴롭히다 □ 파산자라는 치욕은 아마도 그의 여생 동안 계속 따라다니며 괴롭힐 것 같다. **3** 가산명사 단골 장소 □ 해협 제도는 영국과 프랑스 요트 조종자들이 모두 좋아하는 여름의 단골 장소이다. **4** 타동사 (귀신이) 나타나다, 출몰하다 □ 그의 망령은 장난감 북을 치면서 여러 방에 나타난다고 한다.

F

G

haunt|ed /hɔ́ntɪd/ **1** ADJ A **haunted** building or other place is one where a ghost regularly appears. □ *Tracy said the cabin was haunted.* **2** ADJ Someone who has a **haunted** expression looks very worried or troubled. □ *She looked so haunted, I almost didn't recognize her.*

1 형용사 귀신이 나오는 □ 트레이시는 그 오두막에 귀신이 나온다고 말했다. **2** 형용사 불안한, 시달린 □ 그녀가 너무 불안해 보였는지, 나는 그녀인지 거의 알아보지 못했다.

H

I

haunt|ing /hɔ́ntɪŋ/ ADJ **Haunting** sounds, images, or words remain in your thoughts because they are very beautiful or sad. □ *...the haunting calls of wild birds in the mahogany trees.* • **haunt|ing|ly** ADV □ *Each one of these ancient towns is hauntingly beautiful.*

형용사 뇌리에서 잊혀지지 않는, 끊임없이 떠오르는 □ 뇌리에서 잊혀지지 않는 마호가니 숲속 야생 새들의 울음소리 • 뇌리에서 잊혀지지 않을 정도로 부사 □ 고대 시대의 이 마을들은 각각 모두 아름다워 뇌리에서 잊혀지지 않는다.

J

K

┌─────────────────────────────────┐
                           have

  ① AUXILIARY VERB USES
  ② USED WITH NOUNS DESCRIBING ACTIONS
  ③ OTHER VERB USES AND PHRASES
  ④ MODAL PHRASES
└─────────────────────────────────┘

L

① have ♦♦♦ /həv, STRONG hæv/ (**has, having, had**)

In spoken English, forms of **have** are often shortened, for example **I have** is shortened to **I've** and **has not** is shortened to **hasn't**.

구어체 영어에서 have의 형태가 I have는 I've로, has not은 hasn't로 종종 축약된다.

M

1 AUX You use the forms **have** and **has** with a past participle to form the present perfect tense of verbs. □ *Alex has already gone.* □ *What have you found so far?* □ *Frankie hasn't been feeling well for a long time.* **2** AUX You use the form **had** with a past participle to form the past perfect tense of verbs. □ *When I met her, she had just returned from a job interview.* **3** AUX **Have** is used in question tags. □ *You haven't sent her away, have you?* **4** AUX You use **have** when you are confirming or contradicting a statement containing "have," "has," or "had," or answering a question. □ *"You'd never seen the Marilyn Monroe film?" — "No I hadn't."* **5** AUX The form **having** with a past participle can be used to introduce a clause in which you mention an action which had already happened before another action began. □ *He arrived in San Francisco, having left New Jersey on January 19th.*

1 준조동사 (현재 완료 시제로) -하였다 □ 알렉스는 벌써 떠났다. □ 이제껏 무엇을 찾은 거야? □ 프랭키는 오랫동안 몸 상태가 좋지 못했다. **2** 준조동사 (과거 완료 시제로) -했었다 □ 내가 그녀를 만났을 때 그녀는 막 취업 면접에서 돌아온 참이다. **3** 준조동사 부가 의문문에 쓰임 □ 그녀를 멀리 떠나보내지 않았지, 그렇지? **4** 준조동사 have 동사를 사용한 상대방의 말에 대한 대꾸에 쓰임 □ "마릴린 먼로 영화를 본 적이 없었어?" "응, 없었는데." **5** 준조동사 -해서 □ 그는 1월 19일에 뉴저지를 떠나서 샌프란시스코에 도착했다.

N

O

P

Q

┌───────────────────────────────────┐
| **Thesaurus**   *have*의 참조어 |
| |
| v.   own, possess ③ **1** |
| suffer from ③ **10** |
└───────────────────────────────────┘

R

② have ♦♦♦ /hæv/ (**has, having, had**)

Have is used in combination with a wide range of nouns, where the meaning of the combination is mostly given by the noun.

have는 다양한 종류의 명사와 결합하여 쓰이는데 그 결합체의 의미는 주로 명사에 의해 결정된다.

S

1 V-T You can use **have** followed by a noun to talk about an action or event, when it would be possible to use the same word as a verb. For example, you can say "I had a look at the photos" instead of "I looked at the photos." [no passive] □ *I went out and had a walk around.* □ *She rested for a while, then had a wash and changed her clothes.* **2** V-T In normal spoken or written English, people use **have** with a wide range of nouns to talk about actions and events, often instead of a more specific verb. For example people are more likely to say "we had ice cream" or "he's had a shock" than "we ate ice cream," or "he's suffered a shock." [no passive] □ *Come and have a meal with us tonight.* □ *We will be having a meeting to decide what to do.*

1 타동사 -을 하다; 나는 그 사진을 보았다 □ 나는 나가서 주위를 좀 걸었다. □ 그녀는 잠시 동안 휴식을 취한 뒤 씻고 옷을 갈아입었다. **2** 타동사 먹다; 겪다; 하다 □ 오늘 저녁에 우리와 같이 밥 먹으러 와. □ 우리는 무엇을 할지에 대해서 결정하는 회의를 할 것이다.

T

U

V

③ have ♦♦♦ /hæv/ (**has, having, had**)

For meanings **1-4**, people often use **have gotten** in spoken American English or **have got** in spoken British English, instead of **have**. In this case, **have** is pronounced as an auxiliary verb. For more information and examples of the use of "have got" and "have gotten," see **got**.

의미 **1**부터 **4**까지는 종종 have 대신 구어체 미국영어에서는 have gotten으로, 구어체 영국영어에서는 have got으로 쓴다. 이 경우 have는 조동사로 발음된다. have got과 have gotten의 용례와 자세한 내용은 got을 참조.

W

X

→Please look at category **18** to see if the expression you are looking for is shown under another headword. **1** V-T You use **have** to say that someone or something owns a particular thing, or when you are mentioning one of their qualities or characteristics. [no passive] □ *Oscar had a new bicycle.* □ *I want to have my own business.* □ *She had no job and no money.* □ *You have beautiful eyes.* □ *Do you*

1 타동사 가지다, 지니다, 있다 □ 오스카는 새 자전거를 가졌다. □ 나는 내 소유의 사업체를 가지고 싶다. □ 그녀는 직업도 없었고 돈도 없었다. □ 당신은 눈이 예쁘다. □ 형제나 자매가 있습니까? **2** 타동사 -을 것이 있다 □ 그는 할 일이 많았다. **3** 타동사 -이 있다,

Y

Z

have any brothers and sisters? **2** v-T If you **have** something **to** do, you are responsible for doing it or must do it. [no passive] ❑ *He had plenty of work to do.* **3** v-T You can use **have** instead of "there is" to say that something exists or happens. For example, you can say "**you have no alternative**" instead of "there is no alternative," or "**he had a good view from his window**" instead of "there was a good view from his window." [no passive] ❑ *He had two tenants living with him.* **4** v-T If you **have** something such as a part of your body in a particular position or state, it is in that position or state. [no passive] ❑ *Mary had her eyes closed.* ❑ *They had the curtains open.* **5** v-T If you **have** something done, someone does it for you or you arrange for it to be done. [no passive] ❑ *I had your rooms cleaned and aired.* ❑ *They had him killed.* **6** v-T If someone **has** something unpleasant happen to them, it happens to them. [no passive] ❑ *We had our money stolen.* **7** v-T If you **have** someone do something, you persuade, cause, or order them to do it. [no passive] ❑ *The bridge is not as impressive as some guides would have you believe.* **8** v-T If someone **has** you **by** a part of your body, they are holding you there and they are trying to hurt you or force you to go somewhere. [no passive] ❑ *He had her by the arm and he was screaming at her.* **9** v-T If you **have** something from someone, they give it to you. [no passive] ❑ *You can have my ticket.* ❑ *My wife has just had a baby boy.* **10** v-T If you **have** an illness or disability, you suffer from it. [no passive] ❑ *I had a headache.* **11** v-T If a woman **has** a baby, she gives birth to it. If she **is having** a baby, she is pregnant. [no passive] **12** v-T You can use **have** in expressions such as "**I won't have it**" or "**I'm not having that,**" to mean that you will not allow or put up with something. [with neg] ❑ *I'm not having any of that nonsense.* **13** PHRASE You can use **has it** in expressions such as "**rumor has it that**" or "**as legend has it**" when you are quoting something that you have heard, but you do not necessarily think it is true. [VAGUENESS] ❑ *Rumor has it that tickets were being sold for $300.* **14** PHRASE If someone **has it in for** you, they do not like you and they want to make life difficult for you. [INFORMAL] ❑ *He's always had it in for the Dawkins family.* **15** PHRASE If you **have it in** you, you have abilities and skills which you do not usually use and which only show themselves in a difficult situation. ❑ *"You were brilliant!" he said. "I didn't know you had it in you."* **16** PHRASE To **have it off with** someone or **have it away with** someone means to have sex with them. [BRIT, INFORMAL, VULGAR] ❑ *He reckons she's having it off with the gardener.* **17** PHRASE If you **have it out** or **have things out with** someone, you discuss a problem or disagreement very openly with them, even if it means having an argument, because you think this is the best way to solve the problem. ❑ *Why not have it out with your critic, discuss the whole thing face to face?* **18** to **be had** →see **had**. to **have had it** →see **had**

④ have ◆◆◇ /hæv, hæf/ (**has, having, had**) **1** PHRASE You use **have to** when you are saying that something is necessary or required, or must happen. If you do not **have to** do something, it is not necessary or required. ❑ *He had to go to Germany.* ❑ *You have to be careful what you say on telly.* **2** PHRASE You can use **have to** in order to say that you feel certain that something is true or will happen. ❑ *There has to be some kind of way out.*

ha|ven /heɪvᵊn/ (**havens**) N-COUNT A **haven** is a place where people or animals feel safe, secure, and happy. ❑ *...Lake Baringo, a freshwater haven for a mixed variety of birds.* →see also **safe haven**

haven't /hævᵊnt/ Haven't is the usual spoken form of 'have not.'

hav|oc /hævək/ **1** N-UNCOUNT Havoc is great disorder, and confusion. ❑ *Rioters caused havoc in the center of the town.* **2** PHRASE If one thing **plays havoc with** another or **wreaks havoc on** it, it prevents it from continuing or functioning as normal, or damages it. ❑ *The weather played havoc with airline schedules.*

hawk /hɔk/ (**hawks**) **1** N-COUNT A **hawk** is a large bird with a short, hooked beak, sharp claws, and very good eyesight. Hawks catch and eat small birds and animals. **2** N-COUNT In politics, if you refer to someone as a **hawk**, you mean that they believe in using force and violence to achieve something, rather than using more peaceful or diplomatic methods. Compare **dove**. ❑ *Both hawks and doves have expanded their conditions for ending the war.* **3** PHRASE If you **watch** someone **like a hawk**, you observe them very carefully, usually to make sure that they do not make a mistake or do something you do not want them to do. ❑ *If we hadn't watched him like a hawk, he would have gone back to London.*

hay /heɪ/ **1** N-UNCOUNT Hay is grass which has been cut and dried so that it can be used to feed animals. ❑ *...bales of hay.* **2** PHRASE If you say that someone **is making hay** or **is making hay while the sun shines**, you mean that they are taking advantage of a situation that is favorable to them while they have the chance to. ❑ *We shared a prescience of the coming war, and were determined to make hay while we could.*

hay fe|ver N-UNCOUNT If someone is suffering from **hay fever**, they sneeze and their eyes itch, because they are allergic to grass or flowers.

haz|ard /hæzərd/ (**hazards, hazarding, hazarded**) **1** N-COUNT A **hazard** is something which could be dangerous to you, your health or safety, or your plans or reputation. ❑ *A new report suggests that chewing-gum may be a health hazard.* **2** v-T If you **hazard** or if you **hazard a guess**, you make a suggestion about something which is only a guess and which you know might be wrong. ❑ *I would hazard a guess that they'll do fairly well in the next election.*

haz|ard|ous /hæzərdəs/ ADJ Something that is **hazardous** is dangerous, especially to people's health or safety. ❑ *They have no way to dispose of the hazardous waste they produce.*

haze /heɪz/ (**hazes**) **1** N-VAR Haze is light mist, caused by particles of water or dust in the air, which prevents you from seeing distant objects clearly. Haze often forms in hot weather. ❑ *They vanished into the haze near the horizon.* **2** N-SING

당신에게 다른 대안이 있다; 그의 창에서 보면 전망이 좋았다 ❑ 그와 함께 사는 세입자가 두 명 있었다. **4** 타동사 −한 상태이다 ❑ 메리는 눈을 감고 있었다. ❑ 그들은 커튼을 열어 두고 있었다. **5** 타동사 −하게 하다 ❑ 나는 네 방들을 청소하고 환기시켰다. ❑ 그들이 그를 살해하게 했다. **6** 타동사 당하다 ❑ 우리는 돈을 소매치기 당했다. **7** 타동사 시키다, −하게 하다 ❑ 그 다리는 당신이 여러 여행 안내서를 보고 받았을 느낌만큼 인상적이지 않다. **8** 타동사 잡다 ❑ 그는 그녀의 팔을 잡고 그녀에게 소리치고 있었다. **9** 타동사 받다 ❑ 내 티켓을 너에게 줄게. ❑ 성함을 말씀해 주시겠어요? ❑ 내 아내가 막 아들을 낳았다. **10** 타동사 앓다 ❑ 나는 두통이 있었다. **11** 타동사 아이를 낳다; 임신하다 ❑ 내 아내가 막 아들을 낳았다. **12** 타동사 허락하다; 허락할 수 없다, 참을 수 없다 ❑ 나는 그런 허튼소리는 참을 수 없다. **13** 구 −라고 하다; 소문에 −라고 한다; 전설에 의하면 −라고 한다 [점잖다] ❑ 소문에 표가 300달러에 팔리고 있었다고 한다. **14** 구 앙심을 품다 [비격식체] ❑ 그는 항상 도킨스 가족에게 앙심을 품어 왔다. **15** 구 소질이 있다, 역량이 있다 ❑ "탁월했어!"라고 그는 말했다. "나는 너에게 그러한 역량이 있는지 몰랐어." **16** 구 −와 간 때가지 가다 [영국영어, 비격식체, 비속어] ❑ 그는 그녀가 정원사와 갈 때까지 간 사이라고 생각한다. **17** 구 −와 토론으로 결말을 내다, −와 애기를 해서 결말을 짓다 ❑ 당신을 비판한 비평가와 마주 보며 결판이 날 때까지 토론을 해 보는 게 어떨까요?

1 구 −해야 한다 ❑ 그는 독일에 가야만 했다. ❑ 텔레비전에서 말을 할 때는 신중해야 한다. **2** 구 틀림이 없다 ❑ 어떤 것이든 틀림없이 탈출구가 있을 것이다.

가산명사 안식처, 피난처 ❑ 여러 종류의 새들에게 민물 안식처인 배링고 호수

have not의 축약형

1 불가산명사 대혼란 ❑ 폭도들은 도심에서 대혼란을 야기했다. **2** 구 −을 혼란시키다, −을 파괴하다 ❑ 날씨 때문에 항공 스케줄이 엉망이 되었다.

1 가산명사 매 **2** 가산명사 강경론자, 주전론자, 매파 ❑ 강경론자들과 평화론자들 모두 전쟁을 종식시킬 조건들을 늘렸다. **3** 구 매섭게 지켜보다 ❑ 우리가 그를 매섭게 지켜보지 않았다면, 그는 런던으로 다시 갔을 것이다.

1 불가산명사 건초 ❑ 건초 뭉치들 **2** 구 호기를 놓치지 않다 ❑ 우리는 전쟁이 발발할 것이라는 선견지명이 있었고 우리가 할 수 있을 때 기회를 살리기로 결심했다.

불가산명사 건초열

1 가산명사 위험 ❑ 새로운 보고에 의하면 껌을 씹는 것이 건강에 위험할 수도 있다고 한다. **2** 타동사 사실에 입각하지 않은 견해를 말하다, 감히 말하다 ❑ 근거는 없지만 나는 그들이 다음 선거에서는 상당히 선전할 것으로 예상한다.

형용사 위험한 ❑ 그들은 자기들이 만들어 내는 위험한 쓰레기를 처리할 방법이 없다.

1 가산명사 또는 불가산명사 안개, 아지랑이 ❑ 그들은 지평선 가까이 아지랑이 속으로 사라졌다. **2** 단수명사 흐릿한 열기, 흐릿한 김 [문예체] ❑ 댄은 뿌연 담배

A

If there is a **haze of** something such as smoke or steam, you cannot see clearly through it. [LITERARY] ❑ *Dan smiled at him through a haze of smoke and steaming coffee.*

B

ha|zel /ˈheɪzəl/ (hazels) **1** N-VAR A **hazel** is a small tree which produces nuts that you can eat. **2** COLOR **Hazel** eyes are greenish-brown in color.

C

ha|zy /ˈheɪzi/ (hazier, haziest) **1** ADJ **Hazy** weather conditions are those in which things are difficult to see, because of light mist, hot air, or dust. ❑ *The air was thin and crisp, filled with hazy sunshine and frost.* **2** ADJ If you are **hazy about** ideas or details, or if they are **hazy**, you are uncertain or confused about them. ❑ *I'm a bit hazy about it.* **3** ADJ If things seem **hazy**, you cannot see things clearly, for example because you are feeling ill. ❑ *My vision has grown so hazy.*

연기와 커피에서 피어나는 김 사이로 그를 보며 웃었다.

1 가산명사 또는 불가산명사 개암나무 **2** 색채어 담갈색의

1 형용사 흐릿한 ❑ 흐릿한 햇빛과 서리로 가득 찬 공기는 희박했지만 상쾌하였다. **2** 형용사 애매한, 모호한 ❑ 나는 그것에 대해서는 좀 애매하다. **3** 형용사 (눈이) 침침한 ❑ 내 시력이 너무 침침해졌다.

D

E

he ♦♦♦ /hi, STRONG hi/

He is a third person singular pronoun. **He** is used as the subject of a verb.

he는 3인칭 단수대명사이다. he는 동사의 주어로 쓰인다.

F

1 PRON-SING You use **he** to refer to a man, boy, or male animal. ❑ *He could never quite remember all our names.* **2** PRON-SING In written English, **he** is sometimes used to refer to a person without saying whether that person is a man or a woman. Some people dislike this use and prefer to use "he or she" or "they." ❑ *The teacher should encourage the child to proceed as far as he can, and when he is stuck, ask for help.*

1 단수대명사 그는, 그가 ❑ 그는 결코 우리의 이름 모두를 기억하지는 못했다. **2** 단수대명사 그는 ❑ 교사는 아이가 가능한 한 많이 진행해 나갈 수 있도록, 그리고 막히게 되는 경우에는 도움을 구할 수 있도록 용기를 북돋워 주어야 한다.

G

head ♦♦♦ /hed/ (heads, heading, headed)

Head is used in a large number of expressions which are explained under other words in the dictionary. For example, the expression "off the top of your head" is explained at "top."

이 사전에서 head가 포함된 많은 표현들이 다른 표제어에서 설명된다. 예를 들어, 'off the top of your head'는 'top'에서 설명된다.

H

1 N-COUNT Your **head** is the top part of your body, which has your eyes, mouth, and brain in it. ❑ *She turned her head away from him.* **2** N-COUNT You can use **head** to refer to your mind and your mental abilities. ❑ *...an exceptional analyst who could do complex math in his head.* **3** N-SING The **head of** a line of people or vehicles is the front of it, or the first person or vehicle in the line. ❑ *...the head of the queue.* **4** V-T If someone or something **heads** a line or procession, they are at the front of it. ❑ *The parson, heading the procession, had just turned right towards the churchyard.* **5** V-T If something **heads** a list or group, it is at the top of it. ❑ *Running a business heads the list of ambitions among the 1,000 people interviewed by Good Housekeeping magazine.* **6** N-COUNT The **head** of something long and thin is the end which is wider than or a different shape from the rest, and which is often considered to be the most important part. ❑ *There should be no exposed screw heads.* **7** N-COUNT The **head** of a school is the teacher who is in charge of a school. [mainly BRIT] ❑ *She is full of admiration for the head and teachers.* **8** N-COUNT The **head** of a company or organization is the person in charge of it and in charge of the people in it. ❑ *Heads of government from more than 100 countries gather in Geneva tomorrow.* **9** V-T If you **head** a department, company, or organization, you are the person in charge of it. ❑ *...Michael Williams, who heads the department's Office of Civil Rights.* **10** ADV If you toss a coin and it comes down **heads**, you can see the side of the coin which has a picture of a head on it. ❑ *"We might toss up for it," suggested Ted. "If it's heads, then we'll talk."* **11** V-T/V-I If you **are heading** for a particular place, you are going towards that place. In American English, you can also say that you **are headed** for a particular place. ❑ *He headed for the bus stop.* ❑ *It is not clear how many of them will be heading back to Saudi Arabia tomorrow.* **12** V-T/V-I If something or someone **is heading for** a particular result, the situation they are in is developing in a way that makes that result very likely. In American English, you can also say that something or someone **is headed for** a particular result. ❑ *The latest talks aimed at ending the civil war appear to be heading for deadlock.* **13** V-T If a piece of writing **is headed** a particular title, it has that title written at the beginning of it. [usu passive] ❑ *One chapter is headed, "Beating the Test".* **14** V-T If you **head** a ball in soccer, you hit it with your head in order to make it go in a particular direction. ❑ *He headed the ball across the face of the goal.* **15** →see also **heading** **16** PHRASE You use a **head** or **per head** after stating a cost or amount in order to indicate that that cost or amount is for each person in a particular group. ❑ *This simple chicken dish costs less than £1 a head.* **17** PHRASE If you have a **head for** something, you can deal with it easily. For example, if you have a **head for figures**, you can do arithmetic easily, and if you have a **head for heights**, you can climb to a great height without feeling afraid. ❑ *I don't have a head for business.* **18** PHRASE If you **get** a fact or idea **into** your **head**, you suddenly realize or think that it is true and you usually do not change your opinion about it. ❑ *Once they get an idea into their heads, they never give up.* **19** PHRASE If you say that someone has **got** or **gotten** something **into** their **head**, you mean that they have finally understood or accepted it, and you are usually criticizing them because it has taken them a long time to do this. ❑ *Managers have at last got it into their heads that they can no longer rest content with inefficient operations.* **20** PHRASE If alcoholic drink **goes to** your **head**, it makes you feel drunk. ❑ *That wine was strong, it went to your head.* **21** PHRASE If you say that something such as praise or success **goes to** someone's **head**, you are criticizing them because you think that it makes them too proud or confident. [DISAPPROVAL] ❑ *Ford is definitely not a man to let a little success go to his head.* **22** PHRASE If you are **head over heels** or **head over heels in love**, you are very much in love. ❑ *I was very attracted to men and fell head over heels many times.* **23** PHRASE If you **keep** your **head**, you remain calm in a difficult situation. If you **lose** your **head**, you panic or do not remain calm in a difficult situation. ❑ *She was able to keep her head and not panic.* **24** PHRASE If you **knock** something **on the head**, you stop it. [BRIT, INFORMAL] ❑ *When we stop enjoying ourselves we'll knock it on the head.* **25** PHRASE Phrases such as **laugh** your **head off** and **scream** your **head off** can be used to emphasize that someone is laughing or screaming a lot or very loudly. [EMPHASIS] ❑ *He carried on telling a joke, laughing his head off.* **26** PHRASE If something such as an idea, joke, or comment goes **over** someone's **head**, it is too difficult for them to

1 가산명사 머리, 고개 ❑ 그녀는 그에게서 고개를 돌렸다. **2** 가산명사 두뇌, 머리 ❑ 머리 속에서 복잡한 계산을 할 수 있는 매우 뛰어난 분석가 **3** 단수명사 맨 앞, 선두 ❑ 줄의 맨 앞 **4** 타동사 맨 앞에 있다, 선두에 있다 ❑ 행렬의 선두에 있던 목사가 교회의 묘지 쪽으로 막 우회전한 참이었다. **5** 타동사 맨 위에 있다 ❑ 사업체를 경영하는 것이 굿 하우스키핑 잡지가 인터뷰한 사람 천 명의 열망을 나타낸 리스트 맨 위에 있다. **6** 가산명사 머리 부분, 헤드 ❑ 나사 머리 부분이 드러나서는 안 된다. **7** 가산명사 교장 [주로 영국영어] ❑ 그녀는 교장 선생님과 선생님에 대한 존경심이 가득하다. **8** 가산명사 우두머리, 총재 ❑ 100개 국가의 정부 수반이 내일 제네바에 모인다. **9** 타동사 -를 이끌다, -를 지휘하다 ❑ 인권 사무국을 이끌고 있는 마이클 윌리엄스 **10** 부사 (동전의) 앞면 ❑ "동전을 던져서 정하자."라고 테드가 제안했다. "앞면이 나오면, 우리가 말할 것이다." **11** 타동사/자동사 향하다 ❑ 그는 버스 정류장으로 향했다. ❑ 그들은 중 몇 명이 내일 사우디아라비아로 되돌아갈 것인지는 분명하지 않다. **12** 타동사/자동사 (결과를 향해) 나아가다 ❑ 내란의 종결이 목적이었던 최근의 회담들이 교착 상태로 나아가는 것을 듯하다. **13** 타동사 표제가 붙다 ❑ 한 장(章)은 "테스트 때려잡기"라는 제목이 붙어 있다. **14** 타동사 머리로 받다, 헤딩하다 ❑ 그가 골대 정면을 가로질러 공을 헤딩했다. **16** 구 한 사람당, 1인당 ❑ 이렇게 간단한 닭요리는 1인분에 1파운드도 안 든다. **17** 구 -에 능하다 ❑ 숫자에 능하다, 높은 곳에 강하다 ❑ 나는 사업에 재능이 없다. **18** 구 깨닫다, 떠오르다 ❑ 그들은 일단 머리에 어떤 아이디어가 떠오르면 결코 단념하지 않는다. **19** 구 이해하다 ❑ 비효율적인 경영에 더 이상 안주할 수 없다는 것을 경영자들은 마침내 겨우 알게 되었다. **20** 구 취하게 하다 ❑ 저 포도주는 독해서, 너를 취하게 만들었다. **21** 구 자만하게 하다 [탐탁잖음] ❑ 포드는 작은 성공에 자만할 사람이 절대로 아니다. **22** 구 사랑에 폭 빠진 ❑ 나는 남자들에게 매우 끌렸고 여러 번 사랑에 폭 빠졌다. **23** 구 침착하다; 냉정을 잃다 ❑ 그녀는 당황하지 않고 침착할 수 있었다. **24** 구 그만두다, 중단하다 [영국영어, 비격식체] ❑ 우리가 재미가 없으면 그때 그만둘 것이다. **25** 구 정신없이 웃다; 정신없이 비명을 지르다 [강조] ❑ 그는 정신없이 웃으면서 계속 농담을 했다. **26** 구 이해되지 않는 ❑ 그 생각의 많은 것들이 내 머리로는 도저히 이해가 되지 않았던 걸 인정한다. **27** 구 상의도 없이 ❑ 그는 선임 장교들과 상의도 없이 가려고 했다고 훈계를 들었다. **28** 구 (안 좋은 일이) 고개를 들다 ❑ 그가 다시 이사 오고 일주일 정도 뒤에 한 가지 안 좋은 문제가 고개를 들었다. **29** 구 물긋나무로 서다 ❑ 그가 골대 상태로 요가를 하는 그가 사진에 찍혔다. **30** 구 이해하다, 앞뒤를 분간하다 [비격식체] ❑ 나는 그 망할 영화를 전혀 이해하지 못했다. **31** 구 그 생각이 드는 ❑ 그는 갑자기 오스트레일리아로 가서 아들과 함께 있고 싶은 생각이 들었다. **32** 구 극에 달하다 ❑ 이러한 문제들은 방송국 기자 다섯 명이 해고당한 9월에 극에 달했다. **33** 구 이마를 맞대고 상의하다 ❑ 그래서 모두가 이마를 맞대고 상의하여 결국에는 우호적인 합의를 이루었다. **34** 구 지속은 면하다, 근근이 하다 ❑ 우리가 겨우 빚은 안 지고 근근이 꾸려 나가는 현금 유동 상태가 그리 썩 좋지는 않다. **35** 구 차별이 있다, 감원이 있다 ❑ 그룹의 문제점들로 인해서 감원을 고려하게 되었다.

understand. ❏ *I admit that a lot of the ideas went way over my head.* **26 PHRASE** If someone does something **over** another person's **head**, they do it without asking them or discussing it with them, especially when they should do so because the other person is in a position of authority. ❏ *He was reprimanded for trying to go over the heads of senior officers.* **27 PHRASE** If you say that something unpleasant or embarrassing **rears its ugly head** or **raises its ugly head**, you mean that it occurs, often after not occurring for some time. ❏ *There was a problem which reared its ugly head about a week after she moved back in.* **28 PHRASE** If you **stand on** your **head**, you balance upside down with the top of your head and your hands on the ground. ❏ *He was photographed standing on his head doing yoga.* **29 PHRASE** If you say that you cannot **make head nor tail of** something or you cannot **make head or tail of** it, you are emphasizing that you cannot understand it at all. [INFORMAL] ❏ *I couldn't make head nor tail of the damn film.* **30 PHRASE** If somebody **takes it into** their **head to** do something, especially something strange or foolish, they suddenly decide to do it. ❏ *He suddenly took it into his head to go out to Australia to stay with his son.* **31 PHRASE** If a problem or disagreement **comes to a head** or **is brought to a head**, it becomes so bad that something must be done about it. ❏ *These problems came to a head in September when five of the station's journalists were sacked.* **32 PHRASE** If two or more people **put** their **heads together**, they talk about a problem they have and try to solve it. ❏ *So everyone put their heads together and eventually an amicable arrangement was reached.* **33 PHRASE** If you **keep** your **head above water**, you just avoid getting into difficulties; used especially to talk about business. ❏ *We are keeping our head above water, but our cash flow position is not too good.* **34 PHRASE** If you say that **heads will roll** as a result of something bad that has happened, you mean that people will be punished for it, especially by losing their jobs. ❏ *The group's problems have led to speculation that heads will roll.* →see **body**

Thesaurus	head의 참조어
N.	brain, mind **2**
	beginning, front **3**
	director, leader **8**
V.	lead **4**
	command, control, govern, manage **9**

head|ache /hɛdeɪk/ (**headaches**) **1** N-COUNT If you have a **headache**, you have a pain in your head. ❏ *I have had a terrible headache for the last two days.* **2** N-COUNT If you say that something is a **headache**, you mean that it causes you difficulty or worry. ❏ *The airline's biggest headache is the increase in the price of aviation fuel.*

head count (**head counts**) N-COUNT If you do a **head count**, you count the number of people present. You can also use **head count** to talk about the number of people that are present at an event, or that an organization employs. ❏ *The troops rushed back onto the chopper and took off - but a head count showed one man was missing.*

head|er /hɛdər/ (**headers**) N-COUNT A **header** is text such as a name or a page number that can be automatically displayed at the top of each page of a printed document. Compare **footer**. [COMPUTING] ❏ *...page formatting like headers, footers and page numbers.*

head|hunt /hɛdhʌnt/ (**headhunts, headhunting, headhunted**) V-T If someone who works for a particular company **is headhunted**, they leave that company because another company has approached them and offered them another job with better pay and higher status. ❏ *He was headhunted by Barkers last October to build an advertising team.*

head|hunter /hɛdhʌntər/ (**headhunters**) also **head-hunter** N-COUNT A **headhunter** is a person who tries to persuade someone to leave their job and take another job which has better pay and more status. ❏ *...a headhunter for a European bank.*

head|ing /hɛdɪŋ/ (**headings**) N-COUNT A **heading** is the title of a piece of writing, which is written or printed at the top of the page. ❏ *...helpful chapter headings.* →see also **head**

head|light /hɛdlaɪt/ (**headlights**) N-COUNT A vehicle's **headlights** are the large powerful lights at the front. ❏ *Darkness fell and the few cars coming in the opposite direction dipped their headlights as they passed.*

head|line ♦◇◇ /hɛdlaɪn/ (**headlines, headlining, headlined**) **1** N-COUNT A **headline** is the title of a newspaper story, printed in large letters at the top of the story, especially on the front page. ❏ *The Sydney Morning Herald carried the headline: "Sorry Ma'am, Most Australians Want a Republic."* **2** N-PLURAL **The headlines** are the main points of the news which are read on radio or television. ❏ *I'm Claudia Polley with the news headlines.* **3** V-T If a newspaper or magazine article **is headlined** a particular thing, that is the headline that introduces it. [usu passive] ❏ *The article was headlined "Tell us the truth."* **4** PHRASE Someone or something that **hits the headlines** or **grabs the headlines** gets a lot of publicity from the media. ❏ *El Salvador first hit the world headlines at the beginning of the 1980s.*

head|long /hɛdlɔŋ, BRIT hɛdlɒŋ/ **1** ADV If you move **headlong** in a particular direction, you move there very quickly. [ADV after v] ❏ *He ran headlong for the open door.* **2** ADV If you fall or move **headlong**, you fall or move with your head furthest forward. [ADV after v] ❏ *She missed her footing and fell headlong down the stairs.* **3** ADV If you rush **headlong into** something, you do it quickly without thinking about it. [ADV after v] ❏ *Do not leap headlong into decisions.* ● ADJ **Headlong** is also an adjective. [ADJ n] ❏ *...the headlong rush to independence.*

head|master /hɛdmɑstər, -mæst-/ (**headmasters**) N-COUNT A **headmaster** is a man who is the head teacher of a school. [mainly BRIT]

1 가산명사 두통 ❏ 나는 지난 이틀 동안 심한 두통이 있었다. **2** 가산명사 골칫거리, 걱정거리 ❏ 그 항공사의 가장 큰 골칫거리는 항공 연료 값의 인상이다.

가산명사 인원 수 (세기) ❏ 군대는 헬리콥터로 다시 급히 올라타 이륙했는데, 인원을 확인하니 한 사람이 없었다.

가산명사 머리글, (텍스트의) 상단 [컴퓨터] ❏ 머리글, 바닥글, 쪽 번호와 같은 페이지 구성 형태

타동사 스카우트되다 ❏ 그는 지난 10월에 홍보 팀을 구성하려고 바커스에 스카우트되었다.

가산명사 인재 스카우트 담당자 ❏ 유럽 은행의 인재 스카우트 담당자

가산명사 표제, 제목 ❏ 도움이 되는 장(章)별 소제목들

가산명사 헤드라이트 ❏ 날이 어두워졌고 반대 방향에서 오는 몇 대의 차가 지나가면서 헤드라이트를 아래쪽으로 낮추었다.

1 가산명사 표제, 헤드라인 ❏ 시드니 모닝 헤럴드는 '죄송합니다, 마마. 대부분의 오스트레일리아 사람들은 공화국을 원합니다'라는 헤드라인을 실었다. **2** 복수명사 주요 뉴스 ❏ 저는 클라우디아 폴리입니다. 주요 뉴스를 말씀드리겠습니다. **3** 타동사 표제가 붙다 ❏ 그 기사에는 '우리에게 진실을 말해 달라'라는 표제가 붙어 있었다. **4** 구 표제를 장식하다 ❏ 엘살바도르는 1980년대 초에 처음 세계 언론의 표제를 장식하기 시작하였다.

1 부사 곤두박질치듯 ❏ 그는 열린 문으로 곤두박질치듯 달려갔다. **2** 부사 곤두박질로 ❏ 그녀는 발을 헛디디고 계단 아래로 곤두박질쳐 떨어졌다. **3** 부사 무턱대고, 성급하게 ❏ 무턱대고 성급하게 결정하지 말아라. ● 형용사 성급한 ❏ 무턱대고 독립하려고 달려듦

가산명사 (남자) 교장 [주로 영국영어]

A

head|mistress /hɛdmɪstrɪs/ (**headmistresses**) N-COUNT A **headmistress** is a woman who is the head teacher of a school. [mainly BRIT]

가산명사 (여자) 교장 [주로 영국영어]

head of state (**heads of state**) N-COUNT A **head of state** is the leader of a country, for example a president, king, or queen. ❑ *Which country's head of state is Queen Beatrix van Oranje Nassau?*

가산명사 국가 원수, 국가 주석 ❑ 베아트릭스 밴 오란여 낫소 여왕이 어느 나라 국가 주석인가?

B

head-on **1** ADV If two vehicles hit each other **head-on**, they hit each other with their fronts pointing toward each other. [ADV after v] ❑ *The car collided head-on with a van.* ● ADJ **Head-on** is also an adjective. [ADJ n] ❑ *Their car was in a head-on smash with a truck.* **2** ADJ A **head-on** conflict or approach is direct, without any attempt to compromise or avoid the issue. [ADJ n] ❑ *The only victors in a head-on clash between the president and the assembly would be the hardliners on both sides.* ● ADV **Head-on** is also an adverb. [ADV after v] ❑ *Once again, I chose to confront the issue head-on.*

1 부사 정면으로 ❑ 그 차가 밴과 정면으로 충돌했다. ● 형용사 정면의 ❑ 그들의 차는 트럭과 정면충돌했다. **2** 형용사 정면의 ❑ 대통령과 국회 사이의 정면충돌의 유일한 승리자는 양 측의 강경론자들이 될 것이다. ● 부사 정면으로 ❑ 다시 한 번 더, 나는 그 문제에 정면으로 대응하는 것을 택했다.

C

D

head|phones /hɛdfoʊnz/ N-PLURAL **Headphones** are a pair of padded speakers which you wear over your ears in order to listen to a radio, CD player, or tape recorder without other people hearing it. [also *a pair of* N] ❑ *...while out cycling one evening and listening to your program on headphones.*

복수명사 헤드폰 ❑ 어느 날 저녁 나가서 자전거를 타면서 당신의 프로그램을 헤드폰으로 들으며

E

head|quarters ♦◇◇ /hɛdkwɔrtərz/ N-SING-COLL The **headquarters** of an organization is its main offices. ❑ *...fraud squad officers from London's police headquarters.*

단수명사-집합 본부 ❑ 런던 경찰 본부의 사기 분과 팀 경찰들

F

head|rest /hɛdrɛst/ (**headrests**) N-COUNT A **headrest** is the part of the back of a seat on which you can lean your head, especially one on the front seat of a car.

가산명사 머리 받침

G

head|set /hɛdsɛt/ (**headsets**) **1** N-COUNT A **headset** is a small pair of headphones that you can use for listening to a radio or recorded music, or for using a telephone. ❑ *During the race Mr. Taylor talks to the driver using a headset.* **2** N-COUNT A **headset** is a piece of equipment that you wear on your head so you can see computer images or images from a camera in front of your eyes. ❑ *Soon the wearer of a virtual reality headset will be able to be "present" at sporting or theatrical events staged thousands of miles away.*

1 가산명사 (소형) 헤드폰, 헤드셋 ❑ 경기 중에 테일러 씨는 헤드셋을 이용해서 운전자에게 말한다. **2** 가산명사 헤드셋 ❑ 곧 가상 세계의 헤드셋을 쓴 사람은 수천 마일 떨어진 곳에서 일어나는 스포츠나 연극 이벤트에 '참석할' 수 있게 될 것이다.

H

I

head start (**head starts**) N-COUNT If you have a **head start on** other people, you have an advantage over them in something such as a competition or race. ❑ *A good education gives your child a head start in life.*

가산명사 유리한 스타트 ❑ 좋은 교육은 당신의 아이에게 삶의 시발점에서 우위를 준다.

J

head|strong /hɛdstrɒŋ, BRIT hɛdstrɒŋ/ ADJ If you refer to someone as **headstrong**, you are slightly critical of the fact that they are determined to do what they want. ❑ *He's young, very headstrong, but he's a good man underneath.*

형용사 고집이 센 ❑ 그는 어리고, 매우 고집이 세지만 실은 좋은 사람이다.

K

head teach|er (**head teachers**) also **headteacher** N-COUNT A **head teacher** is a teacher who is in charge of a school. [BRIT]

가산명사 교장 선생님 [영국영어]

L

head|way /hɛdweɪ/ PHRASE If you **make headway**, you progress towards achieving something. ❑ *There was concern in the city that police were making little headway in the investigation.*

구 진척되다 ❑ 그 도시 사람들은 경찰이 그 조사를 하는 데 거의 진척이 없다고 걱정했다.

M

heady /hɛdi/ (**headier, headiest**) ADJ A **heady** drink, atmosphere, or experience strongly affects your senses, for example by making you feel drunk or excited. ❑ *...in the heady days just after their marriage.*

형용사 취하게 하는, 황홀한 ❑ 그들이 결혼을 막 한 뒤의 황홀한 나날

N

heal ♦◇◇ /hil/ (**heals, healing, healed**) **1** V-T/V-I When a broken bone or other injury **heals** or if someone or something **heals** it, it becomes healthy and normal again. ❑ *Within six weeks the bruising had gone, but it was six months before it all healed.* **2** V-T/V-I If you **heal** something such as a rift or a wound, or if it **heals**, the situation is put right so that people are friendly or happy again. ❑ *Today Sophie and her sister have healed the family rift and visit their family every weekend.*

1 타동사/자동사 낫다, 치유되다 ❑ 6주 안에 멍든 것은 사라졌으나 6개월이 돼서야 완전히 나았다. **2** 타동사/자동사 해소하다, 화해시키다 ❑ 요즘 소피와 여동생은 가족 간의 불화를 해소했고 주말마다 가족을 방문한다.

O

P

heal|er /hilər/ (**healers**) N-COUNT A **healer** is a person who heals people, especially a person who heals through prayer and religious faith.

가산명사 치료사

Q

health ♦♦♦ /hɛlθ/ **1** N-UNCOUNT A person's **health** is the condition of their body and the extent to which it is free from illness or is able to resist illness. ❑ *Tea contains caffeine. It's bad for your health.* **2** N-UNCOUNT **Health** is a state in which a person is not suffering from any illness and is feeling well. ❑ *In the hospital they nursed me back to health.* **3** N-UNCOUNT The **health** of something such as an organization or a system is its success and the fact that it is working well. ❑ *There's no way to predict the future health of the banking industry.*

1 불가산명사 건강 ❑ 차에는 카페인이 들어 있다. 당신의 건강에 나쁘다. **2** 불가산명사 건강한 상태 ❑ 병원에서 그들은 나를 다시 건강해지도록 간호했다. **3** 불가산명사 건전성, 건강성 ❑ 금융 산업의 앞으로의 건전성을 예상할 방법은 없다.

R

S

healthy ♦◇◇ /hɛlθi/ (**healthier, healthiest**) **1** ADJ Someone who is **healthy** is well and is not suffering from any illness. ❑ *Most of us need to lead more balanced lives to be healthy and happy.* ● **healthily** /hɛlθɪli/ ADV ❑ *What I really want is to live healthily for as long as possible.* **2** ADJ Something that is **healthy** is good for your health. ❑ *...a healthy diet.* **3** ADJ A **healthy** organization or system is successful. ❑ *...an economically healthy socialist state.* **4** ADJ A **healthy** amount of something is a large amount that shows success. ❑ *He predicts a continuation of healthy profits in the current financial year.* **5** ADJ If you have a **healthy** attitude about something, you show good sense. ❑ *She has a refreshingly healthy attitude to work.*

1 형용사 건강한 ❑ 우리들 대부분은 건강하고 행복하기 위해 더욱 균형 잡힌 삶을 영위할 필요가 있다. ● 건강하게 부사 ❑ 내가 정말로 원하는 것은 가능한 한 오래도록 건강하게 사는 것이다. **2** 형용사 몸에 좋은 ❑ 몸에 좋은 식품 **3** 형용사 성공한, 탄탄한 ❑ 경제적으로 성공한 사회주의 국가 **4** 형용사 상당한 ❑ 그는 현 회계 연도에 상당한 수익이 계속되리라 예상한다. **5** 형용사 건전한 ❑ 그녀는 일에 대해 신선하게 보일 정도로 건전한 태도를 보인다.

T

U

V

Thesaurus

*healthy*의 참조어

ADJ.   fit, lively, well **1**
         beneficial, nutritious, wholesome **2**

W

Word Partnership

*healthy*의 연어

N.   healthy **baby** **1**
       healthy **appetite**, healthy **diet/food**, healthy **glow**,
       healthy **lifestyle**, healthy **skin** **2**
       healthy **attitude about** *something* **5**

X

Y

Z

heap /hip/ (**heaps**, **heaping**, **heaped**) **1** N-COUNT A **heap** of things is a pile of them, especially a pile arranged in a rather messy way. ❑ *...a heap of bricks.*

> A **heap** of things is usually untidy, and often has the shape of a hill or mound. ❑ *Now, the house is a heap of rubble.* A **stack** is usually tidy, and often consists of flat objects placed directly on top of each other. ❑ *...a neat stack of dishes.* A **pile** of things can be tidy or untidy. ❑ *...a neat pile of clothes.*

2 V-T If you **heap** things in a pile, you arrange them in a large pile. ❑ *Mrs. Madrigal heaped more carrots onto Michael's plate.* ● PHRASAL VERB **Heap up** means the same as **heap**. ❑ *Off to one side, the militia was heaping up wood for a bonfire.* **3** V-T If you **heap** praise or criticism **on** someone or something, you give them a lot of praise or criticism. ❑ *The head of the navy heaped scorn on both the methods and motives of the conspirators.* **4** QUANT **Heaps of** something or a **heap of** something is a large quantity of it. [INFORMAL] ❑ *You have heaps of time.*

hear ♦♦♦ /hɪər/ (**hears**, **hearing**, **heard**) /hɜrd/ **1** V-T When you **hear** a sound, you become aware of it through your ears. ❑ *She heard no further sounds.* ❑ *They heard the protesters shout: "No more fascism!"* **2** V-T If you **hear** something such as a lecture or a piece of music, you listen to it. ❑ *You can hear commentary on the match in about half an hour's time.* ❑ *I don't think you've ever heard Doris talking about her emotional life before.* **3** V-T When a judge or a court of law **hears** a case, or evidence in a case, they listen to it officially in order to make a decision about it. [FORMAL] ❑ *The jury has heard evidence from defense witnesses.* **4** V-I If you **hear from** someone, you receive a letter or telephone call from them. ❑ *Drop us a line, it's always great to hear from you.* **5** V-T/V-I If you **hear** some news or information about something, you find out about it by someone telling you, or from the radio or television. ❑ *My mother heard of this school through Leslie.* ❑ *He had heard that the trophy had been sold.* **6** V-T/V-I If you **have heard of** something or someone, you know about them, but not in great detail. [no cont] ❑ *Many people haven't heard of reflexology.*

> Do not confuse **hear** and **listen**. You use **hear** to talk about sounds that you are aware of because they reach your ears. You often use **can** with **hear**. ❑ *I can hear him yelling and swearing.* If you want to say that someone is paying attention to something they can hear, you say that they **are listening to** it. ❑ *He turned on the radio and listened to the news.* Note that **listen** is not followed directly by an object. You must always say that you listen **to** something. However, **listen** can also be used on its own without an object. ❑ *I was laughing too much to listen.*

7 PHRASE If you say that you **have heard** something **before**, you mean that you are not interested in it, or do not believe it, or are not surprised about it, because you already know about it or have experienced it. ❑ *Furness shrugs wearily. He has heard it all before.* **8** PHRASE If you say that you **can't hear yourself think**, you are complaining and emphasizing that there is a lot of noise, and that it is disturbing you or preventing you from doing something. [INFORMAL, EMPHASIS] ❑ *For God's sake shut up. I can't hear myself think!* **9** PHRASE If you say that you **won't hear of** someone doing something, you mean that you refuse to let them do it. ❑ *I've always wanted to be an actor but Dad wouldn't hear of it.*

Thesaurus	*hear*의 참조어
v.	detect, listen **1** **5**

hear|ing ♦♦◇ /hɪərɪŋ/ (**hearings**) **1** N-UNCOUNT A person's or animal's **hearing** is the sense which makes it possible for them to be aware of sounds. ❑ *His mind still seemed clear and his hearing was excellent.* **2** N-COUNT A **hearing** is an official meeting which is held in order to collect facts about an incident or problem. ❑ *After more than two hours of pandemonium, the judge adjourned the hearing until next Tuesday.* **3** PHRASE If someone gives you **a fair hearing** or **a hearing**, they listen to you when you give your opinion about something. ❑ *Weber gave a fair hearing to anyone who held a different opinion.* **4** PHRASE If someone says something **in** your **hearing** or **within** your **hearing**, you can hear what they say because they are with you or near you. ❑ *No one spoke disparagingly of her father in her hearing.*

Word Partnership	*hearing*의 연어
N.	hearing **impairment/loss 1**
	court hearing **2**
v.	hold a hearing, testify at/before a hearing **2**

heart ♦♦◇ /hɑrt/ (**hearts**) **1** N-COUNT Your **heart** is the organ in your chest that pumps the blood around your body. People also use **heart** to refer to the area of their chest that is closest to their heart. ❑ *The bullet had passed less than an inch from Andrea's heart.* **2** N-COUNT You can refer to someone's **heart** when you are talking about their deep feelings and beliefs. [LITERARY] ❑ *Alik's words filled her heart with pride.* **3** N-VAR You use **heart** when you are talking about someone's character and attitude toward other people, especially when they are kind and generous. [APPROVAL] ❑ *She loved his brilliance and his generous heart.* **4** N-SING **The heart of** something is the most central and important part of it. ❑ *The heart of the problem is supply and demand.* **5** N-SING **The heart of** a place is its

---

1 가산명사 더미 ❑ 벽돌 더미

> heap은 대개 정돈되어 있지 않은 상태로 수북이 쌓여 있는 것이다. ❑ 이제, 그 집은 파편 더미다. stack은 보통 정돈되어 있고, 흔히 납작한 물체들을 층층이 위로 쌓아 올린 것이다. ❑ ... 가지런히 포개져 있는 접시들. 물건의 pile은 정리되어 있을 수도 있고, 그렇지 않을 수도 있다. ❑ ...단정하게 포개져 있는 옷

2 타동사 쌓아올리다 ❑ 마드리갈 부인은 마이클의 접시 위에 더 많은 당근을 수북이 놓아 주었다. ● 구동사 쌓아올리다 ❑ 한쪽에서는, 민병들이 모닥불을 피우기 위해 장작을 쌓아올리고 있었다. **3** 타동사 (찬사, 비판을) 퍼붓다 ❑ 해군 대장은 반역자들의 방법과 동기 모두에 대해서 경멸을 퍼부었다. **4** 수량사 다수, 다량 [비격식체] ❑ 당신은 시간이 많다.

1 타동사 듣다 ❑ 그녀는 더 이상 어떤 소리도 듣지 못했다. ❑ 그들은 "이제 파시즘은 그만!"이라고 시위자들이 소리치는 것을 들었다. **2** 타동사 듣다 ❑ 약 30분 있으면 그 경기에 대한 해설을 들을 수 있다. ❑ 도리스가 이전에 자신의 정서적인 생활에 대해서 말하는 것을 들어 본 적이 없을 것이다. **3** 타동사 심리하다, 청취하다 [격식체] ❑ 배심원들은 피고 측 증인들의 증언을 들었다. **4** 자동사 소식을 듣다, 연락을 받다 ❑ 우리에게 몇 자 적어 보내 줘, 너한테서 소식을 들으면 항상 너무 좋아. **5** 타동사/자동사 (뉴스 등을) 듣다 ❑ 어머니는 레슬리를 통해서 이 학교에 대해 들었다. ❑ 그는 트로피가 팔렸다고 들었다. **6** 타동사/자동사 들어서 알고 있다 ❑ 많은 사람들이 반사 요법에 대해서 들어보지 못했다.

> hear와 listen을 혼동하지 않도록 하라. 귀에 들리기 때문에 의식하는 소리에 대해 말할 때는 hear를 쓴다. hear는 흔히 can과 함께 쓴다. ❑ 내 귀에 그가 고함지르고 욕하는 소리가 들린다. 누가 자기가 들을 수 있는 것에 주의를 기울인다고 말할 때는 그들이 그것에 listen to한다고 표현한다. ❑ 그는 라디오를 켜고 뉴스를 들었다. listen 다음에는 바로 목적어가 따라오지 않음을 유의하라. 항상 listen to something이라고 표현한다. 그렇지만, listen이 목적어 없이 그냥 쓰일 수도 있다. ❑ 나는 너무 많이 웃느라 듣지를 못했다.

7 구 이미 들은 얘기이다 ❑ 퍼니스는 지겨워서 어깨를 으쓱했다. 모든 것이 그가 이미 들은 얘기들이었다. **8** 구 (시끄러워) 집중할 수 없다 [비격식체, 강조] ❑ 제발 조용히 해. 시끄러워서 제대로 집중할 수가 없어! **9** 구 -을 들어주지 않다, -을 허락하지 않다 ❑ 나는 항상 배우가 되고 싶었지만, 아버지는 그것을 허락하려 하지 않았다.

1 불가산명사 청각, 청력 ❑ 그의 정신은 여전히 멀쩡해 보였고 그의 청력은 훌륭했다. **2** 가산명사 심리, 청문회 ❑ 두 시간이 넘는 혼란 상태가 이어진 후, 판사는 다음 화요일까지 심리를 연기했다. **3** 구 경청 ❑ 웨버는 다른 의견을 가진 모든 사람의 말을 경청하였다. **4** 구 -가 듣는 범위 안에, -가 듣는 데서 ❑ 아무도 그녀가 듣는 데서는 그녀의 아버지를 업신여기는 말은 하지 않았다.

1 가산명사 심장 ❑ 총알은 앤드리아의 심장에서 1인치도 못 미치는 곳을 관통했다. **2** 가산명사 마음, 감정 [문예체] ❑ 앨릭의 말은 그녀의 마음을 자신감에 가득 차게 했다. **3** 가산명사 또는 불가산명사 인정, 마음씨 [마음에 듦] ❑ 그녀는 그의 명석함과 후한 마음씨를 사랑했다. **4** 단수명사 -의 본질, -의 핵심 ❑ 문제의 핵심은 공급과 수요이다. **5** 단수명사 중심 ❑ 런던의 웨스트엔드 중심에 있는 사람이 많은 치과 **6** 가산명사 하트 ❑ 하트 모양의 초콜릿 **7** 불가산명사-집합 (카드의) 하트 ● 가산명사 하트

center. ❑ ...a busy dentists' practice in the heart of London's West End. ◳ N-COUNT A **heart** is a shape that is used as a symbol of love: ♥. ❑ ...heart-shaped chocolates. ◳ N-UNCOUNT-COLL **Hearts** is one of the four suits in a pack of playing cards. Each card in the suit is marked with one or more symbols in the shape of a heart. ● N-COUNT A **heart** is a playing card of this suit. ❑ West had to decide whether to play a heart. ◳ PHRASE If you feel or believe something **with all** your **heart**, you feel or believe it very strongly. [EMPHASIS] ❑ My own family I loved with all my heart. ◳ PHRASE If you say that someone is a particular kind of person **at heart**, you mean that that is what they are really like, even though they may seem very different. ❑ He was a very gentle boy at heart. ◳ PHRASE If you say that someone has your interests or your welfare **at heart**, you mean that they are concerned about you and that is why they are doing something. ❑ She told him she only had his interests at heart. ◳ PHRASE If someone **breaks** your **heart**, they make you very sad and unhappy, usually because they end a love affair or close relationship with you. [LITERARY] ❑ I fell in love on holiday but the girl broke my heart. ◳ PHRASE If something **breaks** your **heart**, it makes you feel very sad and depressed, especially because people are suffering but you can do nothing to help them. ❑ It really breaks my heart to see them this way. ◳ PHRASE If you know something such as a poem **by heart**, you have learned it so well that you can remember it without having to read it. ❑ Mack knew this passage by heart. ◳ PHRASE If someone has a **change of heart**, their attitude toward something changes. ❑ Several brokers have had a change of heart about prospects for the company. ◳ PHRASE If something such as a subject or project is **close to** your **heart** or **near to** your **heart**, it is very important to you and you are very interested in it and concerned about it. ❑ This is a subject very close to my heart. ◳ PHRASE If you can do something **to** your **heart's content**, you can do it as much as you want. ❑ I was delighted to be able to eat my favorite dishes to my heart's content. ◳ CONVENTION You can say "**cross my heart**" when you want someone to believe that you are telling the truth. You can also ask "**cross your heart?**", when you are asking someone if they are really telling the truth. [SPOKEN] ❑ And I won't tell any of the other girls anything you tell me about it. I promise, cross my heart. ◳ PHRASE If you say something **from the heart** or **from the bottom of** your **heart**, you sincerely mean what you say. ❑ He spoke with confidence, from the heart. ◳ PHRASE If you want to do something but do **not have the heart** to do it, you do not do it because you know it will make someone unhappy or disappointed. ❑ We knew all along but didn't have the heart to tell her. ◳ PHRASE If you believe or know something **in** your **heart of hearts**, that is what you really believe or think, even though it may sometimes seem that you do not. ❑ I know in my heart of hearts that I am the right man for that mission. ◳ PHRASE If your **heart isn't in** the thing you are doing, you have very little enthusiasm for it, usually because you are depressed or are thinking about something else. ❑ I tried to learn some lines but my heart wasn't really in it. ◳ PHRASE If you **lose heart**, you become sad and depressed and are no longer interested in something, especially because it is not progressing as you would like. ❑ He appealed to his countrymen not to lose heart. ◳ PHRASE If your **heart is in** your **mouth**, you feel very excited, worried, or frightened. ❑ My heart was in my mouth when I walked into her office. ◳ PHRASE If you **open** your **heart** or **pour out** your **heart** to someone, you tell them your most private thoughts and feelings. ❑ She opened her heart to millions yesterday and told how she came close to suicide. ◳ PHRASE If you say that someone's **heart is in the right place**, you mean that they are kind, considerate, and generous, although you may disapprove of other aspects of their character. ❑ He's rich, handsome, funny, and his heart is in the right place. ◳ PHRASE If you have **set** your **heart on** something, you want it very much or want to do it very much. ❑ He had always set his heart on a career in the fine arts. ◳ PHRASE If you **take heart from** something, you are encouraged and made to feel optimistic by it. ❑ Investors and dealers also took heart from the better than expected industrial production figures. ◳ PHRASE If you **take** something **to heart**, for example someone's behavior, you are deeply affected and upset by it. ❑ If someone says something critical I take it to heart. →see **donor**

heart|ache /hɑːrteɪk/ (**heartaches**) also **heart-ache** N-VAR **Heartache** is very great sadness and emotional suffering. ❑ ...after suffering the heartache of her divorce from her first husband.

heart at|tack (**heart attacks**) N-COUNT If someone has a **heart attack**, their heart begins to beat very irregularly or stops completely. ❑ He died of a heart attack brought on by overwork.

heart|beat /hɑːrtbiːt/ (**heartbeats**) N-SING Your **heartbeat** is the regular movement of your heart as it pumps blood around your body. ❑ Your baby's heartbeat will be monitored continuously.

heart|break /hɑːrtbreɪk/ (**heartbreaks**) N-VAR **Heartbreak** is very great sadness and emotional suffering, especially after the end of a love affair or close relationship. ❑ ...suffering and heartbreak for those close to the victims.

heart|break|ing /hɑːrtbreɪkɪŋ/ ADJ Something that is **heartbreaking** makes you feel extremely sad and upset. ❑ This year we won't even be able to buy presents for our grandchildren. It's heartbreaking.

heart|brok|en /hɑːrtbroʊkən/ ADJ Someone who is **heartbroken** is very sad and emotionally upset. ❑ Was your daddy heartbroken when they got a divorce?

heart|en /hɑːrtᵊn/ (**heartens, heartening, heartened**) V-T If someone **is heartened by** something, it encourages them and makes them cheerful. ❑ He will have been heartened by the telephone opinion poll published yesterday. ● **heart|ened** ADJ [v-link ADJ, oft ADJ by n, ADJ that] ❑ I feel heartened by her progress. ● **heart|en|ing** ADJ ❑ This is heartening news.

heart fail|ure N-UNCOUNT **Heart failure** is a serious medical condition in which someone's heart does not work as well as it should, sometimes stopping completely so that they die. ❑ He remained in a critical condition after suffering heart failure.

놀이 ❑ 웨스트는 하트 놀이를 할지 말지를 결정해야 했다. ◳ 구 진심으로, 중심으로 [강조] ❑ 내가 진심으로 사랑한 나의 가족 ◳ 구 내심으로는, 실제로는 ❑ 그는 실제로는 매우 친절한 소년이었다. ◳ 구 마음속에 ❑ 그녀는 그에게 자기 마음속에는 그를 위한 생각뿐이라고 말했다. ◳ 구 비탄에 잠기게 하다 [문예체] ❑ 나는 휴가 동안 사랑에 빠졌으나 그 소녀는 내 마음을 찢어 놓았다. ◳ 구 상심시키다, 가슴을 찢어 놓다 ❑ 그들을 이런 식으로 보니 내 마음이 정말 찢어질 듯이 아프다. ◳ 구 암기하여, 외워서 ❑ 맥은 이 구절을 외워서 알고 있었다. ◳ 구 태도의 변화 ❑ 여러 중개인들이 이 회사의 전망에 대해 태도의 변화를 보여 왔다. ◳ 구 소중한, 중요한 ❑ 이것은 내게 매우 중요한 주제이다. ◳ 구 마음껏 ❑ 나는 좋아하는 음식을 마음껏 먹을 수 있어서 기뻤다. ◳ 관용 표현 가슴에 십자가를 긋네; 맹세하다 [구어체] ❑ 그리고 네가 그것에 대해 말한 어떤 것도 다른 여자 아이들에게 말하지 않겠어. 약속할게, 맹세해. ◳ 구 진심으로 ❑ 그는 진심으로 자신 있게 말했다. ◳ 구 차마 -하지 못하다 ❑ 우리는 처음부터 알고 있었지만 차마 그녀에게 말하지 못했다. ◳ 구 마음속 가장 깊은 곳에서부터, 아주 솔직히 ❑ 나는 아주 솔직히 내가 그 일에 적임자라는 것을 안다. ◳ 구 -할 열의가 없다 ❑ 나는 몇 줄 배우려고 애써 보았지만 사실은 열의가 안 생겼다. ◳ 구 낙담하다, 원기를 잃다 ❑ 그는 동포들에게 낙담하지 말라고 호소했다. ◳ 구 몹시 놀라다, 혼비백산하다 ❑ 나는 그녀의 사무실에 들어갔을 때 기절초풍하는 줄 알았다. ◳ 구 마음속을 터놓다 ❑ 그녀는 어제 수백만 사람들에게 마음을 터놓고 어떻게 자살할 뻔했는지를 말했다. ◳ 구 마음은 착하다 ❑ 그는 부자에다, 잘생겼고, 재미있고, 마음도 착하다. ◳ 구 -을 열망하다 ❑ 그는 항상 순수 예술의 길을 열망했다. ◳ 구 용기를 얻다 ❑ 투자자들과 거래자들도 산업 생산 수치가 기대했던 것보다 더 나아서 용기를 얻었다. ◳ 구 속이 상하다, 맘에 걸리다 ❑ 누군가 비판적으로 말하면 나는 속이 상한다.

가산명사 또는 불가산명사 슬픔, 비탄 ❑ 그녀가 첫 남편과의 이혼으로 상심을 겪은 후에

가산명사 심장 마비 ❑ 그는 과로로 인한 심장 마비로 죽었다.

단수명사 심장 박동 ❑ 당신 아이의 심장 박동은 계속해서 관찰될 것이다.

가산명사 또는 불가산명사 상심 ❑ 희생자들과 가까운 사람들의 고통과 상심

형용사 가슴 아프게 하는 ❑ 올해는 손주들에게 선물을 사 줄 수조차 없을 것이다. 정말 가슴이 찢어진다.

형용사 비탄에 젖은, 상심한 ❑ 이혼했을 때 너의 아빠는 상심하셨니?

타동사 용기를 얻다 ❑ 어제 공표된 전화 여론 조사에 그는 용기를 얻게 될 것이다. ● 용기를 얻은 형용사 ❑ 나는 그녀의 발전에 용기를 얻는다. ● 고무적인 형용사 ❑ 이것은 고무적인 소식이다.

불가산명사 심장 마비, 심부전 ❑ 심장 마비를 겪고 나서 그는 계속 중태 상태였다.

heart|felt /ˈhɑrtfɛlt/ ADJ **Heartfelt** is used to describe a deep or sincere feeling or wish. ❑ *My heartfelt sympathy goes out to all the relatives.*

형용사 마음에서 우러난 ❑모든 친지들께 진심 어린 조의를 표합니다.

hearth /hɑrθ/ (**hearths**) N-COUNT The **hearth** is the floor of a fireplace, which sometimes extends into the room. ❑ *It was winter and there was a huge fire roaring in the hearth.*

가산명사 화로 ❑때는 겨울이어서 화로에서는 큰 불이 타오르고 있었다.

heart|land /ˈhɑrtlænd/ (**heartlands**) ◼ N-COUNT Journalists use **heartland** or **heartlands** to refer to the area or region where a particular set of activities or beliefs is most significant. ❑ *...his six-day bus tour around the industrial heartland of America.* ◼ N-COUNT The most central area of a country or continent can be referred to as its **heartland** or **heartlands**. [WRITTEN] ❑ *For many, the essence of French living is to be found in the rural heartlands.*

◼ 가산명사 핵심 지역 ❑미국의 산업 핵심 지역을 둘러보는 그의 엿새 동안의 버스 관광 ◼ 가산명사 중심부 [문어체] ❑많은 사람들에게 프랑스 생활의 진수는 시골 중심부에서 발견될 수 있다.

hearty /ˈhɑrti/ (**heartier, heartiest**) ◼ ADJ **Hearty** people or actions are loud, cheerful, and energetic. ❑ *Wade was a hearty, bluff, athletic sort of guy.* ● **heart|i|ly** ADV [ADV after v] ❑ *He laughed heartily.* ◼ ADJ **Hearty** feelings or opinions are strongly felt or strongly held. ❑ *With the last sentiment, Arnold was in hearty agreement.* ● **heart|i|ly** ADV ❑ *...most Afghans are heartily sick of war.* ◼ ADJ A **hearty** meal is large and very satisfying. ❑ *The men ate a hearty breakfast.* ● **heart|i|ly** ADV [ADV after v] ❑ *He ate heartily but would drink only beer.*

◼ 형용사 활기찬 ❑웨이드는 활기차고 솔직하면서 운동선수같은 남자였다. ● 실컷, 마음껏 부사 ❑그는 실컷 웃었다. ◼ 형용사 마음으로부터의, 진심 어린 ❑마지막 생각에 아놀드는 진심으로 동의했다. ● 진심으로 부사 ❑대부분의 아프간 사람들은 전쟁에 정말 진력이 나 있다. ◼ 형용사 배부른 ❑그 남자들은 아침을 배부르게 먹었다. ● 많이, 실컷 부사 ❑그는 먹는 것은 실컷 먹었지만 마시는 건 맥주만 마셨다.

heat ◆◇◇ /hit/ (**heats, heating, heated**) ◼ V-T When you **heat** something, you raise its temperature, for example by using a flame or a special piece of equipment. ❑ *Meanwhile, heat the tomatoes and oil in a pan.* ◼ N-UNCOUNT **Heat** is warmth or the quality of being hot. ❑ *The seas store heat and release it gradually during cold periods.* ◼ N-UNCOUNT **The heat** is very hot weather. [also the n] ❑ *As an asthmatic, he cannot cope with the heat and humidity.* ◼ N-UNCOUNT The **heat** of something is the temperature of something that is warm or that is being heated. ❑ *Adjust the heat of the barbecue by opening and closing the air vents.* ◼ N-SING You use **heat** to refer to a source of heat, for example a burner on a stove or the heating system of a house. ❑ *Immediately remove the pan from the heat.* ◼ N-UNCOUNT You use **heat** to refer to a state of strong emotion, especially of anger or excitement. ❑ *It was all done in the heat of the moment and I have certainly learned by my mistake.* ◼ N-SING **The heat of** a particular activity is the point when there is the greatest activity or excitement. ❑ *Last week, in the heat of the election campaign, the Prime Minister left for America.* ◼ N-COUNT A **heat** is one of a series of races or competitions. The winners of a heat take part in another race or competition, against the winners of other heats. ❑ *...the heats of the men's 100m breaststroke.*

◼ 타동사 가열하다, 데우다 ❑그 동안에 프라이팬에 토마토와 기름을 넣고 가열하시오. ◼ 불가산명사 열 ❑바다는 열을 저장했다가 추운 기간 동안에 서서히 열을 방출한다. ◼ 불가산명사 더위 ❑천식 환자라서 그는 더위와 습기를 견딜 수 없다. ◼ 불가산명사 온도, 뜨거운 정도 ❑공기 통풍구를 열고 닫아서 바비큐의 온도를 조절하시오. ◼ 단수명사 (화사, 난방용) 불, 난방열 ❑즉각 불에서 프라이팬을 내리시오. ◼ 불가산명사 흥기, 열기 ❑그 모든 것을 순간적인 혈기에 이끌려 했는데 나는 확실히 실수를 통해서 배웠다. ◼ 단수명사 최고조 ❑지난 주 선거 유세가 최고조에 달한 상태에서 수상은 미국으로 떠났다. ◼ 가산명사 예선 ❑남자 100미터 평영 예선

▶**heat up** ◼ PHRASAL VERB When you **heat** something **up**, especially food which has already been cooked and allowed to go cold, you make it hot. ❑ *Freda heated up a pie for me but I couldn't eat it.* ◼ PHRASAL VERB When a situation **heats up**, things start to happen much more quickly and with increased interest and excitement among the people involved. ❑ *Then in the last couple of years, the movement for democracy began to heat up.* ◼ PHRASAL VERB When something **heats up**, it gradually becomes hotter. ❑ *In the summer when her mobile home heats up like an oven, the car is Annemarie's refuge.* →see fire, pan

◼ 구동사 데우다 ❑프리다가 나를 위해 파이를 데웠지만 나는 먹을 수가 없었다. ◼ 구동사 열기가 고조되다 ❑그리고 나서 지난 2년 동안에 민주화 운동의 열기가 고조되기 시작했다. ◼ 구동사 가열되다 ❑자신의 이동식 주택이 오븐처럼 뜨거운 여름에는 자동차가 안네마리의 피난처이다.

heat|ed /hitɪd/ ◼ ADJ A **heated** discussion or quarrel is one where the people involved are angry and excited. ❑ *It was a very heated argument and they were shouting at each other.* ◼ ADJ If someone gets **heated about** something, they get angry and excited about it. [v-link ADJ about/over n] ❑ *You will understand that people get a bit heated about issues such as these.* ● **heat|ed|ly** ADV [ADV with v] ❑ *The crowd continued to argue heatedly about the best way to tackle the problem.*

◼ 형용사 격한, 격앙된 ❑그것은 아주 격한 논쟁이었고 그들은 서로 고함을 질렀다. ◼ 형용사 -에 대해 흥분한 ❑당신은 사람들이 이와 같은 사안들에 대해서는 좀 흥분한다는 것을 알게 될 것이다. ● 격렬하게 부사 ❑군중들은 그 문제를 처리할 최선의 방법에 대해 격렬하게 논쟁을 계속했다.

heat|er /hitər/ (**heaters**) N-COUNT A **heater** is a piece of equipment or a machine which is used to raise the temperature of something, especially of the air inside a room or a car. ❑ *There's an electric heater in the bedroom.*

가산명사 난방기, 히터 ❑침실에는 전기 난방기 한 대가 있다.

heath|er /hɛðər/ N-UNCOUNT **Heather** is a low, spreading plant with small purple, pink, or white flowers that grows wild in Europe on high land with poor soil.

불가산명사 헤더 (히스 속의 식물)

heat|ing /hitɪŋ/ ◼ N-UNCOUNT **Heating** is the process of heating a building or room, considered especially from the point of view of how much this costs. ❑ *You can still find cottages for £150 a week, including heating.* ◼ N-UNCOUNT **Heating** is the system and equipment that is used to heat a building. ❑ *I wish I knew how to turn on the heating.* →see central heating

◼ 불가산명사 난방 ❑난방을 포함해서 일주일에 150파운드 정도면 작은 전원주택을 얻을 수 있다. ◼ 불가산명사 난방 장치 ❑난방 장치를 켜는 방법을 알면 좋겠는데.

heave /hiv/ (**heaves, heaving, heaved**) ◼ V-T If you **heave** something heavy or difficult to move somewhere, you push, pull, or lift it using a lot of effort. ❑ *It took five strong men to heave it up a ramp and lower it into place.* ● N-COUNT **Heave** is also a noun. ❑ *It took only one heave to hurl him into the river.* ◼ V-I If something **heaves**, it moves up and down with large regular movements. ❑ *His chest heaved, and he took a deep breath.* ◼ V-I If you **heave**, or if your stomach **heaves**, you vomit or feel sick. ❑ *He gasped and heaved and vomited again.* ◼ V-T If you **heave a sigh**, you give a big sigh. ❑ *Mr. Collier heaved a sigh and got to his feet.* ◼ to heave **a sigh of relief** →see sigh

◼ 타동사 (힘겹게) 들어올리다 ❑그것을 경사로 위로 들어올리고 제자리에 내려놓는 데 힘센 남자 다섯 명이 필요했다. ● 가산명사 들어올림 ❑한 번에 그를 들어올려 강물 속으로 던져 버렸다. ◼ 자동사 들썩거리다 ❑가슴을 들썩거리며 그는 숨을 깊이 들이쉬었다. ◼ 자동사 (구역질로) 웩웩거리다, (속이) 울렁거리다 ❑그는 숨을 헐떡거리며 웩웩거리더니 다시 토했다. ◼ 타동사 (한숨을) 쉬다 ❑콜리어 씨는 한숨을 푹 내쉬면서 벌떡 일어섰다.

heav|en ◆◇◇ /hɛvən/ (**heavens**) ◼ N-PROPER In some religions, **heaven** is said to be the place where God lives, where good people go when they die, and where everyone is always happy. It is usually imagined as being high up in the sky. ❑ *I believed that when I died I would go to heaven and see God.* ◼ N-UNCOUNT You can use **heaven** to refer to a place or situation that you like very much. [INFORMAL] ❑ *We went touring in Wales and Ireland. It was heaven.* ◼ EXCLAM You say "**Good heavens!**" or "**Heavens!**" to express surprise or to emphasize that you agree or disagree with someone. [SPOKEN, FEELINGS] ❑ *Good Heavens! That explains a lot!* ◼ PHRASE You say "**Heaven help** someone" when you are worried that something bad is going to happen to them, often because you disapprove of what they are doing or the way they are behaving. [SPOKEN, DISAPPROVAL] ❑ *If this makes sense to our leaders, then heaven help us all.* ◼ PHRASE You can say "**Heaven knows**" to emphasize that you do not know something, or that you

◼ 고유명사 천국, 천당 ❑나는 죽으면 천국에 가서 하느님을 볼 것이라고 믿었다. ◼ 불가산명사 낙원 [비격식체] ❑우리는 웨일스와 아일랜드를 여행했다. 그곳은 낙원이었다. ◼ 감탄사 저런!, 맞아 [구어체, 감정 게임] ❑맞아! 그렇구나! ◼ 구 신의 가호가 있기를 [구어체, 탐탁찮음] ❑만일 우리 지도자들이 이렇게 생각한다면, 우리 모두에게 신의 가호가 있기를. ◼ 구 신만이 안다, 아무도 모른다 [구어체, 강조] ❑그들이 그 안에 무엇을 넣었는지 아무도 모른다. ◼ 구 맹세코 [구어체, 강조] ❑맹세코 그들에게는 돈이 충분히 있다. ◼ 구 비가 갑자기 쏟아지다 ❑경기가 시작되자마자 비가 갑자기 쏟아져서 시합은 중단되었다.

a b c d e f g h i j k l m n o p q r s t u v w x y z

A

find something very surprising. [SPOKEN, EMPHASIS] ❏ *Heaven knows what they put in it.* **6** PHRASE You can say "**Heaven knows**" to emphasize something that you feel or believe very strongly. [SPOKEN, EMPHASIS] ❏ *Heaven knows they have enough money.* **7** PHRASE If **the heavens open**, it suddenly starts raining very heavily. ❏ *The match had just begun when the heavens opened and play was suspended.* **8 for heaven's sake** →see **sake**. **thank heavens** →see **thank**

B

heaven|ly /ˈhevənli/ **1** ADJ **Heavenly** things are things that are connected with the religious idea of heaven. ❏ *...heavenly beings whose function it is to serve God.* **2** ADJ Something that is **heavenly** is very pleasant and enjoyable. [INFORMAL] ❏ *The idea of spending two weeks with him may seem heavenly.*

C

heavy ♦♦◇ /ˈhevi/ (**heavier, heaviest, heavies**) **1** ADJ Something that is **heavy** weighs a lot. ❏ *These scissors are awfully heavy.* • **heavi|ness** N-UNCOUNT ❏ *...a sensation of warmth and heaviness in the muscles.* **2** ADJ You use **heavy** to ask or talk about how much someone or something weighs. [how ADJ, as ADJ as, ADJ-compar than] ❏ *How heavy are you?* **3** ADJ **Heavy** means great in amount, degree, or intensity. ❏ *Heavy fighting has been going on.* ❏ *He worried about her heavy drinking.* • **heavi|ly** ADV ❏ *It has been raining heavily all day.* • **heavi|ness** N-UNCOUNT ❏ *...the heaviness of the blood loss.* **4** ADJ A **heavy** meal is large in amount and often difficult to digest. ❏ *He had been feeling drowsy, the effect of an unusually heavy meal.* **5** ADJ Something that is **heavy with** things is full of them or loaded with them. [LITERARY] [v-link ADJ with n] ❏ *The air is heavy with moisture.* **6** ADJ If a person's breathing is **heavy**, it is very loud and deep. ❏ *Her breathing became slow and heavy.* • **heavi|ly** ADV [ADV after v] ❏ *She sank back on the pillow and closed her eyes, breathing heavily as if asleep.* **7** ADJ A **heavy** movement or action is done with a lot of force or pressure. [ADJ n] ❏ *...a heavy blow on the back of the skull.* • **heavi|ly** ADV [ADV after v] ❏ *I sat down heavily on the ground beside the road.* **8** ADJ A **heavy** machine or piece of military equipment is very large and very powerful. [ADJ n] ❏ *...government militia backed by tanks and heavy artillery.* **9** ADJ If you describe a period of time or a schedule as **heavy**, you mean it involves a lot of work. ❏ *It's been a heavy day and I'm tired.* **10** ADJ **Heavy** work requires a lot of strength or energy. ❏ *The business is thriving and Philippa employs two full-timers for the heavy work.* **11** ADJ If you say that something is **heavy on** another thing, you mean that it uses a lot of that thing or too much of that thing. [v-link ADJ on n] ❏ *Tanks are heavy on fuel, destructive to roads and difficult to park.* **12** ADJ Air or weather that is **heavy** is unpleasantly still, hot, and damp. ❏ *The outside air was heavy and moist and sultry.* **13** ADJ A situation that is **heavy** is serious and difficult to cope with. [INFORMAL] ❏ *I don't want any more of that heavy stuff.* **14** N-COUNT A **heavy** is a large strong man who is employed to protect a person or place, often by using violence. [INFORMAL] ❏ *They had employed heavies to evict shop squatters from neighboring sites.*

Thesaurus   *heavy*의 참조어

ADJ.   forceful, powerful **7** **8**
        complex, difficult, tough **13**

---

heavy-duty ADJ A **heavy-duty** piece of equipment is very strong and can be used a lot. ❏ *...a heavy duty plastic bag.*

heavy-handed ADJ If you say that someone's behavior is **heavy-handed**, you mean that they are too forceful or too rough. [DISAPPROVAL] ❏ *...heavy-handed police tactics.*

heavy in|dus|try (**heavy industries**) N-VAR **Heavy industry** is industry in which large machines are used to produce raw materials or to make large objects. ❏ *...the policy of redirecting investment to heavy industries like steel and energy.* →see **industry**

heavy|weight /ˈheviweɪt/ (**heavyweights**) **1** N-COUNT A **heavyweight** is a boxer weighing more than 175 pounds and therefore in the heaviest class. **2** N-COUNT If you refer to a person or organization as a **heavyweight**, you mean that they have a lot of influence, experience, and importance in a particular field, subject, or activity. ❏ *He was a political heavyweight.*

He|brew /ˈhibru/ **1** N-UNCOUNT **Hebrew** is a language that was spoken by Jews in former times. A modern form of Hebrew is spoken now in Israel. ❏ *He is a fluent speaker of Hebrew.* **2** ADJ **Hebrew** means belonging to or relating to the Hebrew language or people. ❏ *...the respected Hebrew newspaper Haarez.*

heck|le /ˈhekəl/ (**heckles, heckling, heckled**) V-T/V-I If people in an audience **heckle**, or heckle public speakers or performers, they interrupt them, for example by making rude remarks. ❏ *They heckled him and interrupted his address with angry questions.* • N-COUNT **Heckle** is also a noun. ❏ *The offending comment was in fact a heckle from an audience member.* • **heck|ling** N-UNCOUNT ❏ *The ceremony was disrupted by unprecedented heckling and slogan-chanting.* • **heck|ler** /ˈheklər/ (**hecklers**) N-COUNT ❏ *As he began his speech, a heckler called out asking for his opinion on gun control.*

hec|tare /ˈhektɛər/ (**hectares**) N-COUNT A **hectare** is a measurement of an area of land which is equal to 10,000 square meters, or 2.471 acres.

hec|tic /ˈhektɪk/ ADJ A **hectic** situation is one that is very busy and involves a lot of rushed activity. ❏ *Despite his hectic work schedule, Benny has rarely suffered poor health.*

he'd /id, STRONG hid/ **1** **He'd** is the usual spoken form of "he had," especially when "had" is an auxiliary verb. ❏ *He'd never learnt to read.* **2** **He'd** is a spoken form of "he would." ❏ *He'd come into the clubhouse every day.*

hedge /hedʒ/ (**hedges, hedging, hedged**) **1** N-COUNT A **hedge** is a row of bushes or small trees, usually along the edge of a garden, field, or road. **2** V-I If you **hedge against** something unpleasant or unwanted that might affect you, especially losing money, you do something which will protect you from

---

1 형용사 천국의, 거룩한 ❏ 하느님을 섬기는 역할을 하는 거룩한 존재들 **2** 형용사 멋진, 천국 같은 [비격식체] ❏ 그와 함께 2주일을 보낸다는 것은 정말 멋진 생각처럼 보일지 모른다.

1 형용사 무거운 ❏ 이 가위들은 엄청나게 무겁다. • 무거움 불가산명사 ❏ 근육의 온기와 무게감 **2** 형용사 무게가 -인 ❏ 몸무게가 얼마나 나가요? **3** 형용사 대량의, 심한 ❏ 격렬한 전투가 계속되고 있다. ❏ 그는 그녀의 폭음을 걱정했다. • 심하게 부사 ❏ 하루 종일 비가 심하게 내렸다. • 심함 불가산명사 ❏ 심한 출혈 **4** 형용사 많은 (식사량), 기름진 ❏ 그는 나른해졌는데 평소와 달리 밥을 많이 먹었기 때문이었다. **5** 형용사 -가 많은, -로 무거운 [문예체] ❏ 공기에 습기가 많다. **6** 형용사 (숨소리가) 깊은 ❏ 그녀의 숨소리가 느려지고 깊어졌다. • 깊게 부사 ❏ 그녀가 베개에 드러누워 눈을 감더니 마치 잠든 것처럼 숨을 깊이 쉬었다. **7** 형용사 격렬한, 강한 ❏ 두개골 후면에 가해진 강한 타격 • 털썩 부사 ❏ 나는 길가 땅바닥에 털썩 주저앉았다. **8** 형용사 중장비의 ❏ 탱크와 중포병대의 지원을 받는 정부 의용군 **9** 형용사 빡빡한 ❏ 빡빡한 하루여서 나는 피곤했다. **10** 형용사 힘든 ❏ 사업이 번창해서 필리파는 힘든 일을 위해 두 명의 상근자를 고용한다. **11** 형용사 -을 대량으로 소비하는 ❏ 탱크는 연료를 과도하게 소비하고 도로를 파괴하며 주차하기도 어렵다. **12** 형용사 후텁지근한 ❏ 바깥 공기가 후텁지근하고 습하고 찌는 듯하다. **13** 형용사 심각한 [비격식체] ❏ 나는 그런 심각한 일은 더 이상 원하지 않아. **14** 가산명사 정호원, 덩치 (큰 사람) [비격식체] ❏ 그들은 이웃 부지들에서 불법 노점상들을 쫓아내기 위해 덩치 큰 철거반원들을 고용했었다.

형용사 매우 튼튼한 ❏ 아주 튼튼한 비닐 가방

형용사 고압적인, 거친 [탐탁찮음] ❏ 경찰의 고압적인 작전

가산명사 또는 불가산명사 중공업 ❏ 투자를 철강 또는 에너지 같은 중공업으로 전환하는 정책

1 가산명사 헤비급 권투 선수 **2** 가산명사 중진, 유력자 ❏ 그는 정치적 중진이었다.

1 불가산명사 헤브라이 어 ❏ 그는 헤브라이 어를 유창하게 한다. **2** 형용사 헤브라이 어의; 헤브라이 사람의, 유태인의 ❏ 높이 평가받는 유태계 신문 하레즈

타동사/자동사 야유하다 ❏ 그들은 그를 야유했고 성난 질문을 해서 그의 연설을 방해했다. • 가산명사 야유 ❏ 감정을 상하게 하는 그 논평은 실제로는 한 청중의 야유였다. • 야유 불가산명사 ❏ 그 예식은 전례 없는 야유와 구호를 외치는 소리 때문에 중단되었다. • 야유꾼 가산명사 ❏ 그가 연설을 시작하자 한 야유꾼이 총기 단속에 대한 그의 의견을 요청하며 소리를 질렀다.

가산명사 헥타르

형용사 매우 분주한, 정신없는 ❏ 베니는 정신없이 바쁜 작업 일정에도 불구하고 건강이 나빠진 적이 좀처럼 없다.

1 he had의 축약형 ❏ 그는 읽기를 배운 적이 전혀 없었다. **2** he would의 축약형 ❏ 그는 클럽 회관에 매일 나오곤 했다.

1 가산명사 생나무 울타리 **2** 자동사 대비하다 ❏ 보험을 들어 질병에 대비할 수 있다. **3** 가산명사 -에 대한 방지책, 방비 ❏ 금은 전통적으로 인플레에 대비하는 방지책이다. **4** 구 (분산 투자로) 위험을 줄이다 ❏ 호커

it. □ *You can hedge against illness with insurance.* ⒊ N-COUNT Something that is a **hedge against** something unpleasant will protect you from its effects. □ *Gold is traditionally a hedge against inflation.* ⒋ PHRASE If you **hedge** your **bets**, you reduce the risk of losing a lot by supporting more than one person or thing in a situation where they are opposed to each other. □ *Hawker Siddeley tried to hedge its bets by diversifying into other fields.*

시들리는 다른 분야들로 사업을 다각화시켜서 위험을 줄이려 했다.

hedge fund (**hedge funds**) N-COUNT A **hedge fund** is an investment fund that invests large amounts of money using methods that involve a lot of risk. [BUSINESS]

가산명사 헤지 펀드 [경제]

hedge|hog /hɛdʒhɒg, BRIT hɛdʒhɒg/ (**hedgehogs**) N-COUNT A **hedgehog** is a small brown animal with sharp spikes covering its back.

가산명사 고슴도치

hedge|row /hɛdʒroʊ/ (**hedgerows**) N-VAR A **hedgerow** is a row of bushes, trees, and plants, usually growing along a bank bordering a country lane or between fields. □ *He crouched behind a low hedgerow.*

가산명사 또는 불가산명사 생나무 울타리 □ 그는 낮은 생나무 울타리 뒤에 웅크렸다.

he|don|ism /hid°nɪzəm/ N-UNCOUNT **Hedonism** is the belief that gaining pleasure is the most important thing in life. [FORMAL] □ *...the life of hedonism that she embraced in her youth.*

불가산명사 쾌락주의 [격식체] □ 그녀가 젊었을 때 만끽했던 쾌락주의 생활

he|don|is|tic /hid°nɪstɪk/ ADJ **Hedonistic** means relating to hedonism. [FORMAL] □ *...an eccentric and flamboyant nobleman with a hedonistic lifestyle*

형용사 쾌락주의의 [격식체] □ 쾌락주의적 생활 방식을 지닌 별나고 이채로운 귀족

heed /hid/ (**heeds, heeding, heeded**) ⒈ V-T If you **heed** someone's advice or warning, you pay attention to it and do what they suggest. [FORMAL] □ *But few at the conference in London last week heeded his warning.* ⒉ PHRASE If you **take heed of** what someone says or if you **pay heed to** them, you pay attention to them and consider carefully what they say. [FORMAL] □ *But what if the government takes no heed?*

⒈ 타동사 -에 주의를 기울이다, -을 마음에 두다 [격식체] □ 그러나 지난 주 런던 학회에서 그의 경고에 주의를 기울이는 사람은 거의 없었다. ⒉ 구 -에 주의를 기울이다 [격식체] □ 그러나 정부가 주의를 기울이지 않으면 어떻게 될까?

heel /hil/ (**heels**) ⒈ N-COUNT Your **heel** is the back part of your foot, just below your ankle. □ *He had an operation on his heel in America last week.* ⒉ N-COUNT The **heel** of a shoe is the raised part on the bottom at the back. □ *...the shoes with the high heels.* ⒊ PHRASE If you **dig** your **heels in** or **dig in** your **heels**, you refuse to do something such as change your opinions or plans, especially when someone is trying very hard to make you do so. □ *It was really the British who, by digging their heels in, prevented any last-minute deal.* ⒋ PHRASE If you say that one event follows **hard on the heels** of another or **hot on the heels** of another, you mean that one happens very quickly or immediately after another. □ *Unfortunately, bad news has come hard on the heels of good.* ⒌ PHRASE If you say that someone is **hot on** your **heels**, you are emphasizing that they are chasing you and are not very far behind you. [EMPHASIS] □ *They sped through the American southwest with the law hot on their heels.* ⒍ PHRASE If you are **kicking** your **heels**, you are having to wait around with nothing to do, so that you get bored or impatient. [BRIT, INFORMAL] □ *The authorities wouldn't grant us permission to fly all the way down to San Francisco, so I had to kick my heels at Tunis Airport.* ⒎ **head over heels** →see **head**. to **drag** your **heels** →see **drag** →see **foot**

⒈ 가산명사 뒤꿈치 □ 그는 지난 주 미국에서 발뒤꿈치에 수술을 했다. ⒉ 가산명사 뒷굽 □ 뒷굽이 높은 신발 ⒊ 구 요지부동이다 □ 요지부동으로 막판 협상을 막은 것은 사실 영국인들이었다. ⒋ 구 -의 바로 뒤를 이어 □ 불행하게도 좋은 소식의 바로 뒤를 이어 나쁜 소식이 왔다. ⒌ 구 -을 바싹 뒤쫓아 [강조] □ 그들은 경찰이 바싹 뒤쫓고 있는 가운데 빠른 속도로 미국 남서부를 통과했다. ⒍ 구 지루하게 기다리다 [영국영어, 비격식체] □ 당국이 멀리 샌프란시스코까지 비행할 수 있는 허가를 승인하지 않으려고 해서 나는 튀니스 공항에서 지루하게 기다려야 했다.

hefty /hɛfti/ (**heftier, heftiest**) ⒈ ADJ **Hefty** means large in size, weight, or amount. [INFORMAL] □ *She was quite a hefty woman.* ⒉ ADJ A **hefty** movement is done with a lot of force. [INFORMAL] □ *Max grabs Sascha's hair and she retaliates by giving him a hefty push.*

⒈ 형용사 큰; 무거운; 많은 [비격식체] □ 그녀는 몸집이 아주 큰 여자였다. ⒉ 형용사 강한, 센 [비격식체] □ 맥스가 사샤의 머리를 잡자 그녀가 응수하며 그를 한 번 세게 밀었다.

height ♦◇◇ /haɪt/ (**heights**) ⒈ N-VAR The **height** of a person or thing is their size or length from the bottom to the top. □ *Her weight is about normal for her height.* □ *I am 5'6" in height.* ⒉ N-UNCOUNT **Height** is the quality of being tall. □ *She admits that her height is intimidating for some men.* ⒊ N-VAR A particular **height** is the distance that something is above the ground or above something else mentioned. □ *At the speed and height at which he was moving, he was never more than half a second from disaster.* ⒋ N-COUNT A **height** is a high position or place above the ground. □ *I'm not afraid of heights.* ⒌ N-SING When an activity, situation, or organization is at its **height**, it is at its most successful, powerful, or intense. □ *During the early sixth century emigration from Britain to Brittany was at its height.* ⒍ N-SING If you say that something is **the height of** a particular quality, you are emphasizing that it had that quality to the greatest degree possible. [EMPHASIS] □ *The hip-hugging black and white polka-dot dress was the height of fashion.* ⒎ N-PLURAL If something reaches great **heights**, it becomes very extreme or intense. □ *...the mid-1980s, when prices rose to absurd heights.* →see **area**

⒈ 가산명사 또는 불가산명사 키; 높이 □ 그녀의 몸무게는 키에 비해서 거의 정상이다. □ 나는 키가 5피트 6인치이다. ⒉ 불가산명사 큰 키 □ 그녀는 자기의 큰 키가 어떤 남자들에게는 위협적이라는 것을 인정한다. ⒊ 가산명사 또는 불가산명사 고도, 높이 □ 그가 운항하던 속도와 고도에서는 하마터면 0.5초 차이로 참사가 일어날 뻔했었다. ⒋ 가산명사 고지, 높은 곳 □ 나는 높은 곳이 무섭지 않다. ⒌ 단수명사 한창때, 절정 □ 절정에 이르러 □ 6세기 초반 동안에 영국에서 브르타뉴로의 이주가 절정이었다. ⒍ 단수명사 극치 [강조] □ 허리춤이 낮은 검정색 흰색 물방울 무늬 드레스가 최고 유행이었다. ⒎ 복수명사 절정 □ 물가가 터무니없이 높았던 1980년대 중반

Thesaurus   *height*의 참조어

| N. | altitude, elevation ⒊ |
| | peak ⒌ |

Word Partnership   *height*의 연어

ADJ.	**average** height, **medium** height, **the right** height ⒈
V.	**reach a** height ⒈ ⒌
N.	height **and weight**, height **and width** ⒈
	the height **of** *someone's* **career** ⒌
	the height **of fashion/popularity/style** ⒍

---

height|en /haɪt°n/ (**heightens, heightening, heightened**) V-T/V-I If something **heightens** a feeling or if the feeling **heightens**, the feeling increases in degree or intensity. □ *The move has heightened tension in the state.* □ *Cross's interest heightened.*

타동사/자동사 고조시키다; 고조되다 □ 그 조처는 그 주 내에 긴장을 고조시켰다. □ 크로스의 관심이 높아졌다.

heir /ɛər/ (**heirs**) N-COUNT An **heir** is someone who has the right to inherit a person's money, property, or title when that person dies. □ *...the heir to the throne.*

가산명사 상속인, 후계자 □ 왕위 계승자

a b c d e f g h i j k l m n o p q r s t u v w x y z

A

heir|ess /ɛərɪs/ (heiresses) N-COUNT An **heiress** is a woman or girl who has the right to inherit property or a title, or who has inherited it, especially when this involves great wealth. ◻ ...the heiress to a jewelry empire.

가산명사 여자 상속인, 여자 후계자 ◻ 보석 왕국의 상속녀

B

held /hɛld/ **Held** is the past tense and past participle of **hold**.

hold의 과거 및 과거 분사

heli|cop|ter ◆◇◇ /hɛlɪkɒptər/ (helicopters) N-COUNT A **helicopter** is an aircraft with long blades on top that go around very fast. It is able to stay still in the air and to move straight upward or downward. →see **fly**

가산명사 헬리콥터

C

heli|pad /hɛlɪpæd/ (helipads) N-COUNT A **helipad** is a place where helicopters can land and take off. ◻ Each house had a helipad for a fast evacuation.

가산명사 헬기 이착륙장 ◻ 모든 주택에 신속한 대피를 위한 헬기 이착륙장이 있었다.

D

hell ◆◇◇ /hɛl/ (hells) **1** N-PROPER; N-COUNT In some religions, **hell** is the place where the Devil lives, and where wicked people are sent to be punished when they die. Hell is usually imagined as being under the ground and full of flames. ◻ I've never believed. Not in heaven or hell or God or Satan until now. **2** N-VAR If you say that a particular situation or place is **hell**, you are emphasizing that it is extremely unpleasant. [EMPHASIS] ◻ ...the hell of the Siberian labor camps.

E

3 EXCLAM **Hell** is used by some people when they are angry or excited, or when they want to emphasize what they are saying. This use could cause offence. [EMPHASIS] ◻ "Hell, no!" the doctor snapped. **4** PHRASE You can use **as hell** after adjectives or some adverbs to emphasize the adjective or adverb. [INFORMAL, EMPHASIS] ◻ The men might be armed, but they sure as hell weren't trained. **5** PHRASE If someone does something **for the hell of it**, or **just for the hell of it**, they do it for fun or for no particular reason. [INFORMAL] ◻ I started shouting in German, just for the hell of it. **6** PHRASE You can use **from hell** after a noun when you are emphasizing that something or someone is extremely unpleasant or evil. [INFORMAL] ◻ He's a child from hell. **7** PHRASE If you tell someone to **go to hell**, you are angrily telling them to go away and leave you alone. [INFORMAL, VULGAR, FEELINGS] ◻ "Well, you can go to hell!" He swept out of the room. **8** PHRASE If you say that someone can **go to hell**, you are emphasizing angrily that you do not care about them and that they will not stop you doing what you want. [INFORMAL, VULGAR, EMPHASIS] ◻ Peter can go to hell. It's my money and I'll leave it to who I want. **9** PHRASE If you say that someone **is going hell for leather**, you are emphasizing that they are doing something or are moving very quickly and perhaps carelessly. [INFORMAL, EMPHASIS] ◻ The first horse often goes hell for leather, hits a few fences but gets away with it. **10** PHRASE Some people say **like hell** to emphasize that they strongly disagree with you or are strongly opposed to what you say. [INFORMAL, EMPHASIS] ◻ "I'll go myself." — "Like hell you will!" **11** PHRASE Some people use **like hell** to emphasize how strong an action or quality is. [INFORMAL, EMPHASIS] ◻ It hurts like hell. **12** PHRASE If you say that **all hell breaks loose**, you are emphasizing that a lot of arguing or fighting suddenly starts. [INFORMAL, EMPHASIS] ◻ He had an affair, I found out, and then all hell broke loose. **13** PHRASE If you talk about **a hell of a lot** of something, or **one hell of a lot** of something, you mean that there is a large amount of it. [INFORMAL, EMPHASIS] ◻ The manager took a hell of a lot of money out of the club. **14** PHRASE Some people use **a hell of** or **one hell of** to emphasize that something is very good, very bad, or very big. [INFORMAL, EMPHASIS] ◻ Whatever the outcome, it's going to be one hell of a fight. **15** PHRASE Some people use **the hell out of** for emphasis after verbs such as "scare," "irritate," and "beat." [INFORMAL, EMPHASIS] ◻ I patted the top of her head in the condescending way I knew irritated the hell out of her. **16** PHRASE If you say **there'll be hell to pay**, you are emphasizing that there will be serious trouble. [INFORMAL, EMPHASIS] ◻ There would be hell to pay when Ferguson and Tony found out about it. **17** PHRASE To **play hell with** something means to have a bad effect on it or cause great confusion. In British English, you can also say that one person or thing **plays merry hell with** another. [INFORMAL] ◻ Lord Beaverbrook, to put it bluntly, played hell with the war policy of the R.A.F. **18** PHRASE People sometimes use **the hell** for emphasis in questions, after words such as "what," "where," and "why," often in order to express anger. [INFORMAL, VULGAR, EMPHASIS] ◻ Where the hell have you been? **19** PHRASE If you **go through hell**, or if someone **puts you through hell**, you have a very difficult or unpleasant time. [INFORMAL] ◻ All of you seem to have gone through hell making this record. **20** PHRASE If you say you **hope to hell** or **wish to hell that** something is true, you are emphasizing that you strongly hope or wish it is true. [INFORMAL, EMPHASIS] ◻ I hope to hell you're right. **21** PHRASE You can say "**what the hell**" when you decide to do something in spite of the doubts that you have about it. [INFORMAL, FEELINGS] ◻ What the hell, I thought, at least it will give the lazy old man some exercise. **22** PHRASE If you say "**to hell with**" something, you are emphasizing that you do not care about something and that it will not stop you from doing what you want to do. [INFORMAL, EMPHASIS] ◻ To hell with this, I'm getting out of here.

F

G

H

I

J

K

L

M

N

O

P

Q

R

S

T

U

he'll /hɪl, hil/ **He'll** is the usual spoken form of "he will." ◻ By the time he's twenty he'll know everyone worth knowing in Washington.

V

hel|lo ◆◇◇ /hɛloʊ/ (hellos) also **hallo, hullo 1** CONVENTION You say "**Hello**" to someone when you meet them. [FORMULAE] ◻ Hello, Trish. I won't shake hands, because I'm filthy. ● N-COUNT **Hello** is also a noun. ◻ The salesperson greeted me with a warm hello. **2** CONVENTION You say "**Hello**" to someone at the beginning of a telephone conversation, either when you answer the phone or before you give your name or say why you are phoning. [FORMULAE] ◻ A moment later, Cohen picked up the phone. "Hello?" **3** CONVENTION You can call "**hello**" to attract someone's attention. ◻ Very softly, she called out: "Hello? Who's there?"

W

X

hel|met /hɛlmɪt/ (helmets) N-COUNT A **helmet** is a hat made of a strong material which you wear to protect your head. →see **army, football, skateboarding**

가산명사 헬멧

Y

help ◆◆◆ /hɛlp/ (helps, helping, helped) **1** V-T/V-I If you **help** someone, you make it easier for them to do something, for example by doing part of the work for them or by giving them advice or money. ◻ He has helped to raise a lot of

Z

가산명사 헬기 이착륙장 ◻ 모든 주택에 신속한 대피를 위한 헬기 이착륙장이 있었다.

1 고유명사; 가산명사 지옥 ◻ 나는 믿은 적이 없어. 천국이든 지옥이든 신이든 악마든, 지금까지는 아무것도. **2** 가산명사 또는 불가산명사 지옥 [강조] ◻ 생지옥 같은 시베리아 강제 노동 수용소들 **3** 감탄사 빌어먹을! [강조] ◻ "빌어먹을, 안 돼!"라고 의사는 잘라 말했다. **4** 구 죽어라고, 정말이지 [비격식체, 강조] ◻ 그 남자들은 무장은 했는지 모르지만 정말 훈련은 죽어라고 되어 있지 않았다. **5** 구 그냥 장난삼아서 [비격식체] ◻ 나는 그냥 장난삼아서 독일어로 고함을 지르기 시작했다. **6** 구 지긋지긋한 [비격식체, 강조] ◻ 그는 지긋지긋한 아이다. **7** 구 꺼져 줘!, 신경 꺼! [비격식체, 비속어, 감정 개입] ◻ "그만 신경 끄시지!"라고 그는 방에서 휙 나가며 말했다. **8** 구 ~ 따윈 상관하지 마 [비격식체, 비속어, 강조] ◻ 피터 따윈 상관하지 마. 그건 내 돈이고 내가 원하는 사람에게 맡길 거야. **9** 구 천방으로, 절대 빠르게 [비격식체, 강조] ◻ 첫 번째 말은 흔히 전속력으로 질주하여 울타리에 부딪치곤 하지만 별 문제 없이 넘어간다. **10** 구 지독하게 [비격식체, 강조] ◻ "내가 갈게" "그러기도 하겠다." **11** 구 지독하게 [비격식체, 강조] ◻ 지독하게 아프다. **12** 구 난리가 나다 [비격식체, 강조] ◻ 그가 바람을 피웠고 내가 알게 되었고 그 다음에 난리가 났다. **13** 구 엄청나게 많은 [비격식체, 강조] ◻ 지배인이 클럽에서 엄청난 돈을 빼돌렸다. **14** 구 굉장한, 지독한 [비격식체, 강조] ◻ 결과가 어떻든지 그것은 지독한 싸움이 될 것이다. **15** 구 몹시 [비격식체, 강조] ◻ 나는 잘난 체하며 그녀의 정수리를 토닥거렸는데 나는 내가 그러면 그녀가 성이 나 죽으려고 할 것이라는 것을 알고 있었다. **16** 구 굳게 아파질 것이다 [비격식체, 강조] ◻ 퍼거슨과 토니가 그것을 알게 된 때 골치 아파질 것이었다. **17** 구 ~을 망쳐놓다, ~을 엉망으로 만들다 [비격식체] ◻ 비버브룩 경이, 단도직입적으로 말하자면, 영국 공군의 전략 정책을 망쳐 놓았다. **18** 구 도대체 [비격식체, 비속어, 강조] ◻ 도대체 어디 갔었니? **19** 구 죽도록 고생하다; 죽도록 고생시키다 [비격식체] ◻ 여러분 모두 이 음반을 만드느라 죽을 고생을 한 것 같군요. **20** 구 제발 ~이면 좋겠다 [비격식체, 강조] ◻ 제발 네가 옳다면 좋겠다. **21** 구 어쨌든 [비격식체, 감정 개입] ◻ 어쨌든 내 생각엔 그것이 적어도 그 게으른 노인에게 운동은 될 것이다. **22** 구 ~ 따윈 상관없다, ~을 집어치워라 [비격식체, 강조] ◻ 이 따윈 집어치워. 난 여기서 나갈 거야.

he will의 축약형 ◻ 스무 살이 될 즈음이면 그는 워싱턴에서 알아 두어야 할 모든 사람을 알게 될 것이다.

1 관용 표현 안녕하시오 [의례적인 표현] ◻ 안녕하시오, 트리쉬. 내가 지저분해서 악수하지 않겠소. ● 가산명사 인사 ◻ 판매원은 따뜻한 인사로 나를 맞이했다. **2** 관용 표현 여보세요 [의례적인 표현] ◻ 잠시 후 코언은 전화를 받았다. "여보세요?" **3** 관용 표현 여보세요 ◻ 아주 나지막하게 그녀가 불렀다. "여보세요? 거기 누구세요?"

가산명사 헬멧

1 타동사/자동사 돕다 ◻ 그는 많은 돈을 모으도록 도왔다. ◻ 당신은 물론 그들에게 직접 기부를 함으로써 도울 수 있다. ● 불가산명사 도움 ◻ 도움에

money. ❑ *You can of course help by giving them a donation directly.* ● N-UNCOUNT **Help** is also a noun. ❑ *Thanks very much for your help.* ② V-T/V-I If you say that something **helps**, or **helps** a situation, you mean that it makes something easier to do or get, or that it improves a situation to some extent. ❑ *Building more motorways and by-passes will help the environment by reducing pollution and traffic jams in towns and cities.* ③ V-T If you **help** someone go somewhere or move in some way, you give them support so that they can move more easily. ❑ *Martin helped Tanya over the rail.* ④ N-SING If you say that someone or something has been **a help** or has been some **help**, you mean that they have helped you to solve a problem. [a N, also no det] ❑ *Thank you. You've been a great help already.* ⑤ N-UNCOUNT **Help** is action taken to rescue a person who is in danger. You shout "**help!**" when you are in danger in order to attract someone's attention so that they can come and rescue you. ❑ *He was screaming for help.* ⑥ N-UNCOUNT In computing, **help**, or the **help** menu, is a file that gives you information and advice, for example about how to use a particular program. [COMPUTING] ❑ *If you get stuck, click on Help.* ⑦ V-T If you **help yourself** to something, you serve yourself or you take it for yourself. If someone tells you to **help yourself**, they are telling you politely to serve yourself anything you want or to take anything you want. ❑ *There's bread on the table. Help yourself.* ⑧ V-T If someone **helps themselves to** something, they steal it. [INFORMAL] ❑ *Has somebody helped himself to some film star's diamonds?* ⑨ PHRASE If you **can't help** the way you feel or behave, you cannot control it or stop it happening. You can also say that you **can't help yourself.** ❑ *I can't help feeling sorry for the poor man.* ⑩ PHRASE If you say you **can't help** thinking something, you are expressing your opinion in an indirect way, often because you think it seems rude. [VAGUENESS] ❑ *I can't help feeling that this may just be another of her schemes.* ⑪ PHRASE If someone or something **is of help**, they make a situation easier or better. ❑ *Can I be of help to you?* →see donor

---

Thesaurus　　　help의 참조어

V.	aid, assist, support; (*ant.*) hinder ① ③
N.	aid, assistance, guidance, support ① ④

Word Partnership　　　help의 연어

ADJ.	**financial** help, **professional** help ①
V.	**ask for** help, **get** help, **need** help, **want to** help ①
	try to help ① ③ ⑤
	cry/scream/shout for help ⑤
	can't help **thinking/feeling** *something* ⑨ ⑩

▶**help out** PHRASAL VERB If you **help** someone **out**, you help them by doing some work for them or by lending them some money. ❑ *I help out with the secretarial work.* ❑ *All these presents came to more money than I had, and my mother had to help me out.*

help|er /hɛlpər/ (**helpers**) N-COUNT A **helper** is a person who helps another person or group with a job they are doing. ❑ *Phyllis and her helpers provided us with refreshment.*

help|ful /hɛlpful/ ① ADJ If you describe someone as **helpful**, you mean that they help you in some way, such as doing part of your job for you or by giving you advice or information. ● The staff in the London office are helpful but only have limited information. ● **help|ful|ly** ADV [ADV with v] ❑ *They had helpfully provided us with instructions on how to find the house.* ② ADJ If you describe information or advice as **helpful**, you mean that it is useful for you. ❑ *The catalog includes helpful information on the different bike models available.* ③ ADJ Something that is **helpful** makes a situation more pleasant or more easy to tolerate. ❑ *It is often helpful to have your spouse in the room when major news is expected.*

help|less /hɛlpləs/ ADJ If you are **helpless**, you do not have the strength or power to do anything useful or to control or protect yourself. ❑ *Parents often feel helpless, knowing that all the cuddles in the world won't stop the tears.* ● **help|less|ly** ADV ❑ *Their son watched helplessly as they vanished beneath the waves.* ● **help|less|ness** N-UNCOUNT ❑ *I remember my feelings of helplessness.*

help|line /hɛlplaɪn/ (**helplines**) N-COUNT A **helpline** is a special telephone service that people can call to get advice about a particular subject. ❑ *...Greece's first helpline for gamblers who need counselling.*

hem /hɛm/ (**hems, hemming, hemmed**) N-COUNT A **hem** on something such as a piece of clothing is an edge that is folded over and stitched down to prevent threads coming loose. The **hem** of a skirt or dress is the bottom edge. ❑ *She lifted the hem of her dress and brushed her knees.*

▶**hem in** ① PHRASAL VERB If a place **is hemmed in by** mountains or **by** other places, it is surrounded by them. ❑ *Manchester is hemmed in by greenbelt countryside and by housing and industrial areas.* ② PHRASAL VERB If someone **is hemmed in** or if someone **hems** them **in**, they are prevented from moving or changing, for example because they are surrounded by people or obstacles. ❑ *The company's competitors complain that they are hemmed in by rigid, legal contracts.*

hemi|sphere /hɛmɪsfɪər/ (**hemispheres**) N-COUNT A **hemisphere** is one half of the earth. ❑ *...the depletion of the ozone layer in the northern hemisphere.*

hemo|philia /himəfɪliə/ [BRIT **haemophilia**] N-UNCOUNT **Hemophilia** is a medical condition in which a person's blood does not thicken or clot properly when they are injured, so they continue bleeding.

감사드립니다. ② 타동사/자동사 도움이 되다 ❑ 올바른 스타일의 수영복은 원하는 대로 감추거나 극소화하거나 강조하는 데 도움이 될 수 있다. ❑ 고속도로와 우회 도로를 더 많이 건설하면 읍내와 도시의 오염과 교통 정체를 줄여 환경에 도움이 될 것이다. ③ 타동사 기들다, 도와주다 ❑ 마틴은 타냐가 난간 위로 올라가는 것을 도와주었다. ④ 단수명사 도움 ❑ 고맙습니다. 당신은 이미 큰 도움이 되었습니다. ⑤ 불가산명사 도와주세요! ❑ 그는 소리 질러 도움을 요청하고 있었다. ⑥ 불가산명사 (컴퓨터) 도움말 [컴퓨터] ❑ 막히면 도움말을 클릭하시오. ⑦ 타동사 (음식을 덜어) 먹다, 마음대로 가져가다 ❑ 테이블 위에 빵이 있어요. 드시지요. ⑧ 타동사 -을 슬쩍하다 [비격식체] ❑ 누군가가 어느 영화배우의 다이아몬드를 슬쩍 했나? ⑨ 구 -을 피할 수 없다 ❑ 그 가엾은 남자에 대해 동정을 금할 수 없다. ⑩ 구 -하지 않을 수 없다 [짐작투] ❑ 이것이 그녀의 또 다른 계획의 하나일 것이라는 느낌을 갖지 않을 수 없다. ⑪ 구 도움이 되다 ❑ 제가 도움이 될 수 있을까요?

구동사 도와주다 ❑ 나는 비서 일을 도와준다. ❑ 이런 선물들 총 비용이 내가 가진 돈보다 더 들게 되어 어머니가 도움을 주셔야 했다.

가산명사 도우미 ❑ 필리스와 그녀의 도우미들이 우리들에게 다과를 제공했다.

① 형용사 도움이 되는 ❑ 런던 사무소 직원들은 도움은 되지만 제한된 정보만을 가지고 있다. ● 도움이 되는 부사 ❑ 그들은 우리에게 그 집을 어떻게 찾을 수 있는지 도움이 되도록 설명해 주었다. ② 형용사 유용한 ❑ 그 카탈로그에는 구입할 수 있는 여러 자전거 모델에 관한 유용한 정보가 들어 있다. ③ 형용사 도움이 되는 ❑ 중요한 소식이 있을 것 같을 때는 방에 배우자와 함께 있는 것이 흔히 도움이 된다.

형용사 속수무책인, 무력한 ❑ 부모들은 아무리 안아 주어도 눈물을 그치게 할 수 없음을 알고는 흔히 무력감을 느끼게 된다. ● 속수무책으로 부사 ❑ 그들의 아들은 그들이 파도 속으로 사라지는 것을 속수무책으로 바라보았다. ● 무력함, 속수무책인 불가산명사 ❑ 나는 나의 무력감을 기억한다.

가산명사 도움 전화 서비스 ❑ 상담을 필요로 하는 도박꾼들을 위한 그리스 최초의 도움 전화 서비스

가산명사 가두리, 옷단 ❑ 그녀는 드레스의 치맛단을 들어올리고 무릎을 털었다.

① 구동사 둘러싸이다 ❑ 맨체스터는 녹지대 전원과 주택 및 산업 지역으로 둘러싸여 있다. ② 구동사 속박되다; 속박하다 ❑ 그 회사의 경쟁사들은 자기들이 엄중한 법률적 계약에 속박되어 있다고 불평한다.

가산명사 반구 ❑ 북반구의 오존층 감소

[영국영어 haemophilia] 불가산명사 혈우병

A

hemo|phili|ac /hiːməfɪliæk/ (**hemophiliacs**) [BRIT **haemophiliac**] N-COUNT A **hemophiliac** is a person who suffers from haemophilia. ❑ ...a hemophiliac who contracted the AIDS virus through a blood transfusion.

[영국영어 haemophiliac] 가산명사 혈우병 환자 ❑ 수혈을 통해서 에이즈 바이러스에 걸린 혈우병 환자

B

hem|or|rhage /hɛmərɪdʒ/ (**hemorrhages, hemorrhaging, hemorrhaged**) [BRIT **haemorrhage**] ◼ N-VAR A **hemorrhage** is serious bleeding inside a person's body. ❑ Shortly after his admission into the hospital he had a massive brain hemorrhage and died. ◼ V-I If someone **is hemorrhaging**, there is serious bleeding inside their body. ❑ I hemorrhaged badly after the birth of all three of my sons. ● **hem|or|rhag|ing** N-UNCOUNT ❑ A post mortem showed he died from shock and hemorrhaging.

[영국영어 haemorrhage] ◼ 가산명사 또는 불가산명사 출혈 ❑ 그는 병원으로 이송된 직후에 심한 뇌출혈을 일으켜 죽었다. ◼ 자동사 출혈이 있다, 심하게 피를 흘리다 ❑ 나는 세 명의 아들 모두를 낳을 때마다 출산 후 출혈이 매우 심했다. ● 출혈 불가산명사 ❑ 부검을 통해서 그는 쇼크와 출혈로 죽었다고 밝혀졌다.

C

hen /hɛn/ (**hens**) N-COUNT A **hen** is a female chicken. People often keep hens in order to eat or sell their eggs.

가산명사 암탉

D

E

hence /hɛns/ ◼ ADV You use **hence** to indicate that the statement you are about to make is a consequence of what you have just said. [FORMAL] [ADV cl/group] ❑ The trade imbalance is likely to rise again in 1990. Hence a new set of policy actions will be required soon. ◼ ADV You use **hence** in expressions such as "**several years hence**" or "**six months hence**" to refer to a time in the future, especially a long time in the future. [FORMAL] [amount ADV] ❑ The gases that may be warming the planet will have their main effect many years hence.

◼ 부사 그러므로 [격식체] ❑ 무역 불균형이 1990년에 다시 발생할 것 같다. 그러므로 일단의 새로운 정책 행위가 곧 필요할 것이다. ◼ 부사 지금부터; 향후 몇 년; 향후 6개월 [격식체] ❑ 지구를 온난하게 만들고 있을지도 모를 가스들이 지금부터 수년 후에 본격적인 영향을 끼칠 것이다.

F

G

hence|forth /hɛnsfɔrθ/ ADV **Henceforth** means from this time onwards. [FORMAL] [ADV with cl] ❑ Henceforth, parties which fail to get 5% of the vote will not be represented in parliament.

부사 이제부터, 금후 [격식체] ❑ 금후 투표의 5퍼센트를 얻지 못하는 정당은 의회를 구성할 수 없을 것이다.

H

hepa|ti|tis /hɛpətaɪtɪs/ N-UNCOUNT **Hepatitis** is a serious disease which affects the liver.

불가산명사 간염

I

her ♦♦♦ /hər, STRONG hɜr/

Her is a third person singular pronoun. **Her** is used as the object of a verb or a preposition. **Her** is also a possessive determiner.

---

her는 3인칭 단수대명사이다. her는 동사나 전치사의 목적어 또는 소유 한정사로도 쓰인다.

J

◼ PRON-SING You use **her** to refer to a woman, girl, or female animal. [V PRON, prep PRON] ❑ I went in the room and told her I had something to say to her. ● DET **Her** is also a possessive determiner. ❑ Liz travelled round the world for a year with her boyfriend James. ◼ PRON-SING In written English, **her** is sometimes used to refer to a person without saying whether that person is a man or a woman. Some people dislike this use and prefer to use "him or her" or "them." [V PRON, prep PRON] ❑ Talk to your baby, play games, and show her how much you enjoy her company. ● DET **Her** is also a possessive determiner. ❑ The non-drinking, non-smoking model should do nothing to risk her reputation. ◼ PRON-SING **Her** is sometimes used to refer to a country or nation. [FORMAL or WRITTEN] [V PRON, prep PRON] ● DET **Her** is also a possessive determiner. ❑ Our reporter looks at reactions to Britain's apparently deep-rooted distrust of her EU partner.

◼ 단수대명사 그녀를; 그녀에게 ❑ 나는 방에 들어가서 그녀에게 할 말이 있다고 했다. ● 한정사 그녀의 ❑ 리즈는 자기 남자 친구인 제임스와 1년 동안 세계 일주를 했다. ◼ 단수대명사 그 사람을; 그 사람에게 (문어체에서 성구별 없이 앞에 나온 사람을 가리킴) ❑ 당신 아기에게 이야기하고 놀이도 하고 같이 있어서 얼마나 좋은지를 보여 주시오. ● 한정사 그 사람의 ❑ 음주와 흡연을 하지 않는 그 모델은 자기의 평판을 위태롭게 할 어떤 것도 하지 않을 것이다. ◼ 단수대명사 그 나라를; 그 나라에게 [격식체 또는 문어체] ❑ 한정사 그 나라의 ❑ 저희 기자가 영국이 유럽 연합 상대국에 대해 갖고 있는 분명 뿌리 깊은 불신에 대한 반응들을 알아봅니다.

K

L

M

her|ald /hɛrəld/ (**heralds, heralding, heralded**) ◼ V-T Something that **heralds** a future event or situation is a sign that it is going to happen or appear. [FORMAL] ❑ ...the sultry evening that heralded the end of the baking hot summer. ◼ N-COUNT Something that is a **herald** of a future event or situation is a sign that it is going to happen or appear. [FORMAL] ❑ I welcome the report as a herald of more freedom. ◼ V-T If an important event or action **is heralded by** people, announcements are made about it so that it is publicly known and expected. [FORMAL] [usu passive] ❑ Janet Jackson's new album has been heralded by a massive media campaign.

◼ 타동사 예고하다 [격식체] ❑ 타는 듯이 뜨거운 여름의 종말을 예고하는 무더운 저녁 ◼ 가산명사 에고, 전조 [격식체] ❑ 나는 그 보고서를 더 많은 자유를 예고하는 것으로 환영하는 바이다. ◼ 타동사 예고되다, 광고되다 [격식체] ❑ 재닛 잭슨의 새 앨범은 대대적인 언론 광고를 통해 예고되어 왔다.

N

O

P

herb /ɜrb, BRIT hɜːˀb/ (**herbs**) N-COUNT A **herb** is a plant whose leaves are used in cooking to add flavor to food, or as a medicine. ❑ ...beautiful, fragrant herbs such as basil and coriander.

가산명사 향초, 약초, 허브 ❑ 바질이나 코리엔더 같은 예쁘고 향기로운 허브

Q

herb|al /ɜrbəl, BRIT hɜːˀbəl/ (**herbals**) ADJ **Herbal** means made from or using herbs. [ADJ n] ❑ ...herbal remedies for colds.

형용사 약초의 ❑ 약초를 이용한 감기 치료법

R

herd /hɜrd/ (**herds, herding, herded**) ◼ N-COUNT A **herd** is a large group of animals of one kind that live together. ❑ Chobe is also renowned for its large herds of elephant and buffalo. ◼ N-SING If you say that someone has joined **the herd** or follows **the herd**, you are criticizing them because you think that they behave just like everyone else and do not think for themselves. [DISAPPROVAL] ❑ They are individuals; they will not follow the herd. ◼ V-T If you **herd** people somewhere, you make them move there in a group. ❑ He began to herd the prisoners out. ◼ V-T If you **herd** animals, you make them move along as a group. ❑ Stefano used a motorcycle to herd the sheep.

◼ 가산명사 (동물) 떼 ❑ 초베는 또한 거대한 코끼리 떼와 물소 떼로도 유명하다. ◼ 단수명사 무리, 우중(愚衆) [탐탁찮음] ❑ 그들은 개성이 있는 사람들이다. 우매한 무리를 따르지는 않을 것이다. ◼ 타동사 (사람들) 몰고 가다 ❑ 그는 수감자들을 밖으로 몰아내기 시작했다. ◼ 타동사 (동물 떼를) 몰다 ❑ 스테파노는 양 떼를 모는 데 오토바이를 이용했다.

S

T

here ♦♦♦ /hɪər/ ◼ ADV You use **here** when you are referring to the place where you are. ❑ I'm here all by myself and I know I'm going to get lost. ❑ Well, I can't stand here chatting all day. ◼ ADV You use **here** when you are pointing toward a place that is near you, in order to draw someone else's attention to it. ❑ ...if you will just sign here. ◼ ADV You use **here** in order to indicate that the person or thing that you are talking about is near you or is being held by you. ❑ My friend here writes for radio. ◼ ADV If you say that you are **here to** do something, that is your role or function. [be ADV to-inf] ❑ I'm here to help you. ◼ ADV You use **here** in order to draw attention to something or someone who has just arrived in the place where you are, or to draw attention to the place you have just arrived at. ❑ "Here's the taxi," she said politely. ◼ ADV You use **here** to refer to a particular point or stage of a situation or subject that you have come to or that you are dealing with. ❑ It's here that we come up against the difference of approach. ◼ ADV You use **here** to refer to a period of time, a situation, or an event that is present or happening now. ❑ Economic recovery is here. ◼ ADV You use **here** at the beginning of a sentence in order to draw attention to something or to introduce something. [ADV be n/wh] ❑ Now here's what I want you to do. ◼ ADV You use **here** when you are offering or giving something to someone. [ADV be n] ❑ Here's your coffee, just the way you like it. ❑ Here's some letters I want you to sign. ◼ CONVENTION You say "**here we are**" when you have just found something

◼ 부사 여기 ❑ 나는 여기 홀로 있으며 길을 잃게 될 것을 안다. ❑ 자, 하루 종일 여기서 잡담이나 하며 서 있을 순 없지. ◼ 부사 여기에 ❑ 여기에 서명만 해 주시면 ◼ 부사 여기 있는 ❑ 여기 있는 내 친구는 라디오 작가이다. ◼ 부사 -하려고 있는 ❑ 나는 너를 돕기 위해 있다. ◼ 부사 -여기 ❑ "여기 택시가 왔어요."라고 그녀가 공손하게 말했다. ◼ 부사 이 점에서, 여기서 ❑ 우리의 접근 방식의 차이가 나는 것은 바로 이 점에서이다. ◼ 부사 지금 진행되는 ❑ 경제 회복이 현재 진행 중이다. ◼ 부사 이것이 되는 ❑ 자, 이것이 내가 당신이 해주길 바라는 것이다. ◼ 부사 자, 여기에 ❑ 자, 여기 네 커피이고 네가 맛있게 탄 커피야. ❑ 자, 여기 사인해 주실 편지들입니다. ◼ 관용 표현 자, 찾았다, 여기 있군 ❑ 나는 사람을 샅샅이 뒤져서 아만다의 폴더를 찾았다. "자, 찾았어." ◼ 관용 표현 자, 시작한다, 자, 간다 ❑ 컬버 박사는 염려스러운 듯 "자, 놓는다."라고 중얼거리고 어린 소녀에게 주사를 놓았다. ◼ 구 또 시작이군 [비격식체] ❑ "경찰이다! 문 열어!" "이거 원, 또 시작이군."이라고 나는 생각했다. ◼ 구 바로 지금, 현시점에서 [강조] ❑ 나는 바로 지금

U

V

W

X

Y

Z

Word Web   hero

Odysseus is a **hero** from Greek **mythology**. He is a warrior. He shows great courage in battle. He faces many **dangers** and temptations. However he knows he must return home after the Trojan War*. During his **epic** journey home, Odysseus faces many trials. He must survive wild storms at sea and fight a monster. He must also resist the temptations of sirens and outwit the goddess Circe*. At home Penelope, Odysseus' wife, **defends** their home and **protects** their son. She remains **loyal** and **brave** through many trials. She is the **heroine** of the story.

Trojan War: a legendary war between Greece and Troy.
Circe: a Greek goddess.

Odysseus saves his men from the Cyclops.

that you have been looking for. ❑ *I rummaged through the drawers and came up with Amanda's folder. "Here we are."* ⓫ CONVENTION You say "**here goes**" when you are about to do or say something difficult or unpleasant. ❑ *Dr. Culver nervously muttered "Here goes," and gave the little girl an injection.* ⓬ PHRASE You use expressions such as "**here we go**" and "**here we go again**" in order to indicate that something is happening again in the way that you expected, especially something unpleasant. [INFORMAL] ❑ *"Police! Open up!" — "Oh well," I thought, "here we go."* ⓭ PHRASE You use **here and now** to emphasize that something is happening at the present time, rather than in the future or past, or that you would like it to happen at the present time. [EMPHASIS] ❑ *I'm a practicing physician trying to help people here and now.* ⓮ PHRASE If something happens **here and there**, it happens in several different places. ❑ *I do a bit of teaching here and there.* ⓯ CONVENTION You use expressions such as "**here's to us**" and "**here's to your new job**" before drinking a toast in order to wish someone success or happiness. [FORMULAE] ❑ *He raised his glass. "Here's to neighbors."*

he|redi|tary /hɪrɛdɪteri/ ❶ ADJ A **hereditary** characteristic or illness is passed on to a child from its parents before it is born. ❑ *Cystic fibrosis is the commonest fatal hereditary disease.* ❷ ADJ A title or position in society that is **hereditary** is one that is passed on as a right from parent to child. ❑ *...the position of the head of state is hereditary.*

her|esy /hɛrɪsi/ (**heresies**) ❶ N-VAR **Heresy** is a belief or action that most people think is wrong, because it disagrees with beliefs that are generally accepted. ❑ *It might be considered heresy to suggest such a notion.* ❷ N-VAR **Heresy** is a belief or action which seriously disagrees with the principles of a particular religion. ❑ *He said it was a heresy to suggest that women should not conduct services.*

her|it|age /hɛrɪtɪdʒ/ (**heritages**) N-VAR A country's **heritage** is all the qualities, traditions, or features of life there that have continued over many years and have been passed on from one generation to another. ❑ *The historic building is as much part of our heritage as the paintings.*

her|mit /hɜrmɪt/ (**hermits**) N-COUNT A **hermit** is a person who lives alone, away from people and society. ❑ *I've spent the past ten years living like a hermit.*

her|nia /hɜrniə/ (**hernias**) N-VAR A **hernia** is a medical condition which is often caused by strain or injury. It results in one of your internal organs sticking through a weak point in the surrounding tissue.

hero ◆◇◇ /hɪəroʊ/ (**heroes**) ❶ N-COUNT The **hero** of a book, play, or story is the main male character, who usually has good qualities. ❑ *The hero of Doctor Zhivago dies in 1929.* ❷ N-COUNT A **hero** is someone, especially a man, who has done something brave, new, or good, and who is therefore greatly admired by a lot of people. ❑ *He called Mr. Mandela a hero who had inspired millions.* ❸ N-COUNT If you describe someone as your **hero**, you mean that you admire them a great deal, usually because of a particular quality or skill that they have. ❑ *My boyhood hero was Bobby Charlton.* →see **myth** →see Word Web: **hero**

he|ro|ic /hɪroʊɪk/ (**heroics**) ❶ ADJ If you describe a person or their actions as **heroic**, you admire them because they show extreme bravery. ❑ *His heroic deeds were celebrated in every corner of India.* ● **he|roi|cal|ly** /hɪroʊɪkli/ ADV [ADV with v] ❑ *He had acted heroically during the liner's evacuation.* ❷ ADJ If you describe an action or event as **heroic**, you admire it because it involves great effort or determination to succeed. [APPROVAL] ❑ *The company has made heroic efforts at cost reduction.* ● **he|roi|cal|ly** ADV ❑ *Single parents cope heroically in doing the job of two people.* ❸ ADJ **Heroic** means being or relating to the hero of a story. ❑ *...the book's central, heroic figure.* ❹ N-PLURAL **Heroics** are actions involving bravery, courage, or determination. ❑ *...the man whose aerial heroics helped save the helicopter pilot.* ❺ N-PLURAL If you describe someone's actions or plans as **heroics**, you think that they are foolish or dangerous because they are too difficult or brave for the situation in which they occur. [SPOKEN, DISAPPROVAL] ❑ *He said his advice was: "No heroics, stay within the law."*

hero|in /hɛroʊɪn/ N-UNCOUNT **Heroin** is a powerful drug which some people take for pleasure, but which they can become addicted to.

hero|ine /hɛroʊɪn/ (**heroines**) ❶ N-COUNT The **heroine** of a book, play, or story is the main female character, who usually has good qualities. ❑ *The heroine is a senior TV executive.* ❷ N-COUNT A **heroine** is a woman who has done something brave, new, or good, and who is therefore greatly admired by a lot of people. ❑ *The national heroine of the day was Xing Fen, winner of the first Gold medal*

사람들을 도우려고 애쓰는 개업 의사이다. ⓮ 구 여기저기에 ❑ 나는 여기저기에서 조금씩 가르친다. ⓯ 관용 표현 우리를 위하여; 너의 새 직장을 위하여 [의례적인 표현] ❑ 그가 잔을 들었다. "이웃을 위하여!"

❶ 형용사 유전성의 낭포성 섬유증은 가장 흔한 치명적인 유전성 질병이다. ❷ 형용사 세습의 ❑ 국가수반의 지위는 세습된다.

❶ 가산명사 또는 불가산명사 이단 ❑ 그런 생각을 제안하면 이단으로 간주될지도 모른다. ❷ 가산명사 또는 불가산명사 이교, 이단 ❑ 그는 여자가 예배를 주관해서는 안 된다고 하는 것은 이단이라고 말했다.

가산명사 또는 불가산명사 유산 ❑ 그 역사적 건물은 회화 작품들과 마찬가지로 우리 유산의 일부이다.

가산명사 은자(隱者) ❑ 나는 지난 10년을 은자처럼 살며 지냈다.

가산명사 또는 불가산명사 헤르니아, 탈장

❶ 가산명사 주인공 ❑ 닥터 지바고의 주인공은 1929년에 죽는다. ❷ 가산명사 영웅 ❑ 그는 만델라 씨를 수백만의 사람들을 고무시킨 영웅이라 불렀다. ❸ 가산명사 우상, 영웅 ❑ 내 소년기의 우상은 바비 찰튼이었다.

❶ 형용사 영웅적인 ❑ 그의 영웅적인 행위는 인도 방방곡곡에서 칭송받았다. ● 영웅적으로 부사 ❑ 그는 여객선 승객들을 대피시키는 동안 영웅적으로 행동했었다. ❷ 형용사 과감한, 극도의 [마음에 듦] ❑ 그 회사는 비용 절감에 극도의 노력을 기울여 왔다. ● 과감하게 부사 ❑ 혼자 사는 부모들은 두 사람 몫의 일을 과감하게 해 나간다. ❸ 형용사 주인공의 ❑ 그 책의 중심이 되는, 주인공인 인물 ❹ 복수명사 용기 있는 행위 ❑ 운항 도중 용기 있는 행위로 헬기 조종사를 구하는 데 도움을 준 남자 ❺ 복수명사 만용 [구어체, 탐탁찮음] ❑ 그는 '만용은 금물, 법을 지켜라'라는 것이 자기의 조언이라고 말했다.

불가산명사 헤로인

❶ 가산명사 여주인공 ❑ 그 여주인공은 원로 텔레비전 간부이다. ❷ 가산명사 여걸, 여장부 ❑ 그날의 국가적 영웅은 올림픽에서 첫 번째 금메달을 딴 싱 펜이었다. ❸ 가산명사 경모의 대상이 되는 여자, 우상 ❑ 나의 우상은 엘리자베스 테일러였다.

of the Games. **3** N-COUNT If you describe a woman as your **heroine**, you mean that you admire her greatly, usually because of a particular quality or skill that she has. ❑ *My heroine was Elizabeth Taylor.* →see **hero**

hero|ism /hɛroʊɪzəm/ N-UNCOUNT **Heroism** is great courage and bravery. ❑ *...individual acts of heroism.*

불가산명사 용기 ❑ 개인의 용기 있는 행동들

her|ring /hɛrɪŋ/

The plural can be either **herring** or **herrings**.

복수는 herring 또는 herrings이다.

N-VAR A **herring** is a long silver-colored fish. Herring live in large groups in the sea. ❑ *...a shoal of herring.* ● N-UNCOUNT **Herring** is a piece of this fish eaten as food. ❑ *...a tin of herring.*

가산명사 또는 불가산명사 청어 ❑ 청어 떼 ● 불가산명사 청어 살 ❑ 청어 통조림

hers /hɜrz/

Hers is a third person possessive pronoun.

hers는 3인칭 소유대명사이다.

1 PRON-POSS You use **hers** to indicate that something belongs or relates to a woman, girl, or female animal. ❑ *His hand as it shook hers was warm and firm.* ❑ *Professor Camm was a great friend of hers.* **2** PRON-POSS In written English, **hers** is sometimes used to refer to a person without saying whether that person is a man or a woman. Some people dislike this use and prefer to use "his or hers" or "theirs." ❑ *The author can report other people's results which more or less agree with hers.*

1 소유대명사 그녀의 것 ❑ 그녀와 악수를 하는 그의 손은 따뜻하고 믿음직스러웠다. ❑ 캄 교수는 그녀의 아주 좋은 친구였다. **2** 소유대명사 그 사람의 것 ❑ 그 작가는 자신의 결과와 어느 정도 일치하는 다른 사람들의 결과를 보고할 수도 있다.

her|self ♦♦♦ /hərsɛlf/

Herself is a third person singular reflexive pronoun. **Herself** is used when the object of a verb or preposition refers to the same person as the subject of the verb, except in meaning **3**.

herself는 3인칭 단수 재귀대명사이다. herself는 **3** 의미일 때 외에는 동사나 전치사의 목적어가 동사의 주어와 같은 사람을 지칭할 때 쓰인다.

1 PRON-REFL You use **herself** to refer to a woman, girl, or female animal. [v PRON, prep PRON] ❑ *She let herself out of the room.* ❑ *Jennifer believes she will move out on her own when she is financially able to support herself.* **2** PRON-REFL In written English, **herself** is sometimes used to refer to a person without saying whether that person is a man or a woman. Some people dislike this use and prefer to use "himself or herself" or "themselves." ❑ *How can anyone believe stories for which she feels herself to be in no way responsible?* **3** PRON-REFL-EMPH You use **herself** to emphasize the person or thing that you are referring to. **Herself** is sometimes used instead of "her" as the object of a verb or preposition. [EMPHASIS] ❑ *She herself was not a keen gardener.*

1 재귀대명사 그녀 자신 ❑ 그녀는 방에서 나왔다. ❑ 제니퍼는 스스로 재정적으로 부양할 수 있을 때 독립해서 나올 것이라고 믿는다. **2** 재귀대명사 그 사람 자신 ❑ 스스로 일말의 책임감도 못 느끼는 사람의 말을 어떻게 믿겠는가? **3** 강조 재귀대명사 그녀 자신 [강조] ❑ 그녀 자신도 그다지 열정 있는 정원사는 아니었다.

he's /ɪz, STRONG hiz/ **He's** is the usual spoken form of "he is" or "he has," especially when "has" is an auxiliary verb. ❑ *He's working maybe twenty-five hours a week.*

he is나 he has의 축약형 ❑ 그는 아마 한 주에 스물다섯 시간 일할 것이다.

hesi|tant /hɛzɪt³nt/ ADJ If you are **hesitant about** doing something, you do not do it quickly or immediately, usually because you are uncertain, embarrassed, or worried. ❑ *She was hesitant about coming forward with her story.* ● **hesi|tan|cy** /hɛzɪtənsi/ N-UNCOUNT ❑ *A trace of hesitancy showed in Dr. Stockton's eyes.* ● **hesi|tant|ly** ADV [ADV with v] ❑ *"Would you do me a favor?" she asked hesitantly.*

형용사 주저하는, 망설이는 ❑ 그녀는 자신의 이야기를 들고 나오는 데 대해 주저하고 있었다. ● 망설임, 주저 불가산명사 ❑ 스톡톤 박사의 눈에 망설이는 기색이 보였다. ● 망설이며, 주저하며 부사 ❑ "부탁 하나 들어주시겠어요?"라고 그녀가 주저하며 물었다.

hesi|tate /hɛzɪteɪt/ (**hesitates, hesitating, hesitated**) **1** V-I If you **hesitate**, you do not speak or act for a short time, usually because you are uncertain, embarrassed, or worried about what you are going to say or do. ❑ *The telephone rang. Catherine hesitated, debating whether to answer it.* ● **hesi|ta|tion** /hɛzɪteɪʃ³n/ (**hesitations**) N-VAR ❑ *Asked if he would go back, Mr. Searle said after some hesitation, "I'll have to think about that."* **2** V-T If you **hesitate to** do something, you delay doing it or are unwilling to do it, usually because you are not certain it would be right. If you do not **hesitate to** do something, you do it immediately. ❑ *Some parents hesitate to take these steps because they suspect that their child is exaggerating.* **3** V-T You can use **hesitate** in expressions such as "**don't hesitate to call me**" or "**don't hesitate to contact us**" when you are telling someone that they should do something as soon as it needs to be done and that they should not worry about disturbing other people. [only imper, with neg] ❑ *In the event of difficulties, please do not hesitate to contact our Customer Service Department.*

1 자동사 망설이다, 우물쭈물하다 ❑ 전화가 울렸다. 캐서린은 전화를 받을지 말지를 생각하며 망설였다. ● 망설임 가산명사 또는 불가산명사 ❑ 되돌아 가거나 질문을 받고 서얼 씨는 잠시 망설인 후 "그것에 대해서는 생각해 봐야겠어요."라고 말했다. **2** 타동사 주저하다 ❑ 몇몇의 부모은 아이들이 과장을 하고 있는지 의심하기 때문에 이러한 절차를 밟는 것에 주저한다. **3** 타동사 주저하다; 주저하지 마시고 전화하세요; 망설이지 말고 연락하세요 ❑ 어려운 일이 있는 경우, 주저하지 마시고 고객 서비스 부서로 연락하시기 바랍니다.

Thesaurus   hesitate의 참조어

v.   delay, falter, pause, wait **1** **2**

hesi|ta|tion /hɛzɪteɪʃ³n/ (**hesitations**) **1** N-VAR **Hesitation** is an unwillingness to do something, or a delay in doing it, because you are uncertain, worried, or embarrassed about it. ❑ *He promised there would be no more hesitations in pursuing reforms.* →see also **hesitate** **2** PHRASE If you say that you **have no hesitation in** doing something, you are emphasizing that you will do it immediately or willingly because you are certain that it is the right thing to do. [EMPHASIS] ❑ *The board said it had no hesitation in unanimously rejecting the offer.* **3** PHRASE If you say that someone does something **without hesitation**, you are emphasizing that they do it immediately and willingly. [EMPHASIS] ❑ *The great majority of players would, of course, sign the contract without hesitation.*

1 가산명사 또는 불가산명사 주저 ❑ 그는 개혁을 추구하는 데 더 이상 주저하는 일은 없을 것이라고 약속했다. **2** 구 서슴없다 [강조] ❑ 그 위원회는 서슴없이 만장일치로 그 제안을 거부한다고 말했다. **3** 구 서슴없이 [강조] ❑ 물론 대다수의 선수들은 서슴없이 그 계약에 서명할 것이다.

hetero|sex|ual /hɛtəroʊsɛkʃuəl/ (**heterosexuals**) **1** ADJ A **heterosexual** relationship is a sexual relationship between a man and a woman. ❑ *These show more people got Aids last year from heterosexual sex than homosexual sex.* **2** ADJ Someone who is **heterosexual** is sexually attracted to people of the opposite sex. ❑ *It doesn't matter whether people are heterosexual or homosexual.* ● N-COUNT **Heterosexual** is also a noun. ❑ *In Denmark the age of consent is fifteen for both heterosexuals and homosexuals.* ● **hetero|sexu|al|ity** /hɛtəroʊsɛkʃuælɪti/ N-UNCOUNT ❑ *...a challenge to the assumption that heterosexuality was "normal."*

1 형용사 이성애의 ❑ 이러한 것들은 지난해 동성끼리의 성교에서보다 이성끼리의 성교에서 에이즈에 걸린 사람이 더 많았다는 것을 보여 준다. **2** 형용사 이성애의 ❑ 사람들이 이성애자인지 동성애자인지는 중요하지 않다. ● 가산명사 이성애자 ❑ 덴마크에서는 본인의 의사로 성관계를 갖더라도 법적으로 문제가 안 되는 연령이 이성애자와 동성애자 모두 15세이다. ● 이성애 불가산명사 ❑ 이성애가 '정상'이라는 가정에 대한 도전

hexa|gon /hɛksəgɒn/, BRIT hɛksəgən/ (**hexagons**) N-COUNT A **hexagon** is a shape that has six straight sides.

가산명사 6각형

hex|ago|nal /hɛksǽgən°l/ ADJ A **hexagonal** object or shape has six straight sides.

hey /heɪ/ CONVENTION In informal situations, you say or shout "**hey**" to attract someone's attention, or to show surprise, interest, or annoyance. [FEELINGS] ❑ "Hey! Look out!" shouted Patty.

hey|day /héɪdeɪ/ N-SING Someone's **heyday** is the time when they are most powerful, successful, or popular. ❑ In its heyday, the studio's boast was that it had more stars than there are in heaven.

hi ♦◇◇ /haɪ/ CONVENTION In informal situations, you say "**hi**" to greet someone. [FORMULAE] ❑ "Hi, Liz," she said shyly.

hic|cup /híkʌp/ (**hiccups, hiccuping** or **hiccupping, hiccuped** or **hiccupped**) also **hiccough** ■ N-COUNT You can refer to a small problem or difficulty as a **hiccup**, especially if it does not last very long or is easily put right. ❑ A recent sales hiccup is nothing to panic about. ■ N-UNCOUNT When you have **hiccups**, you make repeated sharp sounds in your throat, often because you have been eating or drinking too quickly. ❑ A young baby may frequently get a bout of hiccups during or soon after a feed. ■ V-I When you **hiccup**, you make repeated sharp sounds in your throat. ❑ She was still hiccuping from the egg she had swallowed whole.

hid /hɪd/ **Hid** is the past tense of **hide**.

hid|den /híd°n/ ■ **Hidden** is the past participle of **hide**. ■ ADJ **Hidden** facts, feelings, activities, or problems are not easy to notice or discover. ❑ Under all the innocent fun, there are hidden dangers, especially for children. ■ ADJ A **hidden** place is difficult to find. ❑ As you descend, suddenly you see at last the hidden waterfall.

hid|den agen|da (**hidden agendas**) N-COUNT If you say that someone has a **hidden agenda**, you are criticizing them because you think they are secretly trying to achieve or cause a particular thing, while they appear to be doing something else. [DISAPPROVAL] ❑ He accused foreign nations of having a hidden agenda to harm French influence.

hide ♦◇◇ /haɪd/ (**hides, hiding, hid, hidden**) ■ V-T If you **hide** something or someone, you put them in a place where they cannot easily be seen or found. ❑ He hid the bicycle in the hawthorn hedge. ■ V-T/V-I If you **hide** or if you **hide yourself**, you go somewhere where you cannot easily be seen or found. ❑ At their approach the little boy scurried and hid. ■ V-T If you **hide** your face, you press your face against something or cover your face with something, so that people cannot see it. ❑ She hid her face under the collar of his jacket and she started to cry. ■ V-T If you **hide** what you feel or know, you keep it a secret, so that no one knows about it. ❑ Lee tried to hide his excitement. ■ V-T If something **hides** an object, it covers it and prevents it from being seen. ❑ The man's heavy moustache hid his upper lip completely. ■ N-VAR A **hide** is the skin of a large animal such as a cow, horse, or elephant, which can be used for making leather. ❑ ...the process of tanning animal hides. ■ →see also **hidden, hiding**

Thesaurus
hide의 참조어

V.   camouflage, conceal, cover, lock up; (ant.) expose, reveal ■-■

Word Partnership
hide의 연어

ADV.   **nowhere to** hide ■ ■
V.   **attempt/try to** hide ■ ■ ■ ■
   run and hide ■
N.   hide *your* face ■
   hide **a fact/secret**, hide *your* **fear/feelings/tears/disappointment** ■

---

hid|eous /hídiəs/ ■ ADJ If you say that someone or something is **hideous**, you mean that they are very ugly or unattractive. ❑ She saw a hideous face at the window and screamed. ■ ADJ You can describe an event, experience, or action as **hideous** when you mean that it is very unpleasant, painful, or difficult to bear. ❑ His family was subjected to a hideous attack by the gang.

hid|eous|ly /hídiəsli/ ■ ADV You use **hideously** to emphasize that something is very ugly or unattractive. [EMPHASIS] ❑ Everything is hideously ugly. ■ ADV You can use **hideously** to emphasize that something is very unpleasant or unacceptable. [EMPHASIS] [ADV adj/-ed] ❑ ...a hideously complex program.

hid|ing /háɪdɪŋ/ ■ N-UNCOUNT If someone is **in hiding**, they have secretly gone somewhere where they cannot be seen or found. ❑ Gray is thought to be in hiding near the France/Italy border. ■ PHRASE If you say that someone who is trying to achieve something is **on a hiding to nothing**, you are emphasizing that they have absolutely no chance of being successful. [BRIT, INFORMAL, EMPHASIS] ❑ As regards commercial survival, a car manufacturer capable of making only 50,000 cars a year is on a hiding to nothing.

hier|ar|chi|cal /haɪ̍ərɑ́rkɪkˀl/ ADJ A **hierarchical** system or organization is one in which people have different ranks or positions, depending on how important they are. ❑ ...the traditional hierarchical system of military organization.

hier|ar|chy /háɪ̍ərɑ̀rki/ (**hierarchies**) ■ N-VAR A **hierarchy** is a system of organizing people into different ranks or levels of importance, for example in society or in a company. ❑ Like most other American companies with a rigid hierarchy, workers and managers had strictly defined duties. ■ N-COUNT-COLL The **hierarchy** of an organization such as the Church is the group of people who manage and

---

형용사 6각형의

관용 표현 이이 [감정 개입] ❑ "어이! 조심해!"라고 패티가 소리쳤다.

단수명사 전성기 ❑ 전성기에 그 스튜디오의 자랑은 그곳에 하늘보다 더 많은 스타가 있다는 것이었다.

관용 표현 안녕 [의례적인 표현] ❑ "안녕, 리즈."라고 그녀는 수줍게 말했다.

■ 가산명사 일시적인 문제 ❑ 최근의 일시적인 판매 하락은 전혀 당황할 필요가 없는 것이다. ■ 불가산명사 딸꾹질 ❑ 어린 아기가 젖을 먹는 중에나 직후에 딸꾹질을 몇 차례 하는 것은 흔히 일어날 수 있는 일이다. ■ 자동사 딸꾹질하다 ❑ 그녀는 달걀 전체를 삼킨 것 때문에 아직도 딸꾹질을 하고 있었다.

hide의 과거

■ hide의 과거 분사 ■ 형용사 보이지 않는, 숨은 ❑ 모든 순수한 재미 이면에는, 특히 아이들의 경우, 보이지 않는 위험이 있다. ■ 형용사 감춰진 ❑ 내려갈 때 바로 마침내 감춰져 있던 폭포가 갑자기 눈에 들어온다.

가산명사 숨은 의도 [탐탁찮음] ❑ 그는 타 국가들이 프랑스 영향력에 해를 끼치려는 숨은 의도를 가지고 있다고 비난하였다.

■ 타동사 숨기다, 감추다 ❑ 그는 산사나무 울타리 안으로 자전거를 숨겼다. ■ 타동사/자동사 숨다 ❑ 그들이 가까이 다가오자 그 작은 소년은 황급히 달아나 숨었다. ■ 타동사 가리다 ❑ 그녀는 그의 재킷 칼라 아래 얼굴을 파묻고 울기 시작했다. ■ 타동사 감추다 ❑ 리는 흥분을 감추려 했다. ■ 타동사 닫다 ❑ 그 남자는 풍성한 콧수염이 윗입술을 완전히 덮고 있었다. ■ 가산명사 또는 불가산명사 가죽 ❑ 동물의 가죽을 무두질하는 과정

■ 형용사 추악한 ❑ 그녀는 창문에서 추악한 얼굴을 보고 소리 질렀다. ■ 형용사 소름끼치는, 몸서리쳐지는 ❑ 그의 가족은 깡패들의 몸서리쳐지는 공격을 당했다.

■ 부사 소름끼치게 [강조] ❑ 모든 것이 아주 끔찍하게 추악하다. ■ 부사 진저리날 정도로 [강조] ❑ 진저리날 정도로 복잡한 프로그램

■ 불가산명사 은신 ❑ 그레이는 프랑스와 이딜리아 국경 근처에 은신하고 있는 것으로 생각된다. ■ 구 전혀 가망이 없는 [영국영어, 비격식체, 강조] ❑ 상업적으로 생존 여부를 고려해볼 때, 1년에 5만 대만을 생산할 수 있는 자동차 제조 회사는 전혀 가망이 없다.

형용사 계급의, 서열의 ❑ 군대 조직의 전통적인 서열 제도

■ 가산명사 또는 불가산명사 위계질서, 서열 ❑ 경직된 위계 구조를 가지고 있는 대부분의 다른 미국 회사들과 마찬가지로, 근로자와 관리자들은 엄격하게 임무가 명시되어 있었다. ■ 가산명사·집합 (교회) 지도층 ❑ 오늘날 교회 지도층에서는 교회도 국가의 사회적,

control it. ❑ *The church hierarchy today feels the church should reflect the social and political realities of the country.*

hi-fi /ˈhaɪ faɪ/ (**hi-fis**) N-VAR A **hi-fi** is a set of equipment on which you play CDs and tapes, and which produces stereo sound of very good quality.

정치적 현실을 반영해야 한다고 생각한다.

가산명사 또는 불가산명사 하이파이 장치, 스테레오

Word Link *est ≈ most : cold**est**, high**est**, larg**est***

---

high ♦♦♦ /haɪ/ (**higher**, **highest**, **highs**) **1** ADJ Something that is **high** extends a long way from the bottom to the top when it is upright. You do not use **high** to describe people, animals, or plants. ❑ *...a house, with a high wall all around it.* ❑ *Mount Marcy is the highest mountain in the Adirondacks.* ● ADV **High** is also an adverb. [ADV after v] ❑ *...wagons packed high with bureaus, bedding, and cooking pots.*

1 형용사 높은 ❑ 높은 담으로 빙 둘러싸인 집 ❑ 마르시 산은 애디론댁 산맥에서 가장 높은 산이다. ● 부사 높이 ❑ 서랍장, 침구, 조리용 냄비들을 높이 실은 마차들

The word you should use to describe people, animals, or plants is **tall**, not "high". ❑ *She was rather tall for a woman.* **Tall** is also used to describe buildings such as skyscrapers, and other things whose height is much greater than their width. ❑ *...tall pine trees...a tall glass vase.*

사람이나 동물, 식물을 묘사할 때는 high가 아니라, tall을 써야 한다. ❑ 그녀는 여자치곤 키가 컸다. 고층 빌딩 같은 건물과 높이가 훨씬 더 큰 다른 사물을 묘사할 때도 tall을 쓴다. ❑ ...키 큰 소나무....키 큰 유리 꽃병
---

2 ADJ You use **high** to talk or ask about how much something upright measures from the bottom to the top. [amount ADJ, n ADJ, how ADJ, as ADJ as, ADJ-compar than] ❑ *...an elegant bronze horse only nine inches high.* ❑ *The grass in the yard was waist high.* **3** ADJ If something is **high**, it is a long way above the ground, above sea level, or above a person or thing. ❑ *I looked down from the high window.* ❑ *The sun was high in the sky, blazing down on us.* ● ADV **High** is also an adverb. [ADV after v] ❑ *...being able to run faster or jump higher than other people.* ● PHRASE If something is **high up**, it is a long way above the ground, above sea level, or above a person or thing. ❑ *His farm was high up in the hills.* **4** ADJ You can use **high** to indicate that something is great in amount, degree, or intensity. ❑ *The European country with the highest birth rate is Ireland.* ❑ *Official reports said casualties were high.* ● ADV **High** is also an adverb. [ADV after v] ❑ *He expects the unemployment figures to rise even higher in coming months.* ● PHRASE You can use phrases such as **"in the high 80s"** to indicate that a number or level is, for example, more than 85 but not as much as 90. **5** ADJ If a food or other substance is **high in** a particular ingredient, it contains a large amount of that ingredient. [v-link ADJ in n] ❑ *Don't indulge in rich sauces, fried food and thick pastry as these are high in fat.* **6** N-COUNT If something reaches a **high of** a particular amount or degree, that is the greatest it has ever been. [oft N of amount] ❑ *Traffic from Jordan to Iraq is down to a dozen loaded trucks a day, compared with a high of 200 a day.* **7** ADJ If you say that something is a **high** priority or is **high on** your list, you mean that you consider it to be one of the most important things you have to do or deal with. ❑ *The party has not made the issue a high priority.* **8** ADJ Someone who is **high in** a particular profession or society, or has a **high** position, has a very important position and has great authority and influence. [v-link ADJ in n, ADJ n] ❑ *Was there anyone particularly high in the administration who was an advocate of a different policy?* ❑ *...corruption in high places.* ● PHRASE Someone who is **high up in** a profession or society has a very important position. ❑ *His cousin is somebody quite high up in the navy.* **9** ADV If you aim **high**, you try to obtain or to achieve the best that you can. [ADV after v] ❑ *You should not be afraid to aim high in the quest for an improvement in your income.* **10** ADJ If someone has a **high** reputation, or people have a **high** opinion of them, people think they are very good in some way, for example at their work. ❑ *People have such high expectations of you.* **11** ADJ If the quality or standard of something is **high**, it is very good indeed. ❑ *This is high quality stuff.* **12** ADJ A **high** sound or voice is close to the top of a particular range of notes. ❑ *Her high voice really irritated Maria.* **13** ADJ If your spirits are **high**, you feel happy and excited. ❑ *Her spirits were high with the hope of seeing Nick in minutes rather than hours.* **14** ADJ If someone is **high on** drink or drugs, they are affected by the alcoholic drink or drugs they have taken. [INFORMAL] [v-link ADJ, usu ADJ on n] ❑ *He was too high on drugs and alcohol to remember them.* **15** N-COUNT A **high** is a feeling or mood of great excitement or happiness. [INFORMAL] ❑ *"I'm still on a high," she said after the show.* **16** PHRASE If you say that something came from **on high**, you mean that it came from a person or place of great authority. ❑ *Orders had come from on high that extra care was to be taken during this week.* **17** PHRASE If you say that you were left **high and dry**, you are emphasizing that you were left in a difficult situation and were unable to do anything about it. [EMPHASIS] ❑ *Schools with better reputations will be flooded with applications while poorer schools will be left high and dry.* **18** PHRASE If you refer to the **highs and lows of** someone's life or career, you are referring to both the successful or happy times, and the unsuccessful or bad times. ❑ *Here, she talks about the highs and lows of her life.* **19** PHRASE If you say that you looked **high and low** for something, you are emphasizing that you looked for it in every place that you could think of. [EMPHASIS] ❑ *...and I rambled around the apartment looking high and low for an aspirin or pain-killer.*

2 형용사 높이가 -인 ❑ 높이가 9인치밖에 안 되는 우아한 청동 말 ❑ 뜰의 잔디가 허리 정도의 높이까지 자라 있었다. **3** 형용사 높은, 고지의 ❑ 나는 높은 창문에서 아래로 내려다보았다. ❑ 하늘 높이 떠 있는 태양이 우리를 향해 내리쬐고 있었다. ● 부사 높이 ❑ 다른 사람보다 더 빠르게 달리고 더 높이 점프할 수 있음 ● 구 높은 곳의 ❑ 그의 농장은 높은 산간 지역에 있었다. **4** 형용사 많은; 심한; 강력한 ❑ 가장 높은 출생률을 보이는 유럽 국가는 아일랜드이다. ❑ 공식 보고에 따르면 사상자가 많았다고 한다. ● 부사 높이 ❑ 그는 실업 수치가 다음 몇 개월 동안 훨씬 더 높이 올라갈 것이라고 예상한다. ● 구 80대 후반 **5** 형용사 -이 많은, 고(高)- ❑ 기름진 소스, 튀긴 음식, 그리고 두툼한 패스트리는 지방이 많이 너무 많이 먹지 말아라. **6** 가산명사 최고치, 최고 수준 ❑ 요르단에서부터 이라크까지의 교통량이 1일 최대치가 짐을 실은 화물차 200대인 것에 비교해 볼 때 현재는 1일 12대까지 내려가 있는 상태이다. **7** 형용사 높은 순위의, 우선순위의 ❑ 그 정당은 그 문제를 최우선시 하지 않았다. **8** 형용사 고위의, 높은 ❑ 비교적 높은 지위를 가진 정부 인물들 중에서 다른 정책을 옹호하는 사람이 있었는가? ❑ 높은 직책에서의 부패 ● 구 고위직의, 요직의 ❑ 그의 사촌은 해군에서 꽤나 중요한 인물이다. **9** 부사 높이 ❑ 소득 개선을 추구할 때는 목표를 높이 잡는 것을 두려워하면 안 된다. **10** 형용사 높은, 좋은 ❑ 사람들이 너에게 아주 큰 기대를 가지고 있다. **11** 형용사 좋은 ❑ 이것은 품질이 좋은 물건이다. **12** 형용사 고음의, 높은 ❑ 그녀의 고음의 목소리가 마리아를 정말로 짜증나게 했다. **13** 형용사 들뜬, 기분이 좋은 ❑ 그녀는 몇 시간이 아니라 몇 분 후에 닉을 본다는 희망에 마음이 들떠 있었다. **14** 형용사 취한, 몽롱한 [비격식체] ❑ 그는 마약과 술로 너무 정신이 몽롱해서 그들을 기억할 수 없었다. **15** 가산명사 행복감 [비격식체] ❑ "저는 여전히 행복합니다."라고 그녀는 자기 인생의 기복에 대해서 말했다. **16** 구 고위직에, 높은 자리에 ❑ 이번 주에 특별한 주의가 필요하다는 지시가 높은 분들로부터 내려온 상태였다. **17** 구 곤경에 빠져 [강조] ❑ 평판이 좋지 못한 학교들은 곤경에 빠지는 반면, 평판이 좋은 학교들은 지원서가 넘칠 것이다. **18** 구 부침(浮沈), 기복 ❑ 자, 그녀가 자기 인생의 기복에 대해서 말한다. **19** 구 모든 곳에, 구석구석 [강조] ❑ 그리고 나는 아스피린이나 진통제를 찾으려고 아파트를 구석구석 뒤졌다.

Thesaurus *high의 참조어*

| ADJ. | tall **1** **2** |
| | lofty; (ant.) low **3** |

---

high-class ADJ If you describe something as **high-class**, you mean that it is of very good quality or of superior social status. ❑ *...a high-class jeweler's.*

형용사 고급의, 상류의 ❑ 고급 보석 가게

high-end ADJ **High-end** products, especially electronic products, are the most expensive of their kind. ❑ *...high-end personal computers and computer workstations.*

형용사 최고가의 ❑ 최고가의 개인용 컴퓨터와 컴퓨터 워크스테이션

high|er /ˈhaɪər/ ADJ A **higher** degree or diploma is a qualification of an advanced standard or level. [ADJ n] ❑ *...a higher diploma in hotel management.* →see also **high**

형용사 고등의, 고급의 ❑ 호텔 경영 고급 과정 학위증서

high|er edu|ca|tion N-UNCOUNT **Higher education** is education at universities and colleges. ❑ *...students in higher education.*

불가산명사 고등 교육, 대학 교육 ❑ 고등 교육을 받는 학생들

high-flying ADJ A **high-flying** person is successful or is likely to be successful in their career. ❑ *...her high-flying newspaper-editor husband.*

형용사 성공한; 유망한 ❑ 그녀의 성공한 신문 편집장인 남편

high|lands /ˈhaɪləndz/ N-PLURAL **Highlands** are mountainous areas of land.

복수명사 고원, 산악 지역

high|light ♦♦◇ /ˈhaɪlaɪt/ (highlights, highlighting, highlighted) **1** V-T If someone or something **highlights** a point or problem, they emphasize it or make you think about it. ❑ *Last year Collins wrote a moving ballad which highlighted the plight of the homeless.* **2** V-T To **highlight** a piece of text means to mark it in a different color, either with a special type of pen or on a computer screen. ❑ *Highlight the chosen area by clicking and holding down the left mouse button.* **3** N-COUNT The **highlights** of an event, activity, or period of time are the most interesting or exciting parts of it. ❑ *...a match that is likely to prove one of the highlights of the tournament.*

1 타동사 강조하다 ❑ 지난해 콜린스는 노숙자들의 역경을 강조하는 감동적인 발라드를 작곡했다. **2** 타동사 눈에 띄게 하다, 하이라이트 처리하다 ❑ 왼쪽 마우스 버튼을 클릭한 뒤 계속 눌러서 선택한 부분을 하이라이트 처리하시오. **3** 가산명사 가장 흥미 있는 부분, 하이라이트 ❑ 토너먼트에서 가장 재미있는 경기 중 하나가 될 것 같은 경기

Word Partnership highlight의 연어

| N. | highlight concerns/problems, highlight differences **1** |
| | highlight of *someone's* career **3** |

---

high|ly ♦♦◇ /ˈhaɪli/ **1** ADV **Highly** is used before some adjectives to mean "very." [ADV adj] ❑ *Mr. Singh was a highly successful salesman.* ❑ *It seems highly unlikely that she ever existed.* **2** ADV You use **highly** to indicate that someone has an important position in an organization or set of people. [ADV -ed] ❑ *...a highly placed government advisor.* **3** ADV If someone is **highly** paid, they receive a large salary. [ADV -ed] ❑ *He was the most highly paid member of staff.* **4** ADV If you think **highly** of something or someone, you think they are very good indeed. ❑ *Daphne and Michael thought highly of the school.*

1 부사 매우 ❑ 싱 씨는 매우 성공한 판매원이었다. ❑ 그녀가 존재했을 가능성은 거의 없어 보인다. **2** 부사 높은 지위에 ❑ 고위직에 있는 정부 자문 위원 **3** 부사 고액의 ❑ 그는 봉급을 가장 많이 받는 직원이었다. **4** 부사 높이 평가하여 ❑ 다프네와 마이클은 그 학교를 아주 좋게 생각했다.

Word Partnership highly의 연어

V.	highly recommended, highly respected **1**
ADJ.	highly addictive, highly competitive, highly contagious,
	highly controversial, highly critical, highly educated,
	highly intelligent, highly qualified, highly skilled,
	highly successful, highly technical, highly trained,
	highly unlikely, highly visible **1**
	highly paid **3**

High|ness /ˈhaɪnɪs/ (Highnesses) N-VOC Expressions such as "**Your Highness**" or "**His Highness**" are used to address or refer to a member of the royal family other than a king or queen. [POLITENESS] ❑ *That would be best, Your Highness.*

호격명사 전하 [공손체] ❑ 그것이 최선일 것 같습니다, 전하.

high-pitched ADJ A **high-pitched** sound is shrill and high in pitch. ❑ *A woman squealed in a high-pitched voice.*

형용사 고음의, (소리가) 새된 ❑ 한 여자가 새된 소리로 길게 비명을 질렀다.

high-powered 1 ADJ A **high-powered** machine or piece of equipment is very powerful and efficient. ❑ *...high powered lasers.* **2** ADJ Someone who is **high-powered** or has a **high-powered** job has a very important and responsible job which requires a lot of ability. ❑ *...a high-powered lawyer.*

1 형용사 고성능의 ❑ 고성능 레이저 **2** 형용사 영향력이 큰 ❑ 영향력이 큰 변호사

high-profile ADJ A **high-profile** person or a **high-profile** event attracts a lot of attention or publicity. ❑ *...one of football's high-profile chairmen.*

형용사 세간의 주목을 받는 ❑ 세간의 주목을 받는 축구 관계자 중 한 명

high-rise (high-rises) ADJ **High-rise** buildings are modern buildings which are very tall and have many levels or floors. [ADJ n] ❑ *...high-rise office buildings.* ● N-COUNT A **high-rise** is a high-rise building. ❑ *That big high-rise above us is where Brian lives.*

형용사 고층의 ❑ 고층 사무실 빌딩들 ● 가산명사 고층 건물 ❑ 우리 위에 있는 저 큰 고층 건물이 브라이언이 사는 곳이다.

high school (high schools) **1** N-VAR; N-IN-NAMES In the United States, a **high school** is a school for children usually aged between fourteen and eighteen. ❑ *...an 18-year-old inner-city kid who dropped out of high school.* **2** N-VAR; N-IN-NAMES In Britain, a **high school** is a school for children aged between eleven and eighteen. ❑ *...Sunderland High School.* →see **graduation**

1 가산명사 또는 불가산명사; 이름명사 (미국의) 고등학교 ❑ 고등학교를 중퇴한 열여덟 살의 빈민가 아이 **2** 가산명사 또는 불가산명사; 이름명사 (영국의) 중등학교 ❑ 선더랜드 중등학교

high street (high streets) **1** N-COUNT; N-IN-NAMES The **high street** of a town is the main street where most of the stores and banks are. [mainly BRIT; AM **Main Street**] ❑ *Vegetarian restaurants and health food shops are springing up in every high street.* **2** ADJ **High street** banks and businesses are companies which have branches in the main shopping areas of most towns. [mainly BRIT] [ADJ n] ❑ *The scanners are available from high street stores.*

1 가산명사; 이름명사 시내, 번화가 [주로 영국영어; 미국영어 main street] ❑ 채식주의자 레스토랑과 건강식품점이 모든 번화가에 생기고 있다. **2** 형용사 번화가의, 시내의 [주로 영국영어] ❑ 그 스캐너들은 시내 상점에서 구입할 수 있다.

high-tech /ˌhaɪ ˈtɛk/ also **high tech** also **hi tech** ADJ **High-tech** activities or equipment involve or result from the use of high technology. ❑ *...such high-tech industries as computers or telecommunications.*

형용사 첨단 기술의 ❑ 컴퓨터와 텔레커뮤니케이션과 같은 첨단 기술 산업

high tech|nol|ogy N-UNCOUNT **High technology** is the practical use of advanced scientific research and knowledge, especially in relation to electronics and computers, and the development of new advanced machines and equipment. ❑ *...a limited war using high technology.*

불가산명사 첨단 기술 ❑ 첨단 기술을 이용한 국지전

high|way /ˈhaɪweɪ/ (highways) N-COUNT A **highway** is a main road, especially one that connects towns or cities. [mainly AM] ❑ *I crossed the highway, dodging the traffic.* →see **traffic**

가산명사 주요 간선 도로 [주로 미국영어] ❑ 나는 교통 체증을 피해서 주요 간선 도로를 건넜다.

hi|jack /ˈhaɪdʒæk/ (hijacks, hijacking, hijacked) **1** V-T If someone **hijacks** a plane or other vehicle, they illegally take control of it by force while it is traveling from one place to another. ❑ *Two men tried to hijack a plane on a flight from Riga to Murmansk.* ● N-COUNT **Hijack** is also a noun. ❑ *Every minute during the hijack seemed like a week.* ● **hi|jack|ing** (hijackings) N-COUNT ❑ *Car hijackings are running at a rate of nearly 50 a day.* **2** V-T If you say that someone **has hijacked** something, you disapprove of the way in which they have taken control of it when they had no right to do so. [DISAPPROVAL] ❑ *A peaceful demonstration had been hijacked by anarchists intent on causing trouble.*

1 타동사 (비행기 등을) 납치하다 ❑ 두 남자가 리가에서 무르만스크로 향하는 비행기를 납치하려고 했다. ● 납치 가산명사 ❑ 납치 기간 동에는 1분 1분이 일주일처럼 느껴졌다. ● 납치 가산명사 ❑ 자동차 납치가 하루에 거의 50건씩 발생하고 있다. **2** 타동사 강탈하다 [탐탁잖음] ❑ 평화적인 시위는 문제를 일으키기로 작정한 무정부주의자들에 의해 난장판으로 변했다.

A

hi|jack|er /ˈhaɪdʒækər/ (**hijackers**) N-COUNT A **hijacker** is a person who hijacks a plane or other vehicle.

가산명사 탈취범, 납치범

hike /haɪk/ (**hikes, hiking, hiked**) ◆ N-COUNT A **hike** is a long walk in the country, especially one that you go on for pleasure. ❑ *The site is reached by a 30-minute hike through dense forest.* ◆ V-I If you **hike**, you go for a long walk in the country. ❑ *You could hike through the Fish River Canyon – it's entirely up to you.* ● **hik|ing** N-UNCOUNT ❑ *...some harder, more strenuous hiking on cliff pathways.* ◆ N-COUNT A **hike** is a sudden or large increase in prices, rates, taxes, or quantities. [INFORMAL] ❑ *...a sudden 1.75 percent hike in Italian interest rates.* ◆ V-T To **hike** prices, rates, taxes, or quantities means to increase them suddenly or by a large amount. [INFORMAL] ❑ *It has now been forced to hike its rates by 5.25 percent.* ● PHRASAL VERB **Hike up** means the same as **hike**. ❑ *The insurers have started hiking up premiums by huge amounts.*

◆ 가산명사 하이킹, 도보 여행 ❑ 그 장소는 울창한 숲 속을 통해 30분간 도보로 가야 도착한다. ◆ 자동사 하이킹하다, 도보 여행 하다 ❑ 피쉬 리버 캐니언을 따라 하이킹할 수도 있다. 그것은 전적으로 당신에게 달려 있다. ● 하이킹, 도보 여행 불가산명사 ❑ 절벽을 따라 난 길로 걸어가는 더 힘들고 더 많은 노력이 필요한 하이킹 ◆ 가산명사 (대폭) 인상 [비격식체] ❑ 이탈리아 금리의 갑작스러운 1.75퍼센트 인상 ◆ 타동사 인상하다 [비격식체] ❑ 지금까지 요금을 5.25퍼센트 인상하는 것이 불가피했다. ● 구동사 인상하다 ❑ 보험업자들이 프리미엄을 거액으로 인상하기 시작했다.

B

C

D

E

hik|er /ˈhaɪkər/ (**hikers**) N-COUNT A **hiker** is a person who is going for a long walk in the countryside for pleasure.

가산명사 하이커, 도보 여행자

hi|lari|ous /hɪˈlɛəriəs/ ADJ If something is **hilarious**, it is extremely funny and makes you laugh a lot. ❑ *We thought it was hilarious when we first heard about it.* ● **hi|lari|ous|ly** ADV ❑ *She found it hilariously funny.*

형용사 아주 재미있는, 아주 웃기는 ❑ 우리가 처음 그것에 대해서 들었을 때 아주 재미있다고 생각했다. ● 아주 재미있게 부사 ❑ 그녀는 그것이 배꼽이 빠질 정도로 웃기다고 생각했다.

F

G

hill ◆◇◇ /hɪl/ (**hills**) ◆ N-COUNT; N-IN-NAMES A **hill** is an area of land that is higher than the land that surrounds it. ❑ *...the shady street that led up the hill to the office building.* ◆ PHRASE If you say that someone is **over the hill**, you are saying rudely that they are old and no longer fit, attractive, or capable of doing useful work. [INFORMAL, DISAPPROVAL] ❑ *He doesn't take kindly to suggestions that he is over the hill.*

◆ 가산명사 구릉, 언덕; 이름명사 ❑ 사무실 건물로 가는 언덕으로 통하는 그늘진 거리 ◆ 구 한창때가 지난, 전성기를 지난 [비격식체, 탐탁찮음] ❑ 그의 전성기가 지났다는 것을 은연중에 내비치면 그는 기분 나빠한다.

H

hilly /ˈhɪli/ (**hillier, hilliest**) ADJ A **hilly** area has many hills. ❑ *The areas where the fighting is taking place are hilly and densely wooded.*

형용사 구릉이 많은 ❑ 싸움이 일어나고 있는 지역은 언덕이 많고 빽빽한 숲이 있는 곳이다.

I

him ◆◆◆ /hɪm/

> **Him** is a third person singular pronoun. **Him** is used as the object of a verb or a preposition.

him은 3인칭 단수대명사이다. him은 동사 또는 전치사의 목적어로 쓰인다.

J

◆ PRON-SING You use **him** to refer to a man, boy, or male animal. [v PRON, prep PRON] ❑ *John's aunt died suddenly and left him a surprisingly large sum.* ❑ *Is Sam there? Let me talk to him.* ◆ PRON-SING In written English, **him** is sometimes used to refer to a person without saying whether that person is a man or a woman. Some people dislike this use and prefer to use "him or her" or "them." [v PRON, prep PRON] ❑ *If the child encounters "hear," we should show him that this is the base word in "hearing" and "hears."*

◆ 단수대명사 그를; 그에게 ❑ 존의 고모가 갑자기 돌아가시면서 그에게 꽤 많은 돈을 남겨 주었다. ❑ 샘 있어요? 그와 잠시 얘기할 수 있도록 해주세요. ◆ 단수대명사 그 사람을; 그 사람에게 ❑ 아이가 '들다'라는 단어를 접하게 되면, 우리는 그에게 그것이 '듣는'이나 '듣는다'의 기본형이라는 것을 알려주어야 한다.

K

L

him|self ◆◆◆ /hɪmˈsɛlf/

> **Himself** is a third person singular reflexive pronoun. **Himself** is used when the object of a verb or preposition refers to the same person as the subject of the verb, except in meaning ◆.

himself는 3인칭 단수 재귀대명사이다. himself는 ◆ 의미일 때 외에는 동사나 전치사의 목적어가 동사의 주어와 같은 사람을 지칭할 때 쓰인다.

M

◆ PRON-REFL You use **himself** to refer to a man, boy, or male animal. [v PRON, prep PRON] ❑ *He poured himself a whisky and sat down in the chair.* ❑ *William went away muttering to himself.* ◆ PRON-REFL In written English, **himself** is sometimes used to refer to a person without saying whether that person is a man or a woman. Some people dislike this use and prefer to use "himself or herself" or "themselves." [v PRON, prep PRON] ❑ *The child's natural way of expressing himself is play.* ◆ PRON-REFL-EMPH You use **himself** to emphasize the person or thing that you are referring to. **Himself** is sometimes used instead of "him" as the object of a verb or preposition. [EMPHASIS] ❑ *The Prime Minister himself is on a visit to Peking.*

◆ 재귀대명사 그 자신 ❑ 그는 자기가 마실 위스키를 한 잔 따라서 의자에 앉았다. ❑ 윌리엄은 혼잣말을 중얼거리면서 떠나갔다. ◆ 재귀대명사 자신 ❑ 아이가 자신을 표현하는 자연스러운 방법이 놀이다. ◆ 강조 재귀대명사 자신이 직접 [강조] ❑ 수상 자신이 직접 베이징을 방문하고 있는 중이다.

N

O

P

hind /haɪnd/ ADJ An animal's **hind** legs are at the back of its body. [ADJ n] ❑ *Suddenly the cow kicked up its hind legs.*

형용사 뒤쪽의 ❑ 갑자기 그 암소가 뒷다리로 걸어갔다.

Q

hin|der /ˈhɪndər/ (**hinders, hindering, hindered**) ◆ V-T If something **hinders** you, it makes it more difficult for you to do something or make progress. ❑ *Further investigation was hindered by the loss of all documentation on the case.* ◆ V-T If something **hinders** your movement, it makes it difficult for you to move forward or move around. ❑ *A thigh injury increasingly hindered her mobility.*

◆ 타동사 방해하다 ❑ 사건과 관련된 문서가 모두 소실되었기 때문에 더 조사하는 것은 어려웠다. ◆ 타동사 방해가 되다 ❑ 허벅지 부상으로 그녀는 점점 더 움직이기 어려워졌다.

R

hin|drance /ˈhɪndrəns/ (**hindrances**) N-COUNT A **hindrance** is a person or thing that makes it more difficult for you to do something. ❑ *The higher rates have been a hindrance to economic recovery.*

가산명사 방해 ❑ 높은 금리가 경제 회복에 방해가 되어 왔다.

S

hind|sight /ˈhaɪndsaɪt/ N-UNCOUNT **Hindsight** is the ability to understand and realize something about an event after it has happened, although you did not understand or realize it at the time. ❑ *With hindsight, we'd all do things differently.*

불가산명사 나중에 생각나는 묘안, 사건이 지난 후 생기는 통찰력 ❑ 만약 지금의 통찰력이 그 당시에 있었다면 우리는 모든 것을 달리했을 것이다.

T

Hin|du /ˈhɪndu/ (**Hindus**) ◆ N-COUNT A **Hindu** is a person who believes in Hinduism and follows its teachings. ◆ ADJ **Hindu** is used to describe things that belong or relate to Hinduism. ❑ *...a Hindu temple.* →see **religion**

◆ 가산명사 힌두교도 ◆ 형용사 힌두교의 ❑ 힌두교 사원

U

Hin|du|ism /ˈhɪnduɪzəm/ N-UNCOUNT **Hinduism** is an Indian religion. It has many gods and teaches that people have another life on earth after they die.

불가산명사 힌두교

V

hinge /hɪndʒ/ (**hinges, hinging, hinged**) N-COUNT A **hinge** is a piece of metal, wood, or plastic that is used to join a door to its frame or to join two things together so that one of them can swing freely. ❑ *The top swung open on well-oiled hinges.*

가산명사 경첩, 연결부 ❑ 기름칠이 잘 된 연결부에 달린 뚜껑이 확 열렸다.

W

▸**hinge on** PHRASAL VERB Something that **hinges on** one thing or event depends entirely on it. ❑ *The plan hinges on a deal being struck with a new company.*

구동사 ~에 전적으로 달려 있다 ❑ 그 계획은 새 회사와 맺는 계약에 전적으로 달려 있다.

X

hint ◆◇◇ /hɪnt/ (**hints, hinting, hinted**) ◆ N-COUNT A **hint** is a suggestion about something that is made in an indirect way. ❑ *I'd dropped a hint about having an exhibition of his work up here.* ● PHRASE If you **take a hint**, you understand something that is suggested to you indirectly. ❑ *"I think I hear the telephone ringing." — "Okay, I can take a hint."* ◆ V-I If you **hint at** something, you suggest it

◆ 가산명사 암시 ❑ 여기에서 그의 작품 전시회를 갖는다고 내가 넌지시 말했었다. ● 구 (암시를) 알아채다 ❑ "전화 소리가 들리는 것 같다." "좋아. 무슨 말인지 알겠어." ◆ 자동사 넌지시 비치다, 빗대어 말하다 ❑ 그녀는 쇼핑하러 가자고 제안하며 뭔가 한턱

Y

Z

in an indirect way. □ *She suggested a trip to the shops and hinted at the possibility of a treat of some sort.* ❸ N-COUNT A **hint** is a helpful piece of advice, usually about how to do something. □ *Here are some helpful hints to make your journey easier.* ❹ N-SING A **hint of** something is a very small amount of it. □ *She added only a hint of vermouth to the gin.*

Word Partnership	hint의 연어
V.	take a hint ❶
	drop a hint, give a hint ❶ ❸
ADJ.	broad hint ❶
	helpful hint ❸

hip ♦♢♢ /hɪp/ (hips) ❶ N-COUNT Your **hips** are the two areas at the sides of your body between the tops of your legs and your waist. □ *Tracey put her hands on her hips and sighed.* ❷ N-COUNT You refer to the bones between the tops of your legs and your waist as your **hips**. □ *Eventually, surgeons replaced both hips and both shoulders.* ❸ ADJ If you say that someone is **hip**, you mean that they are very modern and follow all the latest fashions, for example in clothes and ideas. [INFORMAL] □ *...a hip young character with tight-cropped blond hair and stylish glasses.* ❹ EXCLAM If a large group of people want to show their appreciation or approval of someone, one of them says "**Hip hip**" and they all shout "**hooray**." ❺ PHRASE If you say that someone **shoots from the hip** or **fires from the hip**, you mean that they react to situations or give their opinion very quickly, without stopping to think. □ *Judges don't have to shoot from the hip. They have the leisure to think, to decide.*

hip|pie /hɪpi/ (hippies) also **hippy** N-COUNT **Hippies** were young people in the 1960s and 1970s who rejected conventional ways of living, dressing, and behaving, and tried to live a life based on peace and love. Hippies often had long hair and many took drugs.

hire ♦♢♢ /haɪər/ (hires, hiring, hired) ❶ V-T/V-I If you **hire** someone, you employ them or pay them to do a particular job for you. □ *Sixteen of the contestants have hired lawyers and are suing the organisers.* □ *He will be in charge of all hiring and firing at PHA.* ❷ V-T If you **hire** something, you pay money to the owner so that you can use it for a period of time. [mainly BRIT; AM usually **rent**] □ *To hire a car you must produce a passport and a current driving license.* ❸ N-UNCOUNT You use **hire** to refer to the activity or business of hiring something. [mainly BRIT; AM usually **rental**] □ *They booked our hotel, and organised car hire.* ❹ PHRASE If something is **for hire**, it is available for you to hire. [mainly BRIT; AM usually **for rent**] □ *Fishing tackle is available for hire and tuition can be arranged.*

Do not confuse **hire**, **rent**, and **let**. If you make a series of payments to use something for a long time, you say that you **rent** it. □ *...the apartment he had rented... He rented a TV.* You can say that you **rent** or **rent out** a house or room to someone when they pay you money to live there. □ *We rented our house to a college professor.* In British English, it is more common to say that you **let** it. □ *They were letting a room to a school teacher.* Americans also use **rent** when you pay a sum of money to use something for a short time. □ *He rented a car for the weekend.* In British English, if you pay a sum of money to use something for a short time, you usually say that you **hire** it. □ *He was unable to hire another car.* American English uses **hire** mainly to talk about giving jobs to people. □ *We hired a new waitress this week.*

▶**hire out** PHRASAL VERB If you **hire out** something such as a car or a person's services, you allow them to be used in return for payment. □ *Companies hiring out narrow boats report full order books.*

hire pur|chase N-UNCOUNT **Hire purchase** is a way of buying goods gradually. You make regular payments until you have paid the full price and the goods belong to you. The abbreviation **HP** is often used. [BRIT; AM usually **installment plan**] [oft N n] □ *...the serious problem of hire purchase and credit card debts.*

his ♦♦♦

The determiner is pronounced /hɪz/. The pronoun is pronounced /hɪz/.

His is a third person singular possessive determiner. **His** is also a possessive pronoun.

❶ DET You use **his** to indicate that something belongs or relates to a man, boy, or male animal. □ *Brian splashed water on his face, then brushed his teeth.* □ *He spent a large part of his career in Hollywood.* ● PRON-POSS **His** is also a possessive pronoun. □ *He had taken advice, but the decision was his.* ❷ DET In written English, **his** is sometimes used to refer to a person without saying whether that person is a man or a woman. Some people dislike this use and prefer to use "his or her" or "their." □ *Formerly, the relations between a teacher and his pupils were dominated by fear on the part of the pupils.* ● PRON-POSS **His** is also a possessive pronoun. □ *The student going to art or drama school will be even more enthusiastic about further education than the university student. His is not a narrow mind, but one eager to grasp every facet of anything he studies.*

His|pan|ic /hɪspænɪk/ (Hispanics) ADJ A **Hispanic** person is a citizen of the United States of America who originally came from Latin America, or whose family originally came from Latin America. □ *...a group of Hispanic doctors in*

낼 것 같은 가능성을 넌지시 비쳤다. ❸ 가산명사 조언 □ 여행을 더 수월하게 해 줄 조언 몇 가지가 여기에 있다. ❹ 단수명사 약간 □ 그녀는 진에 베르무트를 약간만 넣었다.

❶ 가산명사 엉덩이 □ 트레이시는 손을 엉덩이 위에 얹으며 한숨을 쉬었다. ❷ 가산명사 엉덩이 뼈 □ 결국 외과 의사들은 엉덩이뼈와 어깨뼈를 모두 교체했다. ❸ 형용사 최신 유행에 정통한, 멋진 [비격식체] □ 바짝 자른 금발 머리에 세련된 안경을 쓴 최신 유행에 정통한 젊은이 ❹ 감탄사 자자 (함성을 선도하는 소리) ❺ 구 즉각적인 행동을 하다, 생각 없이 행동하다 □ 판사들은 성급하게 결정을 내릴 필요가 없다. 그들은 충분히 생각하고 결정할 여유를 가지고 있다.

가산명사 히피

❶ 타동사/자동사 고용하다 □ 열여섯 명의 참가자들이 변호사를 고용하여 주최 측에 소송을 제기하고 있다. □ 그는 주택 관리국에서 모든 고용과 해고 업무를 맡을 것이다. ❷ 타동사 세내다, (요금을 내고 빌리다 [주로 영국영어; 미국영어 대개 rent] □ 자동차를 빌리기 위해서는 여권과 현재 유효한 운전면허증을 제시해야 한다. ❸ 불가산명사 임대 [주로 영국영어; 미국영어 대개 rental] □ 그들은 우리 호텔을 예약해 주고 자동차 임대까지 준비해 주었다. ❹ 구 임대용의 [주로 영국영어; 미국영어 대개 for rent] □ 낚시 도구는 임대 가능하고 강습도 받을 수 있다.

hire, rent, let을 혼동하지 않도록 하라. 장기간 어떤 것을 사용하기 위해 연속적으로 돈을 지불한다면, 그것을 rent한다고 표현한다. □ ...그가 세 낸 아파트... 그는 텔레비전을 빌렸다. 집이나 방을, 돈을 지불하고 거기서 살고자하는 사람에게 rent하거나 rent out한다고 쓸 수 있다. □ 우리는 대학 교수에게 집을 세놓았다. 영국 영어에서는 이럴 때 let을 쓰는 것이 더 일반적이다. □ 그들은 학교 교사에게 방을 세 놓고 있었다. 미국인들은 단기간 무엇을 사용하기 위해 돈을 지불할 때도 rent를 쓴다. □ 그는 주말 동안 차를 빌렸다. 영국 영어에서는 단기간 무엇을 사용하기 위해 돈을 지불할 때는, 대개 hire를 사용한다. □ 그는 차를 한 대 더 빌릴 수가 없었다. 미국 영어에서는 사람들을 일자리에 고용할 때 주로 hire를 쓴다. □ 우리는 이번 주에 새 여종업원을 고용했다.

구동사 임대하다 □ 운항용 거룻배 임대 회사들은 주문이 꽉 찼다고 말한다.

불가산명사 할부 구입 [영국영어; 미국영어 대개 installment plan] □ 할부 구입과 신용 카드 부채라는 심각한 문제

한정사는 /hɪz /로 발음되고, 대명사는 /hɪz /로 발음된다.

his는 3인칭 단수 소유한정사이며 소유대명사이기도 하다.

❶ 한정사 그의 □ 브라이언은 얼굴에 물을 끼얹고 나서 이를 닦았다. □ 그는 활동 기간 대부분을 할리우드에서 보냈다. ● 소유대명사 그의 것 □ 그가 조언을 받아들였지만 결정은 그 자신이 한 것이었다. ❷ 한정사 그 사람의 □ 이전에는 사제 관계가 주로 학생 측이 갖는 두려움에 의해 지배되었다. ● 소유대명사 그 사람의 것 □ 예술 학교나 연극 학교로 가는 학생은 일반 대학생보다 후속 교육에 대해서 더 열정적일 것이다. 그는 마음이 편협한 것이 아니라 배우는 내용의 모든 측면을 알고자 하는 열망이 있는 것이다.

형용사 라틴 아메리카 출신의, 히스패닉의 □ 워싱턴에 있는 라틴 아메리카 출신 의사 집단 ● 가산명사 라틴 아메리카 사람, 히스패닉 □ 식당에서 천한 일은 대부분

a b c d e f g h i j k l m n o p q r s t u v w x y z

A

Washington. • N-COUNT A **Hispanic** is someone who is Hispanic. ❑ *Most menial labour in the restaurant industry is done by Hispanics.*

히스패닉 계 사람들이 한다.

B

hiss /hɪs/ (**hisses, hissing, hissed**) **1** V-I To **hiss** means to make a sound like a long "s." ❑ *The tires of Lenny's bike hissed over the wet pavement as he slowed down.* ❑ *My cat hissed when I stepped on its tail.* • N-COUNT **Hiss** is also a noun. ❑ *...the hiss of water running into the burned pan.* • **hiss**|**ing** N-UNCOUNT ❑ *...a silence broken only by a steady hissing from above my head.* **2** V-I If people **hiss at** someone such as a performer or a person making a speech, they express their disapproval or dislike of that person by making long loud "s" sounds. ❑ *One had to listen hard to catch the words of the President's speech as the delegates booed and hissed.* • N-COUNT **Hiss** is also a noun. ❑ *After a moment the barracking began. First came hisses, then shouts.*

1 자동사 쉬이 하는 소리를 내다 ❑ 레니가 자전거 속도를 줄이자 바퀴가 젖은 노면 위를 구르며 쉬이 하는 소리를 냈다. ❑ 내가 꼬리를 밟자 우리 고양이가 쉬잇 하는 소리를 냈다. • 가산명사 쉬이 하는 소리 ❑ 탄 냄비 안으로 물이 흘러 들어가서 나는 쉬이 하는 소리 • 쉬이 하는 소리 불가산명사 ❑ 머리 위에서 쉬이 하고 나는 소리 외에는 아주 고요한 **2** 자동사 우우 하는 야유 ❑ 대표들이 야유를 해 대는 소리 때문에 대통령의 연설을 제대로 알아듣기 위해서는 귀를 바싹 기울여야 했다. • 가산명사 우우 하는 야유 ❑ 잠시 후에 야유가 나오기 시작했다. 처음에는 우우 하는 소리가 나왔으나, 곧 고함이 터져 나왔다.

C

D

E

his|**to**|**rian** /hɪstɔriən/ (**historians**) N-COUNT A **historian** is a person who specializes in the study of history, and who writes books and articles about it. →see **history**

가산명사 역사가, 사학자

F

his|**tor**|**ic** ◆◇◇ /hɪstɔrɪk, BRIT hɪstɒrɪk/ ADJ Something that is **historic** is important in history, or likely to be considered important at some time in the future. ❑ *...the historic changes in Eastern Europe.*

형용사 역사적인 ❑ 동유럽의 역사적으로 중요한 변화

G

his|**tori**|**cal** ◆◇◇ /hɪstɔrɪkᵊl, BRIT hɪstɒrɪkᵊl/ **1** ADJ **Historical** people, situations, or things existed in the past and are considered to be a part of history. [ADJ n] ❑ *...an important historical figure.* ❑ *...the historical impact of Western capitalism on the world.* • **his**|**tori**|**cal**|**ly** ADV ❑ *Historically, royal marriages have been cold, calculating affairs.* **2** ADJ **Historical** books, movies, or pictures describe or represent people, situations, or things that existed in the past. [ADJ n] ❑ *He is writing a historical novel about nineteenth-century France.* **3** ADJ **Historical** information, research, and discussion is related to the study of history. [ADJ n] ❑ *...historical records.*

1 형용사 역사의 ❑ 중요한 역사적 인물 ❑ 역사적으로 서구 자본주의가 세계에 끼친 영향 • 역사적으로 부사 ❑ 역사적으로 왕실의 결혼은 냉정하고 정략적으로 행해진 일이었다. **2** 형용사 역사에 근거한, 역사상의 ❑ 그는 19세기 프랑스에 관한 역사 소설을 쓰고 있다. **3** 형용사 역사에 관한 ❑ 역사 기록들

H

I

Word Partnership historical의 연어

N. historical **events**, historical **figure**, historical **impact**, historical **significance** **1**
historical **detail/fact**, historical **records**, historical **research** **3**

J

K

his|**to**|**ry** ◆◆◆ /hɪstəri, -tri/ (**histories**) **1** N-UNCOUNT You can refer to the events of the past as **history**. You can also refer to the past events which concern a particular topic or place as its history. ❑ *The Catholic Church has played a prominent role throughout Polish history.* ❑ *...the most evil mass killer in history.* • PHRASE Someone who **makes history** does something that is considered to be important and significant in the development of the world or of a particular society. ❑ *Willy Brandt made history by visiting East Germany in 1970.* • PHRASE If someone or something **goes down in history**, people in the future remember them because of particular actions that they have done or because of particular events that have happened. ❑ *Bradley will go down in history as Los Angeles' longest serving mayor.* **2** N-UNCOUNT **History** is a subject studied in schools, colleges, and universities that deals with events that have happened in the past. ❑ *...a lecturer in history at Birmingham University.* **3** N-COUNT A **history** is an account of events that have happened in the past. ❑ *...his magnificent history of broadcasting in Canada.* **4** N-COUNT If a person or a place has **a history of** something, it has been very common or has happened frequently in their past. ❑ *He had a history of drink problems.* **5** N-COUNT Someone's **history** is the set of facts that are known about their past. ❑ *He couldn't get a new job because of his medical history.* **6** PHRASE If you are telling someone about an event and say **the rest is history**, you mean that you do not need to tell them what happened next because everyone knows about it already. ❑ *We met at college, the rest is history.* →see Word Web: **history**

1 불가산명사 역사 ❑ 천주교회는 폴란드 전 역사상 큰 역할을 해 왔다. ❑ 역사상 가장 악독한 대량 학살자 • 구 역사적인 일을 하다 ❑ 빌리 브란트는 1970년에 동독을 방문하는 역사적인 일을 했다. • 구 역사에 남다 ❑ 브래들리는 로스앤젤레스 시장을 가장 오래 한 사람으로 역사에 남을 것이다. **2** 불가산명사 역사학 ❑ 버밍엄 대학의 역사학 강사 **3** 가산명사 연혁, 연대기 ❑ 그의 뛰어난 캐나다 방송사 **4** 가산명사 -의 전력 ❑ 그는 음주로 문제를 일으킨 전력이 있었다. **5** 가산명사 내력, 병력 ❑ 그는 병력 때문에 새로운 직장을 얻을 수가 없었다. **6** 구 나머지는 알려져 있는 그대로이다 ❑ 우리는 대학 때 만났고, 나머지는 알려져 있는 그대로이다.

L

M

N

O

P

Q

R

Word Partnership history의 연어

N. **the course of** history, **world** history **1**
family history **1** **5**
life history **5**
V. **go down in** history, **make** history **1**
teach history **2**

S

T

hit ◆◆◆ /hɪt/ (**hits, hitting**)

The form **hit** is used in the present tense and is the past and past participle.

hit은 현재, 과거 및 과거 분사로 쓴다.

U

V

1 V-T If you **hit** someone or something, you deliberately touch them with a lot of force, with your hand or an object held in your hand. ❑ *Find the exact grip that allows you to hit the ball hard.* **2** V-T When one thing **hits** another, it touches it with a lot of force. ❑ *The car had apparently hit a traffic sign before skidding out of control.* **3** V-T If a bomb or missile **hits** its target, it reaches it. ❑ *...multiple-warhead missiles that could hit many targets at a time.* • N-COUNT **Hit** is also a noun. ❑ *First a house took a direct hit and then the rocket exploded.* **4** V-T If something **hits** a person, place, or thing, it affects them very badly. [JOURNALISM] ❑ *The plan to charge motorists to use the freeway is going to hit me hard.* ❑ *About two hundred people died in the earthquake which hit northern Peru.* **5** V-T When a feeling or an idea **hits** you, it suddenly affects you or comes into your mind. ❑ *It hit me that I had a choice.* **6** V-T If you **hit** a particular high or low point on a scale of something such as success or health, you reach it. [JOURNALISM] ❑ *He admits to having hit the lowest point in his life.* **7** N-COUNT If a CD, movie, or play is a **hit**, it is very popular and successful. ❑ *The song became a massive hit in 1945.* **8** N-COUNT A **hit** is a single

1 타동사 때리다, 치다 ❑ 공을 강하게 칠 수 있도록 그립 위치를 정확히 잡아라. **2** 타동사 부딪치다, 충돌하다 ❑ 아마도 그 차가 미끄러지며 중심을 잃기 전에 교통 표지판에 부딪쳤던 듯하다. **3** 타동사 명중하다, 맞다 ❑ 한번에 여러 목표물을 맞출 수 있는 복수 탄두 미사일 • 가산명사 명중 ❑ 처음에 주택 한 채가 직격탄을 맞았고 그 다음에 로켓이 폭발하였다. **4** 타동사 타격을 주다, 영향을 끼치다 [언론] ❑ 고속도로를 이용하는 운전자들에게 통행료를 부과하는 계획은 내게 심한 타격을 줄 것이다. ❑ 북부 페루를 강타한 지진으로 약 200명의 사람들이 죽었다. **5** 타동사 -에게 문득 떠오르다 ❑ 나에게 선택권이 있다는 생각이 문득 떠올랐다. **6** 타동사 이르다, 도달하다 [언론] ❑ 그는 삶의 밑바닥까지 가 봤음을 인정한다. **7** 가산명사 성공하다, 히트 치다 ❑ 그

W

X

Y

Z

Word Web   history

3800 BC
The wheel is
invented.

31 BC
Roman Empire
founded.

1200 AD
Incan empire is
founded.

1969
Humans land
on the Moon.

2600 BC
The Pyramid of
Giza is built.

700 AD
The Great Wall of
China is started.

1492
Columbus sails for
America.

Open any history textbook and you will find **timelines**. They show important dates for **ancient civilizations**—when **empires** appeared and disappeared, and when **wars** were fought. But, how much of what we read in **history** books is **fact**? **Accounts** of the **past** are often based on how archeologists interpret the **artifacts** they find. **Scholars** often rely on the **records** of the people who were in power. These **historians** included certain facts and left out others. Historians today look beyond official records. They research primary source **documents** such as **diaries**. They describe **events** from different **points of view**.

visit to a website. [COMPUTING] ❑ *Our small company has had 78,000 hits on its Internet pages.* **9** N-COUNT If someone who is searching for information on the Internet gets a **hit**, they find a website where there is that information. **10** PHRASE If two people **hit it off**, they like each other and become friendly as soon as they meet. [INFORMAL] ❑ *They hit it off straight away, Daddy and Walter.* **11** to **hit the headlines** →see **headline**. to **hit home** →see **home**. to **hit the nail on the head** →see **nail**. to **hit the roof** →see **roof**

Thesaurus   hit의 참조어

v.   bang, beat, knock, pound, slap, smack, strike **1**
N.   success, triumph; *(ant.)* failure **7**

▶**hit on** or **hit upon** **1** PHRASAL VERB If you **hit on** an idea or a solution to a problem, or **hit upon** it, you think of it. ❑ *After running through the numbers in every possible combination, we finally hit on a solution.* **2** PHRASAL VERB If someone **hits on** you, they speak or behave in a way that shows they want to have a sexual relationship with you. [INFORMAL] ❑ *She was hitting on me and I was surprised and flattered.*

Word Partnership   hit의 연어

N.   hit **a ball**, hit **a button**, hit **the brakes 1**
earthquakes/famine/storms hit *someplace* **4**
a hit *movie/show/song* **7**

hit-and-run **1** ADJ A **hit-and-run** accident is an accident in which the driver of a vehicle hits someone and then drives away without stopping. [ADJ n] ❑ *...the victim of a hit-and-run accident.* **2** ADJ A **hit-and-run** attack on an enemy position relies on surprise and speed for its success. [ADJ n] ❑ *The rebels appear to be making hit-and-run guerrilla style attacks on military targets.*

hitch /hɪtʃ/ (**hitches, hitching, hitched**) **1** N-COUNT A **hitch** is a slight problem or difficulty which causes a short delay. ❑ *After some technical hitches the show finally got under way.* **2** V-T/V-I If you **hitch, hitch** a lift, or **hitch** a ride, you hitchhike. [INFORMAL] ❑ *There was no garage in sight, so I hitched a lift into town.* **3** V-T If you **hitch** something **to** something else, you hook it or fasten it there. ❑ *Last night we hitched the horse to the cart and moved here.*

hitch|hike /hɪtʃhaɪk/ (**hitchhikes, hitchhiking, hitchhiked**) V-I If you **hitchhike**, you travel by getting lifts from passing vehicles without paying. ❑ *Neff hitchhiked to New York during his Christmas vacation.* ● **hitch|hiker** (**hitchhikers**) N-COUNT ❑ *On my way to Vancouver one Friday night I picked up a hitchhiker.*

hi tech →see **high-tech**

hither|to /hɪðərtu/ ADV You use **hitherto** to indicate that something was true up until the time you are talking about, although it may no longer be the case. [FORMAL] ❑ *The polytechnics have hitherto been at an unfair disadvantage in competing for pupils and money.*

hit list (**hit lists**) **1** N-COUNT If someone has a **hit list of** people or things, they are intending to take action concerning those people or things. ❑ *Some banks also have a hit list of people whom they threaten to sue for damages.* **2** N-COUNT A **hit list** is a list that someone makes of people they intend to have killed. ❑ *...a group of killers instructed by the deputy minister to attack people on his hit list.*

HIV ♦◇◇ /eɪtʃ aɪ viː/ **1** N-UNCOUNT **HIV** is a virus which reduces people's resistance to illness and can cause AIDS. **HIV** is an abbreviation for "human immunodeficiency virus." **2** PHRASE If someone is **HIV positive**, they are infected with the HIV virus, and may develop AIDS. If someone is **HIV negative**, they are not infected with the virus.

노래는 1945년에 엄청난 히트를 쳤다. **8** 가산명사 조회수 [컴퓨터] ❑ 우리 작은 회사의 인터넷 홈페이지는 7만 8천 번의 조회수를 기록했다. **9** 가산명사 찾고자 하던 웹사이트 **10** 구 보자마자 죽이 맞다 [비격식체] ❑ 아버지와 월터는 처음부터 죽이 맞았다.

1 구동사 생각나다, 떠오르다 ❑ 모든 가능한 숫자의 조합을 다 살펴본 후에 마침내 해결책이 떠올랐다. **2** 구동사 추파를 던지다 [비격식체] ❑ 그녀가 계속 내게 추파를 던져서 나는 놀랍기도 하고 우쭐하기도 했다.

1 형용사 뺑소니의 ❑ 뺑소니 사고 피해자 **2** 형용사 치고 빠지는 ❑ 반군은 군사 목표물을 대상으로 치고 빠지는 게릴라식 공격을 하고 있는 것으로 보인다.

1 가산명사 문제, 장애 ❑ 몇 번의 기술적인 문제가 있은 후에 마침내 쇼가 시작됐다. **2** 타동사/자동사 히치하이크를 하다, 지나가는 차에 편승하다 [비격식체] ❑ 근방에 정비소가 보이지 않아 나는 시내까지 히치하이크를 했다. **3** 타동사 매다, 걸다 ❑ 지난밤 우리는 마차에 말을 메고 여기로 옮겨 왔다.

자동사 히치하이크를 하다, 편승하다 ❑ 네프는 크리스마스 휴가 때 뉴욕까지 히치하이크를 했다. ● 자동차 편승자 가산명사 ❑ 나는 어느 금요일 밤 밴쿠버로 가는 길에 한 사람을 편승시켜 주었다.

부사 지금까지는 [격식체] ❑ 기술 대학들은 학생 모집 및 재정적인 경쟁에서 지금까지는 부당하게 불리한 입장이었다.

1 가산명사 정리 대상 명단, 정리 대상 사항 ❑ 일부 은행들은 그들이 손해 배상 소송을 하겠다고 위협하는 대상자들로 구성된 정리 대상자 명단도 가지고 있다. **2** 가산명사 히치명단을 하다, 편승하다 ❑ 자기의 살해 대상 명단에 있는 사람들을 공격하라는 차관의 지시를 받은 일단의 살인 청부업자들

1 불가산명사 인체 면역 결핍 바이러스 **2** 구 에이치 아이 브이 양성이다; 에이치 아이 브이 음성이다

A

hive /haɪv/ (hives, hiving, hived) **1** N-COUNT A **hive** is a structure in which bees are kept, which is designed so that the beekeeper can collect the honey that they produce. **2** N-COUNT If you describe a place as a **hive of** activity, you approve of the fact that there is a lot of activity there or that people are busy working there. [APPROVAL] ❑ *In the morning the house was a hive of activity.*

1 가산명사 꿀벌통 **2** 가산명사 북새통, (활동) 중심지 [마음에 듦] ❑ 아침이면 집은 북새통이었다.

B

▶**hive off** PHRASAL VERB If someone **hives off** part of a business, they transfer it to new ownership, usually by selling it. [mainly BRIT] ❑ *Klockner plans to hive off its loss-making steel businesses.*

구동사 매각 처분하다 [주로 영국영어] ❑ 크록크너는 손실을 내는 철강 사업체들을 매각 처분할 계획이다.

C

hoard /hɔrd/ (hoards, hoarding, hoarded) **1** V-T/V-I If you **hoard** things such as food or money, you save or store them, often in secret, because they are valuable or important to you. ❑ *They've begun to hoard food and gasoline and save their money.* **2** N-COUNT A **hoard** is a store of things that you have saved and that are valuable or important to you or you do not want other people to have. ❑ *The case involves a hoard of silver and jewels valued at up to $40m.*

1 타동사/자동사 모아 두다, 저장하다 ❑ 그들은 식품과 휘발유를 몰래 축적하고 돈을 저축하기 시작했다. **2** 가산명사 비축물, 저장물, 비장(秘藏) ❑ 그 사건은 4천만 달러에 달하는 비장의 은과 보석이 관련되어 있다.

D

E

hoard|ing /hɔrdɪŋ/ (hoardings) N-COUNT A **hoarding** is a very large board at the side of a road or on the side of a building, which is used for displaying advertisements and posters. [BRIT; AM billboard] ❑ *An advertising hoarding on the platform caught her attention.*

가산명사 간판 [영국영어; 미국영어 billboard] ❑ 플랫폼의 간판이 그녀의 주의를 끌었다.

F

hoarse /hɔrs/ (hoarser, hoarsest) ADJ If your voice is **hoarse** or if you are **hoarse**, your voice sounds rough and unclear, for example because your throat is sore. ❑ *"So what do you think?" she said in a hoarse whisper.* ● **hoarse|ly** ADV ❑ *"Thank you," Maria said hoarsely.*

형용사 목쉰, 쉰 목소리의 ❑ "그럼, 당신은 어떻게 생각합니까?"라고 그녀가 목쉰 소리로 속삭였다. ● 쉰 목소리로 부사 ❑ "고맙습니다."라고 마리아가 쉰 목소리로 말했다.

G

hoax /hoʊks/ (hoaxes) N-COUNT A **hoax** is a trick in which someone tells people a lie, for example that there is a bomb somewhere when there is not, or that a picture is genuine when it is not. ❑ *He denied making the hoax call but was convicted after a short trial.*

가산명사 거짓, 속임 ❑ 그는 거짓 전화한 것을 부인했으나 간단한 재판 후 유죄 선고를 받았다.

H

hob /hɒb/ (hobs) N-COUNT A **hob** is a surface on top of a cooker or set into a work surface, which can be heated in order to cook things on it. [BRIT; AM burner] ❑ *Put the pan on the hob, add the flour and cook for 1 minute.*

가산명사 열판 [영국영어; 미국영어 burner] ❑ 프라이팬을 열판 위에 올려놓고 밀가루를 넣고 1분간 조리하시오.

I

hob|ble /hɒbºl/ (hobbles, hobbling, hobbled) V-I If you **hobble**, you walk in an awkward way with small steps, for example because your foot is injured. ❑ *He got up slowly and hobbled over to the coffee table.*

자동사 절뚝거리다 ❑ 그는 천천히 일어나서 절뚝거리며 커피 탁자로 갔다.

J

hob|by /hɒbi/ (hobbies) N-COUNT A **hobby** is an activity that you enjoy doing in your spare time. ❑ *My hobbies are letter writing, music, photography, and tennis.*

가산명사 취미 ❑ 내 취미는 편지 쓰기, 음악, 사진, 테니스 등이다.

K

Thesaurus	hobby의 참조어
N.	activity, craft, interest, pastime

L

hock|ey /hɒki/ **1** N-UNCOUNT **Hockey** is a game played on ice between two teams of 11 players who use long curved sticks to hit a small rubber disk, called a puck, and try to score goals. [mainly AM; BRIT usually ice hockey] ❑ *...a new hockey arena.* **2** N-UNCOUNT **Hockey** is an outdoor game played between two teams of 11 players who use long curved sticks to hit a small ball and try to score goals. [mainly BRIT; AM usually field hockey] ❑ *She played hockey for the national side.*

1 불가산명사 아이스하키 [주로 미국영어; 영국영어 대개 ice hockey] ❑ 새 아이스하키 경기장 **2** 불가산명사 하키 [주로 영국영어; 미국영어 대개 field hockey] ❑ 그녀는 국가 대표팀 하키 선수였다.

M

N

hoe /hoʊ/ (hoes, hoeing, hoed) **1** N-COUNT A **hoe** is a gardening tool with a long handle and a small square blade, which you use to remove small weeds and break up the surface of the soil. **2** V-T If you **hoe** a field or crop, you use a hoe on the weeds or soil there. ❑ *I have to feed the chickens and hoe the potatoes.*

1 가산명사 괭이 **2** 타동사 괭이질하다 ❑ 나는 닭 모이를 주고 괭이로 감자를 캐야 한다.

O

P

hog /hɔg, BRIT hɒg/ (hogs, hogging, hogged) **1** N-COUNT A **hog** is a pig. In American English, **hog** can refer to any kind of pig, but in British English, it usually refers to a large male pig that has been castrated. ❑ *We picked the corn by hand and we fed it to the hogs and the cows.* **2** V-T If you **hog** something, you take all of it in a greedy or impolite way. [INFORMAL] ❑ *Have you done hogging the bathroom?* **3** PHRASE If you **go the whole hog**, you do something bold or extravagant in the most complete way possible. [INFORMAL] ❑ *Well, I thought, I've already lost half my job, I might as well go the whole hog and lose it completely.*

1 가산명사 돼지, (영국 영어) 거세한 수퇘지 ❑ 우리는 손으로 옥수수를 따서 돼지와 소에게 먹였다. **2** 타동사 제 몫 이상을 갖다 [비격식체] ❑ 이제야 화장실 다 썼니? **3** 구 갈 데까지 가다 [비격식체] ❑ 글쎄, 나는 이미 직장을 반쯤 잃었다고 생각했지. 갈 데까지 가 보고 완전히 잃는 편이 나을지도 모르겠어.

Q

R

hoist /hɔɪst/ (hoists, hoisting, hoisted) **1** V-T If you **hoist** something heavy somewhere, you lift it or pull it up there. ❑ *Hoisting my suitcase on to my shoulder, I turned and headed toward my hotel.* **2** V-T If something heavy **is hoisted** somewhere, it is lifted there using a machine such as a crane. ❑ *A twenty-foot steel pyramid is to be hoisted into position on top of the tower.* **3** N-COUNT A **hoist** is a machine for lifting heavy things. ❑ *He uses a hydraulic hoist to unload two empty barrels.* **4** V-T If you **hoist** a flag or a sail, you pull it up to its correct position by using ropes. ❑ *A group forced their way through police cordons and hoisted their flag on top of the disputed monument.*

1 타동사 들어올리다 ❑ 여행 가방을 어깨에 올려 메고 나는 돌아서서 호텔로 향했다. **2** 타동사 들어올려지다 ❑ 20피트짜리 철제 피라미드가 탑 꼭대기에 올라앉혀질 것이다. **3** 가산명사 들어올리는 장치, 호이스트 ❑ 그는 유압 호이스트를 사용하여 비어 있는 두 개의 큰 통을 내린다. **4** 타동사 감아올리다 ❑ 한 무리의 사람들이 경찰 저지선을 뚫고 나아가서 문제의 기념비 꼭대기에 그들의 깃발을 세웠다.

S

T

U

hold
① PHYSICALLY TOUCHING, SUPPORTING, OR CONTAINING
② HAVING OR DOING
③ CONTROLLING OR REMAINING
④ PHRASES
⑤ PHRASAL VERBS

V

W

X

① **hold** ♦♦♦ /hoʊld/ (holds, holding, held) **1** V-T When you **hold** something, you carry or support it, using your hands or your arms. ❑ *Hold the knife at an angle.* ● N-COUNT **Hold** is also a noun. ❑ *He released his hold on the camera.* **2** N-UNCOUNT **Hold** is used in expressions such as **grab hold of**, **catch hold of**, and **get hold of**, to indicate that you close your hand tightly around something, for example to stop something moving or falling. ❑ *I was woken up by someone grabbing hold of my sleeping bag.* ❑ *A doctor and a nurse caught hold of his arms.* **3** V-T When you **hold** someone, you put your arms around them, usually

1 타동사 (손에) 들다, 갖고 있다 ❑ 나이프를 비스듬히 들어라. ● 가산명사 잡음 ❑ 그가 카메라를 잡은 손을 놓았다. **2** 불가산명사 -을 꽉 잡다 ❑ 나는 누군가가 내 침낭을 꽉 잡아서 잠을 깼다. ❑ 의사와 간호사가 그의 양팔을 꽉 잡았다. **3** 타동사 껴안다 ❑ 그가 그녀를 꼭 끌어안기만 한다면 좋을 텐데. **4** 타동사 붙잡아 놓다 ❑ 그는 그런 다음 경찰이 도착할 때까지 그 남자의 팔을 조른 채 붙잡고 있었다. **5** 가산명사 붙잡음 ❑ 그

Y

Z

because you want to show them how much you like them or because you want to comfort them. ❑ *If only he would hold her close to him.* ◳ V-T If you **hold** someone in a particular position, you use force to keep them in that position and stop them from moving. ❑ *He then held the man in an armlock until police arrived.* ❺ N-COUNT A **hold** is a particular way of keeping someone in a position using your own hands, arms, or legs. ❑ *The man wrestled the Indian to the ground, locked in a hold he couldn't escape.* ❻ V-T When you **hold** a part of your body, you put your hand on or against it, often because it hurts. ❑ *Soon she was crying bitterly about the pain and was holding her throat.* ❼ V-T When you **hold** a part of your body in a particular position, you put it into that position and keep it there. ❑ *Hold your hands in front of your face.* ❽ V-T If one thing **holds** another in a particular position, it keeps it in that position. ❑ *...the wooden wedge which held the heavy door open.* ❾ V-T If one thing is used to **hold** another, it is used to store it. ❑ *Two knife racks hold her favorite knives.* ❿ N-COUNT In a ship or airplane, a **hold** is a place where cargo or luggage is stored. ❑ *A fire had been reported in the cargo hold.* ⓫ V-T If a place **holds** something, it keeps it available for reference or for future use. ❑ *The Small Firms Service holds an enormous amount of information on any business problem.* ⓬ V-T If something **holds** a particular amount of something, it can contain that amount. [no cont] ❑ *One CD-ROM disk can hold over 100,000 pages of text.*

Thesaurus
hold의 참조어

v. carry, support ① ❶
cradle, embrace, hug ① ❸
hang on to, restrain ① ❹

---

② **hold** ♦♦♦ /houɪd/ (**holds, holding, held**)

Hold is often used to indicate that someone or something has the particular thing, characteristic, or attitude that is mentioned. Therefore it takes most of its meaning from the word that follows it.

❶ V-T **Hold** is used with words and expressions indicating an opinion or belief, to show that someone has a particular opinion or believes that something is true. [no cont] ❑ *He held firm opinions which usually conflicted with my own.* ❑ *Current thinking holds that obesity is more a medical than a psychological problem.* ❷ V-T **Hold** is used with words such as "fear" or "mystery" to indicate someone's feelings toward something, as if those feelings were a characteristic of the thing itself. [no passive] ❑ *Death doesn't hold any fear for me.* ❸ V-T **Hold** is used with nouns such as "office," "power," and "responsibility" to indicate that someone has a particular position of power or authority. ❑ *She has never held ministerial office.* ❹ V-T **Hold** is used with nouns such as "permit," "degree," or "ticket" to indicate that someone has a particular document that allows them to do something. ❑ *Applicants should normally hold a good Honours degree.* ❑ *He did not hold a firearm certificate.* ❺ V-T **Hold** is used with nouns such as "party," "meeting," "talks," "election," and "trial" to indicate that people are organizing a particular activity. ❑ *The country will hold democratic elections within a year.* ● **hold**ing N-UNCOUNT ❑ *They also called for the holding of multi-party general elections.* ❻ V-RECIP **Hold** is used with nouns such as "conversation," "interview," and "talks" to indicate that two or more people meet and discuss something. ❑ *The Prime Minister is holding consultations with his colleagues to finalise the deal.* ❑ *The engineer and his son held frequent consultations concerning technical problems.* ❼ V-T **Hold** is used with nouns such as "shares" and "stock" to indicate that someone owns a particular proportion of a business. ❑ *The group said it continues to hold 1,774,687 Vons shares.* →see also **holding** ❽ V-T **Hold** is used with nouns such as "attention" or "interest" to indicate that what you do or say keeps someone interested or listening to you. ❑ *If you want to hold someone's attention, look them directly in the eye but don't stare.* ❾ V-T If you **hold** someone responsible, liable, or accountable for something, you will blame them if anything goes wrong. ❑ *It's impossible to hold any individual responsible.*

③ **hold** ♦♦♦ /houɪd/ (**holds, holding, held**) ❶ V-T If someone **holds** you in a place, they keep you there as a prisoner and do not allow you to leave. ❑ *The inside of a van was as good a place as any to hold a kidnap victim.* ❑ *Somebody is holding your wife hostage.* ❷ V-T If people such as an army or a violent crowd **hold** a place, they control it by using force. ❑ *Demonstrators have been holding the square since Sunday.* ❸ N-SING If you have a **hold over** someone, you have power or control over them, for example because you know something about them which you can use to threaten them or because you are in a position of authority. ❑ *He had ordered his officers to keep an exceptionally firm hold over their men.* ❹ V-T/V-I If you ask someone to **hold**, or to **hold the line**, when you are answering a telephone call, you are asking them to wait for a short time, for example so that you can find the person they want to speak to. [no passive] ❑ *Could you hold the line and I'll just get my pen.* ❺ V-T If you **hold** telephone calls for someone, you do not allow people who phone to speak to that person, but take messages instead. ❑ *He tells his secretary to hold his calls.* ❻ V-T/V-I If something **holds** at a particular value or level, or **is held** there, it is kept at that value or level. ❑ *OPEC production is holding at around 21.5 million barrels a day.* ❼ V-T If you **hold** a sound or musical note, you continue making it. ❑ *...a voice which hit and held every note with perfect ease and clarity.* ❽ V-T If you **hold** something such as a train or an elevator, you delay it. ❑ *A London Underground spokesman defended the decision to hold the train until police arrived.* ❾ V-I If an offer or invitation still **holds**, it is still available for you to accept. ❑ *Does your offer still hold?* ❿ V-I If a good situation **holds**, it continues and does not get worse or fail. ❑ *Our luck couldn't hold forever.* ⓫ V-I If an argument or theory **holds**, it is true or valid, even after close examination. ❑ *Today, most people think that argument no longer holds.* ● PHRASAL VERB **Hold up** means the same as **hold**. ❑ *Democrats say arguments against the bill won't hold up.* ⓬ V-I If part of a structure **holds**, it does not fall or break although there is a lot of force or pressure on it. ❑ *How long would the roof hold?* ⓭ V-I If

---

남자는 인디언을 땅에 넘어뜨려 꼼짝 못하게 꽉 붙잡았다. ❻ 타동사 -을 움켜쥐다 ❑ 곧 그녀가 아파서 몹시 울며 목을 움켜쥐었다. ❼ 타동사 (몸의 일부를 어떤 자세로) 두다 ❑ 손을 얼굴 앞에 두어라. ❽ 타동사 지탱하다 ❑ 묵직한 문이 열려 있게 지탱하고 있는 나무 쐐기 ❾ 타동사 담고 있다, 지니고 있다 ❑ 칼 시렁 두 개에 그녀가 좋아하는 칼들이 꽂혀 있다. ❿ 가산명사 짐칸 ❑ 짐칸에서 화재가 났다는 보고가 있었다. ⓫ 타동사 보유하다 ❑ 소기업 서비스에는 어떤 사업상의 문제에 대해서도 엄청난 양의 정보가 마련되어 있다. ⓬ 타동사 수용하다, 담고 있다 ❑ 시디롬 디스크 한 장에는 10만 쪽 이상 분량의 문서를 담을 수 있다.

---

hold는 사람 또는 사물이 언급되는 특정한 무엇, 특징, 태도를 소유하고 있음을 나타낼 때 쓴다. 그래서 hold는 뒤에 오는 단어로부터 대부분의 의미를 취한다.

❶ 타동사 (견해 등을) 가지고 있다 ❑ 그는 통상 나와는 상충되는 확고한 의견을 가지고 있었다. ❑ 요즘 견해에 따르면 비만은 심리적 문제라기보다 의학적 문제라고 한다. ❷ 타동사 (어떤 느낌을) 주다 ❑ 죽음은 나에게 어떤 두려움도 주지 않는다. ❸ 타동사 (권력 등을) 차지하다 ❑ 그녀는 한번도 장관직에 앉은 적이 없다. ❹ 타동사 소지하다, 갖다 ❑ 지원자는 대개 상급 우등 학위를 소지해야 한다. ❑ 그는 화기 소지 면허를 갖고 있지 않았다. ❺ 타동사 (파티 등을) 열다 ❑ 그 나라는 일년 안에 민주적 선거를 실시할 것이다. ● 실시 불가산명사 ❑ 그들은 다당 총선거 실시도 요구했다. ❻ 상호동사 (인터뷰 등을) 하다 ❑ 수상은 그 협정을 결말짓기 위해 동료들과 협의를 하고 있다. ❑ 기술자와 그의 아들은 기술적인 문제에 대해 자주 협의를 했다. ❼ 타동사 보유하다 ❑ 그 그룹은 본즈 주식 1,774,687주를 계속 보유한다고 말했다. ❽ 타동사 (주의 등을) 끌다 ❑ 누군가의 주의를 끌고 싶으면 그 사람의 눈을 똑바로 보되 너무 빤히 쳐다보지는 말아라. ❾ 타동사 (책임 등을) 지게 하다 ❑ 어떤 개인에게 책임지게 하는 것은 불가능하다.

---

❶ 타동사 억류하다 ❑ 밴의 내부는 유괴된 사람을 억류하기에 어떤 장소보다도 좋았다. ❑ 누군가가 당신 부인을 인질로 잡고 있다. ❷ 타동사 점거하다 ❑ 시위자들이 일요일부터 광장을 점거하고 있다. ❸ 단수명사 지배, 통제 ❑ 그는 장교들에게 각자 병사들에 대해 확고한 지휘권을 유지하도록 명령했다. ❹ 타동사/자동사 끊지 않고 기다리다 ❑ 끊지 말고 기다리시면 펜을 가져오겠습니다. ❺ 타동사 (전화를) 대신 받다 ❑ 그는 비서에게 자기 전화를 대신 받게 시킨다. ❻ 타동사/자동사 (수준을) 유지하다 ❑ 오펙 생산이 하루에 2,150만 배럴 정도를 유지하고 있다. ❼ 타동사 (음을) 지속시키다 ❑ 모든 음을 더할 나위 없이 수월하고 깨끗하게 지속적으로 내는 목소리 ❽ 타동사 지체시키다 ❑ 런던 지하철 대변인은 경찰이 도착할 때까지 열차를 지체시킨 결정을 옹호했다. ❾ 자동사 유효하다 ❑ 당신의 제안이 아직 유효한가요? ❿ 자동사 지속되다 ❑ 우리의 행운이 영원히 지속될 수는 없었다. ⓫ 자동사 타당하다 ❑ 오늘날 대부분의 사람들은 그 주장이 더 이상 타당하지 않다고 생각한다. ● 구.동사 타당하다 ❑ 민주당원들은 그 법안에 반대하는 주장들이 타당하지 않다고 말한다. ⓬ 자동사 지탱하다, 견디다 ❑ 지붕이 얼마나 오래 견딜까요? ⓭ 자동사 적용되다 ❑ 이런 법률들은 대학에도 적용된다. ⓮ 자동사 고수하다, 지키다 [격식체] ❑ 대통령이 이 약속을 지킬 수 있을 것인가? ⓯ 타동사 (약속 등을) 지키게 하다 ❑ "나는 당신을 그와 결혼하게 하지 않을 거요." "그 약속 안 어기게 할게요."

laws or rules **hold**, they exist and remain in force. ❑ *These laws also hold for universities.* ⑭ V-I If you **hold to** a promise or to high standards of behavior, you keep that promise or continue to behave according to those standards. [FORMAL] ❑ *Will the President be able to hold to this commitment?* ⑮ V-T If someone or something **holds** you **to** a promise or **to** high standards of behavior, they make you keep that promise or those standards. ❑ *"I won't make you marry him."* — *"I'll hold you to that."*

④ **hold** ♦♦♦ /hoʊld/ (**holds, holding, held**) →Please look at category ⑬ to see if the expression you are looking for is shown under another headword.
❶ PHRASE If you **hold forth on** a subject, you speak confidently and for a long time about it, especially to a group of people. ❑ *Barry was holding forth on something.* ❷ PHRASE If you **get hold of** an object or information, you obtain it, usually after some difficulty. ❑ *It is hard to get hold of guns in this country.* ❸ PHRASE If you **get hold of** a fact or a subject, you learn about it and understand it well. [BRIT, INFORMAL] ❑ *He first had to get hold of some basic facts.* ❹ PHRASE If you **get hold of** someone, you manage to contact them. ❑ *The only electrician we could get hold of was miles away.* ❺ CONVENTION If you say **"Hold it,"** you are telling someone to stop what they are doing and to wait. ❑ *Hold it! Don't move!* ❻ PHRASE If you put something **on hold**, you decide not to do it, deal with it, or change it now, but to leave it until later. ❑ *He put his retirement on hold to work 16 hours a day, seven days a week to find a solution.* ❼ PHRASE If you **hold your own**, you are able to resist someone who is attacking or opposing you. ❑ *The Frenchman held his own against the challenger.* ❽ PHRASE If you can do something well enough to **hold your own**, you do not appear foolish when you are compared with someone who is generally thought to be very good at it. ❑ *She can hold her own against almost any player.* ❾ PHRASE If you **hold still**, you do not move. ❑ *Can't you hold still for a second?* ❿ PHRASE If something **takes hold**, it gains complete control or influence over a person or thing. ❑ *She felt a strange excitement taking hold of her.* ⓫ PHRASE If you **hold tight**, you put your hand around or against something in order to prevent yourself from falling over. A bus driver might say "Hold tight!" to you if you are standing on a bus when it is about to move. ❑ *He held tight to the rope.* ⓬ PHRASE If you **hold tight**, you do not immediately start a course of action that you have been planning or thinking about. ❑ *The unions have circulated their branches, urging members to hold tight until a national deal is struck.* ⓭ to **hold** something **at bay** →see **bay**. to **hold** something **in check** →see **check**. to **hold fast** →see **fast**. to **hold the fort** →see **fort**. to **hold** your **ground** →see **ground**. to **hold** someone **to ransom** →see **ransom**. to **hold sway** →see **sway**

⑤ **hold** ♦♦♦ /hoʊld/ (**holds, holding, held**)

▶**hold against** PHRASAL VERB If you **hold** something **against** someone, you let their actions in the past influence your present attitude toward them and cause you to deal severely or unfairly with them. ❑ *Bernstein lost the case, but never held it against Grundy.*

▶**hold back** ❶ PHRASAL VERB If you **hold back** or if something **holds** you **back**, you hesitate before you do something because you are not sure whether it is the right thing to do. ❑ *The Bush administration had several reasons for holding back.* ❷ PHRASAL VERB To **hold** someone or something **back** means to prevent someone from doing something, or to prevent something from happening. ❑ *Stagnation in home sales is holding back economic recovery.* ❸ PHRASAL VERB If you **hold** something **back**, you keep it in reserve to use later. ❑ *Farmers apparently hold back produce in the hope that prices will rise.* ❹ PHRASAL VERB If you **hold** something **back**, you do not include it in the information you are giving about something. ❑ *You seem to be holding something back.* ❺ PHRASAL VERB If you **hold back** something such as tears or laughter, or if you **hold back**, you make an effort to stop yourself from showing how you feel. ❑ *She kept trying to hold back her tears.*

▶**hold down** ❶ PHRASAL VERB If you **hold down** a job or a place on a team, you manage to keep it. ❑ *He never could hold down a job.* ❷ PHRASAL VERB If you **hold** someone **down**, you keep them under control and do not allow them to have much freedom or power or many rights. ❑ *Everyone thinks there is some vast conspiracy wanting to hold down the younger generation.*

▶**hold off** ❶ PHRASAL VERB If you **hold off** doing something, you delay doing it or delay making a decision about it. ❑ *The hospital staff held off taking Rosenbaum in for an X-ray.* ❷ PHRASAL VERB If you **hold off** a challenge in a race or competition, you do not allow someone to pass you. ❑ *Between 1987 and 1990, Steffi Graf largely held off Navratilova's challenge for the crown.*

▶**hold on** or **hold onto** ❶ PHRASAL VERB If you **hold on**, or **hold onto** something, you keep your hand on it or around it, for example to prevent the thing from falling or to support yourself. ❑ *His right arm was extended up beside his head, still holding on to a coffee cup.* ❑ *He was struggling to hold onto a rock on the face of the cliff.* ❷ PHRASAL VERB If you **hold on**, you manage to achieve success or avoid failure in spite of great difficulties or opposition. ❑ *This Government deserved to lose power a year ago. It held on.* ❸ PHRASAL VERB If you ask someone to **hold on**, you are asking them to wait for a short time. [SPOKEN] ❑ *The manager asked him to hold on while he investigated.*

▶**hold out** ❶ PHRASAL VERB If you **hold out** your hand or something you have in your hand, you move your hand away from your body, for example to shake hands with someone. ❑ *"I'm Nancy Drew," she said, holding out her hand.* ❷ PHRASAL VERB If you **hold out for** something, you refuse to accept something which you do not think is good enough or large enough, and you continue to demand more. ❑ *I should have held out for a better deal.* ❸ PHRASAL VERB If you say that someone **is holding out** on you, you think that they are refusing to give you information that you want. [INFORMAL] ❑ *He had always believed that kids could sense it when you held out on them.* ❹ PHRASAL VERB If you **hold out**, you manage to resist an enemy or opponent in difficult circumstances and refuse

❶ 구 장황하게 지껄이다 ❑ 배리는 무엇인가에 대해 장황하게 지껄이고 있었다. ❷ 구 -을 손에 넣다 ❑ 이 나라에서는 총기를 입수하기가 어렵다. ❸ 구 -을 파악하다 [영국영어, 비격식체] ❑ 그는 우선 몇 가지 기본적인 사실들을 파악해야 했다. ❹ 구 -와 연락하다 ❑ 우리가 연락할 수 있는 유일한 전기 기사는 몇 마일 떨어져 있었다. ❺ 관용 표현 꼼짝 마 있어 / 멈춰 있어! 움직이지 마! ❻ 구 보류 상태로 ❑ 그는 퇴직을 보류하고 해결책을 찾기 위하여 하루 16시간씩 일주일에 7일 일한다. ❼ 구 지지 않고 버티다 ❑ 그 프랑스인은 도전자에 지지 않고 버텼다. ❽ 구 뒤지지 않다, 굴하지 않다 ❑ 그녀는 거의 어떤 선수에도 뒤지지 않는다. ❾ 구 가만히 있다 ❑ 잠깐만 가만히 있을 수 없니? ❿ 구 장악하다, 사로잡다 ❑ 그녀는 자기를 사로잡는 묘한 흥분을 느꼈다. ⓫ 구 꽉 잡다; 꽉 잡으세요! ❑ 그는 로프를 꽉 잡았다. ⓬ 구 때를 기다리다 ❑ 노동조합들은 각 지부를 순회하며 전국적인 협정이 타결될 때까지 회원들에게 때를 기다리도록 권고했다.

구동사 ...은 이유로 -을 원망하다 ❑ 번스타인은 소송에서 졌으나 그 때문에 그룬디를 원망하지는 않았다.

❶ 구동사 망설이다; 망설이게 하다 ❑ 부시 행정부가 망설이는 데는 여러 가지 이유가 있었다. ❷ 구동사 방해하다, 제지하다 ❑ 내수 판매의 침체가 경제 회복을 가로막고 있다. ❸ 구동사 비축해 두다 ❑ 농민들이 값이 오르리라는 기대에 농산물을 비축해 두고 있는 것이 분명하다. ❹ 구동사 숨기다 ❑ 당신은 무엇인가를 숨기고 있는 것처럼 보인다. ❺ 구동사 억제하다, 자제하다 ❑ 그녀는 계속 눈물을 참으려고 애썼다.

❶ 구동사 (지위 등을) 유지하다 ❑ 그는 결코 한 직장에 머무르지 못했다. ❷ 구동사 -을 억압하다 ❑ 모두들 젊은 세대를 억압하려는 어떤 큰 음모가 있다고 생각한다.

❶ 구동사 지체시키다 ❑ 병원 직원들이 엑스레이 촬영을 하기 위한 로젠바움의 입원을 지체시켰다. ❷ 구동사 (앞서지 못하게) 막다 ❑ 1987년부터 1990년 사이에 스테피 그라프는 나브라틸로바의 우승을 향한 도전을 대부분 막아냈다.

❶ 구동사 -을 꼭 잡고 있다 ❑ 그의 오른팔은 머리 옆으로 뻗은 채 아직도 커피 잔을 쥐고 있었다. ❑ 그는 절벽 면의 바위를 떨어지지 않으려고 안간힘을 쓰고 있었다. ❷ 구동사 견디어 내다, 버티다 ❑ 이 정부는 일년 전에 정권을 잃는 것이 마땅했는데 버텨냈다. ❸ 구동사 잠시 기다리다 [구어체] ❑ 매니저는 그에게 알아보는 동안 잠시 기다려 달라고 요청했다.

❶ 구동사 내밀다 ❑ "낸시 드루입니다."라고 그녀가 손을 내밀면서 말했다. ❷ 구동사 -을 고수하다, -을 끝까지 요구하다 ❑ 나는 끝까지 더 좋은 조건을 요구했어야 했다. ❸ 구동사 -에게 정보를 주지 않다 [비격식체] ❑ 아이들은 자기들에게 비밀로 하는 것이 있으면 그걸 느낄 수 있다고 그는 항상 믿었다. ❹ 구동사 저항하다, 버티다 ❑ 죄수 한 명이 교도소 지붕 위에서 계속 버티고 있었다. ❺ 구동사 (희망을) 품다 ❑ 그는 여전히 그들이 다시 가정을 이룰 것이라는 희망을 품고 있다.

to give in. ❏ *One prisoner was still holding out on the roof of the jail.* **5** PHRASAL VERB If you **hold out** hope of something happening, you hope that in the future something will happen as you want it to. ❏ *He still holds out hope that they could be a family again.*

▶**hold up** **1** PHRASAL VERB If you **hold up** your hand or something you have in your hand, you move it upward into a particular position and keep it there. ❏ *She held up her hand stiffly.* **2** PHRASAL VERB If one thing **holds up** another, it is placed under the other thing in order to support it and prevent it from falling. ❏ *Mills have iron pillars all over the place holding up the roof.* **3** PHRASAL VERB To **hold up** a person or process means to make them late or delay them. ❏ *Why were you holding everyone up?* **4** PHRASAL VERB If someone **holds up** a place such as a bank or a store, they point a weapon at someone there to make them give them money or valuable goods. ❏ *A thief ran off with hundreds of pounds yesterday after holding up a petrol station.* **5** PHRASAL VERB If you **hold up** something such as someone's behavior, you make it known to other people, so that they can criticize or praise it. ❏ *He had always been held up as an example to the younger ones.* **6** PHRASAL VERB If something such as a type of business **holds up** in difficult conditions, it stays in a reasonably good state. ❏ *Children's wear is one area that is holding up well in the recession.* **7** PHRASAL VERB If an argument or theory **holds up**, it is true or valid, even after close examination. ❏ *I'm not sure if the argument holds up, but it's stimulating.* **8** →see also **hold-up**

If you **cancel** or **call off** an arrangement or an appointment, you stop it from happening. ❏ *His failing health forced him to cancel the meeting... The European Community has threatened to call off peace talks.* If you **postpone** or **put off** an arrangement or an appointment, you make another arrangement for it to happen at a later time. ❏ *Elections have been postponed until next year... The Senate put off a vote on the nomination for one week.* If you **delay** something that has been arranged, you make it happen later than planned. ❏ *Space agency managers decided to delay the launch of the space shuttle.* If something **delays** you or **holds** you **up**, you start or finish what you are doing later than you planned. ❏ *He was delayed in traffic... Delivery of equipment had been held up by delays and disputes.*

---

hold|er ♦◇◇ /hoʊldər/ (**holders**) **1** N-COUNT A **holder** is someone who owns or has something. ❏ *This season the club has had 73,500 season-ticket holders.* **2** N-COUNT A **holder** is a container in which you put an object, usually in order to protect it or to keep it in place. ❏ *...a toothbrush holder.*

Word Partnership	*holder*의 연어
N.	**cup** holder, **pot** holder **2**

hold|ing /hoʊldɪŋ/ (**holdings**) N-COUNT If you have a **holding** in a company, you own shares in it. [BUSINESS] ❏ *That would increase Olympia & York's holding to 35%.*

hold|ing com|pa|ny (**holding companies**) N-COUNT A **holding company** is a company that has enough shares in one or more other companies to be able to control the other companies. [BUSINESS] ❏ *...a Montreal-based holding company with interests in telecommunications, gas and natural resources.*

hold-up (**hold-ups**) **1** N-COUNT A **hold-up** is a situation in which someone is threatened with a weapon in order to make them hand over money or valuables. ❏ *What could have happened? A hold-up? There'd been no gunshot or scream.* **2** N-COUNT A **hold-up** is something which causes a delay. ❏ *...bureaucratic hold-ups and legal wrangles over the contract.* **3** N-COUNT A **hold-up** is the stopping or very slow movement of traffic, sometimes caused by an accident which happened earlier. ❏ *They arrived late due to a freeway hold-up.*

hole ♦♦◇ /hoʊl/ (**holes**) **1** N-COUNT A **hole** is a hollow space in something solid, with an opening on one side. ❏ *He took a shovel, dug a hole, and buried his once-prized possessions.* **2** N-COUNT A **hole** is an opening in something that goes right through it. ❏ *...kids with holes in the knees of their jeans.* **3** N-COUNT A **hole** is the home or hiding place of a mouse, rabbit, or other small animal. ❏ *...a rabbit hole.* **4** N-COUNT A **hole** in a law, theory, or argument is a fault or weakness that it has. ❏ *There were some holes in that theory, some unanswered questions.* **5** N-COUNT A **hole** is also one of the nine or eighteen sections of a golf course. ❏ *I played nine holes with Gary Player today.* **6** PHRASE If you say that you are **in a hole**, you mean that you are in a difficult or embarrassing situation. [INFORMAL] ❏ *He admitted that the government was in "a dreadful hole."* **7** PHRASE If you get **a hole in one** in golf, you get the golf ball into the hole with a single stroke. ❏ *All they ever dream about is getting a hole in one.* **8** PHRASE If you **pick holes in** an argument or theory, you find weak points in it so that it is no longer valid. [INFORMAL] ❏ *He then goes on to pick holes in the article before reaching his conclusion.*

Word Partnership	*hole*의 연어
ADJ.	**deep** hole **1**
	big/huge/small hole, **gaping** hole **1 2**
V.	**dig a** hole, **fill/plug a** hole **1**
	cut/punch a hole in *something*, **drill/bore a** hole in *something* **1 2**

---

1 구동사 위로 치켜들다 ❏ 그녀는 뻣뻣하게 손을 치켜들었다. **2** 구동사 떠받치다 ❏ 제분소에는 사방에 지붕을 떠받치는 철제 기둥들이 있다. **3** 구동사 가로막다 ❏ 너는 왜 모든 사람들을 가로막고 있었니? **4** 구동사 강탈하다 ❏ 도둑 한 명이 어제 주유소를 털어 수백 파운드를 가지고 달아났다. **5** 구동사 -을 본보기로 들다 ❏ 그는 항상 젊은이들에게 본보기가 되었었다. **6** 구동사 지탱하다, 유지하다 ❏ 아동복은 불경기에도 잘 유지되는 영역이다. **7** 구동사 타당하다 ❏ 그 주장이 타당한지는 확실하지 않지만 아주 흥미롭기는 하다.

합의나 약속을 cancel 또는 call off하면, 그것이 일어나지 않도록 하는 것이다. ❏ 그는 건강이 나빠져서 회의를 취소해야 했다... 유럽 공동체가 평화 협상을 취소하겠다고 협박해 왔다. 어떤 조치나 약속을 연기(postpone 또는 put off)하면, 그것이 더 뒤의 어느 시기에 일어날 수 있도록 새로운 약속을 하는 것이다. ❏ 선거가 내년으로 연기되었다... 상원이 지명 투표를 일주일 동안 연기했다. 이미 약속된 것을 delay하면, 그것이 계획했던 것보다 나중에 일어나도록 하는 것이다. ❏ 우주항공 센터 관리자들이 우주선 발사를 연기하기로 결정했다. 무슨 일이 당신을 delay하거나 당신을 hold up하면, 일의 시작이나 마무리를 계획보다 늦게 하는 것이다. ❏ 그 사람은 차가 막혀서 늦었다... 장비 배달이 일정 연기와 의견 충돌 때문에 지연되었었다.

---

1 가산명사 보유자, 소지인 ❏ 이번 시즌에는 클럽에는 정기권 소지자가 73,500명이 있었다. **2** 가산명사 용기, 통 ❏ 칫솔통

가산명사 보유 지분 [경제] ❏ 그렇게 하면 올림피아 앤드 요크사의 보유 지분이 35퍼센트까지 증가할 것이다.

가산명사 지주 회사 [경제] ❏ 통신, 가스, 천연자원에 관여하고 있는 몬트리올 소재 지주 회사

1 가산명사 무장 강도 (사건) ❏ 무슨 일이 일어났을까? 무장 강도 사건일까? 총성이나 비명이 없었는데. **2** 가산명사 지연 ❏ 그 계약을 둘러싼 관료주의적 지연들과 법률적 논쟁 **3** 가산명사 교통 정체 ❏ 그들은 고속도로 정체로 인해 늦게 도착했다.

1 가산명사 구멍, 구덩이 ❏ 그는 삽을 들고 구덩이를 파서 한때 소중했던 소지품들을 묻었다. **2** 가산명사 구멍 ❏ 무릎에 구멍 난 청바지를 입고 있는 아이들 **3** 가산명사 (짐승의) 굴 ❏ 토끼 굴 **4** 가산명사 결함, 흠 ❏ 그 이론에는 몇 가지 결함이, 해답이 제시되지 않은 몇 가지 의문 사항들이 있었다. **5** 가산명사 (골프 코스의) 홀 ❏ 나는 오늘 개리 플레이어와 아홉 홀을 돌았다. **6** 구 궁지에 빠져 있는 [비격식체] ❏ 그는 정부가 '끔찍한 궁지'에 빠져 있다고 인정했다. **7** 구 홀인원 ❏ 그들이 늘 꿈꾸는 것은 홀인원을 하는 것이다. **8** 구 -에서 결함을 찾아내다 [비격식체] ❏ 그런 뒤 그는 결론에 이르기 전에 기사에서 결함들을 찾아낸다.

holi|day ♦♦◇ /hɒlɪdeɪ/ (holidays, holidaying, holidayed) **1** N-COUNT A **holiday** is a day when people do not go to work or school because of a religious or national festival. ❑ *New Year's Day is a public holiday throughout Britain.* →see also **bank holiday** **2** N-COUNT A **holiday** is a period of time during which you relax and enjoy yourself away from home. People sometimes refer to their holiday as their **holidays**. [BRIT; AM **vacation**] [also on/from N] ❑ *I've just come back from a holiday in the United States.* ❑ *We rang Duncan to ask where he was going on holiday.* **3** N-PLURAL **The holidays** are the time when children do not have to go to school. [BRIT; AM **vacation**] ❑ *...the first day of the school holidays.* **4** N-UNCOUNT If you have a particular number of days' or weeks' **holiday**, you do not have to go to work for that number of days or weeks. [BRIT; AM **vacation**] ❑ *Every worker will be entitled to four weeks' paid holiday a year.* **5** V-I If you **are holidaying** in a place away from home, you are on holiday there. [BRIT; AM **vacation**] [oft cont] ❑ *Sampling the local cuisine is one of the delights of holidaying abroad.*

holi|day|maker /hɒlɪdeɪmeɪkər/ (holidaymakers) N-COUNT A **holidaymaker** is a person who is away from their home on holiday. [BRIT; AM **vacationer**]

ho|lism /hoʊlɪzəm/ N-UNCOUNT **Holism** is the belief that everything in nature is connected in some way. [FORMAL] ❑ *Nature by itself, he writes, runs on "principles of balance and holism."*

ho|lis|tic /hoʊlɪstɪk/ ADJ **Holistic** means based on the principles of holism. [FORMAL] ❑ *...practitioners of holistic medicine.*

hol|ler /hɒlər/ (hollers, hollering, hollered) V-T/V-I If you **holler**, you shout loudly. [mainly AM, INFORMAL] ❑ *The audience whooped and hollered.* ❑ *"Watch out!" he hollered.* ● N-COUNT **Holler** is also a noun. ❑ *She spun round as the man, with a holler, burst through the door.* ● PHRASAL VERB **Holler out** means the same as **holler**. ❑ *I hollered out the names.*

hol|low /hɒloʊ/ (hollows, hollowing, hollowed) **1** ADJ Something that is **hollow** has a space inside it, as opposed to being solid all the way through. ❑ *...a hollow tree.* **2** ADJ A surface that is **hollow** curves inward. ❑ *He looked young, dark and sharp-featured, with hollow cheeks.* **3** N-COUNT A **hollow** is an area that is lower than the surrounding surface. ❑ *Below him the town lay warm in the hollow of the hill.* **4** ADJ If you describe a statement, situation, or person as **hollow**, you mean they have no real value, worth, or effectiveness. ❑ *Any threat to bring in the police is a hollow one.* ● **hol|low|ness** N-UNCOUNT ❑ *One month before the deadline we see the hollowness of these promises.* **5** ADJ If someone gives a **hollow** laugh, they laugh in a way that shows that they do not really find something amusing. [ADJ n] ❑ *Murray Pick's hollow laugh had no mirth in it.* **6** ADJ A **hollow** sound is dull and echoing. [ADJ n] ❑ *...the hollow sound of a gunshot.* **7** V-T If something **is hollowed**, its surface is made to curve inward or downward. [usu passive] ❑ *The mule's back was hollowed by the weight of its burden.*

Thesaurus	hollow의 참조어
ADJ.	empty, solid **1**
	empty, meaningless; *(ant.)* meaningful, worthwhile **4 5**

hol|ly /hɒli/ (hollies) N-VAR **Holly** is an evergreen tree or shrub which has hard, shiny leaves with sharp points, and red berries in winter.

holo|caust /hɒləkɔːst, hoʊlə-/ (holocausts) **1** N-VAR A **holocaust** is an event in which there is a lot of destruction and many people are killed, especially one caused by war. ❑ *A nuclear holocaust seemed a very real possibility in the '50s.* **2** N-SING **The holocaust** is used to refer to the killing by the Nazis of millions of Jews during the Second World War. ❑ *...an Israeli-based fund for survivors of the holocaust and their families.*

holy ♦◇◇ /hoʊli/ (holier, holiest) ADJ If you describe something as **holy**, you mean that it is considered to be special because it is connected with God or a particular religion. ❑ *To them, as to all Tibetans, this is a holy place.*

hom|age /hɒmɪdʒ, ɒm-/ N-UNCOUNT **Homage** is respect shown towards someone or something you admire, or to a person in authority. [usu N to n] ❑ *Palace has released two marvellous films that pay homage to our literary heritage.*

home ♦♦♦ /hoʊm/ (homes) **1** N-COUNT Someone's **home** is the house or apartment where they live. [oft poss N, also at N] ❑ *Last night they stayed at home and watched TV.* ❑ *The General divided his time between his shabby offices in Carlton Gardens and his home in Hampstead.*

> When people move to a new **home**, they often hold a **housewarming** party. Friends and neighbors usually bring gifts for the house such as plants, soap, kitchen towels, and other non-personal items to welcome the new people to the neighborhood and make them feel welcome.

2 N-UNCOUNT You can use **home** to refer in a general way to the house, town, or country where someone lives now or where they were born, often to emphasize that they feel they belong in that place. ❑ *She gives frequent performances of her work, both at home and abroad.* ❑ *His father worked away from home for much of Jim's first five years.* **3** ADV **Home** means to or at the place where you live. ❑ *His wife wasn't feeling too well and she wanted to go home.* ❑ *I'll telephone you as soon as I get home.* **4** ADJ **Home** means made or done in the place where you live. [ADJ n] ❑ *...cheap but healthy home cooking.* **5** ADJ **Home** means relating to your own country as opposed to foreign countries. [ADJ n] ❑ *Europe's software companies still have a growing home market.* **6** N-COUNT A **home** is a large house or institution where a number of people live and are cared for, instead of living in their own houses or apartments. They usually live there because they are too old or ill to take care of themselves or for their families to care for them.

---

1 가산명사 휴일 ❑ 1월 1일은 영국 전역에서 공휴일이다. **2** 가산명사 휴가 [영국영어; 미국영어 vacation] ❑ 나는 미국에서 휴가를 보내고 막 돌아왔다. ❑ 우리는 던컨에게 전화를 걸어 휴가 때 어디로 가느냐고 물었다. **3** 복수명사 방학 [영국영어; 미국영어 vacation] ❑ 방학 첫날 **4** 불가산명사 휴가 [영국영어; 미국영어 vacation] ❑ 모든 근로자는 일년에 4주간 유급 휴가를 받게 될 것이다. **5** 자동사 휴가를 보내다 [영국영어; 미국영어 vacation] ❑ 지역 특유의 요리를 시식하는 것은 외국에서 휴가를 보내는 즐거움 중 하나이다.

가산명사 휴가객, 휴양객 [영국영어; 미국영어 vacationer]

불가산명사 전체론 [격식체] ❑ 자연은 스스로 '균형과 전체의 원리'에 따라 움직인다고 그는 쓰고 있다.

형용사 전체론적인 [격식체] ❑ 심신 통합적 치료법 의사들

타동사/자동사 고함지르다 [주로 미국영어, 비격식체] ❑ 관객들이 '우' 하고 외치며 고함을 질렀다. ❑ "조심해!"라고 그가 외쳤다. ● 가산명사 고함, 외침 ❑ 그 남자가 고함치며 문을 박차고 들어오자 그녀는 획 돌아보았다. ● 구동사 고함지르다 ❑ 나는 그 이름들을 소리쳐 불렀다.

1 형용사 속이 빈 ❑ 속이 빈 나무 **2** 형용사 우묵한 ❑ 그는 어려 보였는데 얼굴이 까맣고 윤곽이 뚜렷하며 볼이 홀쭉했다. **3** 가산명사 우묵한 곳 ❑ 그의 발아래 읍내가 언덕 우묵한 곳에 아늑하게 자리 잡고 있었다. **4** 형용사 내실이 없는, 허울뿐의 ❑ 경찰을 부르겠다는 어떤 협박도 허울뿐이다. ● 불가산명사 공허함 ❑ 최종 기한을 한달 남기고 우리는 이런 약속들의 공허함을 알게 된다. **5** 형용사 공허한 ❑ 머리 픽의 공허한 웃음에는 명랑함이 없었다. **6** 형용사 공허하게 울리는 ❑ 공허하게 울리는 총성 **7** 타동사 움푹 꺼지다 ❑ 노새의 등이 무거운 짐 무게로 휘청해져 있었다.

가산명사 또는 불가산명사 호랑가시나무

1 가산명사 또는 불가산명사 대학살 ❑ 핵무기에 의한 대학살이 1950년대에는 아주 현실적으로 가능한 일로 보였다. **2** 단수명사 나치의 유태인 대학살, 홀로코스트 ❑ 홀로코스트의 생존자와 그들의 가족을 위한 이스라엘인들의 기금

형용사 신성한 ❑ 모든 티베트 사람들에게와 마찬가지로 그들에게 이곳은 성소이다.

불가산명사 경의, 충성 ❑ 팰리스 사는 우리의 문학적 전통에 경의를 표하는 멋진 영화 2편을 개봉했다.

1 가산명사 자택, 집 ❑ 지난밤 그들은 집에 머무르며 텔레비전을 보았다. ❑ 장군은 칼튼 가에 있는 초라한 사무실과 햄스테드에 있는 집을 오가며 지냈다.

새 집으로 이사를 가면 흔히 housewarming 파티(집들이)를 한다. 친구와 이웃은 대개 화초, 비누, 키친타월, 다른 가정 용품 같은 선물을 가져가서 새로 온 사람들을 이웃으로 환영해 주고 그들이 환대를 받는 기분이 들도록 해준다.

2 불가산명사 생가, 고향, 본국 ❑ 그녀는 본국과 외국에서 자기 작품 공연을 자주 한다. ❑ 짐의 아버지는 짐이 태어난 후 5년 동안 거의 대부분을 일 때문에 집을 떠나 있었다. **3** 부사 집으로 ❑ 그의 아내가 몸이 안 좋아 집에 가고 싶어 했다. ❑ 집에 도착하자마자 전화해 줄게. **4** 형용사 가정의 ❑ 값싸지만 건강에 좋은 가정 요리 **5** 형용사 본국의 ❑ 유럽의 소프트웨어 회사들은 아직 성장하고 있는 내수 시장을 가지고 있다. **6** 가산명사 요양소, 보육원 ❑ 그것은 장애아들을 위한 보육원이다. **7** 가산명사 가정, 세대 ❑ 그녀는 하여튼 해리엇에게 평화롭고 애정이 넘치는 가정을 만들어 주었다. **8** 단수명사 발상지, 본고장 ❑ 이곳 프랑스의 남서부

It's going to be a home for handicapped children. ◼ N-COUNT You can refer to a family unit as a **home**. ❑ *She had, at any rate, provided a peaceful and loving home for Harriet.* ◼ N-SING If you refer to the **home of** something, you mean the place where it began or where it is most typically found. ❑ *This south-west region of France is the home of claret.* ◼ N-COUNT If you find a **home for** something, you find a place where it can be kept. ❑ *The equipment itself is getting smaller, neater and easier to find a home for.* ◼ ADV If you press, drive, or hammer something **home**, you explain it to people as forcefully as possible. [ADV after v] ❑ *It is now up to all of us to debate this issue and press home the argument.* ◼ N-UNCOUNT When a sports team plays **at home**, they play a game on their own ground, rather than on the opposing team's ground. ❑ *I scored in both games against Barcelona; we drew at home and beat them away.* ● ADJ **Home** is also an adjective. [ADJ n] ❑ *All three are Chelsea fans, and attend all home games together.* ◼ PHRASE If you feel **at home**, you feel comfortable in the place or situation that you are in. ❑ *He spoke very good English and appeared pleased to see us, and we soon felt quite at home.* ◼ PHRASE To **bring** something **home** to someone means to make them understand how important or serious it is. ❑ *Their sobering conversation brought home to everyone present the serious and worthwhile work the Red Cross does.* ◼ PHRASE If you say that someone is, in American English **home free**, or in British English **home and dry**, you mean that they have been successful or that they are certain to be successful. ❑ *The prime minister and the moderates are not yet home and dry.* ◼ PHRASE If a situation or what someone says **hits home** or **strikes home**, people accept that it is real or true, even though it may be painful for them to realize. ❑ *Did the reality of war finally hit home?* ◼ PHRASE You can say **a home away from home** in American English or **a home from home** in British English to refer to a place in which you are as comfortable as in your own home. [APPROVAL] ❑ *The café seems to be her home away from home these days.* ◼ CONVENTION If you say to a guest "**Make yourself at home**," you are making them feel welcome and inviting them to behave in an informal, relaxed way. [POLITENESS] ❑ *Take off your jacket and make yourself at home.* ◼ PHRASE If you say that something is **nothing to write home about**, you mean that it is not very interesting or exciting. [INFORMAL] ❑ *So a dreary Monday afternoon in Walthamstow is nothing to write home about, right?* ◼ PHRASE If something that is thrown or fired **strikes home**, it reaches its target. [WRITTEN] ❑ *Only two torpedoes struck home.*

Thesaurus   home의 참조어

N.   dwelling, house, residence ① ◼
      birthplace ① ◼

Word Partnership   home의 연어

V.   bring/take *someone/something* home, build a home,
     buy a home, call/phone home, come home, drive home,
     feel at home, fly home, get home, go home, head for home,
     leave home, return home, ride home, sit *at* home, stay *at* home,
     walk home, work at home ① ◼ ◼ ◼
ADJ.   new home ① ◼ ◼
     close to home ① ◼ ◼ ◼

▶**home in** ◼ PHRASAL VERB If you **home in on** one particular aspect of something, you give all your attention to it. ❑ *The critics immediately homed in on the group's essential members.* ◼ PHRASAL VERB If something such as a missile **homes in on** something else, it is aimed at that thing and moves toward it. ❑ *Two rockets homed in on it from behind without a sound.*

home|coming /hoʊmkʌmɪŋ/ (**homecomings**) ◼ N-VAR Your **homecoming** is your return to your home or your country after being away for a long time. ❑ *Her homecoming was tinged with sadness.* ◼ N-UNCOUNT **Homecoming** is a day or weekend each year when former students of a particular school, college, or university go back to it to meet each other again and go to dances and sports events. [AM] ❑ *...a recent Penn State graduate who was back for Homecoming weekend.*

home-grown ADJ **Home-grown** fruit and vegetables have been grown in your garden, rather than on a farm, or in your country rather than abroad. ❑ *Martinelli reminds visitors often that he uses 100 percent home-grown fruit from California's Bajaro Valley.*

home|land /hoʊmlænd/ (**homelands**) ◼ N-COUNT Your **homeland** is your native country. [mainly WRITTEN] ❑ *Many are planning to return to their homeland.* ◼ N-COUNT The **homelands** were regions within South Africa in which black South Africans had a limited form of self-government.

home|less ◆◇◇ /hoʊmlɪs/ ADJ **Homeless** people have nowhere to live. ❑ *...the growing number of homeless families.* ● N-PLURAL The **homeless** are people who are homeless. ❑ *...shelters for the homeless.* ● **home|less|ness** N-UNCOUNT ❑ *The only way to solve homelessness is to provide more homes.*

home|ly /hoʊmli/ ◼ ADJ If you describe a room or house as **homely**, you like it because you feel comfortable and relaxed there. [mainly BRIT, APPROVAL] [AM usually **homey**] ❑ *We try and provide a very homely atmosphere.* ◼ ADJ If you say that someone is **homely**, you mean that they are not very attractive to look at. [AM] ❑ *The man was homely, overweight, and probably only two or three years younger than Lou.*

home-made ADJ Something that is **home-made** has been made in someone's home, rather than in a store or factory. ❑ *The bread, pastry and mayonnaise are home-made.*

지역은 클라레 적포도주의 본고장이다. ◼ 가산명사 보관소 ❑ 장비 자체가 작아지고 산뜻해지며 보관하기 쉽게 되어 가고 있다. ◼ 부사 철저히 ❑ 이 문제를 토론하고 그 논지를 철저히 파고드는 것이 이제 우리 모두가 해야 할 일이다. ◼ 불가산명사 (스포츠 팀의) 홈, 본거지 ❑ 나는 바르셀로나와 두 번의 경기에서 모두 득점을 했다. 우리는 홈경기에서는 비겼고 원정 경기에서 이겼다. ● 형용사 홈그라운드의 ❑ 3명 모두 첼시 팬이며, 모든 홈그라운드 경기에 함께 참석한다. ◼ 구 마음 편히 ❑ 그는 영어를 아주 잘했고 우리를 만나 기쁜 듯해서 우리는 곧 마음이 아주 편해졌다. ◼ 구 -을 절실히 느끼게 하다 ❑ 듣는 사람을 진지하게 만드는 그들의 대화는 참석한 모든 사람들에게 적십자가 하는 진지하고 보람 있는 일을 절실히 느끼게 했다. ◼ 구 성공을 거둔, 성공이 확실한 ❑ 수상과 온건주의자들은 아직 성공을 거두지 못했다. ◼ 구 정곡을 찌르다, 급소를 찌르다 ❑ 전쟁의 현실이 마침내 절실하게 느껴졌는가? ◼ 구 제 집처럼 마음이 편한 안식처 ❑ 그 카페가 요즘 그녀에게 마음 편한 안식처인 것 같다. ◼ 관용 표현 편하게 하세요 [공손체] ❑ 양복 상의를 벗으시고 편하게 하세요. ◼ 구 특별하지 못한 것, 하찮은 것 [비격식체] ❑ 그래서 월텀스토우에서의 지루한 월요일 오후는 특별한 게 아니었단 말이지, 그렇지? ◼ 구 명중하다 [문어체] ❑ 두 발의 어뢰만이 명중했다.

◼ 구동사 모든 주의를 집중하다 ❑ 비평가들은 즉각 그 그룹의 핵심 회원들에게 주의를 집중했다. ◼ 구동사 (미사일 등이) 목표를 향하여 나아가다 ❑ 두 발의 로켓이 그것을 향해 뒤에서 소리 없이 날아왔다.

◼ 가산명사 또는 불가산명사 귀향, 귀국 ❑ 그녀의 귀향에는 슬픔이 깃들어 있었다. ◼ 불가산명사 연례 동창회 [미국영어] ❑ 주말 연례 동창회를 위해 온 펜실베이니아 주립 대학의 최근 졸업생

형용사 집에서 기른, 국내에서 생산된 ❑ 마티넬리는 자기가 캘리포니아의 바자로 계곡에서 생산된 100퍼센트 국내산 과일만을 사용한다는 것을 방문자들에게 자주 상기시킨다.

◼ 가산명사 본국, 고국 [주로 문어체] ❑ 많은 사람들이 본국으로 돌아갈 계획을 하고 있다. ◼ 가산명사 (남아프리카공화국의) 흑인 자치구

형용사 노숙자인 ❑ 늘어 가는 노숙자 가족의 수 ● 복수명사 노숙자 ❑ 노숙자 쉼터 ● 불가산명사 ❑ 노숙 문제를 해결할 유일한 방법은 집을 더 많이 제공하는 것이다.

◼ 형용사 가정적인, 자기 집 같은 [주로 영국영어, 마음에 듦] [미국영어 대개 homey] ❑ 우리는 아주 가정적인 분위기를 제공하기 위해 애씁니다. ◼ 형용사 평범하게 생긴, 수수한 [미국영어] ❑ 그 남자는 평범하게 생겼고, 너무 살이 쪘으며, 아마 루보다 겨우 두세 살 정도나 어릴 것이다.

형용사 집에서 만든 ❑ 빵, 파스트리, 마요네즈는 집에서 만들었다.

A

Home Of|fice N-PROPER The **Home Office** is the department of the British Government which is responsible for things such as the police, broadcasting, and making decisions about people who want to come to live in Britain. ❑ ...*a Home Office minister.*

고유명사 (영국의) 이민국 ❑ 이민국 정무 위원

B

homeo|path /hoʊmioʊpæθ/ (homeopaths) N-COUNT A **homeopath** is someone who treats illness by homeopathy. [BRIT also **homoeopath**] ❑ *The homeopath will test various strengths of medicines on the patient.*

가산명사 동종 요법 치료사 [영국영어 homoeopath] ❑ 동종 요법 치료사는 환자에게 약제를 다양한 강도로 시험해 볼 것이다.

C

homeo|path|ic /hoʊmioʊpæθɪk/ [BRIT also **homoeopathic**] ADJ **Homeopathic** means relating to or used in homeopathy. ❑ ...*homeopathic remedies.*

[영국영어 homoeopathic] 형용사 동종 요법의 ❑ 동종 요법 치료법

homeopa|thy /hoʊmiɒpəθi/ [BRIT also **homoeopathy**] N-UNCOUNT **Homeopathy** is a way of treating an illness in which the patient is given very small amounts of a drug that produces signs of the illness in healthy people.

[영국영어 homoeopathy] 불가산명사 동종 요법

D

home|page /hoʊmpeɪdʒ/ (homepages) N-COUNT On the Internet, a person's or organization's **homepage** is the main page of information about them, which often contains links to other pages about them. ❑ ...*the homepage of a new sex education website.*

가산명사 홈페이지 ❑ 새 성교육 웹사이트의 홈페이지

E

Home Sec|re|tary (Home Secretaries) N-COUNT The **Home Secretary** is the member of the British government who is in charge of the Home Office.

가산명사 (영국의) 내무 장관

F

home shop|ping N-UNCOUNT **Home shopping** is shopping that people do by ordering goods from their homes, using catalogs, television channels, or computers. [oft N n] ❑ ...*America's most successful home-shopping channel.*

불가산명사 홈쇼핑 ❑ 미국에서 가장 성공한 홈쇼핑 채널

G

home|sick /hoʊmsɪk/ ADJ If you are **homesick**, you feel unhappy because you are away from home and are missing your family, friends, and home very much. ❑ *She's feeling a little homesick.* ● **home|sick|ness** N-UNCOUNT ❑ *There were inevitable bouts of homesickness.*

형용사 향수병에 걸린 ❑ 그녀는 집을 좀 그리워한다. ● 향수병 불가산명사 ❑ 어쩔 수 없는 향수병을 수차례 겪었다.

H

home|stead /hoʊmstɛd/ (homesteads) 1 N-COUNT A **homestead** is a farmhouse, together with the land around it. 2 N-COUNT In United States history, a **homestead** was a piece of government land in the west, which was given to someone so they could settle there and develop a farm. [AM]

1 가산명사 농가 2 가산명사 (미국 정부에서 불하했던) 자작 농장 [미국영어]

I

home|work /hoʊmwɜrk/ 1 N-UNCOUNT **Homework** is schoolwork that teachers give to students to do at home in the evening or on the weekend. ❑ *Have you done your homework, Gemma?* 2 N-UNCOUNT If you **do your homework**, you find out what you need to know in preparation for something. ❑ *Before you go near a stockbroker, do your homework.*

1 불가산명사 숙제 ❑ 제마야, 숙제 다 했니? 2 불가산명사 사전 조사 ❑ 주식 중매인에게 가기 전에 사전 조사를 하시오.

J

K

homey /hoʊmi/ ADJ If you describe a room or house as **homey**, you like it because you feel comfortable and relaxed there. [mainly AM, INFORMAL, APPROVAL] [BRIT usually **homely**] ❑ ...*a large, homey dining room.*

형용사 가정적인, 자기 집 같은 [주로 미국영어, 비격식체, 마음에 듦] [영국영어 대개 homely] ❑ 크고 안락한 식당방

L

M

homi|ci|dal /hɒmɪsaɪdᵊl, hoʊmɪ-/ ADJ **Homicidal** is used to describe someone who is dangerous because they are likely to kill someone. ❑ *That man is a homicidal maniac.*

형용사 살인을 저지를 것 같은 ❑ 저 남자는 살인이라도 저지를 정신병자이다.

N

Word Link	cide ≈ killing : geno*cide*, homi*cide*, pesti*cide*

homi|cide /hɒmɪsaɪd, hoʊmɪ-/ (homicides) N-VAR **Homicide** is the illegal killing of a person. [mainly AM; BRIT usually **murder**] ❑ *The police arrived at the scene of the homicide.*

가산명사 또는 불가산명사 살인 [주로 미국영어, 영국영어 대개 murder] ❑ 경찰이 살인 현장에 도착했다.

O

homoeo|path|ic /hoʊmioʊpæθɪk/ →see **homeopathic**

homoeopa|thy /hoʊmiɒpəθi/ →see **homeopathy**

P

homo|geneous /hɒmədʒiːniəs, hoʊ-/ also **homogenous** /həmɒdʒənəs/ ADJ **Homogeneous** is used to describe a group or thing which has members or parts that are all the same. [FORMAL] ❑ *The unemployed are not a homogeneous group.*

형용사 동질의, 균질의 [격식체] ❑ 실업자들은 동질 집단이 아니다.

Q

homo|pho|bia /hɒməfoʊbiə/ N-UNCOUNT **Homophobia** is a strong and unreasonable dislike of homosexual people, especially homosexual men.

불가산명사 동성애 혐오

R

ho|mo|pho|bic /hɒməfoʊbɪk/ ADJ **Homophobic** means involving or related to a strong and unreasonable dislike of homosexual people, especially homosexual men. ❑ *I'm not homophobic in any way and certainly don't condemn gay relationships.*

형용사 동성애를 혐오하는 ❑ 나는 동성애를 조금도 혐오하지 않으며 물론 동성애 관계를 비난하지도 않는다.

S

homo|sex|ual ♦◇◇ /hoʊmoʊsɛkʃuəl, BRIT hɒmoʊsekʃuəl/ (homosexuals) 1 ADJ A **homosexual** relationship is a sexual relationship between people of the same sex. ❑ ...*partners in a homosexual relationship.* 2 ADJ Someone who is **homosexual** is sexually attracted to people of the same sex. ❑ *A fraud trial involving two homosexual lawyers was abandoned.* ● N-COUNT **Homosexual** is also a noun. ❑ *The judge said that discrimination against homosexuals is deplorable.* ● **homo|sex|ual|ity** /hoʊmoʊsɛkʃuæliti, BRIT hɒmoʊsekʃuæliti/ N-UNCOUNT ❑ ...*a place where gays could openly discuss homosexuality.*

T

1 형용사 동성애의 ❑ 동성애 관계를 맺고 있는 파트너들 2 형용사 동성애를 하는 ❑ 동성애자 변호사 2명이 관련된 사기 재판이 포기되었다. ● 가산명사 동성애자 ❑ 판사는 동성애자에 대한 차별이 유감이라고 말했다. ● 동성애 불가산명사 ❑ 동성애자들이 공공연하게 동성애를 논의할 수 있는 장소

U

V

hone /hoʊn/ (hones, honing, honed) V-T If you **hone** something, for example a skill, technique, idea, or product, you carefully develop it over a long period of time so that it is exactly right for your purpose. ❑ *Leading companies spend time and money on honing the skills of senior managers.*

타동사 도야하다, 연마하다 ❑ 선두 기업들은 고급 관리자들의 기술을 연마하는 데 시간과 돈을 투자한다.

W

X

hon|est ♦◇◇ /ɒnɪst/ 1 ADJ If you describe someone as **honest**, you mean that they always tell the truth, and do not try to deceive people or break the law. ❑ *I know she's honest and reliable.* ● **hon|est|ly** ADV [ADV after v] ❑ *She fought honestly for a just cause and for freedom.* 2 ADJ If you are **honest** in a particular situation, you tell the complete truth or give your sincere opinion, even if this is not very pleasant. ❑ *I was honest about what I was doing.* ❑ *He had been honest with her and she had tricked him!* ● **hon|est|ly** ADV [ADV with v] ❑ *It came as a shock to hear an old friend speak so honestly about Ted.* 3 ADV You say "**honest**" before or after a statement to emphasize that you are telling the truth and that you want people to believe you. [INFORMAL, EMPHASIS] [ADV with cl] ❑ *I'm not sure, honest.*

Y

1 형용사 정직한 ❑ 나는 그녀가 정직하고 믿을 수 있다는 걸 안다. ● 정직하게 부사 ❑ 그녀는 정의로운 대의와 자유를 위해서 정직하게 싸웠다. 2 형용사 솔직한, 거짓 없는 ❑ 나는 내가 하고 있는 일을 솔직히 말했다. ❑ 그는 그녀에게 거짓 없이 대했으나 그녀는 그를 속여 왔던 것이다! ● 솔직히 부사 ❑ 오랜 친구 한 명이 테드에 대해 그렇게 솔직히 말하는 것을 들으니 충격적이었다. 3 부사 정말로, 틀림없이 [비격식체, 강조] ❑ 잘 모르겠어, 정말로. 4 구 정말로, 맹세코 [비격식체, 강조] ❑ 나는 우리가 이것을 하지

Z

4 PHRASE Some people say "**honest to God**" to emphasize their feelings or to emphasize that something is really true. [INFORMAL, EMPHASIS] ❑ *I wish we weren't doing this, Lillian, honest to God, I really do.* 5 PHRASE You can say "**to be honest**" before or after a statement to indicate that you are telling the truth about your own opinions or feelings, especially if you think these will disappoint the person you are talking to. [FEELINGS] ❑ *To be honest the house is not quite our style.*

앉았으면 해. 릴리안, 정말로, 난 그랬으면 좋겠어. 5 구 정직하게 말하면, 솔직하게 말하면 [감정 개입] ❑ 솔직하게 말하면 그 집은 그다지 우리 스타일이 아니다.

Thesaurus   honest의 참조어

ADJ.	fair, genuine, sincere, true, truthful, upright; (ant.) dishonest 1
	candid, frank, straight, truthful 2

---

hon|est|ly /ɒnɪstli/ 1 ADV You use **honestly** to emphasize that you are referring to your, or someone else's, true beliefs or feelings. [EMPHASIS] [ADV before v] ❑ *But did you honestly think we wouldn't notice?* 2 ADV You use **honestly** to emphasize that you are telling the truth and that you want people to believe you. [SPOKEN, EMPHASIS] [ADV with cl] ❑ *Honestly, I don't know anything about it.* 3 ADV You use **honestly** to indicate that you are annoyed or impatient. [SPOKEN, FEELINGS] [ADV with cl] ❑ *Honestly, Nev! Must you be quite so crude!* 4 →see also **honest**

1 부사 솔직히 [강조] ❑ 그렇지만 넌 솔직히 우리가 그걸 알아차리지 못할 거라고 생각했어? 2 부사 솔직히 [구어체, 강조] ❑ 솔직히, 나는 그것에 대해서 아무것도 모른다. 3 부사 참, 정말 참 [구어체, 감정 개입] ❑ 거 참, 네브! 자네 정말 그렇게 저질분하게 굴어야 하겠나?

hon|es|ty /ɒnɪsti/ N-UNCOUNT **Honesty** is the quality of being honest. ❑ *They said the greatest virtues in a politician were integrity, correctness, and honesty.* ● PHRASE You say **in all honesty** when you are saying something that might be disappointing or upsetting, and you want to soften its effect by emphasizing your sincerity. [EMPHASIS]

불가산명사 정직 ❑ 정치인의 최고의 가치는 성실, 정확 그리고 정직이라고 그들은 말했다. ● 구 솔직히 말해서, 싶은 [강조]

hon|ey /hʌni/ (honeys) 1 N-VAR **Honey** is a sweet, sticky, yellowish substance that is made by bees. 2 N-VOC You call someone **honey** as a sign of affection. [mainly AM] ❑ *Honey, I don't really think that's a good idea.*

1 가산명사 또는 불가산명사 벌꿀, 꿀 2 호격명사 여보, 자기 [주로 미국영어] ❑ 자기야, 그것은 좋은 생각 같지 않아.

Honey is a term commonly used to express affection between two people. Other words used in a similar way include: **dear**, **darling**, **sweetheart**, or **angel**. Sometimes these words are used by adults when speaking to a child.

honey는 두 사람 사이에서 애정을 표현할 때 흔히 쓰는 말이다. 비슷하게 쓰이는 다른 말로는 dear, darling, sweetheart, angel 등이 있다. 가끔은 어른이 아이에게 말을 할 때에도 이런 표현을 쓴다.

---

honey|moon /hʌnimun/ (honeymoons, honeymooning, honeymooned) 1 N-COUNT A **honeymoon** is a vacation taken by a man and a woman who have just gotten married. ❑ *The next time I went abroad was on my honeymoon.* 2 V-I When a recently-married couple **honeymoon** somewhere, they go there on their honeymoon. ❑ *They honeymooned in Venice.* 3 N-COUNT You can use **honeymoon** to refer to a period of time after the start of a new job or new government when everyone is pleased with the person or people concerned and is nice to them. ❑ *Brett is enjoying a honeymoon period with both press and public.* →see **wedding**

1 가산명사 신혼여행 ❑ 그 다음에 내가 해외로 나간 것은 신혼여행 때였다. 2 자동사 신혼여행을 가다 ❑ 그들은 베니스로 신혼여행을 갔다. 3 가산명사 밀월, 행복한 시기 ❑ 브렛은 언론과 대중 양측과 함께 밀월을 즐기고 있다.

honk /hɒŋk/ (honks, honking, honked) V-T/V-I If you **honk** the horn of a vehicle or if the horn **honks**, you make the horn produce a short loud sound. ❑ *Drivers honked their horns in solidarity with the peace marchers.* ❑ *Horns honk. An angry motorist shouts.* ● N-COUNT **Honk** is also a noun. ❑ *She pulled to the right with a honk.*

타동사/자동사 (경적을) 울리다; (경적이) 울리다 ❑ 운전기사들은 평화 시위자들과 연대하여 경적을 울렸다. ❑ 경적이 울린다. 화난 운전자가 소리친다. ● 가산명사 경적 ❑ 그녀는 경적을 울리며 차를 오른쪽으로 몰고 갔다.

hon|or ♦◇◇ /ɒnər/ (honors, honoring, honored) [BRIT **honour**] 1 N-UNCOUNT **Honor** means doing what you believe to be right and being confident that you have done what is right. ❑ *The officers died faithful to Poland and to the honor of a soldier.* 2 N-COUNT An **honor** is a special award that is given to someone, usually because they have done something good or because they are greatly respected. ❑ *He was showered with honors – among them an Oscar.* 3 V-T If someone **is honored**, they are given public praise or an award for something they have done. [usu passive] ❑ *Diego Maradona was honored with an award presented by Argentina's soccer association.* 4 N-SING If you describe doing or experiencing something as an **honor**, you mean you think it is something special and desirable. ❑ *Five other cities including Manchester had been competing for the honor of staging the Games.* 5 V-T PASSIVE If you say that you **would be honored to** do something, you are saying very politely and formally that you would be pleased to do it. If you say that you **are honoured by** something, you are saying that you are grateful for it and pleased about it. [POLITENESS] ❑ *Ms. Payne said she was honored to accept the appointment and looked forward to its challenges.* 6 V-T To **honor** someone means to treat them or regard them with special attention and respect. ❑ *Her Majesty later honored the headmaster with her presence at lunch.* 7 V-T If you **honor** an arrangement or promise, you do what you said you would do. ❑ *The two sides agreed to honor a new ceasefire.* 8 N-VOC Judges, and mayors in the United States, are sometimes called **your honor** or referred to as **his honor** or **her honor**. [poss N; poss PRON] ❑ *I bring this up, your honor, because I think it is important to understand the background of the defendant.* 9 N-UNCOUNT **Honors** is a type of university degree which is of a higher standard than a pass or ordinary degree. [BRIT] ❑ *...an honors degree in business studies.* 10 PHRASE If something is arranged **in honor of** a particular event, it is arranged in order to celebrate that event. ❑ *The Foundation is holding a dinner at the Museum of American Art in honor of the opening of their new show.* 11 PHRASE If something is arranged or happens in someone's **honor**, it is done specially to show appreciation of them. ❑ *Mr. Mandela will attend an outdoor concert in his honor in the center of Paris.*

[영국영어 honour] 1 불가산명사 명예 ❑ 그 장교들은 폴란드에 충성하고 군인으로서의 명예를 지키며 죽었다. 2 가산명사 훈장, 명예상 ❑ 그는 상 복이 터졌는데, 그 중에는 오스카상도 있었다. 3 타동사 영광을 누리다, 상을 받다 ❑ 디에고 마라도나는 아르헨티나 축구 협회에서 수여하는 상을 수상하는 영광을 누렸다. 4 단수명사 영예 ❑ 맨체스터를 포함한 다른 다섯 도시들이 올림픽을 유치하는 영예를 얻기 위해 경쟁하고 있었다. 5 수동 타동사 매우 고맙게 여기다, 영광스럽게 여기다 [공손체] ❑ 페인 씨는 그 일을 맡게 되어 매우 영광이고 그 일에 도전하는 것이 매우 기대된다고 말했다. 6 타동사 경의를 표하다 ❑ 나중에 여왕 폐하가 점심 식사에 참석하여 교장에게 경의를 표했다. 7 타동사 이행하다, 지키다 ❑ 두 측이 새로운 휴전 협정을 이행하기로 동의했다. 8 호격명사 각하, 귀하 ❑ 판사님, 저는 이것이 피고 측의 배경을 이해하는 데 중요하다고 생각하여 이를 제기합니다. 9 불가산명사 우등 학위 [영국영어] ❑ 경영학과의 우등 학위 ❑ ...경영학과의 우등 학위 10 구 -을 기념하여, -을 축하하여 ❑ 그 재단은 새로운 전시회의 개막을 기념하여 미국 미술품 박물관에서 만찬을 개최할 예정이다. 11 구 -에게 경의를 표하는 ❑ 만델라 씨는 파리 도심에서 자신을 위해 열리는 야외 음악회에 참가할 것이다.

Thesaurus   honor의 참조어

N.	award, distinction, recognition 2
V.	commend, praise, recognize 3

a b c d e f g h i j k l m n o p q r s t u v w x y z

Word Partnership honor의 연어

N.	code of honor, sense of honor **1**
	honor a ceasefire **7**
	honor the memory of *someone/something* **9** **10**
ADJ.	great/highest honor **2** **4**

hon|or|able /ɒnrəbəl/ [BRIT **honourable**] ADJ If you describe people or actions as **honorable**, you mean that they are good and deserve to be respected and admired. ❑ *He argued that the only honorable course of action was death.*
● **hon|or|ably** /ɒnrəbli/ ADV ❑ *He also felt she had not behaved honorably in the leadership election.*

hon|or|ary /ɒnrɛəri, BRIT ɒnrəri/ **1** ADJ An **honorary** title or membership of a group is given to someone without their needing to have the necessary qualifications, usually their public achievements. [ADJ n] ❑ *He will be awarded the honorary degree in a ceremony at Newcastle University.* **2** ADJ **Honorary** is used to describe an official job that is done without payment. [ADJ n] ❑ *...the honorary secretary of the Cheshire Beekeepers' Association.*

hon|our /ɒnər/ →see **honor**

hon|our|able /ɒnrəbəl/ →see **honorable**

hood /hʊd/ (**hoods**) **1** N-COUNT A **hood** is a part of a coat which you can pull up to cover your head. It is in the shape of a triangular bag attached to the neck of the coat at the back. ❑ *He drew up the hood of his anorak.* **2** N-COUNT The **hood** of a car is the metal cover over the engine at the front. [AM; BRIT **bonnet**] ❑ *He raised the hood of McKee's truck.*

hood|ed /hʊdɪd/ **1** ADJ A **hooded** piece of clothing or furniture has a hood. ❑ *...a blue, hooded anorak.* **2** ADJ A **hooded** person is wearing a hood or a piece of clothing pulled down over their face, so they are difficult to recognize. [ADJ n] ❑ *The class was held hostage by a hooded gunman.*

hoof /huf, hʊf/ (**hoofs** or **hooves**) N-COUNT The **hooves** of an animal such as a horse are the hard lower parts of its feet. ❑ *The horses' hooves often could not get a proper grip.*

hook ♦♢♢ /hʊk/ (**hooks, hooking, hooked**) **1** N-COUNT A **hook** is a bent piece of metal or plastic that is used for catching or holding things, or for hanging things up. ❑ *One of his jackets hung from a hook.* **2** V-T/V-I If you **hook** one thing to another, you attach it there using a hook. If something **hooks** somewhere, it can be hooked there. ❑ *Paul hooked his tractor to the car and pulled it to safety.* **3** V-T If you **hook** your arm, leg, or foot round an object, you place it like a hook round the object in order to move it or hold it. ❑ *She latched on to his arm, hooking her other arm around a tree.* **4** V-T If you **hook** a fish, you catch it with a hook on the end of a line. ❑ *At the first cast I hooked a huge fish, probably a tench.* **5** N-COUNT A **hook** is a short sharp blow with your fist that you make with your elbow bent, usually in a boxing match. ❑ *Lewis desperately needs to keep clear of Ruddock's big left hook.* **6** V-T/V-I If you **are hooked into** something, or **hook into** something, you get involved with it. [mainly AM] ❑ *I'm guessing again now because I'm not hooked into the political circles.* **7** V-I If you **hook into** the Internet, you make a connection with the Internet on a particular occasion so that you can use it. ❑ *...an interactive media tent where people will be able to hook into the Internet.* ● PHRASAL VERB **Hook up** means the same as **hook**. ❑ *...a UK firm that lets Britons hook up to the Internet.* **8** PHRASE If someone gets **off the hook** or is let **off the hook**, they manage to get out of the awkward or unpleasant situation that they are in. [INFORMAL] ❑ *Government officials accused of bribery and corruption get off the hook with monotonous regularity.* **9** PHRASE If you take a phone **off the hook**, you take the receiver off the part that it normally rests on, so that the phone will not ring. ❑ *I'd taken my phone off the hook in order to get some sleep.* **10** PHRASE If your phone **is ringing off the hook**, so many people are trying to telephone you that it is ringing constantly. [AM] ❑ *Since war broke out, the phones at donation centers have been ringing off the hook.*

▸ **hook up** **1** →see **hook 7** **2** PHRASAL VERB When someone **hooks up** a computer or other electronic machine, they connect it to other similar machines or to a central power supply. ❑ *...technicians who hook up computer systems and networks.* ❑ *He brought it down, hooked it up, and we got the generator going.*

Word Partnership hook의 연어

V.	bait a hook, hang *something* from a hook **1**
ADJ.	sharp hook **1**

hooked /hʊkt/ **1** ADJ If you describe something as **hooked**, you mean that it is shaped like a hook. ❑ *He was thin and tall, with a hooked nose.* **2** ADJ If you are **hooked on** something, you enjoy it so much that it takes up a lot of your interest and attention. [INFORMAL] [v-link ADJ, oft ADJ on n] ❑ *Many of the leaders have become hooked on power and money.* **3** ADJ If you are **hooked on** a drug, you are addicted to it. [INFORMAL] [v-link ADJ, oft ADJ on n] ❑ *He spent a number of years hooked on cocaine, heroin, and alcohol.*

hook|er /hʊkər/ (**hookers**) N-COUNT A **hooker** is a prostitute. [mainly AM, INFORMAL]

hoo|li|gan /huligən/ (**hooligans**) N-COUNT If you describe people, especially young people, as **hooligans**, you are critical of them because they behave in a noisy and violent way in a public place. [DISAPPROVAL] ❑ *...riots involving football hooligans.*

[영국영어 honourable] 형용사 명예로운, 존경할 만한 ❑ 그는 명예를 지킬 수 있는 유일한 방책은 죽음뿐이라고 주장하였다. ● 존경받을 만하게, 훌륭하게 부사 ❑ 그도 그녀가 대표자 선거에서 훌륭하게 처신하지 않았다고 생각했다.

1 형용사 명예의 ❑ 그는 뉴캐슬 대학 학위 수여식에서 명예 학위를 받을 것이다. **2** 형용사 무보수의 ❑ 체셔 양봉가 협회에서 무보수로 일하는 총무

1 가산명사 두건, 모자 ❑ 그는 파카의 모자를 끌어올렸다. **2** 가산명사 (자동차 앞) 덮개, 보닛 [미국영어; 영국영어 bonnet] ❑ 그는 맥키의 트럭 보닛을 들어올렸다.

1 형용사 모자가 달린; 덮개가 달린 ❑ 모자 달린 파란색 파카 **2** 형용사 모자를 푹 내려쓴, 두건을 뒤집어쓴 ❑ 그 학급은 모자를 푹 눌러쓴 총잡이에게 인질로 잡혔다.

가산명사 말굽 ❑ 말굽은 종종 단단히 붙지 않을 수 있다.

1 가산명사 갈고리, 훅 ❑ 그의 재킷 중 하나가 고리에 걸려 있었다. **2** 타동사/자동사 고리로 걸다; 고리로 연결되다, 붙다 ❑ 폴은 고리를 걸어 자기 트랙터를 그 자동차에 연결시키고 그것을 안전한 곳으로 끌어내었다. **3** 타동사 (갈고리 모양으로) 구부려 걸다 ❑ 그녀는 한쪽 팔을 나무에 걸면서 그의 팔을 꽉 잡았다. **4** 타동사 -을 낚싯바늘로 낚다 ❑ 내가 처음으로 낚시 바늘을 던져서 큰 물고기를 잡았는데 아마도 잉어였던 것 같다. **5** 가산명사 (권투의) 훅 ❑ 루이스는 러독의 강한 왼쪽 훅을 결사적으로 피해야 한다. **6** 타동사/자동사 끌려 들어가다, 연루되다 [주로 미국영어] ❑ 나는 이제는 정치 집단들에 직접 연관되어 있는 것이 아니기 때문에 다시 추측을 해 보고 있다. **7** 자동사 접속하다 ❑ 사람들이 인터넷에 접속할 수 있는 인터액티브 미디어 텐트 ● 구동사 접속하다 ❑ 영국 사람들이 인터넷에 접속할 수 있게 해 주는 영국 회사 **8** 구 궁지에서 벗어난 [비격식체] ❑ 수뢰와 부패 혐의로 기소된 정부 공무원들은 어김없이 궁지에서 벗어난다. **9** 구 (전화기) 제자리에 안 놓여 ❑ 나는 잠을 좀 자려고 수화기를 내려놓았다. **10** 구 (전화가) 끊임없이 오는 [미국영어] ❑ 전쟁이 발발한 이후에, 기부금 센터의 전화가 쉴 새 없이 울리고 있다.

2 구동사 -와 연결하다 ❑ 컴퓨터 시스템과 네트워크를 연결해 주는 기술자들 ❑ 그가 그것을 내려 연결하자, 우리 발전기가 작동되었다.

1 형용사 갈고리 모양의 ❑ 그는 매부리코에 마르고 키가 컸다. **2** 형용사 -에 푹 빠진 [비격식체] ❑ 지도자들 중 많은 이들이 권력과 돈에 푹 빠지게 되었다. **3** 형용사 -에 중독된 [비격식체] ❑ 그는 코카인, 헤로인, 그리고 알코올에 중독된 채 여러 해를 보냈다.

가산명사 매춘부 [주로 미국영어, 비격식체]

가산명사 불량배, 훌리건 (공공장소에서 난동을 부리는 관중) [탐탁찮음] ❑ 축구 훌리건을 포함한 난동꾼들

hoo|li|gan|ism /ˈhuːlɪɡənɪzəm/ N-UNCOUNT **Hooliganism** is the behavior and actions of hooligans. ❑ *...police investigating football hooliganism.*

불가산명사 (훌리건들의) 난동 ❑ 축구장에서 훌리건들이 일으킨 난동을 조사하고 있는 경찰

hoop /huːp/ (**hoops**) **1** N-COUNT A **hoop** is a large ring made of wood, metal, or plastic. ❑ *A boy came towards them, rolling an iron hoop.* **2** PHRASE If someone makes you **jump through hoops**, they make you do lots of difficult or boring things in order to please them or achieve something. ❑ *He had the duty receptionist almost jumping through hoops for him. But to no avail.*

1 가산명사 둥근 테, 고리 ❑ 한 소년이 굴렁쇠를 굴리며 그들을 향해 왔다. **2** 구 온갖 재주를 부리다 ❑ 그는 그 사람을 만족시키기 위해 담당 접대부원에게 거의 온갖 재주를 다 부리게 했다. 그러나 아무 소용이 없었다.

hoot /huːt/ (**hoots, hooting, hooted**) **1** V-T/V-I If you **hoot** the horn on a vehicle or if it **hoots**, it makes a loud noise on one note. [mainly BRIT] ❑ *I never hoot my horn when I pick a girl up for a date.* ❑ *Somewhere in the distance a siren hooted.* ● N-COUNT **Hoot** is also a noun. [AM usually **honk, toot**] ❑ *Mortlake strode on, ignoring the car, in spite of a further warning hoot.* **2** V-I If you **hoot**, you make a loud high-pitched noise when you are laughing or showing disapproval. ❑ *The protesters chanted, blew whistles and hooted at the name of Governor Pete Wilson.* ● N-COUNT **Hoot** is also a noun. ❑ *His confession was greeted with derisive hoots.* **3** PHRASE If you say that you **don't give a hoot** or **don't care two hoots about** something, you are emphasizing that you do not care at all about it. [INFORMAL, EMPHASIS] ❑ *Alan doesn't care two hoots about Irish politics.*

1 타동사/자동사 (경적을) 울리다; (경적이) 울리다 [주로 영국영어] ❑ 나는 데이트하러 차로 여자를 태우러 갈 때 경적을 절대로 울리지 않는다. ❑ 멀리 어디선가에서 사이렌이 울렸다. ● 가산명사 경적 소리 [미국영어 대개 honk, toot] ❑ 모트레이크는 그 차를 무시하고 터널에서 들리는 경적 소리에도 불구하고 계속 앞으로 걸어갔다. **2** 자동사 큰 소리로 외치다, 야유하다 ❑ 주지사 피트 윌슨의 이름이 나오자 시위자들은 구호를 외치고 휘파람을 불며 야유했다. ● 가산명사 야유 소리 ❑ 그의 고백에 비웃는 야유 소리가 나왔다. **3** 구 조금도 개의치 않다 [비격식체, 강조] ❑ 앨런은 아일랜드 정치에 대해서는 조금도 신경쓰지 않는다.

hoo|ver /ˈhuːvər/ (**hoovers, hoovering, hoovered**) **1** N-COUNT A **Hoover** is a vacuum cleaner. [BRIT, TRADEMARK] **2** V-T If you **hoover** a room or a carpet, you clean it using a vacuum cleaner. [BRIT] ❑ *She hoovered the study and the sitting-room.* ● **hoo|ver|ing** N-UNCOUNT [also the N] ❑ *I finished off the hoovering upstairs.*

1 가산명사 진공청소기 [영국영어, 상표] **2** 타동사 진공청소기로 청소하다 [영국영어] ❑ 그녀는 서재와 거실을 진공청소기로 청소했다. ● 진공청소기로 청소함 불가산명사 ❑ 나는 진공청소기로 위층 청소를 끝마쳤다.

hooves /huːvz/ **Hooves** is a plural of **hoof**.

hoof의 복수

hop /hɒp/ (**hops, hopping, hopped**) **1** V-I If you **hop**, you move along by jumping on one foot. ❑ *I hopped down three steps.* ● N-COUNT **Hop** is also a noun. ❑ *"This really is a catching rhythm, huh?" he added, with a few little hops.* **2** V-I When birds and some small animals **hop**, they move along by jumping on both feet. ❑ *A small brown fawn hopped across the trail in front of them.* ● N-COUNT **Hop** is also a noun. ❑ *The rabbit got up, took four hops and turned round.* **3** V-I If you **hop** somewhere, you move there quickly or suddenly. [INFORMAL] ❑ *My wife and I were the first to arrive and hopped on board.* **4** N-COUNT A **hop** is a short, quick journey, usually by plane. [INFORMAL] ❑ *It is a three-hour drive from Geneva but can be reached by a 20-minute hop in a private helicopter.* **5** N-COUNT **Hops** are flowers that are dried and used for making beer. **6** PHRASE If you are caught **on the hop**, you are surprised by someone doing something when you were not expecting them to and so you are not prepared for it. [BRIT, INFORMAL] ❑ *His plans almost caught security chiefs and hotel staff on the hop.*

1 자동사 깡충깡충 뛰다, 깡충거리다 ❑ 나는 계단 세 개를 껑충 뛰어 내려갔다. ● 가산명사 깡충거림 ❑ "이거 정말 매혹적인 리듬이다. 그렇지?"라고 몇 번 깡충거리면서 그가 덧붙였다. **2** 자동사 깡충거리다, 깡충깡충 뛰다 ❑ 작은 갈색 사슴 한 마리가 그들 앞에서 깡충거리며 길을 가로질러 갔다. ● 가산명사 깡충거림 ❑ 토끼가 일어나서 네 번 깡충거리더니 몸을 돌렸다. **3** 자동사 재빨리 이동하다 [비격식체] ❑ 아내와 나는 제일 먼저 도착해서 승선했다. **4** 가산명사 짧은 여행 [비격식체] ❑ 그곳은 제네바에서 차로 3시간 운전해야 가는 거리이지만 개인 헬리콥터로는 20분간의 짧은 비행만으로 도착할 수 있는 거리이다. **5** 가산명사 (식물) 홉 **6** 구 허둥지둥하는, 허둥거리는 [영국영어, 비격식체] ❑ 그의 계획은 자칫 보안 경비 과장들과 호텔 직원들을 허둥지둥하게 만들 뻔했다.

hope ♦♦♦ /hoʊp/ (**hopes, hoping, hoped**) **1** V-T/V-I If you **hope** that something is true, or if you **hope** for something, you want it to be true or to happen, and you usually believe that it is possible or likely. ❑ *She had decided she must go on as usual, follow her normal routine, and hope and pray.* ❑ *He hesitates before leaving, almost as though he had been hoping for conversation.* **2** V-T/V-I If you say that you cannot **hope for** something, or if you talk about the only thing that you can **hope to** get, you mean that you are in a bad situation, and there is very little chance of improving it. [with brd-neg] ❑ *Things aren't ideal, but that's the best you can hope for.* ● N-VAR **Hope** is also a noun. ❑ *The only hope for underdeveloped countries is to become, as far as possible, self-reliant.* **3** N-UNCOUNT **Hope** is a feeling of desire and expectation that things will go well in the future. ❑ *Now that he has become President, many people once again have hope for genuine changes in the system.* ❑ *But Kevin hasn't given up hope of being fit.* **4** N-COUNT If someone wants something to happen, and considers it likely or possible, you can refer to their **hopes of** that thing, or to their **hope that** it will happen. ❑ *They have hopes of increasing trade between the two regions.* ❑ *My hope is that, in the future, I will go over there and marry her.* **5** N-COUNT If you think that the help or success of a particular person or thing will cause you to be successful or to get what you want, you can refer to them as your **hope**. ❑ *Roemer represented the best hope for a businesslike climate in Louisiana.* **6** PHRASE If you are in a difficult situation and do something and **hope for the best**, you hope that everything will happen in the way you want, although you know that it may not. ❑ *Some companies are cutting costs and hoping for the best.* **7** PHRASE If you tell someone not to **get** their **hopes up**, or not to **build** their **hopes up**, you are warning them that they should not become too confident of progress or success. ❑ *There is no reason for people to get their hopes up over this mission.* **8** PHRASE If you say that someone has **not** got **a hope in hell of** doing something, you are emphasizing that they will not be able to do it. [INFORMAL, EMPHASIS] ❑ *Everybody knows they haven't got a hope in hell of forming a government anyway.* **9** PHRASE If you have **high hopes** or **great hopes that** something will happen, you are confident that it will happen. ❑ *I had great hopes that Derek Randall might play an important part.* **10** PHRASE If you **hope against hope that** something will happen, you hope that it will happen, although it seems impossible. ❑ *She glanced about the hall, hoping against hope that Richard would be waiting for her.* **11** PHRASE You use "**I hope**" in expressions such as "**I hope you don't mind**" and "**I hope I'm not disturbing you**," when you are being polite and want to make sure that you have not offended someone or disturbed them. [POLITENESS] ❑ *I hope you don't mind me coming to see you.* **12** PHRASE You say "**I hope**" when you want to warn someone not to do something foolish or dangerous. ❑ *You're not trying to see him, I hope?* **13** PHRASE

1 타동사/자동사 바라다, 희망하다 ❑ 그녀는 계속 평소와 같이 지내며, 평소의 일과를 따르고, 희망을 가지고 기도를 해야겠다고 결심했다. ❑ 그는 마치 대화를 하고 싶었던 것처럼 떠나기 전에 망설이고 있다. **2** 타동사/자동사 기대하다 ❑ 상황이 이상적이지는 않지만, 당신이 기대할 수 있는 최선의 상황이다. ● 가산명사 또는 불가산명사 희망, 바람 ❑ 후진국들의 유일한 바람은 가능한 한 최대한 자립하게 되는 것이다. **3** 불가산명사 기대 ❑ 이제 그가 대통령이 되었으므로, 많은 사람들이 다시 한 번 제도의 진정한 변화에 대한 기대를 갖는다. ❑ 그러나 케빈은 몸이 좋아지리라는 희망을 포기하지 않았다. **4** 가산명사 희망, 기대치 ❑ 그들은 그 두 지역 간의 무역이 증가할 것이라는 기대를 가지고 있다. ❑ 나의 희망은 장차 그곳으로 가서 그녀와 결혼하는 것이다. **5** 가산명사 희망, 희망을 주는 것 ❑ 로에머는 루이지애나에 사업하기 좋은 환경을 만들 가망성이 가장 높은 사람이었다. **6** 구 낙관하다, 희망을 잃지 않다 ❑ 몇몇 회사들은 원가를 절감하며 희망을 잃지 않고 있다. **7** 구 지나치게 낙관하다 ❑ 사람들이 그 일에 대해서 지나치게 낙관할 이유가 없다. **8** 구 -의 가망은 전혀 없다 [비격식체, 강조] ❑ 그들이 어떻게든 정부를 구성할 가망은 전혀 없다는 것을 모두 안다. **9** 구 큰 기대, 강한 확신 ❑ 나는 데릭 랜덜이 중요한 역할을 하리라는 높은 기대를 가지고 있었다. **10** 구 혹시나 하는 희망을 버리지 않다, 헛된 기대를 하다 ❑ 그녀는 혹시라도 리처드가 자기를 기다리고 있을지도 모른다는 헛된 기대를 하면서 홀을 힐끗 둘러보았다. **11** 구 생각하다, 바라다 [공손체] ❑ 제가 당신을 만나려 오는데 방해가 되지 않기를 바랍니다. **12** 구 설마 -는 아니겠지 ❑ 설마 내가 그를 만나려고 하는 건 아니겠지? **13** 구 기대하고 ❑ 그는 공과 대학에 입학하는 것을 기대하며 공부를 하고 있었다. **14** 구 희망을 품고 살다 ❑ 나는 언젠가 그녀가 나에게 말을 할 것이라는 희망만 품고 살고 있다. **15** 관용 표현 절망적이다, 전혀 가망이 없다 [비격식체, 감정 개입] ❑ 업계는 이번 회계 연도에 주문이 10퍼센트까지 증대할 것이라고 추정한다. 전혀 가망 없는 일이다.

A

If you do one thing **in the hope of** another thing happening, you do it because you think it might cause or help the other thing to happen, which is what you want. ❑ *He was studying in the hope of being admitted to an engineering college.* ⓮ PHRASE If you **live in hope** that something will happen, you continue to hope that it will happen, although it seems unlikely, and you realize that you are being foolish. ❑ *I just live in hope that one day she'll talk to me.* ⓯ CONVENTION If you say "**Some hope**," or "**Not a hope**," you think there is no possibility that something will happen, although you may want it to happen. [INFORMAL, FEELINGS] ❑ *The industry reckons it will see orders swell by 10% this financial year. Some hope.*

Thesaurus　　　*hope*의 참조어

| V. | aspire, desire, dream, wish ❶ |
| N. | ambition, aspiration, desire, dream, wish ❹ |

Word Partnership　　　*hope*의 연어

V.	**give** *someone* hope, **give up** *all* hope, **hold out** hope, **lose** *all* hope ❸ ❹
ADJ.	**faint** hope, **false** hope, **little** hope ❶ ❸ ❹
N.	**glimmer of** hope ❸

---

hope|ful /hoʊpfəl/ (**hopefuls**) ❶ ADJ If you are **hopeful**, you are fairly confident that something that you want to happen will happen. ❑ *I am hopeful this misunderstanding will be rectified very quickly.* ● **hope|ful|ly** ADV [ADV with v] ❑ *"Am I welcome?" He smiled hopefully, leaning on the door.* ❷ ADJ If something such as a sign or event is **hopeful**, it makes you feel that what you want to happen will happen. ❑ *The result of the election is yet another hopeful sign that peace could come to the Middle East.* ❸ ADJ A **hopeful** action is one that you do in the hope that you will get what you want to get. [ADJ n] ❑ *We've chartered the aircraft in the hopeful anticipation that the government will allow them to leave.* ❹ N-COUNT If you refer to someone as a **hopeful**, you mean that they are hoping and trying to achieve success in a particular career, election, or competition. ❑ *His soccer skills continue to be put to good use in his job as football coach to young hopefuls.*

hope|ful|ly /hoʊpfəli/ ADV You say **hopefully** when mentioning something that you hope will happen. Some careful speakers of English think that this use of hopefully is not correct, but it is very frequently used. [ADV with cl/group] ❑ *Hopefully, you won't have any problems after reading this.*

hope|less /hoʊplɪs/ ❶ ADJ If you feel **hopeless**, you feel very unhappy because there seems to be no possibility of a better situation or success. ❑ *He had not heard her cry before in this uncontrolled, hopeless way.* ● **hope|less|ly** ADV ❑ *I looked around hopelessly.* ● **hope|less|ness** N-UNCOUNT ❑ *She had a feeling of hopelessness about the future.* ❷ ADJ Someone or something thing that is **hopeless** is certain to fail or be unsuccessful. ❑ *I don't believe your situation is as hopeless as you think. If you love each other, you'll work it out.* ❸ ADJ If someone is **hopeless at** something, they are very bad at it. [INFORMAL] ❑ *I'd be hopeless at working for somebody else.* ❹ ADJ You use **hopeless** to emphasize how bad or inadequate something or someone is. [EMPHASIS] ❑ *Argentina's economic policies were a hopeless mess.* ● **hope|less|ly** ADV ❑ *They were on the other side of Berlin and Harry was hopelessly lost.*

horde /hɔrd/ (**hordes**) N-COUNT If you describe a crowd of people as a **horde**, you mean that the crowd is very large and excited and, often, rather frightening or unpleasant. ❑ *This attracts hordes of tourists to Las Vegas.*

ho|ri|zon /həraɪzⁿn/ (**horizons**) ❶ N-SING The **horizon** is the line in the far distance where the sky seems to meet the land or the sea. ❑ *A grey smudge appeared on the horizon. That must be Calais, thought Fay.* ❷ N-COUNT Your **horizons** are the limits of what you want to do or of what you are interested or involved in. ❑ *As your horizons expand, these new ideas can give a whole new meaning to life.* ❸ PHRASE If something is **on the horizon**, it is almost certainly going to happen or be done quite soon. ❑ *With breast cancer, as with many common diseases, there is no obvious breakthrough on the horizon.*

hori|zon|tal /hɒrɪzɒntⁿl, BRIT hɒrɪzɒntⁿl/ ADJ Something that is **horizontal** is flat and level with the ground, rather than at an angle to it. ❑ *The board consists of vertical and horizontal lines.* ● N-SING **Horizontal** is also a noun. ❑ *Do not raise your left arm above the horizontal.* ● **hori|zon|tal|ly** ADV ❑ *The wind was cold and drove the snow at him almost horizontally.* →see **graph**

hor|mo|nal /hɔrmoʊnⁿl/ ADJ **Hormonal** means relating to or involving hormones. ❑ *...our individual hormonal balance.*

hor|mone /hɔrmoʊn/ (**hormones**) N-COUNT A **hormone** is a chemical, usually occurring naturally in your body, that makes an organ of your body do something. ❑ *...the male sex hormone testosterone.* →see **emotion**

horn /hɔrn/ (**horns**) ❶ N-COUNT On a vehicle such as a car, the **horn** is the device that makes a loud noise as a signal or warning. ❑ *He sounded the car horn.* ❷ N-COUNT The **horns** of an animal such as a cow or deer are the hard pointed things that grow from its head. ❑ *A mature cow has horns.* ❸ N-COUNT A **horn** is a musical instrument of the brass family. It is a long circular metal tube, wide at one end, which you play by blowing. ❑ *He started playing the horn when he was eight.* ❹ N-COUNT A **horn** is a simple musical instrument consisting of a metal tube that is wide at one end and narrow at the other. You play it by blowing into it. ❑ *...a hunting horn.* ❺ PHRASE If two people **lock horns**, they argue about something. ❑ *During his six years in office, Seidman has often locked horns with lawmakers.*

---

❶ 형용사 기대하고 있는, 바라는 ❑ 나는 이러한 오해가 빨리 풀리기를 바란다. ● 희망을 갖고, 기대를 하며 부사 ❑ "들어가도 될까요?" 그는 문에 기대어, 기대를 하며 웃었다. ❷ 형용사 희망적인 ❑ 그 선거 결과는 중동 지역에 평화가 올 수 있다는 또 다른 희망적인 신호이다. ❸ 형용사 희망을 걸고 하는 ❑ 정부가 그들이 떠나는 것을 허락해 주리라는 희망적인 기대를 안고 우리는 비행기를 전세 냈다. ❹ 가산명사 기대주, 유망주 ❑ 그의 축구 기술은 젊은 유망주들의 축구 코치로서의 그의 직업에 계속해서 매우 유용하다.

부사 원하건대 ❑ 바라건대, 당신이 이것을 읽은 뒤에는 어떤 문제도 없을 것이다.

❶ 형용사 희망이 없는, 절망적인 ❑ 그는 이전에는 그녀가 이렇게 자제를 하지 못하고 절망적으로 우는 소리를 들어 본 적이 없었다. ● 절망적으로 부사 ❑ 나는 절망적으로 주위를 둘러보았다. ● 절망 불가산명사 ❑ 그녀는 미래에 대해서 절망감을 느끼고 있었다. ❷ 형용사 절망적인 ❑ 나는 당신들이 생각하는 만큼 당신들의 상황이 절망적이라고 생각하지 않는다. 만일 당신들이 서로 사랑한다면 그것을 극복해 낼 수 있을 것이다. ❸ 형용사 서툰 [비격식체] ❑ 내가 다른 누군가를 위해 일하는 데는 서툴 것이다. ❹ 형용사 적절치 못한 [강조] ❑ 아르헨티나의 경제 정책은 아주 뒤죽박죽이었다. ● 적절치 못하게 부사 ❑ 그들은 베를린 반대편에 있었는데 해리가 적절치 못하게 길을 잃었던 것이다.

가산명사 떼, 무리 ❑ 이것이 라스베가스로 관광객 무리를 끌어들인다.

❶ 단수명사 지평선, 수평선 ❑ 흐릿한 회색빛 점 하나가 지평선에 나타났다. 저것이 틀림없이 칼레일 거라고 페이는 생각했다. ❷ 가산명사 한계, 범위 ❑ 당신의 관심 범위를 넓힐수록, 이렇게 새로운 생각들이 삶에 전반적으로 새로운 의미를 부여할 수 있다. ❸ 구 조짐이 보이, 일어나리 하여 ❑ 여러 흔한 질병에 대해서도 그러하듯이, 유방암에 대해서도 뚜렷한 해결책이 나타날 조짐이 없다.

형용사 수평의, 가로로 된 ❑ 그 게시판은 세로줄과 가로줄로 되어 있다. ● 단수명사 수평 ❑ 왼팔을 수평이 되도록만 올려라. ● 수평으로 부사 ❑ 바람은 차가웠는데, 그 바람이 그를 향해 거의 수평으로 눈을 휘몰고 왔다.

형용사 호르몬의 ❑ 개개인의 호르몬 균형

가산명사 호르몬 ❑ 남성 호르몬 테스토스테론

❶ 가산명사 경적 ❑ 그는 자동차 경적을 울렸다. ❷ 가산명사 뿔 ❑ 완전히 자란 소는 뿔을 가지고 있다. ❸ 가산명사 호른 (악기) ❑ 그는 여덟 살 때 호른을 연주하기 시작했다. ❹ 가산명사 나팔 ❑ 사냥용 나팔 ❺ 구 논쟁하다 ❑ 공직에 있던 6년 동안 시드맨은 입법자들과 자주 논쟁을 벌였다.

horo|scope /hɔrəskoup, BRIT hɒrəskoup/ (**horoscopes**) N-COUNT Your **horoscope** is a prediction of events which some people believe will happen to you in the future. Horoscopes are based on the position of the stars when you were born. ❑ *I always read my horoscope in The Sun and follow the advice.*

hor|ren|dous /hɔrendəs, hɒ-, hə-, BRIT hɒrendəs/ ❶ ADJ Something that is **horrendous** is very unpleasant or shocking. ❑ *He described it as the most horrendous experience of his life.* ❷ ADJ Some people use **horrendous** to describe something that is so big or great that they find it extremely unpleasant. [INFORMAL] ❑ *...the usually horrendous traffic jams.* ● **hor|ren|dous|ly** ADV ❑ *Many outings can now be horrendously expensive for parents with a young family.*

hor|ri|ble /hɔrəbᵊl, hɒr-, BRIT hɒrɪbᵊl/ ❶ ADJ If you describe something or someone as **horrible**, you do not like them at all. [INFORMAL] ❑ *The record sounds horrible.* ● **hor|ri|bly** /hɔrɪbli, hɒr-, BRIT hɒrɪbli/ ADV [ADV with v] ❑ *When trouble comes they behave selfishly and horribly.* ❷ ADJ You can call something **horrible** when it causes you to feel great shock, fear, and disgust. ❑ *Still the horrible shrieking came out of his mouth.* ● **hor|ri|bly** ADV [ADV with v] ❑ *A two-year-old boy was horribly murdered.* ❸ ADJ **Horrible** is used to emphasize how bad something is. [EMPHASIS] [ADJ n] ❑ *That seems like a horrible mess that will drag on for years.* ● **hor|ri|bly** ADV ❑ *Our plans have gone horribly wrong.*

hor|rid /hɔrɪd, hɒr-, BRIT hɒrɪd/ ❶ ADJ If you describe something as **horrid**, you mean that it is very unpleasant indeed. [INFORMAL] ❑ *What a horrid smell!* ❷ ADJ If you describe someone as **horrid**, you mean that they behave in a very unpleasant way towards other people. [INFORMAL] ❑ *I must have been a horrid little girl.*

hor|rif|ic /hɔrɪfɪk, hɒ-, hə-, BRIT hərɪfɪk/ ❶ ADJ If you describe a physical attack, accident, or injury as **horrific**, you mean that it is very bad, so that people are shocked when they see it or think about it. ❑ *I have never seen such horrific injuries.* ● **hor|rif|ical|ly** ADV [ADV with v] ❑ *He had been horrifically assaulted before he died.* ❷ ADJ If you describe something as **horrific**, you mean that it is so big that it is extremely unpleasant. ❑ *...piling up horrific extra amounts of money on top of your original debt.* ● **hor|rif|ical|ly** ADV [ADV adj] ❑ *Opera productions are horrifically expensive.*

hor|ri|fy /hɔrɪfaɪ, hɒr-, BRIT hɒrɪfaɪ/ (**horrifies**, **horrifying**, **horrified**) V-T If someone **is horrified**, they feel shocked or disgusted, usually because of something that they have seen or heard. ❑ *His family were horrified by the change.*

hor|ri|fy|ing /hɔrɪfaɪɪŋ, hɒr-/ ADJ If you describe something as **horrifying**, you mean that it is shocking or disgusting. ❑ *These were horrifying experiences.*

hor|ror ♦♢♢ /hɔrər, hɒr-, BRIT hɒrəʳ/ (**horrors**) ❶ N-UNCOUNT **Horror** is a feeling of great shock, fear, and worry caused by something extremely unpleasant. ❑ *I felt numb with horror.* ❷ N-SING If you have a **horror** of something, you are afraid of it or dislike it very much. ❑ *...his horror of death.* ❸ N-SING The **horror of** something, especially something that hurts people, is its very great unpleasantness. ❑ *...the horror of this most bloody of civil wars.* ❹ N-COUNT You can refer to extremely unpleasant or frightening experiences as **horrors**. ❑ *Can you possibly imagine all the horrors we have undergone since I last wrote you?* ❺ ADJ A **horror** film or story is intended to be very frightening. ❑ *...a psychological horror film.* ❻ ADJ You can refer to an account of a very unpleasant experience or event as a **horror** story. [ADJ n] ❑ *...a horror story about lost luggage while flying.*

horse ♦♦♢ /hɔrs/ (**horses**) ❶ N-COUNT A **horse** is a large animal which people can ride. Some horses are used for pulling plows and carts. ❑ *A small man on a grey horse had appeared.* ❷ PHRASE If you hear something **from the horse's mouth**, you hear it from someone who knows that it is definitely true. ❑ *He has got to hear it from the horse's mouth. Then he can make a judgment as to whether his policy is correct or not.*
→see Word Web: **horse**

horse|back /hɔrsbæk/ ❶ N-UNCOUNT If you do something **on horseback**, you do it while riding a horse. ❑ *In remote mountain areas, voters arrived on horseback.* ❷ ADJ A **horseback** ride is a ride on a horse. [ADJ n] ❑ *...a horseback ride into the mountains.* ● ADV **Horseback** is also an adverb. ❑ *Many people in this area ride horseback.*

horse|man /hɔrsmən/ (**horsemen**) N-COUNT A **horseman** is a man who is riding a horse, or who rides horses well. ❑ *Gerald was a fine horseman.*

horse|power /hɔrspaʊər/ N-UNCOUNT **Horsepower** is a unit of power used for measuring how powerful an engine is. ❑ *...a 300-horsepower engine.*

horse|shoe /hɔrsʃu/ (**horseshoes**) ❶ N-COUNT A **horseshoe** is a piece of metal shaped like a U, which is fixed with nails to the bottom of a horse's foot in order to protect it. ❷ N-COUNT A **horseshoe** is an object in the shape of a horseshoe which is used as a symbol of good luck, especially at a wedding.

가산명사 별점, 점성술, 운세 ❑ 나는 '더 선' 지에 나오는 별자리 운세를 항상 읽고 그 충고를 따른다.

❶ 형용사 끔찍한 ❑ 그는 그것을 그의 삶에서 가장 끔찍했던 경험이라고 묘사했다. ❷ 형용사 엄청난 [비격식체] ❑ 평상시와 같은 엄청난 교통 체증 ● 끔찍하게, 엄청나게 부사 ❑ 이제 어린 아이가 있는 부모들이 자주 나들이를 나가는 것은 엄청나게 돈이 많이 드는 일이 될 수 있다.

❶ 형용사 아주 싫은 [비격식체] ❑ 이 음반 소리 정말 마음에 안 든다. ● 정떨어지게, 혐오스럽게 부사 ❑ 문제가 발생하면 그들은 이기적이고 정떨어지게 행동한다. ❷ 형용사 무서운, 끔찍한 ❑ 끔찍하게 부사 ❑ 두 살 된 남자 아이가 끔찍하게 살해되었다. ❸ 형용사 지독한 [강조] ❑ 그것은 오랫동안 질질 끌게 될 지독한 혼란 같다. ● 지독히 부사 ❑ 우리의 계획들이 지독히도 잘못되어 왔다.

❶ 형용사 역겨운, 진저리나는 [비격식체] ❑ 정말 역겨운 냄새야! ❷ 형용사 짖궂은, 밉살스러운 [비격식체] ❑ 나는 틀림없이 밉살맞은 어린 여자 애였을 것이다.

❶ 형용사 무시무시한, 끔찍한 ❑ 나는 그렇게 끔찍한 부상을 본 적이 없다. ● 무시무시하게 부사 ❑ 그는 죽기 전에 무시무시하게 폭행을 당했었다. ❷ 형용사 엄청난 ❑ 본래 있던 빚더미 위에 엄청난 액수를 더하기 ● 엄청나게 부사 ❑ 오페라 제작은 엄청나게 비용이 많이 든다.

타동사 끔찍해 하다, 진저리나다 ❑ 그의 가족은 그 변화에 진저리가 났다.

형용사 진저리나는, 역겨운 ❑ 이것들은 진저리나는 경험들이었다.

❶ 불가산명사 두려움 ❑ 나는 두려움에 몸이 마비되는 것을 느꼈다. ❷ 단수명사 -에 대한 공포 ❑ 죽음에 대한 그의 공포 ❸ 단수명사 무시무시함 ❑ 이렇게 피로 얼룩진 무시무시한 내전 ❹ 가산명사 끔찍한 일 ❑ 내가 당신에게 마지막으로 편지를 써 보내고 난 후 우리가 겪었던 그 모든 끔찍한 일들을 당신이 상상이나 할 수 있을까? ❺ 형용사 공포물의 ❑ 심리 공포 영화 ❻ 형용사 끔찍한 ❑ 비행 중 잃어버린 짐에 대한 끔찍한 이야기

❶ 가산명사 말 ❑ 회색 말을 타고 작은 남자가 나타났었다. ❷ 구 확실한 출처에서, 믿을 수 있는 소식통으로부터 ❑ 그는 믿을 수 있는 소식통으로부터 그것을 들어야 한다. 그러면 그가 자기 방침이 옳은지 그른지에 대해 판단을 할 수 있다.

❶ 불가산명사 말을 타고, 기마로 ❑ 멀리 있는 산간 지방에서는 투표자들이 말을 타고 도착했다. ❷ 형용사 말 등의 ❑ 산 속으로 말을 타고 들어감 ● 부사 말을 타고 ❑ 이 지역의 많은 사람들이 말을 탄다.

가산명사 기수 ❑ 제럴드는 멋진 기수였다.

불가산명사 마력 ❑ 300마력짜리 엔진

❶ 가산명사 (말굽) 편자 ❷ 가산명사 편자 모양의 물건

Word Web   horse

The earliest use of **horses** was as a source of meat for prehistoric man. Then, around 4000 BC, groups began to carry goods on **horseback**. These people also probably milked the mares. Later on, early farmers used a primitive form of **bridle** to help guide their horses. In the Middle Ages, knights used horses in battle. Special **saddles** and stirrups helped them stay on the horse during combat. In the 1800s, **cowboys** had to move large herds of cattle thousands of miles. Some spent weeks at a time with only a horse for company.

horse-trading also **horsetrading** ◻ N-UNCOUNT If you describe discussions or negotiations as **horse-trading**, you disapprove of them because they are unofficial and involve compromises. [BRIT, MAINLY JOURNALISM, DISAPPROVAL] ◻ ...the anger and distaste many people feel at the political horse-trading involved in forming a government. ◻ N-UNCOUNT When negotiation or bargaining is forceful and shows clever and careful judgment, you can describe it as **horse-trading**. [AM] ◻ ...an adroit piece of political horse-trading by Senator Orrin Hatch.

◻ 불가산명사 (비공식적인) 흥정 [영국영어, 주로 언론, 탐탁찮음] ◻ 정부를 구성하는 일에 관련된 정치적 흥정에 대해서 많은 사람들이 느끼는 분노와 혐오 ◻ 불가산명사 빈틈없는 협상 [미국영어] ◻ 상원 의원 오린 해치가 빈틈없이 능숙하게 해 낸 정치적 협상 한 가지

hor|ti|cul|tur|al /hɔrtɪkʌltʃərˀl/ ADJ **Horticultural** means concerned with horticulture. ◻ The horticultural show will take place in the old covered Victorian Market.

형용사 원예학의, 원예의 ◻ 원예 전시회는 지붕이 있는 구 빅토리안 마켓에서 열릴 것이다.

hor|ti|cul|ture /hɔrtɪkʌltʃər/ N-UNCOUNT **Horticulture** is the study and practice of growing plants.

불가산명사 원예학, 원예

hose /hoʊz/ (**hoses, hosing, hosed**) ◻ N-COUNT A **hose** is a long, flexible pipe made of rubber or plastic. Water is directed through a hose in order to do things such as put out fires, clean cars, or water gardens. ◻ You've left the garden hose on. ◻ N-COUNT A **hose** is a pipe made of rubber or plastic, along which a liquid or gas flows, for example from one part of an engine to another. ◻ Water in the engine compartment is sucked away by a hose. ◻ V-T If you **hose** something, you wash or water it using a hose. ◻ We wash our cars and hose our gardens without even thinking of the water that uses. →see **scuba diving**

◻ 가산명사 호스 ◻ 당신은 정원의 호스를 잠그지 않았군요. ◻ 가산명사 호스 ◻ 엔진 부분 내부의 물은 호스로 뽑아낸다. ◻ 타동사 호스로 물을 뿌린다 ◻ 우리는 사용되는 물은 생각조차 하지 않고 세차를 하고 정원에 호수로 물을 주었다.

hos|pice /hɒspɪs/ (**hospices**) N-COUNT; N-IN-NAMES A **hospice** is a special hospital for people who are dying, where their practical and emotional needs are dealt with as well as their medical needs. ◻ ...a hospice for cancer patients.

가산명사; 이름명사 호스피스 (말기 환자를 위한 병원) ◻ 암 환자들을 위한 호스피스

hos|pi|table /hɒspɪtəbˀl, hɒspɪt-/ ◻ ADJ A **hospitable** person is friendly, generous, and welcoming to guests or people they have just met. ◻ The locals are hospitable and welcoming. ◻ ADJ A **hospitable** climate or environment is one that encourages the existence or development of particular people or things. ◻ Even in summer this place did not look exactly hospitable: in winter, conditions must have been exceedingly harsh.

◻ 형용사 환대하는, 친절한 ◻ 지역 주민들은 친절하고 호의적이다. ◻ 형용사 쾌적한 ◻ 여름에도 이곳은 그다지 쾌적해 보이지 않았다. 겨울에는 사정이 더 심했을 것이다.

Word Link   hosp, host ≈ guest : hospital, hospitality, hostage

hos|pi|tal ♦♦♦ /hɒspɪtˀl/ (**hospitals**) N-VAR A **hospital** is a place where people who are ill are cared for by nurses and doctors. ◻ ...a children's hospital with 120 beds.
→see Word Web: **hospital**

가산명사 또는 불가산명사 병원 ◻ 120개의 병상을 갖춘 소아 병원

Word Partnership   hospital의 연어

v.   **admit** someone **to** a hospital, **bring/rush/take** someone **to** a hospital, **end up in** a hospital, **go to** a hospital, **visit** someone **in** a hospital

hos|pi|tal|ity /hɒspɪtælɪti/ ◻ N-UNCOUNT **Hospitality** is friendly, welcoming behavior towards guests or people you have just met. ◻ Every visitor to Georgia is overwhelmed by the kindness, charm and hospitality of the people. ◻ N-UNCOUNT **Hospitality** is the food, drink, and other privileges which some companies provide for their visitors or clients at major sports events or other public events. ◻ ...corporate hospitality tents.

◻ 불가산명사 환대, 친절 ◻ 조지아를 방문하는 모든 방문객이 사람들의 친절, 매력, 그리고 환대에 압도된다. ◻ 불가산명사 (무료) 다과 ◻ 고객에게 다과를 제공하는 텐트

hos|pi|tal|ize /hɒspɪtəlaɪz/ (**hospitalizes, hospitalizing, hospitalized**) [BRIT also **hospitalise**] V-T If someone **is hospitalized**, they are sent or admitted to a hospital. ◻ [usu passive] ◻ Most people do not have to be hospitalized for asthma or pneumonia. ● **hos|pi|tal|za|tion** /hɒspɪtələzeɪʃˀn/ N-UNCOUNT ◻ Occasionally hospitalization is required to combat dehydration.

[영국영어 hospitalise] 타동사 입원하다 ◻ 대부분의 사람들은 천식이나 폐렴에 걸려도 입원할 필요가 없다. ● 입원 불가산명사 ◻ 탈수 현상 때문에 때로는 입원까지 해야 할 경우가 있다.

host ♦♦♦ /hoʊst/ (**hosts, hosting, hosted**) ◻ N-COUNT The **host** at a party is the person who has invited the guests and provides the food, drink, or entertainment. ◻ Apart from my host, I didn't know a single person there. ◻ V-T If someone **hosts** a party, dinner, or other function, they have invited the guests and provide the food, drink, or entertainment. ◻ Tonight she hosts a ball for 300 guests. ◻ N-COUNT A country, city, or organization that is the **host** of an event provides the facilities for that event to take place. ◻ Barcelona was chosen to be host of the 1992 Olympic games. ◻ V-T If a country, city, or organization **hosts** an event, they provide the facilities for the event to take place. ◻ Cannes hosts the annual film festival. ◻ PHRASE If a person or country **plays host to** an event or an important visitor, they host the event or the visit. ◻ The Prime Minister played host to French Premier Jacques Chirac. ◻ N-COUNT The **host** of a radio or television show is the person who introduces it and talks to the people who appear in it.

◻ 가산명사 주인, 주최자 ◻ 나를 초대한 주인을 제외하고는 나는 그곳의 단 한 사람도 알지 못했다. ◻ 타동사 주최하다 ◻ 오늘 밤 그녀는 300명의 손님에게 댄스파티를 주최한다. ◻ 가산명사 개최지, 개최국 ◻ 바르셀로나는 1992년 올림픽 개최지로 뽑혔다. ◻ 타동사 개최하다 ◻ 칸은 매년 그 영화제를 개최한다. ◻ 구 - 을 맞이하다 ◻ 수상이 자크 시락 프랑스 대통령을 맞이하였다. ◻ 가산명사 사회자, 진행자 ◻ 나는 생방송 라디오 프로그램의 사회자이다. ◻ 타동사 사회를 보다, (프로그램을) 진행하다 ◻ 그녀는 또 세인트 피터스버그 라디오 프로그램의 사회도 본다. ◻ 수량사 많은 ◻ 많은 문제들 때문에 영불 해협 터널의 개통이 연기될지도 모른다.

Word Web   hospital

Children's **Hospital** in Boston has one of the best pediatric **wards** in the country. Its Advanced Fetal Care Center can even treat babies before they are born. The hospital records about 18,000 inpatient admissions every year. It also has over 150 **outpatient** programs and handles more than 300,000 **emergency cases**. The staff includes 700 **residents** and fellows. Many of its **physicians** teach at nearby Harvard University. The hospital also employs excellent **researchers**. Their work led to the discovery of **vaccines** for **polio** and **measles**. The hospital has also led the way in liver, heart, and lung **transplants** in children.

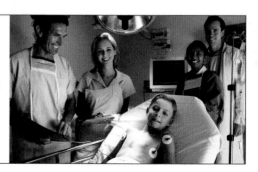

❏ *I am host of a live radio programme.* ◷ V-T The person who **hosts** a radio or television show introduces it and talks to the people who appear in it. ❏ *She also hosts a show on St Petersburg Radio.* ◷ QUANT A **host of** things is a lot of them. ❏ *A host of problems may delay the opening of the Channel Tunnel.* ◷ N-COUNT A **host** or a **host computer** is the main computer in a network of computers, which controls the most important files and programs. ❏ *Subscribers dial directly from their computers into the BBS host computer.*

◧ 가산명사 호스트 컴퓨터 ❏ 가입자들은 자기 컴퓨터에서 비비에스 호스트 컴퓨터로 직접 전화를 건다.

Word Link   *hosp, host ≈ guest : hospital, hospitality, hostage*

---

hos|tage ♦♢◌ /hɒstɪdʒ/ (**hostages**) ◧ N-COUNT A **hostage** is someone who has been captured by a person or organization and who may be killed or injured if people do not do what that person or organization demands. ❏ *It is hopeful that two hostages will be freed in the next few days.* ◪ PHRASE If someone **is taken hostage** or **is held hostage**, they are captured and kept as a hostage. ❏ *He was taken hostage while on his first foreign assignment as a television journalist.* ◫ N-VAR If you say you are **hostage** to something, you mean that your freedom to take action is restricted by things that you cannot control. ❏ *With the reduction in foreign investments, the government will be even more a hostage to the whims of the international oil price.*

◧ 가산명사 인질 ❏ 인질 두 명이 며칠 내로 풀려나리라는 희망이 있다. ◪ 구 인질로 잡히다, 납치되다 ❏ 그는 텔레비전 기자로 첫 해외 업무를 수행하던 중에 인질로 잡혔다. ◫ 가산명사 또는 불가산명사 −의 볼모, −에 발목이 잡힘 ❏ 해외 투자의 감소로, 정부는 국제 유가의 변덕스러운 변화에 더욱 발목이 잡힐 수밖에 없을 것이다.

hos|tel /hɒstəl/ (**hostels**) N-COUNT A **hostel** is a large house where people can stay cheaply for a short period of time. Hostels are usually owned by local government authorities or charities. [mainly BRIT] ❏ *...a hostel for the homeless.* →see also **youth hostel**

가산명사 호스텔 [주로 영국영어] ❏ 노숙자들을 위한 호스텔

host|ess /hoʊstɪs/ (**hostesses**) N-COUNT The **hostess** at a party is the woman who has invited the guests and provides the food, drink, or entertainment. ❏ *The hostess introduced them.*

가산명사 여주인 ❏ 여주인이 그들을 소개했다.

hos|tile /hɒstaɪl, BRIT hɒstaɪl/ ◧ ADJ If you are **hostile to** another person or an idea, you disagree with them or disapprove of them, often showing this in your behavior. ❏ *Many people felt he would be hostile to the idea of foreign intervention.* ❏ *The West has gradually relaxed its hostile attitude to this influential state.* ◪ ADJ Someone who is **hostile** is unfriendly and aggressive. ❏ *Drinking may make a person feel relaxed and happy, or it may make her hostile, violent, or depressed.* ◫ ADJ **Hostile** situations and conditions make it difficult for you to achieve something. ❏ *...some of the most hostile climatic conditions in the world.* ◳ ADJ A **hostile** takeover bid is one that is opposed by the company that is being bid for. [BUSINESS] ❏ *Soon after he arrived, Kingfisher launched a hostile bid for Dixons.* ◵ ADJ In a war, you use **hostile** to describe your enemy's forces, organizations, weapons, land, and activities. [ADJ n] ❏ *The city is encircled by a hostile army.*

◧ 형용사 반대하는 ❏ 많은 사람들은 그가 외국의 개입이라는 아이디어에 반대할 것이라고 생각했다. ❏ 이 영향력 있는 국가에 대해 서양은 적대적인 태도를 점차 누그러뜨려 왔다. ◪ 형용사 비우호적인, 적대적인 ❏ 음주는 긴장을 풀어 주고 기분을 좋게 해 줄 수도 있지만, 적대적, 폭력적이 되게 하거나 의기소침하게 만들 수도 있다. ◫ 형용사 어려운, 혹독한 ❏ 세계에서 가장 혹독한 기후 지역 중 일부 ◳ 형용사 적대적 (인수) [경제] ❏ 그가 도착한 후, 곧 킹피셔는 딕슨스에 대한 적대적 인수에 착수했다. ◵ 형용사 적의, 적군의 ❏ 그 도시는 적군에게 포위되어 있다.

Word Partnership   *hostile의 연어*

ADV.	**increasingly** hostile ◧-◫
N.	hostile **attitude/feelings/intentions** ◧
	hostile **act/action**, hostile **environment** ◫
	hostile **takeover** ◳

---

hos|til|ities /hɒstɪlɪtiz/ N-PLURAL You can refer to fighting between two countries or groups who are at war as **hostilities**. [FORMAL] ❏ *The authorities have urged people to stock up on fuel in case hostilities break out.*

복수명사 전투 [격식체] ❏ 당국은 사람들에게 전투가 벌어질 경우를 대비해서 연료를 비축하도록 촉구했다.

hos|til|ity /hɒstɪlɪti/ ◧ N-UNCOUNT **Hostility** is unfriendly or aggressive behavior towards people or ideas. ❏ *The last decade has witnessed a serious rise in the levels of racism and hostility to Black and ethnic groups.* ◪ N-UNCOUNT Your **hostility** to something you do not approve of is your opposition to it. ❏ *There is hostility among traditionalists to this method of teaching history.*

◧ 불가산명사 적대 행위 ❏ 지난 10년 동안 흑인과 소수 민족에 대한 인종 차별주의와 적대 행위가 심각한 수준으로 증가해 왔다. ◪ 불가산명사 반대 ❏ 이러한 역사 교수법에 대해서 전통주의자들 사이에 반대가 있다.

hot ♦♦♢ /hɒt/ (**hotter, hottest, hots, hotting, hotted**) ◧ ADJ Something that is **hot** has a high temperature. ❏ *When the oil is hot, add the sliced onion.* ❏ *What he needed was a hot bath and a good sleep.* ◪ ADJ **Hot** is used to describe the weather or the air in a room or building when the temperature is high. ❏ *It was too hot even for a gentle stroll.* ◫ ADJ If you are **hot**, you feel as if your body is at an unpleasantly high temperature. ❏ *I was too hot and tired to eat more than a few mouthfuls.*

◧ 형용사 뜨거운 ❏ 기름이 뜨거워지면, 썰어 놓은 양파를 넣으세요. ❏ 그에게 필요한 것은 따뜻한 물에 목욕을 하고 한숨 푹 자는 것이었다. ◪ 형용사 더운 ❏ 날씨가 가볍게 산책을 하기에도 너무 더웠다. ◫ 형용사 열이 나는 ❏ 나는 너무 열이 나고 피곤해서 몇 숟갈밖에 먹지 못했다.

> In informal English, if you want to emphasize how hot the weather is, you can say that it is **boiling** or **scorching**. In winter, if the temperature is above average, you can say that it is **mild**. In general, **hot** suggests a higher temperature than **warm**, and **warm** things are usually pleasant. ❏ *...a warm evening.*

> 비격식체 영어에서는, 날씨가 얼마나 더운지를 강조하고 싶으면, boiling이나 scorching을 쓸 수 있다. 겨울에 기온이 평균보다 높으면, 날씨가 mild하다고 할 수 있다. 대체로, hot은 warm보다 더 기온이 높은 것을 나타내고, warm한 것은 대개 쾌적하다. ❏ ...따스한 저녁

◳ ADJ You can say that food is **hot** when it has a strong, burning taste caused by chilies, pepper, or ginger. ❏ *...hot curries.* ◵ ADJ A **hot** issue or topic is one that is very important at the present time and is receiving a lot of publicity. [JOURNALISM] ❏ *The role of women in war has been a hot topic of debate in America since the Gulf conflict.* ◶ ADJ **Hot** news is new, recent, and fresh. [INFORMAL] ❏ *...eight pages of the latest movies, video releases and the hot news from Tinseltown.* ◷ ADJ You can use **hot** to describe something that is very exciting and that many people want to see, use, obtain, or become involved with. [INFORMAL] ❏ *When I was in Chicago my a friend got me a ticket for the hottest show in town: the Monet Exhibition at the Art Institute.* ◸ ADJ A **hot** contest is one that is intense and involves a great deal of activity and determination. [INFORMAL] ❏ *It took hot competition from abroad, however, to show us just how good Scottish cashmere really is.* ◹ ADJ If a person or team is the **hot** favorite, people think that they are the one most likely to

◳ 형용사 매운 ❏ 매운 카레 ◵ 형용사 (쟁점 등이) 뜨거운 [언론] ❏ 전쟁에서 여성의 역할은 걸프전 이후 미국 내에서 뜨거운 논란거리가 되어 왔다. ◶ 형용사 최신의 [비격식체] ❏ 최신 영화, 출시된 비디오, 할리우드의 최신 소식을 다룬 여덟 페이지 ◷ 형용사 인기 있는 [비격식체] ❏ 1990년에 내가 시카고에 있었을 때 내 친구가 나한테 당시 가장 인기 있던 전람회 표를 한 장 주었다. 그것은 아트 인스티튜트에서 열리는 모네 전시회였다. ◸ 형용사 치열한, 열띤 [비격식체] ❏ 외국 제품들과 치열한 경쟁이 있었으나 그것은 우리에게 그저 스코틀랜드산 캐시미어가 정말 얼마나 좋은지를 보여 주었을 뿐이다. ◹ 형용사 강력한, 유망한 ❏ 애틀랜틱 시티가 그

win a race or competition. [ADJ n] ❑ *Atlantic City is the hot favorite to stage the fight.* ⓾ ADJ Someone who has a **hot** temper gets angry very quickly and easily. ❑ *His hot temper was making it increasingly difficult for others to work with him.* ⓫ PHRASE If someone **blows hot and cold**, they keep changing their attitude towards something, sometimes being very enthusiastic and at other times expressing no interest at all. ❑ *The media, meanwhile, has blown hot and cold on the affair.* ⓬ PHRASE If you are **hot and bothered**, you are so worried and anxious that you cannot think clearly or behave sensibly. ❑ *Ray was getting very hot and bothered about the idea.* ⓭ PHRASE If you say that one person **has the hots for** another, you mean that they feel a strong sexual attraction to that person. [INFORMAL] ❑ *I've had the hots for him ever since he came to college.* →see **weather**

승부의 개최지로 가장 유력한 곳이다. ⓾ 형용사 화를 잘 내는, 성마른 ❑ 그의 성마른 성질 때문에 다른 사람들이 점점 더 그와 함께 일하는 것을 힘들어하게 되었다. ⓫ 구 이랬다 저랬다 하다, 좋다고 했다가 싫다고 하곤 하다 ❑ 그러는 동안 대중 매체에서는 그 문제에 대해 계속 이랬다 저랬다 했다. ⓬ 구 안절부절못하는 ❑ 레이는 그 생각 때문에 점점 더 안절부절못했다. ⓭ 구 성적 매력을 느끼다 [비격식체] ❑ 나는 그가 대학에 들어왔을 때부터 줄곧 그에게 성적 매력을 느껴 왔다.

Thesaurus   hot의 참조어

ADJ.   swelltering; *(ant.)* chilly, cold ② ③
        spicy; *(ant.)* bland, mild ④
        cool, popular; *(ant.)* unpopular ⑦

▶**hot up** PHRASAL VERB When something **hots up**, it becomes more active or exciting. [BRIT] ❑ *The bars rarely hot up before 1 a.m. or the night-clubs before 2 a.m.*

구동사 활기를 띠다 [영국영어] ❑ 술집은 새벽 1시가 되어야, 나이트클럽은 새벽 2시가 되어야 완자지껄해진다.

hot but|ton (**hot buttons**) N-COUNT A **hot button** is a subject or problem that people have very strong feelings about. [mainly AM, JOURNALISM] [oft N n] ❑ *Abortion is still one of the hot button issues of U.S. life.*

가산명사 뜨거운 논란거리 [주로 미국영어, 언론] ❑ 낙태는 여전히 미국 생활에서 뜨거운 논란거리 중의 하나이다.

hot dog (**hot dogs**) N-COUNT A **hot dog** is a long bread roll with a hot sausage inside it.

가산명사 핫도그

ho|tel ♦♦◇ /hoʊtɛl/ (**hotels**) N-COUNT A **hotel** is a building where people stay, for example on vacation, paying for their rooms and sometimes their meals.

가산명사 호텔

In addition to **hotels**, there are several other types of accommodation for travelers and tourists. A **bed and breakfast** or **B & B** is a private home that rents out rooms and serves only breakfast. A **motel** is similar in size to a hotel but particularly is designed for those traveling by car, so the parking lot is very convenient. **Youth hostels** provide dormitories for young people who want low-priced lodgings.

→see Word Web: **hotel**

hotel(호텔) 외에도 여행객을 위한 여러 형태의 숙박시설이 있다. bed and breakfast 또는 B & B(비 앤 비)는 가정집이면서 방을 빌려주고 아침식사만 제공한다. motel(모텔)은 호텔과 규모는 비슷하나 특히 자동차 여행객을 위해 만들어져서 주차장이 아주 편리하다. youth hostel(유스 호스텔)은 싼 가격의 숙박을 원하는 젊은 사람들을 위한 공동 숙소이다.

Word Partnership   hotel의 연어

N.   hotel **guest**, hotel **reservation**, hotel **room**
V.   **check into a** hotel, **check out of a** hotel, **stay at a** hotel
ADJ.   **luxury** hotel, **new** hotel

---

ho|tel|ier /oʊtɛlyeɪ, BRIT hoʊtɛliər/ (**hoteliers**) N-COUNT A **hotelier** is a person who owns or manages a hotel.

가산명사 호텔 경영자

hot key (**hot keys**) N-COUNT A **hot key** is a key, or a combination of keys, on a computer keyboard that you can press in order to make something happen, without having to type the full instructions. [COMPUTING] ❑ *All macros can be set to run when a hot key is pressed.*

가산명사 (컴퓨터) 단축키 [컴퓨터] ❑ 모든 매크로는 단축키를 누르면 실행할 수 있다.

hot|line /hɒtlaɪn/ (**hotlines**) also **hot line** ⓵ N-COUNT A **hotline** is a telephone line that the public can use to contact an organization about a particular subject. Hotlines allow people to obtain information from an organization or to give the organization information. ❑ *...a telephone hotline for gardeners seeking advice.* ② N-COUNT A **hotline** is a special, direct telephone line between the heads of government in different countries. ❑ *They have discussed setting up a military hotline between Hanoi and Bangkok.*

⓵ 가산명사 전화 상담 서비스 ❑ 조언을 구하는 정원사들을 위한 전화 상담 서비스 ② 가산명사 (정부 수뇌 간의) 긴급 직통 전화 ❑ 그들은 하노이와 방콕 간에 군사 긴급 직통 전화를 설치하는 것에 대해 논의했다.

hot link (**hot links**) N-COUNT A **hot link** is a word or phrase in a hypertext document that can be selected in order to access additional information. [COMPUTING] ❑ *Each of these pages has hot links to other documents throughout the network.*

가산명사 핫링크 [컴퓨터] ❑ 각각의 페이지는 네트워크 전반에 걸쳐 다른 문서들과 핫링크로 연결되어 있다.

hot|ly /hɒtli/ ⓵ ADV If people discuss, argue, or say something **hotly**, they speak in a lively or angry way, because they feel strongly. [ADV with v] ❑ *The bank hotly denies any wrongdoing.* ② ADV If you are being **hotly** pursued, someone is trying hard to catch you and is close behind you. [ADV with v] ❑ *He'd snuck out of America hotly pursued by the CIA.*

⓵ 부사 강력히 ❑ 그 은행은 어떤 범법 행위도 강력히 부인한다. ② 부사 바싹, 맹렬히 ❑ 그는 시아이에이(CIA)가 바싹 뒤쫓는데도 미국을 교묘히 빠져나갔다.

hound /haʊnd/ (**hounds, hounding, hounded**) ⓵ N-COUNT A **hound** is a type of dog that is often used for hunting or racing. ❑ *Rainey's chief interest in life is hunting with hounds.* ② V-T If someone **hounds** you, they constantly disturb or speak to you in an annoying or upsetting way. ❑ *Newcomers are constantly*

⓵ 가산명사 사냥개 ❑ 레이니는 삶의 주된 관심사가 사냥개를 데리고 사냥을 하는 것이다. ② 타동사 따라다니며 괴롭히다 ❑ 새로 온 사람들이 조언을 해달라고 끊임없이 따라다니며 그들을 괴롭혔다.

Word Web   hotel

When making **reservations** at a **hotel**, most people request a **single** or a **double** room. Sometimes the **clerk** invites the person to **upgrade** to a **suite**. When arriving at the hotel, the first person to greet the **guest** is the bellhop. He will put the person's suitcases on a **luggage cart**. The guest then goes to the **front desk** and **checks in**. The clerk often describes **amenities** such as a fitness club or **spa**. Most hotels provide **room service** for late night snacks. There is often a concierge to help arrange dinners and other entertainment outside of the hotel.

hounding them for advice. **3** V-T If someone **is hounded out of** a job or place, they are forced to leave it, often because other people are constantly criticizing them. [usu passive] □ *There is a general view around that he has been hounded out of office by the press.*

3 타동사 내쫓기다 □ 그가 언론 때문에 현직에서 물러났다는 것이 일반적인 견해이다.

hour ♦♦♦ /aʊər/ (**hours**) **1** N-COUNT An **hour** is a period of sixty minutes. □ *They waited for about two hours.* □ *I only slept about half an hour that night.* **2** N-PLURAL People say that something takes or lasts **hours** to emphasize that it takes or lasts a very long time, or what seems like a very long time. [EMPHASIS] □ *Getting there would take hours.* **3** N-SING A clock that strikes the **hour** strikes when it is exactly one o'clock, two o'clock, and so on. □ *She'd heard a clock somewhere strike the hour as she'd slipped from her room.* **4** N-SING You can refer to a particular time or moment as a particular **hour**. [LITERARY] □ *...the hour of his execution.* **5** N-COUNT If you refer, for example, to someone's **hour of** need or **hour of** happiness, you are referring to the time in their life when they were or are experiencing that condition or feeling. [LITERARY] □ *He recalled her devotion to her husband during his hour of need.* **6** N-PLURAL You can refer to the period of time during which something happens or operates each day as the **hours** during which it happens or operates. □ *...the hours of darkness.* □ *Phone us on this number during office hours.* **7** N-PLURAL If you refer to the **hours** involved in a job, you are talking about how long you spend each week doing it and when you do it. □ *I worked quite irregular hours.* **8** →see **rush hour** **9** PHRASE If you do something **after hours**, you do it outside normal business hours or the time when you are usually at work. □ *...a local restaurant where steel workers unwind after hours.* **10** PHRASE If you say that something happens **at all hours of** the day or night, you disapprove of it happening at the time that it does or as often as it does. [DISAPPROVAL] □ *She didn't want her fourteen-year-old daughter coming home at all hours of the morning.* **11** PHRASE If something happens **in the early hours** or **in the small hours**, it happens in the early morning after midnight. □ *Gibbs was arrested in the early hours of yesterday morning.* **12** PHRASE If something happens **on the hour**, it happens every hour at, for example, nine o'clock, ten o'clock, and so on, and not at any number of minutes past an hour. □ *During this war in the Persian Gulf, NPR will have newscasts every hour on the hour.* **13** PHRASE Something that happens **out of hours** happens at a time that is not during the usual hours of business or work. [mainly BRIT] □ *Teachers refused to run out of hours sports matches because they weren't being paid.*

1 가산명사 한 시간 □ 그들은 약 두 시간 정도 기다렸다. □ 나는 그날 밤 거의 반 시간밖에 자지 못했다. **2** 복수명사 오랜 시간 [강조] □ 거기에 가는 데는 오래 걸릴 거야. **3** 단수명사 시각 □ 그녀는 방에서 나오면서 어디선가 시계가 시각을 알리는 소리를 들었다. **4** 단수명사 (~ 하는) 시간, 순간 [문어체] □ 그의 처형 시간. **5** 가산명사 때, 시기 [문어체] □ 그는 자기가 어려웠던 시기에 그녀가 남편에게 헌신했던 것을 상기했다. **6** 복수명사 (하루 중 특정한) 시간, 무렵 □ 밤 시간 근무 시간에 이 번호로 전화하세요. **7** 복수명사 근무 시간 □ 나는 근무 시간이 상당히 불규칙했다. **8** 구 근무 시간 후에, 폐점 후에 □ 철강 회사 근로자들이 퇴근 후 쉬러 오는 지역 식당 **10** 구 매를 가리지 않고, 언제고 [탐탁찮음] □ 그녀는 열네 살 먹은 딸이 때를 가리지 않고 새벽에 집에 돌아오는 것을 원치 않았다. **11** 구 이른 새벽에 □ 깁스는 어제 아침 이른 새벽에 체포되었다. **12** 구 매 시 정각에 □ 이 전쟁이 진행되는 동안, 엔피알은 매 시 정각에 뉴스 방송을 내보낼 것이다. **13** 구 근무 시간 외에 [주로 영국영어] □ 교사들은 수당이 지불되지 않기 때문에 근무 시간 외 스포츠 시합을 여는 데 반대했다.

hour|ly /aʊərli/ **1** ADJ An **hourly** event happens once every hour. [ADJ n] □ *He flipped on the radio for the hourly news broadcast.* ● ADV **Hourly** is also an adverb. [ADV after v] □ *The hospital issued press releases hourly.* **2** ADJ Your **hourly** earnings are the money that you earn in one hour. [ADJ n] □ *They have little prospect of finding new jobs with the same hourly pay.*

1 형용사 매 시간의 □ 그는 매 시간 방송되는 뉴스를 들으려고 라디오를 켰다. ● 부사 매시, 시간마다 □ 그 병원은 매 시간 보도 자료를 배포했다. **2** 형용사 시간낭, 한 시간마다 □ 그들은 시간당 급여가 같은 새 직장을 구할 가망이 거의 없다.

house ♦♦♦ (**houses**, **housing**, **housed**)

> The noun and adjective are pronounced /haʊs/. The verb is pronounced /haʊz/. The form **houses** is pronounced /haʊzɪz/.

1 N-COUNT A **house** is a building in which people live, usually the people belonging to one family. □ *She has moved to a small house and is living off her meagre savings.* **2** N-SING You can refer to all the people who live together in a house as **the house**. □ *If he set his alarm clock for midnight, it would wake the whole house.* **3** N-COUNT **House** is used in the names of types of places where people go to eat and drink. □ *...a steak house.* **4** N-COUNT **House** is used in the names of types of companies, especially ones which publish books, lend money, or design clothes. □ *Many of the clothes come from the world's top fashion houses.* **5** N-IN-NAMES **House** is sometimes used in the names of office buildings and large private homes or expensive houses. [mainly BRIT] □ *I was to go to the very top floor of Bush House in Aldwych.* **6** N-COUNT You can refer to one of the two bodies of the U.S. Congress as a **House**. The House of Representatives is sometimes referred to as **the House**. In Britain, a **House** is one of the two bodies of Parliament. □ *Some members of the House and Senate worked all day yesterday.* **7** ADJ A restaurant's **house** wine is the cheapest wine it sells, which is not listed by name on the wine list. [ADJ n] □ *Tweed ordered a carafe of the house wine.* **8** V-T To **house** someone means to provide a house or apartment for them to live in. □ *...homes that house up to nine people.* **9** V-T A building or container that **houses** something is the place where it is located or from where it operates. [no cont] □ *The château itself is open to the public and houses a museum of motorcycles and cars.* **10** V-T If you say that a building **houses** a number of people, you mean that is the place where they live or where they are staying. [no cont] □ *The building will house twelve boys and eight girls.* **11** →see also **clearinghouse, White House** **12** PHRASE If a person or their performance or speech **brings the house down**, the audience claps, laughs, or shouts loudly because the performance or speech is very impressive or amusing. [INFORMAL] □ *It's really an amazing dance. It just always brings the house down.* **13** PHRASE If two people **get on like a house on fire**, they quickly become close friends, for example because they have many interests in common. [INFORMAL] □ *I went over and struck up a conversation, and we got on like a house on fire.* **14** PHRASE If you are given something in a restaurant or bar **on the house**, you do not have to pay for it. □ *The owner knew about the engagement and brought them glasses of champagne on the house.* **15** PHRASE If someone **gets** their **house in order**, **puts** their **house in order**, or **sets** their **house in order**, they arrange their affairs and solve their problems. □ *He's got his house in order and made some tremendous decisions.*
→see Picture Dictionary: **house**

명사와 형용사는 /haʊs/로 발음되고, 동사는 /haʊz/로 발음된다. houses 형태는 /haʊzɪz/로 발음된다.

1 가산명사 집, 가옥, 주택 □ 그녀는 작은 집으로 이사했고 얼마 안 되는 자신의 저축으로 생계를 잇고 있다. **2** 단수명사 집안 식구, 가족 □ 그가 만약 자명종 시계를 자정에 맞추어 놓으면, 온 식구를 다 깨우게 될 것이다. **3** 가산명사 식당, ~집 □ 스테이크 집 **4** 가산명사 (중략사 등) 회사 □ 그 옷들 중 다수는 세계 일류 의류 회사 제품이다. **5** 이름명사 회관, 저택 [주로 영국영어] □ 나는 알드위치에 있는 부시회관 꼭대기 층에 갈 예정이었다. **6** 가산명사 (미국) 의회; (미국) 하원; (영국) 상원 또는 하원 □ 몇몇 하원 의원과 상원 의원은 어제 온종일 일했다. **7** 형용사 가장 값싼 □ 트위드는 하우스 와인 한 병을 주문했다. **8** 타동사 숙소를 제공하다 □ 아홉 명까지 수용하는 집들 **9** 타동사 수용하다, 장소를 제공하다 □ 그 성은 일반인에게 개방되어 있고, 그 성에는 오토바이와 자동차 박물관이 있다. **10** 타동사 숙박시키다, 거주시키다 □ 그 건물에는 12명의 소년과 8명의 소녀가 머물게 될 것이다. **11** 구 만장의 갈채를 받다, 지붕이 떠나가라 박수갈채를 받다 [비격식체] □ 그것은 정말 멋진 춤이다. 항상 지붕이 떠나가라 박수갈채를 받는다. [비격식체] **13** 구 금세 친해지다 □ 나는 건너가서 대화를 시작했고, 우리는 금세 친해졌다. **14** 구 무료로, 판매자 부담으로 □ 주인이 약혼에 대해 알고 그들에게 샴페인 몇 잔을 공짜로 제공했다. **15** 구 신변을 정리하다, 문제를 해결하다 □ 그는 주변 문제를 정리하고 엄청난 결정들을 내렸다.

Thesaurus	*house*의 참조어
N.	dwelling, home, place, residence **1**

Picture Dictionary — house

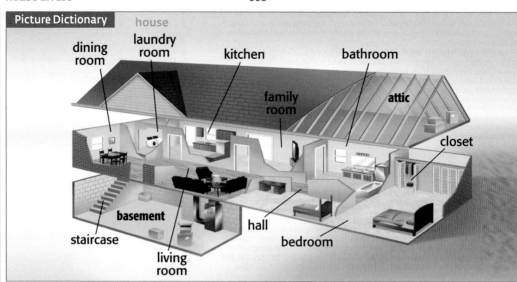

dining room, laundry room, kitchen, bathroom, family room, attic, closet, basement, hall, bedroom, staircase, living room

Word Partnership   *house*의 연어

ADJ.	empty house, expensive house, little house, new/old house ■
N.	house prices, a room in a house ■
V.	break into a house, build a house, buy a house, find a house, live in a house, own a house, rent a house, sell a house ■

house ar|rest N-UNCOUNT If someone is **under house arrest**, they are officially ordered not to leave their home, because they are suspected of being involved in an illegal activity. ❑ *The main opposition leaders had been arrested or placed under house arrest.*

불가산명사 가택 연금 ❑ 주요 야당 대표들이 체포되거나 가택 연금되었다.

house|hold ♦◇◇ /ha͟ʊshoʊld/ (households) ■ N-COUNT A **household** is all the people in a family or group who live together in a house. ❑ *...growing up in a male-only household.* ■ N-SING The **household** is your home and everything that is connected with taking care of it. ❑ *...household chores.* ■ ADJ Someone or something that is a **household** name or word is very well known. [ADJ n] ❑ *Today, fashion designers are household names.*

■ 가산명사 가족, 식구 ❑ 남자들만 사는 집안에서 자라남 ■ 단수명사 가사, 집안 일 ❑ 허드레 가사일 ■ 형용사 잘 알려진, 일상적인 ❑ 오늘날 패션 디자이너들은 널리 알려져 있다.

house|hold|er /ha͟ʊshoʊldər/ (householders) N-COUNT The **householder** is the person who owns or rents a particular house. ❑ *Millions of householders are eligible to claim the new council tax benefit.*

가산명사 가구주 ❑ 수백만의 가구주들이 새 지방세 면제를 신청할 자격이 있다.

house|keep|er /ha͟ʊskipər/ (housekeepers) N-COUNT A **housekeeper** is a person whose job is to cook, clean, and take care of a house for its owner.

가산명사 가정부

house|keep|ing /ha͟ʊskipɪŋ/ ■ N-UNCOUNT **Housekeeping** is the work and organization involved in running a home, including the shopping and cleaning. ❑ *I thought that cooking and housekeeping were unimportant, easy tasks.* ■ N-UNCOUNT **Housekeeping** is the money that you use to buy food, cleaning materials, and other things that you need in your home. [BRIT] ❑ *...the housekeeping money Jim gave her each week.*

■ 불가산명사 가사, 살림 ❑ 나는 요리와 살림이 하찮고 쉬운 일이라고 생각했다. ■ 불가산명사 가계비, 생활비 [영국영어] ❑ 짐이 그녀에게 매주 주는 생활비

House of Com|mons N-PROPER The **House of Commons** is the part of parliament in Britain or Canada whose members are elected. The building where they meet is also called **the House of Commons**. ❑ *The House of Commons has overwhelmingly rejected demands to bring back the death penalty for murder.* →see **government**

고유명사 (영국, 캐나다의) 하원, 하원 의사당 ❑ 하원은 살인에 대한 처벌로 사형을 다시 도입하자는 요구를 압도적으로 거부했다.

House of Lords N-PROPER The **House of Lords** is the part of the parliament in Britain whose members have not been elected. The building where they meet is also called **the House of Lords**. ❑ *The legislation has majority support in the House of Commons but has twice been rejected by the House of Lords.* →see **government**

고유명사 (영국 의회의) 상원, 상원 의사당 ❑ 그 법안은 하원에서 다수의 지지를 받았지만 상원에서 두 번 부결되었다.

House of Rep|re|sen|ta|tives N-PROPER The **House of Representatives** is the less powerful of the two parts of Congress in the United States, or the equivalent part of the system of government in some other countries. ❑ *The House of Representatives approved a new budget plan.* →see **government**

고유명사 (미국 의회의) 하원 ❑ 하원은 새 예산안을 승인했다.

Houses of Par|lia|ment N-PROPER-COLL In Britain, the **Houses of Parliament** are the British parliament, which consists of two parts, the House of Commons and the House of Lords. The buildings where the British parliament does its work are also called **the Houses of Parliament**. ❑ *...issues aired in the Houses of Parliament.*

고유명사-집합 (영국의 상하 양원으로 구성된) 의회, 국회 의사당 ❑ 의회에서 발표된 안건들

house|wife /ha͟ʊswaɪf/ (housewives) N-COUNT A **housewife** is a married woman who does not have a paid job, but instead takes care of her home and children. ❑ *Married at nineteen, she was a traditional housewife and mother of four children.*

가산명사 주부 ❑ 열아홉 살에 결혼해서, 그녀는 전통적인 가정주부이자 네 아이의 어머니였다.

Homemaker is the preferred term in the US for a woman who takes care of her home and children full time. **Housewife** is not the modern term in the US, although it is still quite common in the UK.

미국에서 가사와 자녀를 전업으로 돌보는 여성을 지칭할 때 선호하는 말은 homemaker(전업 주부)이다. housewife는 미국에서는 현대식 표현이 아니지만 영국에서는 여전히 흔히 쓴다.

house|work /ˈhaʊswɜrk/ N-UNCOUNT **Housework** is the work such as cleaning, washing, and ironing that you do in your home. ☐ *Men are doing more housework, but only just.*

불가산명사 가사, 집안일 ☐ 남자가 전보다 집안일을 더 많이 하고 있지만, 아주 조금일 뿐이다.

hous|ing ♦♦◇ /ˈhaʊzɪŋ/ N-UNCOUNT You refer to the buildings in which people live as **housing** when you are talking about their standard, price, or availability. ☐ *...a shortage of affordable housing.*

불가산명사 주택 ☐ 가용 주택의 부족

hous|ing es|tate (**housing estates**) N-COUNT A **housing estate** is a large number of houses or flats built close together at the same time. [BRIT]

가산명사 주택단지 [영국영어]

hov|er /ˈhʌvər, BRIT ˈhɒvəʳ/ (**hovers, hovering, hovered**) **1** V-I To **hover** means to stay in the same position in the air without moving forward or backward. Many birds and insects can hover by moving their wings very quickly. ☐ *Beautiful butterflies hovered above the wild flowers.* **2** V-I If you **hover**, you stay in one place and move slightly in a nervous way, for example because you cannot decide what to do. ☐ *Judith was hovering in the doorway.* **3** V-I If you **hover**, you are in an uncertain situation or state of mind. ☐ *She hovered on the brink of death for three months as doctors battled to save her.* **4** V-I If a something such as a price, value, or score **hovers** around a particular level, it stays at more or less that level and does not change much. ☐ *In September 1989 the exchange rate hovered around 140 yen to the dollar.*

1 자동사 (제자리에서) 공중에 떠 있다, (공중에서) 맴돈다 ☐ 아름다운 나비들이 야생화 위를 맴돌고 있었다. **2** 자동사 배회하다, 서성거리다 ☐ 주디스는 문간에서 서성거리고 있었다. **3** 자동사 기로에 서다 ☐ 그녀는 의사들이 그녀를 구하려고 애쓰는 석 달 동안 죽음의 기로에 서 있었다. **4** 자동사 맴돌다 ☐ 1989년 9월에는 환율이 달러 당 140엔 근처에서 맴돌았다.

hover|craft /ˈhʌvərkræft, BRIT ˈhɒvəʳkrɑːft/

hovercraft은 단수형 및 복수형이다.

| **Hovercraft** is both the singular and the plural form. |

N-COUNT A **hovercraft** is a vehicle that can travel across land and water. It floats above the land or water on a cushion of air. [also *by* N] ☐ *Travelling at speeds of up to thirty-five knots, these hovercraft can easily outpace most boats.*

가산명사 호버크라프트 (압축 공기를 분출하여 수면 위로 날아가는 배) ☐ 이 호버크라프트들은 35노트까지의 속력으로 달리기 때문에 대부분의 보트들을 쉽게 앞지를 수 있다.

how ♦♦♦ /haʊ/

| The conjunction is pronounced /haʊ/. |

접속사는 /haʊ/로 발음된다.

1 QUEST You use **how** to ask about the way in which something happens or is done. ☐ *How do I make payments into my account?* ☐ *How do you manage to keep the place so tidy?* ● CONJ **How** is also a conjunction. ☐ *I don't want to know how he died.* **2** CONJ You use **how** after certain adjectives and verbs to introduce a statement or fact, often something that you remember or expect other people to know about. ☐ *It's amazing how people collect so much stuff over the years.* ☐ *It's funny how I never seem to get a thing done on my day off.* **3** QUEST You use **how** to ask questions about the quantity or degree of something. [QUEST *much/many*, QUEST adj/adv] ☐ *How much money are we talking about?* ☐ *How many full-time staff have we got?* ☐ *How long will you be staying?* ☐ *How old is your son now?* **4** QUEST You use **how** when you are asking someone whether something was successful or enjoyable. ☐ *How was your trip down to Orlando?* ☐ *How did your date go?* **5** QUEST You use **how** to ask about someone's health or to find out someone's news. ☐ *Hi! How are you doing?* ☐ *How's Rosie?*

1 의문사 어떻게, 어떤 식으로 ☐ 제 구좌로 어떻게 불입합니까? ☐ 당신은 어떻게 그렇게 정리정돈을 잘하십니까? ● 접속사 어떻게 -하는지 ☐ 나는 그가 어떻게 죽었는지 알고 싶지 않다. **2** 접속사 어떻게 -하는지 ☐ 사람들이 몇 년 동안 그토록 많은 물건을 어떻게 모으는지 놀랍다. ☐ 나는 쉬는 날이면 어떻게 한 가지 일도 못 하게 되는지 정말 우습다. **3** 의문사 얼마나, 어느 정도 ☐ 액수가 얼마나 되는 겁니까? ☐ 우리 정규 직원이 몇 명이나 됩니까? ☐ 얼마나 오래 계실 겁니까? ☐ 아들이 지금 몇 살이지요? **4** 의문사 어떠한 ☐ 올란도 여행은 어떠셨나요? ☐ 데이트는 어땠어? **5** 의문사 어떠한 ☐ 안녕? 어떻게 지내니? ☐ 로지는 어떻게 지내니?

| You do not use **how** to ask questions about the appearance or character of someone or something. You use an expression with **what** and **like**. For example, if you ask "**How is Susan?**," you are asking about her health. If you want to know about her appearance, you ask "**What does Susan look like?**" If you want to know about her personality, you ask "**What is Susan like?**" |

| 사람이나 사물의 모습이나 성격에 대해 질문할 때는 how를 쓰지 않는다. 대신 what과 like로 된 표현을 사용한다. 예를 들어, "How is Susan?"이라고 물으면, 그녀의 건강 상태에 대해 묻는 것이다. 그녀의 생김새에 대해 알고 싶다면, "What does Susan look like?"라고 질문한다. 그녀의 성격에 대해 알고 싶다면, "What is Susan like?"라고 질문한다. |

6 ADV You use **how** to emphasize the degree to which something is true. [EMPHASIS] [ADV adj/adv] ☐ *I didn't realize how heavy that shopping was going to be.* **7** ADV You use **how** in exclamations to emphasize an adjective, adverb, or statement. [EMPHASIS] [ADV adj/adv/cl] ☐ *How strange that something so simple as a walk on the beach could suddenly mean so much.* **8** QUEST You use **how** in expressions such as "**How can you...**" and "**How could you...**" to indicate that you disapprove of what someone has done or that you find it hard to believe. [DISAPPROVAL] [QUEST *can/could*] ☐ *How can you drink so much beer, Luke?* **9** QUEST You use **how** in expressions such as "**How about...**" or "**How would you like...**" when you are making an offer or a suggestion. ☐ *How about a cup of coffee?* **10** CONVENTION If you ask someone "**How about you?**" you are asking them what they think or want. ☐ *Well, I enjoyed that. How about you two?* **11** PHRASE You use **how about** to introduce a new subject which you think is relevant to the conversation you have been having. ☐ *Are your products and services competitive? How about marketing?* **12** PHRASE You ask "**How come?**" or "**How so?**" when you are surprised by something and are asking why it happened or was said. [INFORMAL] ☐ *"They don't say a single word to each other." — "How come?"*

6 부사 얼마나 [강조] ☐ 나는 쇼핑한 것이 얼마나 무거울 지 생각하지 못했다. **7** 부사 정말로, 참으로 [강조] ☐ 해변가를 산책하는 것과 같이 아주 단순한 일이 갑자기 그토록 의미심장하게 될 수 있다는 것이 정말로 신기하다. **8** 의문사 도대체 ☐ 루크, 자넨 어떻게 그렇게 많은 맥주를 마실 수 있나? **9** 의문사 -은 어떠세요?, -하는 것은 어떠세요? ☐ 커피 한 잔 어때요? **10** 관용 표현 당신 생각은 어때요? ☐ 글쎄, 난 좋았어. 너희 둘은 어땠니? **11** 구 -은 어떤가요?, -에 대해서는 어떻게 생각하시나요? ☐ 귀사의 상품과 서비스는 경쟁력이 있습니까? 마케팅은 어떤가요? **12** 구 어째서?, 왜?, 어째서 그런가? [비격식체] ☐ "그들은 서로 한 마디도 하지 않는다." "어째서?"

how|ever ♦♦♦ /haʊˈevər/ **1** ADV You use **however** when you are adding a comment which is surprising or which contrasts with what has just been said. [ADV with cl] ☐ *This was not an easy decision. It is, however, a decision that we feel is dictated by our duty.* **2** ADV You use **however** before an adjective or adverb to emphasize that the degree or extent of something cannot change a situation. [EMPHASIS] ☐ *You should always strive to achieve more, however well you have done before.* ☐ *However hard she tried, nothing seemed to work.* **3** CONJ You use **however** when you want to say that it makes no difference how something is done. ☐ *However we adopt healthcare reform, it isn't going to save major amounts of money.* **4** ADV You use **however** in expressions such as **or however long it takes** and **or however many there were** to indicate that the figure you have just mentioned may not be accurate. [VAGUENESS] ☐ *Wait 30 to 60 minutes or however long it takes.* **5** QUEST You can use **however** to ask in an emphatic way how something has happened or what someone has done, when you are very surprised by it. Some speakers of English think that this form is incorrect and prefer to use "how ever." [EMPHASIS] ☐ *However did you find this place in such weather?*

1 부사 그렇지만, 하지만 ☐ 이것은 쉽지 않은 결정이었다. 그렇지만 그것은 어쩐지 의무감에서 내린 것 같은 결정이다. **2** 부사 아무리 -할지라도, 아무리 -해도 [강조] ☐ 여러분은 항상 더 많이 성취하려고 노력해야 합니다. 이전에 아무리 잘 해냈다 할지라도. ☐ 그녀가 아무리 애써도 아무것도 안 되는 것 같았다. **3** 접속사 아무리 -해도, 어떤 식으로 -하더라도 ☐ 어떤 식으로 우리가 의료 서비스를 개혁하더라도, 큰 비용이 절감되지는 않을 것이다. **4** 부사 또는 얼마가 걸리든지; 또는 몇 개가 되든지 [짐작컨] ☐ 30분에서 60분 또는 얼마가 걸리든지 기다려라. **5** 의문사 대체 어떻게 [강조] ☐ 이런 날씨에 대체 어떻게 이 곳을 찾아왔습니까?

howl /haʊl/ (howls, howling, howled) **1** V-I If an animal such as a wolf or a dog **howls**, it makes a long, loud, crying sound. ❑ *Somewhere in the streets beyond a dog suddenly howled, baying at the moon.* ● N-COUNT **Howl** is also a noun. ❑ *The dog let out a savage howl and, wheeling round, flew at him.* **2** V-I If a person **howls**, they make a long, loud cry expressing pain, anger, or unhappiness. ❑ *He howled like a wounded animal as blood spurted from the gash.* ● N-COUNT **Howl** is also a noun. ❑ *With a howl of rage, he grabbed the neck of a broken bottle and advanced.* **3** V-I When the wind **howls**, it blows hard and makes a loud noise. ❑ *The wind howled all night, but I slept a little.* **4** V-T If you **howl** something, you say it in a very loud voice. [INFORMAL] ❑ *"Get away, get away, get away," he howled.* **5** V-I If you **howl with** laughter, you laugh very loudly. ❑ *Joe, Pink, and Booker howled with delight.* ● N-COUNT **Howl** is also a noun. ❑ *His stories caused howls of laughter.* →see **laugh**

1 자동사 (늑대 등이) 짖다 ❑ 거리 저 너머 어디선가 개 한 마리가 갑자기 달을 보고 짖었다. ● 가산명사 짖는 소리 ❑ 개가 사납게 짖으며 방향을 바꾸어 그를 향해 돌진했다. **2** 자동사 울부짖다, 악쓰다 ❑ 깊은 상처에서 피가 솟구치자 그는 상처 입은 짐승처럼 울부짖었다. ● 가산명사 울부짖음 ❑ 분노로 울부짖으며, 그는 깨진 병의 목을 움켜잡고 다가왔다. **3** 자동사 (바람이) 윙윙거리다 ❑ 바람이 밤새 윙윙거렸지만 나는 조금 잤다. **4** 타동사 외치다 [비격식체] ❑ "저리 가, 저리 가, 저리 가." 라고 그가 외쳤다. **5** 자동사 큰소리로 껄껄 웃다 ❑ 조우와 핑크와 부커는 기분이 좋아 껄껄 웃었다. ● 가산명사 큰 웃음 ❑ 그의 이야기에 웃음바다가 되었다.

HP /eɪtʃ piː/ N-UNCOUNT **HP** is an abbreviation for **hire purchase**. [BRIT] ❑ *I have never bought anything on HP.*

불가산명사 hire purchase의 약자, 할부 [영국영어] ❑ 나는 할부로 무엇을 사 본 적이 없다.

HQ /eɪtʃ kjuː/ (HQs) N-VAR **HQ** is an abbreviation for **headquarters**. ❑ *The regimental HQ is a tiny office manned by two retired officers.*

가산명사 또는 불가산명사 headquarters의 약자, 본부 ❑ 연대본부는 2명의 퇴역 장교가 근무하는 작은 사무실이다.

hr (hrs) **hr** is a written abbreviation for **hour**. ❑ *Let this cook on low for another 1 hr 15 mins.*

hour의 약자 ❑ 이것을 약한 불로 1시간 15분 더 익히시오.

HR /eɪtʃ ɑːr/ In a company or other organization, the **HR** department is the department with responsibility for the recruiting, training, and welfare of the staff. **HR** is an abbreviation for "human resources." [BUSINESS]

human resources의 약자, 인적 자원 관리 [경제]

HTML /eɪtʃ tiː em el/ N-UNCOUNT **HTML** is a system of codes for producing documents for the Internet. **HTML** is an abbreviation for "hypertext markup language." [COMPUTING] ❑ *...HTML documents.*

불가산명사 hypertext markup language의 약자, 하이퍼텍스트 표기 체계 [컴퓨터] ❑ HTML 문서들

HTTP /eɪtʃ tiː tiː piː/ N-UNCOUNT **HTTP** is a way of formatting and transmitting messages on the Internet. **HTTP** is an abbreviation for "hypertext transfer protocol." [COMPUTING]

불가산명사 hypertext transfer protocol의 약자, 인터넷의 하이퍼텍스트 통신 방식 [컴퓨터]

hub /hʌb/ (hubs) **1** N-COUNT You can describe a place as a **hub** of an activity when it is a very important center for that activity. ❑ *The island's social hub is the Cafe Sport.* **2** N-COUNT The **hub** of a wheel is the part at the center.

1 가산명사 (활동) 중심지, 중추 ❑ 그 섬의 사교 중심지는 카페 스포츠이다. **2** 가산명사 바퀴통 (바퀴살이 모이는 중심부)

hud|dle /hʌdəl/ (huddles, huddling, huddled) **1** V-I If you **huddle** somewhere, you sit, stand, or lie there holding your arms and legs close to your body, usually because you are cold or frightened. ❑ *Mr. Pell huddled in a corner with his notebook on his knees.* **2** V-I If people **huddle together** or **huddle round** something, they stand, sit, or lie close to each other, usually because they all feel cold or frightened. ❑ *Tired and lost, we huddled together.* **3** V-RECIP If people **huddle** in a group, they gather together to discuss something quietly or secretly. ❑ *Off to one side, Sticht, Macomber, Jordan, and Kreps huddled to discuss something.* ❑ *The president has been huddling with his most senior aides.* **4** N-COUNT A **huddle** is a small group of people or things that are standing very close together or lying on top of each other, usually in a disorganized way. ❑ *We lay there: a huddle of bodies, gasping for air.*

1 자동사 움츠리다, 웅크리다 ❑ 펠 씨는 노트북을 무릎에 올려놓고 한 구석에 웅크리고 앉았다. **2** 자동사 웅송그리고 붙어 있다 ❑ 지치고 길을 잃어서 우리는 웅송그리며 붙어 있었다. **3** 상호동사 (비밀 논의를 위해) 모이다 ❑ 스틱트와 매콤버, 조단과 크렙스는 한 편에 나와 모여 뭔가를 상의했다. ❑ 대통령은 자기 최고 보좌관들과 은밀히 논의해 왔다. **4** 가산명사 (어지럽게 모인) 무리; (어지럽게 쌓은) 더미 ❑ 우리는 거기에 누워 있었다. 뒤죽박죽 서로 얽혀 숨을 헐떡이며.

huff /hʌf/ (huffs, huffing, huffed) **1** V-T If you **huff**, you indicate that you are annoyed or offended about something, usually by the way that you say something. ❑ *"This," huffed Mr. Buthelezi, "was discrimination."* **2** PHRASE If someone is **in a huff**, they are behaving in a bad-tempered way because they are annoyed and offended. [INFORMAL] ❑ *He was so disappointed that he drove off in a huff.*

1 타동사 벌컥 성을 내다, 발끈 하다 ❑ "이건 차별이야."라고 버럭지는 발끈 해서 말했다. **2** 구 벌컥 성을 내며, 발끈 하여 [비격식체] ❑ 그는 너무 실망해서 발끈 하고 차를 몰고 가버렸다.

hug /hʌg/ (hugs, hugging, hugged) **1** V-RECIP When you **hug** someone, you put your arms around them and hold them tightly, for example because you like them or are pleased to see them. You can also say that two people **hug** each other or that they hug. ❑ *She had hugged him exuberantly and invited him to dinner the next day.* ● N-COUNT **Hug** is also a noun. ❑ *She leapt out of the back seat, and gave him a hug.* **2** V-T If you **hug** something, you hold it close to your body with your arms tightly around it. ❑ *Shaerl trudged toward them, hugging a large box.* **3** V-T Something that **hugs** the ground or a stretch of land or water stays very close to it. [WRITTEN] ❑ *The road hugs the coast for hundreds of miles.*

1 상호동사 껴안다, 포옹하다 ❑ 그녀는 그를 열정적으로 껴안았고 다음날 저녁 식사에 초대했다. ● 가산명사 껴안음, 포옹 ❑ 그녀는 뒷좌석에서 뛰어나와 그를 껴안았다. **2** 타동사 안다, 품에 안다 ❑ 쉐를이 커다란 상자를 안고 그들을 향해 터벅터벅 걸어왔다. **3** 타동사 (길 등이) ~을 따라 나 있다 [문어체] ❑ 그 도로는 수백 마일에 걸쳐 해변을 끼고 나 있다.

Thesaurus　　　　hug의 참조어

　v.　　cling, embrace, hold **1** **2**

---

huge ♦♦♢ /hjuːdʒ/ (huger, hugest) **1** ADJ Something or someone that is **huge** is extremely large in size. ❑ *...a tiny little woman with huge black glasses.* **2** ADJ Something that is **huge** is extremely large in amount or degree. ❑ *I have a huge number of ties because I never throw them away.* ● **huge|ly** ADV ❑ *In summer this hotel is a hugely popular venue for wedding receptions.* **3** ADJ Something that is **huge** exists or happens on a very large scale, and involves a lot of different people or things. ❑ *Another team is looking at the huge problem of debts between companies.*

1 형용사 거대한, 커다란 ❑ 커다란 검은 안경을 쓴 몸집이 아주 작은 여자 **2** 형용사 막대한, 엄청난 ❑ 나는 넥타이가 엄청나게 많이 있는데 결코 버리지 않기 때문이다. ● 매우, 엄청나게 부사 ❑ 여름에 이 호텔은 결혼 피로연 장소로 매우 인기 있는 장소이다. **3** 형용사 엄청난, 막대한 ❑ 다른 팀은 기업 간의 엄청난 부채 문제를 살펴보고 있다.

hull /hʌl/ (hulls) N-COUNT The **hull** of a boat or tank is the main body of it. ❑ *The hull had suffered extensive damage to the starboard side.*

가산명사 선체, 차체 ❑ 선체가 우현 쪽으로 심한 손상을 입었었다.

hul|lo /hʌloʊ/ →see **hello**

hum /hʌm/ (hums, humming, hummed) **1** V-I If something **hums**, it makes a low continuous noise. ❑ *The birds sang, the bees hummed.* ● N-SING **Hum** is also a noun. ❑ *...the hum of traffic.* **2** V-T/V-I When you **hum**, or **hum** a tune, you sing it with your lips closed. ❑ *She was humming a merry little tune.* **3** V-I If you say that a place **hums**, you mean that it is full of activity. ❑ *The place is really beginning to hum.*

1 자동사 윙윙거리다 ❑ 새들이 노래하고, 벌들이 윙윙거렸다. ● 단수명사 윙윙거리는 소리 ❑ 차들이 웅웅거리는 소리 **2** 타동사/자동사 콧노래를 부르다 ❑ 그녀는 흥겨운 가락을 콧노래로 흥얼거리고 있었다. **3** 자동사 북적거리다, 활기가 넘치다 ❑ 그 곳은 정말 활기가 넘치기 시작한다.

hu|man ♦♦♦ /hjuːmən/ (humans) **1** ADJ **Human** means relating to or concerning people. [ADJ n] ❑ *...the human body.* **2** N-COUNT You can refer to

1 형용사 인간의, 사람의 ❑ 인체 **2** 가산명사 인간 ❑ 인간과 마찬가지로 고양이와 개는 잡식 동물이다.

people as **humans**, especially when you are comparing them with animals or machines. ❑ *Like humans, cats and dogs are omnivores.* ❸ ADJ **Human** feelings, weaknesses, or errors are ones that are typical of humans rather than machines. ❑ *...an ever growing risk of human error.* →see **primate**

❸ 형용사 인간의, 사람의 ❑ 인간이 실수할 위험이 점점 커짐

Word Partnership   human의 연어

N.   human **behavior**, human **body**, human **brain**, human **dignity**, human **life** ❶
human **error**, human **weakness** ❸

---

hu|man be|ing (**human beings**) N-COUNT A **human being** is a man, woman, or child. ❑ *The treatment will be tried out on human beings only after it has been shown to be safe and foolproof in animals.*

가산명사 인간 ❑ 그 치료법은 동물 실험을 통해 안전하고 절대 잘못되지 않는다는 것이 증명된 후에야 비로소 인간에게 사용될 것이다.

Word Link   man ≈ human being : foreman, humane, woman

---

hu|mane /hyuːmeɪn/ ❶ ADJ **Humane** people act in a kind, sympathetic way toward other people and animals, and try to do them as little harm as possible. ❑ *In the mid-nineteenth century, Dorothea Dix began to campaign for humane treatment of the mentally ill.* ● **hu|mane|ly** ADV [ADV with v] ❑ *Our horse had to be humanely destroyed after breaking his right foreleg.* ❷ ADJ **Humane** values and societies encourage people to act in a kind and sympathetic way toward others, even toward people they do not agree with or like. ❑ *...the humane values of socialism.*

❶ 형용사 인도적인, 자비로운 ❑ 19세기 중반, 도로시아 딕스는 정신질환자들을 인도적으로 대우하자는 캠페인을 시작했다. ● 인도적으로, 자비롭게 부사 ❑ 우리 말은 오른쪽 앞다리가 부러진 후 더 이상 고통 받지 않도록 도살해야만 했다. ❷ 형용사 인도적인 ❑ 사회주의의 인도적 가치

hu|man|ism /hyuːmənɪzəm/ N-UNCOUNT **Humanism** is the belief that people can achieve happiness and live well without religion. ● **hu|man|ist** (**humanists**) N-COUNT ❑ *He is a practical humanist, who believes in the dignity of mankind.*

불가산명사 인본주의 ● 인본주의자 가산명사 ❑ 그는 실천적 인본주의자로 인류의 존엄성을 믿는다.

hu|mani|tar|ian /hyuːmænɪteəriən/ ADJ If a person or society has **humanitarian** ideas or behavior, they try to avoid making people suffer or they help people who are suffering. ❑ *Air bombardment raised criticism on the humanitarian grounds that innocent civilians might suffer.*

형용사 인도주의적인 ❑ 공중 폭격은 무고한 시민들이 다칠 수 있다는 인도적인 이유로 비난을 초래했다.

hu|man|ity /hyuːmænɪti/ (**humanities**) ❶ N-UNCOUNT All the people in the world can be referred to as **humanity**. ❑ *They face charges of committing crimes against humanity.* ❷ N-UNCOUNT A person's **humanity** is their state of being a human being, rather than an animal or an object. [FORMAL] ❑ *He was under discussion and it made him feel deprived of his humanity.* ❸ N-UNCOUNT **Humanity** is the quality of being kind, thoughtful, and sympathetic towards others. ❑ *Her speech showed great maturity and humanity.* ❹ N-PLURAL The **humanities** are the subjects such as history, philosophy, and literature which are concerned with human ideas and behavior. ❑ *The number of students majoring in the humanities has declined by about half.*

❶ 불가산명사 인류, 인간 ❑ 그들은 인류에 대한 범죄를 저질렀다는 혐의를 받고 있다. ❷ 불가산명사 인간성 [격식체] ❑ 그가 논의의 대상이어서 그 일로 그는 자신의 인간성을 박탈당한 기분이 들었다. ❸ 불가산명사 인간애, 자비 ❑ 그녀의 연설은 대단한 성숙미와 인간애를 보여 주었다. ❹ 복수명사 인문학 ● 인문학을 전공하는 학생 수가 거의 절반으로 줄어들었다.

hu|man na|ture N-UNCOUNT **Human nature** is the natural qualities and ways of behavior that most people have. ❑ *It seems to be human nature to worry.*

불가산명사 인간의 천성, 인간의 본성 ❑ 걱정하는 것은 인간의 천성인 것 같다.

hu|man race N-SING The **human race** is the same as **mankind**. ❑ *Can the human race carry on expanding and growing the same way that it is now?*

단수명사 인류 ❑ 인류가 지금과 마찬가지로 계속 번창하고 성장할 수 있을까?

hu|man re|sources N-UNCOUNT In a company or other organization, the department of **human resources** is the department with responsibility for the recruiting, training, and welfare of the staff. The abbreviation **HR** is often used. [BUSINESS] ❑ *...Geoff May, the firm's head of human resources.*

불가산명사 인적 자원 관리, 인사 관리 [경제] ❑ 그 회사의 인사 관리 부장인 제오프 메이

hu|man rights ◆◇◇ N-PLURAL **Human rights** are basic rights which many societies believe that all people should have. ❑ *In the treaty both sides pledge to respect human rights.*

복수명사 인권 ❑ 그 협정에서 양측 모두 인권을 존중하겠다고 서약한다.

hum|ble /hʌmbəl/ (**humbler, humblest, humbles, humbling, humbled**) ❶ ADJ A **humble** person is not proud and does not believe that they are better than other people. ❑ *He gave a great performance, but he was very humble.* ● **hum|bly** [ADV with v] ❑ *"I'm a lucky man, undeservedly lucky," he said humbly.* ❷ ADJ People with low social status are sometimes described as **humble**. ❑ *Spyros Latsis started his career as a humble fisherman in the Aegean.* ❸ ADJ A **humble** place or thing is ordinary and not special in any way. ❑ *There are restaurants, both humble and expensive, that specialize in noodles.* ❹ ADJ People use **humble** in a phrase such as **in my humble opinion** as a polite way of emphasizing what they think, even though they do not feel humble about it. [POLITENESS] ❑ *It is, in my humble opinion, perhaps the best steak restaurant in Great Britain.* ● **hum|bly** ADV [ADV before v] ❑ *So may I humbly suggest we all do something next time.* ❺ PHRASE If you **eat humble pie**, you speak or behave in a way which tells people that you admit you were wrong about something. ❑ *Anson was forced to eat humble pie and publicly apologise to her.* ❻ V-T If you **humble** someone who is more important or powerful than you, you defeat them easily. ❑ *Honda won fame in the 1980s as the little car company that humbled the industry giants.* ❼ V-T If something or someone **humbles** you, they make you realize that you are not as important or good as you thought you were. ❑ *Ted's words humbled me.* ● **hum|bling** ADJ ❑ *Giving up an addiction is a humbling experience.*

❶ 형용사 겸손한, 겸허한 ❑ 그는 아주 멋진 공연을 했지만, 매우 겸손했다. ● 겸손하게, 겸허하게 부사 ❑ "나는 운이 좋은 남자야, 과분하게 운이 좋아."라고 그는 겸손하게 말했다. ❷ 형용사 비천한, 보잘것없는 ❑ 스파이로스 랏시스는 에게 해의 보잘것없는 어부로 인생의 첫발을 내딛었다. ❸ 형용사 변변찮은 ❑ 국수를 전문으로 하는 식당은 저렴한 곳도 있고 비싼 곳도 있다. ❹ 형용사 변변찮은; 제 소견으로는 [공손체] ❑ 그곳은, 제 소견으로는, 영국에서 제일 가는 스테이크 식당일 겁니다. ● 겸손하게, 황송하게 부사 ❑ 그래서 저는 우리 모두 다음에는 무언가를 해 보자고 감히 제안합니다. ❺ 구 굴욕을 참다, 백배 사죄하다 ❑ 앤슨은 굴욕을 참고 공개적으로 그녀에게 사과해야만 했다. ❻ 타동사 제치다, 콧대를 꺾다 ❑ 혼다는 1980년대에 거대 기업들의 콧대를 꺾은 작은 자동차 회사로서 명성을 얻었다. ❼ 타동사 겸허하게 만들다 ❑ 테드의 말은 나를 겸허하게 만들었다. ● 겸허하게 만드는 형용사 ❑ 중독을 끊는다는 것은 스스로를 겸허하게 만드는 경험이다.

hu|mid /hyuːmɪd/ ADJ You use **humid** to describe an atmosphere or climate that is very damp, and usually very hot. ❑ *Visitors can expect hot and humid conditions.* →see **weather**

형용사 습한, 눅눅한 ❑ 방문객들은 덥고 습한 날씨를 예측할 수 있다.

hu|mid|ity /hyuːmɪdɪti/ ❶ N-UNCOUNT You say there is **humidity** when the air feels very heavy and damp. ❑ *The heat and humidity were insufferable.* ❷ N-UNCOUNT **Humidity** is the amount of water in the air. ❑ *The humidity is relatively low.* →see **forecast**

❶ 불가산명사 습기, 눅눅함 ❑ 더위와 습기는 견딜 수 없을 정도였다. ❷ 불가산명사 습도 ❑ 습도는 상대적으로 낮다.

a
b
c
d
e
f
g
h
i
j
k
l
m
n
o
p
q
r
s
t
u
v
w
x
y
z

A

Word Link   ate ≈ causing to be : complicate, humiliate, motivate

hu|mil|i|ate /hyumɪlieɪt/ (humiliates, humiliating, humiliated) V-T To **humiliate** someone means to say or do something which makes them feel ashamed or stupid. ❑ She had been beaten and humiliated by her husband. ● **hu|mili|at|ed** ADJ ❑ I have never felt so humiliated in my life.

타동사 굴욕감을 주다, 창피를 주다 ❑ 그녀는 남편에게 맞고 굴욕을 당했다. ● 수치스러운, 굴욕감을 느끼는 형용사 ❑ 내 생전 이렇게 수치스러웠던 적이 없었다.

hu|mil|i|at|ing /hyumɪlieɪtɪŋ/ ADJ If something is **humiliating**, it embarrasses you and makes you feel ashamed and stupid. ❑ The Conservatives have suffered a humiliating defeat.

형용사 굴욕적인, 면목 없는 ❑ 보수당은 굴욕적인 패배를 당했다.

hu|milia|tion /hyumɪlieɪʃªn/ (humiliations) ■ N-UNCOUNT **Humiliation** is the embarrassment and shame you feel when someone makes you appear stupid, or when you make a mistake in public. ❑ She faced the humiliation of discussing her husband's affair. ■ N-COUNT A **humiliation** is an occasion or a situation in which you feel embarrassed and ashamed. ❑ The result is a humiliation for the prime minister.

■ 불가산명사 굴욕, 수치 ❑ 그녀는 남편의 외도에 대해 이야기하는 수치를 감수했다. ■ 가산명사 굴욕, 수치스러운 상황 ❑ 그 결과는 수상에게 굴욕이다.

hu|mil|ity /hyumɪlɪti/ N-UNCOUNT Someone who has **humility** is not proud and does not believe they are better than other people. ❑ ...a deep sense of humility.

불가산명사 겸손, 겸양 ❑ 깊은 겸양심

hu|mor ♦◇◇ /hyumər/ (humors, humoring, humored) [BRIT **humour**] ■ N-UNCOUNT You can refer to the amusing things that people say as their **humor**. ❑ Her humor and determination were a source of inspiration to others. →see also **sense of humor** ■ N-UNCOUNT **Humor** is a quality in something that makes you laugh, for example in a situation, in someone's words or actions, or in a book or movie. ❑ He felt sorry for the man but couldn't ignore the humor of the situation. ■ N-VAR If you are **in** a good **humor**, you feel cheerful and happy, and are pleasant to people. If you are **in** a bad **humor**, you feel bad-tempered and unhappy, and are unpleasant to people. ❑ Christina was still not clear why he had been in such ill humor. ■ N-UNCOUNT If you do something with good **humor**, you do it cheerfully and pleasantly. ❑ Hugo bore his illness with great courage and good humor. ■ V-T If you **humor** someone who is behaving strangely, you try to please them or pretend to agree with them, so that they will not become upset. ❑ She disliked Dido but was prepared to tolerate her for a weekend in order to humor her husband. →see **laugh**

[영국영어 humour] ■ 불가산명사 유머, 해학 ❑ 그녀의 유머와 결단력은 다른 사람들을 고무시키는 원천이었다. ■ 불가산명사 우스꽝스러움 ❑ 그녀는 그 남자가 안됐다고 느꼈지만 그 상황이 우스꽝스러운 것은 어쩔 수 없었다. ■ 가산명사 또는 불가산명사 기분 ❑ 크리스티나는 그가 왜 그렇게 기분이 나빴는지 아직도 잘 알지 못했다. ■ 불가산명사 기질, 성질 ❑ 휴고는 대단한 용기와 낙천적인 성격으로 병을 견뎌 냈다. ■ 타동사 비위를 맞추다, 달래다 ❑ 그녀는 디도를 좋아하지 않았지만 남편의 기분을 맞추려고 주말 동안 그녀를 너그럽게 봐주기로 했다.

Word Partnership   humor의 연어

N.   **brand of** humor, **sense of** humor ■
ADJ.   **good** humor ■ ■

hu|mor|ous /hyumərəs/ ADJ If someone or something is **humorous**, they are amusing, especially in a clever or witty way. ❑ He was quite humorous, and I liked that about him. ● **hu|mor|ous|ly** ADV ❑ He looked at me humorously as he wrestled with the door.

형용사 익살스러운, 해학적인 ❑ 그는 상당히 익살스러웠고, 나는 그의 그런 면이 좋았다. ● 익살스럽게, 우스꽝스럽게 부사 ❑ 그는 문과 씨름하면서 나를 우스꽝스럽게 쳐다보았다.

hu|mour /hyumər/ →see **humor**

hump /hʌmp/ (humps, humping, humped) ■ N-COUNT A **hump** is a small hill or raised area. ❑ The path goes over a large hump by a tree before running near a road. ■ N-COUNT A camel's **hump** is the large lump on its back. ❑ Camels rebuild fat stores in their hump. ■ V-T If you **hump** something heavy, you carry it from one place to another with great difficulty. [BRIT, INFORMAL] ❑ Charlie humped his rucksack up the stairs to his flat.

■ 가산명사 작은 언덕 ❑ 그 소로는 나무 옆 제법 큰 언덕을 넘어가면 도로 옆으로 나 있다. ■ 가산명사 (낙타 등의) 혹 ❑ 낙타는 혹 속에 지방을 다시 축적한다. ■ 타동사 (힘들게) 나르다 [영국영어, 비격식체] ❑ 찰리는 자기 아파트까지 배낭을 지고 계단을 힘겨워 올라갔다.

hunch /hʌntʃ/ (hunches, hunching, hunched) ■ N-COUNT If you have a **hunch** about something, you are sure that it is correct or true, even though you do not have any proof. [INFORMAL] ❑ I had a hunch that Susan and I would work well together. ■ V-I If you **hunch** forward, you raise your shoulders, put your head down, and lean forward, often because you are cold, ill, or unhappy. ❑ He got out his map of Yorkshire and hunched over it to read the small print. ■ V-T If you **hunch** your shoulders, you raise them and lean forward slightly. ❑ Wes hunched his shoulders and leaned forward on the edge of the counter.

■ 가산명사 예감, 육감 [비격식체] ❑ 나는 수잔과 내가 잘 될 것이라는 예감이 들었다. ■ 자동사 숙이다 ❑ 그는 요크셔 지도를 꺼내서 작은 활자를 읽으려고 지도 위로 몸을 숙였다. ■ 타동사 구부리다 ❑ 웨스는 어깨를 구부려서 카운터의 가장자리에 대고 몸을 앞으로 기댔다.

hun|dred ♦♦♦ /hʌndrɪd/ (hundreds)

The plural form is **hundred** after a number, or after a word or expression referring to a number, such as "several" or "a few."

숫자 또는 'several', 'a few'와 같이 수를 지칭하는 단어나 표현 뒤에서 복수형은 hundred이다.

■ NUM A **hundred** or **one hundred** is the number 100. ❑ According to one official more than a hundred people have been arrested. ■ QUANT If you refer to **hundreds of** things or people, you are emphasizing that there are very many of them. [EMPHASIS] [QUANT of pl-n] ❑ Hundreds of tree species face extinction. ● PRON You can also use **hundreds** as a pronoun. ❑ Hundreds have been killed in the fighting and thousands made homeless. ■ PHRASE You can use **a hundred percent** or **one hundred percent** to emphasize that you agree completely with something or that it is completely right or wrong. [INFORMAL, EMPHASIS] ❑ Are you a hundred percent sure it's your neighbor?

■ 수사 100, 백 ❑ 한 공무원에 따르면 100명 이상의 사람들이 체포되었다고 한다. ■ 수량사 수백의, 많은 [강조] ❑ 수백 종의 수목들이 멸종에 직면하고 있다. ● 대명사 수백, 수백 명 ❑ 그 전투로 수백 명이 사망했고 수천 명이 집을 잃었다. ■ 구 백 퍼센트, 완전히 [비격식체, 강조] ❑ 그 사람이 네 이웃이라는 것이 백 퍼센트 확실하니?

hun|dredth ♦◇◇ /hʌndrɪdθ/ (hundredths) ■ ORD The **hundredth** item in a series is the one that you count as number one hundred. ❑ The bank celebrates its hundredth anniversary in December. ■ FRACTION A **hundredth of** something is one of a hundred equal parts of it. ❑ Mitchell beat Lewis by three-hundredths of a second.

■ 서수 백 번째 ❑ 그 은행은 12월에 백 주년 기념식을 거행한다. ■ 분수 100분의 1 ❑ 미첼은 0.03초 차이로 루이스를 이겼다.

hung /hʌŋ/ ■ **Hung** is the past tense and past participle of most of the senses of **hang**. ■ ADJ A **hung** jury is the situation that occurs when a jury is unable to reach a decision because there is not a clear majority of its members in favor of any one decision. In British English you can also talk about a **hung** parliament or a **hung** council. ❑ In the event of a hung Parliament he would still fight for everything in the manifesto.

■ hang의 과거 및 과거 분사 ■ 형용사 (과반수 찬성표를 얻지 못해) 결정을 못 하는 ❑ 의회가 결정을 내리지 못할 경우에도 그는 성명서에 있는 모든 것을 위해 싸울 것이다.

hun|ger /hʌŋgər/ (hungers, hungering, hungered) **1** N-UNCOUNT **Hunger** is the feeling of weakness or discomfort that you get when you need something to eat. ❑ *Hunger is the body's signal that levels of blood sugar are too low.* **2** N-UNCOUNT **Hunger** is a severe lack of food which causes suffering or death. ❑ *Three hundred people in this town are dying of hunger every day.* **3** N-SING If you have a **hunger for** something, you want or need it very much. [WRITTEN] [also no det, with supp, oft N for n] ❑ *Geffen has a hunger for success that seems bottomless.* **4** V-I If you say that someone **hungers for** something or **hungers after** it, you are emphasizing that they want it very much. [FORMAL, EMPHASIS] ❑ *But Jules was not eager for classroom learning, he hungered for adventure.*

hun|ger strike (hunger strikes) N-VAR If someone goes **on hunger strike** or goes **on a hunger strike**, they refuse to eat as a way of protesting about something. ❑ *The protesters have been on hunger strike for 17 days.*

hun|gry /hʌŋgri/ (hungrier, hungriest) **1** ADJ When you are **hungry**, you want some food because you have not eaten for some time and have an uncomfortable or painful feeling in your stomach. ❑ *My friend was hungry, so we drove to a shopping mall to get some food.* ● **hun|gri|ly** /hʌŋgrɪli/ ADV [ADV with v] ❑ *James ate hungrily.* **2** PHRASE If people **go hungry**, they do not have enough food to eat. ❑ *They brought her meat so that she never went hungry.* **3** ADJ If you say that someone is **hungry** for something, you are emphasizing that they want it very much. [LITERARY, EMPHASIS] ❑ *I left Oxford in 1961 hungry to be a critic.* ● COMB in ADJ **Hungry** is also a combining form. ❑ *...power-hungry politicians.* ● **hun|gri|ly** ADV [ADV with v] ❑ *He looked at her hungrily. What eyes! What skin!*

hunk /hʌŋk/ (hunks) **1** N-COUNT A **hunk of** something is a large piece of it. ❑ *...a thick hunk of bread.* **2** N-COUNT If you refer to a man as a **hunk**, you mean that he is big, strong, and sexually attractive. [INFORMAL, APPROVAL] ❑ *...a blond, blue-eyed hunk.*

hunt ♦◊◊ /hʌnt/ (hunts, hunting, hunted) **1** V-I If you **hunt for** something or someone, you try to find them by searching carefully or thoroughly. ❑ *A forensic team was hunting for clues.* ● N-COUNT **Hunt** is also a noun. ❑ *The couple had helped in the hunt for the toddlers.* **2** V-T If you **hunt** a criminal or an enemy, you search for them in order to catch or harm them. ❑ *Detectives have been hunting him for seven months.* ● N-COUNT **Hunt** is also a noun. ❑ *Despite a nationwide hunt for the kidnap gang, not a trace of them was found.* **3** V-I When people or animals **hunt**, they chase and kill wild animals for food or as a sport. ❑ *As a child I learned to hunt and fish.* ● N-COUNT **Hunt** is also a noun. ❑ *He set off for a nineteen-day moose hunt in Nova Scotia.* **4** V-I In Britain, when people **hunt**, they ride horses over fields with dogs called hounds and try to catch and kill foxes, as a sport. ❑ *She liked to hunt as often as she could.* ● N-COUNT **Hunt** is also a noun. ❑ *The hunt was held on land owned by the Duke of Marlborough.* **5** PHRASE If a team or competitor is **in the hunt for** something, they still have a chance of winning it. ❑ *We're still in the hunt for the League title and we want to go all the way in the Cup.* **6** →see also **hunting, witch-hunt**

▶**hunt down** PHRASAL VERB If you **hunt down** a criminal or an enemy, you find them after searching for them. ❑ *Last December they hunted down and killed one of the gangsters.*

hunt|er ♦◊◊ /hʌntər/ (hunters) **1** N-COUNT A **hunter** is a person who hunts wild animals for food or as a sport. ❑ *The hunters stalked their prey.* **2** N-COUNT People who are searching for things of a particular kind are often referred to as **hunters**. ❑ *...job-hunters.* →see also **headhunter**

hunt|ing /hʌntɪŋ/ **1** N-UNCOUNT **Hunting** is the chasing and killing of wild animals by people or other animals, for food or as a sport. ❑ *Deer hunting was banned in Scotland in 1959.* **2** N-UNCOUNT **Hunting** is the activity of searching for a particular thing. ❑ *Job hunting should be approached as a job in itself.* ● COMB in N-UNCOUNT **Hunting** is also a combining form. ❑ *Lee has divided his time between flat-hunting and traveling.*

hur|dle /hɜrdᵊl/ (hurdles, hurdling, hurdled) **1** N-COUNT A **hurdle** is a problem, difficulty, or part of a process that may prevent you from achieving something. ❑ *Two-thirds of candidates fail at this first hurdle and are packed off home.* **2** N-COUNT-COLL **Hurdles** is a race in which people have to jump over a number of obstacles that are also called hurdles. You can use **hurdles** to refer to one or more races. ❑ *Davis won the 400 m hurdles in a new Olympic time of 49.3 sec.* **3** V-T/V-I If you **hurdle**, you jump over something while you are running. ❑ *He crossed the lawn and hurdled the short fence.*

hurl /hɜrl/ (hurls, hurling, hurled) **1** V-T If you **hurl** something, you throw it violently and with a lot of force. ❑ *Groups of angry youths hurled stones at police.* ❑ *Simon caught the grenade and hurled it back.* **2** V-T If you **hurl** abuse or insults **at** someone, you shout insults at them aggressively. ❑ *How would you handle being locked in the back of a cab while the driver hurled abuse at you?*

hur|ri|cane /hɜrɪkeɪn, hɑr-, BRIT hʌrɪkən/ (hurricanes) N-COUNT A **hurricane** is an extremely violent wind or storm. →see **disaster** →see Word Web: **hurricane**

hur|ried /hɜrid, hɑr-, BRIT hʌrid/ **1** ADJ A **hurried** action is done quickly, because you do not have much time to do it in. ❑ *...a hurried breakfast.* ● **hur|ried|ly** ADV [ADV with v] ❑ *...students hurriedly taking notes.* **2** ADJ A **hurried** action is done suddenly, in reaction to something that has just happened. ❑ *Downing Street denied there had been a hurried overnight redrafting of the text.* ● **hur|ried|ly** ADV [ADV with v] ❑ *The moment she saw it, she blushed and hurriedly left the room.* **3** ADJ Someone who is **hurried** does things more quickly than they should because they do not have much time to do them. ❑ *Parisians on the street often looked worried, hurried, and unfriendly.*

1 불가산명사 공복감, 배고픔 **2** 공복감은 혈당치가 너무 낮다는 신체의 신호이다. **2** 불가산명사 기아, 굶주림 **3** 이 마을에서 300명이 매일 굶어 죽어 가고 있다. **3** 단수명사 갈망, 열망 [문어체] **3** 제펜의 성공을 향한 갈망은 끝이 없는 것 같다. **4** 자동사 갈망하다 [격식체, 강조] **3** 그러나 줄스는 학교 수업에 열심이 아니었다. 그는 모험을 갈망했다.

가산명사 또는 불가산명사 단식 투쟁 **3** 시위자들은 17일 동안 단식 투쟁을 하고 있다.

1 형용사 배고픈 **3** 내 친구가 배가 고파서 우리는 뭘 좀 사려고 쇼핑몰로 차를 몰고 갔다. ● 시장한 듯이 부사 **3** 제임스가 시장하게 먹었다. **2** 구 굶주리다 **3** 그들이 그녀에게 고기를 갖다 주어서 그녀는 전혀 굶주리지 않았다. **3** 형용사 -을 갈망하는 [문예체, 강조] **3** 나는 비평가가 되기를 갈망하며 1961년에 옥스퍼드 대학을 떠났다. ● 복합형-형용사 -에 굶주린 **3** 권력에 굶주린 정치가들 ● 갈망하듯 부사 **3** 그가 그녀를 갈망하듯 바라보았다. 저 눈! 저 피부!

1 가산명사 큰 덩어리 **3** 두툼한 빵 한 덩이 **2** 가산명사 섹시한 남자 [비격식체, 마음에 듦] **3** 금발에 푸른 눈의 섹시남

1 자동사 찾다, 뒤지다 **3** 법의학 팀이 단서를 찾고 있었다. ● 가산명사 수색 **3** 그 남녀가 어린 꼬마들을 찾는 데 도움을 주었었다. **2** 타동사 추격하다 **3** 형사들이 그를 7개월 동안 추격해 오고 있다. ● 가산명사 추적 **3** 그 유괴단을 찾기 위한 전국적인 추적에도 불구하고 아무 흔적도 발견되지 않았다. **3** 자동사 사냥하다 **3** 나는 어렸을 때 사냥과 낚시를 배웠다. ● 가산명사 사냥 **3** 그는 노바스코샤로 19일 여정의 큰 사슴 사냥을 떠났다. **4** 자동사 여우 사냥을 하다 **3** 그녀는 가능하면 자주 여우 사냥하기를 좋아했다. ● 가산명사 여우 사냥 **3** 여우사냥은 말보로 공작의 영지에서 열렸다. **5** 구 승산이 있는 **3** 우리는 아직 예선전에서 우승할 승산이 있고 에프 에이(FA)컵 대회 끝까지 가기를 원한다.

구동사 추적하여 잡다 **3** 지난 12월에 그들은 갱단 한 명을 추적한 끝에 사살했다.

1 가산명사 사냥꾼 **3** 사냥꾼들이 사냥감 쪽으로 몰래 다가갔다. **2** 가산명사 -을 찾는 사람 **3** 일자리를 구하는 사람들

1 불가산명사 수렵, 사냥 **3** 스코틀랜드에서 사슴 사냥은 1959년에 금지되었다. **2** 불가산명사 추구, 찾기 **3** 구직 구하기는 그 자체가 하나의 일로 여겨져야 한다. ● 복합형-불가산명사 -찾기 **3** 리는 자기 시간을 아파트 구하기와 여행에 양분해 왔다.

1 가산명사 장애, 곤란 **3** 지원자들의 3분의 2가 첫 번째 난관을 극복하지 못하고 짐을 싸서 집으로 돌아간다. **2** 가산명사-집합 허들 **3** 데이비스는 400미터 허들에서 49.3초의 올림픽 신기록을 세우며 우승했다. **3** 타동사/자동사 뛰어넘다 **3** 그는 잔디밭을 가로질러 가서 얕은 담을 뛰어넘었다.

1 타동사 획 던지다 **3** 성난 젊은이들 무리가 경찰에게 돌을 획 던졌다. **3** 사이먼은 수류탄을 받아 다시 획 던졌다. **2** 타동사 퍼붓다 **3** 택시 기사가 당신에게 욕을 퍼붓는 동안 그 택시의 뒷좌석에 앉아 있는데 문이 잠겨 있는 상황이라면 어떻게 대처하겠습니까?

가산명사 허리케인, 태풍

1 형용사 서두르는 **3** 서둘러 먹은 아침 ● 서둘러 부사 **3** 서둘러 필기하는 학생들 **2** 형용사 황급한 **3** 영국 정부는 그 문건을 밤중에 황급히 고쳐 썼다는 것을 부정했다. ● 황급하게 부사 **3** 그녀는 그것을 보자마자, 얼굴을 붉히며 황급히 그 방을 나갔다. **3** 형용사 서두르는 **3** 길에서 보면 파리 사람들은 보통 근심이 있는 것 같고, 서두르며, 불친절한 인상을 보인다.

a b c d e f g h i j k l m n o p q r s t u v w x y z

Word Web   hurricane

A **hurricane** is a tropical **cyclone** that develops in the Atlantic or Caribbean. When a hurricane develops in the Pacific it is known as a **typhoon**. A hurricane is a violent storm. It begins as a tropical depression. It becomes a **tropical storm** when its winds reach 39 miles per hour (mph). When wind speeds reach 74 mph, a distinct **eye** forms in the center. Then the storm is officially a hurricane. It has heavy rains and very high winds. When a hurricane makes landfall or moves over cool water, it loses some of its power.

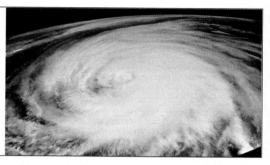

hur|ry /hɜ́ri, hʌ́r-, BRIT hʌ́ri/ (**hurries, hurrying, hurried**) **1** V-I If you **hurry** somewhere, you go there as quickly as you can. ❑ *Claire hurried along the road.* **2** V-I If you **hurry to** do something, you start doing it as soon as you can, or try to do it quickly. ❑ *Mrs. Hardie hurried to make up for her tactlessness by asking her guest about his holiday.* **3** N-SING If you are **in a hurry** to do something, you need or want to do something quickly. If you do something **in a hurry**, you do it quickly or suddenly. ❑ *Kate was in a hurry to grow up, eager for knowledge and experience.* **4** V-T To **hurry** something means the same as to **hurry up** something. ❑ *...the president's attempt to hurry the process of independence.* **5** V-T If you **hurry** someone to a place or into a situation, you try to make them go to that place or get into that situation quickly. ❑ *They say they are not going to be hurried into any decision.* **6** PHRASE If you say to someone "**There's no hurry**" or "**I'm in no hurry**" you are telling them that there is no need for them to do something immediately. ❑ *I'll need to talk with you, but there's no hurry.* **7** PHRASE If you are **in no hurry to** do something, you are very unwilling to do it. ❑ *I love it here so I'm in no hurry to go anywhere.*

Thesaurus   hurry의 참조어

v.   run, rush; (*ant.*) slow down, relax **1**

▶**hurry along** →see **hurry up 2**

▶**hurry up** **1** PHRASAL VERB If you tell someone to **hurry up**, you are telling them do something much more quickly than they were doing. ❑ *Franklin told How to hurry up and take his bath; otherwise, they'd miss their train.* **2** PHRASAL VERB If you **hurry** something **up** or **hurry** it **along**, you make it happen faster or sooner than it would otherwise have done. ❑ *...if you're not a traditionalist and you want to hurry up the process.*

hurt ♦♦◇ /hɜ́rt/ (**hurts, hurting, hurt**) **1** V-T If you **hurt yourself** or **hurt** a part of your body, you feel pain because you have injured yourself. ❑ *Yasin had seriously hurt himself while trying to escape from the police.* **2** V-I If a part of your body **hurts**, you feel pain there. ❑ *His collar bone only hurt when he lifted his arm.* **3** ADJ If you are **hurt**, you have been injured. ❑ *His comrades asked him if he was hurt.* **4** V-T If you **hurt** someone, you cause them to feel pain. ❑ *I didn't mean to hurt her, only to keep her still.* **5** V-T If someone **hurts** you, they say or do something that makes you unhappy. ❑ *He is afraid of hurting Bessy's feelings.* **6** ADJ If you are **hurt**, you are upset because of something that someone has said or done. ❑ *Yes, I was hurt, jealous.* **7** V-I If you say that you **are hurting**, you mean that you are experiencing emotional pain. [only cont] ❑ *I am lonely and I am hurting.* **8** V-T To **hurt** someone or something means to have a bad effect on them or prevent them from succeeding. ❑ *The combination of hot weather and decreased water supplies is hurting many industries.* **9** N-VAR A feeling of **hurt** is a feeling that you have when you think that you have been treated badly and judged unfairly. ❑ *I was full of jealousy and hurt.* **10** PHRASE If you say **It won't hurt to** do something or **It never hurts to** do something, you are recommending an action which you think is helpful or useful. [INFORMAL] ❑ *It never hurts to ask.*

Thesaurus   hurt의 참조어

v.   harm, injure, wound **1**
       ache, smart, sting **2**
ADJ.   injured **3**
       upset **5 6**

Word Partnership   hurt의 연어

ADV.   **badly/seriously** hurt **1 3**
V.   **get** hurt **3**
       feel hurt **6**
N.   hurt *someone's* **chances**, hurt **the economy**,
       hurt *someone's* **feelings**, hurt **sales** **8**

hurt|ful /hɜ́rtfəl/ ADJ If you say that someone's comments or actions are **hurtful**, you mean that they are unkind and upsetting. ❑ *Her comments can only be very hurtful to Mrs. Green's family.*

1 자동사 서둘러 가다 ❑ 클레어는 길을 따라 서둘러 갔다. **2** 자동사 서둘러 하다 ❑ 하디 부인은 자신이 눈치 없었음을 만회하기 위해서 서둘러 손님에게 휴가가 어땠는지를 물었다. **3** 단수명사 서두름, 급함 ❑ 케이트는 지식과 경험에 대한 열의를 보이면서 빨리 어른이 되고 싶어 했다. **4** 타동사 서두르다, 재촉하다 ❑ 독립의 절차를 재촉하려는 대통령의 노력 **5** 타동사 서둘러 ~ 하게 하다 ❑ 그들은 서둘러 결정하지는 않을 것이라고 말한다. **6** 구 서두를 필요는 없다 ❑ 내가 너와 할 말이 좀 있지만, 서두를 필요는 없다. **7** 구 하나도 급할 게 없는 ❑ 나는 여기가 너무 좋아서 다른 데로 가는 것은 하나도 급할 게 없다.

1 구동사 서두르다 ❑ 프랭클린은 하우에게 서둘러 목욕을 하라면서, 서두르지 않으면 기차를 놓칠 것이라고 말했다. **2** 구동사 재촉하다 ❑ 만일 당신이 전통주의자가 아니고 그 과정을 재촉하기를 원한다면,

1 타동사 다치다 ❑ 야신은 경찰에게서 도망치려 하다가 심하게 다쳤다. **2** 자동사 아프다 ❑ 그는 팔을 들어올릴 때에만 쇄골에서 통증을 느꼈다. **3** 형용사 부상을 입은 ❑ 그의 동료가 그에게 부상을 입었는지 물었다. **4** 타동사 다치게 하다, 아프게 하다 ❑ 나는 그녀를 다치게 할 의도는 아니었고, 단지 그녀를 조용히 시키려고 했을 뿐이었다. **5** 타동사 감정을 상하게 하다 ❑ 그는 베시의 감정을 상하게 할까 봐 걱정한다. **6** 형용사 감정이 상한 ❑ 그래, 나는 상처도 받고, 질투도 났어. **7** 자동사 괴롭다 ❑ 나는 외롭고 괴롭다. **8** 타동사 방해하다 ❑ 더운 날씨에 물 공급 감소가 겹쳐 많은 산업이 어려움을 겪고 있다. **9** 가산명사 또는 불가산명사 속상함 ❑ 나는 잔뜩 질투가 나고 속이 상했다. **10** 구 나쁠 건 없다, 손해 볼 건 없다 [비격식체] ❑ 물어봐서 나쁠 건 없다.

형용사 감정을 상하게 하는 ❑ 그녀의 논평은 그런 여자 가족들의 감정을 크게 상하게 할 뿐이다.

hur|tle /hɜrt°l/ (hurtles, hurtling, hurtled) V-I If someone or something **hurtles** somewhere, they move there very quickly, often in a rough or violent way. ❑ *A pretty young girl came hurtling down the stairs.*

자동차 큰 소리 내며 급히 움직이다 ❑ 예쁜 어린 소녀가 쿵쾅거리며 계단을 급히 내려왔다.

hus|band ♦♦♦ /hʌzbənd/ (husbands) N-COUNT A woman's **husband** is the man she is married to. ❑ *Eva married her husband Jack in 1957.* →see **family**, **love**

가산명사 남편 ❑ 에바는 남편 잭과 1957년에 결혼했다.

hush /hʌʃ/ (hushes, hushing, hushed) ■ CONVENTION You say "Hush!" to someone when you are asking or telling them to be quiet. ❑ *Hush, my love, it's all right.* ② V-T/V-I If you **hush** someone or if they **hush**, they stop speaking or making a noise. ❑ *She tried to hush her noisy father.* ③ N-SING You say there is a **hush** in a place when everything is quiet and peaceful, or suddenly becomes quiet. [also no det] ❑ *A hush fell over the crowd and I knew something terrible had happened.*

■ 관용 표현 쉿, 조용히 ❑ 쉿, 내 사랑, 다 괜찮아. ② 타동사/자동사 조용하게 시키다; 조용히 하다 ❑ 그녀는 시끄러운 아버지를 조용히 시키려 했다. ③ 단수명사 조용해짐, 잠잠해짐 ❑ 군중들이 갑자기 조용해졌고, 나는 끔찍한 일이 일어났다는 것을 알았다.

▶**hush up** PHRASAL VERB If someone **hushes** something **up**, they prevent other people from knowing about it. ❑ *The scandal has been discussed by the politburo, although the authorities have tried to hush it up.*

구동사 쉬쉬하다 ❑ 당국에서는 그 추문을 쉬쉬하려고 해 왔지만, 그것을 공산당 정치국이 계속 논의했다.

hushed /hʌʃt/ ■ ADJ A **hushed** place is peaceful and much quieter and calmer than usual. ❑ *The house seemed muted, hushed as if it had been deserted.* ② ADJ A **hushed** voice or **hushed** conversation is very quiet. ❑ *At first we spoke in hushed voices and crept about in order not to alarm them.*

■ 형용사 조용해진, 숨을 죽인 ❑ 그 집은 마치 아무도 없는 것처럼 모두 숨을 죽인 듯이 고요했다. ② 형용사 숨죽인 ❑ 처음에 우리는 그들을 놀라게 하지 않으려고 숨죽여 말하며 살금살금 움직였다.

hus|tle /hʌs°l/ (hustles, hustling, hustled) ■ V-T If you **hustle** someone, you try to make them go somewhere or do something quickly, for example by pulling or pushing them along. ❑ *The guards hustled Harry out of the car.* ② V-I If you **hustle**, you go somewhere or do something as quickly as you can. ❑ *You'll have to hustle if you're to get home for supper.* ③ V-I If someone **hustles**, they try to earn money or gain an advantage from a situation, often by using dishonest or illegal means. [mainly AM] ❑ *We're expected to hustle and fight for what we want.* ④ N-UNCOUNT **Hustle** is busy, noisy activity. ❑ *Shell Cottage provides the perfect retreat from the hustle and bustle of London.*

■ 타동사 우격다짐으로 하다 ❑ 경비들은 해리를 우격다짐으로 차에서 끌어냈다. ② 자동사 서둘러 가다, 서둘러 하다 ❑ 집에 가서 저녁 식사를 하려면, 서둘러야 할 것이다. ③ 자동사 부정한 수단으로 돈을 벌다, 불법적으로 이익을 얻다 [주로 미국영어] ❑ 우리가 원하는 것을 얻기 위해서는 부정한 방법도 동원하고 싸울 수도 있어야 한다. ④ 불가산명사 부산함 ❑ 쉘 코티지는 런던의 온갖 부산함으로부터 벗어난 완벽한 휴식처가 되어 준다.

hut /hʌt/ (huts) ■ N-COUNT A **hut** is a small house with only one or two rooms, especially one which is made of wood, mud, grass, or stones. ② N-COUNT A **hut** is a small wooden building in someone's garden, or a temporary building used by builders or repair workers.

■ 가산명사 오두막 ② 가산명사 (정원의) 간이 연장 창고; (건설 현장의) 가건물

hy|brid /haɪbrɪd/ (hybrids) ■ N-COUNT A **hybrid** is an animal or plant that has been bred from two different species of animal or plant. [TECHNICAL] ❑ *All these brightly colored hybrids are so lovely in the garden.* ● ADJ **Hybrid** is also an adjective. [ADJ n] ❑ *...the hybrid corn seed.* ② N-COUNT You can use **hybrid** to refer to anything that is a mixture of other things, especially two other things. ❑ *...a hybrid of solid and liquid fuel.* ● ADJ **Hybrid** is also an adjective. [ADJ n] ❑ *...a hybrid system.* →see **car**

■ 가산명사 잡종 [과학 기술] ❑ 이렇게 밝은 색의 잡종 화초들을 정원에 심으면 정말 보기 좋다. ● 형용사 잡종의 ❑ 잡종 옥수수씨 ② 가산명사 혼합물 ❑ 고체와 액체 연료의 혼합물 ● 형용사 혼합의, 혼성의 ❑ 혼성 조직

hy|drau|lic /haɪdrɔlɪk, -drɒl-, BRIT haɪdrɒlɪk/ ADJ **Hydraulic** equipment or machinery involves or is operated by a fluid that is under pressure, such as water or oil. [ADJ n] ❑ *The boat has no fewer than five hydraulic pumps.*

형용사 수력의 ❑ 그 배에는 수력 펌프가 무려 다섯 개나 있다.

hy|dro|gen /haɪdrədʒ°n/ N-UNCOUNT **Hydrogen** is a colorless gas that is the lightest and commonest element in the universe.

불가산명사 수소

hy|giene /haɪdʒin/ N-UNCOUNT **Hygiene** is the practice of keeping yourself and your surroundings clean, especially in order to prevent illness or the spread of diseases. ❑ *Be extra careful about personal hygiene.*

불가산명사 위생 ❑ 개인 위생에 각별히 신경 쓰시오.

hy|gien|ic /haɪdʒɛnɪk, BRIT haɪdʒiːnɪk/ ADJ Something that is **hygienic** is clean and unlikely to cause illness. ❑ *...a white, clinical-looking kitchen that was easy to keep clean and hygienic.*

형용사 위생적인 ❑ 깨끗하고 위생적인 상태를 유지하기 쉬운 진료실같이 하얀 부엌

hymn /hɪm/ (hymns) ■ N-COUNT A **hymn** is a religious song that Christians sing in church. ❑ *I like singing hymns.* ② N-COUNT If you describe a movie, book, or speech as a **hymn** to something, you mean that it praises or celebrates that thing. [MAINLY JOURNALISM] ❑ *...a hymn to freedom and rebellion.*

■ 가산명사 찬송가, 성가 ❑ 나는 찬송가 부르는 것을 좋아한다. ② 가산명사 찬가 [주로 언론] ❑ 자유와 도전 정신에 부치는 찬가

hype /haɪp/ (hypes, hyping, hyped) ■ N-UNCOUNT **Hype** is the use of a lot of publicity and advertising to make people interested in something such as a product. [DISAPPROVAL] ❑ *We are certainly seeing a lot of hype by some companies.* ② V-T To **hype** a product means to advertise or praise it a lot. [DISAPPROVAL] ❑ *We had to hype the film to attract the financiers.* ● PHRASAL VERB **Hype up** means the same as **hype**. ❑ *The media seems obsessed with hyping up individuals or groups.*

■ 불가산명사 과대 광고 [탐탁찮음] ❑ 우리는 확실히 일부 회사들의 과대 광고를 많이 보고 있다. ② 타동사 과대 광고하다 [탐탁찮음] ❑ 우리는 투자자들을 끌기 위해 그 영화를 과대 광고해야만 했다. ● 구동사 과대 광고하다 ❑ 대중 매체는 강박적으로 개인이나 단체를 과대 광고하는 것 같다.

Word Link ┆ **hyper** ≈ *above, over* : **hyper**active, **hyper**inflation, **hyper**link

---

hyper|ac|tive /haɪpəræktɪv/ ADJ Someone who is **hyperactive** is unable to relax and is always moving around or doing things. ❑ *His research was used in planning treatments for hyperactive children.*

형용사 과다 활동의, 과민한 ❑ 그의 연구는 과다 활동 아동들을 위한 치료 계획에 사용되었다.

hyper|in|fla|tion /haɪpərɪnfleɪʃ°n/ also **hyper-inflation** N-UNCOUNT **Hyperinflation** is very severe inflation. ❑ *In the hyperinflation of 1922-23 a dollar could be bought for 4.2 billion marks.*

불가산명사 극심한 인플레이션, 초인플레이션 ❑ 1922년에서 1923년 사이의 초인플레이션 중에는 42만 마르크를 줘야 1달러를 살 수 있었다.

hyper|link /haɪpərlɪŋk/ (hyperlinks, hyperlinking, hyperlinked) ■ N-COUNT In an HTML document, a **hyperlink** is a link to another part of the document or to another document. Hyperlinks are shown as words with a line under them. [COMPUTING] ❑ *...Web pages full of hyperlinks.* ② V-T If a document or file is **hyperlinked**, it contains hyperlinks. [COMPUTING] [usu passive] ❑ *The database is fully hyperlinked both within the database and thousands of external links.*

■ 가산명사 하이퍼링크 [컴퓨터] ❑ 하이퍼링크로 가득한 웹페이지 ② 타동사 하이퍼링크 되다 [컴퓨터] ❑ 이 데이터베이스는 내부적으로도 완전히 하이퍼링크 된 상태이며 수천 개의 외부 링크와도 하이퍼링크 되어 있다.

hyper|text /haɪpərtɛkst/ N-UNCOUNT In computing, **hypertext** is a way of connecting pieces of text so that you can go quickly and directly from one to another. [COMPUTING] ❑ *...information embroidered with colorful graphics and tied together by hypertext links.*

불가산명사 하이퍼텍스트 [컴퓨터] ❑ 현란한 그래픽으로 치장되고 하이퍼텍스트 링크들과 연결된 정보

a b c d e f g **h** i j k l m n o p q r s t u v w x y z

Word Web   hypnosis

Hypnosis is a **mental** state somewhere between wakefulness and sleep. When hypnotized, a person's mind is **alert** and **calm** at the same time. Scientists believe this kind of **trance** helps the **conscious** mind relax. This gives the hypnotist access to the **subconscious** mind. Some hypnotists are entertainers. They do things like getting **subjects** on stage to bark like dogs. **Hypnotherapists**, on the other hand, use the trance state to help people. For example, the therapist may suggest that smoking will make the person feel nauseous. This idea stays in the subconscious mind and helps the subject give up cigarettes.

hy|phen /haɪfᵊn/ (**hyphens**) N-COUNT A **hyphen** is the punctuation sign used to join words together to make a compound, as in "left-handed." People also use a hyphen to show that the rest of a word is on the next line.

가산명사 하이픈, 연자(連字) 부호 (-)

hyp|no|sis /hɪpnoʊsɪs/ **1** N-UNCOUNT **Hypnosis** is a state in which a person seems to be asleep but can still see, hear, or respond to things said to them. ❑ *Bevin is now an adult and has re-lived her birth experience under hypnosis.* **2** N-UNCOUNT **Hypnosis** is the art or practice of hypnotizing people.
→see Word Web: **hypnosis**

1 불가산명사 최면 상태 ❑ 베빈은 현재 성인인데 최면 상태에서 탄생을 다시 경험했다. **2** 불가산명사 최면, 최면술

hyp|not|ic /hɪpnɒtɪk/ **1** ADJ If someone is in a **hypnotic** state, they have been hypnotized. ❑ *The hypnotic state actually lies somewhere between being awake and being asleep.* **2** ADJ Something that is **hypnotic** holds your attention or makes you feel sleepy, often because it involves repeated sounds, pictures, or movements. ❑ *His songs are often both hypnotic and reassuringly pleasant.*

1 형용사 최면 상태의, 최면에 걸린 ❑ 최면 상태는 사실 깨어 있는 상태와 잠들어 있는 상태 사이에 있다. **2** 형용사 잠이 오게 하는, 최면이 걸리게 만드는 ❑ 그의 노래는 최면 효과도 있고 마음도 편안하게 해 준다.

hyp|no|tism /hɪpnətɪzəm/ N-UNCOUNT **Hypnotism** is the practice of hypnotizing people. ❑ *Dulcy also saw a psychiatrist who used hypnotism to help her deal with her fear.* ● **hyp|no|tist** (**hypnotists**) N-COUNT ❑ *He was put into a trance by a police hypnotist.*

불가산명사 최면술 ❑ 덜시는 최면술을 사용해서 두려움을 극복하도록 도와준 정신과 의사의 진료를 받기도 하였다. ● 최면술사 가산명사 ❑ 경찰 소속 최면술사가 그에게 최면을 걸었다.

hyp|no|tize /hɪpnətaɪz/ (**hypnotizes, hypnotizing, hypnotized**) [BRIT also **hypnotise**] **1** V-T If someone **hypnotizes** you, they put you into a state in which you seem to be asleep but can still see, hear, or respond to things said to you. ❑ *A hypnotherapist will hypnotize you and will stop you from smoking.* **2** V-T If you **are hypnotized by** someone or something, you are so fascinated by them that you cannot think of anything else. [usu passive] ❑ *He's hypnotized by that black hair and that white face.*

[영국영어 hypnotise] **1** 타동사 최면을 걸다 ❑ 최면술사가 당신에게 최면을 걸어 담배를 끊게 할 것이다. **2** 타동사 -에 매료되다 ❑ 그는 그 검은 머리와 흰 얼굴에 매료되었다.

hy|poc|ri|sy /hɪpɒkrɪsi/ (**hypocrisies**) N-VAR If you accuse someone of **hypocrisy**, you mean that they pretend to have qualities, beliefs, or feelings that they do not really have. [DISAPPROVAL] ❑ *He accused newspapers of hypocrisy in their treatment of the story.*

가산명사 또는 불가산명사 위선 [탐탁찮음] ❑ 그는 그 이야기를 보도하는 신문들의 위선적인 태도를 비난하였다.

hypo|crite /hɪpəkrɪt/ (**hypocrites**) N-COUNT If you accuse someone of being a **hypocrite**, you mean that they pretend to have qualities, beliefs, or feelings that they do not really have. [DISAPPROVAL] ❑ *The magazine wrongly suggested he was a liar and a hypocrite.*

가산명사 위선자 [탐탁찮음] ❑ 그 잡지는 그가 거짓말쟁이이자 위선자라는 잘못된 암시를 주었다.

hypo|criti|cal /hɪpəkrɪtɪkᵊl/ ADJ If you accuse someone of being **hypocritical**, you mean that they pretend to have qualities, beliefs, or feelings that they do not really have. [DISAPPROVAL] ❑ *It would be hypocritical to say I travel at 70mph simply because that is the law.*

형용사 위선적인 [탐탁찮음] ❑ 내가 시속 70마일의 속도로 다니는 것은 단지 그것이 법으로 정해져 있기 때문이라고 말하면 위선적일 것이다.

hypo|der|mic /haɪpədɜrmɪk/ (**hypodermics**) ADJ A **hypodermic** needle or syringe is a medical instrument with a hollow needle, which is used to give injections. [ADJ n] ● N-COUNT **Hypodermic** is also a noun. ❑ *He held up a hypodermic to check the dosage.*

형용사 피하 주사의 ● 가산명사 피하 주사 ❑ 그는 투약량을 확인하기 위해 피하 주사를 들어올렸다.

hy|poth|esis /haɪpɒθɪsɪs/ (**hypotheses**) N-VAR A **hypothesis** is an idea which is suggested as a possible explanation for a particular situation or condition, but which has not yet been proved to be correct. [FORMAL] ❑ *Work will now begin to test the hypothesis in rats.* →see **science**

가산명사 또는 불가산명사 가설 [격식체] ❑ 그 가설을 쥐로 실험하기 위한 작업이 이제 시작될 것이다.

hypo|theti|cal /haɪpəθɛtɪkᵊl/ ADJ If something is **hypothetical**, it is based on possible ideas or situations rather than actual ones. ❑ *Let's look at a hypothetical situation in which Carol, a recovering cocaine addict, gets invited to a party.* ● **hypo|theti|cal|ly** /haɪpəθɛtɪkli/ ADV ❑ *He was invariably willing to discuss the possibilities hypothetically.*

형용사 가정의 ❑ 회복 중인 코카인 중독자인 캐롤이 파티에 초대된다는 상황을 가정해 봅시다. ● 가설적으로, 가정상 부사 ❑ 그는 거의 언제나 기꺼이 그 가능성들을 가정하여 논의하고자 했다.

hys|ter|ec|to|my /hɪstərɛktəmi/ (**hysterectomies**) N-COUNT A **hysterectomy** is a surgical operation to remove a woman's womb. ❑ *I had to have a hysterectomy.*

가산명사 자궁 절제 ❑ 나는 자궁 절제 수술을 받아야 했다.

hys|te|ria /hɪstɪəriə, BRIT hɪstɪəriə/ N-UNCOUNT **Hysteria** among a group of people is a state of uncontrolled excitement, anger, or panic. ❑ *No one could help getting carried away by the hysteria.*

불가산명사 히스테리, 병적 흥분 상태 ❑ 그 광기에 휩쓸리는 것은 아무도 어쩔 수 없었다.

hys|teri|cal /hɪstɛrɪkᵊl/ **1** ADJ Someone who is **hysterical** is in a state of uncontrolled excitement, anger, or panic. ❑ *Police and bodyguards had to form a human shield around him as the almost hysterical crowds struggled to approach him.* ● **hys|teri|cal|ly** /hɪstɛrɪkli/ ADV ❑ *I don't think we can go round screaming hysterically: "Ban these dogs. Muzzle all dogs."* **2** ADJ **Hysterical** laughter is loud and uncontrolled. [INFORMAL] ❑ *The young woman burst into hysterical laughter.* ● **hys|teri|cal|ly** ADV [ADV with v] ❑ *She says she hasn't laughed as hysterically since she was 13.* **3** ADJ If you describe something or someone as **hysterical**, you think that they are very funny and they make you laugh a lot. [INFORMAL] ❑ *Paul*

1 형용사 히스테리의 ❑ 거의 히스테리 상태에 빠진 군중들이 그에게 다가오려고 몸부림치자 경찰과 경호원들은 그를 둘러싸는 인간 방패를 만들어야 했다. ● 히스테리적으로 부사 ❑ 나는 우리가 "이 개들을 금지하시오. 모든 개에게 재갈을 물리시오."라고 히스테리적으로 소리지르며 돌아다닐 수는 없다고 생각한다. **2** 형용사 발작적인, 터져 나오는 [비격식체] ❑ 그 젊은 여자는 발작적인 웃음을 터뜨렸다. ● 발작하듯이, 폭발하듯이 부사 ❑ 그녀는 열세 살

Mazursky was Master of Ceremonies, and he was pretty hysterical. ● **hys|teri|cal|ly** ADV [ADV adj] ❑ *It wasn't supposed to be a comedy but I found it hysterically funny.*

hys|ter|ics /hɪstɛrɪks/ ■ N-PLURAL If someone is **in hysterics** or is having **hysterics**, they are in a state of uncontrolled excitement, anger, or panic. [INFORMAL] ❑ *I'm sick of your having hysterics, okay?* ② N-PLURAL You can say that someone is **in hysterics** or is having **hysterics** when they are laughing loudly in an uncontrolled way. [INFORMAL] ❑ *He'd often have us all in absolute hysterics.*

이후로는 이렇게 발작하듯이 웃어 본 적이 없었다고 말한다. ③ 형용사 아주 웃기는 [비격식체] ❑ 폴 마주르스키가 사회자였는데, 그가 상당히 웃겼다. ● 아주 웃기게 부사 ❑ 그것은 코미디로 만든 것이 아니었지만, 나는 그것이 정말 웃겼다.

■ 복수명사 히스테리를 부림, 히스테리 상태 [비격식체] ❑ 네가 히스테리 부리는 데 질렸어, 알겠어? ② 복수명사 우스워 죽음, 포복절도함 [비격식체] ❑ 그는 자주 우리 모두를 포복절도하게 만들곤 했다.

Ii

I, i /aɪ/ (**I's, i's**) N-VAR I is the ninth letter of the English alphabet.

I ◆◆◇ /aɪ/ PRON-SING A speaker or writer uses I to refer to himself or herself. I is a first person singular pronoun. I is used as the subject of a verb. [PRON v] ❑ *Jim and I are getting married.*

ibid. CONVENTION **Ibid.** is used in books and journals to indicate that a piece of text taken from somewhere else is from the same source as the previous piece of text.

ice ◆◆◇ /aɪs/ (**ices, icing, iced**) ◼ N-UNCOUNT Ice is frozen water. ❑ *Glaciers are moving rivers of ice.* ◻ V-T If you **ice** a cake, you cover it with icing. ❑ *I've made the cake. I've iced and decorated it.* ◼ →see also **iced, icing** ◼ PHRASE If you **break the ice** at a party or meeting, or in a new situation, you say or do something to make people feel relaxed and comfortable. ❑ *That sort of approach should go a long way toward breaking the ice.* ◼ PHRASE If you say that something **cuts no ice with** you, you mean that you are not impressed or influenced by it. ❑ *That sort of romantic attitude cuts no ice with money-men.* ◼ PHRASE If someone puts a plan or project **on ice**, they delay doing it. ❑ *There would be a three-month delay while the deal would be put on ice.* ◼ PHRASE If you say that someone is **on thin ice** or **is skating on thin ice**, you mean that they are doing something risky which may have serious or unpleasant consequences. ❑ *I had skated on thin ice on many assignments and somehow had, so far, got away with it.* →see **crystal**

ice|berg /aɪsbɜrg/ (**icebergs**) N-COUNT An iceberg is a large tall mass of ice floating in the sea. **the tip of the iceberg** →see **tip**

ice cream (**ice creams**) also **ice-cream** ◼ N-MASS Ice cream is a very cold sweet food which is made from frozen cream or a substance like cream and has a flavor such as vanilla, chocolate, or strawberry. ❑ *I'll get you some ice cream.* ◻ N-COUNT An **ice cream** is an amount of ice cream sold in a small container or a cone made of a thin cookie. ❑ *Do you want an ice cream?* →see **dessert**

iced /aɪst/ ◼ ADJ An **iced** drink has been made very cold, often by putting ice in it. [ADJ n] ❑ *...iced tea.* ◻ ADJ An **iced** cake is covered with a layer of icing. ❑ *We were all given little iced cakes.*

ice hock|ey also **ice-hockey** N-UNCOUNT Ice hockey is a game played on ice between two teams of 11 players who use long curved sticks to hit a small rubber disk, called a puck, and try to score goals. [mainly BRIT; AM usually **hockey**]

ice-skate (**ice-skates**) N-COUNT Ice-skates are boots with a thin metal blade underneath that people wear to move quickly on ice.

ice-skating also **ice skating** V-I If you go **ice-skating**, you move around on ice wearing ice-skates. This activity is also a sport. [only cont] ❑ *They took me ice-skating on a frozen lake.* ● N-UNCOUNT **Ice-skating** is also a noun. ❑ *I love watching ice-skating on television.*

ici|cle /aɪsɪkᵊl/ (**icicles**) N-COUNT An icicle is a long pointed piece of ice hanging down from a surface. It forms when water comes slowly off the surface, and freezes as it falls.

ic|ing /aɪsɪŋ/ ◼ N-UNCOUNT Icing is a sweet substance made from powdered sugar that is used to cover and decorate cakes. ❑ *Paul made five-year-old Michelle a birthday cake with yellow icing.* ◻ PHRASE If you describe something as **the icing on the cake**, you mean that it makes a good thing even better, but it is not essential. ❑ *Paul's two goals were the icing on the cake for what was a very good team display.*

icon /aɪkɒn/ (**icons**) ◼ N-COUNT If you describe something or someone as an **icon**, you mean that they are important as a symbol of a particular thing. ❑ *...only Marilyn has proved as enduring a fashion icon.* ◻ N-COUNT An **icon** is a picture of Christ, his mother, or a saint painted on a wooden panel. ❑ *...a painter of religious icons.* ◼ N-COUNT An **icon** is a picture on a computer screen representing a particular computer function. If you want to use it, you move the cursor onto the icon using a mouse. [COMPUTING] ❑ *Kate clicked on the mail icon on her computer screen.* →see **writing**

icy /aɪsi/ (**icier, iciest**) ◼ ADJ If you describe something as **icy** or **icy cold**, you mean that it is extremely cold. ❑ *An icy wind blew hard across the open spaces.* ◻ ADJ An **icy** road has ice on it. ❑ *The roads were icy.* ◼ ADJ If you describe a person or their behavior as **icy**, you mean that they are not affectionate or friendly, and they show their dislike or anger in a quiet, controlled way. [DISAPPROVAL] ❑ *His response was icy.*

ID /aɪ di/ (**IDs**) N-VAR If you have **ID** or an **ID**, you are carrying a document such as an identity card or driver's license which proves that you are a particular person. ❑ *I had no ID on me so the police couldn't establish I was the owner of the car.*

가산명사 또는 불가산명사 영어 알파벳의 아홉 번째 글자

단수대명사 나는, 내가 ❑ 짐과 나는 결혼할 것이다.

관용 표현 이전과 같은 책에

◼ 불가산명사 얼음 ❑ 빙하는 얼음이 흐르는 강이다. ◻ 타동사 당의(糖衣)를 입히다 ❑ 나는 케익을 만들었다. 당의를 입히고 장식했다. ◼ 구 서먹서먹한 분위기를 없애다 ❑ 그러한 접근법이라면 서먹서먹한 분위기를 다소 없앨 수 있을 것이다. ◼ 구 먹혀들지 않다 ❑ 그러한 종류의 낭만적인 태도는 금융가들에게 먹혀들지 않는다. ◼ 구 보류하여, 동결하여 ❑ 거래를 보류하고 있는 동안 3개월의 유예 기간이 있을 것이다. ◼ 구 살얼음을 밟고; 살얼음을 위를 걷고 있다 ❑ 나는 살얼음을 밟듯 많은 과제들을 맡아 왔었는데 그 때까지는 그럭저럭 어떻게 꾸려 나왔었다.

가산명사 빙산

◼ 물질명사 아이스크림 ❑ 너에게 아이스크림을 갖다 줄게. ◻ 가산명사 아이스크림 ❑ 아이스크림 먹고 싶어?

◼ 형용사 얼음으로 차게 한 ❑ 아이스 티 ◻ 형용사 당의(糖衣)를 입힌 ❑ 우리는 모두 당의를 입힌 작은 케익을 받았다.

불가산명사 아이스하키 [주로 영국영어; 미국영어 대개 hockey]

가산명사 스케이트화

자동사 스케이트를 타다 ❑ 그들은 스케이트를 타러 얼음이 언 호수로 나를 데려갔다. ● 불가산명사 아이스 스케이팅 ❑ 나는 텔레비전에서 아이스 스케이팅 보는 것을 좋아한다.

가산명사 고드름

◼ 불가산명사 당의(糖衣), 아이싱 ❑ 폴은 다섯 살이 되는 마이클에게 노란색 아이싱으로 장식된 생일 케익을 만들어 주었다. ◻ 구 금상첨화 ❑ 팀의 아주 훌륭한 기량 발휘에 폴이 골을 두 개 넣어 금상첨화였다.

◼ 가산명사 우상, 상징 ❑ 마릴린만이 지속적인 유행의 상징임이 증명되었다. ◻ 가산명사 성상(聖像) ❑ 종교적 성상을 그리는 화가 ◼ 가산명사 아이콘 [컴퓨터] ❑ 케이트는 컴퓨터 화면의 메일 아이콘을 클릭했다.

◼ 형용사 얼음처럼 차가운 ❑ 확 트인 공간에 얼음처럼 차가운 바람이 심하게 불었다. ◻ 형용사 빙판의 ❑ 도로가 빙판이었다. ◼ 형용사 쌀쌀한, 냉담한 [탐탁잖음] ❑ 그의 반응은 쌀쌀했다.

가산명사 또는 불가산명사 신분증 ❑ 내가 신분증을 가지고 있지 않아서 경찰은 내가 그 차의 주인이라는 것을 확인할 수가 없었다.

I'd /aɪd/ ■ **I'd** is the usual spoken form of "I had," especially when "had" is an auxiliary verb. □ *I felt absolutely certain that I'd seen her before.* ■ **I'd** is the usual spoken form of "I would." □ *There are some questions I'd like to ask.*

idea ♦♦♦ /aɪdiə/ (ideas) ■ N-COUNT An **idea** is a plan, suggestion, or possible course of action. □ *It's a good idea to keep a stock of slimmers' meals for when you're too busy or tired to cook.* □ *I really like the idea of helping people.* ■ N-COUNT An **idea** is an opinion or belief about what something is like or should be like. □ *Some of his ideas about democracy are entirely his own.* ■ N-SING If someone gives you an **idea of** something, they give you information about it without being very exact or giving a lot of detail. □ *This table will give you some idea of how levels of ability in a foreign language can be measured.* ■ N-SING If you have an **idea of** something, you know about it to some extent. □ *No one has any real idea how much the company will make next year.* ■ N-SING If you have an **idea that** something is the case, you think that it may be the case, although you are not certain. [VAGUENESS] □ *I had an idea that he joined the army later, after university, but I may be wrong.* ■ N-SING **The idea** of an action or activity is its aim or purpose. □ *The idea is to lend money to homeowners who are unable to move because their houses are worth less than their mortgages.* ■ N-COUNT If you have the **idea of** doing something, you intend to do it. □ *He sent for a number of books he admired with the idea of re-reading them.*

Thesaurus		idea의 참조어
N.	plan, suggestion ■	
	belief, concept, opinion, thought, viewpoint ■	

Word Partnership		idea의 연어
ADJ.	bad idea, bright idea, brilliant idea, great idea ■	
	crazy idea, different idea, dumb idea, interesting idea, new idea, original idea ■ ■ ■	
	the main idea, the whole idea ■ ■ ■	
V.	get an idea, have an idea ■ ■-■	

| Word Link | ide, ideo ≈ idea : ideal, idealize, ideology |

ideal ♦◇◇ /aɪdiəl/ (ideals) ■ N-COUNT An **ideal** is a principle, idea, or standard that seems very good and worth trying to achieve. □ *The party has drifted too far from its socialist ideals.* ■ N-SING Your **ideal** of something is the person or thing that seems to you to be the best possible example of it. □ *Her features were almost the opposite of the Japanese ideal of beauty in those days.* ■ ADJ The **ideal** person or thing for a particular task or purpose is the best possible person or thing for it. □ *She decided that I was the ideal person to take over the job.* ■ ADJ An **ideal** society or world is the best possible one that you can imagine. [ADJ n] □ *We do not live in an ideal world.*

ideal|ise /aɪdiəlaɪz/ →see **idealize**

ideal|ism /aɪdiəlɪzəm/ N-UNCOUNT **Idealism** is the beliefs and behavior of someone who has ideals and who tries to base their behavior on these ideals. □ *She never lost her respect for the idealism of the 1960s.* ● **ideal|ist** (idealists) N-COUNT □ *He is not such an idealist that he cannot see the problems.*

ideal|is|tic /aɪdiəlɪstɪk/ ADJ If you describe someone as **idealistic**, you mean that they have ideals, and base their behavior on these ideals, even though this may be impractical. □ *Idealistic young people died for a future that was stolen from them as soon as it became possible.*

ideal|ize /aɪdiəlaɪz/ (idealizes, idealizing, idealized) [BRIT also **idealise**] V-T If you **idealize** something or someone, you think of them, or represent them to other people, as being perfect or much better than they really are. □ *People idealize the past.*

ideal|ly /aɪdiəli/ ■ ADV If you say that **ideally** a particular thing should happen or be done, you mean that this is what you would like to happen or be done, but you know that this may not be possible or practical. [ADV with cl/group] □ *People should, ideally, be persuaded to eat a diet with much less fat or oil.* ■ ADV If you say that someone or something is **ideally** suited, **ideally** located, or **ideally** qualified, you mean that they are as well suited, located, or qualified as they could possibly be. □ *They were an extremely happy couple, ideally suited.*

| Word Link | ident ≈ same : identical, identification, unidentified |

iden|ti|cal /aɪdɛntɪkᵊl/ ADJ Things that are **identical** are exactly the same. □ *The two parties fought the last election on almost identical manifestos.* ● **iden|ti|cal|ly** /aɪdɛntɪkli/ ADV □ *...nine identically dressed female dancers.* →see **clone**

iden|ti|fi|able /aɪdɛntɪfaɪəbᵊl/ ADJ Something or someone that is **identifiable** can be recognized. □ *In the corridor were four dirty, ragged bundles, just identifiable as human beings.*

iden|ti|fi|ca|tion /aɪdɛntɪfɪkeɪʃᵊn/ (identifications) ■ N-VAR The **identification** of something is the recognition that it exists, is important, or is true. □ *Early identification of a disease can prevent death and illness.* ■ N-VAR Your **identification** of a particular person or thing is your ability to name them because you know them or recognize them. □ *Officials are awaiting positive identification before charging the men with war crimes.* ■ N-UNCOUNT If someone asks you for some **identification**, they want to see something such as a driver's license, which proves who you are. □ *The woman who was on passport*

Korean column:

■ I had의 구어체 □ 나는 그녀를 이전에 본 적이 있다고 분명히 확신했다. ■ I would의 구어체 □ 여쭙고 싶은 질문이 몇 가지 있습니다.

■ 가산명사 생각 □ 당신이 너무 바쁘거나 피곤해서 요리할 수 없을 때를 대비해서 다이어트 식품을 비축해 두는 것은 좋은 생각이다. □ 나는 사람들을 도와준다는 생각이 정말로 마음에 든다. ■ 가산명사 의견, 신념 □ 민주주의에 대해서 그가 가지고 있는 신념 중 몇 가지는 완전히 그만의 생각이다. ■ 단수명사 개념 □ 이 표를 보면 외국어 능력의 여러 단계를 어떻게 측정할 수 있는지에 대해 개념을 갖게 될 것이다. ■ 단수명사 지식, 의식 □ 그 회사가 내년에 얼마나 흑자를 냈는지에 대해서는 아무도 모른다. ■ 단수명사 (막연한) 생각, 느낌 [짐작투] □ 나는 그가 대학 졸업 후 나중에 군대에 입대하였다는 생각을 했지만, 내가 틀렸을지도 모른다. ■ 단수명사 목적 □ 저당 융자금보다 집값이 적게 나가기 때문에 이사할 수 없는 집주인들에게 돈을 빌려주는 데 그 목적이 있다. ■ 가산명사 의도 □ 그는 예전에 그가 좋아했던 책을 다시 읽겠다는 생각에 그 책들을 보내 달라는 요청을 하였다.

■ 가산명사 이상 □ 그 정당은 사회주의 이상에서 너무 많이 벗어났다. ■ 단수명사 (사람, 물건 등의) 이상적인 것, 전형 □ 그녀의 모습은 그 당시 일본 미인의 전형과는 거의 반대다. ■ 형용사 이상적인, 최상의 □ 그녀는 내가 그 일을 맡을 최적의 사람이라고 결정했다. ■ 형용사 이상적인 □ 우리는 이상적인 세계에 살고 있지 않다.

불가산명사 이상주의 □ 그녀는 1960년대의 이상주의에 대한 존경심을 결코 잃지 않았다. ● 이상주의자 가산명사 □ 그는 그 문제들을 볼 수 없을 정도의 이상주의자는 아니다.

형용사 이상주의의 □ 이상주의적인 젊은이들은 자신들에게 가능하게 되자마자 강탈당한 미래를 갈망했다.

[영국영어 idealise] 타동사 이상화하다 □ 사람들은 과거를 이상화한다.

■ 부사 이상적으로 □ 이상적으로 보면 사람들이 훨씬 적은 지방이나 기름이 함유된 식사를 하도록 설득해야 한다. ■ 부사 완벽하게, 아주 잘 □ 그들은 완벽하게 어울리는 아주 행복한 부부였다.

형용사 똑같은, 동일한 □ 그 두 정당은 지난번 선거에서 거의 똑같은 정책을 가지고 싸웠다. ● 똑같이 부사 □ 똑같이 옷을 입은 아홉 명의 여성 댄서들

형용사 신원을 확인할 수 있는 □ 복도에서는 겨우 사람이란 걸 알아볼 수 있을 정도로 지저분한 넝마 뭉치 같은 사람 넷이 있었다.

■ 가산명사 또는 불가산명사 확인, 검증 □ 질병의 조기 확인으로 죽거나 병드는 걸 예방할 수 있다. ■ 가산명사 또는 불가산명사 신원 확인 □ 당국에서는 그 남자들을 전범으로 고발하기 전에 일단 긍정적인 신원 확인을 기다리고 있다. ■ 불가산명사 신분증 □ 여권 검사대에 있는 그 여자가 나에게 다른 신분증이 있는지 물었다. ■ 가산명사 또는 불가산명사 밀접성 □ 가톨릭교와 스페인과의 밀접성 ■ 불가산명사

A

control asked me if I had any further identification. ◆ N-VAR The **identification of** one person or thing **with** another is the close association of one with the other. ❑ ...the identification of Spain with Catholicism. ◆ N-UNCOUNT **Identification with** someone or something is the feeling of sympathy and support for them. ❑ Marilyn had an intense identification with animals.

동일시, 감정 이입 ❑ 마릴린은 동물에 대한 동일시가 강했다.

B

iden|ti|fy ◆◆◇ /aɪdɛntɪfaɪ/ (**identifies, identifying, identified**) ◆ V-T If you can **identify** someone or something, you are able to recognize them or distinguish them from others. ❑ There are a number of distinguishing characteristics by which you can identify a Hollywood epic. ◆ V-T If you **identify** someone or something, you name them or say who or what they are. ❑ Police have already identified around 10 murder suspects. ◆ V-T If you **identify** something, you discover or notice its existence. ❑ Scientists claim to have identified chemicals produced by certain plants which have powerful cancer-combating properties. ◆ V-T If a particular thing **identifies** someone or something, it makes them easy to recognize, by making them different in some way. ❑ She wore a little nurse's hat on her head to identify her. ◆ V-I If you **identify with** someone or something, you feel that you understand them or their feelings and ideas. ❑ She would only play a role if she could identify with the character. ◆ V-T If you **identify** one person or thing **with** another, you think that they are closely associated or involved in some way. ❑ Moore really hates to play the sweet, passive women that audiences have identified her with.

C

D

E

F

■ 타동사 식별하다 ❑ 할리우드 대작임을 식별할 수 있게 하는 뚜렷한 특징들이 몇 가지 있다. ② 타동사 신원을 밝히다, 거명하다 ❑ 경찰은 이미 살인 용의자 10명 정도의 신원을 밝힌 상태이다. ③ 타동사 규명하다 ❑ 과학자들은 강력한 항암 성분을 가진 특정 식물들이 생산하는 화학 물질을 규명했다고 주장한다. ④ 타동사 알아보기 쉽게 하다 ❑ 그녀는 알아보기 쉽게 작은 간호사 모자를 머리에 쓰고 있었다. ⑤ 자동사 공감하다 ❑ 그녀는 등장인물에게 감정 이입을 할 수 있는 경우에만 역할을 맡을 것이다. ⑥ 타동사 -와 동일시하다 ❑ 무어는 관객들이 자기와 동일시하는 착하고 순종적인 여자 역을 연기하는 것을 정말로 싫어한다.

G

iden|tity ◆◆◇ /aɪdɛntɪti/ (**identities**) ◆ N-COUNT Your **identity** is who you are. ❑ Abu is not his real name, but it's one he uses to disguise his identity. ◆ N-VAR The **identity** of a person or place is the characteristics they have that distinguish them from others. ❑ I wanted a sense of my own identity.

■ 가산명사 신원, 정체 ❑ 아부는 그의 본명이 아니고, 그가 신원을 감추기 위해 사용하는 이름이다. ② 가산명사 또는 불가산명사 개성, 고유성 ❑ 나는 나만의 개성을 원했다.

H

I

Word Partnership   identity의 연어

N.	identity **theft** ■
	identity **crisis, sense of** identity ②
ADJ.	**ethnic** identity, **national** identity, **personal** identity ②

J

K

iden|tity card (**identity cards**) N-COUNT An **identity card** is a card with a person's name, photograph, date of birth, and other information on it. In some countries, people are required to carry identity cards in order to prove who they are.

가산명사 신분증

L

ideo|logi|cal /aɪdiəlɒdʒɪkᵊl, ɪdi-/ ADJ **Ideological** means relating to principles or beliefs. ❑ Others left the party for ideological reasons. ● ideo|logi|cal|ly /aɪdiəlɒdʒɪkli, ɪdi-/ ADV ❑ ...an ideologically sound organisation.

형용사 이념의 ❑ 다른 사람들은 이념적인 이유들로 그 정당을 떠났다. ● 이념적으로 부사 ❑ 이념적으로 건전한 기관

M

Word Link   ide, ideo ≈ idea : ideal, idealize, ideology

ideol|ogy /aɪdiɒlədʒi, ɪdi-/ (**ideologies**) N-VAR An **ideology** is a set of beliefs, especially the political beliefs on which people, parties, or countries base their actions. ❑ ...capitalist ideology.

가산명사 또는 불가산명사 이념, 이데올로기 ❑ 자본주의 이념

N

idi|om /ɪdiəm/ (**idioms**) ◆ N-COUNT A particular **idiom** is a particular style of something such as music, dance, or architecture. [FORMAL] ❑ McCartney was also keen to write in a classical idiom, rather than a pop one. ◆ N-COUNT An **idiom** is a group of words which have a different meaning when used together from the one they would have if you took the meaning of each word separately. [TECHNICAL] ❑ Proverbs and idioms may become worn with over-use.

O

■ 가산명사 스타일 [격식체] ❑ 맥카트니는 또한 팝보다는 고전적인 스타일로 곡을 쓰고 싶어했다. ② 가산명사 관용어구, 숙어 [과학 기술] ❑ 속담과 숙어는 너무 많이 사용되면 진부해질 수 있다.

P

id|iot /ɪdiət/ (**idiots**) N-COUNT If you call someone an **idiot**, you are showing that you think they are very stupid or have done something very stupid. [DISAPPROVAL] ❑ I knew I'd been an idiot to stay there.

가산명사 바보, 멍청이 [탐탁찮음] ❑ 그곳에 머무르다니 내가 바보였다는 것을 알았다.

Q

idle /aɪdᵊl/ (**idles, idling, idled**) ◆ ADJ If people who were working are **idle**, they have no jobs or work. [v-link ADJ] ❑ 4,000 workers have been idle for 12 of the first 27 weeks of this year. ② ADJ If machines or factories are **idle**, they are not working or being used. [v-link ADJ] ❑ Now the machine is lying idle. ③ ADJ If you say that someone is **idle**, you disapprove of them because they are not doing anything and you think they should be. [DISAPPROVAL] ❑ ...idle bureaucrats who spent the day reading newspapers. ● idly ADV [ADV with v] ❑ We were not idly sitting around. ④ ADJ **Idle** is used to describe something that you do for no particular reason, often because you have nothing better to do. [ADJ n] ❑ Brian kept up the idle chatter for another five minutes. ● idly ADV ❑ We talked idly about magazines and baseball. ⑤ ADJ You refer to an **idle** threat or boast when you do not think the person making it will or can do what they say. [ADJ n] ❑ It was more of an idle threat than anything. ⑥ V-T To **idle** a factory or other place of work means to close it down because there is no work to do or because the workers are on strike. [AM, BUSINESS; BRIT usually **shut down**] ❑ Officials say some of the idle assembly plants will resume production after the Labor Day holiday. ⑦ V-T To **idle** workers means to stop them working. [AM, BUSINESS; BRIT **lay off**] ❑ The strike has idled about 55,000 machinists. ⑧ V-I If an engine or vehicle **is idling**, the engine is running slowly and quietly because it is not in gear, and the vehicle is not moving. ❑ Beyond a stand of trees a small plane idled.

R

S

T

U

V

■ 형용사 놀고 있는, 일이 없는 ❑ 4천 명의 노동자들이 올해의 첫 27주 중에 12주 동안 놀고 있다. ② 형용사 놀고 있는, 사용하지 않는 ❑ 현재 그 기계는 방치돼 놀고 있다. ③ 형용사 게으른, 빈둥거리는 [탐탁찮음] ❑ 신문이나 읽으면서 하루를 보냈던 나태한 관료들 ● 빈둥거리며 부사 ❑ 우리는 빈둥거리며 앉아 있지 않았다. ④ 형용사 하릴없는 ❑ 브라이언은 다시 5분 동안 하릴없이 잡담을 계속 늘어놓았다. ● 하릴없이 부사 ❑ 우리는 하릴없이 잡지와 야구에 대해서 이야기를 했다. ⑤ 형용사 실속 없는 ❑ 그것은 단순히 말뿐인 위협이었다. ⑥ 타동사 휴업하다, 놀리다 [미국영어, 경제; 영국영어 대개 shut down] ❑ 관계자들에 따르면 노동절 휴일 이후에는 현재 휴업 중인 조립 공장 중 몇 개는 생산을 재개할 것이다. ⑦ 타동사 놀리다 [미국영어, 경제; 영국영어 lay off] ❑ 파업으로 인해 기계 기사 5만 5천 명이 놀고 있다. ⑧ 자동사 공회전하다 ❑ 나무들이 무리지어 서 있는 곳 너머에 작은 비행기 한 대가 공회전을 하고 있었다.

W

Thesaurus   idle의 참조어

ADJ.	inactive, jobless, unemployed ■
	lazy, passive, wasteful; (ant.) busy, productive ③

X

Y

idol /aɪdᵊl/ (**idols**) ◆ N-COUNT If you refer to someone such as a movie, pop, or sports star as an **idol**, you mean that they are greatly admired or loved by their fans. ❑ A great cheer went up from the crowd as they caught sight of their idol. ② N-COUNT An **idol** is a statue or other object that is worshiped by people who believe that it is a god.

Z

■ 가산명사 우상 ❑ 그들의 우상이 눈에 띄자 무리에서는 큰 환호성이 터져 나왔다. ② 가산명사 우상, 신상(神像)

idol|ize /ˈaɪdəlaɪz/ (**idolizes**, **idolizing**, **idolized**) [BRIT also **idolise**] V-T If you **idolize** someone, you admire them very much. ❑ *Naomi idolized her father as she was growing up.*

idyl|lic /aɪˈdɪlɪk, BRIT ɪdɪlɪk/ ADJ If you describe something as **idyllic**, you mean that it is extremely pleasant, simple, and peaceful without any difficulties or dangers. ❑ *...an idyllic setting for a summer romance.*

i.e. /ˈaɪ ˈi/ **i.e.** is used to introduce a word or sentence which makes what you have just said clearer or gives details. ❑ *His every utterance was directed to the intellect, i.e., to the mind.*

if ♦♦♦ /ɪf/

Often pronounced /ɪf/ at the beginning of the sentence.

1 CONJ You use **if** in conditional sentences to introduce the circumstances in which an event or situation might happen, might be happening, or might have happened. ❑ *She gets very upset if I exclude her from anything.* ❑ *You can go if you want.* **2** CONJ You use **if** in indirect questions where the answer is either "yes" or "no." ❑ *He asked if I had left with you, and I said no.* **3** CONJ You use **if** to suggest that something might be slightly different from what you are stating in the main part of the sentence, for example that there might be slightly more or less of a particular quality. ❑ *Sometimes, that standard is quite difficult, if not impossible, to achieve.* **4** CONJ You use **if**, usually with "can," "could," "may," or "might," at a point in a conversation when you are politely trying to make a point, change the subject, or interrupt another speaker. ❑ *If I could just make another small point about the weightlifters in the Olympics.* **5** CONJ You use **if** at or near the beginning of a clause when politely asking someone to do something. [POLITENESS] ❑ *I wonder if you'd be kind enough to give us some information, please?* **6** PHRASE You use **if not** in front of a word or phrase to indicate that your statement does not apply to that word or phrase, but to something closely related to it that you also mention. ❑ *She understood his meaning, if not his words, and took his advice.* **7** CONJ You use **if** to introduce a subordinate clause in which you admit a fact which you regard as less important than the statement in the main clause. ❑ *If there was any disappointment it was probably temporary.* **8** PHRASE You use **if ever** with past tenses when you are introducing a description of a person or thing, to emphasize how appropriate it is. [EMPHASIS] ❑ *I became a distraught, worried mother, a useless role if ever there was one.* **9** PHRASE You use **if only** with past tenses to introduce what you think is a fairly good reason for doing something, although you realize it may not be a very good one. ❑ *She always writes me once a month, if only to scold me because I haven't answered her last letter yet.* **10** PHRASE You use **if only** to express a wish or desire, especially one that cannot be fulfilled. [FEELINGS] ❑ *If only you had told me that some time ago.* **11** PHRASE You use **as if** when you are making a judgment about something that you see or notice. Your belief or impression might be correct, or it might be wrong. ❑ *The whole room looks as if it has been lovingly put together over the years.* **12** PHRASE You use **as if** to describe something or someone by comparing them with another thing or person. ❑ *He points two fingers at his head, as if he were holding a gun.* **13** PHRASE You use **as if** to emphasize that something is not true. [SPOKEN, EMPHASIS] ❑ *Getting my work done! My God! As if it mattered.*

ig|nite /ɪgˈnaɪt/ (**ignites**, **igniting**, **ignited**) **1** V-T/V-I When you **ignite** something or when it **ignites**, it starts burning or explodes. ❑ *The bombs ignited a fire which destroyed some 60 houses.* **2** V-T If something or someone **ignites** your feelings, they cause you to have very strong feelings about something. [LITERARY] ❑ *There was one teacher who really ignited my interest in words.*

ig|ni|tion /ɪgˈnɪʃən/ (**ignitions**) **1** N-VAR In a car engine, the **ignition** is the part where the fuel is ignited. ❑ *The device automatically disconnects the ignition.* **2** N-SING Inside a car, **the ignition** is the part where you turn the key so that the engine starts. ❑ *Abruptly he turned the ignition key and started the engine.* **3** N-UNCOUNT **Ignition** is the process of something starting to burn. ❑ *The ignition of methane gas killed eight men.*

ig|no|rance /ˈɪgnərəns/ N-UNCOUNT **Ignorance of** something is lack of knowledge about it. ❑ *I am beginning to feel embarrassed by my complete ignorance of non-European history.*

ig|no|rant /ˈɪgnərənt/ **1** ADJ If you describe someone as **ignorant**, you mean that they do not know things they should know. If someone is **ignorant of** a fact, they do not know it. ❑ *People don't like to ask questions for fear of appearing ignorant.* **2** ADJ People are sometimes described as **ignorant** when they do something that is not polite or kind. Some people think that it is not correct to use **ignorant** with this meaning. ❑ *I met some very ignorant people who called me all kinds of names.*

ig|nore ♦♦◊ /ɪgˈnɔr/ (**ignores**, **ignoring**, **ignored**) **1** V-T If you **ignore** someone or something, you pay no attention to them. ❑ *She said her husband ignored her.* **2** V-T If you say that an argument or theory **ignores** an important aspect of a situation, you are criticizing it because it fails to consider that aspect or to take it into account. ❑ *Such arguments ignore the question of where ultimate responsibility lay.*

Word Partnership	*ignore*의 연어
N.	ignore **advice**, ignore **a warning** **1**
V.	**choose to** ignore *someone/something*, **try to** ignore *someone/something*
ADJ.	**hard to** ignore, **impossible to** ignore **1**

[영국영어 idolise] 타동사 숭배하다, 우상시하다 ❑ 나오미는 자라면서 아버지를 우상시켰다.

형용사 전원풍의, 목가의 ❑ 여름날의 사랑을 위한 전원풍 배경

즉, 바꿔 말하면 ❑ 그의 모든 발언은 지성을, 즉 이성을 향한 것이었다.

문장의 시작 부분에서는 흔히 /ɪf/로 발음된다.

1 접속사 만일, 만약 ❑ 만일 내가 어느 것에서든 그녀를 제외시키면 그녀는 매우 속상해한다. ❑ 네가 원한다면 가도 좋다. **2** 접속사 ―인지 아닌지 ❑ 그는 내가 함께 떠나는지를 물었고 나는 아니라고 말했다. **3** 접속사 ―하더라도, ―이긴 하지만 ❑ 가끔씩 그런 수준은, 불가능하진 않지만, 성취하기가 매우 어렵다. **4** 접속사 ―해도 되나면 ❑ 제가 올림픽에 참가한 역도 선수들에 대해서 또 다른 사소한 점 하나를 지적해도 된나면. **5** 접속사 ―인지 [공손히] ❑ 우리에게 정보를 알려 주실 수 있을까요? **6** 구 ―은 아닐지라도 ❑ 그녀는 그의 말 자체는 아니었지만 그가 의미하는 바를 이해했고 그래서 그의 충고를 받아들였다. **7** 접속사 ―라면 ❑ 실망한 것이 있다면, 그것은 아마도 일시적이었을 것이다. **8** 구 진정 ―한, 그야말로 ―한 [강조] ❑ 나는 노심초사하는 걱정꾼 엄마가 되었는데 그야말로 아무 쓸모없는 역할이었다. **9** 구 단지 ―때문이라도 ❑ 그녀는 단지 지난번 자기가 보낸 편지에 대해 내가 답장을 안 한 것을 꾸짖기 위해서라도 한 달에 한 번씩은 꼭 내게 편지를 쓴다. **10** 구 ―하기만 하면 좋을 텐데 [감정 개입] ❑ 네가 나에게 그 말을 좀 전에 했더라면 좋았을 텐데. **11** 구 마치 ―인 것처럼 ❑ 방 전체가 마치 여러 해 동안 애정을 기울여 꾸며 온 것처럼 보인다. **12** 구 마치 ―인 것처럼 ❑ 그가 마치 총을 들고 있는 것처럼 손가락 두 개로 자기 머리를 가리킨다. **13** 구 마치 ―인 것처럼 [구어체, 강조] ❑ 내 일을 끝내라고! 맙소사! 마치 중요한 일인 것처럼.

1 타동사/자동사 불을 붙이다, 점화하다; 불이 붙다, 점화되다 ❑ 폭탄이 터져 그 불길에 약 60 채의 집이 전소되었다. **2** 타동사 (감정의) 불을 붙이다, 타오르게 하다 [문예체] ❑ 내가 정말로 언어에 흥미를 가지도록 해 준 선생님이 한 분 계셨다.

1 가산명사 또는 불가산명사 점화 장치 ❑ 그 장치는 자동적으로 점화 스위치를 차단한다. **2** 단수명사 시동 장치 ❑ 갑작스럽게 그가 시동 장치에 열쇠를 넣고 돌려 엔진에 시동을 걸었다. **3** 불가산명사 발화, 점화 ❑ 메탄가스에 불이 붙어 8명이 죽었다.

불가산명사 무지 ❑ 내가 유럽 이외의 역사에 대해서는 전혀 모르고 있다는 사실이 부끄럽게 여겨지기 시작한다.

1 형용사 무지한, 무식한 ❑ 사람들은 무식해 보이는 것이 두려워서 질문하기를 좋아하지 않는다. **2** 형용사 무례한 ❑ 나를 별의별 이름으로 부르던 아주 무례한 사람들을 몇 명을 만났다.

1 타동사 무시하다 ❑ 그녀는 남편이 자신을 무시한다고 말했다. **2** 타동사 간과하다, 소홀히 여기다 ❑ 그러한 주장은 궁극적 책임이 어디에 있는지에 대한 물음을 간과하는 것이다.

a b c d e f g h i j k l m n o p q r s t u v w x y z

ill ◆◇◇ /ɪl/ (**ills**) **1** ADJ Someone who is **ill** is suffering from a disease or a health problem. ❑ *In November 1941 Payne was seriously ill with pneumonia.* ● N-PLURAL People who are ill in some way can be referred to as, for example, **the mentally ill**. ❑ *I used to work with the mentally ill.*

1 형용사 병든, 아픈 ❑ 1941년 11월에 페인은 폐렴을 심하게 앓았다. ● 복수명사 병든 사람들 ❑ 나는 한 때 정신 질환을 앓고 있는 사람들과 함께 일을 했다.

> The words **ill** and **sick** are very similar in meaning, but are used in slightly different ways. Ill is generally not used before a noun, and can be used in verbal expressions such as **fall ill** and **be taken ill**. ❑ *He fell ill shortly before Christmas... One of the jury members was taken ill.* **Sick** is often used before a noun. ❑ *...sick children.* In British English, **ill** is a slightly more polite, less direct word than **sick**. **Sick** often suggests the actual physical feeling of being ill, for example nausea or vomiting. ❑ *I spent the next 24 hours in bed, groaning and being sick.* In American English, **sick** is often used where British people would say **ill**. ❑ *Some people get hurt in accidents or get sick.*

> ill과 sick은 뜻이 아주 비슷하지만 조금 다르게 쓰인다. ill은 보통 명사 앞에는 쓰이지 않고 fall ill과 be taken ill과 같은 동사구에서 쓰일 수 있다. ❑ 그는 성탄절 직전에 병이 났다... 배심원 한 명이 병이 났다. sick은 흔히 명사 앞에 쓰인다. ❑ ...아픈 아이들. 영국 영어에서는, ill이 sick보다 약간 더 공손하고, 완곡한 말이다. sick은 흔히 병으로 인한 실제 신체상의 느낌, 예를 들면, 메스꺼림이나 구토 같은 것을 의미한다. ❑ 나는 이후 24시간을 아파서 신음하며 누워 있었다. 영국 사람들은 ill을 쓸 곳에 미국 영어에서는 흔히 sick을 사용한다. ❑ 어떤 사람들은 사고로 다치거나 병이 든다.

2 N-COUNT Difficulties and problems are sometimes referred to as **ills**. [FORMAL] ❑ *His critics maintain that he's responsible for many of Algeria's ills.* **3** N-UNCOUNT **Ill** is evil or harm. [LITERARY] ❑ *They say they mean you no ill.* **4** ADV **Ill** means the same as "badly." [FORMAL] [ADV with v] ❑ *The company's conservative instincts sit ill with competition.* **5** ADJ You can use **ill** in front of some nouns to indicate that you are referring to something harmful or unpleasant. [FORMAL] [ADJ n] ❑ *She had brought ill luck into her family.* **6** PHRASE If you say that someone **can ill afford to** do something, or **can ill afford** something, you mean that they must prevent it from happening because it would be harmful or embarrassing to them. [FORMAL] ❑ *It's possible he won't play but I can ill afford to lose him.* **7** PHRASE If you **fall ill** or **are taken ill**, you suddenly become ill. ❑ *Shortly before Christmas, he was mysteriously taken ill.* **8** to **speak ill of** someone →see **speak**

2 가산명사 문제들 [격식체] ❑ 그를 비판하는 사람들은 그가 알제리의 문제 중 많은 것에 대해 책임이 있다고 주장한다. **3** 불가산명사 해악 [문어체] ❑ 그들은 너에게 전혀 해악을 끼칠 의도가 없다고 말한다. **4** 부사 나쁘게 [격식체] ❑ 그 회사의 보수적인 성향이 경쟁에서는 나쁘게 작용한다. **5** 형용사 나쁜 [격식체] ❑ 그녀는 가족에게 불운을 가져왔다. **6** 구 -할 형편이 아니다 [격식체] ❑ 그가 시합을 하지 않을 가능성이 있지만, 나는 그 없이 할 수 있는 형편이 아니다. **7** 구 갑자기 병에 걸리다 ❑ 크리스마스 조금 전에, 그는 이상하게도 갑자기 병에 걸렸다.

Word Partnership ill의 연어

ADV.	**critically** ill, **mentally** ill, **physically** ill, **seriously** ill, **terminally** ill, **very** ill **1**
V.	**become** ill, **feel** ill, **look** ill **1**

I'll /aɪl/ **I'll** is the usual spoken form of "I will" or "I shall." ❑ *I'll be leaving town in a few weeks.*

I will 또는 I shall의 구어체 ❑ 나는 몇 주 후에 도시를 떠날 것이다.

Word Link il ≈ not : il**legal**, il**literate**, il**logical**

---

il|legal ◆◇◇ /ɪliːgᵊl/ (**illegals**) **1** ADJ If something is **illegal**, the law says that it is not allowed. ❑ *It is illegal to intercept radio messages.* ❑ *...illegal drugs.* ● il**legal|ly** ADV [ADV with v] ❑ *They were yesterday convicted of illegally using a handgun.* **2** ADJ **Illegal** immigrants or workers have traveled into a country or are working without official permission. [ADJ n] ● N-COUNT Illegal immigrants or workers are sometimes referred to as **illegals**. ❑ *...a clothing factory where many other illegals also worked.*

1 형용사 불법의 ❑ 무선 메시지를 가로채는 것은 불법이다. ❑ 불법 마약 ● 불법적으로 부사 ❑ 그들은 불법적으로 권총을 사용한 죄로 어제 유죄 판결을 받았다. **2** 형용사 불법의 ● 가산명사 불법 체류자 ❑ 또 다른 많은 불법 체류자들이 일했던 옷 공장

il|legi|ti|mate /ɪlidʒɪtɪmɪt/ **1** ADJ A person who is **illegitimate** was born of parents who were not married to each other. ❑ *...Charles's illegitimate son Jemmy.* **2** ADJ **Illegitimate** is used to describe activities and institutions that are not in accordance with the law or with accepted standards of what is right. ❑ *He realized that, otherwise, the election would have been dismissed as illegitimate by the international community.*

1 형용사 사생아인 ❑ 찰스의 사생아 아들인 제미 **2** 형용사 위법의, 비합법의 ❑ 그렇지 않았다면 그 선거는 국제 사회에 의해 위법이라고 기각될 뻔했다는 것을 그는 알았다.

ill-fated ADJ If you describe something as **ill-fated**, you mean that it ended or will end in an unsuccessful or unfortunate way. ❑ *England's footballers are back home after their ill-fated trip to Algeria.*

형용사 불운한 ❑ 잉글랜드 축구 선수들이 불운했던 알제리 원정 경기를 마치고 집으로 돌아오고 있다.

ill health N-UNCOUNT Someone who suffers from **ill health** has an illness or keeps being ill. ❑ *He was forced to retire because of ill health.*

불가산명사 건강이 좋지 않음 ❑ 그는 건강이 좋지 않아서 퇴직해야 했다.

il|lic|it /ɪlɪsɪt/ ADJ An **illicit** activity or substance is not allowed by law or the social customs of a country. ❑ *Dante clearly condemns illicit love.*

형용사 위법의, 금기된 ❑ 단테는 분명히 금기된 사랑을 비난한다.

Word Link liter ≈ letter : il**liter**ate, **liter**al, **liter**ary

---

il|lit|er|ate /ɪlɪtərɪt/ (**illiterates**) ADJ Someone who is **illiterate** does not know how to read or write. ❑ *A large percentage of the population is illiterate.* ● N-COUNT An **illiterate** is someone who is illiterate. ❑ *...an educational center for illiterates.*

형용사 문맹의 ❑ 인구의 많은 비율이 문맹이다. ● 가산명사 문맹자 ❑ 문맹자 교육 센터

ill|ness ◆◇◇ /ɪlnɪs/ (**illnesses**) **1** N-UNCOUNT **Illness** is the fact or experience of being ill. ❑ *If your child shows any signs of illness, take her to the doctor.* **2** N-COUNT An **illness** is a particular disease such as measles or pneumonia. ❑ *She returned to her family home to recover from an illness.* →see Word Web: illness

1 불가산명사 병 ❑ 아이가 조금이라도 병의 증후를 보이면 아이를 병원에 데려가라. **2** 가산명사 병, 질병 ❑ 그녀는 병에서 회복하기 위해 가족이 있는 집으로 돌아왔다.

Thesaurus illness의 참조어

N.	ailment, disease, sickness; (*ant.*) health **1** **2**

Word Partnership illness의 연어

N.	**signs**/**symptoms** of *an* illness **1** **2**
ADJ.	**mental** illness, **serious** illness, **terminal** illness **1** **2** **long**/**short** illness, **mysterious** illness, **sudden** illness **2**
V.	**suffer** from an illness, **treat** an illness **1** **2** **diagnose** an illness, **have** an illness **2**

Word Web — illness

Most **infectious diseases** pass from person to person. However, some people have **contracted viruses** from animals. During the 2002 SARS **epidemic**, doctors discovered that the disease came from birds. SARS caused over 800 deaths in 32 countries. The disease had to be stopped quickly. Hospitals **quarantined** SARS patients. Medical workers used **symptoms** such as **fever, chills**, and a **cough** to help **diagnose** the disease. **Treatment** was not simple. By the time the symptoms appeared, the disease had already caused a lot of damage. **Patients** received oxygen and physical therapy to help clear the lungs.

Word Link — il ≈ not : illegal, illiterate, illogical

il|log|i|cal /ɪlɒdʒɪkᵊl/ ADJ If you describe an action, feeling, or belief as **illogical**, you are critical of it because you think that it does not result from a logical and ordered way of thinking. [DISAPPROVAL] ❑ It is illogical to oppose the repatriation of economic migrants.

형용사 비논리적인, 불합리한 [탐탁잖음] ❑ 경제적 이주민들의 송환에 반대하는 것을 불합리하다.

il|lu|mi|nate /ɪluːmɪneɪt/ (illuminates, illuminating, illuminated) **1** V-T To **illuminate** something means to shine light on it and to make it brighter and more visible. [FORMAL] ❑ No streetlights illuminated the street. **2** V-T If you **illuminate** something that is unclear or difficult to understand, you make it clearer by explaining it carefully or giving information about it. [FORMAL] ❑ Instead of formulas and charts, the two instructors use games and drawings to illuminate their subject. • il|lu|mi|nat|ing ADJ ❑ It is illuminating to compare how different sections of the national press have treated the story.

1 타동사 조명하다, 밝게 비추다 [격식체] ❑ 길을 밝게 비춰 주는 가로등이 하나도 없었다. **2** 타동사 설명하다 [격식체] ❑ 그 두 교사는 그들의 주제를 설명하기 위해서 공식이나 차트 대신에 그림과 게임을 이용하고 있다. • 분명히 보여 주는, 계몽적인 형용사 ❑ 국가 언론의 다른 분야들에서는 그 이야기를 어떻게 다루어 왔는지를 비교해 보면 좀 더 분명히 알 수 있을 것이다.

il|lu|mi|na|tion /ɪluːmɪneɪʃᵊn/ (illuminations) **1** N-UNCOUNT **Illumination** is the lighting that a place has. [FORMAL] ❑ The only illumination came from a small window high in the opposite wall. **2** N-PLURAL **Illuminations** are colored lights which are put up in towns, especially at Christmas, in order to make them look attractive, especially at night. [mainly BRIT] ❑ ...the famous Blackpool illuminations.

1 불가산명사 조명 [격식체] ❑ 불빛이라곤 반대쪽 벽 높이 나 있는 작은 창문에서 들어오는 것뿐이었다. **2** 복수명사 전등 장식, 일류미네이션 [주로 영국영어] ❑ 블랙풀의 유명한 전등 장식

il|lu|sion /ɪluːʒᵊn/ (illusions) **1** N-VAR An **illusion** is a false idea or belief. ❑ No one really has any illusions about winning the war. **2** N-COUNT An **illusion** is something that appears to exist or be a particular thing but does not actually exist or is in reality something else. ❑ Floor-to-ceiling windows can look stunning, giving the illusion of extra height.

1 가산명사 또는 불가산명사 환상 ❑ 전쟁에서 승리할 것이라는 환상을 가진 사람은 사실 아무도 없다. **2** 가산명사 환각, 환영 ❑ 바닥에서 천장에 이르는 창문은 너무나 근사하고 전체적인 방의 높이를 더 높아 보이게 하기도 한다.

Word Partnership — illusion의 연어

v.   be under an illusion **1**
   create an illusion, give an illusion about/of/that
   something **1** **2**

il|lus|trate ♦◇◇ /ɪləstreɪt/ (illustrates, illustrating, illustrated) **1** V-T If you say that something **illustrates** a situation that you are drawing attention to, you mean that it shows that the situation exists. ❑ The example of the United States illustrates this point. ❑ The incident graphically illustrates how parlous their position is. **2** V-T If you use an example, story, or diagram to **illustrate** a point, you use it show that what you are saying is true or to make your meaning clearer. ❑ Let me give another example to illustrate this difficult point. • il|lus|tra|tion /ɪləstreɪʃᵊn/ N-UNCOUNT ❑ Here, by way of illustration, are some extracts from our new catalog. **3** V-T If you **illustrate** a book, you put pictures, photographs or diagrams into it. ❑ She went on to art school and is now illustrating a book. • il|lus|tra|tion N-UNCOUNT ❑ ...the world of children's book illustration. →see **animation**

1 타동사 보여 주다, 설명하다 ❑ 미국의 예가 이러한 점을 보여 준다. ❑ 그 사건은 그들의 위치가 얼마나 위험한가를 생생하게 보여 준다. **2** 타동사 예를 들다, 예증하다 ❑ 이 어려운 부분을 분명히 보여 줄 수 있도록 다른 예를 들어보겠다. • 예증, 실례(實例) 불가산명사 ❑ 실례로 저희 새 카탈로그에서 뽑은 몇 가지 사례가 여기 있습니다. **3** 타동사 삽화를 넣다, 삽화를 그리다 ❑ 그녀는 미술 대학에 다녔고 지금은 책에 삽화를 그리는 일을 하고 있다. • 삽화 불가산명사 ❑ 어린이 책 삽화의 세계

il|lus|tra|tion ♦◇◇ /ɪləstreɪʃᵊn/ (illustrations) **1** N-COUNT An **illustration** is an example or a story which is used to make a point clear. ❑ An illustration of China's dynamism is that a new company is formed in Shanghai every 11 seconds. **2** N-COUNT An **illustration** in a book is a picture, design, or diagram. ❑ She looked like a princess in a nineteenth-century illustration. **3** →see also **illustrate**

1 가산명사 실례(實例) ❑ 중국의 역동성을 보여 주는 실례가 상하이에서는 새로운 회사가 11초마다 하나씩 생긴다는 것이다. **2** 가산명사 삽화 ❑ 그녀는 19세기 삽화에 나오는 공주처럼 보였다.

il|lus|tri|ous /ɪlʌstriəs/ ADJ If you describe someone as an **illustrious** person, you mean that they are extremely well known because they have a high position in society or they have done something impressive. ❑ ...the most illustrious scientists of the century.

형용사 저명한, 유명한 ❑ 금세기 가장 저명한 과학자들

I'm /aɪm/ **I'm** is the usual spoken form of "I am." ❑ I'm sorry.

I am의 구어체 ❑ 미안합니다.

im|age ♦♦◇ /ɪmɪdʒ/ (images) **1** N-COUNT If you have an **image** of something or someone, you have a picture or idea of them in your mind. ❑ The image of art theft as a gentleman's crime is outdated. **2** N-COUNT The **image** of a person, group, or organization is the way that they appear to other people. ❑ The Prime Minister knows that his personal image is his greatest political asset. **3** N-COUNT An **image** is a picture of someone or something. [FORMAL] ❑ ...photographic images of young children. **4** N-COUNT An **image** is a poetic description of something. [FORMAL] ❑ The natural images in the poem are meant to be suggestive of realities beyond themselves. **5** PHRASE If you **are the image of** someone else, you look very much like them. ❑ Marianne's son was the image of his father. **6** spitting image →see **spit** →see **copy, eye, photography, television**

1 가산명사 상(像), 생각 ❑ 예술 작품을 훔치는 것은 신사적인 범죄라는 식의 생각은 시대에 뒤떨어진 것이다. **2** 가산명사 모습, 이미지 ❑ 수상은 자신의 개인적인 이미지가 자신의 가장 큰 정치적 자산이라는 것을 알고 있다. **3** 가산명사 사진 [격식체] ❑ 어린 아이들의 모습을 담은 사진 **4** 가산명사 심상 [격식체] ❑ 그 시에 쓰인 자연과 관련된 심상들은 실재를 초월한 실재를 암시하도록 의도된 것이다. **5** 구 -을 꼭 닮다 ❑ 마리앤의 아들은 자기 아버지를 꼭 닮았다.

Word Partnership   image의 연어

ADJ.	**corporate** image, **negative/positive** image, **public** image 🔢
N.	**body** image, **self**-image 🔢 🔢
	image **on a screen** 🔢
V.	**project an** image 🔢 🔢
	display an image 🔢

im|age|ry /ɪmɪdʒri/ 🔢 N-UNCOUNT You can refer to the descriptions in something such as a poem or song, and the pictures they create in your mind, as its **imagery**. [FORMAL] ❏ ...the nature imagery of the ballad. 🔢 N-UNCOUNT You can refer to pictures and representations of things as **imagery**, especially when they act as symbols. [FORMAL] ❏ This is an ambitious and intriguing movie, full of striking imagery.

🔢 불가산명사 심상, 이미지들 [격식체] ❏ 발라드에 나오는 자연의 이미지들 🔢 불가산명사 형상 [격식체] ❏ 이것은 놀라운 형상들로 가득한, 호기심을 자극하는 야심찬 영화이다.

im|agi|nable /ɪmædʒɪnəbəl/ 🔢 ADJ You use **imaginable** after a superlative such as "best" or "worst" to emphasize that something is extreme in some way. [EMPHASIS] [adj-superl n ADJ, adj-superl ADJ n] ❏ ...their imprisonment under some of the most horrible circumstances imaginable. 🔢 ADJ You use **imaginable** after a word like "every" or "all" to emphasize that you are talking about all the possible examples of something. You use **imaginable** after "no" to emphasize that something does not have the quality mentioned. [EMPHASIS] [ADJ n, n ADJ] ❏ Parents encourage every activity imaginable.

🔢 형용사 상상할 수 있는 [강조] ❏ 상상할 수 있는 가장 끔찍한 상황 속에 그들이 감금되어 있음 🔢 형용사 상상할 수 있는, 생각할 수 있는 [강조] ❏ 부모들은 생각할 수 있는 모든 활동을 장려한다.

im|agi|nary /ɪmædʒɪneri, BRIT ɪmædʒɪnəri/ ADJ An **imaginary** person, place, or thing exists only in your mind or in a story, and not in real life. ❏ Lots of children have imaginary friends. →see **fantasy**

형용사 상상의, 가상의 ❏ 많은 아이들에게는 상상 속의 친구들이 있다.

im|agi|na|tion ♦♦◇ /ɪmædʒɪneɪʃⁿn/ (**imaginations**) 🔢 N-VAR Your **imagination** is the ability that you have to form pictures or ideas in your mind of things that are new and exciting, or things that you have not experienced. ❏ Antonia is a woman with a vivid imagination. 🔢 N-COUNT Your **imagination** is the part of your mind which allows you to form pictures or ideas of things that do not necessarily exist in real life. ❏ Long before I ever went there, Africa was alive in my imagination. 🔢 PHRASE If you say that someone or something **captured** your **imagination**, you mean that you thought they were interesting or exciting when you saw them or heard them for the first time. ❏ Italian football captured the imagination of the nation last season. 🔢 not **by any stretch of the imagination** →see **stretch** →see **fantasy**

🔢 가산명사 또는 불가산명사 상상력 ❏ 안토니아는 생생한 상상력을 가진 여자이다. 🔢 가산명사 상상, 마음 ❏ 내가 아프리카로 가기 오래전부터 그곳은 나의 상상 속에 살아 있었다. 🔢 구 흥미를 끌다 ❏ 이탈리아 축구는 지난 시즌 전 국민적인 흥미를 끌었다.

Word Partnership   imagination의 연어

PREP.	**beyond** (*someone's*) imagination 🔢
ADJ.	**active** imagination, **lively** imagination, **vivid** imagination 🔢
N.	**lack of** imagination 🔢

im|agi|na|tive /ɪmædʒɪnətɪv/ ADJ If you describe someone or their ideas as **imaginative**, you are praising them because they are easily able to think of or create new or exciting things. [APPROVAL] ❏ ...an imaginative writer. ● **im|agi|na|tive|ly** ADV [ADV with v] ❏ The hotel is decorated imaginatively and attractively.

형용사 상상력이 뛰어난 [마음에 듦] ❏ 상상력이 뛰어난 작가 ● 풍부한 상상력을 발휘하여 부사 ❏ 그 호텔은 풍부한 상상력을 발휘하여 매력적으로 장식되어 있다.

im|ag|ine ♦♦◇ /ɪmædʒɪn/ (**imagines, imagining, imagined**) 🔢 V-T If you **imagine** something, you think about it and your mind forms a picture or idea of it. ❏ He could not imagine a more peaceful scene. ❏ Can you imagine how she must have felt when Mary Brent turned up with me in tow? 🔢 V-T If you **imagine** that something is the case, you think that it is the case. ❏ I imagine you're referring to Jean-Paul Sartre. 🔢 V-T If you **imagine** something, you think that you have seen, heard, or experienced that thing, although actually you have not. ❏ Looking back on it now, I realized that I must have imagined the whole thing.

🔢 타동사 마음에 품다, 상상하다 ❏ 그는 이보다 더 평화로운 장면을 상상할 수 없었다. ❏ 메리 브렌트가 나를 데리고 나타났을 때 네가 어떤 기분이었을지 상상할 수 있어? 🔢 타동사 생각하다 ❏ 장 폴 사르트르를 말하시는 모양이군요. 🔢 타동사 상상하다, -같은 느낌이 든다 ❏ 지금 그것에 대해 되돌아보니, 그 모두가 틀림없이 내 상상이었을 것이라는 깨달음이 든다.

Thesaurus   imagine의 참조어

V.	picture, see, visualize 🔢
	believe, guess, think 🔢

Word Partnership   imagine의 연어

V.	**can/can't/could/couldn't** imagine *something*, **try to** imagine 🔢 🔢
ADJ.	**difficult/easy/hard/impossible to** imagine 🔢 🔢

Word Link   im ≈ not : imbalance, immature, impossible

im|bal|ance /ɪmbæləns/ (**imbalances**) N-VAR If there is an **imbalance** in a situation, the things involved are not the same size, or are not the right size in proportion to each other. ❏ ...the imbalance between the two sides in this war.

가산명사 또는 불가산명사 불균형 ❏ 이 전쟁에서 양측 사이의 불균형

im|bue /ɪmbyu/ (**imbues, imbuing, imbued**) V-T If someone or something **is imbued** with an idea, feeling, or quality, they become filled with it. [FORMAL] ❏ The film is imbued with the star's rebellious spirit.

타동사 고취되다, -로 채워지다 [격식체] ❏ 그 영화는 그 배우의 반항적인 기질로 가득 차 있다.

IMF /aɪ ɛm ɛf/ N-PROPER The **IMF** is an international agency which tries to promote trade and improve economic conditions in poorer countries, sometimes by lending them money. **IMF** is an abbreviation for "International Monetary Fund."

고유명사 국제 통화 기금

imi|tate /ɪmɪteɪt/ (imitates, imitating, imitated) ◼ V-T If you **imitate** someone, you copy what they do or produce. ❏ *...a genuine German musical which does not try to imitate the American model.* ◻ V-T If you **imitate** a person or animal, you copy the way they speak or behave, usually because you are trying to be funny. ❏ *Clarence screws up his face and imitates the Colonel again.*

imi|ta|tion /ɪmɪteɪʃⁿn/ (imitations) ◼ N-COUNT An **imitation** of something is a copy of it. ❏ *...the most accurate imitation of Chinese architecture in Europe.* ◻ N-UNCOUNT **Imitation** means copying someone else's actions. ❏ *They discussed important issues in imitation of their elders.* ◼ ADJ **Imitation** things are not genuine but are made to look as if they are. [ADJ n] ❏ *...a complete set of Dickens bound in imitation leather.* ◼ N-COUNT If someone does an **imitation** of another person, they copy the way they speak or behave, sometimes in order to be funny. ❏ *He gave his imitation of Queen Elizabeth's royal wave.*

im|macu|late /ɪmækyʊlɪt/ ◼ ADJ If you describe something as **immaculate**, you mean that it is extremely clean, tidy, or neat. ❏ *Her front room was kept immaculate.* ● **im|macu|late|ly** ADV ❏ *As always he was immaculately dressed.* ◻ ADJ If you say that something is **immaculate**, you are emphasizing that it is perfect, without any mistakes or bad parts at all. [EMPHASIS] ❏ *...goalkeeper Peter Schmeichel, who was immaculate under first-half pressure.* ● **im|macu|late|ly** ADV [ADV with v] ❏ *The orchestra plays immaculately.*

im|ma|te|ri|al /ɪmətɪəriəl/ ADJ If you say that something is **immaterial**, you mean that it is not important or not relevant. [v-link ADJ] ❏ *Whether we like him or not is immaterial.*

| **Word Link** | im ≈ not : imbalance, immature, impossible |

im|ma|ture /ɪmətʃʊər, -tʊər, BRIT ɪmətyʊəʳ/ ◼ ADJ Something or someone that is **immature** is not yet completely grown or fully developed. ❏ *She is emotionally immature.* ◻ ADJ If you describe someone as **immature**, you are being critical of them because they do not behave in a sensible or responsible way. [DISAPPROVAL] ❏ *She's just being childish and immature.*

Thesaurus	immature의 참조어
ADJ.	undeveloped; *(ant.)* mature ◼
	childish, foolish, juvenile; *(ant.)* mature ◻

im|me|di|ate ♦♢♢ /ɪmiːdiɪt/ ◼ ADJ An **immediate** result, action, or reaction happens or is done without any delay. ❏ *These tragic incidents have had an immediate effect.* ◻ ADJ **Immediate** needs and concerns exist at the present time and must be dealt with quickly. ❏ *Relief agencies say the immediate problem is not a lack of food, but transportation.* ◼ ADJ The **immediate** person or thing comes just before or just after another person or thing in a sequence. [ADJ n] ❏ *In the immediate aftermath of the riots, a mood of hope and reconciliation sprang up.* ◼ ADJ You use **immediate** to describe an area or position that is next to or very near a particular place or person. [ADJ n] ❏ *Only a handful had returned to work in the immediate vicinity.* ◼ ADJ Your **immediate** family are the members of your family who are most closely related to you, for example your parents, children, brothers, and sisters. [ADJ n] ❏ *The presence of his immediate family is obviously having a calming effect on him.*

Word Partnership	immediate의 연어
N.	immediate **action**, immediate **plans**, immediate **reaction**, immediate **response**, immediate **results** ◼
	immediate **future** ◼
	immediate **surroundings** ◼
	immediate **family** ◼

im|me|di|ate|ly ♦♦♢ /ɪmiːdiɪtli/ ◼ ADV If something happens **immediately**, it happens without any delay. [ADV with v] ❏ *He immediately flung himself to the floor.* ◻ ADV If something is **immediately** obvious, it can be seen or understood without any delay. [ADV adj] ❏ *The cause of the accident was not immediately apparent.* ◼ ADV **Immediately** is used to indicate that someone or something is closely and directly involved in a situation. [ADV adj/-ed] ❏ *The man immediately responsible for this misery is the province's governor.* ◼ ADV **Immediately** is used to emphasize that something comes next, or is next to something else. [ADV prep/adj] ❏ *They wish to begin immediately after dinner.* ◼ CONJ If one thing happens **immediately** something else happens, it happens after that event, without any delay. [mainly BRIT] ❏ *Immediately I've done it I feel completely disgusted with myself.*

Thesaurus	immediately의 참조어
ADV.	at once, now, right away; *(ant.)* later ◼

im|mense /ɪmens/ ADJ If you describe something as **immense**, you mean that it is extremely large or great. ❏ *...an immense cloud of smoke.*

im|mense|ly /ɪmensli/ ADV You use **immensely** to emphasize the degree or extent of a quality, feeling, or process. [EMPHASIS] ❏ *I enjoyed this movie immensely.*

im|merse /ɪmɜrs/ (immerses, immersing, immersed) ◼ V-T If you **immerse** yourself in something that you are doing, you become completely involved in

---

◼ 타동사 따라 하다 ◻ 미국식 모델을 따라 하려고 애쓰지 않는 진정한 독일 뮤지컬 ◻ 타동사 흉내 내다 ◻ 클라렌스는 그의 얼굴을 찡그리고 다시 대령 흉내를 낸다.

◼ 가산명사 모방한 것 ◻ 유럽에서 중국 건축 양식을 가장 정확하게 모방한 것 ◻ 그들은 어른들을 모방하는 것에 대한 중요한 쟁점들을 토론했다. ◼ 형용사 모조품 ◻ 모조 가죽으로 장정한 디킨스 전집 ◼ 가산명사 모방, 흉내 ◻ 그는 엘리자베스 여왕이 여왕답게 손을 흔드는 모습을 흉내 내었다.

◼ 형용사 아주 깔끔한, 티 하나 없이 깨끗한 ◻ 그녀의 거실은 티 한점 없이 깨끗하게 정돈되어 있었다. ● 아주 깨끗하게, 아주 깔끔하게 부사 ◻ 늘 그렇듯이 그는 아주 깨끗하게 차려입고 있었다. ◻ 형용사 완벽한, 오류 하나 없는 [강조] ◻ 전반전의 부담에도 깔끔한 수비력을 보여 준 골키퍼 피터 슈마이켈 ● 완벽하게, 흠 하나 없이 부사 ◻ 그 오케스트라는 완벽하게 연주를 한다.

형용사 중요하지 않은; 관계가 없는 ◻ 우리가 그를 좋아하든 싫어하든 그것은 관계가 없다.

◼ 형용사 성숙하지 못한, 미발달한 ◻ 그녀는 정서적으로 성숙하지 못한다. ◻ 형용사 미숙한, 유치한 [탐탁잖음] ◻ 그녀는 마냥 철없고 유치하게 굴고 있다.

◼ 형용사 즉시의, 즉각의 ◻ 이러한 비극적인 사건들은 즉각적인 영향을 주곤 하였다. ◻ 형용사 현재의, 당면한 ◻ 구제 기관들은 현재 당면한 문제는 식량의 부족이 아니라 운송 수단의 부족이라고 말한다. ◼ 형용사 바로 앞의; 바로 뒤의 ◻ 폭동의 직접적인 여파로 희망과 화해의 분위기가 형성되었다. ◼ 형용사 바로 이웃의 ◻ 바로 인근에 있는 극소수만이 직장으로 되돌아왔다. ◼ 형용사 직계의 ◻ 직계 가족이 있으니까 분명히 그가 평온함을 느끼는 것 같다.

◼ 부사 즉시 ◻ 그는 즉시 바닥으로 몸을 던졌다. ◻ 부사 바로 ◻ 그 사고의 원인이 바로 분명해지진 않았다. ◼ 부사 직접, 직접적으로 ◻ 이러한 재난을 직접적으로 책임져야 할 사람은 그 지역의 주지사이다. ◼ 부사 바로 ◻ 그들은 저녁 식사 후 바로 시작하기를 바란다. ◼ 접속사 즉시, 곧 [주로 영국영어] ◻ 나는 그것을 하고 바로 나 자신에게 정나미가 떨어졌다.

형용사 광대한, 거대한 ◻ 거대한 연기구름

부사 거대하게, 엄청나게 [강조] ◻ 나는 이 영화를 엄청 재미있게 봤다.

◼ 타동사 몰두하다 ◻ 그들은 책무 때문에 원하는 만큼 현행 문제들에 몰두하지 못한다. ● 몰두한, 빠져든

it. ❑ *Their commitments do not permit them to immerse themselves in current affairs as fully as they might wish.* ● **im|mersed** ADJ [v-link ADJ in n] ❑ *He's really becoming immersed in this work.* ❷ V-T If something **is immersed** in a liquid, someone puts it into the liquid so that it is completely covered. [usu passive] ❑ *The electrodes are immersed in liquid.*

형용사 ❑ 그는 정말로 자신의 일에 빠져들고 있다. ❷ 타동사 담그다 ❑ 그 전극들은 용액 안에 담겨 있다.

Word Link	migr ≈ moving, changing : *emigrant*, *immigrant*, *migrant*

im|mi|grant ♦◇◇ /ɪmɪgrənt/ (**immigrants**) N-COUNT An **immigrant** is a person who has come to live in a country from some other country. Compare **emigrant**. ❑ *...illegal immigrants.* →see **culture**

가산명사 이주민, 이민 ❑ 불법 이민자들

im|mi|gra|tion ♦◇◇ /ɪmɪgreɪʃⁿn/ ❶ N-UNCOUNT **Immigration** is the coming of people into a country in order to live and work there. ❑ *The government has decided to tighten its immigration policy.* ❷ N-UNCOUNT **Immigration** or **immigration control** is the place at a port, airport, or international border where officials check the passports of people who wish to come into the country. ❑ *First, you have to go through immigration and customs.*

❶ 불가산명사 이주, 이민 ❑ 정부는 이민 정책을 강화하기로 결정했다. ❷ 불가산명사 출입국 관리, 입국 심사 ❑ 우선, 당신은 입국 심사와 세관을 거쳐야 한다.

im|mi|nent /ɪmɪnənt/ ADJ If you say that something is **imminent**, especially something unpleasant, you mean it is almost certain to happen very soon. ❑ *There appeared no imminent danger.*

형용사 임박한, 절박한 ❑ 절박한 위험은 없는 것 같았다.

im|mo|bi|liz|er /ɪmoʊbɪlaɪzər/ (**immobilizers**) N-COUNT An **immobilizer** is a device on a car which prevents it from starting unless a special key is used, so that no one can steal the car. [BRIT also **immobiliser**]

가산명사 (자동차 도난 방지용) 핸들 고정 장치 [영국영어 immobiliser]

im|mor|al /ɪmɔːrⁿl, BRIT ɪmɒrⁿl/ ADJ If you describe someone or their behavior as **immoral**, you believe that their behavior is morally wrong. [DISAPPROVAL] ❑ *...those who think that birth control and abortion are immoral.*

형용사 부도덕한 [탐탁잖음] ❑ 피임과 낙태가 부도덕하다고 생각하는 사람들

im|mor|tal /ɪmɔːrtⁿl/ (**immortals**) ❶ ADJ Someone or something that is **immortal** is famous and likely to be remembered for a long time. ❑ *...Wuthering Heights, Emily Bronte's immortal love story.* ● N-COUNT An **immortal** is someone who is immortal. ❑ *He called Moore "one of the immortals of soccer."* ● **im|mor|tal|ity** /ɪmɔːrtælɪti/ N-UNCOUNT ❑ *Some people want to achieve immortality through their works.* ❷ ADJ Someone or something that is **immortal** will live or last forever and never die or be destroyed. ❑ *The pharaohs, after all, were considered gods and therefore immortal.* ● N-COUNT An **immortal** is an immortal being. ❑ *...porcelain figurines of the Chinese immortals.* ● **im|mor|tal|ity** N-UNCOUNT ❑ *The Greeks accepted belief in the immortality of the soul.* ❸ ADJ If you refer to someone's **immortal** words, you mean that what they said is well-known, and you are usually about to quote it. [ADJ n] ❑ *Everyone knows Teddy Roosevelt's immortal words, "Speak softly and carry a big stick."*

❶ 형용사 불후의 ❑ 에밀리 브론테가 쓴 불후의 러브 스토리인 폭풍의 언덕 ❑ 그는 무어를 '축구 사상 불후의 인물들 중 한 명'이라고 불렀다. ● 불후의 명성; 영생 불가산명사 ❑ 어떤 사람들은 작품을 통해서 불후의 명성을 얻고자 한다. ❷ 형용사 불사의, 영원한 ❑ 결국 파라오들은 신이라고 여겨졌고 그래서 죽지 않는다고 여겨졌다. ● 가산명사 불사신 ❑ 도자기로 만들어진 중국 불사신들 ● 불멸, 불사 불가산명사 ❑ 그리스인들은 영혼 불멸의 믿음을 받아들였다. ❸ 형용사 불후의 ❑ 테디 루즈벨트의 '말은 부드럽게, 징계는 엄하게'라는 불후의 명언은 모든 사람이 다 알고 있다.

im|mor|tal|ize /ɪmɔːrtⁿlaɪz/ (**immortalizes, immortalizing, immortalized**) [BRIT also **immortalise**] V-T If someone or something **is immortalized** in a story, movie, or work of art, they appear in it, and will be remembered for it. [WRITTEN] ❑ *His original interior design is immortalized in at least seven movies and television shows.*

[영국영어 immortalise] 타동사 불후의 명성을 남기다 [문어체] ❑ 그의 독창적인 인테리어 디자인은 적어도 일곱 개의 영화와 텔레비전 쇼를 통해 후대에 영원히 남게 되었다.

im|mune ♦◇◇ /ɪmjuːn/ ❶ ADJ If you are **immune to** a particular disease, you cannot be affected by it. [v-link ADJ, usu ADJ to n] ❑ *Most adults are immune to Rubella.* ● **im|mun|ity** /ɪmjuːnɪti/ N-UNCOUNT ❑ *Birds in outside cages develop immunity to airborne bacteria.* ❷ ADJ If you are **immune** to something that happens or is done, you are not affected by it. [v-link ADJ, usu ADJ to n] ❑ *Higher education is no longer immune to state budget cuts.* ❸ ADJ Someone or something that is **immune from** a particular process or situation is able to escape it. [v-link ADJ, usu ADJ from n] ❑ *Members of the Bundestag are immune from prosecution for corruption.* ● **im|mun|ity** N-UNCOUNT ❑ *The police are offering immunity to witnesses who help identify the murderers.*

❶ 형용사 면역의, 면역성이 있는 ❑ 대부분의 어른들은 풍진에 면역성이 있다. ● 면역, 면역성 불가산명사 ❑ 옥외에 있는 둥지 속의 새들은 공중에 떠다니는 박테리아에 대해 면역성을 기르게 된다. ❷ 형용사 영향을 받지 않는 ❑ 고등 교육은 더 이상 주 예산 삭감의 영향을 받지 않는다. ❸ 형용사 면책된 ❑ 독일 하원 의원들은 부패 비리 사건에 대해 면책 특권을 가진다. ● 면책 불가산명사 ❑ 경찰은 살인자들의 신원을 밝히는 것을 도와주는 목격자들에게 면책을 제의하고 있다.

Word Partnership	immune의 연어
N.	immune **disorder**, immune **response** ❶
	immune **from attack**, immune **from prosecution** ❸

im|mune sys|tem (**immune systems**) N-COUNT Your **immune system** consists of all the organs and processes in your body which protect you from illness and infection. ❑ *His immune system completely broke down and he became very ill.*

가산명사 면역 체계 ❑ 그의 면역 체계가 완전히 무너져서 병을 앓게 되었다.

im|mun|ize /ɪmjənaɪz/ (**immunizes, immunizing, immunized**) [BRIT also **immunise**] V-T If people or animals **are immunized**, they are made immune to a particular disease, often by being given an injection. [usu passive] ❑ *We should require that every student is immunized against hepatitis B.* ❑ *The monkeys used in those experiments had previously been immunized with a vaccine made from killed infected cells.* ● **im|mun|iza|tion** /ɪmjənaɪzeɪʃⁿn/ (**immunizations**) N-VAR ❑ *...universal immunization against childhood diseases.*

[영국영어 immunise] 타동사 예방 접종 주사를 맞다 ❑ 우리는 학생 모두가 비형 간염 예방 접종 주사를 맞도록 요구해야 한다. ❑ 그 실험들에 사용된 원숭이들은 감염된 후 파괴된 세포들로 만든 백신으로 이전에 면역 주사를 맞았다. ● 예방 접종 가산명사 또는 불가산명사 ❑ 전반적인 유년기 질병에 대한 예방 접종

im|pact ♦◇◇ (**impacts, impacting, impacted**)

The noun is pronounced /ɪmpækt/. The verb is pronounced /ɪmpækt/ or /ɪmpækt/.

명사는 /ɪmpækt /로, 동사는 /ɪmpækt / 또는 /ɪmpækt /로 발음된다.

❶ N-COUNT The **impact** that something has **on** a situation, process, or person is a sudden and powerful effect that it has on them. ❑ *They say they expect the meeting to have a marked impact on the future of the country.* ❷ N-VAR An **impact** is the action of one object hitting another, or the force with which one object hits another. ❑ *The plane is destroyed, a complete wreck: the pilot must have died on impact.* ❸ V-T/V-I To **impact on** a situation, process, or person means to affect them. ❑ *Such schemes mean little unless they impact on people.* ❹ V-T/V-I If one object

❶ 가산명사 영향, 효과 ❑ 그들은 이 회의가 나라의 미래에 현저한 영향을 끼치기를 기대한다고 말한다. ❷ 가산명사 또는 불가산명사 충격 ❑ 비행기는 산산조각으로 부서져 있다. 조종사는 충돌 시 죽은 것이 틀림없었다. ❸ 타동사/자동사 -에 영향을 주다 ❑ 사람들에게 영향을 주지 않는다면 그러한 계획들은 별 의미가 없다. ❹ 타동사/자동사 충돌하다, 세게

impacts on another, it hits it with great force. [FORMAL] ❑ ...*the sharp tinkle of metal impacting on stone.*

부딪치다 [격식체] ❑ 금속이 돌에 세게 부딪치면서 짤랑거리는 날카로운 소리

Word Partnership	*impact*의 연어
ADJ.	**historical** impact, **important** impact 🔟
V.	**have an** impact, **make an** impact 🔟
	die on impact 🔁
PREP.	**on** impact 🔁

im|pair /ɪmpɛər/ (**impairs, impairing, impaired**) V-T If something **impairs** something such as an ability or the way something works, it damages it or makes it worse. [FORMAL] ❑ *Consumption of alcohol impairs your ability to drive a car or operate machinery.* ● **im|paired** ADJ ❑ *The blast left him with permanently impaired hearing.*

타동사 해치다, 손상시키다 [격식체] ❑ 알코올의 섭취는 차를 운전하거나 기계를 작동하는 능력을 해친다. ● 손상된, 못 쓰게 된 형용사 ❑ 그 폭발로 그는 청력을 완전히 잃었다.

im|pair|ment /ɪmpɛərmənt/ (**impairments**) N-VAR If someone has an **impairment,** they have a condition which prevents their eyes, ears, or brain from working properly. ❑ *He has a visual impairment in the right eye.*

가산명사 또는 불가산명사 장애 ❑ 그는 오른쪽 눈에 시각 장애가 있다.

im|part /ɪmpɑrt/ (**imparts, imparting, imparted**) 🔟 V-T If you **impart** information **to** people, you tell it to them. [FORMAL] ❑ *The ability to impart knowledge and command respect is the essential qualification for teachers.* 🔁 V-T To **impart** a particular quality to something means to give it that quality. [FORMAL] ❑ *She managed to impart great elegance to the unpretentious dress she was wearing.*

🔟 타동사 말하다, 알리다 [격식체] ❑ 지식을 전수하고 존경을 받을 수 있는 능력은 교사의 필수적인 자격 요건이다. 🔁 타동사 주다, 부여하다 [격식체] ❑ 그녀는 입고 있던 소박한 옷을 굉장히 우아해 보이게 만들고 있었다.

im|par|tial /ɪmpɑrʃ°l/ ADJ Someone who is **impartial** is not directly involved in a particular situation, and is therefore able to give a fair opinion or decision about it. ❑ *Careers officers offer impartial advice, guidance, and information to all pupils.* ● **im|par|tial|ity** /ɪmpɑrʃiælɪti/ N-UNCOUNT ❑ ...*a justice system lacking impartiality by democratic standards.* ● **im|par|tial|ly** ADV [ADV with v] ❑ *He has vowed to oversee the elections impartially.*

형용사 공평한, 공정한 ❑ 진로 지도 교사들은 모든 학생들에게 공평한 조언, 지도, 그리고 정보를 제공한다. ● 공평, 공정 불가산명사 ❑ 민주적 기준에서 본다면 공정성이 부족한 사법 제도 ● 공평하게, 공정하게 부사 ❑ 그는 선거를 공정하게 감독할 것을 서약했다.

im|passe /ɪmpæs/ N-SING If people are in a difficult position in which it is impossible to make any progress, you can refer to the situation as an **impasse.** ❑ *The company says it has reached an impasse in negotiations with the union.*

단수명사 막다른 골목, 난국 ❑ 그 회사는 노동조합과의 협상에서 막다른 골목에 봉착했다고 전한다.

im|pas|sioned /ɪmpæf°nd/ ADJ An **impassioned** speech or piece of writing is one in which someone expresses their strong feelings about an issue in a forceful way. [WRITTEN] ❑ *He made an impassioned appeal for peace.*

형용사 열정적인, 열렬한 [문어체] ❑ 그는 평화를 열렬히 호소했다.

im|pas|sive /ɪmpæsɪv/ ADJ If someone is **impassive** or their face is **impassive,** they are not showing any emotion. [WRITTEN] ❑ *He searched Hill's impassive face for some indication that he understood.* ● **im|pas|sive|ly** ADV [ADV with v] ❑ *The lawyer looked impassively at him and said nothing.*

형용사 무심한, 무표정한 [문어체] ❑ 힐이 이해했는지 파악하기 위해 그는 힐의 무표정한 얼굴을 유심히 살폈다. ● 무표정하게 부사 ❑ 그 변호사는 그를 무표정하게 바라보며 아무 말도 하지 않았다.

im|pa|tient /ɪmpeɪʃ°nt/ 🔟 ADJ If you are **impatient,** you are annoyed because you have to wait too long for something. [v-link ADJ] ❑ *The public are increasingly impatient with Labour's failure to deliver better public services.* ● **im|pa|tient|ly** ADV [ADV with v] ❑ *People have been waiting impatiently for a chance to improve the situation.* ● **im|pa|tience** /ɪmpeɪʃ°ns/ N-UNCOUNT ❑ *There is considerable impatience with the slow pace of political change.* 🔁 ADJ If you are **impatient,** you are easily irritated by things. ❑ *Beware of being too impatient with others.* ● **im|pa|tient|ly** ADV [ADV with v] ❑ *"Come on, David," Harry said impatiently.* ● **im|pa|tience** N-UNCOUNT ❑ *There was a hint of impatience in his tone.* 🔟 ADJ If you are **impatient to** do something or **impatient for** something to happen, you are eager to do it or for it to happen and do not want to wait. [v-link ADJ, ADJ to-inf, ADJ for n] ❑ *He didn't want to tell Mr. Morrisson why he was impatient to get home.* ● **im|pa|tience** N-UNCOUNT ❑ *She showed impatience to continue the climb.*

🔟 형용사 참지 못하는, 안달하는 ❑ 사람들은 더 나은 공공 서비스를 제공하지 못하는 노동당에 대해서 점점 조바심을 내고 있다. ● 안달하며, 초조하게 부사 ❑ 사람들은 상황을 호전시킬 기회를 조바심을 내며 기다려 왔다. ● 성급함, 조급함 불가산명사 ❑ 느린 속도의 정치적 변화에 대한 조급함이다. 🔁 형용사 성마른, 조급한 ❑ 다른 사람들에게 너무 조급하게 굴지 않도록 해라. ● 조급하게 부사 ❑ "어서, 데이비드."라고 해리가 조급증을 내며 말했다. ● 조급증, 안달 불가산명사 ❑ 그의 목소리에 약간 성급한 짜증기가 섞여 있었다. 🔟 형용사 ~하고 싶어 안달하는 ❑ 그는 자기가 왜 그렇게도 집에 가고 싶어 하는지를 모리슨 씨에게 말하고 싶지 않았다. ● 안달 불가산명사 ❑ 그녀는 등산을 계속하고 싶어 안달이 나 있었다.

im|pec|cable /ɪmpɛkəb°l/ ADJ If you describe something such as someone's behavior or appearance as **impeccable,** you are emphasizing that it is perfect and has no faults. [EMPHASIS] ❑ *She had impeccable taste in clothes.* ● **im|pec|cably** /ɪmpɛkəbli/ ADV ❑ *He was charming, considerate and impeccably mannered.*

형용사 결점이 없는, 나무랄 데 없는 [강조] ❑ 그녀는 옷에 대해 나무랄 데 없는 미적 감각을 가지고 있었다. ● 나무랄 데 없이 부사 ❑ 그는 매력적이고, 사려가 깊고, 나무랄 데 없이 점잖았다.

im|pede /ɪmpid/ (**impedes, impeding, impeded**) V-T If you **impede** someone or something, you make their movement, development, or progress difficult. [FORMAL] ❑ *Debris and fallen rock are impeding the progress of the rescue workers.*

타동사 방해하다, 훼방 놓다 [격식체] ❑ 파편과 떨어진 암석들이 구조 작업대의 진행을 방해하고 있다.

im|pedi|ment /ɪmpɛdɪmənt/ (**impediments**) 🔟 N-COUNT Something that is an **impediment** to a person or thing makes their movement, development, or progress difficult. [FORMAL] ❑ *He was satisfied there was no legal impediment to the marriage.* 🔁 N-COUNT Someone who has a speech **impediment** has a disability which makes speaking difficult. ❑ *John's slight speech impediment made it difficult for his mother to understand him.*

🔟 가산명사 방해, 장애물 [격식체] ❑ 그는 그 결혼에 어떠한 법률상의 장애도 없음에 만족했다. 🔁 가산명사 장애 ❑ 존은 약간 언어 장애가 있어서 어머니가 그를 이해하기 힘들었다.

im|pend|ing /ɪmpɛndɪŋ/ ADJ An **impending** event is one that is going to happen very soon. [FORMAL] [ADJ n] ❑ *On the morning of the expedition I awoke with a feeling of impending disaster.*

형용사 임박한 [격식체] ❑ 탐험 날 아침에 나는 재난이 곧 닥칠 것이라는 예감과 함께 잠에서 깨어났다.

im|pen|etrable /ɪmpɛnɪtrəb°l/ 🔟 ADJ If you describe something such as a barrier or a forest as **impenetrable,** you mean that it is impossible or very difficult to get through. ❑ ...*the Caucasus range, an almost impenetrable barrier between Europe and Asia.* 🔁 ADJ If you describe something such as a book or a theory as **impenetrable,** you are emphasizing that it is impossible or very difficult to understand. [EMPHASIS] ❑ *His philosophical work is notoriously impenetrable.*

🔟 형용사 관통할 수 없는, 뚫고 들어갈 수 없는 ❑ 유럽과 아시아 사이에 놓여 있는 거의 관통할 수 없는 장벽인 카프카스 산맥 🔁 형용사 이해할 수 없는 [강조] ❑ 그의 철학적인 작품은 이해하기 어렵기로 악명이 높다.

im|pera|tive /ɪmpɛrətɪv/ (**imperatives**) 🔟 ADJ If it is **imperative** that something is done, that thing is extremely important and must be done. [FORMAL] ❑ *It was imperative that he act as naturally as possible.* 🔁 N-COUNT An **imperative** is something that is extremely important and must be done. [FORMAL] ❑ *The most important political imperative is to limit the number of U.S. casualties.* 🔟 N-SING In grammar, a clause that is in **the imperative,** or in **the**

🔟 형용사 중요한, 필수적인 [격식체] ❑ 그는 반드시 가능한 한 자연스럽게 행동해야 했다. 🔁 가산명사 긴급한 과제 [격식체] ❑ 가장 중요한 정치적 과제는 미국인 사상자 수를 제한하는 것이다. 🔟 단수명사 명령법 🔟 가산명사 명령형

imperative mood, contains the base form of a verb and usually has no subject. Examples are "Go away" and "Please be careful." Clauses of this kind are typically used to tell someone to do something. ◳ N-COUNT An **imperative** is a verb in the base form that is used, usually without a subject, in an imperative clause.

im|per|fect /ɪmpɜrfɪkt/ ADJ Something that is **imperfect** has faults and is not exactly as you would like it to be. [FORMAL] ◻ We live in an imperfect world.

형용사 결함이 있는, 불완전한 [격식체] ◻ 우리는 불완전한 세계에 살고 있다.

im|per|fec|tion /ɪmpərfɛkʃən/ (**imperfections**) ◳ N-VAR An **imperfection** in someone or something is a fault, weakness, or undesirable feature that they have. ◻ He concedes that there are imperfections in the socialist system. ◳ N-COUNT An **imperfection** in something is a small mark or damaged area which may spoil its appearance. ◻ Optical scanners ensure that imperfections in the cloth are located and removed.

◳ 가산명사 또는 가산명사 결점, 단점 ◻ 그는 사회주의 체제에 결점이 있다는 것을 인정한다. ◳ 가산명사 흠 ◻ 광학 스캐너는 천에 나 있는 흠집의 위치를 확실히 찾아내고 제거한다.

im|pe|ri|al /ɪmpɪəriəl/ ◳ ADJ **Imperial** is used to refer to things or people that are or were connected with an empire. [ADJ n] ◻ ...the Imperial Palace in Tokyo. ◳ ADJ The **imperial** system of measurement uses inches, feet, and yards to measure length, ounces and pounds to measure weight, and pints and gallons to measure volume. [ADJ n] ◻ ...shopkeepers who trade in imperial measures.

◳ 형용사 제국의, 황제의 ◻ 동경에 있는 황궁 ◳ 형용사 (도량형이) 영국 법정 표준의 ◻ 영국 법정 표준 도량형에 따라 거래하는 소매상인들

im|pe|ri|al|ism /ɪmpɪəriəlɪzəm/ N-UNCOUNT **Imperialism** is a system in which a rich and powerful country controls other countries, or a desire for control over other countries. ◻ ...nations or groups which have been victims of imperialism.

불가산명사 제국주의 ◻ 제국주의의 희생자들이었던 국가나 집단

im|pe|ri|al|ist /ɪmpɪəriəlɪst/ (**imperialists**) ADJ **Imperialist** means relating to or based on imperialism. ◻ The developed nations have all benefited from their imperialist exploitation. ● N-COUNT An **imperialist** is someone who has imperialist views. ◻ He claims that imperialists are trying to re-establish colonial rule in the country.

형용사 제국주의자의 ◻ 선진국들은 모두 제국주의를 통한 착취로 이익을 봤다. ● 가산명사 제국주의자 ◻ 그는 제국주의자들이 그 나라에서 식민지 통치를 다시 수립하려 한다고 주장한다.

im|per|son|al /ɪmpɜrsənəl/ ◳ ADJ If you describe a place, organization, or activity as **impersonal**, you mean that it is not very friendly and makes you feel unimportant because it involves or is used by a large number of people. [DISAPPROVAL] ◻ Before then many children were cared for in large impersonal orphanages. ◳ ADJ If you describe someone's behavior as **impersonal**, you mean that they do not show any emotion about the person they are dealing with. ◻ We must be as impersonal as a surgeon with his knife. ◳ ADJ An **impersonal** room or statistic does not give any information about the character of the person to whom it belongs or relates. ◻ The rest of the room was neat and impersonal.

◳ 형용사 개인에 대한 배려가 없는, 비인격적인 [탐탁찮음] ◻ 그 이전에는 많은 아이들이 개개인에게는 신경을 쓰지 못하는 대규모 고아원에서 보살핌을 받았다. ◳ 형용사 인간의 감정이 없는, 비인간적인, 냉정한 ◻ 수술용 칼을 들고 있는 외과 의사만큼이나 우리는 냉정해져야 한다. ◳ 형용사 개인 정보를 알 수 없는 ◻ 그 방에서 그 외 나머지는 깔끔했고 누가 쓰는지 알 수가 없었다.

im|per|son|ate /ɪmpɜrsəneɪt/ (**impersonates, impersonating, impersonated**) V-T If someone **impersonates** a person, they pretend to be that person, either to deceive people or to make people laugh. ◻ He was returned to prison in 1977 for impersonating a police officer. ● **im|per|so|na|tion** /ɪmpɜrsəneɪʃən/ (**impersonations**) N-COUNT ◻ She excelled at impersonations of his teachers, which provided great amusement for him.

타동사 -인 체하다 ◻ 그는 경찰관을 사칭한 죄로 1977년에 다시 교도소로 보내졌다. ● 흉내 냄, 사칭(詐稱) 가산명사 ◻ 그녀는 그의 선생님들을 흉내를 내는 데 뛰어났는데, 그게 그에게는 무척 재미있었다.

im|per|ti|nent /ɪmpɜrtɪnənt/ ADJ If someone talks or behaves in a rather impolite and disrespectful way, you can say that they are being **impertinent**. ◻ Would it be impertinent to ask where exactly you were?

형용사 건방진, 무례한 ◻ 당신이 정확히 어디에 계셨는지 물어보면 결례가 될까요?

im|pe|tus /ɪmpɪtəs/ N-UNCOUNT Something that gives a process **impetus** or an **impetus** makes it happen or progress more quickly. [also a N, oft N for n] ◻ This decision will give renewed impetus to the economic regeneration of east London.

불가산명사 추진력, 활력 ◻ 이러한 결정이 런던 동부의 경제 부흥에 새로운 활력을 불어넣을 것이다.

im|pla|ca|ble /ɪmplækəbəl/ ADJ If you say that someone is **implacable**, you mean that they have very strong feelings of hostility or disapproval which nobody can change. ◻ ...the threat of invasion by a ruthless and implacable enemy. ● **im|pla|ca|bly** ADV ◻ His union was implacably opposed to the privatization of the company.

형용사 달랠 수 없는, 철천지한을 품은 ◻ 철천지한을 품은 가차 없는 적의 침입 위협 ● 가차 없이 부사 ◻ 그의 노동조합은 회사의 민영화에 극심하게 반대했다.

im|plant (**implants, implanting, implanted**)

The verb is pronounced /ɪmplænt/. The noun is pronounced /ɪmplænt/.

동사는 /ɪmplænt/로 발음되고, 명사는 /ɪmplænt/로 발음된다.

◳ V-T To **implant** something into a person's body means to put it there, usually by means of a medical operation. ◻ Two days later, they implanted the fertilized eggs back inside me. ◳ N-COUNT An **implant** is something that is implanted into a person's body. ◻ They felt a woman had a right to choose to have a breast implant. ◳ V-I When an egg or embryo **implants in** the womb, it becomes established there and can then develop. ◻ Non-identical twins are the result of two fertilized eggs implanting in the uterus at the same time. ◳ V-T If you **implant** an idea or attitude **in** people, you make it become accepted or believed. ◻ The diagram implanted a dangerous prejudice firmly in the minds of countless economics students.

◳ 타동사 이식하다 ◻ 이틀이 지난 뒤 그들은 수정된 난자를 내 몸 안에 이식했다. ◳ 가산명사 이식 ◻ 그들은 여성에게 유방 이식 수술을 선택할 권리가 있다고 생각했다. ◳ 자동사 (자궁에) 착상되다 ◻ 이란성 쌍둥이는 수정된 난자 두 개가 동시에 자궁에 착상된 결과이다. ◳ 타동사 (마음에) 심다, 불어넣다 ◻ 그 도표는 많은 경제학과 학생들의 마음에 위험한 편견을 확고히 심어 놓았다.

im|ple|ment ♦◇◇ (**implements, implementing, implemented**)

The verb is pronounced /ɪmplɪmɛnt/ or /ɪmplɪmənt/. The noun is pronounced /ɪmplɪmənt/.

동사는 /ɪmplɪmɛnt/ 또는 /ɪmplɪmənt/로, 명사는 /ɪmplɪmənt/로 발음된다.

◳ V-T If you **implement** something such as a plan, you ensure that what has been planned is done. ◻ The government promised to implement a new system to control financial loan institutions. ● **im|ple|men|ta|tion** /ɪmplɪmɛnteɪʃən, -mɛn-/ N-UNCOUNT ◻ Very little has been achieved in the implementation of the peace agreement signed last January. ◳ N-COUNT An **implement** is a tool or other piece of equipment. [FORMAL] ◻ ...writing implements.

◳ 타동사 이행하다, 수행하다 ◻ 정부는 금융 대출 기관을 통제하는 새로운 시스템을 구축하겠다고 약속했다. ● 이행, 수행 불가산명사 ◻ 지난 1월에 체결된 평화 조약은 거의 이행된 것이 없다. ◳ 가산명사 연장, 도구 [격식체] ◻ 필기도구들

im|pli|cate /ˈɪmplɪkeɪt/ (**implicates, implicating, implicated**) v-t To **implicate** someone means to show or claim that they were involved in something wrong or criminal. ❑ *He was obliged to resign when one of his own aides was implicated in a financial scandal.* ● **im|pli|ca|tion** N-UNCOUNT ❑ *Implication in a murder finally brought him to the gallows.*

im|pli|ca|tion ♦♢♢ /ˌɪmplɪˈkeɪʃən/ (**implications**) **1** N-COUNT The **implications of** something are the things that are likely to happen as a result. ❑ *The Attorney General was aware of the political implications of his decision to prosecute.* **2** N-COUNT The **implication** of a statement, event, or situation is what it implies or suggests is the case. ❑ *The implication was obvious: vote for us or it will be very embarrassing for you.* ● PHRASE If you say that something is the case **by implication**, you mean that a statement, event, or situation implies that it is the case. ❑ *Now his authority and, by implication, that of the whole management team are under threat as never before.* **3** →see also **implicate**

Word Partnership	*implication*의 연어
ADJ.	**clear** implication, **important** implication, **obvious** implication **2**

im|plic|it /ɪmˈplɪsɪt/ **1** ADJ Something that is **implicit** is expressed in an indirect way. ❑ *It is taken as an implicit warning to the Moroccans not to continue or repeat the military actions they began a week ago.* ● **im|plic|it|ly** ADV [ADV with v] ❑ *An inquest jury implicitly criticized the Home Office's administration of Armley Jail by returning an open verdict on a teenager who was found hanging in his cell.* **2** ADJ If a quality or element is **implicit in** something, it is involved in it or is shown by it. [FORMAL] [v-link ADJ in n] ❑ *Implicit in snobbery is timidity – being afraid to take a risk for fear of what your posh friends may think.* **3** ADJ If you say that someone has an **implicit** belief or faith in something, you mean that they have complete faith in it and no doubts at all. ❑ *He had implicit faith in the noble intentions of the Emperor.* ● **im|plic|it|ly** ADV [ADV after v] ❑ *I trust him implicitly.*

im|plore /ɪmˈplɔr/ (**implores, imploring, implored**) v-t If you **implore** someone **to** do something, you ask them to do it in a forceful, emotional way. ❑ *Opposition leaders this week implored the president to break the deadlock in parliament.*

im|ply ♦♢♢ /ɪmˈplaɪ/ (**implies, implying, implied**) **1** v-t If you **imply that** something is the case, you say something which indicates that it is the case in an indirect way. ❑ *"Are you implying that I have something to do with those attacks?"* she asked coldly. **2** v-t If an event or situation **implies** that something is the case, it makes you think it likely that it is the case. ❑ *Exports in June rose 1.5%, implying that the economy was stronger than many investors had realized.*

Do not confuse **imply** and **infer**. If you **imply** that something is the case, you suggest that it is the case without actually saying so. ❑ *Rose's lawyer implied that he had married her for her money.* If you **infer** that something is the case, you decide that it must be the case because of what you know, but without actually being told. ❑ *From this simple statement I could infer a lot about his wife.* Note that some English speakers use **infer** with the same meaning as **imply**, but this is considered incorrect by careful speakers.

Thesaurus	*imply*의 참조어
v.	hint, suggest **1**

Word Partnership	*imply*의 연어
v.	**not mean to** imply **1**
	seem to imply **2**
ADV.	**not necessarily** imply **1** **2**

im|po|lite /ˌɪmpəˈlaɪt/ ADJ If you say that someone is **impolite**, you mean that they are rather rude and do not have good manners. ❑ *The Count acknowledged the two newcomers as briefly as was possible without being impolite.*

Word Link	port ≈ carrying : ex**port**, im**port**, **port**able

im|port ♦♦♢ (**imports, importing, imported**)

The verb is pronounced /ɪmˈpɔrt/ or /ɪmˈpɔrt/. The noun is pronounced /ˈɪmpɔrt/.

1 v-t/v-i To **import** products or raw materials means to buy them from another country for use in your own country. ❑ *Britain last year spent nearly £5000 million more on importing food than selling abroad.* ❑ *To import from Russia, a Ukrainian firm needs Russian roubles.* ● N-UNCOUNT **Import** is also a noun. [also n in pl] ❑ *Germany, however, insists on restrictions on the import of Polish coal.* ● **im|por|ta|tion** /ˌɪmpɔrˈteɪʃən/ N-UNCOUNT ❑ *...restrictions concerning the importation of birds.* **2** N-COUNT **Imports** are products or raw materials bought from another country for use in your own country. ❑ *...French farmers protesting about what they say are cheap imports from other European countries.* **3** N-UNCOUNT The **import** of something is its importance. [FORMAL] ❑ *Such arguments are of little import.* **4** v-t If you **import** files or information into one type of software from another type, you open them in a format that can be used in the new software. [COMPUTING] ❑ *You can import files from Microsoft Word 5.1 or MacWrite II.*

타동사 연루시키다, 말려들게 하다 ❑ 그의 측근들 중 한 명이 금융 스캔들에 연루되었을 때 그는 할 수 없이 사임하게 되었다. ● 연루, 연화 불가산명사 ❑ 살인에 연루되어 그는 결국 교수형에 처해졌다.

1 가산명사 귀결; 함의 ❑ 법무부 장관은 기소하겠다는 자신의 결정이 정치적으로 어떤 파장을 일으킬지 알고 있었다. **2** 가산명사 암시 ❑ 암시는 명백했다. 그것은 우리에게 투표해라, 그러지 않으면 매우 곤란해질 거라는 것이었다. ● 구 그에 연락지어; 함축적으로 ❑ 현재 그의 권위와, 그에 따라 경영 팀 전체의 권위가, 전례 없는 위험을 받고 있다.

1 형용사 암시적인 ❑ 그것은 모로코 인들에게 일 주 전에 시작한 군사적 행동을 계속하거나 되풀이하지 말라는 암시적인 경고로 받아들여진다. ● 암시적으로, 완곡적으로 부사 ❑ 배심원은 감방에서 목을 맨 상태로 발견된 십대 한 명에 대해 사인 불명이란 판결을 내림으로써 암리 교도소에 대한 내부의 관리를 암시적으로 비판했다. **2** 형용사 내포된, 내재하는 [격식체] ❑ 속물근성에 내재되어 있는 것은 소심함, 즉 상류층 친구들이 어떻게 생각할지 두려워서 위험을 무릅쓰지 못하는 마음이다. **3** 형용사 절대적인, 맹목적인 ❑ 그는 황제의 고귀한 의도에 맹목적인 믿음을 가지고 있었다. ● 절대적으로, 맹목적으로 부사 ❑ 나는 그를 절대적으로 신뢰한다.

타동사 애원하다, 간청하다 ❑ 야당 지도자들은 이번 주에 국회의 교착 상태를 깨기를 대통령에게 간청했다.

1 타동사 넌지시 말하다, 함축하다 ❑ "당신은 내가 그 공격 사건들과 관계가 있다고 말하고 있는 건가요?"라고 그녀가 차갑게 물었다. **2** 타동사 암시하다 ❑ 6월에 수출은 1.5퍼센트 늘었는데 이것은 많은 투자자들이 생각했던 것보다 경제가 건실하다는 것을 암시했다.

imply와 infer를 혼동하지 않도록 하라. 무엇이 어떻다고 imply하는 것은 실제로 그렇다고 말하지 않고 암시하는 것이다. ❑ 로즈의 변호사는 그가 돈 때문에 그녀와 결혼했다는 듯한 말을 했다. 무엇이 어떻다고 infer하는 것은, 실제로 듣지는 못했지만, 알고 있는 사실에 비추어 틀림없이 그렇다는 결론을 내리는 것이다. ❑ 이 단순한 진술로부터 나는 그의 아내에 대해 많은 것을 추론할 수 있었다. 어떤 영어 사용자들은 imply와 같은 의미로 infer를 사용하지만 주의 깊은 사람들은 그것을 틀린 것으로 간주함을 유의하라.

형용사 무례한, 버릇없는 ❑ 백작은 새로 온 그 두 사람에게 무례하지 않을 정도로만 가능한 한 짧게 인사를 했다.

동사는 /ɪmˈpɔrt/ 또는 /ɪmˈpɔrt/로 발음되고, 명사는 /ˈɪmpɔrt/로 발음된다.

1 타동사/자동사 수입하다, 들여오다 ❑ 영국은 작년 한 해 식품을 해외로 수출하는 것보다 수입하는 데 거의 50억 파운드를 더 썼다. ❑ 우크라이나 회사는 러시아로부터 수입을 하기 위해 러시아의 루블화가 필요하다. ● 수입 불가산명사 ❑ 그러나 독일은 폴란드 석탄의 수입을 제한한다는 입장을 굽히지 않는다. ● 수입 불가산명사 ❑ 조류의 수입에 관한 규제 **2** 가산명사 수입품 ❑ 다른 유럽 국가들로부터 들여오는 소위 값싼 수입품에 대한 시위를 하는 프랑스 농부들 **3** 불가산명사 중요성 [격식체] ❑ 그러한 주장은 별로 중요하지 않다. **4** 타동사 가져오다 [컴퓨터] ❑ 마이크로소프트 워드 5.1 또는 맥라이트 2에서 파일을 가져올 수 있다.

A
B
C
D
E
F
G
H
I
J
K
L
M
N
O
P
Q
R
S
T
U
V
W
X
Y
Z

im|por|tance ♦♦♢ /ɪmpɔ́rtⁿns/ ① N-UNCOUNT The **importance** of something is its quality of being significant, valued, or necessary in a particular situation. ❑ *China has been stressing the importance of its ties with third world countries.* ② N-UNCOUNT **Importance** means having influence, power, or status. ❑ *Obviously a man of his importance is going to be missed.*

① 불가산명사 중요성, 중대성 ❑ 중국은 제3 세계 국가들과의 연대의 중요성을 강조해 왔다. ② 불가산명사 유력함, 영향력 ❑ 분명히 그 정도의 유력 인사가 빠지면 많이 아쉬워할 것이다.

> ## Word Partnership *importance*의 연어
>
> | | |
> |---|---|
> | ADJ. | **critical** importance, **enormous** importance, **growing/increasing** importance, **utmost** importance ① |
> | V. | **place less/more** importance **on** *something*, **recognize the** importance, **understand the** importance ① |
> | N. | **self**-importance, **sense of** importance ② |

im|por|tant ♦♦♦ /ɪmpɔ́rtⁿnt/ ① ADJ Something that is **important** is very significant, is highly valued, or is necessary. ❑ *The planned general strike represents an important economic challenge to the government.* ❑ *It's important to answer her questions as honestly as you can.* ● im|por|tant|ly ADV ❑ *I was hungry, and, more importantly, my children were hungry.* ② ADJ Someone who is **important** has influence or power within a society or a particular group. ❑ *...an important figure in the media world.*

① 형용사 중요한, 중대한 ❑ 계획된 총파업은 정부에게는 중대한 경제적 도전이다. ❑ 할 수 있는 한 정직하게 그녀의 질문에 대답하는 것이 중요하다. ● 중요하게 부사 ❑ 나도 배가 고팠지만, 그것보다 더욱 중요한 것은 내 아이들이 배가 고픈 것이었다. ② 형용사 유력한, 권위 있는 ❑ 언론계의 유력 인사

> You do not use **important** to say that an amount or quantity is very large. Instead, you use words such as **large**, **considerable**, or **substantial**. ❑ *...a large sum of money....a man with considerable influence... The armed forces face substantial cuts.*

important는 양이 많다는 뜻을 나타내는 데는 사용되지 않는다. 대신에 large나 considerable, substantial을 사용한다. ❑ ...많은 액수의 돈...상당한 영향력을 가진 사람... 군대는 상당한 인원 감축에 직면해 있다.

> ## Thesaurus *important*의 참조어
>
> | | |
> |---|---|
> | ADJ. | critical, essential, principal, significant; (ant.) unimportant ① |
> | | distinguished, high-ranking ② |

im|port|er /ɪmpɔ́rtər/ (importers) N-COUNT An **importer** is a country, firm, or person that buys goods from another country for use in their own country. ❑ *He made his money first as an importer of exotic food in west London.*

가산명사 수입업자 ❑ 그는 런던의 서부에서 이국적인 식품의 수입업자로 처음 돈을 벌었다.

im|pose ♦♦♢ /ɪmpóuz/ (imposes, imposing, imposed) ① V-T If you **impose** something on people, you use your authority to force them to accept it. ❑ *Britain was the first country to impose fines on airlines which bring passengers without proper immigration papers.* ❑ *A third of companies reviewing pay since last August have imposed a pay freeze of up to a year.* ● im|po|si|tion /ɪmpəzɪ́ʃⁿn/ N-UNCOUNT ❑ *Cambridge cyclists are attempting to fight the imposition of a day-time ban on cycling in the city center.* ② V-T If you **impose** your opinions or beliefs **on** other people, you try and make people accept them as a rule or as a model to copy. ❑ *Parents of either sex should beware of imposing their own tastes on their children.* ③ V-T If something **imposes** strain, pressure, or suffering **on** someone, it causes them to experience it. ❑ *The filming imposed an additional strain on her as she had little or no experience of using such a camera.* ④ V-I If someone **imposes** on you, they unreasonably expect you to do something for them which you do not want to do. ❑ *I was afraid you'd simply feel we were imposing on you.* ● im|po|si|tion N-COUNT ❑ *I know this is an imposition. But please hear me out.* ⑤ V-T If someone **imposes** themselves **on** you, they force you to accept their company although you may not want to. ❑ *I didn't want to impose myself on my married friends.*

① 타동사 부과하다 ❑ 영국은 적절한 이민 서류 없이 승객을 태운 항공사들에게 벌금을 부과한 첫 번째 국가였다. ❑ 지난 8월부터의 임금을 검토하는 회사의 3분의 1이 일 년까지의 임금 동결을 부과했다. ● 부과 불가산명사 ❑ 케임브리지의 자전거 이용객들은 도시 중심지에서 낮 시간 동안 자전거 사용을 금지한 명령에 대해 투쟁하려고 하고 있다. ② 타동사 강요하다 ❑ 아버지든 어머니든 자녀들에게 자기 자신의 기호를 강요하는 것을 경계해야 한다. ③ 타동사 부과하다, (부담 등을) 지우다 ❑ 그녀는 그러한 카메라를 사용한 경험이 거의 또는 전혀 없었기 때문에 그것을 촬영하는 일은 그녀에게 또 다른 부담이 되었다. ④ 자동사 강요하다, 억지를 부리다 ❑ 나는 우리가 당신에게 억지를 부리고 있다고 생각할까 봐 걱정했다. ● 강요, 억지 가산명사 ❑ 나는 이것이 억지라는 것을 안다. 그렇지만 내 이야기를 끝까지 들어 달라. ⑤ 타동사 받아들이도록 강요하다 ❑ 나는 결혼한 친구들에게 나를 끼워 달라고 강요하고 싶지 않았다.

> ## Word Partnership *impose*의 연어
>
> | | |
> |---|---|
> | N. | impose **a fine**, impose **limits**, impose **order**, impose **a penalty**, impose **restrictions**, impose **sanctions**, impose **a tax** ① |

im|pos|ing /ɪmpóuzɪŋ/ ADJ If you describe someone or something as **imposing**, you mean that they have an impressive appearance or manner. ❑ *He was an imposing man.*

형용사 인상적인, 장대한 ❑ 그는 장대한 사람이었다.

> ## Word Link *im ≈ not : imbalance, immature, impossible*

im|pos|si|ble ♦♦♢ /ɪmpɑ́sɪbⁿl/ ① ADJ Something that is **impossible** cannot be done or cannot happen. ❑ *It was impossible for anyone to get in because no one knew the password.* ❑ *He thinks the tax is impossible to administer.* ● N-SING The **impossible** is something which is impossible. ❑ *They were expected to do the impossible.* ● im|pos|si|bly ADV [ADV adj] ❑ *Mathematical physics is an almost impossibly difficult subject.* ● im|pos|si|bil|ity /ɪmpɑ́sɪbɪ́lɪti/ (impossibilities) N-VAR ❑ *...the impossibility of knowing absolute truth.* ② ADJ An **impossible** situation or an **impossible** position is one that is very difficult to deal with. [ADJ n] ❑ *The Government was now in an almost impossible position.* ③ ADJ If you describe someone as **impossible**, you are annoyed that their bad behavior or strong views make them difficult to deal with. [DISAPPROVAL] ❑ *The woman is impossible, thought Frannie.*

① 형용사 불가능한 ❑ 아무도 비밀 번호를 모르므로 누군가가 들어가는 것은 불가능했다. ❑ 그는 그 세금을 관리하는 것이 불가능하다고 생각한다. ● 단수명사 불가능한 일 ❑ 그들은 불가능한 일을 하도록 요구받았다. ● 불가능하게 부사 ❑ 수리 물리학은 거의 불가능할 정도로 어려운 과목이다. ● 불가능 (성) 가산명사 또는 불가산명사 ❑ 절대적 진리를 아는 것의 불가능성 ② 형용사 다루기 힘든, 어쩔 수 없는 ❑ 정부는 이제 거의 어쩔 수 없는 지경에 처해 있었다. ③ 형용사 어쩔 수 없는, 구제 불능인 [탐탁찮음] ❑ 그 여자는 구제 불능이군, 하고 프래니는 생각했다.

> ## Thesaurus *impossible*의 참조어
>
> | | |
> |---|---|
> | ADJ. | unreasonable, unworkable; (ant.) possible ② |
> | | absurd, difficult, trying ③ |

> ## Word Partnership *impossible*의 연어
>
> | | |
> |---|---|
> | V. | impossible **to describe**, impossible **to find**, impossible **to ignore**, impossible **to prove**, impossible **to say/tell**, **seem** impossible ① |
> | N. | **an** impossible **task** ① ② |
> | ADV. | **absolutely** impossible, **almost** impossible, **nearly** impossible ① ② |

im|po|tence /ˈɪmpətəns/ ■ N-UNCOUNT **Impotence** is a lack of power to influence people or events. □ ...a sense of impotence in the face of deplorable events. ■ N-UNCOUNT **Impotence** is a man's sexual problem in which his penis fails to get hard or stay hard. □ Impotence affects 10 million men in the U.S. alone.

im|po|tent /ˈɪmpətənt/ ■ ADJ If someone feels **impotent**, they feel that they have no power to influence people or events. □ The aggression of a bully leaves people feeling hurt, angry and impotent. ■ ADJ If a man is **impotent**, he is unable to have sex normally, because his penis fails to get hard or stay hard. □ At the age of 40, 19 per cent of men are impotent.

im|pound /ɪmˈpaʊnd/ (impounds, impounding, impounded) V-T If something **is impounded** by police officers, customs officers, or other officials, they officially take possession of it because a law or rule has been broken. □ The ship was impounded under the terms of the UN trade embargo.

im|pov|er|ish /ɪmˈpɒvərɪʃ/ (impoverishes, impoverishing, impoverished) ■ V-T Something that **impoverishes** a person or a country makes them poor. □ We need to reduce the burden of taxes that impoverish the economy. ● **im|pov|er|ished** ADJ □ The goal is to lure businesses into impoverished areas by offering them tax breaks. ■ V-T A person or thing that **impoverishes** something makes it worse in quality. □ A top dressing of fertilizer should be added to improve growth as mint impoverishes the soil quickly.

im|prac|ti|cal /ɪmˈpræktɪkəl/ ■ ADJ If you describe an object, idea, or course of action as **impractical**, you mean that it is not sensible or realistic, and does not work well in practice. □ Once there were regularly scheduled airlines, it became impractical to make a business trip by ocean liner. ■ ADJ If you describe someone as **impractical**, you mean that they do not have the abilities or skills to do practical work such as making, repairing, or organizing things. □ Geniuses are supposed to be difficult, eccentric, and hopelessly impractical.

im|press ◆◇◇ /ɪmˈpres/ (impresses, impressing, impressed) ■ V-T/V-I If something **impresses** you, you feel great admiration for it. □ What impressed him most was their speed. ● **im|pressed** ADJ [v-link ADJ, oft ADJ by/with n] □ I was very impressed by one young man at my lectures. ■ V-T If you **impress** something **on** someone, you make them understand its importance or degree. □ I had always impressed upon the children that if they worked hard they would succeed in life. □ I've impressed upon them the need for more professionalism. ■ V-T If something **impresses itself on** your mind, you notice and remember it. □ But this change has not yet impressed itself on the minds of the British public. ■ V-T If someone or something **impresses** you **as** a particular thing, usually a good one, they gives you the impression of being that thing. □ Billy Sullivan had impressed me as a fine man.

im|pres|sion ◆◇◇ /ɪmˈpreʃən/ (impressions) ■ N-COUNT Your **impression** of a person or thing is what you think they are like, usually after having seen or heard them. Your **impression** of a situation is what you think is going on. □ What were your first impressions of college? □ My impression is that they are totally out of control. ■ N-SING If someone gives you a particular **impression**, they cause you to believe that something is the case, often when it is not. □ I don't want to give the impression that I'm running away from the charges. ■ N-COUNT An **impression** is an amusing imitation of someone's behavior or way of talking, usually someone well-known. □ ...doing impressions of Sean Connery and James Mason. ■ N-COUNT An **impression** of an object is a mark or outline that it has left after being pressed hard onto a surface. □ ...the world's oldest fossil impressions of plant life. ■ PHRASE If someone or something **makes an impression**, they have a strong effect on people or a situation. □ The type of aid coming in makes no immediate impression on the horrific death rates. ■ PHRASE If you are **under the impression that** something is the case, you believe that it is the case, usually when it is not actually the case. □ He had apparently been under the impression that a military coup was in progress.

Word Partnership	impression의 연어
ADJ.	**favorable** impression, **first** impression, **good** impression ■
	strong impression ■ ■
	the wrong impression ■
V.	**have** an impression ■ ■
	get the impression **that**, **give the** impression **that** ■

im|pres|sive ◆◇◇ /ɪmˈpresɪv/ ADJ Something that is **impressive** impresses you, for example because it is great in size or degree, or is done with a great deal of skill. □ It is an impressive achievement. ● **im|pres|sive|ly** ADV □ ...an impressively bright and energetic American woman called Cathie Gould.

im|print (imprints, imprinting, imprinted)

The noun is pronounced /ˈɪmprɪnt/. The verb is pronounced /ɪmˈprɪnt/.

■ N-COUNT If something leaves an **imprint** on a place or on your mind, it has a strong and lasting effect on it. □ Few cities in America bear the imprint of Japanese money more than Los Angeles. ■ V-T When something **is imprinted on** your memory, it is firmly fixed in your memory so that you will not forget it. □ As I arrived, the shimmering skyline of domes and minarets was imprinted on my memory. ■ N-COUNT An **imprint** is a mark or outline made by the pressure of one object on another. □ It was the imprint of his little finger on a box of poisoned chocolates that finally sealed his fate. ■ V-T If a surface **is imprinted with** a mark or design, that mark or design is printed on the surface or pressed into it. [usu passive] □ The firm carries a variety of binders that can be imprinted with your message or logo.

im|pris|on /ɪmˈprɪzən/ (imprisons, imprisoning, imprisoned) V-T If someone is **imprisoned**, they are locked up or kept somewhere, usually in prison as a

■ 불가산명사 무력, 무능 □ 통탄할 만한 사건들을 직면했을 때의 무력감 ■ 불가산명사 발기 부전으로 미국에서만 천만 명의 남자들이 고생하고 있다.

■ 형용사 무력한, 무능력한 □ 약자에 대한 공격은 사람들의 마음을 다치게 하고, 분노와 무력감을 느끼게 한다. ■ 형용사 성교 불능의, 발기 부전의 □ 40세가 되면 남성의 1.9퍼센트가 발기 부전이 된다.

타동사 압수되다 □ 그 배는 유엔 통상 금지 조처에 의해 압수되었다.

■ 타동사 가난하게 하다, 피폐시키다 □ 우리는 경제를 피폐하게 하는 세금의 부담을 줄일 필요가 있다. ● 가난해진 형용사 □ 세금 감면 혜택을 주어 빈곤 지역에 기업 투자를 유치하는 것이 목표이다. ■ 타동사 저하시키다, 황폐화시키다 □ 박하가 토지를 빠르게 황폐화시키므로 성장을 향상시키려면 비료를 토양 표면에 뿌려 주어야 한다.

■ 형용사 비현실적인, 비실용적인 □ 일단 정기 항공편이 생기자, 정기 여객선으로 출장을 가는 것은 비실용적인 것이 되었다. ■ 형용사 비실용적인, 비현실적인 □ 천재들은 다루기 힘들고 괴상하며 대책이 없을 정도로 비현실적이라고 여겨진다.

■ 타동사/자동사 감명을 주다, 감동시키다 □ 그를 가장 감동시킨 것은 그들의 속력이었다. ● 감명 받은, 감동 받은 형용사 □ 나는 내 강의를 듣던 젊은 청년 한 명에게 매우 감동을 받았다. ■ 타동사 중요성을 인식시켜 □ 나는 항상 아이들에게 열심히 공부하면 인생에서 성공할 것이라는 인식을 심어 주곤 했었다. □ 나는 그들에게 더욱 전문적일 필요가 있다고 인식시켜 주었다. ■ 타동사 새겨지다, 인식되다 □ 그러나 이러한 변화는 아직 영국 대중에게 인식되지 않았다. ■ 타동사 인상을 주다 □ 빌리 설리번은 나에게 훌륭한 사람이라는 인상을 주었다.

■ 가산명사 인상 □ 대학의 첫 인상은 어땠어? □ 내가 받은 인상은 그들이 완전히 통제 불가라는 것이다. ■ 단수명사 인상 □ 나는 혐의로부터 도망치고 있다는 인상을 주고 싶지 않다. ■ 가산명사 흉내, 성대모사 □ 숀 코네리와 제임스 메이슨의 성대모사하기 ■ 가산명사 (눌러서 생긴) 자국, 흔적 □ 세계에서 가장 오래된 식물 화석의 흔적 ■ 구 영향을 주다 □ 이런 종류의 원조 도입은 끔찍한 사망률에 즉각적인 영향을 주지는 못한다. ■ 구 ―라고 생각하고 있는 □ 그는 분명히 군사 쿠데타가 진행 중이라고 생각하고 있었다.

형용사 인상적인, 강한 인상을 주는 □ 그것은 눈부신 성과이다. ● 인상적으로 부사 □ 캐시 골드라고 하는, 인상적일 정도로 총명하고 활기 넘치는 미국 여성

명사는 /ˈɪmprɪnt/로 발음되고, 동사는 /ɪmˈprɪnt/로 발음된다.

■ 가산명사 강한 영향 □ 미국에서 로스앤젤레스만큼 일본 자본의 강한 영향을 드러내는 도시는 없다. ■ 타동사 각인되다 □ 내가 도착했을 때, 둥근 지붕과 뾰족탑들이 빈쩍거리며 만들어 내는 스카이라인이 나의 기억에 각인되었다. ■ 가산명사 흔적, (눌러 생긴) 자국 □ 마침내 그의 운명을 결정지은 것은 어느 독이 든 초콜릿 박스에 남겨진 그의 새끼손가락 자국이었다. ■ 타동사 ―가 찍혀 있다 □ 그 회사는 당신의 메시지나 로고를 찍을 수 있는 여러 바인더를 팔고 있다.

타동사 감금되다, 투옥되다 □ 그 지방 목사는 반국가적인 선동 혐의로 18개월 동안 투옥되었다.

A

punishment for a crime or for political opposition. ❑ *The local priest was imprisoned for 18 months on charges of anti-state agitation.*

im|pris|on|ment /ɪmprɪzˀnmənt/ N-UNCOUNT **Imprisonment** is the state of being imprisoned. ❑ *She was sentenced to seven years' imprisonment.*

불가산명사 투옥, 감금 ❑ 그녀는 7년 금고형을 받았다.

B

im|prob|able /ɪmprɒbəbˀl/ ◼ ADJ Something that is **improbable** is unlikely to be true or to happen. ❑ *Ordered arrangements of large groups of atoms and molecules are highly improbable.* ● im|prob|abil|ity (**improbabilities**) N-VAR ❑ *...the improbability of such an outcome.* ◼ ADJ If you describe something as **improbable**, you mean it is strange, unusual, or ridiculous. ❑ *On the face of it, their marriage seems an improbable alliance.* ● im|prob|ably ADV ❑ *The sea is an improbably pale turquoise.*

◼ 형용사 사실 같지 않은, 일어날 것 같지 않은 ❑ 원자와 분자가 크게 무리지어 질서 정연하게 배열된 형태로 나타날 가능성은 매우 희박하다. ● 사실 같지 않음 가산명사 또는 불가산명사 ❑ 그러한 결과의 불가능성 ◼ 형용사 기이한, 그럴듯하지 않은 ❑ 언뜻 보기에는, 그들의 결혼은 선뜻 이해가 안 가는 결합이다. ● 기이한 정도로 부사 ❑ 이 바다는 기이한 정도로 열은 청록색을 띤다.

C

D

im|promp|tu /ɪmprɒmptu, BRIT ɪmprɒmptyu:/ ADJ An **impromptu** action is one that you do without planning or organizing it in advance. ❑ *This afternoon the Palestinians held an impromptu press conference.*

형용사 준비 없는, 즉석의 ❑ 오늘 오후 팔레스타인 사람들은 즉석으로 기자 회견을 했다.

E

im|prop|er /ɪmprɒpər/ ◼ ADJ **Improper** activities are illegal or dishonest. [FORMAL] ❑ *25 officers were investigated following allegations of improper conduct during the murder inquiry.* ● im|prop|er|ly ADV [ADV with v] ❑ *I acted neither fraudulently nor improperly.* ◼ ADJ **Improper** conditions or methods of treatment are not suitable or good enough for a particular purpose. [FORMAL] [ADJ n] ❑ *The improper use of medicine could lead to severe adverse reactions.* ● im|prop|er|ly ADV [ADV with v] ❑ *The study confirmed many reports that doctors were improperly trained.*

F

◼ 형용사 불법의, 부도덕한 [격식체] ❑ 25명의 경찰관들이 살인 사건 조사 중 행해진 부당 행위에 관한 혐의에 따라 조사를 받았다. ● 불법적으로 부사 ❑ 나는 사기지도, 불법적으로 행동하지도 않았다. ◼ 형용사 부적당한, 부적절한 [격식체] ❑ 약을 부적절하게 사용하면 심한 부작용을 일으킬 수 있다. ● 부적당하게, 부적절하게 부사 ❑ 그 연구는 의사들이 부적절하게 훈련을 받는다는 많은 보도들을 뒷받침했다.

G

H

im|prove ◆◆◇ /ɪmpruv/ (**improves, improving, improved**) ◼ V-T/V-I If something **improves** or if you **improve** it, it gets better. ❑ *Within a month, both the texture and condition of your hair should improve.* ◼ V-T/V-I If a skill you have **improves** or you **improve** a skill, you get better at it. ❑ *Their French has improved enormously.* ◼ V-I If you **improve** after an illness or an injury, your health gets better or you get stronger. ❑ *He had improved so much the doctor had cut his dosage.* ◼ V-I If you **improve on** a previous achievement of your own or of someone else, you achieve a better standard or result. ❑ *We need to improve on our performance against France.*

I

◼ 타동사/자동사 개선되다; 개선시키다 ❑ 한 달 안에 당신의 머릿결과 상태 모두 개선될 것이다. ◼ 타동사/자동사 향상되다; 향상시키다 ❑ 그들의 불어 실력은 크게 향상되었다. ◼ 자동사 건강이 증진되다 ❑ 그의 건강이 크게 호전되어서 의사가 그의 투약용량을 줄였다. ◼ 자동사 -보다 낫다 ❑ 우리가 대프랑스 전에서 보인 성적을 개선할 필요가 있다.

J

K

Word Partnership	improve의 연어
ADV.	**significantly** improve, improve **slightly** ◼-◼
V.	**continue to** improve, **expected to** improve ◼-◼
	need to improve, **try to** improve ◼ ◼ ◼

L

M

im|prove|ment ◆◇◇ /ɪmpruvmənt/ (**improvements**) ◼ N-VAR If there is an **improvement in** something, it becomes better. If you make **improvements to** something, you make it better. ❑ *...the dramatic improvements in organ transplantation in recent years.* ◼ N-COUNT If you say that something is **an improvement on** a previous thing or situation, you mean that it is better than that thing. ❑ *The new Prime Minister is an improvement on his predecessor.*

N

◼ 가산명사 또는 불가산명사 향상, 개선 ❑ 최근 몇 년간 극적인 향상을 보여 온 장기 이식 ◼ 가산명사 -보다 개선됨 ❑ 신임 수상은 전임자보다 낫다.

O

Thesaurus	improvement의 참조어
N.	advancement, progress ◼ ◼

P

Word Partnership	improvement의 연어
N.	**home** improvement, **self-**improvement, **signs of** improvement ◼
ADJ.	**gradual** improvement ◼
	big improvement, **dramatic** improvement, **marked** improvement,
	significant improvement, **slight** improvement ◼ ◼

Q

R

S

im|pro|vise /ɪmprəvaɪz/ (**improvises, improvising, improvised**) ◼ V-T/V-I If you **improvise**, you make or do something using whatever you have or without having planned it in advance. ❑ *You need a wok with a steaming rack for this; if you don't have one, improvise.* ❑ *The vet had improvised a harness.* ◼ V-T/V-I When performers **improvise**, they invent music or words as they play, sing, or speak. ❑ *I asked her what the piece was and she said, "Oh, I'm just improvising."* ❑ *Uncle Richard intoned a chapter from the Bible and improvised a prayer.*

T

◼ 타동사/자동사 즉석에서 만들다 ❑ 이것을 만들려면 아주 뜨거운 조리대에 중국 요리 냄비를 걸어야 한다. 만일 그런 것이 없다면, 즉석에서 다른 수단을 강구하라. ❑ 그 수의사는 마구를 즉석에서 만들었다. ◼ 타동사/자동사 즉흥 연주를 하다, 즉석에서 하다 ❑ 내가 그녀에게 그 곡이 무엇인지 물었더니 그녀는 "아, 그냥 즉흥 연주를 하고 있는데요."라고 말했다. ❑ 리처드 삼촌이 성경의 한 구절을 봉독하고 즉석에서 기도를 했다.

U

V

im|pu|dent /ɪmpyədənt/ ADJ If you describe someone as **impudent**, you mean they are rude or disrespectful, or do something they have no right to do. [FORMAL, DISAPPROVAL] ❑ *Some of them spoke pleasantly and were well behaved, while others were impudent and insulting.*

형용사 무례한, 뻔뻔스러운 [격식체, 탐탁찮음] ❑ 그들 중 몇몇은 즐겁게 말하고 예의 바르게 행동했던 반면, 다른 사람들은 뻔뻔스러웠고 무례했다.

W

| Word Link | puls ≈ driving, pushing : compulsion, expulsion, impulse |

X

im|pulse /ɪmpʌls/ (**impulses**) ◼ N-VAR An **impulse** is a sudden desire to do something. ❑ *Unable to resist the impulse, he glanced at the sea again.* ◼ N-COUNT An **impulse** is a short electrical signal that is sent along a wire or nerve or through the air, usually as one of a series. ❑ *It works by sending a series of electrical impulses which are picked up by hi-tech sensors.* ◼ ADJ An **impulse** buy or **impulse** purchase is something that you decide to buy when you see it, although you had not planned to buy it. [ADJ n] ❑ *The curtains were an impulse buy.* ◼ PHRASE If

Y

Z

◼ 가산명사 또는 불가산명사 충동, 욕구 ❑ 충동을 억제할 수 없어서 그는 다시 바다를 힐끗 쳐다보았다. ◼ 가산명사 충격, 임펄스 ❑ 최첨단 센서에 의해서 감지되는 일련의 전기 충격을 보냄으로써 그것은 작동한다. ◼ 형용사 충동적인 (구매) ❑ 그 커튼은 충동구매로 산 것이었다. ◼ 구 충동적으로 ❑ 손은 생각이 빠르고 충동적으로 행동한다.

you do something **on impulse**, you suddenly decide to do it, without planning it. ❑ *Sean's a fast thinker, and he acts on impulse.*

Word Partnership	*impulse*의 연어

ADJ.	**first** impulse, **strong** impulse, **sudden** impulse ■
V.	**control an** impulse, **resist an** impulse ■
	act on impulse ▣

im·pul·sive /ɪmpʌlsɪv/ ADJ If you describe someone as **impulsive**, you mean that they do things suddenly without thinking about them carefully first. ❑ *He is too impulsive to be a responsible prime minister.* ● **im·pul·sive·ly** ADV [ADV with v] ❑ *He studied her face for a moment, then said impulsively: "Let's get married."*

im·pure /ɪmpyʊər/ ADJ A substance that is **impure** is not of good quality because it has other substances mixed with it. ❑ *...diarrhea, dysentery, and other diseases borne by impure water.*

im·pu·ri·ty /ɪmpyʊərɪti/ (**impurities**) N-COUNT **Impurities** are substances that are present in small quantities in another substance and make it dirty or of an unacceptable quality. ❑ *The air in the factory is filtered to remove impurities.*

형용사 충동적인 ❑ 그는 책임감 있는 수상이 되기에는 너무나 충동적이다. ● 충동적으로 부사 ❑ 그는 그녀의 얼굴을 잠시 동안 유심히 보고 나서는 "우리 결혼합시다."라고 충동적으로 말했다.

형용사 불순한, 불순물이 든 ❑ 깨끗하지 않은 물 때문에 생기는 설사, 이질, 그리고 다른 질병들

가산명사 불순물 ❑ 그 공장의 공기는 불순물을 제거하기 위해 정화한다.

---

in

① POSITION OR MOVEMENT
② INCLUSION OR INVOLVEMENT
③ TIME AND NUMBERS
④ STATES AND QUALITIES
⑤ OTHER USES AND PHRASES

① in ♦♦♦

The preposition is pronounced /ɪn/. The adverb is pronounced /ɪn/.

전치사는 /ɪn/으로 발음되고, 부사는 /ɪn/으로 발음된다.

In addition to the uses shown below, **in** is used after some verbs, nouns, and adjectives in order to introduce extra information. **In** is also used with verbs of movement such as "walk" and "push," and in phrasal verbs such as "give in" and "dig in."

in은 아래 용법 외에도 추가 정보를 나타내기 위해 일부의 동사, 명사, 형용사 뒤에 쓴다. in은 'walk', 'push'와 같은 이동 동사와도 함께 쓰며 'give in', 'dig in'과 같은 구동사에도 쓰인다.

■ PREP Someone or something that is **in** something else is enclosed by it or surrounded by it. If you put something in a container, you move it so that it is enclosed by the container. ❑ *He was in his car.* ② PREP If something happens in a place, it happens there. ❑ *...spending a few days in a hotel.* ③ ADV If you **are in**, you are present at your home or place of work. [be ADV] ❑ *My flatmate was in at the time.* ④ ADV When someone comes **in**, they enter a room or building. [ADV after v] ❑ *She looked up anxiously as he came in.* ⑤ ADV If a train, boat, or plane has come **in** or is **in**, it has arrived at a station, port, or airport. ❑ *We'd be watching every plane coming in from Melbourne.* ⑥ ADV When the sea or tide comes **in**, the sea moves towards the shore rather than away from it. ❑ *She thought of the tide rushing in, covering the wet sand.* ⑦ PREP Something that is in a window, especially a store window, is just behind the window so that you can see it from outside. ❑ *There was a camera for sale in the window.* ⑧ PREP When you see something in a mirror, the mirror shows an image of it. ❑ *I couldn't bear to see my reflection in the mirror.* ⑨ PREP If you are dressed **in** a piece of clothing, you are wearing it. ❑ *He was a big man, smartly dressed in a suit and tie.* ⑩ PREP Something that is covered or wrapped **in** something else has that thing over or round its surface. ❑ *His legs were covered in mud.* ⑪ PREP If there is something such as a crack or hole **in** something, there is a crack or hole on its surface. ❑ *There was a deep crack in the ceiling above him.*

■ 전치사 - 안에 ❑ 그는 자기 자동차 안에 있었다. ② 전치사 -에서 ❑ 호텔에서 며칠을 보내기 ③ 부사 (집이나 사무실에) 있다 ❑ 그때 나의 룸메이트가 집에 있었다. ④ 부사 안으로 ❑ 그가 들어왔을 때 그녀는 걱정스럽게 쳐다보았다. ⑤ 부사 도착하여 ❑ 우리는 멜버른에서 도착하는 모든 비행기를 지켜보고 있을 것이다. ⑥ 부사 (조수가) 밀려와 ❑ 그녀는 젖은 모래를 뒤덮으며 빠르게 들어오는 밀물을 생각했다. ⑦ 전치사 쇼윈도에 (진열된) ❑ 쇼윈도에 팔려고 내놓은 카메라가 있었다. ⑧ 전치사 -에 ❑ 나는 거울에 비친 내 모습을 볼 수가 없었다. ⑨ 전치사 -을 입고 있는 ❑ 그는 거구였는데, 말쑥하게 양복을 입고 넥타이를 매고 있었다. ⑩ 전치사 -로 둘러싸인 ❑ 그의 다리는 온통 진흙투성이였다. ⑪ 전치사 -에 ❑ 그의 머리 위 천장에 깊이 금이 가 있었다.

② in ♦♦♦ /ɪn/ ■ PREP If something is **in** a book, movie, play, or picture, you can read it or see it there. ❑ *Don't stick too precisely to what it says in the book.* ② PREP If you are **in** something such as a play or a race, you are one of the people taking part. ❑ *Alf offered her a part in the play he was directing.* ③ PREP Something that is in a group or collection is a member of it or part of it. ❑ *The New England team are the worst in the league.* ④ PREP You use **in** to specify a general subject or field of activity. ❑ *...those working in the defense industry.*

■ 전치사 -에 ❑ 너무 꼼꼼하게 그 책에 쓰여 있는 것을 고수하지 말아라. ② 전치사 -에 참가한 ❑ 알프는 그녀에게 자신이 감독하고 있는 연극의 배역을 제안했다. ③ 전치사 -에서 ❑ 뉴잉글랜드 팀은 그 리그에서 최하 팀이다. ④ 전치사 -에서 ❑ 경비 업체에서 일하는 사람들

③ in ♦♦♦ /ɪn/ ■ PREP If something happens **in** a particular year, month, or other period of time, it happens during that time. ❑ *...that early spring day in April 1949.* ❑ *Export orders improved in the last month.* ② PREP If something happens **in** a particular situation, it happens while that situation is going on. ❑ *His father had been badly wounded in the last war.* ③ PREP If you do something **in** a particular period of time, that is how long it takes you to do it. [PREP amount] ❑ *He walked two hundred and sixty miles in eight days.* ④ PREP If something will happen **in** a particular length of time, it will happen after that length of time. [PREP amount] ❑ *I'll have some breakfast ready in a few minutes.* ⑤ PREP You use **in** to indicate roughly how old someone is. For example, if someone is in their fifties, they are between 50 and 59 years old. [PREP poss pl-num] ❑ *...young people in their twenties.* ⑥ PREP You use **in** to indicate roughly how many people or things do something. ❑ *...men who came there in droves.* ⑦ PREP You use **in** to express a ratio, proportion, or probability. [num PREP num] ❑ *Last year, one in five boys left school without a qualification.*

■ 전치사 -에, - 동안에 ❑ 1949년 4월의 그 이른 봄날 ❑ 수출 주문은 지난달에 증가했다. ② 전치사 -에, -에서 ❑ 그의 아버지는 지난 전쟁에서 심하게 부상당했었다. ③ 전치사 - 동안 ❑ 그는 8일 동안 260마일을 걸었다. ④ 전치사 - 후에 ❑ 몇 분 후에 아침을 준비해 놓을게요. ⑤ 전치사 나이가 -인 ❑ 20대 젊은이들 ⑥ 전치사 -로 ❑ 떼를 지어 그곳에 온 남자들 ⑦ 전치사 -에 ❑ 지난해, 5명에 한 명의 비율로 남학생들이 아무런 자격을 못 따고 학교를 떠났다.

④ in ♦♦♦ /ɪn/ ■ PREP If something or someone is **in** a particular state or situation, that is their present state or situation. [v-link PREP n] ❑ *The economy was in trouble.* ❑ *Dave was in a hurry to get back to work.* ② PREP You use **in** to indicate the feeling or desire which someone has when they do something, or which causes them to do it. ❑ *Simpson looked at them in surprise.* ③ PREP If a

■ 전치사 -한 상태인 ❑ 경제가 위기에 빠져 있었다. ❑ 데이브는 일하러 돌아가기 위해 서두르고 있었다. ② 전치사 (감정이) -한 ❑ 심슨은 놀라며 그들을 바라보았다. ③ 전치사 -에게 있는 ❑ 폭력은 그의 천성이 아니다. ④ 전치사 -에, -에게 ❑ 그는 내가

particular quality or ability is **in** you, you naturally have it. ❑ *Violence is not in his nature.* ❹ PREP You use **in** when saying that someone or something has a particular quality. ❑ *He had all the qualities I was looking for in a partner.* ❺ PREP You use **in** to indicate how someone is expressing something. ❑ *Information is given to the patient verbally and in writing.* ❻ PREP You use **in** in expressions such as **in a row** or **in a ball** to describe the arrangement or shape of something. ❑ *The cards need to be laid out in two rows.* ❼ PREP If something is **in** a particular color, it has that color. ❑ *...white flowers edged in pink.* ❽ PREP You use **in** to specify which feature or aspect of something you are talking about. ❑ *The movie is nearly two hours in length.* ❑ *There is a big difference in the amounts that banks charge.*

파트너에게서 찾고 있는 모든 자질을 다 가지고 있었다. ❺ 전치사 -로 ❑ 정보는 환자에게 말로도 또 글로도 전달된다. ❻ 전치사 (어떤) 형태로 ❑ 카드를 두 줄로 펼쳐 놓을 필요가 있다. ❼ 전치사 (색깔을) 띠다 ❑ 가장자리가 분홍색인 흰 꽃 ❽ 전치사 -가, -의 ❑ 그 영화는 상영 시간이 거의 2시간이다. ❑ 은행들이 청구하는 액수가 큰 차이가 있다.

⑤ in ♦♦♦ (ins)

Pronounced /ɪn/ for meanings ❶ and ❸ to ❽, and /ɪn/ for meaning ❷.

❶과, ❸부터 ❽까지의 의미일 때는 /ɪn/으로 발음되고, ❷의 의미일 때는 /ɪn/으로 발음된다.

❶ ADJ If you say that something is **in**, or is the **in** thing, you mean it is fashionable or popular. [INFORMAL] ❑ *A few years ago jogging was the in thing.* ❷ PREP You use **in** with a present participle to indicate that when you do something, something else happens as a result. [PREP -ing] ❑ *He shifted uncomfortably on his feet. In doing so he knocked over Steven's briefcase.* ❸ PHRASE If you say that someone **is in for** a shock or a surprise, you mean that they are going to experience it. ❑ *You might be in for a shock at the sheer hard work involved.* ❹ PHRASE If someone **has it in for** you, they dislike you and try to cause problems for you. [INFORMAL] ❑ *The other kids had it in for me.* ❺ PHRASE If you are **in on** something, you are involved in it or know about it. ❑ *I don't know. I wasn't in on that particular argument.* ❻ PHRASE If you **are in with** a person or group, they like you and accept you, and are likely to help you. [INFORMAL] ❼ PHRASE You use **in that** to introduce an explanation of a statement you have just made. ❑ *I'm lucky in that I've got four sisters.* ❽ PHRASE The **ins and outs** of a situation are all the detailed points and facts about it. ❑ *...the ins and outs of high finance.*

❶ 형용사 유행하는 [비격식체] ❑ 몇 년 전에는 조깅이 유행했었다. ❷ 전치사 -할 때 ❑ 그는 불편한듯 체중을 한쪽 발에서 다른 쪽 발로 옮겼다. 그렇게 하면서 그는 스티븐의 서류 가방을 넘어뜨렸다. ❸ 구 -하도록 되어 있다 ❑ 얼마나 힘든 일이 관련되는지 알면 놀라 자빠질지도 모른다. ❹ 구 -에게 앙심을 품다 [비격식체] ❑ 나머지 아이들이 나에게 앙심을 품었다. ❺ 구 -에 관계하다, -에 알고 있다 ❑ 나는 잘 모른다. 나는 그 논쟁에 관여하지 않았다. ❻ 구 -의 마음에 들다 [비격식체] ❼ 구 -이라는 점에서, -이므로 ❑ 나는 자매가 네 명이나 있으니 운이 좋다. ❽ 구 세부 사항 ❑ 고급 금융의 세부 내용

Word Link	in ≈ not : *inability, inaccurate, inadequate*

in|abil|ity /ɪnəbɪlɪti/ N-UNCOUNT If you refer to someone's **inability to** do something, you are referring to the fact that they are unable to do it. ❑ *Her inability to concentrate could cause an accident.*

불가산명사 - 할 수 없음, 무능 ❑ 그녀가 집중하지 못하는 것이 사고를 유발할 수도 있다.

in|ac|ces|sible /ɪnəksɛsɪbªl/ ❶ ADJ An **inaccessible** place is very difficult or impossible to reach. ❑ *...people living in remote and inaccessible parts of China.* ❷ ADJ If something is **inaccessible**, you are unable to see, use, or buy it. ❑ *Ninety-five per cent of its magnificent collection will remain inaccessible to the public.* ❸ ADJ Someone or something that is **inaccessible** is difficult or impossible to understand or appreciate. [DISAPPROVAL] ❑ *...language that is inaccessible to working people.*

❶ 형용사 접근하기 어려운, 접근할 수 없는 ❑ 중국의 접근하기 어려운 벽지에 사는 사람들 ❷ 형용사 이용할 수 없는, 접근 불가능한 ❑ 그 어마어마한 소장품 중 95퍼센트가 일반 대중은 볼 수 없는 상태로 남을 것이다. ❸ 형용사 이해하기 힘든, 난해한 [탐탁찮음] ❑ 노동자들이 이해할 수 없는 언어

in|ac|cu|ra|cy /ɪnækyərəsi/ (inaccuracies) N-VAR The **inaccuracy** of a statement or measurement is the fact that it is not accurate or correct. ❑ *He was disturbed by the inaccuracy of the answers.*

가산명사 또는 불가산명사 부정확함 ❑ 그는 대답이 정확하지 않아서 걱정스러웠다.

in|ac|cu|rate /ɪnækyərət/ ADJ If a statement or measurement is **inaccurate**, it is not accurate or correct. ❑ *The book is both inaccurate and exaggerated.*

형용사 부정확한, 틀린 ❑ 그 책은 부정확하고 과장되었다.

in|ac|tion /ɪnækʃªn/ N-UNCOUNT If you refer to someone's **inaction**, you disapprove of the fact that they are doing nothing. [DISAPPROVAL] ❑ *He is bitter about the inaction of the other political parties.*

불가산명사 게으름 [탐탁찮음] ❑ 그는 다른 정당들이 아무 것도 하지 않는 것에 화가 나 있다.

in|ac|tive /ɪnæktɪv/ ADJ Someone or something that is **inactive** is not doing anything or is not working. ❑ *He certainly was not politically inactive.* ● **in|ac|tiv|ity** /ɪnæktɪvɪti/ N-UNCOUNT ❑ *The players have comparatively long periods of inactivity.*

형용사 활동하지 않는, 가만히 있는 ❑ 그는 분명히 정치적으로 가만히 있지 않았다. ● 활동 정지 불가산명사 ❑ 그 선수들은 비교적 오랜 동안 활동을 쉬고 있다.

in|ad|equa|cy /ɪnædɪkwəsi/ (inadequacies) ❶ N-VAR The **inadequacy** of something is the fact that there is not enough of it, or that it is not good enough. ❑ *...the inadequacy of the water supply.* ❷ N-UNCOUNT If someone has feelings of **inadequacy**, they feel that they do not have the qualities and abilities necessary to do something or to cope with life in general. ❑ *...his deep-seated sense of inadequacy.*

❶ 가산명사 또는 불가산명사 불충분함, 부적합함 ❑ 물 공급 부족 ❷ 불가산명사 부적합함, 무능 ❑ 그의 뿌리 깊은 무능감

in|ad|equate /ɪnædɪkwɪt/ ❶ ADJ If something is **inadequate**, there is not enough of it or it is not good enough. ❑ *Supplies of food and medicines are inadequate.* ● **in|ad|equate|ly** ADV [ADV with v] ❑ *The projects were inadequately funded.* ❷ ADJ If someone feels **inadequate**, they feel that they do not have the qualities and abilities necessary to do something or to cope with life in general. ❑ *I still feel inadequate, useless and mixed up.*

❶ 형용사 불충분한, 부족한 ❑ 식량과 의약품 공급이 부족하다. ● 불충분하게, 부족하게 부사 ❑ 그 사업은 자금이 충분히 지원되지 않았다. ❷ 형용사 부적합한, 무능한 ❑ 난 여전히 무능하고, 쓸모없고, 혼란스러운 느낌이다.

Word Partnership	inadequate의 연어
N.	inadequate **funding**, inadequate **supply**, inadequate **training** ❶
ADV.	**woefully** inadequate ❶ ❷
V.	**feel** inadequate ❷

in|ad|vert|ent /ɪnədvɜrtənt/ ADJ An **inadvertent** action is one that you do without realizing what you are doing. ❑ *The government has said it was an inadvertent error.* ● **in|ad|vert|ent|ly** ADV [ADV with v] ❑ *You may have inadvertently pressed the wrong button.*

형용사 고의가 아닌, 의도하지 않은 ❑ 정부는 그것이 의도하지 않은 실수라고 했다. ● 부주의로, 잘못해서 부사 ❑ 당신이 부주의로 엉뚱한 버튼을 눌렀을지도 모릅니다.

in|ap|pro|pri|ate /ɪnəproupriɪt/ ❶ ADJ Something that is **inappropriate** is not useful or suitable for a particular situation or purpose. ❑ *There is no suggestion that clients have been sold inappropriate policies.* ❷ ADJ If you say that someone's speech or behavior in a particular situation is **inappropriate**, you are criticizing it because you think it is not suitable for that situation. [DISAPPROVAL] ❑ *I feel the remark was inappropriate for such a serious issue.*

❶ 형용사 부적당한, 어울리지 않는 ❑ 고객들에게 부적당한 보험을 팔았을 가능성은 없다. ❷ 형용사 부적절한 [탐탁찮음] ❑ 나는 그 말이 그렇게 심각한 사안에 부적절했다고 생각한다.

in|as|much as /ɪnəzmʌtʃ æz/ PHRASE You use **inasmuch as** to introduce a statement which explains something you have just said, and adds to it. [FORMAL] ❑ *We were doubly lucky inasmuch as my friend was living on the island and spoke Greek fluently.*

구 _이므로, _하는 한은 [격식체] ❑ 내 친구가 그 섬에 살고 있었고 또 그리스 어를 유창하게 해서 운이 곱으로 좋았다.

in|augu|ral /ɪnɔːgyərəl/ ADJ An **inaugural** meeting or speech is the first meeting of a new organization or the first speech by the new leader of an organization or a country. [ADJ n] ❑ *In his inaugural address, the President appealed for national unity.*

형용사 취임의 ❑ 취임 연설에서, 대통령은 국가적 결속을 호소했다.

in|augu|rate /ɪnɔːgyəreɪt/ (**inaugurates**, **inaugurating**, **inaugurated**) ◼ V-T When a new leader **is inaugurated**, they are formally given their new position at an official ceremony. [USU passive] ❑ *The new President will be inaugurated on January 20.* ● **in|augu|ra|tion** /ɪnɔːgyəreɪʃ°n/ (**inaugurations**) N-VAR ❑ *...the inauguration of the new Governor.* ◼ V-T When a new building or institution **is inaugurated**, it is declared open in a formal ceremony. [USU passive] ❑ *A new center for research on toxic waste was inaugurated today at Imperial College.* ● **in|augu|ra|tion** N-COUNT ❑ *They later attended the inauguration of the University.* ◼ V-T If you **inaugurate** a new system or service, you start it. [FORMAL] ❑ *Pan Am inaugurated the first scheduled international flight.*

◼ 타동사 취임하다 ❑ 신임 대통령이 1월 20일에 취임식을 거행할 것이다. ● 취임 가산명사 또는 불가산명사 ❑ 새 주지사의 취임 ◼ 타동사 준공식을 거행하다 ❑ 새 독성 폐기물 연구 센터가 오늘 임피리얼 대학에서 준공식을 가졌다. ● 준공식 가산명사 ❑ 그들은 후에 그 대학 준공식에 참석했다. ◼ 타동사 (새로운 서비스를) 개시하다 [격식체] ❑ 팬암 사는 최초의 국제 정기 항공편의 막을 열었다.

in box also **in-box** (**in boxes**) N-COUNT An **in box** is a shallow container used in offices to put letters and documents in before they are dealt with. [AM; BRIT **in tray**]

가산명사 미결 서류함 [미국영어; 영국영어 in tray]

inc. In written advertisements, **inc.** is an abbreviation for **including**. ❑ *The hotel offers a two-night break for £210 per person, inc. breakfast and dinner.*

including의 약자 ❑ 그 호텔은 아침 식사와 저녁 식사를 포함하여 1인당 210파운드에 2박 휴가를 제공합니다.

Inc. ◆◇◇ **Inc.** is an abbreviation for **Incorporated** when it is used after a company's name. [AM, BUSINESS] ❑ *...BP America Inc.*

유한 책임 회사, 주식회사 [미국영어, 경제] ❑ 비피 미국 주식회사

in|ca|pable /ɪnkeɪpəb°l/ ◼ ADJ Someone who is **incapable of** doing something is unable to do it. [V-link ADJ of -ing/n] ❑ *She seemed incapable of making the decision.* ◼ ADJ An **incapable** person is weak or stupid. ❑ *He lost his job for allegedly being incapable.*

◼ 형용사 -할 능력이 없는, -할 수 없는 ❑ 그녀는 그 결정을 내릴 능력이 없어 보였다. ◼ 형용사 무능한 ❑ 그는 무능해서 실직했다고들 한다.

in|car|cer|ate /ɪnkɑːrsəreɪt/ (**incarcerates**, **incarcerating**, **incarcerated**) V-T If people **are incarcerated**, they are kept in a prison or other place. [FORMAL] ❑ *They were incarcerated for the duration of the war.* ● **in|car|cera|tion** N-UNCOUNT ❑ *...her mother's incarceration in a psychiatric hospital.*

타동사 투옥되다, 감금되다 [격식체] ❑ 그들은 전쟁 기간 동안 투옥되어 있었다. ● 투옥, 감금 불가산명사 ❑ 그녀 모친의 정신 병원 감금

in|car|na|tion /ɪnkɑːrneɪʃ°n/ (**incarnations**) ◼ N-COUNT If you say that someone is the **incarnation of** a particular quality, you mean that they represent that quality or are typical of it in an extreme form. ❑ *The regime was the very incarnation of evil.* ◼ N-COUNT An **incarnation** is an instance of being alive on earth in a particular form. Some religions believe that people have several incarnations in different forms. ❑ *She began recalling a series of previous incarnations.*

◼ 가산명사 화신 ❑ 그 정권은 악의 화신 그 자체였다. ◼ 가산명사 생, 삶 ❑ 그녀는 일련의 전생에 대해 기억해 내기 시작했다.

in|cen|di|ary /ɪnsendieri, BRIT ɪnsendɪəri/ (**incendiaries**) ◼ ADJ **Incendiary** weapons or attacks are ones that cause large fires. [ADJ n] ❑ *Five incendiary devices were found in her house.* ◼ N-COUNT An **incendiary** is an incendiary bomb. ❑ *A shower of incendiaries struck the Opera House.*

◼ 형용사 불을 내는, 방화의 ❑ 다섯 개의 방화용 장비가 그녀의 집에서 발견되었다. ◼ 가산명사 소이탄 ❑ 소이탄이 오페라 하우스에 비 오듯 떨어졌다.

in|cense (**incenses**, **incensing**, **incensed**)

The noun is pronounced /ɪnsens/. The verb is pronounced /ɪnsens/.

명사는 /ɪnsens/로 발음되고, 동사는 /ɪnsens/로 발음된다.

◼ N-UNCOUNT **Incense** is a substance that is burned for its sweet smell, often as part of a religious ceremony. ◼ V-T If you say that something **incenses** you, you mean that it makes you extremely angry. ❑ *This proposal will incense conservation campaigners.* ● **in|censed** ADJ ❑ *Mom was incensed at his lack of compassion.*

◼ 불가산명사 향 ◼ 타동사 몹시 화나게 하다 ❑ 이 제안은 자연 보호 운동가들을 몹시 성나게 할 것이다. ● 매우 화난 형용사 ❑ 엄마는 그가 공감해 주지 않아 무척 화가 났다.

in|cen|tive /ɪnsentɪv/ (**incentives**) N-VAR If something is an **incentive to** do something, it encourages you to do it. ❑ *There is little or no incentive to adopt such measures.*

가산명사 또는 불가산명사 동기, 유인 ❑ 그러한 조치를 취할 동기가 거의 또는 전혀 없다.

in|ces|sant /ɪnses°nt/ ADJ An **incessant** process or activity is one that continues without stopping. ❑ *Incessant rain made conditions almost intolerable.* ● **in|ces|sant|ly** ADV ❑ *Dee talked incessantly about herself.*

형용사 끊임없는, 쉴 새 없는 ❑ 끊임없이 내리는 비로 거의 못 견딜 지경이 되었다. ● 끊임없이, 쉴 새 없이 부사 ❑ 디는 자기 자신에 대해 쉴 새 없이 말했다.

in|cest /ɪnsest/ N-UNCOUNT **Incest** is the crime of two members of the same family having sexual intercourse, for example a father and daughter, or a brother and sister. ❑ *Oedipus, according to ancient Greek legend, killed his father and committed incest with his mother.*

불가산명사 근친상간 ❑ 오디푸스는, 고대 그리스 전설에 따르면, 자기 아버지를 죽이고 어머니와 근친상간을 범했다.

inch ◆◇◇ /ɪntʃ/ (**inches**, **inching**, **inched**) ◼ N-COUNT An **inch** is an imperial unit of length, approximately equal to 2.54 centimeters. There are twelve inches in a foot. ❑ *...18 inches below the surface.* ◼ V T To **inch** somewhere means to move there very slowly and carefully, or to make something do this. ❑ *...a climber inching up a vertical wall of rock.* ❑ *He inched the van forward.* ◼ PHRASE If you say that someone looks **every inch** a certain type of person, you are emphasizing that they look exactly like that kind of person. [EMPHASIS] ❑ *He looks every inch the City businessman, with his grey suit, dark blue shirt and blue tie.*

◼ 가산명사 인치 (2.54센티미터) ❑ 표면에서 18인치 아래 ◼ 타동사/자동사 조금씩 움직이다 ● 수직의 암벽을 조금씩 올라가는 등반가 ❑ 그는 밴을 조금씩 앞으로 움직였다. ◼ 구 철두철미하게, 완벽하게 [강조] ❑ 그는 회색 정장과 암청색 셔츠와 파란 넥타이를 매고, 완벽하게 런던의 사업가로 보인다.

in|ci|dence /ɪnsɪdəns/ (**incidences**) N-VAR The **incidence of** something bad, such as a disease, is the frequency with which it occurs, or the occasions when it occurs. ❑ *The incidence of breast cancer increases with age.*

가산명사 또는 불가산명사 발생률, 빈도 ❑ 유방암 발병률은 나이가 들수록 증가한다.

in|ci|dent ◆◆◇ /ɪnsɪdənt/ (**incidents**) N-COUNT An **incident** is something that happens, often something that is unpleasant. [FORMAL] [also without N] ❑ *These incidents were the latest in a series of disputes between the two nations.*

가산명사 사건, 일어난 일 [격식체] ❑ 이 사건들은 두 나라 사이의 일련의 분쟁 중에서 가장 최근의 것이었다.

Thesaurus	*incident*의 참조어
N.	episode, event, fact, happening, occasion, occurrence

A

in|ci|den|tal /ɪnsɪdɛntᵊl/ ADJ If one thing is **incidental** to another, it is less important than the other thing or is not a major part of it. ❑ *The playing of music proved to be incidental to the main business of the evening.*

형용사 부차적인, 지엽적인 ❑ 음악 연주는 그날 저녁의 주요 행사에 부수적인 것으로 드러났다.

B

in|ci|den|tal|ly /ɪnsɪdɛntli/ **1** ADV You use **incidentally** to introduce a point which is not directly relevant to what you are saying, often a question or extra information that you have just thought of. [ADV with cl] ❑ *"I didn't ask you to come. Incidentally, why have you come?"* **2** ADV If something occurs only **incidentally**, it is less important than another thing or is not a major part of it. [ADV with v] ❑ *The letter mentioned my great-aunt and uncle only incidentally.*

1 부사 말이 난 김에, 덧붙여 말하자면 ❑ "난 너보고 와 달라고 하지 않았어. 말이 난 김에 말인데, 왜 왔어?" **2** 부사 부차적으로, 지엽적으로 ❑ 편지에서 우리 고모할머니와 할아버지는 지엽적으로만 언급되었다.

C

D

in|cin|er|ate /ɪnsɪnəreɪt/ (**incinerates, incinerating, incinerated**) V-T When authorities **incinerate** garbage or waste material, they burn it completely in a special container. ❑ *They were incinerating hazardous waste without a license.* ● **in|cin|era|tion** /ɪnsɪnəreɪʃᵊn/ N-UNCOUNT ❑ *South Pacific nations have protested against the incineration of the weapons.*

타동사 소각하다 ❑ 그들은 허가 없이 유독 산업 폐기물을 소각하고 있었다. ● 소각 불가산명사 ❑ 남태평양 국가들이 무기의 소각에 항의했다.

in|cin|era|tor /ɪnsɪnəreɪtər/ (**incinerators**) N-COUNT An **incinerator** is a special large container for burning garbage at a very high temperature.

가산명사 소각로

E

F

in|ci|sive /ɪnsaɪsɪv/ ADJ You use **incisive** to describe a person, their thoughts, or their speech when you approve of their ability to think and express their ideas clearly, briefly, and forcefully. [APPROVAL] ❑ *He is a very shrewd operator with an incisive mind.*

형용사 날카로운, 예리한; 통렬한 [마음에 듦] ❑ 그는 머리가 비상하고 아주 능란한 수단가이다.

G

in|cite /ɪnsaɪt/ (**incites, inciting, incited**) V-T If someone **incites** people **to** behave in a violent or illegal way, they encourage people to behave in that way, usually by making them excited or angry. ❑ *He incited his fellow citizens to take their revenge.* ❑ *The party agreed not to incite its supporters to violence.*

타동사 자극하다, 선동하다 ❑ 그는 자국민들이 복수를 하도록 선동하였다. ❑ 그 당은 지지자들을 선동하여 폭력을 일으키지 않기로 동의했다.

H

in|cite|ment /ɪnsaɪtmənt/ (**incitements**) N-VAR If someone is accused of **incitement to** violent or illegal behavior, they are accused of encouraging people to behave in that way. ❑ *British law forbids incitement to murder.*

가산명사 또는 불가산명사 자극, 선동 ❑ 영국법은 살인 교사를 금한다.

I

incl. **1** In written advertisements, **incl.** is an abbreviation for **including.** ❑ *...blood pressure monitor with batteries, case and 1 year warranty incl.* **2** In written advertisements, **incl.** is an abbreviation for **inclusive.** ❑ *Open 19th July-6th September, Sun to Thurs incl.*

1 including의 약자 ❑ 배터리와 가방, 1년 보증을 포함하는 혈압계 **2** inclusive의 약자 ❑ 개장 7월 19일– 9월 6일, 일요일부터 목요일까지

J

in|cli|na|tion /ɪnklɪneɪʃᵊn/ (**inclinations**) N-VAR An **inclination** is a feeling that makes you want to act in a particular way. ❑ *He had neither the time nor the inclination to think of other things.* ❑ *She showed no inclination to go.*

가산명사 또는 불가산명사 기분, 의향 ❑ 그는 다른 것을 생각할 시간도 의향도 없었다. ❑ 그녀는 갈 의향을 보이지 않았다.

K

L

Word Link	*clin ≈ leaning : de*cline, in*cline, re*cline

in|cline (**inclines, inclining, inclined**)

The verb is pronounced /ɪnklaɪn/. The noun is pronounced /ɪnklaɪn/.

동사는 /ɪnklaɪn/으로 발음되고, 명사는 /ɪnklaɪn/으로 발음된다.

M

N

1 V-T/V-I If you **incline to** think or act in a particular way, or if something **inclines** you **to** it, you are likely to think or act in that way. [FORMAL] ❑ *...the factors which incline us towards particular beliefs.* ❑ *Those who fail incline to blame the world for their failure.* **2** V-T If you **incline** your head, you bend your neck so that your head is leaning forward. [WRITTEN] ❑ *Jack inclined his head very slightly.* **3** N-COUNT An **incline** is land that slopes at an angle. [FORMAL] ❑ *He came to a halt at the edge of a steep incline.*

1 타동사/자동사 마음이 내키다; 마음이 내키게 하다 [격식체] ❑ 특정한 견해들로 마음이 기울게 하는 요인들 ❑ 실패하는 사람들은 자기들의 실패에 대해서 세상을 탓하는 경향이 있다. **2** 타동사 (머리를) 숙이다 [문어체] ❑ 잭은 머리를 아주 조금 숙였다. **3** 가산명사 비탈, 경사면 [격식체] ❑ 그는 가파른 비탈의 가장자리에서 멈췄다.

O

P

in|clined /ɪnklaɪnd/ **1** ADJ If you are **inclined to** behave in a particular way, you often behave in that way, or you want to do so. [v-link ADJ, ADJ to-inf, ADJ to n, so ADJ] ❑ *Nobody felt inclined to argue with Smith.* ❑ *He was inclined to self-pity.* **2** ADJ If you say that you are **inclined to** have a particular opinion, you mean that you hold this opinion but you are not expressing it strongly. [VAGUENESS] [v-link ADJ to-inf] ❑ *I am inclined to agree with Alan.* **3** ADJ Someone who is mathematically **inclined** or artistically **inclined**, for example, has a natural talent for mathematics or art. [adv ADJ] ❑ *...the needs of academically inclined pupils.* **4** →see also **incline**

1 형용사 –할 마음이 내키는; –하는 성향이 있는 ❑ 아무도 스미스와 언쟁할 마음이 내키지 않았다. ❑ 그는 자기 연민을 하는 경향이 있었다. **2** 형용사 –할 마음이 드는 [짐작투] ❑ 나는 앨런에게 동의할 생각이 있다. **3** 형용사 – 성향을 타고난 ❑ 학문적인 성향을 타고난 학생들의 요구

Q

R

Word Partnership	*inclined의 연어*
v.	inclined **to agree**, inclined **to believe** *someone/something*, inclined **to think 2**

S

T

in|clude ♦♦♦ /ɪnklud/ (**includes, including, included**) **1** V-T If one thing **includes** another thing, it has the other thing as one of its parts. ❑ *The trip has been extended to include a few other events.* **2** V-T If someone or something **is included in** a large group, system, or area, they become a part of it or are considered a part of it. ❑ *I had worked hard to be included in a project like this.*

1 타동사 포함하다 ❑ 그 여행은 몇 가지 다른 행사를 포함하도록 확대되었다. **2** 타동사 포함되다, 일원이 되다 ❑ 나는 이와 같은 프로젝트의 일원이 되기 위해 열심히 노력했었다.

U

in|clud|ed ♦♦◇ /ɪnkludɪd/ ADJ You use **included** to emphasize that a person or thing is part of the group of people or things that you are talking about. [EMPHASIS] [n ADJ, v-link ADJ] ❑ *All of us, myself included, had been totally committed to the Party.*

형용사 포함된 [강조] ❑ 나를 포함한 우리 모두는 그 당에 전적으로 헌신했었다.

V

W

in|clud|ing ♦♦♦ /ɪnkludɪŋ/ PREP You use **including** to introduce examples of people or things that are part of the group of people or things that you are talking about. [PREP n/-ing] ❑ *A number of international stars, including Joan Collins, are expected to attend.*

전치사 –을 포함하여 ❑ 조안 콜린스를 포함하여 많은 세계적 스타들이 참석할 것으로 예상된다.

X

in|clu|sion /ɪnkluʒᵊn/ (**inclusions**) N-VAR **Inclusion** is the act of making a person or thing part of a group or collection. ❑ *...a confident performance which justified his inclusion in the team.*

가산명사 또는 불가산명사 포함 ❑ 팀에 그를 합류시키는 것을 정당화한 자신만만한 실적

Y

in|clu|sive /ɪnklusɪv/ **1** ADJ If a price is **inclusive**, it includes all the charges connected with the goods or services offered. If a price is **inclusive of** postage and packing, it includes the charge for this. ❑ *...all prices are inclusive of delivery.* ● ADV **Inclusive** is also an adverb. [amount ADV] ❑ *The outpatient program costs $105*

1 형용사 일체를 포함한, (우송료와 포장비를) 포함한 ❑ 모든 가격에는 배송료가 포함된다. ● 부사 포함하여 ❑ 외래 환자 프로그램은 모든 것을 포함하여 하루에 105달러이다. **2** 형용사 포함하여, 함께 넣어 ❑ 또한

Z

per day, all inclusive. →see also **all-inclusive** ◨ ADJ After stating the first and last item in a set of things, you can add **inclusive** to make it clear that the items stated are included in the set. [n ADJ] ❏ *You are also invited to join us on our prayer days (this year, June 6 to June 14 inclusive).* ◧ ADJ If you describe a group or organization as **inclusive**, you mean that it allows all kinds of people to belong to it, rather than just one kind of person. ❏ *The academy is far more inclusive now than it used to be.*

우리 기도 주간에 함께 하시도록 당신을 초대합니다(올해는 6월 6일부터 6월 14일 당일까지). ◧ 형용사 (다양한 사람들에게) 개방적인 ❏ 대학이 예전보다는 훨씬 개방적이 되었다.

in|co|her|ent /ɪnkoʊhɪərənt/ ◨ ADJ If someone is **incoherent**, they are talking in a confused and unclear way. ❏ *The man was almost incoherent with fear.* ◧ ADJ If you say that something such as a policy is **incoherent**, you are criticizing it because the different parts of it do not fit together properly. [DISAPPROVAL] ❏ *...an incoherent set of objectives.*

◨ 형용사 말에 두서가 없는 ❏ 그 남자는 겁이 나서 말에 두서가 없었다. ◧ 형용사 일관성이 없는 [탐탁찮음] ❏ 일관성이 없는 일련의 목표들

in|come ♦♦◇ /ɪnkʌm/ (incomes) N-VAR A person's or organization's **income** is the money that they earn or receive, as opposed to the money that they have to spend or pay out. [BUSINESS] ❏ *Many families on low incomes will be unable to afford to buy their own home.*

가산명사 또는 불가산명사 수입, 소득 [경제] ❏ 소득이 낮은 많은 가정이 자신들의 집을 구입할 수 없을 것이다.

Word Partnership		income의 연어
ADJ.	**average** income, **fixed** income, **large/small** income, **a second** income, **steady** income, **taxable** income	
N.	**loss of** income, **source of** income	
V.	**earn *an*** income, **supplement *your*** income	

in|come sup|port N-UNCOUNT In Britain, **income support** is money that the government gives regularly to people with no income or very low incomes. ❏ *People on income support do not have to pay council tax.*

불가산명사 (영국의) 소득 지원 ❏ 소득 지원을 받는 사람들은 지방세를 내지 않아도 된다.

in|come tax (income taxes) N-VAR **Income tax** is a certain percentage of your income that you have to pay regularly to the government. [BUSINESS] ❏ *You pay income tax on all your earnings, not just your salary.*

가산명사 또는 불가산명사 소득세 [경제] ❏ 소득세는 봉급뿐 아니라 모든 소득에 대해서 낸다.

in|com|ing /ɪnkʌmɪŋ/ ◨ ADJ An **incoming** message or phone call is one that you receive. [ADJ n] ❏ *We keep a tape of incoming calls.* ◧ ADJ An **incoming** plane or passenger is one that is arriving at a place. [ADJ n] ❏ *The airport was closed for incoming flights.* ◩ ADJ An **incoming** official or government is one that has just been appointed or elected. [ADJ n] ❏ *...the problems confronting the incoming government.*

◨ 형용사 걸려 오는 ❏ 우리는 걸려 오는 전화를 녹음해 둔다. ◧ 형용사 도착하는 ❏ 공항이 도착하는 비행 편에 대해 폐쇄되었다. ◩ 형용사 신임의 ❏ 새로 들어서는 정부가 직면하는 문제들

in|com|pa|ra|ble /ɪnkɒmpərəbᵊl/ ◨ ADJ If you describe someone or something as **incomparable**, you mean that they are extremely good or impressive. ❏ *...a play starring the incomparable Edith Evans.* ◧ ADJ You use **incomparable** to emphasize that someone or something has a good quality to a great degree. [FORMAL, EMPHASIS] [ADJ n] ❏ *...an area of incomparable beauty.*

◨ 형용사 비할 바 없는 ❏ 견줄 데 없이 출중한 에디스 에반스가 주연하는 연극 ◧ 형용사 비길 데 없는 [격식체, 강조] ❏ 비길 데 없이 아름다운 지역

in|com|pat|ible /ɪnkəmpætɪbᵊl/ ◨ ADJ If one thing or person is **incompatible with** another, they are very different in important ways, and do not suit each other or agree with each other. ❏ *They feel strongly that their religion is incompatible with the political system.* ● in|com|pat|ibil|ity /ɪnkəmpætɪbɪlɪti/ N-UNCOUNT ❏ *Incompatibility between the mother's and the baby's blood groups may cause jaundice.* ◧ ADJ If one type of computer or computer system is **incompatible with** another, they cannot use the same programs or be linked up together. ❏ *This made its mini-computers incompatible with its mainframes.*

◨ 형용사 성격이 맞지 않는, 양립할 수 없는 ❏ 그들은 자기들의 종교가 정치 체제와 맞지 않는다고 절실히 느끼고 있다. ● 살병, 부적화성 불가산명사 ❏ 엄마와 아기 혈액형이 서로 맞지 않을 경우 황달을 일으킬 수도 있다. ◧ 형용사 호환되지 않는 ❏ 이것 때문에 소형 컴퓨터들이 주 컴퓨터들과 호환되지 않게 되었다.

in|com|pe|tence /ɪnkɒmpɪtəns/ N-UNCOUNT If you refer to someone's **incompetence**, you are criticizing them because they are unable to do their job or a task properly. [DISAPPROVAL] ❏ *The incompetence of government officials is appalling.*

불가산명사 무능력 [탐탁찮음] ❏ 정부 관리들의 무능력은 끔찍할 지경이다.

in|com|pe|tent /ɪnkɒmpɪtənt/ (incompetents) ADJ If you describe someone as **incompetent**, you are criticizing them because they are unable to do their job or a task properly. [DISAPPROVAL] ❏ *He wants the power to sack incompetent teachers.* ● N-COUNT An **incompetent** is someone who is incompetent. ❏ *The Prince turned furiously on his staff. "I'm surrounded by incompetents!"*

형용사 무능한 [탐탁찮음] ❏ 그는 무능한 교사들을 해고할 수 있는 권한을 원한다. ● 가산명사 무능력자 ❏ 왕자는 보좌진을 보며 화가 치밀어 성을 냈다. "내 주위엔 무능력자들만 있어!"

Word Partnership		incompetent의 연어
ADJ.	**corrupt and** incompetent, **lazy and** incompetent	
N.	incompetent **leadership**, incompetent **management**	

in|com|plete /ɪnkəmplit/ ADJ Something that is **incomplete** is not yet finished, or does not have all the parts or details that it needs. ❏ *The clearing of rubbish and drains is still incomplete.*

형용사 불완전한, 불충분한 ❏ 쓰레기와 배수관 청소가 아직 다 끝나지 않았다.

in|com|pre|hen|sible /ɪnkɒmprɪhensɪbᵊl/ ADJ Something that is **incomprehensible** is impossible to understand. ❏ *...incomprehensible mathematics puzzles.*

형용사 불가해한 ❏ 불가해한 수학 난제들

in|con|ceiv|able /ɪnkənsivəbᵊl/ ADJ If you describe something as **inconceivable**, you think it is very unlikely to happen or be true. ❏ *It was inconceivable to me that Toby could have been my attacker.*

형용사 생각조차 못 할 ❏ 토비가 나를 공격한 사람이었을 수도 있다는 것은 내겐 생각조차 못 할 일이었다.

in|con|clu|sive /ɪnkənklusɪv/ ◨ ADJ If research or evidence is **inconclusive**, it has not proved anything. ❏ *Research has so far proved inconclusive.* ◧ ADJ If a contest or conflict is **inconclusive**, it is not clear who has won or who is winning. ❏ *The past two elections were inconclusive.*

◨ 형용사 결론에 이르지 못한 ❏ 연구는 지금까지 결론에 이르지 못한 것으로 판명 났다. ◧ 형용사 확정이 나지 않은 ❏ 지난 두 선거로는 결정이 나지 않았다.

in|con|gru|ous /ɪnkɒŋgruəs/ ADJ Someone or something that is **incongruous** seems strange when considered together with other aspects of a situation. [FORMAL] ❏ *She was small and fragile and looked incongruous in an army uniform.* ● in|con|gru|ous|ly ADV ❏ *...a town of Western-style buildings perched incongruously in a high green valley.*

형용사 어울리지 않는, 부조리한 [격식체] ❏ 그녀는 작고 허약했으며 군복이 어색해 보였다. ● 어울리지 않게 부사 ❏ 높은 초록의 계곡에 어울리지 않게 자리 잡고 있는 서양식 건물이 들어선 마을

A

in|con|sid|er|ate /ɪnkənsɪdərɪt/ ADJ If you accuse someone of being **inconsiderate**, you mean that they do not take enough care over how their words or actions will affect other people. [DISAPPROVAL] ❏ *Does your partner spend hours in the bathroom in a way you feel is inconsiderate?*

형용사 사려가 없는, 경솔한 [탐탁찮음] ❏ 당신의 배우자가 너무하다 싶을 정도로 욕실에서 많은 시간을 보냅니까?

B

in|con|sist|en|cy /ɪnkənsɪstənsi/ (**inconsistencies**) **1** N-UNCOUNT If you refer to someone's **inconsistency**, you are criticizing them for not behaving in the same way every time a similar situation occurs. [DISAPPROVAL] ❏ *His worst fault was his inconsistency.* **2** N-VAR If there are **inconsistencies** in two statements, one cannot be true if the other is true. ❏ *We were asked to investigate the alleged inconsistencies in his evidence.*

1 불가산명사 일관성이 없음 [탐탁찮음] ❏ 그의 최악의 과실은 일관성이 없는 것이었다. **2** 가산명사 또는 불가산명사 모순점 ❏ 우리는 그의 증거에서 진위가 의심스러운 모순점들을 조사하도록 요청받았다.

C

in|con|sist|ent /ɪnkənsɪstənt/ **1** ADJ If you describe someone as **inconsistent**, you are criticizing them for not behaving in the same way every time a similar situation occurs. [DISAPPROVAL] ❏ *You are inconsistent and unpredictable.* **2** ADJ Someone or something that is **inconsistent** does not stay the same, being sometimes good and sometimes bad. ❏ *We had a terrific start to the season, but recently we've been inconsistent.* **3** ADJ If two statements are **inconsistent**, one cannot possibly be true if the other is true. ❏ *The evidence given in court was inconsistent with what he had previously told them.* **4** ADJ If something is **inconsistent with** a set of ideas or values, it does not fit in well with them or match them. [v-link ADJ with n] ❏ *This legislation is inconsistent with what they call Free Trade.*

1 형용사 일관성이 없는 [탐탁찮음] ❏ 당신은 일관성이 없고 예측할 수 없어요. **2** 형용사 변덕스러운, 들쭉날쭉한 ❏ 우리는 시즌을 향한 출발은 무척 좋았으나 최근에 들쭉날쭉했다. **3** 형용사 모순된 ❏ 법정에 제출한 증거가 그가 그들에게 전에 말한 것과 모순되었다. **4** 형용사 ~와 상반되는 ❏ 이 법은 소위 말하는 자유 무역과 상반된다.

D

E

F

G

in|con|ti|nence /ɪnkɒntɪnəns/ N-UNCOUNT **Incontinence** is the inability to prevent urine or feces coming out of your body. ❏ *Incontinence is not just a condition of old age.*

불가산명사 요실금 ❏ 요실금은 노인들에게만 생기는 병이 아니다.

H

in|con|ti|nent /ɪnkɒntɪnənt/ ADJ Someone who is **incontinent** is unable to prevent urine or feces coming out of their body. ❏ *His diseased bladder left him incontinent.*

형용사 요실금의 ❏ 그는 방광에 병이 생겨 요실금이 되었다.

I

in|con|ven|ience /ɪnkənviniəns/ (**inconveniences, inconveniencing, inconvenienced**) **1** N-VAR If someone or something causes **inconvenience**, they cause problems or difficulties. ❏ *We apologize for any inconvenience caused during the repairs.* **2** V-T If someone **inconveniences** you, they cause problems or difficulties for you. ❏ *He promised to be quick so as not to inconvenience them any further.*

1 가산명사 또는 불가산명사 불편 ❏ 수리하는 동안 끼친 불편에 대해서 사과드립니다. **2** 타동사 불편을 끼치다 ❏ 그는 그들에게 더 이상 불편을 끼치지 않도록 빨리 하겠다고 약속했다.

J

K

in|con|ven|ient /ɪnkənviniənt/ ADJ Something that is **inconvenient** causes problems or difficulties for someone. ❏ *Can you come at 10.30? I know it's inconvenient for you, but I must see you.*

형용사 불편한 ❏ 10시 30분에 올 수 있나요? 불편하리라는 것을 알지만 당신을 보아야겠어요.

L

in|cor|po|rate /ɪnkɔrpəreɪt/ (**incorporates, incorporating, incorporated**) **1** V-T If one thing **incorporates** another thing, it includes the other thing. [FORMAL] ❏ *The new cars will incorporate a number of major improvements.* **2** V-T If someone or something is **incorporated into** a large group, system, or area, they become a part of it. [FORMAL] ❏ *The agreement would allow the rebels to be incorporated into a new national police force.*

1 타동사 포함하다 [격식체] ❏ 새 자동차에는 많은 중요한 개선 사항들이 포함될 것이다. **2** 타동사 통합되다, 합병되다 [격식체] ❏ 그 협정은 반군들이 새 국가 경찰대로 편입되는 것을 허용할 것이다.

M

N

In|cor|po|rat|ed /ɪnkɔrpəreɪtɪd/ ADJ **Incorporated** is used after a company's name to show that it is a legally established company in the United States. [AM, BUSINESS] [n ADJ] ❏ *...MCA Incorporated.*

형용사 유한 책임의 [미국영어, 경제] ❏ 엠시에이 주식회사

O

in|cor|rect /ɪnkərɛkt/ **1** ADJ Something that is **incorrect** is wrong and untrue. ❏ *He denied that his evidence about the telephone call was incorrect.* ● **in|cor|rect|ly** ADV [ADV with v] ❏ *The magazine suggested, incorrectly, that he was planning to announce his retirement.* **2** ADJ Something that is **incorrect** is not the thing that is required or is most suitable in a particular situation. ❏ *...injuries caused by incorrect posture.* ● **in|cor|rect|ly** ADV [ADV with v] ❏ *He was told that the doors had been fitted incorrectly.*

1 형용사 부정확한, 틀린 ❏ 그는 전화 통화에 대한 자기의 증거가 틀리다는 것을 부인했다. ● 부정확하게, 틀리게 부사 ❏ 그 잡지는 그가 은퇴를 발표할 계획을 하고 있다는 내용을 시사했는데 잘못된 것이었다. **2** 형용사 적절치 않은, 올바르지 않은 ❏ 올바르지 않은 자세에 의한 부상 ● 올바르지 않게 부사 ❏ 그는 문들이 잘못 맞추어졌다고 들었다.

P

Q

R

Word Link

cresc, creas ≈ growing : crescent, decrease, increase

S

in|crease ♦♦♦ (**increases, increasing, increased**)

The verb is pronounced /ɪnkris/. The noun is pronounced /ɪnkris/.

동사는 /ɪnkris/로 발음되고, 명사는 /ɪnkris/로 발음된다.

T

1 V-T/V-I If something **increases** or you **increase** it, it becomes greater in number, level, or amount. ❏ *The population continues to increase.* ❏ *Japan's industrial output increased by 2%.* **2** N-COUNT If there is an **increase** in the number, level, or amount of something, it becomes greater. ❏ *...a sharp increase in productivity.* **3** PHRASE If something is **on the increase**, it is happening more often or becoming greater in number or intensity. ❏ *Crime is on the increase.*

1 타동사/자동사 늘다, 증가하다; 늘리다, 증가시키다 ❏ 인구가 계속 늘고 있다. ❏ 일본의 산업 생산이 2퍼센트 증가했다. **2** 가산명사 증가, 증대 ❏ 생산성의 급격한 증대 **3** 구 증가하고 있는, 증대하고 있는 ❏ 범죄가 증가하고 있다.

U

V

Thesaurus

increase의 참조어

V.	expand, extend, raise; *(ant.)* decrease, reduce **1**
N.	gain, hike, raise, rise; *(ant.)* decrease, reduction **2**

W

X

Word Partnership

increase의 연어

ADV.	increase **dramatically**, increase **rapidly** **1**
N.	**population** increase, **price** increase, **salary** increase **1**
	increase **in crime**, increase **in demand**, increase **in size**, increase **in spending**, increase **in temperature**, increase **in value** **2**
ADJ.	**big** increase, **marked** increase, **sharp** increase **1 2**

Y

Z

in|creas|ing|ly ◆◇○ /ɪnkrisɪŋli/ ADV You can use **increasingly** to indicate that a situation or quality is becoming greater in intensity or more common. ❑ *He was finding it increasingly difficult to make decisions.* ❑ *The U.S. has increasingly relied on Japanese capital.*

부사 점점, 더욱 더 ❑ 그는 결정을 내리기가 점점 어려워짐을 깨닫고 있었다. ❑ 미국은 일본 자본에 점점 더 의존해 왔다.

Word Partnership   increasingly의 연어

ADJ.	increasingly **clear**, increasingly **common**, increasingly **complex**, increasingly **difficult**, increasingly **important**, increasingly **popular**

Word Link   cred ≈ to believe : *cred*entials, *cred*ibility, in*cred*ible

in|cred|ible ◆◇○ /ɪnkrɛdɪbəl/ **1** ADJ If you describe something or someone as **incredible**, you like them very much or are impressed by them, because they are extremely or unusually good. [APPROVAL] ❑ *The wildflowers will be incredible after this rain.* ● **in|cred|ibly** /ɪncrɛdɪbli/ ADV [ADV adj/adv] ❑ *Their father was incredibly good-looking.* **2** ADJ If you say that something is **incredible**, you mean that it is very unusual or surprising, and you cannot believe it is really true, although it may be. ❑ *It seemed incredible that people would still want to play football during a war.* ● **in|cred|ibly** ADV ❑ *Incredibly, some people don't like the name.* **3** ADJ You use **incredible** to emphasize the degree, amount, or intensity of something. [EMPHASIS] ❑ *We import an incredible amount of cheese from the Continent.* ● **in|cred|ibly** ADV [ADV adj/adv] ❑ *It was incredibly hard work.*

1 형용사 놀랄 정도로 멋진 [마음에 듦] ❑ 이 비가 그치면 야생화가 엄청나게 멋질 것이다. ● 놀랄 정도로 부사 ❑ 그들의 아버지는 놀랄 정도로 미남이었다. **2** 형용사 믿어지지 않는 ❑ 사람들이 전쟁 중에도 미식축구를 하기를 원한다는 것이 믿어지지 않아 보였다. ● 믿을 수 없을 만큼 부사 ❑ 믿을 수 없게도, 일부 사람들은 그 이름을 좋아하지 않는다. **3** 형용사 엄청난 [강조] ❑ 우리는 유럽 대륙으로부터 엄청난 양의 치즈를 수입한다. ● 엄청나게 부사 ❑ 그것은 엄청나게 힘든 일이었다.

Word Partnership   incredible의 연어

N.	incredible **discovery**, incredible **prices** **1**
ADV.	incredible **experience** **1**-**3**
	absolutely incredible **1**-**3**

in|credu|lous /ɪnkrɛdʒələs/ ADJ If someone is **incredulous**, they are unable to believe something because it is very surprising or shocking. ❑ *"He made you do it?" Her voice was incredulous.* ● **in|credu|lous|ly** ADV [ADV with v] ❑ *"You told Pete?" Rachel said incredulously. "I can't believe it!"*

형용사 쉽사리 믿지 않는, 의심하는 듯한 ❑ "그가 그것을 하도록 시켰나요?" 그녀의 목소리가 의심하는 듯했다. ● 믿어지지 않는 듯이 부사 ❑ "피트에게 말했니?"라고 레이첼이 믿어지지 않는 듯이 말했다. "믿을 수 없어."

in|cre|ment /ɪnkrɪmənt/ (**increments**) **1** N-COUNT An **increment in** something or an increase in the value of something is an amount by which it increases. [FORMAL] ❑ *The average yearly increment in labor productivity in industry was 4.5 per cent.* **2** N-COUNT An **increment** is an amount by which your salary automatically increases after a fixed period of time. [FORMAL] ❑ *Many teachers qualify for an annual increment.*

1 가산명사 증대, 증가 [격식체] ❑ 산업의 노동 생산성 연간 평균 증가율은 4.5퍼센트였다. **2** 가산명사 봉급 인상액 [격식체] ❑ 많은 선생님들이 연간 봉급 인상을 받을 자격이 있다.

in|crimi|nate /ɪnkrɪmɪneɪt/ (**incriminates, incriminating, incriminated**) V-T If something **incriminates** you, it suggests that you are responsible for something bad, especially a crime. ❑ *He claimed that the drugs had been planted to incriminate him.* ● **in|crimi|nat|ing** ADJ ❑ *Police had reportedly searched his flat and found incriminating evidence.*

타동사 죄를 씌우다 ❑ 그는 누군가 자기에게 죄를 씌우기 위해 마약을 자기 소지품에 숨겼다고 주장했다. ● 혐의를 입증하는 형용사 ❑ 보도에 따르면 경찰이 그의 아파트를 수색해서 혐의를 입증하는 증거를 발견했다고 한다.

in|cu|bate /ɪnkyəbeɪt, ɪŋ/ (**incubates, incubating, incubated**) V-T/V-I When birds **incubate** their eggs or when they **incubate**, they keep the eggs warm until the baby birds come out. ❑ *The birds returned to their nests and continued to incubate the eggs.* ● **in|cu|ba|tion** /ɪnkyəbeɪʃᵊn, ɪŋ/ N-UNCOUNT ❑ *Male albatrosses share in the incubation of eggs.*

타동사/자동사 (알을) 품다 ❑ 새들이 자기들 둥지로 돌아와서 계속 알을 품었다. ● 알을 품음 불가산명사 ❑ 수컷 신천옹은 암컷과 함께 알을 품는다.

in|cum|bent /ɪnkʌmbənt/ (**incumbents**) **1** N-COUNT An **incumbent** is someone who holds an official post at a particular time. [FORMAL] ❑ *In general, incumbents have a 94 per cent chance of being re-elected.* ● **Incumbent** is also an adjective. [ADJ n] ❑ *...the only candidate who defeated an incumbent senator.* **2** ADJ If it is **incumbent upon** you **to** do something, it is your duty or responsibility to do it. [FORMAL] [it v-link ADJ upon/on n to-inf] ❑ *It is incumbent upon all of us as loyal citizens to make an extra effort.*

1 가산명사 재직자, 현직자 [격식체] ❑ 일반적으로 현직자가 다시 선출될 가능성이 94퍼센트이다. ● 형용사의 현직 상원 의원을 물리친 유일한 후보 **2** 형용사 의무인 [격식체] ❑ 특별한 노력을 더 하는 것이 충성된 국민으로서 우리 모두의 의무이다.

in|cur /ɪnkɜr/ (**incurs, incurring, incurred**) V-T If you **incur** something unpleasant, it happens to you because of something you have done. [WRITTEN] ❑ *The government had also incurred huge debts.*

타동사 초래하다 [문어체] ❑ 정부는 엄청난 부채 또한 지게 되었다.

Word Link   able ≈ able to be : in*cur*able, infl*at*able, port*able*

in|cur|able /ɪnkyʊərəbᵊl/ **1** ADJ If someone has an **incurable** disease, they cannot be cured of it. ❑ *He is suffering from an incurable skin disease.* ● **in|cur|ably** /ɪnkyʊərəbli/ ADV [ADV adj] ❑ *...youngsters who are disabled, or incurably ill.* **2** ADJ You can use **incurable** to indicate that someone has a particular quality or attitude and will not change. [ADJ n] ❑ *Poor old William is an incurable romantic.* ● **in|cur|ably** ADV [ADV adj] ❑ *I know you think I'm incurably nosey, but the truth is I'm concerned about you.*

1 형용사 불치의 ❑ 그는 불치의 피부병에 걸려 있다. ● 치유할 수 없게 부사 ❑ 불구이거나 불치병에 걸린 아이들 **2** 형용사 고치기 어려운, 구제 불능의 ❑ 불쌍한 윌리엄 노인은 못 말리게 낭만적인 사람이다. ● 구제 불능의 만큼, 못 말리게 부사 ❑ 네가 나를 못 말리게 참견이 심하다고 생각한다는 것을 알고 있지만 사실은 네가 걱정이 돼서 그래.

in|debt|ed /ɪndɛtɪd/ **1** ADJ If you say that you are **indebted to** someone for something, you mean that you are very grateful to them for something. [v-link ADJ to n] ❑ *I am deeply indebted to him for his help.* **2** ADJ **Indebted** countries, organizations, or people are ones that owe money to other countries, organizations, or people. ❑ *America's treasury secretary identified the most heavily indebted countries.*

1 형용사 ~에게 신세를 진, ~의 덕택인 ❑ 나는 그에게 도움을 많이 받았다. **2** 형용사 부채가 있는 ❑ 미국 재무 장관이 가장 부채가 많은 국가들을 밝혔다.

in|de|cen|cy /ɪndisᵊnsi/ **1** N-UNCOUNT If you talk about the **indecency** of something or someone, you are indicating that you find them morally or sexually offensive. ❑ *...the indecency of their language.* **2** N-UNCOUNT In law, an act of **indecency** is an illegal sexual act. ❑ *They were found guilty of acts of gross indecency.*

1 불가산명사 무례; 외설 ❑ 그들 언어의 추잡함 **2** 불가산명사 외설죄 ❑ 그들은 끔찍한 외설죄를 저지른 것으로 밝혀졌다.

a b c d e f g h i j k l m n o p q r s t u v w x y z

A

in|de|cent /ɪndiːsᵊnt/ **1** ADJ If you describe something as **indecent**, you mean that it is shocking and offensive, usually because it relates to sex or nakedness. ❑ *He accused Mrs. Moore of making an indecent suggestion.* ● **in|de|cent|ly** ADV ❑ *...an indecently short skirt.* **2** ADJ If you describe the speed or amount of something as **indecent**, you are indicating, often in a humorous way, that it is much quicker or larger than is usual or desirable. ❑ *The opposition says the legislation was drafted with indecent haste.* ● **in|de|cent|ly** ADV ❑ *...an indecently large office.*

1 형용사 상스러운, 외설의 ❑ 그는 무어 부인을 외설적인 제안을 했다고 고소했다. ● 상스럽게 부사 ❑ 상스러울 정도로 짧은 스커트 **2** 형용사 터무니없는 ❑ 야당은 그 법이 터무니없이 성급하게 초안이 작성되었다고 말한다. ● 터무니없이 부사 ❑ 터무니없이 큰 사무실

B

C

in|de|ci|sion /ɪndɪsɪʒᵊn/ N-UNCOUNT If you say that someone suffers from **indecision**, you mean that they find it very difficult to make decisions. ❑ *After months of indecision, the government gave the plan the go-ahead on Monday.*

불가산명사 우유부단, 주저 ❑ 몇 달 동안의 주저 끝에 정부는 월요일에 그 계획을 허가했다.

D

in|de|ci|sive /ɪndɪsaɪsɪv/ **1** ADJ If you say that someone is **indecisive**, you mean that they find it very difficult to make decisions. ❑ *He was criticized as a weak and indecisive leader.* **2** ADJ An **indecisive** result in a contest or election is one which is not clear or definite. ❑ *The outcome of the battle was indecisive.*

1 형용사 우유부단한 ❑ 그는 나약하고 우유부단한 지도자라고 비난받았다. **2** 형용사 뚜렷하지 않은, 결정적이지 않은 ❑ 전투의 결과는 뚜렷하지 않았다.

E

F

in|deed ♦♦◇ /ɪndiːd/ **1** ADV You use **indeed** to confirm or agree with something that has just been said. [EMPHASIS] ❑ *Later, he admitted that the payments had indeed been made.* ❑ *"Did you know him?" — "I did indeed."* **2** ADV You use **indeed** to introduce a further comment or statement which strengthens the point you have already made. [EMPHASIS] [ADV with cl] ❑ *We have nothing against diversity; indeed, we want more of it.* **3** ADV You use **indeed** at the end of a clause to give extra force to the word "very," or to emphasize a particular word. [EMPHASIS] [adj ADV] ❑ *The engine began to sound very loud indeed.*

1 부사 실로, 참으로 [강조] ❑ 나중에 그는 실제로 지불이 되었다고 시인했다. ❑ "그를 알고 있었나요?" "그렇고 말고요." **2** 부사 게다가, 그뿐 아니라 [강조] ❑ 우리는 다양성에 거부감이 없으며, 그뿐 아니라 더 많은 다양성을 원한다. **3** 부사 정말, 대단히 [강조] ❑ 엔진이 정말 크게 소리를 내기 시작했다.

G

H

in|defi|nite /ɪndɛfɪnɪt/ **1** ADJ If you describe a situation or period as **indefinite**, you mean that people have not decided when it will end. ❑ *The trial was adjourned for an indefinite period.* **2** ADJ Something that is **indefinite** is not exact or clear. ❑ *...at some indefinite time in the future.*

1 형용사 불명확한, 정해지지 않은 ❑ 재판이 무기한 연기되었다. **2** 형용사 막연한 ❑ 미래의 어떤 막연한 시기에

I

in|defi|nite ar|ti|cle (indefinite articles) N-COUNT The words "a" and "an" are sometimes called **the indefinite article**.

가산명사 부정 관사

J

in|defi|nite|ly /ɪndɛfɪnɪtli/ ADV If a situation will continue **indefinitely**, it will continue for ever or until someone decides to change it or end it. [ADV with v] ❑ *The visit has now been postponed indefinitely.*

부사 무기한으로 ❑ 방문은 이제 무기한으로 연기되었다.

K

in|dem|ni|fy /ɪndɛmnɪfaɪ/ (indemnifies, indemnifying, indemnified) V-T To **indemnify** someone against something bad happening means to promise to protect them, especially financially, if it happens. [FORMAL] ❑ *They agreed to indemnify the taxpayers against any loss.*

타동사 보상하다; 배상하다 [격식체] ❑ 그들은 납세자들의 모든 손실에 대해 배상하기로 동의했다.

L

in|dem|ni|ty /ɪndɛmnɪti/ N-UNCOUNT If something provides **indemnity**, it provides insurance or protection against damage or loss. [FORMAL] ❑ *Political exiles had not been given indemnity from prosecution.*

불가산명사 배상; 보장 [격식체] ❑ 정치적 망명자들은 기소 면책 보장을 받지 못했었다.

M

Word Link	ence ≈ state, condition : dependence, excellence, independence

N

in|de|pend|ence ♦♦◇ /ɪndɪpɛndəns/ **1** N-UNCOUNT If a country has or gains **independence**, it has its own government and is not ruled by any other country. ❑ *In 1816, Argentina declared its independence from Spain.* **2** N-UNCOUNT Someone's **independence** is the fact that they do not rely on other people. ❑ *He was afraid of losing his independence.*

1 불가산명사 독립, 자주 ❑ 1816년에 아르헨티나는 스페인으로부터 독립을 선언했다. **2** 불가산명사 독립심, 자립정신 ❑ 그는 자기의 독립심을 잃을까 두려워했다.

O

Word Partnership	independence의 연어
N.	**a struggle for** independence **1**
ADJ.	**economic/financial** independence **1** **2**
V.	**fight for** independence, **gain** independence **1**

P

Q

in|de|pend|ent ♦♦♦ /ɪndɪpɛndənt/ (independents) **1** ADJ If one thing or person is **independent of** another, they are separate and not connected, so the first one is not affected or influenced by the second. ❑ *Your questions should be independent of each other.* ❑ *We're going independent from the university and setting up our own group.* ● **in|de|pend|ent|ly** ADV ❑ *...several people working independently in different areas of the world.* **2** ADJ If someone is **independent**, they do not need help or money from anyone else. ❑ *Phil was now much more independent of his parents.* ● **in|de|pend|ent|ly** ADV ❑ *...helping disabled students to live and study as independently as possible.* **3** ADJ **Independent** countries and states are not ruled by other countries but have their own government. ❑ *Papua New Guinea became independent from Australia in 1975.* **4** ADJ An **independent** organization or other body is one that controls its own finances and operations, rather than being controlled by someone else. [ADJ n] ❑ *...an independent television station.* **5** ADJ An **independent** school does not receive money from the government or local council, but from the fees paid by its students' parents or from charities. [BRIT] ❑ *He taught chemistry at a leading independent school.* **6** ADJ An **independent** inquiry or opinion is one that involves people who are not connected with a particular situation, and should therefore be fair. [ADJ n] ❑ *The government ordered an independent inquiry into the affair.* **7** ADJ An **independent** politician is one who does not represent any political party. ❑ *There's been a late surge of support for an independent candidate.* ● N-COUNT An **independent** is an independent politician. ❑ *Mr. Vassiliou, standing as an independent, succeeded in convincing a significant number of voters of his argument.*

R

S

T

U

V

W

1 형용사 독자적인, 독립적인 ❑ 당신의 질문들은 서로 별개여야 한다. ❑ 우리는 대학교로부터 독립하여 우리 자신의 그룹을 세우려고 한다. ● 독자적으로 부사 ❑ 세계 다른 지역에서 독자적으로 일하고 있는 몇몇 사람들 **2** 형용사 자활하는, 독립한 ❑ 필은 이제 부모로부터 한층 더 독립한 상태였다. ● 독립적으로 부사 ❑ 장애인 학생들이 가능한 한 독립적으로 생활하고 공부할 수 있도록 도와주는 **3** 형용사 독립한, 자주의 ❑ 파푸아뉴기니는 1975년에 호주로부터 독립되었다. **4** 형용사 독립의 ❑ 독립 텔레비전 방송국 (정부 보조가 없는) 사립의 [영국영어] ❑ 그는 일류 사립학교에서 화학을 가르쳤다. **6** 형용사 공정한, 독립적인 ❑ 정부는 그 사건에 대한 공정한 조사를 명령했다. **7** 형용사 무소속의 ❑ 무소속 후보에 대한 지지가 막판에 급증했다. ● 가산명사 무소속 정치인 ❑ 무소속 후보로 출마하는 바실리우 씨는 상당수의 유권자들에게 자기의 주장을 납득시키는 데 성공했다.

X

in|dex ♦◇◇ /ɪndɛks/ (indices, indexes, indexing, indexed)

The usual plural is **indexes**, but the form **indices** can be used for meaning **1**.

대개 복수형은 indexes이지만, indices를 **1** 의미로 쓸 수 있다.

Y

1 N-COUNT An **index** is a system by which changes in the value of something and the rate at which it changes can be recorded, measured, or interpreted. ❑ *The UK retail price index for October is expected to show an increase of 0.8 per cent.*

1 가산명사 지수 ❑ 영국의 10월 소매 물가 지수는 0.8퍼센트의 증가를 보일 것으로 예상된다. **2** 가산명사 색인, 찾아보기 ❑ 특별한 주제별 색인

Z

② N-COUNT An **index** is an alphabetical list that is printed at the back of a book and tells you on which pages important topics are referred to. ❑ *There's even a special subject index.* ③ V-T If you **index** a book or a collection of information, you make an alphabetical list of the items in it. ❑ *A quarter of this vast archive has been indexed and made accessible to researchers.* ④ V-T If a quantity or value **is indexed to** another, a system is arranged so that it increases or decreases whenever the other one increases or decreases. [usu passive] ❑ *Minimum pensions and wages are to be indexed to inflation.* ⑤ →see also **card index**

index-linked ADJ **Index-linked** interest rates or payments change as inflation or the cost of living changes. [mainly BRIT] ❑ *...civil servants and politicians whose own pensions are index linked.*

in|di|cate ◆◇◇ /ɪ́ndɪkeɪt/ (**indicates, indicating, indicated**) ① V-T If one thing **indicates** another, the first thing shows that the second is true or exists. ❑ *A survey of retired people has indicated that most are independent and enjoying life.* ❑ *Our vote today indicates a change in United States policy.* ② V-T If you **indicate** an opinion, an intention, or a fact, you mention it in an indirect way. ❑ *Mr. Rivers has indicated that he may resign.* ③ V-T If you **indicate** something to someone, you show them where it is, especially by pointing to it. [FORMAL] ❑ *He indicated a chair. "Sit down."* ④ V-T If one thing **indicates** something else, it is a sign of that thing. ❑ *Dreams can help indicate your true feelings.* ⑤ V-T If a technical instrument **indicates** something, it shows a measurement or reading. ❑ *The needles that indicate your height are at the top right-hand corner.* ⑥ V-T/V-I When drivers **indicate**, they make lights flash on one side of their vehicle to show that they are going to turn in that direction. [mainly BRIT; AM **signal**] ❑ *He told us when to indicate and when to change gear.*

Thesaurus   *indicate*의 참조어
v.   demonstrate, hint, mean, reveal, show ① ②

Word Partnership   *indicate*의 연어
N.   **polls** indicate, **records** indicate, **reports** indicate, **results** indicate, **statistics** indicate, **studies** indicate, **surveys** indicate ①
       indicate **a change in** *something* ① ②

in|di|ca|tion ◆◇◇ /ɪ̀ndɪkéɪʃⁿn/ (**indications**) N-VAR An **indication** is a sign which suggests, for example, what people are thinking or feeling. ❑ *He gave no indication that he was ready to compromise.*

Word Partnership   *indication*의 연어
ADJ.   **a clear** indication, **a strong** indication
v.   **give an** indication

in|dica|tive /ɪndɪ́kətɪv/ ADJ If one thing is **indicative of** another, it suggests what the other thing is likely to be. [FORMAL] ❑ *His action is indicative of growing concern about the shortage of skilled labour.*

in|di|ca|tor /ɪ́ndɪkeɪtər/ (**indicators**) ① N-COUNT An **indicator** is a measurement or value which gives you an idea of what something is like. ❑ *...vital economic indicators, such as inflation, growth and the trade gap.* ② N-COUNT A car's **indicators** are the flashing lights that tell you when it is going to turn left or right. [mainly BRIT; AM usually **turn signals**] ❑ *I flashed the indicator, ignored the mirror and spun the wheel.*

Word Partnership   *indicator*의 연어
ADJ.   **economic** indicator, **good** indicator, **important** indicator, **reliable** indicator ①

in|di|ces /ɪ́ndɪsiz/ **Indices** is a plural form of **index**.

in|dict /ɪndáɪt/ (**indicts, indicting, indicted**) V-T If someone **is indicted for** a crime, they are officially charged with it. [mainly AM, LEGAL] [usu passive] ❑ *He was later indicted on corruption charges.*

in|dict|ment /ɪndáɪtmənt/ (**indictments**) ① N-COUNT If you say that one thing is **an indictment of** another thing, you mean that it shows how bad the other thing is. ❑ *It's a sad indictment of society that policeman are regarded as easy targets by thugs.* ② N-VAR An **indictment** is a formal accusation that someone has committed a crime. [mainly AM, LEGAL] ❑ *Prosecutors may soon seek an indictment on racketeering and fraud charges.*

in|die /ɪ́ndi/ (**indies**) ① ADJ **Indie** music refers to rock or pop music produced by new bands working with small, independent record companies. [ADJ n] ❑ *...a multi-racial indie band.* ● N-COUNT An **indie** is an indie band or record company. ❑ *The fact is that the indies are selling a lot more records than the majors.* ② ADJ **Indie** films are produced by small independent companies rather than by major studios. [ADJ n] ❑ *With a role in the indie movie Happiness, her career is now swimming along.* ● N-COUNT An **indie** is an indie film or film company. ❑ *The indies have been complaining about lack of access to the BBC.*

in|dif|fer|ence /ɪndɪ́fərəns/ N-UNCOUNT If you accuse someone of **indifference to** something, you mean that they have a complete lack of interest in it. ❑ *...his callous indifference to the plight of his son.*

in|dif|fer|ent /ɪndɪ́fərənt/ ① ADJ If you accuse someone of being **indifferent to** something, you mean that they have a complete lack of interest in it. ❑ *People*

있다. ③ 타동사 색인을 달다 ❑ 이 거대한 수집 문서의 4분의 1에 색인을 달아서 연구자들이 이용할 수 있게 했다. ④ 타동사 -에 연동되다 ❑ 최소 연금과 임금은 인플레에 연동되어져야 한다.

형용사 물가 지수 연동제의 [주로 영국영어]
❑ 자신들의 연금은 물가 지수에 연동되는 공무원과 정치인들

① 타동사 나타내다, 보여 주다 ❑ 은퇴한 사람들을 조사해 보니 대부분이 독립적으로 즐거운 삶을 살고 있는 것으로 나타났다. ❑ 오늘 우리의 투표는 미국 정책의 변화를 보여 준다. ② 타동사 암시하다, 은연 중 나타내다 ❑ 리버스 씨는 사임할 수도 있다는 것을 암시했다. ③ 타동사 가리키다 [격식체] ❑ 그는 의자를 가리켰다. "앉으시지요." ④ 타동사 -의 징조를 나타내다 ❑ 꿈은 당신의 진짜 감정을 보여주는 데 도움이 될 수 있다. ⑤ 타동사 표시하다 ❑ 당신의 키를 표시해 주는 바늘이 오른쪽 모서리 위에 있다. ⑥ 타동사/자동사 방향 지시등을 켜다 [주로 영국영어; 미국영어 signal] ❑ 그는 우리에게 언제 방향 지시등을 켜고 언제 기어를 바꾸는지 말해 주었다.

가산명사 또는 불가산명사 암시, 표시 ❑ 그는 타협할 준비가 되어 있다는 표시를 하지 않았다.

형용사 -을 표시하는, -을 암시하는 [격식체] ❑ 그의 조치는 숙련공 부족에 대해 점점 커져 가는 우려를 표시한 것이다.

① 가산명사 지표 ❑ 인플레, 성장, 무역 수지 적자와 같은 중요한 경제 지표들 ② 가산명사 방향 지시등 [주로 영국영어; 미국영어 대개 turn signals] ❑ 나는 방향 지시등을 켜고, 후사경을 보지 않고 핸들을 돌렸다.

index의 복수형

타동사 기소되다 [주로 미국영어, 법률] ❑ 그는 나중에 부패 혐의로 기소되었다.

① 가산명사 고발, 비난 ❑ 폭력 범죄자들이 경찰을 쉬운 표적으로 삼는다는 것은 통탄스러운 사회상을 고발하는 것과 마찬가지이다. ② 가산명사 또는 불가산명사 기소, 고발 [주로 미국영어, 법률] ❑ 검찰은 아마도 공갈과 사기 혐의로 곧 기소하려고 할 것이다.

① 형용사 인디 (음악) ❑ 다인종 인디 밴드 ● 가산명사 인디 밴드; 인디 음반사 ❑ 사실은 인디 음반사들이 거대 음반사들보다 훨씬 장사를 잘하고 있다. ② 형용사 독립 영화사가 만든 ❑ 독립 영화 해피니스에서 배역을 맡은 그녀는 이제 잘나가는 배우이다. ● 가산명사 독립 영화; 독립 영화사 ❑ 독립 영화사들은 비비시를 이용하기 어려운 것을 불평해 왔다.

불가산명사 무관심 ❑ 아들이 처한 곤경에 대한 그의 냉담한 무관심

① 형용사 무관심한 ❑ 사람들은 다른 사람들의 고통에 무관심하게 되었다. ● 무관심하게 부사 ❑ "중요한 것은

have become indifferent to the suffering of others. ● **in|dif|fer|ent|ly** ADV [ADV after v] ❑ "Not that it matters," said Tench indifferently. ◻2 ADJ If you describe something or someone as **indifferent**, you mean that their standard or quality is not very good, and often quite bad. ❑ She had starred in several very indifferent movies. ● **in|dif|fer|ent|ly** ADV [ADV with v] ❑ ...an eight-year-old girl who reads tolerably and writes indifferently.

in|dig|enous /ɪndɪdʒɪnəs/ ADJ **Indigenous** people or things belong to the country in which they are found, rather than coming there or being brought there from another country. [FORMAL] ❑ ...the country's indigenous population.

in|di|ges|tion /ɪndɪdʒestʃ⁰n, -daɪ-/ N-UNCOUNT If you have **indigestion**, you have pains in your stomach and chest that are caused by difficulties in digesting food.

Word Link	dign ≈ proper, worthy : dignity, dignitary, indignant

in|dig|nant /ɪndɪgnənt/ ADJ If you are **indignant**, you are shocked and angry, because you think that something is unjust or unfair. ❑ He is indignant at suggestions that they were secret agents. ❑ MPs were indignant that the government had not consulted them. ● **in|dig|nant|ly** ADV [ADV with v] ❑ "That is not true," Erica said indignantly.

in|dig|na|tion /ɪndɪgneɪʃ⁰n/ N-UNCOUNT **Indignation** is the feeling of shock and anger which you have when you think that something is unjust or unfair. ❑ She was filled with indignation at the conditions under which miners were forced to work.

in|dig|nity /ɪndɪgnɪti/ (**indignities**) N-VAR If you talk about **the indignity of** doing something, you mean that it makes you feel embarrassed or unimportant. [FORMAL] ❑ Later, he suffered the indignity of having to flee angry protesters.

in|di|rect /ɪndaɪrekt, -dɪr-/ ◻1 ADJ An **indirect** result or effect is not caused immediately and obviously by a thing or person, but happens because of something else that they have done. ❑ Businesses are feeling the indirect effects from the recession that's going on elsewhere. ● **in|di|rect|ly** ADV ❑ Drugs are indirectly responsible for the violence. ◻2 ADJ An **indirect** route or journey does not use the shortest or easiest way between two places. ❑ The goods went by a rather indirect route. ◻3 ADJ **Indirect** remarks and information suggest something or refer to it, without actually mentioning it or stating it clearly. ❑ His remarks amounted to an indirect appeal for economic aid. ● **in|di|rect|ly** ADV [ADV with v] ❑ He referred indirectly to the territorial dispute.

in|di|rect dis|course N-UNCOUNT **Indirect discourse** is speech which tells you what someone said, but does not use the person's actual words; for example, "They said you didn't like it," "I asked him what his plans were," and "Citizens complained about the smoke."

in|di|rect ob|ject (**indirect objects**) N-COUNT An **indirect object** is an object which is used with a transitive verb to indicate who benefits from an action or gets something as a result. For example, in "She gave him her address," "him" is the indirect object. Compare **direct object**.

in|di|rect speech N-UNCOUNT **Indirect speech** is the same as **indirect discourse**. [mainly BRIT]

in|dis|crimi|nate /ɪndɪskrɪmɪnɪt/ ADJ If you describe an action as **indiscriminate**, you are critical of it because it does not involve any careful thought or choice. [DISAPPROVAL] ❑ The indiscriminate use of fertilizers is damaging to the environment. ● **in|dis|crimi|nate|ly** ADV ❑ The men opened fire indiscriminately.

in|dis|pen|sable /ɪndɪspensəb⁰l/ ADJ If you say that someone or something is **indispensable**, you mean that they are absolutely essential and other people or things cannot function without them. ❑ She was becoming indispensable to him.

in|dis|put|able /ɪndɪspyutəb⁰l/ ADJ If you say that something is **indisputable**, you are emphasizing that it is true and cannot be shown to be untrue. [EMPHASIS] ❑ It is indisputable that birds in the UK are harboring this illness.

in|dis|tin|guish|able /ɪndɪstɪŋgwɪʃəb⁰l/ ADJ If one thing is **indistinguishable from** another, the two things are so similar that it is difficult to know which is which. ❑ Replica weapons are indistinguishable from the real thing.

in|di|vid|ual ◆◆◇ /ɪndɪvɪdʒu⁰l/ (**individuals**) ◻1 ADJ **Individual** means relating to one person or thing, rather than to a large group. [ADJ n] ❑ ...waiting for the group to decide rather than making individual decisions. ● **in|di|vid|ual|ly** ADV ❑ ...cheeses which come in individually wrapped segments. ◻2 N-COUNT An **individual** is a person. ❑ ...anonymous individuals who are doing good things within our community. ◻3 ADJ If you describe someone or something as **individual**, you mean that you admire them because they are very unusual and do not try to imitate other people or things. [APPROVAL] ❑ It was really all part of her very individual personality.

Thesaurus	individual의 참조어	
N.	human being, person ◻2	
ADJ.	distinctive, original, unique ◻3	

in|di|vidu|al|ity /ɪndɪvɪdʒuælɪti/ N-UNCOUNT The **individuality** of a person or thing consists of the qualities that make them different from other people or things. ❑ People should be free to express their individuality.

in|di|vidu|al|ize /ɪndɪvɪdʒuəlaɪz/ (**individualizes, individualizing, individualized**) V-T To **individualize** a thing or person means to make them different from other things or people and to give them a recognizable identity. [FORMAL; BRIT also **individualise**] ❑ You can individualize a document by adding comments in the margins. ● **in|di|vidu|al|ized** ADJ ❑ Doctors feel that a more individualized approach to patients should now be adopted.

그게 아니야."라고 텐치는 무관심하게 말했다. ◻2 형용사 썩 좋지 않은, 그저 그런 ❑ 그녀는 그저 그런 영화 몇 편에서 주연을 했었다. ● 썩 좋지 않게, 그저 그렇게 부사 ❑ 어지간히 읽을 줄은 알지만, 쓰는 것은 그저 그런 여덟 살짜리 여자 아이

형용사 토착의 [격식체] ❑ 그 나라의 토착 인구

불가산명사 소화 불량

형용사 분노한, 분개한 ❑ 그는 그들이 비밀 요원이었다는 시사하는 말들을 대해 분개하고 있다. ❑ 하원 의원들은 정부가 자신들과 상의하지 않았다는 것에 분개했다. ● 분노하여, 분개하여 부사 ❑ "그것은 사실이 아니야."라고 에리카는 분개하여 말했다.

불가산명사 분개, 분노 ❑ 그녀는 광부들이 일해야 했던 작업 환경에 대한 분노심이 가득했다.

가산명사 또는 불가산명사 모욕, 수모 [격식체] ❑ 나중에 그는 성난 시위자들로부터 달아나야 하는 수모를 겪었다.

◻1 형용사 간접적인 ❑ 사업들은 다른 곳에서 진행되고 있는 불경기의 간접적인 영향을 받고 있다. ● 간접적으로 부사 ❑ 마약은 폭력의 간접적인 원인이 된다. ◻2 형용사 (길을) 돌아가는 ❑ 상품은 다소 돌아가는 경로로 배송되었다. ◻3 형용사 우회적인, 직접적이 아닌 ❑ 그의 말은 결국 경제적 원조를 우회적으로 요청하는 것과 같았다. ● 우회적으로 부사 ❑ 그는 영토 분쟁을 우회적으로 언급했다.

불가산명사 간접 화법

가산명사 간접 목적어

불가산명사 간접 화법 [주로 영국영어]

형용사 분별없는 [탐탁찮음] ❑ 무분별한 비료 사용이 환경에 해를 주고 있다. ● 무분별하게 부사 ❑ 그 남자들은 무차별 사격을 개시했다.

형용사 필수의 ❑ 그녀는 그에게 있어서 없어서는 안 되는 사람이 되고 있었다.

형용사 의문의 여지가 없는 [강조] ❑ 영국의 새들이 이 병을 가지고 있다는 것은 의문의 여지가 없다.

형용사 분간할 수 없는 ❑ 모형 무기는 진짜와 구별할 수 없다.

◻1 형용사 개인의 ❑ 개개인의 결정보다는 그룹이 결정하기를 기다림 ● 개별적으로 부사 ❑ 조각이 따로따로 포장된 치즈 ◻2 가산명사 개인 ❑ 우리 공동체 안에서 선행을 하고 있는 이름 모를 개개인들 ◻3 형용사 개성 있는 [마음에 듦] ❑ 그것은 사실 그녀의 독특한 개성의 일부분이었다.

불가산명사 개성 ❑ 사람들에게는 자신들의 개성을 표출할 자유가 있어야 한다.

타동사 -을 차별화하다, -에 개성을 주다 [격식체; 영국영어 individualise] ❑ 여백에 주석을 닮으로써 문서를 자신의 것으로 만들 수 있다. ● 개별화 된 형용사 ❑ 이제는 각 환자들을 개인으로 대우하는 방식이 도입되어야 한다고 의사들은 생각한다.

in|door /ˈɪndɔr/ ADJ **Indoor** activities or things are ones that happen or are used inside a building and not outside. [ADJ n] ❑ *No smoking in any indoor facilities.*

형용사 실내의 ❑ 모든 건물 실내에서는 금연

in|doors /ˈɪndɔrz/ ADV If something happens **indoors**, it happens inside a building. ❑ *I think perhaps we should go indoors.*

부사 건물 안에서 ❑ 실내로 들어가는 것이 좋을 것 같다.

in|duce /ɪnˈdus, BRIT ɪnˈdjuːs/ (induces, inducing, induced) **1** V-T To **induce** a state or condition means to cause it. ❑ *Doctors said surgery could induce a heart attack.* **2** V-T If you **induce** someone **to** do something, you persuade or influence them to do it. ❑ *More than 4,000 teachers were induced to take early retirement.*

1 타동사 일으키다 ❑ 수술이 심장 마비를 일으킬 수 있다고 의사들은 말했다. **2** 타동사 권유하다 ❑ 4천 명 이상의 교사들이 조기 퇴임하도록 권고를 받았다.

in|duce|ment /ɪnˈdusmənt, BRIT ɪnˈdjuːsmənt/ (inducements) N-COUNT If someone is offered an **inducement to** do something, they are given or promised gifts or benefits in order to persuade them to do it. ❑ *They offer every inducement to foreign businesses to invest in their states.*

가산명사 유인책, 혜택 ❑ 그들은 외국 회사들이 자기들 주에 투자하도록 온갖 혜택을 제공한다.

in|duc|tion /ɪnˈdʌkʃn/ (inductions) N-VAR **Induction** is a procedure or ceremony for introducing someone to a new job, organization, or way of life. ❑ *...an induction course for new members.*

가산명사 또는 불가산명사 안내, 소개 ❑ 새로운 회원들을 위한 안내 코스

in|dulge /ɪnˈdʌldʒ/ (indulges, indulging, indulged) **1** V-T/V-I If you **indulge in** something or if you **indulge yourself**, you allow yourself to have or do something that you know you will enjoy. ❑ *Only rarely will she indulge in a glass of wine.* ❑ *He returned to Britain so that he could indulge his passion for football.* **2** V-T If you **indulge** someone, you let them have or do what they want, even if this is not good for them. ❑ *He did not agree with indulging children.*

1 타동사/자동사 빠지다, 탐닉하다 ❑ 그녀는 와인을 매우 드물게 한 잔씩 즐긴다. ❑ 그는 축구에 대한 열정에 몰두하기 위하여 영국으로 돌아왔다. **2** 타동사 ─을 제멋대로 하게 놔두다, 오냐오냐하다 ❑ 그는 아이들이 제멋대로 하게 놔두는 것에 동의하지 않았다.

Word Partnership	*indulge의 연어*
ADV.	**freely** indulge **1**
PREP.	indulge **in** *something* **1**
N.	indulge **children** **2**

in|dul|gence /ɪnˈdʌldʒns/ (indulgences) N-VAR **Indulgence** means treating someone with special kindness, often when it is not a good thing. ❑ *The king's indulgence towards his sons angered the business community.*

가산명사 또는 불가산명사 지나친 관용, 오냐오냐하며 대함 ❑ 아들들에 대한 왕의 지나친 관용은 재계를 성나게 했다.

in|dul|gent /ɪnˈdʌldʒnt/ ADJ If you are **indulgent**, you treat a person with special kindness, often in a way that is not good for them. ❑ *His indulgent mother was willing to let him do anything he wanted.* ● **in|dul|gent|ly** ADV ❑ *Ned smiled at him indulgently and said, "Come on over when you feel like it."*

형용사 오냐오냐하는, 지나치게 관대한 ❑ 아들을 응석받이로 키우는 그의 어머니는 그가 원하는 것이면 뭐든 하게 놔뒀다. ● 오냐오냐하며, 응석을 다 받아 주듯 부사 ❑ 네드는 그를 보고 응석을 다 받아 주듯 너그럽게 웃으며 "마음 내키면 언제든지 와라."라고 말했다.

in|dus|trial ◆◇◇ /ɪnˈdʌstriəl/ **1** ADJ You use **industrial** to describe things which relate to or are used in industry. ❑ *...industrial machinery and equipment.* **2** ADJ An **industrial** city or country is one in which industry is important or highly developed. ❑ *...ministers from leading western industrial countries.*

1 형용사 산업의, 공업의 ❑ 산업 기계와 장비 **2** 형용사 산업이 발달한, 공업이 발달한 ❑ 선두적인 서양 산업 국가들의 장관들

Word Partnership	*industrial의 연어*
N.	industrial **machinery**, industrial **production**, industrial **products** **1**
	industrial **area**, industrial **city**, industrial **country** **2**

in|dus|trial ac|tion N-UNCOUNT If workers take **industrial action**, they join together and do something to show that they are unhappy with their pay or working conditions, for example refusing to work. [mainly BRIT, BUSINESS] ❑ *Prison officers will decide next week whether to take industrial action over staffing levels.*

불가산명사 노동 쟁의 [주로 영국영어, 경제] ❑ 교도소 관리들은 다음 주에 인력 보충에 대한 노동 쟁의를 할지에 대해서 결정할 것이다.

in|dus|trial es|tate (industrial estates) N-COUNT An **industrial estate** is the same as an **industrial park**. [BRIT]

가산명사 공업 단지, 산업단지 [영국영어]

in|dus|tri|al|ist /ɪnˈdʌstriəlɪst/ (industrialists) N-COUNT An **industrialist** is a powerful businessperson who owns or controls large industrial companies or factories. ❑ *...prominent Japanese industrialists.*

가산명사 자본가 ❑ 저명한 일본인 자본가들

in|dus|tri|al|ize /ɪnˈdʌstriəlaɪz/ (industrializes, industrializing, industrialized) [BRIT also industrialise] V-T/V-I When a country **industrializes** or **is industrialized**, it develops a lot of industries. ❑ *Energy consumption rises as countries industrialize.* ● **in|dus|tri|al|iza|tion** /ɪnˌdʌstriəlɪˈzeɪʃn/ N-UNCOUNT ❑ *Industrialization began early in Spain.*

[영국영어 industrialise] 타동사/자동사 산업화되다, 공업화되다 ❑ 나라가 산업화될수록 에너지 소비는 늘어난다. ● 산업화, 공업화 불가산명사 ❑ 산업화는 일찍이 스페인에서 시작되었다.

in|dus|trial park (industrial parks) N-COUNT An **industrial park** is an area which has been specially planned for a lot of factories. [AM; BRIT **industrial estate**]

가산명사 공업 단지, 산업 단지 [미국영어; 영국영어 industrial estate]

in|dus|trial re|la|tions N-PLURAL **Industrial relations** refers to the relationship between employers and employees in industry, and the political decisions and laws that affect it. [BUSINESS] ❑ *The offer is seen as an attempt to improve industrial relations.*

복수명사 노사 관계 [경제] ❑ 그 제안은 노사 관계를 개선하기 위한 시도로 보인다.

in|dus|try ◆◆◆ /ˈɪndəstri/ (industries) **1** N-UNCOUNT **Industry** is the work and processes involved in collecting raw materials, and making them into products in factories. ❑ *British industry suffers through insufficient investment in research.* **2** N-COUNT A particular **industry** consists of all the people and activities involved in making a particular product or providing a particular service. ❑ *...the motor vehicle and textile industries.* **3** N-COUNT If you refer to a social or political activity as an **industry**, you are criticizing it because you think it involves a lot of people in unnecessary or useless work. [DISAPPROVAL] ❑ *Some Afro-Caribbeans are rejecting the whole race relations industry.* **4** N-UNCOUNT **Industry** is the fact of working very hard. [FORMAL] ❑ *No one doubted his ability, his industry or his integrity.* **5** →see also **cottage industry, service industry** →see Word Web: **industry**.

1 불가산명사 산업, 공업 ❑ 연구에 대한 투자 부족으로 영국의 산업은 어려움을 겪고 있다. **2** 가산명사 제조업 ❑ 자동차와 직물 제조업 **3** 가산명사 소위 ─라는 사업 [빈정댐] ❑ 일부 카리브 흑인들은 소위 사회 내 인종 관계 개선 사업이라는 것을 전면적으로 거부하고 있다. **4** 불가산명사 근면, 부지런함 [격식체] ❑ 아무도 그의 능력, 근면함, 또는 성실함을 의심하지 않았다.

Word Web   industry

There are three general categories of **industry**. Primary industry involves **extracting raw materials** from the environment. Examples include **agriculture**, **forestry**, and **mining**. Secondary industry involves **refining** raw materials to make new **products**. It also includes **assembling** parts created by other **manufacturers**. There are two types of secondary industry—**light industry** (such as **textile weaving**) and **heavy industry** (such as shipbuilding). Tertiary industry deals with **services** which don't involve a concrete product. Some examples are **banking**, **tourism**, and education. Recently, computers have created millions of jobs in the **information technology** field. Some researchers describe this as a fourth type of industry.

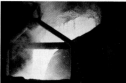

in|ed|ible /ɪnedɪbªl/ ADJ If you say that something is **inedible**, you mean you cannot eat it, for example because it tastes bad or is poisonous. ❑ *Detainees complained of being given food which is inedible.*

형용사 먹을 수 없는, 식용에 적합하지 않은 ❑ 억류자들은 먹을 수도 없는 음식을 받고 있다고 불평했다.

in|ef|fec|tive /ɪnɪfɛktɪv/ ADJ If you say that something is **ineffective**, you mean that it has no effect on a process or situation. ❑ *Economic reform will continue to be painful and ineffective.*

형용사 효과가 없는 ❑ 경제 개혁은 앞으로도 고통스러우면서도 실효를 거두지 못할 것이다.

in|ef|fec|tual /ɪnɪfɛktʃuəl/ ADJ If someone or something is **ineffectual**, they fail to do what they are expected to do or are trying to do. ❑ *The mayor had become ineffectual in the struggle to clamp down on drugs.* ● **in|ef|fec|tu|al|ly** ADV ❑ *Her voice trailed off ineffectually.*

형용사 효과가 없는, 헛된 ❑ 마약을 단속하려는 그 시장의 노력은 헛된 것이 되었다. ● 소용없이, 헛되게 부사 ❑ 아무런 소용도 없이 그녀의 목소리가 점점 잦아들었다.

in|ef|fi|cient /ɪnɪfɪʃªnt/ ADJ **Inefficient** people, organizations, systems, or machines do not use time, energy, or other resources in the best way. ❑ *Their communication systems are inefficient in the extreme.* ● **in|ef|fi|cien|cy** (**inefficiencies**) N-VAR ❑ *The inefficiency of the distribution system has led to the loss of millions of tons of food.* ● **in|ef|fi|cient|ly** ADV [ADV with v] ❑ *Energy prices have been kept low, so energy is used inefficiently.*

형용사 비능률적인, 비효율적인 ❑ 그들의 의사소통 체계는 극히 비능률적이다. ● 비능률, 비효율 가산명사 또는 불가산명사 ❑ 비효율적인 분배 체계가 수백만 톤의 식량 손실을 가져왔다. ● 비능률적으로, 비효율적으로 부사 ❑ 에너지 가격이 낮게 유지되었고, 그래서 에너지가 비효율적으로 사용되고 있다.

in|ept /ɪnɛpt/ ADJ If you say that someone is **inept**, you are criticizing them because they do something with a complete lack of skill. [DISAPPROVAL] ❑ *He was inept and lacked the intelligence to govern.*

형용사 서투른, 능력이 없는 [탐탁잖음] ❑ 그는 능력이 없었고 통치하기에 지력이 부족했다.

in|equal|ity /ɪnɪkwɒlɪti/ (**inequalities**) N-VAR **Inequality** is the difference in social status, wealth, or opportunity between people or groups. ❑ *People are concerned about corruption and social inequality.*

가산명사 또는 불가산명사 불균등, 불평등 ❑ 사람들은 부패와 사회적 불평등을 우려하고 있다.

Word Partnership   inequality의 연어

ADJ. **economic** inequality, **growing/increasing** inequality, **racial** inequality, **social** inequality
N. **gender** inequality, **income** inequality

in|ert /ɪnɜrt/ **1** ADJ Someone or something that is **inert** does not move at all. ❑ *He covered the inert body with a blanket.* **2** ADJ If you describe something as **inert**, you are criticizing it because it is not very lively or interesting. [DISAPPROVAL] ❑ *The novel itself remains oddly inert.*

1 형용사 움직이지 않는 ❑ 그는 움직임이 없는 그 시신을 담요로 덮었다. **2** 형용사 흥미 없는, 생동감이 없는 [탐탁잖음] ❑ 그 소설은 이상하게도 계속 흥미가 없다.

in|er|tia /ɪnɜrʃə/ N-UNCOUNT If you have a feeling of **inertia**, you feel very lazy and unwilling to move or be active. ❑ *He resented her inertia, her lack of energy and self-direction.*

불가산명사 무력감 ❑ 그는 그녀의 무력감, 에너지와 자제력 부족에 화를 냈다.

in|es|cap|able /ɪnɪskeɪpəbªl/ ADJ If you describe a fact, situation, or activity as **inescapable**, you mean that it is difficult not to notice it or be affected by it. ❑ *The inescapable conclusion is that he was trying to avenge the death of his friend.* ● **in|es|cap|ably** /ɪnɪskeɪpəbli/ ADV ❑ *It is inescapably clear that they won't turn round.*

형용사 모면할 수 없는, 불가피한 ❑ 필연적인 결론은 그가 친구의 죽음에 대해 복수를 하려고 했다는 것이다. ● 불가피하게 부사 ❑ 그들이 바뀌지 않으리라는 것은 누가 봐도 분명하다.

in|evi|tabil|ity /ɪnɛvɪtəbɪlɪti/ (**inevitabilities**) N-VAR The **inevitability** of something is the fact that it is certain to happen and cannot be prevented or avoided. ❑ *We are all bound by the inevitability of death.*

가산명사 또는 불가산명사 불가피성, 필연성 ❑ 우리 모두는 죽음의 필연성에 매여 있다.

in|evi|table /ɪnɛvɪtəbªl/ ADJ If something is **inevitable**, it is certain to happen and cannot be prevented or avoided. ❑ *If the case succeeds, it is inevitable that other trials will follow.* ● N-SING The **inevitable** is something which is inevitable. ❑ *"It's just delaying the inevitable," he said.*

형용사 피할 수 없는, 필연적인 ❑ 그 소송이 승소한다면 다른 재판들이 뒤따르리라는 것은 분명하다. ● 단수명사 피할 수 없는 것 ❑ "그것은 단지 피할 수 없는 것을 뒤로 미룰 뿐이다."라고 그는 말했다.

in|evi|tably /ɪnɛvɪtəbli/ ADV If something will **inevitably** happen, it is certain to happen and cannot be prevented or avoided. ❑ *Technological changes will inevitably lead to unemployment.*

부사 불가피하게, 필연적으로 ❑ 기술의 변화는 불가피하게 실업을 야기할 것이다.

in|exo|rable /ɪnɛksərəbªl/ ADJ You use **inexorable** to describe a process which cannot be prevented from continuing or progressing. [FORMAL] ❑ *...the seemingly inexorable rise in unemployment.* ● **in|exo|rably** /ɪnɛksərəbli/ ADV [ADV with v] ❑ *Spending on health is growing inexorably.*

형용사 멈출 수 없는, 계속되는 [격식체] ❑ 계속될 것 같은 실업의 증가 ● 계속 부사 ❑ 건강에 들이는 돈은 계속 증가하고 있다.

in|ex|pen|sive /ɪnɪkspɛnsɪv/ ADJ Something that is **inexpensive** does not cost very much. ❑ *There is a large variety of good inexpensive restaurants.*

형용사 값싼, 비용이 안 드는 ❑ 값싸면서도 괜찮은 음식점들이 아주 다양하게 있다.

in|ex|pe|ri|ence /ɪnɪkspɪəriəns/ N-UNCOUNT If you refer to someone's **inexperience**, you mean that they have little knowledge or experience of a particular situation or activity. ❑ *Critics attacked the youth and inexperience of his staff.*

불가산명사 무경험, 미숙 ❑ 비평가들은 그의 부원들이 어리고 미숙하다고 비난했다.

in|ex|pe|ri|enced /ɪnɪkspɪ́əriənst/ ADJ If you are **inexperienced**, you have little knowledge or experience of a particular situation or activity. ❑ *Routine tasks are often delegated to inexperienced young doctors.*

형용사 경험이 없는, 미숙한 ❑ 일상적인 업무들은 보통 경험이 없는 젊은 의사들에게 맡겨진다.

in|ex|pli|ca|ble /ɪnɛksplɪ́kəbəl, ɪnɪksplɪ́k-/ ADJ If something is **inexplicable**, you cannot explain why it happens or why it is true. ❑ *His behavior was extraordinary and inexplicable.* ● **in|ex|pli|ca|bly** /ɪnɛksplɪ́kəbli, ɪnɪksplɪ́k-/ ADV ❑ *She suddenly and inexplicably announced her retirement.*

형용사 불가사의한 ❑ 그의 행동은 엉뚱했고 불가사의했다. ● 불가해하게 부사 ❑ 그녀는 갑자기 이해할 수 없게도 사퇴를 발표했다.

in|ex|tri|ca|bly /ɪnɛkstrɪ́kəbli, ɪnɪkstrɪ́k-/ ADV If two or more things are **inextricably** linked, they cannot be considered separately. [FORMAL] [ADV with v] ❑ *Our survival is inextricably linked to the survival of the rainforest.*

부사 얽혀 [격식체] ❑ 우리의 생존은 열대 우림의 생존에 밀접하게 연결되어 있다.

in|fa|mous /ɪ́nfəməs/ ADJ **Infamous** people or things are well-known because of something bad. [FORMAL] ❑ *He was infamous for his anti-feminist attitudes.*

형용사 악명 높은 [격식체] ❑ 그는 반페미니스트적인 태도로 악명이 높았다.

> A **famous** person or thing is known to more people than a **well-known** one. A **notorious** person or thing is famous because they are connected with something bad or undesirable. **Infamous** is not the opposite of **famous**. It has a similar meaning to **notorious**, but is a stronger word. Someone or something that is **notable** is important or interesting.

> famous한 사람이나 사물은 well-known한 사람이나 사물보다 더 많은 사람들에게 알려져 있다. notorious한 사람이나 사물은 나쁘거나 바람직하지 않은 것과 연관되어 있기 때문에 유명하다. infamous는 '유명하다(famous)'의 반대말이 아니라, '악명 높다(notorious)'와 비슷한 뜻이지만 더 강한 말이다. notable한 사람이나 사물은 중요하거나 흥미로움을 나타낸다.

in|fan|cy /ɪ́nfənsi/ ■ N-UNCOUNT **Infancy** is the period of your life when you are a baby or very young child. ❑ *...the development of the mind from infancy onwards.* ② N-UNCOUNT If something is **in its infancy**, it is new and has not developed very much. ❑ *Computing science was still in its infancy.*

■ 불가산명사 유년 시대, 유아기 ❑ 유아기부터 계속 이루어지는 정신의 발전 ② 불가산명사 초기에 ❑ 컴퓨터 과학은 아직도 초기 단계였다.

in|fant /ɪ́nfənt/ (**infants**) ■ N-COUNT An **infant** is a baby or very young child. [FORMAL] ❑ *...holding the infant in his arms.* ❑ *They are saying that he is tiring of playing daddy to their infant son.* ② N-COUNT **Infants** are children between the ages of five and seven, who go to an infant school. [BRIT] ❑ *This entertainment will be most suitable for lower juniors, infants, and pre-school children.* ● N-UNCOUNT You use **the infants** to refer to a school or class for such children. ❑ *You've been my best friend ever since we started in the infants.* ③ ADJ **Infant** means designed especially for very young children. [ADJ n] ❑ *...an infant carrier in the back of a car.* ④ ADJ An **infant** organization or system is new and has not developed very much. [ADJ n] ❑ *The infant company was based in Germany.* →see **age**, **child**

■ 가산명사 갓난아기, 유아 [격식체] ❑ 그가 두 팔로 갓난아이를 안고 ❑ 그들은 그가 어린 아들의 아빠 노릇을 하는 데 지쳐 있다고 말하고 있다. ② 가산명사 아동, 소아 [영국영어] ❑ 이 오락은 초등학교 저학년생, 아동, 그리고 유치원 아이들에게 가장 적당할 것이다. ● 불가산명사 유치원, 유아 반 ❑ 너는 우리가 유치원에 들어갔을 때부터 계속 나의 단짝친구였다. ③ 형용사 유아용의 ❑ 차 뒷좌석의 유아용 좌석 ④ 형용사 초기의 ❑ 그 신생 회사는 독일을 본거지로 했다.

in|fan|try /ɪ́nfəntri/ N-UNCOUNT-COLL **Infantry** are soldiers who fight on foot rather than in tanks or on horses. ❑ *...an infantry division.*

불가산명사-집합 보병 ❑ 보병 사단

in|fect ◆◇◇ /ɪnfɛ́kt/ (**infects, infecting, infected**) ■ V-T To **infect** people, animals, or plants means to cause them to have a disease or illness. ❑ *A single mosquito can infect a large number of people.* ❑ *...objects used by an infected person.* ● **in|fec|tion** /ɪnfɛ́kʃən/ N-UNCOUNT ❑ *...plants that are resistant to infection.* ② V-T To **infect** a substance or area means to cause it to contain harmful germs or bacteria. ❑ *The birds infect the milk.* ③ V-T When people, places, or things **are infected** by a feeling or influence, it spreads to them. ❑ *For an instant I was infected by her fear.* ❑ *He thought they might infect others with their bourgeois ideas.* ④ V-T If a virus **infects** a computer, it affects the computer by damaging or destroying programs. [COMPUTING] ❑ *This virus infected thousands of computers across the U.S. and Europe within days.*

■ 타동사 감염시키다 ❑ 한 마리의 모기가 많은 수의 사람들을 감염시킬 수 있다. ❑ 감염된 사람이 사용한 물건들 ● 감염 불가산명사 ❑ 감염에 내성이 있는 식물들 ② 타동사 감염시키다, 오염시키다 ❑ 그 조류에 의해 우유가 오염된다. ③ 타동사 퍼지다, 감염되다 ❑ 일순간 그녀의 공포가 내게도 감염되었다. ❑ 그들이 다른 사람들에게 부르주아적 생각을 감염시킬 수 있다고 그는 생각했다. ④ 타동사 침입하다, 데이터를 오염시키다 [컴퓨터] ❑ 이 바이러스는 며칠 안에 미국과 유럽 전 지역에서 수천 대의 컴퓨터에 침입하여 피해를 주었다.

Word Partnership	infect의 연어
N.	**bacteria** infect, infect **cells**, infect **people** ■ ②
	viruses infect, infect **with a virus** ■ ④
PRON.	infect **others** ■ ②

in|fec|tion ◆◇◇ /ɪnfɛ́kʃən/ (**infections**) N-COUNT An **infection** is a disease caused by germs or bacteria. ❑ *Ear infections are common in pre-school children.* →see also **infect**
→see **diagnosis**

가산명사 전염병 ❑ 귀 전염병은 취학 전 아이들에게 흔하다.

Word Partnership	infection의 연어
N.	**cases of** infection, **rates of** infection, **risk of** infection, **symptoms of** infection
V.	**cause an** infection, **have an** infection, **prevent** infection, **spread an** infection

in|fec|tious /ɪnfɛ́kʃəs/ ■ ADJ A disease that is **infectious** can be caught by being near a person who has it. Compare **contagious**. ❑ *...infectious diseases such as measles.* ② ADJ If a feeling is **infectious**, it spreads to other people. ❑ *She radiates an infectious enthusiasm for everything she does.* →see **illness**

■ 형용사 전염의 ❑ 홍역과 같은 전염병 ② 형용사 퍼지기 쉬운, 전염성이 강한 ❑ 그녀는 어떤 일을 하든 전염성이 강한 열정을 발산한다.

in|fer /ɪnfɜ́r/ (**infers, inferring, inferred**) ■ V-T If you **infer** that something is the case, you decide that it is true on the basis of information that you already have. ❑ *I inferred from what she said that you have not been well.* ② V-T Some people use **infer** to mean "imply," but many people consider this use to be incorrect. ❑ *The police inferred, though they didn't exactly say it, that they found her behavior rather suspicious.*

■ 타동사 추론하다, 추정하다 ❑ 나는 그녀의 말에서 당신이 잘 지내지 못하고 있다고 추정했다. ② 타동사 함축하다, 암시하다 ❑ 경찰은 정확하게 그렇다고 말하지는 않았지만 그녀의 행동을 꽤 의심스럽게 생각한다고 넌지시 비추었다.

> Do not confuse **infer** and **imply**. If you **infer** that something is the case, you decide that it must be the case because of what you know, but without actually being told. ❑ *From this simple statement I could infer a lot about his wife.* If you imply that something is the case, you suggest that it is the case without actually saying so. ❑ *Rose's lawyer implied that he had married her for her money.*

> infer와 imply를 혼동하지 않도록 하라. 무엇이 어떻다고 infer하는 것은, 실제로 듣지는 못했지만, 알고 있는 사실에 비추어 틀림없이 그렇다는 결론을 내리는 것이다. ❑ 이 단순한 진술로부터 나는 그의 아내에 대해 많은 것을 추론할 수 있었다. 무엇이 어떻다고 imply하는 것은 실제로 그렇다고 말하지 않고 암시하는 것이다. ❑ 로즈의 변호사는 그가 돈 때문에 그녀와 결혼했다는 듯한 말을 했다.

a b c d e f g h i j k l m n o p q r s t u v w x y z

in|fer|ence /ˈɪnfərəns/ (**inferences**) ◼ N-COUNT An **inference** is a conclusion that you draw about something by using information that you already have about it. ❑ *There were two inferences to be drawn from her letter.* ◼ N-UNCOUNT **Inference** is the act of drawing conclusions about something on the basis of information that you already have. ❑ *It had an extremely tiny head and, by inference, a tiny brain.*

◼ 가산명사 추론 ❑ 그녀의 편지에서 이끌어 낼 수 있는 추론이 두 가지가 있었다. ◼ 불가산명사 추론, 추리 ❑ 그것은 지극히 머리가 작았고 그에 따라 추론되듯이 뇌도 아주 작았다.

in|fe|ri|or /ɪnˈfɪəriər/ (**inferiors**) ◼ ADJ Something that is **inferior** is not as good as something else. ❑ *The cassettes were of inferior quality.* ❑ *This resulted in overpriced and often inferior products.* ◼ ADJ If one person is regarded as **inferior to** another, they are regarded as less important because they have less status or ability. ❑ *He preferred the company of those who were intellectually inferior to himself.* ● N-COUNT **Inferior** is also a noun. ❑ *It was a gentleman's duty always to be civil, even to his inferiors.* ● **in|fe|ri|or|ity** /ɪnfɪəriˈɒrɪti, BRIT ɪnfɪəriˈɒrɪti/ N-UNCOUNT ❑ *I found it difficult to shake off a sense of social inferiority.*

◼ 형용사 질이 떨어지는, 지적으로 열등한 ❑ 그 카세트는 질이 조금 떨어졌다. ❑ 이것으로 인해 너무 비싸면서 대개는 질이 떨어지는 상품이 생겼다. ◼ 형용사 ~보다 낮은, 열등한 ❑ 그는 자신보다 지적으로 열등한 사람들과의 모임을 선호했다. ● 가산명사 낮은 위치의 사람 ❑ 자신보다 낮은 위치의 사람들에게까지 항상 공손해야 하는 것이 신사의 의무였다. ● 하위, 열등 불가산명사 ❑ 나는 사회적 열등감을 떨쳐 내기 어렵다는 것을 알았다.

> **Thesaurus**   inferior의 참조어
>
> ADJ.   mediocre, second-rate; (ant.) superior ◼

in|fer|tile /ɪnˈfɜrtəl, BRIT ɪnˈfɜːtaɪl/ ◼ ADJ A person or animal that is **infertile** is unable to produce babies. ❑ *According to one survey, one woman in eight is infertile.* ● **in|fer|til|ity** /ɪnfərˈtɪlɪti/ N-UNCOUNT ❑ *Male infertility is becoming commonplace.* ◼ ADJ **Infertile** soil is of poor quality so that plants cannot grow in it. ❑ *The polluted waste is often dumped, making the surrounding land infertile.*

◼ 형용사 불임의, 아이를 낳을 수 없는 ❑ 어느 한 조사에 의하면, 8명의 여자 중 1명이 불임이다. ● 불임 불가산명사 ❑ 남성의 불임이 평범한 일이 되고 있다. ◼ 형용사 불모의, 메마른 ❑ 오염된 쓰레기가 자주 버려져서 주변의 땅을 불모지로 만든다.

in|fest /ɪnˈfɛst/ (**infests, infesting, infested**) ◼ V-T When creatures such as insects or rats **infest** plants or a place, they are present in large numbers and cause damage. ❑ *...pests like aphids which infest cereal crops.* ● **in|fest|ed** ADJ ❑ *The prison is infested with rats.* ◼ V-T If you say that people or things you disapprove of or regard as dangerous **are infesting** a place, you mean that there are large numbers of them in that place. [DISAPPROVAL] ❑ *Crime and drugs are infesting the inner cities.* ● **in|fest|ed** ADJ ❑ *The road further south was infested with bandits.*

◼ 타동사 득시글거리다, 들끓다 ❑ 곡물에 들끓는 진딧물과 같은 해충들 ● 득시글거리는, 들끓는 형용사 ❑ 그 감옥에는 쥐가 우글거린다. ◼ 타동사 만연하다 [탐탁찮음] ❑ 범죄와 마약이 도심에 만연해 있다. ● 만연한, 들끓는 형용사 ❑ 더 멀리 남쪽으로 난 길에는 산적들이 들끓었다.

in|fi|del|ity /ɪnfɪˈdɛlɪti/ (**infidelities**) N-VAR **Infidelity** occurs when a person who is married or in a steady relationship has sex with another person. ❑ *George turned a blind eye to his partner's infidelities.*

가산명사 또는 불가산명사 간통, 부정(不貞) ❑ 조지는 배우자의 부정을 모르는 체했다.

in|fil|trate /ɪnˈfɪltreɪt/ (**infiltrates, infiltrating, infiltrated**) ◼ V-T/V-I If people **infiltrate** a place or organization, or **infiltrate into** it, they enter it secretly in order to spy on it or influence it. ❑ *Activists had infiltrated the student movement.* ● **in|fil|tra|tion** /ɪnfɪlˈtreɪʃᵊn/ N-VAR ❑ *...an inquiry into alleged infiltration by the far left group.* ◼ V-T To **infiltrate** people **into** a place or organization means to get them into it secretly in order to spy on it or influence it. ❑ *He claimed that some countries have been trying to infiltrate their agents into the Republic.*

◼ 타동사/자동사 침투하다, 잠입하다 ❑ 활동가들이 학생운동에 침투했었다. ● 침투, 잠입 가산명사 또는 불가산명사 ❑ 극좌익 그룹의 잠입 혐의에 대한 조사 ◼ 타동사 침투시키다, 잠입시키다 ❑ 일부 국가들이 그 공화국으로 스파이를 침투시키려 하고 있다고 그는 주장했다.

in|fi|nite /ˈɪnfɪnɪt/ ◼ ADJ If you describe something as **infinite**, you are emphasizing that it is extremely great in amount or degree. [EMPHASIS] ❑ *...an infinite variety of landscapes.* ❑ *With infinite care, John shifted position.* ● **in|fi|nite|ly** ADV [ADV adj/adv] ❑ *His design was infinitely better than anything I could have done.* ◼ ADJ Something that is **infinite** has no limit, end, or edge. ❑ *...an infinite number of atoms.* ● **in|fi|nite|ly** ADV [ADV with v] ❑ *A centimeter can be infinitely divided into smaller units.*

◼ 형용사 엄청난, 무한한 [강조] ❑ 무한히 다양한 풍경들 ❑ 존은 엄청 조심하며 자리를 옮겼다. ● 엄청, 무한히 부사 ❑ 그의 디자인은 내가 할 수 있는 그 어떤 것보다도 엄청 더 좋았다. ◼ 형용사 무한한 ❑ 무한개의 원자 ● 무한히 부사 ❑ 센티미터는 더 작은 단위로 무한히 나눌 수 있다.

in|fini|tive /ɪnˈfɪnɪtɪv/ (**infinitives**) N-COUNT The **infinitive** of a verb is the basic form, for example "do," "be," "take," and "eat." The infinitive is often used with "to" in front of it.

가산명사 부정사

in|fin|ity /ɪnˈfɪnɪti/ ◼ N-UNCOUNT **Infinity** is a number that is larger than any other number and can never be given an exact value. [also a N of n] ❑ *These permutations multiply towards infinity.* ◼ N-UNCOUNT **Infinity** is a point that is further away than any other point and can never be reached. ❑ *...the darkness of a starless night stretching to infinity.*

◼ 불가산명사 무한대 ❑ 이 순열들은 무한대로 증가한다. ◼ 불가산명사 무한대 ❑ 무한대로 펼쳐져 있는 별 하나 없는 어두운 밤

> **Word Link**   firm ≈ making strong : af*firm*, con*firm*, in*firm*

in|firm /ɪnˈfɜrm/ ADJ A person who is **infirm** is weak or ill, and usually old. [FORMAL] ❑ *She moved with her aging, infirm husband into a retirement center.* ● N-PLURAL **The infirm** are people who are infirm. ❑ *We are here to protect and assist the weak and infirm.*

형용사 허약한, 노쇠한 [격식체] ❑ 그녀는 늙고 쇠약한 남편과 함께 양로원으로 들어갔다. ● 복수명사 ❑ 우리는 노쇠한 분들을 보호하고 돕기 위해 여기에 왔다.

in|fir|ma|ry /ɪnˈfɜrməri/ (**infirmaries**) ◼ N-COUNT An **infirmary** is a place in a school or other institution that is used to take care of people who are sick or injured. ◼ N-COUNT; N-IN-NAMES Some hospitals are called **infirmaries**. ❑ *Mrs. Hardie had been taken to the infirmary in an ambulance.*

◼ 가산명사 양호실 ◼ 가산명사; 이름명사 병원 ❑ 하디 부인은 응급차에 실려 병원으로 이송되었다.

> **Word Link**   flam ≈ burning : *flame*, *flam*mable, in*flame*

in|flame /ɪnˈfleɪm/ (**inflames, inflaming, inflamed**) V-T If something **inflames** a situation or **inflames** people's feelings, it makes people feel even more strongly about something. [JOURNALISM] ❑ *The General holds the rebels responsible for inflaming the situation.*

타동사 (사태를) 악화시키다; (감정을) 자극하다 [언론] ❑ 장군은 반군들에게 사태를 악화시킨 책임을 지우고 있다.

in|flamed /ɪnˈfleɪmd/ ADJ If part of your body is **inflamed**, it is red or swollen, usually as a result of an infection, injury, or illness. [FORMAL] ❑ *Symptoms include red, itchy, and inflamed skin.*

형용사 빨갛게 부어오른 [격식체] ❑ 증상은 피부가 붉게 되고 가려우면서 빨갛게 부어오르는 것이다.

in|flam|mable /ɪnˈflæməbᵊl/ ADJ An **inflammable** material or chemical catches fire and burns easily. ❑ *A highly inflammable liquid escaped into the drilling equipment.*

형용사 가연성의, 불타기 쉬운 ❑ 가연성이 높은 액체가 드릴 장비로 새어 들어갔다.

in|flam|ma|tion /ɪnfləˈmeɪʃᵊn/ (**inflammations**) N-VAR An **inflammation** is a painful redness or swelling of a part of your body that results from an infection, injury, or illness. [FORMAL] ❑ *The drug can cause inflammation of the liver.*

가산명사 또는 불가산명사 염증 [격식체] ❑ 그 약물은 간의 염증을 유발할 수 있다.

in|flam|ma|tory /ɪnflæmətɔri, BRIT ɪnflæmətəri/ **1** ADJ If you accuse someone of saying or doing **inflammatory** things, you mean that what they say or do is likely to make people react very angrily. [DISAPPROVAL] ❑ ...nationalist policies that are too drastic and inflammatory. **2** ADJ An **inflammatory** condition or disease is one in which the patient suffers from inflammation. [FORMAL] [ADJ n] ❑ ...the inflammatory reactions that occur in asthma.

1 형용사 선동적인 [탐탁찮음] ❑ 지나치게 대립적이고 선동적인 민족주의적 정책들 **2** 형용사 염증성의 [격식체] ❑ 천식에서 일어나는 염증 반응

Word Link   able ≈ able to be : incurable, inflatable, portable

---

in|flat|able /ɪnfleɪtəbəl/ (**inflatables**) **1** ADJ An **inflatable** object is one that you fill with air when you want to use it. ❑ The children were playing on the inflatable castle. **2** N-COUNT An **inflatable** is an inflatable object, especially a small boat. ❑ Lifeboats were launched 12 times in four hours at Dover as kids on inflatables drifted out to sea.

1 형용사 부풀게 할 수 있는 ❑ 그 아이들은 공기를 주입할 수 있는 성을 가지고 놀고 있었다. **2** 가산명사 부풀릴 수 있는 물건 ❑ 도버에서는 부풀린 튜브를 탄 아이들이 바다로 떠내려가서 구명보트가 4시간 동안 12번 출동했다.

in|flate /ɪnfleɪt/ (**inflates, inflating, inflated**) **1** V-T/V-I If you **inflate** something such as a balloon or tire, or if it **inflates**, it becomes bigger as it is filled with air or a gas. ❑ Stuart jumped into the sea and inflated the liferaft. **2** V-T/V-I If you say that someone **inflates** the price of something, or that the price **inflates**, you mean that the price increases. ❑ The promotion of a big release can inflate a film's final cost. ● **in|flat|ed** ADJ ❑ They had to buy everything at inflated prices at the ranch store. **3** V-T If someone **inflates** the amount or effect of something, they say it is bigger, better, or more important than it really is, usually so that they can profit from it. ❑ They inflated their clients' medical injuries and treatment to defraud insurance companies.

1 타동사/자동사 부풀리다 ❑ 스튜어트는 바다로 뛰어들어 구명정을 부풀렸다. **2** 타동사/자동사 (가격을) 올리다; 부풀다 ❑ 대작 개봉을 앞두고 벌이는 판촉 때문에 영화의 마지막 제작 경비가 늘어날 수 있다. ● (가격이) 부풀린 형용사 ❑ 목장 가게에서 모든 것을 부풀린 가격으로 그들이 사야 했다. **3** 타동사 부풀리다, 과장하다 ❑ 그들은 보험 회사들을 속이려고 의뢰인들의 부상과 치료를 부풀렸다.

in|fla|tion ♦♦◇ /ɪnfleɪʃən/ N-UNCOUNT **Inflation** is a general increase in the prices of goods and services in a country. [BUSINESS] ❑ ...rising unemployment and high inflation.

불가산명사 인플레이션 [경제] ❑ 증가하는 실업과 높은 인플레이션

Word Partnership   inflation의 연어

ADJ.	high/low inflation
N.	inflation **fears**, **increase in** inflation, inflation **rate**
V.	**control** inflation, **reduce** inflation

---

in|fla|tion|ary /ɪnfleɪʃəneri, BRIT ɪnfleɪʃənri/ ADJ **Inflationary** means connected with inflation or causing inflation. [BUSINESS] ❑ The bank is worried about mounting inflationary pressures.

형용사 인플레이션의, 인플레이션을 일으키는 [경제] ❑ 은행은 증가하는 인플레이션 압박을 걱정하고 있다.

in|flec|tion /ɪnflɛkʃən/ (**inflections**) N-VAR An **inflection** in someone's voice is a change in its tone or pitch as they are speaking. [WRITTEN] ❑ The man's voice was devoid of inflection.

가산명사 또는 불가산명사 억양, 이조 [문어체] ❑ 그 남자의 목소리에는 억양이 없었다.

in|flex|ible /ɪnflɛksɪbəl/ **1** ADJ Something that is **inflexible** cannot be altered in any way, even if the situation changes. ❑ Workers insisted the new system was too inflexible. ● **in|flex|ibil|ity** /ɪnflɛksɪbɪliti/ N-UNCOUNT ❑ The snag about an endowment mortgage is its inflexibility. ❑ Marvin's father was exceptional for the inflexibility of his rules. **2** ADJ If you say that someone is **inflexible**, you are criticizing them because they refuse to change their mind or alter their way of doing things. [DISAPPROVAL] ❑ His opponents viewed him as stubborn, dogmatic, and inflexible. ● **in|flex|ibil|ity** N-UNCOUNT ❑ Joyce was irritated by the inflexibility of her colleagues.

1 형용사 확고한, 경직된 ❑ 노동자들은 새로운 제도가 너무나 경직되어 있다고 주장했다. ● 확고함, 경직성 불가산명사 ❑ 양도성 저당 융자의 문제는 그것의 경직성이다. ❑ 마빈의 아버지는 유별나게 자신의 규칙에 관해서는 확고하였다. **2** 형용사 융통성 없는, 완고한 [탐탁찮음] ❑ 그의 상대들은 그를 고집 세고 독단적이며 융통성 없다고 보았다. ● 완고함 불가산명사 ❑ 조이스는 동료들의 완고함에 짜증이 났다.

Word Link   flict ≈ striking : affliction, conflict, inflict

---

in|flict /ɪnflɪkt/ (**inflicts, inflicting, inflicted**) V-T To **inflict** harm or damage **on** someone or something means to make them suffer it. ❑ ...the damage being inflicted on Britain's industries by the recession.

타동사 –을 가하다 ❑ 경기 침체로 영국 산업이 입은 타격

in|flu|ence ♦♦◇ /ɪnfluəns/ (**influences, influencing, influenced**) **1** N-UNCOUNT **Influence** is the power to make other people agree with your opinions or do what you want. ❑ I have rather a large influence over a good many people. ❑ He denies exerting any political influence over them. **2** V-T If you **influence** someone, you use your power to make them agree with you or do what you want. ❑ He is trying to improperly influence a witness. **3** N-COUNT To have an **influence on** people or situations means to affect what they do or what happens. ❑ Van Gogh had a major influence on the development of modern painting. **4** V-T If someone or something **influences** a person or situation, they have an effect on that person's behavior or that situation. ❑ We became the best of friends and he influenced me deeply. **5** N-COUNT Someone or something that is a good or bad **influence on** people has a good or bad effect on them. ❑ I thought Sue would be a good influence on you. **6** PHRASE If you are **under the influence of** someone or something, you are being affected or controlled by them. ❑ He was arrested on suspicion of driving under the influence of alcohol.

1 불가산명사 영향력 ❑ 나는 제법 많은 사람들에게 꽤나 큰 영향력을 가지고 있다. ❑ 그는 그들에게 어떠한 정치적인 영향력도 행사하지 않았다고 한다. **2** 타동사 영향을 행사하다, 좌우하다 ❑ 그는 목격자에게 부당하게 영향력을 행사하려고 하고 있다. **3** 가산명사 영향 ❑ 반 고흐는 현대 미술 발전에 지대한 영향을 끼쳤다. **4** 타동사 영향을 주다 ❑ 우리는 가장 친한 친구 사이가 되었고 그는 나에게 많은 영향을 주었다. **5** 가산명사 영향 ❑ 나는 수가 너에게 좋은 영향을 줄 것이라고 생각했다. **6** 구 –의 영향을 받아 ❑ 그는 술에 취한 채 운전한 혐의로 체포되었다.

Word Partnership   influence의 연어

ADJ.	**political** influence **1**
	considerable influence, **important** influence, **major** influence, **powerful** influence, **strong** influence **1**-**3**
	bad/good influence **5**
N.	influence **behavior**, influence **opinion**, influence **people** **2** **4**

---

in|flu|en|tial /ɪnfluɛnʃəl/ ADJ Someone or something that is **influential** has a lot of influence over people or events. ❑ It helps to have influential friends. ❑ He had been influential in shaping economic policy.

형용사 영향력 있는 ❑ 그것은 영향력 있는 친구들을 사귈 수 있게 해 준다. ❑ 그는 경제 정책을 계획하는 데 영향력을 발휘했었다.

in|flux /ɪnflʌks/ (**influxes**) N-COUNT An **influx of** people or things into a place is their arrival there in large numbers. ❑ ...problems caused by the influx of refugees.

가산명사 유입, 쇄도 ❑ 난민 유입으로 발생되는 문제들

info /ˈɪnfoʊ/ N-UNCOUNT **Info** is information. [INFORMAL] ❑ *For more info phone 414-3935.*

불가산명사 정보 [비격식체] ❑ 더 문의하실 내용은 414-3935로 전화하세요.

in|form ♦♢♢ /ɪnˈfɔrm/ (**informs, informing, informed**) **1** V-T If you **inform** someone **of** something, you tell them about it. ❑ *They would inform him of any progress they had made.* ❑ *My daughter informed me that she was pregnant.* **2** V-I If someone **informs on** a person, they give information about the person to the police or another authority, which causes the person to be suspected or proved guilty of doing something bad. ❑ *Thousands of American citizens have informed on these organized crime syndicates.* **3** V-T If a situation or activity **is informed** by an idea or a quality, that idea or quality is very noticeable in it. [FORMAL] ❑ *All great songs are informed by a certain sadness and tension.*

1 타동사 알려 주다 ❑ 그들은 모든 진척 상황을 그에게 알려 주곤 했다. ❑ 딸은 나에게 임신했다고 말했다. **2** 자동사 -를 고발하다 ❑ 수천 명의 미국 시민들이 이 조직적인 범죄 단체들을 고발해 왔다. **3** 타동사 가득 차다 [격식체] ❑ 모든 위대한 노래는 어떤 비애와 긴장감으로 가득 차 있다.

Word Partnership inform의 연어

N. inform **parents**, inform **people**, inform **the police**, inform **readers**, inform *someone* **in writing** **1**
---

in|for|mal /ɪnˈfɔrməl/ **1** ADJ **Informal** speech or behavior is relaxed and friendly rather than serious, very correct, or official. ❑ *She is refreshingly informal.* ● **in|for|mal|ly** ADV [ADV after v] ❑ *She was always there at half past eight, chatting informally to the children.* **2** ADJ An **informal** situation is one which is relaxed and friendly and not very serious or official. ❑ *The house has an informal atmosphere.* **3** ADJ **Informal** clothes are casual and suitable for wearing when you are relaxing, but not on formal occasions. ❑ *For lunch, dress is informal.* ● **in|for|mal|ly** ADV ❑ *Everyone dressed informally in shorts or faded jeans, and baggy sweatshirts.* **4** ADJ You use **informal** to describe something that is done unofficially or casually without planning. ❑ *The two leaders will retire to Camp David for informal discussions.* ● **in|for|mal|ly** ADV ❑ *He began informally to handle Ted's tax affairs for him.*

1 형용사 격식을 차리지 않은, 탁 터놓은 ❑ 그녀가 신선할 정도로 격식을 차리지 않고 있다. ● 격식을 차리지 않고 부사 ❑ 그녀는 8시 반이면 항상 거기 와서 아이들과 가볍게 대화를 나누었다. **2** 형용사 격식을 차리지 않은, 친근한 ❑ 그 집은 분위기가 친근하다. **3** 형용사 평상복의 ❑ 점심 식사 때 옷은 평상복차림으로 해. ❑ 평상복으로 부사 ❑ 모두가 반바지 또는 물 빠진 청바지와 헐렁한 면 티를 입은 평상복차림이었다. **4** 형용사 비공식의 ❑ 두 지도자는 비공식 회담을 위해 캠프 데이비드로 갈 것이다. ● 비공식적으로 부사 ❑ 그는 테드를 위해 비공식적으로 그의 세금 문제를 다루기 시작했다.

Thesaurus informal의 참조어

ADJ. natural, relaxed; (ant.) formal **1** **2**
unofficial; (ant.) formal **2** **4**
casual; (ant.) formal **3**
---

in|form|ant /ɪnˈfɔrmənt/ (**informants**) **1** N-COUNT An **informant** is someone who gives another person a piece of information. [FORMAL] ❑ *On the basis of data furnished by her informants, Mead concluded that adolescents in Samoa had complete sexual freedom.* **2** N-COUNT An **informant** is the same as an **informer**.

1 가산명사 정보 제공자, 정보원 [격식체] ❑ 미이드는 정보 제공자들로부터 입수한 데이터를 기초로 하여 사모아의 청소년들이 완전한 성적 자유를 가지고 있다고 결론지었다. **2** 가산명사 정보 제공자, 정보원

in|for|ma|tion ♦♦♦ /ˌɪnfərˈmeɪʃən/ N-UNCOUNT **1** **Information** about someone or something consists of facts about them. ❑ *Pat refused to give her any information about Sarah.* ❑ *Each center would provide information on technology and training.* **2** N-UNCOUNT **Information** consists of the facts and figures that are stored and used by a computer program. [COMPUTING] ❑ *Pictures are scanned into a form of digital information that computers can recognize.* **3** N-UNCOUNT **Information** is a service which you can telephone to find out someone's telephone number. [AM; BRIT **directory enquiries**] ❑ *He called information, and they gave him the number.*

1 불가산명사 정보 ❑ 패트는 그녀에게 사라에 대한 어떠한 정보도 주려고 하지 않았다. ❑ 각각의 센터는 기술과 훈련에 대한 정보를 제공할 것이다. **2** 불가산명사 데이터, 정보 [컴퓨터] ❑ 그림들은 컴퓨터가 인식할 수 있는 디지털 정보의 형태로 스캔된다. **3** 불가산명사 (전화번호) 안내 [미국영어; 영국영어 directory enquiries] ❑ 그가 안내에 전화를 걸었고 그들이 그에게 그 전화번호를 알려 주었다.

Note that **information** is only ever used as an uncount noun. You cannot say "an information" or "informations." However, you can say a **piece of information** or an **item of information** when you are referring to a particular fact that someone has informed you of.

information은 언제나 불가산 명사로만 사용된다는 점을 유의하라. an information이나 informations라고는 쓸 수 없다. 그러나 누가 알려준 특정한 사실을 언급할 때는 a piece of information 또는 an item of information이라고 할 수 있다.

Word Partnership information의 연어

ADJ. **additional** information, **background** information, **classified** information, **important** information, **new** information, **personal** information **1**
V. **find** information, **get** information, **have** information, **need** information, **provide** information, **want** information **1** **retrieve** information, **store** information **2**
---

in|for|ma|tion tech|nol|o|gy N-UNCOUNT **Information technology** is the theory and practice of using computers to store and analyze information. The abbreviation **IT** is often used. ❑ *...the information technology industry.* →see **industry**

불가산명사 정보 기술 ❑ 정보 기술 산업

in|forma|tive /ɪnˈfɔrmətɪv/ ADJ Something that is **informative** gives you useful information. ❑ *Both men termed the meeting friendly and informative.*

형용사 정보를 주는, 유익한 ❑ 두 사람 모두 그 회담이 호의적이고 유익했다고 말했다.

in|formed /ɪnˈfɔrmd/ **1** ADJ Someone who is **informed** knows about a subject or what is happening in the world. ❑ *Informed people know the company is shaky.* →see also **well-informed** **2** ADJ When journalists talk about **informed** sources, they mean people who are likely to give correct information because of their private or special knowledge. [ADJ n] ❑ *According to informed sources, those taken into custody include at least one major-general.* **3** ADJ An **informed** guess or decision is one that is likely to be good, because it is based on definite knowledge or information. [ADJ n] ❑ *Science is now enabling us to make more informed choices about how we use common drugs.* **4** →see also **inform**

1 형용사 유식한, 견문이 넓은 ❑ 아는 사람들은 그 회사가 흔들리고 있다는 것을 알고 있다. **2** 형용사 소식통의, 정보통의 ❑ 소식통에 의하면, 구속된 사람들 중에는 군의 소장도 적어도 한 명 포함되어 있다. **3** 형용사 정보에 입각한 ❑ 과학 덕분에 이제 우리가 더 많은 정보를 갖고 사용할 일반 약품을 선택할 수 있게 되었다.

in|form|er /ɪnˈfɔrmər/ (**informers**) N-COUNT An **informer** is a person who tells the police that someone has done something illegal. ❑ *...two men suspected of being police informers.*

가산명사 정보 제공자, 정보원 ❑ 경찰 정보원이라는 의심을 받고 있는 두 사람

info|tain|ment /ˌɪnfoʊˈteɪnmənt/ N-UNCOUNT **Infotainment** is used to refer to radio or television programs that are intended both to entertain people and to give information. The word is formed from "information" and "entertainment." ❑ *...TV3's cheapo line-up of imports and infotainment.*

불가산명사 인포테인먼트, 오락성 정보 프로그램 ❑ 수입 프로그램과 오락성 정보 프로그램으로 짜여진 티브이3의 싸구려 편성표

infra|struc|ture /ˈɪnfrəstrʌktʃər/ (**infrastructures**) N-VAR The **infrastructure** of a country, society, or organization consists of the basic facilities such as transportation, communications, power supplies, and buildings, which enable it to function. ❑ *...improvements in the country's infrastructure.*

가산명사 또는 불가산명사 하부 구조, 사회 기반 시설 ❑ 국가 사회 기반 시설의 개선

in|fringe /ɪnˈfrɪndʒ/ (**infringes, infringing, infringed**) ❑ V-T If someone **infringes** a law or a rule, they break it or do something which disobeys it. ❑ *The film exploited his image and infringed his copyright.* ❷ V-T/V-I If something **infringes** on people's rights, it interferes with these rights and does not allow people the freedom they are entitled to. ❑ *They rob us, they infringe our rights, they kill us.*

❶ 타동사 어기다, 침해하다 ❑ 그 회사는 그의 이미지를 부당하게 이용했고 그의 저작권을 침해했다. ❷ 타동사/자동사 침해하다 ❑ 그들은 우리를 약탈하고, 우리의 권리를 침해하고, 우리를 죽인다.

in|fringe|ment /ɪnˈfrɪndʒmənt/ (**infringements**) ❶ N-VAR An **infringement** is an action or situation that interferes with your rights and the freedom you are entitled to. ❑ *...infringement of privacy.* ❷ N-VAR An **infringement of** a law or rule is the act of breaking it or disobeying it. ❑ *There might have been an infringement of the rules.*

❶ 가산명사 또는 불가산명사 침해 ❑ 사생활 침해 ❷ 가산명사 또는 불가산명사 위반 ❑ 규칙 위반이 있었을 수도 있다.

in|furi|ate /ɪnˈfyʊərieɪt/ (**infuriates, infuriating, infuriated**) V-T If something or someone **infuriates** you, they make you extremely angry. ❑ *Jimmy's presence had infuriated Hugh.*

타동사 격분시키다 ❑ 지미가 참석해서 휴를 노발대발하게 만들었다.

in|furi|at|ing /ɪnˈfyʊərieɪtɪŋ/ ADJ Something that is **infuriating** annoys you very much. ❑ *A man of indecision is infuriating to watch.*

형용사 아주 짜증스럽게 하는 ❑ 우유부단한 사람을 지켜보는 것은 아주 짜증나는 일이다.

in|fuse /ɪnˈfyuz/ (**infuses, infusing, infused**) V-T To **infuse** a quality **into** someone or something, or to **infuse** them **with** a quality, means to fill them with it. [FORMAL] ❑ *Many of the girls seemed to be infused with excitement on seeing the snow.*

타동사 불어넣다 [격식체] ❑ 많은 소녀들은 눈을 보자 흥분에 휩싸이는 것 같았다.

in|gen|ious /ɪnˈdʒinyəs/ ADJ Something that is **ingenious** is very clever and involves new ideas, methods, or equipment. ❑ *...a truly ingenious invention.*

형용사 독창적인 ❑ 정말 독창적인 발명품

in|genu|ity /ˌɪndʒəˈnuɪti, BRIT ˌɪndʒəˈnyuːɪti/ N-UNCOUNT **Ingenuity** is skill at working out how to achieve things or skill at inventing new things. ❑ *Inspecting the nest can be difficult and may require some ingenuity.*

불가산명사 독창성 ❑ 둥지를 조사하는 것은 어려울 수 있고 약간의 독창성을 요구할 수도 있다.

in|grained /ɪnˈgreɪnd/ ADJ **Ingrained** habits and beliefs are difficult to change or remove. ❑ *Morals tend to be deeply ingrained.*

형용사 깊이 배어든, 뿌리 깊은 ❑ 윤리 의식은 뿌리 깊이 배어 있기 쉽다.

in|gre|di|ent ♦◇◇ /ɪnˈgridiənt/ (**ingredients**) ❶ N-COUNT **Ingredients** are the things that are used to make something, especially all the different foods you use when you are cooking a particular dish. ❑ *Mix in the remaining ingredients.* ❷ N-COUNT An **ingredient** of a situation is one of the essential parts of it. ❑ *The meeting had all the ingredients of high political drama.*

❶ 가산명사 성분, 요소 ❑ 남은 재료에 섞어 넣으세요. ❷ 가산명사 요인, 구성 요소 ❑ 이 회의에는 고도의 정치 드라마에 필요한 모든 구성 요소가 다 들어 있었다.

	Word Partnership	*ingredient*의 연어
ADJ.	**active** ingredient, **a common** ingredient, **secret** ingredient ❶ **important** ingredient, **key** ingredient, **main** ingredient ❶ ❷	

in|hab|it /ɪnˈhæbɪt/ (**inhabits, inhabiting, inhabited**) V-T If a place or region **is inhabited** by a group of people or a species of animal, those people or animals live there. ❑ *The valley is inhabited by the Dani tribe.* ❑ *...the people who inhabit these islands.*

타동사 거주하다; 서식하다 ❑ 그 골짜기에는 대니 부족이 거주하고 있다. ❑ 이들 섬에 거주하는 사람들

in|hab|it|ant /ɪnˈhæbɪtənt/ (**inhabitants**) N-COUNT The **inhabitants** of a place are the people who live there. ❑ *...the inhabitants of Glasgow.*

가산명사 주민, 거주자 ❑ 글래스고 주민들

in|hale /ɪnˈheɪl/ (**inhales, inhaling, inhaled**) V-T/V-I When you **inhale**, you breathe in. When you **inhale** something such as smoke, you take it into your lungs when you breathe in. ❑ *He took a long slow breath, inhaling deeply.* →see **respiratory**

타동사/자동사 들이마시다 ❑ 그는 깊게 숨을 들이마시면서 길고 천천히 숨을 쉬었다.

in|her|ent /ɪnˈhɛrənt, -ˈhɪər-/ ADJ The **inherent** qualities of something are the necessary and natural parts of it. ❑ *Stress is an inherent part of dieting.* ● **in|her|ent|ly** ADV ❑ *Soft drinks aren't inherently unhealthy. You just have to be aware that you're drinking sugar and water, a little bit of flavoring.*

형용사 본질적인 ❑ 스트레스는 다이어트에 본질적인 부분이다. ● 본래부터, 본질적으로 부사 ❑ 탄산음료가 본질적으로 건강에 해롭지는 않다. 그저 향료를 조금 탄 설탕물을 마시는 것이라는 점을 알고 있기만 하면 된다.

in|her|it /ɪnˈhɛrɪt/ (**inherits, inheriting, inherited**) ❶ V-T If you **inherit** money or property, you receive it from someone who has died. ❑ *He has no son to inherit his land.* ❷ V-T If you **inherit** something such as a task, problem, or attitude, you get it from the people who used to have it, for example because you have taken over their job or been influenced by them. ❑ *The Endara government inherited an impossibly difficult situation from its predecessors.* ❸ V-T If you **inherit** a characteristic or quality, you are born with it, because your parents or ancestors also had it. ❑ *We inherit from our parents many of our physical characteristics.* ❑ *Her children have inherited her love of sport.*

❶ 타동사 물려받다, 상속 받다 ❑ 그는 자기 땅을 물려받을 아들이 없다. ❷ 타동사 인계받다 ❑ 엔다라 정부는 불가능할 정도로 어려운 상황을 그 이전 정부에게서 물려받았다. ❸ 타동사 (유전으로) 물려받다 ❑ 우리는 부모님으로부터 많은 신체적인 특징을 물려받는다. ❑ 아이들은 그녀의 스포츠에 대한 애정을 물려받았다.

in|her|it|ance /ɪnˈhɛrɪtⁿns/ (**inheritances**) ❶ N-VAR An **inheritance** is money or property which you receive from someone who has died. ❑ *She feared losing her inheritance to her stepmother.* ❷ N-COUNT If you get something such as job, problem, or attitude from someone who used to have it, you can refer to this as an **inheritance**. ❑ *...starvation and disease over much of Europe and Asia, which was Truman's inheritance as President.* ❸ N-SING Your **inheritance** is the particular characteristics or qualities which your family or ancestors had and which you are born with. ❑ *Eye color shows more than your genetic inheritance.*

❶ 가산명사 또는 불가산명사 유산 ❑ 그녀는 자신의 유산을 새모에게 빼앗길 것을 두려워했다. ❷ 가산명사 물려받음, 계승 ❑ 유럽과 아시아에 만연한 기아와 질병, 그것을 대통령이 된 트루먼이 물려받은 것이다. ❸ 단수명사 유전적 성질, 타고난 것 ❑ 눈 색깔은 당신이 유전적으로 타고난 것 이상을 보여 준다.

in|her|it|ance tax (**inheritance taxes**) N-COUNT An **inheritance tax** is a tax which has to be paid on the money and property of someone who has died.

가산명사 상속세

in|hib|it /ɪnˈhɪbɪt/ (**inhibits, inhibiting, inhibited**) ❶ V-T If something **inhibits** an event or process, it prevents it or slows it down. ❑ *The high cost of borrowing is inhibiting investment by industry in new equipment.* ❷ V-T To **inhibit** someone from doing something means to prevent them from doing it, although they want to do it or should be able to do it. ❑ *Officers will be inhibited from doing their duty.*

❶ 타동사 제지하다, 억제하다 ❑ 높은 융자 수수료가 산업체의 새로운 설비 투자를 억제하고 있다. ❷ 타동사 금하다, 못 하게 막다 ❑ 경찰들의 임무 수행이 금지될 것이다.

in|hib|it|ed /ɪnˈhɪbɪtɪd/ ADJ If you say that someone is **inhibited**, you mean they find it difficult to behave naturally and show their feelings, and that you think

형용사 억눌린, 억압된 [탐탁찮음] ❑ 남자들은 서로 접촉하는 것에 대해 여자들보다 억압되어 있다.

this is a bad thing. [DISAPPROVAL] ❑ *Men are more inhibited about touching each other than women.*

in|hi|bi|tion /ɪnɪbɪʃᵊn/ (inhibitions) N-VAR **Inhibitions** are feelings of fear or embarrassment that make it difficult for you to behave naturally. ❑ *The whole point about dancing is to stop thinking and lose all your inhibitions.*

가산명사 또는 불가산명사 억압감, 억제감 ❑ 춤의 핵심은 생각을 그만두고 자신의 모든 억압된 감정을 풀어 놓는 것이다.

in-house ADJ **In-house** work or activities are done by employees of an organization or company, rather than by workers outside the organization or company. ❑ *A lot of companies do in-house training.* ● ADV **In-house** is also an adverb. ❑ *The magazine is still produced in-house.*

형용사 조직 내의, 사내의 ❑ 많은 기업이 사내 연수를 한다. ● 부사 조직 내에서, 사내에서 ❑ 그 잡지는 여전히 사내에서 출판된다.

in|hu|man /ɪnhyumən/ ◼ ADJ If you describe treatment or an action as **inhuman**, you mean that it is extremely cruel. ❑ *The detainees are often held in cruel and inhuman conditions.* ◼ ADJ If you describe someone or something as **inhuman**, you mean that they are strange or bad because they do not seem human in some way. ❑ *...those inhuman shrieks that rent the air and chilled my heart.*

◼ 형용사 비인간적인, 잔인한 ❑ 억류자들은 종종 잔인하고 비인간적인 환경에 처해진다. ◼ 형용사 인간이 아닌, 사람의 것이 아닌 ❑ 허공을 가르며 내 심장을 얼어붙게 한 괴이한 비명 소리

in|hu|mane /ɪnhyumeɪn/ ADJ If you describe something as **inhumane**, you mean that it is extremely cruel. ❑ *He was kept under inhumane conditions.*

형용사 무자비한, 몰인정한 ❑ 그는 무자비한 상황에 처해 있었다.

in|itial ◆◇◇ /ɪnɪʃᵊl/ (initials, initialing, initialed) [BRIT, sometimes AM initialling, initialled] ◼ ADJ You use **initial** to describe something that happens at the beginning of a process. [ADJ n] ❑ *The initial reaction has been excellent.* ◼ N-COUNT **Initials** are the capital letters which begin each word of a name. For example, if your full name is Michael Dennis Stocks, your initials will be M.D.S. ❑ *...a silver Porsche car with her initials JB on the side.* ◼ V-T If someone **initials** an official document, they write their initials on it, for example to show that they have seen it or that they accept or agree with it. ❑ *Would you mind initialing this voucher?*

[영국영어, 미국영어 가끔 initialling, initialled] ◼ 형용사 최초의, 초기의 ❑ 초기 대응은 아주 훌륭했다. ◼ 가산명사 머리글자 ❑ 그녀의 이름 머리글자인 제이비가 옆면에 새겨진 은빛 포르셰 차 ◼ 타동사 머리글자로 서명하다 ❑ 이 상품권에 머리글자로 서명해 주시겠습니까?

Word Partnership   initial의 연어

N.	initial **diagnosis**, initial **estimate**, initial **investment**, initial **phase**, initial **reaction**, initial **results**, initial **stages** ◼

in|itial|ly ◆◇◇ /ɪnɪʃəli/ ADV **Initially** means soon after the beginning of a process or situation, rather than in the middle or at the end of it. ❑ *Forecasters say the gales may not be as bad as they initially predicted.*

부사 처음에, 초기에 ❑ 기상 통보관들은 강풍이 처음에 예상했던 것만큼 심하지 않을 것 같다고 말한다.

in|iti|ate /ɪnɪʃieɪt/ (initiates, initiating, initiated) ◼ V-T If you **initiate** something, you start it or cause it to happen. ❑ *They wanted to initiate a discussion on economics.* ◼ V-T If you **initiate** someone **into** something, you introduce them to a particular skill or type of knowledge and teach them about it. ❑ *He initiated her into the study of other cultures.* ◼ V-T If someone is **initiated into** something such as a religion, secret society, or social group, they become a member of it by taking part in ceremonies at which they learn its special knowledge or customs. ❑ *In many societies, young people are formally initiated into their adult roles.*

◼ 타동사 시작하다, 착수하다 ❑ 그들은 경제에 대한 토론을 먼저 시작하고 싶어 했다. ◼ 타동사 ...을 -로 이끌다, ...에게 -을 전수하다 ❑ 그가 그녀를 타문화 연구를 하도록 이끌었다. ◼ 타동사 -에 가입하다, -에 입회하다 ❑ 많은 사회에서, 젊은이들은 예식을 거쳐 정식으로 성인으로 편입하게 된다.

in|tia|tion /ɪnɪʃieɪʃᵊn/ (initiations) ◼ N-UNCOUNT The **initiation** of something is the starting of it. ❑ *They announced the initiation of a rural development programme.* ◼ N-VAR Someone's **initiation into** a particular group is the act or process by which they officially become a member, often involving special ceremonies. ❑ *This was my initiation into the peace movement.*

◼ 불가산명사 발족, 개시 ❑ 그들은 농촌 개발 프로그램의 발족을 선언했다. ◼ 가산명사 또는 불가산명사 입회, 가입, 입문 ❑ 이렇게 해서 나는 평화 운동에 입문했다.

in|itia|tive ◆◇◇ /ɪnɪʃiətɪv, -ʃᵊtɪv/ (initiatives) ◼ N-COUNT An **initiative** is an important act or statement that is intended to solve a problem. ❑ *Government initiatives to help young people have been inadequate.* ◼ N-SING In a fight or contest, if you have **the initiative**, you are in a better position than your opponents to decide what to do next. ❑ *We have the initiative; we intend to keep it.* ◼ N-UNCOUNT If you have **initiative**, you have the ability to decide what to do next and to do it, without needing other people to tell you what to do. ❑ *She was disappointed by his lack of initiative.* ◼ PHRASE If you **take the initiative** in a situation, you are the first person to act, and are therefore able to control the situation. ❑ *We are the only power willing to take the initiative in the long struggle to end the war.*

◼ 가산명사 발의, 솔선 ❑ 젊은이들을 도우려는 정부의 발의가 적절치 못했다. ◼ 단수명사 주도, 주도권 ❑ 우리가 주도권을 가지고 있고, 그것을 지키고자 한다. ◼ 불가산명사 독창력 ❑ 그녀는 그가 독창력이 부족한 것에 실망했다. ◼ 구 선도하다, 주도하다 ❑ 우리는 그 전쟁을 끝내려는 긴 투쟁을 기꺼이 선도해 가는 유일한 세력이다.

Word Partnership   initiative의 연어

ADJ.	**diplomatic** initiative, **political** initiative ◼
V.	**have the** initiative, **seize the** initiative ◼
	take the initiative ◼

in|ject /ɪndʒɛkt/ (injects, injecting, injected) ◼ V-T To **inject** someone with a substance such as a medicine means to put it into their body using a device with a needle called a syringe. ❑ *His son was injected with strong drugs.* ❑ *The technique consists of injecting healthy cells into the weakened muscles.* ◼ V-T If you **inject** a new, exciting, or interesting quality **into** a situation, you add it. ❑ *She kept trying to inject a little fun into their relationship.* ◼ V-T If you **inject** money or resources **into** a business or organization, you provide more money or resources for it. [BUSINESS] ❑ *He said that in order to protect depositors, the insurance fund would inject $750M into the banks.*

◼ 타동사 주사하다, 주입하다 ❑ 그의 아들은 강력한 약물 주사를 맞았다. ❑ 그 기술은 약화된 근육에 건강한 세포를 주입하는 것으로 이루어져 있다. ◼ 타동사 도입하다, 가미하다 ❑ 그녀는 그들의 관계에 약간의 재미를 가미하려고 애써 왔다. ◼ 타동사 (돈 등을) 투입하다 [경제] ❑ 그는 예금자들을 보호하기 위해 보험기금에서 7억 5천만 달러를 은행에 투입할 것이라고 말했다.

Word Partnership   inject의 연어

N.	inject **a drug**, inject **insulin** ◼
	inject **humor**, inject **life** ◼

in|jec|tion /ɪndʒɛkʃᵊn/ (injections) ◼ N-COUNT If you have an **injection**, a doctor or nurse puts a medicine into your body using a device with a needle called a syringe. [also by N] ❑ *They gave me an injection to help me sleep.* ◼ N-COUNT An **injection of** money or resources into an organization is the act of

◼ 가산명사 주사 ❑ 그들은 내가 잠들 수 있도록 주사를 놓았다. ◼ 가산명사 투입, 제공 [경제] ❑ 이 사업들 중 일부에 자금을 대기 위해 현금 투입이 필요하다.

providing it with more money or resources, to help it become more efficient or profitable. [BUSINESS] ❑ *An injection of cash is needed to fund some of these projects.*

in|junc|tion /ɪndʒʌŋkʃⁿn/ (**injunctions**) **1** N-COUNT An **injunction** is a court order, usually one telling someone not to do something. [LEGAL] ❑ *He took out a court injunction against the newspaper demanding the return of the document.* **2** N-COUNT An **injunction to** do something is an order or strong request to do it. [FORMAL] ❑ *We hear endless injunctions to managers to build commitment and a sense of community among their staff.*

■ 가산명사 (법원의) 금지 명령 [법률] ❑ 그는 서류 반환을 요구하는 신문사에 대항하여 법원의 금지 명령을 받아 냈다. **2** 가산명사 명령, 훈령 [격식체] ❑ 우리는 일에 헌신하고 직원 사이에 유대감을 키우라는 관리자들에게 주는 끊임없는 훈령을 듣는다.

in|jure /ɪndʒər/ (**injures, injuring, injured**) V-T/V-I If you **injure** a person or animal, you damage some part of their body. ❑ *A number of bombs have exploded, seriously injuring at least five people.* →see **war**

타동사/자동사 상처를 입히다, 다치게 하다 ❑ 많은 폭탄이 폭발하면서 적어도 다섯 명이 중상을 입었다.

Word Partnership	*injure*의 연어
ADV.	**seriously** injure
PRON.	injure *yourself*, injure *someone*
V.	**kill or** injure

in|jured ◆◇◇ /ɪndʒərd/ **1** ADJ An **injured** person or animal has physical damage to part of their body, usually as a result of an accident or fighting. ❑ *The other injured man had a superficial stomach wound.* ● N-PLURAL **The injured** are people who are injured. ❑ *Army helicopters tried to evacuate the injured.* **2** ADJ If you have **injured** feelings, you feel upset because you believe someone has been unfair or unkind to you. ❑ *...a look of injured pride.*

■ 형용사 부상당한, 다친 ❑ 다른 한 부상자는 복부에 찰과상을 입었다. ● 복수명사 부상자들 ❑ 육군 헬기들이 부상자들을 후송하려고 애썼다. **2** 형용사 감정이 상한, 상처받은 ❑ 자존심 상한 표정

Word Partnership	*injured*의 연어
ADJ.	**dead/killed and** injured **1**
ADV.	**badly** injured, **critically** injured, **seriously** injured **1**
N.	injured **in an accident/attack**, injured **people 1**
V.	**get** injured, **rescue the** injured **1**

in|ju|ry ◆◇◇ /ɪndʒəri/ (**injuries**) **1** N-VAR An **injury** is damage done to a person's or an animal's body. ❑ *Four police officers sustained serious injuries in the explosion.*

■ 가산명사 또는 불가산명사 상해, 손상 ❑ 네 명의 경찰관이 폭발 사고로 중상을 입었다.

Note that when someone is hurt accidentally, for example, in a car crash or when they are playing sports, you do not use the word **wound**. You use **injury** instead. ❑ *A man and his baby were injured in the explosion... Many of the deaths that occur in cycling are due to head injuries.* In more formal English, **injury** can also be an uncount noun. ❑ *Two teenagers escaped serious injury when their car rolled down an embankment.* **Wound** is normally restricted to soldiers who are injured in battle, or to deliberate acts of violence against a particular person. ❑ *...stab wounds*

누가 사고로, 예를 들어 자동차 충돌 사고나 운동을 하다가 다친 경우에는 wound를 쓰지 않고 injury를 쓰는 것에 유의하라. ❑ 그 폭발 사고로 남자 한 명과 그의 아기가 부상을 입었다... 자전거를 타다가 생기는 사망 사고 중 많은 경우가 머리 부상 때문이다. 비교적 격식을 갖춘 영어에서는 injury가 불가산 명사로도 쓰인다. ❑ 십대 두 명이 그들이 탄 차가 강둑에서 굴러 떨어졌지만 중상을 면했다. wound는 보통 전투에서 부상당한 군인이나 특정인에 대한 고의적인 폭력 행위에 국한되어 쓰인다. ❑ ...칼에 찔린 상처

2 N-VAR If someone suffers **injury to** their feelings, they are badly upset by something. If they suffer **injury to** their reputation, their reputation is seriously harmed. [LEGAL] ❑ *She was awarded £3,500 for injury to her feelings.* **3** to **add insult to injury** →see **insult**

2 가산명사 또는 불가산명사 침해, 명예 훼손 [법률] ❑ 그녀는 자신의 심적인 침해에 대한 보상으로 3,500파운드를 받았다.

Word Partnership	*injury*의 연어
ADJ.	**bodily** injury, **internal** injury, **minor** injury, **personal** injury, **serious** injury, **severe** injury **1**
V.	**escape** injury, **suffer an** injury **1**

in|jus|tice /ɪndʒʌstɪs/ (**injustices**) **1** N-VAR **Injustice** is a lack of fairness in a situation. ❑ *They'll continue to fight injustice.* **2** PHRASE If you say that someone has **done** you **an injustice**, you mean that they have been unfair in the way that they have judged you or treated you. ❑ *Calling them a bunch of capricious kids with half-formed ideas does them an injustice.*

■ 가산명사 또는 불가산명사 불공평, 불의 ❑ 그들은 불의에 맞서 싸움을 계속할 것이다. **2** 구 부당한 대우를 하다 ❑ 그들을 생각이 모자라는 변덕쟁이 아이들 떼거리라고 부르는 것은 부당하다.

ink /ɪŋk/ (**inks**) N-MASS **Ink** is the colored liquid used for writing or printing. ❑ *The letter was handwritten in black ink.* →see **drawing**

물질명사 잉크, 먹 ❑ 그 편지는 검은색 잉크를 사용해서 손으로 쓴 것이었다.

in|laid /ɪnleɪd/ ADJ An object that is **inlaid** has a design on it which is made by putting materials such as wood, gold, or silver into the surface of the object. ❑ *...a box delicately inlaid with little triangles.*

형용사 상감 세공한, 한, 아로새긴 ❑ 작은 삼각형들이 섬세하게 상감 세공된 상자

in|land

The adverb is pronounced /ɪnlǽnd/. The adjective is pronounced /ɪnlænd/.

부사는 /ɪnlǽnd /로 발음되고, 형용사는 /ɪnlænd /로 발음된다.

1 ADV If something is situated **inland**, it is away from the coast, toward or near the middle of a country. If you go **inland**, you go away from the coast, toward the middle of a country. ❑ *The vast majority live further inland.* ❑ *It's about 15 minutes' drive inland from Cannes.* **2** ADJ **Inland** areas, lakes, and places are not on the coast, but in or near the middle of a country. [ADJ n] ❑ *...a rather quiet inland town.*

■ 부사 내륙에, 내륙으로 ❑ 대다수가 더 깊은 내륙 지방에 산다. ❑ 그곳은 칸에서 내륙으로 차로 15분 정도 거리다. **2** 형용사 내륙의 ❑ 꽤 조용한 내륙 도시

In|land Rev|enue N-PROPER In Britain, **the Inland Revenue** is the government authority which collects income tax and some other taxes.

고유명사 (영국의) 국세청

in-laws N-PLURAL Your **in-laws** are the parents and close relatives of your husband or wife. ❑ *...meals with the in-laws.*

복수명사 인척 ❑ 인척들과의 식사

A

Word Link

let ≈ little : booklet, droplet, inlet

in|let /ˈɪnlɛt, -lɪt/ (inlets) N-COUNT An **inlet** is a narrow strip of water which goes from a sea or lake into the land. ❑ *A tiny fishing village by a rocky inlet.*

가산명사 내포(內浦), 작은 만 ❑ 바위가 많은 내포의 자그마한 어촌 마을

in|mate /ˈɪnmeɪt/ (inmates) N-COUNT The **inmates** of a prison or mental hospital are the prisoners or patients who are living there. ❑ *Muslims make up the fourth largest group of inmates in prisons in England and Wales.*

가산명사 재소자, 입원 환자 ❑ 회교도들이 잉글랜드와 웨일즈 지방의 감옥에서 네 번째로 많은 재소자 그룹을 이루고 있다.

inn /ˈɪn/ (inns) N-COUNT; N-IN-NAMES An **inn** is a small hotel, bar, or restaurant, usually one in the country. ❑ *...the Waterside Inn.*

가산명사; 이름명사 여관 ❑ 워터사이드 여관

in|nate /ɪˈneɪt/ ADJ An **innate** quality or ability is one which a person is born with. ❑ *Americans have an innate sense of fairness.* ● **in|nate|ly** ADV [ADV adj] ❑ *I believe everyone is innately psychic.*

형용사 타고난, 천부의 ❑ 미국인들은 공명정대한 정신을 타고났다. ● 천부적으로, 선천적으로 부사 ❑ 나는 누구나 천부적으로 예지력이 있다고 믿는다.

in|ner ♦♦♦ /ˈɪnər/ ❶ ADJ The **inner** parts of something are the parts which are contained or are enclosed inside the other parts, and which are closest to the center. [ADJ n] ❑ *She got up and went into an inner office.* ❷ ADJ Your **inner** feelings are feelings which you have but do not show to other people. [ADJ n] ❑ *Loving relationships that a child makes will give him an inner sense of security.*

❶ 형용사 안쪽의, 내부의 ❑ 그녀는 일어나서 안쪽 사무실로 들어갔다. ❷ 형용사 내적인, 은밀한 ❑ 아이가 만들어 주는 정다운 관계가 그에게 내적 안정감을 줄 것이다.

in|ner cir|cle (inner circles) N-COUNT An **inner circle** is a small group of people within a larger group who have a lot of power, influence, or special information. ❑ *Among Mr. Blair's inner circle of advisers are Derek Scott and Roger Liddle.*

가산명사 중추부, 핵심층 ❑ 블레어 총리의 측근 고문들 중에 대럭 스콧과 로저 리들이 있다.

in|ner city (inner cities) N-COUNT You use **inner city** to refer to the areas in or near the center of a large city where people live and where there are often social and economic problems. ❑ *No one could deny that problems of crime in the inner city exist.* →see **city**

가산명사 도심부, 도심의 빈민 지역 ❑ 도심 빈민 지역에 범죄 문제가 있다는 것을 아무도 부인할 수 없을 것이다.

in|no|cence /ˈɪnəsəns/ ❶ N-UNCOUNT **Innocence** is the quality of having no experience or knowledge of the more complex or unpleasant aspects of life. ❑ *...the sweet innocence of youth.* ❷ N-UNCOUNT If someone proves their **innocence**, they prove that they are not guilty of a crime. ❑ *He claims he has evidence which could prove his innocence.*

❶ 불가산명사 순수함, 때 묻지 않음 ❑ 젊음의 감미로운 순수함 ❷ 불가산명사 무죄, 결백 ❑ 그는 자신의 무죄를 입증할 수 있는 증거를 가지고 있다고 주장한다.

in|no|cent ♦♦♦ /ˈɪnəsənt/ (innocents) ❶ ADJ If someone is **innocent**, they did not commit a crime which they have been accused of. ❑ *He was sure that the man was innocent of any crime.* ❷ ADJ If someone is **innocent**, they have no experience or knowledge of the more complex or unpleasant aspects of life. ❑ *They seemed so young and innocent.* ● N-COUNT An **innocent** is someone who is innocent. ❑ *She had always regarded Ian as a hopeless innocent where women were concerned.* ● **in|no|cent|ly** ADV ❑ *The baby gurgled innocently on the bed.* ❸ ADJ **Innocent** people are those who are not involved in a crime or conflict, but are injured or killed as a result of it. ❑ *All those wounded were innocent victims.* ❹ ADJ An **innocent** question, remark, or comment is not intended to offend or upset people, even if it does so. ❑ *It was probably an innocent question, but Michael got flustered, anyway.*

❶ 형용사 무죄의, 결백한 ❑ 그는 그 남자가 아무 죄도 없다고 확신했다. ❷ 형용사 순수한, 때 묻지 않은 ❑ 그들은 너무나 젊고 순수해 보였다. ● 가산명사 순진한 사람 ❑ 그녀는 언제나 이언을 여자에 관한 한 대책 없이 순진한 사람으로 여겨 왔었다. ● 순진하게, 천진하게 부사 ❑ 아기가 침대에 누워 천진하게 옹알거렸다. ❸ 형용사 죄 없는, 무고한 ❑ 모든 부상자들은 죄 없는 희생자들이었다. ❹ 형용사 무해한, 악의 없는 ❑ 그것은 아마도 악의 없는 질문이었겠지만 마이클은 어쨌든 당황했다.

Word Partnership   innocent의 연어

V.	**plead** innocent, **presumed** innocent, **proven** innocent ❶
N.	innocent **man/woman** ❶
	innocent **children** ❷
	innocent **bystander**, innocent **civilians**, innocent **people**, innocent **victim** ❸
ADV.	**perfectly** innocent ❹

in|no|cent|ly /ˈɪnəsəntli/ ADV If you say that someone does or says something **innocently**, you mean that they are pretending not to know something about a situation. [ADV with v] ❑ *I tried to catch Chrissie's eye to find out what she was playing at, but she only smiled back at me innocently.* →see also **innocent**

부사 모르는 척하고 ❑ 나는 크리시가 무슨 의도가 있는지 알아내기 위해 눈을 맞춰 보려고 했지만, 그녀는 짐짓 모르는 척하고 내게 미소만 지었다.

in|nocu|ous /ɪˈnɒkjuəs/ ADJ Something that is **innocuous** is not at all harmful or offensive. [FORMAL] ❑ *Both mushrooms look innocuous but are in fact deadly.*

형용사 무해한, 무독성의 [격식체] ❑ 두 버섯이 모두 독성이 없어 보이지만 사실은 치명적이다.

Word Link

nov ≈ new : innovate, novel, renovate

in|no|vate /ˈɪnəveɪt/ (innovates, innovating, innovated) V-I To **innovate** means to introduce changes and new ideas in the way something is done or made. ❑ *What sets Rice apart from most engineers is his constant desire to innovate and experiment.*

자동사 혁신하다, 쇄신하다 ❑ 라이스가 대부분의 기술자들과 다른 점은 혁신하고 실험하려는 그의 끊임없는 열망이다.

in|no|va|tion /ˌɪnəˈveɪʃən/ (innovations) ❶ N-COUNT An **innovation** is a new thing or a new method of doing something. ❑ *They produced the first vegetarian beanburger – an innovation which was rapidly exported to Britain.* ❷ N-UNCOUNT **Innovation** is the introduction of new ideas, methods, or things. ❑ *We must promote originality, inspire creativity and encourage innovation.* →see **inventor**

❶ 가산명사 신개발품, 신기술 ❑ 그들은 최초의 채식용 콩버거를 만들었는데 이것은 빠른 속도로 영국으로 수출된 신개발품이었다. ❷ 불가산명사 혁신, 기술 혁신 ❑ 우리는 독창성을 증진시키고, 창의성을 북돋우고, 기술 혁신을 장려해야 한다.

in|no|va|tive /ˈɪnəveɪtɪv/ ❶ ADJ Something that is **innovative** is new and original. ❑ *...products which are cheaper, more innovative and more reliable than those of their competitors.* ❷ ADJ An **innovative** person introduces changes and new ideas. ❑ *He was one of the most creative and innovative engineers of his generation.* →see **technology**

❶ 형용사 혁신적인 ❑ 경쟁사들 것보다 더 저렴하고, 더 혁신적이며, 더 신뢰할 수 있는 제품들 ❷ 형용사 혁신적인 ❑ 그는 자기 세대에서 가장 창의적이고 혁신적인 기술자 중 한 사람이었다.

in|no|va|tor /ˈɪnəveɪtər/ (innovators) N-COUNT An **innovator** is someone who introduces changes and new ideas. ❑ *He is an innovator in this field.*

가산명사 혁신가, 개혁가 ❑ 그는 이 분야의 혁신가이다.

in|nu|en|do /ˌɪnjuˈɛndoʊ/ (innuendoes or innuendos) N-VAR **Innuendo** is indirect reference to something rude or unpleasant. ❑ *The report was based on rumors, speculation, and innuendo.*

가산명사 또는 불가산명사 빈정대는 말, 빗대는 말 ❑ 그 보고서는 소문과 억측, 그리고 빈정거림에 근거한 것이었다.

Word Link	numer ≈ number : in**numer**able, **numer**ical, **numer**ous

in|nu|mer|able /ɪnuməräbᵊl, BRIT ɪnyuːmərəbᵊl/ ADJ **Innumerable** means very many, or too many to be counted. [FORMAL] ❑ *He has invented innumerable excuses, told endless lies.*

형용사 무수한, 셀 수 없이 많은 [격식체] ❑ 그는 무수한 핑계를 대고 끊임없이 거짓말을 했다.

in|or|di|nate /ɪnɔrdᵊnɪt/ ADJ If you describe something as **inordinate**, you are emphasizing that it is unusually or excessively great in amount or degree. [FORMAL, EMPHASIS] ❑ *They spend an inordinate amount of time talking.*
● in|or|di|nate|ly ADV ❑ *He is inordinately proud of his wife's achievements.*

형용사 지나친, 과도한 [격식체, 강조] ❑ 그들은 이야기하느라 지나치게 많은 시간을 보낸다.
● 지나치게, 과도하게 부사 ❑ 그는 자기 아내의 공적에 대해 지나치게 자랑스러워한다.

in|or|gan|ic /ɪnɔrgænɪk/ ADJ **Inorganic** substances are substances such as stone and metal that do not come from living things. ❑ *...roofing made from organic and inorganic fibres.*

형용사 무생물의, 무기성의 ❑ 유기물 섬유와 무기물 섬유로 만든 지붕재

in|put /ɪnpʊt/ (inputs, inputting)

The form **input** is used in the present tense and is the past tense and past participle.

1 N-VAR **Input** consists of information or resources that a group or project receives. ❑ *It's up to the teacher to provide a variety of types of input in the classroom.* **2** N-UNCOUNT **Input** is information that is put into a computer. [COMPUTING] ❑ *The x-ray detectors feed the input into computer programs.* **3** V-T If you **input** information into a computer, you feed it in, for example by typing it on a keyboard. [COMPUTING] ❑ *The computer acts as a word processor where the text of a speech can be input at any time.*

input은 동사의 현재, 과거, 과거 분사로 쓴다.

1 가산명사 또는 불가산명사 정보, 자료 ❑ 교실에서 다양한 종류의 자료를 제공하는 것은 교사에게 달려 있다. **2** 불가산명사 (컴퓨터) 데이터, 정보 [컴퓨터] ❑ 엑스레이 탐지기가 컴퓨터 프로그램에 정보를 입력한다. **3** 타동사 (컴퓨터에 정보를) 입력하다 [컴퓨터] ❑ 컴퓨터는 말로 한 텍스트가 언제든지 입력될 수 있는 문서 작성기 역할을 한다.

in|put de|vice (input devices) N-COUNT An **input device** is a piece of computer equipment such as a keyboard which enables you to put information into a computer. [COMPUTING] ❑ *The officers use stylus pen-based input devices to write their reports onto touch-sensitive screens.*

가산명사 (컴퓨터) 입력 장치 [컴퓨터] ❑ 사무원들은 철필이 달린 입력 장치를 써서 촉각 감응 장치가 되어 있는 스크린에 보고서를 쓴다.

input/output **1** N-UNCOUNT **Input/output** refers to the information that is passed into or out of a computer. [COMPUTING] ❑ *...input/output delays.* **2** N-UNCOUNT **Input/output** refers to the hardware or software that controls the passing of information into or out of a computer. [COMPUTING] ❑ *... an input/output system.*

1 불가산명사 입출력 [컴퓨터] ❑ 입출력 지연 **2** 불가산명사 입출력 기계, 입출력 통제 프로그램 [컴퓨터] ❑ 입출력 시스템

in|quest /ɪnkwest/ (inquests) **1** N-COUNT When an **inquest** is held, a public official hears evidence about someone's death in order to find out the cause. ❑ *The inquest into their deaths opened yesterday in Enniskillen.* **2** N-COUNT You can refer to an investigation by the people involved into the causes of a defeat or failure as an **inquest**. ❑ *His plea came last night as party chiefs held an inquest into the election disaster.*

1 가산명사 사인 심리 ❑ 그들의 사인에 관한 심리가 어제 에니스킬렌에서 열렸다. **2** 가산명사 감사, 조사 ❑ 선거 참패에 대해 당 지도부가 감사를 벌이자 어젯밤 그가 탄원을 해 왔다.

in|quire /ɪnkwaɪər/ (inquires, inquiring, inquired)

in BRIT usually use, and in AM sometimes use **enquire**

1 V-T/V-I If you **inquire** about something, you ask for information about it. [FORMAL] ❑ *"What are you doing there?" she inquired.* ❑ *He called them several times to inquire about job possibilities.* **2** V-I If you **inquire into** something, you investigate it carefully. ❑ *Inspectors were appointed to inquire into the affairs of the company.*

enquire은 대개 영국영어에서, 가끔 미국영어에서 쓴다.
1 타동사/자동사 묻다, 문의하다 [격식체] ❑ "거기서 뭐하니?" 하고 그녀가 물었다. ❑ 그는 일자리 가능성을 알아보기 위해 그들에게 여러 번 전화를 했다. **2** 자동사 자세히 조사하다 ❑ 그 회사의 추문을 조사하기 위해 조사관들이 선임되었다.

Thesaurus	inquire의 참조어
v.	ask, question, quiz **1**

in|quir|ing /ɪnkwaɪərɪŋ/ also enquiring **1** ADJ [ADJ n] ❑ *All this helps children to develop an inquiring attitude to learning.* **2** ADJ If someone has an **inquiring** expression on their face, they are showing that they want to know something. [WRITTEN] [ADJ n] ❑ *"That's right," she said in reply to his inquiring glance.*
● in|quir|ing|ly ADV ◆◇◇ ❑ *She looked at me inquiringly. "Well?"*

1 형용사 묻는; 탐구적인 ❑ 이 모두가 아이들이 배움에 있어서 탐구하는 태도를 기르는 데 도움이 된다. **2** 형용사 호기심에 찬, 알고 싶어 하는 [문어체] ❑ "맞아."라고 그의 호기심에 찬 눈길을 보고 그녀가 대답했다. ● 호기심에 가득 차서 부사 ❑ 그녀는 호기심에 가득 차서 나를 쳐다보았다. "그래서?"

in|quiry ◆◇◇ /ɪnkwaɪəri/ (inquiries)

The spelling **enquiry** is usually used in British English, and sometimes used in American English. **Inquiry** is sometimes pronounced /ɪŋkwɪri/ in American English.

1 N-COUNT An **inquiry** is a question which you ask in order to get some information. ❑ *He made some inquiries and discovered she had gone to the Continent.* **2** N-COUNT An **inquiry** is an official investigation. ❑ *This is the most difficult and shocking murder inquiry I have had to open in the last 25 years.* **3** N-UNCOUNT **Inquiry** is the process of asking about or investigating something in order to find out more about it. ❑ *The investigation has suddenly switched to a new line of inquiry.*

철자 enquiry은 대개 영국영어에서 쓰며, 가끔 미국영어에서도 쓴다. inquiry는 미국영어에서 가끔 /ɪŋkwɪri/로 발음된다.
1 가산명사 문의, 질문 ❑ 그는 여기저기 알아보고 나서 그녀가 유럽으로 가 버렸다는 것을 알았다. **2** 가산명사 심리, 조사 ❑ 이것은 내가 지난 25년간 한 것 중 가장 어렵고 충격적인 살인 사건 조사이다. **3** 불가산명사 탐문, 조사 ❑ 그 조사는 돌연 새로운 방향의 탐문으로 선회했다.

Word Partnership	inquiry의 연어
N.	**board of** inquiry, **the outcome of an** inquiry **2**
V.	**conduct an** inquiry, **hold an** inquiry **2**
ADJ.	**scientific** inquiry **3**

in|quisi|tive /ɪnkwɪzɪtɪv/ ADJ An **inquisitive** person likes finding out about things, especially secret things. ❑ *Barrow had an inquisitive nature.*

형용사 꼬치꼬치 알려고 하는, 캐묻기 좋아하는 ❑ 배로우는 캐묻기 좋아하는 성격이었다.

in|roads /ɪnroʊdz/ PHRASE If one thing **makes inroads into** another, the first thing starts affecting or destroying the second. ❑ *In Italy, as elsewhere, television has made deep inroads into cinema.*

구 ~을 잠식하다, ~에 침입하다 ❑ 다른 곳과 마찬가지로 이태리에서도 텔레비전이 영화를 깊이 잠식해 들어왔다.

Word Link	san ≈ health : in**san**e, **san**e, **san**itation

in|sane /ɪnseɪn/ **1** ADJ Someone who is **insane** has a mind that does not work in a normal way, with the result that their behavior is very strange. ❑ *Some*

1 형용사 제정신이 아닌, 미친 ❑ 어떤 사람들은 그것을 견디지 못하고 그냥 미쳐 버린다. **2** 형용사

A
people simply can't take it and they just go insane. ☑ ADJ If you describe a decision or action as **insane**, you think it is very foolish or excessive. [DISAPPROVAL] ☐ *He asked me what I thought and I said, "Listen, this is completely insane."* ● **in|sane|ly** ADV ☐ *I would be insanely jealous if Bill left me for another woman.*

미친 듯한, 말도 안 되는 [탐탁잖음] ☐ 그가 내게 어떻게 생각하는지 물어서 나는 "이봐, 이건 완전히 미친 짓이야."라고 대답했다. ● 미친 듯이 부사 ☐ 빌이 다른 여자 때문에 나를 떠난다면 나는 미친 듯이 질투가 날 것이다.

B
in|san|ity /ɪnsænɪti/ ☐ N-UNCOUNT **Insanity** is the state of being insane. ☐ *The defense pleaded insanity, but the defendant was found guilty and sentenced.* ☑ N-UNCOUNT If you describe a decision or an action as **insanity**, you think it is very foolish. [DISAPPROVAL] ☐ *...the final financial insanity of the 1980s.*

C
☐ 불가산명사 정신 이상 ☐ 피고 측은 정신 이상을 이유로 내세웠지만 피고인은 유죄 판결이 나서 선고를 받았다. ☑ 불가산명사 어리석은 것, 미친 짓 [탐탁잖음] ☐ 1980년대 최후의 금융 광풍

D
| **Word Link** | *sat, satis* ≈ *enough : dis*satis*faction, in*satis*ble, satis*fy |

in|sa|tia|ble /ɪnseɪʃəbəl, -fiə-/ ADJ If someone has an **insatiable** desire for something, they want as much of it as they can possibly get. ☐ *A section of the reading public has an insatiable appetite for dirty stories about the famous.*

E
형용사 만족을 모르는, 탐욕스러운 ☐ 독서 인구의 일부는 유명인들의 추문에 대해 끝없는 욕구를 지니고 있다.

F
in|scribe /ɪnskraɪb/ (**inscribes, inscribing, inscribed**) ☐ V-T If you **inscribe** words **on** an object, you write or carve the words on the object. ☐ *Some galleries commemorate donors by inscribing their names on the walls.* ☑ V-T If you **inscribe** something in the front of a book or on a photograph, you write it there, often before giving it to someone. ☐ *On the back I had inscribed the words: "Here's to Great Ideas! John."*

☐ 타동사 ~에 새기다, 파다 ☐ 어떤 미술관들은 벽에 기증자들의 이름을 새겨 그들을 기념한다. ☑ 타동사 (증정하기 전에) 적어 넣다 ☐ 뒷면에 나는 이 말을 적어 넣었다. "위대한 착상을 축하하며! 존."

G
in|scrip|tion /ɪnskrɪpʃən/ (**inscriptions**) ☐ N-COUNT An **inscription** is writing carved into something made of stone or metal, for example a gravestone or medal. ☐ *The silver medal bears the sovereign's head and the inscription "For distinguished service."* ☑ N-COUNT An **inscription** is something written by hand in the front of a book or on a photograph. ☐ *The inscription reads: "To Emma, with love from Harry."*

H
☐ 가산명사 묘비명, 새김글 ☐ 그 은메달에는 군주의 두상과 '수훈'이라는 글자가 새겨져 있다. ☑ 가산명사 헌사(獻辭) ☐ 헌사(獻辭)에는 다음과 같이 적혀 있었다. "에마에게, 사랑하는 해리가"

I
in|sect /ɪnsɛkt/ (**insects**) N-COUNT An **insect** is a small animal that has six legs. Most insects have wings. Ants, flies, butterflies, and beetles are all insects. →see flower

가산명사 곤충, 벌레

in|sec|ti|cide /ɪnsɛktɪsaɪd/ (**insecticides**) N-MASS **Insecticide** is a chemical substance that is used to kill insects. ☐ *Spray the plants with insecticide.* →see farm

J
물질명사 살충제 ☐ 식물에 살충제를 뿌리시오.

K
in|se|cure /ɪnsɪkyʊər/ ☐ ADJ If you are **insecure**, you lack confidence because you think that you are not good enough or are not loved. ☐ *Most mothers are insecure about their performance as mothers.* ● **in|se|cu|rity** /ɪnsɪkyʊərɪti/ (**insecurities**) N-VAR ☐ *She is always assailed by self-doubt and emotional insecurity.* ☑ ADJ Something that is **insecure** is not safe or protected. ☐ *...low-paid, insecure jobs.* ● **in|se|cu|rity** N-UNCOUNT ☐ *...the increase in crime, which has created feelings of insecurity in the population.*

☐ 형용사 불안한, 자신이 없는 ☐ 대부분의 엄마들은 엄마로서 자신의 역할을 하는 것에 불안해한다. ● 불안, 근심 가산명사 또는 불가산명사 ☐ 그녀는 항상 자신감 상실과 정서적 불안에 시달린다. ☑ 형용사 불안정한 ☐ 급료가 낮고 불안정한 직업들 ● 불안정, 불안 불가산명사 ☐ 주민의 불안감을 가져온 범죄의 증가

L

M
in|sen|si|tive /ɪnsɛnsɪtɪv/ ☐ ADJ If you describe someone as **insensitive**, you are criticizing them for being unaware of or unsympathetic to other people's feelings. [DISAPPROVAL] ☐ *I feel my husband is very insensitive about my problem.* ● **in|sen|si|tiv|ity** /ɪnsɛnsɪtɪvɪti/ N-UNCOUNT ☐ *I was ashamed and appalled at my clumsiness and insensitivity towards her.* ☑ ADJ Someone who is **insensitive to** a situation or to a need does not think or care about it. ☐ *...women's and Latino organizations that say he is insensitive to civil rights.* ● **in|sen|si|tiv|ity** N-UNCOUNT ☐ *...insensitivity to the environmental consequences.* ☒ ADJ Someone who is **insensitive to** a physical sensation is unable to feel it. ☐ *He had become insensitive to cold.*

N
☐ 형용사 둔감한, 감각이 둔한 [탐탁잖음] ☐ 나는 남편이 내 문제에 아주 둔감하다는 느낌이 든다. ● 둔감 불가산명사 ☐ 나는 그녀에 대한 나의 서투름과 둔감함에 부끄럽고 섬뜩했다. ☑ 형용사 무신경한, 무감각한 ☐ 그가 인권에 신경을 쓰지 않는다고 말하는 여성 및 남미계 단체들 ● 무신경, 무감각 불가산명사 ☐ 환경에 끼치는 영향에 무신경함 ☒ 형용사 무감각한 ☐ 그는 추위에 무감각해져 있었다.

O

P
in|sepa|rable /ɪnsɛpərəbəl/ ☐ ADJ If one thing is **inseparable from** another, the things are so closely connected that they cannot be considered separately. ☐ *He firmly believes liberty is inseparable from social justice.* ● **in|sepa|rably** ADV ☐ *In his mind, religion and politics were inseparably intertwined.* ☑ ADJ If you say that two people are **inseparable**, you are emphasizing that they are very good friends and spend a great deal of time together. [EMPHASIS] ☐ *She and Kristin were inseparable.*

Q
☐ 형용사 나눌 수 없는, 불가분의 ☐ 그는 자유와 사회 정의는 분리될 수 ☐ 없다고 굳게 믿는다. ● 밀접하게 부사 ☐ 그의 마음속에는 종교와 정치가 밀접하게 얽혀 있었다. ☑ 형용사 떨어질 수 없는 [강조] ☐ 그녀와 크리스틴은 떨어질 수 없는 사이였다.

R
in|sert (**inserts, inserting, inserted**)

The verb is pronounced /ɪnsɜrt/. The noun is pronounced /ɪnsɜrt/.

동사는 /ɪnsɜrt/로 발음되고, 명사는 /ɪnsɜrt/로 발음된다.

S

T
☐ V-T If you **insert** an object **into** something, you put the object inside it. ☐ *He took a small key from his pocket and slowly inserted it into the lock.* ● **in|ser|tion** /ɪnsɜrʃən/ (**insertions**) N-VAR ☐ *...the first experiment involving the insertion of a new gene into a human being.* ☑ V-T If you **insert** a comment into a piece of writing or a speech, you include it. ☐ *They joined with the monarchists to insert a clause calling for a popular vote on the issue.* ● **in|ser|tion** N-VAR ☐ *He saw no point whatsoever in recording an item for insertion in the programme.* ☒ N-COUNT An **insert** is something that is inserted somewhere, especially an advertisement on a piece of paper that is placed between the pages of a book or magazine. ☐ *Since Sunday is the preferred day for advertising inserts, it accounts for a growing proportion of newspaper revenues.*

U
☐ 타동사 끼워 넣다, 삽입하다 ☐ 그는 주머니에서 작은 열쇠를 꺼내서 천천히 자물쇠에 끼워 넣었다. ● 삽입, 부착 가산명사 또는 불가산명사 ☐ 인체에 새로운 유전자 삽입을 수반하는 첫 실험 ☑ 타동사 써넣다, 포함하다 ☐ 그들은 그 문제에 대한 일반 투표를 요구하는 조항을 넣기 위해 군주주의자들과 손을 잡았다. ● 포함 가산명사 또는 불가산명사 ☐ 그는 프로그램에 삽입하기 위한 항목을 녹음하는 이유를 전혀 납득할 수 없었다. ☒ 가산명사 삽입 광고물 ☐ 일요일이 삽입 광고물을 넣기에 선호되는 날이어서 일요판 신문이 신문료 총수입에서 점점 큰 비중을 차지한다.

V

W
in-service ADJ If people working in a particular profession are given **in-service** training, they attend special courses to improve their skills or to learn about new developments in their field. [ADJ n] ☐ *...in-service courses for people such as doctors, teachers, and civil servants.*

형용사 현직의 ☐ 현직 의사, 교사, 공무원과 같은 사람들을 위한 연수 과정들

X
in|side ♦♦◇ /ɪnsaɪd/ (**insides**)

The preposition is usually pronounced /ɪnsaɪd/.

전치사는 대개 /ɪnsaɪd/로 발음된다.

Y
The form **inside of** can also be used as a preposition. This form is more usual in American English.

inside of도 전치사로 쓸 수 있다. 미국영어에서는 이 형태가 더 일반적으로 쓰인다.

Z
☐ PREP Something or someone that is **inside** a place, container, or object is in it or is surrounded by it. ☐ *Inside the passport was a folded slip of paper.* ● ADV **Inside**

☐ 전치사 ~의 안쪽에, ~의 내부에 ☐ 여권 안에 접은 종이쪽지가 있었다. ● 부사 내부에, 내부로 ☐ 그

is also an adverb. ❏ *The couple chatted briefly on the doorstep before going inside.* ● ADJ **Inside** is also an adjective. [ADJ n] ❏ *...four-berth inside cabins with en suite bathroom and shower.* ❷ N-COUNT The **inside** of something is the part or area that its sides surround or contain. ❏ *The doors were locked from the inside.* ● ADJ **Inside** is also an adjective. [ADJ n] ❏ *The popular papers all have photo features on their inside pages.* ● ADV **Inside** is also an adverb. [adj ADV] ❏ *The potato cakes can be shallow or deep-fried until crisp outside and meltingly soft inside.* ❸ ADV You can say that someone is **inside** when they are in prison. [INFORMAL] ❏ *They've both done prison time – he's been inside three times.* ❹ ADJ **Inside** information is obtained from someone who is involved in a situation and therefore knows a lot about it. [ADJ n] ❏ *Sloane used inside diplomatic information to make himself rich.* ❏ *Keith Vass, editor, denies he had inside knowledge.* ❺ PREP If you are **inside** an organization, you belong to it. ❏ *75 percent of chief executives come from inside the company.* ● ADJ **Inside** is also an adjective. [ADJ n] ❏ *...a recent book about the inside world of pro football.* ● N-SING **Inside** is also a noun. ❏ *McAvoy was convinced he could control things from the inside but he lost control.* ❻ N-PLURAL Your **insides** are your internal organs, especially your stomach. [INFORMAL] ❏ *Every pill made my insides turn upside down.* ❼ ADV If you say that someone has a feeling **inside**, you mean that they have it but have not expressed it. ❏ *There is nothing left inside – no words, no anger, no tears.* ● PREP **Inside** is also a preposition. ❏ *He felt a great weight of sorrow inside him.* ● N-SING **Inside** is also a noun. ❏ *What is needed is a change from the inside, a real change in outlook and attitude.* ❽ PREP If you do something **inside** a particular time, you do it before the end of that time. [PREP amount] ❏ *They should have everything working inside an hour.* ❾ PHRASE If something such as a piece of clothing is **inside out**, the part that is normally inside now faces outward. ❏ *Her umbrella blew inside out.* ❿ PHRASE If you say that you know something or someone **inside out**, you are emphasizing that you know them extremely well. [EMPHASIS] ❏ *He knew the game inside out.*

Thesaurus   inside의 참조어

PREP.	in; *(ant.)* outside ❶
N.	interior, middle; *(ant.)* exterior ❷

in|sid|er /ɪnsaɪdər/ (**insiders**) N-COUNT An **insider** is someone who is involved in a situation and who knows more about it than other people. ❏ *An insider said, "Katharine has told friends it is time to end her career."*

in|sid|er trad|ing also **insider dealing** N-UNCOUNT **Insider trading** or **insider dealing** is the illegal buying or selling of a company's shares by someone who has secret or private information about the company. [BUSINESS] ❏ *...a friend of Ms. Stewart's who is accused of insider trading in shares of his own company.*

in|sidi|ous /ɪnsɪdiəs/ ADJ Something that is **insidious** is unpleasant or dangerous and develops gradually without being noticed. ❏ *The changes are insidious, and will not produce a noticeable effect for 15 to 20 years.*

in|sight /ɪnsaɪt/ (**insights**) ❶ N-VAR If you gain **insight** or an **insight into** a complex situation or problem, you gain an accurate and deep understanding of it. ❏ *The project would give scientists new insights into what is happening to the earth's atmosphere.* ❷ N-UNCOUNT If someone has **insight**, they are able to understand complex situations. ❏ *He was a man of forceful character, with considerable insight and diplomatic skills.*

in|sig|nifi|cance /ɪnsɪgnɪfɪkəns/ N-UNCOUNT **Insignificance** is the quality of being insignificant. ❏ *These prices pale into insignificance when compared with what was paid for two major works by the late Alfred Stieglitz.*

in|sig|nifi|cant /ɪnsɪgnɪfɪkənt/ ADJ Something that is **insignificant** is unimportant, especially because it is very small. ❏ *In 1949 Bonn was a small, insignificant city.*

in|sin|cere /ɪnsɪnsɪər/ ADJ If you say that someone is **insincere**, you are being critical of them because they say things they do not really mean, usually pleasant, admiring, or encouraging things. [DISAPPROVAL] ❏ *Some people are so terribly insincere you can never tell if they are telling the truth.*

in|sist ♦♦◇ /ɪnsɪst/ (**insists, insisting, insisted**) ❶ V-T/V-I If you **insist that** something should be done, you say so very firmly and refuse to give in about it. If you **insist on** something, you say firmly that it must be done or provided. ❏ *My family insisted that I should not give in, but stay and fight.* ❏ *She insisted on being present at all the interviews.* ❷ V-T/V-I If you **insist that** something is the case, you say so very firmly and refuse to say otherwise, even though other people do not believe you. ❏ *The president insisted that he was acting out of compassion, not political opportunism.* ❏ *"It's not that difficult," she insists.*

Word Partnership   insist의 연어

V.	**continue to** insist ❶ ❷
N.	**critics** insist, **leaders/officials** insist, **people** insist ❶ ❷

in|sist|ence /ɪnsɪstəns/ N-UNCOUNT Someone's **insistence** on something is the fact that they insist that it should be done or insist that it is the case. ❏ *...Raeder's insistence that naval uniform be worn.*

in|sist|ent /ɪnsɪstənt/ ❶ ADJ Someone who is **insistent** keeps insisting that a particular thing should be done or is the case. ❏ *Stalin was insistent that the war would be won and lost in the machine shops.* ● **in|sist|ent|ly** ADV [ADV with v] ❏ *"What is it?" his wife asked again, gently but insistently.* ❷ ADJ An **insistent** noise or rhythm keeps going on for a long time and holds your attention. ❏ *...the insistent rhythms of the Caribbean and Latin America.*

커플은 안으로 들어가기 전에 문간에서 잠시 이야기를 나누었다. ● 형용사 내부의 ❏ 개별 욕실과 샤워 시설이 딸린 침대 네 개짜리 안쪽 선실 ❷ 가산명사 안쪽, 내부 ❏ 문들이 안쪽에서 잠겨 있었다. ● 형용사 안쪽의 ❏ 대중 일간지에는 모두 안쪽 면에 특집 사진난이 있다. ● 부사 안쪽에, 안쪽으로 ❏ 감자 케이크는 바깥쪽은 바삭바삭하고 안쪽은 살살 녹을 정도로 부드럽게 될 때까지 기름에 지지거나 튀기면 된다. ❸ 부사 감옥에 갇혀 [비격식체] ❏ 그들은 둘 다 옥살이를 했다. 그는 감옥에 세 번 갔다 왔다. ❹ 형용사 내밀한, 비밀의 ❏ 슬로안은 기밀 외교 정보를 이용해서 부자가 되었다. 편집자인 키스 배스는 자기에게 내부 정보가 있었다는 것을 부인한다. ❺ 전치사 – 소속의 ❏ 중역의 75퍼센트가 회사 내부 출신이다. ● 형용사 내부의 ❏ 프로 미식축구의 내부 세계에 관한 최근 서적 ● 단수명사 내부 ❏ 맥아보이는 자기가 내부에서 일을 통제할 수 있을 것이라고 확신했지만 장악할 수 없었다. ❻ 복수명사 배, 뱃속 [비격식체] ❏ 알약은 먹을 때마다 내 뱃속을 뒤집어 놓았다. ❼ 부사 마음속으로 ❏ 마음속에 남은 것은 없다. 할 말도 분노도, 눈물도, 아무 것도. ● 전치사 –의 속에 ❏ 그는 마음속으로 깊은 슬픔을 느꼈다. ● 단수명사 내심, 본성 ❏ 정말 필요한 것은 본성의 변화, 즉 사고방식과 마음가짐에 있어서의 진실한 변화이다. ❽ 전치사 – 이내에 ❏ 그들은 한 시간 내에 모든 것이 제대로 돌아가도록 만들어야 한다. ❾ 구 뒤집어져서 ❏ 그녀의 우산이 바람에 뒤집어졌다. ❿ 구 샅샅이, 속속들이 [강조] ❏ 그는 그 게임을 샅샅이 알고 있었다.

가산명사 내막에 밝은 사람, 내부자 ❏ 한 내부자가 말했다. "캐서린이 친구들에게 이제 일을 그만둬야 할 때라고 말했다."

불가산명사 내부자 거래 [경제] ❏ 자기 자신의 회사 주식 내부 거래로 고발된 스튜어트 씨의 친구

형용사 잠행성의, 모르는 사이에 진행하는 ❏ 변화는 아주 서서히 진행되어 15 내지 20년 동안은 눈에 띄는 결과를 보이지 않을 것이다.

❶ 가산명사 또는 불가산명사 통찰, 통찰력 ❏ 그 프로젝트는 과학자들에게 지구의 대기에서 일어나고 있는 일에 대한 새로운 통찰력을 제공할 것이다. ❷ 불가산명사 식견 ❏ 그는 상당한 식견과 외교적 수완을 가진 성격이 강한 사람이었다.

불가산명사 하찮음, 무의미 ❏ 고 알프레드 스티그릿츠의 주요 두 작품에 지불한 것에 비하면 이런 가격들은 하찮아진다.

형용사 하찮은, 사소한 ❏ 1949년에 본은 작고 하찮은 도시였다.

형용사 위선적인 [탐탁잖음] ❏ 어떤 사람들은 몹시 위선적이라서 진실을 말하고 있는지 여부를 전혀 알 수 없다.

❶ 타동사/자동사 강요하다, 우기다 ❏ 내 가족은 내가 굴복하지 말고 버티며 싸울 것을 강하게 요구했다. ❏ 그녀는 모든 인터뷰에 참석하겠다고 우겼다. ❷ 타동사/자동사 주장하다, 고집하다 ❏ 대통령은 정치적 기회주의에서가 아니라 깊은 동정심에서 행동한다고 주장했다. ❏ "그건 그렇게 어렵지 않아."라고 그녀가 주장한다.

불가산명사 강요, 주장 ❏ 해군 제복을 입어야 한다는 래더의 주장

❶ 형용사 강요하는, 주장하는 ❏ 스탈린은 그 전쟁은 장비 공장에서 승패가 가려질 것이라고 주장했다. ● 끈질기게, 고집스럽게 부사 ❏ "그게 뭐예요?"라고 그의 부인이 부드럽지만 끈덕지게 다시 물었다. ❷ 형용사 지속적인 ❏ 카리브 해와 남미의 지속적인 리듬들

a b c d e f g h i j k l m n o p q r s t u v w x y z

in|so|far as /ɪnsəfɑːr æz, ɪnsoʊ-/ PHRASE You use **insofar as** to introduce a statement which explains and adds to something you have just said. [FORMAL] ❑ *We are entering a period of less danger insofar as the danger of nuclear war between the superpowers is less.*

구 ﹏하는 한에 있어서 [격식체] ❑ 초강대국 사이의 핵전쟁 위험이 적어지고 있는 한 우리는 위험이 덜한 시기로 접어들고 있다.

in|so|lent /ɪnsələnt/ ADJ If you say that someone is being **insolent**, you mean they are being rude to someone they ought to be respectful to. ❑ *...her insolent stare.*

형용사 무례한, 거만한 ❑ 그녀의 무례한 응시

in|sol|uble /ɪnsɒlyəbəl/ ❶ ADJ An **insoluble** problem is so difficult that it is impossible to solve. ❑ *I pushed the problem aside; at present it was insoluble.* ❷ ADJ If a substance is **insoluble**, it does not dissolve in a liquid. ❑ *Carotenes are insoluble in water and soluble in oils and fats.*

❶ 형용사 해결할 수 없는 ❑ 나는 그 문제를 제쳐놓았다. 현재로선 해결할 수 없었다. ❷ 형용사 불용해성의 ❑ 카로틴은 물에 용해되지 않고 기름과 유지에 용해된다.

in|sol|ven|cy /ɪnsɒlvənsi/ (**insolvencies**) N-VAR **Insolvency** is the state of not having enough money to pay your debts. [FORMAL, BUSINESS] ❑ *...eight mortgage companies, seven of which are on the brink of insolvency.*

가산명사 또는 불가산명사 변제 불능, 지불 불능 [격식체, 경제] ❑ 지불 불능 상태 직전에 있는 일곱 개의 회사를 포함한 여덟 개의 모기지 회사

in|sol|vent /ɪnsɒlvənt/ ADJ A person or organization that is **insolvent** does not have enough money to pay their debts. [FORMAL, BUSINESS] ❑ *Two years later, the bank was declared insolvent.*

형용사 지불 불능의, 파산한 [격식체, 경제] ❑ 2년 후, 그 은행은 지급 불능이라고 선고받았다.

in|som|nia /ɪnsɒmniə/ N-UNCOUNT Someone who suffers from **insomnia** finds it difficult to sleep. →see **sleep**

불가산명사 불면증

in|spect ♦◇◇ /ɪnspɛkt/ (**inspects, inspecting, inspected**) ❶ V-T If you **inspect** something, you look at every part of it carefully in order to find out about it or check that it is all right. ❑ *Elaine went outside to inspect the playing field.* ● **in|spec|tion** /ɪnspɛkʃən/ (**inspections**) N-VAR ❑ *"Excellent work," he said when he had completed his inspection of the painted doors.* ❷ V-T When an official **inspects** a place or a group of people, they visit it and check it carefully, for example in order to find out whether regulations are being obeyed. ❑ *The Public Utilities Commission inspects us once a year.* ● **in|spec|tion** N-VAR ❑ *Officers making a routine inspection of the vessel found fifty kilograms of cocaine.*

❶ 타동사 (세밀히) 조사하다, 검사하다 ❑ 일레인은 운동장을 점검하기 위해 밖으로 나갔다. ● 조사, 검사 가산명사 또는 불가산명사 ❑ "아주 잘 되었군요."라고 그는 페인트칠을 한 문들을 점검하고 나서 말했다. ❷ 타동사 감사하다, 검열하다 ❑ 공익 기업 위원회가 일 년에 한 번 우리를 감사한다. ● 감사, 검열 가산명사 또는 불가산명사 ❑ 그 선박을 의례적으로 검열하던 경찰들이 코카인 50킬로그램을 찾아냈다.

<table>
<tr><td colspan="2">**Word Partnership**   *inspect*의 연어</td></tr>
<tr><td>N.</td><td>inspect **damage**, inspect **records**, inspect **sites**, inspect **weapons** ❶ ❷</td></tr>
</table>

in|spec|tor ♦◇◇ /ɪnspɛktər/ (**inspectors**) ❶ N-COUNT An **inspector** is a person, usually employed by a government agency, whose job is to find out whether people are obeying official regulations. ❑ *The mill was finally shut down by state safety inspectors.* ❷ N-COUNT; N-TITLE; N-VOC In the United States, an **inspector** is an officer in the police who is next in rank to a superintendent or police chief. ❑ *San Francisco police inspector Tony Camileri.* ❸ N-COUNT; N-TITLE; N-VOC In Britain, an **inspector** is an officer in the police who is higher in rank than a sergeant and lower in rank than a superintendent. ❑ *Last week gunmen attacked Mogadishu airport killing a police inspector.*

❶ 가산명사 검열관 ❑ 그 공장은 마침내 정부 안전 검열관에 의해 폐쇄되었다. ❷ 가산명사; 경칭명사; 호격명사 (미국의) 경감 ❑ 샌프란시스코 경찰 경감 토니 카밀레리 ❸ 가산명사; 경칭명사; 호격명사 (영국의) 경감 ❑ 지난 주 무장 괴한들이 모가디슈 공항을 공격하여 경감 한 명을 죽였다.

in|spi|ra|tion /ɪnspɪreɪʃən/ (**inspirations**) ❶ N-UNCOUNT **Inspiration** is a feeling of enthusiasm you get from someone or something, which gives you new and creative ideas. ❑ *My inspiration comes from poets like Baudelaire and Jacques Prévert.* ❷ N-SING If you describe someone or something good as **an inspiration**, you mean that they make you or other people want to do or achieve something. [APPROVAL] ❑ *Powell's unusual journey to high office is an inspiration to millions.* ❸ N-SING If something or someone is **the inspiration for** a particular book, work of art, or action, they are the source of the ideas in it or act as a model for it. ❑ *India's myths and songs are the inspiration for her books.* ❹ N-COUNT If you suddenly have an **inspiration**, you suddenly think of an idea of what to do or say. ❑ *Alison had an inspiration. "Wouldn't it be good if we made a tunnel out of hardboard."*

❶ 불가산명사 영감 ❑ 나의 영감은 보들레르와 자크 프레베르와 같은 시인들로부터 온다. ❷ 단수명사 고무시키는 사람, 고무시키는 것 [마음에 듦] ❑ 파월의 범상치 않은 고위직 진출이 수백만 사람들을 고무시킨다. ❸ 단수명사 영감의 근원 ❑ 인도의 신화와 노래가 그녀의 책들이 나오게 된 영감의 원천이다. ❹ 가산명사 신통한 생각, 기발한 착상 ❑ 앨리슨에게 기발한 생각이 들었다. "우리가 하드보드로 터널을 만든다면 좋지 않을까."

<table>
<tr><td colspan="2">**Word Partnership**   *inspiration*의 연어</td></tr>
<tr><td>V.</td><td>provide *an* inspiration ❶-❸
draw inspiration from *someone/something*, find inspiration ❶ ❸
have an inspiration ❹</td></tr>
<tr><td>N.</td><td>source of inspiration ❶-❸</td></tr>
</table>

<table>
<tr><td>**Word Link**   spir ≈ breath : a**spir**e, in**spir**e, re**spir**atory</td></tr>
</table>

in|spire /ɪnspaɪər/ (**inspires, inspiring, inspired**) ❶ V-T If someone or something **inspires** you **to** do something new or unusual, they make you want to do it. ❑ *Our challenge is to motivate those voters and inspire them to join our cause.* ❷ V-T If someone or something **inspires** you, they give you new ideas and a strong feeling of enthusiasm. ❑ *In the 1960s, the electric guitar virtuosity of Jimi Hendrix inspired a generation.* ❸ V-T If a book, work of art, or action **is inspired by** something, that thing is the source of the ideas in it. [usu passive] ❑ *The book was inspired by a real person, namely Tamara de Treaux.* ● **-inspired** COMB in ADJ ❑ *...Mediterranean-inspired ceramics in bright yellow and blue.* ❹ V-T Someone or something that **inspires** a particular emotion or reaction in people makes them feel this emotion or reaction. ❑ *The car's performance is effortless and its handling is precise and quickly inspires confidence.*

❶ 타동사 고무시키다 ❑ 우리의 도전은 그 유권자들을 자극하고 고무시켜 우리의 대의에 동참시키는 일이다. ❷ 타동사 영감을 불어넣다 ❑ 1960년대에 지미 헨드릭스의 현란한 전자 기타 연주 솜씨는 한 세대에게 영감을 불어넣었다. ❸ 타동사 영감을 받다 ❑ 그 책은 실제 인물, 즉 타마라 드 트로에게서 영감을 받았다. ● ~에 영감을 받은 복합형·형용사 ❑ 지중해에서 영감을 받은 선명한 노란색과 푸른색의 도자기들 ❹ 타동사 불어넣다, 고취하다 ❑ 이 자동차는 부드럽게 움직이고, 핸들링이 정확하여 금방 자신감을 불어넣는다.

<table>
<tr><td colspan="2">**Word Partnership**   *inspire*의 연어</td></tr>
<tr><td>N.</td><td>inspire **people** ❶ ❷
ability to inspire ❶ ❷ ❹
inspire **affection**, inspire **confidence**, inspire **fear** ❹</td></tr>
</table>

in|spir|ing /ɪnspaɪərɪŋ/ ADJ Something or someone that is **inspiring** is exciting and makes you feel strongly interested and enthusiastic... ❑ *She was a very strong, impressive character and one of the most inspiring people I've ever met.*

형용사 고무적인, 영감을 불어넣어 주는 ❑ 그녀는 매우 강하고 인상적인 성격이었으며, 내가 만난 사람 중 가장 강한 영감을 주는 사람들 중 한 명이었다.

Word Link　　stab ≈ steady : de*stab*ilize, e*stab*lish, in*stab*ility

---

in|stabil|ity /ɪnstəbɪlɪti/ (**instabilities**) N-UNCOUNT **Instability** is the quality of being unstable. ❑ *...unpopular policies, which resulted in social discontent and political instability.*

불가산명사 불안정 ❑ 인기가 없는 정책들, 이들이 사회적 불만족과 정치적 불안정을 낳았다.

in|stall ♦♢♢ /ɪnstɔl/ (**installs, installing, installed**) [BRIT also **instal**] ■ V-T If you **install** a piece of equipment, you fit it or put it somewhere so that it is ready to be used. ❑ *They had installed a new phone line in the apartment.* • in|stal|la|tion N-UNCOUNT ❑ *Hundreds of lives could be saved if the installation of alarms was more widespread.* ■ V-T If someone **is installed** in a new job or important position, they are officially given the job or position, often in a special ceremony. ❑ *A new Catholic bishop was installed in Galway yesterday.* ❑ *Professor Sawyer was formally installed as President last Thursday.* • in|stal|la|tion N-UNCOUNT ❑ *He sent a letter inviting Naomi to attend his installation as chief of his tribe.* ■ V-T If you **install yourself** in a particular place, you settle there and make yourself comfortable. [FORMAL] ❑ *Before her husband's death she had installed herself in a modern villa.*

[영국영어 instal] ■ 타동사 설치하다 ❑ 그들은 아파트에 새 전화선을 설치했었다. ● 설치 불가산명사 ❑ 경보기가 좀 더 광범위하게 설치된다면 수백 명의 목숨을 구할 수 있을 것이다. ■ 타동사 –에 임명되다 ❑ 어제 골웨이에 새 가톨릭 주교가 임명되었다. ❑ 소이어 교수는 지난주 목요일에 총장으로 공식 임명되었다. ● 임명, 취임 불가산명사 ❑ 그는 나오미에게 자신의 부족의 족장 취임식에 참석을 초청하는 편지를 보냈다. ■ 타동사 –에 자리 잡다 [격식체] ❑ 남편이 사망하기 전에 그녀는 현대식 빌라에 자리 잡았었다.

Word Partnership　　*install*의 연어

ADJ.	**easy to** install ■
N.	install **equipment**, install **machines**, install **software** ■

---

in|stal|la|tion /ɪnstəleɪʃⁿn/ (**installations**) N-COUNT An **installation** is a place that contains equipment and machinery which are being used for a particular purpose. ❑ *The building was turned into a secret military installation.* →see also **install**

가산명사 시설 ❑ 그 건물은 비밀 군사 시설로 전환되었다.

in|stall|ment /ɪnstɔlmənt/ (**installments**) [BRIT **instalment**] ■ N-COUNT If you pay for something in **installments**, you pay small sums of money at regular intervals over a period of time, rather than paying the whole amount at once. ❑ *Some pay by check or credit card, but no one buys on the installment plan.* ❑ *Upper-bracket taxpayers who elected to pay their tax increase in installments must pay the third installment by April 15.* ■ N-COUNT An **installment** of a story or plan is one of its parts that are published or carried out separately one after the other. ❑ *The next installment of this four-part series deals with the impact of the war on the continent of Africa.*

[영국영어 instalment] ■ 가산명사 할부, 분납 ❑ 몇몇은 수표나 신용 카드로 지불하지만, 아무도 할부로는 사지 않는다. ❑ 세금 증액분을 분할 납부할 것을 선택한 고액 납세자들은 4월 15일까지 3기분 분납금을 납부해야 한다. ■ 가산명사 (연재물 등의) 1회분 ❑ 이 4부작 시리즈물의 다음 회는 아프리카 대륙에 끼친 전쟁의 영향을 다룬다.

in|stall|ment plan (**installment plans**) N-COUNT An **installment plan** is a way of buying goods gradually. You make regular payments to the seller until, after some time, you have paid the full price and the goods belong to you. [AM; BRIT **hire purchase**]

가산명사 할부 구매 [미국영어; 영국영어 hire purchase]

in|stance ♦♦♢ /ɪnstəns/ (**instances**) ■ PHRASE You use **for instance** to introduce a particular event, situation, or person that is an example of what you are talking about. ❑ *In sub-Saharan Africa today, for instance, gross investment accounts for roughly 15% of national income.* ■ N-COUNT An **instance** is a particular example or occurrence of something. ❑ *...an investigation into a serious instance of corruption.* ■ PHRASE You say **in the first instance** to mention something that is the first step in a series of actions. ❑ *In the first instance your child will be seen by an ear, nose, and throat specialist.*

■ 구 예를 들면 ❑ 예를 들면 오늘날 사하라 사막 이남의 아프리카에서는 총투자 금액이 대체로 국민소득의 15퍼센트에 달한다. ■ 가산명사 사례, 실례 ❑ 중대한 부패 사례에 대한 조사 ■ 구 첫째로, 우선 ❑ 우선 당신 아이를 눈, 코, 목 전문의가 진찰할 것입니다.

in|stant ♦♢♢ /ɪnstənt/ (**instants**) ■ N-COUNT An **instant** is an extremely short period of time. ❑ *For an instant, Catherine was tempted to flee.* ■ N-SING If you say that something happens **at** a particular **instant**, you mean that it happens at exactly the time you have been referring to, and you are usually suggesting that it happens quickly or immediately. ❑ *At that instant the museum was plunged into total darkness.* ■ PHRASE To do something **the instant** something else happens means to do it immediately. [EMPHASIS] ❑ *I had bolted the door the instant I had seen the bat.* ■ ADJ You use **instant** to describe something that happens immediately. ❑ *Mr. Porter's book was an instant hit.* • in|stant|ly ADV ❑ *The man was killed instantly.* ■ ADJ **Instant** food is food that you can prepare very quickly, for example by just adding water. [ADJ n] ❑ *He was stirring instant coffee into two mugs of hot water.*

■ 가산명사 순간, 찰나 ❑ 일순간, 캐서린은 달아나고 싶은 유혹을 느꼈다. ■ 단수명사 바로 그 순간 ❑ 바로 그 순간 박물관이 완전 어둠에 잠겼다. ■ 구 –하자마자 [강조] ❑ 나는 박쥐를 보자마자 문을 잠갔다. ■ 형용사 즉각적인, 순간적인 ❑ 포터 씨의 책은 즉각 히트를 쳤다. ● 즉시, 순식간에 부사 ❑ 그 남자는 즉사했다. ■ 형용사 인스턴트 (식품) ❑ 그는 인스턴트 커피를 뜨거운 물이 담긴 물잔 두 개에 넣고 저었다.

Thesaurus　　*instant*의 참조어

N.	minute, second, split second ■

Word Partnership　　*instant*의 연어

PREP.	**for an** instant, **in an** instant ■
ADJ.	**the next** instant ■ ■
N.	instant **access**, instant **messaging**, instant **success** ■

---

in|stan|ta|neous /ɪnstənteɪniəs/ ADJ Something that is **instantaneous** happens immediately and very quickly. ❑ *Death was not instantaneous because none of the bullets hit the heart.* • in|stan|ta|neous|ly ADV [ADV with v] ❑ *Airbags inflate instantaneously on impact to form a cushion between the driver and the steering column.*

형용사 즉시의, 순간적인 ❑ 총알이 모두 심장을 피해 갔기 때문에 즉사하지는 않았다. ● 즉시, 순간적으로 부사 ❑ 에어백은 충돌 시 순식간에 운전자와 운전대 사이에 쿠션 형태로 부풀어 오른다.

in|stead ♦♦♢ /ɪnstɛd/ ■ PHRASE If you do one thing **instead of** another, you do the first thing and not the second thing, as the result of a choice or a change of behavior. ❑ *They raised prices and cut production, instead of cutting costs.* ■ ADV If you do not do something, but do something else **instead**, you do the second

■ 구 – 대신에 ❑ 그들은 비용을 줄이는 대신에 가격을 올리고 생산을 줄였다. ■ 부사 대신에 ❑ 그는 와인을 집었지만 정작 마시지는 않고, 대신 조안나가 있는 테이블 건너 쪽으로 밀어 버렸다.

a b c d e f g h i j k l m n o p q r s t u v w x y z

A

thing and not the first thing, as the result of a choice or a change of behavior. [ADV with cl] ❏ *He reached for the wine but did not drink, pushed it, instead, across the table towards Joanna.*

B

in|sti|gate /ɪnstɪgeɪt/ (**instigates, instigating, instigated**) V-T Someone who **instigates** an event causes it to happen. ❏ *Jenkinson instigated a refurbishment of the old gallery.* ● **in|sti|ga|tion** /ɪnstɪgeɪʃ°n/ N-UNCOUNT ❏ *The talks are taking place at the instigation of Germany.*

타동사 부추기다, ~하게 하다 ❏ 젠킨슨은 그 낡은 갤러리를 재단장하도록 하였다. ● 부추김, 선동 불가산명사 ❏ 독일의 주도로 그 회담이 이루어지고 있다.

C

in|sti|ga|tor /ɪnstɪgeɪtər/ (**instigators**) N-COUNT The **instigator** of an event is the person who causes it to happen. ❏ *He was accused of being the main instigator of the coup.*

가산명사 선동자, 주동자 ❏ 그는 쿠데타의 주동자로 기소되었다.

D

in|still /ɪnstɪl/ (**instills, instilling, instilled**) [BRIT **instil**] V-T If you **instill** an idea or feeling in someone, especially over a period of time, you make them think it or feel it. ❏ *The tough thing is trying to instill a winning attitude in the kids.*

[영국영어 instil] 타동사 서서히 불어넣다, 주입하다 ❏ 아이들에게 승부 근성을 갖게 하는 것은 힘든 일이다.

E

in|stinct /ɪnstɪŋkt/ (**instincts**) ■ N-VAR **Instinct** is the natural tendency that a person or animal has to behave or react in a particular way. ❏ *I didn't have as strong a maternal instinct as some other mothers.* ■ N-COUNT If you have an **instinct for** something, you are naturally good at it or able to do it. ❏ *He seems to have an instinct for smart advertising and marketing.* ■ N-VAR If it is your **instinct to** do something, you feel that it is right to do it. ❏ *I should've gone with my first instinct, which was not to do the interview.* ■ N-VAR **Instinct** is a feeling that you have that something is the case, rather than an opinion or idea based on facts. ❏ *There is scientific evidence to support our instinct that being surrounded by plants is good for health.*

■ 가산명사 또는 불가산명사 본능 ❏ 나는 다른 어머니들처럼 강한 모성 본능이 없었다. ■ 가산명사 타고난 재능, 소질 ❏ 그는 광고와 마케팅에 타고난 재능이 있는 것 같다. ■ 가산명사 또는 불가산명사 직감 ❏ 나는 인터뷰를 하지 않겠다는 첫 직감을 따랐어야 했다. ■ 가산명사 또는 불가산명사 직관 ❏ 식물에 둘러싸여 있는 것이 건강에 좋다는 우리의 직관을 뒷받침해 주는 과학적 증거가 있다.

F

G

H

Word Partnership *instinct의 연어*

N.	**survival** instinct ■
ADJ.	**basic** instinct, **maternal** instinct, **natural** instinct ■

I

J

in|stinc|tive /ɪnstɪŋktɪv/ ADJ An **instinctive** feeling, idea, or action is one that you have or do without thinking or reasoning. ❏ *It's an absolutely instinctive reaction – if a child falls you pick it up.* ● **in|stinc|tive|ly** ADV [ADV with v] ❏ *Jane instinctively knew all was not well with her 10-month old son.*

형용사 본능의, 본능적인 ❏ 아이가 넘어지면 일으켜 세워 주는 것은 전적으로 본능적인 반응이다. ● 본능적으로 부사 ❏ 제인은 십 개월 된 아들에게 무슨 일이 있다는 것을 본능적으로 알았다.

K

L

in|sti|tute ♦♦◇ /ɪnstɪtut, BRIT ɪnstɪtjuːt/ (**institutes, instituting, instituted**) ■ N-COUNT; N-IN-NAMES An **institute** is an organization set up to do a particular type of work, especially research or teaching. You can also use **institute** to refer to the building the organization occupies. ❏ *...the National Cancer Institute.* ■ V-T If you **institute** a system, rule, or course of action, you start it. [FORMAL] ❏ *We will institute a number of measures to better safeguard the public.*

■ 가산명사; 이름명사 연구소, 학회 ❏ 국립 암 연구소 ■ 타동사 시작하다, 제정하다 [격식체] ❏ 우리는 일반 대중을 더욱 잘 보호하기 위하여 많은 조치들을 취할 것이다.

M

N

in|sti|tu|tion ♦♦◇ /ɪnstɪtuʃ°n, BRIT ɪnstɪtjuːʃ°n/ (**institutions**) ■ N-COUNT; N-IN-NAMES An **institution** is a large important organization such as a university, church, or bank. ❏ *...the Institution of Civil Engineers.* ■ N-COUNT; N-IN-NAMES An **institution** is a building where certain people are cared for, for example people who are mentally ill or children who have no parents. ❏ *Larry has been in an institution since he was four.* ■ N-COUNT An **institution** is a custom or system that is considered an important or typical feature of a particular society or group, usually because it has existed for a long time. ❏ *I believe in the institution of marriage.* ■ N-UNCOUNT The **institution** of a new system is the act of starting it or bringing it in. ❏ *There was never an official institution of censorship in Albania.*

■ 가산명사; 이름명사 기관 ❏ 토목 공학 대학 ■ 가산명사; 이름명사 시설, 정신 병원, 고아원 ❏ 래리는 네 살 때부터 고아원에 있었다. ■ 가산명사 제도, 관례 ❏ 나는 결혼 제도를 믿는다. ■ 불가산명사 실립, 제정 ❏ 알바니아에는 공식적인 검열 제도가 존재한 적이 없었다.

O

P

Q

in|sti|tu|tion|al /ɪnstɪtuʃən°l, BRIT ɪnstɪtjuːʃən°l/ ■ ADJ **Institutional** means relating to a large organization, for example a university, bank, or church. [ADJ n] ❏ *NATO remains the United States' chief institutional anchor in Europe.* ■ ADJ **Institutional** means relating to a building where people are cared for or held. [ADJ n] ❏ *Outside the protected environment of institutional care he could not survive.* ■ ADJ An **institutional** value or quality is considered an important and typical feature of a particular society or group, usually because it has existed for a long time. [ADJ n] ❏ *...social and institutional values.*

■ 형용사 공공 기관의 ❏ 나토는 여전히 유럽에 있는 미국 주요 기관의 보루이다. ■ 형용사 시설의 ❏ 보호 시설의 보호 환경 밖에서는 그가 살아갈 수가 없을 것이다. ■ 형용사 제도적, 관례적 ❏ 사회 제도적 가치들

R

S

in|sti|tu|tion|al|ize /ɪnstɪtuʃən°laɪz, BRIT ɪnstɪtjuːʃənəlaɪz/ (**institutionalizes, institutionalizing, institutionalized**) [BRIT also **institutionalise**] ■ V-T If someone such as a sick, mentally ill, or old person is **institutionalized**, they are sent to stay in a special hospital or home, usually for a long period. [usu passive] ❏ *She became seriously ill and had to be institutionalized for a lengthy period.* ■ V-T To **institutionalize** something means to establish it as part of a culture, social system, or organization. ❏ *The goal is to institutionalize family planning into community life.*

[영국영어 institutionalise] ■ 타동사 시설에 수용되다 ❏ 그녀는 병을 심각하게 앓게 되어서 장기간 시설에 수용되어야 했다. ■ 타동사 제도화하다 ❏ 가족계획을 공동체 삶에 제도화하는 것이 목표이다.

T

U

V

Word Link *struct ≈ building : construct, destructive, instruct*

W

in|struct /ɪnstrʌkt/ (**instructs, instructing, instructed**) ■ V-T If you **instruct** someone to do something, you formally tell them to do it. [FORMAL] ❏ *The family has instructed solicitors to sue Thomson for compensation.* ❏ *"Go and have a word with her, Ken," Webb instructed.* ■ V-T Someone who **instructs** people in a subject or skill teaches it to them. ❏ *He instructed family members in nursing techniques.*

■ 타동사 지시하다 [격식체] ❏ 그 가족은 보상 문제로 톰슨을 고소하라고 변호사들에게 공식적으로 요청하였다. ❏ "가서 그녀에게 말을 해라, 켄."이라고 웹이 지시했다. ■ 타동사 가르치다, 교육하다 ❏ 그는 가족 구성원들에게 간호 기술을 가르쳤다.

X

in|struc|tion ♦♦◇ /ɪnstrʌkʃ°n/ (**instructions**) ■ N-COUNT An **instruction** is something that someone tells you to do. ❏ *Two lawyers were told not to leave the building but no reason for this instruction was given.* ■ N-UNCOUNT If someone gives you **instruction** in a subject or skill, they teach it to you. [FORMAL] ❏ *Each candidate is given instruction in safety.* ■ N-PLURAL **Instructions** are clear and

■ 가산명사 지시, 명령 ❏ 변호사 두 명에게 그 건물을 떠나지 말라는 말은 했으나 그러한 지시를 하는 이유는 말해 주지 않았다. ■ 불가산명사 교육, 가르치는 것 [격식체] ❏ 각 후보자에게 안전 관련 교육을 해 준다. ■ 복수명사 설명 ❏ 이 책은 다양한

Y

Z

detailed information on how to do something. ❏ *This book gives instructions for making a wide range of skin and hand creams.*

종류의 스킨과 핸드크림 만드는 법을 설명해 준다.

Thesaurus
*instruction*의 참조어

N.	direction, order **1**
	education, learning **2**

Word Partnership
*instruction*의 연어

ADJ.	**explicit** instruction **1** **2**
N.	**classroom** instruction, instruction **manual** **2**
V.	**give** instruction, **provide** instruction, **receive** instruction **2**

in|struc|tive /ɪnstrʌktɪv/ ADJ Something that is **instructive** gives useful information. ❏ *...an entertaining and instructive documentary.*

형용사 교훈적인 ❏ 재미있으면서 교훈적인 다큐멘터리

in|struc|tor /ɪnstrʌktər/ (**instructors**) N-COUNT An **instructor** is someone who teaches a skill such as driving or skiing. In American English, **instructor** can also be used to refer to a schoolteacher or to a university teacher of low rank. ❏ *I recommend that you drive under tuition from an approved driving instructor.*

가산명사 교사, 강사 ❏ 공인된 운전 교습 강사에게 교육을 받으며 운전하는 것을 추천한다.

Thesaurus
*instructor*의 참조어

N.	leader, professor, teacher

in|stru|ment ♦◇◇ /ɪnstrəmənt/ (**instruments**) **1** N-COUNT An **instrument** is a tool or device that is used to do a particular task, especially a scientific task. ❏ *...instruments for cleaning and polishing teeth.* **2** N-COUNT A musical **instrument** is an object such as a piano, guitar, or flute, which you play in order to produce music. ❏ *Learning a musical instrument introduces a child to an understanding of music.* **3** N-COUNT An **instrument** is a device that is used for making measurements of something such as speed, height, or sound, for example on a ship or plane or in a car. ❏ *The design of crucial instruments on the control panel will have to be improved.* **4** N-COUNT Something that is an **instrument** for achieving a particular aim is used by people to achieve that aim. ❏ *The veto has been a traditional instrument of diplomacy for centuries.* →see **concert, drum, orchestra**

1 가산명사 기구, 기계 ❏ 치아를 깨끗하게 닦아 주는 기구 **2** 가산명사 악기 ❏ 악기를 배우는 것은 아이에게 음악을 이해하게 해 준다. **3** 가산명사 측량 장치 ❏ 제어판에 있는 중요 장치들의 설계를 개선해야 할 것이다. **4** 가산명사 수단, 방법 ❏ 거부권은 수세기 동안 외교의 전통적인 수단이었다.

in|stru|men|tal /ɪnstrəmɛntəl/ (**instrumentals**) **1** ADJ Someone or something that is **instrumental in** a process or event helps to make it happen. ❏ *In his first years as chairman he was instrumental in raising the company's wider profile.* **2** ADJ **Instrumental** music is performed by instruments and not by voices. [ADJ n] ❏ *...a cassette recording of vocal and instrumental music.* ● N-COUNT **Instrumentals** are pieces of instrumental music. ❏ *After a couple of brief instrumentals, he puts his guitar down.*

1 형용사 도움이 되는 ❏ 회장으로 지낸 초기에 그는 회사의 지명도를 높이는 데 공헌을 했다. **2** 형용사 기악의 ❏ 성악과 기악의 카세트 녹음 ● 가산명사 기악곡 ❏ 짧은 기악곡 두어 개를 연주한 후에, 그는 기타를 내려놓는다.

in|suf|fi|cient /ɪnsəfɪʃənt/ ADJ Something that is **insufficient** is not large enough in amount or degree for a particular purpose. [FORMAL] ❏ *He decided there was insufficient evidence to justify criminal proceedings.* ● in|suf|fi|cient|ly ADV [ADV adj/-ed] ❏ *Food that is insufficiently cooked can lead to food poisoning.*

형용사 불충분한 [격식체] ❏ 형사 소송을 정당화할 증거가 불충분하다고 그는 결정했다. ● 불충분하게 부사 ❏ 덜 익힌 음식은 식중독을 유발할 수 있다.

in|su|lar /ɪnsələr, BRIT ɪnsyʊlɑːr/ ADJ If you say that someone is **insular**, you are being critical of them because they are unwilling to meet new people or to consider new ideas. [DISAPPROVAL] ❏ *The old image of the insular, xenophobic Brit has altered dramatically with this new Euro-conscious generation.* ● in|su|lar|ity /ɪnsəlærɪti, BRIT ɪnsyʊlærɪti/ N-UNCOUNT ❏ *But at least they have started to break out of their old insularity.*

형용사 편협한 [탐탁찮음] ❏ 편협하고 외국인을 혐오한다는 영국 사람들의 옛 이미지는 새로이 유럽을 인지하는 세대의 등장과 더불어 급속하게 변하였다. ● 편협함 불가산명사 ❏ 그러나 적어도 그들은 이전의 편협함을 깨기 시작했다.

in|su|late /ɪnsəleɪt, BRIT ɪnsyʊleɪt/ (**insulates, insulating, insulated**) **1** V-T If a person or group **is insulated from** the rest of society or from outside influences, they are protected from them. ❏ *They wonder if their community is no longer insulated from big city problems.* ● in|su|la|tion N-UNCOUNT ❏ *They lived in happy insulation from brutal facts.* **2** V-T To **insulate** something such as a building means to protect it from cold or noise by covering it or surrounding it in a thick layer. ❏ *It will take almost 25 years to insulate the homes of the six million households that require this assistance.* ❏ *Is there any way we can insulate our home from the noise?* **3** V-T If a piece of equipment **is insulated**, it is covered with rubber or plastic to prevent electricity passing through it and giving the person using it an electric shock. ❏ *In order to make it safe, the element is electrically insulated.*

1 타동사 차단되다, 격리되다 ❏ 그들은 자신들의 공동체가 더 이상 대도시 문제로부터 자유로운지에 대해 의문이 들었다. ● 차단, 격리 불가산명사 ❏ 그들은 냉혹한 사실로부터 격리되어 행복하게 살았다. **2** 타동사 단열하다, 방음하다 ❏ 이러한 도움이 필요한 600만 가구의 주택에 단열 공사를 하는 데는 거의 25년이 소요될 것이다. ❏ 그 소음이 안 들리게 우리 집에 방음 장치를 할 수 있는 방법이 있는가? **3** 타동사 절연되다 ❏ 안전을 위해서 그 성분은 절연 처리 되었다.

in|su|la|tion /ɪnsəleɪʃən, BRIT ɪnsyʊleɪʃən/ N-UNCOUNT **Insulation** is a thick layer of a substance that keeps something warm, especially a building. ❏ *High electricity bills point to a poor heating system or bad insulation.* →see also **insulate**

불가산명사 단열재 ❏ 전기료가 많이 나오는 것을 볼 때 난방 시설이 나쁘거나 좋지 않은 단열재를 사용하는 듯하다.

in|su|lin /ɪnsəlɪn, BRIT ɪnsyʊlɪn/ N-UNCOUNT **Insulin** is a substance that most people produce naturally in their body and which controls the level of sugar in their blood. ❏ *Sufferers from the more severe form of diabetes have faulty insulin-producing cells.*

불가산명사 인슐린 ❏ 증세가 심한 당뇨를 앓고 있는 사람들은 인슐린을 생성하는 세포에 문제가 있다.

in|sult (**insults, insulting, insulted**)

The verb is pronounced /ɪnsʌlt/. The noun is pronounced /ɪnsʌlt/.

동사는 /ɪnsʌlt /로 말음되고, 명사는 /ɪnsʌlt /로 발음된다.

1 V-T If someone **insults** you, they say or do something that is rude or offensive. ❏ *I did not mean to insult you.* ● in|sult|ed ADJ ❏ *I mean, I was a bit insulted that they thought I needed bribing to shut up.* **2** N-COUNT An **insult** is a rude remark, or something a person says or does which insults you. ❏ *Their behavior was an insult to the people they represent.* **3** PHRASE You say **to add insult to injury** when mentioning an action or fact that makes an unfair or unacceptable situation even worse. ❏ *The driver of the car that killed Smith got a £250 fine and*

1 타동사 모욕하다, 무례하게 대하다 ❏ 당신을 모욕하려고 한 것은 아니었다. ● 모욕당한 형용사 ❏ 내 말은, 그들이 내 입을 막기 위해서 뇌물이 필요할 것이라고 생각했다는 것 자체가 조금은 모욕감을 주었다는 것이다. **2** 가산명사 모욕, 모욕적 언동 ❏ 그들의 행동은 그들이 대표하는 사람들에 대한 모욕이었다. **3** 구 엎친 데 덮치기로, 설상가상으로

A

five penalty points on his license. To add insult to injury, he drove away from court in his own car.

□ 스미스를 죽인 그 차의 운전자는 250파운드의 벌금과 운전면허에 벌점 5점을 받았다. 유가족에게 더욱 상처를 준 것은 그가 법정에서 나와 자신의 차를 몰고 유유히 갔다는 사실이었다.

B

in|sult|ing /ɪnsʌltɪŋ/ ADJ Something that is **insulting** is rude or offensive. □ The article was politically insensitive and possibly insulting to the families of British citizens.

형용사 모욕적인, 무례한 □ 그 기사는 정치적으로 냉담했고, 아마도 영국 시민들의 가족에게는 모욕적으로 보일 가능성이 있었다.

C

in|sur|ance ♦♦◇ /ɪnʃʊərəns/ (insurances) ■ N-VAR **Insurance** is an arrangement in which you pay money to a company, and they pay money to you if something unpleasant happens to you, for example if your property is stolen or damaged, or if you get a serious illness. □ The house was a total loss and the insurance company promptly paid us the policy limit. ■ N-VAR If you do something as **insurance against** something unpleasant happening, you do it to protect yourself in case the unpleasant thing happens. □ Attentive proofreading is the only insurance against the kind of omissions described in this section.

D

E

■ 가산명사 또는 불가산명사 보험 □ 그 집은 완전히 유실되었고 보험 회사는 즉각적으로 우리에게 보험 한도액을 지불해 주었다. ■ 가산명사 또는 불가산명사 보호 수단, 보증 □ 꼼꼼한 교정 작업만이 이 부분에 지적된 누락 사항들을 바로잡을 수 있는 유일한 수단이다.

F

<table>
<tr><td colspan="2">**Word Partnership**   insurance의 연어</td></tr>
<tr><td>N.</td><td>insurance **claim**, insurance **company**, insurance **coverage**, insurance **payments**, insurance **policy** ■</td></tr>
<tr><td>V.</td><td>**buy/purchase** insurance, **carry** insurance, **sell** insurance ■</td></tr>
</table>

G

in|sur|ance ad|just|er (insurance adjusters) N-COUNT An **insurance adjuster** is the same as a **claims adjuster**. [AM, BUSINESS; BRIT **loss adjuster**]

가산명사 보험 손해 사정인 [미국영어, 경제; 영국영어 loss adjuster]

H

in|sure /ɪnʃʊər/ (insures, insuring, insured) ■ V-T/V-I If you **insure** yourself or your property, you pay money to an insurance company so that, if you become ill or if your property is damaged or stolen, the company will pay you a sum of money. □ For protection against unforeseen emergencies, you insure your house, your furnishings and your car. □ While many people insure against death, far fewer take precautions against long-term loss of income because of sickness. ■ V-T/V-I If you **insure yourself against** something unpleasant that might happen in the future, you do something to protect yourself in case it happens, or to prevent it happening. □ All the electronics in the world cannot insure against accidents, though. ■ →see also **ensure**

I

■ 타동사/자동사 보험을 들다 □ 예측할 수 없는 긴급 사태를 대비하여, 집과 가구 그리고 차에 대한 보험을 든다. □ 사망에 대비해서 보험을 드는 사람은 많은 반면, 병으로 인한 장기간 소득 손실에 대비하는 사람은 훨씬 적다. ■ 타동사/자동사 지키다, 안전하게 하다 □ 그러나 세계의 모든 전자 기술이 사고로부터 안전할 수는 없다.

J

K

<table>
<tr><td colspan="2">**Word Partnership**   insure의 연어</td></tr>
<tr><td>N.</td><td>insure *your* car/health/house/property ■
insure *your* safety ■</td></tr>
<tr><td>ADJ.</td><td>**difficult** to insure, **necessary** to insure ■ ■</td></tr>
</table>

L

M

in|sur|er /ɪnʃʊərər/ (insurers) N-COUNT An **insurer** is a company that sells insurance. [BUSINESS]

가산명사 보험 회사 [경제]

N

in|sur|gen|cy /ɪnsɜrdʒənsi/ (insurgencies) N-VAR An **insurgency** is a violent attempt to oppose a country's government carried out by citizens of that country. [FORMAL] □ Both countries were threatened with communist insurgencies in the 1960s.

가산명사 또는 불가산명사 반란 [격식체] □ 양국 모두 1960년대에 공산주의 반란의 위협을 받고 있었다.

O

in|sur|rec|tion /ɪnsərekʃⁿn/ (insurrections) N-VAR An **insurrection** is violent action that is taken by a large group of people against the rulers of their country, usually in order to remove them from office. [FORMAL] □ They were plotting to stage an armed insurrection if negotiations with the government should fail.

가산명사 또는 불가산명사 반란, 폭동 [격식체] □ 정부와의 협상이 실패한다면 그들은 무장 반란을 실행하려는 음모를 꾸미고 있었다.

P

in|tact /ɪntækt/ ADJ Something that is **intact** is complete and has not been damaged or changed. □ Customs men put dynamite in the water to destroy the cargo, but most of it was left intact.

형용사 손상되지 않은 □ 세관 담당자들은 화물을 폭파하기 위해서 물속에 다이너마이트를 설치했으나, 화물의 대부분은 손상되지 않았다.

Q

in|take /ɪnteɪk/ (intakes) ■ N-SING Your **intake** of a particular kind of food, drink, or air is the amount that you eat, drink, or breathe in. □ Your intake of alcohol should not exceed two units per day. ■ N-COUNT The people who are accepted into an organization or place at a particular time are referred to as a particular **intake**. □ ...one of this year's intake of students.

■ 단수명사 흡입, 섭취 □ 알코올 섭취량은 하루에 두 단위를 초과해서는 안 된다. ■ 가산명사 신입 회원, 새로 온 사람 □ 올해의 신입생 중 한 명

R

<table>
<tr><td colspan="2">**Word Partnership**   intake의 연어</td></tr>
<tr><td>N.</td><td>**alcohol** intake, **total** intake ■</td></tr>
<tr><td>V.</td><td>**increase** *your* intake, **limit** *your* intake, **reduce** *your* intake ■</td></tr>
</table>

S

T

in|tan|gi|ble /ɪntændʒɪbⁿl/ (intangibles) ADJ Something that is **intangible** is abstract or is hard to define or measure. □ ...the intangible and non-material dimensions of our human and social existence. ● N-PLURAL You can refer to intangible things as **intangibles**. □ That approach fails to take into consideration intangibles such as pride of workmanship, loyalty and good work habits.

U

형용사 실체가 없는, 무형의 □ 인간적, 사회적 존재로서 우리가 가지는 무형의 비물질적 차원 ● 복수명사 만질 수 없는 것, 무형 자산 □ 그러한 접근법으로는 기량에 대한 자부심, 충성도, 이로운 작업 습관 등과 같은 무형 자산들을 고려하지 못하게 된다.

V

in|te|gral /ɪntɪgrəl/ ADJ Something that is an **integral** part of something is an essential part of that thing. □ Rituals and festivals form an integral part of every human society.

형용사 필수의 □ 종교 의식과 축제는 모든 인간 사회의 필수적인 부분을 형성한다.

W

in|te|grate ♦◇◇ /ɪntɪgreɪt/ (integrates, integrating, integrated) ■ V-T/V-I If someone **integrates** into a social group, or is **integrated** into it, they behave in such a way that they become part of the group or are accepted into it. □ He didn't integrate successfully into the Italian way of life. □ Integrating the kids with the community, finding them a role, is essential. ● in|te|grat|ed ADJ □ He thinks we are living in a fully integrated, supportive society. ● in|te|gra|tion /ɪntɪgreɪʃⁿn/ N-UNCOUNT □ Americans overwhelmingly support the integration of disabled people into mainstream society. ■ V-T/V-I When races **integrate** or when schools and organizations **are integrated**, people who are black or belong to ethnic minorities can join white people in their schools and organizations. [AM] □ In some of the school cases, plaintiffs and the local NAACP had come to us because they

X

Y

Z

■ 타동사/자동사 통합되다; 통합하다 □ 그는 이탈리아 삶의 방식에 성공적으로 통합되지 못했다. □ 아이들을 공동체에 통합시키고, 역할을 찾아 주는 것이 필수적이다. ● 통합된 형용사 □ 그는 우리가 완전히 통합되고, 사람을 보살펴 주는 사회에 살고 있다고 생각한다. ● 통합, 융화 불가산명사 □ 미국인들은 장애인들이 주류 사회에 통합되는 것을 압도적으로 지지한다. ■ 타동사/자동사 인종 차별이 철폐되다 [미국영어] □ 일부 학교들의 경우에, 원고와 미국 유색 인종 향상 의회는 인종 차별 철폐를 원해서 우리를 만나러 왔었다. ● 인종

wanted to integrate. ● **in|te|grat|ed** ADJ [ADJ n] ❑ *...a black honor student in Chicago's integrated Lincoln Park High School.* ● **in|te|gra|tion** N-UNCOUNT ❑ *Lots of people in Chicago don't see that racial border. They see progress towards integration.* ❸ V-RECIP If you **integrate** one thing **with** another, or one thing **integrates with** another, the two things become closely linked or form part of a whole idea or system. You can also say that two things **integrate**. ❑ *Integrating the pound with other European currencies could cause difficulties.* ❑ *Ann wanted the conservatory to integrate with the kitchen.* ● **in|te|grat|ed** ADJ ❑ *There is, he said, a lack of an integrated national transport policy.* ● **in|te|gra|tion** N-UNCOUNT ❑ *With Germany, France has been the prime mover behind closer European integration.*

통합적인, 인종 차별을 하지 않는 형용사 ❑ 인종 통합형 고교인 시카고 링컨 파크 고등학교의 흑인 우등생 ● 인종 통합 불가산명사 ❑ 시카고의 많은 사람들은 그러한 인종 간의 장벽을 느끼지 않는다. 그들은 인종 통합으로 나아가고 있다고 느끼고 있다. ❸ 상호동사 통합하다 ❑ 파운드를 다른 유럽의 화폐와 통합하는 것은 어려움을 야기할 수 있다. ❑ 앤은 온실과 부엌을 통합하기를 바랐다. ● 통합된 형용사 ❑ 통합된 국가적 운송 정책이 부족하다고 그가 말했다. ● 통합, 합병 불가산명사 ❑ 독일과 함께 프랑스는 긴밀한 유럽 통합을 이끄는 주도 세력이었다.

Thesaurus   *integrate*의 참조어

V.   assimilate, combine, consolidate, incorporate, synthesize, unite; (*ant.*) separate ❶ ❸

Word Partnership   *integrate*의 연어

N.   integrate **schools** ❷
      integrate **efforts**, integrate **information/knowledge** ❸

---

in|te|grat|ed /ˈɪntɪɡreɪtɪd/ ADJ An **integrated** institution is intended for use by all races or religious groups. ❑ *We believe that pupils of integrated schools will have more tolerant attitudes.* →see also **integrate**

형용사 인종 통합형 ❑ 인종 통합형 학교의 학생들이 더욱 관대한 태도를 가질 것이라고 우리는 생각한다.

in|teg|rity /ɪnˈtɛɡrɪti/ ❶ N-UNCOUNT If you have **integrity**, you are honest and firm in your moral principles. ❑ *I have always regarded him as a man of integrity.* ❷ N-UNCOUNT The **integrity** of something such as a group of people or a text is its state of being a united whole. [FORMAL] ❑ *Separatist movements are a threat to the integrity of the nation.*

❶ 불가산명사 성실 ❑ 나는 항상 그를 성실한 사람으로 생각해 왔다. ❷ 불가산명사 통합 [격식체] ❑ 분리주의 운동은 국가 통합에 위협적인 것이다.

Word Partnership   *integrity*의 연어

N.   **honesty and** integrity, **a man of** integrity, **sense of** integrity ❶
ADJ. **moral** integrity, **personal** integrity ❶
      structural integrity, **territorial** integrity ❷

---

in|tel|lect /ˈɪntɪlɛkt/ (**intellects**) ❶ N-VAR **Intellect** is the ability to understand or deal with ideas and information. ❑ *Do the emotions develop in parallel with the intellect?* ❷ N-VAR **Intellect** is the quality of being very intelligent or clever. ❑ *Her intellect is famed far and wide.*

❶ 가산명사 또는 불가산명사 지성, 지력 ❑ 감성이 지성과 나란히 발달하는가? ❷ 가산명사 또는 불가산명사 지능, 지성 ❑ 그녀의 명석함은 널리 알려져 있다.

in|tel|lec|tual ♦◇◇ /ˌɪntɪlɛktʃuəl/ (**intellectuals**) ❶ ADJ **Intellectual** means involving a person's ability to think and to understand ideas and information. [ADJ n] ❑ *High levels of lead could damage the intellectual development of children.* ● **in|tel|lec|tual|ly** ADV ❑ *...intellectually satisfying work.* ❷ N-COUNT An **intellectual** is someone who spends a lot of time studying and thinking about complicated ideas. ❑ *Teachers, artists and other intellectuals urged political parties to launch a united movement against the government.* ● ADJ **Intellectual** is also an adjective. ❑ *They were very intellectual and witty.*

❶ 형용사 지성의, 지력의 ❑ 높은 수치의 납은 아이들의 지능 발달에 해를 끼칠 수 있다. ● 지적으로 부사 ❑ 지적으로 만족스러운 일 ❷ 가산명사 지식인 ❑ 교사, 예술가, 그리고 다른 지식인들이 정부를 상대로, 연합 운동을 벌일 것을 각 정당들에게 촉구하였다. ● 형용사 지적인 ❑ 그들은 매우 지적이고 재치가 넘쳤다.

Word Partnership   *intellectual*의 연어

N.   intellectual **ability**, intellectual **activity**, intellectual **freedom**, intellectual **interests** ❶

---

in|tel|li|gence ♦◇◇ /ɪnˈtɛlɪdʒəns/ ❶ N-UNCOUNT **Intelligence** is the quality of being intelligent or clever. ❑ *She's a woman of exceptional intelligence.* ❷ N-UNCOUNT **Intelligence** is the ability to think, reason, and understand instead of doing things automatically or by instinct. ❑ *Nerve cells, after all, do not have intelligence of their own.* ❸ N-UNCOUNT **Intelligence** is information that is gathered by the government or the army about their country's enemies and their activities. ❑ *Why was military intelligence so lacking?*

❶ 불가산명사 지능 ❑ 그녀는 매우 뛰어난 지능을 가진 여성이다. ❷ 불가산명사 지적 능력 ❑ 무엇보다, 신경 세포에는 지적 능력이 없다. ❸ 불가산명사 정보, 첩보 ❑ 어째서 군사 정보 쪽이 그렇게 부실했나요?

Word Partnership   *intelligence*의 연어

N.   **human** intelligence ❷
      intelligence **agent**, intelligence **expert**, **military** intelligence, **secret** intelligence ❸

---

in|tel|li|gent ♦◇◇ /ɪnˈtɛlɪdʒənt/ ❶ ADJ A person or animal that is **intelligent** has the ability to think, understand, and learn things quickly and well. ❑ *Susan's a very bright and intelligent woman who knows her own mind.* ● **in|tel|li|gent|ly** ADV ❑ *They are incapable of thinking intelligently about politics.* ❷ ADJ Something that is **intelligent** has the ability to think and understand instead of doing things automatically or by instinct. ❑ *Within a few years an intelligent computer will certainly be an indispensable diagnostic tool for every doctor in the country.*

❶ 형용사 머리가 좋은 ❑ 수잔은 스스로의 마음을 잘 아는 매우 명석하고 머리가 좋은 여성이다. ● 총명하게, 똑똑하게 부사 ❑ 그들은 정치에 대해서 똑똑하게 생각하지 못한다. ❷ 형용사 자체 정보 처리 능력을 갖춘, 지능을 가진 ❑ 몇 년 안에 지능을 가진 컴퓨터가 확실히 국내 모든 의사들을 도와주는 필수 진찰 도구가 될 것이다.

Thesaurus   *intelligent*의 참조어

ADJ.   bright, clever, sharp, smart; (*ant.*) dumb, stupid ❶

---

in|tel|li|gible /ɪnˈtɛlɪdʒɪbəl/ ADJ Something that is **intelligible** can be understood. ❑ *The language of Darwin was intelligible to experts and non-experts alike.*

형용사 이해할 수 있는 ❑ 다윈의 언어는 전문가와 비전문가가 모두 이해할 수 있었다.

a b c d e f g h i j k l m n o p q r s t u v w x y z

in|tend ♦♦◇ /ɪntɛnd/ (intends, intending, intended) **1** V-T If you **intend** to do something, you have decided or planned to do it. ❑ She intends to do A levels and go to university. ❑ I didn't intend coming to Germany to work. **2** V-T If something **is intended** for a particular purpose, it has been planned to fulfill that purpose. If something **is intended** for a particular person, it has been planned to be used by that person or to affect them in some way. [usu passive] ❑ This money is intended for the development of the tourist industry. ❑ Columns are usually intended in architecture to add grandeur and status. **3** V-T If you **intend** a particular idea or feeling in something that you say or do, you want to express it or want it to be understood. ❑ He didn't intend any sarcasm. ❑ Burke's response seemed a little patronizing, though he undoubtedly hadn't intended it that way.

1 타동사 작정이다, -할 생각이다 ❑ 그녀는 대입 자격시험을 봐서 대학에 들어갈 생각이다. ❑ 나는 일하러 독일에 온 것이 아니었다. **2** 타동사 의도되다 ❑ 이 돈은 관광 산업의 발달에 사용될 예정이다. ❑ 기둥들은 보통 건축물에 웅장함과 위신을 더할 의도로 세워진다. **3** 타동사 -을 뜻하다 ❑ 그는 빈정댈 의도가 아니었다. ❑ 물론 그가 의도했던 것은 아니었지만, 버크의 반응은 다소 거만해 보였다.

Word Partnership *intend*의 연어

V.	intend **to be**, intend **to continue**, intend **to do**, intend **to go**, intend **to leave**, intend **to make**, intend **to return**, intend **to say**, intend **to stay** **1**

---

in|tense ♦♦◇ /ɪntɛns/ **1** ADJ **Intense** is used to describe something that is very great in strength or degree. ❑ He was sweating from the intense heat. ❑ Stevens's murder was the result of a deep-seated and intense hatred. ● **in|tense|ly** ADV ❑ The fast-food business is intensely competitive. ● **in|ten|sity** /ɪntɛnsɪti/ (intensities) N-VAR ❑ The attack was anticipated but its intensity came as a shock. **2** ADJ If you describe an activity as **intense**, you mean that it is very serious and concentrated, and often involves doing a great deal in a short time. ❑ The battle for third place was intense. **3** ADJ If you describe the way someone looks at you as **intense**, you mean that they look at you very directly and seem to know what you are thinking or feeling. ❑ I felt so self-conscious under Luke's mother's intense gaze. ● **in|tense|ly** ADV [ADV with v] ❑ He sipped his drink, staring intensely at me. **4** ADJ If you describe a person as **intense**, you mean that they appear to concentrate very hard on everything that they do, and they feel and show their emotions in a very extreme way. ❑ I know he's an intense player, but he does enjoy what he's doing. ● **in|ten|sity** N-UNCOUNT ❑ His intensity and the ferocity of his feelings alarmed me.

1 형용사 강렬한, 극심한 ❑ 그는 극심한 더위로 땀을 흘리고 있었다. ❑ 스티븐스의 살인은 뿌리 깊은 극심한 증오의 결과였다. ● 강렬하게 부사 ❑ 패스트푸드 사업은 경쟁이 극심하다. ● 강렬함 가산명사 또는 불가산명사 ❑ 공격은 예상한 것이었으나 그 강도는 충격적이었다. **2** 형용사 격렬한 ❑ 3등을 차지하기 위한 싸움은 치열했다. **3** 형용사 강렬한 ❑ 나는 루크 어머니의 강렬한 눈빛에 안절부절못했었다. ● 강렬하게 부사 ❑ 그는 나를 강렬히 응시하며 술을 조금씩 마셨다. **4** 형용사 지독한, 열정적인 ❑ 나는 그가 열정적인 선수라는 것을 알고 있지만, 그는 정말로 현재 자신이 하고 있는 일을 즐기고 있다. ● 지독함, 강렬함 불가산명사 ❑ 그의 강렬하고도 격렬한 감정이 나를 놀라게 했다.

Word Partnership *intense*의 연어

N.	intense **concentration**, intense **feelings**, intense **pain**, intense **pressure** **1**
	intense **activity**, intense **competition**, intense **debate**, intense **fighting**, intense **relationship** **2**
	intense **scrutiny** **2** **3**

Word Link *ify ≈ making : clarify, diversify, intensify*

in|ten|si|fy /ɪntɛnsɪfaɪ/ (intensifies, intensifying, intensified) V-T/V-I If you **intensify** something or if it **intensifies**, it becomes greater in strength, amount, or degree. ❑ Britain is intensifying its efforts to secure the release of three British hostages.

타동사/자동사 강화하다, 증대하다 ❑ 영국은 영국인 인질 세 명을 무사히 석방시키기 위한 노력을 강화하고 있다.

in|ten|sive /ɪntɛnsɪv/ **1** ADJ **Intensive** activity involves concentrating a lot of effort or people on one particular task in order to try to achieve a great deal in a short time. ❑ ...after several days and nights of intensive negotiations. ● **in|ten|sive|ly** ADV [ADV with v] ❑ Ruth's parents opted to educate her intensively at home. **2** ADJ **Intensive** farming involves producing as many crops or animals as possible from your land, usually with the aid of chemicals. ❑ ...intensive methods of rearing poultry. ● **in|ten|sive|ly** ADV [ADV with v] ❑ Will they farm the rest of their land less intensively?

1 형용사 집중적인 ❑ 수일 밤낮으로 진행된 집중적인 협상 후에 ● 집중적으로 부사 ❑ 루스의 부모는 그녀를 집에서 집중적으로 교육시키는 쪽을 택했다. **2** 형용사 집약적인 ❑ 집약적 가금류 사육 방법 ● 집약적으로 부사 ❑ 그들은 나머지 땅을 덜 집약적으로 경작할 것인가?

Word Partnership *intensive*의 연어

N.	intensive **efforts**, intensive **negotiations**, intensive **program**, intensive **study**, intensive **training**, intensive **treatment** **1**

---

in|ten|sive care N-UNCOUNT If someone is **in intensive care**, they are being given extremely thorough care in a hospital because they are very ill or very badly injured. ❑ She spent the night in intensive care after the operation.

불가산명사 집중 치료 ❑ 그녀는 수술 후 중환자실에서 하룻밤을 보냈다.

in|tent /ɪntɛnt/ (intents) **1** ADJ If you are **intent on** doing something, you are eager and determined to do it. [v-link ADJ on/upon -ing/n] ❑ The rebels are obviously intent on keeping up the pressure. **2** ADJ If someone does something in an **intent** way, they pay great attention to what they are doing. [WRITTEN] ❑ She looked from one intent face to another. ● **in|tent|ly** ADV [ADV after v] ❑ He listened intently, then slammed down the receiver. **3** N-VAR A person's **intent** is their intention to do something. [FORMAL] ❑ The timing of this strong statement of intent on arms control is crucial. **4** PHRASE You say **to all intents and purposes** to suggest that a situation is not exactly as you describe it but the effect is the same as if it were. ❑ To all intents and purposes he was my father.

1 형용사 벼르고 있는 ❑ 반란군은 분명히 계속 압박을 가하려고 벼르고 있을 것이다. **2** 형용사 전념하고 있는 [문어체] ❑ 그녀는 열심히 지켜보는 얼굴들을 차례차례 바라보았다. ● 집중하여, 전념하여 부사 ❑ 그는 열심히 듣다가 수화기를 쾅 내려놓았다. **3** 가산명사 또는 불가산명사 의도, 목적 [격식체] ❑ 군비 통제에 대한 이와 같은 강력한 의지를 표명하는 시기가 중요하다. **4** 구 사실상, 실제로는 ❑ 사실상 그는 나의 아버지였다.

in|ten|tion ♦♦◇ /ɪntɛnʃ°n/ (intentions) **1** N-VAR An **intention** is an idea or plan of what you are going to do. ❑ The company has every intention of keeping share price high. ❑ It is my intention to remain in my position until a successor is elected. **2** PHRASE If you say that you **have no intention of** doing something, you are emphasizing

1 가산명사 또는 불가산명사 의도, 계획 ❑ 회사는 어떻게든 주가를 높게 유지하려고 한다. ❑ 후임자가 선출될 때까지 내 자리에 남아 있는 것이 나의 계획이다. **2** 구 -할 의사가 전혀 없다; 반드시 -할

that you are not going to do it. If you say that you **have every intention of** doing something, you are emphasizing that you intend to do it. [EMPHASIS] ❏ *We have no intention of buying American jets.*

것이다 [강조] ❏ 우리는 미국 제트기를 살 의사가 전혀 없다.

Word Partnership   intention의 연어

ADJ.	**clear** intention, **original** intention **1**
V.	**express** *your* intention, **state** *your* intention **1**
	have every intention **of**, **have no** intention **of 2**

---

in|ten|tion|al /ɪntenʃənᵊl/ ADJ Something that is **intentional** is deliberate. ❏ *Women who are the victims of intentional discrimination will be able to get compensation.* ● **in|ten|tion|al|ly** ADV ❏ *I've never intentionally hurt anyone.*

형용사 고의적인, 의도적인 ❏ 의도적인 차별로 피해를 입은 여성들은 보상을 받을 수 있을 것이다. ● 고의적으로, 의도적으로 부사 ❏ 나는 누구에게도 고의로 상처 준 적이 없다.

in|ter|act /ɪntərækt/ (**interacts, interacting, interacted**) **1** V-RECIP When people **interact with** each other or **interact**, they communicate as they work or spend time together. ❏ *While the other children interacted and played together, Ted ignored them.* ● **in|ter|ac|tion** /ɪntərækʃᵊn/ (**interactions**) N-VAR ❏ *This can sometimes lead to somewhat superficial interactions with other people.* **2** V-I When people **interact with** computers, or when computers **interact with** other machines, information or instructions are exchanged. ❏ *Millions of people want new, simplified ways of interacting with a computer.* ● **in|ter|ac|tion** (**interactions**) N-VAR ❏ *...experts on human-computer interaction.* **3** V-RECIP When one thing **interacts with** another or two things **interact**, the two things affect each other's behavior or condition. ❏ *You have to understand how cells interact.* ● **in|ter|ac|tion** N-VAR ❏ *...the interaction between physical and emotional illness.*

1 상호동사 어울리다, 교류하다 ❏ 다른 아이들이 함께 어울리며 노는 동안, 테드는 그들을 무시했다. ● 교류 가산명사 또는 불가산명사 ❏ 이는 때로 다른 사람들과 다소 피상적인 교류로 이어질 수 있다. **2** 자동사 상호 작용하다, 교류하다 ❏ 수백만 명의 사람들이 컴퓨터와 교류할 수 있는 새롭고 간단한 방식들을 바란다. ● 상호 작용, 교류 가산명사 또는 불가산명사 ❏ 인간과 컴퓨터 교류의 전문가 **3** 상호동사 상호 작용하다 ❏ 어떻게 세포들이 상호 작용을 하는지 이해해야 한다. ● 상호 작용 가산명사 또는 불가산명사 ❏ 육체적인 병과 심리적인 병 사이의 상호 작용

in|ter|ac|tive /ɪntəræktɪv/ **1** ADJ An **interactive** computer program or television system is one which allows direct communication between the user and the machine. ❏ *This will make videogames more interactive than ever.* ● **in|ter|ac|tiv|ity** /ɪntəræktɪviti/ N-UNCOUNT ❏ *Cable & Wireless was the first cable broadcast company to offer interactivity.* **2** ADJ If you describe a group of people or their activities as **interactive**, you mean that the people communicate with each other. ❏ *There is little evidence that this encouraged flexible, interactive teaching in the classroom.*

1 형용사 쌍방향의 ❏ 이것으로 비디오 게임의 쌍방향성이 이전보다 더욱 강화될 것이다. ● 쌍방향성 불가산명사 ❏ 케이블 앤 와이어리스는 쌍방향성을 제공하는 첫 유선 방송 회사였다. **2** 형용사 토론식의 ❏ 이것이 교실에서 유연하면서도 서로 토론하는 방식의 교육을 장려한다는 증거가 거의 없다.

in|ter|cept /ɪntərsept/ (**intercepts, intercepting, intercepted**) V-T If you **intercept** someone or something that is traveling from one place to another, you stop them before they get to their destination. ❏ *Gunmen intercepted him on his way to the airport.* ● **in|ter|cep|tion** /ɪntərsepʃᵊn/ (**interceptions**) N-VAR ❏ *...the interception of a ship off the west coast of Scotland.*

타동사 방해하다, 차단하다 ❏ 그는 공항으로 가는 도중에 무장 괴한들에게 납치되었다. ● 방해, 차단 가산명사 또는 불가산명사 ❏ 스코틀랜드의 서부 해안 근방에서 선박을 나포함

Word Link   inter ≈ between : *inter*change, *inter*connect, *inter*nal

---

in|ter|change (**interchanges, interchanging, interchanged**)

The noun is pronounced /ɪntərtʃeɪndʒ/. The verb is pronounced /ɪntərtʃeɪndʒ/.

명사는 /ɪntərtʃeɪndʒ /로 발음되고, 동사는 /ɪntərtʃeɪndʒ /로 발음된다.

1 N-VAR If there is an **interchange** of ideas or information among a group of people, each person talks about his or her ideas or gives information to the others. ❏ *What made the meeting exciting was the interchange of ideas from different disciplines.* **2** V-RECIP If you **interchange** one thing **with** another, or you **interchange** two things, each thing takes the place of the other or is exchanged for the other. You can also say that two things **interchange**. ❏ *She likes to interchange her furnishings at home with the stock in her shop.* ❏ *Your task is to interchange words so that the sentence makes sense.* ● N-VAR **Interchange** is also a noun. ❏ *...the interchange of matter and energy at atomic or sub-atomic levels.* **3** N-COUNT An **interchange** on a highway, freeway, or road is a place where it joins a main road or another highway or freeway. ❏ *...Sudley Road in Manassas, near the interchange with Interstate 66.*

1 가산명사 또는 불가산명사 교환, 주고받기 ❏ 그 회의를 흥미롭게 한 것은 다양한 학문간 견해의 교환이었다. **2** 상호동사 교체하다; 교체되다 ❏ 그녀는 자기 상점에 들여놓은 가구와 집안의 가구를 교체하는 것을 좋아한다. ❏ 당신의 일은 그 문장이 의미가 통하도록 단어를 교체하는 것이다. ● 가산명사 또는 불가산명사 교체 ❏ 원자 또는 소립자 단계에서의 물질과 에너지의 교체 **3** 가산명사 교차로 ❏ 66번 고속도로와 교차로 근방, 마나사스에 있는 서들리 로드

in|ter|change|able /ɪntərtʃeɪndʒəbᵊl/ ADJ Things that are **interchangeable** can be exchanged with each other without it making any difference. ❏ *His greatest innovation was the use of interchangeable parts.* ● **in|ter|change|ably** ADV [ADV after v] ❏ *These expressions are often used interchangeably, but they do have different meanings.*

형용사 상호 대체 가능한, 호환성이 있는 ❏ 그의 위대한 기술 혁신은 호환성 있는 부품을 사용하는 것이었다. ● 상호 대체 가능하게 부사 ❏ 이러한 표현들이 자주 서로 대체 가능한 것처럼 쓰이나 사실은 의미가 다르다.

in|ter|com /ɪntərkɒm/ (**intercoms**) N-COUNT An **intercom** is a small box with a microphone which is connected to a loudspeaker in another room. You use it to talk to the people in the other room. ❏ *I pushed a button on my intercom and told Viktor Ilyushin that I needed to see him.*

가산명사 내부 통화 장치, 인터폰 ❏ 나는 인터폰을 눌러서 빅토르 일류신에게 좀 보자고 말했다.

in|ter|con|nect /ɪntərkənekt/ (**interconnects, interconnecting, interconnected**) V-RECIP Things that **interconnect** or **are interconnected** are connected to or with each other. You can also say that one thing **interconnects with** another. ❏ *The causes are many and may interconnect.*

상호동사 서로 연결되다; 서로 연결하다 ❏ 원인들은 다양하며 상호 연관되어 있을 수도 있다.

in|ter|con|nec|tion /ɪntərkənekʃᵊn/ (**interconnections**) N-VAR If you say that there is an **interconnection** between two or more things, you mean that they are very closely connected. [FORMAL] ❏ *...the alarming interconnection of drug abuse and AIDS infection.*

가산명사 또는 불가산명사 상호 연관성 [격식체] ❏ 약물 남용과 에이즈 감염 사이의 우려스러운 상호 관련성

in|ter|con|ti|nen|tal /ɪntərkɒntɪnentᵊl/ ADJ **Intercontinental** is used to describe something that exists or happens between continents. [ADJ n] ❏ *...intercontinental flights.*

형용사 대륙 간의, 대륙을 잇는 ❏ 대륙을 잇는 항공기

in|ter|course /ɪntərkɔrs/ **1** N-UNCOUNT **Intercourse** is the act of having sex. [FORMAL] ❏ *...sexual intercourse.* **2** N-UNCOUNT Social **intercourse** is communication between people as they spend time together. [OLD-FASHIONED] ❏ *There was social intercourse between the old and the young.*

1 불가산명사 성교 [격식체] ❏ 성행위 **2** 불가산명사 교제, 친교 [구식어] ❏ 늙은 사람들과 젊은 사람들 사이에 사회적 교류가 있었다.

in|ter|de|pend|ence /ɪntərdɪpendəns/ N-UNCOUNT **Interdependence** is the condition of a group of people or things that all depend on each other. ❏ *...the interdependence of nations.*

불가산명사 상호 의존성 ❏ 국가들의 상호 의존성

in|ter|de|pend|ent /ɪntərdɪpɛndənt/ ADJ People or things that are **interdependent** all depend on each other. ❑ *We live in an increasingly interdependent world.*

형용사 상호 의존적인 ❑ 우리는 점점 더 상호 의존적인 세계에서 살고 있다.

inter|dict /ɪntərdɪkt/ (**interdicts, interdicting, interdicted**) V-T If an armed force **interdicts** something or someone, they stop them and prevent them from moving. If they **interdict** a route, they block it or cut it off. [AM, FORMAL] ❑ *Troops could be ferried in to interdict drug shipments.*

타동사 금지하다; 차단하다 [미국영어, 격식체] ❑ 마약 수송을 차단하기 위해 군대가 투입될 수도 있다.

in|ter|est ♦♦♦ /ɪntrɪst, -tərɪst/ (**interests, interesting, interested**)
■ N-UNCOUNT If you have an **interest** in something, you want to learn or hear more about it. [also a N] ❑ *There has been a lively interest in the elections in the last two weeks.* ❑ *She'd liked him at first, but soon lost interest.* ② N-COUNT Your **interests** are the things that you enjoy doing. ❑ *Encourage your child in her interests and hobbies even if they're things that you know little about.* ③ V-T If something **interests** you, it attracts your attention so that you want to learn or hear more about it or continue doing it. ❑ *That passage interested me because it seems to parallel very closely what you're doing in the novel.* ④ V-T If you are trying to persuade someone to buy or do something, you can say that you are trying to **interest** them in it. ❑ *In the meantime I can't interest you in a new car, I suppose?* ⑤ N-COUNT If something is in the **interests** of a particular person or group, it will benefit them in some way. ❑ *Did those directors act in the best interests of their club?* ⑥ N-COUNT You can use **interests** to refer to groups of people who you think use their power or money to benefit themselves. ❑ *The government accused unnamed "foreign interests" of inciting the trouble.* ⑦ N-COUNT A person or organization that has an **interest** in a company or in a particular type of business owns shares in this company or this type of business. [BUSINESS] ❑ *Her other business interests include a theme park in Scandinavia and hotels in the West Country.* ⑧ N-COUNT If a person, country, or organization has an **interest** in a possible event or situation, they want that event or situation to happen because they are likely to benefit from it. ❑ *The West has an interest in promoting democratic forces in Eastern Europe.* ⑨ N-UNCOUNT **Interest** is extra money that you receive if you have invested a sum of money. **Interest** is also the extra money that you pay if you have borrowed money or are buying something on credit. ❑ *Does your current account pay interest?* ⑩ →see also **interested, interesting, compound interest, self-interest, vested interest** ⑪ PHRASE If you do something **in the interests of** a particular result or situation, you do it in order to achieve that result or maintain that situation. ❑ *...a call for all businessmen to work together in the interests of national stability.* to have someone's **interests at heart** →see **heart** →see **bank, interest rate**

■ 불가산명사 흥미, 관심 ❑ 지난 두 주 동안 선거에 대한 관심이 활발했다. ❑ 처음에는 그녀가 그를 좋아했지만, 곧 흥미를 잃었다. ② 가산명사 흥밋거리 ❑ 당신이 잘 모르는 것이더라도 아이가 흥미를 갖거나 취미로 삼는 것이 있으면 그것을 장려해라. ③ 타동사 흥미를 끌다, 관심을 끌다 ❑ 제가 그 구절에 관심을 가진 것은 그것이 당신이 소설 속에서 하는 것과 매우 유사해 보였기 때문입니다. ④ 타동사 흥미를 갖게 하다 ❑ 그동안 혹시 신차를 구매할 의향은 없으신지요? ⑤ 가산명사 이익 ❑ 그 이사들이 클럽에 가장 이익이 되는 방향으로 행동했는가? ⑥ 가산명사 이익 단체 ❑ 정부는 익명의 '외국 이익 단체'가 그 사태를 부추겼다고 비난했다. ⑦ 가산명사 지분, 이권 [경제] ❑ 그녀는 스칸디나비아의 놀이 공원과 서부 지역의 호텔 사업에도 이권을 갖고 있다. ⑧ 가산명사 이익, 이득 ❑ 동유럽에 민주 세력을 조성하는 것이 서유럽의 이익에 부합한다. ⑨ 불가산명사 이자 ❑ 귀 은행의 보통 예금에도 이자가 붙습니까? ⑪ 구 -을 위하여 ❑ 국가의 안정을 위하여 모든 재계 관계자들이 협상할 것을 요청함

Word Partnership	interest의 연어
V.	**attract** interest, **express** interest, **lose** interest ■
	earn interest, **pay** interest ⑨
N.	**level of** interest, **places of** interest, **self**-interest ■
	conflict of interest ⑦ ⑧
	interest **charges**, interest **expenses**, interest **payments** ⑨
ADJ.	**great** interest, **little** interest, **strong** interest ■ ⑧

in|ter|est|ed ♦♦◇ /ɪntərɛstɪd, -trɪstɪd/ ■ ADJ If you are **interested in** something, you think it is important and want to learn more about it or spend time doing it. ❑ *I thought she might be interested in Paula's proposal.* ② ADJ An **interested** party or group of people is affected by or involved in a particular event or situation. [ADJ n] ❑ *The success was only possible because all the interested parties eventually agreed to the idea.*

■ 형용사 흥미를 가진, 호기심이 생긴 ❑ 나는 폴라의 제안에 그녀가 흥미를 가질 수도 있겠다고 생각했다. ② 형용사 이해관계가 있는 ❑ 오로지 모든 이해 당사자들이 결국 그 생각에 동의했기 때문에 성공할 수 있었다.

Word Partnership	interested의 연어
ADV.	**really** interested, **very** interested ■
V.	**become** interested, interested **in buying**, **get** interested,
	interested **in getting**, interested **in helping**,
	interested **in learning**, interested **in making**, **seem** interested ■

Word Web   interest rate

Borrowers have several options when choosing a **mortgage** to purchase a new home. The most common home **loan** is the **fixed rate** mortgage. With this loan the interest rate does not change, so the borrower pays the same amount of principal and interest each month. The interest on an **adjustable rate** mortgage does change. With an **interest only** mortgage, the borrower pays only the interest every month and owes the **lender** the entire **principal** amount at the end of the period.

interest-free ADJ An **interest-free** loan has no interest charged on it. ❑ *He was offered a £10,000 interest-free loan.* ● ADV **Interest-free** is also an adverb. [ADV after v] ❑ *Customers allowed the banks to use their money interest-free.*

형용사 무이자의 ❑ 그는 10,000파운드의 무이자 대출을 제안 받았다. ● 부사 무이자로 ❑ 손님들은 은행이 그들의 돈을 무이자로 사용하도록 했다.

in|ter|est|ing ♦♦♦ /ɪntərɪstɪŋ, -trɪstɪŋ/ ADJ If you find something **interesting**, it attracts your attention, for example because you think it is exciting or unusual. ❑ *It was interesting to be in a different environment.*

형용사 흥미로운, 관심을 끄는 ❑ 다른 환경에 있는 것은 흥미로웠다.

Thesaurus	*interesting*의 참조어	
ADJ.	absorbing, compelling, unusual; (*ant.*) boring	

Word Partnership	*interesting*의 연어	
ADV.	**especially** interesting, **really** interesting, **very** interesting	
N.	interesting **idea**, interesting **people**, interesting **point**, interesting **question**, interesting **story**, interesting **things**	

in|ter|est|ing|ly /ɪntərɪstɪŋli, -trɪstɪŋli/ ADV You use **interestingly** to introduce a piece of information that you think is interesting or unexpected. [ADV with cl] ❑ *Interestingly enough, a few weeks later, Benjamin remarried.*

부사 흥미롭게도 ❑ 매우 흥미롭게도, 몇 주 뒤에 벤자민은 재혼했다.

in|ter|est rate (**interest rates**) N-COUNT The **interest rate** is the amount of interest that must be paid. It is expressed as a percentage of the amount that is borrowed or gained as profit. [BUSINESS] ❑ *The Finance Minister has renewed his call for lower interest rates.*
→see Word Web: **interest rate**

가산명사 이자율, 금리 [경제] ❑ 재무 장관은 금리 인하를 거듭 요청했다.

inter|face /ɪntərfeɪs/ (**interfaces, interfacing, interfaced**) **1** N-COUNT The **interface** between two subjects or systems is the area in which they affect each other or have links with each other. ❑ *...a witty exploration of that interface between bureaucracy and the working world.* **2** N-COUNT If you refer to the user **interface** of a particular piece of computer software, you are talking about its presentation on screen and how easy it is to operate. [COMPUTING] ❑ *...the development of better user interfaces.* **3** V-RECIP If one thing **interfaces with** another, or if two things **interface**, they have connections with each other. If you **interface** one thing with another, you connect the two things. [FORMAL] ❑ *...the way we interface with the environment.* ❑ *He had interfaced all this machinery with a master computer.*

1 가산명사 접점, 중간지점 ❑ 관료 사회와 노동계 간의 그런 접점에 대한 재치 있는 탐구 **2** 가산명사 인터페이스 [컴퓨터] ❑ 더 나은 사용자 인터페이스의 개발 **3** 상호동사 연결되다, 조화상 이루다; 연결시키다, 조화시키다 [격식체] ❑ 환경과 조화하는 방법 ❑ 그는 모든 기계를 중앙 컴퓨터에 연결시켰다.

inter|fere /ɪntərfɪər/ (**interferes, interfering, interfered**) **1** V-I If you say that someone **interferes in** a situation, you mean they get involved in it although it does not concern them and their involvement is not wanted. [DISAPPROVAL] ❑ *I wish everyone would stop interfering and just leave me alone.* **2** V-I Something that **interferes with** a situation, activity, or process has a damaging effect on it. ❑ *Smoking and drinking interfere with your body's ability to process oxygen.*

1 자동사 간섭하다 [탐탁잖음] ❑ 모든 사람들이 간섭하지 말고 그냥 나를 혼자 내버려두면 좋겠다. **2** 자동사 방해하다, 지장을 주다 ❑ 흡연과 음주는 신체의 산소 처리 능력에 지장을 준다.

Word Partnership	*interfere*의 연어	
N.	**ability to** interfere, **right to** interfere **1**	
V.	**try to** interfere, **not want to** interfere **1**	

inter|fer|ence /ɪntərfɪərəns/ **1** N-UNCOUNT **Interference** by a person or group is their unwanted or unnecessary involvement in something. [DISAPPROVAL] ❑ *Airlines will be able to set cheap fares without interference from the government.* **2** N-UNCOUNT When there is **interference**, a radio signal is affected by other radio waves or electrical activity so that it cannot be received properly. ❑ *...electrical interference.*

1 불가산명사 간섭, 방해 [탐탁잖음] ❑ 항공사들은 정부의 간섭 없이 싼 운임을 책정할 수 있을 것이다. **2** 불가산명사 전파 방해, 혼신 ❑ 전기 방해

in|ter|im ♦♦♦ /ɪntərɪm/ **1** ADJ **Interim** is used to describe something that is intended to be used until something permanent is done or established. [ADJ n] ❑ *She was sworn in as head of an interim government in March.* **2** PHRASE **In the interim** means until a particular thing happens or until a particular thing happened. [FORMAL] ❑ *But, in the interim, we obviously have a duty to maintain law and order.*

1 형용사 임시의 ❑ 그녀는 3월에 임시 정부 대표로 취임 선서를 했다. **2** 구 그 사이에, 당분간 [격식체] ❑ 그러나 당분간 우리에게 법과 질서를 유지할 의무가 분명히 있다.

in|te|ri|or ♦♦♦ /ɪntɪəriər/ (**interiors**) **1** N-COUNT The **interior** of something is the inside part of it. ❑ *The interior of the house was furnished with heavy, old-fashioned pieces.* **2** ADJ You use **interior** to describe something that is inside a building or vehicle. [ADJ n] ❑ *The interior walls were painted green.* **3** N-SING The **interior** of a country or continent is the central area of it. ❑ *The Yangzi river would give access to much of China's interior.* **4** ADJ A country's **interior** minister, ministry, or department deals with affairs within that country, such as law and order. [ADJ n] ❑ *The French Interior Minister has intervened in a scandal over the role of a secret police force.* **5** N-SING A country's minister or ministry of **the interior** deals with affairs within that country, such as law and order. ❑ *An official from the Ministry of the Interior said six people had died.*

1 가산명사 내부 ❑ 그 집의 내부에는 육중하고 고풍스런 가구들이 비치되어 있었다. **2** 형용사 내부의 ❑ 내부 벽은 초록색으로 칠해져 있었다. **3** 단수명사 내륙 ❑ 양쯔 강을 통해서 중국 내륙의 대부분 지역으로 접근할 수 있다. **4** 형용사 내무부의 ❑ 프랑스 내무부 장관이 비밀경찰의 역할에 대한 스캔들에 개입해 왔다. **5** 단수명사 내무부의 ❑ 내무부의 한 관리가 여섯 사람이 죽었다고 말했다.

Thesaurus	*interior*의 참조어	
N.	inside; (*ant.*) exterior, outside **1**	

inter|lude /ɪntərlud/ (**interludes**) N-COUNT An **interlude** is a short period of time when an activity or situation stops and something else happens. ❑ *Superb musical interludes were provided by Sinclair.*

가산명사 사이, 막간 ❑ 싱클레어가 화려한 뮤지컬 막간극을 제공했다.

Word Link	*med* ≈ middle : inter*med*iary, *med*ia, *med*iate	

inter|medi|ary /ɪntərmidieri/ (**intermediaries**) N-COUNT An **intermediary** is a person who passes messages or proposals between two people or groups. ❑ *She wanted him to act as an intermediary in the dispute with Moscow.*

가산명사 중개자 ❑ 러시아 정부와의 분쟁에서 그녀는 그가 중개자 역할을 해 주기를 원했다.

inter|medi|ate /ɪntərmidiɪt/ (**intermediates**) ◼ ADJ An **intermediate** stage, level, or position is one that occurs between two other stages, levels, or positions. ❑ You should consider breaking the journey with intermediate stopovers at airport hotels. ◻ ADJ **Intermediate** learners of something have some knowledge or skill but are not yet advanced. ❑ The Badminton Club holds coaching sessions for beginners and intermediate players on Friday evenings. ● N-COUNT An **intermediate** is an intermediate learner. ❑ The ski school coaches beginners, intermediates, and advanced skiers.

■ 형용사 중간의 ❑ 중간 중간에 공항 호텔에 머무는 방식으로 전체 여정을 나눠 보는 것도 고려해 볼 만하다. ◻ 형용사 중급의 ❑ 배드민턴 클럽은 금요일 저녁마다 초보자와 중급자를 위한 강습을 연다. ● 가산명사 중급자 ❑ 스키 강습 학교는 초급자, 중급자, 상급자들을 지도한다.

in|ter|mi|nable /ɪntɜrmɪnəbəl/ ADJ If you describe something as **interminable**, you are emphasizing that it continues for a very long time and indicating that you wish it was shorter or would stop. [EMPHASIS] ❑ ...an interminable meeting. ● **in|ter|mi|nably** ADV ❑ He talked to me interminably about his first wife.

형용사 영구히 계속되는, 그칠 줄 모르는 [강조] ❑ 끝없이 계속된 회의 ● 끝없이 계속되어 부사 ❑ 그는 나에게 자기 첫 부인에 대해서 끝없이 말했다.

inter|mis|sion /ɪntərmɪʃən/ (**intermissions**) N-COUNT An **intermission** is a short break between two parts of a concert, show, or movie. ❑ ...during the intermission of the musical "Steppin' Out". ● N-COUNT In American English, you can also use **intermission** to refer to a short break between two parts of a game, or say that something happens at, after, or during **intermission**. [also prep N] ❑ Fraser did not perform until after intermission.

가산명사 중간 휴식 시간 ❑ 뮤지컬 '스테핑 아웃'의 중간 휴식 시간에 ● 가산명사 중간 휴식 시간 ❑ 프레이저는 휴식 시간이 지난 후까지 연주를 하지 않았다.

inter|mit|tent /ɪntərmɪtənt/ ADJ Something that is **intermittent** happens occasionally rather than continuously. ❑ After three hours of intermittent rain, the game was abandoned. ● **inter|mit|tent|ly** ADV ❑ The talks went on intermittently for three years.

형용사 때때로 끊기는, 간헐적인 ❑ 비가 세 시간 동안 간헐적으로 내린 후에 시합은 취소되었다. ● 간헐적으로 부사 ❑ 그 회담은 3년 동안 간헐적으로 열렸다.

in|tern (**interns, interning, interned**)

The verb is pronounced /ɪntɜrn/. The noun is pronounced /ɪntɜrn/.

동사는 /ɪntɜrn/으로 발음되고, 명사는 /ɪntɜrn/으로 발음된다.

■ V-T If someone **is interned**, they are put in prison or in a prison camp for political reasons. [usu passive] ❑ He was interned as an enemy alien at the outbreak of the Second World War. ◻ N-COUNT An **intern** is an advanced student or a recent graduate, especially in medicine, who is being given practical training under supervision. [AM] ❑ ...a medical intern.

■ 타동사 구금되다, 억류되다 ❑ 그는 제2차 세계 대전이 발발했을 때 외국 적군으로 구금되었다. ◻ 가산명사 인턴 [미국영어] ❑ 인턴 의사

Word Link   inter ≈ between : **inter**change, **inter**connect, **inter**nal

in|ter|nal ♦◇◇ /ɪntɜrnəl/ ■ ADJ **Internal** is used to describe things that exist or happen inside a country or organization. [ADJ n] ❑ The country stepped up internal security. ❑ We now have a Europe without internal borders. ● **in|ter|nal|ly** ADV ❑ The state is not a unified and internally coherent entity. ◻ ADJ **Internal** is used to describe things that exist or happen inside a particular person, object, or place. [ADJ n] ❑ The doctor said the internal bleeding had been massive. ● **in|ter|nal|ly** ADV ❑ Evening primrose oil is used on the skin as well as taken internally.

■ 형용사 국내의, 기관 내의 ❑ 그 나라는 국내 안보를 강화시켰다. ❑ 이제는 내부의 국경선이 없는 하나의 유럽이 되었다. ● 국내에서 부사 ❑ 국가라는 것은 통일되고 내부적으로 통합된 개체가 아니다. ◻ 형용사 체내의, 내부의 ❑ 그 의사는 내출혈이 상당했었다고 말했다. ● 체내에서 부사 ❑ 달맞이꽃 기름은 체내 복용에도 사용될 뿐만 아니라 피부에 바르는 데도 사용된다.

inter|na|tion|al ♦♦♦ /ɪntərnæʃənəl/ (**internationals**) ■ ADJ **International** means between or involving different countries. ❑ ...an international agreement against exporting arms to that country. ❑ There are only two internationally recognized certificates in Teaching English as a Foreign Language. ◻ N-COUNT In sports, an **international** is a game that is played between teams representing two different countries. ❑ ...the midweek international against England. ▣ N-COUNT An **international** is a member of a country's sports team. [BRIT] ❑ The two players, both former England internationals, had been at the club for 16 years.

■ 형용사 국가 간의, 국제적인 ❑ 그 나라에 무기 수출을 반대하는 국제적인 협약 ● 국제적으로 부사 ❑ 외국어로 영어를 가르치는 데 국제적으로 공인된 자격증은 오직 둘뿐이다. ◻ 가산명사 국제 경기 [영국영어] ❑ 잉글랜드와의 주중 국제 경기 ▣ 가산명사 국제 경기 출전자 [영국영어] ❑ 모두 전 잉글랜드 팀 국제 경기 출전 선수들이었던 그 두 명의 선수는 16년 동안 그 팀에 있었었다.

In|ter|net /ɪntərnɛt/ also **internet** N-PROPER The **Internet** is the computer network which allows computer users to connect with computers all over the world, and which carries e-mail.
→see Word Web: Internet

고유명사 인터넷

In|ter|net café (**Internet cafés**) N-COUNT An **Internet café** is a café with computers where people can pay to use the Internet.

가산명사 인터넷 카페, 피시방

in|tern|ship /ɪntɜrnʃɪp/ (**internships**) N-COUNT An **internship** is the position held by an intern, or the period of time when someone is an intern. [AM] ❑ She vanished from Washington after ending an internship at the Bureau of Prisons.

가산명사 수련 과정, 견습 기간 [미국영어] ❑ 그녀는 교도국에서 수련 과정을 마친 후 워싱턴에서 사라졌다.

inter|per|son|al /ɪntərpɜrsənəl/ ADJ **Interpersonal** means relating to relationships between people. [ADJ n] ❑ Training in interpersonal skills is essential.

형용사 대인 관계의 ❑ 대인 관계 기술 훈련이 필수적이다.

in|ter|pret /ɪntɜrprɪt/ (**interprets, interpreting, interpreted**) ■ V-T If you **interpret** something in a particular way, you decide that this is its meaning or significance. ❑ The whole speech might well be interpreted as a coded message to the Americans. ❑ The judge quite rightly says that he has to interpret the law as it's been

■ 타동사 해석하다, 이해하다 ❑ 연설 전체가 미국인들에게 보내는 암호화된 메시지로 해석될 수도 있다. ❑ 판사는 자기는 법을 판례대로 해석해야 한다고 아주 적절하게 말했다. ◻ 타동사/자동사 통역하다

Word Web   Internet

The **Internet** allows information to be shared around the world. The **World Wide Web** allows users to access **servers** anywhere. **User names** and **passwords** give access and protect information. **E-mail** travels through **networks**. **Websites** are created by companies and individuals to share information. **Web pages** can include images, words, sound, and video. Some organizations built private **intranets**. These groups have to guard the **gateway** between their system and the larger Internet. **Hackers** can break into computer networks. They sometimes steal information or damage the system. **Webmasters** usually build **firewalls** for protection.

passed. ② V-T/V-I If you **interpret** what someone is saying, you translate it immediately into another language. ❑ *The chambermaid spoke little English, so her husband came with her to interpret.* →see **dream**

❑ 객실 담당 여종업원이 영어를 거의 못해서, 그녀의 남편이 통역해 주러 같이 왔다.

Word Partnership   *interpret의 연어*

N.	interpret **data**, interpret **the meaning of** *something*, interpret **results**, **ways to** interpret ❶
ADJ.	**difficult to** interpret ❶ ❷

---

in|ter|pre|ta|tion /ɪntɜrprɪteɪʃⁿn/ (**interpretations**) ❶ N-VAR An **interpretation** of something is an opinion about what it means. ❑ *The opposition Conservative Party put a different interpretation on the figures.* ❷ N-COUNT A performer's **interpretation** of something such as a piece of music or a role in a play is the particular way in which they choose to perform it. ❑ *...her full-bodied interpretation of the role of Micaela.*

❶ 가산명사 또는 불가산명사 해석, 설명 ❑ 야당인 보수당이 그 수치에 대해 다른 해석을 내놓았다. ❷ 가산명사 (연주자 등의) 작품 해석 ❑ 미카엘라 역에 대한 그녀의 농익은 연기

Word Partnership   *interpretation의 연어*

N.	**data** interpretation, interpretation **of results** ❶
ADJ.	**correct** interpretation, **literal** interpretation, **open to** interpretation, **strict** interpretation ❶

---

in|ter|pret|er /ɪntɜrprɪtər/ (**interpreters**) N-COUNT An **interpreter** is a person whose job is to translate what someone is saying into another language. ❑ *Speaking through an interpreter, Aristide said that Haitians had hoped coups were behind them.*

가산명사 통역, 통역사 ❑ 통역을 통해 말하면서, 아리스티드는 하이티 사람들이 쿠데타가 반복되지 않기를 희망해 왔다고 말했다.

in|ter|ro|gate /ɪntɛrəgeɪt/ (**interrogates, interrogating, interrogated**) V-T If someone, especially a police officer, **interrogates** someone, they question them thoroughly for a long time in order to get some information from them. ❑ *I interrogated everyone even slightly involved.*

타동사 심문하다 ❑ 나는 조금이라도 연루된 사람들은 모두 심문했다.

in|ter|ro|ga|tion /ɪntɛrəgeɪʃⁿn/ (**interrogations**) N-VAR An **interrogation** is the act of interrogating someone. ❑ *...the right to silence in police interrogations.*

가산명사 또는 불가산명사 심문 ❑ 경찰 심문에 대한 묵비권

Word Link   **rupt ≈ breaking : dis**rupt, e**rupt**, inter**rupt**

in|ter|rupt /ɪntərʌpt/ (**interrupts, interrupting, interrupted**) ❶ V-T/V-I If you **interrupt** someone who is speaking, you say or do something that causes them to stop. ❑ *Turkin tapped him on the shoulder. "Sorry to interrupt, Colonel."* ● in|ter|rup|tion /ɪntərʌpʃⁿn/ (**interruptions**) N-VAR ❑ *The sudden interruption stopped Beryl in mid-flow.* ❷ V-T If someone or something **interrupts** a process or activity, they stop it for a period of time. ❑ *He has rightly interrupted his holiday in Spain to return to London.* ● in|ter|rup|tion N-VAR ❑ *...interruptions in the supply of food and fuel.* ❸ V-T If something **interrupts** a line, surface, or view, it stops it from being continuous or makes it look irregular. ❑ *Taller plants interrupt the views from the house.*

❶ 타동사/자동사 (말하는 도중에) 방해하다, 중단시키다 ❑ 터킨이 그의 어깨를 툭툭 쳤다. "방해해서 미안한데, 대령." ● 방해 가산명사 또는 불가산명사 ❑ 갑작스런 방해로 베릴은 도중에 말을 멈추었다. ❷ 타동사 중단시키다 ❑ 그가 런던으로 돌아가기 위해 스페인에서 휴가를 중단한 건 잘한 일이다. ● 중단 가산명사 또는 불가산명사 ❑ 식량과 연료 공급의 중단 ❸ 타동사 방해하다, 가로막다 ❑ 키가 더 큰 초목들이 그 집의 전망을 가로막는다.

Word Link   **sect ≈ cutting : dis**sect, inter**sect**, **section**

inter|sect /ɪntərsɛkt/ (**intersects, intersecting, intersected**) ❶ V-RECIP If two or more lines or roads **intersect**, they meet or cross each other. You can also say that one line or road **intersects** another. ❑ *The orbit of this comet intersects the orbit of the Earth.* ❷ V-RECIP If one thing **intersects with** another or if two things **intersect**, the two things have a connection at a particular point. ❑ *...the ways in which historical events intersect with individual lives.*

❶ 상호동사 교차하다, 가로지르다 ❑ 이 혜성의 궤도는 지구의 궤도를 가로지른다. ❷ 상호동사 교차하다, 만나다 ❑ 역사적 사건들이 개인의 삶과 교차하는 방식들

inter|sec|tion /ɪntərsɛkʃⁿn/ (**intersections**) N-COUNT An **intersection** is a place where roads or other lines meet or cross. ❑ *...at the intersection of two main canals.*

가산명사 교차점, 교차로 ❑ 두 개의 주요 운하가 만나는 교차점

inter|spersed /ɪntərspɜrst/ ADJ If one group of things are **interspersed with** another or **interspersed among** another, the second things occur between or among the first things. [v-link ADJ prep, usu ADJ with n, ADJ among n] ❑ *...a series of bursts of gunfire, interspersed with single shots.*

형용사 드문드문 섞인, 산재한 ❑ 연속된 연발 사격 사이에 갑자기 섞이는 단발들

inter|state /ɪntərsteɪt/ (**interstates**) ❶ ADJ **Interstate** means between states, especially the states of the United States. [ADJ n] ❑ *...interstate highways.* ❷ N-COUNT In the United States, an **interstate** is a major road linking states. [also N num] ❑ *...the southbound lane of Interstate 75.*

❶ 형용사 (미국의) 주 사이의 ❑ 주간 고속도로 ❷ 가산명사 주간 고속도로 ❑ 75번 주간 고속도로 남행 차선

in|ter|val /ɪntərvⁿl/ (**intervals**) ❶ N-COUNT An **interval** between two events or dates is the period of time between them. ❑ *The ferry service between Burnham and Wallasea Island has restarted after an interval of 12 years.* ❷ N-COUNT An **interval** during a concert, show, movie, or game is a short break between two of the parts. [mainly BRIT; AM usually **intermission**] ❑ *During the interval, wine was served.* ❸ PHRASE If something happens **at intervals**, it happens several times with gaps or pauses in between. ❑ *She woke him for his medicines at intervals throughout the night.* ❹ PHRASE If things are placed **at** particular **intervals**, there are spaces of a particular size between them. ❑ *Several red and white barriers marked the road at intervals of about a mile.*

❶ 가산명사 (시간의) 간격 ❑ 버넘과 월라시 섬 간의 페리 운항이 12년 만에 재개되었다. ❷ 가산명사 (연주회 등의) 중간 휴식 시간 [주로 영국영어; 미국영어 대개 intermission] ❑ 막간에 와인이 제공되었다. ❸ 구 의례적인, 이따금 ❑ 그녀는 약을 주려고 밤새 몇 번씩 그를 깨웠다. ❹ 구 -의 간격으로 ❑ 몇몇 적색과 흰색 장애물로 도로에 1마일 정도씩의 간격을 표시해 놓았었다.

inter|vene /ɪntərviːn/ (**intervenes, intervening, intervened**) ❶ V-I If you **intervene in** a situation, you become involved in it and try to change it. ❑ *The situation calmed down when police intervened.* ❷ V-T/V-I If you **intervene**, you interrupt a conversation in order to add something to it. ❑ *Hattie intervened and told me to stop it.* ❸ V-T/V-I If an event **intervenes**, it happens suddenly in a way that stops, delays, or prevents something from happening. ❑ *The South African mailboat arrived on Friday mornings unless bad weather intervened.*

❶ 자동사 간섭하다, 개입하다 ❑ 경찰이 개입하자 그 사태가 진정되었다. ❷ 타동사/자동사 (대화에) 끼어들다 ❑ 해티가 끼어들어 내게 그만두라고 말했다. ❸ 타동사/자동사 (어떤 일이) 방해하다 ❑ 악천후로 지장을 받지 않으면 남아프리카 우편선은 매주 금요일 아침에 도착했다.

A

B

C

D

E

F

G

H

I

inter|ven|ing /ɪntərvi:nɪŋ/ **1** ADJ An **intervening** period of time is one that separates two events or points in time. [ADJ n] ❑ *During those intervening years Bridget had married her husband Robert.* **2** ADJ An **intervening** object or area comes between two other objects or areas. [ADJ n] ❑ *They had scoured the intervening miles of moorland.*

inter|ven|tion ♦♢♢ /ɪntərvenʃən/ (**interventions**) N-VAR **Intervention** is the act of intervening in a situation. ❑ *...the role of the United States and its intervention in the internal affairs of many countries.*

inter|view ♦♦♢ /ɪntərvju:/ (**interviews, interviewing, interviewed**) **1** N-VAR An **interview** is a formal meeting at which someone is asked questions in order to find out if they are suitable for a job or a course of study. ❑ *The interview went well.* **2** V-T If you **are interviewed** for a particular job or course of study, someone asks you questions about yourself to find out if you suitable for it. [usu passive] ❑ *When Wardell was interviewed, he was impressive, and on that basis, he was hired.* **3** N-COUNT An **interview** is a conversation in which a journalist puts questions to someone such as a famous person or politician. ❑ *The trouble began when Allan gave an interview to the Chicago Tribune newspaper last month.* **4** V-T When a journalist **interviews** someone such as a famous person, they ask them a series of questions. ❑ *I seized the chance to interview Chris Hani about this issue.* **5** V-T When the police **interview** someone, they ask them questions about a crime that has been committed. ❑ *The police interviewed the driver, but had no evidence to go on.*

Word Partnership	*interview*의 연어
N.	**job** interview **1**
	(tele)phone interview **1** **3**
	radio/magazine/newspaper/television interview **3**
V.	**conduct an** interview, **give an** interview, **request an** interview **1** **3**

J

inter|view|ee /ɪntərvju:i:/ (**interviewees**) N-COUNT An **interviewee** is a person who is being interviewed. ❑ *Is there any interviewee who stands out as memorable?*

K

inter|view|er /ɪntərvju:ər/ (**interviewers**) N-COUNT An **interviewer** is a person who is asking someone questions at an interview. ❑ *Being a good interviewer, however, requires much preparation and skill.*

L

in|tes|tine /ɪntestɪn/ (**intestines**) N-COUNT Your **intestines** are the tubes in your body through which food passes when it has left your stomach. ❑ *This area is always tender to the touch if the intestines are not functioning properly.*

M

in|ti|ma|cy /ɪntɪməsi/ **1** N-UNCOUNT **Intimacy** between two people is a very close personal relationship between them. ❑ *...a means of achieving intimacy with another person.* **2** N-UNCOUNT You sometimes use **intimacy** to refer to sex or a sexual relationship. ❑ *The truth was he did not feel like intimacy with any woman.*

N

in|ti|mate (**intimates, intimating, intimated**)

The adjective is pronounced /ɪntɪmət/. The verb is pronounced /ɪntɪmeɪt/.

O

P

1 ADJ If you have an **intimate** friendship with someone, you know very well and like them a lot. ❑ *I discussed with my intimate friends whether I would immediately have a baby.* ● **in|ti|mate|ly** ADV ❑ *He did not feel he had got to know them intimately.* **2** ADJ If two people are in an **intimate** relationship, they are involved with each other in a loving or sexual way. ❑ *...their intimate moments with their boyfriends.* ● **in|ti|mate|ly** ADV [ADV after v] ❑ *You have to be willing to get to know yourself and your partner intimately.* **3** ADJ An **intimate** conversation or detail, for example, is very personal and private. ❑ *He wrote the intimate details of his family life.* ● **in|ti|mate|ly** ADV [ADV after v] ❑ *It was the first time they had attempted to talk intimately.* **4** ADJ If you use **intimate** to describe an occasion or the atmosphere of a place, you like it because it is quiet and pleasant, and seems suitable for close conversations between friends. [APPROVAL] ❑ *...an intimate candlelit dinner for two.* **5** ADJ An **intimate** connection between ideas or organizations, for example, is a very strong link between them. ❑ *...an intimate connection between madness and wisdom.* ● **in|ti|mate|ly** ADV [ADV after v] ❑ *Scientific research and conservation are intimately connected.* **6** ADJ An **intimate** knowledge of something is a deep and detailed knowledge of it. ❑ *He surprised me with his intimate knowledge of Kierkegaard and Schopenhauer.* ● **in|ti|mate|ly** ADV ❑ *...a golden age of musicians whose work she knew intimately.* **7** V-T If you **intimate** something, you say it in an indirect way. [FORMAL] ❑ *He went on to intimate that he was indeed contemplating a shake-up of the company.*

Q

R

S

T

U

Word Partnership	*intimate*의 연어
N.	intimate **friend 1**
	intimate **relationship 2**
	intimate **details 3**
	intimate **atmosphere 4**

V

W

X

Y

in|timi|date /ɪntɪmɪdeɪt/ (**intimidates, intimidating, intimidated**) V-T If you **intimidate** someone, you deliberately make them frightened enough to do what you want them to do. ❑ *Jones had set out to intimidate and dominate Paul.* ● **in|timi|da|tion** /ɪntɪmɪdeɪʃən/ N-UNCOUNT ❑ *...an inquiry into allegations of intimidation during last week's vote.*

Z

in|timi|dat|ed /ɪntɪmɪdeɪtɪd/ ADJ Someone who feels **intimidated** feels frightened and lacks confidence because of the people they are with or the situation they are in. ❑ *Women can come in here and not feel intimidated.*

1 형용사 ~ 사이의, 중간에 낀 ❑ 그 사이의 몇 년 동안 브리지트는 현 남편인 로버트와 결혼했다. **2** 형용사 중간의 ❑ 그들은 그 중간 몇 마일의 황무지를 철저히 조사했다.

가산명사 또는 불가산명사 간섭, 개입 ❑ 여러 나라의 내정에 대한 미국의 역할과 개입

1 가산명사 또는 불가산명사 인터뷰, 면접 ❑ 면접은 잘 되었다. **2** 타동사 면접을 보다 ❑ 워델은 면접 때 인상적이었으며, 그 때문에 고용되었다. **3** 가산명사 회견, 대담 ❑ 말썽은 앨런이 지난달 시카고 트리뷴지와 회견을 했을 때 생겼다. **4** 타동사 회견을 하다 ❑ 나는 이 문제에 대해 크리스 하니와 기자 회견할 기회를 포착했다. **5** 타동사 심문하다 ❑ 경찰이 그 운전사를 심문했지만 이렇다 할 단서를 찾지 못했다.

가산명사 피면접자 ❑ 기억에 남을 만큼 뛰어난 피면접자가 있습니까?

가산명사 면접관 ❑ 그러나 훌륭한 면접관이 되려면 많은 준비와 기술이 필요하다.

가산명사 창자, 소장 ❑ 만일 소장이 제대로 기능을 하지 않으면 이 부위가 항상 만져 보면 아프다.

1 불가산명사 친밀함, 친교 ❑ 타인과 친교를 맺기 위한 방법 **2** 불가산명사 육체관계 ❑ 사실은 그가 어떤 여자와도 육체적 관계를 맺고 싶지 않다는 것이었다.

형용사는 /ɪntɪmət/로 발음되고, 동사는 /ɪntɪmeɪt/로 발음된다.

1 형용사 친밀한, 친숙한 ❑ 나는 내가 지금 당장 아이를 가질 것인가에 대해 친한 친구들과 의논했다. ● 친밀하게 부사 ❑ 그는 자기가 그들과 친해져야겠다는 생각이 들지 않았다. **2** 형용사 깊은 관계의, 육체관계의 ❑ 그들이 남자 친구들과 애정을 나누는 순간들 ● (육체적으로) 깊이 부사 ❑ 당신은 기꺼이 당신의 짝과 육체적으로 깊은 관계를 맺고자 해야 합니다. **3** 형용사 일신상의, 극히 개인적인 ❑ 그는 자기 가족의 극히 개인적인 사항에 대해 썼다. ● 친밀하게 부사 ❑ 그게 그들이 친밀하게 대화를 나누려는 최초의 시도였다. **4** 형용사 아늑한, 친밀감이 드는 [마음에 듦] ❑ 아늑하게 촛불을 켠 둘만의 저녁 식사 **5** 형용사 밀접한 ❑ 광기와 지혜 사이의 밀접한 관련성 ● 밀접하게 부사 ❑ 과학적 연구와 환경 보존은 밀접하게 관련되어 있다. **6** 형용사 상세한, 깊은 ❑ 그는 키에르케고르와 쇼펜하우어에 대한 깊은 지식으로 나를 놀라게 했다. ● 상세하게, 깊이 부사 ❑ 그녀가 작품을 상세하게 알고 있는 음악가들의 황금기 **7** 타동사 암시하다, 넌지시 알리다 [격식체] ❑ 그는 실제로 회사의 재편성을 고려하고 있다는 것을 암시하기까지 했다.

타동사 겁주다, 위협하다 ❑ 존스는 폴을 겁주고 위압하기 시작했었다. ● 위협, 위협 불가산명사 ❑ 지난주 투표에서 위협이 있었다는 혐의에 대한 조사

형용사 겁먹은 ❑ 여자들이 겁먹지 않고 여기에 들어올 수 있다.

in|timi|dat|ing /ɪntɪmɪdeɪtɪŋ/ ADJ If you describe someone or something as **intimidating**, you mean that they are frightening and make people lose confidence. ❑ *He was a huge, intimidating figure.*

형용사 위협적인, 집주는 ❑ 그는 거대하고 위협적인 인물이었다.

into ♦♦♦ /ɪntu/

> Pronounced /ɪntu/ or /ɪntu/, particularly before pronouns and for meaning [14].

특히 대명사 앞이거나 [14]의 의미일 때는 /ɪntu/ 또는 /ɪntu/로 발음된다.

> In addition to the uses shown below, **into** is used after some verbs and nouns in order to introduce extra information. **Into** is also used with verbs of movement, such as "walk" and "push," and in phrasal verbs such as "enter into" and "talk into."

into는 아래 용법 외에도 추가 정보를 나타내기 위해 일부의 동사나 명사 뒤에 쓴다. into는 'walk', 'push'와 같은 이동 동사와도 함께 쓰며 'enter into', 'talk into'와 같은 구동사에도 쓰인다.

1 PREP If you put one thing **into** another, you put the first thing inside the second. ❑ *Combine the remaining ingredients and put them into a dish.* **2** PREP If you go **into** a place or vehicle, you move from being outside it to being inside it. ❑ *I have no idea how he got into Iraq.* **3** PREP If one thing goes **into** another, the first thing moves from the outside to the inside of the second thing, by breaking or damaging the surface of it. ❑ *The rider came off and the handlebar went into his neck.* **4** PREP If one thing gets **into** another, the first thing enters the second and becomes part of it. ❑ *Poisonous smoke had got into the water supply.* **5** PREP If you are walking or driving a vehicle and you bump **into** something or crash **into** something, you hit it accidentally. ❑ *A train from Kent plowed into the barrier at the end of the platform.* **6** PREP When you get **into** a piece of clothing, you put it on. ❑ *She could change into a different outfit in two minutes.* **7** PREP If someone or something gets **into** a particular state, they start being in that state. [V PREP n, n PREP n] ❑ *I slid into a depression.* **8** PREP If you talk someone **into** doing something, you persuade them to do it. [V n PREP n/-ing] ❑ *Gerome tried to talk her into taking an apartment in Paris.* **9** PREP If something changes **into** something else, it then has a new form, shape, or nature. ❑ *...to turn a nasty episode into a little bit of a joke.* **10** PREP If something is cut or split **into** a number of pieces or sections, it is divided so that it becomes several smaller pieces or sections. ❑ *Sixteen teams are taking part, divided into four groups.* **11** PREP An investigation **into** a subject or event is concerned with that subject or event. [n PREP n] ❑ *It would provide hundreds of millions of dollars for research into alternative energy sources.* **12** PREP If you move or go **into** a particular career or business, you start working in it. ❑ *In the early 1980s, it was easy to get into the rental business.* **13** PREP If something continues **into** a period of time, it continues until after that period of time has begun. ❑ *He had three children, and lived on into his sixties.* **14** PREP If you are very interested in something and like it very much, you can say that you are **into** it. [INFORMAL] [v-link PREP n] ❑ *I'm into electronics myself.*

❑ 전치사 - 속에, - 안에 ❑ 남은 재료들을 다 섞어 접시에 담으시오. ❑ 전치사 - 안으로, - 속으로 ❑ 나는 그가 어떻게 이라크에 들어 갔는지 모르겠다. ❑ 전치사 - 속으로, - 안으로 ❑ 타고 가던 사람이 나가떨어지고 핸들이 그의 목에 꽂혔다. ❑ 전치사 - 속으로 섞여 ❑ 유독한 연기가 상수원 속으로 섞여 들어갔다. ❑ 전치사 -에 부딪혀 ❑ 켄트 발 기차가 승강장 끝에 있는 방책을 들이받았다. ❑ 전치사 -을 입어 ❑ 그녀는 2분 만에 다른 옷으로 갈아입을 수 있었다. ❑ 전치사 -에 ❑ 나는 우울증에 빠져들었다. ❑ 전치사 (대화를 통해) -하게 하는 ❑ 제롬은 파리에 아파트를 구하도록 그녀를 설득하려고 했다. ❑ 전치사 -으로 (변하여) ❑ 추잡한 일화를 약간의 농담거리로 바꾸는 것 ❑ 전치사 -으로 (나뉘어) ❑ 16개 팀이 네 그룹으로 나뉘어 참가한다. ❑ 전치사 -에 관한 ❑ 그것은 대체 에너지원에 관한 연구에 수억 달러를 마련해 줄 것이다. ❑ 전치사 -에 (종사하여) ❑ 1980년대 초에는 대여업에 종사하기가 쉬웠다. ❑ 전치사 -까지 ❑ 그는 자녀가 셋 있었고, 60까지 살았다. ❑ 전치사 -에 열중하여 [비격식체] ❑ 내 자신이 전자 공학에 심취하고 있다.

in|tol|er|able /ɪntɒlərəbəl/ ADJ If you describe something as **intolerable**, you mean that it is so bad or extreme that no one can bear it or tolerate it. ❑ *They felt this would put intolerable pressure on them.* ● **in|tol|er|ably** /ɪntɒlərəbli/ ADV ❑ *...intolerably cramped conditions.*

형용사 참을 수 없는, 과도한 ❑ 그들은 이것이 자신들에게 과도한 압력을 줄 것이라고 생각했다. ● 참을 수 없이 부사 ❑ 견딜 수 없이 비좁은 상태

in|tol|er|ance /ɪntɒlərəns/ N-UNCOUNT **Intolerance** is unwillingness to let other people act in a different way or hold different opinions from you. [DISAPPROVAL] ❑ *...his intolerance of any opinion other than his own.*

불가산명사 편협함 [탐탁찮음] ❑ 자기 의견 외에는 용납하지 못하는 그의 편협함

in|tol|er|ant /ɪntɒlərənt/ ADJ If you describe someone as **intolerant**, you mean that they do not accept behavior and opinions that are different from their own. [DISAPPROVAL] ❑ *...intolerant attitudes toward non-Catholics.*

형용사 편협한, 옹졸한 [탐탁찮음] ❑ 비천주교도에 대한 편협한 태도

in|toxi|cat|ed /ɪntɒksɪkeɪtɪd/ **1** ADJ Someone who is **intoxicated** is drunk. [FORMAL] ❑ *He appeared intoxicated, police said.* **2** ADJ If you are **intoxicated by** or **with** something such as a feeling or an event, you are so excited by it that you find it hard to think clearly and sensibly. [LITERARY] [v-link ADJ by/with n] ❑ *They seem to have become intoxicated by their success.*

❑ 형용사 술 취한 [격식체] ❑ 그가 술에 취한 듯했다고 경찰이 말했다. ❑ 형용사 도취된 [문예체] ❑ 그들이 자신들의 성공에 도취되었던 것 같다.

in|trac|table /ɪntræktəbəl/ **1** ADJ **Intractable** people are very difficult to control or influence. [FORMAL] ❑ *What may be done to reduce the influence of intractable opponents?* **2** ADJ **Intractable** problems or situations are very difficult to deal with. [FORMAL] ❑ *The economy still faces intractable problems.*

❑ 형용사 완고한, 고집스러운 [격식체] ❑ 완고한 반대자들의 영향력을 줄이기 위해 무엇을 할 수 있을까? ❑ 형용사 다루기 힘든 [격식체] ❑ 경제는 여전히 난제들에 직면해 있다.

in|tra|net /ɪntrənɛt/ (**intranets**) N-COUNT An **intranet** is a network of computers, similar to the Internet, within a particular company or organization. →see **Internet**

가산명사 인트라넷

in|tran|si|gence /ɪntrænsɪdʒəns/ N-UNCOUNT If you talk about someone's **intransigence**, you mean that they refuse to behave differently or to change their attitude to something. [FORMAL, DISAPPROVAL] ❑ *He often appeared angry and frustrated by the intransigence of both sides.*

불가산명사 비타협적태도, 타협하지 않음 [격식체, 탐탁찮음] ❑ 그는 양측 모두의 비타협적인 태도에 종종 화가 나고 좌절하는 것 같았다.

in|tran|si|gent /ɪntrænsɪdʒənt/ ADJ If you describe someone as **intransigent**, you mean that they refuse to behave differently or to change their attitude to something. [FORMAL, DISAPPROVAL] ❑ *They put pressure on the Government to change its intransigent stance.*

형용사 비타협적인, 양보하지 않는 [격식체, 탐탁찮음] ❑ 그들은 정부에 비타협적인 자세를 바꾸도록 압력을 넣었다.

in|tran|si|tive /ɪntrænsɪtɪv/ ADJ An **intransitive** verb does not have an object.

형용사 자동사의

intra|venous /ɪntrəviːnəs/ ADJ **Intravenous** foods or drugs are taken into people's bodies through their veins, rather than their mouths. [MEDICAL] [ADJ n] ❑ *...an intravenous drip.* ● **intra|venous|ly** ADV [ADV after v] ❑ *Premature babies have to be fed intravenously.*

형용사 정맥 내의, 정맥 주사의 [의학] ❑ 정맥 주사 점적 장치 ● 정맥 주사로 부사 ❑ 미숙아들은 정맥 주사로 영양 공급을 받아야 한다.

in tray (**in trays**) also **in-tray** N-COUNT An **in tray** is a shallow container used in offices to put letters and documents in before they are dealt with. Compare **out tray**. [mainly BRIT; AM usually **in box**] ❑ *He went through his in-tray until he came to the report he'd been looking for.*

가산명사 미결 서류함 [주로 영국영어; 미국영어 대개 in box] ❑ 그는 자기가 찾고 있던 서류를 발견할 때까지 미결 서류함을 뒤졌다.

in|trep|id /ɪntrɛpɪd/ ADJ An **intrepid** person acts in a brave way. ❑ *...an intrepid space traveler.*

형용사 용감한, 대담한 ❑ 대담한 우주 여행가

a b c d e f g h i j k l m n o p q r s t u v w x y z

in|tri|ca|cy /ɪntrɪkəsi/ N-UNCOUNT **Intricacy** is the state of being made up of many small parts or details. ❑ *Garments are priced from $100 to several thousand dollars, depending on the intricacy of the work.*

불가산명사 복잡함 ❑ 의상은 공정의 복잡성에 따라 100달러에서 수천 달러까지 가격이 매겨진다.

in|tri|cate /ɪntrɪkət/ ADJ You use **intricate** to describe something that has many small parts or details. ❑ *...the production of carpets with highly intricate patterns.* ● **in|tri|cate|ly** ADV ❑ *...intricately carved sculptures.*

형용사 복잡한 ❑ 아주 복잡한 무늬가 있는 카펫 생산 ● 복잡하게 부사 ❑ 복잡한 모양으로 깎은 조각들

in|trigue (intrigues, intriguing, intrigued)

The noun is pronounced /ɪntrig/. The verb is pronounced /ɪntrig/.

명사는 /ɪntrig /로 발음되고, 동사는 /ɪntrig /로 발음된다.

1 N-VAR **Intrigue** is the making of secret plans to harm or deceive people. ❑ *...political intrigue.* **2** V-T If something, especially something strange, **intrigues** you, it interests you and you want to know more about it. ❑ *The novelty of the situation intrigued him.*

1 가산명사 또는 불가산명사 음모, 술책 ❑ 정치적 음모 **2** 타동사 호기심을 자극하다 ❑ 상황이 진기해서 그는 호기심이 발동했다.

in|trigued /ɪntrigd/ ADJ If you are **intrigued by** something, especially something strange, it interests you and you want to know more about it. ❑ *I would be intrigued to hear others' views.*

형용사 흥미를 느끼는 ❑ 나는 다른 사람들의 의견을 흥미 있게 듣고 싶다.

in|tri|guing /ɪntrigɪŋ/ ADJ If you describe something as **intriguing**, you mean that it is interesting or strange. ❑ *This intriguing book is both thoughtful and informative.* ● **in|tri|guing|ly** ADV ❑ *...the intriguingly-named newspaper Le Canard Enchaîné (The Chained Duck).*

형용사 흥미로운, 호기심을 자극하는 ❑ 이 흥미로운 책은 내용 정리가 잘 되어 있는 동시에 유익하다. ● 호기심을 자극하게 부사 ❑ 르 까나르 앙셰네라는, 호기심을 자극하는 이름의 신문

in|trin|sic /ɪntrɪnsɪk/ ADJ If something has **intrinsic** value or **intrinsic** interest, it is valuable or interesting because of its basic nature or character, and not because of its connection with other things. [FORMAL] [ADJ n] ❑ *Diamonds have little intrinsic value and their price depends almost entirely on their scarcity.* ● **in|trin|si|cal|ly** /ɪntrɪnsɪkli/ ADV ❑ *Sometimes I wonder if people are intrinsically evil.*

형용사 본래의, 고유의 [격식체] ❑ 다이아몬드는 고유의 가치는 거의 없고 그 가격은 거의 전적으로 그 희소성에 달려 있다. ● 원래, 본질적으로 부사 ❑ 때때로 나는 사람이 본질적으로 사악한 것이 아닐까 생각한다.

in|tro|duce ♦♦◊ /ɪntrədus, BRIT ɪntrədyuːs/ (introduces, introducing, introduced) **1** V-T To **introduce** something means to cause it to enter a place or exist in a system for the first time. ❑ *The Government has introduced a number of other money-saving moves.* ● **in|tro|duc|tion** N-UNCOUNT ❑ *What he is better remembered for is the introduction of the moving assembly-line in Detroit in 1913.* **2** V-T If you **introduce** someone **to** something, you cause them to learn about it or experience it for the first time. ❑ *He introduced us to the delights of natural food.* ● **in|tro|duc|tion** N-SING ❑ *His introduction to League football would have been gentler if he had started at a smaller club.* **3** V-T If you **introduce** one person **to** another, or you **introduce** two people, you tell them each other's names, so that they can get to know each other. If you **introduce yourself** to someone, you tell them your name. ❑ *Tim, may I introduce you to my uncle's secretary, Mary Waller?* ❑ *We haven't been introduced. My name is Nero Wolfe.* ● **in|tro|duc|tion** (introductions) N-VAR ❑ *With considerable shyness, Elaine performed the introductions.* **4** V-T The person who **introduces** a television or radio program speaks at the beginning of it, and often between the different items in it, in order to explain what the program or the items are about. ❑ *"Health Matters" is introduced by Dick Oliver on BBC World Service.*

1 타동사 도입하다, 시작하다 ❑ 정부는 많은 경비 절약 조치를 도입했다. ● 도입 불가산명사 ❑ 그는 1913년 디트로이트에서 처음으로 이동 조립 라인을 도입한 것으로 더 잘 기억된다. **2** 타동사 입문시키다, 처음 경험하게 하다 ❑ 그는 우리에게 자연식의 즐거움을 처음 맛보게 해 주었다. ● 입문 단수명사 ❑ 만일 그가 좀 더 작은 구단에서 시작했더라면 리그 축구로 입문하는 게 더 순조로웠을 것이다. **3** 타동사 소개하다 ❑ 팀, 우리 삼촌의 비서인 매리 월러 씨를 소개합니다. ❑ 우리는 서로 소개받은 적이 없습니다. 제 이름은 네로 울프입니다. ● 소개 가산명사 또는 불가산명사 ❑ 무척 수줍어하면서, 일레인은 소개를 했다. **4** 타동사 (프로그램의 서두에) 해설하다 ❑ '건강 문제'는 비비시 세계 방송에서 딕 올리버가 서두에 해설을 한다.

Word Partnership introduce의 연어

N.	introduce **a bill**, introduce **changes**, introduce **legislation**, introduce **reform 1**
V.	**allow me to** introduce, **let me** introduce, **want to** introduce **3 4**

in|tro|duc|tion /ɪntrədʌkʃ⁰n/ (introductions) **1** N-COUNT The **introduction to** a book or talk is the part that comes at the beginning and tells you what the rest of the book or talk is about. ❑ *Ellen Malos, in her introduction to "The Politics of Housework," provides a summary of the debates.* **2** N-COUNT If you refer to a book as an **introduction to** a particular subject, you mean that it explains the basic facts about that subject. ❑ *On balance, the book is a friendly, down-to-earth introduction to physics.* **3** N-COUNT You can refer to a new product as an **introduction** when it becomes available in a place for the first time. ❑ *There are two among their recent introductions that have greatly impressed me.* **4** →see also **introduce**

1 가산명사 (책 등의) 서두, 머리말 ❑ '가사의 정치학'의 머리말에서 엘런 말로스는 그 논쟁을 요약해 놓았다. **2** 가산명사 입문서, 개론서 ❑ 모든 것을 고려할 때, 그 책은 읽기가 쉽고, 실제적인 물리학 입문서이다. **3** 가산명사 출시품 ❑ 그들의 최근 출시품 중에서 두 가지가 내게 아주 인상적이었다.

in|tro|duc|tory /ɪntrədʌktəri/ **1** ADJ An **introductory** remark, talk, or part of a book gives a small amount of general information about a particular subject, often before a more detailed explanation. [ADJ n] ❑ *...an introductory course in religion and theology.* **2** ADJ An **introductory** offer or price on a new product is something such as a free gift or a low price that is meant to attract new customers. [BUSINESS] [ADJ n] ❑ *...just out on the shelves at an introductory price of £2.99.*

1 형용사 입문의, 소개의 ❑ 종교와 신학에 대한 입문 강좌 **2** 형용사 출시 기념의, 출시 할인의 [경제] ❑ 2.99파운드의 출시 할인 가격에 막 상점에 나온

in|trude /ɪntrud/ (intrudes, intruding, intruded) **1** V-I If you say that someone **is intruding into** a particular place or situation, you mean that they are not wanted or welcome there. ❑ *The press has been blamed for intruding into people's personal lives in an unacceptable way.* **2** V-I If something **intrudes on** your mood or your life, it disturbs it or has an unwanted effect on it. ❑ *Do you feel anxious when unforeseen incidents intrude on your day?* **3** V-I If someone **intrudes into** a place, they go there even though they are not allowed to be there. ❑ *An American officer on the scene said no one had intruded into the space he was defending.*

1 자동사 ~에 간섭하다 ❑ 언론은 사람들의 사생활을 용납할 수 없는 방식으로 침해한다고 비난을 받아 왔다. **2** 자동사 끼어들다, 방해하다 ❑ 예기치 않은 사건들이 당신의 일상에 끼어들면 불안해집니까? **3** 자동사 침범하다 ❑ 현장에 있던 한 미국인 경찰은 아무도 그가 지키고 있던 곳에 침입하지 않았다고 말했다.

in|trud|er /ɪntrudər/ (intruders) N-COUNT An **intruder** is a person who goes into a place where they are not supposed to be. ❑ *Christopher says he surprised intruders in his flat and fought them off.*

가산명사 침입자 ❑ 크리스토퍼는 본인이 자기 아파트 침입자들을 기습하여 격퇴했다고 말한다.

in|tru|sion /ɪntruʒ⁰n/ (intrusions) **1** N-VAR If someone disturbs you when you are in a private place or having a private conversation, you can call this event an **intrusion**. ❑ *I hope you don't mind this intrusion, Jon.* **2** N-VAR An **intrusion** is something that disturbs your mood or your life in a way you do not like. ❑ *I felt it was a grotesque intrusion into our lives.*

1 가산명사 또는 불가산명사 방해 ❑ 이렇게 방해하는 것을 양해해 주시기 바래요, 존. **2** 가산명사 또는 불가산명사 침해 ❑ 나는 그것이 우리 생활을 괴이하게 침해한다는 느낌이 들었다.

in|tru|sive /ɪntruːsɪv/ ADJ Something that is **intrusive** disturbs your mood or your life in a way you do not like. ❑ *The cameras were not an intrusive presence.*

형용사 훼방을 놓는 ❑ 카메라들이 훼방꾼이 되지는 않았다.

in|tui|tion /ɪntuˈɪʃⁿn, BRIT ɪntyuːɪʃⁿn/ (**intuitions**) N-VAR Your **intuition** or your **intuitions** are unexplained feelings you have that something is true even when you have no evidence or proof of it. ❑ *Her intuition was telling her that something was wrong.*

가산명사 또는 불가산명사 직관 ❑ 그녀는 직관적으로 무엇인가 잘못되었다는 것을 알았다.

in|tui|tive /ɪntuˈɪtɪv, BRIT ɪntyuːətɪv/ ADJ If you have an **intuitive** idea or feeling about something, you feel that it is true although you have no evidence or proof of it. ❑ *A positive pregnancy test soon confirmed her intuitive feelings.* ● **in|tui|tive|ly** ADV ❑ *He seemed to know intuitively that I must be missing my mother.*

형용사 직관적인 ❑ 임신 검사 양성 반응이 곧 그녀의 직관적인 느낌이 맞다는 것을 확인해 주었다. ● 직관적으로 부사 ❑ 내가 어머니를 그리워하고 있음에 틀림없다는 것을 그는 직관적으로 알고 있는 것 같았다.

in|un|date /ɪnʌndeɪt/ (**inundates, inundating, inundated**) 〖1〗 V-T If you say that you **are inundated with** things such as letters, demands, or requests, you are emphasizing that you receive so many of them that you cannot deal with them all. [EMPHASIS] ❑ *Her office was inundated with requests for tickets.* 〖2〗 V-T If an area of land **is inundated**, it becomes covered with water. [usu passive] ❑ *Their neighborhood is being inundated by the rising waters of the Colorado River.*

〖1〗 타동사 쇄도하다 [강조] ❑ 그녀의 사무실에는 표를 구하려는 요청이 쇄도했다. 〖2〗 타동사 범람하다 ❑ 그들의 이웃 지역이 불어나는 콜로라도 강물로 범람하고 있다.

in|vade /ɪnveɪd/ (**invades, invading, invaded**) 〖1〗 V-T/V-I To **invade** a country means to enter it by force with an army. ❑ *In autumn 1944 the allies invaded the Italian mainland at Anzio and Salerno.* 〖2〗 V-T If you say that people or animals **invade** a place, you mean that they enter it in large numbers, often in a way that is unpleasant or difficult to deal with. ❑ *People invaded the streets in victory processions almost throughout the day.*

〖1〗 타동사/자동사 침략하다 ❑ 1944년 가을에 연합군은 이태리 본토의 안지오와 살레르노를 침공했다. 〖2〗 타동사 밀어닥치다 ❑ 사람들이 거의 하루 종일 승전 행진을 하며 거리로 몰려들었다.

in|vad|er /ɪnveɪdər/ (**invaders**) 〖1〗 N-COUNT **Invaders** are soldiers who are invading a country. ❑ *The invaders were only finally crushed when troops overcame them at Glenshiel in June 1719.* 〖2〗 N-COUNT You can refer to a country or army that has invaded or is about to invade another country as an **invader**. ❑ *...action against a foreign invader.*

〖1〗 가산명사 침략자 ❑ 침략군은 1719년 6월 글렌쉬엘에서 군대가 그들을 무찔렀을 때에야 마침내 격파되었다. 〖2〗 가산명사 침략국, 침략군 ❑ 외국 침략국에 대항한 조치

in|va|lid (**invalids**)

> The noun is pronounced /ɪnvəlɪd/. The adjective is pronounced /ɪnvælɪd/ and is hyphenated in|val|id.

명사는 /ɪnvəlɪd /로 발음되고, 형용사는 /ɪnvælɪd /로 발음되며 invallid로 분철된다.

〖1〗 N-COUNT An **invalid** is someone who needs to be cared for because they have an illness or disability. ❑ *I hate being treated as an invalid.* 〖2〗 ADJ If an action, procedure, or document is **invalid**, it cannot be accepted, because it breaks the law or some official rule. ❑ *The trial was stopped and the results declared invalid.* 〖3〗 ADJ An **invalid** argument or conclusion is wrong because it is based on a mistake. ❑ *We think that those arguments are rendered invalid by the hard facts on the ground.*

〖1〗 가산명사 병약자 ❑ 나는 병약자 취급을 받고 싶지 않다. 〖2〗 형용사 무효의 ❑ 재판이 중지되었고 관결은 무효라고 발표되었다. 〖3〗 형용사 타당성이 없는 ❑ 우리는 그러한 주장들이 명백한 사실들에 비추어 보아 타당성이 없다고 생각한다.

in|vali|date /ɪnvælɪdeɪt/ (**invalidates, invalidating, invalidated**) V-T If something **invalidates** something such as a law, contract, or election, it causes it to be considered illegal. ❑ *An official decree invalidated the vote in the capital.*

타동사 무효로 하다 ❑ 법령 포고로 수도에서의 투표가 무효가 되었다.

in|valu|able /ɪnvælyəbⁿl/ ADJ If you describe something as **invaluable**, you mean that it is extremely useful. ❑ *I was able to gain invaluable experience over that year.*

형용사 매우 귀중한 ❑ 나는 그해에 걸쳐 매우 소중한 경험을 얻을 수 있었다.

in|vari|ably /ɪnveəriəbli/ ADV If something **invariably** happens or is **invariably** true, it always happens or is always true. ❑ *They almost invariably get it wrong.*

부사 변함없이, 항상 ❑ 그들은 거의 언제나 그것을 잘못한다.

in|va|sion ♦◇◇ /ɪnveɪʒⁿn/ (**invasions**) 〖1〗 N-VAR If there is an **invasion** of a country, a foreign army enters it by force. ❑ *...seven years after the Roman invasion of Britain.* 〖2〗 N-VAR If you refer to the arrival of a large number of people or things as an **invasion**, you are emphasizing that they are unpleasant or difficult to deal with. ❑ *...this year's annual invasion of flies, wasps and ants.* 〖3〗 N-VAR If you describe an action as an **invasion**, you disapprove of it because it affects someone or something in a way that is not wanted. [DISAPPROVAL] ❑ *Is reading a child's diary always a gross invasion of privacy?*

〖1〗 가산명사 또는 불가산명사 침입, 침략 ❑ 로마의 영국 침공 후 7년 〖2〗 가산명사 또는 불가산명사 내습, 쇄도 ❑ 올해의 파리, 말벌, 개미의 연례적인 내습 〖3〗 가산명사 또는 불가산명사 침해 [탐탁잖음] ❑ 아이의 일기를 읽는 것이 항상 심각한 사생활 침해인가?

in|va|sive /ɪnveɪsɪv/ 〖1〗 ADJ You use **invasive** to describe something undesirable which spreads very quickly and which is very difficult to stop from spreading. ❑ *They found invasive cancer during a routine examination.* 〖2〗 ADJ An **invasive** medical procedure involves operating on a patient or examining the inside of their body. ❑ *Many people find the idea of any kind of invasive surgery unbearable.*

〖1〗 형용사 급성의 ❑ 그들은 정기 검사에서 급성인 암을 발견했다. 〖2〗 형용사 수술을 통한 ❑ 많은 사람들이 어떤 종류든 검사를 위해 수술을 한다는 생각을 끔찍하게 여긴다.

in|vent /ɪnvɛnt/ (**invents, inventing, invented**) 〖1〗 V-T If you **invent** something such as a machine or process, you are the first person to think of it or make it. ❑ *He invented the first electric clock.* 〖2〗 V-T If you **invent** a story or excuse, you try to make other people believe that it is true when in fact it is not. ❑ *I stood still, trying to invent a plausible excuse.*

〖1〗 타동사 발명하다 ❑ 그가 최초의 전기 시계를 발명했다. 〖2〗 타동사 꾸며 내다, 날조하다 ❑ 나는 그럴듯한 변명을 꾸며 내려고 애쓰면서 가만히 서 있었다.

Thesaurus　　　　*invent*의 참조어

v.　　come up with, concoct, devise, originate 〖1〗〖2〗
　　　fabricate, make up 〖2〗

---

in|ven|tion /ɪnvɛnʃⁿn/ (**inventions**) 〖1〗 N-COUNT An **invention** is a machine, device, or system that has been invented by someone. ❑ *The spinning wheel was a Chinese invention.* 〖2〗 N-UNCOUNT **Invention** is the act of inventing something that has never been made or used before. ❑ *...the invention of the telephone.* 〖3〗 N-VAR If you refer to someone's account of something as an **invention**, you think that it is untrue and that they have made it up. ❑ *The story was certainly a favorite one, but it was undoubtedly pure invention.* 〖4〗 N-UNCOUNT **Invention** is the ability to invent things or to have clever and

〖1〗 가산명사 발명품 ❑ 물레는 중국 사람의 발명품이었다. 〖2〗 불가산명사 발명 ❑ 전화의 발명 〖3〗 가산명사 또는 불가산명사 날조, 허구 ❑ 그 이야기는 정말 인기가 있었으나 틀림없이 완전히 날조된 것이었다. 〖4〗 불가산명사 독창성 ❑ 그런 독창성과 수학적 능력이 있으니 아마 그는 컴퓨터 업계에서 일자리를 제의받을 것이다.

original ideas. ❑ *Perhaps, with such powers of invention and mathematical ability, he will be offered a job in computers.*

in|ven|tive /ɪnˈvɛntɪv/ ADJ An **inventive** person is good at inventing things or has clever and original ideas. ❑ *It inspired me to be more inventive with my own cooking.* ● **in|ven|tive|ness** N-UNCOUNT ❑ *He has surprised us before with his inventiveness.*

형용사 독창적인, 창의적인 ❑ 그것으로 나는 좀 더 창의적으로 요리를 해야겠다는 자극을 받았다.
● 독창성 불가산명사 ❑ 그는 일전에 독창성으로 우리를 놀라게 한 적이 있다.

in|ven|tor /ɪnˈvɛntər/ (**inventors**) N-COUNT An **inventor** is a person who has invented something, or whose job is to invent things. ❑ *...Alexander Graham Bell, the inventor of the telephone.*
→see Word Web: **inventor**

가산명사 발명가 ❑ 전화 발명가인 알렉산더 그레이엄 벨

in|ven|tory /ˈɪnvəntɔri, BRIT ˈɪnvəntri/ (**inventories**) **1** N-COUNT An **inventory** is a written list of all the objects in a particular place. ❑ *Before starting, he made an inventory of everything that was to stay.* **2** N-VAR An **inventory** is a supply or stock of something. [AM] ❑ *...one inventory of twelve sails for each yacht.*

1 가산명사 (상품 등의) 목록 ❑ 시작하기 전에 그는 남겨 두어야 할 모든 것의 목록을 만들었다.
2 가산명사 또는 불가산명사 재고품 [미국영어] ❑ 각 요트마다 12개씩의 돛 재고 물량

in|vert /ɪnˈvɜrt/ (**inverts, inverting, inverted**) V-T If you **invert** something, you turn it the other way up or back to front. [FORMAL] ❑ *Invert the cake onto a serving plate.*

타동사 전도시키다, 뒤집다 [격식체] ❑ 케이크을 차림용 큰 접시에 뒤집어 얹으시오.

in|vert|ed com|mas **1** N-PLURAL **Inverted commas** are punctuation marks that are used in writing to show where speech or a quotation begins and ends. They are usually written or printed as ' ' or " ". Inverted commas are also sometimes used around the titles of books, plays, or songs, or around a word or phrase that is being discussed. [BRIT; AM **quotation marks**] **2** PHRASE If you say **in inverted commas** after a word or phrase, you are indicating that it is inaccurate or unacceptable in some way, or that you are quoting someone else. [BRIT] ❑ *They're asked to make objective, in inverted commas, evaluations of these statements.*

1 복수명사 따옴표, 인용 부호 [영국영어; 미국영어 quotation marks] **2** 구 인용 부호로 문맥에 맞지 않거나 인용을 했다는 것을 나타내기 위한 표시 [영국영어] ❑ 그들은 이 보고서에 관해, 인용 부호로 표시된, 객관적인 평가를 내려 달라는 요청을 받았다.

in|vest ♦♦◇ /ɪnˈvɛst/ (**invests, investing, invested**) **1** V-T/V-I If you **invest in** something, or if you **invest** a sum of money, you use your money in a way that you hope will increase its value, for example by paying it into a bank, or buying shares or property. ❑ *They intend to invest directly in shares.* ❑ *He invested all our profits in gold shares.* **2** V-T/V-I When a government or organization **invests in** something, it gives or lends money for a purpose that it considers useful or profitable. ❑ *...the British government's failure to invest in an integrated transport system.* ❑ *...the European Investment Bank, which invested £100 million in Canary Wharf.* **3** V-T/V-I If you **invest in** something useful, you buy it, because it will help you to do something more efficiently or more cheaply. ❑ *The company has invested a six-figure sum in an electronic order-control system which is used to keep shops stocked.* **4** V-T If you **invest** time or energy in something, you spend a lot of time or energy on something that you consider to be useful or likely to be successful. ❑ *I would rather invest time in Rebecca than in the kitchen.* **5** V-T To **invest** someone **with** rights or responsibilities means to give them those rights or responsibilities legally or officially. [FORMAL] ❑ *The constitution had invested him with certain powers and he was determined to deploy them.* →see **stock market**

1 타동사/자동사 투자하다, 운용하다 ❑ 그들은 직접 주식에 투자할 작정이다. ❑ 그는 우리의 이익 전부를 금 생산 관련주에 투자했다. **2** 타동사/자동사 투자하다, 돈을 들이다 ❑ 영국 정부의 통합 수송 체계 투자 실패 ❑ 카나리 부두에 1억 파운드를 투자한 유럽 투자 은행 **3** 타동사/자동사 투자하다, 돈을 쓰다 ❑ 그 회사는 여섯 자리 수치의 금액을 상점의 상품 재고를 유지하게 해 주는 전자 주문 제어 시스템에 투자했다. **4** 타동사 바치다, ~을 위해 쓰다 ❑ 나는 부엌보다 레베카를 위해 시간을 쓰겠다. **5** 타동사 부여하다, 주다 [격식체] ❑ 헌법은 그에게 특정한 권력을 부여했고 그는 그것을 사용하기로 결심했다.

Word Partnership   *invest의 연어*

N.	invest **in a company**, invest **in stocks** **1**
	invest **funds/money** **1** **2**
	invest **energy**, invest **time** **4**
ADV.	invest **heavily** **1**-**3**

---

in|ves|ti|gate ♦♦◇ /ɪnˈvɛstɪgeɪt/ (**investigates, investigating, investigated**) V-T/V-I If someone, especially an official, **investigates** an event, situation, or claim, they try to find out what happened or what is the truth. ❑ *Gas officials are investigating the cause of an explosion which badly damaged a house in Hampshire.* ● **in|ves|ti|ga|tion** /ɪnˌvɛstɪˈgeɪʃⁿn/ (**investigations**) N-VAR ❑ *He ordered an investigation into the affair.*

타동사/자동사 조사하다, 수사하다 ❑ 가스 담당 공무원들이 햄프셔에서 가옥을 심하게 파손한 폭발 사고의 원인을 조사하고 있다. ● 조사, 수사 가산명사 또는 불가산명사 ❑ 그는 그 사건을 조사하라고 명령했다.

Word Partnership   *investigate의 연어*

ADV.	**fully** investigate, investigate **further**
N.	investigate **complaints**, investigate **a crime**, **police** investigate, investigate **the possibility of** *something*

---

in|ves|ti|ga|tive /ɪnˈvɛstɪgeɪtɪv, BRIT ɪnˈvɛstɪgətɪv/ ADJ **Investigative** work, especially journalism, involves investigating things. ❑ *...an investigative reporter.*

형용사 조사의, (부정) 폭로 보도의 ❑ 부정 폭로 전문 기자

Word Web   inventor

In the 1920s, Thomas Midgley, Jr.* developed two important chemical compounds. He was the **inventor** of leaded gasoline and Freon* gas. He found that a lead compound added to gasoline gave cars more power. Freon gas replaced the poisonous gases originally used in refrigerators. Both **products** were very popular when they first appeared. But over time, both **innovations** created new problems. **Research** has shown that leaded gas causes lead poisoning—particularly in children. Freon gas is harmful to the ozone layer around the earth. Scientists believe this contributes to global warming, skin cancer, and other serious problems.

Thomas Midgley, Jr. (1889-1944): an American engineer and chemist.
Freon: a trade name for a chemical compound.

in|ves|ti|ga|tor /ɪnvɛstɪgeɪtər/ (**investigators**) N-COUNT An **investigator** is someone who carries out investigations, especially as part of their job. ❑ ...*the insurance investigator who came to interview me.*

in|vest|ment ◆◇◇ /ɪnvɛstmənt/ (**investments**) **1** N-UNCOUNT **Investment** is the activity of investing money. ❑ *He said the government must introduce tax incentives to encourage investment.* **2** N-VAR An **investment** is an amount of money that you invest, or the thing that you invest it in. ❑ ...*an investment of twenty-eight million pounds.* **3** N-COUNT If you describe something you buy as an **investment**, you mean that it will be useful, especially because it will help you to do a task more cheaply or efficiently. ❑ *When selecting boots, fine, quality leather will be a wise investment.* **4** N-UNCOUNT **Investment** of time or effort is the spending of time or effort on something in order to make it a success. ❑ *I worry about this big investment of time and money and effort not working.*

Word Partnership	investment의 연어
N.	**capital** investment **1** **2**
	investment **advisor**, investment **banker**, investment **company**, investment **fund**, investment **opportunity**, investment **plan** **2**
V.	**encourage** investment, **stimulate** investment **1**
	make an investment **2** **3**
ADJ.	**long-term/short-term** investment **2** **4**

in|ves|tor ◆◇◇ /ɪnvɛstər/ (**investors**) N-COUNT An **investor** is a person or organization that buys stocks or shares, or pays money into a bank in order to receive a profit. ❑ *The main investor in the project is the French bank Credit National.*

in|vig|or|at|ing /ɪnvɪgəreɪtɪŋ/ ADJ If you describe something as **invigorating**, you mean that it makes you feel more energetic. ❑ ...*the bright Finnish sun and invigorating northern air.*

Word Link	vict, vinc ≈ conquering : convict, convince, invincible

in|vin|cible /ɪnvɪnsɪbᵊl/ **1** ADJ If you describe an army or sports team as **invincible**, you believe that they cannot be defeated. ❑ *You couldn't help feeling the military's fire power was invincible.* **2** ADJ If someone has an **invincible** belief or attitude, it cannot be changed. ❑ *He also had an invincible faith in the medicinal virtues of garlic.*

in|vis|ible /ɪnvɪzɪbᵊl/ **1** ADJ If you describe something as **invisible**, you mean that it cannot be seen, for example because it is transparent, hidden, or very small. ❑ *The lines were so finely etched as to be invisible from a distance.* ● **in|vis|ibly** /ɪnvɪzɪbli/ ADV [ADV with v] ❑ *A thin coil of smoke rose almost invisibly into the sharp, bright sky.* **2** ADJ You can use **invisible** when you are talking about something that cannot be seen but has a definite effect. In this sense, **invisible** is often used before a noun which refers to something that can usually be seen. [ADJ n] ❑ *All the time you are in doubt about the cause of your illness, you are fighting against an invisible enemy.* ● **in|vis|ibly** ADV [ADV with v] ❑ ...*the tradition that invisibly shapes things in the present.* **3** ADJ If you say that you feel **invisible**, you are complaining that you are being ignored by other people. If you say that a particular problem or situation is **invisible**, you are complaining that it is not being considered or dealt with. ❑ *It was strange, how invisible a clerk could feel.* ● **in|vis|ibil|ity** /ɪnvɪzɪbɪliti/ N-UNCOUNT ❑ *She takes up the issue of the invisibility of women and women's concerns in society.* **4** ADJ In stories, **invisible** people or things have a magic quality which makes people unable to see them. ❑ ...*The Invisible Man.* **5** ADJ In economics, **invisible** earnings are the money that a country makes as a result of services such as banking and tourism, rather than by producing goods. [BUSINESS] [ADJ n] ❑ *The revenue from tourism is the biggest single item in the country's invisible earnings.*

in|vi|ta|tion /ɪnvɪteɪʃᵊn/ (**invitations**) **1** N-COUNT An **invitation** is a written or spoken request to come to an event such as a party, a meal, or a meeting. ❑ ...*an invitation to lunch.* ❑ *The Syrians have not yet accepted an invitation to attend.* **2** N-COUNT An **invitation** is the card or paper on which an invitation is written or printed. ❑ *Hundreds of invitations are being sent out this week.* **3** N-SING If you believe that someone's action is likely to have a particular result, especially a bad one, you can refer to the action as an **invitation to** that result. ❑ *Don't leave your shopping on the back seat of your car – it's an open invitation to a thief.*

Word Partnership	invitation의 연어
V.	**accept an** invitation, **decline an** invitation **1**
	get/receive an invitation **1** **2**

in|vite ◆◆◇ (**invites, inviting, invited**)

The verb is pronounced /ɪnvaɪt/. The noun is pronounced /ɪnvaɪt/.

1 V-T If you **invite** someone to something such as a party or a meal, you ask them to come to it. ❑ *She invited him to her 26th birthday party in New Jersey.* ❑ *Barron invited her to accompany him to the races.* **2** V-T If you **are invited to** do something, you are formally asked or given permission to do it. ❑ *At a future date, managers will be invited to apply for a management buy-out.* ❑ *If a new leader emerged, it would then be for the Queen to invite him to form a government.* **3** V-T If something you say or do **invites** trouble or criticism, it makes trouble or criticism more likely. ❑ *Their refusal to compromise will inevitably invite more criticism from the UN.* **4** N-COUNT An

가산명사 조사자, 수사관 ❑ 나를 면담하러 왔던 보험 조사관

1 불가산명사 투자, 출자 ❑ 그는 정부가 투자를 장려하기 위한 세제 혜택을 도입해야 한다고 말했다. **2** 가산명사 또는 불가산명사 투자액 ❑ 2천 8백만 파운드의 투자액 **3** 가산명사 투자 대상, 투자 부츠를 고를 때는, 질 좋은 고급 가죽을 고르는 것이 현명한 투자이다. **4** 불가산명사 (시간, 노력 등의) 투입 ❑ 나는 시간과 돈과 노력을 이렇게 많이 투입하고 성과가 없는 것을 염려한다.

가산명사 투자자 ❑ 이 사업의 주요 투자자는 프랑스 은행인 크레디트 내셔널이다.

형용사 기운을 북돋우는 ❑ 빛나는 핀란드의 태양과 기운을 북돋우는 북부의 공기

1 형용사 무적의, 불굴의 ❑ 당신은 그 군대의 화력이 천하무적이라는 느낌을 갖지 않을 수 없을 것이다. **2** 형용사 완강한, 굳센 ❑ 그는 또한 마늘의 약효에 대해 굳센 믿음을 가지고 있었다.

1 형용사 눈에 보이지 않는 ❑ 그 선은 너무 가늘게 새겨져 있어서 멀리서는 보이지 않는다. ● 눈에 안 보이게 부사 ❑ 가늘고 구불구불한 연기가 거의 눈에 띄지 않게 청명하고 밝은 하늘로 올라갔다. **2** 형용사 모습을 드러내지 않는, 얼굴을 보이지 않는 ❑ 자신의 병이이 무엇인지 의아해하는 내내 당신은 보이지 않는 적과 싸우고 있는 것이다. ● 모습을 드러내지 않고 부사 ❑ 현재에도 보이지 않게 상황을 규정하는 전통 **3** 형용사 무시당하는 ❑ 그것은 이상했다. 그 점원이 얼마나 무시당하는 기분일까. ● 무시당하는 것, 간과되는 것 불가산명사 ❑ 그녀는 사회에서의 여성에 대한 무시와 여성들의 관심사라는 쟁점을 택했다. **4** 형용사 투명한 ❑ 투명 인간 **5** 형용사 무역 외 수입의 [경제] ❑ 관광 소득이 이 나라 무역 외 수입 중 가장 큰 단일 항목이다.

1 가산명사 초대, 초청 ❑ 점심 초대 ❑ 시리아 사람들은 아직 참가 초청을 수락하지 않았다. **2** 가산명사 초대장, 초청장 ❑ 수백 통의 초청장이 이번 주에 발송될 것이다. **3** 단수명사 자초, 유인 ❑ 산 물건들을 차 뒷좌석에 두지 마시오. 그것은 도난을 자초하는 것입니다.

동사는 /ɪnvaɪt /으로 발음되고, 명사는 /ɪnvaɪt/ 으로 발음된다.

1 타동사 초대하다, 초청하다 ❑ 그녀는 뉴저지에서 열리는 자신의 스물여섯 살 생일 파티에 그를 초대했다. ❑ 배런은 경주에 함께 가자고 그녀를 초대했다. **2** 타동사 요청받다 ❑ 장래에, 관리자들이 경영권 인수를 신청하도록 요청받을 것이다. ❑ 새 지도자가 나타나면, 여왕이 그에게 새 정부를 구성하도록 요청할 것이다. **3** 타동사 초래하다 ❑ 그들의 타협 거부가 불가피하게 유엔으로부터 더

a b c d e f g h i j k l m n o p q r s t u v w x y z

invite is an invitation to something such as a party or a meal. [INFORMAL] ❑ *They haven't got an invite to the wedding.*

많은 비난을 초래할 것이다. ◼️ 가산명사 초대 [비격식체] ❑ 그들은 결혼식 초대를 받지 못했다.

Word Partnership | *invite*의 연어
N. | invite **someone** to dinner, invite **friends**, invite **people** ◼️
| invite **criticism**, invite **questions** ◼️

---

in|vit|ing /ɪnvaɪtɪŋ/ ADJ If you say that something is **inviting**, you mean that it has good qualities that attract you or make you want to experience it. ❑ *The February air was soft, cool, and inviting.* ● **in|vit|ing|ly** ADV ❑ *The waters of the tropics are invitingly clear.* →see also **invite**

형용사 마음을 끄는, 유혹적인 ◼️ 2월의 공기는 부드럽고 시원하며 유혹적이다. ● 유혹하듯 부사 ❑ 열대의 바다는 매혹적일 정도로 맑다.

in|voice /ɪnvɔɪs/ (**invoices, invoicing, invoiced**) ◼️ N-COUNT An **invoice** is a document that lists goods that have been supplied or services that have been done, and says how much money you owe for them. ❑ *We will then send you an invoice for the total course fees.* ◼️ V-T If you **invoice** someone, you send them a bill for goods or services you have provided them with. ❑ *The agency invoices the client who then pays the full amount to the agency.*

◼️ 가산명사 청구서, 송장 ❑ 그러면 전체 수강료에 대한 청구서를 보내드리겠습니다. ◼️ 타동사 청구서를 보내다 ❑ 대리점이 고객에게 청구서를 보내면 고객은 대리점에 전액을 지불한다.

in|voke /ɪnvoʊk/ (**invokes, invoking, invoked**) ◼️ V-T If you **invoke** a law, you state that you are taking a particular action because that law allows or tells you to. ❑ *The judge invoked an international law that protects refugees.* ◼️ V-T If you **invoke** something such as a principle, a saying, or a famous person, you refer to them in order to support your argument. ❑ *He invoked memories of Britain's near-disastrous disarmament in the 1930s to argue that the project could not be postponed.* ◼️ V-T If something such as a piece of music **invokes** a feeling or an image, it causes someone to have the feeling or to see the image. Many people consider this use to be incorrect. ❑ *"Appalachian Spring" by Aaron Copland invoked the atmosphere of the wide open spaces of the prairies.*

◼️ 타동사 (법에) 호소하다, 발동하다 ❑ 그 판사는 난민을 보호하는 국제법을 발동했다. ◼️ 타동사 상기시키다 ❑ 그 계획이 지연되어서는 안 된다고 주장하기 위해 그는 1930년대 영국에서 재난을 초래할 뻔했던 무장 해제의 기억을 상기시켰다. ◼️ 타동사 떠오르게 하다, 연상시키다 ❑ 아론 코프랜드의 '애팔래치아의 봄'은 대평원의 드넓게 펼쳐진 공간의 분위기를 떠오르게 한다.

Word Link | vol ≈ will : bene**vol**ent, in**vol**untary, **vol**unteer

---

in|vol|un|tary /ɪnvɒləntəri, BRIT ɪnvɒləntri/ ◼️ ADJ If you make an **involuntary** movement or exclamation, you make it suddenly and without intending to because you are unable to control yourself. ❑ *Another surge of pain in my ankle caused me to give an involuntary shudder.* ● **in|vol|un|tari|ly** /ɪnvɒləntɛərɪli, BRITɪnvɒləntrɪli/ ADV [ADV with v] ❑ *His left eyelid twitched involuntarily.* ◼️ ADJ You use **involuntary** to describe an action or situation which is forced on someone. ❑ *...insurance policies that cover death, accident, sickness and involuntary unemployment.*

◼️ 형용사 저도 모르는, 부지불식간의 ❑ 또 다시 밀려오는 발목의 통증 때문에 나는 나도 모르게 몸을 떨었다. ● 저도 모르게, 무의식중에 부사 ❑ 그의 왼쪽 눈꺼풀이 저도 모르게 씰룩거렸다. ◼️ 형용사 본의 아닌, 자의가 아닌 ❑ 사망, 사고, 질병, 비자발적인 실업을 포괄하는 보험

in|volve ♦♦◇ /ɪnvɒlv/ (**involves, involving, involved**) ◼️ V-T If a situation or activity **involves** something, that thing is a necessary part or consequence of it. ❑ *Running a kitchen involves a great deal of discipline and speed.* ◼️ V-T If a situation or activity **involves** someone, they are taking part in it. ❑ *If there was a cover-up, it involved people at the very highest levels of government.* ◼️ V-T If you say that someone **involves** themselves **in** something, you mean that they take part in it, often in a way that is unnecessary or unwanted. ❑ *I seem to have involved myself in something I don't understand.* ◼️ V-T If you **involve** someone else in something, you get them to take part in it. ❑ *Noel and I do everything together, he involves me in everything.* ◼️ V-T If one thing **involves** you **in** another thing, especially something unpleasant or inconvenient, the first thing causes you to do or deal with the second. ❑ *A late booking may involve you in extra cost.*

◼️ 타동사 수반하다, 필요로 하다 ❑ 조리부를 운영하는 것은 상당한 기강과 속도를 필요로 한다. ◼️ 타동사 연루시키다 ❑ 만일 은폐가 있었다면, 그것은 정부의 최고위층과 연루되어 있었다. ◼️ 타동사 -에 연루되다, -에 말려들다 ❑ 나는 내가 이해하지 못하는 어떤 것에 말려든 것 같다. ◼️ 타동사 -에 끌어들이다, -에 관련시키다 ❑ 노엘과 나는 모든 일을 함께 하는데, 그가 나를 만사에 끌어들인다. ◼️ 타동사 -을 감수하게 하다 ❑ 늦게 예약하면 추가 비용을 감수해야 될지 모릅니다.

in|volved ♦♦◇ /ɪnvɒlvd/ ◼️ ADJ If you are **involved in** a situation or activity, you are taking part in it or have a strong connection with it. [v-link ADJ, usu ADJ in/with n] ❑ *If she were involved in business, she would make a strong chief executive.* ◼️ ADJ If you are **involved in** something, you give a lot of time, effort, or attention to it. [v-link ADJ, usu ADJ in n] ❑ *The family were deeply involved in Jewish culture.* ◼️ ADJ The things **involved** in something such as a job or system are the necessary parts or consequences of it. [v-link ADJ, oft ADJ in n] ❑ *We believe the time and hard work involved in completing such an assignment are worthwhile.* ◼️ ADJ If a situation or activity is **involved**, it has a lot of different parts or aspects, often making it difficult to understand, explain, or do. ❑ *The operations can be quite involved, requiring many procedures in order to restructure the anatomy.* ◼️ ADJ If one person is **involved with** another, especially someone they are not married to, they are having a sexual or romantic relationship. ❑ *During a visit to Kenya in 1928 he became romantically involved with a married woman.*

◼️ 형용사 관여된 ❑ 만일 그녀가 사업에 관여한다면, 강력한 최고 경영자가 될 것이다. ◼️ 형용사 열중한 ❑ 그 가족은 유대인 문화에 깊이 빠져 있었다. ◼️ 형용사 수반되는, 필요한 ❑ 우리는 그러한 과업을 완수하는 데 수반되는 시간과 노력이 가치 있는 것이라고 믿습니다. ◼️ 형용사 복잡한, 뒤얽힌 ❑ 그 수술은 인체 구조를 복구하기 위해 많은 과정을 거쳐야 하기 때문에 매우 복잡할 수도 있다. ◼️ 형용사 (남녀가) 관계에 빠진 ❑ 1928년 케냐를 방문하는 동안 그는 한 유부녀와 연애 관계에 빠졌다.

Word Partnership | *involved*의 연어
ADJ. | **directly** involved, **personally** involved ◼️ ◼️
N. | involved **in an accident**, **people** involved, involved **in planning**, involved **in politics**, involved **in a process** ◼️ ◼️
| **risks** involved, **work** involved ◼️

---

in|volve|ment ♦◇◇ /ɪnvɒlvmənt/ (**involvements**) ◼️ N-UNCOUNT Your **involvement in** or **with** something is the fact that you are taking part in it. ❑ *She disliked his involvement with the group and disliked his friends.* ◼️ N-UNCOUNT **Involvement** is the enthusiasm that you feel when you care deeply about something. ❑ *Ben has always felt a deep involvement with animals.* ◼️ N-VAR An **involvement** is a close relationship between two people, especially if they are not married to each other. ❑ *They were very good friends but there was no romantic involvement.*

◼️ 불가산명사 참가, 관여 ❑ 그녀는 그가 그 단체에 참가하는 것도 싫어했고 그의 친구들도 싫어했다. ◼️ 불가산명사 애착 ❑ 벤은 항상 동물에 대해 깊은 애착을 느껴 왔다. ◼️ 가산명사 또는 불가산명사 깊은 관계 ❑ 그들은 아주 친한 친구였지만 연애하는 사이는 아니었다.

Word Partnership | *involvement*의 연어
N. | **community** involvement ◼️
ADJ. | **active** involvement, **direct** involvement, **parental** involvement ◼️
| **romantic** involvement ◼️

Word Link

ward ≈ in the direction of : backward, forward, inward

in|ward /ɪnwərd/ **1** ADJ Your **inward** thoughts or feelings are the ones that you do not express or show to other people. [ADJ n] ❑ *I sighed with inward relief.* ● **in|ward|ly** ADV ❑ *Sara, while remaining outwardly amiable toward all concerned, was inwardly furious.* **2** ADJ An **inward** movement is one towards the inside or center of something. [ADJ n] ❑ *...a sharp, inward breath like a gasp.* **3** ADV If something moves or faces **inward**, it moves or faces toward the inside or center of something. [ADV after v] ❑ *He pushed open the front door, which swung inward with a groan.*

The form **inwards** can also be used for meaning **1**.

in|ward in|vest|ment N-UNCOUNT **Inward investment** is the investment of money in a country by companies from outside that country. [BUSINESS] ❑ *There is also evidence that exchange-rate uncertainty may have boosted inward investment from the rest of Europe.*

iodine /aɪədaɪn, BRIT aɪədi:n/ N-UNCOUNT **Iodine** is a dark-colored substance used in medicine and photography.

IOU /aɪ oʊ yu/ (**IOUs**) N-COUNT An **IOU** is a written promise that you will pay back some money that you have borrowed. **IOU** is an abbreviation for "I owe you."

IQ /aɪ kyu/ (**IQs**) N-VAR Your **IQ** is your level of intelligence, as indicated by a special test that you do. **IQ** is an abbreviation for "intelligence quotient." ❑ *His IQ is above average.*

irate /aɪreɪt/ ADJ If someone is **irate**, they are very angry about something. ❑ *The owner was so irate he almost threw me out of the place.*

IRC /aɪ ɑr si/ N-UNCOUNT **IRC** is a way of having conversations with people who are using the Internet, especially people you do not know. **IRC** is an abbreviation for "Internet Relay Chat."

iris /aɪrɪs/ (**irises**) N-COUNT The **iris** is the round colored part of a person's eye. →see **eye**, **muscle**

iron ♦♢♢ /aɪərn/ (**irons**, **ironing**, **ironed**) **1** N-UNCOUNT **Iron** is an element which usually takes the form of a hard, dark gray metal. It is used to make steel, and also forms part of many tools, buildings, and vehicles. Very small amounts of iron occur in your blood and in food. ❑ *The huge, iron gate was locked.* ❑ *...the highest grade iron ore deposits in the world.* **2** N-COUNT An **iron** is an electrical device with a flat metal base. You heat it until the base is hot, then rub it over clothes to remove creases. **3** V-T If you **iron** clothes, you remove the creases from them using an iron. ❑ *She used to iron his shirts.* ● **iron|ing** N-UNCOUNT ❑ *I managed to get all the ironing done this morning.* **4** ADJ You can use **iron** to describe the character or behavior of someone who is very firm in their decisions and actions, or who can control their feelings well. [ADJ n] ❑ *...a man of icy nerve and iron will.* **5** ADJ **Iron** is used in expressions such as **an iron hand** and **iron discipline** to describe strong, harsh, or unfair methods of control which do not allow people much freedom. [ADJ n] ❑ *He died in 1985 after ruling Albania with an iron fist for 40 years.* **6** PHRASE If someone has a lot of **irons in the fire**, they are involved in several different activities or have several different plans. ❑ *Too many irons in the fire can sap your energy and prevent you from seeing which path to take.*

Word Partnership

iron의 연어

ADJ.	**cast** iron **1**
	a hot iron **2**
N.	iron **bar**, iron **gate** **1**
	iron **a shirt** **3**
	an iron fist/hand **5**

▶**iron out** PHRASAL VERB If you **iron out** difficulties, you resolve them and bring them to an end. ❑ *"It was in the beginning, when we were still ironing out problems," a company spokesman said.*

iron|ic /aɪrɒnɪk/ or **ironical** /aɪrɒnɪkᵊl/ **1** ADJ When you make an **ironic** remark, you say something that you do not mean, as a joke. ❑ *At the most solemn moments he will flash a mocking smile or make an ironic remark.* **2** ADJ If you say that it is **ironic** that something should happen, you mean that it is odd or amusing because it involves a contrast. ❑ *Does he not find it ironic that the sort of people his movie celebrates hardly ever watch this kind of movie?*

ironi|cal|ly /aɪrɒnɪkli/ **1** ADV You use **ironically** to draw attention to a situation which is odd or amusing because it involves a contrast. [ADV with cl] ❑ *Ironically, for a man who hated war, he would have made a superb war cameraman.* **2** ADV If you say something **ironically**, you do not mean it and are saying it as a joke. [ADV with v] ❑ *Classmates at West Point had ironically dubbed him Beauty.*

iro|ny /aɪrəni, aɪər-/ (**ironies**) **1** N-UNCOUNT **Irony** is a subtle form of humor which involves saying things that you do not mean. ❑ *They find only irony in the narrator's concern.* **2** N-VAR If you talk about the **irony** of a situation, you mean that it is odd or amusing because it involves a contrast. ❑ *The irony is that many officials in Washington agree in private that their policy is inconsistent.*

Word Partnership

irony의 연어

ADJ.	**bitter** irony **1**
	ultimate irony **1** **2**
N.	**hint of** irony, **sense of** irony, **trace of** irony **1**
	irony **of a situation** **2**

1 형용사 마음속의 ❑ 나는 속으로 안도의 한숨을 쉬었다. ● 마음속으로 부사 ❑ 겉보기에는 관계자 모두에게 상냥했지만 사라는 속으로 화가 치밀고 있었다. **2** 형용사 안쪽으로 향하는, 내부의 ❑ 숨이 멎을 것처럼 갑자기 들이쉬는 호흡 **3** 부사 안쪽으로 ❑ 그가 현관문을 밀자 문이 삐걱거리며 안쪽으로 휙 열렸다.

inwards도 **1** 의미에 쓸 수 있다.

불가산명사 본국 투자 [경제] ❑ 불안정한 환율이 그 외 유럽 국가들로부터의 본국 투자를 부추겼을지도 모른다는 증거도 있다.

불가산명사 요오드

가산명사 약식 차용 증서

가산명사 또는 불가산명사 지능 지수 ❑ 그의 지능 지수는 보통 이상이다.

형용사 노한, 성난 ❑ 주인이 몹시 노해서 거의 나를 거기서 쫓아낼 기세였다.

불가산명사 인터넷 릴레이 채팅

가산명사 홍채

1 불가산명사 철 ❑ 거대한 철문이 잠겨 있었다. ❑ 세계 최고 품질의 철광석 매장지 **2** 가산명사 다리미 **3** 타동사 다리다, 다림질하다 ❑ 전에는 그녀가 그의 셔츠를 다렸다. ● 다림질 불가산명사 ❑ 나는 오늘 아침에 간신히 다림질을 모두 마쳤다. **4** 형용사 강철 같은, 굳은 ❑ 얼음 같은 담력과 강철 같은 의지를 갖춘 남자 **5** 형용사 냉혹한; 가혹한 통치; 혹독한 훈련 ❑ 그는 40년간 알바니아를 철권통치한 후 1985년에 수도 있다. **6** 구 해결해야 할 문제들 ❑ 너무 많은 일을 병행하면 기력이 약해질 수도 있고 무엇을 선택해야 할지 잘 보지 못할 수 있다.

구동사 해결하다 ❑ "시작은, 그러니까 우리가 아직 문제를 해결하고 있는 와중이었는데."라고 회사 대변인이 말했다.

1 형용사 반어적인 ❑ 가장 엄숙한 순간에 그는 조롱조의 웃음을 흘끗 보내거나 반어적인 말을 할 것이다. **2** 형용사 역설적인 ❑ 그는 자신의 영화가 찬양하는 부류의 사람들이 이런 종류의 영화를 거의 보지 않는다는 것을 역설적이라고 생각하지 않는 것일까?

1 부사 역설적으로 ❑ 역설적으로, 전쟁을 증오하는 남자이던 그는 뛰어난 전쟁 사진 기자가 될 수도 있었을 것이다. **2** 부사 반어적으로 ❑ 육군 사관학교의 동급생들은 반어적으로 그를 '미인'이라는 별명으로 불렀다.

1 불가산명사 반어, 풍자 ❑ 그들은 해설자가 풍자에만 관심이 있다는 것을 발견한다. **2** 가산명사 또는 불가산명사 역설, 아이러니 ❑ 역설적인 것은 워싱턴의 많은 관리들이 개인적으로는 그들의 정책에 일관성이 없다는 사실에 동의한다는 것이다.

Word Link	ir ≈ not : **ir**rational, **ir**regular, **ir**responsible

Word Link ir ≈ not : **ir**rational, **ir**regular, **ir**responsible

ir|ra|tion|al /ɪræʃənºl/ ADJ If you describe someone's feelings and behavior as **irrational**, you mean they are not based on logical reasons or clear thinking. ❏ ...an irrational fear of science. ● **ir|ra|tion|al|ly** ADV ❏ My husband is irrationally jealous over my past loves. ● **ir|ra|tion|al|ity** /ɪræʃºnælɪti/ N-UNCOUNT ❏ ...the irrationality of his behavior.

형용사 비이성적인, 불합리한 ❏ 과학에 대한 불합리한 두려움 ● 비이성적으로 부사 ❏ 내 남편은 내 과거의 사랑에 대해 비이성적으로 질투심을 느낀다. ● 불합리 불가산명사 ❏ 그의 행동의 불합리성

ir|rec|on|cil|able /ɪrekənsaɪləbºl/ ❶ ADJ If two things such as opinions or proposals are **irreconcilable**, they are so different from each other that it is not possible to believe or have both of them. [FORMAL] ❏ These old concepts are irreconcilable with modern life. ❷ ADJ An **irreconcilable** disagreement or conflict is so serious that it cannot be settled. [FORMAL] ❏ ...an irreconcilable clash of personalities.

❶ 형용사 양립할 수 없는, 조화되지 않는 [격식체] ❏ 이러한 케케묵은 개념들은 현대의 생활과 양립할 수 없다. ❷ 형용사 타협이 불가능한 [격식체] ❏ 타협이 불가능한 성격상의 충돌

ir|regu|lar /ɪregyələr/ (**irregulars**) ❶ ADJ If events or actions occur at **irregular** intervals, the periods of time between them are of different lengths. ❏ Cars passed at irregular intervals. ❏ She was taken to hospital suffering from an irregular heartbeat. ● **ir|regu|lar|ly** ADV [ADV with v] ❏ He was eating irregularly, steadily losing weight. ● **ir|regu|lar|ity** /ɪregyəlærɪti/ (**irregularities**) N-VAR ❏ ...a dangerous irregularity in her heartbeat. ❷ ADJ Something that is **irregular** is not smooth or straight, or does not form a regular pattern. ❏ He had bad teeth, irregular and discolored. ● **ir|regu|lar|ly** ADV ❏ Located off-center in the irregularly shaped lake was a fountain. ● **ir|regu|lar|ity** N-VAR ❏ ...treatment of abnormalities or irregularities of the teeth. ❸ ADJ **Irregular** behavior is dishonest or not in accordance with the normal rules. ❏ ...the minister accused of irregular business practices. ● **ir|regu|lar|ity** N-VAR ❏ ...charges arising from alleged financial irregularities. ❹ ADJ An **irregular** verb, noun, or adjective has different forms from most other verbs, nouns, or adjectives in the language. For example, "break" is an irregular verb because its past form is "broke," not "breaked."

❶ 형용사 불규칙한 ❏ 자동차들이 불규칙한 간격을 두고 지나갔다. ❏ 그녀는 불규칙적인 심장 박동 때문에 병원으로 실려 갔다. ● 불규칙하게 부사 ❏ 그는 불규칙하게 식사를 해서 꾸준히 체중이 줄고 있었다. ● 불규칙함 가산명사 또는 불가산명사 ❏ 그녀 심장 박동의 위태로운 불규칙성 ❷ 형용사 고르지 않은 ❏ 그는 치아가 좋지 않았는데, 치열이 고르지 않고 변색되어 있었다. ● 고르지 않게 부사 ❏ 울퉁불퉁하게 생긴 호수 가운데쯤에 분수가 하나 있었다. ● 고르지 않음 가산명사 또는 불가산명사 ❏ 치아의 기형이나 고르지 않은 치열에 대한 치료 ❸ 형용사 잘못된, 부정한 ❏ 부정 업무 행위로 비난받는 성직자 ● 부정행위 가산명사 또는 불가산명사 ❏ 추정되는 회계 부정행위에서 기인하는 혐의들 ❹ 형용사 불규칙 변화의

ir|rel|evance /ɪrelɪvºns/ (**irrelevances**) ❶ N-UNCOUNT If you talk about **the irrelevance of** something, you mean that it is irrelevant. ❏ ...the utter irrelevance of the debate. ❷ N-COUNT If you describe something as an **irrelevance**, you have a low opinion of it because it is not important in a situation. ❏ The Patriotic Front has been a political irrelevance since it was abandoned by its foreign backers.

❶ 불가산명사 무관함 ❏ 토론과 전혀 무관함 ❷ 가산명사 별 볼일 없는 존재 ❏ 애국 연합 전선은 외국인 후원자들이 손을 뗀 이후 정치적으로 별 볼일 없는 존재가 되어 왔다.

ir|rel|evant /ɪrelɪvºnt/ ❶ ADJ If you describe something such as a fact or remark as **irrelevant**, you mean that it is not connected with what you are discussing or dealing with. ❏ ...irrelevant details. ❷ ADJ If you say that something is **irrelevant**, you mean that it is not important in a situation. ❏ The choice of subject matter is irrelevant.

❶ 형용사 관련 없는 ❏ 관련 없는 세부 사항들 ❷ 형용사 중요하지 않은 ❏ 주제 선택은 중요하지 않다.

ir|resist|ible /ɪrɪzɪstɪbºl/ ❶ ADJ If you describe something such as a desire or force as **irresistible**, you mean that it is so powerful that it makes you act in a certain way, and there is nothing you can do to prevent this. ❏ It proved an irresistible temptation to Hall to go back. ● **ir|resist|ibly** ADV [ADV with v] ❏ I found myself irresistibly drawn to Steve's world. ❷ ADJ If you describe something or someone as **irresistible**, you mean that they are so good or attractive that you cannot stop yourself from liking them or wanting them. [INFORMAL] ❏ The music is irresistible. ● **ir|resist|ibly** ADV [ADV adj] ❏ She had a gamine charm which men found irresistibly attractive.

❶ 형용사 저항할 수 없는 ❏ 돌아간다는 것은 홀에게는 저항할 수 없는 유혹이었음이 드러났다. ● 불가항력으로 부사 ❏ 나는 스티브의 세계에 불가항력으로 끌리고 있는 나 자신을 발견했다. ❷ 형용사 홀딱 반하게 하는, 푹 빠지게 하는 [비격식체] ❏ 그 음악을 들으면 푹 빠지게 된다. ● 홀딱 반할 만큼 부사 ❏ 그녀의 사내아이 같은 매력에 남자들은 그녀가 홀딱 반할 만큼 매력적이라고 느꼈다.

ir|re|spec|tive /ɪrɪspektɪv/ PHRASE If you say that something happens or should happen **irrespective of** a particular thing, you mean that it is not affected by or should not be affected by that thing. [FORMAL] ❏ ...their commitment to a society based on equality for all citizens irrespective of ethnic origin.

구 ~에 관계없이 [격식체] ❏ 민족적 출신에 관계없이 모든 시민들의 평등에 기반을 둔 사회를 세우겠다는 그들의 서약

ir|re|spon|sible /ɪrɪspɒnsɪbºl/ ADJ If you describe someone as **irresponsible**, you are criticizing them because they do things without properly considering their possible consequences. [DISAPPROVAL] ❏ I felt that it was irresponsible to advocate the legalization of drugs. ● **ir|re|spon|sibly** /ɪrɪspɒnsɪbli/ ADV ❏ They resent the implication that they have behaved irresponsibly. ● **ir|re|spon|sibil|ity** /ɪrɪspɒnsɪbɪlɪti/ N-UNCOUNT ❏ I can only wonder at the irresponsibility of people who advocate such destruction to our environment.

형용사 무책임한 [탐탁찮음] ❏ 나는 마약 합법화를 옹호하는 것은 무책임한 행위라고 느꼈다. ● 무책임하게 부사 ❏ 그들은 자신들이 무책임하게 행동했다는 암시를 불쾌해 한다. ● 무책임함 불가산명사 ❏ 나는 그러한 환경 파괴를 옹호하는 사람들의 무책임함이 놀라울 뿐이다.

Word Link vere ≈ fear, awe : irre**ver**ent, re**ver**e, re**ver**ence

ir|rev|er|ent /ɪrevºrənt/ ADJ If you describe someone as **irreverent**, you mean that they do not show respect for people or things that are generally respected. [APPROVAL] ❏ Taylor combined great knowledge with an irreverent attitude to history. ● **ir|rev|er|ence** N-UNCOUNT ❏ His irreverence for authority marks him out as a troublemaker.

형용사 불손한 [마음에 듦] ❏ 테일러는 굉장한 지식을 역사에 대한 불손한 태도와 결합시켰다. ● 불손함 불가산명사 ❏ 권위에 대한 불손함 때문에 그는 말썽꾸러기로 보인다.

ir|re|vers|ible /ɪrɪvɜrsɪbºl/ ADJ If a change is **irreversible**, things cannot be changed back to the way they were before. ❏ She could suffer irreversible brain damage if she is not treated in seven days.

형용사 되돌릴 수 없는 ❏ 7일 안에 치료를 안 받으면 그녀는 되돌릴 수 없는 뇌 손상을 겪을 수 있다.

ir|revo|cable /ɪrevəkəbºl/ ADJ If a decision, action, or change is **irrevocable**, it cannot be changed or reversed. [FORMAL] ❏ He said the decision was irrevocable. ● **ir|revo|cably** /ɪrevəkəbli/ ADV ❏ My relationships with friends have been irrevocably altered by their reactions to my illness.

형용사 번복할 수 없는, 돌이킬 수 없는 [격식체] ❏ 그는 그 결정은 번복할 수 없다고 말했다. ● 돌이킬 수 없게 부사 ❏ 친구들과의 관계는 내 질병에 대한 그들의 반응으로 돌이킬 수 없게 변해 버렸다.

ir|ri|gate /ɪrɪgeɪt/ (**irrigates**, **irrigating**, **irrigated**) V-T To **irrigate** land means to supply it with water in order to help crops grow. ❏ None of the water from Lake Powell is used to irrigate the area. ● **ir|ri|ga|tion** /ɪrɪgeɪʃºn/ N-UNCOUNT ❏ The agricultural land is hilly and the irrigation poor. →see **dam**

타동사 물을 대다, 관개하다 ❏ 파웰호의 물은 그 지역에 물을 대는 데 전혀 쓰이지 않는다. ● 물을 댐, 관개 불가산명사 ❏ 농경지는 구릉이 많고 관개 시설은 열악하다.

ir|ri|table /ɪrɪtəbºl/ ADJ If you are **irritable**, you are easily annoyed. ❏ He had been waiting for over an hour and was beginning to feel irritable. ● **ir|ri|tably** /ɪrɪtəbli/ ADV [ADV with v] ❏ "Why are you whispering?" he asked irritably. ● **ir|ri|tabil|ity** /ɪrɪtəbɪlɪti/ N-UNCOUNT ❏ Patients usually suffer from memory loss, personality changes, and increased irritability.

형용사 성마른, 짜증내는 ❏ 그는 한 시간이 넘도록 기다리고 있었고 짜증이 나려 하고 있었다. ● 성마르게, 짜증내며 부사 ❏ "왜 속삭이는 거야?"라고 그가 성마르게 물었다. ● 성마름, 짜증냄 불가산명사 ❏ 환자들은 대개 기억 상실, 성격 변화와 짜증이 느는 것을 경험한다.

ir|ri|tant /ˈɪrɪtənt/ (**irritants**) **1** N-COUNT If you describe something as an **irritant**, you mean that it keeps annoying you. [FORMAL] ❑ *He said the issue was not a major irritant.* **2** N-COUNT An **irritant** is a substance which causes a part of your body to itch or become sore. [FORMAL] ❑ *Many pesticides are irritants.*

ir|ri|tate /ˈɪrɪteɪt/ (**irritates, irritating, irritated**) **1** V-T If something **irritates** you, it keeps annoying you. ❑ *Their attitude irritates me.* ● **ir|ri|tat|ed** ADJ ❑ *Not surprisingly, her teacher is getting irritated with her.*

> **Angry** is normally used to talk about someone's mood or feelings on a particular occasion. If someone is often angry, you can describe them as **bad-tempered**. ❑ *She's a bad-tempered young lady.* If someone is very angry, you can describe them as **furious**. ❑ *Senior police officers are furious at the blunder.* If they are less angry, you can describe them as **annoyed** or **irritated**. ❑ *The Premier looked annoyed but calm....a man irritated by the barking of his neighbor's dog.* Typically, someone is **irritated** by something because it happens constantly or continually. If someone is often irritated, you can describe them as **irritable**.

2 V-T If something **irritates** a part of your body, it causes it to itch or become sore. ❑ *Wear rubber gloves while chopping chillies as they can irritate the skin.*

ir|ri|tat|ing /ˈɪrɪteɪtɪŋ/ **1** ADJ Something that is **irritating** keeps annoying you. ❑ *They also have the irritating habit of interrupting.* ● **ir|ri|tat|ing|ly** ADV ❑ *They can be irritatingly indecisive at times.* **2** ADJ An **irritating** substance can cause your body to itch or become sore. ❑ *In heavy concentrations, ozone is irritating to the eyes, nose and throat.*

ir|ri|ta|tion /ˌɪrɪˈteɪʃən/ (**irritations**) **1** N-UNCOUNT **Irritation** is a feeling of annoyance, especially when something is happening that you cannot easily stop or control. ❑ *He tried not to let his irritation show as he blinked in the glare of the television lights.* **2** N-COUNT An **irritation** is something that keeps annoying you. ❑ *Don't allow a minor irritation in the workplace to mar your ambitions.* **3** N-VAR **Irritation** in a part of your body is a feeling of sharp pain and discomfort there. ❑ *These oils may cause irritation to sensitive skins.*

IRS /ˌaɪ ɑr ˈɛs/ N-PROPER In the United States, **the IRS** is the government authority which collects taxes. **IRS** is an abbreviation for "Internal Revenue Service."

is /ɪz/ **Is** is the third person singular of the present tense of **be**. **Is** is often added to other words and shortened to '-'s.

ISDN /ˌaɪ ɛs di ˈɛn/ N-UNCOUNT **ISDN** is a telephone network that can send voice and computer messages. **ISDN** is an abbreviation for "Integrated Service Digital Network." ❑ *...an ISDN phone line.*

Is|lam ◆◇◇ /ˈɪslɑm, BRIT ɪzˈlɑːm/ N-UNCOUNT **Islam** is the religion of the Muslims, which was started by Mohammed. ❑ *He converted to Islam at the age of 16.* **2** N-UNCOUNT Some people use **Islam** to refer to all the countries where Islam is the main religion. ❑ *...relations between Islam and the West.* →see **religion**

Is|lam|ic ◆◇◇ /ɪsˈlæmɪk, -ˈlɑ-/ ADJ **Islamic** means belonging or relating to Islam. [ADJ n] ❑ *...Islamic law.* →see **religion**

is|land ◆◆◇ /ˈaɪlənd/ (**islands**) N-COUNT; N-IN-NAMES An **island** is a piece of land that is completely surrounded by water. ❑ *...the Canary Islands.*

is|land|er /ˈaɪləndər/ (**islanders**) N-COUNT **Islanders** are people who live on an island. ❑ *The islanders endured centuries of exploitation.*

isle /ˈaɪl/ (**isles**) N-COUNT; N-IN-NAMES An **isle** is an island; often used as part of an island's name, or in literary English. ❑ *...the Isle of Man.*

isn't /ˈɪzənt/ **Isn't** is the usual spoken form of "is not."

iso|late /ˈaɪsəleɪt/ (**isolates, isolating, isolated**) **1** V-T To **isolate** a person or organization means to cause them to lose their friends or supporters. ❑ *This policy could isolate the country from the other permanent members of the United Nations Security Council.* ● **iso|lat|ed** ADJ ❑ *They are finding themselves increasingly isolated within the teaching profession.* ● **iso|la|tion** /ˌaɪsəˈleɪʃən/ N-UNCOUNT ❑ *Diplomatic isolation could lead to economic disaster.* **2** V-T If you **isolate yourself**, or if something **isolates** you, you become physically or socially separated from other people. ❑ *When he was thinking out a problem Tweed's habit was never to isolate himself in his room.* ❑ *His radicalism and refusal to compromise isolated him.* **3** V-T If you **isolate** something such as an idea or a problem, you separate it from others that it is connected with, so that you can concentrate on it or consider it on its own. ❑ *Our anxieties can also be controlled by isolating thoughts, feelings and memories.* **4** V-T To **isolate** a substance means to obtain it by separating it from other substances using scientific processes. [TECHNICAL] ❑ *We can use genetic engineering techniques to isolate the gene that is responsible.* **5** V-T To **isolate** a sick person or animal means to keep them apart from other people or animals, so that their illness does not spread. ❑ *Patients will be isolated from other people for between three days and one month after treatment.*

iso|lat|ed /ˈaɪsəleɪtɪd/ **1** ADJ An **isolated** place is a long way away from large towns and is difficult to reach. ❑ *Many of the refugee villages are in isolated areas.* **2** ADJ If you feel **isolated**, you feel lonely and without friends or help. ❑ *Some patients may become very isolated and depressed.* **3** ADJ An **isolated** example is an example of something that is not very common. [ADJ n] ❑ *They said the allegations related to an isolated case of cheating.*

iso|la|tion /ˌaɪsəˈleɪʃən/ **1** N-UNCOUNT **Isolation** is the state of feeling alone and without friends or help. ❑ *Many deaf people have feelings of isolation and*

---

1 가산명사 방해물, 신경을 거스르는 것 [격식체] ❑ 그는 이 문제가 신경을 거스르는 주요한 요소는 아니라고 말했다. **2** 가산명사 자극성 물질, 자극제 [격식체] ❑ 많은 농약이 자극성 물질이다.

1 타동사 짜증나게 하다 ❑ 그들의 태도가 나를 짜증나게 한다. ● 짜증나는 형용사 ❑ 놀랄 것도 없이 그녀의 선생님은 그녀에게 짜증이 나고 있다.

> angry는 보통 특정한 경우에 어떤 사람의 기분이나 감정을 얘기할 때 쓴다. 누가 자주 화를 내면, 그 사람은 bad-tempered라고 할 수 있다. ❑ 그녀는 성질이 나쁜 젊은 여자다. 누가 아주 화가 났으면, furious하다고 표현할 수 있다. ❑ 고참 경찰들이 그 중대한 실수에 격노했다. angry보다 덜한 경우에는 annoyed나 irritated를 써서 표현할 수 있다. ❑ 수상은 불쾌해 하는 것 같았으나 침착했다....이웃집 개 짖는 소리에 짜증이 난 남자. 대체로 누가 무엇에 의해 irritated되는 것은 그것이 끊임없이 계속 일어나기 때문이다. 누가 자주 짜증을 내면, 그 사람을 irritable(짜증을 잘 내는)하다고 표현할 수 있다.

2 타동사 자극하다 ❑ 고추는 피부를 자극할 수 있으니 고추를 다질 때는 고무장갑을 끼세요.

1 형용사 짜증스러운 ❑ 그들 역시 말을 가로막는 성가신 버릇이 있다. ● 짜증스럽게 부사 ❑ 그들은 때때로 짜증날 정도로 우유부단할 때도 있다. **2** 형용사 자극하는 ❑ 심하게 농축된 오존은 눈과 코, 목에 자극적이다.

1 불가산명사 짜증, 성가심 ❑ 그는 텔레비전에서 나오는 빛의 번쩍임에 눈을 깜빡거리면서 자신의 짜증이 드러나지 않도록 애썼다. **2** 가산명사 골칫거리 ❑ 직장에서의 대수롭지 않은 골칫거리 때문에 당신의 큰 뜻을 해치지 마십시오. **3** 가산명사 또는 불가산명사 자극 ❑ 이런 기름들은 민감성 피부에 자극을 유발할 수도 있습니다.

고유명사 (미국) 국세청

be 동사의 3인칭 단수 현재형; is의 축약형

불가산명사 종합 정보 통신망 ❑ 종합 정보 통신망을 이용한 전화선

1 불가산명사 이슬람교, 회교 ❑ 그는 열여섯 살에 이슬람교로 개종했다. **2** 불가산명사 회교국 ❑ 회교국과 서방의 관계

형용사 이슬람교의, 회교국의 ❑ 회교 율법

가산명사; 이름명사 섬 ❑ 카나리 제도

가산명사 섬 주민들 ❑ 그 섬 주민들은 수백 년에 걸친 착취를 견뎠다.

가산명사; 이름명사 섬 ❑ 맨 섬

is not의 축약형

1 타동사 고립시키다 ❑ 이 정책으로 그 나라가 국제 연합 안전 보장 이사회의 타 상임 이사국들로부터 고립될 수도 있다. ● 고립된 형용사 ❑ 그들은 교직이라는 테두리 안에서 자신들이 더욱 고립되어 가고 있는 것을 깨닫게 되고 있다. ● 고립 불가산명사 ❑ 외교적 고립이 경제 파탄으로 이어질 수도 있다. **2** 타동사 격리하다, 고립시키다 ❑ 트위드가 어떤 문제를 생각하고 있을 때 그의 버릇은 절대 자신의 방에 혼자 있지 않는 것이었다. ❑ 자신의 급진주의와 타협 거부로 인해 그는 고립되었다. **3** 타동사 분리하다 ❑ 우리의 근심은 사고와 감정과 기억을 분리시킴으로써 통제할 수도 있다. **4** 타동사 분리하다 [과학 기술] ❑ 유전자 공학 기술을 이용해서 문제가 되는 유전자를 분리해낼 수 있다. **5** 타동사 격리하다 ❑ 환자들은 치료를 받고 난 후 적어도 사흘에서 한 달까지 다른 사람들에게서 격리될 것이다.

1 형용사 외딴 ❑ 난민촌 다수가 외딴 지역에 있다. **2** 형용사 홀로 버려진, 외로운 ❑ 어떤 환자들은 홀로 버려졌다고 느끼게 되고 매우 우울해질 수도 있다. **3** 형용사 단발성의 ❑ 그들은 단발성 사기 사건과 관련된 주장을 했다.

1 불가산명사 고립, 고독 ❑ 많은 청각 장애인들이 고립감과 외로움을 느낀다. **2** 구 따로 떼어서,

A

loneliness. →see also **isolate** **2** PHRASE If something is considered **in isolation from** other things that it is connected with, it is considered separately, and those other things are not considered. ❑ *Punishment cannot, therefore, be discussed in isolation from social and political theory.* **3** PHRASE If someone does something **in isolation**, they do it without other people being present or without their help. ❑ *Malcolm, for instance, works in isolation but I have no doubts about his abilities.*

분리하여 ❑ 그러므로 징계란 사회적, 정치적 이론과 따로 떼어서 논의할 수 없다. **3** 구 혼자서, 고립되어 ❑ 예를 들면, 말콤은 혼자서 일하지만 나는 그의 능력을 믿어 의심치 않는다.

B

ISP /ˌaɪ ɛs ˈpi/ (**ISPs**) N-COUNT An **ISP** is a company that provides Internet and e-mail services. **ISP** is an abbreviation for "Internet service provider."

가산명사 인터넷 서비스 제공자

C

is|sue ♦♦♦ /ˈɪʃu/ (**issues, issuing, issued**) **1** N-COUNT An **issue** is an important subject that people are arguing about or discussing. ❑ *Agents will raise the issue of prize-money for next year's world championships.* ❑ *A key issue for higher education in the 1990's is the need for greater diversity of courses.* **2** N-SING If something is **the issue**, it is the thing you consider to be the most important part of a situation or discussion. ❑ *I was earning a lot of money, but that was not the issue.* ❑ *Do not draw it on the chart, however, as this will confuse the issue.* **3** N-COUNT An **issue** of something such as a magazine or newspaper is the version of it that is published, for example, in a particular month or on a particular day. ❑ *The growing problem is underlined in the latest issue of the Lancet.* **4** V-T If you **issue** a statement or a warning, you make it known formally or publicly. ❑ *Last night he issued a statement denying the allegations.* ❑ *The government issued a warning that the strikers should end their action or face dismissal.* **5** V-T If you **are issued with** something, it is officially given to you. [usu passive] ❑ *On your appointment you will be issued with a written statement of particulars of employment.* ● N-UNCOUNT **Issue** is also a noun. ❑ *...a standard army issue rifle.* **6** PHRASE The question or point **at issue** is the question or point that is being argued about or discussed. ❑ *The problems of immigration were not the question at issue.* **7** PHRASE If you **make an issue of** something, you try to make other people think about it or discuss it, because you are concerned or annoyed about it. ❑ *It seemed the Colonel had no desire to make an issue of the affair.* **8** PHRASE If you **take issue with** someone or something they said, you disagree with them, and start arguing about it. ❑ *I will not take issue with the fact that we have a recession.* →see **philosophy**

1 가산명사 쟁점, 논점 ❑ 스포츠 에이전트들이 내년 세계 챔피언 대회의 상금에 관한 쟁점을 제기할 것이다. ❑ 1990년대의 고등 교육을 위한 중요한 논점은 더욱 다양한 교과 과정의 필요성이다. **2** 단수명사 핵심, 초점 ❑ 나는 돈을 많이 벌고 있었지만 그건 중요하지 않았다. ❑ 그렇지만, 이게 핵심을 혼동시킬 테니 그것을 車트에 그리지는 말아. **3** 가산명사 (출판물의) 호, 쇄 ❑ 심각해지는 그 문제는 랜싯 최신호에서 중요하게 다루고 있다. **4** 타동사 공포하다, 발표하다 ❑ 어젯밤 그는 그 혐의들을 부인하는 성명을 발표했다. ❑ 정부는 파업노동자들이 파업을 끝내지 않으면 해고시키겠다는 경고를 발표했다. **5** 타동사 지급받다, 배급받다 ❑ 임용되는 날 당신은 서면으로 된 고용 상세 진술서를 지급받게 됩니다. ● 불가산명사 지급, 배급 ❑ 표준 규격의 군 배급 라이플총 **6** 구 쟁점이 되고 있는 ❑ 이민 문제는 쟁점이 되고 있는 현안은 아니었다. **7** 구 -을 문제로 삼다 ❑ 연대장은 그 사건을 문제 삼고 싶은 생각이 전혀 없는 것 같았다. **8** 구 -와 논쟁을 벌이다, -에 이의를 제기하다 ❑ 나는 지금이 불경기라는 사실에 이의를 제기하지는 않겠어.

D

E

F

G

H

I

J

Word Partnership *issue의 연어*

V.	become an issue, debate an issue, discuss an issue, raise an issue, vote on an issue **1**
	address an/the issue, deal with an/the issue **1 2**
ADJ.	complicated issue, controversial issue, difficult issue, legal issue, political issue, sensitive issue, serious issue, unresolved issue **1**
	big issue, critical issue, important issue, major issue **1 2**
	current issue, recent issue **1 3**
N.	election issue, safety issue, security issue **1**
	issue an appeal, issue a statement, issue a warning **4**

K

L

M

N

---

is|sue price (**issue prices**) N-COUNT The **issue price** of shares is the price at which they are offered for sale when they first become available to the public. [BUSINESS] ❑ *Shares in the company slipped below their issue price on their first day of trading.*

가산명사 발행 가격 [경제] ❑ 그 회사 주식은 거래 첫날 발행 가격 아래로 떨어졌다.

O

it ♦♦♦ /ɪt/

P

It is a third person singular pronoun. **It** is used as the subject or object of a verb, or as the object of a preposition.

it은 3인칭 단수대명사이다. it은 동사의 주어나 목적어, 또는 전치사의 목적어로 쓰인다.

Q

1 PRON-SING You use **it** to refer to an object, animal, or other thing that has already been mentioned. ❑ *It's a wonderful city, really. I'll show it to you if you want.* ❑ *My wife has become crippled by arthritis. She is embarrassed to ask the doctor about it.* **2** PRON-SING You use **it** to refer to a child or baby whose sex you do not know or whose sex is not relevant to what you are saying. ❑ *She could, if she wanted, compel him, through a court of law, to support the child after it was born.* **3** PRON-SING You use **it** to refer in a general way to a situation that you have just described. ❑ *He was through with sports, not because he had to be but because he wanted it that way.* **4** PRON-SING You use **it** before certain nouns, adjectives, and verbs to introduce your feelings or point of view about a situation. ❑ *It was nice to see Steve again.* ❑ *It's a pity you never got married, Sarah.* **5** PRON-SING You use **it** in passive clauses which report a situation or event. ❑ *It has been said that stress causes cancer.* **6** PRON-SING You use **it** with some verbs that need a subject or object, although there is no noun that it refers to. ❑ *Of course, as it turned out, three-fourths of the people in the group were psychiatrists.* **7** PRON-SING You use **it** as the subject of "be," to say what the time, day, or date is. ❑ *It's three o'clock in the morning.* ❑ *It was a Monday, so she was at home.* **8** PRON-SING You use **it** as the subject of a link verb to describe the weather, the light, or the temperature. ❑ *It was very wet and windy the day I drove over the hill to Milland.* **9** PRON-SING You use **it** when you are telling someone who you are, or asking them who they are, especially at the beginning of a phone call. You also use **it** in statements and questions about the identity of other people. ❑ *"Who is it?" he called. —"It's your neighbor."* **10** PRON When you are emphasizing or drawing attention to something, you can put that thing immediately after **it** and a form of the verb "be." [EMPHASIS] ❑ *It's really the poor countries that don't have an economic base that have the worst environmental records.* **11** PHRASE You use **it** in expressions such as **it's not that** or **it's not simply that** when you are giving a reason for something and are suggesting that there are several other reasons. ❑ *It's not that I didn't want to be with my family.* **12** **if it wasn't for** →see **be**

1 단수대명사 그것 (앞서 언급된 사물이나 동물) ❑ 그 곳은 정말이지 멋진 도시야. 원한다면 그 곳을 보여 줄게. ❑ 내 아내가 관절염으로 다리를 절게 되었는데, 그녀는 그것에 관해 의사에게 묻는 걸 민망해해. **2** 단수대명사 그 아이 (성별을 모를 때) , 그 아기 ❑ 그녀는, 자신이 그러기를 원했다면, 사법 재판소의 힘을 빌어 그로 하여금 아이가 태어난 후 그 아이를 부양하도록 할 수 있었다. **3** 단수대명사 앞서 제시된 상황을 가리킴 ❑ 그는 운동을 그만두었는데, 그래야만 해서가 아니고 자신이 그러기를 원했기 때문이었다. **4** 단수대명사 느낌이나 견해를 나타내는 문장의 주어 ❑ 스티브를 다시 만나게 기분 좋았다. ❑ 결혼을 안 했다니 참 안 되었구려, 사라. **5** 단수대명사 상황, 사건을 전하는 수동태 문장의 주어 ❑ 스트레스가 암을 유발한다고 알려져 왔다. **6** 단수대명사 형식주어 및 형식목적어 ❑ 물론, 밝혀진 대로 그 단체에 속한 사람들의 4분의 3은 정신과 의사였다. **7** 단수대명사 시간, 요일, 날짜를 가리키는 비인칭주어 ❑ 새벽 3시야. ❑ 월요일이어서 그녀는 집에 있었다. **8** 단수대명사 날씨, 명암, 기온을 가리키는 비인칭주어 ❑ 내가 언덕을 넘어 밀랜드까지 차를 몰고 간 그 날은 무척 날이 궂고 바람이 불었다. **9** 단수대명사 전화 통화 등에서 누구인지 말할 때 쓰임 ❑ "누구세요?"라고 그가 소리쳤다. "이웃 사람입니다." **10** 대명사 강조용법의 주어로 쓰임 [강조] ❑ 최악의 환경 기록들을 보유한 곳은 바로 경제적 기반이 없는 정말로 가난한 나라들이야. **11** 구 -때문은 아니다 ❑ 단지 - 때문은 아니다 ❑ 내가 가족들과 함께 지내고 싶지 않았기 때문은 아니다.

R

S

T

U

V

W

X

Y

Z

IT /ˌaɪ ˈti/ **IT** is an abbreviation for **information technology**. ❑ *....people with IT skills.*

정보 기술 ❑ 정보기술 기량을 갖춘 사람들

ital|ic /ɪtǽlɪk/ (**italics**) **1** N-PLURAL **Italics** are letters which slope to the right. Italics are often used to emphasize a particular word or sentence. The examples in this dictionary are printed in italics. ❑ *...a novel written entirely in italics.* **2** ADJ **Italic** letters slope to the right. [ADJ n] ❑ *She addressed them by hand in her beautiful italic script.*

1 복수명사 이탤릭체 ❑ 모조리 이탤릭체로 쓰인 소설 **2** 형용사 이탤릭체의 ❑ 그녀는 멋진 이탤릭체 필체로 그들의 주소를 적었다.

itch /ɪtʃ/ (**itches, itching, itched**) **1** V-I When a part of your body **itches**, you have an unpleasant feeling on your skin that makes you want to scratch. ❑ *When someone has hay fever, the eyes and nose will stream and itch.* ● N-COUNT **Itch** is also a noun. ❑ *Scratch my back – I've got an itch.* ● **itch|ing** N-UNCOUNT ❑ *It may be that the itching is caused by contact with irritant material.* **2** V-T/V-I If you **are itching** to do something, you are very eager or impatient to do it. [INFORMAL] [usu cont] ❑ *I was itching to get involved.* ● N-SING **Itch** is also a noun. ❑ *...cable TV viewers with an insatiable itch to switch from channel to channel.*

1 자동사 가렵다, 근질거리다 ❑ 건초열에 걸리면 눈물과 콧물이 흐르고 눈과 코가 근질거린다. ● 가산명사 가려움, 근질근질함 ❑ 등을 긁어 줘. 가려워. ● 가려움, 근질근질함 불가산명사 ❑ 가려움 증세는 자극적인 물질과의 접촉 때문에 생긴 것일 수 있다. **2** 타동사/자동사 ~하고 싶어 근질거리다 [비격식체] ❑ 나는 거기 참여하고 싶어 근질거렸다. ● 단수명사 참을 수 없는 욕망, 근질거림 ❑ 채널을 이리저리 바꾸고 싶어 온몸이 근질대는, 만족을 모르는 케이블 텔레비전 시청자들

itchy /ɪtʃi/ **1** ADJ If a part of your body or something you are wearing is **itchy**, you have an unpleasant feeling on your skin that makes you want to scratch. [INFORMAL] ❑ *...itchy, sore eyes.* **2** PHRASE If you have **itchy feet**, you have a strong desire to leave a place and to travel. [INFORMAL] ❑ *The thought gave me really itchy feet so within a couple of months I decided to leave.*

1 형용사 가려운 [비격식체] ❑ 가렵고 따가운 두 눈 **2** 구 떠나고 싶어 발바닥이 근질거림, 여행하고 싶은 욕망 [비격식체] ❑ 그 생각에 정말 발바닥이 근질근질해진 나는 채 두 달도 못 되어 떠나기로 결심했다.

it'd /ɪtəd/ **1** **It'd** is a spoken form of "it would." ❑ *It'd be better for a place like this to remain closed.* **2** **It'd** is a spoken form of "it had," especially when "had" is an auxiliary verb. ❑ *Marcie was watching the news. It'd just started.*

1 it would의 축약형 ❑ 이런 장소는 계속 폐쇄해 두는 편이 낫겠다. **2** it had의 축약형 ❑ 마시는 뉴스를 시청하고 있었는데, 뉴스는 이제 막 시작한 참이었다.

item ◆◇◇ /ɑitəm/ (**items**) **1** N-COUNT An **item** is one of a collection or list of objects. ❑ *The most valuable item on show will be a Picasso drawing.* **2** N-COUNT An **item** is one of a list of things for someone to do, deal with, or talk about. ❑ *The other item on the agenda is the tour.* **3** N-COUNT An **item** is a report or article in a newspaper or magazine, or on television or radio. ❑ *There was an item in the paper about him.* **4** N-SING If you say that two people are an **item**, you mean that they are having a romantic or sexual relationship. [INFORMAL] ❑ *She and Gino were an item.*

1 가산명사 품목 ❑ 진열품 중 가장 값진 품목은 피카소 그림일 것이다. **2** 가산명사 항목 ❑ 협의 사항의 다른 항목은 시찰이다. **3** 가산명사 기사 ❑ 신문에 그에 관한 기사가 있었다. **4** 단수명사 연인 사이 [비격식체] ❑ 그녀와 지노는 연인 사이였다.

Thesaurus   item의 참조어

N.   issue, subject, task **2**
      article, story **3**
      a couple **4**

Word Partnership   item의 연어

N.   item **of clothing 1**
      agenda item (or item **on an agenda**) **2**
      newspaper item **3**

---

item|ize /ɑitəmaɪz/ (**itemizes, itemizing, itemized**) [BRIT also **itemise**] V-T If you **itemize** a number of things, you make a list of them. ❑ *The report will itemize the cost of various improvements.*

[영국영어 itemise] 타동사 조목별로 작성하다 ❑ 그 보고서는 여러 가지 개수 공사비용을 항목별로 작성할 것이다.

itin|er|ary /ɑitɪnərɛri, BRIT ɑitɪnərəri/ (**itineraries**) N-COUNT An **itinerary** is a plan of a journey, including the route and the places that you will visit. ❑ *The next place on our itinerary was Silistra.*

가산명사 여행 일정 ❑ 우리 여행 일정에 따르면 다음 장소는 실리스트라였다.

it'll /ɪtəl/ **It'll** is a spoken form of "it will." ❑ *It's ages since I've seen her so it'll be nice to meet her in town on Thursday.*

it will의 축약형 ❑ 내가 그녀를 본 지 오래되었으니 목요일에 시내에서 그녀를 만나면 참 반가울 것이다.

its ◆◆◆ /ɪts/

> **Its** is a third person singular possessive determiner.

DET You use **its** to indicate that something belongs or relates to a thing, place, or animal that has just been mentioned or whose identity is known. You can use **its** to indicate that something belongs or relates to a child or baby. ❑ *The British Labor Party concludes its annual conference today in Brighton.*

> Do not confuse **its** and **it's**. **Its** means "belonging to it." **It's** is short for "it is" or "it has." ❑ *The horse raised its head... It's hot in here... It's stopped raining.*

> its는 3인칭 단수 소유한정사이다.

한정사 그것의; 그 아이의 ❑ 영국 노동당은 오늘 브라이튼에서 자체 연례 협의회를 마쳤다.

> its와 it's를 혼동하지 않도록 하라. its는 it의 소유격이고, it's는 it is 또는 it has의 준말이다. ❑ 말이 머리를 들었다... 이 안은 덥다... 비가 그쳤다.

it's /ɪts/ **1** **It's** is the usual spoken form of "it is." ❑ *It's the best news I've heard in a long time.* **2** **It's** is the usual spoken form of "it has," especially when "has" is an auxiliary verb. ❑ *It's been such a long time since I played.*

1 it is의 축약형 ❑ 그것은 오랫동안 들어온 소식 중 가장 좋은 소식이다. **2** it has의 축약형 ❑ 연주를 해 본 지 정말 오래 되었다.

it|self ◆◆◆ /ɪtsɛlf/ **1** PRON-REFL **Itself** is used as the object of a verb or preposition when it refers to something that is the same thing as the subject of the verb. [v PRON, prep PRON] ❑ *Scientists have discovered remarkable new evidence showing how the body rebuilds itself while we sleep.* **2** PRON-REFL-EMPH You use **itself** to emphasize the thing you are referring to. [EMPHASIS] ❑ *I think life itself is a learning process.* **3** PRON-REFL-EMPH If you say that someone is, for example, politeness **itself** or kindness **itself**, you are emphasizing they are extremely polite or extremely kind. [EMPHASIS] [n PRON] ❑ *I am never really happy staying in a hotel, although the management here have been kindness itself.*

1 재귀대명사 그것 자체, 스스로 ❑ 과학자들은 어떻게 우리 몸이 수면 중에 스스로를 회복하는지를 보여 주는 주목할 만한 새로운 증거를 발견했다. **2** 강조 재귀대명사 그 자체 [강조] ❑ 나는 인생 자체가 학습 과정이라고 생각한다. **3** 강조 재귀대명사 바로 그 자체 [강조] ❑ 여기 관리자들은 바로 친절함 그 자체이지만 나는 호텔에서 지내는 것이 정말로 행복해지지는 않다.

I've /aɪv/ **I've** is the usual spoken form of "I have," especially when "have" is an auxiliary verb. ❑ *I've been invited to meet with the American Ambassador.*

I have의 축약형 ❑ 나는 미국 대사를 만나도록 초청받았다.

IVF /aɪ vi ɛf/ N-UNCOUNT **IVF** is a method of helping a woman to have a baby in which an egg is removed from one of her ovaries, fertilized outside her body, and then replaced in her womb. **IVF** is an abbreviation for "in vitro fertilization." ❑ *When she first underwent IVF it was still a relatively new procedure.*

불가산명사 시험관 아기 시술, 체외 수정 ❑ 그녀가 처음 시험관 아기 시술을 받았을 때는 그 시술이 아직 비교적 새로운 처치였다.

ivo|ry /ˈaɪvəri/ ■ N-UNCOUNT **Ivory** is a hard cream-colored substance which forms the tusks of elephants. It is valuable and can be used for making carved ornaments. ❑ *...the international ban on the sale of ivory.* ■ COLOR **Ivory** is a creamy-white color. ❑ *...small ivory flowers.*

■ 불가산명사 상아 ❑ 상아 판매에 대한 국제적 금지령
■ 색채어 상아색의 ❑ 작은 상아색 꽃들

ivy /ˈaɪvi/ (**ivies**) N-VAR **Ivy** is an evergreen plant that grows up walls or along the ground.

가산명사 또는 불가산명사 담쟁이덩굴

Jj

J, j /dʒeɪ/ (**J's, j's**) N-VAR **J** is the tenth letter of the English alphabet.
가산명사 또는 불가산명사 영어 알파벳의 열 번째 글자

jab /dʒæb/ (**jabs, jabbing, jabbed**) **1** V-T/V-I If you **jab** one thing into another, you push it there with a quick, sudden movement and with a lot of force. ❑ *He saw her jab her thumb on a red button – a panic button.* ❑ *Stern jabbed at me with his glasses.* **2** N-COUNT A **jab** is a sudden, sharp punch. ❑ *He was simply too powerful for his opponent, rocking him with a steady supply of left jabs.* **3** N-COUNT A **jab** is an injection of something into your blood to prevent illness. [BRIT, INFORMAL] ❑ *...painful anti malaria jabs.*
1 타동사/자동사 쿡 찌르다, 쭉 누르다 ❑ 그는 그녀가 엄지손가락으로 비상 버튼인 빨간 버튼을 쿡 누르는 것을 보았다. ❑ 스턴은 안경으로 나를 쿡쿡 찔렀다. **2** 가산명사 빠른 펀치, 잽 ❑ 꾸준히 왼쪽 잽을 날리면서 상대방을 뒤흔들었던 그는 너무나도 강한 상대였다. **3** 가산명사 주사, 예방 접종 [영국영어, 비격식체] ❑ 고통스러운 말라리아 예방 접종

jack /dʒæk/ (**jacks**) **1** N-COUNT A **jack** is a device for lifting a heavy object off the ground, for example a car. ❑ *The jack slips and the car crushes Ken underneath.* **2** N-COUNT A **jack** is a playing card whose value is between a ten and a queen. A jack is usually represented by a picture of a young man. ❑ *...the jack of spades.*
1 가산명사 들어올리는 기계, 잭 ❑ 잭이 미끄러지자 아래에 있는 켄은 차에 깔리게 된다. **2** 가산명사 (카드놀이) 잭 ❑ 스페이드 잭

jack|et ♦◇◇ /dʒækɪt/ (**jackets**) **1** N-COUNT A **jacket** is a short coat with long sleeves. ❑ *...a black leather jacket.* **2** N-COUNT Potatoes baked in their **jackets** are baked with their skin on. ❑ *For baking whole in their jackets, use large potatoes of 225g to 275g each (8-10oz).* **3** N-COUNT The **jacket** of a book is the paper cover that protects the book. [mainly AM] ❑ *A beautiful naked girl gazes from the jacket of this book.* **4** N-COUNT A record **jacket** is the cover in which a record is kept. [AM; BRIT **sleeve**] ❑ *He used to read the backs of the record jackets.* **5** →see also **clothing, dinner jacket, straitjacket**
1 가산명사 재킷, 상의 ❑ 검정 가죽 재킷 **2** 가산명사 (감자) 껍질 ❑ 감자를 껍질 채 통째로 구울 때는 하나에 225–275그램(8–10온스) 정도 되는 큰 감자를 사용하세요. **3** 가산명사 (책의) 커버, 표지 [주로 미국영어] ❑ 책 표지에 나체인 아름다운 소녀가 쳐다보고 있다. **4** 가산명사 음반 표지, 음반 재킷 [미국영어; 영국영어 sleeve] ❑ 그는 음반 재킷의 뒷면을 읽곤 했었다.

jack|pot /dʒækpɒt/ (**jackpots**) **1** N-COUNT A **jackpot** is the most valuable prize in a game or lottery, especially when the game involves increasing the value of the prize until someone wins it. ❑ *A nurse who gambled £6 in a slot machine walked away with the biggest ever jackpot of more than £5 million.* **2** PHRASE If you **hit the jackpot**, you have a great success, for example by winning a lot of money or having a piece of good luck. [INFORMAL] ❑ *The National Theatre hit the jackpot with its first musical, Guys and Dolls.*
1 가산명사 최고 상금 ❑ 슬롯머신에 6파운드를 걸었던 한 간호사가 5백만 파운드나 되는, 역대 최고의 대박을 터뜨렸다. **2** 구 대성공을 거두다 [비격식체] ❑ 내셔널 시어터는 그곳의 첫 번째 뮤지컬인 '아가씨와 건달들'로 대성공을 거두었다.

Ja|cuz|zi /dʒəkuzi/ (**Jacuzzis**) N-COUNT A **Jacuzzi** is a large circular bath which is fitted with a device that makes the water move around. [TRADEMARK]
가산명사 자쿠지 (공기방울 욕조) [상표]

jade /dʒeɪd/ **1** N-UNCOUNT **Jade** is a hard stone, usually green in color, that is used for making jewelry and ornaments. ❑ *The Burmese jade choker featured in the catalog was very beautiful.* **2** COLOR Something that is **jade** or **jade green** is bright green in color. ❑ *Amy had bought a soft, jade green cashmere jacket for Helen.*
1 불가산명사 비취, 옥(玉) ❑ 카탈로그에 있는 버마산(産) 옥 목걸이는 매우 아름다웠다. **2** 색채어 비취색 ❑ 에이미는 부드러운 비췻빛 초록 캐시미어 재킷을 헬렌에게 사 주었다.

jad|ed /dʒeɪdɪd/ ADJ If you are **jaded**, you feel bored, tired, and not enthusiastic, for example because you have had too much of the same thing. ❑ *We had both become jaded, disinterested, and disillusioned.*
형용사 지겨운, 지친 ❑ 우리 둘 모두 지겨움, 무관심, 환멸을 느끼기 시작했다.

jag|ged /dʒægɪd/ ADJ Something that is **jagged** has a rough, uneven shape or edge with lots of sharp points. ❑ *...jagged black cliffs.*
형용사 톱날같은 ❑ 삐죽삐죽한 검은 절벽

jail ♦◇◇ /dʒeɪl/ (**jails, jailing, jailed**) [BRIT also **gaol**] **1** N-VAR A **jail** is a place where criminals are kept in order to punish them, or where people waiting to be tried are kept. ❑ *Three prisoners escaped from a jail.* **2** V-T If someone **is jailed**, they are put into jail. [usu passive] ❑ *He was jailed for twenty years.*
[영국영어 gaol] **1** 가산명사 또는 불가산명사 교도소, 감옥 ❑ 죄수 세 명이 교도소를 탈출했다. **2** 타동사 (감옥에) 수감되다 ❑ 그는 20년 동안 감옥에 수감되었다.

jam /dʒæm/ (**jams, jamming, jammed**) **1** N-MASS **Jam** is a sweet food that is made by cooking fruit with a large amount of sugar until it is thickened. It is usually spread on bread. [mainly BRIT; AM usually **jelly**] ❑ *...home-made jam.* **2** V-T If you **jam** something somewhere, you push or put it there roughly. ❑ *Pete jammed his hands into his pockets.* **3** V-T/V-I If something such as a part of a machine **jams**, or if something **jams** it, the part becomes fixed in position and is unable to move freely or work properly. ❑ *The second time he fired his gun jammed.* ❑ *A rope jammed the boat's propeller.* **4** V-T If vehicles **jam** a road, there are so many of them that they cannot move. ❑ *Hundreds of departing motorists jammed roads that had been closed during the height of the storm.* ● N-COUNT **Jam** is also a noun. ❑ *400 trucks may sit in a jam for ten hours waiting to cross the limited number of bridges.* ● **jammed** ADJ ❑ *Nearby roads and the dirt track to the beach were jammed with cars.* **5** V-T/V-I If a lot of people **jam** a place, or **jam into** a place, they are pressed tightly together so that they can hardly move. ❑ *Hundreds of people jammed the boardwalk to watch.* ● **jammed** ADJ ❑ *The stadium was jammed and they had to turn away hundreds of disappointed fans.* **6** V-T To **jam** a radio or electronic signal means to interfere with it and prevent it from being received or heard clearly. ❑ *They will try to jam the transmissions electronically.* ● **jam|ming** N-UNCOUNT ❑ *The plane is used for electronic jamming and radar detection.* **7** V-T If callers **are jamming** telephone lines, there are so many callers that the people answering the telephones find it difficult to deal with them all. ❑ *Hundreds of callers jammed the BBC switchboard for more than an hour.* →see **traffic**
1 물질명사 잼 [주로 영국영어; 미국영어 대개 jelly] ❑ 집에서 만든 잼 **2** 타동사 쑤셔 넣다 ❑ 피트는 손을 주머니에 쑤셔 넣었다. **3** 타동사/자동사 움직이지 않다 ❑ 두 번째 쐈을 때 그의 총은 작동하지 않았다. ❑ 밧줄이 보트의 프로펠러를 움직이지 못하게 했다. **4** 타동사 막다, (차가 도로를) 메우다 ❑ 폭풍이 한창일 때 떠나려는 수백 명의 자동차 운전자들이 통행이 금지되었던 도로를 가득 메웠다. ● 가산명사 교통 정체 ❑ 400대의 트럭이 제한된 수의 다리를 건너려고 기다리며 10시간 동안 교통이 정체된 가운데 서 있을 수도 있다. ● 꽉 막힌 형용사 ❑ 해변으로 가는 근처 도로와 비포장도로는 차로 꽉 막혀 있었다. **5** 타동사/자동사 가득 메우다 ❑ 수백 명의 사람들이 구경을 하느라 바닷가를 따라 널빤지를 깐 길을 가득 메웠다. ● 꽉 찬 형용사 ❑ 경기장은 사람들로 꽉 찼고, 입장하지 못해 낙담한 수백 명의 팬들은 되돌아가야만 했다. **6** 타동사 방해하다 ❑ 그들은 전송되는 내용에 대해서 전파 방해를 시도할 것이다. ● 전파 방해 불가산명사 ❑ 비행기는 전파 교란 및 레이더 탐지에 이용된다. **7** 타동사 (통화량 폭주로) 회선을 마비시키다 ❑ 수백 통의 전화가 걸려 와 한 시간 넘게 비비시의 전화 교환대가 마비되었다.

Word Partnership *jam*의 연어

N. jam **jar, strawberry** jam **1**
traffic jam **4**

Jan. Jan. is a written abbreviation for **January**.

1월

jan|gle /dʒæŋgᵊl/ (jangles, jangling, jangled) V-T/V-I When objects strike against each other and make an unpleasant ringing noise, you can say that they **jangle** or **are jangled**. ❑ *Her bead necklaces and bracelets jangled as she walked.*

타동사/자동사 쨍그렁거리다 ❑ 그녀가 길을 때 그녀의 구슬 목걸이와 팔찌가 쨍그렁거렸다.

jani|tor /dʒænɪtər/ (janitors) N-COUNT A **janitor** is a person whose job is to take care of a building. [mainly AM] ❑ *Ed Roberts had been a school janitor for a long time.*

가산명사 수위, 문지기 [주로 미국영어] ❑ 에드 로버츠는 오랫동안 학교 수위를 했었다.

Janu|ary ♦♦♦ /dʒænyueri, BRIT dʒænyəri/ (Januaries) N-VAR **January** is the first month of the year in the Western calendar. ❑ *We always have snow in January.*

가산명사 또는 불가산명사 1월 ❑ 1월에는 항상 눈이 내린다.

jar /dʒɑr/ (jars, jarring, jarred) **1** N-COUNT A **jar** is a glass container with a lid that is used for storing food. ❑ *...yellow cucumbers in great glass jars.* **2** N-COUNT You can use **jar** to refer to a jar and its contents, or to the contents only. ❑ *She opened up a glass jar of plums.* **3** V-T/V-I If something **jars on** you, you find it unpleasant, disturbing, or shocking. ❑ *Sometimes a light remark jarred on her father.* ❑ *...televised congressional hearings that jarred the nation's faith in the presidency.* ● **jar|ring** ADJ ❑ *In the context of this chapter, Dore's comments strike a jarring note.* **4** V-T/V-I If an object **jars**, or if something **jars** it, the object moves with a fairly hard shaking movement. ❑ *The ship jarred a little.* →see **can**

1 가산명사 병, 단지 ❑ 큰 유리병에 들어 있는 누르스름한 오이들 **2** 가산명사 단지 (의 양) ❑ 그녀는 자두가 들어 있는 유리병 하나를 열었다. **3** 타동사/자동사 불쾌감을 주다, 신경을 거스르다 ❑ 때로는 가벼운 한 마디가 그녀의 아버지를 불쾌하게 했다. ❑ 대통령 직에 대한 국민의 신뢰를 상하게 한, 텔레비전으로 생중계된 국회 청문회 ● 신경에 거슬리는 형용사 ❑ 이 장의 맥락에서 도어의 논평은 신경에 거슬린다. **4** 타동사/자동사 덜컹거리다, 요동하다 ❑ 그 배는 조금 흔들렸다.

jar|gon /dʒɑrgən/ N-UNCOUNT You use **jargon** to refer to words and expressions that are used in special or technical ways by particular groups of people, often making the language difficult to understand. ❑ *The manual is full of the jargon and slang of self-improvement courses.*

불가산명사 특수 용어, 전문 용어 ❑ 그 안내서는 자기 계발 코스의 특수 용어와 은어들로 가득하다.

jaun|ty /dʒɔnti/ (jauntier, jauntiest) ADJ If you describe someone or something as **jaunty**, you mean that they are full of confidence and energy. ❑ *...a jaunty little man.* ● **jaun|ti|ly** /dʒɔntɪli/ ADV ❑ *He walked jauntily into the cafe.*

형용사 발랄한, 쾌활한 ❑ 발랄한 작은 남자 ● 발랄하게, 쾌활하게 부사 ❑ 그는 카페 안으로 발랄하게 걸어 들어갔다.

Java /dʒɑvə/ N-UNCOUNT **Java** is a computer programming language. It is used especially in creating websites. [TRADEMARK] ❑ *...applications written in Java.*

불가산명사 자바 언어 [상표] ❑ 자바 언어로 만들어진 응용 프로그램

jave|lin /dʒævlɪn/ (javelins) **1** N-COUNT A **javelin** is a long spear that is used in sports competitions. Competitors try to throw the javelin as far as possible. **2** N-SING You can refer to the competition in which the javelin is thrown as **the javelin**. ❑ *...Steve Backley who won the javelin.*

1 가산명사 (스포츠용) 투창 **2** 단수명사 투창 경기 ❑ 투창 경기에서 이긴 스티브 백클리

jaw /dʒɔ/ (jaws) **1** N-COUNT Your **jaw** is the lower part of your face below your mouth. The movement of your jaw is sometimes considered to express a particular emotion. For example, if your **jaw drops**, you are very surprised. ❑ *He thought for a moment, stroking his well-defined jaw.* **2** N-COUNT A person's or animal's **jaws** are the two bones in their head which their teeth are attached to. ❑ *...a forest rodent with powerful jaws.* **3** N-PLURAL If you talk about the **jaws of** something unpleasant such as death or hell, you are referring to a dangerous or unpleasant situation. ❑ *A family dog rescued a newborn boy from the jaws of death.*

1 가산명사 턱 ❑ 그는 윤곽이 뚜렷한 턱을 만지며 잠시 동안 생각했다. **2** 가산명사 턱뼈 ❑ 강한 턱뼈를 가지고 있는 야생 설치 동물 **3** 복수명사 손아귀 ❑ 애완견이 갓난 사내아이를 죽음의 손아귀에서 구했다.

jaw-dropping ADJ Something that is **jaw-dropping** is extremely surprising, impressive, or shocking. [mainly BRIT, INFORMAL, JOURNALISM] ❑ *One insider who has seen the report said it was pretty jaw-dropping stuff.*

형용사 입을 다물 수 없게 만드는 [주로 영국영어, 비격식체, 언론] ❑ 그 보고서를 본 내부 사람 한 명은 그것이 입을 다물 수 없게 만드는 것이었다고 말했다.

jazz ♦♦♦ /dʒæz/ N-UNCOUNT **Jazz** is a style of music that was invented by African American musicians in the early part of the twentieth century. Jazz music has very strong rhythms and often involves improvisation. ❑ *The pub has live jazz on Sundays.* →see **genre**

불가산명사 재즈 ❑ 그 술집은 일요일마다 라이브 재즈 음악을 제공한다.

jeal|ous /dʒɛləs/ **1** ADJ If someone is **jealous**, they feel angry or bitter because they think that another person is trying to take a lover or friend, or a possession, away from them. ❑ *She got insanely jealous and there was a terrible fight.* ● **jeal|ous|ly** ADV [ADV with v] ❑ *The formula is jealously guarded.* **2** ADJ If you are **jealous of** another person's possessions or qualities, you feel angry or bitter because you do not have them. ❑ *She was jealous of his wealth.* ● **jeal|ous|ly** ADV [ADV after v] ❑ *Gloria eyed them jealously.*

1 형용사 질투하는; 경계하는 ❑ 그녀는 질투심으로 제정신이 아니었고 끔찍한 싸움이 있었다. ● 질투심이 가득하여; 경계하여 부사 ❑ 그 제조법은 철저하게 보호되고 있다. **2** 형용사 시기하는 ❑ 그녀는 그의 부를 시기했다. ● 시기하여 부사 ❑ 글로리아는 그들을 시샘하며 주시했다.

jeal|ousy /dʒɛləsi/ **1** N-UNCOUNT **Jealousy** is the feeling of anger or bitterness which someone has when they think that another person is trying to take a lover or friend, or a possession, away from them. ❑ *At first his jealousy only showed in small ways – he didn't mind me talking to other guys.* **2** N-UNCOUNT **Jealousy** is the feeling of anger or bitterness which someone has when they wish that they could have the qualities or possessions that another person has. ❑ *Her beauty causes envy and jealousy.*

1 불가산명사 질투 ❑ 처음에는 그의 질투심이 조금밖에 안 드러났고, 그는 내가 다른 남자들과 이야기하는 것에는 신경을 쓰지 않았다. **2** 불가산명사 시기 ❑ 그녀의 아름다움은 질투심과 시기심을 야기한다.

jeans /dʒinz/ N-PLURAL **Jeans** are casual pants that are usually made of strong blue cotton cloth called denim. [also *a pair of* N] ❑ *...a young man in jeans and a worn T-shirt.* →see **clothing**

복수명사 진, 청바지 ❑ 청바지와 낡은 티셔츠를 입은 젊은 남자

Jeep /dʒip/ (Jeeps) N-COUNT A **Jeep** is a type of car that can travel over rough ground. [TRADEMARK] ❑ *...a U.S. Army Jeep.*

가산명사 지프 [상표] ❑ 미군 지프

jeer /dʒɪər/ (jeers, jeering, jeered) **1** V-T/V-I To **jeer at** someone means to say or shout rude and insulting things to them to show that you do not like or respect them. ❑ *Marchers jeered at white passers-by, but there was no violence, nor any arrests.* ❑ *Demonstrators have jeered the mayor as he arrived for a week-long visit.* ● **jeer|ing** N-UNCOUNT ❑ *There was constant jeering and interruption from the floor.* **2** N-COUNT **Jeers** are rude and insulting things that people shout to show they do not like or respect someone. ❑ *...the heckling and jeers of his audience.*

1 타동사/자동사 조소하다, 야유하다 ❑ 시위대는 지나가는 백인들에게 야유를 보냈지만, 폭력 행위나 체포는 없었다. ❑ 시장이 일주일 일정으로 방문하였을 때 시위 참가자들은 그에게 야유를 보냈다. ● 야유, 조소 불가산명사 ❑ 방청석의 야유와 방해가 계속되었다. **2** 가산명사 야유 ❑ 청중들의 그에 대한 조롱과 야유

Jell-O N-UNCOUNT **Jell-O** is a transparent, usually colored food that is eaten as a dessert. It is made from gelatine, fruit juice, and sugar. [AM, TRADEMARK; BRIT **jelly**] ❑ *...a bowl of Jell-O.* →see **dessert**

불가산명사 젤로 [미국영어, 상표; 영국영어 jelly] ❑ 젤로 한 그릇

jel|ly /dʒɛli/ (jellies) **1** N-MASS **Jelly** is a sweet food that is made by cooking fruit or fruit juice with a large amount of sugar until it is thickened. It is usually spread on bread. ❑ *I had two peanut butter and jelly sandwiches.* **2** N-VAR A **jelly** is a transparent substance that is not completely solid. ❑ *She opened the jar of petroleum jelly and scooped out a little.* **3** N-MASS **Jelly** is a transparent, usually

1 물질명사 젤리, 잼 ❑ 나는 땅콩버터와 젤리를 바른 샌드위치 두 개를 먹었다. **2** 불가산명사 젤리 상태 ❑ 그녀는 바셀린 통을 열어서 조금 떠냈다. **3** 물질명사 젤리 [영국영어; 미국영어 Jell-o] ❑ 식탁 가운데에 젤리가 담긴 큰 그릇이 있었다.

colored food that is eaten as a dessert. It is made from gelatine, fruit juice, and sugar. [BRIT; AM Jell-O] ❏ *In the middle of the table stood a large bowl of jelly.*

jeop|ard|ize /dʒɛpərdaɪz/ (**jeopardizes, jeopardizing, jeopardized**) [BRIT also **jeopardise**] V-T To **jeopardize** a situation or activity means to do something that may destroy it or cause it to fail. ❏ *He has jeopardized the future of his government.*

[영국영어 jeopardise] 타동사 위태롭게 하다 ❏ 그는 그의 정부의 미래를 위태롭게 해 왔다.

jeop|ardy /dʒɛpərdi/ PHRASE If someone or something is in **jeopardy**, they are in a dangerous situation where they might fail, be lost, or be destroyed. ❏ *A series of setbacks have put the whole project in jeopardy.*

구 위험에 빠져, 위태로운 ❏ 일련의 저해 요소들로 프로젝트 전체가 위험에 빠졌다.

jerk /dʒɜrk/ (**jerks, jerking, jerked**) V-T/V-I If you **jerk** something or someone in a particular direction, or they **jerk** in a particular direction, they move a short distance very suddenly and quickly. ❏ *Mr. Griffin jerked forward in his chair.* ❏ *"This is Brady Coyne," said Sam, jerking his head in my direction.* ● N-COUNT **Jerk** is also a noun. ❏ *He indicated the bedroom with a jerk of his head.*

타동사/자동사 –을 홱 움직이다, 갑자기 움직이다 ❏ 그리핀 씨가 의자에 앉은 채로 홱 앞으로 나왔다. ❏ "이 분은 브래디 코인입니다."라고 샘이 머리를 내 쪽으로 홱 돌리면서 말했다. ● 가산명사 급격한 동작, 홱 잡아당김 ❏ 그는 머리를 홱 돌려서 침실을 가리켰다.

jerky /dʒɜrki/ (**jerkier, jerkiest**) ADJ **Jerky** movements are very sudden and quick, and do not flow smoothly. ❏ *Mr. Griffin made a jerky gesture.* ● **jerk|i|ly** /dʒɜrkɪli/ ADV [ADV with v] ❏ *Using his stick heavily, he moved jerkily towards the car.*

형용사 갑자기 움직이는, 씰룩거리는 ❏ 그리핀 씨가 갑자기 홱 하고 움직였다. ● 갑자기 움직이며, 씰룩거리며 부사 ❏ 그는 지팡이를 무겁게 움직이며 씰룩씰룩 그 차를 향해 나아갔다.

jer|sey ◆◇◇ /dʒɜrzi/ (**jerseys**) **1** N-COUNT A **jersey** is a knitted piece of clothing that covers the upper part of your body and your arms and does not open at the front. Jerseys are usually worn over a shirt or blouse. [OLD-FASHIONED] ❏ *His grey jersey and trousers were sodden with the rain.* **2** N-VAR **Jersey** is a knitted, slightly stretchy fabric used especially to make women's clothing. ❏ *Sheila had come to dinner in a black jersey top.*

1 가산명사 스웨터 [구식어] ❏ 그의 회색 스웨터와 바지는 비에 흠뻑 젖어 있었다. **2** 가산명사 또는 불가산명사 니트 ❏ 실라는 검정 니트 상의를 입고 저녁 식사를 하러 왔다.

Jesus ◆◇◇ /dʒiːzəs/ **1** N-PROPER **Jesus** or **Jesus Christ** is the name of the man who Christians believe was the son of God, and whose teachings are the basis of Christianity. **2** EXCLAM **Jesus** is used by some people to express surprise, shock, or annoyance. This use could cause offense. [FEELINGS]

1 고유명사 예수, 예수 그리스도 **2** 감탄사 세상에, 맙소사 [감정 개입]

jet ◆◇◇ /dʒɛt/ (**jets, jetting, jetted**) **1** N-COUNT A **jet** is an aircraft that is powered by jet engines. [also by N] ❏ *Her private jet landed in the republic on the way to Japan.* ❏ *He had arrived from Jersey by jet.* **2** V-I If you **jet** somewhere, you travel there in a fast plane. ❏ *He and his wife, Val, will be jetting off on a two-week holiday in America.* **3** N-COUNT A **jet** of liquid or gas is a strong, fast, thin stream of it. ❏ *A jet of water poured through the windows.* →see **flight**, **fly**

1 가산명사 제트기 ❏ 그녀의 개인 제트기는 일본으로 가는 도중에 그 공화국에 착륙했다. ❏ 그는 저지에서 제트기로 도착했다. **2** 자동사 제트기로 가다 ❏ 그와 그의 부인 밸은 미국에서 2주간의 휴가를 보내기 위해 제트기로 출발할 예정이다. **3** 가산명사 분출 ❏ 창문을 통해 물줄기가 쏟아져 들어왔다.

jet en|gine (**jet engines**) N-COUNT A **jet engine** is an engine in which hot air and gases are forced out at the back. Jet engines are used for most modern aircraft.

가산명사 제트 엔진

jet lag [BRIT also **jetlag**] N-UNCOUNT If you are suffering from **jet lag**, you feel tired and slightly confused after a long trip by airplane, especially after traveling between places that have a time difference of several hours. ❏ *...the best way to avoid jet lag.*

[영국영어 jetlag] 불가산명사 시차로 인한 피로 ❏ 시차로 인한 피로를 예방하는 가장 좋은 방법

jet ski (**jet skis**) N-COUNT A **jet ski** is a small machine like a motorcycle that is powered by a jet engine and can travel on the surface of water. [TRADEMARK]

가산명사 제트 스키 [상표]

jet|ti|son /dʒɛtɪsən, -zən/ (**jettisons, jettisoning, jettisoned**) **1** V-T If you **jettison** something, for example an idea or a plan, you deliberately reject it or decide not to use it. ❏ *The Government seems to have jettisoned the plan.* **2** V-T To **jettison** something that is not needed or wanted means to throw it away or get rid of it. ❏ *The crew jettisoned excess fuel and made an emergency landing.*

1 타동사 포기하다, 폐기하다 ❏ 정부는 그 계획을 폐기한 것으로 보인다. **2** 타동사 버리다 ❏ 승무원들은 남은 연료를 버리고 비상 착륙을 하였다.

jet|ty /dʒɛti/ (**jetties**) N-COUNT A **jetty** is a wide stone wall or wooden platform where boats stop to let people get on or off, or to load or unload goods.

가산명사 부두

Jew ◆◇◇ /dʒuː/ (**Jews**) N-COUNT A **Jew** is a person who believes in and practices the religion of Judaism.

가산명사 유대인

jew|el /dʒuːəl/ (**jewels**) **1** N-COUNT A **jewel** is a precious stone used to decorate valuable things that you wear, such as rings or necklaces. ❏ *...a golden box containing precious jewels.* **2** N-COUNT If you describe something or someone as a **jewel**, you mean that they are better, more beautiful, or more special than other similar things or than other people. ❏ *Walk down Castle Street and admire our little jewel of a cathedral.* **3** PHRASE If you refer to an achievement or thing as the **jewel in** someone's **crown**, you mean that it is considered to be their greatest achievement or the thing they can be most proud of. ❏ *His achievement is astonishing and this book is the jewel in his crown.*

1 가산명사 보석 ❏ 귀한 보석이 들어 있는 금 상자 **2** 가산명사 소중한 사람, 보배 ❏ 캐슬 스트리트를 따라 걸어 내려와서 우리의 보배인 작은 대성당을 감상해 보세요. **3** 구 가장 눈부신 것, 가장 좋은 것 ❏ 그의 성과는 놀랄 만한 것이고 이 책은 그의 최고 걸작이다.

jew|el|er /dʒuːələr/ (**jewelers**) [BRIT **jeweller**] **1** N-COUNT A **jeweler** is a person who makes, sells, and repairs jewelry and watches. **2** N-COUNT A **jeweler** or a **jeweler's** is a store where jewelry and watches are made, sold, and repaired. ❏ *Emily had been to the jeweler's and ordered a man's toilet set in silver.* →see **diamond**

[영국영어 jeweller] **1** 가산명사 보석 세공인, 보석 상인 **2** 가산명사 보석 가게 ❏ 에밀리는 보석 가게에 가서 은으로 된 남성화장 도구를 주문했다.

jew|el|ry /dʒuːəlri/ [BRIT **jewellery**] N-UNCOUNT **Jewelry** is ornaments that people wear, for example rings, bracelets, and necklaces. It is often made of a valuable metal such as gold, and sometimes decorated with precious stones. ❏ *Discover a full selection of fine watches and jewelry at these two Upper Manhattan stores.* →see Picture Dictionary: **jewelry**

[영국영어 jewellery] 불가산명사 장신구 ❏ 상부 맨해튼의 이 두 개의 상점에서 정선된 멋진 시계와 장신구를 발견하세요.

Jew|ish ◆◇◇ /dʒuːɪʃ/ ADJ **Jewish** means belonging or relating to the religion of Judaism or to Jews. ❏ *...the Jewish festival of Passover.* →see **religion**

형용사 유대인의 ❏ 유대인의 유월절 축제

jibe /dʒaɪb/ (**jibes, jibing, jibed**)

The spelling **gibe** is also used for meanings **1** and **2**.

철자 gibe도 **1**과 **2** 의미로 쓴다.

1 N-COUNT A **jibe** is a rude or insulting remark about someone that is intended to make them look foolish. ❏ *...a cheap jibe about his loss of hair.* **2** V-T To **jibe** means to say something rude or insulting which is intended to make another person look foolish. [WRITTEN] ❏ *"No doubt he'll give me the chance to fight him again," he jibed, tongue in cheek.* **3** V-RECIP If numbers, statements, or events **jibe**, they are exactly the same as each other or they are consistent with each other. [mainly AM] ❏ *The numbers don't jibe.*

1 가산명사 비웃음, 조롱 ❏ 그의 탈모 증상에 대한 조롱 **2** 타동사 조롱하다 [문어체] ❏ "분명히 내가 그와 다시 싸울 수 있는 기회가 있을 것이야."라고 그는 장난삼아 조롱했다. **3** 상호동사 일치하다 [주로 미국영어] ❏ 숫자가 일치하지 않는다.

jig /dʒɪg/ (**jigs, jigging, jigged**) **1** N-COUNT A **jig** is a lively dance. ❏ *She danced an*

1 가산명사 지그춤 ❏ 그녀는 아일랜드 식 지그춤을

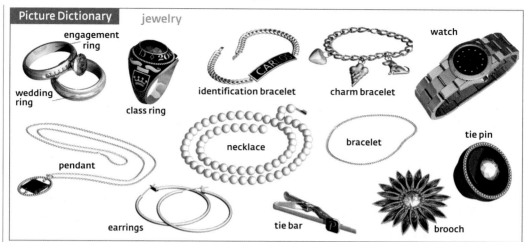

Picture Dictionary — jewelry

engagement ring
wedding ring
class ring
identification bracelet
charm bracelet
watch
necklace
pendant
bracelet
tie pin
earrings
tie bar
brooch

Irish jig. ■ V-I To **jig** means to dance or move energetically, especially bouncing up and down. ❑ *You didn't just jig about by yourself, I mean you danced properly.*

jig|saw /d͡ʒɪɡsɔː/ (**jigsaws**) ■ N-COUNT A **jigsaw** or **jigsaw puzzle** is a picture on cardboard or wood that has been cut up into odd shapes. You have to make the picture again by putting the pieces together correctly. ❑ *We have a family tradition of doing a big jigsaw over the Christmas holiday.* ❷ N-COUNT You can describe a complicated situation as a **jigsaw**. ❑ *...the jigsaw of high-level diplomacy.*

jin|gle /d͡ʒɪŋɡəl/ (**jingles, jingling, jingled**) ■ V-T/V-I When something **jingles** or when you **jingle** it, it makes a gentle ringing noise, like small bells. ❑ *Brian put his hands in his pockets and jingled some change.* ● N-SING **Jingle** is also a noun. ❑ *...the jingle of money in a man's pocket.* ❷ N-COUNT A **jingle** is a short, simple tune, often with words, which is used to advertise a product or program on radio or television. ❑ *...advertising jingles.*

jit|ters /d͡ʒɪtərz/ N-PLURAL If you have the **jitters**, you feel extremely nervous, for example because you have to do something important or because you are expecting important news. [INFORMAL] ❑ *Officials feared that any public announcements would only increase market jitters.*

jit|tery /d͡ʒɪtəri/ ADJ If someone is **jittery**, they feel nervous or are behaving nervously. [INFORMAL] ❑ *Foreign investors have become jittery about the country's economy.*

job ♦♦♦ /d͡ʒɒb/ (**jobs**) ■ N-COUNT A **job** is the work that someone does to earn money. ❑ *Once I'm in America I can get a job.* ❑ *Thousands have lost their jobs.* ❷ N-COUNT A **job** is a particular task. ❑ *He said he hoped that the job of putting together a coalition wouldn't take too much time.* ❸ N-COUNT The **job** of a particular person or thing is their duty or function. ❑ *Their main job is to preserve health rather than treat illness.* ❑ *His next job is to get us to the World Cup finals.* ❹ N-SING If you say that someone is doing a good **job**, you mean that they are doing something well. In British English, you can also say that they are making a good **job** of something. ❑ *We could do a far better job of managing it than they have.* ❺ N-SING If you say that you have **a job** doing something, you are emphasizing how difficult it is. [EMPHASIS] ❑ *He may have a hard job selling that argument to investors.* ❻ PHRASE If you refer to work as **jobs for the boys**, you mean that the work is unfairly given to someone's friends, supporters, or relations, even though they may not be the best qualified people to do it. [BRIT, DISAPPROVAL] ❑ *The Party has been accused of creating a "jobs for the boys" system of government.* ❼ PHRASE If someone is **on the job**, they are actually doing a particular job or task. ❑ *The top pay scale after five years on the job would reach $5.00 an hour.* ❽ **it's a good job** →see job. **the job in hand** →see hand

Thesaurus   *job*의 참조어

N.   employment, occupation, profession, vocation, work ■
      assignment, duty, obligation, task ❷ ❸

job de|scrip|tion (**job descriptions**) N-COUNT A **job description** is a written account of all the duties and responsibilities involved in a particular job or position. ❑ *...the job description for the position of division general manager.*

job|less /d͡ʒɒbləs/ ADJ Someone who is **jobless** does not have a job, although they would like one. ❑ *One in four people are now jobless in inner areas like Tottenham and Peckham.* ● N-PLURAL The **jobless** are people who are jobless. ❑ *They joined the ranks of the jobless.*

job share (**job shares, job sharing, job shared**) V-I If two people **job share**, they share the same job by working part-time, for example one person working in the mornings and the other in the afternoons. ❑ *They both want to job share.*

jock|ey /d͡ʒɒki/ (**jockeys, jockeying, jockeyed**) ■ N-COUNT A **jockey** is someone who rides a horse in a race. ❷ V-I If you say that someone **is jockeying for** something, you mean that they are using whatever methods they can in

---

추었다. ❷ 자동사 격렬하게 움직이다; 힘차게 춤추다 ❑ 내 말은, 네가 네 멋대로 흔들어 댄 게 아니라, 제대로 춤을 췄다는 것이야.

■ 가산명사 조각 그림 맞추기 ❑ 우리 집안에는 크리스마스 휴일 동안 큰 조각 그림 맞추기를 하는 전통이 있다. ❷ 가산명사 복잡한 상황 ❑ 고위급 외교의 복잡한 상황

■ 타동사/자동사 딸랑딸랑 울리다; 짤랑거리다 ❑ 브라이언은 손을 주머니에 넣고 동전을 짤랑거렸다. ● 단수명사 딸랑딸랑 소리, 짤랑거리는 소리 ❑ 한 남자의 주머니에 든 돈이 짤랑거리는 소리 ❷ 가산명사 짧은 광고 문구 ❑ 광고 문구들

복수명사 불안, 초조 [비격식체] ❑ 당국에서는 어떤 형태의 공식 발표도 시장의 불안감만 증가시킬 것이라고 두려워하였다.

형용사 불안해하는, 안절부절못하는 [비격식체] ❑ 외국 투자자들은 그 나라 경제에 대하여 불안해하기 시작했다.

■ 가산명사 직장 ❑ 일단 내가 미국에 가면 직장을 가질 수 있다. ❑ 수천 명이 직장을 잃었다. ❷ 가산명사 (특정한) 일 ❑ 그는 연합체를 구성하는 일이 시간이 많이 걸리지 않기를 바란다고 말했다. ❸ 가산명사 의무, 일 ❑ 그들의 주된 일은 병을 고치는 것이라기보다는 건강을 지키는 것이다. ❑ 그의 다음 일은 우리를 월드컵 결승으로 이끄는 것이다. ❹ 단수명사 (일을) 함 ❑ 우리는 그들보다 그것을 관리하는 일을 훨씬 더 잘 할 수 있다. ❺ 단수명사 어려움 [강조] ❑ 그는 투자자들에게 그 주장을 납득시키려면 상당히 어려움을 겪을지도 모른다. ❻ 구 연줄로 얻은 자리 [영국영어, 탐탁찮음] ❑ 그 정당은 정부의 체제를 '연줄에 의한 자리 배치' 체제로 만들었다고 비난을 받아 왔다. ❼ 구 근무 중에 ❑ 5년 근무 후 최고 급료는 시간당 5달러에 달한다.

가산명사 직무 내용 설명서 ❑ 지부 총지배인 자리의 직무 내용에 대한 설명서

형용사 무직의, 실직의 ❑ 토튼햄과 페크햄 같은 도심지 지역에서 4명 중 1명은 현재 실직 상태이다. ● 복수명사 실직자, 실업자 ❑ 그들은 실직자의 대열에 합류하였다.

자동사 동일 업무를 시간제로 분담해서 근무하다 ❑ 그 둘 모두 동일 업무의 시간제 분담 근무를 원한다.

■ 가산명사 기수 ❷ 자동사 모든 수단을 동원하다 ❑ 두 경쟁 정당은 이미 정권을 잡기 위해 모든 수단을 동원하고 있다. ● 구 유리한 입장에 서려고 획책하다

order to get it or do it before their competitors can get it or do it. ❑ *The rival political parties are already jockeying for power.* ● PHRASE If someone **is jockeying for position**, they are using whatever methods they can in order to get into a better position than their rivals.

jog /dʒɒg/ (jogs, jogging, jogged) ❶ V-I If you **jog**, you run slowly, often as a form of exercise. ❑ *I got up early the next morning to jog.* ● N-COUNT **Jog** is also a noun. ❑ *He went for another early morning jog.* ● **jogging** N-UNCOUNT ❑ *It isn't the walking and jogging that got his weight down.* ❷ V-T If you **jog** something, you push or bump it slightly so that it moves. ❑ *Avoid jogging the camera.* ❸ PHRASE If something or someone **jogs** your memory, they cause you to suddenly remember something that you had forgotten. ❑ *Police have planned a reconstruction of the crime tomorrow in the hope this will jog the memory of passers-by.*

jog|ger /dʒɒgər/ (joggers) N-COUNT A **jogger** is a person who jogs as a form of exercise.

join ♦♦♦ /dʒɔɪn/ (joins, joining, joined) ❶ V-T If one person or vehicle **joins** another, they move or go to the same place, for example so that both of them can do something together. ❑ *His wife and children moved to join him in their new home.* ❷ V-T If you **join** an organization, you become a member of it or start work as an employee of it. ❑ *He joined the Army five years ago.* ❸ V-T/V-I If you **join** an activity that other people are doing, you take part in it or become involved with it. ❑ *Telephone operators joined the strike and four million engineering workers are also planning action.* ❑ *The pastor requested the women present to join him in prayer.* ❹ V-T If you **join** a line, you stand at the end of it so that you are part of it. ❑ *It is advised that fans seeking autographs join the line before practice starts.* ❺ V-T To **join** two things means to fix or fasten them together. ❑ *The opened link is used to join the two ends of the chain.* ❑ *...the conjunctiva, the skin which joins the eye to the lid.* ❻ V-T If something such as a line or path **joins** two things, it connects them. ❑ *...a global highway of cables joining all the continents together.* ❼ V-RECIP If two roads or rivers **join**, they meet or come together at a particular point. ❑ *Do you know the highway to Tulsa? The airport road joins it.* ❽ N-COUNT A **join** is a place where two things are fastened or fixed together. ❑ *Looking down, she saw she was standing on the join between a blue and a red carpet tile.* ❾ **join forces** →see **force**

▶**join in** PHRASAL VERB If you **join in** an activity, you take part in it or become involved in it. ❑ *I hope that everyone will be able to join in the fun.*

▶**join up** ❶ PHRASAL VERB If someone **joins up**, they become a member of the army, the navy, or the air force. ❑ *When hostilities broke out he returned to England and joined up.* ❷ PHRASAL VERB-RECIP If one person or organization **joins up with** another, they start doing something together. ❑ *Councils are joining up with their European counterparts in a number of special interest groups.*

joint ♦♦◇ /dʒɔɪnt/ (joints) ❶ ADJ **Joint** means shared by or belonging to two or more people. [ADJ n] ❑ *She and Frank had never gotten around to opening a joint account.* ● **joint|ly** ADV [ADV with v] ❑ *The Port Authority is an agency jointly run by New York and New Jersey.* ❷ N-COUNT A **joint** is a part of your body such as your elbow or knee where two bones meet and are able to move together. ❑ *Her joints ache if she exercises.* ❸ N-COUNT A **joint** is the place where two things are fastened or fixed together. ❑ *...the joint between the inner and outer panels.* ❹ N-COUNT A **joint** is a fairly large piece of meat which is suitable for roasting. [BRIT; AM **roast**] ❑ *He carved the joint of beef.* ❺ N-COUNT You can refer to a cheap place where people go for some form of entertainment as a **joint**. [INFORMAL] ❑ *They had come to the world's most famous pick-up joint.* ❻ N-COUNT A **joint** is a cigarette which contains cannabis or marijuana. [INFORMAL] ❑ *He's smoking a joint.* ❼ PHRASE If something puts someone's **nose out of joint**, it upsets or offends them because it makes them feel less important or less valued. [INFORMAL] ❑ *Barry had his nose put out of joint by Lucy's aloof sophistication.*

Word Partnership	*joint*의 연어
N.	joint **account**, joint **agreement**, joint **effort**, joint **resolution**, joint **statement** ❶

joint-stock company (joint-stock companies) N-COUNT A **joint-stock company** is a company that is owned by the people who have bought shares in that company. [BUSINESS]

joke ♦◇◇ /dʒoʊk/ (jokes, joking, joked) ❶ N-COUNT A **joke** is something that is said or done to make you laugh, for example a funny story. ❑ *No one told worse jokes than Claus.* ❷ V-T/V-I If you **joke**, you tell funny stories or say amusing things. ❑ *She would joke about her appearance.* ❑ *Lorna was laughing and joking with Trevor.* ❸ N-COUNT A **joke** is something untrue that you tell another person in order to amuse yourself. ❑ *It was probably just a joke to them, but it wasn't funny to me.* ❹ V-T/V-I If you **joke**, you tell someone something that is not true in order to amuse yourself. ❑ *Don't get defensive, Charlie. I was only joking.* ❺ N-SING If you say that something or someone is **a joke**, you think they are ridiculous and do not deserve respect. [INFORMAL, DISAPPROVAL] ❑ *It's ridiculous, it's pathetic, it's a joke.* ❻ PHRASE If you say that an annoying or worrying situation is **beyond a joke**, you are emphasizing that it is worse than you think is fair or reasonable. [BRIT, EMPHASIS] ❑ *I'm not afraid of a fair fight but this is beginning to get beyond a joke.* ❼ PHRASE If you **make a joke of** something, you laugh at it even though it is in fact rather serious or sad. ❑ *I wish I had your courage, Michael, to make a joke of it like that.* ❽ PHRASE If you describe a situation as **no joke**, you are emphasizing that it is very difficult or unpleasant. [INFORMAL, EMPHASIS] ❑ *Two hours on a bus is no joke, is it.* ❾ PHRASE If you say that **the joke is on** a particular person, you mean that they have been made to look very foolish by

---

❶ 자동사 천천히 뛰다, 조깅하다 ❑ 나는 다음 날 아침 조깅을 하려고 일찍 일어났다. ● 가산명사 조깅 ❑ 그는 또 새벽 조깅을 하러 나갔다. ● 조깅 불가산명사 ❑ 그의 몸무게를 줄게 한 것은 걷기와 조깅이 아니다. ❷ 타동사 살짝 건드리다 ❑ 카메라를 건들지 않도록 조심해라. ❸ 구 기억나게 하다, 일깨우다 ❑ 경찰들은 사건 당시의 행인들의 기억을 되살릴 수 있으리라는 기대를 가지고 내일 범죄의 재연을 계획하였다.

가산명사 조깅하는 사람

❶ 타동사 합류하다 ❑ 그의 부인과 아이들은 새 집에서 그와 같이 살기 위해 이사했다. ❷ 타동사 가입하다, 등록하다 ❑ 그는 5년 전 육군에 입대했다. ❸ 타동사/자동사 참가하다 ❑ 전화 교환원들이 파업에 참가하였고 400만 기술공들이 또한 참여하려 하고 있다. ❑ 목사는 그 자리에 있던 여자들에게 같이 기도를 하자고 요청하였다. ❹ 타동사 (줄을) 서다 ❑ 사인을 받으실 팬들은 연습이 시작되기 전에 줄을 서 주시기 바랍니다. ❺ 타동사 결합하다, 접합하다 ❑ 끝이 맞물려 있지 않은 고리는 사슬의 양 끝을 접합하는 데 사용된다. ❑ 눈과 눈꺼풀을 연결시키는 피부인 결막. ❻ 타동사 연결하다 ❑ 전 대륙을 연결시켜 주는 전 세계의 케이블 통신망 ❼ 상호동사 만나다 ❑ 툴사로 가는 고속도로를 알고 있어? 공항로가 그 도로와 만나. ❽ 가산명사 접합, 연결 ❑ 내려다보니 그녀는 자신이 파란 카펫 타일과 빨간 카펫 타일 사이의 접합 부분에 서 있다는 것을 알았다.

구동사 참가하다, 가담하다 ❑ 나는 모두가 이 여흥에 참여할 수 있었으면 좋겠다.

❶ 구동사 군에 입대하다 ❑ 전쟁이 일어나자 그는 영국으로 돌아와 군에 입대했다. ❷ 상호 구동사 연합하다 ❑ 위원회들은 수많은 이익 단체를 구성하여 유럽의 위원회들과 연합하고 있다.

❶ 형용사 공동의, 합동의 ❑ 그녀와 프랭크는 같이 공동 계좌를 개설할 기회가 한 번도 없었다. ● 공동으로 부사 ❑ 항만 관리 위원회는 뉴욕과 뉴저지가 공동으로 운영하는 기관이다. ❷ 가산명사 관절 ❑ 그녀는 운동을 하면 관절에 통증을 느낀다. ❸ 가산명사 접합 부분 ❑ 안쪽 판유리와 바깥 판유리 사이의 접합 부분 ❹ 가산명사 큰 고깃덩이 [영국영어; 미국영어 roast] ❑ 그는 큰 쇠고기 덩어리를 썰었다. ❺ 가산명사 저렴한 유흥업소 [비격식체] ❑ 그들은 세계에서 가장 유명한 매음 유흥 지역에 가게 되었다. ❻ 가산명사 마리화나 [비격식체] ❑ 그는 마리화나를 피고 있다. ❼ 구 기분이 잡치게 만들다 [비격식체] ❑ 배리는 루시가 냉랭하게 교양을 떠는 것에 기분이 잡쳤다.

가산명사 합자 회사 [경제]

❶ 가산명사 농담, 우스개 ❑ 클로스보다 더 심한 농담을 한 사람은 없었다. ❷ 타동사/자동사 농담하다 ❑ 그녀는 자신의 외모에 대해 농담을 하곤 했다. ❑ 로나는 트레버와 웃으며 농담을 하고 있었다. ❸ 가산명사 농담거리 ❑ 그것이 그들에게는 단지 농담거리였을 뿐이었지만, 나에게는 웃긴 일이 아니었다. ❹ 타동사/자동사 농담하다, 우스갯소리를 하다 ❑ 방어적인 자세를 취하지 마, 찰리. 난 그냥 농담한 것뿐이었어. ❺ 단수명사 웃음거리 [비격식체, 탐탁잖음] ❑ 그것은 말도 안 되고 터무니없는 웃음거리일 뿐이다. ❻ 구 웃을 일이 아닌, 생각보다 안 좋은 [영국영어, 강조] ❑ 공평한 승부가 겁나는 것은 아니지만, 이건 점점 말이 안 되는 일이 되고 있다. ❼ 구 웃어넘기다 ❑ 그런 것을 웃어넘길 수 있는 당신의 용기가 나는 부럽다고 있으면 좋겠습니다, 마이클. ❽ 구 장난이 아닌 일 [비격식체, 강조] ❑ 버스로 두 시간은 장난이 아니다, 정말로. ❾ 구 ~가 도로 웃음거리가 되다 ❑ "이번에는 내가 웃음거리가 됐군. 근데 별로 웃을 일이 아냐."라고 그는 말했다. ❿ 관용 표현

a
b
c
d
e
f
g
h
i
j
k
l
m
n
o
p
q
r
s
t
u
v
w
x
y
z

something. ❑ *"For once," he said, "the joke's on me. And it's not very funny."* 10 CONVENTION You say **you're joking** or **you must be joking** to someone when they have just told you something that is so surprising or unreasonable that you find it difficult to believe. [SPOKEN, FEELINGS] ❑ *You're joking. Are you serious?*

농담하고 있는 거지, 농담일 거야 [구어체, 감정 개입] ❑ 농담이겠지. 설마 진심이야?

Word Partnership *joke*의 연어

ADJ. **bad** joke, **cruel** joke, **dirty** joke, **funny** joke, **good** joke, **old** joke 1
V. **crack a** joke, **make a** joke, **play a** joke, **tell a** joke 2 4

jok|er /dʒoʊkər/ (**jokers**) 1 N-COUNT Someone who is a **joker** likes making jokes or doing amusing things. ❑ *He is, by nature, a joker, a witty man with a sense of fun.* 2 N-COUNT The **joker** in a pack of playing cards is the card which does not belong to any of the four suits. 3 N-COUNT You can call someone a **joker** if you think they are behaving in a stupid or dangerous way. [INFORMAL, DISAPPROVAL] ❑ *Keep your eye on these jokers, you never know what they will come up with.* 4 PHRASE If you describe someone or something as **the joker in the pack**, you mean that they are different from the other people or things in their group, and can be unpredictable. ❑ *Franco Moschino is described as the joker in the pack of Italian fashion.*

1 가산명사 재담꾼 ❑ 그는 천성적으로 유머 감각이 있는 재담꾼이며 익살꾼이다. 2 가산명사 (카드놀이) 조커 3 가산명사 요주의 인물 [비격식체, 탐탁찮음] ❑ 이 요주의 인물들을 잘 감시해라. 무슨 짓을 꾸밀지 모르니까. 4 구 예측 불허의 인물 ❑ 프랑코 모스키노는 이탈리아 패션계에서 예측 불허의 인물로 묘사된다.

jol|ly /dʒɒli/ (**jollier, jolliest**) 1 ADJ Someone who is **jolly** is happy and cheerful in their appearance or behavior. ❑ *She was a jolly, kindhearted woman.* 2 ADJ A **jolly** event is lively and enjoyable. ❑ *She had a very jolly time in Korea.*

1 형용사 명랑한 ❑ 그녀는 명랑하고 마음씨 고운 여자였다. 2 형용사 즐거운 ❑ 그녀는 한국에서 매우 즐거운 시간을 보냈다.

jolt /dʒoʊlt/ (**jolts, jolting, jolted**) 1 V-T/V-I If something **jolts** or if something **jolts** it, it moves suddenly and quite violently. ❑ *The wagon jolted again.* ❑ *The train jolted into motion.* ● N-COUNT **Jolt** is also a noun. ❑ *We were worried that one tiny jolt could worsen her injuries.* 2 V-T If something **jolts** someone, it gives them an unpleasant surprise or shock. ❑ *A stinging slap across the face jolted her.* ● N-COUNT **Jolt** is also a noun. ❑ *Then my husband left me. It gave me the jolt I needed.*

1 타동사/자동사 크게 흔들리다; 거칠게 흔들다 ❑ 마차가 다시 덜커덕 하고 흔들렸다. ❑ 열차는 덜커덕하며 움직이기 시작하였다. ● 가산명사 급격한 충격, 갑작스런 흔들림 ❑ 우리는 아주 작은 충격 하나라도 그녀의 상처를 더 악화시킬까 봐 걱정을 했다. 2 타동사 ~에게 충격을 주다 ❑ 호되게 빰을 맞은 그녀는 너무나 충격을 받았다. ● 가산명사 충격 ❑ 그리고 나서 남편이 나를 떠났다. 충격은 그것으로 충분했다.

jos|tle /dʒɒsᵊl/ (**jostles, jostling, jostled**) 1 V-T/V-I If people **jostle** you, they bump against you or push you in a way that annoys you, usually because you are in a crowd and they are trying to get past you. ❑ *You get 2,000 people jostling each other and bumping into furniture.* ❑ *We spent an hour jostling with the crowds as we did our shopping.* 2 V-I If people or things **are jostling for** something such as attention or a reward, they are competing with other people or things in order to get it. ❑ *...the contenders who have been jostling for the top job.*

1 타동사/자동사 떠밀다 ❑ 서로 떠밀며 가구에 부딪치는 사람들이 2천 명이 있다. ❑ 우리는 쇼핑할 때 사람들과 부딪치며 1시간을 보냈다. 2 자동사 ~을 위해 겨루다 ❑ 최고의 일자리를 얻기 위해 겨루어 온 경쟁자들

jot /dʒɒt/ (**jots, jotting, jotted**) V-T If you **jot** something short such as an address somewhere, you write it down so that you will remember it. ❑ *Could you just jot his name on there?* ● PHRASAL VERB **Jot down** means the same as **jot**. ❑ *Keep a pad handy to jot down queries as they occur.*

타동사 적어 두다, 메모하다 ❑ 그의 이름을 저기에 간단히 적어 주시겠어요? ● 구동사 적어 두다, 메모하다 ❑ 의문점이 생길 때마다 바로 적어 둘 수 있는 메모장을 가지고 다녀라.

jour|nal ♦♦◊ /dʒɜrnᵊl/ (**journals**) 1 N-COUNT A **journal** is a magazine, especially one that deals with a specialized subject. ❑ *All our results are published in scientific journals.* 2 N-COUNT A **journal** is a daily or weekly newspaper. The word journal is often used in the name of the paper. ❑ *He was a newspaperman for The New York Times and some other journals.* 3 N-COUNT A **journal** is an account which you write of your daily activities. ❑ *Sara confided to her journal.*

1 가산명사 잡지; 학술지 ❑ 우리가 얻은 모든 결과가 과학 학술지에 출판되었다. 2 가산명사 신문 ❑ 그는 뉴욕타임스를 비롯한 다른 신문의 신문 기자였다. 3 가산명사 일기 ❑ 사라는 일기장에 속마음을 털어놓았다.

jour|nal|ism /dʒɜrnəlɪzəm/ N-UNCOUNT **Journalism** is the job of collecting news and writing about it for newspapers, magazines, television, or radio. ❑ *He began a career in journalism, working for the North London Press Group.*

불가산명사 언론계 ❑ 그는 북런던 프레스 그룹에서 일하면서 언론인의 길을 걷기 시작했다.

jour|nal|ist ♦♦◊ /dʒɜrnəlɪst/ (**journalists**) N-COUNT A **journalist** is a person whose job is to collect news and write about it for newspapers, magazines, television, or radio. →see **newspaper**

가산명사 기자

jour|ney ♦◊◊ /dʒɜrni/ (**journeys, journeying, journeyed**) 1 N-COUNT When you make a **journey**, you travel from one place to another. ❑ *There is an express service from Paris which completes the journey to Bordeaux in under 4 hours.* 2 N-COUNT You can refer to a person's experience of changing or developing from one state of mind to another as a **journey**. ❑ *My films try to describe a journey of discovery, both for myself and the watcher.* 3 V-I If you **journey** somewhere, you travel there. [FORMAL] ❑ *In February 1935, Naomi journeyed to the United States for the first time.*

1 가산명사 여행, 여정 ❑ 파리에서 보르도까지의 여정을 4시간도 못 돼 갈 수 있는 급행 노선이 있다. 2 가산명사 노정 ❑ 나의 영화는 나 자신과 시청자 모두를 위한 발견의 노정을 묘사하고자 한다. 3 자동사 여행하다 [격식체] ❑ 1935년 2월에 나오미는 처음으로 미국으로 여행을 했다.

The noun **travel** is used to talk about the general activity of traveling. It is either uncount or plural. You cannot say "a travel," you would use the word **trip** or **journey** instead. ❑ *First-class rail travel to Paris or Brussels is included* ❑ *We were going to go on a trip to Florida together.*

명사 travel은 일반적인 여행 행위에 대해 말할 때 쓰는데, 불가산 명사나 복수로 쓴다. a travel이라고는 하지 않고, 대신 trip이나 journey를 쓸 수 있다. ❑ 파리나 브뤼셀로 가는 일등칸 기차 여행이 포함되어 있다. ❑ 우리는 플로리다로 함께 여행을 가려고 했다.

Thesaurus *journey*의 참조어

N. adventure, trip, visit, voyage 1
V. cruise, fly, go, travel 3

Word Partnership *journey*의 연어

V. **begin a** journey, **complete a** journey, **make a** journey 1 2
N. **end of a** journey, **first/last leg of a** journey 1 2
journey **of discovery** 2

joy ♦◊◊ /dʒɔɪ/ (**joys**) 1 N-UNCOUNT **Joy** is a feeling of great happiness. ❑ *Salter shouted with joy.* 2 N-COUNT A **joy** is something or someone that makes you feel happy or gives you great pleasure. ❑ *Spending evenings outside is one of the joys of summer.* 3 N-UNCOUNT If you get no **joy**, you do not have success or luck in

1 불가산명사 기쁨 ❑ 살터는 기뻐서 소리를 질렀다. 2 가산명사 기쁨 ❑ 야외에서 저녁 시간을 보내는 것은 여름이 주는 기쁨의 하나이다. 3 불가산명사 행운, 만족 [영국영어, 비격식체] ❑ 그들은 투표 자체에서

achieving what you are trying to do. [BRIT, INFORMAL] ❑ *They expect no joy from the vote itself.* **4** PHRASE If you say that someone **is jumping for joy**, you mean that they are very pleased or happy about something. ❑ *He jumped for joy on being told the news.* →see **emotion**

행운을 기대하지 않는다. **4** 구 뛸 듯이 기뻐하다 ❑ 그는 그 소식을 듣고 뛸 듯이 기뻐했다.

Word Partnership   joy의 연어

ADJ.	**filled with** joy, **great** joy, **pure** joy, **sheer** joy **1**
N.	**tears of** joy **1**
V.	**bring** *someone* joy, **cry/weep for** joy, **feel** joy **1**

Word Link   joy ≈ being glad : en*joy*, *joy*ful, *joy*ous

joy|ful /dʒɔɪfəl/ **1** ADJ Something that is **joyful** causes happiness and pleasure. [FORMAL] ❑ *A wedding is a joyful celebration of love.* **2** ADJ Someone who is **joyful** is extremely happy. [FORMAL] ❑ *We're a very joyful people; we're very musical people and we love music.* ● **joy|ful|ly** ADV ❑ *They greeted him joyfully.*

1 형용사 기쁜 [격식체] ❑ 결혼식은 기쁘게 사랑을 축하하는 것이다. **2** 형용사 매우 행복한 [격식체] ❑ 우리는 매우 행복한 사람들이다. 우리는 아주 음악적인 사람들로 음악을 사랑한다. ● 기쁘게 부사 ❑ 그들은 기쁜 마음으로 그를 맞았다.

joy|ous /dʒɔɪəs/ ADJ **Joyous** means extremely happy. [LITERARY] ❑ *She had made their childhood so joyous and carefree.* ● **joy|ous|ly** ADV ❑ *Sarah accepted joyously.*

형용사 매우 행복한 [문예체] ❑ 그 분은 그들이 매우 행복하고 근심 없는 어린 시절을 보내게 해 주었다. ● 행복하게, 기꺼이 부사 ❑ 사라는 기꺼이 받아들였다.

joy|rider /dʒɔɪraɪdər/ (**joyriders**) also **joy rider** N-COUNT A **joyrider** is someone who steals cars in order to drive around in them at high speed. ❑ *...a car crash caused by joyriders.*

가산명사 자동차 탈취 폭주족 ❑ 자동차 탈취 폭주족이 일으킨 교통사고

joy|stick /dʒɔɪstɪk/ (**joysticks**) N-COUNT In some computer games, the **joystick** is the lever which the player uses in order to control the direction of the things on the screen.

가산명사 조이 스틱

JPEG /dʒeɪpɛg/ (**JPEGs**) also **Jpeg** N-UNCOUNT **JPEG** is a standard file format for compressing pictures so they can be stored or sent by e-mail more easily. **JPEG** is an abbreviation for "Joint Photographic Experts Group." [COMPUTING] ❑ *...JPEG images.* ● N-COUNT A **JPEG** is a JPEG file or picture. ❑ *You can add edge enhancement or smooth to a Jpeg, or vary the color depth.*

불가산명사 제이페그 파일 [컴퓨터] ❑ 제이페그 이미지 파일들 ● 가산명사 제이페그 파일 ❑ 제이페그 파일을 색조리를 장식하거나 매끈하게 만들 수도 있고, 색조를 다양하게 할 수 있다.

ju|bi|lant /dʒubɪlənt/ ADJ If you are **jubilant**, you feel extremely happy because of a success. ❑ *Ferdinand was jubilant after making an impressive comeback from a month on the injured list.*

형용사 환희에 넘친 ❑ 페르디난드는 부상자 명단에 오른 지 한 달 만에 멋진 모습으로 돌아와 환희에 넘쳤다.

ju|bi|lee /dʒubɪli/ (**jubilees**) N-COUNT A **jubilee** is a special anniversary of an event, especially the 25th or 50th anniversary. ❑ *...Queen Victoria's jubilee.*

가산명사 기념제, 기념일 ❑ 빅토리아 여왕 기념제

Ju|da|ism /dʒudiɪzəm, -deɪ-/ N-UNCOUNT **Judaism** is the religion of the Jewish people. It is based on the Old Testament of the Bible and the Talmud.

불가산명사 유대교

judge ♦♢♢ /dʒʌdʒ/ (**judges, judging, judged**) **1** N-COUNT; N-TITLE A **judge** is the person in a court of law who decides how the law should be applied, for example how criminals should be punished. ❑ *The judge adjourned the hearing until next Tuesday.* **2** N-COUNT A **judge** is a person who decides who will be the winner of a competition. ❑ *A panel of judges is now selecting the finalists.* **3** V-T/V-I If you judge something such as a competition, you decide who or what is the winner. ❑ *Colin Mitchell will judge the entries each week.* **4** V-T If you **judge** something or someone, you form an opinion about them after you have examined the evidence or thought carefully about them. ❑ *It will take a few more years to judge the impact of these ideas.* ❑ *I am ready to judge any book on its merits.* ❑ *It's for other people to judge how much I have improved.* **5** V-T If you **judge** something, you guess its amount, size, or value or you guess what it is. ❑ *It is important to judge the weight of your washing load correctly.* ❑ *I judged him to be about forty.* **6** N-COUNT If someone is a good **judge of** something, they understand it and can make sensible decisions about it. If someone is a bad **judge of** something, they cannot do this. ❑ *I'm a pretty good judge of character.* **7** PHRASE You use **judging by, judging from**, or **to judge from** to introduce the reasons why you believe or think something. ❑ *Judging by the opinion polls, he seems to be succeeding.* ❑ *Judging from the way he laughed as he told it, it was meant to be humorous.* →see **trial**

1 가산명사; 경칭명사 판사, 재판관 ❑ 판사는 다음 화요일까지 심리를 연기하였다. **2** 가산명사 심판, 심사 위원 ❑ 심사 위원들이 지금 최종 결승 진출자를 선정하고 있다. **3** 타동사/자동사 심사하다 ❑ 콜린 미첼이 매주 참가자를 심사할 것이다. **4** 타동사 판단하다 ❑ 이러한 생각의 여파를 판단하려면 몇 년은 더 걸려야 할 것이다. ❑ 나는 어떤 책이든 좋은 책인지를 판단할 준비가 되어 있다. ❑ 내가 얼마나 발전했는지는 다른 사람이 판단하는 것이다. **5** 타동사 가늠하다, 어림잡다 ❑ 세탁물의 무게를 제대로 가늠하는 것이 중요하다. ❑ 나는 그가 어림잡아 마흔 살쯤 되는 것으로 보았다. **6** 가산명사 판단 ❑ 나는 사람들의 성격을 꽤 잘 알아맞힌다. **7** 구 _으로 판단하건대, _으로 미루어 보아 ❑ 여론 조사를 보아하니 그가 성공할 것 같다. ❑ 그가 그것을 말하면서 웃는 것으로 보아, 그 말은 재미있으라고 한 말이었다.

Word Partnership   judge의 연어

N.	**decision by/of** a judge, **trial** judge **1**
V.	judge **approves** *something*, judge **asks** *something*, judge **decides** *something*, judge **denies a motion/request**, judge **grants** *something*, judge **orders** *something*, judge **rules** *something*, judge **says** *something*, judge **sentences** *someone* **1**

---

judg|ment ♦♢♢ /dʒʌdʒmənt/ (**judgments**) [BRIT also **judgement**] **1** N-VAR A **judgment** is an opinion that you have or express after thinking carefully about something. ❑ *In your judgment, what has changed over the past few years?* **2** N-UNCOUNT **Judgment** is the ability to make sensible guesses about a situation or sensible decisions about what to do. ❑ *I respect his judgement and I'll follow any advice he gives me.* **3** N-VAR A **judgment** is a decision made by a judge or by a court of law. ❑ *The industry was awaiting a judgment from the European Court.* **4** PHRASE If something is **against** your **better judgment**, you believe that it would be more sensible or better not to do it. ❑ *Against our better judgment, we buy the products of manufacturers whose claims seem too good to be true.* **5** PHRASE If you **pass judgment** on someone or something, you give your opinion about it, especially if you are making a criticism. ❑ *They won't pass judgment on their friends or family.* **6** PHRASE If you **reserve judgment** on something, you refuse to give

[영국영어 judgement] **1** 가산명사 또는 불가산명사 판단 ❑ 당신의 판단으로는, 지난 몇 년 동안 무엇이 변했습니까? **2** 불가산명사 판단력 ❑ 나는 그의 판단력을 존중하고 그가 해 주는 조언은 무엇이든 따를 것이다. **3** 가산명사 또는 불가산명사 재판, 판결 ❑ 업계는 유럽 법원의 판결을 기다리고 있었다. **4** 구 이게 아닌데 싶으면서도 ❑ 우리는 이게 아닌데 싶으면서도 너무 번드르해서 사실 같지 않은 주장을 하는 제조사들의 제품을 산다. **5** 구 의견을 말하다, 비판을 하다 ❑ 그들은 친구나 가족에 대해서는 의견을 말하지 않을 것이다. **6** 구 판단을 유보하다 ❑ 나는 그들 중요 세부 사항들을 좀 볼 때까지 그런다고 뭐가 달라질지에 대한 판단을 유보해야 한다고 생각한다.

a b c d e f g h i j k l m n o p q r s t u v w x y z

an opinion about it until you know more about it. □ *I think I'd have to reserve judgment on whether it'll make any difference until I see some of those key details.*

Word Partnership   *judgment*의 연어

V.	**make a** judgment, **rush to** judgment **1**
	exercise judgment, **trust** *someone's* judgment, **use** judgment **2**
ADJ.	**bad** judgment, **good** judgment, **poor** judgment **2**

---

judg|men|tal /dʒʌdʒmɛntəl/ [BRIT also **judgemental**] ADJ If you say that someone is **judgmental**, you are critical of them because they form opinions of people and situations very quickly, when it would be better for them to wait until they know more about the person or situation. [DISAPPROVAL] □ *We tried not to seem critical or judgmental while giving advice that would protect him from ridicule.*

ju|di|cial /dʒudɪʃəl/ ADJ **Judicial** means relating to the legal system and to judgments made in a court of law. [ADJ n] □ *...an independent judicial inquiry.* □ *The last judicial hanging in Britain was in 1964.* ● **ju|di|cial|ly** ADV [ADV with v] □ *Even if the amendment is passed it can be defeated judicially.*

ju|di|ci|ary /dʒudɪʃieri, BRIT dʒuːdɪʃəri/ N-SING **The judiciary** is the branch of authority in a country which is concerned with law and the legal system. [FORMAL] □ *The judiciary must think very hard before jailing non-violent offenders.*

ju|di|cious /dʒudɪʃəs/ ADJ If you describe an action or decision as **judicious**, you approve of it because you think that it shows good judgment and sense. [FORMAL, APPROVAL] □ *The President authorizes the judicious use of military force to protect our citizens.* ● **ju|di|cious|ly** ADV [ADV with v] □ *Modern fertilizers should be used judiciously.*

judo /dʒudoʊ/ N-UNCOUNT **Judo** is a sport in which two people fight and try to throw each other to the ground. □ *He was also a black belt in judo.*

jug /dʒʌg/ (**jugs**) N-COUNT A **jug** is a cylindrical container with a handle and is used for holding and pouring liquids. ● N-COUNT A **jug** of liquid is the amount that the jug contains. □ *...a jug of water.*

jug|gle /dʒʌgəl/ (**juggles, juggling, juggled**) **1** V-T If you **juggle** lots of different things, for example your work and your family, you try to give enough time or attention to all of them. □ *The management team meets several times a week to juggle budgets and resources.* **2** V-T/V-I If you **juggle**, you entertain people by throwing things into the air, catching each one and throwing it up again so that there are several of them in the air at the same time. □ *Soon she was juggling five eggs.* ● **jug|gling** N-UNCOUNT □ *He can perform an astonishing variety of acts, including mime and juggling.*

jug|gler /dʒʌglər/ (**jugglers**) N-COUNT A **juggler** is someone who juggles in order to entertain people.

juice ♦◇◇ /dʒus/ (**juices**) **1** N-MASS **Juice** is the liquid that can be obtained from a fruit. □ *...fresh orange juice.* **2** N-PLURAL The **juices** of a piece of meat are the liquid that comes out of it when you cook it. □ *When cooked, drain off the juices and put the meat in a processor or mincer.*

Word Partnership   *juice*의 연어

N.	**bottle of** juice, **fruit** juice, **glass of** juice **1**

---

juicy /dʒusi/ (**juicier, juiciest**) **1** ADJ If food is **juicy**, it has a lot of juice in it and is very enjoyable to eat. □ *...a thick, juicy steak.* **2** ADJ **Juicy** gossip or stories contain details about people's lives, especially details which are normally kept private. [INFORMAL] □ *It provided some juicy gossip for a few days.*

Jul. **Jul.** is a written abbreviation for **July**.

July ♦♦♦ /dʒulaɪ/ (**Julys**) N-VAR **July** is the seventh month of the year in the Western calendar. □ *In late July 1914, he and Violet spent a few days with friends near Berwick-upon-Tweed.*

jum|ble /dʒʌmbəl/ (**jumbles, jumbling, jumbled**) **1** N-COUNT A **jumble** of things is a lot of different things that are all mixed together in a disorganized or confused way. □ *The shoreline was made up of a jumble of huge boulders.* **2** V-T/V-I If you **jumble** things, they become mixed together so that they are untidy or are not in the correct order. □ *He's making a new film by jumbling together bits of his other movies.* ● PHRASAL VERB To **jumble up** means the same as to **jumble**. □ *They had jumbled it all up into a heap.* □ *The bank scrambles all that money together, jumbles it all up and lends it out to hundreds and thousands of borrowers.* **3** N-UNCOUNT **Jumble** is old or unwanted things that people give away to charity. [BRIT; AM **rummage**] □ *She expects me to drive round collecting jumble for the church.*

jum|bo /dʒʌmboʊ/ (**jumbos**) **1** ADJ **Jumbo** means very large; used mainly in advertising and in the names of products. [ADJ n] □ *...a jumbo box of tissues.* **2** N-COUNT A **jumbo** or a **jumbo jet** is a very large jet aircraft that can carry several hundred passengers. □ *...a British Airways jumbo.* →see **fly**

jump ♦♦◇ /dʒʌmp/ (**jumps, jumping, jumped**) **1** V-T/V-I If you **jump**, you bend your knees, push against the ground with your feet, and move quickly upward into the air. □ *I jumped over the fence.* □ *I'd jumped seventeen feet six in the long jump, which was a school record.* ● N-COUNT **Jump** is also a noun. □ *The longest jumps by a man and a woman were witnessed in Sestriere, Italy, yesterday.* **2** V-T/V-I If you **jump** from something above the ground, you deliberately push yourself into the air so that you drop toward the ground. □ *He jumped out of a third-floor window.* **3** V-T If you **jump** something such as a fence, you move quickly up and through the air over or across it. □ *He jumped the first fence beautifully.* **4** V-I If you

---

[영국영어 judgemental] 형용사 섣부른 판단의 [탐탁찮음] □ 우리는 그가 조롱을 당하지 않도록 보호할 수 있는 조언을 해 주는 동안 비판적이거나 섣부른 판단을 한다는 인상을 주지 않기 위해 노력했다.

형용사 사법의 □ 독립적인 사법 조사 □ 영국에서 재판에 의한 교수형이 마지막으로 행해진 것은 1964년이었다. ● 사법적으로 부사 □ 개정안이 통과된다고 해도 사법적으로 무효 처리될 수 있다.

단수명사 사법부 [격식체] □ 사법부는 비폭력 범죄자를 투옥하기 전에 고심해야 할 것이다.

형용사 현명한 [격식체, 마음에 듦] □ 대통령은 우리의 국민들을 보호하기 위해 군사력을 현명하게 사용하는 것을 허용한다. ● 현명하게 부사 □ 현대의 비료는 현명하게 사용해야 한다.

불가산명사 유도 □ 그는 또한 유도 유단자였다.

가산명사 주전자 ● 가산명사 한 주전자 분량 □ 물 한 주전자

1 타동사 동시에 다루다 □ 관리 팀은 예산과 자원을 동시에 다루기 위해 일주일에 여러 번 만난다. **2** 타동사/자동사 요술을 부리다, 재주 부리다 □ 곧 그녀는 계란 다섯 개로 재주를 부리고 있었다. ● 재주 부리기 불가산명사 □ 그는 무언극과 재주 부리기를 포함해서 놀라울 정도로 다양한 묘기를 부릴 수 있다.

가산명사 요술이나 재주를 부리는 사람

1 물질명사 주스 □ 신선한 오렌지 주스 **2** 복수명사 육즙 □ 다 익으면 육즙은 버리고 고기를 가공 기계나 믹서에 넣어라.

1 형용사 즙이 많은 □ 두툼하고 즙이 많은 스테이크 **2** 형용사 재미있는 [비격식체] □ 그것은 며칠간 재미있는 소문거리가 되었다.

7월

가산명사 또는 불가산명사 7월 □ 1914년 7월 말에 그와 바이올렛은 버위커폰트위드에서 친구들과 며칠을 보냈다.

1 가산명사 뒤범벅 □ 그 해안선은 마구 뒤섞인 거대한 바위들로 이뤄져 있었다. **2** 타동사/자동사 뒤섞다 □ 그는 자기의 다른 영화들에서 딴 온갖 장면을 함께 뒤섞어 새로운 영화를 만들고 있다. ● 구동사 뒤섞다 □ 그들은 그것을 모두 한 덩어리로 뒤섞어 놓았다. □ 은행은 그 돈을 전부 끌어 모은 다음 잔뜩 뒤섞고는 수백 수천 명의 대출자들에게 빌려 준다. **3** 불가산명사 (중고품) 자선 바자 [영국영어; 미국영어 rummage] □ 그녀는 내가 교회 자선 바자를 위한 물건을 받으러 돌아다니길 원한다.

1 형용사 특대의 □ 특대 티슈 박스 **2** 가산명사 점보기 □ 영국 항공 점보기

1 타동사/자동사 뛰다, 뛰어오르다 □ 나는 울타리를 뛰어넘었다. □ 나는 멀리뛰기에서 학교 최고 기록인 17.5피트를 기록했었다. ● 가산명사 도약 □ 어제 이태리의 세스트리에르에서 여자 및 남자 멀리뛰기 최고 기록이 나왔다. **2** 타동사/자동사 뛰다, 뛰어내리다 □ 그는 3층 창문에서 뛰어내렸다. **3** 타동사 뛰어넘다 □ 그는 첫 번째 장애물을 우아하게 뛰어넘었다. **4** 자동사 재빨리 달려가다 □ 아담은 소녀의 비명에 자리에서 재빨리 일어나 달려갔다.

jump somewhere, you move there quickly and suddenly. ❑ *Adam jumped from his seat at the girl's cry.* **5** V-I If something **makes** you **jump**, it makes you make a sudden movement because you are frightened or surprised. ❑ *The phone shrilled, making her jump.* **6** V-T/V-I If an amount or level **jumps**, it suddenly increases or rises by a large amount in a short time. ❑ *Sales jumped from $94 million to over $101 million.* ❑ *The number of crimes jumped by ten per cent last year.* ● N-COUNT **Jump** is also a noun. ❑ *A big jump in energy conservation could be achieved without much disruption of anyone's standard of living.* **7** V-T If someone **jumps** a queue, they move to the front of it and are served or dealt with before it is their turn. [BRIT] ❑ *The prince refused to jump the queue for treatment at the local hospital.* **8** V-I If you **jump at** an offer or opportunity, you accept it quickly and eagerly. [no cont] ❑ *Members of the public would jump at the chance to become part owners of the corporation.* **9** V-I If someone **jumps on** you, they quickly criticize you if you do something that they do not approve of. ❑ *A lot of people jumped on me about that, you know.* **10** PHRASE If you **get a jump on** something or someone or **get the jump on** them, you gain an advantage over them. [AM] ❑ *Helicopters helped fire crews get a jump on the blaze.* **11** to **jump on the bandwagon** →see **bandwagon**. to **jump bail** →see **bail**. to **jump the gun** →see **gun**. to **jump for joy** →see **joy**

Thesaurus | *jump*의 참조어

v.	bound, hop, leap, lunge **1**
	dive, leap, parachute **2**
	hurdle **3**
	startle **5**
	increase, rise; *(ant.)* decline **6**

Word Partnership | *jump*의 연어

ADJ.	**big** jump **1 6**
N.	jump to *your* **feet 4**
	jump **in** prices, jump **in** sales **6**

---

jump|er /dʒʌmpər/ (**jumpers**) **1** N-COUNT If you refer to a person or a horse as a particular kind of **jumper**, you are describing how good they are at jumping or the way that they jump. ❑ *He is a terrific athlete and a brilliant jumper.* **2** N-COUNT A **jumper** is a sleeveless dress that is worn over a blouse or sweater. [AM; BRIT **pinafore**] ❑ *She wore a checkered jumper and had ribbons in her hair.* **3** N-COUNT A **jumper** is a warm knitted piece of clothing which covers the upper part of your body and your arms. [BRIT; AM **sweater**] ❑ *With her simple jumper and skirt, Isabel looked like a young girl again.*

jump-start (**jump-starts, jump-starting, jump-started**) also **jump start 1** V-T To **jump-start** a vehicle which has a dead battery means to make the engine start by getting power from the battery of another vehicle, using special cables called jumper cables. ❑ *He was huddled with John trying to jump-start his car.* ● N-COUNT **Jump-start** is also a noun. ❑ *I drove out to give him a jump-start because his battery was dead.* **2** V-T To **jump-start** a system or process that has stopped working or progressing means to do something that will make it start working quickly or effectively. ❑ *The EU is trying to jump-start the peace process.* ● N-COUNT **Jump-start** is also a noun. ❑ *...attempts to give the industry a jump start.*

Jun. Jun. is a written abbreviation for **June.**

junc|tion /dʒʌŋkʃⁿn/ (**junctions**) N-COUNT; N-IN-NAMES A **junction** is a place where roads or railroad lines join. [BRIT; AM usually **intersection**] ❑ *Follow the road to a junction and turn left.*

June ♦♦♦ /dʒuːn/ (**Junes**) N-VAR **June** is the sixth month of the year in the Western calendar. ❑ *He spent two and a half weeks with us in June 1986.* ❑ *I am moving out on June 5.*

jun|gle /dʒʌŋgᵊl/ (**jungles**) **1** N-VAR A **jungle** is a forest in a tropical country where large numbers of tall trees and plants grow very close together. ❑ *...the mountains and jungles of Papua New Guinea.* **2** N-SING If you describe a place as **a jungle**, you are emphasizing that it is full of lots of things and very messy. [EMPHASIS] ❑ *...a jungle of stuffed sofas, stuffed birds, knick-knacks, potted plants.* **3** N-SING If you describe a situation as **a jungle**, you dislike it because it is complicated and difficult to get what you want from it. [DISAPPROVAL] ❑ *Social security law and procedure remain a jungle of complex rules.*

jun|ior ♦♦◇◇ /dʒuːniər/ (**juniors**) **1** ADJ A **junior** official or employee holds a low-ranking position in an organization or profession. ❑ *Junior and middle-ranking civil servants have pledged to join the indefinite strike.* ● N-COUNT **Junior** is also a noun. ❑ *The Lord Chancellor has said legal aid work is for juniors when they start out in the law.* **2** N-SING If you are someone's **junior**, you are younger than they are. ❑ *She now lives with actor Denis Lawson, 10 years her junior.* **3** N-IN-NAMES **Junior** is sometimes used after the name of the younger of two men in a family who have the same name, sometimes in order to prevent confusion. The abbreviation **Jr.** is also used. [AM] ❑ *His son, Arthur Ochs Junior, is expected to succeed him as publisher.* **4** N-COUNT In the United States, a student in the third year of high school or college is called a **junior**. ❑ *Their youngest daughter Amy's a junior at the University of Evansville in Indiana.*

Word Partnership | *junior*의 연어

N.	junior **executive**, junior **officer**, junior **partner**, junior **senator 1**

---

5 자동사 펄쩍 뛰다 ❑ 전화가 날카로운 소리를 내자 그녀가 놀라서 펄쩍 뛰었다. **6** 타동사/자동사 급증하다 ❑ 판매가 9천 4백만 달러에서 1억 1백만 달러로 급증했다. ❑ 범죄 건수가 작년에 10퍼센트 급증했다. ● 가산명사 급증 ❑ 어느 누구의 생활수준도 침해를 안 하면서도 엄청난 양의 에너지를 절약하는 것이 가능하다. **7** 타동사 새치기하다 [영국영어] ❑ 왕자는 인근 병원에서 치료를 받기 위해 새치기하기를 거부했다. **8** 자동사 냉큼 받아들이다 ❑ 대중은 회사의 부분적인 소유자가 될 수 있는 기회에 냉큼 달려들 것이다. **9** 자동사 힐난하다 ❑ 많은 사람들이 그것 가지고 나를 힐난한 것 있지. **10** 구 우위를 점하다 [미국영어] ❑ 헬리콥터 덕분에 소방대원들이 불길을 잡을 수 있었다.

1 가산명사 도약하는 사람, 말 ❑ 그는 훌륭한 선수이자 뛰어난 도약 선수이다. **2** 가산명사 점퍼스커트 [미국영어; 영국영어 pinafore] ❑ 그녀는 체크무늬 점퍼스커트를 입고 머리에 리본을 달고 있었다. **3** 가산명사 잠바, 스웨터 [영국영어; 미국영어 sweater] ❑ 단순한 잠바와 치마를 입으니 이사벨은 다시 어린 소녀처럼 보였다.

1 타동사 점프 스타트를 하다 ❑ 다른 차의 배터리를 자신의 차에 연결하여 시동을 걸려는 존과 그는 바짝 달라붙어 있었다. ● 가산명사 점프 스타트 ❑ 그의 배터리가 다 되어서 나는 그의 차에 점프 스타트를 해 주러 차를 몰고 그가 있는 곳으로 나갔다. **2** 타동사 힘을 불어넣다 ❑ 유럽 연합이 그 평화 협상에 힘을 불어넣으려 하고 있다. ● 가산명사 힘을 불어넣기 ❑ 산업에 힘을 불어넣기 위한 노력

6월

가산명사; 이름명사 교차점 [영국영어; 미국영어 대개 intersection] ❑ 교차점이 나올 때까지 길을 따라간 다음 좌회전을 해라.

가산명사 또는 불가산명사 6월 ❑ 그는 1986년 6월에 2주 반을 우리와 같이 보냈다. ❑ 나는 6월 5일에 이사 나간다.

1 가산명사 또는 불가산명사 밀림 ❑ 파푸아 뉴기니의 산과 밀림 **2** 단수명사 혼잡한 곳 [강조] ❑ 속을 채워 넣은 소파, 박제 새, 자질구레한 장신구, 화분 등의 아수라장 **3** 단수명사 미로 [탐탁찮음] ❑ 사회 복지법과 절차는 여전히 복잡한 규칙들의 미로이다.

1 형용사 하급의 ❑ 하급 및 중간 계급 공무원들이 무기한 농성에 동참하기로 약속했다. ● 가산명사 하급자 ❑ 대법관은 법률 보조 업무는 하급자들이 처음 법조계에 발을 디딜 때 하는 것이라고 했다. **2** 단수명사 손아랫사람 ❑ 그녀는 지금 자기보다 열 살 아래인 배우 데니스 로슨과 같이 산다. **3** 이름명사 2세 [미국영어] ❑ 그의 아들인 아더 오크스 2세가 출판 발행인으로 그의 자리를 이을 것으로 예상된다. **4** 가산명사 3학년생 ❑ 그들의 막내딸인 에이미는 인디애나의 에반스빌 대학 3학년에 재학 중이다.

A B C D E F G H I J K L M N O P Q R S T U V W X Y Z

jun|ior high (junior highs) N-COUNT; N-IN-NAMES In the United States, **junior high** is the school that young people attend between the ages of 11 or 12 and 14 or 15. □ ...Benjamin Franklin Junior High.

가산명사; 이름명사 (미국) 중학교 □ 벤자민 프랭클린 중학교

jun|ior high school (junior high schools) N-COUNT; N-IN-NAMES **Junior high school** is the same as **junior high**. □ He dropped out of Junior High School.

가산명사; 이름명사 중학교 □ 그는 중학교를 중퇴했다.

jun|ior school (junior schools) N-VAR; N-IN-NAMES In England and Wales, a **junior school** is a school for children between the ages of about seven and eleven. □ ...Middleton Road Junior School.

가산명사 또는 불가산명사; 이름명사 (영국과 웨일스) 초등학교 □ 미들턴 로드 초등학교

junk /dʒʌŋk/ (junks, junking, junked) **1** N-UNCOUNT **Junk** is old and used goods that have little value and that you do not want any more. □ Rose finds her furniture in junk shops. **2** V-T If you **junk** something, you get rid of it or stop using it. [INFORMAL] □ Consumers will not have to junk their old cassettes to use the new format.

1 불가산명사 폐물, 쓰레기 □ 로즈는 가구를 중고품 가게에서 산다. **2** 타동사 버리다 [비격식체] □ 고객들은 새로운 포맷을 사용하기 위해서 옛날 카세트를 버릴 필요가 없다.

junk bond (junk bonds) N-COUNT If a company issues **junk bonds**, it borrows money from investors, usually at a high rate of interest, in order to finance a particular deal, for example the setting up or the taking over of another company. [BUSINESS]

가산명사 쓰레기 채권, 정크본드 [경제]

junk food (junk foods) N-MASS If you refer to food as **junk food**, you mean that it is quick and easy to prepare but is not good for your health. □ Sharon fears that her love of junk food may have contributed to her cancer.

물질명사 정크 푸드, 불량 식품 □ 샤론이 자신이 정크 푸드를 너무 많이 먹은 것도 암이 발병한 부분적인 이유가 됐을 것이라고 우려한다.

junkie /dʒʌŋki/ (junkies) **1** N-COUNT A **junkie** is a drug addict. [INFORMAL] □ ...those desperate junkies who have tried every known drug. **2** N-COUNT You can use **junkie** to refer to someone who is very interested in a particular activity, especially when they spend a lot of time on it. [INFORMAL] □ ...a computer junkie.

1 가산명사 마약 중독자 [비격식체] □ 아는 모든 마약을 시도해 본 절망적인 마약 중독자들 **2** 가산명사 -광(狂), 심취한 사람 [비격식체] □ 컴퓨터 중독자

junk mail N-UNCOUNT **Junk mail** is advertisements and publicity materials that you receive through the post which you have not asked for and which you do not want. □ We still get junk mail for the previous occupants.

불가산명사 잡동사니 우편물 □ 우리는 전 입주자 명의의 잡동사니 우편물을 아직도 받는다.

ju|ris|dic|tion /dʒʊərɪsdɪkʃⁿn/ (jurisdictions) **1** N-UNCOUNT **Jurisdiction** is the power that a court of law or an official has to carry out legal judgments or to enforce laws. [FORMAL] □ The British police have no jurisdiction over foreign bank accounts. **2** N-COUNT A **jurisdiction** is a state or other area in which a particular court and system of laws has authority. [LEGAL] □ In the UK, unlike in most other European jurisdictions, there is no right to strike.

1 불가산명사 관할권 [격식체] □ 영국 경찰은 해외 은행 계좌에 대해서는 아무런 관할권이 없다. **2** 가산명사 사법권 [법률] □ 다른 대부분 유럽 국가의 사법권 내에서와는 달리 영국에서는 파업을 할 수 있는 권리가 없다.

ju|ror /dʒʊərər/ (jurors) N-COUNT A **juror** is a member of a jury. □ The foreman was asked by the clerk whether the jurors had reached verdicts on which they all agreed.

가산명사 배심원 □ 서기가 배심장에게 배심원들이 만장일치의 평결을 얻었는지 물었다.

jury ♦♢♢ /dʒʊəri/ (juries) **1** N-COUNT-COLL In a court of law, the **jury** is the group of people who have been chosen from the general public to listen to the facts about a crime and to decide whether the person accused is guilty or not. [also by N] □ The jury convicted Mr. Hampson of all offences. **2** N-COUNT-COLL A **jury** is a group of people who choose the winner of a competition. □ I am not surprised that the Booker Prize jury included it on their shortlist. **3** PHRASE If you say that **the jury is out** or that **the jury is still out** on a particular subject, you mean that people in general have still not made a decision or formed an opinion about that subject. □ The jury is out on whether or not this is true. →see trial

1 가산명사-집합 배심원단 □ 배심원단은 햄슨 씨의 모든 혐의에 대해 유죄 판결을 내렸다. **2** 가산명사-집합 심사 위원단 □ 나는 부커상 심사 위원단이 그것을 최종 심사 대상에 포함한 것이 놀랍지 않다. **3** 구 판단이 유보되다 □ 이것이 사실인지 아닌지는 아직 판단이 유보된 상태이다.

	Word Partnership	jury의 연어
N.	jury **duty**, **trial by** jury **1**	
V.	jury **convicts 1**	
	jury **announces 1 2**	
ADJ.	**hung** jury **1**	

just

① ADVERB USES
② ADJECTIVE USE

① just ♦♦♦ /dʒʌst/ →Please look at category **17** to see if the expression you are looking for is shown under another headword. **1** ADV You use **just** to say that something happened a very short time ago, or is starting to happen at the present time. For example, if you say that someone **has just arrived**, you mean that they arrived a very short time ago. [ADV before v] □ I've just bought a new house. □ The two had only just met. **2** ADV If you say that you are **just** doing something, you mean that you are doing it now and will finish it very soon. If you say that you are **just about to** do something, or **just going to** do it, you mean that you will do it very soon. □ I'm just making the sauce for the cauliflower. □ I'm just going to walk down the lane now and post some letters. **3** ADV You can use **just** to emphasize that something is happening at exactly the moment of speaking or at exactly the moment that you are talking about. □ Randall would just now be getting the Sunday paper. □ Just then the phone rang. **4** ADV You use **just** to indicate that something is no more important, interesting, or difficult, than you say it is, especially when you want to correct a wrong idea that someone may get or has already gotten. [EMPHASIS] [ADV group/cl] □ It's just a suggestion. □ It's not just a financial matter. **5** ADV You use **just** to emphasize that you are talking about a small part, not the whole of an amount. [EMPHASIS] [ADV n] □ That's just one example of the kind of experiments you can do. **6** ADV You use **just** to emphasize how small an amount is or how short a length of time is. [EMPHASIS] [ADV amount] □ Stephanie and David redecorated a room in just three days. **7** ADV You can use **just** in front of a verb to indicate that the result of something is unfortunate or undesirable and is likely to make the situation worse rather than better. [ADV before v] □ Leaving like I did just made

1 부사 방금, 막 □ 나는 막 집을 새로 샀다. □ 둘은 갓 만난 상태였다. **2** 부사 바로, 막 □ 나는 막 콜리플라워용 소스를 만드는 중이다. □ 나는 지금 바로 걸어 내려가서 편지를 몇 통 부칠 것이다. **3** 부사 바로 지금 [강조] □ 랜달은 바로 지금쯤 일요 신문을 받아 보고 있을 것이다. □ 바로 그때 전화가 울렸다. **4** 부사 단지 [강조] □ 그것은 단지 제안이다. □ 그것은 단순한 재정적 사안이 아니다. **5** 부사 단지 [강조] □ 그것은 할 수 있는 실험의 단 한 가지 예에 불과하다. **6** 부사 겨우 [강조] □ 스테파니와 데이비드는 방을 겨우 3일만에 재단장했다. **7** 부사 -할 뿐이니 □ 내가 그렇게 떠나서 상황은 악화되기만 했다. **8** 부사 간신히 □ 거실의 불빛으로 그녀의 손을 간신히 볼 수 있었다. □ 콜린의 목소리였지만 간신히 알아들을 수 있었다. **9** 부사 어쩌면 □ 남은 수법이지만 어쩌면 통할지도 모른다. **10** 부사 작정, 존경, 확신 등을 강조하기 위한 표현 [강조] □ 그녀는 그저 긴장을 풀려고 하지를 않아. **11** 부사 잠깐만 [구어체] □ "들어보내 줘, 다이." "알았어, 잠깐만." **12** 부사 잠깐만 [구어체] □ 어, 잠깐만, 그 전체에 나는 완전히 동의할 수 없어. **13** 부사 - 눈에 선하게, 귀에 쟁쟁하게 □ 그녀가 자신의 친구들에게 "나는 그의 어머님이 원망스러워"라고 말하는 것이 귀에 쟁쟁하게 들린다. **14** 부사 꼭 바라 [강조] □ 그럴듯한 겉모습 뒤를 보면 그들은 우리와

it worse. **8** ADV You use **just** to indicate that what you are saying is the case, but only by a very small degree or amount. ❑ *Her hand was just visible by the light from the sitting room.* ❑ *It was Colin's voice, only just audible.* **9** ADV You use **just** with "might," "may," and "could," when you mean that there is a small chance of something happening, even though it is not very likely. [ADV with modal] ❑ *It's an old trick but it just might work.* **10** ADV You use **just** to emphasize the following word or phrase, in order to express feelings such as annoyance, admiration, or certainty. [EMPHASIS] ❑ *She just won't relax.* **11** ADV You use **just** in expressions such as **just a minute** and **just a moment** to ask someone to wait for a short time. [SPOKEN] [ADV n] ❑ *"Let me in, Di." — "Okay. Just a minute."* **12** ADV You can use **just** in expressions such as **just a minute** and **just a moment** to interrupt someone, for example in order to disagree with them, explain something, or calm them down. [SPOKEN] [ADV n] ❑ *Well, now just a second, I don't altogether agree with the premise.* **13** ADV If you say that you can **just** see or hear something, you mean that it is easy for you to imagine seeing or hearing it. [ADV before v] ❑ *I can just hear her telling her friends, "Well, I blame his mother!"* **14** ADV You use **just** in expressions such as **just like**, **just as...as**, and **just the same** when you are emphasizing the similarity between two things or two people. [EMPHASIS] ❑ *Behind the facade they are just like the rest of us.* ❑ *He worked just as hard as anyone.* **15** PHRASE You use **just about** to indicate that what you are talking about is so close to being the case that it can be regarded as being the case. ❑ *There are those who believe that Nick Price is just about the best golfer in the world.* **16** PHRASE You use **just about** to indicate that what you are talking about is in fact the case, but only by a very small degree or amount. ❑ *I can just about tolerate it at the moment.* **17** just my luck →see **luck**. not just →see **not**. just now →see **now**. only just →see **only**. it just goes to show →see **show**

다를 것이 전혀 없다. ❑ 그는 어느 누구 못지않게 열심히 일했다. **15** 구 거의 ❑ 닉 프라이스가 거의 세계 최고의 골퍼라고 생각하는 사람들이 있다. **16** 구 기우 ❑ 나는 지금 겨우 참고 있다.

Thesaurus   *just*의 참조어

ADV.   barely ① **1**
          now, presently ① **2 3**
          only, merely ① **4 5 6**

---

② **just** /dʒʌst/ ADJ If you describe a situation, action, or idea as **just**, you mean that it is right or acceptable according to particular moral principles, such as respect for all human beings. [FORMAL] ❑ *In a just society there must be a system whereby people can seek redress through the courts.* ● **just**|**ly** ADV [ADV with v] ❑ *They were not treated justly in the past.*

형용사 공정한 [격식체] ❑ 공정한 사회에서는 사람들이 법정을 통해 구제를 받을 수 있는 제도가 있어야 한다. ● 공정하게 부사 ❑ 과거에 그들은 공정한 대우를 받지 못했다.

jus|**tice** ◆◆◇ /dʒʌstɪs/ (**justices**) **1** N-UNCOUNT **Justice** is fairness in the way that people are treated. ❑ *He has a good overall sense of justice and fairness.* ❑ *He only wants freedom, justice and equality.* **2** N-UNCOUNT The **justice** of a cause, claim, or argument is its quality of being reasonable, fair, or right. ❑ *We are a minority and must win people round to the justice of our cause.* **3** N-UNCOUNT **Justice** is the legal system that a country uses in order to deal with people who break the law. ❑ *Many in Toronto's black community feel that the justice system does not treat them fairly.* **4** N-COUNT A **justice** is a judge. [AM] ❑ *Thomas will be sworn in today as a justice on the Supreme Court.* **5** N-TITLE **Justice** is used before the names of judges. ❑ *A preliminary hearing was due to start today before Mr. Justice Hutchison, but was adjourned.* **6** PHRASE If a criminal is **brought to justice**, he or she is punished for a crime by being arrested and tried in a court of law. ❑ *They demanded that those responsible be brought to justice.* **7** PHRASE To **do justice** to a person or thing means to reproduce them accurately and show how good they are. ❑ *The photograph I had seen didn't do her justice.* **8** PHRASE If you **do justice to** someone or something, you deal with them properly and completely. ❑ *No one article can ever do justice to the topic of fraud.* **9** PHRASE If you **do yourself justice**, you do something as well as you are capable of doing it. ❑ *I don't think he could do himself justice playing for England.* **10** PHRASE If you describe someone's treatment or punishment as **rough justice**, you mean that it is not given according to the law. [BRIT] ❑ *Trial by television makes for very rough justice indeed.*

1 불가산명사 정의 ❑ 그는 정의와 공평함에 대해 건실하면서도 포괄적인 개념을 가지고 있다. ❑ 그가 원하는 것은 단지 자유, 정의, 평등이다. **2** 불가산명사 정당함 ❑ 우리는 소수이고 우리 대의의 정당함에 대해 사람들을 설득하고 끌어들여야 한다. **3** 불가산명사 사법 ❑ 토론토 흑인 사회 내의 많은 이들이 사법 제도가 자신들을 공평하게 대하지 않는다고 생각한다. **4** 가산명사 판사 [미국영어] ❑ 토머스는 오늘 선서를 하고 대법관으로 취임할 것이다. **5** 경칭명사 판사 ❑ 허치슨 판사가 주관하는 예심이 오늘 열리기로 되어 있었으나 연기되었다. **6** 구 법의 심판을 받다 ❑ 그들은 책임자들이 법의 심판을 받아야 한다고 요구했다. **7** 구 정확하게 새 모습을 보여 주다 ❑ 내가 본 사진에서는 그녀가 실물보다 못했다. **8** 구 제대로 다루다 ❑ 어떠한 기사도 하나의 기사가 사기라는 주제를 제대로 다루지는 못한다. **9** 구 역량을 충분히 발휘하다 ❑ 내 생각에 그가 영국을 위해서 뛰면 역량을 충분히 발휘하기 힘들 것 같다. **10** 구 대강의 정의 [영국영어] ❑ 텔레비전으로 재판을 치르면 정의가 너무 대충 구현된다.

Word Partnership   *justice*의 연어

ADJ.   **racial** justice, **social** justice **1**
        criminal justice, **equal** justice **3**

V.   **seek** justice **1**

N.   **obstruction of** justice, justice **system 3**

---

jus|**ti**|**fi**|**able** /dʒʌstɪfaɪəbəl/ ADJ An action, situation, emotion, or idea that is **justifiable** is acceptable or correct because there is a good reason for it. ❑ *The violence of the revolutionary years was justifiable on the grounds of political necessity.* ● **jus**|**ti**|**fi**|**ably** /dʒʌstɪfaɪəbli/ ADV ❑ *He was justifiably proud of his achievements.*

형용사 정당화할 수 있는 ❑ 혁명기의 폭력은 정치적 필요라는 근거로 정당화할 수 있었다. ● 정당하게 부사 ❑ 그는 자신의 업적에 대해 자랑스러워할 만했다.

jus|**ti**|**fi**|**ca**|**tion** /dʒʌstɪfɪkeɪʃən/ (**justifications**) N-VAR A **justification for** something is an acceptable reason or explanation for it. ❑ *To me the only justification for a zoo is educational.*

가산명사 또는 불가산명사 정당한 이유, 정당화 ❑ 내 생각에 동물원이 정당할 수 있는 유일한 이유는 그 교육적인 측면에 있다.

jus|**ti**|**fied** /dʒʌstɪfaɪd/ **1** ADJ If you describe a decision, action, or idea as **justified**, you think it is reasonable and acceptable. ❑ *In my opinion, the decision was wholly justified.* **2** ADJ If you think that someone is **justified in** doing something, you think that their reasons for doing it are good and valid. [v-link ADJ in -ing] ❑ *He's absolutely justified in resigning. He was treated shamefully.*

1 형용사 타당한 ❑ 내 생각에 그 결정은 전적으로 타당했다. **2** 형용사 -에 있어 정당한 ❑ 그가 사직하는 것은 전적으로 정당한 처사였다. 그는 너무도 불명예스러운 대우를 받았다.

jus|**ti**|**fy** ◆◇◇ /dʒʌstɪfaɪ/ (**justifies**, **justifying**, **justified**) **1** V-T To **justify** a decision, action, or idea means to show or prove that it is reasonable or

1 타동사 정당화하다 ❑ 어떠한 논리도 전쟁을 정당화할 수 없다. **2** 타동사 문단을 정렬하다

A

necessary. ❑ *No argument can justify a war.* **2** V-T To **justify** printed text means to adjust the spaces between the words so that each line of type is exactly the same length. ❑ *Click on this icon to align or justify text at both the left and right margins.* →see also **left-justify**

❑ 텍스트의 왼쪽과 오른쪽 여백을 맞추려면 이 아이콘을 클릭하세요.

B

just|ly /dʒʌstli/ ADV You use **justly** to show that you approve of someone's attitude towards something, because it seems to be based on truth or reality. [APPROVAL] ❑ *Australians are justly proud of their native wildlife.* →see also **just**

부사 합당하게 [마음에 듦] 호주 사람들은 고유 야생 생태계를 충분히 자랑스러워할 만하다.

C

D

jut /dʒʌt/ (**juts, jutting, jutted**) **1** V-I If something **juts out**, it sticks out above or beyond a surface. ❑ *The northern end of the island juts out like a long, thin finger into the sea.* **2** V-T/V-I If you **jut** a part of your body, especially your chin, or if it **juts**, you push it forward in an aggressive or determined way. ❑ *His jaw jutted stubbornly forward; he would not be denied.* ❑ *Gwen jutted her chin forward, her nose in the air, and did not bother to answer the teacher.*

1 자동사 튀어나오다, 돌출하다 ❑ 섬의 북단은 길고 가는 손가락처럼 바다로 돌출해 있다. **2** 타동사/자동사 내밀다; 튀어나오다 ❑ 그는 고집스럽게 턱을 앞으로 내밀었다. 거부하는 것은 용납하지 않겠다는 것이었다. ❑ 그웬은 턱과 코를 치켜세우고 선생님께 대답조차도 안 했다.

E

ju|venile /dʒuvən⁹l, -naɪl/ (**juveniles**) **1** N-COUNT A **juvenile** is a child or young person who is not yet old enough to be regarded as an adult. [FORMAL] ❑ *The number of juveniles in the general population has fallen by a fifth in the past 10 years.* **2** ADJ **Juvenile** activity or behavior involves young people who are not yet adults. [ADJ n] ❑ *Juvenile crime is increasing at a terrifying rate.*

1 가산명사 청소년 [격식체] ❑ 지난 10년 사이에 전체 인구 중 청소년의 수가 5분의 1이 줄었다. **2** 형용사 청소년의 ❑ 청소년 범죄가 무서운 속도로 증가하고 있다.

F

G

jux|ta|pose /dʒʌkstəpoʊz/ (**juxtaposes, juxtaposing, juxtaposed**) V-T If you **juxtapose** two contrasting objects, images, or ideas, you place them together or describe them together, so that the differences between them are emphasized. [FORMAL] ❑ *The technique Mr. Wilson uses most often is to juxtapose things for dramatic effect.* ❑ *Contemporary photographs are juxtaposed with a sixteenth-century, copper Portuguese mirror.*

타동사 병치하다 [격식체] ❑ 윌슨 씨가 가장 자주 사용하는 기교는 극적 효과를 위해 사물들을 병치하는 것이다. ❑ 현대 사진들이 16세기 포르투갈 산 구리거울과 나란히 놓여 있다.

H

jux|ta|po|si|tion /dʒʌkstəpəzɪʃⁿn/ (**juxtapositions**) N-VAR The **juxtaposition of** two contrasting objects, images, or ideas is the fact that they are placed together or described together, so that the differences between them are emphasized. [FORMAL] ❑ *This juxtaposition of brutal reality and lyrical beauty runs through Park's stories.*

가산명사 또는 불가산명사 병치 [격식체] ❑ 파크의 이야기들 속에는 잔인한 현실과 서정적 아름다움의 이런 병치가 줄곧 계속된다.

I

J

K

L

M

N

O

P

Q

R

S

T

U

V

W

X

Y

Z

Kk

K, k /keɪ/ (K's, k's) N-VAR K is the eleventh letter of the English alphabet.

가산명사 또는 불가산명사 영어 알파벳의 열한 번째 글자

kan|ga|roo /kæŋgəru/ (**kangaroos**) N-COUNT A **kangaroo** is a large Australian animal which moves by jumping on its back legs. Female kangaroos carry their babies in a pouch on their stomach.

가산명사 캥거루

ka|ra|te /kərɑti/ N-UNCOUNT **Karate** is a Japanese sport or way of fighting in which people fight using their hands, elbows, feet, and legs.

불가산명사 가라데, 공수도

keel /kil/ (**keels, keeling, keeled**) ☐ N-COUNT The **keel** of a boat is the long, specially shaped piece of wood or steel along the bottom of it. ☐ *It was luck the keel hit the rock first or it would have ripped a hole in the hull.* ☐ PHRASE If you say that someone or something is **on an even keel**, you mean that they are working or progressing smoothly and steadily, without any sudden changes. ☐ *Jason had helped him out with a series of loans, until he could get back on an even keel.*

☐ 가산명사 (배의) 용골 ☐ 용골이 먼저 암초에 부딪친 것은 운이 좋았다. 아니면 선체에 구멍이 났을 것이다. ☐ 구 원활히, 안정되어 ☐ 제이슨은 그가 다시 안정될 때까지, 여러 번 대출을 받도록 도와주었었다.

▶**keel over** PHRASAL VERB If someone **keels over**, they collapse because they are tired or ill. [INFORMAL] ☐ *He then keeled over and fell flat on his back.*

구동사 쓰러지다, 졸도하다 [비격식체] ☐ 그는 그리고 나서 쓰러져 바닥에 완전히 드러누웠다.

keen ♦♢♢ /kin/ (**keener, keenest**) ☐ ADJ If you say that someone has a **keen** mind, you mean that they are very clever and aware of what is happening around them. [ADJ n] ☐ *They described him as a man of keen intellect.* ● **keen|ly** ADV ☐ *They're keenly aware that whatever they decide will set a precedent.* ☐ ADJ If you have a **keen** eye or ear, you are able to notice things that are difficult to detect. ☐ *...an amateur artist with a keen eye for detail.* ● **keen|ly** ADV [ADV with v] ☐ *Charles listened keenly.* ☐ ADJ A **keen** interest or emotion is one that is very intense. ☐ *He had retained a keen interest in the progress of the work.* ● **keen|ly** ADV ☐ *She remained keenly interested in international affairs.* ☐ ADJ A **keen** fight or competition is one in which the competitors are all trying very hard to win, and it is not easy to predict who will win. ☐ *There is expected to be a keen fight in the local elections.* ● **keen|ly** ADV ☐ *The contest should be very keenly fought.* ☐ ADJ If you are **keen on** doing something, you very much want to do it. If you are **keen that** something should happen, you very much want it to happen. [mainly BRIT] [v-link ADJ, ADJ on -ing/n, ADJ that, ADJ to-inf] ☐ *You're not keen on going, are you?* ☐ *Both companies were keen on a merger.* ● **keen|ness** N-UNCOUNT ☐ *...Doyle's keenness to please.* ☐ ADJ If you are **keen on** something, you like it a lot and are very enthusiastic about it. [mainly BRIT] [v-link ADJ on n] ☐ *I wasn't too keen on physics and chemistry.* ● **keen|ness** N-UNCOUNT ☐ *...his keenness for the arts.* ☐ ADJ You use **keen** to indicate that someone has a lot of enthusiasm for a particular activity and spends a lot of time doing it. [mainly BRIT] [ADJ n, v-link ADJ on n/-ing] ☐ *She was a keen amateur photographer.* ☐ ADJ If you describe someone as **keen**, you mean that they have an enthusiastic nature and are interested in everything that they do. [mainly BRIT] ☐ *He's a very keen student and works very hard.* ● **keen|ness** N-UNCOUNT ☐ *...the keenness of the students.* ☐ ADJ If you are a **keen** supporter of a cause, movement, or idea, you support it enthusiastically. [mainly BRIT] [ADJ n] ☐ *He's been a keen supporter of the Labour Party all his life.* ☐ ADJ **Keen** prices are low and competitive. [mainly BRIT] ☐ *The company negotiates very keen prices with their suppliers.* ● **keen|ly** ADV [ADV -ed] ☐ *The shops also offer a keenly priced curtain-making service.* ☐ PHRASE If you say that someone is **mad keen on** something, you are emphasizing that they are very enthusiastic about it. [BRIT, INFORMAL, EMPHASIS] ☐ *So you're not mad keen on science then?*

☐ 형용사 빈틈없는, 예리한 ☐ 그들은 그를 예리한 지성의 소유자로 묘사했다. ● 매우 잘, 통렬하게 부사 ☐ 그들은 자기들이 어떤 결정을 내리든 그것이 선례가 되리라는 것을 잘 알고 있다. ☐ 형용사 예리한, 민감한 ☐ 세부적인 것을 예리하게 볼 줄 아는 아마추어 화가 ● 예리하게 부사 ☐ 찰스는 예리하게 귀를 기울여 들었다. ☐ 형용사 강렬한, 대단한 ☐ 그는 그 일의 진행에 큰 관심을 가지고 있었다. ● 대단히 부사 ☐ 그녀는 국제 문제에 계속 깊은 관심을 가지고 있었다. ☐ 형용사 격심한, 격렬한 ☐ 지방 선거에서 격렬한 열전이 예상된다. ● 격렬하게 부사 ☐ 그 경기는 아주 격렬하게 처러질 것이다. ☐ 형용사 열망하는, 열심인 [주로 영국영어] ☐ 너는 꼭 가고 싶은 것은 아니지, 그렇지? ☐ 두 기업이 모두 합병을 열망하고 있었다. ☐ 그녀는 여전히 연락하고 지내기를 열망한다. ● 열망 불가산명사 ☐ 다른 사람을 즐겁게 해 주려는 도일의 열망 ☐ 형용사 ~에 열중하는, ~을 무척 좋아하는 [주로 영국영어] ☐ 나는 물리학과 화학을 그다지 좋아하지 않았다. ● 열중, 애호 불가산명사 ☐ 그의 예술 애호 ☐ 형용사 열렬한 [주로 영국영어] ☐ 그녀는 열렬한 아마추어 사진작가였다. ☐ 형용사 열정적인, 열심히 하는 [주로 영국영어] ☐ 그는 아주 열정적인 학생으로 아주 열심히 공부를 한다. ● 열정 불가산명사 ☐ 그 학생들의 열정 ☐ 형용사 열렬한 [주로 영국영어] ☐ 그는 평생 노동당을 열렬히 지지해 왔다. ☐ 형용사 (가격이) 경쟁력 있는, 싼 [주로 영국영어] ☐ 그 회사는 공급업자들과 아주 싼 가격으로 협상한다. ● 싸게 부사 ☐ 그 상점들은 싼값에 커튼을 제작해 주기도 한다. ☐ 구 ~에 완전히 미친 [영국영어, 비격식체, 강조] ☐ 그러면 당신은 과학에 완전히 미쳐 있진 않나요?

keep ♦♦♦ /kip/ (**keeps, keeping, kept**) ☐ V-LINK If someone **keeps** or **is kept** in a particular state, they remain in it. ☐ *The noise kept him awake.* ☐ *To keep warm they burnt wood in a rusty oil barrel.* ☐ V-T/V-I If you **keep** or you **are kept** in a particular position or place, you remain in it. ☐ *Keep away from the doors while the train is moving.* ☐ *He kept his head down, hiding his features.* ☐ V-T/V-I If you **keep off** something or **keep away from** it, you avoid it. If you **keep** out of something, you avoid getting involved in it. ☐ *I managed to stick to the diet and keep off sweet foods.* ☐ V-T If someone or something **keeps** you **from** a particular action, they prevent you from doing it. ☐ *Embarrassment has kept me from doing all sorts of things.* ☐ V-T If you **keep** something **from** someone, you do not tell them about it. ☐ *She knew that Gabriel was keeping something from her.* ☐ V-T If you **keep** doing something, you do it repeatedly or continue to do it. ☐ *I keep forgetting it's December.* ● PHRASAL VERB **Keep on** means the same as **keep**. ☐ *Did he give up or keep on trying?* ☐ V-T **Keep** is used with some nouns to indicate that someone does something for a period of time or continues to do it. For example, if you **keep a grip on** something, you continue to hold or control it. ☐ *Until last year, the regime kept a tight grip on the country.* ☐ V-T If you **keep** something, you continue to have it in your possession and do not throw it away, give it away, or sell it. ☐ *"I like this dress," she said. "Keep it. You can have it," said Daphne.* ☐ V-T If you **keep** something in a particular place, you always have it or store it in that

☐ 연결동사 (어떤 상태에) 계속 있다 ☐ 소음 때문에 그는 계속 깨어 있었다. ☐ 온기를 유지하려고 그들은 녹슨 기름통에 나무를 땠다. ☐ 타동사/자동사 (어떤 위치나 장소에) 계속 있다 ☐ 기차가 달리는 동안에는 문가에 가지 마시오. ☐ 그는 계속 고개를 숙여 자기 얼굴 모습을 숨겼다. ☐ 타동사/자동사 ~을 피하다, -하기를 피하다 ☐ 나는 용케 다이어트를 계속하고 단 음식들을 피했다. ☐ 타동사 방해하다, 막다 ☐ 당황해서 나는 아무 것도 할 수 없었다. ☐ 타동사 숨기다, 말하지 않다 ☐ 그녀는 가브리엘이 자기에게 무언가를 숨기고 있다는 것을 알았다. ☐ 타동사 계속해서 -하다 ☐ 나는 12월이라는 것을 자꾸 잊어버린다. ● 구동사 계속해서 -하다 ☐ 그가 포기했니 아니면 계속 시도했니? ☐ 타동사 계속하다, 지속하다 ☐ 작년까지, 그 정권이 나라를 철저히 통제했다. ☐ 타동사 보존하다, 간직하다 ☐ "난 이 옷이 마음에 들어."라고 그녀가 말했다. "가져, 가져도 돼."라고 대프니가 말했다. ☐ 타동사 보관하다, 저장하다 ☐ 그녀는 자기 돈을 매트리스 밑에 보관했다. ☐ 타동사 (약속을) 지키다 ☐ 나는 네가 우리 집에 와서

place so that you can use it whenever you need it. ❑ *She kept her money under the mattress.* 🔟 V-T When you **keep** something such as a promise or an appointment, you do what you said you would do. ❑ *I'm hoping you'll keep your promise to come for a long visit.* 🔢 V-T If you **keep** a record of a series of events, you write down details of it so that they can be referred to later. ❑ *Eleanor began to keep a diary.* 🔢 V-T If you **keep** yourself or **keep** someone else, you support yourself or the other person by earning enough money to provide food, clothing, money, and other necessary things. ❑ *She could just about afford to keep her five kids.* ❑ *I just cannot afford to keep myself.* 🔢 N-SING Someone's **keep** is the cost of food and other things that they need in their daily life. ❑ *Ray will earn his keep on local farms while studying.* 🔢 V-T If you **keep** animals, you own them and take care of them. ❑ *I've brought you some eggs. We keep chickens.* 🔢 V-T If someone or something **keeps** you, they delay you and make you late. ❑ *Sorry to keep you, Jack.* 🔢 V-I If food **keeps** for a certain length of time, it stays fresh and suitable to eat for that time. ❑ *Whatever is left over may be put into the refrigerator, where it will keep for 2-3 weeks.* 🔢 V-I You can say or ask how someone **is keeping** as a way of saying or asking whether they are well. [only cont] ❑ *She hasn't been keeping too well lately.* 🔢 N-COUNT A **keep** is the main tower of a medieval castle, in which people lived. ❑ *...the first stone-built castle keep in Britain.* 🔢 PHRASE If you **keep at it**, you continue doing something that you have started, even if you are tired and would prefer to stop. ❑ *It may take a number of attempts, but it is worth keeping at it.* 🔢 PHRASE If you **keep going**, you continue moving along or doing something that you have started, even if you are tired and would prefer to stop. ❑ *She forced herself to keep going.* 🔢 PHRASE If one thing is **in keeping with** another, it is suitable in relation to that thing. If one thing is **out of keeping with** another, you mean that it is not suitable in relation to that thing. ❑ *His office was in keeping with his station and experience.* 🔢 PHRASE If you **keep it up**, you continue working or trying as hard as you have been in the past. ❑ *There are fears that he will not be able to keep it up when he gets to the particularly demanding third year.* 🔢 PHRASE If you **keep** something **to yourself**, you do not tell anyone else about it. ❑ *I have to tell someone. I can't keep it to myself.* 🔢 PHRASE If you **keep yourself to yourself** or **keep to yourself**, you stay on your own most of the time and do not mix socially with other people. ❑ *He was a quiet man who kept himself to himself.* 🔢 to **keep** someone **company** →see **company**. to keep a straight face →see **face**. to **keep your head** →see **head**. to **keep pace** →see **pace**. to **keep the peace** →see **peace**. to **keep a secret** →see **secret**. to **keep time** →see **time**. to **keep track** →see **track**

▶**keep down** 🔟 PHRASAL VERB If you **keep** the number, size, or amount of something **down**, you do not let it get bigger or go higher. ❑ *The prime aim is to keep inflation down.* 🔢 PHRASAL VERB If someone **keeps** a group of people **down**, they prevent them from getting power and status and being completely free. ❑ *No matter what a woman tries to do to improve her situation, there is some barrier or attitude to keep her down.* 🔢 PHRASAL VERB If you **keep** food or drink **down**, you manage to swallow it properly and not vomit, even though you feel sick. ❑ *I tried to give her something to drink but she couldn't keep it down.*

▶**keep on** 🔟 →see **keep 6** 🔢 PHRASAL VERB If you **keep** someone **on**, you continue to employ them, for example after they are old enough to retire or after other employees have lost their jobs. ❑ *Sometimes they keep you on a bit longer if there's no one quite ready to step into your shoes.*

▶**keep to** 🔟 PHRASAL VERB If you **keep to** a rule, plan, or agreement, you do exactly what you are expected or supposed to do. ❑ *You've got to keep to the speed limit.* 🔢 PHRASAL VERB If you **keep to** something such as a path or river, you do not move away from it as you go somewhere. ❑ *Please keep to the paths.* 🔢 PHRASAL VERB If you **keep to** a particular subject, you talk only about that subject, and do not talk about anything else. ❑ *Let's keep to the subject, or you'll get me too confused.* 🔢 PHRASAL VERB If you **keep** something **to** a particular number or quantity, you limit it to that number or quantity. ❑ *Keep costs to a minimum.*

▶**keep up** 🔟 PHRASAL VERB If you **keep up with** someone or something that is moving near you, you move at the same speed. ❑ *She shook her head and started to walk on. He kept up with her.* 🔢 PHRASAL VERB To **keep up with** something that is changing means to be able to cope with the change, usually by changing at the same rate. ❑ *The union called the strike to press for wage increases which keep up with inflation.* 🔢 PHRASAL VERB If you **keep up with** your work or with other people, you manage to do or understand all your work, or to do or understand it as well as other people. ❑ *Penny tended to work through her lunch hour in an effort to keep up with her work.* 🔢 PHRASAL VERB If you **keep up with** what is happening, you make sure that you know about it. ❑ *She did not bother to keep up with the news.* 🔢 PHRASAL VERB If you **keep** something **up**, you continue to do it or provide it. ❑ *I was so hungry all the time that I could not keep the diet up for longer than a month.* 🔢 PHRASAL VERB If you **keep** something **up**, you prevent it from growing less in amount, level, or degree. ❑ *There will be a major incentive among TV channels to keep standards up.* 🔢 →see also **keep 22**

keep|er /kiːpər/ (**keepers**) 🔟 N-COUNT In football, a **keeper** is a play in which the quarterback keeps the ball. [AM] 🔢 N-COUNT In soccer, the **keeper** is the same as the **goalkeeper**. [BRIT, INFORMAL] 🔢 N-COUNT A **keeper** at a zoo is a person who takes care of the animals.

ken|nel /kɛnˀl/ (**kennels**) 🔟 N-COUNT **Kennels** or a **kennels** or a **kennel** is a place where dogs are bred and trained, or cared for when their owners are away. ❑ *The guard dog was now in kennels as it was not aggressive.* 🔢 N-COUNT A **kennel** is a small building made especially for a dog to sleep in. [mainly BRIT; AM usually **doghouse**] ❑ *A sick dog will hide in its kennel and not eat for days.*

kept /kɛpt/ **Kept** is the past tense and past participle of **keep**.

kerb /kɜːrb/ (**kerbs**) [AM **curb**] N-COUNT The **kerb** is the raised edge of a sidewalk or pavement which separates it from the road. ❑ *Stewart stepped off the kerb.*

오래 머물겠다는 약속을 지키길 바라고 있어. 🔟 타동사 (일기 등을) 쓰다 ❑ 엘리너는 일기를 쓰기 시작했다. 🔢 타동사 부양하다, 먹여 살리다 ❑ 그녀는 자기의 다섯 자녀를 겨우 부양할 수 있을 정도였다. ❑ 나는 내 자신을 부양할 정도도 안돼. 🔢 단수명사 생활비 ❑ 레이는 학교에 다니면서 동네 농장에서 생활비를 벌 것이다. 🔢 타동사 (가축 등을) 기르다 ❑ 네게 계란을 좀 가져왔어. 우린 닭을 치거든. 🔢 타동사 붙들어 두다 ❑ 붙들어 두어서 미안해, 잭. 🔢 자동사 (음식이 상하지 않고) 유지되다 ❑ 남는 것은 뭐든 냉장고에 넣어 둘 수 있는데, 거기 두면 2-3주 정도는 간다. 🔢 자동사 (어떻게) 지내다 ❑ 그녀는 최근에 그다지 잘 지내지 못했다. 🔢 가산명사 (성의) 본성(本城), 중심 탑 ❑ 영국 최초의 석조 본성. 🔢 구 꾸준히 해내다 ❑ 여러 번 시도해야 할지도 모르지만, 그것은 애써 해 볼 만한 가치가 있다. 🔢 구 계속하다 ❑ 그녀는 억지로 계속 해 나갔다. 🔢 구 -와 맞는, -와 어울리는; -와 맞지 않는 ❑ 그의 직책은 그의 신분과 경륜에 걸맞았다. 🔢 구 (곤란한 무릅쓰고) 계속하다 ❑ 그가 특히 노력을 요하는 3년째가 되면 계속 버텨 낼 수 없을 것이라는 우려가 있다. 🔢 구 (정보 등을) 혼자만 알다, 비밀로 하다 ❑ 난 누군가에게 얘기해야만 해. 혼자만 알고 있을 수 없어. 🔢 구 교제를 피하다, 사람들과 어울리지 않다 ❑ 그는 사람들과 안 어울리는 조용한 사람이었다.

🔟 구동사 억제하다, 늘리지 않다 ❑ 급선무는 인플레를 억제하는 것이다. 🔢 구동사 억압하다 ❑ 여성이 자신의 지위를 향상시키기 위해 무엇을 하더라도, 그들을 억압하는 장애나 사고방식이 있다. 🔢 구동사 (음식물 등을) 삼키다, 넘기다 ❑ 나는 그녀에게 마실 것을 주려고 했지만 그녀는 넘기지를 못했다.

🔢 구동사 계속 고용해 두다 ❑ 당신 자리를 메울 사람이 마땅하지 않을 때로 좀 더 오래 고용하기도 한다.

🔟 구동사 (규칙 등을) 지키다, 고수하다 ❑ 제한 속도를 지켜야 한다. 🔢 구동사 (길 등을) 따라 나아가다, 벗어나지 않고 따라가다 ❑ 길을 따라 가시오. 🔢 구동사 (주제에서) 벗어나지 않다 ❑ 주제에서 벗어나지 맙시다. 안 그러면 제가 너무 혼란스러워져요. 🔢 구동사 (수나 양을) 제한하다 ❑ 비용을 최소로 제한하시오.

🔟 구동사 보조를 맞추다 ❑ 그녀는 머리를 흔들고 걷기 시작했다. 그는 그녀와 보조를 맞추었다. 🔢 구동사 (시류에) 뒤처지지 않다 ❑ 노동조합은 인플레에 걸맞은 임금 인상을 요구하는 파업을 지시했다. 🔢 구동사 (일을) 때맞추어 해내다; (다른 사람을) 뒤처지지 않다 ❑ 페니는 자기 일을 때맞추어 해내려고 점심시간 내내 일하곤 했다. 🔢 구동사 (소식 등을) 알고 있다 ❑ 그녀는 애써 뉴스를 다 알려고 하지 않았다. 🔢 구동사 계속하다, 계속 조달하다 ❑ 나는 항상 너무도 배가 고파서 다이어트를 한 달 이상은 계속할 수 없었다. 🔢 구동사 (수준 등을) 유지하다 ❑ 텔레비전 방송사에는 수준을 유지하게 하는 주요한 자극 요인이 있을 것이다.

🔟 가산명사 키퍼 (미식축구에서 쿼터백이 공을 갖고 달리는 공격법) [미국영어] 🔢 가산명사 (축구) 골키퍼 [영국영어, 비격식체] 🔢 가산명사 사육사

🔟 가산명사 개 사육장 ❑ 그 감시견은 난폭하지 않아서 이제 사육장에 들어가 있었다. 🔢 가산명사 개 집 [주로 영국영어; 미국영어 대개 doghouse] ❑ 병든 개는 제 집에 숨어서 며칠씩 먹지도 않는다.

keep의 과거 및 과거 분사

[미국영어 curb] 가산명사 (인도와 차도 사이의) 연석 ❑ 스튜어트는 연석 아래로 발을 내디뎠다.

kero|sene /kɛrəsin/ N-UNCOUNT Kerosene is a clear, strong-smelling liquid which is used as a fuel, for example in heaters and lamps. [mainly AM; BRIT usually **paraffin**] ❑ ...a kerosene lamp. →see **dry cleaning**

불가산명사 등유, 등불용 석유 [주로 미국영어; 영국영어 대개 paraffin] ❑ 등유 램프.

ket|tle /kɛtᵊl/ (**kettles**) ◼ N-COUNT A **kettle** is a metal pot for boiling or cooking things in. [mainly AM; BRIT **pan**] ❑ Put the meat into a small kettle. ◼ N-COUNT A **kettle** is a covered container that you use for boiling water. It has a handle, and a spout for the water to come out of. [mainly BRIT] ❑ I'll put the kettle on and make us some tea. ● N-COUNT A **kettle** of water is the amount of water contained in a kettle. [AM usually **teakettle**] ❑ Pour a kettle of boiling water over the onions. ◼ PHRASE If you say that something is **a different kettle of fish**, you mean that it is very different from another related thing that you are talking about. [INFORMAL] ❑ Playing for the reserve team is a totally different kettle of fish.

◼ 가산명사 솥 [주로 미국영어; 영국영어 pan] ❑ 고기를 작은 솥에 담으시오. ◼ 가산명사 주전자 [주로 영국영어] ❑ 내가 주전자를 불에 올려 차를 끓일게. ● 가산명사 한 주전자 (분량) [미국영어 대개 teakettle] ❑ 양파에 끓는 물 한 주전자를 부으시오. ◼ 구 별 문제, 다른 사항 [비격식체] ❑ 예비 팀에서 뛰는 것은 전혀 다른 문제이다.

key ♦♦◇ /ki/ (**keys, keying, keyed**) ◼ N-COUNT A **key** is a specially shaped piece of metal that you place in a lock and turn in order to open or lock a door, or to start or stop the engine of a vehicle. ❑ They put the key in the door and entered. ◼ N-COUNT The **keys** on a computer keyboard or typewriter are the buttons that you press in order to operate it. ❑ Finally, press the Delete key. ◼ N-COUNT The **keys** of a piano or organ are the long narrow pieces of wood or plastic that you press in order to play it. ❑ ...the black and white keys on a piano keyboard. ◼ N-VAR In music, a **key** is a scale of musical notes that starts on one specific note. ❑ ...the key of A minor. ◼ N-COUNT The **key** on a map or diagram or in a technical book is a list of the symbols or abbreviations used and their meanings. ❑ You will find a key at the front of the book. ◼ ADJ The **key** person or thing in a group is the most important one. [ADJ n] ❑ He is expected to be the key witness at the trial. ◼ N-COUNT The **key to** a desirable situation or result is the way in which it can be achieved. ❑ The key to success is to be ready from the start. →see **graph**

◼ 가산명사 열쇠 ❑ 그들은 문에 열쇠를 꽂고 들어갔다. ◼ 가산명사 (컴퓨터) 키 ❑ 마지막으로, 삭제키를 누르시오. ◼ 가산명사 (피아노나 오르간의) 건, 키 ❑ 피아노 건반의 검은 건과 흰 건들 ◼ 가산명사 또는 불가산명사 (음악) 조 ❑ 가단조 ◼ 가산명사 기호 줄이, 약어표 ❑ 책 맨 앞에 약어표가 있다. ◼ 형용사 핵심의 ❑ 그가 재판에서 핵심 증인이 될 것으로 예상된다. ◼ 가산명사 비결 ❑ 성공의 비결은 시작부터 만반의 준비를 갖추는 것이다.

Thesaurus
key의 참조어

N. code, explanation, guide ◼

ADJ. critical, important, major, vital ◼

Word Partnership
key의 연어

V. turn a key ◼

N. key **component**, key **decision**, key **factor**, key **figure**, key **ingredient**, key **issue**, key **official**, key **player**, key **point**, key **question**, key **role**, key **word** ◼

key **to success** ◼

▶**key in** PHRASAL VERB If you **key** something **in**, you put information into a computer or you give the computer a particular instruction by typing the information or instruction on the keyboard. ❑ Brian keyed in his personal code.

구동사 입력하다 ❑ 브라이언은 자신의 개인 코드를 입력했다.

key|board /kibord/ (**keyboards**) ◼ N-COUNT The **keyboard** of a typewriter or computer is the set of keys that you press in order to operate it. ❑ He was in his office, battering the keyboard of his computer as if it were an old manual typewriter. ◼ N-COUNT The **keyboard** of a piano or organ is the set of black and white keys that you press in order to play it. ❑ Tanya's hands rippled over the keyboard. ◼ N-COUNT People sometimes refer to musical instruments that have a keyboard as **keyboards**. ❑ ...Sean O'Hagan on keyboards. →see **computer** →see Picture Dictionary: **keyboard**

◼ 가산명사 자판 ❑ 그는 사무실에서 자기 컴퓨터의 자판을 마치 옛날 수동 타자기인 것처럼 세게 두드려 대고 있었다. ◼ 가산명사 건반 ❑ 타냐의 손이 건반 위를 물결치듯 흘러갔다. ◼ 가산명사 키보드, 건반 악기 ❑ 키보드 연주에 손 오허건

key card (**key cards**) N-COUNT A **key card** is a small plastic card which you can use instead of a key to open a door or barrier, for example in some hotels and parking lots. ❑ The electronic key card to Julie's room would not work.

가산명사 카드 키 ❑ 줄리 방의 전자 카드 키가 작동하지 않았다.

a
b
c
d
e
f
g
h
i
j
k
l
m
n
o
p
q
r
s
t
u
v
w
x
y
z

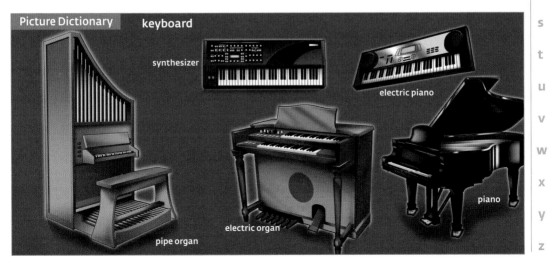

Picture Dictionary keyboard

synthesizer

electric piano

piano

electric organ

pipe organ

key|note /kiːnoʊt/ (**keynotes**) N-COUNT The **keynote** of a policy, speech, or idea is the main theme of it or the part of it that is emphasized the most. ▢ He would be setting out his plans for the party in a keynote speech.

가산명사 (연설 등의) 요지, 기조 ▢ 그는 기조연설에서 당을 위한 자신의 계획을 설명할 것이다.

key|pad /kiːpæd/ (**keypads**) N-COUNT The **keypad** on a modern telephone is the set of buttons that you press in order to operate it. Some other machines, such as ATMs, also have a keypad. ▢ Two presses on the keypad, after the call has started, switches the loudspeaker on.

가산명사 (전화기 등의) 숫자판 ▢ 통화가 시작된 후, 숫자판을 두 번 누르면 스피커가 켜진다.

key|stone /kiːstoʊn/ (**keystones**) N-COUNT A **keystone of** a policy, system, or process is an important part of it, which is the basis for later developments. ▢ The government's determination to beat inflation has so far been the keystone of its economic policy.

가산명사 초석, 기반 ▢ 인플레를 잡겠다는 정부의 결의가 지금까지 경제 정책의 기반이 되어 왔다.

key|stroke /kiːstroʊk/ (**keystrokes**) N-COUNT A **keystroke** is one touch of one of the keys on a computer or typewriter keyboard. ▢ With a few keystrokes, Rebecca was connected to her computer at Liberty Air Service.

가산명사 (타자기 자판의) 키 누르기 ▢ 자판의 키를 몇 번 눌러서 레베카는 리버티 항공사의 자기 컴퓨터에 접속되었다.

kg kg is an abbreviation for **kilogram** or **kilograms**.

kilogram 또는 kilograms의 약자

kha|ki /kæki, BRIT kɑːki/ **1** N-UNCOUNT **Khaki** is a strong material of a greenish brown color, used especially to make uniforms for soldiers. ▢ On each side of me was a figure in khaki. **2** COLOR Something that is **khaki** is greenish brown in color. ▢ He was dressed in khaki trousers.

1 불가산명사 카키색 군복용 천 ▢ 내 양 쪽에 군복을 입은 사람이 한 명씩 있었다. **2** 색채어 카키색, 녹갈색 ▢ 그는 카키색 바지를 입고 있었다.

kick ♦♦◇ /kɪk/ (**kicks, kicking, kicked**) **1** V-T/V-I If you **kick** someone or something, you hit them forcefully with your foot. ▢ He kicked the door hard. ▢ He threw me to the ground and started to kick. ● N-COUNT **Kick** is also a noun. ▢ He suffered a kick to the knee. **2** V-T When you **kick** a ball or other object, you hit it with your foot so that it moves through the air. ▢ I went to kick the ball and I completely missed it. ▢ He kicked the ball away. ● N-COUNT **Kick** is also a noun. ▢ Schmeichel swooped to save the first kick from Borisov. **3** V-T/V-I If you **kick** or if you **kick** your legs, you move your legs with very quick, small, and forceful movements, once or repeatedly. ▢ They were dragged away struggling and kicking. ▢ First he kicked the left leg, then he kicked the right. ● PHRASAL VERB **Kick out** means the same as kick. ▢ As its rider tried to free it, the horse kicked out and rolled over, crushing her. **4** V-T If you **kick** your legs, you lift your legs up very high one after the other, for example when you are dancing. ▢ ...kicking his legs like a Can Can dancer. **5** V-T If you **kick** a habit, you stop doing something that is bad for you and that you find difficult to stop doing. [INFORMAL] ▢ She's kicked her drug habit and learned that her life has value. **6** N-SING If something gives you **a kick**, it makes you feel very excited or very happy for a short period of time. [INFORMAL] ▢ I got a kick out of seeing my name in print. **7** PHRASE If you say that someone **kicks** you **when** you **are down**, you think they are behaving unfairly because they are attacking you when you are in a weak position. ▢ In the end I just couldn't kick Jimmy when he was down. **8** PHRASE If you say that someone does something **for kicks**, you mean that they do it because they think it will be exciting. [INFORMAL] ▢ They made a few small bets for kicks. **9** PHRASE If you say that someone is dragged **kicking and screaming into** a particular course of action, you are emphasizing that they are very unwilling to do what they are being made to do. [EMPHASIS] ▢ He had to be dragged kicking and screaming into action. **10** PHRASE If you describe an event as **a kick in the teeth**, you are emphasizing that it is very disappointing and upsetting. [INFORMAL, EMPHASIS] ▢ We've been struggling for years and it's a real kick in the teeth to see a new band make it ahead of us. **11** to **kick up a fuss** →see **fuss**

1 타동사/자동사 차다 ▢ 그는 문을 세게 걷어찼다. ▢ 그는 나를 바닥에 던지고 발로 차기 시작했다. ● 가산명사 차기, 발길질 ▢ 그는 무릎을 걷어 채였다. **2** 타동사 차다 ▢ 나는 공을 차려 나갔지만 완전히 놓쳤다. ▢ 그는 공을 멀리 차냈다. ● 가산명사 공차기, 킥 ▢ 슈마이헬은 보리소프가 첫 번째 찬 볼을 잡으려고 내리덮쳤다. **3** 타동사/자동사 발길질하다 ▢ 그들은 끌려가면서 버둥거리고 발길질을 해댔다. ▢ 처음에 그는 왼다리로 차고, 그 다음에 오른다리로 찼다. ● 구동사 발길질하다 ▢ 기수가 풀어 주려고 하자, 말은 발길질을 하고, 뒹굴며 그녀를 깔아뭉갰다. **4** 타동사 (다리를) 높이 차서 올리다 ▢ 그가 캉캉춤 댄서처럼 다리를 높이 차면서 **5** 타동사 (나쁜 습관을) 끊다 [비격식체] ▢ 그녀는 마약하던 습관을 끊고 자신의 삶이 소중함을 배웠다. **6** 단수명사 자극, 흥분 [비격식체] ▢ 나는 내 이름이 인쇄된 것을 보고 흥분했다. **7** 구 약점을 악용하다, 일진 데 덮치다 ▢ 결국 난 넘어진 지미에게 발길질을 할 수는 없었다. **8** 구 재미 삼아, 스릴을 맛보려고 [비격식체] ▢ 그들은 재미삼아 약간씩 돈을 걸었다. **9** 구 억지로, 강제로 [강조] ▢ 그는 억지로 시켜야만 일을 했다. **10** 구 참담함, 쓰라림 [비격식체, 강조] ▢ 우리는 몇 년을 노력해 왔는데, 새 악단이 우리보다 앞서 나가는 것을 보니 정말 참담했다.

Thesaurus kick의 참조어

V. abandon, give up, quit, stop; (ant.) start, take up **5**

N. enjoyment, excitement, fun, thrill **6**

Word Partnership kick의 연어

N. kick **a door 1**
kick **a ball**, **penalty** kick **2**
kick **a habit**, kick **smoking 5**

▶**kick off 1** PHRASAL VERB In soccer or football, when the players **kick off**, they start a game by kicking the ball. ▢ Liverpool kicked off an hour ago. **2** PHRASAL VERB In football, when the players **kick off**, they resume a game by kicking the ball. **3** PHRASAL VERB If an event, game, series, or discussion **kicks off**, or **is kicked off**, it begins. ▢ The shows kick off on October 24th. ▢ The Mayor kicked off the party. **4** PHRASAL VERB If you **kick off** your shoes, you shake your feet so that your shoes come off. ▢ She stretched out on the sofa and kicked off her shoes. **5** PHRASAL VERB To **kick** someone **off** an area of land means to force them to leave it. [INFORMAL] ▢ We can't kick them off the island.

1 구동사 (축구나 미식축구) 경기를 시작하다 ▢ 리버풀이 한 시간 전에 경기를 시작했다. **2** 구동사 (미식축구에서 경기를) 속개하다 **3** 구동사 (토론 등이) 시작되다 ▢ 공연은 10월 24일에 시작한다. ▢ 시장이 파티를 시작했다. **4** 구동사 (신발을) 차서 벗다 ▢ 그녀는 소파에 쭉 뻗고 누워서 신발을 벗어던졌다. **5** 구동사 -에서 쫓아내다 [비격식체] ▢ 우리는 그들을 섬에서 쫓아낼 수 없다.

▶**kick out** PHRASAL VERB To **kick** someone **out of** a place means to force them to leave it. [INFORMAL] ▢ The country's leaders kicked five foreign journalists out of the country. →see also **kick 3**

구동사 -에서 쫓아내다 [비격식체] ▢ 그 나라의 지도자들이 5명의 외신 기자들을 추방했다.

kickoff (**kickoffs**) [BRIT **kick-off**] **1** N-VAR In football or soccer, the **kickoff** is the time at which a particular game starts. ▢ Hakan Sukur netted the goal just 10.8 seconds after the kickoff. **2** N-COUNT In football, a **kickoff** is the kick that begins a play, for example at the beginning of a half or after a touchdown or goal has been scored. [AM] ▢ Gunn fumbled away the opening kickoff for the second straight week. **3** N-SING The **kickoff** of an event or activity is its beginning. [INFORMAL] ▢ This Memorial Day weekend marks the kickoff of the summer vacation season for Americans.

[영국영어 kick-off] **1** 가산명사 또는 불가산명사 (미식축구 또는 축구에서) 경기 시작 시간 ▢ 하칸 수쿠르가 경기 시작 10.8초 만에 골을 넣었다. **2** 가산명사 (미식축구에서) 킥오프 [미국영어] ▢ 건은 둘째 주 내내 킥오프 볼을 놓쳤다. **3** 단수명사 시작, 개시 [비격식체] ▢ 이번 전몰장병 기념일 주말이 미국인들에게는 여름휴가 시즌의 시작이다.

kick-start (**kick-starts, kick-starting, kick-started**) also **kickstart 1** V-T To **kick-start** a process that has stopped working or progressing is to take a

1 타동사 부양하다 ▢ 대통령은 금리를 큰 폭으로 인하하여 경기를 부양하기로 결정했다. ● 가산명사

course of action that will quickly start it going again. ❑ *The President has chosen to kick-start the economy by slashing interest rates.* ● N-COUNT **Kick-start** is also a noun. ❑ *The housing market needs a kick-start.* ② V-T If you **kick-start** a motorcycle, you press the lever that starts it with your foot. ❑ *He lifted the bike off its stand and kick-started it.*

kid ◆◆◇ /kɪd/ (**kids, kidding, kidded**) ① N-COUNT You can refer to a child as a **kid**. [INFORMAL] ❑ *They've got three kids.* ② N-COUNT A **kid** is a young goat. ③ V-T/V-I If you **are kidding**, you are saying something that is not really true, as a joke. [INFORMAL] [usu cont] ❑ *I'm not kidding, Frank. There's a cow out there, just standing around.* ❑ *I'm just kidding.* ④ V-T If you **kid** someone, you tease them. ❑ *He liked to kid Ingrid a lot.* ⑤ V-T If people **kid themselves**, they allow themselves to believe something that is not true because they wish that it was true. ❑ *We're kidding ourselves, Bill. We're not winning, we're not even doing well.* ⑥ PHRASE You can say "**you've got to be kidding**" or "**you must be kidding**" to someone if they have said something that you think is ridiculous or completely untrue. [INFORMAL, FEELINGS] ❑ *You've got to be kidding! I can't live here!*

① 가산명사 아이, 어린이 [비격식체] ❑ 그들은 아이가 셋이다. ② 가산명사 새끼 염소 ③ 타동사/자동사 농담하다 [비격식체] ❑ 농담이 아니야, 프랭크. 저쪽에 소 한 마리가 있는데 그냥 서 있지. ❑ 그냥 농담이야. ④ 타동사 놀리다 ❑ 그는 잉그리드를 놀려 주는 것을 아주 좋아했다. ⑤ 타동사 속이다 ❑ 우린 우리 자신을 속이고 있어, 빌. 우리는 이기고 있지 않아. 제대로 하지도 못하고 있어. ⑥ 구 농담하지 마, 장난하지 마 [비격식체, 감정 개입] ❑ 장난하지 마! 난 여기에 살 수 없어!

Word Partnership   *kid*의 연어

N.	kid **brother/sister** ①
ADJ.	**fat** kid, **friendly** kid, **good** kid, **little** kid, **new** kid, **nice** kid, **poor** kid, **skinny** kid, **smart** kid, **tough** kid, **young** kid ①
V.	**raise a** kid ①

---

kid|nap /kɪdnæp/ (**kidnaps, kidnapping, kidnapped**) [AM also **kidnaped, kidnaping**] ① V-T/V-I To **kidnap** someone is to take them away illegally and by force, and usually to hold them prisoner in order to demand something from their family, employer, or government. ❑ *Police in Brazil uncovered a plot to kidnap him.* ❑ *They were middle-class university students, intelligent and educated, yet they chose to kidnap and kill.* ● **kid|nap|per** (**kidnappers**) N-COUNT ❑ *His kidnappers have threatened that they will kill him unless three militants are released from prison.* ● **kid|nap|ping** (**kidnappings**) N-VAR ❑ *Two youngsters have been arrested and charged with kidnapping.* ② N-VAR **Kidnap** or a **kidnap** is the crime of taking someone away by force. ❑ *Stewart denies attempted murder and kidnap.*

[미국영어 kidnaped, kidnaping] ① 타동사/자동사 유괴하다, 납치하다 ❑ 브라질 경찰이 그를 납치하려는 음모를 적발했다. ❑ 그들은 중산층 대학생들로 지적이고 교양이 있었는데, 납치하고 살해할 생각을 했다. ● 유괴범, 납치범 가산명사 ❑ 그의 납치범들은 3명의 투사를 감옥에서 석방하지 않으면 그를 죽이겠다고 협박했다. ● 유괴, 납치 가산명사 또는 불가산명사 ❑ 두 청소년이 체포되고 유괴 혐의로 기소되었다. ② 가산명사 또는 불가산명사 유괴, 납치 ❑ 스튜어트는 살인 미수와 유괴 혐의를 부인한다.

kid|ney /kɪdni/ (**kidneys**) ① N-COUNT Your **kidneys** are the organs in your body that take waste matter from your blood and send it out of your body as urine. ❑ *...a kidney transplant.* ② N-VAR **Kidneys** are the kidneys of an animal, for example a lamb, calf, or pig, that are eaten as meat. ❑ *...lambs' kidneys.* →see **donor**

① 가산명사 신장 ❑ 신장 이식 ② 가산명사 또는 불가산명사 콩팥 ❑ 양의 콩팥

kill ◆◆◆ /kɪl/ (**kills, killing, killed**) ① V-T/V-I If a person, animal, or other living thing **is killed**, something or someone causes them to die. ❑ *More than 1,000 people have been killed by the armed forces.* ❑ *He had attempted to kill himself on several occasions.* ● **kill|ing** N-UNCOUNT ❑ *There is tension in the region following the killing of seven civilians.* ② N-COUNT The act of killing an animal after hunting it is referred to as **the kill**. ❑ *After the kill, they were looking forward to a meal.* ③ V-T If someone or something **kills** a project, activity, or idea, they completely destroy or end it. ❑ *His objective was to kill the space station project altogether.* ● PHRASAL VERB **Kill off** means the same as **kill**. ❑ *He would soon launch a second offensive, killing off the peace process.* ④ V-T If something **kills** pain, it weakens it so that it is no longer as strong as it was. ❑ *He was forced to take opium to kill the pain.* ⑤ V-T If you say that something **is killing** you, you mean that it is causing you physical or emotional pain. [INFORMAL] [only cont] ❑ *My feet are killing me.* ⑥ V-T If you say that you **kill yourself to** do something, you are emphasizing that you make a great effort to do it, even though it causes you a lot of trouble or suffering. [INFORMAL, EMPHASIS] ❑ *You shouldn't always have to kill yourself to do well.* ⑦ V-T If you say that you will **kill** someone for something they have done, you are emphasizing that you are extremely angry with them. [EMPHASIS] ❑ *Tell Richard I'm going to kill him when I get hold of him.* ⑧ V-T If you say that something will not **kill** you, you mean that it is not really as difficult or unpleasant as it might seem. [INFORMAL] ❑ *Three or four more weeks won't kill me!* ⑨ V-T If you **are killing** time, you are doing something because you have some time available, not because you really want to do it. ❑ *I'm just killing time until I can talk to the other witnesses.*

① 타동사/자동사 목숨을 잃다 ❑ 1,000명 이상의 사람들이 군대에 의해서 목숨을 잃었다. ❑ 그는 여러 차례 자살하려고 시도했다. ● 살해 불가산명사 ❑ 7명의 시민이 살해당한 후 그 지역에는 긴장이 감돈다. ② 가산명사 (사냥한 동물을) 죽이기 ❑ 사냥감을 죽인 후 그들은 식사를 고대했다. ③ 타동사 (계획 등을) 폐기하다 ❑ 그의 목표는 우주정거장 계획을 완전히 폐기하는 것이었다. ● 구동사 (계획 등을) 폐기하다 ❑ 그는 평화 진행 절차를 폐기하면서 곧 두 번째 공격을 가할 것이다. ④ 타동사 (통증을) 없애다 ❑ 그는 통증을 없애기 위해 아편을 맞아야 했다. ⑤ 타동사 (육체적 또는 정신적으로) 죽을 지경이 되게 하다 [비격식체] ❑ 난 다리가 아파 죽겠다. ⑥ 타동사 죽도록 ~하다 [비격식체, 강조] ❑ 항상 죽도록 잘 하려고 할 필요는 없다. ⑦ 타동사 죽여버리다 ❑ 리처드에게 내가 잡으면 죽여 버린다고 해. ⑧ 타동사 심한 고통을 주다 [비격식체] ❑ 3-4주 정도 더 해도 안 죽어! ⑨ 타동사 (남는 시간을) 보내다 ❑ 나는 다른 목격자들에게 얘기할 수 있을 때까지 그냥 시간을 보내고 있다.

There are several words which mean similar things to **kill**. To **murder** someone means to kill them deliberately. **Assassinate** is used to talk about the murder of an important person, often for political reasons. If a large number of people are murdered, the words **slaughter** or **massacre** are sometimes used. **Slaughter** can also be used to talk about killing animals for their meat.

---

kill과 뜻이 비슷한 단어가 몇 개 있다. 누구를 murder하는 것은 일부러 죽인다는 의미이다. assassinate는 흔히 정치적 이유로 요인을 살해하는 것을 말할 때 쓰인다. 많은 사람들이 살해당하는 경우에는 가끔 slaughter나 massacre가 쓰이기도 한다. slaughter는 고기를 얻으려고 짐승을 도축하는 것을 말할 때도 쓴다.

⑩ PHRASE If you say that you will do something **if it kills** you, you are emphasizing that you are determined to do it even though it is extremely difficult or painful. [EMPHASIS] ❑ *I'll make this marriage work if it kills me.* ⑪ PHRASE If you say that you **killed yourself laughing**, you are emphasizing that you laughed a lot because you thought something was extremely funny. [INFORMAL, EMPHASIS] ❑ *I eventually got to the top about an hour after everyone else, and they were all killing themselves laughing.* ⑫ PHRASE If you **move in for the kill** or if you **close in for the kill**, you take advantage of a changed situation in order to do something that you have been preparing to do. ❑ *Seeing his chance, Dennis moved in for the kill.* ⑬ **dressed to kill** →see **dressed**. **to be killed outright** →see **outright** →see **war**

⑩ 구 죽어도 [강조] ❑ 나는 죽어도 이 결혼 생활이 잘 되도록 할 것이다. ⑪ 구 우스워 죽다 [비격식체, 강조] ❑ 내가 마침내 다른 사람보다 한 시간 정도 후에 정상에 이르자 그들이 모두 우스워 죽으려 했다. ⑫ 구 결정타를 가할 준비를 하다 ❑ 호기임을 알고 데니스는 결정타를 가할 준비를 했다.

Thesaurus   *kill*의 참조어

V.	execute, murder, put down, wipe out ①

▶kill off ■ →see kill 3 ■ PHRASAL VERB If you say that a group or an amount of something **has been killed off**, you mean that all of them or all of it have been killed or destroyed. ❏ *Their natural predators have been killed off.* ❏ *It is an effective treatment for the bacteria and does kill it off.*

■ 구동사 절멸하다 ❏ 그들의 천적들이 절멸했다. ❏ 그것은 세균에 효과적인 치료법이며 세균을 박멸시킨다.

kill|er ♦♢♢ /kɪlər/ (**killers**) ■ N-COUNT A **killer** is a person who has killed someone, or who intends to kill someone. ❏ *The police are searching for his killers.* ■ N-COUNT You can refer to something that causes death or is likely to cause death as a **killer**. ❏ *Heart disease is the biggest killer of men in most developed countries.*

■ 가산명사 살인자, 살해범 ❏ 경찰이 그를 살해한 자들을 찾고 있다. ■ 가산명사 목숨을 앗아가는 것 ❏ 대부분의 선진국에서 심장병은 남성 사망의 가장 큰 원인이다.

kill|ing ♦♢♢ /kɪlɪŋ/ (**killings**) ■ N-COUNT A **killing** is an act of deliberately killing a person. ❏ *This is a brutal killing.* ■ PHRASE If you **make a killing**, you make a large profit very quickly and easily. [INFORMAL] ❏ *They have made a killing on the deal.*

■ 가산명사 살해, 살인 ❏ 이건 잔인한 살인이다. ■ 구 한몫 잡다 [비격식체] ❏ 그들은 그 거래로 한몫 잡았다.

kilo /kiːloʊ/ (**kilos**) N-COUNT A **kilo** is the same as a **kilogram**. ❏ *He'd lost ten kilos in weight.*

가산명사 킬로 ❏ 그는 몸무게가 10킬로 빠졌다.

Word Link   kilo ≈ thousand : kilobyte, kilogram, kilometer

---

kilo|byte /kɪləbaɪt/ (**kilobytes**) N-COUNT In computing, a **kilobyte** is one thousand bytes of data.

가산명사 킬로바이트

kilo|gram /kɪləgræm/ (**kilograms**) [BRIT also **kilogramme**] N-COUNT A **kilogram** is a metric unit of weight. One kilogram is a thousand grams, or a thousandth of a metric ton, and is equal to 2.2 pounds. ❏ *...a parcel weighing around 4.5 kilograms.*

[영국영어 kilogramme] 가산명사 킬로그램 ❏ 약 4.5킬로그램 무게의 소포

kilo|hertz /kɪləhɜːrts/

Kilohertz is both the singular and the plural form.

kilohertz는 단수형 및 복수형이다.

N-COUNT A **kilohertz** is a unit of measurement of radio waves. One kilohertz is a thousand hertz. ❏ *Their instruments detected very faint radiowaves at a frequency of 3 kilohertz.*

가산명사 킬로헤르츠 ❏ 그들의 장비는 3킬로헤르츠 주파수의 아주 약한 전파를 탐지했다.

Word Link   meter ≈ measuring : kilometer, meter, perimeter

---

kilo|meter ♦♢♢ /kɪləmiːtər, kɪlɒmɪtər/ (**kilometers**) [BRIT **kilometre**] N-COUNT A **kilometer** is a metric unit of distance or length. One kilometer is a thousand meters and is equal to 0.62 miles. ❏ *...only one kilometer from the border.*

[영국영어 kilometre] 가산명사 킬로미터 ❏ 국경에서 단지 1킬로미터

kilo|watt /kɪləwɒt/ (**kilowatts**) N-COUNT A **kilowatt** is a unit of power. One kilowatt is a thousand watts. ❏ *...a prototype system which produces 25 kilowatts of power.*

가산명사 킬로와트 ❏ 25킬로와트의 전력을 생산하는 전형적인 시스템

kin /kɪn/ N-PLURAL Your **kin** are your relatives. [DIALECT or OLD-FASHIONED] ❏ *She has gone to live with her husband's kin.* →see also **next of kin**

복수명사 친족, 친척 [방언 또는 구식어] ❏ 그녀는 시가 쪽 사람들과 같이 살러 갔다.

---

kind

① NOUN USES AND PHRASES
② ADJECTIVE USES

---

① **kind** ♦♦♦ /kaɪnd/ (**kinds**) ■ N-COUNT If you talk about a particular **kind of** thing, you are talking about one of the types or sorts of that thing. ❏ *The party needs a different kind of leadership.* ❏ *Had Jamie ever been in any kind of trouble?* ■ N-COUNT If you refer to someone's **kind**, you are referring to all the other people that are like them or that belong to the same class or set. [DISAPPROVAL] ❏ *I can take care of your kind.* ■ PHRASE You can use **all kinds of** to emphasize that there are a great number and variety of particular things or people. [EMPHASIS] ❏ *Adoption can fail for all kinds of reasons.* ■ PHRASE You use **kind of** when you want to say that something or someone can be roughly described in a particular way. [SPOKEN, VAGUENESS] ❏ *It was kind of sad, really.* ■ PHRASE You can use **of a kind** to indicate that something is not as good as it might be expected to be, but that it seems to be the best that is possible or available. ❏ *She finds solace of a kind in alcohol.* ■ PHRASE If you refer to someone or something as **one of a kind**, you mean that there is nobody or nothing else like them. [APPROVAL] ❏ *She's a very unusual woman, one of a kind.* ■ PHRASE If you refer, for example, to **two, three,** or **four of a kind**, you mean two, three, or four similar people or things that seem to go well or belong together. ❏ *They were two of a kind, from the same sort of background.* ■ PHRASE If you respond **in kind**, you react to something that someone has done to you by doing the same thing to them. ❏ *They hurled defiant taunts at the riot police, who responded in kind.* ■ PHRASE If you pay a debt **in kind**, you pay it in the form of goods or services and not money. ❏ *...benefits in kind.*

■ 가산명사 종류 ❏ 그 당은 다른 종류의 지도력을 필요로 한다. ❏ 제이미에게 혹시라도 어떤 문제가 있었나요? ■ 가산명사 부류 [탐탁찮음] ❏ 내가 너 같은 부류는 다룰 수 있지. ■ 구 온갖 종류의 [강조] ❏ 입양은 온갖 이유로 실패할 수 있다. ■ 구 약간 [구어체, 짐작투] ❏ 그건 약간 슬펐어, 정말. ■ 구 일종의, 그나마 ❏ 그녀는 술에서 그나마 위안을 찾는다. ■ 구 유별난 사람, 유별난 것 [마음에 듦] ❏ 그녀는 아주 보기 드문 여자로 유별나다. ■ 구 비슷한 부류 ❏ 그들은 같은 종류의 배경을 가진 비슷한 부류였다. ■ 구 같은 방법으로 ❏ 그들은 경찰 기동대에 도전하듯 욕설을 퍼부었고, 기동대도 같은 방식으로 응수했다. ■ 구 물품으로, 현물로 ❏ 현물로 주는 수당

② **kind** /kaɪnd/ (**kinder, kindest**) ■ ADJ Someone who is **kind** behaves in a gentle, caring, and helpful way towards other people. ❏ *I must thank you for being so kind to me.* ● **kind|ly** ADV [ADV after v] ❏ *"You seem tired this morning, Jenny,"* she said kindly. ■ ADJ You can use **kind** in expressions such as **please be so kind as to** and **would you be kind enough to** in order to ask someone to do something in a firm but polite way. [POLITENESS] [v-link ADJ] ❏ *Please be so kind as to see to it that all the alterations are made at once!* ■ →see also **kindly, kindness**

■ 형용사 친절한, 다정한 ❏ 저에게 정말 친절하게 해 주셔서 감사합니다. ● 친절하게 부사 ❏ "오늘 아침 피곤해 보이는데, 제니"라고 그녀는 상냥하게 말했다. ■ 형용사 ~좀 해 주세요; ~좀 해 주시겠어요 [공손체] ❏ 모든 것이 한번에 변경될 수 있도록 꼭 좀 챙겨 봐 주세요.

Thesaurus   kind의 참조어

N.	sort, type ① ■
ADJ.	affectionate, considerate, gentle ② ■

---

kin|der|gar|ten /kɪndərgɑːrtʰn/ (**kindergartens**) N-COUNT A **kindergarten** is an informal kind of school for very young children, where they learn things by playing. In the United States, kindergarten is for children between the ages of five or six. It prepares them to go into the first grade. [also in/to/at N] ❏ *She's in kindergarten now.*

가산명사 유치원 ❏ 그 애는 지금 유치원에 다닌다.

kind|ly /ˈkaɪndli/ **1** ADJ A **kindly** person is kind, caring, and sympathetic. ❑ *He was a stern critic but an extremely kindly man.* **2** ADV If someone **kindly** does something for you, they act in a thoughtful and helpful way. [ADV before v] ❑ *He kindly carried our picnic in a rucksack.* **3** ADV If someone asks you to **kindly** do something, they are asking you in a way which shows that they have authority over you, or that they are angry with you. [FORMAL] [ADV before v] ❑ *Will you kindly obey the instructions I am about to give?* **4** →see also **kind**

1 형용사 인정 많은 ❑ 그는 엄격한 비평가였지만 몸시도 인정이 많은 남자였다. **2** 부사 친절하게 ❑ 그는 친절하게도 배낭에 우리 소풍 짐을 지고 갔다. **3** 부사 쾌히, 기꺼이 [격식체] ❑ 제가 이제 내리려는 지시에 기꺼이 따라 주시겠습니까?

Word Link   ness ≈ state, condition : conscious*ness*, happi*ness*, kind*ness*

kind|ness /ˈkaɪndnɪs/ N-UNCOUNT **Kindness** is the quality of being gentle, caring, and helpful. ❑ *We have been treated with such kindness by everybody.*

불가산명사 친절, 호의 ❑ 모든 사람들이 우리를 아주 친절하게 대해 주었다.

king ♦♦◇ /kɪŋ/ (**kings**) **1** N-TITLE; N-COUNT A **king** is a man who is the most important member of the royal family of his country, and who is considered to be the Head of State of that country. ❑ *...the king and queen of Spain.* **2** N-COUNT If you describe a man as **the king of** something, you mean that he is the most important person doing that thing or he is the best at doing it. ❑ *He was the king of the cowboys.* **3** N-COUNT A **king** is a playing card with a picture of a king on it. ❑ *...the king of diamonds.* **4** N-COUNT In chess, the **king** is the most important piece. When you are in a position to capture your opponent's king, you win the game. →see **chess**

1 경칭명사; 가산명사 왕, 국왕 ❑ 스페인의 왕과 왕비 **2** 가산명사 거물, -왕 ❑ 그는 카우보이의 황제였다. **3** 가산명사 (카드) 킹 ❑ 다이아몬드 킹 **4** 가산명사 (체스) 킹

king|dom /ˈkɪŋdəm/ (**kingdoms**) **1** N-COUNT A **kingdom** is a country or region that is ruled by a king or queen. ❑ *The kingdom's power declined.* **2** N-SING All the animals, birds, and insects in the world can be referred to together as the animal **kingdom**. All the plants can be referred to as the plant **kingdom**. ❑ *The animal kingdom is full of fine and glorious creatures.* →see **plant**

1 가산명사 왕국 ❑ 그 왕국의 힘이 쇠퇴했다. **2** 단수명사 -계 ❑ 동물계에는 멋지고 아름다운 동물들이 많다.

ki|osk /ˈkiːɒsk/ (**kiosks**) **1** N-COUNT A **kiosk** is a small building or structure from which people can buy things such as sandwiches and newspapers through an open window. ❑ *I was getting cigarettes at the kiosk.* **2** N-COUNT A **kiosk** or a **telephone kiosk** is a public telephone booth. [BRIT] ❑ *He phoned me from a kiosk.*

1 가산명사 키오스크, 간이 상점 ❑ 나는 간이 상점에서 담배를 사고 있었다. **2** 가산명사 공중전화 박스 [영국영어] ❑ 그는 공중전화로 내게 전화를 걸었다.

kiss ♦◇◇ /kɪs/ (**kisses, kissing, kissed**) **1** V-RECIP If you **kiss** someone, you touch them with your lips to show affection or sexual desire, or to greet them or say goodbye. ❑ *She leaned up and kissed him on the cheek.* ❑ *Her parents kissed her goodbye as she set off from their home.* ● N-COUNT **Kiss** is also a noun. ❑ *I put my arms around her and gave her a kiss.* **2** V-T If you say that something **kisses** another thing, you mean that it touches that thing very gently. ❑ *The wheels of the aircraft kissed the runway.* **3** PHRASE If you **blow** someone **a kiss** or **blow a kiss**, you touch the palm of your hand lightly with your lips, and then blow across your hand toward the person, in order to show them your affection. ❑ *Maria blew him a kiss.* **4** PHRASE If you say that you **kiss** something **goodbye** or **kiss goodbye to** something, you accept the fact that you are going to lose it, although you do not want to. [INFORMAL] ❑ *I felt sure I'd have to kiss my dancing career goodbye.* →see Word Web: **kiss**

1 상호동사 키스하다, 입 맞추다 ❑ 그녀는 몸을 위로 젖혀 그의 볼에 키스했다. ❑ 그녀의 부모는 그녀가 집에서 떠날 때 그녀에게 작별 키스를 했다. ● 가산명사 키스, 입맞춤 ❑ 나는 그녀를 팔로 껴안고 그녀에게 키스를 했다. **2** 타동사 가볍게 닿다 ❑ 비행기의 바퀴들이 활주로에 가볍게 닿았다. **3** 구 -에게 키스를 불어 보내다 ❑ 마리아는 그에게 키스를 불어 보냈다. **4** 구 단념하다 [비격식체] ❑ 나는 무용수의 길을 포기해야만 한다는 확신이 들었다.

Word Partnership   kiss의 연어

ADJ.	**big** kiss, **first** kiss, **quick** kiss **1**
V.	**give** *someone* a kiss, **plant** a kiss **on** *someone*, **want to** kiss *someone* **1**
N.	kiss *someone* **on the cheek/lips/mouth**, kiss (*someone*) **goodbye/goodnight, hug and** kiss **1**

kit /kɪt/ (**kits, kitting, kitted**) **1** N-COUNT A **kit** is a group of items that are kept together, often in the same container, because they are all used for similar purposes. ❑ *Make sure you keep a well-stocked first aid kit ready to deal with any emergency.* **2** N-COUNT A **kit** is a set of parts that can be put together in order to make something. ❑ *Her popular potholder is also available in do-it-yourself kits.* **3** N-UNCOUNT **Kit** is special clothing and equipment that you use when you take part in a particular activity, especially a sport. [mainly BRIT] ❑ *I forgot my gym kit.* **4** PHRASE If someone **gets** their **kit off** or **takes** their **kit off**, they take off all their clothes. If they **keep** their **kit on**, they do not take off all their clothes, even though people may be expecting them to. [BRIT, INFORMAL] ❑ *I don't like taking my kit off on screen.*

1 가산명사 도구 한 벌, 용구 한 세트 ❑ 모든 응급 사태에 대처할 수 있도록 잘 갖추어진 구급상자를 반드시 구비하시오. **2** 가산명사 조립 용품 한 벌 ❑ 그녀가 좋아하는 뜨거운 냄비를 들 때 쓰는 장갑은 손수 만들기 세트로도 구입할 수 있다. **3** 불가산명사 복장과 장비 [주로 영국영어] ❑ 나는 운동복과 장비를 잊어버렸다. **4** 구 옷을 벗다; 옷을 벗지 않다 [영국영어, 비격식체] ❑ 나는 영화에서 옷을 벗고 싶지 않다.

Word Web   kiss

Some anthropologists believe mothers invented the **kiss**. They chewed a bit of food and then used their lips to place it in their child's mouth. Others believe that primates started the practice. There are many types of kisses. Kisses express affection or accompany a greeting or a goodbye. Friends and family members exchange social kisses on the **lips** or sometimes on the **cheek**. When people are about to kiss they pucker their lips. In European countries, friends kiss each other lightly on both cheeks. And in the Middle East, a kiss between two political figures indicates a pledge of mutual support.

a
b
c
d
e
f
g
h
i
j
k
l
m
n
o
p
q
r
s
t
u
v
w
x
y
z

A

▶**kit out** PHRASAL VERB If someone or something **is kitted out**, they have everything they need at a particular time, such as clothing, equipment, or furniture. [BRIT, INFORMAL] ❑ *She was kitted out with winter coat, skirts, jumpers, nylon stockings.*

구동사 만반의 준비를 갖추다 [영국영어, 비격식체] ❑ 그녀는 겨울 외투, 스커트, 스웨터, 나일론 스타킹 등 만반의 준비를 갖추고 있었다.

B

kitch|en ♦♦◇ /kɪtʃⁿn/ (kitchens) N-COUNT A **kitchen** is a room that is used for cooking and for household jobs such as washing dishes. →see **house**

가산명사 부엌, 주방

C

kite /kaɪt/ (kites) **1** N-COUNT A **kite** is an object, usually used as a toy, which is flown in the air. It consists of a light frame covered with paper or cloth and a long string attached which you hold while the kite is flying. ❑ *Willy asks if I've ever flown a kite before.* **2** PHRASE If you say that someone is **as high as a kite**, you mean that they are very excited or that they are greatly affected by alcohol or drugs. ❑ *I felt so strange on the steroid injections. I was as high as a kite some of the time.*

1 가산명사 연 ❑ 윌리는 내가 전에 연을 날려 본 적이 있는지 묻는다. **2** 구 공중에 붕 뜬 기분인 ❑ 스테로이드 주사를 맞으니 아주 묘한 느낌이었다. 한동안 공중에 붕 뜨는 기분이었다.

D

E

kitsch /kɪtʃ/ N-UNCOUNT You can refer to a work of art or an object as **kitsch** if it is showy and thought by some people to be in bad taste. ❑ *...a hideous ballgown verging on the kitsch.* ● ADJ **Kitsch** is also an adjective. ❑ *Blue and green eyeshadow has long been considered kitsch.*

불가산명사 천박한 것 ❑ 천박하다고 할 만한 야회복 ● 형용사 천박한 ❑ 푸른색과 녹색 아이섀도는 오랫동안 천박한 것으로 여겨져 왔다.

F

kit|ten /kɪtⁿn/ (kittens) N-COUNT A **kitten** is a very young cat.

가산명사 새끼 고양이

kit|ty /kɪti/ (kitties) **1** N-COUNT A **kitty** is an amount of money gathered from several people, which is meant to be spent on things that these people will share or use together. ❑ *You haven't put any money in the kitty for three weeks.* **2** N-COUNT A **kitty** is the total amount of money which is bet in a gambling game, and which is taken by the winner or winners. ❑ *Each month the total prize kitty is £13.5 million.*

G

1 가산명사 공동 적립금 ❑ 너는 3주 동안 공동 적립금에 한 푼도 넣지 않았다. **2** 가산명사 (도박의) 판돈 ❑ 매달 당첨금 총액이 1,350만 파운드이다.

H

kiwi /kiwi/ (kiwis) A **kiwi** is the same as a **kiwi fruit**.

키위

I

kiwi fruit (kiwi fruits)

> Kiwi fruit can also be used as the plural form.

> kiwi fruit도 복수형으로 쓸 수 있다.

N-VAR A **kiwi fruit** is a fruit with a brown hairy skin and green flesh.

가산명사 또는 불가산명사 키위

J

km (kms) km is a written abbreviation for **kilometer**.

킬로미터

knack /næk/ (knacks) N-COUNT A **knack** is a particularly clever or skillful way of doing something successfully, especially something which most people find difficult. ❑ *He's got the knack of getting people to listen.*

가산명사 솜씨, 재주 ❑ 그는 사람들이 귀를 기울이게 만드는 기교를 가지고 있다.

K

knap|sack /næpsæk/ (knapsacks) N-COUNT A **knapsack** is a canvas or leather bag that you carry on your back or over your shoulder, for example when you are walking in the countryside.

가산명사 배낭

L

knead /nid/ (kneads, kneading, kneaded) **1** V-T When you **knead** dough or other food, you press and squeeze it with your hands so that it becomes smooth and ready to bake. ❑ *Lightly knead the mixture on a floured surface.* **2** V-T If you **knead** a part of someone's body, you press or squeeze it with your fingers. ❑ *She felt him knead the aching muscles.*

M

1 타동사 반죽하다 ❑ 가루를 입힌 표면에 대고 혼합물을 가볍게 반죽하세요. **2** 타동사 주무르다 ❑ 그녀는 그가 아픈 근육을 주무르고 있는 것을 느꼈다.

knee ♦◇◇ /ni/ (knees, kneeing, kneed) **1** N-COUNT Your **knee** is the place where your leg bends. ❑ *He will receive physiotherapy on his damaged left knee.* **2** N-COUNT If something or someone is **on your knee** or **on your knees**, they are resting or sitting on the upper part of your legs when you are sitting down. ❑ *He sat with the package on his knees.* **3** N-PLURAL If you are on your **knees**, your legs are bent and your knees are on the ground. ❑ *She fell to the ground on her knees and prayed.* **4** V-T If you **knee** someone, you hit them using your knee. ❑ *Ian kneed him in the groin.* **5** PHRASE If a country or organization is **brought to its knees**, it is almost completely destroyed by someone or something. ❑ *The country was being brought to its knees by the loss of 2.4 million manufacturing jobs.* →see **body**

N

O

1 가산명사 무릎 ❑ 그는 다친 왼쪽 무릎에 물리 치료를 받을 것이다. **2** 가산명사 무릎 위에 ❑ 그는 무릎 위에 꾸러미를 얹어 놓고 앉아 있었다. **3** 복수명사 무릎을 꿇고 ❑ 그녀는 무릎을 꿇고 앉아 기도를 했다. **4** 타동사 무릎으로 치다 ❑ 이안은 그의 사타구니를 무릎으로 쳤다. **5** 구 무릎을 꿇다, 거의 파탄나다 ❑ 제조업계 일자리 240만 개를 잃고 그 나라는 휘청거리고 있었다.

P

Q

Word Partnership knee의 연어

N.	knee **injury** **1**
ADJ.	**left/right** knee **1**
V.	**bend your** knees, knees **buckle** **1**
	fall on your knees **3**

R

S

kneel /nil/ (kneels, kneeling, kneeled, knelt)

> The forms **kneeled** and **knelt** can both be used for the past tense and past participle.

> kneeled와 knelt 모두 과거 및 과거 분사로 쓸 수 있다.

T

V-I When you **kneel**, you bend your legs so that your knees are touching the ground. ❑ *She knelt by the bed and prayed.* ❑ *Other people were kneeling, but she just sat.* ● PHRASAL VERB **Kneel down** means the same as **kneel**. ❑ *She kneeled down beside him.*

자동사 무릎을 꿇다 ❑ 그녀는 침대 옆에 무릎을 꿇고 기도했다. ❑ 다른 사람들은 무릎을 꿇고 있었지만 그녀는 그냥 앉아 있었다. ● 구동사 무릎을 꿇다 ❑ 그녀는 그 옆에 무릎을 꿇었다.

U

knew /nu, BRIT nyuː/ **Knew** is the past tense of **know**.

know의 과거

V

knick|ers /nɪkərz/

> The form **knicker** is used as a modifier.

> knicker는 수식어구로 쓴다.

W

1 N-PLURAL **Knickers** are a piece of underwear worn by women and girls which have holes for the legs and elastic around the waist to hold them up. [BRIT; AM **panties**] [also **a pair of** N] ❑ *She bought Ann two bras and six pairs of knickers.* **2** PHRASE If someone is **getting** their **knickers in a twist** about something, they are getting annoyed or upset about it without good reason. [BRIT, HUMOROUS, INFORMAL] ❑ *The company, which makes its money on 3,000 grocery lines has its knickers in a twist about Sunday trading.*

X

1 복수명사 팬티 [영국영어; 미국영어 panties] ❑ 그녀는 앤에게 브래지어 두 개와 팬티 여섯 장을 사 주었다. **2** 구 괜히 성내다 [영국영어, 해학체, 비격식체] ❑ 3천 개의 식료품점에서 돈을 버는 그 회사가 일요일의 영업을 두고 괜히 성을 내고 있다.

Y

knife ♦◇◇ /naɪf/ (knives, knifes, knifing, knifed)

> Knives is the plural form of the noun and knifes is the third person singular of the present tense of the verb.

> knives는 명사의 복수형이고, knifes는 동사의 현재시제 3인칭 단수이다.

Z

1 N-COUNT A **knife** is a tool for cutting or a weapon and consists of a flat piece of metal with a sharp edge on the end of a handle. ❑ ...a knife and fork. **2** V-T To **knife** someone means to attack and injure them with a knife. ❑ Dawson takes revenge on the man by knifing him to death. **3** PHRASE If you have been in a place where there was a very tense atmosphere, you can say that you **could have cut** the atmosphere **with a knife**. [mainly BRIT] ❑ Officials hung the flag upside down. You could have cut the atmosphere with a knife. **4** PHRASE If a lot of people want something unpleasant to happen to someone, for example if they want them to lose their job, you can say that **the knives are out for** that person. [mainly BRIT] ❑ The Party knives are out for the leader. **5** PHRASE If you **twist the knife** or if you **turn the knife in** someone's **wound**, you do or say something to make an unpleasant situation they are in even more unpleasant. ❑ Hearing his own plans was like having a knife turned in his wound.

knight /naɪt/ (**knights, knighting, knighted**) **1** N-COUNT In medieval times, a **knight** was a man of noble birth, who served his king or lord in battle. ❑ ...King Arthur's faithful knight, Gawain. **2** V-T If someone **is knighted**, they are given a knighthood. [usu passive] ❑ He was knighted in the Queen's birthday honours list in June 1988. **3** N-COUNT In chess, a **knight** is a piece which is shaped like a horse's head. **4** PHRASE If you refer to someone as a **knight in shining armor**, you mean that they are kind and brave, and likely to rescue you from a difficult situation. ❑ The love songs tricked us all into believing in happy endings and knights in shining armor. →see **chess**

knight|hood /naɪthʊd/ (**knighthoods**) N-COUNT A **knighthood** is a title that is given to a man by a British king or queen for his achievements or his service to his country. A man who has been given a knighthood can put "Sir" in front of his name instead of "Mr." ❑ When he finally received his knighthood in 1975 Chaplin was 85.

knit /nɪt/ (**knits, knitting, knitted**) **1** V-T/V-I If you **knit** something, especially an article of clothing, you make it from wool or a similar thread by using two knitting needles or a machine. ❑ I had endless hours to knit and sew. ❑ I have already started knitting baby clothes. ● COMB in ADJ **Knit** is also a combining form. [ADJ n] ❑ Ferris wore a heavy knit sweater. **2** V-T If someone or something **knits** things or people **together**, they make them fit or work together closely and successfully. ❑ The best thing about sport is that it knits the whole family close together. ● COMB in ADJ **Knit** is also a combining form. ❑ ...a closer-knit family. **3** V-I When broken bones **knit**, the broken pieces grow together again. ❑ The bone hasn't knitted together properly.

Word Partnership		*knit*의 연어
N.	knit **a sweater** **1**	
ADV.	knit **together** **2**	

knit|ting /nɪtɪŋ/ **1** N-UNCOUNT **Knitting** is something, such as an article of clothing, that is being knitted. ❑ She had been sitting with her knitting at her fourth-floor window. **2** N-UNCOUNT **Knitting** is the action or process of knitting. ❑ Take up a relaxing hobby, such as knitting.

knives /naɪvz/ **Knives** is the plural of **knife**.

knob /nɒb/ (**knobs**) **1** N-COUNT A **knob** is a round handle on a door or drawer which you use in order to open or close it. ❑ He turned the knob and pushed against the door. **2** N-COUNT A **knob** is a round switch on a piece of machinery or equipment. ❑ ...the volume knob. **3** N-COUNT A **knob of** butter is a small amount of it. [mainly BRIT] ❑ Top the steaming hot potatoes with a knob of butter.

knock ♦♢♢ /nɒk/ (**knocks, knocking, knocked**) **1** V-I If you **knock on** something such as a door or window, you hit it, usually several times, to attract someone's attention. ❑ She went directly to Simon's apartment and knocked on the door. ● N-COUNT **Knock** is also a noun. ❑ They heard a knock at the front door. ● **knock|ing** N-SING [also no det] ❑ They were wakened by a loud knocking at the door. **2** V-T If you **knock** something, you touch or hit it roughly, especially so that it falls or moves. ❑ She accidentally knocked the tea tin off the shelf. ● N-COUNT **Knock** is also a noun. ❑ The bags have tough exterior materials to protect against knocks, rain and dust. **3** V-T If someone **knocks** two rooms or buildings **into** one, or **knocks** them **together**, they make them form one room or building by removing a wall. ❑ They decided to knock the two rooms into one. **4** V-T To **knock** someone into a particular position or condition means to hit them very hard so that they fall over or become unconscious. ❑ The third wave was so strong it knocked me backwards. **5** V-T To **knock** a particular quality or characteristic **out of** someone means to make them lose it. [no cont] ❑ The stories of his links with the actress had knocked the fun out of him. **6** V-T If you **knock** something or someone, you criticize them and say unpleasant things about them. [INFORMAL] ❑ I'm not knocking them: if they want to do it, it's up to them. **7** N-COUNT If someone receives a **knock**, they have an unpleasant experience which prevents them from achieving something or which causes them to change their attitudes or plans. ❑ I can remember it feeling a real knock to my self-confidence that they said I wasn't academically up to being a teacher. **8** to **knock** something **on the head** →see **head**. to **knock** someone or something **into shape** →see **shape**

Thesaurus		*knock*의 참조어
V.	rap, tap **1**	
	bash, hit, strike **4**	
	criticize, denounce; (ant.) praise **6**	

1 N-가산명사 나이프 ❑ 나이프와 포크 **2** V-T동사 칼로 찌르다 ❑ 도손은 그를 칼로 찔러 죽여 복수를 한다. **3** 구 분위기가 꽁꽁 얼어 있는, 온통 살얼음판이다 [주로 영국영어] ❑ 공무원들이 국기를 거꾸로 달았다. 분위기가 온통 살얼음판이었다. **4** 구 적의의 노골적으로 드러내다 [주로 영국영어] ❑ 당내에서 당수에 대해 노골적으로 적대적인 태도를 보이고 있다. **5** 구 한 번 찔린 곳을 또 찌르는 격이다 ❑ 그가 자기 자신의 계획을 듣는 것은 한 번 찔린 곳을 또 찔리는 것과 같았다.

1 N-가산명사 기사 ❑ 아서 왕의 충실한 기사 가웨인. **2** V-T동사 기사 작위를 수여받다 ❑ 그는 1988년 6월에 여왕 탄신일 기념 영예의 리스트에 포함되어 기사 작위를 받았다. **3** N-가산명사 (체스) 나이트 **4** 구 백마 탄 왕자 ❑ 그 사랑 노래들은 우리 모두에게 행복한 결말과 백마 탄 왕자의 등장을 믿게 하였다.

N-가산명사 기사의 작위 ❑ 채플린이 마침내 1975년에 기사 작위를 받았을 때 그의 나이는 85세였다.

1 V-T동사/V-I자동사 (털실로) 짜다, 뜨다 ❑ 나는 뜨개질을 하고 바느질을 하는 데 수많은 시간을 보냈다. ❑ 나는 이미 아기 옷을 뜨기 시작했다. ● 복합형-형용사 털실로 짠, 니트의 ❑ 페리스는 털실로 짠 두꺼운 스웨터를 입고 있었다. **2** V-T동사 밀착시키다, 결합시키다 ❑ 스포츠의 가장 좋은 점은 온 가족을 긴밀하게 결합시켜 준다는 것이다. ● 복합형-형용사 결합된 ❑ 더욱 친밀해진 가족 **3** V-I자동사 (부러진 뼈가) 접합되다 ❑ 뼈가 제대로 접합되지 않았다.

1 N-불가산명사 뜨개질감 ❑ 그녀는 4층 창문가에 뜨개질감을 두고 앉아 있었다. **2** N-불가산명사 뜨개질하기 ❑ 뜨개질을 하는 것과 같이 마음을 차분하게 하는 취미를 가져라.

*knife*의 복수형

1 N-가산명사 (문, 서랍 등의) 손잡이 ❑ 그는 문의 손잡이를 돌리고 문을 밀었다. **2** N-가산명사 (둥그런) 스위치 ❑ 볼륨 스위치 **3** N-가산명사 작은 덩어리 [주로 영국영어] ❑ 김이 나는 뜨거운 감자 위에 버터 한 덩어리를 얹어라.

1 V-I자동사 노크하다 ❑ 그녀는 곧바로 사이먼의 아파트로 가서 문에 노크를 했다. ● N-가산명사 노크 단수명사 ❑ 그들은 현관문에서 노크 소리를 들었다. ● 노크 ❑ 문을 두드리는 큰 노크 소리에 그들은 잠에서 깼다. **2** V-T동사 치다, 건드리다 ❑ 그녀가 실수로 차가 든 깡통을 쳐서 선반에서 떨어뜨렸다. ● N-가산명사 건드리기, 치기 ❑ 그 가방은 외피가 외부 충격, 비, 먼지를 견딜 수 있는 단단한 소재로 만들어져 있다. **3** V-T동사 칸막이 벽을 없애다 ❑ 그들은 벽을 없애고 방을 하나로 만들기로 결정했다. **4** V-T동사 때려눕히다; 의식을 잃게 하다 ❑ 세 번째 파도는 너무나 강해서 나는 뒤로 쓰러졌다. **5** V-T동사 ~을 잃게 만들다 ❑ 그와 그 여배우와의 관계에 대한 이야기들을 들으니 그에 대한 흥미가 떨어졌었다. **6** V-T동사 비판하다, 헐뜯다 [비격식체] ❑ 나는 그들을 비판하는 것이 아니다. 그들이 하고 싶다면, 그건 그들이 결정할 일이다. **7** N-가산명사 타격 ❑ 나는 그들이 내가 교사가 되기에 학문적 역량이 부족하다는 말을 했을 때 그것이 내 자존심에 큰 타격으로 느껴지던 것을 기억하고 있다.

	Word Partnership	*knock*의 연어
N.	knock **at/on a door** 1	
ADJ.	**loud** knock 1	
	knock *someone* **unconscious** 4	
V.	**answer** a knock, **hear** a knock 1	

►**knock about** →see **knock around**

►**knock around** 1 PHRASAL VERB If someone **knocks around** or **knocks about** somewhere, they spend time there, experiencing different situations or just passing time. ❑ ...reporters who knock around in troubled parts of the world. ❑ They knock around on weekends in grubby sweaters and pants. 2 PHRASAL VERB If someone **knocks** you **around** or **knocks** you **about**, they hit or kick you several times. [mainly BRIT, INFORMAL] ❑ He lied to me constantly and started knocking me around.

1 구동사 돌아다니다 4 세계의 분쟁 지역들을 돌아다니는 기자들 2 그들은 주말이면 지저분한 스웨터와 바지를 입고 나돌아 다닌다. 2 구동사 마구 때리다, 마구 차다 [주로 영국영어, 비격식체] 2 그는 계속해서 거짓말을 하더니 나를 마구 때리기 시작하였다.

►**knock back** PHRASAL VERB If an event, situation, or person **knocks** you **back**, they prevent you from progressing or achieving something. [mainly BRIT] ❑ It seemed as though every time we got rolling something came along to knock us back.

구동사 훼방하다 [주로 영국영어] 2 우리 일에 속도가 붙으려고 할 때마다 뭔가 나타나 발목을 잡는 것처럼 보였다.

►**knock down** 1 PHRASAL VERB If someone **is knocked down** or **is knocked over** by a vehicle or its driver, they are hit by a car and fall to the ground, and are often injured or killed. ❑ He fell off the curb at an intersection and was knocked down by a car. ❑ A drunk driver knocked down and killed two girls. 2 PHRASAL VERB To **knock down** a building or part of a building means to demolish it. ❑ Why doesn't he just knock the wall down? 3 PHRASAL VERB To **knock down** a price or amount means to decrease it. [mainly AM; BRIT usually **bring down**] ❑ The market might abandon the stock, and knock down its price.

1 구동사 (차에) 치이다 2 그는 교차로에서 도로 갓돌 밖으로 넘어져 차에 치였다. 2 음주 운전자가 여자 아이 두 명을 차로 치어 죽였다. 2 구동사 헐물다 2 왜 그는 그 벽을 그냥 허물지 않을까? 3 구동사 인하하다, 줄이다 [주로 미국영어; 영국영어 대개 bring down] 2 시장은 그 주식을 포기하고 가격을 인하할지도 모른다.

►**knock off** 1 PHRASAL VERB To **knock off** an amount from a price, time, or level means to reduce it by that amount. ❑ Udinese have knocked 10% off admission prices. 2 PHRASAL VERB If you **knock** something **off** a list or document, you remove it. ❑ Tighter rules for benefit entitlement have knocked many people off the unemployment register. 3 PHRASAL VERB When you **knock off**, you finish work at the end of the day or before a break. [INFORMAL] ❑ If I get this report finished I'll knock off early.

1 구동사 줄이다, 낮추다 2 우디네세는 입장료를 10퍼센트 낮췄다. 2 구동사 빼다, 제거하다 3 생활 보조금 수혜 자격 관련 법률 강화로 인하여 많은 사람들이 실업 수당 수령자 명부에서 빠졌다. 3 구동사 (일을) 마치다 [비격식체] 2 이 보고서를 끝내면 집에 일찍 갈 수 있을 것이다.

►**knock out** 1 PHRASAL VERB To **knock** someone **out** means to cause them to become unconscious or to go to sleep. ❑ The three drinks knocked him out. 2 PHRASAL VERB If a person or team **is knocked out** of a competition, they are defeated in a game, so that they take no more part in the competition. ❑ Henri Leconte has been knocked out in the quarter-finals of the Geneva Open. →see also **knockout** 3 PHRASAL VERB If something **is knocked out** by enemy action or bad weather, it is destroyed or stops functioning because of it. ❑ Our bombers have knocked out the mobile launchers.

1 구동사 정신을 잃게 만들다, 곯아떨어지게 만들다 2 술 석 잔을 마시고 그는 나가떨어졌다. 2 구동사 탈락되다 2 앙리 르콩트는 제네바 오픈 준준결승에서 탈락되었다. 3 구동사 파괴하다 2 우리 측의 폭격기들이 이동 발사대를 파괴했다.

knock-on ADJ If there is a **knock-on** effect, one action or event causes several other events to happen one after the other. [BRIT] [ADJ n] ❑ The cut in new car prices has had a knock-on effect on the price of used cars.

형용사 연쇄적인 [영국영어] 2 새 차 가격 인하는 중고차 가격에도 연쇄 효과를 주었다.

knock|out /nɒkaʊt/ (knockouts) also **knock-out** 1 N-COUNT In boxing, a **knockout** is a situation in which a boxer wins the fight by making his opponent fall to the ground and be unable to stand up before the referee has counted to ten. [also by N] ❑ Lennox Lewis ended the scheduled 12-round fight with a knockout in the eighth round. 2 ADJ A **knockout** blow is an action or event that completely defeats an opponent. [ADJ n] ❑ He delivered a knockout blow to all of his rivals. 3 ADJ A **knockout** competition is one in which the players or teams that win continue playing until there is only one winner left. [mainly BRIT; AM **elimination**] [ADJ n] ❑ ...the European Cup, a knockout competition between the top teams in Europe.

1 가산명사 녹아웃, 케이오 2 레녹스 루이스는 12라운드로 계획된 시합을 8라운드만에 케이오로 끝마쳤다. 2 형용사 맹렬한 2 그는 모든 경쟁자들에게 맹렬한 일격을 가했다. 3 형용사 승자만이 진출하는, 토너먼트의 [주로 영국영어; 미국영어 elimination] 2 유럽의 최고 팀들 간의 토너먼트식 경기인 유럽 컵

knot /nɒt/ (knots, knotting, knotted) 1 N-COUNT If you tie a **knot** in a piece of string, rope, cloth, or other material, you pass one end or part of it through a loop and pull it tight. ❑ One lace had broken and been tied in a knot. 2 V-T If you **knot** a piece of string, rope, cloth, or other material, you pass one end or part of it through a loop and pull it tight. ❑ He knotted the laces securely together. ❑ He knotted the bandanna around his neck. 3 N-COUNT If you feel a **knot** in your stomach, you get an uncomfortable tight feeling in your stomach, usually because you are afraid or excited. ❑ There was a knot of tension in his stomach. 4 V-T/V-I If your stomach **knots** or if something **knots** it, it feels tight because you are afraid or excited. ❑ I felt my stomach knot with apprehension. 5 V-T/V-I If part of your face or your muscles **knot**, they become tense, usually because you are worried or angry. ❑ His forehead knotted in a frown. 6 N-COUNT A **knot** in a piece of wood is a small hard area where a branch grew. ❑ A typical joiner rejects half his wood because of knots or cracks. 7 N-COUNT A **knot** is a unit of speed. The speed of ships, aircraft, and winds is measured in knots. ❑ They travel at speeds of up to 30 knots. →see **rope**

1 가산명사 매듭 2 신발 끈 하나가 떨어져서 매듭으로 묶여져 있었다. 2 타동사 매듭을 묶다, 매다 2 그는 신발 끈을 단단히 맸다. 2 그는 목에 스카프를 맸다. 3 가산명사 조이는 듯한 느낌 2 그는 긴장하여 배가 조였다. 4 타동사/자동사 조이다, 줄이다 2 나는 두려움에 가슴을 졸였다. 5 타동사/자동사 (얼굴, 근육 등이) 긴장하다 2 그는 긴장하여 이마가 찌푸려졌다. 6 가산명사 나무옹이 2 대부분의 목수들은 재료로 나오는 나무의 절반을 옹이나 벌어진 것 때문에 안 쓴다. 7 가산명사 노트 (속도의 단위) 2 그들은 최고 30노트까지의 속력으로 달린다.

know ♦♦♦ /noʊ/ (knows, knowing, knew, known) 1 V-T/V-I If you **know** a fact, a piece of information, or an answer, you have it correctly in your mind. [no cont] ❑ I don't know the name of the place. ❑ "People like doing things for nothing." — "I know they do." ❑ I don't know what happened to her husband. ❑ "How did he meet your mother?" — "I don't know." 2 V-T If you **know** someone, you are familiar with them because you have met them and talked to them before. [no cont] ❑ Gifford was a friend. I'd known him for nine years. 3 V-T If you say that you **know of** something, you mean that you have heard about it but you do not necessarily have a lot of information about it. [no cont] ❑ We know of the incident but have no further details. ❑ The president admitted that he did not know of any rebels having surrendered so far. 4 V-T/V-I If you **know about** a subject, you have studied it or

1 타동사/자동사 알다 2 나는 그 장소의 이름을 모른다. 2 "사람들은 보수 없이 일하는 것을 좋아해." "나도 그들이 그러는 걸 알지." 2 나는 그녀 남편에게 무슨 일이 일어났는지 모른다. 2 "어떻게 그는 네 어머니를 만났지?" "모르겠어." 2 타동사 (사람을) 알다, 면식이 있다 2 기포드는 친구였다. 나는 9년 동안 그를 알고 지냈다. 3 자동사 -에 대해 알고 있다, -에 대해 들어 봤다 2 우리는 그 사건에 대해 들어서 알고는 있지만, 더 이상 세부적인 사항은 모른다. 2 대통령은 지금까지 항복한 반란군이 있다는 이야기는 못 들었다고 인정했다. 4 타동사/자동사

taken an interest in it, and understand part or all of it. [no cont] ❑ *Hire someone with experience, someone who knows about real estate.* ◼ V-T If you **know** a language, you have learned it and can understand it. [no cont] ❑ *It helps to know French and Creole if you want to understand some of the lyrics.* ◼ V-T If you **know** something such as a place, a work of art, or an idea, you have visited it, seen it, read it, or heard about it, and so you are familiar with it. [no cont] ❑ *No matter how well you know Paris, it is easy to get lost.* ◼ V-T If you **know how** to do something, you have the necessary skills and knowledge to do it. [no cont] ❑ *The health authorities now know how to deal with the disease.* ◼ V-T/V-I You can say that someone **knows that** something is happening when they become aware of it. [no cont] ❑ *Then I saw a gun under the hall table so I knew that something was wrong.* ◼ V-T If you **know** something or someone, you recognize them when you see them or hear them. [no cont] ❑ *Would she know you if she saw you on the street?* ◼ V-T If someone or something **is known as** a particular name, they are called by that name. [no cont] ❑ *The disease is more commonly known as Mad Cow Disease.* ❑ *He was the only boy in the school who was known by his Christian name and not his surname.* ◼ V-T If you **know** someone or something **as** a person or thing that has particular qualities, you consider that they have those qualities. ❑ *Lots of people knew her as a very kind woman.* ◼ →see also **knowing, known** ◼ PHRASE If you talk about a thing or system **as we know it**, you are referring to the form in which it exists now and which is familiar to most people. ❑ *He planned to end the welfare system as we know it.* ◼ PHRASE If you **get to know** someone, you find out what they are like by spending time with them. ❑ *The new neighbors were getting to know each other.* ◼ PHRASE People use expressions such as **goodness knows**, **Heaven knows**, and **God knows** when they do not know something and want to suggest that nobody could possibly know it. [INFORMAL] ❑ *"Who's he?" — "God knows."* ◼ CONVENTION You say "**I know**" to show that you agree with what has just been said. ❑ *"This country is so awful." — "I know, I know."* ◼ PHRASE You can use **I don't know** to indicate that you do not completely agree with something or do not really think that it is true. ❑ *"He should quite simply resign." — "I don't know about that."* ◼ PHRASE You can say "**I don't know about you**" to indicate that you are going to give your own opinion about something and you want to find out if someone else feels the same. ❑ *I don't know about the rest of you, but I'm hungry.* ◼ PHRASE You use **I don't know** in expressions which indicate criticism of someone's behavior. For example, if you say that you **do not know how** someone can do something, you mean that you cannot understand or accept them doing it. [DISAPPROVAL] ❑ *I don't know how he could do this to his own daughter.* ◼ PHRASE If you are **in the know** about something, especially something that is not known about or understood by many people, you have information about it. ❑ *It was gratifying to be in the know about important people.* ◼ CONVENTION You can use expressions such as **you know what I mean** and **if you know what I mean** to suggest that the person listening to you understands what you are trying to say, and so you do not have to explain any more. [SPOKEN] ❑ *None of us stayed long. I mean, the atmosphere wasn't – well, you know what I mean.* ◼ CONVENTION You say "**You never know**" or "**One never knows**" to indicate that it is not definite or certain what will happen in the future, and to suggest that there is some hope that things will turn out well. [VAGUENESS] ❑ *You never know, I might get lucky.* ◼ CONVENTION You say "**Not that I know of**" when someone has asked you whether or not something is true and you think the answer is "no" but you cannot be sure because you do not know all the facts. [VAGUENESS] ❑ *"Is he married?" — "Not that I know of."* ◼ CONVENTION You use **you know** to emphasize or to draw attention to what you are saying. [SPOKEN, EMPHASIS] ❑ *The conditions in there are awful, you know.* ◼ PHRASE You can say "**You don't know**" in order to emphasize how strongly you feel about the remark you are going to make. [SPOKEN, EMPHASIS] ❑ *You don't know how good it is to speak to somebody from home.* ◼ to **know best** →see **best**. to **know better** →see **better**. to **know** something **for a fact** →see **fact**. **as far as I know** →see **far**. **not to know the first thing about** something →see **first**. to **know full well** →see **full**. to **let** someone **know** →see **let**. to **know** your **own mind** →see **mind**. to **know the ropes** →see **rope**

Thesaurus   know의 참조어

| v. | comprehend, recognize, understand ◼ ◼ |
| | be acquainted, be familiar with ◼ ◼ ◼ |

know-how ◆◇◇ [AM **knowhow**] N-UNCOUNT **Know-how** is knowledge of the methods or techniques of doing something, especially something technical or practical. [INFORMAL] ❑ *He hasn't got the know-how to run a farm.*

know|ing /nˈoʊɪŋ/ ADJ A **knowing** gesture or remark is one that shows that you understand something, for example the way that someone is feeling or what they really mean, even though it has not been mentioned directly. ❑ *Ron gave her a knowing smile.* ● **know|ing|ly** ADV ❑ *He smiled knowingly.*

know|ing|ly /nˈoʊɪŋli/ ADV If you **knowingly** do something wrong, you do it even though you know it is wrong. [ADV before v] ❑ *He repeated that he had never knowingly taken illegal drugs.*

know-it-all (**know-it-alls**) N-COUNT If you say that someone is a **know-it-all**, you are critical of them because they think that they know a lot more than other people. [AM, INFORMAL, DISAPPROVAL] [BRIT **know-all**] ❑ *Don't act like a know-it-all. You listen to your mother.*

knowl|edge ◆◆◇ /nˈɒlɪdʒ/ ◼ N-UNCOUNT **Knowledge** is information and understanding about a subject which a person has, or which all people have. ❑ *She disclaims any knowledge of her husband's business concerns.* ◼ PHRASE If you say that something is true **to your knowledge** or **to the best of** your **knowledge**,

---

알다, 이해하다 ❑ 경력이 있고 부동산에 대해서 아는 사람을 고용하라. ◼ 타동사 (언어를) 알다 ❑ 그 노래들의 가사를 이해하려면 불어와 크레올을 아는 것이 도움이 된다. ◼ 타동사 알고 있다, 익숙하다 ❑ 파리에 대해서 아무리 잘 알고 있어도 길을 잃기 쉽다. ◼ 타동사 (방법을) 알다 ❑ 보건 당국은 그 질병을 치료하는 방법을 이제는 알고 있다. ◼ 타동사/자동사 알다 ❑ 그때 나는 홀 탁자 아래에 권총이 있는 것을 보았기에 뭔가 잘못되었다는 것을 알았다. ◼ 타동사 알아보다, 식별하다 ❑ 거리에서 보면 그녀가 당신을 알아볼 수 있을까요? ◼ 타동사 (-으로) 알려지다 ❑ 그 병은 광우병으로 더 흔히 알려져 있다. ❑ 그는 그 학교에서 유일하게 성이 아닌 세례명으로 알려져 있는 소년이었다. ◼ 타동사 ...을 -로 알다 ❑ 많은 사람들이 그녀를 매우 친절한 여자로 알고 있다. ◼ 구 우리가 아는 대로의 ❑ 그는 우리가 지금까지 알고 있던 복지 제도를 종식시키려는 계획을 세웠다. ◼ 구 알게 되다 ❑ 새로운 이웃들은 서로를 알아 가고 있었다. ◼ 구 아무도 모른다 ❑ "그는 누구야?" "누가 알겠어." ◼ 관용 표현 맞다 ❑ "이 나라는 아주 끔찍해." "맞아, 맞아." ◼ 구 글쎄 ❑ "그는 그냥 사퇴해야 해." "글쎄." ◼ 구 당신은 어떤지 모르겠다 ❑ 나머지 여러분은 어떤지 모르겠습니다만, 저는 배고프네요. ◼ 구 이해할 수가 없다 [탐탁찮음] ❑ 어떻게 그가 자기 친딸에게 이런 짓을 할 수 있는지 이해할 수가 없다. ◼ 구 잘 알고 있는 ❑ 중요한 사람들에 대해 잘 알고 있어서 만족스러웠다. ◼ 관용 표현 무슨 말인지 알지? [구어체] ❑ 그러니까 분위기가 좀, 무슨 말인지 알지? ◼ 관용 표현 글쎄, 그건 모르지 [짐작투] ❑ 혹시 알아, 내가 운이 좋을지. ◼ 관용 표현 내가 알기로는 아니다 [짐작투] ❑ "그가 결혼했어?" "내가 알기로는 안 했어." ◼ 관용 표현 있잖아, 알다시피 [구어체, 강조] ❑ 있잖아, 그곳의 상태는 정말 끔찍해. ◼ 구 넌 모를 거야 [구어체, 강조] ❑ 같은 고향 사람과 이야기하는 것이 얼마나 좋은지 넌 모를 거야.

[미국영어 knowhow] 불가산명사 전문적인 지식, 실제적인 지식 [비격식체] ❑ 그는 농장을 경영하는 전문적인 지식이 없었다.

형용사 아는 듯한 ❑ 론이 그녀에게 뭔가 아는 듯한 미소를 지어 보였다. ● 아는 듯이 부사 ❑ 그가 아는 체하며 웃었다.

부사 알고서도 ❑ 그는 절대 불법 마약인 줄 알면서 한 적은 없었다고 반복해서 말했다.

가산명사 아는 체하는 사람, 똑똑한 체하는 사람 [미국영어, 비격식체, 탐탁찮음] [영국영어 know-all] ❑ 똑똑한 체 굴지 마. 엄마 말을 들어.

◼ 불가산명사 지식 ❑ 그녀는 남편의 사업에 관해서는 전혀 아는 바가 없다고 주장한다. ◼ 구 - 가 알고 있는 한 ❑ 내가 알고 있는 한 알렉은 총을 소지한 적이 없었다.

a b c d e f g h i j k l m n o p q r s t u v w x y z

you mean that you believe it to be true but it is possible that you do not know all the facts. ❑ *Alec never carried a gun to my knowledge.*

Thesaurus	*knowledge의 참조어*
N.	comprehension, consciousness, education, intelligence, wisdom; (*ant.*) ignorance ■

Word Partnership	*knowledge의 연어*
ADJ.	**background** knowledge, **common** knowledge, **general** knowledge, **prior** knowledge, **scientific** knowledge, **useful** knowledge, **vast** knowledge ■
N.	knowledge **base** ■
V.	**acquire** knowledge, **gain** knowledge, **have** knowledge, **lack** knowledge, **require** knowledge, **test** *your* knowledge, **use** *your* knowledge ■

knowl|edge|able /nɒlɪdʒəbəl/ ADJ Someone who is **knowledgeable** has or shows a clear understanding of many different facts about the world or about a particular subject. ❑ *Do you think you are more knowledgeable about life than your parents were at your age?*

형용사 정통한, 박식한 ❑ 여러분은 부모님이 여러분이 인생에 대해 더 많이 알고 있다고 생각합니까?

known /noʊn/ ■ **Known** is the past participle of **know**. ◨ ADJ You use **known** to describe someone or something that is clearly recognized by or familiar to all people or to a particular group of people. [ADJ n, v-link ADJ prep, v-link adv ADJ] ❑ *...He was a known drug dealer.* ◨ ADJ If someone or something is **known for** a particular achievement or feature, they are familiar to many people because of that achievement or feature. [v-link ADJ for n/-ing] ❑ *He is better known for his film and TV work.* ◨ PHRASE If you **let it be known that** something is the case, or you **let** something **be known**, you make sure that people know it or can find out about it. ❑ *The Prime Minister has let it be known that he is against it.*

■ know의 과거 분사 ◨ 형용사 알려진 ❑ 그는 알려진 마약상이었다. ◨ 형용사 -로 알려진 ❑ 그는 영화와 텔레비전 작품으로 더 잘 알려져 있다. ◨ 구 모두가 알게 하다 ❑ 수상은 자기가 그것을 반대한다는 것을 모두가 알도록 했다.

knuck|le /nʌkəl/ (knuckles) N-COUNT Your **knuckles** are the rounded pieces of bone that form lumps on your hands where your fingers join your hands, and where your fingers bend. ❑ *Brenda's knuckles were white as she gripped the arms of the chair.* **a rap on the knuckles** →see **rap** →see **hand**

가산명사 손가락 관절 ❑ 브렌다가 의자 팔걸이를 불잡았을 때 그녀의 손가락 관절은 하얗게 핏기가 가셔 있었다.

Ko|ran /kɔrɑn/ N-PROPER The **Koran** is the sacred book on which the religion of Islam is based.

고유명사 코란

kph /keɪ pi eɪtʃ/ **kph** is written after a number to indicate the speed of something such as a vehicle. **kph** is an abbreviation for "kilometers per hour."

시속, kilometers per hour의 축약형

KW also **kW** **KW** is a written abbreviation for **kilowatt**.

킬로와트, kilowatt의 축약형

L l

L, l /ɛl/ (**L's, l's**) N-VAR **L** is the twelfth letter of the English alphabet.

lab /læb/ (**labs**) N-COUNT A **lab** is the same as a **laboratory**.

la|bel ♦◇◇ /ˈleɪbəl/ (**labels, labeling, labeled**) [BRIT, sometimes AM **labelling, labelled**] **1** N-COUNT A **label** is a piece of paper or plastic that is attached to an object in order to give information about it. ❑ *He peered at the label on the bottle.* **2** V-T If something **is labeled**, a label is attached to it giving information about it. [usu passive] ❑ *It requires foreign frozen-food imports to be clearly labeled.* ❑ *The produce was labeled "Made in China."* **3** V-T If you say that someone or something **is labeled as** a particular thing, you mean that people generally describe them that way and you think that this is unfair. [DISAPPROVAL] [usu passive] ❑ *It won't be labeled in any way as a military expedition.* ❑ *It does not matter whether these duties are labeled as duties or tasks.* →see **graph**

가산명사 또는 불가산명사 영어 알파벳의 열두 번째 글자

가산명사 실험실, 연구소

[영국영어, 미국영어 가끔 labelling, labelled] **1** 가산명사 라벨, 꼬리표 ❑ 그는 병에 붙은 라벨을 자세히 들여다보았다. **2** 타동사 라벨이 붙어 있다 ❑ 외국산 냉동식품에는 라벨이 확실히 붙어 있어야 한다. ❑ 그 농산물에는 '중국산'이라고 라벨이 붙어 있었다. **3** 타동사 불리다 [탐탁찮음] ❑ 그것은 어떤 식으로든 군의 원정이라고 불리지 않을 것이다. ❑ 이 임무들이 임무로 불리든 과제로 불리든 상관없다.

Thesaurus	*label*의 참조어
N.	sticker, tag **1**
V.	brand, characterize, classify **3**

la|bor ♦♦♦ /ˈleɪbər/ (**labors, laboring, labored**) [BRIT **labour**] **1** N-UNCOUNT **Labor** is very hard work, usually physical work. [also N in pl, oft supp N] ❑ *... the labor of hauling the rocks away.* **2** V-I Someone who **labors** works hard using their hands. ❑ *...he will be laboring 14-hundred meters below ground.* **3** V-T/V-I If you **labor to** do something, you do it with difficulty. ❑ *Scientists labored for months to unravel the mysteries of Neptune and still remain baffled.* **4** N-UNCOUNT **Labor** is used to refer to the workers of a country or industry, considered as a group. ❑ *We have a problem of skilled labor.* ❑ *Employers want cheap labor and consumers want cheap houses.* **5** N-UNCOUNT The work done by a group of workers or by a particular worker is referred to as their **labor**. ❑ *He exhibits a profound humility in the low rates he pays himself for his labor.* **6** N-PROPER-COLL In Britain, people use **Labour** to refer to the **Labour Party**. ❑ *He believes that, historically, Labour has been most successful as the party that helped people get on in life.* **7** ADJ A **Labour** politician or voter is a member of a Labour Party or votes for a Labour Party. ❑ *...a Labour MP.* **8** N-UNCOUNT **Labor** is the last stage of pregnancy, in which the baby is gradually pushed out of the womb by the mother. ❑ *Her labor had lasted ten hours before the doctor arranged a Cesarean section.* →see **factory**

[영국영어 labour] **1** 불가산명사 노역 ❑ 바위들을 저만치 운반하는 노역 ❑ 그는 지하 천 사백 미터 지점에서 일을 하게 될 것이다. **3** 타동사/자동사 애쓰다 ❑ 과학자들이 수개월간 해왕성의 신비를 벗기려고 애썼지만 여전히 미궁으로 남아 있다. **4** 불가산명사 노동자 ❑ 우리는 숙련된 노동자들에 관한 문제를 안고 있다. ❑ 고용주는 저임금 노동자를 원하고 소비자는 저렴한 주택을 원한다. **5** 불가산명사 노고 ❑ 그는 자신의 노고에 대해 낮게 평가함으로써 지극한 겸손함을 나타낸다. **6** 고유명사-집합 (영국의) 노동당 ❑ 그는 역사적으로 노동당이 사람들이 삶을 잘 영위할 수 있도록 지원한 당으로써 가장 성공한 당이라고 믿는다. **7** 형용사 노동당의 ❑ 노동당 소속의 하원의원 **8** 불가산명사 진통 ❑ 그녀의 진통이 10시간 동안 계속되자 의사가 제왕 절개술을 준비하기로 결정했다.

Thesaurus	*labor*의 참조어
N.	effort, employment, work; (*ant.*) leisure, rest **1 5**
	employees, help, workforce, working people; (*ant.*) management **4**
V.	exert *yourself*, strain, struggle, work; (*ant.*) relax, rest **2 3**

Word Link	*labor* ≈ working : col**labor**ate, e**labor**ate, **labor**atory

la|bora|tory ♦◇◇ /ˈlæbrətɔri, BRIT ləbɒrətri/ (**laboratories**) **1** N-COUNT A **laboratory** is a building or a room where scientific experiments, analyses, and research are carried out. ❑ *...a brain research laboratory at Columbia University.* **2** N-COUNT A **laboratory** in a school, college, or university is a room containing scientific equipment where students are taught science subjects such as chemistry. ❑ *...my old school chemistry laboratory.* →see Word Web: **laboratory**

1 가산명사 연구실 ❑ 컬럼비아 대학 내 두뇌 연구 연구실 **2** 가산명사 실험실 ❑ 내가 전에 다녔던 학교의 화학 실험실

Word Partnership	*laboratory*의 연어
N.	laboratory **conditions**, **research** laboratory, laboratory **technician**, laboratory **test** **1**
	laboratory **equipment**, laboratory **experiment** **1 2**

la|bor|er /ˈleɪbərər/ (**laborers**) [BRIT **labourer**] N-COUNT A **laborer** is a person who does a job which involves a lot of hard physical work. ❑ *She still lives on the farm where he worked as a laborer.*

[영국영어 labourer] 가산명사 인부, 노동자 ❑ 그녀는 아직도 그가 인부로 일했던 농장에서 살고 있다.

la|bor force (**labor forces**) N-COUNT The **labor force** consists of all the people who are able to work in a country or area, or all the people who work for a particular company. [BUSINESS] ❑ *He says the reduction of the labor force could be significant.*

가산명사 노동력 [경제] ❑ 그는 노동력 감소가 심각할 수도 있다고 말한다.

labor-intensive ADJ **Labor-intensive** industries or methods of making things involve a lot of workers. Compare **capital-intensive**. [BUSINESS] ❑ *For labor-intensive businesses like garments, factory labor is cheap.*

형용사 노동집약적 [경제] ❑ 의류업과 같은 노동집약적 산업은 공장 노임이 싸다.

A
B
C
D
E

Word Web laboratory

The discovery of the life-saving drug penicillin was a fortunate accident. While cleaning up his **laboratory**, a **researcher** named Alexander Fleming* noticed that the bacteria in one petri dish had been killed by some kind of **mold**. He took a **sample** and found that it was a form of penicillin. Fleming and others did further **research** and **published** their **findings** in 1928, but few people took notice. However, ten years later a team at Oxford University read Fleming's **study** and began animal and human **experiments**. Within a decade, companies were manufacturing 650 billion units of penicillin a month!

Alexander Fleming (1881-1955): a Scottish biologist and pharmacologist.

F
G
H
I
J
K
L
M
N
O
P
Q
R
S
T
U
V
W
X
Y
Z

la|bo|ri|ous /ləbɔ̱riəs/ ADJ If you describe a task or job as **laborious**, you mean that it takes a lot of time and effort. ❑ *Keeping the garden tidy all year round can be a laborious task.* ● **la|bo|ri|ous|ly** ADV [ADV with v] ❑ *...the embroidery she'd worked on so laboriously during the long winter nights.*

형용사 힘든 ❑ 일년 내내 정원을 깔끔하게 유지하는 것은 힘든 일일 것이다. ● 힘들게 부사 ❑ 그 기나긴 겨울밤들 동안 그녀가 아주 힘들게 놓아 온 자수

la|bor mar|ket (**labor markets**) N-COUNT When you talk about **the labor market**, you are referring to all the people who are able to work and want jobs in a country or area, in relation to the number of jobs there are available in that country or area. [BUSINESS] ❑ *In a tight labor market, demand by employers exceeds the available supply of workers.*

가산명사 노동 시장 [경제] ❑ 경직된 노동 시장에서는 고용주의 요구가 노동자들이 제공할 수 있는 수준을 초과한다.

la|bor re|la|tions [BRIT **labour relations**] N-PLURAL **Labor relations** refers to the relationship between employers and employees in industry, and the political decisions and laws that affect it. ❑ *We have to balance good labor relations against the need to cut costs.*

[영국영어 labour relations] 복수명사 노사 관계 ❑ 우리는 비용 절감의 필요성과 건전한 노사 관계 사이의 균형을 유지해야 한다.

la|bor un|ion (**labor unions**) N-COUNT A **labor union** is an organization that represents the rights and interests of workers to their employers, for example in order to improve working conditions or wages. [AM; BRIT **trade union**] ❑ *...NYSUT, the state's largest labor union.*

가산명사 노동조합 [미국영어; 영국영어 trade union] ❑ 그 주(州)의 최대 노동조합인 엔와이에스유티

la|bour /le̱ɪbər/ →see **labor**

la|bour|er /le̱ɪbərər/ →see **laborer**

La|bour Par|ty ♦♦◇ N-PROPER In Britain, **the Labour Party** is the main left-of-center party. It believes that wealth and power should be shared fairly and public services should be free for everyone. ❑ *The Labour Party and the teaching unions condemned the idea.*

고유명사 (영국의) 노동당 ❑ 노동당과 교원노조들이 그 견해를 비판했다.

lab|y|rinth /læ̱bɪrɪnθ/ (**labyrinths**) **1** N-COUNT If you describe a place as a **labyrinth**, you mean that it is made up of a complicated series of paths or passages, through which it is difficult to find your way. [LITERARY] ❑ *...the labyrinth of corridors.* **2** N-COUNT If you describe a situation, process, or area of knowledge as a **labyrinth**, you mean that it is very complicated. [FORMAL] ❑ *...a labyrinth of conflicting political and sociological interpretations.*

1 가산명사 미로 [문예체] ❑ 미로 같은 회랑 **2** 가산명사 복잡함, 미로 (같은 것) [격식체] ❑ 상충하는 정치 및 사회적 해석의 복잡함

lace /le̱ɪs/ (**laces, lacing, laced**) **1** N-UNCOUNT **Lace** is a very delicate cloth which is made with a lot of holes in it. It is made by twisting together very fine threads of cotton to form patterns. ❑ *She finally found the perfect gown, a beautiful creation trimmed with lace.* **2** N-COUNT **Laces** are thin pieces of material that are put through special holes in some types of clothing, especially shoes. The laces are tied together in order to tighten the clothing. ❑ *Barry was sitting on the bed, tying the laces of an old pair of running shoes.* **3** V-T If you **lace** something such as a pair of shoes, you tighten the shoes by pulling the laces through the holes, and usually tying them together. ❑ *I have a good pair of skates, but no matter how tightly I lace them, my ankles wobble.* ● PHRASAL VERB **Lace up** means the same as **lace**. ❑ *He sat on the steps, and laced up his boots.* **4** V-T To **lace** food or drink with a substance such as alcohol or a drug means to put a small amount of the substance into the food or drink. ❑ *She laced his food with sleeping pills.*

1 불가산명사 레이스 ❑ 그녀는 드디어 더할 나위 없는 드레스를 찾았는데 가선이 레이스로 장식된 아름다운 옷이었다. **2** 가산명사 끈 ❑ 배리는 침대에 앉아서, 오래된 운동화의 끈을 매고 있었다. **3** 타동사 끈을 매다 ❑ 나는 좋은 스케이트 한 켤레가 있는데 아무리 끈을 꽉 매도 발목이 흔들거린다. ● 구동사 끈을 매다 ❑ 그는 계단에 앉아 부츠의 끈을 매었다. **4** 타동사 타다, 가미하다 ❑ 그녀는 그의 음식에 수면제를 탔다.

lack ♦♦◇ /læ̱k/ (**lacks, lacking, lacked**) **1** N-UNCOUNT If there is a **lack** of something, there is not enough of it or it does not exist at all. [also a N, usu N of n] ❑ *Despite his lack of experience, he got the job.* ❑ *The charges were dropped for lack of evidence.* **2** V-T/V-I If you say that someone or something **lacks** a particular quality or that a particular quality **is lacking** in them, you mean that they do not have any or enough of it. ❑ *It lacked the power of the Italian cars.* ❑ *He lacked the judgment and political acumen for the post of chairman.* **3** PHRASE If you say there is **no lack of** something, you are emphasizing that there is a great deal of it. [EMPHASIS] ❑ *He said there was no lack of things for them to talk about.*

1 불가산명사 부족, 결핍 ❑ 경험이 부족함에도, 그는 그 일자리를 얻었다. ❑ 그 혐의는 증거 부족으로 기각되었다. **2** 타동사/자동사 결여되어 있다 ❑ 그것에는 이탈리아 차들이 가지는 힘이 결여되어 있었다. ❑ 그는 회장직을 수행하기에는 판단력과 정치적 통찰력이 결여되어 있었다. **3** 구 ~가 넘치는 [강조] ❑ 그는 그들이 이야기할 거리가 넘쳐난다고 말했다.

Thesaurus lack의 참조어

N. absence, shortage; (*ant.*) abundance **1**

V. be without, miss, need, require, want; (*ant.*) have, own **2**

Word Partnership lack의 연어

N. lack *of* **confidence**, lack *of* **control**, lack *of* **enthusiasm**,
lack *of* **evidence**, lack **of exercise**, lack *of* **experience**, lack *of* **food**,
lack *of* **information**, lack *of* **knowledge**, lack *of* **money**,
lack *of* **progress**, lack *of* **resources**, lack *of* **skills**, lack *of* **sleep**,
lack *of* **support**, lack *of* **trust**, lack *of* **understanding** **1** **3**

lack|ing /lǽkɪŋ/ ADJ If something or someone **is lacking in** a particular quality, they do not have any of it or enough of it. [v-link ADJ, usu ADJ in n] ❏ ...*if your hair is lacking in lustre and feeling dry.* ❏ *She felt nervous, increasingly lacking in confidence about herself.*

형용사 _이 걸어되어 있다, _이 부족하다 ❏ 여러분의 머리에 윤기가 없고 건조하다면 ❏ 그녀는 불안했고, 점점 더 자신감이 부족해졌다.

lack|luster /lǽklʌstər/ (BRIT **lacklustre**) ADJ If you describe something or someone as **lackluster**, you mean that they are not exciting or energetic. ❏ *He has already been blamed for his party's lackluster performance during the election campaign.*

[영국영어 lacklustre] 형용사 활기 없는 ❏ 그는 선거 운동 기간 중의 활기 없는 당 운영에 대해 이미 비난을 받고 있다.

lac|quer /lǽkər/ (**lacquers**) N-MASS **Lacquer** is a special liquid which is painted on wood or metal in order to protect it and to make it shiny. ❏ *We put on the second coating of lacquer.*

물질명사 래커, 옻칠 ❏ 우리는 래커를 두 번째 입혔다.

lacy /léɪsi/ (**lacier, laciest**) ADJ **Lacy** things are made from lace or have pieces of lace attached to them. ❏ ...*lacy nightgowns.*

형용사 레이스로 된, 레이스의 ❏ 레이스가 달린 잠옷

lad ◆◇◇ /lǽd/ (**lads**) ▮ N-COUNT; N-VOC A **lad** is a young man or boy. [INFORMAL] ❏ *When I was a lad his age I would laugh at the strangest things.* ▮ N-PLURAL Some men refer to their male friends or colleagues as **the lads**. [BRIT, INFORMAL] ❏ ...*having a drink with the lads.*

▮ 가산명사; 호격명사 젊은이, 소년 [비격식체] ❏ 내가 그 젊은이 또래였다면 가장 별스러운 일에도 콧방귀를 뀌었을 것이다. ▮ 복수명사 녀석들, 동료들 [영국영어, 비격식체] ❏ 동료들과 술 한 잔 하며

lad|der /lǽdər/ (**ladders**) ▮ N-COUNT A **ladder** is a piece of equipment used for climbing up something or down from something. It consists of two long pieces of wood, metal, or rope with steps fixed between them. ❏ *He climbed the ladder to the next deck.* ▮ N-SING You can use **the ladder** to refer to something such as a society, organization, or system which has different levels that people can progress up or drop down. ❏ *If they want to climb the ladder of success they should be given that opportunity.* ▮ N-COUNT A **ladder** is a hole or torn part in a woman's stocking or pantyhose, where some of the vertical threads have broken, leaving only the horizontal threads. [mainly BRIT; AM **run**] ❏ *There was a ladder in her stocking.*

▮ 가산명사 사다리 ❏ 그가 사다리를 타고 옆 갑판으로 올라갔다. ▮ 단수명사 (성공으로 향하는) 계단, 출세의 수단 ❏ 그들이 성공에 이르는 계단을 오르고 싶어 한다면 그들에게 그러한 기회가 주어져야 한다. ▮ 가산명사 (스타킹의 주로) 올이 풀린 곳 [주로 영국영어; 미국영어 run] ❏ 그녀의 스타킹이 올이 풀렸었다.

lad|dish /lǽdɪʃ/ ADJ If you describe someone as **laddish**, you mean that they behave in a way that people think is typical of young men, for example by being rough and noisy, drinking a lot of alcohol, and having a bad attitude toward women. [DISAPPROVAL] ❏ *Their manager is unconcerned at the laddish image and the drinking that goes with it.*

형용사 거친, 사내 특유의 [탐탁잖음] ❏ 그들의 매니저는 거친 이미지와 이에 동반되는 음주에 대해서는 걱정하지 않는다.

lad|en /léɪdən/ ▮ ADJ If someone or something is **laden with** a lot of heavy things, they are holding or carrying them. [LITERARY] ❏ *I came home laden with cardboard boxes.* ❏ *The following summer the peach tree was laden with fruit.* ▮ ADJ If you describe a person or thing as **laden with** something, particularly something bad, you mean that they have a lot of it. [v-link ADJ with n] ❏ *We're so laden with guilt.*

▮ 형용사 잔뜩 실은 [문예체] ❏ 나는 마분지 상자를 잔뜩 싣고 집에 왔다. ❏ 그 다음 해 여름 그 복숭아나무에는 열매가 주렁주렁 열렸다. ▮ 형용사 시달리는 ❏ 우리는 죄책감에 몹시 시달리고 있다.

lady ◆◆◇ /léɪdi/ (**ladies**) ▮ N-COUNT You can use **lady** when you are referring to a woman, especially when you are showing politeness or respect. ❏ *She's a very sweet old lady.* ❏ ...*a cream-colored lady's shoe.* ▮ N-TITLE In Britain, **Lady** is a title used in front of the names of some female members of the nobility, or the wives of knights. ❏ *Cockburn's arrival coincided with that of Sir Iain and Lady Noble.* ▮ N-SING People sometimes refer to a public toilet for women as **the ladies**. [BRIT, INFORMAL] ❏ *At Temple station, Charlotte rushed into the Ladies.* ▮ N-VOC **"Lady"** is sometimes used by men as a form of address when they are talking to a woman that they do not know, especially in stores and on the street. [AM, INFORMAL, POLITENESS] ❏ *What seems to be the trouble, lady?*

▮ 가산명사 부인, 여자분, 숙녀 ❏ 그녀는 매우 상냥한 노부인이다. ❏ 크림색의 숙녀화 ▮ 경칭명사 (작위 귀족) 부인, 영부 ❏ 콕번 씨는 우연히도 아인 경, 그리고 노블 부인과 함께 도착했다. ▮ 단수명사 여자 화장실 [영국영어, 비격식체] ❏ 템플역에서, 샬롯은 여자 화장실로 급히 뛰어 들어갔다. ▮ 호격명사 부인, 사모님 [미국영어, 비격식체, 공손체] ❏ 부인, 무슨 문제라도 있으신가요?

lag /lǽg/ (**lags, lagging, lagged**) ▮ V-I If one thing or person **lags behind** another thing or person, their progress is slower than that of the other thing or person. ❏ *Western banks still lag behind financial institutions in most other regions of the country.* ❏ *The restructuring of the pattern of consumption in Britain also lagged behind.* ▮ N-COUNT A time **lag** or a **lag** of a particular length of time is a period of time between one event and another related event. ❏ *There's a time lag between infection with HIV and developing AIDS.*

▮ 자동사 뒤처지다, 꾸물거리다 ❏ 서구 은행들은 아직도 이 나라의 다른 대부분 지역에 있는 금융 기관들에 비해 뒤처져 있다. ❏ 영국은 소비 형태 개혁 역시 뒤떨어져 있었다. ▮ 가산명사 지연, 시차 ❏ 인체 면역 결핍 바이러스에 감염되면 어느 정도 시간이 지난 뒤에 에이즈가 발병한다.

la|ger /lάːgər/ (**lagers**) N-MASS **Lager** is a type of light beer. [BRIT] ❏ ...*a pint of lager.* ● N-COUNT A glass of lager can be referred to as a **lager**. ❏ *Liz and Darren shared a lager and danced a little.*

물질명사 라거 (맥주) [영국영어] ❏ 1파인트의 라거 ● 가산명사 라거 한 잔 ❏ 리즈와 다렌은 라거 한 잔을 나눠 마시고 잠깐 춤을 추었다.

la|goon /ləgúːn/ (**lagoons**) N-COUNT A **lagoon** is an area of calm sea water that is separated from the ocean by a line of rock or sand.

가산명사 석호

laid /léɪd/ **Laid** is the past tense and past participle of **lay**.

lay의 과거 및 과거 분사

laid-back ADJ If you describe someone as **laid-back**, you mean that they behave in a calm relaxed way as if nothing will ever worry them. [INFORMAL] ❏ *Everyone here has a really laid-back attitude.*

형용사 느긋한 [비격식체] ❏ 여기 있는 사람들은 모두 다 정말 태도가 느긋하다.

lain /léɪn/ **Lain** is the past participle of **lie**.

lie의 과거 분사

laissez-faire /léɪseɪ fɛər, lɛs-/ N-UNCOUNT **Laissez-faire** is the policy which is based on the idea that governments and the law should not interfere with business, finance, or the conditions of people's working lives. [BUSINESS] ❏ ...*the doctrine of laissez-faire and unbridled individualism.*

불가산명사 자유방임주의 [경제] ❏ 자유방임주의와 구속 없는 개인주의 정책

lake ◆◇◇ /léɪk/ (**lakes**) N-COUNT A **lake** is a large area of fresh water, surrounded by land. ❏ *They can go fishing in the lake.* →see **river** →see Word Web: **lake**

가산명사 호수 ❏ 그들은 그 호수로 낚시하러 갈 수도 있다.

lamb /lǽm/ (**lambs**) ▮ N-COUNT A **lamb** is a young sheep. ● N-UNCOUNT **Lamb** is the flesh of a lamb eaten as food. ❏ *Laura was basting the leg of lamb.* ▮ **mutton dressed as lamb** →see **mutton**

▮ 가산명사 새끼 양 ● 불가산명사 새끼 양의 고기 ❏ 로라는 양 다리 고기에 육수를 바르고 있었다.

lame /léɪm/ (**lamer, lamest**) ▮ ADJ If someone is **lame**, they are unable to walk properly because of damage to one or both of their legs. ❏ *He was aware that she was lame in one leg.* ● N-PLURAL **The lame** are people who are lame. ❏ ... *the wounded and the lame of the last war.* ▮ ADJ If you describe an excuse, argument, or remark as **lame**, you mean that it is poor or weak. ❏ *He mumbled some lame excuse about having gone to sleep.* ● **lame|ly** ADV [ADV with v] ❏ *"Lovely house," I said lamely.*

▮ 형용사 절룩거리는 ❏ 그는 그녀가 한쪽 다리를 절룩거린다는 것을 깨달았다. ● 복수명사 절름발이 ❏ 지난 전쟁으로 인한 부상자들과 절름발이들 ▮ 형용사 변변찮은 ❏ 그는 잠을 자러 간 것에 대해 변변찮은 변명을 몇 마디 중얼거렸다. ● 변변찮게 부사 ❏ "멋진 집이네요." 나는 변변찮게 말했다.

a b c d e f g h i j k l m n o p q r s t u v w x y z

Word Web   lake

Several forces create **lakes**. The movement of a glacier can carve out a deep **basin** in the soil. The Great Lakes between the U.S. and Canada are **glacial** lakes. Very deep lakes appear when large pieces of the earth's crust suddenly shift. Lake Baikal in Russia is over a mile deep. When a volcano erupts, it creates a **crater**. Crater Lake in Oregon is the perfectly round remains of a volcanic cone. It contains **water** from melted snow and rain. Erosion also creates lakes. When the wind blows away sand, the hole left behind forms a natural lake **bed**.

la|ment /ləmɛnt/ (**laments, lamenting, lamented**) ◼ V-T/V-I If you **lament** something, you express your sadness, regret, or disappointment about it. [mainly FORMAL OR WRITTEN] ❑ *Ken began to lament the death of his only son.* ❑ *He laments their position in Villa El Salvador are suspicious of the police.* ◼ N-COUNT Someone's **lament** is an expression of their sadness, regret, or disappointment about something. [mainly FORMAL OR WRITTEN] ❑ *She spoke of the professional woman's lament that a woman's judgment is questioned more than a man's.* ◼ N-COUNT A **lament** is a poem, song, or piece of music which expresses sorrow that someone has died. ❑ *...Shelley's lament for the death of Keats.*

lamp /læmp/ (**lamps**) N-COUNT A **lamp** is a light that works by using electricity or by burning oil or gas. ❑ *She switched on the bedside lamp.*

LAN /læn/ (**LANs**) N-COUNT A **LAN** is a group of personal computers and associated equipment that are linked by cable, for example in an office building, and that share a communications line. **LAN** is an abbreviation for **local area network**. [COMPUTING] ❑ *You can take part in multiplayer games either on a LAN network or via the internet.*

land ♦♦♦ /lænd/ (**lands, landing, landed**) ◼ N-UNCOUNT **Land** is an area of ground, especially one that is used for a particular purpose such as farming or building. ❑ *Good agricultural land is in short supply.* ❑ *...160 acres of land.* ◼ N-COUNT You can refer to an area of land which someone owns as their **land** or their **lands**. ❑ *Their home is on his father's land.* ◼ N-SING If you talk about **the land**, you mean farming and the way of life in farming areas, in contrast to life in the cities. ❑ *Living off the land was hard enough at the best of times.* ◼ N-UNCOUNT **Land** is the part of the world that consists of ground, rather than sea or air. [also the N] ❑ *It isn't clear whether the plane went down over land or sea.* ◼ N-COUNT You can use **land** to refer to a country in a poetic or emotional way. [LITERARY] ❑ *...America, land of opportunity.*

Country is the most usual word to use when you are talking about the major political units that the world is divided into. **State** is used when you are talking about politics or government institutions. ❑ *...the new German state created by the unification process....Italy's state-controlled telecommunications company.* **State** can also refer to a political unit within a particular country. ❑ *...the state of California.* **Nation** is often used when you are talking about a country's inhabitants, and their cultural or ethnic background. ❑ *Wales is a proud nation with its own traditions... A senior government spokesman will address the nation.* **Land** is a less precise and more literary word, which you can use, for example, to talk about the feelings you have for a particular country. ❑ *She was fascinated to learn about this strange land at the edge of Europe.*

◼ V-I When someone or something **lands**, they come down to the ground after moving through the air or falling. ❑ *He was sent flying into the air and landed 20ft away.* ◼ V-T/V-I When someone **lands** a plane, ship, or spacecraft, or when it **lands**, it arrives somewhere after a journey. ❑ *The jet landed after a flight of just under three hours.* ❑ *He landed his troops on the western shore.* ◼ V-T/V-I If you **land in** an unpleasant situation or place or if something **lands** you in it, something causes you to be in it. [INFORMAL] ❑ *He landed in a psychiatric ward.* ◼ V-T If someone or something **lands** you **with** a difficult situation, they cause you to have to deal with the difficulties involved. [mainly BRIT, INFORMAL] ❑ *The other options simply complicate the situation and could land him with more expense.* ◼ V-I If something **lands** somewhere, it arrives there unexpectedly, often causing problems. [INFORMAL] ❑ *Two days later the book had already landed on his desk.* ◼ to **land on** your **feet** →see **foot**
→see **continents, earth**

Thesaurus   land의 참조어

N.	acreage, area, country, real estate ◼
V.	arrive, touch down; (ant.) take off ◼ ◼

Word Partnership   land의 연어

N.	**acres of** land, **area of** land, **desert** land, land **development**, land **management**, land **ownership**, **piece of** land, **plot of** land, **strip of** land, land **use** ◼ ◼
ADJ.	**agricultural** land, **fertile** land, **flat** land, **private** land, **public** land, **vacant** land, **vast** land ◼ ◼
V.	**buy** land, **own** land, **sell** land ◼ ◼

◼ 타동사/자동사 애도하다, 안타까워하다 [주로 격식체 또는 문어체] ❑ 켄은 외아들의 죽음을 애도하기 시작했다. ❑ 그는 '빌라 엘 살바도르' 사람들이 경찰을 의혹의 눈초리로 보고 있다고 안타까워한다. ◼ 가산명사 애도, 비애 [주로 격식체 또는 문어체] ❑ 그녀는 여성의 판단이 남성의 판단보다 더 문제시되는 전문직 여성의 비애에 대해서 말했다. ◼ 가산명사 애가 ❑ 키이츠의 죽음에 부치는 셜리의 애가

가산명사 전등, 등불 ❑ 그녀는 침대 옆의 등을 켰다.

가산명사 근거리 통신망 [컴퓨터] ❑ 근거리 통신망이나 인터넷을 통해 다자간 게임에 참여할 수 있다.

◼ 불가산명사 토지 ❑ 기름진 농토가 부족하다. ◼ 160에이커의 토지 ◼ 가산명사 사유지 ❑ 그들의 집은 그 사람 아버지 소유의 사유지에 있다. ◼ 단수명사 경작, 토지 ❑ 땅을 갈아먹고 사는 일은 사정이 가장 좋은 때에도 어렵기만 했다. ◼ 불가산명사 육지 ❑ 그 비행기가 육지에 추락했는지 바다에 추락했는지는 확실치 않다. ◼ 가산명사 나라 [문예체] ❑ 미국, 기회의 나라

country는 세계를 나누는 주요 정치 단위에 대해 얘기할 때 쓰는 가장 일반적인 말이다. state는 정치나 정부 기관에 대해 얘기할 때 쓴다. ❑ ...통일 과정에 의해 만들어진 새 독일 정부.... 정부가 관장하는 이태리 통신 회사. state는 특정 국가 내의 정치 단위를 가리킬 수도 있다. ❑ ...캘리포니아 주. nation은 한 나라의 거주자, 거주자의 문화적 또는 인종적 배경을 얘기할 때 흔히 쓴다. ❑ 웨일스는 고유의 전통을 지닌 자부심이 있는 나라이다... 정부 고위 대변인이 국민에게 연설할 것이다. land는 덜 정확하고 더 문학적인 말이며, 예를 들면 특정한 국가에 대한 감정을 얘기할 때 쓸 수 있다. ❑ 그녀는 유럽의 가장자리에 있는 이 낯선 땅에 대해 배우는 데 매료되었다.

◼ 자동사 땅에 닿다 ❑ 그는 공중에 냅다 던져져 20피트 떨어진 곳에 떨어졌다. ◼ 타동사/자동사 착륙시키다, 상륙시키다; 착륙하다, 상륙하다 ❑ 그 제트기는 근 세 시간의 비행 후 착륙했다. ❑ 그는 서쪽 해안에 병력을 상륙시켰다. ◼ 타동사/자동사 (곤경에) 빠지다; (곤경에) 빠뜨리다 [비격식체] ❑ 그는 정신병동에 처넣어졌다. ◼ 타동사 떠맡기다 [주로 영국영어, 비격식체] ❑ 다른 선택을 한다면 단지 상황만 복잡해지고 그가 추가 비용을 떠맡을 수도 있다. ◼ 자동사 놓이다 [비격식체] ❑ 이틀 후에 그 책은 이미 그의 책상 위에 놓여 있었다.

land|fill /lǽndfɪl/ (landfills) **1** N-UNCOUNT **Landfill** is a method of getting rid of very large amounts of garbage by burying it in a large deep hole. ❑ *...the environmental costs of landfill.* **2** N-COUNT A **landfill** is a large deep hole in which very large amounts of garbage are buried. ❑ *The rubbish in modern landfills does not rot.*

불가산명사 쓰레기 매립 ❑ 쓰레기 매립에 따른 환경적 손실 **2** 가산명사 매립지 ❑ 요즘 매립지에서는 쓰레기가 썩지 않는다.

land|ing /lǽndɪŋ/ (landings) **1** N-COUNT In a house or other building, the **landing** is the area at the top of the staircase which has rooms leading off it. ❑ *I ran out onto the landing.* **2** N-VAR A **landing** is an act of bringing an aircraft or spacecraft down to the ground. ❑ *I had to make a controlled landing into the sea.* **3** N-COUNT When a **landing** takes place, troops are unloaded from boats or aircraft at the beginning of a military invasion or other operation. ❑ *American forces have begun a big landing.*

1 가산명사 층계참 ❑ 나는 층계참 쪽으로 내달렸다. **2** 가산명사 또는 불가산명사 착륙 ❑ 나는 바다 속으로 유도 착륙을 해야 했다. **3** 가산명사 상륙 ❑ 미군이 대규모 상륙을 막 시작했다.

land|lady /lǽndleɪdi/ (landladies) N-COUNT Someone's **landlady** is the woman who allows them to live or work in a building which she owns, in return for rent. ❑ *We had been made homeless by our landlady.*

가산명사 (여자) 집주인 ❑ 우리는 집주인에게서 쫓겨나 집 없는 신세가 되었었다.

land|lord /lǽndlɔrd/ (landlords) N-COUNT Someone's **landlord** is the man who allows them to live or work in a building which he owns, in return for rent. ❑ *His landlord doubled the rent.*

가산명사 (남자) 집주인 ❑ 그의 집주인이 집세를 두 배로 올렸다.

land|mark /lǽndmɑrk/ (landmarks) **1** N-COUNT A **landmark** is a building or feature which is easily noticed and can be used to judge your position or the position of other buildings or features. ❑ *The Ambassador Hotel is a Los Angeles landmark.* **2** N-COUNT You can refer to an important stage in the development of something as a **landmark**. ❑ *...a landmark arms control treaty.*

1 가산명사 주요 지형지물 ❑ 앰배서더 호텔은 로스앤젤레스에서 주요 지형지물이다. **2** 가산명사 획기적인 사건 ❑ 획기적인 군축 협정

land|scape ♦◇◇ /lǽndskeɪp/ (landscapes, landscaping, landscaped) **1** N-VAR The **landscape** is everything you can see when you look across an area of land, including hills, rivers, buildings, trees, and plants. ❑ *...Arizona's desert landscape.*

1 가산명사 또는 불가산명사 풍경 ❑ 애리조나의 황량한 풍경

> Do not confuse **landscape**, **scenery**, **countryside**, and **nature**. With **landscape**, the emphasis is on the physical features of the land, while **scenery** includes everything you can see when you look out over an area of land. ❑ *...the landscape of steep woods and distant mountains....unattractive urban scenery.* **Countryside** is land which is away from towns and cities. ❑ *...3,500 acres of mostly flat countryside.* **Nature** includes the landscape, the weather, animals, and plants. ❑ *These creatures roamed the Earth as the finest and rarest wonders of nature.*

> landscape, scenery, countryside, nature를 혼동하지 않도록 하라. scenery는 어떤 지역에서 눈에 보이는 모든 것을 포함하는 반면, landscape는 땅의 물리적 특징을 강조한다. ❑ *...우뚝 서 있는 숲과 멀리 산이 보이는 경치....볼품없는 도회지풍 경치.* countryside는 중소 도시나 대도시에서 떨어져 있는 땅이다. ❑ *... 대부분이 평지인 3,500에이커의 시골 지역.* nature는 경치, 날씨, 동물, 식물을 포함한다. ❑ *이 생물체들은 가장 멋지고 가장 희귀한 자연의 경이로서 지구상을 활보했다.*

2 N-COUNT A **landscape** is all the features that are important in a particular situation. ❑ *June's events completely altered the political landscape.* **3** N-COUNT A **landscape** is a painting which shows a scene in the countryside. ❑ *Kenna's latest series of landscapes is on show at the Zelda Cheatle Gallery.* **4** V-T If an area of land is **landscaped**, it is changed to make it more attractive, for example by adding streams or ponds and planting trees and bushes. ❑ *The gravel pits have been landscaped and planted to make them attractive to wildfowl.* ❑ *They had landscaped their property with trees, shrubs, and lawns.* ● **land|scap|ing** N-UNCOUNT ❑ *The landowner insisted on a high standard of landscaping.* →see **painting**

2 가산명사 판 ❑ 6월에 있는 행사들은 정치판을 완전히 바꾸었다. **3** 가산명사 풍경화 ❑ 케나의 최근 풍경화 연작들이 젤다 치틀 갤러리에서 전시 중입니다. **4** 타동사 조경하다 ❑ 그 자갈 구덩이를 조경을 하고 나무도 심어서 야생 조류가 좋아하도록 만들었다. ❑ 그들은 나무, 관목, 그리고 잔디로 소유지를 조경하였다. ● 조경 불가산명사 ❑ 그 토지 소유자는 조경을 매우 고급스럽게 해야 한다고 우겼다.

land|slide /lǽndslaɪd/ (landslides) **1** N-COUNT A **landslide** is a victory in an election in which a person or political party gets far more votes or seats than their opponents. ❑ *He won last month's presidential election by a landslide.* **2** N-COUNT A **landslide** is a large amount of earth and rocks falling down a cliff or the side of a mountain. ❑ *The storm caused landslides and flooding in Savona.* →see **disaster**

1 가산명사 압승 ❑ 그는 지난달 대통령 선거에서 압승을 거두었다. **2** 가산명사 산사태 ❑ 그 태풍으로 사보나에 여러 건의 산사태와 홍수가 발생했다.

lane ♦◇◇ /leɪn/ (lanes) **1** N-COUNT A **lane** is a narrow road, especially in the country. ❑ *...a quiet country lane.* **2** N-IN-NAMES **Lane** is also used in the names of roads, either in cities or in the country. ❑ *...The Dorchester Hotel, Park Lane.* **3** N-COUNT A **lane** is a part of a main road which is marked by the edge of the road and a painted line, or by two painted lines. ❑ *The lorry was traveling at 20mph in the slow lane.* **4** N-COUNT At a swimming pool or racing track, a **lane** is a long narrow section which is marked by lines or ropes. ❑ *...after being disqualified for running out of his lane in the 200 meters.* **5** N-COUNT A **lane** is a route that is frequently used by aircraft or ships. ❑ *The collision took place in the busiest shipping lanes in the world.* →see **traffic**

1 가산명사 (좁은) 길, 오솔길 ❑ 시골의 조용한 오솔길 **2** 이름명사 가(街) (거리 이름) ❑ 파크 가에 위치한 도체스터 호텔 **3** 가산명사 차선 ❑ 그 화물차는 서행 차선에서 시속 20마일로 주행하고 있었다. **4** 가산명사 (수영장 등의) 레인 ❑ 200미터 달리기에서 그가 자신의 레인을 벗어나서 달리다 실격당한 후 **5** 가산명사 항로 ❑ 그 충돌 사고는 전 세계적으로 가장 교통량이 많은 해상 항로에서 발생했다.

lan|guage ♦♦◇ /lǽŋgwɪdʒ/ (languages) **1** N-COUNT A **language** is a system of communication which consists of a set of sounds and written symbols which are used by the people of a particular country or region for talking or writing. ❑ *...the English language.* ❑ *Students are expected to master a second language.* **2** N-UNCOUNT **Language** is the use of a system of communication which consists of a set of sounds or written symbols. ❑ *Students examined how children acquire language.* **3** N-UNCOUNT You can refer to the words used in connection with a particular subject as **the language of** that subject. ❑ *...the language of business.* **4** N-UNCOUNT You can refer to someone's use of rude words or swearing as **bad language** when you find it offensive. ❑ *Television companies tend to censor bad language in feature films.* **5** N-UNCOUNT The **language** of a piece of writing or speech is the style in which it is written or spoken. ❑ *...a booklet summarizing it in plain language.* ❑ *The tone of his language was diplomatic and polite.* **6** N-VAR You can use **language** to refer to various means of communication involving recognizable symbols, nonverbal sounds, or actions. ❑ *Some sign languages are very sophisticated means of communication.* →see **culture**, **English**

1 가산명사 언어 ❑ 영어 ❑ 학생들이 제 2 언어에 숙달하게 될 것으로 기대된다. **2** 불가산명사 언어 ❑ 학생들은 아이들이 어떻게 언어를 습득하는지를 조사했다. **3** 불가산명사 (특정 분야의) 언어, 용어 ❑ 상업 언어 **4** 불가산명사 저속한 말, 욕설 ❑ 텔레비전 방송국들은 장편 영화에 나오는 저속한 말들을 검열하는 편이다. **5** 불가산명사 문체, 말씨 ❑ 평이한 문체로 그것을 요약한 소책자 ❑ 그의 어조는 외교적이고 공손했다. **6** 가산명사 또는 불가산명사 의사 전달 수단 ❑ 일부 수화는 매우 정교한 의사소통 수단이다.

Thesaurus	*language*의 참조어	
N.	communication, dialect, lexicon **1 2 6**	
	jargon, slang, terminology **3 5**	
	swear **4**	

Word Partnership language의 연어

V.	know a language, learn a language, speak a language, study a language, teach a language, understand a language, use a language **1**
N.	language acquisition, language **barrier**, child language, language of children, language classes, language comprehension, language development, proficiency in a language, language skills **1 2** body language, computer language, sign language **6**
ADJ.	a different language, foreign language, native language, official language, second language, universal language **1** bad language, foul language, vulgar language **4** plain language, simple language, technical language **5**

lan|guid /lǽŋgwɪd/ ADJ If you describe someone as **languid**, you mean that they show little energy or interest and are very slow and casual in their movements. [LITERARY] ❑ *He's a large, languid man with a round and impassive face.* ● **lan|guid|ly** ADV ❑ *We sat about languidly after dinner.*

형용사 심드렁한, 나른한 [문예체] ❑ 그는 큰 몸집에 표정 없는 동그란 얼굴을 한 심드렁한 남자이다. ● 심드렁하게, 나른하게 부사 ❑ 우리는 저녁을 먹고 그냥 나른하게 앉아 있었다.

lan|guish /lǽŋgwɪʃ/ (languishes, languishing, languished) **1** V-I If someone **languishes** somewhere, they are forced to remain and suffer in an unpleasant situation. ❑ *Pollard continues to languish in prison.* **2** V-I If something **languishes**, it is not successful, often because of a lack of effort or because of a lot of difficulties. ❑ *Without the founder's drive and direction, the company gradually languished.*

1 자동사 괴로운 시간을 보내다, 고생하다 ❑ 폴라드는 계속 감옥에서 괴로운 생활을 하고 있다. **2** 자동사 부진하다, 쇠하다 ❑ 설립자의 추진력과 지도력이 없어지자 그 회사는 차츰 부진해졌다.

lan|tern /lǽntərn/ (lanterns) N-COUNT A **lantern** is a lamp in a metal frame with glass sides and with a handle on top so you can carry it.

가산명사 손전등, 제등

lap ♦◇◇ /lǽp/ (laps, lapping, lapped) **1** N-COUNT If you have something on your **lap** when you are sitting down, it is on top of your legs and near to your body. ❑ *She waited quietly with her hands in her lap.* **2** N-COUNT In a race, a competitor completes a **lap** when they have gone round a course once. ❑ *...that last lap of the race.* **3** V-T In a race, if you **lap** another competitor, you go past them while they are still on the previous lap. ❑ *He was caught out while lapping a slower rider.* **4** N-COUNT A **lap** of a long journey is one part of it, between two points where you stop. ❑ *I had thought we might travel as far as Oak Valley, but we only managed the first lap of the journey.* **5** V-T/V-I When water **laps** against something such as the shore or the side of a boat, it touches it gently and makes a soft sound. [WRITTEN] ❑ *...the water that lapped against the pillars of the boathouse.* ❑ *With a rising tide the water was lapping at his chin before rescuers arrived.* ● **lap|ping** N-UNCOUNT ❑ *The only sound was the lapping of the waves.* **6** V-T When an animal **laps** a drink, it uses short quick movements of its tongue to take liquid up into its mouth. ❑ *It lapped milk from a dish.* ● PHRASAL VERB **Lap up** means the same as **lap**. ❑ *She poured some water into a plastic bowl. Faust, her Great Dane, lapped it up with relish.*

1 가산명사 무릎 (앉았을 때 넓적다리 위의 공간) ❑ 그녀는 무릎 위에 양손을 올린 채 조용히 기다렸다. **2** 가산명사 한 바퀴 ❑ 그 경주의 마지막 한 바퀴 **3** 타동사 한 바퀴 앞서다 ❑ 그가 자기보다 느린 기수를 한 바퀴 앞서다가 실수를 했다. **4** 가산명사 여정, (긴 여행길의) 한 단계 ❑ 나는 우리가 오크 밸리까지는 이동할 수 있을 거라고 생각했었지만 겨우 첫 번째 여정만 이동했다. **5** 타동사/자동사 찰싹거리다 [문예체] ❑ 보트 창고의 기둥에 찰싹거리는 바닷물 ❑ 구조대원들이 도착하기 전에 썰물이 밀려들면서 바닷물이 그의 턱에 찰싹거렸다. ● 찰싹거리는 소리 불가산명사 ❑ 들리는 것이라고는 파도가 찰싹거리는 소리뿐이었다. **6** 타동사 핥아먹다 ❑ 그것이 접시에 있던 우유를 핥아먹었다. ● 구동사 핥아먹다 ❑ 그녀는 플라스틱 사발에 물을 약간 따랐다. 그녀가 기르는 그레이트데인 종인 파우스트가 그 물을 맛있게 핥아먹었다.

▶**lap up** PHRASAL VERB If you say that someone **laps up** something such as information or attention, you mean that they accept it eagerly, usually when you think they are being foolish in believing that it is sincere. ❑ *Their audience will lap up whatever they throw at them.* →see **lap 6**

구동사 덥석덥석 받아들이다 ❑ 청중들은 그들이 쏟아 놓는 것은 무엇이든 덥석덥석 받아들일 것이다.

la|pel /ləpɛ́l/ (lapels) N-COUNT The **lapels** of a jacket or coat are the two top parts at the front that are folded back on each side and join on to the collar. ❑ *He sports a small red flower in his lapel.*

가산명사 (상의의 접힌) 옷깃 ❑ 그는 옷깃에 작은 빨간 꽃 한 송이를 자랑스럽게 꽂고 있다.

Word Link lapse ≈ falling : col*lapse*, e*lapse*, *lapse*

lapse /lǽps/ (lapses, lapsing, lapsed) **1** N-COUNT A **lapse** is a moment or instance of bad behavior by someone who usually behaves well. ❑ *On Friday he showed neither decency nor dignity. It was an uncommon lapse.* **2** N-COUNT A **lapse of** something such as concentration or judgment is a temporary lack of that thing, which can often cause you to make a mistake. ❑ *I had a little lapse of concentration in the middle of the race.* ❑ *He was a genius and because of it you could accept lapses of taste.* **3** V-I If you **lapse into** a quiet or inactive state, you stop talking or being active. ❑ *He muttered something unintelligible and lapsed into silence.* **4** V-I If someone **lapses into** a particular way of speaking, or behaving, they start speaking or behaving in that way, usually for a short period. ❑ *She lapsed into a girlish voice to deliver a nursery rhyme.* ● N-COUNT **Lapse** is also a noun. ❑ *Her lapse into German didn't seem peculiar. After all, it was her native tongue.* **5** N-SING A **lapse of** time is a period that is long enough for a situation to change or for people to have a different opinion about it. ❑ *...the restoration of diplomatic relations after a lapse of 24 years.* **6** V-I If a period of time **lapses**, it passes. ❑ *New products and production processes are transferred to the developing countries only after a substantial amount of time has lapsed.* **7** V-I If a situation or legal contract **lapses**, it is allowed to end rather than being continued, renewed, or extended. ❑ *Her membership of the Labour Party has lapsed.* **8** V-T/V-I If a member of a particular religion **lapses**, they stop believing in it or stop following its rules and practices. ❑ *I lapsed in my 20s, returned to it, then lapsed again, while writing the life of historical Jesus.*

1 가산명사 일탈 ❑ 금요일에 그에게서는 체면도 품위도 찾아 볼 수 없었다. 그건 좀처럼 그가 하지 않던 일탈이다. **2** 가산명사 (순간적으로) 깜빡함 ❑ 나는 경주 도중 집중력을 약간 잃었다. ❑ 그는 천재였으니까 그것 때문에 네가 그의 감식력이 깜빡깜빡해도 용인할 수 있었던 거야. **3** 자동사 -한 상태에 빠지다 ❑ 그녀가 알아들을 수 없는 말을 뭐라고 중얼거리더니 조용해졌다. **4** 자동사/자동사 ❑ 그녀는 동요를 읊어 주기 위해 목소리를 잠깐 어린 여자아이처럼 내었다. ● 가산명사 잠깐씩 -함 ❑ 그녀가 잠깐씩 독일어를 하는 것은 이상해 보이지 않았다. 따지고 보면, 독일어는 그녀의 모국어였다. **5** 단수명사 (시간의) 경과 ❑ 24년이 경과한 후 외교 관계 복원 **6** 자동사 (시간이) 경과하다 ❑ 상당한 시간이 경과한 후라야만 신제품 및 새 제조공정이 개발도상국으로 이전된다. **7** 자동사 소멸되다 ❑ 그녀의 노동당원 자격은 소멸되었다. **8** 타동사/자동사 (특정 종교를) 그만 믿다 ❑ 나는 20대에 그 종교를 그만 믿었다가 다시 믿게 되었는데, 역사적인 예수의 생애를 집필하면서 다시 그만 믿게 되었다.

lap|top /lǽptɒp/ (laptops) N-COUNT A **laptop** or a **laptop computer** is a small portable computer. ❑ *She used to work at her laptop until four in the morning.*

가산명사 휴대용 컴퓨터, 노트북 컴퓨터 ❑ 그녀는 새벽 4시까지 자신의 휴대용 컴퓨터로 작업을 하곤 했다.

Word Link　　　est ≈ most : cold**est**, high**est**, larg**est**

large ♦♦♦ /lɑrdʒ/ (**larger**, **largest**) **1** ADJ A **large** thing or person is greater in size than usual or average. ❑ *The pike lives mainly in large rivers and lakes.* ❑ *In the largest room about a dozen children and seven adults are sitting on the carpet.* **2** ADJ A **large** amount or number of people or things is more than the average amount or number. ❑ *The gang finally fled with a large amount of cash and jewelry.* ❑ *There are a large number of centers where you can take full-time courses.* **3** ADJ **Large** is used to indicate that a problem or issue which is being discussed is very important or serious. ❑ *...the already large problem of under-age drinking.*

> **Large**, **big**, and **great** are all used to talk about size. In general, **large** is more formal than **big** and **great** is more formal than **large**. **Large** and **big** are normally used to describe objects, but you can also use **big** to suggest that something is important or impressive. ❑ *...his influence over the big advertisers.* You normally use **great** to emphasize the importance of someone or something. ❑ *...the great English architect, Inigo Jones.* However, you can also use **great** to suggest that something is impressive because of its size. ❑ *The great bird of prey was a dark smudge against the sun.* You can use **large** or **great**, but not **big**, to describe amounts. ❑ *...a large amount of blood on the floor....the coming of tourists in great numbers.* Both **big** and **great** can be used to emphasize the intensity of something, although **great** is more formal. ❑ *It gives me great pleasure to welcome you... Most of them act like big fools.*

4 PHRASE You use **at large** to indicate that you are talking in a general way about most of the people mentioned. ❑ *I think the chances of getting reforms accepted by the community at large remain extremely remote.* **5** PHRASE If you say that a dangerous person, thing, or animal is **at large**, you mean that they have not been captured or made safe. ❑ *The man who tried to have her killed is still at large.* **6** **to a large extent** →see **extent**

Thesaurus　　　*large*의 참조어

ADJ.　　big, sizable, spacious, substantial; (*ant.*) small **1**

large|ly ♦♦◇ /lɑrdʒli/ **1** ADV You use **largely** to say that a statement is not completely true but is mostly true. ❑ *The fund is largely financed through government borrowing.* ❑ *I largely work with people who already are motivated.* **2** ADV **Largely** is used to introduce the main reason for a particular event or situation. [ADV prep] ❑ *Retail sales dipped 6/10ths of a percent last month, largely because Americans were buying fewer cars.*

large-scale also **large scale** **1** ADJ A **large-scale** action or event happens over a very wide area or involves a lot of people or things. [ADJ n] ❑ *...a large scale military operation.* **2** ADJ A **large-scale** map or diagram represents a small area of land or a building or machine on a scale that is large enough for small details to be shown. [ADJ n] ❑ *...a large-scale map of the county.*

lar|va /lɑrvə/ (**larvae**) /lɑrvi/ N-COUNT A **larva** is an insect at the stage of its life after it has developed from an egg and before it changes into its adult form. ❑ *The eggs quickly hatch into larvae.*

la|ser /leɪzər/ (**lasers**) N-COUNT A **laser** is a narrow beam of concentrated light produced by a special machine. It is used for cutting very hard materials, and in many technical fields such as surgery and telecommunications. ❑ *...new laser technology.*
→see Word Web: **laser**

la|ser print|er (**laser printers**) N-COUNT A **laser printer** is a computer printer that produces clear words and pictures by using laser beams.

lash /læʃ/ (**lashes**, **lashing**, **lashed**) **1** N-COUNT Your **lashes** are the hairs that grow on the edge of your upper and lower eyelids. ❑ *...sombre grey eyes, with unusually long lashes.* **2** V-T If you **lash** two or more things together, you tie one of them firmly to the other. ❑ *Secure the anchor by lashing it to the rail.* ❑ *The shelter is built by lashing poles together to form a small dome.* **3** V-T/V-I If wind, rain, or water **lashes** someone or something, it hits them violently. [WRITTEN] ❑ *The worst winter storms of the century lashed the east coast of North America.* **4** V-T/V-I If someone **lashes** you or **lashes into** you, they speak very angrily to you, criticizing you or saying you have done something wrong. ❑ *She*

1 형용사 큰 ❑ 강꼬치류들은 주로 큰 강이나 호수에 서식한다. ❑ 가장 큰 방 안에서 아이들 10여 명과 어른 7명이 카펫 위에 앉아 있다. **2** 형용사 많은 ❑ 그 폭력단은 결국 많은 돈과 보석을 가지고 달아났다. ❑ 하루 종일 강좌를 들을 수 있는 센터들이 많이 있다. **3** 형용사 중대한 ❑ 이미 중대한 문제로 떠오른 미성년자 음주

large, big, great은 모두 크기를 말할 때 쓴다. 일반적으로 large가 big보다, great이 large보다 더 격식체이다. large와 big은 보통 사물을 묘사할 때 쓰지만, big은 무엇이 중요하거나 인상적임을 시사할 때에도 쓴다. **2** 주요 광고주들에 대한 그의 영향력. 사람이나 사물의 중요성을 강조할 때는 보통 great을 쓴다. ❑ ...위대한 영국 건축가 이니고 존스. 그러나 great은 사물이 그 크기 때문에 인상적임을 시사할 때도 쓸 수 있다. ❑ 그 거대한 맹금은 햇빛을 배경으로 하나의 흐릿한 검은 점처럼 보였다. 양을 나타낼 때는 large나 great은 쓸 수 있지만 big은 못 쓴다. ❑ ...바닥 위의 많은 양의 피.... 수많은 여행객의 방문. big과 great은 어떤 것의 강도를 강조할 때에도 쓸 수 있는데 great이 더 격식체이다. ❑ 이렇게 환영 인사를 드리게 되어 정말 기쁩니다... 그들 대부분은 엄청난 바보처럼 행동한다.

4 구 대부분이, 대체로 ❑ 나는 그 공동체 대부분이 개혁을 수락할 가능성은 매우 희박하다고 생각한다. **5** 구 잡히지 않은 ❑ 그녀를 죽이려고 한 그 남자가 아직도 잡히지 않았다.

1 부사 대개 ❑ 그 자금은 대개 정부차관을 통해 조달된다. ❑ 나는 대개 이미 동기 부여가 되어 있는 사람들과 일을 한다. **2** 부사 주로 ❑ 지난달에 소매가 0.6퍼센트 하락했는데, 주로 미국인들의 자동차 구입이 적어졌기 때문이다.

1 형용사 대규모의 ❑ 대규모 군사 작전 **2** 형용사 대축척의 ❑ 그 지방의 대축척 지도

가산명사 애벌레 ❑ 그 알들은 금방 애벌레로 부화한다.

가산명사 레이저 ❑ 신 레이저 기술

가산명사 레이저 프린터

1 가산명사 속눈썹 ❑ 유난히 속눈썹이 긴 짙은 잿빛 눈 **2** 타동사 묶다 ❑ 닻을 난간에 단단히 고정시켜라. ❑ 그 피신처는 나무막대기들을 함께 묶어 작게 둥근 천장처럼 만들어서 지었다. **3** 타동사/자동사 휘몰아치다 [문어체] ❑ 금세기 최악의 겨울 폭풍이 북아메리카의 동부 해안에 휘몰아쳤다. **4** 타동사/자동사 몰아세우다 ❑ 그녀는 그를 몰아세울 말을 생각해 내느라 잠시 동안 조용해졌다. **5** 가산명사 채찍 ❑ 그 마을 사람들은

Word Web　　　laser

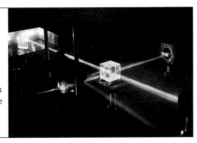

Lasers are an amazing form of technology. Laser **beams** read **CDs** and **DVDs**. They can create three-dimensional holograms. Laser **light shows** add excitement at concerts. **Fiber optic cables** carry intense flashes of laser light. This allows a single cable to transmit thousands of email and phone messages at the same time. Laser **scanners** read prices from **bar codes**. Lasers are also used as scalpels in **surgery**, and to remove hair, birthmarks and tattoos. Dentists use them to remove cavities. Laser eye surgery has become very popular. In manufacturing, lasers make precise cuts in everything from fabric to steel.

A

went quiet for a moment while she summoned up the words to lash him. **5** N-COUNT A **lash** is a blow with a whip, especially a blow on someone's back as a punishment. ❑ *The villagers sentenced one man to five lashes for stealing a ham from his neighbor.*

B

▶**lash out** **1** PHRASAL VERB If you **lash out**, you attempt to hit someone quickly and violently with a weapon or with your hands or feet. ❑ *Riot police fired in the air and lashed out with clubs to disperse hundreds of demonstrators.*
2 PHRASAL VERB If you **lash out** at someone or something, you speak to them or about them very angrily or critically. ❑ *As a politician Jefferson frequently lashed out at the press.*

C

D

lass /læs/ (**lasses**) N-COUNT; N-VOC A **lass** is a young woman or girl. [mainly SCOTTISH OR NORTHERN ENGLISH] ❑ *Anne is a Lancashire lass from Longton, near Preston.*

E

last ♦♦♦ /læst/ (**lasts, lasting, lasted**) **1** DET You use **last** in expressions such as **last Friday, last night**, and **last year** to refer, for example, to the most recent Friday, night, or year. ❑ *I got married last July.* ❑ *He never made it home at all last night.* **2** ADJ The **last** event, person, thing, or period of time is the most recent one. [det ADJ] ❑ *Much has changed since my last visit.* ❑ *I split up with my last boyfriend three years ago.* ● PRON **Last** is also a pronoun. ❑ *The next tide, it was announced, would be even higher than the last.* **3** ADV If something **last** happened on a particular occasion, that is the most recent occasion on which it happened. [ADV with v] ❑ *When were you there last?* ❑ *The house is a little more dilapidated than when I last saw it.* **4** ORD The **last** thing, person, event, or period of time is the one that happens or comes after all the others of the same kind. ❑ *This is his last chance as prime minister.* ❑ *...the last three pages of the chapter.* ● PRON **Last** is also a pronoun. ❑ *It wasn't the first time that this particular difference had divided them and it wouldn't be the last.* **5** ADV If you do something **last**, you do it after everyone else does, or after you do everything else. [ADV after v] ❑ *I testified last.* ❑ *I was always picked last for the football team at school.* **6** PRON If you are **the last to** do or know something, everyone else does or knows it before you. [PRON to-inf] ❑ *She was the last to go to bed.* **7** ADJ **Last** is used to refer to the only thing, person, or part of something that remains. [det ADJ] ❑ *Jed nodded, finishing off the last piece of pizza.* ● N-SING **Last** is also a noun. ❑ *He finished off the last of the wine.* **8** ADJ You can use **last** to indicate that something is extremely undesirable or unlikely. [EMPHASIS] [det ADJ] ❑ *The last thing I wanted to do was teach.* ● PRON **Last** is also a pronoun. [PRON to-inf] ❑ *I would be the last to say that science has explained everything.* **9** PRON **The last** you see of someone or **the last** you hear of them is the final time that you see them or talk to them. [the PRON that] ❑ *She disappeared shouting, "To the river, to the river!" And that was the last we saw of her.* **10** V-T/V-I If an event, situation, or problem **lasts** for a particular length of time, it continues to exist or happen for that length of time. ❑ *The marriage had lasted for less than two years.* ❑ *The games lasted only half the normal time.* **11** V-T/V-I If something **lasts** for a particular length of time, it continues to be able to be used for that time, for example because there is some of it left or because it is in good enough condition. ❑ *You only need a very small blob of glue, so one tube lasts for ages.* ❑ *The repaired sail lasted less than 24 hours.* **12** →see also **lasting** **13** PHRASE If you say that something has happened **at last** or **at long last** you mean it has happened after you have been hoping for it for a long time. ❑ *I'm so glad that we've found you at last!* ❑ *Here, at long last, was the moment he had waited for.* **14** PHRASE You use expressions such as **the night before last, the election before last** and **the leader before last** to refer to the period of time, event, or person that came immediately before the most recent one in a series. ❑ *It was the dog he'd heard the night before last.* **15** PHRASE You can use phrases such as the **last but one**, the **last but two**, or the **last but three**, to refer to the thing or person that is, for example, one, two, or three before the final person or thing in a group or series. [BRIT] ❑ *It's the last but one day in the athletics programme.* **16** PHRASE You can use expressions such as **the last I heard** and **the last she heard** to introduce a piece of information that is the most recent that you have on a particular subject. ❑ *The last I heard, Joe and Irene were still happily married.* **17** PHRASE If you **leave** something or someone **until last**, you delay using, choosing, or dealing with them until you have used, chosen, or dealt with all the others. ❑ *I have left my best wine until last.* **18** **the last straw** →see **straw**. **last thing** →see **thing**

F

G

H

I

J

K

L

M

N

O

P

Q

R

last-ditch ADJ A **last-ditch** action is done only because there are no other ways left to achieve something or to prevent something happening. It is often done without much hope that it will succeed. [ADJ n] ❑ *...a last-ditch attempt to prevent civil war.*

S

T

last|ing /læstɪŋ/ ADJ You can use **lasting** to describe a situation, result, or agreement that continues to exist or have an effect for a very long time. ❑ *We are well on our way to a lasting peace.* →see also **last**

U

last|ly /læstli/ **1** ADV You use **lastly** when you want to make a final point, ask a final question, or mention a final item that is connected with the other ones you have already asked or mentioned. [ADV with cl/group] ❑ *Lastly, I would like to ask about your future plans.* **2** ADV You use **lastly** when you are saying what happens after everything else in a series of actions or events. [ADV cl] ❑ *They wash their hands, arms and faces, and lastly, they wash their feet.* →see **last**

V

last-minute →see **minute**

W

X

latch /lætʃ/ (**latches, latching, latched**) **1** N-COUNT A **latch** is a fastening on a door or gate. It consists of a metal bar which you lift in order to open the door. ❑ *You left the latch off the gate and the dog escaped.* **2** N-COUNT A **latch** is a lock on a door which locks automatically when you shut the door, so that you need a key in order to open it from the outside. ❑ *...a key clicked in the latch of the front door.*

Y

Z

▶**latch onto** or **latch on** **1** PHRASAL VERB If someone **latches onto** a person or an idea or **latches on**, they become very interested in the person or idea, often

---

이웃에서 햄 한 조각을 훔친 죄로 한 남자를 채찍으로 5번 내리치기로 판결을 내렸다.

1 구동사 후려치다, 갈기다 ❑ 진압 경찰이 수백 명의 시위 군중을 해산하기 위해 공중에 총을 발포하고 곤봉을 휘둘렀다. **2** 구동사 혹평하다, 몰아세우다 ❑ 정치인으로서, 제퍼슨은 언론을 자주 혹평했다.

가산명사; 호격명사 처녀, 아가씨 [주로 스코틀랜드 또는 북부영어] ❑ 애니는 프레스톤 인근 롱톤에서 온 랭커셔 처녀이다.

1 한정사 지난 ❑ 나는 지난 7월에 결혼했다. ❑ 그는 간밤에 결코 집까지 가지 못했다. **2** 형용사 최근의, 지난번의, 이 앞의 ❑ 최근에 내가 방문한 이후로 많은 변화가 있었다. ❑ 나는 지난번 남자 친구와 3년 전에 헤어졌다. ● 대명사 최근의 것, 이 앞의 것, 지난번 것 ❑ 다음에 다가올 물살은 지난번 것보다 훨씬 높을 것이라고 발표되었다. **3** 부사 마지막으로 ❑ 마지막으로 거기에 간 게 언제였지? ❑ 그 집은 내가 마지막으로 봤을 때보다 조금 더 퇴락했다. **4** 서수 마지막의 ❑ 이것은 그가 총리로서 갖는 마지막 기회이다. ❑ 이 장의 마지막 세 페이지 ● 대명사 마지막 이 특징한 차이점으로 인해 그들이 갈라선 것은 그때가 처음이 아니고 마지막도 아닐 것이다. **5** 부사 마지막으로 ❑ 내가 마지막으로 증언했다. ❑ 나는 언제나 마지막에 학교 축구부원으로 뽑혔다. **6** 대명사 마지막 사람 ❑ 그녀가 맨 나중에 잠자리에 들었다. **7** 형용사 마지막 남은 ❑ 제드가 고개를 끄덕이더니 마지막 남은 피자 조각을 마저 먹었다. ● 단수명사 마지막 남은 것 ❑ 그가 마지막 남은 포도주를 마저 마셨다. **8** 형용사 가장 -할 것 같지 않은 [강조] ❑ 내가 가장 하고 싶지 않은 일이 가르치는 일이었다. ● 대명사 결코 -하지 않을 사람 ❑ 나는 결코 과학이 모든 것을 설명했다고는 말하지 않을 것이다. **9** 대명사 마지막 ❑ 그녀는 "강으로, 강으로!"라고 외치면서 사라졌다. 그리고 그것이 우리가 그녀를 본 마지막이었다. **10** 타동사/자동사 지속되다, 계속되다 ❑ 그 결혼은 채 두 해도 지속되지 못했다. ❑ 그 경기가 단지 정규 시간의 절반 동안만 지속되었다. **11** 타동사/자동사 (얼마 동안) 가다, 쓰이다 ❑ 풀이 아주 조금만 있으면 되니까 한 통이면 오래 갈 거야. ❑ 그 수리된 돛은 24시간을 채 못 갔다. **13** 구 마침내, 드디어 ❑ 마침내 우리가 너희들을 찾다니 정말 기뻐. ❑ 드디어 그가 기다려 왔던 순간이 다가왔다. **14** 구 지지난 밤; 지지난 선거; 지지난번 지도자 ❑ 그가 지지난 밤에 짖는 소리를 들었던 그 개였다. **15** 구 끝에서 두 번째, 끝에서 세 번째; 끝에서 네 번째 [영국영어] ❑ 오늘이 육상 경기 일정 중 끝에서 두 번째 날이다. **16** 구 내가 최근에 들은 바, 그녀가 최근에 들은 바 ❑ 내가 최근에 들은 바로는 조와 아이린이 여전히 행복한 결혼 생활을 한다고 했어. **17** 구 -을 마지막까지 두다 ❑ 나는 가장 좋은 포도주를 마지막까지 손대지 않았다.

형용사 최후의, 막판으로 내몰린 ❑ 내전을 막기 위한 최후의 시도

형용사 지속적인, 항구적인 ❑ 우리는 항구적 평화를 향해 순탄히 가고 있다.

1 부사 마지막으로 ❑ 마지막으로, 저는 여러분들의 장래 계획에 대해 묻고 싶습니다. **2** 부사 마지막으로, 마지막에 ❑ 그들은 손, 팔, 얼굴을 씻고 마지막에 발을 씻는다.

1 가산명사 빗장 ❑ 네가 문에서 빗장을 벗겨 놓아서 개가 도망쳤다. **2** 가산명사 자동 잠금장치 ❑ 현관의 자동 잠금장치에 찰칵 하고 열쇠 들어가는 소리가 났다.

1 구동사 들러붙다 [비격식체] ❑ 롭은 나에게 들러붙어 있었다. 그는 나를 졸졸 따라다녔고, 내

finding them so useful that they do not want to leave them. [INFORMAL] ❑ *Rob had latched onto me. He followed me around, sat beside me at lunch, and usually ended up working with me.* **2** PHRASAL VERB If one thing **latches onto** another, or if it **latches on**, it attaches itself to it and becomes part of it. ❑ *These are substances which specifically latch onto the protein on the cell membrane.*

late ♦♦♦ /leɪt/ (**later, latest**) **1** ADV **Late** means near the end of a day, week, year, or other period of time. ❑ *It was late in the afternoon.* ❑ *His autobiography was written late in life.* ● ADJ **Late** is also an adjective. [ADJ n] ❑ *The talks eventually broke down in late spring.* ❑ *He was in his late 20s.* **2** ADJ If it is **late**, it is near the end of the day or it is past the time that you feel something should have been done. [v-link ADJ] ❑ *It was very late and the streets were deserted.* ● **late|ness** N-UNCOUNT ❑ *A large crowd had gathered despite the lateness of the hour.* **3** ADV **Late** means after the time that was arranged or expected. ❑ *Steve arrived late.* ❑ *The talks began some fifteen minutes late.* ● ADJ **Late** is also an adjective. ❑ *His campaign got off to a late start.* ❑ *The train was 40 minutes late.* ● **late|ness** N-UNCOUNT ❑ *He apologized for his lateness.* **4** ADV **Late** means after the usual time that a particular event or activity happens. [ADV after v] ❑ *We went to bed very late.* ● ADJ **Late** is also an adjective. [ADJ n] ❑ *They had a late lunch in a cafe.* **5** ADJ You use **late** when you are talking about someone who is dead, especially someone who has died recently. [det ADJ] ❑ *...my late husband.* **6** →see also **later, latest** **7** PHRASE If an action or event is **too late**, it is useless or ineffective because it occurs after the best time for it. ❑ *It was too late to turn back.* **8** **a late night** →see **night**

Thesaurus	late의 참조어
ADJ.	belated, overdue; (ant.) early **3 4**
	deceased; (ant.) living **5**

late|ly /leɪtli/ ADV You use **lately** to describe events in the recent past, or situations that started a short time ago. ❑ *Dad's health hasn't been too good lately.* ❑ *"Have you talked to her lately?" — "Not lately, really."*

la|tent /leɪtᵊnt/ ADJ **Latent** is used to describe something which is hidden and not obvious at the moment, but which may develop further in the future. ❑ *Advertisements attempt to project a latent meaning behind an overt message.*

lat|er ♦♦♦ /leɪtər/ **1** **Later** is the comparative of **late**. **2** ADV You use **later** to refer to a time or situation that is after the one that you have been talking about or after the present one. ❑ *He resigned ten years later.* ● PHRASE You use **later on** to refer to a time or situation that is after the one that you have been talking about or after the present one. ❑ *Later on I'll be speaking to Patty Davis.* **3** ADJ You use **later** to refer to an event, period of time, or other thing which comes after the one that you have been talking about or after the present one. [ADJ n, the ADJ, the ADJ of n] ❑ *At a later news conference, he said differences should not be dramatized.* ❑ *The competition should have been re-scheduled for a later date.* **4** ADJ You use **later** to refer to the last part of someone's life or career or the last part of a period of history. [ADJ n] ❑ *He found happiness in later life.* ❑ *...the later part of the 20th century.* **5** →see also **late**

You use **after**, **afterwards**, and **later** to talk about things that happen following the time when you are speaking, or following a particular event. Expressions such as "not long" and "shortly" can also be used with **after**. ❑ *After dinner she spoke to him... I returned to England after visiting India... Shortly after, she called me.* **Afterwards** can be used when you do not need to mention the particular time or event. ❑ *Afterwards we went to a night club.* You can also use words such as "soon" and "shortly" with **afterwards**. ❑ *Soon afterwards, he came to the clinic.* You can use **later** to refer to a time or situation that follows the time when you are speaking. ❑ *I'll go and see her later.* "A little," "much," and "not much" can also be used with **later**. ❑ *A little later, the lights went out... I learned all this much later.* You can use **after**, **afterwards**, or **later** following a phrase that mentions a period of time, in order to say when something happens. ❑ *...five years after his death... She wrote about it six years afterwards... Ten minutes later he left the house.*

lat|er|al /lætərəl/ ADJ **Lateral** means relating to the sides of something, or moving in a sideways direction. ❑ *McKinnon estimated the lateral movement of the bridge to be between four and six inches.*

lat|est ♦♦◇ /leɪtɪst/ **1** **Latest** is the superlative of **late**. **2** ADJ You use **latest** to describe something that is the most recent thing of its kind. ❑ *...her latest book.* **3** ADJ You can use **latest** to describe something that is very new and modern and is better than older things of a similar kind. ❑ *Crooks are using the latest laser photocopiers to produce millions of fake banknotes.* ❑ *I got to drive the latest model.* **4** →see also **late** **5** PHRASE You use **at the latest** in order to indicate that something must happen at or before a particular time and not after that time. [EMPHASIS] ❑ *She should be back by ten o'clock at the latest.*

lathe /leɪð/ (**lathes**) N-COUNT A **lathe** is a machine which is used for shaping wood or metal.

Lat|in ♦♦◇ /lætɪn, -tᵊn/ **1** N-UNCOUNT **Latin** is the language which the ancient Romans used to speak. **2** ADJ **Latin** countries are countries where Spanish, or perhaps Portuguese, Italian, or French, is spoken. You can also use **Latin** to refer to things and people that come from these countries. ❑ *Cuba was one of the least Catholic of the Latin countries.* →see **English**

옆에서 점심을 먹고, 결국 대개는 나와 함께 일을 하게 되었다. **2** 구동사 달라붙다 ❑ 이것들은 특히 세포막의 단백질에 달라붙는 물질들이다.

1 부사 늦게 ❑ 늦은 오후였다. ❑ 그의 자서전은 만년에 쓰였다. ● 형용사 늦은 ❑ 그 회담은 늦은 봄에 결국 결렬되었다. ❑ 그는 20대 후반이었다. **2** 형용사 늦은 ❑ 시간이 매우 늦어서 거리에는 사람들이 없었다. ● 지체 불가산명사 ❑ 시간이 지체되었는데도 많은 군중이 모여들었다. **3** 부사 (약속보다) 늦게 ❑ 스티브는 늦게 도착했다. ❑ 회담은 약 15분 늦게 시작되었다. ● 형용사 늦은 ❑ 그의 선거 운동은 뒤늦게 시작되었다. ❑ 그 기차는 40분 늦었다. ● 지각 불가산명사 ❑ 그는 자신이 지각한 것에 대해 사과했다. **4** 부사 (일상적인 시각보다) 늦게 ❑ 우리는 매우 늦게 잠자리에 들었다. ● 형용사 늦은 ❑ 그들은 한 카페에서 늦은 점심을 했다. **5** 형용사 사망한, 고(故) ❑ 사망한 내 남편 **7** 구 너무 늦은 ❑ 이미 너무 늦어 돌이킬 수 없었다.

부사 최근에 ❑ 아빠의 건강이 최근에 썩 좋지는 않았다. ❑ "최근에 그녀와 얘기해 봤어?" "최근엔 안 했어, 정말이야."

형용사 숨어 있는, 잠재된 ❑ 광고는 밖으로 드러내는 메시지 이면에 숨은 의미를 전달하려고 한다.

late의 비교급 **2** 부사 후에 ❑ 그는 십 년 후에 사임했다. ● 구 나중에 ❑ 나중에 패티 데이비스에게 말할게요. **3** 형용사 나중의, 후의, 더 뒤의 ❑ 나중의 기자 회견에서, 그는 차이점들을 과장해서는 안 된다고 말했다. ❑ 그 경기는 더 뒤로 일정을 재조정했어야 했다. **4** 형용사 만년의, 늘그막의, 마지막 부분의 ❑ 그는 만년에 행복을 찾았다. ❑ 20세기가 끝나갈 무렵

말을 하는 시점 이후나 특정한 사건 이후에 일어나는 일을 얘기할 때 after, afterwards, later를 쓴다. after와 함께는 not long이나 shortly 같은 표현도 쓸 수 있다. ❑ 저녁 식사 후에 그녀는 그에게 말했다... 나는 인도를 방문하고 영국으로 돌아왔다... 바로 얼마 후에 그녀가 내게 전화를 했다. afterwards는 특정한 시간이나 사건을 언급할 필요가 없을 때 쓸 수 있다. ❑ 나중에 우리는 나이트클럽에 갔다. afterwards와 함께는 soon이나 shortly 같은 말을 쓸 수 있다. ❑ 그 뒤에 곧, 그가 진료소로 왔다. 말하는 시점 이후의 어떤 시점이나 상황을 가리킬 때는 later를 쓸 수 있다. ❑ 내가 나중에 그녀를 보러 갈게. later와 함께는 a little, much, not much를 쓸 수 있다. ❑ 조금 후에, 불이 꺼졌다... 나는 이 모든 것을 훨씬 나중에 알게 되었다. 어떤 일이 언제 일어났는지를 말하려면 일정 기간을 언급하는 구 뒤에 after, afterwards, later를 쓰면 된다. ❑ ...그가 사망한 뒤 5년 후... 그녀는 6년 후에 그것에 대한 글을 썼다... 10분 뒤에 그는 집을 떠났다.

형용사 측면의, 좌우의 ❑ 맥키논은 그 교량의 측면운동 폭이 4인치에서 6인치라고 산정했다.

late의 최상급 **2** 형용사 최근의 ❑ 그녀의 최근 저서 **3** 형용사 최신의 ❑ 사기꾼들이 최신식 레이저 복사기를 이용하여 수백만 장의 위조지폐를 만들고 있다. ❑ 나는 최신 모델의 자동차를 몰기 시작했다. **5** 구 늦어도 [강조] ❑ 그녀는 늦어도 10시까지는 돌아와야 한다.

가산명사 선반 (기계)

1 불가산명사 라틴어 **2** 형용사 라틴계의 ❑ 쿠바는 라틴계 국가 중에서 가톨릭 신자가 가장 적은 나라 중 하나였다.

A

Lat|in Ameri|can /lætɪn əmɛrɪkən/ ADJ **Latin American** means belonging or relating to the countries of South America, Central America, and Mexico. **Latin American** also means belonging or relating to the people of culture of these countries. ❑ *Leaders of eight Latin American countries are meeting in Caracas, Venezuela, today.*

형용사 라틴 아메리카의, 라틴 아메리카인의 ❑ 오늘 라틴 아메리카 8개국 지도자들이 베네수엘라의 카라카스에서 회담을 열고 있다.

B

lati|tude /lætɪtud, BRIT lætɪtyuːd/ (**latitudes**) **1** N-VAR The **latitude** of a place is its distance from the equator. Compare **longitude**. ❑ *In the middle to high latitudes rainfall has risen steadily over the last 20-30 years.* ● ADJ **Latitude** is also an adjective. ❑ *The army must cease military operations above 36 degrees latitude north.* **2** N-UNCOUNT **Latitude** is freedom to choose the way in which you do something. [FORMAL] ❑ *He would be given every latitude in forming a new government.*

1 가산명사 또는 불가산명사 위도 ❑ 중위도에서 고위도 지역의 강우량이 지난 20~30년 동안 가파르게 증가했다. ● 형용사 위도의 ❑ 군대는 북위 36도 위의 지역에서는 군사 작전을 중지해야 한다. **2** 불가산명사 재량권 [격식체] ❑ 그에게 새 정부 수립을 위한 모든 재량권이 주어질 것이다.

C

D

lat|ter ◆◇◇ /lætər/ **1** PRON When two people, things, or groups have just been mentioned, you can refer to the second of them as **the latter**. [the PRON] ❑ *He tracked down his cousin and uncle. The latter was sick.* ● ADJ **Latter** is also an adjective. [ADJ n] ❑ *There are the people who speak after they think and the people who think while they're speaking. Mike definitely belongs in the latter category.* **2** ADJ You use **latter** to describe the later part of a period of time or event. [ADJ n] ❑ *He is getting into the latter years of his career.*

1 대명사 후자 ❑ 그는 사촌과 삼촌을 찾아내었다. 삼촌은 아픈 상태였다. ● 형용사 후자의 ❑ 사람들 중엔 생각한 후 말을 하는 사람이 있는가 하면 말하면서 생각하는 사람이 있다. 마이크는 확실히 후자의 부류에 속한다. **2** 형용사 후반의 ❑ 그는 직장 생활 후반부로 접어들고 있다.

E

F

> **The latter** should only be used to refer to the second of two items which have already been mentioned: ❑ *Given the choice between working for someone else and being on call day and night for the family business, she'd prefer the latter.* The last of three or more items can be referred to as **the last-named**. Compare this with **the former** which is used to talk about the first of two things already mentioned.

> the latter는 이미 언급된 두 가지 중의 두 번째 것을 지칭할 때만 써야 한다: ❑ 남 밑에서 일하는 것과 밤낮으로 대기하며 집안에서 하는 사업에 종사하는 것 중에서 고르라고 한다면, 그녀는 후자를 택할 것이다. 세 개 또는 그 이상의 항목에서 마지막 것은 the last-named로 가리킬 수 있다. 이와 같은 내용을 이미 언급된 두 개 중 첫 번째 것을 말할 때 쓰는 the former와 비교해 보라.

G

H

I

lat|tice /lætɪs/ (**lattices**) N-COUNT A **lattice** is a pattern or structure made of strips of wood or another material which cross over each other diagonally leaving holes in between. ❑ *We were crawling along the narrow steel lattice of the bridge.*

가산명사 격자 ❑ 우리는 교량의 좁다란 강철 격자를 따라 기어가고 있었다.

J

laugh ◆◆◆ /læf/ (**laughs, laughing, laughed**) **1** V-T/V-I When you **laugh**, you make a sound with your throat while smiling and show that you are happy or amused. People also sometimes laugh when they feel nervous or are being unfriendly. ❑ *He was about to offer an explanation, but she was beginning to laugh.* ❑ *The British don't laugh at the same jokes as the French.* ● N-COUNT **Laugh** is also a noun. ❑ *Lysenko gave a deep rumbling laugh at his own joke.* **2** V-I If people **laugh at** someone or something, they mock them or make jokes about them. ❑ *I thought they were laughing at me because I was ugly.* **3** PHRASE If you do something **for a laugh** or **for laughs**, you do it as a joke or for fun. ❑ *They were persuaded onstage for a laugh by their mates.* **4** PHRASE If you describe a situation as **a laugh, a good laugh**, or **a bit of a laugh**, you think that it is fun and do not take it too seriously. [mainly BRIT, INFORMAL] ❑ *Working there's great. It's quite a good laugh actually.* **5** to **laugh** your **head off** →see **head** →see Word Web: **laugh**

1 타동사/자동사 웃다 ❑ 그가 막 설명을 하려 하는데, 그녀가 웃기 시작했다. ❑ 영국 사람들은 프랑스 사람들이 듣고 웃는 것과 똑같은 농담에 웃지 않는다. ● 가산명사 웃음 ❑ 리센코는 자기가 농담을 해 놓고 우렁차게 웃었다. **2** 자동사 ~을 보고 비웃다 ❑ 나는 내가 못 생겨서 그들이 나를 보고 비웃는다고 생각했다. **3** 구 재미 삼아 ❑ 그들은 동료들이 재미 삼아 하는 권유에 무대 위로 올라갔다. **4** 구 신나는 일; 패 신나는 일; 좀 신나는 일 [주로 영국영어, 비격식체] ❑ 거기서 일하는 건 정말 좋아. 사실 꽤 신나는 일이야.

K

L

M

N

Thesaurus *laugh*의 참조어

v. chuckle, crack up, giggle, howl; (*ant.*) cry **1**

O

P

Word Partnership *laugh*의 연어

V. **begin/start to** laugh, **hear** *someone* laugh, **make** *someone* laugh, **try to** laugh **1**

ADJ. **big** laugh, **good** laugh, **hearty** laugh, **little** laugh **1**

Q

R

▶**laugh off** PHRASAL VERB If you **laugh off** a difficult or serious situation, you try to suggest that it is amusing and unimportant, for example by making a joke about it. ❑ *Frank turned to laugh off his aunt's worry.*

구동사 웃어넘기다 ❑ 프랭크는 이모의 걱정을 웃어넘기려 했다.

S

laugh|ter ◆◇◇ /læftər/ N-UNCOUNT **Laughter** is the sound of people laughing, for example because they are amused or happy. ❑ *Their laughter filled the corridor.* ❑ *He delivered the line perfectly, and everybody roared with laughter.* →see **laugh**

불가산명사 웃음소리 ❑ 그들의 웃음소리가 복도에 가득했다. ❑ 그가 그 대사를 완벽하게 전달해서 모두 박장대소를 했다.

T

Word Partnership *laughter*의 연어

V. **burst into** laughter, **hear** laughter, **roar with** laughter

N. **burst of** laughter, **sound of** laughter

ADJ. **hysterical** laughter, **loud** laughter, **nervous** laughter

U

V

W

Word Web laugh

There is an old saying, "**Laughter** is the best medicine." New scientific research supports the idea that **humor** really is good for your health. For example, laughing 100 times provides the same exercise benefits as a 15-minute bike ride. When a person **bursts out laughing**, levels of stress hormones in the bloodstream immediately drop. And laughter is more than just a sound. **Howling with laughter** gives face, stomach, leg, and back muscles a good workout. From polite **giggles** to noisy guffaws, laughter allows the release of anger, sadness, and fear. And that has to be good for you.

X

Y

Z

launch ♦♦◊ /lɔntʃ/ (**launches, launching, launched**) **1** V-T To **launch** a rocket, missile, or satellite means to send it into the air or into space. ❑ *NASA plans to launch a satellite to study cosmic rays.* ● N-VAR **Launch** is also a noun. ❑ *This morning's launch of the space shuttle Columbia has been delayed.* **2** V-T To **launch** a ship or a boat means to put it into water, often for the first time after it has been built. ❑ *There was no time to launch the lifeboats because the ferry capsized with such alarming speed.* ● N-COUNT **Launch** is also a noun. ❑ *The launch of a ship was a big occasion.* **3** V-T To **launch** a large and important activity, for example a military attack, means to start it. ❑ *The police have launched an investigation into the incident.* ❑ *The President was on holiday when the coup was launched.* ● N-COUNT **Launch** is also a noun. ❑ *...the launch of a campaign to restore law and order.* **4** V-T If a company **launches** a new product, it makes it available to the public. ❑ *...powerful allies to help the company launch a low-cost "network computer."* ● N-COUNT **Launch** is also a noun. ❑ *The company's spending has also risen following the launch of a new Sunday magazine.*
→see **satellite**

▶**launch into** PHRASAL VERB If you **launch into** something such as a speech, task, or fight, you enthusiastically start it. ❑ *Horrigan launched into a speech about the importance of new projects.*

laun|der /lɔndər/ (**launders, laundering, laundered**) **1** V-T When you **launder** clothes, sheets, and towels, you wash and iron them. [OLD-FASHIONED] ❑ *How many guests who expect clean towels every day in an hotel launder their own every day at home?* **2** V-T To **launder** money that has been obtained illegally means to process it through a legitimate business or to send it abroad to a foreign bank, so that when it comes back nobody knows that it was illegally obtained. ❑ *The House voted today to crack down on banks that launder drug money.* ● **laun|der|er** N-COUNT ❑ *...a businessman and self-described money launderer.*

laun|dry /lɔndri/ (**laundries**) **1** N-UNCOUNT **Laundry** is used to refer to clothes, sheets, and towels that are about to be washed, are being washed, or have just been washed. ❑ *I'll do your laundry.* ❑ *...the room where I hang the laundry.* **2** N-COUNT A **laundry** is a firm that washes and irons clothes, sheets, and towels for people. ❑ *We had to have the washing done at the laundry.*

> A business where people go to wash their clothes for themselves is called a **Laundromat**. The machines are operated by inserting coins so another name for these is **coin laundry**. In the UK, the usual word is **launderette**.

3 N-COUNT A **laundry** or a **laundry room** is a room in a house, hotel, or institution where clothes, sheets, and towels are washed. ❑ *He worked in the laundry at Oxford prison.* →see **soap**

lau|rel /lɔrəl/, BRIT lɒrəl/ (**laurels**) **1** N-VAR A **laurel** or a **laurel tree** is a small evergreen tree with shiny leaves. The leaves are sometimes used to make decorations such as wreaths. **2** PHRASE If someone is **resting on** their **laurels**, they appear to be satisfied with the things they have achieved and have stopped putting effort into what they are doing. [DISAPPROVAL] ❑ *The committee's chairman accused NASA of resting on its laurels after making it to the moon.*

lava /lɑvə, lævə/ (**lavas**) N-MASS **Lava** is the very hot liquid rock that comes out of a volcano. ❑ *Mexico's Mount Colima began spewing lava and ash last night.* →see **volcano**

lava|tory /lævətɔri, BRIT lævətri/ (**lavatories**) N-COUNT A **lavatory** is the same as a **toilet**. [mainly BRIT] ❑ *...the ladies' lavatory at the University of London.*

lav|en|der /lævɪndər/ (**lavenders**) N-UNCOUNT **Lavender** is a garden plant with sweet-smelling, bluish-purple flowers.

lav|ish /lævɪʃ/ (**lavishes, lavishing, lavished**) **1** ADJ If you describe something as **lavish**, you mean that it is very elaborate and impressive and a lot of money has been spent on it. ❑ *...a lavish party to celebrate Bryan's fiftieth birthday.* ● He staged the most lavish productions of Mozart. ● **lav|ish|ly** ADV [ADV with v] ❑ *...the train's lavishly furnished carriages.* **2** ADJ If you say that spending, praise, or the use of something is **lavish**, you mean that someone spends a lot or that something is praised or used a lot. ❑ *Critics attack his lavish spending and flamboyant style.* **3** ADJ If you say that someone is **lavish** in the way they behave, you mean that they give, spend, or use a lot of something. ❑ *American reviewers are lavish in their praise of this book.* ● **lav|ish|ly** ADV [ADV with v] ❑ *Entertaining in style needn't mean spending lavishly.* **4** V-T If you **lavish** money, affection, or praise **on** someone or something, you spend a lot of money on them or give them a lot of affection or praise. ❑ *Prince Sadruddin lavished praise on Britain's contributions to world diplomacy.*

law ♦♦♦ /lɔ/ (**laws**) **1** N-SING The **law** is a system of rules that a society or government develops in order to deal with crime, business agreements, and social relationships. You can also use the **law** to refer to the people who work in this system. ❑ *Obscene and threatening phone calls are against the law.* ❑ *They are seeking permission to begin criminal proceedings against him for breaking the law on financing political parties.* **2** N-UNCOUNT **Law** is used to refer to a particular branch of the law, such as **criminal law** or **company law**. ❑ *He was a professor of criminal law at Harvard University law school.* ❑ *Under international law, diplomats living in foreign countries are exempt from criminal prosecution.* **3** N-COUNT A **law** is one of the rules in a system of law which deals with a particular type of agreement, relationship, or crime. ❑ *...the country's liberal political asylum law.* **4** N-PLURAL The **laws of** an organization or activity are its rules, which are used to organize and control it. ❑ *...the laws of the Church of England.* **5** N-COUNT A **law** is a rule or set of rules for good behavior which is considered right and important by the majority of people for moral, religious, or emotional reasons. ❑ *...inflexible moral laws.* **6** N-COUNT A **law** is a natural process in which a particular event or thing always leads to a particular result. ❑ *The laws of nature are absolute.*

1 타동사 발사하다 □ 미 항공우주국은 우주선(宇宙線)을 연구하기 위한 위성 발사를 계획하고 있다. ● 가산명사 또는 불가산명사 발사 □ 오늘 아침으로 예정된 우주 왕복선 콜럼비아호의 발사가 연기되었다. **2** 타동사 물에 띄우다, 진수시키다 □ 정기 운항선이 엄청난 속도로 전복되어서 구명정을 띄울 시간이 없었다. ● 가산명사 진수 □ 배를 진수시키는 것은 큰 행사였다. **3** 타동사 착수하다 □ 경찰이 그 사건에 대한 조사에 착수했다. □ 대통령이 휴가 중에 쿠데타가 일어났다. ● 가산명사 착수, 출범 □ 법질서 회복 운동 출범 **4** 타동사 출시하다 □ 그 기업의 저렴한 '네트워크 컴퓨터' 출시를 돕는 막강한 제휴들 ● 가산명사 출시 □ 새 일요판 잡지 출간 후 그 기업의 지출도 또한 증가했다.

구동사 (싸움 등을) 기세 좋게 시작하다 □호리건은 신규 계획의 중요성에 대한 연설을 기세 좋게 시작했다.

1 타동사 세탁하다 [구식어] □ 매일 깨끗한 수건을 기대하는 호텔 투숙객들 중에 얼마나 많은 사람들이 자기 집 수건을 매일 세탁할까? **2** 타동사 돈세탁하다 □ 의회는 오늘 마약 자금을 돈세탁하는 은행들에 대해 엄벌 조치하기로 결의했다. ● 세탁업자 가산명사 □ 기업인이자 자칭 돈세탁업자

1 불가산명사 세탁물, 빨래 □ 내가 네 빨래 해 줄게. □ 내가 세탁물을 너는 그 방 **2** 가산명사 세탁소 □ 우리는 그 세탁소에 빨래를 맡겨야만 했다.

> 사람들이 가서 직접 빨래를 하는 빨래방을 Laundromat이라고 한다. 이런 곳에서는 동전을 넣어 기계를 돌리기 때문에 이런 곳을 다른 이름으로 coin laundry라고도 한다. 영국에서는 흔히 launderette라고 한다.

3 가산명사 세탁실 □ 그는 옥스퍼드 교도소 세탁실에서 일했다.

1 가산명사 또는 불가산명사 월계수 **2** 구 이미 얻은 결과에 안주하여 더 이상 노력하지 않다 [탐탁잖음] □ 위원회 위원장은 나사가 달 착륙 성공 이후 그 성과에 안주하여 더 이상 노력하지 않고 있다고 비난했다.

물질명사 용암 □ 멕시코의 콜리마 산이 어젯밤 용암과 화산재를 내뿜기 시작했다.

가산명사 화장실 [주로 영국영어] □ 런던 대학교에 있는 숙녀용 화장실

불가산명사 라벤더

1 형용사 성대한 □ 브라이언의 50세 생일을 축하하기 위한 성대한 파티 □ 그는 모차르트의 가장 성대한 작품들을 무대에 올렸다. ● 성대하게, 호화롭게 부사 □ 호화스러운 가구로 꾸며진 그 기차의 객차들 **2** 형용사 헤픈 □ 그는 헤픈 씀씀이와 과시적인 스타일로 비난을 받고 있다. ● 후하게 후한, 헤픈 □ 미국 평론가들은 이 책에 대해 점수를 후하게 줬다. ● 후하게, 헤프게 부사 □ 멋을 부린다는 것이 꼭 헤픈 씀씀이를 뜻하는 것은 아니다. **3** 형용사 후하게 주다 **4** 타동사 후하게 주다 □ 사루딘 왕자는 영국이 세계 외교에 기여한 바에 대해 칭찬을 후하게 했다.

1 단수명사 법 □ 음란 전화와 협박 전화는 위법이다. □ 그들은 그를 정치 자금법 위반 혐의로 조사하기 위해 조사 착수를 허가해 줄 것을 요청하고 있다. **2** 불가산명사 법률; 형법; 회사법 □ 그는 하버드 법대의 형법 교수였다. □ 해외 주재 외교관들은 국제법에 의해 형사 소추 예외 대상이다. **3** 가산명사 법 □ 그 나라의 관대한 정치 망명법 **4** 복수명사 규정 □ 영국 국교회의 규정 **5** 가산명사 규범 □ 완고한 노년규범 **6** 가산명사 법칙 □ 자연의 법칙은 절대적이다. **7** 가산명사 법칙 □ 중력의 법칙 **8** 불가산명사 법조계 □ 법조계에서 일하는 것은 젊은이들에게 점점 더 매력적으로 비춰지고 있다. **9** 불가산명사 법학 □ 그는 법학을 공부했다. **10** 구 초법적인 [탐탁잖음] □ 의회의 야당 의원 중 한 명은 정부가 초법적인 존재가 되려 하고 있다고 비난했다. **11** 구 법률에 의해 □ 모든 식당은 가격을 밖에 게시하도록 법률로 정해져 있다.

a
b
c
d
e
f
g
h
i
j
k
l
m
n
o
p
q
r
s
t
u
v
w
x
y
z

7 N-COUNT A **law** is a scientific rule that someone has invented to explain a particular natural process. ☐ ...*the law of gravity.* **8** N-UNCOUNT **Law** or **the law** is all the professions which deal with advising people about the law, representing people in court, or giving decisions and punishments. ☐ *A career in law is becoming increasingly attractive to young people.* **9** N-UNCOUNT **Law** is the study of systems of law and how laws work. ☐ *He studied law.* **10** PHRASE If you accuse someone of thinking they are **above the law**, you criticize them for thinking that they are so clever or important that they do not need to obey the law. [DISAPPROVAL] ☐ *One opposition member of parliament accuses the government of wanting to be above the law.* **11** PHRASE If you have to do something **by law** or if you are not allowed to do something **by law**, the law states that you have to do it or that you are not allowed to do it. ☐ *By law all restaurants must display their prices outside.* **12** Sod's law →see sod

형용사 법을 준수하는 ☐ "저는 법을 준수하는 선량한 시민과 그들의 재산을 보호해 줄 수 있게 되기를 간절히 바라고 있습니다."라고 총리는 말했다.

law-abiding ADJ A **law-abiding** person always obeys the law and is considered to be good and honest because of this. ☐ *The Prime Minister said: "I am anxious that the law should protect decent law-abiding citizens and their property."*

불가산명사 법herzfel ☐ 법질서가 파괴된다면 군이 개입을 시도할지도 모른다.

law and or|der N-UNCOUNT When there is **law and order** in a country, the laws are generally accepted and obeyed, so that society there functions normally. ☐ *If there were a breakdown of law and order, the army might be tempted to intervene.*

law|ful /lɔfəl/ ADJ If an activity, organization, or product is **lawful**, it is allowed by law. [FORMAL] ☐ *The detention of the fugitive was lawful.* ● **law|ful|ly** ADV [ADV with v] ☐ *Amnesty International is trying to establish whether the police acted lawfully in shooting him.*

형용사 합법적인 [격식체] ☐ 그 도망범을 유치한 것은 합법적이었다. ● 합법적으로 부사 ☐ 국제 사면 위원회는 경찰이 그에게 총을 쐈을 때 합법적 절차를 따랐는지를 밝히려고 노력 중이다.

law|less /lɔlɪs/ **1** ADJ **Lawless** actions break the law, especially in a wild and violent way. ☐ *The government recognized there were problems in urban areas but these could never be an excuse for lawless behavior.* ● **law|less|ness** N-UNCOUNT ☐ *Lawlessness is a major problem.* **2** ADJ A **lawless** place or time is one where people do not respect the law. ☐ ...*lawless inner-city streets plagued by muggings, thefts, assaults and even murder.*

1 형용사 무법의 ☐ 정부가 도시 지역에 여러 문제가 있다는 것을 인정하기는 했지만, 절대로 이것들이 무법 행위의 사유가 될 수는 없었다. ● 무법, 불법 불가산명사 ☐ 무법 사태는 중대한 문제이다. **2** 형용사 무법천지의 ☐ 강도, 절도, 성폭행, 심지어는 살인이 난무하는 무법천지의 도심 거리

lawn /lɔn/ (**lawns**) N-VAR A **lawn** is an area of grass that is kept cut short and is usually part of someone's garden or backyard, or part of a park. ☐ *They were sitting on the lawn under a large beech tree.*

가산명사 또는 불가산명사 잔디밭 ☐ 그들은 커다란 너도밤나무 아래 잔디밭에 앉아 있었다.

lawn|mow|er /lɔnmoʊər/ (**lawnmowers**) also lawn mower N-COUNT A **lawnmower** is a machine for cutting grass on lawns.

가산명사 제초기, 잔디 깎는 기계

law|suit /lɔsut/ (**lawsuits**) N-COUNT A **lawsuit** is a case in a court of law which concerns a dispute between two people or organizations. [FORMAL] ☐ *The dispute culminated last week in a lawsuit against the government.*

가산명사 소송 [격식체] ☐ 그 논쟁은 지난 주에 정부를 대상으로 한 소송으로 절정에 다다랐다.

law|yer ♦♦◇ /lɔɪər, lɔyər/ (**lawyers**) N-COUNT A **lawyer** is a person who is qualified to advise people about the law and represent them in court. ☐ *Prosecution and defense lawyers are expected to deliver closing arguments next week.* →see trial

가산명사 변호사 ☐ 원고 측 변호사와 피고 측 변호사는 다음 주에 최후 변론을 하게 될 것이다.

In both British and American English, **lawyer** is a general term for someone who is qualified in law and represents people in legal matters. American **lawyers** can prepare cases and can also represent their clients in court. Another American word commonly used for **lawyer** is **attorney**. In Britain, a **solicitor** prepares legal documents such as wills and contracts, and also prepares cases that are heard in court. **Solicitors** can also represent their clients, especially in lower courts. In higher courts, the argument for each side is usually presented by a **barrister**. In Scotland, a **barrister** is usually called an **advocate**.

영국 영어와 미국 영어 둘 다에서 lawyer는 자격을 갖추고 법률문제를 대리해 주는 사람을 가리키는 일반적인 용어이다. 미국의 lawyer는 소송 사건을 준비하고 법정에서 그들의 의뢰인을 대변한다. lawyer 대신 흔히 쓰이는 다른 미국식 단어는 attorney이다. 영국에서는 solicitor가 유언장이나 계약서 같은 법률 서류를 작성하고 법정에서 심리될 소송 사건을 준비한다. solicitor가 의뢰인을 대변하기도 하는데 특히 하급 법원에서 그렇게 한다. 상급 법원에서는 양측의 주장을 barrister가 대변한다. 스코틀랜드에서는 barrister가 보통 advocate라 불린다.

Word Link   lax ≈ allowing, loosening : *lax, laxative, relax*

lax /læks/ (**laxer, laxest**) ADJ If you say that a person's behavior or a system is **lax**, you mean they are not careful or strict about maintaining high standards. ☐ *One of the problem areas is lax security for airport personnel.* ☐ *There have been allegations from survivors that safety standards had been lax.* ● **lax|ity** N-UNCOUNT ☐ *The laxity of export control authorities has made a significant contribution to the problem.*

형용사 허술한, 해이한 ☐ 여러 가지 문제되는 분야 중 하나는 공항 직원들에 대한 보안이 허술한 것이다. ☐ 생존자로부터 안전 기준이 허술했다는 혐의가 제기되어 왔다. ● 허술함, 해이함 불가산명사 ☐ 수출 관리 당국의 해이함이 이 문제를 일으키는 데 크게 일조를 했다.

laxa|tive /læksətɪv/ (**laxatives**) N-MASS A **laxative** is something you eat or drink that makes you go to the toilet. ☐ *Foods that ferment quickly in the stomach are excellent natural laxatives.*

물질명사 변비약, 관장약, 하제 ☐ 위에서 빨리 발효되는 음식은 뛰어난 천연 변비약이다.

lay

① VERB AND NOUN USES
② ADJECTIVE USES

① lay ♦♦◇ /leɪ/ (**lays, laying, laid**)

In standard English, the form **lay** is also the past tense of the verb **lie** in some meanings. In informal English, people sometimes use the word **lay** instead of **lie** in those meanings.

표준 영어의 일부 의미에서 lay가 동사 lie의 과거 시제인데, 비격식체 영어에서는 가끔 lie 대신 lay를 그런 의미로 쓴다.

Do not confuse the verb **lay** with the verb **lie**. Because **lay** is used to talk about putting something in a particular place or position, it is related to the verb **lie**. If someone **lays** something somewhere, it **lies** there. The past tense and past participle of **lay** are both **laid** and it is usually a transitive verb. ☐ *They laid him on the floor.* However, **lie** is an intransitive verb with the past tense **lay** and the past participle **lain**. ☐ *I lay on the floor with my legs in the air.*

동사 lay와 lie를 혼동하지 않도록 하라. lay가 사물을 특정한 장소나 위치에 놓는 것을 말할 때 쓰이므로, 동사 lie와 관련이 있기는 하다. 누가 무엇을 어디에 놓으면(lay), 그것은 거기에 놓여 있게(lie) 되는 것이다. lay의 과거와 과거분사는 둘 다 laid이고, lay는 보통 타동사로 쓰인다. ☐ 그들은 그를 바닥에 눕혔다. 그러나 lie는 자동사로서, 과거는 lay이고, 과거분사는 lain이다. ☐ 나는 다리를 위로 들고 바닥에 누워 있었다.

→Please look at category **7** to see if the expression you are looking for is shown under another headword. **1** V-T If you **lay** something somewhere, you put it there in a careful, gentle, or neat way. ❑ *Lay a sheet of newspaper on the floor.* ❑ *Mothers routinely lay babies on their backs to sleep.* **2** V-T If you **lay** something such as carpets, cables, or foundations, you put them into their permanent position. ❑ *A man came to lay the saloon carpet.* **3** V-T/V-I When a female bird **lays** an egg, it produces an egg by pushing it out of its body. ❑ *My canary has laid an egg.* **4** V-T **Lay** is used with some nouns to talk about making official preparations for something. For example, if you **lay the basis** for something or **lay plans** for it, you prepare it carefully. ❑ *Diplomats meeting in Chile have laid the groundwork for far-reaching environmental regulations.* **5** V-T **Lay** is used with some nouns in expressions about accusing or blaming someone. For example, if you **lay the blame** for a mistake on someone, you say it is their fault, or if the police **lay charges** against someone, they officially accuse that person of a crime. ❑ *She refused to lay the blame on any one party.* **6** V-T If you **lay** the table or **lay** the places at a table, you arrange the knives, forks, and other things that people need on the table before a meal. [mainly BRIT; AM usually **set**] ❑ *The butler always laid the table.* **7** to **lay** something **at** someone's **door** →see **door**. to **lay a finger on** someone →see **finger**. to **lay your hands on** something →see **hand**. to **lay siege to** something →see **siege**

▶**lay aside** **1** PHRASAL VERB If you **lay** something **aside**, you put it down, usually because you have finished using it or want to save it to use later. ❑ *He finished the tea and laid the cup aside.* **2** PHRASAL VERB If you **lay aside** a feeling or belief, you reject it or give it up in order to progress with something. ❑ *Perhaps the opposed parties will lay aside their sectional interests and rise to this challenge.*

▶**lay down** **1** PHRASAL VERB If you **lay** something **down**, you put it down, usually because you have finished using it. ❑ *Daniel finished the article and laid the newspaper down on his desk.* **2** PHRASAL VERB If rules or people in authority **lay down** what people should do or must do, they officially state what they should or must do. ❑ *The Companies Act lays down a set of minimum requirements.* **3** PHRASAL VERB If someone **lays down** their weapons, they stop fighting a battle or war and make peace. ❑ *The drug-traffickers have offered to lay down their arms.*

▶**lay off** PHRASAL VERB If workers **are laid off**, they are told by their employers to leave their job, usually because there is no more work for them to do. [BUSINESS] ❑ *100,000 federal workers will be laid off to reduce the deficit.* →see also **layoff**

▶**lay on** PHRASAL VERB If you **lay on** something such as food, entertainment, or a service, you provide or supply it, especially in a generous or grand way. [mainly BRIT] ❑ *They laid on a superb evening.*

▶**lay out** **1** PHRASAL VERB If you **lay out** a group of things, you spread them out and arrange them neatly, for example so that they can all be seen clearly. ❑ *Grace laid out the knives and forks at the lunch-table.* **2** PHRASAL VERB To **lay out** ideas, principles, or plans means to explain or present them clearly, for example in a document or a meeting. ❑ *Maxwell listened closely as Johnson laid out his plan.* **3** →see also **layout**

② **lay** /leɪ/ **1** ADJ You use **lay** to describe people who are involved with a Christian church but are not members of the clergy or are not monks or nuns. [ADJ n] ❑ *Edwards is a Methodist lay preacher and social worker.* **2** ADJ You use **lay** to describe people who are not experts or professionals in a particular subject or activity. [ADJ n] ❑ *It is difficult for a lay person to gain access to medical libraries.*

lay|er ♦◇◇ /leɪər/ (**layers, layering, layered**) **1** N-COUNT A **layer** of a material or substance is a quantity or piece of it that covers a surface or that is between two other things. ❑ *...the depletion of the ozone layer.* **2** N-COUNT If something such as a system or an idea has many **layers**, it has many different levels or parts. ❑ *Critics and the public puzzle out the layers of meaning in his photos.* **3** V-T If you **layer** something, you arrange it in layers. ❑ *Layer half the onion slices on top of the potatoes.*

Word Partnership	*layer의 연어*	
ADJ.	**bottom/top** layer, **lower/upper** layer, **outer** layer, **protective** layer, **single** layer, **thick/thin** layer **1**	
N.	layer **of dust**, layer **of fat**, **ozone** layer, layer **of skin**, **surface** layer **1**	

lay|man /leɪmən/ (**laymen**) N-COUNT A **layman** is a person who is not trained, qualified, or experienced in a particular subject or activity. ❑ *The mere mention of the words "heart failure," can conjure up, to the layman, the prospect of imminent death.*

lay|off /leɪɔf, BRIT leɪɒf/ (**layoffs**) N-COUNT When there are **layoffs** in a company, people are made unemployed because there is no more work for them in the company. [BUSINESS] ❑ *It will close more than 200 stores nationwide resulting in the layoffs of an estimated 2,000 employees.*

lay|out /leɪaʊt/ (**layouts**) N-COUNT The **layout** of a garden, building, or piece of writing is the way in which the parts of it are arranged. ❑ *He tried to recall the layout of the farmhouse.*

lazy /leɪzi/ (**lazier, laziest**) **1** ADJ If someone is **lazy**, they do not want to work or make any effort to do anything. ❑ *Lazy and incompetent police officers are letting the public down.* ● **la|zi|ness** N-UNCOUNT ❑ *Current employment laws will be changed to reward effort and punish laziness.* **2** ADJ You can use **lazy** to describe an activity or event in which you are very relaxed and which you do or take part in

1 타동사 놓다; 깔다; 눕히다 ❑ 바닥에 신문지 한 장을 깔아라. ❑ 엄마들은 아기를 보통 반듯이 눕혀 재운다. **2** 타동사 깔다, 설치하다 ❑ 한 남자가 살롱 카펫을 깔려고 왔다. **3** 타동사/자동사 (알을) 낳다 ❑ 우리 카나리아가 알을 한 개 낳았다. **4** 타동사 마련하다; 기초를 마련하다; 계획을 마련하다 ❑ 칠레에서 있었던 외교관 회의는 폭넓은 환경 규약을 마련하기 위한 초석을 놓았다. **5** 타동사 -하다; 비난하다; 기소하다 ❑ 그녀는 어느 한 정당을 비난하기를 거부했다. **6** 타동사 상을 보다, 밥상을 차리다 [주로 영국영어; 미국영어 대개 set] ❑ 집사가 항상 상을 보았다.

1 구동사 내려놓다 ❑ 그는 차를 다 마시고, 찻잔을 내려놓았다. **2** 구동사 제쳐 놓다, 제쳐 두다 ❑ 아마 야당들이 자신들의 파당적 이해관계를 제쳐 두고 잘 대처할 것이다.

1 구동사 내려놓다 ❑ 다니엘은 기사를 다 읽고 신문을 책상 위에 내려놓았다. **2** 구동사 규정하다 ❑ 회사법은 최소 요구 조건을 규정하고 있다. **3** 구동사 (무기를) 내려놓다 ❑ 마약 밀매상들은 무기를 버리겠다고 제안해 왔다.

구동사 정리 해고당하다 [경제] ❑ 적자를 줄이기 위해 10만 명의 연방 노동자들을 정리 해고할 것이다.

구동사 한턱 내다 [주로 영국영어] ❑ 그들은 정말 근사한 저녁 시간을 마련해 주었다.

1 구동사 정리하다 ❑ 그레이스는 점심 식탁에 나이프와 포크를 가지런히 올려놓았다. **2** 구동사 (계획 등을) 설명하다 ❑ 존이 자신의 계획에 대해 설명할 때 맥스웰은 주의를 기울여 들었다.

1 형용사 평신도 ❑ 에드워즈는 감리교의 평신도 전도사이자 사회 복지사이다. **2** 형용사 문외한의, 일반 보통 사람의 ❑ 전문가가 아닌 일반 보통 사람이 의학 도서관을 이용하기는 쉽지 않다.

1 가산명사 키, 층 ❑ 오존층의 파괴 **2** 가산명사 계층, 중위 ❑ 비평가와 관람객들은 그는 사진에 겹겹이 숨겨져 있는 의미를 풀어낸다. **3** 타동사 켜켜이 쌓다 ❑ 채 썬 양파 절반을 감자 위에 켜켜이 얹어 놓아라.

가산명사 문외한 ❑ 단지 '심장마비'라고 말만 해도 문외한들은 당장 죽게 되겠구나 하고 받아들일 수도 있다.

가산명사 정리 해고 [경제] ❑ 전국적으로 200개 이상의 분점들이 문을 닫을 것이고 그 결과 약 2,000명의 종업원들이 정리 해고될 것이다.

가산명사 배치, 레이아웃 ❑ 그는 그 농가의 배치를 기억해 내려고 애썼다.

1 형용사 게으른 ❑ 게으르고 무능한 경찰관들이 사람들을 실망시키고 있다. ● 게으름 불가산명사 ❑ 현재의 고용법은 노력하는 사람에게는 보상하고 나태한 사람에게는 불이익을 주는 쪽으로 바뀔 것이다. **2** 형용사 나른한 ❑ 그녀가 최근에 발표한 소설은

a
b
c
d
e
f
g
h
i
j
k
l
m
n
o
p
q
r
s
t
u
v
w
x
y
z

without making much effort. [ADJ n] ❏ *Her latest novel is perfect for a lazy summer's afternoon reading.* ● **la|zi|ly** /leɪzɪli/ ADV [ADV with v] ❏ *Liz went back into the kitchen, stretching lazily.*

나른한 여름 오후 읽을거리로 안성맞춤이다.
● 나른하게 부사 ❏ 리즈는 부엌으로 다시 들어가며 나른하게 기지개를 폈다.

lb **lb** is a written abbreviation for **pound**, when it refers to weight. ❏ *The baby was born three months early at 3 lb 5 oz.*

무게 단위 파운드의 약어 ❏ 그 아기는 예정보다 3개월 일찍 3파운드 5온스의 체중으로 태어났다.

LCD /ɛl si di/ (**LCDs**) N-COUNT An **LCD** is a display of information on a screen, which uses liquid crystals that become visible when electricity is passed through them. **LCD** is an abbreviation for "liquid crystal display." ❏ *...a color LCD screen.*

가산명사 액정 화면 ❏ 칼라 액정 화면

---
lead

① BEING AHEAD OR TAKING SOMEONE SOMEWHERE
② SUBSTANCES

---

① **lead** ♦♦♦ /lid/ (**leads, leading, led**) →Please look at category **16** to see if the expression you are looking for is shown under another headword. **1** V-T/V-I If you **lead** a group of people, you walk or ride in front of them. ❏ *John Major and the Duke of Edinburgh led the mourners.* ❏ *He walks with a stick but still leads his soldiers into battle.* **2** V-T If you **lead** someone to a particular place or thing, you take them there. ❏ *He took Dickon by the hand to lead him into the house.* ❏ *She confessed to the killing and led police to his remains.* **3** V-I If a road, gate, or door **leads** somewhere, you can get there by following the road or going through the gate or door. ❏ *...the door that led to the yard.* ❏ *...a hallway leading to the living room.* **4** V-T/V-I If you **are leading** at a particular point in a race or competition, you are winning at that point. ❏ *He's leading in the presidential race.* ❏ *So far Fischer leads by five wins to two.* **5** N-SING If you have **the lead** or are **in the lead** in a race or competition, you are winning. ❏ *Harvard took the lead from the start and remained composed and unperturbed by the repeated challenges.* **6** V-T If one company or country **leads** others in a particular activity such as scientific research or business, it is more successful or advanced than they are in that activity. ❏ *In 1920, the United States led the world in iron and steel manufacturing.* **7** V-T If you **lead** a group of people, an organization, or an activity, you are in control or in charge of the people or the activity. ❏ *He led the country between 1949 and 1984.* **8** N-COUNT If you give a **lead**, you do something new or develop new ideas or methods that other people consider to be a good example or model to follow. ❏ *...the need for the president to give a moral lead.* ❏ *The American and Japanese navies took the lead in the development of naval aviation.* **9** V-T You can use **lead** when you are saying what kind of life someone has. For example, if you **lead** a busy life, your life is busy. ❏ *She led a normal, happy life with her sister and brother.* **10** V-I If something **leads to** a situation or event, usually an unpleasant one, it begins a process which causes that situation or event to happen. ❏ *Ethnic tensions among the republics could lead to civil war.* **11** V-T If something **leads** you **to** do something, it influences or affects you in such a way that you do it. ❏ *His abhorrence of racism led him to write The Algiers Motel Incident.* **12** V-T You can say that one point or topic in a discussion or piece of writing **leads** you **to** another in order to introduce a new point or topic that is linked with the previous one. ❏ *Well, I think that leads me to the real point.* **13** N-COUNT A **lead** is a piece of information or an idea which may help people to discover the facts in a situation where many facts are not known, for example in the investigation of a crime or in a scientific experiment. ❏ *The inquiry team is also following up possible leads after receiving 400 calls from the public.* **14** N-COUNT A dog's **lead** is a long, thin chain or piece of leather which you attach to the dog's collar so that you can control the dog. [mainly BRIT; AM usually **leash**] ❏ *An older man came out with a little dog on a lead.* **15** N-COUNT A **lead** in a piece of equipment is a piece of wire covered in plastic which supplies electricity to the equipment or carries it from one part of the equipment to another. ❏ *...a lead that plugs into a socket on the camcorder.* **16** →see also **leading. to lead** someone **astray** →see **astray. to lead the way** →see **way**

1 타동사/자동사 지휘하다, 인도하다 ❏ 존 메이저 수상과 에든버러 공작이 조문객들을 인도했다. ❏ 그는 지팡이를 짚고 걸어 다니지만, 여전히 전투에서 부하들을 지휘한다. **2** 타동사 안내하다, 데리고 가다 ❏ 그는 딕콘의 손을 잡고 집안으로 안내하였다. ❏ 그녀는 살인을 자백하고, 경찰을 피살자 유해가 있는 곳으로 데리고 갔다. **3** 자동사 (길, 문 등이) 연결되다 ❏ 뜰로 연결되는 문 ❏ 거실로 연결되는 복도 **4** 타동사/자동사 앞서고 있다, 우세를 보이고 있다 ❏ 그가 대통령 선거전에서 우세를 보이고 있다. ❏ 지금까지는 피셔가 5대 2로 앞서고 있다. **5** 단수명사 (경주나 경쟁에서) 앞섬 ❏ 하버드는 시작부터 앞서더니 계속된 도전에도 동요하지 않고 침착했다. **6** 타동사 주도하다 ❏ 1920년에 미국은 세계 철강 산업을 주도했었다. **7** 타동사 이끌다 ❏ 그는 1949년에서 1984년까지 그 나라를 이끌었다. **8** 가산명사 솔선수범, 선도 ❏ 대통령이 도덕적으로 솔선수범해야 할 필요성 ❏ 미국과 일본의 해군이 해군 비행 전술의 발달을 선도했다. **9** 타동사 (어떠한 삶을) 살다 ❏ 그녀는 언니, 오빠와 함께 평범하고 행복한 삶을 살았다. **10** 자동사 (어떠한 일로) 이어지다, (어떠한 일로) 번지다 ❏ 그 공화국들 간의 종족 갈등이 내전으로 번질 수도 있다. **11** 타동사 -하게 하다 ❏ 그는 인종주의에 대한 혐오감에 '알제 모텔 사건'을 집필하게 되었다. **12** 타동사 (내용을) 이어 주다 ❏ 음, 그것을 통해 본격적인 문제로 들어가게 되는 것 같군. **13** 가산명사 단서 ❏ 조사 팀은 또한 사람들에게서 400통의 전화를 받은 후 가능한 단서들을 추적하고 있다. **14** 가산명사 개줄 [주로 영국영어; 미국영어 대개 leash] ❏ 나이 든 남자가 개줄에 묶은 조그만 개를 데리고 나왔다. **15** 가산명사 도선 ❏ 캠코더의 소켓에 연결되는 도선

Thesaurus   *lead*의 참조어

v.   escort, guide, precede; *(ant.)* follow ① **1 2**
       govern, head, manage ① **7**

▶**lead up to** **1** PHRASAL VERB The events that **led up to** a particular event happened one after the other until that event occurred. ❏ *Alan Tomlinson has reconstructed the events that led up to the deaths.* **2** PHRASAL VERB If someone **leads up to** a particular subject, they gradually guide a conversation to a point where they can introduce it. ❏ *I'm leading up to something quite important.*

1 구동사 (사건을) 부르다; (사건에) 이르게 하다 ❏ 앨런 톰린슨은 그 죽음을 부른 사건들을 재현해 냈다. **2** 구동사 이끌다, 유도하다 ❏ 제가 상당히 중요한 내용을 말씀드리려고 합니다.

② **lead** /lɛd/ (**leads**) **1** N-UNCOUNT **Lead** is a soft, gray, heavy metal. ❏ *...drinking water supplied by old-fashioned lead pipes.* **2** N-COUNT The **lead** in a pencil is the center part of it which makes a mark on paper. ❏ *He grabbed a pencil, and the lead immediately broke.* →see **mineral, plumbing**

1 불가산명사 납 ❏ 구식의 납 파이프를 통해 공급되는 식수 **2** 가산명사 (연필) 심 ❏ 그가 연필을 꽉 움켜잡자 바로 심이 부러졌다.

lead|er ♦♦♦ /lidər/ (**leaders**) **1** N-COUNT The **leader** of a group of people or an organization is the person who is in control of it or in charge of it. ❏ *We now need a new leader of the party and a new style of leadership.* **2** N-COUNT The **leader** at a particular point in a race or competition is the person who is winning at that point. ❏ *The leaders came in two minutes clear of the field.*

1 가산명사 지도자 ❏ 지금 우리는 당에 새 지도자와 새로운 스타일의 리더십이 필요하다. **2** 가산명사 선두 주자, 선두 ❏ 선두 그룹은 후발 그룹을 2분 간의 격차로 앞서며 필드에 들어왔다.

lead|er|board /lidərbɔrd/ N-SING The **leaderboard** is a board that shows the names and positions of the leading competitors in a competition, especially a golf tournament. ❏ *I'm delighted to be on top of the leaderboard in a tournament that has so many star names playing.*

단수명사 리더보드 (골프 등에서 경기자의 경기 실적을 알려 주는 판) ❏ 이렇게 많은 스타 선수들이 함께 하는 경기에서 리더보드 맨 위에 제 이름이 올랐다는 것이 정말 기쁩니다.

lead|er|ship ♦♦◇ /líːdərʃɪp/ (leaderships) **1** N-COUNT You refer to people who are in control of a group or organization as the **leadership**. □ *He is expected to hold talks with both the Croatian and Slovenian leaderships.* **2** N-UNCOUNT Someone's **leadership** is their position or state of being in control of a group of people. □ *He praised her leadership during the crisis.*

lead|ing ♦♦◇ /líːdɪŋ/ **1** ADJ The **leading** person or thing in a particular area is the one which is most important or successful. [ADJ n] □ *...a leading member of Bristol's Sikh community.* **2** ADJ The **leading** role in a play or movie is the main role. A **leading** lady or man is an actor who plays this role. [ADJ n] □ *...an offer to play the leading role in an Alan Bennett play.* **3** ADJ The **leading** group, vehicle, or person in a race or procession is the one that is at the front. [ADJ n] □ *The leading car came to a halt.*

Word Partnership leading의 연어

N. leading **advocate**, leading **cause of death**, leading **expert**, leading **manufacturer** **1**
leading **candidate**, leading **contender**, leading **in the polls**, leading **in a race**, leading **runner**, leading **scorer** **3**

lead|ing ar|ti|cle (leading articles) **1** N-COUNT A **leading article** in a newspaper is the most important story in it. [AM; BRIT **lead**] **2** N-COUNT A **leading article** in a newspaper is a piece of writing which gives the editor's opinion on an important news item. [BRIT; AM **editorial**] □ *A leading article in the Independent urges justice rather than military action.*

lead|ing edge N-SING The **leading edge of** a particular area of research or development is the area of it that seems most advanced or sophisticated. □ *I think Israel tends to be at the leading edge of technological development.* ● **leading-edge** ADJ □ *...leading-edge technology.*

lead time (lead times) **1** N-COUNT **Lead time** is the time between the original design or idea for a particular product and its actual production. [BUSINESS] □ *They aim to cut production lead times to under 18 months.* **2** N-COUNT **Lead time** is the period of time that it takes for goods to be delivered after someone has ordered them. [BUSINESS] □ *Lead times on new equipment orders can run as long as three years.*

leaf ♦◇◇ /líːf/ (leaves, leafs, leafing, leafed) **1** N-COUNT The **leaves** of a tree or plant are the parts that are flat, thin, and usually green. Many trees and plants lose their leaves in the winter and grow new leaves in the spring. [usu pl, also in/into N] □ *In the garden, the leaves of the horse chestnut had already fallen.* **2** N-COUNT A **leaf** is one of the pieces of paper of which a book is made. □ *He flattened the wrappers and put them between the leaves of his book.*
→see **tea**

▶**leaf through** PHRASAL VERB If you **leaf through** something such as a book or magazine, you turn the pages without reading or looking at them very carefully. □ *Most patients derive enjoyment from leafing through old picture albums.*

leaf|let /líːflɪt/ (leaflets) N-COUNT A **leaflet** is a little book or a piece of paper containing information about a particular subject. □ *Campaigners handed out leaflets on passive smoking.*

leafy /líːfi/ **1** ADJ **Leafy** trees and plants have lots of leaves on them. □ *His two-story brick home was graced with a patio and surrounded by tall, leafy trees.* **2** ADJ You say that a place is **leafy** when there are lots of trees and plants there. □ *...semi-detached homes with gardens in leafy suburban areas.*
→see **vegetable**

league ♦♦◇ /líːg/ (leagues) **1** N-COUNT A **league** is a group of people, clubs, or countries that have joined together for a particular purpose, or because they share a common interest. □ *...the League of Nations.* **2** N-COUNT A **league** is a group of teams that play the same sport or activity against each other. □ *...the American League series between the Boston Red Sox and World Champion Oakland Athletics.* **3** N-COUNT You use the word **league** to make comparisons between different people or things, especially in terms of their quality. □ *Her success has taken her out of my league.* **4** PHRASE If you say that someone is **in league with** another person to do something bad, you mean that they are working together to do that thing. □ *There is no evidence that the broker was in league with the fraudulent vendor.*

Word Partnership league의 연어

N. league **leader**, league **record**, league **schedule** **2**
V. **lead** the league **2**
PREP. **in league with** *someone* **4**

leak ♦◇◇ /líːk/ (leaks, leaking, leaked) **1** V-T/V-I If a container **leaks**, there is a hole or crack in it which lets a substance such as liquid or gas escape. You can also say that a container **leaks** a substance such as liquid or gas. □ *The roof leaked.* □ *The pool's fiberglass sides had cracked and the water had leaked out.* ● N-COUNT **Leak** is also a noun. □ *It's thought a gas leak may have caused the blast.* **2** N-COUNT A **leak** is a crack, hole, or other gap that a substance such as a liquid or gas can pass through. □ *...a leak in the radiator.* **3** V-T/V-I If a secret document or piece of information **leaks** or **is leaked**, someone lets the public know about it. □ *Mr Ashton accused police of leaking information to the press.* □ *We don't know how the transcript leaked.* ● N-COUNT **Leak** is also a noun. □ *More serious leaks, possibly involving national security, are likely to be investigated by the police.*

A

● PHRASAL VERB **Leak out** means the same as **leak**. ❏ *More details are now beginning to leak out.*

누설하다 ❏ 더 자세한 내용들이 누출되기 시작하고 있다.

B

Thesaurus
*leak*의 참조어

V.	discharge, drip, ooze, seep, trickle **1**
	come out, divulge, pass on **3**
N.	crack, hole, opening **2**

C

D

Word Partnership
*leak*의 연어

V.	**cause** a leak **1**
N.	**fuel** leak, **gas** leak, **oil** leak, leak **in the roof, water** leak **1**
	leak **information**, leak **news**, leak **a story** **3**

E

F

leak|age /líːkɪdʒ/ (**leakages**) N-VAR A **leakage** is an amount of liquid or gas that is escaping from a pipe or container by means of a crack, hole, or other fault. ❏ *A leakage of kerosene has polluted water supplies.*

가산명사 또는 불가산명사 누출량 ❏ 누출된 석유가 상수도를 오염시켰다.

lean ♦♢♢ /líːn/ (**leans, leaning, leaned, leaner, leanest**)

G

American English uses the form **leaned** as the past tense and past participle. British English uses either **leaned** or **leant**.

미국영어에서 과거 및 과거 분사로 leaned를 쓴다. 영국영어에서는 leaned 또는 leant를 쓴다.

H

I

J

K

1 V-I When you **lean** in a particular direction, you bend your body in that direction. ❏ *Eileen leaned across and opened the passenger door.* **2** V-T/V-I If you **lean on** or **against** someone or something, you rest against them so that they partly support your weight. If you **lean** an object **on** or **against** something, you place the object so that it is partly supported by that thing. ❏ *She was feeling tired and was glad to lean against him.* ❏ *Lean the plants against a wall and cover the roots with peat.* **3** ADJ If you describe someone as **lean**, you mean that they are thin but look strong and healthy. [APPROVAL] ❏ *Like most athletes, she was lean and muscular.* **4** ADJ If meat is **lean**, it does not have very much fat. ❏ *It is a beautiful meat, very lean and tender.* **5** ADJ If you describe an organization as **lean**, you mean that it has become more efficient and less wasteful by getting rid of staff, or by dropping projects which are unprofitable. ❏ *The value of the pound will force British companies to be leaner and fitter.* **6** ADJ If you describe periods of time as **lean**, you mean that people have less of something such as money or are less successful than they used to be. ❏ *...the lean years of the 1930s.*

1 자동사 몸을 굽히다 ❏ 에일린은 몸을 굽혀 승객실 문을 열었다. **2** 타동사/자동사 기대다 ❏ 그녀는 피곤감을 느꼈고, 그에게 기댈 수 있다는 것이 기뻤다. ❏ 식물들을 벽에 기대게 하고 뿌리를 토탄으로 덮어 주어라. **3** 형용사 군살이 없는 [마음에 듦] ❏ 대부분의 운동선수들과 같이, 그녀는 군살이 없는 단단한 몸매였다. **4** 형용사 기름기가 별로 없는 ❏ 기름기도 없고 부드러운 아주 좋은 고기이다. **5** 형용사 군살을 뺀 ❏ 파운드 화 가치 때문에 영국 회사들은 군살을 더 빼고 조직을 더 탄탄하게 만들어야 할 것이다. **6** 형용사 어려운 (시절) ❏ 1930년대의 어려웠던 시절

L

Thesaurus
*lean*의 참조어

V.	bend, incline, prop, tilt **1**
	recline, rest **2**
ADJ.	angular, slender, slim, wiry **3**

M

N

Word Partnership
*lean*의 연어

ADJ.	**long and** lean, **tall and** lean **3**
N.	lean **body** **3**
	lean **beef**, lean **meat** **4**

O

P

▶**lean on** or **lean upon** PHRASAL VERB If you **lean on** someone or **lean upon** them, you depend on them for support and encouragement. ❏ *She leaned on him to help her to solve her problems.*

구동사 -에게 기대다, -의 도움을 바라다 ❏ 그녀는 자신의 문제를 해결하는 데 그가 도움을 주기를 바랬다.

Q

leap ♦♢♢ /líːp/ (**leaps, leaping, leaped** or **leapt**)

R

British English usually uses the form **leapt** as the past tense and past participle. American English usually uses **leaped**.

영국영어에서 대개 과거 및 과거 분사로 leapt를 쓴다. 미국영어에서는 leaped를 쓴다.

S

T

U

1 V-I If you **leap**, you jump high in the air or jump a long distance. ❏ *...the federal agents leaped from their hiding places.* ❏ *The newsreels show him leaping into the air.* ● N-COUNT **Leap** is also a noun. ❏ *Smith took Britain's fifth medal of the championships with a leap of 2.37 meters.* **2** V-I If you **leap** somewhere, you move there suddenly and quickly. ❏ *The two men leaped into the jeep and roared off.* **3** V-I If a vehicle **leaps** somewhere, it moves there in a short sudden movement. ❏ *The car leaped forward.* **4** N-COUNT A **leap** is a large and important change, increase, or advance. [JOURNALISM] ❏ *The result has been a giant leap in productivity.* ❏ *...the leap in the unemployed from 35,000 to 75,000.* **5** V-I If you **leap to** a particular place or position, you make a large and important change, increase, or advance. ❏ *Warwicks leap to third in the table, 31 points behind leaders Essex.*

1 자동사 뛰다, 뛰어오르다 ❏ 연방 정부 요원들이 자신들의 은신처에서 뛰어올랐다. ❏ 그 단편 뉴스 영화는 그가 공중으로 뛰어오르는 장면을 보여 준다. ● 가산명사 도약 ❏ 스미스는 2.37미터를 뛰어넘어서 영국에게 다섯 번째 메달을 안겨 주었다. **2** 자동사 날쌔게 움직이다 ❏ 두 남자는 지프차에 뛰어올라 핑음을 내며 달아났다. **3** 자동사 급발진하다 ❏ 차가 급발진했다. **4** 가산명사 급변; 급증; 도약 [언론] ❏ 그 결과로 생산성이 크게 높아졌다. ❏ 실업자 수가 3만 5천에서 7만 5천으로 급증한 **5** 자동사 급변하다; 급증하다; 도약하다 ❏ 1위인 에섹스를 31점차로 따라잡으면서 워릭이 3위로 도약했다.

V

Word Partnership
*leap*의 연어

ADJ.	**big** leap, **giant** leap, **sudden** leap **1** **2** **4**
N.	leap **to your feet** **2**
V.	**make** a leap, **take** a leap **4**

W

X

Y

Z

leap|frog /líːpfrɒg, BRIT líːpfrɒg/ (**leapfrogs, leapfrogging, leapfrogged**) **1** N-UNCOUNT **Leapfrog** is a game which children play, in which a child bends over, while others jump over their back. ❏ *Little men, dressed in what looked like leather clothes, were playing leapfrog and doing somersaults in my yard.* **2** V-T/V-I If one group of people **leapfrogs** into a particular position or **leapfrogs** someone else, they use the achievements of another person or group in order to make advances of their own. ❏ *It is already obvious that all four American systems have leapfrogged over the European versions.*

1 불가산명사 등 짚고 뛰어넘기 ❏ 가죽옷처럼 보이는 옷을 입은 작은 남자들이 내 뜰에서 등 짚고 뛰어넘기와 재주넘기를 하며 놀고 있었다. **2** 타동사/자동사 뛰어넘다, 앞지르다 ❏ 네 가지의 미국 시스템 모두가 이미 유럽 버전을 뛰어넘었음이 분명하다.

leap year (**leap years**) N-COUNT A **leap year** is a year which has 366 days. The extra day is February 29th. There is a leap year every four years. →see **year**

learn ♦♦♦ /lɜrn/ (**learns, learning, learned**)

> American English uses the form **learned** as the past tense and past participle. British English uses either **learned** or **learnt**.

■ V-T/V-I If you **learn** something, you obtain knowledge or a skill through studying or training. ❑ *Their children were going to learn English.* ❑ *He is learning to play the piano.* ● **learning** N-UNCOUNT ❑ *...a bilingual approach to the learning of English.* ■ V-T/V-I If you **learn** of something, you find out about it. ❑ *It was only after his death that she learned of his affair with Betty.* ❑ *It didn't come as a shock to learn that the fuel and cooling systems are the most common causes of breakdown.* ■ V-T If people **learn to** behave or react in a particular way, they gradually start to behave in that way as a result of a change in attitudes. ❑ *You have to learn to face your problem.* ■ V-T/V-I If you **learn from** an unpleasant experience, you change the way you behave so that it does not happen again or so that, if it happens again, you can deal with it better. ❑ *I am convinced that he has learned from his mistakes.* ■ V-T If you **learn** something such as a poem or a role in a play, you study or repeat the words so that you can remember them. ❑ *He learned this song as an inmate at a Texas prison.* ■ →see also **learned, learning** ■ to **learn** something **the hard way** →see **hard**. to **learn the ropes** →see **rope**

Thesaurus   learn의 참조어
v.   master, pick up, study ■
       discover, find out, understand ■

Word Partnership   learn의 연어
v.   learn **to drive**, learn **to read**, learn **to speak**, learn **to swim**, learn **to use** *something*, learn **to write** ■
       have to learn, **must** learn, **need to** learn, **try to** learn, **want to** learn ■-■
       learn **to cope with** *someone/something* ■
N.   learn **a language**, learn **a secret**, learn **a skill**, learn **things**, learn **the truth** ■
       children learn, **opportunity to** learn, **people** learn, learn **in school**, **students** learn ■ ■
       learn **from experience**, learn **a lesson**, learn **from mistakes** ■ ■
ADJ.   **eager to** learn ■-■ ■

learn|ed /lɜrnɪd/ ■ ADJ A **learned** person has gained a lot of knowledge by studying. ❑ *He is a serious scholar, a genuinely learned man.* ■ →see also **learn**

learn|er /lɜrnər/ (**learners**) N-COUNT A **learner** is someone who is learning about a particular subject or how to do something. ❑ *Learner drivers must be supervised by adults who are at least 21 years old.*

learn|ing /lɜrnɪŋ/ N-UNCOUNT **Learning** is the process of gaining knowledge through studying. ❑ *The brochure described the library as the focal point of learning on the campus.* →see also **learn**

learn|ing curve (**learning curves**) N-COUNT A **learning curve** is a process where people develop a skill by learning from their mistakes. A steep learning curve involves learning very quickly. [usu sing] ❑ *Both he and the crew are on a steep learning curve.*

lease ♦♦♦ /lis/ (**leases, leasing, leased**) ■ N-COUNT A **lease** is a legal agreement by which the owner of a building, a piece of land, or something such as a car allows someone else to use it for a period of time in return for money. ❑ *He took up a 10 year lease on the house at Rossie Priory.* ■ V-T If you **lease** property or something such as a car from someone or if they **lease** it **to** you, they allow you to use it in return for regular payments of money. ❑ *He went to Toronto, where he leased an apartment.* ❑ *She hopes to lease the building to students.*

lease|hold /lishoʊld/ ADJ If a building or land is described as **leasehold**, it is allowed to be used in return for payment according to the terms of a lease. [mainly BRIT] ❑ *I went into a leasehold property at four hundred and fifty pounds rent per year.*

leash /liʃ/ (**leashes**) N-COUNT A dog's **leash** is a long thin piece of leather or a chain, which you attach to the dog's collar so that you can keep the dog under control. ❑ *All dogs in public places should be on a leash.*

least ♦♦♦ /list/

> **Least** is often considered to be the superlative form of **little**.

■ PHRASE You use **at least** to say that a number or amount is the smallest that is possible or likely and that the actual number or amount may be greater. The forms **at the least** and **at the very least** are also used. ❑ *About two-thirds of adults consult their doctor at least once a year.* ■ PHRASE You use **at least** to say that something is the minimum that is true or possible. The forms **at the least** and **at the very least** are also used. ❑ *She could take a nice holiday at least.* ❑ *His possession of classified documents in his home was, at the very least, a violation of Navy security regulations.* ■ PHRASE You use **at least** to indicate an advantage that exists in spite of the disadvantage or bad situation that has just been mentioned. ❑ *We've no idea what his state of health is but at least we know he is still alive.* ■ PHRASE You use **at least** to indicate that you are correcting or changing something that you have just said. ❑ *It's*

가산명사 윤년

미국영어에서 과거 및 과거 분사로 learned를 쓴다. 영국영어에서는 learned 또는 learnt를 쓴다.

■ 타동사/자동사 배우다 ❑ 그들의 자녀들은 영어를 배울 예정이었다. ❑ 그는 피아노를 배우고 있다. ● 학습 불가산명사 ❑ 이중 언어 접근법적 영어 학습 ■ 타동사/자동사 알아내다 ❑ 그가 죽은 후에서야 그녀는 그와 베티와의 관계를 알게 되었다. ❑ 연료와 냉각 장치가 고장의 주 원인이라는 것을 알아낸 것은 그다지 충격적이지 않았다. ■ 타동사 배우다, –한 줄 알게 되다 ❑ 너 자신의 문제를 직시하는 법을 배워야 해. ■ 타동사/자동사 배우다 ❑ 나는 그가 실수로부터 뭔가를 배웠으리라고 확신한다. ■ 타동사 외다 ❑ 그는 이 노래를 텍사스 교도소 수감 시절에 외웠다.

■ 형용사 학식이 있는 ❑ 그는 진지한 학자이고, 진정으로 학식이 있는 사람이다.

가산명사 학습자 ❑ 운전 연습자는 21세 이상인 성인의 지도를 받아야 합니다.

불가산명사 학습 ❑ 그 소책자에는 도서관이 캠퍼스 학습의 중심점으로 묘사되어 있다.

가산명사 학습 곡선 ❑ 그와 승무원들은 아주 빨리 배우고 있다.

■ 가산명사 임대 계약 ❑ 그는 로시 수도원에 있는 그 집을 10년 계약으로 임대했다. ■ 타동사 임대하다 ❑ 그는 토론토로 가서 아파트를 한 채 빌렸다. ❑ 그녀는 그 빌딩을 학생들에게 임대하기를 바라고 있다.

형용사 임대된 [주로 영국영어] ❑ 나는 연 450파운드에 임대된 건물로 들어갔다.

가산명사 개줄 ❑ 공공장소에서는 개를 줄에 묶어 다녀야 한다.

least가 종종 little의 최상급 형태로 간주된다.

■ 구 최소한, 적어도 ❑ 최소 반 파인트 이상의 우유를 매일 마시는 걸 목표로 삼아라. ❑ 성인 중 약 3분의 2는 일 년에 최소 한 번 이상 의사를 찾아간다. ■ 구 최소한 ❑ 적어도 그녀는 멋진 휴일을 보낼 수 있었다. ❑ 그가 비밀문서를 집에 보관하고 있었다는 것은, 아무리 최소로 보아도 해군 보안 규정 위반 사항이다. ■ 구 최소한 ❑ 우리는 그의 건강 상태가 어떤지 전혀 모르고 있지만, 최소한 그가 아직 살아 있다는 것은 알고 있다. ■ 구 적어도 ❑ 연구 자금을 받는 것이 어렵지는 않아. 적어도 항상 어려운 것은 아냐. ■ 형용사 최소 ❑ 나는 가능한 한 사람들을 불쾌하게 만들지 않으려고 노력한다. ● 대명사 최소 ❑ 교육 예산을 보면 일본은

A

not difficult to get money for research or at least it's not always difficult. ⑤ ADJ You use **the least** to mean a smaller amount than anyone or anything else, or the smallest amount possible. [the ADJ n] ❑ I try to offend the least amount of people possible. ● PRON **Least** is also a pronoun. ❑ On education funding, Japan performs best but spends the least per student. ● ADV **Least** is also an adverb. [the ADV after v] ❑ Damming the river may end up benefitting those who need it the least. ⑥ ADV You use **least** to indicate that someone or something has less of a particular quality than most other things of its kind. [ADV adj/adv] ❑ He was one of the least warm human beings I had ever met. ⑦ ADJ You use **the least** to emphasize the smallness of something, especially when it hardly exists at all. [EMPHASIS] [the ADJ n] ❑ I don't have the least idea of what you're talking about. ⑧ ADV You use **least** to indicate that something is true or happens to a smaller degree or extent than anything else or at any other time. [ADV with v] ❑ He had a way of throwing Helen off guard with his charm when she least expected it. ⑨ ADJ You use **least** in structures where you are emphasizing that a particular situation or event is much less important or serious than other possible or actual ones. [EMPHASIS] [ADJ of def-n] ❑ Having to get up at three o'clock every morning was the least of her worries. ⑩ PRON You use **the least** in structures where you are stating the minimum that should be done in a situation, and suggesting that more should really be done. [the PRON cl] ❑ Well, the least you can do, if you won't help me yourself, is to tell me where to go instead.

학생 1인당 지출을 최소로 하지만 효과는 가장 크다.
● 부사 최소로, 가장 덜 ❑ 그 강에 댐을 쌓으면 결국 그 댐을 가장 덜 필요로 하는 사람들이 혜택을 볼 것이다. ⑥ 부사 가장 적게, 가장 덜 ❑ 그는 내가 만나 본 사람 중 가장 인간미가 없는 사람 중 하나였다. ⑦ 형용사 최소한도 [강조] ❑ 나는 네가 무슨 말을 하는지 전혀 모르겠어. ⑧ 부사 가장 적게, 가장 적게 ❑ 그는 헬렌이 전혀 예상하지 못하고 있을 때 자신의 매력으로 그녀를 무장 해제시키는 재주를 가지고 있었다. ⑨ 형용사 가장 하찮은 [강조] ❑ 매일 새벽 3시에 일어나야 한다는 것은 그녀에게 걱정거리도 아니었다. ⑩ 대명사 최소 ❑ 음, 네가 나를 도와주지 않겠다면, 대신 내가 어디를 가야 하는지는 최소한 알려 줄 수 있는 것 같은데.

Thesaurus   least의 참조어

ADJ.   fewest, lowest, minimum, smallest ⑤

leath|er ◆◇◇ /lɛðər/ (**leathers**) N-MASS **Leather** is treated animal skin which is used for making shoes, clothes, bags, and furniture. ❑ He wore a leather jacket and dark trousers.

물질명사 가죽 ❑ 그는 가죽 잠바와 진한 색 바지를 입고 있었다.

leave ◆◆◆ /liv/ (**leaves, leaving, left**) ① V-T/V-I If you **leave** a place or person, you go away from that place or person. ❑ He would not be allowed to leave the country. ❑ My flight leaves in less than an hour. ② V-T/V-I If you **leave** an institution, group, or job, you permanently stop attending that institution, being a member of that group, or doing that job. ❑ He left school with no qualifications. ❑ I am leaving to concentrate on writing fiction. ③ V-T/V-I If you **leave** your husband, wife, or some other person with whom you have had a close relationship, you stop living with them or you end the relationship. ❑ He'll never leave you. You need have no worry. ④ V-T If you **leave** something or someone in a particular place, you let them remain there when you go away. If you **leave** something or someone with a person, you let them remain with that person so they are safe while you are away. ❑ I left my bags in the car. ❑ From the moment that Philippe had left her in the bedroom at the hotel, she had heard nothing of him. ⑤ V-T If you **leave** a message or an answer, you write it, record it, or give it to someone so that it can be found or passed on. ❑ You can leave a message on our answering machine. ❑ I left my phone number with several people. ⑥ V-T If you **leave** someone doing something, they are doing that thing when you go away from them. ❑ Salter drove off, leaving Callendar surveying the scene. ⑦ V-T If you **leave** someone **to** do something, you go away from them so that they do it on their own. If you **leave** someone **to** himself or herself, you go away from them and allow them to be alone. ❑ I'll leave you to get to know each other. ❑ Diana took the hint and left them to it. ⑧ V-T To **leave** an amount of something means to keep it available after the rest has been used or taken away. ❑ He always left a little food for the next day. ⑨ V-T To **leave** someone **with** something, especially when that thing is unpleasant or difficult to deal with, means to make them have it or make them responsible for it. ❑ ...a crash which left him with a broken collar-bone. ⑩ V-T If an event **leaves** people or things in a particular state, they are in that state when the event has finished. ❑ ...violent disturbances which have left at least ten people dead. ⑪ V-T If you **leave** food or drink, you do not eat or drink it, often because you do not like it. ❑ If you don't like the cocktail you ordered, just leave it and try a different one. ⑫ V-T If something **leaves** a mark, effect, or sign, it causes that mark, effect, or sign to remain as a result. ❑ A muscle tear will leave a scar after healing. ⑬ V-T If you **leave** something in a particular state, position, or condition, you let it remain in that state, position, or condition. ❑ He left the album open on the table. ❑ I've left the car lights on. ⑭ V-T If you **leave** a space or gap in something, you deliberately make that space or gap. ❑ Leave a gap at the top and bottom so air can circulate. ⑮ V-T If you **leave** a job, decision, or choice **to** someone, you give them the responsibility for dealing with it or making it. ❑ Affix the blue airmail label and leave the rest to us. ❑ The judge should not have left it to the jury to decide. ⑯ V-T To **leave** someone **with** a particular course of action or the opportunity to do something means to let it be available to them, while restricting them in other ways. ❑ He was left with no option but to resign. ⑰ V-T If you **leave** something **until** a particular time, you delay doing it or dealing with it until then. ❑ Don't leave it all until the last minute. ● PHRASE If you **leave** something **too late**, you delay doing it so that when you eventually do it, it is useless or ineffective. ⑱ V-T If you **leave** a particular subject, you stop talking about it and start discussing something else. ❑ I think we'd better leave the subject of Nationalism. ⑲ V-T If you **leave** property or money **to** someone, you arrange for it to be given to them after you have died. ❑ He died two and a half years later, leaving everything to his wife. ⑳ N-UNCOUNT **Leave** is a period of time when you are not working at your job, because you are on vacation, or for some other reason. If you are **on leave**, you are not working at your job. ❑ Why don't you take a few days' leave? ❑ ...maternity leave. ㉑ →see also **left** ㉒ PHRASE If you **leave** someone or something **alone**, or if you **leave** them **be**, you do not pay them any attention or bother them. ❑ Some people need to confront a traumatic past; others find it better to leave it alone. ㉓ PHRASE If something continues **from where** it **left off**, it starts happening again at the point where it had previously

① 타동사/자동사 떠나다 ❑ 그의 출국은 허가되지 않을 것이다. ❑ 내가 탈 비행기는 한 시간 있으면 출발한다. ② 타동사/자동사 그만 두다, 탈퇴하다 ❑ 그는 아무런 자격도 못 딴 채 학교를 그만두었다. ❑ 나는 소설 창작에 전념하기 위해 사직할 것이다. ③ 타동사/자동사 떠나다 ❑ 그는 절대 널 떠나지 않을 거야. 걱정할 필요 없어. ④ 타동사 남겨 두다; 맡겨 두다 ❑ 나는 차에다 가방을 놓고 내렸다. ❑ 필립이 그녀를 호텔 방에 남겨 두고 간 이후로, 그녀는 그의 소식을 전혀 듣지 못한 상태였다. ⑤ 타동사 (메시지 등을) 남기다 ❑ 자동 응답기에 메시지를 남기셔도 됩니다. ❑ 나는 내 전화번호를 여러 사람에게 알려 주었다. ⑥ 타동사 -하게 두다 ❑ 캘린더가 현장을 조사하게 남겨 두고 솔터는 차를 몰고 갔다. ⑦ 타동사 놔두다 ❑ 서로 얘기하시도록 저는 이만 가 볼게요. ❑ 다이애나는 힌트를 알아차리고 그들에게 그것을 맡겨 두었다. ⑧ 타동사 남겨 두다 ❑ 그는 다음 날을 위해 항상 음식을 조금 남겨 둔다. ⑨ 타동사 안겨 주다 ❑ 그에게 쇄골 골절을 안겨 준 충돌 사고 ⑩ 타동사 (상태를) 초래하다; (상태에) 이르게 하다 ❑ 최소 열 명 이상의 사망자를 낸 난동 ⑪ 타동사 (음식을) 남기다 ❑ 주문하신 칵테일이 마음에 안 드시면 그냥 남겨 두시고 다른 것을 시키세요. ⑫ 타동사 (흔적 등을) 남기다 ❑ 근육 파열은 치료 후에도 흉터가 남는다. ⑬ 타동사 (-한 상태로) 두다 ❑ 그는 사진첩을 탁자 위에 펼쳐 두었다. ❑ 내가 차의 전등을 켜 두었다. ⑭ 타동사 (공간 등을) 남겨 놓으세요. ❑ 공기가 순환할 수 있게 위와 아래 사이에 틈을 남겨 놓으세요. ⑮ 타동사 -에게 맡기다, -가 하도록 내버려 두다 ❑ 파란색 항공 우편 라벨을 붙이시고 그 나머지는 저희에게 맡기세요. ❑ 재판관은 그 사안을 배심원이 결정하게 내버려 두어서는 안 된다. ⑯ 타동사 ...이 -하게 하다 ❑ 그는 사임할 수밖에 다른 방도가 없었다. ⑰ 타동사 미루다 ❑ 그 모두를 마지막 순간까지 미루지는 말라. ● 구 미루다가 제때를 놓치다, 너무 미루다 ⑱ 타동사 (주제를) 바꾸다 ❑ 주제를 민족주의에서 다른 주제로 바꾸는 것이 좋을 것 같은데요. ⑲ 타동사 (유산을) 남기다 ❑ 그는 모든 재산을 부인에게 남기고 이 년 반 후에 죽었다. ⑳ 불가산명사 휴가, 휴직 ❑ 며칠 동안 휴가를 갖는 게 어때? ❑ 출산 휴가 ㉒ 구 내버려 두다 ❑ 어떤 사람들은 정신적 충격을 준 과거를 대면할 필요가 있고, 어떤 사람들은 그것을 그냥 내버려 두는 것이 더 좋을 수도 있다. ㉓ 구 이전에 멈춘 거기서 ❑ 경찰들이 사라지면 폭력은 발생하던 그 자리에서 다시 일어난다.

stopped. ❑ *As soon as the police disappear the violence will take up from where it left off.*
② **take it or leave it** →see **take**

▶**leave behind** **①** PHRASAL VERB If you **leave** someone or something **behind**, you go away permanently from them. ❑ *"I'd go and live there and leave England behind," says Brown.* **②** PHRASAL VERB If you **leave behind** an object or a situation, it remains after you have left a place. ❑ *I don't want to leave anything behind.* **③** PHRASAL VERB If a person, country, or organization **is left behind**, they remain at a lower level than others because they are not as quick at understanding things or developing. ❑ *We're going to be left behind by the rest of the world.* ❑ *People are concerned about getting left behind right now.*

▶**leave off** PHRASAL VERB If someone or something **is left off** a list, they are not included on that list. ❑ *She has been deliberately left off the guest list.*

▶**leave out** PHRASAL VERB If you **leave** someone or something **out** of an activity, collection, discussion, or group, you do not include them in it. ❑ *Some would question the wisdom of leaving her out of the team.* ❑ *If you prefer mild flavors reduce or leave out the chilli.*

leaves /livz/ **Leaves** is the plural form of **leaf**, and the third person singular form of **leave**.

lec|tern /lɛktərn/ (**lecterns**) N-COUNT A **lectern** is a high sloping desk on which someone puts their notes when they are standing up and giving a lecture.

lec|ture ♦◇◇ /lɛktʃər/ (**lectures, lecturing, lectured**) **①** N-COUNT A **lecture** is a talk someone gives in order to teach people about a particular subject, usually at a university or college. ❑ *...a series of lectures by Professor Eric Robinson.* **②** V-I If you **lecture on** a particular subject, you give a lecture or a series of lectures about it. ❑ *She then invited him to Atlanta to lecture on the history of art.* **③** V-T If someone **lectures** you about something, they criticize you or tell you how they think you should behave. ❑ *He used to lecture me about getting too much sun.* ❑ *Chuck would lecture me, telling me to get a haircut.* ● N-COUNT **Lecture** is also a noun. ❑ *Our captain gave us a stern lecture on safety.*

lec|tur|er /lɛktʃərər/ (**lecturers**) **①** N-COUNT A **lecturer** is a teacher at a university or college. ❑ *...a lecturer in law at Southampton University.* **②** N-COUNT A **lecturer** is a person who gives lectures.

led /lɛd/ **Led** is the past tense and past participle of **lead**.

ledge /lɛdʒ/ (**ledges**) **①** N-COUNT A **ledge** is a piece of rock on the side of a cliff or mountain, which is in the shape of a narrow shelf. ❑ *...like a wounded bird seeking refuge on a mountain ledge.* **②** N-COUNT A **ledge** is a narrow shelf along the bottom edge of a window. ❑ *Dorothy had climbed onto the ledge outside his window.*

ledg|er /lɛdʒər/ (**ledgers**) N-COUNT A **ledger** is a book in which a company or organization writes down the amounts of money it spends and receives. [BUSINESS]

leek /lik/ (**leeks**) N-VAR **Leeks** are long thin vegetables which smell like onions. They are white at one end, have long light green leaves, and are eaten cooked.

leer /lɪər/ (**leers, leering, leered**) V-I If someone **leers** at you, they smile in an unpleasant way, usually because they are sexually interested in you. [DISAPPROVAL] ❑ *...men standing around, swilling beer and occasionally leering at passing females.*

---

left
① REMAINING
② DIRECTION AND POLITICAL GROUPINGS

---

① **left** ♦◇◇ /lɛft/ **①** **Left** is the past tense and past participle of **leave**. **②** ADJ If there is a certain amount of something **left**, or if you have a certain amount of it **left**, it remains when the rest has gone or been used. [v-link ADJ, v n ADJ] ❑ *Is there any gin left?* ❑ *They still have six games left to play.* ● PHRASE If there is a certain amount of something **left over**, or if you have it **left over**, it remains when the rest has gone or been used. ❑ *So much income is devoted to monthly mortgage payments that nothing is left over.*

② **left** ♦♦♦ /lɛft/

The spelling **Left** is also used for meanings **③** and **④**.

① N-SING The **left** is one of two opposite directions, sides, or positions. If you are facing north and you turn to the left, you will be facing west. In the word "to," the "t" is to the left of the "o." ❑ *In Britain cars drive on the left.* ❑ *...the brick wall to the left of the conservatory.* ● ADV **Left** is also an adverb. [ADV after v] ❑ *Turn left at the crossroads into Clay Lane.* **②** ADJ Your **left** arm, leg, or ear, for example, is the one which is on the left side of your body. Your **left** shoe or glove is the one which is intended to be worn on your left foot or hand. [ADJ n] ❑ *Ferdinand landed awkwardly on top of Delgado's right boot and twisted his left leg.* **③** N-SING-COLL You can refer to people who support the political ideals of socialism as **the**

---

① 구동사 영원히 떠나다 ❑ "저는 거기 가서 살 거고, 잉글랜드에 다시는 돌아오지 않겠어요."라고 브라운이 말한다. **②** 구동사 남겨 두다 ❑ 난 아무 것도 남겨 두고 싶지 않아. **③** 구동사 뒤처지다 ❑ 우리는 세계 나머지 국가들에게 뒤처질 것이다. ❑ 사람들은 지금 당장 뒤처질까 봐 걱정하고 있다.

구동사 세외되다 ❑ 초대인 명단에서 그녀의 이름을 고의로 누락시켰다.

구동사 빼다 ❑ 몇몇 사람들은 그녀를 팀에서 빼는 방안에 대해 이의를 제기할 것이다. ❑ 부드러운 맛을 좋아하신다면 고추를 조금만 넣으시거나 빼세요.

leaf의 복수형

가산명사 강의대

① 가산명사 강의 ❑ 에릭 로빈슨 교수의 강의 시리즈 **②** 자동사 강의하다 ❑ 그러다가 그녀가 예술사에 대해 강의를 해 달라고 그를 애틀란타로 초대했다. **③** 타동사 훈계하다, 잔소리하다 ❑ 그는 내가 햇볕을 너무 많이 쬔다고 잔소리를 하곤 했다. ❑ 척은 머리를 깎으라고 내게 잔소리를 할 것이다. ● 가산명사 훈계, 잔소리 ❑ 선장은 우리에게 안전에 관해서 엄하게 훈계를 했다.

① 가산명사 교수, 대학 강사 ❑ 사우샘프턴 대학의 법학 강사 **②** 가산명사 강의자, 강연자

lead의 과거, 과거 분사

① 가산명사 바위턱 ❑ 산속 바위턱에서 쉴 곳을 찾아다니는 상처 입은 새처럼 **②** 가산명사 창문턱 ❑ 도로시는 그의 창문 밖 창문턱으로 올라갔다.

가산명사 회계 장부 [경제]

가산명사 또는 불가산명사 대파

자동사 음흉하게 웃다 [탐탁찮음] ❑ 맥주를 꿀꺽꿀꺽 마시며 지나가는 여자들에게 가끔 음흉스런 웃음을 지어 보이며 서 있는 남자들

① leave의 과거, 과거 분사 **②** 형용사 남은 ❑ 진 남은 것 있어? ❑ 그들은 아직도 여섯 경기를 남겨 놓고 있다. ● 구 남다 ❑ 수입 중에서 많은 돈을 주택 융자 상환금에 다 갖다 바쳐서 남는 게 없다.

철자 Left도 **③**과 **④** 의미로 쓴다.

① 단수명사 왼쪽 ❑ 영국에서는 차가 도로 왼쪽으로 다닌다. ❑ 온실방 왼쪽에 있는 벽돌벽 ● 부사 왼쪽으로, 왼쪽에 ❑ 저 사거리에서 왼쪽으로 도서서 클레이 레인 쪽으로 가세요. **②** 형용사 왼쪽의 ❑ 페르디난드가 잘못해서 델갈도의 오른쪽 부츠 위로 발을 디디는 바람에 자기 왼발을 삐었다. **③** 단수명사·집합 좌파; 우파 ❑ 전통적인 좌파 정당들 **④** 단수명사 좌경화 ❑ 1979년에 대처가 선거에서 처음 승리한 후, 노동당은 급격히 좌경화됐다.

left. They are often contrasted with **the right,** who support the political ideals of capitalism and conservatism. ❑ ...*the traditional parties of the Left.* ◼ N-SING If you say that a person or political party has moved **to the left,** you mean that their political beliefs have become more left-wing. ❑ *After Mrs Thatcher's first election victory in 1979, Labour moved sharply to the left.*

left-click (**left-clicks, left-clicking, left-clicked**) V-I To **left-click** or to **left-click on** something means to press the left-hand button on a computer mouse. [COMPUTING] ❑ *When the menu has popped up you should left-click on one of the choices to make it operate.*

자동사 왼쪽 클릭 [컴퓨터] ❑ 메뉴창이 뜨면 여러 항목 중 하나를 선택해 왼쪽 클릭을 하셔야 작동이 됩니다.

left-hand ADJ If something is on the **left-hand** side of something, it is positioned on the left of it. [ADJ n] ❑ *The Japanese drive on the left-hand side of the road.*

형용사 왼쪽의 ❑ 일본에서는 차가 길 왼쪽으로 다닌다.

left-handed ADJ Someone who is **left-handed** uses their left hand rather than their right hand for activities such as writing and sports and for picking things up. ❑ *There is a place in London that supplies practically everything for left-handed people.*

형용사 왼손잡이의 ❑ 런던에 왼손잡이 용품 일체를 취급하는 전문점이 있다.

left|ist /lɛftɪst/ (**leftists**) N-COUNT Socialists and Communists are sometimes referred to as **leftists.** ❑ *Two of the men were leftists and two were centrists.*

가산명사 좌익 ❑ 그 사람들 중 두 명은 좌익이었고, 두 명은 중도주의자였다.

left-justify (**left-justifies, left-justifying, left-justified**) V-T If printed text is **left-justified,** each line begins at the same distance from the left-hand edge of the page or column. ❑ *The data in the cells should be left-justified.*

타동사 왼쪽 여백을 맞추다 ❑ 셀 안의 데이터들은 왼쪽 여백을 맞춰 정렬해야 합니다.

left|over /lɛftoʊvər/ (**leftovers**) also **left-over** ◼ N-PLURAL You can refer to food that has not been eaten after a meal as **leftovers.** ❑ *Refrigerate any leftovers.* ◻ You use **leftover** to describe an amount of something that remains after the rest of it has been used or eaten. [ADJ n] ❑ *...leftover pieces of wallpaper.*

◼ 복수명사 남은 음식 ❑ 남은 음식들은 냉장고에 보관해라. ◻ 형용사 쓰고 남은, 먹다 남은 ❑ 쓰고 남은 벽지들

left-wing also **left wing** ◼ ADJ **Left-wing** people have political ideas that are based on socialism. ❑ *They said they would not be voting for him because he was too left-wing.* ◻ N-SING The **left wing** of a group of people, especially a political party, consists of the members of it whose beliefs are closer to socialism than are those of its other members. ❑ *The left-wing of the party is confident that the motion will be carried.*

◼ 형용사 좌익의 ❑ 그들은 그가 급진 좌파라서 그에게 표를 주지 않을 것이라고 했다. ◻ 단수명사 좌파 ❑ 그 정당의 좌파들은 그 재정 신청이 받아들여질 것이라고 믿고 있다.

leg ♦♦◇ /lɛg/ (**legs**) ◼ N-COUNT A person or animal's **legs** are the long parts of their body that they use to stand on. ❑ *He was tapping his walking stick against his leg.* ◻ N-COUNT The **legs** of a pair of pants are the parts that cover your legs. ❑ *He moved on through wet grass that soaked his trouser legs.* ◼ N-COUNT A **leg** of lamb, pork, chicken, or other meat is a piece of meat that consists of the animal's or bird's leg, especially the thigh. ❑ *...a chicken leg.* ◼ N-COUNT The **legs** of a table, chair, or other piece of furniture are the parts that rest on the floor and support the furniture's weight. ❑ *His ankles were tied to the legs of the chair.* ◼ N-COUNT A **leg** of a long journey is one part of it, usually between two points where you stop. ❑ *The first leg of the journey was by boat to Lake Naivasha in Kenya.* ◼ N-COUNT A **leg** of a sports competition is one of a series of games that are played to find an overall winner. [mainly BRIT] ❑ *They will televise both legs of Leeds' European Cup clash with Rangers.* ◼ PHRASE If you **are pulling** someone's **leg,** you are teasing them by telling them something shocking or worrying as a joke. [INFORMAL] ❑ *Of course I won't tell them; I was only pulling your leg.* →see **body**

◼ 가산명사 다리 ❑ 그는 지팡이로 자기 다리를 톡톡 치고 있었다. ◻ 가산명사 바지 가랑이 ❑ 그는 젖은 잔디 위를 지나느라 바지 가랑이가 다 젖었다. ◼ 가산명사 다리 (살) ❑ 닭다리 ◼ 가산명사 (가구의) 다리 ❑ 그의 두 발목은 의자 다리에 묶여 있었다. ◼ 가산명사 여정의 일부 ❑ 그 여행의 첫 부분은 보트를 타고 케냐에 있는 나이바샤 호수에 가는 것이었다. ◼ 가산명사 시합, 경기 (일련의 경기 중 일부), 여러 경기를 가진 후 종합 결과로 승자를 가리는 경기 [주로 영국영어] ❑ 리즈와 레인저스가 붙는 유러피안 컵 두 경기가 다 텔레비전으로 중계방송될 것이다. ◼ 구 놀리다 [비격식체] ❑ 물론 걔들한테 안 이를게. 그냥 장난쳤던 것뿐이야.

	Word Partnership	*leg*의 연어
V.	amputate a/*your* leg, break a/*your* leg, lose a/*your* leg ◼	
ADJ.	front leg, hind leg, left/right leg, lower leg ◼ broken leg ◼ ◼	
N.	leg bones, leg injury, leg muscles, leg pain ◼ final/first/last/second leg of a journey/trip/tour ◼	

lega|cy /lɛgəsi/ (**legacies**) ◼ N-COUNT A **legacy** is money or property which someone leaves to you when they die. ❑ *You could make a real difference to someone's life by leaving them a generous legacy.* ◻ N-COUNT A **legacy of** an event or period of history is something which is a direct result of it and which continues to exist after it is over. ❑ *...a program to overcome the legacy of inequality and injustice created by Apartheid.*

◼ 가산명사 유산 ❑ 엄청난 재산을 남겨 줘서 다른 사람의 인생을 확 바꿔 놓을 수도 있어. ◻ 가산명사 유산, 잔재 ❑ 인종 격리 정책이 남겨 놓은 불평등과 불의의 잔재를 청산하기 위한 프로그램

le|gal ♦♦◇ /liɡ'l/ ◼ ADJ **Legal** is used to describe things that relate to the law. [ADJ n] ❑ *He vowed to take legal action.* ❑ *...the British legal system.* ● **le|gal|ly** ADV ❑ *It could be a bit problematic, legally speaking.* ◻ ADJ An action or situation that is **legal** is allowed or required by law. ❑ *What I did was perfectly legal.*

◼ 형용사 법의, 법적인 ❑ 그는 법적 절차를 밟겠다고 맹세했다. ❑ 영국의 법체계 ● 법적으로 부사 ❑ 법률상으로 말하자면 그건 문제될 소지가 약간 있어. ◻ 형용사 합법적인 ❑ 내가 한 일은 전적으로 합법적이었다.

	Word Partnership	*legal*의 연어
N.	legal **action**, legal **advice**, legal **battle**, legal **bills**, legal **costs/expenses**, legal **defense**, legal **department**, legal **documents**, legal **expert**, legal **fees**, legal **guardian**, legal **issue**, legal **liability**, legal **matters**, legal **obligation**, legal **opinion**, legal **problems/troubles**, legal **procedures/proceedings**, legal **profession**, legal **responsibility**, legal **rights**, legal **services**, legal **status**, legal **system** ◼	
ADV.	**perfectly** legal ◻	

le|gal|ity /liɡæliti/ N-UNCOUNT If you talk about **the legality of** an action or situation, you are talking about whether it is legal or not. ❑ *The auditor has questioned the legality of the contracts.*

불가산명사 합법성 ❑ 회계 감사원은 그 계약의 합법성에 대해 의문을 던졌다.

le|gal|ize /líːgəlaɪz/ (**legalizes, legalizing, legalized**) [BRIT also **legalise**] V-T If something **is legalized**, a law is passed that makes it legal. ❏ *Divorce was legalized in 1981.*

[영국영어 legalise] 타동사 합법화되다 ❏ 이혼은 1981년에 합법화됐다.

legal ten|der N-UNCOUNT **Legal tender** is money, especially a particular coin or banknote, which is officially part of a country's currency at a particular time. ❏ *The French franc was no longer legal tender after midnight last night.*

불가산명사 법정 통화 ❏ 어젯밤 자정 이후로 프랑스 프랑은 더 이상 법정 통화가 아니다.

leg|end /lédʒ³nd/ (**legends**) ■ N-VAR A **legend** is a very old and popular story that may be true. ❏ *...the legends of ancient Greece.* ■ N-COUNT If you refer to someone as a **legend**, you mean that they are very famous and admired by a lot of people. [APPROVAL] ❏ *...blues legends John Lee Hooker and B.B. King.* →see **fantasy**

■ 가산명사 또는 불가산명사 전설 ❏ 고대 그리스 전설 ■ 가산명사 전설적인 인물 [마음에 듦] ❏ 블루스의 전설적인 인물들인 존 리 후커와 비 비 킹

leg|end|ary /lédʒ³ndɛri, BRIT lédʒ³ndri/ ■ ADJ If you describe someone or something as **legendary**, you mean that they are very famous and that many stories are told about them. ❏ *...the legendary Jazz singer Adelaide Hall.* ■ ADJ A **legendary** person, place, or event is mentioned or described in an old legend. ❏ *The hill is supposed to be the resting place of the legendary King Lud.*

■ 형용사 전설적인 ❏ 전설적인 재즈 가수 애들레이드 홀 ■ 형용사 전설상의 ❏ 그 언덕은 전설에 나오는 루드 왕이 영면한 곳으로 여겨진다.

leg|gings /léɡɪŋz/ N-PLURAL **Leggings** are close-fitting pants, usually made out of a stretchy fabric, that are worn by women and girls. [also *a pair of* N] ❏ *She is wearing tight, black leggings and a baggy green jersey.*

복수명사 레깅스, 퀼바지 ❏ 그녀는 몸에 짝 달라붙는 검은색 레깅스와 헐렁한 녹색 저지 스웨터를 입고 있었다.

le|gion /líːdʒ³n/ (**legions**) N-COUNT A **legion** is a large group of soldiers who form one section of an army. ❏ *...the Sudan-based troops of the Libyan Islamic Legion.*

가산명사 군단 ❏ 수단에 기지를 두고 있는 리비아 이슬람 군단 병력들

leg|is|late /lédʒɪsleɪt/ (**legislates, legislating, legislated**) V-T/V-I When a government or state **legislates**, it passes a new law. [FORMAL] ❏ *Most member countries have already legislated against excessive overtime.* ❏ *You cannot legislate to change attitudes.*

타동사/자동사 법을 제정하다 [격식체] ❏ 대부분의 회원국들은 과도한 초과 노동 금지법을 이미 제정했다. ❏ 태도를 바꾸기 위해 법을 제정할 수는 없다.

leg|is|la|tion ◆◇◇ /lédʒɪsléɪ³n/ N-UNCOUNT **Legislation** consists of a law or laws passed by a government. [FORMAL] ❏ *...a letter calling for legislation to protect women's rights.*

불가산명사 법률 제정 [격식체] ❏ 여권 보호를 위한 법률 제정을 청원하는 서한

<table>
<tr><td colspan="2">**Word Partnership**   *legislation*의 연어</td></tr>
<tr><td>ADJ.</td><td>**federal** legislation, **new** legislation</td></tr>
<tr><td>V.</td><td>**draft** legislation, **enact** legislation, **introduce** legislation, **oppose** legislation, **pass** legislation, **support** legislation, **veto** legislation</td></tr>
</table>

leg|is|la|tive /lédʒɪsleɪtɪv, BRIT lédʒɪslətɪv/ ADJ **Legislative** means involving or relating to the process of making and passing laws. [FORMAL] [ADJ n] ❏ *Today's hearing was just the first step in the legislative process.*

형용사 입법의 [격식체] ❏ 오늘의 청문회는 입법 절차의 첫 번째 단계였을 뿐이다.

leg|is|la|tor /lédʒɪsleɪtər/ (**legislators**) N-COUNT A **legislator** is a person who is involved in making or passing laws. [FORMAL] ❏ *...an attempt to get US legislators to change the system.*

가산명사 입법자, 국회의원 [격식체] ❏ 미국 입법자들로 하여금 그 제도를 바꾸게 하려는 시도

leg|is|la|ture /lédʒɪsleɪtʃər, BRIT lédʒɪslətʃəʳ/ (**legislatures**) N-COUNT The **legislature** of a particular state or country is the group of people in it who have the power to make and pass laws. [FORMAL] ❏ *The proposals before the legislature include the creation of two special courts to deal exclusively with violent crimes.*

가산명사 입법부 [격식체] ❏ 입법부에 상정된 법안 중에는 강력 범죄만을 전담하는 두 개의 특수 법원을 설립하는 것이 포함되어 있다.

le|giti|mate /lɪdʒítɪmɪt/ ■ ADJ Something that is **legitimate** is acceptable according to the law. ❏ *The French government has condemned the coup in Haiti and has demanded the restoration of the legitimate government.* ● **le|giti|ma|cy** /lɪdʒítɪməsi/ N-UNCOUNT ❏ *The opposition parties do not recognize the political legitimacy of his government.* ● **le|giti|mate|ly** ADV [ADV with v] ❏ *The government has been legitimately elected by the people.* ■ ADJ If you say that something such as a feeling or claim is **legitimate**, you think that it is reasonable and justified. ❏ *That's a perfectly legitimate fear.* ● **le|giti|ma|cy** N-UNCOUNT ❏ *Sampras beat Carl-Uwe Steeb by 6-1, 6-2, 6-1 to underline the legitimacy of his challenge for the title.* ● **le|giti|mate|ly** ADV [ADV with v] ❏ *They could quarrel quite legitimately with some of my choices.*

■ 형용사 합법적인 ❏ 프랑스 정부는 아이티의 쿠데타를 비난하고 합법적인 정권 회복을 요청했다. ● 합법성 불가산명사 ❏ 야당은 그의 정부의 정치적 합법성을 인정하지 않는다. ● 합법적으로 부사 ❏ 정부는 국민에 의해 합법적으로 선출되었다. ■ 형용사 정당한, 타당한 ❏ 그러한 두려움은 전적으로 정당한 것이다. ● 정당한 불가산명사 ❏ 샘프라스는 칼-우베 슈텝을 6-1, 6-2, 6-1로 이겨 그가 우승에 도전할 자격이 충분히 있음을 입증했다. ● 정당하게 부사 ❏ 그들은 나의 선택 몇 개에 대해 충분히 이의를 제기할 자격이 있다.

lei|sure /líːʒər, léʒ-, BRIT léʒəʳ/ ■ N-UNCOUNT **Leisure** is the time when you are not working and you can relax and do things that you enjoy. ❏ *...a relaxing way to fill my leisure time.* ■ PHRASE If someone does something **at leisure** or **at their leisure**, they enjoy themselves by doing it when they want to, without hurrying. ❏ *You will be able to stroll at leisure through the gardens.*

■ 불가산명사 여가 ❏ 나의 여가 시간을 편하게 메울 수 있는 방식 ■ 구 여유롭게, 느긋하게 ❏ 정원을 여유롭게 거닐 수 있을 것이다.

<table>
<tr><td colspan="2">**Word Partnership**   *leisure*의 연어</td></tr>
<tr><td>N.</td><td>leisure **activity**, leisure **class**, leisure **goods**, leisure **hours**, leisure **time** ■</td></tr>
</table>

lei|sure cen|tre (**leisure centres**) N-COUNT A **leisure centre** is a large public building containing different facilities for leisure activities, such as a sports hall, a swimming pool, and rooms for meetings. [BRIT] ❏ *Ask your local leisure centre about organized running groups in your area.*

가산명사 레저 센터 [영국영어] ❏ 자신이 사는 지역에 조직화된 달리기 동호회가 있는지 지역 레저 센터에 문의해라.

lei|sure|ly /líːʒərli, léʒ-, BRIT léʒəʳli/ ADJ A **leisurely** action is done in a relaxed and unhurried way. ❏ *Lunch was a leisurely affair.* ● ADV **Leisurely** is also an adverb. [ADV with v] ❏ *We walked leisurely into the hotel.*

형용사 여유로운, 느긋한 ❏ 점심은 여유롭게 먹었다. ● 부사 여유롭게, 느긋하게 ❏ 우리는 느긋하게 호텔 안으로 들어갔다.

lem|on /lémən/ (**lemons**) N-VAR A **lemon** is a bright yellow fruit with very sour juice. Lemons grow on trees in warm countries. ❏ *...a slice of lemon.* ❏ *...oranges, lemons, and other citrus fruits.* →see **fruit**

가산명사 또는 불가산명사 레몬 ❏ 레몬 한 조각 ❏ 오렌지, 레몬과 그 외 감귤류 과일

lem|on|ade /lémənéɪd/ (**lemonades**) ■ N-UNCOUNT **Lemonade** is a drink that is made from lemons, sugar, and water. ❏ *He was pouring ice and lemonade into tall glasses.* ■ N-COUNT **Lemonade** is a colorless, sweet, carbonated drink. [mainly BRIT] ❏ *Top up the jug with ice-cold fizzy lemonade or ginger ale.*

■ 불가산명사 레모네이드 ❏ 그는 큰 잔에 얼음과 레모네이드를 붓고 있었다. ■ 가산명사 탄산 레모네이드 [주로 영국영어] ❏ 피처 윗부분에 아주 차가운 탄산 레모네이드나 진저에일을 부어라.

A B C D E F G H I J K L M N O P Q R S T U V W X Y Z

lend ◆◇◇ /lɛnd/ (**lends, lending, lent**) **1** V-T/V-I When people or organizations such as banks **lend** you money, they give it to you and you agree to pay it back at a future date, often with an extra amount as interest. ❑ *The bank is reassessing its criteria for lending money.* ❑ *The government will lend you money at incredible rates, between zero percent and 3 percent.* ● **lending** N-UNCOUNT ❑ *...a financial institution that specializes in the lending of money.* **2** V-T If you **lend** something that you own, you allow someone to have it or use it for a period of time. ❑ *Will you lend me your jacket for a little while?* **3** V-T If you **lend** your support **to** someone or something, you help them with what they are doing or with a problem that they have. ❑ *He was approached by the organizers to lend support to a benefit concert.* **4** V-T If something **lends itself to** a particular activity or result, it is easy for it to be used for that activity or to achieve that result. ❑ *The room lends itself well to summer eating with its light, airy atmosphere.* **5** →see also **lent 6** to **lend a hand** →see hand →see bank

Do not confuse **lend** and **borrow**. You say that you **borrow** something **from** another person. However, if you allow someone to **borrow** something that belongs to you, you say that you **lend** it **to** them. **Lend** is often followed by two objects. ❑ *Betty lent him some blankets... He lent Tim the money.* Both **borrow** and **lend** can be used without objects. ❑ *The poor had to borrow from the rich... Banks will not lend to them.* The noun related to **lend** is **loan**. ❑ *...a government loan of $3m.* **Loan** can also be used as a verb in the same way as **lend**, especially in American English. ❑ *I'll loan you fifty dollars.*

1 타동사/자동사 대출하다 ❑ 은행은 금전 대출 기준을 재검토하고 있다. ❑ 정부는 0퍼센트에서 3퍼센트 사이의 믿어지지 않는 이율로 대출을 해 줄 것이다. ● 빌려 주기 불가산명사 ❑ 금전 대출을 전문으로 하는 금융 기관 **2** 타동사 빌려 주다 ❑ 네 재킷을 잠시만 빌려 줄래? **3** 타동사 (원조 등을) 제공하다 ❑ 주최 측이 그에게 찾아와 자선 공연에 도움을 제공해 달라고 부탁했다. **4** 타동사 ~에 알맞다 ❑ 밝고 통풍이 잘 돼서 그 방은 여름에 식사하는 데 알맞다.

lend와 borrow를 혼동하지 않도록 하라. 다른 사람으로부터(from) 무엇을 빌린다(borrow)고 말한다. 그러나 누가 당신의 것을 빌리도록(borrow) 허락하는 경우에는, 당신이 그에게 그것을 빌려준다(lend)고 말한다. lend 뒤에는 종종 목적어가 두 개 온다. ❑ 베티가 그에게 담요를 빌려 주었다... 그는 팀에게 그 돈을 빌려주었다. borrow와 lend 모두 목적어 없이 쓸 수 있다. ❑ 가난한 사람은 부자에게서 돈을 빌려야 했다... 은행에서 그들에게 돈을 빌려주지 않을 것이다. lend와 관련된 명사는 loan이다. ❑ ...공채 300만 달러. loan은 특히 미국영어에서 lend와 마찬가지로 동사로도 쓸 수 있다. ❑ 내가 50달러를 빌려줄게.

Word Partnership   lend의 연어
N.	lend **money 1**
	lend **support 3**

lend|er /lɛndər/ (**lenders**) N-COUNT A **lender** is a person or an institution that lends money to people. [BUSINESS] ❑ *...the six leading mortgage lenders.* →see **interest rate**

가산명사 대출자, 대출 기관 [경제] ❑ 상위 6개 주택 담보 대출 기관들

lend|ing rate (**lending rates**) N-COUNT The **lending rate** is the rate of interest that you have to pay when you are repaying a loan. [BUSINESS] ❑ *The bank left its lending rates unchanged.*

가산명사 대출 이자율 [경제] ❑ 은행은 대출 이자율을 바꾸지 않았다.

length ◆◆◇ /lɛŋθ/ (**lengths**) **1** N-VAR The **length** of something is the amount that it measures from one end to the other along the longest side. ❑ *It is about a meter in length.* ❑ *...the length of the fish.* **2** N-VAR The **length** of something such as a piece of writing is the amount of writing that is contained in it. ❑ *...a book of at least 100 pages in length.* **3** N-VAR The **length** of an event, activity, or situation is the period of time from beginning to end for which something lasts or during which something happens. ❑ *The exact length of each period may vary.* **4** N-COUNT A **length** of rope, cloth, wood, or other material is a piece of it that is intended to be used for a particular purpose or that exists in a particular situation. ❑ *...a 30ft length of rope.* **5** N-UNCOUNT The **length of** something is its quality of being long. ❑ *Many have been surprised at the length of time it has taken him to make up his mind.* **6** →see also **full-length 7** at arm's length →see arm →see ratio

1 가산명사 또는 불가산명사 길이 ❑ 그것은 길이가 약 1미터 된다. ❑ 물고기의 길이 **2** 가산명사 또는 불가산명사 길이 ❑ 길이가 최소한 100페이지 되는 책 **3** 가산명사 또는 불가산명사 길이 ❑ 정확한 길이는 시대마다 다를 수 있다. **4** 가산명사 길이 ❑ 30피트 길이의 밧줄 **5** 불가산명사 길이 ❑ 그가 마음을 정하는 데 걸린 그 긴 시간에 많은 사람들이 놀랐다.

Word Partnership   length의 연어
N.	length **and width 1**
	length **of** *your* **stay**, length **of time**, length **of treatment 3 5**
ADJ.	**average** length, **entire** length **1 4**

length|en /lɛŋθən/ (**lengthens, lengthening, lengthened**) **1** V-T/V-I When something **lengthens** or when you **lengthen** it, it increases in length. ❑ *The evening shadows were lengthening.* **2** V-T/V-I When something **lengthens** or when you **lengthen** it, it lasts for a longer time than it did previously. ❑ *Vacations have lengthened and the work week has shortened.*

1 타동사/자동사 길어지다; 늘이다 ❑ 저녁 그림자가 길어지고 있었다. **2** 타동사/자동사 길어지다; 늘이다 ❑ 휴가는 길어지고 한 주의 업무 시간은 줄어들었다.

length|wise /lɛŋθwaɪz/ or **lengthways** /lɛŋθweɪz/ ADV **Lengthwise** or **lengthways** means in a direction or position along the length of something. [ADV after v] ❑ *She tore off two sections of paper towel and folded them lengthwise.*

부사 세로의, 길이로 ❑ 그녀가 종이 타월 두 칸을 뜯은 후 세로로 접었다.

length|y /lɛŋθi/ (**lengthier, lengthiest**) **1** ADJ You use **lengthy** to describe an event or process which lasts for a long time. ❑ *...a lengthy meeting.* **2** ADJ A **lengthy** report, article, book, or document contains a lot of speech, writing, or other material. ❑ *...a lengthy report from the Council of Ministers.*

1 형용사 긴 ❑ 긴 회의 **2** 형용사 긴 ❑ 장관 회의에서 작성된 긴 보고서

Word Partnership   lengthy의 연어
N.	lengthy **period 1**
	lengthy **description**, lengthy **discourse**, lengthy **discussion**, lengthy **report 1 2**

le|ni|ent /liniənt, linyənt/ ADJ When someone in authority is **lenient**, they are not as strict or severe as expected. ❑ *He believes the government already is lenient with drug traffickers.* ● **le|ni|ent|ly** ADV [ADV after v] ❑ *Many people believe reckless drivers are treated too leniently.*

형용사 관대한 ❑ 그는 정부가 마약 밀거래자들에 대해 이미 관대하다고 생각한다. ● 관대하게 부사 ❑ 많은 사람들이 난폭 운전자들이 너무 관대한 처분을 받는다고 생각한다.

lens ◆◇◇ /lɛnz/ (**lenses**) **1** N-COUNT A **lens** is a thin curved piece of glass or plastic used in things such as cameras, telescopes, and pairs of glasses. You look through a lens in order to make things look larger, smaller, or clearer. ❑ *...a camera lens.* **2** N-COUNT In your eye, the **lens** is the part behind the pupil that focuses light and helps you to see clearly. ❑ *...degenerative changes in the lens of the eye.* **3** →see also **contact lens** →see eye

1 가산명사 렌즈 ❑ 카메라 렌즈 **2** 가산명사 수정체 ❑ 눈의 수정체의 퇴화

lent /lɛnt/ Lent is the past tense and past participle of **lend**.

leopard /lɛpərd/ (**leopards**) N-COUNT A **leopard** is a type of large, wild cat. Leopards have yellow fur and black spots, and live in Africa and Asia.

lesbian ♦◇◇ /lɛzbiən/ (**lesbians**) ADJ **Lesbian** is used to describe homosexual women. ❑ *Many of her best friends were lesbian.* ● N-COUNT A **lesbian** is a woman who is lesbian. ❑ *...a youth group for lesbians, gays, and bisexuals.*

less ♦♦♦ /lɛs/

> Less is often considered to be the comparative form of **little**.

1 DET You use **less** to indicate that there is a smaller amount of something than before or than average. You can use "a little," "a lot," "a bit," "far," and "much" in front of **less**. ❑ *People should eat less fat to reduce the risk of heart disease.* ❑ *...a dishwasher that uses less water and electricity than older machines.* ● PRON **Less** is also a pronoun. ❑ *Borrowers are striving to ease their financial position by spending less and saving more.* ● QUANT **Less** is also a quantifier. [QUANT of def-n-uncount/sing] ❑ *Last year less of the money went into high-technology companies.* **2** PHRASE You use **less than** before a number or amount to say that the actual number or amount is smaller than this. ❑ *Motorways actually cover less than 0.1 percent of the countryside.* **3** ADV You use **less** to indicate that something or someone has a smaller amount of a quality than they used to or than is average or usual. ❑ *I often think about those less fortunate than me.* ❑ *Other amenities, less commonly available, include a library and exercise room.* **4** ADV If you say that something is **less** one thing **than** another, you mean that it is like the second thing rather than the first. [ADV group than group/cl] ❑ *At first sight it looked less like a capital city than a mining camp.* **5** ADV If you do something **less** before or **less** than someone else, you do it to a smaller extent or not as often. [ADV with v] ❑ *We are eating more and exercising less.* **6** PREP When you are referring to amounts, you use **less** in front of a number or quantity to indicate that it is to be subtracted from another number or quantity already mentioned. ❑ *...Boyton Financial Services Fees: £750, less £40.*

> You use **less** to talk about amounts that cannot be counted. ❑ *...less meat.* When you are talking about things that can be counted, you should use **fewer**. ❑ *...fewer potatoes.*

7 PHRASE You use **less than** to say that something does not have a particular quality. For example, if you describe something as **less than** perfect, you mean that it is not perfect at all. [EMPHASIS] ❑ *Her greeting was less than enthusiastic.* **8 couldn't care less** →see **care. more or less** →see **more**

lessen /lɛs²n/ (**lessens, lessening, lessened**) V-T/V-I If something **lessens** or you **lessen** it, it becomes smaller in size, amount, degree, or importance. ❑ *He is used to a lot of attention from his wife, which will inevitably lessen when the baby is born.* ● **lessening** N-UNCOUNT ❑ *...increased trade and a lessening of tension on the border.*

lesser /lɛsər/ **1** ADJ You use **lesser** in order to indicate that something is smaller in extent, degree, or amount than another thing that has been mentioned. [ADJ n, the ADJ of n] ❑ *No medication works in isolation but is affected to a greater or lesser extent by many other factors.* ● ADV **Lesser** is also an adverb. [ADV -ed] ❑ *...lesser known works by famous artists.* **2** ADJ You can use **lesser** to refer to something or someone that is less important than other things or people of the same type. [ADJ n, the ADJ of n] ❑ *They pleaded guilty to lesser charges of criminal damage.* **3 the lesser of two evils** →see **evil**

lesson ♦◇◇ /lɛs²n/ (**lessons**) **1** N-COUNT A **lesson** is a fixed period of time when people are taught about a particular subject or taught how to do something. ❑ *It would be his last French lesson for months.* **2** N-COUNT You use **lesson** to refer to an experience which acts as a warning to you or an example from which you should learn. ❑ *There's still one lesson to be learned from the crisis – we all need to better understand the thinking of the other side.* ● PHRASE If you say that you are going to **teach** someone a **lesson**, you mean that you are going to punish them for something that they have done so that they do not do it again.

Thesaurus   *lesson의 참조어*

N.   class, course, instruction, session **1**

Word Partnership   *lesson의 연어*

ADJ.   **private** lesson **1**
       hard lesson, **important** lesson, **painful** lesson, **valuable** lesson **2**
V.   **get a** lesson, **give a** lesson **1 2**
       learn a lesson, **teach** *someone* a lesson **2**

---

let ♦♦♦ /lɛt/ (**lets, letting**)

> The form **let** is used in the present tense and is the past tense and past participle.

1 V-T If you **let** something happen, you allow it to happen without doing anything to stop or prevent it. ❑ *People said we were interfering with nature, and that we should just let the animals die.* ❑ *I can't let myself be distracted by those things.* **2** V-T If you **let** someone do something, you give them your permission to do it. ❑ *I love sweets but Mom doesn't let me have them very often.* **3** V-T If you **let** someone into, out of, or through a place, you allow them to enter, leave, or go through it, for example by opening a door or making room for them. ❑ *I had to get up at seven o'clock this morning to let them into the building because they had lost their keys.* **4** V-T You use **let me** when you are introducing something you want to say. [only imper] ❑ *Let me tell you what I saw last night.* ❑ *Let me explain why.* **5** V-T You

---

lend의 과거형 및 과거 분사

가산명사 표범

형용사 레즈비언인 ❑ 그녀의 가장 친한 친구들 중 많은 이들이 레즈비언이었다. ● 가산명사 레즈비언 ❑ 레즈비언, 게이, 양성애자를 위한 청년 단체

less가 종종 little의 비교급 형태로 간주된다.

1 한정사 덜 ❑ 심장병의 가능성을 낮추기 위해 사람들은 지방을 덜 먹어야 한다. ❑ 옛날 기계보다 물과 전기를 덜 사용하는 식기 세척기 ● 대명사 보다 적은 것 ❑ 채무자들은 덜 쓰고 더 저축함으로써 자신들의 재정적 처지를 개선하고자 노력 중이다. ● 수량사 보다 적은 ❑ 작년보다 적은 돈이 첨단 기술 기업 쪽으로 들어갔다. **2** 구 보다 작은 ❑ 자동차 도로는 실제로 전원 지역의 0.1퍼센트도 안 되는 면적을 차지한다. **3** 부사 덜 ❑ 나는 나보다 축복을 덜 받은 사람들에 대해 자주 생각한다. ❑ 이보다 드물긴 하지만 다른 편의 시설로는 도서관과 체력 단련실이 있다. **4** 부사 ...보다는 ...처럼 보이다 ❑ 첫눈에 그곳은 수도라기보다는 광산촌처럼 보였다. **5** 부사 덜 ❑ 우리는 과거보다 더 많이 먹고 운동을 덜 하고 있다. **6** 전치사 ...보다 적은 ❑ 보이튼 금융 서비스 수수료: 400파운드가 더 적은 750파운드임

셀 수 없는 양에 대해 말할 때는 less를 쓴다. ❑ ...더 적은 양의 고기. 셀 수 있는 것에 대해 말할 때는 fewer를 사용해야 한다. ❑ ...더 적은 수의 감자.

7 구 ...보다 못한 [강조] ❑ 그녀의 인사는 그다지 반가워 보이지 않았다.

타동사/자동사 준다; 줄이다 ❑ 그는 아내로부터 많은 관심을 받는 것에 익숙해져 있으나 아기가 태어나면 그 관심은 어쩔 수 없이 줄어들 것이다. ● 감소 불가산명사 ❑ 국경 지역에서의 무역의 증가와 긴장의 감소

1 형용사 더 작은 ❑ 어떤 약도 독립적인 변수로 작용하지 않으며 다른 여러 요인에 의해 많든 작든 간에 영향을 받는다. ● 부사 더 적게 ❑ 유명한 화가들의 덜 알려진 작품들 **2** 형용사 더 못한 ❑ 그들은 형사상 침해라는 비교적 가벼운 혐의에 대해서는 유죄를 인정했다.

1 가산명사 수업 ❑ 그것은 몇 달 동안 그의 마지막 불어 수업이 될 것이었다. **2** 가산명사 교훈 ❑ 그 위기로부터 얻을 수 있는 교훈이 아직도 하나가 있다. 즉 그것은 우리 모두 상대편의 생각을 더 잘 이해할 필요가 있다는 것이다. ● 구 따끔하게 혼내다

let은 동사의 현재, 과거, 과거 분사로 쓴다.

1 타동사 놔두다 ❑ 사람들은 우리가 자연의 섭리에 걸고 있다며 그 동물들이 그냥 죽도록 놔둬야 한다고 했다. ❑ 그런 것들에 정신 팔릴 여유가 없다. **2** 타동사 허용하다 ❑ 나는 단 것을 좋아하지만 엄마는 내가 그것을 자주 못 먹게 한다. **3** 타동사 들여보내 주다; 가게 하다 ❑ 나는 그들이 열쇠를 잃어버려서 그들을 건물 안으로 들여 준다고 오늘 아침 7시에 일어나야 했다. **4** 타동사 ...해 줄게 ❑ 내가 어젯밤에 뭘 봤는지 얘기해 줄게. ❑ 왜 그런지 설명해 줄게. **5** 타동사 ...을 해 드릴게요 [공손체] ❑ 코트를

use **let me** when you are offering politely to do something. [POLITENESS] [only imper] ❏ *Let me take your coat.* ⑥ V-T You say **let's** or, in more formal English, **let us**, to direct the attention of the people you are talking to towards the subject that you want to consider next. [only imper] ❏ *Let us look at these views in more detail.* ⑦ V-T You say **let's** or, in formal English, **let us**, when you are making a suggestion that involves both you and the person you are talking to, or when you are agreeing to a suggestion of this kind. [only imper] ❏ *I'm bored. Let's go home.* ⑧ V-T Someone in authority, such as a teacher, can use **let's** or, in more formal English, **let us**, in order to give a polite instruction to another person or group of people. [POLITENESS] [only imper] ❏ *Let's have some hush, please.* ⑨ V-T You can use **let** when you are saying what you think someone should do, usually in a way that you think is unreasonable or wrong. [only imper] ❏ *Let him get his own cup of tea.* ⑩ V-T If you **let** your house or land **to** someone, you allow them to use it in exchange for money that they pay you regularly. [mainly BRIT] ❏ *She is thinking of letting her house to an American serviceman.* ● PHRASAL VERB **Let out** means the same as **let**. [AM **rent**] ❏ *I couldn't sell the London flat, so I let it out to pay the mortgage.*

> Do not confuse **let**, **rent**, and **hire**. You can say that you **rent** a house or room to someone when you pay you money to live there. ❏ *We rented our house to a college professor.* You can also say that you **let** a house or room to someone. ❏ *They were letting a room to a school teacher.* In British English, if you pay a sum of money to use something for a short time, you say that you **hire** it. In American English, it is more common to say that you **rent** it. ❏ *He was unable to hire another car... He rented a car for the weekend.* If you make a series of payments to use something for a long time, you say that you **rent** it. ❏ *...the apartment he had rented... He rented a TV.*

⑪ PHRASE **Let alone** is used after a statement, usually a negative one, to indicate that the statement is even more true of the person, thing, or situation that you are going to mention next. [EMPHASIS] ❏ *It is incredible that the 12-year-old managed to even reach the pedals, let alone drive the car.* ⑫ PHRASE If you **let go of** someone or something, you stop holding them. ❏ *She let go of Mona's hand and took a sip of her drink.* ⑬ PHRASE If you **let** someone or something **go**, you allow them to leave or escape. ❏ *They held him for three hours and then let him go.* ⑭ PHRASE When someone leaves a job, either because they are told to or because they want to, the employer sometimes says that they are **letting** that person **go**. [BUSINESS] ❏ *I've assured him I have no plans to let him go.* ⑮ PHRASE If you say that you did not know what you were **letting yourself in for** when you decided to do something, you mean you did not realize how difficult, unpleasant, or expensive it was going to be. ❏ *He got the impression that Miss Hawes had no idea of what she was letting herself in for.* ⑯ PHRASE If you **let** someone **know** something, you tell them about it or make sure that they know about it. ❏ *They want to let them know that they are safe.* ⑰ to **let fly** →see **fly**. to **let** your **hair down** →see **hair**. to **let** someone **off the hook** →see **hook**. to **let it be known** →see **known**.

Thesaurus   *let*의 참조어

v.   allow, approve, permit; *(ant.)* prevent, stop ① ②

▶**let down** ① PHRASAL VERB If you **let** someone **down**, you disappoint them, by not doing something that you have said you will do or that they expected you to do. ❏ *Don't worry, Xiao, I won't let you down.* ● **let down** ADJ [v-link ADJ] ❏ *The company now has a large number of workers who feel badly let down.* ② PHRASAL VERB If something **lets** you **down**, it is the reason you are not as successful as you could have been. ❏ *Many believe it was his shyness and insecurity which let him down.*

▶**let in** ① PHRASAL VERB If an object **lets in** something such as air, light, or water, it allows air, light, or water to get into it, for example because the object has a hole in it. ❏ *...balconies shaded with lattice-work which lets in air but not light.*

▶**let off** ① PHRASAL VERB If someone in authority **lets** you **off** a task or duty, they give you permission not to do it. [mainly BRIT] ❏ *I realized that having a new baby lets you off going to boring dinner-parties.* ② PHRASAL VERB If you **let** someone **off**, you give them a lighter punishment than they expect or no punishment at all. ❏ *Because he was a Christian, the judge let him off.* ③ PHRASAL VERB If you **let off** an explosive or a gun, you explode or fire it. ❏ *A resident of his neighborhood had let off fireworks to celebrate the Revolution.*

▶**let out** ① PHRASAL VERB If something or someone **lets** water, air, or breath **out**, they allow it to flow out or escape. ❏ *It lets sunlight in but doesn't let heat out.* ② PHRASAL VERB If you **let out** a particular sound, you make that sound. [WRITTEN] ❏ *When she saw him, she let out a cry of horror.* ③ →see also **let** ⑩

▶**let up** PHRASAL VERB If an unpleasant, continuous process **lets up**, it stops or becomes less intense. ❏ *The traffic in this city never lets up, even at night.*

le|thal /líːθ³l/ ① ADJ A substance that is **lethal** can kill people or animals. ❏ *...a lethal dose of sleeping pills.* ② ADJ If you describe something as **lethal**, you mean that it is capable of causing a lot of damage. ❏ *Shearer was the most lethal striker in British football.*

le|thar|gic /lɪθάːrdʒɪk/ ADJ If you are **lethargic**, you do not have much energy or enthusiasm. ❏ *He felt too miserable and lethargic to get dressed.*

받아 드릴게요. ⑥ 타동사 - 하자 ❏ 이 관점들을 보다 자세히 살펴봅시다. ⑦ 타동사 - 하자 ❏ 지루하다. 집에 가자. ⑧ 타동사 - 하자 [공손체] ❏ 좀 조용히 합시다. ⑨ 타동사 - 을 하도록 하다 ❏ 자기가 마실 차는 스스로 타게 해. ⑩ 타동사 임대하다 [주로 영국영어] ❏ 그녀는 미국 군인에게 집을 세 놓는 것을 고려하고 있다. ● 구동사 임대하다 [미국영어 rent] ❏ 나는 런던 아파트를 팔 수가 없어서 주택 담보 대출을 갚기 위해 그것을 세를 놓았다.

let, rent, hire를 혼동하지 않도록 하라. 집이나 방을, 돈을 지불하고 거기서 살고자 하는 사람에게 rent 한다고 할 수 있다. ❏ 우리는 대학 교수에게 집을 세놓았다. 집이나 방을 누구에게 세놓는다(let a house or room to someone)고 할 수도 있다. ❏ 그들은 학교 교사에게 방을 세 놓고 있었다. 영국 영어에서는 단기간 무엇을 사용하기 위해 돈을 지불할 때는, 대개 hire를 사용한다. 미국 영어에서는 rent하는 것이 더 일반적이다. ❏ 그는 차를 한 대 더 빌릴 수가 없었다... 그는 주말 동안 차를 빌렸다. 장기간 어떤 것을 사용하기 위해 연속적으로 돈을 지불한다면, 그것을 rent한다고 표현한다. ❏ ...그가 세 낸 아파트... 그는 텔레비전을 빌렸다.

⑪ 구 -은 고사하고, -은 물론이고 [강조] ❏ 열두 살짜리가 차를 모는 것은 물론이고 페달에 발이 닿았다는 것 자체가 믿어지지 않는다. ⑫ 구 놓아 주다 ❏ 그녀는 모나의 손을 놔주고 술을 한 잔 마셨다. ⑬ 구 놓아 주다, 가도록 하다 ❏ 그들은 그를 3시간 동안 붙잡고 있다가 놓아 주었다. ⑭ 구 해고하다; 사직을 허용하다 [경제] ❏ 나는 그에게 그를 해고할 생각이 전혀 없다고 안심시켰다. ⑮ 구 -에 맞닥뜨리다 ❏ 그는 호스 양이 자신이 어떤 일에 맞닥뜨리게 될지에 대해 전혀 개념이 없다는 인상을 받았다. ⑯ 구 알리다 ❏ 그들은 자기들이 안전하다는 것을 그들에게 알리고 싶어 한다.

---

① 구동사 실망시키다 ❏ 걱정하지 마, 샤오. 너를 실망시키지 않을게. ● 실망한 형용사 ❏ 회사 근로자 중 상당수가 상당히 실망감을 느끼고 있다. ② 구동사 좌절시키다 ❏ 많은 사람들은 그가 수줍음과 불안감 때문에 좌절당했다고 생각한다.

① 구동사 들여보내다 ❏ 공기는 들여보내지만 빛을 차단하는 격자무늬 차일을 친 발코니

① 구동사 -에서 빼 주다 [주로 영국영어] ❏ 나는 새 아기를 가지면 지루한 디너파티에 가야 되는 의무로부터 면제된다는 것을 깨달았다. ② 구동사 가볍게 처벌하다 ❏ 그가 기독교인이었기 때문에 판사가 그에게 가벼운 벌을 주었다. ③ 구동사 쏘다, 폭발시키다 ❏ 그의 이웃 중 하나가 혁명을 기념하기 위해 폭죽을 터뜨렸었다.

① 구동사 내보내다 ❏ 그것은 햇빛은 들여보내지만 열을 내보내지는 않는다. ② 구동사 (소리를) 내다 [문어체] ❏ 그녀가 그를 보고 공포에 찬 비명을 질렀다.

구동사 완화되다, 수그러들다 ❏ 이 도시의 교통은 절대로, 심지어는 저녁에도, 완화되는 법이 없다.

① 형용사 치명적인 ❏ 치사량의 수면제 ② 형용사 파괴적인 ❏ 시어러는 영국 축구에서 가장 파괴적인 공격수였다.

형용사 무기력한 ❏ 그는 기분이 너무 비참하고 기운도 없어서 옷을 입을 수도 없었다.

leth|ar|gy /lɛθərdʒi/ N-UNCOUNT **Lethargy** is the condition or state of being lethargic. ☐ *Symptoms include tiredness, paleness, and lethargy.*

불가산명사 무기력 ☐ 피로, 창백함, 무기력감 등의 증상이 있다.

let's ♦♢♢ /lɛts/ **Let's** is the usual spoken form of "let us."

let us의 축약형

let|ter ♦♦♦ /lɛtər/ (**letters**) **1** N-COUNT If you write a **letter** to someone, you write a message on paper and send it to them, usually through the mail. [also by N] ☐ *I had received a letter from a very close friend.* ☐ *...a letter of resignation.* **2** N-COUNT **Letters** are written symbols which represent one of the sounds in a language. ☐ *...the letters of the alphabet.* **3** →see also **covering letter, newsletter**

1 가산명사 편지 ☐ 내가 매우 친한 친구로부터 편지를 받았었다. ☐ 사직서 **2** 가산명사 글자 ☐ 알파벳의 글자들

let|ter|box /lɛtərbɒks/ (**letterboxes**) also **letter box** N-COUNT A **letterbox** is a rectangular hole in a door or a small box at the entrance to a building into which letters and small parcels are delivered. Compare **post box**. [mainly BRIT; AM usually **mailbox**] ☐ *They shouted at her through the letterbox.*

가산명사 우편물통, (문에 있는) 우편물 투입구 [주로 영국영어; 미국영어 대개 mailbox] ☐ 그들은 우편물 투입구로 그녀에게 소리를 질렀다.

let|ter|ing /lɛtərɪŋ/ N-UNCOUNT **Lettering** is writing, especially when you are describing the type of letters used. ☐ *...a small blue sign with white lettering.*

불가산명사 글자 쓰기 ☐ 흰 글씨가 있는 작고 푸른 표지판

let|tuce /lɛtɪs/ (**lettuces**) N-VAR A **lettuce** is a plant with large green leaves that is the basic ingredient of many salads.

가산명사 또는 불가산명사 상추, 양상추

leu|ke|mia /lukimiə/ [BRIT **leukaemia**] N-UNCOUNT **Leukemia** is a disease of the blood in which the body produces too many white blood cells.

[영국영어 leukaemia] 불가산명사 백혈병

lev|el ♦♦♦ /lɛvəl/ (**levels, leveling, leveled**) [BRIT, sometimes AM **levelling, levelled**] **1** N-COUNT A **level** is a point on a scale, for example a scale of amount, quality, or difficulty. ☐ *If you don't know your cholesterol level, it's a good idea to have it checked.* ☐ *We do have the lowest level of inflation for some years.* **2** N-SING The **level** of a river, lake, or ocean or the **level** of liquid in a container is the height of its surface. ☐ *The water level of the Mississippi River is already 6.5 feet below normal.* →see also **sea level** **3** N-SING If something is at a particular **level**, it is at that height. ☐ *Liz sank down until the water came up to her chin and the bubbles were at eye level.* **4** ADJ If one thing is **level with** another thing, it is at the same height as it. [v-link ADJ, oft ADJ with n] ☐ *He leaned over the counter so his face was almost level with the boy's.* **5** ADJ When something is **level**, it is completely flat with no part higher than any other. ☐ *The floor was level, but the ceiling sloped toward his head.* **6** ADV If you draw **level** with someone or something, you get closer to them until you are by their side. [mainly BRIT] [ADV after v] ☐ *Just before we drew level with the gates, he slipped out of the jeep and disappeared into the crowd.* ● ADJ **Level** is also an adjective. [v-link ADJ, oft ADJ with n] ☐ *He waited until they were level with the door before he pivoted around sharply and punched Graham hard on the side of the head.* **7** V-T If an accusation or criticism **is leveled at** someone, they are accused of doing wrong or they are criticized for something they have done. ☐ *Allegations of corruption were levelled at him and his family.* **8** →see also **A level** **9** a **level playing field** →see **playing field**

[영국영어, 미국영어 가끔 levelling, levelled] **1** 가산명사 수치 ☐ 본인의 콜레스테롤 수치를 모른다면 알아보는 것이 좋다. ☐ 근 몇 년 사이 사실 물가 인상률이 가장 낮다. **2** 단수명사 수위 ☐ 미시시피 강의 수위가 이미 정상보다 6.5피트 낮다. **3** 단수명사 높이 ☐ 리즈는 물이 턱까지 올라오고 거품이 눈높이로 올라올 때까지 물 속으로 들어갔다. **4** 형용사 높이가 같은 ☐ 그는 자기 얼굴이 소년의 얼굴과 높이가 같아질 정도로 카운터 너머로 몸을 숙였다. **5** 형용사 평평한 ☐ 바닥은 평평했지만 천장은 그의 머리 쪽으로 비스듬히 기울어져 있었다. **6** 부사 옆으로 나란히 [주로 영국영어] ☐ 우리가 문에 다다르기 직전에 그가 지프차 밖으로 빠져 나가 군중 속으로 사라졌다. ● 형용사 옆으로 나란한 ☐ 그들이 문과 거의 나란하게 될 때까지 기다렸다가 그가 갑자기 돌아서서 그림의 옆머리를 주먹으로 세게 때렸다. **7** 타동사 겨냥되다, 향하다 ☐ 그와 그의 가족을 겨냥한 부패 혐의들이 있었다.

Thesaurus   level의 참조어

ADJ.   even, flat, horizontal, smooth; (*ant.*) uneven **5**

Word Partnership   level의 연어

ADJ.   **basic** level, **intermediate** level, **top** level, **upper** level **1**
      high/low level **1** **3**

N.   level **of activity**, **cholesterol** level, **college** level, **comfort** level, level **of difficulty**, **energy** level, **noise** level, **reading** level, **skill** level, **stress** level, level **of violence** **1**
      eye level, **ground** level, **street** level **3**

▶**level off** or **level out** **1** PHRASAL VERB If a changing number or amount **levels off** or **levels out**, it stops increasing or decreasing at such a fast speed. ☐ *The figures show evidence that murders in the nation's capital are beginning to level off.* **2** PHRASAL VERB If an aircraft **levels off** or **levels out**, it travels horizontally after having been traveling in an upward or downward direction. ☐ *The aircraft leveled out at about 30,000 feet.*

1 구동사 (수나 양이) 안정되다 ☐ 그 나라 수도에서의 살인 건수가 점점 안정되어 가고 있다는 증거가 수치에서 드러난다. **2** 구동사 수평 비행하다 ☐ 비행기는 30,000피트에서 수평 비행을 했다.

lev|el cross|ing (**level crossings**) N-COUNT A **level crossing** is a place where a railroad track crosses a road at the same level. [BRIT; AM **grade crossing, railroad crossing**]

가산명사 평면 교차 [영국영어; 미국영어 grade crossing, railroad crossing]

lev|er /lɛvər, also lɛvər, BRIT liːvəʳ/ (**levers, levering, levered**) **1** N-COUNT A **lever** is a handle or bar that is attached to a piece of machinery and which you push or pull in order to operate the machinery. ☐ *Push the tiny lever on the lock and let the door lock itself.* →see also **gear lever** **2** N-COUNT A **lever** is a long bar, one end of which is placed under a heavy object so that when you press down on the other end you can move the object. ☐ *He examined the machine, worked a lever that lifted the lid.* **3** V-T If you **lever** something in a particular direction, you move it there, especially by using a lot of effort. ☐ *Neighbors eventually levered open the door with a crowbar.*

1 가산명사 레버 ☐ 자물쇠의 작은 레버를 누른 후 문이 자동적으로 잠기도록 놔둬라. **2** 가산명사 지렛대 ☐ 그는 기계를 살펴보고 지렛대를 움직여 뚜껑을 열었다. **3** 타동사 힘들어 움직이다 ☐ 이웃들은 결국 쇠지레를 이용해서 문을 힘겹게 열었다.

lev|er|age /lɛvərɪdʒ, BRIT liːvərɪdʒ/ (**leverages, leveraging, leveraged**) **1** N-UNCOUNT **Leverage** is the ability to influence situations or people so that you can control what happens. ☐ *His function as a Mayor affords him the leverage to get things done through attending committee meetings.* **2** V-T To **leverage** a company or investment means to use borrowed money in order to buy it or pay for it. [BUSINESS] ☐ *He might feel that leveraging the company at a time when he sees tremendous growth opportunities would be a mistake.*

1 불가산명사 영향력 ☐ 위원회 회의에 참석하여 결과가 나오도록 이끌 수 있는 영향력이 시장인 그에게 주어진다. **2** 타동사 -에 차입금을 이용하여 투자하다 [경제] ☐ 그가 보기에 그 회사가 엄청난 성장 기회를 보이는 시점에 차입금으로 투자하는 것은 실수라고 그가 여길지도 모른다.

levy /lɛvi/ (**levies, levying, levied**) **1** N-COUNT A **levy** is a sum of money that you have to pay, for example as a tax to the government. ☐ *...an annual motorway*

1 가산명사 부담금, 부과액 ☐ 모든 운전자들에게 매년 부과되는 고속도로 통행료 **2** 타동사 부과하다

A

levy on all drivers. ◻ **2** V-T If a government or organization **levies** a tax or other sum of money, it demands it from people or organizations. ◻ *They levied religious taxes on Christian commercial transactions.*

◻ 기독교인의 상업적 거래에 그들은 종교세를 부과했다.

B

lia|bil|ity /laɪəbɪlɪti/ (**liabilities**) **1** N-COUNT If you say that someone or something is **a liability**, you mean that they cause a lot of problems or embarrassment. ◻ *As the president's prestige continues to fall, they're clearly beginning to consider him a liability.* **2** N-COUNT A company's or organization's **liabilities** are the sums of money which it owes. [BUSINESS or LEGAL] ◻ *The company had assets of $138 million and liabilities of $120.5 million.* **3** →see also **liable**

1 가산명사 문제의 소지 ◻ 대통령의 명성이 계속 추락하자 그들이 분명히 그를 문제의 소지로 여기기 시작하고 있다. **2** 가산명사 부채 [경제 또는 법률] ◻ 그 회사는 자산 1억 3천 800만 달러에 1억 2천 50만 달러의 부채를 가지고 있다.

C

lia|ble /laɪəbᵊl/ **1** PHRASE When something **is liable to** happen, it is very likely to happen. ◻ *Only a small minority of the mentally ill are liable to harm themselves or others.* **2** ADJ If people or things are **liable to** something unpleasant, they are likely to experience it or do it. [v-link ADJ to n] ◻ *She will grow into a woman particularly liable to depression.* **3** ADJ If you are **liable for** something such as a debt, you are legally responsible for it. [v-link ADJ, usu ADJ for n] ◻ *The airline's insurer is liable for damages to the victims' families.* ● lia|bil|ity /laɪəbɪlɪti/ N-UNCOUNT ◻ *The company does not accept liability for fragile, valuable, or perishable articles.*

1 구 -할 가능성이 있다 ◻ 정신병자의 소수만이 자신이나 남을 해칠 가능성이 있다. **2** 형용사 -할 경향이 있는 ◻ 그녀는 훗날 특히 우울증에 빠지는 성향이 있는 여자로 성장할 것이다. **3** 형용사 책임이 있는 ◻ 항공사의 보험 회사가 피해자들 가족의 손해에 대해 책임을 진다. ● 책임 불가산명사 ◻ 쉽게 깨지는 것, 고가의 물건, 상하기 쉬운 물품 등에 대해서는 회사가 어떠한 책임도 지지 않는다.

D

E

li|aise /liˈeɪz/ (**liaises, liaising, liaised**) V-RECIP When organizations or people **liaise**, or when one organization **liaises with** another, they work together and keep each other informed about what is happening. [mainly BRIT] ◻ *Detectives are liaising with Derbyshire police following the bomb explosion early today.* ◻ *The three groups will all liaise with each other to help the child.*

상호동사 공조하다 [주로 영국영어] ◻ 오늘 아침 일찍 발생한 폭탄 폭발 사건 후 형사들이 더비셔 경찰과 공조 수사를 하고 있다. ◻ 세 단체는 그 아이를 돕기 위해 서로 공조할 것이다.

F

G

li|ai|son /liˈeɪzɒn, BRIT liˈeɪzɒn/ N-UNCOUNT **Liaison** is cooperation and the exchange of information between different organizations or between different sections of an organization. ◻ *Liaison between police forces and the art world is vital to combat art crime.*

불가산명사 공조 ◻ 미술품 범죄에 대처하기 위해서는 경찰과 미술계의 공조가 필수적이다.

H

I

Word Link   ar, er ≈ one who acts as : buyer, liar, seller

J

liar /laɪər/ (**liars**) N-COUNT If you say that someone is a **liar**, you mean that they tell lies. ◻ *He was a liar and a cheat.*

가산명사 거짓말쟁이 ◻ 그는 거짓말쟁이이자 사기꾼이었다.

K

li|bel /laɪbᵊl/ (**libels, libeling, libeled**) [BRIT, sometimes AM **libelling, libelled**] **1** N-VAR **Libel** is a written statement which wrongly accuses someone of something, and which is therefore against the law. Compare **slander**. [LEGAL] ◻ *Warren sued him for libel over the remarks.* **2** V-T To **libel** someone means to write or print something in a book, newspaper, or magazine which wrongly damages that person's reputation and is therefore against the law. [LEGAL] ◻ *The newspaper which libeled him had already offered compensation.*

[영국영어, 미국영어 가끔 libelling, libelled] **1** 가산명사 또는 불가산명사 명예 훼손 [법률] ◻ 워렌은 그 발언을 두고 그를 명예 훼손으로 고소했다. **2** 타동사 명예를 훼손하다 [법률] ◻ 그의 명예를 훼손했던 그 신문은 그에게 이미 보상금을 지급한 상태였다.

L

Word Link   liber ≈ free : liberal, liberate, liberty

M

lib|er|al ♦♦◇ /lɪbərəl, lɪbrəl/ (**liberals**) **1** ADJ Someone who has **liberal** views believes people should have a lot of freedom in deciding how to behave and think. ◻ *She is known to have liberal views on divorce and contraception.* ● N-COUNT **Liberal** is also a noun. ◻ *...a nation of free-thinking liberals.* **2** ADJ A **liberal** system allows people or organizations a lot of political or economic freedom. ◻ *...a liberal democracy with a multiparty political system.* ● N-COUNT **Liberal** is also a noun. ◻ *These kinds of price controls go against all the financial principles of the free market liberals.* **3** ADJ A **Liberal** politician or voter is a member of a Liberal Party or votes for a Liberal Party. [ADJ n] ◻ *The Liberal leader has announced his party's withdrawal from the ruling coalition.* ● N-COUNT **Liberal** is also a noun. ◻ *The Liberals hold twenty-three seats in parliament.* **4** ADJ **Liberal** means giving, using, or taking a lot of something, or existing in large quantities. ◻ *As always he is liberal with his jokes.* ● lib|er|al|ly ADV [ADV with v] ◻ *Chemical products were used liberally over agricultural land.*

1 형용사 개방적인 ◻ 그녀는 이혼과 피임에 대해 개방적인 사고를 가진 것으로 알려졌다. ● 가산명사 진보주의자 ◻ 자유로운 사고를 가진 진보주의자들의 나라 **2** 형용사 자유로운 ◻ 복수 정당 정치 체계를 갖춘 자유 민주 국가 ● 가산명사 자유주의자 ◻ 이런 종류의 가격 통제는 시장자유주의자들의 모든 재정적 원칙에 역행한다. **3** 형용사 진보당의 ◻ 진보당 당수가 자기 당은 여권 연합으로부터 탈퇴한다고 발표했다. ● 가산명사 진보당원 ◻ 자유당은 국회 의석 23개를 차지하고 있다. **4** 형용사 풍성한 ◻ 여느 때처럼 그는 많은 농담을 한다. ● 풍성하게 부사 ◻ 농지에 화학제품을 거침없이 이용했다.

N

O

P

Q

Lib|er|al Demo|crat Par|ty N-PROPER **The Liberal Democrat Party** is the third largest political party in Britain and the main center party. It believes in improving the constitution and the voting system and in providing good welfare services.

고유명사 (영국) 자유 민주당

R

lib|er|al|ize /lɪbərəlaɪz, lɪbrəl-/ (**liberalizes, liberalizing, liberalized**) [BRIT also **liberalise**] V-T/V-I When a country or government **liberalizes**, or **liberalizes** its laws or its attitudes, it becomes less strict and allows people more freedom in their actions. ◻ *...authoritarian states that have recently, and only now begun to liberalize.* ● lib|er|ali|za|tion /lɪbərəlaɪzeɪᵊn, lɪbrəl-/ N-UNCOUNT ◻ *...the liberalization of divorce laws in the late 1960s.*

[영국영어 liberalise] 타동사/자동사 자유화하다 ◻ 이제 자유화를 실시하기 시작한 독재 국가들 ● 자유화 불가산명사 ◻ 1960년대 말에 실시된 이혼법의 자유화

S

T

lib|er|ate ♦♦◇ /lɪbəreɪt/ (**liberates, liberating, liberated**) **1** V-T To **liberate** a place or the people in it means to free them from the political or military control of another country, area, or group of people. ◻ *They planned to march on and liberate the city.* ● lib|era|tion /lɪbəreɪᵊn/ N-UNCOUNT ◻ *...a mass liberation movement.* **2** V-T To **liberate** someone **from** something means to help them escape from it or overcome it, and lead a better way of life. ◻ *He asked how committed the leadership was to liberating its people from poverty.* ● lib|er|at|ing ADJ ◻ *If you have the chance to spill your problems out to a therapist it can be a very liberating experience.* ● lib|era|tion N-UNCOUNT ◻ *...the women's liberation movement.*

1 타동사 해방하다 ◻ 그들은 계속 행군하여 도시를 해방할 계획이었다. ● 해방 불가산명사 ◻ 대대적인 해방 운동 **2** 타동사 해방하다 ◻ 그는 국민들을 빈곤으로부터 해방시키는 데 지도층이 얼마나 강한 의지를 가지고 있는지를 요청했다. ● 해방하는 형용사 ◻ 기회가 있어서 고민을 심리 상담사에게 모두 털어낸다면 그것은 속이 확 뚫리는 경험이 될 것이다. ● 해방 불가산명사 ◻ 여성 해방 운동

U

V

W

Thesaurus   liberate의 참조어

   V.   emancipate, free, let out, release; (ant.) confine **1**

X

Y

lib|er|ty ♦♦◇ /lɪbərti/ (**liberties**) **1** N-VAR **Liberty** is the freedom to live your life in the way that you want, without interference from other people or the authorities. ◻ *...the ideal of equality and the appreciation of liberty.* **2** N-UNCOUNT

1 가산명사 또는 불가산명사 자유 ◻ 평등의 이상과 자유의 존중 **2** 불가산명사 자유 ◻ 차를 세 대 훔쳐 법정에서 세 개의 유죄 판정을 받으면 자유가 3개월간

Z

Liberty is the freedom to go wherever you want, which you lose when you are a prisoner. ❑ *Why not say that three convictions before court for stealing cars means three months' loss of liberty.* **3** PHRASE If someone is **at liberty to** do something, they have been given permission to do it. ❑ *The island's in the Pacific Ocean; I'm not at liberty to say exactly where, because we're still negotiating for its purchase.*

박탈당한다고 차라리 말하자. **3** 구 자유가 있는 ❑ 섬은 태평양에 있습니다. 아직도 구매를 위해 흥정을 하고 있기 때문에 정확히 어디에 있는지는 말할 수 없습니다.

Thesaurus	*liberty*의 참조어

N. freedom, independence, privilege **1** **2**

Word Partnership	*liberty*의 연어

N. **human** liberty, **individual** liberty **1**
ADJ. **personal** liberty, **religious** liberty **1**

li|brar|ian /laɪbrɛəriən/ (**librarians**) N-COUNT A **librarian** is a person who is in charge of a library or who has been specially trained to work in a library. →see **library**

가산명사 사서

li|brary ◆◇◇ /laɪbreri, BRIT laɪbrəri/ (**libraries**) **1** N-COUNT A public **library** is a building where things such as books, newspapers, videos, and music are kept for people to read, use, or borrow. ❑ *...the local library.* **2** N-COUNT A private **library** is a collection of things such as books or music, that is normally only used with the permission of the owner. ❑ *My thanks go to the British School of Osteopathy, for the use of their library.*
→see Word Web: **library**

1 가산명사 도서관 ❑ 지역 도서관 **2** 가산명사 도서관 ❑ 서고를 사용할 수 있게 해 준 영국 정골 요법 대학에 감사를 드립니다.

lice /laɪs/ **Lice** is the plural of **louse**.

*louse*의 복수

li|cence /laɪsᵊns/ →see **license**

li|cense ◆◇◇ /laɪsᵊns/ (**licenses, licensing, licensed**) **1** N-COUNT A **license** is an official document which gives you permission to do, use, or own something. [BRIT **licence**] ❑ *The judge fined the man and suspended his license.* ❑ *The company has applied to the FDA for a license to sell the drug.* **2** N-UNCOUNT If you say that something gives someone **license** or **a license to** act in a particular way, you mean that it gives them an excuse to behave in an irresponsible or excessive way. [DISAPPROVAL] [BRIT **licence**] [also a N, N to-inf] ❑ *Partition would give license to other aggressors in other conflicts.* **3** V-T To **license** a person or activity means to give official permission for the person to do something or for the activity to take place. ❑ *...a proposal that would require the state to license guns the way it does cars.*

1 가산명사 면허 [영국영어 licence] ❑ 판사는 그에게 벌금을 부과하고 면허를 정지했다. ❑ 그 회사는 식약청에 그 약품의 판매 허가를 신청했다. **2** 불가산명사 허가 [탐탁잖음] [영국영어 licence] ❑ 분리가 이루어지면 다른 분쟁 지역의 다른 공격자들에게 지나친 자유를 주게 될 것이다. **3** 타동사 허가하다 ❑ 주가 자동차에 대해서 면허를 주듯이 총기에 대해서도 면허를 주자는 제안

Thesaurus	*license*의 참조어

N. certificate, permission, permit, warrant **1**

Word Partnership	*license*의 연어

ADJ. **valid** license **1**
N. **driver's** license, license **fees**, **hunting** license, **liquor** license, **marriage** license, **pilot's** license, **software** license **1**
V. **get/obtain a** license, **renew a** license, **revoke a** license **1**

li|censed /laɪsᵊnst/ **1** ADJ If you are **licensed to** do something, you have official permission from the government or from the authorities to do it. ❑ *There were about 250 people on board, about 100 more than the ferry was licensed to carry.* **2** ADJ If something that you own or use is **licensed**, you have official permission to own it or use it. ❑ *While searching the house they discovered an unlicensed shotgun and a licensed rifle.* **3** ADJ If a place such as a restaurant or hotel is **licensed**, it has been given a license to sell alcoholic drinks. [BRIT] ❑ *...licensed premises.*

1 형용사 인가된 ❑ 그 연락선에는 인가받은 수보다 100여 명을 초과한 250명이 타고 있었다. **2** 형용사 허가된 ❑ 그 집을 수색하면서 그들은 무허가 산탄총 1정과 허가된 소총 1정을 발견했다. **3** 형용사 주류 판매 허가를 받은 [영국영어] ❑ 주류 판매 허가를 받은 업소

li|cense num|ber (**license numbers**) N-COUNT The **license number** of a car or other road vehicle is the series of letters and numbers that are shown at the front and back of it. [AM; BRIT **registration number**] ❑ *...a maroon 1992 Ford Taurus, license number 2YMT 804.*

가산명사 차량 번호 [미국영어; 영국영어 registration number] ❑ 적갈색의 1992년형 포드 토러스, 차량 번호 2YMT 804

li|cense plate (**license plates**) N-COUNT A **license plate** is a sign on the front and back of a vehicle that shows its license number. [AM; BRIT **number plate**] ❑ *...a car with Austrian license plates.*

가산명사 차량 번호판 [미국영어; 영국영어 number plate] ❑ 오스트리아 차량 번호판을 단 차

Word Web	library

Public libraries are changing. You can still **borrow** and **return books, magazines**, DVDs, CDs, and other **media** free of charge. However, many new **services** are now available. Websites often allow you to search the library's **catalog** of books and **periodicals**. Many libraries have computers with Internet access for the public. Some offer literacy classes, tutoring, and homework assistance. You can still wander through the **fiction** section to find a good **novel**. You can also search the nonfiction **bookshelves** for an interesting **biography**. And if you need help, the **librarian** is still there to answer your questions.

a
b
c
d
e
f
g
h
i
j
k
l
m
n
o
p
q
r
s
t
u
v
w
x
y
z

lick /lɪk/ (licks, licking, licked) **1** V-T When people or animals **lick** something, they move their tongue across its surface. ❑ *She folded up her letter, licking the envelope flap with relish.* ● N-COUNT **Lick** is also a noun. ❑ *He wouldn't lend the lollipop he was licking. Kevin, who was a year older, wanted a lick.* **2** to **lick into shape** →see **shape**

1 타동사 핥다 ❑ 그녀는 편지를 접고는 봉투 덮개 부분에 흐뭇하게 침을 발랐다. ● 가산명사 핥기 ❑ 그는 핥고 있던 막대 사탕을 빌려 주려고 하지 않았다. 한 살 많은 케빈은 그것을 한 번 핥아먹고 싶었다.

lid /lɪd/ (lids) N-COUNT A **lid** is the top of a box or other container which can be removed or raised when you want to open the container. ❑ *She lifted the lid of the box and displayed the contents.* →see **can**

가산명사 뚜껑 ❑ 그녀는 상자의 뚜껑을 열고 내용물을 보여 주었다.

Word Partnership   lie의 연어

ADJ.	lie **awake** ① **1**
	lie **flat** ① **2**
	lie **hidden** ① **4**
N.	lie **on** *your* **back**, lie **on the beach**, lie **in/on a bed**,
	lie **on a couch/sofa** ① **1**
	lie **on the floor**, lie **on the ground** ① **1** **2**
	lie **in ruins** ① **4**
V.	**tell** a **lie** ① **1**
PREP.	lie **about** *something*; lie **to** *someone* ② **2**

---
lie

① POSITION OR SITUATION
② THINGS THAT ARE NOT TRUE

---

① lie ♦♦◇ /laɪ/ (lies, lying, lay, lain) →Please look at category **8** to see if the expression you are looking for is shown under another headword. **1** V-I If you **are lying** somewhere, you are in a horizontal position and are not standing or sitting. ❑ *There was a child lying on the ground.* **2** V-I If an object **lies** in a particular place, it is in a flat position in that place. ❑ *...a newspaper lying on a nearby couch.* **3** V-I If you say that a place **lies** in a particular position or direction, you mean that it is situated there. ❑ *The islands lie at the southern end of the Kurile chain.* **4** V-LINK You can use **lie** to say that something is or remains in a particular state or condition. For example, if something **lies forgotten**, it has been and remains forgotten. ❑ *The picture lay hidden in the archives for over 40 years.* **5** V-T/V-I You can use **lie** to say what position a competitor or team is in during a competition. [mainly BRIT] ❑ *I was going well and was lying fourth.* **6** V-I You can talk about where something such as a problem, solution, or fault **lies** to say what you think it consists of, involves, or is caused by. ❑ *Television chiefs were trying to persuade him that the problem lay with the family and the school system rather than with television.* **7** V-I You use **lie** in expressions such as **lie ahead**, **lie in store**, and **lie in wait** when you are talking about what someone is going to experience in the future, especially when it is something unpleasant or difficult. [BRIT also **lie about**] ❑ *She'd need all her strength and bravery to cope with what lay in store.* **8** to **lie in state** →see **state**. to **take** something **lying down** →see **take**

1 자동사 누워 있다 ❑ 바닥에 아이가 누워 있었다. **2** 자동사 놓여 있다 ❑ 근처 소파에 놓여 있는 신문 **3** 자동사 위치하다, 있다 ❑ 그 섬들은 쿠릴 열도 남단에 있다. **4** 연결동사 ~한 상태에 있다; 잊히진 상태이다 ❑ 그 그림은 보관소에 40년 동안 감춰져 있었다. **5** 타동사/자동사 (등수가) 위이다 [주로 영국영어] ❑ 나는 잘 해서 4위를 기록하고 있었다. **6** 자동사 ~에 있다 ❑ 텔레비전 방송 국장들은 문제가 텔레비전보다는 가족과 학교 제도에 놓여 있다고 그를 설득하려 하고 있었다. **7** 자동사 (불쾌한 것이) 기다리고 있다, 앞에 놓여 있다 [영국영어 lie about] ❑ 앞에 기다리고 있는 일에 대응하려면 그녀는 자신이 지닌 모든 힘과 용기가 필요할 것이다.

Do not confuse the verb **lie** with the verb **lay**. Because **lay** is used to talk about putting something in a particular place or position, it is related to the verb **lie**. If someone **lays** something somewhere, it **lies** there. The past tense of **lie** is **lay** and the past participle is **lain**. It is an intransitive verb. ❑ *I lay on the floor with my legs in the air.* However, **lay**, whose past tense and past participle are both **laid**, is usually a transitive verb. ❑ *They laid him on the floor.*

동사 lie와 lay를 혼동하지 않도록 하라. lay가 사물을 특정한 장소나 위치에 놓는 것을 말할 때 쓰이므로, 동사 lie와 관련이 있기는 한다. 누가 무엇을 어디에 놓으면(lay), 그것은 거기에 놓여 있게(lie) 되는 것이다. lie의 과거는 lay이고, 과거분사는 lain이다. lie는 자동사이다. ❑ 나는 다리를 위로 들고 바닥에 누워 있었다. ❑ 그들은 그를 바닥에 눕혔다. 그러나 lay는 타동사로서, 과거와 과거분사는 laid이다.

Thesaurus   lie의 참조어

V.	recline, rest; *(ant.)* stand ① **1** **2**
	deceive, distort, fake, falsify, mislead ② **2**
N.	dishonesty ② **1**

▶**lie around** PHRASAL VERB If things are left **lying around** or **lying about**, they are not put away but left casually somewhere where they can be seen. ❑ *People should be careful about their possessions and not leave them lying around.*

구동사 아무 데나 두다 ❑ 사람들은 자기 물건을 아무 데나 두지 말고 조심해야 한다.

▶**lie behind** PHRASAL VERB If you refer to what **lies behind** a situation or event, you are referring to the reason the situation exists or the event happened. ❑ *It seems that what lay behind the clashes was disagreement over the list of candidates.*

구동사 배후에 있다 ❑ 그 충돌 이면에는 후보자 명단을 둘러싼 불화가 있었던 듯하다.

▶**lie down** PHRASAL VERB When you **lie down**, you move into a horizontal position, usually in order to rest or sleep. ❑ *Why don't you go upstairs and lie down for a bit?*

구동사 눕다 ❑ 위층에 올라가서 잠시 눕지 그래?

② lie ♦♦◇ /laɪ/ (lies, lying, lied) **1** N-COUNT A **lie** is something that someone says or writes which they know is untrue. ❑ *"Who else do you work for?" — "No one." — "That's a lie."* ❑ *I've had enough of your lies.* **2** V-I If someone **is lying**, they are saying something which they know is untrue. ❑ *I know he's lying.* ● **lying** N-UNCOUNT *Lying is something that I will not tolerate.* **3** →see also **lying**

1 가산명사 거짓말 ❑ "또 누굴 위해서 일하나?" "더 없어요." "거짓말 하지 마." ❑ 네 거짓말은 이제 지겨워. **2** 자동사 거짓말하고 있다 ❑ 그가 거짓말하고 있다는 것을 안다. ● 거짓말 불가산명사 ❑ 나는 거짓말은 절대로 용납할 수 없다.

lieu /lu, BRIT lyuː/ **1** PHRASE If you do, get, or give one thing **in lieu of** another, you do, get, or give it instead of the other thing, because the two things are considered to have the same value or importance. [FORMAL] ❑ *He left what little furniture he owned to his landlord in lieu of rent.* **2** PHRASE If you do, get, or give something **in lieu**, you do, get, or give it instead of something else, because the two things are considered to have the same value or importance. [mainly BRIT, FORMAL] ❑ *...an increased salary or time off in lieu.*

1 구 대신에 [격식체] ❑ 그는 집세 대신에 자신이 가진 얼마 안 되는 가구를 집주인에게 남겼다. **2** 구 대신에 [주로 영국영어, 격식체] ❑ 급료 인상 혹은 그 대신의 근로 시간 축소

lieu|ten|ant /lu:tenənt, BRIT leftenənt/ (**lieutenants**) N-COUNT; N-TITLE A **lieutenant** is a person who holds a junior officer's rank in the army, navy, marines, or air force, or in the American police force. ❑ *Lieutenant Campbell ordered the man at the wheel to steer for the gunboat.*

가산명사; 경칭명사 중위 ❑ 캠벨 중위는 타륜을 잡은 병사에게 포함을 향해 가라고 지시했다.

life ♦♦♦ /laɪf/ (**lives** /laɪvz/) N-UNCOUNT **Life** is the quality which people, animals, and plants have when they are not dead, and which objects and substances do not have. ❑ *...a baby's first minutes of life.* ❑ *Amnesty International opposes the death penalty as a violation of the right to life.* ② N-UNCOUNT You can use **life** to refer to things or groups of things which are alive. ❑ *Is there life on Mars?* ③ N-COUNT If you refer to someone's **life**, you mean their state of being alive, especially when there is a risk or danger of them dying. ❑ *Your life is in danger.* ❑ *A nurse began to try to save his life.* ④ N-COUNT Someone's **life** is the period of time during which they are alive. ❑ *He spent the last fourteen years of his life in retirement.* ⑤ N-COUNT You can use **life** to refer to a period of someone's life when they are in a particular situation or job. ❑ *Interior designers spend their working lives keeping up to date with the latest trends.* ⑥ N-COUNT You can use **life** to refer to particular activities which people regularly do during their lives. ❑ *My personal life has had to take second place to my career.* ⑦ N-UNCOUNT You can use **life** to refer to the things that people do and experience that are characteristic of a particular place, group, or activity. ❑ *How did you adjust to college life?* ❑ *...he abhors the wheeling-and-dealing associated with conventional political life.* ⑧ N-UNCOUNT A person, place, book, or movie that is full of **life** gives an impression of excitement, energy, or cheerfulness. [APPROVAL] ❑ *The town itself was full of life and character.* ⑨ N-UNCOUNT If someone is sentenced to **life**, they are sentenced to stay in prison for the rest of their life or for a very long time. [INFORMAL] ❑ *He could get life in prison, if convicted.* ⑩ N-COUNT The **life** of something such as a machine, organization, or project is the period of time that it lasts for. ❑ *The repairs did not increase the value or the life of the equipment.* ⑪ PHRASE If you **bring** something **to life** or if it **comes to life**, it becomes interesting or exciting. ❑ *The cold, hard cruelty of two young men is vividly brought to life in this true story.* ⑫ PHRASE If you say that someone **is fighting for** their **life**, you mean that they are in a very serious condition and may die as a result of an accident or illness. [JOURNALISM] ❑ *A horrifying robbery that left a man fighting for his life.* ⑬ PHRASE **For life** means for the rest of a person's life. ❑ *He was jailed for life in 1966 for the murder of three policemen.* ❑ *She may have been scarred for life.* ⑭ PHRASE If someone **takes** another person's **life**, they kill them. If someone **takes** their own **life**, they kill themselves. [FORMAL] ❑ *Before execution, he admitted to taking the lives of at least 35 more women.* ⑮ PHRASE You can use expressions such as **to come to life**, **to spring to life**, and **to roar into life** to indicate that a machine or vehicle suddenly starts working or moving. [LITERARY] ❑ *To his great relief the engine came to life.* ⑯ a matter of **life and death** →see **death** →see **earth**

❶ 불가산명사 생명 ❑ 아기의 탄생 후 첫 순간들 ❑ 국제 사면 기구는 사형 제도가 생명에 대한 권리를 위반하는 것이라며 반대한다. ❷ 불가산명사 생물 ❑ 화성에 생물이 있나? ❸ 가산명사 목숨 ❑ 네 목숨이 위험에 처해 있어. ❑ 한 간호원이 그의 목숨을 구하려는 시도를 시작했다. ❹ 가산명사 삶 ❑ 그는 은퇴한 뒤 자신의 삶의 마지막 14년을 보냈다. ❺ 가산명사 삶 ❑ 인테리어 디자이너들은 최신 동향들을 따라가면서 직업적인 삶을 보낸다. ❻ 가산명사 삶 ❑ 내 사생활은 내 일 다음 자리를 차지해 와야 했다. ❼ 불가산명사 생활 ❑ 대학 생활에는 어떻게 적응했니? ❑ 전통적인 정치 생활에 연관된 온갖 처세술을 그는 혐오한다. ❽ 불가산명사 생기 [마음에 듦] ❑ 그 마을 자체가 생기와 개성으로 넘쳐 났다. ❾ 불가산명사 종신형 [비격식체] ❑ 유죄 판결을 받는다면 그는 종신형을 선고받을 수도 있다. ❿ 가산명사 수명 ❑ 수리로 장비의 가치나 수명이 늘어나지는 않았다. ⓫ 구 생기를 불어넣다; 생기가 돈다 ❑ 두 청년의 냉혹하고 가차 없는 잔혹함이 이 실화에서 생생하게 구현되고 있다. ⓬ 구 목숨이 경각에 달려 있다 [언론] ❑ 끔찍한 강도사건 때문에 한 남자의 목숨이 경각에 달려 있게 되었다. ⓭ 구 남은 평생 동안, 여생 동안 ❑ 그는 경찰 3명을 살해한 죄로 1966년에 종신형으로 수감되었다. ❑ 그녀가 평생 지워지지 않는 상처를 입었을 수도 있다. ⓮ 구 생명을 앗다, 죽이다; 자살하다 [격식체] ❑ 사형당하기 전에 그는 최소한 여성 35명의 목숨을 더 앗았다는 것을 인정했다. ⓯ 구 가동되다 [문예체] ❑ 아주 다행히도 엔진에 시동이 걸렸다.

life as|sur|ance N-UNCOUNT **Life assurance** is the same as **life insurance**. [BRIT] ❑ *...a life assurance policy.*

불가산명사 생명 보험 [영국영어] ❑ 생명 보험 증권

life|boat /laɪfboʊt/ (**lifeboats**) ❶ N-COUNT A **lifeboat** is a medium-sized boat that is sent out from a port or harbor in order to rescue people who are in danger at sea. ❷ N-COUNT A **lifeboat** is a small boat that is carried on a ship, which people on the ship use to escape when the ship is in danger of sinking. ❑ *The captain ordered all passengers and crew into lifeboats.*

❶ 가산명사 구명정 ❷ 가산명사 구명정 ❑ 선장은 모든 승객과 선원에게 구명정에 타라고 명령했다.

life cy|cle (**life cycles**) ❶ N-COUNT The **life cycle** of an animal or plant is the series of changes and developments that it passes through from the beginning of its life until its death. ❑ *...a plant that completes its life cycle in a single season.* ❷ N-COUNT The **life cycle** of something such as an idea, product, or organization is the series of developments that take place in it from its beginning until the end of its usefulness. ❑ *Each new product would have a relatively long life cycle.* →see **plant**

❶ 가산명사 생명의 주기 ❑ 한 철 안에 생명의 주기를 마치는 식물 ❷ 가산명사 수명 ❑ 각 신제품은 비교적 긴 수명을 가질 것이다.

life|guard /laɪfgɑrd/ (**lifeguards**) N-COUNT A **lifeguard** is a person who works at a beach or swimming pool and rescues people when they are in danger of drowning.

가산명사 안전 요원, 인명 구조원

life in|sur|ance N-UNCOUNT **Life insurance** is a form of insurance in which a person makes regular payments to an insurance company, in return for a sum of money to be paid to them after a period of time, or to their family if they die. ❑ *I have also taken out a life insurance policy on him just in case.*

불가산명사 생명 보험 ❑ 나는 만약에 대비해 그를 생명 보험에 가입시켰다.

life|less /laɪflɪs/ ❶ ADJ If a person or animal is **lifeless**, they are dead, or are so still that they appear to be dead. ❑ *Their cold-blooded killers had then dragged their lifeless bodies upstairs to the bathroom.* ❷ ADJ If you describe an object or a machine as **lifeless**, you mean that they are not living things, even though they may resemble living things. ❑ *It was made of plaster, hard and white and lifeless, bearing no resemblance to human flesh.* ❸ ADJ A **lifeless** place or area does not have anything living or growing there at all. ❑ *Dry stone walls may appear stark and lifeless, but they provide a valuable habitat for plants and animals.*

❶ 형용사 죽은, 죽은 듯한 ❑ 그 후 그들의 냉혹한 살인자들이 그들의 이미 죽은 시신을 위층 화장실로 끌고 간 상태였다. ❷ 형용사 생기 없는 ❑ 그것은 석고로 만들어져 딱딱하고 하얗고 생기가 없었으며 인간의 육신과 전혀 비슷한 점이 없었다. ❸ 형용사 생명이 없는 ❑ 건조한 돌담이 황량하고 생명이 없는 것처럼 보일지 몰라도 그것들은 식물과 동물들에게 귀중한 서식처를 제공한다.

life|line /laɪflaɪn/ (**lifelines**) N-COUNT A **lifeline** is something that enables an organization or group to survive or to continue with an activity. ❑ *Information about the job market can be a lifeline for those who are out of work.*

가산명사 생명선 ❑ 구인 시장에 대한 정보는 직장이 없는 이들에게 생명선이 될 수도 있다.

life|long /laɪflɒŋ, BRIT laɪflɒŋ/ ADJ **Lifelong** means existing or happening for the whole of a person's life. [ADJ n] ❑ *...her lifelong friendship with Naomi.*

형용사 평생의 ❑ 그녀가 평생 나오미와 나누었던 우정

life|span /laɪfspæn/ (**lifespans**) also **life span** ❶ N-VAR The **lifespan** of a person, animal, or plant is the period of time for which they live or are normally expected to live. ❑ *A 15-year lifespan is not uncommon for a dog.* ❷ N-COUNT The **lifespan** of a product, organization, or idea is the period of time for which it is expected to work properly or to last. ❑ *Most boilers have a lifespan of 15 to 20 years.*

❶ 가산명사 또는 불가산명사 수명 ❑ 개에게 수명 15년은 이례적인 일이 아니다. ❷ 가산명사 수명 ❑ 대부분 보일러의 수명은 15년에서 20년 정도이다.

life|style /ˈlaɪfstaɪl/ (**lifestyles**) also **life-style, life style** ◼ N-VAR The **lifestyle** of a particular person or group of people is the living conditions, behavior, and habits that are typical of them or are chosen by them. ❑ *They enjoyed an income and lifestyle that many people would envy.* ◼ ADJ **Lifestyle** magazines, television programs, and products are aimed at people who wish to be associated with glamorous and successful lifestyles. [ADJ n] ❑ *This year people are going for luxury and buying lifestyle products.* ◼ ADJ **Lifestyle** drugs are drugs that are intended to improve people's quality of life rather than to treat particular medical disorders. [ADJ n] ❑ *"I see anti-depressants as a lifestyle drug," says Dr Charlton.*

◼ 가산명사 또는 불가산명사 생활 방식 ❑ 그들은 많은 사람들이 부러워할 수입과 생활 방식을 영위하고 있었다. ◼ 형용사 호사스러운, 고급의 ❑ 올해 사람들 사이에서 사치와 호사스러운 제품이 유행하고 있다. ◼ 형용사 삶의 질을 개선하는 ❑ "제가 보기에 항우울제는 삶의 질을 개선하는 약입니다."라고 찰튼 박사는 말한다.

life|time /ˈlaɪftaɪm/ (**lifetimes**) N-COUNT A **lifetime** is the length of time that someone is alive. ❑ *During my lifetime I haven't got around to much traveling.* ❑ *...a trust fund to be administered throughout his wife's lifetime.*

가산명사 생애 ❑ 나는 사는 동안 여행을 별로 하지 못했다. ❑ 그의 아내가 생존해 있는 동안 지급될 신탁 기금

lift ◆◆◇ /lɪft/ (**lifts, lifting, lifted**) ◼ V-T If you **lift** something, you move it to another position, especially upward. ❑ *The Colonel lifted the phone and dialed his superior.* ● PHRASAL VERB **Lift up** means the same as **lift**. ❑ *She put her arms around him and lifted him up.*

◼ 타동사 들다 ❑ 대령은 수화기를 들고 상관에게 전화를 걸었다. ❑ 구동사 들다 ❑ 그녀는 그를 두 팔로 안아서 들어올렸다.

> Do not confuse **lift** and **carry**. When you **carry** something, you move it from one place to another without letting it touch the ground. When you **lift** something, you move it upwards using your hands or a machine. After you have lifted it, you may **carry** it to a different place.

> lift와 carry를 혼동하지 않도록 하라. 무엇을 carry하면, 그것을 땅에 닿지 않게 해서 한 장소에서 다른 장소로 옮기는 것이다. 무엇을 lift하면 손이나 기계로 그것을 위로 들어올리는 것이다. 무엇을 들어올린(lift) 다음에, 그것을 다른 장소로 carry할 수 있다.

◼ V-T If you **lift** your eyes or your head, you look up, for example when you have been reading and someone comes into the room. ❑ *When he finished he lifted his eyes and looked out the window.* ◼ V-T If people in authority **lift** a law or rule that prevents people from doing something, they end it. ❑ *The European Commission has urged France to lift its ban on imports of British beef.* ◼ V-T/V-I If something **lifts** your spirits or your mood, or if they **lift**, you start feeling more cheerful. ❑ *He used his incredible sense of humor to lift my spirits.* ◼ N-COUNT A **lift** is a device that carries people or goods up and down inside tall buildings. [BRIT; AM **elevator**] ❑ *They took the lift to the fourth floor.* ◼ N-COUNT If you give someone a **lift** somewhere, you take them there in your car as a favor to them. ❑ *He had a car and often gave me a lift home.* ◼ V-T If a government or organization **lifts** people or goods in or out of an area, it transports them there by aircraft, especially when there is a war. ❑ *The army lifted people off rooftops where they had climbed to escape the flooding.* ◼ V-T To **lift** something means to increase its amount or to increase the level or the rate at which it happens. ❑ *The bank lifted its basic home loans rate to 10.99% from 10.75%.* ◼ to **lift a finger** →see **finger**

◼ 타동사 들다 ❑ 일이 끝나자 그는 눈을 들어 창 밖을 바라보았다. ◼ 타동사 없애다, 끝내다 ❑ 유럽 연합은 프랑스에게 영국 소고기 수입 금지 조치를 풀라고 재촉했다. ◼ 타동사/자동사 나아지게 하다; 나아지다 ❑ 그는 내 기분을 풀어 주기 위해 놀라운 유머 감각을 발휘했다. ◼ 가산명사 승강기 [영국영어; 미국영어 elevator] ❑ 그들은 승강기를 타고 4층으로 갔다. ◼ 가산명사 태워 줌 ❑ 그에겐 차가 있어서 그가 가끔 나를 집까지 태워 줬다. ◼ 타동사 비행기로 수송하다 ❑ 홍수를 피하기 위해 지붕 위로 올라간 사람들을 육군이 비행기로 이동시켰다. ◼ 타동사 인상하다 ❑ 은행은 기본 주택 대출 이자율을 10.75퍼센트에서 10.99퍼센트로 인상했다.

Thesaurus
lift의 참조어

v.　hoist, pick up; (*ant.*) drop, lower, put down ◼
cancel, repeal, terminate ◼
boost, enhance, raise ◼

Word Partnership
lift의 연어

N.　lift *your* arm, lift *your* hand, lift **weights** ◼
lift **a ban**, lift **a blockade**, lift **an embargo**, lift **restrictions**,
lift **sanctions**, lift **a siege** ◼

---

liga|ment /ˈlɪɡəmənt/ (**ligaments**) N-COUNT A **ligament** is a band of strong tissue in a person's body which connects bones. ❑ *He suffered torn ligaments in his knee.*

가산명사 인대 ❑ 그는 무릎의 인대가 찢어졌다.

---

light
① BRIGHTNESS OR ILLUMINATION
② NOT GREAT IN WEIGHT, AMOUNT, OR INTENSITY
③ UNIMPORTANT OR NOT SERIOUS

Word Link
light ≈ shining: day*light*, en*light*en, *light*

---

①light ◆◆◇ /laɪt/ (**lights, lighting, lit, lighted, lighter, lightest**)

> The form **lit** is the usual past tense and past participle, but the form **lighted** is also used.

> lit이 대개 과거 및 과거 분사이지만 lighted도 쓴다.

→Please look at category ◼ to see if the expression you are looking for is shown under another headword. ◼ N-UNCOUNT **Light** is the brightness that lets you see things. Light comes from sources such as the sun, moon, lamps, and fire. [also the N] ❑ *Cracks of light filtered through the shutters.* ❑ *...ultraviolet light.* ◼ N-COUNT A **light** is something such as an electric lamp which produces light. ❑ *The janitor comes round to turn the lights out.* ◼ N-PLURAL You can use **lights** to refer to a set of traffic lights. ❑ *...the heavy city traffic with its endless delays at lights and crossings.* ◼ V-T If a place or object **is lit** by something, it has light shining on it. ❑ *It was dark and a giant moon lit the road so brightly you could see the landscape clearly.* ❑ *The room was lit by only the one light.* ◼ ADJ If it is **light**, the sun is providing light at the beginning or end of the day. ❑ *It was still light when we arrived at Lalong Creek.* ◼ ADJ If a room or building is **light**, it has a lot of natural light in it, for example because it has large windows. ❑ *It is a light room with tall windows.* ● **light|ness** N-UNCOUNT ❑ *The dark green spare bedroom is in total contrast to the lightness of the large main bedroom.* ◼ V-T/V-I If you **light** something such as a cigarette or fire, or if it **lights**, it starts burning. ❑ *Stephen hunched down to light*

◼ 불가산명사 빛 ❑ 셔터의 갈라진 틈을 통해 빛이 새어 들어왔다. ❑ 자외선 ◼ 가산명사 불 ❑ 수위가 돌아다니며 불을 끈다. ◼ 복수명사 신호등 ❑ 신호등과 교차로에서 끝없이 지체되는 혼잡한 도시 교통 ◼ 타동사 비춰지다 ❑ 날은 어두웠는데 커다란 달이 길을 너무 밝게 비춰 주어서 경치를 선명하게 볼 수 있었다. ❑ 그 방에는 불이 단지 그것 하나만 켜져 있었다. ◼ 형용사 해가 떠 있는 ❑ 우리가 라롱 계곡에 도착했을 때는 아직도 해가 떠 있었다. ◼ 형용사 밝은 ❑ 큰 창을 가진 밝은 방이다. ● 밝기 불가산명사 ❑ 짙은 녹색으로 꾸며진 예비 침실은 밝은 큰 안방과 완전히 대조적이다. ◼ 타동사/자동사 불을 붙이다; 불이 붙다 ❑ 스티븐은 몸을 수그리고 담배에 불을 붙였다. ❑ 혹시 숯에 불이 붙지 않는다면 특수 액체 스프레이를 사용한 후 긴 양초로 불을 붙여라. ◼ 가산명사 방식 ❑ 그는 뉴욕을 보다 좋게 그리기 위해 최근 몇 달간 열심히

a cigarette. ❑ *If the charcoal does fail to light, use a special liquid spray and light it with a long taper.* ⑧ N-COUNT If something is presented in a particular **light**, it is presented so that you think about it in a particular way or so that it appears to be of a particular nature. ❑ *He has worked hard in recent months to portray New York in a better light.* ⑨ →see also **lighter, lighting** ⑩ PHRASE If something **comes to light** or is **brought to light**, it becomes obvious or is made known to a lot of people. ❑ *Nothing about this sum has come to light.* ⑪ PHRASE If someone in authority gives you **a green light**, they give you permission to do something. ❑ *The food industry was given a green light to extend the use of these chemicals.* ⑫ PHRASE If something is possible **in the light of** particular information, it is only possible because you have this information. ❑ *In the light of this information it is now possible to identify a number of key issues.* ⑬ PHRASE If you **set light to** something, you make it start burning. [mainly BRIT; AM usually **set fire to**] ❑ *They had poured fuel through the door of the flat and had then set light to it.* ⑭ PHRASE To **shed light on, throw light on,** or **cast light on** something means to make it easier to understand, because more information is known about it. ❑ *A new approach offers an answer, and may shed light on an even bigger question.* ⑮ **all sweetness and light** →see **sweetness**
→see **laser, light bulb**

노력했다. ⑩ 구 드러나다 ❑ 이 합계에 대해서 드러난 것은 아무것도 없다. ⑪ 구 청신호 ❑ 식품 업계는 이 화학 물질의 사용을 확대해도 된다는 청신호를 받았다. ⑫ 구 ~에 비춰 볼 때 ❑ 이 정보에 비춰 볼 때 이제 많은 주요 사안들을 규명하는 것이 가능하다. ⑬ 구 ~에 불을 붙이다 [주로 영국영어; 미국영어 대개 set fire to] ❑ 그들은 아파트 문 사이로 연료를 부은 다음 그것에 불을 붙였다. ⑭ 구 설명하다, 밝히다 ❑ 새로운 접근 방식이 답을 제공하고 훨씬 더 큰 의문에 대해서도 설명해 줄 수 있을지 모른다.

N.	gleam, glow, radiance, shine ①⑪
ADJ.	bright, sunny ①⑤⑥

▶**light up** ⑪ PHRASAL VERB If you **light** something **up** or if it **lights up**, it becomes bright, usually when you shine light on it. ❑ *...a keypad that lights up when you pick up the handset.* ② PHRASAL VERB If your face or your eyes **light up** you suddenly look very surprised or happy. ❑ *Sue's face lit up with surprise.*

⑪ 구동사 불을 켜다; 불이 켜지다 ❑ 수화기를 들면 불이 켜지는 번호판 ② 구동사 환해지다 ❑ 수의 얼굴이 화들짝 놀라는 표정을 지었다.

---

② **light** ◆◇◇ /laɪt/ (**lighter, lightest**) ⑪ ADJ Something that is **light** does not weigh very much, or weighs less than you would expect it to. ❑ *Modern tennis rackets are now apparently 20 per cent lighter.* ❑ *...weight training with light weights.* ● **light|ness** N-UNCOUNT [usu with supp] ❑ *The toughness, lightness, strength, and elasticity of whalebone gave it a wide variety of uses.* ② ADJ Something that is **light** is not very great in amount, degree, or intensity. ❑ *It's a Sunday like any other with the usual light traffic in the city.* ❑ *Trading was very light ahead of yesterday's auction.* ● **light|ly** ADV ❑ *Put the onions in the pan and cook until lightly browned.* ③ ADJ Something that is **light** is very pale in color. ❑ *He is light haired with gray eyes.* ● COMB in COLOR **Light** is also a combining form. ❑ *We know he has a light green van.* ④ ADJ A **light** sleep is one that is easily disturbed and in which you are often aware of the things around you. If you are a **light** sleeper, you are easily woken when you are asleep. [ADJ n] ❑ *She had drifted into a light sleep.* ● **light|ly** ADV [ADV after v] ❑ *He was dozing lightly in his chair.* ⑤ ADJ A **light** meal consists of food that is easy to digest. ❑ *...a light, healthy lunch.* ● **light|ly** ADV [ADV after v] ❑ *She found it impossible to eat lightly.* ⑥ ADJ **Light** work does not involve much physical effort. ❑ *He was on the training field for some light work yesterday.* ⑦ ADJ If you describe the result of an action or a punishment as **light**, you mean that it is less serious or severe than you expected. ❑ *She confessed her astonishment at her light sentence when her father visited her at the jail.* ● **light|ly** ADV [ADV after v] ❑ *One of the accused got off lightly in exchange for pleading guilty to withholding information from Congress.* ⑧ ADJ Movements and actions that are **light** are graceful or gentle and are done with very little force or effort. ❑ *Use a light touch when applying cream or makeup.* ● **light|ly** ADV [ADV with v] ❑ *He kissed her lightly on the mouth.* ● **light|ness** N-UNCOUNT ❑ *She danced with a grace and lightness that were breathtaking.*
⑨ →see also **lighter**

⑪ 형용사 가벼운 ❑ 현대 테니스 채들은 분명히 20퍼센트 더 가볍다. ❑ 가벼운 역기를 들고 하는 웨이트 트레이닝 ● 가벼움 불가산명사 ❑ 고래 뼈는 질기고 가볍고 강하고 신축성이 있어서 쓰임새가 매우 다양했다. ② 형용사 가벼운 ❑ 다른 여느 일요일처럼 도시의 교통이 한산한 일요일이다. ❑ 어제 경매 이전에는 거래가 매우 소량으로 이루어지고 있었다. ● 가볍게, 약간 부사 ❑ 양파를 팬에 넣고 약간 갈색이 될 때까지 익혀라. ③ 형용사 옅은 ❑ 그는 옅은 색의 머리에 회색 눈을 하고 있다. ● 복합형-색채로 옅은 ❑ 우리는 그가 옅은 녹색 밴을 가지고 있는 것을 안다. ④ 형용사 옅은 ❑ 그녀가 깜빡 옅은 잠에 빠져 있었다. ● 얕게 부사 ❑ 그는 의자에서 가볍게 졸고 있었다. ⑤ 형용사 가벼운 ❑ 가볍고 건강에 좋은 점심 ● 가볍게 부사 ❑ 그녀는 가볍게 먹는 것이 불가능했다. ⑥ 형용사 가벼운 ❑ 그는 어제 가볍게 운동을 한다고 훈련장에 나가 있었다. ⑦ 형용사 가벼운 ❑ 그녀는 아버지가 교도소로 면회하러 왔을 때 자신의 가벼운 형기에 대한 놀라움을 고백했다. ● 가볍게 부사 ❑ 피고 중 한 명은 하원에 정보를 제공하지 않은 것에 대해 유죄를 인정한 대가로 가벼운 처벌을 받았다. ⑧ 형용사 가벼운 ❑ 크림이나 화장품을 바를 때는 가볍게 발라라. ● 가볍게 부사 ❑ 그는 그녀의 입에 가볍게 입을 맞추었다. ● 가벼움 불가산명사 ❑ 그녀는 숨 막힐 정도로 우아하고 가볍게 춤을 추었다.

③ **light** ◆◇◇ /laɪt/ (**lighter, lightest**) →Please look at category ④ to see if the expression you are looking for is shown under another headword. ⑪ ADJ If you describe things such as books, music, and movies as **light**, you mean that they entertain you without making you think very deeply. ❑ *He doesn't like me reading light novels.* ❑ *...light classical music.* ② ADJ If you say something in a **light** way, you sound as if you think that something is not important or serious. ❑ *Talk to him in a friendly, light way about the relationship.* ● **light|ly** ADV [ADV after v] ❑ *"Once a detective, always a detective," he said lightly.* ● **light|ness** N-UNCOUNT ❑ *"I'm not an authority on them," Jessica said with forced lightness.* ③ PHRASE If you **make light of** something, you treat it as though it is not serious or important, when in fact it is. ❑ *Roberts attempted to make light of his discomfort.* ④ →see also **lighter**

⑪ 형용사 가벼운, 딱딱하지 않은 ❑ 그는 내가 가벼운 소설 따위나 읽는 것을 좋아하지 않는다. ❑ 가벼운 고전 음악 ② 형용사 가벼운 ❑ 그 관계에 대해 상냥하고 가벼운 어투로 그에게 말을 건네 보세요. ● 가볍게 부사 ❑ "한 번 형사는 영원히 형사야." 그가 쾌활하게 말했다. ● 가벼움 불가산명사 ❑ "나는 그런 일들에 대해서는 잘 모릅니다." 제시카가 억지로 가볍게 말했다. ③ 구 ~을 얕보다; 무시하다 ❑ 로버츠는 자신의 불안을 무시하고자 애썼다.

light bulb (**light bulbs**) N-COUNT A **light bulb** or **bulb** is the round glass part of an electric light or lamp which light shines from.
→see Word Web: **light bulb**

가산명사 전구

light|en /ˈlaɪtən/ (**lightens, lightening, lightened**) ⑪ V-T/V-I When something **lightens** or when you **lighten** it, it becomes less dark in color. ❑ *The sky began to lighten.* ② V-T If someone **lightens** a situation, they make it less serious or less boring. ❑ *Anthony felt the need to lighten the atmosphere.* ③ V-T/V-I If your attitude or mood **lightens**, or if someone or something **lightens** it, they make you feel more cheerful, happy, and relaxed. ❑ *As they approached the outskirts of the city, Ella's mood visibly lightened.*

⑪ 타동사/자동사 밝아지다; 밝게 하다 ❑ 하늘이 밝아오기 시작했다. ② 타동사 누그러뜨리다, 가볍게 하다 ❑ 앤소니는 분위기를 좀 밝게 해야겠다고 느꼈다. ③ 타동사/자동사 (마음이) 가벼워지다; 기운을 북돋우다 ❑ 시 외곽에 가까워지자, 엘라의 기분이 눈에 띄게 가벼워졌다.

light|er /ˈlaɪtər/ (**lighters**) N-COUNT A **lighter** is a small device that produces a flame which you can use to light cigarettes, cigars, and pipes.

가산명사 라이터

Word Web   light bulb

The incandescent **light bulb** has changed little since the 1870s. It consists of a **glass** globe containing an inert gas, such as argon, some wires, and a filament. **Electricity** flows through the wires and the tungsten filament. The filament heats up and **glows**. Light bulbs aren't very efficient. They give off more heat than **light**. **Fluorescent** lights are much more efficient. They contain liquid mercury and argon gas. A layer of phosphorus covers the inside of the tube. When electricity begins to flow, the mercury becomes a gas and **emits** ultraviolet light. This causes the phosphorus coating to **shine**.

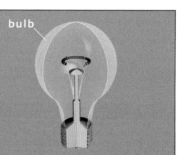

bulb

Word Link   light ≈ not heavy : light**en**, light**est**, light**hearted**

light|hearted /laɪthɑrtɪd/ [BRIT **light-hearted**] **1** ADJ Someone who is **lighthearted** is cheerful and happy. ❑ *I was amazingly lighthearted and peaceful.* **2** ADJ Something that is **lighthearted** is intended to be entertaining or amusing, and not at all serious. ❑ *There have been many attempts, both light-hearted and serious, to locate the Loch Ness Monster.*

light|house /laɪthaʊs/ (**lighthouses**) N-COUNT A **lighthouse** is a tower containing a powerful flashing lamp that is built on the coast or on a small island. Lighthouses are used to guide ships or to warn them of danger.

light in|dus|try (**light industries**) N-VAR **Light industry** is industry in which only small items are made, for example household goods and clothes. ❑ *State and local officials are hoping to bring some light industry to the site.* →see **industry**

light|ing /laɪtɪŋ/ N-UNCOUNT The **lighting** in a place is the way that it is lit, for example by electric lights, by candles, or by windows, or the quality of the light in it. ❑ *...the bright fluorescent lighting of the laboratory.* ❑ *The whole room is bathed in soft lighting.* →see **concert**, **eye**, **photography**

light|ning /laɪtnɪŋ/ **1** N-UNCOUNT **Lightning** is the very bright flashes of light in the sky that happen during thunderstorms. ❑ *One man died when he was struck by lightning.* ❑ *Another flash of lightning lit up the cave.* **2** ADJ **Lightning** describes things that happen very quickly or last for only a short time. [ADJ n] ❑ *Driving today demands lightning reflexes.* →see **storm**, **wave** →see Word Web: **lightning**

light|weight /laɪtweɪt/ (**lightweights**) also **light-weight** **1** ADJ Something that is **lightweight** weighs less than most other things of the same type. ❑ *...lightweight denim.* **2** N-UNCOUNT **Lightweight** is a category in some sports, such as boxing, judo, or rowing, based on the weight of the athlete. ❑ *By the age of sixteen he was the junior lightweight champion of Poland.* **3** N-COUNT If you describe someone as a **lightweight**, you are critical of them because you think that they are not very important or skillful in a particular area of activity. [DISAPPROVAL] ❑ *Hill considered Sam a lightweight, a real amateur.* ● ADJ **Lightweight** is also an adjective. ❑ *Some of the discussion in the book is lightweight and unconvincing.*

light year (**light years**) **1** N-COUNT A **light year** is the distance that light travels in a year. ❑ *...a star system millions of light years away.* **2** N-COUNT You can say that two things are **light years** apart to emphasize a very great difference or a very long distance or period of time between them. [INFORMAL, EMPHASIS] ❑ *She says the French education system is light years ahead of the English one.* →see **galaxy**

lik|able /laɪkəbəl/ →see **likeable**

like
① PREPOSITION AND CONJUNCTION USES
② VERB USES
③ NOUN USES AND PHRASES

① **like** ♦♦♦ /laɪk, laɪk/ (**likes**) **1** PREP If you say that one person or thing is **like** another, you mean that they share some of the same qualities or features. ❑ *He looks like Father Christmas.* ❑ *It's a bit like going to the dentist; it's never as bad as*

[영국영어 light-hearted] **1** 형용사 명랑한, 낙천적인 ❑ 나는 놀라우리만큼 기분이 좋고 편안했다. **2** 형용사 가벼운, 재미 삼은 ❑ 재미 삼아서든 진지하게든, 네스호의 괴수를 찾아내려는 시도가 허다하게 계속되어 왔다.

가산명사 등대

가산명사 또는 불가산명사 경공업 ❑ 주 정부와 지방 관리들은 그 부지에 일부 경공업을 들여오기를 희망하고 있다.

불가산명사 조명; 채광 ❑ 실험실의 밝은 형광등 조명 ❑ 방 전체가 부드러운 불빛에 잠겨 있었다.

1 불가산명사 번개 ❑ 한 남자가 번개에 맞아 숨졌다. ❑ 또 한 번 번개가 번쩍 하면서 동굴 속을 밝혔다. **2** 형용사 전광석화처럼, 번개 같은 ❑ 요즘은 운전을 하려면 전광석화 같은 반사 능력을 갖추고 있어야 한다.

1 형용사 경량의, 가벼운 ❑ 가벼운 데님 천 **2** 불가산명사 라이트급 ❑ 이미 열여섯 살 무렵에 그는 폴란드의 주니어 라이트급 챔피언이었다. **3** 가산명사 하찮은 사람 [탐탁찮음] ❑ 힐은 샘을 하찮은 완전 풋내기로만 여겼다. ● 형용사 하찮은 ❑ 그 책에 담긴 논의 중 일부는 별 쓸모가 없는 데다 설득력도 갖추고 있지 못하다.

1 가산명사 광년 ❑ 수백만 광년 떨어진 행성계 **2** 가산명사 시간적이나 공간적으로 매우 거리가 있음을 강조하는 표현 [비격식체, 강조] ❑ 프랑스의 교육 시스템이 영국보다 훨씬 앞서 있다고 그녀는 말한다.

1 전치사 -와 같이 ❑ 그는 흡사 산타클로스 할아버지처럼 보인다. ❑ 그건 치과에 가는 것과 거의 비슷해. 네가 두려워하는 것처럼 끔찍한 일이 전혀

Word Web   lightning

Lightning originates in storm clouds. Strong winds cause tiny **particles** within the clouds to rub together violently. This creates **positive charges** on some particles and **negative charges** on others. The negatively charged particles sink to the bottom of the cloud. There they are attracted by the positively charged surface of the earth. Gradually a large negative charge accumulates in a cloud. When it is large enough, a **bolt** of lightning strikes the earth. When a bolt branches out, the result is called **forked lightning**. Sheet lightning occurs when the bolt **discharges** within a cloud, instead of on the earth.

you fear. ❑ It's nothing like what happened in the mid-seventies. ② PREP If you talk about what something or someone is **like**, you are talking about their qualities or features. ❑ What was Bulgaria like? ❑ What did she look like? ③ PREP You can use **like** to introduce an example of the set of things or people that you have just mentioned. [n PREP n/-ing] ❑ The neglect that large cities like New York have received over the past 12 years is tremendous. ④ PREP You can use **like** to say that someone or something is in the same situation as another person or thing. ❑ It also moved those who, like me, are too young to have lived through the war. ⑤ PREP If you say that someone is behaving **like** something or someone else, you mean that they are behaving in a way that is typical of that kind of thing or person. **Like** is used in this way in many fixed expressions, for example **to cry like a baby** and **to watch someone like a hawk**. [v PREP n] ❑ I was shaking all over, trembling like a leaf. ⑥ CONJ **Like** is sometimes used as a conjunction in order to say that something appears to be the case when it is not. Some people consider this use to be incorrect. ❑ His arms look like they might snap under the weight of his gloves. ⑦ CONJ **Like** is sometimes used as a conjunction in order to indicate that something happens or is done in the same way as something else. Some people consider this use to be incorrect. ❑ People are strolling, buying ice cream for their children, just like they do every Sunday. ❑ He spoke exactly like I did. ⑧ PREP You can use **like** in negative expressions such as **nothing like it** and **no place like it** to emphasize that there is nothing as good as the situation, thing, or person mentioned. [EMPHASIS] [with neg] ❑ There's nothing like candlelight for creating a romantic mood. ⑨ PREP You can use **like** in expressions such as **nothing like** to make an emphatic negative statement. [EMPHASIS] [with neg] ❑ Three hundred million dollars will be nothing like enough.

Thesaurus   like의 참조어

ADJ.	alike, comparable, similar; (ant.) different ① ①
V.	admire, appreciate, enjoy; (ant.) dislike ② ①

---

② **like** ♦♦♦ /laɪk/ (**likes**, **liking**, **liked**) ① V-T If you **like** something or someone, you think they are interesting, enjoyable, or attractive. [no cont] ❑ He likes baseball. ❑ I just didn't like being in crowds. ❑ Do you like to go swimming? ② V-T If you ask someone how they **like** something, you are asking them for their opinion of it and whether they enjoy it or find it pleasant. [no cont, no passive] ❑ How do you like America? ③ V-T If you say that you **like to** do something or that you like something to be done, you mean that you prefer to do it or prefer it to be done as part of your normal life or routine. [no cont, no passive] ❑ I like to get to airports in good time. ④ V-T If you say that you **would like** something or **would like** to do something, you are indicating a wish or desire that you have. [no cont, no passive] ❑ I'd like a bath. ⑤ V-T If you ask someone if they **would like** something or **would like** to do something, you are making a polite offer or invitation. [POLITENESS] [no cont, no passive] ❑ Here's your change. Would you like a bag? ❑ Perhaps while you wait you would like a drink at the bar. ⑥ V-T If you say to someone that you **would like** something or you **would like** them to do something, or ask them if they **would like** to do it, you are politely telling them what you want or what you want them to do. [POLITENESS] [no cont, no passive] ❑ I'd like an explanation. ❑ We'd like you to look around and tell us if anything is missing.

③ **like** ♦♦♦ /laɪk/ (**likes**) ① N-UNCOUNT You can use **like** in expressions such as **like attracts like**, when you are referring to two or more people or things that have the same or similar characteristics. ❑ You have to make sure you're comparing like with like. ② N-PLURAL Someone's **likes** are the things that they enjoy or find pleasant. ❑ I thought that I knew everything about Jemma: her likes and dislikes, her political viewpoints. ③ →see also **liking** ④ PHRASE You say **if you like** when you are making or agreeing to an offer or suggestion in a casual way. ❑ You can stay here if you like. ⑤ PHRASE You say **like this**, **like that**, or **like so** when you are showing someone how something is done. ❑ It opens and closes, like this. ⑥ PHRASE You use **like this** or **like that** when you are drawing attention to something that you are doing or that someone else is doing. ❑ I'm sorry to intrude on you like this. ⑦ PHRASE You use the expression **something like** with an amount, number, or description to indicate that it is approximately accurate. ❑ They can get something like £3,000 a year.

-like /-laɪk/ COMB in ADJ **-like** combines with nouns to form adjectives which describe something as being similar to the thing referred to by the noun. ❑ ...beautiful purple-red petunia-like flowers. ❑ ...a tiny worm-like creature.

like|able /laɪkəbᵊl/ also **likable** ADJ Someone or something that is **likeable** is pleasant and easy to like. ❑ He was a bright guy, a likeable guy.

like|li|hood /laɪklihʊd/ ① N-UNCOUNT The **likelihood** of something happening is how likely it is to happen. ❑ The likelihood of infection is minimal. ② N-SING If something is a **likelihood**, it is likely to happen. ❑ But the likelihood is that people would be willing to pay if they were certain that their money was going to a good cause.

like|ly ♦♦♦ /laɪkli/ (**likelier**, **likeliest**) ① ADJ You use **likely** to indicate that something is probably the case or will probably happen in a particular situation. ❑ Experts say a "yes" vote is still the likely outcome. ❑ If this is your first baby, it's far more likely that you'll get to the hospital too early. ● ADV **Likely** is also an adverb. [ADV with cl/group] ❑ Profit will most likely have risen by about £25 million. ② ADJ If someone or something is **likely to** do a particular thing, they will very probably do it. [v-link ADJ to-inf] ❑ In the meantime the war of nerves seems likely to continue.

(Korean column)

아니거든. ❑ 그 일을 70년대 중반에 일어났던 사건에 비할 바가 아니지. ② 전치사 what과 함께 의문문에 쓰여 성이나 특색을 묻는 표현을 만든다. ❑ 불가리아에서는 어땠어요? 그 나라는 어떻게 생겼어요? ③ 전치사 이를테면 ~와 같은 ❑ 뉴욕과 같은 대도시들이 지난 12년 동안 견디어 온 무관심은 엄청나다. ④ 전치사 ~처럼, ~같이 ❑ 그것은 나처럼 너무 어려서 생전 전쟁을 한 번도 겪어 보지 못했던 사람들까지도 감동시켰다. ⑤ 전치사 ~마냥, ~처럼 ❑ 나는 온몸을 사시나무 떨듯 떨고 있었다. ⑥ 접속사 마치 ~인 것처럼 ❑ 그의 두 팔은 그가 긴 장갑 무게에 눌려 툭 부러질 것처럼 보인다. ⑦ 접속사 ~처럼, ~와 비슷하게 ❑ 매주 일요일마다 으레 그래 왔듯이 사람들이 자녀들에게 아이스크림을 사 주면서 산책하고 있다. ❑ 그는 내가 말한 바 그대로 똑같이 말했다. ⑧ 전치사 ~만한 [강조] ❑ 로맨틱한 분위기를 조성하는 데는 촛불만한 게 없죠. ⑨ 전치사 nothing 등의 부정어와 함께 '견고 ~않다'는 뜻을 만든다. [강조] ❑ 3억 달러로는 결코 충분치 않을 것이다.

① 타동사 좋아하다 ❑ 그는 야구를 좋아한다. ❑ 난 그저 군중 속에 있는 게 싫었어. ❑ 너 수영하러 갈래? ② 타동사 how와 함께 쓰여 '~은 어때?'라는 식으로 상대방의 의견을 묻는다. ❑ 미국은 어때요? ③ 타동사 ~하고 싶다, ~이면 좋겠다 ❑ 나는 때맞춰 공항에 도착하고 싶다. ④ 타동사 ~하고 싶다 ❑ 목욕을 좀 하고 싶은데. ⑤ 타동사 공손하게 제안이나 권유를 할 때 쓰는 표현 [공손체] ❑ 거스름돈 여기 있습니다. 가방에 담아 드릴까요? ⑥ 타동사 공손하게 부탁을 하거나 자신이 원하는 바를 말할 때 쓰는 표현 [공손체] ❑ 해명이 필요한 것 같습니다. ❑ 한번 둘러보시고 혹시 없어진 게 있으면 말씀해 주시기 바랍니다.

① 불가산명사 비슷한 것; 비슷한 사람 ❑ 비슷한 대상끼리 비교하고 있는지 반드시 확인해 보아야만 한다. ② 복수명사 좋아하는 것, 기호 ❑ 나는 제마가 무엇을 좋아하고 무엇을 싫어하는지, 어떤 정치적 견해를 갖고 있는지 등등 그녀에 대해 모든 것을 알고 있다고 생각했다. ③ 구 좋다면, 그렇게 하고 싶다면 ❑ 당신만 괜찮으시다면 여기 머무르셔도 됩니다. ⑤ 구 이렇게; 저렇게; 그렇게 ❑ 그것은 이와 같이 열리고 닫힌다. ⑥ 구 이런 식으로, 저런 식으로 ❑ 이런 식으로 너를 방해해서 미안해. ⑦ 구 대략 ❑ 그들은 일 년에 대략 3천 파운드 정도를 받을 수 있다.

복합형-형용사 ~와 같은 ❑ 아름다운 홍자색의 피튜니아 같은 꽃들 ❑ 조그맣고 벌레같은 생물체

형용사 마음에 드는, 호감이 가는 ❑ 그는 근사하고 호감이 가는 사내였다.

① 불가산명사 가능성 ❑ 감염 가능성은 아주 희박하다. ② 단수명사 있음직한 일 ❑ 하지만 자신들이 낸 돈이 좋은 목적으로 쓰이리라는 것을 확신한다면, 사람들은 기꺼이 돈을 내려 할 수도 있다.

① 형용사 있음직한, 가능한 ❑ 찬성 표결이 여전히 결과로 나올 만하다고 전문가들은 말한다. ❑ 이번이 초산이라면, 병원에 너무 일찍 도착하는 게 될 것 같은데요. ● 부사 아마, 십중팔구 ❑ 수익이 2천 5백만 파운드 가량 증가할 가능성이 크다. ② 형용사 ~할 것 같은 ❑ 그러는 동안 신경전은 계속될 듯 하다.

like-minded ADJ Like-minded people have similar opinions, ideas, attitudes, or interests. □ ...the opportunity to mix with hundreds of like-minded people.

형용사 비슷한 생각의, 비슷한 취미의 □ 비슷한 생각을 가진 사람들 수백 명과 어울릴 수 있는 기회

lik|en /ˈlaɪkən/ (likens, likening, likened) V-T If you **liken** one thing or person **to** another thing or person, you say that they are similar. □ She likens marriage to slavery.

타동사 비유하다, 견주다 □ 그녀는 결혼을 노예 제도에 비유한다.

like|ness /ˈlaɪknɪs/ (likenesses) **1** N-SING If two things or people have a **likeness to** each other, they are similar to each other. □ These myths have a startling likeness to one another. **2** N-COUNT A **likeness of** someone is a picture or sculpture of them. □ The museum displays wax likenesses of every US president. **3** N-COUNT If you say that a picture of someone is a good **likeness**, you mean that it looks just like them. □ She says the artist's impression is an excellent likeness of her abductor.

1 단수명사 비슷함, 닮음 □ 이 신화들은 놀라우리만큼 서로 비슷하다. **2** 가산명사 초상, 조각 □ 그 박물관에서는 역대 모든 미국 대통령들을 본뜬 밀랍 인형을 전시한다. **3** 가산명사 꼭 닮은 것 □ 그녀는 그 화가가 자신을 유괴했던 사람과 인상이 꼭 닮았다고 말한다.

Word Link wise ≈ in the direction or manner of : clockwise, likewise, otherwise

like|wise /ˈlaɪkwaɪz/ **1** ADV You use **likewise** when you are comparing two methods, states, or situations and saying that they are similar. □ All attempts by the Socialists to woo him back were spurned. Similar overtures from the right have likewise been rejected. **2** ADV If you do something and someone else does **likewise**, they do the same or a similar thing. [ADV after v] □ He lent money, made donations and encouraged others to do likewise.

1 부사 똑같이, 마찬가지로 □ 그를 설득해서 돌아오게 하려고 사회주의자들이 여러 번 시도는 했으나 모두 퇴짜를 맞았다. 우익 쪽에서도 그에게 비슷한 제안을 건네 보았으나, 역시 거절당했다. **2** 부사 똑같이 □ 그는 돈을 빌려 주고 기부를 했으며, 다른 사람들에게도 그렇게 하도록 격려했다.

lik|ing /ˈlaɪkɪŋ/ **1** N-SING If you have **a liking for** something or someone, you like them. □ She had a liking for good clothes. □ He bought me records to encourage my liking for music. **2** PHRASE If something is, for example, too fast **for** your **liking**, you would prefer it to be slower. If it is not fast enough **for** your **liking**, you would prefer it to be faster. □ He had become too powerful for their liking. **3** PHRASE If something is **to** your **liking**, it suits your interests, tastes, or wishes. □ London was more to his liking than Rome.

1 단수명사 좋아함, 기호, 취미 □ 그녀는 멋진 옷을 좋아했다. □ 그는 내가 음악을 좋아하는 것을 알고 격려차 내게 음반을 사 주었다. **2** 구 ~의 기호에 비추어 볼 때 □ 그들이 보기에는, 그가 지나치게 강력해져 있었다. **3** 구 ~의 마음에 드는 □ 로마보다 런던이 더 그의 마음에 들었다.

li|lac /ˈlaɪlək, -læk, -lək/ (lilacs)

Lilac can also be used as the plural form.

1 N-VAR A **lilac** or a **lilac tree** is a small tree which has sweet-smelling purple, pink, or white flowers in large, cone-shaped groups. □ Lilacs grew against the side wall. **2** COLOR Something that is **lilac** is pale pinkish-purple in color. □ All shades of mauve, lilac, lavender and purple were fashionable.

lilac도 복수형으로 쓸 수 있다.

1 가산명사 또는 불가산명사 라일락 □ 라일락이 옆 담에 기대어 자랐다. **2** 색채어 연보라색 □ 담자색과 연보라색, 옅은 자주색과 보라색 등의 색조가 온통 유행이었다.

lily /ˈlɪli/ (lilies) N-VAR A **lily** is a plant with large flowers that are often white.

가산명사 또는 불가산명사 백합

limb /ˈlɪm/ (limbs) **1** N-COUNT Your **limbs** are your arms and legs. □ She would be able to stretch out her cramped limbs and rest for a few hours. **2** PHRASE If someone goes **out on a limb**, they do something they strongly believe in even though it is risky or extreme, and is likely to fail or be criticized by other people. □ They can see themselves going out on a limb, voting for a very controversial energy bill.

1 가산명사 수족; 손발 □ 그녀는 쥐가 난 손발을 내뻗고 몇 시간 동안이나마 쉴 수 있을 것이다. **2** 구 위태로운 상황에; 비난받기 쉬운 □ 그들은 상황이 좋지 않음을 알면서도 매우 논란이 많은 에너지 법안에 찬성표를 던진다.

lim|bo /ˈlɪmboʊ/ N-UNCOUNT If you say that someone or something is **in limbo**, you mean that they are in a situation where they seem to be caught between two stages and it is unclear what will happen next. □ The negotiations have been in limbo since mid-December.

불가산명사 중간 상태; 어정쩡한 상태 □ 협상은 12월 중순 이래로 어정쩡한 상태에 머물러 왔다.

lime /ˈlaɪm/ (limes) **1** N-VAR A **lime** is a green fruit that tastes like a lemon. Limes grow on trees in tropical countries. □ ...peeled slices of lime. **2** N-COUNT A **lime** is a large tree with pale green leaves. It is often planted in parks in towns and cities. [BRIT; AM **linden**] □ ...dilapidated avenues of limes. **3** N-UNCOUNT **Lime** is a substance containing calcium. It is found in soil and water. □ If your soil is very acid, add lime.

1 가산명사 또는 불가산명사 라임 □ 껍질을 벗겨 얇게 썬 라임 몇 조각 **2** 가산명사 보리수 [영국영어; 미국영어 linden] □ 보리수가 늘어선 황폐한 길 **3** 불가산명사 석회 □ 토양이 강산성이라면, 땅에 석회를 뿌려 보세요.

lime|light /ˈlaɪmlaɪt/ N-UNCOUNT If someone is in the **limelight**, a lot of attention is being paid to them, because they are famous or because they have done something very unusual or exciting. □ Tony has now been thrust into the limelight, with a high-profile job.

불가산명사 세상의 이목, 집중적인 관심 □ 토니는 이제 고위직에 올라 세상의 주목을 한 몸에 받게 되었다.

lime|stone /ˈlaɪmstoʊn/ (limestones) N-MASS **Limestone** is a whitish-colored rock which is used for building and for making cement. □ ...high limestone cliffs.

물질명사 석회암 □ 높은 석회암 절벽

lim|it ♦♢♢ /ˈlɪmɪt/ (limits, limiting, limited) **1** N-COUNT A **limit** is the greatest amount, extent, or degree of something that is possible. □ Her love for him was being tested to its limits. □ There is no limit to how much fresh fruit you can eat in a day. **2** N-COUNT A **limit** of a particular kind is the largest or smallest amount of something such as time or money that is allowed because of a rule, law, or decision. □ The three-month time limit will be up in mid-June. **3** N-COUNT The **limit** of an area is its boundary or edge. □ ...the city limits of Baghdad. **4** N-PLURAL The **limits** of a situation are the facts involved in it which make only some actions or results possible. □ She has to work within the limits of a fairly tight budget. **5** V-T If you **limit** something, you prevent it from becoming greater than a particular amount or degree. □ He limited payments on the country's foreign debt. **6** V-T If you **limit yourself** to something, or if someone or something **limits** you, the number of things that you have or do is reduced. □ It is now accepted that men should limit themselves to 20 units of alcohol a week. ● **lim|it|ing** ADJ □ The conditions laid down to me were not too limiting. **7** V-T If something **is limited to** a particular place or group of people, it exists only in that place, or is had or done only by that group. [usu passive] □ The protests were not limited to New York. **8** →see also **limited 9** PHRASE If an area or a place is **off limits**, you are not allowed to go there. □ A one-mile area around the wreck is still off limits.

1 가산명사 한계; 극한 □ 그에 대한 그녀의 사랑이 한계치까지 시험당하고 있었다. □ 신선한 과일이라면 하루에 얼마든지 먹을 수 있다. **2** 가산명사 한도 □ 석 달로 주어진 기한이 6월 중순경에 끝난다. **3** 가산명사 경계 □ 바그다드 시 경계 **4** 복수명사 제약 □ 그녀는 상당히 빠듯한 예산이라는 제약을 안고 작업을 해 나가야 한다. **5** 타동사 제한하다 □ 그는 자국이 진 외채 상환을 제한했다. **6** 타동사 제한하다 □ 일주일에 섭취하는 알코올 양을 20유닛으로 제한해야 한다는 설이 이제는 받아들여진다. ● 제한하는 형용사 □ 나에게 주어진 조건이 특별히 제한적이었거나 하지는 않았다. **7** 타동사 국한되다 □ 뉴욕 이외의 다른 곳들에서도 항의가 잇따랐다. **9** 구 출입 금지의 □ 그 난파선 근처 1마일 내 주변 지역은 여전히 출입 금지 지역이다.

Thesaurus limit의 참조어

N.	ceiling, maximum **1**
	border, edge, perimeter **3**
V.	check, confine, reduce, restrict **5 6**

Word Partnership	*limit*의 연어	
ADJ.	**lower** limit, **upper** limit **1** **2**	
	legal limit **2**	
PREP.	**beyond the** limit, **over the** limit **2**	
N.	**credit** limit, **term** limit, **time** limit **2**	
	limit **the amount of** *something*, limit **benefits**, limit **damage**,	
	limit **growth**, limit **the number of** *something* **5**	

lim|ta|tion /lɪmɪteɪʰn/ (limitations) **1** N-UNCOUNT The **limitation** of something is the act or process of controlling or reducing it. ❑ *All the talk had been about the limitation of nuclear weapons.* **2** N-VAR A **limitation on** something is a rule or decision which prevents that thing from growing or extending beyond certain limits. ❑ *...a limitation on the tax deductions for people who make more than $100,000 a year.* **3** N-PLURAL If you talk about the **limitations** of someone or something, you mean that they can only do some things and not others, or cannot do something very well. ❑ *I realized how possible it was to overcome your limitations, to achieve well beyond what you believe yourself capable of.* **4** N-VAR A **limitation** is a fact or situation that allows only some actions and makes others impossible. ❑ *This drug has one important limitation. Its effects only last six hours.*

lim|it|ed ♦♢♢ /lɪmɪtɪd/ **1** ADJ Something that is **limited** is not very great in amount, range, or degree. ❑ *They may only have a limited amount of time to get their points across.* **2** ADJ A **limited** company is one whose owners are legally responsible for only a part of any money that it may owe if it goes bankrupt. [BRIT, BUSINESS; AM **incorporated**] [ADJ n, n ADJ] ❑ *They had plans to turn the club into a limited company.*

lim|it|ed edi|tion (limited editions) N-COUNT A **limited edition** is a work of art, such as a book which is only produced in very small numbers, so that each one will be valuable in the future. ❑ *The limited edition of 300 copies was edited by Rebekah Scott.*

lim|it|less /lɪmɪtlɪs/ ADJ If you describe something as **limitless**, you mean that there is or appears to be so much of it that it will never be exhausted. ❑ *...a cheap and potentially limitless supply of energy.*

lim|ou|sine /lɪməzin/ (limousines) N-COUNT A **limousine** is a large and very comfortable car. Limousines are usually driven by a chauffeur and are used by very rich or important people.

limp /lɪmp/ (limps, limping, limped, limper, limpest) **1** V-I If a person or animal **limps**, they walk with difficulty or in an uneven way because one of their legs or feet is hurt. ❑ *I wasn't badly hurt, but I injured my thigh and had to limp.* ● N-COUNT **Limp** is also a noun. ❑ *A stiff knee following surgery forced her to walk with a limp.* **2** ADJ If you describe something as **limp**, you mean that it is soft or weak when it should be firm or strong. ❑ *She was told to reject applicants with limp handshakes.* ● **limp|ly** ADV [ADV with v] ❑ *Flags and bunting hung limply in the still, warm air.* **3** ADJ If someone is **limp**, their body has no strength and is not moving, for example because they are asleep or unconscious. ❑ *He carried her limp body into the room and laid her on the bed.*

line ♦♦♦ /laɪn/ (lines, lining, lined) **1** N-COUNT A **line** is a long thin mark which is drawn or painted on a surface. ❑ *Draw a line down that page's center.* ❑ *...a dotted line.* **2** N-COUNT The **lines** on someone's skin, especially on their face, are long thin marks that appear there as they grow older. ❑ *He has a large, generous face with deep lines.* **3** N-COUNT A **line** of people or things is a number of them arranged one behind the other or side by side. ❑ *The sparse line of spectators noticed nothing unusual.* **4** N-COUNT A **line** of people or vehicles is a number of them that are waiting one behind another, for example in order to buy something or to go in a particular direction. ❑ *Children clutching empty bowls form a line.* **5** N-COUNT A **line** of a piece of writing is one of the rows of words, numbers, or other symbols in it. ❑ *The next line should read: Five days, 23.5 hours.* **6** N-VAR You can refer to a long piece of wire, string, or cable as a **line** when it is used for a particular purpose. ❑ *She put her washing on the line.* ❑ *...a piece of fishing-line.* **7** N-COUNT A **line** is a connection which makes it possible for two people to speak to each other on the telephone. ❑ *The telephone lines went dead.* ❑ *It's not a very good line. Shall we call you back, Susan?* **8** N-COUNT You can use **line** to refer to a telephone number which you can call in order to get information or advice. ❑ *...the 24-hour information line.* **9** N-COUNT A **line** is a route, especially a dangerous or secret one, along which people move or send messages or supplies. ❑ *The American continent's geography severely limited the lines of attack.* ❑ *Negotiators say they're keeping communication lines open.* **10** N-COUNT The **line** in which something or someone moves is the particular route that they take, especially when they keep moving straight ahead. ❑ *Walk in a straight line.* **11** N-COUNT A **line** is a particular route, involving the same stations, roads, or stops along which a train or bus service regularly operates. ❑ *They've got to ride all the way to the end of the line.* **12** N-COUNT A railroad **line** consists of the pieces of metal and wood which form the track that the trains travel along. ❑ *Floods washed out much of the railroad line.* **13** N-COUNT A shipping, air, or bus **line** is a company which provides services for transporting people or goods by sea, air, or bus. [BUSINESS] ❑ *The Foreign Office offered to pay the shipping line all the costs of diverting the ship to Bermuda.* **14** N-COUNT A state or county **line** is a boundary between two states or counties. [AM] ❑ *...the California state line.* **15** N-COUNT You can use **lines** to refer to the set of physical defenses or the soldiers that have been established along the boundary of an area occupied by an army. ❑ *Their unit was shelling the German lines only seven miles away.* **16** N-COUNT The particular **line** that a person has toward a problem is the attitude that they have toward it. For example, if someone takes a **hard line** on something, they have a firm

1 불가산명사 제한 ❑ 모든 회담은 핵무기 제한에 대한 것이었다. **2** 가산명사 불가산명사 한도, 제한 ❑ 연간 10만 달러 이상을 버는 사람들에 대한 세금 공제 한도 **3** 복수명사 한계 ❑ 어떻게 네가 한계를 극복하고 스스로 가능하다고 믿는 것 이상을 이루어내는 일이 가능했는지 깨달았다. **4** 가산명사 또는 불가산명사 제약 ❑ 이 약은 제약이 한 가지 있다. 약효가 6시간 동안만 지속된다.

1 형용사 한정된 ❑ 그들은 제한된 시간 내에 자신들의 취지를 전달해야만 할 것이다. **2** 형용사 유한 책임의 [영국영어, 경제; 미국영어 incorporated] ❑ 그들은 그 조직을 유한 책임 회사로 전환시키고자 계획하고 있었다.

가산명사 한정판 ❑ 300부만 찍어 낸 한정판은 레베카 스콧이 편집했다.

형용사 무한한 ❑ 에너지를 값싸게 무한정 공급할 수 있는 방법

가산명사 리무진

1 자동사 절뚝거리다 ❑ 나는 중상은 아니었지만 허벅지를 다쳐서 절뚝거리고 다녀야 했다. ● 가산명사 발을 절기, 절뚝거림 ❑ 그녀는 수술 이후에 무릎이 뻣뻣해져서 발을 절며 걸어야 했다. **2** 형용사 아무지지 못한, 이완된 ❑ 그녀는 악수를 야무지지 못하게 하는 지원자는 퇴짜를 놓으라고 들었다. ● 아무지지 못하게, 이완되게 ❑ 깃발과 장막이 고요하고 따뜻한 대기 속에 어설프게 걸려 있었다. **3** 형용사 생기 없는, 맥없는 ❑ 그는 맥없이 축 늘어진 그녀를 방 안으로 옮겨 침대에 뉘었다.

1 가산명사 선, 줄 ❑ 그 페이지 중앙에 선을 하나 그어라. ❑ 점선 **2** 가산명사 주름 ❑ 그는 크고 너그러운 얼굴에 깊은 주름이 있다. **3** 가산명사 줄 ❑ 드문드문 늘어선 구경꾼들은 아무런 낌새도 채지 못했다. **4** 가산명사 줄 ❑ 아이들이 빈 그릇을 움켜쥔 채 한 줄로 늘어서 있다. **5** 가산명사 줄, 행 ❑ 다음 행은 아마 이렇게 될 것이다. 5일간, 23.5시간. **6** 가산명사 또는 불가산명사 줄, 끈 ❑ 그녀는 빨랫줄에 세탁물을 널었다. ❑ 낚싯줄 토막 **7** 가산명사 전화 회선; 통화 연결 ❑ 전화가 끊어졌다. ❑ 통화 연결 상태가 좋지 않아. 우리가 나중에 다시 걸까, 수잔? **8** 가산명사 (특정 정보 등을 제공하는) 전화 ❑ 24시간 안내 전화 **9** 가산명사 통로, 경로 ❑ 남북아메리카 대륙의 지형상, 공격 작전을 감행할 만한 통로가 매우 부족했다. ❑ 교섭을 진행하고 있는 사람들은 대화 통로를 열어 놓고 있다고 말한다. **10** 가산명사 진로, 길 ❑ 일직선으로 걸으시오. **11** 가산명사 노선 ❑ 그들은 노선 종점까지 내처 타고 가야만 한다. **12** 가산명사 선로 ❑ 상당 부분의 철도 선로가 홍수로 씻겨 내려갔다. **13** 가산명사 운수 회사 [경제] ❑ 외무성은 배가 버뮤다로 방향을 돌리는 데 드는 모든 비용을 그 해운 회사에 지불하겠다고 제의했다. **14** 가산명사 경계 [미국영어] ❑ 캘리포니아 주 경계 **15** 가산명사 전선, 방어선 ❑ 그들의 부대는 불과 7마일 떨어진 독일 전선을 포격하고 있었다. **16** 가산명사 방침 ❑ 여당인 보수당 쪽 의원 40명이 정부의 뜻을 거슬러 정부 방침에 반대표를 던졌다. **17** 가산명사 (생각 등의) 진전 과정 ❑ 이전 장에서 우리가 논의했던 내용은 이러한 사고의 연장선상이다. **18** 복수명사 ...와 비슷한, ...식의 ❑ "이야, 이 커피, 맛이 환상적인데!" 하는 식으로 커피에 대한 갖은 칭찬이 줄줄이 이어졌다. ❑ 그가 이미 그와 비슷한 말을 했었다. **19** 복수명사 방침, 주의 ❑ 소수 민족주의에 근거를 둔 소위 자치 공화국들 **20** 가산명사 분야, 직업 [경제] ❑ 그래서 너희 아버지 직업이 뭐였지? **21** 가산명사 공정식, 작업 라인 ❑ 세 가지 종류의 각기 다른 제품을 생산할 수 있는 작업 라인 **22** 가산명사

strict policy which they refuse to change. ❑ *Forty members of the governing Conservative party rebelled, voting against the government line.* 🔳 N-COUNT You can use **line** to refer to the way in which someone's thoughts or activities develop, particularly if it is logical. ❑ *Our discussion in the previous chapter continues this line of thinking.* 🔳 N-PLURAL If you say that something happens **along** particular **lines**, or **on** particular **lines**, you are giving a general summary or approximate account of what happens, which may not be correct in every detail. ❑ *There followed an assortment of praise for the coffee along the lines of "Hey, this coffee is fantastic!"* ❑ *He'd said something on those lines already.* 🔳 N-PLURAL If something is organized **on** particular **lines**, or **along** particular **lines**, it is organized according to that method or principle. ❑ *...so-called autonomous republics based on ethnic lines.* 🔳 N-COUNT Your **line of** business or work is the kind of work that you do. [BUSINESS] ❑ *So what was your father's line of business?* 🔳 N-COUNT In a factory, a **line** is an arrangement of workers or machines where a product passes from one worker to another until it is finished. ❑ *...a production line capable of producing three different products.* 🔳 N-COUNT You can use **line** when you are referring to a number of people who are ranked according to status. ❑ *Nicholas Paul Patrick was seventh in the line of succession to the throne.* 🔳 N-COUNT A particular **line** of people or things is a series of them that has existed over a period of time, when they have all been similar in some way, or done similar things. ❑ *We were part of a long line of artists.* 🔳 V-T If people or things **line** a road, room, or other place, they are present in large numbers along its edges or sides. ❑ *Thousands of local people lined the streets and clapped as the procession went by.* 🔳 V-T If you **line** a wall, container, or other object, you put a layer of something such as leaves or paper on the inside surface of it in order to make it stronger, warmer, or cleaner. ❑ *Scoop the blanket weed out and use it to line hanging baskets.* 🔳 →see also **lining, bottom line, front line, picket line** 🔳 PHRASE If you **draw the line at** a particular activity, you refuse to do it, because you disapprove of it or because it is more extreme than what you normally do. ❑ *Letters have come from prisoners, declaring that they would draw the line at hitting an old lady.* 🔳 PHRASE If you do something or if it happens to you **in the line of duty**, you do it or it happens as part of your regular work or as a result of it. ❑ *More than 3,000 police officers were wounded in the line of duty last year.* 🔳 PHRASE If you refer to a method as **the first line of**, for example, defense or treatment, you mean that it is the first or most important method to be used in dealing with a problem. ❑ *Residents have the responsibility of being the first line of defense against wildfires.* 🔳 PHRASE If one object is **in line with** others, or moves **into line with** others, they are arranged in a line. You can also say that a number of objects are **in line** or move **into line**. ❑ *The device itself was right under the vehicle, almost in line with the gear lever.* 🔳 PHRASE If one thing is **in line with** another, or is brought **into line with** it, the first thing is, or becomes, similar to the second, especially in a way that has been planned or expected. ❑ *The structure of our schools is now broadly in line with the major countries of the world.* ❑ *This brings the law into line with most medical opinion.* 🔳 PHRASE If you **keep** someone **in line** or bring them **into line**, you make them obey you, or you make them behave in the way you want them to. ❑ *All this was just designed to frighten me and keep me in line.* 🔳 PHRASE If a machine or piece of equipment comes **on line**, it starts operating. If it is **off line**, it is not operating. ❑ *The new machine will go on line in June 2006.* 🔳 PHRASE If you do something **on line**, you do it using a computer or a computer network. ❑ *They can order their requirements on line.* →see also **online** 🔳 to **sign on the dotted line** →see **dotted, mathematics, train**

Thesaurus	*line*의 참조어
N.	cable, rope, wire 🔳

▶**line up** 🔳 PHRASAL VERB If people **line up** or if you **line** them **up**, they move so that they are standing in a line. ❑ *The senior leaders lined up behind him in orderly rows.* ❑ *The gym teachers lined us up against the cement walls.* 🔳 PHRASAL VERB If you **line** things **up**, you move them into a straight row. ❑ *I would line up my toys on this windowsill and play.* 🔳 PHRASAL VERB-RECIP If you **line** one thing **up with** another, or one thing **lines up with** another, the first thing is moved into its correct position in relation to the second. You can also say that two things **line up**, or **are lined up**. ❑ *You have to line the car up with the ones beside you.* ❑ *Gas cookers are adjustable in height to line up with your kitchen work top.* 🔳 PHRASAL VERB If you **line up** an event or activity, you arrange for it to happen. If you **line** someone **up** for an event or activity, you arrange for them to be available for that event or activity. ❑ *She lined up executives, politicians and educators to serve on the board of directors.* 🔳 →see also **line-up**

lin|ear /lɪniər/ 🔳 ADJ A **linear** process or development is one in which something changes or progresses straight from one stage to another, and has a starting point and an ending point. ❑ *Her novel subverts the conventions of linear narrative. It has no neat chronology and no tidy denouement.* 🔳 ADJ A **linear** shape or form consists of straight lines. ❑ *...the sharp, linear designs of the seventies and eighties.* 🔳 ADJ **Linear** movement or force occurs in a straight line rather than in a curve. ❑ *...linear movement toward a goal.*

line man|ag|er (line managers) N-COUNT Your **line manager** is the person at work who is in charge of your department, group, or project. [mainly BRIT, BUSINESS] ❑ *I believe that my wife is having an affair with her line manager.*

lin|en /lɪnɪn/ (linens) 🔳 N-MASS **Linen** is a kind of cloth that is made from a plant called flax. It is used for making clothes and things such as tablecloths and sheets. ❑ *...a white linen suit.* 🔳 N-UNCOUNT **Linen** is tablecloths, sheets, pillowcases, and similar things made of cloth that are used in the home. [also N in pl] ❑ *...embroidered bed linen.*

lin|er /laɪnər/ (liners) N-COUNT A **liner** is a large ship in which people travel long distances, especially on vacation. ❑ *...luxury ocean liners.*

서열 ❑ 니콜라스 폴 패트릭은 왕위 승계 서열 7순위였다. 🔳 가산명사 대열 ❑ 우리는 예술가들로 이루어진 긴 대열의 일부였다. 🔳 자동사 -을 따라 죽 늘어서다 ❑ 행렬이 지나갈 때 수천 명의 지역 주민들이 도로를 따라 늘어서서 박수를 쳤다. 🔳 타동사 안을 바르다; 안을 대다 ❑ 수북이 난 잡초를 한 삽 떠서 걸이 화분의 안을 바르는 데 쓰세요. 🔳 구 (-까지는) 하지 않다 ❑ 노파를 때리는 일까지는 차마 하지 않겠노라고 선언하는 편지를 죄수들이 보내왔다. 🔳 구 근무 중 ❑ 작년에 3천 명 이상의 경찰관이 근무 중 부상을 입었다. 🔳 구 1차적인 (방어나 대응) ❑ 산불을 1차적으로 막아야 할 책임은 주민들에게 있다. 🔳 구 -와 일렬로, -와 줄을 맞추어 ❑ 그 장치는 기어 레버와 거의 일렬로 차 바로 밑에 있었다. 🔳 구 -와 비슷한; -와 일치되게 ❑ 현재 우리나라의 학교 체계는 세계 주요 국가들과 거의 비슷하다. ❑ 이 점에서 법은 대부분의 의학적 견해와 일치한다. 🔳 구 복종시키다, 시키는 대로 하게 하다 ❑ 이 모든 일은 나를 겁주어서 말을 듣게 하려고 계획된 것이었다. 🔳 구 가동하는; 가동하지 않는 ❑ 새 기계는 2006년 6월에 가동될 것이다. 🔳 구 전산망으로 ❑ 그들은 전산망으로 필요한 것들을 주문할 수 있다.

🔳 구동사 한 줄로 서다; 한 줄로 세우다 ❑ 원로 지도자들이 그의 뒤에 정렬해서 줄을 섰다. ❑ 체육 교사들이 우리를 시멘트 벽 앞의 한 줄로 세웠다. 🔳 구동사 한 줄로 늘어놓다 ❑ 내가 이 창턱에 장난감들을 일렬로 세워 놓고 놀곤 했었지. 🔳 상호 구동사 정렬시키다; 정렬하다 ❑ 당신은 옆에 있는 차들에 맞춰서 그 차를 정렬시켜야 한다. ❑ 가스레인지의 높이를 주방 조리대에 맞추어 조절할 수 있습니다. 🔳 구동사 준비하다, 전용을 짜다 ❑ 그녀는 이사회 일을 볼 사람들을 간부들과 정치가, 교육자 등으로 구성했다.

🔳 형용사 선형의, 일렬의 ❑ 그녀가 쓴 소설은 전형적인 일렬적 서사 구조를 뒤엎는다. 그 소설 어디에서도 정연한 연대기적 전후 관계나 깔끔한 대단원을 찾아볼 수 없다. 🔳 형용사 직선의 ❑ 직선으로만 이루어진 70, 80년대의 날카로운 디자인들 🔳 형용사 직선적인 ❑ 목표를 향해 똑바로 나아가기

가산명사 직속 상사 [주로 영국영어, 경제] ❑ 나는 아내가 직속 상사와 바람을 피우고 있다고 믿는다.

🔳 물질명사 아마포, 리넨 ❑ 흰색 리넨 정장 🔳 불가산명사 리넨 제품 (식탁보, 침구류) ❑ 수가 놓인 침구류

가산명사 정기선 ❑ 호화로운 대양 항로 정기 운항선

lines|man /ˈlaɪnzmən/ (**linesmen**) N-COUNT A **linesman** is an official who assists the referee or umpire in games such as football and tennis by indicating when the ball goes over the lines around the edge of the field or court.

가산명사 (구기 종목) 선심(線審)

line-up (**line-ups**) N-COUNT A **line-up** is a group of people or a series of things that have been gathered together to be part of a particular event. ❑ *Ryan Giggs is likely to be in Wales's starting line-up for their World Cup qualifying match.*

가산명사 진용, 구성 ❑ 라이언 긱스가 웨일스 팀의 월드컵 예선 경기 선발 명단에 들 것 같다.

lin|ger /ˈlɪŋɡər/ (**lingers**, **lingering**, **lingered**) **1** V-I When something such as an idea, feeling, or illness **lingers**, it continues to exist for a long time, often much longer than expected. ❑ *The scent of her perfume lingered on in the room.* ❑ *He was ashamed. That feeling lingered, and he was never comfortable in church after that.* **2** V-I If you **linger** somewhere, you stay there for a longer time than is necessary, for example because you are enjoying yourself. ❑ *Customers are welcome to linger over coffee until around midnight.*

1 자동사 질질 끌다; 좀처럼 없어지지 않다 ❑ 그녀의 향수 냄새가 방 안에 계속 남아 있었다. ❑ 그는 부끄러웠다. 그런 기분은 좀처럼 없어지지 않았고, 그 이후로 그는 교회에서 편안함을 느낄 수 없었다. **2** 자동사 오래 머무르다 ❑ 고객들께서는 커피를 마시면서 자정 무렵까지 마음대로 머물러 계실 수 있습니다.

lin|gerie /ˈlɒnʒəreɪ, ˌlæn-, BRIT ˈlænʒəri/ N-UNCOUNT **Lingerie** is women's underwear and nightclothes. ❑ *...a new range of lingerie.*

불가산명사 란제리, 여성 속옷류 ❑ 란제리 신제품류

lin|guist /ˈlɪŋɡwɪst/ (**linguists**) **1** N-COUNT A **linguist** is someone who is good at speaking or learning foreign languages. ❑ *He had a scholarly air and was an accomplished linguist.* **2** N-COUNT A **linguist** is someone who studies or teaches linguistics. ❑ *Many linguists have looked at language in this way.*

1 가산명사 외국어에 능한 사람 ❑ 그는 학자적인 풍모를 지녔고 외국어에 능통했다. **2** 가산명사 언어학자 ❑ 많은 언어학자들이 언어를 이런 시각에서 보아 왔다.

lin|guis|tic /lɪŋˈɡwɪstɪk/ (**linguistics**) **1** ADJ **Linguistic** abilities or ideas relate to language or linguistics. ❑ *...linguistic skills.* **2** N-UNCOUNT **Linguistics** is the study of the way in which language works. ❑ *Modern linguistics emerged as a distinct field in the nineteenth century.*

1 형용사 어학의, 언어의 ❑ 언어 능력 **2** 불가산명사 언어학 ❑ 현대 언어학은 19세기에 독자적인 한 연구 분야로 떠올랐다.

lin|ing /ˈlaɪnɪŋ/ (**linings**) **1** N-VAR The **lining** of something such as a piece of clothing or a curtain is a layer of cloth attached to the inside of it in order to make it thicker or warmer, or in order to make it hang better. ❑ *...a padded satin jacket with quilted lining.* **2** N-COUNT The **lining** of your stomach or other organ is a layer of tissue on the inside of it. ❑ *...a bacterium that attacks the lining of the stomach.* **3** →see also **line**

1 가산명사 또는 불가산명사 안감 ❑ 누비 안감을 덧댄 공단 재킷 **2** 가산명사 내벽 ❑ 위 내벽을 공격하는 박테리아

link ♦♦♢ /lɪŋk/ (**links**, **linking**, **linked**) **1** N-COUNT If there is a **link between** two things or situations, there is a relationship between them, for example because one thing causes or affects the other. ❑ *...the link between smoking and lung cancer.* **2** V-T If someone or something **links** two things or situations, there is a relationship between them, for example because one thing causes or affects the other. ❑ *The UN Security Council has linked any lifting of sanctions to compliance with the ceasefire terms.* ❑ *The study further strengthens the evidence linking smoking with early death.* →see also **index-linked** **3** N-COUNT A **link between** two things or places is a physical connection between them. ❑ *...the high-speed rail link between London and the Channel Tunnel.* ❑ *The new road schemes include a link between Chelmsford and the M25.* **4** V-T If two places or objects **are linked** or something **links** them, there is a physical connection between them. ❑ *...the Rama Road, which links the capital, Managua, with the Caribbean coast.* ❑ *The campus is linked by regular bus services to Coventry.* **5** N-COUNT A **link** between two people, organizations, or places is a friendly or business connection between them. ❑ *Kiev hopes to cement close links with Bonn.* ❑ *In 1984 the long link between AC Cars and the Hurlock family was severed.* **6** N-COUNT A **link** to another person or organization is something that allows you to communicate with them or have contact with them. ❑ *She was my only link with the past.* ❑ *The Red Cross was created to provide a link between soldiers in battle and their families at home.* **7** V-T If you **link** one person or thing to another, you claim that there is a relationship or connection between them. ❑ *Criminologist Dr Ann Jones has linked the crime to social circumstances.* ❑ *They've linked her with various men, including magnate Donald Trump.* **8** N-COUNT In computing, a **link** is a connection between different documents, or between different parts of the same document, using hypertext. ❑ *Available in English, French, German, and Italian, it has links to other relevant tourism sites.* ● V-T **Link** is also a verb. ❑ *Certainly, Andreessen didn't think up using hypertext to link Internet documents.* **9** N-COUNT A **link** is one of the rings in a chain. ❑ *...a chain of heavy gold links.* **10** V-T If you **link** one thing with another, you join them by putting one thing through the other. ❑ *She linked her arm through his.* ● PHRASE If two or more people **link arms**, or if one person **links arms** with another, they stand next to each other, and each person puts their arm round the arm of the person next to them. ❑ *It was so slippery that some of the walkers linked arms and proceeded very carefully.* **11** →see also **link-up**

1 가산명사 관련 ❑ 흡연과 폐암 사이의 관련 **2** 타동사 관련짓다, 결부하다 ❑ 유엔 안전 보장 이사회는 정전 협정에 응하느냐 여부를 제재 완화와 결부시켜 왔다. ❑ 그 연구는 흡연이 조기 사망과 관련 있음을 보여 주는 증거에 신빙성을 더해 준다. **3** 가산명사 연결 ❑ 런던과 해저 터널 사이를 잇는 고속 철도 ❑ 새 도로 계획에는 첼름스퍼드와 엠25번 도로를 잇는 연결 도로도 포함된다. **4** 타동사 연결되다; 연결하다 ❑ 수도인 마나과와 카리브 해 연안을 잇는 라마 도로 ❑ 캠퍼스는 코벤트리까지 정기 버스 노선이 있습니다. **5** 가산명사 관계, 친분 ❑ 키예프는 본과 친밀한 관계를 다지기를 바란다. ❑ 1984년에 에이시 자동차와 허록 집안 간의 오랜 친분 관계가 끊어지고 말았다. **6** 가산명사 (비유적) 연결 고리 ❑ 그녀는 지난 시절과 나를 이어주는 유일한 연결 고리였다. ❑ 적십자는 전장에 있는 병사들이 고향에 있는 가족들과 연락을 취할 수 있도록 해 주기 위해 만들어졌다. **7** 타동사 관련이 있다고 주장하다 ❑ 범죄학자 앤 존스 박사는 범죄가 사회적인 환경과 관련이 있다고 주장해 왔다. ❑ 그들은 그녀가 거물 도널드 트럼프를 비롯한 여러 남자들과 연루되어 있다고 주장해 왔다. **8** 가산명사 (컴퓨터) 링크 ❑ 영어, 프랑스 어, 독일어, 그리고 이탈리아 어로도 이용이 가능하며, 관련이 있는 다른 여행 사이트에 링크도 되어 있다. ● 타동사 (컴퓨터) 링크하다 ❑ 분명히, 앤드리슨은 인터넷 문서를 링크하기 위해 하이퍼텍스트를 사용하는 것은 생각해 내지 못했다. **9** 가산명사 (사슬의) 고리 ❑ 고리가 굵은 묵직한 금목걸이 **10** 타동사 (끼워서) 잇다 ❑ 그녀는 그의 팔짱을 꼈다. ● 구 팔짱을 끼다 ❑ 바닥이 아주 미끄러워서 몇몇 행인들은 서로 팔짱을 끼고 아주 조심스럽게 걸어갔다.

Word Partnership	*link*의 연어
ADJ.	**direct** link, **possible** link, **vital** link **1 3 5 6**
	strong/weak link **1 5 6**
V.	**establish** a link, **find** a link **1 3 5 6**
	attempt to link **2 4 7 10**
	click on a link **8**

▶**link up** **1** PHRASAL VERB-RECIP If you **link up with** someone, you join them for a particular purpose. ❑ *They linked up with a series of local anti-nuclear and anti-apartheid groups.* **2** PHRASAL VERB If one thing **is linked up to** another, the two things are connected to each other. ❑ *The television screens of the next century will be linked up to an emerging world telecommunications grid.*

1 상호 구동사 연합하다 ❑ 그들은 일련의 반핵 및 반인종차별 단체와 연합을 했다. **2** 구동사 연결되다 ❑ 다음 세기의 텔레비전 스크린은 새로 떠오르고 있는 전 세계 원거리 통신망에 연결될 것이다.

link-up (**link-ups**) **1** N-COUNT A **link-up** is a connection between two machines or communication systems. ❑ *...a live satellite link-up with Bonn.* **2** N-COUNT A **link-up** is a relationship or partnership between two organizations. ❑ *...new link-ups between school and commerce.*

1 가산명사 연결 ❑ 독일의 도시, 본과의 실황 위성 연결 **2** 가산명사 연합, 제휴 ❑ 새로운 산학 협동 연계

A

lion /laɪən/ (lions) N-COUNT A **lion** is a large wild member of the cat family that is found in Africa. Lions have yellowish fur, and male lions have long hair on their head and neck.

가산명사 사자

B

lion's share N-SING If a person, group, or project gets **the lion's share of** something, they get the largest part of it, leaving very little for other people. ❑ Military and nuclear research have received the lion's share of public funding.

단수명사 가장 큰 몫 ❑ 군사 및 핵 분야의 연구가 가장 많은 공공 자금을 지원받아 왔다.

C

lip ◇◇◇ /lɪp/ (lips) N-COUNT Your **lips** are the two outer parts of the edge of your mouth. ❑ Wade stuck the cigarette between his lips. →see **face**, **kiss**

가산명사 입술 ❑ 웨이드는 입술 사이에 담배를 끼워 물었다.

D

lip|stick /lɪpstɪk/ (lipsticks) N-MASS **Lipstick** is a colored substance in the form of a stick which women put on their lips. ❑ She was wearing red lipstick. →see **makeup**

물질명사 립스틱 ❑ 그녀는 빨간 립스틱을 바르고 있었다.

E

li|queur /lɪkɜr, -kyuər, BRIT lɪkyʊər/ (liqueurs) N-MASS A **liqueur** is a strong alcoholic drink with a sweet taste. You drink it after a meal. ❑ ...liqueurs such as Grand Marnier and Kirsch.

물질명사 리큐어 (달콤하고 독한 술) ❑ 그랑 마니에르나 키르슈 같은 리큐어

F

liq|uid /lɪkwɪd/ (liquids) **1** N-MASS A **liquid** is a substance which is not solid but which flows and can be poured, for example water. ❑ Drink plenty of liquid. ❑ Boil for 20 minutes until the liquid has reduced by half. **2** ADJ A **liquid** substance is in the form of a liquid rather than being solid or a gas. ❑ Wash in warm water with liquid detergent. ❑ ...liquid nitrogen. **3** ADJ **Liquid** assets are the things that a person or company owns which can be quickly turned into cash if necessary. [BUSINESS] ❑ The bank had sufficient liquid assets to continue operations. →see **matter**

1 물질명사 액체 ❑ 물 종류를 많이 마셔라. ❑ 국물이 절반 정도로 졸아들 때까지 20분 동안 끓여라. **2** 형용사 액체의 ❑ 액체 세제로 더운물에 세탁하세요. ❑ 액화 질소 **3** 형용사 현금화하기 쉬운, 유동적인 [경제] ❑ 그 은행은 영업을 계속해 나가기에 충분한 유동 자산을 보유하고 있었다.

G

H

liq|ui|date /lɪkwɪdeɪt/ (liquidates, liquidating, liquidated) **1** V-T To **liquidate** a company is to close it down and sell all its assets, usually because it is in debt. [BUSINESS] ❑ A unanimous vote was taken to liquidate the company. ● **liq|ui|da|tion** /lɪkwɪdeɪʃʳn/ (liquidations) N-VAR ❑ The company went into liquidation. **2** V-T If a company **liquidates** its assets, its property such as buildings or machinery is sold in order to get money. [BUSINESS] ❑ The company closed down operations and began liquidating its assets in January.

1 타동사 (회사를) 청산하다 [경제] ❑ 투표 결과 전원이 그 회사를 정리해야 한다는 데에 찬성했다. ● 청산 가산명사 또는 불가산명사 ❑ 그 회사는 청산되었다. **2** 타동사 (자산을) 정리하다 [경제] ❑ 그 회사는 1월에 영업을 중지하고 자산을 정리하기 시작했다.

I

J

liq|ui|da|tor /lɪkwɪdeɪtər/ (liquidators) N-COUNT A **liquidator** is a person who is responsible for settling the affairs of a company that is being liquidated. [BUSINESS] ❑ ...the failed company's liquidators.

가산명사 청산인 [경제] ❑ 파산한 그 회사의 청산인

K

li|quid|ity /lɪkwɪdɪti/ N-UNCOUNT In finance, a company's **liquidity** is the amount of cash or liquid assets it has easily available. [BUSINESS] ❑ The company maintains a high degree of liquidity.

불가산명사 유동성 [경제] ❑ 그 회사는 유동 자산을 넉넉하게 보유하고 있다.

L

liq|uid|iz|er /lɪkwɪdaɪzər/ (liquidizers) N-COUNT A **liquidizer** is an electric machine that you use to liquidize food. [mainly BRIT; BRIT also **liquidiser**]

가산명사 (요리용) 믹서기 [주로 영국영어; 영국영어 liquidiser]

M

liq|uor /lɪkər/ (liquors) N-MASS Strong alcoholic drinks such as whiskey, vodka, and gin can be referred to as **liquor**. [AM; BRIT **spirits**] ❑ The room was filled with cases of liquor.

물질명사 독한 증류주, 술 [미국영어; 영국영어 spirits] ❑ 그 방안에 술이 담긴 상자들이 가득 차 있었다.

N

liq|uor store (liquor stores) N-COUNT A **liquor store** is a store which sells beer, wine, and other alcoholic drinks. [AM; BRIT **off-licence**]

가산명사 주류 판매점 [미국영어; 영국영어 off-licence]

O

list ◇◇◇ /lɪst/ (lists, listing, listed) **1** N-COUNT A **list** of things such as names or addresses is a set of them which all belong to a particular category, written down one below the other. ❑ We are making a list of the top ten men we would not want to be married to. ❑ There were six names on the list. →see also **hit list**, **mailing list**, **waiting list** **2** N-COUNT A **list** of things is a set of them that you think of as being in a particular order. ❑ High on the list of public demands is to end military control of broadcasting. ❑ The criminal judicial system always comes up at the top of the list of voters' concerns in focus groups. **3** V-T To **list** several things such as reasons or names means to write or say them one after another, usually in a particular order. ❑ The pupils were asked to list the sports they loved most and hated most. **4** V-T To **list** something in a particular way means to include it in that way in a list or report. ❑ A medical examiner has listed the deaths as homicides. **5** V-T/V-I If a company **is listed**, or if it **lists**, on a stock exchange, it obtains an official quotation for its shares so that people can buy and sell them. [BUSINESS] ❑ It will list on the London Stock Exchange next week with a value of 130 million pounds. **6** →see also **listed**

1 가산명사 목록, 명단 ❑ 우리는 가장 결혼하고 싶지 않은 남자 열 명의 목록을 만들고 있는 중이다. ❑ 그 명단에는 여섯 명의 이름이 올라 있었다. **2** 가산명사 일련 ❑ 대중이 가장 강력하게 요구하는 것 중 하나가 군부가 방송을 더 이상 통제하지 않는 것이다. ❑ 형사 재판 제도는 초점 집단 내 유권자들이 언제나 관심을 기울이는 주제 중 하나이다. **3** 타동사 열거하다, 나열하다 ❑ 학생들은 가장 좋아하는 운동과 가장 싫어하는 운동을 나열해 보라는 질문을 받았다. **4** 타동사 목록에 올리다 ❑ 검시관이 사인을 살인으로 기록했다. **5** 타동사/자동사 상장되다 [경제] ❑ 그 회사는 다음 주 런던 증권 거래소에 평가액 1억 3천만 파운드로 상장될 것이다.

P

Q

R

S

	Word Partnership	list의 연어
V.	add *someone/something* to a list, list **includes**, make a list **1 2**	
N.	list **of** candidates, list **of** demands, guest list, list **of** ingredients, list **of** items, list **of** names, price list, list **of** questions, reading list, list **of** things, wine list, wish list, list **of** words **1 2**	
ADJ.	complete list, long list, short list **1 2**	

T

U

list|ed /lɪstɪd/ ADJ In Britain, a **listed** building is protected by law against being destroyed or altered because it is historically or architecturally important. ❑ About 2 percent of the population lives in a listed building.

형용사 문화재로 등록된 ❑ 인구의 약 2퍼센트가 문화재로 등록된 건물에 산다.

V

list|ed com|pa|ny (listed companies) N-COUNT A **listed company** is a company whose shares are quoted on a stock exchange. [BUSINESS] ❑ Some of Australia's largest listed companies are expected to announce huge interim earnings this week.

가산명사 상장 회사 [경제] ❑ 호주 최대의 몇몇 상장 회사들이 이번 주에 막대한 잠정 소득을 발표할 것으로 예상된다.

W

X

lis|ten ◇◇◇ /lɪsʳn/ (listens, listening, listened) **1** V-I If you **listen to** someone who is talking or **to** a sound, you give your attention to them or it. ❑ He spent his time listening to the radio. ● **lis|ten|er** (listeners) N-COUNT ❑ One or two listeners had fallen asleep while the President was speaking. **2** V-I If you **listen for** a sound, you keep alert and are ready to hear it if it occurs. ❑ We listen for footsteps approaching. ● PHRASAL VERB **Listen out** means the same as **listen**. [BRIT] ❑ I didn't really listen out for the lyrics. **3** V-I If you **listen to** someone, you do what they advise you to do, or you believe them. ❑ Anne, you need to listen to me this time.

1 자동사 귀를 기울이다, 듣다 ❑ 그는 라디오를 들으며 시간을 보냈다. ● 청취자, 청취 가산명사 ❑ 대통령이 연설하는 동안 청중 한두 명이 잠들어 버리고 말았다. **2** 자동사 소리가 들리는지 귀를 기울이다 ❑ 우리는 다가오는 발소리가 나는지 들어 보려고 귀를 쫑긋 세운다. ● 구동사 귀를 기울이다 [영국영어] ❑ 나는 사실 가사에는 귀를 기울이지 않았다. **3** 자동사 듣다, 따르다 ❑ 앤, 이번에는 내 말을

Y

Z

4 CONVENTION You say **listen** when you want someone to pay attention to you because you are going to say something important. ❑ *Listen, I finish at one.*

Thesaurus   *listen*의 참조어

v.   catch, tune in; *(ant.)* ignore **1**
       heed, mind; *(ant.)* ignore **3**

Word Partnership   *listen*의 연어

v.   listen **to** *someone's* **voice** **1**
       sit *up* **and** listen, **willing to** listen **1**–**3**

Do not confuse **listen** and **hear**. If you want to say that someone is paying attention to something they can hear, you say that they **are listening to** it. ❑ *He turned on the radio and listened to the news.* Note that **listen** is not followed directly by an object. You must always say that you **listen to** something. However, **listen** can also be used on its own without an object. ❑ *I was laughing too much to listen.* You use **hear** to talk about sounds that you are aware of because they reach your ears. You often use **can** with **hear**. ❑ *I can hear him yelling and swearing.*

따라 줘야겠어. **4** 관용 표현 들어 봐, 이봐 ❑ 들어 봐, 난 1시에 끝나.

listen과 hear를 혼동하지 않도록 하라. 누가 자기가 들을 수 있는 것에 주의를 기울인다고 말할 때는 그들이 그것에 listen을 한다고 표현한다. ❑ *그는 라디오를 켜고 뉴스를 들었다.* listen 다음에는 바로 목적어가 따라오지 않음을 유의하라. 항상 listen to something이라고 표현한다. 그렇지만, listen이 목적어 없이 그냥 쓰일 수도 있다. ❑ *나는 너무 많이 웃느라 듣지를 못했다.* 귀에 들리기 때문에 의식하는 소리에 대해 말할 때는 hear를 쓴다. hear는 흔히 can과 함께 쓴다. ❑ *내 귀에 그가 고함지르고 욕하는 소리가 들린다.*

▶**listen in** PHRASAL VERB If you **listen in** to a private conversation, you secretly listen to it. ❑ *He assigned federal agents to listen in to Martin Luther King's phone calls.*

구동사 엿듣다 ❑ *그는 연방 첩보원을 배치해서 마틴 루터 킹의 전화 통화를 엿들게 했다.*

lis|ten|er /lɪsnər/ (listeners) **1** N-COUNT A **listener** is a person who listens to the radio or to a particular radio program. ❑ *I'm a regular listener to her show.* **2** N-COUNT If you describe someone as a good **listener**, you mean that they listen carefully and sympathetically to you when you talk, for example about your problems. ❑ *Dr Brian was a good listener.* **3** →see also **listen**
→see **radio**

1 가산명사 청취자 ❑ *나는 그녀가 진행하는 쇼의 고정 청취자이다.* **2** 가산명사 남의 말을 잘 들어 주는 사람 ❑ *브라이언 박사는 다른 사람의 말을 잘 들어 주었다.*

list|less /lɪstlɪs/ ADJ Someone who is **listless** has no energy or enthusiasm. ❑ *He was listless and pale and wouldn't eat much.* ● **list|less|ly** ADV [ADV with v] ❑ *Usually, you would just sit listlessly, too hot to do anything else.*

형용사 얼이 없는, 멍한 ❑ *그는 핼쑥한 얼굴로 멍하게 있는 데다 잘 먹지도 않았다.* ● 얼이 없이, 멍하게 부사 ❑ *그 밖의 또 다른 일을 하기에는 너무 더워서 너는 대개 그저 멍하게 앉아 있곤 했다.*

list price (list prices) N-COUNT The **list price** of an item is the price which the manufacturer suggests that a storekeeper should charge for it. ❑ *...a small car with a list price of £18,000.*

가산명사 소매가격 ❑ *소매가격이 18,000파운드인 소형차*

lit /lɪt/ **Lit** is a past tense and past participle of **light**.

light의 과거 및 과거 분사

li|ter /lɪtər/ (liters) [BRIT litre] N-COUNT A **liter** is a metric unit of volume that is a thousand cubic centimeters. It is equal to 2.11 American pints or 1.76 British pints. ❑ *...a 13-thousand liter water tank.* ❑ *It is sold to the public at eight cents a liter.*

[영국영어 litre] 가산명사 리터 ❑ *1만 3천 리터짜리 물탱크* ❑ *그것은 일반인에게는 리터당 8센트에 판매된다.*

lit|er|a|cy /lɪtərəsi/ N-UNCOUNT **Literacy** is the ability to read and write. ❑ *Many adults have some problems with literacy and numeracy.*

불가산명사 읽고 쓰는 능력 ❑ *다수의 성인들이 읽고 쓰는 능력과 기본 계산력에 다소 문제가 있다.*

Word Link   liter ≈ letter : il**liter**ate, **liter**al, **liter**ary

---

lit|er|al /lɪtərəl/ **1** ADJ The **literal** sense of a word or phrase is its most basic sense. ❑ *In many cases, the people there are fighting, in a literal sense, for their homes.* **2** ADJ A **literal** translation is one in which you translate each word of the original work rather than giving the meaning of each expression or sentence using words that sound natural. ❑ *A literal translation of the name Tapies is "walls."*

1 형용사 글자 그대로의, 사전적인 ❑ *그곳의 많은 사람들이 말 그대로 순전히 살아 나갈 터전을 지키기 위해 싸우고 있다.* **2** 형용사 글자 그대로의, 직역의 ❑ *Tapies라는 이름을 직역하면 '벽'이 된다.*

lit|er|al|ly /lɪtərəli/ **1** ADV You can use **literally** to emphasize an exaggeration. Some careful speakers of English think that this use is incorrect. [EMPHASIS] ❑ *We've got to get the economy under control or it will literally eat us up.* **2** ADV You use **literally** to emphasize that what you are saying is true, even though it seems exaggerated or surprising. [EMPHASIS] ❑ *Putting on an opera is a tremendous enterprise involving literally hundreds of people.* **3** ADV If a word or expression is translated **literally**, its most simple or basic meaning is translated. ❑ *The word "volk" translates literally as "folk."*

1 부사 말 그대로, 완전히 [강조] ❑ *우리는 경제를 잘 관리해야만 한다. 그렇지 않으면 그녀가 말 그대로 우리를 잡아먹어 버릴 것이다.* **2** 부사 정말로 [강조] ❑ *오페라 한 편을 상연하는 것은 말 그대로 수백 명의 인력을 동원하는 엄청난 기획이다.* **3** 부사 글자 뜻 그대로 ❑ *'volk'라는 단어를 직역하면, 'folk'가 된다.*

lit|er|ary ◆◇◇ /lɪtəreri, BRIT lɪtərəri/ **1** ADJ **Literary** means concerned with or connected with the writing, study, or appreciation of literature. ❑ *Her literary criticism focuses on the way great literature suggests ideas.* ❑ *She's the literary editor of the "Sunday Review".* **2** ADJ **Literary** words and expressions are often unusual in some way and are used to create a special effect in a piece of writing such as a poem, speech, or novel. ❑ *...archaic, literary words from the Tang dynasty.*

1 형용사 문학의 ❑ *그녀의 문학 비평은 저명한 문학 작품들이 어떻게 사상을 개진하는지에 초점을 맞추고 있다.* ❑ *그녀는 '선데이 리뷰' 지의 문학 담당이다.* **2** 형용사 문어적인 ❑ *당 왕조 시기의 고대 문어*

lit|er|ate /lɪtərɪt/ ADJ Someone who is **literate** is able to read and write. ❑ *Over one-quarter of the adult population are not fully literate.* →see also **computer-literate**

형용사 글을 읽고 쓸 줄 아는 ❑ *성인 인구 전체의 4분의 1 이상이 읽고 쓰는 능력을 완전히 갖추지 못하고 있다.*

lit|era|ture ◆◇◇ /lɪtərətʃər, -tʃʊr, BRIT lɪtrətʃə/ (literatures) **1** N-VAR Novels, plays, and poetry are referred to as **literature**, especially when they are considered to be good or important. ❑ *...classic works of literature.* ❑ *I have spent my life getting to know diverse literatures of different epochs.* **2** N-UNCOUNT The **literature** on a particular subject of study is all the books and articles that have been published about it. ❑ *The literature on immigration policy is almost unrelievedly critical of the state.* **3** N-UNCOUNT **Literature** is written information produced by people who want to sell you something or give you advice. ❑ *I am sending you literature from two other companies that provide a similar service.*

1 가산명사 또는 불가산명사 문학 ❑ *고전 문학 작품* ❑ *나는 여러 시대의 다양한 문학을 경험하는 데 내 일생을 바쳐 왔다.* **2** 불가산명사 문헌 ❑ *이민 정책에 대해 다루는 문헌은 거의 변함없이 정부에 대해 비판적이다.* **3** 불가산명사 인쇄물, 정보지 ❑ *비슷한 서비스를 제공하는 각기 다른 두 회사의 정보지를 보내 드립니다.*

liti|ga|tion /lɪtɪgeɪʃən/ N-UNCOUNT **Litigation** is the process of fighting or defending a case in a civil court of law. ❑ *The settlement ends more than four years of litigation on behalf of the residents.*

불가산명사 소송 ❑ *거주자들의 이익을 대변하여 4년 넘게 끌어 온 소송이 마무리된다.*

a
b
c
d
e
f
g
h
i
j
k
l
m
n
o
p
q
r
s
t
u
v
w
x
y
z

li|tre /líːtər/ →see liter

lit|ter /líɪtər/ (litters, littering, littered) **1** N-UNCOUNT **Litter** is garbage or trash that is left lying around outside. ❑ *If you see litter in the corridor, pick it up.* **2** V-T If a number of things **litter** a place, they are scattered around it or over it. ❑ *Glass from broken bottles litters the pavement.* ● **lit|tered** ADJ [v-link ADJ prep] ❑ *The entrance hall is littered with toys and wellington boots.* **3** ADJ If something is **littered with** things, it contains many examples of it. [v-link ADJ with n] ❑ *History is littered with men and women spurred into achievement by a father's disregard.* **4** N-COUNT A **litter** is a group of animals born to the same mother at the same time. ❑ *...a litter of pups.*

1 불가산명사 쓰레기 ❑ 복도에서 쓰레기를 보면 주워라. **2** 타동사 어지럽게 널려 있다, -에 흩어져 있다 ❑ 깨진 유리병 조각이 보도 위에 널려 있다. ● 어지럽게 널린 형용사 ❑ 현관 입구에 장난감과 장화가 어지럽게 널려 있다. **3** 형용사 -가 많이 있는 ❑ 아버지의 무관심에 오히려 자극을 받아 위업을 이룬 남녀들이 역사상 많이 존재한다. **4** 가산명사 (동물의) 한배 새끼 ❑ 함께 태어난 강아지들

---

little

① DETERMINER, QUANTIFIER, AND ADVERB USES
② ADJECTIVE USES

---

① lit|tle ♦♦♦ /líɪtᵊl/ **1** DET You use **little** to indicate that there is only a very small amount of something. You can use "so," "too," and "very" in front of **little**. ❑ *I had little money and little free time.* ❑ *I find that I need very little sleep these days.* ● QUANT **Little** is also a quantifier. [QUANT of def-n] ❑ *Little of the existing housing is of good enough quality.* ● PRON **Little** is also a pronoun. ❑ *He ate little, and drank less.* ❑ *In general, employers do little to help the single working mother.* **2** ADV **Little** means not very often or to only a small extent. [ADV with v] ❑ *On their way back to Marseille they spoke very little.* **3** DET **A little** of something is a small amount of it, but not very much. You can also say **a very little**. ❑ *Mrs Caan needs a little help getting her groceries home.* ❑ *A little food would do us all some good.* ● PRON **Little** is also a pronoun. ❑ *They get paid for it. Not much. Just a little.* ● QUANT **Little** is also a quantifier. [QUANT of def-n-uncount/sing] ❑ *Pour a little of the sauce over the chicken.* **4** ADV If you do something **a little**, you do it for a short time. [ADV after v] ❑ *He walked a little by himself in the garden.* **5** ADV **A little** or **a little bit** means to a small extent or degree. ❑ *He complained a little of a nagging pain between his shoulder blades.* ❑ *He was a little bit afraid of his father's reaction.*

1 한정사 거의 없는 ❑ 나는 돈도 없지만 여가 시간도 거의 없다. ● 수량사 소량의 ❑ 지금까지 존재하는 주택 중에서 딱히 품질이 뛰어나다고 할 만한 게 거의 없다. ● 대명사 조금 ❑ 그는 음식을 조금밖에 먹지 않았고, 술은 거의 입에 대지도 않았다. ❑ 일반적으로, 혼자 벌어서 아이를 키우는 독신모를 돕기 위해 고용주들이 하는 일이란 거의 없다. **2** 부사 거의 - 아닌 ❑ 마르세유로 돌아오면서 그들은 거의 말을 하지 않았다. **3** 한정사 약간의, 조금의 ❑ 칸 부인이 식료품을 집까지 가져가는 데 약간의 도움을 필요로 한다. ❑ 약간의 음식이라도 우리 모두에게 어느 정도씩은 도움이 될 것이다. ● 대명사 약간, 조금 ❑ 그들은 그 일에 대해 받는다. 많지는 않아. 단지 약간의 돈이지. ● 수량사 약간, 조금 ❑ 닭 요리 위에 소스를 약간 부어 주세요. **4** 부사 잠시 동안 ❑ 그는 잠시 동안 뜰 안을 홀로 거닐었다. **5** 부사 약간, 조금 ❑ 그는 견갑골 사이에서 약간의 통증이 가시지 않고 계속된다고 호소했다. ❑ 그는 아버지가 어떤 반응을 보이실까 약간 걱정스러워 했다.

You can use the adjective **little** to talk about things that are small. ❑ *...a little house...little children.* However, **little** is not normally used to emphasize or draw attention to the fact that something is small. For instance, you do not usually say "The town is little" or "I have a very little car," but you can say "The town is small" or "I have a very small car." **Little** is a less precise word than **small**, and may be used to suggest the speaker's feelings or attitude toward the person or thing being described. For that reason, **little** is often used after another adjective. ❑ *What a nice little house you've got here!... Shut up, you horrible little boy!* **Little** and **a little** are both used as determiners in front of uncount nouns, but they do not have the same meaning. For example, if you say "**I have a little money**," this is a positive statement and you are saying that you have some money. However, if you say "**I have little money**," this is a negative statement and you are saying that you have almost no money.

어떤 작은 것에 대해 말할 때 형용사 little을 쓸 수 있다. ❑ ...작은 집...어린 아이들. 그러나, 보통 어떤 것이 작다는 사실을 강조하거나 그 사실에 주의를 끌 때는 little을 쓰지 않는다. 예를 들어, 일반적으로 "The town is little."이나 "I have a very little car."라고는 하지 않고, "The town is small." 혹은 "I have a very small car."라고 쓴다. little은 small보다 정확하지 못한 단어로, 묘사하고 있는 사람이나 사물에 대한 화자의 느낌이나 태도를 나타내는 데 쓰인다. 그러한 이유로 little은 흔히 다른 형용사 뒤에 쓰인다. ❑ 당신은 이곳에 정말 자그마하고 멋진 집을 가지고 있군요!... 입 닥쳐, 이 끔찍한 애새끼! little과 a little은 둘 다 불가산명사 앞에서 한정사로 쓰이지만, 뜻이 같지는 않다. 예를 들어, I have a little money라고 하면, 이것은 긍정적인 진술로 돈을 좀 가지고 있다는 뜻이다. 그러나, I have little money라고 하면, 이것은 부정적인 진술로 돈이 거의 없다는 뜻이다.

---

② lit|tle ♦♦♦ /líɪtᵊl/ (littler, littlest)

The comparative **littler** and the superlative **littlest** are sometimes used in spoken English for meanings **1**, **3**, and **4**, but otherwise the comparative and superlative forms of the adjective **little** are not used.

비교급 littler와 최상급 littlest는 가끔 구어체 영어에서 의미 **1**, **3**, **4**로 쓰이지만, 그 밖의 경우에는 형용사 little의 비교급, 최상급 형태는 쓰지 않는다.

---

1 ADJ **Little** things are small in size. **Little** is slightly more informal than **small**. ❑ *We sat around a little table, eating and drinking wine.* **2** ADJ You use **little** to indicate that someone or something is small, in a pleasant and attractive way. [ADJ n] ❑ *She's got the nicest little house not far from the library.* ❑ *...a little old lady.* **3** ADJ Your **little** sister or brother is younger than you are. [ADJ n] ❑ *Whenever Daniel's little sister was asked to do something she always had a naughty reply.* **4** ADJ **A little** distance, period of time, or event is short in length. [ADJ n] ❑ *Just go down the road a little way, turn left, and cross the bridge.* ❑ *Why don't we just wait a little while and see what happens.* **5** ADJ **A little** sound or gesture is quick. [ADJ n] ❑ *I had a little laugh to myself.* ❑ *She stood up quickly, giving a little cry of astonishment.* **6** ADJ You use **little** to indicate that something is not serious or important. [ADJ n] ❑ *...irritating little habits.*

1 형용사 작은 ❑ 우리는 작은 탁자에 둘러앉아 식사를 하고 포도주도 마셨다. **2** 형용사 아담한 ❑ 그녀는 도서관에서 과히 멀지 않은 곳에 자리 잡고 있는 그 아담하면서도 아주 멋진 집을 얻었다. ❑ 아담한 체구의 노부인 **3** 형용사 어린, 연소한 ❑ 다니엘의 여동생에게 뭔가를 하라고 좀 시키면, 그 애는 항상 심술궂게 반항하기 일쑤였다. **4** 형용사 짧은 ❑ 그 길을 조금만 따라 내려가다가 좌회전한 다음, 다리를 건너세요. ❑ 잠시만 기다리면서 무슨 일이 벌어지는지 보는 게 어떨까? **5** 형용사 짧은, 잠시의 ❑ 나는 혼자서 살짝 웃었다. ❑ 그녀는 깜짝 놀라서 외마디 비명을 지르며 벌떡 일어섰다. **6** 형용사 사소한, 대수롭지 않은 ❑ 신경을 거슬리게 하는 사소한 습관들

─── live ───

① VERB USES
② ADJECTIVE USES

① **live** ♦♦♦ /lɪv/ (lives, living, lived) →Please look at category **7** to see if the expression you are looking for is shown under another headword. **1** V-I If someone **lives** in a particular place or with a particular person, their home is in that place or with that person. □ *She has lived here for 10 years.* □ *Where do you live?* **2** V-T/V-I If you say that someone **lives** in particular circumstances or that they **live** a particular kind of life, you mean that they are in those circumstances or that they have that kind of life. □ *We lived quite grandly.* □ *Compared to people living only a few generations ago, we have greater opportunities to have a good time.* **3** V-I If you say that someone **lives for** a particular thing, you mean that it is the most important thing in their life. □ *He lived for his work.* **4** V-T/V-I To **live** means to be alive. If someone **lives to** a particular age, they stay alive until they are that age. □ *He's got a terrible disease and will not live long.* □ *He lived to be 103.* **5** V-I If people **live by** doing a particular activity, they get the money, food, or clothing they need by doing that activity. [no cont] □ *...the last indigenous people to live by hunting.* **6** →see also **living** **7** to **live hand to mouth** →see **hand**

> When you are talking about someone's home, the verb **live** has a different meaning in the continuous tenses than it does in the simple tenses. For example, if you say "**I'm living in Boston**," this suggests that the situation is temporary and you may soon move to a different place. If you say "**I live in Boston**," this suggests that Boston is your permanent home.

▶**live down** PHRASAL VERB If you are unable to **live down** a mistake, failure, or bad reputation, you are unable to make people forget about it. □ *Labour was also unable to live down its reputation as the party of high taxes.*

▶**live off** PHRASAL VERB If you **live off** another person, you rely on them to provide you with money. □ *...a man who all his life had lived off his father.*

▶**live on** or **live off** **1** PHRASAL VERB If you **live on** or **live off** a particular amount of money, that amount of money is one in which you buy things. □ *They are earning between $20 and $30 a day. It's enough to live on but not enough to save much.* **2** PHRASAL VERB If you **live on** or **live off** a particular source of income, that is where you get the money that you need. □ *The proportion of Americans living on welfare rose.* **3** PHRASAL VERB If an animal **lives on** or **lives off** a particular food, this is the kind of food that it eats. □ *The fish live on the plankton.*

▶**live on** PHRASAL VERB If someone **lives on**, they continue to be alive for a long time after a particular point in time or after a particular event. □ *I know my life has been cut short by this terrible virus but Daniel will live on after me.*

▶**live up to** PHRASAL VERB If someone or something **lives up to** what they were expected to be, they are as good as they were expected to be. □ *Sales have not lived up to expectations this year.*

② **live** ♦♦◇ /laɪv/ **1** ADJ **Live** animals or plants are alive, rather than being dead or artificial. [ADJ n] □ *...a protest against the company's tests on live animals.* **2** ADJ A **live** television or radio program is one in which an event or performance is broadcast at exactly the same time as it happens, rather than being recorded first. □ *Murray was a guest on a live radio show.* □ *They watch all the live matches.* ● ADV **Live** is also an adverb. [ADV after v] □ *It was broadcast live in 50 countries.* **3** ADJ A **live** performance is given in front of an audience, rather than being recorded and then broadcast or shown in a movie. □ *The Rainbow has not hosted live music since the end of 1981.* □ *A live audience will pose the questions.* ● ADV **Live** is also an adverb. [ADV after v] □ *Kat Bjelland has been playing live with her new band.* **4** ADJ A **live** wire or piece of electrical equipment is directly connected to a source of electricity. □ *The plug broke, exposing live wires.* **5** ADJ **Live** bullets are made of metal, rather than rubber or plastic, and are intended to kill people rather than injure them. □ *They trained in the jungle using live ammunition.*

Thesaurus	*live*의 참조어
v.	dwell, inhabit, occupy, reside ① **1**
	exist ① **4**
	manage, survive ① **5**
ADJ.	alive, active, living, vigorous ② **1**

live-in ♦◇◇ /lɪv ɪn/ **1** ADJ A **live-in** partner is someone who lives in the same house as the person they are having a sexual relationship with, but is not married to them. [ADJ n] □ *She shared the apartment with her live-in partner.* **2** ADJ A **live-in** servant or other domestic worker sleeps and eats in the house where they work. [ADJ n] □ *I have a live-in nanny for my youngest daughter.*

live|li|hood /laɪvlihʊd/ (livelihoods) N-VAR Your **livelihood** is the job or other source of income that gives you the money to buy the things you need. □ *...fishermen who depend on the seas for their livelihood.*

live|ly /laɪvli/ (livelier, liveliest) **1** ADJ You can describe someone as **lively** when they behave in an enthusiastic and cheerful way. □ *She had a sweet, lively personality.* ● **live|li|ness** N-UNCOUNT □ *Amy could sense his liveliness even from where she stood.* **2** ADJ A **lively** event or a **lively** discussion, for example, has lots of interesting and exciting things happening or being said in it. □ *It turned out to*

1 자동사 살다 □ 그녀는 이곳에 십 년 동안 살았다. □ 어디 살아요? **2** 타동사/자동사 살다 □ 우리는 꽤 화려하게 살았다. □ 우리는 겨우 몇 세대 전에 살았던 사람들에 비해 즐거운 시간을 보낼 수 있는 기회가 훨씬 많다. **3** 자동사 -을 위해 살다 □ 그는 인생에서 일이 제일 중요했다. **4** 타동사/자동사 살아 있다 □ 그는 끔찍한 병에 걸려서 오래 못 살 것이다. □ 그는 103세까지 살았다. **5** 자동사 -을 하며 생계를 잇다 □ 사냥으로 생계를 이어간 마지막 토착 민족

누군가가 사는 곳을 말할 때, 동사 live는 진행시제를 사용하면 단순시제를 사용할 때와 뜻이 다르다. 예를 들어, "I'm living in Boston."이라고 하면, 이것은 이 상황이 일시적이며 조만간 다른 곳으로 이사 갈지도 모른다는 의미이다. 만일 "I live in Boston."이라고 말하면, 이것은 보스턴이 장기적인 거주지라는 뜻이다.

구동사 불명예를 씻다 □ 또한 노동당은 높은 세금을 징수한 당이라는 오명을 떨쳐 버릴 수 없었다.

구동사 -에게 얹혀산다 □ 평생 아버지에게 얹혀 산 남자

1 구동사 -으로 생활하다 □ 그들은 하루에 20–30달러를 번다. 그 돈으로 먹고 사는 데는 문제가 없지만 제대로 저축하기에는 부족하다. **2** 구동사 -을 수입원으로 하다 □ 복지 수당을 받아 사는 미국인의 비율이 증가했다. **3** 구동사 -을 먹고 살다 □ 물고기는 플랑크톤을 먹고 산다.

구동사 살아남다 □ 이 끔찍한 바이러스 때문에 내가 오래 못 산다는 것을 알아요. 하지만 다니엘은 내가 죽은 뒤에도 계속 살겠죠.

구동사 (기대에) 부응하다 □ 올해 매출이 기대에 미치지 못했다.

1 형용사 살아 있는 □ 그 회사가 살아 있는 동물을 대상으로 실험하는 것에 대한 항의 **2** 형용사 생방송의 □ 머레이가 생방송 라디오 프로그램에 출연했다. □ 그들은 생방송 경기라면 모조리 본다. ● 부사 생방송으로 □ 이는 50개국에서 생방송되었다. **3** 형용사 라이브의, 실황의 □ 1981년 말 이후로 레인보우에서 라이브 음악 공연이 열린 적이 없었다. □ 관중이 즉석에서 질문을 할 것이다. ● 부사 라이브로, 실황으로 □ 캣 비엘란드는 새 밴드를 결성한 후 라이브 공연을 해 왔다. **4** 형용사 전기가 흐르고 있는 □ 플러그가 깨지면서 전기가 흐르고 있는 전선이 노출되었다. **5** 형용사 실탄의 □ 그들은 정글에서 실탄을 사용하며 훈련했다.

1 형용사 동거하는 □ 그녀는 아파트에서 애인과 동거했다. **2** 형용사 집에서 함께 사는 (일꾼) □ 유모가 집에 같이 살면서 우리 막내딸을 봐 주고 있다.

가산명사 또는 불가산명사 생계 □ 생계를 바다에 의존하는 어민들

1 형용사 명랑한, 활발한 □ 그녀는 사랑스럽고 활발한 성격을 지니고 있었다. ● 명사형, 활발함 불가산명사 □ 에이미는 자신이 서 있는 곳에서도 그의 명랑한 기운을 느낄 수 있었다. **2** 형용사 활발한, 활기찬 □ 활발한 토론으로 매우 흥미로운 회의가 되었다.

a b c d e f g h i j k l m n o p q r s t u v w x y z

be a very interesting session with a lively debate. ● **live|li|ness** N-UNCOUNT *Some may enjoy the liveliness of such a restaurant for a few hours a day or week.* ◼ ADJ Someone who has a **lively** mind is intelligent and interested in a lot of different things. ❑ *She was a very well educated girl with a lively mind, a girl with ambition.*

● 환기 불가산명사 ❑ 어떤 사람은 하루 혹은 일주일에 몇 시간씩은 이런 식당에서 활기찬 기운을 만끽할 수도 있을 것이다. ◼ 형용사 지적 호기심이 강한 ❑ 그녀는 배운 것이 많고 지적 호기심이 강하며 야망을 가진 소녀였다.

Word Partnership lively의 연어

ADV.	**very** lively ◼-◼
N.	lively **atmosphere**, lively **conversation**, lively **debate**, lively **discussion**, lively **music**, lively **performance** ◼
	lively **imagination**, lively **interest**, lively **sense of humor** ◼

liv|en /ˈlaɪvən/ (livens, livening, livened)
▶**liven up** ◼ PHRASAL VERB If a place or event **livens up**, or if something **livens it up**, it becomes more interesting and exciting. ❑ *How could we decorate the room to liven it up?* ❑ *The multicolored rag rug was chosen to liven up the grey carpet.* ◼ PHRASAL VERB If people **liven up**, or if something **livens** them up, they become more cheerful and energetic. ❑ *Talking about her daughters livens her up.*

◼ 구동사 활기를 띠다; 활기를 불어넣다 ❑ 어떤 색을 칠하면 방이 환해 보일까? ❑ 여러 가지 색깔의 카펫을 환하게 반쳐 주기 위해서 알록달록한 깔개를 골랐다. ◼ 구동사 생기를 띠다; 생기를 불어넣다 ❑ 그녀는 딸에 대한 이야기가 나오면 생기를 띤다.

liv|er /ˈlɪvər/ (livers) ◼ N-COUNT Your **liver** is a large organ in your body which processes your blood and helps to clean unwanted substances out of it. ❑ *Three weeks ago, it was discovered the cancer had spread to his liver.* ◼ N-VAR **Liver** is the liver of some animals, especially lambs, pigs, and cows, which is cooked and eaten. ❑ *...grilled calves' liver.* →see **donor**

◼ 가산명사 간 ❑ 삼 주 전에 암이 그의 간까지 퍼진 것이 발견되었다. ◼ 가산명사 또는 불가산명사 간 ❑ 송아지 간 구이

lives ◼ **Lives** is the plural of **life**. ◼ **Lives** is the third person singular form of **live**.

◼ life의 복수 ◼ live의 3인칭 단수형

live|stock /ˈlaɪvstɒk/ N-UNCOUNT-COLL Animals such as cattle and sheep which are kept on a farm are referred to as **livestock**. ❑ *The heavy rains and flooding killed scores of livestock.*

불가산명사-집합 가축 ❑ 폭우와 홍수로 수십 마리의 가축이 폐사했다.

liv|id /ˈlɪvɪd/ ADJ Someone who is **livid** is extremely angry. [INFORMAL] ❑ *I am absolutely livid about it.*

형용사 노발대발한, 격분한 [비격식체] ❑ 나는 그 일에 너무도 화가 난다.

liv|ing ♦♢♢ /ˈlɪvɪŋ/ (livings) ◼ N-COUNT The work that you do for a **living** is the work that you do in order to earn the money that you need. ❑ *Father never talked about what he did for a living.* ◼ N-UNCOUNT You use **living** when you are talking about the quality of people's daily lives. ❑ *Olivia has always been a model of healthy living.* ◼ ADJ You use **living** to talk about the places where people relax when they are not working. [ADJ n] ❑ *The spacious living quarters were on the second floor.*

◼ 가산명사 생계, 생계 수단 ❑ 아버지는 자신의 직업에 대해 단 한 번도 말씀하지 않으셨다. ◼ 불가산명사 생활 ❑ 올리비아는 지금까지 항상 건강한 생활의 모범이었다. ◼ 형용사 생활하는, 거주하는 ❑ 널찍한 생활공간이 2층에 있었다.

living room (living rooms) also **living-room** N-COUNT The **living room** in a house is the room where people sit and relax. ❑ *We were sitting on the couch in the living room watching TV.* →see **house**

가산명사 거실 ❑ 우리는 거실 소파에 앉아 텔레비전을 보고 있었다.

liz|ard /ˈlɪzərd/ (lizards) N-COUNT A **lizard** is a reptile with short legs and a long tail. →see **desert**

가산명사 도마뱀

load ♦♢♢ /loʊd/ (loads, loading, loaded) ◼ V-T If you **load** a vehicle or a container, you put a large quantity of things into it. ❑ *The three men seemed to have finished loading the truck.* ❑ *Mr. Dambar had loaded his plate with lasagne.* ● PHRASAL VERB **Load up** means the same as **load**. ❑ *I've just loaded my truck up.* ❑ *The giggling couple loaded up their red sports car and drove off.* ◼ N-COUNT A **load** is something, usually a large quantity or heavy object, which is being carried. ❑ *He drove by with a big load of hay.* ◼ QUANT If you refer to **a load of** people or things or **loads of** them, you are emphasizing that there are a lot of them. [INFORMAL, EMPHASIS] [QUANT of n-uncount/pl-n] ❑ *I've got loads of money.* ❑ *...a load of kids.* ◼ V-T When someone **loads** a weapon such as a gun, they put a bullet or missile in it so that it is ready to use. ❑ *I knew how to load and handle a gun.* ❑ *He carried a loaded gun.* ◼ V-T To **load** a camera or other piece of equipment means to put film, tape, or data into it so that it is ready to use. ❑ *A photographer from the newspaper was loading his camera with film.* ◼ N-COUNT You can refer to the amount of work you have to do as a **load**. ❑ *She's taking some of the load off the secretaries.* ◼ N-COUNT The **load** of a system or piece of equipment, especially a system supplying electricity or a computer, is the extent to which it is being used at a particular time. ❑ *An efficient bulb may lighten the load of power stations.* ◼ N-SING The **load on** something is the amount of weight that is pressing down on it or the amount of strain that it is under. ❑ *Some of these chairs have flattened feet which spread the load on the ground.* ◼ →see also **loaded**. **a load off** your **mind** →see **mind** →see **photography**

◼ 타동사 싣다, 잔뜩 올려놓다 ❑ 그 남자들 세 명이 트럭에 짐을 다 실은 것 같았다. ❑ 담바 씨는 접시에 라자냐를 가득 담았다. ● 구동사 싣다, 잔뜩 올려놓다 ❑ 방금 트럭에 짐을 다 실었다. ❑ 그 커플은 킥킥거리며 빨간 스포츠카에 짐을 잔뜩 싣고 출발했다. ◼ 가산명사 짐, 화물 ❑ 그는 건초를 가득 싣고 차를 몰고 지나갔다. ◼ 수량사 많은 [비격식체, 강조] ❑ 나는 돈이 엄청 많아. ❑ 엄청 많은 아이들 ◼ 타동사 장전하다 ❑ 나는 총을 장전하고 사용할 줄 안다. ❑ 그는 장전된 총을 가지고 다녔다. ◼ 타동사 넣다 ❑ 신문사 사진 기자가 카메라에 필름을 넣고 있었다. ◼ 가산명사 작업량, 업무량 ❑ 그녀는 비서들의 업무량을 줄여 주고 있다. ◼ 가산명사 작업량, 부하 ❑ 전력 효율이 높은 전구가 생기면 발전량을 줄일 수도 있다. ◼ 단수명사 하중 ❑ 이 의자 중 몇 개는 하중을 바닥에 분산시킬 수 있도록 다리 밑이 납작하다.

Thesaurus load의 참조어

V.	fill, pack, pile up, stack; (ant.) unload ◼
N.	bundle, cargo, freight, shipment ◼

Word Partnership load의 연어

N.	load **a truck** ◼
V.	**carry** a load, **handle** a load, **lighten** a load, **take on** a load ◼ ◼
ADJ.	**big** load, **full** load, **heavy** load ◼ ◼

load|ed /ˈloʊdɪd/ ◼ ADJ A **loaded** question or word has more meaning or purpose than it appears to have, because the person who uses it hopes it will cause people to respond in a particular way. ❑ *That's a loaded question.* ◼ ADJ If something is **loaded with** a particular characteristic, it has that characteristic to a very great degree. ❑ *The President's visit is loaded with symbolic significance.* ◼ ADJ If you say that something is **loaded in favor of** someone, you

◼ 형용사 함축적인, 의의가 있는 ❑ 함축적인 질문이다. ◼ 형용사 -로 가득한 ❑ 대통령의 방문에는 상징적인 의미가 가득 담겨 있다. ◼ 형용사 -에 지나치게 우호적인; -에 지나치게 적대적인 [탐탁찮음] ❑ 언론이 현 정부에 지나치게 우호적이다.

mean it works unfairly to their advantage. If you say it is **loaded against** them, you mean it works unfairly to their disadvantage. [DISAPPROVAL] ❑ *The press is loaded in favor of this present government.*

loaf /lo͞of/ (**loaves**) N-COUNT A **loaf** of bread is bread which has been shaped and baked in one piece. It is usually large enough for more than one person and can be cut into slices. ❑ *...a loaf of crusty bread.*

가산명사 덩어리 ❑ 껍질이 딱딱한 빵 한 덩어리

loan ♦♦◇ /lo͞on/ (**loans, loaning, loaned**) **1** N-COUNT A **loan** is a sum of money that you borrow. ❑ *The country has no access to foreign loans or financial aid.* ❑ *The president wants to make it easier for small businesses to get bank loans.* →see also **bridge loan, soft loan 2** N-SING If someone gives you a **loan of** something, you borrow it from them. ❑ *I am in need of a loan of a bike for a few weeks.* **3** V-T If you **loan** something to someone, you lend it to them. ❑ *He had kindly offered to loan us all the plants required for the exhibit.* ● PHRASAL VERB **Loan out** means the same as **loan**. ❑ *It is common practice for clubs to loan out players to sides in the lower divisions.* **4** PHRASE If something is **on loan**, it has been borrowed. ❑ *...impressionist paintings on loan from the National Gallery.* →see **bank, interest rate**

1 가산명사 대출, 차관 ❑ 그 나라가 외국 차관이나 재정 보조를 받을 길이 없다. ❑ 대통령은 중소기업이 은행 대출을 더욱 쉽게 받을 수 있는 환경을 만들고 싶어 한다. **2** 단수명사 빌림, 차용 ❑ 나는 몇 주 동안 자전거를 빌려야 한다. **3** 타동사 빌려 주다 ❑ 그는 친절하게도 전시회에 필요한 화분을 전부 우리에게 빌려 주겠다고 했다. ● 구동사 빌려 주다 ❑ 구단이 하위 리그 팀에게 선수를 빌려 주는 일은 흔한 관행이다. **4** 구 빌린 ❑ 국립 미술관에서 빌린 인상주의 작품

loath /lo͞oθ/ also **loth** ADJ If you are **loath to** do something, you do not want to do it. [v-link ADJ to-inf] ❑ *The new finance minister seems loth to cut income tax.*

형용사 ~하기 싫어하는 ❑ 새 재무 장관은 소득세 삭감을 싫어하는 것으로 보인다.

loathe /lo͞oð/ (**loathes, loathing, loathed**) V-T If you **loathe** something or someone, you dislike them very much. ❑ *The two men loathe each other.*

타동사 혐오하다, 질색하다 ❑ 그 두 남자는 서로를 몹시 싫어한다.

loath|ing /ˈlo͞oðɪŋ/ N-UNCOUNT **Loathing** is a feeling of great dislike and disgust. ❑ *She looked at him with loathing.*

불가산명사 혐오, 질색 ❑ 그녀는 질색하며 그를 쳐다보았다.

loaves /lo͞ovz/ **Loaves** is the plural of **loaf**.

loaf의 복수형

lob|by ♦◇◇ /ˈlɒbi/ (**lobbies, lobbying, lobbied**) **1** V-T/V-I If you **lobby** someone such as a member of a government or council, you try to persuade them that a particular law should be changed or that a particular thing should be done. ❑ *Carers from all over the UK lobbied Parliament last week to demand a better financial deal.* **2** N-COUNT A **lobby** is a group of people who represent a particular organization or campaign, and try to persuade a government or council to help or support them. ❑ *Agricultural interests are some of the most powerful lobbies in Washington.* **3** N-COUNT In a hotel or other large building, the **lobby** is the area near the entrance that usually has corridors and staircases leading off it. ❑ *I met her in the lobby of the museum.*

1 타동사/자동사 로비하다 ❑ 영국 전역의 간병인들이 지난 주 더 나은 재정 지원을 요구하며 의회를 대상으로 로비활동을 벌였다. **2** 가산명사 로비 단체 ❑ 농민 단체는 워싱턴 정가에서 가장 강력한 로비 단체 중 하나이다. **3** 가산명사 로비 ❑ 나는 박물관 로비에서 그녀를 만났다.

lob|ster /ˈlɒbstər/ (**lobsters**) N-VAR A **lobster** is a sea creature that has a hard shell, two large claws, and eight legs. ❑ *She sold me a couple of live lobsters.* ● N-UNCOUNT **Lobster** is the flesh of a lobster eaten as food. ❑ *...lobster on a bed of fresh vegetables.*

가산명사 또는 불가산명사 바닷가재 ❑ 그녀는 나에게 살아 있는 바닷가재 두 마리를 팔았다. ● 불가산명사 바닷가재, 랍스터 요리 ❑ 싱싱한 야채 위에 놓인 바닷가재

lo|cal ♦♦♦ /ˈlo͞okªl/ (**locals**) **1** ADJ **Local** means existing in or belonging to the area where you live, or to the area that you are talking about. [ADJ n] ❑ *We'd better check on the match in the local paper.* ❑ *Some local residents joined the students' protest.* ● N-COUNT The **locals** are local people. ❑ *Camping is a great way to meet the locals as the Portuguese themselves are enthusiastic campers.* ● **lo|cal|ly** ADV ❑ *We've got cards which are drawn and printed and designed by someone locally.* **2** ADJ **Local** government is elected by people in one area of a country and controls aspects such as education, housing, and transportation within that area. ❑ *Education comprises two-thirds of all local council spending.* **3** ADJ A **local** anesthetic or condition affects only a small area of your body. [MEDICAL] ❑ *The procedure was done under local anesthetic in the physician's office.*

1 형용사 지역의, 현지의 ❑ 지역 신문에서 경기를 확인해 보는 편이 낫겠는걸. ❑ 일부 현지 주민들도 학생 시위에 참여했다. ● 가산명사 지역민, 현지인 ❑ 포르투갈 사람들이 열렬한 캠핑광이기 때문에 캠핑을 하는 것은 현지인을 만날 수 있는 훌륭한 방법이다. ● 지역에서, 현지에서 부사 ❑ 우리에게는 지역 주민이 직접 그리고 인쇄하고 디자인한 카드가 있다. **2** 형용사 지방의 ❑ 교육이 지방 의회 예산의 2/3를 차지한다. **3** 형용사 국부의 [의학] ❑ 수술은 국부 마취로 진료실에서 했다.

lo|cal area net|work (**local area networks**) N-COUNT A **local area network** is a group of computers and associated equipment that are linked by cable, for example in an office building, and that share a communications line. The abbreviation **LAN** is also used. [COMPUTING] ❑ *Users can easily move files between PCs connected by local area networks or the internet.*

가산명사 랜 (근거리 통신망) [컴퓨터] ❑ 사용자들은 랜이나 인터넷으로 연결된 피시 간에 파일을 쉽게 옮길 수 있다.

lo|cal author|ity ♦◇◇ (**local authorities**) N-COUNT A **local authority** is the same as a **local government**.

가산명사 지방 정부

lo|cal gov|ern|ment (**local governments**) **1** N-UNCOUNT **Local government** is the system of electing representatives to be responsible for the administration of public services and facilities in a particular area. ❑ *...careers*

1 불가산명사 지방 자치 ❑ 지방 자치와 관련된 일 **2** 가산명사 지방 정부, 지방 자치 단체 [미국영어; 영국영어 local authority]

in local government. **2** N-COUNT A **local government** is an organization that is officially responsible for all the public services and facilities in a particular area. [AM; BRIT **local authority**]

lo|cal|ity /loʊkælɪti/ (**localities**) N-COUNT A **locality** is a small area of a country or city. [FORMAL] ❑ *Following the discovery of the explosives the president cancelled his visit to the locality.*

lo|cate /loʊkeɪt, BRIT loʊkeɪt/ (**locates, locating, located**) **1** V-T If you **locate** something or someone, you find out where they are. [FORMAL] ❑ *The scientists want to locate the position of the gene on a chromosome.* **2** V-T/V-I If you **locate** something in a particular place, you put it there or build it there. [FORMAL] ❑ *Atlanta was voted the best city in which to locate a business by more than 400 chief executives.* **3** V-I If you **locate** in a particular place, you move there or open a business there. [mainly AM, BUSINESS] ❑ *...tax breaks for businesses that locate in run-down neighborhoods.*

lo|cat|ed /loʊkeɪtɪd, BRIT loʊkeɪtɪd/ ADJ If something is **located** in a particular place, it is present or has been built there. [FORMAL] [v-link ADJ prep, adv ADJ] ❑ *A boutique and beauty salon are conveniently located within the grounds.*

lo|ca|tion ♦◇◇ /loʊkeɪʃ°n/ (**locations**) **1** N-COUNT A **location** is the place where something happens or is situated. ❑ *The first thing he looked at was his office's location.* **2** N-COUNT The **location** of someone or something is their exact position. ❑ *She knew the exact location of The Eagle's headquarters.* **3** N-VAR A **location** is a place away from a studio where a movie or part of a movie is made. ❑ *...an art movie with dozens of exotic locations.*

Word Partnership	location의 연어
ADJ.	**central** location, **convenient** location **1**
	exact location, **present** location, **specific** location **2**
V.	**pinpoint** a location **1 2**

loch /lɒx, lɒk/ (**lochs**) N-COUNT A **loch** is a large area of water in Scotland that is completely or almost completely surrounded by land. ❑ *...twenty miles north of Loch Ness.*

lock ♦◇◇ /lɒk/ (**locks, locking, locked**) **1** V-T When you **lock** something such as a door, drawer, or case, you fasten it, usually with a key, so that other people cannot open it. ❑ *Are you sure you locked the front door?* **2** N-COUNT The **lock** on something such as a door or a drawer is the device which is used to keep it shut and prevent other people from opening it. Locks are opened with a key. ❑ *At that moment he heard Gill's key turning in the lock of the door.* **3** V-T If you **lock** something or someone in a place, room, or container, you put them there and fasten the lock. ❑ *Her maid locked the case in the safe.* **4** V-T/V-I If you **lock** something in a particular position or if it **locks** there, it is held or fitted firmly in that position. ❑ *He leaned back in the swivel chair and locked his fingers behind his head.* **5** N-COUNT On a canal or river, a **lock** is a place where walls have been built with gates at each end so that boats can move to a higher or lower section of the canal or river, by gradually changing the water level inside the gates. ❑ *As the lock filled, the ducklings rejoined their mother to wait for another vessel to go through.* **6** N-COUNT A **lock** of hair is a small bunch of hairs on your head that grow together and curl or curve in the same direction. ❑ *She brushed a lock of hair off his forehead.*

Word Partnership	lock의 연어
N.	lock a **car**, lock a **door**, lock a **room** **1**
	door lock, lock and **key** **2**
V.	**change** a lock, **open** a lock **2**

▶**lock away** **1** PHRASAL VERB If you **lock** something **away** in a place or container, you put or hide it there and fasten the lock. ❑ *She meticulously cleaned the gun and locked it away in its case.* **2** PHRASAL VERB To **lock** someone **away** means to put them in prison or a secure mental hospital. ❑ *Locking them away is not sufficient, you have to give them treatment.*

▶**lock out** **1** PHRASAL VERB If someone **locks** you **out** of a place, they prevent you entering it by locking the doors. ❑ *His wife locked him out of their bedroom after the argument.* **2** PHRASAL VERB In an industrial dispute, if a company **locks** its workers **out**, it closes the factory or office in order to prevent the employees coming to work. [BUSINESS] ❑ *The company locked out the workers, and then the rest of the work force went on strike.*

▶**lock up** **1** PHRASAL VERB If you **lock** something **up** in a place or container, you put or hide it there and fasten the lock. ❑ *Give away any food you have on hand, or lock it up and give the key to the neighbors.* **2** PHRASAL VERB To **lock** someone **up** means to put them in prison or a secure psychiatric hospital. ❑ *Mr Milner persuaded the federal prosecutors not to lock up his client.* **3** PHRASAL VERB When you **lock up** a building or car or **lock up**, you make sure that all the doors and windows are locked so that nobody can get in. ❑ *Don't forget to lock up.*

lock|er /lɒkər/ (**lockers**) N-COUNT A **locker** is a small metal or wooden cabinet with a lock, where you can put your personal possessions, for example in a school, place of work, or sports club.

lock|out (**lockouts**) [BRIT **lock-out**] N-COUNT A **lockout** is a situation in which employers close a place of work and prevent workers from entering it until the workers accept the employer's new proposals on pay or conditions of work. [BUSINESS] ❑ *The lockout could resume if no new contract agreement is signed.*

가산명사 작은 지역 [격식체] ❑ 그 지역에서 폭발물이 발견됨에 따라 대통령의 방문이 취소되었다.

1 타동사 위치를 알아내다 [격식체] ❑ 과학자들은 그 유전자가 염색체 어디에 있는지 알아내고 싶어 한다. **2** 타동사/자동사 놓다, 두다 [격식체] ❑ 400명 이상의 최고 경영자가 사업을 하기에 가장 좋은 도시로 애틀란타를 뽑았다. **3** 자동사 자리 잡다 [주로 미국영어, 경제] ❑ 황폐한 지역에 자리 잡은 사업장이 받는 세금 우대

형용사 위치한 [격식체] ❑ 고급 옷가게와 미용실이 구내에 있어서 편리하다.

1 가산명사 위치, 장소 ❑ 그가 처음 살펴본 것은 사무실 위치였다. **2** 가산명사 위치, 소재 ❑ 그녀는 이글 본사의 정확한 위치를 알고 있었다. **3** 가산명사 또는 불가산명사 야외 촬영지, 로케이션 ❑ 해외 수십 곳에서 촬영된 예술 영화

가산명사 (스코틀랜드의) 호수 ❑ 네스 호 북쪽으로 20마일

1 타동사 잠그다 ❑ 앞문 잠근 것 확실해? **2** 가산명사 자물쇠 ❑ 그 순간 그는 질이 열쇠로 문을 여는 소리를 들었다. **3** 타동사 잠궈 두다, 가둬 놓다 ❑ 그녀의 가정부가 그 케이스를 금고 안에 잠궈 두었다. **4** 타동사/자동사 고정시키다 ❑ 그는 회전의자 뒤로 몸을 기대면서 양손으로 깍지를 껴 머리 뒤에 고정시켰다. **5** 가산명사 수문식 독 ❑ 수문식 독에 물이 차자, 오리 새끼들이 엄마와 함께 배가 또 지나가기를 기다렸다. **6** 가산명사 머리 타래 ❑ 그녀가 그의 이마 뒤로 머리카락을 쓸어 넘겼다.

1 구동사 자물쇠를 채워 보관하다 ❑ 그녀는 치밀하게 총을 닦아서 케이스에 넣어 잠궈 두었다. **2** 구동사 가둬 놓다 ❑ 병원에 가둬 두는 것이 다가 아니다. 그들에게 치료를 해 주어야 한다.

1 구동사 들어가지 못하게 하다 ❑ 그렇게 다툰 이후에 아내는 그가 침실에 들어오지 못하게 했다. **2** 구동사 공장이나 사무실을 폐쇄하다 [경제] ❑ 회사가 일부 노동자들에게 공장을 폐쇄하자, 나머지 노동자들이 파업에 돌입했다.

1 구동사 자물쇠를 채워 보관하다 ❑ 가지고 있는 식품을 주거나, 용기에 넣어서 자물쇠를 채운 뒤 열쇠를 이웃에게 주어라. **2** 구동사 가둬 놓다 ❑ 밀너 씨가 의뢰인을 투옥시키지 말아 달라고 연방 정부 검찰을 설득했다. **3** 구동사 문을 잠그다 ❑ 문 잠그는 것 잊지 마.

가산명사 사물함

[영국영어 lock-out] 가산명사 공장 폐쇄 [경제] ❑ 새로운 계약 협상안이 타결되지 않으면 공장 폐쇄가 재개될 수도 있다.

lo|cust /loʊkəst/ (**locusts**) N-COUNT **Locusts** are large insects that live mainly in hot countries. They fly in large groups and eat crops. ❑ ...a swarm of locusts.

가산명사 메뚜기 ❑ 메뚜기 떼

lodge /lɒdʒ/ (**lodges, lodging, lodged**) ◼ N-COUNT A **lodge** is a house or hut in the country or in the mountains where people stay on vacation, especially when they want to shoot or fish. ❑ ...a Victorian hunting lodge. ◪ N-COUNT A **lodge** is a small house at the entrance to the grounds of a large house. ❑ I drove out of the gates, past the keeper's lodge. ◉ V-T If you **lodge** a complaint, protest, accusation, or claim, you officially make it. ❑ He has four weeks in which to lodge an appeal. ◮ V-T/V-I If you **lodge** somewhere, such as in someone else's house or if you **are lodged** there, you live there, usually paying rent. ❑ ...the story of the farming family she lodged with as a young teacher. ◵ V-T/V-I If an object **lodges** somewhere, it becomes stuck there. ❑ The bullet lodged in the sergeant's leg, shattering his thigh bone. ◶ →see also **lodging**

◼ 가산명사 작은 별장, 산장 ❑ 빅토리아 양식의 사냥을 위한 산장 ◪ 가산명사 문간채, 수위실 ❑ 나는 수위실을 지나 정문 밖으로 차를 몰았다. ◉ 타동사 제기하다, 제출하다 ❑ 그는 4주 내에 항소할 수 있다. ◮ 타동사/자동사 하숙하다, 묵다 ❑ 젊은 시절 그녀가 선생님이었을 때 살던 하숙집 농부 가족의 이야기 ◵ 타동사/자동사 박히다, 꽂히다 ❑ 총알이 하사관 다리에 박혀 허벅지뼈를 으스러뜨렸다.

Word Partnership   lodge의 연어

| N. | **country** lodge, **hunting** lodge, **ski** lodge ◼ |

---

lodg|er /lɒdʒər/ (**lodgers**) N-COUNT A **lodger** is a person who pays money to live in someone else's house. ❑ Jennie took in a lodger to help with the mortgage.

가산명사 하숙인 ❑ 제니는 주택 융자금 상환 부담을 덜기 위해 하숙인을 들였다.

lodg|ing /lɒdʒɪŋ/ (**lodgings**) N-UNCOUNT If you are provided with **lodging** or **lodgings**, you are provided with a place to stay for a period of time. You can use **lodgings** to refer to one or more of these places. [also N in pl] ❑ He was given free lodging in a three-room flat.

불가산명사 숙박, 숙소 ❑ 그는 방 세 개짜리 아파트로 무료 숙소를 제공받았다.

loft /lɔft, BRIT lɒft/ (**lofts**) ◼ N-COUNT A **loft** is the space inside the sloping roof of a house or other building, where things are sometimes stored. ❑ A loft conversion can add considerably to the value of a house. ◪ N-COUNT A **loft** is an apartment in the upper part of a building, especially a building such as a warehouse or factory that has been converted for people to live in. Lofts are usually large and not divided into separate rooms. ❑ ...Andy Warhol's New York loft.

◼ 가산명사 다락 ❑ 다락방을 개조하면 집의 가치가 크게 뛴다. ◪ 가산명사 창고나 공장 위층을 개조한 원룸 형식의 대형 아파트 ❑ 앤디 워홀의 뉴욕 아파트

lofty /lɔfti, BRIT lɒfti/ (**loftier, loftiest**) ◼ ADJ A **lofty** ideal or ambition is noble, important, and admirable. ❑ It was a bank that started out with grand ideas and lofty ideals. ◪ ADJ A **lofty** building or room is very high. [FORMAL] ❑ ...a light, lofty apartment in the suburbs of Salzburg. ◉ ADJ If you say that someone behaves in a **lofty** way, you are critical of them for behaving in a proud and rather unpleasant way, as if they think they are very important. [DISAPPROVAL] ❑ ...the lofty disdain he often expresses for his profession.

◼ 형용사 고매한 ❑ 그것은 원대한 계획과 고매한 이상을 가지고 시작한 은행이었다. ◪ 형용사 매우 높은 [격식체] ❑ 잘츠부르크 교외의 환한 고층 아파트 ◉ 형용사 거만한 [탐탁찮음] ❑ 그가 종종 자신의 직업에 대해 표현하는 거만한 경멸감

log /lɔg, BRIT lɒg/ (**logs, logging, logged**) ◼ N-COUNT A **log** is a piece of a thick branch or of the trunk of a tree that has been cut so that it can be used for fuel or for making things. ❑ He dumped the logs on the big stone hearth. ◪ N-COUNT A **log** is an official written account of what happens each day, for example on board a ship. ❑ The family made an official complaint to a ship's officer, which was recorded in the log. ◉ V-T If you **log** an event or fact, you record it officially in writing or on a computer. ❑ They log everyone and everything that comes in and out of here.

◼ 가산명사 나무토막 ❑ 그는 커다란 돌 벽난로에 나무토막을 쏟아 넣었다. ◪ 가산명사 일지 ❑ 가족은 항해사에게 정식으로 불만을 호소했으며, 이는 일지에 기록되었다. ◉ 타동사 기록하다 ❑ 그들은 이곳을 드나드는 사람들이나 물건을 모두 기록했다.

▶**log in** or **log on** PHRASAL VERB When someone **logs in** or **logs on**, or **logs into** a computer system, they start using the system, usually by typing their name or identity code and a password. ❑ Customers pay to log on and gossip with other users.

구동사 로그인하다, 접속하다 ❑ 이용자들은 요금을 내고 접속 및 채팅을 할 수 있다.

▶**log out** or **log off** PHRASAL VERB When someone who is using a computer system **logs out** or **logs off**, they finish using the system by typing a particular command. ❑ If a computer user fails to log off, the system is accessible to all.

구동사 로그아웃하다 ❑ 사용자가 로그아웃을 하지 않으면, 누구나 그 시스템을 사용할 수 있게 된다.

log|ic /lɒdʒɪk/ ◼ N-UNCOUNT **Logic** is a method of reasoning that involves a series of statements, each of which must be true if the statement before it is true. ❑ Apart from criminal investigation techniques, students learn forensic medicine, philosophy and logic. ◪ N-UNCOUNT The **logic** of a conclusion or an argument is its quality of being correct and reasonable. ❑ I don't follow the logic of your argument. ◉ N-UNCOUNT A particular kind of **logic** is the way of thinking and reasoning about things that is characteristic of a particular type of person or particular field of activity. ❑ The plan was based on sound commercial logic. →see **philosophy**

◼ 불가산명사 논리학 ❑ 학생들은 범죄 수사 기법 말고도 법의학, 철학, 논리학 등을 배운다. ◪ 가산명사 논리적으로 ❑ 당신 주장의 논리가 뭔지 모르겠어요. ◉ 불가산명사 논리 ❑ 그 계획은 탄탄한 상업 논리에 기초한 것이었다.

log|i|cal /lɒdʒɪkᵊl/ ◼ ADJ In a **logical** argument or method of reasoning, each step must be true if the step before it is true. ❑ Only when each logical step has been checked by other mathematicians will the proof be accepted. ● **logi|cal|ly** /lɒdʒɪkli/ ADV ❑ My professional training has taught me to look at things logically. ◪ ADJ The **logical** conclusion or result of a series of facts or events is the only one which can come from it, according to the rules of logic. ❑ If the climate gets drier, then the logical conclusion is that even more drought will occur. ● **logi|cal|ly** ADV [ADV with v] ❑ From that it followed logically that he would not be meeting Hildegarde. ◉ ADJ Something that is **logical** seems reasonable or sensible in the circumstances. ❑ Connie suddenly struck her as a logical candidate. ❑ There was a logical explanation. ● **logi|cal|ly** ADV ❑ This was the one possibility I hadn't taken into consideration, though logically I should have done.

◼ 형용사 논리적인 ❑ 논리적 단계 하나하나가 다른 수학자들의 검증을 받아야만, 증명이 인정될 것이다. ● 논리적으로 부사 ❑ 나는 직업상 상황을 논리적으로 봐야 한다는 훈련을 받았다. ◪ 형용사 논리적으로 당연한 ❑ 기후가 건조해지면, 당연히 가뭄이 더욱 빈번해질 것이다. ● 당연히 부사 ❑ 그렇기 때문에 당연히 그는 힐데가드를 만나지 않을 것이다. ◉ 형용사 마땅한, 타당한 ❑ 그녀는 갑자기 코니가 마땅한 후보라는 생각이 들었다. ❑ 타당한 해명이 있었다. ● 마땅히 부사 ❑ 이는 내가 마땅히 고려해야 했지만, 실제로 생각지 못한 가능성이었다.

log|ic bomb (**logic bombs**) N-COUNT A **logic bomb** is an unauthorized program that is inserted into a computer system so that when it is started it affects the operation of the computer. [COMPUTING] ❑ Viruses and logic bombs can doubtless do great damage under some circumstances.

가산명사 논리 폭탄 [컴퓨터] ❑ 바이러스나 논리 폭탄은 특정 상황에서는 확실히 큰 피해를 낳을 수 있다.

lo|gis|tics /loʊdʒɪstɪks/ N-UNCOUNT-COLL If you refer to the **logistics** of doing something complicated that involves a lot of people or equipment, you are referring to the skillful organization of it so that it can be done successfully and efficiently. ❑ The skills and logistics of getting such a big show on the road pose enormous practical problems.

불가산명사-집합 준비, 조직 ❑ 그렇게 규모가 큰 순회공연을 올리기 위한 기술과 준비에는 어마어마한 현실적인 문제가 따른다.

a b c d e f g h i j k l m n o p q r s t u v w x y z

A

logo /loʊgoʊ/ (**logos**) N-COUNT The **logo** of a company or organization is the special design or way of writing its name that it puts on all its products, stationery, or advertisements. ❏ ...the famous MGM logo of the roaring lion. →see **advertising**

가산명사 로고 ❏ 영화 제작 배급사 엠지엠의 유명한 로고인 포효하는 사자

B

loi|ter /lɔɪtər/ (**loiters, loitering, loitered**) V-I If you **loiter** somewhere, you remain there or walk up and down without any real purpose. ❏ Unemployed young men loiter at the entrance of the factory.

자동사 어슬렁거리다, 빈둥거리다 ❏ 젊은 실업자들이 공장 입구에서 어슬렁거린다.

C

D

lone /loʊn/ ❶ ADJ If you talk about a **lone** person or thing, you mean that they are alone. [ADJ n] ❏ A lone woman motorist waited for six hours for help yesterday because of a name mix-up. ❷ ADJ A **lone** parent is a parent who is caring for her or his child or children and who is not married or living with a partner. [mainly BRIT] [ADJ n] ❏ Ninety per cent of lone parent families are headed by mothers.

❶ 형용사 혼자의 ❏ 어제 성명 착오 때문에 여성 운전자가 도움을 받기 위해 혼자서 6시간이나 기다렸다. ❷ 형용사 배우자가 없는 [주로 영국영어] ❏ 한 부모 가정의 90퍼센트은 편모 가정이다.

E

lone|li|ness /loʊnlinɪs/ N-UNCOUNT **Loneliness** is the unhappiness that is felt by someone because they do not have any friends or do not have anyone to talk to. ❏ I have so many friends, but deep down, underneath, I have a fear of loneliness.

불가산명사 외로움, 고독 ❏ 나는 친구들이 그처럼 많아도, 가슴 깊은 곳에는 외로움에 대한 두려움이 자리 잡고 있다.

F

G

lone|ly /loʊnli/ (**lonelier, loneliest**) ❶ ADJ Someone who is **lonely** is unhappy because they are alone or do not have anyone they can talk to. ❏ ...lonely people who just want to talk. ❷ ADJ A **lonely** situation or period of time is one in which you feel unhappy because you are alone or do not have anyone to talk to. ❏ I desperately needed something to occupy me during those long, lonely nights. ❸ ADJ A **lonely** place is one where very few people come. ❏ It felt like the loneliest place in the world.

❶ 형용사 외로운, 고독한 ❏ 단지 이야기가 하고 싶은 외로운 사람들 ❷ 형용사 외로운, 고독한 ❏ 나는 그 길고 외로운 여러 밤 동안 열중할 수 있는 뭔가가 간절히 필요했다. ❸ 형용사 인적이 드문 ❏ 그곳은 세상에서 가장 인적이 드문 곳 같았다.

H

lon|er /loʊnər/ (**loners**) N-COUNT If you describe someone as a **loner**, you mean they prefer to be alone rather than with a group of people. ❏ I'm very much a loner – I never go out.

가산명사 혼자 있는 것을 즐기는 사람 ❏ 나는 정말 혼자 있는 걸 좋아해. 절대로 나가지 않지.

I

J

┌─────────────────────────────┐
│   **long**   │
│ ① TIME   │
│ ② DISTANCE AND SIZE   │
│ ③ PHRASES   │
│ ④ VERB USES   │
└─────────────────────────────┘

K

L

① long ♦♦♦ /lɔŋ, BRIT lɒŋ/ (**longer** /lɔŋgər, BRIT lɒŋgəʳ/ (**longest** /lɔŋgɪst, BRIT lɒŋgɪst/ ❶ ADV **Long** means a great amount of time or for a great amount of time. ❏ Repairs to the cable did not take too long. ❏ Have you known her parents long? ❏ I learned long ago to avoid these invitations. ● PHRASE The expression **for long** is used to mean "for a great amount of time." ❏ "Did you live there?" — "Not for long." ❷ ADJ A **long** event or period of time lasts for a great amount of time or takes a great amount of time. ❏ We had a long meeting with the attorney general. ❏ She is planning a long holiday in Egypt and America. ❸ ADV You use **long** to ask or talk about amounts of time. ❏ How long have you lived around here? ❏ He has been on a diet for as long as any of his friends can remember. ● ADJ **Long** is also an adjective. [how ADJ, amount ADJ] ❏ How long is the usual stay in hospital? ❹ ADJ A **long** speech, book, movie, or list contains a lot of information or a lot of items and takes a lot of time to listen to, read, watch, or deal with. ❏ He was making quite a long speech. ❺ ADJ If you describe a period of time or work as **long**, you mean it lasts for more hours or days than is usual, or seems to last for more time than it actually does. ❏ Go to sleep. I've got a long day tomorrow. ❏ She was a TV reporter and worked long hours. ❻ ADJ If someone has a **long** memory, they are able to remember things that happened far back in the past. ❏ Mr Assad, who has a long memory, will not have forgotten that meeting. ❼ ADV **Long** is used in expressions such as **all year long, the whole day long,** and **your whole life long** to say and emphasize that something happens for the whole of a particular period of time. [EMPHASIS] [n ADV] ❏ We played that record all night long.

❶ 부사 오래 ❏ 케이블을 고치는 데 그다지 오래 걸리지 않았다. ❏ 그녀의 부모님을 알고 지낸 지 오래됐나요? ❏ 나는 오래전에 이런 초청은 피하라고 배웠다. ● 구 오랫동안 ❏ "거기서 오래 살았어?" "그렇게 오래 살진 않았어." ❷ 형용사 긴 ❏ 우리는 검찰 총장과 만나 오랫동안 이야기했다. ❏ 그녀는 이집트와 미국에서 긴 휴가를 보낼 계획이다. ❸ 부사 오래 ❏ 이 근방에서 얼마나 오래 사셨어요? ❏ 친구들의 기억에 그는 항상 다이어트를 하고 있었다. ● 형용사 오래 ❏ 병원에 보통 얼마나 오래 입원하나요? ❹ 형용사 긴 ❏ 그가 상당히 긴 연설을 하고 있었다. ❺ 형용사 오래 걸리는, 길게 느껴지는 ❏ 자자. 난 내일 할 일이 많아. ❏ 그녀는 텔레비전 리포터였으며 긴 검정 일이 많았다. ❻ 형용사 기억력이 좋은 ❏ 아사드 씨는 기억력이 좋아서 그 회의를 잊지 않을 것이다. ❼ 부사 내내; 일년 내내; 하루 종일; 평생토록 [강조] ❏ 우리는 밤새도록 그 음반을 틀었다.

M

N

O

P

Q

R

② long ♦♦♦ /lɔŋ, BRIT lɒŋ/ (**longer** /lɔŋgər, BRIT lɒŋgəʳ/ (**longest** /lɔŋ, BRIT lɒŋgɪst/ ❶ ADJ Something that is **long** measures a great distance from one end to the other. ❏ ...a long table. ❏ Lucy was 27, with long dark hair. ❷ ADJ A **long** distance is a great distance. A **long** journey or route covers a great distance. ❏ His destination was Chobham Common, a long way from his Cotswold home. ❏ The long journey tired him. ❸ ADJ A **long** piece of clothing covers the whole of someone's legs or more of their legs than usual. Clothes with **long** sleeves cover the whole of someone's arms. [ADJ n] ❏ She is wearing a long black dress. ❹ ADJ You use **long** to talk or ask about the distance something measures from one end to the other. [amount ADJ, how ADJ, as ADJ as, ADJ-compar than] ❏ An eight-week-old embryo is only an inch long. ❏ How long is the tunnel? ● COMB in ADJ **Long** is also a combining form. ❏ ...a three-foot-long gash in the tanker's side. →see **ratio**

❶ 형용사 긴 ❏ 긴 탁자 ❏ 루시는 스물일곱에 머리카락 길고 까맸다. ❷ 형용사 먼 ❏ 그의 목적지는 코츠월드 집에서 멀리 떨어진 초뱀커먼이었다. ❏ 그는 먼 거리를 여행해서 피곤했다. ❸ 형용사 긴 ❏ 그녀는 긴 검정 드레스를 입고 있다. ❹ 형용사 길이가 _인 ❏ 8주 된 태아의 키는 1인치 정도밖에 안 된다. ❏ 터널이 얼마나 길어요? ● 복합형-형용사 길이 _의 ❏ 유조선 측면에 생긴 길이 3피트의 홈집

S

T

U

③ long ♦♦♦ /lɔŋ, BRIT lɒŋ/ (**longer** /lɔŋgər, BRIT lɒŋgəʳ/ →Please look at category ❺ to see if the expression you are looking for is shown under another headword. ❶ PHRASE If you say that something is the case **as long as** or **so long as** something else is the case, you mean that it is only the case if the second thing is the case. ❏ The interior minister said he would still support them, as long as they didn't break the rules. ❷ PHRASE If you say that someone **won't be long**, you mean that you think they will arrive or be back soon. If you say that it **won't be long** before something happens, you mean that you think it will happen soon. ❏ "What's happened to her?" — "I'm sure she won't be long." ❸ PHRASE If you say that something will happen or happened **before long**, you mean that it will happen or it happened soon. ❏ German interest rates will come down before long. ❹ PHRASE Something that is **no longer** the case used to be the case but is not the case now. You can also say that something is not the case **any longer**. ❏ Food shortages are no longer a problem. ❏ She could no longer afford to keep him at school. ❺ **at long last** →see **last**. **in the long run** →see **run**. **a long shot** →see **shot**. **in the long term** →see **term**. **to go a long way** →see **way**

❶ 구 _하는 한 ❏ 내무부 장관은 그들이 규율을 어기지 않는 한, 계속 지지하겠다고 밝혔다. ❷ 구 금방 올 거야 ❏ "그녀는 도대체 어떻게 된 거야?" "분명히 금방 올 거야." ❸ 구 머지않아, 곧 ❏ 독일 금리가 머지않아 내려갈 것이다. ❹ 구 더 이상 _하지 않는, 더 이상 _가 아닌 ❏ 식량 부족은 이제 문제가 아니다. ❏ 그녀는 더 이상 그를 학교에 보낼 형편이 못 됐다.

V

W

X

Y

Z

④ **long** /lɒŋ, BRIT lɒŋ/ (longs, longing, longed) V-T/V-I If you **long for** something, you want it very much. □ *Steve longed for the good old days.* □ *I'm longing to meet her.* →see also **longing**

타동사/자동사 간절히 원하다 □ 스티브는 마냥 좋던 지난 시절로 돌아가고 싶었다. □ 나는 그녀를 꼭 만나고 싶어.

long-distance ■ ADJ **Long-distance** is used to describe travel between places that are far apart. [ADJ n] □ *Trains are reliable, cheap and best for long-distance journeys.* ■ ADJ **Long-distance** is used to describe communication that takes place between people who are far apart. □ *He received a long-distance phone call from his girlfriend in Colorado.*

■ 형용사 장거리의 □ 기차는 장거리 여행 시 저렴하고 믿을 수 있는 최선의 수단이다. ■ 형용사 장거리의 □ 그는 콜로라도에 있는 여자 친구로부터 장거리 전화를 받았다.

long-haul ADJ **Long-haul** is used to describe things that involve transporting passengers or goods over long distances. Compare **short-haul**. [ADJ n] □ *...learning how to avoid the unpleasant side-effects of long-haul flights.*

형용사 장거리의 □ 장거리 비행 시 발생하는 불쾌한 증상을 피하는 방법을 배우기

long·ing /lɒŋɪŋ, BRIT lɒŋɪŋ/ (longings) N-VAR If you feel **longing** or a **longing for** something, you have a rather sad feeling because you want it very much. □ *He felt a longing for the familiar.*

가산명사 또는 불가산명사 그리움, 갈망 □ 그는 익숙한 것들이 몹시도 그리웠다.

lon·gitude /lɒndʒɪtud, BRIT lɒndʒɪtyuːd/ (longitudes) N-VAR The **longitude** of a place is its distance to the west or east of a line passing through Greenwich, England. Compare **latitude**. □ *He noted the latitude and longitude, then made a mark on the admiralty chart.* ● ADJ **Longitude** is also an adjective. □ *A similar feature is found at 13 degrees North between 230 degrees and 250 degrees longitude.*

가산명사 또는 불가산명사 경도 □ 그는 위도와 경도를 적은 후에 해도에 위치를 표시했다. ● 형용사 경도의 □ 경도 230도와 250도 사이 북위 13도 지점에서 비슷한 지형을 볼 수 있다.

long-lost ADJ You use **long-lost** to describe someone or something that you have not seen for a long time. [ADJ n] □ *For me it was like meeting a long-lost sister. We talked, and talked, and talked.*

형용사 오랫동안 보지 못한 □ 나에게는 마치 오랫동안 보지 못한 여동생을 만나는 것 같았다. 우리는 이야기하고 또 이야기했다.

long-range ■ ADJ A **long-range** piece of military equipment or vehicle is able to hit or detect a target a long way away or to travel a long way in order to do something. □ *He is very keen to reach agreement with the US on reducing long-range nuclear missiles.* ■ ADJ A **long-range** plan or prediction relates to a period extending a long time into the future. □ *Eisenhower was intensely aware of the need for long-range planning.*

■ 형용사 장거리의 □ 그는 미국과 장거리 핵 미사일 감축 협정을 맺는 데 매우 열중하고 있다. ■ 형용사 장기적인 □ 아이젠하워는 장기적인 계획 수립의 필요성을 너무나도 잘 알고 있었다.

long-running (longest-running) ADJ Something that is **long-running** has been in existence, or has been performed, for a long time. [ADJ n] □ *...a long-running trade dispute.*

형용사 장기간에 걸친 □ 오래된 무역 분쟁

long-standing ADJ A **long-standing** situation has existed for a long time. □ *They are on the brink of resolving their long-standing dispute over money.*

형용사 오랫동안 계속된 □ 그들은 오랫동안 계속된 금전 문제 해결을 눈앞에 두고 있다.

long-suffering ADJ Someone who is **long-suffering** patiently puts up with a lot of trouble or unhappiness, especially when it is caused by someone else. □ *He went back to Yorkshire to join his loyal, long-suffering wife.*

형용사 참을성 있는, 인내심이 강한 □ 그는 요크셔로 가서 충실하고 인내심이 강한 아내 곁으로 돌아갔다.

long-term ◆◇◇ (longer-term) ■ ADJ Something that is **long-term** has continued for a long time or will continue for a long time in the future. □ *They want their parents to have access to affordable long-term care.* ■ N-SING When you talk about what happens in **the long term**, you are talking about what happens over a long period of time, either in the future or after a particular event. □ *In the long term the company hopes to open in Moscow and other major cities.* →see **memory**

■ 형용사 장기적인 □ 그들은 부모님이 장기적으로 저렴하게 이용할 수 있는 요양 시설이 있었으면 한다. ■ 단수명사 장기간 □ 장기적으로 모스크바를 비롯한 다른 주요 도시에 지사를 여는 것이 회사의 꿈이다.

long-time ◆◇◇ ADJ You use **long-time** to describe something that has existed or been a particular thing for a long time. [ADJ n] □ *Newcomers had to pay far more in taxes than long-time land owners.*

형용사 오랫동안의 □ 땅을 소유한 지 오래된 지주보다 얼마 안 된 지주가 훨씬 더 많은 세금을 내야 했다.

loo /luː/ (loos) N-COUNT A **loo** is a toilet. [BRIT, INFORMAL] □ *I asked if I could go to the loo.*

가산명사 화장실 [영국영어, 비격식체] □ 나는 화장실에 가도 되는지 물었다.

---

look

① USING YOUR EYES OR YOUR MIND
② APPEARANCE

---

① **look** ◆◆◆ /lʊk/ (looks, looking, looked) →Please look at category ⑫ to see if the expression you are looking for is shown under another headword. ■ V-I If you **look** in a particular direction, you direct your eyes in that direction, especially so that you can see what is there or see what something is like. □ *I looked down the hallway to room number nine.* □ *If you look, you'll see what was a lake.* ● N-SING **Look** is also a noun. □ *Lucille took a last look in the mirror.* ■ V-I If you **look at** a book, newspaper, or magazine, you read it fairly quickly or read part of it. □ *You've just got to look at the last bit of Act Three.* ● N-SING **Look** is also a noun. □ *A quick look at Monday's British newspapers shows that there's plenty of interest in foreign news.* ■ V-I If you **look at** someone in a particular way, you look at them with your expression showing what you are feeling or thinking. □ *She looked at him earnestly. "You don't mind?"* ● N-COUNT **Look** is also a noun. □ *He gave her a blank look, as if he had no idea who she was.* ■ V-I If you **look for** something, for example something that you have lost, you try to find it. □ *I'm looking for a child. I believe your husband can help me find her.* □ *I looked everywhere for ideas.* ● N-SING **Look** is also a noun. □ *Go and have another look.* ■ V-I If you are **looking for** something such as the solution to a problem or a new method, you want it and are trying to obtain it or think of it. □ *The working group will be looking for practical solutions to the problems faced by doctors.* ■ V-I If you **look at** a subject, problem, or situation, you think about it or study it, so that you know all about it and can consider what should be done in relation to it. □ *Next term we'll be looking at the Second World War period.* □ *Anne Holker looks at the pros and cons of making changes to your property.* ● N-SING **Look** is also a noun. □ *A close look at the statistics reveals a troubling picture.* ■ V-I If you **look at** a person, situation, or subject from a particular point of view, you judge them or consider them from that point of view. □ *Brian had learned to look at her with new*

■ 자동사 보다 □ 복도 아래로 9번 방이 보였다. □ 보시면 언젠가는 호수였던 것이 보일 거예요. ● 단수명사 봄 □ 루실이 마지막으로 거울을 봤다. ■ 자동사 보다, 대충 읽다 □ 너는 3막 마지막 부분만 좀 보면 돼. ● 단수명사 봄, 대충 읽기 □ 월요일 자 영국 신문을 대강 보면 해외 뉴스에 관심이 많다는 점을 알 수 있다. ■ 자동사 바라보다 □ 그녀는 그를 진지하게 바라봤다. "괜찮겠어요?" ● 가산명사 바라봄 □ 그는 그녀가 누구인지 전혀 모르겠다는 듯이 그녀를 멍하게 바라보았다. ■ 자동사 찾아보다 □ 아이를 찾고 있어요. 딸을 찾는 데 남편분의 도움이 필요해요. □ 나는 아이디어를 찾아 모든 곳을 뒤졌다. ● 단수명사 찾아봄 □ 가서 한 번 더 찾아 봐. ■ 자동사 찾아보다 □ 실무진이 의사들의 문제에 대한 실질적인 해답을 찾아볼 것이다. ■ 자동사 살펴보다 □ 다음 학기에는 2차 세계 대전 기간을 살펴보겠어요. □ 앤 홀커는 재산 변경의 장단점을 살펴보고 있습니다. ● 단수명사 살펴봄 □ 통계를 자세히 살펴보면 걱정스러운 상황이 드러난다. ■ 자동사 판단하다, 바라보다 □ 브라이언은 그녀를 새로운 존경심을 가지고 바라보게 되었다. ■ 관용 표현 뭐, 있잖아, 저기, 있잖아요 □ 저, 있잖아. 미안해. 진심이 아니었어. ● 타동사/자동사 ― 좀 봐 □시간 좀 봐! 이따가 저녁에 이야기하자. 괜찮지? □ 그러니까 내 말은 텔레비전을 보는 사람은 많은데 책을 읽는 사람은 거의 없다는 거야. ⑩ 자동사 ―향하다, ―가 내다보이다

respect. **8** CONVENTION You say **look** when you want someone to pay attention to you because you are going to say something important. [only imper] ❑ *Look, I'm sorry. I didn't mean it.* **9** V-T/V-I You can use **look** to draw attention to a particular situation, person, or thing, for example because you find it very surprising, significant, or annoying. [only imper] ❑ *Hey, look at the time! We'll talk about it tonight. All right?* ❑ *I mean, look at how many people watch television and how few read books.* **10** V-I If something such as a building or window **looks** somewhere, it has a view of a particular place. ❑ *The castle looks over private parkland.* ● PHRASAL VERB **Look out** means the same as **look**. ❑ *Nine windows looked out over the sculpture gardens.* **11** EXCLAM If you say or shout "**look out!**" to someone, you are warning them that they are in danger. ❑ *"Look out!" somebody shouted, as the truck started to roll toward the sea.* **12** to **look down** your **nose at** someone →see **nose**

□ 성에서 개인 녹지가 내다보인다. ● 구동사 _향이다, _가 내다보이다 □ 창문 아홉 개가 조각 공원 쪽으로 나있다. **11** 감탄사 조심해 □ "조심해!" 트럭이 바다 쪽으로 구르기 시작하자 누군가 소리쳤다.

> If you want to say that someone is paying attention to something they can see, you say that they **are looking at** it or **watching** it. In general, you **look at** something that is not moving, while you **watch** something that is moving or changing. ❑ *I asked him to look at the picture above his bed... He watched Blake run down the stairs.* **Look** is never followed directly by an object. You must always use **at** or some other preposition. ❑ *I looked toward the plane.* You use **see** to talk about things that you are aware of because a visual impression reaches your eyes. You often use **can** in this case. ❑ *I can see the fax here on the desk.*

> 누군가가 자신이 볼 수 있는 어떤 것에 주의를 기울이고 있다고 말하려면, look이나 watch를 써서 they are looking at 또는 they are watching it이라고 한다. 대개, 움직이거나 변하는 것은 watch하는 반면에, 움직이지 않는 것은 look at한다. □ 나는 그에게 그의 침대 위에 걸려 있는 그림을 보라고 했다... 그는 블레이크가 계단을 달려 내려가는 것을 지켜보았다. look 다음에는 절대 바로 목적어가 오지 않는다. 항상 at이나 다른 전치사를 써야 한다. □ 나는 비행기 쪽을 쳐다보았다. 시각적 인상이 눈에 들어와서 의식하게 되는 것에 대해 말할 때는 see를 쓴다. 이런 경우에는 흔히 can을 쓴다. □ 난 여기 책상 위에 팩스가 보인다.

Thesaurus — *look*의 참조어

N.	gaze, glance, glimpse, stare ① **1**
V.	gaze, glance, observe, stare, view, watch ① **1**
	examine, inspect, investigate, observe, study, survey ① **6**
V-LINK.	appear, seem ② **1**

▶**look after** **1** PHRASAL VERB If you **look after** someone or something, you do what is necessary to keep them healthy, safe, or in good condition. ❑ *I love looking after the children.* **2** PHRASAL VERB If you **look after** something, you are responsible for it and deal with it or make sure it is all right, especially because it is your job to do so. ❑ *...the farm manager who looks after the day-to-day organization.*

1 구동사 돌보다 □ 나는 아이 보는 것을 좋아한다. **2** 구동사 책임지다 □ 일상적인 조직 활동을 책임지고 있는 농장 매니저

▶**look around** PHRASAL VERB If you **look around** or **look round** a building or place, you walk round it and look at the different parts of it. ❑ *Look around the showrooms.*

구동사 둘러보다 □ 전시실을 둘러보세요.

▶**look back** PHRASAL VERB If you **look back**, you think about things that happened in the past. ❑ *Looking back, I am staggered how easily it was all arranged.*

구동사 뒤돌아보다 □ 뒤돌아보면 그 모든 일이 너무나 쉽게 마련된 것이 놀랍다.

▶**look down on** PHRASAL VERB To **look down on** someone means to consider that person to be inferior or unimportant, usually when this is not true. ❑ *I wasn't successful, so they looked down on me.*

구동사 깔보다, 깔보다 □ 내가 그다지 성공하지 못했기 때문에 그들은 나를 깔봤다.

▶**look forward to** **1** PHRASAL VERB If you **look forward to** something that is going to happen, you want it to happen because you think you will enjoy it. ❑ *He was looking forward to working with the new Prime Minister.* **2** PHRASAL VERB If you say that someone **is looking forward** to something useful or positive, you mean they expect it to happen. ❑ *He now says that he's looking forward to increased trade after the war.*

1 구동사 기대하다 □ 그는 신임 총리와 함께 일하기를 기대하고 있었다. **2** 구동사 기대하다 □ 그는 이제 전후 무역 증가를 기대하고 있다고 말한다.

> Do not confuse **look forward to**, **expect**, and **wait for**. When you **look forward to** something that is going to happen, you feel happy because you think you will enjoy it. ❑ *I'll bet you're looking forward to your holidays... I always looked forward to seeing her.* When you are **expecting** someone or something, you think that the person or thing is going to arrive or that the thing is going to happen. ❑ *I sent a postcard so they were expecting me... We are expecting rain.* When you **wait for** someone or something, you stay in the same place until the person arrives or the thing happens. ❑ *Soft drinks were served while we waited for him... We got off the plane and waited for our luggage.*

> look forward to, expect, wait for를 혼동하지 않도록 하라. 일어날 무엇을 look forward to하면, 그것이 즐거울 것이라고 생각해서 기분이 좋음을 나타낸다. □ 너는 틀림없이 휴가를 고대하고 있을 거야... 나는 항상 그녀를 보게 되기를 고대했다. 누구를 또는 무엇을 expect하면, 그 사람 또는 그것이 도착하거나 그것이 일어날 것이라고 생각한다. □ 내가 엽서를 보내서 그들은 나를 기다리고 있었다... 우리는 비가 오리라고 생각하고 있다. 누구를 또는 무엇을 wait for하면 그 사람이 도착하거나 그것이 일어날 때까지 같은 장소에 머무르는 것이다. □ 우리가 그를 기다리는 동안 위스키가 제공되었다... 우리는 비행기에서 내려 짐을 기다렸다.

▶**look into** PHRASAL VERB If a person or organization **is looking into** a possible course of action, a problem, or a situation, they are finding out about it and examining the facts relating to it. ❑ *He had once looked into buying his own island off Nova Scotia.*

구동사 알아보다, 조사하다 □ 그는 예전에 노바스코샤 연안에 섬을 사려고 이것저것 알아봤었다.

▶**look on** PHRASAL VERB If you **look on** while something happens, you watch it happening without taking part yourself. ❑ *About 150 local people looked on in silence as the two coffins were taken into the church.*

구동사 지켜보다 □ 관 두 개가 교회로 운구되는 동안 150명가량의 주민들이 침묵 속에서 지켜보았다.

▶**look on** or **look upon** PHRASAL VERB If you **look on** or **look upon** someone or something in a particular way, you think of them in that way. ❑ *A lot of people looked on him as a healer.* ❑ *A lot of people look on it like that.*

구동사 생각하다, 간주하다 □ 많은 사람들이 그를 의사로 생각했다. □ 많은 사람들이 그런 식으로 생각했다.

▶**look out** →see **look** 10

▶**look out for** PHRASAL VERB If you **look out for** something, you pay attention to things so that you notice it if or when it occurs. ❑ *Look out for special deals.*

구동사 살피다 □ 특별한 거래가 있나 살펴라.

▶**look round** →see **look around**

▶**look through** 1 PHRASAL VERB If you **look through** a group of things, you examine each one so that you can find or choose the one that you want. ❏ *Peter starts looking through the mail as soon as the door shuts.* 2 PHRASAL VERB If you **look through** something that has been written or printed, you read it. ❏ *He happened to be looking through the medical book "Gray's Anatomy" at the time.*

1 구동사 하나하나 살피다 ❏ 피터는 문이 닫히자마자 메일을 하나하나 살펴보기 시작했다. 2 구동사 읽다 ❏ 그는 그때 마침 "그레이의 해부학"이라는 의학 서적을 읽고 있었다.

▶**look to** 1 PHRASAL VERB If you **look to** someone or something for a particular thing that you want, you expect or hope that they will provide it. ❏ *The difficulties women encounter with their doctors partly explain why so many of us are looking to alternative therapies.* 2 PHRASAL VERB If you **look to** something that will happen in the future, you think about it. ❏ *Looking to the future, though, we asked him what the prospects are for a vaccine to prevent infection in the first place.*

1 구동사 의지하다 ❏ 의사의 진찰을 받을 때 부딪치는 문제들도 우리 여성들 상당수가 대체 요법에 의지하는 이유 중 하나이다. 2 구동사 생각하다 ❏ 그래도 미래를 생각하면서, 우리는 전염병을 처음부터 예방할 수 있는 백신이 나올 전망에 관해 그에게 물었다.

▶**look up** 1 PHRASAL VERB If you **look up** a fact or a piece of information, you find it out by looking in something such as a reference book or a list. ❏ *I looked your address up in the personnel file.* 2 PHRASAL VERB If you **look** someone **up**, you visit them after not having seen them for a long time. ❏ *I'll try to look him up, ask him a few questions.*

1 구동사 찾아내다, 찾아서 보다 ❏ 인사과 서류에서 네 주소를 찾았어. 2 구동사 방문하다 ❏ 그를 방문해서 몇 가지 물어 볼 생각이야.

▶**look up to** PHRASAL VERB If you **look up to** someone, especially someone older than you, you respect and admire them. ❏ *You're a popular girl, Grace, and a lot of the younger ones look up to you.*

구동사 존경하다, 우러러보다 ❏ 그레이스, 너는 인기 있는 사람이야. 너보다 어린 아이들이 널 우러러 본다고.

② **look** ◆◆◇ /lʊk/ (**looks, looking, looked**) 1 V-LINK You use **look** when describing the appearance of a person or thing or the impression that they give. ❏ *Sheila was looking miserable.* ❏ *They look like stars to the naked eye.* ❏ *He looked as if he was going to smile.* 2 N-SING If someone or something has a particular **look**, they have a particular appearance or expression. ❏ *She had the look of someone deserted and betrayed.* ❏ *When he came to decorate the kitchen, Kenneth opted for a friendly rustic look.* 3 N-PLURAL When you refer to someone's **looks**, you are referring to how beautiful or ugly they are, especially how beautiful they are. ❏ *I never chose people just because of their looks.* 4 V-LINK You use **look** when indicating what you think will happen in the future or how a situation seems to you. ❏ *He had lots of time to think about the future, and it didn't look good.* ❏ *So far it looks like Warner Brothers' gamble is paying off.* ❏ *The Europeans had hoped to win, and, indeed, had looked like winning.* 5 PHRASE You use expressions such as **by the look of him** and **by the looks of it** when you want to indicate that you are giving an opinion based on the appearance of someone or something. ❏ *He was not a well man by the look of him.* 6 PHRASE If you **don't like the look of** something or someone, you feel that they may be dangerous or cause problems. ❏ *I don't like the look of those clouds.* 7 PHRASE If you ask **what** someone or something **looks like**, you are asking for a description of them.

1 연결동사 보이다 ❏ 셰일라는 비참해 보였다. ❏ 이들은 육안으로 보면 별처럼 보인다. ❏ 그는 금방 웃을 것처럼 보였다. 2 단수명사 모양, 모습, 표정 ❏ 그녀는 버림받고 배신당한 사람처럼 보였다. ❏ 그가 부엌을 꾸미러 왔을 때 케네스는 따뜻하고 소박한 디자인을 선택했다. 3 복수명사 외모 ❏ 나는 외모만 보고 사람을 고르지 않는다. 4 연결동사 보이다 ❏ 그는 오랫동안 미래에 관해 생각해 보았지만, 미래가 그다지 밝아 보이지는 않았다. ❏ 지금까지는 워너 브라더스의 모험이 성과를 거두고 있는 것으로 보인다. ❏ 유럽 인들은 이기기를 바랬고 실제로 이길 것처럼 보였다. 5 구 겉모습만 봐서는 ❏ 그는 겉모습만 봐서는 건강해 보이지 않았다. 6 구 불길해 보이다 ❏ 구름이 불길해 보여. 7 구 생김새

look|out /lʊkaʊt/ (**lookouts**) 1 N-COUNT A **lookout** is a place from which you can see clearly in all directions. ❏ *Troops tried to set up a lookout post inside a refugee camp.* 2 N-COUNT A **lookout** is someone who is watching for danger in order to warn other people about it. ❏ *Next came a brief spell as a lookout and minder to a local housebreaker.* 3 PHRASE If someone **keeps a lookout**, especially on a boat, they look around all the time in order to make sure there is no danger. ❏ *He denied that he'd failed to keep a proper lookout that night.*

1 가산명사 망루 ❏ 군인들이 난민 수용소 안쪽에 망루를 세우려고 했다. 2 가산명사 망보는 사람, 감시인 ❏ 그 다음에는 주택 침입자 감시인으로 잠깐 일했다. 3 구 망보다 ❏ 그는 그날 밤 제대로 망을 보지 못한 사실을 부인했다.

loom /luːm/ (**looms, looming, loomed**) 1 V-I If something **looms over** you, it appears as a large or unclear shape, often in a frightening way. ❏ *Vincent loomed over me, as pale and grey as a tombstone.* 2 V-I If a worrying or threatening situation or event **is looming**, it seems likely to happen soon. [JOURNALISM] ❏ *Another government spending crisis is looming in the United States.* ❏ *The threat of renewed civil war looms ahead.* 3 N-COUNT A **loom** is a machine that is used for weaving thread into cloth.

1 자동사 모습을 드러내다 ❏ 빈센트가 묘비처럼 창백한 잿빛 모습을 드러냈다. 2 자동사 다가오다 [언론] ❏ 미국 정부의 재정 위기가 또다시 다가오고 있다. ❏ 내전 재개 위협이 다가오고 있다. 3 가산명사 베틀

loony /luːni/ (**loonies**) N-COUNT If you refer to someone as a **loony**, you mean that they behave in a way that seems mad, strange, or eccentric. Some people consider this use offensive. [INFORMAL, DISAPPROVAL] ❏ *At first they all thought I was a loony.*

가산명사 미치광이 [비격식체, 탐탁찮음] ❏ 그들 모두 처음에는 나를 미치광이라고 생각했다.

loop /luːp/ (**loops, looping, looped**) 1 N-COUNT A **loop** is a curved or circular shape in something long, for example in a piece of string. ❏ *Mrs. Morrell reached for a loop of garden hose.* 2 V-T If you **loop** something such as a piece of rope around an object, you tie a length of it in a loop around the object, for example in order to fasten it to the object. ❏ *He looped the rope over the wood.* 3 V-I If something **loops** somewhere, it goes there in a circular direction that makes the shape of a loop. ❏ *The enemy was looping around the south side.*

1 가산명사 고리 모양 ❏ 모렐 부인은 동그랗게 말린 정원 호스로 손을 뻗었다. 2 타동사 묶다, 매듭짓다 ❏ 그는 나무에 밧줄을 묶었다. 3 자동사 돌아가다 ❏ 적군이 남쪽 방면을 돌아가고 있었다.

loop|hole /luːphoʊl/ (**loopholes**) N-COUNT A **loophole** in the law is a small mistake which allows people to do something that would otherwise be illegal. ❏ *It is estimated that 60,000 shops open every Sunday and trade by exploiting some loophole in the law to avoid prosecution.*

가산명사 허점 ❏ 대략 6만 개의 상점이 법의 허점을 이용해 기소는 피하면서 일요일마다 문을 열고 장사하는 것으로 추산된다.

loose ◆◇◇ /luːs/ (**looser, loosest**) 1 ADJ Something that is **loose** is not firmly held or fixed in place. ❏ *If a tooth feels very loose, your dentist may recommend that it's taken out.* ❏ *Two wooden beams had come loose from the ceiling.* ● **loose|ly** ADV [ADV with v] ❏ *Tim clasped his hands together and held them loosely in front of his belly.* 2 ADJ Something that is **loose** is not attached to anything, or held or contained in anything. ❏ *Frank emptied a handful of loose change on the table.* 3 ADJ If people or animals break **loose** or are set **loose**, they are no longer held, tied, or kept somewhere and can move around freely. [ADJ after v, ADJ n, v-link ADJ] ❏ *She broke loose from his embrace and crossed to the window.* 4 ADJ Clothes that are **loose** are rather large and do not fit closely. ❏ *A pistol wasn't that hard to hide under a loose shirt.* ● **loose|ly** ADV ❏ *His shirt hung loosely over his thin shoulders.* 5 ADJ If your hair is **loose**, it hangs freely around your shoulders and is not tied back. ❏ *She was still in her nightdress, with her hair hanging loose over her shoulders.* 6 ADJ A

1 형용사 헐거운, 느슨한 ❏ 이가 흔들리면, 의사가 빼라고 할 수도 있다. ❏ 지붕에 고정되어 있는 나무들보 두 개가 헐거워져 있었다. ● 헐겁게, 느슨하게 부사 ❏ 팀은 양손으로 두 손을 끼고 배 위에 느슨하게 올려놓았다. 2 형용사 매여 있지 않은, 흩어진 ❏ 프랭크는 동전 한 움큼을 탁자 위에 이리저리 쏟아 놓았다. 3 형용사 풀린, 벗어난, 도망친 ❏ 그녀는 그의 품을 벗어나 창문 쪽으로 건너갔다. 4 형용사 헐렁한 ❏ 헐렁한 셔츠 속에 권총을 숨기는 것은 그리 어렵지 않았다. ● 헐렁하게 부사 ❏ 그의 마른 어깨 위로 셔츠가 헐렁하게 걸쳐져 있었다. 5 형용사 풀린, 늘어뜨린 ❏ 그녀는 여전히 잠옷을 입고 머리를 어깨 위로 늘어뜨리고 있었다. 6 형용사 느슨한, 유동적인

loose grouping, arrangement, or organization is flexible rather than strictly controlled or organized. ❑ *Murray and Alison came to some sort of loose arrangement before he went home.* ● **loose|ly** ADV [ADV with v] ❑ *The investigation had aimed at a loosely organized group of criminals.* ◻ PHRASE If a person or an animal is **on the loose**, they are free because they have escaped from a person or place. ❑ *Up to a thousand prisoners may be on the loose inside the jail.* ◻ a **loose cannon** →see **cannon**. **all hell breaks loose** →see **hell**

□ 그가 집에 가기 전에 머레이와 앨리슨은 일종의 잠정적인 합의를 보았다. ❑ 느슨하게, 유동적으로 부사 □ 범죄자로 구성된 느슨한 조직이 수사 표적이었다. ◻ 구 자유롭게 움직이는 □ 천 명에 달하는 수감자들이 교도소 내에서 자유롭게 움직이고 있을지도 모른다.

Do not confuse **loose** and **lose**. **Loose** is usually an adjective. If something is **loose**, it is not properly fixed or held in place. ❑ *...the loose floorboards on the landing....a loose tooth.* If you let an animal **loose**, you release it from where it was kept. ❑ *He brought a pair of white rats into church, and let them loose on the floor.* **Lose** is a verb. If you **lose** something, you no longer have it and cannot find it. ❑ *I've lost my wallet.* The past participle and past tense of **lose** are both **lost**.

loose와 lose를 혼동하지 않도록 하라. loose는 대개 형용사로 쓰인다. 어떤 것이 loose하면, 그것이 어디에 제대로 고정되어 있거나 붙어 있지 않은 것이다. □ ...층계참의 헐거운 마룻널....흔들리는 이. 동물을 let loose하면, 그것을 갇혀 있던 곳에서부터 풀어 주는 것이다. □ 그는 흰 쥐 한 쌍을 교회로 가져와서 바닥에 풀어 주었다. lose는 동사다. 무엇을 lose하면, 더 이상 그것을 가지고 있지 않고 찾을 수 없는 것이다. □ 나는 지갑을 잃어버렸다. lose의 과거와 과거분사는 둘 다 lost이다.

Thesaurus   *loose*의 참조어

ADJ.   slack, wobbly ◻
     free ◻
     baggy ◻

Word Partnership   *loose*의 연어

V.   **break** loose, **cut** *someone/something* loose, **set** *someone/something* loose, **turn** *someone/something* loose ◻
   hang loose ◻◻◻◻
   come loose ◻◻◻
N.   loose **coalition**, loose **confederation** ◻

loose end (**loose ends**) ◻ N-COUNT A **loose end** is part of a story, situation, or crime that has not yet been explained. ❑ *There are some annoying loose ends in the plot.* ◻ PHRASE If you are **at loose ends**, you are bored because you do not have anything to do and cannot think of anything that you want to do. In British English, you say that you are **at a loose end**. [INFORMAL] ❑ *She had woken feeling at loose ends.*

◻ 가산명사 결말이 나지 않은 부분 □ 줄거리 중에 결말이 나지 않아 거슬리는 부분이 몇 군데나 있다. ◻ 구 따분한, 의욕이 없는 [비격식체] □ 그녀는 따분함을 느끼며 깨어났다.

loos|en /lˈuːsˀn/ (**loosens, loosening, loosened**) ◻ V-T If someone **loosens** restrictions or laws, for example, they make them less strict or severe. ❑ *Many business groups have been pressing the Federal Reserve to loosen interest rates.* ● **loos|en|ing** N-SING ❑ *Domestic conditions did not justify a loosening of monetary policy.* ◻ V-T/V-I If someone or something **loosens** the ties between people or groups of people, or if the ties **loosen**, they become weaker. ❑ *The Federal Republic must loosen its ties with the United States.* ❑ *The deputy leader is cautious about loosening the links with the unions.* ◻ V-T/V-I If you **loosen** your clothing or something that is tied or fastened, you undo it slightly so that it is less tight or less firmly held in place. ❑ *He reached up to loosen the scarf around his neck.* ❑ *Loosen the bolt so the bars can be turned.* ◻ V-T/V-I If you **loosen** your grip on something, or if your grip **loosens**, you hold it less tightly. ❑ *Harry loosened his grip momentarily and Anna wriggled free.* ◻ V-T/V-I If a government or organization **loosens** its grip on a group of people or an activity, or if its grip **loosens**, it begins to have less control over it. ❑ *There is no sign that the Party will loosen its tight grip on the country.*

◻ 타동사 완화하다 □ 많은 기업체들이 연방 준비 은행에게 금리를 완화하라고 압력을 가하고 있다. ● 완화 단수명사 □ 국내 사정을 고려한다면 재정 정책의 완화는 부당한 것이다. ◻ 타동사/자동사 (관계를) 늦추다, (관계가) 늦춰지다 □ 연방 공화국은 미국과의 관계를 늦출 필요가 있다. □ 부대표는 노조와의 유대를 늦추는 것에 대해 조심스럽다. ◻ 타동사/자동사 느슨하게 하다 □ 그는 손을 올려 목에 두른 스카프를 느슨하게 풀었다. □ 볼트를 풀어 빗장을 돌려라. ◻ 타동사/자동사 풀다; 풀어지다 □ 해리가 손에서 힘을 잠깐 푼 순간 안나가 몸을 비틀어 몸을 빼냈다. ◻ 타동사/자동사 완화하다; 완화되다 □ 당이 국가에 대해 통제를 완화해 줄 것이라는 어떠한 징조도 없다.

▶ **loosen up** ◻ PHRASAL VERB If a person or situation **loosens up**, they become more relaxed and less tense. ❑ *Relax, smile; loosen up in mind and body and behavior.* ❑ *Things loosened up, in politics and the economy.* ◻ PHRASAL VERB If you **loosen up** your body, or if it **loosens up**, you do simple exercises to get your muscles ready for a difficult physical activity, such as running or playing sports. ❑ *Squeeze the foot with both hands, again to loosen up tight muscles.*

◻ 구동사 긴장을 풀다; 긴장이 풀리다 □ 긴장을 풀고 웃어라. 마음과 몸과 행동에 있어 모든 긴장을 풀어라. □ 정치와 경제에 있어 사정이 수월해졌다. ◻ 구동사 몸을 풀다; 몸이 풀어지다 □ 긴장한 근육을 풀어 주기 위해 발을 양손으로 주물러라.

loot /luːt/ (**loots, looting, looted**) ◻ V-T/V-I If people **loot** stores or houses, they steal things from them, for example during a war or riot. ❑ *The trouble began when gangs began breaking windows and looting shops.* ● **loot|ing** N-UNCOUNT ❑ *In the country's largest cities there has been rioting and looting.* ◻ V-T If someone **loots** things, they steal them, for example during a war or riot. ❑ *The town has been plagued by armed thugs who have looted food supplies and terrorized the population.*

◻ 타동사/자동사 약탈하다 □ 갱단이 창문을 깨고 가게를 약탈하기 시작하면서 문제가 발생했다. ● 약탈 불가산명사 □ 나라의 가장 큰 도시들에서 폭동과 약탈이 있었다. ◻ 타동사 약탈하다 □ 마을은 식량 자원을 약탈하고 주민들을 위협해 온 무장 폭도들에게 계속 시달리고 있다.

lop|sided /lˈɒpsaɪdɪd/ also **lop-sided** ADJ Something that is **lopsided** is uneven because one side is lower or heavier than the other. ❑ *His suit had shoulders that made him look lopsided.*

형용사 한쪽으로 기울어진 □ 양복 때문에 그의 어깨가 한쪽으로 기울어진 것처럼 보였다.

lord ◆◇◇ /lˈɔːrd/ (**lords**) ◻ N-COUNT; N-TITLE In Britain, a **lord** is a man who has a high rank in the nobility, for example an earl, a viscount, or a marquis. ❑ *She married a lord and lives in this huge house in the Cotswolds.* ◻ N-VOC In Britain, judges, bishops, and some male members of the nobility are addressed as "**my Lord**." [POLITENESS] ❑ *My lord, I am instructed by my client to claim that the evidence has been tampered with.* ◻ N-TITLE In Britain, **Lord** is used in the titles of some officials of very high rank. ❑ *He was Lord Chancellor from 1970 until 1974.* ◻ N-PROPER-COLL **The Lords** is the same as **the House of Lords**. ❑ *It's very likely the bill will be defeated in the Lords.* ◻ N-PROPER In the Christian church, people refer to God and to Jesus Christ as the **Lord**. [usu the N; N-VOC] ❑ *I know the Lord will look after him.* ❑ *She prayed now. "Lord, help me to find courage."* ◻ EXCLAM **Lord** is used in exclamations such as "good Lord!" and "oh Lord!" to express surprise, shock, frustration, or annoyance about something. [FEELINGS] ❑ *"Good lord, that's what he is: he's a policeman."*

◻ 가산명사; 경칭명사 (영국의) 귀족 □ 그녀는 귀족과 결혼해서 코츠월드에 있는 이 큰 집에서 살았다. ◻ 호격명사 각하 [공존체] □ 각하, 제 의뢰인으로부터 증거가 조작되었다고 주장하라는 지시를 받았습니다. ◻ 경칭명사 영국의 일부 고위 관직에 붙는 명칭 □ 그는 1970년부터 1974년까지 재무장관이었다. ◻ 고유명사-집합 (영국) 상원 □ 법안이 상원에서 부결될 가능성이 높다. ◻ 고유명사 하느님 □ 하느님께서 그들을 돌볼 것이라는 것을 안다. □ "하느님, 저에게 용기를 주세요."라고 그녀는 이제 기도했다. ◻ 감탄사 하느님; 맙소사 [감정 개입] □ 하느님 맙소사, 그의 직업이 다름 아닌 경찰이로군."

lor|ry /lˈɒri, BRIT lˈɒri/ (**lorries**) N-COUNT A **lorry** is a large vehicle that is used to transport goods by road. [BRIT; AM **truck**] ❑ *...a seven-ton lorry.*

가산명사 트럭 [영국영어; 미국영어 truck] □ 7톤 트럭

lose ♦♦♦ /luːz/ (**loses**, **losing**, **lost**) **1** V-T/V-I If you **lose** a contest, a fight, or an argument, you do not succeed because someone does better than you and defeats you. □ *A C Milan lost the Italian Cup Final.* □ *The government lost the argument over the pace of reform.* **2** V-T If you **lose** something, you do not know where it is, for example because you have forgotten where you put it. □ *I lost my keys.* **3** V-T You say that you **lose** something when you no longer have it because it has been taken away from you or destroyed. □ *I lost my job when the company moved to another state.* □ *He lost his licence for six months.* **4** V-T If someone **loses** a quality, characteristic, attitude, or belief, they no longer have it. □ *He lost all sense of reason.* □ *The government had lost all credibility.* **5** V-T If you **lose** an ability, you stop having that ability because of something such as an accident. □ *They lost their ability to hear.* **6** V-T If someone or something **loses** heat, their temperature becomes lower. □ *Babies lose heat much faster than adults.* **7** V-T If you **lose** blood or fluid from your body, it leaves your body so that you have less of it. □ *The victim suffered a dreadful injury and lost a lot of blood.* **8** V-T If you **lose** weight, you become less heavy, and usually look thinner. □ *I have lost a lot of weight.* **9** V-T If someone **loses** their life, they die. □ *...the ferry disaster in 1987, in which 192 people lost their lives.* **10** V-T If you **lose** a close relative or friend, they die. □ *My Grandma lost her brother in the war.* **11** V-T If things **are lost**, they are destroyed in a disaster. [usu passive] □ *...the famous Nankin pottery that was lost in a shipwreck off the coast of China.* **12** V-T If you **lose** time, something slows you down so that you do not make as much progress as you hoped. □ *They claim that police lost valuable time in the early part of the investigation.* **13** V-T If you **lose** an opportunity, you do not take advantage of it. □ *If you don't do it soon you're going to lose the opportunity.* □ *They did not lose the opportunity to say what they thought of events.* **14** V-T If you **lose yourself in** something or if you **are lost in** it, you give a lot of attention to it and do not think about anything else. □ *Michael held on to her arm, losing himself in the music.* **15** V-T If a business **loses** money, it earns less money than it spends, and is therefore in debt. [BUSINESS] □ *His shops stand to lose millions of pounds.* **16** V-T If something **loses** you a contest or **loses** you something that you had, it causes you to fail or to no longer have what you had. □ *My own stupidity lost me the match.* **17** →see also **lost.** **18** PHRASE If you **lose** your **way**, you become lost when you are trying to go somewhere. □ *The men lost their way in a sandstorm.* **19** to **lose** your **balance** →see **balance.** to **lose contact** →see **contact.** to **lose face** →see **face.** to **lose** your **grip** →see **grip.** to **lose** your **head** →see **head.** to **lose heart** →see **heart.** to **lose** your **mind** →see **mind.** to **lose** your **nerve** →see **nerve.** to **lose sight of** →see **sight.** to **lose** your **temper** →see **temper.** to **lose touch** →see **touch.** to **lose track of** →see **track**

Do not confuse **lose** and **loose**. Lose is a verb. If you lose something, you no longer have it and cannot find it. □ *I've lost my wallet.* The past participle and past tense of **lose** are both **lost. Loose** is usually an adjective. If something is **loose**, it is not properly fixed or held in place. □ *...the loose floorboards on the landing....a loose tooth.* If you let an animal **loose**, you release it from where it was kept. □ *He brought a pair of white rats into church, and let them loose on the floor.*

▶**lose out** PHRASAL VERB If you **lose out**, you suffer a loss or disadvantage because you have not succeeded in what you were doing. □ *We both lost out.* □ *Laura lost out to Tom.*

los|er /luːzər/ (**losers**) **1** N-COUNT The **losers** of a game, contest, or struggle are the people who are defeated or beaten. □ *...the Dallas Cowboys and Buffalo Bills, the winners and losers of this year's Super Bowl.* ● PHRASE If someone is a **good loser**, they accept that they have lost a game or contest without complaining. If someone is a **bad loser**, they hate losing and complain about it. □ *I'm sure the prime minister will turn out to be a good loser.* **2** N-COUNT If you refer to someone as a **loser**, you have a low opinion of them because you think they are always unsuccessful. [INFORMAL, DISAPPROVAL] □ *They've only been trained to compete with other men, so a successful woman can make them feel like a real loser.* **3** N-COUNT People who are **losers** as the result of an action or event, are in a worse situation because of it or do not benefit from it. □ *Some of Britain's top business leaders of the 1980s became the country's greatest losers in the recession.*

loss ♦♦◇ /lɒs, BRIT lɒs/ (**losses**) **1** N-VAR **Loss** is the fact of no longer having something or having less of it than before. □ *...loss of sight.* □ *...hair loss.* **2** N-VAR **Loss** of life occurs when people die. □ *...a terrible loss of human life.* **3** N-UNCOUNT The **loss** of a relative or friend is their death. □ *They took the time to talk about the loss of Thomas and how their grief was affecting them.* **4** N-VAR If a business makes a **loss**, it earns less than it spends. □ *In 1986 Rover made a loss of nine hundred million pounds.* □ *The company said it will stop producing fertilizer in 1990 because of continued losses.* **5** N-UNCOUNT **Loss** is the feeling of sadness you experience when someone or something you like is taken away from you. □ *Talk to others about your feelings of loss and grief.* **6** N-COUNT A **loss** is the disadvantage you suffer when a valuable and useful person or thing leaves or is taken away. □ *She said his death was a great loss to herself.* **7** N-UNCOUNT The **loss** of something such as heat, blood, or fluid is the gradual reduction of it or of its level in a system or in someone's body. □ *...blood loss.* □ *...a rapid loss of heat from the body.* **8** PHRASE If a business produces something **at a loss**, they sell it at a price which is less than it cost them to produce it or buy it. [BUSINESS] □ *Timber owners have often produced lumber at a loss and survived these down cycles in demand.* **9** PHRASE If you say that you are **at a loss**, you mean that you do not know

---

1 타동사/자동사 지다 □ 에이시 밀란이 이태리컵 결승전에서 졌다. **2** 타동사 패배하다 □ 정부는 개혁의 속도에 관한 논쟁에서 패배했다. **2** 타동사 잃어버리다 □ 나는 열쇠를 잃어버렸다. **3** 타동사 잃다 □ 회사가 다른 주로 이사 갈 때 나는 직장을 잃었다. □ 그는 6개월 동안 면허를 잃었다. **4** 타동사 잃다 □ 그는 모든 이성을 잃었다. □ 정부는 모든 신용을 잃었었다. **5** 타동사 잃다 □ 그들은 청각을 잃었다. **6** 타동사 빼앗기다 □ 아기들은 어른들보다 체온을 훨씬 빨리 빼앗긴다. **7** 타동사 빼앗기다, 잃다 □ 피해자는 심한 부상을 입고 많은 피를 흘렸다. **8** 타동사 (살을) 빼다 □ 나는 살을 많이 뺐다. **9** 타동사 잃다 □ 192명이 목숨을 잃은 1987년의 연락선 사고 **10** 타동사 여의다 □ 할머니께서는 남동생을 전쟁 때 여의셨다. **11** 타동사 소실되다 □ 중국 연안의 난파 사고로 소실된 유명한 난징 자기 **12** 타동사 빼앗기다 □ 그들은 조사의 초기에 경찰이 귀중한 시간을 뺏겼다고 주장한다. **13** 타동사 놓치다 □ 곧 하지 않으면 기회를 놓칠 것이다. □ 그들은 행사에 대해 생각하는 바를 말할 기회를 놓치지 않았다. **14** 타동사 몰입하다 □ 마이클은 그녀의 팔을 계속 붙잡은 채 음악에 몰입해 들어갔다. **15** 타동사 잃다 [경제] □ 그의 가게들은 수백만 파운드를 잃을 처지에 있다. **16** 타동사 지도록 만들다; 잃도록 하다 □ 내 우둔함 때문에 경기에서 졌다. **18** 구 길을 잃다 □ 그 남자들은 모래 폭풍 속에서 길을 잃었다.

lose와 loose를 혼동하지 않도록 하라. lose는 동사다. 무엇을 lose하면, 더 이상 그것을 가지고 있지 않고 찾을 수 없는 것이다. □ 나는 지갑을 잃어버렸다. lose의 과거와 과거분사는 둘 다 lost이다. loose는 대개 형용사로 쓰인다. 어떤 것이 loose하면, 그것이 어디에 제대로 고정되어 있거나 붙어 있지 않은 것이다. □ ...층계참의 헐거운 바닥널....흔들리는 이. 동물을 let loose하면, 그것을 간혀 있던 곳에서부터 풀어 주는 것이다. □ 그는 흰 쥐 한 쌍을 교회로 가져와서 바닥에 풀어 주었다.

구동사 손해를 입다, 실패하다 □ 우리 둘 다 손해를 입었다. □ 로라는 톰에게 졌다.

1 가산명사 패자 □ 올해 슈퍼볼의 승자와 패자인 댈러스 카우보이스와 버펄로 빌스 ● 구 깨끗이 승복하는 패자; 굳소리 많은 패자 □ 수상리 패하면 깨끗이 물러날 것이라고 믿는다. **2** 가산명사 실패자, 패배자 [비격식체, 탐탁찮음] □ 그들은 다른 남자들하고만 경쟁하도록 훈련을 받았기 때문에 성공적인 여성을 만나면 스스로 인생의 패배자라고 느낄 수도 있다. **3** 가산명사 손해를 보는 사람 □ 영국에서 1980년대에 가장 성공한 기업들 중 일부는 불경기에 가장 쓴 맛을 봤다.

1 가산명사 또는 불가산명사 상실 □ 시력의 상실 □ 머리가 빠짐 **2** 가산명사 또는 불가산명사 손실 □ 끔찍한 인명 손실 **3** 불가산명사 여읨 □ 그들은 그 시간에 토머스의 죽음과 그에 따른 슬픔이 그들에게 어떤 영향을 미치고 있는지에 대해 이야기했다. **4** 가산명사 또는 불가산명사 손실 □ 1986년에 로버는 9억 파운드의 손실을 봤다. □ 회사는 지속되는 손실 때문에 1990년에 비료의 생산을 중단할 것이라고 했다. **5** 불가산명사 상실감 □ 당신의 상실감과 슬픔에 대해 다른 사람들에게 이야기하라. **6** 가산명사 상실, 빼앗김 □ 그녀는 그의 죽음으로 너무나 큰 것을 잃었다고 했다. **7** 불가산명사 손실 □ 혈액 손실 □ 체온의 급격한 손실 **8** 구 손해를 보며 [경제] □ 목재소 주인들은 흔히 손해를 보면서도 목재를 생산하면서 수요가 하강 곡선을 긋는 이런 시기를 견뎌 냈다. **9** 구 어찌할 바를 모르는 □ 다음에 뭘 해야 할지 몰랐다.

a b c d e f g h i j k l m n o p q r s t u v w x y z

what to do in a particular situation. ❑ *I was at a loss for what to do next.*
→see **disaster**

Word Partnership   *loss*의 연어

ADJ.	**great/huge/substantial** loss **1**-**7**
	tragic loss **2** **3**
	net loss **4**
N.	loss **of appetite**, loss **of control**, loss **of income**, loss **of a job** **1**
	blood loss, **hair** loss, **hearing** loss, **memory** loss, **weight** loss **7**

loss adjust|er (**loss adjusters**) also **loss adjustor** N-COUNT A **loss adjuster** is someone who is employed by an insurance company to decide how much money should be paid to a person making a claim. [BRIT, BUSINESS; AM **insurance adjuster, claims adjuster**]

loss lead|er (**loss leaders**) also **loss-leader** N-COUNT A **loss leader** is an item that is sold at such a low price that it makes a loss in the hope that customers will be attracted by it and buy other goods at the same store. [BUSINESS] ❑ *Hoskins does not expect a huge profit from the cookies, viewing them more as a loss leader.*

lost ♦♦◇◇ /lɒst, BRIT lɒst/ **1** **Lost** is the past tense and past participle of **lose**. **2** ADJ If you are **lost** or if you get **lost**, you do not know where you are or are unable to find your way. ❑ *Barely had I set foot in the street when I realised I was lost.* **3** ADJ If something is **lost**, or gets **lost**, you cannot find it, for example because you have forgotten where you put it. ❑ *...a lost book.* ❑ *He was scrabbling for his pen, which had got lost somewhere under the sheets of paper.* **4** ADJ If you feel **lost**, you feel very uncomfortable because you are in an unfamiliar situation. ❑ *Of the funeral he remembered only the cold, the waiting, and feeling very lost.* **5** ADJ If you describe something as **lost**, you mean that you no longer have it or it no longer exists. ❑ *...their lost homeland.* ❑ *The sense of community is lost.* **6** ADJ You use **lost** to refer to a period or state of affairs that existed in the past and no longer exists. [ADJ n] ❑ *He seemed to pine for his lost youth.* ❑ *They are links to a lost age.* **7** ADJ If something is **lost**, it is not used properly and is considered wasted. ❑ *Fox is not bitter about the lost opportunity to compete in the Games.*

Thesaurus   *lost*의 참조어

ADJ.	adrift **2** **4**
	missing **3**

lost and found **1** N-SING **Lost and found** is the place where lost property is kept. [AM; BRIT **lost property**] ❑ *Excuse me, can you tell me where the lost and found is?* **2** ADJ **Lost and found** things are things which someone has lost and which someone else has found. ❑ *...the shelf where they stored lost-and-found articles.*

lot ♦♦♦ /lɒt/ (**lots**) **1** QUANT A **lot** of something or **lots** of it is a large amount of it. A **lot** of people or things, or **lots** of them, is a large number of them. [QUANT of n] ❑ *A lot of our land is used to grow crops for export.* ❑ *I remember a lot of things.* ❑ *He drank lots of milk.* ● PRON **Lot** is also a pronoun. ❑ *I personally prefer to be in a town where there's lots going on.* ❑ *I learned a lot from him about how to run a band.* **2** ADV A **lot** means to a great extent or degree. ❑ *Matthew's out quite a lot doing his research.* ❑ *I like you, a lot.* **3** ADV If you do something **a lot**, you do it often or for a long time. [ADV after v] ❑ *They went out a lot, to the Cafe Royal or the The Ivy.* **4** N-COUNT You can use **lot** to refer to a set or group of things or people. ❑ *He bought two lots of 1,000 shares in the company during August and September.* **5** N-SING You can refer to a specific group of people as a particular **lot**. [INFORMAL] ❑ *Future generations are going to think that we were a pretty boring lot.* **6** N-SING You can use **the lot** to refer to the whole of an amount that you have just mentioned. [INFORMAL] ❑ *This may turn out to be the best football game of the lot.* **7** N-SING Your **lot** is the kind of life you have or the things that you have or experience. ❑ *She tried to accept her marriage as her lot in life but could not.* **8** N-COUNT A **lot** is a small area of land that belongs to a person or company. [AM] ❑ *If oil or gold are discovered under your lot, you can sell the mineral rights.* →see also **parking lot** **9** N-COUNT A **lot** in an auction is one of the objects or groups of objects that are being sold. ❑ *The receivers are keen to sell the stores as one lot.* **10** PHRASE If people **draw lots** to decide who will do something, they each take a piece of paper from a container. One or more pieces of paper is marked, and the people who take marked pieces are chosen. ❑ *For the first time in a World Cup finals, lots had to be drawn to decide who would finish second and third.*

loth /loʊθ/ →see **loath**

lo|tion /loʊʃⁿ/ (**lotions**) N-MASS A **lotion** is a liquid that you use to clean, improve, or protect your skin or hair. ❑ *...suntan lotion.*

lot|tery /lɒtəri/ (**lotteries**) **1** N-COUNT A **lottery** is a type of gambling game in which people buy numbered tickets. Several numbers are then chosen, and the people who have those numbers on their tickets win a prize. ❑ *...the national lottery.* **2** N-SING If you describe something as a **lottery**, you mean that what happens depends entirely on luck or chance. ❑ *The stockmarket is a lottery.* →see Word Web: **lottery**

loud ♦♦◇◇ /laʊd/ (**louder, loudest**) **1** ADJ If a noise is **loud**, the level of sound is very high and it can be easily heard. Someone or something that is **loud** produces a lot of noise. ❑ *Suddenly there was a loud bang.* ❑ *His voice became harsh and loud.* ● ADV **Loud** is also an adverb. [ADV after v] ❑ *She wonders whether Paul's hearing is OK because he turns the television up very loud.* ● **loud|ly** ADV [ADV with v] ❑ *His footsteps echoed loudly in the tiled hall.* **2** ADJ If you describe something, especially a piece of clothing, as **loud**, you dislike it because it has very bright colors or very large, bold patterns which look unpleasant. [DISAPPROVAL] ❑ *He*

가산명사 보험배상조정관 [영국영어, 경제; 미국영어 insurance adjuster, claims adjuster]

가산명사 미끼상품 [경제] ❑ 호스킨스는 쿠키로부터 커다란 수익을 기대하지 않으며 오히려 그것을 미끼상품으로 여긴다.

lose의 과거 및 과거 분사 **2** 형용사 길을 잃은 ❑ 거리에 발을 들여 놓는 순간 내가 길을 잃었다는 것을 깨달았다. **3** 형용사 사라진, 잃은 ❑ 사라진 책 ❑ 여러 장의 종이에 묻혀 어딘가로 사라진 펜을 찾기 위해 남자는 이리저리 뒤졌다. **4** 형용사 어쩔 바를 모르는 ❑ 장례식에 대해서 그가 기억하는 것이라고는 추위와 기다림과 어쩔 바를 몰랐던 기분밖에 없다. **5** 형용사 잃어버린 ❑ 그들의 잃어버린 고향 ❑ 공동체 의식이 사라진다. **6** 형용사 지나간 **6** 그는 지나간 젊은 시절을 그리워하는 것 같았다. ❑ 그것들은 지나간 시대를 잇는 고리이다. **7** 형용사 허비한 ❑ 폭스는 올림픽 경기에 출전할 수 있는 기회를 허비한 것에 대해 씁쓸하게 생각하지 않는다.

1 단수명사 분실물 센터 [미국영어; 영국영어 lost property] ❑ 죄송한데 분실물 센터가 어디 있나요? **2** 형용사 분실 ❑ 그들이 분실물을 보관했던 선반

1 수량사 많은 ❑ 우리의 많은 땅이 수출용 농작물을 재배하는 데 쓰인다. ❑ 나는 많은 것을 기억한다. ❑ 그는 우유를 많이 마셨다. ● 대명사 많은 ❑ 많은 일이 벌어지는 도시에 있는 것을 개인적으로 선호한다. ❑ 밴드를 어떻게 운영해야 하는지에 대해 그로부터 많은 것을 배웠다. **2** 부사 많이 ❑ 매튜는 현장 연구를 하느라 많이 나가 있다. ❑ 나는 너를 많이 좋아한다. **3** 부사 많이 ❑ 그들은 카페 로열이나 아이비 같은 데를 많이 나갔다. **4** 가산명사 묶음, 그룹 ❑ 그는 8월과 9월에 그 회사의 주식을 1,000주씩 두 번 샀다. **5** 단수명사 족속 [비격식체] ❑ 미래의 후손들은 우리가 꽤나 재미없는 족속이었다고 생각할 것이다. **6** 단수명사 개중 [비격식체] ❑ 이것이 어쩌면 개중에 가장 훌륭한 축구 경기가 될지도 모른다. **7** 단수명사 운명 ❑ 그녀는 결혼이 자신의 팔자라고 받아들이려고 노력했으나 그럴 수가 없었다. **8** 가산명사 부지 [미국영어] ❑ 만약 자신의 땅에서 석유나 금이 발견된다면 채굴권을 가질 수 있다. **9** 가산명사 하나의 경매물품 ❑ 재산 관리인들은 그 가게들을 묶어서 팔기를 간절히 원한다. **10** 구 제비뽑기 하다 ❑ 월드컵 결승 사상 처음으로 2위와 3위를 결정하기 위해 제비뽑기를 해야 했다.

물질명사 로션 ❑ 선탠로션

1 가산명사 복권 ❑ 전국적으로 실시되는 복권 **2** 단수명사 도박 ❑ 주식 시장은 도박판과 같다.

1 형용사 소리가 큰, 시끄러운 ❑ 갑자기 펑 하는 큰 소리가 들렸다. ❑ 그의 목소리가 크고 거칠었다. ● 부사 소리가 크게, 큰 소리로 ❑ 폴은 텔레비전의 소리를 매우 크게 틀기 때문에 그녀는 폴의 청력이 괜찮은지 궁금해한다. ● 크게, 큰 소리로 부사 ❑ 그의 발자국 소리가 타일로 덮인 복도에서 크게 울려 퍼졌다. **2** 형용사 요란한 [탐탁찮음] ❑ 그는 목걸이에 요란한 옷을 입고 사람들을 놀라키는 것을 좋아한다.

Word Web   lottery

People **gamble** for many different reasons. Some want to become rich. Some find it entertaining or exciting. Others need more **money** to live. **Lotteries** have become a popular form of **betting**. Most places have a lottery. **Winners** can choose between a **lump sum** payment and annual **payouts**. Either way, they usually have to pay the government about half their **winnings** in taxes. The **odds** of **winning** a lottery are very tiny. There is often only about one chance in 20 million of winning the **jackpot**. Studies have shown that poor people are the most likely to **play** the lottery.

---

liked to shock with his gold chains and loud clothes. ❸ PHRASE If you say or read something **out loud**, you say it or read it so that it can be heard, rather than just thinking it. ❏ *Even Ford, who seldom smiled, laughed out loud a few times.* ❹ **for crying out loud** →see **cry**

❸ 구 소리 내어 ❏ 거의 웃음이 없는 포드조차 여러 번 소리 내어 웃었다.

Thesaurus   loud의 참조어

| ADJ. | deafening, noisy, piercing; (ant.) quiet, soft ❶ |
| | flashy, gaudy, tasteless ❷ |

Word Partnership   loud의 연어

N.	loud **bang**, loud **crash**, loud **explosion**, loud **music**, loud **noise**, loud **voice** ❶
ADJ.	loud **and clear** ❶
V.	**laugh** out loud, **read** out loud, **say** *something* out loud, **think** out loud ❸

loud|speaker /la͟ʊdspiːkər/ (**loudspeakers**) also **loud speaker** N-COUNT A **loudspeaker** is a piece of equipment, for example part of a radio or hi-fi system, through which sound comes out.

가산명사 스피커

lounge /la͟ʊndʒ/ (**lounges, lounging, lounged**) ❶ N-COUNT In a hotel, club, or other public place, a **lounge** is a room where people can sit and relax. ❏ *I spoke to her in the lounge of a big Johannesburg hotel where she was attending a union meeting.* ❷ N-COUNT In an airport, a **lounge** is a very large room where people can sit and wait for aircraft to arrive or leave. ❏ *Instead of taking me to the departure lounge they took me right to my seat on the plane.* ❸ N-COUNT In a house, a **lounge** is a room where people sit and relax. [mainly BRIT] ❏ *The Holmbergs were sitting before a roaring fire in the lounge, sipping their cocoa.* ❹ V-I If you **lounge** somewhere, you sit or lie there in a relaxed or lazy way. ❏ *They ate and drank and lounged in the shade.*

❶ 가산명사 휴게실, 라운지 ❏ 나는 그녀가 노동조합 회의에 참석하느라 있었던 요하네스버그의 큰 호텔 휴게실에서 그녀와 이야기했다. ❷ 가산명사 출발 대기장 ❏ 그들은 나를 출발 대기장으로 데려가지 않고 바로 비행기 안 내 자리로 데려갔다. ❸ 가산명사 거실 [주로 영국영어] ❏ 홈버그 가족은 거실에서 훨훨 타는 난로 앞에 앉아 코코아를 마시고 있었다. ❹ 자동사 편안히 쉬다 ❏ 그들은 그늘에서 먹고 마시며 편안히 쉬었다.

louse /la͟ʊs/ (**lice**) N-COUNT **Lice** are small insects that live on the bodies of people or animals and bite them in order to feed off their blood.

가산명사 이

lousy /la͟ʊzi/ (**lousier, lousiest**) ❶ ADJ If you describe something as **lousy**, you mean that it is of very bad quality or that you do not like it. [INFORMAL] ❏ *He blamed Fiona for a lousy weekend.* ❏ *At Billy's Cafe, the menu is limited and the food is lousy.* ❷ ADJ If you describe someone as **lousy**, you mean that they are very bad at something they do. [INFORMAL] ❏ *I was a lousy secretary.* ❸ ADJ If you describe the number or amount of something as **lousy**, you mean it is smaller than you think it should be. [INFORMAL] ❏ *The pay is lousy.* ❹ ADJ If you feel **lousy**, you feel very ill. [INFORMAL] [feel/look ADJ] ❏ *I wasn't actually sick but I felt lousy.*

❶ 형용사 형편없는 [비격식체] ❏ 형편없는 주말을 보낸 것을 그는 피오나 탓으로 돌렸다. ❏ 빌리스 카페는 메뉴가 몇 가지 없고 음식은 형편없다. ❷ 형용사 형편없는 [비격식체] ❏ 나는 형편없는 비서였다. ❸ 형용사 형편없는 [비격식체] ❏ 봉급은 형편없다. ❹ 형용사 몸이 안 좋은 [비격식체] ❏ 실제로 아픈 것은 아니었지만 기분이 아주 안 좋았다.

lout /la͟ʊt/ (**louts**) N-COUNT If you describe a man or boy as a **lout**, you are critical of them because they behave in an impolite or aggressive way. [DISAPPROVAL] ❏ *...a drunken lout.*

가산명사 망나니 [탐탁찮음] ❏ 술 취한 망나니

lov|able /lʌ͟vəbəl/ ADJ If you describe someone as **lovable**, you mean that they have attractive qualities, and are easy to like. ❏ *His vulnerability makes him even more lovable.*

형용사 사랑스러운 ❏ 그는 약한 면이 있어서 훨씬 더 사랑스럽다.

love ◆◆◇ /lʌ͟v/ (**loves, loving, loved**) ❶ V-T If you **love** someone, you feel romantically or sexually attracted to them, and they are very important to you. ❏ *Oh, Amy, I love you.* ❷ N-UNCOUNT **Love** is a very strong feeling of affection toward someone who you are romantically or sexually attracted to. ❏ *Our love for each other has been increased by what we've been through together.* ❏ *...a old fashioned love story.* ❸ V-T You say that you **love** someone when their happiness is very important to you, so that you behave in a kind and caring way towards them. ❏ *You'll never love anyone the way you love your baby.* ❹ N-UNCOUNT **Love** is the feeling that a person's happiness is very important to you, and the way you show this feeling in your behavior toward them. ❏ *My love for all my children is unconditional.* ❺ V-T If you **love** something, you like it very much. ❏ *We loved the food so much, especially the fish dishes.* ❏ *...one of these people that loves to be in the outdoors.* ❻ V-T You can say that you **love** something when you consider that it is important and want to protect or support it. ❏ *I love my country as you love yours.* ❼ N-UNCOUNT **Love** is a strong liking for something, or a belief that it is important. ❏ *This is no way to encourage a love of literature.* ❽ N-COUNT Your **love** is someone or something that you love. ❏ *"She is the love of my life," he said.* ❾ V-T If you **would love to** have or do something, you very much want to have it or do it. ❏ *I would love to play for England again.* ❏ *I would love a hot*

❶ 타동사 사랑하다 ❏ 오, 에이미, 사랑해. ❷ 불가산명사 사랑 ❏ 우리는 함께 겪은 일로 해서 서로에 대한 사랑이 더 커졌다. ❏ 전형적인 사랑 이야기 ❸ 타동사 사랑하다 ❏ 자기 아이를 사랑하는 것만큼은 어느 누구도 사랑할 수 없을 것이다. ❹ 불가산명사 사랑 ❏ 내 아이들에 대한 나의 사랑은 무조건적이다. ❺ 타동사 매우 좋아하다 ❏ 우리는 그 음식을, 특히 생선 요리를 너무 좋아했다. ❏ 야외에 있는 것을 너무 좋아하는 사람들 중 하나 ❻ 타동사 사랑하다 ❏ 네가 네 나라를 사랑하듯이 나도 내 나라를 사랑한다. ❼ 불가산명사 애정 ❏ 이렇게 해서는 문학에 대한 애정을 키울 수 없다. ❽ 가산명사 연인; 애호품 ❏ "그녀는 내 인생의 연인이다."라고 그는 말했다. ❾ 타동사 ~했으면 정말 좋겠다 ❏ 잉글랜드를 위해 정말로 다시 뛰고 싶다. ❏ 뜨거운 목욕을 하고 깨끗한 옷을 입으면 정말 좋겠다. ❿ 호격명사 자기 [영국영어, 비격식체, 감정 개입] ❏ 그렇다면 당신 말을 믿을게, 자기. ⓫ 수사 (테니스) 영점 ❏ 그는 오스트리아의 토머스 머스터를 세트 스코어 3대 0으로 이겼다.

bath and clean clothes. **10** N-VOC Some people use **love** as an affectionate way of addressing someone. [BRIT, INFORMAL, FEELINGS] ❑ *Well, I'll take your word for it then, love.* **11** NUM In tennis, **love** is a score of zero. ❑ *He beat Thomas Muster of Austria three sets to love.* **12** CONVENTION You can use expressions such as "**love**," "**love from**," and "**all my love**," followed by your name, as an informal way of ending a letter to a friend or relative. ❑ *...with love from Grandma and Grandpa.* **13** N-UNCOUNT If you send someone your **love**, you ask another person, who will soon be speaking or writing to them, to tell them that you are thinking about them with affection. ❑ *Please give her my love.* **14** →see also **loving** **15** PHRASE If you **fall in love with** someone, you start to be in love with them. ❑ *I fell in love with him because of his kind nature.* **16** PHRASE If you **fall in love with** something, you start to like it very much. ❑ *Working with Ford closely, I fell in love with the cinema.* **17** PHRASE If you **are in love with** someone, you feel romantically or sexually attracted to them, and they are very important to you. ❑ *Laura had never before been in love.* ❑ *I've never really been in love with anyone.* **18** PHRASE If you are **in love with** something, you like it very much. ❑ *He had always been in love with the enchanted landscape of the West.* **19** PHRASE When two people **make love**, they have sex. ❑ *Have you ever made love to a girl before?* →see **emotion**
→see Word Web: **love**

Thesaurus   love의 참조어

v.	adore, cherish; *(ant.)* dislike, hate **1** **3**
N.	adoration, devotion; *(ant.)* hate **2** **4**

Word Partnership   love의 연어

N.	love **a girl/guy**, love **your husband/wife**, love **a man/woman**, love **and marriage** **1** **3**
	love **of books**, love **of life**, love **music**, love **of nature** **7**
ADJ.	**passionate** love, **romantic** love, **sexual** love **2**
	great love, **true** love **2** **4** **8**

love af|fair (**love affairs**) **1** N-COUNT A **love affair** is a romantic and usually sexual relationship between two people who love each other but who are not married or living together. ❑ *...a stressful love affair with a married man.* **2** N-SING If you refer to someone's **love affair with** something, you mean that they like it a lot and are very enthusiastic about it. ❑ *...the American love affair with firearms.*

love life (**love lives**) N-COUNT Someone's **love life** is the part of their life that consists of their romantic and sexual relationships. ❑ *His love life was complicated, and involved intense relationships.*

love|ly ♦♢♢ /lʌvli/ (**lovelier, loveliest**) **1** ADJ If you describe someone or something as **lovely**, you mean that they are very beautiful and therefore pleasing to look at or listen to. ❑ *You look lovely, Marcia.* ❑ *He had a lovely voice.* ● **love|li|ness** N-UNCOUNT ❑ *You are a vision of loveliness.* **2** ADJ If you describe something as **lovely**, you mean that it gives you pleasure. [mainly SPOKEN] ❑ *Mary! How lovely to see you!* ❑ *It's a lovely day.* **3** ADJ If you describe someone as **lovely**, you mean that they are friendly, kind, or generous. [mainly BRIT] ❑ *Laura is a lovely young woman.*

lov|er ♦♢♢ /lʌvər/ (**lovers**) **1** N-COUNT Someone's **lover** is someone who they are having a sexual relationship with but who are not married to. ❑ *Every Thursday she would meet her lover Leon.* **2** N-COUNT If you are a **lover** of something such as animals or the arts, you enjoy them very much and take great pleasure in them. ❑ *She is a great lover of horses and horse racing.*

Word Partnership   lover의 연어

ADJ.	**former** lover, **great** lover, **jealous** lover, **married** lover **1**
N.	**animal** lover, **music** lover, **nature** lover **2**

lov|ing /lʌvɪŋ/ **1** ADJ Someone who is **loving** feels or shows love to other people. ❑ *Jim was a most loving husband and father.* ● **lov|ing|ly** ADV ❑ *Brian gazed lovingly at Mary Ann.* **2** ADJ **Loving** actions are done with great enjoyment and care. ❑ *The house has been restored with loving care.* ● **lov|ing|ly** ADV ❑ *I lifted the box and ran my fingers lovingly over the top.*

low ♦♦♦ /loʊ/ (**lower, lowest, lows**) **1** ADJ Something that is **low** measures only a short distance from the bottom to the top, or from the ground to the top. ❑ *...the low garden wall that separated the front garden from next door.* ❑ *The country,*

---

12 관용 표현 편지의 맺음말 ❑ 사랑하는 할머니와 할아버지로부터 **13** 불가산명사 안부 ❑ 그녀에게 안부를 전해 주세요. **15** 구 사랑에 빠지다, 아주 좋아하게 되다 ❑ 나는 그의 착한 성품 때문에 그와 사랑에 빠졌다. **16** 구 사랑에 빠지다 ❑ 포드와 가까이 일하면서 나는 영화와 사랑에 빠졌다. **17** 구 사랑하다 ❑ 로라는 여태껏 사랑해 본 적이 없다. ❑ 나는 진정 누구를 사랑해 본 적이 없다. **18** 구 사랑하다 ❑ 그는 서부의 신비로운 경치를 항상 사랑했다. **19** 구 성관계를 가지다 ❑ 여자와 성관계를 가져 본 적이 있니?

1 가산명사 정사, 연애 ❑ 유부남과의 힘든 연애 **2** 단수명사 열광 ❑ 총기에 대한 미국의 열광

가산명사 애정 생활 ❑ 그의 애정 생활은 복잡하면서도 격렬했다.

1 형용사 아름다운, 너무 좋은 ❑ 아름답다, 마셔. ❑ 그는 목소리가 너무 좋았다. ● 아름다움 불가산명사 ❑ 너는 아름다움 그 자체야. **2** 형용사 좋은 [주로 구어체] ❑ 메리! 만나서 너무 반갑다! ❑ 정말 날씨 좋다. **3** 형용사 사랑스러운 [주로 영국영어] ❑ 로라는 정말 사랑스러운 젊은 여성이다.

1 가산명사 연인 ❑ 매주 목요일 그녀는 연인인 레온을 만나곤 했다. **2** 가산명사 애호가 ❑ 그녀는 말과 경마의 대단한 애호가이다.

1 형용사 다정한 ❑ 짐은 매우 다정한 남편이자 아버지였다. ● 다정하게 부사 ❑ 브라이언은 메리 앤을 다정하게 바라봤다. **2** 형용사 애정 어린 ❑ 그 집은 애정 어린 손길로 복원되었다. ● 애정을 갖고 부사 ❑ 나는 상자를 들고 애정 어린 손으로 뚜껑을 쓸어 보았다.

1 형용사 낮은 ❑ 앞마당을 옆집과 구분하는 낮은 정원 담장으로 낮은 구릉지로 이루어진 그 지역은 아름다웠다. **2** 형용사 낮은 ❑ 그는 낮은 들보에 머리를 부딪쳤다.

Word Web   love

Until the Middle Ages, **romance** was not an important part of **marriage**. Parents decided who their children would marry. Often social class and political connections were the deciding factor. No one expected a couple to **fall in love**. However, during the Middle Ages, poets and musicians began to write about love in a new way. These **romantic** poems and songs describe a new type of courtship. In them, the man **woos** a woman for her **affection**. This is the basis for the modern idea of a romantic **bond** between **husband** and **wife**.

with its low, rolling hills was beautiful. **2** ADJ If something is **low**, it is close to the ground, to sea level, or to the bottom of something. ❑ *He bumped his head on the low beams.* ❑ *It was late afternoon and the sun was low in the sky.* **3** ADJ When a river is **low**, it contains less water than usual. ❑ *...pumps that guarantee a constant depth of water even when the supplying river is low.* **4** ADJ You can use **low** to indicate that something is small in amount or that it is at the bottom of a particular scale. You can use phrases such as **in the low 80s** to indicate that a number or level is less than 85 but not as little as 80. ❑ *British casualties remained remarkably low.* ❑ *They are still having to live on very low incomes.* **5** ADJ **Low** is used to describe people who are not considered to be very important because they are near the bottom of a particular scale or system. ❑ *She refused to promote Colin above the low rank of "legal adviser."* **6** N-COUNT If something reaches a **low** of a particular amount or degree, that is the smallest it has ever been. ❑ *Prices dropped to a low of about $1.12 in December.* **7** ADJ If the quality or standard of something is **low**, it is very poor. ❑ *A school would not accept low-quality work from any student.* ❑ *The inquiry team criticises staff at the psychiatric hospital for the low standard of care.* **8** ADJ If a food or other substance is **low in** a particular ingredient, it contains only a small amount of that ingredient. [v-link ADJ in n] ❑ *They look for foods that are low in calories.* ● COMB in ADJ **Low** is also a combining form. ❑ *...low-sodium tomato sauce.* **9** ADJ If you have a **low** opinion of someone or something, you disapprove of them or dislike them. ❑ *The majority of sex offenders have a low opinion of themselves.* **10** ADJ You can use **low** to describe negative feelings and attitudes. ❑ *We are all very tired and morale is low.* **11** ADJ If a sound or noise is **low**, it is deep. ❑ *Then suddenly she gave a low, choking moan and began to tremble violently.* **12** ADJ If someone's voice is **low**, it is quiet or soft. ❑ *Her voice was so low he had to strain to catch it.* **13** ADJ A light that is **low** is not bright or strong. ❑ *Their eyesight is poor in low light.* **14** ADJ If a radio, oven, or light is on **low**, it has been adjusted so that only a small amount of sound, heat, or light is produced. ❑ *She turned her little kitchen radio on low.* ❑ *Buy a dimmer switch and keep the light on low, or switch it off altogether.* **15** ADJ If you are **low on** something or if a supply of it is **low**, there is not much of it left. [v-link ADJ, usu ADJ on n] ❑ *We're a bit low on bed linen.* **16** ADJ If you are **low**, you are depressed. [INFORMAL] ❑ *"I didn't ask for this job, you know," he tells friends when he is low.* **17** →see also **lower** **18** to look **high and low** →see **high**. **low profile** →see **profile**. to be running **low** →see **run**

Thesaurus   *low*의 참조어

ADJ.   bottom **2**
          inferior, second-rate, shoddy **7**

---

low|er ♦◇◇ /loʊər/ (**lowers**, **lowering**, **lowered**) **1** ADJ You can use **lower** to refer to the bottom one of a pair of things. [ADJ n, the ADJ] ❑ *She bit her lower lip.* ❑ *...the lower of the two holes.* **2** ADJ You can use **lower** to refer to the bottom part of something. [ADJ n] ❑ *Use a small cushion to help give support to the lower back.* **3** ADJ You can use **lower** to refer to people or things that are less important than similar people or things. [ADJ n, the ADJ] ❑ *Already the awards are causing resentment in the lower ranks of council officers.* ❑ *The nation's highest court reversed the lower court's decision.* **4** V-T If you **lower** something, you move it slowly downward. ❑ *Two reporters had to help lower the coffin into the grave.* ❑ *Sokolowski lowered himself into the black leather chair.* ● **low|er|ing** N-UNCOUNT ❑ *...the extinguishing of the Olympic flame and the lowering of the flag.* **5** V-T If you **lower** something, you make it less in amount, degree, value, or quality. ❑ *The Central Bank has lowered interest rates by 2 percent.* ● **low|er|ing** N-UNCOUNT ❑ *...a package of social measures which included the lowering of the retirement age.* **6** V-T If someone **lowers** their head or eyes, they look downward, for example because they are sad or embarrassed. ❑ *She lowered her head and brushed past photographers as she went back inside.* **7** V-T If you say that you would not **lower yourself** by doing something, you mean that you would not behave in a way that would make you or other people respect you less. [oft with brd-neg] ❑ *Don't lower yourself, don't be the way they are.* **8** V-T/V-I If you **lower** your voice or if your voice **lowers**, you speak more quietly. ❑ *The man moved closer, lowering his voice.* **9** →see also **low**

low|er|case also **lower-case**, **lower case** N-UNCOUNT **Lowercase** letters are small letters, not capital letters. ❑ *It was printed in lowercase.*

low-key ADJ If you say that something is **low-key**, you mean that it is on a small scale rather than involving a lot of activity or being made to seem impressive or important. ❑ *The wedding will be a very low-key affair.*

low|ly /loʊli/ (**lowlier**, **lowliest**) ADJ If you describe someone or something as **lowly**, you mean that they are low in rank, status, or importance. ❑ *...lowly bureaucrats pretending to be senators.*

low-paid ADJ If you describe someone or their job as **low-paid**, you mean that their work earns them very little money. ❑ *...low-paid workers.*

low-tech /loʊ tɛk/ ADJ **Low-tech** machines or systems are ones that do not use modern or sophisticated technology. ❑ *...a simple form of low-tech electric propulsion.*

loy|al /lɔɪəl/ ADJ Someone who is **loyal** remains firm in their friendship or support for a person or thing. [APPROVAL] ❑ *They had remained loyal to the president.* ● **loy|al|ly** ADV [ADV with v] ❑ *They have loyally supported their party and their leader.* →see **hero**

loy|al|ty /lɔɪəlti/ (**loyalties**) **1** N-UNCOUNT **Loyalty** is the quality of staying firm in your friendship or support for someone or something. ❑ *I have sworn an oath of loyalty to the monarchy.* **2** N-COUNT **Loyalties** are feelings of friendship, support, or duty towards someone or something. ❑ *She had developed strong loyalties to the Manet family.*

1 늦은 오후였고 태양은 하늘에 낮게 떠 있었다. **3** 형용사 (수위가) 낮은 ❑ 물을 공급하는 강의 수위가 낮더라도 물 깊이가 일정하게 해 주는 펌프 시설 **4** 형용사 낮은 ❑ 영국 측 사상자 수는 놀라울 정도로 낮았다. ❑ 그들은 여전히 매우 낮은 수입으로 살아야 한다. **5** 형용사 낮은 ❑ 그녀는 콜린을 '법률 고문'이라는 낮은 직급 이상으로 승진시키길 거부했다. **6** 가산명사 저점 ❑ 물가가 12월에 약 1.12달러의 저점까지 떨어졌다. **7** 형용사 질 낮은 ❑ 학교는 어떤 학생으로부터도 질 낮은 과제물은 받지 않을 것이다. ❑ 조사팀은 간호 수준이 열악하다고 그 정신 병원의 직원들을 비판한다. **8** 형용사 ~이 낮은 ❑ 그들은 칼로리가 낮은 음식을 찾는다. ● 복합형_형용사 ~이 작은, 저~ ❑ 저 나트륨 토마토 소스 **9** 형용사 낮은 ❑ 대부분의 성 범죄자들은 자존감이 낮다. **10** 형용사 기운 없는, 저조한 ❑ 우리는 모두 지쳤고 사기는 낮다. **11** 형용사 낮은 ❑ 그러더니 그녀가 갑자기 목에 뭐가 걸린 듯 낮은 신음 소리를 내며 심하게 떨기 시작했다. **12** 형용사 낮은, 조용한 ❑ 그녀의 목소리가 너무 낮아서 그는 알아듣기 위해 애를 써야 했다. **13** 형용사 약한 ❑ 조명이 약한 데서는 그들이 잘 못 본다. **14** 형용사 약한, 낮은, 작은 ❑ 그녀는 작은 부엌 라디오를 작게 틀었다. ❑ 불 밝기 조절 스위치를 사서 불빛을 약하게 해 놓든지 아니면 아예 소등해버려라. **15** 형용사 불가산명사 ❑ 침구가 약간 부족하다. **16** 형용사 우울한 [비격식체] ❑ "내가 이 자리를 달라고 한 적이 없다는 것을 너도 알잖아."라고 그는 우울할 때면 친구들에게 이야기한다.

1 형용사 (둘 중) 아래의 ❑ 그녀는 아랫입술을 깨물었다. ❑ 두 구멍 중 밑의 구멍 **2** 형용사 아래의 ❑ 작은 방석을 써서 허리 아래 부분을 받쳐 주어라. **3** 형용사 하급의 ❑ 그 상들 때문에 이미 시 의회 하급 직원들 사이에 불만이 생기고 있다. ❑ 국가의 최상급 법원이 하급 법원의 판결을 뒤집었다. **4** 타동사 낮추다, 내리다 ❑ 두 명의 기자가 관을 무덤 속으로 내리는 것을 도와야 했다. ❑ 소코로브스키는 검은 가죽 의자에 앉았다. ● 낮춤 불가산명사 ❑ 올림픽 성화를 끄고 깃발을 내림 **5** 타동사 낮추다 ❑ 중앙은행이 금리를 2퍼센트 낮추었다. ❑ 낮춤 불가산명사 ❑ 청년 단축을 포함한 사회 정책 패키지 **6** 타동사 숙이다, 떨구다 ❑ 그녀는 안으로 다시 들어가면서 고개를 떨구고 사진사들을 스쳐 지나갔다. **7** 타동사 격하시키다 ❑ 그들처럼 스스로 가치 떨어지는 짓은 하지 말아라. **8** 타동사/자동사 낮추다 ❑ 남자가 목소리를 낮추며 가까이 다가왔다.

불가산명사 소문자 ❑ 그것은 소문자로 인쇄되어 있었다.

형용사 수수한 ❑ 결혼식은 굉장히 수수하게 처리될 것이다.

형용사 낮은 ❑ 상원의원인 양 행세하는 하급 관료들

형용사 저임금의 ❑ 저임금 노동자들

형용사 단순 기술의 ❑ 간단하고 단순한 전기 추진력 형태

형용사 충성스러운, 충실한 [마음에 듦] ❑ 그들은 계속 대통령에게 충성을 다 했었다. ● 충성스레, 충실히 부사 ❑ 그들은 당과 당의장을 충실히 지지했다.

1 불가산명사 충성 ❑ 나는 군주께 충성을 맹세했다. **2** 가산명사 유대감 ❑ 그녀는 마네 가족에 대해 강한 유대감을 갖게 된 상태였다.

loyalty card (**loyalty cards**) N-COUNT A **loyalty card** is a plastic card that some stores give to regular customers. Each time the customer buys something from the store, points are electronically stored on their card and can be exchanged later for goods or services.

가산명사 (우수 고객용) 실적 카드

LPG /ɛl pi dʒi/ N-UNCOUNT **LPG** is a type of fuel consisting of hydrocarbon gases in liquid form. **LPG** is an abbreviation for "liquefied petroleum gas."

불가산명사 액화 석유 가스

Ltd ◆◇◇ **Ltd** is a written abbreviation for **limited** when it is used after the name of a company. Compare **plc**. [BRIT, BUSINESS] ❑ ...Times Newspapers Ltd.

(유한 책임의) 회사 [영국영어, 경제] ❑ 타임즈 신문 주식회사

lu|bri|cate /lubrɪkeɪt/ (**lubricates, lubricating, lubricated**) V-T If you **lubricate** something such as a part of a machine, you put a substance such as oil on it so that it moves smoothly. [FORMAL] ❑ Mineral oils are used to lubricate machinery. ● **lu|bri|ca|tion** /lubrɪkeɪʃⁿn/ N-UNCOUNT ❑ Use a touch of linseed oil for lubrication.

타동사 윤활유를 바르다 [격식체] ❑ 기계에 바르는 윤활유로는 광유(鑛油)가 사용된다. ● 매끄럽게 하기 불가산명사 ❑ 윤활제로는 아마씨 기름을 조금만 쳐라.

lu|cid /lusɪd/ **1** ADJ **Lucid** writing or speech is clear and easy to understand. ❑ ...a lucid account of the history of mankind. ● **lu|cid|ly** ADV [ADV with v] ❑ Both of them had the ability to present complex matters lucidly. ● **lu|cid|ity** /lusɪdɪti/ N-UNCOUNT ❑ His writings were marked by an extraordinary lucidity and elegance of style. **2** ADJ If someone is **lucid**, they are thinking clearly again after a period of illness or confusion. [FORMAL] ❑ He wasn't very lucid, he didn't quite know where he was. ● **lu|cid|ity** N-UNCOUNT ❑ The pain had lessened in the night, but so had his lucidity.

1 형용사 명쾌한, 명료한 ❑ 인류의 역사에 대한 명쾌한 설명 ● 명쾌하게 부사 ❑ 그들 둘 다 복잡한 것들을 명쾌하게 설명할 수 있는 능력을 가지고 있었다. ● 명쾌함 불가산명사 ❑ 그의 글은 뛰어나게 명쾌하고 우아한 문체가 돋보였다. **2** 형용사 정신이 맑은 [격식체] ❑ 그는 정신이 맑지 못했고 자신이 어디 있는지 잘 알지 못했다. ● 본정신 불가산명사 ❑ 밤새 고통은 덜해졌으나 그의 의식도 덜 맑아졌다.

luck ◆◇◇ /lʌk/ **1** N-UNCOUNT **Luck** or **good luck** is success or good things that happen to you, that do not come from your own abilities or efforts. ❑ I knew I needed a bit of luck to win. ❑ The Sri Lankans have been having no luck with the weather. **2** N-UNCOUNT **Bad luck** is lack of success or bad things that happen to you, that have not been caused by yourself or other people. ❑ I had a lot of bad luck during the first half of this season. **3** CONVENTION If you ask someone the question "**Any luck?**" or "**No luck?**," you want to know if they have been successful in something they were trying to do. [INFORMAL] ❑ "Any luck?" — "No." **4** CONVENTION You can say "**Bad luck**," or "**Hard luck**," to someone when you want to express sympathy to them. [INFORMAL, FORMULAE] ❑ Bad luck, man, just bad luck. **5** CONVENTION If you say "**Good luck**" or "**Best of luck**" to someone, you are telling them that you hope they will be successful in something they are trying to do. [INFORMAL, FORMULAE] ❑ He kissed her on the cheek. "Best of luck!" **6** PHRASE You can say someone **is in luck** when they are in a situation where they can have what they want or need. ❑ You're in luck. The doctor's still in. **7** PHRASE If you say that someone **is out of luck**, you mean that they cannot have something which they can normally have. ❑ "What do you want, Roy? If it's money, you're out of luck."

1 불가산명사 행운 ❑ 이기기 위해선 운이 필요하리라는 것을 알았다. ❑ 스리랑카는 최근에 날씨가 계속 안 좋았다. **2** 불가산명사 액운, 불운 ❑ 올 시즌 초반에 운이 너무 안 좋았다. **3** 관용 표현 잘 됐어?, 잘 안 됐어? ❑ "잘 됐어?" ❑ "아니." **4** 관용 표현 막하군, 안 됐다 [비격식체, 의례적인 표현] ❑ 막하군, 참 막해. **5** 관용 표현 행운을 빌어 [비격식체, 의례적인 표현] ❑ 그는 그녀의 볼에 입을 맞추며 "행운을 빌어!"라고 했다. **6** 구 운이 좋다 ❑ 운이 좋으신데요. 의사 선생님이 아직 퇴근을 안 했습니다. **7** 구 운이 없다 ❑ "원하는 게 뭐야, 로이? 만약 돈이라면 딴 데를 알아봐."

Word Partnership   luck의 연어

ADJ.	**good** luck, **just** luck, **pure** luck, **sheer** luck **1**
V.	**bring** someone luck, **need a little** luck, **need some** luck, **wish** someone luck **1**
	have any/bad/better/good/no luck **1** **2**

luck|ily /lʌkɪli/ ADV You add **luckily** to a statement to indicate that it is good that a particular thing happened or is the case because otherwise the situation would have been difficult or unpleasant. [ADV with cl] ❑ Luckily, we both love football.

부사 다행히 ❑ 다행히 우리 둘 다 축구를 좋아한다.

lucky ◆◇◇ /lʌki/ (**luckier, luckiest**) **1** ADJ You say that someone is **lucky** when they have something that is very desirable or when they are in a very desirable situation. ❑ I am luckier than most. I have a job. ❑ He is incredibly lucky to be alive. **2** ADJ Someone who is **lucky** seems to always have good luck. ❑ Some people are born lucky aren't they? **3** ADJ If you describe an action or experience as **lucky**, you mean that it was good or successful, and that it happened by chance and not as a result of planning or preparation. ❑ They admit they are now desperate for a lucky break. **4** ADJ A **lucky** object is something that people believe helps them to be successful. ❑ He did not have on his other lucky charm, a pair of green socks. **5** PHRASE If you say that someone **will be lucky to** do or get something, you mean that they are very unlikely to do or get it, and will definitely not do or get any more than that. ❑ You'll be lucky if you get any breakfast. ❑ Those remaining in work will be lucky to get the smallest of pay increases.

1 형용사 운이 좋은 ❑ 나는 대부분의 사람들보다 운이 좋다. 나에겐 직장이 있으니까. ❑ 그가 살아 있다니 운이 매우 좋다. **2** 형용사 운이 좋은 ❑ 어떤 사람들은 운을 타고 나, 안 그래? **3** 형용사 행운의 ❑ 그들은 운이 풀리기를 절실히 기다리고 있음을 인정한다. **4** 형용사 행운의 ❑ 그는 자신의 다른 행운의 부적인 녹색 양말을 신고 있지 않았다. **5** 구 -만 해도 다행일 것이라 ❑ 아침 식사만이라도 할 수 있다면 다행일 것이라. ❑ 아직도 직장에 남아 있는 사람들은 최소한이라도 봉급이 인상된다면 다행으로 알아야 할 것이다.

Word Partnership   lucky의 연어

ADV.	lucky **enough**, **pretty** lucky, **really** lucky, **so** lucky, **very** lucky **1**
V.	**be** lucky, **feel** lucky, **get** lucky, lucky **to get** something, lucky **to have** something **1**
N.	lucky **break**, lucky **guess** **3**

lu|cra|tive /lukrətɪv/ ADJ A **lucrative** activity, job, or business deal is very profitable. ❑ Thousands of ex-army officers have found lucrative jobs in private security firms.

형용사 돈이 되는, 수지맞는 ❑ 수천 명의 전직 장교들이 민간 경비 업체에서 수지맞는 직장을 찾았다.

lu|di|crous /ludɪkrəs/ ADJ If you describe something as **ludicrous**, you are emphasizing that you think it is foolish, unreasonable, or unsuitable. [EMPHASIS] ❑ It was ludicrous to suggest that the visit could be kept secret. ● **lu|di|crous|ly** ADV ❑ By Western standards the prices are ludicrously low.

형용사 어처구니없는, 터무니없는 [강조] ❑ 그 방문이 비밀로 붙여질 수 있다고 생각하는 것은 터무니없는 것이었다. ● 어처구니없이, 터무니없이 부사 ❑ 서양 기준으로 보면 가격이 터무니없이 낮다.

lug /lʌg/ (**lugs, lugging, lugged**) V-T If you **lug** a heavy or awkward object somewhere, you carry it there with difficulty. [INFORMAL] ❑ Nobody wants to lug around huge suitcases full of clothes.

타동사 힘들게 끌다 [비격식체] ❑ 옷으로 꽉 찬 큰 여행 가방을 힘들게 끌고 다니고 싶어 하는 사람은 없다.

lug|gage /lʌɡɪdʒ/ N-UNCOUNT **Luggage** is the suitcases and bags that you take with you when travel. ☐ *Leave your luggage in the hotel.*
→see **hotel**

불가산명사 짐 ☐ 짐은 호텔에 두십시오.

> **Luggage** is an uncount noun. You can have **a piece of luggage** or **some luggage** but you cannot have "a luggage" or "some luggages." In British English, people normally use **luggage** when they are talking about everything that travelers carry. **Baggage** is a more technical word and is used for example when discussing airports or travel insurance. In American English, **luggage** refers to empty bags and suitcases and **baggage** refers to bags and suitcases with their contents. Both British and American speakers can refer to everything that travelers carry as their **bags**. American speakers can also call an individual suitcase a **bag**.

> luggage는 불가산 명사이다. 그래서 a piece of luggage나 some luggage라고 할 수는 있지만 a luggage나 some luggages라 할 수는 없다. 영국 영어에서든 미국 영어에서든 여행자가 가지고 다니는 모든 짐을 다 가리켜 luggage라고 할 수 있다. 영국 영어에서는 여행자가 가지고 다니는 짐을 통틀어 가리킬 때는 보통 luggage라고 하고, baggage는 좀 더 전문적인 용어로서 공항이나 여행 보험 등과 관련된 논의를 할 때 쓴다. 미국 영어에서는 luggage는 빈 가방을 가리키고 baggage는 내용물이 든 가방을 가리킨다.

lug|gage rack (**luggage racks**) ◼ N-COUNT A **luggage rack** is a shelf for putting luggage on, on a vehicle such as a train or bus. ◼ N-COUNT A **luggage rack** is a metal frame that is fixed on top of a car and used for carrying large objects. [AM; BRIT **roof rack**]

◼ 가산명사 화물용 선반 ◼ 가산명사 승용차 지붕에 짐을 싣기 위해 붙인 금속 틀 [미국영어; 영국영어 roof rack]

luke|warm /lukwɔrm/ ◼ ADJ Something, especially a liquid, that is **lukewarm** is only slightly warm. ☐ *Wash your face with lukewarm water.* ◼ ADJ If you describe a person or their attitude as **lukewarm**, you mean that they are not showing much enthusiasm or interest. ☐ *Economists have never been more than lukewarm towards him.*

◼ 형용사 미지근한 ☐ 미지근한 물로 얼굴을 씻어라. ◼ 형용사 미온적인, 미적지근한 ☐ 경제학자들은 그를 미온적인 태도 이상으로 대한 적이 없다.

lull /lʌl/ (**lulls, lulling, lulled**) ◼ N-COUNT A **lull** is a period of quiet or calm in a longer period of activity or excitement. ☐ *There was a lull in political violence after the election of the current president.* ◼ V-T If you **are lulled into** feeling safe, someone or something causes you to feel safe at a time when you are not safe. ☐ *It is easy to be lulled into a false sense of security.* ☐ *I had been lulled into thinking the publicity would be a trivial matter.*

◼ 가산명사 일시적인 고요, 소강상태 ☐ 현 대통령 선출 이후에 정치적 폭력이 잠깐 수그러들었다. ◼ 타동사 (안심하라고) 속다 ☐ 쉬이 속아 넘어가서 거짓된 안정감을 갖게 된다. ☐ 유명세는 사소한 일일 것이라고 나는 잘못 생각하게 되었었다.

lum|ber /lʌmbər/ (**lumbers, lumbering, lumbered**) ◼ N-UNCOUNT **Lumber** consists of trees and large pieces of wood that have been roughly cut up. [mainly AM] ☐ *It was made of soft lumber, spruce by the look of it.* ◼ V-I If someone or something **lumbers** from one place to another, they move there very slowly and clumsily. ☐ *He turned and lumbered back to his chair.*

◼ 불가산명사 목재 [주로 미국영어] ☐ 그것은 부드러운 목재, 외관상으로는 전나무로 만들어진 것처럼 보였다. ◼ 자동사 어기적어기적 간다 ☐ 그는 돌아서서 어기적어기적 자기 의자로 다시 갔다.

▶**lumber with** PHRASAL VERB If you **are lumbered with** someone or something, you have to deal with them or take care of them even though you do not want to and this annoys you. [BRIT, INFORMAL, DISAPPROVAL] ☐ *I was lumbered with the job of taking charge of all the money.*

구동사 —을 억지로 떠맡다 [영국영어, 비격식체, 탐탁찮음] ☐ 모든 돈을 관리하는 직책이 나에게 억지로 떠넘겨졌다.

lu|mi|nous /lumɪnəs/ ADJ Something that is **luminous** shines or glows in the dark. ☐ *The luminous dial on the clock showed five minutes to seven.*

형용사 야광의 ☐ 시계의 야광 숫자판이 7시 5분 전을 가리켰다.

lump /lʌmp/ (**lumps, lumping, lumped**) ◼ N-COUNT A **lump of** something is a solid piece of it. ☐ *The potter shaped and squeezed the lump of clay into a graceful shape.* ☐ *...a lump of wood.* ◼ N-COUNT A **lump** on or in someone's body is a small, hard swelling that has been caused by an injury or an illness. ☐ *I've got a lump on my shoulder.* ◼ N-COUNT A **lump of** sugar is a small cube of it. ☐ *...a nugget of rough gold about the size of a lump of sugar.* ◼ →see also **lump sum** ◼ PHRASE If you say that you have a **lump in** your **throat**, you mean that you have a tight feeling in your throat because of a strong emotion such as sorrow or gratitude. ☐ *I stood there with a lump in my throat and tried to fight back tears.*

◼ 가산명사 덩어리 ☐ 도공은 찰흙 덩어리를 모양을 잡고 쥐어 짜듯해서 우아한 모양으로 만들었다. ☐ 나무 덩어리 ◼ 가산명사 혹 ☐ 나는 어깨에 혹이 있다. ◼ 가산명사 덩어리 ☐ 각설탕 한 개만한 크기의 가공되지 않은 금덩어리 ◼ 구 목이 메인 ☐ 나는 목이 메인 채 거기 서서 눈물을 참으려고 애썼다.

▶**lump together** PHRASAL VERB If a number of different people or things **are lumped together**, they are considered as a group rather than separately. ☐ *Policemen and prostitutes, bankers and butchers are all lumped together in the service sector.*

구동사 같이 묶어지다 ☐ 경찰, 윤락녀, 은행원, 정육업자들이 모두 서비스 분야로 함께 분류된다.

lump sum (**lump sums**) N-COUNT A **lump sum** is an amount of money that is paid as a large amount on a single occasion rather than as smaller amounts on several separate occasions. ☐ *...a tax-free lump sum of £50,000 at retirement age.* →see **lottery**

가산명사 일시불 ☐ 정년에 세금 공제 없이 일시불로 받는 5만 파운드

lumpy /lʌmpi/ (**lumpier, lumpiest**) ADJ Something that is **lumpy** contains lumps or is covered with lumps. ☐ *When the rice isn't cooked properly it goes lumpy and gooey.*

형용사 덩어리진 ☐ 쌀이 제대로 안 익으면 덩어리가 지고 끈적해진다.

lu|nar /lunər/ ADJ **Lunar** means relating to the moon. [ADJ n] ☐ *The vast volcanic slope was eerily reminiscent of a lunar landscape.* →see **eclipse**

형용사 달의 ☐ 거대한 화산 등성이를 바라보니 기분 나쁘게도 달의 표면이 연상되었다.

lu|na|tic /lunætɪk/ (**lunatics**) ◼ N-COUNT If you describe someone as a **lunatic**, you think they behave in a dangerous, stupid, or annoying way. [INFORMAL, DISAPPROVAL] ☐ *Her son thinks she's an absolute raving lunatic.* ◼ ADJ If you describe someone's behavior or ideas as **lunatic**, you think they are very foolish and possibly dangerous. [DISAPPROVAL] ☐ *...the operation of the market taken to lunatic extremes.* ◼ N-COUNT People who were mentally ill used to be called **lunatics**. [OLD-FASHIONED] ☐ *...the lunatics in the Bedlam asylum.*

◼ 가산명사 미치광이 [비격식체, 탐탁찮음] ☐ 여자의 아들 생각에 그녀는 완전히 발광한 미치광이이다. ◼ 형용사 정신 나간 [탐탁찮음] ☐ 시장 자유주의를 비정상적인 극한까지 끌고 간 경우 ◼ 가산명사 정신병자 [구식어] ☐ 베들럼 정신 병원의 정신병자들

lunch ♦♦◇ /lʌntʃ/ (**lunches, lunching, lunched**) ◼ N-VAR **Lunch** is the meal that you have in the middle of the day. ☐ *Shall we meet somewhere for lunch?* ☐ *He did not enjoy business lunches.* →see **meal** ◼ V-I When you **lunch**, you have lunch, especially at a restaurant. [FORMAL] ☐ *Only the extremely rich could afford to lunch at the Mirabelle.* →see **meal**

◼ 가산명사 또는 불가산명사 점심 ☐ 점심 식사라도 같이 할까요? ☐ 그는 사업상 하는 점심을 좋아하지 않았다. ◼ 자동사 점심 식사하다 [격식체] ☐ 엄청난 부자들만이 미라벨에서 점심 식사를 할 수 있을 것이다.

Word Partnership	*lunch*의 연어
ADJ.	**free** lunch, **good** lunch, **hot** lunch, **late** lunch ◼
V.	**break for** lunch, **bring** *your* lunch, **buy** *someone* lunch, **eat** lunch, **go** *somewhere* **for** lunch, **go to** lunch, **have** lunch, **serve** lunch ◼

lunch|eon /lʌntʃən/ (**luncheons**) N-COUNT A **luncheon** is a formal lunch, for example to celebrate an important event or to raise money for charity. ☐ *Earlier this month, a luncheon for former UN staff was held in Vienna.*

가산명사 점심 만찬 ☐ 이번 달 초, 전 국제 연합 직원들을 위한 점심 만찬이 빈에서 치뤄졌다.

a b c d e f g h i j k l m n o p q r s t u v w x y z

lunch|time /ˈlʌntʃtaɪm/ (lunchtimes) also lunch time N-VAR Lunchtime is the period of the day when people have their lunch. ❑ Could we meet at lunchtime?

가산명사 또는 불가산명사 점심 시간 ❑ 점심 때 만날 수 있을까요?

lung /lʌŋ/ (lungs) N-COUNT Your lungs are the two organs inside your chest which fill with air when you breathe in. ❑ ...a smoker who died of lung cancer. →see **donor, respiratory**

가산명사 폐 ❑ 폐암으로 사망한 흡연자

lunge /lʌndʒ/ (lunges, lunging, lunged) ❑ V-I If you lunge in a particular direction, you move in that direction suddenly and clumsily. ❑ He lunged at me, grabbing me violently. ● N-COUNT Lunge is also a noun. ❑ The attacker knocked on their door and made a lunge for Wendy when she answered.

자동사 갑자기 덤비다, 돌진하다 ❑ 그가 내게 덤벼들더니 나를 거칠게 잡았다. ● 가산명사 돌진 ❑ 범인은 그들의 집 문을 두드리고 웬디가 문을 열자 그녀에게 갑자기 덤벼들었다.

lurch /lɜːrtʃ/ (lurches, lurching, lurched) ❑ V-I To lurch means to make a sudden movement, especially forward, in an uncontrolled way. ❑ As the car sped over a pothole she lurched forward. ❑ Henry looked, stared, and lurched to his feet. ● N-COUNT Lurch is also a noun. ❑ The car took a lurch forward. ❑ V-I If you say that a person or organization lurches from one thing to another, you mean they move suddenly from one course of action or attitude to another in an uncontrolled way. [DISAPPROVAL] ❑ The state government has lurched from one budget crisis to another. ● N-COUNT Lurch is also a noun. ❑ The property sector was another casualty of the lurch towards higher interest rates.

❑ 자동사 휘청거리다, 쏠리다 ❑ 차가 큰 구덩이를 빠른 속도로 지나가자 그녀는 몸이 앞으로 쏠렸다. ❑ 헨리는 보고 쏘아보고 하다가 휘청거리며 일어섰다. ● 가산명사 휘청함, 쏠림 ❑ 차가 앞으로 휘청했다. ❑ 자동사 휘청거리다 [탐탁찮음] ❑ 주정부는 연이어 예산 위기를 겪으면서 계속 휘청거리고 있다. ● 가산명사 휘청거림 ❑ 금리가 휘청하고 오르는 바람에 또 피해를 본 것이 부동산 부문이다.

lure /lʊr, BRIT lyʊəʳ/ (lures, luring, lured) ❑ V-T To lure someone means to trick them into a particular place or to trick them into doing something that they should not do. ❑ He lured her to his home and shot her with his father's gun. ❑ They did not realise that they were being lured into a trap. ❑ N-COUNT A lure is an attractive quality that something has, or something that you find attractive. ❑ The excitement of hunting big game in Africa has been a lure to Europeans for 200 years.

❑ 타동사 유인하다 ❑ 그는 그녀를 집으로 유인한 후 아버지의 총으로 그녀를 쐈다. ❑ 그들은 덫으로 유인당하고 있다는 것을 인식하지 못했다. ❑ 가산명사 매력 ❑ 아프리카에서 큰 사냥감을 사냥할 수 있는 흥분은 200년 동안 유럽 인들에게 매력적인 일이었다.

lu|rid /ˈlʊrɪd, BRIT lyʊərɪd/ ❑ ADJ If you say that something is lurid, you are critical of it because it involves a lot of violence, sex, or shocking detail. [DISAPPROVAL] ❑ ...lurid accounts of Claire's sexual exploits. ❑ ADJ If you describe something as lurid, you do not like it because it is very brightly colored. [DISAPPROVAL] ❑ She took care to paint her toe nails a lurid red or orange.

❑ 형용사 끔찍한, 충격적인 [탐탁찮음] ❑ 클레어의 성적 편력에 대한 충격적인 이야기 ❑ 형용사 요란한 [탐탁찮음] ❑ 그녀는 신경 써서 요란한 붉은색이나 주황색으로 발톱을 칠했다.

lurk /lɜːrk/ (lurks, lurking, lurked) ❑ V-I If someone lurks somewhere, they wait there secretly so that they cannot be seen, usually because they intend to do something bad. ❑ He thought he saw someone lurking above the chamber during the address. ❑ V-I If something such as a danger, doubt, or fear lurks somewhere, it exists but is not obvious or easily recognized. ❑ Hidden dangers lurk in every family saloon car.

❑ 자동사 잠복하다 ❑ 연설 도중 방 위에 누군가가 숨어 있는 것을 봤다고 그는 생각했다. ❑ 자동사 잠재해 있다 ❑ 숨은 위험이 모든 가족 세단에 잠재해 있다.

lus|cious /ˈlʌʃəs/ ❑ ADJ If you describe a woman or something about her as luscious, you mean that you find her or this thing sexually attractive. ❑ ...a luscious young blonde. ❑ ADJ Luscious food is juicy and very good to eat. ❑ ...a small apricot tree which bore luscious fruit.

❑ 형용사 관능적인 ❑ 관능적인 젊은 금발 여자 ❑ 형용사 맛있는, 즙이 많은 ❑ 즙이 많은 열매가 열리던 작은 살구나무

lush /lʌʃ/ (lusher, lushest) ❑ ADJ Lush fields or gardens have a lot of very healthy grass or plants. ❑ ...the lush green meadows bordering the river. ❑ ADJ If you describe a place or thing as lush, you mean that it is very luxurious. [v-link ADJ] ❑ The Carlton-intercontinental hotel is lush, plush, and very non-backpacker.

❑ 형용사 무성한, 우거진 ❑ 강 주변의 우거진 푸른 초원 ❑ 형용사 호화로운 ❑ 칼튼-인터컨티넨탈 호텔은 호화롭고 고급스러우며 배낭여행객이 쉽게 갈 수 있는 곳이 절대 아니다.

lust /lʌst/ ❑ N-UNCOUNT Lust is a feeling of strong sexual desire for someone. ❑ His relationship with Angie was the first which combined lust with friendship. ❑ N-UNCOUNT A lust for something is a very strong and eager desire to have it. ❑ It was Fred's lust for glitz and glamor that was driving them apart.

❑ 불가산명사 색정 ❑ 그와 앤지의 관계는 처음으로 색정과 우정이 결합된 것이었다. ❑ 불가산명사 욕정 ❑ 그들이 멀어진 것은 화려한 것에 대한 프레드의 욕정 때문이었다.

luxu|ri|ous /lʌgˈʒʊəriəs/ ❑ ADJ If you describe something as luxurious, you mean that it is very comfortable and expensive. ❑ Our honeymoon was two days in Las Vegas at a luxurious hotel called Le Mirage. ● luxu|ri|ous|ly ADV ❑ The dining-room is luxuriously furnished and carpeted. ❑ ADJ Luxurious means feeling or expressing great pleasure and comfort. ❑ Amy tilted her wine in her glass with a luxurious sigh. ● luxu|ri|ous|ly ADV [ADV after v] ❑ Liz laughed, stretching luxuriously.

❑ 형용사 사치스러운, 호화로운 ❑ 우리는 신혼여행으로 라스베가스의 르 미라주라는 고급 호텔에서 이틀을 보냈다. ● 호화롭게 부사 ❑ 식당은 호화로운 가구와 카펫으로 치장되어 있다. ❑ 형용사 아주 기분 좋은 ❑ 에이미는 아주 만족스러운 한숨을 내쉬며 와인을 기울여 술잔에 부었다. ● 아주 기분 좋게 부사 ❑ 리즈는 웃으며 기분 좋게 기지개를 폈다.

luxu|ry ◆◇◇ /ˈlʌkʃəri, lʌgzə-/ (luxuries) ❑ N-UNCOUNT Luxury is very great comfort, especially among beautiful and expensive surroundings. ❑ By all accounts he leads a life of considerable luxury. ❑ N-COUNT A luxury is something expensive which is not necessary but which gives you pleasure. ❑ A week by the sea is a luxury they can no longer afford. ❑ ADJ A luxury item is something expensive which is not necessary but which gives you pleasure. [ADJ n] ❑ He could not afford luxury food on his pay. ❑ N-SING A luxury is a pleasure which you do not often have the opportunity to enjoy. ❑ Hot baths are my favorite luxury.

❑ 불가산명사 사치, 호화 ❑ 그는 모든 면에서 상당히 호화로운 삶을 산다. ❑ 가산명사 사치품 ❑ 해변에서 일주일을 보내는 것은 그들이 더 이상 감당할 수 없는 사치이다. ❑ 형용사 사치스러운 ❑ 그는 자신의 월급으로는 사치스러운 식품은 살 형편이 안 되었다. ❑ 단수명사 사치 ❑ 뜨거운 전신 목욕은 내가 좋아하는 사치이다.

Thesaurus	luxury의 참조어
N.	comfort, splendor ❑
	extra, extravagance, treat ❑ ❑

ly|ing /ˈlaɪɪŋ/ Lying is the present participle of lie.

lie의 현재 분사

lynch /lɪntʃ/ (lynches, lynching, lynched) V-T If an angry crowd of people lynch someone, they kill that person by hanging them, without letting them have a trial, because they believe that that person has committed a crime. ❑ They were about to lynch him when reinforcements from the army burst into the room and rescued him. ● lynch|ing (lynchings) N-VAR ❑ Some towns found that lynching was the only way to drive away bands of outlaws.

타동사 린치를 가하다 ❑ 그들이 그에게 린치를 가하려는 순간 육군 지원 병력이 방안으로 뛰어 들어와 그를 구해 줬다. ● 린치 가산명사 또는 불가산명사 ❑ 무법자 집단을 몰아낼 수 있는 유일한 방법은 린치밖에 없음을 어떤 마을들은 깨달았다.

lyr|ic /ˈlɪrɪk/ (lyrics) ❑ ADJ Lyric poetry is written in a simple and direct style, and usually expresses personal emotions such as love. [ADJ n] ❑ ...Lawrence's splendid short stories and lyric poetry. ❑ N-COUNT The lyrics of a song are its words. ❑ ...Kurt Weill's Broadway opera with lyrics by Langston Hughes.

❑ 형용사 서정적인 ❑ 로렌스의 뛰어난 단편 소설과 서정시 ❑ 가산명사 가사 ❑ 랭스턴 휴스가 작사를 쓴 쿠르트 바일의 브로드웨이 오페라

M, m /ɛm/ (**M's, m's**) N-VAR **M** is the thirteenth letter of the English alphabet.

가산명사 또는 불가산명사 영어 알파벳의 열세 번째 글자

ma'am /mæm/ N-VOC People sometimes say **ma'am** as a very formal and polite way of addressing a woman whose name they do not know or a woman of superior rank. [mainly AM, POLITENESS] ❏ *Would you repeat that please, ma'am?*

호격명사 사모님, 부인 [주로 미국영어, 공손체] ❏ 다시 말씀해 주시겠습니까, 사모님?

ma|ca|bre /məkɑbrə/ ADJ You describe something such as an event or story as **macabre** when it is strange and horrible or upsetting, usually because it involves death or injury. ❏ *Police have made a macabre discovery.*

형용사 섬뜩한 ❏ 경찰이 섬뜩한 것을 발견해 냈다.

ma|chete /məʃɛti/ (**machetes**) N-COUNT A **machete** is a large knife with a broad blade.

가산명사 날이 넓은 큰 칼

ma|chine ♦♦◇ /məʃin/ (**machines, machining, machined**) ◼ N-COUNT A **machine** is a piece of equipment which uses electricity or an engine in order to do a particular kind of work. [also by N] ❏ *I put the coin in the machine and pulled the lever.* ◻ V-T If you **machine** something, you make it or work on it using a machine. [usu passive] ❏ *The material is machined in a factory.* ❏ *...machined brass zinc alloy gears.* ◼ N-COUNT You can use **machine** to refer to a large and well-controlled system or organization. ❏ *...Nazi Germany's military machine.* ◼ →see also **vending machine**

◼ 가산명사 기계, 기계 장치 ❏ 나는 그 기계에 동전을 넣고 손잡이를 당겼다. ◻ 타동사 (기계로) 가공하다 ❏ 그 자재는 공장에서 기계로 가공된다. ❏ 기계 가공된 황동 아연 합금 기어 ◼ 가산명사 기구, 조직 ❏ 나치 독일의 군사 조직

Thesaurus
machine의 참조어

N. appliance, computer, gadget, mechanism ◼
organization, structure, system ◼

Word Partnership
machine의 연어

V. **design a** machine, **invent a** machine, **use a** machine ◼
ADJ. **heavy** machine, **new** machine, machine **washable** ◼
N. machine **oil**, machine **parts**, machine **shop**, **Xerox** machine ◼

---

ma|chine gun (**machine guns**) also **machine-gun** N-COUNT A **machine gun** is a gun which fires a lot of bullets one after the other very quickly. ❏ *...a burst of machine-gun fire.*

가산명사 기관총 ❏ 기총 소사

ma|chin|ery /məʃinəri/ ◼ N-UNCOUNT You can use **machinery** to refer to machines in general, or machines that are used in a factory or on a farm. ❏ *...quality tools and machinery.* ◻ N-SING The **machinery** of a government or organization is the system and all the procedures that it uses to deal with things. ❏ *The machinery of democracy could be created quickly.*

◼ 불가산명사 기계류 ❏ 질 좋은 연장과 기계류 ◻ 단수명사 체제, 조직 ❏ 민주주의 체제가 신속하게 만들어질 수도 있을 것이다.

ma|chin|ist /məʃinist/ (**machinists**) N-COUNT A **machinist** is a person whose job is to operate a machine, especially in a factory. ❏ *His father is a machinist in an aerospace plant.*

가산명사 기사, 기계공 ❏ 그의 아버지는 항공 우주 산업 공장의 기사이다.

macho /mɑtʃoʊ, BRIT mætʃoʊ/ ADJ You use **macho** to describe men who are very conscious and proud of their masculinity. [INFORMAL] ❏ *...displays of macho bravado.*

형용사 남성 우월적인, 남자다움을 과시하는 [비격식체] ❏ 남성적 허세의 과시

mack|er|el /mækərəl, mækrəl/

Mackerel is both the singular and the plural form.

N-VAR A **mackerel** is a sea fish with a dark, patterned back. ❏ *Almiro's boat had sailed out to the middle of the bay to fish for mackerel.* ● N-UNCOUNT **Mackerel** is this fish eaten as food. ❏ *...piles of smoked mackerel.*

mackerel은 단수형 및 복수형이다.

가산명사 또는 불가산명사 고등어 ❏ 알미로의 배는 고등어 낚시를 하러 만 한가운데로 항해해 나갔었다. ● 불가산명사 ❏ 훈제 고등어 여러 더미

mac|ro|eco|nom|ic /mækroʊikənɒmɪk, -ɛk-/ also **macro-economic** ADJ **Macroeconomic** means relating to the major, general features of a country's economy, such as the level of inflation, unemployment, or interest rates. [BUSINESS] ❏ *...the attempt to substitute low inflation for full employment as a goal of macro-economic policy.*

형용사 거시 경제의 [경제] ❏ 거시 경제 정책 목표를 완전 고용에서 낮은 물가상승률로 대체하려는 시도

mad ♦◇◇ /mæd/ (**madder, maddest**) ◼ ADJ If you say that someone is **mad**, you mean that they are very angry. [INFORMAL] ❏ *You're just mad at me because I don't want to go.* ◻ ADJ You use **mad** to describe people or things that you think are very foolish. [DISAPPROVAL] ❏ *You'd be mad to work with him again.* ● **madness** N-UNCOUNT ❏ *It is political madness.* ◼ ADJ Someone who is **mad** has a mind that does not work in a normal way, with the result that their behavior is very strange. ❏ *She was afraid of going mad.* ● **madness** N-UNCOUNT ❏ *He was driven to the brink of madness.* ◼ ADJ If you are **mad about** something or someone, you like them very much indeed. In British English, you say you are **mad on** something or someone. [INFORMAL] [v-link ADJ about/on N] ❏ *She's not as mad about sport as I am.* ❏ *He's mad about you.* ● COMB in ADJ **Mad** is also a combining form. ❏ *...his football-mad son.* ◼ ADJ **Mad** behavior is wild and uncontrolled.

◼ 형용사 몹시 화난 [비격식체] ❏ 너는 내가 가고 싶어 하지 않는다고 나한테 화낸 것뿐이야. ◻ 형용사 바보 같은, 무모한 [탐탁찮음] ❏ 또 다시 그 사람하고 같이 일한다면 넌 바보야. ● 바보짓 불가산명사 ❏ 그것은 정치적으로 바보짓이다. ◼ 형용사 미친, 실성한 ❏ 그녀는 미쳐 갈까봐 두려웠다. ● 미침, 실성 불가산명사 ❏ 그는 실성하기 직전의 지경까지 몰려갔다. ◼ 형용사 열중하는, 푹 빠진 [비격식체] ❏ 그녀는 나만큼 운동에 열중하지는 않는다. ❏ 그는 너에게 푹 빠져 있어. ● 복합형-형용사 -에 열중한 ❏ 그의 축구에 빠져 있는 아들 ◼ 형용사 격한, 미친 듯한 ❏ 게임은 다 하는 데 딱 한 시간만 주어지므로

A

❏ *You only have an hour to complete the game so it's a mad dash against the clock.* ● **mad|ly** ADV [ADV with v] ❏ *Down in the streets people were waving madly.* **6** PHRASE If you say that someone or something **drives** you **mad**, you mean that you find them extremely annoying. [INFORMAL] ❏ *There are certain things he does that drive me mad.* **7** PHRASE If you do something **like mad**, you do it very energetically or enthusiastically. [INFORMAL] ❏ *He was weight training like mad.* **8** →see also **madly. mad keen** →see **keen**

B

치열한 시간 다툼이 된다. ● 격렬하게, 미친 듯이 부사 ❏ 거리에서는 사람들이 미친 듯이 손을 흔들고 있었다. **6** 구 ~를 화가 나 미치게 만들다 [비격식체] ❏ 그가 하는 어떤 일을 보면 난 화가 나 죽겠어. **7** 구 미친 듯이, 맹렬히 [비격식체] ❏ 그는 맹렬히 웨이트 트레이닝을 하고 있었다.

C

Thesaurus   *mad*의 참조어

ADJ.	angry, furious **1**
	crazy, foolish, senseless **2**
	deranged, insane **3**

D

Word Partnership   *mad*의 연어

N.	mad **as hell 1**
	mad **dog**, mad **scientist 3**
	mad **dash**, mad **rush 5**
V.	**get** mad, **make** *someone* mad **1**
	go mad **3**

E

F

G

mad|am /mædəm/ also **Madam** N-VOC People sometimes say **Madam** as a very formal and polite way of addressing a woman whose name they do not know or a woman of superior rank. For example, a store clerk might address a woman customer as **Madam**. [POLITENESS] ❏ *Try them on, madam.*

호격명사 사모님 [공손체] ❏ 한 번 입어 보세요, 사모님.

H

mad|den /mæd³n/ (**maddens, maddening, maddened**) V-T To **madden** a person or animal means to make them very angry. ❏ *The swine were maddening farmers by guzzling their lettuces.*

타동사 성나게 하다 ❏ 돼지들이 상추를 뜯어먹어서 농부들을 성나게 하고 있었다.

I

mad|den|ing /mæd³nɪŋ/ ADJ If you describe something as **maddening**, you mean that it makes you feel angry, irritated, or frustrated. ❏ *Shopping in the January sales can be maddening.* ● **mad|den|ing|ly** ADV ❏ *The service is maddeningly slow.*

형용사 화나게 하는, 골치 아픈 ❏ 1월 세일 때 쇼핑을 하는 일은 골치 아플 수도 있다. ● 화가 날 정도로 부사 ❏ 서비스가 화가 날 정도로 느리다.

J

K

made /meɪd/ **1 Made** is the past tense and past participle of **make. 2** ADJ If something is **made of** or **made out of** a particular substance, that substance was used to build it. [v-link ADJ of/out of n] ❏ *The top of the table is made of glass.* **3** PHRASE If you say that someone **has it made** or **has got it made**, you mean that they are certain to be rich or successful. [INFORMAL] ❏ *When I was at school, I thought I had it made.*

1 make의 과거, 과거 분사 **2** 형용사 ~로 만들어진 ❏ 그 탁자의 윗면은 유리로 만들어졌다. **3** 구 성공할 것이 확실하다 [비격식체] ❏ 나는 학교 다닐 때, 꼭 성공할 거라고 생각했다.

L

M

made-up ♦◇◇ also **made up 1** ADJ If you are **made-up**, you are wearing makeup such as powder or eye shadow. [v-link ADJ, adv ADJ n] ❏ *She was beautifully made-up, beautifully groomed.* **2** ADJ A **made-up** word, name, or story is invented, rather than really existing or being true. ❏ *It looks like a made-up word.*

1 형용사 화장한 ❏ 그녀는 예쁘게 화장을 했고 멋지게 차려입고 있었다. **2** 형용사 만들어 낸 ❏ 그것은 만들어 낸 말인 것 같다.

N

mad|ly /mædli/ **1** ADV You can use **madly** to indicate that one person loves another a great deal. ❏ *She has fallen madly in love with him.* **2** ADV You can use **madly** in front of an adjective in order to emphasize the quality expressed by the adjective. [mainly BRIT, EMPHASIS] [ADV adj] ❏ *Inside it is madly busy.*

1 부사 미친 듯이 ❏ 그녀는 그와 미친 듯이 사랑에 빠져 버렸다. **2** 부사 몹시 [주로 영국영어, 강조] ❏ 안쪽은 몹시 바쁘다.

O

mag /mæg/ (**mags**) N-COUNT A **mag** is the same as a magazine. [INFORMAL] ❏ *...a well-known glossy mag.*

가산명사 잡지 [비격식체] ❏ 광택 지질의 유명한 대중 잡지

P

maga|zine ♦♦◇ /mæɡəzin, BRIT mæɡəziːn/ (**magazines**) **1** N-COUNT A **magazine** is a publication with a paper cover which is issued regularly, usually every week or every month, and which contains articles, stories, photographs, and advertisements. ❏ *Her face is on the cover of a dozen or more magazines.* **2** N-COUNT In an automatic gun, the **magazine** is the part that contains the bullets. ❏ *The corporal ignored him, sliding the empty magazine from his weapon and replacing it with a fresh one.* →see **advertising, library**

1 가산명사 잡지 ❏ 그녀의 얼굴이 십 수 개 잡지의 표지에 실렸다. **2** 가산명사 탄창 ❏ 상병은 그를 무시하고, 빈 탄창을 총에서 빼 낸 다음 새 탄창으로 갈아 끼웠다.

Q

R

mag|got /mæɡət/ (**maggots**) N-COUNT **Maggots** are creatures that look like very small worms and turn into flies.

가산명사 구더기

S

mag|ic ♦◇◇ /mædʒɪk/ **1** N-UNCOUNT **Magic** is the power to use supernatural forces to make impossible things happen, such as making people disappear or controlling events in nature. ❏ *They believe in magic.* ❏ *...the use of magic to combat any adverse powers or influences.* **2** N-UNCOUNT You can use **magic** when you are referring to an event that is so wonderful, strange, or unexpected that it seems as if supernatural powers have caused it. You can also say that something happens **as if by magic** or **like magic**. ❏ *All this was supposed to work magic.* **3** ADJ You use **magic** to describe something that does things, or appears to do things, by magic. [ADJ n] ❏ *So it's a magic potion?* **4** N-UNCOUNT **Magic** is the art and skill of performing mysterious tricks to entertain people, for example by making things appear and disappear. ❏ *His secret hobby: performing magic tricks.* **5** N-UNCOUNT If you refer to **the magic of** something, you mean that it has a special mysterious quality which makes it seem wonderful and exciting to you and which makes you feel happy. ❏ *It infected them with some of the magic of a lost age.* ● ADJ **Magic** is also an adjective. ❏ *Then came those magic moments in the rose-garden.* **6** N-UNCOUNT If you refer to a person's **magic**, you mean a special talent or ability that they have, which you admire or consider very impressive. ❏ *The 32-year-old Jamaican-born fighter believes he can still regain some of his old magic.* **7** ADJ You can use expressions such as **the magic number** and **the magic word** to indicate that a number or word is the one which is significant or desirable in a particular situation. [the ADJ n] ❏ *...their quest to gain the magic number of 270 electoral votes on Election Day.* **8** ADJ **Magic** is used in expressions such as **there is no magic formula** and **there is no magic solution** to say that someone will have to make an effort to solve a problem, because it will not

T

U

V

W

X

Y

Z

1 불가산명사 마법 ❏ 그들은 마법을 믿는다. ❏ 악한 힘이나 영향력에 맞서 싸우기 위해 마법을 쓰는 것 **2** 불가산명사 마법, 놀라운 일 ❏ 이 모든 것은 놀라운 일을 일으키게 되어 있었다. **3** 형용사 마법의 ❏ 그럼 그것은 마법의 약인가? **4** 불가산명사 마술 ❏ 그의 숨겨진 취미: 마술 시연 **5** 불가산명사 신비한 매력 ❏ 그것은 그들을 사라진 시대의 신비한 매력에 젖게 했다. ● 형용사 매력적인; 마법과 같은 ❏ 그러자 장미 화원에 마법과 같은 순간이 찾아왔다. **6** 불가산명사 놀라운 능력 ❏ 자메이카 태생인 서른두 살의 그 권투선수는 여전히 예전의 놀라운 능력을 되찾을 수 있다고 믿는다. **7** 형용사 마법의 숫자인; 마법을 거는 낱말 ❏ 대통령 선거일에 마법의 숫자인 270명의 선거인단을 확보하기 위한 그들의 원정 **8** 형용사 마법의 공식 같은 것은 없다; 마법의 해결책 같은 것은 없다 ❏ 히트 상품을 제조하는 마법의 공식 같은 것은 없다.

Word Web   magnet

Magnets have a north **pole** and a south pole. One side has a **negative charge** and the other side has a **positive** charge. The negative side of a magnet **attracts** the positive side of another magnet. This is where the phrase "opposites attract" comes from. Two sides that have the same charge will **repel** each other. The earth itself is a huge magnet, with a North Pole and a South Pole. A **compass** uses a **magnetized** needle to indicate directions. The "north" end of the needle always points toward the earth's North Pole.

solve itself. [ADJ n, with neg] ❑ *There is no magic formula for producing winning products.*

Thesaurus   *magic*의 참조어

N.   enchantment, illusion, sorcery, witchcraft **1**

mag|i|cal /mǽdʒɪkʰl/ **1** ADJ Something that is **magical** seems to use magic or to be able to produce magic. ❑ *...the story of Sin-Sin, a little boy who has magical powers.* ● **mag|i|cal|ly** /mǽdʒɪkli/ ADV [ADV with v] ❑ *During the holiday season the town is magically transformed into a Christmas wonderland.* **2** ADJ You can say that a place or object is **magical** when it has a special mysterious quality that makes it seem wonderful and exciting. ❑ *The beautiful island of Cyprus is a magical place to get married.*

ma|gi|cian /mədʒɪ́ʃʰn/ (**magicians**) N-COUNT A **magician** is a person who entertains people by doing magic tricks.

mag|is|trate /mǽdʒɪstreɪt/ (**magistrates**) N-COUNT A **magistrate** is an official who acts as a judge in law courts which deal with minor crimes or disputes. ❑ *She will face a local magistrate on Tuesday.*

mag|nate /mǽgneɪt, -nɪt/ (**magnates**) N-COUNT A **magnate** is someone who has earned a lot of money from a particular business or industry. ❑ *...a multimillionaire shipping magnate.*

mag|net /mǽgnɪt/ (**magnets**) **1** N-COUNT If you say that something is a **magnet** or is like a **magnet**, you mean that people are very attracted by it and want to go to it or look at it. ❑ *Prospect Park, with its vast lake, is a magnet for all health freaks.* **2** N-COUNT A **magnet** is a piece of iron or other material which attracts iron toward it. ❑ *It's possible to hang a nail from a magnet and then use that nail to pick up another nail.*
→see Word Web: **magnet**

mag|net|ic /mægnétɪk/ **1** ADJ If something metal is **magnetic**, it acts like a magnet. ❑ *...magnetic particles.* **2** ADJ You use **magnetic** to describe something that is caused by or relates to the force of magnetism. ❑ *The electrically charged gas particles are affected by magnetic forces.* **3** ADJ You use **magnetic** to describe tapes and other objects which have a coating of a magnetic substance and contain coded information that can be read by computers or other machines. ❑ *...her magnetic strip ID card.* **4** ADJ If you describe something as **magnetic**, you mean that it is very attractive to people because it has unusual, powerful, and exciting qualities. ❑ *...the magnetic effect of the prosperous German economy on would-be immigrants.*

mag|net|ism /mǽgnɪtɪzəm/ **1** N-UNCOUNT Someone or something that has **magnetism** has unusual, powerful, and exciting qualities which attract people to them. ❑ *There was no doubting the animal magnetism of the man.* **2** N-UNCOUNT **Magnetism** is the natural power of some objects and substances, especially iron, to attract other objects toward them. ❑ *...his research in electricity and magnetism.*

mag|ni|fi|ca|tion /mǽgnɪfɪkéɪʃʰn/ (**magnifications**) **1** N-UNCOUNT **Magnification** is the act or process of magnifying something. ❑ *The man was tall, his figure shortened by the magnification of Lenny's binoculars.* **2** N-VAR **Magnification** is the degree to which a lens, mirror, or other device can magnify an object, or the degree to which the object is magnified. ❑ *The electron microscope uses a beam of electrons to produce images at high magnifications.*

mag|nifi|cent /mægnɪ́fɪsənt/ ADJ If you say that something or someone is **magnificent**, you mean that you think they are extremely good, beautiful, or impressive. ❑ *...a magnificent country house in wooded grounds.* ● **mag|nifi|cence** N-UNCOUNT ❑ *I shall never forget the magnificence of the Swiss mountains and the beauty of the lakes.* ● **mag|nifi|cent|ly** ADV ❑ *The team played magnificently throughout the competition.*

mag|ni|fy /mǽgnɪfaɪ/ (**magnifies, magnifying, magnified**) **1** V-T To **magnify** an object means to make it appear larger than it really is, by means of a special lens or mirror. ❑ *This version of the Digges telescope magnifies images 11 times.* ❑ *A lens would magnify the picture so it would be like looking at a large TV screen.* **2** V-T To **magnify** something means to increase its effect, size, loudness, or intensity. ❑ *Poverty and human folly magnify natural disasters.* **3** V-T If you **magnify** something, you make it seem more important or serious than it really is. ❑ *They do not grasp the broad situation and spend their time magnifying ridiculous details.*

mag|ni|tude /mǽgnɪtud, BRIT mǽgnɪtyuːd/ **1** N-UNCOUNT If you talk about the **magnitude** of something, you are talking about its great size, scale, or importance. ❑ *An operation of this magnitude is going to be difficult.* **2** PHRASE You can use **order of magnitude** when you are giving an approximate idea of the amount or importance of something. ❑ *America and Russia do not face a problem of the same order of magnitude as Japan.*

1 형용사 마법의, 요술의 ❑ 마법의 힘을 지닌 어린 아이 신신의 이야기 ● 마법처럼 부사 ❑ 휴가철 동안에 그 읍은 마법에 걸린 것처럼 동화 속의 크리스마스 나라로 바뀐다. **2** 형용사 매력적인, 매혹적인 ❑ 아름다운 키프로스 섬은 매혹적인 결혼 장소이다.

가산명사 마술사

가산명사 치안 판사 ❑ 그녀는 화요일에 지역 치안 판사와 대면할 것이다.

가산명사 거물, -왕 ❑ 대부호 해운왕

1 가산명사 마음을 끄는 것, 자석과 같은 것 ❑ 거대한 호수를 갖춘 프로스펙트 파크는 건강이라면 사족을 못 쓰는 사람들의 마음을 끈다. **2** 가산명사 자석, 자철 ❑ 못 하나를 자석에 붙인 다음 그 못을 가지고 다른 못을 집어 올릴 수 있다.

1 형용사 자성을 띤 ❑ 자성을 띤 미립자 **2** 형용사 자기의, 자력의 ❑ 대전(帶電)된 기체 입자는 자기력의 영향을 받는다. **3** 형용사 마그네틱의 ❑ 마그네틱 띠가 입혀진 그녀의 신분증 **4** 형용사 마음을 끄는, 매력 있는 ❑ 번영하는 독일 경제가 이민 희망자들의 마음을 끄는 효과

1 불가산명사 마음을 끄는 힘 ❑ 그 남자에게 동물적인 매력이 있음은 의심할 여지가 없었다. **2** 불가산명사 자기, 자력 ❑ 전기와 자기에 대한 그의 연구

1 불가산명사 확대, 과장 ❑ 레니가 가진 쌍안경의 확대 작용으로 인해 작아보였지만, 그 남자는 키가 컸다. **2** 가산명사 또는 불가산명사 배율 ❑ 전자 현미경은 전자 광선을 이용하여 고배율의 상을 만들어 낸다.

형용사 훌륭한, 멋진 ❑ 우거진 숲 속에 있는 멋진 전원주택 ● 웅대함, 훌륭함 불가산명사 ❑ 스위스의 웅대한 산과 아름다운 호수를 결코 잊지 못할 것이다. ● 훌륭히 부사 ❑ 그 팀은 대회 내내 훌륭한 경기를 펼쳤다.

1 타동사 확대하다 ❑ 딕스 사의 이 망원경은 상을 11배로 확대한다. ❑ 렌즈를 이용하면 커다란 텔레비전 화면을 보는 것처럼 그림이 확대될 것이다. **2** 타동사 증대시키다 ❑ 가난과 인간의 어리석음이 자연재해를 증대시킨다. **3** 타동사 과장하다 ❑ 그들은 사태를 폭넓게 이해하지 못하고 터무니없이 사소한 일을 과장하는 데 시간을 허비한다.

1 불가산명사 크기; 중요성 ❑ 이 정도로 큰 규모의 사업 진행은 어려워질 것이다. **2** 구 규모, 정도 ❑ 미국과 러시아는 일본과 같은 규모의 문제에 직면해 있지는 않다.

mag|pie /mǽgpaɪ/ (**magpies**) N-COUNT A **magpie** is a large black and white bird with a long tail.

가산명사 까치

ma|hog|a|ny /məhɒ́gəni/ N-UNCOUNT **Mahogany** is a dark reddish-brown wood that is used to make furniture. ❑ ...*mahogany tables and chairs.*

불가산명사 마호가니 ❑ 마호가니재로 만든 탁자와 의자들

maid /meɪd/ (**maids**) N-COUNT A **maid** is a woman who works as a servant in a hotel or private house. ❑ *A maid brought me breakfast at half past eight.*

가산명사 하녀; 호텔 여종업원 ❑ 호텔 여종업원이 여덟 시 반에 내게 아침 식사를 가져다주었다.

maid|en /méɪd³n/ (**maidens**) ■ N-COUNT A **maiden** is a young girl or woman. [LITERARY] ❑ ...*stories of noble princes and their brave deeds on behalf of beautiful maidens.* ② ADJ The **maiden** voyage or flight of a ship or aircraft is the first official journey that it makes. [ADJ n] ❑ *In 1912, the Titanic sank on her maiden voyage.*

■ 가산명사 처녀 [문예체] ❑ 고귀한 왕자들과 그들이 아름다운 처녀들을 위해 행한 용감한 행동에 대한 이야기들 ② 형용사 처녀 (항해 또는 비행) ❑ 1912년에, 타이타닉 호는 처녀항해 도중 침몰했다.

maid|en name (**maiden names**) N-COUNT A married woman's **maiden name** is her parents' surname, which she used before she got married and started using her husband's surname. ❑ *The marriage broke up in 1997 and she reverted to her maiden name of Boreman.*

가산명사 (여성의) 결혼 전의 성 ❑ 1997년에 결혼이 파탄 나서 그녀는 결혼 전의 성인 보어먼을 다시 썼다.

mail ♦♢♢ /meɪl/ (**mails, mailing, mailed**) ■ N-SING The **mail** is the public service or system by which letters and parcels are collected and delivered. [the N, also by N] ❑ *Your check is in the mail.* ② N-UNCOUNT You can refer to letters and parcels that are delivered to you as **mail**. [also the N] ❑ *There was no mail except the usual junk addressed to the occupier.* ③ V-T If you **mail** a letter or parcel to someone, you send it to them by putting it in a mailbox or taking it to a post office. [mainly AM; BRIT usually **post**] ❑ *Last year, he mailed the documents to French journalists.* ❑ *He mailed me the contract.* ④ V-T To **mail** a message to someone means to send it to them by means of e-mail or a computer network. ❑ ...*if a report must be electronically mailed to an office by 9 am the next day.* ● N-UNCOUNT **Mail** is also a noun. ❑ *If you have any problems then send me some mail.* ⑤ →see also **mailing, e-mail, electronic mail, junk mail, surface mail**

■ 단수명사 우편 ❑ 네 수표는 우편으로 보냈어. ② 불가산명사 우편물 ❑ 거주자 앞으로 온 흔한 잡동사니들을 제외하고는 아무 우편물도 없었다. ③ 타동사 우편으로 보내다 [주로 미국영어; 영국영어 대개 **post**] ❑ 작년에 그는 프랑스 기자들에게 우편으로 그 서류들을 보냈다. ❑ 그는 내게 우편으로 계약서를 보냈다. ④ 타동사 이메일로 보내다 ❑ 보고서를 다음날 오전 9시까지 이메일로 사무실에 보내야 한다면 ● 불가산명사 이메일 ❑ 문제가 있으면 저한테 이메일을 보내세요.

> ### Word Partnership   mail의 연어
>
> | | |
> |---|---|
> | PREP. | **by** mail, **in the** mail, **through the** mail ■ |
> | N. | mail **carrier**, **fan** mail ② |
> | V. | **deliver** mail, **get** mail, **open** mail, **read** mail, **receive** mail, **send** mail ② |

mail|box /méɪlbɒks/ (**mailboxes**) ■ N-COUNT A **mailbox** is a box outside your house where your letters are delivered. [AM] ❑ *The next day there was a letter in her mailbox.* ② N-COUNT A **mailbox** is a metal box in a public place, where you put letters and small parcels to be collected. They are then sorted and delivered. [mainly AM; BRIT **post box**] ❑ *And with a trembling hand, he dropped the letters into the mailbox.* ③ N-COUNT On a computer, your **mailbox** is the file where your e-mail is stored. ❑ *The prank crammed his mailbox with computer-delivered electronic junk mail.*

■ 가산명사 우편함 [미국영어] ❑ 다음날 그녀의 우편함에 편지가 한 통 와 있었다. ② 가산명사 우체통 [주로 미국영어; 영국영어 post box] ❑ 그리고 떨리는 손으로, 그는 편지들을 우체통에 넣었다. ③ 가산명사 (컴퓨터) 메일 박스 ❑ 그 장난으로 인해 그의 메일 박스에는 컴퓨터로 전송된 광고성 이메일이 가득 했다.

mail|ing /méɪlɪŋ/ (**mailings**) ■ N-UNCOUNT **Mailing** is the activity of sending things to people through the postal service. [also N in pl] ❑ *The newsletter was printed towards the end of June in readiness for mailing.* ② N-COUNT A **mailing** is something that is sent to people through the postal service. ❑ *The seniors organizations sent out mailings to their constituencies.*

■ 불가산명사 우송 ❑ 그 소식지는 우송에 대비해서 6월 말경에 간행되었다. ② 가산명사 우편물 ❑ 노인 단체에서 지역 유권자들에게 우편물을 보냈다.

mail|ing list (**mailing lists**) N-COUNT A **mailing list** is a list of names and addresses that a company or organization keeps, so that they can send people information or advertisements. ❑ *Place your name on our mailing list now.*

가산명사 우편물 수취인 명부 ❑ 지금 저희 우편물 수취인 명부에 이름을 올리세요.

mail|man /méɪlmæn/ (**mailmen**) N-COUNT A **mailman** is a man whose job is to collect and deliver letters and parcels that are sent by mail. [AM; BRIT usually **postman**]

가산명사 우편물 집배원 [미국영어; 영국영어 대개 postman]

mail merge N-UNCOUNT **Mail merge** is a word processing procedure which enables you to combine a document with a data file, for example a list of names and addresses, so that copies of the document are different for each person it is sent to. [COMPUTING] ❑ *He sent every member of staff a mail-merge letter wishing them a merry Christmas!*

불가산명사 (컴퓨터) 메일 머지 [컴퓨터] ❑ 그는 모든 직원들에게 즐거운 성탄절을 기원하는 같은 내용의 편지를 보냈다.

mail or|der (**mail orders**) ■ N-UNCOUNT **Mail order** is a system of buying and selling goods. You choose the goods you want from a company by looking at their catalog, and the company sends them to you by mail. ❑ *The toys are available by mail order from Opi Toys.* ② N-COUNT **Mail orders** are goods that have been ordered by mail order. [mainly AM] ❑ *I supervise the packing of all mail orders.*

■ 불가산명사 통신 판매 ❑ 그 장난감들은 오피 완구에서 통신 판매로 구입하실 수 있습니다. ② 가산명사 통신 판매 상품 [주로 미국영어] ❑ 내가 모든 통신 판매 상품의 포장을 관리한다.

mail|shot /méɪlʃɒt/ (**mailshots**) N-COUNT A **mailshot** is a letter advertising something or appealing for money for a particular charity. Mailshots are sent out to a large number of people at once. [BRIT] ❑ *I have received a mailshot for a product which I would like your opinion of.*

가산명사 (광고용 등) 대량 우편물 [영국영어] ❑ 제가 어떤 상품의 광고 우편물을 받았는데 그에 대해 당신의 의견을 듣고 싶습니다.

maim /meɪm/ (**maims, maiming, maimed**) V-T To **maim** someone means to injure them so badly that part of their body is permanently damaged. ❑ *Mines have been scattered in rice paddies and jungles, maiming and killing civilians.*

타동사 불구로 만들다 ❑ 지뢰가 논과 정글 여기저기에 산재해 있어서 민간인들을 불구로 만들거나 목숨을 앗아 왔다.

main ♦♦♦ /meɪn/ (**mains**) ■ ADJ The **main** thing is the most important one of several similar things in a particular situation. [det ADJ] ❑ ...*one of the main tourist areas of Amsterdam.* ❑ *My main concern now is to protect the children.* ② PHRASE If you say that something is true **in the main**, you mean that it is generally true, although there may be exceptions. ❑ *Tourists are, in the main, sympathetic people.* ③ N-COUNT The **mains** are the pipes which supply gas or water to buildings, or which take sewage away from them. ❑ ...*the water supply from the mains.* ④ N-PLURAL The **mains** are the wires which supply electricity to

■ 형용사 주요한, 주된 ❑ 암스테르담의 주요 관광지 중 한 곳 ❑ 지금 나의 주된 관심사는 아이들을 보호하는 것이다. ② 구 대개는, 주로 ❑ 관광객들은 대개 인정이 많은 사람들이다. ③ 가산명사 (수도 등의) 본관 ❑ 급수 본관을 통한 물공급 ④ 복수명사 (전기용) 본선; 전원 [주로 영국영어] ❑ 전원에 플러그를 끼우는 앰프

buildings, or the place where the wires end inside the building. [mainly BRIT]
❑ ...amplifiers which plug into the mains.

Thesaurus   main의 참조어

ADJ.   chief, major, primary, principal; (ant.) minor **1**

main|frame /**meɪnfreɪm**/ (**mainframes**) N-COUNT A **mainframe** or **mainframe computer** is a large powerful computer which can be used by many people at the same time and which can do very large or complicated tasks. ❑ I downloaded the whole thing into the hospital mainframe before I left work today.

가산명사 (컴퓨터) 메인프레임 ❑ 내가 오늘 퇴근하기 전에 병원 메인프레임 컴퓨터에다 모든 것을 내려받았다.

main|land /**meɪnlænd**/ N-SING You can refer to the largest part of a country or continent as **the mainland** when contrasting it with the islands around it. ❑ She was going to Nanaimo to catch the ferry to the mainland.

단수명사 대륙, 본토 ❑ 그녀는 본토로 가는 연락선을 타기 위해 나나이모로 가고 있었다.

main|ly ♦♦◇ /**meɪnli**/ **1** ADV You use **mainly** when mentioning the main reason or thing involved in something. ❑ The stockmarket scandal is refusing to go away, mainly because there's still no consensus over how it should be dealt with. **2** ADV You use **mainly** when you are referring to a group and stating something that is true of most of it. [ADV with group] ❑ The African half of the audience was mainly from Senegal or Mali.

1 부사 주로 ❑ 주식 시장의 스캔들은 사라지지 않고 있는데, 그 주된 이유는 그것을 어떻게 다루어야 하는지에 대해 아직 의견이 일치되지 않기 때문이다. **2** 부사 대체로 ❑ 관객들 중 아프리카 쪽에서 온 절반은 대체로 세네갈이나 말리에서 온 사람들이었다.

main road (**main roads**) N-COUNT A **main road** is an important road that leads from one town or city to another. ❑ Troops had barricaded the main road from the airport.

가산명사 간선 도로 ❑ 군대가 공항에서 들어오는 간선 도로에 바리케이드를 쳤다.

main|stream /**meɪnstrim**/ (**mainstreams**) N-COUNT People, activities, or ideas that are part of the **mainstream** are regarded as the most typical, normal, and conventional because they belong to the same group or system as most others of their kind. ❑ ...people outside the economic mainstream. →see **culture**

가산명사 주류 ❑ 경제적 주류 밖의 사람들

Main Street **1** N-PROPER In small towns in the United States, the street where most of the stores are is often called **Main Street**. ❑ Almost all the stores and restaurants along Main Street were shut for the season. **2** N-UNCOUNT **Main Street** is used by journalists to refer to the ordinary people of America who live in small towns rather than big cities or are not very rich. [AM] ❑ This financial crisis had a much greater impact on Main Street.

1 고유명사 (미국) 중심가 ❑ 중심가를 따라 나 있는 거의 모든 상점과 식당들이 그 기간 동안 폐쇄되었다. **2** 불가산명사 지방 시민들; 중산층 [미국영어] ❑ 이러한 재정 위기는 중산층에 훨씬 더 큰 충격을 주었다.

main|tain ♦♦◇ /**meɪnteɪn**/ (**maintains, maintaining, maintained**) **1** V-T If you **maintain** something, you continue to have it, and do not let it stop or grow weaker. ❑ France maintained close contacts with Jordan during the Gulf War. **2** V-T If you say that someone **maintains that** something is true, you mean that they have stated their opinion strongly but not everyone agrees with them or believes them. ❑ He has maintained that the money was donated for international purposes. ❑ "Not all feminism has to be like this," Jo maintains. **3** V-T If you **maintain** something **at** a particular rate or level, you keep it at that rate or level. ❑ The government was right to maintain interest rates at a high level. **4** V-T If you **maintain** a road, building, vehicle, or machine, you keep it in good condition by regularly checking it and repairing it when necessary. ❑ The house costs a fortune to maintain. **5** V-T If you **maintain** someone, you provide them with money and other things that they need. ❑ ...the basic costs of maintaining a child.

1 타동사 지속하다, 유지하다 ❑ 프랑스는 걸프 전쟁 중에 요르단과 긴밀한 연락을 유지했다. **2** 타동사 주장하다 ❑ 그는 그 돈을 국제적인 용도로 기부했다고 주장해 왔다. ❑ "모든 페미니즘이 이와 같아야만 하는 것은 아니다."라고 조는 주장한다. **3** 타동사 유지하다 ❑ 금리를 높은 수준으로 유지한 정부가 옳았다. **4** 타동사 유지하다, 정비하다 ❑ 그 집은 유지하는 데 큰 돈이 든다. **5** 타동사 부양하다 ❑ 아이를 부양하는 데 드는 기본 비용

Thesaurus   maintain의 참조어

V.   carry on, continue; (ant.) neglect **1**
       look after, protect, repair **4**

Word Partnership   maintain의 연어

N.   maintain **friendship**, maintain **law**, maintain **a relationship** **1**
V.   **need to** maintain, **pledge to** maintain, **try to** maintain **1**-**5**

main|te|nance /**meɪntɪnəns**/ **1** N-UNCOUNT The **maintenance** of a building, vehicle, road, or machine is the process of keeping it in good condition by regularly checking it and repairing it when necessary. ❑ ...maintenance work on government buildings. ❑ The window had been replaced last week during routine maintenance. **2** N-UNCOUNT **Maintenance** is money that someone gives regularly to another person to pay for the things that the person needs. ❑ ...the government's plan to make absent fathers pay maintenance for their children. **3** N-UNCOUNT If you ensure the **maintenance of** a state or process, you make sure that it continues. ❑ ...the maintenance of peace and stability in Asia.

1 불가산명사 정비 ❑ 정부 건물에 대한 정비 작업 ❑ 그 창문은 지난주 정기 정비 중에 갈아 끼웠다. **2** 불가산명사 생활비 ❑ 집을 떠나 있는 아버지들이 자녀들의 생활비를 지급하도록 하는 정부의 계획 **3** 불가산명사 유지, 지속 ❑ 아시아의 평화와 안정 유지

maize /**meɪz**/ N-UNCOUNT **Maize** is a tall plant which produces long objects covered with yellow seeds called corn. It is often grown as a food crop. [BRIT; AM **corn**] ❑ ...vast fields of maize.

불가산명사 옥수수 [영국영어; 미국영어 corn] ❑ 드넓은 옥수수 밭

ma|jes|tic /**mədʒestɪk**/ ADJ If you describe something or someone as **majestic**, you think they are very beautiful, dignified, and impressive. ❑ ...a majestic country home that once belonged to the Astor family. ● **ma|jes|ti|cal|ly** /**mədʒestɪkli**/ ADV ❑ She rose majestically to her feet.

형용사 웅장한, 장엄한, 당당한 ❑ 한때 애스터 가문 소유였던 웅장한 전원주택 ● 웅장하게, 장엄하게 부사 당당하게 ❑ 그녀는 당당하게 일어났다.

ma|jes|ty /**mædʒɪsti**/ (**majesties**) **1** N-VOC; PRON You use majesty in expressions such as **Your Majesty** or **Her Majesty** when you are addressing or referring to a King or Queen. [POLITENESS] [poss PRON] ❑ His Majesty requests your presence in the royal chambers. **2** N-UNCOUNT **Majesty** is the quality of being beautiful, dignified, and impressive. ❑ ...the majesty of the mainland mountains.

1 호격명사; 대명사 폐하 [공손체] ❑ 국왕 폐하께서 귀하게 궁실로 출두하라 하십니다. **2** 불가산명사 장엄함, 웅장함, 당당함 ❑ 대륙 산맥의 장엄함

ma|jor ♦♦♦ /**meɪdʒər**/ (**majors, majoring, majored**) **1** ADJ You use **major** when you want to describe something that is more important, serious, or significant than others in a group or situation. [ADJ n] ❑ The major

1 형용사 주요한 ❑ 머물지 떠날지를 결정하는 데 있어서 주요한 요소는 보통 직업상의 문제였다. ❑ 그곳 당국에게는 약물 남용이 오랫동안 주요한 문제가 되어

factor in the decision to stay or to leave was usually professional. ❑ *Drug abuse has long been a major problem for the authorities there.* **2** N-COUNT; N-TITLE; N-VOC A **major** is an officer who is one rank above captain in the United States army, air force, or marines, or in the British army. ❑ *I was a major in the war, you know.* **3** N-COUNT At a university or college in the United States, a student's **major** is the main subject that they are studying. ❑ *English majors would be asked to explore the roots of language.* **4** N-COUNT At a university or college in the United States, if a student is, for example, a geology **major**, geology is the main subject they are studying. ❑ *She was named the outstanding undergraduate history major at the University of Oklahoma.* **5** V-I If a student at a university or college in the United States **majors in** a particular subject, that subject is the main one they study. ❑ *He majored in finance at Claremont Men's College in California.* **6** ADJ In music, a **major** scale is one in which the third note is two tones higher than the first. [n ADJ, ADJ n] ❑ *...Mozart's Symphony No 35 in D Major.* **7** N-COUNT A **major** is a large or important company. [BUSINESS] ❑ *Neither oil-producing countries nor oil majors need fear being unable to sell their crude.* **8** N-PLURAL The **majors** are groups of professional sports teams that compete against each other, especially in baseball. [mainly AM] ❑ *I knew what I could do in the minor leagues, I just wanted a chance to prove myself in the majors.* **9** N-COUNT A **major** is an important sports competition, especially in golf or tennis. ❑ *Sarazen became the first golfer to win all four majors.*

Thesaurus	*major*의 참조어
ADJ.	chief, critical, crucial, key, main, principal; *(ant.)* little, minor, unimportant **1**

majority ♦♦◇ /mədʒɒrɪti, BRIT mədʒɒrɪti/ (**majorities**) **1** N-SING-COLL The **majority** of people or things in a group is more than half of them. ❑ *The majority of my patients come to me from out of town.* ● PHRASE If a group is **in a majority** or **in the majority**, they form more than half of a larger group. ❑ *Surveys indicate that supporters of the treaty are still in the majority.* **2** N-COUNT A **majority** is the difference between the number of votes or seats that the winner gets in an election, and the number of votes or seats that the next person or party gets. ❑ *Members of parliament approved the move by a majority of ninety-nine.* **3** ADJ **Majority** is used to describe opinions, decisions, and systems of government that are supported by more than half the people involved. [ADJ n] ❑ *...her continuing disagreement with the majority view.* **4** N-UNCOUNT **Majority** is the state of legally being an adult. In most states in the United States and in Britain, people reach their majority at the age of eighteen. ❑ *The age of majority in Romania is eighteen.*

Word Partnership	*majority*의 연어
ADJ.	**overwhelming** majority, **vast** majority **1** **2**
N.	majority **of people**, majority **of the population** **1**
	majority **leader** **2**
	majority **opinion**, majority **rule**, majority **vote** **3**

major league (**major leagues**) **1** N-PLURAL The **major leagues** are groups of professional sports teams that compete against each other, especially in American baseball. ❑ *Chandler was instrumental in making Jackie Robinson the first black player in the major leagues.* **2** ADJ **Major league** means connected with the major leagues in baseball. ❑ *I'm doomed to live in a town with no major league baseball.* **3** ADJ **Major league** people or institutions are important or successful. ❑ *James Hawes's books have achieved cult status, and his first film boasts major-league stars.* **4** PHRASE If someone **moves into the major league** or **makes it into the major league**, they become very successful in their career. [JOURNALISM] ❑ *Once a girl has made it into the major league every detail is mapped out by her agency.*

make
① CARRYING OUT AN ACTION
② CAUSING OR CHANGING
③ CREATING OR PRODUCING
④ LINK VERB USES
⑤ ACHIEVING OR REACHING
⑥ STATING AN AMOUNT OR TIME
⑦ PHRASAL VERBS

① **make** ♦♦♦ /meɪk/ (**makes, making, made**)

Make is used in a large number of expressions which are explained under other words in this dictionary. For example, the expression "to make sense" is explained at "sense."

1 V-T You can use **make** with a wide range of nouns to indicate that someone performs an action or says something. For example, if you **make** a suggestion, you suggest something. ❑ *I'd just like to make a comment.* ❑ *I made a few phone calls.* **2** V-T You can use **make** with certain nouns to indicate that someone does something well or badly. For example, if you **make** a success of something, you do it successfully, and if you **make** a mess of something, you do it very badly. ❑ *Apparently he made a mess of his audition.* **3** V-T/V-I If you **make as if to** do something or **make to** do something, you behave in a way that makes it seem that you are just about to do it. [WRITTEN] ❑ *Mary made as if to protest, then hesitated.* **4** PHRASE If you **make do with** something, you use or have it instead

---

왔다. **2** 가산명사; 경칭명사; 호격명사 소령 ❑ 알다시피, 나는 전쟁 때 소령이었다. **3** 가산명사 전공 ❑ 영어 전공들에 언어의 뿌리를 탐구할 것을 요구할 수도 있다. **4** 가산명사 전공자 ❑ 그녀는 오클라호마 대학에서 역사학 전공 우수 학부생으로 거명되었다. **5** 자동사 전공하다 ❑ 그는 캘리포니아에 있는 클레어몬트 남자 대학에서 재정학을 전공했다. **6** 형용사 장조의 ❑ 모차르트의 교향곡 제 35번 라장조 **7** 가산명사 거대 기업 [경제] ❑ 산유국이나 거대 석유 기업 양쪽 모두 원유를 팔지 못할까봐 걱정할 필요가 없다. **8** 복수명사 메이저리그 [주로 미국영어] ❑ 나는 내가 마이너리그에서는 뭘 할 수 있는지를 알고 있었다. 나는 그저 메이저리그에서 스스로의 인기를 증명할 수 있는 기회를 잡고 싶었다. **9** 가산명사 주요 대회 ❑ 사라젠은 네 개 주요 대회를 석권한 최초의 골프 선수가 되었다.

1 단수명사-집합 대부분, 대다수 ❑ 내 환자들 대부분은 시 외곽에서 온다. ● 구 다수를 점하는 ❑ 조사에 의하면 그 조약을 지지하는 사람이 여전히 다수를 점하는 것으로 나타난다. **2** 가산명사 득표 차 ❑ 국회의원들은 아흔아홉 표 차로 그 조치에 찬성했다. **3** 형용사 다수의 ❑ 다수 의견에 대한 그녀의 계속되는 반대 **4** 불가산명사 성년 ❑ 루마니아에서 성년 나이는 열여덟 살이다.

1 복수명사 메이저리그 ❑ 챈들러는 재키 로빈슨이 메이저 리그 최초의 흑인 선수가 되는 데 중요한 역할을 했다. **2** 형용사 메이저리그의 ❑ 나는 메이저리그 야구팀이 없는 도시에 살 운명이다. **3** 형용사 유력한, 일류의 ❑ 제임스 호스의 저서는 숭배의 대상이 되는 지위에까지 올랐고, 그의 첫 영화에는 일류 스타들이 등장한다. **4** 구 성공하다, 출세하다 [언론] ❑ 여자 연예인이 일단 인기를 끌면 그녀가 소속된 대행사가 모든 세부 계획을 짠다.

이 사전에서 make가 포함된 많은 표현들이 다른 표제어에서 설명된다. 예를 들어, 'to make sense'는 'sense'에서 설명된다.

1 타동사 (행위, 말 등을) 하다 ❑ 그저 한 말씀드리고 싶습니다. ❑ 몇 차례 전화를 걸었다. **2** 타동사 ~을 어떻게 하다 ❑ 분명히 그는 오디션을 망쳤다. **3** 타동사/자동사 막 ~할 것처럼 하다 [문어체] ❑ 메리는 막 항의할 것처럼 하다가 주저했다. **4** 구 (대용품 등으로) 변통하다 ❑ 원본을 살 여유가 있다면 왜 복사본으로 때우죠?

of something else that you do not have, although it is not as good. ❑ *Why make do with a copy if you can afford the genuine article?*

Thesaurus	*make*의 참조어
v.	build, compose, create, fabricate, produce; *(ant.)* destroy ③ 🕦

② **make** ♦♦♦ /meɪk/ (**makes, making, made**)→Please look at category 🔟 to see if the expression you are looking for is shown under another headword. 🕦 v-T If something **makes** you do something, it causes you to do it. ❑ *Grit from the highway made him cough.* ❑ *The white tips of his shirt collar made him look like a choirboy.* 🔁 v-T If you **make** someone do something, you force them to do it. ❑ *You can't make me do anything.* 🔃 v-T You use **make** to talk about causing someone or something to be a particular thing or to have a particular quality. For example, to **make** someone a star means to cause them to become a star, and to **make** someone angry means to cause them to become angry. ❑ *...James Bond, the role that made him a star.* ❑ *She made life very difficult for me.* 🔄 v-T If you say that one thing or person **makes** another seem, for example, small, stupid, or good, you mean that they cause them to seem small, stupid, or good in comparison, even though they are not. ❑ *They live in fantasy worlds which make Euro Disney seem uninventive.* 🔅 v-T If you **make** yourself understood, heard, or known, you succeed in getting people to understand you, hear you, or know that you are there. ❑ *Aron couldn't speak Polish. I made myself understood with difficulty.* 🔆 v-T If you **make** someone something, you appoint them to a particular job, role, or position. ❑ *He made her a director in his numerous companies.* 🔇 v-T If you **make** something **into** something else, you change it in some way so that it becomes that other thing. ❑ *We made it into a beautiful home.* 🔈 v-T To **make** a total or score a particular amount means to increase it to that amount. ❑ *This makes the total cost of the bulb and energy £27.* 🔉 v-T When someone **makes** a friend or an enemy, someone becomes their friend or their enemy, often because of a particular thing they have done. ❑ *Lorenzo was a natural leader who made friends easily.* 🔟 to **make friends** →see **friend**

③ **make** ♦♦♦ /meɪk/ (**makes, making, made**) 🕦 v-T To **make** something means to produce, construct, or create it. ❑ *She made her own bread.* ❑ *Having curtains made professionally can be costly.* 🔁 v-T If you **make** a note or list, you write something down in that form. ❑ *Mr. Perry made a note in his book.* 🔃 v-T If you **make** rules or laws, you decide what these should be. ❑ *The police don't make the laws, they merely enforce them.* 🔄 v-T If you **make** money, you get it by working for it, by selling something, or by winning it. ❑ *I think every business's goal is to make money.* 🔅 N-COUNT The **make** of something such as a car or radio is the name of the company that made it. ❑ *The only car parked outside is a black Saab – a different make.*

The **brand** of a product such as jeans, tea, or soap is its name, which can also be the name of the company that makes or sells it. The **make** of a car or electrical appliance such as a radio or washing machine is the name of the company that produces it. If you talk about what **type** of product or service you want, you are talking about its quality and what features it should have. You can also talk about **types** of people or of abstract things. ❑ *...which type of coffeemaker to choose....a new type of bank account....looking for a certain type of actor.* A **model** of car or of some other devices is a name that is given to a particular **type**, for example, Ford Escort or Nissan Micra. Note that **type** can also be used informally to mean either **make** or **model**. For example, if someone asks what **type** of car you have got, you could reply "an SUV," "a Ford," or perhaps "an Escort."

④ **make** ♦♦♦ /meɪk/ (**makes, making, made**) 🕦 V-LINK You can use **make** to say that someone or something has the right qualities for a particular task or role. For example, if you say that someone will **make** a good politician, you mean that they have the right qualities to be a good politician. ❑ *She'll make a good actress, if she gets the right training.* ❑ *You've a very good idea there. It will make a good book.* 🔁 V-LINK If people **make** a particular pattern such as a line or a circle, they arrange themselves in this way. ❑ *A group of people made a circle around the Pentagon.* 🔃 V-LINK You can use **make** to say what two numbers add up to. ❑ *Four twos make eight.*

⑤ **make** ♦♦♦ /meɪk/ (**makes, making, made**) 🕦 v-T If someone **makes** a particular team or **makes** a particular high position, they do so well that they are put in that team or get that position. ❑ *The athletes are just happy to make the British team.* 🔁 v-T If you **make** a place in or by a particular time, you get there in or by that time, often with some difficulty. ❑ *The engine is gulping two tons of fuel an hour in order to make New Orleans by nightfall.* 🔃 PHRASE If you **make** it somewhere, you succeed in getting there, especially in time to do something. ❑ *So you did make it to America, after all.* ❑ *...the hostages who never made it home.* 🔄 PHRASE If you **make** it, you are successful in achieving something difficult, or in surviving through a very difficult period. ❑ *I believe I have the talent to make it.* 🔅 PHRASE If you cannot **make** it, you are unable to attend an event that you have been invited to. ❑ *He hadn't been able to make it to our dinner.*

⑥ **make** ♦♦♦ /meɪk/ (**makes, making, made**) 🕦 v-T You use **make** it when saying what you calculate or guess an amount to be. ❑ *"How many shots she got left?" — "I make it two."* 🔁 v-T You use **make** it when saying what time your watch says it is. ❑ *I make it nearly nine o'clock.*

⑦ **make** ♦♦♦ /meɪk/ (**makes, making, made**)

🕦 타동사 -하게 만들다 ❑ 그는 큰길에서 날려 온 먼지 때문에 기침을 했다. ❑ 그는 끝부분이 흰색으로 된 셔츠 깃 때문에 합창단원처럼 보였다. 🔁 타동사 -하게 하다 ❑ 당신은 나에게 어떤 일도 시킬 수 없어. 🔃 타동사 -을...로 만들다; -을...하게 만들다 ❑ 그를 스타로 만들어 준 역할인 제임스 본드 ❑ 그녀 때문에 나는 사는 게 아주 힘들었다. 🔄 타동사 -을...로 보이게 하다 ❑ 그들은 유로 디즈니조차 초라해 보일만한 환상의 세계에 산다. 🔅 타동사 (다른 사람이 자신을) -하게 하다 ❑ 애런은 폴란드 어를 할 줄 몰랐다. 나는 간신히 내 뜻을 전했다. 🔆 타동사 (직위 등에) 임명하다 ❑ 그는 그녀를 자신의 수많은 회사 중 한 곳의 중역 자리에 앉혔다. 🔇 타동사 -을...로 만들다 ❑ 우리는 그곳을 아름다운 집으로 만들었다. 🔈 타동사 (총액 등이) -에 이르게 하다 ❑ 이렇게 하면 전구와 전력에 드는 총비용이 27파운드가 됩니다. 🔉 타동사 (친구나 적을) 만들다 ❑ 로렌조는 쉽게 친구를 사귀는 타고난 지도자였다.

🕦 타동사 만들다 ❑ 그녀는 자기 스스로 생활비를 벌었다. ❑ 전문가에게 커튼을 주문 제작하면 비용이 많이 들 수 있다. 🔁 타동사 작성하다 ❑ 페리 씨는 책에다 메모를 했다. 🔃 타동사 (법 등을) 제정하다 ❑ 경찰은 법을 제정하지 않고 다만 집행할 뿐이다. 🔄 타동사 (돈을) 벌다 ❑ 모든 사업의 목표는 돈을 버는 것이라고 생각한다. 🔅 가산명사 상표, 제조자 ❑ 밖에 주차된 유일한 차는 다른 제조사 차인 검은색 사브이다.

청바지, 차, 비누와 같은 상품의 brand는 그 상품의 이름인데, 상품명이 그것을 만들거나 파는 회사명일 수도 있다. 자동차 또는 라디오나 세탁기 같은 전기제품의 make는 그것을 생산하는 회사명이다. 원하는 상품이나 서비스의 type을 얘기할 때는 그 상품이나 서비스가 지녀야 할 품질이나 특성을 말하는 것이다. 사람이나 추상적 사물에 대해서도 type을 말할 수 있다. ❑ ...어떤 종류의 커피 메이커를 선택할지....새로운 종류의 은행 계좌....어떤 특정한 유형의 배우를 찾는. 자동차나 다른 일부 장치의 model은 특정 type에 붙여진 이름으로, 예를 들면 포드 에스코트나 닛산 마이크라와 같은 것이다. type은 또한 비격식체로 make나 model을 뜻할 수도 있다. 예를 들어 어떤 type의 자동차를 가지고 있느냐고 누가 물으면, '스포츠 유틸리티 차량,' 또는 '포드,' 또는 '에스코트'라고 대답할 수 있다.

🕦 연결동사 -이 되다, -이 될 자격이 있다 ❑ 그녀는 적절한 훈련을 받으면 훌륭한 배우가 될 것이다. ❑ 아주 좋은 아이디어를 가지고 있구나. 좋은 책이 되겠어. 🔁 연결동사 (대형을) 이루다 ❑ 한 무리의 사람들이 미 국방부를 둥글게 둘러쌌다. 🔃 연결동사 (계산 결과) -이 되다 ❑ 4 곱하기 2는 8이다.

🕦 타동사 -에 들다; -에 오르다 ❑ 선수들은 영국 대표팀에 들게 되어 기쁠 뿐이다. 🔁 타동사 도착하다 ❑ 그 기관차는 해질녘까지 뉴올리언스에 닿기 위해 시간당 2톤의 연료를 소비하고 있다. 🔃 구 -에 도착하다 ❑ 그래서 결국 미국에 도착하긴 했구나. 🔄 구 결코 집으로 돌아가지 못한 인질들 ❑ 나는 내 자신이 그 일을 해 낼 재능이 있다고 믿는다. 🔅 구 참석하다 ❑ 그는 우리의 저녁 식사에 오지 못했었다.

🕦 타동사 (계산 결과) -이 되다 ❑ "그 여자 몇 발이나 남았지?" "내 계산으로는 두 발." 🔁 타동사 (시간이) -이다 ❑ 내 시계로는 거의 아홉 시가 다 되었다.

a b c d e f g h i j k l m n o p q r s t u v w x y z

▶**make for** ◼ PHRASAL VERB If you **make for** a place, you move toward it. ❑ *He rose from his seat and made for the door.* ◻ PHRASAL VERB If something **makes for** another thing, it causes or helps to cause that thing to happen or exist. [INFORMAL] ❑ *A happy parent makes for a happy child.*

◼ 구동사 -을 향하여 가다 ❑ 그는 자리에서 일어나 문 쪽으로 갔다. ◻ 구동사 -에 이바지하다, -을 조장하다 [비격식체] ❑ 행복한 부모가 행복한 아이를 만들게 된다.

▶**make of** PHRASAL VERB If you ask a person what they **make of** something, you want to know what their impression, opinion, or understanding of it is. ❑ *Nancy wasn't sure what to make of Mick's apology.*

구동사 -을 이해하다, -을 받아들이다 ❑ 낸시는 믹의 사과를 어떻게 받아들여야 할지 잘 알 수가 없었다.

▶**make off** PHRASAL VERB If you **make off**, you leave somewhere as quickly as possible, often in order to escape. ❑ *They broke free and made off in a stolen car.*

구동사 (급히) 떠나다, 도망치다 ❑ 그들은 탈출해서 훔친 차를 타고 도망쳤다.

▶**make out** ◼ PHRASAL VERB If you **make** something **out**, you manage with difficulty to see or hear it. ❑ *I could just make out a tall, pale, shadowy figure tramping through the undergrowth.* ❑ *She thought she heard a name. She couldn't make it out, though.* ◻ PHRASAL VERB If you try to **make** something **out**, you try to understand it or decide whether or not it is true. ❑ *I couldn't make it out at all.* ❑ *It is hard to make out what criteria are used.* ▣ PHRASAL VERB If you **make out that** something is the case or **make** something **out to** be the case, you try to cause people to believe that it is the case. ❑ *They were trying to make out that I'd actually done it.* ❑ *I don't think it was as glorious as everybody made it out to be.* ▤ PHRASAL VERB If you **make out** a case **for** something, you try to establish or prove that it is the best thing to do. ❑ *You could certainly make out a case for this point of view.* ▥ PHRASAL VERB When you **make out** a check, receipt, or order form, you write all the necessary information on it. ❑ *I'll make the check out to you and put it in the mail this afternoon.* ▦ PHRASAL VERB-RECIP If two people **are making out**, they are engaged in sexual activity. [mainly AM, INFORMAL] ❑ *...pictures of the couple making out in their underwear on the beach.*

◼ 구동사 (힘겹게) 알아보다, 알아듣다 ❑ 키 크고 창백하며 희미한 사람 모습이 덤불 사이로 터벅터벅 걷고 있는 것을 겨우 알아볼 수 있었다. ❑ 그녀는 무슨 이름을 들은 것 같았다. 하지만 그 이름을 알아들을 수는 없었다. ◻ 구동사 이해하다 ❑ 나는 그것을 전혀 이해할 수 없었다. ❑ 어떤 기준이 사용되는지도 이해하기 힘들다. ▣ 구동사 믿게 하다, 주장하다 ❑ 그들은 사람들에게 실제로 그 일을 저지른 것이 나라고 믿게 하려 했다. ❑ 그 일이 모든 이들이 주장하는 것만큼 영예롭지는 않았다고 생각한다. ▤ 구동사 -를 내세우다 ❑ 너는 물론 이런 견해를 내세울지도 모른다. ▥ 구동사 작성하다; 수표를 작성하다 ❑ 네 앞으로 수표를 써서 오늘 오후에 우편으로 보내 줄게. ▦ 상호 구동사 성교하다 [주로 미국영어, 비격식체] ❑ 해변에서 속옷 차림으로 사랑을 나누고 있는 남녀를 찍은 사진들

▶**make up** ◼ PHRASAL VERB The people or things that **make up** something are the members or parts that form that thing. ❑ *North Africans make up the largest and poorest immigrant group in the country.* ❑ *Women officers make up 13 percent of the police force.* ◻ PHRASAL VERB If you **make up** something such as a story or excuse, you invent it, sometimes in order to deceive people. ❑ *I think it's very unkind of you to make up stories about him.* ▣ PHRASAL VERB If you **make up** an amount, you add something to it so that it is as large as it should be. ❑ *Less than half of the money that students receive is in the form of grants, and loans have made up the difference.* ❑ *The team had six professionals and made the number up with five amateurs.* ▤ PHRASAL VERB If you **make up** time or hours, you work some extra hours because you have previously taken some time off work. ❑ *They'll have to make up time lost during the strike.* ▥ PHRASAL VERB-RECIP If two people **make up** or **make it up** after a quarrel or disagreement, they become friends again. ❑ *She came back and they made up.* ▦ PHRASAL VERB If you **make up** something such as food or medicine, you prepare it by mixing or putting different things together. ❑ *Prepare the soufflé dish before making up the soufflé mixture.* ▧ PHRASAL VERB If you **make up** a bed, you put sheets and blankets on it so that someone can sleep there. ❑ *Her mother made up a bed in her old room.*

◼ 구동사 구성하다, 이루다 ❑ 북부 아프리카인들이 그 나라에서 가장 규모가 크고 가장 가난한 이민자 집단을 이룬다. ❑ 여성 경찰관이 경찰력의 13퍼센트를 차지한다. ◻ 구동사 만들어 내다, 날조하다 ❑ 그에 관한 이야기를 지어내다니 당신 참 너무하는 것 같군요. ▣ 구동사 (수량 등을) 채우다, 벌충하다 ❑ 학생들이 받는 돈의 절반 미만이 보조금 형식이고, 차액은 융자로 채워져 왔다. ❑ 그 팀은 프로 선수 6명을 보유했고 아마추어 선수 5명으로 수를 채웠다. ▤ 구동사 (부족한 시간을) 메우다, 벌충하다 ❑ 그들은 파업 중에 일하지 못한 시간을 벌충해야 할 것이다. ▥ 상호 구동사 화해하다 ❑ 그녀가 돌아와서 그들은 화해를 했다. ▦ 구동사 (섞거나 조합해서) 만들다 ❑ 수플레를 만들기 전에 그릇을 준비하세요. ▧ 구동사 (잠자리를) 보다 ❑ 그녀가 이전에 쓰던 방에 어머니께서 잠자리를 보아주셨다.

mak|er ◆◇◇ /ˈmeɪkər/ (makers) ◼ N-COUNT The **maker** of a product is the firm that manufactures it. ❑ *...Japan's two largest car makers.* ◻ N-COUNT You can refer to the person who makes something as its **maker**. ❑ *...the makers of news and current affairs programmes.*

◼ 가산명사 제조사 ❑ 일본 최대의 자동차 제조사 두 곳 ◻ 가산명사 제작자 ❑ 뉴스와 시사 프로그램 제작자들

make|shift /ˈmeɪkʃɪft/ ADJ **Makeshift** things are temporary and usually of poor quality, but they are used because there is nothing better available. ❑ *...the cardboard boxes and makeshift shelters of the homeless.*

형용사 임시변통의 ❑ 노숙자들의 판지 상자와 임시 거처

makeup ◆◇◇ also **make-up** ◼ N-UNCOUNT **Makeup** consists of things such as lipstick, eye shadow, and powder which some women put on their faces to make themselves look more attractive or which actors use to change or improve their appearance. ❑ *Normally she wore little makeup, but this evening was clearly an exception.* ◻ N-UNCOUNT Someone's **make-up** is their nature and the various qualities in their character. ❑ *There was some fatal flaw in his makeup, and as time went on he lapsed into long silences or became off-hand.* ▣ N-UNCOUNT The **make-up** of something consists of its different parts and the way these parts are arranged. ❑ *The ideological make-up of the unions is now radically different from what it had been.*
→see Word Web: makeup

◼ 불가산명사 화장, 분장; 화장품 ❑ 그녀는 보통 화장을 거의 안 했지만 오늘 저녁은 분명 예외였다. ◻ 불가산명사 성질, 기질 ❑ 그의 기질에는 중대한 결함이 있어서, 시간이 갈수록 그는 긴 침묵에 빠져들거나 무뚝뚝해졌다. ▣ 불가산명사 구조, 조직 ❑ 이제는 노조의 이상적인 구조가 이전과는 현격히 다르다.

mak|ing /ˈmeɪkɪŋ/ (makings) ◼ N-UNCOUNT The **making** of something is the act or process of producing or creating it. ❑ *...Salomon's book about the making of this movie.* ◻ PHRASE If you describe a person or thing as something **in the making**, you mean that they are going to become known or recognized as that thing. ❑ *Her drama teacher is confident Julie is a star in the making.* ▣ PHRASE If something **is the making of** a person or thing, it is the reason that they become successful or become very much better than they used to be. ❑ *This discovery may yet be the making of him.* ▤ PHRASE If you say that a person or thing **has the makings of** something, you mean it seems possible or likely that they will become that thing, as they have the necessary qualities. ❑ *Godfrey had the*

◼ 불가산명사 제작, 제작 과정 ❑ 이 영화의 제작 과정에 대한 살라몬의 책 ◻ 구 발단 중의, -이 되어 가는 ❑ 줄리의 연극 선생은 그녀가 스타가 될 것임을 확신한다. ▣ 구 -의 성공 요인이다 ❑ 이와 같은 발견이 머지않아 그의 성공 요인이 될지도 모른다. ▤ 구 -의 소질이 있다 ❑ 고드프리는 기자로 성공할 소질이 있었다. ▥ 구 스스로 조달한, 자립자금의 ❑ 그 대학의 재정 문제 중 일부는 스스로 조달한 것이다.

Word Web makeup

The women of ancient Egypt were among the first to **wear makeup**. They **applied foundation** to lighten their skin and used kohl as **eye shadow** to darken their eyelids. Greek women used charcoal as an **eyeliner** and **rouge** on their cheeks. In 14th century Europe, the most popular **cosmetic** was wheat flour. Women whitened their faces to show their social class. A light **complexion** indicated the woman didn't have to work outdoors. **Cosmetics** containing lead and arsenic sometimes caused illness and death. Makeup use increased in the early 1900s. Suddenly many women could afford mass-produced **lipstick, mascara,** and **face powder**.

makings of a successful journalist. ⑤ PHRASE If you say that something such as a problem you have is **of** your **own making**, you mean you have caused or created it yourself. ❏ *Some of the university's financial troubles are of its own making.*

Word Link | mal ≈ bad : malaria, malfunction, malice

ma|laria /məlɛ́əriə/ N-UNCOUNT **Malaria** is a serious disease carried by mosquitoes which causes periods of fever.

불가산명사 말라리아

male ◆◇◇ /meɪl/ (**males**) ❶ ADJ Someone who is **male** is a man or a boy. ❏ *Many women achievers appear to pose a threat to their male colleagues.* ❏ *The London City Ballet has engaged two male dancers from the Bolshoi.* ❷ N-COUNT Men and boys are sometimes referred to as **males** when they are being considered as a type. ❏ *...the remains of a Caucasian male, aged 65-70.* ❸ ADJ **Male** means relating to, belonging to, or affecting men rather than women. [ADJ n] ❏ *The rate of male unemployment in Britain is now the third worst in Europe.* ❏ *...male violence.* ❹ N-COUNT You can refer to any creature that belongs to the sex that cannot lay eggs or have babies as a **male**. ❏ *Males and females take turns brooding the eggs.* ● ADJ **Male** is also an adjective. ❏ *After mating the male wasps tunnel through the sides of their nursery.*

❶ 형용사 남성의, 남자의 ❏ 성공한 많은 여성들이 남성 동료들에게는 위협이 되는 것처럼 보인다. ❏ 런던 시립 발레단이 볼쇼이 발레단으로부터 남자 무용수 2명을 고용했다. ❷ 가산명사 남성, 남자 ❏ 65세에서 70세 사이의 백인 남성 유골 ❸ 형용사 남성의, 남자의 ❏ 영국의 남성 실업률은 현재 유럽에서 세 번째로 높다. ❏ 남성 폭력 ❹ 가산명사 수컷 ❏ 수컷과 암컷이 번갈아 가며 알을 품는다. ● 형용사 수컷의 ❏ 짝짓기 후에 수컷 장수말벌들은 알들이 자랄 방의 옆면을 파고 들어간다.

mal|func|tion /mælfʌ́ŋkʃ³n/ (**malfunctions, malfunctioning, malfunctioned**) V-I If a machine or part of the body **malfunctions**, it fails to work properly. [FORMAL] ❏ *The radiation can damage microprocessors and computer memories, causing them to malfunction.* ● N-COUNT **Malfunction** is also a noun. ❏ *There must have been a computer malfunction.*

자동사 제대로 작동하지 않다 [격식체] ❏ 발생하는 열 때문에 마이크로프로세서와 컴퓨터 메모리가 손상되어 오작동을 일으킬 수 있다. ● 가산명사 오작동 ❏ 틀림없이 컴퓨터 오작동이 있었다.

mal|ice /mǽlɪs/ N-UNCOUNT **Malice** is behavior that is intended to harm people or their reputations, or cause them embarrassment and upset. ❏ *There was a strong current of malice in many of his portraits.*

불가산명사 악의, 적의 ❏ 그가 그린 다수의 초상화에는 악의적인 기운이 강하게 담겨 있었다.

ma|li|cious /məlɪ́ʃəs/ ADJ If you describe someone's words or actions as **malicious**, you mean that they are intended to harm people or their reputation, or cause them embarrassment and upset. ❏ *That might merely have been malicious gossip.* ● **ma|li|cious|ly** ADV ❏ *...his maliciously accurate imitation of Hubert de Burgh.*

형용사 악의 있는, 심술궂은 ❏ 그것은 단순히 악의가 담긴 가십에 불과했을지도 모른다. ● 악의적으로, 심술궂게 부사 ❏ 그가 악의적으로 똑같이 내는 허버트 드 버그 흉내

ma|lig|nant /məlɪ́gnənt/ ❶ ADJ A **malignant** tumor or disease is out of control and likely to cause death. [MEDICAL] ❏ *She developed a malignant breast tumor.* ❷ ADJ If you say that someone is **malignant**, you think they are cruel and like to cause harm. ❏ *He said that we were evil, malignant and mean.*

❶ 형용사 악성의 [의학] ❏ 그녀는 악성 유방 종양에 걸렸다. ❷ 형용사 악의 있는 ❏ 그는 우리를 가리켜 사악하고 악의에 차 있으며 비열하다고 말했다.

mall /mɔl/ (**malls**) N-COUNT A **mall** is a very large enclosed shopping area. ❏ *The mall also has a hypermarket and 10 cafes and restaurants.*

가산명사 쇼핑센터 ❏ 그 쇼핑센터에는 대형 슈퍼마켓과 10개의 카페와 음식점이 있다.

mal|let /mǽlɪt/ (**mallets**) N-COUNT A **mallet** is a wooden hammer with a square head.

가산명사 나무 메

mal|nu|tri|tion /mælnutrɪ́ʃ³n, BRIT mælnyu:trɪ́ʃ³n/ N-UNCOUNT If you are suffering from **malnutrition**, you are physically weak and extremely thin because they have not eaten enough food. ❏ *Infections are more likely in those suffering from malnutrition.*

불가산명사 영양실조 ❏ 영양실조를 겪는 사람들 사이에서 감염 가능성이 더 크다.

mal|prac|tice /mǽlpræktɪs/ (**malpractices**) N-VAR If you accuse someone of **malpractice**, you are accusing them of being careless or of breaking the law or the rules of their profession. [FORMAL] ❏ *There were only one or two serious allegations of malpractice.*

가산명사 또는 불가산명사 배임 행위 [격식체] ❏ 한두 건의 심각한 배임 혐의 밖에 없었다.

malt /mɔlt/ (**malts**) ❶ N-UNCOUNT **Malt** is a substance made from grain that has been soaked in water and then dried in a hot oven. Malt is used in the production of whiskey, beer, and other alcoholic drinks. ❏ *German beer has traditionally been made from just four ingredients – hops, malt, yeast and water.* ❷ N-COUNT A **malt** is a drink made from malted milk and sometimes other flavorings. [AM] ❏ *...a chocolate malt.*

❶ 불가산명사 맥아, 엿기름 ❏ 독일 맥주는 전통적으로 네 가지 성분만으로 만들어져 왔다. 그것은 홉, 맥아, 이스트, 그리고 물이다. ❷ 가산명사 맥아 분유 [미국영어] ❏ 초콜릿이 든 맥아 분유

mam|mal /mǽm³l/ (**mammals**) N-COUNT **Mammals** are animals such as humans, dogs, lions, and whales. In general, female mammals give birth to babies rather than laying eggs, and feed their young with milk. →see **pet**, **whale**

가산명사 포유동물

mam|moth /mǽməθ/ (**mammoths**) ❶ ADJ You can use **mammoth** to emphasize that a task or change is very large and needs a lot of effort to achieve. [EMPHASIS] ❏ *...the mammoth task of relocating the library.* ❷ N-COUNT A **mammoth** was an animal like an elephant, with very long tusks and long hair, that lived a long time ago but no longer exists.

❶ 형용사 거대한 [강조] ❏ 도서관을 이전하는 거대한 작업 ❷ 가산명사 매머드

man ◆◆◆ /mæn/ (**men, mans, manning, manned**) ❶ N-COUNT A **man** is an adult male human being. ❏ *He had not expected the young man to reappear before evening.* ❏ *I have always regarded him as a man of integrity.* ❷ N-VAR **Man** and **men** are sometimes used to refer to all human beings, including both males and females. Some people dislike this use. ❏ *The chick initially has no fear of man.* ❸ N-COUNT If you say that a man is, for example, **a gambling man** or **an outdoors man**, you mean that he likes gambling or outdoor activities. ❏ *Are you a gambling man, Mr. Graham?* ❹ N-COUNT If you say that a man is, for example, **a Harvard man** or **a Yale man**, you mean that he went to that university. ❏ *Stewart, a Yale man, was invited to stay on and write the script.* ❺ N-COUNT If you refer to a particular company's or organization's **man**, you mean a man who works for that company or organization. [JOURNALISM] ❏ *...the Daily Telegraph's man in Abu Dhabi.* ❻ N-SING Some people refer to a woman's husband, lover, or boyfriend as her **man**. [INFORMAL] ❏ *...if they see your man cuddle you in the kitchen or living room.* ❼ N-VOC In very informal social situations, **man** is sometimes used as a greeting or form of address to a man. [FORMULAE] ❏ *Hey wow, man! Where d'you get those boots?* ❽ V-T If you **man** something such as a place or machine, you operate it or are in charge of it. ❏ *French soldiers manned*

❶ 가산명사 (성인) 남자 ❏ 그는 그 젊은 남자가 저녁 전에 다시 나타나리라고 예상치 못했다. ❏ 나는 항상 그를 성실한 사람이라고 생각해 왔다. ❷ 가산명사 또는 불가산명사 인간, 사람 ❏ 병아리는 처음에는 사람을 두려워하지 않는다. ❸ 가산명사 -를 좋아하는 남자, 도박을 좋아하는 남자; 바깥 활동을 좋아하는 남자 ❏ 도박 좋아하세요, 그레이엄 씨? ❹ 가산명사 어떤 대학을 나온 남자; 하버드 출신 남자; 예일 대학 출신 남자 ❏ 예일 대학을 나온 스튜어트는 계속 남아서 원고를 써 달라는 권유를 받았다. ❺ 가산명사 (소속원) 사람 [언론] ❏ 아부다비 주재 데일리 텔레그래프 소속 기자 ❻ 단수명사 남편; 애인, 남자 친구 ❏ 당신 애인이 주방이나 거실에서 당신을 껴안고 있는 것을 그들이 본다면 ❼ 호격명사 어이, 이봐 [의례적인 표현] ❏ 와 이런, 이봐! 그 장화 어디서 났어? ❽ 타동사 -의 임무를 맡다, 관리하다 ❏ 프랑스 군인들이 수도의 도로 방책을 관리했다. ❾ 고객 고충 처리부에서 전화 업무를 담당하는 사람 ❿ 구 -하기에 충분한 용기나 능력이

roadblocks in the capital city. ❏ ...the person manning the phone at the complaints department. **9** →see also **manned, no-man's land** **10** PHRASE If you say that a man is **man enough** to do something, you mean that he has the necessary courage or ability to do it. ❏ I told him that he should be man enough to admit he had done wrong. **11** PHRASE If you describe a man as **a man's man**, you mean that he has qualities which make him popular with other men rather than with women. ❏ Very much a man's man, he enjoyed drinking and jesting with his cronies. **12** PHRASE If you say that a man **is his own man**, you approve of the fact that he makes his decisions and his plans himself, and does not depend on other people. [APPROVAL] ❏ Be your own man. Make up your own mind. **13** PHRASE If you say that a group of men are, do, or think something **to a man**, you are emphasizing that every one of them is, does, or thinks that thing. [EMPHASIS] ❏ To a man, the surveyors blamed the government. →see **age**

man|age ♦♦◇ /mænɪdʒ/ (**manages, managing, managed**) **1** V-T If you **manage** an organization, business, or system, or the people who work in it, you are responsible for controlling them. ❏ Within two years he was managing the store. ❏ There is a lack of confidence in the government's ability to manage the economy. **2** V-T If you **manage** time, money, or other resources, you deal with them carefully and do not waste them. ❏ In a busy world, managing your time is increasingly important. **3** V-T If you **manage** to do something, especially something difficult, you succeed in doing it. ❏ Somehow, he'd managed to persuade Kay to buy one for him. ❏ I managed to pull myself up onto a wet, sloping ledge. **4** V-I If you **manage**, you succeed in coping with a difficult situation. ❏ She had managed perfectly well without medication for three years. **5** V-T If you say that you can **manage** an amount of time or money for something, you mean that you can afford to spend that time or money on it. ❏ I try to manage about five hours on my bike a week. **6** V-T If you say that someone **managed** a particular response, such as a laugh or a greeting, you mean that it was difficult for them to do it because they were feeling sad or upset. ❏ He looked dazed as he spoke to reporters, managing only a weak smile. **7** CONVENTION You say "**I can manage**" or "**I'll manage**" as a way of refusing someone's offer of help and insisting on doing something by yourself. ❏ I know you mean well, but I can manage by myself.

1 타동사 관리하다 ❏ 2년 내에 그는 매장 관리자가 되었다. ❏ 정부의 경제 관리 능력에 대한 신뢰가 부족하다. **2** 타동사 관리하다 ❏ 바쁜 세상에서는, 시간 관리가 갈수록 중요해진다. **3** 타동사 이럭저럭 -해내다, 간신히 -하다 ❏ 그럭저럭, 그는 케이를 설득해서 자신에게 하나를 사 주도록 했었다. ❏ 나는 가까스로 비에 젖은 경사진 바위 턱에 몸을 올려놓았다. **4** 자동사 잘 헤쳐 나가다 ❏ 그녀는 3년 동안 약물 치료 없이도 굉장히 잘 헤쳐 나갔었다. **5** 타동사 변통하다; 할애하다 ❏ 나는 일주일에 다섯 시간 정도를 자전거에 할애하려고 노력한다. **6** 타동사 억지로 -하다, 간신히 -하다 ❏ 기자들에게 이야기할 때 그는 명해 보였고, 억지로 가벼운 미소를 지을 뿐이었다. **7** 관용 표현 내가 처리할 수 있다 ❏ 네가 좋은 뜻으로 그러는 건 알지만, 나 혼자 처리할 수 있어.

man|age|able /mænɪdʒəbəl/ ADJ Something that is **manageable** is of a size, quantity, or level of difficulty that people are able to deal with. ❏ He will now try to cut down the task to a manageable size.

형용사 다루기 쉬운 ❏ 그는 이제 그 일을 다루기 쉬운 규모로 줄이려고 할 것이다.

man|age|ment ♦♦◇ /mænɪdʒmənt/ (**managements**) **1** N-UNCOUNT **Management** is the control and organizing of a business or other organization. ❏ The zoo needed better management rather than more money. ❏ The dispute is about wages, working conditions and the management of the mining industry. **2** N-VAR-COLL You can refer to the people who control and organize a business or other organization as the **management**. [BUSINESS] ❏ The management is doing its best to improve the situation. ❏ We need to get more women into top management. **3** N-UNCOUNT **Management** is the way people control different parts of their lives. ❏ ...her management of her professional life.

1 불가산명사 경영, 운영 ❏ 그 동물원은 추가 자금보다는 운영 개선이 필요하였다. ❏ 그 쟁의는 임금과 작업 조건, 그리고 광산업 경영에 대한 것이다. **2** 가산명사 또는 불가산명사·집합 경영진 [경제] ❏ 경영진은 사태 개선을 위해 최선을 다하고 있다. ❏ 최고 경영진에 더 많은 여성을 들일 필요가 있다. **3** 불가산명사 관리 ❏ 그녀의 직업 생활 관리

man|age|ment buy|out (**management buyouts**) N-COUNT A **management buyout** is the buying of a company by its managers. The abbreviation **MBO** is also used. [BUSINESS] ❏ Dozens of company boards are now discreetly sounding out venture capitalists to see if they will support management buyouts.

가산명사 경영자 인수 (기존 전문 경영인에 의한 기업 인수) [경제] ❏ 현재 수십 개의 기업 이사회가 경영자 매수 지원에 대한 벤처 투자가들의 의사를 신중하게 타진하고 있다.

man|ag|er ♦♦◇ /mænɪdʒər/ (**managers**) **1** N-COUNT A **manager** is a person who is responsible for running part of or the whole of a business organization. ❏ The chef, staff, and managers are all Chinese. **2** N-COUNT The **manager** of a pop star or other entertainer is the person who takes care of their business interests. ❏ ...the star's manager and agent, Anne Chudleigh. **3** N-COUNT The **manager** of a sports team is the person responsible for training the players and organizing the way they play. In American English, **manager** is only used for baseball; in other sports, **coach** is used instead. ❏ The team expects to have a new manager before the winter meetings. →see **concert, restaurant**

1 가산명사 관리자, 지배인 ❏ 주방장과 직원, 지배인 모두가 중국인입니다. **2** 가산명사 매니저 ❏ 그 인기 스타의 매니저이자 에이전트인 앤 처들리 **3** 가산명사 감독 ❏ 그 팀은 동계 시합 이전에 새 감독을 영입할 계획이다.

man|ag|er|ess /mænɪdʒərɪs/ (**manageresses**) N-COUNT The **manageress** of a store, restaurant, or other small business is the woman who is responsible for running it. Some women object to this word and prefer to be called a "manager." ❏ ...the manageress of a betting shop.

가산명사 여지배인 ❏ 도박장 여지배인

있는 사람 ❏ 나는 자신이 잘못했다는 것을 인정할 수 있는 용기가 있어야 한다고 그에게 얘기했다. **11** 구 여자들보다 남자들에게 인기 있는 남자 ❏ 여자들보다 남자들에게 인기가 아주 좋던 그는 친구들과 술을 마시고 시시덕거리는 걸 즐겼다. **12** 구 주체성이 있다 [마음에 듦] ❏ 주체성을 가져. 스스로 결정을 내리라고. **13** 구 만장일치로, 모두 다 [강조] ❏ 조사관들은 한 목소리로 정부를 비난했다.

mana|gerial /mænɪdʒɪəriºl/ ADJ **Managerial** means relating to the work of a manager. □ ...*his managerial skills.* □ ...*a managerial career.*

형용사 경영상의, 관리의 □ 그가 지닌 경영 기술 □ 경영직

man|aging di|rec|tor (**managing directors**) N-COUNT The **managing director** of a company is the most important working director, and is in charge of the way the company is managed. [mainly BRIT, BUSINESS; AM usually **chief executive officer**]

가산명사 최고 경영자 [주로 영국영어, 경제; 미국영어 대개 chief executive officer]

man|date /mændeɪt/ (**mandates, mandating, mandated**) **1** N-COUNT If a government or other elected body has a **mandate** to carry out a particular policy or task, they have the authority to carry it out as a result of winning an election or vote. □ *The President and his supporters are almost certain to read this vote as a mandate for continued economic reform.* **2** N-COUNT If someone is given a **mandate** to carry out a particular policy or task, they are given the official authority to do it. □ *How much longer does the independent prosecutor have a mandate to pursue this investigation?* **3** N-COUNT You can refer to the fixed length of time that a country's leader or government remains in office as their **mandate**. [FORMAL] □ ...*his intention to leave politics once his mandate ends.* **4** V-T When someone **is mandated to** carry out a particular policy or task, they are given the official authority to do it. [FORMAL] [usu passive] □ *He'd been mandated by the West African Economic Community to go in and to enforce a ceasefire.* **5** V-T To **mandate** something means to make it mandatory. [AM] □ *The proposed initiative would mandate a reduction of carbon dioxide of 40%.* □ *Sixteen years ago, Quebec mandated that all immigrants send their children to French schools.*

1 가산명사 권한 □ 대통령과 그의 지지자들이 이번 표결 결과를 경제 개혁을 계속해도 좋다는 권한 부여로 해석할 것이 거의 틀림없다. **2** 가산명사 권한 □ 특별 검사가 이번 수사를 계속할 수 있는 권한을 얼마나 더 오랫동안 갖게 됩니까? **3** 가산명사 임기 [격식체] □ 임기가 끝나자마자 정계를 떠나려는 그의 의도 **4** 타동사 권한을 부여받다 [격식체] □ 그는 서아프리카 경제 공동체로부터 개입하여 휴전을 선언하는 권한을 공동체로부터 부여받았다. **5** 타동사 의무화하다 [미국영어] □ 이번에 제안된 방안에서는 이산화탄소 배출량 40퍼센트 감소를 의무화하고 있다. □ 16년 전 퀘벡은 이민 가족 자녀들이 모두 프랑스계 학교를 다니도록 의무화했다.

man|da|tory /mændətɔri/ **1** ADJ If an action or procedure is **mandatory**, people have to do it, because it is a rule or a law. [FORMAL] □ ...*the mandatory retirement age of 65.* **2** ADJ If a crime carries a **mandatory** punishment, that punishment is fixed by law for all cases, in contrast to crimes for which the judge or magistrate has to decide the punishment for each particular case. [FORMAL] □ ...*the mandatory life sentence for murder.*

1 형용사 의무적인, 강제적인 [격식체] □ 법정 퇴직 연령인 예순다섯 살 **2** 형용사 법에서 정한 [격식체] □ 살인죄에 대한 법정 종신형

mane /meɪn/ (**manes**) N-COUNT The **mane** on a horse or lion is the long thick hair that grows from its neck. □ *The horse's mane can be washed at the same time as his body.*

가산명사 (말이나 사자의) 갈기 □ 말의 갈기는 몸뚱이와 동시에 씻길 수 있다.

ma|neu|ver /mənuvər/ (**maneuvers, maneuvering, maneuvered**) [BRIT **manoeuvre**] **1** V-T/V-I If you **maneuver** something into or out of an awkward position, you skillfully move it there. □ *That will allow them to maneuver the satellite into the shuttle's cargo bay.* □ *I manoeuvred my way among the tables to the back corner of the place.* ● N-VAR **Maneuver** is also a noun. □ *The chopper shot upward in a maneuver matched by the other pilot.* **2** V-T/V-I If you **maneuver** a situation, you change it in a clever and skillful way so that you can benefit from it. □ *The president has tried to maneuver the campaign away from himself.* ● N-COUNT **Maneuver** is also a noun. □ *The company announced a series of maneuvers to raise cash and reduce debt.* **3** N-PLURAL Military **maneuvers** are training exercises which involve the movement of soldiers and equipment over a large area. □ *Allied troops begin maneuvers tomorrow to show how quickly forces could be mobilized in case of a new invasion.*

[영국영어 manoeuvre] **1** 타동사/자동사 요령껏 움직이다 □ 이것을 사용해서 위성을 우주왕복선 화물실에 요령껏 넣을 수 있을 것이다. □ 나는 테이블 사이를 요령껏 빠져나와 뒤쪽 구석으로 갔다. ● 가산명사 또는 불가산명사 요령껏 움직임 □ 헬기가 공중에 치솟자 다른 헬기 조종사도 요령껏 같은 궤도를 그리며 치솟았다. **2** 타동사/자동사 요령 있게 처리하다 □ 대통령은 요령 있게 선거 운동과 거리를 두려고 노력해 왔다. ● 가산명사 요령, 묘책 □ 회사가 자금 조달 및 부채 감면을 위한 일련의 묘책을 발표했다. **3** 복수명사 기동 훈련 □ 연합군이 내일 기동 훈련을 시작해 새로 침공이 있을 시에 군이 얼마나 빨리 동원될 수 있는지 보여 줄 것이다.

man|gle /mæŋgºl/ (**mangles, mangling, mangled**) V-T If a physical object **is mangled**, it is crushed or twisted very forcefully, so that it is difficult to see what its original shape was. [usu passive] □ *His body was crushed and mangled beyond recognition.*

타동사 뭉개지다, 으스러지다 □ 그의 몸은 형체를 알아볼 수 없을 정도로 으스러져 있었다.

man|go /mæŋgoʊ/ (**mangoes** or **mangos**) N-VAR A **mango** is a large sweet yellowish fruit which grows on a tree in hot countries. □ *Peel, stone, and dice the mango.* ● N-COUNT A **mango** is the tree that this fruit grows on. □ ...*orchards of lime and mango trees.*

가산명사 또는 불가산명사 망고 □ 망고의 껍질을 벗겨 씨를 빼낸 후 깍두기 모양으로 썰어라. ● 가산명사 망고나무 □ 라임과 망고 과수원

Word Link   hood ≈ state, condition : adult**hood**, child**hood**, man**hood**

---

man|hood /mænhʊd/ N-UNCOUNT **Manhood** is the state of being a man rather than a boy. □ *They were failing lamentably to help their sons grow from boyhood to manhood.*

불가산명사 성년, 성인 □ 그들은 안타깝게도 아들이 어린아이를 벗어나 성인으로 자라도록 하지 못했다.

man-hour (**man-hours**) N-COUNT A **man-hour** is the average amount of work that one person can do in an hour. **Man-hours** are used to estimate how long jobs take, or how many people are needed to do a job in a particular time. □ *The restoration took almost 4,000 man-hours over four years.*

가산명사 1인 1시간 노동량 (한 사람이 한 시간 동안 평균 할 수 있는 노동량) □ 그 복구 작업에는 거의 4년에 걸쳐 4천 시간의 노동력이 들었다.

ma|nia /meɪniə/ (**manias**) **1** N-COUNT If you say that a person or group has a **mania for** something, you mean that they enjoy it very much or spend a lot of time on it. □ *The mania for dinosaurs began in the late 1800s.* **2** N-UNCOUNT **Mania** is a mental illness which causes the sufferer to become very worried or concerned about something. [also N in pl] □ ...*the treatment of mania.*

1 가산명사 열광, 열풍 □ 공룡 열풍은 1800년대 말에 시작되었다. **2** 불가산명사 조급증, 조증(躁症) □ 조급증 치료

ma|ni|ac /meɪniæk/ (**maniacs**) **1** N-COUNT A **maniac** is a crazy person who is violent and dangerous. □ *The cabin looked as if a maniac had been let loose there.* **2** ADJ If you describe someone's behavior as **maniac**, you are emphasizing that it is extremely foolish and uncontrolled. [EMPHASIS] [ADJ n] □ *He could not maintain his maniac speed for much longer.* **3** N-COUNT If you call someone, for example, a religious **maniac** or a sports **maniac**, you are critical of them because they have such a strong interest in religion or sport. [DISAPPROVAL] □ *My mom is turning into a religious maniac.*

1 가산명사 미치광이 □ 오두막은 마치 미치광이가 방금 전까지 날뛰던 곳처럼 보였다. **2** 형용사 미친 듯한, 통제 불능의 [강조] □ 그는 미친 듯이 빠른 속도를 그다지 오래 유지할 수 없었다. **3** 가산명사 광신도, 열성팬 [탐탁찮음] □ 우리 어머니가 광신도로 변하고 있다.

man|ic /mænɪk/ **1** ADJ If you describe someone as **manic**, you mean that they do things extremely quickly or energetically, often because they are very excited or anxious about something. □ *He was really manic.* ● **man|ic|al|ly** /mænɪkli/ ADV □ *We cleaned the house manically over the weekend.* **2** ADJ If you describe someone's smile, laughter, or sense of humor as **manic**, you mean that it seems excessive or strange, as if they were insane. □ ...*a manic grin.*

1 형용사 정신없이 움직이는 □ 그는 정말이지 정신없이 움직였다. ● 정신없이 부사 □ 우리는 주말에 정신없이 집을 청소했다. **2** 형용사 정신 나간 듯한 □ 정신 나간 듯이 씩 웃음

mani|cure /mǽnɪkyʊər/ (manicures, manicuring, manicured) V-T If you **manicure** your hands or nails, you care for them by softening your skin and cutting and polishing your nails. ❑ *He was surprised to see how carefully she had manicured her broad hands.* ● N-COUNT **Manicure** is also a noun. ❑ *I have a manicure occasionally.*

타동사 손을 관리하다, 손톱을 손질하다 ❑ 그는 그녀가 넓적한 손을 세심하게 관리한 것을 보고 놀랐다. ● 가산명사 손 관리, 손톱 손질 ❑ 나는 종종 손 관리를 받는다.

mani|fest /mǽnɪfɛst/ (manifests, manifesting, manifested) **1** ADJ If you say that something is **manifest**, you mean that it is clearly true and that nobody would disagree with it if they saw it or considered it. [FORMAL] ❑ *...the manifest failure of the policies.* ● **mani|fest|ly** ADV ❑ *She manifestly failed to last the mile and a half of the race.* **2** V-T If you **manifest** a particular quality, feeling, or illness, or if it **manifests itself**, it becomes visible or obvious. [FORMAL] ❑ *He manifested a pleasing personality on stage.* ❑ *The virus needs two weeks to manifest itself.* ● ADJ **Manifest** is also an adjective. ❑ *The same alarm is manifest everywhere.*

1 형용사 명백한, 분명한 [격식체] ❑ 명백한 정책 실패 ● 명백하게, 분명히 부사 ❑ 그녀가 1.5마일 경주 완주에 실패했음에 틀림없었다. **2** 타동사 보이다; 나타나다 [격식체] ❑ 그는 무대에서 유쾌한 모습을 보였다. ❑ 그 바이러스는 감염 후 2주가 지나야 증상이 나타난다. ● 형용사 나타나는 ❑ 똑같은 우려가 모든 곳에서 나타난다.

mani|fes|ta|tion /mænɪfesteɪʃⁿn/ (manifestations) N-COUNT A **manifestation of** something is one of the different ways in which it can appear. [FORMAL] ❑ *Different animals in the colony had different manifestations of the disease.*

가산명사 나타남, 발현 [격식체] ❑ 그 지역에서 같은 질병이 동물마다 다른 형태로 나타났다.

mani|fes|to /mænɪféstoʊ/ (manifestos or manifestoes) N-COUNT A **manifesto** is a statement published by a person or group of people, especially a political party, or a government, in which they say what their aims and policies are. ❑ *The Tories are currently drawing up their election manifesto.*

가산명사 성명서 ❑ 토리당이 현재 선거 관련 성명서를 작성 중이다.

ma|nipu|late /mənɪpyəleɪt/ (manipulates, manipulating, manipulated) **1** V-T If you say that someone **manipulates** people, you disapprove of them because they skillfully force or persuade people to do what they want. [DISAPPROVAL] ❑ *He is a very difficult character. He manipulates people.* ❑ *She's always borrowing my clothes and manipulating me to give her vast sums of money.* ● **ma|nipu|la|tion** /mənɪpyəleɪʃⁿn/ (manipulations) N-VAR ❑ *...repeated criticism or manipulation of our mind.* **2** V-T If you say that someone **manipulates** an event or situation, you disapprove of them because they use or control it for their own benefit, or cause it to develop in the way they want. [DISAPPROVAL] ❑ *She was unable, for once, to control and manipulate events.* ● **ma|nipu|la|tion** N-VAR ❑ *...accusations of political manipulation.* **3** V-T If you **manipulate** something that requires skill, such as a complicated piece of equipment or a difficult idea, you operate it or process it. ❑ *The technology uses a pen to manipulate a computer.* ● **ma|nipu|la|tion** N-VAR ❑ *...science that requires only the simplest of mathematical manipulations.* **4** V-T If someone **manipulates** your bones or muscles, they skillfully move and press them with their hands in order to push the bones into their correct position or make the muscles less stiff. ❑ *The way he can manipulate my leg has helped my arthritis so much.* ● **ma|nipu|la|tion** N-VAR ❑ *A permanent cure will only be effected by acupuncture, chiropractic, or manipulation.*

1 타동사 마음대로 주무르다, 조종하다 [탐탁찮음] ❑ 그는 정말 상대하기 어려운 사람이다. 사람을 마음대로 갖고 논다. ❑ 그녀는 항상 내 옷을 빌려 입고 나를 조종해서 상당한 액수의 돈을 받아간다. ● 주무름, 조종 가산명사 또는 불가산명사 **2** 타동사 조종하다 ❑ 우리 정신을 거듭 비판하거나 조종함 **2** 타동사 조종하다, 조작하다 [탐탁찮음] ❑ 그녀는 그때만큼은 일들을 통제하고 조종할 수 없었다. ● 조종, 조작 가산명사 또는 불가산명사 **3** 정치 공작 혐의 **3** 타동사 조작하다 ❑ 이 기술에서는 펜을 사용해 컴퓨터를 조작한다. ● 조작 가산명사 또는 불가산명사 ❑ 아주 간단한 수학적인 조작만 알면 되는 과학 **4** 타동사 교정하다, 안마하다, 주무르다 ❑ 그가 내 다리를 주무르는 방법이 관절염 완화에 큰 도움이 됐다. ● 교정, 안마 가산명사 또는 불가산명사 ❑ 침, 교정, 안마 등으로만 완치가 가능하다.

ma|nipu|la|tive /mənɪpyʊlətɪv, -leɪtɪv/ ADJ If you describe someone as **manipulative**, you disapprove of them because they skillfully force or persuade people to act in the way that they want. [DISAPPROVAL] ❑ *He described Mr. Long as cold, calculating, and manipulative.*

형용사 교활한 [탐탁찮음] ❑ 그는 롱 씨가 차갑고 계산적이며 교활한 사람이라고 했다.

man|kind /mǽnkaɪnd/ N-UNCOUNT You can refer to all human beings as **mankind** when considering them as a group. Some people dislike this use. ❑ *...the evolution of mankind.*

불가산명사 인류 ❑ 인류의 진화

man|ly /mǽnli/ (manlier, manliest) ADJ If you describe a man's behavior or appearance as **manly**, you approve of it because it shows qualities that are considered typical of a man, such as strength or courage. [APPROVAL] ❑ *He set himself manly tasks and expected others to follow his example.* ● **man|li|ness** N-UNCOUNT ❑ *He has no doubts about his manliness.*

형용사 남자다운 [마음에 듦] ❑ 그는 남자다운 일을 골라 하면서 다른 사람들이 자신을 모범으로 삼기를 기대했다. ● 남자다움 불가산명사 ❑ 그는 자신의 남자다움을 추호도 의심하지 않는다.

man-made ADJ **Man-made** things are created or caused by people, rather than occurring naturally. ❑ *Man-made and natural disasters have disrupted the Government's economic plans.* ❑ *...man-made lakes.*

형용사 인공의 ❑ 인재와 천재로 정부의 경제 계획에 차질이 생겼다. ❑ 인공 호수

man man|age|ment N-UNCOUNT **Man management** involves controlling and organizing the people who work in a business or organization. [BUSINESS] ❑ *Team captains need to have effective man-management skills.*

불가산명사 인사 관리 [경제] ❑ 팀장은 인사 관리 기술이 뛰어날 필요가 있다.

manned /mǽnd/ ADJ A **manned** vehicle such as a spacecraft has people in it who are operating its controls. ❑ *In thirty years from now the United States should have a manned spacecraft on Mars.* →see also **man**

형용사 유인의 ❑ 지금으로부터 30년 후 미국이 화성에 유인 우주선을 보낼 것이다.

man|ner ♦◇◇ /mǽnər/ (manners) **1** N-SING The **manner** in which you do something is the way that you do it. ❑ *She smiled again in a friendly manner.* ❑ *I'm a professional and I have to conduct myself in a professional manner.* **2** N-SING Someone's **manner** is the way in which they behave and talk when they are with other people, for example whether they are polite, confident, or bad-tempered. ❑ *His manner was self-assured and brusque.* ● **-mannered** COMB in ADJ ❑ *Forrest was normally mild-mannered, affable, and untalkative.* **3** N-PLURAL If someone has **good manners**, they are polite and observe social customs. If someone has **bad manners**, they are impolite and do not observe these customs. ❑ *He dressed well and had impeccable manners.* ❑ *The manners of many doctors were appalling.*

1 단수명사 방식 ❑ 그녀는 다시 친절하게 미소를 보냈다. ❑ 나는 전문가이므로 전문가답게 처신해야 한다. **2** 단수명사 매너, 태도 ❑ 그는 자신감 넘치고 통명스러운 태도를 보였다. ● -한 태도의 복합형-형용사 ❑ 포레스트는 평상시에 태도가 상냥하고 말이 적으며 온화한 사람이었다. **3** 복수명사 예의 바름; 무례함 ❑ 그는 옷을 잘 차려입고 흠잡을 데 없이 예의가 발랐다. ❑ 상당수의 의사들이 예의라고는 전혀 모르는 듯했다.

Word Partnership	manner의 연어
ADJ.	**effective** manner, **efficient** manner **1**
	abrasive manner, **abrupt** manner, **appropriate** manner, **businesslike** manner, **different** manner, **friendly** manner, **usual** manner **1** **2**

ma|noeu|vre /mənúːvər/ →see **maneuver**

man|or /mǽnər/ (manors) N-COUNT A **manor** is a large private house in the country, usually built in the Middle Ages, and also includes the land and smaller buildings around it. [BRIT] ❑ *Thieves broke into the manor at night.*

가산명사 (중세) 저택 [영국영어] ❑ 밤 사이에 도둑이 저택에 침입했다.

man|power /mǽnpaʊər/ N-UNCOUNT Workers are sometimes referred to as **manpower** when they are being considered as a part of the process of producing goods or providing services. ❏ ...the shortage of skilled manpower in the industry.

불가산명사 인력, 노동력 ❏ 산업 내의 고급 인력 부족

man|sion /mǽnʃ*n/ (**mansions**) N-COUNT A **mansion** is a very large house. ❏ ...an eighteenth century mansion in Hampshire.

가산명사 저택 ❏ 햄프셔에 위치한 18세기 저택

man|slaugh|ter /mǽnslɔːtər/ N-UNCOUNT **Manslaughter** is the illegal killing of a person by someone who did not intend to kill them. [LEGAL] ❏ A judge accepted her plea that she was guilty of manslaughter, not murder.

불가산명사 과실 치사 [법률] ❏ 자신의 죄는 살인이 아닌 과실 치사라는 그녀의 주장을 판사가 받아들였다.

mantel|piece /mǽnt*lpɪs/ (**mantelpieces**) also **mantlepiece** N-COUNT A **mantelpiece** is a wood or stone shelf which is the top part of a border around a fireplace. ❏ On the mantelpiece are a pair of bronze Ming vases.

가산명사 벽난로 위의 선반 ❏ 벽난로 위에는 명조 청동 화병 두 개가 놓여 있다.

man|tra /mǽntrə/ (**mantras**) ◪ N-COUNT A **mantra** is a word or phrase repeated by Buddhists and Hindus when they meditate, or to help them feel calm. ◫ N-COUNT You can use **mantra** to refer to a statement or a principle that people repeat very often because they think it is true, especially when you think that it not true or is only part of the truth. ❏ Listening to customers is now part of the mantra of new management in public services. But how many public bodies really do it?

◪ 가산명사 염불; 기도문 ◫ 가산명사 주문 ❏ '고객의 소리를 들어라' 역시 이제 공공 서비스 부문 새 운영진의 주문이 되었다. 하지만 실제로 이를 실천하는 공공 기관이 몇이나 될까?

Word Link   manu ≈ hand : manual, manufacture, manure

manu|al /mǽnyuəl/ (**manuals**) ◪ ADJ **Manual** work is work in which you use your hands or your physical strength rather than your mind. ❏ ...skilled manual workers. ◫ ADJ **Manual** is used to talk about movements which are made by someone's hands. [FORMAL] [ADJ n] ❏ ...toys designed to help develop manual dexterity. ◧ ADJ **Manual** means operated by hand, rather than by electricity or a motor. [ADJ n] ❏ There is a manual pump to get rid of the water. ● **manu|al|ly** ADV [ADV with v] ❏ The device is manually operated, using a simple handle. ◨ N-COUNT A **manual** is a book which tells you how to do something or how a piece of machinery works. ❏ ...the instruction manual.

◪ 형용사 육체노동의 ❏ 숙련 육체 노동자 ◫ 형용사 손의 [격식체] ❏ 손재주 개발을 돕는 장난감 ◧ 형용사 수동의 ❏ 물을 빼낼 수 있는 수동식 펌프가 있다. ● 수동으로 부사 ❏ 장치는 간단한 손잡이를 통해 수동으로 작동된다. ◨ 가산명사 사용 설명서 ❏ 사용 설명서

manu|fac|ture ♦◇◇ /mǽnyəfǽktʃər/ (**manufactures, manufacturing, manufactured**) ◪ V-T To **manufacture** something means to make it in a factory, usually in large quantities. [BUSINESS] ❏ They manufacture the class of plastics known as thermoplastic materials. ◫ The first three models are being manufactured at the factory in Ashton-under-Lyne. ● N-UNCOUNT **Manufacture** is also a noun. ❏ ...the manufacture of nuclear weapons. ● **manu|fac|tur|ing** N-UNCOUNT ❏ ...management headquarters for manufacturing in China. ◫ N-COUNT In economics, **manufactures** are goods or products which have been made in a factory. [BUSINESS] ❏ ...a long-term rise in the share of manufactures in non-oil exports. ◧ V-T If you say that someone **manufactures** information, you are criticizing them because they invent information that is not true. [DISAPPROVAL] ❏ According to the prosecution, the officers manufactured an elaborate story.

◪ 타동사 생산하다, 제조하다 [경제] ❏ 그들은 열가소성 물질로 알려진 플라스틱 제품을 생산한다. ◫ 처음 세 모델이 애슈턴언더라인 공장에서 생산되고 있다. ● 불가산명사 생산, 제조 ❏ 핵무기 생산 ● 생산, 제조 불가산명사 ❏ 중국 내 생산 관리 본부 ◫ 가산명사 공산품 [경제] ❏ 비석유 수출 부문에서 공산품 비중의 장기적인 증가 ◧ 타동사 날조하다 [탐탁찮음] ❏ 검찰에 따르면 경찰들이 이야기를 철저하게 조작했다고 한다.

manu|fac|tur|er ♦◇◇ /mǽnyəfǽktʃərər/ (**manufacturers**) N-COUNT A **manufacturer** is a business or company which makes goods in large quantities to sell. [BUSINESS] ❏ ...the world's largest doll manufacturer. →see **industry**

가산명사 생산업체, 제조업체 [경제] ❏ 세계에서 가장 큰 인형 제조업체

ma|nure /mənʊər, BRIT mənyʊər/ (**manures**) N-MASS **Manure** is animal feces, sometimes mixed with chemicals, that is spread on the ground in order to make plants grow healthy and strong. ❏ ...bags of manure.

물질명사 거름, 비료 ❏ 비료 몇 포대

Word Link   script ≈ writing : manuscript, scripture, transcript

manu|script /mǽnyəskrɪpt/ (**manuscripts**) N-COUNT A **manuscript** is a handwritten or typed document, especially a writer's first version of a book before it is published. [also in N] ❏ He had seen a manuscript of the book.

가산명사 친필의, 원고의 ❏ 그는 책의 원고를 본 적이 있었다.

many ♦♦♦ /mέni/ ◪ DET You use **many** to indicate that you are talking about a large number of people or things. ❏ I don't think many people would argue with that. ❏ Not many films are made in Finland. ● PRON **Many** is also a pronoun. ❏ We stood up, thinking through the possibilities. There weren't many. ● QUANT **Many** is also a quantifier. [QUANT of def-pl-n] ❏ So, once we have cohabited, why do many of us feel the need to get married? ❏ It seems there are not very many of them left in the sea. ● ADJ **Many** is also an adjective. [det ADJ, v-link ADJ] ❏ Among his many hobbies was the breeding of fine horses. ◫ ADV You use **many** in expressions such as "not many," "not very many," and "too many" when replying to questions about numbers of things or people. [ADV as reply] ❏ "How many of the songs that dealt with this theme became hit songs?" — "Not very many." ◧ PREDET You use **many** followed by "a" and a noun to emphasize that there are a lot of people or things involved in something. [EMPHASIS] ❏ Many a mother tries to act out her unrealized dreams through her daughter. ◨ DET You use **many** after "how" to ask questions about numbers or quantities. You use **many** after "how" in reported clauses to talk about numbers or quantities. ❏ How many years have you been here? ● PRON **Many** is also a pronoun. [how PRON] ❏ How many do you smoke a day? ◩ DET You use **many** with "as" when you are comparing numbers of things or people. ❏ I've always entered as many photo competitions as I can. ● PRON **Many** is also a pronoun. [as PRON] ❏ Let the child try on as many as she likes. ◪ PRON You use **many** to mean "many people." ❏ Iris Murdoch was regarded by many as a supremely good and serious writer. ◪ N-SING **The many** means a large group of people, especially the ordinary people in society, considered as separate from a particular small group. ❏ The printing press gave power to a few to change the world for the many.

◪ 한정사 많은 ❏ 그 문제에 관해서 뭐라고 할 사람이 별로 없을 것 같아요. ❏ 핀란드에서 제작되는 영화가 많지 않다. ● 대명사 많은 것; 많은 사람 ❏ 우리는 일어서며 가능한 상황들을 짚어 보았다. 많지는 않았다. ● 수량사 많은 것; 많은 사람 ❏ 그렇다면 일단 동거를 시작한 사람 중 상당수가 결혼의 필요성을 느끼는 이유는 무엇일까? ❏ 이것이 바다에 많이 남아 있지 않은 것으로 보인다. ● 형용사 많은 ❏ 좋은 말을 키우는 것도 그의 다양한 취미 중 하나였다. ◫ 부사 수를 묻는 대답에 사용 ❏ "이 문제를 다룬 노래 중에 히트한 곡이 몇 개나 되나요?" "그렇게 많지 않아요." ◧ 전치 한정사 'many a 명사'의 확대로 많다는 것을 강조 [강조] ❏ 딸을 통해 자신이 이루지 못한 꿈을 실현시키려는 어머니들이 많다. ◨ 한정사 얼마나 많은, 몇 ─ 의문에서 쓰여 넌이나 살았습니까? ● 대명사 몇 개 ❏ 하루에 담배를 몇 개피나 피우세요? ◩ 한정사 ─한 만큼의 ❏ 나는 항상 가능한 한 많은 사진전에 참가해 왔다. ● 대명사 ─한 만큼 ❏ 아이가 입어 보고 싶은 만큼 입어 보게 하라. ◪ 대명사 많은 사람들 ❏ 아이리스 머독은 많은 사람들로부터 아주 뛰어나고 진지한 작가로 여겨졌다. ◪ 단수명사 대다수의 사람, 대중 ❏ 인쇄 매체는 소수가 대다수의 사람들을 위해 세상을 바꿀 수 있는 힘을 주었다.

You only use **many** to talk about things that can be counted. ❏ They owned many cars. You should use **much** if you want to talk about things that cannot be counted. ❏ ...too much water.

many는 셀 수 있는 것에 대해 말할 때만 쓴다. ❏ 그들은 차를 많이 소유하고 있었다. 셀 수 없는 것에 대해 말할 때는 much를 써야 한다. ❏ ...너무 많은 물

map 836

A

8 PHRASE You use **as many as** before a number to suggest that it is surprisingly large. [EMPHASIS] ❑ *New York City police say that as many as four and a half million people watched today's parade.*

map ◆◇◇ /mæp/ (maps, mapping, mapped) **1** N-COUNT A **map** is a drawing of a particular area such as a city, a country, or a continent, showing its main features as they would appear if you looked at them from above. ❑ *He unfolded the map and set it on the floor.* **2** V-T To **map** an area means to make a map of it. ❑ *...a spacecraft which is using radar to map the surface of Venus.*

B

C

Word Partnership	*map*의 연어
ADJ.	**detailed** map **1**
V.	**draw a** map, **look at a** map, **open a** map, **read a** map **1**

D

▶**map out** PHRASAL VERB If you **map out** something that you are intending to do, you work out in detail how you will do it. ❑ *I went home and mapped out my strategy.* ❑ *I cannot conceive of anybody writing a play by sitting down and mapping it out.*

E

ma|ple /meɪpᵊl/ (maples) N-VAR A **maple** or a **maple tree** is a tree with five-pointed leaves which turn bright red or gold in the fall. ● N-UNCOUNT **Maple** is the wood of this tree. ❑ *...a solid maple worktop.*

F

mar /mɑr/ (mars, marring, marred) V-T To **mar** something means to spoil or damage it. ❑ *A number of problems marred the smooth running of this event.*

G

Mar. **Mar.** is a written abbreviation for **March**.

mara|thon /mærəθɒn, BRIT mærəθən/ (marathons) **1** N-COUNT A **marathon** is a race in which people run a distance of 26 miles, which is about 42 km. ❑ *...running in his first marathon.* **2** ADJ If you use **marathon** to describe an event or task, you are emphasizing that it takes a long time and is very tiring. [EMPHASIS] [ADJ n] ❑ *People make marathon journeys to buy glass here.*

H

I

mar|ble /mɑrbᵊl/ (marbles) **1** N-UNCOUNT **Marble** is a type of very hard rock which feels cold when you touch it and which shines when it is cut and polished. Statues and parts of buildings are sometimes made of marble. ❑ *The house has a superb staircase made from oak and marble.* **2** N-COUNT **Marbles** are sculptures made of marble. ❑ *...marbles and bronzes from the Golden Age of Athens.* **3** N-UNCOUNT **Marbles** is a children's game played with small balls, usually made of colored glass. You roll a ball along the ground and try to hit an opponent's ball with it. ❑ *On the far side of the street, two boys were playing marbles.* **4** N-COUNT A **marble** is one of the small balls used in the game of marbles. ❑ *...a glass marble.*

J

K

L

march ◆◇◇ /mɑrtʃ/ (marches, marching, marched) **1** V-T/V-I When soldiers **march** somewhere, or when a commanding officer **marches** them somewhere, they walk there with very regular steps, as a group. ❑ *A Scottish battalion was marching down the street.* ❑ *Captain Ramirez called them to attention and marched them off to the main camp.* ● N-COUNT **March** is also a noun. ❑ *After a short march, the column entered the village.* **2** V-I When a large group of people **march** for a cause, they walk somewhere together in order to express their ideas or to protest about something. ❑ *The demonstrators then marched through the capital chanting slogans and demanding free elections.* ● N-COUNT **March** is also a noun. ❑ *Organizers expect up to 300,000 protesters to join the march.* ● **march|er** (marchers) N-COUNT ❑ *Fights between police and marchers lasted for three hours.* **3** V-I If you say that someone **marches** somewhere, you mean that they walk there quickly and in a determined way, for example because they are angry. ❑ *He marched into the kitchen without knocking.* **4** V-T If you **march** someone somewhere, you force them to walk there with you, for example by holding their arm tightly. ❑ *They were marched through a crocodile-infested area and, if they slowed down, were beaten with sticks.* **5** N-SING **The march of** something is its steady development or progress. ❑ *It is easy to feel trampled by the relentless march of technology.* **6** N-COUNT A **march** is a piece of music with a regular rhythm that you can march to. ❑ *A military band played Russian marches and folk tunes.*

M

N

O

P

Q

R

March ◆◆◇ (Marches) N-VAR **March** is the third month of the year in the Western calendar. ❑ *I flew to Milan in early March.* ❑ *She was born in Austria on March 6, 1920.*

S

mar|ga|rine /mɑrdʒərɪn, BRIT mɑːdʒəriːn/ (margarines) N-MASS **Margarine** is a yellow substance made from vegetable oil or animal fat that is similar to butter. You spread it on bread or use it for cooking.

T

mar|gin ◆◇◇ /mɑrdʒɪn/ (margins) **1** N-COUNT A **margin** is the difference between two amounts, especially the difference in the number of votes or points between the winner and the loser in an election or other contest. ❑ *They could end up with a 50-point winning margin.* **2** N-COUNT The **margin** of a written or printed page is the empty space at the side of the page. ❑ *She added her comments in the margin.* **3** N-VAR If there is a **margin** for something in a situation, there is some freedom to choose what to do or decide how to do it. ❑ *The money is collected in a straightforward way with little margin for error.* **4** N-COUNT The **margin** of a place or area is the extreme edge of it. ❑ *...the low coastal plain along the western margin.* **5** N-PLURAL To be **on the margins** of a society, group, or activity means to be among the least typical or least important parts of it. ❑ *Students have played an important role in the past, but for the moment, they're on the margins.* **6** →see also **profit margin**

U

V

W

X

Y

Word Partnership	*margin*의 연어
ADJ.	**comfortable** margin, **large** margin, **slim** margin **1**
	narrow margin, **wide** margin **1 2**
N.	margin **for error 3**

Z

---

8 구 무리 [강조] ❑ 뉴욕 시 경찰에 따르면 무려 450만 명이 오늘 퍼레이드를 지켜봤다고 한다.

1 가산명사 지도 ❑ 그는 지도를 펴서 바닥에 놓았다. **2** 타동사 지도를 만들다 ❑ 금성 표면 지도를 제작하기 위해 레이더를 사용하고 있는 우주선

구동사 구체적인 계획을 세우다 ❑ 나는 집으로 돌아와 구체적인 전략을 세웠다. ❑ 난 가만히 앉아서 궁리만으로 각본을 쓰는 사람은 도저히 상상이 안 돼.

가산명사 또는 불가산명사 단풍나무 ● 불가산명사 단풍나무 ❑ 단단한 단풍나무로 만든 작업대

타동사 망치다 ❑ 문제가 많이 생겨 행사의 순조로운 진행을 망쳤다.

3월

1 가산명사 마라톤 ❑ 그의 첫 마라톤 출전 **2** 형용사 장시간에 걸친, 마라톤 같은 [강조] ❑ 사람들이 유리를 사기 위해 장시간에 걸쳐 여기까지 온다.

1 불가산명사 대리석 ❑ 이 집 계단은 오크재와 대리석을 사용한 최고급 계단이다. **2** 가산명사 대리석 조각 ❑ 아테네 황금시대의 대리석 및 청동 조각품들 **3** 불가산명사 구슬치기 ❑ 길 저 건너편에서 사내아이 둘이 구슬치기를 하고 있었다. **4** 가산명사 구슬 ❑ 유리구슬

1 타동사/자동사 행군하다; 행군시키다 ❑ 스코틀랜드 대대가 길을 따라 행군하고 있었다. ❑ 라미레즈 대장은 군인들에게 차렷 자세를 시킨 뒤 막사까지 행군을 명했다. ● 가산명사 행군 ❑ 짧은 행군 뒤에 종대가 마을로 진입했다. **2** 자동사 가두 행진을 벌이다 ❑ 그 후 시위자들은 구호를 외치고 자유선거를 요구하면서 수도 전역에 걸쳐 가두 행진을 벌였다. ● 가산명사 가두 행진 ❑ 관계자들은 약 30만 명이 가두 행진에 참여할 것으로 예상한다. ● 가두 행진 시위자 가산명사 ❑ 경찰과 가두 행진 중인 시위대들 사이의 충돌이 3시간 동안 계속됐다. **3** 자동사 씩씩거리며 가다 ❑ 그는 노크도 하지 않고 부엌으로 씩씩거리며 들어갔다. **4** 타동사 끌고 가다 ❑ 그들은 악어 출몰 지역을 끌려 다니면서 걷는 속도가 떨어지면 막대기로 맞았다. **5** 단수명사 발달, 진보 ❑ 급격한 기술 발달 때문에 중압감을 느끼기 쉽다. **6** 가산명사 행진곡 ❑ 군악대가 러시아 행진곡과 민요를 연주했다.

가산명사 또는 불가산명사 3월 ❑ 나는 3월 초에 비행기를 타고 밀라노에 갔다. ❑ 그녀는 1920년 3월 6일 오스트리아에서 태어났다.

물질명사 마가린

1 가산명사 차, 차이 ❑ 그들이 50점 앞선 상태에서 끝낼 수도 있다. **2** 가산명사 여백 ❑ 그녀는 여백에 자신의 의견을 덧붙였다. **3** 가산명사 또는 불가산명사 여지 ❑ 오차의 여지가 거의 없는 직접적인 방식으로 돈이 회수되었다. **4** 가산명사 가장자리 ❑ 서부 가장자리를 따라 낮게 자리 잡은 해안 평원 **5** 복수명사 주변 ❑ 과거에는 학생들이 중요한 역할을 했지만 현재는 주변으로 밀려나 있다.

mar|gin|al /mɑrdʒɪnᵊl/ (**marginals**) **1** ADJ If you describe something as **marginal**, you mean that it is small or not very important. ❑ *This is a marginal improvement on October.* **2** ADJ If you describe people as **marginal**, you mean that they are not involved in the main events or developments in society because they are poor or have no power. ❑ *The tribunals were established for the well-integrated members of society and not for marginal individuals.* **3** ADJ In political elections, a **marginal** seat or constituency is one which is usually won or lost by only a few votes, and is therefore of great interest to politicians and journalists. [BRIT] ❑ *...the views of voters in five marginal seats.* ● N-COUNT A **marginal** is a marginal seat. [BRIT] ❑ *The votes in the marginals are those that really count.* **4** ADJ **Marginal** activities, costs, or taxes are not the main part of a business or an economic system, but often make the difference between its success or failure, and are therefore important to control. [BUSINESS] ❑ *The analysts applaud the cuts in marginal businesses, but insist the company must make deeper sacrifices.*

mar|gin|al|ly /mɑrdʒɪnᵊli/ ADV **Marginally** means to only a small extent. ❑ *Sales last year were marginally higher than in 1991.*

ma|ri|jua|na /mærɪwɑnə/ N-UNCOUNT **Marijuana** is a drug which is made from the dried leaves and flowers of the hemp plant, and which can be smoked.

ma|ri|na /mərinə/ (**marinas**) N-COUNT A **marina** is a small harbor for small boats that are used for leisure.

mari|nade /mærɪneɪd/ (**marinades, marinading, marinaded**) **1** N-COUNT A **marinade** is a sauce of oil, vinegar, spices, and herbs, which you pour over meat or fish before you cook it, in order to add flavor, or to make the meat or fish softer. ❑ *Fish is already tender and moist, so a marinade is just added for flavor.* **2** V-T/V-I To **marinade** means the same as to **marinate**. ❑ *Leave to marinade for 24 hours.*

mari|nate /mærɪneɪt/ (**marinates, marinating, marinated**) V-T/V-I If you **marinate** meat or fish, or if it **marinates**, you keep it in a mixture of oil, vinegar, spices, and herbs before cooking it, so that it can develop a special flavor. ❑ *Marinate the chicken for at least 4 hours.*

Word Link
mar ≈ sea : *marine, maritime, submarine*

ma|rine ♦◇◇ /mərin/ (**marines**) **1** N-COUNT A **marine** is a member of an armed force, for example the U.S. Marine Corps or the Royal Marines, who is specially trained for military duties at sea as well as on land. ❑ *A small number of Marines were wounded.* **2** ADJ **Marine** is used to describe things relating to the sea or to the animals and plants that live in the sea. [ADJ n] ❑ *...breeding grounds for marine life.* **3** ADJ **Marine** is used to describe things relating to ships and their movement at sea. [ADJ n] ❑ *...a solicitor specializing in marine law.* →see **ship**

mari|tal /mærɪtᵊl/ ADJ **Marital** is used to describe things relating to marriage. [ADJ n] ❑ *Caroline was keen to make her marital home in London to be near her family.*

mari|tal sta|tus N-UNCOUNT Your **marital status** is whether you are married, single, or divorced. [FORMAL] ❑ *How well off you are in old age is largely determined by race, sex, and marital status.*

mari|time /mærɪtaɪm/ ADJ **Maritime** is used to describe things relating to the sea and to ships. [ADJ n] ❑ *...the largest maritime museum of its kind.*

mark ♦♦◇ /mɑrk/ (**marks, marking, marked**) **1** N-COUNT A **mark** is a small area of something such as dirt that has accidentally gotten onto a surface or piece of clothing. ❑ *The dogs are always rubbing against the wall and making dirty marks.* **2** V-T/V-I If something **marks** a surface, or if the surface **marks**, the surface is damaged by marks or a mark. ❑ *Leather overshoes were put on the horses' hooves to stop them marking the turf.* **3** N-COUNT A **mark** is a written or printed symbol, for example a letter of the alphabet. ❑ *He made marks with a pencil.* **4** V-T If you **mark** something with a particular word or symbol, you write that word or symbol on it. ❑ *The bank marks the check "certified."* ❑ *Mark them with a symbol.* **5** N-COUNT A **mark** is a point that is given for a correct answer or for doing something well in an exam or competition. A **mark** can also be a written symbol such as a letter that indicates how good a student's or competitor's work or performance is. ❑ *...a simple scoring device of marks out of 10, where "1" equates to "Very poor performance."* ❑ *Candidates who answered "b" could be awarded half marks for demonstrating some understanding of the process.* **6** N-PLURAL If you get good or high **marks** for doing something, they have done it well. If they get poor or low **marks**, they have done it badly. ❑ *You have to give her top marks for moral guts.* **7** V-T When a teacher **marks** a student's work, the teacher decides how good it is and writes a number or letter on it to indicate this opinion. ❑ *He was marking essays in his small study.* ● **mark|ing** N-UNCOUNT ❑ *For the rest of the lunchbreak I do my marking.* **8** N-COUNT A particular **mark** is a particular number, point, or stage which has been reached or might be reached, especially a significant one. ❑ *Unemployment is rapidly approaching the one million mark.* **9** N-COUNT The **mark of** something is the characteristic feature that enables you to recognize it. ❑ *The mark of a civilized society is that it looks after its weakest members.* **10** N-SING If you say that a type of behavior or an event is **a mark of** a particular quality, feeling, or situation, you mean that it shows that that quality, feeling, or situation exists. ❑ *It was a mark of his unfamiliarity with Hollywood that he didn't understand that an agent was paid out of his client's share.* **11** V-T If something **marks** a place or position, it shows where something else is or where it used to be. ❑ *A huge crater marks the spot where the explosion happened.* **12** V-T An event that **marks** a particular stage or point is a sign that something different is about to happen. ❑ *The announcement marks the end of an extraordinary period in European history.* **13** V-T If you do something to **mark** an event or occasion, you do it to show that you are aware of the importance of the event or occasion. ❑ *Hundreds of thousands of people took to the streets to mark the occasion.* **14** V-T

---

1 형용사 작은, 사소한 ❑ 이로써 10월의 조금 개선되었다. **2** 형용사 주변적인 ❑ 이 특별 법정이 사회에 잘 융화된 사람들을 위해 설립된 것이지 주변인들을 위한 것은 아니었다. **3** 형용사 접전의 [영국영어] ❑ 접전 지역 다섯 곳 유권자들의 견해 ● 가산명사 접전 지역 [영국영어] ❑ 접전 지역의 표가 정말 중요한 표이다. **4** 형용사 한계의 [경제] ❑ 경제 전문가들은 한계사업 축소에 대해선 칭찬을 아끼지 않으면서도 회사가 더 큰 희생을 감수해야 한다고 주장한다.

부사 약간 ❑ 작년 매출이 1991년보다 약간 높았다.

불가산명사 마리화나, 대마초

가산명사 나루

1 가산명사 양념장 ❑ 생선살이 이미 부드럽고 촉촉하니까 양념장은 맛을 돋우는 데만 사용한다. **2** 타동사/자동사 양념장에 재다 ❑ 24시간 동안 마리네이드에 재어 둔다.

타동사/자동사 양념장에 재다 ❑ 닭을 최소 4시간 동안 양념장에 재어 두어라.

1 가산명사 해병 대원 ❑ 해병 대원 몇 명이 부상을 입었다. **2** 형용사 해양의 ❑ 해양 생물 번식지 **3** 형용사 해상의, 선박의 ❑ 해상법 전문 법무사

형용사 결혼의 ❑ 캐롤린은 런던 신혼집을 친정집 근처에 마련하고 싶어 안달이었다.

불가산명사 혼인 여부 [격식체] ❑ 노년 생활이 얼마나 풍요로운가는 대체로 인종, 성별, 혼인 여부 등으로 결정된다.

형용사 해상의 ❑ 같은 부류 중에 가장 큰 해상 박물관

1 가산명사 자국, 흔적 ❑ 개들이 허구한 날 몸을 벽에 비벼 대서 더러운 자국을 낸다. **2** 타동사/자동사 자국을 남기다, 흔적을 남기다 ❑ 말발굽에 가죽 덧신을 신겨서 잔디에 말발굽 자국이 남지 않도록 했다. **3** 가산명사 표시 ❑ 그가 연필로 표시를 몇 개 했다. **4** 타동사 표시하다 ❑ 수표에 '지급 보증'이라고 표시한다. ❑ 기호를 사용해서 표시하라. **5** 가산명사 점수 ❑ 1점이 '매우 서투름'을 뜻하는 10점 만점의 점수 체계 ❑ 'b'라고 답한 응시자들은 과정에 대해 어느 정도 이해하고 있다는 것을 보여 주기 때문에 반점을 받을 수도 있다. **6** 복수명사 점수 ❑ 당신은 그녀의 도덕적 용기에 최고점을 줘야 한다. **7** 타동사 성적을 매기다, 채점하다 ❑ 그는 작은 서재에서 작문 성적을 매기고 있었다. ● 채점 불가산명사 ❑ 나는 남은 점심시간 동안 채점을 한다. **8** 가산명사 지점, 수준 ❑ 실업자 수가 백만 명 선에 빠르게 가까워지고 있다. **9** 가산명사 특징 ❑ 문명사회의 특징은 가장 약한 사회 구성원을 보살핀다는 데 있다. **10** 단수명사 표시 ❑ 에이전트가 고객 몫의 일부를 지급받는 사실을 이해 못하는 것은 그가 할리우드를 잘 모른다는 표시이다. **11** 타동사 위치를 보여 주다 ❑ 커다란 구멍이 폭발이 일어난 지점을 보여 주고 있다. **12** 타동사 상징하다 ❑ 이번 발표는 유럽 역사상 특별했던 한 시기의 끝을 상징한다. **13** 타동사 기념하다 ❑ 수십만 명의 사람들이 거리로 뛰쳐나와 행사를 기념했다. **14** 타동사 ─한 유형의 사람이다 ❑ 낙태와 페미니즘에 대한 반대로 볼 때 그녀는 확고한 전통주의자다. **16** 구 징후이다 ❑ 영향을 미치다 ❑ 수년간의 경험을 통해 받은 영향으로 그녀는 처음 보는 사람에게 말을 걸고 싶은 적이 한 번도 없었다. **17** 구 두각을 나타내다 ❑ 그녀가 영화계에서 두각을 나타낸 것은 1960년대였다. **18** 구 빛나다, 부정확한 ❑ 저것이 겉으로 보이는 것처럼 그다지 엉뚱한 비교는 아니다.

Something that **marks** someone **as** a particular type of person indicates that they are that type of person. ❑ *Her opposition to abortion and feminism mark her as a convinced traditionalist.* **15** →see also **marked, marking, punctuation mark, question mark** **16** PHRASE If someone or something **leaves** their **mark** or **leaves a mark**, they have a lasting effect on another person or thing. ❑ *Years of conditioning had left their mark on her, and she never felt inclined to talk to strange men.* **17** PHRASE If you **make** your **mark** or **make a mark**, you become noticed or famous by doing something impressive or unusual. ❑ *She made her mark in the film industry in the 1960s.* **18** PHRASE If something such as a claim or estimate is **wide of the mark**, it is incorrect or inaccurate. ❑ *That comparison isn't as wide of the mark as it seems.*

	Thesaurus	mark의 참조어
N.	dot, smudge **1**	
	attribute, feature, label, quality, trait **9**	
V.	dent, scratch **2**	

▶**mark down** **1** PHRASAL VERB If you **mark** something **down**, you write it down. ❑ *I tend to forget things unless I mark them down.* **2** PHRASAL VERB To **mark** an item **down** or **mark** its price **down** means to reduce its price. ❑ *A toy store has marked down the Sonic Hedgehog computer game.*

1 구동사 적어 두다 ❑ 나는 뭐든 적어 놓지 않으면 자꾸 잊어버린다. **2** 구동사 가격을 내리다 ❑ 한 장난감 가게가 컴퓨터 게임 '고슴도치 소닉'의 가격을 내렸다.

▶**mark off** PHRASAL VERB If you **mark off** a piece or length of something, you make it separate, for example by putting a line on it or around it. ❑ *He used a rope to mark off the circle.*

구동사 따로 표시해 두다 ❑ 그는 밧줄을 사용해 원에 표시를 해 두었다.

▶**mark up** PHRASAL VERB If you **mark** something **up**, you increase its price. ❑ *You can sell it to them at a set wholesale price, allowing them to mark it up for retail.* →see also **mark-up**

구동사 가격을 올리다 ❑ 물건을 도매가에 팔아서 구매자가 나중에 소매가로 가격을 올릴 수 있게 할 수 있다.

marked ♦◇◇ /mɑrkt/ ADJ A **marked** change or difference is very obvious and easily noticed. ❑ *There has been a marked increase in crimes against property.* ● **mark|ed|ly** /mɑrkɪdli/ ADV *America's current economic downturn is markedly different from previous recessions.*

형용사 현저한, 두드러진 ❑ 재산을 노린 범죄가 현저하게 증가했다. ● 현저하게, 두드러지게 부사 ❑ 미국의 현 경기 침체는 이전 불경기와는 현저하게 다르다.

mark|er /mɑrkər/ (**markers**) **1** N-COUNT A **marker** is an object which is used to show the position of something, or is used to help someone remember something. ❑ *He put a marker in his book and followed her out.* **2** N-COUNT A **marker** or a **marker pen** is a pen with a thick tip made of felt, which is used for drawing and for coloring things. ❑ *Draw your child's outline with a heavy black marker or crayon.*

1 가산명사 표시 도구 ❑ 그는 책에 책갈피를 끼워 놓고 그녀를 따라 나갔다. **2** 가산명사 매직펜 ❑ 검정색 굵은 매직이나 크레용으로 아이 얼굴의 윤곽을 그리시오.

mar|ket ♦♦♦ /mɑrkɪt/ (**markets, marketing, marketed**) **1** N-COUNT A **market** is a place where goods are bought and sold, usually outdoors. ❑ *He sold boots on a market stall.* **2** N-COUNT The **market** for a particular type of thing is the number of people who want to buy it, or the area of the world in which it is sold. [BUSINESS] ❑ *The foreign market was increasingly crucial.* **3** N-SING The **market** refers to the total amount of a product that is sold each year, especially when you are talking about the competition between the companies who sell that product. [BUSINESS] ❑ *The two big companies control 72% of the market.* **4** ADJ If you talk about a **market** economy, or the **market** price of something, you are referring to an economic system in which the prices of things depend on how many are available and how many people want to buy them, rather than prices being fixed by governments. [BUSINESS] [ADJ n] ❑ *Their ultimate aim was a market economy for Hungary.* ❑ *He must sell the house for the current market value.* **5** V-T To **market** a product means to organize its sale, by deciding on its price, where it should be sold, and how it should be advertised. [BUSINESS] ❑ *...if you marketed our music the way you market pop music.* **6** N-SING The **job market** or the **labor market** refers to the people who are looking for work and the jobs available for them to do. [BUSINESS] ❑ *Every year, 250,000 people enter the job market.* **7** N-SING The stock market is sometimes referred to as **the market**. [BUSINESS] ❑ *The market collapsed last October.* **8** →see also **black market, market forces, open market** **9** PHRASE If you say that it is **a buyer's market**, you mean that it is a good time to buy a particular thing, because there is a lot of it available, so its price is low. If you say that it is a **seller's market**, you mean that very little of it is available, so its price is high. [BUSINESS] ❑ *Don't be afraid to haggle: for the moment, it's a buyer's market.* **10** PHRASE If you are **in the market for** something, you are interested in buying it. ❑ *If you're in the market for a new radio, you'll see that the latest models are very different.* **11** PHRASE If something is **on the market**, it is available for people to buy. If it comes **onto the market**, it becomes available for people to buy. [BUSINESS] ❑ *...putting more empty offices on the market.* **12** PHRASE If you **price** yourself **out of the market**, you try to sell goods or services at a higher price than other people, with the result that no one buys them from you. [BUSINESS] ❑ *At £150,000 for a season, he really is pricing himself out of the market.*

1 가산명사 시장 ❑ 그는 시장 좌판에서 부츠를 팔았다. **2** 가산명사 시장 [경제] ❑ 해외 시장이 갈수록 중요해졌다. **3** 단수명사 시장 [경제] ❑ 두 대기업의 시장 점유율은 총 72퍼센트이다. **4** 형용사 시장의 [경제] ❑ 그들의 최종 목표는 헝가리의 시장 경제 정착이었다. ❑ 그는 시가에 집을 팔아야만 한다. **5** 타동사 마케팅하다 [경제] ❑ 만약 당신이 대중음악과 같은 방식으로 우리 음악을 마케팅하면 **6** 단수명사 구직 시장; 노동 시장 [경제] ❑ 매년 25만 명이 구직 시장에 뛰어든다. **7** 단수명사 주식 시장 [경제] ❑ 지난 10월 주가가 폭락했다. **9** 구 매수자 시장; 매도자 시장 [경제] ❑ 흥정을 두려워하지 말라. 당분간은 매수자 시장이다. **10** 구 ~을 사려고 하는 ❑ 지금 새 라디오를 구매하려는 사람이라면 최신 모델들이 상당히 다르다는 점을 알게 될 것이다. **11** 구 시장에 나와 있는 [경제] ❑ 시장에 빈 사무실을 더 내놓는 **12** 구 터무니없이 비싼 가격을 요구해 빌려주다 [경제] ❑ 그는 한 시즌에 15만 파운드라는 터무니없이 높은 가격을 제시해 거절을 자초하고 있다.

mar|ket|able /mɑrkɪtəbʰl/ ADJ Something that is **marketable** is able to be sold because people want to buy it. [BUSINESS] ❑ *What began as an attempt at artistic creation has turned into a marketable commodity.*

형용사 시장성이 있는 [경제] ❑ 예술 창작품으로 시작된 것이 시장성 있는 상품으로 바뀌었다.

mar|ket|eer /mɑrkɪtɪər/ (**marketeers**) N-COUNT A **marketeer** is the same as a **marketer**. →see also **free-marketeer** [BUSINESS]

가산명사 마케팅 전문가 [경제]

mar|ket|er /mɑrkɪtər/ (**marketers**) N-COUNT A **marketer** is someone whose job involves marketing. [BUSINESS] ❑ *As a marketer I understood what makes people buy things.*

가산명사 마케팅 전문가 [경제] ❑ 나는 마케팅 전문가로서 무엇이 사람들로 하여금 물건을 사게끔 하는지 알고 있었다.

mar|ket forces N-PLURAL When politicians and economists talk about **market forces**, they mean the economic factors that affect the availability of goods and the demand for them, without any help or control by governments. [BUSINESS] ❑ *...opening the economy to market forces and increasing the role of private enterprise.*

복수명사 시장의 힘, 시장 원리 [경제] ❑ 경제를 시장 원리에 맡기고 민간 기업의 역할을 증진시키는 것

mar|ket|ing ♦○○ /mɑrkɪtɪŋ/ N-UNCOUNT **Marketing** is the organization of the sale of a product, for example, deciding on its price, the areas it should be supplied to, and how it should be advertised. [BUSINESS] ❑ ...*expert advice on production and marketing*.

불가산명사 마케팅 [경제] ❑ 생산과 마케팅에 대한 전문가 조언

mar|ket lead|er (**market leaders**) N-COUNT A **market leader** is a company that sells more of a particular product or service than most of its competitors do. [BUSINESS] ❑ *We are becoming one of the market leaders in the fashion industry*.

가산명사 시장 선두 주자 [경제] ❑ 우리는 패션업계의 시장 선두 주자 대열에 합류하고 있다.

market|place /mɑrkɪtpleɪs/ (**marketplaces**) also **market place** ■ N-COUNT The **marketplace** refers to the activity of buying and selling products. [BUSINESS] ❑ *It's our hope that we will play an increasingly greater role in the marketplace and, therefore, supply more jobs*. ◼ N-COUNT A **marketplace** is a small area in a town or city where goods are bought and sold, often outdoors. ❑ *The marketplace was jammed with a noisy crowd of buyers and sellers*.

■ 가산명사 매매 [경제] ❑ 매매 활동에서 점점 더 큰 역할을 함으로써 더 많은 일자리를 제공하는 것이 우리의 희망이다. ◼ 가산명사 시장, 장터 ❑ 상인들과 장보러 나온 사람들이 시끌벅적하니 시장을 가득 메웠다.

mar|ket re|search N-UNCOUNT **Market research** is the activity of collecting and studying information about what people want, need, and buy. [BUSINESS] ❑ *A new all-woman market research company has been set up to find out what women think about major news and issues*.

불가산명사 시장 조사 [경제] ❑ 전원 여성으로 구성된 새로운 시장 전문 회사가 주요 뉴스와 이슈에 관한 여성들의 의견 조사를 목적으로 탄생했다.

mar|ket share (**market shares**) N-VAR A company's **market share** in a product is the proportion of the total sales of that product that is produced by that company. [BUSINESS] ❑ *Ford has been gaining market share this year at the expense of GM and some Japanese car manufacturers*.

가산명사 또는 불가산명사 시장 점유율 [경제] ❑ 올해 지엠과 몇몇 일본 자동차 제조업체의 입지가 줄어들면서 포드의 시장 점유율이 꾸준히 상승했다.

mar|ket test (**market tests, market testing, market tested**) ■ N-COUNT If a company carries out a **market test**, it asks a group of people to try a new product or service and give their opinions on it. [BUSINESS] ❑ *Results from market tests in the U.S. and Europe show little enthusiasm for the product*. ◼ V-T If a new product or service **is market tested**, a group of people are asked to try it and then asked for their opinions on it. [BUSINESS] ❑ *These nuts have been market tested and found to be most suited to the Australian palate*. ● **mar|ket test|ing** N-UNCOUNT ❑ *They learnt a lot from the initial market testing exercise*.

■ 가산명사 시험 판매 [경제] ❑ 미국과 유럽 시험 판매에서 제품에 대한 반응이 시들했다. ◼ 타동사 시험 판매되다 [경제] ❑ 이 견과류에 대한 시험 판매 결과 호주 사람의 입맛에 가장 잘 맞는 것으로 드러났다. ● 시험 판매 불가산명사 ❑ 그들은 첫 시험 판매 과정에서 많은 것을 배웠다.

mark|ing /mɑrkɪŋ/ (**markings**) N-COUNT **Markings** are colored lines, shapes, or patterns on the surface of something, which help to identify it. ❑ *A plane with Danish markings was over-flying his vessel*. →see also **mark**

가산명사 마크, 로고 ❑ 덴마크 마크가 붙은 비행기가 그의 배 상공을 날아가고 있었다.

mark-up (**mark-ups**) [AM also **markup**] N-COUNT A **mark-up** is an increase in the price of something, for example the difference between its cost and the price that it is sold for. ❑ *We all know that most wine in restaurants is over-priced: a mark-up of 200 percent on cost is considered normal*.

[미국영어 markup] 가산명사 가격 인상, 이윤 ❑ 음식점에서 판매되는 와인 대부분의 가격이 지나치게 비싸다는 것은 모두가 아는 사실이다. 원가의 2백 퍼센트 정도 이윤이 붙는 것이 보통이다.

mar|ma|lade /mɑrməleɪd/ (**marmalades**) N-MASS **Marmalade** is a food made from oranges, lemons, or grapefruit that is similar to jam. It is eaten on bread or toast at breakfast.

물질명사 마멀레이드

ma|roon /mərun/ (**maroons, marooning, marooned**) ■ COLOR Something that is **maroon** is dark reddish-purple in color. ❑ ...*maroon velvet curtains*. ◼ V-T If someone **is marooned** somewhere, they are left in a place that is difficult for them to escape from. [usu passive] ❑ *He found himself marooned on a bare gray mountainside*.

■ 색채어 적갈색 ❑ 적갈색 벨벳 커튼 ◼ 타동사 고립되다 ❑ 그는 잿빛 민둥산 중턱에 고립되고 말았다.

mar|riage ♦♦◇ /mærɪdʒ/ (**marriages**) ■ N-COUNT A **marriage** is the relationship between a husband and wife. ❑ *In a good marriage, both husband and wife work hard to solve any problems that arise*. ❑ *When I was 35 my marriage broke up*. ◼ N-VAR A **marriage** is the act of marrying someone, or the ceremony at which this is done. ❑ *I opposed her marriage to Darryl*. →see **love, wedding**

■ 가산명사 결혼 생활 ❑ 모범적인 결혼 생활을 하는 부부는 문제가 발생하면 남편과 아내 모두 이를 해결하려 열심히 노력으로 끝난다. ❑ 내가 서른다섯 살 때 결혼 생활이 파탄으로 끝났다. ◼ 가산명사 또는 불가산명사 결혼, 결혼식 ❑ 나는 그녀와 다릴의 결혼을 반대했다.

> Do not confuse **marriage** and **wedding**. A **wedding** is a ceremony in which a man and woman get married. It usually includes a meal or other celebration that takes place after the ceremony itself. ❑ *It wasn't a formal wedding*. This ceremony can also be called a **marriage**. ❑ ...*the day of my marriage*. **Marriage** can also be used to refer to the relationship between a husband and wife. ❑ *It has been a happy marriage*.

> marriage와 wedding을 혼동하지 않도록 하라. wedding은 남자와 여자가 결혼하는 예식이다. 이는 보통 예식 그 자체가 끝난 후에 열리는 식사와 다른 축하 행사를 포함한다. ❑ 그것은 격식을 차린 결혼식이 아니었다. 이러한 결혼 예식을 marriage라고 부를 수도 있다. ❑ ...내 결혼식 날. marriage는 남편과 아내 사이의 관계를 지칭할 때도 쓸 수 있다. ❑ 행복한 결혼생활이었다.

mar|ried ♦♦◇ /mærɪd/ ■ ADJ If you are **married**, you have a husband or wife. ❑ *We have been married for 14 years*. ❑ *She is married to an Englishman*. ◼ ADJ **Married** means relating to marriage or to people who are married. [ADJ n] ❑ *For the first ten years of our married life we lived in a farmhouse*. ◼ ADJ If you say that someone is **married to** their work or another activity, you mean that they are very involved with it and have little interest in anything else. [v-link ADJ to n] ❑ *I'm not married to my job*.

■ 형용사 결혼한, 기혼의 ❑ 우리가 결혼한 지 14년이 되었다. ❑ 그녀는 영국 사람과 결혼했다. ◼ 형용사 결혼의 ❑ 우리는 결혼 첫 10년 동안 농장에서 살았다. ◼ 형용사 ~에 푹 빠진, ~에 중독된 ❑ 나는 일에만 푹 빠져있지 않아.

mar|ry ♦♦◇ /mæri/ (**marries, marrying, married**) ■ V-RECIP When two people **get married** or **marry**, they legally become husband and wife in a special ceremony. **Get married** is less formal and more commonly used than **marry**. ❑ *I thought he would change after we got married*. ❑ *They married a month after they met*. ❑ *He wants to marry her*. ◼ V-T When a priest or official **marries** two people, he or she conducts the ceremony in which the two people legally become husband and wife. ❑ *The local vicar has agreed to marry us in the chapel on the estate*.

■ 상호동사 결혼하다 ❑ 나는 남편이 일단 결혼하면 바뀔 거라고 생각했다. ❑ 그들은 만난 지 한 달 만에 결혼했다. ❑ 그는 그녀와 결혼하고 싶어 한다. ◼ 타동사 주례를 맡다 ❑ 교구 목사님이 마을 예배당에서 있을 우리 결혼식의 주례를 맡아 주기로 했다.

marsh /mɑrʃ/ (**marshes**) N-VAR A **marsh** is a wet, muddy area of land. →see **wetland**

가산명사 또는 불가산명사 늪, 습지

mar|shal /mɑrʃ°l/ (**marshals, marshaling, marshaled**) [BRIT, sometimes AM **marshalling, marshalled**] ■ V-T If you **marshal** people or things, you gather them together and arrange them for a particular purpose. ❑ *The company turned its attention to marshaling its creditors' approval*. ◼ N-COUNT A **marshal** is an official who helps to organize a public event, especially a sports event. ❑ *The grand prix is controlled by well-trained marshals*. ◼ N-COUNT In the United States and some other countries, a **marshal** is a police officer, often one who is responsible for a particular area. ❑ *A federal marshal was killed in a shoot-out*. ◼ N-COUNT A

[영국영어, 미국영어 가끔 marshalling, marshalled] ■ 타동사 집결하다, 동원하다 ❑ 회사가 채권자들의 지지 모으기로 눈을 돌렸다. ◼ 가산명사 진행 요원 ❑ 그랑프리상은 고도의 훈련을 받은 진행 요원이 관리한다. ◼ 가산명사 보안관 ❑ 연방 보안관 한 명이 총격전으로 사망했다. ◼ 가산명사 소방서장 [미국영어] ❑ 옆집에서 가스 누출로 폭파 사고가 일어났다며 소방서장이 그녀에게 집 밖으로 나가라고

a b c d e f g h i j k l m n o p q r s t u v w x y z

marshal is an officer in a fire department. [AM] ❑ *She was ordered out of her home by a fire marshal because the house next door had an explosion from a leaking gas main.* ⑤ N-COUNT; N-TITLE In Britain and some other countries, a **marshal** is an officer who has the highest rank in an army or air force. ❑ *...Air Chief Marshal Sir Kenneth Cross.*

말했다. ⑤ 가산명사 육군 대장; 공군 대장 ❑ 케네스 크로스 공군 대장

mart /mɑrt/ (**marts**) N-COUNT A **mart** is a place such as a market where things are bought and sold. [AM] ❑ *...the flower mart.*

가산명사 시장 [미국영어] ❑ 꽃 시장

mar|tial /mɑrʃ°l/ **Martial** is used to describe things relating to soldiers or war. [FORMAL] ❑ *The paper was actually twice banned under the martial regime.* →see also **court martial**

형용사 군의, 전쟁의 [격식체] ❑ 이 신문은 사실 군사 정권하에서 두 번 정간됐었다.

mar|tial art (**martial arts**) N-COUNT A **martial art** is one of the methods of fighting, often without weapons, that come from the Far East, for example kung fu, karate, or judo.

가산명사 무술

mar|tial law N-UNCOUNT **Martial law** is control of an area by soldiers, not the police. ❑ *The military leadership have lifted martial law in several more towns.*

불가산명사 계엄령 ❑ 군 지도부가 몇 개 지역에서 추가로 계엄령을 해제했다.

mar|tyr /mɑrtər/ (**martyrs, martyring, martyred**) ① N-COUNT A **martyr** is someone who is killed or made to suffer greatly because of their religious or political beliefs, and is admired and respected by people who share those beliefs. ❑ *...a glorious martyr to the cause of liberty.* ② V-T If someone **is martyred**, they are killed or made to suffer greatly because of their religious or political beliefs. [usu passive] ❑ *St Pancras was martyred in 304 AD.* ③ N-COUNT If you refer to someone as a **martyr**, you disapprove of the fact that they pretend to suffer, or exaggerate their suffering, in order to get sympathy or praise from other people. [DISAPPROVAL] ❑ *When are you going to quit acting like a martyr?* ④ N-COUNT If you say that someone is a **martyr** to something, you mean that they suffer as a result of it. ❑ *Ellsworth was a martyr to his sense of honor and responsibility.*

① 가산명사 순교자 ❑ 자유를 위해 명예롭게 목숨 바친 순교자 ② 타동사 순교하다 ❑ 세인트 판크라스는 기원후 304년에 순교했다. ③ 가산명사 순교자인 척하는 사람 [탐탁잖음] ❑ 도대체 언제쯤 순교자 행세를 그만둘 거야? ④ 가산명사 ~로 고통받는 사람 ❑ 엘스워스는 체면과 책임감으로 시달렸다.

mar|vel /mɑrv°l/ (**marvels, marveling, marveled**) [BRIT, sometimes AM **marvelling, marvelled**] ① V-T/V-I If you **marvel** at something, you express your great surprise, wonder, or admiration. ❑ *Her fellow members marveled at her seemingly infinite energy.* ❑ *Sara and I read the story and marveled.* ② N-COUNT You can describe something or someone as a **marvel** to indicate that you think that they are wonderful. ❑ *The whale, like the dolphin, has become a symbol of the marvels of creation.*

[영국영어, 미국영어 가끔 marvelling, marvelled] ① 타동사/자동사 놀라다, 경탄하다 ❑ 동료 위원들은 끝이 없어 보이는 그녀의 에너지에 경탄했다. ❑ 사라와 나는 그 이야기를 읽고 놀랐다. ② 가산명사 경이 ❑ 돌고래와 마찬가지로 고래도 경이로운 창조물의 상징이 되었다.

mar|vel|ous /mɑrvələs/ [BRIT **marvellous**] ADJ If you describe someone or something as **marvelous**, you are emphasizing that they are very good. ❑ *It's the most marvelous piece of music.* ● **mar|vel|ous|ly** ADV ❑ *We want people to think he's doing marvelously.*

[영국영어 marvellous] 형용사 훌륭한 ❑ 이는 가장 훌륭한 음악 작품이다. ● 훌륭히 부사 ❑ 우리는 사람들이 그가 일을 훌륭히 하고 있다고 생각하길 바란다.

Marx|ism /mɑrksɪzəm/ N-UNCOUNT **Marxism** is a political philosophy based on the writings of Karl Marx which stresses the importance of the struggle between different social classes.

불가산명사 마르크스주의

Marx|ist /mɑrksɪst/ (**Marxists**) ① ADJ **Marxist** means based on Marxism or relating to Marxism. ❑ *...a Marxist state.* ② N-COUNT A **Marxist** is a person who believes in Marxism or who is a member of a Marxist party. ❑ *...a 78-year-old former Marxist.*

① 형용사 마르크스주의의 ❑ 마르크스주의 국가 ② 가산명사 마르크스주의자 ❑ 과거 마르크스주의자였던 일흔여덟 살 된 노인

mas|cara /mæskærə, BRIT mæskɑːrə/ (**mascaras**) N-MASS **Mascara** is a substance used as makeup to make eyelashes darker. ❑ *...water-resistant mascaras.* →see **makeup**

물질명사 마스카라 ❑ 물에 지워지지 않는 마스카라

mas|cot /mæskɒt/ (**mascots**) N-COUNT A **mascot** is an animal, toy, or symbol which is associated with a particular organization or event, and which is thought to bring good luck. ❑ *...the official mascot of the Barcelona Games.*

가산명사 마스코트 ❑ 바르셀로나 올림픽 공식 마스코트

mas|cu|line /mæskyəlɪn/ ① ADJ **Masculine** qualities and things relate to or are considered typical of men, in contrast to women. ❑ *...masculine characteristics like a husky voice and facial hair.* ② ADJ If you say that someone or something is **masculine**, you mean that they have qualities such as strength or confidence which are considered typical of men. ❑ *...her aggressive, masculine image.* ③ ADJ In some languages, a **masculine** noun, pronoun, or adjective has a different form from a feminine or neuter one, or behaves in a different way.

① 형용사 남성적인 ❑ 허스키한 목소리, 수염과 같은 남성적인 특징 ② 형용사 남성적인 ❑ 그녀의 공격적이고 남성적인 이미지 ③ 형용사 남성형의

mas|cu|lin|ity /mæskyəlɪnɪti/ ① N-UNCOUNT A man's **masculinity** is the fact that he is a man. ❑ *...a project on the link between masculinity and violence.* ② N-UNCOUNT **Masculinity** means the qualities, especially sexual qualities, which are considered to be typical of men. ❑ *The old ideas of masculinity do not work for most men.*

① 불가산명사 남자임 ❑ 남성과 폭력의 연관관계에 대한 연구 프로젝트 ② 불가산명사 남성성, 남자다움 ❑ 예전에 남성성을 상징하던 것들이 요즘 남성에게는 별로 들어맞지 않는다.

mash /mæʃ/ (**mashes, mashing, mashed**) V-T If you **mash** food that is solid but soft, you crush it so that it forms a soft mass. ❑ *Mash the bananas with a fork.*

타동사 으깨다 ❑ 포크로 바나나를 으깨라.

mask ♦◇◇ /mæsk/ (**masks, masking, masked**) ① N-COUNT A **mask** is a piece of cloth or other material, which you wear over your face so that people cannot see who you are, or so that you look like someone or something else. ❑ *The gunman, whose mask had slipped, fled.* ② N-COUNT A **mask** is a piece of cloth or other material that you wear over all or part of your face to protect you from germs or harmful substances. ❑ *You must wear goggles and a mask that will protect you against the fumes.* ③ N-COUNT If you describe someone's behavior as a **mask**, you mean that they do not show their real feelings or character. ❑ *His mask of detachment cracked, and she saw for an instant an angry and violent man.* ④ N-COUNT A **mask** is a thick cream or paste made of various substances, which you spread over your face and leave for some time in order to improve your skin. ❑ *This mask leaves your complexion feeling soft and supple.* ⑤ V-T If you **mask** your feelings, you deliberately do not show them in your behavior, so that people cannot know what you really feel. ❑ *Dena lit a cigarette, trying to mask her agitation.* ⑥ V-T If one thing **masks** another, it prevents people from noticing or recognizing the other thing. ❑ *He was squinting through the smoke that masked the enemy.* ⑦ →see also **gas mask** →see **scuba diving, theater**

① 가산명사 복면, 가면 ❑ 복면이 벗겨진 저격수가 달아났다. ② 가산명사 마스크 ❑ 연기를 차단해 줄 고글과 마스크를 꼭 써야 한다. ③ 가산명사 가장 ❑ 태연한 척 하던 그의 본 모습이 드러나면서, 그녀는 일순간 그가 화를 내며 폭력적으로 바뀌는 것을 보았다. ④ 가산명사 얼굴 팩 ❑ 이 팩을 사용하면 피부가 부드럽고 유연해집니다. ⑤ 타동사 감추다 ❑ 데나는 마음의 동요를 감추려는 듯 담배에 불을 붙였다. ⑥ 타동사 가리다 ❑ 그는 적군을 가리고 있는 연기를 눈살을 찌푸리며 바라보고 있었다.

masked /mæskt/ ADJ If someone is **masked**, they are wearing a mask. ❑ *Masked youths threw stones and fire-bombs.*

maso|chism /mǽsəkɪzəm/ ❶ N-UNCOUNT **Masochism** is behavior in which someone gets sexual pleasure from their own pain or suffering. ❑ *The tendency towards masochism is however always linked with elements of sadism.* ● **maso|chist** (**masochists**) N-COUNT ❑ *...consensual sexual masochists.* ❷ N-UNCOUNT If you describe someone's behavior as **masochism**, you mean that they seem to be trying to get into a situation which causes them suffering or great difficulty. ❑ *Once you have tasted life in southern California, it takes a peculiar kind of masochism to return to a British winter.* ● **maso|chist** N-COUNT ❑ *Anybody who enjoys this is a masochist.*

maso|chis|tic /mæsəkɪstɪk/ ❶ ADJ **Masochistic** behavior involves a person getting sexual pleasure from their own pain or suffering. ❑ *...his masochistic tendencies.* ❷ ADJ If you describe someone's behavior as **masochistic**, you mean that they seem to be trying to get into a situation which causes them suffering or great difficulty. ❑ *It seems masochistic, somehow.*

ma|son /meɪsᵊn/ (**masons**) N-COUNT A **mason** is a person who is skilled at making things or building things with stone. In American English, **masons** are people who work with stone or bricks.

ma|son|ry /meɪsənri/ N-UNCOUNT **Masonry** is bricks or pieces of stone which have been stuck together with cement as part of a wall or building. ❑ *...a huge blast that sent pieces of masonry flying through the air.*

mas|quer|ade /mæskəreɪd/ (**masquerades, masquerading, masqueraded**) ❶ V-I To **masquerade as** someone or something means to pretend to be that person or thing, particularly in order to deceive other people. ❑ *He masqueraded as a doctor and fooled everyone.* ❷ N-COUNT A **masquerade** is an attempt to deceive people about the true nature or identity of something. ❑ *He told a news conference that the elections would be a masquerade.*

mass ◆◇◇ /mæs/ (**masses, massing, massed**) ❶ N-SING A **mass of** things is a large number of them grouped together. ❑ *On his desk is a mass of books and papers.* ❷ N-SING A **mass of** something is a large amount of it. ❑ *She had a mass of auburn hair.* ❸ QUANT **Masses of** something means a great deal of it. [INFORMAL] [QUANT of n-uncount/pl-n] ❑ *There's masses of work for her to do.* ❹ ADJ **Mass** is used to describe something which involves or affects a very large number of people. [ADJ n] ❑ *...ideas on combating mass unemployment.* ❑ *All the lights went off, and mass hysteria broke out.* ❺ N-COUNT A **mass of** a solid substance, a liquid, or a gas is an amount of it, especially a large amount which has no definite shape. ❑ *...before it cools and sets into a solid mass.* ❻ N-PLURAL If you talk about **the masses**, you mean the ordinary people in society, in contrast to the leaders or the highly educated people. ❑ *His music is commercial. It is aimed at the masses.* ❼ N-SING The **mass of** people are most of the people in a country, society, or group. ❑ *The 1939-45 world war involved the mass of the population.* ❽ V-T/V-I When people or things **mass**, or when you **mass** them, they gather together into a large crowd or group. ❑ *Shortly after the workers went on strike, police began to mass at the shipyard.* ❾ N-SING If you say that something is **a mass of** things, you mean that it is covered with them or full of them. ❑ *His body was a mass of sores.* ❿ N-VAR In physics, the **mass** of an object is the amount of physical matter that it has. [TECHNICAL] ❑ *Astronomers know that Pluto and Triton have nearly the same size, mass, and density.* ⓫ N-VAR **Mass** is a Christian church ceremony, especially in a Roman Catholic or Orthodox church, during which people eat bread and drink wine in order to remember the last meal of Jesus Christ. ❑ *She attended a convent school and went to Mass each day.* ⓬ →see also **massed**
→see transportation

Word Partnership	*mass*의 연어

N.   mass **communication**, mass **destruction**, mass **evacuation**, mass **execution**, mass **exodus**, mass **grave**, mass **hysteria**, mass **killings**, mass **layoffs**, mass **mailing**, mass **migration**, mass **protest**, mass **unemployment** ❹
bone mass, muscle mass ❺

---

mas|sa|cre /mǽsəkər/ (**massacres, massacring, massacred**) ❶ N-VAR A **massacre** is the killing of a large number of people at the same time in a violent and cruel way. ❑ *Maria lost her 62-year-old mother in the massacre.* →see **kill** ❷ V-T If people **are massacred**, a large number of them are attacked and killed in a violent and cruel way. ❑ *300 civilians are believed to have been massacred by the rebels.*

mas|sage /məsɑːʒ, BRIT mǽsɑːʒ/ (**massages, massaging, massaged**) ❶ N-VAR **Massage** is the action of squeezing and rubbing someone's body, as a way of making them relax or reducing their pain. ❑ *Alex asked me if I wanted a massage.* ❷ V-T If you **massage** someone or a part of their body, you squeeze and rub their body, in order to make them relax or reduce their pain. ❑ *She continued massaging her right foot, which was bruised and aching.* ❸ V-T If you say that someone **massages** statistics, figures, or evidence, you are criticizing them for changing or presenting the facts in a way that misleads people. [DISAPPROVAL] ❑ *Their governments have no reason to "massage" the statistics.*

masse →see en masse

massed /mæst/ ADJ **Massed** is used to describe a large number of people who have been brought together for a particular purpose. [ADJ n] ❑ *He could not escape the massed ranks of newsmen who spotted him crossing the lawn.*

형용사 가면을 쓴, 복면한, 마스크를 쓴 ❑ 마스크를 쓴 젊은이들이 돌과 화염병을 던졌다.

❶ 불가산명사 마조히즘 (피학대 성욕도착증) ❑ 하지만 마조히즘적 성향은 항상 사디스틱한 요소와 결부되어 있다. ● 마조히스트 가산명사 ❑ 합의에 의한 성적 마조히스트 ❷ 불가산명사 자기 학대, 피학적 성향 ❑ 일단 캘리포니아 남부 생활을 맛본 사람이 겨울철 영국 생활을 다시 시작하기 위해선 특이한 종류의 자기 학대가 필요하다. ● 자신을 학대하는 사람 가산명사 ❑ 이를 즐기는 사람은 모두 자신을 학대하는 사람이다.

❶ 형용사 마조히즘적인 ❑ 그의 마조히즘적인 성향 ❷ 형용사 자기 학대적인, 피학적인 ❑ 어쨌든 이는 피학적으로 보인다.

가산명사 석공

불가산명사 벽돌, 콘크리트 조각 ❑ 콘크리트 조각을 사방으로 날려 보낸 대규모 폭발

❶ 자동사 가장하다, 변장하다 ❑ 그는 의사로 가장해서 모든 사람들을 속였다. ❷ 가산명사 속임수, 겉치레 ❑ 그는 기자 회견에서 선거가 속임수에 불과할 것이라고 말했다.

❶ 단수명사 더미 ❑ 그의 책상 위에는 책과 서류가 잔뜩 쌓여 있다. ❷ 단수명사 많은 양 ❑ 그녀의 머리는 적갈색에 숱이 많았다. ❸ 수량사 방대한, 상당한 [비격식체] ❑ 그녀가 해야 할 일이 산더미같이 쌓여 있다. ❹ 형용사 대량의, 집단의 ❑ 대량 실업 해결 방안 ❑ 불이 전부 꺼지자, 집단 히스테리가 나타났다. ❺ 가산명사 덩어리 ❑ 이것이 냉각되어 고체 덩어리로 굳기 전에 ❻ 복수명사 대중, 서민 ❑ 그는 상업적이며 대중을 겨냥한 음악을 한다. ❼ 단수명사 대다수 ❑ 인구의 대다수가 1939년부터 1945년까지의 세계 대전을 경험했다. ❽ 타동사/자동사 모이다; 모으다 ❑ 노조가 파업에 돌입하고 얼마 지나지 않아 경찰이 조선소에 모여들기 시작했다. ❾ 단수명사 _투성이 ❑ 그의 몸은 상처투성이였다. ❿ 가산명사 또는 불가산명사 질량 [과학 기술] ❑ 천문학자들은 명왕성과 해왕성이 크기와 질량, 밀도가 거의 똑같다는 것을 안다. ⓫ 가산명사 또는 불가산명사 미사 ❑ 그녀는 수녀원에서 하는 학교에 다녔고 매일 미사에 갔다.

❶ 가산명사 또는 불가산명사 대학살 ❑ 마리아는 그 대학살로 예순두 살 되신 어머니를 잃었다. ❷ 타동사 학살당하다 ❑ 3백 명의 민간인들이 반군들에 의해서 대량 학살당했다고 믿고 있다.

❶ 가산명사 또는 불가산명사 마사지 ❑ 알렉스는 마사지를 받고 싶냐고 나에게 물었다. ❷ 타동사 마사지하다 ❑ 그녀는 멍들고 쑤시는 오른발을 계속 마사지했다. ❸ 타동사 (수치 등을) 조작하다 [탐탁찮음] ❑ 그들의 정부가 그 통계치를 '조작'할 이유가 전혀 없다.

형용사 밀집한 ❑ 그는 자신이 잔디밭을 횡단하는 것을 목격한 밀집해 있는 취재 기자들을 피할 수가 없었다.

A

mas|sive ♦◇◇ /mǽsɪv/ **1** ADJ Something that is **massive** is very large in size, quantity, or extent. [EMPHASIS] ❑ There was evidence of massive fraud. ❑ ...massive air attacks. ● **mas|sive|ly** ADV ❑ ...a massively popular game. **2** ADJ If you describe a medical condition as **massive**, you mean that it is extremely serious. [ADJ n] ❑ He died six weeks later of a massive heart attack.

1 형용사 엄청난, 대규모의 [강조] ❑ 대규모 사기에 대한 증거가 있었다. ❑ 대규모 공습 ● 엄청나게, 대규모로 부사 ❑ 엄청나게 인기 있는 경기 **2** 형용사 심각한 ❑ 그는 심각한 심장마비로 6주 후에 숨졌다.

B

mass mar|ket (mass markets) 1 N-COUNT **Mass market** is used to refer to the large numbers of people who want to buy a particular product. [BUSINESS] ❑ They now have access to the mass markets of China, Japan, and the UK. **2** ADJ **Mass-market** products are designed and produced for selling to large numbers of people. [BUSINESS] [ADJ n] ❑ ...mass-market paperbacks.

1 가산명사 일반 수요자 [경제] ❑ 그들은 이제 중국, 일본, 영국에 있는 일반 수요자에게 물건을 팔 수 있다. **2** 형용사 문제는 일반 수요자용의 [경제] ❑ 일반 수요자용 종이 표지 책들

C

mass me|dia N-SING-COLL You can use the **mass media** to refer to the various ways, especially television, radio, newspapers, and magazines, by which information and news is given to large numbers of people. ❑ ...mass media coverage of the issue.

단수명사-집합 매스미디어 ❑ 그 화제에 대한 매스미디어의 보도

D

mass-pro|duce (mass-produces, mass-producing, mass-produced) V-T If someone **mass-produces** something, they make it in large quantities, usually by machine. This means that the product can be sold cheaply. [BUSINESS] ❑ ...the invention of machinery to mass-produce footwear. ● **mass-produced** ADJ [ADJ n] ❑ In 1981 it launched the first mass-produced mountain bike.

타동사 대량 생산하다 [경제] ❑ 신발류를 대량 생산하기 위한 기계의 발명 ● 대량 생산의 형용사 ❑ 1981년 그 회사는 최초로 산악자전거를 대량 생산 체제로 만들기 시작했다.

E
F

mass pro|duc|tion also **mass-production** N-UNCOUNT **Mass production** is the production of something in large quantities, especially by machine. [BUSINESS] ❑ ...equipment that would allow the mass production of baby food. →see Word Web: **mass production**

불가산명사 대량 생산 [경제] ❑ 유아식 대량 생산이 가능한 설비

G

mast /mǽst/ **(masts) 1** N-COUNT The **masts** of a boat are the tall upright poles that support its sails. **2** N-COUNT A radio **mast** is a tall upright structure that is used to transmit radio or television signals.

1 가산명사 돛대들 **2** 가산명사 (라디오 등의) 송신탑

H

mas|ter ♦♦◇ /mǽstər/ **(masters, mastering, mastered) 1** N-COUNT A servant's **master** is the man that he or she works for. ❑ My master ordered me not to deliver the message except in private. **2** N-COUNT If you say that someone is a **master** of a particular activity, you mean that they are extremely skilled at it. ❑ She was a master of the English language. ● ADJ **Master** is also an adjective. [ADJ n] ❑ ...a master craftsman. **3** N-VAR If you are **master** of a situation, you have complete control over it. ❑ Jackson remained calm and always master of his passions. **4** V-T If you **master** something, you learn how to do it properly or you succeed in understanding it completely. ❑ Duff soon mastered the skills of radio production. **5** V-T If you **master** a difficult situation, you succeed in controlling it. ❑ When you have mastered one situation you have to go on to the next. →see also **headmaster 6** N-COUNT A famous male painter of the past is often called a **master**. ❑ ...a portrait by the Dutch master, Vincent Van Gogh. **7** ADJ A **master** copy of something such as a film or a tape recording is an original copy that can be used to produce other copies. [ADJ n] ❑ Keep one as a master copy for your own reference and circulate the others. **8** N-SING A **master's degree** can be referred to as a **master's**. ❑ I've a master's in economics.

1 가산명사 주인 ❑ 내 주인이 그 전갈을 반드시 은밀히 전달하라고 명령했다. **2** 가산명사 달인, 명인 ❑ 그녀는 영어의 달인이었다. ● 형용사 숙련된 ❑ 숙련된 장인 **3** 가산명사 또는 불가산명사 (상황을) 잘 제어하는 사람 ❑ 잭슨은 침착하며 항상 자신의 열정을 잘 다스렸다. **4** 타동사 통달하다, 숙달되다 ❑ 더프는 곧 라디오 제작 기술을 완전히 익혔다. **5** 타동사 잘 처리하다 ❑ 한 가지 상황을 잘 처리하면 그 다음 문제로 넘어가야 한다. **6** 가산명사 대가 ❑ 네덜란드의 대화가인 빈센트 반 고흐가 그린 초상화 **7** 형용사 원본의 ❑ 당신이 참고할 수 있도록 한 장은 원본으로 가지고 있고, 나머지 사본들을 회람시키세요. **8** 단수명사 석사 학위 ❑ 나는 경제학 석사 학위를 가지고 있다.

I
J
K
L
M

Thesaurus　　　master의 참조어

N.　owner; (ant.) servant, slave **1**
　　artist, expert, professional **2**
V.　learn, study, understand **4**

N
O
P

Word Partnership　　　master의 연어

N.　lord and master, master and slave **1**
　　master chef, master craftsman, master criminal,
　　master of disguise, master spy, Zen master **2 4**
　　master a skill **4**
　　master drawings **7**

Q
R

master|mind /mǽstərmaɪnd/ **(masterminds, masterminding, masterminded) 1** V-T If you **mastermind** a difficult or complicated activity, you plan it in detail and then make sure that it happens successfully. ❑ The finance minister will continue to mastermind Poland's economic reform. **2** N-COUNT The **mastermind behind** a difficult or complicated plan, often a criminal one, is the person who is responsible for planning and organizing it. ❑ He was the mastermind behind the plan to acquire the explosives.

1 타동사 (주도면밀하게) 지휘하다 ❑ 재무 장관이 폴란드의 경제 개혁을 지속적으로 주도면밀하게 지휘할 것이다. **2** 가산명사 배후 조종자 ❑ 그가 폭발물 입수 계획의 배후 조종자였다.

S
T

master|piece /mǽstərpis/ **(masterpieces) 1** N-COUNT A **masterpiece** is an extremely good painting, novel, movie, or other work of art. ❑ His book, I must add, is a masterpiece. **2** N-COUNT An artist's, writer's, or composer's **masterpiece**

1 가산명사 걸작 ❑ 내가 부언하건대, 그의 저서는 걸작이다. **2** 가산명사 대표작 ❑ 열여섯 개의 언어로 번역된 '인간의 운명'은 아마도 그의 대표작일 것이다.

U
V

Word Web　　　mass production

Up until 1913, the automobile was an expensive, custom-made product. But that year Henry Ford* created the first moving **assembly line** in his car **factory**. This changed the manufacturing process forever. It also introduced the world to **mass production**. For the first time, workers stayed in one place. Their work came to them on a conveyor belt. And Ford's cars used only standardized parts. These things helped **streamline** the process. Today's assembly lines look quite different. The **components** still move along on a conveyor belt. However, **robots** have taken over much of the work.

Henry Ford (1863-1947): an American automobile manufacturer.

W
X
Y
Z

is the best work that they have ever produced. ❏ *"Man's Fate," translated into sixteen languages, is probably his masterpiece.* ❸ N-COUNT A **masterpiece** is an extremely clever or skillful example of something. ❏ *The whole thing was a masterpiece of crowd management.*

mas|ter plan (**master plans**) N-COUNT A **master plan** is a clever plan that is intended to help someone succeed in a very difficult or important task. ❏ *...the master plan for the reform of the economy.*

mas|ter's de|gree (**master's degrees**) also Master's degree N-COUNT A **master's degree** is a university degree such as an MA or an MS which is of a higher level than a first degree and usually takes one or two years to complete.

mas|tery /ˈmæstəri/ N-UNCOUNT If you show **mastery** of a particular skill or language, you show that you have learned or understood it completely and have no difficulty using it. ❏ *He doesn't have mastery of the basic rules of grammar.*

mas|tur|bate /ˈmæstərbeɪt/ (**masturbates, masturbating, masturbated**) V-RECIP If someone **masturbates**, they stroke or rub their own genitals in order to get sexual pleasure. [v] ❏ *Do women masturbate as often as men?*

mat /mæt/ (**mats**) ❶ N-COUNT A **mat** is a small piece of something such as cloth, card, or plastic which you put on a table to protect it from plates or cups. ❏ *The food is served on polished tables with mats.* ❷ N-COUNT A **mat** is a small piece of carpet or other thick material which is put on the floor for protection, decoration, or comfort. ❏ *There was a letter on the mat.* ❸ →see also **matt**

match ♦♦♦ /mætʃ/ (**matches, matching, matched**) ❶ N-COUNT A **match** is an organized game of tennis, soccer, cricket, or some other sport. ❏ *He was watching a soccer match.* ❷ N-COUNT A **match** is a small wooden stick with a substance on one end that produces a flame when you rub it along the rough side of a matchbox. ❏ *...a packet of cigarettes and a box of matches.* ❸ V-RECIP If something of a particular color or design **matches** another thing, they have the same color or design, or have a pleasing appearance when they are used together. ❏ *"The shoes are too tight." — "Well, they do match your dress."* ❏ *All the chairs matched.* ● PHRASAL VERB **Match up** means the same as **match**. ❏ *The pillow cover can match up with the sheets.* ❹ V-RECIP If something such as an amount or a quality **matches with** another amount or quality, they are both the same or equal. If you **match** two things, you make them the same or equal. ❏ *Their strengths in memory and spatial skills matched.* ❏ *Our value system does not match with their value system.* ❺ V-RECIP If one thing **matches** another, they are connected or suit each other in some way. ❏ *The students are asked to match the books with the authors.* ❏ *It can take time and effort to match buyers and sellers.* ● PHRASAL VERB-RECIP **Match up** means the same as **match**. ❏ *The consultant seeks to match up jobless professionals with small companies in need of expertise.* ❏ *They compared the fat intake of groups of vegetarians and meat eaters, and matched their diets up with levels of harmful blood fats.* ❻ N-SING If a combination of things or people is a good **match**, they have a pleasing effect when placed or used together. ❏ *Helen's choice of lipstick was a good match for her skin-tone.* ❼ V-T If you **match** something, you are as good as it or equal to it, for example in speed, size, or quality. ❏ *They played some fine attacking football, but I think we matched them in every department.* ❽ →see also **matched, matching**
→see **fire**

Word Partnership	*match*의 연어	
N.	**boxing** match, **chess** match, **tennis** match, **wrestling** match	❶
ADJ.	**bad** match, **good** match, **perfect** match	❻
V.	**strike a** match	❷

matched /mætʃt/ ❶ ADJ If you say that two people are well **matched**, you mean that they have qualities that will enable them to have a good relationship. [adv ADJ] ❏ *My parents were not very well matched.* ❷ ADJ In sports and other competitions, if the two opponents or teams are well **matched**, they are both of the same standard in strength or ability. [adv ADJ] ❏ *Two well-matched sides conjured up an entertaining game.*

match|ing /ˈmætʃɪŋ/ ADJ **Matching** is used to describe things which are of the same color or design. [ADJ n] ❏ *...a coat and a matching handbag.*

mate ♦♢♢ /meɪt/ (**mates, mating, mated**) ❶ N-COUNT Someone's wife, husband, or sexual partner can be referred to as their **mate**. ❏ *He has found his ideal mate.* ❷ N-COUNT An animal's **mate** is its sexual partner. ❏ *The males guard their mates zealously.* ❸ V-RECIP When animals **mate**, a male and a female have sex in order to produce young. ❏ *This allows the pair to mate properly and stops the hen staying in the nest-box.* ❏ *They want the males to mate with females.* ❹ N-COUNT You can refer to someone's friends as their **mates**, especially when you are talking about a man and his male friends. [BRIT, INFORMAL] ❏ *He's off drinking with his mates.* ❺ N-VOC Some men use **mate** as a way of addressing other men when they are talking to them. [BRIT, INFORMAL] ❏ *Come on mate, things aren't that bad.* ❻ →see also **classmate, roommate, running mate**

ma|te|ri|al ♦♦♢ /məˈtɪəriəl/ (**materials**) ❶ N-VAR A **material** is a solid substance. ❏ *...electrons in a conducting material such as a metal.* ❷ N-MASS **Material** is cloth. ❏ *...the thick material of her skirt.* ❸ N-PLURAL **Materials** are the things you need for a particular activity. ❏ *The builders ran out of materials.* ❹ N-UNCOUNT Ideas or information that are used as a basis for a book, play, or film can be referred to as **material**. ❏ *In my version of the story, I added some new material.* ❺ ADJ **Material** things are related to possessions or money, rather than to more abstract things such as ideas or values. ❏ *Every room must have been stuffed with material things.* ● **ma|te|ri|al|ly** ADV ❏ *He has tried to help this child materially and spiritually.* ❻ ADJ **Material** evidence or information is directly relevant and

❸ 가산명사 절묘한 사례 ❏ 그 모든 것은 군중 관리의 절묘한 사례였다.

가산명사 종합 계획 ❏ 경제 개혁을 위한 종합 계획

가산명사 석사 학위

불가산명사 숙달, 통달 ❏ 그는 기초 문법 규칙에 숙달해 있지 않다.

상호동사 자위행위를 하다 ❏ 여자들도 남자들처럼 자주 자위행위를 하니?

❶ 가산명사 (식탁용) 받침 ❏ 잘 닦여진 식탁 위에 받침을 깔고 음식을 내놓는다. ❷ 가산명사 바닥 매트 ❏ 매트 위에 편지가 한 통 놓여 있었다.

❶ 가산명사 경기 ❏ 그는 축구 경기를 관람하고 있었다. ❷ 가산명사 성냥 ❏ 담배 한 갑과 성냥 한 통 ❸ 상호동사 어울리다 ❏ "신발이 너무 끼어." "음, 네 드레스와는 잘 어울리는데." ❏ 모든 의자가 잘 어울렸다. ● 구동사 어울리다 ❏ 그 베갯잇이 홑이불과 잘 어울릴 수 있다. ❹ 상호동사 대등하다; 동일시하다 ❏ 그들의 기억력과 공간 지각력은 대등했다. ❏ 우리의 가치 체계가 그들의 가치 체계와 대등하지 않다. ❺ 상호동사 연결시키다 ❏ 학생들에게 책과 그에 맞는 저자를 서로 연결시키도록 한다. ❏ 매도자와 매수자를 서로 연결시키는 데는 시간과 노력이 들 수 있다. ● 상호 구동사 연결시키다 ❏ 그 상담자는 직장이 없는 전문가와 전문 기술을 필요로 하는 소규모 회사를 연결시키는 것을 모색 중이다. ❏ 그들은 채식주의자와 육류 섭취자 집단의 지방 섭취량을 비교해서, 그들이 섭취하는 음식과 혈액 내 해로운 지방 수치를 연결시켰다. ❻ 단수명사 조화 ❏ 헬렌이 고른 립스틱이 그녀의 피부색과 잘 어울렸다. ❼ 타동사 -에 필적하다 ❏ 그들은 공격적인 축구를 훌륭히 해냈지만, 내 생각에는 우리가 모든 부분에서 그들에게 필적했던 것 같다.

❶ 형용사 어울리는 ❏ 우리 부모님은 그렇게 썩 잘 어울리지는 않으셨다. ❷ 형용사 필적하는, 엇비슷한 ❏ 서로 실력이 엇비슷한 두 팀이 흥미로운 경기를 해냈다.

형용사 어울리는 ❏ 코트와 그에 어울리는 핸드백

❶ 가산명사 짝 ❏ 그는 이상적인 짝을 찾았다. ❷ 가산명사 (동물의) 짝 ❏ 수컷들은 그들의 짝을 열심히 지킨다. ❸ 상호동사 짝짓기하다 ❏ 이렇게 하면 암탉을 닭장 밖으로 나오게 하여 그 닭 한 쌍이 원활하게 짝짓기를 할 수 있다. ❏ 그들은 그 수컷들이 야생 암컷들과 교미하기를 원한다. ❹ 가산명사 동료 [영국영어, 비격식체] ❏ 그는 동료들과 술 마시는 것을 끊었다. ❺ 호격명사 이보게 [영국영어, 비격식체] ❏ 여보게, 진정해. 사정이 그렇게 나빠진 않다구.

❶ 가산명사 또는 불가산명사 물질 ❏ 금속과 같은 전도체의 전자 ❷ 물질명사 천 ❏ 그녀의 두꺼운 치맛감 ❸ 복수명사 자재, 원료 ❏ 그 건축업자들은 건축 자재를 다 써버렸다. ❹ 불가산명사 소재 ❏ 내가 그 이야기를 고쳐 쓰면서 새로운 소재를 약간 더 추가했다. ❺ 형용사 세속적인, 물질적인 ❏ 모든 방이 세속적인 것들로 채워졌음에 틀림없다. ● 물질적으로 부사 ❏ 그는 이 아이를 물심양면으로 도와주려고 애써왔다. ❻ 형용사 관결에 큰 영향을 주는 [격식체] ❏ 판결에 큰 영향을 줄 증거의 성격이나

important in a legal or academic argument. [FORMAL] [ADJ n] ❏ *The nature and availability of material evidence was not to be discussed.*

입수 가능성은 토의되지 않을 예정이었다.

Word Partnership

*material*의 연어

ADJ. **classified** material, **instructional** material,
sensitive material 🚹 🌀
genetic material, **hazardous** material 🚹
new material, **original** material 🙎 🗷
raw materials 🗟

---

ma|teri|al|ism /mətɪəriəlɪzəm/ N-UNCOUNT **Materialism** is the attitude of someone who attaches a lot of importance to money and wants to possess a lot of material things. ❏ *...the rising consumer materialism in society at large.* 🙎 N-UNCOUNT **Materialism** is the belief that only physical matter exists, and that there is no spiritual world. ❏ *Scientific materialism thus triumphed over ignorance and superstition.*

🚹 불가산명사 물질 만능주의 ❏ 사회 전반적으로 증가하는 소비자 물질 만능주의 🙎 불가산명사 유물론 ❏ 그래서 과학적 유물론이 무지와 속설을 눌렀다.

ma|teri|al|ize /mətɪəriəlaɪz/ (materializes, materializing, materialized) [BRIT also **materialise**] 🚹 V-I If a possible or expected event does not **materialize**, it does not happen. [usu with brd-neg] ❏ *A rebellion by radicals failed to materialize.* 🙎 V-I If a person or thing **materializes**, they suddenly appear, after they have been invisible or in another place. ❏ *Tamsin materialized at her side, notebook at the ready.*

[영국영어 materialise] 🚹 자동사 실현되다 ❏ 급진파들의 반란은 실현되지 못했다. 🙎 자동사 불쑥 나타나다 ❏ 탐신이 공책을 준비해 들고 그녀 옆에 불쑥 나타났다.

ma|ter|nal /mətɜrnəl/ 🚹 ADJ **Maternal** is used to describe feelings or actions which are typical of those of a kind mother toward her child. ❏ *She had little maternal instinct.* 🙎 ADJ **Maternal** is used to describe things that relate to the mother of a baby. [ADJ n] ❏ *Maternal smoking can damage the unborn child.* 🗟 ADJ A **maternal** relative is one who is related through a person's mother rather than their father. [ADJ n] ❏ *Her maternal grandfather was Mayor of Karachi.*

🚹 형용사 어머니다운 ❏ 그녀는 모성 본능이 별로 없었다. 🙎 형용사 어머니의 ❏ 산모의 흡연은 태아에게 해로울 수 있다. 🗟 형용사 어머니 쪽의 ❏ 그녀의 외할아버지께서는 카라치 시장이셨다.

ma|ter|nity /mətɜrniti/ ADJ **Maternity** is used to describe things relating to the help and medical care given to a woman when she is pregnant and when she gives birth. [ADJ n] ❏ *Your job will be kept open for your return after maternity leave.*

형용사 임산부를 위한 ❏ 출산 휴가가 끝난 후에 복직할 수 있도록 당신 자리를 그대로 두겠습니다.

math /mæθ/ N-UNCOUNT **Math** is the same as **mathematics**. [AM; BRIT **maths**] ❏ *He studied math in college.* →see **mathematics**

불가산명사 수학 [미국영어; 영국영어 maths] ❏ 그는 대학에서 수학을 공부했다.

math|emati|cal /mæθəmætɪkəl/ 🚹 ADJ Something that is **mathematical** involves numbers and calculations. [ADJ n] ❏ *...mathematical calculations.* ● math|emati|cal|ly /mæθəmætɪkli/ ADV ❏ *...a mathematically complicated formula.* 🙎 ADJ If you have **mathematical** abilities or a **mathematical** mind, you are clever at doing calculations or understanding problems that involve numbers. ❏ *...a mathematical genius.* ● math|emati|cal|ly ADV [ADV -ed/adj] ❏ *Anyone can be an astrologer as long as they are mathematically minded.* →see **mathematics, ratio**

🚹 형용사 수학적인 ● 수학적 계산 ● 수학적으로 부사 ❏ 수학적으로 복잡한 공식 🙎 형용사 수학을 잘하는 ❏ 수학 천재 ● 수학적으로 부사 ❏ 수학적 사고방식만 지니고 있다면 누구든지 천문학자가 될 수 있다.

math|ema|ti|cian /mæθəmətɪʃən/ (mathematicians) 🚹 N-COUNT A **mathematician** is a person who is trained in the study of numbers and calculations. ❏ *The risks can be so complex that banks hire mathematicians to puzzle them out.* 🙎 N-COUNT A **mathematician** is a person who is good at doing calculations and using numbers. ❏ *I'm not a very good mathematician.* →see **mathematics, ratio**

🚹 가산명사 수학자 ❏ 손실 위험이 그리 간단한 문제가 아니어서 은행은 그것을 풀 수 있는 수학자들을 고용한다. 🙎 가산명사 수학을 잘하는 사람, 숫자에 밝은 사람 ❏ 나는 계산을 잘 못한다.

math|emat|ics /mæθəmætɪks/ 🚹 N-UNCOUNT **Mathematics** is the study of numbers, quantities, or shapes. ❏ *...a professor of mathematics at Boston College.* 🙎 N-UNCOUNT **The mathematics of** a problem is the calculations that are involved in it. ❏ *Once you understand the mathematics of debt you can work your way out of it.* →see Word Web: **mathematics**

🚹 불가산명사 수학 ❏ 보스턴 대학의 수학 교수 🙎 불가산명사 계산 ❏ 일단 네가 진 빚이 얼마인지 계산이 되면, 그 빚을 갚기 위한 방법을 강구할 수 있다.

maths /mæθs/ N-UNCOUNT **Maths** is the same as **mathematics**. [BRIT; AM **math**] ❏ *He taught science and maths.*

불가산명사 수학 [영국영어; 미국영어 math] ❏ 그는 과학과 수학을 가르쳤다.

mati|nee /mætˀneɪ, BRIT mætɪneɪ/ (matinees) N-COUNT A **matinee** is a performance of a play or a showing of a movie which takes place in the afternoon.

가산명사 (연극 등의) 낮 공연

ma|trix /meɪtrɪks/ (matrices) 🚹 N-COUNT A **matrix** is the environment or context in which something such as a society develops and grows. [FORMAL] ❏ *...the matrix of their culture.* 🙎 N-COUNT In mathematics, a **matrix** is an arrangement of numbers, symbols, or letters in rows and columns which is used in solving mathematical problems.

🚹 가산명사 모체, 기반 [격식체] ❏ 그들의 문화적 모체 🙎 가산명사 (수학) 행렬

Word Web   mathematics

At first prehistoric people **counted** things they could see—for example, four sheep. Later they began to use **numbers** with abstract **quantities** like time—for example, two days. This led to the development of basic **arithmetic**—addition, subtraction, **multiplication**, and **division**. When people discovered how to use written numerals, they could do more complex **mathematical calculations**. **Mathematicians** developed new types of **math** to **measure** land and keep financial records. **Algebra** and **geometry** developed in the Middle East between 2,000 and 3,000 years ago. Algebra uses letters to represent possible **quantities**. Geometry deals with the relationships among **lines**, **angles**, and **shapes**.

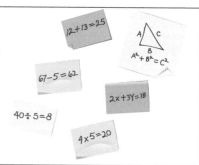

matt /mæt/

The spellings **matte** or **mat** in American English, and **matte** in British English are also used.

ADJ A matt color, paint, or surface is dull rather than shiny. ❏ ...*a creamy white matt emulsion.*

철자 matte 또는 mat은 미국영어에서 쓰며, 영국영어에서는 matte도 쓴다.

형용사 뿌연 ❏ 크림색의 희뿌연 우유 같은 액체

mat|ter ♦♦♦ /mætər/ (**matters, mattering, mattered**) **1** N-COUNT A **matter** is a task, situation, or event which you have to deal with or think about, especially one that involves problems. ❏ *It was clear that she wanted to discuss some private matter.* ❏ *Business matters drew him to Paris.* **2** N-PLURAL You use **matters** to refer to the situation you are talking about, especially when something is affecting the situation in some way. [no det] ❏ *We have no objection to this change, but doubt that it will significantly improve matters.* ❏ *If it would facilitate matters, I would be happy to come to New York.* **3** N-SING If you say that a situation is **a matter of** a particular thing, you mean that that is the most important thing to be done or considered when you are involved in the situation or explaining it. ❏ *History is always a matter of interpretation.* ❏ *Observance of the law is a matter of principle for us.* **4** N-UNCOUNT Printed **matter** consists of books, newspapers, and other texts that are printed. Reading **matter** consists of things that are suitable for reading, such as books and newspapers. ❏ *...the Government's plans to levy VAT on printed matter.* **5** N-UNCOUNT **Matter** is the physical part of the universe consisting of solids, liquids, and gases. ❏ *A proton is an elementary particle of matter that possesses a positive charge.* **6** N-UNCOUNT You use **matter** to refer to a particular type of substance. ❏ *...waste matter from industries.* **7** N-SING You use **matter** in expressions such as "**What's the matter?**" or "**Is anything the matter?**" when you think that someone has a problem and you want to know what it is. ❏ *Carole, what's the matter? You don't seem happy.* **8** N-SING You use **matter** in expressions such as "**a matter of weeks**" when you are emphasizing how small an amount is or how short a period of time it is. [EMPHASIS] ❏ *Within a matter of days she was back at work.* **9** V-T/V-I If you say that something does not **matter**, you mean that it is not important to you because it does not have an effect on you or on a particular situation. [no cont, usu with brd-neg] ❏ *A lot of the food goes on the floor but that doesn't matter.* ❏ *As long as staff are smart, it does not matter how long their hair is.* **10** →see also **subject matter** **11** PHRASE If you say that something is **another matter** or **a different matter**, you mean that it is very different from the situation that you have just discussed. ❏ *Being responsible for one's own health is one thing, but being responsible for another person's health is quite a different matter.* **12** PHRASE If you are going to do something **as a matter of** urgency or priority, you are going to do it as soon as possible, because it is important. ❏ *Your doctor and health visitor can help a great deal and you need to talk about it with them as a matter of urgency.* **13** PHRASE If something is **no easy matter**, it is difficult to do it. ❏ *Choosing the color for the drawing-room walls was no easy matter.* **14** PHRASE If someone says **that's the end of the matter** or **that's an end to the matter**, they mean that a decision that has been taken must not be changed or discussed any more. ❏ *"He's moving in here," Maria said. "So that's the end of the matter."* **15** PHRASE You use **the fact of the matter is** or **the truth of the matter is** to introduce a fact which supports what you are saying or which is not widely known, for example because it is a secret. ❏ *The fact of the matter is that most people consume far more protein than they actually need.* **16** CONVENTION You say "**it doesn't matter**" to tell someone who is apologizing to you that you are not angry or upset, and that they should not worry. ❏ *"Did I wake you?" — "Yes, but it doesn't matter."* **17** PHRASE If you say that something **makes matters worse**, you mean that it makes a difficult situation even more difficult. ❏ *Don't let yourself despair; this will only make matters worse.* **18** PHRASE You use **no matter** in expressions such as "**no matter how**" and "**no matter what**" to say that something is true or happens in all circumstances. ❏ *No matter what your age, you can lose weight by following this program.* **19** a matter of **life and death** →see **death**. as a matter of course →see **course**. **as a matter of fact** →see **fact** →see Word Web: **matter**

1 가산명사 문제 ❏ 그녀가 개인적인 문제를 얘기하고 싶어 하는 것이 분명했다. ❏ 사업상 문제로 그는 파리로 갔다. **2** 복수명사 (문제가 되는) 상황, 사정 ❏ 우리는 이 개혁에 대해 반대하지는 않지만 그것이 상황을 충분히 향상시킬지는 의심스럽다. ❏ 만약 그렇게 해서 사정이 용이해진다면, 내가 뉴욕으로 기꺼이 갈 텐데. **3** 단수명사 (중요한) 문제 ❏ 역사는 항상 해석하는 것이 중요한 문제이다. ❏ 우리가 법을 준수하는 것은 원칙에 관한 문제이다. **4** 불가산명사 자료 ❏ 인쇄물에 부가 가치세를 부과하려는 정부안 **5** 불가산명사 물질 ❏ 양자는 양전하를 가지고 있는 물질의 기본적인 미립자이다. **6** 불가산명사 물질 ❏ 산업 폐기물 **7** 단수명사 문제; 무슨 일이야?; 무슨 문제 있어? ❏ 캐롤, 무슨 일이야? 기분이 안 좋아 보이는 걸. **8** 단수명사 거우; 거우 몇 주일 [강조] ❏ 거우 며칠 후에 그녀가 일에 복귀했다. **9** 타동사/자동사 중요하다 ❏ 음식이 바닥에 많이 떨어지지만 그것은 중요하지 않다. ❏ 직원들이 똑똑하기만 하다면 그들의 머리 길이는 중요하지 않다. **11** 구 별개의 문제 ❏ 자기 자신의 건강에 대해 책임지는 것과 다른 사람의 건강에 대해 책임지는 것은 전혀 별개의 문제이다. **12** 구 - 의 문제로서 ❏ 당신 주치의와 방문 간호사가 많이 도와주겠지만 당신도 그들에게 가능한 한 빨리 그것에 대해 말할 필요가 있다. **13** 구 쉽지 않은 문제 ❏ 응접실 벽의 색을 고르는 것은 쉽지 않은 문제였다. **14** 구 그것은 이미 결정된 사항이다, 더 이상 왈가왈부하지 마 ❏ "그 사람이 이리로 이사 올 거야."라고 마리아가 말했다. "그러니까 이제 더 이상 왈가왈부하지 마." **15** 구 사실은 ❏ 사실은 대부분의 사람들이 실제 필요한 양보다 훨씬 더 많은 단백질을 섭취하고 있다. **16** 관용 표현 괜찮아 ❏ "나 때문에 깼니?" "응, 하지만 괜찮아." **17** 구 상황을 악화시키다 ❏ 절망하지 마, 그러면 상황을 더 악화시킬 뿐이야. **18** 구 아무리 -라 할지라도 ❏ 당신이 아무리 나이가 들었다 해도 이 프로그램을 따라 하면 체중을 줄일 수 있습니다.

matter-of-fact ADJ If you describe a person as **matter-of-fact**, you mean that they show no emotions such as enthusiasm, anger, or surprise, especially in a situation where you would expect them to be emotional. ❏ *John was doing his best to give Francis the news in a matter-of-fact way.* ● **matter-of-factly** ADV [ADV after v] ❏ *"She thinks you're a spy," Scott said matter-of-factly.*

형용사 사무적인 ❏ 존은 프란시스에게 사무적인 투로 그 소식을 알리려고 무진 애를 쓰고 있었다. ● 사무적인 투로 부사 ❏ "그녀는 내가 스파이라고 생각해."라며 스코트는 사무적인 투로 말했다.

mat|tress /mætrɪs/ (**mattresses**) N-COUNT A **mattress** is the large, flat object which is put on a bed to make it comfortable to sleep on.

가산명사 매트리스

Word Web   matter

Matter exists in three states—**solid**, **liquid**, and **gas**. When a solid becomes hot enough, it **melts** and becomes a liquid. When a liquid is hot enough, it **evaporates** into a gas. The process also works the other way around. A gas which becomes very cool will **condense** into a liquid. And a liquid that is cooled enough will freeze and become a solid. Other changes in **state** are possible. Sublimation describes what happens when a solid, dry ice, turns directly into a gas, carbon dioxide. And did you know that glass is actually a liquid, not a solid?

solid   liquid   gas

a b c d e f g h i j k l m n o p q r s t u v w x y z

ma|ture /mətyʊ̯ər, -tʊ̯ər, -tʃʊ̯ər/ (**matures, maturing, matured, maturer, maturest**) **1** V-I When a child or young animal **matures**, it becomes an adult. ❑ *You will learn what to expect as your child matures physically.* **2** V-I When something **matures**, it reaches a state of complete development. ❑ *When the trees matured they were cut in certain areas.* **3** V-I If someone **matures**, they become more fully developed in their personality and emotional behavior. ❑ *They have matured way beyond their age.* **4** ADJ If you describe someone as **mature**, you think that they are fully developed and balanced in their personality and emotional behavior. [APPROVAL] ❑ *They are emotionally mature and should behave responsibly.* **5** V-T/V-I If something such as wine or cheese **matures** or **is matured**, it is left for a time to allow its full flavor or strength to develop. ❑ *Unlike wine, brandy matures only in wood, not glass.* **6** ADJ **Mature** cheese or wine has been left for a time to allow its full flavor or strength to develop. ❑ *Grate some mature cheddar cheese.* **7** V-I When an investment such as an insurance policy or bond **matures**, it reaches the stage when the company pays you back the money you have saved, and the interest your money has earned. [BUSINESS] ❑ *These bonuses will be paid when your savings plan matures in ten years' time.* **8** ADJ If you say that someone is **mature** or of **mature** years, you are saying politely that they are middle-aged or old. [POLITENESS] ❑ *...a man of mature years who had been in the job for longer than most of the members could remember.*

ma|tur|ity /mətyʊ̯əriti, -tʊ̯ər-, -tʃʊ̯ər-/ (**maturities**) **1** N-UNCOUNT **Maturity** is the state of being fully developed or adult. ❑ *Humans experience a delayed maturity; we arrive at all stages of life later than other mammals.* **2** N-UNCOUNT Someone's **maturity** is their quality of being fully developed in their personality and emotional behavior. ❑ *Her speech showed great maturity and humanity.* **3** N-VAR When an investment such as an insurance policy or bond reaches **maturity**, it reaches the stage when the company pays you back the money you have saved, and the interest your money has earned. [BUSINESS] ❑ *Customers are told what their policies will be worth on maturity, not what they are worth today.*

Thesaurus · *maturity*의 참조어

N.　　adulthood, manhood, womanhood **1**

---

maul /mɔl/ (**mauls, mauling, mauled**) V-T If you **are mauled** by an animal, you are violently attacked by it and badly injured. ❑ *He had been mauled by a bear.*

mav|er|ick /mævərɪk/ (**mavericks**) N-COUNT If you describe someone as a **maverick**, you mean that they are unconventional and independent, and do not think or behave in the same way as other people. ❑ *He was too much of a maverick ever to hold high office.* ● ADJ **Maverick** is also an adjective. [ADJ n] ❑ *...a maverick group of scientists, who oppose the prevailing medical opinion on the disease.*

max. /mæks/ ADJ **Max.** is an abbreviation for **maximum**, and is often used after numbers or amounts. [NUM ADJ, ADJ n] ❑ *I'll give him eight out of 10, max.*

Word Link · maxim ≈ greatest : maxim, maximize, maximum

---

max|im /mæksɪm/ (**maxims**) N-COUNT A **maxim** is a rule for good or sensible behavior, especially one in the form of a saying. ❑ *I believe in the maxim "if it ain't broke, don't fix it."*

max|im|ize /mæksɪmaɪz/ (**maximizes, maximizing, maximized**) [BRIT also **maximise**] **1** V-T If you **maximize** something, you make it as great in amount or importance as you can. ❑ *In order to maximize profit the firm would seek to maximize output.* **2** V-T If you **maximize** a window on a computer screen, you make it as large as possible. ❑ *Click on the square icon to maximize the window.*

maxi|mum ♦◇◇ /mæksɪməm/ **1** ADJ You use **maximum** to describe an amount which is the largest that is possible, allowed, or required. [ADJ n] ❑ *Under planning law the maximum height for a fence or hedge is 2 meters.* ● N-SING **Maximum** is also a noun. ❑ *The law provides for a maximum of two years in prison.* **2** ADJ You use **maximum** to indicate how great an amount is. [ADJ n] ❑ *...the maximum amount of information.* ❑ *It was achieved with minimum fuss and maximum efficiency.* **3** ADV If you say that something is a particular amount **maximum**, you mean that this is the greatest amount it should be or could possibly be, although a smaller amount is acceptable or very possible. [amount ADV] ❑ *We need an extra 6g a day maximum.*

Thesaurus · *maximum*의 참조어

ADJ.　　greatest, largest, most; *(ant.)* minimum **1 2**

Word Partnership · *maximum*의 연어

N.　　maximum **benefit**, maximum **charge**, maximum **efficiency**, maximum **fine**, maximum **flexibility**, maximum **height**, maximum **penalty**, maximum **rate**, maximum **sentence**, maximum **speed** **1**

---

may ♦♦♦ /meɪ/

May is a modal verb. It is used with the base form of a verb.

1 MODAL You use **may** to indicate that something will possibly happen or be true in the future, but you cannot be certain. [VAGUENESS] ❑ *We may have some rain today.* ❑ *I may be back next year.* **2** MODAL You use **may** to indicate that there is a possibility that something is true, but you cannot be certain. [VAGUENESS]

---

1 자동사 성장하다 ❑ 당신 아이가 신체적으로 성장함에 따라 무엇을 기대해야 할지 알게 될 것이다. **2** 자동사 완전히 자라다 ❑ 어떤 지역에서는 그 나무들이 완전히 자라면, 그것을 베었다. **3** 자동사 성숙하다 ❑ 그들은 나이에 비해서 훨씬 성숙했다. **4** 형용사 성숙한 [마음에 듦] ❑ 그들은 정서적으로 성숙하므로 책임감 있게 행동할 것이다. **5** 타동사/자동사 숙성하다 ❑ 포도주와는 달리 브랜디는 유리가 아닌 목통속에서만 숙성된다. **6** 형용사 숙성한 ❑ 숙성한 체다 치즈를 강판에 갈아라. **7** 자동사 (보험 등이) 만기가 되다 [경제] ❑ 당신의 저축이 십 년 만기가 될 때 이 보너스가 지불될 것입니다. **8** 형용사 중년의 [공손체] ❑ 대부분의 직원들이 기억할 수 있었던 것보다 더 오랫동안 그 직장을 다녔던 중년의 남자

1 불가산명사 성장, 장성 ❑ 인간은 더디게 장성한다. 즉, 우리는 다른 포유동물보다 모든 성장 단계에 더 늦게 도달한다. **2** 불가산명사 성숙 ❑ 그녀는 연설을 통하여 상당한 성숙미와 인간미를 보여 주었다. **3** 가산명사 또는 불가산명사 만기 [경제] ❑ 고객들에게는 그들의 보험이 지금 이 순간이 아니라, 만기가 되었을 때 어떤 가치가 있을 것인가를 알려준다.

타동사 크게 다치다 ❑ 그는 곰에게 크게 다쳤었다.

가산명사 독불장군 ❑ 그는 너무나 독불장군이어서 고위직에 한번도 오르지 못했다. ● 형용사 독자적인 ❑ 그 질병에 대한 일반적인 의학적 의견에 반대하는 독자적인 과학자 집단

형용사 최고의, 최대의 ❑ 나는 그에게 최고인 10점에서 8점을 줄 것이다.

가산명사 격언 ❑ 나는 "부서지지 않은 것은 수리하지 말라."라는 격언이 맞는다고 생각한다.

[영국영어 maximise] **1** 타동사 극대화하다, 최대화하다 ❑ 그 회사가 이윤을 극대화하려면 생산을 최대화할 수 있는 방법을 모색해야 할 것이다. **2** 타동사 (컴퓨터 화면을) 최대로 하다 ❑ 창의 크기를 최대로 하려면 네모 아이콘을 클릭해라.

1 형용사 최대한의 ❑ 개발 법안에 따르면 울타리의 최고 허용 높이는 2미터이다. ● 단수명사 최고, 최대 ❑ 법에 따르면 최고 징역 2년이다. **2** 형용사 최대의 ❑ 정보의 최대량 ❑ 가장 적게 야단스럽고 가장 효율적인 방법으로 그 일을 달성했다. **3** 부사 최대한으로 ❑ 우리는 하루에 최대 6그램이 더 필요하다.

may는 조동사이며 동사 원형과 함께 쓴다.

1 법조동사 -일 지도 모른다 [짐작투] ❑ 오늘 비가 좀 올지도 모른다. ❑ 나는 내년에 돌아올지도 모른다. **2** 법조동사 -일 수도 있다 [짐작투] ❑ 민권 담당자들은 다른 인종 차별적 폭력 사건들이 수백 건에 달할 수도

❑ *Civil rights officials say there may be hundreds of other cases of racial violence.* **3** MODAL You use **may** to indicate that something is sometimes true or is true in some circumstances. ❑ *A vegetarian diet may not provide enough calories for a child's normal growth.* **4** MODAL You use **may have** with a past participle when suggesting that it is possible that something happened or was true, or when giving a possible explanation for something. [VAGUENESS] ❑ *He may have been to some of those places.* **5** MODAL You use **may** in statements where you are accepting the truth of a situation, but contrasting it with something that is more important. ❑ *I may be almost 50, but there's not a lot of things I've forgotten.* **6** MODAL You use **may** when you are mentioning a quality or fact about something that people can make use of if they want to. ❑ *The bag has narrow straps, so it may be worn over the shoulder or carried in the hand.* **7** MODAL You use **may** to indicate that someone is allowed to do something, usually because of a rule or law. You use **may not** to indicate that someone is not allowed to do something. ❑ *Any two persons may marry in Scotland provided that both persons are at least 16 years of age on the day of their marriage.* **8** MODAL You use **may** when you are giving permission to someone to do something, or when asking for permission. [FORMAL] ❑ *Mr. Hobbs? May we come in?* **9** MODAL You use **may** when you are making polite requests. [FORMAL, POLITENESS] ❑ *I'd like the use of your living room, if I may.* **10** MODAL You use **may** when you are mentioning the reaction or attitude that you think someone is likely to have to something you are about to say. ❑ *You know, Brian, whatever you may think, I work hard for a living.* **11** MODAL If you do something so that a particular thing **may** happen, you do it so that there is an opportunity for that thing to happen. ❑ *...the need for an increase in the numbers of surgeons so that patients may be treated as soon as possible.* **12** **may as well** →see **well**

May ♦♦♦ /meɪ/ (**Mays**) N-VAR **May** is the fifth month of the year in the Western calendar. ❑ *University examinations are held in early May.*

may|be ♦♦◇ /ˈmeɪbi/ **1** ADV You use **maybe** to express uncertainty, for example when you do not know that something is definitely true, or when you are mentioning something that may possibly happen in the future in the way you describe. [VAGUENESS] [ADV with cl/group] ❑ *Maybe she is in love.* ❑ *I do think about having children, maybe when I'm 40.* **2** ADV You use **maybe** when you are making suggestions or giving advice. **Maybe** is also used to introduce polite requests. [POLITENESS] [ADV with cl/group] ❑ *Maybe we can go to the movies or something.* ❑ *Maybe you'd better tell me what this is all about.* **3** ADV You use **maybe** to indicate that, although a comment is partly true, there is also another point of view that should be considered. [ADV cl] ❑ *Maybe there is jealousy, but I think the envy is more powerful.* **4** ADV You can say **maybe** as a response to a question or remark, when you do not want to agree or disagree. [ADV as reply] ❑ *"Is she coming back?" — "Maybe. No one hears from her."* **5** ADV You use **maybe** when you are making a rough guess at a number, quantity, or value, rather than stating it exactly. [VAGUENESS] [ADV amount] ❑ *The men were maybe a hundred feet away and coming closer.* **6** ADV People use **maybe** to mean "sometimes," particularly in a series of general statements about what someone does, or about something that regularly happens. [ADV with cl/group] ❑ *They'll come to the bar for a year, or maybe even two, then they'll find another favorite spot.*

may|hem /ˈmeɪhem/ N-UNCOUNT You use **mayhem** to refer to a situation that is not controlled or ordered, when people are behaving in a disorganized, confused, and often violent way. ❑ *Their arrival caused mayhem as crowds of refugees rushed towards them.*

may|on|naise /ˈmeɪəneɪz/ N-UNCOUNT **Mayonnaise** is a thick pale sauce made from egg yolks and oil. It is used in salads.

mayor ♦◇◇ /ˈmeɪər, mɛər/ (**mayors**) N-COUNT The **mayor** of a town or city is the person who has been elected to represent it for a fixed period of time or, in some places, to run its government. ❑ *...the new Mayor of New York.*

maze /meɪz/ (**mazes**) **1** N-COUNT A **maze** is a complex system of passages or paths between walls or hedges and is designed to confuse people who try to find their way through it, often as a form of amusement. ❑ *The palace has extensive gardens, a maze, and tennis courts.* **2** N-COUNT A **maze of** streets, rooms, or tunnels is a large number of them that are connected in a complicated way, so that it is difficult to find your way through them. ❑ *The children lead me through the maze of alleys to the edge of the city.* **3** N-COUNT You can refer to a set of ideas, topics, or rules as a **maze** when a large number of them are related to each other in a complicated way that makes them difficult to understand. ❑ *The book tries to steer you through the maze of alternative therapies.*

MBO /ˌɛm bi ˈoʊ/ N-COUNT An **MBO** is the buying of a company by its managers. **MBO** is an abbreviation for **management buyout**. [BUSINESS] ❑ *...the largest MBO ever undertaken by Australian financial investors.*

MD /ˌɛm ˈdi/ (**MDs**) N-COUNT **MD** is an abbreviation for **managing director**. [mainly BRIT, BUSINESS] ❑ *He's going to be the MD of the Park Lane company.*

me ♦♦♦ /mi, STRONG mi/ PRON-SING A speaker or writer uses **me** to refer to himself or herself. **Me** is a first person singular pronoun. **Me** is used as the object of a verb or a preposition. [V PRON, prep PRON] ❑ *I had to make important decisions that would affect me for the rest of my life.* ❑ *He asked me to go to Cambridge with him.*

mead|ow /ˈmɛdoʊ/ (**meadows**) N-COUNT A **meadow** is a field which has grass and flowers growing in it.

mea|ger /ˈmiɡər/ [BRIT **meagre**] ADJ If you describe an amount or quantity of something as **meager**, you are critical of it because it is very small or not enough. [DISAPPROVAL] ❑ *The rations that they gave us were meager and inadequate.*

meal ♦♦◇ /mil/ (**meals**) **1** N-COUNT A **meal** is an occasion when people sit down and eat, usually at a regular time. ❑ *She sat next to him throughout the meal.* **2** N-COUNT A **meal** is the food you eat during a meal. ❑ *The waiter offered him red*

있다고 말한다. **3** 법조동사 -일 수도 있다 ❑ 채식은 아동의 정상적인 성장에 필요한 충분한 열량을 제공하지 못할 수도 있다. **4** 법조동사 -었을 수도 있다 [짐작투] ❑ 그가 그 곳 중 몇 군데는 가 봤을 수도 있다. **5** 법조동사 - 인지는 모르지만 ❑ 내가 쉰 살이 다 되었다고는 하지만 내가 잊은 것이 많지는 않다. **6** 법조동사 -할 수도 있다 ❑ 그 가방은 끈이 가늘어서 어깨에 맬 수도 있고 손에 들 수도 있다. **7** 법조동사 -할 수 있다 ; - 할 수 없다 스코틀랜드에서는 결혼식 당일에 두 사람 모두 최하 열여섯 살만 되면 누구든지 결혼할 수 있다. **8** 법조동사 -해도 쥐니다 [격식체] ❑ 홉스 씨? 저희가 들어가도 될까요? **9** 법조동사 - 해도 되다 [격식체, 공손체] ❑ 괜찮으시다면, 댁의 거실을 쓰고 싶습니다. **10** 법조동사 -할 것 같다 ❑ 있잖아, 브라이언, 네가 어떻게 생각하든, 나는 살기 위해 열심히 일 하고 있어. **11** 법조동사 -할 수 있도록 ❑ 환자들이 가능한 한 빨리 치료를 받을 수 있도록 의사들의 수를 늘릴 필요성

가산명사 또는 불가산명사 5월 ❑ 대학 시험은 5월 초에 실시된다.

1 부사 아마도 [짐작투] ❑ 아마도 그녀가 사랑에 빠진 것 같아. ❑ 아마 마흔 살쯤엔 아이를 가져볼까 하고 생각은 하고 있어. **2** 부사 어쩌면 [공손체] ❑ 어쩌면 영화를 보든지, 아니면 다른 것을 할 수도 있을 거야. ❑ 이것이 다 무슨 일인지 내게 말해 주는 게 좋을 것 같은데. **3** 부사 아마 ❑ 아마 질투도 있겠지만, 내 생각으로는 부러움이 더 클 것 같다. **4** 부사 글쎄 ❑ "그녀가 돌아 올 거래?" "글쎄, 누구도 그녀에게서 연락을 받은 사람은 없어." **5** 부사 약 [짐작투] ❑ 그 남자들은 약 백 피트 앞에서 점점 가까이 오고 있었다. **6** 부사 때로는 ❑ 그들은 1년 동안, 때로는 2년 동안까지 그 술집에 오다가, 그런 다음에는 또 다른 흥미 있는 장소를 찾을 것이다.

불가산명사 대혼란 ❑ 그들이 도착할 때 피난민들이 그들에게 돌진함으로써 대혼란을 야기했다.

불가산명사 마요네즈

가산명사 시장 ❑ 신임 뉴욕 시장

1 가산명사 미로 ❑ 그 궁전에는 광활한 정원과 미로와 테니스장이 있다. **2** 가산명사 복잡한 길 ❑ 그 아이들이 나를 복잡한 골목길을 통과해서 도시의 변두리로 데리고 간다. **3** 가산명사 복잡함 ; 복잡한 것 ❑ 이 책은 대체 요법의 복잡한 미로 속에서 당신에게 길을 안내하고자 합니다.

가산명사 경영자에 의한 회사 인수 [경제] ❑ 호주 금융 투자자들이 지금까지 했던 것 중에서 가장 큰 규모의 경영자에 의한 회사 인수

가산명사 전무이사 [주로 영국영어, 경제] ❑ 그는 파크레인 회사의 전무이사가 될 예정이다.

단수대명사 나; 나를, 나에게 ❑ 나는 남은 인생 동안 나에게 영향을 주게 될 중요한 결정을 해야 했다. ❑ 그가 나에게 케임브리지에 같이 가자고 했다.

가산명사 초원

[영국영어 meagre] 형용사 빈약한 [탐탁잖음] ❑ 그들이 우리에게 준 일일 배급량은 빈약하고 부적절했다.

1 가산명사 식사 ❑ 그녀는 식사하는 동안 내내 그 남자 옆에 앉아 있었다. **2** 가산명사 음식 ❑ 웨이터는 그에게 음식과 함께 적포도주나 백포도주를 대접했다.

a b c d e f g h i j k l m n o p q r s t u v w x y z

Word Web   meal

Mealtime customs vary widely around the world. In the Middle East, popular **breakfast** foods include pita bread, olives and white cheese. In China, favorite **fast food** breakfast items are steamed buns and fried breadsticks. The continental breakfast in Europe consists of bread, butter, jam, and a hot drink. In many places **lunch** is a light **meal**, perhaps a **sandwich**. But in Germany, it is the main meal of the day. In most places, **dinner** is the name of the meal eaten in the evening. However, some people say they eat dinner at noon and supper at night.

wine or white wine with his meal. **3** PHRASE If you have a **square meal**, you have a large healthy meal. ❏ *The troops are very tired. They haven't had a square meal for four or five days.* →see **restaurant**
→see Word Web: **meal**

The first meal of the day is called **breakfast**. The most common word for the midday meal is **lunch**, but in some parts of Britain, and in some contexts, **dinner** is used as well. ❏ *He seldom has lunch at all....school dinners....Christmas dinner.* However, **dinner** is used mainly to refer to a meal in the evening. ❏ *...a celebratory dinner in the evening.* In British English, it may also suggest a formal or special meal. **Supper** and **tea** are sometimes also used to refer to the evening meal, though for some people, **supper** is a snack in the late evening and **tea** is a light meal in the afternoon.

Thesaurus   meal의 참조어

N.   breakfast, dinner, lunch, supper **1**

Word Partnership   meal의 연어

V.   enjoy a meal, miss a meal, skip a meal **1**
cook a meal, eat a meal, have a meal, order a meal, prepare a meal, serve a meal **2**

ADJ.   big meal, delicious meal, good meal, hot meal, large meal, simple meal, well-balanced meal **2**

mean

① VERB USES
② ADJECTIVE USES
③ NOUN USE

① **mean** ♦♦♦ /miːn/ (**means, meaning, meant**) →Please look at category **18** to see if the expression you are looking for is shown under another headword. **1** V-T If you want to know what a word, code, signal, or gesture **means**, you want to know what it refers to or what its message is. [no cont] ❏ *In modern Welsh, "glas" means "blue."* ❏ *What does "evidence" mean?* **2** V-T If you ask someone what they **mean**, you are asking them to explain exactly what or who they are referring to or what they are intending to say. [no cont] ❏ *Do you mean me?* ❏ *Let me illustrate what I mean with an old story.* **3** V-T If something **means** something to you, it is important to you in some way. [no cont] ❏ *The idea that she witnessed this shameful incident meant nothing to him.* **4** V-T If one thing **means** another, it shows that the second thing exists or is true. [no cont] ❏ *An enlarged prostate does not necessarily mean cancer.* **5** V-T If one thing **means** another, the first thing leads to the second thing happening. [no cont] ❏ *It would almost certainly mean the end of NATO.* **6** V-T If doing one thing **means** doing another, it involves doing the second thing. ❏ *Children universally prefer to live in peace and security, even if that means living with only one parent.* **7** V-T If you say that you **mean** what you are saying, you are telling someone that you are serious about it and are not joking, exaggerating, or just being polite. [no cont] ❏ *He says you're fired if you're not back at work on Friday. And I think he meant it.* **8** V-T If you say that someone **meant to** do something, you are saying that they did it deliberately. [no cont] ❏ *I didn't mean to hurt you.* ❏ *If that sounds harsh, it is meant to.* **9** V-T If you say that someone **did not mean any** harm, offense, or disrespect, you are saying that they did not intend to upset or offend them or to cause problems, even though they may in fact have done so. [no cont, with brd-neg] ❏ *I'm sure he didn't mean any harm.* **10** V-T If you **mean to** do something, you intend or plan to do it. [no cont] ❏ *Summer is the perfect time to catch up on the new books you meant to read.* **11** V-T If you say that something **was meant to** happen, you believe that it was made to happen by God or fate, and did not just happen by chance. [usu passive, no cont] ❏ *John was constantly reassuring me that we were meant to be together.* **12** PHRASE You say "**I mean**" when making clearer something that you have just said. [SPOKEN] ❏ *It was his idea. Gordon's, I mean.* **13** PHRASE You can use "**I mean**" to introduce a statement, especially one that justifies something that you have just said. [SPOKEN] ❏ *I'm sure he wouldn't mind. I mean, I was the one who asked him.* **14** PHRASE You say **I mean** when correcting something that you have just said. [SPOKEN] ❏ *It was law or classics – I mean English or classics.* **15** PHRASE If you **know what it means** to do something, you know everything that is involved in a particular activity or experience, especially the effect that it has on you. ❏ *I know what it means to lose a child under such tragic circumstances.* **16** PHRASE If a name, word, or phrase **means something to** you, you have heard

3 구 푸짐한 식사 ❏ 그 군대는 매우 지쳐 있다. 그들은 4-5일 동안 푸짐한 식사를 하지 못했다.

하루의 첫 식사는 breakfast라고 부른다. 한낮에 먹는 식사에 대해 가장 흔히 쓰는 말은 lunch이지만, 영국의 어떤 지방이나 어떤 상황에서는, dinner도 쓴다. ❏ 그는 좀처럼 점심을 먹는 일이 없다....학교 급식....크리스마스 만찬. 그렇지만, dinner는 주로 저녁 식사를 가리킬 때 쓴다. ❏ ...저녁의 축하 만찬. 영국 영어에서는 dinner가 격식을 갖춘 또는 특별한 식사를 말하기도 한다. 비록 어떤 사람들에게는, supper가 늦은 밤에 먹는 야식이고 tea가 가벼운 오후 식사를 뜻하지만, supper와 tea도 가끔 저녁 식사를 가리킬 때 쓴다.

1 타동사 의미하다 ❏ 현대 웨일스 어로 'glas'는 '파란색'을 의미한다. ❏ 'evidence'가 무슨 뜻이죠? **2** 타동사 의미하다; 의도하다 ❏ 나 말이에요? ❏ 옛날이야기를 예로 들어서 내가 말하려는 것을 설명해 줄게. **3** 타동사 의미가 갖다 ❏ 그녀가 이런 창피한 사건을 목격했다는 것도 그에게는 아무런 의미가 없었다. **4** 타동사 -라는 뜻이다 ❏ 전립선이 확대되었다고 해서 그것이 반드시 암이라는 뜻은 아니다. **5** 타동사 -로 이어지다, 의미하다 ❏ 그것은 거의 확실하게 나토의 해체로 이어질 것이다. **6** 타동사 (결과로) - 하게 되다 ❏ 아이들은 비록 부모 중 한 분과만 살게 된다 할지라도, 보편적으로 평화롭고 안전하게 살기를 더 원한다. **7** 타동사 진심으로 말하다, 농담이 아니다 ❏ 그는 네가 금요일에 다시 회사에 나오지 않으면 해고할 거래. 그리고 내 생각엔 그가 농담한 게 아닌 것 같에. **8** 타동사 의도적으로 하다 ❏ 너를 기분 상하게 할 의도는 없었어. ❏ 그것이 귀에 거슬린다면, 그렇게 하려고 의도했기 때문이다. **9** 타동사 의도를 품다 ❏ 나는 그가 악의가 있었던 것은 아니라고 확신한다. **10** 타동사 계획하다 ❏ 여름은 당신이 읽으려고 계획했던 신간 도서를 모두 읽을 수 있는 절호의 기회이다. **11** 타동사 - 할 운명이다 ❏ 우리는 함께 있어야 할 운명이라고 존이 나를 끈질기게 확신시키고 있었다. **12** 구 내 말 뜻은 [구어체] ❏ 이것은 그 사람 생각이었어, 내 말 뜻은, 고든의 생각이었다고. **13** 구 글쎄 [구어체] ❏ 그 사람은 분명히 신경 안 쓸 거야. 글쎄, 내가 직접 그 사람에게 물어봤다니까. **14** 구 그게 아니라 [구어체] ❏ 법이거나 고전이었어. 아, 그게 아니라 영어이거나 고전이었다고. **15** 구 충분히 이해하다 ❏ 그렇게 참담한 상황에서 아이를 잃는다는 것이 어떤 것인지 나는 충분히 이해한다. **16** 구 들어본 적이 있다 ❏ "아, 개어드너"라며 마치 전에 들어본 적이 있는 것처럼 그가 말했다. **17** 구 - 라는 말이니? (의문문) ❏ 어떤 사고? 크리스티나의 사고 말이니?

it before and you know what it refers to. ☐ *"Oh, Gairdner," he said, as if that meant something to him.* 🔟 PHRASE You use "**you mean**" in a question to check that you have understood what someone has said. ☐ *What accident? You mean Christina's?* 🔟 →see also **meaning, means, meant. if you know what I mean** →see **know**

② **mean** /miːn/ (**meaner, meanest**) 🔟 ADJ If you describe someone as **mean**, you are being critical of them because they are unwilling to spend much money or to use very much of a particular thing. [mainly BRIT, DISAPPROVAL] [AM **cheap, stingy**] ☐ *Don't be mean with fabric, otherwise curtains will end up looking skimpy.* ● **mean**|**ness** N-UNCOUNT ☐ *This very careful attitude to money can sometimes border on meanness.* 🔟 ADJ If you describe an amount as **mean**, you are saying that it is very small. [BRIT, DISAPPROVAL] ☐ *...the meanest grant possible from the local council.* 🔟 ADJ If someone is being **mean**, they are being unkind to another person, for example by not allowing them to do something. ☐ *The little girls had locked themselves in upstairs because Mack had been mean to them.* 🔟 ADJ If you describe a person or animal as **mean**, you are saying that they are very bad-tempered and cruel. [mainly AM] ☐ *The state's former commissioner of prisons once called Leonard the meanest man he'd ever seen.*

③ **mean** /miːn/ N-SING The **mean** is a number that is the average of a set of numbers. ☐ *Take a hundred and twenty values and calculate the mean.* →see also **means**

me|**ander** /miˈændər/ (**meanders, meandering, meandered**) 🔟 V-I If a river or road **meanders**, it has a lot of bends, rather than going in a straight line from one place to another. ☐ *We took a gravel road that meandered through farmland.* 🔟 V-I If you **meander** somewhere, you move slowly and not in a straight line. ☐ *We meandered through a landscape of mountains, rivers, and vineyards.*

mean|**ing** ♦◇◇ /miːnɪŋ/ (**meanings**) 🔟 N-VAR The **meaning** of a word, expression, or gesture is the thing or idea that it refers to or represents and which can be explained using other words. ☐ *I hadn't a clue to the meaning of "activism."* 🔟 N-VAR The **meaning** of what someone says or of something such as a book or film is the thoughts or ideas that are intended to be expressed by it. ☐ *Unsure of the meaning of this remark, Ryle chose to remain silent.* 🔟 N-UNCOUNT If an activity or action has **meaning**, it has a purpose and is worthwhile. ☐ *Art has real meaning when it helps people to understand themselves.*

mean|**ing**|**ful** /miːnɪŋfəl/ 🔟 ADJ If you describe something as **meaningful**, you mean that it is serious, important, or useful in some way. ☐ *She believes these talks will be the start of a constructive and meaningful dialogue.* 🔟 ADJ A **meaningful** look or gesture is one that is intended to express something, usually to a particular person, without anything being said. [ADJ n] ☐ *Upon the utterance of this word, Dan and Harry exchanged a quick, meaningful look.* ● **mean**|**ing**|**ful**|**ly** ADV ☐ *He glanced meaningfully at the other policeman, then he went up the stairs.*

mean|**ing**|**less** /miːnɪŋlɪs/ 🔟 ADJ If something that someone says or writes is **meaningless**, it has no meaning, or appears to have no meaning. ☐ *The sentence "kicked the ball the man" is meaningless.* 🔟 ADJ Something that is **meaningless** in a particular situation is not important or relevant. ☐ *Fines are meaningless to guys earning millions.* 🔟 ADJ If something that you do is **meaningless**, it has no purpose and is not at all worthwhile. ☐ *They seek strong sensations to dull their sense of a meaningless existence.*

means ♦◇◇ /miːnz/ 🔟 N-COUNT A **means** of doing something is a method, instrument, or process which can be used to do it. **Means** is both the singular and the plural form for this use. ☐ *The move is a means to fight crime.* ☐ *The army had perfected the use of terror as a means of controlling the population.* 🔟 N-PLURAL You can refer to the money that someone has as their **means**. [FORMAL] ☐ *...a person of means.* 🔟 PHRASE If you do something **by means of** a particular method, instrument, or process, you do it using that method, instrument, or process. ☐ *This is a two year course taught by means of lectures and seminars.* 🔟 CONVENTION You can say "**by all means**" to tell someone that you are very willing to allow them to do something. [FORMULAE] ☐ *"Can I come and have a look at your house?" — "Yes, by all means."*

meant /ment/ 🔟 **Meant** is the past tense and past participle of **mean**. 🔟 ADJ You use **meant to** to say that something or someone was intended to be or do a particular thing, especially when they have failed to be or to do it. [v-link ADJ

🔟 형용사 인색한 [주로 영국영어, 탐탁잖음] [미국영어 cheap, stingy] ☐ 커튼 감에 너무 인색하지 마라, 그렇지 않으면 커튼이 꽉 쬐어 보일 거야. ● 인색함 불가산명사 ☐ 돈 쓰는 것에 대해 너무 조심하는 이런 태도가 때로는 인색함에 가까울 수 있다. 🔟 형용사 아주 작은 [영국영어, 탐탁잖음] ☐ 지방 의회로부터 받을 수 있는 쥐꼬리만한 보조금 🔟 형용사 심술궂은 ☐ 맥이 그 여자애들에게 심술궂게 굴었기 때문에 그들은 2층에 올라가 꼼짝하지 않았다. 🔟 형용사 비열한 [주로 미국영어] ☐ 언젠가 주 교도소의 선임 소장이 레너드를 그가 만나본 사람 중에 가장 비열한 사람이라고 말했다.

단수명사 중간값 ☐ 120개의 수치를 잡아서 중간값을 계산해라.

🔟 자동사 구불구불하다 ☐ 우리는 경작지 사이로 구불구불 난 자갈길로 들어섰다. 🔟 자동사 이리저리 간다 ☐ 우리는 산과 강과 포도밭이 그림처럼 어우러진 곳을 이리저리 걸었다.

🔟 가산명사 또는 불가산명사 의미 ☐ 나는 'activism'의 의미를 알 수가 없었다. 🔟 가산명사 또는 불가산명사 의도 ☐ 이 말의 의도에 확신할 수 없어서 라일은 잠자코 있기로 했다. 🔟 불가산명사 가치 ☐ 예술은 사람들이 자기 스스로를 이해할 수 있도록 도와줄 수 있을 때 진정한 가치가 있다.

🔟 형용사 의미 있는 ☐ 그녀는 이런 회담이 건설적이고 의미 있는 대화의 시발점이 될 것이라고 생각한다. 🔟 형용사 의미심장한 ☐ 이 말이 나오자마자, 댄과 해리가 서로 재빨리 의미심장한 눈길을 주고받았다. ● 의미심장하게 부사 ☐ 그는 다른 경찰관을 의미심장하게 힐끗 쳐다보더니 위층으로 올라갔다.

🔟 형용사 의미 없는 ☐ "kicked the ball the man" 이라는 문장은 아무런 의미가 없다. 🔟 형용사 의미 없는, 중요하지 않은 ☐ 수백만 달러를 버는 사람들에게는 벌금이 아무 의미가 없다. 🔟 형용사 무가치한 ☐ 그들은 자신들이 무가치한 존재라는 생각을 떨쳐버릴 수 있도록 강력히 감각적인 것을 찾고 있다.

🔟 가산명사 수단 ☐ 그 조치는 범죄와 싸우기 위한 하나의 수단이다. ☐ 육군은 주민 통제의 수단으로서 테러를 십분 활용했다. 🔟 복수명사 재산 [격식체] ☐ 재산가 🔟 구 -을 통해 ☐ 이것은 강연과 세미나를 통해 배우는 2년 과정의 강좌이다. 🔟 관용 표현 물론 [의례적인 표현] ☐ "당신 집을 한 번 봐도 좋겠습니까?" "예, 물론이지요."

🔟 mean의 과거, 과거 분사 🔟 형용사 – 하기로 되어 있는 ☐ 나는 더 이상 말할 수 없어. 그것은 중대한 비밀이거든. ☐ 모든 것이 사무적으로 되어 있었다.

A

to-inf] ❑ *I can't say any more, it's meant to be a big secret.* ❑ *Everything is meant to be businesslike.* **3** ADJ If something **is meant for** particular people or for a particular situation, it is intended for those people or for that situation. [v-link ADJ for n] ❑ *Fairy tales weren't just meant for children.* ❑ *The seeds were not meant for human consumption.* **4** PHRASE If you say that something **is meant to** happen, you mean that it is expected to happen or that it ought to happen. ❑ *The peculiar thing about getting engaged is that you're meant to announce it to everyone.* **5** PHRASE If you say that something **is meant to** have a particular quality or characteristic, you mean that it has a reputation for being like that. ❑ *Spurs are meant to be one of the top teams in the world.*

meantime /ˈmiːntaɪm/ **1** PHRASE **In the meantime** or **meantime** means in the period of time between two events. ❑ *Eventually your child will leave home to lead her own life as a fully independent adult, but in the meantime she relies on your support.* **2** PHRASE **For the meantime** means for a period of time from now until something else happens. ❑ *The Prime Minister has, for the meantime, seen off the challenge of the opposition.*

meanwhile ◆◇◇ /ˈmiːnwaɪl/ **1** ADV **Meanwhile** means while a particular thing is happening. [ADV with cl] ❑ *Brush the aubergines with oil, add salt and pepper, and bake till soft. Meanwhile, heat the remaining oil in a heavy pan.* **2** ADV **Meanwhile** means in the period of time between two events. [ADV with cl] ❑ *You needn't worry; I'll be ready to greet them. Meanwhile I'm off to discuss the Fowlers' party with Felix.* **3** ADV You use **meanwhile** to introduce a different aspect of a particular situation, especially one that is completely opposite to the one previously mentioned. [ADV with cl] ❑ *Personally, he had always found his wife's mother a bit annoying. The mother-daughter relationship, meanwhile, was close, and he understandably felt like an outsider.*

measles /ˈmiːzəlz/ N-UNCOUNT **Measles** is an infectious illness that gives you a high temperature and red spots on your skin. [also the N] →see **hospital**

measurable /ˈmeʒərəbəl/ **1** ADJ If you describe something as **measurable**, you mean that it is large enough to be noticed or to be significant. [FORMAL] ❑ *Both leaders seemed to expect measurable progress.* **2** ADJ Something that is **measurable** can be measured. ❑ *Economists emphasize measurable quantities – the number of jobs, the per capita income.*

measure ◆◆◇ /ˈmeʒər/ (measures, measuring, measured) **1** V-T If you **measure** the quality, value, or effect of something, you discover or judge how great it is. ❑ *I continued to measure his progress against the charts in the doctor's office.* **2** V-T If you **measure** a quantity that can be expressed in numbers, such as the length of something, you discover it using a particular instrument or device, for example a ruler. ❑ *Measure the length and width of the gap.* **3** V-T If something **measures** a particular length, width, or amount, that is its size or intensity, expressed in numbers. [no cont] ❑ *It measures two-hundred-thirty-eight meters from side to side.* **4** N-SING A **measure of** a particular quality, feeling, or activity is a fairly large amount of it. [FORMAL] ❑ *With the exception of Juan, each attained a measure of success.* **5** N-SING If you say that one aspect of a situation is **a measure of** that situation, you mean that it shows that the situation is very serious or has developed to a very great extent. ❑ *That is a measure of how bad things have become at the bank.* **6** N-COUNT When someone, usually a government or other authority, takes **measures** to do something, they carry out particular actions in order to achieve a particular result. [FORMAL] ❑ *The government warned that police would take tougher measures to contain the trouble.* **7** N-COUNT A **measure of** a strong alcoholic drink such as brandy or whiskey is an amount of it in a glass. In bars, a **measure** is an official standard amount. ❑ *He poured himself another generous measure of malt.* **8** N-COUNT In music, a **measure** is one of the several short parts of the same length into which a piece of music is divided. [AM; BRIT **bar**] ❑ *Malcolm wanted to mix the beginning of a sonata, then add Beethoven for a few measures, then go back to Bach.* **9** →see also **tape measure** **10** PHRASE If you say that something has changed or that it has affected you **beyond measure**, you are emphasizing that it has done this to a great extent. [EMPHASIS] ❑ *Mankind's knowledge of the universe has increased beyond measure.* →see **mathematics**

▶**measure up** PHRASAL VERB If you do not **measure up to** a standard or to someone's expectations, you are not good enough to achieve the standard or fulfil the person's expectations. ❑ *It was fatiguing sometimes to try to measure up to her standard of perfection.*

Word Partnership	*measure*의 연어
N.	measure **intelligence**, measure **performance**, measure **progress** **1** **tests** measure **1**-**3**
	emergency measure, **safety** measure, **security** measure **6**
V.	**adopt a** measure, **approve a** measure, **support a** measure, **veto a** measure **6**
ADJ.	**drastic** measure, **economic** measure **6**

measurement /ˈmeʒərmənt/ (measurements) **1** N-COUNT A **measurement** is a result, usually expressed in numbers, that you obtain by measuring something. ❑ *We took lots of measurements.* **2** N-VAR **Measurement** of something is the process of measuring it in order to obtain a result expressed in numbers. ❑ *Tests include measurement of height, weight, and blood pressure.* **3** N-VAR The **measurement** of the quality, value, or effect of something is the activity of deciding how great it is. ❑ *The measurement of intelligence has been the greatest achievement of twentieth-century scientific psychology.* **4** N-PLURAL Your **measurements** are the size of your waist, chest, hips, and other parts of your body, which you need to know when you are buying clothes. ❑ *I know all her measurements and find it easy to buy stuff she likes.*

3 형용사 ~를 위한 ❑ 동화는 단지 아이들만을 위한 것이 아니었다. ❑ 그 씨앗은 인간이 먹기 위한 것은 아니었다. **4** 구 ~하기로 되어 있다 ❑ 약혼하는 데 있어서 특이한 것은 모든 사람에게 그 사실을 선언하기로 되어 있다는 것이다. **5** 구 마땅히 ~ 하다 ❑ 스퍼스는 마땅히 전 세계에서 최고의 팀 중 하나가 될 것이다.

1 구 그 동안은 ❑ 당신의 아이가 결국에는 완전히 독립된 성인으로서 자신의 삶을 위해 집을 떠나겠지만, 그 동안은 당신의 보살핌을 필요로 한다. **2** 구 당장은 ❑ 총리가 야당이 제기한 난제를 당장은 해결했다.

1 부사 그러는 동안 ❑ 가지에 기름을 살짝 바르고 소금과 후추를 뿌린 후 부드러워질 때까지 구워라. 그러는 동안 두꺼운 팬에 남아 있는 기름을 달궈라. **2** 부사 그 사이에 ❑ 넌 걱정할 필요 없어. 내가 그들을 맞이할 준비가 될 거야. 그 사이에 난 펠릭스와 파울러의 파티에 대해서 상의하러 갈게. **3** 부사 한편으로는 ❑ 그는 개인적으로 자기 장모가 좀 짜증스럽다고 늘 생각했다. 한편으로는, 어머니와 딸의 관계가 가까웠고, 그렇다 보니 자연히 그는 자신이 이방인인 것처럼 느껴졌다.

불가산명사 홍역

1 형용사 상당히 큰 [격식체] ❑ 두 지도자들은 모두 상당히 큰 진전을 기대하는 것 같았다. **2** 형용사 측정할 수 있는 ❑ 경제학자들은 일자리의 수나 1인당 소득과 같은 측정할 수 있는 수치를 강조한다.

1 타동사 측정하다 ❑ 나는 의사의 차트와 비교해 가며 그의 진행 상태를 계속 측정했다. **2** 타동사 자로 재다 ❑ 빈틈의 길이와 폭을 자로 재시오. **3** 타동사 (수치가) ~이다 ❑ 좌우의 길이가 238미터이다. **4** 단수명사 상당한 양 [격식체] ❑ 후안만 빼고는 각기 상당한 성공을 이루었다. **5** 단수명사 척도 ❑ 그것이 그 은행에서 어떻게 일이 잘못되고 있는지를 보여 주는 척도이다. **6** 가산명사 조치 [격식체] ❑ 경찰이 그 소란을 진압하기 위해서 더 강력한 조치를 취할 것이라고 정부는 경고했다. **7** 가산명사 일정량 ❑ 그는 자기가 마실 위스키를 또 한 잔 가득 따랐다. **8** 가산명사 (음악) 소절 [미국영어; 영국영어 bar] ❑ 말콤은 소나타의 도입 부분을 섞은 다음 베토벤 곡을 몇소절을 더 넣고, 다시 바흐 곡으로 돌아가고 싶어 했다. **10** 구 상당히 많이 [강조] ❑ 우주에 대한 인류의 지식이 상당히 많이 증가했다.

구동사 기대에 미치다 ❑ 그녀의 완벽한 수준에 맞추는 것이 때로는 피곤한 일이었다.

1 가산명사 치수 ❑ 우리는 많은 치수를 쟀다. **2** 가산명사 또는 불가산명사 측정 ❑ 검진은 키, 몸무게, 혈압 측정을 포함한다. **3** 가산명사 또는 불가산명사 측정 ❑ 지능을 측정할 수 있게 된 것은 20세기 과학 심리학이 이룬 가장 큰 성과였다. **4** 복수명사 신체 치수 ❑ 나는 그녀 신체 치수를 모두 알고 있어서 그녀가 좋아하는 물건을 사기 쉽다.

meat ◆◇◇ /mi:t/ (**meats**) N-MASS **Meat** is flesh taken from a dead animal that people cook and eat. ❑ *Meat and fish are relatively expensive.* ❑ *...imported meat products.* →see **vegetarian**
→see Word Web: **meat**

물질명사 고기 ❑ 고기와 생선은 비교적 비싸다. ❑ 수입산 육류 제품

meaty /mi:ti/ (**meatier, meatiest**) **1** ADJ Food that is **meaty** contains a lot of meat. ❑ *...a pleasant lasagne with a meaty sauce.* **2** ADJ You can describe something such as a piece of writing or a part in a movie as **meaty** if it contains a lot of interesting or important material. ❑ *The short, meaty reports are those he likes best.*

1 형용사 고기가 많은 ❑ 고기가 많이 들어간 소스를 얹은 맛 좋은 라자냐 **2** 형용사 내용이 충실한 ❑ 간략하고도 내용이 충실한 보고서가 그가 제일 좋아하는 것이다.

me|chan|ic /mɪkænɪk/ (**mechanics**) **1** N-COUNT A **mechanic** is someone whose job is to repair and maintain machines and engines, especially car engines. ❑ *If you smell something unusual (gas fumes or burning, for instance), take the car to your mechanic.* **2** N-PLURAL The **mechanics of** a process, system, or activity are the way in which it works or the way in which it is done. ❑ *What are the mechanics of this new process?* **3** N-UNCOUNT **Mechanics** is the part of physics that deals with the natural forces that act on moving or stationary objects. ❑ *He has not studied mechanics or engineering.*

1 가산명사 기계 정비 기사 ❑ 만약 이상한 냄새가 나거든 (예를 들어, 가스 냄새나 타는 냄새), 차를 정비 기사에게로 가져가라. **2** 복수명사 기술 ❑ 이 새로운 공정의 기술은 무엇입니까? **3** 불가산명사 역학 ❑ 그는 역학이나 공학 공부를 하지 않았다.

me|chani|cal /mɪkænɪkᵊl/ **1** ADJ A **mechanical** device has parts that move when it is working, often using power from an engine or from electricity. ❑ *...a small mechanical device that taps out the numbers.* ❑ *...the oldest working mechanical clock in the world.* ● **me|chani|cal|ly** /mɪkænɪkli/ ADV [ADV with v] ❑ *The air was circulated mechanically.* **2** ADJ **Mechanical** means relating to machines and engines and the way they work. [ADV n] ❑ *...mechanical engineering.* ● **me|chani|cal|ly** ADV [ADV adj/-ed] ❑ *The car was mechanically sound, he decided.* **3** ADJ If you describe a person as **mechanical**, you mean they are naturally good at understanding how machines work. ❑ *He was a very mechanical person, who knew a lot about sound.* ● **me|chani|cal|ly** ADV [ADV -ed] ❑ *I'm not mechanically minded.* **4** ADJ If you describe someone's action as **mechanical**, you mean that they do it automatically, without thinking about it. ❑ *It is real prayer, and not mechanical repetition.* ● **me|chani|cal|ly** ADV [ADV with v] ❑ *He nodded mechanically, his eyes fixed on the girl.*

1 형용사 기계적인, 자동적인 ❑ 숫자를 입력하는 작은 기계 장치 ❑ 아직도 작동하는 세상에서 제일 오래된 자동 괘종시계 ● 자동적으로 부사 ❑ 공기가 자동적으로 순환되었다. **2** 형용사 기계적인 ❑ 기계 공학 ● 기계적으로 부사 ❑ 그 자동차는 기계가 튼튼하다고 그는 판단했다. **3** 형용사 기계에 대해 잘 아는 ❑ 그는 기계에 아주 밝아서 소리에 대해서도 잘 알았다. ● 기계적으로 부사 ❑ 나는 기계에 대해서는 관심이 없다. **4** 형용사 기계적인 ❑ 그것은 기계적인 반복이 아니라 진정한 기도이다. ● 기계적으로 부사 ❑ 그는 두 눈을 그 소녀에게 고정시킨 채, 그저 기계적으로 고개만 끄덕였다.

mecha|nism ◆◇◇ /mɛkənɪzəm/ (**mechanisms**) **1** N-COUNT In a machine or piece of equipment, a **mechanism** is a part, often consisting of a set of smaller parts, which performs a particular function. ❑ *...the locking mechanism.* **2** N-COUNT A **mechanism** is a special way of getting something done within a particular system. ❑ *There's no mechanism for punishing arms exporters who break the rules.* **3** N-COUNT A **mechanism** is a part of your behavior that is automatic and that helps you to survive or to cope with a difficult situation. ❑ *...a survival mechanism, a means of coping with intolerable stress.*

1 가산명사 기계 장치 ❑ 잠금장치 **2** 가산명사 메커니즘, (정해진) 절차 ❑ 법을 어기고 무기를 수출하는 사람들을 처벌하기 위한 메커니즘이 없다. **3** 가산명사 심리 기제 ❑ 견딜 수 없을 정도의 스트레스를 해결하는 수단인 생존 기제

mecha|nize /mɛkənaɪz/ (**mechanizes, mechanizing, mechanized**) [BRIT also **mechanise**] V-T If someone **mechanizes** a process, they cause it to be done by a machine or machines, when it was previously done by people. ❑ *Only gradually are technologies being developed to mechanize the task.* ● **mecha|ni|za|tion** /mɛkənaɪzeɪʃᵊn/ N-UNCOUNT ❑ *Mechanization happened years ago on the farms of Islay.*

[영국영어 mechanise] 타동사 기계화하다 ❑ 그 작업을 기계화할 수 있는 기술은 아주 점진적으로 발달하고 있다. ● 기계 불가산명사 ❑ 이슬레이 농장에서는 수년 전에 기계화가 이루어졌다.

med|al ◆◇◇ /mɛdᵊl/ (**medals**) N-COUNT A **medal** is a small metal disk which is given as an award for bravery or as a prize in a sports event. ❑ *Dufour was awarded his country's highest medal for bravery.*

가산명사 훈장, 메달 ❑ 두포는 국가 최고의 무공훈장을 받았다.

med|dle /mɛdᵊl/ (**meddles, meddling, meddled**) V-I If you say that someone **meddles** in something, you are criticizing the fact that they try to influence or change it without being asked. [DISAPPROVAL] ❑ *Already some people are asking whether scientists have any right to meddle in such matters.* ❑ *If only you hadn't felt compelled to meddle.*

자동사 간섭하다 [탐탁잖음] ❑ 이미 일부 사람들은 과학자들이 그런 문제에 간섭할 권리가 있는지에 대해 묻고 있는 중이다. ❑ 네가 무리하게 참견하지 않았더라면 좋았을 텐데.

Word Link   med ≈ middle : inter**med**iary, **med**ia, **med**iate

---

me|dia ◆◆◇ /mi:diə/ **1** N-SING-COLL You can refer to television, radio, newspapers, and magazines as **the media**. ❑ *It is hard work and not a glamorous job as portrayed by the media.* ❑ *They are wondering whether bias in the news media contributed to the president's defeat.* →see also **mass media, multimedia 2** **Media** is a plural of **medium**. →see **library**

1 단수명사-집합 대중 매체, 매스컴 ❑ 그것은 힘든 일이며 대중 매체에서 묘사하는 것처럼 매력적인 직업이 아니다. ❑ 그들은 보도 매체의 편향된 보도가 대통령이 패배한 일부 원인이 된 것이 아닐까 생각하고 있다. **2** medium의 복수

me|dia cir|cus (**media circuses**) N-COUNT If an event is described as a **media circus**, a large group of people from the media is there to report on it and take photographs. [DISAPPROVAL] ❑ *...the couple married in the Caribbean to avoid a media circus.*

가산명사 지나친 취재 열기 [탐탁잖음] ❑ 그 부부는 지나친 취재 열기를 피해 카리브 해에서 결혼을 했다.

me|di|aeval /mɛdiiːvᵊl, mɪdiiːvᵊl, BRIT mɛdiiːvᵊl/ →see **medieval**

me|di|ate /mi:dieɪt/ (**mediates, mediating, mediated**) V-T/V-I If someone **mediates between** two groups of people, or **mediates** an agreement **between**

타동사/자동사 중재하다 ❑ 젤다와 그녀의 어머니 사이에서 중재한 사람이 바로 우리 엄마였다. ❑ 국제

Word Web   meat

The English language has different words for animals and the **meat** that comes from them. In the year 1066 AD the Anglo-Saxons of England lost a major battle to the French-speaking Normans. As a result, the Normans became the ruling class and the Anglo-Saxons worked on farms. The Anglo-Saxons tended the animals. They tended **sheep, cows, chickens**, and **pigs** in the fields. The wealthier Normans, who purchased and ate the meat from these animals, used different words. They bought "mouton," which became the word **mutton**, "bouef," which became **beef**, "poulet," which became **poultry**, and "porc," which became **pork**.

<table>
<tr><td>A</td><td></td></tr>
</table>

them, they try to settle an argument between them by talking to both groups and trying to find things that they can both agree to. ❑ *My mom was the one who mediated between Zelda and her mom.* ❑ *United Nations officials have mediated a series of peace meetings between the two sides.* ● me|di|a|tion /miːdieɪʃ³n/ N-UNCOUNT ❑ *The agreement provides for United Nations mediation between the two sides.* ● me|di|a|tor (mediators) N-COUNT ❑ *An archbishop has been acting as mediator between the rebels and the authorities.*

연합 관리들이 양측 간의 연속된 평화 회담을 중재해 왔다. ● 중재 불가산명사 ❑ 그 협정에 따라 국제 연합이 양측 간의 중재를 마련할 수 있다. ● 중재자 가산명사 ❑ 대주교가 반군들과 당국 간에 중재자의 역할을 해 오고 있다.

med|i|cal ♦♦♢ /mɛdɪk³l/ (medicals) **1** ADJ **Medical** means relating to illness and injuries and to their treatment or prevention. [ADJ n] ❑ *Several police officers received medical treatment for cuts and bruises.* ● medi|cal|ly /mɛdɪkli/ ADV ❑ *Therapists cannot prescribe drugs as they are not necessarily medically qualified.* **2** N-COUNT A **medical** is a thorough examination of your body by a doctor, for example before you start a new job. ❑ *I'm fine, sir. I had a medical only last week.*

1 형용사 의료의, 의학의 ❑ 경관 몇 명이 자상 및 타박상으로 치료를 받았다. ● 의학적으로 부사 ❑ 치료사들이 반드시 의학적으로 자격을 갖춘 것은 아니므로 약을 처방할 수 없다. **2** 가산명사 건강 진단 ❑ 저는 건강합니다, 선생님. 바로 지난주에 건강 진단을 받았거든요.

Word Partnership   medical의 연어

N.	medical **advice**, medical **attention**, medical **bills**, medical **care**, medical **center**, medical **doctor**, medical **emergency**, medical **practice**, medical **problems**, medical **research**, medical **science**, medical **supplies**, medical **tests**, medical **treatment** **1**

medi|ca|tion /mɛdɪkeɪʃ³n/ (medications) N-VAR **Medication** is medicine that is used to treat and cure illness. ❑ *When somebody comes for treatment I always ask them if they are on any medication.*

가산명사 또는 불가산명사 약물, 의약품 ❑ 누군가가 치료를 받으러 오면 나는 혹시 먹고 있는 약이 있는지를 항상 묻는다.

me|dici|nal /mədɪsən³l/ ADJ **Medicinal** substances or substances with **medicinal** effects can be used to treat and cure illnesses. ❑ *...medicinal plants.*

형용사 의학의 ❑ 약용 식물

medi|cine ♦♢♢ /mɛdɪsɪn, BRIT mɛds³n/ (medicines) **1** N-UNCOUNT **Medicine** is the treatment of illness and injuries by doctors and nurses. ❑ *He pursued a career in medicine.* ❑ *I was interested in alternative medicine and becoming an aromatherapist.* **2** N-MASS **Medicine** is a substance that you drink or swallow in order to cure an illness. ❑ *People in hospitals are dying because of shortage of medicine.*
→see Word Web: medicine

1 불가산명사 의료, 의학 ❑ 그는 의료 분야의 직업을 갖기 위한 교육을 받았다. ❑ 나는 대체 의학과 방향 요법 치료사가 되는 것에 흥미를 느꼈다. **2** 물질명사 의약품 ❑ 의약품 부족으로 병원에서 사람들이 죽어간다.

Word Partnership   medicine의 연어

V.	**practice** medicine, **study** medicine **1** **give** *someone* medicine, **take** medicine, **use** medicine **2**

me|di|eval /miːdiiːv³l, mɪdiːv³l, BRIT mɛdiiːv³l/ [BRIT also mediaeval] ADJ Something that is **medieval** relates to or was made in the period of European history between the end of the Roman Empire in A.D. 476 and about A.D. 1500. ❑ *...a medieval castle.*

[영국영어 mediaeval] 형용사 중세의 ❑ 중세의 성채

me|dio|cre /miːdioʊkər/ ADJ If you describe something as **mediocre**, you mean that it is of average quality but you think it should be better. [DISAPPROVAL] ❑ *His school record was mediocre.*

형용사 그저 그런, 보통의 [탐탁찮음] ❑ 그의 학교 성적은 그저 그랬다.

me|di|oc|rity /miːdiɒkrɪti/ N-UNCOUNT If you refer to the **mediocrity** of something, you mean that it is of average quality but you think it should be better. [DISAPPROVAL] ❑ *...the mediocrity of most contemporary literature.*

불가산명사 평범함, 보통밖에 안 됨 [탐탁찮음] ❑ 현대 문학 작품 대다수에서 보여 지는 평범함

medi|tate /mɛdɪteɪt/ (meditates, meditating, meditated) **1** V-I If you **meditate on** something, you think about it very carefully and deeply for a long time. ❑ *On the day her son began school, she meditated on the uncertainties of his future.* **2** V-I If you **meditate** you remain in a silent and calm state for a period of time, as part of a religious training or so that you are more able to deal with the problems and difficulties of everyday life. ❑ *I was meditating, and reached a higher state of consciousness.*

1 자동사 ~에 대해 곰곰이 생각하다 ❑ 아들이 처음으로 등교한 날, 그녀는 불확실한 아들의 미래에 대해 곰곰이 생각했다. **2** 자동사 명상하다 ❑ 명상하던 중에 나는 보다 높은 차원의 정신세계에 도달했다.

medi|ta|tion /mɛdɪteɪʃ³n/ N-UNCOUNT **Meditation** is the act of remaining in a silent and calm state for a period of time, as part of a religious training, or so that you are more able to deal with the problems and difficulties of everyday life. ❑ *Many busy executives have begun to practice yoga and meditation.*

불가산명사 명상 ❑ 쉴 틈 없는 중역들 다수가 요가와 명상을 시작했다.

Medi|ter|ra|nean /mɛdɪtəreɪniən/ **1** N-PROPER The **Mediterranean** is the sea between southern Europe and North Africa. ❑ *You have the choice of night fishing in the Mediterranean, or wind-surfing on a lake in the Creuse.* **2** N-PROPER The **Mediterranean** refers to the southern part of Europe, which is next to the

1 고유명사 지중해 ❑ 지중해에서의 밤낚시와 크루즈에 있는 호수에서의 윈드서핑 중에서 선택하실 수 있습니다. **2** 고유명사 지중해 연안 ❑ 바르셀로나는 지중해 연안에서 가장 역동적이고 번창한 도시 중

Word Web   medicine

Western **medicine** began in ancient Greece. The Greek philosopher Hippocrates separated medicine from religion and **disease** from supernatural explanations. He is also responsible for the Hippocratic oath which describes a **physician's** duties. During the Middle Ages, Andreas Vesalius helped to advance medicine through his **research** on anatomy. Another major step forward was Friedrich Henle's development of **germ** theory. An understanding of germs led to Joseph Lister's demonstrations of the effective use of **antiseptics**, and Alexander Fleming's discovery of the **antibiotic** penicillin.

400 BC	1500	1790	1840	1860	1900	1920
400 BC Hippocrates the Hippocratic oath	1500s Andreas Vesalius anatomy	1790s Friedrich Henle germ theory	1840s Charles Jackson anesthetic	1860s Joseph Lister antiseptic	1900s Karl Landsteiner blood type system	1920s Alexander Fleming antibiotics

Important Medical Advances

Mediterranean Sea. ❑ *Barcelona has become one of the most dynamic and prosperous cities in the Mediterranean.*

me|di|um ♦♢♢ /míːdiəm/ (mediums, media)

> The plural of the noun can be either **mediums** or **media** for meanings ◢ and ◣. The form **mediums** is the plural for meaning ◖.

◢ ADJ If something is of **medium** size, it is neither large nor small, but approximately half way between the two. ❑ *A medium dose produces severe nausea within hours.* ◣ ADJ You use **medium** to describe something which is average in degree or amount, or approximately half way along a scale between two extremes. ❑ *Foods that contain only medium levels of sodium are bread, cakes, milk, butter, and margarine.* ● ADV **Medium** is also an adverb. [ADV adj] ❑ *Toast by stirring in a medium-hot skillet for a few minutes.* ◥ COMB IN COLOR If something is of a **medium** color, it is neither light nor dark, but approximately half way between the two. ❑ *Andrea has medium brown hair, gray eyes, and very pale skin.* ◤ N-COUNT A **medium** is a way or means of expressing your ideas or of communicating with people. ❑ *In Sierra Leone, English is used as the medium of instruction for all primary education.* ◢ N-COUNT A **medium** is a substance or material which is used for a particular purpose or in order to produce a particular effect. ❑ *Blood is the medium in which oxygen is carried to all parts of the body.* ◖ N-COUNT A **medium** is a person who claims to be able to contact and speak to people who are dead, and to pass messages between them and people who are still alive. ❑ *Bruce Willis says he has been talking to his dead brother through a medium.* ◗ →see also **media**

medium-term N-SING The **medium-term** is the period of time which lasts a few months or years beyond the present time, in contrast with the short term or the long term. ❑ *Economists had been arguing that the medium-term economic prospects remained poor.*

meek /miːk/ (meeker, meekest) ADJ If you describe a person as **meek**, you think that they are gentle and quiet, and likely to do what other people say. ❑ *He was a meek, mild-mannered fellow.* ● **meek|ly** ADV [ADV with v] ❑ *Most have meekly accepted such advice.*

meet ♦♦♦ /miːt/ (meets, meeting, met) ◢ V-RECIP If you **meet** someone, you happen to be in the same place as them and start talking to them. You may know the other person, but be surprised to see them, or you may not know them at all. ❑ *I have just met the man I want to spend the rest of my life with.* ❑ *He's the kindest and sincerest person I've ever met.* ● PHRASAL VERB-RECIP **Meet up** means the same as **meet**. ❑ *Last night, when he was parking my automobile, he met up with a buddy he had at Oxford.* ◣ V-RECIP If two or more people **meet**, they go to the same place, which they have earlier arranged to do, so that they can talk or do something together. ❑ *We could meet for a drink after work.* ● PHRASAL VERB-RECIP **Meet up** means the same as **meet**. ❑ *We tend to meet up for lunch once a week.* ◥ V-T If you **meet** someone, you are introduced to them and begin talking to them and getting to know them. ❑ *Hey, Terry, come and meet my Dad.* ◤ V-T You use **meet** in expressions such as "**Pleased to meet you**" and "**Nice to have met you**" when you want to politely say hello or goodbye to someone you have just met for the first time. [FORMULAE] ❑ *"Jennifer," Miss Mallory said, "this is Leigh Van-Voreen." — "Pleased to meet you," Jennifer said.* ◢ V-T If you **meet** someone off their train, plane, or bus, you go to the station, airport, or bus stop in order to be there when they arrive. ❑ *Mama met me at the station.* ❑ *Lili and my father met me off the boat.* ◖ V-I When a group of people such as a committee **meet**, they gather together for a particular purpose. ❑ *Officials from the two countries will meet again soon to resume negotiations.* ◗ V-I If you **meet with** someone, you have a meeting with them. [mainly AM] ❑ *Most of the lawmakers who met with the president yesterday said they backed the mission.* ◘ V-T/V-I If something such as a suggestion, proposal, or new book **meets with** or **is met with** a particular reaction, it gets that reaction from people. ❑ *The idea met with a cool response from various quarters.* ❑ *We hope today's offer will meet with your approval too.* ◙ V-T If something **meets** a need, requirement, or condition, it is good enough to do what is required. ❑ *He suggested that the current arrangements for the care of severely mentally ill people are inadequate to meet their needs.* ◢◢ V-T If you **meet** something such as a problem or challenge, you deal with it satisfactorily or do what is required. ❑ *British manufacturing failed to meet the crisis of the 1970s.* ◢◣ V-T If you **meet** the cost of something, you provide the money that is needed for it. ❑ *The government said it will help meet some of the cost of the damage.* ◢◥ V-T If you **meet** a situation, attitude, or problem, you experience it or become aware of it. ❑ *I honestly don't know how I will react the next time I meet a potentially dangerous situation.* ◢◤ V-I You can say that someone **meets with** success or failure when they are successful or unsuccessful. ❑ *Attempts to find civilian volunteers have met with embarrassing failure.* ◢◢ V-RECIP When a moving object **meets** another object, it hits or touches it. ❑ *You sense the stresses in the hull each time the keel meets the ground.* ◢◖ V-RECIP If your eyes **meet** someone else's, you both look at each other at the same time. [WRITTEN] ❑ *As he came closer, his eyes met mine for an instant.* ◢◗ V-RECIP If two areas **meet**, especially two areas of land or sea, they are next to one another. ❑ *It is one of the rare places in the world where the desert meets the sea.* ◢◘ V-RECIP The place where two lines **meet** is the place where they join together. ❑ *Parallel lines will never meet no matter how far extended.* ◢◙ to **make ends meet** →see **end**. to **meet** someone **halfway** →see **halfway**

Thesaurus		*meet*의 참조어
v.	bump into, encounter, run into	◢
	get together	◣
	gather	◖
	comply with, follow, fulfill	◙

하나로 성장했다.

이 명사의 복수는 ◢ 또는 ◣ 의미로는 mediums 또는 media를 쓸 수 있다. mediums는 ◖ 의미의 복수이다.

◢ 형용사 절반쯤의, 중간의 ❑ 1회 복용량의 절반쯤만 복용해도 몇 시간 안에 심한 메스꺼움을 느끼게 된다. ◣ 형용사 적당한 ❑ 적당량의 나트륨염만 들어간 식품에는 빵, 케이크, 우유, 버터, 마가린이 있다. ● 부사 적당하게 ❑ 적당하게 달궈진 프라이팬에 넣고 몇 분 동안 저어가며 노릇하게 익혀라. ◥ 복합형-색채어 중간색의, 보통의 ❑ 안드레아는 머리카락이 보통 갈색이고 눈은 회색이고 피부는 무척 창백하다. ◤ 가산명사 방법, 수단 ❑ 시에라리온에서는 영어가 모든 초등 교육의 교수 방편으로 쓰인다. ◢ 가산명사 매체 ❑ 혈액은 산소를 신체 모든 부위로 나르는 매체이다. ◖ 가산명사 영매 ❑ 브루스 윌리스는 영매를 통해 죽은 동생과 이야기를 나눠왔다고 말한다.

단수명사 중기 ❑ 경제학자들은 중기 경제 전망이 여전히 어둡다고 주장해 오고 있었다.

형용사 얌전한 ❑ 그는 얌전하고 온순한 사람이었다. ● 얌전히 부사 ❑ 대부분은 그런 권고를 얌전히 받아들였다.

◢ 상호동사 (우연히) 만나다, 마주치다 ❑ 난 이제 막 내 남은 생을 함께 하고픈 남자를 만났다. ❑ 그 사람은 내가 지금껏 만난 사람들 중 가장 친절하고 더할 나위 없이 진실한 사람이다. ● 상호 구동사 (우연히) 만나다, 마주치다 ❑ 어제 밤 그는 내 차를 주차하던 중에 자신의 옥스퍼드 대학 시절 친구와 마주쳤다. ◣ 상호동사 (약속해서) 만나다 ❑ 퇴근 후에 만나서 술 한 잔 하면 어떨까? ● 상호 구동사 (약속해서) 만나다 ❑ 우리는 일주일에 한 번씩 만나서 점심을 먹곤 한다. ◥ 타동사 만나다, 아는 사이가 되다 ❑ 어이, 테리, 여기 와서 우리 아빠께 인사드려. ◤ 타동사 처음 만나서 만나서 반갑습니다 [의례적인 표현] ❑ "제니퍼, 이 분이 리 밴 보린 씨이네."라고 맬러리 양이 말했다. "만나서 반가워요."라고 제니퍼가 인사했다. ◢ 타동사 마중 나가다 ❑ 엄마가 역으로 나를 마중 나오셨다. ❑ 릴리와 아버지가 선착장으로 나를 마중 나왔다. ◖ 자동사 만나다, 회담하다 ❑ 양국 관료들이 곧 다시 만나서 협상을 재개할 것이다. ◗ 자동사 -와 면담하다 [주로 미국영어] ❑ 어제 대통령을 방문했던 국회의원 중 대다수가 그 임무를 지지한다고 밝혔다. ◘ 타동사/자동사 -을 받다 ❑ 그 견해는 여러 방면에서 냉담한 반응을 받았다. ❑ 오늘 우리가 한 제안에 대해 당신의 승인 역시 받게 되기를 바랍니다. ◙ 타동사 충족시키다 ❑ 그는 중증 정신 장애를 앓고 있는 사람들을 보살피기 위한 현재의 조치가 그들의 필요를 충족시키기에 불충분함을 시사했다. ◢◢ 타동사 잘 대처하다 ❑ 영국의 제조업 분야는 1970년대의 위기에 잘 대처하지 못했다. ◢◣ 타동사 대다 ❑ 정부가 손실액 지불을 일부 원조하겠다고 밝혔다. ◢◥ 타동사 부딪치다, 만나다 ❑ 위험할 수도 있는 상황에 다시 부딪친다면 나는 어떻게 대응할지 솔직히 모르겠다. ◢◤ 자동사 -을 겪다, 만나다 ❑ 민간인 지원자를 찾으려는 시도는 당혹스러울 정도로 실패를 겪었다. ◢◢ 상호동사 닿다 ❑ 용골이 바닥에 닿을 때마다 선체 안에서 중압감이 느껴집니다. ◢◖ 상호동사 눈길이 마주치다 [문어체] ❑ 그가 가까이 다가서면서 일순간 그의 눈이 내 눈과 마주쳤다. ◢◗ 상호동사 접하다 ❑ 그곳은 세계의 희귀한 장소 중 하나로 사막이 바다와 접하는 곳이다. ◢◘ 상호동사 교차하다 ❑ 평행선은 아무리 연장해도 절대 교차하지 않는다.

▶**meet up** →see **meet 1, 2**

meet|ing ♦♦♦ /mi̱tɪŋ/ (**meetings**) **1** N-COUNT A **meeting** is an event in which a group of people come together to discuss things or make decisions. ❑ *Can we have a meeting to discuss that?* ● N-SING You can also refer to the people at a meeting as **the meeting**. ❑ *The meeting decided that further efforts were needed.* **2** N-COUNT When you meet someone, either by chance or by arrangement, you can refer to this event as a **meeting**. ❑ *In January, 37 years after our first meeting, I was back in the studio with Denis.*

1 가산명사 회의 ❑ 우리가 회의를 열어서 그 문제를 논의할 수 있을까? ● 단수명사 회의 참석자들 ❑ 회의 참석자들은 더 많은 노력이 필요하다고 결의했다. **2** 가산명사 만남 ❑ 우리의 첫 만남 이후 37년 만인 1월에 나는 데니스와 함께 작업실로 돌아왔다.

Word Partnership	*meeting*의 연어
N.	meeting **agenda, board** meeting, **business** meeting **1**
V.	**attend** a meeting, **call** a meeting, **go to** a meeting, **have** a meeting, **hold** a meeting **1**
	plan a meeting, **schedule** a meeting **1 2**

mega|byte /me̱gəbaɪt/ (**megabytes**) N-COUNT In computing, a **megabyte** is one million bytes of data. ❑ *...256 megabytes of memory.*

가산명사 메가바이트 ❑ 256메가바이트의 메모리

mel|an|choly /me̱lənkɒli/ ADJ You describe something that you see or hear as **melancholy** when it gives you an intense feeling of sadness. ❑ *The only sounds were the distant, melancholy cries of the sheep.*

형용사 구슬픈, 우울한 ❑ 들리는 소리라고는 멀리서 양들이 구슬프게 우는 소리뿐이었다.

mel|low /me̱loʊ/ (**mellower, mellowest, mellows, mellowing, mellowed**) **1** ADJ **Mellow** is used to describe things that have a pleasant, soft, rich color, usually red, orange, yellow, or brown. ❑ *...the softer, mellower light of evening.* **2** ADJ A **mellow** sound or flavor is pleasant, smooth, and rich. ❑ *His voice was deep and mellow and his speech had a soothing and comforting quality.* **3** V-T/V-I If someone **mellows** or if something **mellows** them, they become kinder or less extreme in their behavior, especially as a result of growing older. ❑ *He became a taciturn man, a man not easy to live with. Later, when the older children married and had children of their own, he mellowed a little.* ● ADJ **Mellow** is also an adjective. ❑ *Is she more mellow and tolerant?*

1 형용사 아늑한, 부드러운 ❑ 더 차분하고 더 아늑한 저녁 빛 **2** 형용사 감미로운 ❑ 그의 음성은 그윽하고 감미로웠고 그의 말에는 사람의 마음을 진정시키고 위안을 주는 데가 있었다. **3** 타동사/자동사 원만해지다, 원숙해지다; 원만하게 하다, 원숙하게 하다 ❑ 그는 함께 살기에 쉽지 않은 과묵한 사람이 되었는데, 나중에 자녀들이 결혼해서 아이를 낳은 후에는 약간 원만해졌다. ● 형용사 원숙한 ❑ 그녀가 좀더 원숙하고 관대해졌니?

melo|dra|ma /me̱lədrɑːmə/ (**melodramas**) N-VAR A **melodrama** is a story or play in which there are a lot of exciting or sad events and in which people's emotions are very exaggerated.

가산명사 또는 불가산명사 멜로드라마, 통속극

melo|dra|mat|ic /me̱lədrəmæ̱tɪk/ ADJ **Melodramatic** behavior is behavior in which someone treats a situation as much more serious than it really is. ❑ *"Don't you think you're being rather melodramatic?"* Jane asked.

형용사 감상적이고 과장된, 멜로드라마 같은 ❑ "네가 좀 멜로드라마 같이 군다는 생각이 안 드니?"라고 제인이 물었다.

melo|dy /me̱lədi/ (**melodies**) N-COUNT A **melody** is a tune. [FORMAL] ❑ *I whistle melodies from Beethoven and Vivaldi and the more popular classical composers.*

가산명사 선율, 곡조 [격식체] ❑ 나는 베토벤과 비발디, 그 외에도 유명한 고전 음악 작곡가들의 선율을 휘파람으로 분다.

mel|on /me̱lən/ (**melons**) N-VAR A **melon** is a large fruit which is sweet and juicy inside and has a hard green or yellow skin. ❑ *...some juicy slices of melon.*

가산명사 또는 불가산명사 메론 ❑ 과즙이 많은 메론 몇 조각

melt /me̱lt/ (**melts, melting, melted**) **1** V-T/V-I When a solid substance **melts** or when you **melt** it, it changes to a liquid, usually because it has been heated. ❑ *The snow had melted, but the lake was still frozen solid.* ❑ *Meanwhile, melt the white chocolate in a bowl suspended over simmering water.* **2** V-I If something such as your feelings **melt**, they suddenly disappear and you no longer feel them. [LITERARY] ❑ *His anxiety about the outcome melted, to return later but not yet.* ● PHRASAL VERB **Melt away** means the same as **melt**. ❑ *When he heard these words, Shinran felt his inner doubts melt away.* **3** V-I If a person or thing **melts into** something such as darkness or a crowd of people, they become difficult to see, for example because they are moving away from you or are the same color as the background. [LITERARY] ❑ *The youths dispersed and melted into the darkness.* →see **matter**

1 타동사/자동사 녹다; 녹이다 ❑ 눈은 녹았지만, 호수는 여전히 꽁꽁 얼어 있었다. ❑ 그러는 동안, 흰색 초콜릿을 사발에 넣고 보글보글 끓는 물 위에서 녹이시오. **2** 자동사 사라지다, 누그러지다 [문예체] ❑ 결과에 대한 그의 근심은 사라졌고, 나중에 또 걱정하게 되겠지만 아직은 아니었다. ● 구동사 사라지다, 누그러지다 ❑ 그가 이러한 말들을 들었을 때, 쉰란은 마음속에 품고 있던 의심이 사라짐을 느꼈다. **3** 자동사 -로 녹아들다, -로 사라지다 [문예체] ❑ 젊은이들이 흩어져서 어둠 속으로 사라졌다.

Thesaurus	*melt*의 참조어
V.	dissolve, soften, thaw **1**
	disappear, fade **2 3**

melt|down /me̱ltdaʊn/ (**meltdowns**) **1** N-VAR If there is **meltdown** in a nuclear reactor, the fuel rods start melting because of a failure in the system, and radiation starts to escape. ❑ *Scientists warned that emergency cooling systems could fail and a reactor meltdown could occur.* **2** N-UNCOUNT The **meltdown** of a company, organization, or system is its sudden and complete failure. [JOURNALISM] ❑ *Urgent talks are going on to prevent the market going into financial meltdown during the summer.*

1 가산명사 또는 불가산명사 (원자로의) 용해, (금속의) 용융 ❑ 과학자들은 비상 냉각 시스템이 제대로 작동하지 않아 원자로가 용해될 수도 있다고 경고했다. **2** 불가산명사 파국 [언론] ❑ 이번 여름 경기가 경제적 파국으로 치닫는 것을 방지하기 위해 긴급회담이 열리고 있다.

melt|ing pot (**melting pots**) N-COUNT A **melting pot** is a place or situation in which people or ideas of different kinds gradually get mixed together. ❑ *The republic is a melting pot of different nationalities.*

가산명사 다양한 인종과 문화가 뒤섞인 장소, 용광로 ❑ 그 공화국은 다양한 국적을 가진 사람들이 뒤섞여 사는 용광로 같은 곳이다.

The term **melting pot** is used to picture the mixing of various immigrant traditions together into one American culture. In places where the cultures do not blend but exist intact side by side, this phenomenon has been described as a **mosaic**.

melting pot(용광로)은 이민자들의 다양한 전통이 모여 하나의 미국 문화 속으로 혼합되어가는 모습을 묘사한 말이다. 문화가 서로 섞이지 않고 나란히 공존하는 곳에서는 이런 현상을 mosaic이라고 한다.

mem|ber ♦♦♦ /me̱mbər/ (**members**) **1** N-COUNT A **member** of a group is one of the people, animals, or things belonging to that group. ❑ *He refused to name the members of staff involved.* **2** N-COUNT A **member** of an organization such as a club or a political party is a person who has officially joined the organization. ❑ *The support of our members is of great importance to the Association.* **3** ADJ A **member country** or **member state** is one of the countries that has joined an international organization or group. [ADJ n] ❑ *...the member countries of the European Free Trade Association.* **4** N-COUNT A **member** or **Member** is a person who has been elected to a legislature or parliament. ❑ *He was elected to Parliament as the Member for Leeds.*

1 가산명사 일원, 구성원 ❑ 그는 연루된 직원들의 이름을 대지 않으려 했다. ❑ 그들의 훈련 부족 때문에 사회 구성원들이 위험에 빠질 수도 있다. **2** 가산명사 회원 ❑ 우리 회원들의 지지는 협회에 아주 중요합니다. **3** 형용사 회원국 ❑ 유럽 자유 무역 연합의 회원국들 **4** 가산명사 의원 ❑ 그는 리즈 지역 국회의원으로 선출되었다.

Mem|ber of Con|gress (**Members of Congress**) N-COUNT A **Member of Congress** is a person who has been elected to the United States Congress. ❑ ...*the party's only black member of Congress.*

가산명사 (미국) 하원의원 ❑ 그 정당 소속의 유일한 흑인 하원의원

Mem|ber of Par|lia|ment (**Members of Parliament**) N-COUNT A **Member of Parliament** is a person who has been elected by the people in a particular area to represent them in a country's parliament. The abbreviation **MP** is often used. ❑ ...*the Member of Parliament for Torbay.* →see **government**

가산명사 하원의원 ❑ 토베이가 지역구인 하원의원

mem|ber|ship ♦◇◇ /mɛmbərʃɪp/ (**memberships**) ◼ N-UNCOUNT **Membership** of an organization is the state of being a member of it. ❑ ...*his membership of the Communist Party.* ◼ N-VAR-COLL The **membership** of an organization is the people who belong to it, or the number of people who belong to it. ❑ *The European Builders Confederation has a membership of over 350,000 building companies.*

◼ 불가산명사 회원 자격 ❑ 그의 공산당 회원 자격 ◼ 가산명사 또는 불가산명사-집합 회원 전원, 회원 총수 ❑ 유럽 건축업자 동맹에는 삼십 오만 개 이상의 건축 회사가 회원으로 있다.

mem|brane /mɛmbreɪn/ (**membranes**) N-COUNT A **membrane** is a thin piece of skin which connects or covers parts of a person's or animal's body. ❑ ...*inflammation of the thin membrane that lines the heart.*

가산명사 피막 ❑ 심장을 두르는 얇은 피막에 생긴 염증

memo /mɛmoʊ/ (**memos**) N-COUNT A **memo** is a short official note that is sent by one person to another within the same company or organization. ❑ *He sent out a memo expressing his disagreement with their decisions.*

가산명사 메모 ❑ 그는 그들의 결정에 동의하지 않는다는 메모를 보냈다.

mem|oir /mɛmwar/ (**memoirs**) N-PLURAL A person's **memoirs** are a written account of the people who they have known and events that they remember. ❑ *If you've read my earlier memoirs you'll know all about it.*

복수명사 회고록 ❑ 나의 이전 회고록을 네가 읽어 봤다면 그것에 관해 모두 알고 있을 것이다.

memo|ra|bilia /mɛmərəbɪliə/ N-PLURAL **Memorabilia** are things that you collect because they are connected with a person or organization in which you are interested. ❑ ...*the country's leading dealer in Beatles memorabilia.*

복수명사 기념품, 기억할 만한 것 ❑ 그 나라에서 손꼽히는, 비틀스 기념품 거래인

memo|rable /mɛmərəbəl/ ADJ Something that is **memorable** is worth remembering or likely to be remembered, because it is special or very enjoyable. ❑ ...*the perfect setting for a nostalgic memorable day.*

형용사 기억할 만한 ❑ 향수를 불러일으키는, 기억할 만한 날에 어울리는 완벽한 설정

memo|ran|dum /mɛmərændəm/ (**memoranda** or **memorandums**) ◼ N-COUNT A **memorandum** is a written report that is prepared for a person or committee in order to provide them with information about a particular matter. ❑ ...*a memorandum from the Ministry of Defence on its role.* ◼ N-COUNT A **memorandum** is a short official note that is sent by one person to another within the same company or organization. ❑ ...*a memorandum sent to all senior UN personnel.* [FORMAL]

◼ 가산명사 기록 ❑ 국방부에서 낸 국방부 역할에 관한 기록 ◼ 가산명사 짧은 공식 문서 ❑ 유엔 고위 관리 모두에게 전달된 짧은 공식 문서 [격식체]

| **Word Link** | *memor ≈ memory : com**memor**ate, **memor**ial, **memor**y* |

me|mo|rial /mɪmɔriəl/ (**memorials**) ◼ N-COUNT A **memorial** is a structure built in order to remind people of a famous person or event. ❑ *Building a memorial to Columbus has been his lifelong dream.* ◼ ADJ A **memorial** event, object, or prize is in honor of someone who has died, so that they will be remembered. [ADJ n] ❑ *A memorial service is being held for her at St Paul's Church.* ◼ N-COUNT If you say that something will be a **memorial** to someone who has died, you mean that it will continue to exist and remind people of them. ❑ *The museum will serve as a memorial to the millions who passed through Ellis Island.*

◼ 가산명사 기념관, 기념물 ❑ 콜럼버스 기념관을 세우는 것이 그가 평생 간직해 온 꿈이다. ◼ 형용사 추도의, 추모의 ❑ 그녀의 추도식이 세인트 폴 성당에서 열릴 예정이다. ◼ 가산명사 -을 추모하는 것, -에 대한 추모비 ❑ 그 박물관은 엘리스 섬을 거쳐 간 수백만 명의 사람들에게 바치는 추모비가 될 것이다.

memo|rize /mɛməraɪz/ (**memorizes**, **memorizing**, **memorized**) [BRIT also **memorise**] V-T If you **memorize** something, you learn it so that you can remember it exactly. ❑ *He studied his map, trying to memorize the way to Rose's street.*

[영국영어 memorise] 타동사 기억하다, 암기하다 ❑ 그는 자신의 지도를 자세히 살펴보면서 로즈가 사는 거리로 가는 길을 암기하려고 했다.

memo|ry ♦♦◇ /mɛməri/ (**memories**) ◼ N-VAR Your **memory** is your ability to remember things. ❑ *All the details of the meeting are fresh in my memory.* ❑ *But locals with long memories thought this was fair revenge for the injustice of 1961.* ◼ N-COUNT A **memory** is something that you remember from the past. ❑ *She cannot bear to watch the film because of the bad memories it brings back.* ❑ *Her earliest memory is of singing at the age of four to wounded soldiers.* ◼ N-COUNT A computer's **memory** is the part of the computer where information is stored, especially for a short time before it is transferred to disks or magnetic tapes. [COMPUTING] ❑ *The data are stored in the computer's memory.* ◼ N-SING If you talk about the **memory** of someone who has died, especially someone who was loved or respected, you are referring to the thoughts, actions, and ceremonies by which they are remembered. [usu with poss, also *in* N *of* n] ❑ *She remained devoted to his memory.* ◼ PHRASE If you do something **from memory**, for example speak the words of a poem or play a piece of music, you do it without looking at it, because you know it very well. ❑ *Many members of the church sang from memory.* ◼ PHRASE If you say that something is, for example, the best, worst, or first thing of its kind **in living memory**, you are emphasizing that it is the only thing of that kind that people can remember. [EMPHASIS] ❑ *The floods are the worst in living memory.* ◼ PHRASE If you **lose your memory**, you forget things that you used to know. ❑ *His illness caused him to lose his memory.* ◼ to **commit** something **to memory**
→see **commit**
→see Word Web: **memory**

◼ 가산명사 또는 불가산명사 기억, 기억력 ❑ 내 기억으로는 그 모임에 대한 세세한 일까지 모두 생생하다. ❑ 그러나 아직까지 기억하고 있는 지역 주민들은 이것을 1961년의 부당함에 대한 온당한 보복으로 여겼다. ◼ 가산명사 기억, 추억 ❑ 그 영화를 보면 나쁜 기억이 되살아나서 그녀는 그것을 차마 보지 못한다. ❑ 그녀의 가장 어릴 적 기억은 네 살 때 부상병들에게 노래를 불러 주던 것이다. ◼ 가산명사 기억 장치 [컴퓨터] ❑ 데이터가 컴퓨터의 기억 장치에 저장된다. ◼ 단수명사 기억, 추모, 애도 ❑ 그녀는 계속 여전히 그를 추모하는 데 전념했다. ◼ 구 외워서 ❑ 많은 교회 신도들이 노래를 외워서 불렀다. ◼ 구 사람들의 기억에 남아 [강조] ❑ 그 홍수들은 사람들의 기억에 최악으로 남아 있다. ◼ 구 기억을 잃다 ❑ 병으로 인해 그는 기억을 잃었다.

Word Partnership	*memory*의 연어
ADJ.	**collective** memory, **conscious** memory, **failing** memory, **fresh in *your*** memory, **long-/short-term** memory, **poor** memory, **in recent** memory ◼
	bad memory, **good** memory ◼ ◼
	happy memory, **painful** memory, **sad** memory, **vivid** memory ◼
N.	**computer** memory, **random access** memory, memory **storage** ◼

Word Web   memory

Scientists divide **memory** into three types. **Short-term** memory holds small amounts of information for a short time. The information is then **forgotten**. Short-term memory lasts from two to thirty seconds. Working memory organizes items in the short-term memory. For example, adding up several numbers in your mind involves working memory. **Long-term** memory can last for years. Several things influence long-term memory. You remember an event with meaningful **associations** better than a routine event. **Rehearsing** the information also helps preserve a long-term memory. In addition, mnemonics can help you **remember** the most important details.

men /mɛn/ **Men** is the plural of **man**.

man의 복수

men|ace /mɛnɪs/ (**menaces, menacing, menaced**) **1** N-COUNT If you say that someone or something is a **menace** to other people or things, you mean that person or thing is likely to cause serious harm. ❏ *In my view you are a menace to the public.* **2** N-COUNT You can refer to someone or something as a **menace** when you want to say that they cause you trouble or annoyance. [INFORMAL] ❏ *You're a menace to my privacy, Kenworthy.* **3** N-UNCOUNT **Menace** is a quality or atmosphere that gives you the feeling that you are in danger or that someone wants to harm you. ❏ *There is a pervading sense of menace.* **4** V-T If you say that one thing **menaces** another, you mean that the first thing is likely to cause the second thing serious harm. ❏ *The European states retained a latent capability to menace Britain's own security.*

1 가산명사 위협적인 사람, 위협적인 것 ❏ 내가 보기에 너는 사회에 위협적인 인물이야. **2** 가산명사 골칫거리 [비격식체] ❏ 켄워디, 넌 내 사생활에 있어 골칫거리야. **3** 불가산명사 위협, 위기 ❏ 위기감이 퍼지고 있다. **4** 타동사 위협하다 ❏ 유럽 국가들은 영국의 안보를 위협할 만한 잠재력을 보유하고 있었다.

men|ac|ing /mɛnɪsɪŋ/ ADJ If someone or something looks **menacing**, they give you a feeling that they are likely to cause you harm or put you in danger. ❏ *The strong dark eyebrows give his face an oddly menacing look.* ● **men|ac|ing|ly** ADV ❏ *A group of men suddenly emerged from a doorway and moved menacingly forward to block her way.*

형용사 위협적인 ❏ 진한 눈썹 때문에 그의 얼굴은 묘하게도 위협적인 인상을 준다. ● 위협하듯 부사 ❏ 일단의 남자들이 문간에서 갑자기 나타나서 위협하듯 앞으로 걸어 나와 그녀의 길을 가로막았다.

mend /mɛnd/ (**mends, mending, mended**) **1** V-T If you **mend** something that is broken or not working, you repair it, so that it works properly or can be used. ❏ *They took a long time to mend the roof.* **2** V-T/V-I If a person or a part of their body **mends** or **is mended**, they get better after they have been ill or have had an injury. ❏ *I'm feeling a good bit better. The cut aches, but it's mending.* **3** V-T If you try to **mend** divisions between people, you try to end the disagreements or quarrels between them. ❏ *He sent Evans as his personal envoy to discuss ways to mend relations between the two countries.* **4** PHRASE If a relationship or situation is **on the mend** after a difficult or unsuccessful period, it is improving. [INFORMAL] ❏ *More evidence that the economy was on the mend was needed.* **5** PHRASE If you are **on the mend** after an illness or injury, you are recovering from it. [INFORMAL] ❏ *The baby had been poorly but seemed on the mend.* **6** PHRASE If someone who has been behaving badly **mends** their **ways**, they begin to behave well. ❏ *He has promised drastic disciplinary action if they do not mend their ways.*

1 타동사 수리하다 ❏ 그들이 지붕을 수리하는 데 오래 걸렸다. **2** 타동사/자동사 나아지다; 낫게 하다 ❏ 훨씬 좋아진 걸 느껴. 베인 상처가 아프지만 나아지고 있어. **3** 타동사 개선하다 ❏ 그는 자신의 개인 특사 자격으로 에반스를 보내어 양국 간의 관계를 개선할 방안에 대해 논의하도록 했다. **4** 구 호전되어 [비격식체] ❏ 경제가 호전되고 있다는 증거가 더 필요했다. **5** 구 나아지고 있는 [비격식체] ❏ 아기는 계속 건강이 좋지 않았지만 나아지고 있는 것처럼 보였다. **6** 구 행실을 고치다 ❏ 그는 그들이 행실을 고치지 않으면 강경한 징계 처분을 내리겠다고 약속했다.

me|nial /miniəl, minyəl/ ADJ **Menial** work is very boring, and the people who do it have a low status and are usually badly paid. ❏ *...low paid menial jobs, such as cleaning and domestic work.*

형용사 천한 ❏ 청소나 집안일 따위의 천한 저임금 일자리

men|in|gi|tis /mɛnɪndʒaɪtɪs/ N-UNCOUNT **Meningitis** is a serious infectious illness which affects your brain and spinal cord.

불가산명사 수막염, 뇌막염

meno|pause /mɛnəpɔz/ N-SING **Menopause** is the time during which a woman gradually stops menstruating, usually when she is about fifty years old. [BRIT sometimes **the menopause**] ❏ *... alternative therapies to fight the symptoms of menopause.* ● **meno|pau|sal** ADJ ❏ *A menopausal woman of average build and height requires 1600 – 2400 calories daily.*

단수명사 폐경기 [영국영어 가끔 the menopause] ❏ 폐경기 증상에 대처하기 위한 대체 치료 ● 폐경기의 형용사 ❏ 평균 신장과 체격을 가진 여성이 폐경기에 이르면 하루 1,600에서 2,400 칼로리가 필요하다.

men|strual /mɛnstruəl/ ADJ **Menstrual** means relating to menstruation. [ADJ n] ❏ *...the menstrual cycle.*

형용사 월경의 ❏ 월경 주기

men|stru|ate /mɛnstrueɪt/ (**menstruates, menstruating, menstruated**) V-I When a woman **menstruates**, a flow of blood comes from her womb. Women menstruate once a month unless they are pregnant or have reached menopause. [FORMAL] ❏ *Lean hard-training women athletes may menstruate less frequently or not at all.* ● **men|strua|tion** /mɛnstrueɪʃən/ N-UNCOUNT ❏ *Menstruation may cease when a woman is anywhere between forty-five and fifty years of age.*

자동사 월경을 치르다 [격식체] ❏ 격렬한 운동을 하는 마른 여자 운동선수들은 월경 횟수가 적어지거나 아예 월경을 하지 않을 수도 있다. ● 월경 불가산명사 ❏ 여성이 마흔다섯 살에서 쉰 살이 되면 월경이 멈출 것이다.

mens|wear /mɛnzwɛər/ N-UNCOUNT **Menswear** is clothing for men. ❏ *...the menswear industry.*

불가산명사 남성의류 ❏ 남성의류 산업

men|tal ♦◇◇ /mɛntəl/ **1** ADJ **Mental** means relating to the process of thinking. [ADJ n] ❏ *The intellectual environment has a significant influence on the mental development of the children.* ● **men|tal|ly** ADV ❏ *I think you are mentally tired.* **2** ADJ **Mental** means relating to the state or the health of a person's mind. [ADJ n] ❏ *The mental state that had created her psychosis was no longer present.* ● **men|tal|ly** ADV ❏ *...an inmate who is mentally disturbed.* **3** ADJ A **mental** act is one that involves only thinking and not physical action. [ADJ n] ❏ *Practise mental arithmetic when you go out shopping.* ● **men|tal|ly** ADV [ADV with v] ❏ *This technique will help people mentally organize information.* →see **hypnosis**

1 형용사 정신의 ❏ 지적 환경은 아동의 정신 발달에 중대한 영향을 끼친다. ● 정신적으로 부사 ❏ 네가 정신적으로 지쳤다는 생각이 든다. **2** 형용사 정신의 ❏ 정신병을 유발한 그녀의 정신 상태가 더 이상은 존재하지 않았다. ● 정신적으로 부사 ❏ 정신적으로 불안한 재소자 **3** 형용사 머리를 쓰는 ❏ 쇼핑할 때는 늘 암산을 해 보세요. ● 머리를 써서 부사 ❏ 이 기법은 사람들이 머리를 써서 정보를 정리하는 데 도움이 될 것이다.

men|tal|ity /mɛntæliti/ (**mentalities**) N-COUNT Your **mentality** is your attitudes and your way of thinking. ❏ *...a criminal mentality.*

가산명사 정신 상태 ❏ 범죄자의 정신 상태

men|tion ♦♦◇ /mɛnʃən/ (**mentions, mentioning, mentioned**) **1** V-T If you **mention** something, you say something about it, usually briefly. ❏ *She did not mention her mother's absence.* ❏ *I may not have mentioned it to her.* ❏ *I had mentioned that I didn't really like contemporary music.* **2** N-VAR A **mention** is a reference to

1 타동사 (간단히) 말하다, 언급하다 ❏ 그녀는 어머니께서 안 계신다는 사실을 말하지 않았다. ❏ 내가 그녀에게 그걸 말하지 않았을 수도 있어. ❏ 나는 사실은 현대 음악을 좋아하지 않는다고 말해 왔던

something or someone. ❑ *The statement made no mention of government casualties.*
3 V-T If someone **is mentioned** in writing, a reference is made to them by name, often to criticize or praise something that they have done. [usu passive] ❑ *I was absolutely outraged that I could be even mentioned in an article of this kind.*
4 N-VAR A special or honorable **mention** is formal praise that is given for an achievement that is very good, although not usually the best of its kind. ❑ *Two of the losers deserve special mention: Caroline Swaithes, of Kings Norton, and Maria Pons, of Valencia.* **5** CONVENTION People sometimes say "**don't mention it**" as a polite reply to someone who has just thanked them for doing something. [FORMULAE] ❑ *"Thank you very much." — "Don't mention it."*

> If you **mention** something, you say it, but only briefly, especially when you have not talked about it before. ❑ *He mentioned that he might go to New York.* If you **comment** on a situation, or make a **comment** about it, you give your opinion on it. ❑ *Mr. Cook has not commented on these reports... I was wondering whether you had any comments.* If you **remark** on something, or make a **remark** about it, you say what you think or what you have noticed, often in a casual way. ❑ *Visitors remark on how well the children look... General Sutton's remarks about the conflict.*

Word Partnership   *mention*의 연어

V.	**fail to** mention, **forget to** mention, **neglect to** mention **1**
	make *no* mention **of** *someone/something* **2**
ADJ.	**honorable** mention, **special** mention **4**

men|tor /mɛntɔr/ (**mentors, mentoring, mentored**) **1** N-COUNT A person's **mentor** is someone who gives them help and advice over a period of time, especially help and advice related to their job. ❑ *Leon Sullivan was my mentor and my friend.* **2** V-T To **mentor** someone means to give them help and advice over a period of time, especially help and advice related to their job. ❑ *He had mentored scores of younger doctors.*

menu /mɛnyu/ (**menus**) **1** N-COUNT In a restaurant or café or at a formal meal, the **menu** is a list of the meals and drinks that are available. ❑ *A waiter offered him the menu.* **2** N-COUNT A **menu** is the food that you serve at a meal. ❑ *Try out the menu on a few friends.* **3** N-COUNT On a computer screen, a **menu** is a list of choices. Each choice represents something that you can do using the computer. ❑ *Hold down the Shift key and press F7 to display the Print menu.*

MEP /ɛm i pi/ (**MEPs**) N-COUNT An **MEP** is a person who has been elected to the European Parliament. **MEP** is an abbreviation for "Member of the European Parliament." ❑ *...Tuesday's secret ballot of Europe's 626 MEPs.*

mer|ce|nary /mɜrsəneri, BRIT mɜːˈsənri/ (**mercenaries**) **1** N-COUNT A **mercenary** is a soldier who is paid to fight by a country or group that they do not belong to. ❑ *...the recruitment of foreign mercenaries.* **2** ADJ If you describe someone as **mercenary**, you are criticizing them because you think that they are only interested in the money that they can get from a particular person or situation. [DISAPPROVAL] ❑ *"I hate to sound mercenary," Labane said, "but am I getting paid to be in this opus of yours?"*

mer|chan|dise /mɜrtʃəndaɪz, -daɪs/ N-UNCOUNT **Merchandise** is goods that are bought, sold, or traded. [FORMAL] ❑ *...a mail-order company that provides merchandise for people suffering from allergies.*

mer|chan|dis|er /mɜrtʃəndaɪzər/ (**merchandisers**) N-COUNT A **merchandiser** is a person or company that sells goods to the public. [AM, BUSINESS; BRIT **retailer**] ❑ *In 1979, Liquor Barn thrived as a discount merchandiser.*

mer|chan|dis|ing /mɜrtʃəndaɪzɪŋ/ **1** N-UNCOUNT **Merchandising** consists of goods that are toys as toys and clothes that are linked with something such as a movie, sports team, or pop group. ❑ *We are selling the full range of World Cup merchandising.* **2** N-UNCOUNT **Merchandising** is used to refer to the way stores and businesses organize the sale of their products, for example the way they are displayed and the prices that are chosen. [mainly AM, BUSINESS] ❑ *Company executives say revamped merchandising should help Macy's earnings to grow.*

mer|chant ♦♢♢ /mɜrtʃənt/ (**merchants**) **1** N-COUNT A **merchant** is a person who buys or sells goods in large quantities, especially one who imports and exports them. ❑ *Any knowledgeable wine merchant would be able to advise you.* **2** N-COUNT A **merchant** is a person who owns or runs a store, or other business. [AM; BRIT usually **retailer, shopkeeper**] ❑ *The family was forced to live on credit from local merchants.* **3** ADJ **Merchant** seamen or ships are involved in carrying goods for trade. [ADJ n] ❑ *There's been a big reduction in the size of the British merchant fleet in recent years.*

mer|chant bank (**merchant banks**) N-COUNT A **merchant bank** is a bank that deals mainly with firms, investment, and foreign trade, rather than with the public. [BUSINESS]

mer|chant bank|er (**merchant bankers**) N-COUNT A **merchant banker** is someone who works for a merchant bank. [BUSINESS]

mer|ci|ful|ly /mɜrsɪfəli/ ADV You can use **mercifully** to show that you are glad that something good has happened, or that something bad has not happened or has stopped. [FEELINGS] ❑ *Mercifully, a friend came to the rescue.*

mer|ci|less /mɜrsɪlɪs/ ADJ If you describe someone as **merciless**, you mean that they are very cruel or determined and do not show any concern for the effect their actions have on other people. ❑ *...the merciless efficiency of a modern police state.* ● **mer|ci|less|ly** ADV ❑ *We teased him mercilessly.*

mer|cu|ry /mɜrkyəri/ N-UNCOUNT **Mercury** is a silver-colored liquid metal that is used especially in thermometers and barometers.

터였다. **2** 가산명사 또는 불가산명사 언급 ❑ 성명서에서는 정부 측 사상자에 대한 어떤 언급도 없었다. **3** 타동사 (이름이) 언급되다 ❑ 나는 이런 기사에 내 이름이 언급될 수 있다는 사실에 이루 말할 수 없이 격분했다. **4** 가산명사 또는 불가산명사 언급, 거명 ❑ 패자 중 두 명은 특별히 거명할 만하다. 바로 킹스 노턴의 캐롤라인 스웨이스와 발렌시아의 마리아 폰스이다. **5** 관용 표현 별말씀요 [의례적인 표현] ❑ "정말 감사합니다." "별말씀요."

> 특히 이전에 무엇에 대해 이야기한 적이 없으면서 그것을 mention하면, 그것에 대해 간략하게 얘기하는 것이다. ❑ 그는 뉴욕에 갈지도 모른다고 언급했다. 어떤 상황에 대해서 comment하거나 make a comment하면, 그것에 대한 의견을 말하는 것이다. ❑ 쿡 씨는 이 보고서들에 대해 논평을 하지 않았다... 논평할 것이 있는지 궁금해 하던 참이었습니다. 무엇에 대해 remark한다고 하면, 생각하는 바나 인지한 바를 흔히 가볍게 말하는 것이다. ❑ 방문객들은 그 아이들이 얼마나 좋아 보이는지에 대해 말한다... 그 분쟁에 대한 서튼 장군의 발언

1 가산명사 조언자 ❑ 레온 술리반은 내 조언자이자 친구였다. **2** 타동사 조언하다 ❑ 그는 수십 명의 젊은 의사들에게 조언을 해 오고 있었다.

1 가산명사 단표, 메뉴판 ❑ 웨이터가 그에게 메뉴판을 건네주었다. **2** 가산명사 요리 ❑ 불가산명사 판매 촉진 명에게 맞보게 하세요. **3** 가산명사 (컴퓨터) 메뉴, 기능 선택표 ❑ 쉬프트 키를 누른 채로 F7을 누르면 인쇄 메뉴가 나타난다.

가산명사 유럽 의회 의원 ❑ 유럽 의회 의원 626명이 참여한 화요일의 비밀 투표

1 가산명사 용병 ❑ 해외 용병 모집 **2** 형용사 돈만 밝히는 [탐탁찮은] ❑ "돈만 밝히는 것처럼 보이고 싶지는 않지만 당신의 이 작품에 내 이야기가 들어가면 돈을 받게 되는 겁니까?"라고 라바네가 물었다.

불가산명사 상품 [격식체] ❑ 알레르기 환자를 위한 상품을 판매하는 통신 판매 회사

가산명사 상인, 상점 [미국영어, 경제; 영국영어 retailer] ❑ 1979년에 '리쿼르 반'이 할인 상점으로 번창했다.

1 불가산명사 관련 상품 ❑ 우리는 모든 종류의 월드컵 관련 상품을 판매하고 있다. **2** 불가산명사 판매 촉진 방안 [주로 미국영어, 경제] ❑ 회사 중역들은 개선된 판매 촉진 방안이 메이시스 백화점의 수익 증가에 보탬이 될 것이라고 말한다.

1 가산명사 도매상인; 무역상인 ❑ 정통한 와인 무역상이라면 누구든 너에게 조언해 줄 수 있을 거야. **2** 가산명사 상인 [미국영어; 영국영어 대개 retailer, shopkeeper] ❑ 그 가족은 먹고 살기 위해 동네 상인들에게 외상을 져야 했다. **3** 형용사 무역의 ❑ 최근 몇 년 간 영국 상선의 규모가 크게 줄었다.

가산명사 머천트 뱅크 [경제]

가산명사 머천트 뱅크 직원 [경제]

부사 다행히도 [감정 개입] ❑ 다행히도 친구가 와서 구출해 주었다.

형용사 무자비한 ❑ 효율성이라는 이름으로 행해지는 근대 경찰국가의 무자비함 ● 무자비하게 부사 ❑ 우리는 그를 무자비하게 괴롭혔다.

불가산명사 수은

mer|cy /mɜrsi/ (**mercies**) **1** N-UNCOUNT If someone in authority shows **mercy**, they choose not to harm someone they have power over, or they forgive someone they have the right to punish. □ *Neither side took prisoners or showed any mercy.* **2** ADJ **Mercy** is used to describe a special journey to help someone in great need, such as people who are sick or made homeless by war. [JOURNALISM] [ADJ n] □ *She vanished nine months ago while on a mercy mission to West Africa.* **3** N-COUNT If you refer to an event or a situation as **a mercy**, you mean that it makes you feel happy or relieved, usually because it stops something unpleasant from happening. □ *It really was a mercy that he'd gone so rapidly at the end.* **4** PHRASE If one person or thing is **at the mercy of** another, the first person or thing is in a situation where they cannot prevent themselves being harmed or affected by the second. □ *Buildings are left to decay at the mercy of vandals and the weather.*

	Word Partnership	mercy의 연어
V.	beg for mercy, call for mercy, have mercy on *someone*, show mercy **1**	
N.	mercy of God **1**	
PREP.	at the mercy of *someone/something* **4**	

mere ♦◇◇ /mɪər/ (**merest**)

> **Mere** does not have a comparative form. The superlative form **merest** is used to emphasize how small something is, rather than in comparisons.

1 ADJ You use **mere** to emphasize how unimportant or inadequate something is, in comparison to the general situation you are describing. [EMPHASIS] [ADJ n] □ *...successful exhibitions which go beyond mere success.* □ *There is more to good health than the mere absence of disease.* **2** ADJ You use **mere** to indicate that a quality or action that is usually unimportant has a very important or strong effect. [ADJ n] □ *The mere mention of food had triggered off hunger pangs.* **3** ADJ You use **mere** to emphasize how small a particular amount or number is. [EMPHASIS] [a ADJ amount] □ *Sixty percent of teachers are women, but a mere 5 percent of women are heads and deputies.*

mere|ly ♦◇◇ /mɪərli/ **1** ADV You use **merely** to emphasize that something is only what you say and not better, more important, or more exciting. [EMPHASIS] □ *Michael is now merely a good friend.* □ *Francis Watson was far from being merely a furniture expert.* **2** ADV You use **merely** to emphasize that a particular amount or quantity is very small. [ADV amount] □ *The brain accounts for merely three percent of body weight.* **3** PHRASE You use **not merely** before the less important of two contrasting statements, as a way of emphasizing the more important statement. [EMPHASIS] □ *The team needs players who want to play cricket for England, not merely any country that will have them.*

Word Link	merg ≈ sinking : emerge, merge, submerge

merge /mɜrdʒ/ (**merges, merging, merged**) **1** V-RECIP If one thing **merges with** another, or **is merged with** another, they combine or come together to make one whole thing. You can also say that two things **merge**, or **are merged**. □ *Bank of America merged with a rival bank.* □ *The rivers merge just north of a vital irrigation system.* □ *The two countries merged into one.* **2** V-RECIP If one sound, color, or object **merges** into another, the first changes so gradually into the second that you do not notice the change. □ *Like a chameleon, he could merge unobtrusively into the background.* □ *His features merged with the darkness.*

mer|ger ♦◇◇ /mɜrdʒər/ (**mergers**) N-COUNT A **merger** is the joining together of two separate companies or organizations so that they become one. [BUSINESS] □ *...a merger between two of Britain's biggest trades unions.*

mer|it /mɛrɪt/ (**merits, meriting, merited**) **1** N-UNCOUNT If something has **merit**, it has good or worthwhile qualities. □ *The argument seemed to have considerable merit.* **2** N-PLURAL The **merits** of something are its advantages or other good points. □ *They have been persuaded of the merits of peace.* **3** V-T If someone or something **merits** a particular action or treatment, they deserve it. [FORMAL] □ *He said he had done nothing wrong to merit a criminal investigation.*

mer|maid /mɜrmeɪd/ (**mermaids**) N-COUNT In fairy tales and legends, a **mermaid** is a woman with a fish's tail instead of legs, who lives in the sea.

mer|ri|ly /mɛrɪli/ **1** ADV If you say that someone **merrily** does something, you are critical of the fact that they do it without realizing that there are a lot of problems which they have not thought about. [DISAPPROVAL] [ADV with v] □ *There they were, merrily describing their 16-hour working days while simultaneously claiming to be happily married.* **2** ADV If you say that something is happening **merrily**, you mean that it is happening fairly quickly, and in a pleasant or satisfactory way. [ADV with v] □ *The ferry cut merrily through the water.*

mer|ry /mɛri/ (**merrier, merriest**) **1** ADJ If you describe someone's character or behavior as **merry**, you mean that they are happy and cheerful. [OLD-FASHIONED] □ *From the house come the bursts of merry laughter.* ● **mer|ri|ly** ADV [ADV after v] □ *Chris threw back his head and laughed merrily.* **2** CONVENTION Just before Christmas and on Christmas Day, people say "**Merry Christmas**" to other people to express the hope that they will have a happy time. [FORMULAE] □ *Merry Christmas, everyone.* □ **to play merry hell** →see **hell**

merry-go-round (**merry-go-rounds**) **1** N-COUNT A **merry-go-round** is a circular platform at a carnival or amusement park on which there are model animals or vehicles for people to ride on as it turns around. **2** N-COUNT You can refer to a continuous series of activities as a **merry-go-round**. [usu sing, oft N of n] □ *...a merry-go-round of teas, fetes, musical events and the like.*

1 불가산명사 자비, 용서 ▪어느 쪽도 죄수를 데려가거나 자비를 베풀지 않았다. **2** 형용사 구제 [언론] □ 그녀는 9개월 전에 자취를 감추었는데 서아프리카에서 구제 사업을 하던 중이었다. **3** 가산명사 다행, 고마운 일 □ 결국엔 그가 그렇게 빨리 가버리다니 참 다행이었다. **4** 구 ~의 손에 넘겨져, ~에 좌우되어 □ 건물들은 혹독한 날씨와 파괴자들의 손에 넘겨져 퇴락해질 일만 남았다.

mere는 비교급 형태가 없다. 최상급 merest는 비교보다는 사물이 얼마나 작은지를 강조할 때 쓴다.

1 형용사 단순한 [강조] □ 단순한 성공을 뛰어넘는 성공적인 전시회들 □ 건강에는 단순히 병이 없다는 것 말고 무언인가가 더 있다. **2** 형용사 조금의 □ 음식 이야기가 조금만 나와도 고통스런 허기가 느껴졌다. **3** 형용사 불과한 [강조] □ 교사의 60퍼센트가 여성이지만, 그 중 5퍼센트에 불과한 여교사만이 교장 혹은 교감 직을 맡고 있다.

1 부사 단지, 그저 그런 [강조] □ 마이클은 지금으로선 단지 좋은 친구이다. □ 프랜시스 왓슨은 절대 그저 그런 가구 전문가가 아니었다. **2** 부사 겨우 [강조] □ 뇌의 무게는 몸무게의 겨우 3퍼센트밖에 안 된다. **3** 구 단순히 ~기 아닌 [강조] □ 그 팀은 어디든 단순히 자신들을 받아 주는 나라를 위해서가 아니라 잉글랜드를 위해 크리켓을 하고 싶어 하는 선수가 필요하다.

1 상호동사 합병하다, 합치다; 합병되다, 합쳐지다 □ 뱅크 오브 아메리카가 한 경쟁 은행과 합병하였다. □ 그 강들은 긴요한 관개 시스템의 북쪽 지점에서 정확히 합쳐진다. □ 양국이 하나로 합쳐졌다. **2** 상호동사 스며들다 □ 마치 카멜레온처럼, 그는 눈에 띄지 않게 주위 배경에 스며들 수 있다. □ 그의 모습이 어둠 속으로 스며들었다.

가산명사 합병 [경제] □ 영국 최대 노조 중 두 곳의 합병

1 불가산명사 가치 □ 그 주장에는 상당한 가치가 있는 것으로 보였다. **2** 복수명사 우수성, 이점 □ 그들은 평화가 가져다주는 이점을 믿게 되었다. **3** 타동사 받을 만하다 [격식체] □ 그는 자신이 범죄 수사를 받을 만한 나쁜 짓을 한 적이 없다고 말했다.

가산명사 인어

1 부사 (생각 없이) 들떠서 [탐탁잖음] □ 거기서 그들은 자신들이 하루에 16시간 일하던 시절에 대해 생각 없이 들떠서 얘기하면서 결혼 생활이 행복하다고 일제히 주장하고 있었다. **2** 부사 시원하게 □ 연락선이 시원하게 물길을 가르며 나아갔다.

1 형용사 명랑한, 유쾌한 [구식어] □ 그 집에서 명랑한 웃음소리가 터져 나왔다. ● 명랑하게, 유쾌하게 부사 □ 크리스가 고개를 뒤로 젖히고 유쾌하게 웃었다. **2** 관용 표현 즐거운 성탄절입니다, 메리 크리스마스 [의례적인 표현] □ 여러분, 성탄절을 즐겁게 보내세요.

1 가산명사 회전목마 **2** 가산명사 정신없이 돌아감 □ 정신없이 이어지는 다과회와 축제, 음악 행사 등

mesh /mɛʃ/ (meshes, meshing, meshed) **1** N-VAR **Mesh** is material like a net made from wire, thread, or plastic. ❑ *The ground-floor windows are obscured by wire mesh.* **2** V-RECIP If two things or ideas **mesh** or **are meshed**, they go together well or fit together closely. ❑ *Their senses of humor meshed perfectly.* ❑ *This of course meshes with the economic philosophy of those on the right.*

1 가산명사 또는 불가산명사 망 ❑ 1층 창문이 철망에 가려져 있다. **2** 상호동사 어울리다, 맞물리다; 어울리게 하다, 맞물리게 하다 ❑ 그들의 유머 감각은 완벽하게 어울렸다. ❑ 이것은 당연히 보수층의 경제 철학과 맞물린다.

mes|mer|ize /mɛzməraɪz/ (mesmerizes, mesmerizing, mesmerized) [BRIT also **mesmerise**] V-T If you **are mesmerized** by something, you are so interested in it or so attracted to it that you cannot think about anything else. ❑ *He was absolutely mesmerized by Pavarotti on television.*

[영국영어 mesmerise] 타동사 매료되다 ❑ 그는 텔레비전에 나오는 파바로티에게 완전히 매료되었다.

mess ♦♦◇ /mɛs/ (messes, messing, messed) **1** N-SING If you say that something is **a mess**, you think that it is not neat. [also no det] ❑ *The house is a mess.* **2** N-VAR If you say that a situation is **a mess**, you mean that it is full of trouble or problems. You can also say that something is **in a mess.** ❑ *I've made such a mess of my life.* ❑ *...the many reasons why the economy is in such a mess.* **3** N-VAR A **mess** is something liquid or sticky that has been accidentally dropped on something. ❑ *I'll clear up the mess later.* **4** N-COUNT The **mess** at a military base or military barracks is the building in which members of the armed forces can eat or relax. ❑ *...a party at the officers' mess.*

1 단수명사 어수선함 ❑ 집 안이 어수선하다. **2** 가산명사 또는 불가산명사 엉망, 혼란 ❑ 내가 내 삶을 이렇게 엉망으로 만들었다. ❑ 경제가 이런 혼란에 빠지게 된 여러 가지 이유 **3** 가산명사 또는 불가산명사 흘린 것, 더러운 것 ❑ 흘린 것은 내가 나중에 치울게. **4** 가산명사 (군대의) 회당 ❑ 장교 클럽에서 열린 파티

▶**mess around 1** PHRASAL VERB If you **mess around** or **mess about**, you spend time doing things without any particular purpose or without achieving anything. ❑ *We were just messing around playing with paint.* **2** PHRASAL VERB If you say that someone **is messing around with** or **messing about with** something, you mean that they are interfering with it in a harmful way. ❑ *"Don't be stupid,"* Max snapped. *"You don't want to go messing around with bears."* **3** PHRASAL VERB If someone **is messing around** or **messing about**, they are behaving in a joking or silly way. ❑ *I thought she was messing about.* **4** PHRASAL VERB If you **mess** someone **around** or **mess** them **about**, you treat them badly, for example by not being honest with them, or by continually changing plans which affect them. [mainly BRIT] ❑ *I think they've been messed around far too much.*

1 구동사 빈둥거리다 ❑ 우리는 물감을 가지고 놀며 그저 빈둥거리고 있었다. **2** 구동사 쓸데없이 참견하다 ❑ "어리석게 굴지마."하고 맥스가 딱딱거렸다. "난폭한 사람들에게 괜히 참견했다가는 좋지 않아." **3** 구동사 어리석게 굴다 ❑ 그녀가 어리석게 구는 것 같았어. **4** 구동사 아무렇게나 대하다 [주로 영국영어] ❑ 내 생각엔 그 사람들이 지나치게 소홀한 대접을 받아온 것 같아.

▶**mess up 1** PHRASAL VERB If you **mess** something **up** or if you **mess up**, you cause something to fail or be spoiled. [INFORMAL] ❑ *When politicians mess things up, it is the people who pay the price.* ❑ *He had messed up one career.* **2** PHRASAL VERB If you **mess up** a place or a thing, you make it dirty or not neat. [INFORMAL] ❑ *I hope they haven't messed up your video tapes.*

1 구동사 망쳐 놓다, 실패하다 [비격식체] ❑ 정치가들이 일을 망쳐 놓으면, 국민들이 그 대가를 치른다. ❑ 그는 자신의 경력 한 가지를 망쳤다. **2** 구동사 엉망진창으로 만들다 [비격식체] ❑ 그들이 네 비디오테이프를 엉망진창으로 만들지 않았으면 좋겠다.

▶**mess with** PHRASAL VERB If you tell someone not to **mess with** a person or thing, you are warning them not to get involved with that person or thing. ❑ *You are messing with people's religion and they don't like that.*

구동사 참견하다 ❑ 네가 사람들의 종교에 참견을 하고 있는데 그들은 그걸 좋아하지 않아.

Word Partnership	*mess*의 연어
v.	clean up a mess, leave a mess, make a mess **1**-**3**
	get into a mess **2**

mes|sage ♦♦◇ /mɛsɪdʒ/ (messages, messaging, messaged) **1** N-COUNT A **message** is a piece of information or a request that you send to someone or leave for them when you cannot speak to them directly. ❑ *I got a message you were trying to reach me.* **2** N-COUNT The **message** that someone is trying to communicate, for example in a book or play, is the idea or point that they are trying to communicate. ❑ *The report's message was unequivocal.* ❑ *I no longer want to stay friendly with her but I don't know how to get the message across.* **3** V-T/V-I If you **message** someone, you send them a message electronically using a computer or another device such as a cellphone. ❑ *People who message a lot feel unpopular if they don't get many back.*

1 가산명사 전갈, 메시지 ❑ 네가 내게 연락하려 한다는 전갈을 받았어. **2** 가산명사 취지, 의도 ❑ 그 보고서의 취지는 명백했다. ❑ 난 더 이상 그녀와 친구로 지내고 싶지 않지만 어떻게 내 의도를 전해야 할지 모르겠어. **3** 타동사/자동사 전자통신을 하다 ❑ 전자통신을 많이 하는 사람들은 회신이 많지 않으면 자신이 인기가 없다고 느낀다.

Word Partnership	*message*의 연어
ADJ.	clear message, important message, urgent message **1** **2**
	powerful message, simple message, strong message, wrong message **2**
v.	give *someone* a message, leave a message, read a message, take a message **1**
	deliver a message, get a message, hear a message, send a message **1** **2**
	get a message across, spread a message **2**

mes|sag|ing /mɛsɪdʒɪŋ/ N-UNCOUNT **Messaging** is the sending of written or spoken messages using a computer or another electronic device such as a cellphone. ❑ *Messaging allows real-time communication by keyboard with up to five people at any one time.*

불가산명사 전자통신 ❑ 전자통신을 하면 한번에 최대 다섯 사람과 자판을 통해 실시간 의사소통이 가능하다.

mes|sen|ger /mɛsɪndʒər/ (messengers) N-COUNT A **messenger** takes a message to someone, or takes messages regularly as their job. [also by N] ❑ *There will be a messenger at the Airport to collect the photographs from our courier.*

가산명사 배달원, 전령 ❑ 공항에 배달원이 나와 있다가 우리 안내원에게서 사진을 수거할 것입니다.

Messrs /mɛsərz/ N-TITLE **Messrs** is used before the names of two or more men as part of the name of a business. [BRIT] ❑ *The repairs were hopefully to be put in hand by Messrs Clegg & Sons of Balham.*

경칭명사 상사 (인명이 포함된 회사명에 쓰임) [영국영어] ❑ 바라건대 '클레그 앤 썬즈오브발함 상사'가 복구 직업을 맡을 예정이었다.

messy /mɛsi/ (messier, messiest) **1** ADJ A **messy** person or activity makes things dirty or not neat. ❑ *She was a good, if messy, cook.* **2** ADJ Something that is **messy** is dirty or not neat. ❑ *Don't worry if this first coat of paint looks messy.* **3** ADJ If you describe a situation as **messy**, you are emphasizing that it is confused or complicated, and therefore unsatisfactory. ❑ *John had been through a messy divorce himself.*

1 형용사 지저분한, 깔끔하지 못한 ❑ 그녀는 깔끔하진 않았지만 좋은 요리사였다. **2** 형용사 지저분한 ❑ 페인트 초벌칠이 지저분해 보여도 걱정하지 마세요. **3** 형용사 복잡하게 꼬여 있는 ❑ 존은 직접 복잡하기 짝이 없는 과정을 통해 이혼을 했다.

met /mɛt/ **Met** is the past tense and past participle of **meet**.

meet의 과거 및 과거 분사

a b c d e f g h i j k l m n o p q r s t u v w x y z

Word Web   metal

In their natural state, most **metals** are not pure. They are usually combined with other materials in mixtures known as **ores**. Almost all metals are **shiny**. Many metals share these special properties–they are ductile, meaning that they can be made into **wire**; they are malleable and can be formed into thin, flat sheets; they are also good **conductors** of heat and electricity. Except for **copper** and **gold**, metals are generally gray or silver in color.

copper

aluminum

gold

meta|bol|ic /mɛtəbɒlɪk/ ADJ **Metabolic** means relating to a person's or animal's metabolism. [ADJ n] ❑ *People who have inherited a low metabolic rate will gain weight.*

형용사 신진대사의 ❑ 선천적으로 신진대사가 저조한 사람들은 살이 찌기 마련이다.

Word Link   *meta ≈ beyond, change : metabolism, metamorphosis, metaphor*

me|tabo|lism /mɪtæbəlɪzəm/ (**metabolisms**) N-VAR Your **metabolism** is the way that chemical processes in your body cause food to be used in an efficient way, for example to make new cells and to give you energy. ❑ *If you skip breakfast, your metabolism slows down.*

가산명사 또는 불가산명사 신진대사 ❑ 아침식사를 거르면 신진대사가 느려진다.

met|al ♦♦◇ /mɛtˀl/ (**metals**) N-MASS **Metal** is a hard substance such as iron, steel, gold, or lead. ❑ *...pieces of furniture in wood, metal and glass.*
→see can, mineral
→see Word Web: metal

물질명사 금속 ❑ 목재, 금속 및 유리로 제작된 가구 몇 점

me|tal|lic /mɪtælɪk/ 🔢 ADJ A **metallic** sound is like the sound of one piece of metal hitting another. ❑ *There was a metallic click and the gates swung open.* 🔢 ADJ **Metallic** paint or colors shine like metal. ❑ *He had painted all the wood with metallic silver paint.* 🔢 ADJ Something that tastes **metallic** has a bitter unpleasant taste. ❑ *There was a metallic taste at the back of his throat.* 🔢 ADJ **Metallic** means consisting entirely or partly of metal. ❑ *Even the smallest metallic object, whether a nail file or cigarette lighter, is immediately confiscated.*

🔢 형용사 금속성의 ❑ 찰칵 하는 금속성 소리가 나더니 대문이 활짝 열렸다. 🔢 형용사 금속 느낌이 나는 ❑ 그가 금속 느낌이 나는 은색 페인트로 목재 전부를 칠했다. 🔢 형용사 비릿한 ❑ 그는 목구멍 뒤쪽에서 비릿한 맛을 느꼈다. 🔢 형용사 금속제의 ❑ 손톱 소제용 줄이나 담배 라이터 같은 아무리 작은 금속 제품이라도 즉각 압수당한다.

meta|mor|pho|sis /mɛtəmɔrfəsɪs/ (**metamorphoses**) N-VAR When a **metamorphosis** occurs, a person or thing develops and changes into something completely different. [FORMAL] ❑ *...his metamorphosis from a Republican to a Democrat.*

가산명사 또는 불가산명사 변모, 변신 [격식체] ❑ 공화당원에서 민주당원으로의 그의 변신

meta|phor /mɛtəfɔr/ (**metaphors**) 🔢 N-VAR A **metaphor** is an imaginative way of describing something by referring to something else which is the same in a particular way. For example, if you want to say that someone is very shy and frightened of things, you might say that they are a mouse. ❑ *...the avoidance of "violent expressions and metaphors" like "kill two birds with one stone."* 🔢 N-VAR If one thing is a **metaphor for** another, it is intended or regarded as a symbol of it. ❑ *The divided family remains a powerful metaphor for a society that continued to tear itself apart.* 🔢 PHRASE If you **mix** your **metaphors**, you use two conflicting metaphors. People do this accidentally, or sometimes deliberately as a joke. ❑ *To mix yet more metaphors, you were trying to run before you could walk, and I've clipped your wings.*

🔢 가산명사 또는 불가산명사 은유 ❑ '돌 하나로 새 두 마리 죽이기'와 같은 '과격한 표현과 은유'를 피함 🔢 가산명사 또는 불가산명사 비유, 상징 ❑ 가정 파괴는 여전히 한 사회가 해체를 계속했다는 사실을 보여 주는 강력한 상징이다. 🔢 구 비유에 비유를 섞어 쓰다 ❑ 더 많은 비유를 섞어 써 보자면, 너는 걸음마도 떼기 전에 뛰려고 했고 난 너의 날개를 잘라버린 거지.

meta|phor|ical /mɛtəfɔrɪkˀl, BRIT mɛtəfɒrɪkˀl/ ADJ You use the word **metaphorical** to indicate that you are not using words with their ordinary meaning, but are describing something by means of an image or symbol. ❑ *It turns out Levy is talking in metaphorical terms.* ● **meta|phor|ical|ly** ADV ❑ *You're speaking metaphorically, I hope.*

형용사 은유적인, 비유적인 ❑ 알고 보니 레비가 은유적인 표현으로 말하고 있다. ● 은유적으로, 비유적으로 부사 ❑ 네가 지금 비유적으로 말하고 있는 것이길 바래.

mete /mit/ (**metes**, **meting**, **meted**)
▶ **mete out** PHRASAL VERB To **mete out** a punishment means to order that someone should be punished in a certain way. [FORMAL] ❑ *His father meted out punishment with a slipper.*

구동사 (벌을) 내리다 [격식체] ❑ 그의 아버지는 슬리퍼로 벌을 내렸다.

me|teor /mitiər/ (**meteors**) N-COUNT A **meteor** is a piece of rock or metal that burns very brightly when it enters the earth's atmosphere from space.
→see Word Web: meteor

가산명사 유성, 별똥별

me|teor|ite /mitiərait/ (**meteorites**) N-COUNT A **meteorite** is a large piece of rock or metal from space that has landed on Earth.

가산명사 운석

me|teoro|logi|cal /mitiərəlɒdʒɪkˀl/ ADJ **Meteorological** means relating to meteorology. [ADJ n] ❑ *...adverse meteorological conditions.*

형용사 기상학의, 기상의 ❑ 기상 악조건

me|teor|ol|ogy /mitiərɒlədʒi/ N-UNCOUNT **Meteorology** is the study of the processes in the Earth's atmosphere that cause particular weather conditions, especially in order to predict the weather. ● **me|teor|olo|gist** /mitiərɒlədʒɪst/

불가산명사 기상학 ● 기상학자 가산명사 ❑ 기상학자들이 앞으로 2, 3일 동안 비가 약하게 내릴 것이라고 예측했다.

Word Web   meteor

As an asteroid flies through **space**, small pieces called meteoroids sometimes break off. When a meteoroid enters the earth's **atmosphere**, we call it a **meteor**. As the earth passes through asteroid belts we see spectacular meteor showers. Meteors that reach the earth are called meteorites. Scientists believe a huge meteorite struck the earth about 65 million years ago. It left a pit in Mexico called the Chicxulub **Crater**. It's about 150 miles wide. The crash caused earthquakes and tsunamis. It may also have produced a change in the earth's environment. Some believe this event caused the dinosaurs to die out.

(**meteorologists**) N-COUNT ❑ *Meteorologists have predicted mild rains for the next few days.*

Word Link
meter ≈ measuring : kilometer, **meter, peri**meter

me|ter /miːtər/ (**meters, metering, metered**) **1** N-COUNT A **meter** is a device that measures and records something such as the amount of gas or electricity that you have used. ❑ *He was there to read the electricity meter.* **2** V-T To **meter** something such as gas or electricity means to use a meter to measure how much of it people use, usually in order to calculate how much they have to pay. ❑ *Only a third of these households thought it reasonable to meter water.* **3** N-COUNT A **meter** is the same as a **parking meter**. **4** N-COUNT A **meter** is a metric unit of length equal to 100 centimeters. [BRIT **metre**] ❑ *She's running the 1,500 meters here.*

me|thane /mɛθeɪn, BRIT miːθeɪn/ N-UNCOUNT **Methane** is a colorless gas that has no smell. Natural gas consists mostly of methane.

meth|od ♦♦◇ /mɛθəd/ (**methods**) N-COUNT A **method** is a particular way of doing something. ❑ *The pill is the most efficient method of birth control.*

Thesaurus
method의 참조어

N. manner, procedure, process, system, technique

Word Partnership
method의 연어

ADJ. **alternative/traditional** method, **best** method, **effective** method, **new** method, **preferred** method, **scientific** method
N. method **of payment, teaching** method
V. **develop a** method, **use a** method

me|thod|i|cal /məθɒdɪkəl/ ADJ If you describe someone as **methodical**, you mean that they do things carefully, thoroughly, and in order. ❑ *Da Vinci was methodical in his research, carefully recording his observations and theories.* ● me|thod|i|cal|ly /məθɒdɪkli/ ADV [ADV with v] ❑ *She methodically put the things into her suitcase.*

meth|od|ol|ogy /mɛθədɒlədʒi/ (**methodologies**) N-VAR A **methodology** is a system of methods and principles for doing something, for example for teaching or for carrying out research. [FORMAL] ❑ *Teaching methodologies vary according to the topic.* ● meth|odo|logi|cal /mɛθədəlɒdʒɪkəl/ ADJ ❑ *...theoretical and methodological issues raised by the study of literary texts.*

me|ticu|lous /mətɪkyələs/ ADJ If you describe someone as **meticulous**, you mean that they do things very carefully and with great attention to detail. ❑ *He was so meticulous about everything.* ● me|ticu|lous|ly /mətɪkyələsli/ ADV ❑ *The flat had been meticulously cleaned.*

me|tre ♦♦◇ /miːtər/ →see meter

met|ric /mɛtrɪk/ ADJ **Metric** means relating to the metric system. ❑ *Around 180,000 metric tons of food aid is required.*

met|ro /mɛtroʊ/ (**metros**) also Metro N-COUNT The **metro** is the subway system in some cities, for example in Paris. ❑ *A new metro runs under the square, carrying hundreds of thousands who used to cycle to work.* →see transportation

Word Link
poli ≈ city : metropolis, **poli**ce, **poli**cy

me|tropo|lis /mətrɒpəlɪs/ (**metropolises**) N-COUNT A **metropolis** is the largest, busiest, and most important city in a country or region. ❑ *Even Lhasa was a small provincial town compared to the bustling metropolis of Chengdu.*

met|ro|poli|tan /mɛtrəpɒlɪtən/ (**metropolitans**) ADJ **Metropolitan** means belonging to or typical of a large busy city. [ADJ n] ❑ *...the metropolitan district of Miami.* ❑ *...a dozen major metropolitan hospitals.*

mg **mg** is a written abbreviation for **milligram** or **milligrams**. ❑ *...300 mg of calcium.*

mice /maɪs/ **Mice** is the plural of **mouse**.

mi|crobe /maɪkroʊb/ (**microbes**) N-COUNT A **microbe** is a very small living thing, which you can only see if you use a microscope. ❑ *...a type of bacteria that include the microbes responsible for tuberculosis and leprosy.*

Word Link
micro ≈ small : microchip, **micro**fiber, **micro**scope

micro|chip /maɪkroʊtʃɪp/ (**microchips**) N-COUNT A **microchip** is a very small piece of silicon inside a computer. It has electronic circuits on it and can hold large quantities of information or perform mathematical and logical operations.

micro|cosm /maɪkrəkɒzəm/ (**microcosms**) N-COUNT A **microcosm** is a small society, place, or activity which has all the typical features of a much larger one and so seems like a smaller version of it. [FORMAL] [oft N of n, also in N] ❑ *Kitchell says the city was a microcosm of all American culture during the '60s.*

micro|cred|it /maɪkroʊkrɛdɪt/ N-UNCOUNT **Microcredit** is credit in the form of small loans offered to local businesses, especially in developing countries. [BUSINESS] ❑ *...a microcredit scheme which provides credit to small businesses.*

micro|fiber /maɪkroʊfaɪbər/ (**microfibers**) [BRIT **microfibre**] N-VAR **Microfibers** are extremely light artificial fibres that are used to make cloth. ❑ *...woven in great looking and durable microfiber.*

1 가산명사 계량기, 미터 ❑ 그는 전기 계량기를 읽기 위해 거기 가 있었다. **2** 타동사 계량하다 ❑ 이들 세대 중 삼분의 일에 해당하는 세대들만 수도 계량이 합리적이라고 생각했다. **3** 가산명사 주차 요금 징수기 **4** 가산명사 미터 [영국영어 metre] ❑ 그녀는 지금 1,500미터 경주를 달리고 있다.

불가산명사 메탄

가산명사 방법 ❑ 그 알약이 피임에 가장 효과적인 방법이다.

형용사 조직적인, 질서 정연한 ❑ 다빈치는 연구에 있어 조직적이었고, 관찰 결과와 이론을 주의 깊게 기록했다. ● 조직적으로, 질서 정연하게 부사 ❑ 그녀는 질서 정연하게 소지품을 여행 가방에 넣었다.

가산명사 또는 불가산명사 방법론 [격식체] ❑ 교수 방법론은 주제에 따라 다양하다. ● 방법론적인 형용사 ❑ 문학 작품의 원문 연구에 의해 제기된 이론적이고 방법론적인 문제

형용사 꼼꼼한 ❑ 그는 매사에 아주 꼼꼼했다. ● 꼼꼼하게 부사 ❑ 아파트가 꼼꼼하게 치워져 있었다.

형용사 미터법의 ❑ 약 180,000미터 톤에 이르는 구호 식품이 필요하다.

가산명사 지하철 ❑ 그 광장 아래로 새로운 지하철이 운행하면서 이전에 자전거로 출퇴근했던 수십만 시민을 실어 나른다.

가산명사 대도시, 중심도시 ❑ 북적대는 대도시인 청두에 비하면 라사조차도 작은 지방 도시였다.

형용사 대도시의 ❑ 대도시 지역인 마이애미 ❑ 10여 개의 주요 대도시 병원들

밀리그램 ❑ 칼슘 300밀리그램

mouse의 복수

가산명사 미생물, 병원균 ❑ 결핵과 나병의 원인이 되는 병원균을 포함한 일종의 박테리아

가산명사 마이크로칩, 반도체 집적 회로 소자

가산명사 축소판 [격식체] ❑ 키첼은 1960년대엔 그 도시가 모든 미국 문화의 축소판이었다고 말한다.

불가산명사 무담보 소액 대출 [경제] ❑ 소규모 사업자들에게 신용 대부를 제공하는 무담보 소액 대출 계획

[영국영어 microfibre] 가산명사 또는 불가산명사 초미세 합성 섬유, 극세사, 마이크로 파이버 ❑ 모양도 훌륭하고 내구성이 강한 초미세 합성 섬유로 짜여진

micro|organism /maɪkroʊˈɔːrɡənɪzəm/ (**microorganisms**) also **micro-organism** N-COUNT A **microorganism** is a very small living thing which you can only see if you use a microscope. →see **fungus**

가산명사 미생물

micro|phone /maɪkrəfoʊn/ (**microphones**) N-COUNT A **microphone** is a device that is used to make sounds louder or to record them on a tape recorder. →see **concert**

가산명사 확성기, 마이크

micro|pro|ces|sor /maɪkroʊprˈoʊsɛsər/ (**microprocessors**) N-COUNT In a computer, the **microprocessor** is the main microchip, which controls its most important functions. [COMPUTING]

가산명사 마이크로프로세서, 초소형 중앙 처리 장치 [컴퓨터]

Word Link   micro ≈ small : microchip, microfiber, microscope

---

micro|scope /maɪkrəskoʊp/ (**microscopes**) N-COUNT A **microscope** is a scientific instrument which makes very small objects look bigger so that more detail can be seen.

가산명사 현미경

micro|scop|ic /maɪkrəskˈɒpɪk/ **1** ADJ **Microscopic** objects are extremely small, and usually can be seen only through a microscope. ❑ ...microscopic fibres of protein. **2** ADJ A **microscopic** examination is done using a microscope. [ADJ n] ❑ Microscopic examination of a cell's chromosomes can reveal the sex of the fetus.

1 형용사 극히 미세한 ❑ 극히 미세한 단백질 섬유 조직 **2** 형용사 현미경을 사용하는 ❑ 현미경을 사용한 세포 염색체 조사를 통해 태아의 성을 알 수 있다.

micro|wave /maɪkroʊweɪv/ (**microwaves, microwaving, microwaved**) **1** N-COUNT A **microwave** or a **microwave oven** is an oven which cooks food very quickly by electromagnetic radiation rather than by heat. **2** V-T To **microwave** food or drink means to cook or heat it in a microwave oven. ❑ Steam or microwave the vegetables until tender. →see **cook**

1 가산명사 전자레인지 ❑ 타동사 전자레인지에 넣고 돌리다 ❑ 야채가 연해질 때까지 찌거나 전자레인지에 넣고 돌리세요.

mid-air /mɪd ˈɛər/ N-UNCOUNT If something happens in **mid-air**, it happens in the air, rather than on the ground. ❑ The bird stopped and hovered in mid-air.

불가산명사 공중, 상공 ❑ 새가 공중에서 멈추더니 빙빙 맴돌았다.

mid|day /mɪddeɪ/ **1** N-UNCOUNT **Midday** is twelve o'clock in the middle of the day. ❑ At midday everyone would go down to Reg's Cafe. **2** N-UNCOUNT **Midday** is the middle part of the day, from late morning to early afternoon. ❑ People were beginning to tire in the midday heat.

1 불가산명사 정오 ❑ 정오에 모든 사람들이 레그스 카페로 내려오곤 했다. **2** 불가산명사 한낮 ❑ 사람들이 한낮의 더위에 지치기 시작하고 있었다.

mid|dle ♦♦♦ /mɪd²l/ (**middles**) **1** N-COUNT The **middle** of something is the part of it that is furthest from its edges, ends, or outside surface. ❑ Howard stood in the middle of the room sipping a cup of coffee. ❑ They had a volleyball court in the middle of the courtyard. **the middle of nowhere** →see **nowhere** **2** ADJ The **middle** object in a row of objects is the one that has an equal number of objects on each side. [ADJ n] ❑ The middle button of his uniform jacket was strained over his belly. **3** N-SING The **middle** of an event or period of time is the part that comes after the first part and before the last part. ❑ I woke up in the middle of the night and could hear a tapping on the window. ● ADJ **Middle** is also an adjective. [ADJ n] ❑ The month began and ended quite dry, but the middle fortnight saw nearly 100mm of rain fall nationwide. **4** PHRASE If you are **in the middle of** doing something, you are busy doing it. ❑ It's a bit hectic. I'm in the middle of cooking for nine people.

1 가산명사 한가운데, 중앙 ❑ 하워드는 커피 한 잔을 홀짝이며 방 한가운데에 서 있었다. ❑ 안뜰 중앙에 배구 코트가 있었다. **2** 형용사 가운데의 ❑ 그가 입고 있는 제복 상의의 가운데 단추 부분이 그의 배 위로 팽팽하게 당겼다. **3** 단수명사 중도, 한창때 ❑ 나는 한밤중에 잠에서 깨어 창문을 톡톡 두드리는 소리를 들을 수 있었다. ● 형용사 가운데의 ❑ 이 달 초와 말에는 매우 건조했지만, 가운데 2주 동안은 전국적으로 거의 100밀리미터의 강우량을 보였다. **4** 구 ~하는 중에 ❑ 꽤 바빠. 9인분의 요리를 하는 중이거든.

mid|dle age N-UNCOUNT **Middle age** is the period in your life when you are no longer young but have not yet become old. Middle age is usually considered to take place between the ages of 40 and 60. ❑ Men tend to put on weight in middle age.

불가산명사 중년 ❑ 남자들은 중년이 되면 몸무게가 느는 경향이 있다.

middle-aged **1** ADJ If you describe someone as **middle-aged**, you mean that they are neither young nor old. People between the ages of 40 and 60 are usually considered to be middle-aged. ❑ ...middle-aged, married businessmen. **2** ADJ If you describe someone's activities or interests as **middle-aged**, you are critical of them because you think they are typical of a middle-aged person, for example by being conventional or old-fashioned. [DISAPPROVAL] ❑ Her novels are middle-aged and boring. →see **age**

1 형용사 중년의 ❑ 중년의 기혼 사업가들 **2** 형용사 시대에 뒤떨어진, 노티가 나는 [탐탁찮음] ❑ 그녀가 쓴 소설은 시대에 뒤떨어지고 따분하다.

mid|dle class ♦♢♢ (**middle classes**) N-COUNT-COLL The **middle class** or **middle classes** are the people in a society who are not working class or upper class. Business people, managers, doctors, lawyers, and teachers are usually regarded as middle class. ❑ ...the expansion of the middle class in the late 19th century. ● ADJ **Middle class** is also an adjective. ❑ He is rapidly losing the support of blue-collar voters and of middle-class conservatives.

가산명사-집합 중산층 ❑ 19세기 말의 중산층 팽창 ● 형용사 중산층의 ❑ 그는 생산직 유권자들과 중산층 보수파로부터 급속히 지지를 잃고 있다.

Mid|dle East ♦♦♢ N-PROPER The **Middle East** is the area around the eastern Mediterranean that includes Iran and all the countries in Asia to the west and southwest of Iran. ❑ The two great rivers of the Middle East rise in the mountains of Turkey.

고유명사 중동 ❑ 중동의 거대한 두 강은 터키의 산맥에서 발원한다.

middle|man /mɪd²lmæn/ (**middlemen**) **1** N-COUNT A **middleman** is a person or company which buys things from the people who produce them and sells them to the people who want to buy them. [BUSINESS] ❑ Why don't they cut out the middleman and let us do it ourselves? **2** N-COUNT A **middleman** is a person who helps in negotiations between people who are unwilling to meet each other directly. ❑ The two sides would only meet indirectly, through middlemen.

1 가산명사 중간 상인 [경제] ❑ 왜 그들은 그 중개인을 거치지 않고 우리 스스로 그 일을 하도록 하지 않을까? **2** 가산명사 중재자 ❑ 양측은 중재자를 통해서 간접적으로만 만날 것이다.

mid|dle man|age|ment N-UNCOUNT **Middle management** refers to managers who are below the top level of management, and who are responsible for controlling and running an organization rather than making decisions about how it operates. [BUSINESS] ❑ The proportion of women in middle management has risen to 40%.

불가산명사 중간 관리자 [경제] ❑ 중간 관리자 중 여성의 비율이 40퍼센트로 증가했다.

middle-of-the-road **1** ADJ If you describe someone's opinions or policies as **middle-of-the-road**, you mean that they are neither left-wing nor right-wing, and not at all extreme. ❑ Consensus need not be weak, nor need it result in middle-of-the-road policies. **2** ADJ If you describe something or someone as **middle-of-the-road**, you mean that they are ordinary or unexciting. ❑ I actually don't want to be a middle-of-the-road person, married with a mortgage.

1 형용사 중도의 ❑ 합의의 정도가 불충분해서도 안 되고, 그 결과가 중도성향의 정책일 필요도 없다. **2** 형용사 평범한 ❑ 사실 나는 주택 융자금에 얽매여 사는 보통 사람이 되고 싶지 않다.

Mid|lands /mɪdləndz/ N-PROPER-COLL The **Midlands** is the region or area in the central part of a country, in particular the central part of England. ❑ ...an engineering company in the Midlands.

고유명사-집합 (특히 잉글랜드의) 중부지방 ❑ 중부지방의 토목 회사

mid|night ♦♦♦ /mɪdnaɪt/ **1** N-UNCOUNT **Midnight** is twelve o'clock in the middle of the night. ❑ *It was well after midnight by the time Anne returned to her apartment.* **2** ADJ **Midnight** is used to describe something which happens or appears at midnight or in the middle of the night. [ADJ n] ❑ *It is totally out of the question to postpone the midnight deadline.* **3** PHRASE If someone **is burning the midnight oil**, they are staying up very late in order to study or do some other work. ❑ *Chris is asleep after burning the midnight oil trying to finish his article.*

mid-range /mɪd reɪndʒ/ ADJ You can use **mid-range** to describe products or services which are neither the most expensive nor the cheapest of their type. [ADJ n] ❑ *...the price of a mid-range family car.*

midst /mɪdst/ **1** PHRASE If you are **in the midst of** doing something, you are doing it at the moment. ❑ *We are in the midst of one of the worst recessions for many, many years.* **2** PHRASE If something happens **in the midst of** an event, it happens during it. ❑ *Eleanor arrived in the midst of a blizzard.* **3** PHRASE If someone or something is **in the midst of** a group of people or things, they are among them or surrounded by them. ❑ *Many were surprised to see him exposed like this in the midst of a large crowd.*

mid|way /mɪdweɪ/ also **mid-way** **1** ADV If something is **midway between** two places, it is between them and the same distance from each of them. [ADV prep] ❑ *The studio is midway between his aunt's old home and his cottage.* ● ADJ **Midway** is also an adjective. ❑ *The vineyard is close to the midway point between Gloucester, Hereford and Worcester.* **2** ADV If something happens **midway through** a period of time, it happens during the middle part of it. ❑ *He crashed midway through the race.* ● ADJ **Midway** is also an adjective. [ADJ n] ❑ *They were denied an obvious penalty before the midway point of the first half.*

mid|week /mɪdwik/ ADJ **Midweek** describes something that happens in the middle of the week. [ADJ n] ❑ *Enjoy the peace and beauty of midweek walks in the Palo Alto.* ● ADV **Midweek** is also an adverb. ❑ *They'll be able to go up to London midweek.*

mid|wife /mɪdwaɪf/ (**midwives**) N-COUNT A **midwife** is a nurse who is trained to deliver babies and to advise pregnant women. ❑ *You don't have to call the midwife as soon as labour starts.*

---

might

① MODAL USES
② NOUN USES

---

① might ♦♦♦ /maɪt/

Might is a modal verb. It is used with the base form of a verb.

→Please look at category **11** to see if the expression you are looking for is shown under another headword. **1** MODAL You use **might** to indicate that something will possibly happen or be true in the future, but you cannot be certain. [VAGUENESS] ❑ *There's a report today that smoking might be banned totally in most buildings.* ❑ *I might well regret it later.* **2** MODAL You use **might** to indicate that there is a possibility that something is true, but you cannot be certain. [VAGUENESS] ❑ *She and Simon's father had not given up hope that he might be alive.* ❑ *You might be right.* **3** MODAL You use **might** to indicate that something could happen or be true in particular circumstances. [VAGUENESS] ❑ *America might sell more cars to the islands if they were made with the steering wheel on the right.* **4** MODAL You use **might have** with a past participle to indicate that it is possible that something happened or was true, or when giving a possible explanation for something. ❑ *I heard what might have been an explosion.* **5** MODAL You use **might have** with a past participle to indicate that something was a possibility in the past, although it did not actually happen. ❑ *If she had had to give up riding she might have taken up sailing competitively.* **6** MODAL You use **might** in statements where you are accepting the truth of a situation, but contrasting it with something that is more important. ❑ *They might not have two cents to rub together, but at least they have a kind of lifestyle that is different.* **7** MODAL You use **might** when you are saying emphatically that someone ought to do the thing mentioned, especially when they are annoyed because they have not done it. [EMPHASIS] ❑ *You might have told me that before!* **8** MODAL You use **might** to make a suggestion or to give advice in a very polite way. [POLITENESS] ❑ *They might be wise to stop advertising on television.* **9** MODAL You use **might** as a polite way of interrupting someone, asking a question, making a request, or introducing what you are going to say next. [FORMAL, SPOKEN, POLITENESS] ❑ *Might I make a suggestion?* ❑ *Might I ask what you're doing here?* **10** MODAL You use **might** in expressions such as **I might have known** and **I might have guessed** to indicate that you are not surprised at a disappointing event or fact. ❑ *I might have known I'd find you with some little slut.* **11** **might as well** →see **well**

② might /maɪt/ **1** N-UNCOUNT **Might** is power or strength. [FORMAL] ❑ *The might of the army could prove a decisive factor.* **2** PHRASE If you do something **with all** your **might**, you do it using all your strength and energy. ❑ *She swung the hammer at his head with all her might.*

mightn't /maɪtᵊnt/ **Mightn't** is a spoken form of "might not."

might've /maɪtəv/ **Might've** is the usual spoken form of "might have," especially when "have" is an auxiliary verb.

mighty /maɪti/ (**mightier**, **mightiest**) ADJ **Mighty** is used to describe something that is very large or powerful. [LITERARY] ❑ *There was a flash and a mighty bang.*

---

1 불가산명사 자정 ❑ 족히 자정이 넘은 시간에 앤이 자기 아파트로 돌아왔다. **2** 형용사 자정의, 심야의 ❑ 자정 마감 시간을 연기하는 것은 전적으로 불가능하다. **3** 구 밤늦게까지 일하다 ❑ 크리스는 기사를 끝내려고 밤늦게까지 일을 한 후에 잠이 들어 있다.

형용사 중간 가격의 ❑ 중간 가격의 가족형 승용차

1 구 –의 한가운데서, 한창 –하는 중인 ❑ 우리는 수년 동안 여러 차례 있었던 최악의 불경기의 한가운데 있다. **2** 구 –하는 가운데 ❑ 엘리너는 심한 눈보라의 가운데 도착했다. **3** 구 가운데에 ❑ 큰 무리 가운데서 이렇게 그가 노출된 것을 보고 많은 사람들이 놀랐다.

1 부사 중간쯤에 ❑ 그 작업실은 그의 이모의 옛날 집과 자신의 작은집 중간쯤에 위치하고 있다. ● 형용사 중간쯤의 ❑ 그 포도원은 글로스터, 헤리퍼드, 우스터 사이의 중간 지점에 가깝다. **2** 부사 중반에 ❑ 그는 경주 중반에 사고를 당했다. ● 형용사 중반의 ❑ 그들은 전반전 중반 이전에 상대방이 분명히 페널티 반칙을 했음에도 유리한 판정을 받지 못했다.

형용사 한 주 중반의 ❑ 팰러 앨토에서 주 중반에 평화롭고 아름다운 산책을 즐기십시오. ● 부사 한 주의 중반에 ❑ 그들은 주 중반에 런던으로 갈 수 있을 것이다.

가산명사 조산사 ❑ 진통이 시작되자마자 조산사를 부를 필요는 없습니다.

---

might은 조동사이며 동사 원형과 함께 쓴다.

1 법조동사 –할 수도 있다, –할지도 모른다 [짐작투] ❑ 오늘 흡연이 대부분의 건물에서 전면적으로 금지될 수도 있다는 보도가 나왔다. ❑ 내가 나중에 그 일에 대해 상당히 후회할지도 몰라. **2** 법조동사 –일 수도 있다 [짐작투] ❑ 사이먼의 아버지는 그가 생존해 있을 수도 있다는 희망을 버리지 않았었다. ❑ 네가 옳을 수도 있다. **3** 법조동사 –한 수 있을 것이다 [짐작투] ❑ 미국은 핸들을 오른쪽에 설치한다면 그 섬들에 더 많은 차를 판매할 수 있을 것이다. **4** 법조동사 –했을 것이다 ❑ 나는 무언가 폭발하는 듯한 소리를 들었다. **5** 법조동사 –했을지도 모른다 ❑ 그녀가 말 타기를 포기했어야만 했다면 남들에게 뒤지지 않게끔 요트 조정에 열중했을지도 모른다. **6** 법조동사 –일지도 모른다 ❑ 그들이 돈이 없을지는 모르지만, 적어도 남들과는 다른 생활 방식으로 살아가고 있다. **7** 법조동사 –했어야 했다 [강조] ❑ 너는 이전에 나에게 그 말을 해줬어야 했다. **8** 법조동사 –해야 할 텐데 [공손체] ❑ 그들이 텔레비전 광고를 중단하는 것이 현명할 텐데. **9** 법조동사 –해도 될까? [격식체, 구어체, 공손체] ❑ 제가 제안 하나 해도 될까요? ❑ 당신이 지금 여기서 무엇을 하고 있는지 여쭤봐도 될까요? **10** 법조동사 –일지도 모르니; 짐작 못한 것도 아니다 ❑ 당신이 어린 매춘부 같은 애와 있으리라는 것을 내가 짐작 못한 건 아니야.

1 불가산명사 힘 [격식체] ❑ 그 군대의 병력이 결정적인 요소로 판명될 수 있다. **2** 구 힘껏, 전력을 다하여 ❑ 그녀는 그의 머리를 향해 망치를 힘껏 휘둘렀다.

might not의 구어체형

might have의 구어체형

형용사 강력한, 엄청난 [문예체] ❑ 번쩍하는 불빛과 함께 엄청난 소리가 쿵 하고 났다.

:

mi|graine /ˈmaɪɡreɪn, BRIT ˈmiːɡreɪn/ (**migraines**) N-VAR A **migraine** is an extremely painful headache that makes you feel very ill. ❑ *Her mother suffered from migraines.*

가산명사 또는 불가산명사 편두통 ❑ 그녀의 어머니께서는 편두통으로 고생하셨다.

Word Link   migr ≈ moving, changing : e*migr*ant, im*migr*ant, *migr*ant

---

mi|grant /ˈmaɪɡrənt/ (**migrants**) **1** N-COUNT A **migrant** is a person who moves from one place to another, especially in order to find work. ❑ *The government divides asylum-seekers into economic migrants and genuine refugees.* **2** N-COUNT **Migrants** are birds, fish, or animals that migrate from one part of the world to another. ❑ *Migrant birds shelter in the reeds.*

1 가산명사 이주자 ❑ 정부는 망명 희망자들을 경제적인 이유로 온 이주자와 진정한 난민으로 분류했다. **2** 가산명사 철새 ❑ 철새는 갈대밭에 머문다.

mi|grate /ˈmaɪɡreɪt, BRIT maɪˈɡreɪt/ (**migrates, migrating, migrated**) **1** V-I If people **migrate**, they move from one place to another, especially in order to find work or to live somewhere for a short time. ❑ *People migrate to cities like Jakarta in search of work.* ● **mi|gra|tion** /maɪˈɡreɪʃ³n/ (**migrations**) N-VAR ❑ *...the migration of Soviet Jews to Israel.* **2** V-I When birds, fish, or animals **migrate**, they move at a particular season from one part of the world or from one part of a country to another, usually in order to breed or to find new feeding grounds. ❑ *Most birds have to fly long distances to migrate.* ● **mi|gra|tion** N-VAR ❑ *...the migration of animals in the Serengeti.*

1 자동사 이주하다 ❑ 사람들은 일을 찾아서 자카르타 같은 도시로 이주한다. ● 이주 가산명사 또는 불가산명사 ❑ 소련 내 거주했던 유태인들이 이스라엘로 이주 철 따라 이동하다 ❑ 대부분의 새들은 철 따라 이동하기 위해 머나먼 거리를 날아야 한다. ● 이동 가산명사 또는 불가산명사 ❑ 세렝게티 내 동물들의 이동

mike /maɪk/ (**mikes**) N-COUNT A **mike** is the same as a **microphone**. [INFORMAL]

가산명사 마이크 [비격식체]

mil /mɪl/ NUM **Mil** means the same as **million**. [INFORMAL] ❑ *Zhamnov, 22, signed for $1.25 mil over three years.*

수사 백만 [비격식체] ❑ 스물두 살인 잠노프는 3년간 백 25만 달러의 계약을 했다.

mild ♦♢♢ /maɪld/ (**milder, mildest**) **1** ADJ **Mild** is used to describe something such as a feeling, attitude, or illness that is not very strong or severe. ❑ *Teddy turned to Mona with a look of mild confusion.* ● **mild|ly** ADV ❑ *Josephine must have had the disease very mildly as she showed no symptoms.* **2** ADJ A **mild** person is gentle and does not get angry easily. ❑ *He is a mild man, who is reasonable almost to the point of blandness.* ● **mild|ly** ADV [ADV after v] ❑ *"I'm not meddling," Kenworthy said mildly, "I'm just curious."* **3** ADJ **Mild** weather is pleasant because it is neither extremely hot nor extremely cold. ❑ *The area is famous for its very mild winter climate.*

1 형용사 약간의; 순한; (병세 등이) 가벼운 ❑ 테디는 약간 혼란스러운 표정으로 모나를 돌아보았다. ● 약간, 가볍게 부사 ❑ 증상이 없었던 것으로 보아, 조세핀은 그 병에 아주 가볍게 걸렸던 것이 분명하다. **2** 형용사 온순한 ❑ 그는 온순한 사람으로, 거의 재미없다고 할 정도로 합리적이다. ● 온순하게 부사 ❑ "나는 끼어드는 게 아냐. 그냥 궁금해서 그래."라고 켄워디가 온순하게 말했다. **3** 형용사 온화한 ❑ 그 지역은 겨울날씨가 무척 온화하기로 유명하다.

> In informal English, if you want to emphasize how hot the weather is, you can say that it is **boiling** or **scorching**. In winter, if the temperature is above average, you can say that it is **mild**. In general, **hot** suggests a higher temperature than **warm**, and **warm** things are usually pleasant. ❑ *...a warm evening.*

> 비격식체 영어에서는, 날씨가 얼마나 더운지를 강조하고 싶으면, boiling이나 scorching을 쓸 수 있다. 겨울에 기온이 평균보다 높으면, 날씨가 mild하다고 할 수 있다. 대체로, hot은 warm보다 더 기온이 높은 것을 나타내고, warm한 것은 대개 쾌적하다. ❑ ...따스한 저녁

4 ADJ You describe food as **mild** when it does not taste or smell strong, sharp, or bitter, especially when you like it because of this. ❑ *This cheese has a soft, mild flavor.* **5** →see also **mildly**

4 형용사 담백한 ❑ 이 치즈는 부드럽고 담백한 향이 납니다.

Thesaurus   mild의 참조어

ADJ.   slight **1**
     friendly, gentle, kind, warm **2**
     comfortable, pleasant, warm; (ant.) harsh, severe **3**

---

mild|ly /ˈmaɪldli/ **1** →see **mild** **2** PHRASE You use **to put it mildly** to indicate that you are describing something in language that is much less strong, direct, or critical than what you really think. ❑ *But not all the money, to put it mildly, has been used wisely.*

2 구 조심스럽게 말하면 ❑ 그러나, 조심스럽게 말하자면, 그 돈이 모두 현명하게 쓰여진 건 아니다.

Word Link   mill ≈ thousand : *mil*e, *mill*ennium, *mill*ion

---

mile ♦♦♢ /maɪl/ (**miles**) **1** N-COUNT A **mile** is a unit of distance equal to 1760 yards or approximately 1.6 kilometers. ❑ *They drove 600 miles across the desert.* ❑ *She lives just half a mile away.* **2** N-PLURAL **Miles** is used, especially in the expression **miles away**, to refer to a long distance. ❑ *If you enroll at a gym that's miles away, you won't be visiting it as often as you should.* **3** N-COUNT **Miles** or **a mile** is used with the meaning "very much" in order to emphasize the difference between two things or qualities, or the difference between what you aimed to do and what you actually achieved. [INFORMAL, EMPHASIS] ❑ *You're miles better than most of the performers we see nowadays.* ❑ *With a Labour candidate in place they won by a mile.*

1 가산명사 마일 ❑ 그들은 차를 타고 사막을 가로질러 600마일을 갔다. ❑ 그녀는 겨우 반 마일 떨어진 곳에 산다. **2** 복수명사 상당한 거리 ❑ 상당히 멀리 있는 체육관에 등록하면, 가야 할 만큼 자주 가게 되지 않을 것이다. **3** 가산명사 훨씬; 크게 [비격식체, 강조] ❑ 너는 요즘 우리가 보는 대부분의 연기자들보다 훨씬 우수하다. ❑ 노동당 후보가 확실한 자리를 지키고 있었기 때문에, 그들이 큰 차이로 승리했다.

Word Partnership   mile의 연어

ADJ.   mile **high**, mile **long**, **nautical** mile, **square** mile, mile **wide** **1**

---

mile|age /ˈmaɪlɪdʒ/ (**mileages**) **1** N-UNCOUNT **Mileage** refers to the distance that you have traveled, measured in miles. ❑ *While most of their mileage may be in and around town, they still want motorways for longer trips.* **2** N-UNCOUNT The **mileage** of a vehicle is the number of miles that it can travel using one gallon or liter of fuel. ❑ *They are willing to pay up to $500 more for cars that get better mileage.* **3** N-UNCOUNT The **mileage** in a particular course of action is its usefulness in getting you what you want. ❑ *It's obviously important to get as much mileage out of the convention as possible.*

1 불가산명사 주행 거리 ❑ 그들이 보통 주행하는 길은 마을 안팎이지만 그래도 더 멀리 갈 때는 고속도로를 원한다. **2** 불가산명사 연비 ❑ 그들은 차량의 연비 향상을 원하며 그래서 추가로 최대 500달러를 지불할 용의가 있다. **3** 불가산명사 이익 ❑ 그 협약에서 가능한 한 많은 이익을 얻는 것이 명백히 중요하다.

mile|stone /ˈmaɪlstoʊn/ (**milestones**) N-COUNT A **milestone** is an important event in the history or development of something or someone. ❑ *He said the launch of the party represented a milestone in Zambian history.*

가산명사 획기적인 사건 ❑ 그는 그 정당의 창립이 잠비아 역사상 획기적인 사건이라고 말했다.

mi|lieu /ˈmiːljuː, mil-, BRIT miːˈljɜː/ (**milieux** or **milieus**) N-COUNT Your **milieu** is the group of people or activities that you live among or are familiar with. [FORMAL] ❑ *They stayed, safe and happy, within their own social milieu.*

가산명사 환경 [격식체] ❑ 그들은 자신들의 사회적 환경 내에서 안전하고 행복하게 머물렀다.

mili|tant ◆◇◇ /mɪlɪtənt/ (militants) ADJ You use **militant** to describe people who believe in something very strongly and are active in trying to bring about political or social change, often in extreme ways that other people find unacceptable. ❑ *Militant mineworkers in the Ukraine have voted for a one-day stoppage next month.* ● N-COUNT **Militant** is also a noun. ❑ *Even now we could not be sure that the militants would not find some new excuse to call a strike the following winter.* ● **mili|tan|cy** N-UNCOUNT ❑ *…the rise of trade union militancy.*

형용사 강경한 ❑ 우크라이나의 강경 광산 노동자들이 다음 달에 하루 동안 파업하기로 결의했다. ● 가산명사 강경파 ❑ 심지어 지금도 우리는 다가오는 겨울에 강경파들이 구실이 없어서 파업을 못할 것이라고는 확신할 수 없다. ● 호전성 불가산명사 ❑ 커져가는 산별 노조의 호전성

Word Link   *milit ≈ soldier : de**milit**arize, **milit**ary, **milit**ia*

mili|tary ◆◆◆ /mɪlɪteri, BRIT mɪlɪtri/ (militaries) **1** ADJ **Military** means relating to the armed forces of a country. ❑ *Military action may become necessary.* ❑ *The president is sending in almost 20,000 military personnel to help with the relief efforts.* ● **mili|tari|ly** ADV ❑ *They remain unwilling to intervene militarily in what could be an unending war.* **2** N-COUNT-COLL **The military** are the armed forces of a country, especially officers of high rank. ❑ *The bombing has been far more widespread than the military will admit.* **3** ADJ **Military** means well-organized, controlled, or neat, in a way that is typical of a soldier. ❑ *Your working day will need to be organized with military precision.*
→see **army**

1 형용사 군대의, 군사적인 ❑ 군사적인 조치가 필요하게 될지도 모른다. ❑ 대통령은 구조 활동의 지원을 위해 2만여 명에 달하는 군 병력을 보낼 것이다. ● 군사적으로 부사 ❑ 그들은 끝이 보이지 않을 것 같은 전쟁에 군사적으로 개입하는 것을 여전히 꺼리고 있다. **2** 가산명사·집합 군 당국, 군부 ❑ 폭격은 군 당국이 인정하려는 것보다 훨씬 넓은 지역에 가해졌다. **3** 형용사 군인다운 ❑ 근무일은 군인다운 정확성을 가지고 짜여질 필요가 있을 것이다.

mili|tia /mɪlɪʃə/ (militias) N-COUNT A **militia** is an organization that operates like an army but whose members are not professional soldiers. ❑ *The troops will not attempt to disarm the warring militias.*
→see **army**

가산명사 무장 조직, 민병 ❑ 군대가 전투 중인 무장 조직을 무장 해제시키려고 하지는 않을 것이다.

milk ◆◇◇ /mɪlk/ (milks, milking, milked) **1** N-UNCOUNT **Milk** is the white liquid produced by cows, goats, and some other animals, which people drink and use to make butter, cheese, and yogurt. ❑ *He popped out to buy a pint of milk.* **2** V-T If someone **milks** a cow or goat, they get milk from it, using either their hands or a machine. ❑ *Farm-workers milked cows by hand.* **3** N-UNCOUNT **Milk** is the white liquid produced by women to feed their babies. ❑ *Milk from the mother's breast is a perfect food for the human baby.* **4** N-MASS Liquid products for cleaning your skin or making it softer are sometimes referred to as **milks**. ❑ *Sales of cleansing milks, creams, and gels have doubled over the past decade.* **5** V-T If you say that someone **milks** something, you mean that they get as much benefit or profit as they can from it, without caring about the effects this has on other people. [DISAPPROVAL] ❑ *A few people tried to milk the insurance companies.* **6** →see also **skim milk, dairy**

1 불가산명사 우유 ❑ 그는 우유 1파인트를 사려고 뛰어나갔다. **2** 타동사 젖을 짜다 ❑ 농장 일꾼이 손으로 소젖을 짰다. **3** 불가산명사 모유 ❑ 모유가 아기에게는 완전식품이다. **4** 물질명사 유제 ❑ 지난 십 년간 세안용 유제, 크림 및 젤의 판매가 두 배로 증가했다. **5** 타동사 최대한 이익을 뽑아내다, ~을 착취하다 [탐탁찮음] ❑ 많은 사람들이 보험 회사들에게서 최대한 이익을 뽑아내려 한다.

milky /mɪlki/ (milkier, milkiest) **1** ADJ If you describe something as **milky**, you mean that it is pale white in color. You can describe other colors as **milky** when they are very pale. ❑ *A milky mist filled the valley.* **2** ADJ Drinks or food that are **milky** contain a lot of milk. ❑ *…his big cup of milky coffee.*

1 형용사 우윳빛의 ❑ 우윳빛 안개가 계곡을 가득 메웠다. **2** 형용사 우유를 넣은 ❑ 우유를 넣은 커피가 담긴 그의 큰 컵

mill ◆◇◇ /mɪl/ (mills, milling, milled) **1** N-COUNT A **mill** is a building in which grain is crushed to make flour. ❑ *There was an old mill that really did grind corn.* **2** N-COUNT A **mill** is a small device used for grinding something such as coffee beans or pepper into powder. ❑ *…a pepper mill.* **3** N-COUNT A **mill** is a factory used for making and processing materials such as steel, wool, or cotton. ❑ *…a steel mill.* **4** V-T To **mill** something such as wheat or pepper means to grind it in a mill. [BRIT also **mill about**] ❑ *They do not have the capacity to mill the maize.*

1 가산명사 제분소 ❑ 그곳엔 정말 옥수수를 빻던 오래된 제분소가 하나 있었다. **2** 가산명사 분쇄기 ❑ 후추 분쇄기 **3** 가산명사 제조 공장 ❑ 제철소 **4** 타동사 제분하다 [영국영어 mill about] ❑ 그들은 옥수수를 제분할 능력이 없다.

▶**mill around** PHRASAL VERB When a crowd of people **mill around** or **mill about**, they move around within a particular place or area, so that the movement of the whole crowd looks very confused. ❑ *Quite a few people were milling about, but nothing was happening.*

구동사 맴돌다 ❑ 상당수의 사람들이 맴돌고 있었지만, 아무 일도 일어나지 않았다.

Word Link   *enn ≈ year : cent**enn**ial, mill**enn**ium, per**enn**ial*

Word Link   *mill ≈ thousand : **mil**e, **mill**ennium, **mill**ion*

mil|len|nium /mɪleniəm/ (millenniums or millennia) **1** N-COUNT A **millennium** is a period of one thousand years, especially one which begins and ends with a year ending in "000," for example the period from the year 1000 to the year 2000. [FORMAL] ❑ *…the dawn of a new millennium.* **2** N-SING Many people refer to the year 2000 as **the Millennium**. ❑ *…the eve of the Millennium.*

1 가산명사 천년 [격식체] ❑ 새 천년의 여명 **2** 단수명사 새 천년, 밀레니엄 ❑ 새 천년의 전야

Word Link   *milli ≈ thousandth : **milli**gram, **milli**liter, **milli**meter*

mil|li|gram /mɪlɪgræm/ (milligrams) [BRIT also **milligramme**] N-COUNT A **milligram** is a unit of weight that is equal to a thousandth of a gram. ❑ *…0.5 milligrams of mercury.*

[영국영어 milligramme] 가산명사 밀리그램 ❑ 0.5밀리그램의 수은

mil|li|liter /mɪlɪlitər/ (milliliters) [BRIT **millilitre**] N-COUNT A **milliliter** is a unit of volume for liquids and gases that is equal to a thousandth of a liter. ❑ *…100 milliliters of blood.*

[영국영어 millilitre] 가산명사 밀리리터 ❑ 100밀리리터의 혈액

mil|li|meter /mɪlɪmitər/ (millimeters) [BRIT **millimetre**] N-COUNT A **millimeter** is a metric unit of length that is equal to a tenth of a centimeter or a thousandth of a meter. ❑ *The creature is a tiny centipede, just 10 millimeters long.*

[영국영어 millimetre] 가산명사 밀리미터 ❑ 그 생명체는 아주 작은 지네로, 길이가 겨우 10밀리미터이다.

mil|lion ◆◆◆ /mɪlyən/ (millions)

The plural form is **million** after a number, or after a word or expression referring to a number, such as "several" or "a few."

숫자 또는 'several', 'a few'와 같이 수를 지정하는 단어나 표현 뒤에서 복수형은 million이다.

1 NUM A **million** or one **million** is the number 1,000,000. ❑ *Up to five million people a year visit the county.* **2** QUANT-PLURAL If you talk about **millions of** people or things, you mean that there is a very large number of them but you do not know or do not want to say exactly how many. [QUANT of pl-n] ❑ *The programme was viewed on television in millions of homes.*

1 수사 백만 ❑ 연간 5백만 명에 이르는 사람들이 그 자치구를 방문했다. **2** 복수수량사 수백만의 ❑ 수백만 가구가 그 프로그램을 텔레비전으로 시청하였다.

mil|lion|aire /mɪlyənɛ́ər/ (**millionaires**) N-COUNT A **millionaire** is a very rich person who has money or property worth at least a million pounds or dollars. ❏ *By the time he died, he was a millionaire.*

가산명사 백만장자 ❏ 사망할 무렵이 되었을 때 그는 백만장자였다.

mil|lionth ♦♢◇ /mɪ́lyənθ/ (**millionths**) **1** ORD The **millionth** item in a series is the one you count as number one million. ❏ *Last year the millionth truck rolled off the assembly line.* **2** FRACTION A **millionth of** something is one of a million equal parts of it. ❏ *The bomb must explode within less than a millionth of a second.*

1 서수 백만 번째의 ❏ 지난해 그 조립 라인에서 백만 번째 트럭이 출고되었다. **2** 분수 100만 분의 1 ❏ 그 폭탄은 100만 분의 1초보다 짧은 시간 안에 폭발해야 한다.

Word Link	mim ≈ copying : mimic, mime, pantomime

mime /maɪm/ (**mimes, miming, mimed**) **1** N-VAR **Mime** is the use of movements and gestures in order to express something or tell a story without using speech. ❏ *Music, mime, and strong visual imagery play a strong part in the productions.* **2** V-T/V-I If you **mime** something, you describe or express it using mime rather than speech. ❏ *It featured a solo dance in which a woman in a short overall mimed a lot of dainty housework.* **3** V-T/V-I If you **mime**, you pretend to be singing or playing an instrument, although the music is in fact coming from a CD or cassette. ❏ *Richey's not miming, he's playing very quiet guitar.* ❏ *In concerts, the group mime their songs.*

1 가산명사 또는 불가산명사 마임 ❏ 음악, 마임 그리고 강렬한 시각적 이미지가 그 작품에서 두드러진 역할을 한다. **2** 타동사/자동사 마임으로 보여 주다 ❏ 그것은 한 여성이 짧은 작업복을 입고 수많은 세세한 집안일을 하는 것을 마임으로 보여 주는 독무를 특징으로 한다. **3** 타동사/자동사 (노래나 연주를) 시늉만 하다, 립싱크하다 ❏ 리치가 연주를 하는 척 하고 있는 것이 아니라 아주 조용히 기타를 치고 있어. ❏ 콘서트에서, 그 그룹은 립싱크한다.

mim|ic /mɪ́mɪk/ (**mimics, mimicking, mimicked**) **1** V-T If you **mimic** the actions or voice of a person or animal, you imitate them, usually in a way that is meant to be amusing or entertaining. ❏ *He could mimic anybody, and he often reduced Isabel to helpless laughter.* **2** V-T If someone or something **mimics** another person or thing, they try to be like them. ❏ *The computer doesn't mimic human thought; it reaches the same ends by different means.* **3** N-COUNT A **mimic** is a person who is able to mimic people or animals. ❏ *At school I was a good mimic.*

1 타동사 흉내 내다 ❏ 그는 누구든 흉내 낼 수 있어서 종종 이사벨을 속수무책으로 웃게 만들었다. **2** 타동사 -을 닮으려고 노력하다 ❏ 컴퓨터는 인간의 사고를 닮으려고 하는 게 아니라 다른 방법을 통해 동일한 목표에 도달한다. **3** 가산명사 흉내 내는 사람 ❏ 학창 시절에 나는 흉내를 잘 내었다.

min. Min. is a written abbreviation for **minimum**, or for **minutes** or **minute**.

최소; 분

mince /mɪns/ (**minces, mincing, minced**) **1** V-T If you **mince** food such as meat or vegetables, you cut or grind it up into very small pieces, usually in a machine. ❏ *Perhaps I'll buy lean meat and mince it myself.* **2** N-UNCOUNT **Mince** is meat which has been cut or ground up into very small pieces using a machine. [BRIT; AM **ground beef, hamburger meat**] ❏ *Brown the mince in a frying pan.*

1 타동사 다지다, 갈다 ❏ 아마 살코기를 사서 내가 직접 갈 거야. **2** 불가산명사 다진 고기 [영국영어; 미국영어 ground beef, hamburger meat] ❏ 다진 고기를 프라이팬에 넣고 노릇노릇하게 볶아라.

---

mind

① NOUN USES
② VERB USES

① mind ♦♦♦ /maɪnd/ (**minds**) →Please look at category **33** to see if the expression you are looking for is shown under another headword. **1** N-COUNT You refer to someone's **mind** when talking about their thoughts. For example, if you say that something is **in your mind**, you mean that you are thinking about it, and if you say that something is **at the back of your mind**, you mean that you are aware of it, although you are not thinking about it very much. ❏ *I'm trying to clear my mind of all this.* ❏ *There was no doubt in his mind that the man was serious.* **2** N-COUNT Your **mind** is your ability to think and reason. ❏ *You have a good mind.* ❏ *Studying stretched my mind and got me thinking about things.* **3** N-COUNT If you have a particular type of **mind**, you have a particular way of thinking which is part of your character, or a result of your education or professional training. ❏ *Andrew, you have a very suspicious mind.* ❏ *The key to his success is his logical mind.* **4** N-COUNT You can refer to someone as a particular kind of **mind** as a way of saying that they are clever, intelligent, or imaginative. ❏ *She moved to London, meeting some of the best minds of her time.* **5** →see also **frame of mind, state of mind 6** PHRASE If you tell someone to **bear** something **in mind** or to **keep** something **in mind**, you are reminding or warning them about something important which they should remember. ❏ *Bear in mind that petrol stations are scarce in the more remote areas.* **7** PHRASE If you **cast** your **mind back to** a time in the past, you think about what happened then. ❏ *Cast your mind back to 1978, when Forest won the title.* **8** PHRASE If you **change** your **mind**, or if someone or something **changes** your **mind**, you change a decision you have made or an opinion that you had. ❏ *I was going to vote for him, but I changed my mind and voted for Reagan.* **9** PHRASE If something **comes to mind** or **springs to mind**, you think of it without making any effort. ❏ *Integrity and honesty are words that spring to mind when talking of the man.* **10** PHRASE If you say that an idea or possibility never **crossed** your **mind**, you mean that you did not think of it. ❏ *It had never crossed his mind that there might be a problem.* **11** PHRASE If you see something **in** your **mind's eye**, you imagine it and have a clear picture of it in your mind. ❏ *In his mind's eye, he can imagine the effect he's having.* **12** PHRASE If you say that you **have a good mind to** do something or **have half a mind to** do it, you are threatening or announcing that you have a strong desire to do it, although you probably will not do it. ❏ *He raged on about how he had a good mind to resign.* **13** PHRASE If you ask someone what they **have in mind**, you want to know in more detail about an idea or wish they have. ❏ *"Maybe we could celebrate tonight." — "What did you have in mind?"* **14** PHRASE If you do something **with** a particular thing **in mind**, you do it with that thing as your aim or as the reason or basis for your action. ❏ *These families need support. With this in mind a group of 35 specialists met last weekend.* **15** PHRASE If you say that something such as an illness is **all in the mind**, you mean that it relates to someone's feelings or attitude, rather than having any physical cause. ❏ *It could be a virus, or it could be all in the mind.* **16** PHRASE If you **know** your **own mind**, you are sure about your opinions, and are not easily influenced by other people. ❏ *She knows her own mind and won't let anyone talk her into something she doesn't want to do.* **17** PHRASE If you say that someone **is losing their mind**, you mean that they are becoming mad. ❏ *Sometimes I feel I'm losing my mind.* **18** PHRASE If you **make up** your **mind** or make your **mind up**, you decide which of a number of possible things you will want or do. ❏ *Once he made up his mind to*

1 가산명사 생각; 내 생각으로는; 내 심중은 ❏ 나는 이 모든 것에 대해 생각을 정리하려고 노력 중이야. ❏ 그가 생각할 때 그 남자가 진지했다는 것은 의심의 여지가 없었다. **2** 가산명사 지적 능력 ❏ 너는 지적 능력이 뛰어나. ❏ 공부를 통해 내 지적 능력이 확대되었고 사물에 대해 생각하게 되었다. **3** 가산명사 사고방식 ❏ 앤드류, 너는 사고방식이 매우 의심스러워. ❏ 그의 성공 비결은 논리적인 사고방식이다. **4** 가산명사 지성인, 지성 ❏ 그녀는 런던으로 이사했고, 자신의 생애 중 최고의 지성을 몇 명 만나게 되었다. **6** 구 명심하다 ❏ 더 외진 곳에는 주유소가 드물다는 것을 명심해라. **7** 구 -을 회상하다 ❏ 1978년, 포레스트가 그 타이틀을 땄을 때를 회상해 보세요. **8** 구 마음을 바꾸다; 마음을 바꾸게 하다 ❏ 그에게 투표하려고 했으나, 마음을 바꿔 레이건에게 투표를 했다. **9** 구 마음속에 떠오르다 ❏ 그 사람에 대한 얘기를 할 때는 청렴과 정직이란 단어가 저절로 마음속에 떠오른다. **10** 구 마음속에 떠오르다, 생각나다 ❏ 그는 문제일 수도 있다는 생각을 전혀 하지 못했다. **11** 구 마음속으로 ❏ 그는 마음속으로 자신이 미치고 있는 영향력을 상상할 수 있다. **12** 구 -할 생각이 많이 나다 ❏ 그는 화를 내며 얼마나 자기가 사임하고 싶은지 모른다고 소리를 질렀다. **13** 구 (마음속으로) 계획하다 ❏ "아마 우리가 오늘밤 축하할 수 있을 거야." "넌 뭘 계획하고 있었니?" **14** 구 -을 염두에 두고 ❏ 그 가족들은 원조를 필요로 한다. 이것을 염두에 두고 35명의 전문가로 구성된 단체가 지난 주말에 모임을 가졌다. **15** 구 그렇다고 생각하기 때문이든 ❏ 그것이 진짜 바이러스 때문일 수도 있고, 아니면 그냥 그렇다고 생각하기 때문일 수도 있다. **16** 구 자신의 의지가 분명하다 ❏ 그녀는 의지가 분명하기 때문에 그 누구 때문에도 자신이 바라지 않는 일을 하지는 않을 것이다. **17** 구 제정신을 잃다, 미치다 ❏ 때때로 난 내가 제정신을 잃어 간다고 느낀다. **18** 구 결심하다 ❏ 일단 그가 뭔가를 하려고 결심하면, 그 무엇도 그를 막지 못했다. ❏ 같은 생각을 가진 다른 장애인 요트 조종사들과 접촉해 보면 도움이 될 것이다. **20** 구 마음이 홀가분한, 마음의 짐을 덜 ❏ 의료 보험 혜택을 볼 수 있다는 사실에 그녀는 마음이 홀가분하다. **21** 구 마음에 걸리다 ❏ 이 경기가 한 내내 마음에 걸린다. **22** 구 -에 신경 쓰다 ❏ 학창 시절에 난 항상 문제를 일으켰으며, 학업엔 전혀 신경을 안 썼다. **23** 구 열린 마음 ❏ 제가 열린 마음을 가지려고 애쓰고 있습니다만, 그 문제를 달리 보는 건 어렵습니다. **24** 구 -에 마음을 열다 ❏ 그것은 또한 그의 호기심을 자극했고 그가 타 문화에 대해 마음을 열게 했다. **25** 구 정신 나간 [비격식체, 탐탁찮음] ❏ 너 지금 뭐하니?

do something, there was no stopping him. **19** PHRASE If a number of people are **of one mind**, **of like mind**, or **of the same mind**, they all agree about something. ❏ *Contact with other disabled yachtsmen of like mind would be helpful.* **20** PHRASE If you say that something that happens is a **load off** your **mind** or a **weight off** your **mind**, you mean that it causes you to stop worrying, for example because it solves a problem that you had. ❏ *Knowing that she had medical insurance took a great load off her mind.* **21** PHRASE If something is **on** your **mind**, you are worried or concerned about it and think about it a lot. ❏ *This game has been on my mind all week.* **22** PHRASE If your **mind is on** something or you **have** your **mind on** something, you are thinking about that thing. ❏ *At school I was always in trouble – my mind was never on my work.* **23** PHRASE If you have **an open mind**, you avoid forming an opinion or making a decision until you know all the facts. ❏ *It's hard to see it any other way, though I'm trying to keep an open mind.* **24** PHRASE If something **opens** your **mind to** new ideas or experiences, it makes you more willing to accept them or try them. ❏ *She also stimulated his curiosity and opened his mind to other cultures.* **25** PHRASE If you say that someone is **out of their mind**, you mean that they are mad or very foolish. [INFORMAL, DISAPPROVAL] ❏ *What are you doing? Are you out of your mind?* **26** PHRASE If you say that someone is **out of their mind with** a feeling such as worry or fear, you are emphasizing that they are extremely worried or afraid. [INFORMAL, EMPHASIS] ❏ *I was out of my mind with fear. I didn't know what to do.* **27** PHRASE If you say that someone is, for example, **bored out of their mind**, **scared out of their mind**, or **stoned out of their mind**, you are emphasizing that they are extremely bored, scared, or affected by drugs. [INFORMAL, EMPHASIS] ❏ *That was one of the most depressing experiences of my life. I was bored out of my mind after five minutes.* **28** PHRASE If you **put** your **mind to** something, you start making an effort to do it. ❏ *You could do fine in the world if you put your mind to it.* **29** PHRASE If you can **read** someone's **mind**, you know what they are thinking without them saying anything. ❏ *Don't expect others to read your mind.* **30** PHRASE To **put** someone's **mind at rest** or **set** their **mind at rest** means to stop them worrying about something. ❏ *It may be advisable to have a blood test to put your mind at rest.* **31** PHRASE If you say that nobody **in** their **right mind** would do a particular thing, you are emphasizing that it is an irrational thing to do and you would be surprised if anyone did it. [EMPHASIS] ❏ *No one in her right mind would make such a major purchase without asking questions.* **32** PHRASE If you **set** your **mind on** something or **have** your **mind set on** it, you are determined to do it or obtain it. ❏ *When my wife sets her mind on something, she invariably finds a way to achieve it.* **33** PHRASE If something **slips** your **mind**, you forget it. ❏ *I was going to mention it, but it slipped my mind.* **34** PHRASE If you **speak** your **mind**, you say firmly and honestly what you think about a situation, even if this may offend or upset people. ❏ *Martina Navratilova has never been afraid to speak her mind.* **35** PHRASE If something **sticks in** your **mind**, it remains firmly in your memory. ❏ *I've always been fond of poetry and one piece has always stuck in my mind.* **36** PHRASE If something **takes** your **mind off** a problem or unpleasant situation, it helps you to forget about it for a while. ❏ *"How about a game of tennis?" suggested Alan. "That'll take your mind off things."* **37** PHRASE You say or write **to my mind** to indicate that the statement you are making is your own opinion. ❏ *There are scenes in this play which to my mind are incredibly violent.* **38** PHRASE If you are **of two minds**, you are uncertain about what to do, especially when you have to choose between two courses of action. The expression **in two minds** is also used in British English. ❏ *He was of two minds about this plan.* ▸ to **give** someone **a piece of** your **mind** →see **piece**

② **mind** ◆◇◇ /maɪnd/ (**minds, minding, minded**) **1** V-T/V-I If you do not **mind** something, you are not annoyed or bothered by it. [usu with brd-neg] ❏ *I don't mind the noise during the day.* ❏ *I hope you don't mind me calling in like this, without an appointment.* **2** V-T/V-I You use **mind** in the expressions "**do you mind?**" and "**would you mind?**" as a polite way of asking permission or asking someone to do something. [POLITENESS] ❏ *Do you mind if I ask you one more thing?* ❏ *Would you mind waiting outside for a moment?* **3** V-T If someone does not **mind** what happens or what something is like, they do not have a strong preference for any particular thing. [with brd-neg] ❏ *I don't mind what we play, really.* **4** V-T If you tell someone to **mind** something, you are warning them to be careful not to hurt themselves or other people, or damage something. [mainly BRIT; AM usually **watch**] [usu imper] ❏ *Mind that bike!* **5** V-T You use **mind** when you are reminding someone to do something or telling them to be careful not to do something. [mainly BRIT; AM usually **make sure, take care**] [only imper] ❏ *Mind you don't burn those sausages.* **6** V-T If you **mind** a child or something such as a store or luggage, you look after it, usually while the person who owns it or is usually responsible for it is somewhere else. [mainly BRIT; AM usually **take care of, watch**] ❏ *Jim Coulters will mind the store while I'm away.* **7** CONVENTION If you are offered something or offered a choice and you say "**I don't mind**," you are saying politely that you will be happy with any of the things offered. [BRIT, FORMULAE] ❏ *"Which one of these do you want?" — "I don't mind."* **8** PHRASE People use the expression **if you don't mind** when they are rejecting an offer or saying that they do not want to do something, especially when they are annoyed. [FEELINGS] ❏ *"Sit down." — "I prefer standing for a while, if you don't mind."* **9** PHRASE You use **mind you** to emphasize a piece of information that you are adding, especially when the new information explains what you have said or contrasts with it. Some people use **mind** in a similar way. [EMPHASIS] ❏ *They pay full rates. Mind you, they can afford it.* **10** CONVENTION You say **never mind** when you are emphasizing that something is not serious or important, especially when someone is upset about it or is saying they are sorry. [EMPHASIS] ❏ *Her voice trembled. "Oh, Sylvia, I'm so sorry." — "Never mind."* **11** PHRASE You use **never mind** to tell someone that they need not do something or worry about something, because it is not important or because you will do it yourself. ❏ *"Was his name David?" — "No I don't think it was, but never mind, go on."* ❏ *Dorothy, come on. Never mind your shoes. They'll soon dry off.* **12** PHRASE You use **never mind** after a statement, often a negative one, to indicate that the statement is even more true of the person, thing, or situation that you are going to mention

정신 나갔니? **26** 구 ~으로 제정신이 아닌 [비격식체, 강조] ❏ 나는 두려워서 내 정신이 아니었어. 어쩌해야 할 지 몰랐어. **27** 구 지무워서 죽으러 하는; 무서워서 혼이 나간; 약에 취해 정신이 나간 [비격식체, 강조] ❏ 그것은 내 생애 가장 침울한 경험 중 하나였다. 나는 5분 후가 되자 지루해 죽을 지경이었다. **28** 구 ~에 마음을 쓰다 ❏ 네가 그것에 마음을 쓴다면 세상일을 잘 해낼 수 있을 거야. **29** 구 ~의 마음을 알아주다 ❏ 다른 사람들이 네 마음을 알아주기를 기대하지 마. **30** 구 ~을 안심시키다 ❏ 네가 안심하고 싶으면 혈액 검사를 받아 보는 것이 현명할 거야. **31** 구 제정신으로 [강조] ❏ 그녀가 제정신이라면 아무런 질문 없이 그렇게 많이 구매하지 않을 것이다. **32** 구 ~하기로 결심하다 ❏ 내 아내는 뭔가 결심을 하면, 틀림없이 그것을 이뤄내는 방법을 찾는다. **33** 구 깜빡 잊다 ❏ 내가 그것을 말하려던 참인데, 깜빡 잊었다. **34** 구 시숨없이 생각을 말하다 ❏ 마르티나 나브라틸로바는 서슴없이 자신의 생각을 말하는 것을 결코 두려워하지 않았다. **35** 구 마음속에 뚜렷이 남아 있다 ❏ 나는 항상 시를 좋아했는데 그 중에서 한 편이 마음속에 뚜렷이 남아 있다. **36** 구 한동안 잊게 해 주다 ❏ "테니스 한 게임 어때?"라고 알렌이 제안했다. "한동안 이런저런 일들을 잊게 해 줄 거야." **37** 구 내 생각에는 ❏ 내 생각에는 이 연극에 대단히 폭력적인 장면들이 있다. **38** 구 양단간에 결정을 못 내리다 ❏ 그는 이 계획에 관해 이럴까 저럴까 결정을 못했다.

1 타동사/자동사 싫어하다, 폐로 여기다 ❏ 나는 낮 동안에는 소음에 개의치 않는다. ❏ 약속 없이 이렇게 방문하는 것이 폐가 되지 않았으면 합니다. **2** 타동사/자동사 괜찮을까요? (공손체) ❏ 제가 한 가지 더 여쭤봐도 될까요? ❏ 잠깐만 밖에서 기다려 주시겠습니까? **3** 타동사 상관하다 ❏ 나는 우리가 뭐하고 놀든 상관없어, 정말이야. **4** 타동사 ~에 조심하다 [주로 영국영어; 미국영어 대개 watch] ❏ 그 자전거 조심해! **5** 타동사 주의하다 [주로 영국영어; 미국영어 대개 make sure, take care] ❏ 그 소시지가 타지 않게 주의하세요. **6** 타동사 돌보다, 돌보다 [주로 영국영어; 미국영어 대개 take care of, watch] ❏ 내가 없는 동안 짐 코울터스가 가게를 봐줄 거야. **7** 관용 표현 아무 거나 좋다 [영국영어, 의례적인 표현] ❏ "이 중에서 어떤 걸 원하세요?" "아무거나 좋아요." **8** 구 괜찮으시다면 [감정 개입] ❏ "앉아요." "괜찮으시다면, 전 좀 서 있겠습니다." **9** 구 잘 들어 [강조] ❏ 그들이 전체 요금을 지불해. 잘 들어, 그들은 그럴 여유가 있어. **10** 관용 표현 걱정하지 말아라, 괜찮아요 [강조] ❏ 그녀는 떨리는 목소리로 말했다. "오, 실비아, 정말 미안하군요." "괜찮아요." **11** 구 신경 쓰지 말아라 ❏ "그 사람 이름이 데이비드였니?" "아니, 아닌 것 같지만 신경 쓰지 말고 계속해." ❏ 자, 도로시. 네 신발에 신경 쓰지 마. 곧 마를 테니까. **12** 구 ~은 말할 것도 없고 [강조] ❏ 다른 사람을 납득시키는 것은 말할 것도 없고 나 자신도 그걸 믿지 않을 거야. **13** 구 ~라면 좋겠다 ❏ 커피 한 잔 했으면 좋겠어.

a b c d e f g h i j k l **m** n o p q r s t u v w x y z

next. [EMPHASIS] ❑ *I'm not going to believe it myself, never mind convince anyone else.* ⓭ PHRASE If you say that you **wouldn't mind** something, you mean that you would quite like it. ❑ *I wouldn't mind a coffee.*

mind|er /ˈmaɪndər/ (**minders**) ■ N-COUNT A **minder** is a person whose job is to protect someone, especially someone famous. [mainly BRIT, INFORMAL] ❑ *Prince William arrived with his minders.* ■ N-COUNT A **minder** is the same as a **childminder**. [BRIT]

■ 가산명사 경호원 [주로 영국영어, 비격식체] ❑ 윌리엄 왕자가 경호원들과 함께 도착했다. ■ 가산명사 보모 [영국영어]

mind|ful /ˈmaɪndfəl/ ADJ If you are **mindful of** something, you think about it and consider it when taking action. [FORMAL] [v-link ADJ, usu ADJ of n] ❑ *We must be mindful of the consequences of selfishness.*

형용사 염두에 두는 [격식체] ❑ 우리는 이기심이 가져올 결과를 염두에 두어야 한다.

mind|less /ˈmaɪndlɪs/ ■ ADJ If you describe a violent action as **mindless**, you mean that it is done without thought and will achieve nothing. [mainly BRIT, DISAPPROVAL] ❑ *...a plot that mixes blackmail, extortion and mindless violence.* ■ ADJ If you describe a person or group as **mindless**, you mean that they are stupid or do not think about what they are doing. [DISAPPROVAL] ❑ *She wasn't at all the mindless little wife so many people perceived her to be.* ● **mind|less|ly** ADV [ADV with v] ❑ *I was annoyed with myself for having so quickly and mindlessly lost thirty dollars.* ■ ADJ If you describe an activity as **mindless**, you mean that it is so dull that people do it or take part in it without thinking. [DISAPPROVAL] ❑ *...the mindless repetitiveness of some tasks.* ● **mind|less|ly** ADV [ADV with v] ❑ *I spent many hours in it mindlessly banging a tennis ball against the wall.*

■ 형용사 무분별한 [주로 영국영어, 탐탁찮음] ❑ 협박, 갈취, 그리고 무분별한 폭력으로 얼룩진 음모 ■ 형용사 어리석은 [탐탁찮음] ❑ 그녀는 그렇게 많은 사람들이 생각했던 것처럼 어리석고 하찮은 아내가 결코 아니었다. ● 어리석게 부사 ❑ 나는 바보같이 그렇게 순식간에 삼십 달러를 잃은 것에 대해 나 자신에게 화가 났다. ■ 형용사 생각 없는 [탐탁찮음] ❑ 생각 없이 되풀이하는 몇 가지 일들 ● 생각 없이 부사 ❑ 나는 벽에 대고 테니스공을 팡팡 치면서 생각 없이 여러 시간을 그 안에서 보냈다.

--- mine ---

① PRONOUN USE
② NOUN AND VERB USES

① **mine** ♦♦♦ /maɪn/ PRON-POSS **Mine** is the first person singular possessive pronoun. A speaker or writer uses **mine** to refer to something that belongs or relates to himself or herself. ❑ *Her right hand is inches from mine.* ❑ *That wasn't his fault, it was mine.*

소유대명사 내 것 ❑ 그녀의 오른손이 내 손 바로 옆에 있다. ❑ 그것은 그의 잘못이 아니라, 제 잘못이었습니다.

② **mine** /maɪn/ (**mines, mining, mined**) ■ N-COUNT A **mine** is a place where deep holes and tunnels are dug under the ground in order to obtain a mineral such as coal, diamonds, or gold. ❑ *...coal mines.* ■ V-T When a mineral such as coal, diamonds, or gold **is mined**, it is obtained from the ground by digging deep holes and tunnels. [usu passive] ❑ *The pit is being shut down because it no longer has enough coal that can be mined economically.* ■ N-COUNT A **mine** is a bomb which is hidden in the ground or in water and which explodes when people or things touch it. ■ V-T If an area of land or water **is mined**, mines are placed there which will explode when people or things touch them. ❑ *The approaches to the garrison have been heavily mined.* ■ →see also **mining** →see **diamond**

■ 가산명사 광산 ❑ 탄광 ■ 타동사 채광되다 ❑ 그 탄갱은 채광하기에 더 이상 수지타산이 안 맞아서 폐쇄된다. ■ 가산명사 지뢰 ■ 타동사 지뢰 매설되다 ❑ 그 주둔지로 가는 길목에는 지뢰가 잔뜩 매설되어 있다.

mine|field /ˈmaɪnfiːld/ (**minefields**) ■ N-COUNT A **minefield** is an area of land or water where explosive mines have been hidden. ■ N-COUNT If you describe a situation as a **minefield**, you are emphasizing that there are a lot of hidden dangers or problems, and people need to behave with care because things could easily go wrong. [EMPHASIS] ❑ *The whole subject is a political minefield.*

■ 가산명사 지뢰밭 ■ 가산명사 (비유적) 지뢰밭 [강조] ❑ 그 주제 전체가 정치적 지뢰밭이나 마찬가지이다.

min|er ♦♢♢ /ˈmaɪnər/ (**miners**) N-COUNT A **miner** is a person who works underground in mines in order to obtain minerals such as coal or diamonds.

가산명사 광부

min|er|al /ˈmɪnərəl/ (**minerals**) N-COUNT A **mineral** is a substance such as tin, salt, or sulfur that is formed naturally in rocks and in the earth. Minerals are also found in small quantities in food and drink. →see Word Web: **mineral**

가산명사 광물; 무기질

min|er|al wa|ter (**mineral waters**) N-MASS **Mineral water** is water that comes out of the ground naturally and is considered healthy to drink.

물질명사 광천수

min|gle /ˈmɪŋɡəl/ (**mingles, mingling, mingled**) ■ V-RECIP If things such as sounds, smells, or feelings **mingle**, they become mixed together but are usually still recognizable. ❑ *Now the cheers and applause mingled in a single sustained roar.* ■ V-RECIP At a party, if you **mingle with** the other people there, you move around and talk to them. ❑ *Go out of your way to mingle with others at the wedding.* ❑ *Guests ate and mingled.*

■ 상호동사 섞이다 ❑ 이제 응원 소리와 박수 소리가 섞여서 지속적인 하나의 함성이 되었다. ■ 상호동사 어울리다 ❑ 결혼식에 가서 애써 다른 사람들과 어울려 보렴. ❑ 손님들은 식사하며 서로 어울렸다.

Word Link mini ≈ very small : miniature, minibar, minibus

min|ia|ture /ˈmɪniətʃər, -tʃʊər, BRIT ˈmɪnɪtʃər/ (**miniatures**) ■ ADJ **Miniature** is used to describe something which is very small, especially a smaller version of something which is normally much bigger. [ADJ n] ❑ *Rosehill Farm has been selling miniature roses since 1979.* ■ PHRASE If you describe one thing as another thing **in miniature**, you mean that it is much smaller in size or scale than the

■ 형용사 축소 모형의, 미니어처의 ❑ 로즈힐 팜에서는 축소 모형 장미를 1979년부터 판매해 오고 있다. ■ 구 축소판의 ❑ 에콰도르는 남미를 완벽하게 소개하는 나라이다. 이 나라는 남미의 축소판이다. ■ 가산명사 세밀화

Word Web mineral

The **extraction** of **minerals** from ore is an ancient process. Neolithic man discovered **copper** around 8000 BC. Using fire and charcoal, they **reduced** the ore to its pure **metal** form. About 4,000 years later, Egyptians learned to pour molten copper into molds and **metallurgy** was born. **Silver** ore often contains large amounts of copper and **lead**. Silver **refineries** often use the **smelting** process to remove these impurities. Most **gold** does not exist as an ore. Instead, veins of gold run through the earth. Refiners use solvents such as cyanide to obtain pure gold.

other thing, but is otherwise exactly the same. ❏ *Ecuador provides a perfect introduction to South America; it's a continent in miniature.* ◼ N-COUNT A **miniature** is a very small detailed painting, often of a person.

Word Link   mini ≈ very small : mini**ature**, mini**bar**, mini**bus**

mini**bar** /ˈmɪnibɑːr/ (minibars) N-COUNT In a hotel room, a **minibar** is a small refrigerator containing alcoholic drinks.

가산명사 객실용 소형 냉장고, 미니 바

mini**bus** /ˈmɪnibʌs/ (minibuses) also mini-bus N-COUNT A **minibus** is a large van which has seats in the back for passengers, and windows along its sides. [also *by N*] ❏ *He was then taken by minibus to the military base.*

가산명사 소형 버스 ❏ 그는 그리고 나서 소형 버스에 태워져 그 군기지로 이송되었다.

mini**disc** /ˈmɪnidɪsk/ (minidiscs) N-COUNT A **minidisc** is a small compact disc which you can record music or data on. [TRADEMARK]

가산명사 소형 디스크 [상표]

mini**dish** /ˈmɪnidɪʃ/ (minidishes) N-COUNT A **minidish** is a small satellite dish that can receive signals from communications satellites for media such as television programs and the Internet.

가산명사 소형 위성 안테나

Word Link   minim ≈ smallest : minim**al**, minim**ize**, minim**um**

mini**mal** /ˈmɪnɪməl/ ADJ Something that is **minimal** is very small in quantity, value, or degree. ❏ *The cooperation between the two is minimal.*

형용사 최소의 ❏ 양측의 협력은 최소로 이뤄지고 있다.

mini**mal**ism /ˈmɪnɪməlɪzəm/ N-UNCOUNT **Minimalism** is a style in which a small number of very simple things are used to create a particular effect. ❏ *In her own home, she replaced austere minimalism with cosy warmth and color.*

불가산명사 미니멀리즘 ❏ 그녀는 자신의 집은 엄격한 미니멀리즘 대신 포근함을 주는 분위기와 색깔로 바꾸었다.

mini**mal**ist /ˈmɪnɪməlɪst/ (minimalists) ◼ N-COUNT A **minimalist** is an artist or designer who uses minimalism. ❏ *He was influenced by the minimalists in the 1970s.* ◼ ADJ **Minimalist** is used to describe ideas, artists, or designers that are influenced by minimalism. ❏ *The two designers settled upon a minimalist approach.*

◼ 가산명사 미니멀리스트 ❏ 그는 1970년대에 미니멀리스트들의 영향을 받았다. ◼ 형용사 미니멀리즘의 ❏ 그 두 디자이너는 미니멀리즘 방식에 합의했다.

mini**mize** /ˈmɪnɪmaɪz/ (minimizes, minimizing, minimized) [BRIT also minimise] ◼ V-T If you **minimize** a risk, problem, or unpleasant situation, you reduce it to the lowest possible level, or prevent it from increasing beyond that level. ❏ *Concerned people want to minimize the risk of developing cancer.* ◼ V-T If you **minimize** something, you make it seem smaller or less significant than it really is. ❏ *Some have minimized the importance of ideological factors.* ◼ V-T If you **minimize** a window on a computer screen, you make it very small, because you do not want to use it. ❏ *Click the square icon again to minimize the window.*

[영국영어 minimise] ◼ 타동사 최소화하다 ❏ 사람들은 우려를 나타내며 암 발병 위험률을 최소화하기를 바란다. ◼ 타동사 경시하다 ❏ 일부 사람들은 이념적 요인의 중요성을 경시했다. ◼ 타동사 최소화하다 ❏ 창을 최소화하려면 사각 아이콘을 다시 누르세요.

mini**mum** ◆◇◇ /ˈmɪnɪməm/ ◼ ADJ You use **minimum** to describe an amount which is the smallest that is possible, allowed, or required. [ADJ n] ❏ *He was only five feet nine, the minimum height for a policeman.* ● N-SING **Minimum** is also a noun. ❏ *This will take a minimum of one hour.* ◼ ADJ You use **minimum** to state how small an amount is. [ADJ n] ❏ *The basic needs of life are available with minimum effort.* ● N-SING **Minimum** is also a noun. ❏ *With a minimum of fuss, she produced the grandson he had so desperately wished for.* ◼ ADV If you say that something is a particular amount **minimum**, you mean that this is the smallest amount it should be or could possibly be, although a larger amount is acceptable or very possible. [amount ADV] ❏ *You're talking over a thousand pounds minimum for one course.*

◼ 형용사 최소한의 ❏ 그의 키는 겨우 5.9피트였는데, 경관 자격 최소 신장이었을 것이다. ◼ 단수명사 최소 ❏ 이것은 최소 한 시간은 소요될 것이다. ◼ 형용사 최소의 ❏ 생활에 기본적으로 필요한 것은 최소의 노력으로 얻을 수 있다. ● 단수명사 최소 ❏ 거의 아단 피우지 않고, 그녀는 그가 그렇게도 원했었던 손자를 낳았다. ◼ 부사 최소로 ❏ 한 과정에 최소한 천 파운드 이상이 든다는 말이죠.

Word Partnership   minimum의 연어

| ADJ. | **absolute** minimum, **bare** minimum ◼ ◼ |
| N. | minimum **age**, minimum **balance**, minimum **payment**, minimum **purchase**, minimum **requirement**, minimum **salary** ◼ |

mini**mum wage** N-SING The **minimum wage** is the lowest wage that an employer is allowed to pay an employee, according to a law or agreement. ❏ *Some of them earn below the minimum wage.* →see **factory**

단수명사 최저임금 ❏ 그들 중 일부의 소득은 최저 임금에 못 미친다.

min**ing** /ˈmaɪnɪŋ/ N-UNCOUNT **Mining** is the industry and activities connected with getting valuable or useful minerals from the ground, for example coal, diamonds, or gold. ❏ *...traditional industries such as coal mining and steel making.* →see **industry**, **tunnel**

불가산명사 광산업 ❏ 탄광업, 제철업과 같은 전통적인 산업들

min**ister** ◆◆◆ /ˈmɪnɪstər/ (ministers) ◼ N-COUNT A **minister** is a member of the clergy, especially in Protestant churches. ❏ *His father was a Baptist minister.* ◼ N-COUNT A **minister** is a person who officially represents their government in a foreign country and has a lower rank than an ambassador. ❏ *He concluded a deal with the Danish minister in Washington.* ◼ N-COUNT In Britain and some other countries, a **minister** is a person who is in charge of a particular government department. ❏ *When the government had come to power, he had been named minister of culture.* →see **government**

◼ 가산명사 목사 ❏ 그의 아버지는 침례교 목사였다. ◼ 가산명사 공사 ❏ 워싱턴에서 그는 덴마크 공사와 협정을 체결하였다. ◼ 가산명사 장관 ❏ 그 정부가 들어섰을 때, 그는 문화부 장관으로 임명되었다.

min**ister**ial /ˌmɪnɪˈstɪəriəl/ ADJ You use **ministerial** to refer to people, events, or jobs that are connected with government ministers. [ADJ n] ❏ *The prime minister's initial ministerial appointments haven't pleased all his supporters.*

형용사 장관의 ❏ 수상의 초기 장관 임명에 모든 지지자들이 만족한 것은 아니었다.

min**istry** ◆◆◇ /ˈmɪnɪstri/ (ministries) N-COUNT In Britain and some other countries, a **ministry** is a government department which deals with a particular thing or area of activity, for example trade, defense, or transportation. ❏ *...the Ministry of Justice.*

가산명사 (정부의) 부 ❏ 법무부

mink /ˈmɪŋk/ (minks)

| **Mink** can also be used as the plural form. |

mink도 복수형으로 쓸 수 있다.

◼ N-COUNT A **mink** is a small animal with highly valued fur. ❏ *...a proposal for a ban on the hunting of foxes, mink, and hares.* ● N-UNCOUNT **Mink** is the fur of a mink. ❏ *...a mink coat.* ◼ N-COUNT A **mink** is a coat or other garment made from the fur of a mink. ❏ *Some people like to dress up in minks and diamonds.*

◼ 가산명사 밍크 ❏ 여우, 밍크, 산토끼 사냥 금지안 ● 불가산명사 밍크 모피 ❏ 밍크코트 ◼ 가산명사 밍크코트, 밍크로 만든 옷 ❏ 일부 사람들은 밍크코트와 다이아몬드로 치장하기 좋아한다.

mi|nor ♦♢♢ /maɪnər/ (minors) **1** ADJ You use **minor** when you want to describe something that is less important, serious, or significant than other things in a group or situation. ❑ *She is known in Italy for a number of minor roles in films.* **2** ADJ A **minor** illness or operation is not likely to be dangerous to someone's life or health. ❑ *Sarah had been plagued continually by a series of minor illnesses since her mid teens.* **3** N-COUNT A **minor** is a person who is still legally a child. In most states in the United States and in Britain, people are minors until they reach the age of eighteen. ❑ *The approach has virtually ended cigarette sales to minors.*

1 형용사 비중이 적은 ❑ 그녀는 영화에서 수많은 단역을 해 온 것으로 이탈리아에서 알려져 있다. **2** 형용사 대수롭지 않은, 사소한 ❑ 사라는 십대 중반부터 이런저런 잔병에 계속 시달려왔었다. **3** 가산명사 미성년자 ❑ 그 방식이 미성년자에 대한 담배 판매를 사실상 중지시켰다.

Thesaurus	minor의 참조어
ADJ.	insignificant, lesser, small, unimportant; (ant.) important, major, significant **1**

Word Partnership	minor의 연어
N.	minor **adjustment**, minor **damage**, minor **detail**, minor **problem 1**
	minor **illness**, minor **injury**, minor **operation**, minor **surgery 2**
ADV.	**relatively** minor **1 2**

mi|nor|ity ♦♦♢ /maɪnɒriti, maɪ-, BRIT mɪnɒriti/ (minorities) **1** N-SING If you talk about a **minority** of people or things in a larger group, you are referring to a number of them that forms less than half of the larger group, usually much less than half. ❑ *Local authority nursery provision covers only a tiny minority of working mothers.* ● PHRASE If people are **in a minority** or **in the minority**, they belong to a group of people or things that form less than half of a larger group. ❑ *Even in the 1960s, politically active students and academics were in a minority.* **2** N-COUNT A **minority** is a group of people of the same race, culture, or religion who live in a place where most of the people around them are of a different race, culture, or religion. ❑ *...the region's ethnic minorities.*

1 단수명사 소수 ❑ 지방 당국의 탁아 조항은 아이를 가진 직장 여성 중 극소수에게만 적용된다. ● 구 소수 집단 ❑ 심지어 1960년대에도, 정치적으로 적극적인 학생들과 대학 교수들은 소수 집단이었다. **2** 가산명사 소수 민족 ❑ 그 지역의 소수 민족들

Word Partnership	minority의 연어
N.	minority **leader**, minority **party 1**
	minority **applicants**, minority **community**, minority **group**, minority **population**, minority **students**, minority **voters**, minority **women 2**

mint /mɪnt/ (mints, minting, minted) **1** N-UNCOUNT **Mint** is a herb with fresh-tasting leaves. ❑ *Garnish with mint sprigs.* **2** N-COUNT A **mint** is a candy with a peppermint flavor. Some people suck mints in order to make their breath smell fresher. ❑ *She popped a mint into her mouth.* **3** N-COUNT **The mint** is the place where the official coins of a country are made. ❑ *In 1965 the mint stopped putting silver in dimes.* **4** V-T To **mint** coins or medals means to make them in a mint. ❑ *...the right to mint coins.* →see **money**

1 불가산명사 박하 ❑ 박하 잔가지로 고명을 얹으세요. **2** 가산명사 박하사탕 ❑ 그녀는 박하사탕을 얼른 입속에 넣었다. **3** 가산명사 조폐국 ❑ 1965년 조폐국이 10센트 은화 생산을 중단했다. **4** 타동사 주조하다 ❑ 동전 주전권

Word Link	min ≈ small, less : diminish, minus, minute

mi|nus /maɪnəs/ (minuses) **1** CONJ You use **minus** to show that one number or quantity is being subtracted from another. ❑ *One minus one is zero.* **2** ADJ **Minus** before a number or quantity means that the number or quantity is less than zero. [ADJ amount] ❑ *The aircraft was subjected to temperatures of minus 65 degrees and plus 120 degrees.* **3** Teachers use **minus** in grading work in schools and colleges. "B minus" is not as good as "B", but is a better grade than "C." ❑ *I'm giving him a B minus.* **4** PREP To be **minus** something means not to have that thing. ❑ *The film company collapsed, leaving Chris jobless and minus his life savings.* **5** N-COUNT A **minus** is a disadvantage. [INFORMAL] ❑ *The minuses far outweigh that possible gain.*

1 접속사 뺀 ❑ 1 빼기 1은 0이다. **2** 형용사 마이너스의, 0보다 작은 ❑ 그 항공기는 마이너스 65도와 플러스 120도의 온도에 놓였었다. **3** 마이너스(성적) ❑ 난 그에게 비 마이너스(B-)를 줄 것이다. **4** 전치사 –이 없는 ❑ 그 영화사가 망하자 크리스는 직장을 잃었고 노후 대비 저축도 잃었다. **5** 가산명사 불리한 점 [비격식체] ❑ 불리한 점들이 가능한 이득보다 훨씬 중대하다.

Thesaurus	minus의 참조어
PREP.	without **4**
N.	deficiency, disadvantage, drawback **5**

Word Link	cule ≈ small : minuscule, molecule, ridicule

mi|nus|cule /mɪnɪskyul/ ADJ If you describe something as **minuscule**, you mean that it is very small. ❑ *The film was shot in 17 days, a minuscule amount of time.*

형용사 정말 작은 ❑ 그 영화는 17일 만에 촬영되었는데, 그것은 정말 짧은 기간이었다.

minute

① NOUN AND VERB USES
② ADJECTIVE USE

① mi|nute ♦♦♦ /mɪnɪt/ (minutes, minuting, minuted) **1** N-COUNT A **minute** is one of the sixty parts that an hour is divided into. People often say "a minute" or "minutes" when they mean a short length of time. ❑ *The pizza will then take about twenty minutes to cook.* ❑ *Bye Mom, see you in a minute.* **2** N-PLURAL The **minutes** of a meeting are the written records of the things that are discussed or decided at it. ❑ *He'd been reading the minutes of the last meeting.* **3** V-T When someone **minutes** something that is discussed or decided at a meeting, they make a written record of it. ❑ *You don't need to minute that.* **4** CONVENTION People often use expressions such as **wait a minute** or **just a minute** when they want to stop you doing or saying something. ❑ *Wait a minute, folks, something is wrong here.* **5** PHRASE If you say that something will or may happen **at any minute** or

1 가산명사 (시간) 분 ❑ 그 피자는 그리고 나서 조리되기까지 약 20분 걸릴 것이다. ❑ 엄마 안녕, 곧 다시 만나요. **2** 복수명사 의사록 ❑ 그는 지난번 회의의 의사록을 읽고 있는 중이었다. **3** 타동사 기록하다 ❑ 그건 기록할 필요없어. **4** 관용 표현 잠깐 기다려 ❑ 여보게들, 잠깐 기다려, 여기 뭔가 이상한데. **5** 구 당장이라도 [강조] ❑ 당장이라도 비가 내릴 것 같았다. **6** 구 최후의 ❑ 그는 아마 최후의 순간까지 기다릴 것이다. **7** 구 하자마자 [강조] ❑ 네가 이걸 하자마자, 주체할 수 없게 될 거야.

any minute now, you are emphasizing that it is likely to happen very soon. [EMPHASIS] ❑ *It looked as though it might rain at any minute.* ⑥ PHRASE A **last-minute** action is one that is done at the latest time possible. ❑ *He will probably wait until the last minute.* ⑦ PHRASE If you say that something happens **the minute** something else happens, you are emphasizing that it happens immediately after the other thing. [EMPHASIS] ❑ *The minute you do this, you'll lose control.*

Word Link	min ≈ small, less : di**min**ish, **min**us, **min**ute

② mi|nute /maɪnut, BRIT maɪnyuːt/ (**minutest**) ADJ If you say that something is **minute**, you mean that it is very small. ❑ *Only a minute amount is needed.*

형용사 아주 작은 ❑ 아주 작은 양만 있으면 돼.

Word Partnership		*minute*의 연어
DET.	a minute **or two**, **another** minute, **each** minute, **every** minute, **half** a minute ① ❶	
	any minute **now**, **at any** minute ① ❺	
V.	**take** a minute ① ❶	
	wait a minute ① ❹	
N.	minute **detail**, minute **quantity of** *something* ②	

mir|a|cle /mɪrəkªl/ (**miracles**) ❶ N-COUNT If you say that a good event is a **miracle**, you mean that it is very surprising and unexpected. ❑ *It is a miracle no one was killed.* ❷ ADJ A **miracle** drug or product does something that was thought almost impossible. [JOURNALISM] [ADJ n] ❑ *...the miracle drugs that keep his 94-year-old mother healthy.* ❸ N-COUNT A **miracle** is a wonderful and surprising event that is believed to be caused by God. ❑ *...Jesus's ability to perform miracles.*

❶ 가산명사 경이적인 일, 기적 ❑ 아무도 죽지 않은 건 기적이다. ❷ 형용사 기적과 같은 [언론] ❑ 아흔네 살 된 그의 어머니를 건강하게 지켜주는 기적과 같은 약 ❸ 가산명사 기적 ❑ 기적을 행하시는 예수의 능력

mi|rac|u|lous /mɪrækyələs/ ❶ ADJ If you describe a good event as **miraculous**, you mean that it is very surprising and unexpected. ❑ *The horse made a miraculous recovery to finish a close third.* ● mi|rac|u|lous|ly ADV ❑ *Miraculously, the guards escaped death or serious injury.* ❷ ADJ If someone describes a wonderful event as **miraculous**, they believe that the event was caused by God. ❑ *...miraculous healing.*

❶ 형용사 놀라운 ❑ 그 말이 놀랍게 만회를 하여 아슬아슬하게 삼등으로 들어왔다. ● 경이롭게도 부사 ❑ 경이롭게도, 그 보초들은 죽지도 않고 중상도 입지 않았다. ❷ 형용사 기적적인 ❑ 기적적인 치유

mir|ror ♦◇◇ /mɪrər/ (**mirrors, mirroring, mirrored**) ❶ N-COUNT A **mirror** is a flat piece of glass which reflects light, so that when you look at it you can see yourself reflected in it. ❑ *He went into the bathroom absent-mindedly and looked at himself in the mirror.* ❷ V-T If something **mirrors** something else, it has similar features to it, and therefore seems like a copy or representation of it. ❑ *Despite the fact that I have tried to be objective, the book inevitably mirrors my own interests and experiences.* ❸ V-T If you see something reflected in water, you can say that the water **mirrors** it. [LITERARY] ❑ *...the sudden glitter where a newly-flooded field mirrors the sky.*

❶ 가산명사 거울 ❑ 그는 멍한 상태로 욕실로 가서 거울에 비친 자신을 바라보았다. ❷ 타동사 반영하다 ❑ 난 객관적이고자 했지만, 그 책에는 불가피하게 내 개인적인 관심과 경험이 반영되어 있다. ❸ 타동사 비추다 [문예체] ❑ 최근 물속에 잠긴 들판에 하늘이 반사되어 갑작스레 반짝임

Word Partnership		*mirror*의 연어
N.	**reflection** in a mirror ❶	
PREP.	**in front of** a mirror ❶	
V.	**glance** in a mirror, **look** in a mirror, **reflect** in a mirror, **see** in a mirror ❶	

mis|be|have /mɪsbɪheɪv/ (**misbehaves, misbehaving, misbehaved**) V-I If someone, especially a child, **misbehaves**, they behave in a way that is not acceptable to other people. ❑ *When the children misbehaved she was unable to cope.*

자동사 버릇없이 굴다 ❑ 아이들이 버릇없이 굴면 그녀는 속수무책이었다.

mis|cal|cu|late /mɪskælkyəleɪt/ (**miscalculates, miscalculating, miscalculated**) V-T/V-I If you **miscalculate**, you make a mistake in judging a situation or in making a calculation. ❑ *It's clear that he has badly miscalculated the mood of the people.* ● mis|cal|cu|la|tion /mɪskælkyəleɪʃ°n/ (**miscalculations**) N-VAR ❑ *The coup failed because of miscalculations by the plotters.*

타동사/자동사 잘못 헤아리다, 오판하다 ❑ 그가 사람들의 심중을 굉장히 잘못 헤아렸던 것이 분명하다. ● 오산 가산명사 또는 불가산명사 ❑ 그 쿠데타는 음모자들의 오산으로 인해 실패했다.

mis|car|riage /mɪskærɪdʒ, -kær-/ (**miscarriages**) N-VAR If a pregnant woman has a **miscarriage**, her baby dies and she gives birth to it before it is properly formed. ❑ *No one had any idea she had had a miscarriage.*

가산명사 또는 불가산명사 유산 ❑ 그녀가 유산을 했다는 사실을 아무도 몰랐다.

mis|cel|la|neous /mɪsəleɪniəs/ ADJ A **miscellaneous** group consists of many different kinds of things or people that are difficult to put into a particular category. [ADJ n] ❑ *...a hoard of miscellaneous junk.*

형용사 잡다한 ❑ 한 더미의 잡다한 고물들

mis|chief /mɪstʃɪf/ ❶ N-UNCOUNT **Mischief** is playing harmless tricks on people or doing things you are not supposed to do. It can also refer to the desire to do this. ❑ *The little lad was a real handful. He was always up to mischief.* ❷ N-UNCOUNT **Mischief** is behavior that is intended to cause trouble for people. It can also refer to the trouble that is caused. ❑ *The more sinister explanation is that he is about to make mischief in the Middle East again.*

❶ 불가산명사 장난 ❑ 그 어린 녀석은 정말 골칫덩어리였는데 항상 장난을 치려했다. ❷ 불가산명사 해를 끼침; 해악 ❑ 더 나쁘게 설명하자면 그가 다시 한 번 중동 지역에 해를 끼치려고 한다는 것이다.

mis|chie|vous /mɪstʃɪvəs/ ❶ ADJ A **mischievous** person likes to have fun by playing harmless tricks on people or doing things they are not supposed to do. ❑ *She rocks back and forth on her chair like a mischievous child.* ● mis|chie|vous|ly ADV ❑ *Kathryn winked mischievously.* ❷ ADJ A **mischievous** act or suggestion is intended to cause trouble. ❑ *A statement issued after the meeting speaks of a mischievous campaign by the press to divide the ANC.* ● mis|chie|vous|ly ADV ❑ *That does not require "massive" military intervention, as some have mischievously claimed.*

❶ 형용사 장난을 좋아하는 ❑ 그녀는 장난꾸러기 아이처럼 의자에 앉아 몸을 앞뒤로 흔들어댄다. ● 장난스럽게 부사 ❑ 캐스린이 장난스럽게 윙크했다. ❷ 형용사 악의적인 ❑ 그 회담 후 발표된 성명은 아프리카 민족 회의를 분열시키려는 언론사들의 악의적인 캠페인에 대한 내용을 담고 있다. ● 악의적으로 부사 ❑ 그것은 일부 사람들이 악의적으로 주장하고 있는 것처럼 '대규모' 군사 개입을 필요로 하지는 않는다.

a b c d e f g h i j k l m n o p q r s t u v w x y z

A

mis|con|cep|tion /mɪskənsɛpʃᵊn/ (**misconceptions**) N-COUNT A **misconception** is an idea that is not correct. ❑ *It is a misconception that Peggy was fabulously wealthy.*

가산명사 오해, 잘못된 생각 ❑ 페기가 엄청난 부자였다는 것은 오해이다.

B

mis|con|duct /mɪskɒndʌkt/ N-UNCOUNT **Misconduct** is bad or unacceptable behavior, especially by a professional person. ❑ *A psychologist was found guilty of serious professional misconduct yesterday.*

불가산명사 과오 ❑ 한 심리학자가 중대한 직무상의 과오로 어제 유죄 판결을 받았다.

C

mis|de|mean|or /mɪsdɪminər/ (**misdemeanors**) [BRIT **misdemeanour**]
❶ N-COUNT A **misdemeanor** is an act that some people consider to be wrong or unacceptable. [FORMAL] ❑ *...a school where caning was the regular punishment for serious misdemeanor.* ❷ N-COUNT In the United States and other countries where the legal system distinguishes between very serious crimes and less serious ones, a **misdemeanor** is a less serious crime. [LEGAL] ❑ *Under state law, it is a misdemeanor to possess a firearm on school premises.*

[영국영어 misdemeanour] ❶ 가산명사 비행 [격식체] ❑ 학생들이 중대한 비행을 저지르면 회초리로 때리는 것이 통상적인 징계였던 학교 ❷ 가산명사 경범죄 [법률] ❑ 주정부 법에 의해 학교 경내에서 총기 소지는 경범죄이다.

D

E

mis|er|able /mɪzərəbᵊl/ ❶ ADJ If you are **miserable**, you are very unhappy. ❑ *I took a series of badly paid secretarial jobs which made me really miserable.* ● **mis|er|ably** /mɪzərəbli/ ADV ❑ *He looked miserably down at his plate.* ❷ ADJ If you describe a place or situation as **miserable**, you mean that it makes you feel unhappy or depressed. ❑ *There was nothing at all in this miserable place to distract him.* ❸ ADJ If you describe the weather as **miserable**, you mean that it makes you feel depressed, because it is raining or dull. ❑ *On a grey, wet, miserable day our teams congregated in Port Hamble.* ❹ ADJ If you describe someone as **miserable**, you mean that you do not like them because they are bad-tempered or unfriendly. [ADJ n] ❑ *He always was a miserable man. He never spoke to me nor anybody else, not even to pass the time of day.* ❺ ADJ You can describe a quantity or quality as **miserable** when you think that it is much smaller or worse than it ought to be. [EMPHASIS] ❑ *Our speed over the ground was a miserable 2.2 knots.* ● **mis|er|ably** ADV [ADV adj] ❑ *...the miserably inadequate supply of books now provided for schools.* ❻ ADJ A **miserable** failure is a very great one. [EMPHASIS] [ADJ n] ❑ *The film was a miserable commercial failure both in Italy and in the United States.* ● **mis|er|ably** ADV [ADV with v] ❑ *Some manage it. Some fail miserably.*

❶ 형용사 비참한 ❑ 나는 형편없는 급여의 비서직을 연달아 맡게 되었고, 그 때문에 아주 비참했다. ● 비참하게 부사 ❑ 그는 자기 접시를 비참하게 내려다보았다. ❷ 형용사 비참한 ❑ 이 비참한 곳에서 그를 즐겁게 해 주는 것은 아무것도 없었다. ❸ 형용사 (날씨가) 우중충한 ❑ 흐리고 비도 오는 우중충한 어느 날 우리 팀은 포트 햄블에 모였다. ❹ 형용사 고약한 ❑ 그는 언제나 성격이 괴팍한 사람이었다. 그는 낮 동안 시간 보내기 삼아서라도 나에게나 그 누구에게도 말을 걸지 않았다. ❺ 형용사 고작, 형편없는 [강조] ❑ 땅에서 우리의 속도는 고작 2.2노트였다. ● 볼품없이, 형편없이 부사 ❑ 현재 학교에 제공되는 책들의 형편없이 부족한 물량 ❻ 형용사 처참한 (실패) [강조] ❑ 그 영화는 이탈리아와 미국에서 상업적으로 처참하게 실패했다. ● 처참하게 부사 ❑ 몇몇은 겨우 버티고, 몇몇은 처참하게 실패한다.

F

G

H

I

Thesaurus *miserable*의 참조어

ADJ. unhappy, wretched ❶

J

K

L

mis|ery /mɪzəri/ (**miseries**) ❶ N-VAR **Misery** is great unhappiness. ❑ *All that money brought nothing but sadness and misery and tragedy.* ❷ N-UNCOUNT **Misery** is the way of life and unpleasant living conditions of people who are very poor. ❑ *A tiny, educated elite profited from the misery of their two million fellow countrymen.* ❸ PHRASE If someone **makes** your **life a misery**, they behave in an unpleasant way towards you over a period of time and make you very unhappy. ❑ *I would really like living here if it wasn't for the gangs of kids who make our lives a misery.* ❹ PHRASE If you **put** someone **out of** their **misery**, you tell them something that they are very anxious to know. [INFORMAL] ❑ *Please put me out of my misery. How do you do it?* ❺ PHRASE If you **put** an animal **out of** its **misery**, you kill it because it is sick or injured and cannot be cured or healed. ❑ *He notes grimly that the Watsons have called the vet to put their dog out of its misery.*

❶ 가산명사 또는 불가산명사 불행 ❑ 그 돈이 가져다준 것은 슬픔, 불행, 비극뿐이었다. ❷ 불가산명사 비참함 ❑ 교육을 받은 극소수의 엘리트들은 200만 동포의 불행으로부터 이득을 봤다. ❸ 구 사는 걸 불행하게 만들다 ❑ 우리를 불행하게 만드는 애들만 아니라면 난 정말 여기 살고 싶다. ❹ 구 궁금해 죽겠는 것을 알려 주다 [비격식체] ❑ 난 궁금해 죽겠어. 그거 어떻게 해? ❺ 구 (동물을) 안락사시키다 ❑ 그는 왓슨 가족이 수의사를 불러 자기들의 개를 안락사시켰다고 우울하게 말한다.

M

N

O

mis|fit /mɪsfɪt/ (**misfits**) N-COUNT A **misfit** is a person who is not easily accepted by other people, often because their behavior is very different from that of everyone else. ❑ *I have been made to feel a social and psychological misfit for not wanting children.*

가산명사 부적응자 ❑ 나는 아이를 갖고 싶은 마음이 없는 것 때문에 내가 사회적·심리적 부적응자인 것처럼 느껴야 했다.

P

mis|for|tune /mɪsfɔrtʃən/ (**misfortunes**) N-VAR A **misfortune** is something unpleasant or unlucky that happens to someone. ❑ *She seemed to enjoy the misfortunes of others.*

가산명사 또는 불가산명사 불운, 불행 ❑ 그녀는 남의 불행을 즐기는 것처럼 보였다.

Q

mis|giv|ing /mɪsgɪvɪŋ/ (**misgivings**) N-VAR If you have **misgivings** about something that is being suggested or done, you feel that it is not quite right, and are worried that it may have unwanted results. ❑ *She had some misgivings about what she was about to do.*

가산명사 또는 불가산명사 염려, 걱정 ❑ 그녀는 지금 막 하려는 일에 대해 걱정하고 있었다.

R

S

mis|guid|ed /mɪsgaɪdɪd/ ADJ If you describe an opinion or plan as **misguided**, you are critical of it because you think it is based on an incorrect idea. You can also describe people as misguided. [DISAPPROVAL] ❑ *In a misguided attempt to be funny, he manages only offensiveness.*

형용사 잘못된, 오도된 [탐탁찮음] ❑ 그는 사람들을 웃기려고 했는데, 잘못해서 불쾌하게만 만들었다.

T

mis|han|dle /mɪshændᵊl/ (**mishandles, mishandling, mishandled**) V-T If you say that someone **has mishandled** something, you are critical of them because you think they have dealt with it badly. [DISAPPROVAL] ❑ *He completely mishandled an important project purely through lack of attention.* ● **mis|han|dling** N-UNCOUNT ❑ *...the Government's mishandling of the economy.*

타동사 잘못 다루다 [탐탁찮음] ❑ 그녀는 순전히 부주의로 중요한 프로젝트를 완전히 망쳐 버렸다. ● 실책 불가산명사 ❑ 정부의 경제 실책

U

mis|hap /mɪshæp/ (**mishaps**) N-VAR A **mishap** is an unfortunate but not very serious event that happens to someone. ❑ *After a number of mishaps she did manage to get back to Germany.*

가산명사 또는 불가산명사 불상사 ❑ 여러 불상사를 겪은 후 그녀는 독일로 겨우 돌아갔다.

V

W

mis|in|for|ma|tion /mɪsɪnfərmeɪʃᵊn/ N-UNCOUNT **Misinformation** is wrong information which is given to someone, often in a deliberate attempt to make them believe something which is not true. ❑ *This was a deliberate piece of misinformation.*

불가산명사 허위 정보 ❑ 이건 고의적인 허위 정보였어.

X

Word Link *mis ≈ bad* : *mis*interpret, *mis*judge, *mis*leading

---

Y

mis|in|ter|pret /mɪsɪntɜrprɪt/ (**misinterprets, misinterpreting, misinterpreted**) V-T If you **misinterpret** something, you understand it wrongly. ❑ *He was amazed that he'd misinterpreted the situation so completely.* ● **mis|in|ter|pre|ta|tion** /mɪsɪntɜrprɪteɪʃᵊn/ (**misinterpretations**) N-VAR ❑ *...a misinterpretation of the aims and ends of socialism.*

타동사 잘못 해석하다, 오해하다 ❑ 그는 자신이 그 상황을 완전히 오해하고 있었다는 것을 알고는 경악을 금치 못했다. ● 오해, 잘못된 해석 가산명사 또는 불가산명사 ❑ 사회주의의 목적과 취지에 대한 잘못된 해석

Z

Word Link	mis ≈ bad : *mis*interpret, *mis*judge, *mis*leading

mis|judge /mɪsdʒʌdʒ/ (**misjudges, misjudging, misjudged**) V-T If you say that someone **has misjudged** a person or situation, you mean that they have formed an incorrect idea or opinion about them, and often that they have made a wrong decision as a result of this. ❑ *Perhaps I had misjudged him, and he was not so predictable after all.*

타동사 오판하다, 잘못 보다 ❑ 내가 그를 잘못 봤을 수도 있겠지만, 그는 어쨌든 예측 불허였다.

mis|lead /mɪslid/ (**misleads, misleading, misled**) V-T If you say that someone **has misled** you, you mean that they have made you believe something which is not true, either by telling you a lie or by giving you a wrong idea or impression. ❑ *It's this legend which has misled scholars.*

타동사 오도하다 ❑ 이 전설이 학자들을 오도한 것이다.

mis|lead|ing /mɪslidɪŋ/ ADJ If you describe something as **misleading**, you mean that it gives you a wrong idea or impression. ❑ *It would be misleading to say that we were friends.* ● **mis|lead|ing|ly** ADV ❑ *The data had been presented misleadingly.*

형용사 오해를 살 수 있는 ❑ 우리가 친구라고 한다면 오해를 살 수도 있을 거야. ● 오해를 살 수 있게 부사 ❑ 그 자료는 오해를 사기 쉽게 발표됐다.

mis|led /mɪslɛd/ **Misled** is the past tense and past participle of **mislead**.

mislead의 과거, 과거 분사

mis|man|age /mɪsmænɪdʒ/ (**mismanages, mismanaging, mismanaged**) V-T To **mismanage** something means to manage it badly. ❑ *75% of voters think the President has mismanaged the economy.*

타동사 잘못 관리하다 ❑ 유권자의 75퍼센트가 대통령이 경제를 잘못 관리했다고 생각한다.

mis|man|age|ment /mɪsmænɪdʒmənt/ N-UNCOUNT Someone's **mismanagement** of a system or organization is the bad way they have dealt with it or organized it. ❑ *His gross mismanagement left the company desperately in need of restructuring.*

불가산명사 잘못 관리함 ❑ 그가 행한 총체적 부실 경영으로 그 회사를 재정비해야 할 지경에 이르렀다.

mis|placed /mɪspleɪst/ ADJ If you describe a feeling or action as **misplaced**, you are critical of it because you think it is inappropriate, or directed towards the wrong thing or person. [DISAPPROVAL] ❑ *A telling sign of misplaced priorities is the concentration on health not environmental issues.*

형용사 잘못 주어진 [탐탁찮음] ❑ 우선순위가 잘못 되었다는 명백한 징후 하나는 환경이 아니라 보건에만 관심이 쏠리고 있다는 것이다.

mis|read /mɪsrid/ (**misreads, misreading**)

The form **misread** is used in the present tense, and is the past tense and past participle, when it is pronounced /mɪsrɛd/.

misread 형태는 현재형이면서 과거형이기도 하고 과거 분사이기도 하다. 과거형 및 과거 분사일 때는 /mɪsrɛd/로 발음된다.

◼ V-T If you **misread** a situation or someone's behavior, you do not understand it properly. ❑ *The government largely misread the mood of the electorate.* ● **mis|read|ing** (**misreadings**) N-COUNT ❑ *...a misreading of opinion in France.* ◾ V-T If you **misread** something that has been written or printed, you look at it and think that it says something that it does not say. ❑ *His chauffeur misread his route and took a wrong turning.*

◼ 타동사 잘못 파악하다 ❑ 정부는 유권자들의 분위기를 한참 잘못 파악하고 있었다. ● 잘못 파악함 가산명사 ❑ 프랑스의 여론을 잘못 파악함 ◾ 타동사 잘못 읽다 ❑ 그의 운전기사는 길을 잘못 읽어서 엉뚱한 곳으로 차를 돌렸다.

mis|rep|re|sent /mɪsrɛprɪzɛnt/ (**misrepresents, misrepresenting, misrepresented**) V-T If someone **misrepresents** a person or situation, they give a wrong or inaccurate account of what the person or situation is like. ❑ *He said that the press had misrepresented him as arrogant and bullying.* ❑ *Hollywood films misrepresented us as drunks, maniacs, and murderers.* ● **mis|rep|re|sen|ta|tion** /mɪsrɛprɪzɛnteɪʃ°n/ (**misrepresentations**) N-VAR ❑ *I wish to point out your misrepresentation of the facts.*

타동사 잘못 묘사하다 ❑ 그는 언론이 자신을 오만하며 약자를 괴롭히는 사람으로 잘못 묘사하고 있다고 말했다. ❑ 할리우드 영화는 우리를 주정뱅이에 미치광이 그리고 살인자로 잘못 묘사했다. ● 잘못 묘사한 가산명사 또는 불가산명사 ❑ 저는 당신이 잘못 묘사한 사실들을 지적하고 싶습니다.

---

miss

① USED AS A TITLE OR A FORM OF ADDRESS
② VERB AND NOUN USES

① **Miss** ♦♦♦ /mɪs/ (**Misses**) ◼ N-TITLE You use **Miss** in front of the name of a girl or unmarried woman when you are speaking to her or referring to her. ❑ *It was nice talking to you, Miss Ellis.* ◾ N-VOC In some schools, children address their women teachers as **Miss**. [mainly BRIT] ❑ *"Smith!" — "Yes, Miss?"*

◼ 경칭명사 - 양, 미스 - ❑ 얘기 즐거웠습니다, 엘리스 양. ◾ 호격명사 선생님 (학생들이 여교사를 부를 때) [주로 영국영어] ❑ "스미스!" "예, 선생님?"

In English-speaking countries **Miss** is used in front of the name of an unmarried woman when you are speaking or referring to her. **Mrs.** is used before the name of a married woman. Some women who do not think it is important to let people know whether they are married or not, choose to call themselves **Ms.** instead. Just like **Mr.**, used for men, Ms. does not tell you whether a person is married or single.

영어권에서 Miss는 대화 상대방이나 언급하고 있는 여성이 미혼일 때 그 이름 앞에 사용하고, Mrs.는 기혼 여성의 이름 앞에 사용한다. 다른 사람들이 자기가 결혼을 했는지 안 했는지를 아는 것이 중요하지 않다고 생각하는 일부 여성들은 자기를 Ms.라고 부르기를 선택한다. 남성에게 붙이는 Mr.와 마찬가지로 Ms.도 이것만 가지고는 기혼인지 미혼인지를 알 수 없다.

② **miss** ♦♦♢ /mɪs/ (**misses, missing, missed**) →Please look at category ◉ to see if the expression you are looking for is shown under another headword. ◼ V-T/V-I If you **miss** something, you fail to hit it, for example when you have thrown something at it or you have shot a bullet at it. ❑ *She hurled the ashtray across the room, narrowly missing my head.* ● N-COUNT **Miss** is also a noun. ❑ *After more misses, they finally put two arrows into the lion's chest.* ◾ V-T/V-I In sports, if you **miss** a shot, you fail to get the ball in the goal, net, or hole. ❑ *He scored four of the goals but missed a penalty.* ● N-COUNT **Miss** is also a noun. ❑ *Striker Alan Smith was guilty of two glaring misses.* ◉ V-T If you **miss** something, you fail to notice it. ❑ *From this vantage point he watched, his searching eye never missing a detail.* ◈ V-T If you **miss** the meaning or importance of something, you fail to understand or appreciate it. ❑ *One BBC correspondent had totally missed the point of the question.* ◍ V-T If you **miss** a chance or opportunity, you fail to take advantage of it. ❑ *It was too good an opportunity to miss.* ◎ V-T If you **miss** someone who is no longer with you or who has died, you feel sad and wish that they were still with you. ❑ *Your mama and I are gonna miss you at Christmas.* ● V-T If you **miss** something, you feel sad because you no longer have it or are no longer doing or experiencing it. ❑ *I could happily move back into a flat if it wasn't for the fact that I'd miss my garden.* ◐ V-T If you **miss** something such as a plane or train, you arrive too late to catch it. ❑ *He missed the last bus home.* ◑ V-T If you **miss** something such as a meeting or an activity, you do not go to it or take part in it. ❑ *It's a pity*

◼ 타동사/자동사 빗맞히다, 못 맞히다 ❑ 그녀가 방 저편에서 재떨이를 내던졌는데 하마터면 내 머리에 맞을 뻔했다. ● 가산명사 빗맞힘, 못 맞힘 ❑ 몇 번 더 빗맞힌 후에, 그들은 마침내 사자의 가슴에 화살 두 대를 꽂을 수 있었다. ◾ 타동사/자동사 (득점 기회를) 놓치다 ❑ 그는 네 골을 넣었지만, 페널티 킥 하나를 놓쳤다. ● 가산명사 (득점 기회) 놓침 ❑ 스트라이커 앨런 스미스는 절호의 찬스를 허망하게 놓치는 잘못을 저질렀다. ◉ 타동사 알아차리지 못 하다 ❑ 이렇게 유리한 위치에서 바라볼 수 있어서, 그의 눈은 세세한 것 하나도 놓치지 않았다. ◈ 타동사 이해하지 못하다 ❑ 한 비비시통신원은 그 질문의 뜻에 대한 요점을 전혀 이해하지 못하고 있었다. ◍ 타동사 (기회를) 놓치다 ❑ 놓치기에는 너무 아까운 기회였다. ◎ 타동사 그리워하다 ❑ 크리스마스가 되면 너희 엄마랑 나는 네가 그리울 거야. ● 타동사 -이 없어져 섭섭해 하다 ❑ 내가 정원이 그립지만 않다면 아파트로 다시 이사해서도 행복할 거야. ◐ 타동사 (비행기 등을) 놓치다 ❑ 그는 집으로 가는 막차를 놓쳤다. ◑ 타동사 빠지다, 참석하지 못하다 ❑ 마쿠와 내가 저번 주 수업에 빠져야 해서 유감이다. ❑ 맨날 하는 재방송

Makku and I had to miss our lesson last week. ❑ *You won't be missing much on TV tonight apart from the usual repeats.* ⑩ →see also **missing**. to **miss the boat** →see **boat**

> 말고는 오늘 텔레비전을 안 봐도 놓치는 게 별로 없을 거야.

Word Partnership   miss의 연어

N.	miss **the point** ② ④
	miss **a chance**, miss **an opportunity** ② ⑤
	miss **a class**, miss **school** ② ⑨
ADV.	miss *someone/something* terribly ② ⑥ ⑦

▶**miss out** ❶ PHRASAL VERB If you **miss out on** something that would be enjoyable or useful to you, you are not involved in it or do not take part in it. ❑ *We're missing out on a tremendous opportunity.* ❷ PHRASAL VERB If you **miss out** something or someone, you fail to include them. [BRIT; AM **leave out**] ❑ *There should be an apostrophe here, and look, you've missed out the word "men" altogether!*

> ❶ 구동사 놓치다 ❑ 우리는 엄청난 기회를 놓치고 있다. ❷ 구동사 빠뜨리다 [영국영어; 미국영어 leave out] ❑ 여기 아포스트로피를 붙여야지, 그리고 봐, 'men'도 다 빠뜨렸잖아.

mis-sell /mɪs sɛl/ (**mis-sells, mis-selling, mis-sold**) V-T To **mis-sell** something such as a pension or an insurance policy means to sell it to someone even though you know that it is not suitable for them. [BUSINESS] ❑ *The company has been accused of mis-selling products to thousands of elderly investors.*

> 타동사 속여 팔다 [경제] ❑ 그 회사는 수천 명의 노인 투자자들에게 상품을 속여 판 혐의로 고발당했다.

Word Link   miss ≈ sending : dismiss, missile, missionary

mis|sile ♦◇◇ /mɪsˀl, BRIT mɪsaɪl/ (**missiles**) ❶ N-COUNT A **missile** is a tube-shaped weapon that travels long distances through the air and explodes when it reaches its target. ❑ *The authorities offered to stop firing missiles if the rebels agreed to stop attacking civilian targets.* ❷ N-COUNT Anything that is thrown as a weapon can be called a **missile**. ❑ *The football supporters began throwing missiles, one of which hit the referee.*

> ❶ 가산명사 미사일 ❑ 당국은 반군이 민간인에 대한 공격을 멈춘다면 미사일 공격을 중지하겠다고 제안했다. ❷ 가산명사 던지는 무기 ❑ 축구 응원단들이 물건들을 던지기 시작했는데, 그 중 하나에 심판이 맞았다.

miss|ing ♦◇◇ /mɪsɪŋ/ ❶ ADJ If something is **missing** or has **gone missing**, it is not in its usual place, and you cannot find it. ❑ *It was only an hour or so later that I discovered that my gun was missing.* ❷ ADJ If a part of something is **missing**, it has been removed or has come off, and has not been replaced. ❑ *Three buttons were missing from his shirt.* ❸ ADJ If you say that something is **missing**, you mean that it has not been included, and you think that it should have been. ❑ *She had given me an incomplete list. One name was missing from it.* ❹ ADJ Someone who is **missing** cannot be found, and it is not known whether they are alive or dead. ❑ *Five people died in the explosion and more than one thousand were injured. One person is still missing.* ● PHRASE If a member of the armed forces is **missing in action**, they have not returned from a battle, their body has not been found, and they are not thought to have been captured.

> ❶ 형용사 없어진 ❑ 겨우 한 시간 정도 지나서, 나는 내 총이 없어진 것을 알아차렸다. ❷ 형용사 세거진, 떨어져 나간 ❑ 그의 셔츠에서 단추 세 개가 떨어져 나가고 없었다. ❸ 형용사 누락된 ❑ 그녀는 나에게 미완성 명단을 줬다. 그 명단에서는 한 사람의 이름이 누락돼 있었다. ❹ 형용사 실종된 ❑ 그 폭발 사고로 5명이 사망했고, 천 명 이상이 부상을 입었다. 한 사람은 아직 실종 상태이다. ● 구 작전 중 실종

Word Partnership   missing의 연어

ADV.	still missing ❶-❹
N.	missing piece ❶ ❷
	missing information, missing ingredient ❸
	missing children, missing girl, missing people, missing soldiers ❹

mis|sion ♦♦◇ /mɪʃən/ (**missions**) ❶ N-COUNT A **mission** is an important task that people are given to do, especially one that involves traveling to another country. ❑ *Salisbury sent him on a diplomatic mission to North America.* ❷ N-COUNT A **mission** is a group of people who have been sent to a foreign country to carry out an official task. ❑ *...a senior member of a diplomatic mission.* ❸ N-COUNT A **mission** is a special journey made by a military airplane or spacecraft. ❑ *...a bomber that crashed during a training mission in the west Texas mountains.* ❹ N-SING If you say that you have a **mission**, you mean that you have a strong commitment and sense of duty to do or achieve something. ❑ *He viewed his mission in life as protecting the weak from the evil.* ❺ N-COUNT A **mission** is the activities of a group of Christians who have been sent to a place to teach people about Christianity. ❑ *They say God spoke to them and told them to go on a mission to the poorest country in the Western Hemisphere.*

> ❶ 가산명사 임무, 사명 ❑ 솔즈베리는 그에게 외교 임무를 줘서 북미로 보냈다. ❷ 가산명사 사절단 ❑ 외교 사절단의 고위 멤버 ❸ 가산명사 비행 작전, 특무 비행 ❑ 서부 텍사스 산악 지대에서 훈련 비행을 하다 추락한 폭격기 ❹ 단수명사 사명 ❑ 그는 약한 자로부터 약자를 보호하는 것을 평생의 사명으로 여겼다. ❺ 가산명사 선교 ❑ 그들은 하나님께서 서반구에서 가장 가난한 나라에 선교하러 가라고 자신들에게 명하셨다고 말한다.

Word Partnership   mission의 연어

ADJ.	dangerous mission, secret mission, successful mission ❶
N.	combat mission, rescue mission, suicide mission, training mission ❶ ❸
	peacekeeping mission ❶ ❷
V.	accomplish a mission, carry out a mission ❶ ❸ ❹

mis|sion|ary /mɪʃəneri/ (**missionaries**) ❶ N-COUNT A **missionary** is a Christian who has been sent to a foreign country to teach people about Christianity. ❑ *My mother would still like me to be a missionary in Africa.* ❷ ADJ **Missionary** is used to describe the activities of missionaries. [ADJ n] ❑ *You should be in missionary work.* ❸ ADJ If you refer to someone's enthusiasm for an activity or belief as **missionary** zeal, you are emphasizing that they are very enthusiastic about it. [EMPHASIS] [ADJ n] ❑ *She had a kind of missionary zeal about bringing culture to the masses.*

> ❶ 가산명사 선교사 ❑ 우리 어머니께서는 아직도 내가 아프리카 선교사가 되었으면 하신다. ❷ 형용사 선교 (활동) ❑ 너는 선교 활동을 해야지. ❸ 형용사 뜨거운 (열정) [강조] ❑ 그녀는 대중에게 문화를 보급하는 데 일종의 뜨거운 열정을 가지고 있었다.

mis|sion state|ment (**mission statements**) N-COUNT A company's or organization's **mission statement** is a document which states what they aim to achieve and the kind of service they intend to provide. [BUSINESS] ❑ *Our mission statement is to be the best design firm in the world.*

> 가산명사 사훈(社訓) [경제] ❑ 세계 최고의 디자인 회사가 되는 것이 우리의 사훈이다.

mis|spend /mɪsspɛnd/ (**misspends, misspending, misspent**) v-T If you say that time or money **has been misspent**, you disapprove of the way in which it has been spent. [DISAPPROVAL] ❏ *Much of the money was grossly misspent.*

mist /mɪst/ (**mists, misting, misted**) **1** N-VAR Mist consists of a large number of tiny drops of water in the air, which make it difficult to see very far. ❏ *Thick mist made flying impossible.* **2** V-T/V-I If a piece of glass **mists** or **is misted**, it becomes covered with tiny drops of moisture, so that you cannot see through it easily. ❏ *The windows misted, blurring the stark streetlight.* • PHRASAL VERB Mist over and mist up mean the same as **mist**. ❏ *The front windshield was misting over.*

mis|take ♦♦◇ /mɪsteɪk/ (**mistakes, mistaking, mistook, mistaken**) **1** N-COUNT If you make a **mistake**, you do something which you did not intend to do, or which produces a result that you do not want. [oft N of -ing, also by N] ❏ *They made the big mistake of thinking they could seize its border with a relatively small force.* ❏ *There must be some mistake.* **2** N-COUNT A **mistake** is something or part of something which is incorrect or not right. ❏ *Her mother sighed and rubbed out another mistake in the crossword puzzle.* **3** V-T If you **mistake** one person or thing for another, you wrongly think that they are the other person or thing. ❏ *When they first occurs it is often mistaken for a summer cold.* **4** V-T If you **mistake** something, you fail to recognize or understand it. ❏ *The government completely mistook the feeling of the country.* **5** PHRASE You can say **there is no mistaking** something when you are emphasizing that you cannot fail to recognize or understand it. [EMPHASIS] ❏ *There's no mistaking the eastern flavor of the food.*

Word Partnership	mistake의 연어
ADJ.	**fatal** mistake, **honest** mistake, **tragic** mistake **1**
	big mistake, **common** mistake, **costly** mistake, **huge** mistake, **serious** mistake, **terrible** mistake **1 2**
V.	**admit** a mistake, **correct** a mistake, **fix** a mistake, **make** a mistake, **realize** a mistake **1 2**

mis|tak|en /mɪsteɪkən/ **1** ADJ If you are **mistaken about** something, you are wrong about it. [v-link ADJ, oft ADJ about n] ❏ *I see I was mistaken about you.* • PHRASE You use expressions such as **if I'm not mistaken** and **unless I'm very much mistaken** as a polite way of emphasizing the statement you are making, especially when you are confident that it is correct. [EMPHASIS] ❏ *I think Alfred wanted to marry Jennifer, if I am not mistaken.* **2** ADJ A **mistaken** belief or opinion is incorrect. [ADJ n] ❏ *I had a mistaken view of what was happening.* • **mis|tak|en|ly** ADV [ADV with v] ❏ *He says they mistakenly believed the standard licenses they held were sufficient.*

Word Partnership	mistaken의 연어
V.	**if I'm not** mistaken **1**
N.	mistaken **belief**, mistaken **impression**, mistaken **notion** **2**

mis|ter /mɪstər/ N-VOC Men are sometimes addressed as **mister**, especially by children and especially when the person talking to them does not know their name. [INFORMAL] ❏ *Look, Mister, we know our job, so don't try to tell us what to do.*

mis|took /mɪstʊk/ **Mistook** is the past tense and past participle of **mistake**.

mis|tress /mɪstrɪs/ (**mistresses**) N-COUNT A married man's **mistress** is a woman who is not his wife and with whom he is having a sexual relationship. [OLD-FASHIONED] ❏ *Tracy was his mistress for three years.*

mis|trust /mɪstrʌst/ (**mistrusts, mistrusting, mistrusted**) **1** N-UNCOUNT **Mistrust** is the feeling that you have towards someone who you do not trust. ❏ *There was mutual mistrust between the two men.* **2** V-T If you **mistrust** someone or something, you do not trust them. ❏ *It frequently appears that Bell mistrusts all journalists.*

misty /mɪsti/ ADJ On a **misty** day, there is a lot of mist in the air. ❏ *It's a bit misty this morning.*

mis|under|stand /mɪsʌndərstænd/ (**misunderstands, misunderstanding, misunderstood**) v-T If you **misunderstand** someone or something, you do not understand them properly. ❏ *They have simply misunderstood what rock and roll is.* →see also **misunderstood** • CONVENTION You can say **don't misunderstand me** when you want to correct a wrong impression that you think someone may have gotten about what you are saying.

mis|under|stand|ing /mɪsʌndərstændɪŋ/ (**misunderstandings**) **1** N-VAR A **misunderstanding** is a failure to understand something properly, for example a situation or a person's remarks. ❏ *There has been some misunderstanding of our publishing aims.* **2** N-COUNT You can refer to a disagreement or slight quarrel as a **misunderstanding**. [FORMAL] ❏ *...a little misunderstanding with the police.*

mis|under|stood /mɪsʌndərstʊd/ **1** **Misunderstood** is the past tense and past participle of **misunderstand**. **2** ADJ If you describe someone or something as **misunderstood**, you mean that people do not understand them and have a wrong impression or idea of them. ❏ *Eric is very badly misunderstood.*

mis|use (**misuses, misusing, misused**)

The noun is pronounced /mɪsyus/. The verb is pronounced /mɪsyuz/.

1 N-VAR The **misuse** of something is incorrect, careless, or dishonest use of it. ❏ *...the misuse of power and privilege.* **2** V-T If someone **misuses** something, they use it incorrectly, carelessly, or dishonestly. ❏ *She misused her position in the appointment of 26,000 party supporters to government jobs.*

타동사 잘못 사용되다 [탐탁찮음] ❏ 그 돈의 대부분은 완전히 잘못 사용됐다.

1 가산명사 또는 불가산명사 안개 ❏ 짙은 안개로 인해 비행이 불가능했다. **2** 타동사/자동사 김이 서리다 ❏ 창에 김이 서려서 밝은 가로등 불빛이 번져 보였다. • 구동사 김이 서리다 ❏ 차 앞 유리에 김이 서려 있었다.

1 가산명사 실수 ❏ 상대적으로 적은 수의 병력으로 국경을 장악할 수 있다고 생각한 것은 그들이 범한 심각한 실수였다. ❏ 뭔가 잘못 된 게 있을 거야. **2** 가산명사 착오 ❏ 그녀의 어머니는 한숨을 쉬신 후, 십자 낱말 맞추기에서 또 잘못 쓴 글을 지웠다. **3** 타동사 착각하다 ❏ 건초열이 처음에 발병하면, 사람들은 대부분 여름 감기로 착각한다. **4** 타동사 파악하지 못하다, 이해하지 못하다 ❏ 정부는 국민의 기분을 전혀 파악하지 못하고 있었다. **5** 구 분명히 ─이다 [강조] ❏ 이건 분명히 동양 음식의 맛이야.

1 형용사 틀린 ❏ 내가 너에 대해 틀린 거 알아. • 구 내가 잘못 안 게 아니라면 [강조] ❏ 내가 잘못 안 게 아니라면, 앨프레드는 제니퍼랑 결혼하고 싶어 하는 것 같아. **2** 형용사 잘못된 ❏ 나는 그때 일어나는 일을 잘못 파악하고 있었다. • 잘못 부사 ❏ 그는 그 사람들이 그들이 갖고 있는 표준 면허면 충분하다고 잘못 믿고 있었다고 말한다.

호격명사 아저씨 [비격식체] ❏ 이 보세요, 아저씨, 우리 일은 우리가 잘 알고 있으니까 우리더러 어떻게 하라는 얘기하려 들지 마세요.

mistake의 과거, 과거 분사

가산명사 정부 [구식어] ❏ 트레이시는 3년 동안 그의 정부였다.

1 불가산명사 불신 ❏ 그 두 남자는 서로 불신하고 있었다. **2** 타동사 불신하다 ❏ 벨이 기자들은 모두 불신한다는 것을 자주 눈치 챌 수 있다.

형용사 안개 낀 ❏ 오늘 아침은 안개가 조금 끼어 있다.

타동사 오해하다 ❏ 그들은 단지 록앤롤이 뭔지 오해해 왔을 뿐이다. • 관용 표현 오해가 없었으면 해

1 가산명사 또는 불가산명사 오해 ❏ 우리 출판 목적에 대해 몇 가지 오해가 있었다. **2** 가산명사 마찰 [격식체] ❏ 경찰과의 가벼운 마찰

1 misunderstand의 과거, 과거 분사 **2** 형용사 오해를 받는 ❏ 에릭은 아주 심하게 오해를 받고 있다.

명사는 /mɪsyus/로 발음되고, 동사는 /mɪsyuz/로 발음된다.

1 가산명사 또는 불가산명사 오용, 남용 ❏ 권력과 특전 남용 **2** 타동사 오용하다, 남용하다 ❏ 그녀는 자신의 지위를 남용하여 2만 6천 명의 정당 지지자에게 정부 일자리를 주었다.

A

mite /maɪt/ (**mites**) N-COUNT **Mites** are very tiny creatures that live on plants, for example, or in animals' fur. ❑ ...*an itching skin disorder caused by parasitic mites.*

가산명사 진드기 ❑ 기생하는 진드기로 인해 발생한 피부 가려움증

mitigate /ˈmɪtɪɡeɪt/ (**mitigates, mitigating, mitigated**) V-T To **mitigate** something means to make it less unpleasant, serious, or painful. [FORMAL] ❑ ...*ways of mitigating the effects of an explosion.*

타동사 완화하다, 누그러뜨리다 [격식체] ❑ 폭발의 여파를 줄이는 방법

B

mitigating /ˈmɪtɪɡeɪtɪŋ/ ADJ **Mitigating** circumstances or factors make a bad action, especially a crime, easier to understand and excuse, and may result in the person responsible being punished less severely. [FORMAL] [ADJ n] ❑ *The judge found that in her case there were mitigating circumstances.*

형용사 참작할 [격식체] ❑ 판사는 그녀의 경우 정상 참작의 여지가 있다고 판결했다.

C

D

mix ♦♢♢ /mɪks/ (**mixes, mixing, mixed**) ◘ V-RECIP If two substances **mix** or if you **mix** one substance **with** another, you stir or shake them together, or combine them in some other way, so that they become a single substance. ❑ *Oil and water don't mix.* ❑ *A quick stir will mix them thoroughly.* ❑ *Mix the cinnamon with the rest of the sugar.* ◙ V-T If you **mix** something, you prepare it by mixing other things together. ❑ *He had spent several hours mixing cement.* ◗ N-VAR A **mix** is a powder containing all the substances that you need in order to make something such as a cake or a sauce. When you want to use it, you add liquid. ❑ *For speed we used packets of pizza dough mix.* ◖ N-COUNT A **mix of** different things or people is two or more of them together. ❑ *The story is a magical mix of fantasy and reality.* ◎ V-RECIP If two things or activities do not **mix**, it is not a good idea to have them or do them together, because the result would be unpleasant or dangerous. [usu with brd-neg] ❑ *Politics and sport don't mix.* ❑ ...*some of these pills that don't mix with drink.* ◢ V-RECIP If you **mix with** other people, you meet them and talk to them. You can also say that people **mix**. ❑ *I ventured the idea that the secret of staying young was to mix with older people.* ❑ *People are supposed to mix, do you understand?* ◿ →see also **mixed**. to **mix** your **metaphors** →see **metaphor**

E

F

G

H

◙ 상호동사 섞이다; 섞다 ❑ 물과 기름은 서로 섞이지 않는다. ❑ 빨리 저으면 그것들은 충분히 섞일 겁니다. ❑ 계피 가루를 설탕 남은 것과 섞어라. ◙ 타동사 섞다, 개다 ❑ 그는 시멘트를 개는 데 여러 시간을 보냈다. ◗ 가산명사 또는 불가산명사 믹스 (가루) ❑ 빨리 하기 위해 우리는 피자 반죽 믹스를 여러 포대 사용했다. ◖ 가산명사 어우러짐 ❑ 그 이야기는 환상과 현실이 환상적으로 잘 어우러진 작품이다. ◎ 상호동사 어울리다 ❑ 정치와 스포츠는 어울리지 않는다. ❑ 술과 함께 복용하면 안 되는 이 알약 중 몇 가지 ◢ 상호동사 어울리다; 어우러지다 ❑ 나는 젊음을 유지하는 비결은 나이 든 사람들과 어울리는 것이라고 과감하게 말했다. ❑ 사람이란 서로 어우러져야 하는 거야, 내 말 알겠어?

Word Partnership mix의 연어

| N. | mix **ingredients**, mix **with water** ◙ ◗ |
| ADV. | mix **thoroughly**, mix **together** ◙ ◗ |

I

J

K

►**mix up** ◙ PHRASAL VERB If you **mix up** two things or people, you confuse them, so that you think that one of them is the other one. ❑ *People often mix me up with other actors.* ❑ *Depressed people may mix up their words.* ◙ PHRASAL VERB If you **mix up** a number of things, you put things of different kinds together or place things so that they are not in order. ❑ *I like to mix up designer clothes.* ❑ *Part of the plan was that the town should not fall into office, industrial, and residential zones, but mix the three up together.* ◗ →see also **mixed up**

◙ 구동사 혼동하다 ❑ 사람들은 나를 종종 다른 배우와 혼동한다. ❑ 의기소침해 있는 사람은 자신들이 한 말을 혼동할 수도 있다. ◙ 구동사 섞다 ❑ 나는 유명 디자이너가 디자인한 옷들을 섞어 입는 것을 좋아한다. ❑ 계획 중의 일부분은 그 도시를 사무 지구나 산업 지구, 주거 지구로 만드는 것이 아니라 이 셋을 합친 지역으로 만든다는 것이었다.

L

M

mixed ♦♢♢ /mɪkst/ ◙ ADJ If you have **mixed** feelings about something or someone, you feel uncertain about them because you can see both good and bad points about them. ❑ *I came home from the meeting with mixed feelings.* ◙ ADJ A **mixed** group of people consists of people of many different types. ❑ *I found a very mixed group of individuals some of whom I could relate to and others with whom I had very little in common.* ◗ ADJ **Mixed** is used to describe something that involves people from two or more different races. ❑ *Sally had attended a racially mixed school.* ◖ ADJ **Mixed** education or accommodations are intended for both males and females. ❑ *Girls who have always been at a mixed school know how to stand up for themselves.* ◎ ADJ **Mixed** is used to describe something which includes or consists of different things of the same general kind. [ADJ n] ❑ ...*a teaspoon of mixed herbs.*

N

◙ 형용사 착잡한, 복잡한 ❑ 나는 그 모임을 마친 후 착잡한 심정으로 집에 왔다. ◙ 형용사 다양한 종류의 사람으로 구성된 ❑ 나는 몇몇은 나와 연관을 지을 수 있고, 몇몇은 나와는 공통점이 거의 없는, 정말 다양한 종류의 사람들로 구성된 그룹을 발견했어. ◗ 형용사 여러 인종이 섞여 있는, 혼혈의 ❑ 샐리는 여러 인종이 섞여 있는 학교를 다녔다. ◖ 형용사 남녀 공학의, 남녀 공용의 ❑ 계속 남녀 공학 학교를 다닌 여자애들은 자기 자신을 지켜내는 법을 안다. ◎ 형용사 혼합의 ❑ 혼합 허브 한 스푼

O

P

mixed econo|my (**mixed economies**) N-COUNT A **mixed economy** is an economic system in which some companies are owned by the state and some are not. [BUSINESS] ❑ *The African National Congress today dropped its doctrine of nationalizing industry in favor of a mixed economy.*

가산명사 혼합 경제 [경제] ❑ 아프리카 민족회의는 오늘 혼합 경제를 위해 산업 국유화 정책을 포기했다.

Q

mixed up ◙ ADJ If you are **mixed up**, you are confused, often because of emotional or social problems. ❑ *I think he's a rather mixed up kid.* ◙ ADJ To be **mixed up in** something bad, or **with** someone you disapprove of, means to be involved in it or with them. [v-link ADJ in/with n] ❑ *Why did I ever get mixed up with you?*

R

◙ 형용사 가치관이 혼돈된 ❑ 그 애는 약간 가치관이 혼돈된 애 같아. ◙ 형용사 말려 들어가는 ❑ 왜 내가 너 같은 아이한테 말려 들어갔지?

S

mix|er /ˈmɪksər/ (**mixers**) ◙ N-COUNT A **mixer** is a machine used for mixing things together. ❑ ...*an electric mixer.* ◙ N-COUNT A **mixer** is a nonalcoholic drink such as fruit juice that you mix with strong alcohol such as gin. ❑ *At the Tropicana you buy a bottle of rum with your ticket, and order ice and mixers from the waiters at the table.* ◗ N-COUNT If you say that someone is a good **mixer**, you mean that they are good at talking to people and making friends. ❑ *Cooper was a good mixer, he was popular.* ◖ N-COUNT A **mixer** is a piece of equipment that is used to make changes to recorded music or film. ❑ ...*a three channel audio mixer.*

T

◙ 가산명사 혼합기, 믹서 ❑ 전기 믹서 ◙ 가산명사 (주류) 희석용 음료 ❑ 트로피카나에서 티켓으로 럼주 1병을 사고, 테이블에 앉아 웨이터에게 얼음과 희석용 음료를 주문했다. ◗ 가산명사 사교가 ❑ 쿠퍼는 훌륭한 사교가였고, 인기가 있었다. ◖ 가산명사 (녹음된 음악 등의) 조절 장치, 믹싱 기계 ❑ 세 개의 채널이 있는 음향 믹싱 기계

U

mix|ture ♦♢♢ /ˈmɪkstʃər/ (**mixtures**) ◙ N-SING A **mixture of** things consists of several different things together. ❑ *They looked at him with a mixture of horror, envy, and awe.* ◙ N-COUNT A **mixture** is a substance that consists of other substances which have been stirred or shaken together. ❑ ...*a mixture of water and sugar and salt.*

V

◙ 단수명사 혼합 ❑ 그들은 공포와 부러움과 경외심이 섞인 눈으로 그를 바라보았다. ◙ 가산명사 혼합물 ❑ 설탕, 소금, 물을 혼합한 것

W

Thesaurus mixture의 참조어

| N. | blend, collection, combination, variety ◙ |
| | blend, compound, fusion ◙ |

X

ml ml is a written abbreviation for **milliliter** or **milliliters**. ❑ *Boil the sugar and 100 ml of water.*

밀리리터 ❑ 물 100 밀리리터에 설탕을 넣고 끓이세요.

Y

mm ♦♢♢ mm is an abbreviation for **millimeter** or **millimeters**. ❑ ...*a 135mm lens.*

밀리미터 ❑ 135밀리 렌즈

moan /moʊn/ (**moans, moaning, moaned**) ◙ V-T/V-I If you **moan**, you make a low sound, usually because you are unhappy or in pain. ❑ *Tony moaned in his*

Z

◙ 타동사/자동사 신음하다 ❑ 토니는 자면서 신음을 하며 옆으로 돌아누웠다. ● 가산명사 신음 ❑ 그녀는

sleep and then turned over on his side. ● N-COUNT **Moan** is also a noun. ❑ *Suddenly she gave a low, choking moan and began to tremble violently.* ● V-T/V-I To **moan** means to complain or speak in a way which shows that you are very unhappy. [DISAPPROVAL] ❑ *I used to moan if I didn't get at least six hours' sleep at night.* ❑ *...moaning about the weather.* ● N-COUNT A **moan** is a complaint. [INFORMAL] ❑ *They have been listening to people's moans and praise.*

mob /mɒb/ (**mobs, mobbing, mobbed**) ● N-COUNT A **mob** is a large, disorganized, and often violent crowd of people. ❑ *The inspectors watched a growing mob of demonstrators gathering.* ● N-SING People sometimes use **the mob** to refer in a disapproving way to the majority of people in a country or place, especially when these people are behaving in a violent or uncontrolled way. [DISAPPROVAL] ❑ *If they continue like this there is a danger of the mob taking over.* ● V-T If you say that someone **is being mobbed by** a crowd of people, you mean that the people are trying to talk to them or get near them in an enthusiastic or threatening way. [usu passive] ❑ *Her car was mobbed by the media.*

Word Link   mobil ≈ moving : *auto*mobile, mobile, mobilize

mo|bile ◆◇◇ /moʊbᵊl, BRIT moʊbaɪl/ (**mobiles**) ● ADJ You use **mobile** to describe something large that can be moved easily from place to place. ❑ *...the four-hundred seat mobile theater.* ● ADJ If you are **mobile**, you can move or travel easily from place to place, for example because you are not physically disabled or because you have your own transportation. ❑ *I'm still very mobile.* ● **mo|bil|ity** /moʊbɪlɪti/ N-UNCOUNT ❑ *Two cars gave them the freedom and mobility to go their separate ways.* ● ADJ In a **mobile** society, people move easily from one job, home, or social class to another. ❑ *We're a very mobile society, and people move after they get divorced.* ● **mo|bil|ity** N-UNCOUNT ❑ *Prior to the nineteenth century, there were almost no channels of social mobility.* ● N-COUNT A **mobile** is a decoration which you hang from a ceiling. It usually consists of several small objects which move as the air around them moves. ● N-COUNT A **mobile** is the same as a **mobile phone**. →see cellphone

Thesaurus   mobile의 참조어

ADJ.   movable, portable; (ant.) stationery ●

Word Partnership   mobile의 연어

N.   mobile **communications**, mobile **device**, mobile **service** ●

mo|bile phone (**mobile phones**) N-COUNT A **mobile phone** is a telephone that you can carry with you and use to make or receive calls wherever you are. [BRIT; AM **cellphone, cellular phone**]

mo|bi|lize /moʊbɪlaɪz/ (**mobilizes, mobilizing, mobilized**) [BRIT also **mobilise**] ● V-T/V-I If you **mobilize** support or **mobilize** people to do something, you succeed in encouraging people to take action, especially political action. If people **mobilize**, they prepare to take action. ❑ *The best hope is that we will mobilize international support and get down to action.* ● **mo|bi|li|za|tion** /moʊbɪlɪzeɪʃᵊn/ N-UNCOUNT ❑ *...the rapid mobilization of international opinion in support of the revolution.* ● V-T If you **mobilize** resources, you start to use them or make them available for use. ❑ *If you could mobilize the resources, you could get it done.* ● **mo|bi|li|za|tion** N-UNCOUNT ❑ *...the mobilization of resources for education.* ● V-T/V-I If a country **mobilizes**, or **mobilizes** its armed forces, or if its armed forces **mobilize**, they are given orders to prepare for a conflict. [JOURNALISM or MILITARY] ❑ *Sudan even threatened to mobilize in response to the ultimatums.* ● **mo|bi|li|za|tion** N-UNCOUNT ❑ *...a demand for full-scale mobilization to defend the republic.*

mock /mɒk/ (**mocks, mocking, mocked**) ● V-T If someone **mocks** you, they show or pretend that they think you are foolish or inferior, for example by saying something funny about you, or by imitating your behavior. ❑ *I thought you were mocking me.* ● ADJ You use **mock** to describe something which is not real or genuine, but which is intended to be very similar to the real thing. [ADJ n] ❑ *"It's tragic!" swoons Jeffrey in mock horror.* ● N-COUNT **Mocks** are practice exams that you take as part of your preparation for real exams. [BRIT, INFORMAL] ❑ *Bridget went from a D in her mocks to a B in the real thing.*

mock|ery /mɒkəri/ N-UNCOUNT If someone mocks you, you can refer to their behavior or attitude as **mockery**. ❑ *Was there a glint of mockery in his eyes?* ● N-SING If something makes **a mockery of** something, it makes it appear worthless and foolish. ❑ *This action makes a mockery of the Government's continuing protestations of concern.*

mock|ing /mɒkɪŋ/ ADJ A **mocking** expression or **mocking** behavior indicates that you think someone or something is stupid or inferior. ❑ *She gave a mocking smile.*

mod|al /moʊdᵊl/ (**modals**) N-COUNT In grammar, a **modal** or a **modal auxiliary** is a word such as "can" or "would" which is used with a main verb to express ideas such as possibility, intention, or necessity. [TECHNICAL]

Word Link   mod ≈ measure, manner : mode, model, modern

mode /moʊd/ (**modes**) ● N-COUNT A **mode** of life or behavior is a particular way of living or behaving. [FORMAL] ❑ *...the capitalist mode of production.* ● N-COUNT A **mode** is a particular style in art, literature, or dress. ❑ *...a slightly more elegant and formal mode of dress.* ● N-COUNT On some cameras or electronic

갑자기 낮고 숨이 넘어갈 것 같은 신음 소리를 내며 마구 몸을 떨기 시작했다. ❷ 타동사/자동사 불평하다 [탐탁찮음] ❑ 밤에 최소 6시간 이상 자지 못했을 때면 나는 불평을 하곤 했다. ❑ 날씨에 대한 불평 ❸ 가산명사 불평 [비격식체] ❑ 그들은 사람들의 불평과 칭찬을 들어왔다.

❶ 가산명사 군중 ❑ 시찰관들은 점점 더 많은 시위대가 모여드는 것을 지켜보았다. ❷ 단수명사 폭도 [탐탁찮음] ❑ 그들이 계속 이렇게 한다면 폭도들이 접수할 위험도 있다. ❸ 타동사 둘러싸이다 ❑ 그녀의 차는 기자들에게 둘러싸였다.

❶ 형용사 이동식의 ❑ 4백 개의 좌석이 있는 이동식 극장 ❷ 형용사 이동 능력을 가진, 움직일 수 있는 ❑ 난 여전히 어디든지 갈 수 있어. ● 이동성 불가산명사 ❑ 두 대의 차로 그들은 각자 가고 싶은 곳을 갈 수 있는 자유와 이동성을 갖게 되었다. ❸ 형용사 유동적인 (사회) ❑ 우리는 정말 유동적인 사회에 살고 있어서, 사람들은 이동을 한 후에 다른 곳으로 이사를 간다. ● (사회) 유동성 불가산명사 ❑ 19세기 이전에는 사회적인 이동 통로가 거의 없었다. ❹ 가산명사 모빌 ❺ 가산명사 휴대폰

가산명사 휴대폰 [영국영어; 미국영어 cellphone, cellular phone]

[영국영어 mobilise] ❶ 타동사/자동사 동원하다 ❑ 우리가 국제적 지원을 동원해서 행동에 착수할 수 있게 되는 것이 가장 바라는 바이다. ● 동원 불가산명사 ❑ 혁명을 지지하는 국제 여론의 신속한 형성 ❷ 타동사 (자원을) 동원하다 ❑ 그 자원을 동원할 수 있다면, 그 일을 해낼 수 있을 거야. ● (자원) 개발, (자원) 동원 불가산명사 ❑ 교육 자원 개발 ❸ 타동사/자동사 (군대를) 동원하다; (군대가) 동원되다 [언론 또는 군사] ❑ 수단은 최후통첩에 대한 대응으로 군대를 동원하겠다는 협박까지 했다. ● 동원 불가산명사 ❑ 공화국을 지켜 내기 위해 군대를 총동원하자는 요구

❶ 타동사 조롱하다, 흉내 내며 놀리다 ❑ 나는 네가 날 조롱하고 있다고 생각했어. ❷ 형용사 거짓된, 꾸민 ❑ "이건 비극이야!"라고 제프리는 거짓으로 놀란 척하며 졸도했다. ❸ 가산명사 모의고사 [영국영어, 비격식체] ❑ 브리짓은 성적이 모의고사 때는 D였다가 본고사에서 B로 올랐다.

❶ 불가산명사 조롱 ❑ 그가 조롱 섞인 눈빛을 잠깐 보이지 않았어? ❷ 단수명사 조롱거리 ❑ 이러한 조치는 정부가 그 문제에 관해 계속 단언해 온 것을 조롱거리로 만든다.

형용사 비웃는, 조롱하는 ❑ 그녀는 비웃음을 지어 보였다.

가산명사 조동사 [과학 기술]

❶ 가산명사 양식, 형태 [격식체] ❑ 자본주의적 생산 양식 ❷ 가산명사 양식, 스타일 ❑ 약간 더 우아하고 격식을 차린 스타일의 드레스 ❸ 가산명사 모드 ❑ 카메라가 수동 모드로 되어 있을 때

A devices, the different **modes** available are the different programs or settings that you can choose when you use them. ❑ *...when the camera is in manual mode.*

Word Link mod ≈ measure, manner : *mode, model, modern*

mod|el ♦♦◇ /mɒdᵊl/ (models, modeling, modeled) [BRIT, sometimes AM **modelling, modelled**] **1** N-COUNT A **model** of an object is a physical representation that shows what it looks like or how it works. The model is often smaller than the object it represents. ❑ *...an architect's model of a wooden house.* ❑ *I made a model out of paper and glue.* ● ADJ **Model** is also an adjective. [ADJ n] ❑ *...a model railway.* **2** N-COUNT A **model** is a system that is being used and that people might want to copy in order to achieve similar results. [FORMAL] ❑ *...the Chinese model of economic reform.* **3** N-COUNT A **model** of a system or process is a theoretical description that can help you understand how the system or process works, or how it might work. [TECHNICAL] ❑ *Darwin eventually put forward a model of biological evolution.* **4** V-T If someone such as a scientist **models** a system or process, they make an accurate theoretical description of it in order to understand or explain how it works. [TECHNICAL] ❑ *I have moved from trying to model and understand the distribution and evolution of water vapor.* **5** N-COUNT If you say that someone or something is **a model of** a particular quality, you are showing approval of them because they have that quality to a large degree. [APPROVAL] ❑ *A model of good manners, he has conquered any inward fury.* **6** ADJ You use **model** to express approval of someone when you think that they perform their role or duties extremely well. [APPROVAL] [ADJ n] ❑ *As a girl she had been a model pupil.* **7** V-T If one thing **is modeled on** another, the first thing is made so that it is like the second thing in some way. ❑ *The quota system was modeled on those operated in America and continental Europe.* **8** V-T If you **model** yourself **on** someone, you copy the way that they do things, because you admire them and want to be like them. ❑ *You have been modeling yourself on others all your life.* **9** N-COUNT A particular **model** of a machine is a particular version of it. ❑ *To keep the cost down, opt for a basic model.* **10** N-COUNT An artist's **model** is a person who stays still in a particular position so that the artist can make a picture or sculpture of them. ❑ *...the model for his portrait of Mary Magdalene, the Marchesa Attavanti.* **11** V-I If someone **models** for an artist, they stay still in a particular position so that the artist can make a picture or sculpture of them. ❑ *Tullio has been modeling for Sandra for eleven years.* **12** N-COUNT A fashion **model** is a person whose job is to display clothes by wearing them. ❑ *...Paris's top fashion model.* **13** V-T/V-I If someone **models** clothes, they display them by wearing them. ❑ *She began modeling in Paris aged 15.* ● **mod|el|ing** N-UNCOUNT ❑ *She was being offered a modeling contract.* **14** V-T/V-I If you **model** shapes or figures, you make them out of a substance such as clay or wood. ❑ *There she began to model in clay.* **15** →see also **role model** →see **forecast**

The **brand** of a product such as jeans, tea, or soap is its name, which can also be the name of the company that makes or sells it. The **make** of a car or electrical appliance such as a radio or washing machine is the name of the company that produces it. If you talk about what **type** of product or service you want, you are talking about its quality and what features it should have. You can also talk about **types** of people or of abstract things. ❑ *...which type of coffeemaker to choose....a new type of bank account....looking for a certain type of actor.* A **model** of car or of some other devices is a name that is given to a particular **type**, for example, Ford Escort or Nissan Micra. Note that **type** can also be used informally to mean either **make** or **model**. For example, if someone asks what **type** of car you have got, you could reply "an SUV," "a Ford," or perhaps "an Escort."

Word Partnership   *model의 연어*

V.	build a model, make a model **1**
	base *something* on a model, follow a model, serve as a model **1**-**3**
N.	business model **3**
ADJ.	basic model, current model, latest model, new model, standard model **3** **9**

mo|dem /moʊdəm, -dɛm/ (modems) N-COUNT A **modem** is a device which uses a telephone line to connect computers or computer systems. [COMPUTING] [also by N] ❑ *He sent his work to his publishers by modem.*

mod|er|ate ♦◇◇ (moderates, moderating, moderated)

The adjective and noun are pronounced /mɒdərət/. The verb is pronounced /mɒdəreɪt/.

1 ADJ **Moderate** political opinions or policies are not extreme. ❑ *He was an easygoing man of very moderate views.* **2** ADJ You use **moderate** to describe people or groups who have moderate political opinions or policies. ❑ *...a moderate Democrat.* ● N-COUNT A **moderate** is someone with moderate political opinions. ❑ *If he presents himself as a radical he risks scaring off the moderates whose votes he so desperately needs.* **3** ADJ You use **moderate** to describe something that is neither large nor small in amount or degree. ❑ *While a moderate amount of stress can be beneficial, too much stress can exhaust you.* ● **mod|er|ate|ly** ADV ❑ *Both are moderately large insects, with a wingspan of around four centimeters.* **4** ADJ A **moderate** change in something is a change that is not great. ❑ *Most drugs offer either no real improvement or, at best, only moderate improvements.* ● **mod|er|ate|ly** ADV [ADV after v] ❑ *Share prices on the Tokyo Exchange declined moderately.* **5** V-T/V-I If you **moderate** something or if it **moderates**, it becomes less extreme or

[영국영어, 미국영어 가끔 modelling, modelled]
1 가산명사 모형 ❑ 건축가가 만든 목조 가옥 모형 ❑ 나는 종이와 풀로 모형을 만들었다. ● 형용사 모형의 ❑ 철도 모형 **2** 가산명사 ...식 모델 [격식체] ❑ 중국식 경제 개혁 모델 **3** 가산명사 모델 [과학 기술] ❑ 다윈은 마침내 생물학적 진화로 모델을 내놓았다. **4** 타동사 구축하다 [과학 기술] ❑ 나는 수증기의 분포와 변화 과정을 구축하고 이해하려던 것에서 관심을 돌렸다. **5** 가산명사 모형 [마음에 듦] ❑ 모범적일 정도로 매너가 좋은 그는, 마음속의 분노를 잘 다스려 왔다. **6** 형용사 모범의 [마음에 듦] ❑ 어렸을 때 그녀는 모범생이었다. **7** 타동사 본뜨다, 본따다 ❑ 할당제도는 미국과 유럽에서 시행되던 것을 본떠 만들었다. **8** 타동사 본받다, 본뜨다 ❑ 너는 평생 동안 다른 사람들을 본받아 왔다. **9** 가산명사 (기계의) 모델, (기계의) 사양 ❑ 가격을 낮추려면 기본 사양을 선택하세요. **10** 가산명사 모델 ❑ 그가 그린 마리아 막달레나 초상화의 모델인 마르케사 앗타반티 **11** 자동사 모델을 하다 ❑ 툴리오는 11년 동안 샌드라의 모델을 해 오고 있다. **12** 가산명사 모델 ❑ 파리 최고의 패션모델 **13** 타동사/자동사 (의상) 모델을 하다 ❑ 그녀는 열다섯 살 때 모델 일을 시작했다. ● 모델 일 불가산명사 ❑ 그녀는 모델 계약을 제안받은 상태였다. **14** 타동사/자동사 (모형 등을) 만들다 ❑ 거기서 그녀는 찰흙으로 모형을 만들기 시작했다.

청바지, 차, 비누와 같은 상품의 brand는 그 상품의 이름인데, 상품명이 그것을 만들거나 파는 회사명일 수도 있다. 자동차 또는 라디오나 세탁기 같은 전기 제품의 make는 그것을 생산하는 회사명이다. 원하는 상품이나 서비스의 type을 얘기하는 것은 그 상품이나 서비스가 지녀야 할 품질이나 특성을 말하는 것이다. 사람이나 추상적 사물에 대해서도 type을 말할 수 있다. ❑ ...어떤 종류의 커피 메이커를 선택할지...새로운 종류의 은행 계좌....어떤 특정한 유형의 배우를 찾는. 자동차나 다른 일부 장치의 model은 특정 type에 붙여진 이름으로, 예를 들면 포드 에스코트나 니산 마이크라와 같은 것이다. type은 또한 비격식체로 make나 model을 뜻할 수도 있다. 예를 들어 어떤 type의 자동차를 가지고 있느냐고 누가 물으면, '스포츠 유틸리티 차량,' 또는 '포드,' 또는 '에스코트'라고 대답할 수 있다.

가산명사 모뎀 [컴퓨터] ❑ 그는 출판사에 작업한 것을 모뎀으로 보냈다.

형용사와 명사는 /mɒdərət /로 발음되고, 동사는 /mɒdəreɪt /로 발음된다.

1 형용사 온건한 ❑ 그는 아주 온건한 견해를 갖고 있는 느긋한 사람이었다. **2** 형용사 온건한 ❑ 온건파 민주당원 ● 가산명사 온건파 ❑ 그가 자신을 급진주의자로 표방한다면 절대적으로 지지가 필요한 온건한 유권자들이 겁을 먹고 이탈할 위험이 있다. **3** 형용사 적정한, 적당한 ❑ 적정한 수준의 스트레스는 도움이 될 수도 있지만, 과도하면 당신을 지치게 만들 수 있습니다. ● 적당하게, 중간 정도의 부사 ❑ 둘 다 날개폭이 4센티미터 내외의 중간 정도 크기의 곤충이다. **4** 형용사 약간의, 보통의 ❑ 대부분의 약들은 진정한 효과를 주지는 못하고, 잘 봐야 약간 낫게 해 줄 뿐이다. ● 약간 부사 ❑ 도쿄 시장에서 주식값이 약간 하락했다. **5** 타동사/자동사 완화하다, 누그러뜨리다,

violent and easier to deal with or accept. ❑ *They are hoping that once in office he can be persuaded to moderate his views.* ● mod|era|tion /mɒdəreɪʃ³n/ N-UNCOUNT ❑ *A moderation in food prices helped to offset the first increase in energy prices.*

악화되다 ❑ 그들은 그가 일단 관직에 앉게 되면 그를 설득해서 온건한 견해를 갖도록 할 수 있으리라고 희망하고 있다. ● 완화, 안정 불가산명사 ❑ 식료품 가격 안정으로 에너지 가격의 첫 인상분이 상쇄되었다.

Word Partnership   *moderate*의 연어

N.   moderate **approach**, moderate **position**, moderate **view** ◼
     moderate **exercise**, moderate **heat**, moderate **prices**,
     moderate **speed** ◼
     moderate **amount** ◼
     moderate **growth**, moderate **improvement** ◼

---

mod|era|tion /mɒdəreɪʃ³n/ ◼ N-UNCOUNT If you say that someone's behavior shows **moderation**, you approve of them because they act in a way that you think is reasonable and not extreme. [APPROVAL] ❑ *The United Nations Secretary General called on all parties to show moderation.* ● PHRASE If you say that someone does something such as eat, drink, or smoke **in moderation**, you mean that they do not eat, drink, or smoke too much or more than is reasonable. ◼ →see also **moderate**

◼ 불가산명사 중용, 절제 [마음에 듦] ❑ 유엔 사무총장은 모든 해당국들에게 자제해 줄 것을 요청했다. ● 구 적당히

Word Link   mod ≈ measure, manner : *mode*, *model*, *modern*

---

mod|ern ♦♦◇ /mɒdərn/ (**moderns**) ◼ ADJ **Modern** means relating to the present time, for example the present decade or present century. [ADJ n] ❑ *We had a long talk about the problem of materialism in modern society.* ◼ ADJ Something that is **modern** is new and involves the latest ideas or equipment. ❑ *In many ways, it was a very modern school for its time.* ◼ ADJ People are sometimes described as **modern** when they have opinions or ways of behavior that have not yet been accepted by most people in a society. ❑ *She is very modern in outlook.* ◼ ADJ **Modern** is used to describe styles of art, dance, music, and architecture that have developed in recent times, in contrast to classical styles. [ADJ n] ❑ *She'd been a professional dancer with a modern dance company in New York.*

◼ 형용사 현대의 ❑ 우리는 현대 사회의 물질주의가 가져오는 문제점에 대해 오랜 시간 얘기했다. ◼ 형용사 신식의 ❑ 그 학교는 여러 면에서 당시로서는 아주 신식 학교였다. ◼ 형용사 신식의, 신구적인 ❑ 그녀는 생각이 아주 신식이다. ◼ 형용사 현대의 ❑ 그녀는 뉴욕에 있는 현대 무용단에서 직업 무용가로 일해 왔다.

Thesaurus   *modern*의 참조어

ADJ.   contemporary, current, present ◼ ◼
       state-of-the-art; (ant.) out of date ◼

Word Partnership   *modern*의 연어

N.   modern **civilization**, modern **culture**, modern **era**, modern **life**,
     modern **science**, modern **society**, modern **times**, modern **warfare** ◼
     modern **conveniences**, modern **equipment**, modern **methods**,
     modern **techniques**, modern **technology** ◼
     modern **art**, modern **dance**, modern **literature**, modern **music** ◼

---

mod|ern|ize /mɒdərnaɪz/ (**modernizes, modernizing, modernized**) [BRIT also **modernise**] V-T To **modernize** something such as a system or a factory means to change it by replacing old equipment or methods with new ones. ❑ *...plans to modernize the refinery.* ● mod|ern|i|za|tion /mɒdərnaɪzeɪʃ³n/ N-UNCOUNT ❑ *...a five-year modernization programme.*

[영국영어 modernise] 타동사 현대화하다 ❑ 정제소를 현대화하기 위한 계획 ● 현대화 불가산명사 ❑ 현대화 5개년 계획

mod|est ♦◇◇ /mɒdɪst/ ◼ ADJ A **modest** house or other building is not large or expensive. ❑ *They had spent the night at a modest hotel.* ◼ ADJ You use **modest** to describe something such as an amount, rate, or improvement which is fairly small. ❑ *Swiss unemployment rose to the still modest rate of 0.7%.* ● mod|est|ly ADV ❑ *Britain's balance of payments improved modestly last month.* ◼ ADJ If you say that someone is **modest**, you approve of them because they do not talk much about their abilities or achievements. [APPROVAL] ❑ *He's modest, as well as being a great player.* ● mod|est|ly ADV [ADV with v] ❑ *"You really must be very good at what you do." — "I suppose I am," Kate said modestly.*

◼ 형용사 적당한 수준의, 수수한 ❑ 그들은 그날 밤을 적당한 수준의 호텔에서 묵었다. ◼ 형용사 미미한 ❑ 스위스의 실업률이 0.7퍼센트까지 올랐으나 아직은 미미한 수준이었다. ● 미미하게 부사 ❑ 영국의 무역 수지는 지난달에 미미하나마 호전되었다. ◼ 형용사 겸손한 [마음에 듦] ❑ 그는 훌륭한 선수일 뿐만 아니라 겸손하기도 하다. ● 겸손하게 부사 ❑ "네가 하는 일은 정말 아주 잘 해야 돼." "당연히 그래야 한다고 생각해요."라고 케이트가 겸손하게 말했다.

Word Partnership   *modest*의 연어

N.   modest **home/house** ◼
     modest **amount**, modest **fee**, modest **income**, modest **increase** ◼

---

mod|es|ty /mɒdɪsti/ ◼ N-UNCOUNT Someone who shows **modesty** does not talk much about their abilities or achievements. [APPROVAL] ❑ *His modesty does him credit, for the food he produces speaks for itself.* ◼ N-UNCOUNT You can refer to the **modesty** of something such as a place or amount when it is fairly small. ❑ *The modesty of the town itself comes as something of a surprise.* ◼ N-UNCOUNT If someone, especially a woman, shows **modesty**, they are cautious about the way they dress and behave because they are aware that other people may view them in a sexual way. ❑ *There were shrieks of embarrassment, mingled with giggles, from some of the girls as they struggled to protect their modesty.*

◼ 불가산명사 겸손 [마음에 듦] ❑ 그의 겸손은 칭찬받아 마땅하다. 그가 만드는 음식이 모든 걸 말해 주고 있으니. ◼ 불가산명사 작음 ❑ 그 읍내 자체는 놀라울 정도로 아담하다. ◼ 불가산명사 정숙함 ❑ 여자애들이 정숙하려 애쓰는 가운데 몇 명이 당혹스러운 비명을 지르며 킬킬거리기도 했다.

mod|ify /mɒdɪfaɪ/ (**modifies, modifying, modified**) V-T If you **modify** something, you change it slightly, usually in order to improve it. ❑ *The club members did agree to modify their recruitment policy.* ● modi|fi|ca|tion /mɒdɪfɪkeɪʃ³n/ (**modifications**) N-VAR ❑ *Relatively minor modifications were required.*

타동사 수정하다, 개조하다 ❑ 클럽 회원들은 모집 정책을 수정하는 데 적극 동의했다. ● 수정, 개조 가산명사 또는 불가산명사 ❑ 비교적 사소한 수정이 필요했다.

a
b
c
d
e
f
g
h
i
j
k
l
m
n
o
p
q
r
s
t
u
v
w
x
y
z

A

mod|u|lar /mɒdʒələr/ **1** ADJ In building, **modular** means relating to the construction of buildings in parts called modules. ❑ *They ended up buying a prebuilt modular home on a two-acre lot.* **2** ADJ **Modular** means relating to the teaching of courses at a college or university in units called modules. [BRIT] ❑ *The course is modular in structure.*

1 형용사 (건축이) 모듈식의 ❑그들은 결국 2 에이커짜리 대지에 이미 지어 놓은 모듈식 주택을 샀다. **2** 형용사 (대학 과정이) 모듈식의 [영국영어] ❑ 그 과정은 모듈 구조로 되어 있다.

B

mod|ule /mɒdʒul/ (**modules**) **1** N-COUNT A **module** is a part of a spacecraft which can operate by itself, often away from the rest of the spacecraft. ❑ *A rescue plan could be achieved by sending an unmanned module to the space station.* **2** N-COUNT A **module** is one of the separate parts of a course taught at a college or university. [BRIT] ❑ *These courses cover a twelve-week period and are organized into three four-week modules.*

1 가산명사 모듈 (모체에서 분리된 소형 우주선) ❑구출 계획은 무인 우주선을 우주 정거장에 보내는 것으로 달성될 수 있다. **2** 가산명사 모듈 (강좌 구성 단위) [영국영어] ❑이 강좌들은 12주짜리인데, 4주짜리 모듈 3개로 구성되어 있다.

C

moist /mɔɪst/ (**moister, moistest**) ADJ Something that is **moist** is slightly wet. ❑ *The soil is reasonably moist after the September rain.*

형용사 촉촉한, 습기가 있는 ❑9월에 비가 내린 후, 흙이 적당히 촉촉해졌다.

D

mois|ten /mɔɪsᵊn/ (**moistens, moistening, moistened**) V-T To **moisten** something means to make it slightly wet. ❑ *She took a sip of water to moisten her dry throat.*

타동사 촉촉하게 하다, 축이다 ❑그녀는 마른 목을 축이려고 물을 한 모금 마셨다.

E

mois|ture /mɔɪstʃər/ N-UNCOUNT **Moisture** is tiny drops of water in the air, on a surface, or in the ground. ❑ *When the soil is dry, more moisture is lost from the plant.*

불가산명사 습기, 수분 ❑흙이 메말라 있으면 식물이 더 많은 수분을 뺏긴다.

F

mois|tur|ize /mɔɪstʃəraɪz/ (**moisturizes, moisturizing, moisturized**) [BRIT also **moisturise**] V-T/V-I If you **moisturize** your skin, you rub cream into it to make it softer. If a cream **moisturizes** your skin, it makes it softer. ❑ *...products to moisturize, protect, and firm your skin.*

[영국영어 moisturise] 타동사/자동사 수분을 공급하다 ❑피부에 수분을 공급하고, 보호하며 탱탱하게 만들어 주는 제품

G

mold /moʊld/ (**molds, molding, molded**) [BRIT **mould**] **1** N-COUNT A **mold** is a hollow container that you pour liquid into. When the liquid becomes solid, it takes the same shape as the mould. ❑ *He makes plastic reusable molds.* **2** N-COUNT If a person fits into or is cast in a **mold** of a particular kind, they have the characteristics, attitudes, behavior, or lifestyle that are typical of that type of person. ❑ *He could never be accused of fitting the mold.* ● PHRASE If you say that someone **breaks the mold**, you mean that they do completely different things from what has been done before or from what is usually done. **3** V-T If you **mold** a soft substance such as plastic or clay, you make it into a particular shape or into an object. ❑ *He would dampen the clay and begin to mold it into an entirely different shape.* **4** V-T To **mold** someone or something means to change or influence them over a period of time so that they develop in a particular way. ❑ *It was a very safe, long childhood with Diane, and she really molded my ideas a lot.* **5** V-T/V-I When something **molds** to an object or when you **mold** it there, it fits round the object tightly so that the shape of the object can still be seen. ❑ *It looked as though the plastic wrap was molded to the fruit.* **6** N-MASS **Mold** is a soft gray, green, or blue substance that sometimes forms in spots on old food or on damp walls or clothes. ❑ *She discovered black and green mold growing in her hall closet.* →see **fungus, laboratory**

[영국영어 mould] **1** 가산명사 거푸집, 틀, 주형 ❑그는 재사용 가능한 플라스틱 틀을 만든다. **2** 가산명사 틀, 유형 ❑절대 그를 틀에 박힌 사람이라고 비난할 수는 없을 것이다. ● 구 틀을 깨다 **3** 타동사 빚다 ❑그는 찰흙을 물에 축여서 완전히 다른 모양으로 빚기 시작할 것이다. **4** 타동사 영향을 끼치다, 성격을 형성하다 ❑나는 아주 안전하고 오랫동안 어린 시절을 다이앤과 함께 보냈고, 그녀는 정말 내 사고 형성에 많은 영향을 끼쳤다. **5** 타동사/자동사 꼭 달라붙다; 꼭 달라붙게 하다 ❑비닐 포장지가 과일에 딱 달라붙어 있는 것처럼 보였다. **6** 물질명사 곰팡이 ❑그녀는 현관에 있는 벽장 속에 검은색과 녹색의 곰팡이가 피어 있는 것을 발견했다.

H

I

J

K

L

M

mole /moʊl/ (**moles**) **1** N-COUNT A **mole** is a natural dark spot or small dark lump on someone's skin. ❑ *Researchers studied moles on those aged between 12 and 50.* **2** N-COUNT A **mole** is a small animal with black fur that lives underground. **3** N-COUNT A **mole** is a member of a government or other organization who gives secret information to the press or to a rival organization. ❑ *He had been recruited by the Russians as a mole and trained in Moscow.*

1 가산명사 검은 점, 사마귀 ❑연구자들은 12세에서 50세 사이의 사람들의 사마귀를 연구했다. **2** 가산명사 두더지 **3** 가산명사 스파이 ❑그는 러시아인들에게 스파이로 채용되어서 모스크바에서 훈련받았다.

N

O

mo|lecu|lar /məlɛkyələr/ ADJ **Molecular** means relating to or involving molecules. [ADJ n] ❑ *...the molecular structure of fuel.*

형용사 분자의, 분자로 된 ❑연료의 분자식

P

| **Word Link** | cule ≈ small : minuscule, molecule, ridicule |

Q

mol|ecule /mɒlɪkyul/ (**molecules**) N-COUNT A **molecule** is the smallest amount of a chemical substance which can exist by itself. ❑ *...the hydrogen bonds between water molecules.* →see **element**

가산명사 분자 ❑물분자 속의 수소 결합

R

mo|lest /məlɛst/ (**molests, molesting, molested**) V-T A person who **molests** someone, especially a woman or a child, interferes with them in a sexual way against their will. ❑ *He was accused of sexually molesting a female colleague.*

타동사 성희롱하다, 성추행하다 ❑그는 여자 동료를 성희롱했다고 고소당했다.

S

mol|ten /moʊltᵊn/ ADJ **Molten** rock, metal, or glass has been heated to a very high temperature and has become a hot thick liquid. ❑ *The molten metal is poured into the mold.* →see **volcano**

형용사 용해된, 녹은 ❑녹은 금속을 거푸집 안으로 붓는다.

T

mom /mɒm/ (**moms**) N-FAMILY Your **mom** is your mother. [AM, INFORMAL; BRIT **mum**] ❑ *We waited for Mom and Dad to get home.*

친족명사 엄마 [미국영어, 비격식체; 영국영어 mum] ❑우리는 엄마 아빠가 집에 도착하기를 기다렸다.

U

mo|ment ♦♦♦ /moʊmənt/ (**moments**) **1** N-COUNT You can refer to a very short period of time, for example a few seconds, as a **moment** or **moments**. ❑ *In a moment he was gone.* ❑ *In moments, I was asleep once more.* **2** N-COUNT A particular **moment** is the point in time at which something happens. ❑ *At this moment a car stopped at the house.* **3** PHRASE If you say that something will or may happen **at any moment** or **any moment now**, you are emphasizing that it is likely to happen very soon. [EMPHASIS] ❑ *He'll be here to see you any moment now.* **4** PHRASE You use expressions such as **at the moment, at this moment,** and **at the present moment** to indicate that a particular situation exists at the time when you are speaking. ❑ *At the moment, no one is talking to me.* ❑ *He's touring South America at this moment in time.* **5** PHRASE You use **for the moment** to indicate that something is true now, even if it will not be true in the future. ❑ *For the moment, a potential crisis appears to have been averted.* **6** PHRASE If you say that someone or something **has** their **moments,** you are indicating that there are times when they are successful or interesting, but that this does not happen very often. ❑ *The film has its moments.* **7** PHRASE If someone does something at **the last moment,** they do it at the latest time possible. ❑ *They*

1 가산명사 순식간, 잠깐 ❑그는 순식간에 사라졌다. ❑잠시 후 나는 다시 잠이 들었다. **2** 가산명사 ❑그 순간 차 한 대가 그 집 앞에 멈춰 섰다. **3** 구 금방이라도 [강조] ❑그가 금방이라도 널 보러 올 거야. **4** 구 현재, 이제 ❑이제 아무도 나와 얘기하지 않는다. ❑그는 지금 현재 남미를 여행 중이다. **5** 구 지금으로서는 ❑현재로서는 잠재적 위기를 일단 모면한 것 같아 보인다. **6** 구 제때를 만나다 ❑그 영화는 제때를 만났다. **7** 구 마지막 순간 ❑그들은 마지막 순간에 맘을 바꿔서 가지 않겠다고 했다. **8** 구 갑자기 [강조] ❑그가 갑자기 울다가 그 다음엔 웃고 도무지 종잡을 수가 없다. **9** 구 한창 잘 나가다 ❑그는 요즘 한창 잘 나가, 안 그래? **10** 구 -하자마자 [강조] ❑나는 눈을 감자마자 잠들었다.

V

W

X

Y

Z

changed their minds at the last moment and refused to go. **8** PHRASE You use the expression **the next moment**, or expressions such as "**one moment** he was there **, the next** he was gone," to emphasize that something happens suddenly, especially when it is very different from what was happening before. [EMPHASIS] ❑ *He is unpredictable, weeping one moment, laughing the next.* **9** PHRASE You use **of the moment** to describe someone or something that is or was especially popular at a particular time, especially when you want to suggest that their popularity is unlikely to last long or did not last long. ❑ *He's the man of the moment, isn't he?* **10** PHRASE If you say that something happens **the moment** something else happens, you are emphasizing that it happens immediately after the other thing. [EMPHASIS] ❑ *The moment I closed my eyes, I fell asleep.* **11** spur of the moment →see spur

---

Word Partnership   *moment*의 연어

ADV.	a moment **ago**, just a moment **1**
N.	moment **of silence**, moment **of thought 1**
V.	**stop for** a moment, **take a** moment, **think for a** moment, **wait a** moment **1**
ADJ.	**an awkward** moment, **a critical** moment, **the right** moment **2**

---

mo|men|tari|ly /moʊmənteɛrɪli/ **1** ADV **Momentarily** means for a short time. ❑ *She paused momentarily when she saw them.* **2** ADV **Momentarily** means very soon. [AM] ❑ *The younger hunters stand up, all eyes turned towards the woods, towards the exact spot from which the pack will momentarily appear.*

mo|men|tary /moʊmənteri, BRIT moʊməntəri/ ADJ Something that is **momentary** lasts for a very short period of time, for example for a few seconds or less. ❑ *...a momentary lapse of concentration.*

mo|men|tous /moʊmentəs/ ADJ If you refer to a decision, event, or change as **momentous**, you mean that it is very important, often because of the effects that it will have in the future. ❑ *...the momentous decision to send in the troops.*

mo|men|tum /moʊmentəm/ **1** N-UNCOUNT If a process or movement gains **momentum**, it keeps developing or happening more quickly and keeps becoming less likely to stop. ❑ *This campaign is really gaining momentum.* **2** N-UNCOUNT In physics, **momentum** is the mass of a moving object multiplied by its speed in a particular direction. [TECHNICAL] →see **motion**

Word Partnership   *momentum*의 연어

V.	**build** momentum, **gain** momentum, **gather** momentum, **have** momentum, **lose** momentum, **maintain** momentum **1 2**

---

mom|my /mɒmi/ (**mommies**) N-FAMILY Some people, especially young children, call their mother **mommy**. [AM, INFORMAL; BRIT **mummy**] ❑ *Be very good and very quiet and help your mommy.*

Mon. Mon. is a written abbreviation for **Monday**. ❑ *...Mon. Oct. 19.*

mon|arch /mɒnərk, -ɑrk/ (**monarchs**) N-COUNT The **monarch** of a country is the king, queen, emperor, or empress.

mon|chist /mɒnərkɪst/ (**monarchists**) ADJ If someone has **monarchist** views, they believe that their country should have a monarch, such as a king or queen. ❑ *A monarchist party is running in the forthcoming elections.* ● N-COUNT A **monarchist** is someone with monarchist views. ❑ *The Queen's responses to "Mr. Chretien" will be studied by republicans and monarchists alike here.*

mon|ar|chy /mɒnərki/ (**monarchies**) **1** N-VAR A **monarchy** is a system in which a country has a monarch. ❑ *...a serious debate on the future of the monarchy.* **2** N-COUNT A **monarchy** is a country that has a monarch. ❑ *Britain is a constitutional monarchy.* **3** N-COUNT The **monarchy** is used to refer to the monarch and his or her family. ❑ *The monarchy has to create a balance between its public and private lives.*

mon|as|tery /mɒnəsteri, BRIT mɒnəstri/ (**monasteries**) N-COUNT A **monastery** is a building or collection of buildings in which monks live.

Mon|day ♦♦♦ /mʌndeɪ, -di/ (**Mondays**) N-VAR **Monday** is the day after Sunday and before Tuesday. ❑ *I went back to work on Monday.* ❑ *The first meeting of the group took place last Monday.*

mon|etar|ism /mɒnɪtərɪzəm, BRIT mʌnɪtərɪzəm/ N-UNCOUNT **Monetarism** is an economic policy that involves controlling the amount of money that is available and in use in a country at any one time. [BUSINESS]

mon|etar|ist /mɒnɪtərɪst, BRIT mʌnɪtərɪst/ (**monetarists**) ADJ **Monetarist** policies or views are based on the theory that the amount of money that is available and in use in a country at any one time should be controlled. [BUSINESS] ❑ *...tough monetarist policies.* ● N-COUNT A **monetarist** is someone with monetarist views. ❑ *Such a policy, monetarists claim, encourages steady growth and price stability.*

mon|etary ♦♦◇ /mɒnɪteri, BRIT mʌnɪtri/ ADJ **Monetary** means relating to money, especially the total amount of money in a country. [BUSINESS] [ADJ n] ❑ *Some countries tighten monetary policy to avoid inflation.*

mon|ey ♦♦♦ /mʌni/ (**monies** or **moneys**) **1** N-UNCOUNT **Money** is the coins or bank notes that you use to buy things, or the sum that you have in a bank account. ❑ *A lot of the money that you pay at the cinema goes back to the film distributors.* ❑ *Players should be allowed to earn money from advertising.* **2** N-PLURAL

---

1 부사 잠깐 ❑ 그녀가 그들을 보고는 잠깐 멈췄다. **2** 부사 곧 [미국영어] ❑ 그 젊은 사냥꾼들은 숲으로, 곧 한 무리의 동물이 튀어나올 정확한 지점으로 눈을 돌려서 섰다.

형용사 순간적인 ❑ 집중이 순간적으로 흐트러짐

형용사 중대한 ❑ 중대한 파병 결정

1 불가산명사 탄력 ❑ 이 운동은 정말로 점점 더 탄력이 붙고 있다. **2** 불가산명사 운동량 [과학 기술]

친족명사 엄마 [미국영어, 비격식체; 영국영어 mummy] ❑ 얌전하게 조용히 있고, 엄마를 좀 도와드리렴.

월 ❑ 10월 19일 월요일

가산명사 군주

형용사 군주제를 주장하는 ❑ 다가오는 선거에 군주제를 주장하는 정당 하나가 참가한다. ● 가산명사 군주제주의자 ❑ 여기 공화정주의자나 군주제주의자를 막론하고 크레티안 총리에게 전달된 여왕의 답변들을 연구할 것이다.

1 가산명사 또는 불가산명사 군주제 ❑ 군주제의 미래에 대한 심각한 논쟁 **2** 가산명사 군주국 ❑ 영국은 입헌 군주국이다. **3** 가산명사 왕족, 황족 ❑ 왕족들은 자신들의 공적인 삶과 사적인 삶 사이에서 균형을 맞춰야 한다.

가산명사 수도원

가산명사 또는 불가산명사 요일 ❑ 나는 월요일에 업무에 복귀했다. ❑ 그 그룹은 첫 모임을 지난 월요일에 가졌다.

불가산명사 통화주의 [경제]

형용사 통화주의의 [경제] ❑ 강력한 통화주의 정책 ● 가산명사 통화주의자 ❑ 그런 정책은 지속적인 성장과 물가 안정을 가져올 것이라고 통화주의자들은 주장한다.

형용사 통화의, 재정의 [경제] ❑ 몇몇 나라들은 인플레이션을 막기 위해서 통화 정책을 강화한다.

1 불가산명사 돈 ❑ 극장에 내는 많은 돈은 영화 배급사에게 되돌아간다. ❑ 선수들이 광고로 돈을 벌 수 있도록 허용해야 한다. **2** 복수명사 금전, 금액 [격식체] ❑ 우리는 갚아야 할 나머지 금액에 대해 상환

Monies is used to refer to several separate sums of money that form part of a larger amount that is received or spent. [FORMAL] ❑ *We drew up a schedule of payments for the rest of the monies owed.* ❸ →see also **pocket money** ❹ PHRASE If you say that someone **has money to burn**, you mean that they have more money than they need or that they spend their money on things that you think are unnecessary. ❑ *He was a high-earning broker with money to burn.* ❺ PHRASE If you are **in the money**, you have a lot of money to spend. [INFORMAL] ❑ *If you are one of the lucky callers chosen to play, you could be in the money.* ❻ PHRASE If you **make money**, you obtain money by earning it or by making a profit. ❑ *...the only bit of the firm that consistently made money.* ❼ PHRASE If you say that you want someone to **put** their **money where their mouth is**, you want them to spend money to improve a bad situation, instead of just talking about improving it. ❑ *The government might be obliged to put its money where its mouth is to prove its commitment.* ❽ PHRASE If you say that **the smart money** is on a particular person or thing, you mean that people who know a lot about it think that this person will be successful, or this thing will happen. [JOURNALISM] ❑ *With England not playing, the smart money was on the Germans.* ❾ PHRASE If you say that **money talks**, you mean that if someone has a lot of money, they also have a lot of power. ❑ *The formula in Hollywood is simple – money talks.* ❿ PHRASE If you say that someone is **throwing money at** a problem, you are critical of them for trying to improve it by spending money on it, instead of doing more thoughtful and practical things to improve it. [DISAPPROVAL] ❑ *The Australian government's answer to the problem has been to throw money at it.* ⓫ PHRASE If you **get** your **money's worth**, you get something which is worth the money that it costs or the effort you have put in. ❑ *The fans get their money's worth.* ⓬ **money for old rope** →see **rope**. to **give** someone **a run for** their **money** →see **run**
→see **bank, donor, lottery, salt**
→see Word Web: **money**

일정을 짰다. ❹ 구 돈이 남아돌다 ❑ 그는 돈이 남아도는 고소득 브로커였다. ❺ 구 돈방석에 앉은, 돈에 파묻힌 [비격식체] ❑ 게임에 선발된 행운의 통화자 중 한 명이 되면, 돈방석에 앉으실 수도 있습니다. ❻ 구 돈을 벌다, 이익을 내다 ❑ 그 회사에서 지속적으로 이익을 낸 유일한 분야 ❼ 구 말만 하지 말고 돈을 써서 일이 되게 하다 ❑ 정부가 공약을 지키려면 말만 하지 말고 돈을 투자해야 할 것이다. ❽ 구 전문가 [언론] ❑ 잉글랜드가 탈락함에 따라, 전문가들은 독일이 우승할 것으로 보고 있었다. ❾ 구 돈이 힘이다 ❑ 할리우드의 법칙은 간단해, 즉 돈이 곧 힘이야. ❿ 구 돈을 퍼붓다 [탐탁잖음] ❑ 그 문제에 대한 호주 정부의 해법은 거기에 돈을 퍼붓는 것이었다. ⓫ 구 본전을 뽑다, 본전을 건지다 ❑ 팬들은 밑지지는 않을 것이다.

Thesaurus　　*money*의 참조어

N.　capital, cash, currency, funds, wealth ❶

---

mon|ey laun|der|ing N-UNCOUNT **Money laundering** is the crime of processing stolen money through a legitimate business or sending it abroad to a foreign bank, to hide the fact that the money was illegally obtained. ❑ *Investigators are looking at what they believe may be the largest money-laundering scandal in history.*

불가산명사 돈세탁 ❑ 수사관들이 역사상 가장 큰 규모일지도 모르는 돈세탁 사건을 조사 중이다.

mon|ey|maker /mʌnimeɪkər/ (**moneymakers**) also **money-maker** N-COUNT If you say that a business, product, or investment is a **moneymaker**, you mean that it makes a big profit. [BUSINESS] ❑ *The drug is a big moneymaker for them.*

가산명사 큰 수익원, 돈벌이 되는 일 [경제] ❑ 이 약은 그들에게 효자상품이다.

mon|ey mar|ket (**money markets**) N-COUNT A country's **money market** consists of all the banks and other organizations that deal with short-term loans, capital, and foreign exchange. [BUSINESS] ❑ *On the money markets the dollar was weaker against European currencies.*

가산명사 단기 금융 시장 [경제] ❑ 단기 금융 시장에서 유럽 각국 화폐 대비 달러화 가치가 떨어졌다.

mon|ey or|der (**money orders**) N-COUNT A **money order** is a piece of paper representing a sum of money which you can buy at a post office and send to someone as a way of sending them money by mail. [AM; BRIT **postal order**] ❑ *I sent them a money order for $40.*

가산명사 우편환 [미국영어; 영국영어 postal order] ❑ 나는 그들에게 40달러짜리 우편환을 보냈다.

mon|ey|spin|ner /mʌnispɪər/ (**moneyspinners**) also **money-spinner** N-COUNT If you say that something is a **moneyspinner**, you mean that it earns a lot of money for someone. [INFORMAL] ❑ *The first two stores have proved to be real moneyspinners.*

가산명사 큰 수익원, 돈벌이 되는 일 [비격식체] ❑ 처음 두 상점이 진정한 수익원으로 판명되었다.

mon|ey sup|ply N-UNCOUNT The **money supply** is the total amount of money in a country's economy at any one time. [BUSINESS] ❑ *They believed that controlling the money supply would reduce inflation.*

불가산명사 통화 공급량 [경제] ❑ 그들은 통화 공급량을 조절하면 인플레이션이 감소할 것으로 믿었다.

moni|tor ♦♢♢ /mɒnɪtər/ (**monitors, monitoring, monitored**) ❶ V-T If you **monitor** something, you regularly check its development or progress, and sometimes comment on it. ❑ *Officials had not been allowed to monitor the voting.* ❷ V-T If someone **monitors** radio broadcasts from other countries, they record them or listen carefully to them in order to obtain information. ❑ *Peter Murray is in London and has been monitoring reports out of Monrovia.* ❸ N-COUNT A **monitor** is a machine that is used to check or record things, for example processes or substances inside a person's body. ❑ *The heart monitor shows low levels of consciousness.* ❹ N-COUNT A **monitor** is a screen which is used to display certain kinds of information, for example in airports or television studios. ❑ *He was watching a game of tennis on a television monitor.* ❺ N-COUNT You can refer to a

❶ 타동사 점검하다, 감독하다 ❑ 정부 관리가 투표 과정의 감독을 맡을 수 없도록 되어 있었다. ❷ 타동사 모니터하다 ❑ 피터 머레이는 런던에 살고 있으며 몬로비아 현지 보도를 쭉 모니터해 왔다. ❸ 가산명사 모니터 ❑ 심장박동 모니터에 의식이 거의 없는 것으로 나타난다. ❹ 가산명사 모니터 ❑ 그는 텔레비전 모니터를 통해 테니스 경기를 보고 있었다. ❺ 가산명사 감시자, 모니터 요원 ❑ 정부 모니터 요원들이 계속해서 기자들과 동행할 것이다.

Word Web　　money

Early traders used a system of **barter** which didn't involve **money**. For example, a farmer might trade a cow for a wooden cart. In China, India, and Africa, cowrie shells* became a form of **currency**. The first **coins** were crude lumps of metal. Uniform circular coins appeared in China around 1500 BC. In 1150 AD, the Chinese started using paper bills. In 560 BC, the Lydians (living in what is now Turkey) **minted** three types of coins—a **gold** coin, a **silver** coin, and a mixed metal coin. Their use quickly spread through Asia Minor and Greece.

cowrie shell: a small, shiny, oval shell.

person who checks that something is done correctly, or that it is fair, as a **monitor**. ❏ *Government monitors will continue to accompany reporters.*

Word Partnership	*monitor*의 연어
N.	monitor **activity**, monitor **elections**, monitor **performance**, monitor **progress**, monitor **a situation** 1
	color monitor, **computer** monitor, **video** monitor 4
ADV.	**carefully** monitor, **closely** monitor 1 2

monk /mʌŋk/ (**monks**) N-COUNT A **monk** is a member of a male religious community that is usually separated from the outside world. ❏ *...saffron-robed Buddhist monks.*

가산명사 수사, 수도사 ❏ 샛노란 법의를 입은 스님

mon|key /mʌŋki/ (**monkeys**) 1 N-COUNT A **monkey** is an animal with a long tail which lives in hot countries and climbs trees. 2 N-COUNT If you refer to a child as a **monkey**, you are saying in an affectionate way that he or she is very lively and naughty. [FEELINGS] ❏ *She's such a little monkey.* →see **primate**

1 가산명사 원숭이 2 가산명사 장난꾸러기 [감정 개입] ❏ 정말 장난꾸러기 같은 여자 아이야.

mon|key wrench (**monkey wrenches**) →see **wrench**

mono /mɒnoʊ/ ADJ **Mono** is used to describe a system of playing music in which all the sound is directed through one speaker only. Compare **stereo**. ❏ *This model has a mono soundtrack.*

형용사 모노의, 모노 방식의 ❏ 이 모델의 사운드트랙은 모노 방식이다.

mo|noga|mous /mənɒɡəməs/ 1 ADJ Someone who is **monogamous** or who has a **monogamous** relationship has a sexual relationship with only one partner. ❏ *Do you believe that men are not naturally monogamous?* 2 ADJ **Monogamous** animals have only one sexual partner during their lives or during each mating season. ❏ *Only about 5 percent of mammals are monogamous.*

1 형용사 일부일처의 ❏ 인간의 본성은 일부일처와 무관하다고 생각하십니까? 2 형용사 일부일처의 ❏ 포유동물의 5퍼센트 정도만 일부일처를 따른다.

mo|noga|my /mənɒɡəmi/ 1 N-UNCOUNT **Monogamy** is used to refer to the state or custom of having a sexual relationship with only one partner. ❏ *People still opt for monogamy and marriage.* 2 N-UNCOUNT **Monogamy** is the state or custom of being married to only one person at a particular time. ❏ *In many non-Western societies, however, monogamy has never dominated.*

1 불가산명사 (성적) 일부일처제 ❏ 사람들은 여전히 일부일처제와 결혼을 선호한다. 2 불가산명사 (사회적) 일부일처제 ❏ 하지만 상당수의 비서구 사회에서는 일부일처제가 우세했던 적이 없다.

Word Link	*mono* ≈ *one* : mono**lithic**, mono**logue**, mono**poly**

mono|lith|ic /mɒnəlɪθɪk/ 1 ADJ If you refer to an organization or system as **monolithic**, you are critical of it because it is very large and very slow to change, and does not seem to have different parts with different characters. [DISAPPROVAL] ❏ *...an authoritarian and monolithic system.* 2 ADJ If you describe something such as a building as **monolithic**, you do not like it because it is very large and plain with no character. [DISAPPROVAL] ❏ *...a huge monolithic concrete building.*

1 형용사 획일적인 [탐탁찮음] ❏ 권위적이고 획일적인 시스템 2 형용사 밋밋한 [탐탁찮음] ❏ 크고 밋밋한 콘크리트 빌딩

mono|logue /mɒnəlɔɡ, BRIT mɒnəlɒɡ/ (**monologues**) 1 N-COUNT If you refer to a long speech by one person during a conversation as a **monologue**, you mean it prevents other people from talking or expressing their opinions. ❏ *Morris ignored the question and continued his monologue.* 2 N-VAR A **monologue** is a long speech which is spoken by one person as an entertainment, or as part of an entertainment such as a play. ❏ *...a monologue based on the writing of Quentin Crisp.*

1 가산명사 일방적인 대화 ❏ 모리스는 질문을 무시하고 자기가 할 말만 계속했다. 2 가산명사 또는 불가산명사 독백, 1인극 ❏ 퀜틴 크리스프의 원작을 각색한 1인극

mo|nopo|lize /mənɒpəlaɪz/ (**monopolizes, monopolizing, monopolized**) [BRIT also **monopolise**] 1 V-T If you say that someone **monopolizes** something, you mean that they have a very large share of it and prevent other people from having a share. ❏ *They are controlling so much cocoa that they are virtually monopolizing the market.* ● **mo|nopo|li|za|tion** /mənɒpəlaɪzeɪʃ⁰n/ N-UNCOUNT ❏ *...the monopolization of a market by a single supplier.* 2 V-T If something or someone **monopolizes** you, they demand a lot of your time and attention, so that there is very little time left for anything or anyone else. ❏ *He would monopolize her totally, to the exclusion of her brothers and sisters.*

[영국영어 monopolise] 1 타동사 독점하다 ❏ 그들의 코코아 시장 점유율이 너무나 높아서 사실상 독점하고 있다고 볼 수 있다. ● 독점 불가산명사 ❏ 단 하나의 공급 업체에 의한 시장 독점 2 타동사 독차지하다 ❏ 그가 전적으로 그녀를 독차지해서 정작 그녀의 형제나 자매는 소외되곤 했었다.

mo|nopo|ly /mənɒpəli/ (**monopolies**) 1 N-VAR If a company, person, or state has a **monopoly on** something such as an industry, they have complete control over it, so that it is impossible for others to become involved in it. [BUSINESS] ❏ *...Russian moves to end a state monopoly on land ownership.* 2 N-COUNT A **monopoly** is a company which is the only one providing a particular product or service. [BUSINESS] ❏ *...a state-owned monopoly.* 3 N-SING If you say that someone does not have a **monopoly on** something, you mean that they are not the only person who has that thing. ❏ *Women do not have a monopoly on feelings of betrayal.*

1 가산명사 또는 불가산명사 독점 [경제] ❏ 정부의 토지소유 독점을 끝내기 위해 러시아가 취한 조치 2 가산명사 독점 기업 [경제] ❏ 국유 독점 기업 3 단수명사 독차지, 전유 ❏ 배신감이 여성의 전유물은 아니다.

mo|noto|nous /mənɒt⁰nəs/ ADJ Something that is **monotonous** is very boring because it has a regular, repeated pattern which never changes. ❏ *It's monotonous work, like most factory jobs.*

형용사 단조로운 ❏ 이는 대부분의 공장 일처럼 단조로운 작업이다.

mon|soon /mɒnsun/ (**monsoons**) 1 N-COUNT The **monsoon** is the season in Southern Asia when there is a lot of very heavy rain. ❏ *...the end of the monsoon.* 2 N-PLURAL Monsoon rains are sometimes referred to as **the monsoons**. ❏ *In Bangladesh, the monsoons have started.* →see **disaster**

1 가산명사 몬순 (동남아의 우기) ❏ 몬순의 끝 2 복수명사 몬순 때 오는 비 ❏ 방글라데시에서 몬순비가 내리기 시작했다.

mon|ster /mɒnstər/ (**monsters**) 1 N-COUNT A **monster** is a large imaginary creature that looks very ugly and frightening. ❏ *Both movies are about a monster in the bedroom closet.* 2 N-COUNT A **monster** is something which is extremely large, especially something which is difficult to manage or which is unpleasant. ❏ *...the monster which is now the London marathon.* 3 ADJ **Monster** means extremely and surprisingly large. [INFORMAL, EMPHASIS] [ADJ n] ❏ *...a monster weapon.* 4 N-COUNT If you describe someone as a **monster**, you mean that they are cruel, frightening, or evil. ❏ *Galbraith said that her husband was a depraved monster who threatened and humiliated her.*

1 가산명사 괴물 ❏ 두 영화 모두 침실 벽장에 사는 괴물 이야기를 담고 있다. 2 가산명사 괴물 (같은 것) ❏ 이제는 거대한 괴물이 되어버린 런던 마라톤 3 형용사 거대한 [비격식체, 강조] ❏ 거대한 무기 4 가산명사 극악무도한 사람, 괴물 ❏ 갤브레이스는 남편이 자신을 위협하고 모욕하는 등 저열하고 극악무도한 사람이었다고 말했다.

A

mon|strous /mɒnstrəs/ ■ ADJ If you describe a situation or event as **monstrous**, you mean that it is extremely shocking or unfair. ❑ *She endured the monstrous behavior for years.* ● **mon|strous|ly** ADV [ADV after v] ❑ *Your husband's family has behaved monstrously.* ■ ADJ If you describe an unpleasant thing as **monstrous**, you mean that it is extremely large in size or extent. [EMPHASIS]

B

❑ *A group of men are erecting a monstrous copper edifice.* ● **mon|strous|ly** ADV [ADV adj/-ed] ❑ *It would be monstrously unfair.* ■ ADJ If you describe something as **monstrous**, you mean that it is extremely frightening because it appears unnatural or ugly. ❑ *...the film's monstrous fantasy figure.*

C

month ♦♦♦ /mʌnθ/ (**months**) ■ N-COUNT A **month** is one of the twelve periods of time that a year is divided into, for example January or February. ❑ *The trial is due to begin next month.* ❑ *...an exhibition which opens this month at London's Design Museum.* ■ N-COUNT A **month** is a period of about four weeks. ❑ *She was here for a month.* ❑ *Over the next several months I met most of her family.* →see **year**

D

E

month|ly ♦♦♦ /mʌnθli/ (**monthlies**) ■ ADJ A **monthly** event or publication happens or appears every month. [ADJ n] ❑ *Many people are now having trouble making their monthly house payments.* ❑ *Kidscape runs monthly workshops for teachers.* ● ADV **Monthly** is also an adverb. [ADV after v] ❑ *In some areas the property price can rise monthly.* ■ N-COUNT You can refer to a publication that is published monthly as a **monthly**. ❑ *...Scallywag, a London satirical monthly.* ■ ADJ **Monthly** quantities or rates relate to a period of one month. [ADJ n] ❑ *Consumers are charged a monthly fee above their basic cable costs.*

F

G

monu|ment /mɒnyəmənt/ (**monuments**) ■ N-COUNT A **monument** is a large structure, usually made of stone, which is built to remind people of an event in history or of a famous person. ❑ *...a newly restored monument commemorating a 119-year-old tragedy.* ■ N-COUNT A **monument** is something such as a castle or bridge which was built a very long time ago and is regarded as an important part of a country's history. ❑ *...the ancient monuments of England, Scotland, and Wales.* ■ N-COUNT If you describe something as a **monument** to someone's qualities, you mean that it is a very good example of the results or effects of those qualities. ❑ *By his international achievements he leaves a fitting monument to his beliefs.*

H

I

J

monu|men|tal /mɒnyəmɛntˀl/ ■ ADJ You can use **monumental** to emphasize the large size or extent of something. [EMPHASIS] ❑ *It had been a monumental blunder to give him the assignment.* ■ ADJ If you describe a book or musical work as **monumental**, you are emphasizing that it is very large and impressive, and is likely to be important for a long time. [EMPHASIS] ❑ *...his monumental work on Chinese astronomy.* ■ ADJ A **monumental** building or sculpture is very large and impressive. [ADJ n] ❑ *I take no real interest in monumental sculpture.*

K

L

M

mood ♦♦♦ /muːd/ (**moods**) ■ N-COUNT Your **mood** is the way you are feeling at a particular time. If you are in a good **mood**, you feel cheerful. If you are in a bad **mood**, you feel angry and impatient. ❑ *He is clearly in a good mood today.* ❑ *Lily was in one of her aggressive moods.* ● PHRASE If you say that you are in the **mood for** something, you mean that you want to do it or have it. If you say that you are in **no mood to** do something, you mean that you do not want to do it or have it. ❑ *After a day of air and activity, you should be in the mood for a good meal.* ■ N-COUNT If someone is in a **mood**, the way they are behaving shows that they are feeling angry and impatient. ❑ *She was obviously in a mood.* ■ N-SING The **mood** of a group of people is the way that they think and feel about an idea, event, or question at a particular time. ❑ *The government seemed to be in tune with the popular mood.* ■ N-COUNT The **mood** of a place is the general impression that you get of it. ❑ *First set the mood with music.*

N

O

P

Word Partnership	mood의 연어
ADJ.	**bad/good** mood, **depressed** mood, **foul** mood, **positive** mood, **tense** mood ■
N.	mood **change**, mood **disorder**, mood **swings** ■
V.	**create** a mood, **set** a mood ■ ■

Q

R

S

moody /muːdi/ (**moodier**, **moodiest**) ■ ADJ If you describe someone as **moody**, you mean that their feelings and behavior change frequently, and in particular that they often become depressed or angry without any warning. ❑ *David's mother was unstable and moody.* ● **mood|ily** /muːdɪli/ ADV ❑ *He sat and stared moodily out the window.* ● **mood|iness** N-UNCOUNT ❑ *His moodiness may have been caused by his poor health.* ■ ADJ If you describe a picture, movie, or piece of music as **moody**, you mean that it suggests particular emotions, especially sad ones. ❑ *...moody black and white photographs.*

T

U

moon ♦♦♦ /muːn/ (**moons**) ■ N-SING The **moon** is the object that you can often see in the sky at night. It goes around the Earth once every four weeks, and as it does so its appearance changes from a circle to part of a circle. [usu the N, also full/new N] ❑ *...the first man on the moon.* ■ N-COUNT A **moon** is an object similar to a small planet that travels around a planet. ❑ *...Neptune's large moon.* →see **eclipse**, **satellite**, **solar system**, **tide** →see Word Web: **moon**

V

W

A **blue moon** is the name given to the second full moon occurring within one calendar month. It happens at long intervals so the phrase "Once in a blue moon" means "not often."

X

Y

moon|light /muːnlaɪt/ (**moonlights**, **moonlighting**, **moonlighted**) ■ N-UNCOUNT **Moonlight** is the light that comes from the moon at night. ❑ *They walked along the road in the moonlight.* ■ V-I If someone **moonlights**, they have a second job in addition to their main job, often without informing

Z

■ 형용사 극악무도한 ❑ 그녀는 그 극악무도한 태도를 수년간 참았다. ● 극악무도하게, 끔찍하게 부사 ❑ 너희 시댁이 지금까지 끔찍하게 굴었잖아. ■ 형용사 거대한, 굉장한 [강조] ❑ 한 무리의 사람들이 거대한 구릿빛 건물을 세우고 있다. ● 어마어마하게, 굉장히 부사 ❑ 이는 굉장히 부당한 처사가 될 것이다. ■ 형용사 괴물 같은 ❑ 영화에 등장하는 괴물 같은 상상의 인물

■ 가산명사 달 ❑ 재판은 다음 달에 시작될 예정이다. ❑ 이번 달 런던 디자인 박물관에서 열리는 전시회 ■ 가산명사 한 달 ❑ 그녀는 한 달 동안 여기에 있었다. ❑ 나는 그 후 몇 달에 걸쳐 그녀의 가족 대부분을 만났다.

■ 형용사 한 달에 한 번 있는, 매월의 ❑ 요즘 많은 사람들이 매월 집세를 내는 데 어려움을 겪고 있다. ❑ 키즈스케이프는 매월 교사를 위한 워크숍을 연다. ● 부사 매월 ❑ 일부 지역에서는 부동산 가격이 매월 오를 수 있다. ■ 가산명사 월간지 ❑ 런던 풍자 월간지 스캘리왝 ■ 형용사 한 달의 ❑ 소비자들은 기본적인 케이블 설치비용 외에 매달 사용료를 내야 한다.

■ 가산명사 기념비, 기념물 ❑ 새로 복원된, 119년 전의 비극을 기리는 기념비 ■ 가산명사 유물 ❑ 잉글랜드와 스코틀랜드, 웨일스의 고대 유물 ■ 가산명사 기념비적 업적 ❑ 그가 국제무대에서 이룬 성과는 그의 믿음을 잘 보여 주는 업적으로 남을 것이다.

■ 형용사 엄청난 [강조] ❑ 그에게 그 일을 맡긴 것은 엄청난 실수였다. ■ 형용사 기념비적인, 역사적인 [강조] ❑ 그가 중국 천문학에 남긴 기념비적인 업적 ■ 형용사 거대한 ❑ 나는 커다란 조각에는 전혀 관심이 없다.

■ 가산명사 기분 ❑ 확실히 오늘 그의 기분이 좋아 보인다. ❑ 릴리의 기분이 공격적인 상태에 있었다. ● 구 - 할 기분이 나는; -할 기분이 아닌 ❑ 하루 종일 바깥 공기를 마시고 움직이고 나면 맛있는 식사를 하고 싶을 것이다. ■ 가산명사 기분이 안 좋은 ❑ 그녀는 분명 기분이 안 좋아 보였다. ■ 단수명사 분위기, 정서 ❑ 정부가 국민 정서를 따라가고 있는 것으로 보였다. ■ 가산명사 분위기 ❑ 먼저 음악으로 분위기를 조성하라.

■ 형용사 변덕스러운, 우울한 ❑ 데이비드의 어머니는 감정의 기복이 심한 분이셨다. ● 시무룩하게 부사 ❑ 그는 시무룩하게 창 밖을 내다보며 앉아 있었다. ● 자주 우울해 함 불가산명사 ❑ 그가 건강이 나빠서 쉽게 우울해진 것인지도 모른다. ■ 형용사 감성적인, 슬픈 ❑ 감수성을 자극하는 흑백 사진

■ 단수명사 달 ❑ 최초로 달에 착륙한 사람. ■ 가산명사 위성 ❑ 해왕성의 큰 위성

blue moon은 한 달 안에 보름달이 뜨는 날이 두 번 있을 때, 두 번째로 뜨는 보름달을 일컫는 말이다. 이 현상은 아주 오랜 간격을 두고 일어나기 때문에 'once in a blue moon'이라는 표현은 '드물게'를 뜻한다.

■ 불가산명사 달빛 ❑ 그들은 달빛 속에서 길을 따라 걸었다. ■ 자동사 부업하다 ❑ 부업으로 택시 운전을 하고 있었던 기술자

Word Web   moon

Scientists believe the **moon** is about five billion years old. They think a large asteroid hit the earth. A big piece of the earth broke off. It went flying into **space**. However, Earth's **gravity** caught it and it began to circle the earth. This piece became our moon. The moon orbits the earth once a month. It also **rotates** on its **axis** every thirty days. The moon has no **atmosphere**, so meteoroids constantly crash into it. When a meteoroid hits the surface of the **moon**, it makes a **crater**. Craters cover the surface of the moon.

their main employers or the tax office. ❑ *...an engineer who was moonlighting as a taxi driver.*

moor /mʊər/ (moors, mooring, moored) **1** N-VAR A **moor** is an area of open and usually high land with poor soil that is covered mainly with grass and heather. [mainly BRIT] ❑ *Colliford is higher, right up on the moors.* **2** V-T/V-I If you **moor** a boat somewhere, you stop and tie it to the land with a rope or chain so that it cannot move away. ❑ *She had moored her barge on the right bank of the river.* **3** N-COUNT The **Moors** were a Muslim people who established a civilization in North Africa and Spain between the 8th and the 15th century A.D. **4** →see also **mooring**

mooring /mʊərɪŋ/ (moorings) **1** N-COUNT A **mooring** is a place where a boat can be tied so that it cannot move away, or the object it is tied to. ❑ *Free moorings will be available.* **2** N-PLURAL **Moorings** are the ropes, chains, and other objects used to moor a boat. ❑ *He cut the engine and grabbed the mooring lines.*

moorland /mʊərlænd/ (moorlands) N-UNCOUNT **Moorland** is land which consists of moors. [also N in pl] ❑ *...rugged Yorkshire moorland.*

moose /muːs/

> **Moose** is both the singular and the plural form.

N-COUNT A **moose** is a large type of deer. Moose have big flat horns called antlers and are found in Northern Europe, Asia, and North America. Some British speakers use **moose** to refer to the North American variety of this animal, and **elk** to refer to the European and Asian varieties.

mop /mɒp/ (mops, mopping, mopped) **1** N-COUNT A **mop** is a piece of equipment for washing floors. It consists of a sponge or many pieces of string attached to a long handle. **2** V-T If you **mop** a surface such as a floor, you clean it with a mop. ❑ *There was a woman mopping the stairs.* **3** V-T If you **mop** sweat from your forehead or **mop** your forehead, you wipe it with a piece of cloth. ❑ *He mopped perspiration from his forehead.*

▶ **mop up** PHRASAL VERB If you **mop up** a liquid, you clean it with a cloth so that the liquid is absorbed. ❑ *A waiter mopped up the mess as best he could.* ❑ *When the washing machine spurts out water at least we can mop it up.* **2** PHRASAL VERB If you **mop up** something that you think is undesirable or dangerous, you remove it or deal with it so that it is no longer a problem. ❑ *The infantry divisions mopped up remaining centers of resistance.*

mope /moʊp/ (mopes, moping, moped) V-I If you **mope**, you feel miserable and do not feel interested in doing anything. ❑ *Get on with life and don't sit back and mope.*

moped /moʊpɛd/ (mopeds) N-COUNT A **moped** is a small motorcycle which you can also pedal like a bicycle. [mainly BRIT]

moral ♦◇◇ /mɒrəl, BRIT mɒrəl/ (morals) **1** N-PLURAL **Morals** are principles and beliefs concerning right and wrong behavior. ❑ *...Western ideas and morals.* **2** ADJ **Moral** means relating to beliefs about what is right or wrong. [ADJ n] ❑ *She describes her own moral dilemma in making the film.* ● **morally** ADV ❑ *When, if ever, is it morally justifiable to allow a patient to die?* **3** ADJ **Moral** courage or duty is based on what you believe is right or acceptable, rather than on what the law says should be done. [ADJ n] ❑ *The Government had a moral, if not a legal duty to pay compensation.* **4** ADJ A **moral** person behaves in a way that is believed by most people to be good and right. ❑ *The people who will be on the committee are moral, cultured, competent people.* ● **morally** ADV [ADV with v] ❑ *Art is not there to improve you morally.* **5** ADJ If you give someone **moral** support, you encourage them in what they are doing by expressing approval. [ADJ n] ❑ *Moral as well as financial support was what the West should provide.* **6** N-COUNT The **moral** of a story or event is what you learn from it about how you should or should not behave. ❑ *I think the moral of the story is let the buyer beware.* **7** **moral victory** →see **victory** →see **philosophy**

1 가산명사 또는 불가산명사 황야, 황폐한 산간 지대 [주로 영국영어] ❑ 콜리포드는 산간 지대 황무지 바로 위 조금 높은 곳에 있다. **2** 타동사/자동사 정박시키다, 잡아매다 ❑ 그녀는 강 오른쪽 둑에 배를 매어 놓았었다. **3** 가산명사 무어인

1 가산명사 계류장, 정박지 ❑ 계류장을 무료로 사용할 수 있을 것이다. **2** 복수명사 계선비 ❑ 그가 엔진을 끄고 계류용 밧줄을 잡았다.

불가산명사 산간 황무지 ❑ 바위투성이인 요크셔 산간 지대 황무지

moose는 단수형 및 복수형이다.

가산명사 무스, 큰 사슴

1 가산명사 대걸레 **2** 타동사 대걸레로 닦다 ❑ 한 여자가 대걸레로 계단을 닦고 있었다. **3** 타동사 닦다 ❑ 그는 이마에서 땀을 닦아냈다.

1 구동사 닦아내다 ❑ 웨이터가 최선을 다해 더러워진 것을 닦아냈다. ❑ 세탁기에서 물이 튀어나올 때 최소한 우리가 닦아 낼 수는 있다. **2** 구동사 세거하다, 해결하다 ❑ 보병 사단이 남아 있는 저항 세력의 중심지를 소탕했다.

자동사 맥없이 침울해하다, 의욕을 못 느끼다 ❑ 정신 차리고 살 생각 해. 가만히 앉아서 침울해하지 말고.

가산명사 전동 자전거 [주로 영국영어]

1 복수명사 도덕관념, 사회 규범 ❑ 서구 사회의 사상과 도덕관념 **2** 형용사 윤리의, 도덕의 ❑ 그녀는 영화를 만들면서 부딪친 윤리적 딜레마에 대해 묘사한다. ● 윤리적으로, 도덕적으로 부사 ❑ 만약의 경우이긴 합니다만, 환자가 죽도록 놔두는 것이 윤리적으로 정당할 때는 언제입니까? **3** 형용사 도덕적인 ❑ 법적인 의무는 아니더라도 윤리적인 측면에서 정부는 보상해야 할 의무가 있었다. **4** 형용사 도덕적인 ❑ 위원회에 포함될 이들은 도덕적이며 교양 있고, 실력 있는 사람들이다. ● 도덕적으로 부사 ❑ 예술은 인간의 도덕성 향상을 위해 있는 것이 아니다. **5** 형용사 정신적인, 마음의 ❑ 서구 사회는 금전적인 지원뿐만이 아니라 정신적인 지지도 보내야 했다. **6** 가산명사 교훈 ❑ 나는 이 이야기의 교훈이 구매자의 경각심 환기라고 생각한다.

mo|rale /mərǽl/ N-UNCOUNT **Morale** is the amount of confidence and cheerfulness that a group of people have. ❏ *Many pilots are suffering from low morale.*

불가산명사 사기, 의욕 ❏ 조종사 상당수가 사기 저하에 시달리고 있다.

mo|ral|ity /mərǽliti/ (**moralities**) **1** N-UNCOUNT **Morality** is the belief that some behavior is right and acceptable and that other behavior is wrong. ❏ *...standards of morality and justice in society.* **2** N-COUNT A **morality** is a system of principles and values concerning people's behavior, which is generally accepted by a society or by a particular group of people. ❏ *...a morality that is sexist.* **3** N-UNCOUNT The **morality of** something is how right or acceptable it is. ❏ *...the arguments about the morality of blood sports.*

1 불가산명사 도덕 ❏ 사회의 도덕과 정의에 대한 기준 **2** 가산명사 사회 규범 ❏ 성차별적인 사회 규범 **3** 불가산명사 도덕성 ❏ 피를 동반하는 과격 스포츠의 도덕성에 대한 논쟁

mora|to|rium /mɔ̀rətɔ́riəm/, BRIT mɒ̀rətɔ́riəm/ (**moratoriums** or **moratoria**) N-COUNT A **moratorium on** a particular activity or process is the stopping of it for a fixed period of time, usually as a result of an official agreement. ❏ *The House voted to impose a one-year moratorium on nuclear testing.*

가산명사 일시 중단, 모라토리엄 ❏ 하원이 핵 실험을 1년 간 중단시키기 위해 투표를 했다.

mor|bid /mɔ́rbɪd/ ADJ If you describe a person or their interest in something as **morbid**, you mean that they are very interested in unpleasant things, especially death, and you think this is strange. [DISAPPROVAL] ❏ *Some people have a morbid fascination with crime.* ● **mor|bid|ly** ADV ❏ *There's something morbidly fascinating about the thought.*

형용사 병적인, 괴상한 [탐탁잖음] ❏ 어떤 사람들은 범죄에 병적으로 심취한다. ● 병적으로, 괴상하게 부사 ❏ 그 같은 생각에는 뭔가 괴상하게 사람을 빨아들이는 힘이 있다.

more ♦♦♦ /mɔ́r/

> **More** is often considered to be the comparative form of **much** and **many**.

> more가 종종 much와 many의 비교급 형태로 간주된다.

1 DET You use **more** to indicate that there is a greater amount of something than before or than average, or than something else. You can use "a little," "a lot," "a bit," "far," and "much" in front of **more**. ❏ *More and more people are surviving heart attacks.* ❏ *He spent more time perfecting his dance moves instead of gym work.* ● PRON **More** is also a pronoun. ❏ *As the level of work increased from light to heavy, workers ate more.* ● QUANT **More** is also a quantifier. [QUANT of def-n] ❏ *Employees may face increasing pressure to take on more of their own medical costs in retirement.* **2** PHRASE You use **more than** before a number or amount to say that the actual number or amount is even greater. ❏ *The Afghan authorities say the airport had been closed for more than a year.* **3** ADV You use **more** to indicate that something or someone has a greater amount of a quality than they used to or than is average or usual. [ADV adj/adv] ❏ *Prison conditions have become more brutal.* **4** ADV If you say that something is **more** one thing **than** another, you mean that it is like the first thing rather than the second. ❏ *He's more like a film star than a life-guard, really.* ❏ *Sue screamed, not loudly, more in surprise than terror.* **5** ADV If you do something **more** than before or **more** than someone else, you do it to a greater extent or more often. ❏ *When we are tired, tense, depressed or unwell, we feel pain much more.* **6** ADV You can use **more** to indicate that something continues to happen for a further period of time. [ADV after v] ❏ *Things might have been different if I'd talked a bit more.* ● PHRASE You can use **some more** to indicate that something continues to happen for a further period of time. **7** ADV You use **more** to indicate that something is repeated. For example, if you do something "once more," you do it again once. ❏ *This train would stop twice more in the suburbs before rolling southeast toward Munich.* **8** DET You use **more** to refer to an additional thing or amount. You can use "a little," "a lot," "a bit," "far" and "much" in front of **more**. ❏ *They needed more time to consider whether to hold an inquiry.* ● ADJ **More** is also an adjective. [ADJ n] ❏ *We stayed in Danville two more days.* ● PRON **More** is also a pronoun. ❏ *Oxfam has appealed to western nations to do more to help the refugees.* **9** ADV You use **more** in conversations when you want to draw someone's attention to something interesting or important that you are about to say. [ADV adv/adj] ❏ *Over the past few decades, continental Europe's economies have converged in several areas. More interestingly, there has been convergence in economic growth rates.* **10** PHRASE You can use **more and more** to indicate that something is becoming greater in amount, extent, or degree all the time. ❏ *Her life was heading more and more where she wanted it to go.* **11** PHRASE If something is **more or less** true, it is true in a general way, but is not completely true. [VAGUENESS] ❏ *The Conference is more or less over.* **12** PHRASE If something is **more than** a particular thing, it has greater value or importance than this thing. ❏ *He's more than a coach, he's a friend.* **13** PHRASE You use **more than** to say that something is true to a greater degree than is necessary or than average. ❏ *Lithuania produces more than enough food to feed itself.* **14** PHRASE You can use **what is more** or **what's more** to introduce an extra piece of information which supports or emphasizes the point you are making. [EMPHASIS] ❏ *Many more institutions, especially banks, were allowed to lend money for mortgages, and what was more, banks could lend out more money than they actually held.* **15** **all the more** →see **all**. **any more** →see **any**

1 한정사 더 많은 ❏ 심장 마비를 겪고도 살아나는 사람이 증가하고 있다. ❏ 그는 운동 대신에 춤 스텝을 연습하며 더 많은 시간을 보냈다. ● 대명사 더 많은 것; 더 많은 사람 ❏ 작업 강도가 낮았다가 높아지면서 일꾼들이 더 많은 일을 먹었다. ● 수량사 더 많은 것; 더 많은 사람 ❏ 퇴직 후 의료비 가운데 직장인의 본인 부담 분 증가 압력이 더욱 커질지도 모른다. **2** 구 -보다 많이 ❏ 아프간 당국은 공항이 1년 이상 봉쇄됐었다고 말한다. **3** 부사 더, 더욱 ❏ 교도소 환경이 더욱 험악해졌다. **4** 부사 오히려, 차라리 ❏ 정말이지 그는 구조 요원이라기보다 영화배우처럼 보인다. ❏ 형용사 수가 비명을 질렀다. 소리는 크지 않았고 무서워서라기보다 놀라서였다. **5** 부사 더 많이 ❏ 사람이 피곤하거나 긴장하고, 우울하고, 몸이 아플 때 고통을 훨씬 더 많이 느낀다. **6** 부사 더, 더 오래 ❏ 내가 조금 더 오래 이야기했더라면 상황이 달라졌을지도 모른다. ● 구 더, 더 오래 **7** 부사 -번 더 ❏ 이 기차는 뮌헨을 향해 동남쪽으로 가기 이전에 교외 지역에서 두 번 더 정차할 것이다. **8** 한정사 더 많은 ❏ 그들은 조사 여부를 결정하기 위해 시간이 더 필요했다. ● 형용사 추가의 ❏ 우리는 댄빌에서 이틀 더 묵었다. ● 대명사 더 많은 것; 더 많은 사람 ❏ 옥스팜은 서부 선진국이 난민 구호를 위해 더 많은 일을 할 것을 촉구했다. **9** 부사 더 ❏ 지난 몇 십 년 동안 유럽 대륙 각국의 경제가 몇몇 부문에서 통합되어 왔다. 더 재미있는 사실은 경제 성장률에서도 이같은 현상이 일어났다는 것이다. **10** 구 점점 더, 더욱 더 ❏ 인생이 점점 더 그녀가 원하는 방향으로 가고 있었다. **11** 구 다소, 어느 정도 [짐작투] ❏ 회의가 어느 정도 끝났다. **12** 구 -이상인 ❏ 그는 코치 이상인 친구 같은 존재이다. **13** 구 -하고도 남는, 여유 있는 ❏ 리투아니아는 자급하고도 남을 정도의 식량을 생산한다. **14** 구 게다가, 더욱이 [강조] ❏ 그 외에 더 많은 금융 기관, 특히 은행의 주택 담보 대출이 허용되었으며, 게다가 은행은 실제로 보유하고 있는 액수보다 더 많은 돈을 빌려 줄 수 있었다.

more|over ♦◇◇ /mɔ̀rouvər/ ADV You use **moreover** to introduce a piece of information that adds to or supports the previous statement. [FORMAL] [ADV with cl (not last in cl)] ❏ *She saw that there was indeed a man immediately behind her. Moreover, he was observing her strangely.*

부사 게다가 [격식체] ❏ 그녀는 정말로 자기 바로 뒤에 한 남자가 있는 것을 보았다. 게다가, 그는 그녀를 이상하게 눈빛으로 관찰하고 있었다.

morgue /mɔ́rg/ (**morgues**) N-COUNT A **morgue** is a building or a room in a hospital where dead bodies are kept before they are buried or cremated, or before they are identified or examined.

가산명사 시체 공시소, 영안실

morn|ing ♦♦♦ /mɔ́rnɪŋ/ (**mornings**) **1** N-VAR The **morning** is the part of each day between the time that people usually wake up and 12 o'clock noon or lunchtime. ❏ *During the morning your guide will take you around the city.* ❏ *On Sunday morning Bill was woken by the telephone.* **2** N-SING If you refer to a particular time in the morning, you mean a time between 12 o'clock midnight and 12 o'clock noon. ❏ *I often stayed up until two or three in the morning.* **3** PHRASE If you say that something will happen in the morning, you mean that it will happen during the morning of the following day. ❏ *I'll fly it to London in the morning.* **4** PHRASE If you say that something happens morning, noon and night, you mean that it

1 가산명사 또는 불가산명사 아침, 오전 ❏ 오전에는 가이드가 도시 이곳저곳을 안내해 드릴 겁니다. ❏ 일요일 아침 빌은 전화벨 소리에 잠이 깼다. **2** 단수명사 자정부터 정오까지 ❏ 나는 종종 새벽 두세 시까지 깨어 있는다. **3** 구 아침에, 오전에 ❏ 저는 아침에 런던행 비행기를 탈 거예요. **4** 구 밤낮없이, 항상 ❏ 매일매일 밤낮없이 이 게임을 하면 건강해진다.

happens all the time. ❑ *You get fit by playing the game, day in, day out, morning, noon and night.*

Thesaurus	morning의 참조어

N. dawn, light, sunrise ▪

mo|rose /mərous/ ADJ Someone who is **morose** is miserable, bad-tempered, and not willing to talk very much to other people. ❑ *She was morose, pale, and reticent.* ● **mo|rose|ly** ADV ❑ *One elderly man sat morosely at the bar.*

형용사 뚱한, 침울한 ❑ 그녀는 뚱하고 생기 없고 과묵한 사람이었다. ● 뚱하게, 침울하게 부사 ❑ 할아버지 한 분이 바에 침울한 표정으로 앉아 있었다.

mor|phine /mɔrfin/ N-UNCOUNT **Morphine** is a drug used to relieve pain.

불가산명사 모르핀

mor|sel /mɔrsˀl/ (**morsels**) N-COUNT A **morsel** is a very small amount of something, especially a very small piece of food. ❑ *...a delicious little morsel of meat.*

가산명사 소량, 조각 ❑ 자그마한 맛있는 고기 한 조각

mor|tal /mɔrtˀl/ (**mortals**) ▪ ADJ If you refer to the fact that people are **mortal**, you mean that they have to die and cannot live forever. ❑ *A man is deliberately designed to be mortal. He grows, he ages, and he dies.* ● **mor|tal|ity** /mɔrtǽliti/ N-UNCOUNT ❑ *She has suddenly come face to face with her own mortality.* ▪ N-COUNT You can describe someone as a **mortal** when you want to say that they are an ordinary person. ❑ *Tickets seem unobtainable to the ordinary mortal.* ▪ ADJ You can use **mortal** to show that something is very serious or may cause death. [ADJ n] ❑ *The police were defending themselves and others against mortal danger.* ● **mor|tal|ly** ADV ❑ *He falls, mortally wounded.* ▪ ADJ You can use **mortal** to emphasize that a feeling is extremely great or severe. [EMPHASIS] [ADJ n] ❑ *When self-esteem is high, we lose our mortal fear of jealousy.* ● **mor|tal|ly** ADV [ADV -ed/adj/adv] ❑ *Candida admits to having been "mortally embarrassed."*

▪ 형용사 죽어야 할 운명의, 필멸의 ❑ 인간은 언제나 반드시 죽도록 만들어졌다. 자라고, 나이 들고, 죽는 것이다. ● 죽어야 할 운명, 필멸 불가산명사 ❑ 그녀는 갑자기 자신의 죽음과 맞닥뜨렸다. ▪ 가산명사 인간 ❑ 보통 사람들은 표를 구할 방법이 없는 것 같다. ▪ 형용사 치명적인 ❑ 경찰이 스스로와 다른 이들을 치명적인 위험으로부터 방어하고 있었다. ● 치명적으로 부사 ❑ 그는 치명상을 입고 쓰러진다. ▪ 형용사 커다란, 심한 [강조] ❑ 우리는 자부심이 강할 때 시기심에 의한 큰 공포는 버리게 된다. ● 크게, 심하게 부사 ❑ 캔디다는 '크게 당황했었다'고 인정한다.

mor|tal|ity /mɔrtǽliti/ N-UNCOUNT The **mortality** in a particular place or situation is the number of people who die. ❑ *The nation's infant mortality rate has reached a record low.*

불가산명사 사망률 ❑ 전국 유아 사망률이 사상 최저치로 떨어졌다.

mor|tar /mɔrtər/ (**mortars**) ▪ N-COUNT A **mortar** is a big gun which fires missiles high into the air over a short distance. ❑ *The two sides exchanged fire with artillery, mortars and small arms.* ▪ N-UNCOUNT **Mortar** is a mixture of sand, water, and cement or lime which is put between bricks to hold them together. ❑ *...the mortar between the bricks.* ▪ N-COUNT A **mortar** is a bowl in which you can crush things such as herbs, spices, or grain using a rod called a pestle. ❑ *Use a mortar and pestle to crush the heads, shells and claws.*

▪ 가산명사 박격포 ❑ 양 진영이 대포, 박격포, 총을 들고 교전을 벌였다. ▪ 불가산명사 회반죽 ❑ 벽돌 사이의 회반죽 ▪ 가산명사 막자사발 ❑ 머리와 껍질과 다리는 막자사발과 막자를 사용해 빻아라.

mort|gage ♦♦◇ /mɔrgɪdʒ/ (**mortgages, mortgaging, mortgaged**) ▪ N-COUNT A **mortgage** is a loan of money which you get from a bank or savings and loan association in order to buy a house. ❑ *...an increase in mortgage rates.* ▪ V-T If you **mortgage** your house or land, you use it as a guarantee to a company in order to borrow money from them. ❑ *They had to mortgage their home to pay the bills.* →see **interest rate**

▪ 가산명사 주택 담보 대출, 모기지론 ❑ 주택담보 대출 금리 인상 ▪ 타동사 저당 잡히다 ❑ 그들은 공과금을 내기 위해 집을 저당 잡혀야 했다.

mor|ti|cian /mɔrtɪʃˀn/ (**morticians**) N-COUNT A **mortician** is a person whose job is to deal with the bodies of people who have died and to arrange funerals. [mainly AM]

가산명사 장의사 [주로 미국영어]

mor|tu|ary /mɔrtʃueri, BRIT mɔːtʃuəri/ (**mortuaries**) N-COUNT A **mortuary** is a building or a room in a hospital where dead bodies are kept before they are buried or cremated, or before they are identified or examined.

가산명사 시체 공시소, 영안실

mo|sa|ic /mouzeɪɪk/ (**mosaics**) N-VAR A **mosaic** is a design which consists of small pieces of colored glass, pottery, or stone set in concrete or plaster. ❑ *...a Roman villa which once housed a fine collection of mosaics.*

가산명사 또는 불가산명사 모자이크 ❑ 한때 아름다운 모자이크 작품 일체를 간직하고 있던 로마 저택

Mos|lem /mɒzləm, mʊzlɪm/ →see **Muslim**

mosque /mɒsk/ (**mosques**) N-COUNT A **mosque** is a building where Muslims go to worship.

가산명사 이슬람 사원

mos|qui|to /məskitoʊ/ (**mosquitoes** or **mosquitos**) N-COUNT **Mosquitos** are small flying insects which bite people and animals in order to suck their blood.

가산명사 모기

moss /mɔs, BRIT mɒs/ (**mosses**) N-MASS **Moss** is a very small soft green plant which grows on damp soil, or on wood or stone. ❑ *...ground covered over with moss.*

물질명사 이끼 ❑ 이끼 덮인 땅

most ♦♦♦ /moʊst/

Most is often considered to be the superlative form of **much** and **many**.

most가 종종 much와 many의 최상급 형태로 간주된다.

▪ QUANT You use **most** to refer to the majority of a group of things or people or the largest part of something. [QUANT of def-n] ❑ *Most of the houses in the capital don't have piped water.* ❑ *By stopping smoking you are undoing most of the damage smoking has caused.* ● DET **Most** is also a determiner. ❑ *Most people think the Queen has done a good job over the last 50 years.* ● PRON **Most** is also a pronoun. ❑ *Seventeen civilians were hurt. Most are students who had been attending a twenty-first birthday party.* ▪ ADJ You use **the most** to mean a larger amount than anyone or anything else, or the largest amount possible. [the ADJ n] ❑ *The President himself won the most votes.* ● PRON **Most** is also a pronoun. ❑ *The most they earn in a day is ten roubles.* ▪ ADV You use **most** to indicate that something is true or happens to a greater degree or extent than anything else. [ADV with v] ❑ *What she feared most was becoming like her mother.* ❑ *...Professor Morris, the person he most hated.* ● PHRASE You use **most of all** to indicate that something happens or is true to a greater extent than anything else. ▪ ADV You use **most** to indicate that someone or something has a greater amount of a particular quality than most other things of its kind. [ADV adj/adv] ❑ *Her children had the best, most elaborate birthday parties in the neighborhood.* ❑ *He was one of the most influential performers of modern jazz.* ▪ ADV If you do something **the most**, you do it to the greatest extent possible or with the greatest frequency. [the ADV after v] ❑ *What question are you asked the most?* ▪ ADV You use **most** in conversations when you want to draw someone's attention to something very interesting or

▪ 수량사 대부분 ❑ 수도의 주택 대부분이 수돗물 공급을 받지 못한다. ❑ 당신이 담배를 끊음으로써 흡연이 일으킨 피해 대부분을 되돌리고 있는 것이다. ● 한정사 대부분의 ❑ 대부분의 사람들은 여왕이 지난 50년 동안 일을 잘했다고 생각한다. ● 대명사 대부분 ❑ 민간인 17명이 다쳤다. 대부분은 21번째 생일 파티에 참석한 학생들이다. ▪ 형용사 가장 많은 ❑ 대통령이 가장 많은 표를 얻었다. ● 대명사 가장 많은 것 ❑ 그들이 하루 동안 가장 많이 번 금액은 10루블이다. ▪ 부사 가장 ❑ 그녀가 가장 두려워한 것은 어머니처럼 되는 것이었다. ❑ 가장 싫어한 사람인 모리스 교수 ● 구 무엇보다도 ▪ 부사 가장 ❑ 그녀의 아이들은 동네에서 가장 좋고 가장 공들인 생일 파티를 열었다. ❑ 그는 가장 영향력 있는 모던 재즈 음악가 중 하나였다. ▪ 부사 가장 많이 ❑ 가장 많이 받는 질문이 뭐죠? ▪ 부사 가장 ❑ 가장 놀라운 것은 상당수의 사람들이 투표할 생각이 없다고 말했다는 것이다.

A

important that you are about to say. [ADV adv/adj] ❏ *Most surprisingly, quite a few said they don't intend to vote at all.*

> Note that you can say "**Most children love candy**," but you cannot say "Most of children love candy." However, when a pronoun is used, you can say "**Most of them love candy.**"

> "Most children love candy"라고는 하지만, "Most of children love candy"라고는 쓰지 않음을 유의하라. 그러나 대명사를 쓸 경우에는, "Most of them love candy"라고 할 수 있다.

B

☑ PHRASE You use **at most** or **at the most** to say that a number or amount is the maximum that is possible and that the actual number or amount may be smaller. ❏ *Poach the pears in apple juice or water and sugar for perhaps ten minutes at most.* ☑ PHRASE If you **make the most of** something, you get the maximum use or advantage from it. ❏ *Happiness is the ability to make the most of what you have.*

☑ 구 기껏해야, 많아야, 최대한 ❏ 배를 사과 주스나 설탕물에 담가 최대한 10분 정도 익혀라. ☑ 구 최대한 활용하다 ❏ 행복이란 자신이 가진 것을 최대한 활용할 줄 아는 능력이다.

C

most|ly ◆◇◇ /mo͟ʊstli/ ADV You use **mostly** to indicate that a statement is generally true, for example true about the majority of a group of things or people, true most of the time, or true in most respects. [ADV with cl/group] ❏ *I am working with mostly highly motivated people.* ❏ *Cars are mostly metal.*

부사 대개, 주로 ❏ 나는 주로 의욕이 많은 사람들과 함께 일한다. ❏ 차는 대부분 금속으로 되어 있다.

D

mo|tel /mo͟ʊte̱l/ (**motels**) N-COUNT A **motel** is a hotel intended for people who are traveling by car.

가산명사 모텔

E

moth /mɒθ, BRIT mɒθ/ (**moths**) N-COUNT A **moth** is an insect like a butterfly which usually flies about at night.

가산명사 나방

F

moth|er ◆◆◆ /mʌ͟ðər/ (**mothers, mothering, mothered**) ☑ N-FAMILY Your **mother** is the woman who gave birth to you. You can also call someone your **mother** if she brings you up as if she was this woman. ❏ *She sat on the edge of her mother's bed.* ❏ *She's an English teacher and a mother of two children.* ☑ V-T If a woman **mothers** a child, she looks after it and brings it up, usually because she is its mother. ❏ *Colleen had dreamed of mothering a large family.* ☑ V-T If you **mother** someone, you treat them with great care and affection, as if they were a small child. ❏ *Stop mothering me.* →see **family**

☑ 친족명사 어머니, 엄마 ❏ 그녀는 어머니의 침대 가장자리에 앉았다. ❏ 그녀는 영어 선생님이며 두 자녀를 둔 어머니이다. ☑ 타동사 어머니로서 자식을 돌보다, 어머니가 되다 ❏ 콜린은 아이 많은 집 엄마가 되는 꿈을 꿨다. ☑ 타동사 어머니처럼 굴다, 아이 돌보듯 하다 ❏ 절 아이 취급하지 말아요.

G

H

moth|er|hood /mʌ͟ðərhʊd/ N-UNCOUNT **Motherhood** is the state of being a mother. ❏ *...women who try to combine work and motherhood.*

불가산명사 어머니임 ❏ 일과 어머니로서의 역할을 함께 하려는 여성들

I

mother-in-law (**mothers-in-law**) N-COUNT Someone's **mother-in-law** is the mother of their husband or wife. →see **family**

가산명사 시어머니; 장모

J

moth|er|ly /mʌ͟ðərli/ ADJ **Motherly** feelings or actions are like those of a kind mother. ❏ *It was an incredible display of motherly love and forgiveness.*

형용사 어머니 같은 ❏ 이는 어머니 같은 사랑과 용서를 훌륭하게 보여 주었다.

K

mo|tif /mo͟ʊti̱f/ (**motifs**) N-COUNT A **motif** is a design which is used as a decoration or as part of an artistic pattern. ❏ *...a rose motif.*

가산명사 모티브, 문양 ❏ 장미 문양

L

Word Link mot ≈ moving : *mot*ion, *mot*ivate, pro*mot*e

M

mo|tion ◆◇◇ /mo͟ʊʃən/ (**motions, motioning, motioned**) ☑ N-UNCOUNT **Motion** is the activity or process of continually changing position or moving from one place to another. ❏ *...the laws governing light, sound, and motion.* ❏ *One group of muscles sets the next group in motion.* ☑ N-COUNT A **motion** is an action, gesture, or movement. ❏ *He made a neat chopping motion with his hand.* ☑ N-COUNT A **motion** is a formal proposal or statement in a meeting, debate, or trial, which is discussed and then voted on or decided on. ❏ *The conference is now debating the motion and will vote on it shortly.* ❏ *Opposition parties are likely to bring a no-confidence motion against the government.* ☑ V-T/V-I If you **motion** to someone, you move your hand or head as a way of telling them to do something or telling them where to go. ❏ *She motioned for the locked front doors to be opened.* ❏ *He stood aside and motioned Don to the door.* ☑ →see also **slow motion** ☑ PHRASE If you say that someone **is going through the motions**, you think they are only saying or doing something because it is expected of them without being interested, enthusiastic, or sympathetic. ❏ *"You really don't care, do you?" she said quietly. "You're just going through the motions."* ☑ PHRASE If a process or event is **in motion**, it is happening. If it is **set in motion**, it is happening or beginning to happen. ❏ *His job as England manager begins in earnest now his World Cup campaign is in motion.* ☑ PHRASE If someone **sets the wheels in motion**, they take the necessary action to make something start happening. ❏ *I have set the wheels in motion to sell Endsleigh Court.* →see Word Web: **motion**

☑ 불가산명사 운동, 움직임 ❏ 빛, 소리, 운동을 지배하는 법칙 ❏ 한 덩어리의 근육이 다음 근육을 움직이게 한다. ☑ 가산명사 동작 ❏ 그가 손으로 깔끔하게 내리치는 동작을 취했다. ☑ 가산명사 동의, 발의 ❏ 현재 동의안이 회의에서 논의되고 있으며 곧 투표에 부쳐질 것이다. ❏ 야당이 정부에 대한 불신임 투표 동의안을 상정할 가능성이 크다. ☑ 타동사/자동사 손짓하다, 신호를 보내다 ❏ 그녀는 잠긴 앞문을 열라고 신호를 보냈다. ❏ 그는 옆으로 비켜서서 돈에게 문 쪽을 가리켰다. ☑ 구 시늉만 하다 ❏ "진짜 신경 써서 하는 거 아니지?" 그녀가 조용히 말했다. "넌 지금 시늉만 하는 거야." ☑ 구 진행 중인, 일어나기 시작한 ❏ 그의 월드컵 작전이 진행되면서 잉글랜드 팀 매니저로서의 본격적인 활동도 시작되고 있다. ☑ 구 필요한 절차를 마치다, 궤도에 올리다 ❏ 엔드슬레이 저택 매각에 필요한 모든 절차를 마쳤다.

N

O

P

Q

R

S

Word Partnership motion의 연어

ADJ.	**constant** motion, **full** motion, **perpetual** motion ☑
	circular motion, **smooth** motion ☑ ☑
	quick motion ☑
V.	**set** *something* **in** motion ☑ ☑ ☑

T

U

Word Web motion

Newton's three laws of **motion** describe how **forces** affect the movement of objects. This is the first law: an object at **rest** won't move unless a force makes it move. Similarly, a moving object keeps its **momentum** unless something stops it. The second law describes **acceleration**. The **rate** of acceleration depends on two things: how strong the push on the object is, and how much the object weighs. The third law says that for every **action** there is an equal and opposite **reaction**. When one object **exerts** a force on another, the second object pushes back with an equal force.

V

W

X

Y

Z

mo|tion|less /mouˈʃənlɪs/ ADJ Someone or something that is **motionless** is not moving at all. ❑ *He has this ability of being able to remain as motionless as a statue, for hours on end.*

mo|tion pic|ture (**motion pictures**) N-COUNT A **motion picture** is a movie made for movie theaters. [mainly AM] ❑ *It was there that I saw my first motion picture.*

Word Link	ate ≈ causing to be : complic*ate*, humili*ate*, motiv*ate*

Word Link	mot ≈ moving : *mot*ion, *mot*ivate, pro*mot*e

mo|ti|vate ♦♢♢ /mouˈtɪveɪt/ (**motivates, motivating, motivated**) **1** V-T If you **are motivated** by something, especially an emotion, it causes you to behave in a particular way. ❑ *They are motivated by a need to achieve.* ● **mo|ti|vat|ed** ADJ ❑ *...highly motivated employees.* ● **mo|ti|va|tion** /mouˈtɪveɪʃ°n/ N-UNCOUNT ❑ *His poor performance may be attributed to lack of motivation rather than to reading difficulties.* **2** V-T If someone **motivates** you to do something, they make you feel determined to do it. ❑ *How do you motivate people to work hard and efficiently?* ● **mo|ti|va|tion** N-UNCOUNT ❑ *Given parental motivation we are optimistic about the ability of people to change.*

Word Partnership	*motivate*의 연어
N.	motivate **an audience**, motivate **consumers**, motivate **employees**, motivate **people**, motivate **students** **2**

mo|ti|va|tion /mouˈtɪveɪʃ°n/ (**motivations**) N-COUNT Your **motivation** for doing something is what causes you to want to do it. ❑ *Money is my motivation.*

mo|tive /mouˈtɪv/ (**motives**) N-COUNT Your **motive** for doing something is your reason for doing it. ❑ *Police have ruled out robbery as a motive for the killing.*

Word Partnership	*motive*의 연어
PREP.	motive **behind** *something*, motive **for** *something*
ADJ.	**possible** motive, **primary** motive, **ulterior** motive

mo|tor ♦♢♢ /mouˈtər/ (**motors**) **1** N-COUNT The **motor** in a machine, vehicle, or boat is the part that uses electricity or fuel to produce movement, so that the machine, vehicle, or boat can work. ❑ *She got in and started the motor.* **2** ADJ **Motor** vehicles and boats have a gasoline or diesel engine. [ADJ n] ❑ *Theft of motor vehicles is up 15.9%.* **3** ADJ **Motor** is used to describe activities relating to vehicles such as cars and buses. [mainly BRIT; AM usually **automotive, automobile**] [ADJ n] ❑ *...the future of the British motor industry.* **4** →see also **motoring**

motor|bike /mouˈtərbaɪk/ (**motorbikes**) also **motor-bike** **1** N-COUNT A **motorbike** is a lighter, less powerful motorcycle. [AM] **2** N-COUNT A **motorbike** is the same as a **motorcycle**. [BRIT]

motor|cycle /mouˈtərsaɪk°l/ (**motorcycles**) N-COUNT A **motorcycle** is a vehicle with two wheels and an engine.

motor|cyclist /mouˈtərsaɪklɪst/ (**motorcyclists**) N-COUNT A **motorcyclist** is a person who rides a motorcycle.

mo|tor|ing /mouˈtərɪŋ/ ADJ **Motoring** means relating to cars and driving. [mainly BRIT; AM usually **driving, automobile**] [ADJ n] ❑ *...a three-month sentence for motoring offences.*

mo|tor|ist /mouˈtərɪst/ (**motorists**) N-COUNT A **motorist** is a person who drives a car. [mainly BRIT; AM **driver**] ❑ *Police urged motorists to take extra care on the roads.*

mo|tor|ized /mouˈtəraɪzd/ [BRIT also **motorised**] **1** ADJ A **motorized** vehicle has an engine. ❑ *Around 1910 motorized carriages were beginning to replace horse-drawn cabs.* **2** ADJ A **motorized** group of soldiers is equipped with motor vehicles. ❑ *...motorized infantry and artillery.*

motor|way /mouˈtərweɪ/ (**motorways**) N-VAR A **motorway** is a major road that has been specially built for fast travel over long distances. Motorways have several lanes and special places where traffic gets on and leaves. [BRIT; AM usually **freeway**] ❑ *...the M1 motorway.*

mot|to /mɒtou/ (**mottoes** or **mottos**) N-COUNT A **motto** is a short sentence or phrase that expresses a rule for sensible behavior, especially a way of behaving in a particular situation. ❑ *The regiment's motto is "Nemo nos impune lacessit" (No one provokes us with impunity).*

mould /mould/ →see **mold**

mound /maund/ (**mounds**) **1** N-COUNT A **mound** of something is a large rounded pile of it. ❑ *The bulldozers piled up huge mounds of dirt.* **2** N-COUNT In baseball, the **mound** is the raised area where the pitcher stands when he or she throws the ball. ❑ *He went to the mound to talk with a struggling pitcher who spoke only Spanish.*

mount ♦♢♢ /maunt/ (**mounts, mounting, mounted**) **1** V-T If you **mount** a campaign or event, you organize it and make it take place. ❑ *The ANC announced it was mounting a major campaign of mass political protests.* **2** V-I If something **mounts**, it increases in intensity. ❑ *For several hours, tension mounted.* **3** V-I If something **mounts**, it increases in quantity. ❑ *The uncollected garbage mounts in city streets.* ● PHRASAL VERB To **mount up** means the same as to **mount**. ❑ *Her medical bills mounted up.* **4** V-T If you **mount** the stairs or a platform, you go up the stairs or go up onto the platform. [FORMAL] ❑ *Llewelyn was mounting the*

형용사 움직이지 않는 ❑ 그는 조각상처럼 몇 시간 동안 계속 움직이지 않고 버틸 수 있는 능력을 가졌다.

가산명사 영화 [주로 미국영어] ❑ 그곳이 바로 내가 처음으로 영화를 본 곳이다.

1 타동사 자극받다, 동기를 부여받다 ❑ 그들은 뭔가 성취해야 할 필요 때문에 움직인다. ● 의욕 있는 형용사 ❑ 의욕이 강한 직원들 ● 의욕 불가산명사 ❑ 그가 성적이 나쁜 이유는 읽기 능력이 부족해서라기보다 의욕이 없기 때문일지도 모른다. **2** 타동사 동기를 부여하다, 의욕이 생기게 하다 ❑ 어떻게 하면 사람들이 열심히 또 효율적으로 일하게 할 수 있을까? ● 동기 부여 불가산명사 ❑ 부모로부터 동기 부여만 있다면, 우리는 인간의 변화 능력에 대해 낙관적으로 생각한다.

가산명사 동기, 원동력 ❑ 나를 움직이는 힘은 돈이다.

가산명사 동기, 목적 ❑ 경찰은 살인 동기에서 금품 갈취를 배제했다.

1 가산명사 모터 ❑ 그녀는 차 안으로 들어가 시동을 걸었다. **2** 형용사 모터가 달린, 내연 기관이 달린 ❑ 자동차 절도가 15.9퍼센트 증가했다. **3** 형용사 자동차의 [주로 영국영어; 미국영어 대개 automotive, automobile] ❑ 영국 자동차 산업의 미래

1 가산명사 소형 오토바이, 스쿠터 [미국영어] **2** 가산명사 오토바이 [영국영어]

가산명사 오토바이

가산명사 오토바이 운전자

형용사 자동차와 관련된, 운전과 관련된 [주로 영국영어; 미국영어 대개 driving, automobile] ❑ 교통법 위반에 대한 3개월형

가산명사 운전자 [주로 영국영어; 미국영어 driver] ❑ 운전자에게 도로상에서 더욱 조심하도록 경찰이 촉구했다.

[영국영어 motorised] **1** 형용사 엔진이 달린 ❑ 대략 1910년에 자동차가 마차를 대체하기 시작했다. **2** 형용사 동력설비를 갖춘 ❑ 동력설비를 갖춘 보병대와 포병대

가산명사 또는 불가산명사 고속도로 [영국영어; 미국영어 대개 freeway] ❑ 고속도로 M1

가산명사 좌우명, 모토 ❑ 연대의 좌우명은 '우리를 자극하는 자는 반드시 응징한다.'이다.

1 가산명사 무더기 ❑ 불도저가 거대한 흙무더기를 쌓아올렸다. **2** 가산명사 마운드 ❑ 그는 마운드로 가 스페인 어밖에 몰라서 힘들어하는 투수와 이야기했다.

1 타동사 조직하다, 벌이다 ❑ 아프리카 민족 회의(ANC)가 대규모 집단 정치시위를 벌이고 있다고 발표했다. **2** 자동사 높아지다 ❑ 몇 시간 동안 긴장이 높아졌다. **3** 자동사 늘어나다 ❑ 도시 길거리에 미수거 쓰레기가 늘어나고 있다. ● 구동사 늘어나다 ❑ 그녀의 의료비용은 늘어나 갔다. **4** 타동사 오르다 [격식체] ❑ 르웰린이 망루로 통하는 계단을 올라가고 있었다. **5** 타동사/자동사 타다 ❑ 안전 헬멧을 쓴 남자가

stairs up into the keep. **5** V-T/V-I If you **mount** a horse or motorcycle, you climb on to it so that you can ride it. ❑ *A man in a crash helmet was mounting a motorbike.* **6** V-T If you **mount** an object **on** something, you fix it there firmly. ❑ *Her husband mounts the work on velour paper and makes the frame.* ● **-mounted** COMB in ADJ ❑ *...a wall-mounted electric fan.* **7** V-T If you **mount** an exhibition or display, you organize and present it. ❑ *The gallery has mounted an exhibition of art by Irish women painters.* **8** N-IN-NAMES **Mount** is used as part of the name of a mountain. ❑ *...Mount Everest.* **9** →see also **mounted**

오토바이를 타고 있었다. **6** 타동사 고정시키다, 설치하다 ❑ 그녀의 남편이 벨루어 종이에 작품을 고정시키고 틀을 만든다. ● -에 고정된, -에 설치된 복합형-형용사 ❑ 벽에 단 선풍기 **7** 타동사 열다 ❑ 미술관이 아일랜드 여성 화가 작품 전시회를 열었다. **8** 이름명사 산 이름에 고유 명사처럼 사용 ❑ 에베레스트 산

mountain ♦♦◇ /ma͟ʊnt³n, BRIT ma͟ʊntɪn/ (**mountains**) **1** N-COUNT A **mountain** is a very high area of land with steep sides. ❑ *Ben Nevis, in Scotland, is Britain's highest mountain.* **2** QUANT If you talk about a **mountain of** something, or **mountains of** something, you are emphasizing that there is a large amount of it. [INFORMAL, EMPHASIS] [QUANT of pl-n/n-uncount] ❑ *They are faced with a mountain of bureaucracy.* **3** PHRASE If you say that someone has **a mountain to climb**, you mean that it will be difficult for them to achieve what they want to achieve. [JOURNALISM] ❑ *"We had a mountain to climb after the second goal went in," said Crosby.* →see Picture Dictionary: mountain

1 가산명사 산 ❑ 스코틀랜드에 있는 벤네비스는 영국에서 가장 높은 산이다. **2** 수량사 산더미 [비격식체, 강조] ❑ 그들이 처리해야 할 행정 절차가 산더미 같다. **3** 구 넘어야 할 산, 고비 [언론] ❑ "두 번째 골이 터진 후로 우리는 고비를 맞았다."라고 크로스비가 말했다.

mountain bike (**mountain bikes**) N-COUNT A **mountain bike** is a type of bicycle that is suitable for riding over rough ground. It has a strong frame and thick tires.

가산명사 산악자전거

mountaineer /ma͟ʊntᵊnɪ͟ər/ (**mountaineers**) N-COUNT A **mountaineer** is a person who is skillful at climbing the steep sides of mountains.

가산명사 등반가

mountainous /ma͟ʊntᵊnəs/ **1** ADJ A **mountainous** place has a lot of mountains. ❑ *...the mountainous region of Campania.* **2** ADJ You use **mountainous** to emphasize that something is great in size, quantity, or degree. [EMPHASIS] [ADJ n] ❑ *The plan is designed to reduce some of the company's mountainous debt.*

1 형용사 산이 많은, 산악성의 ❑ 캄파니아 산악 지대 **2** 형용사 산더미 같은 [강조] ❑ 그 계획은 산더미 같은 회사 부채의 일부를 줄이기 위해 고안된 것이다.

mountainside /ma͟ʊntᵊnsaɪd/ (**mountainsides**) N-COUNT A **mountainside** is one of the steep sides of a mountain. ❑ *The couple trudged up the dark mountainside.*

가산명사 산허리, 산중턱 ❑ 그 둘은 어두운 산허리를 힘겹게 올라갔다.

mounted /ma͟ʊntɪd/ ADJ **Mounted** police or soldiers ride horses when they are on duty. [ADJ n] ❑ *A dozen mounted police rode into the square.* →see also **mount**

형용사 말을 탄 ❑ 기마경찰 12명이 광장으로 달려갔다.

mourn /mɔ͟rn/ (**mourns, mourning, mourned**) **1** V-T/V-I If you **mourn** someone who has died or **mourn for** them, you are very sad that they have died and show your sorrow in the way that you behave. ❑ *Joan still mourns her father.* ❑ *He mourned for his valiant one.* **2** V-T/V-I If you **mourn** something or **mourn for** it, you regret that you no longer have it and show your regret in the way that you behave. ❑ *We mourned the loss of our cities.*

1 타동사/자동사 애도하다 ❑ 조앤은 아직까지도 아버지의 죽음을 슬퍼한다. ❑ 그는 용맹한 부하들의 죽음을 애도했다. **2** 타동사/자동사 한탄하다, 아쉬워하다 ❑ 우리는 도시를 잃고 한탄했다.

mourner /mɔ͟rnər/ (**mourners**) N-COUNT A **mourner** is a person who attends a funeral, especially as a relative or friend of the dead person. ❑ *Weeks after his death, mourners still gather outside the house.* →see **funeral**

가산명사 조문객, 애도자 ❑ 그가 운명한지 몇 주가 지났는데도 아직 조문객들이 집 밖에 모여든다.

mournful /mɔ͟rnfəl/ **1** ADJ If you are **mournful**, you are very sad. ❑ *He looked mournful, even near to tears.* ● **mournfully** ADV ❑ *He stood mournfully at the gate waving bye bye.* **2** ADJ A **mournful** sound seems very sad. ❑ *...the mournful wail of bagpipes.*

1 형용사 구슬픈 ❑ 그는 금방이라도 눈물을 흘릴 것처럼 매우 슬퍼 보였다. ● 구슬프게 부사 ❑ 그가 탑승구 옆에서 슬픈 모습으로 손을 흔들며 서 있었다. **2** 형용사 구슬픈 ❑ 백파이프의 구슬픈 소리

mouse /ma͟ʊs/ (**mice**) **1** N-COUNT A **mouse** is a small furry animal with a long tail. ❑ *...a mouse running in a wheel in its cage.* **2** N-COUNT A **mouse** is a device that is connected to a computer. By moving it over a flat surface and pressing its buttons, you can move the cursor around the screen and do things without

1 가산명사 쥐 ❑ 우리에 갇혀 쳇바퀴 속을 돌고 있는 쥐 **2** 가산명사 마우스 ❑ 메시지 작성은 끝났다. 이제 그녀가 해야 할 일은 마우스를 클릭하는 것뿐이었다.

Picture Dictionary   mountain

ridge   pass   peak   cliff   summit   glacier

using the keyboard. ❑ *Her message had been written, all she had to do was click the mouse.*

mouse mat (mouse mats) also **mousemat** N-COUNT A **mouse mat** is the same as **mouse pad** [BRIT]

가산명사 마우스 패드 [영국영어]

mouse pad (mouse pads) also **mousepad** N-COUNT A **mouse pad** is a flat piece of plastic or some other material that you rest the mouse on while using a computer. [mainly AM]

가산명사 마우스 패드 [주로 미국영어]

mousse /muːs/ (**mousses**) ◾ N-VAR **Mousse** is a sweet light food made from eggs and cream. It is often flavored with fruit or chocolate. ❑ *... a rich chocolate mousse.* ◿ N-MASS **Mousse** is a soft substance containing a lot of tiny bubbles, for example one that you can put in your hair to make it easier to shape into a particular style. ❑ *He had even put mousse in his hair.* →see **dessert**

◾ 가산명사 또는 불가산명사 (음식) 무스 ❑ 풍부한 맛의 초콜릿 무스 ◿ 물질명사 무스 ❑ 그는 머리에 무스도 바르고 있었다.

mous|tache /mʊstæʃ, BRIT məstɑːʃ/ →see **mustache**

mouth (**mouths, mouthing, mouthed**)

| The noun is pronounced /maʊθ/. The verb is pronounced /maʊð/. The plural of the noun and the third person singular of the verb are both pronounced /maʊðz/. |

명사는 /maʊθ/로 발음되고, 동사는 /maʊð/로 발음된다. 명사의 복수형이거나 동사의 3인칭 단수형은 모두 /maʊðz/로 발음된다.

◾ N-COUNT Your **mouth** is the area of your face where your lips are or the space behind your lips where your teeth and tongue are. ❑ *She clamped her hand against her mouth.* ● **-mouthed** /-maʊðd/ COMB in ADJ ❑ *He straightened up and looked at me, open-mouthed.* ◿ N-COUNT You can say that someone has a particular kind of **mouth** to indicate that they speak in a particular kind of way or that they say particular kinds of things. ❑ *I've always had a loud mouth, I refuse to be silenced.* ● **-mouthed** COMB in ADJ ❑ *Simon, their smart-mouthed teenage son.* ◼ N-COUNT The **mouth** of a cave, hole, or bottle is its entrance or opening. ❑ *By the mouth of the tunnel he bent to retie his lace.* ● **-mouthed** COMB in ADJ ❑ *He put the flowers in a wide-mouthed blue vase.* ◾ N-COUNT The **mouth** of a river is the place where it flows into the sea. ❑ *...the town at the mouth of the River Dart.* ◗ V-T If you **mouth** something, you form words with your lips without making any sound. ❑ *I mouthed a goodbye and hurried in behind Momma.* ◙ PHRASE If you have a number of **mouths to feed**, you have the responsibility of earning enough money to feed and take care of that number of people. ❑ *He had to feed his family on the equivalent of four hundred pounds a month and, with five mouths to feed, he found this very hard.* ◚ PHRASE If you say that someone does not **open** their **mouth**, you are emphasizing that they never say anything at all. [EMPHASIS] ❑ *Sometimes I hardly dare open my mouth.* ◛ PHRASE If you **keep** your **mouth shut** about something, you do not talk about it, especially because it is a secret. ❑ *You wouldn't be here now if she'd kept her mouth shut.* ◜ to **live hand to mouth** →see **hand**. **heart in** your **mouth** →see **heart**. **from the horse's mouth** →see **horse**. to **put** your **money where** your **mouth is** →see **money**. **shut** your **mouth** →see **shut**. **word of mouth** →see **word**
→see **face, respiratory**

◾ 가산명사 입 ❑ 그녀는 손으로 입을 꽉 막았다. ● 입이 –한 복합형-형용사 ❑ 그는 일어서서 입을 벌린 채로 나를 바라보았다. ◿ 가산명사 말 ❑ 나는 원래 말이 많은 사람이다. 입 다물고 있지 않겠다. ● –하게 말하는 복합형-형용사 ❑ 말을 똑똑하게 잘하는 그들의 십대 아들 사이먼 ◼ 가산명사 입구, 주둥이 ❑ 그가 터널 입구에서 신발끈을 고쳐 매려고 몸을 굽혔다. ● 입구가 –한, 주둥이가 –한 복합형-형용사 ❑ 그는 주둥이가 넓은 푸른색 꽃병에 꽃을 꽂았다. ◾ 가산명사 어귀 ❑ 다트 강어귀에 있는 마을 ◗ 타동사 소리 없이 입 모양으로 말하다 ❑ 나는 입 모양으로만 작별 인사를 하고 재빨리 엄마 뒤로 갔다. ◙ 구 먹여 살려야 할 사람 ❑ 그는 한 달에 400파운드 정도밖에 벌어 가족을 부양해야 했는데 다섯 식구를 먹여 살려야 했으니 이것이 너무나도 힘들었다. ◚ 구 입을 열다, 말하다 [강조] ❑ 나는 가끔 입을 열 엄두조차 내지 못한다. ◛ 구 입 다물다, 비밀을 지키다 ❑ 그녀가 입을 다물었더라면 네가 지금 이 자리에 없을 것이다.

Word Partnership   *mouth*의 연어

| ADJ. | **big** mouth ◾ ◿ |
| V. | **close** *your* mouth, **keep** *your* mouth **closed/shut**, **shut** *your* mouth ◾ ◛ |

mouth|ful /maʊθfʊl/ (**mouthfuls**) ◾ N-COUNT A **mouthful of** drink or food is the amount that you put or have in your mouth. ❑ *She gulped down a mouthful of coffee.* ◿ N-SING If you describe a long word or phrase as a **mouthful**, you mean that it is difficult to say. [INFORMAL] ❑ *It's called the Pan-Caribbean Disaster Preparedness and Prevention Project, which is quite a mouthful.*

◾ 가산명사 한 입 가득 ❑ 그녀가 커피를 한 입 가득 들이켰다. ◿ 단수명사 발음하기 어려운 [비격식체] ❑ 이 계획은 '카리브 전역 재해 방지 예방 프로젝트'라는 발음하기도 어려운 긴 이름으로 불린다.

mouth|piece /maʊθpiːs/ (**mouthpieces**) ◾ N-COUNT The **mouthpiece** of a telephone is the part that you speak into. ❑ *He shouted into the mouthpiece.* ◿ N-COUNT The **mouthpiece** of a musical instrument or other device is the part that you put into your mouth. ❑ *He showed him how to blow into the ivory mouthpiece.* ◼ N-COUNT The **mouthpiece** of an organization or person is someone who informs other people of the opinions and policies of that organization or person. ❑ *Their mouthpiece is the vice-president.* →see **scuba diving**

◾ 가산명사 송화기 ❑ 그는 전화기에 대고 소리쳤다. ◿ 가산명사 마우스피스 (악기 등의 입술이 닿는 부분) ❑ 그가 그 남자에게 상아 마우스피스를 부는 방법을 보여 줬다. ◼ 가산명사 대변인 ❑ 그들의 대변인은 부통령이다.

Word Link   *mov* ≈ *moving* : *movable, movement, movie*

mov|able /muːvəbᵊl/ also **moveable** ADJ Something that is **movable** can be moved from one place or position to another. ❑ *It's a vinyl doll with movable arms and legs.*

형용사 움직일 수 있는 ❑ 이것은 팔과 다리를 움직일 수 있는 플라스틱 인형이다.

move ◆◆◆ /muːv/ (**moves, moving, moved**) ◾ V-T/V-I When you **move** something or when it **moves**, its position changes and it does not remain still. ❑ *She moved the sheaf of papers into position.* ❑ *A traffic warden asked him to move his car.* ❑ *The train began to move.* ◿ V-I When you **move**, you change your position or go to a different place. ❑ *She waited for him to get up, but he didn't move.* ❑ *He moved around the room, putting his possessions together.* ● N-COUNT **Move** is also a noun. ❑ *The doctor made a move towards the door.* ◼ V-I If you **move**, you act or you begin to do something. ❑ *Industrialists must move fast to take advantage of new opportunities in Eastern Europe.* ◾ N-COUNT A **move** is an action that you take in order to achieve something. ❑ *The one point cut in interest rates was a wise move.* ❑ *It may also be a good move to suggest she talks things over.* ◗ V-T/V-I If a person or company **moves**, they leave the building where they have been living or working, and they go to live or work in a different place, taking their possessions with them. ❑ *Two people in love are a home wherever they are, no matter how often they move.* ❑ *She had often considered moving to London.* ● N-COUNT **Move** is also a noun. ❑ *Modigliani announced his move to Montparnasse in 1909.* ◙ V-T If people in authority **move** someone, they make that person go from one place

◾ 타동사/자동사 옮기다; 움직이다 ❑ 그녀가 종이 다발을 제자리에 놓았다. ❑ 교통경찰이 그에게 차를 올리라고 말했다. ❑ 기차가 움직이기 시작했다. ◿ 자동사 움직이다 ❑ 그녀는 그가 일어나기를 기다렸지만 그는 움직이지 않았다. ❑ 그가 방 안을 돌아다니면서 자기 물건을 챙겼다. ● 가산명사 움직임 ❑ 의사가 문을 향해 움직였다. ◼ 자동사 움직이다, 행동하다 ❑ 기업인들은 빠르게 움직여 동유럽에서의 새로운 기회를 이용해야 한다. ◾ 가산명사 조치, 수단 ❑ 금리 1퍼센트 인하는 현명한 조치였다. ❑ 그녀에게 문제를 솔직하게 이야기해 보라고 제안하는 것도 좋은 방법일 수 있다. ◗ 타동사/자동사 이사하다, 이전하다 ❑ 사랑에 빠진 두 사람은 어디에 있건 얼마나 자주 이사를 하건 제집처럼 느낀다. ❑ 그녀는 런던으로 이사할 생각을 했었다. ● 가산명사 이사, 이전 ❑ 모딜리아니가 1909년에 몽파르나스로 거처를 옮긴다고 발표했다. ◙ 타동사 발령하다 ❑ 상부에서

or job to another one. ❑ *His superiors moved him to another parish.* **7** V-T/V-I If you **move from** one job or interest **to** another, you change to it. ❑ *He moved from being an extramural tutor to being a lecturer in social history.* ● N-COUNT **Move** is also a noun. ❑ *His move to the chairmanship means he will take a less active role in day-to-day management.* **8** V-I If you **move to** a new topic in a conversation, you start talking about something different. ❑ *Let's move to another subject, Dan.* **9** V-T If you **move** an event or the date of an event, you change the time at which it happens. ❑ *The club has moved its meeting to Saturday, January 22nd.* **10** V-I If you **move** toward a particular state, activity, or opinion, you start to be in that state, do that activity, or have that opinion. ❑ *The Labour Party has moved to the right and become like your Democratic Party.* ● N-COUNT **Move** is also a noun. ❑ *His move to the left was not a sudden leap but a natural working out of ideas.* **11** V-I If a situation or process **is moving**, it is developing or progressing, rather than staying still. [usu cont] ❑ *Events are moving fast.* **12** V-T If you say that you will not **be moved**, you mean that you have come to a decision and nothing will change your mind. [usu passive, with neg] ❑ *Everyone thought I was mad to go back, but I wouldn't be moved.* **13** V-T If something **moves** you **to** do something, it influences you and causes you to do it. ❑ *It was punk that first moved him to join a band seriously.* **14** V-T If something **moves** you, it has an effect on your emotions and causes you to feel sadness or sympathy for another person. ❑ *These stories surprised and moved me.* ● **moved** ADJ [v-link ADJ] ❑ *Those who listened to him were deeply moved.* **15** V-I If you say that someone **moves** in a particular society, circle, or world, you mean that they know people in a particular social class or group and spend most of their time with them. ❑ *She moves in high-society circles in London.* **16** V-T At a meeting, if you **move** a motion, you formally suggest it so that everyone present can vote on it. ❑ *Somebody needs to move an amendment.* **17** N-COUNT A **move** is an act of putting a chess piece or other counter in a different position on a board when it is your turn to do so in a game. ❑ *With no idea of what to do for my next move, my hand hovered over the board.* **18** PHRASE If you say that one **false move** will cause a disaster, you mean that you or someone else must not make any mistakes because the situation is so difficult or dangerous. ❑ *He knew one false move would end in death.* **19** PHRASE If you **make a move**, you prepare or begin to leave one place and go somewhere else. ❑ *He glanced at his wristwatch. "I suppose we'd better make a move."* **20** PHRASE If you **make a move**, you take a course of action. ❑ *The week before the deal was supposed to close, fifteen Japanese banks made a move to pull out.* **21** PHRASE If you are **on the move**, you are going from one place to another. ❑ *Jack never wanted to stay in one place for very long, so they were always on the move.* **22** to **move the goalposts** →see goalpost. to **move a muscle** →see muscle

▶ **move in 1** PHRASAL VERB When you **move in** somewhere, you begin to live there as your home. ❑ *Her house was in perfect order when she moved in.* ❑ *Her husband had moved in with a younger woman.* **2** PHRASAL VERB If police, soldiers, or attackers **move in**, they go toward a place or person in order to deal with or attack them. ❑ *There were violent and chaotic scenes when police moved in to disperse the crowd.* **3** PHRASAL VERB If someone **moves in on** an area of activity which was previously only done by a particular group of people, they start becoming involved with it for the first time. ❑ *Organized crime is moving in on e-commerce.*

▶ **move off** PHRASAL VERB When you **move off**, you start moving away from a place. ❑ *Gil waved his hand and the car moved off.*

▶ **move on 1** PHRASAL VERB When you **move on** somewhere, you leave the place where you have been staying or waiting and go there. ❑ *Mr. Brooke moved on from Paris to Belgrade.* **2** PHRASAL VERB If someone such as a police officer **moves** you **on**, they order you to stop standing in a particular place and to go somewhere else. ❑ *Eventually the police were called to move them on.* **3** PHRASAL VERB If you **move on**, you finish or stop one activity and start doing something different. ❑ *She ran this shop for ten years before deciding to move on to fresh challenges.*

▶ **move out** PHRASAL VERB If you **move out**, you stop living in a particular house or place and go to live somewhere else. ❑ *The harassment had become too much to tolerate and he decided to move out.*

▶ **move over 1** PHRASAL VERB If you **move over to** a new system or way of doing something, you change to it. ❑ *The government is having to introduce some difficult changes, particularly in moving over to a market economy.* **2** PHRASAL VERB If someone **moves over**, they leave their job or position in order to let someone else have it. ❑ *They said Mr. Jenkins should make balanced programs about the Black community or move over and let someone else who can.* **3** PHRASAL VERB If you **move over**, you change your position in order to make room for someone else. ❑ *Move over and let me drive.*

▶ **move up 1** PHRASAL VERB If you **move up**, you change your position, especially in order to be nearer someone or to make room for someone else. ❑ *Move up, John, and let the lady sit down.* **2** PHRASAL VERB If someone or something **moves up**, they go to a higher level, grade, or class. ❑ *Share prices moved up.*

move|able /mˈuːvəbᵊl/ →see movable

| **Word Link** | ment ≈ state, condition : agreement, management, movement |

| **Word Link** | mov ≈ moving : movable, movement, movie |

move|ment ♦♦◇ /mˈuːvmənt/ (**movements**) **1** N-COUNT A **movement** is a group of people who share the same beliefs, ideas, or aims. ❑ *It's part of a broader Hindu nationalist movement that's gaining strength throughout the country.* **2** N-VAR **Movement** involves changing position or going from one place to another. ❑ *They actually monitor the movement of the fish going up river.* ❑ *There was*

그를 다른 교구로 발령했다. **7** 타동사/자동사 바꾸다 ❑ 그는 시간 강사에서 사회학 전임 강사로 일을 바꿨다. ● 가산명사 바꿈 ❑ 그가 회장이 된다는 것은 실제적인 경영에서의 역할이 그만큼 줄어들기 됨을 뜻한다. **8** 자동사 주제를 바꾸다 ❑ 댄, 이제 다른 이야기로 넘어가 보죠. **9** 타동사 날짜를 바꾸다 ❑ 클럽이 회의 날짜를 1월 22일 토요일로 바꿨다. **10** 자동사 변하다 ❑ 노동당이 우파 성향을 띠기 시작하면서 당신들의 민주당처럼 되었다. ● 가산명사 변화 ❑ 그의 좌경화는 갑작스러운 변화가 아니라 자연스러운 사상의 전환이었다. **11** 자동사 움직이고 있다, 진행되고 있다 ❑ 상황이 빠르게 진행되고 있다. **12** 타동사 흔들리다 ❑ 내가 돌아가는 것을 모두들 미친 짓이라고 생각했지만 나는 흔들리지 않았다. **13** 타동사 -하도록 영향을 주다 ❑ 그가 처음으로 진지하게 밴드 활동을 하게 된 계기는 펑크 때문이었다. **14** 타동사 감동시키다 ❑ 나는 이들 이야기를 읽고 놀라고 감동했다. ● 감동받은 형용사 ❑ 그의 이야기를 들은 사람들은 깊이 감동받았다. **15** 자동사 활동하다, 어울리다 ❑ 그녀는 런던 상류 사회 사람들과 어울린다. **16** 타동사 동의하다, 제안하다 ❑ 누군가 수정을 제안해야 한다. **17** 가산명사 (체스) 수, 말의 움직임 ❑ 다음 수를 어디에 놔야 할지 알 수가 없어 내 손이 체스판 위에 멈춰 있었다. **18** 구 실수 ❑ 그는 한 번의 실수로 죽을 수도 있다는 사실을 알고 있었다. **19** 구 슬슬 떠나다, 슬슬 움직여 보다 ❑ 그가 손목시계를 보며 말했다. "우리 이제 슬슬 가봐야 하겠는걸." **20** 구 조치를 취하다 ❑ 계약 성사를 일주일 앞두고 일본 은행 15개가 철회 조치를 취했다. **21** 구 이동 중인 ❑ 잭이 한 곳에 오래 머물려 하지 않아서 그들은 항상 옮겨 다녔다.

1 구동사 이사 오다 ❑ 그녀가 이사 왔을 때 집이 완벽하게 정리돼있었다. ❑ 그녀의 남편이 젊은 여자를 데리고 들어와 있었다. **2** 구동사 개입하다 ❑ 경찰이 군중을 해산시키기 위해 개입했을 때 폭력이 난무하는 혼란이 벌어지고 있었다. **3** 구동사 새로 진출하다 ❑ 조직범죄가 전자 상거래 쪽으로 새로 진출하고 있다.

구동사 떠나기 시작하다 ❑ 길이 손을 흔들었다. 차가 떠나기 시작했다.

1 구동사 떠나다 ❑ 브룩 씨는 파리를 떠나 베오그라드로 향했다. **2** 구동사 이동시키다 ❑ 결국 경찰을 불러 그들을 이동시켰다. **3** 구동사 다른 일을 시작하다 ❑ 그녀는 새로운 도전을 해보기로 결심하기 전에 10년 동안 이 가게를 운영했다.

구동사 이사 가다 ❑ 견딜 수 없을 정도로 괴롭힘을 당한 나머지 그는 이사 가기로 결심했다.

1 구동사 -로 전환하다 ❑ 정부가 특히 시장 경제로 전환하는 과정에서 몇 가지 어려운 변화를 도입해야 할 것이다. **2** 구동사 자리를 내주다 ❑ 젠킨스 씨가 흑인 사회에 대한 균형 있는 프로그램을 만들든지, 아니면 그렇게 할 수 있는 다른 누군가에게 자리를 넘기든지 해야 한다고 그들이 말했다. **3** 구동사 비키다 ❑ 비켜 봐. 내가 운전할게.

1 구동사 자리를 좁히다 ❑ 존, 숙녀분이 앉을 수 있게 자리 좀 좁혀봐. **2** 구동사 올라가다, 상승하다 ❑ 주가가 상승했다.

1 가산명사 운동 ❑ 이는 전국적으로 힘을 얻고 있는 힌두 민족주의 운동의 일부이다. **2** 가산불가산명사 움직임, 이동 ❑ 그들은 강을 거슬러 올라가는 물고기의 움직임을 실제로 관찰했다. ❑ 뒷문 쪽에서 무언가가 움직였다. **3** 가산명사 또는

movement behind the window in the back door. ▣ N-VAR A **movement** is a planned change in position that an army makes during a battle or military exercise. ❑ *There are reports of fresh troop movements across the border.* ▣ N-VAR **Movement** is a gradual development or change of an attitude, opinion, or policy. ❑ *...the movement towards democracy in Latin America.* ▣ N-PLURAL Your **movements** are everything which you do or plan to do during a period of time. ❑ *I want a full account of your movements the night Mr. Gower was killed.*

불가산명사 움직임, 이동 ▣ 군대가 국경을 넘어 다시 움직이는 중이라는 보도가 있다. ▣ 가산명사 또는 불가산명사 이행, 동향 ❑ 라틴아메리카의 민주주의로의 이행 ▣ 복수명사 행적 ❑ 가우어 씨가 살해되던 날 밤 당신의 행적을 자세하게 알고 싶습니다.

Word Partnership   *movement*의 연어

N.	**freedom** movement, **labor** movement, **leader of a** movement, **peace** movement, **reform** movement ▣
ADJ.	**environmental** movement, **political** movement ▣
	rapid movement, **slow** movement, **sudden** movement ▣

---

mov|er /muːvər/ (**movers**) PHRASE The **movers and shakers** in a place or area of activity are the people who have most power or influence. ❑ *It is the movers and shakers of the record industry who will decide which bands make it.*

구 유력 인사 ❑ 성공하는 밴드를 결정하는 사람들은 바로 음반업계의 유력 인사들이다.

Word Link   *mov ≈ moving : movable, movement, movie*

---

movie ♦♦◇ /muːvi/ (**movies**) ▣ N-COUNT A **movie** is a series of moving picture that have been recorded so that they can be shown in a theater or on television. A movie tells a story, or shows a real situation. [AM, also BRIT, INFORMAL] ❑ *In the first movie Tony Curtis ever made he played a grocery clerk.*

▣ 가산명사 영화 [미국, 영국영어, 비격식체] ❑ 토니 커티스는 맨 첫 영화에서 식료품점 점원을 연기했다.

An **Oscar** is the nickname for the golden statue given as the prize to those films considered the best each year. Also known as the **Academy Awards**, these prizes also recognize the talent of actors, writers, designers and other staff members. Not only American movies but also foreign films are included.

Oscar(오스카)는 매년 최고로 선정된 영화에 상으로 주는 황금상의 별칭이다. Academy Awards(아카데미상)라고도 알려진 이 상은 배우, 작가, 디자이너 및 다른 제작 관련자들의 재능을 인정해 주며, 미국 영화뿐만 아니라 외국 영화도 수상에 포함한다.

▣ N-PLURAL You can talk about **the movies** when you are talking about seeing a movie in a movie theater. [mainly AM; BRIT usually **the cinema**] ❑ *He took her to the movies.* →see DVD

▣ 복수명사 영화 관람 [주로 미국영어; 영국영어 대개 the cinema] ❑ 그는 그녀를 데리고 영화를 보러 갔다.

Word Partnership   *movie*의 연어

ADJ.	**bad/good** movie, **favorite** movie, **new/old** movie, **popular** movie ▣
N.	**scene in a** movie, movie **screen**, movie **set**, movie **studio**, **television/TV** movie ▣
V.	**go to a** movie, **see a** movie, **watch a** movie ▣

---

movie|goer /muːvigoʊər/ (**moviegoers**) also **movie-goer** N-COUNT A **moviegoer** is a person who often goes to the movies. [AM; BRIT usually **cinema-goer, film-goer**] ❑ *What is it about Tom Hanks that moviegoers find so appealing?*

가산명사 영화팬 [미국영어; 영국영어 대개 cinema-goer, film-goer] ❑ 영화팬들이 톰 행크스의 어떤 면을 그렇게 매력적이라고 생각하는 걸까?

movie star (**movie stars**) N-COUNT A **movie star** is a famous actor or actress who appears in movies. [mainly AM; BRIT usually **film star**]

가산명사 영화배우 [주로 미국영어; 영국영어 대개 film star]

movie thea|ter (**movie theaters**) N-COUNT A **movie theater** is a place where people go to watch movies for entertainment. [AM; BRIT **cinema**]

가산명사 영화관 [미국영어; 영국영어 cinema]

mov|ing /muːvɪŋ/ ▣ ADJ If something is **moving**, it makes you feel strongly an emotion such as sadness, pity, or sympathy. ❑ *It is very moving to see how much strangers can care for each other.* ● **mov|ing|ly** ADV [ADV with v] ❑ *You write very movingly of your sister Amy's suicide.* ▣ ADJ A **moving** model or part of a machine moves or is able to move. [ADJ n] ❑ *It also means there are no moving parts to break down.*

▣ 형용사 감동적인 ❑ 낯선 사람들이 서로를 얼마나 아낄 수 있는지를 보는 것은 정말 감동적이다. ● 감동적으로 부사 ❑ 언니 에이미의 자살에 대한 당신의 글은 정말 감동적이에요. ▣ 형용사 움직이는 ❑ 이는 움직이는 부분은 고장 나는 게 없다는 뜻이다.

mow /moʊ/ (**mows, mowing, mowed, mown**)

The past participle can be either **mowed** or **mown**.

과거 분사는 mowed 또는 mown이다.

V-T/V-I If you **mow** an area of grass, you cut it using a machine called a lawn mower. ❑ *He continued to mow the lawn and do other routine chores.*

타동사/자동사 잔디를 깎다 ❑ 그는 계속해서 잔디를 깎고 다른 일상적이고 자질구레한 일들을 했다.

▶**mow down** PHRASAL VERB If someone **is mown down**, they are killed violently by a vehicle or gunfire. ❑ *She was mown down on a pedestrian crossing.*

구동사 깔려 죽다; 총살되다 ❑ 그녀는 횡단보도에서 차에 깔려 죽었다.

mow|er /moʊər/ (**mowers**) ▣ N-COUNT A **mower** is the same as a **lawnmower**. ▣ N-COUNT A **mower** is a machine that has sharp blades for cutting something such as corn or wheat.

▣ 가산명사 잔디 깎는 기계, 예초기 ▣ 가산명사 수확기

MP ♦♦◇ /ɛm piː/ (**MPs**) N-COUNT In Britain, an **MP** is a person who has been elected to represent the people from a particular area in the House of Commons. **MP** is an abbreviation for **Member of Parliament**. ❑ *Several Conservative MPs have voted against the government.* →see government

가산명사 (영국) 하원의원 ❑ 보수당 하원의원 몇 명이 정부에 반대하는 표를 던졌다.

MP3 /ɛm piː θriː/ N-UNCOUNT **MP3** is a kind of technology which enables you to record and play music from the Internet.

불가산명사 엠피쓰리3

MPEG /ɛmpɛg/ N-UNCOUNT **MPEG** is a standard file format for compressing video images so that they can be stored or sent by e-mail more easily. **MPEG** is an abbreviation for "Motion Picture Experts Group." [COMPUTING]

불가산명사 디지털 동영상 압축 기술 [컴퓨터]

mph mph is written after a number to indicate the speed of something such as a vehicle. **mph** is an abbreviation for "miles per hour." ❑ *Inside these zones, traffic speeds are restricted to 20 mph.*

시속 _마일 ❑ 이 구역 내의 차량 제한 속도는 시속 20마일이다.

Mr. ♦♦♦ /mɪstər/ [BRIT **Mr**] ▣ N-TITLE **Mr.** is used before a man's name when you are speaking or referring to him. ❑ *...Mr. Grant.* ❑ *...Mr. Bob Price.* ▣ N-VOC **Mr.** is sometimes used in front of words such as "President" and "Chairman" to address the man who holds the position mentioned. ❑ *Mr. President, you're aware of the system.* ▣ →see also **Messrs**

[영국영어 Mr] ▣ 경칭명사 (남자 이름) 씨 ❑ 그랜트 씨 ❑ 보브 프라이스 씨 ▣ 호격명사 관직명 앞에 써서 호칭으로 사용 ❑ 대통령님, 대통령께서는 이 시스템에 대해 알고 계십니다.

a
b
c
d
e
f
g
h
i
j
k
l
m
n
o
p
q
r
s
t
u
v
w
x
y
z

A B C D E F G H I J K L **M** N O P Q R S T U V W X Y Z

Mrs. ♦♦♦ /mɪsɪz/ [BRIT **Mrs**] N-TITLE **Mrs.** is used before the name of a married woman when you are speaking or referring to her. ❑ *Hello, Mrs. Miles.* ❑ *...Mrs. Anne Pritchard.*

[영영영어 Mrs] 경칭명사 - 씨 부인, - 여사 ❑ 마일스 부인, 안녕하세요. ❑ 앤 프리챠드 여사

Ms. ♦♦♦ /mɪz/ [BRIT **Ms**] N-TITLE **Ms.** is used, especially in written English, before a woman's name when you are speaking to her or referring to her. If you use **Ms.**, you are not specifying if the woman is married or not. ❑ *...Ms. Brown.*

[영영영어 Ms] 경칭명사 (여자 이름) 씨 ❑ 브라운 씨

MSP /ɛm ɛs piː/ (**MSPs**) N-COUNT An **MSP** is someone who has been elected as a member of the Scottish Parliament. **MSP** is an abbreviation for "Member of the Scottish Parliament." ❑ *... a committee of MSPs.*

가산명사 스코틀랜드 의회 의원 ❑ 스코틀랜드 의원 위원회

much ♦♦♦ /mʌtʃ/ **1** ADV You use **much** to indicate the great intensity, extent, or degree of something such as an action, feeling, or change. **Much** is usually used with "so," "too," and "very," and in negative clauses with this meaning. [ADV after v] ❑ *She laughs too much.* ❑ *Thank you very much.* **2** ADV If something does not happen **much**, it does not happen very often. ❑ *He said that his father never talked much about the war.* ❑ *Gwen had not seen her Daddy all that much, because mostly he worked on the ships.* **3** ADV You use **much** in front of "too" or comparative adjectives and adverbs in order to emphasize that there is a large amount of a particular quality. [EMPHASIS] ❑ *The skin is much too delicate.* **4** ADV If one thing is **much** the same as another thing, it is very similar to it. ❑ *The day ended much as it began.* **5** DET You use **much** to indicate that you are referring to a large amount of a substance or thing. ❑ *They are grown on the hillsides in full sun, without much water.* ❑ *Japan has been reluctant to offer much aid to Russia.* ● PRON **Much** is also a pronoun. ❑ *...eating too much and drinking too much.* ● QUANT **Much** is also a quantifier. [QUANT of def-n-uncount/def-sing-n] ❑ *Much of the time we do not notice that we are solving problems.* **6** ADV You use **much** in expressions such as **not much**, **not very much**, and **too much** when replying to questions about amounts. [ADV as reply] ❑ *"Can you hear it where you live?" He shook his head. "Not much."* **7** QUANT If you do not see much of someone, you do not see them very often. [with brd-neg, QUANT of n-proper/pron] ❑ *I don't see much of Tony nowadays.* **8** DET You use **much** in the expression **how much** to ask questions about amounts or degrees, and also in reported clauses and statements to give information about the amount or degree of something. ❑ *How much money can I afford?* ● ADV **Much** is also an adverb. ❑ *She knows how much this upsets me but she persists in doing it.* ● PRON **Much** is also a pronoun. [how PRON] ❑ *How much do you earn?* **9** DET You use **much** in the expression **as much** when you are comparing amounts. ❑ *I shall try, with as much patience as is possible, to explain yet again.* ❑ *Their aim will be to produce as much milk as possible.*

1 부사 많이, 대단히 ❑ 그녀는 너무 많이 웃는다. ❑ 대단히 감사합니다. **2** 부사 자주, 많이 ❑ 아버지가 전쟁에 대해 자주 이야기하지 않았다고 그가 말했다. ❑ 그웬은 아버지를 그리 자주 보지 못했다. 아버지가 주로 배에서 일하셨기 때문이다. **3** 부사 매우, 지나치게 [강조] ❑ 피부가 지나치게 민감하다. **4** 부사 아주 ❑ 하루가 시작할 때와 아주 비슷하게 끝났다. **5** 한정사 많은 ❑ 이들은 햇볕은 흠뻑 내리쬐되 물은 별로 많지 않은 산허리에서 자란다. ❑ 일본은 러시아에 대한 대규모 지원을 꺼려해 왔다. ● 대명사 많은 ❑ 너무 많이 먹고 너무 많이 마시는 것 ● 수량사 상당 부분, 많은 양 ❑ 상당 시간 동안 우리는 문제를 풀고 있다는 사실조차 자각하지 못한다. **6** 부사 many을 묻는 질문에 대한 대답에 사용 ❑ "네가 사는 곳에서 그게 들리니?" 그가 고개를 저었다. "잘 안 들려." **7** 수량사 자주 ❑ 나는 요즘 토니를 자주 못 봐. **8** 한정사 'how much 명사' 구문으로 양이나 정도를 묻는 의문문에서 사용 ❑ 내가 돈이 얼마나 있지? ● 부사 'how much' 형태로 부사로도 쓰임 ❑ 그녀는 자기 행동이 나를 얼마나 짜증나게 하는지 알면서도 계속 그런다. ● 대명사 'how much' 형태로 정도를 나타내는 대명사처럼 사용 ❑ 당신은 얼마나 법니까? **9** 한정사 -만큼 많은 ❑ 가능한 한 모든 인내력을 동원해서 다시 한 번 설명해 볼게. ❑ 그들의 목표는 가능한 한 많은 양의 우유 생산일 것이다.

You should use **much** if you want to talk about things that cannot be counted. ❑ *...too much water.* You only use **many** to talk about things that can be counted. ❑ *They owned many cars.*

셀 수 없는 것에 대해 말할 때는 much를 써야 한다. ❑ *...너무 많은 물.* many는 셀 수 있는 것에 대해 말할 때만 쓴다. ❑ 그들은 차를 많이 소유하고 있었다.

---

10 PHRASE You use **much as** to introduce a fact which makes something else you have just said or will say rather surprising. ❑ *Much as they hope to go home tomorrow, they're resigned to staying until the end of the year.* **11** PHRASE You use **as much** in expressions such as **"I thought as much"** and **"I guessed as much"** after you have just been told something and you want to say that you already believed or expected it to be true. ❑ *You're waiting for a woman – I thought as much.* **12** PHRASE You use **as much as** before an amount to suggest that it is surprisingly large. [EMPHASIS] ❑ *The organizers hope to raise as much as £6m for charity.* **13** PHRASE You use **much less** after a statement, often a negative one, to indicate that the statement is more true of the person, thing, or situation that you are going to mention next. ❑ *They are always short of water to drink, much less to bathe in.* **14** PHRASE If you say that something is **not so much** one thing as another, you mean that it is more like the second thing than the first. ❑ *I don't really think of her as a daughter so much as a very good friend.* **15** PHRASE You use **so much so** to indicate that your previous statement is true to a very great extent, and therefore it has the result mentioned. ❑ *He himself believed in freedom, so much so that he would rather die than live without it.* **16** PHRASE If a situation or action is **too much for** you, it is so difficult, tiring, or upsetting that you cannot cope with it. ❑ *His inability to stay at one job for long had finally proved too much for her.* **17** PHRASE You use **very much** to emphasize that someone or something has a lot of a particular quality, or that the description you are about to give is particularly accurate. [EMPHASIS] ❑ *...a man very much in charge of himself.* **18 a bit much →**see **bit**

10 구 -이긴 하지만 ❑ 그들은 당장 내일이라도 집에 돌아가고 싶지 하지만 연말까지 머무는 것을 기정사실로 받아들이고 있다. **11** 구 그러리라고 생각하다 ❑ 당신은 여자를 기다리고 있군요. 그러리라고 생각했어요. **12** 구 무려, -만큼이나 [강조] ❑ 준비위원들은 자선기금으로 무려 6백만 파운드를 모으고 싶어 한다. **13** 구 -은 더욱 아니다, -은 말할 것도 없이 ❑ 그들은 항상 마실 물이 부족하다. 목욕할 물은 말할 것도 없이 오히려... 이다 **14** 구 -라기 보다 오히려... ❑ 나는 사실 그 애를 딸이라기보다 아주 좋은 친구로 생각한다. **15** 구 너무나 그렇기 때문에 -하다 ❑ 그 자신이 자유를 그토록 믿었기 때문에 자유없이 사느니 차라리 죽을 마음이었다. **16** 구 지나친, 무리한 ❑ 그가 한 직장에서 오래 머물지 못하는 것이 결국 그녀에게는 견디기 힘든 일이었다. **17** 구 매우 [강조] ❑ 매우 자립심이 강한 사람

muck /mʌk/ N-UNCOUNT **Muck** is dirt or some other unpleasant substance. [INFORMAL] ❑ *This congealed muck was interfering with the filter and causing the flooding.*

불가산명사 오물 [비격식체] ❑ 오물이 굳어서 필터를 막아 물이 넘치게 하고 있었다.

mu|cus /mjuːkəs/ N-UNCOUNT **Mucus** is a thick liquid that is produced in some parts of your body, for example the inside of your nose. ❑ *...the thin layer of mucus that helps protect the delicate lining of the rectum.*

불가산명사 점액 ❑ 직장 내부를 감싸고 있는 섬세한 막의 보호를 돕는 얇은 점액 층

mud /mʌd/ N-UNCOUNT **Mud** is a sticky mixture of earth and water. ❑ *His uniform was crumpled, untidy, splashed with mud.*

불가산명사 진흙 ❑ 그의 유니폼은 구겨지고 지저분했으며 진흙 범벅이었다.

mud|dle /mʌdəl/ (**muddles, muddling, muddled**) **1** N-VAR If people or things are **in a muddle**, they are in a state of confusion or disorder. ❑ *My thoughts are all in a muddle.* ❑ *We are going to get into a hopeless muddle.* **2** V-T If you **muddle** things or people, you get them mixed up, so that you do not know which is which. ❑ *Already, one or two critics have begun to muddle the two names.* ● PHRASAL VERB **Muddle up** means the same as **muddle**. ❑ *The question muddles up three separate issues.* ● **mud|dled up** ADJ ❑ *I know that I am getting my words muddled up.*

1 가산명사 또는 불가산명사 엉망, 뒤죽박죽 ❑ 내 머릿속이 여러 생각으로 뒤죽박죽이다. ❑ 우리는 손도 못 쓰게 엉망진창인 상태에 빠질 것이다. **2** 타동사 혼동하다, 뒤섞다 ❑ 이미 비평가 한두 명이 그 두 이름을 혼동하기 시작했다. ● 구동사 혼동하다 ❑ 이 질문은 서로 다른 세 가지 사안을 혼동하고 있다. ● 혼동된, 뒤섞인 형용사 ❑ 저도 제가 말을 두서없이 하고 있는 것 같습니다.

▶**muddle through** PHRASAL VERB If you **muddle through**, you manage to do something even though you do not have the proper equipment or do not really know how to do it. ❑ *We will muddle through and just play it day by day.* ❑ *The BBC may be able to muddle through the next five years like this.*

구동사 그럭저럭 해내다 ❑ 우리는 하루하루를 그럭저럭 살아갈 것이다. ❑ 비비시가 향후 5년 동안에도 지금처럼 그럭저럭 버틸 수 있을지 모른다.

▶**muddle up** →see **muddle 2**

mud|dled /mʌdˀld/ ADJ If someone is **muddled**, they are confused about something. ❑ *I'm afraid I'm a little muddled. I'm not exactly sure where to begin.*

형용사 혼동된, 혼란스러운 ❑ 제가 조금 혼란스러워요. 정확히 어디서부터 시작해야 할지 모르겠어요.

mud|dy /mʌdi/ (muddier, muddiest, muddies, muddying, muddied) **1** ADJ Something which is **muddy** contains mud or is covered in mud. ❑ *...a muddy track.* **2** V-T If you **muddy** something, you cause it to be muddy. ❑ *The ground still smelled of rain and they muddied their shoes.* **3** V-T If someone or something **muddies** a situation or issue, they cause it to seem less clear and less easy to understand. ❑ *It's difficult enough without muddying the issue with religion.* ● PHRASE If someone or something **muddies the waters**, they cause a situation or issue to seem less clear and less easy to understand.

1 형용사 진흙투성이의 ❑ 진흙 길 **2** 타동사 진흙으로 더럽히다 ❑ 땅에서는 아직 비 냄새가 났고 그들의 신발에는 진흙이 묻었다. **3** 타동사 흐리게 하다, 혼란스럽게 하다 ❑ 종교까지 가세해 혼란스럽게 하지 않더라도 그것은 이미 충분히 어려운 문제이다. ● 구 흐리게 하다, 혼란스럽게 하다

muf|fle /mʌfˀl/ (muffles, muffling, muffled) V-T If something **muffles** a sound, it makes it quieter and more difficult to hear. ❑ *Blake held his handkerchief over the mouthpiece to muffle his voice.*

타동사 소리를 죽이다 ❑ 블레이크가 목소리를 죽이기 위해 손수건을 전화기에 대고 있었다.

mug /mʌg/ (mugs, mugging, mugged) **1** N-COUNT A **mug** is a large deep cup with straight sides and a handle, used for hot drinks. ❑ *He spooned instant coffee into two of the mugs.* ● N-COUNT A **mug** of something is the amount of it contained in a mug. ❑ *He had been drinking mugs of coffee to keep himself awake.* **2** N-COUNT Someone's **mug** is their face. [INFORMAL] ❑ *He managed to get his ugly mug on the telly.* **3** V-T If someone **mugs** you, they attack you in order to steal your money. ❑ *I was walking out to my car when this guy tried to mug me.* ● **mug|ging** (muggings) N-VAR ❑ *Bank robberies, burglaries, and muggings are reported almost daily in the press.* **4** N-COUNT If you say that someone is a **mug**, you mean that they are stupid and easily deceived by other people. [BRIT, INFORMAL, DISAPPROVAL] ❑ *He's a mug as far as women are concerned.*

1 가산명사 머그잔 ❑ 그가 머그잔 두 개에 인스턴트커피를 떠 넣었다. ● 가산명사 머그컵 하나 분량 ❑ 그는 잠을 깨기 위해 커피를 머그컵으로 몇 잔 마시는 참이었다. **2** 가산명사 얼굴 [비격식체] ❑ 그가 용케 못생긴 자기 얼굴을 텔레비전 화면에 비쳤다. **3** 타동사 (돈을 빼앗기 위해) 공격하다 ❑ 내가 차로 걸어가던 중이었는데 이 남자가 나를 공격하려 했다. ● 명사 가산명사 또는 불가산명사 ❑ 은행 강도, 주거 침입, 폭력 강도 등의 범죄가 거의 매일 언론에 보도된다. **4** 가산명사 바보, 숙맥 [영국영어, 비격식체, 탐탁찮음] ❑ 그는 여자에 관해서라면 숙맥이다.

mug|ger /mʌgər/ (muggers) N-COUNT A **mugger** is a person who attacks someone violently in a street in order to steal money from them. ❑ *...hiding places for muggers and thieves.*

가산명사 길거리 강도 ❑ 길거리 강도와 도둑의 은신처

mug|gy /mʌgi/ ADJ **Muggy** weather is unpleasantly warm and damp. ❑ *It was muggy and overcast.*

형용사 찌는 듯한, 후텁지근한 ❑ 날이 후텁지근하고 구름이 잔뜩 끼었다.

mule /myul/ (mules) **1** N-COUNT A **mule** is an animal whose parents are a horse and a donkey. **2** N-COUNT A **mule** is a shoe or slipper which is open around the heel.

1 가산명사 노새 **2** 가산명사 뮬 (뒤축 없는 슬리퍼)

mull /mʌl/ (mulls, mulling, mulled) V-T/V-I If you **mull** something, you think about it for a long time before deciding what to do. [AM] ❑ *Last month, a federal grand jury began mulling evidence in the case.*

타동사/자동사 숙고하다 [미국영어] ❑ 지난달 연방 대배심원이 그 사건의 증거를 심의하기 시작했다.

▶**mull over** PHRASAL VERB If you **mull** something **over**, you think about it for a long time before deciding what to do. ❑ *McLaren had been mulling over an idea to make a movie.*

구동사 숙고하다 ❑ 맥라렌이 영화 제작을 놓고 곰곰이 생각을 해오던 참이었다.

Word Link	multi ≈ many : *multi*cultural, *multi*media, *multi*national

multi|cul|tur|al /mʌltikʌltʃərəl/ also **multi-cultural** ADJ **Multicultural** means consisting of or relating to people of many different nationalities and cultures. ❑ *...children growing up in a multicultural society.*

형용사 다문화적인 ❑ 다문화 사회에서 자란 아이들

multi|lat|er|al /mʌltilætərˀl/ ADJ **Multilateral** means involving at least three different groups of people or nations. ❑ *Many want to abandon the multilateral trade talks in Geneva.*

형용사 다자간의 ❑ 많은 이들이 제네바에서 열리는 다자 무역 회담의 철회를 원한다.

multi|me|dia /mʌltimidiə/ **1** N-UNCOUNT You use **multimedia** to refer to computer programs and products which involve sound, pictures, and film, as well as text. ❑ *...the case of an insurance company using multimedia to improve customer service in its branches.* **2** N-UNCOUNT In education, **multimedia** is the use of television and other different media in a lesson, as well as books. ❑ *I am making a multimedia presentation for my science project.*

1 불가산명사 멀티미디어 ❑ 보험 회사가 지정한 고객 서비스 향상을 위해 멀티미디어를 사용한 사례 **2** 불가산명사 멀티미디어 ❑ 나는 멀티미디어를 사용해 과학 프로젝트 프레젠테이션을 준비하고 있다.

multi|na|tion|al /mʌltinæʃənˀl/ (multinationals) also **multi-national** **1** ADJ A **multinational** company has branches or owns companies in many different countries. ● N-COUNT **Multinational** is also a noun. ❑ *...multinationals such as Ford and IBM.* **2** ADJ **Multinational** armies, organizations, or other groups involve people from several different countries. ❑ *The U.S. troops would be part of a multinational force.* **3** ADJ **Multinational** countries or regions have a population that is made up of people of several different nationalities. ❑ *We live in a multinational country.*

1 형용사 다국적 기업의 ● 가산명사 다국적 기업 ❑ 포드나 아이비엠 같은 다국적 기업 **2** 형용사 다국적의 ❑ 미군이 다국적군에 포함될 것이다. **3** 형용사 다민족의 ❑ 우리는 다민족 국가에 산다.

multi|ple /mʌltɪpˀl/ (multiples) **1** ADJ You use **multiple** to describe things that consist of many parts, involve many people, or have many uses. ❑ *He died of multiple injuries.* **2** N-COUNT If one number is a **multiple** of a smaller number, it can be exactly divided by that smaller number. ❑ *Their numerical system, derived from the Babylonians, was based on multiples of the number six.* **3** N-COUNT A **multiple** or a **multiple store** is a store with a lot of branches in different towns. [BRIT] ❑ *It made it almost impossible for the smaller retailer to compete against the multiples.* →see **copy**

1 형용사 복합적인, 다중의, 다양한 ❑ 그는 복합 부상으로 사망했다. **2** 가산명사 ~의 배수 ❑ 그들의 수 체계는 바빌로니아 인들로부터 유래된 것으로 6의 배수에 기초한 것이었다. **3** 가산명사 체인점 [영국영어] ❑ 이 때문에 작은 소매점이 체인점과 경쟁하는 것이 거의 불가능해졌다.

multiple choice ADJ In a **multiple choice** test or question, you have to choose the answer that you think is right from several possible answers that are listed on the question paper. ❑ *The multiple-choice questions must be answered within a strict time limit.*

형용사 객관식의 ❑ 객관식 문제는 엄격히 정해진 시간 내에 풀어야 한다.

multi|pli|ca|tion /mʌltɪplɪkeɪʃˀn/ **1** N-UNCOUNT **Multiplication** is the process of calculating the total of one number multiplied by another. ❑ *There will be simple tests in addition, subtraction, multiplication and division.* **2** N-UNCOUNT The **multiplication** of things of a particular kind is the process or fact of them increasing in number or amount. ❑ *Increasing gravity is known to speed up the multiplication of cells.* →see **mathematics**

1 불가산명사 곱셈 ❑ 덧셈, 뺄셈, 곱셈, 나눗셈을 묻는 간단한 시험이 있을 것이다. **2** 불가산명사 증가, 증식 ❑ 중력이 증가하면 세포 증식이 빨라진다고 알려져 있다.

a b c d e f g h i j k l m n o p q r s t u v w x y z

multi|plic|ity /mʌltɪplɪsɪti/ QUANT A **multiplicity of** things is a large number or a large variety of them. [FORMAL] [QUANT of pl-n] ❑ ...a writer who uses a multiplicity of styles.

수량사 여러 가지, 가지각색 [격식체] ❑ 여러 가지 문체를 구사하는 작가

multi|ply /mʌltɪplaɪ/ (multiplies, multiplying, multiplied) **1** V-T/V-I When something **multiplies** or when you **multiply** it, it increases greatly in number or amount. ❑ Such disputes multiplied in the eighteenth and nineteenth centuries. **2** V-I When animals and insects **multiply**, they increase in number by giving birth to large numbers of young. ❑ These creatures can multiply quickly. **3** V-T If you **multiply** one number by another, you add the first number to itself as many times as is indicated by the second number. For example 2 multiplied by 3 is equal to 6. ❑ What do you get if you multiply six by nine?

1 타동사/자동사 급격히 증가하다; 급격히 늘리다 ❑ 18세기와 19세기에 이 같은 논쟁이 급격히 증가했다. **2** 자동사 번식하다 ❑ 이들 생물체는 빠르게 번식할 수 있다. **3** 타동사 곱하다 ❑ 6에 9를 곱하면 얼마가 나오지?

multi|ra|cial /mʌltɪreɪʃəl/ also **multi-racial** ADJ **Multiracial** means consisting of or involving people of many different nationalities and cultures. ❑ We live in a multiracial society.

형용사 다인종의 ❑ 우리는 다인종 사회에 산다.

multi|task|ing /mʌltɪtæskɪŋ/ also **multi-tasking** N-UNCOUNT **Multitasking** is a situation in which a computer or person does more than one thing at the same time. ❑ Often women are so good at multitasking that it appears it's all effortless.

불가산명사 여러 가지 일을 동시에 수행함 ❑ 여성들이 한꺼번에 여러 가지 일을 너무 훌륭히 해내서 전혀 힘들어 보이지 않을 때가 자주 있다.

multi|tude /mʌltɪtud, BRIT mʌltɪtjuːd/ (multitudes) **1** QUANT A **multitude of** things or people is a very large number of them. [FORMAL] ❑ There are a multitude of small quiet roads to cycle along. ❑ Addiction to drugs can bring a multitude of other problems. ● PHRASE If you say that something covers or hides **a multitude of sins**, you mean that it hides something unattractive or does not reveal the true nature of something. **2** N-COUNT You can refer to a very large number of people as a **multitude**. [WRITTEN] ❑ ...surrounded by a noisy multitude. **3** N-COUNT-COLL You can refer to the great majority of people in a particular country or situation as **the multitude** or **the multitudes**. ❑ The hideous truth was hidden from the multitude.

1 수량사 다수의 ❑ 자전거 타기에 좋은 작고 조용한 길이 많이 있다. ❑ 마약 중독은 다른 문제를 많이 일으킬 수 있다. ● 구 바람직하지 못한 실상 **2** 가산명사 군중, 많은 사람 [문어체] ❑ 시끌벅적한 사람들에 둘러싸여 **3** 가산명사-집합 일반인, 대다수의 사람들 ❑ 그 추악한 진실을 대다수의 사람들에게 숨겼다.

mum ♦◊◊ /mʌm/ (mums) N-FAMILY Your **mum** is your mother. [BRIT, INFORMAL; AM mom] ❑ He misses his mum. ❑ Mum and Dad are coming for lunch.

친족명사 엄마 [영국영어, 비격식체; 미국영어 mom] ❑ 그는 엄마가 그립다. ❑ 엄마, 아빠께서 점심식사 하러 오신다.

mum|ble /mʌmbəl/ (mumbles, mumbling, mumbled) V-T/V-I If you **mumble**, you speak very quietly and not at all clearly with the result that the words are difficult to understand. ❑ Her grandmother mumbled in her sleep. ❑ He mumbled a few words. ● N-COUNT **Mumble** is also a noun. ❑ He could hear the low mumble of Navarro's voice.

타동사/자동사 중얼거리다 ❑ 그녀의 할머니가 잠꼬대를 했다. ❑ 그가 몇 마디 중얼거렸다. ● 가산명사 중얼거림 ❑ 그는 나바로가 낮게 중얼거리는 소리를 들을 수 있었다.

mum|my /mʌmi/ (mummies) **1** N-FAMILY Some people, especially young children, call their mother **mummy**. [BRIT, INFORMAL; AM **mommy**] ❑ I want my mummy. **2** N-COUNT A **mummy** is a dead body which was preserved long ago by being rubbed with special oils and wrapped in cloth. ❑ ...an Egyptian mummy.

1 친족명사 엄마 [영국영어, 비격식체; 미국영어 mommy] ❑ 우리 엄마 데려와 줘. **2** 가산명사 미이라 ❑ 이집트 미이라

munch /mʌntʃ/ (munches, munching, munched) V-T/V-I If you **munch** food, you eat it by chewing it slowly, thoroughly, and rather noisily. ❑ Luke munched the chicken sandwiches. ❑ Across the table, his son Benjie munched appreciatively.

타동사/자동사 우적우적 먹다 ❑ 루크가 치킨 샌드위치를 우적우적 씹어 먹었다. ❑ 식탁 건너편에서는 아들 벤지가 맛있게 밥을 먹고 있었다.

mun|dane /mʌndeɪn/ ADJ Something that is **mundane** is very ordinary and not at all interesting or unusual. ❑ Be willing to do mundane tasks with good grace. ● N-SING You can refer to mundane things as the **mundane**. ❑ It's an attitude that turns the mundane into something rather more interesting and exciting.

형용사 평범한, 일상적인 ❑ 일상적인 일을 즐겁게 하는 자세를 가져라. ● 단수명사 평범한 것, 일상적인 것 ❑ 평범한 일을 뭔가 더 재미있고 신나는 일로 바꾸는 것은 바로 так태도다.

mu|nici|pal /myunɪsɪpəl/ ADJ **Municipal** means associated with or belonging to a city or town that has its own local government. [ADJ n] ❑ The municipal authorities gave the go-ahead for the march. ❑ ...next month's municipal elections.

형용사 지방 자치의 ❑ 지방 자치 당국이 그 시위에 대한 허가를 내주었다. ❑ 다음달의 지방 자치 선거

mu|nici|pal|ity /myunɪsɪpælɪti/ (municipalities) **1** N-COUNT In Britain, a **municipality** is a city or town which is governed by its own locally-appointed officials. You can also refer to a city's or town's local government as a **municipality**. **2** N-COUNT In the United States, a **municipality** is a city or town that is incorporated and can elect its own government, which is also called a **municipality**.

1 가산명사 지방 자치체, 지방 당국 **2** 가산명사 지방 자치체

mu|ni|tions /myunɪʃənz/ N-PLURAL **Munitions** are military equipment and supplies, especially bombs, shells, and guns. ❑ ...the shortage of men and munitions.

복수명사 군수품, 탄약 ❑ 인력과 군수품 부족

mu|ral /myʊərəl/ (murals) N-COUNT A **mural** is a picture painted on a wall. ❑ ...a mural of Tangier bay.

가산명사 벽화 ❑ 탕헤르만 벽화

mur|der ♦♦◊ /mɜrdər/ (murders, murdering, murdered) **1** N-VAR **Murder** is the deliberate and illegal killing of a person. ❑ The three accused, aged between 19 and 20, are charged with attempted murder. ❑ She refused to testify, unless the murder charge against her was dropped. →see kill **2** V-T To **murder** someone means to commit the crime of killing them deliberately. ❑ ...a thriller about two men who murder a third to see if they can get away with it. **3** PHRASE If you say that someone **gets away with murder**, you are complaining that they can do whatever they like without anyone trying to control them or punish them. [INFORMAL, DISAPPROVAL] ❑ His charm and the fact that he is so likeable often allows him to get away with murder.

1 가산명사 또는 불가산명사 살인 ❑ 19세에서 20세 사이의 피고인 3명은 살인 미수 혐의를 받고 있다. ❑ 그녀는 자신의 살인 죄목이 취하되지 않는 한 증언하지 않겠다고 했다. **2** 타동사/자동사 살해하다 ❑ 한 사람을 죽이려고 토키기 않으려는 두 남자를 다룬 스릴러 영화 **3** 구 제멋대로 하다 [비격식체, 탐탁찮음] ❑ 그가 매력 있고 너무나 호감이 가는 사람이라는 사실 때문에 종종 제멋대로 구는 게 허용되기도 한다.

mur|der|er /mɜrdərər/ (murderers) N-COUNT A **murderer** is a person who has murdered someone. ❑ One of these men may have been the murderer.

가산명사 살인자 ❑ 이 남자들 중 하나가 살인자였을지도 모른다.

murky /mɜrki/ (murkier, murkiest) **1** ADJ A **murky** place or time of day is dark and rather unpleasant because there is not enough light. ❑ The large lamplit room was murky with woodsmoke. **2** ADJ **Murky** water or fog is so dark and dirty that you cannot see through it. ❑ ...the deep, murky waters of Loch Ness. **3** ADJ If you describe something as **murky**, you mean that the details of it are not clear or that it is difficult to understand. ❑ The law here is a little bit murky. **4** ADJ If you describe an activity or situation as **murky**, you suspect that it is dishonest or

1 형용사 어두컴컴한 ❑ 램프 켜진 큰 방은 장작 연기로 어두컴컴했다. **2** 형용사 짙은, 뿌연 ❑ 네스 호의 깊고 뿌연 물 **3** 형용사 불분명한, 애매한 ❑ 법이 이 부분에서 약간 불분명하다. **4** 형용사 음침한, 음흉한 [영국영어, 탐탁찮음] ❑ 그들을 권력 밖으로 밀어내려는 음흉한 음모가 있어 왔다.

morally wrong. [BRIT, DISAPPROVAL] ❑ *There has been a murky conspiracy to keep them out of power.*

mur|mur /mɜrmər/ (**murmurs, murmuring, murmured**) ◼ V-T If you **murmur** something, you say it very quietly, so that not many people can hear what you are saying. ❑ *He turned and murmured something to the professor.* ❑ *"How lovely," she murmured.* ◻ N-COUNT A **murmur** is something that is said which can hardly be heard. ❑ *They spoke in low murmurs.* ◻ N-SING A **murmur** is a continuous low sound, like the noise of a river or of voices far away. ❑ *The piano music mixes with the murmur of conversation.* ◻ N-COUNT A **murmur** of a particular emotion is a quiet expression of it. ❑ *The promise of some basic working rights draws murmurs of approval.* ◻ N-COUNT A **murmur** is an abnormal sound which is made by the heart and which shows that there is probably something wrong with it. ❑ *The doctor said James had now developed a heart murmur.* ◻ PHRASE If someone does something **without a murmur**, they do it without complaining. ❑ *Then came the bill and my friend paid up without a murmur.*

mus|cle ◆◇◇ /mʌsəl/ (**muscles, muscling, muscled**) ◼ N-VAR A **muscle** is a piece of tissue inside your body which connects two bones and which you use when you make a movement. ❑ *Keeping your muscles strong and in tone helps you to avoid back problems.* ◻ N-UNCOUNT If you say that someone has **muscle**, you mean that they have power and influence, which enables them to do difficult things. ❑ *Eisenhower used his muscle to persuade Congress to change the law.* ◻ PHRASE If a group, organization, or country **flexes its muscles**, it does something to impress or frighten people, in order to show them that it has power and is considering using it. ❑ *The Fair Trade Commission has of late been flexing its muscles, cracking down on cases of corruption.* ◻ PHRASE If you say that someone did not **move a muscle**, you mean that they stayed absolutely still. ❑ *He stood without moving a muscle, unable to believe what his eyes saw so plainly.* →see **nervous system**
→see Word Web: **muscle**

▸**muscle in** PHRASAL VERB If someone **muscles in on** something, they force their way into a situation where they have no right to be and where they are not welcome, in order to gain some advantage for themselves. [DISAPPROVAL] ❑ *Cohen complained that Kravis was muscling in on his deal.*

Word Partnership	*muscle*의 연어
N.	muscle **aches**, muscle **mass**, muscle **pain**, muscle **tone** ◼
V.	**contract** a muscle, **flex** a muscle, **pull** a muscle ◼

mus|cu|lar /mʌskyələr/ ◼ ADJ **Muscular** means involving or affecting your muscles. [ADJ n] ❑ *As a general rule, all muscular effort is enhanced by breathing in as the effort is made.* ◻ ADJ If a person or their body is **muscular**, they are very fit and strong, and have firm muscles which are not covered with a lot of fat. ❑ *Like most female athletes, she was lean and muscular.*

muse /myuz/ (**muses, musing, mused**) V-T/V-I If you **muse** on something, you think about it, usually saying or writing what you are thinking at the same time. [WRITTEN] ❑ *Many of the papers muse on the fate of the President.* ❑ *"As a whole," she muses, "the 'organized church' turns me off."* ● **mus|ing** (**musings**) N-COUNT ❑ *His musings were interrupted by Montagu who came and sat down next to him.*

mu|seum ◆◇◇ /myuziəm/ (**museums**) N-COUNT A **museum** is a building where a large number of interesting and valuable objects, such as works of art or historical items, are kept, studied, and displayed to the public. ❑ *For months Malcolm had wanted to visit the Parisian art museums.*

mush|room /mʌʃrum/ (**mushrooms, mushrooming, mushroomed**) ◼ N-VAR **Mushrooms** are fungi that you can eat. They have short stems and round tops. ❑ *There are many types of wild mushrooms.* ◻ V-I If something such as an industry or a place **mushrooms**, it grows or comes into existence very quickly. ❑ *The media training industry has mushroomed over the past decade.*
→see **fungus**

mu|sic ◆◆◆ /myuzɪk/ ◼ N-UNCOUNT **Music** is the pattern of sounds produced by people singing or playing instruments. ❑ *...classical music.* ◻ N-UNCOUNT **Music** is the art of creating or performing music. ❑ *He went on to study music, specialising in the clarinet.* ◻ N-UNCOUNT **Music** is the symbols written on paper which represent musical sounds. ❑ *He's never been able to read music.* ◻ PHRASE If something that you hear is **music to** your **ears**, it makes you feel very happy. [FEELINGS] ❑ *Popular support – it's music to the ears of any politician.* ◻ PHRASE If you **face the music**, you put yourself in a position where you will be criticized or

[Korean translations column]

◼ 타동사 중얼거리다 ❑ 그는 돌아서서 교수님께 뭐라고 중얼거렸다. ❑ "너무 사랑스러워."라고 그녀가 중얼거렸다. ◻ 가산명사 중얼거림 ❑ 그들이 낮게 중얼거리며 말했다. ◻ 단수명사 (중얼거리듯) 낮은 소리 ❑ 피아노 소리가 나직한 대화 소리와 섞인다. ◻ 가산명사 감정의 조용한 표출 ❑ 몇 가지 기본적인 노동권에 대한 약속이 조용한 지지를 받고 있다. ◻ 가산명사 심장 잡음 ❑ 의사는 제임스한테서 심장 잡음이 들린다고 말했다. ◻ 구 불평하지 않고 ❑ 그리고는 계산서가 나왔고 내 친구가 불평하지 않고 돈을 냈다.

◼ 가산명사 또는 불가산명사 근육 ❑ 근육 단련은 요통 예방에 좋다. ◻ 불가산명사 영향력 ❑ 아이젠하워는 자신의 영향력을 이용해 의회가 그 법률을 바꾸도록 설득했다. ◻ 구 힘을 과시하다 ❑ 공정 거래 위원회는 최근 부패 사건들을 단속하면서 힘을 과시해 왔다. ◻ 구 꼼짝하다 ❑ 그는 자신이 두 눈으로 똑똑히 목격한 것이 믿기지 않아 꼼짝도 하지 않고 서 있었다.

구동사 끼어들다 [탐탁찮음] ❑ 코렌은 크라비스가 자기 거래에 끼어들고 있다고 불평했다.

◼ 형용사 근육의 ❑ 일반적으로 근육을 움직일 때 숨을 들이쉬면 근육 활동이 촉진된다. ◻ 형용사 근육질의, 근육이 발달된 ❑ 대부분의 여성 선수들처럼 그녀는 마르고 근육이 발달됐다.

타동사/자동사 생각에 잠겨 말하다; 생각에 잠겨 쓰다 [문어체] ❑ 각종 신문에서 대통령의 운명에 대해 숙고를 하고 있다. ❑ "대체로 조직적인 교회에는 흥미 없어."라고 그녀가 생각에 잠겨 말했다. ● 숙고, 묵상 가산명사 ❑ 몬터규가 옆에 와서 앉는 바람에 그의 생각이 중단되었다.

가산명사 박물관 ❑ 몇 달 동안 말콤은 파리에 있는 미술 박물관들을 방문하고 싶어했다.

◼ 가산명사 또는 불가산명사 버섯 ❑ 여러 종류의 야생 버섯이 있다. ◻ 자동사 급격히 늘어나다 ❑ 언론인 훈련 산업이 지난 10년간 급격히 성장했다.

◼ 불가산명사 음악 ❑ 고전 음악 ◻ 불가산명사 음악 ❑ 그는 클라리넷을 전공하며 계속 음악 공부를 했다. ◻ 불가산명사 악보 ❑ 그는 전에 악보를 볼 수없었다. ◻ 구 기분 좋게 들리다 [감정 개입] ❑ 대중의 지지란 모든 정치인에게 듣기 좋은 소리이다. ◻ 구 잘못에 대한 책임을 지다, 당당히 비판받다 ❑ 조만간 내 잘못에 대한 책임을 지겠다.

Word Web	**muscle**

There are three types of **muscles** in the body. Voluntary or skeletal muscles produce external movements. Involuntary or smooth muscles provide internal movement within the body. For example, the smooth muscles in the **iris** of the eye adjust the size of the pupil. This controls how much light enters the eye. **Cardiac** muscles are found only in the heart. They work constantly but never get tired. When we **exercise**, voluntary muscles **contract** and then **relax**. With repeated **workouts**, we can **build** these muscles and increase their **strength**. If we don't exercise, these muscles can atrophy and become **weak**.

A punished for something you have done. ❑ *Sooner or later, I'm going to have to face the music.*
→see Word Web: **music**

mu·si·cal ◆◇◇ /myúzɪkªl/ (musicals) ■ ADJ You use **musical** to indicate that something is connected with playing or studying music. [ADJ n] ❑ *We have a wealth of musical talent in this region.* ● **mu·si·cal·ly** /myúzɪkli/ ADV ❑ *Musically there is a lot to enjoy.* ■ N-COUNT A **musical** is a play or movie that uses singing and dancing in the story. ❑ *...London's smash hit musical Miss Saigon.* ■ ADJ Someone who is **musical** has a natural ability and interest in music. ❑ *I came from a musical family.* ■ ADJ Sounds that are **musical** are light and pleasant to hear. ❑ *He had a soft, almost musical voice.*

■ 형용사 음악의, 음악적인 ❑ 이 지역에는 음악 천재들이 많이 산다. ● 음악적으로 부사 ❑ 음악적으로 즐길 만한 것이 많다. ■ 가산명사 뮤지컬 ❑ 런던 뮤지컬 대 성공작 미스 사이공 ■ 형용사 음악에 재능이 있는 ❑ 나는 음악가 집안에서 태어났다. ■ 형용사 음악처럼 듣기 좋은 ❑ 그는 부드럽고 음악처럼 듣기 좋은 목소리를 지니고 있었다.

mu·si·cal in·stru·ment (musical instruments) N-COUNT A **musical instrument** is an object such as a piano, guitar, or violin which you play in order to produce music. ❑ *The drum is one of the oldest musical instruments.*

가산명사 악기 ❑ 드럼은 가장 오래된 악기 중 하나이다.

Word Link   *ician ≈ person who works at : mus*ician*, pediatr*ician*, phys*ician

mu·si·cian ◆◇◇ /myuzíʃªn/ (musicians) N-COUNT A **musician** is a person who plays a musical instrument as their job or hobby. ❑ *He was a brilliant musician.*
→see concert, DVD, music, orchestra

가산명사 음악가 ❑ 그는 뛰어난 음악가였다.

Mus·lim ◆◆◇ /mʌzlɪm, BRIT mʊzlɪm/ (Muslims) ■ N-COUNT A **Muslim** is someone who believes in Islam and lives according to its rules. ■ ADJ **Muslim** means relating to Islam or Muslims. ❑ *...Iran and other Muslim countries.*

■ 가산명사 이슬람교도 ■ 형용사 이슬람교의 ❑ 이란을 비롯한 다른 이슬람 국가들

mus·lin /mʌzlɪn/ (muslins) N-MASS **Muslin** is very thin cotton cloth. ❑ *...white muslin curtains.*

물질명사 모슬린 ❑ 하얀 모슬린 커튼

mus·sel /mʌsªl/ (mussels) N-COUNT **Mussels** are a kind of shellfish that you can eat from their shells.

가산명사 홍합

must ◆◆◆ /məst, STRONG mʌst/ (musts)

The noun is pronounced /mʌst/.

명사는 /mʌst/로 발음된다.

Must is a modal verb. It is followed by the base form of a verb.

must는 조동사이며 뒤에는 동사 원형이 온다.

■ MODAL You use **must** to indicate that you think it is very important or necessary for something to happen. You use **must not** or **mustn't** to indicate that you think it is very important or necessary for something not to happen. ❑ *What you wear should be stylish and clean, and must definitely fit well.* ❑ *You are going to have to take a certain amount of criticism, but you must cope with it.* ■ MODAL You use **must** to indicate that it is necessary for something to happen, usually because of a rule or law. ❑ *Candidates must satisfy the general conditions for admission.* ❑ *Mr. Allen must pay Mr. Farnham's legal costs.* ■ MODAL You use **must** to indicate that you are fairly sure that something is the case. ❑ *At 29 Russell must be one of the youngest ever Wembley referees.* ❑ *Claire's car wasn't there, so she must have gone to her mother's.* ■ MODAL You use **must**, or **must have** with a past participle, to indicate that you believe that something is the case, because of the available evidence. ❑ *"You must be Emma," said the visitor.* ❑ *Miss Holloway had a weak heart. She must have had a heart attack.* ■ MODAL If you say that one thing **must have** happened in order for something else to happen, you mean that it is necessary for the first thing to have happened before the second thing can happen. ❑ *In order to take that job, you must have left another job.* ■ MODAL You use **must** to express your intention to do something. ❑ *I must be getting back.* ❑ *I must telephone my parents.* ■ MODAL You use **must** to make suggestions or invitations very forcefully. ❑ *You must see a doctor, Frederick.* ■ MODAL You use **must** in remarks and comments where you are expressing sympathy. ❑ *This must be a very difficult job for you.* ■ MODAL You use **must** in conversation in expressions such as "**I must say**" and "**I must admit**" in order to emphasize a point that you are making. [EMPHASIS] ❑ *This came as a surprise, I must say.* ❑ *I must admit I like looking feminine.* ■ MODAL You use **must** in expressions such as "**it must be noted**" and "**it must be remembered**" in order to draw the reader's or listener's attention to what you are about to say. ❑ *It must be noted, however, that not all British and American officers carried out orders.* ■ MODAL You use **must** in

■ 법조동사 -해야 하다; -해서는 안 되다 ❑ 옷은 맵시 있고 깔끔해야 하며 꼭 잘 맞아야 한다. ❑ 당신은 어느 정도의 비판을 받아야 할 것이고 이에 잘 대처해야만 한다. ■ 법조동사 -해야만 하다 ❑ 후보들은 승인을 받기 위한 전반적인 조건을 충족시켜야만 한다. ❑ 알렌 씨는 판햄 씨의 소송비용을 지불해야만 한다. ■ 법조동사 -임에 틀림없다 ❑ 올해 스물아홉 살인 러셀은 틀림없이 역대 웸블리 심판 중 가장 어린 축에 속할 것이다. ❑ 클레어의 차가 거기 없는 것으로 봐서 어머니 집으로 간 게 틀림없다. ■ 법조동사 -인에 틀림없다; -였음에 틀림없다 ❑ "당신이 엠마군요."라고 방문객이 말했다. ❑ 할러웨이 양은 심장이 약했다. 분명히 심장 마비를 일으켰을 것이다. ■ 법조동사 -했어야 하다 ❑ 그 일을 하기 위해서는 다른 일을 그만뒀어야 했어요. ■ 법조동사 -해야 하다, -해야겠다 ❑ 이제 돌아가 봐야겠어요. ❑ 난 부모님께 전화해야 해. ■ 법조동사 -해야 하다 ❑ 프레더릭, 꼭 병원에 가 봐. ■ 법조동사 -인 것이다 ❑ 당신에게 상당히 힘든 일이겠군요. ■ 법조동사 하고 싶은 말을 강조할 때 사용 [강조] ❑ 정말이지 이번 일로 놀랐어요. ❑ 사실 저는 정말 여성스럽게 보이기를 좋아해요. ■ 법조동사 -이야 한다; -임을 주목해야 한다; -임을 기억해야 한다 ❑ 하지만 모든 영국과 미국 장교가 명령을 수행한 것은 아니라는 점에 주목해야 한다. ■ 법조동사 하필이면 -하다 [감정 개입] ❑ 하필 그녀가 끼어드는 게 뭐람? ■ 법조동사 놀라움이나 충격을 나타낼 때 사용 [강조] ❑ "가! 제발 가." "너 지금 농담하는 거 맞지?" ❑ 내가 정말 단단히 미친 게

questions to express your anger or irritation about something that someone has done, usually because you do not understand their behavior. [FEELINGS] ❑ *Why must she interrupt?* 12 MODAL You use **must** in exclamations to express surprise or shock. [EMPHASIS] ❑ *"Go! Please go." — "You must be joking!"* ❑ *I really must be quite mad!* 13 N-COUNT If you refer to something as a **must**, you mean that it is absolutely necessary. [INFORMAL] ❑ *Taking out travel insurance may seem an unnecessary expense, but it is a must.* 14 PHRASE You say "**if you must**" when you know that you cannot stop someone doing something that you think is wrong or stupid. ❑ *If you must be in the sunlight, use the strongest filter cream you can get.* 15 PHRASE You say "**if you must know**" when you tell someone something that you did not want them to know and you want to suggest that you think they were wrong to ask you about it. ❑ *It scared the hell out of her, if you must know. And me, too.*

mus|tache /mʌstæʃ, BRIT məstɑːʃ/ (**mustaches**) also **mustache** N-COUNT A man's **mustache** is the hair that grows on his upper lip. If it is very long, it is sometimes referred to as his **mustaches**. ❑ *The thick beard had gone, replaced by a bushy mustache.*

mus|tard /mʌstərd/ (**mustards**) 1 N-MASS **Mustard** is a yellow or brown paste usually eaten with meat. It tastes hot and spicy. ❑ ...*a pot of mustard.* 2 COLOR **Mustard** is used to describe things that are brownish yellow in color. ❑ *I sat in my father's chair, a mustard-colored recliner.* 3 PHRASE If someone does not **cut the mustard**, their work or their performance is not as good as it should be or as good as it is expected to be. [INFORMAL] ❑ *He just wasn't a good student. He wasn't cutting the mustard and we let him go.*

mus|ter /mʌstər/ (**musters, mustering, mustered**) 1 V-T If you **muster** something such as support, strength, or energy, you gather as much of it as you can in order to do something. ❑ *He traveled around West Africa trying to muster support for his movement.* 2 V-T/V-I When soldiers **muster** or **are mustered**, they gather together in one place in order to take part in a military action. ❑ *The men mustered before their clan chiefs.*

mustn't /mʌsᵊnt/ **Mustn't** is the usual spoken form of "must not."

must've /mʌstəv/ **Must've** is the usual spoken form of "must have," especially when "have" is an auxiliary verb.

mu|tant /myutᵊnt/ (**mutants**) N-COUNT A **mutant** is an animal or plant that is physically different from others of the same species because of a change in its genes. ❑ *New species are merely mutants of earlier ones.*

mu|tate /myuteɪt/ (**mutates, mutating, mutated**) 1 V-T/V-I If an animal or plant **mutates**, or something **mutates** it, it develops different characteristics as the result of a change in its genes. ❑ *The virus mutates in the carrier's body.* ❑ *HIV has proven to possess an ability to mutate into drug-resistant forms.* ● **mu|ta|tion** /myuteɪʃᵊn/ (**mutations**) N-VAR ❑ *Scientists have found a genetic mutation that appears to be the cause of Huntington's disease.* 2 V-I If something **mutates into** something different, it changes into that thing. ❑ *Overnight, the gossip begins to mutate into headlines.*

mute /myut/ (**mutes, muting, muted**) 1 ADJ Someone who is **mute** is silent for a particular reason and does not speak. ❑ *He was mute, distant, and indifferent.* ● ADV **Mute** is also an adverb. [ADV after v] ❑ *He could watch her standing mute by the phone.* 2 ADJ Someone who is **mute** is unable to speak. [OLD-FASHIONED] ❑ *Marianna, the duke's daughter, became mute after a shock.* 3 V-T If someone **mutes** something such as their feelings or their activities, they reduce the strength or intensity of them. ❑ *The corruption does not seem to have muted the country's prolonged economic boom.* ● **mut|ed** ADJ ❑ *The threat contrasted starkly with his administration's previous muted criticism.* 4 V-T If you **mute** a noise or sound, you lower its volume or make it less distinct. ❑ *They begin to mute their voices, not be as assertive.* ● **mut|ed** ADJ ❑ *"Yes," he muttered, his voice so muted I hardly heard his reply.*

mut|ed /myutɪd/ ADJ **Muted** colors are soft and gentle, not bright and strong. ❑ ...*painted in subtle, muted colors.*

mu|ti|late /myutᵊleɪt/ (**mutilates, mutilating, mutilated**) 1 V-T If a person or animal **is mutilated**, their body is severely damaged, usually by someone who physically attacks them. ❑ *More than 30 horses have been mutilated in the last nine months.* ❑ *He tortured and mutilated six young men.* ● **mu|ti|la|tion** /myutᵊleɪʃᵊn/ (**mutilations**) N-VAR ❑ *Amnesty International chronicles cases of torture and mutilation.* 2 V-T If something **is mutilated**, it is deliberately damaged or spoiled. ❑ *Brecht's verdict was that his screenplay had been mutilated.*

mu|ti|ny /myutᵊni/ (**mutinies, mutinying, mutinied**) 1 N-VAR A **mutiny** is a refusal by people, usually soldiers or sailors, to continue obeying a person in authority. ❑ *A series of coup attempts and mutinies within the armed forces destabilized the regime.* 2 V-I If a group of people, usually soldiers or sailors, **mutiny**, they refuse to continue obeying a person in authority. ❑ *Units stationed around the capital mutinied because they had received no pay for nine months.*

mut|ter /mʌtər/ (**mutters, muttering, muttered**) V-T/V-I If you **mutter**, you speak very quietly so that you cannot easily be heard, often because you are complaining about something. ❑ *"God knows," she muttered, "what's happening in that madman's mind."* ❑ *She can hear the old woman muttering about consideration.* ● N-COUNT **Mutter** is also a noun. ❑ *They make no more than a mutter of protest.* ● **mut|ter|ing** (**mutterings**) N-VAR ❑ *He heard muttering from the front of the crowd.*

틀림없어! 13 가산명사 반드시 필요한 것, 필수 [비격식체] ❑ 돈 낭비처럼 보일 수도 있지만 여행자 보험 가입은 필수다. 14 구 꼭 ─해야 한다면 ❑ 꼭 태양빛에 노출되어야 한다면 가능한 한 가장 강한 자외선 차단제를 사용하라. 15 구 굳이 알고 싶다면 ❑ 꼭 알고 싶은 모양인데 그녀가 그 일로 굉장히 겁먹었어. 나도 마찬가지고.

가산명사 콧수염 ❑ 숱이 많던 턱수염이 사라진 대신 덥수룩한 콧수염을 기르고 있었다.

1 물질명사 겨자 ❑ 겨자 한 통 2 색채어 겨자색 ❑ 나는 등받이가 뒤로 젖혀지는, 아버지의 겨자색 의자에 앉았다. 3 구 기준에 닿하다, 기대에 부응하다 [비격식체] ❑ 그는 뛰어난 학생이 아니었어요. 그가 수준 미달이었기 때문에 우리가 그를 보냈어요.

1 타동사 모으다, 불러일으키다 ❑ 그는 서아프리카를 순회하며 자신이 펼치는 운동에 대한 지지를 모으려고 애썼다. 2 타동사/자동사 집합하다; 집합시키다 ❑ 남자들이 각 씨족장 앞에 집합했다.

must not의 축약형

must have의 축약형

가산명사 돌연변이 ❑ 새로운 좋은 이전 종의 돌연변이에 불과하다.

1 타동사/자동사 변이하다; 변이를 일으키다 ❑ 바이러스가 감염자의 몸에서 변이한다. ❑ 에이취아이 브이가 약에 내성을 가진 형태로 변이할 수 있는 능력이 있다는 것이 증명되었다. ● 변이, 돌연변이 가산명사 또는 불가산명사 ❑ 과학자들이 헌팅턴병의 원인으로 보이는 변이 유전자를 발견했다. 2 자동사 ─로 돌변하다 ❑ 하룻밤 사이에 소문이 머리기사로 돌변하기 시작했다.

1 형용사 말없는 ❑ 그는 말이 없고 차가웠으며 무관심했다. ● 부사 말없이 ❑ 그는 그녀가 전화 옆에 조용히 서 있는 모습을 볼 수 있었다. 2 형용사 벙어리의 [구식어] ❑ 공작의 딸 마리아나는 충격적인 일을 겪은 후 벙어리가 되었다. 3 타동사 잠재우다, 약화시키다 ❑ 부패가 국내 경제의 장기 호황을 약화시키지 못한 것으로 보인다. ● 힘없는, 약한 형용사 ❑ 이번 엄포는 그의 내각이 이전에 내놓은 힘없는 비판과 뚜렷한 대조를 이루었다. 4 타동사 소리를 낮추다 ❑ 그들은 태도를 누그러뜨리며 목소리를 낮추기 시작한다. ● 작은 소리의 형용사 ❑ "네." 하고 그가 내가 거의 알아들을 수 없을 정도의 작은 목소리로 대답했다.

형용사 연한 ❑ 은은하고 연한 색으로 칠한

1 타동사 만신창이가 되다, 불구가 되다 ❑ 지난 9개월간 말 서른 마리 이상이 불구가 되었다. ❑ 그는 젊은 남성 6명을 고문해서 불구로 만들었다. ● 신체 상해 가산명사 또는 불가산명사 ❑ 국제 사면 위원회는 고문과 신체 상해 사례를 기록한다. 2 타동사 못쓰게 되다, 망쳐지다 ❑ 브레히트는 누군가 자신의 시나리오를 망쳐놓다고 말했다.

1 가산명사 또는 불가산명사 반란, 항명 ❑ 군 내부에서 쿠데타 시도와 반란이 계속되면서 정권이 흔들리기 시작했다. 2 자동사 반란을 일으키다, 항명하다 ❑ 수도 방위 부대가 9개월간 보수를 받지 못했다는 이유로 반란을 일으켰다.

타동사/자동사 중얼거리다, 투덜대다 ❑ "그 미치광이가 무슨 생각을 하고 있는지는 하늘만 알 거야."라고 그녀가 투덜댔다. ❑ 그녀 귀에 그 노파가 배려 운운하며 중얼대는 말이 들린다. ● 가산명사 중얼거림, 불평 ❑ 그들은 불평 섞인 말 한마디만 내뱉을 뿐이다. ● 중얼거림, 불평 가산명사 또는 불가산명사 ❑ 그는 사람들 앞쪽에서 중얼거리는 소리를 들었다.

A B C D E F G H I J K L M N O P Q R S T U V W X Y Z

mut|ton /mʌtᵊn/ ❶ N-UNCOUNT **Mutton** is meat from an adult sheep that is eaten as food. ❑ ...a leg of mutton. ❷ PHRASE If you describe a woman as **mutton dressed as lamb**, you are criticizing her for trying to look younger than she really is, in a way that you consider unattractive. [BRIT, INFORMAL, DISAPPROVAL] ❑ You become very sensitive about looking like mutton dressed as lamb in your late thirties. →see **meat**

❶ 불가산명사 양고기 ❑ 양고기 다리 부위 ❷ 구 억지로 젊어 보이려는 여자 [영국영어, 비격식체, 탐탁찮음] ❑ 30대 후반에는 억지로 젊게 꾸민 여자처럼 보일까봐 매우 예민해진다.

mu|tu|al ♦◇◇ /myutʃuəl/ ❶ ADJ You use **mutual** to describe a situation, feeling, or action that is experienced, felt, or done by both of two people mentioned. ❑ The East and the West can work together for their mutual benefit and progress. ● **mu|tu|al|ly** ADV ❑ Attempts to reach a mutually agreed solution had been fruitless. →see **exclusive** ❷ ADJ You use **mutual** to describe something such as an interest which two or more people share. ❑ They do, however, share a mutual interest in design. ❸ ADJ If an insurance company or savings bank has **mutual** status, it is not owned by shareholders but by its customers, who receive a share of the profits. [BUSINESS] [ADJ n] ❑ ...a mutual company based in Columbus, Ohio.

❶ 형용사 서로의, 상호의 ❑ 동서양이 상호 이익과 발전을 위해 협력할 수 있다. ● 서로, 상호간에 부사 ❑ 상호 합의된 해결안 도출을 시도했지만 아무런 소용이 없었다. ❷ 형용사 공통의 ❑ 하지만 그들에게는 디자인이라는 공통의 관심사가 있다. ❸ 형용사 상호 회사의 [경제] ❑ 오하이오 주 콜럼버스에 본사를 둔 상호 회사

mu|tu|al fund (**mutual funds**) N-COUNT A **mutual fund** is an organization which invests money in many different kinds of business and which offers units for sale to the public as an investment. [AM, BUSINESS; BRIT **unit trust**]

가산명사 뮤추얼펀드 [미국영어, 경제; 영국영어 unit trust]

muz|zle /mʌzᵊl/ (**muzzles, muzzling, muzzled**) ❶ N-COUNT The **muzzle** of an animal such as a dog is its nose and mouth. ❑ The mongrel presented his muzzle for scratching. ❷ N-COUNT A **muzzle** is an object that is put over a dog's nose and mouth so that it cannot bite people or make a noise. ❑ ...dogs like pit bulls which have to wear a muzzle. ❸ V-T If you **muzzle** a dog or other animal, you put a muzzle over its nose and mouth. ❑ He was convicted of failing to muzzle a pit bull. ❹ V-T If you say that someone **is muzzled**, you are complaining that they are prevented from expressing their views freely. [DISAPPROVAL] ❑ He complained of being muzzled by the chairman. ❺ N-COUNT The **muzzle** of a gun is the end where the bullets come out when it is fired. ❑ Mickey felt the muzzle of a rifle press hard against his neck.

❶ 가산명사 (개 등의) 코와 주둥이 부분 ❑ 똥개가 코를 들이대고 긁기 시작했다. ❷ 가산명사 재갈 ❑ 핏불처럼 재갈을 물려야 하는 개 ❸ 타동사 재갈을 물리다 ❑ 그는 핏불에 재갈을 물리지 않은 혐의가 입증되었다. ❹ 타동사 재갈이 물리다 [탐탁찮음] ❑ 그는 회장이 말하지 못하게 재갈을 물렸다고 불평했다. ❺ 가산명사 총부리 ❑ 미키는 라이플의 총부리가 목을 세게 짓누르는 것을 느꼈다.

my ♦♦♦ /maɪ/

My is the first person singular possessive determiner.

my는 1인칭 단수 소유한정사이다.

❶ DET A speaker or writer uses **my** to indicate that something belongs or relates to himself or herself. ❑ I invited him back to my flat for a coffee. ❷ DET In conversations or in letters, **my** is used in front of a word like "dear" or "darling" to show affection. [FEELINGS] ❑ My sweet Freda. ❸ DET **My** is used in phrases such as "**My God**" and "**My goodness**" to express surprise or shock. [SPOKEN, FEELINGS] ❑ My God, I've never seen you so nervous.

❶ 한정사 나의 ❑ 나는 답례로 내 아파트에서 커피를 한 잔 하자고 그를 초대했다. ❷ 한정사 대화나 편지에서 친근감을 표현하는 데 사용 [감정 개입] ❑ 사랑스러운 프레다에게 ❸ 한정사 놀라움을 나타냄; 하느님 맙소사, 세상에 [구어체, 감정 개입] ❑ 세상에, 너 전에는 이렇게 초조해한 적 없잖아.

myr|i|ad /mɪriəd/ ❶ QUANT A **myriad** or **myriads of** people or things is a very large number or great variety of them. [QUANT of pl-n] ❑ They face a myriad of problems bringing up children. ❷ ADJ **Myriad** means having a large number or great variety. [ADJ n] ❑ The magazine has been celebrating British pop and culture in all its myriad forms.

❶ 수량사 무수한, 다양한 ❑ 그들은 아이를 키우면서 무수한 문제에 직면한다. ❷ 형용사 무수한, 다양한 ❑ 이 잡지는 영국의 팝과 문화를 셀 수 없이 다양한 형태로 알려 왔다.

my|self ♦♦◇ /maɪsɛlf/

Myself is the first person singular reflexive pronoun.

myself는 1인칭 단수 재귀대명사이다.

❶ PRON-REFL A speaker or writer uses **myself** to refer to himself or herself. **Myself** is used as the object of a verb or preposition when the subject refers to the same person. [v PRON, prep PRON] ❑ I asked myself what I would have done in such a situation. ❷ PRON-REFL-EMPH You use **myself** to emphasize a first person singular subject. In more formal English, **myself** is sometimes used instead of "me" as the object of a verb or preposition, for emphasis. [EMPHASIS] ❑ I myself enjoy cinema, poetry, eating out and long walks. ❸ PRON-REFL-EMPH If you say something such as "I did it **myself**," you are emphasizing that you did it, rather than anyone else. [EMPHASIS] ❑ "Where did you get that embroidery?" — "I made it myself."

❶ 재귀대명사 나 자신 ❑ 나는 그 같은 상황에서 어떻게 했을지 나 자신에게 자문해 보았다. ❷ 강조 재귀대명사 바로 나, 나 자신 [강조] ❑ 내 자신이 영화, 시, 외식, 긴 산책을 즐기는 사람이다. ❸ 강조 재귀대명사 내가 직접 [강조] ❑ "그 자수 장식은 어디서 난 거야?" "내가 직접 만들었어."

mys|te|ri|ous /mɪstɪəriəs/ ❶ ADJ Someone or something that is **mysterious** is strange and is not known about or understood. ❑ He died in mysterious circumstances. ❑ A mysterious illness confined him to bed for over a month. ● **mys|te|ri|ous|ly** ADV ❑ A couple of messages had mysteriously disappeared. ❷ ADJ If someone is **mysterious** about something, they deliberately do not talk much about it, sometimes because they want to make people more interested in it. [v-link ADJ, oft ADJ about n] ❑ As for his job – well, he was very mysterious about it. ● **mys|te|ri|ous|ly** ADV [ADV after v] ❑ Asked what she meant, she said mysteriously: "Work it out for yourself."

❶ 형용사 알 수 없는, 불가사의한 ❑ 그가 숨진 상황은 불가사의로 남아 있다. ❑ 그는 알 수 없는 병에 걸려 한 달 넘게 누워 있어야 했다. ● 불가사의하게 부사 ❑ 메시지 두 개가 수수께끼처럼 사라졌었다. ❷ 형용사 말을 아끼는, 비밀스러운 ❑ 그는 자기 직업에 대해 말을 아꼈다. ● 말을 아끼며, 비밀스럽게 부사 ❑ 무슨 뜻이냐고 묻자 그녀는 비밀스럽게 "직접 알아내 보세요."라고 말했다.

mys|tery ♦◇◇ /mɪstəri, mɪstri/ (**mysteries**) ❶ N-COUNT A **mystery** is something that is not understood or known about. ❑ The source of the gunshots still remains a mystery. ❷ N-UNCOUNT If you talk about the **mystery** of someone or something, you are talking about how difficult they are to understand or know about, especially when this gives them a rather strange or magical quality. ❑ She's a lady of mystery. ❸ ADJ A **mystery** person or thing is one whose identity or nature is not known. [ADJ n] ❑ The mystery hero immediately alerted police after spotting a bomb. ❹ N-COUNT A **mystery** is a story in which strange

❶ 가산명사 미스터리, 불가사의 ❑ 발포 근원지는 아직까지 미스터리로 남아 있다. ❷ 불가산명사 신비 ❑ 그녀는 신비로운 여인이다. ❸ 형용사 신비에 싸인, 베일에 싸인 ❑ 베일에 싸인 영웅이 폭탄을 발견하자마자 즉각 경찰에 신고했다. ❹ 가산명사 추리 소설, 미스터리 ❑ 그의 네 번째 소설은 런던을 배경으로 한 살인 추리물이다.

things happen that are not explained until the end. ❑ *His fourth novel is a murder mystery set in London.*

mys|tic /mɪstɪk/ (**mystics**) **1** N-COUNT A **mystic** is a person who practices or believes in religious mysticism. ❑ *...an Indian mystic known as Bhagwan Shree Rajneesh.* **2** ADJ **Mystic** means the same as **mystical**. [ADJ n] ❑ *...mystic union with God.*

mys|ti|cal /mɪstɪkəl/ ADJ Something that is **mystical** involves spiritual powers and influences that most people do not understand. ❑ *That was clearly a deep mystical experience.*

mys|ti|cism /mɪstɪsɪzəm/ N-UNCOUNT **Mysticism** is a religious practice in which people search for truth, knowledge, and closeness to God through meditation and prayer. ❑ *As a younger man Harrison was intrigued by Indian mysticism.*

mys|ti|fy /mɪstɪfaɪ/ (**mystifies, mystifying, mystified**) V-T If you **are mystified** by something, you find it impossible to explain or understand. ❑ *The audience must have been totally mystified by the plot.* ● **mys|ti|fy|ing** ADJ ❑ *I find your attitude a little mystifying, Moira.*

mys|tique /mɪstik/ N-SING If there is a **mystique** about someone or something, they are thought to be special and people do not know much about them. [also N-UNCOUNT] ❑ *His book destroyed the mystique of monarchy.*

myth ♦◇◇ /mɪθ/ (**myths**) **1** N-VAR A **myth** is a well-known story which was made up in the past to explain natural events or to justify religious beliefs or social customs. ❑ *There is a famous Greek myth in which Icarus flew too near to the Sun.* **2** N-VAR If you describe a belief or explanation as a **myth**, you mean that many people believe it but it is actually untrue. ❑ *Contrary to the popular myth, women are not reckless spendthrifts.* →see **fantasy**
→see Word Web: **myth**

mythi|cal /mɪθɪkəl/ **1** ADJ Something or someone that is **mythical** exists only in myths and is therefore imaginary. ❑ *...the Hydra, the mythical beast that had seven or more heads.* **2** ADJ If you describe something as **mythical**, you mean that it is untrue or does not exist. ❑ *...the American West, not the mythical, romanticized West of cowboys and gunslingers, but the real West.*

my|thol|ogy /mɪθɒlədʒi/ (**mythologies**) **1** N-VAR **Mythology** is a group of myths, especially all the myths from a particular country, religion, or culture. ❑ *In Greek mythology, the god Zeus took the form of a swan to seduce Leda.* ● **mytho|logi|cal** /mɪθəlɒdʒɪkəl/ ADJ ❑ *...the mythological beast that was part lion and part goat.* **2** N-VAR You can use **mythology** to refer to the beliefs or opinions that people have about something, when you think that they are false or untrue. ❑ *Altman strips away the pretence and mythology to expose the film industry as a business like any other, dedicated to the pursuit of profit.* →see **hero, myth**

---

1 가산명사 신비주의자 ❑ 바그완 쉬리 라즈니쉬로 알려진 인도 신비주의자 **2** 형용사 초자연적인, 신비로운 ❑ 신과의 초자연적인 합일

형용사 초자연적인, 신비로운 ❑ 이는 명백히 심오한 초자연적인 경험이었다.

불가산명사 신비주의 ❑ 해리슨은 젊은 시절 인도 신비주의에 흥미를 느꼈다.

타동사 어리둥절하다 ❑ 관객이 줄거리를 보고 완전히 어리둥절했음에 틀림없다. ● 어리둥절하게 하는 형용사 ❑ 모이라, 네 태도에 약간 어리둥절하게 하는 면이 있어.

단수명사 신비로운 분위기 ❑ 그의 책이 군주 정치에 대한 환상을 깨뜨렸다.

1 가산명사 또는 불가산명사 신화 ❑ 이카루스가 태양에 너무 가깝게 날아갔다는 내용의 유명한 그리스 신화가 있다. **2** 가산명사 또는 불가산명사 그릇된 통념 ❑ 일반적인 통념과는 달리 여성들은 흥청망청 낭비를 일삼지 않는다.

1 형용사 신화의, 상상의 ❑ 머리를 일곱 개 넘게 가진 신화 속의 괴물, 히드라 **2** 형용사 사실과 다른, 근거 없는 ❑ 미국 서부, 근거 없이 낭만적으로 묘사된 카우보이와 총잡이들이 나오는 서부가 아니라 진짜 서부

1 가산명사 또는 불가산명사 신화 ❑ 그리스 신화에서 제우스 신은 레다를 유혹하기 위해 백조의 모습으로 변신했다. ● 신화의, 신화적인 형용사 ❑ 일부는 사자, 일부는 염소의 모습을 한 신화 속의 동물 **2** 가산명사 또는 불가산명사 허위, 근거 없는 믿음 ❑ 알트만은 가식과 허위를 벗어 던지고 영화 산업이 다른 산업과 마찬가지로 이익 추구에 충실한 사업이라는 점을 까발린다.

Word Web   **myth**

The scholar Joseph Campbell* believed that **mythologies** explain a **culture's** understanding of their world. **Stories, symbols, rituals,** and **myths** explain the **psychological, social,** cosmological, and **spiritual** parts of life. Campbell also believed that artists and philosophers are a culture's mythmakers. He explored **archetypal themes** in myths from many different cultures. He showed how these themes are repeated in many different cultures. For example, the **hero's** journey appeared in ancient Greece in *The Odyssey**, and the same theme appears later in England in King Arthur's* search for the Holy Grail*. A 20th-century version shows up in the film *Star Wars*.

Joseph Campbell (1904–1987): an American professor and author
The Odyssey: an epic poem from ancient Greece
King Arthur: a legendary king of Great Britain
Holy Grail: a cup that legends say Jesus used

Nn

N, n /ɛn/ (**N's, n's**) N-VAR N is the fourteenth letter of the English alphabet.

N.A. also **n/a** CONVENTION N.A. is a written abbreviation for **not applicable** or **not available**.

nag /næg/ (**nags, nagging, nagged**) ◼ V-T/V-I If someone **nags** you, they keep asking you to do something you have not done yet or do not want to do. [DISAPPROVAL] ❑ *The more Sarah nagged her, the more stubborn Cissie became.* ❑ *My girlfriend nagged me to cut my hair.* ● N-COUNT A **nag** is someone who nags. ❑ *Aunt Molly is a nag about regular meals.* ● **nagging** N-UNCOUNT ❑ *Her endless nagging drove him away from home.* ◼ V-T/V-I If something such as a doubt or worry **nags at** you, or **nags** you, it keeps worrying you. ❑ *He could be wrong about her. The feeling nagged at him.* ❑ *...the anxiety that had nagged Amy all through lunch.*

nail /neɪl/ (**nails, nailing, nailed**) ◼ N-COUNT A **nail** is a thin piece of metal with one pointed end and one flat end. You hit the flat end with a hammer in order to push the nail into something such as a wall. ❑ *A mirror hung on a nail above the washstand.* ◼ V-T If you **nail** something somewhere, you fasten it there using one or more nails. ❑ *Frank put the first plank down and nailed it in place.* ❑ *They nail shut the front door.* ◼ N-COUNT Your **nails** are the thin hard parts that grow at the ends of your fingers and toes. ❑ *Keep your nails short and your hands clean.* ◼ V-T To **nail** someone means to catch them and prove that they have been breaking the law. [INFORMAL] ❑ *The prosecution still managed to nail him for robberies at the homes of leading industrialists.* ◼ PHRASE If you say that someone **has hit the nail on the head**, you think they are exactly right about something. ❑ *"I think it would civilize people a bit more if they had decent conditions."* — *"I think you've hit the nail on the head."*

▶**nail down** ◼ PHRASAL VERB If you **nail down** something unknown or uncertain, you find out exactly what it is. ❑ *It would be useful if you could nail down the source of this tension.* ◼ PHRASAL VERB If you **nail down** an agreement, you manage to reach a firm agreement with a definite result. ❑ *The Secretary of State and his Russian counterpart met to try to nail down the elusive accord.*

naïve /naɪiːv, BRIT naɪiːv/ also **naïve** ADJ If you describe someone as **naive**, you think they lack experience and so expect things to be easy or people to be honest or kind. ❑ *It's naive to think that teachers are always tolerant.* ❑ *Their view was that he had been politically naive.* ● **naïvely** ADV ❑ *...naively applying Western solutions to Eastern problems.* ● **naïvety** /naɪiviti/ N-UNCOUNT ❑ *I was alarmed by his naivety and ignorance of international affairs.*

naked /neɪkɪd/ ◼ ADJ Someone who is **naked** is not wearing any clothes. [ADJ n, ADJ after v, v-link ADJ] ❑ *Her naked body was found wrapped in a sheet in a field.* ❑ *They stripped me naked.* ● **nakedness** N-UNCOUNT ❑ *He had pulled the blanket over his body to hide his nakedness.* ◼ ADJ If an animal or part of an animal is **naked**, it has no fur or feathers on it. ❑ *The nest contained eight little mice that were naked and blind.* ◼ ADJ You can describe an object as **naked** when it does not have its normal covering. ❑ *...a naked bulb dangling in a bare room.* ◼ ADJ You can use **naked** to describe unpleasant or violent actions and behavior which are not disguised or hidden in any way. [JOURNALISM] [ADJ n] ❑ *Naked aggression and an attempt to change frontiers by force could not go unchallenged.* ❑ *...violence and the naked pursuit of power.*

Word Partnership	naked의 연어
ADV.	**bare** naked, **completely** naked, **half** naked, **nearly** naked ◼

name ♦♦♦ /neɪm/ (**names, naming, named**) ◼ N-COUNT The **name** of a person, place, or thing is the word or group of words that is used to identify them. ❑ *"What's his name?"* — *"Peter."* ❑ *I don't even know if Sullivan's his real name.*

Your **first name** is the name that your parents chose for you. When you are telling someone your name, this comes first in English-speaking countries. Your **last name**, or **surname**, is the name that you share with other members of your family. In between your first name and your last name you may have a **middle name**, a second name that your parents chose for you. It is only usually used in official circumstances such as registering for a course or signing documents.

◼ V-T When you **name** someone or something, you give them a name, usually at the beginning of their life. ❑ *My mother insisted on naming me Horace.* ❑ *...a man named John T. Benson.* ◼ V-T If you **name** someone or something **after** another person or thing, you give them the same name as that person or thing. ❑ *Why*

가산명사 또는 불가산명사 영어 알파벳의 열네 번째 글자

관용 표현 not applicable 또는 not available의 약자

◼ 타동사/자동사 잔소리하다 [탐탁찮음] ❑ 새러의 잔소리가 심해질수록 씨시는 더욱 고집을 부렸다. ❑ 내 여자친구가 나에게 머리를 자르라고 잔소리를 했다. ● 가산명사 잔소리꾼 ❑ 몰리 고모는 규칙적인 식사를 하라고 항상 잔소리이다. ● 잔소리 불가산명사 ❑ 그녀의 끝없는 잔소리가 그를 집에서 몰아냈다. ◼ 타동사/자동사 괴롭히다 ❑ 그가 그녀에 대해 잘못 생각했을 수도 있다. 그 생각이 그를 괴롭혔다. ❑ 점심 내내 에이미를 괴롭혔던 불안감

◼ 가산명사 못 ❑ 세면대 위에 거울이 못에 걸려 있었다. ◼ 타동사 못을 박다 ❑ 프랭크는 첫 번째 판자를 내려놓고 못을 박아 고정시켰다. ❑ 그들은 앞문에 못을 박아 막아버렸다. ◼ 가산명사 손톱 ❑ 손톱은 항상 짧게 하고 손은 청결히 해라. ◼ 타동사 적발하다 [비격식체] ❑ 검찰 측은 그럼에도 불구하고 주요 사업가들의 집에서 강도짓을 한 그를 적발해 내었다. ◼ 구 핵심을 짚다 ❑ "내 생각엔 사람들에게 올바른 여건만 주어진다면 좀 더 교화될 수 있을 텐데." "네 말이 사안의 핵심을 짚은 것 같아."

◼ 구동사 알아내다 ❑ 이 알력의 원인을 알아낼 수 있다면 유용할 것이다. ◼ 구동사 확정 짓다 ❑ 국무성 장관과 러시아 측 상대방이 난해한 협정을 확정 짓기 위해 만났다.

형용사 순진한, 미숙한 ❑ 교사들이 항상 관대하다고 생각하는 것은 지나치게 순진하다. ❑ 그들의 견해에 그는 정치적으로 미숙했다. ● 순진하게 부사 ❑ 동양의 문제에 서구적 해결책을 순진하게 적용함 ● 순진함 불가산명사 ❑ 그가 국제 문제에 대해 얼마나 무지하고 순진한 안목을 가졌는지 나는 놀랐다.

◼ 형용사 알몸의, 벌거벗은 ❑ 그녀의 벌거벗은 사체가 천에 감긴 채 들판에서 발견되었다. ❑ 그들은 나를 벌거벗겼다. ● 벌거벗음 불가산명사 ❑ 그는 알몸을 감추기 위해 담요를 끌어당겨 덮었다. ◼ 형용사 털이 없는 ❑ 둥지에는 털도 안 나고 눈도 못 뜬 여덟 마리의 새끼 쥐가 있었다. ◼ 형용사 날개가 없는 ❑ 빈 방에 갓도 없이 매달려 있는 전구 ◼ 형용사 적나라한 [언론] ❑ 대놓고 이루어지는 공격과 무력으로 국경을 바꾸려는 시도에 대응 안 할 수 없었다. ❑ 폭력과 적나라한 권력 추구

◼ 가산명사 이름 ❑ "그의 이름은 뭐야?" "피터." ❑ 나도 설리번이 그의 실명인지조차도 몰라.

first name은 부모가 지어준 이름이다. 영어권에서는 다른 사람에게 이름을 알려줄 때 이 first name을 먼저 말한다. last name 또는 surname은 가족의 다른 구성원과 공유하는 부분, 즉 성(姓)이다. 이름과 성 사이에 middle name이 있을 수도 있는데, 이것은 부모가 지어준 두 번째 이름이며, 강좌 등록이나 서류 서명과 같은 공식적인 상황에서만 주로 사용된다.

◼ 타동사 명명하다 ❑ 우리 어머니께서 나를 호레이스라고 불려야 한다고 우기셨다. ❑ 존 티 벤슨이라는 이름의 사내 ◼ 타동사 명명하다 ❑ 왜 아들들 누구에게도 당신의 이름을 붙이지 않았나요?

have you not named any of your sons after yourself? ☐ V-T If you **name** someone, you identify them by stating their name. ☐ *It's nearly thirty years since a journalist was jailed for refusing to name a source.* 🖪 V-T If you **name** something such as a price, time, or place, you say what you want it to be. ☐ *Call Marty, tell him to name his price.* 🖪 V-T If you **name** the person for a particular job, you say who you want to have the job. ☐ *The England manager will be naming a new captain, to replace the injured Bryan Robson.* ☐ *When the chairman of Campbell's retired, McGovern was named as his successor.* 🖪 N-COUNT You can refer to the reputation of a person or thing as their **name**. ☐ *He had a name for good judgement.* 🖪 N-COUNT You can refer to someone as, for example, a famous **name** or a great **name** when they are well-known. [JOURNALISM] ☐ *...some of the most famous names in modeling and show business.* 🖪 →see also **brand name, Christian name, first name, maiden name** 🔟 PHRASE If something is **in** someone's **name**, it officially belongs to them or is reserved for them. ☐ *The house is in my husband's name.* 🔢 PHRASE If someone does something **in the name of** a group of people, they do it as the representative of that group. ☐ *In the United States the majority governs in the name of the people.* 🔢 PHRASE If you do something **in the name of** an ideal or an abstract thing, you do it in order to preserve or promote that thing. ☐ *...one of those rare occasions in history when a political leader risked his own power in the name of the greater public good.* 🔢 PHRASE When you mention someone or something **by name**, or address someone **by name**, you use their name. ☐ *When he walks down 131st street, he greets most people he sees by name.* 🔢 PHRASE You can use **by name** or **by the name of** when you are saying what someone is called. [FORMAL] ☐ *In 1911 he met up with a young Australian by the name of Harry Busteed.* 🔢 PHRASE If someone **calls** you **names**, they insult you by saying unpleasant things to you or about you. ☐ *At my last school they called me names because I was so slow.* 🔢 PHRASE If you **make a name for yourself** or **make** your **name as** something, you become well-known for that thing. ☐ *She was beginning to make a name for herself as a portrait photographer.* →see **Internet**

Word Partnership   name의 연어

N.	name and address, company name, name and number 🛽
ADJ.	common name, full name, real name 🛽
	familiar name, famous name, well-known name 🛽

name‖ly /neɪmli/ ADV You use **namely** to introduce detailed information about the subject you are discussing, or a particular aspect of it. ☐ *A district should serve its clientele, namely students, staff, and parents.*

nan‖ny /næni/ (**nannies**) N-COUNT A **nanny** is a woman who is paid by parents to take care of their child or children.

nap /næp/ (**naps, napping, napped**) 🛽 N-COUNT If you take or have a **nap**, you have a short sleep, usually during the day. ☐ *I might take a little nap.* 🛽 V-I If you **nap**, you sleep for a short period of time, usually during the day. ☐ *An elderly person may nap during the day and then sleep only five hours a night.* 🛽 PHRASE If someone **is caught napping**, something happens when they are not prepared for it, although they should have been. [INFORMAL] ☐ *The security services were clearly caught napping.* →see **sleep**

nap‖kin /næpkɪn/ (**napkins**) N-COUNT A **napkin** is a square of cloth or paper that you use when you are eating to protect your clothes, or to wipe your mouth or hands. ☐ *...taking tiny bites of a hot dog and daintily wiping my lips with a napkin.*

nap‖py /næpi/ (**nappies**) N-COUNT A **nappy** is a piece of soft thick cloth or paper which is fastened around a baby's bottom in order to soak up its urine and feces. [BRIT; AM **diaper**] ☐ *I've learned how to change a nappy.*

nar‖cot‖ic /nɑrkɒtɪk/ (**narcotics**) 🛽 N-COUNT **Narcotics** are drugs such as opium or heroin which make you sleepy and stop you from feeling pain. You can also use **narcotics**, especially in American English, to mean any kind of illegal drugs. ☐ *He was indicted for dealing in narcotics.* 🛽 ADJ If something, especially a drug, has a **narcotic** effect, it makes the person who uses it feel sleepy. ☐ *...hormones that have a narcotic effect on the immune system.*

nar‖rate /næreɪt, BRIT nəreɪt/ (**narrates, narrating, narrated**) 🛽 V-T If you **narrate** a story, you tell it from your own point of view. [FORMAL] ☐ *The three of them narrate the same events from three perspectives.* ● **nar‖ra‖tion** /nəreɪʃᵊn/ N-UNCOUNT ☐ *Its story-within-a-story method of narration is confusing.* ● **nar‖ra‖tor** /næreɪtər, BRIT nəreɪtᵊr/ (**narrators**) N-COUNT ☐ *Jules, the story's narrator, is an actress in her late thirties.* 🛽 V-T The person who **narrates** a film or program speaks the words which accompany the pictures, but does not appear in it. ☐ *She also narrated a documentary about the Kirov Ballet School.* ● **nar‖ra‖tion** N-UNCOUNT ☐ *As soon as the crew gets back from lunch, we can put your narration on it right away.* ● **nar‖ra‖tor** (**narrators**) N-COUNT ☐ *...the narrator of the documentary.*

nar‖ra‖tive /nærətɪv/ (**narratives**) 🛽 N-COUNT A **narrative** is a story or an account of a series of events. ☐ *...a fast-moving narrative.* 🛽 N-UNCOUNT **Narrative** is the description of a series of events, usually in a novel. ☐ *Neither author was very strong on narrative.*

nar‖row ♦♢♢ /nærəʊ/ (**narrower, narrowest, narrows, narrowing, narrowed**) 🛽 ADJ Something that is **narrow** measures a very small distance from one side to the other, especially compared to its length or height. ☐ *...through the town's narrow streets.* ☐ *She had long, narrow feet.* ● **nar‖row‖ness** N-UNCOUNT ☐ *...the narrowness of the river mouth.* 🛽 V-I If something **narrows**, it becomes less wide. ☐ *The wide track narrows before crossing another stream.* 🛽 V-T/V-I If your eyes **narrow** or if you **narrow** your eyes, you almost close them, for example because you are angry or because you are trying to concentrate on something. [WRITTEN] ☐ *Coggins's eyes narrowed angrily. "You think I'd tell you?"* 🛽 ADJ If you describe someone's ideas, attitudes, or beliefs as **narrow**, you disapprove of them because they are restricted in some way, and often ignore the more

🛽 타동사 지명하다 ☐ 정보원을 밝히기를 거부했다는 이유로 언론인이 갑옥에 마지막으로 간 지 거의 30년이 되었다. 🖪 타동사 지정하다 ☐ 마티에게 전화해서 가격을 불러 보라고 해. 🖪 타동사 임명하다 ☐ 잉글랜드 팀의 감독이 부상당한 브라이언 롭슨을 대체하기 위해 새로운 주장을 임명할 것이다. ☐ 캠벨스의 회장이 은퇴했을 때 그의 후임으로 맥거번이 임명되었다. 🖪 가산명사 평판 ☐ 그는 판단력이 좋다는 평판을 들었다. 🖪 가산명사 이름, 명사 [언론] ☐ 모델 및 연예계에서 가장 잘 알려진 이름들 몇몇 🖪 →의 -의 명칭으로 🔟 구 -의 이름으로 ☐ 미국에서는 다수당이 국민의 이름으로 통치한다. 🔢 구 -의 명분하에 ☐ ...의 명분으로 ☐ 집은 제 남편 명의로 되어 있어요. 🔢 구 -의 이름으로 ☐ 미국에서는 다수당이 국민의 이름으로 통치한다. 🔢 구 -의 명분하에 ☐ ...의 명분으로 ☐ 자신의 권력을 내걸었던 몇 안 되는 역사적 사례 중 하나 🔢 구 호명하여 ☐ 그는 131번가를 걸어 다닐 때 만나는 대부분의 사람들과 공공의 대의라는 명분을 위해 인사를 한다. 🔢 구 -라는 이름의 [격식체] ☐ 1911년에 그는 해리 버스티드라는 이름의 젊은 호주 사람을 만났다. 🔢 구 이름을 떨치다 ☐ 내가 지난번에 다닌 학교에선 내가 너무 느리다고 사람들이 나를 놀렸다. 🔢 구 이름을 떨치다 ☐ 그녀는 인물 사진작가로서 점점 이름을 떨치기 시작하였다.

부사 즉 ☐ 학군은 고객, 즉 학생, 직원, 학부모에게 봉사해야 한다.

가산명사 보모

🛽 가산명사 낮잠 ☐ 내가 잠깐 낮잠을 잘지도 모른다. 🛽 자동사 낮잠 자다 ☐ 노인의 경우 낮에 낮잠을 잔 다음 밤에는 3시간만 잘 수도 있다. 🛽 구 방심한 사이 당하다 [비격식체] ☐ 보안 서비스들이 방심한 사이 일을 당한 것이 분명했다.

가산명사 냅킨 ☐ 핫도그를 조금씩 베어 먹으면서 냅킨으로 내 입술을 꼭꼭 닦으며

가산명사 기저귀 [영국영어; 미국영어 diaper] ☐ 기저귀 가는 법을 배웠다.

🛽 가산명사 마취제; 마약 ☐ 그는 마약 거래 혐의로 기소당했다. 🛽 형용사 마취성의 ☐ 면역 체계에 마취성 효과를 가져오는 호르몬

🛽 타동사 서술하다 [격식체] ☐ 그들 셋은 각자의 시선으로 동일한 사건을 서술한다. ● 서술 불가산명사 ☐ 액자식 이야기 서술 방식은 혼란스럽다. ● 내레이터, 서술자 가산명사 ☐ 그 이야기의 내레이터인 줄스는 30대 후반의 여배우다. 🛽 타동사 내레이션을 하다 ☐ 그녀는 또한 키로프 발레 학교에 관한 다큐멘터리의 내레이션을 했다. ● 내레이션 불가산명사 ☐ 제작진이 점심을 먹고 돌아오는 대로 당신의 내레이션을 바로 삽입할 수 있습니다. ● 내레이터, 해설자 가산명사 ☐ 다큐멘터리의 내레이터

🛽 가산명사 이야기 ☐ 속도가 빠른 이야기 🛽 불가산명사 이야기의 서술 ☐ 두 저자 모두 서술이 그다지 강렬하지는 못했다.

🛽 형용사 좁은 ☐ 읍내의 좁은 길을 따라 ☐ 그녀의 발은 길고 좁았다. ● 좁음 불가산명사 ☐ 강어귀가 좁음 🛽 자동사 좁아지다 ☐ 개울을 하나 더 건너기 전에 넓은 산책길은 좁아진다. 🛽 타동사/자동사 (눈이) 실눈이 되다; 실눈을 뜨다 [문어체] ☐ 화가 나 코긴스의 실눈이 되며 말했다. "내가 너한테 말할 것 같아?" 🛽 형용사 편협한 [탐탁찮음] ☐ 가족생활에 대한 편협하고 구식적인 시각 ☐ 그들이 자신들의 기여분을 지나치게 편협하게 잡을 수도 있다. ● 편협함 불가산명사 ☐ 그들의 정신적, 영적 시야의 편협함 🛽 타동사/자동사 좁아지다; 좁히다 ☐ 최근

important aspects of an argument or situation. [DISAPPROVAL] ❏ *...a narrow and outdated view of family life.* ● **nar|row|ly** ADV ❏ *They may define their contribution too narrowly.* ● **nar|row|ness** N-UNCOUNT ❏ *...the narrowness of their mental and spiritual outlook.* **5** V-T/V-I If something **narrows** or if you **narrow** it, its extent or range becomes smaller. → ❏ *Most recent opinion polls suggest that the gap between the two main parties has narrowed.* ● **nar|row|ing** N-SING ❏ *...a narrowing of the gap between rich members and poor.* **6** ADJ If you have a **narrow** victory, you succeed in winning but only by a small amount. ❏ *Delegates have voted by a narrow majority in favor of considering electoral reform.* ● **nar|row|ly** ADV ❏ *She narrowly failed to win enough votes.* ● **nar|row|ness** N-UNCOUNT ❏ *The narrowness of the government's victory reflected deep division within the Conservative Party.* **7** ADJ If you have a **narrow** escape, something unpleasant nearly happens to you. [ADJ n] ❏ *Two police officers had a narrow escape when separatists attacked their vehicles.* ● **nar|row|ly** [ADV with v] ❏ *Five firemen narrowly escaped death when a staircase collapsed beneath their feet.*

Thesaurus	narrow의 참조어	
ADJ.	close, cramped, tight; (ant.) broad, wide **1**	

Word Partnership	narrow의 연어	
ADV.	relatively narrow, too narrow **1**	
N.	narrow band, narrow hallway, narrow opening, narrow path **1**	
	narrow definition, narrow focus, narrow mind, narrow view **4**	

▶**narrow down** PHRASAL VERB If you **narrow down** a range of things, you reduce the number of things included in it. ❏ *What's happened is that the new results narrow down the possibilities.*

narrow-minded ADJ If you describe someone as **narrow-minded**, you are criticizing them because they are unwilling to consider new ideas or other people's opinions. [DISAPPROVAL] ❏ *...a narrow-minded bigot.*

NASA /nǽsə/ N-PROPER **NASA** is the American government organization concerned with spacecraft and space travel. **NASA** is an abbreviation for "National Aeronautics and Space Administration."

na|sal /néɪzᵊl/ **1** ADJ **Nasal** is used to describe things relating to the nose and the functions it performs. [ADJ n] ❏ *...inflamed nasal passages.* **2** ADJ If someone's voice is **nasal**, it sounds as if air is passing through their nose as well as their mouth while they are speaking. ❏ *Her voice was nasal and penetrating.* →see **smell**

nas|ty /nǽsti/ (**nastier**, **nastiest**) **1** ADJ Something that is **nasty** is very unpleasant to see, experience, or feel. ❏ *...an extremely nasty murder.* ● **nas|ti|ness** N-UNCOUNT ❏ *...the nastiness of war.* **2** ADJ If you describe a person or their behavior as **nasty**, you mean that they behave in an unkind and unpleasant way. ❏ *What nasty little snobs you all are.* ❏ *The guards looked really nasty.* ● **nas|ti|ly** ADV [ADV after v] ❏ *She took the money and eyed me nastily.* ● **nas|ti|ness** N-UNCOUNT ❏ *As the years went by his nastiness began to annoy his readers.* **3** ADJ If you describe something as **nasty**, you mean it is unattractive, undesirable, or in bad taste. ❏ *...Emily's nasty little house in Balham.* **4** ADJ A **nasty** problem or situation is very worrisome and difficult to deal with. ❏ *A spokesman said this firm action had defused a very nasty situation.* **5** ADJ If you describe an injury or a disease as **nasty**, you mean that it is serious or looks unpleasant. ❏ *My little granddaughter caught her heel in the spokes of her bicycle – it was a very nasty wound.*

na|tion ♦♦◊ /néɪʃᵊn/ (**nations**) **1** N-COUNT A **nation** is an individual country considered together with its social and political structures. ❏ *Such policies would require unprecedented cooperation between nations.*

Country is the most usual word to use when you are talking about the major political units that the world is divided into. **State** is used when you are talking about politics or government institutions. ❏ *...the new German state created by the unification process....Italy's state-controlled telecommunications company.* **State** can also refer to a political unit within a particular country. ❏ *...the state of California.* **Nation** is often used when you are talking about a country's inhabitants, and their cultural or ethnic background. ❏ *Wales is a proud nation with its own traditions... A senior government spokesman will address the nation.* **Land** is a less precise and more literary word, which you can use, for example, to talk about the feelings you have for a particular country. ❏ *She was fascinated to learn about this strange land at the edge of Europe.*

2 N-SING **The nation** is sometimes used to refer to all the people who live in a particular country. [JOURNALISM] ❏ *It was a story that touched the nation's heart.*

Thesaurus	nation의 참조어	
N.	country, population, republic, society **1**	

na|tion|al ♦♦♦ /nǽʃᵊnᵊl/ (**nationals**) **1** ADJ **National** means relating to the whole of a country or nation rather than to part of it or to other nations. ❏ *...major national and international issues.* ● **na|tion|al|ly** ADV ❏ *...a nationally televised speech.* **2** ADJ **National** means typical of the people or customs of a particular country or nation. [ADJ n] ❏ *...the national characteristics and history of the country.* **3** N-COUNT You can refer to someone who is legally a citizen of a country as a **national** of that country. ❏ *...a Sri-Lankan-born British national.*

대부분의 여론 조사에 의하면 두 주요 정당 사이의 격차가 좁아진 듯 하다. ● 좁아짐 단수명사 ❏ 구성원들 간의 빈부 격차의 축소 **6** 형용사 아슬아슬한, 근소한 ❏ 대의원들의 투표에서 선거법 개정을 실시하자는 측이 근소한 차이로 이겼다. ● 아슬아슬하게 부사 ❏ 그녀는 아슬아슬한 차이로 충분한 표를 얻지 못했다. ● 아슬아슬함 불가산명사 ❏ 정부의 아슬아슬한 승리는 보수당 내부의 깊은 균열을 드러내는 것이었다. **7** 형용사 가까스로 해내 ❏ 분리주의자들이 차량을 공격했을 때 경찰 2명이 가까스로 탈출했다. ● 가까스로 부사 ❏ 소방관 5명이 발밑에서 계단이 무너짐에도 불구하고 가까스로 죽음을 모면했다.

구동사 줄이다 ❏ 결국 새로운 결과들을 통해 가능성들을 줄여 나갈 수 있게 되었다.

형용사 마음이 좁은, 편협한, 옹졸한 [탐탁잖음] ❏ 옹졸할 정도로 편협한 사람

고유명사 미 항공 우주국

1 형용사 코의 ❏ 염증이 생긴 비강 **2** 형용사 비음의 ❏ 그녀의 비음 섞인 목소리는 앙칼졌다.

1 형용사 끔찍한 ❏ 너무도 끔찍한 살인 ● 끔찍함 불가산명사 ❏ 전쟁의 끔찍함 **2** 형용사 성질 더러운, 역겨운 ❏ 정말 역겨운 속물들이군. ❏ 경비원들이 정말 기분 나쁘게 생겼었다. ● 불쾌하게, 기분 나쁘게 부사 ❏ 그녀는 돈을 받으면서 나를 불쾌하게 처다봤다. ● 더러운 성질, 성깔 불가산명사 ❏ 해가 지나면서 그의 못된 심보가 독자들을 점점 짜증나게 했다. **3** 형용사 볼품없는, 흉한 ❏ 발햄에 있는 에밀리의 흉하게 생긴 작은 집 **4** 형용사 다루기 힘든, 아주 곤란한 ❏ 이 단호한 조치로 몹시 곤란한 상황을 돌파했다고 대변인은 말했다. **5** 형용사 심한 ❏ 작은 손녀의 발꿈치가 자전거의 살에 끼었었다. 상당히 심한 상처였다.

1 가산명사 국가 ❏ 그러한 정책은 국가들 사이의 전례 없는 협력을 요구할 것이다.

country는 세계를 나누는 주요 정치 단위에 대해 얘기할 때 쓰는 가장 일반적인 말이다. state는 정치나 정부 기관에 대해 얘기할 때 쓴다. ❏ ...통일 과정에 의해 만들어진 새 독일 정부.... 정부가 관장하는 이태리 통신 회사. state는 특정 국가 내의 정치 단위를 가리킬 수도 있다. ❏ ...캘리포니아 주. nation은 한 나라의 거주자, 거주자의 문화적 또는 인종적 배경을 얘기할 때 흔히 쓴다. ❏ 웨일스는 고유의 전통을 통해 자부심을 지닌 나라이다... 정부 고위 대변인이 국민들에게 연설할 것이다. land는 덜 정확하고 더 문학적인 말이며, 예를 들면 특정한 국가에 대한 감정을 얘기할 때 쓸 수 있다. ❏ 그녀는 유럽의 가장자리에 있는 이 낯선 땅에 대해 배우는 데 매료되었다.

2 단수명사 국민 [언론] ❏ 그것은 전 국민의 심금을 울린 이야기였다.

1 형용사 전국적인, 국가적인 ❏ 주요 국내 및 국제적 사안 ● 전국적으로 부사 ❏ 텔레비전으로 전국에 방영된 연설 **2** 형용사 국가적, 민족적 ❏ 그 나라의 국가적 특성과 역사 **3** 가산명사 시민 ❏ 스리랑카에서 태어난 영국 시민

Na|tion|al Health Ser|vice N-PROPER In Britain, **the National Health Service** is the state system for providing medical care. It is paid for by taxes. ❑ *An increasing number of these treatments are now available on the National Health Service.*

불가산명사 국가 의료 보험 제도 ❑ 이러한 치료를 이제는 국가 의료 보장 제도를 통해 점점 더 많이 받을 수 있다.

na|tion|al in|sur|ance N-UNCOUNT In Britain, **national insurance** is the state system of paying money to people who are ill, unemployed, or retired. It is financed by money that the government collects from people who work, or from their employers. [BUSINESS] ❑ *For example, a worker earning £50,000 will pay national insurance of about £3,086 next year.*

불가산명사 국민 연금 제도 [경제] ❑ 예를 들어 5만 파운드를 버는 근로자는 내년에 3,086파운드의 국민 연금을 납부할 것이다.

na|tion|al|ise /nǽʃənᵊlaɪz/ →see **nationalize**

na|tion|al|ism /nǽʃənᵊlɪzəm/ ◆ N-UNCOUNT **Nationalism** is the desire for political independence of people who feel they are historically or culturally a separate group within a country. ❑ *The rising tide of Slovak nationalism may also help the party to win representation in parliament.* ◾ N-UNCOUNT You can refer to a person's great love for their nation as **nationalism**. It is often associated with the belief that a particular nation is better than any other nation, and in this case is often used showing disapproval. ❑ *This kind of fierce nationalism is a powerful and potentially volatile force.*

◾ 불가산명사 민족주의 ❑ 거세지는 슬로바키아 민족주의 물결 덕분에 당이 의회에서 의석을 얻을 수도 있다. ◾ 불가산명사 애국심 ❑ 이렇게 맹렬한 애국심은 강력하면서도 잠재적 폭발력을 지닌 힘이다.

na|tion|al|ist ◆◇◇ /nǽʃənᵊlɪst/ (**nationalists**) ◾ ADJ **Nationalist** means connected with the desire of a group of people within a country for political independence. [ADJ n] ❑ *The crisis has set off a wave of nationalist feelings in Quebec.* ● N-COUNT A **nationalist** is someone with nationalist views. ❑ *...demands by Slovak nationalists for an independent state.* ◾ ADJ **Nationalist** means connected with a person's great love for their nation. It is often associated with the belief that their nation is better than any other nation, and in this case is often used showing disapproval. [ADJ n] ❑ *Political life has been infected by growing nationalist sentiment.* ● N-COUNT A **nationalist** is someone with nationalist views. ❑ *Some nationalists would like to depict the British monarchy as a purely English institution.*

◾ 형용사 민족주의의 ❑ 그 위기 때문에 퀘벡에서는 민족주의적 여론이 일파만파로 번지고 있다. ● 가산명사 민족주의자 ❑ 독립 국가를 세우자는 슬로바키아 민족주의자들의 요구 ◾ 형용사 국수주의 ❑ 정치 생활이 점점 국수주의적 여론의 영향을 받고 있다. ● 가산명사 국수주의자 ❑ 일부 국수주의자들은 영연방의 왕권을 순수하게 영국에만 국한된 제도로 그리고자 한다.

na|tion|al|is|tic /nǽʃənᵊlɪstɪk/ ADJ If you describe someone as **nationalistic**, you mean they are very proud of their nation. They also often believe that their nation is better than any other nation, and in this case it is often used showing disapproval. ❑ *...Barcelona, a team who are a monument to the nationalistic pride of the Catalan people.*

형용사 국수주의적인 ❑ 카탈로니아 사람들의 국수주의적 자긍심을 대변하는 팀인 바르셀로나 팀

na|tion|al|ity /nǽʃənǽlɪti/ (**nationalities**) ◾ N-VAR If you have the **nationality** of a particular country, you were born there or have the legal right to be a citizen. ❑ *Asked his nationality, he said British.* ◾ N-COUNT You can refer to people who have the same racial origins as a **nationality**, especially when they do not have their own independent country. ❑ *...the many nationalities that comprise Ethiopia.*

◾ 가산명사 또는 불가산명사 국적 ❑ 국적을 묻자 그는 영국인이라고 했다. ◾ 가산명사 민족 ❑ 에티오피아를 구성하는 수많은 민족들

na|tion|al|ize /nǽʃənᵊlaɪz/ (**nationalizes, nationalizing, nationalized**) [BRIT also **nationalise**] V-T If a government **nationalizes** a private company or industry, that company or industry becomes owned by the state and controlled by the government. [BUSINESS] ❑ *In 1987, Garcia introduced legislation to nationalize Peru's banking and financial systems.* ● na|tion|ali|za|tion /nǽʃənᵊlɪzeɪʃn/ (**nationalizations**) N-UNCOUNT ❑ *...the campaign for the nationalization of the coal mines.*

[영국영어 nationalise] 타동사 국유화하다 [경제] ❑ 1987년에 가르시아는 페루의 은행 및 금융 체제를 국유화하기 위한 법을 도입했다. ● 국유화 불가산명사 ❑ 석탄 광산을 국유화하기 위한 운동

na|tion|al park (**national parks**) N-COUNT; N-IN-NAMES A **national park** is a large area of land which is protected by the government because of its natural beauty, plants, or animals, and which the public can usually visit. ❑ *...the Masai Mara game reserve and Amboseli national park.*

가산명사; 이름명사 국립공원 ❑ 마사이 마라 동물 보호 구역과 암보셀리 국립공원

na|tion|wide /neɪʃnwaɪd/ ADJ **Nationwide** activities or situations happen or exist in all parts of a country. ❑ *The rising number of car crimes is a nationwide problem.* ● ADV **Nationwide** is also an adverb. ❑ *The figures show unemployment falling nationwide last month.*

형용사 전국적인 ❑ 자가용 범죄의 증가는 전국적인 문제이다. ● 부사 전국적으로 ❑ 지난달 전국적으로 실업률이 떨어졌음을 이 수치들은 보여 준다.

na|tive ◆◇◇ /neɪtɪv/ (**natives**) ◾ ADJ Your **native** country or area is the country or area where you were born and brought up. [ADJ n] ❑ *It was his first visit to his native country since 1948.* ◾ N-COUNT A **native** of a particular country or region is someone who was born in that country or region. ❑ *Dr. Aubin is a native of St. Blaise.* ● ADJ **Native** is also an adjective. [ADJ n, v-link ADJ to n] ❑ *Joshua Halpern is a native Northern Californian.* ◾ N-COUNT Some European people use **native** to refer to a person living in a non-Western country who belongs to the race or tribe that the majority of people there belong to. This use could cause offense. ❑ *They used force to banish the natives from the more fertile land.* ● ADJ **Native** is also an adjective. [ADJ n] ❑ *Native people were allowed to retain some sense of their traditional culture and religion.* ◾ ADJ Your **native** language or tongue is the first language that you learned to speak when you were a child. [ADJ n] ❑ *She spoke not only her native language, Swedish, but also English and French.* ◾ ADJ Plants or animals that are **native to** a particular region live or grow there naturally and were not brought there. [ADJ n, v-link ADJ to n] ❑ *...a project to create a 50 acre forest of native Caledonian pines.* ● N-COUNT **Native** is also a noun. ❑ *The coconut palm is a native of Malaysia.*

◾ 형용사 출생지인, 자기가 태어난 ❑ 그것은 그가 자신이 태어난 나라를 1948년 이후 처음 방문하는 것이었다. ◾ 가산명사 - 지역 출신인 사람 ❑ 오빈 박사는 세인트 블레이스에서 태어났다. ● 형용사 - 출신의, -에서 태어난 ❑ 조슈아 핼펀은 북부 캘리포니아 출신 주민이다. ◾ 가산명사 원주민 ❑ 비옥한 땅으로부터 원주민들을 추방하기 위해 그들은 무력을 썼다. ● 형용사 원주민의 ❑ 원주민들은 자신들의 전통 문화와 종교를 어느 정도 유지할 수 있도록 허락을 받았다. ◾ 형용사 모국의 ❑ 그녀는 모국어인 스웨덴뿐만 아니라 영어와 불어도 할 줄 알았다. ◾ 형용사 원산의, -에 자생하는 ❑ 칼레도니아 원산 소나무 숲 50에이커를 조성하기 위한 사업 ● 가산명사 특산물, 자생 식물 ❑ 야자수는 말레이시아의 자생 식물이다.

Thesaurus   *native*의 참조어

N.   citizen, resident ◾

Word Partnership   *native*의 연어

N.   native **country**, native **land** ◾
      native **language**, native **tongue** ◾

Na|tive Ameri|can (**Native Americans**) N-COUNT **Native Americans** are people from any of the many groups who were already living in North America before

가산명사 북미 원주민 ❑ 독수리는 북미 원주민에게 가장 신성한 동물이다. ● 형용사 북미 원주민의 ❑ 북미

Europeans arrived. □ *The eagle is the animal most sacred to the Native Americans.* ● ADJ **Native American** is also an adjective. [ADJ n] □ *...a gathering of Native American elders.*

원주민 원로 모임

Native Americans are people from any of the many groups, such as Comanche, Apache and Sioux, who were already living in North America before Europeans, and later Africans and Asians, arrived. They were originally called "Indians" by Westerners, as it was wrongly believed that the discoverer Christopher Columbus had reached the East Indies rather than the continent of North America. You should never use the racist terms "Red Indian" or "redskin."

Native Americans(아메리카 원주민)란, 북미 대륙에 유럽인, 후에는 아프리카 인과 아시아 인들이 들어가기 전부터 살고 있던 코만치, 아파치, 수 종족 등과 같은 여러 종족의 사람들을 가리키는 말이다. 그들을 원래 서양 사람들이 '인디언'이라고 불렀는데, 발견 크리스토퍼 콜럼버스가 북미 대륙을 발견했을 때 그곳을 동인도라고 잘못 생각했기 때문이다. '레드 인디언'이나 '레드스킨'은 인종 차별적인 단어이므로 절대 사용하면 안 된다.

NATO ♦◇◇ /ˈneɪtoʊ/ N-PROPER **NATO** is an international organization which consists of the U.S., Canada, Britain, and other European countries, all of whom have agreed to support one another if they are attacked. **NATO** is an abbreviation for "North Atlantic Treaty Organization." □ *NATO says it will keep a reduced number of modern nuclear weapons to guarantee peace.*

고유명사 북대서양 조약 기구 □ 나토는 평화를 보장하기 위해 현대 핵무기 보유 대수를 계속 감축한 상태로 유지할 것이라고 한다.

natu|ral ♦♦◇ /ˈnætʃərəl, ˈnætʃrəl/ (**naturals**) **1** ADJ If you say that it is **natural** for someone to act in a particular way or for something to happen in that way, you mean that it is reasonable in the circumstances. □ *It is only natural for youngsters to crave the excitement of driving a fast car.* □ *It is only natural that he should resent you.* **2** ADJ **Natural** behavior is shared by all people or all animals of a particular type and has not been learned. □ *...the insect's natural instinct to feed.* **3** ADJ Someone with a **natural** ability or skill was born with that ability and did not have to learn it. □ *She has a natural ability to understand the motives of others.* **4** N-COUNT If you say that someone is **a natural**, you mean that they do something very well and very easily. □ *He's a natural with any kind of engine.* **5** ADJ If someone's behavior is **natural**, they appear to be relaxed and are not trying to hide anything. □ *Bethan's sister was as friendly and natural as the rest of the family.* ● **natu|ral|ly** ADV [ADV after v] □ *For pictures of people behaving naturally, not posing for the camera, it is essential to shoot unnoticed.* ● **natu|ral|ness** N-UNCOUNT □ *The critics praised the reality of the scenery and the naturalness of the acting.* **6** ADJ **Natural** things exist or occur in nature and are not made or caused by people. [ADJ n] □ *The gigantic natural harbour of Poole is a haven for boats.* ● **natu|ral|ly** ADV □ *Nitrates are chemicals that occur naturally in water and the soil.* **7** PHRASE If someone dies **of** or **from natural causes**, they die because they are ill or old rather than because of an accident or violence. □ *According to the Home Office, your brother died of natural causes.* →see **energy**

1 형용사 당연한 □ 젊은이들이 빠른 차를 운전하는 쾌감에 빠져드는 것은 너무나 당연하다. □ 그가 너를 원망하는 것은 지극히 당연하다. **2** 형용사 타고난 □ 먹고 살기 위한 그 곤충의 타고난 본능 **3** 형용사 타고난, 천부적인 □ 그녀는 타인의 동기를 이해하는 타고난 능력을 지녔다. **4** 가산명사 타고난 명수 □ 그녀는 어떤 엔진이든 다룰 줄 아는 타고난 명수이다. **5** 형용사 자연스러운 □ 베탄의 누이는 다른 가족처럼 친절하고 자연스러웠다. ● 자연스럽게 부사 □ 카메라를 보고 자세를 취하지 않고 자연스럽게 행동하는 사람들을 찍기 위해서는 눈치 채지 않게 찍는 것이 중요하다. ● 자연스러움 불가산명사 □ 비평가들은 무대의 사실성과 연기의 자연스러움을 칭찬했다. **6** 형용사 자연의, 천연의 □ 거대한 천연 항구인 풀은 배들을 위한 안식처이다. ● 자연적으로, 천연적으로 부사 □ 질산염은 물과 토양에서 자연적으로 발생하는 화학 물질이다. **7** 구 자연적인 이유로 □ 내무부에 의하면 당신의 형은 자연사했습니다.

Thesaurus natural의 참조어

ADJ. normal **1**
innate, instinctive **2** **3**
genuine, sincere, unaffected **5**
wild; (ant.) artificial **6**

Word Partnership natural의 연어

ADV. **perfectly** natural **1** **2**
N. natural **reaction**, natural **tendency** **2**
natural **beauty**, natural **disaster**, natural **food** **6**

---

natu|ral|ist /ˈnætʃərəlɪst, ˈnætʃrəl-/ (**naturalists**) N-COUNT A **naturalist** is a person who studies plants, animals, insects, and other living things.

가산명사 박물학자

natu|ral|ly ♦◇◇ /ˈnætʃərəli, ˈnætʃrəli/ **1** ADV You use **naturally** to indicate that you think something is very obvious and not at all surprising in the circumstances. □ *When things go wrong, all of us naturally feel disappointed and frustrated.* □ *Naturally these comings and goings excited some curiosity.* **2** ADV If one thing develops **naturally** from another, it develops as a normal consequence or result of it. [ADV after v] □ *A study of yoga leads naturally to meditation.* **3** ADV You can use **naturally** to talk about a characteristic of someone's personality when it is the way that they normally act. [ADV adj] □ *He has a lively sense of humor and appears naturally confident.* **4** ADV If someone is **naturally** good at something, they learn it easily and quickly and do it very well. [ADV adj] □ *Some individuals are naturally good communicators.* **5** PHRASE If something **comes naturally to** you, you find it easy to do and quickly become good at it. □ *Humanitarian work comes naturally to them.*

1 부사 당연히, 자연히 □ 일이 잘 안 될 때, 사람들은 당연히 실망과 좌절을 느끼게 된다. □ 당연히 이러한 왕래는 궁금증을 유발했다. **2** 부사 자연스럽게, 자연히 □ 요가를 배우면 자연스럽게 명상으로 이어진다. **3** 부사 자연스럽게 □ 그는 풍부한 유머 감각을 가졌으며 본연의 자신감이 있어 보인다. **4** 부사 천부적으로 □ 어떤 사람들은 천부적으로 의사 전달을 잘한다. **5** 구 자연스럽게 다가오다 □ 인도적 활동이 그들에게는 아주 자연스럽다.

natu|ral re|sources N-PLURAL **Natural resources** are all the land, forests, energy sources and minerals existing naturally in a place that can be used by people. □ *Angola was a country rich in natural resources.*

복수명사 천연 자원 □ 앙고라는 천연 자원이 풍부한 나라였다.

natu|ral wast|age N-UNCOUNT **Natural wastage** is the process of employees leaving their jobs because they want to retire or move to other jobs, rather than because their employer wants them to leave. [mainly BRIT, BUSINESS; AM usually **attrition**] □ *The company hopes the job cuts will be made through natural wastage and voluntary redundancy.*

불가산명사 자연 감축 [주로 영국영어, 경제; 미국영어 대개 attrition] □ 회사에서는 자연 감축과 명퇴를 통해서 직원 감축을 이룰 수 있기를 희망한다.

na|ture ♦♦◇ /ˈneɪtʃər/ (**natures**) **1** N-UNCOUNT **Nature** is all the animals, plants, and other things in the world that are not made by people, and all the events and processes that are not caused by people. □ *The most amazing thing about nature is its infinite variety.* □ *...grasses that grow wild in nature.*

1 불가산명사 자연 □ 자연의 가장 놀라운 점은 무한한 다양성이다. □ 자연에서 야생으로 자라는 풀들

Do not confuse **nature**, **landscape**, **scenery**, and **countryside**. **Nature** includes the landscape, the weather, animals, and plants. □ *These creatures roamed the Earth as the finest and rarest wonders of nature.* With **landscape**, the emphasis is on the physical features of the land, while **scenery** includes everything

nature, landscape, scenery, countryside를 혼동하지 않도록 하라. nature는 경치, 날씨, 동물, 식물을 포함한다. □ 이 생물체들은 가장 멋지고 가장 희귀한 자연의 경이로서 지구상에 활보했다.

you can see when you look out over an area of land. ❑ ...*the landscape of steep woods and distant mountains....unattractive urban scenery*. **Countryside** is land which is away from towns and cities. ❑ ...*3,500 acres of mostly flat countryside*.

② N-SING The **nature** of something is its basic quality or character. [with supp, oft N N, also by/in N] ❑ *Mr. Sharp would not comment on the nature of the issues being investigated*. ❑ *The rise of a major power is both economic and military in nature*. ③ N-SING Someone's **nature** is their character, which they show by the way they behave. [with poss, also by N] ❑ *Jeya feels that her ambitious nature made her unsuitable for an arranged marriage*. ❑ *She trusted people. That was her nature*. →see also **human nature** ④ PHRASE If you say that something has a particular characteristic **by its nature** or **by its very nature**, you mean that things of that type always have that characteristic. ❑ *Peacekeeping, by its nature, makes pre-planning difficult*. ⑤ PHRASE If you say that something is **in the nature of things**, you mean that you would expect it to happen in the circumstances mentioned. ❑ *Of course, in the nature of things, and with a lot of drinking going on, people failed to notice*. ⑥ PHRASE If you say that one thing is **in the nature of** another, you mean that it is like the other thing. ❑ *There is movement towards, I think, something in the nature of a pluralistic system*. ⑦ PHRASE If a way of behaving is **second nature to** you, you do it almost without thinking because it is easy for you or obvious to you. ❑ *Planning ahead had always come as second nature to her*.

Word Partnership   nature의 연어

V.	love nature, preserve nature ①
N.	love of nature, wonders of nature ①
	nature of life, nature of society, nature of work ②
	nature and nurture ③

naugh|ty /nɔ́ti/ (**naughtier, naughtiest**) ① ADJ If you say that a child is **naughty**, you mean that they behave badly or do not do what they are told. ❑ *Girls, you're being very naughty*. ② ADJ You can describe books, pictures, or words as **naughty** when they are slightly vulgar or related to sex. ❑ *You know what little boys are like with naughty words*.

nau|sea /nɔ́ziə, -ʒə, -siə, -ʃə/ N-UNCOUNT **Nausea** is the condition of feeling sick and the feeling that you are going to vomit. ❑ *I was overcome with a feeling of nausea*.

nau|ti|cal /nɔ́tɪkəl/ ADJ **Nautical** means relating to ships and sailing. ❑ ...*a nautical chart of the region you sail*.

Word Link   nav ≈ ship : naval, navigate, navy

na|val ◆◇◇ /néɪvəl/ ADJ **Naval** means belonging to, relating to, or involving a country's navy. [ADJ n] ❑ *He was the senior serving naval officer*.

na|vel /néɪvəl/ (**navels**) N-COUNT Your **navel** is the small hollow just below your waist at the front of your body. ❑ ...*a girl with a ring in her navel*.

navi|gate /nǽvɪgeɪt/ (**navigates, navigating, navigated**) ① V-T/V-I When someone **navigates** a ship or an aircraft somewhere, they decide which course to follow and steer it there. ❑ *Captain Cook was responsible for safely navigating his ship without accident for 100 voyages*. ❑ *The purpose of the visit was to navigate into an ice-filled fiord*. ● **navi|ga|tion** /nǽvɪgéɪʃən/ (**navigations**) N-VAR ❑ *The expedition was wrecked by bad planning and poor navigation*. ② V-T/V-I When a ship or boat **navigates** an area of water, it sails on or across it. ❑ ...*a lock system to allow sea-going craft to navigate the upper reaches of the river*. ③ V-T/V-I When someone in a car **navigates**, they decide what roads the car should be driven along in order to get somewhere. ❑ *When traveling on fast roads at night it is impossible to drive and navigate at the same time*. ❑ ...*the relief at successfully navigating across the Golden Gate Bridge to arrive here*. ④ V-I When fish, animals, or insects **navigate** somewhere, they find the right direction to go and travel there. ❑ *In tests, the bees navigate back home after being placed in a field a mile away*. ⑤ V-T/V-I If you **navigate** an obstacle, you move carefully in order to avoid hitting the obstacle or hurting yourself. ❑ *He was not able to walk without a cane and could only navigate steps backwards*. ❑ *He's got to learn how to navigate his way around the residence*. →see **star**

navi|ga|tion /nǽvɪgéɪʃən/ N-UNCOUNT You can refer to the movement of ships as **navigation**. ❑ *Pack ice around Iceland was becoming a threat to navigation*. →see also **navigate**
→see Word Web: **navigation**

landscape는 땅의 물리적 특징을 강조하는 반면, scenery는 어떤 지역에서 눈에 보이는 모든 것을 포함한다. ❑ ...우뚝 서 있는 숲과 멀리 산이 보이는 경치....볼품없는 도회지 풍경. countryside는 중소 도시나 대도시에서 떨어져 있는 땅이다. ❑ ...대부분이 평지인 3,500에이커의 시골 지역.

② 단수명사 본질, 성질 ❑ 샤프 씨는 조사 중인 사안의 본질에 대해서는 논평을 하지 않을 것이다. ❑ 강대국의 형성은 본질적으로 경제적이면서도 군사적이다. ③ 단수명사 본성, 천성 ❑ 제야는 자신의 야심찬 본성상 중매결혼은 자기에게 맞지 않다고 생각한다. ❑ 그녀는 사람들을 믿었다. 그것은 그녀의 천성이었다. ④ 구 특성상 ❑ 평화 유지는 그 자체의 특성상 사전 계획이 어렵다. ⑤ 구 정황으로 보아, 당연히 ❑ 물론 정황으로 보아, 또 그 당시 술을 많이 마시고 있었으므로 사람들은 눈치 채지 못했다. ⑥ 구 ~성격의, ~와 비슷한 ❑ 내 생각에 이것은 다원주의적 체계와 비슷한 것을 향한 움직임이다. ⑦ 구 제2의 천성 ❑ 사전에 계획하는 것은 그녀에게 너무나 당연한 것이었다.

① 형용사 버릇없는 ❑ 얘들아, 너무 버릇없게 구는구나. ② 형용사 천박한, 외설스러운 ❑ 남자애들이 외설스러운 말을 가지고 어떻게 하는지 알잖아.

불가산명사 메스꺼움, 욕지기 ❑ 메스꺼움이 치밀어 올랐다.

형용사 항해의 ❑ 항해하는 지역의 해도

형용사 해군의 ❑ 그는 고위 현역 해군 장교였다.

가산명사 배꼽 ❑ 배꼽에 고리를 박은 여자

① 타동사/자동사 조종하다 ❑ 쿡 선장의 휘하에서 배는 100번의 항해를 하는 동안 한 번도 사고가 나지 않았다. ❑ 그 방문의 목적은 얼음으로 덮인 찬 피오르드를 항해하는 것이었다. ● 조종 가산명사 또는 불가산명사 ❑ 탐사는 조악한 계획과 형편없는 조종에 의해 엉망이 되었다. ② 타동사/자동사 항해하다 ❑ 해양 선박이 강의 상류를 항해할 수 있도록 해 주는 수문 체계 ③ 타동사/자동사 길을 찾아내다 ❑ 밤에 빠른 길을 달리는 경우 운전을 하면서 동시에 길을 찾아내는 것은 불가능하다. ❑ 길을 찾아 금문교를 성공적으로 건너서 이곳에 도착했다는 안도감 ④ 자동사 길을 찾아가다 ❑ 실험들에서 보면 벌들은 1마일 떨어진 들판에 놓아두어도 집으로 길을 찾아 돌아온다. ⑤ 타동사/자동사 통과하다, 빠져나가다 ❑ 그는 지팡이가 없이는 걷지 못했고 계단은 뒷걸음질로 다녀야만 했다. ❑ 그는 집 근처 길을 찾아다니는 법을 배워야 한다.

불가산명사 항해 ❑ 아이슬란드 주위의 총빙이 항해에 위협이 되고 있었다.

Word Web   navigation

Early explorers used the **sun** and **stars** to navigate the seas. The sextant allowed later navigators to use these celestial objects to accurately calculate their **position**. By sighting or measuring their position at noon, sailors could determine their latitude. The **compass** helped sailors determine their position at any time of night or day. It also worked in any weather. Today all sorts of travelers use the global positioning system (GPS) to guide their journeys. A **GPS receiver** is connected to a system of 24 **satellites** that can establish a location within a few feet.

compass   sextant   GPS

a b c d e f g h i j k l m n o p q r s t u v w x y z

A

naviga|tor /ˈnævɪɡeɪtər/ (**navigators**) N-COUNT The **navigator** on an aircraft or ship is the person whose job is to work out the direction in which the aircraft or ship should be traveling. ❑ *He became an RAF navigator during the war.*

가산명사 항해사, 조종사 ❑ 그는 전쟁 기간에 영국 공군의 조종사가 되었다.

B

| Word Link | nav ≈ ship : naval, navigate, navy |

navy ♦♦◇ /ˈneɪvi/ (**navies**) **1** N-COUNT A country's **navy** consists of the people it employs to fight at sea, and the ships they use. ❑ *The government announced an order for three Type 23 frigates for the Royal Navy yesterday.* ❑ *Her own son was also in the Navy.* **2** COLOR Something that is **navy** or **navy-blue** is very dark blue. ❑ *When I was a fashion editor, I mostly wore white shirts and black or navy trousers.*

1 가산명사 해군 ❑ 영국 정부는 해군이 쓸 23형 프리깃함 세 척을 주문한다고 어제 발표했다. ❑ 그녀의 아들 또한 해군에 있었다. **2** 색채어 감색 ❑ 내가 패션 잡지 편집자였을 당시 나는 대개 하얀 셔츠에 검정 혹은 감색 바지를 입었다.

Nazi ♦♦◇ /ˈnɑːtsi/ (**Nazis**) **1** N-COUNT The **Nazis** were members of the right-wing political party, led by Adolf Hitler, which held power in Germany from 1933 to 1945. **2** ADJ You use **Nazi** to say that something relates to the Nazis. ❑ *...the rise of the Nazi Party.*

1 가산명사 나치 **2** 형용사 나치의 ❑ 나치당의 발흥

C

D

E

NB /ˌɛn ˈbiː/ You write **NB** to draw someone's attention to what you are about to say or write. ❑ *NB: The opinions stated in this essay do not necessarily represent those of the Church of God Missionary Society.*

주의 ❑ 주의: 이 글에 개진된 의견들이 반드시 하나님의 교회 선교회의 것과 일치하는 것은 아닙니다.

F

near ♦♦♦ /nɪər/ (**nearer, nearest, nears, nearing, neared**) **1** PREP If something is **near** a place, thing, or person, it is a short distance from them. ❑ *Don't come near me.* ❑ *He drew his chair nearer the fire.* ● ADV **Near** is also an adverb. ❑ *He crouched as near to the door as he could.* ❑ *She took a step nearer to the barrier.* ● ADJ **Near** is also an adjective. [ADJ n, the ADJ of n] ❑ *He collapsed into the nearest chair.* ❑ *The nearer of the two barges was perhaps a mile away.* **2** PHRASE If someone or something is **near to** a particular state, they have almost reached it. ❑ *After the war, The House of Hardie came near to bankruptcy.* ❑ *The repairs to the Hafner machine were near to completion.* ● PREP **Near** means the same as **near to**. ❑ *He was near tears.* ❑ *For almost a month he lay near death.* **3** PHRASE If something is similar to something else, you can say that it is **near** to it. ❑ *It combined with the resinous cedar smell of the logs to produce a sickening sensation that was near to nausea.* ● PREP **Near** means the same as **near to**. ❑ *Often her feelings were nearer hatred than love.* **4** ADJ You describe the thing most similar to something as **the nearest** thing **to** it when there is no example of the thing itself. [the ADJ n to n, the ADJ to n] ❑ *It would appear that the legal profession is the nearest thing to a recession-proof industry.* **5** ADV If a time or event draws **near**, it will happen soon. [WRITTEN] ❑ *The time for my departure from Japan was drawing nearer every day.* **6** PREP If something happens **near** a particular time, it happens just before or just after that time. ❑ *Performance is lowest between 3 a.m. and 5 a.m., and reaches a peak near midday.* ❑ *"Since I retired to this place," he wrote near the end of his life, "I have never been out of these mountains."* **7** PREP You use **near** to say that something is a little more or less than an amount or number stated. ❑ *...to increase manufacturing from about 2.5 million cars a year to nearer 4.75 million.* **8** PREP You can say that someone will **not go near** a person or thing when you are emphasizing that they refuse to see them or go there. [EMPHASIS] [with brd-neg] ❑ *He will absolutely not go near a hospital.* **9** ADJ The **near** one of two things is the one that is closer. [det ADJ n] ❑ *...a mighty beech tree on the near side of the little clearing.* **10** ADJ You use **near** to indicate that something is almost the thing mentioned. [ADJ n] ❑ *She was believed to have died in near poverty on the French Riviera.* ● ADV **Near** is also an adverb. [ADV adj] ❑ *...his near fatal accident two years ago.* **11** ADJ In a contest, your **nearest** rival or challenger is the person or team that is most likely to defeat you. [ADJ n] ❑ *He completed the lengthy course some three seconds faster than his nearest rival, Jonathon Ford.* **12** V-T When you **near** a place, you get quite near to it. [LITERARY] [no passive] ❑ *As he neared the stable, he slowed the horse and patted it on the neck.* **13** V-T When someone or something **nears** a particular stage or point, they will soon reach that stage or point. [no passive] ❑ *His age was hard to guess – he must have been nearing fifty.* ❑ *You are nearing the end of your training and you haven't attempted any assessments yet.* **14** V-I You say that an important time or event **nears** when it is going to occur quite soon. [LITERARY] ❑ *As half time neared, Hardyman almost scored twice.* **15** PHRASE You use **near and far** to indicate that you are referring to a very large area or distance. ❑ *People would gather from near and far.* **16** PHRASE If you say that something will happen **in the near future**, you mean that it will happen quite soon. ❑ *The controversy regarding vitamin C is unlikely to be resolved in the near future.* **17** PHRASE You use **nowhere near** and **not anywhere near** to emphasize that something is not the case. [EMPHASIS] ❑ *They are nowhere near good enough.* ❑ *It was nowhere near as painful as David had expected.*

G

H

I

J

K

L

M

N

O

P

Q

R

S

T

1 전치사 근처에, 가까이에 ❑ 내 옆에 오지 마. ❑ 그는 의자를 불 가까이로 당겼다. ● 부사 가까이 ❑ 그는 문에 최대한 가까이 쪼그려 앉았다. ❑ 그녀는 난간을 향해 한 발자국 더 가까이 다가갔다. ● 형용사 가까운 ❑ 그는 가장 가까운 의자에 털썩 주저앉았다. ❑ 거룻배 두 척 중 더 가까운 것이 약 1마일 떨어져 있었다. **2** 구 -에 가까운 ❑ 전쟁후 하디 가문은 거의 파산 지경이 되었다. ❑ 하프너 기계의 수리가 거의 다 되어 가고 있었다. ● 전치사 -에 가까운 ❑ 그는 울기 일보 직전이었다. ❑ 거의 한 달간 그는 사경을 헤매고 있었다. **3** 구 -와 비슷한 ❑ 그것은 통나무의 설송나무 송진 냄새와 결합하여 메스꺼울 정도로 불쾌한 기분을 불러일으켰다. ● 전치사 -와 비슷한 ❑ 그녀의 감정은 대개 사랑보다는 증오에 가까웠다. **4** 형용사 -와 가장 비슷한 ❑ 불황을 모르는 산업이 실제로 존재한다면 아마도 그것에 제일 가까운 것이 법조계일 것이다. **5** 부사 가까이 [문어체] ❑ 내가 일본을 떠날 시일이 하루하루 다가오고 있었다. **6** 전치사 즈음, 무렵 ❑ 새벽 3시에서 5시 사이에 성적이 가장 낮으며 정오경에 가장 좋다. ❑ "내가 이곳으로 은퇴한 이후 나는 이 산을 떠나본 적이 없다."라고 그는 인생의 말기에 썼다. **7** 전치사 가량의 ❑ 차량 생산을 연간 약 250만 대에서 475만 대 가량으로 늘리는 것 **8** 전치사 근처에도 [강조] ❑ 그는 병원 근처에 얼씬도 안 하려고 한다. **9** 형용사 가까운 ❑ 작은 공터에서 우리 쪽으로 서 있는 거대한 너도밤나무 **10** 형용사 거의 -한 ❑ 그녀는 프랑스의 리비에라에서 거의 빈곤 상태에서 죽은 것으로 추정되고 있다. ● 부사 거의 -하게 ❑ 2년 전에 그가 목숨을 잃을 뻔했던 사고 **11** 형용사 필적하는 ❑ 그는 긴 코스에서 가장 가까운 경쟁자인 조나단 포드보다 3초 빠르게 들어왔다. **12** 타동사 다가가다 [문어체] ❑ 그는 마구간에 다가가면서 말의 속도를 늦추고 목을 어루만져 줬다. **13** 타동사 다다르다 ❑ 그는 나이를 짐작하기 어려웠다. 쉰이 다 된 것이 틀림없다. ❑ 당신은 훈련의 막바지에 다다랐는데도 아직 어떠한 평가도 받아보지 않았다구. **14** 자동사 다가오다 [문어체] ❑ 그는 전반전이 다 되어갈 무렵 하디맨이 거의 두 번이나 득점을 할 뻔했다. **15** 구 사방의 ❑ 사방에서 사람들이 모여들곤 했다. **16** 구 가까운 시일 내의 ❑ 비타민 C에 대한 논란은 가까운 시일 내에 해결될 것 같지 않다. **17** 구 어림도 없는, 한참 모자라는 [강조] ❑ 그들의 실력으로는 어림도 없다. ❑ 고통은 데이비드가 예상한 것에 한참 못 미쳤다.

U

near|by ♦♦◇ /ˌnɪərˈbaɪ/ ADV If something is **nearby**, it is only a short distance away. ❑ *He might easily have been seen by someone who lived nearby.* ❑ *The helicopter crashed to earth nearby.* ● ADJ **Nearby** is also an adjective. [ADJ n] ❑ *At a nearby table a man was complaining in a loud voice.*

부사 근처에 ❑ 근처에 사는 누군가가 쉽사리 그를 봤을 것이다. ❑ 헬리콥터는 근처로 추락했다. ● 형용사 근처의 ❑ 근처의 테이블에서 한 남자가 큰 소리로 불평을 하고 있었다.

V

near|ly ♦♦◇ /ˈnɪərli/ **1** ADV **Nearly** is used to indicate that something is not quite the case, or not completely the case. ❑ *Goldsworth stared at me in silence for nearly twenty seconds.* ❑ *Hunter knew nearly all of this already.* ❑ *The beach was nearly empty.* **2** ADV **Nearly** is used to indicate that something will soon be the case. ❑ *It was already nearly eight o'clock.* ❑ *I was nearly asleep.* ❑ *I've nearly finished the words for your song.*

1 부사 거의 ❑ 골스워스는 거의 20초 동안 나를 말없이 쳐다봤다. ❑ 헌터는 이미 거의 모든 것을 알고 있었다. ❑ 해변은 거의 비어 있었다. **2** 부사 거의 ❑ 이미 거의 8시가 다 되어 가고 있었다. ❑ 나는 거의 잠들었다. ❑ 당신의 곡을 위한 작사를 거의 마쳤습니다.

W

near|sighted /ˌnɪərˈsaɪtɪd/ also **near-sighted** ADJ Someone who is **nearsighted** cannot see distant things clearly. [AM, also BRIT, OLD-FASHIONED] ❑ *As you get older, you may become farsighted or near-sighted.* →see **eye**

형용사 근시의 [미국, 영국영어, 구식어] ❑ 나이가 들면서 원시 혹은 근시가 될 수 있다.

X

neat ♦◇◇ /niːt/ (**neater, neatest**) **1** ADJ A **neat** place, thing, or person is organized and clean, and has everything in the correct place. ❑ *So they left him in the neat little house, alone with her memories.* ❑ *Everything was neat and tidy and gleamingly clean.* ● **neat|ly** ADV [ADV with v] ❑ *He folded his paper neatly and sipped his coffee.* ● **neat|ness** N-UNCOUNT ❑ *The grounds were a perfect balance between neatness and natural wildness.* **2** ADJ Someone who is **neat** keeps their home or

1 형용사 정연한, 깔끔한 ❑ 그래서 그들은 그녀를 깔끔한 작은 집에 혼자 추억만을 남겨 두고 떠났다. ❑ 모든 것이 깔끔하고 잘 정돈되어 있으며 광이 날 정도로 깨끗했다. ● 깔끔하게 부사 ❑ 그는 자기 신문을 깔끔하게 접고 커피를 홀짝거렸다. ● 정연함 불가산명사 ❑ 마당은 정돈과 거친 자연미 사이의

Y

Z

possessions organized and clean, with everything in the correct place. □ "That's not like Alf," he said, "leaving papers muddled like that. He's always so neat." ● **neat|ly** ADV [ADV with v] □ I followed her into that room which her mother had maintained so neatly. ● **neat|ness** N-UNCOUNT □ ...a paragon of neatness, efficiency and reliability. ◘ ADJ A **neat** object, part of the body, or shape is quite small and has a smooth outline. □ ...neat handwriting. ● **neat|ly** ADV [ADV -ed] □ She was a small woman, slender and neatly made. ◘ ADJ A **neat** movement or action is done accurately and skillfully, with no unnecessary movements. □ "Did you have any trouble?" Cord asked, driving into a small parking lot and changing the subject in the same neat maneuver. ● **neat|ly** ADV [ADV with v] □ He watched her peel and dissect a pear neatly, no mess, no sticky fingers. ◘ ADJ A **neat** way of organizing, achieving, explaining, or expressing something is clever and convenient. □ It had been such a neat, clever plan. □ Neat solutions are not easily found to these issues. ● **neat|ly** ADV [ADV with v] □ Real people do not fit neatly into these categories. ● **neat|ness** N-UNCOUNT □ He knew full well he had been outflanked, and he appreciated the neatness of it. ◘ ADJ When someone drinks strong alcohol **neat**, they do not add a weaker liquid such as water to it. [mainly BRIT; AM usually **straight**] [v n ADJ, ADJ n] □ He poured himself a brandy and swallowed it neat.

Thesaurus   neat의 참조어

ADJ.   orderly, tidy; (ant.) messy ◼ ◻

---

nec|es|sar|ily ♦◇◇ /nɛsɪsɛərɪli/ ◼ ADV If you say that something is **not necessarily** the case, you mean that it may not be the case or is not always the case. [VAGUENESS] □ Anger is not necessarily the most useful or acceptable reaction to such events. ● CONVENTION If you reply "**Not necessarily**," you mean that what has just been said or suggested may not be true. □ "He was lying, of course." — "Not necessarily." ◻ ADV If you say that something **necessarily** happens or is the case, you mean that it has to happen or be the case and cannot be any different. □ Brookman & Langdon were said to manufacture the most desirable pens and these necessarily command astonishingly high prices.

nec|es|sary ♦♦◇ /nɛsɪsɛri/ ◼ ADJ Something that is **necessary** is needed in order for something else to happen. □ I kept the engine running because it might be necessary to leave fast. □ Make the necessary arrangements. ◻ ADJ A **necessary** consequence or connection must happen or exist, because of the nature of the things or events involved. [ADJ n] □ Scientific work is differentiated from art by its necessary connection with the idea of progress.

Thesaurus   necessary의 참조어

ADJ.   essential, mandatory, obligatory; (ant.) unnecessary ◼
         unavoidable ◻

---

ne|ces|si|tate /nɪsɛsɪteɪt/ (**necessitates**, **necessitating**, **necessitated**) V-T If something **necessitates** an event, action, or situation, it makes it necessary. [FORMAL] □ A prolonged drought had necessitated the introduction of water rationing.

ne|ces|si|ty /nɪsɛsɪti/ (**necessities**) ◼ N-UNCOUNT The **necessity** of something is the fact that it must happen or exist. □ There is agreement on the necessity of reforms. □ As soon as the necessity for action is over the troops must be withdrawn. ● PHRASE If you say that something is **of necessity** the case, you mean that it is the case because nothing else is possible or practical in the circumstances. [FORMAL] □ The assembly line of necessity kept moving. ◻ N-COUNT A **necessity** is something that you must have in order to live properly or do something. □ Water is a basic necessity of life. ◼ N-COUNT A situation or action that is a **necessity** is necessary and cannot be avoided. □ The President pleaded that strong rule from the center was a regrettable, but temporary necessity.

Word Partnership   necessity의 연어

ADJ.   **absolute** necessity ◼-◼
         economic necessity ◻ ◼
         political necessity ◻

---

neck ♦◇◇ /nɛk/ (**necks**) ◼ N-COUNT Your **neck** is the part of your body which joins your head to the rest of your body. □ She threw her arms round his neck and hugged him warmly. ◻ N-COUNT The **neck** of an article of clothing such as a shirt, dress, or sweater is the part which surrounds your neck. □ ...the low, ruffled neck of her blouse. ◼ N-COUNT The **neck** of something such as a bottle or a guitar is the long narrow part at one end of it. □ Catherine gripped the broken neck of the bottle. ◼ PHRASE If you say that someone **is breathing down** your **neck**, you mean that they are watching you very closely and checking everything you do. □ Most farmers have bank managers breathing down their necks. ◼ PHRASE In a competition, especially an election, if two or more competitors are **neck and neck**, they are level with each other and have an equal chance of winning. □ The latest polls indicate that the two main parties are neck and neck. ◼ PHRASE If you **stick** your **neck out**, you bravely say or do something that might be criticized or might turn out to be wrong. [INFORMAL] □ During my political life I've earned myself a reputation as someone who'll stick his neck out, a bit of a rebel. →see **body**

Word Partnership   neck의 연어

N.   **back/nape of the** neck, **head and** neck, neck **injury** ◼
ADJ.   **broken** neck, **long** neck, **stiff** neck, **thick** neck ◼ ◼

완벽한 조화를 이루고 있었다. ◻ 형용사 깔끔한 □ "종이를 저렇게 함부로 두다니 저것은 알프답지 않아. 그는 항상 아주 깔끔하거든."이라고 그는 말했다. ● 깔끔하게 부사 □ 나는 그녀의 어머니가 너무나도 깔끔하게 해 놓은 그 방으로 그녀를 따라 들어갔다. ● 깔끔함 불가산명사 □ 깔끔함, 효율성, 신뢰성의 전형 ◼ 형용사 아담한 □ 아담한 글씨 ● 아담하게 부사 □ 그녀는 날씬하고 체격이 아담한 작은 여자였다. ◼ 형용사 군더더기 없는, 깔끔한 □ "문제가 있었나요?"라고 코드가 작은 주차장에 들어서면서 예의 군더더기 없는 솜씨로 주제를 바꾸면 물었다. ● 깔끔하게 부사 □ 그는 그녀가 깔끔하게 전혀 지저분하게 만들지 않고 손가락에 즙을 흘리지도 않으면서 배 껍질을 깎고 자르는 것을 지켜보았다. ◼ 형용사 깔끔한 □ 참 깔끔하고 기발한 계획이었는데. □ 이런 문제에 대해서는 깔끔한 해결책을 쉽게 찾을 수 없다. ● 깔끔하게 부사 □ 실제 사람들은 이런 분류에 깔끔하게 들어맞지 않는다. ● 깔끔함 불가산명사 □ 그는 자신이 적에게 허를 찔렸다는 것을 잘 알았으며 그 깔끔함에 감탄했다. ◼ 형용사 스트레이트의 [주로 영국영어; 미국영어 대개 straight] □ 그는 자기 잔에 브랜디를 한 잔 따라 스트레이트로 마셨다.

◼ 부사 반드시 [짐작투] □ 이런 일에 대해 화를 내는 것이 반드시 가장 유용하거나 가장 용납할 만한 반응은 아니다. ● 관용 표현 반드시 그렇지는 않다 □ "그는 물론 거짓말을 하고 있었을 거야." "꼭 그렇지는 않아." ◻ 부사 반드시 □ 브룩만 앤 랭던이 가장 뛰어난 펜을 제작한다는 평을 받았고 그래서 이들 펜은 놀라울 정도로 비싸다.

◼ 형용사 필요한 □ 빨리 떠나야 할지도 몰라 시동을 켜 놨다. □ 필요한 준비를 해라. ◻ 형용사 필연적인 □ 과학적인 작업은 진보라는 개념과의 필연적인 연관성 때문에 예술과 차별된다.

타동사 필요로 하다, 요구하다 [격식체] □ 장기화된 가뭄 때문에 물 배급제를 도입할 수밖에 없었다.

◼ 불가산명사 필요 □ 개혁의 필요성에 대한 합의가 있다. □ 작전의 필요성이 사라지는 즉시 병력을 철수해야 한다. ● 구 어쩔 수 없이, 부득불 [격식체] □ 조립 라인은 어쩔 수 없이 계속 가동되었다. ◻ 가산명사 필수품 □ 물은 생명체에겐 기본적인 필수품이다. ◼ 가산명사 필연 □ 중앙의 강력한 통치가 애석하지만 일시적으로는 불가피한 조처라고 대통령은 호소했다.

◼ 가산명사 목 □ 그녀는 그의 목을 두 팔로 감고 따뜻이 껴안았다. ◻ 가산명사 목 부분 □ 그녀 블라우스의 낮고 주름 잡힌 목 부분 ◼ 가산명사 목 □ 캐서린은 깨진 병목을 움켜잡았다. ◼ 구 일일이 감시하다 □ 대부분의 농부들의 경우 은행 간부들의 집요한 주시를 받고 있다. ◼ 구 호각을 이뤄, 막상막하로 □ 최근의 여론 조사에 의하면 두 주요 정당이 호각을 이루고 있다. ◼ 구 위험을 무릅쓰다, 용감하게 굴다 [비격식체] □ 내 정치 경력 동안 나는 위험을 무릅쓰는 사람, 일종의 반항아라는 평판을 얻었다.

neck|lace /nɛklɪs/ (necklaces) N-COUNT A **necklace** is a piece of jewelry such as a chain or a string of beads which someone, usually a woman, wears around their neck. ❑ ...a diamond necklace and matching earrings. →see **jewelry**

가산명사 목걸이 ❑ 다이아몬드 목걸이와 그에 어울리는 귀걸이

nec|tar|ine /nɛktəriːn/ (nectarines) N-COUNT A **nectarine** is a round, juicy fruit which is similar to a peach but has a smooth skin.

가산명사 천도복숭아

need ♦♦♦ /niːd/ (needs, needing, needed)

Need sometimes behaves like an ordinary verb, for example "She needs to know" and "She doesn't need to know" and sometimes like a modal, for example "She need know," "She needn't know," or, in more formal English, "She need not know."

need는 'She needs to know'나 'She doesn't need to know'에서처럼 일반 동사로 쓰이기도 하고 'She need know'나 'She needn't know', 또는 비격식체 영어인 'She need not know'에서처럼 조동사로 쓰이기도 한다.

1 V-T If you **need** something, or **need to** do something, you cannot successfully achieve what you want or live properly without it. [no cont] ❑ He desperately needed money. ❑ I need to make a phone call. ❑ I need you to do something for me. ❑ I need you here, Wally. ● N-COUNT **Need** is also a noun. ❑ Charles has never felt the need to compete with anyone. ❑ ...the child who never had his need for attention and importance satisfied. **2** V-T If an object or place **needs** something done to it, that action should be done to improve the object or place. If a task **needs** doing, it should be done to improve a particular situation. [no cont] ❑ The building needs quite a few repairs. ❑ ...a garden that needs tidying. **3** N-SING If there is a **need for** something, that thing would improve a situation or something cannot happen without it. ❑ Mr. Forrest believes there is a need for other similar schools throughout Britain. ❑ "I think we should see a specialist." — "I don't think there's any need for that." **4** MODAL If you say that someone **needn't** do something, you are telling them not to do it, or advising or suggesting that they should not do it. [with neg] ❑ "I'll put the key in the window." — "You needn't bother," he said gruffly. ❑ Look, you needn't shout. ● V-T **Need** is also a verb. [no cont, with neg] ❑ Well, for Heaven's sake, you don't need to apologize. **5** MODAL If you tell someone that they **needn't** do something, or that something **needn't** happen, you are telling them that that thing is not necessary, in order to make them feel better. [with neg] ❑ You needn't worry. ❑ Loneliness can be horrible, but it need not remain that way. ● V-T **Need** is also a verb. [no cont, with neg] ❑ He replied, with a reassuring smile, "Oh, you don't need to worry about them." **6** MODAL You use **needn't** when you are giving someone permission not to do something. [with neg] ❑ You needn't come again, if you don't want to. ● V-T **Need** is also a verb. [no cont] ❑ You don't need to wait for me. **7** MODAL If someone **needn't have** done something, they didn't need to do it. [with neg] ❑ She could have made the sandwich herself; her mom needn't have bothered to do anything. ❑ I was a little nervous when I announced my engagement to Grace, but I needn't have worried. **8** V-T If someone **didn't need to** do something, it wasn't necessary or useful for them to do it, although they did it. [no cont, with neg] ❑ You didn't need to give me any more money you know, but thank you. **9** MODAL You use **need** in expressions such as **I need hardly say** and **I needn't add** to emphasize that the person you are talking to already knows what you are going to say. [EMPHASIS] ❑ I needn't add that if you fail to do as I ask, you will suffer the consequences. ● V-T **Need** is also a verb. [no cont] ❑ I hardly need to say that I have never lost contact with him. **10** PHRASE People **in need** do not have enough of essential things such as money, food, or good health. ❑ The new Children Act places an enhanced duty on education authorities to provide for children in need. **11** PHRASE If you are **in need of** something, you need it or ought to have it. ❑ I was all right but in need of rest. ❑ He was badly in need of a shave. **12** PHRASE If you say that you will do something, especially an extreme action, **if need be**, you mean that you will do it if it is necessary. In British English, you can also say **if needs be**. ❑ They will now seek permission to take their case to the House of Lords, and, if need be, to the European Court of Human Rights.

1 타동사 필요로 하다 ❑ 그는 돈이 절실히 필요했다. ❑ 나는 전화를 해야 한다. ❑ 네가 나를 위해 뭔가를 해 줘야겠어. ❑ 네가 여기 있으면 좋겠어, 왈리. ● 가산명사 필요, 욕구 ❑ 찰스는 누군가와 경쟁할 필요를 느껴 본 적이 없다. ❑ 관심을 얻고 본인이 중요하다는 느낌을 받고 싶은 욕구가 충족된 적이 없는 아이 **2** 타동사 -이 필요하다; -이 되어야 하다 ❑ 그 건물은 많은 수리가 필요하다. ❑ 정돈이 필요한 정원 **3** 단수명사 필요 ❑ 포레스트 씨는 영국 전역에 비슷한 학교를 세울 필요가 있다고 생각한다. ❑ "전문의에게 가야 할 것 같아." "그럴 필요는 없을 것 같아." **4** 법조동사 -을 할 필요가 없다 ❑ "열쇠를 창문 안에 넣을게." "귀찮게 그럴 필요 없어"라고 그는 통명스레 말했다. ❑ 이봐, 소리를 지를 필요 없어. ● 타동사 -을 할 필요가 있다 ❑ 참, 세상에, 사과할 필요는 없다니까. **5** 법조동사 -을 할 필요가 없다 ❑ 걱정할 필요 없어. ❑ 고독은 끔찍할 수 있지만 꼭 그래야 할 필요는 없다. ● 타동사 -을 할 필요가 있다 ❑ "아, 그들에 대해서는 걱정할 필요 없어요."라고 그는 안심시키려는 듯 미소를 지으며 말했다. **6** 법조동사 -을 할 필요가 없다, -을 하지 않아도 되다 ❑ 원하지 않으면 다시 올 필요가 없다. ● 타동사 -을 할 필요가 있다 ❑ 나를 위해 기다릴 필요는 없다. **7** 법조동사 -을 할 필요가 없었다 ❑ 그녀는 샌드위치를 직접 만들었을 수도 있다. 그녀의 어머니가 굳이 뭘 할 필요는 없었다. ❑ 그레이스와 나의 약혼을 발표했을 때 나는 약간 긴장했었지만 그럴 필요는 없었다. **8** 타동사 -을 할 필요가 없었다 ❑ 나에게 돈을 더 안 줬어도 됐지만 어쨌든 고맙다. **9** 법조동사 -을 할 필요가 없다 [강조] ❑ 내가 요구하는 대로 하지 않으면 후회하게 될 것이라고 굳이 덧붙이지 않아도 되겠지. ● 타동사 -을 할 필요가 있다 ❑ 나는 그와 연락이 두절된 적이 없다는 사실을 굳이 말할 필요가 없다. **10** 구 빈곤한 ❑ 새로운 아동법은 빈곤 아동들을 돕도록 교육 당국에 더 많은 책임을 부과한다. **11** 구 -을 필요로 하는 ❑ 나는 괜찮았지만 휴식이 필요했다. ❑ 그는 면도를 꼭 해야 했다. **12** 구 필요하다면 ❑ 그들은 이제 자신들의 사건을 상원으로 가져가고, 필요하다면 유럽 인권 법원까지 가져갈 수 있도록 허가를 구할 것이다.

Thesaurus   need의 참조어

v.   demand, must have, require **1**

nee|dle /niːdəl/ (needles) **1** N-COUNT A **needle** is a small, very thin piece of polished metal which is used for sewing. It has a sharp point at one end and a hole in the other for a thread to go through. ❑ He took a needle and thread and sewed it up. **2** N-COUNT Knitting **needles** are thin sticks that are used for knitting. They are usually made of plastic or metal and have a point at one end. ❑ ...a pair of knitting needles. **3** N-COUNT A **needle** is a thin hollow metal rod with a sharp point, which is part of a medical instrument called a syringe. It is used to put a drug into someone's body, or to take blood out. ❑ ...the transmission of the aids virus through dirty needles. **4** N-COUNT A **needle** is a thin metal rod with a point which is put into a patient's body during acupuncture. ❑ I gave Kevin a course of acupuncture using six needles strategically placed on the scalp. **5** N-COUNT On an instrument which measures something such as speed or weight, the **needle** is the long strip of metal or plastic on the dial that moves backward and forward, showing the measurement. ❑ She kept looking at the dial on the boiler. The needle had reached 250 degrees. **6** N-COUNT The **needles** of a fir or pine tree are its thin, hard, pointed leaves. ❑ The carpet of pine needles was soft underfoot.

1 가산명사 바늘 ❑ 그는 바늘과 실을 가지고 그것을 꿰맸다. **2** 가산명사 (뜨개질) 바늘 ❑ 뜨개질바늘 한 쌍 **3** 가산명사 (주사기) 바늘 ❑ 불결한 주사 바늘을 통한 에이즈 바이러스 전염 **4** 가산명사 침 ❑ 나는 케빈에게 침 여섯 개를 주요 부위에 놓는 침술 치료를 한 차례 해주었다. **5** 가산명사 (계기판의) 바늘 ❑ 그녀는 계속해서 보일러의 눈금판을 바라보았다. 바늘이 250도에 도달해 있었다. **6** 가산명사 (침엽수의) 잎 ❑ 발밑에 융단처럼 깔린 솔잎이 폭신했다.

need|less /niːdlɪs/ ADJ Something that is **needless** is completely unnecessary. ❑ But his death was so needless. ● **need|less|ly** ADV ❑ Half a million women die needlessly each year during childbirth.

형용사 헛된, 불필요한 ❑ 그러나 그의 죽음은 아주 헛된 것이었다. ● 헛되이, 불필요하게 부사 ❑ 매년 50만의 여성들이 출산 중에 불필요하게 목숨을 잃는다.

needn't /niːdənt/ **Needn't** is the usual spoken form of 'need not.'

need not의 축약형

needy /niːdi/ (needier, neediest) ADJ **Needy** people do not have enough food, medicine, or clothing, or adequate houses. ❑ ...a multinational force aimed at ensuring that food and medicine get to needy Somalis. ● N-PLURAL The **needy** are

형용사 빈곤한, 궁핍한 ❑ 식량과 의약품이 빈곤한 소말리아 인들에게 안전하게 전해지도록 하는 것을 목표로 한 다국적군 ● 복수명사 빈곤한 사람들

people who are needy. ❑ *There will be efforts to get larger amounts of food to the needy.*

ne|gate /nɪɡeɪt/ (negates, negating, negated) **1** V-T If one thing **negates** another, it causes that other thing to lose the effect or value that it had. [FORMAL] ❑ *These weaknesses negated his otherwise progressive attitude towards the staff.* **2** V-T If someone **negates** something, they say that it does not exist. [FORMAL] ❑ *He warned that to negate the results of elections would only make things worse.*

ne|ga|tive ◆◇◇ /nɛɡətɪv/ (negatives) **1** ADJ A fact, situation, or experience that is **negative** is unpleasant, depressing, or harmful. ❑ *The news from overseas is overwhelmingly negative.* ● **nega|tive|ly** ADV [ADV with v] ❑ *This will negatively affect the result over the first half of the year.* **2** ADJ If someone is **negative** or has a **negative** attitude, they consider only the bad aspects of a situation, rather than the good ones. ❑ *When asked for your views about your current job, on no account must you be negative about it.* ● **nega|tive|ly** ADV ❑ *A few weeks later he said that maybe he viewed all his relationships rather negatively.* ● **nega|tiv|ity** /nɛɡətɪvɪti/ N-UNCOUNT ❑ *I loathe negativity. I can't stand people who moan.* **3** ADJ A **negative** reply or decision indicates the answer "no." ❑ *Dr. Velayati gave a vague but negative response.* ● **nega|tive|ly** ADV [ADV after v] ❑ *Upon a negative decision, the applicant loses the protection offered by Belgian law.* ● **nega|tive|ly** ADV [ADV after v] ❑ *60 percent of the sample answered negatively.* **4** N-COUNT A **negative** is a word, expression, or gesture that means "no" or "not." ❑ *In the past we have heard only negatives when it came to following a healthy diet.* **5** ADJ In grammar, a **negative** clause contains a word such as "not," "never," or "no one." **6** ADJ If a medical test or scientific test is **negative**, it shows no evidence of the medical condition or substance that you are looking for. ❑ *So far 57 have taken the test and all have been negative.* **7** HIV **negative** →see HIV **8** N-COUNT In photography, a **negative** is an image that shows dark areas as light and light areas as dark. Negatives are made from camera film, and are used to print photographs. ❑ *...negatives of Diana's wedding dress.* **9** ADJ A **negative** charge or current has the same electrical charge as an electron. ❑ *Stimulate the injury or site of greatest pain with a small negative current.* ● **nega|tive|ly** ADV [ADV -ed] ❑ *As these electrons are negatively charged they will attempt to repel each other.* **10** ADJ A **negative** number, quantity, or measurement is less than zero. ❑ *Patients record a positive score and simple ones score negative numbers.* **11** PHRASE If an answer is **in the negative**, it is "no" or means "no." ❑ *The Council answered those questions in the negative.* →see **lightning**, **magnet**

Word Partnership   *negative*의 연어

N. negative **effect**, negative **experience**, negative **image**, negative **publicity** **1**
    negative **attitude**, negative **thoughts** **1** **2**
    negative **comment**, negative **reaction**, negative **response** **3**

---

nega|tive equity N-UNCOUNT If someone who has borrowed money to buy a house or apartment has **negative equity**, the amount of money they owe is greater than the present value of their home. [BRIT, BUSINESS] ❑ *Also, should there be a downturn in the housing market, Lucy could be left with negative equity.*

ne|glect /nɪɡlɛkt/ (neglects, neglecting, neglected) **1** V-T If you **neglect** someone or something, you fail to take care of them properly. ❑ *The woman denied that she had neglected her child.* ❑ *Feed plants and they grow, neglect them and they suffer.* ● N-UNCOUNT **Neglect** is also a noun. ❑ *The town's old quayside is collapsing after years of neglect.* **2** V-T If you **neglect** someone or something, you fail to give them the amount of attention that they deserve. ❑ *He'd given too much to his career, worked long hours, neglected her.* ● **ne|glect|ed** ADJ [v-link ADJ, ADJ n, ADJ after v] ❑ *The fact that she isn't coming today makes her grandmother feel lonely and neglected.* **3** V-T If you **neglect to** do something that you ought to do or **neglect** your duty, you fail to do it. ❑ *We often neglect to make proper use of our bodies.*

ne|gli|gence /nɛɡlɪdʒəns/ N-UNCOUNT If someone is guilty of **negligence**, they have failed to do something which they ought to do. [FORMAL] ❑ *The soldiers were ordered to appear before a disciplinary council on charges of negligence.*

ne|gli|gent /nɛɡlɪdʒənt/ ADJ If someone in a position of responsibility is **negligent**, they do not do something which they ought to do. ❑ *The jury determined that the airline was negligent in training and supervising the crew.* ● **neg|li|gent|ly** ADV [ADV with v] ❑ *A manufacturer negligently made and marketed a car with defective brakes.*

ne|gli|gible /nɛɡlɪdʒɪbəl/ ADJ An amount or effect that is **negligible** is so small that it is not worth considering or worrying about. ❑ *The pay that the soldiers received was negligible.*

ne|go|ti|able /nɪɡoʊʃiəbəl, -ʃəbəl/ ADJ Something that is **negotiable** can be changed or agreed upon when people discuss it. ❑ *He warned that his economic programme for the country was not negotiable.*

ne|go|ti|ate ◆◆◇ /nɪɡoʊʃieɪt/ (negotiates, negotiating, negotiated) **1** V-RECIP If people **negotiate with** each other or **negotiate** an agreement, they talk about a problem or a situation such as a business arrangement in order to solve the problem or complete the arrangement. ❑ *It is not clear whether the president is willing to negotiate with the democrats.* ❑ *When you have two adversaries negotiating, you need to be on neutral territory.* ❑ *The local government and the army negotiated a truce.* ❑ *Western governments have this week urged him to negotiate and avoid force.* **2** V-T If you **negotiate** an area of land, a place, or an obstacle, you successfully travel across it or around it. ❑ *Frank Mariano negotiates the desert*

❑ 빈곤한 사람들에게 더 많은 양의 식량을 공급하려는 노력이 있을 것이다.

1 타동사 무효로 하다 [격식체] ❑ 그의 직원들에 대한 진보적일 수도 있었을 태도가 이러한 약점들 때문에 빛이 바랬다. **2** 타동사 부정하다, 부인하다 [격식체] ❑ 그는 선거 결과를 부정하는 것은 사태를 악화시킬 뿐이라고 경고했다.

1 형용사 부정적인, 좋지 않은 ❑ 해외로부터 오는 소식은 대단히 좋지 않다. ● 부정적으로 부사 ❑ 이것은 금년 상반기에 걸쳐 그 결과에 부정적인 영향을 미칠 것이다. **2** 형용사 부정적인 ❑ 현재의 직업에 대한 견해를 물어보실 경우 절대 부정적인 말을 하지 마세요. ● 부정적으로 부사 ❑ 수주 후 그는 어쩌면 자신이 모든 관계를 다소 부정적으로 보는 것 같다고 말했다. ● 부정적인, 소극성 불가산명사 ❑ 나는 부정적인 것을 몹시 싫어한다. 불평하는 사람들은 참을 수가 없다. **3** 형용사 부정하는, 부정적인 ❑ 벨라야티 박사는 모호하지만 부정하는 답변을 했다. ● 부정하여, 부정적으로 부사 ❑ 기각 판결에 따라, 신청인은 벨기에 법에 의해 제공되는 보호를 받지 못하게 된다. ● 부정하여, 부정적으로 부사 ❑ 표본 집단의 60퍼센트가 아니라고 답했다. **4** 가산명사 부정어 ❑ 과거에는 건강에 좋은 식이 요법에 대해서라면 뭘 하지 말라는 식의 말만 들어 왔다. **5** 형용사 부정의 **6** 형용사 음성의 ❑ 현재까지 57명이 검사를 받았고 모두가 음성 판정을 받았다. **8** 가산명사 음화 (사진) ❑ 다이애나의 결혼 예복 음화 사진 **9** 형용사 음전기의, 음극의 ❑ 상처나 통증이 심한 부위를 약한 음전류로 자극하세요. ● 음전기로 부사 ❑ 이 전자들이 음전기로 대전되면 서로를 밀어내려고 하게 된다. **10** 형용사 음수의, 마이너스의 ❑ 어려운 텍스트는 플러스 점수를 받고 간단한 것들은 마이너스 점수를 받는다. **11** 구 부정하여, 아니라고 ❑ 위원회는 그와 같은 질문에 아니라고 답했다.

불가산명사 소극 자산 [영국영어, 경제] ❑ 또한, 주택 시장이 침체될 경우에는, 루시는 자산이 마이너스가 될 수도 있다.

1 타동사 소홀히 하다, 제대로 돌보지 않다 ❑ 그 여자는 자신이 아이에게 소홀했다는 것을 부인했다. ❑ 나무에 물 등을 잘 주면 자랄 것이고, 돌보지 않으면 병들 것이다. ● 불가산명사 소홀 ❑ 그 도시의 오래된 부두 지대는 수년간 관리 소홀로 퇴락해 가고 있다. **2** 타동사 간과하다, 소홀히 하다 ❑ 그는 일에 지나치게 많은 신경을 쏟으며 장시간 일을 하면서 그녀를 소홀히 했다. ● 간과된, 무시당한 형용사 ❑ 그녀가 오늘 오지 않는다는 사실에 그녀의 할머니는 외롭고 무시당한 기분을 느낀다. **3** 타동사 (해야 할 일을) 하지 않다, 태만히 하다 ❑ 우리는 종종 우리의 몸을 올바르게 사용하지 않는다.

불가산명사 태만, 부주의 [격식체] ❑ 그 병사들은 근무 태만 혐의로 징계 위원회에 출두하라는 명령을 받았다.

형용사 태만한, 부주의한 ❑ 배심원단은 항공사 측이 승무원들을 훈련시키고 관리하는 데 태만했다고 판결했다. ● 부주의하여, 태만하게 부사 ❑ 생산 회사가 부주의하게 브레이크에 하자가 있는 차를 만들어서 유통시켰다.

형용사 무시해도 좋은, 하찮은 ❑ 그 병사들이 받은 봉급은 하찮은 액수였다.

형용사 협상할 수 있는 ❑ 그는 자신의 국가 경제 계획은 협상할 수 있는 것이 아니라고 경고했다.

1 상호동사 협상하다, 협정하다 ❑ 대통령이 기꺼이 민주당원들과 협상하려 할지는 확실치 않다. ❑ 두 적대자 간의 협상을 중재할 때는 중립적인 위치에 설 필요가 있다. ❑ 지방 정부와 군대는 정전 협정을 맺었다. ❑ 이번 주에 서방 국가들은 그에게 무력을 피하고 협상하라고 촉구해 왔다. **2** 타동사 잘 통과하다 ❑ 프랭크 마리아노는 찌그러진 픽업트럭을 돌아서 사막 지대를 통과한다. ❑ 나는 소형 오토바이를 타고 모퉁이를 잘 통과해서 멈춰 섰다.

a b c d e f g h i j k l m n o p q r s t u v w x y z

terrain in his battered pickup. ❏ *I negotiated the corner on my motorbike and pulled to a stop.*

Word Partnership   *negotiate의 연어*

| V. | **agree to** negotiate, **fail to** negotiate, **refuse to** negotiate, **try to** negotiate **1** |
| N. | negotiate **an agreement**, negotiate **a contract**, negotiate **a deal**, negotiate **a settlement**, negotiate **the terms of** *something* **1** |

---

ne|go|ti|at|ing ta|ble N-SING If you say that people are at **the negotiating table**, you mean that they are having discussions in order to settle a dispute or reach an agreement. ❏ *"We want to settle all matters at the negotiating table," he said.*

ne|go|tia|tion ♦♦◇ /nɪɡoʊʃieɪʃⁿn/ (**negotiations**) N-VAR **Negotiations** are formal discussions between people who have different aims or intentions, especially in business or politics, during which they try to reach an agreement. ❏ *Warren said, "We have had meaningful negotiations and I believe we are very close to a deal."*

Word Partnership   *negotiation의 연어*

N.	**basis for** negotiation, **process of** negotiation
PREP.	negotiation **between**, **under** negotiation
ADJ.	**successful** negotiation

---

ne|go|tia|tor /nɪɡoʊʃieɪtər/ (**negotiators**) N-COUNT **Negotiators** are people who take part in political or financial negotiations. ❏ *On Thursday night the rebels' chief negotiator at the peace talks announced that dialogue had gone as far as it could go.*

neigh|bor ♦◇◇ /neɪbər/ (**neighbors**) [BRIT **neighbour**] **1** N-COUNT Your **neighbor** is someone who lives near you. ❏ *My neighbor spies on me through the crack of my fence.* **2** N-COUNT You can refer to the person who is standing or sitting next to you as your **neighbor**. ❏ *The woman prodded her neighbor and whispered urgently in his ear.* **3** N-COUNT You can refer to something which stands next to something else of the same kind as its **neighbor**. ❏ *...its big oil-rich neighbor.*

neigh|bor|hood /neɪbərhʊd/ (**neighborhoods**) [BRIT **neighbourhood**] **1** N-COUNT A **neighborhood** is one of the parts of a town where people live. ❏ *There is no neighborhood which is really safe.* **2** N-COUNT The **neighborhood** of a place or person is the area or the people around them. ❏ *...a suburban Boston neighborhood close to where I live.* **3** PHRASE **In the neighborhood of** a number means approximately that number. ❏ *The album's now sold something in the neighborhood of 2 million copies.* **4** PHRASE A place **in the neighborhood of** another place is near it. ❏ *...the loss of woodlands in the neighborhood of large towns.*

Word Partnership   *neighborhood의 연어*

| ADJ. | **poor** neighborhood, **residential** neighborhood, **run-down** neighborhood **1 2** |

---

neigh|bor|ing /neɪbərɪŋ/ [BRIT **neighbouring**] ADJ **Neighboring** places or things are near other things of the same kind. [ADJ n] ❏ *He is on his way back to Beijing after a tour of neighboring Asian capitals.*

nei|ther ♦♦◇ /niðər, naɪ-/ **1** CONJ You use **neither** in front of the first of two or more words or expressions when you are linking two or more things which are not true or do not happen. The other thing is introduced by "nor." ❏ *Professor Hisamatsu spoke neither English nor German.* **2** DET You use **neither** to refer to each of two things or people, when you are making a negative statement that includes both of them. ❏ *At first, neither man could speak.* ● QUANT-NEG **Neither** is also a quantifier. ❏ *Neither of us felt like going out.* ● PRON-NEG **Neither** is also a pronoun. ❏ *Both smiled; neither seemed likely to be aware of my absence for long.* **3** CONJ If you say that one person or thing does not do something and **neither** does another, what you say is true of all the people or things that you are mentioning. ❏ *I never learned to swim and neither did they.* **4** CONJ You use **neither** after a negative statement to emphasize that you are introducing another negative statement. [FORMAL] ❏ *I can't ever recall Dad hugging me. Neither did I sit on his knee.*

Do not confuse **neither** and **none**. You use **neither** in negative statements to refer to two people or things. ❏ *Neither had close friends in college.* You use **neither of** in the same way, followed by a pronoun or a noun group. ❏ *Neither of them spoke... Neither of these extremes is desirable.* Note that you can also use **neither** before a singular count noun. ❏ *Neither side can win.* You use **none** in negative statements to refer to three or more people or things. ❏ *None could afford the food.* You use **none of** in the same way, followed by a pronoun or a noun group. ❏ *None of them had learned anything... None of his companions answered.*

Word Partnership   *neither의 연어*

| V. | neither **confirm nor deny** **1** |
| N. | neither **candidate**, neither **man**, neither **party**, neither **side**, neither **team** **2** |

---

neon /niɒn/ **1** ADJ **Neon** lights or signs are made from glass tubes filled with neon gas which produce a bright electric light. [ADJ n] ❏ *In the city squares the neon lights flashed in turn.* **2** N-UNCOUNT **Neon** is a gas which occurs in very small amounts in the atmosphere. ❏ *Inert gases like neon and argon have eight electrons in their outer shell.*

단수명사 협상 테이블 ❏ "우리는 협상 테이블에서 모든 문제를 해결하고 싶습니다."라고 그가 말했다.

가산명사 또는 불가산명사 협상, 교섭, 절충 ❏ 워렌은 말했다. "우리는 의미 있는 교섭을 해 왔으며, 나는 우리가 협정에 매우 가까이 접근해 있다고 믿는다."

가산명사 협상자, 중재관 ❏ 의견 교환이 최대한으로 이루어졌다고 목요일 밤 반란군 측 수석 중재관이 평화 회담에서 공표했다.

[영국영어 neighbour] **1** 가산명사 이웃 사람 ❏ 이웃 사람이 우리 집 울타리의 갈라진 틈을 통해 나를 감시한다. **2** 가산명사 옆 사람 ❏ 그 여자는 옆 사람을 쿡 찌르더니 귀에 대고 다급하게 속삭였다. **3** 가산명사 이웃에 있는 것 ❏ 거대 산유국인 그 이웃 나라

[영국영어 neighbourhood] **1** 가산명사 지구, 구역 ❏ 정말로 안전한 구역은 없다. **2** 가산명사 인근; 근처의 사람들 ❏ 내가 사는 곳에 가까운 보스턴 교외 인근 **3** 구 약, 대략 ❏ 그 음반은 현재까지 약 2백만 장 가까이 팔렸다. **4** 구 -의 근처에 ❏ 대도시 인근 삼림 지대의 감소

[영국영어 neighbouring] 형용사 이웃의, 인접한 ❏ 그는 인접 아시아 국가들의 수도를 순회한 후에 베이징으로 돌아오는 길이다.

1 접속사 -도 ...도 아니다 ❏ 히사마츠 교수는 영어도 독일어도 할 줄 몰랐다. **2** 한정사 (둘 중에서) 어느 쪽의 -도 ...않다 ❏ 처음에는 두 사람 중 어느 쪽도 말을 하지 못했다. ● 부정(否定)수량사 (둘 중의) 어느 쪽도 - 않다 ❏ 우리 둘 중 어느 쪽도 나가고 싶지 않았다. ● 부정(否定)대명사 (둘 중의) 어느 쪽도 - 않다 ❏ 둘 다 모두 웃었다. 둘 중 어느 쪽도 내가 오랫동안 자리를 비운 것을 알아차리지 못하는 것처럼 보였다. **3** 접속사 -도 또한 아니다 ❏ 나는 수영을 배운 적이 없고 그들 또한 그랬다. **4** 접속사 -도 또한 아니다 [격식체] ❏ 아버지가 나를 껴안았던 적이 있었는지 기억나지 않는다. 나는 그의 무릎 위에 앉아보지도 않았다.

neither와 none을 혼동하지 않도록 하라. neither는 부정문에서 두 사람이나 두 개의 사물을 가리킬 때 쓴다. ❏ 두 사람 모두 대학 시절에 가까운 친구가 없었다. neither of도 같은 방식으로 쓰는데 뒤에는 대명사나 명사구가 따라 온다. ❏ 그들은 둘 다 말을 하지 않았다... 이런 양극단은 어느 것도 바람직하지 않다. neither는 가산 명사 단수형 앞에 쓸 수도 있음을 유의하라. ❏ 아무도 편도 이길 수 없다. none은 부정문에서 셋 또는 그 이상의 사람이나 사물을 가리킬 때 쓴다. ❏ 아무도 음식을 살 형편이 안 됐다. none of도 같은 방식으로 쓰는데 뒤에는 대명사나 명사구가 따라 온다. ❏ 그들 누구도 아무것도 배우지 못했다... 그의 동료 아무도 대답하지 않았다.

1 형용사 네온 ❏ 시가지에서는 네온 불빛이 차례로 점멸했다. **2** 불가산명사 네온 ❏ 네온과 아르곤 같은 비활성 기체는 외각에 여덟 개의 전자를 가지고 있다.

neph|ew /nɛfyu/ (**nephews**) N-COUNT Someone's **nephew** is the son of their sister or brother. ❑ *I am planning a 25th birthday party for my nephew.*

가산명사 조카 ❑ 내 조카의 스물다섯 번째 생일 파티를 계획하고 있다.

nerve ♦♦♦ /nɜrv/ (**nerves**) **1** N-COUNT **Nerves** are long thin fibres that transmit messages between your brain and other parts of your body. ❑ *...spinal nerves.* **2** N-PLURAL If you refer to someone's **nerves**, you mean their ability to cope with problems such as stress, worry, and danger. ❑ *Jill's nerves are stretched to breaking point.* **3** N-PLURAL You can refer to someone's feelings of anxiety or tension as **nerves**. ❑ *I just played badly. It wasn't nerves.* **4** N-UNCOUNT **Nerve** is the courage that you need in order to do something difficult or dangerous. ❑ *The brandy made him choke, but it restored his nerve.* **5** PHRASE If someone or something **gets on** your **nerves**, they annoy or irritate you. [INFORMAL] ❑ *Lately he's not done a bloody thing and it's getting on my nerves.* **6** PHRASE If you say that someone **has a nerve** or **has the nerve** to do something, you are criticizing them for doing something which you feel they had no right to do. [INFORMAL, DISAPPROVAL] ❑ *He told his critics they had a nerve complaining about Lithuania.* **7** PHRASE If you **lose** your **nerve**, you suddenly panic and become too afraid to do something that you were about to do. ❑ *The bomber had lost his nerve and fled.* →see **ear**, **eye**, **nervous system**

1 가산명사 신경 ❑ 척추 신경 **2** 복수명사 신경; 냉정 ❑ 질의 신경은 한계점에 이를 정도로 예민해져 있다. **3** 복수명사 긴장; 신경과민 ❑ 그저 경기를 형편없이 했을 뿐이야. 긴장한 건 아니었어. **4** 불가산명사 용기, 담력 ❑ 그는 브랜디를 마시고 목이 메었지만, 용기를 되찾았다. **5** 구 ~의 신경을 거스르다 [비격식체] ❑ 최근에 그는 아무 일도 하지 않았고 그것이 내 신경을 거스르고 있다. **6** 구 뻔뻔스럽게도 ~하다 [비격식체, 탐탁찮음] ❑ 그는 자기를 비판하는 사람들에게 그들이 뻔뻔스럽게도 리투아니아에 대해 불평한다고 말했다. **7** 구 겁에 질리다 ❑ 폭파범은 겁에 질려 달아났다.

> ### Word Partnership   *nerve*의 연어
>
> | | |
> |---|---|
> | N. | nerve **cells**, nerve **damage**, nerve **fibers**, nerve **impulses** **1** |
> | V. | **hit** a nerve, **strike** a nerve, **touch** a nerve **1** |
> | | **get up** the nerve, **got** *a/the* nerve, **have** *a/the* nerve **6** |

nerv|ous ♦♦♦ /nɜrvəs/ ADJ If someone is **nervous**, they are frightened or worried about something that is happening or might happen, and show this in their behavior. ❑ *The party has become deeply nervous about its prospects of winning the next election.* ● **nerv|ous|ly** ADV [ADV with v] ❑ *Brunhilde stood up nervously as the men came into the room.* ● **nerv|ous|ness** N-UNCOUNT ❑ *I smiled warmly so he wouldn't see my nervousness.* **2** ADJ A **nervous** person is very tense and easily upset. ❑ *She was apparently a very nervous woman, and that affected her career.* **3** ADJ A **nervous** illness or condition is one that affects your emotions and your mental state. [ADJ n] ❑ *The number of nervous disorders was rising in the region.*

1 형용사 불안한, 겁내는 ❑ 그 정당은 차기 선거 승리 전망에 대해 몹시 불안해졌다. ● 불안하게 부사 ❑ 남자들이 방에 들어오자 브룬힐데는 불안하게 일어났다. ● 불안함 불가산명사 ❑ 내가 불안해하는 것을 그가 눈치 채지 못하도록 다정하게 미소 지었다. **2** 형용사 신경질적인 ❑ 겉보기에 그녀는 매우 신경질적인 여자였고, 그것이 그녀의 경력에 영향을 미쳤다. **3** 형용사 신경의 ❑ 그 지역에서 신경 질환의 수가 증가하고 있었다.

> ### Word Partnership   *nervous*의 연어
>
> | | |
> |---|---|
> | PREP. | nervous **about** *something* **1** |
> | V. | **become** nervous, **feel** nervous, **get** nervous, **look** nervous, **make** *someone* nervous **1** |
> | ADV. | **increasingly** nervous, **a little** nervous, **too** nervous, **very** nervous **1** **2** |

nerv|ous break|down (**nervous breakdowns**) N-COUNT If someone has a **nervous breakdown**, they become extremely depressed and cannot cope with their normal life. ❑ *His wife would not be able to cope and might suffer a nervous breakdown.*

가산명사 신경 쇠약 ❑ 그의 아내는 이겨내지 못하고 신경 쇠약에 걸릴지도 모른다.

nerv|ous sys|tem (**nervous systems**) N-COUNT Your **nervous system** consists of all the nerves in your body together with your brain and spinal cord. ❑ *So it is possible that the symptoms will not finally go until your nervous system is in a better state.* →see Word Web: **nervous system**

가산명사 신경계 ❑ 따라서 당신의 신경계가 나아지기 전까지는 그런 증상이 완전히 사라지지 않을 수도 있습니다.

nest /nɛst/ (**nests, nesting, nested**) **1** N-COUNT A bird's **nest** is the home that it makes to lay its eggs in. ❑ *I can see an eagle's nest on the rocks.* **2** V-I When a bird **nests** somewhere, it builds a nest and settles there to lay its eggs. ❑ *Some species may nest in close proximity to each other.* **3** N-COUNT A **nest** is a home that a group of insects or other creatures make in order to live in and give birth to their young in. ❑ *Some solitary bees make their nests in burrows in the soil.* →see **bird**

1 가산명사 둥지, 보금자리 ❑ 암벽 위에 독수리 둥지가 보인다. **2** 자동사 보금자리를 짓다, 보금자리에 깃들이다 ❑ 어떤 종들은 서로 가까이에 보금자리를 지을 수도 있다. **3** 가산명사 (곤충 등의) 집, 동우리 ❑ 무리를 짓지 않는 어떤 벌들은 땅 속 굴에다 집을 짓는다.

nes|tle /nɛsᵊl/ (**nestles, nestling, nestled**) **1** V-T/V-I If you **nestle** or **are nestled** somewhere, you move into a comfortable position, usually by pressing against someone or against something soft. ❑ *John took one child into the crook of each arm and let them nestle against him.* **2** V-I If something such as a building **nestles** somewhere, it is in that place and seems safe or sheltered. ❑ *Nearby, nestling in the hills, was the children's home.*

1 타동사/자동사 기대어 눕다; 편히 몸을 눕히다 ❑ 존은 한 팔에 하나씩 아이들을 안고서 자신의 몸에 편히 기대게 했다. **2** 자동사 아늑하게 자리 잡다 ❑ 가까이에는 아이들의 집이 언덕 속에 아늑하게 자리 잡고 있었다.

net
① NOUN AND VERB USES
② ADJECTIVE AND ADVERB USES

① **net** ♦♦♦ /nɛt/ (**nets, netting, netted**) **1** N-UNCOUNT **Net** is a kind of cloth that you can see through. It is made of very fine threads woven together so that there are small equal spaces between them. **2** N-COUNT A **net** is a piece of netting which is used as a protective covering for something, for example to protect vegetables from birds. ❑ *I threw aside my mosquito net, jumped out of bed and drew up the blind.* **3** N-COUNT A **net** is a piece of netting which is used for catching fish, insects, or animals. ❑ *Several fishermen sat on wooden barrels, tending their nets.* **4** V-T If you **net** a fish or other animal, you catch it in a net. ❑ *I'm quite happy to net a fish and then let it go.* **5** V-T If you **net** something, you manage to get it, especially by using skill. ❑ *Two fourth-quarter drives netted a grand total of 21 yards.* **6** V-T If you **net** a particular amount of money, you gain it as profit after all expenses have been paid. ❑ *He netted profit of $1.85 billion from three large sales of stock.* **7** N-SING **The Net** is the same as the **Internet**. **8** →see also **safety net** →see **tennis**

1 불가산명사 망사 **2** 가산명사 (보호용) 그물 ❑ 나는 모기장을 걷어치우고 침대 밖으로 뛰어 나가서 블라인드를 올렸다. **3** 가산명사 (사냥이나 어획용) 그물 ❑ 어부들 몇 명이 나무 통 위에 앉아서 그물을 손질하고 있었다. **4** 타동사 그물로 잡다 ❑ 고기를 그물로 잡은 다음 놓아줘서 아주 즐겁다. **5** 타동사 획득하다 ❑ 4쿼터에 두 번의 전진을 통해 총 21야드를 획득했다. **6** 타동사 순익을 얻다 ❑ 그는 3건의 대량 주식 매각을 통해 18억 5천만 달러의 순이익을 올렸다. **7** 단수명사 인터넷

Word Web   nervous system

The body's **nervous system** is a two-way road which transmits electrochemical messages to and from various parts of the body. Sensory neurons carry information from both inside and outside the body to the central nervous system (CNS) which consists of the **brain** and the **spinal cord**. Motor neurons carry impulses from the CNS to **organs** and to **muscles** such as the muscles in the hand, telling them how to move. Sensory and motor neurons are bound together, creating **nerves** that run throughout the body.

② **net** ♦♦◇ /nɛt/ [BRIT also **nett**] ◢ ADJ A **net** amount is one which remains when everything that should be subtracted has been subtracted. [ADJ n, v-link ADJ of n] ❑ ...*a rise in sales and net profit.* ❑ *Its net assets totaled $165 million.* ● ADV **Net** is also an adverb. ❑ *Balances of £5,000 and above will earn 11 per cent gross, 8.25 per cent net.* ❑ *They pay him around £2 million net.* ◢ ADJ The **net** weight of something is its weight without its container or the material that has been used to wrap it. [ADJ n] ❑ ...*350 mg net weight.* ◢ ADJ A **net** result is a final result after all the details have been considered or included. [ADJ n] ❑ *There has been a net gain in jobs in our country.*

[영국영어 nett] ◢ 형용사 순수한 ❑ 대상과 순이익의 증가 ❑ 그 회사의 순 자산은 총 1억 6천 5백만 달려었다. ● 부사 (제할 것을 다 제하고) 순수하게 ❑ 5천 파운드 이상의 잔고에는 총 11퍼센트, 순수하게는 8.25퍼센트의 이자가 붙는다. ❑ 그들이 그에게 지불하는 돈은 제할 것 다 제하고 2백만 파운드 정도이다. ◢ 형용사 순수한 (중량) ❑ 순 중량 350밀리그램 ◢ 형용사 최종적인, 순수한 ❑ 우리나라에서는 일자리가 순증해 왔다.

Word Partnership   net의 연어

N.	**fishing** net ① ◢
V.	**access** the Net, **surf** the Net ① ◢
N.	net **earnings**, net **income/loss**, net **proceeds**, net **profit**, net **revenue** ② ◢
	net **gain**, net **increase**, net **result** ② ◢ ◢

net|ball /nɛtbɔl/ N-UNCOUNT In Britain and some other countries, **netball** is a game played by two teams of seven players, usually women. Each team tries to score goals by throwing a ball through a net on the top of a pole at each end of the court. ❑ ...*an after-school netball match.*

불가산명사 네트볼 (경기) ❑ 방과 후의 네트 볼 시합

nett /nɛt/ →see **net**

net|tle /nɛtᵊl/ (nettles, nettling, nettled) ◢ N-COUNT **Nettles** are wild plants which have leaves covered with fine hairs that sting you when you touch them. ❑ *The nettles stung their legs.* ◢ V-T If something **nettles** you, you are annoyed or offended by it. ❑ *He was nettled by her manner.*

◢ 가산명사 쐐기풀; 가시가 많은 식물 ❑ 쐐기풀이 그들의 다리를 쩔렀다. ◢ 타동사 화나다 ❑ 그는 그녀의 태도에 화가 났다.

net|work ♦♦◇ /nɛtwɜrk/ (networks, networking, networked) ◢ N-COUNT A **network** of lines, roads, veins, or other long thin things is a large number of them which cross each other or meet at many points. ❑ ...*Strasbourg, with its rambling network of medieval streets.* ◢ N-COUNT A **network of** people or institutions is a large number of them that have a connection with each other and work together as a system. ❑ *Distribution of the food is going ahead using a network of local church people and other volunteers.* ◢ N-COUNT A particular **network** is a system of things which are connected and which operate together. For example, a **computer network** consists of a number of computers that are part of the same system. ❑ ...*a computer network with 154 terminals.* ◢ N-COUNT A radio or television **network** is a company or group of companies that broadcast radio or television programs throughout an area. ❑ *An American network says it has obtained the recordings.* ◢ V-I If you **network**, you try to meet new people who might be useful to you in your job. [BUSINESS] ❑ *In business, it is important to network with as many people as possible on a face to face basis.* →see **Internet**

◢ 가산명사 망상조직 ❑ 중세풍의 도로가 무질서하게 뻗어 얽혀 있는 스트라스부르 ◢ 가산명사 조직망 ❑ 식량 배급은 지방 교회 신도들과 다른 자원 봉사자들의 조직망을 통해 계속되고 있다. ◢ 가산명사 네트워크, 망 ❑ 154개의 단말기로 이루어진 컴퓨터 네트워크 ◢ 가산명사 방송망 ❑ 한 미국 방송사가 녹음테이프를 입수했다고 말했다. ◢ 자동사 인간관계를 형성하다 [경제] ❑ 사업에서는, 가능한 한 많은 사람들과 직접적인 인간관계를 형성하는 것이 중요하다.

Word Partnership   network의 연어

ADJ.	**extensive** network, **nationwide** network, **vast** network, **worldwide** network ◢ ◢
	wireless network ◢
N.	network **administrator**, **computer** network, network **coverage**, network **support** ◢
	broadcast network, **cable** network, **radio** network, **television/TV** network ◢

net|work|ing /nɛtwɜrkɪŋ/ ◢ N-UNCOUNT **Networking** is the process of trying to meet new people who might be useful to you in your job, often through social activities. [BUSINESS] ❑ *If executives fail to exploit the opportunities of networking they risk being left behind.* ◢ N-UNCOUNT You can refer to the things associated with a computer system or the process of establishing such a system as **networking**. ❑ *Managers have learned to grapple with networking, artificial intelligence, computer-aided engineering, and manufacturing.*

◢ 불가산명사 인간관계 형성 [경제] ❑ 만약 임원들이 인간관계를 형성할 수 있는 기회를 이용하지 않는다면, 뒤처질 위험을 무릅쓰는 것이다. ◢ 불가산명사 (컴퓨터) 네트워킹 ❑ 관리자들은 네트워킹과 인공 지능, 컴퓨터 이용 공학 및 생산 등과 씨름하는 법을 배워 왔다.

Word Link   otic ≈ affecting, causing : erotic, neurotic, patriotic

neu|rot|ic /nʊərɒtɪk, BRIT nyʊərɒtɪk/ (neurotics) ADJ If you say that someone is **neurotic**, you mean that they are always frightened or worried about things that you consider unimportant. [DISAPPROVAL] ❑ *He was almost neurotic about being followed.* ● N-COUNT A **neurotic** is someone who is neurotic. ❑ *These patients are not neurotics.*

형용사 신경과민의 [탐탁찮음] ❑ 그는 신경과민에 가까울 정도로 자기 뒤를 누군가가 따라 다닌다고 생각했다. ● 가산명사 신경증 환자 ❑ 이 환자들은 신경증 환자가 아니다.

neu|tral /nutrəl, BRIT nyu:trəl/ (**neutrals**) **1** ADJ If a person or country adopts a **neutral** position or remains **neutral**, they do not support anyone in a disagreement, war, or contest. ❑ *Let's meet on neutral territory.* ● N-COUNT A **neutral** is someone who is neutral. ❑ *It was a good game to watch for the neutrals.* ● **neu|tral|ity** /nutrælɪti, BRIT nyu:trælɪti/ N-UNCOUNT *...a reputation for political neutrality and impartiality.* **2** ADJ If someone speaks in a **neutral** voice or if the expression on their face is **neutral**, they do not show what they are thinking or feeling. ❑ *Isabel put her magazine down and said in a neutral voice, "You're very late, darling."* ● **neu|tral|ity** N-UNCOUNT ❑ *I noticed, behind the neutrality of his gaze, a deep weariness.* **3** ADJ If you say that something is **neutral**, you mean that it does not have any effect on other things because it lacks any significant qualities of its own, or it is an equal balance of two or more different qualities, amounts, or ideas. ❑ *Three in every five interviewed felt that the Budget was neutral and they would be no better off.* **4** N-UNCOUNT **Neutral** is the position between the gears of a vehicle such as a car, in which the gears are not connected to the engine. ❑ *Graham put the van in neutral and jumped out into the road.* **5** ADJ In an electrical device or system, the **neutral** wire is one of the three wires needed to complete the circuit so that the current can flow. The other two wires are called the earth wire and the live or positive wire. ❑ *The earth wire in the house is connected to the neutral wire.* **6** COLOR **Neutral** is used to describe things that have a pale color such as cream or gray, or that have no color at all. ❑ *At the horizon the land mass becomes a continuous pale neutral grey, almost blending with the sky.* **7** ADJ In chemistry, **neutral** is used to describe things that are neither acid nor alkaline. ❑ *Pure water is neutral with a pH of 7.* →see **war**

neu|tral|ize /nutrəlaɪz, BRIT nyu:trəlaɪz/ (**neutralizes, neutralizing, neutralized**) [BRIT also **neutralise**] **1** V-T To **neutralize** something means to prevent it from having any effect or from working properly. ❑ *The U.S. is trying to neutralize the resolution in the UN Security Council.* **2** V-T When a chemical substance **neutralizes** an acid, it makes it less acid. ❑ *Antacids are alkaline and they relieve pain by neutralizing acid in the contents of the stomach.*

nev|er ♦♦♦ /nevər/ **1** ADV **Never** means at no time in the past or at no time in the future. ❑ *I have never lost the weight I put on in my teens.* ❑ *He never has been so free of worry.* ❑ *That was a mistake. We'll never do it again.* **2** ADV **Never** means "not in any circumstances at all." ❑ *I would never do anything to hurt him.* ❑ *Divorce is never easy for children.* **3** PHRASE **Never ever** is an emphatic way of saying "never." [EMPHASIS] ❑ *I never, ever sit around thinking, "What shall I do next?"* **4** ADV **Never** is used to refer to the past and means "not." ❑ *He never achieved anything.* ❑ *I never knew the lad.* **5** **never mind** →see **mind**

never-ending ADJ If you describe something bad or unpleasant as **never-ending**, you are emphasizing that it seems to last a very long time. [EMPHASIS] ❑ *...a never-ending series of scandals rocking the House of Windsor.*

never|the|less ♦◇◇ /nevərðəles/ ADV You use **nevertheless** when saying something that contrasts with what has just been said. [FORMAL] [ADV with cl] ❑ *Although the market has been flattened, residential property costs remain high. Nevertheless, the fall-off in demand has had an impact on resale values.*

new ♦♦♦ /nu, BRIT nyu:/ (**newer, newest**) **1** ADJ Something that is **new** has been recently created, built, or invented or is in the process of being created, built, or invented. ❑ *They've just opened a new hotel in the Stoke area.* ❑ *These ideas are nothing new in America.* **2** ADJ Something that is **new** has not been used or owned by anyone. ❑ *That afternoon she went out and bought a new dress.* ❑ *There are many boats, new and used, for sale.* **3** ADJ You use **new** to describe something which has replaced another thing, for example because you no longer have the old one, or it no longer exists, or it is no longer useful. ❑ *Under the new rules, some factories will cut emissions by as much as 90 percent.* ❑ *I had to find somewhere new to live.* ❑ *Rachel has a new boyfriend.* **4** ADJ **New** is used to describe something that has only recently been discovered or noticed. ❑ *The new planet is about ten times the size of the earth.* **5** ADJ A **new** day or year is the beginning of the next day or year. [ADJ n] ❑ *The start of a new year is a good time to reflect on the many achievements of the past.* **6** ADJ **New** is used to describe someone or something that has recently acquired a particular status or position. [ADJ n] ❑ *...the usual exhaustion of a new mother.* **7** ADJ If you are **new to** a situation or place, or if the situation or place is **new** to you, you have not previously seen it or had any experience with it. [v-link ADJ, oft ADJ to n] ❑ *She wasn't new to the company.* ❑ *His name was new to me then and it stayed in my mind.* **8** ADJ **New** potatoes, carrots, or peas are produced early in the season for such vegetables and are usually small with a sweet flavor. [ADJ n] ❑ *Serve with a green salad and new potatoes.* **9** →see also **brand-new**. **as good as new** →see **good**

Thesaurus *new*의 참조어

ADJ. contemporary, current, latest, modern, novel; (*ant.*) existing, old, past **1**

---

new blood N-UNCOUNT If people talk about bringing **new blood** into an organization or onto a sports team, they are referring to new people who are likely to improve the organization or team. ❑ *We'll get some new blood in there that can really do the job.*

new|born /nuborn, BRIT nyu:bɔ:ˈn/ (**newborns**) ADJ A **newborn** baby or animal is one that has just been born. ❑ *The electronic sensor has been adapted to fit on a newborn baby.* ● N-PLURAL **The newborn** are babies or animals who are newborn. ❑ *Mild jaundice in the newborn is common and often clears without treatment.*

1 형용사 중립의 ❑ 중립 지역에서 만납시다. ● 가산명사 중립자; 중립인 ❑ 어느 편도 들지 않는 사람들이 지켜보기에 좋은 경기였다. ● 중립 불가산명사 ❑ 정치적으로 중립적이며 공명정대하다는 평판 **2** 형용사 담담한 ❑ 이사벨은 잡지를 내려놓으며 담담한 목소리로 말했다. "많이 늦으셨군요, 여보." ● 담담함 불가산명사 ❑ 나는 담담한 그의 시선 이면에서 깊은 권태를 알아차렸다. **3** 형용사 실효가 없는, 어정쩡한 ❑ 인터뷰 대상자 5명 중 3명이 예산안이 실효가 없을 것이며 살림살이가 나아지지 않을 것이라고 생각했다. **4** 불가산명사 중립 (기어) ❑ 그레이엄은 밴의 기어를 중립에 놓고 도로로 뛰어내렸다. **5** 형용사 중성의, 전하가 없는 ❑ 집 안의 접지선은 중성선에 연결되어 있다. **6** 색채어 (색이) 엷은 ❑ 지평선에서 땅덩어리는 끊임없이 엷은 회색빛이 되며 하늘과 뒤섞이다시피 된다. **7** 형용사 중성의 ❑ 순수한 물은 pH 값이 7로 중성이다.

[영국영어 neutralise] **1** 타동사 무력하게 하다 ❑ 미국은 유엔 안전 보장 이사회의 결의를 무력화시키려 하고 있다. **2** 타동사 중화하다 ❑ 제산제는 알칼리성이어서 위의 내용물 속에 든 산을 중화함으로써 통증을 덜어 준다.

1 부사 한번도 ~하지 않아, 다시는 ~하지 않아 ❑ 나는 십대에 찐 살이 한 번도 빠진 적이 없다. ❑ 그가 그처럼 걱정 없었던 적은 버도 없었다. ❑ 그건 실수였습니다. 다시는 그런 일이 없을 겁니다. **2** 부사 결코 ~하지 않아 ❑ 결코 그를 다치게 할 어떤 일도 하지 않을 것이다. ❑ 이혼은 아이들에게는 결코 쉽지 않다. **3** 구 never는 강조한 표현 [강조] ❑ 나는 절대로 "다음에는 뭘 할까"라고 생각하며 빈둥거리지 않는다. **4** 부사 ~않았다 ❑ 그는 아무것도 성취하지 못했다. ❑ 나는 그 젊은이를 모르고 지냈다.

형용사 끝없는 [강조] ❑ 윈저 왕조를 뒤흔드는 끝없이 이어지는 추문들

부사 그럼에도 불구하고 [격식체] ❑ 시장이 잠잠해지긴 했지만, 주거용 부동산 가격은 여전히 높다. 그럼에도 불구하고, 수요의 감소는 재판매 가격에 영향을 미쳐 왔다.

1 형용사 새로운, 새로 나온 ❑ 그들은 스토크 지역에 새 호텔을 막 개장했다. ❑ 이런 생각들은 미국에서는 전혀 새로운 것이 아니다. **2** 형용사 새 신상품의, 아직 안 쓴 ❑ 그 날 오후 그녀는 외출해서 새 옷을 한 벌 샀다. ❑ 팔려고 내놓은 신제품 혹은 중고품 보트가 많이 있다. **3** 형용사 새로운, 새로워진 ❑ 새로운 법규 하에서는, 일부 공장들이 무려 90퍼센트까지 오염 물질 배출을 줄일 것이다. ❑ 새로운 거처를 찾아야만 했다. ❑ 레이첼은 새 남자 친구가 있다. **4** 형용사 새로 발견된 ❑ 새로 발견된 행성은 지구의 약 열 배 크기이다. **5** 형용사 새 ❑ 새해 초는 과거에 성취한 많은 일들을 회고하기에 좋은 시기이다. **6** 형용사 신임의, 새로 온 ❑ 새로 엄마가 된 주부가 흔히 겪는 극도의 피로 **7** 형용사 경험이 없는, 낯선 ❑ 그녀는 그 회사가 낯설지 않았다. ❑ 그의 이름은 당시에는 내게 낯설었는데 내 마음속에 남았다. **8** 형용사 갓 나온, 햇 ❑ 야채샐러드와 햇감자를 곁들여 내세요.

불가산명사 새 인물, (비유적) 새 피 ❑ 실제로 일을 할 수 있는 새 인물을 그 자리에 들일 것이다.

형용사 갓 태어난, 신생의 ❑ 그 전자 감지기는 신생아에게 적합하도록 개조되었다. ● 복수명사 갓난아기; 갓 태어난 새끼 ❑ 갓난아기에게 가벼운 황달은 흔히 있으며 치료를 받지 않고서도 낫는 경우가 많다.

new|comer /nukʌmər, BRIT nyu:kʌmə^r/ (**newcomers**) N-COUNT A **newcomer** is a person who has recently arrived in a place, joined an organization, or started a new activity. ❑ *He must be a newcomer to town and he obviously didn't understand our local customs.*

가산명사 새로 온 사람, 초심자 ❑ 그는 틀림없이 마을에 새로 온 사람으로 우리 지방 풍습을 이해하지 못한 것이 분명하다.

new|found /nufaʊnd, BRIT nyu:faʊnd/ ADJ A **newfound** quality or ability is one that you have got recently. [ADJ n] ❑ *His friends have a newfound sense of patriotism.*

형용사 새로 발견된; 최근에 두드러진 ❑ 그의 친구들은 최근에 애국심을 새로이 가지게 되었다.

new|ly ♦◇◇ /nuli, BRIT nyu:li/ ADV **Newly** is used before a past participle or an adjective to indicate that a particular action is very recent, or that a particular state of affairs has very recently begun to exist. [ADV -ed/adj] ❑ *She was young at the time, and newly married.*

부사 최근에, 새로 ❑ 그녀는 당시 젊고 신혼이었다.

news ♦♦♦ /nuz, BRIT nyu:z/ **1** N-UNCOUNT **News** is information about a recently changed situation or a recent event. ❑ *We waited and waited for news of him.* ❑ *They still haven't had any news about when they'll be able to go home.* **2** N-UNCOUNT **News** is information that is published in newspapers and broadcast on radio and television about recent events in the country or world or in a particular area of activity. [also the n] ❑ *Foreign News is on Page 16.* ❑ *The announcement was made at a news conference.* **3** N-SING **The news** is a television or radio broadcast which consists of information about recent events in the country or the world. ❑ *I heard all about the bombs on the news.* **4** N-UNCOUNT If you say that someone or something is **news**, you mean that they are considered to be interesting and important at the moment, and that people want to hear about them on the radio and television and in newspapers. [INFORMAL] ❑ *A murder was big news.*

1 불가산명사 소식, 기별 ❑ 우리는 그의 소식을 기다리고 또 기다렸다. ❑ 그들은 언제 집에 돌아갈 수 있을지에 대해 여전히 아무런 기별도 받지 못했다. **2** 불가산명사 기사, 뉴스 ❑ 해외 기사는 16면에 있습니다. ❑ 그 발표는 기자 회견에서 이루어졌다. **3** 단수명사 뉴스 프로그램 ❑ 뉴스를 통해 그 폭탄에 대해 전부 들었다. **4** 불가산명사 흥미로운 사건, 흥미로운 인물, 뉴스거리 [비격식체] ❑ 살인은 큰 뉴스거리였다.

> Note that, although **news** looks like a plural, it is often in fact an uncount noun. ❑ *Good news is always worth waiting for.* You cannot say "a news," but you can say a **piece of news** when you are referring to a particular fact or message. ❑ *One of my Dutch colleagues told me a very exciting piece of news.* When you are talking about television and radio news, or newspapers, you can refer to an individual story or report as a **news item**.

> news는 복수형처럼 보이지만 실제로 흔히 불가산 명사라는 점을 유의하라. ❑ 좋은 소식은 항상 기다릴 만한 가치가 있다. a new라고는 할 수 없지만 특정한 사실이나 메시지를 가리킬 때는 a piece of news라고 할 수 있다. ❑ 내 네덜란드 동료 중 한 사람이 내게 아주 흥미로운 소식을 하나 말해 주었다. 텔레비전과 라디오 뉴스 또는 신문에 대해 말할 때는, 각각의 기사나 보도를 a news item이라고 부를 수 있다.

5 PHRASE If you say that something is **bad news**, you mean that it will cause you trouble or problems. If you say that something is **good news**, you mean that it will be useful or helpful to you. ❑ *The drop in travel is bad news for the airline industry.* **6** PHRASE If you say that something **is news to** you, you mean that you did not previously know what you have just been told, especially when you are surprised or annoyed about it. ❑ *I'd certainly tell you if I knew anything, but I don't. What you're saying is news to me.*

5 구 흉보, 좋지 않은 소식; 낭보, 좋은 소식 ❑ 여행 감소는 항공 산업에 좋지 않은 소식이다. **6** 구 금시초문이다 ❑ 내가 뭔가 알고 있다면 틀림없이 너에게 얘기하겠지만, 아는 게 없어. 네가 하는 말은 금시초문인걸.

Word Partnership   news의 연어

ADJ.	**big** news, **grim** news, **sad** news **1**
	latest news **1** **2**
V.	**spread** the news, **tell** *someone* the news **1**
	hear the news **1**-**3**
	listen to the news, **watch** the news **3**
N.	news **headlines**, news **media**, news **report**, news **update** **2**

news agen|cy ♦◇◇ (**news agencies**) N-COUNT A **news agency** is an organization that gathers news stories from a particular country or from all over the world and supplies them to journalists. ❑ *A correspondent for Reuters news agency says he saw a number of demonstrators being beaten.*

가산명사 통신사 ❑ 로이터 통신사의 기자가 다수의 시위 참가자들이 두들겨 맞는 것을 목격했다고 말했다.

news|agent /nuzeɪdʒ°nt, BRIT nyu:zeɪdʒ°nt/ (**newsagents**) **1** N-COUNT A **newsagent** or a **newsagent's** is a small store that sells newspapers and magazines, and things such as cigarettes and candy. [BRIT] ❑ *...Corinne, who now runs a newsagent's with Mike.* **2** N-COUNT A **newsagent** is a person who sells newspapers and magazines, and things such as cigarettes and candy. [BRIT] ❑ *...David Weston, a local newsagent.*

1 가산명사 신문 가판대 [영국영어] ❑ 지금은 마이크와 함께 신문 가판대를 운영하는 코린 **2** 가산명사 신문 가판대 주인 [영국영어] ❑ 지역 신문 가판대 주인인 데이비드 웨스턴

news|caster /nuzkæstər, BRIT nyu:zkɑːstə^r/ (**newscasters**) N-COUNT A **newscaster** is a person who reads the news on the radio or on television. ❑ *...American TV newscaster Barbara Walters.*

가산명사 뉴스 진행자 ❑ 미국 텔레비전 뉴스 진행자 바바라 월터스

news con|fer|ence (**news conferences**) N-COUNT A **news conference** is a meeting held by a famous or important person in which they answer journalists' questions. ❑ *He is due to hold a news conference in about an hour.*

가산명사 기자 회견 ❑ 그는 약 한 시간 있다가 기자 회견을 열기로 되어 있다.

news|group /nuzgrup, BRIT nyu:zgru:p/ (**newsgroups**) N-COUNT A **newsgroup** is an Internet site where people can put information and opinions about a particular subject so they can be read by everyone who looks at the site. ❑ *Surfwatch allows parents to prohibit access to specific web sites, newsgroups and bulletin boards.*

가산명사 (인터넷) 뉴스 그룹 ❑ '서프워치'를 사용하여 부모들은 특정 웹사이트나 뉴스 그룹, 게시판 접속을 차단할 수 있다.

news|letter /nuzlɛtər, BRIT nyu:zlɛtə^r/ (**newsletters**) N-COUNT A **newsletter** is one or more printed sheets of paper containing information about an organization that is sent regularly to its members. ❑ *The organization now has around 18,000 members who receive a quarterly newsletter.*

가산명사 회보 ❑ 그 단체는 현재 계간 회보를 받아 보는 회원을 약 1만 8천 명 정도 보유하고 있다.

news|paper ♦♦◇ /nuzpeɪpər, nus-, BRIT nyu:speɪpə^r/ (**newspapers**) **1** N-COUNT A **newspaper** is a publication consisting of a number of large sheets of folded paper, on which news, advertisements, and other information is printed. ❑ *He was carrying a newspaper.* ❑ *They read their daughter's allegations in the newspaper.*

1 가산명사 신문 ❑ 그는 신문을 한 부 들고 있었다. ❑ 그들은 딸에 대한 혐의 내용을 신문에서 읽었다. **2** 가산명사 신문사 ❑ 그곳은 영국에서 가장 빠르게 성장하고 있는 일간 전국지 발행사이다. **3** 불가산명사

2 N-COUNT A **newspaper** is an organization that produces a newspaper. ❑ *It is Britain's fastest growing national daily newspaper.* **3** N-UNCOUNT **Newspaper** consists of pieces of old newspapers, especially when they are being used for another purpose such as wrapping things up. ❑ *He found two pots, each wrapped in newspaper.* →see **advertising**
→see Word Web: **newspaper**

news|print /nuːzprɪnt, BRIT njuːzprɪnt/ **1** N-UNCOUNT **Newsprint** is the cheap, fairly rough paper on which newspapers are printed. ❑ *...a newsprint warehouse.* **2** N-UNCOUNT **Newsprint** is the text that is printed in newspapers. ❑ *...the acres of newsprint devoted to Madonna in the past seven days.* **3** N-UNCOUNT **Newsprint** is the ink which is used to print newspapers and magazines. ❑ *They get their hands covered in newsprint.*

news|read|er /nuːzriːdər, BRIT njuːzriːdəʳ/ (**newsreaders**) N-COUNT A **newsreader** is a person who reads the news on the radio or on television. [BRIT; AM **newscaster**] ❑ *...British TV newsreader Jon Snow.*

news re|lease (**news releases**) N-COUNT A **news release** is a written statement about a matter of public interest which is given to the press by an organization concerned with the matter. [mainly AM; BRIT usually **press release**] ❑ *In a news release, the company said it had experienced severe financial problems.*

new wave (**new waves**) N-COUNT In the arts or in politics, a **new wave** is a group or movement that deliberately introduces new or unconventional ideas instead of using traditional ones. ❑ *...the new wave of satirical comedy.*

New Year **1** N-UNCOUNT **New Year** or **the New Year** is the time when people celebrate the start of a year. [also *the* N] ❑ *Happy New Year, everyone.* ❑ *The restaurant was closed over the New Year.*

New Year's Eve, the last day of the old year, is known as **Hogmanay** in Scotland, where the festivities are particularly important. Families and friends gather together for the chimes at midnight, and then go "first-footing" – visiting friends and neighbors, and taking along something to drink (often whisky) and a piece of coal which is supposed to bring good luck for the coming year.

---

2 N-SING **The New Year** is the first few weeks of a year. ❑ *Isabel was expecting their baby in the New Year.*

next ♦♦♦ /nɛkst/ **1** ORD The **next** period of time, event, person, or thing is the one that comes immediately after the present one or after the previous one. ❑ *I got up early the next morning.* ❑ *...the next available flight.* ❑ *Who will be the next prime minister?* **2** DET You use **next** in expressions such as **next Friday**, **next day** and **next year** to refer, for example, to the first Friday, day, or year that comes after the present or previous one. ❑ *Let's plan a big night next week.* ❑ *He retires next January.* ● ADJ **Next** is also an adjective. [n ADJ] ❑ *I shall be 26 years old on Friday next.* ● PRON **Next** is also a pronoun. ❑ *He predicted that the region's economy would grow by about six per cent both this year and next.* **3** ADJ **The next** place or person is the one that is nearest to you or that is the first one that you come to. [det ADJ] ❑ *Grace sighed so heavily that Trish could hear it in the next room.* ❑ *The man in the next chair was asleep.* **4** ADV The thing that happens **next** is the thing that happens immediately after something else. ❑ *Next, close your eyes then screw them up tight.* ❑ *I don't know what to do next.* **5** ADV When you next do something, you do it for the first time since you last did it. [ADV before v] ❑ *I next saw him at his house in Berkshire.* **6** ADV You use **next** to say that something has more of a particular quality than all other things except one. For example, the thing that is **next** best is the one that is the best except for one other thing. [ADV adj-superl] ❑ *The one thing he didn't have was a son. I think he's felt that a grandson is the next best thing.* **7** PHRASE You use **after next** in expressions such as **the week after next** to refer to a period of time after the next one. For example, when it is May, the month after next is July. ❑ *...the party's annual conference, to be held in Bournemouth the week after next.* **8** PHRASE If you say that you do something or experience something as much **as the next** person, you mean that you are no different from anyone else in the respect mentioned. [EMPHASIS] ❑ *I enjoy pleasure as much as the next person.* **9** PHRASE If one thing is **next to** another thing, it is at the other side of it. ❑ *She sat down next to him on the sofa.* ❑ *...at the southern end of the Gaza Strip next to the Egyptian border.* **10** PHRASE You use **next to** in order to give the most important aspect of something when comparing it with another aspect. ❑ *Her children were the number two priority in her life next to her career.* **11** PHRASE You use **next to** before a negative, or a word that suggests something

신문지 ❑ 그는 각각 신문지로 싼 두 개의 단지를 발견했다.

1 불가산명사 신문 인쇄용지 ❑ 신문 인쇄용지 창고 **2** 불가산명사 신문에 실린 글 ❑ 지난 7일 간 신문에 실린 마돈나에 대한 엄청난 양의 글들 **3** 불가산명사 신문 인쇄용 잉크 ❑ 그들은 손에 온통 신문 인쇄용 잉크를 묻힌다.

가산명사 뉴스 진행자 [영국영어; 미국영어 newscaster] ❑ 영국 텔레비전 뉴스 진행자 존 스노우

가산명사 보도 자료 [주로 미국영어; 영국영어 대개 press release] ❑ 보도 자료에서, 그 회사는 심각한 재정 문제를 겪었었다고 말했다.

가산명사 (예술 사조 등의) 새로운 흐름 ❑ 풍자 희극의 새로운 흐름

1 불가산명사 설날, 새해 ❑ 모두 새해 복 많이 받으세요. ❑ 그 식당은 설날 연휴 동안 문을 닫았다.

한 해의 맨 마지막 날인 New Year's Eve(섣달 그믐날)를 스코틀랜드에서는 Hogmanay라고 하는데, 명절을 특히 중시하는 스코틀랜드에서는 이날 가족이나 친구들이 함께 모여 제야의 종소리를 듣고, 친구나 이웃집을 새해 새벽에 첫 방문한다. 이것을 first-footing이라고 하는데, 이 때 보통 위스키 같은 마실 것과 새해의 행운을 상징한다고 믿는 석탄 조각을 들고 간다.

---

2 단수명사 연초 ❑ 이사벨은 연초에 출산을 할 예정이었다.

1 서수 다음의 ❑ 나는 다음날 아침 일찍 일어났다. ❑ 탈 수 있는 다음 비행기 편 ❑ 누가 차기 수상이 될 것인가? **2** 한정사 다음에 오는 ❑ 다음 주에 멋진 밤을 한 번 계획해 봅시다. ❑ 그는 내년 1월에 은퇴한다. ● 형용사 다음에 오는 ❑ 나는 다음 주 금요일이면 스물여섯 살이 된다. ● 대명사 다음 사람, 다음 것 ❑ 그는 그 지역의 경제가 올해와 내년에 약 6퍼센트 성장하리라고 내다보았다. **3** 형용사 옆의 ❑ 그레이스가 하도 깊게 한숨을 쉬어서 트리시는 옆방에서 그 소리를 들을 수 있었다. ❑ 옆 의자에 앉은 남자는 잠들어 있었다. **4** 부사 다음에 ❑ 다음에는, 눈을 감고 꽉 찡그리세요. ❑ 다음에는 무슨 일을 해야 할지 모르겠다. **5** 부사 다음번에 ❑ 다음번에는 버크셔에 있는 그의 집에서 그를 보았다. **6** 부사 그 다음으로 ❑ 그가 갖지 못한 단 한 가지는 아들이었다. 손자는 차선이라고 생각해 온 것 같다. **7** 구 다다음의 ❑ 다다음 주에 본머스에서 열릴 예정인 그 정당의 연례회의 **8** 구 누구나와 마찬가지로 [강조] ❑ 나는 누구나와 마찬가지로 유쾌한 일을 좋아한다. **9** 구 –의 곁에 ❑ 그녀는 소파에 앉아 있는 그 옆에 앉았다. ❑ 이집트 국경 옆 가자 지구 남단에 있는 ❑ 그녀의 삶에서 아이들은 일 다음으로 중요한 우선순위였다. **11** 구 거의 ❑ 존은 아직도 담배에 대해 거의 아무것도 몰랐다.

Word Web　　newspaper

Newspapers played an important role in freeing colonial America from British rule. In 1733, John Peter Zenger* began **publishing** the *New York Weekly Journal*. Some **articles** and **editorials** in the paper were critical of the British governor. The governor accused Zenger of libel and put him in prison. At his trial, Zenger's lawyer showed that the newspaper had told the truth. The jury sided with the **journalist**. This trial helped establish freedom of the **press** in America. The U.S. Constitution, signed 40 years later, contains the First Amendment. This is a clear guarantee of the freedom of the press.

John Peter Zenger (1697-1746): an American journalist and printer.

negative, to mean almost, but not completely. ❑ *Johnson still knew next to nothing about tobacco.*

Word Partnership   *next*의 연어

N.	next **election**, next **generation**, next **level**, next **meeting**, next **move**, next **question**, next **step**, next **stop**, next **time**, next **train** ◼
	next **day/hour/month/week/year**, next **day** ◼ ◼
V.	**come** next, **go** next, **happen** next ◼ ◼

---

next door

The adjective is usually spelled **next-door**.

◼ ADV If a room or building is **next door**, it is the next one to the right or left. ❑ *I went next door to the bathroom.* ❑ *...the old lady who lived next door.* ● ADJ **Next door** is also an adjective. [ADJ n] ❑ *...a thud like a cellar door slamming shut in a next-door house.* ● PHRASE If a room or building is **next door to** another one, it is the next one to the left or right. ❑ *The kitchen is right next door to the dining room.* ◼ ADV The people **next door** are the people who live in the house or apartment to the right or left of yours. [n ADV] ❑ *The neighbors thought the family next door had moved.* ● ADJ **Next door** is also an adjective. [ADJ n] ❑ *Even your next-door neighbor didn't see through your disguise.* ◼ PHRASE If you refer to someone as **the boy next door** or **the girl next door**, you mean that they are pleasant and respectable but rather dull. ❑ *He was dependable, straightforward, the boy next door.*

next of kin N-UNCOUNT-COLL **Next of kin** is sometimes used to refer to the person who is your closest relative, especially in official or legal documents. [FORMAL] ❑ *We have notified the next of kin.*

NHS /ɛn eɪtʃ ɛs/ N-SING **NHS** is an abbreviation for **National Health Service**. [the n, n n] ❑ *This vaccine is not normally provided free under the NHS.*

nib│ble /nɪbəl/ (nibbles, nibbling, nibbled) ◼ V-T/V-I If you **nibble** food, you eat it by biting very small pieces of it, for example because you are not very hungry. ❑ *Linda lay face down on a living room couch, nibbling popcorn.* ● N-COUNT **Nibble** is also a noun. ❑ *We each took a nibble.* ◼ V-T/V-I If you **nibble** something, you bite it very gently. ❑ *John found he was kissing and nibbling her ear.* ◼ V-T/V-I When an animal **nibbles** something, it takes small bites of it quickly and repeatedly. ❑ *A herd of goats was nibbling the turf around the base of the tower.* ● PHRASAL VERB **Nibble away** means the same as **nibble**. ❑ *The rabbits nibbled away on the herbaceous plants.* ◼ V-I If one thing **nibbles at** another, it gradually affects, harms, or destroys it. ❑ *It was all going to plan, yet small doubts kept nibbling at the edges of his mind.* ● PHRASAL VERB **Nibble away** means the same as **nibble**. ❑ *Several manufacturers are also nibbling away at Ford's traditional customer base.*

nice ♦♦◇ /naɪs/ (nicer, nicest) ◼ ADJ If you say that something is **nice**, you mean that you find it attractive, pleasant, or enjoyable. ❑ *I think silk ties can be quite nice.* ❑ *It's nice to be here together again.* ● **nice│ly** ADV ❑ *He's just written a book, nicely illustrated and not too technical.* ◼ ADJ If you say that it is **nice** of someone to say or do something, you are saying that they are being kind and thoughtful. This is often used as a way of thanking someone. [it v-link ADJ of n to-inf, v-link ADJ of n] ❑ *It's awfully nice of you to come all this way to see me.* ❑ *"How are your boys?"—"How nice of you to ask."* ◼ ADJ If you say that someone is **nice**, you mean that you like them because they are friendly and pleasant. ❑ *I've met your father and he's rather nice.* ◼ ADJ If you are **nice** to people, you are friendly, pleasant, or polite toward them. [v-link ADJ, oft ADJ to n] ❑ *She met Mr. and Mrs. Ricciardi, who were very nice to her.* ● **nice│ly** ADV [ADV after v] ❑ *He treated you very nicely and acted like a decent guy.* ◼ ADJ When the weather is **nice**, it is warm and pleasant. ❑ *He nodded to us and said, "Nice weather we're having."* ◼ ADJ You can use **nice** to emphasize a particular quality that you like. [EMPHASIS] [ADJ adj n, v-link ADJ and adj, ADJ and adv after v] ❑ *With a nice dark color, the wine is medium to full bodied.* ❑ *I'll explain it nice and simply so you can understand.* ◼ ADJ You can use **nice** when you are greeting people. For example, you can say **"Nice to meet you," "Nice to have met you,"** or **"Nice to see you."** [FORMULAE] [it v-link ADJ to-inf] ❑ *Good morning. Nice to meet you and thanks for being with us this weekend.* ◼ →see also **nicely**

Thesaurus   *nice*의 참조어

ADJ.	friendly, kind, likable, pleasant, polite; (ant.) mean, unpleasant ◼ ◼

Word Partnership   *nice*의 연어

ADJ.	nice **and clean** ◼
V.	**look** nice, nice **to see** *someone/something* ◼
N.	nice **clothes**, nice **guy**, nice **people**, nice **place**, nice **smile** ◼ ◼
	nice **day**, nice **weather** ◼

---

nice│ly /naɪsli/ ◼ ADV If something is happening or working **nicely**, it is happening or working in a satisfactory way or in the way that you want it to. [ADV with v] ❑ *She has a bit of private money, so they manage quite nicely.* →see also **nice** ◼ PHRASE If someone or something **is doing nicely**, they are being successful. ❑ *...another hotel owner who is doing very nicely.*

niche /nɪtʃ, niʃ, BRIT niːʃ/ (niches) ◼ N-COUNT A **niche** in the market is a specific area of marketing which has its own particular requirements,

---

형용사는 대개 철자가 next-door이다.

◼ 부사 바로 옆에, 이웃에 ❑ 나는 옆방인 욕실로 갔다. ❑ 이웃집에 살던 노부인 ● 형용사 이웃의 ❑ 이웃집에서 지하실 문이 세게 닫히는 듯한 쾅 하는 소리 ● 구 -의 옆에 있는 ❑ 주방은 식당 바로 옆에 있습니다. ◼ 부사 옆집에 사는 ● 이웃집 사람들은 옆집에 사는 가족이 이사를 갔다고 생각했다. ● 형용사 옆집의 ❑ 당신 옆집에 사는 이웃조차 당신의 변장을 꿰뚫어보지 못했다. ◼ 구 이웃집 남자; 이웃집 여자 ❑ 그는 신뢰할 수 있고 정직한, 이웃집 남자 같은 사람이었다.

불가산명사-집합 최근친, 가장 가까운 친척 [격식체] ❑ 우리는 제일 가까운 친척에게 통지했다.

단수명사 국민 건강 보험 ❑ 이 백신은 보통 국민 건강 보험상으로는 무상 제공되지 않는다.

◼ 타동사/자동사 조금씩 베어 먹다, 야금거리다 ❑ 린다는 거실 소파에 엎드려 팝콘을 야금거리고 있었다. ◼ 부사 옆집에 사는 ❑ 우리는 각자 조금씩 베어 먹었다. ◼ 타동사/자동사 가볍게 깨물다 ❑ 존은 자신이 그녀의 귀에 입을 맞추고 가볍게 깨물고 있음을 알았다. ◼ 타동사/자동사 조금씩 뜯어먹다, 갉아먹다 ❑ 한 무리의 염소 떼가 탑 아래쪽 주변의 잔디를 뜯고 있었다. ● 구동사 조금씩 뜯어먹다, 갉아먹다 ❑ 토끼들이 초본 식물을 뜯어먹었다. ◼ 자동사 잠식하다 ❑ 모든 것이 계획대로 되어 가고 있었지만, 작은 의혹들이 그의 마음 한 켠을 계속 잠식해 들어갔다. ● 구동사 잠식하다 ❑ 몇몇 제조업체들 또한 포드의 전통적인 고객 기반을 잠식하고 있다.

◼ 형용사 좋은; 기쁜 ❑ 실크 넥타이가 꽤 좋을 것 같다. ❑ 이곳에 다시 함께 있게 된 것은 기쁜 일이다. ● 종게 : 훌륭히 부사 ❑ 그는 훌륭한 삽화가 곁들여지고 너무 전문적이지도 않은 책을 한 권 막 써냈다. ◼ 형용사 (-해 줘서) 감사한 ❑ 저를 보러 이렇게 와 주셔서 정말 감사합니다. ❑ "애들아 어떠니?" "물어봐 줘서 정말 고마워요." ◼ 형용사 다정한, 친절한 ❑ 너의 아버지를 만난 적이 있는데 상당히 다정하시군요. ◼ 형용사 친절한, 다정한 ❑ 그녀는 리치아디 부부를 만났는데, 그들은 그녀에게 매우 친절했다. ● 친절하게 부사 ❑ 그는 너를 매우 친절하게 대했고 예의 바른 사람처럼 행동했다. ◼ 형용사 (날씨가) 좋은, 갠 ❑ 그는 우리에게 고개를 끄덕이며 말했다. "날씨가 정말 좋군." ◼ 형용사 형용사나 부사를 강조하는 표현으로 사용 [강조] ❑ 멋지게 짙은 색상을 띤 그 와인은 중간 내지 진한 맛이다. ❑ 네가 이해할 수 있도록 알기 쉽게 설명해 주지. ◼ 형용사 '만나서 반갑습니다.'와 같은 표현에서 쓴다. [의례적인 표현] ❑ 안녕하세요. 만나서 반갑습니다. 이번 주말에 함께 해 주셔서 감사합니다.

◼ 부사 잘, 좋게 ❑ 그녀에게는 자기 돈이 약간 있기에, 그들은 제법 잘 살아 나간다. ◼ 구 잘 해 나가다, 성공하다 ❑ 크게 성공하고 있는 또 다른 호텔 소유주

◼ 가산명사 틈새시장 [경제] ❑ 우리는 장난감 시장에서 틈새시장을 발견한 것 같다. ◼ 형용사

customers, and products. [BUSINESS] ❏ *I think we have found a niche in the toy market.* ❷ ADJ **Niche** marketing is the practice of dividing the market into specialized areas for which particular products are made. A **niche** market is one of these specialized areas. [BUSINESS] [ADJ n] ❏ *Many media experts see such all-news channels as part of a general move towards niche marketing.* ❸ N-COUNT A **niche** is a hollow area in a wall which has been made to hold a statue, or a natural hollow part in a hill or cliff. ❏ *Above him, in a niche on the wall, sat a tiny veiled Ganesh, the elephant god.* ❹ N-COUNT Your **niche** is the job or activity which is exactly suitable for you. ❏ *Simon Lane quickly found his niche as a busy freelance model maker.*

nick /nɪk/ (**nicks, nicking, nicked**) ❶ V-T If you **nick** something or **nick** yourself, you accidentally make a small cut in the surface of the object or your skin. ❏ *When I pulled out of the space, I nicked the rear bumper of the car in front of me. A sharp blade is likely to nick the skin and draw blood.* ❷ N-COUNT A **nick** is a small cut made in the surface of something, usually in someone's skin. ❏ *The barbed wire had left only the tiniest nick just below my right eye.* ❸ V-T If you **are nicked** by someone, they cheat you, for example by charging you too much money. [AM, INFORMAL] ❏ *College students already are being nicked, but probably don't realize it.* ❹ V-T If someone **nicks** something, they steal it. [mainly BRIT, INFORMAL] ❏ *He smashed a window to get in and nicked a load of silver cups.* ❺ V-T If the police **nick** someone, they arrest them. [mainly BRIT, INFORMAL] ❏ *The police nicked me for carrying an offensive weapon.*

nick|el /nɪkᵊl/ (**nickels**) ❶ N-UNCOUNT **Nickel** is a silver-colored metal that is used in making steel. ❷ N-COUNT In the United States and Canada, a **nickel** is a coin worth five cents. ❏ *...a large glass jar filled with pennies, nickels, dimes, and quarters.*

nick|name /nɪkneɪm/ (**nicknames, nicknaming, nicknamed**) ❶ N-COUNT A **nickname** is an informal name for someone or something. ❏ *Red got his nickname for his red hair.* ❷ V-T If you **nickname** someone or something, you give them an informal name. ❏ *When he got older I nicknamed him Little Alf.*

nico|tine /nɪkitin/ N-UNCOUNT **Nicotine** is the substance in tobacco that people can become addicted to. ❏ *Nicotine produces a feeling of well-being in the smoker.*

niece /nis/ (**nieces**) N-COUNT Someone's **niece** is the daughter of their sister or brother. ❏ *...his niece from America, the daughter of his eldest sister.*

nig|gle /nɪgᵊl/ (**niggles, niggling, niggled**) ❶ V-T/V-I If something **niggles** you, it causes you to worry slightly over a long period of time. [mainly BRIT] ❏ *I realise now that the things which used to niggle and annoy me just don't really matter.* ❏ *It's been niggling at my mind ever since I met Neville in Nice.* ● N-COUNT **Niggle** is also a noun. ❏ *So why is there a little niggle at the back of my mind?* ❷ V-T/V-I If someone **niggles** you, they annoy you by continually criticizing you for what you think are small or unimportant things. [mainly BRIT] ❏ *I don't react anymore when opponents try to niggle me.* ● N-COUNT **Niggle** is also a noun. ❏ *The life we have built together is more important than any minor niggle either of us might have.*

night ♦♦♦ /naɪt/ (**nights**) ❶ N-VAR The **night** is the part of each day when the sun has set and it is dark outside, especially the time when you are sleeping. ❏ *The fighting began in the late afternoon and continued all night.* ❏ *Finally night fell.* ❷ N-COUNT The **night** is the period of time between the end of the afternoon and the time that you go to bed, especially the time when you relax before going to bed. ❏ *So whose party was it last night?* ❸ N-COUNT A particular **night** is a particular evening when a special event takes place, such as a show or a play. ❏ *The first night crowd packed the building.* ❹ PHRASE If it is a particular time **at night**, it is during the time when it is dark and is before midnight. ❏ *It's eleven o'clock at night in Moscow.* ❺ PHRASE If something happens **at night**, it happens regularly during the evening or night. ❏ *He was going to college at night, in order to become an accountant.* ❻ PHRASE If something happens **day and night** or **night and day**, it happens all the time without stopping. ❏ *Dozens of doctors and nurses have been working day and night for weeks.* ❼ PHRASE If you have **an early night**, you go to bed early. If you have **a late night**, you go to bed late. ❏ *I've had a hell of a day, and all I want is an early night.* ❽ **morning, noon and night** →see **morning**

Word Partnership	*night*의 연어
V.	spend a/the night ❶ ❷
	sleep at night, stay out at night, stay the night,
	work at night ❶ ❺
ADJ.	cold night, cool night, dark night, rainy night, warm night ❶
N.	election night, wedding night ❸

night|club /naɪtklʌb/ (**nightclubs**) N-COUNT A **nightclub** is a place where people go late in the evening to drink and dance.

night|life /naɪtlaɪf/ N-UNCOUNT **Nightlife** is all the entertainment and social activities that are available at night in cities and towns, such as nightclubs and theaters. ❏ *Hamburg's energetic nightlife is second to none.*

night|ly /naɪtli/ ADJ A **nightly** event happens every night. [ADJ n] ❏ *I'm sure we watched the nightly news, and then we turned on the movie.* ● ADV **Nightly** is also an adverb. ❏ *She appears nightly on the television news.*

night|mare ♦♢♢ /naɪtmeər/ (**nightmares**) ❶ N-COUNT A **nightmare** is a very frightening dream. ❏ *All the victims still suffered nightmares.* ❷ N-COUNT If you refer to a situation as a **nightmare**, you mean that it is very frightening and

Korean column:

뉴스의 [경제] ❏ 많은 미디어 전문가들은 그와 같은 뉴스 전문 채널을 틈새 마케팅 쪽으로 움직이는 일반적인 추이의 일부로 본다. ❸ 가산명사 (벽면이나 언덕의) 벽감 ❏ 그의 머리 위 벽감 속에는 베일로 가린 조그마한 코끼리 신 가네쉬가 놓여 있었다. ❹ 가산명사 적소 ❏ 사이먼 레인은 재빨리 자신의 적소를 찾아내서 프리랜서 모형 제작자로 바쁘게 일했다.

❶ 타동사 긁다; 긁히다 ❏ 그 자리를 빠져나오다가, 내 앞에 있는 차의 뒤 범퍼를 긁었다. ❏ 예리한 칼날이 피부에 칼자국을 내고 피가 나게 할 것 같다. ❷ 가산명사 긁힌 자국 ❏ 가시철사에 긁혀서 오른쪽 눈 바로 밑에 아주 작게 긁힌 상처만 남았을 뿐이다. ❸ 타동사 속이다, 터무니없는 돈을 요구하다 [미국영어, 비격식체] ❏ 대학생들은 이미 터무니없는 돈을 요구받고 있지만, 대개는 그 사실을 깨닫지 못한다. ❹ 타동사 훔치다 [주로 영국영어, 비격식체] ❏ 그는 창문을 부수고 침입해서 은잔을 잔뜩 훔쳤다. ❺ 타동사 체포하다 [주로 영국영어, 비격식체] ❏ 경찰이 공격용 무기를 휴대했다고 나를 체포했다.

❶ 불가산명사 니켈 ❷ 가산명사 5센트짜리 동전 ❏ 1센트, 5센트, 10센트, 25센트짜리 동전들이 가득 들어 있는 커다란 유리 단지

❶ 가산명사 별명, 애칭 ❏ 레드는 빨간 머리 때문에 그런 별명을 얻었다. ❷ 타동사 ~에게 별명을 붙이다 ❏ 그가 나이를 더 먹자 나는 그에게 '리틀 엘프'라는 별명을 붙였다.

불가산명사 니코틴 ❏ 니코틴은 흡연자들에게 행복감을 일으킨다.

가산명사 조카딸 ❏ 그의 큰누나 딸인, 미국에서 온 조카딸

❶ 타동사/자동사 신경 쓰이게 하다, 괴롭히다 [주로 영국영어] ❏ 나는 이제 나를 귀찮고 짜증나게 했던 일들이 실제로는 중요치 않음을 깨닫는다. ❏ 니스에서 네빌을 만난 이래로 그 일이 오랫동안 내 마음을 괴롭히고 있다. ● 가산명사 신경 쓰임 ❏ 그러면 왜 내 마음속 한 구석에서 자꾸 신경이 쓰이는 걸까? ❷ 타동사/자동사 ~을 탓 잡다 [주로 영국영어] ❏ 상대편이 나에 대해 탈을 잡으려 할 때 나는 더 이상 반응을 하지 않는다. ● 가산명사 허물 ❏ 우리 둘 각자가 가지고 있을지 모르는 그 어떤 사소한 허물보다 우리가 함께 쌓아 올려 온 삶이 더 중요하다.

❶ 가산명사 또는 불가산명사 밤, 야간 ❏ 전투는 오후 늦게 시작되어 밤새도록 계속되었다. ❏ 마침내 밤이 찾아왔다. ❷ 가산명사 저녁 ❏ 그럼 어제 저녁 파티는 누구네 파티였지? ❸ 가산명사 (특정 행사가 있는) 밤 ❏ 첫 날 밤에 군중들이 건물을 가득 메웠다. ❹ 구 밤중에 ❏ 모스크바는 밤 11시이다. ❺ 구 야간에 ❏ 그는 회계사가 되기 위해 야간 대학을 다니고 있었다. ❻ 구 밤낮 없이 ❏ 수많은 의사와 간호사들이 몇 주 동안 밤낮으로 일해 오고 있다. ❼ 구 일찍 잠; 늦게 잠 ❏ 아주 고된 하루를 보냈기에, 내가 원하는 것은 오직 일찍 자는 것뿐이다.

가산명사 나이트클럽

불가산명사 야간 유흥 ❏ 함부르크의 왕성한 야간 유흥은 어디에도 뒤지지 않는다.

형용사 밤마다의 ❏ 나는 우리가 밤 뉴스를 보았고, 그리고 나서 영화를 틀었다고 확신한다. ● 부사 밤마다 ❏ 그녀는 매일 밤 텔레비전 뉴스에 등장한다.

❶ 가산명사 악몽 ❏ 피해자들은 모두 아직도 악몽에 시달렸다. ❷ 가산명사 악몽 같은 일 ❏ 감옥에서 보낸 세월은 악몽과도 같았다. ❸ 가산명사 악몽, 무서

unpleasant. ❑ *The years in prison were a nightmare.* ❸ N-COUNT If you refer to a situation as a **nightmare**, you are saying in a very emphatic way that it is irritating because it causes you a lot of trouble. [EMPHASIS] ❑ *Taking my son Peter to a restaurant was a nightmare.*

성가신 일 [강조] ❑ 내 아들 피터를 식당에 데려가는 것은 악몽이었다.

Word Partnership	nightmare의 연어
ADJ.	**worst** nightmare ❶ ❷
	bureaucratic nightmare, **logistical** nightmare ❸
V.	**become a** nightmare, **turn into a** nightmare ❷ ❸

nil /nɪl/ ❶ N-UNCOUNT If you say that something **is nil**, you mean that it does not exist at all. ❑ *Their legal rights are virtually nil.* ❷ NUM **Nil** means the same as zero. It is usually used to say what the score is in sports such as soccer or rugby. [BRIT] ❑ *They beat the defending champions, Argentina, one-nil in the final.* →see **nought**

❶ 불가산명사 무, 전무 ❑ 그들의 법적 권리는 실질적으로 전무하다. ❷ 수사 영 [영국영어] ❑ 그들은 결승에서 챔피언 타이틀을 가지고 있는 아르헨티나를 1대 0으로 이겼다.

nim|ble /nɪmbᵊl/ (**nimbler, nimblest**) ❶ ADJ Someone who is **nimble** is able to move their fingers, hands, or legs quickly and easily. ❑ *Everything had been stitched by Molly's nimble fingers.* ❷ ADJ If you say that someone has a **nimble mind**, you mean they are clever and can think very quickly. ❑ *A nimble mind backed by a degree in economics gave him a firm grasp of financial matters.*

❶ 형용사 재빠른, 민첩한 ❑ 모든 것이 몰리의 민첩한 손으로 바느질되었다. ❷ 형용사 영리한, 꾀바른 ❑ 영리한 머리에 경제학 학위까지 있는 그는 재정적인 문제들을 확실히 파악했다.

nine ♦♦♦ /naɪn/ (**nines**) NUM **Nine** is the number 9. ❑ *We still sighted nine yachts.*

수사 9, 아홉 ❑ 우리는 여전히 요트 아홉 대를 보았다.

911 /naɪn wʌn wʌn/ NUM **911** is the number that you call in the United States in order to contact the emergency services. ❑ *The women made their first 911 call about a prowler at 12:46 a.m.*

수사 미국에서 응급 상황을 신고할 때 거는 전화번호 ❑ 여자들이 수상한 사람이 있다고 911에 첫 전화를 건 것이 밤 12시 46분이었다.

999 /naɪn naɪn naɪn/ NUM **999** is the number that you call in Britain in order to contact the emergency services. ❑ *...a fire engine answering a 999 call.*

수사 영국에서 응급 상황을 신고할 때 거는 전화번호 ❑ 999 신고에 출동하는 소방차

nine|teen ♦♦♦ /naɪntiːn/ (**nineteens**) NUM **Nineteen** is the number 19. ❑ *They have nineteen days to make up their minds.*

수사 19 ❑ 그들이 마음을 정할 기한이 19일 남았다.

nine|teenth ♦♦◇ /naɪntiːnθ/ ORD The **nineteenth** item in a series is the one that you count as number nineteen. ❑ *...my nineteenth birthday.*

서수 열아홉 번째 ❑ 내 열아홉 번째 생일

nine|ti|eth ♦♦◇ /naɪntiəθ/ ORD The **ninetieth** item in a series is the one that you count as number ninety. ❑ *He celebrates his ninetieth birthday on Friday.*

서수 아흔 번째 ❑ 그는 금요일에 아흔 번째 생일을 맞이한다.

nine|ty ♦♦♦ /naɪnti/ (**nineties**) ❶ NUM **Ninety** is the number 90. ❑ *It was decided she had to stay another ninety days.* ❷ N-PLURAL When you talk about the **nineties**, you are referring to numbers between 90 and 99. For example, if you are in your **nineties**, you are aged between 90 and 99. If the temperature is **in the nineties**, the temperature is between 90 and 99 degrees. ❑ *By this time she was in her nineties and needed help more and more frequently.* ❸ N-PLURAL The **nineties** is the decade between 1990 and 1999. ❑ *These trends only got worse as we moved into the nineties.*

❶ 수사 90 ❑ 그녀가 90일 더 머물러야 한다고 결정되었다. ❷ 복수명사 90대 ❑ 그녀는 이즈음 90대에 접어든 상태였으며 도움을 점점 더 자주 필요로하게 되었다. ❸ 복수명사 90년대 ❑ 이러한 추세는 90년대에 들어서자 더 악화되었다.

ninth ♦♦◇ /naɪnθ/ (**ninths**) ❶ ORD The **ninth** item in a series is the one that you count as number nine. ❑ *...January the ninth.* ❑ *...students in the ninth grade.* ❷ FRACTION A **ninth** is one of nine equal parts of something. ❑ *In Brussels the dollar rose by a ninth of a cent.*

❶ 서수 아홉 번째 ❑ 1월 9일 ❑ 9학년 학생들 ❷ 분수 9분의 1 ❑ 브뤼셀에서 달러가 9분의 1센트 정도 상승했다.

nip /nɪp/ (**nips, nipping, nipped**) ❶ V-T If an animal or person **nips** you, they bite you lightly or squeeze a piece of your skin between their finger and thumb. ❑ *I have known cases where dogs have nipped babies.* ● N-COUNT **Nip** is also a noun. ❑ *Incidents range from a petty nip, which fails to break the skin or draw blood, to serious injuries.* ❷ N-COUNT A **nip** is a small amount of a strong alcoholic drink. ❑ *She had a habit of taking an occasional nip from a flask of cognac.* ❸ V-I If you **nip** somewhere, usually somewhere nearby, you go there quickly or for a short time. [BRIT, INFORMAL] [no passive] ❑ *Should I nip out and get some groceries?* ❑ *Wayne is always nipping down to the corner shop for him.* ❹ to **nip** something **in the bud** →see **bud**

❶ 자동사 살짝 물다; 살짝 꼬집다 ❑ 개가 아기를 깨문 경우들을 안다. ● 가산명사 살짝 깨물기; 살짝 꼬집기 ❑ 피부가 안 찢어지거나 피가 안 날 정도로 살짝 꼬집는 것부터 심각한 상처에 이르기까지 사례는 다양하다. ❷ 가산명사 (독주) 한 모금 ❑ 그녀는 코냑을 휴대용 술병에 담아 다니면서 가끔 한 모금씩 마시는 버릇이 있었다. ❸ 자동사 (급히 또는 잠깐) 다녀오다 [영국영어, 비격식체] ❑ 잠깐 나가서 먹을 거나 뭐 좀 사올까? ❑ 웨인은 항상 그를 위해서 구멍가게에 금방 갔다 오곤 한다.

nip|ple /nɪpᵊl/ (**nipples**) ❶ N-COUNT The **nipples** on someone's body are the two small pieces of slightly hard flesh on their chest. Babies suck milk from their mothers' breasts through their mothers' nipples. ❑ *Sore nipples can inhibit the milk supply.* ❷ N-COUNT A **nipple** is a piece of rubber or plastic which is fitted to the top of a baby's bottle. ❑ *...a white plastic bottle with a rubber nipple.*

❶ 가산명사 유두, 젖꼭지 ❑ 젖꼭지가 아리면 수유를 하지 못할 수도 있다. ❷ 가산명사 고무젖꼭지 ❑ 고무젖꼭지가 달린 흰 플라스틱 병

ni|trate /naɪtreɪt/ (**nitrates**) N-MASS **Nitrate** is a chemical compound that includes nitrogen and oxygen. Nitrates are used as fertilizers in agriculture. ❑ *High levels of nitrate occur in eastern England because of the heavy use of fertilizers.*

물질명사 질산염 ❑ 비료의 과다 사용으로 인하여 영국 동부에서는 질산염이 많이 발생한다.

ni|tro|gen /naɪtrədʒən/ N-UNCOUNT **Nitrogen** is a colorless element that has no smell and is usually found as a gas. It forms about 78% of the earth's atmosphere, and is found in all living things.

불가산명사 질소

no ♦♦♦ /noʊ/ (**noes** or **no's**) ❶ CONVENTION You use **no** to give a negative response to a question. ❑ *"Any problems?" — "No, I'm O.K."* ❷ CONVENTION You use **no** to say that something that someone has just said is not true. ❑ *"We thought you'd emigrated." — "No, no."* ❸ CONVENTION You use **no** to refuse an offer or a request, or to refuse permission. ❑ *"Here, have mine." — "No, this is fine."* ❑ *"Can you just get the message through to Pete for me?" — "No, no I can't."* ❹ EXCLAM You use **no** to indicate that you do not want someone to do something. ❑ *No. I forbid it. You cannot.* ❺ CONVENTION You use **no** to acknowledge a negative statement or to show that you agree and understand it. ❑ *"We're not on the main campus." — "No."* ❑ *"It's not one of my favorite forms of music." — "No."* ❻ CONVENTION You use **no** before correcting what you have just said. ❑ *I was twenty-two – no, twenty-one.* ❼ EXCLAM You use **no** to express shock or disappointment at something you have just been told. [FEELINGS] ❑ *"We went with Sarah and the married man that she's*

❶ 관용 표현 아니다 ❑ "무슨 문제 있나요?" "아뇨, 괜찮아요." ❷ 관용 표현 아니다 ❑ "우린 네가 이민 간 줄 알았어." "아냐, 아냐." ❸ 관용 표현 아니다 ❑ "여기, 내걸 가져." "아냐, 이거면 괜찮아." ❑ "나 대신에 그 메시지를 피트에게 그냥 전해 줄 수 없어?" "아니, 그럴 수 없어." ❹ 감탄사 안 된다 ❑ 안 돼. 허용할 수 없다. 해서는 안 돼. ❺ 관용 표현 부정문에 대한 수긍을 표현할 때 쓰임 ❑ "본 캠퍼스를 벗어난 것 같아." "맞아." ❑ "내가 많이 좋아하는 음악 형태는 아냐." "그래." ❻ 관용 표현 아니다 ❑ 나는 스물두 살이었어. 아니다, 스물한 살이었다. ❼ 감탄사 세상에, 맙소사 [감정 개입] ❑ "우리는 새라와 그녀가 현재 사귀는 유부남과 같이 갔다." "세상에." ❽ 한정사 ─이 없는

currently seeing." — "Oh no." ⃞ DET You use **no** to mean not any or not one person or thing. ⃞ *He had no intention of paying the cash.* ⃞ *No job has more influence on the future of the world.* ⃞ DET You use **no** to emphasize that someone or something is not the type of thing mentioned. [EMPHASIS] ⃞ *He is no singer.* ⃞ *I make it no secret that our worst consultants earn nothing.* ⃞ ADV You can use **no** to make the negative form of a comparative. [ADV compar] ⃞ *It is to start broadcasting no later than the end of 1994.* ⃞ *Yesterday no fewer than thirty climbers reached the summit.* ⃞ DET You use **no** in front of an adjective and noun to make the noun group mean its opposite. ⃞ *Sometimes a bit of selfishness, if it leads to greater self-knowledge, is no bad thing.* ⃞ DET **No** is used in notices or instructions to say that a particular activity or thing is forbidden. ⃞ *The captain turned out the "no smoking" signs.* ⃞ *No talking after lights out.* ⃞ N-COUNT A **no** is a person who has answered "no" to a question or who has voted against something. ⃞ *According to the latest opinion polls, the noes have 50 percent, the yeses 35 percent.* ⃞ PHRASE If you say that **there is no** doing a particular thing, you mean that it is very difficult or impossible to do that thing. ⃞ *There is no going back to the life she had.* ⃞ **not** to **take no for an answer** →see **answer**. **no doubt** →see **doubt**. **no longer** →see **long**. **in no way** →see **way**. **there's no way** →see **way**. **no way** →see **way**

No. (Nos) **No.** is a written abbreviation for **number.** ⃞ *That year he was named the nation's No. 1 college football star.*

no|bil|ity /noʊbɪlɪti/ ⃞ N-SING-COLL The **nobility** of a society are all the people who have titles and belong to a high social class. ⃞ *They married into the nobility and entered the highest ranks of state administration.* ⃞ N-UNCOUNT A person's **nobility** is their noble character and behavior. [FORMAL] ⃞ *...his nobility of character, and his devotion to his country.*

no|ble /noʊbəl/ (**nobler, noblest**) ⃞ ADJ If you say that someone is a **noble** person, you admire and respect them because they are unselfish and morally good. [APPROVAL] ⃞ *He was an upright and noble man who was always willing to help in any way he could.* ● **no|bly** [ADV with v] ⃞ *Eric's sister had nobly volunteered to help with the gardening.* ⃞ ADJ If you say that something is a **noble** idea, goal, or action, you admire it because it is based on high moral principles. [APPROVAL] ⃞ *He had implicit faith in the noble intentions of the Emperor.* ⃞ *We'll always justify our actions with noble sounding theories.* ⃞ ADJ If you describe something as **noble**, you think that its appearance or quality is very impressive, making it superior to other things of its type. ⃞ *...the great parks with their noble trees.* ⃞ ADJ **Noble** means belonging to a high social class and having a title. ⃞ *...rich and noble families.*

no|body ♦♢♢ /noʊbɒdi, -bʌdi/ (**nobodies**) ⃞ PRON-INDEF-NEG **Nobody** means not a single person, or not a single member of a particular group or set. ⃞ *They were shut away in a little room where nobody could overhear.* ⃞ *Nobody realizes how bad things are.* ⃞ N-COUNT If someone says that a person is a **nobody**, they are saying in an unkind way that the person is not at all important. [DISAPPROVAL] ⃞ *A man in my position has nothing to fear from a nobody like you.*

> You do not use **nobody** or **no one** in front of **of** to talk about a particular group of people. The word you need is **none.** *None of his companions answered.*

noc|tur|nal /nɒktɜrnəl/ ⃞ ADJ **Nocturnal** means occurring at night. ⃞ *The dog's main duties will be to accompany me on long nocturnal walks.* ⃞ ADJ **Nocturnal** creatures are active mainly at night. ⃞ *When there is a full moon, this nocturnal rodent is careful to stay in its burrow.*

nod ♦♢♢ /nɒd/ (**nods, nodding, nodded**) ⃞ V-T/V-I If you **nod**, you move your head downward and upward to show that you are answering "yes" to a question, or to show agreement, understanding, or approval. [no passive] ⃞ *"Are you okay?" I asked. She nodded and smiled.* ⃞ *Jacques tasted one and nodded his approval.* ● N-COUNT **Nod** is also a noun. ⃞ *She gave a nod and said, "I see."* ⃞ *"Probably," agreed Hunter, with a slow nod of his head.* ⃞ V-I If you **nod** in a particular direction, you bend your head once in that direction in order to indicate something or to give someone a signal. [no passive] ⃞ *"Does it work?" he asked, nodding at the piano.* ⃞ *She nodded towards the drawing room. "He's in there."* ⃞ V-T/V-I If you **nod**, you bend your head once, as a way of saying hello or goodbye. [no passive] ⃞ *All the girls nodded and said "Hi."* ⃞ *Both of them smiled and nodded at friends.*

▶**nod off** PHRASAL VERB If you **nod off**, you fall asleep, especially when you had not intended to. [INFORMAL] ⃞ *The judge appeared to nod off yesterday while a witness was being cross-examined.*

Word Partnership	nod의 연어
N.	nod **in agreement**, nod *your* **head** ⃞
V.	**give a** nod ⃞

noise ♦♢♢ /nɔɪz/ (**noises**) ⃞ N-UNCOUNT **Noise** is a loud or unpleasant sound. ⃞ *There was too much noise in the room and he needed peace.* ⃞ *The noise of bombs and guns was incessant.* ⃞ N-COUNT A **noise** is a sound that someone or something makes. ⃞ *Sir Gerald made a small noise in his throat.* ⃞ *...birdsong and other animal noises.* ⃞ N-PLURAL If someone **makes noises** of a particular kind about something, they say things that indicate their attitude to it in a rather indirect or vague way. ⃞ *The President took care to make encouraging noises about the future.* ⃞ PHRASE If you say that someone **makes the right noises** or **makes all the right noises**, you think that they are showing concern or enthusiasm about something because they feel they ought to rather than

a
b
c
d
e
f
g
h
i
j
k
l
m
n
o
p
q
r
s
t
u
v
w
x
y
z

⃞ 그는 돈을 지불할 의사가 전혀 없었다. ⃞ 이보다 세계의 미래에 더 큰 영향을 끼치는 직업은 없다. ⃞ 한정사 _의 아닌 [강조] ⃞ 그는 노래를 매우 못 부른다. ⃞ 우리의 최악의 컨설턴트들은 수입이 없다는 것을 나는 결코 숨기지 않는다. ⃞ 부사 비교급의 부정에 쓰임 ⃞ 늦어도 1994년 말부터 방송을 시작할 것이다. ⃞ 어제 최소한 30명의 등반가가 정상에 다다랐다. ⃞ 한정사 _의 아닌 ⃞ 보다 큰 자기 이해에 도달할 수 있다면 약간의 이기주의가 때로는 나쁜 것이 아니다. ⃞ 한정사 _의 안 되는 _을 금하는 ⃞ 기장은 "금연" 표지판을 켰다. ⃞ 소등 이후 잡담 금지 ⃞ 가산명사 반대자; 반대 ⃞ 최근의 여론 조사에 따르면 50퍼센트가 반대하고 35퍼센트가 찬성한다. ⃞ 구 _의 거의 불가능하다 [강조] ⃞ 그녀가 전에 영위하던 삶으로 돌아갈 수 있는 길은 없다.

번호 ⃞ 그 해 그는 전국 최고 미식축구 선수로 선정되었다.

⃞ 단수명사-집합 귀족 계급, 양반 계층 ⃞ 그들은 귀족과 결혼하여 정부의 최고위직까지 올라갔다. ⃞ 불가산명사 고결함 [격식체] ⃞ 그의 고결한 성품과 국가에 대한 헌신

⃞ 형용사 고결한 [마음에 듦] ⃞ 그는 항상 사람들을 최대한 도와주려고 하는 정직하고 고결한 성품의 소유자였다. ● 고결하게 부사 ⃞ 에릭의 누이가 정원 일을 도와주겠다고 훌륭하게 자원했다. ⃞ 형용사 숭고한 [마음에 듦] ⃞ 그는 황제의 숭고한 의도에 대해 암묵적인 신뢰를 품고 있었다. ⃞ 우리는 숭고하게 들리는 이론을 가지고 항상 자신의 행동을 정당화할 것이다. ⃞ 형용사 멋진 ⃞ 멋진 나무들이 있는 거대한 공원들 ⃞ 형용사 귀족의 ⃞ 부유한 귀족 가문들

⃞ 부정(不定)대명사-부정(否定) 아무도 _하지 않는 ⃞ 그들은 아무도 엿들을 수 없는 작은 방에 문을 닫고 있었다. ⃞ 아무도 사태가 얼마나 안 좋은지 모른다. ⃞ 가산명사 보잘것없는 사람 [탐탁잖음] ⃞ 나 같은 지위에 있으면 당신 같은 보잘것없는 사람은 전혀 무서울 것이 없다.

특정한 사람들의 집단에 대해 말할 때 of 앞에 nobody나 no one을 쓰지 않는다. 여기에 필요한 말은 none이다. ⃞ 그의 동료 아무도 대답하지 않았다.

⃞ 형용사 밤의 ⃞ 개의 주요 임무는 긴 야간 산책에 나와 동행하는 것이다. ⃞ 형용사 야행성의 ⃞ 보름달이 떴을 때 이 야행성 설치류는 굴을 떠나지 않도록 조심한다.

⃞ 타동사/자동사 끄덕이다 ⃞ "괜찮아?"라고 내가 물었다. 그녀는 고개를 끄덕이며 미소를 지었다. ⃞ 자크는 하나를 맛보고는 흡족한 듯 고개를 끄덕였다. ● 가산명사 끄덕임 ⃞ 그녀는 고개를 끄덕이며 "알겠어."라고 했다. ⃞ "아마도,"라고 헌터는 동의하며 고개를 천천히 끄덕였다. ⃞ 자동사 까딱이다 ⃞ "작동해?"라고 그가 피아노를 향해 고개를 까닥이며 물었다. ⃞ 그녀는 응접실을 향해 고개를 까딱였다. "그는 저 안에 있어." ⃞ 타동사/자동사 끄덕이며 인사하다 ⃞ 모든 여자 애들이 고개를 끄덕여 인사하며 "안녕."이라고 했다. ⃞ 그들 둘은 웃으며 친구들에게 고개를 끄덕였다.

구동사 졸다 [비격식체] ⃞ 어제 증인이 반대 심문을 받는 동안 판사가 조는 것 같았다.

⃞ 불가산명사 소음 ⃞ 방 안에 소음이 너무 심했는데 그는 정숙이 필요했다. ⃞ 폭탄과 총의 소음은 멈추지 않았다. ⃞ 가산명사 소리 ⃞ 제럴드 경은 목청에서 작은 소리를 냈다. ⃞ 새 소리와 다른 동물 소리 ⃞ 복수명사 (_처럼 들리게) 말을 하다 ⃞ 대통령은 미래에 대해 긍정적으로 들리게 말을 하기 위해 신경을 썼다. ⃞ 구 상황에 맞춰 말을 하다, 겉치레 처신 ⃞ 그러나 연례 당 회의에서 그는 항상 상황에 맞춰 말을 했다.

because they really want to. ❑ *But at the annual party conference he always made the right noises.*

Thesaurus

*noise*의 참조어

N.　boom, crash; *(ant.)* quiet, silence **1**

Word Partnership

*noise*의 연어

N.　**background** noise, noise **level**, noise **pollution**, **traffic** noise **1**
ADJ.　**loud** noise **1** **2**
V.　**hear a** noise, **make** *a* noise **2**

noisy /nɔ́ɪzi/ (**noisier, noisiest**) **1** ADJ A **noisy** person or thing makes a lot of loud or unpleasant noise. ❑ *...my noisy old typewriter.* ● **noisily** ADV ❑ *The students on the grass bank cheered noisily.* **2** ADJ A **noisy** place is full of a lot of loud or unpleasant noise. ❑ *It's a noisy place with film clips showing constantly on one of the cafe's giant screens.* ❑ *The baggage hall was crowded and noisy.* **3** ADJ If you describe someone as **noisy**, you are critical of them for trying to attract attention to their views by frequently and forcefully discussing them. [DISAPPROVAL] ❑ *It might, at last, silence the small but noisy intellectual clique.*

no|mad|ic /noumǽdɪk/ **1** ADJ **Nomadic** people travel from place to place rather than living in one place all the time. ❑ *...the great nomadic tribes of the Western Sahara.* **2** ADJ If someone has a **nomadic** way of life, they travel from place to place and do not have a settled home. ❑ *The daughter of a railway engineer, she at first had a somewhat nomadic childhood.*

no-man's land **1** N-UNCOUNT **No-man's land** is an area of land that is not owned or controlled by anyone, for example the area of land between two opposing armies. ❑ *In Tobruk, leading a patrol in no-man's land, he was blown up by a mortar bomb.* **2** N-SING If you refer to a situation as a **no-man's land** between different things, you mean that it seems unclear because it does not fit into any of the categories. ❑ *The play is set in the dangerous no-man's land between youth and adolescence.*

nomi|nal /nɒmɪnəl/ **1** ADJ You use **nominal** to indicate that someone or something is supposed to have a particular identity or status, but in reality does not have it. ❑ *As he was still not allowed to run a company, his wife became its nominal head.* ● **nomi|nal|ly** ADV ❑ *The Sultan was still nominally the Chief of Staff.* ❑ *Nominally she is the king's prisoner.* **2** ADJ A **nominal** price or sum of money is very small in comparison with the real cost or value of the thing that is being bought or sold. [ADJ n] ❑ *I am prepared to sell my shares at a nominal price.* **3** ADJ In economics, the **nominal** value, rate, or level of something is the one expressed in terms of current prices or figures, without taking into account general changes in prices that take place over time. [ADJ n] ❑ *Inflation would be lower and so nominal rates would be rather more attractive in real terms.*

nomi|nate /nɒmɪneɪt/ (**nominates, nominating, nominated**) **1** V-T If someone **is nominated** for a job or position, their name is formally suggested as a candidate for it. ❑ *Under party rules each candidate has to be nominated by 55 Labour MPs.* ❑ *The Security Council can nominate anyone for secretary-general.* **2** V-T If you **nominate** someone to a job or position, you formally choose them to hold that job or position. ❑ *The EU would nominate two members to the committee.* ❑ *He was nominated by the African National Congress as one of its team at the Groote Sehuur talks.* **3** V-T If someone or something such as an actor or a movie **is nominated** for an award, someone formally suggests that they should be given that award. ❑ *Practically every movie he made was nominated for an Oscar.*

nomi|na|tion /nɒmɪneɪʃən/ (**nominations**) **1** N-COUNT A **nomination** is an official suggestion of someone as a candidate in an election or for a job. ❑ *...his candidacy for the Republican presidential nomination.* **2** N-COUNT A **nomination for** an award is an official suggestion that someone or something should be given that award. ❑ *They say he's certain to get a nomination for best supporting actor.* **3** N-VAR The **nomination** of someone to a particular job or position is their appointment to that job or position. ❑ *They opposed the nomination of a junior officer to the position of Inspector General of Police.*

nomi|nee /nɒmɪniː/ (**nominees**) N-COUNT A **nominee** is someone who is nominated for a job, position, or award. ❑ *His nominee for vice president was elected only after a second ballot.*

non|cha|lant /nɒnʃələnt, BRIT nɒnʃǽlənt/ ADJ If you describe someone as **nonchalant**, you mean that they appear not to worry or care about things and that they seem very calm. ❑ *Clark's mother is nonchalant about her role in her son's latest work.* ❑ *Denis tried to look nonchalant and uninterested.* ● **non|cha|lance** /nɒnʃələns, BRIT nɒnʃǽləns/ N-UNCOUNT ❑ *Affecting nonchalance, I handed her two hundred-dollar bills.* ● **non|cha|lant|ly** ADV ❑ *"Does Will intend to return with us?" Joanna asked as nonchalantly as she could.*

none ♦♦◇ /nʌn/ **1** QUANT **None of** something means not even a small amount of it. **None of** a group of people or things means not even one of them. [QUANT of def-n] ❑ *We knew how to treat her.* ● PRON-INDEF-NEG **None** is also a pronoun. ❑ *I turned to bookshops and libraries seeking information and found none.* ❑ *No one could imagine a great woman painter. None had existed yet.* **2** PHRASE If you say that someone **will have none** of something, or **is having none** of something, you mean that they refuse to accept it. [INFORMAL] ❑ *He knew his own mind and was having none of their attempts to keep him at home.* **3** PHRASE You use **none too** in front of an adjective or adverb in order to emphasize that the quality mentioned is not present. [FORMAL, EMPHASIS] ❑ *He was none too thrilled to hear from me at that hour.* **4** PHRASE You use **none the** to say that someone or something does not have any more of a particular quality than they did

1 형용사 시끄러운 ❑ 나의 시끄러운 고물 타자기 ● 시끄럽게 부사 ❑ 잔디로 뒤덮인 강둑에서 학생들이 와자지껄하게 응원을 했다. **2** 형용사 시끄러운 ❑ 그곳은 여러 개의 거대한 화면 중 한 곳에서는 반드시 영화가 상영되고 있는 시끄러운 카페이다. ❑ 수화물 찾는 곳은 붐비고 시끄러웠다. **3** 형용사 시끄러운 [탐탁잖음] ❑ 그로써 작지만 시끄러운 지식인 모임을 드디어 침묵시킬는지 모른다.

1 형용사 유목민의 ❑ 서부 사하라의 거대한 유목민족 **2** 형용사 방랑하는 ❑ 철도 기술자의 딸로서 그녀는 처음에는 자주 이사를 다니는 유년기를 보냈다.

1 불가산명사 (대치 중인 적군 사이의) 중간 지대 ❑ 토브룩에서 중간 지대의 순찰을 지휘하던 도중 그는 포탄에 맞아 숨졌다. **2** 단수명사 중간적 시기, 애매한 상태 ❑ 연극의 배경은 청년기와 유년기 사이의 위험하고 애매한 시기이다.

1 형용사 명목상의 ❑ 그는 아직도 회사를 경영할 권한이 없었기 때문에 그의 아내가 명목적인 사장이 되었다. ● 명목상으로 부사 ❑ 술탄이 아직도 명목적으로는 참모 총장이었다. ❑ 명목상으로 그녀는 왕의 포로이다. **2** 형용사 명목뿐인, 보잘것없는 ❑ 내 지분을 헐값에 팔 의향이 있다. **3** 형용사 명목상의 ❑ 물가 인상률이 더 낮을 것이기 때문에 명목상의 금리라 하더라도 실질적으로는 그리 나쁘지 않을 것이다.

1 타동사 지명되다, 추천받다 ❑ 당 규약에 따라 각 후보는 노동당 의원 55명의 추천을 받아야 한다. ❑ 안보리는 아무나 사무총장으로 추천할 수 있다. **2** 타동사 임명하다 ❑ 유럽 연합이 그 위원회에 위원 2명을 임명할 것이다. ❑ 그는 그루트 세후르의 회담에 갈 팀의 일원으로 아프리카 민족 회의에서 임명되었다. **3** 타동사 후보에 오르다 ❑ 사실상 그가 만든 영화란 영화는 모두 오스카상 후보에 올랐다.

1 가산명사 후보 지명 ❑ 공화당 대통령 후보 지명을 위한 그의 입후보 **2** 가산명사 입후 지명 ❑ 그가 남우조연상 후보에 오를 것이 확실하다고 한다. **3** 가산명사 또는 불가산명사 임명 ❑ 하급 경관을 경찰 감찰감에 임명한 것을 그들은 반대했다.

가산명사 후보 ❑ 그는 두 번째 표결을 거친 뒤에야 부통령 후보로 선출되었다.

형용사 무심한 ❑ 클라크의 어머님은 본인이 아들의 최신 작품에서 맡은 역할에 대해 무심하다. ❑ 데니스는 무심하고 태연한 척 보이기 위해 노력했다. ● 무심함 불가산명사 ❑ 무심한 척하며 나는 그녀에게 100달러 지폐 두 장을 줬다. ● 무심하게 부사 ❑ "윌이 우리와 같이 돌아갈 생각이야?"라고 조아나는 최대한 무심하게 물었다.

1 수량사 -의 중에서 하나도 아니다, -의 중에서 아무도 아니다 ❑ 우리 중 어느 누구도 여자를 어떻게 대해야 할지 몰랐다. ● 부정(不定)대명사-부정(否定) 아무것도 -않다 ❑ 정보를 찾기 위해 서점과 도서관에 가봤으나 아무것도 찾지 못했다. ❑ 아무도 위대한 여성 화가라는 것을 상상조차 하지 못했다. 아직 그런 사람이 존재한 적이 없었다. **2** 구 -을 거부하다 [비격식체] ❑ 그는 생각이 확실했고 그들 집에 머물게 하려는 그들의 어떤 시도도 거부했다. **3** 구 조금도 [격식체, 강조] ❑ 그는 나로부터 그 시각에 연락받는 것을 조금도 달가워하지 않았다. **4** 구 조금도 -하지 않은 ❑ 또 다른 저축 방식에 돈을 맡기고 나서도

before. ❑ *You could end up committed to yet another savings scheme and none the wiser about managing your finances.* **5** **second to none** →see **second**

본인의 재정 관리에 대해 하나도 현명해진 것이 없을 가능성이 크다.

> Do not confuse **none** and **neither**. You use **none** in negative statements to refer to three or more people or things. ❑ *None could afford the food.* You use **none of** in the same way, followed by a pronoun or a noun group. ❑ *None of them had learned anything... None of his companions answered.* You use **neither** in negative statements to refer to two people or things. ❑ *Neither had close friends in college.* You use **neither of** in the same way, followed by a pronoun or a noun group. ❑ *Neither of them spoke... Neither of these extremes is desirable.* Note that you can also use **neither** before a singular count noun. ❑ *Neither side can win.*

> none과 neither를 혼동하지 않도록 하라. none은 부정문에서 세 사람 이상이나 세 개 이상의 사물을 가리킬 때 쓴다. ❑ 아무도 음식을 살 형편이 안 되었다. none of도 같은 방식으로 쓰는데 뒤에는 대명사나 명사구가 따라 온다. ❑ 그들 누구도 아무것도 배우지 못했다... 그의 동료 아무도 대답하지 않았다. neither는 부정문에서 두 사람이나 두 개의 사물을 가리킬 때 쓴다. ❑ 두 사람 모두 대학 시절에 가까운 친구가 없었다. neither of도 같은 방식으로 쓰는데 뒤에는 대명사나 명사구가 따라 온다. ❑ 그들은 둘 다 말을 하지 않았다... 이런 양극단은 어느 것도 바람직하지 않다. neither는 가산 명사 단수형 앞에 쓸 수도 있음을 유의하라. ❑ 둘 중 아무 편도 이길 수 없다.

PRON.	**none of that/this/those**, **none of them/us** **1**
ADV.	**almost none**, **virtually none**, **none whatsoever** **1**
	none too **3**

none|the|less /nʌnðəles/ ADV **Nonetheless** means the same as **nevertheless**. [FORMAL] [ADV with cl] ❑ *There was still a long way to go. Nonetheless, some progress had been made.*

부사 그렇지만, 그럼에도 불구하고 [격식체] ❑ 아직도 갈 길이 많이 남아 있었다. 그렇지만 약간의 진전은 있었다.

non|executive /nɒnɪgzekyətɪv/ (**nonexecutives**) [BRIT also **non-executive**] **1** ADJ Someone who has a **nonexecutive** position in a company or organization gives advice but is not responsible for making decisions or ensuring that decisions are carried out. [BUSINESS] [ADJ n] ❑ *...nonexecutive directors.* **2** N-COUNT A **nonexecutive** is someone who has a non-executive position in a company or organization. [BUSINESS] ❑ *Seven of its nonexecutives have been on the board for close to a decade.*

[영국영어 non-executive] **1** 형용사 사외의 [경제] ❑ 사외이사 **2** 가산명사 사외이사 [경제] ❑ 그의 사외이사 중 7명이 거의 10년 가까이 이사회에 있었다.

non|existent /nɒnɪgzɪstənt/ [BRIT also **non-existent**] ADJ If you say that something is **nonexistent**, you mean that it does not exist when you feel that it should. ❑ *Hygiene was nonexistent: no running water, no bathroom.*

[영국영어 non-existent] 형용사 존재하지 않는 ❑ 위생이라는 것은 존재하지 않았다. 수돗물도 화장실도 없었다.

no-nonsense **1** ADJ If you describe someone as a **no-nonsense** person, you approve of the fact that they are efficient, direct, and quite tough. [APPROVAL] ❑ *She saw herself as a direct, no-nonsense modern woman.* **2** ADJ If you describe something as a **no-nonsense** thing, you approve of the fact that it is plain and does not have unnecessary parts. [APPROVAL] ❑ *You'll need no-nonsense boots for the jungle.*

1 형용사 허투루 하지 않는, 똑 떨어지는 [마음에 듦] ❑ 그녀는 스스로를 솔직하고 똑 떨어지는 현대 여성이라고 생각했다. **2** 형용사 허식이 없는, 실용적인 [마음에 듦] ❑ 밀림을 위해선 실용적인 장화가 필요할 것이다.

non|payment /nɒnpeɪmənt/ [BRIT also **non-payment**] N-UNCOUNT **Nonpayment** is a failure to pay a sum of money that you owe. ❑ *She faced an end to treatments because of nonpayment of her claim.*

[영국영어 non-payment] 불가산명사 미납, 미불 ❑ 그녀는 의료비를 지불하지 않아 치료 중단을 앞둔 상태였다.

Word Link　　　**non** ≈ **not** : **non**profit, **non**sense, **non**stop

non|profit /nɒnprɒfɪt/ [BRIT also **non-profit**] ADJ A **nonprofit** organization is one which is not run with the aim of making a profit. [BUSINESS] ❑ *Most of that money goes to nonprofit organizations that run programs for the poor.*

[영국영어 non-profit] 형용사 비영리의 [경제] ❑ 그 돈의 대부분은 빈민을 위한 프로그램을 운영하는 비영리 단체에게 간다.

nonprofit-making [BRIT also **non-profit-making**] ADJ A **nonprofit-making** organization or charity is not run with the intention of making a profit. [mainly BRIT, BUSINESS] [usu ADJ n] ❑ *...the Film Theatre Foundation, a nonprofit-making company which raises money for the arts.*

[영국영어 non-profit-making] 형용사 비영리의 [주로 영국영어, 경제] ❑ 예술을 위한 기금을 조성하는 비영리 회사인 영화 연극 재단

non|sense /nɒnsens, -səns/ **1** N-UNCOUNT If you say that something spoken or written is **nonsense**, you mean that you consider it to be untrue or silly. [DISAPPROVAL] ❑ *Most orthodox doctors however dismiss this as complete nonsense.* ❑ *...all that poetic nonsense about love.* **2** N-UNCOUNT You can use **nonsense** to refer to something that you think is foolish or that you disapprove of. [DISAPPROVAL] [also a N, usu supp N] ❑ *Surely it is an economic nonsense to deplete the world of natural resources.* **3** N-UNCOUNT You can refer to spoken or written words that do not mean anything because they do not make sense as **nonsense**. ❑ *...a children's nonsense poem by Charles E Carryl.* **4** →see also **no-nonsense** **5** PHRASE To **make a nonsense of** something or to **make nonsense of** it means to make it seem ridiculous or pointless. ❑ *The fighting made a nonsense of peace pledges made in London last week.*

1 불가산명사 헛소리 [탐탁찮음] ❑ 대부분의 정규 의사들은 이것을 완전 헛소리로 치부한다. ❑ 사랑에 관한 모든 시적 헛소리 **2** 불가산명사 허튼 짓 [탐탁찮음] ❑ 세계의 천연 자원을 고갈시키는 것은 분명히 경제적으로 말도 안 되는 것이다. **3** 불가산명사 말장난 ❑ 찰스 이 캐릴이 쓴 아동용 난센스 시 **5** 구 무의미하게 만들다 ❑ 그 싸움으로 지난 주 런던에서 이루어진 평화의 맹세가 무의미하게 되었다.

Word Partnership　　　*nonsense*의 연어

ADJ.	**absolute nonsense**, **complete nonsense**, **utter nonsense** **1**-**3**
V.	**talk nonsense** **1** **3**

non|smoker /nɒnsmoʊkər/ (**nonsmokers**) also **non-smoker** [BRIT also **non-smoker**] N-COUNT A **nonsmoker** is someone who does not smoke. ❑ *It could be fair to nonsmokers to allow smoking in a building with windows that open.*

[영국영어 non-smoker] 가산명사 비흡연가 ❑ 창문이 열리는 건물에서는 흡연을 허용하는 것이 비흡연가들에게 공평할 수도 있다.

non|stick /nɒnstɪk/ also **non-stick** [BRIT also **non-stick**] ADJ **Nonstick** saucepans, frying pans, or baking pans have a special coating on the inside which prevents food from sticking to them. ❑ *Coat a shallow nonstick baking pan with cooking spray.*

[영국영어 non-stick] 형용사 눌어붙지 않는 ❑ 음식이 달라붙지 않는 얕은 구이용 팬에 요리용 스프레이를 뿌리세요.

non|stop /nɒnstɒp/ also **non-stop** ADJ Something that is **nonstop** continues without any pauses or interruptions. ❑ *Many U.S. cities now have nonstop flights to Aspen.* ❑ *...80 minutes of nonstop music.* ● ADV **Non-stop** is also an adverb. [ADV after v] ❑ *Amy and her group had driven non-stop through Spain.*

형용사 도중에 멈추지 않는 ❑ 많은 미국 도시들에는 이제 애스팬까지 가는 직항편이 있다. ❑ 80분간 중단 없이 음악만 틈 ● 부사 직행으로, 직항으로 ❑ 에이미와 그 일행은 쉬지 않고 차를 몰아 스페인을 통과했다.

Thesaurus　　　*nonstop*의 참조어

ADJ.	**continuous**, **direct**, **uninterrupted**

a
b
c
d
e
f
g
h
i
j
k
l
m
n
o
p
q
r
s
t
u
v
w
x
y
z

non|union /nɒnyunyən/ [BRIT **non-union**] ADJ **Nonunion** workers do not belong to a labor union or trade union. A **non-union** company or organization does not employ workers who belong to a labor union or trade union. [BUSINESS] ❑ *The company originally intended to reopen the factory with nonunion workers.*

[영국영어 non-union] 형용사 노조에 속하지 않은; 노조원을 고용하지 않는 [경제] ❑ 회사는 원래 비노조원들을 이용하여 공장을 재가동하려고 했었다.

noo|dle /nud°l/ (**noodles**) N-COUNT **Noodles** are long, thin, curly strips of pasta. They are used especially in Chinese and Italian cooking.

가산명사 국수

noon /nun/ **1** N-UNCOUNT **Noon** is twelve o'clock in the middle of the day. ❑ *The long day of meetings started at noon.* **2** ADJ **Noon** means happening or appearing in the middle part of the day. [ADJ n] ❑ *The noon sun was fierce.* **3** **morning, noon, and night** →see **morning**

1 불가산명사 정오 ❑ 회의로 꽉 찬 긴 하루는 정오에 시작되었다. **2** 형용사 한낮의 ❑ 한낮의 태양은 맹렬했다.

no one ♦♦◇ [BRIT also **no-one**] PRON-INDEF-NEG **No one** means not a single person, or not a single member of a particular group or set. ❑ *Everyone wants to be a hero, but no one wants to die.*

[영국영어 no-one] 부정(不定)대명사-부정(否定) 아무도 -이 아니다 ❑ 모든 사람은 영웅이 되고 싶어 하지만 아무도 죽기를 원하는 않는다.

noose /nus/ (**nooses**) N-COUNT A **noose** is a circular loop at the end of a piece of rope or wire. A **noose** is tied with a knot that allows it to be tightened, and it is usually used to trap animals or hang people. ❑ *...a horrifying videotape of a man swinging from a noose.*

가산명사 올가미 ❑ 올가미에 남자가 매달려 있는 모습을 담은 끔찍한 비디오테이프

nope /noup/ CONVENTION **Nope** is sometimes used instead of "no" as a negative response. [INFORMAL, SPOKEN] ❑ *"Is she supposed to work today?" — "Nope, tomorrow."*

관용 표현 아니 [비격식체, 구어체] ❑ "그녀는 오늘 일하는 날이야?" "아니, 내일이야."

nor ♦♦◇ /nɔr/ **1** CONJ You use **nor** after "neither" in order to introduce the second alternative or the last of a number of alternatives in a negative statement. ❑ *Neither Mr. Rose nor Mr. Woodhead was available for comment yesterday.* ❑ *I can give you neither an opinion nor any advice.* **2** CONJ You use **nor** after a negative statement in order to indicate that the negative statement also applies to you or to someone or something else. ❑ *"None of us has any idea how long we're going to be here." — "Nor do I."* ❑ *"If my husband has no future," she said, "then nor do my children."* **3** CONJ You use **nor** after a negative statement in order to introduce another negative statement which adds information to the previous one. ❑ *Cooking up a quick dish doesn't mean you have to sacrifice flavor. Nor does fast food have to be junk food.*

1 접속사 -도 아니다 ❑ 로즈 씨에게서도 우드헤드 씨에게도 어제는 코멘트를 듣지 못했다. ❑ 나는 네게 의견도 충고도 줄 수 없다. **2** 접속사 - 또한 아니다 ❑ "우리 중 어느 누구도 우리가 여기에 얼마나 오래 있을지에 대해서 전혀 알지 못해." "나도 마찬가지야." ❑ "나의 남편에게 미래가 없다면 나의 아이들 또한 미래가 없다."라고 그녀는 말했다. **3** 접속사 또한 -도 아니다 ❑ 음식을 급히 준비한다고 해서 반드시 맛이 없어지는 건 아니다. 또한 패스트푸드라고 해서 반드시 불량 식품이라는 법도 없다.

norm /nɔrm/ (**norms**) **1** N-COUNT **Norms** are ways of behaving that are considered normal in a particular society. ❑ *The actions taken depart from what she called the commonly accepted norms of democracy.* **2** N-SING If you say that a situation is **the norm**, you mean that it is usual and expected. ❑ *Families of six or seven are the norm in Borough Park.* **3** N-COUNT A **norm** is an official standard or level that organizations are expected to reach. ❑ *...a Europe-wide environmental protection agency which would establish European norms and co-ordinate national policies to halt pollution.*

1 가산명사 규범 ❑ 취해진 행동들은 그녀가 민주주의의 통상적인 규범이라고 부르는 것에서 벗어난 것이다. **2** 단수명사 표준 ❑ 바로우 파크에서는 6인 혹은 7인 가족이 표준이다. **3** 가산명사 기준 ❑ 유럽 기준을 마련하고 오염을 방지하기 위한 국가 정책을 조정하는 범유럽 환경 보호 기구

nor|mal ♦♦◇ /nɔrm°l/ **1** ADJ Something that is **normal** is usual and ordinary, and is what people expect. ❑ *The two countries resumed normal diplomatic relations.* ❑ *Some of the shops were closed but that's quite normal for a Thursday afternoon.* **2** ADJ A **normal** person has no serious physical or mental health problems. ❑ *Statistics indicate that depressed patients are more likely to become ill than are normal people.*

1 형용사 정상적인, 보통의 ❑ 두 나라는 정상적인 외교 관계를 재개했다. ❑ 일부 가게가 문을 닫았으나 사실 그것은 목요일 오후에는 보통이다. **2** 형용사 정상적인 ❑ 통계에 의하면 우울증 환자가 정상인보다 병에 걸릴 확률이 높다.

Thesaurus   normal의 참조어

ADJ.   ordinary, regular, typical, usual; (*ant.*) abnormal, unusual **1**

Word Partnership   normal의 연어

N.   normal **conditions**, normal **development**, normal **routine** **1**
V.   **return to** normal **1**
ADV.   **back to** normal **1**
      completely normal, **perfectly** normal **1 2**

---

nor|mal|ity /nɔrmæliti/ N-UNCOUNT **Normality** is a situation in which everything is normal. ❑ *A semblance of normality has returned with people going to work and shops re-opening.*

불가산명사 정상 ❑ 사람들이 출근하고 가게를 다시 열면서 정상 생활로 돌아온 것처럼 보인다.

Word Link   ize ≈ making : finalize, minimize, normalize

---

nor|mal|ize /nɔrməlaɪz/ (**normalizes, normalizing, normalized**) [BRIT also **normalise**] **1** V-T/V-I When you **normalize** a situation or when it **normalizes**, it becomes normal. ❑ *Meditation tends to lower or normalize blood pressure.* **2** V-RECIP If people, groups, or governments **normalize** relations, or when relations **normalize**, they become normal or return to normal. ❑ *The two governments were close to normalizing relations.* ❑ *The United States says they are not prepared to join in normalizing ties with their former enemy.* ● **nor|mal|iza|tion** /nɔrməlɪzeɪʃ°n/ N-UNCOUNT ❑ *The two sides would like to see the normalization of diplomatic relations.*

[영국영어 normalise] **1** 타동사/자동사 정상화하다 ❑ 명상은 혈압을 낮추거나 정상화하는 경향이 있다. **2** 상호동사 정상화하다 ❑ 두 정부는 관계를 정상화하는 단계에 거의 다가갔다. ❑ 미국은 이전에 적국이던 국가와 관계를 정상화할 준비가 되어 있지 않다고 한다. ● 정상화 불가산명사 ❑ 양측은 외교 관계의 정상화를 이루고 싶어한다.

nor|mal|ly ♦♦◇ /nɔrməli/ **1** ADV If you say that something **normally** happens or that you **normally** do a particular thing, you mean that it is what usually happens or what you usually do. ❑ *All airports in the country are working normally today.* ❑ *Social progress is normally a matter of struggles and conflicts.* **2** ADV If you do something **normally**, you do it in the usual or conventional way. [ADV after v] ❑ *...failure of the blood to clot normally.*

1 부사 정상적으로, 대개 ❑ 국가의 모든 공항이 오늘 정상적으로 돌아가고 있다. ❑ 사회적 발전은 대개 투쟁과 분쟁의 문제이다. **2** 부사 정상적으로 ❑ 피가 정상적으로 응고하지 않음

north ♦♦♦ /nɔrθ/ also North **1** N-UNCOUNT The **north** is the direction which is on your left when you are looking toward the direction where the sun rises. [also the n] ❑ *In the north the ground becomes very cold as the winter snow and ice covers the ground.* **2** N-SING The **north** of a place, country, or region is the part which is in the north. ❑ *The scheme mostly benefits people in the North and Midlands where rateable values were lowest.* **3** ADV If you go **north**, you travel towards the north. [ADV after v] ❑ *Anita drove north up Pacific Highway.* **4** ADV Something that is **north** of a place is positioned to the north of it. ❑ *That's a little village a few miles*

1 불가산명사 북쪽 ❑ 북쪽에서는 겨울 눈과 얼음이 땅을 뒤덮기 시작하면서 땅이 매우 차가워진다. **2** 단수명사 북부 ❑ 그 계획 덕택에 평가 가치가 가장 낮은 북부와 중부 사람들이 가장 많은 이득을 본다. **3** 부사 북쪽으로 ❑ 아니타는 퍼시픽 고속도로를 따라 북쪽으로 차를 몰고 갔다. **4** 부사 북쪽에 ❑ 그곳은 구 런던 로드 인근인 포츠머스의 북쪽으로 몇 마일 떨어진 작은 마을이다. **5** 형용사 북쪽의 ❑ 산의 북쪽

north of Portsmouth, off the old London Road. **5** ADJ The **north** edge, corner, or part of a place or country is the part which is toward the north. [ADJ n] ❑ ...the north side of the mountain. **6** ADJ "**North**" is used in the names of some countries, states, and regions in the north of a larger area. [ADJ n] ❑ There were demonstrations this weekend in cities throughout North America, Asia, and Europe. **7** ADJ A **north** wind is a wind that blows from the north. [ADJ n] ❑ ...a bitterly cold north wind. **8** N-SING The **North** is used to refer to the richer, more developed countries of the world. [the N] ❑ Malaysia has emerged as the toughest critic of the North's environmental attitudes.

north|east ♦♦◇ /nɔrθist/ [BRIT also **north-east**] **1** N-UNCOUNT The **northeast** is the direction which is halfway between north and east. [also the N] ❑ ...the warm waters of Salt Springs Island to the northeast. **2** N-SING The **northeast** of a place, country, or region is the part which is in the northeast. ❑ The northeast has been particularly hard hit. **3** ADV If you go **northeast**, you travel toward the northeast. [ADV after v] ❑ "We're going northeast," Paula told them, before they started. **4** ADV Something that is **northeast of** a place is positioned to the northeast of it. [ADV of n] ❑ This latest attack was at Careysburg, twenty miles north-east of the capital, Monrovia. **5** ADJ The **northeast** edge, corner, or part of a place is the part which is towards the northeast. [ADJ n] ❑ ... a climate like that of our northeast coast.

north|eastern /nɔrθistərn/ [BRIT also **north-eastern**] ADJ **Northeastern** means in or from the northeast of a region or country. ❑ ...on the northeastern coast of Florida.

nor|ther|ly /nɔrðərli/ ADJ A **northerly** point, area, or direction is to the north or toward the north. ❑ Fetlaw is the most northerly island in the British Isles.

north|ern ♦♦◇ /nɔrðərn/ also **Northern** ADJ **Northern** means in or from the north of a region, state, or country. [ADJ n] ❑ Their two children were immigrants to Northern Ireland from Pennsylvania.

north|ward /nɔrθwərd/ also **northwards** ADV **Northward** or **northwards** means toward the north. ❑ Tropical storm Marco is pushing northward up Florida's coast. ● ADJ **Northward** is also an adjective. [ADJ n] ❑ The northward journey from Jalalabad was no more than 120 miles.

north|west ♦♦◇ /nɔrθwɛst/ [BRIT also **north-west**] **1** N-UNCOUNT The **northwest** is the direction which is halfway between north and west. [also the N] ❑ ... four miles to the northwest. **2** N-SING The **northwest** of a place, country, or region is the part which is toward the northwest. ❑ ...in the extreme northwest of the country. **3** ADV If you go **northwest**, you travel toward the northwest. [ADV after v] ❑ Take the narrow lane going north-west parallel with the railway line. **4** ADV Something that is **northwest of** a place is positioned to the north-west of it. [ADV of n] ❑ Just a couple of hours to the northwest of the capital is the wine-growing area of Hunter Valley. **5** ADJ The **northwest** part of a place, country, or region is the part which is toward the northwest. [ADJ n] ❑ ...the northwest coast of the United States.

north|western /nɔrθwɛstərn/ [BRIT also **north-western**] ADJ **Northwestern** means in or from the northwest of a region or country. ❑ Virtually every river in northwestern Oregon was near flood stage.

nose ♦◇◇ /noʊz/ (**noses, nosing, nosed**) **1** N-COUNT Your **nose** is the part of your face which sticks out above your mouth. You use it for smelling and breathing. ❑ She wiped her nose with a tissue. **2** N-COUNT The **nose** of a vehicle such as a car or aeroplane is the front part of it. ❑ Sue parked off the main street, with the van's nose pointing away from the street. **3** N-COUNT You can refer to your sense of smell as your **nose**. ❑ The river that runs through Middlesbrough became ugly on the eye and hard on the nose. **4** V-T/V-I If a vehicle **noses** in a certain direction or if you **nose** it there, you move it slowly and carefully in that direction. ❑ He could not see the driver as the car nosed forward. ❑ A motorboat nosed out of the mist and nudged into the branches of a tree. **5** PHRASE If you **keep** your **nose clean**, you behave well and stay out of trouble. [INFORMAL] ❑ If you kept your nose clean, you had a job for life. **6** PHRASE If you **follow** your **nose** to get to a place, you go straight ahead or follow the most obvious route. ❑ Just follow your nose and in about five minutes you're at the old railway. **7** PHRASE If you **follow** your **nose**, you do something in a particular way because you feel it should be done like that, rather than because you are following any plan or rules. ❑ You won't have to think, just follow your nose. **8** PHRASE If you say that someone **has a nose for** something, you mean that they have a natural ability to find it or recognize it. ❑ He had a nose for trouble and a brilliant tactical mind. **9** PHRASE If you say that someone or something **gets up** your **nose**, you mean that they annoy you. [BRIT, INFORMAL] ❑ He's just getting up my nose so much at the moment. **10** PHRASE If you say that someone **looks down** their **nose** at something or someone, you mean that they believe they are superior to that person or thing and treat them with disrespect. [DISAPPROVAL] ❑ I don't look down my nose at comedy. **11** PHRASE If you say that you **paid through the nose** for something, you are emphasizing that you had to pay what you consider too high a price for it. [INFORMAL, EMPHASIS] ❑ We don't like paying through the nose for our wine when eating out. **12** PHRASE If someone **pokes** their **nose into** something or **sticks** their **nose into** something, they try to interfere with it even though it does not concern them. [INFORMAL, DISAPPROVAL] ❑ We don't like strangers who poke their noses into our affairs. **13** PHRASE To **rub** someone's **nose in** something that they do not want to think about, such as a failing or a mistake that they have made, means to remind them repeatedly about it. [INFORMAL] ❑ His enemies will attempt to rub his nose in past policy statements. **14** PHRASE If vehicles are **nose to tail**, the front of one vehicle is close behind the back of another. [mainly BRIT; AM **bumper-to-bumper**] ❑ ...a line of about twenty fast-moving trucks driving nose to tail. **15** PHRASE If you **turn up** your **nose at** something, you reject it because you think that it is not good enough for you. ❑ I'm not in a financial position to turn up my nose at several hundred thousand pounds. **16** PHRASE If you do something **under**

6 형용사 (국가 등의 이름) 북- ❑이번 주말에 북아메리카, 아시아, 유럽 등의 여러 도시에서 시위가 있었다. **7** 형용사 북의 ❑살을 에는 듯한 차가운 북풍 **8** 단수명사 선진국 ❑말레이시아는 선진국들의 환경에 대한 태도를 가장 강하게 비판하는 국가로 부상했다.

[영국영어 north-east] **1** 불가산명사 북동쪽 ❑북동쪽에 있는 솔트스프링 섬의 따뜻한 수역 **2** 단수명사 북동부 ❑북동부에 대한 타격이 특히 심했다. **3** 부사 북동쪽으로 ❑"우리는 북동쪽으로 갈 거야."라고 폴라가 출발하기 전에 그들에게 말했다. **4** 부사 북동쪽에 ❑이 최근 공격이 수도인 먼로비아 북동쪽으로 20마일 떨어진 캐리스버그에서 있었다. **5** 형용사 북동쪽의 ❑우리의 북동쪽 해안의 것과 비슷한 기후

[영국영어 north-eastern] 형용사 북동쪽의 ❑플로리다의 북동쪽 해안에서

형용사 북쪽의 ❑페트로는 영국 섬들 중에서 최북단에 위치한 섬이다.

형용사 북쪽의 ❑그들의 두 아이는 펜실베이니아에서 북아일랜드로 온 이민자였다.

부사 북쪽으로 ❑열대성 폭풍 마르코는 플로리다의 해안을 따라 북상하고 있다. ● 형용사 북향의 ❑잘라라바드로부터 북쪽으로 가는 여정은 120마일에 불과했다.

[영국영어 north-west] **1** 불가산명사 북서쪽 ❑북서쪽으로 4마일 **2** 단수명사 북서부 ❑나라의 북서부 끝 북서쪽으로 ❑철도선과 평행되게 북서쪽으로 나 있는 좁은 길을 타세요. **4** 부사 북서쪽에 ❑수도의 북서쪽으로 두어 시간만 가면 헌터 밸리라는 와인 생산 지대가 나온다. **5** 형용사 북서쪽의 ❑미국의 북서쪽 해안

[영국영어 north-western] 형용사 북서쪽의 ❑오레곤 북서부의 거의 모든 강이 홍수 수위에 도달하고 있었다.

1 가산명사 코 ❑여자는 코를 휴지로 닦았다 **2** 가산명사 앞부분 ❑수는 중심가 인근에 밴의 정면이 도로 바깥쪽을 향하도록 주차했다. **3** 가산명사 후각 ❑미들스브로우를 통과하는 강은 보기에 흉해졌고 악취가 나게 되었다. **4** 타동사/자동사 천천히 움직이다 ❑앞으로 천천히 움직이는 차의 운전자를 그는 볼 수가 없었다. ❑모터보트가 안개 속에서 천천히 빠져나오더니 나뭇가지를 밀고 들어갔다. **5** 구 얌전하게 있다 [비격식체] ❑얌전하게만 지낸다면 평생직장을 가질 수 있다. **6** 구 직진하다 ❑직진해서 약 5분 정도 가면 옛날 철길에 도착할 것이다. **7** 구 직감을 따르다 ❑생각하지 말고 직감을 따르세요. **8** 구 -을 직감하는 능력이 있다 ❑그에게는 문제 상황을 직감하는 능력과 탁월한 전략적 머리가 있었다. **9** 구 귀찮게 하다 [영국영어, 비격식체] ❑그는 지금 나를 너무 귀찮게 하고 있어. **10** 구 경멸하다, 깔보다 ❑나는 코미디를 경멸하지 않아. **11** 구 바가지를 쓰다 [비격식체, 강조] ❑우리는 외식을 할 때 와인에 대해 바가지 쓰는 것을 좋아하지 않는다. **12** 구 참견하다 [비격식체, 탐탁잖음] ❑우리는 낯선 사람들이 우리의 일에 참견하는 것을 좋아하지 않는다. **13** 구 좋지 않은 일을 계속 상기시키다 [비격식체] ❑그의 적들은 그의 과거 정책 발언을 계속 문제 삼으며 상기시킬 것이다. **14** 구 꼬리에 꼬리를 물고 [주로 영국영어; 미국영어 bumper-to-bumper] ❑꼬리에 꼬리를 물고 빨리 달리는 20대의 트럭 **15** 구 (경멸하며) 거절하다, 콧방귀를 뀌다 ❑내가 경제적으로 수십만 파운드를 거절한 수 있는 처지가 아니다. **16** 구 면전에서, 바로 코앞에서 ❑우리는 결혼한 지 25년이 되었는데 바로 내 코앞에서 이런 행태를 부리는 것은 더 이상 참을 수 없었다.

A

someone's **nose**, you do it right in front of them, without trying to hide it from them. □ *We've been married 25 years and this carrying on under my nose was the last straw.* **17** to put someone's **nose out of joint** →see joint
→see face respiratory, smell

B

C

D

nose|dive /nouzdaıv/ (**nosedives, nosediving, nosedived**) also **nose-dive 1** V-I
If prices, profits, or exchange rates **nosedive**, they suddenly fall by a large amount. [JOURNALISM] □ *The market suffered from a knock-on effect, causing the value of other shares to nosedive by £2.6 billion.* ● N-SING **Nosedive** is also a noun. □ *The bank yesterday revealed a 30 per cent nosedive in profits.* **2** V-I If something such as someone's reputation or career **nosedives**, it suddenly gets much worse. [JOURNALISM] □ *Since the U.S. invasion the president's reputation has nosedived.*
● N-SING **Nosedive** is also a noun. □ *He told the tribunal his career had "taken a nosedive" since his dismissal last year.*

E

F

nos|tal|gia /nɒstældʒə/ N-UNCOUNT **Nostalgia** is an affectionate feeling you have for the past, especially for a particularly happy time. □ *He might be influenced by nostalgia for the surroundings of his happy youth.*

G

nos|tal|gic /nɒstældʒık/ **1** ADJ **Nostalgic** things cause you to think affectionately about the past. □ *Although we still depict nostalgic snow scenes on Christmas cards, winters are now very much warmer.* **2** ADJ If you feel **nostalgic**, you think affectionately about experiences you had in the past. □ *Many people were nostalgic for the good old days.* ● **nos|tal|gi|cal|ly** /nɒstældʒıkli/ ADV □ *People look back nostalgically on the war period, simply because everyone pulled together.*

H

I

nos|tril /nɒstrıl/ (**nostrils**) N-COUNT Your **nostrils** are the two openings at the end of your nose. □ *Keeping your mouth closed, breathe in through your nostrils.*

J

nosy /nouzi/ (**nosier, nosiest**) also **nosey** ADJ If you describe someone as **nosy**, you mean that they are interested in things which do not concern them. [INFORMAL, DISAPPROVAL] □ *He was having to whisper in order to avoid being overheard by their nosy neighbors.*

K

not ♦♦♦ /nɒt/

L

Not is often shortened to **n't** in spoken English, and added to the auxiliary or modal verb. For example, "did not" is often shortened to "didn't."

M

1 NEG You use **not** with verbs to form negative statements. □ *The sanctions are not working the way they were intended.* □ *I don't trust my father anymore.* **2** NEG You use **not** to form questions to which you expect the answer "yes." □ *Haven't they got enough problems there already?* □ *Didn't I see you at the party last week?* **3** NEG You use **not**, usually in the form **n't**, in questions which imply that someone should have done something, or to express surprise that something is not the case. □ *Why didn't you do it months ago?* □ *Why couldn't he listen to her?* **4** NEG You use **not**, usually in the form **n't**, in question tags after a positive statement. □ *"It's crazy, isn't it?* □ *I've been a great husband, haven't I?* **5** NEG You use **not**, usually in the form **n't**, in polite suggestions. [POLITENESS] □ *Actually we do have a position in mind. Why don't you fill out our application?* **6** NEG You use **not** to represent the negative of a word, group, or clause that has just been used. □ *"Have you found Paula?" — "I'm afraid not, Kate."* **7** NEG You can use **not** in front of "all" or "every" when you want to say something that applies only to some members of the group that you are talking about. □ *Not all the money, to put it mildly, has been used wisely.* **8** NEG If something is **not** always the case, you mean that sometimes it is the case and sometimes it is not. □ *He didn't always win the arguments, but he often was right.* □ *She couldn't always afford a babysitter.* **9** NEG You can use **not** or **not even** in front of "a" or "one" to emphasize that there is none at all of what is being mentioned. [EMPHASIS] □ *...no office, no phone, not even a shelf on which to put my meager belongings.* □ *I sent report after report. But not one word was published.* **10** NEG You can use **not** in front of a word referring to a distance, length of time, or other amount to say that the actual distance, time, or amount is less than the one mentioned. [NEG amount] □ *The tug crossed our stern not fifty yards away.* □ *...a large crowd not ten yards away waiting for a bus.* **11** NEG You use **not** when you are contrasting something that is true with something that is untrue. You use this especially to indicate that people might think that the untrue statement is true. □ *He has his place in the Asian team not because he is white but because he is good.* □ *Training is an investment not a cost.* **12** NEG You use **not** in expressions such as "not only," "not just," and "not simply" to emphasize that something is true, but it is not the whole truth. [EMPHASIS] □ *These movies were not only making money; they were also perceived to be original.* □ *There is always a "black market" not just in Britain but in Europe as a whole.* **13** PHRASE You use **not that** to introduce a negative clause that contradicts something that the previous statement implies. □ *His death took me a year to get over; not that you're ever really over it.* **14** CONVENTION **Not at all** is an emphatic way of saying "No" or of agreeing that the answer to a question is "No." [EMPHASIS] □ *"Sorry. I sound like Abby, don't I?" — "'No. Not at all."* **15** CONVENTION **Not at all** is a polite way of acknowledging a person's thanks. [FORMULAE] □ *"Thank you very much for speaking with us." — "Not at all."* **16** **not half** →see half. **if not** →see if. **more often than not** →see often

N

O

P

Q

R

S

T

U

V

W

X

Y

no|table /noutəbªl/ ADJ Someone or something that is **notable** is important or interesting. □ *The proposed new structure is notable not only for its height, but for its shape.* □ *Mo did not want to be ruled by anyone and it is notable that she never allowed the men in her life to eclipse her.*

Z

---

1 자동사 폭락하다 [언론] □ 시장에서 피해가 연쇄적으로 번져가서 다른 주식들의 가치도 26억 파운드가 폭락했다. ● 단수명사 폭락 □ 은행은 어제 순익이 30퍼센트 폭락했다고 공개했다. **2** 자동사 추락하다 [언론] □ 미국의 침공 이후 대통령의 평판이 급격히 추락했다. ● 단수명사 추락 □ 그는 지난해 자기 항소가 기각된 이후 자기 경력이 급격히 악화되었다고 재판위원회에 말했다.

불가산명사 향수 □ 그가 자신이 행복했던 청년기의 세상에 대해 향수병을 앓고 있을지도 모른다.

1 형용사 향수를 불러일으키는 □ 비록 우리가 아직도 크리스마스카드에는 향수를 불러일으키는 설정을 그리지만 이제 겨울은 훨씬 따뜻해졌다. **2** 형용사 향수에 젖은 □ 많은 사람들이 아름다운 지난 시절을 그리워했다. ● 향수에 젖어서 부사 □ 단지 모든 사람들이 화합을 했다는 이유로 사람들은 전쟁 시기를 그리운 마음으로 회고한다.

가산명사 콧구멍 □ 입을 다물고 콧구멍으로 숨을 쉬세요.

형용사 주제넘은 [비격식체, 탐탁잖음] □ 그들의 주제넘은 이웃들이 엿듣지 못하게 하기 위해 어쩔 수 없이 그는 속삭여야 했다.

구어체 영어에서 not은 종종 n't로 축약되어 보조 동사나 조동사에 덧붙는다. 예를 들면, 'did not'이 종종 'didn't'로 축약된다.

1 부정어 –하지 않는 □ 제재가 그들이 의도했던 대로 작동하고 있지 않다. □ 나는 아버지를 더 이상 믿지 않는다. **2** 부정어 긍정적인 대답을 예상하는 의문문에 쓰임 □ 그들에겐 이미 너무 많은 문제가 있지 않아? □ 내가 너를 지난주 파티에서 보지 않았니? **3** 부정어 어떠한 것을 했어야 했는데 안 한 것을 놀라워하는 의문문에 쓰임 □ 왜 몇 달 전에 그걸 하지 않았어? □ 왜 그는 그녀의 말을 듣지 않았을까? **4** 부정어 부가의문문에 쓰임 □ "너무 황당하지, 그렇지 않아?" □ 나는 훌륭한 남편이었어, 안 그래? **5** 부정어 정유형에 쓰임 [공손체] □ 사실 생각하고 있는 자리가 있어요. 지원서를 작성해 주시겠어요? **6** 부정어 –이 아닌 □ "폴라를 찾았어?" "아쉽게도 못 찾았어, 케이트." **7** 부정어 (all이나 every와 함께 쓰여) 모두가 –인 것은 아닌 □ 분명히 말하자면 그 돈 전부가 현명하게 쓰인 것은 아니다. **8** 부정어 (always와 함께 쓰여) 항상 –인 것은 아닌 □ 그가 항상 논쟁에서 이긴 것은 아니었지만 그가 대개는 옳았다. □ 그녀가 항상 보모를 고용할 형편은 아니었다. **9** 부정어 심지어 –조차 없는 [강조] □ 사무실, 전화, 심지어는 내 얼마 안 되는 물품을 얹어놓을 선반조차 없었다. □ 나는 계속 보고서를 보냈다. 그러나 단 한 단어도 출판되지 않았다. **10** 부정어 –이 채 안되게 □ 예인선이 50야드가 채 안되는 거리를 두고 우리 배의 고물 앞을 지났다. □ 채 10야드도 떨어지지 않은 곳에서 버스를 기다리는 많은 사람들 **11** 부정어 –이 아니라 □ 그는 백인이어서가 아니라 실력이 좋기 때문에 그 아시아 팀의 일원이 되었다. □ 훈련은 비용이 아니라 투자이다. **12** 부정어 –이 아니라 [강조] □ 이 영화들은 돈을 벌고 있을 뿐만 아니라 독창적이라고 인식되고 있었다. □ 영국뿐만 아니라 유럽 어디든 간에 암시장이 항상 있다. **13** 구 –인 것은 아니지만 □ 그의 죽음으로 인한 슬픔을 극복하는 데 1년이 걸렸다. 그것을 완전히 극복한 것은 아니지만. **14** 관용 표현 전혀 [강조] □ "미안, 애비하고 말하는 것이 똑같지?" "아니, 전혀." **15** 관용 표현 천만에 [의례적인 표현] □ "우리와 이야기해 주셔서 너무 감사드립니다." "천만에요."

형용사 주목할 만한 □ 제안된 새로운 구조물은 높이뿐만 아니라 모양으로도 주목할 만하다. □ 모우는 어느 누구로부터도 지배를 받고 싶어 하지 않았는데 자신의 남자들 때문에 본인이 퇴색되는 것을 결코 허용하지 않았다는 것이 주목할 만하다.

A **famous** person or thing is known to more people than a **well-known** one. A **notorious** person or thing is famous because they are connected with something bad or undesirable. **Infamous** is not the opposite of **famous**. It has a similar meaning to **notorious**, but is a stronger word. Someone or something that is **notable** is important or interesting.

no|tably /nˈoʊtəbli/ **1** ADV You use **notably** to specify an important or typical example of something that you are talking about. [ADV group/cl] ❏ *The divorce would be granted when more important problems, notably the fate of the children, had been decided.* **2** ADV You can use **notably** to emphasize a particular quality that someone or something has. [EMPHASIS] [ADV adj/adv] ❏ *Old established friends are notably absent, so it's a good opportunity to make new contacts.*

notch /nˈɒtʃ/ (**notches, notching, notched**) **1** N-COUNT You can refer to a level on a scale of measurement or achievement as a **notch**. [JOURNALISM] ❏ *Average earnings in the economy moved up another notch in August.* ❏ *In this country the good players are pulled down a notch or two.* **2** V-T If you **notch** a success, especially in a sports contest, you achieve it. [JOURNALISM] ❏ *Hoffman escaped a jam to notch his 37th save.* **3** N-COUNT A **notch** is a small V-shaped or circular cut in the surface or edge of something. ❏ *It is a myth that gunslingers in the American west cut notches in the handle of their pistol for each man they shot.*

▸**notch up** PHRASAL VERB If you **notch up** something such as a score or total, you achieve it. [JOURNALISM] ❏ *He had notched up more than 25 victories worldwide.*

note ♦♦◇ /nˈoʊt/ (**notes, noting, noted**) **1** N-COUNT A **note** is a short letter. ❏ *Stevens wrote him a note asking him to come to his apartment.* **2** N-COUNT A **note** is something that you write down to remind yourself of something. ❏ *I knew that if I didn't make a note I would lose the thought so I asked to borrow a pen or pencil.* **3** N-COUNT In a book or article, a **note** is a short piece of additional information. ❏ *See Note 16 on page p. 223.* **4** N-COUNT A **note** is a short document that has to be signed by someone and that gives official information about something. ❏ *Since Mr. Bennett was going to need some time off work, he asked for a sick note.* **5** N-COUNT You can refer to a banknote as a **note**. [BRIT; AM **bill**] ❏ *They exchange travellers cheques at a different rate from notes.* **6** N-COUNT In music, a **note** is the sound of a particular pitch, or a written symbol representing this sound. ❏ *She has a deep voice and doesn't even try for the high notes.* **7** N-SING You can use **note** to refer to a particular quality in someone's voice that shows how they are feeling. ❏ *There is an unmistakable note of nostalgia in his voice when he looks back on the early years of the family business.* **8** N-SING You can use **note** to refer to a particular feeling, impression, or atmosphere. ❏ *Yesterday's testimony began on a note of passionate but civilized disagreement.* ❏ *Somehow he tells these stories without a note of horror.* **9** V-T If you **note** a fact, you become aware of it. ❏ *The White House has noted his promise to support any attack that was designed to enforce the UN resolutions.* ❏ *Suddenly, I noted that the rain had stopped.* **10** V-T If you tell someone to **note** something, you are drawing their attention to it. ❏ *Note the statue to Sallustio Bandini, a prominent Sienese.* **11** V-T If you **note** something, you mention it in order to draw people's attention to it. ❏ *The report notes that export and import volumes picked up in leading economies.* **12** V-T When you **note** something, you write it down as a record of what has happened. ❏ *"He has had his tonsils out and has been ill, too," she noted in her diary.* ❏ *They never noted the building's history of problems.* **13** →see also **noted, promissory note** **14** PHRASE Someone or something that is **of note** is important, worth mentioning, or well-known. ❏ *...politicians of note.* **15** PHRASE If you **take note of** something, you pay attention to it because you think that it is important or significant. ❏ *Take note of the weather conditions.*

Word Partnership   *note*의 연어

v.   **leave a note, send a note 1**
       find a note, read a note, scribble a note, write a note 1 2
       make a note 2
       sound a note, strike a note 6
       take note of *something*15

▸**note down** PHRASAL VERB If you **note down** something, you write it down quickly, so that you have a record of it. ❏ *She had noted down the names and she told me the story simply and factually.* ❏ *If you find a name that's on the list I've given you, note it down.*

note|book /nˈoʊtbʊk/ (**notebooks**) **1** N-COUNT A **notebook** is a small book for writing notes in. ❏ *He brought out a notebook and pen from his pocket.* **2** N-COUNT A **notebook** computer is a small personal computer. ❏ *...a range of notebook computers which allows all your important information to travel safely with you.*

not|ed ♦◇◇ /nˈoʊtɪd/ ADJ To be **noted for** something you do or have means to be well-known and admired for it. ❏ *...a television program noted for its attacks on organized crime.*

nothing ♦♦♦ /nˈʌθɪŋ/ (**nothings**) **1** PRON-INDEF-NEG **Nothing** means not a single thing, or not a single part of something. ❏ *I've done nothing much since coffee time.* ❏ *There is nothing wrong with the car.* **2** PRON-INDEF-NEG You use **nothing** to indicate that something or someone is not important or significant. ❏ *Because he had always had money it meant nothing to him.* ❏ *Do our years together mean nothing?* ● N-COUNT **Nothing** is also a noun. ❏ *It is the picture itself that is the problem; so small, so dull. It's a nothing, really.* **3** PRON-INDEF-NEG If

---

famous한 사람이나 사물은 well-known한 사람이나 사물보다 더 많은 사람들에게 알려져 있다. notorious한 사람이나 사물은 나쁘거나 바람직하지 않은 것과 연관되어 있기 때문에 유명하다. infamous는 '유명하다(famous)'의 반대말이 아니라, '악명 높다(notorious)'와 비슷한 뜻이며 더 강한 말이다. notable한 사람이나 사물은 중요하거나 흥미로움을 나타낸다.

1 부사 그 중에 특히 ❏ 더 중요한 문제들, 그 중에 특히 아이들의 운명이 결정된 이후에 이혼이 허용될 것이다. **2** 부사 눈에 띄게 [강조] ❏ 오랫동안 잘 알아온 친구들이 눈에 띄게 부족해서 새로운 인연을 만들기 좋은 기회이다.

1 가산명사 단계, 등급 [언론] ❏ 경제면에서 평균 수입이 8월 달에 한 단계 더 올라갔다. ❏ 이 나라는 훌륭한 선수들이 한두 등급씩 끌어 내려진다. **2** 타동사 (승리를) 올리다 [언론] ❏ 호프만은 어려운 상황을 벗어나서 서른일곱 번째 세이브를 기록했다. **3** 가산명사 새김눈 ❏ 미국 서부의 총잡이들이 사람을 쏴 죽일 때마다 권총 손잡이에 눈금을 새긴다는 것은 지어낸 이야기이다.

구동사 (점수를) 올리다 [언론] ❏ 그는 전 세계에서 25승 이상을 올렸다.

1 가산명사 짧은 편지 ❏ 스티븐스는 그에게 아파트로 와달라는 내용의 짧은 편지를 썼다. **2** 가산명사 메모 ❏ 내가 만약 메모를 하지 않는다면 그 생각을 잊으리라는 것을 알았기 때문에 펜이나 연필을 빌려 달라고 했다. **3** 가산명사 주석 ❏ 223페이지의 16번 주석 참고. **4** 가산명사 (간단한) 문서 ❏ 베넷 씨는 어느 정도 업무에서 잠깐 손 뗄 시간이 필요했으므로 그는 의사 진단서를 요청했다. **5** 가산명사 지폐 [영국영어; 미국영어 bill] ❏ 그들은 여행자 수표를 지폐와는 다른 환율로 바꿔 준다. **6** 가산명사 음, 소리 ❏ 그녀는 목소리가 저음이라서 고음은 시도조차 하지 않는다. **7** 단수명사 어조 ❏ 그가 가족 사업의 초창기를 되돌아볼 때 그의 목소리에는 드러나게 향수가 어려 있다. **8** 단수명사 분위기, 기색, 느낌 ❏ 어제의 증언은 열정적이지만 차분한 의견을 출발점 삼아 시작했다. ❏ 어쨌든 그는 이 이야기들을 전혀 끔찍한 기색 없이 말한다. **9** 타동사 지목 ❏ 백악관은 유엔의 결의안을 강행하기 위해 시행되는 모든 공격을 지지하겠다는 그의 약속을 주목했다. ❏ 갑자기 나는 비가 그쳤다는 것을 알아차렸다. **10** 타동사 주목하다 ❏ 저명한 시에나 사람인 살루스티오 반디니에 바치는 조상을 주목하세요. **11** 타동사 주목하다 ❏ 주요 경제 국가들의 경우 수출 및 수입 물량이 증가했다는 사실을 보고서는 주목한다. **12** 타동사 기록하다 ❏ "그는 편도선을 제거했고 아프기도 했다."라고 그녀는 일기에 적었다. ❏ 그들은 그 건물에 발생한 문제들의 내력을 기록하지 않았다. **14** 구 저명한 ❏ 저명한 정치인들 **15** 구 주목하다 ❏ 기상 조건을 주목하세요.

구동사 적다 ❏ 그녀는 이름들을 적고 난 뒤 나에게 그 이야기를 간단히 그리고 사실 위주로 들려주었다. ❏ 내가 당신에게 준 명단에 있는 이름을 발견하면 적어두세요.

1 가산명사 수첩 ❏ 그는 주머니에서 수첩과 펜을 꺼냈다. **2** 가산명사 노트북 ❏ 모든 중요한 정보를 안전하게 같이 들고 다닐 수 있게 해 주는 일군의 노트북 제품

형용사 주목받는 ❏ 조직 폭력에 대한 공격으로 주목받는 텔레비전 프로그램

1 부정(否定)대명사-부정(否定) 아무것도 아닌 것 ❏ 휴식 시간 이후 별로 한 것이 없다. ❏ 차는 아무 문제가 없다. **2** 부정(否定)대명사-부정(否定) 하찮은 것, 중요하지 않은 것 (또는 사람) ❏ 그는 항상 돈이 있었기 때문에 그것은 그에게 중요하지 않았다. ❏ 우리가 같이 보낸 시간이 아무 것도 아니란 말이야? ● 가산명사 하찮은 것, 중요하지 않은 것 (또는 사람)

<table>
<tr><td>A</td><td>

you say that something cost **nothing** or is worth **nothing**, you are indicating that it cost or is worth a surprisingly small amount of money. ❑ *The furniture was threadbare; he'd obviously picked it up for nothing.* ④ PRON-INDEF-NEG You use **nothing** before an adjective or "to"-infinitive to say that something or someone does not have the quality indicated. [PRON adj, PRON to-inf] ❑ *Around the lake the countryside generally is nothing special.* ❑ *There was nothing remarkable about him.* ⑤ PRON-INDEF-NEG You can use **nothing** before "so" and an adjective or adverb, or before a comparative, to emphasize how strong or great a particular quality is. [EMPHASIS] [PRON so adj/adv, PRON compar] ❑ *Youngsters learn nothing so fast as how to beat the system.* ❑ *I consider nothing more important in my life than songwriting.* ⑥ PHRASE You can use **all or nothing** to say that either something must be done fully and completely or else it cannot be done at all. ❑ *Either he went through with this thing or he did not; it was all or nothing.* ⑦ PHRASE If you say that something is **better than nothing**, you mean that it is not what is required, but that it is better to have that thing than to have nothing at all. ❑ *After all, 15 minutes of exercise is better than nothing.* ⑧ PHRASE You use **nothing but** in front of a noun, an infinitive without "to," or an "-ing" form to mean "only." ❑ *All that money brought nothing but sadness and misery and tragedy.* ❑ *It did nothing but make us ridiculous.* ⑨ PHRASE If you say that **there is nothing for it** but to take a particular action, you mean that it is the only possible course of action that you can take, even though it might be unpleasant. [BRIT] ❑ *Much depends on which individual ingredients you choose. There is nothing for it but to taste and to experiment for yourself.* ⑩ CONVENTION People sometimes say "**It's nothing**" as a polite response after someone has thanked them for something they have done. [FORMULAE] ❑ *"Thank you for the wonderful dinner." — "It's nothing," Sarah said.* ⑪ PHRASE If you say about a story or report that there is **nothing in it** or **nothing to it**, you mean that it is untrue. ❑ *It's all rubbish and superstition, and there's nothing in it.* ⑫ PHRASE If you say about an activity that there is **nothing to it** or **nothing in it**, you mean that it is extremely easy. ❑ *If you've shied away from making pancakes in the past, don't be put off – there's really nothing in it!* ⑬ PHRASE If you say about a contest or competition that there is **nothing in it**, you mean that two or more of the competitors are level and have an equal chance of winning. ❑ *Until we scored, there was really nothing in it.* ⑭ PHRASE **Nothing of the sort** is used when strongly contradicting something that has just been said. [EMPHASIS] ❑ *"We're going to talk this over in my office." — "We're going to do nothing of the sort."* ⑮ **nothing to write home about** →see **home**. **to stop at nothing** →see **stop**. **to think nothing of** →see **think**

no|tice ♦♦◇ /nˈoʊtɪs/ (**notices, noticing, noticed**) ① V-T/V-I If you **notice** something or someone, you become aware of them. ❑ *He stressed that people should not hesitate to contact the police if they've noticed any strangers in Hankham recently.* ❑ *I noticed that most academics were writing papers during the summer.* ❑ *Luckily, I'd noticed where you left the car.* ② N-COUNT A **notice** is a written announcement in a place where everyone can read it. ❑ *Notices in the waiting room requested that you neither smoke nor spit.* ❑ *A few guest houses had "No Vacancies" notices in their windows.* ③ N-UNCOUNT If you give **notice** about something that is going to happen, you give a warning in advance that it is going to happen. ❑ *Interest is paid monthly. Three months' notice is required for withdrawals.* ❑ *Unions are required to give seven days' notice of industrial action.* ④ N-COUNT A **notice** is a formal announcement in a newspaper or magazine about something that has happened or is going to happen. ❑ *I rang The Globe with news of Blake's death, and put notices in the personal column of The Times.* ⑤ N-COUNT A **notice** is one of a number of letters that are similar or exactly the same which an organization sends to people in order to give them information or ask them to do something. ❑ *Bonus notices were issued each year from head office to local agents.* ⑥ N-COUNT A **notice** is a written article in a newspaper or magazine in which someone gives their opinion of a play, movie, or concert. ❑ *Nevertheless, it's good to know you've had good notices, even if you don't read them.* ⑦ PHRASE **Notice** is used in expressions such as "**at short notice**," "**at a moment's notice**" or "**at twenty-four hours' notice**," to indicate that something can or must be done within a short period of time. ❑ *There's no one available at such short notice to take her class.* ⑧ PHRASE If a situation is said to exist **until further notice**, it will continue for an uncertain length of time until someone changes it. ❑ *The bad news was that all flights to Lanchow had been cancelled until further notice.* ⑨ PHRASE If an employer **gives** an employee **notice**, the employer tells the employee that he or she must leave his or her job within a short fixed period of time. [BUSINESS] ❑ *The next morning I telephoned him and gave him his notice.* ⑩ PHRASE If you **give notice** or **hand in notice** you tell your employer that you intend to leave your job soon, within a set period of time. You can also **give in** your **notice** or **hand in your notice**. [BUSINESS] ❑ *He handed in his notice at the bank and ruined his promising career.* ⑪ PHRASE If you **take notice of** a particular fact or situation, you behave in a way that shows that you are aware of it. ❑ *We want the government to take notice of what we think they should do for single parents.* ⑫ PHRASE If you **take no notice of** someone or something, you do not consider them to be important enough to affect what you think or what you do. ❑ *They took no notice of him, he did not stand out, he was in no way remarkable.*

Thesaurus		*notice의 참조어*
v.	note, observe, perceive, see	①
N.	advertisement, announcement	② ④ ⑤

Word Partnership		*notice의 연어*
N.	notice **a change**, notice **a difference** ①	
v.	**begin to** notice, **fail to** notice, **pretend not to** notice ①	
	receive notice, **serve** notice ③	
	give notice ③ ⑨ ⑩	

</td><td>

❑ 문제는 그림 자체이다. 너무 작고 평범하다. 사실 너무 허술하다. ③ 부정(不定)대명사-부정(否定) 공짜 비슷한 것 ❑ 가구는 초라했다. 거의 공짜로 구한 것이 분명했다. ④ 부정(不定)대명사-부정(否定) ~이 전혀 아니다 ❑ 호수 주위의 시골은 대체로 지극히 평범하다. ❑ 그에 대해서 특별한 것이라고는 없었다. ⑤ 부정(不定)대명사-부정(否定) ~만한 것은 없다 [강조] ❑ 젊은 사람들에겐 체제를 깨부수는 것만큼 빨리 배우는 것이 없다. ❑ 작곡보다 내 인생에서 더 중요한 것은 없다. ⑥ 구 전부이거나 아니거나 ❑ 그가 이것을 하든지 말든지 둘 중에 하나였다. 전부이거나 아니거나였다. ⑦ 구 없는 것보다는 낫다 ❑ 사실 15분이라도 운동을 하는 것이 하지 않는 것보다는 낫다. ⑧ 구 ~만, 오직 ~뿐 ❑ 그 돈이 가져온 것이라고는 슬픔과 불행과 비극뿐이었다. ❑ 그 때문에 우리는 웃음거리로 전락하였다. ⑨ 구 ~을 할 수밖에 없다 [영국영어] ❑ 어떤 재료를 선택하느냐가 매우 중요하다. 스스로 맛을 보고 실험해 보는 수밖에 없다. ⑩ 관용 표현 별 말씀을요 [의례적인 표현] ❑ "너무 맛있는 저녁 식사에 대해 감사드립니다." "별 말씀을요." 사라는 말했다. ⑪ 구 거짓말이다, 사실이 아니다 ❑ 다 헛소리이고 미신이며 거짓말이다. ⑫ 구 매우 쉽다 ❑ 예전에 팬케이크 만드는 걸 겁이 나서 못해 봤다면, 더 이상 미루지 마세요. 그것 같이 쉬운 게 없거든요. ⑬ 구 막상막하다 ❑ 우리가 점수를 얻을 때까지는 비등했다. ⑭ 구 그런 건 전혀 아니다 [강조] ❑ "이것에 대해서 내 사무실에서 이야기를 하죠." "그런 일은 없을 겁니다."

---

① 타동사/자동사 감지하다, 알아채다 ❑ 최근 행크햄에서 낯선 사람을 봤을 경우 주저하지 말고 경찰에 연락을 해야 한다고 그는 강조했다. ❑ 대부분의 학자들이 여름에 논문을 쓴다는 사실을 발견했다. ❑ 다행히 네가 차를 어디다 두는지 내가 봤었다. ② 가산명사 공고, 안내문 ❑ 대기실의 표지판은 금연하고 침을 뱉지 말 것을 요청했다. ❑ 여러 민박집에 "빈 방 없음"이라는 표지가 창문에 붙어 있었다. ③ 불가산명사 통보 ❑ 이자는 매달 붙는다. 출금을 위해선 석 달 전에 통보를 해야 한다. ❑ 노조는 쟁의 행위에 대해 7일 전에 통보해야 한다. ④ 가산명사 공고 ❑ 블레이크의 죽음에 대해 글로브지에 전화를 했고 타임스 지의 인물란에 공고를 실었다. ⑤ 가산명사 공문 ❑ 상여금 공문이 본사에서 지점으로 매년 발송되었다. ⑥ 가산명사 비평문 ❑ 어쨌든 읽지 않는다고 해도 좋은 평을 받는 것은 기분 좋은 일이다. ⑦ 구 예고, 통지 ❑ 그렇게 짧은 기간을 두고 통지를 하면 그녀의 반을 맡을 사람을 구할 수가 없다. ⑧ 구 추가 통지가 있을 때까지 ❑ 안 좋은 소식은 모든 란조우 행 항공편이 추가 통지가 있을 때까지 취소되었다는 것이었다. ⑨ 구 해고를 통지하다 [경제] ❑ 다음날 아침 나는 그에게 전화해 해고를 통지했다. ⑩ 구 사표를 내다 [경제] ❑ 그는 은행에 사표를 제출하고 촉망받는 앞날을 망쳤다. ⑪ 구 주목하다 ❑ 우리는 정부가 한 부모들을 위해 무엇을 해야 하는지에 대한 우리의 생각을 주목해 주길 바란다. ⑫ 구 관심을 두지 않다 ❑ 그들은 그에게 관심을 두지 않았다. 그는 눈에 띄지도 않았으며 전혀 특출하지도 않았다.

</td></tr>
</table>

no|tice|able /nóutɪsəbəl/ ADJ Something that is **noticeable** is very obvious, so that it is easy to see, hear, or recognize. ❑ *It is noticeable that women do not have the rivalry that men have.* ● **no|tice|ably** ADV ❑ *Standards of living were deteriorating rather noticeably.*

형용사 두드러지는 ❑ 여성들에겐 남성들이 가지는 경쟁의식이 없다는 것이 두드러진다. ● 두드러지게 부사 ❑ 생활수준이 꽤 두드러지게 악화되고 있었다.

Word Partnership   noticeable의 연어

ADV.	**barely** noticeable, **hardly** noticeable, **less** noticeable, **more** noticeable
N.	noticeable **change**, noticeable **difference**, noticeable **improvement**

---

no|tice|board /nóutɪsbɔrd/ (**noticeboards**) N-COUNT A **noticeboard** is a board which is usually attached to a wall in order to display notices giving information about something. [BRIT; AM **bulletin board**] ❑ *She added her name to the list on the noticeboard.*

가산명사 게시판 [영국영어; 미국영어 bulletin board] ❑ 그녀는 게시판에 있는 목록에 자신의 이름을 추가했다.

no|ti|fi|ca|tion /nóutɪfɪkeɪʃən/ (**notifications**) N-VAR If you are given **notification** of something, you are officially informed of it. ❑ *Names of the dead and injured are being withheld pending notification of relatives.*

가산명사 또는 불가산명사 통지 ❑ 친척들에게 통지가 이루어질 때까지 사상자의 이름은 공개되지 않고 있다.

no|ti|fy /nóutɪfaɪ/ (**notifies, notifying, notified**) V-T If you **notify** someone of something, you officially inform them about it. [FORMAL] ❑ *The skipper notified the coastguard of the tragedy.* ❑ *Earlier this year they were notified that their homes were to be cleared away.*

타동사 통지하다 [격식체] ❑ 선장은 해안 경비대에게 그 비극을 통지했다. ❑ 올해 초에 그들은 자신들의 집이 철거될 것이라는 통지를 받았다.

no|tion ♦♢♢ /nóuʃən/ (**notions**) N-COUNT A **notion** is an idea or belief about something. ❑ *We each have a notion of just what kind of person we'd like to be.* ❑ *I reject absolutely the notion that privatization of our industry is now inevitable.*

가산명사 생각 ❑ 본인이 어떤 사람이 되고 싶은지에 대해서는 우리 각자 생각을 가지고 있다. ❑ 우리 업계의 민영화가 불가피하다는 생각에 나는 절대적으로 반대한다.

Thesaurus   notion의 참조어

N.	concept, idea, opinion, thought

---

no|to|ri|ety /nóutəraɪɪti/ N-UNCOUNT To achieve **notoriety** means to become well-known for something bad. ❑ *He achieved notoriety as chief counsel to President Nixon in the Watergate break-in.*

불가산명사 악명 ❑ 그는 워터게이트 침입 사건 당시 닉슨 대통령의 자문 대표로서 악명을 얻었다.

no|to|ri|ous /noutɔ́riəs/ ADJ To be **notorious** means to be well-known for something bad. ❑ *...an area notorious for drugs, crime, and violence.* ● **no|to|ri|ous|ly** ADV ❑ *The train company is overstaffed and notoriously inefficient.* ❑ *He worked mainly in New York City where living space is notoriously at a premium.*

형용사 악명 높은 ❑ 마약, 범죄, 폭력 등으로 악명 높은 지역 ● 악명 높게 부사 ❑ 철도 회사는 인원이 남아돌고 비효율적인 것으로 악명이 높다. ❑ 그는 주거 공간이 구하기 힘들기로 악명 높은 뉴욕 시에서 주로 일했다.

A **famous** person or thing is known to more people than a **well-known** one. A **notorious** person or thing is famous because they are connected with something bad or undesirable. **Infamous** is not the opposite of **famous**. It has a similar meaning to **notorious**, but is a stronger word. Someone or something that is **notable** is important or interesting.

famous한 사람이나 사물은 well-known한 사람이나 사물보다 더 많은 사람들에게 알려져 있다. notorious한 사람이나 사물은 나쁘거나 바람직하지 않은 것과 연관되어 있기 때문에 유명하다. infamous는 '유명하다(famous)'의 반대말이 아니라, '악명 높다(notorious)'와 비슷한 뜻이며 더 강한 말이다. notable한 사람이나 사물은 중요하거나 흥미로움을 나타낸다.

---

not|with|stand|ing /nɒtwɪθstændɪŋ, -wɪð-/ PREP If something is true **notwithstanding** something else, it is true in spite of that other thing. [FORMAL] ❑ *He despised William Pitt, notwithstanding the similar views they both held.* ● ADV **Notwithstanding** is also an adverb. [N ADV] ❑ *His relations with colleagues, differences of opinion notwithstanding, were unfailingly friendly.*

전치사 ~에도 불구하고 [격식체] ❑ 둘이 비슷한 견해를 가지고 있음에도 불구하고 그는 윌리엄 피트를 경멸했다. ● 부사 ~에도 불구하고 ❑ 견해 차이에도 불구하고 그와 직장 동료들과의 관계는 틀림없이 우호적이었다.

nought /nɔt/ (**noughts**) NUM **Nought** is the number 0. [mainly BRIT; AM usually **zero**] ❑ *Sales rose by nought point four per cent last month.* ❑ *Houses are graded from nought to ten for energy efficiency.*

수사 영, 0 [주로 영국영어; 미국영어 대개 zero] ❑ 지난달에 판매가 0.4퍼센트 증가했다. ❑ 주택은 에너지 효율성을 기준으로 0부터 10까지 등급이 매겨진다.

noun /naʊn/ (**nouns**) N-COUNT A **noun** is a word such as "car," "love," or "Anne" which is used to refer to a person or thing. →see also **count noun, proper noun**

가산명사 명사

nour|ish /nɜ́rɪʃ, BRIT nʌrɪʃ/ (**nourishes, nourishing, nourished**) V-T To **nourish** a person, animal, or plant means to provide them with the food that is necessary for life, growth, and good health. ❑ *The food she eats nourishes both her and the baby.* ● **nour|ish|ing** ADJ ❑ *Most of these nourishing substances are in the yolk of the egg.*

타동사 영양분을 공급하다 ❑ 그녀가 섭취하는 음식이 본인과 아기에게 영양분을 공급한다. ● 영양가가 있는 형용사 ❑ 이 영양소 중 대부분은 계란의 노른자위에 있다.

nour|ish|ment /nɜ́rɪʃmənt, BRIT nʌrɪʃmənt/ **1** N-UNCOUNT If something provides a person, animal, or plant with **nourishment**, it provides them with the food that is necessary for life, growth, and good health. ❑ *The mother provides the embryo with nourishment and a place to grow.* **2** N-UNCOUNT The action of nourishing someone or something, or the experience of being nourished, can be referred to as **nourishment**. ❑ *Sugar gives quick relief to hunger but provides no lasting nourishment.*

1 불가산명사 자양분 ❑ 엄마는 태아에게 자양분과 자랄 수 있는 곳을 제공한다. **2** 불가산명사 영양 공급 ❑ 설탕은 허기를 금방 해결해 주지만 지속적인 영양 공급원이 되지는 않는다.

Nov. Nov. is a written abbreviation for **November**. ❑ *The first ballot is on Tuesday Nov. 20.*

11월 ❑ 투표는 11월 20일 화요일에 시작한다.

Word Link   nov ≈ new : in**nov**ate, **nov**el, re**nov**ate

---

nov|el ♦♦♢ /nɒ́vəl/ (**novels**) **1** N-COUNT A **novel** is a long written story about imaginary people and events. ❑ *...a novel by Herman Hesse.* **2** ADJ **Novel** things are new and different from anything that has been done, experienced, or made before. ❑ *Protesters found a novel way of demonstrating against steeply rising oil prices.* →see **library**

1 가산명사 소설 ❑ 헤르만 헤세의 소설 **2** 형용사 새로운 ❑ 시위자들은 급격히 오르는 유가를 반대할 수 있는 새로운 방식을 발견했다.

nov|el|ist /nɒ́vəlɪst/ (**novelists**) N-COUNT A **novelist** is a person who writes novels. ❑ *The key to success as a romantic novelist is absolute belief in your story.* →see **fantasy**

가산명사 소설가 ❑ 낭만적 소설가로 성공하는 열쇠는 자신의 이야기를 전적으로 믿는 것이다.

nov|el|ty /nɒ́vəlti/ (**novelties**) **1** N-UNCOUNT **Novelty** is the quality of being different, new, and unusual. ❑ *In the contemporary western world, rapidly changing*

1 불가산명사 새로움 ❑ 현대 서구 세계에서 스타일의 급격한 변화는 새로움과 개인주의에 대한 욕구를

styles cater to a desire for novelty and individualism. ◆2 N-COUNT A **novelty** is something that is new and therefore interesting. ❑ Seeing people queuing for food was a novelty. ◆3 N-COUNT **Novelties** are cheap toys, ornaments, or other objects that are sold as presents or souvenirs. ❑ At Easter, we give them plastic eggs filled with small toys, novelties, and coins.

충족시키기 위한 것이다. ◆2 가산명사 새로운 것 ❑ 식품을 구하기 위해 사람들이 줄을 서는 광경은 새로웠다. ◆3 가산명사 색다른 물건 ❑ 부활절에 우리는 작은 장난감, 특이한 물건, 동전 등을 채운 플라스틱 달걀을 준다.

No|vem|ber ♦♦♦ /nouvɛmbər/ (Novembers) N-VAR **November** is the eleventh month of the year in the Western calendar. ❑ He arrived in London in November 1939.

가산명사 또는 불가산명사 11월 ❑ 그는 1939년 11월에 런던에 도착했다.

nov|ice /nɒvɪs/ (novices) ◆1 N-COUNT A **novice** is someone who has been doing a job or other activity for only a short time and so is not experienced at it. ❑ I'm a novice at these things, Lieutenant. You're the professional. ◆2 N-COUNT In a monastery or convent, a **novice** is a person who is preparing to become a monk or nun.

◆1 가산명사 초보자 ❑ 나는 이런 것에 초보라네, 대위. 자네가 전문가지. ◆2 가산명사 수련 수사; 수련 수녀

now ♦♦♦ /naʊ/ ◆1 ADV You use **now** to refer to the present time, often in contrast to a time in the past or the future. ❑ She's a widow now. ❑ But we are now a much more fragmented society. ● PRON **Now** is also a pronoun. ❑ Now is the time when we must all live as economically as possible. ◆2 ADV If you do something **now**, you do it immediately. ❑ [ADV after v] I'm sorry, but I must go now. ● PRON **Now** is also a pronoun. ❑ Now is your chance to talk to him. ◆3 CONJ You use **now** or **now that** to indicate that an event has occurred and as a result something else may or will happen. ❑ Now you're settled, why don't you take up some serious study? ◆4 ADV You use **now** to indicate that a particular situation is the result of something that has recently happened. ❑ Mrs. Chandra has received one sweater for each of her five children and says that the winter will not be so hard now. ❑ She told me not to repeat it, but now I don't suppose it matters. ◆5 ADV In stories and accounts of past events, **now** is used to refer to the particular time that is being written or spoken about. ❑ She felt a little better now. ❑ It was too late now for Blake to lock his room door. ◆6 ADV You use **now** in statements which specify the length of time up to the present that something has lasted. ❑ They've been married now for 30 years. ❑ They have been missing for a long time now. ◆7 ADV You say "**Now**" or "**Now then**" to indicate to the person or people you are with that you want their attention, or that you are about to change the subject. [SPOKEN] [ADV cl] ❑ "Now then," Max said, "to get back to the point." ❑ Now then, laddie, what's the trouble? ◆8 ADV You use **now** to give a slight emphasis to a request or command. [SPOKEN] [ADV with cl] ❑ Come on now. You know you must be hungry. ❑ Come and sit down here, now. ◆9 ADV You can say "**Now**" to introduce information which is relevant to the part of a story or account that you have reached, and which needs to be known before you can continue. [SPOKEN] [ADV cl] ❑ My son went to Almeria in Southern Spain. Now he and his wife are people who love a quiet holiday. ◆10 ADV You say "**Now**" to introduce something which contrasts with what you have just said. [SPOKEN] [ADV cl] ❑ Now, if it was me, I'd want to do more than just change the locks. ◆11 PHRASE If you say that something happens **now and then** or **every now and again**, you mean that it happens sometimes but not very often or regularly. ❑ My father has a collection of magazines to which I return every now and then. ◆12 PHRASE If you say that something will happen **any day now**, **any moment now**, or **any time now**, you mean that it will happen very soon. ❑ Jim expects to be sent to Europe any day now. ◆13 PHRASE People such as television presenters sometimes use **now for** when they are going to start talking about a different subject or start presenting a new activity. [SPOKEN] ❑ And now for something completely different. ◆14 PHRASE **Just now** means a very short time ago. [SPOKEN] ❑ You looked pretty upset just now. ❑ I spoke just now of being in love. ◆15 PHRASE You use **just now** when you want to say that a particular situation exists at the time when you are speaking, although it may change in the future. [SPOKEN] ❑ I'm pretty busy just now.

◆1 부사 이제 ❑ 그녀는 이제 과부이다. ❑ 하지만 우리는 이제 훨씬 분화된 사회이다. ● 대명사 지금 ❑ 지금이야말로 우리 모두 최대한 경제적으로 살아야 하는 시기이다. ◆2 부사 지금 ❑ 미안하지만 나는 지금 가야 해. ● 대명사 지금 ❑ 지금이 네가 그에게 말을 할 수 있는 기회이다. ◆3 접속사 이제 ❑ 이제 자리를 잡았으니 공부를 제대로 해 보는 것이 어때? ◆4 부사 이제 ❑ 찬드라 부인은 자녀 다섯 명 각각을 위한 스웨터를 하나씩 받았으니 이제 겨울이 그렇게 힘들지는 않을 것이라고 한다. ❑ 그녀는 내게 그것을 발설하지 말라고 했지만 이제는 상관이 없는 것 같다. ◆5 부사 이제 ❑ 그녀는 이제 조금 나은 것 같았다. ❑ 블레이크가 자신의 방문을 잠그기에는 이제 너무 늦어 있었다. ◆6 부사 이제 ❑ 그들은 이제 결혼 생활을 30년간 했다. ❑ 그들이 실종된 지 이제 꽤 되었다. ◆7 부사 자 [구어체] ❑ "자, 주제로 돌아가서." 맥스는 말했다. ❑ 자, 어린 친구, 뭐가 문제인가? ◆8 부사 어서 [구어체] ❑ 자, 어서. 배고플 것 같은데. ❑ 와서 여기 앉아, 어서. ◆9 부사 이제 [구어체] ❑ 아들이 남부 스페인의 알메리아에 갔어. 이제 아들과 며느리는 조용한 휴가를 즐기는 사람들이란 말이야. ◆10 부사 그런데 [구어체] ❑ 그런데 나라면 단순히 자물쇠를 바꾸는 것 이상을 하고 싶을 것 같아. ◆11 구 이따금 ❑ 내가 이따금 뒤져 보는 잡지 모음을 아버지께서 가지고 계셔. ◆12 구 조만간 ❑ 짐은 조만간 유럽으로 파견될 것으로 예상한다. ◆13 구 이제 [구어체] ❑ 이제 완전히 다른 것을 선보이겠다. ◆14 구 방금 [구어체] ❑ 너 방금 상당히 속상해 보이던데. ❑ 나는 방금 사랑에 빠진 것에 대해 이야기했다. ◆15 구 지금 [구어체] ❑ 나 지금 꽤 바빠.

nowa|days /naʊədeɪz/ ADV **Nowadays** means at the present time, in contrast with the past. [ADV with cl] ❑ Nowadays it's acceptable for women to be ambitious. But it wasn't then.

부사 요즘 ❑ 요즘은 여자가 야망을 가지는 것이 용납된다. 하지만 그때는 안 그랬다.

no|where ♦♢♢ /nouwɛər/ ◆1 ADV You use **nowhere** to emphasize that a place has more of a particular quality than any other place, or that it is the only place where something happens or exists. [EMPHASIS] ❑ Nowhere is language a more serious issue than in Hawaii. ❑ This kind of forest exists nowhere else in the world. ◆2 ADV You use **nowhere** when making negative statements to say that a suitable place of the specified kind does not exist. ❑ There was nowhere to hide and nowhere to run. ❑ I have nowhere else to go, nowhere in the world. ◆3 ADV You use **nowhere** to indicate that something or someone cannot be seen or found. ❑ Michael glanced anxiously down the corridor, but Wilfred was nowhere to be seen. ❑ The escaped prisoner was nowhere in sight. ◆4 ADV You can use **nowhere** to refer in a general way to small, unimportant, or uninteresting places. ❑ ...endless paths that led nowhere in particular. ◆5 ADV If you say that something or someone appears **from nowhere** or **out of nowhere**, you mean that they appear suddenly and unexpectedly. [from/out of ADV] ❑ A car came from nowhere, and I had to jump back into the hedge just in time. ◆6 ADV You use **nowhere** to mean not in any part of a text, speech, or argument. [EMPHASIS] ❑ He nowhere offers concrete historical background to support his arguments. ❑ Point taken, but nowhere did we suggest that this yacht's features were unique. ◆7 PHRASE If you say that a place is **in the middle of nowhere**, you mean that it is a long way from other places. ❑ At dusk we pitched camp in the middle of nowhere. ◆8 PHRASE If you use **nowhere near** in front of a word or expression, you are emphasizing that the real situation is very different from, or has not yet reached, the state which that word or expression suggests. [EMPHASIS] ❑ He's nowhere near recovered yet from his experiences.

◆1 부사 아무 데도 -이 없다 [강조] ❑ 하와이에서만큼 언어가 심각한 사안이 되는 곳은 없다. ❑ 이런 종류의 숲은 세상 다른 어느 곳에서도 존재하지 않는다. ◆2 부사 아무 데도 없다 ❑ 숨을 곳도 도망갈 곳도 없었다. ❑ 나는 달리 갈 곳이, 이 세상 어디에도 갈 곳이 없다. ◆3 부사 어디에도 -이 없다 ❑ 마이클은 불안해하며 복도 끝을 쳐다봤으나 윌프레드는 어디에도 보이지 않았다. ❑ 탈옥수는 어디에도 없었다. ◆4 부사 별 볼일 없는 곳 ❑ 딱히 별 볼일 없는 곳으로 이어진 끝없는 길들 ◆5 부사 난데없이 ❑ 차가 난데없이 나타나서 나는 가까스로 생울타리 쪽으로 피해냈다. ◆6 부사 어디에도 -이 없다 [강조] ❑ 그는 어디에서도 자신의 주장을 뒷받침하기 위한 구체적 역사적 배경을 제시하지 않는다. ❑ 요점은 알겠지만 우리는 어디서도 이 요트의 특징들이 독특하다고 말한 적은 없다. ◆7 구 외딴 곳에 ❑ 해질 무렵에 우리는 근처에 인가라곤 없는 곳에 텐트를 쳤다. ◆8 구 -와는 거리가 먼 [강조] ❑ 그는 자신의 경험에서 전혀 회복하지 못했다.

Word Partnership   nowhere의 연어

V.   nowhere **to be found**, nowhere **to be seen**, *have* nowhere **to go**, *have* nowhere **to hide**, *have* nowhere **to run** ◆2 ◆3
go nowhere ◆4

no-win situation (**no-win situations**) N-COUNT If you are in a **no-win situation**, any action you take will fail to benefit you in any way. ❑ *It was a no-win situation. Either she pretended she hated Ned and felt awful or admitted she loved him and felt even worse!*

nu|ance /nuɑns, BRIT nyuːɑːns/ (**nuances**) N-VAR A **nuance** is a small difference in sound, feeling, appearance, or meaning. ❑ *We can use our eyes and facial expressions to communicate virtually every subtle nuance of emotion there is.*

nu|clear ♦♦◇ /nukliər, BRIT nyuːkliəʳ/ ■ ADJ **Nuclear** means relating to the nuclei of atoms, or to the energy released when these nuclei are split or combined. [ADJ n] ❑ *...a nuclear power station.* ❑ *...nuclear energy.* ◻ ADJ **Nuclear** means relating to weapons that explode by using the energy released when the nuclei of atoms are split or combined. [ADJ n] ❑ *They rejected a demand for the removal of all nuclear weapons from UK soil.* →see **energy**

nu|clear re|ac|tor (**nuclear reactors**) N-COUNT A **nuclear reactor** is a machine which is used to produce nuclear energy or the place where this machine and other related machinery and equipment is kept. ❑ *Germany has decided to shut its last Soviet-designed nuclear reactor this weekend for safety reasons.*

nu|cleus /nukliəs, BRIT nyuːkliəs/ (**nuclei**) /nukliaɪ, BRIT nyuːkliaɪ/ ■ N-COUNT The **nucleus** of an atom or cell is the central part of it. ❑ *Neutrons and protons are bound together in the nucleus of an atom.* ◻ N-COUNT **The nucleus of** a group of people or things is the small number of members which form the most important part of the group. ❑ *The Civic Movement could be the nucleus of a centrist party of the future.*

nude /nud, BRIT nyuːd/ (**nudes**) ■ ADJ A **nude** person is not wearing any clothes. [ADJ n, v-link ADJ] ❑ *The occasional nude bather comes here.* ● PHRASE If you do something **in the nude**, you are not wearing any clothes. If you paint or draw someone **in the nude**, they are not wearing any clothes. ❑ *Sleeping in the nude, if it suits you, is not a bad idea.* ◻ N-COUNT A **nude** is a picture or statue of a person who is not wearing any clothes. A **nude** is also a person in a picture who is not wearing any clothes. ❑ *He was one of Australia's most distinguished artists, renowned for his portraits, landscapes and nudes.*

nudge /nʌdʒ/ (**nudges, nudging, nudged**) ■ V-T If you **nudge** someone, you push them gently, usually with your elbow, in order to draw their attention to something. ❑ *I nudged Stan and pointed again.* ● N-COUNT **Nudge** is also a noun. ❑ *She slipped her arm under his and gave him a nudge.* ◻ V-T If you **nudge** someone or something into a place or position, you gently push them there. ❑ *Edna Swinson nudged him into the sitting room.* ● N-COUNT **Nudge** is also a noun. ❑ *McKinnon gave the wheel another slight nudge to starboard.* ◻ V-T If you **nudge** someone into doing something, you gently persuade them to do it. ❑ *Bit by bit Bob had nudged Fritz into selling his controlling interest.* ❑ *Foreigners must use their power not simply to punish the country but to nudge it towards greater tolerance.* ● N-COUNT **Nudge** is also a noun. ❑ *I had a feeling that the challenge appealed to him. All he needed was a nudge.*

nu|dity /nudɪti, BRIT nyuːdɪti/ N-UNCOUNT **Nudity** is the state of wearing no clothes. ❑ *...constant nudity and bad language on TV.*

nui|sance /nusᵊns, BRIT nyuːsᵊns/ (**nuisances**) N-COUNT If you say that someone or something is a **nuisance**, you mean that they annoy you or cause you a lot of problems. ❑ *He could be a bit of a nuisance when he was drunk.* ❑ *Sorry to be a nuisance.* ● PHRASE If someone **makes a nuisance of** themselves, they behave in a way that annoys other people.

null /nʌl/ PHRASE If an agreement, a declaration, or the result of an election is **null and void**, it is not legally valid. ❑ *A spokeswoman said the agreement had been declared null and void.* →see **zero**

numb /nʌm/ (**numbs, numbing, numbed**) ■ ADJ If a part of your body is **numb**, you cannot feel anything there. ❑ *He could feel his fingers growing numb at their tips.* ● **numb|ness** N-UNCOUNT ❑ *I have recently been suffering from pain and numbness in my hands.* ◻ ADJ If you are **numb** with shock, fear, or grief, you are so shocked, frightened, or upset that you cannot think clearly or feel any emotion. ❑ *The mother, numb with grief, has trouble speaking.* ● **numb|ness** N-UNCOUNT ❑ *Many men become more aware of emotional numbness in their 40s.* ◻ V-T If an event or experience **numbs** you, you can no longer think clearly or feel any emotion. ❑ *For a while the shock of Philippe's letter numbed her.* ● **numbed** ADJ ❑ *I'm so numbed with shock that I can hardly think.* ◻ V-T If cold weather, a drug, or a blow **numbs** a part of your body, you can no longer feel anything in it. ❑ *The cold numbed my fingers.* ❑ *An injection of local anesthetic is usually given first to numb the area.*

num|ber ♦♦♦ /nʌmbər/ (**numbers, numbering, numbered**) ■ N-COUNT A **number** is a word such as "two," "nine," or "twelve," or a symbol such as 1, 3, or 47. You use numbers to say how many things you are referring to or where something comes in a series. ❑ *No, I don't know the room number.* ❑ *Stan Laurel was born at number 3, Argyll Street.* ◻ N-COUNT You use **number** with words such as "large" or "small" to say approximately how many things or people there are. ❑ *Quite a considerable number of interviews are going on.* ❑ *I have had an enormous number of letters from single parents.* ◻ N-SING If there are **a number of** things or people, there are several of them. If there are **any number of** things or people, there is a large quantity of them. ❑ *I seem to remember that Sam told a number of lies.* ◻ N-UNCOUNT You can refer to someone's or something's position in a list of the most successful or most popular of a particular type of thing as, for example, **number** one or **number** two. ❑ *Martin now faces the world number one, Jansher Khan of Pakistan.* ❑ *Before you knew it, the single was at Number 90 in the U.S.*

가산명사 승산이 없는 상황, 이럴 수도 저럴 수도 없는 상황 ❑ 승산이 없는 상황이었다. 그녀는 자신이 네드를 싫어한다고 가장하면서 자신의 기분을 망치든지 아니면 그를 사랑한다는 것을 인정하고 더 기분 나빠하는 것밖에 없다!

가산명사 또는 불가산명사 미묘한 차이, 뉘앙스 ❑ 우리는 눈과 표정을 사용하여 감정의 거의 모든 미묘한 차이를 전달할 수 있다.

■ 형용사 핵의 ❑ 핵발전소 ❑ 핵에너지 ◻ 형용사 핵의 ❑ 그들은 영국 영토에서 모든 핵무기를 제거하라는 요구를 거절했다.

가산명사 원자로 ❑ 독일은 안전성의 이유로 이번 주말에 소련이 설계한 마지막 원자로를 폐쇄하기로 결정했다.

■ 가산명사 핵 ❑ 중성자와 양성자가 원자의 핵에 같이 묶여 있다. ◻ 가산명사 구심점, 핵심 ❑ 시민운동이 미래의 중도파 정당의 구심점이 될 수 있다.

■ 형용사 발가벗은 ❑ 이곳에 종종 나체 수영객이 나타난다. ❑ 만약 발가벗고 자는 것이 편하다면 나쁜 생각은 아니다. ◻ 가산명사 나체화, 누드화 ❑ 그는 초상화, 풍경화, 나체화 등으로 유명한 호주의 가장 저명한 화가 중 하나였다.

■ 타동사 팔꿈치로 슬쩍 찌르다 ❑ 나는 팔꿈치로 스탠을 슬쩍 찌르고 다시 손가락으로 가리켰다. ● 가산명사 팔꿈치로 슬쩍 찌르기 ❑ 그녀는 자신의 팔을 그의 팔 밑으로 살짝 밀어 넣으며 팔꿈치로 그를 슬쩍 찔렀다. ◻ 타동사 살살 밀다 ❑ 에드나 스윈슨은 그를 거실로 살살 밀었다. ● 가산명사 살살 밀기 ❑ 맥키넌은 바퀴를 다시 우현 쪽으로 살짝 밀었다. ◻ 타동사 살살 설득하다 ❑ 조금씩 밥은 프릿츠가 그의 지배적 지분을 팔도록 살살 설득했다. ❑ 외국 국가들은 그 나라를 힘을 이용해 간단히 처벌할 것이 아니라 보다 관용이 있는 사회로 나아갈 수 있도록 살살 설득해야 한다. ● 가산명사 살살 설득함 ❑ 그 도전이 그의 구미를 당기는 인상을 받았다. 조금만 더 설득하면 될 것 같았다.

불가산명사 벌거숭이, 알몸 상태 ❑ 텔레비전에 나오는 끝없는 알몸 노출과 욕설

가산명사 골칫덩이 ❑ 그는 술 취하면 좀 골칫덩이가 되는 경향이 있었다. ❑ 골치 아프게 해서 미안해요. ● 구 골칫거리가 되다

구 무효한 ❑ 대변인은 그 협약이 무효 선언되었다고 했다.

■ 형용사 감각을 잃은, (손, 발이) 곱은 ❑ 그는 손가락 끝이 점점 감각을 잃는 것을 느꼈다. ● 무감각, 마비 증세 불가산명사 ❑ 나는 최근 양손의 통증과 마비 증세로 고통받고 있다. ◻ 형용사 (충격으로) 무감각해진 ❑ 슬픔에 무감각해진 그 어머니는 말을 잘 못한다. ● 무감각 불가산명사 ❑ 많은 남자들이 40대가 되면 감정적으로 무감각해지는 것을 보다 더 많이 인식하게 된다. ◻ 타동사 무감각하게 만들다 ❑ 필립의 편지로 받은 충격 때문에 그녀는 한동안 아무 감각을 느낄 수가 없었다. ● 무감각해진 형용사 ❑ 나는 너무 충격을 받아 무감각해져서 생각도 제대로 못하겠다. ◻ 타동사 감각을 잃게 만들다, 마비시키다 ❑ 추위로 손가락이 곱아 감각이 없어졌다. ❑ 그 부위를 마비시키기 위해 대체로 먼저 국소 마취제를 주사한다.

■ 가산명사 숫자, 번호 ❑ 아니, 방 번호를 몰라. ❑ 스탠 로렐은 아가일 가 3번지에 태어났다. ◻ 가산명사 수 ❑ 상당히 많은 인터뷰가 진행되고 있다. ❑ 혼자 아이를 키우는 부모들로부터 엄청난 양의 편지를 받았다. ◻ 단수명사 수 ❑ 샘이 패 많은 거짓말을 했던 걸로 기억난다. ◻ 불가산명사 등위 ❑ 마틴은 이제 세계 1위인 파키스탄의 잰셔 칸과 대적할 것이다. ❑ 부지불식간에 그 싱글은 미국 싱글 차트 90위에 가 있었다. ◻ 타동사 모두 _이 되다 ❑ 그들은 내게 자기들 마을 주민 수가 총 100명이라고 했다. ◻ 가산명사 전화번호 ❑ 이름과 전화번호 목록 ❑ 내 전화번호는 414-3925이다. ◻ 가산명사 곡, 노래 ❑ 1951년에 쓰이고 연주된 노래인 '언포게터블' ◻ 타동사 -에 속하다 [격식체] ❑ 레스터 스완녹톤

A

singles charts. **5** V-T If a group of people or things **numbers** a particular total, that is how many there are. ❑ *They told me that their village numbered 100.* **6** N-COUNT A **number** is the series of numbers that you dial when you are making a telephone call. ❑ *...a list of names and telephone numbers.* ❑ *My number is 414-3925.* **7** N-COUNT You can refer to a short piece of music, a song, or a dance as a **number**. ❑ *..."Unforgettable," a number that was written and performed in 1951.* **8** V-T If someone or something **is numbered among** a particular group, they are believed to belong to that group. [FORMAL] ❑ *The Leicester Swannington Railway is numbered among Britain's railway pioneers.* **9** V-T If you **number** something, you mark it with a number, usually starting at 1. ❑ *He cut his paper up into tiny squares, and he numbered each one.* **10** →see also **serial number**
→see **mathematics**, **zero**

num|ber one (**number ones**) **1** ADJ **Number one** means better, more important, or more popular than anything else of its kind. [INFORMAL] [ADJ n] ❑ *The economy is the number one issue by far.* **2** N-COUNT In popular music, the **number one** is the best-selling recording in any one week, or the group or person who has made that recording. [INFORMAL] ❑ *Paula is the only artist to achieve four number ones from a debut album.*

num|ber plate (**number plates**) also **numberplate** N-COUNT A **number plate** is a sign on the front and back of a vehicle that shows its registration number. [BRIT; AM **license plate**] ❑ *He drove a Rolls-Royce with a personalized number plate.*

Word Link   numer ≈ number : in**numer**able, **numer**ical, **numer**ous

---

nu|meri|cal /nuːˈmerɪkᵊl, BRIT nyuːˈmeːrɪkᵊl/ ADJ **Numerical** means expressed in numbers or relating to numbers. ❑ *Your job is to group them by letter and put them in numerical order.* ● **nu|meri|cal|ly** ADV ❑ *...a numerically coded color chart.*

nu|mer|ous ♦◇◇ /ˈnuːmərəs, BRIT nyuːˈmeːrəs/ ADJ If people or things are **numerous**, they exist or are present in large numbers. ❑ *Sex crimes were just as numerous as they are today.*

Word Partnership   numerous의 연어

N.   numerous **attempts**, numerous **examples**, numerous **occasions**, numerous **problems**, numerous **times**

---

nun /nʌn/ (**nuns**) N-COUNT A **nun** is a member of a female religious community. ❑ *Mr. Thomas was taught by the Catholic nuns whose school he attended to work and study hard.*

nurse ♦◇◇ /nɜːrs/ (**nurses**, **nursing**, **nursed**) **1** N-COUNT; N-TITLE; N-VOC A **nurse** is a person whose job is to care for people who are ill. ❑ *She had spent 29 years as a nurse.* **2** V-T If you **nurse** someone, you care for them when they are ill. ❑ *All the years he was sick my mother had nursed him.* **3** V-T If you **nurse** an illness or injury, you allow it to get better by resting as much as possible. ❑ *We're going to go home and nurse our colds.* **4** V-T If you **nurse** an emotion or desire, you feel it strongly for a long time. ❑ *Jane still nurses the pain of rejection.*

Word Partnership   nurse의 연어

N.   nurse's **aide**, **visiting** nurse **1**

---

nurse|ry /ˈnɜːrsəri/ (**nurseries**) **1** N-COUNT A **nursery** is a place where children who are not old enough to go to school are cared for. [also at/from/to n] ❑ *She puts her baby in this nursery and then goes back to work.* **2** N-VAR **Nursery** is the same as a **nursery school**. ❑ *An affordable nursery education service is an essential basic amenity.* **3** N-COUNT A **nursery** is a room in a family home in which the young children of the family sleep or play. ❑ *He has painted murals in his children's nursery.* **4** N-COUNT A **nursery** is a place where plants are grown in order to be sold. ❑ *The garden, developed over the past 35 years, includes a nursery.*

nurse|ry school (**nursery schools**) N-VAR A **nursery school** is a school for very young children. ❑ *The availability of nursery school places varies widely across London.*

nurs|ing /ˈnɜːrsɪŋ/ N-UNCOUNT **Nursing** is the profession of caring for people who are ill. ❑ *She had no aptitude for nursing.*

nurs|ing home (**nursing homes**) N-COUNT A **nursing home** is a residence for old or sick people. ❑ *Isaac Binger has died in a nursing home in Florida at the age of 87.*

nur|ture /ˈnɜːrtʃər/ (**nurtures**, **nurturing**, **nurtured**) **1** V-T If you **nurture** something such as a young child or a young plant, you care for it while it is growing and developing. [FORMAL] ❑ *Parents want to know the best way to nurture and raise their child to adulthood.* **2** V-T If you **nurture** plans, ideas, or people, you encourage them or help them to develop. [FORMAL] ❑ *She had always nurtured great ambitions for her son.* ❑ *...parents whose political views were nurtured in the sixties.* **3** N-UNCOUNT **Nurture** is care and encouragement that is given to someone while they are growing and developing. ❑ *The human organism learns partly by nature, partly by nurture.*

nut /nʌt/ (**nuts**) **1** N-COUNT The firm shelled fruit of some trees and bushes are called **nuts**. Some nuts can be eaten. ❑ *Nuts and seeds are good sources of vitamin E.* →see also **peanut** **2** N-COUNT A **nut** is a thick metal ring which you screw onto a metal rod called a bolt. Nuts and bolts are used to hold things such as pieces of machinery together. ❑ *If you want to repair the wheels you just undo the four nuts.* **3** N-COUNT If you describe someone as, for example, a baseball **nut** or a health **nut**, you mean that they are extremely enthusiastic about the thing mentioned. [INFORMAL] ❑ *...Annie, the girlfriend who was a true baseball nut.* **4** ADJ If you are **nuts about** something or someone, you like it very much. [INFORMAL, FEELINGS] [v-link ADJ about n] ❑ *They're nuts about the car.*

철도는 영국의 철도를 개척한 기업들 중 하나로 꼽힌다. **9** 타동사 번호를 매기다 ❑ 그는 종이를 작은 사각 쪽지들로 자르고 각각에 번호를 매겼다.

1 형용사 제일의 [비격식체] ❑ 경제가 단연 최우선 사안이다. **2** 가산명사 1위곡 [비격식체] ❑ 폴라는 데뷔 음반에서 네 개의 1위곡을 낸 유일한 가수이다.

가산명사 번호판 [영국영어; 미국영어 license plate] ❑ 그는 개인적으로 주문한 번호판이 달린 롤스로이스를 몰았다.

형용사 숫자의 ❑ 네 일은 그것들을 글자별로 분류한 다음 번호순으로 정돈하는 것이다. ● 숫자로 부사 ❑ 숫자 코드로 분류된 색깔 도표

형용사 다수의 ❑ 성범죄는 그때도 요즘만큼이나 많았다.

가산명사 수녀 ❑ 토머스 씨는 일을 하면서 열심히 공부하기 위해 다닌 학교의 천주교 수녀들로부터 가르침을 받았다.

1 가산명사; 경칭명사; 호격명사 간호사 ❑ 그녀는 29년을 간호사로 보냈다. **2** 타동사 간호하다 ❑ 그가 아팠던 여러 해 동안 우리 어머니께서 그를 간호하셨다. **3** 타동사 (병을) 다스리다 ❑ 우리는 집에 가서 감기가 나을 수 있도록 쉴 것이다. **4** 타동사 (강한 감정을) 품다 ❑ 제인은 아직도 거절당한 고통을 품고 있다.

1 가산명사 아기방 ❑ 그녀는 아기를 이 아기방에 맡기고 다시 일하러 간다. **2** 가산명사 또는 불가산명사 유치원 ❑ 저렴한 유치원 교육 서비스는 필수 기본 시설이다. **3** 가산명사 아이 방 ❑ 그는 아이들의 방에 벽화를 그렸다. **4** 가산명사 묘장, 종묘원 ❑ 지난 35년에 걸쳐 가꿔 온 그 정원에는 묘상이 있다.

가산명사 또는 불가산명사 유치원 ❑ 유치원에 빈 자리가 있는지의 여부는 런던 내에서도 천차만별이다.

불가산명사 간호 ❑ 그녀는 간호에 전혀 적성이 없었다.

가산명사 양로원 ❑ 아이작 빙어는 87세를 일기로 플로리다의 한 양로원에서 사망했다.

1 타동사 키우다, 양육하다 [격식체] ❑ 부모들은 아이를 성인으로 양육하고 키울 수 있는 최선의 방법을 알고 싶어 한다. **2** 타동사 키우다, 양성하다 [격식체] ❑ 그녀는 항상 아들에 대해 엄청난 야망을 키워 왔다. ❑ 정치적 견해가 60년대에 형성된 부모들 **3** 불가산명사 양육 ❑ 개체로서의 한 인간은 한편으로는 천성으로부터 한편으로는 양육으로부터 배운다.

1 가산명사 견과 ❑ 견과와 씨앗은 비타민 E의 좋은 공급원이다. **2** 가산명사 너트 ❑ 바퀴를 수리하고 싶으면 너트 네 개를 풀기만 하면 된다. **3** 가산명사 -광 [비격식체] ❑ 진짜 야구광이었던 여자 친구, 애니. **4** 형용사 열광하는 [비격식체] ❑ 그들은 그 차에 대해 열광한다. **5** 형용사 미친 [비격식체] ❑ 너희들은 미쳤어. **6** 구 꼭지가 돌다 [비격식체] ❑ 내 몸에 멍이 난 것을 보면 우리 아버지가 완전히 꼭지가 돌 거야.

5 ADJ If you say that someone goes **nuts** or is **nuts**, you mean that they go crazy or are very foolish. [INFORMAL] [v-link ADJ] ❑ *You guys are nuts.* **6** PHRASE If someone **goes nuts**, or in British English **does** their **nut**, they become extremely angry. [INFORMAL] ❑ *My father would go nuts if he saw bruises on me.* →see **peanut**

nu|tri|ent /nutriənt, BRIT nyu:triənt/ (**nutrients**) N-COUNT **Nutrients** are substances that help plants and animals to grow. ❑ *In her first book she explained the role of vegetable fibres, vitamins, minerals, and other essential nutrients.* →see **food**

가산명사 영양소 ❑ 그녀는 첫 번째 책에서 채소의 섬유질, 비타민, 광물질 및 기타 필수 영양소의 역할을 설명했다.

nu|tri|tion /nutrɪʃ°n, BRIT nyu:trɪʃ°n/ N-UNCOUNT **Nutrition** is the process of taking food into the body and absorbing the nutrients in those foods. ❑ *There are alternative sources of nutrition to animal meat.*

불가산명사 영양 섭취 ❑ 육류를 대체할 수 있는 영양 공급원이 있다.

nu|tri|tion|al /nutrɪʃənəl, BRIT nyu:trɪʃənəl/ ADJ The **nutritional** content of food is all the substances that are in it which help you to remain healthy. ❑ *It does sometimes help to know the nutritional content of foods.* ● **nu|tri|tion|al|ly** ADV ❑ *...a nutritionally balanced diet.*

형용사 영양의 ❑ 식품의 영양 성분을 아는 것이 사실 도움이 될 때도 있다. ● 영양적으로 부사 ❑ 영양적으로 균형 잡힌 식사

nu|tri|tious /nutrɪʃəs, BRIT nyu:trɪʃəs/ ADJ **Nutritious** food contains substances which help your body to be healthy. ❑ *It is always important to choose enjoyable, nutritious foods.*

형용사 영양가 있는 ❑ 맛있고 영양가 있는 음식을 고르는 것은 항상 중요하다.

ny|lon /naɪlɒn/ N-UNCOUNT **Nylon** is a strong, flexible artificial fiber. ❑ *Europe's largest producer of nylon is based in Belgium.* →see **rope**

불가산명사 나일론 ❑ 유럽 최대 나일론 생산사는 벨기에에 있다.

a
b
c
d
e
f
g
h
i
j
k
l
m
n
o
p
q
r
s
t
u
v
w
x
y
z

Oo

O, o /<u>oʊ</u>/ (O's, o's) N-VAR **O** is the fifteenth letter of the English alphabet.

oak /<u>oʊ</u>k/ (oaks) N-VAR An **oak** or an **oak tree** is a large tree that often grows in woods and forests and has strong, hard wood. ❑ *Many large oaks were felled during the war.* ● N-UNCOUNT **Oak** is the wood of this tree. ❑ *The cabinet was made of oak and was hand-carved.* →see **plant**

OAP /<u>oʊ</u> eɪ pi/ (OAPs) N-COUNT An **OAP** is a person who is old enough to receive an old age pension from the government. **OAP** is an abbreviation for **old age pensioner**. [BRIT] ❑ *...tickets only £6 each and half that for OAPs and kids.*

oar /<u>ɔr</u>/ (oars) N-COUNT **Oars** are long poles with a wide, flat blade at one end which are used for rowing a boat.

oasis /oʊ<u>eɪ</u>sɪs/ (oases) /oʊ<u>eɪ</u>siz/ ◀ N-COUNT An **oasis** is a small area in a desert where water and plants are found. ◀ N-COUNT You can refer to a pleasant place or situation as an **oasis** when it is surrounded by unpleasant ones. ❑ *The immaculately tended gardens are an oasis in the midst of Cairo's urban sprawl.* →see **desert**

oath /<u>oʊ</u>θ/ (oaths) ◀ N-COUNT An **oath** is a formal promise, especially a promise to be loyal to a person or country. ❑ *He took an oath of loyalty to the government.* ◀ N-SING In a court of law, when someone takes **the oath**, they make a formal promise to tell the truth. You can say that someone is **on oath** or **under oath** when they have made this promise. [the N, also on/under N] ❑ *His girlfriend had gone into the witness box and taken the oath.* ❑ *Under oath, Aston finally admitted that he had lied.*

oat|meal /<u>oʊ</u>tmil/ ◀ N-UNCOUNT **Oatmeal** is a kind of flour made by crushing oats. [oft N n] ❑ *...oatmeal cookies.* ◀ N-UNCOUNT **Oatmeal** is a thick sticky food made from oats cooked in water or milk and eaten hot, especially for breakfast. [mainly AM; BRIT usually **porridge**] ◀ COLOR Something that is **oatmeal** is a pale creamy brown color.

oats /<u>oʊ</u>ts/

The form **oat** is used as a modifier.

N-PLURAL **Oats** are a cereal crop or its grains, used for making cookies or a food called oatmeal, or for feeding animals. ❑ *Oats provide good, nutritious food for horses.* →see **grain**

obe|di|ent /oʊb<u>i</u>diənt/ ADJ A person or animal who is **obedient** does what they are told to do. ❑ *He was very respectful at home and obedient to his parents.* ● **obe|di|ence** N-UNCOUNT ❑ *...unquestioning obedience to the law.* ● **obe|di|ent|ly** ADV [ADV with v] ❑ *He was looking obediently at Keith, waiting for orders.*

obese /oʊb<u>i</u>s/ ADJ If someone is **obese**, they are extremely fat. ❑ *Obese people tend to have higher blood pressure than lean people.* ● **obe|sity** /oʊb<u>i</u>sɪti/ N-UNCOUNT ❑ *...the excessive consumption of sugar that leads to problems of obesity.* →see **fat**, **diet**

obey /oʊb<u>eɪ</u>/ (obeys, obeying, obeyed) V-T/V-I If you **obey** a person, a command, or an instruction, you do what you are told to do. ❑ *Cissie obeyed her mother without question.* ❑ *Most people obey the law.*

Word Partnership	*obey*의 연어
N.	obey **a command**, obey **God**, obey **the law**, obey **orders**, obey **the rules**
V.	**refuse to** obey

obitu|ary /oʊb<u>ɪ</u>tʃuɛri, BRIT oʊb<u>ɪ</u>tʃuəri/ (obituaries) N-COUNT Someone's **obituary** is an account of their life and character which is printed in a newspaper or broadcast soon after they die. ❑ *His obituary was published in one edition of his own newspaper before it was discovered that he was alive.*

ob|ject ◆◆◇ (objects, objecting, objected)

The noun is pronounced /<u>ɒ</u>bdʒɪkt/. The verb is pronounced /əbdʒ<u>ɛ</u>kt/.

◀ N-COUNT An **object** is anything that has a fixed shape or form, that you can touch or see, and that is not alive. ❑ *He squinted his eyes as though he were studying an object on the horizon.* ❑ *...an object the shape of a coconut.* ◀ N-COUNT The **object** of what someone is doing is their aim or purpose. ❑ *The object of the exercise is to raise money for the charity.* ❑ *He made it his object in life to find the island.* ◀ N-COUNT The **object of** a particular feeling or reaction is the person or thing it is

---

가산명사 또는 불가산명사 영어 알파벳의 열다섯 번째 글자

가산명사 또는 불가산명사 오크나무 ❑ 전쟁 중에 큰 오크나무들이 많이 베어 넘겨졌다. ● 불가산명사 오크 재목 ❑ 그 진열장은 오크나무로 만들어졌으며 손으로 조각한 것이었다.

가산명사 노령 연금 수령자 [영국영어] ❑ 한 장에 단돈 6파운드며 연금 수령자와 아이들은 그 반값에 살 수 있는 입장권

가산명사 노

◀ 가산명사 오아시스 ◀ 가산명사 안식처, 위안의 장소 ❑ 흠잡을 데 없이 잘 손질된 그 공원들은 불규칙하게 뻗어 나간 카이로 도회지 한가운데 있는 안식처이다.

◀ 가산명사 맹세, 서약 ❑ 그는 정부에 충성을 맹세했다. ◀ 단수명사 (법정의) 선서 ❑ 그의 여자친구가 증인석으로 들어가 선서를 했었다. ❑ 선서한 상태에서, 애스턴은 결국 자신이 거짓말을 했었다고 자백했다.

◀ 불가산명사 오트밀 ❑ 오트밀 쿠키 ◀ 불가산명사 오트밀 죽 [주로 미국영어; 영국영어 대개 porridge] ◀ 색채어 담황갈색

oat은 수식어구로 쓴다.

복수명사 귀리 ❑ 귀리는 말에게 맛있고 영양 많은 먹이가 된다.

형용사 말 잘 듣는, 고분고분한 ❑ 그는 집에서 매우 예의 바르고 부모님의 말을 잘 들었다. ● 복종, 순종 불가산명사 ❑ 법률에 대한 무조건적인 복종 ● 고분고분하게 부사 ❑ 그는 명령을 기다리며 고분고분하게 키스를 바라보고 있었다.

형용사 살찐, 뚱뚱한 ❑ 뚱뚱한 사람들이 마른 사람들보다 혈압이 높은 경향이 있다. ● 비만, 비대 불가산명사 ❑ 비만 문제의 원인이 되는 과도한 설탕 소비

타동사/자동사 -의 말을 듣다, -에 따르다 ❑ 시시는 의심하지 않고 어머니의 말을 들었다. ❑ 대부분의 사람들이 법을 지킨다.

가산명사 부고 기사 ❑ 그가 살아 있다는 사실이 밝혀지기 전에 그 자신 소유의 신문 한 판에 그의 부고 기사가 실렸다.

명사는 /ɒbdʒɪkt/로 발음되고, 동사는 /əbdʒɛkt/로 발음된다.

◀ 가산명사 물체, 사물 ❑ 그는 지평선에 있는 물체를 주시하기라도 하는 것처럼 눈을 가늘게 떴다. ❑ 코코넛 모양의 물체 ◀ 가산명사 목적, 목표 ❑ 그 행사의 목적은 자선기금을 마련하는 것이다. ❑ 그는 그 섬을 찾는 것을 일생의 목표로 삼았다. ◀ 가산명사 대상 ❑ 그녀의 증오의 대상은 스물네 살짜리 모델 로스

directed toward or that causes it. ❑ *The object of her hatred was 24-year-old model Ros French.* ❑ *The object of great interest at the Temple was a large marble tower built in memory of Buddha.* 🔟 N-COUNT In grammar, the **object** of a verb or a preposition is the word or phrase which completes the structure begun by the verb or preposition. →see also **direct object, indirect object** 🔟 V-T/V-I If you **object** to something, you express your dislike or disapproval of it. ❑ *A lot of people will object to the book.* ❑ *Cullen objected that his small staff would be unable to handle the added work.* 🔟 PHRASE If you say that **money is no object** or **distance is no object**, you are emphasizing that you are willing or able to spend as much money as necessary or travel whatever distance is required. [EMPHASIS] ❑ *This was a very impressive program in which money seems to have been no object.*

프렌치였다. ❑ 그 사원에서 커다란 관심의 대상은 부처를 기리기 위해 세운 큰 대리석 탑이었다.
🔟 가산명사 목적어 🔟 타동사/자동사 반대하다, 이의를 제기하다 ❑ 많은 사람들이 그 책에 이의를 제기할 것이다. ❑ 컬렌은 자신의 소수의 직원들이 추가된 업무를 처리하는 것이 불가능하리라고 반대했다. 🔟 구 비용 불문, 비용은 문제가 안 된다; 거리 불문, 거리는 문제가 안 된다 [강조] ❑ 이것은 돈이 얼마가 들어도 상관없을 듯한 아주 인상적인 프로그램이었다.

Thesaurus   object의 참조어

N.	item, thing 🔟
	aim, goal, intent, purpose 🔟
V.	argue, disagree, oppose, protest against 🔟

Word Partnership   object의 연어

ADJ.	**foreign** object, **inanimate** object, **moving** object, **solid** object 🔟
PREP.	object **to *someone*/*something*** 🔟

---

ob|jec|tion /əbdʒɛkʃ°n/ (**objections**) 🔟 N-VAR If you make or raise an **objection** to something, you say that you do not like it or agree with it. ❑ *Some managers have recently raised objection to the PFA handling these negotiations.* 🔟 N-UNCOUNT If you say that you have **no objection to** something, you mean that you are not annoyed or bothered by it. ❑ *I have no objection to banks making money.*

🔟 가산명사 또는 불가산명사 반대, 이의 ❑ 최근 일부 관리자들이 피에프에이(PFA)가 이러한 협상을 처리하는 것에 대해 이의를 제기해 왔다. 🔟 불가산명사 반감 ❑ 은행들이 돈을 버는 것에 대한 반감은 없다.

Word Partnership   objection의 연어

V.	**make an** objection, **raise an** objection, **sustain an** objection 🔟
	have no objection 🔟

---

ob|jec|tive ♦◇◇ /əbdʒɛktɪv/ (**objectives**) 🔟 N-COUNT Your **objective** is what you are trying to achieve. ❑ *Our main objective was the recovery of the child safe and well.* 🔟 ADJ **Objective** information is based on facts. [ADJ n] ❑ *He had no objective evidence that anything extraordinary was happening.* ● **ob|jec|tive|ly** ADV ❑ *We simply want to inform people objectively about events.* ● **ob|jec|tiv|ity** /ɒbdʒɛktɪvɪti/ N-UNCOUNT ❑ *The poll, whose objectivity is open to question, gave the party a 39% share of the vote.* 🔟 ADJ If someone is **objective,** they base their opinions on facts rather than on their personal feelings. ❑ *I believe that a journalist should be completely objective.* ● **ob|jec|tive|ly** ADV ❑ *Try to view situations more objectively, especially with regard to work.* ● **ob|jec|tiv|ity** N-UNCOUNT ❑ *The psychiatrist must learn to maintain an unusual degree of objectivity.*

🔟 가산명사 목적, 목표 ❑ 우리의 주된 목표는 아이를 무사히 되찾는 것이었다. 🔟 형용사 객관적인, 실제의 ❑ 그는 어떤 특별한 일이 벌어지고 있다는 실재적인 증거를 갖고 있지 않았다. ● 객관적으로 부사 ❑ 우리는 그저 사람들에게 사건에 대해 객관적으로 알려 주기를 원할 뿐이다. ● 객관성 불가산명사 ❑ 객관성에 대한 의심을 면하기 힘든 득표 집계 결과 그 당에 39퍼센트의 표가 돌아갔다. 🔟 형용사 객관적인 ❑ 기자라면 마땅히 철저하게 객관적이어야 한다고 생각한다. ● 객관적으로 부사 ❑ 특히 일에 관해서는, 사태를 보다 더 객관적으로 보려고 노력하세요. ● 객관성 불가산명사 ❑ 정신과 의사는 비범할 정도의 객관성을 유지하는 법을 배워야 한다.

Word Partnership   objective의 연어

V.	**achieve an** objective 🔟
ADJ.	**important** objective, **main** objective, **primary** objective 🔟

---

ob|li|ga|tion /ɒblɪgeɪʃ°n/ (**obligations**) 🔟 N-VAR If you have an **obligation to** do something, it is your duty to do that thing. ❑ *When teachers assign homework, students usually feel an obligation to do it.* 🔟 N-VAR If you have an **obligation to** a person, it is your duty to take care of them or protect their interests. ❑ *The United States will do that which is necessary to meet its obligations to its own citizens.* 🔟 PHRASE In advertisements, if a product or a service is available **without obligation**, you do not have to pay for that product or service until you have tried it and are satisfied with it. ❑ *If you are selling your property, why not call us for a free valuation without obligation.*

🔟 가산명사 또는 불가산명사 의무, 책임 ❑ 선생님들이 숙제를 내 주면, 일반적으로 학생들은 그 숙제를 해야 할 의무를 느낀다. 🔟 가산명사 또는 불가산명사 책무 ❑ 미합중국은 자국 시민에 대한 책무를 다하는 데 필요한 일을 할 것이다. 🔟 구 (금전 등의) 의무가 없는 ❑ 가지고 계신 자산을 팔고 계신다면, 저희에게 전화를 걸어서, 꼭 요금을 내지 않아도 되는 무료 평가를 받아 보세요.

Thesaurus   obligation의 참조어

N.	duty, responsibility 🔟 🔟

Word Partnership   obligation의 연어

ADJ.	**legal** obligation, **moral** obligation 🔟 🔟
N.	**sense of** obligation 🔟 🔟
V.	obligation **to pay** 🔟
	feel an obligation, **fulfill an** obligation, **meet an** obligation 🔟 🔟

---

ob|li|ga|tory /əblɪgətɔri, BRIT əblɪgətri/ ADJ If something is **obligatory**, you must do it because of a rule or a law. ❑ *Most women will be offered an ultrasound scan during pregnancy, although it's not obligatory.*

형용사 의무적인, 필수의 ❑ 의무적인 것은 아니지만, 대부분의 여성들이 임신 중에 초음파 검사를 제의받는다.

ob|lige /əblaɪdʒ/ (**obliges, obliging, obliged**) 🔟 V-T If you **are obliged to** do something, a situation, rule, or law makes it necessary for you to do that thing. ❑ *The storm got worse and worse. Finally, I was obliged to abandon the car and continue on foot.* 🔟 V-T/V-I To **oblige** someone means to be helpful to them by doing what they have asked you to do. ❑ *If you ever need help with the babysitting, I'd be glad to oblige.* ❑ *We called up three economists to ask how to eliminate the deficit and they obliged with very straightforward answers.* 🔟 CONVENTION If you tell someone that you **would be obliged** or **should be obliged** if they would do something, you are telling them in a polite but firm way that you want them to do it. [FORMAL, POLITENESS] ❑ *I would be obliged if you could read it to us.*

🔟 타동사 -해야만 하다 ❑ 폭풍우가 갈수록 더 심해졌다. 결국, 나는 차를 버리고 도보로 계속 가야만 했다. 🔟 타동사/자동사 노움이 되어 주다, 은혜를 베풀다 ❑ 아이 보는 일 때문에 도움이 필요하시면, 제가 기꺼이 도움이 되어 드리겠습니다. ❑ 우리는 경제 전문가 3명에게 전화를 걸어 결손을 없애는 방법을 물어보았고, 그들은 고맙게도 아주 솔직한 답변을 해 주었다. 🔟 관용 표현 (-해 주시면) 고맙겠습니다 [격식체, 공손체] ❑ 그것을 우리에게 읽어 주시면 고맙겠습니다.

oblig|ing /əblaɪdʒɪŋ/ ADJ If you describe someone as **obliging**, you think that they are willing and eager to be helpful. [OLD-FASHIONED or WRITTEN, APPROVAL] ❑ *He is an extremely pleasant and obliging man.* ● **oblig|ing|ly** ADV [ADV with v] ❑ *He swung round and strode towards the door. Benedict obligingly held it open.*

형용사 자상한, 친절한 [구어체 또는 문어체, 마음에 듦] ❑ 그는 매우 상냥하고 자상한 남자이다. ● 자상하게, 친절하게 부사 ❑ 그는 빙 돌아서 저 쪽으로 성큼성큼 걸어갔다. 베네딕트는 친절하게 문을 열고 잡아 주었다.

oblique /oʊblik/ ADJ If you describe a statement as **oblique**, you mean that is not expressed directly or openly, making it difficult to understand. ❑ *It was an oblique reference to his mother.* ● **oblique|ly** ADV [ADV with v] ❑ *He obliquely referred to the U.S., Britain, and Saudi Arabia.*

형용사 완곡한, 에두르는 ❑ 그것은 에둘러 그의 어머니를 가리킨 것이었다. ● 완곡하게 부사 ❑ 그는 완곡하게 미국과 영국, 사우디아라비아에 관해 언급했다.

oblit|erate /əblɪtəreɪt/ (**obliterates**, **obliterating**, **obliterated**) **1** V-T If something **obliterates** an object or place, it destroys it completely. ❑ *Their warheads are enough to obliterate the world several times over.* ● **oblit|era|tion** /əblɪtəreɪʃ°n/ N-UNCOUNT ❑ *...the obliteration of three isolated rainforests.* **2** V-T If you **obliterate** something such as a memory, emotion, or thought, you remove it completely from your mind. [LITERARY] ❑ *There was time enough to obliterate memories of how things once were for him.*

1 타동사 말살하다 ❑ 그들이 가진 탄두들은 전 세계를 몇 번이나 말살해 버리기에 충분하다. ● 말살 불가산명사 ❑ 열대 우림 지역 세 곳의 말살 **2** 타동사 완전히 지우다 [문예체] ❑ 한때 사정이 그에게 어떠했던가 하는 기억을 완전히 지워 버릴 시간이 충분히 있었다.

obliv|ion /əblɪviən/ **1** N-UNCOUNT **Oblivion** is the state of not being aware of what is happening around you, for example because you are asleep or unconscious. ❑ *He just drank himself jovially into oblivion.* **2** N-UNCOUNT **Oblivion** is the state of having been forgotten or of no longer being considered important. ❑ *It seems that the so-called new theory is likely to sink into oblivion.* **3** N-UNCOUNT If you say that something is bombed or blasted **into oblivion**, you are emphasizing that it is completely destroyed. [EMPHASIS] ❑ *An entire poor section of town was bombed into oblivion.*

1 불가산명사 의식을 못하는 상태, 인사불성 ❑ 그는 다만 스스로 인사불성 지경에 이르도록 즐겁게 술을 마셨다. **2** 불가산명사 망각, 잊혀짐 ❑ 소위 그 새로운 이론이라는 것은 잊혀져 버릴 것 같다. **3** 불가산명사 완전 소멸 [강조] ❑ 도시의 빈곤 지구 전체가 폭격으로 완전히 소멸되었다.

oblivi|ous /əblɪviəs/ ADJ If you are **oblivious** to something or oblivious of it, you are not aware of it. ❑ *She lay motionless where she was, oblivious to pain.*

형용사 의식하지 못하는 ❑ 그녀는 통증도 의식하지 못한 채 있던 곳에 꼼짝 않고 그대로 누워 있었다.

ob|nox|ious /əbnɒkʃəs/ ADJ If you describe someone as **obnoxious**, you think that they are very unpleasant. [DISAPPROVAL] ❑ *One of the parents was a most obnoxious character. No one liked him.*

형용사 밉살스러운, 아주 불쾌한 [탐탁찮음] ❑ 그 부모 중 한 명은 매우 밉살스러운 사람이었다. 아무도 그를 좋아하지 않았다.

ob|scene /əbsin/ **1** ADJ If you describe something as **obscene**, you mean it offends you because it relates to sex or violence in a way that you think is unpleasant and shocking. ❑ *I'm not prudish but I think these photographs are obscene.* **2** ADJ In legal contexts, books, pictures, or movies which are judged **obscene** are illegal because they deal with sex or violence in a way that is offensive to the general public. ❑ *A city magistrate ruled that the novel was obscene and copies should be destroyed.* **3** ADJ If you describe something as **obscene**, you disapprove of it very strongly and consider it to be offensive or immoral. [DISAPPROVAL] ❑ *It was obscene to spend millions producing unwanted food.*

1 형용사 외설적인 ❑ 내가 얌전빼는 성격은 아니지만 이 사진들은 외설적이라고 생각한다. **2** 형용사 음란한 ❑ 한 시 치안 판사가 그 소설을 음란물로 판정하고 책들을 파기해야 한다는 판결을 내렸다. **3** 형용사 당치 않은, 억거운 [탐탁찮음] ❑ 쓸모없는 식품을 생산하는 데 수백만 달러를 쓰는 것은 당치 않은 일이었다.

ob|scen|ity /əbsenɪti/ (**obscenities**) **1** N-UNCOUNT **Obscenity** is behavior, art, or language that is sexual and offends or shocks people. ❑ *He insisted these photographs were not art but obscenity.* **2** N-VAR An **obscenity** is a very offensive word or expression. ❑ *They shouted obscenities at us and smashed bottles on the floor.*

1 불가산명사 외설 ❑ 그는 이 사진들이 예술이 아니라 외설이라고 주장했다. **2** 가산명사 또는 불가산명사 음란한 말, 외설적인 언사 ❑ 그들이 우리를 향해 외설적인 욕설을 해대며 바닥에 병을 던져 깼다.

ob|scure /əbskyʊər/ (**obscurer**, **obscurest**, **obscures**, **obscuring**, **obscured**) **1** ADJ If something or someone is **obscure**, they are unknown, or are known by only a few people. ❑ *The origin of the custom is obscure.* **2** ADJ Something that is **obscure** is difficult to understand or deal with, usually because it involves so many parts or details. ❑ *The contracts are written in obscure language.* **3** V-T If one thing **obscures** another, it prevents it from being seen or heard properly. ❑ *Trees obscured his vision; he couldn't see much of the Square's southern half.* **4** V-T To **obscure** something means to make it difficult to understand. ❑ *...the jargon that frequently obscures educational writing.*

1 형용사 잘 알려지지 않은 ❑ 그 풍습의 기원은 잘 알려져 있지 않다. **2** 형용사 이해하기 어려운 ❑ 그 계약서는 이해하기 힘든 말들로 작성되어 있다. **3** 타동사 가리다, 막아 감추다 ❑ 나무들이 그의 시야를 가려서, 그는 광장의 남반부 대부분을 볼 수 없었다. **4** 타동사 알기 어렵게 하다, 모호하게 만들다 ❑ 교육적인 글을 자주 이해하기 어렵게 만드는 전문 용어

ob|scu|rity /əbskyʊərɪti/ (**obscurities**) **1** N-UNCOUNT **Obscurity** is the state of being known by only a few people. ❑ *For the lucky few, there's the chance of being plucked from obscurity and thrown into the glamorous world of modeling.* **2** N-VAR **Obscurity** is the quality of being difficult to understand. An **obscurity** is something that is difficult to understand. ❑ *"How can that be?" asked Hunt, irritated by the obscurity of Henry's reply.*

1 불가산명사 잘 알려지지 않음, 무명 ❑ 운 좋은 극소수에게는, 무명의 상태에서 벗어나 매혹적인 모델의 세계로 발탁될 수 있는 기회가 있다. **2** 가산명사 또는 불가산명사 이해하기 힘듦; 이해하기 힘든 것 ❑ "어떻게 그럴 수가 있지?"라고 헨리의 이해하기 힘든 대답에 화가 나서 헌트가 물었다.

ob|ser|vance /əbzɜrv°ns/ (**observances**) N-VAR The **observance** of something such as a law or custom is the practice of obeying or following it. ❑ *Local councils should use their powers to ensure strict observance of laws.*

가산명사 또는 불가산명사 준수, 지킴 ❑ 지방 의회는 엄격한 법 준수를 보장하기 위해 힘을 써야 한다.

ob|ser|vant /əbzɜrv°nt/ ADJ Someone who is **observant** pays a lot of attention to things and notices more about them than most people do. ❑ *That's a marvellous description, Mrs. Drummond. You're unusually observant.*

형용사 관찰력이 예리한 ❑ 그거 놀라운 묘사로군요, 드러먼드 부인. 대단히 관찰력이 예리하시네요.

ob|ser|va|tion /ɒbzərveɪʃ°n/ (**observations**) **1** N-UNCOUNT **Observation** is the action or process of carefully watching someone or something. ❑ *...careful observation of the movement of the planets.* **2** N-COUNT An **observation** is something that you have learned by seeing or watching something and thinking about it. ❑ *This book contains observations about the causes of addictions.* **3** N-COUNT If a person makes an **observation**, they make a comment about something or someone, usually as a result of watching how they behave. ❑ *"You're an obstinate man," she said. "Is that a criticism," I said, "or just an observation?"* **4** N-UNCOUNT **Observation** is the ability to pay a lot of attention to things and to notice more about them than most people do. ❑ *She has good powers of observation.* →see **forecast**, **science**

1 불가산명사 관찰, 관측 ❑ 행성의 운동에 대한 면밀한 관측 **2** 가산명사 관찰 ❑ 이 책에는 여러 가지 중독의 원인에 대한 관찰이 들어 있다. **3** 가산명사 (관찰에 의거한) 의견, 발언 ❑ "당신은 고집불통이야."라고 그녀가 말했다. 내가 말했다. "그건 비난인가 아니면 그냥 지켜보면서 느낀 의견인가?" **4** 불가산명사 관찰력 ❑ 그녀는 뛰어난 관찰력을 가지고 있다.

Word Partnership		*observation*의 연어
PREP.	**by** observation, **through** observation, **under** observation	**1**
ADJ.	**careful** observation	**1**
	direct observation	**1**-**3**
V.	**make an** observation	**3**

ob|ser|va|tory /əbzɜrvətɔri, BRIT əbzɜːˈvətri/ (observatories) N-COUNT An **observatory** is a building with a large telescope from which scientists study things such as the planets by watching them.

가산명사 천문대

Word Link
serv ≈ keeping : conserve, observe, preserve

ob|serve ♦♢♢ /əbzɜrv/ (observes, observing, observed) **1** V-T If you **observe** a person or thing, you watch them carefully, especially in order to learn something about them. □ *Stern also studies and observes the behavior of babies.* □ *Are there any classes I could observe?* **2** V-T If you **observe** someone or something, you see or notice them. [FORMAL] □ *In 1664 Hooke observed a reddish spot on the surface of the planet.* **3** V-T If you **observe** that something is the case, you make a remark or comment about it, especially when it is something you have noticed and thought about a lot. [FORMAL] □ *We observe that the first calls for radical transformation did not begin until the period of the industrial revolution.* **4** V-T If you **observe** something such as a law or custom, you obey it or follow it. □ *Imposing speed restrictions is easy, but forcing motorists to observe them is trickier.* □ *The army was observing a ceasefire.*

1 타동사 관찰하다, 관측하다 □ 스턴은 갓난아이들의 행동 양식 또한 연구 관찰한다. □ 제가 관찰할 수 있는 학급이 있을까요? **2** 타동사 보다, 인지하다 [격식체] □ 1664년에 훅은 그 행성의 표면에서 불그스레한 반점을 보았다. **3** 타동사 (소견을) 말하다 [격식체] □ 급격한 변화에 대한 최초의 요구는 산업 혁명 시기에 이르러서야 시작되었다는 소견을 밝히는 바이다. **4** 타동사 지키다, 준수하다 □ 속도 제한을 부과하기는 쉽지만, 운전자들에게 그것을 지키도록 하는 것은 더 까다로운 일이다. □ 군대는 정전 명령을 준수하고 있었다.

Thesaurus
observe의 참조어

V.　study, watch **1**
detect, notice, spot **2**

Word Partnership
observe의 연어

N.　observe **behavior**, **opportunity to** observe **1** **2**
observe **guidelines**, observe **rules** **4**

---

ob|serv|er ♦♢♢ /əbzɜrvər/ (observers) **1** N-COUNT You can refer to someone who sees or notices something as an **observer**. □ *A casual observer would have taken them to be three men out for an evening stroll.* **2** N-COUNT An **observer** is someone who studies current events and situations, especially in order to comment on them and predict what will happen next. [JOURNALISM] □ *Observers say the events of the weekend seem to have increased support for the opposition.* **3** N-COUNT An **observer** is a person who is sent to observe an important event or situation, especially in order to make sure it happens as it should, or so that they can tell other people about it. □ *The president suggested that a UN observer should attend the conference.*

1 가산명사 보는 사람 □ 그냥 무심코 보는 사람이라면 그들을 저녁 산책 나온 세 남자쯤으로 생각했을 것이다. **2** 가산명사 관찰자, 관측자 [언론] □ 주말의 사건으로 인해 야당에 대한 지지가 늘어난 것 같다고 관측자들은 말한다. **3** 가산명사 입회인, 옵서버 □ 대통령은 유엔 입회인이 회의에 참석할 것을 제안했다.

Word Partnership
observer의 연어

ADJ.　**casual** observer **1**
independent observer, **outside** observer **1**‑**3**

---

ob|sess /əbsɛs/ (obsesses, obsessing, obsessed) V-T/V-I If something **obsesses** you or if you **obsess about** something, you keep thinking about it and find it difficult to think about anything else. □ *A string of scandals is obsessing America.* □ *She stopped drinking but began obsessing about her weight.*

타동사/자동사 사로잡다; 사로잡히다, 집착하다 □ 일련의 추문이 미국을 사로잡고 있다. □ 그녀는 술을 끊었지만 몸무게에 대해 집착하기 시작했다.

ob|sessed /əbsɛst/ ADJ If someone is **obsessed with** a person or thing, they keep thinking about them and find it difficult to think about anything else. □ *He was obsessed with American gangster movies.*

형용사 ～에 사로잡힌 □ 그는 미국 갱 영화에 사로잡혀 있었다.

ob|ses|sion /əbsɛʃ⁰n/ (obsessions) N-VAR If you say that someone has an **obsession** with a person or thing, you think they are spending too much time thinking about them. □ *She would try to forget her obsession with Christopher.*

가산명사 또는 불가산명사 강박 관념, 집착 □ 그녀는 크리스토퍼에 대한 집착을 잊으려 애쓸 것이다.

ob|ses|sive /əbsɛsɪv/ (obsessives) **1** ADJ If someone's behavior is **obsessive**, they cannot stop doing a particular thing or behaving in a particular way. □ *Williams is obsessive about motor racing.* ● **ob|ses|sive|ly** ADV □ *He couldn't help worrying obsessively about what would happen.* **2** N-COUNT An **obsessive** is someone who is obsessive about something or who behaves in an obsessive way. □ *Obsessives, in any area, are invariably as boring as their hobbies.*

1 형용사 강박적인 □ 윌리엄스는 자동차 경주에 강박적으로 빠져 있다. ● 강박적으로 부사 □ 그는 앞으로 일어날 일에 대해 강박적으로 걱정하는 일을 멈출 수가 없었다. **2** 가산명사 강박감에 사로잡힌 사람 □ 어떤 분야에서든, 강박감에 사로잡힌 사람들은 예외 없이 그들의 취미만큼이나 따분하다.

ob|so|lete /ɒbsəlit/ ADJ Something that is **obsolete** is no longer used because something better has been invented. □ *So much equipment becomes obsolete almost as soon as it's made.*

형용사 폐물이 된, 구식의 □ 너무나 많은 장비들이 거의 만들어지자마자 폐물이 된다.

ob|sta|cle /ɒbstək⁰l/ (obstacles) **1** N-COUNT An **obstacle** is an object that makes it difficult for you to go where you want to go, because it is in your way. □ *Most competition cars will only roll over if they hit an obstacle.* **2** N-COUNT You can refer to anything that makes it difficult for you to do something as an **obstacle**. □ *Overcrowding remains a large obstacle to improving conditions.*

1 가산명사 장애물 □ 경기에 참가한 대부분의 자동차들은 장애물에 부딪힌다 해도 그저 전복되기만 할 것이다. **2** 가산명사 장애 □ 지나친 혼잡이 여전히 상황 개선에 커다란 장애 요인이다.

Word Partnership
obstacle의 연어

N.　obstacle **course** **1**
obstacle **to peace** **2**
V.　**be an** obstacle, **hit an** obstacle, **overcome an** obstacle **1** **2**
ADJ.　**big** obstacle, **main** obstacle, **major** obstacle, **serious** obstacle **1** **2**

---

ob|ste|tri|cian /ɒbstətrɪʃ⁰n/ (obstetricians) N-COUNT An **obstetrician** is a doctor who is specially trained to deal with pregnant women and with women who are giving birth. [MEDICAL]

가산명사 산부인과 의사 [의학]

ob|sti|nate /ɒbstɪnɪt/ ADJ If you describe someone as **obstinate**, you are being critical of them because they are very determined to do what they want, and refuse to change their mind or be persuaded to do something else.

1 형용사 완고한, 고집 센 [탐탁찮음] □ 그는 고집 세고 단호하며 포기하려 하지 않는다. ● 완고하게, 끈질기게 부사 □ 나는 끈질기게 내 방 안에서 전화 옆에 앉아

a
b
c
d
e
f
g
h
i
j
k
l
m
n
o
p
q
r
s
t
u
v
w
x
y
z

A B C D E F G H I J K L M N O P Q R S T U V W X Y Z

[DISAPPROVAL] ❑ *He is obstinate and determined and will not give up.* ● **ob|sti|nate|ly** ADV [ADV with v] ❑ *I stayed obstinately in my room, sitting by the telephone.* ● **ob|sti|na|cy** N-UNCOUNT ❑ *I might have become a dangerous man with all that stubbornness and obstinacy built into me.* ② ADJ You can describe things as **obstinate** when they are difficult to move, change, or destroy. ❑ *...rusted farm equipment strewn among the obstinate weeds.* ● **ob|sti|nate|ly** ADV [ADV with v] ❑ *...the door of the shop which obstinately stayed closed when he tried to push it open.*

버텼다. ● 완고한, 고집 불가산명사 ❑ 그런 완고함과 고집이 내 안에 자리 잡은 나는 위험인물이 되었을지도 몰랐다. ② 형용사 제어하기 힘든, 완강한 ❑ 없애기 힘든 잡초 사이에 어수선하게 널려 있는 녹슨 농사 장비 ● 완강히 부사 ❑ 그가 밀어서 열려고 했을 때 닫힌 채로 좀처럼 열리지 않았던 그 상점 문

ob|struct /əbstrʌkt/ (**obstructs, obstructing, obstructed**) ① V-T If something **obstructs** a road or path, it blocks it, stopping people or vehicles getting past. ❑ *A knot of black and white cars obstructed the intersection.* ② V-T To **obstruct** someone or something means to make it difficult for them to move forward by blocking their path. ❑ *A number of local people have been arrested for trying to obstruct lorries loaded with logs.* ③ V-T To **obstruct** progress or a process means to prevent it from happening properly. ❑ *The authorities are obstructing a United Nations investigation.* ④ V-T If someone or something **obstructs** your view, they are positioned between you and the thing you are trying to look at, stopping you from seeing it properly. ❑ *Claire positioned herself so as not to obstruct David's line of sight.*

① 타동사 막다, 차단하다 ❑ 한 무리의 검은색과 흰색 자동차들이 교차로를 막았다. ② 타동사 -의 길을 막다 ❑ 통나무를 실은 화물차들의 길을 막으려 한 혐의로 다수의 지역 주민들이 체포되었다. ③ 타동사 방해하다 ❑ 당국이 유엔 조사를 방해하고 있다. ④ 타동사 (시야를) 가리다 ❑ 클레어는 데이비드의 시야를 가리지 않도록 자리를 잡았다.

ob|struc|tion /əbstrʌkʃⁿn/ (**obstructions**) ① N-COUNT An **obstruction** is something that blocks a road or path. ❑ *John was irritated by drivers parking near his house and causing an obstruction.* ② N-VAR An **obstruction** is something that blocks a passage in your body. ❑ *The boy was suffering from a bowel obstruction and he died.* ③ N-UNCOUNT **Obstruction** is the act of deliberately delaying something or preventing something from happening, usually in business, law, or government. ❑ *Mr. Guest refused to let them in and now faces a criminal charge of obstruction.*

① 가산명사 장애물, 차단물 ❑ 존은 자기 집 근처에 주차를 해서 길을 막는 운전자들 때문에 화가 났다. ② 가산명사 또는 불가산명사 폐색 (물) ❑ 그 소년은 장폐색을 앓다가 죽었다. ③ 불가산명사 방해 ❑ 게스트 씨가 그들을 들어가지 못하게 해서 현재 업무 방해로 형사 고발에 직면해 있다.

ob|tain ♦◇◇ /əbteɪn/ (**obtains, obtaining, obtained**) V-T To **obtain** something means to get it or achieve it. [FORMAL] ❑ *Evans was trying to obtain a false passport and other documents.*

타동사 입수하다, 획득하다 [격식체] ❑ 에반스는 위조 여권과 기타 서류를 입수하려 하고 있었다.

Word Partnership *obtain*의 연어

ADJ.	**able to** obtain, **difficult to** obtain, **easy to** obtain, **unable to** obtain
N.	obtain **approval**, obtain **a copy**, obtain **help**, obtain **information**, obtain **insurance**, obtain **permission**, obtain **weapons**

ob|tuse /əbtus, BRIT əbtyuːs/ ADJ An **obtuse** angle is between 90° and 180°. Compare **acute** angle. [TECHNICAL]

형용사 둔각의 [과학 기술]

ob|vi|ous ♦♦◇ /ɒbviəs/ ① ADJ If something is **obvious**, it is easy to see or understand. ❑ *...the need to rectify what is an obvious injustice.* ② ADJ If you describe something that someone says as **obvious**, you are being critical of it because you think it is unnecessary or shows lack of imagination. [DISAPPROVAL] ❑ *There are some very obvious phrases that we all know or certainly should know better than to use.* ● PHRASE If you say that someone **is stating the obvious**, you mean that they are saying something that everyone already knows and understands.

① 형용사 명백한, 명료한 ❑ 명백한 부정을 바로 잡을 필요 ② 형용사 속이 들여다보는, 뻔한 [탐탁찮음] ❑ 우리 모두가 알고 있거나 사용은 안 해도 정말 잘 알고는 있는 아주 뻔한 문구들이 몇 개 있다. ● 구 다 아는 소리를 하다

Thesaurus *obvious*의 참조어

ADJ.	noticeable, plain, unmistakable ①

Word Partnership *obvious*의 연어

ADV.	**fairly** obvious, **immediately** obvious, **less** obvious, **most** obvious, **painfully** obvious, **quite** obvious, **so** obvious ① ②
N.	obvious **answer**, obvious **choice**, obvious **differences**, obvious **example**, obvious **question**, obvious **reasons**, obvious **solution** ① ②

ob|vi|ous|ly ♦♦◇ /ɒbviəsli/ ① ADV You use **obviously** when you are stating something that you expect the person who is listening to know already. [EMPHASIS] [ADV with cl] ❑ *Obviously, they've had sponsorship from some big companies.* ② ADV You use **obviously** to indicate that something is easily noticed, seen, or recognized. [ADV with cl/group] ❑ *They obviously appreciate you very much.*

① 부사 알다시피 [강조] ❑ 아시다시피, 그들은 몇몇 대기업들로부터 후원을 받아 왔습니다. ② 부사 분명히 ❑ 그들은 분명히 당신에게 대단히 고마워합니다.

oc|ca|sion ♦♦◇ /əkeɪʒⁿn/ (**occasions**) ① N-COUNT An **occasion** is a time when something happens, or a case of it happening. ❑ *I often think fondly of an occasion some years ago at Covent Garden.* ② N-COUNT An **occasion** is an important event, ceremony, or celebration. ❑ *Taking her with me on official occasions has been a challenge.* ③ N-COUNT An **occasion for** doing something is an opportunity for doing it. [FORMAL] ❑ *It is an occasion for all the family to celebrate.* ④ PHRASE If you **have occasion to** do something, it is necessary for you to do it. ❑ *We have had occasion to deal with members of the group on a variety of charges.* ⑤ PHRASE If you say that someone **rose to the occasion**, you mean that they did what was necessary to successfully overcome a difficult situation. ❑ *Inverness, however, rose to the occasion in the second half, producing some of the best football they have played for some time.*

① 가산명사 (특정한) 경우, 때 ❑ 나는 종종 몇 년 전 코벤트 가든에서 있었던 일을 기분 좋게 떠올리곤 한다. ② 가산명사 행사 ❑ 지금까지 내가 그녀를 공식 행사에 데리고 다니기가 힘들었다. ③ 가산명사 -할 기회, 호기 [격식체] ❑ 그것은 온 가족이 경축할 기회이다. ④ 구 -할 필요가 있다 ❑ 여러 가지의 혐의에 대해 그 단체 구성원들을 조처할 필요가 있었다. ⑤ 구 난국에 대처하다 ❑ 하지만 인버네스 팀은 후반전에 근래 들어 최고의 축구 경기를 펼치며 위기를 극복했다.

Word Partnership *occasion*의 연어

ADJ.	**festive** occasion, **historic** occasion, **rare** occasion, **solemn** occasion, **special** occasion ① ②
V.	**mark an** occasion ②
	rise to an occasion ⑤

oc|ca|sion|al ♦◇◇ /əkeɪʒənᵊl/ ADJ **Occasional** means happening sometimes, but not regularly or often. ❏ *I've had occasional mild headaches all my life.*
● **oc|ca|sion|al|ly** ADV ❏ *He still misbehaves occasionally.*

oc|cult /ɒkʌlt, ɒkʌlt/ N-SING The **occult** is the knowledge and study of supernatural or magical forces. ❏ *However, interest in the occult tended more toward ceremonial magic rather than witchcraft.* ● ADJ **Occult** is also an adjective. [ADJ n] ❏ *...organizations which campaign against paganism and occult practice.*

oc|cu|pan|cy /ɒkyəpənsi/ N-UNCOUNT **Occupancy** is the act of using a room, building, or area of land, usually for a fixed period of time. [FORMAL] ❏ *Hotel occupancy has been as low as 40%.*

oc|cu|pant /ɒkyəpənt/ (**occupants**) ◻ N-COUNT The **occupants** of a building or room are the people who live or work there. ❏ *Most of the occupants had left before the fire broke out.* ◻ N-PLURAL You can refer to the people who are in a place such as a room, vehicle, or bed at a particular time as the **occupants**. ❏ *He wanted the occupants of the vehicle to get out.*

oc|cu|pa|tion ♦◇◇ /ɒkyəpeɪʃᵊn/ ◻ N-COUNT Your **occupation** is your job or profession. ❏ *I suppose I was looking for an occupation which was going to be an adventure.* ◻ N-COUNT An **occupation** is something that you spend time doing, either for pleasure or because it needs to be done. ❏ *Parachuting is a dangerous occupation.* ◻ N-UNCOUNT The **occupation** of a country happens when it is entered and controlled by a foreign army. ❏ *...the deportation of Jews from Paris during the German occupation.*

oc|cu|pa|tion|al /ɒkyəpeɪʃᵊnᵊl/ ADJ **Occupational** means relating to a person's job or profession. ❏ *Some received substantial occupational assistance in the form of low- interest loans.*

oc|cu|pi|er /ɒkyəpaɪər/ (**occupiers**) N-COUNT The **occupier** of a house, apartment, or piece of land is the person who lives or works there. [FORMAL] ❏ *One letter was addressed to 'The Occupier'*

oc|cu|py ♦◇◇ /ɒkyəpaɪ/ (**occupies, occupying, occupied**) ◻ V-T The people who **occupy** a building or a place are the people who live or work there. ❏ *There were over 40 tenants, all occupying one wing of the hospital.* ◻ V-T PASSIVE If a room or something such as a seat **is occupied**, someone is using it, so that it is not available for anyone else. ❏ *The hospital bed is no longer occupied by his wife.* ◻ V-T If a group of people or an army **occupies** a place or country, they move into it, using force in order to gain control of it. ❏ *U.S. forces now occupy a part of the country.* ◻ V-T If someone or something **occupies** a particular place in a system, process, or plan, they have that place. ❏ *Many men still occupy more positions of power than women.* ◻ V-T If something **occupies** you, or if you **occupy** yourself, your time, or your mind with it, you are busy doing that thing or thinking about it. ❏ *Her parliamentary career has occupied all of her time.* ❏ *He hurried to take the suitcases and occupy himself with packing the car.* ● **oc|cu|pied** ADJ [v-link ADJ, oft ADJ with n] ❏ *Keep the brain occupied.* ◻ V-T If something **occupies** you, it requires your efforts, attention, or time. ❏ *I had other matters to occupy me, during the day at least.* ◻ V-T If something **occupies** a particular area or place, it fills or covers it, or exists there. ❏ *Even quite small aircraft occupy a lot of space.*

Word Partnership	occupy의 연어
N.	occupy **a house**, occupy **land** ◻ ◻
	occupy **a place** ◻ ◻ ◻ ◻
	occupy **a position** ◻ ◻
	occupy **an area**, forces occupy *someplace*, occupy **space**, troops
	occupy *someplace* ◻ ◻

oc|cur ♦◇◇ /əkɜr/ (**occurs, occurring, occurred**) ◻ V-I When something **occurs**, it happens. ❏ *If headaches only occur at night, lack of fresh air and oxygen is often the cause.* ❏ *The crash occurred when the crew shut down the wrong engine.* ◻ V-I When something **occurs** in a particular place, it exists or is present there. ❏ *The cattle disease occurs more or less anywhere in Africa where the fly occurs.* ◻ V-I If a thought or idea **occurs to** you, you suddenly think of it or realize it. [no passive, no cont] ❏ *It did not occur to me to check my insurance policy.* ❏ *It occurred to me that I could have the book sent to me.*

Thesaurus	occur의 참조어
V.	come about, develop, happen ◻
	dawn on, strike ◻

Word Partnership	occur의 연어
N.	**accidents** occur, **changes** occur, **deaths** occur, **diseases** occur, **events** occur, **injuries** occur, **problems** occur ◻
ADV.	**naturally** occur, **normally** occur, **often** occur, **usually** occur ◻-◻

oc|cur|rence /əkɜrəns, BRIT əkʌrəns/ (**occurrences**) ◻ N-COUNT An **occurrence** is something that happens. [FORMAL] ❏ *Complaints seemed to be an everyday*

형용사 이따금씩의, 때때로의 ❏ 나는 일생 동안 때때로 가벼운 두통을 앓아 왔다. ● 이따금, 때때로 부사 ❏ 그는 아직도 때때로 무례하게 군다.

단수명사 비술(祕術), 오컬트 ❏ 하지만, 비술에 대한 관심은 마법보다는 오히려 의식적인 주술 쪽에 쏠렸다. ● 형용사 비술의; 신비로운 ❏ 이교 신앙과 신비적 의식에 대한 반대 운동을 벌이는 단체들

불가산명사 점유, 사용 [격식체] ❏ 호텔 객실 점유율은 계속 40퍼센트 대에 이를 만큼 낮았다.

◻ 가산명사 거주자, 점유자 ❏ 거주자들 대부분은 화재가 나기 전에 빠져나가고 없었다. ◻ 복수명사 (탈것 등의) 안에 있는 사람 ❏ 그는 그 차에 타고 있는 사람들이 내리기를 원했다.

◻ 가산명사 직업, 일 ❏ 나는 모험 같은 경험이 될 일을 찾고 있었던 것 같다. ◻ 가산명사 일 ❏ 낙하산 강하는 위험한 일이다. ◻ 불가산명사 점령 ❏ 독일의 점령 기간 동안 파리에서 유태인을 국외로 추방함

형용사 직업상의 ❏ 어떤 사람들은 저리 융자의 형태로 실질적인 직업상의 원조를 받았다.

가산명사 거주인, 점유인 [격식체] ❏ 한 통의 편지가 '거주인' 앞으로 보내져 왔다.

◻ 타동사 거주하다, 점유하다 ❏ 40여 명의 세입자가 있었는데, 그들 모두가 병원의 한 쪽 병동을 점유하고 있었다. ◻ 수동 타동사 사용 중이다 ❏ 그 병원 침대는 더 이상 그의 아내가 사용하지 않는다. ◻ 타동사 점령하다 ❏ 미군이 현재 그 나라의 일부를 점령하고 있다. ◻ 타동사 (지위 등을) 차지하다 ❏ 여전히 많은 남자들이 유력한 자리를 여자들보다 더 많이 차지하고 있다. ◻ 타동사 바쁘게 ~을 하다, ~에 시간이나 마음을 쏟다 ❏ 그녀는 의회 일에 모든 시간을 쏟아 왔다. ● 바쁜 형용사 ❏ 두뇌를 계속 바쁘게 하세요. ◻ 타동사 ~의 수고나 주의를 요하다 ❏ 적어도 낮 동안에는 신경 쓸 다른 일이 있었다. ◻ 타동사 (공간을) 차지하다 ❏ 아주 작은 비행기도 큰 공간을 차지한다.

◻ 자동사 일어나다 ❏ 두통이 밤에만 일어난다면, 흔히 신선한 공기와 산소 부족이 그 원인이다. ❏ 승무원이 고장난 엔진을 정지시켰을 때 충돌이 일어났다. ◻ 자동사 존재하다, 나타나다 ❏ 그 우역(牛疫)은 그 파리가 존재하는 아프리카 거의 전 지역에서 발생한다. ◻ 자동사 떠오르다, 생각이 나다 ❏ 보험 증권을 확인해 본다는 생각은 떠오르지 않았다. ❏ 내게 보내온 그 책을 내가 가지고 있을지도 모른다는 생각이 떠올랐다.

◻ 가산명사 사건, 일 [격식체] ❏ 불평불만은 일상적인 일처럼 보였다. ◻ 가산명사 발생 ❏ 관상

occurrence. **2** N-COUNT **The occurrence of** something is the fact that it happens or is present. ❑ *The greatest occurrence of coronary heart disease is in those over 65.*

동맥 질환은 65세 이상의 사람들에게 가장 많이 발생한다.

ocean ♦♢♢ /ˈoʊᵊn/ (**oceans**) **1** N-SING **The ocean** is the sea. ❑ *There were few sights as beautiful as the calm ocean on a warm night.* **2** N-COUNT An **ocean** is one of the five very large areas of sea on the Earth's surface. ❑ *They spent many days cruising the northern Pacific Ocean.* **3** N-COUNT If you say that there is an **ocean of** something, you are emphasizing that there is a very large amount of it. [INFORMAL, EMPHASIS] ❑ *I had cried oceans of tears.* **4** PHRASE If you say that something is **a drop in the ocean**, you mean that it is a very small amount which is unimportant compared to the cost of other things or is so small that it has very little effect on something. [EMPHASIS] ❑ *His fee is a drop in the ocean compared with the real cost of broadcasting.* →see **earth, river, whale** →see Word Web: **ocean**

1 단수명사 바다 ❑ 더운 날 밤의 고요한 바다만큼 아름다운 광경은 별로 없었다. **2** 가산명사 대양 ❑ 그들은 북태평양을 항해하면서 많은 날들을 보냈다. **3** 가산명사 막대한 양 [비격식체, 강조] ❑ 나는 엄청나게 많은 눈물을 흘렸다. **4** 구 (비유적) 바닷물 한 방울, 새 발의 피 [강조] ❑ 그가 받는 수수료는 실제 방송 비용에 비하면 새 발의 피다.

o'clock ♦♢♢ /əˈklɒk/ ADV You use **o'clock** after numbers from one to twelve to say what time it is. For example, if you say that it is 9 o'clock, you mean that it is nine hours after midnight or nine hours after midday. [num ADV] ❑ *The trouble began just after ten o'clock last night.*

부사 _시 ❑ 사태는 지난밤 10시가 막 지나서 시작되었다.

Oct. **Oct.** is a written abbreviation for **October.** ❑ *...Tuesday Oct. 25th.*

10월 ❑ 10월 25일 화요일

Oc|to|ber ♦♦♢ /ɒkˈtoʊbər/ (**Octobers**) N-VAR **October** is the tenth month of the year in the Western calendar. ❑ *Most seasonal hiring is done in early October.* ❑ *The first plane is due to leave on October 2.*

가산명사 또는 불가산명사 10월 ❑ 대부분의 계절적 고용은 10월 초에 이루어진다. ❑ 첫 비행기는 10월 2일에 떠날 예정이다.

oc|to|pus /ˈɒktəpəs/ (**octopuses**) N-VAR An **octopus** is a soft sea creature with eight long arms called tentacles which it uses to catch food. ● N-UNCOUNT **Octopus** is this creature eaten as food. ❑ *...plates of octopus.*

가산명사 또는 불가산명사 문어 ● 불가산명사 문어 ❑ 문어 여러 접시

OD /ˌoʊ ˈdi/ (**OD's, OD'ing, OD'd**) V-I To **OD** means the same as to **overdose.** [INFORMAL] ❑ *His son was a junkie, the kid OD'd a year ago.* ● N-COUNT **OD** is also a noun. ❑ *"I had a friend died of an OD," she said.*

자동사 과다 복용하다 [비격식체] ❑ 그의 아들은 마약 중독자였는데, 1년 전 과다 복용으로 쓰러졌다. ● 가산명사 약물 과다 복용 ❑ "친구 하나가 약물 과다 복용으로 숨졌어."라고 그녀가 말했다.

odd ♦♦♢ /ɒd/ (**odder, oddest**) **1** ADJ If you describe someone or something as **odd**, you think that they are strange or unusual. ❑ *He'd always been odd, but not to this extent.* ❑ *What an odd coincidence that he should have known your family.* ● **odd|ly** ADV [ADV with v] ❑ *...an oddly shaped hill.* **2** ADJ You use **odd** before a noun to indicate that you are not mentioning the type, size, or quality of something because it is not important. [det ADJ] ❑ *...moving from place to place where she could find the odd bit of work.* ❑ *He had various odd cleaning jobs around the place.* **3** ADV You use **odd** after a number to indicate that it is only approximate. [INFORMAL] [num ADV] ❑ *How many pages was it, 500 odd?* ❑ *He has now appeared in sixty odd films.* **4** ADJ **Odd** numbers, such as 3 and 17, are those which cannot be divided exactly by the number two. ❑ *The odd numbers are on the left as you walk up the street.* **5** ADJ You say that two things are **odd** when they do not belong to the same set or pair. ❑ *I'm wearing odd socks today by the way.* **6** PHRASE **The odd man out, the odd woman out,** or **the odd one out** in a particular situation is a person who is different from the other people in it. ❑ *Azerbaijan has been the odd man out, the one republic not to hold democratic elections.* **7** →see also **odds**

1 형용사 기묘한, 이상한 ❑ 그는 항상 이상하긴 했었지만, 이 정도는 아니었다. ❑ 그가 너희 가족을 알고 있었을 거라니 정말 묘한 우연의 일치로군. ● 묘하게, 이상하게 부사 ❑ 이상하게 생긴 언덕 **2** 형용사 이런저런 ❑ 그녀가 이런저런 일거리를 찾을 수 있는 곳으로 여기저기 옮겨 다니면서 ❑ 그는 그곳 주변에서 이런저런 여러 가지 청소 일을 했다. **3** 부사 _여의, _남짓의 [비격식체] ❑ 몇 쪽이나 됐지, 500여 쪽? ❑ 그는 지금까지 60여 편의 영화에 출연했다. **4** 형용사 홀수의 ❑ 길을 걸어 올라가면 홀수 번지 집들은 왼편에 있습니다. **5** 형용사 짝이 안 맞는 ❑ 그나저나 나는 오늘 짝짝이 양말을 신었다. **6** 구 유별난 사람, 튀는 사람 ❑ 아제르바이잔은 유별나게 민주 선거를 시행하지 않는 유일한 공화국이었다.

Word Web ocean

Oceans cover over seventy-five percent of the earth's surface. These huge bodies of saltwater are constantly in motion. On the surface, the wind pushes the water into **waves.** At the same time, **currents** under the surface flow like rivers through the oceans. These currents are affected by the earth's rotation. It shifts them to the right in the northern hemisphere and to the left in the southern hemisphere. Other forces affect the oceans as well. For example, the gravitational pull of the moon and sun cause the **ebb** and **flow** of ocean **tides.**

odd|ity /ɒdɪti/ (**oddities**) N-COUNT An **oddity** is someone or something that is very strange. ❑ Losing my hair made me feel an oddity.

가산명사 기이함; 기이한 사람이나 물건 ❑ 머리가 빠지는 것 때문에 나는 기이한 기분이 들었다.

odd|ly /ɒdli/ ADV You use **oddly** to indicate that what you are saying is true, but that it is not what you expected. ❑ He said no and seemed oddly reluctant to talk about it. ❑ Oddly, Emma says she never considered her face was attractive. →see also **odd**

부사 이상하게 ❑ 그는 아니라고 말했는데 이상하게 그것에 대해 말하길 꺼리는 듯이 보였다. ❑ 이상하게도, 에마는 자신의 얼굴이 매력적이라고 생각해 본 적이 없었다고 말한다.

odds /ɒdz/ ◼ N-PLURAL You refer to how likely something is to happen as the **odds** that it will happen. ❑ What are the odds of finding a parking space right outside the door? ◻ N-PLURAL In betting, **odds** are expressions with numbers such as "10 to 1" and "7 to 2" that show how likely something is thought to be, for example how likely a particular horse is to lose or win a race. ❑ Gavin Jones, who put £25 on Eugene, at odds of 50 to 1, has won £1,250. ◻ PHRASE If someone is **at odds** with someone else, or if two people are **at odds**, they are disagreeing or quarreling with each other. ❑ He was at odds with his Prime Minister. ◼ PHRASE If you say that **the odds are against** something or someone, you mean that they are unlikely to succeed. ❑ He reckoned the odds are against the scheme going ahead. ◼ PHRASE If something happens **against** all **odds**, it happens or succeeds although it seemed impossible or very unlikely. ❑ Some women do manage to achieve business success against all odds. ◼ PHRASE If you say that **the odds are in** someone's **favor**, you mean that they are likely to succeed in what they are doing. ❑ His troops will only engage in a ground battle when all the odds are in their favor. →see **lottery**

◼ 복수명사 가망, 가능성 ❑ 출입구 바로 바깥에서 주차 공간을 찾아낼 가능성이 얼마나 될까? ◻ 복수명사 (경마 등의) 승산(勝算) ❑ 유진에게 25파운드를 걸어서 50대 1의 승산으로 1,250파운드를 딴 가빈 존스 ◼ 구 불화하는 ❑ 그는 수상과 불화 중이었다. ◼ 구 -의 가망이 없다 ❑ 그는 그 계획이 진전될 가망이 없다고 보았다. ◼ 구 온갖 악조건에도 불구하고 ❑ 어떤 여자들은 온갖 악조건에도 불구하고 사업에서 성공을 해내기도 한다. ◼ 구 -의 승산이 있다 ❑ 그의 군대는 승산이 매우 큰 지상전에서만 교전을 벌일 것이다.

Word Partnership	odds의 연어
PREP.	the odds of *something* ◼ ◻
	at odds (with *someone*) ◼
	odds against *something* ◼
	against all odds ◼
V.	odds of winning ◼ ◻
N.	odds in *someone's/something's* favor ◼

odor /oʊdər/ (**odors**) [BRIT **odour**] N-VAR An **odor** is a particular and distinctive smell. ❑ ...the lingering odor of automobile exhaust. →see **smell**, **taste**

[영국영어 odour] 가산명사 또는 불가산명사 냄새 ❑ 가시지 않고 있는 자동차 배기가스 냄새

of ◆◆◆ /əv, STRONG ʌv, BRIT ɒv/

In addition to the uses shown below, **of** is used after some verbs, nouns, and adjectives in order to introduce extra information. **Of** is also used in phrasal prepositions such as "because of," "instead of" and "in spite of," and in phrasal verbs such as "make of" and "dispose of."

of는 아래 용법 외에도 추가 정보를 나타내기 위해 일부의 동사, 명사, 형용사 뒤에 쓴다. 또한 'because of', 'instead of', 'in spite of'와 같은 전치사구 'make of', 'dispose of'와 같은 구동사에도 쓰인다.

◼ PREP You use **of** to combine two nouns when the first noun identifies the feature of the second noun that you want to talk about. [n PREP n] ❑ The average age of the women interviewed was only 21.5. ❑ ...the population of this town. ◻ PREP You use **of** to combine two nouns, or a noun and a present participle, when the second noun or present participle defines or gives more information about the first noun. [n PREP n/-ing] ❑ She let out a little cry of pain. ❑ ...the problem of a national shortage of teachers. ◼ PREP You use **of** after nouns referring to actions to specify the person or thing that is affected by the action or that performs the action. For example, "the kidnapping of the child" refers to an action affecting a child; "the arrival of the next train" refers to an action performed by a train. [n PREP n] ❑ ...the reduction of trade union power inside the party. ❑ ...the assessment of future senior managers. ◼ PREP You use **of** after words and phrases referring to quantities or groups of things to indicate the substance or thing that is being measured. [quant PREP n, n PREP n] ❑ ...dozens of people. ❑ ...a collection of short stories. ◼ PREP You use **of** after the name of someone or something to introduce the institution or place they belong to or are connected with. [n PREP n] ❑ ...the Prince of Wales. ◼ PREP You use **of** after a noun referring to a container for an expression referring to the container and its contents. [n PREP n] ❑ ...a box of tissues. ❑ ...a roomful of people. ◼ PREP You use **of** after a count noun and before an uncount noun when you want to talk about an individual piece or item. [n PREP n] ❑ ...a blade of grass. ❑ Marina ate only one slice of bread. ◼ PREP You use **of** to indicate the materials or things that form something. [n PREP n] ❑ ...local decorations of wood and straw. ❑ ...loose-fitting garments of linen. ◼ PREP You use **of** after a noun which specifies a particular part of something, to introduce the thing that it is a part of. [n PREP n] ❑ ...the other side of the square. ❑ ...the beginning of the year. ◼ PREP You use **of** after some verbs to indicate someone or something else involved in the action. [v PREP n/-ing, v n PREP n/-ing] ❑ He'd been dreaming of her. ❑ Listen, I shall be thinking of you always. ◼ PREP You use **of** after some adjectives to indicate the thing that a feeling or quality relates to. [adj PREP n/-ing] ❑ I have grown very fond of Alec. ❑ His father was quite naturally very proud of him. ◼ PREP You use **of** before a word referring to the person who performed an action when saying what you think about the action. [adj PREP pron/n-proper] ❑ This has been so nice, so terribly kind of you. ◼ PREP If something is **more of** or **less of** a particular thing, it is that thing to a greater or smaller degree. [more/less PREP a n] ❑ Your extra fat may be more of a health risk than you realize. ◼ PREP You use **of** to indicate a characteristic or quality that someone or something has. [n PREP n, adj-superl PREP n] ❑ ...the worth of their music. ❑ She is a woman of enviable beauty. ◼ PREP You use **of** to specify an amount, value, or age. [n PREP amount] ❑ Last Thursday, Nick announced record revenues of $3.4 billion. ❑ ...young people under the age of 16 years. ◼ PREP You use **of** after a noun such as "month" or "year" to indicate the length of time that some state or activity continues. [n PREP n/-ing] ❑ ...eight bruising years of war. ◼ PREP You can use **of** to say what time it is by indicating how many minutes there are before the hour mentioned. [AM] ❑ At about a quarter of eight in the evening Joe Urber calls.

◼ 전치사 -의 ❑ 인터뷰한 여성들의 평균 연령은 겨우 21.5세였다. ❑ 이 소도시의 주민 수 ◻ 전치사 -한; -의 ❑ 그녀는 약간 고통스러운 비명을 질렀다. ❑ 전국적으로 교사가 부족한 문제 ◼ 전치사 -의; -을, -에 대한 ❑ 당내 노동조합 세력의 쇠퇴 ❑ 장래의 고위 관리자들에 대한 평가 ◼ 전치사 -의 (수나 양) ❑ 수십 명의 사람들 ❑ 단편 소설 모음집 ◼ 전치사 소속의 ❑ 웨일스 왕자 ◼ 전치사 -가 든, -의 ❑ 티슈 한 박스 ❑ 방 한가에 가득 찬 사람들 ◼ 전치사 개별 수량 셀 때 단위 명사와 불가산 명사 사이에 쓴다. ❑ 풀잎 한 잎 ❑ 마리나는 빵 한 조각만 먹었다. ◼ 전치사 -로 만든, -로 된 ❑ 나무와 짚으로 만든 토속 장식물 ❑ 리넨으로 만든 헐렁한 옷 ◼ 전치사 -의 ❑ 그 광장의 다른 쪽 편 ❑ 그 해 초 ◼ 전치사 -에 대해서 ❑ 그는 계속 그녀에 대한 꿈을 꾸었었다. ❑ 들어 봐, 나는 항상 너에 대해 생각할 거야. ◼ 전치사 (형용사 뒤에서) -을 ❑ 나는 알렉이 매우 좋아졌다. ❑ 그의 아버지는 아주 당연하게 그를 매우 자랑스러워했다. ◼ 전치사 -가; -의 ❑ 당신이 이렇게 해 주신 것은 정말 친절한 일이었습니다. ◼ 전치사 더 -의; 덜 -임 ❑ 과다 지방은 당신이 자각하는 것보다 더 건강에 위험할 수 있다. ◼ 전치사 -의; -을 지닌 ❑ 그들 음악의 가치 ❑ 그녀는 부럽도록 아름다운 여인이다. ◼ 전치사 (분량 등) -의 ❑ 지난 목요일, 닉은 34억 달러의 기록적인 소득을 발표했다. ❑ 열여섯 살 이하의 어린 사람들 ◼ 전치사 (기간) -의 ❑ 8년 동안의 치열한 전쟁 ◼ 전치사 (시각이) -전 [미국영어] ❑ 저녁 8시 15분 전쯤에 조 어버가 전화를 한다.

of course ♦♦♦ **1** ADV You say **of course** to suggest that something is normal, obvious, or well-known, and should therefore not surprise the person you are talking to. [SPOKEN] [ADV with cl] ❑ *Of course there were lots of other interesting things at the exhibition.* ❑ *"I have read about you in the newspapers of course," Charlie said.* **2** CONVENTION You use **of course** as a polite way of giving permission. [SPOKEN, FORMULAE] ❑ *"Can I just say something about the cup game on Saturday?" — "Yes of course you can."* **3** ADV You use **of course** in order to emphasize a statement that you are making, especially when you are agreeing with or disagreeing with someone. [SPOKEN, EMPHASIS] ❑ *"I expect you're right." — "Of course I'm right."* ❑ *Of course I'm not afraid!* **4** CONVENTION **Of course not** is an emphatic way of saying no. [SPOKEN, EMPHASIS] ❑ *"You're not really seriously considering this thing, are you?" — "No, of course not."*

off ♦♦♦

> The preposition is pronounced /ɔf/. The adverb is pronounced /ɔf/.

> In addition to the uses shown below, **off** is used after some verbs and nouns in order to introduce extra information. **Off** is also used in phrasal verbs such as "get off," "pair off," and "sleep off."

1 PREP If something is taken **off** something else or moves **off** it, it is no longer touching that thing. ❑ *He took his feet off the desk.* ❑ *I took the key for the room off a rack above her head.* • ADV **Off** is also an adverb. [ADV after v] ❑ *Lee broke off a small piece of orange and held it out to him.* **2** PREP When you get **off** a bus, train, or plane, you come out of it or leave it after you have been traveling on it. ❑ *Don't try to get on or off a moving train!* • ADV **Off** is also an adverb. [ADV after v] ❑ *At the next stop the man got off too and introduced himself.* **3** PREP If you keep **off** a street or piece of land, you do not step on it or go there. ❑ *Locking up men does nothing more than keep them off the streets.* • ADV **Off** is also an adverb. [ADV after v] ❑ *...a sign saying "Keep Off."* **4** PREP If something is situated **off** a place such as a coast, room, or road, it is near to it or next to it, but not exactly in it. ❑ *The boat was anchored off the northern coast of the peninsula.* ❑ *Lily lives in a penthouse just off Park Avenue.* **5** ADV If you go **off**, you leave a place. ❑ *He was just about to drive off when the secretary came running out.* ❑ *She was off again. Last year she had been to Kenya. This year it was Goa.* **6** ADV When you take **off** clothing or jewelry that you are wearing, you remove it from your body. [ADV after v] ❑ *He took off his spectacles and rubbed frantically at the lens.* **7** ADV If you have time **off** or a particular day **off**, you do not go to work or school, for example because you are ill or it is a day when you do not usually work. ❑ *The rest of the men had the day off.* ❑ *I'm off tomorrow.* • PREP **Off** is also a preposition. ❑ *He could not get time off work to go on holiday.* **8** PREP If you keep **off** a subject, you deliberately avoid talking about it. ❑ *Keep off the subject of politics.* **9** ADV If something such as an agreement or a sports event is **off**, it is canceled. ❑ *Until Pointon is completely happy, however, the deal's off.* **10** PREP If someone is **off** something harmful such as a drug, they have stopped taking or using it. ❑ *She felt better and the psychiatrist took her off drug therapy.* **11** PREP If you are **off** something, you have stopped liking it. ❑ *I'm off coffee at the moment.* **12** ADV When something such as a machine or electric light is **off**, it is not functioning or in use. When you switch it **off**, you stop it from functioning. ❑ *As he pulled into the driveway, he saw her bedroom light was off.* ❑ *We used sail power and turned the engine off to save our fuel.* **13** PREP If there is money **off** something, its price is reduced by the amount specified. [amount PREP n] ❑ *...Simons Leatherwear, 37 Old Christchurch Road. 20 per cent off all jackets this Saturday.* • ADV **Off** is also an adverb. ❑ *Take $5 off the regular price of any membership.* **14** ADV If something is a long way **off**, it is a long distance away from you. [n/amount ADV] ❑ *Florida was a long way off.* **15** ADV If something is a long time **off**, it will not happen for a long time. [n/amount ADV] ❑ *An end to the crisis seems a long way off.* **16** PREP If you get something **off** someone, you obtain it from them. [SPOKEN] ❑ *I don't really get a lot of information, and if I do I get it off Mark.* **17** ADV If food has gone **off**, it tastes and smells bad because it is no longer fresh enough to be eaten. [mainly BRIT; AM usually **spoiled, bad**] [v-link ADJ] ❑ *Food can be something of a problem. It goes off, and when it's gone off it smells.* **18** PREP If you live **off** a particular kind of food, you eat it in order to live. If you live **off** a particular source of money, you use it to live. [v PREP n] ❑ *Her husband's memories of living off roast chicken and drinking whisky.* **19** PREP If a machine runs **off** a particular kind of fuel or power, it uses that power in order to function. [v PREP n] ❑ *The electric armor runs off the tank's power supply.* **20** PHRASE If something happens **on and off**, or **off and on**, it happens occasionally, or only for part of a period of time, not in a regular or continuous way. ❑ *I was still working on and off as a waitress to support myself.*

offal /ɔfl, BRIT ɒfl/ N-UNCOUNT **Offal** is the internal organs of animals, for example their hearts and livers, when they are cooked and eaten. ❑ *...imports of fresh meat and offal to the EU.*

off-balance also **off balance 1** ADJ If someone or something is **off-balance**, they can easily fall or be knocked over because they are not standing firmly. [v n ADJ, v-link ADJ] ❑ *He tried to use his own weight to push his attacker off but he was off balance.* **2** ADJ If someone is caught **off-balance**, they are extremely surprised or upset by a particular event or piece of news they are not expecting. ❑ *Mullins knocked me off-balance with his abrupt change of subject.*

off-duty ADJ When someone such as a soldier or police officer is **off-duty**, they are not working. ❑ *The place is the haunt of off-duty policemen.*

offence /əfɛns/ →see **offense**

Word Link	fend ≈ striking : defend, fender, offend

offend /əfɛnd/ (**offends, offending, offended**) **1** V-T/V-I If you **offend** someone, you say or do something rude which upsets or embarrasses them. ❑ *He*

---

1 부사 물론 [구어체] ❑ 물론 전시회에는 다른 재미있는 것들이 많이 있었다. ❑ "저는 신문에서 당신에 관한 기사를 읽었습니다."라고 찰리가 말했다. **2** 관용 표현 물론입니다 [구어체, 의례적인 표현] ❑ "토요일의 우승컵 쟁탈전 경기에 대해 좀 이야기해도 될까요?" "예, 물론입니다." **3** 부사 당연히; 물론 [구어체, 강조] ❑ "네가 옳다고 생각해." "당연히 내가 옳지." ❑ 물론 나는 두렵지 않아! **4** 관용 표현 물론 아니다 [구어체, 강조] ❑ "이 일을 정말 심각하게 고려하고 있는 건 아니겠지, 그렇지?" "그럼, 물론 아니지."

전치사는 /ɔf/로 발음되고, 부사는 /ɔf/로 발음된다.

off는 아래 용법 외에도 추가 정보를 나타내기 위해 일부의 동사, 명사 뒤에도 쓴다. 또한 'get off', 'pair off', 'sleep off'와 같은 구동사에도 쓰인다.

1 전치사 -로부터 떨어져 ❑ 그가 책상에서 발을 떼었다. ❑ 나는 그녀의 머리 위에 있는 열쇠걸이에서 그 방 열쇠를 떼어냈다. • 부사 떨어져 ❑ 리가 작은 오렌지 한 조각을 떼어내서 그에게 내밀었다. **2** 전치사 -로부터 ❑ 열차가 달리고 있을 때 타거나 내리려 하지 마세요! • 부사 (탈것에서) 내려 ❑ 다음 정류장에서 그 사람도 내리더니 자기소개를 했다. **3** 전치사 -에 가지 않아 ❑ 사람을 감금한다는 것은 단지 길거리에 다니지 못하게 하는 것일 뿐이다. • 부사 가지 않아 ❑ "출입 금지"라고 쓰인 표지판 **4** 전치사 -의 가까이에 ❑ 그 배는 반도의 북쪽 연안에 정박했다. ❑ 릴리는 파크 애비뉴 바로 옆에 있는 최고층 호화 아파트에 산다. **5** 부사 떠나 ❑ 비서가 달려 나왔을 때 그는 막 차를 몰고 떠나려는 참이었다. ❑ 그녀는 다시 떠났다. 지난해에는 케냐에 갔었다. 올해는 고아였다. **6** 부사 벗어 ❑ 그는 안경을 벗고 미친 듯이 렌즈를 문질렀다. **7** 부사 (근무 등을) 쉬어 ❑ 나머지 사람들은 근무를 쉬었다. ❑ 내일은 쉰다. • 전치사 -을 쉬어 ❑ 그는 일을 쉬고 휴가를 갈 수가 없었다. **8** 전치사 -을 피하여 ❑ 정치와 관련된 화제는 피하세요. **9** 부사 취소되어 ❑ 하지만, 포인톤이 완전히 기뻐할 때까지 그 계약은 취소다. **10** 전치사 -을 끊고 ❑ 그녀가 기분이 나아지자 정신과 의사는 그녀에 대한 약물 요법을 중단했다. **11** 전치사 -이 싫어져, -을 끊고 ❑ 지금은 커피를 마시지 않는다. **12** 부사 (기계 등이) 꺼져 ❑ 차를 몰고 진입로로 들어섰을 때, 그는 그녀의 침실 불이 꺼져 있는 것을 보았다. ❑ 우리는 연료를 아끼기 위해 엔진을 끄고 돛에 바람을 받으며 항해했다. **13** 전치사 -을 할인하여 ❑ 사이먼스 가죽의류, 올드 크라이스트처치 로드 37번지. 이번 토요일 모든 재킷류 20퍼센트 할인. • 부사 할인하여 ❑ 회원 정가에서 5달러를 할인 받으세요. **14** 부사 (거리상으로) 떨어져 ❑ 플로리다는 멀리 떨어져 있었다. **15** 부사 (시간적으로) 떨어져 ❑ 그 위기의 끝은 아직 먼 것 같다. **16** 전치사 -로부터 [구어체] ❑ 나는 사실 정보를 많이 얻지 못하고, 설사 얻는다 해도 마크로부터 얻는다. **17** 형용사 (음식이) 상한 [주로 영국영어; 미국영어 대개 spoiled, bad] ❑ 식품은 하나의 문제가 될 수 있다. 식품은 상하고, 상하면 냄새가 난다. **18** 전치사 -에 의존하여 ❑ 그녀 남편의 추억은 구운 닭고기를 즐겨 먹으며 위스키를 마시던 것에 대한 것이다. **19** 전치사 -을 동력으로 하여 ❑ 이 전기 장갑은 탱크의 전력 공급 장치에서 동력을 얻어 작동한다. **20** 구 단속적으로, 이따금씩 ❑ 나는 여전히 생활비를 벌기 위해 이따금씩 웨이트리스로 일하고 있었다.

불가산명사 (짐승의) 내장 ❑ 유럽 연합으로 들어오는 정육과 내장의 수입

1 형용사 균형을 잃은, 불안정한 ❑ 그는 자신의 몸무게를 이용해서 공격수를 밀어내려고 했지만 균형을 잃었다. **2** 형용사 몹시 놀란, 크게 당황한 ❑ 멀린스는 갑작스럽게 화제를 바꿔서 나를 몹시 당황하게 했다.

형용사 비번의 ❑ 그곳은 비번인 경찰관들이 자주 드나드는 곳이다.

1 타동사/자동사 기분을 상하게 하다 ❑ 그는 자신이 한 말에 대해 사과하고 주민들의 기분을 상하게

apologizes for his comments and says he had no intention of offending the community. ❑ *The survey found almost 90 percent of people were offended by strong swearwords.* ● **of·fend·ed** ADJ [v-link ADJ] ❑ *She is terribly offended, angered and hurt by this.* ② V-I If someone **offends**, they commit a crime. [FORMAL] [no cont] ❑ *In Western countries girls are far less likely to offend than boys.*

of·fend·er /əfɛndər/ (**offenders**) ① N-COUNT An **offender** is a person who has committed a crime. ❑ *The authorities often know that sex offenders will attack again when they are released.* ② N-COUNT You can refer to someone or something which you think is causing a problem as an **offender**. ❑ *The contraceptive pill is the worst offender, but it is not the only drug to deplete the body's vitamin levels.*

of·fense ♦♢♢ /əfɛns/ (**offenses**) [BRIT **offence**] ① N-COUNT An **offense** is a crime that breaks a particular law and requires a particular punishment. ❑ *A first offense carries a fine of $1,000.* ② N-VAR **Offense** or an **offense** is behavior which causes people to be upset or embarrassed. ❑ *He said he didn't mean to give offense.* ③ CONVENTION Some people say "**no offense**" to make it clear that they do not want to upset you, although what they are saying may seem rather rude. [FORMULAE] ❑ *"No offense," she said, "but your sister seems a little gloomy."* ④ PHRASE If someone **takes offense at** something you say or do, they feel upset, often unnecessarily, because they think you are being rude to them. ❑ *Instead of taking offense, the woman smiled.*

Thesaurus   *offense*의 참조어

N.	crime, wrongdoing ①
	attack, insult, snub ②

Word Partnership   *offense*의 연어

V.	**commit an** offense ① ②
	take offense ④
ADJ.	**criminal** offense ①
	serious offense ① ②

---

of·fen·sive ♦♢♢ /əfɛnsɪv/ (**offensives**) ① ADJ Something that is **offensive** upsets or embarrasses people because it is rude or insulting. ❑ *Some friends of his found the play horribly offensive.* ② N-COUNT A military **offensive** is a carefully planned attack made by a large group of soldiers. ❑ *Its latest military offensive against rebel forces is aimed at re-opening important trade routes.* ③ N-COUNT If you conduct an **offensive**, you take strong action to show how angry you are about something or how much you disapprove of something. ❑ *Republicans acknowledged that they had little choice but to mount an all-out offensive on the Democratic nominee.* ④ PHRASE If you **go on the offensive**, go over to the **offensive**, or **take the offensive**, you begin to take strong action against people who have been attacking you. ❑ *The West African forces went on the offensive in response to attacks on them.*

Word Partnership   *offensive*의 연어

N.	offensive **language** ①
	offensive **capability**, **ground** offensive, offensive **operations**, offensive **weapons** ②
V.	**launch an** offensive, **mount an** offensive ② ③
	take the offensive ④

---

of·fer ♦♦♦ /ɒfər, BRIT ɒfər/ (**offers, offering, offered**) ① V-T If you **offer** something to someone, you ask them if they would like to have it or use it. ❑ *He has offered seats at the conference table to the Russian leader and the president of Kazakhstan.* ❑ *The number of companies offering them work increased.* ② V-T If you **offer to** do something, you say that you are willing to do it. ❑ *Peter offered to teach them water-skiing.* ③ N-COUNT An **offer** is something that someone says they will give you or do for you. ❑ *The offer of talks with Moscow marks a significant change from the previous western position.* ❑ *"I ought to reconsider her offer to move in," he mused.* ④ V-T If you **offer** someone information, advice, or praise, you give it to them, usually because you feel that they need it or deserve it. ❑ *They manage a company offering advice on mergers and acquisitions.* ❑ *She offered him emotional and practical support in countless ways.* ⑤ V-T If you **offer** someone something such as love or friendship, you show them that you feel that way toward them. ❑ *The President has offered his sympathy to the Georgian people.* ❑ *It must be better to be able to offer them love and security.* ⑥ V-T If people **offer** prayers, praise, or a sacrifice to God or a god, they speak to or give something to their god. ❑ *Church leaders offered prayers and condemned the bloodshed.* ● PHRASAL VERB **Offer up** means the same as **offer**. ❑ *He should consider offering up a prayer to St Lambert.* ⑦ V-T If an organization **offers** something such as a service or product, it provides it. ❑ *We have been successful because we are offering a quality service.* ❑ *Sainsbury's is offering customers 1p for each shopping bag re-used.* ⑧ N-COUNT An **offer** in a store is a specially low price for a specific product or something extra that you get if you buy a certain product. [oft supp N, also on N] ❑ *This month's offers include a shirt, trousers, and bed covers.* ❑ *Today's special offer gives you a choice of three destinations.* ⑨ V-T If you **offer** a particular amount of money for something, you say that you will pay that much to buy it. ❑ *Whitney has offered $21.50 a share in cash for 49.5 million Prime shares.* ❑ *They are offering farmers $2.15 a bushel for corn.* ⑩ N-COUNT An **offer** is the amount of money that someone says they will pay to buy something. ❑ *The lawyers say no one else will make me an offer.* ⑪ PHRASE If you **have something to offer**, you have a quality or ability that makes you

---

의도는 없었다고 말한다. ❑ 거의 90퍼센트에 달하는 사람들이 심한 욕설 때문에 기분이 상했음이 그 조사를 통해 드러났다. ● 기분이 상한 형용사 ❑ 그녀는 이 일 때문에 몹시 감정이 상하고 화가 났다. ② 자동사 죄를 저지르다 [격식체] ❑ 서방 국가에서 여자 아이들은 남자 아이들보다 범죄를 저지를 확률이 훨씬 낮다.

① 가산명사 범죄자, 위반자 ❑ 성범죄자들이 풀려나면 다시 범죄를 저지르기 마련이라는 사실을 당국에서 알고 있을 때가 많다. ② 가산명사 문젯거리 ❑ 피임약이 가장 큰 문젯거리이지만, 그것만이 체내 비타민 수준을 고갈시키는 약은 아니다.

[영국영어 offence] ① 가산명사 범죄 ❑ 초범에는 1,000달러의 벌금이 부과된다. ② 가산명사 또는 불가산명사 기분을 상하게 하는 것; 모욕 ❑ 그는 기분을 상하게 할 뜻은 없었다고 말했다. ③ 관용 표현 기분 나쁘게 생각하지 마 [의례적인 표현] ❑ "기분 나쁘게 생각 마라." 그녀가 말했다. "하지만 네 누이가 약간 우울해 보이는구나." ④ 구 -에 화를 내다, 감정 상해하다 ❑ 그 여자는 화를 내는 대신 미소를 지었다.

① 형용사 무례한; 모욕적인 ❑ 그의 친구 몇 명이 보기에 그 연극은 끔찍하게 모욕적이었다. ② 가산명사 (군사) 공격 ❑ 반군에 대한 가장 최근의 군사 공격은 중요한 교역 통로를 다시 열기 위한 것이다. ③ 가산명사 공세 ❑ 공화당원들은 민주당 지명자에 대해 전면적인 공세를 펼치는 것 외에 선택의 여지가 별로 없다는 것을 인정했다. ④ 구 공세를 취하다 ❑ 서아프리카 군대는 자신들이 받은 공격에 대응하여 공세를 취했다.

① 타동사 제의하다, 제안하다 ❑ 그는 러시아 지도자와 카자흐스탄 대통령에게 회담 테이블을 제의할 것을 제의했다. ❑ 그들에게 일자리를 제의하는 회사 수가 늘어났다. ② 타동사 제의하다 ❑ 피터는 그들에게 수상 스키를 가르쳐 주겠다고 제의했다. ③ 가산명사 제안, 제의 ❑ 모스크바와의 회담 제안은 이전까지의 서방 측 태도와 중요한 변화를 나타낸다. ❑ "이사장 들어오라는 그녀의 제의를 다시 생각해 봐야겠어."라고 그는 생각에 잠겨 말했다. ④ 타동사 제공하다, 주다 ❑ 그들은 인수 합병에 대한 조언을 제공하는 회사를 운영한다. ❑ 그녀는 무수히 많은 방법으로 정서적 및 실제적 후원을 제공했다. ⑤ 타동사 (감정을) 표현하다 ❑ 대통령은 조지아 주 사람들에게 연민을 표해 왔다. ❑ 그들에게 애정과 안심을 표할 수 있는 것이 틀림없이 더 낫다. ⑥ 타동사 (기도를) 드리다, (신 등에) 바치다 ❑ 교회 지도자들은 기도를 올리고 학살을 규탄했다. ● 구동사 (기도를) 드리다, (신 등에) 바치다 ❑ 그는 성 램버트에게 기도를 드리는 것을 고려해야 한다. ⑦ 타동사 제공하다, 주다 ❑ 우리는 질 좋은 서비스를 제공하고 있기 때문에 번창해 왔다. ❑ '세인스베리스'는 재사용하는 쇼핑백 하나당 1페니를 고객들께 드리고 있습니다. ⑧ 가산명사 특가; 특별 사은품 ❑ 이번 달의 특별 사은품으로는 셔츠, 바지, 침대 커버가 있습니다. ❑ 오늘의 특별 사은품으로 세 곳의 행선지 중 하나를 선택하실 수 있습니다. ⑨ 타동사 (얼마의 값을) 제시하다 ❑ 휘트니는 4천 9백 5십만 주의 프라임사 주식에 대해 주당 현금으로 21.50달러의 값을 제시했다. ❑ 그들은 농부들에게 옥수수 1부셸당 2.15달러의 값을 부르고 있다. ⑩ 가산명사 제시 가격

important, attractive, or useful. ❑ *In your free time, explore all that this incredible city has to offer.* ⑫ PHRASE If there is something **on offer**, it is available to be used or bought. ❑ *They are making trips to check out the merchandise on offer.* ⑬ PHRASE If you are **open to offers**, you are willing to do something if someone will pay you an amount of money that you think is reasonable. ❑ *It seems that while the Kiwis are keen to have him, he is still open to offers.*

of·fer·ing ♦◇◇ /ˈɔfərɪŋ, BRIT ˈɒfərɪŋ/ (**offerings**) ❶ N-COUNT An **offering** is something that is specially produced to be sold. ❑ *It was very, very good, far better than vegetarian offerings in many a posh restaurant.* ❷ N-COUNT An **offering** is a gift that people offer to their God or gods as a form of worship. ❑ *...the holiest of the Shinto rituals, where offerings are made at night to the great Sun.*

of·fer price (**offer prices**) N-COUNT The **offer price** for a particular stock or share is the price that the person selling it says that they want for it. [BUSINESS] ❑ *BET shares closed just above the offer price, up 1.5p at 207p.* →see also **asking price, bid price**

of·fice ♦♦♦ /ˈɔfɪs, BRIT ˈɒfɪs/ (**offices**) ❶ N-COUNT An **office** is a room or a part of a building where people work sitting at desks. ❑ *By the time Flynn arrived at his office it was 5:30.* ❑ *Telephone their head office for more details.* ❷ N-COUNT An **office** is a department of an organization, especially the government, where people deal with a particular kind of administrative work. [N-IN-NAMES] ❑ *Thousands have registered with unemployment offices.* ❑ *...Downing Street's press office.* ❸ N-COUNT An **office** is a small building or room where people can go for information, tickets, or a service of some kind. ❑ *The tourist office operates a useful room-finding service.* ❹ N-COUNT A doctor's or dentist's **office** is a place where a doctor or dentist sees their patients. [AM; BRIT **surgery**] ❑ *The chance of getting AIDS at the doctor's or dentist's office is extremely low.* ❺ N-UNCOUNT If someone holds **office** in a government, they have an important job or position of authority. ❑ *The events to mark the President's ten years in office went ahead as planned.* ❑ *The president shall hold office for five years.* ❻ →see also **box office, post office**
→see Picture Dictionary: **office**

of·fice hours N-PLURAL **Office hours** are the times when an office or similar place is open for business. For example, office hours in the United States and Britain are usually from 9 o'clock and 5 o'clock from Monday to Friday. ❑ *If you have any queries, please call Anne Fisher on 0121-414-6203 during office hours.*

of·fic·er ♦♦♦ /ˈɔfɪsər, BRIT ˈɒfɪsəʳ/ (**officers**) ❶ N-COUNT In the armed forces, an **officer** is a person in a position of authority. ❑ *...a retired British army officer.* ❷ N-COUNT An **officer** is a person who has a responsible position in an organization, especially a government organization. ❑ *...a local authority education officer.* ❸ N-COUNT Members of the police force can be referred to as **officers.** ❑ *...senior officers in the West Midlands police force.* ❹ →see also **police officer, probation officer**

of·fi·cial ♦♦♦ /əˈfɪʃᵊl/ (**officials**) ❶ ADJ **Official** means approved by the government or by someone in authority. ❑ *According to the official figures, over one thousand people died during the revolution.* ❑ *An official announcement is expected in the next few days.* ● **of·fi·cial·ly** ADV ❑ *The election results have still not been officially announced.* ❷ ADJ **Official** activities are carried out by a person in authority as part of their job. [ADJ n] ❑ *The President is in Brazil for an official two-day visit.* ❸ ADJ **Official** things are used by a person in authority as part of their job. [ADJ n] ❑ *...the official residence of the Head of State.* ❹ ADJ If you describe someone's explanation or reason for something as the **official** explanation, you are suggesting that it is probably not true, but is used because the real explanation is embarrassing. [ADJ n] ❑ *The official explanation for the cancellation*

❑ 다른 어떤 사람도 나에게 가격을 제시하지 않을 것이라고 변호사들이 말한다. ⑪구 (매력적인 것을) 갖고 있다 ❑ 여가 시간에, 이 엄청난 도시가 가지고 있는 모든 매력을 탐험해 보세요. ⑫구 매물로 나온 ❑ 그들은 매물로 나온 상품들을 확인하기 위해 출장을 다니고 있다. ⑬구 제안을 수락할 용의가 있는 ❑ 뉴질랜드 사람들이 그를 몹시 원하지만, 그는 아직 다른 제안을 수락할 용의가 있는 것 같다.

❶ 가산명사 (특별한 용도로 판) 상품 ❑ 많은 호화 레스토랑에서 제공하는 채식주의자들을 위한 식사보다 그것이 훨씬 더 좋았습니다. ❷ 가산명사 제물 ❑ 밤중에 태양신에게 제물을 바치는 가장 거룩한 신도 의식

가산명사 (증권) 매도호가 [경제] ❑ 비이티 주식이 1.5포인트 오른 207포인트로 매도호가를 약간 상회하는 선에서 마감되었다.

❶ 가산명사 사무실 ❑ 플린이 그의 사무실에 도착했을 때가 5시 30분이었다. ❑ 더 자세한 문의는 본사로 전화하세요. ❷ 가산명사 부처 ❑ 실업 담당 부처에 수천 명이 등록했다. ❑ 다우닝가의 언론 담당 부처 ❸ 가산명사 사무소 ❑ 관광안내소에서는 유용한 숙박 안내 서비스를 제공한다. ❹ 가산명사 진료실 [미국영어; 영국영어 surgery] ❑ 병원이나 치과 진료실에서 에이즈에 걸릴 확률은 굉장히 낮다. ❺ 불가산명사 공직 ❑ 대통령의 집권 10년을 기념하기 위한 행사는 계획대로 진행되었다. ❑ 대통령은 5년 재직하게 될 것이다.

복수명사 근무 시간 ❑ 문의 사항은 앤 피셔에게 0121-414-6203으로 근무 시간 중에 전화하세요.

❶ 가산명사 장교 ❑ 퇴역한 영국 육군 장교 ❷ 가산명사 공무원 ❑ 지방 정부 교육 담당 공무원 ❸ 가산명사 경찰관 ❑ 웨스트 미들랜드 경찰서의 중견 경찰관들

❶ 형용사 공식적인 ❑ 공식 수치에 따르면, 그 혁명 기간 동안 천 명 이상이 목숨을 잃었다. ❑ 수일 내에 공식 성명이 있을 것이다. ● 공식적으로 부사 ❑ 선거 결과가 아직 공식적으로 발표되지 않았다. ❷ 형용사 공적인 ❑ 대통령은 이틀간의 공식 방문으로 브라질에 체재중이다. ❸ 형용사 공무의 ❑ 국가수반이 거주하는 공관 ❹ 형용사 명목상의 ❑ 그 정당 회의를 취소한 외견상 이유는 회담 장소가 없다는 것이다. ● 외견상으로, 명목상으로는 부사 ❑ 명목상으로는 그 호위병이 우리를 보호하도록 되어 있었지만, 사실은 우리의 일거수일투족을 보고하기 위해 그곳에 있었다.

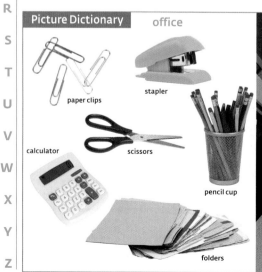

Picture Dictionary office

paper clips

stapler

calculator

scissors

pencil cup

folders

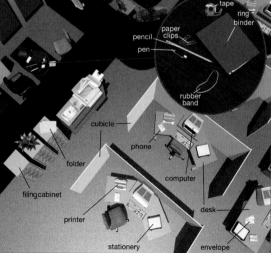

tape

ring binder

paper clips

pencil

pen

rubber band

cubicle

phone

folder

computer

filing cabinet

printer

desk

stationery

envelope

of the party conference is that there are no premises available. ● **of|fi|cial|ly** ADV [ADV with cl/group] □ *Officially, the guard was to protect us. In fact, they were there to report on our movements.* **5** N-COUNT An **official** is a person who holds a position of authority in an organization. □ *A senior UN official hopes to visit Baghdad this month.* **6** N-COUNT An **official** at a sports event is a referee, umpire, or other person who checks that the players follow the rules. □ *Officials suspended the game because of safety concerns.*

Thesaurus   official의 참조어

ADJ.   formal, legitimate, valid; *(ant.)* unauthorized, unofficial **1**
N.   administrator, director, executive, manager **5**

Word Partnership   official의 연어

N.   official **documents**, official **language**, official **report**, official
sources, official **statement 1**
official **duties**, official **visit 2**
administration official, **city** official, **government** official,
military official **5**
ADJ.   **federal** official, **local** official, **senior** official, **top** official **5**

---

off-licence (**off-licences**) N-COUNT An **off-licence** is a store which sells beer, wine, and other alcoholic drinks. [BRIT; AM **liquor store**] □ *I'm going to the off-licence to buy some whisky.*

off|line /ɒflaɪn/ ADJ If a computer is **offline**, it is not connected to the Internet. Compare **online**. [COMPUTING] □ *Initially the system was offline for a number of days.* ● ADV **Offline** is also an adverb. [ADV with v] □ *Most software programs allow you to compose emails offline.* **off line →see line**

off-peak ADJ You use **off-peak** to describe something that happens or that is used at times when there is least demand for it. Prices at off-peak times are often lower than at other times. [ADJ n] □ *Drivers now pay 33 cents during peak hours and 30 cents during off-peak hours.* ● ADV **Off-peak** is also an adverb. [ADV after v] □ *Each tape lasts three minutes and costs 36p per minute off-peak and 48p at all other times.*

off|set /ɒfsɛt, BRIT ɒfsɛt/ (**offsets, offsetting**)

The form **offset** is used in the present tense and is the past tense and past participle of the verb.

V-T If one thing **is offset** by another, the effect of the first thing is reduced by the second, so that any advantage or disadvantage is canceled out. □ *The increase in pay costs was more than offset by higher productivity.*

off|shoot /ɒfʃuːt, BRIT ɒfʃuːt/ (**offshoots**) N-COUNT If one thing is an **offshoot** of another, it has developed from that other thing. □ *Psychology began as a purely academic offshoot of natural philosophy.*

off|shore /ɒfʃɔr, BRIT ɒfʃɔːr/ **1** ADJ **Offshore** means situated or happening in the sea, near to the coast. [ADJ n] □ *...Britain's offshore oil industry.* ● ADV **Offshore** is also an adverb. □ *One day a larger ship anchored offshore.* **2** ADJ **Offshore** investments or companies are located in a place, usually an island, which has fewer tax regulations than most other countries. [BUSINESS] [ADJ n] □ *The island offers a wide range of offshore banking facilities.*

off|side /ɒfsaɪd, BRIT ɒfsaɪd/ also **off-side 1** ADJ In football, a player is **offside** if they cross the line of scrimmage before a play begins. **2** ADJ In games such as soccer or hockey, when an attacking player is **offside**, they have broken the rules by being nearer to the goal than a defending player when the ball is passed to them. □ *The goal was disallowed because Wark was offside.* ● ADV **Offside** is also an adverb. [ADV after v] □ *Wise was standing at least ten yards offside.* ● N-UNCOUNT **Offside** is also a noun. □ *Rush had a 45th-minute goal disallowed for offside.*

off|spring /ɒfsprɪŋ, BRIT ɒfsprɪŋ/

Offspring is both the singular and the plural form.

N-COUNT You can refer to a person's children or to an animal's young as their **offspring**. [FORMAL] □ *Eleanor was now less anxious about her offspring than she had once been.*

of|ten ♦♦♦ /ɒfən, BRIT ɒfən/

Often is usually used before the verb, but it may be used after the verb when it has a word like "less" or "more" before it, or when the clause is negative.

1 ADV If something **often** happens, it happens many times or much of the time. □ *They often spent Christmas at Prescott Hill.* □ *That doesn't happen very often.* **2** ADV You use **how often** to ask questions about frequency. You also use **often** in reported clauses and other statements to give information about the frequency of something. □ *How often do you brush your teeth?*

You do not use **often** to talk about something that happens several times within a short period of time. You do not say, for example, "I often phoned her yesterday." You say **"I phoned her several times yesterday"** or **"I kept phoning her yesterday."**

---

5 가산명사 공직자, 관리 □ 한 유엔 고위 관리가 이번 달에 바그다드를 방문하기를 희망한다. **6** 가산명사 심판 □ 심판들은 안전 문제로 그 경기를 중단시켰다.

가산명사 주류 판매점 [영국영어; 미국영어 liquor store] □ 위스키를 좀 사러 주류 판매점에 갈 거야.

형용사 오프라인의, 인터넷 연결이 안 되는 [컴퓨터] □ 처음 며칠 동안 그 시스템이 인터넷 연결이 안 됐었다. ● 부사 오프라인으로 □ 대부분의 소프트웨어 프로그램은 이메일을 오프라인으로 쓸 수 있도록 하고 있다.

형용사 한산할 때의, 비수기의 □ 운전자들이 이제 한산한 시간대에는 30센트를 내고, 복잡한 시간대에는 33센트를 낸다. ● 부사 비수기에 □ 각 녹음테이프는 3분짜리인데, 비수기에는 1분에 36펜스이고 그 외 다른 때에는 48펜스이다.

offset은 동사의 현재, 과거, 과거 분사로 쓴다.

타동사 상쇄되다 □ 생산 증가가 급여비용 상승을 상쇄하지 못했다.

가산명사 분파 □ 심리학은 순전히 자연철학의 학문적인 분파로서 출발했다.

1 형용사 연안의 □ 영국 연안의 석유 산업 ● 부사 연안에 □ 어느 날 더 큰 배 한 척이 연안에 닻을 내렸다. **2** 형용사 조세 우대의 [경제] □ 그 섬나라는 광범위한 조세 우대 금융 혜택을 제공한다.

1 형용사 (축구) 오프사이드의 **2** 형용사 오프사이드를 범한 □ 와크가 오프사이드를 범해서 득점으로 인정받지 못했다. ● 부사 오프사이드 지점에 □ 와이즈가 적어도 오프사이드 십 야드 지점에 서 있었다. ● 불가산명사 오프사이드 □ 러시가 45분에 넣은 골이 오프사이드로 득점으로 인정되지 않았다.

offspring은 단수형 및 복수형이다.

가산명사 자식, 자손 [격식체] □ 엘리노어는 그때는 옛날에 그랬던 것보다 자식에 대해서 덜 안달했다.

often은 대개 동사 앞에 쓰지만 앞에 'less'나 'more'와 같은 단어가 있거나 절이 부정일 경우에는 동사 뒤에 쓸 수도 있다.

1 부사 자주 □ 그들은 자주 크리스마스를 프레스콧 힐에서 보냈다. □ 그 일은 자주 일어나지는 않는다. **2** 부사 얼마나 자주; 자주 □ 얼마나 자주 이를 닦습니까?

often은 짧은 기간 내에 여러 번 일어나는 것에 대해 말할 때는 쓰지 않는다. 예를 들면, "I often phoned her yesterday."라고 하지 않고 "I phoned her several times yesterday." 또는 "I kept phoning her yesterday."라고 한다.

A

❸ PHRASE If something happens **every so often**, it happens regularly, but with fairly long intervals between each occasion. ❑ *She's going to come back every so often.* **❹** PHRASE If you say that something happens **as often as not**, or **more often than not**, you mean that it happens fairly frequently, and that this can be considered as typical of the kind of situation you are talking about. ❑ *Yet, as often as not, they find themselves the target of persecution rather than praise.*

B

❸ 구 가끔 ❑ 그녀는 가끔 돌아오려고 한다. ❹ 구 상당히 자주 ❑ 하지만, 상당히 자주 그들은 찬사보다는 책망의 대상이 되고 있다.

Thesaurus   *often*의 참조어

ADV.   repeatedly, usually; (ant.) never, rarely, seldom **❶**

C

oh ♦♦◇ /oʊ/ **❶** CONVENTION You use **oh** to introduce a response or a comment on something that has just been said. [SPOKEN] ❑ *"Had you seen the car before?" — "Oh yes, it was always in the drive."* **❷** EXCLAM You use **oh** to express a feeling such as surprise, pain, annoyance, or happiness. [SPOKEN, FEELINGS] ❑ *"Oh!" Kenny blinked. "Has everyone gone?"* **❸** CONVENTION You use **oh** when you are hesitating while speaking, for example because you are trying to estimate something, or because you are searching for the right word. [SPOKEN] ❑ *I've been here, oh, since the end of June.*

D

E

F

❶ 관용 표현 아 [구어체] ❑ "그 차를 전에 본 적이 있었나요?" "아, 예. 그 차는 항상 도로에 서 있었어요." **❷** 감탄사 오 [구어체, 감정 게임] ❑ "오, 다들 갔나요?"라며 케니가 눈을 깜빡거렸다. **❸** 관용 표현 음 [구어체] ❑ 저는 여기에 쭉 있었어요, 음, 6월 말부터.

OHP /oʊ eɪtʃ pi/ (**OHPs**) N-COUNT An **OHP** is the same as an **overhead projector**.

가산명사 투사 환등기, 오버헤드 프로젝터

G

oil ♦♦◇ /ɔɪl/ (**oils, oiling, oiled**) **❶** N-MASS **Oil** is a smooth, thick liquid that is used as a fuel and for making the parts of machines move smoothly. Oil is found underground. ❑ *The company buys and sells about 600,000 barrels of oil a day.* ❑ *...the rapid rise in prices for oil and petrol.* **❷** V-T If you **oil** something, you put oil onto or into it, for example to make it work smoothly or to protect it. ❑ *A crew of assistants oiled and adjusted the release mechanism until it worked perfectly.* **❸** N-MASS **Oil** is a smooth, thick liquid made from plants and is often used for cooking. ❑ *Combine the beans, chopped mint, and olive oil in a large bowl.* **❹** N-MASS **Oil** is a smooth, thick liquid, often with a pleasant smell, that you rub into your skin or add to your bath. ❑ *Try a hot bath with some relaxing bath oil.* **❺** →see also **crude oil, olive oil** **❻** to **burn the midnight oil** →see **midnight** →see **ship** →see Word Web: oil

H

I

J

❶ 물질명사 석유 ❑ 그 회사는 하루 약 60만 배럴의 석유를 사고판다. ❑ 석유와 휘발유 가격의 급상승 **❷** 타동사 윤활유를 치다 ❑ 그것이 잘 작동될 때까지 조수들이 윤활유를 칠하고 해지 장치를 조정했다. **❸** 물질명사 기름 ❑ 큰 그릇에 콩과 잘게 썬 박하를 넣고, 올리브기름을 넣어 잘 버무리세요. **❹** 물질명사 오일 ❑ 뜨거운 물에 몸을 풀어 주는 목욕 오일을 몇 방울 넣고 목욕해 보세요.

oil paint (**oil paints**) N-UNCOUNT **Oil paint** is a thick paint used by artists. It is made from colored powder and linseed oil. [also N in pl]

불가산명사 유성 물감

K

oil paint|ing (**oil paintings**) N-COUNT An **oil painting** is a picture which has been painted using oil paints. ❑ *Several magnificent oil paintings adorn the walls.*

가산명사 유화 ❑ 멋진 유화 몇 점이 벽을 장식하고 있다.

L

oil rig (**oil rigs**) N-COUNT An **oil rig** is a structure on land or in the sea that is used when getting oil from the ground.

가산명사 석유 굴착 장치

oil slick (**oil slicks**) N-COUNT An **oil slick** is a layer of oil that is floating on the sea or on a lake because it has accidentally come out of a ship or container. ❑ *The oil slick is now 35 miles long.*

M

가산명사 기름띠 ❑ 현재 그 기름띠가 35마일에 걸쳐 뻗어 있다.

oily /ɔɪli/ (**oilier, oiliest**) **❶** ADJ Something that is **oily** is covered with oil or contains oil. ❑ *He was wiping his hands on an oily rag.* **❷** ADJ **Oily** means looking, feeling, tasting, or smelling like oil. ❑ *...traces of an oily substance.*

N

❶ 형용사 기름기가 있는 ❑ 그는 기름기 있는 천으로 손을 닦고 있었다. **❷** 형용사 기름 같은 ❑ 기름 같은 물질의 흔적

oint|ment /ɔɪntmənt/ (**ointments**) **❶** N-MASS An **ointment** is a smooth thick substance that is put on sore skin or a wound to help it heal. ❑ *A range of ointments and creams is available for the treatment of eczema.* **❷** PHRASE If you describe someone or something as a **fly in the ointment**, you think they spoil a situation and prevent it from being as successful as you had hoped. ❑ *Rachel seems to be the one fly in the ointment of Caroline's smooth life.*

O

❶ 물질명사 연고 ❑ 습진 치료를 위한 다양한 연고와 크림이 있다. **❷** 구 옥의 티 ❑ 레이첼이 캐럴라인의 평탄한 삶에 유일한 옥의 티처럼 보인다.

okay ♦♦◇ /oʊkeɪ/ (**okays, okaying, okayed**) also **OK, O.K., ok** **❶** ADJ If you say that something is **okay**, you find it satisfactory or acceptable. [INFORMAL] ❑ *...a shooting range where it's OK to use weapons.* ❑ *Is it okay if I come by myself?* ● ADV **Okay** is also an adverb. [ADV after v] ❑ *We seemed to manage okay for the first year or so after David was born.* **❷** ADJ If you say that someone is **okay**, you mean that they are safe and well. [INFORMAL] [v-link adj] ❑ *Check that the baby's okay.* **❸** CONVENTION You can say "**Okay**" to show that you agree to something. [INFORMAL, FORMULAE] ❑ *"Just tell him Sir Kenneth would like to talk to him." — "OK."* **❹** CONVENTION You can say "**Okay?**" to check whether the person you are talking to understands what you have said and accepts it. [INFORMAL] ❑ *We'll get together next week, OK?* **❺** CONVENTION You can use **okay** to indicate that you want to start talking about something else or doing something else. [INFORMAL] ❑ *OK. Now, let's talk some business.* **❻** CONVENTION You can use **okay** to stop someone from arguing with you by showing that you accept the point they are making, though you do not necessarily regard it as very important. [INFORMAL] ❑ *Okay, there is a slight difference.* **❼** V-T If someone in authority **okays**

P

Q

R

S

T

❶ 형용사 괜찮은 [비격식체] ❑ 무기를 사용해도 괜찮은 사격장 ❑ 나 혼자 와도 괜찮니? ● 부사 잘 ❑ 데이비드가 태어난 후 1년 정도는 우리가 잘 해나갔던 것 같았다. **❷** 형용사 괜찮은 [비격식체] ❑ 아기가 괜찮은지 확인하세요. **❸** 관용 표현 알았어 [비격식체, 의례적인 표현] ❑ "그에게 케네스 경이 얘기하고 싶어 한다고만 전해." "알았어." **❹** 관용 표현 알았지? [비격식체] ❑ 우리는 다음 주에 만나는 거야, 알았지? **❺** 관용 표현 자 [비격식체] ❑ 자, 이제 사업 얘기 좀 합시다. **❻** 관용 표현 그래 [비격식체] ❑ 그래, 차이가 좀 있지. **❼** 타동사 허락하다 [비격식체] ❑ 그의 담당 의사가 그 여행을 허락하지 않을 텐데. ● 단수명사 허락 ❑ 그는 새로운 언론 보도 자료 공개를 허락했다.

U

V

Word Web   oil

W

There is a great demand for **petroleum** in the world today. Companies are constantly **drilling oil wells** in oilfields on land and on the ocean floor. Some offshore drilling **oil rigs** or oil platforms sit on a concrete or metal foundation on a man-made island. Others float on a ship. The **crude oil** obtained from these wells goes to **refineries** through **pipelines** or in huge **tanker** ships. At the refinery, the crude oil is processed into a variety of products including **gasoline**, **aviation fuel**, and **plastic**.

X

Y

Z

something, they officially agree to it or allow it to happen. [INFORMAL] □ *His doctor wouldn't OK the trip.* ● N-SING **Okay** is also a noun. □ *He gave the okay to issue a new press release.*

old ♦♦♦ /oʊld/ (**older**, **oldest**) **1** ADJ Someone who is **old** has lived for many years and is no longer young. □ *...a white-haired old man.* ● N-PLURAL **The old** are people who are old. □ *...providing a caring response for the needs of the old and the handicapped.* **2** ADJ You use **old** to talk about how many days, weeks, months, or years someone or something has lived or existed. [amount *old, how* ADJ] *as,* ADJ-compar *than*] □ *He was abandoned by his father when he was three months old.* □ *How old are you now?* □ *Bill was six years older than David.* **3** ADJ Something that is **old** has existed for a long time. □ *She loved the big old house.* □ *These books must be very old.* **4** ADJ Something that is **old** is no longer in good condition because of its age or because it has been used a lot. □ *He took a bunch of keys from the pocket of his old corduroy trousers.* **5** ADJ You use **old** to refer to something that is no longer used, that no longer exists, or that has been replaced by something else. [ADJ n] □ *The old road had disappeared under grass and heather.* **6** ADJ You use **old** to refer to something that used to belong to you, or to a person or thing that used to have a particular role in your life. [poss ADJ n] □ *I'll make up the bed in your old room.* □ *I still have affection for my old school.* **7** ADJ An **old** friend, enemy, or rival is someone who has been your friend, enemy, or rival for a long time. [ADJ n] □ *I called my old friend John Horner.* □ *Mr. Brownson, I assure you King's an old enemy of mine.* **8** ADJ You can use **old** to express affection when talking to or about someone you know. [INFORMAL, FEELINGS] [ADJ n] □ *Are you all right, old chap?* **9** PHRASE You use **any old** to emphasize that the quality or type of something is not important. If you say that a particular thing is **not any old** thing, you are emphasizing how special or famous it is. [INFORMAL, EMPHASIS] □ *Any old paper will do.* **10** PHRASE **In the old days** means in the past, before things changed. □ *In the old days we got a visit from the vet maybe once a year.* **11** PHRASE When people refer to **the good old days**, they are referring to a time in the past when they think that life was better than it is now. □ *He remembers the good old days when everyone in his village knew you and you could leave your door open at night.* **12 good old** →see **good. to settle an old score** →see **score**

Thesaurus	*old*의 참조어
ADJ.	elderly, mature, senior; (*ant.*) young **1**
	ancient, antique, archaic, dated, old-fashioned, outdated, traditional; (*ant.*) new **5**

old age N-UNCOUNT Your **old age** is the period of years toward the end of your life. □ *They worry about how they will support themselves in their old age.*

old age pen|sion|er (**old age pensioners**) also **old-age pensioner** N-COUNT An **old age pensioner** is a person who is old enough to receive an pension from their employer or the government. [BRIT]

old-fashioned 1 ADJ Something such as a style, method, or device that is **old-fashioned** is no longer used, done, or admired by most people, because it has been replaced by something that is more modern. □ *The house was dull, old-fashioned and in bad condition.* **2** ADJ **Old-fashioned** ideas, customs, or values are the ideas, customs, and values of the past. □ *She has some old-fashioned values and can be a strict disciplinarian.*

ol|ive /ˈɒlɪv/ (**olives**) **1** N-VAR **Olives** are small green or black fruit with a bitter taste. Olives are often pressed to make olive oil. □ *...a pile of black olives.* **2** N-COUNT An **olive tree** or an **olive** is a tree on which olives grow. □ *Olives look romantic on a hillside in Provence.* **3** COLOR Something that is **olive** is yellowish-green in color. □ *...glowing colors such as deep red, olive, saffron, and ocher.* ● COMB in COLOR **Olive** is also a combining form. □ *She wore an olive-green T-shirt.* **4** ADJ If someone has **olive** skin, the color of their skin is yellowish brown. □ *They are handsome with dark, shining hair, olive skin, and fine brown eyes.*

ol|ive oil (**olive oils**) N-MASS **Olive oil** is oil that is obtained by pressing olives. It is used for putting on salads or in cooking.

Olym|pic /əˈlɪmpɪk/ (**Olympics**) **1** ADJ **Olympic** means relating to the Olympic Games. [ADJ n] □ *...the reigning Olympic champion.* **2** N-PROPER **The Olympics** are the Olympic Games. □ *I will be in Atlanta for the next Olympics.*

Olym|pic Games N-PROPER-COLL **The Olympic Games** are a set of international sports competitions which take place every four years, each time in a different city. □ *At the 1968 Olympic Games she had won gold medals in races at 200, 400, and 800m.*

om|buds|man /ˈɒmbʊdzmən/ (**ombudsmen**) N-COUNT **The ombudsman** is an independent official who has been appointed to investigate complaints that people make against the government or public organizations. □ *The leaflet explains how to complain to the banking ombudsman.*

ome|let /ˈɒmlɪt, ˈɒməlɪt/ (**omelets**) [BRIT, sometimes AM **omelette**] N-COUNT An **omelet** is a type of food made by beating eggs and cooking them in a flat pan. □ *...a cheese omelet.*

omen /ˈoʊmɛn/ (**omens**) N-COUNT If you say that something is an **omen**, you think it indicates what is likely to happen in the future and whether it will be good or bad. □ *Her appearance at this moment is an omen of disaster.*

omi|nous /ˈɒmɪnəs/ ADJ If you describe something as **ominous**, you mean that it worries you because it makes you think that something unpleasant is going to happen. □ *There was an ominous silence at the other end of the phone.* ● **omi|nous|ly** ADV □ *The bar seemed ominously quiet.*

1 형용사 나이 든, 늙은 **1** 백발의 노인 ● 복수명사 노인들 **1** 노인과 장애인들의 필요에 대해 세심한 반응을 보이는 **2** 형용사 나이가 _인 **1** 그가 생후 3개월 되었을 때 아버지로부터 버림받았다. **1** 넌 지금 몇 살이니? **1** 빌은 데이비드보다 여섯 살 위였다. **3** 형용사 오래된 **1** 그녀는 그 오래된 큰 집을 사랑했다. **1** 이 책들은 틀림없이 굉장히 오래되었을 거야. **4** 형용사 낡은, 헌 **1** 그는 낡은 코듀로이 바지 주머니 속에서 열쇠 꾸러미를 꺼냈다. **5** 형용사 옛날의, 구~ **1** 옛날 길은 풀과 헤더로 우거져서 더 이상 보이지 않았다. **6** 형용사 예전의, 옛날의 **1** 네가 예전에 쓰던 방에 잠자리를 마련해 줄게. **1** 나는 아직도 내 예전 학교에 대해 애정이 있다. **7** 형용사 오랜 **1** 그녀는 오랜 친구인 존 호너에게 전화했다. **1** 브라운슨 씨, 제가 확실히 말씀드리건대 킹은 저의 오랜 원수입니다. **8** 형용사 잘 아는 사람을 친하게 부를 때 씀 [비격식체, 감정 개입] **1** 괜찮니, 이 사람아? **9** 구 어떤 것이든, 아무 거나 [비격식체, 강조] **1** 어떤 종이든 괜찮다. **10** 구 옛날에는 **1** 옛날에는 아마도 1년에 한 번쯤은 수의사가 우리를 방문했었다. **11** 구 더 좋았던 옛날 **1** 그는 마을 사람들을 모두 자신을 알고 밤에도 문을 열어 두고 살았던 그 평화로웠던 옛날을 기억한다.

불가산명사 노년 **1** 그들은 노년에는 어떻게 먹고 살까를 걱정하고 있다.

가산명사 노령 연금 수령자 [영국영어]

1 형용사 구식의 **1** 그 집은 우중충하고 구식이며 상태가 안 좋았다. **2** 형용사 시대에 뒤떨어진, 구식의 **1** 그녀는 다소 시대에 뒤떨어진 가치관을 가지고 있어서 엄격한 규율 엄수자일 수 있다.

1 가산명사 또는 불가산명사 올리브 열매 **1** 아주 많은 검은 올리브 열매 **2** 가산명사 올리브 나무 **1** 프로방스 지역의 언덕 위에 있는 올리브 나무는 낭만적으로 보인다. **3** 색채어 올리브색, 노르스름한 녹색 **1** 진한 빨강, 올리브색, 선황색과 황토색 같은 선명한 색채 ● 복합형-색채어 올리브색의 **1** 그녀는 올리브 그린색 티셔츠를 입고 있었다. **4** 형용사 황갈색의 **1** 그들은 짙은 색의 빛나는 머릿결과 황갈색 피부, 아름다운 갈색 눈동자를 가진 미남이다.

물질명사 올리브기름

1 형용사 올림픽 경기의 **1** 챔피언 자리에 오른 올림픽 우승자 **2** 고유명사 올림픽 경기 **1** 나는 다음 올림픽 경기 때문에 애틀랜타에 가 있을 것이다.

고유명사-집합 올림픽 경기 **1** 1968년 올림픽 경기에서 그녀는 200미터, 400미터, 800미터 달리기에서 금메달을 땄었다.

가산명사 민원 처리 감찰관, 옴부즈맨 **1** 그 전단은 은행 관련 민원 처리 감찰관에게 어떻게 불만을 호소해야 하는지를 설명하고 있다.

[영국영어, 미국영어 가끔 omelette] 가산명사 오믈렛 **1** 치즈 오믈렛

가산명사 징조 **1** 이 순간 그녀의 모습은 재앙의 징조이다.

형용사 불길한 **1** 상대편 전화에서 불길한 침묵이 흘렀다. ● 불길하게 부사 **1** 그 술집은 불길하게 조용한 것 같았다.

omis|sion /oʊmɪʃⁿn/ (**omissions**) **1** N-COUNT An **omission** is something that has not been included or has not been done, either deliberately or accidentally. ❑ *The duke was surprised by his wife's omission from the guest list.* **2** N-VAR **Omission** is the act of not including a particular person or thing or of not doing something. ❑ *...the prosecution's seemingly malicious omission of recorded evidence.*

omit /oʊmɪt/ (**omits, omitting, omitted**) **1** V-T If you **omit** something, you do not include it in an activity or piece of work, deliberately or accidentally. ❑ *Omit the salt in this recipe.* **2** V-T If you **omit to** do something, you do not do it. [FORMAL] ❑ *His new girlfriend had omitted to tell him she was married.*

1 가산명사 생략; 누락 ❑ 그 공작은 손님 명단에서 자기 아내 이름이 누락된 것을 보고 놀랐다.
2 가산명사 또는 불가산명사 생략함 ❑ 검사가 기록되어 있는 증거를 겉으로 보기에도 악의적으로 생략함

1 타동사 빼다, 생략하다; 누락하다 ❑ 이 요리법에서 소금을 빼세요. **2** 타동사 -하지 못하다 [격식체] ❑ 그의 새 여자 친구는 자기가 결혼했다는 사실을 그에게 말하지 못했었다.

Thesaurus
*omit*의 참조어

v.   forget, leave out, miss; (*ant.*) add, include **1**

---

on ◆◆◆

The preposition is pronounced /ɒn/. The adverb and the adjective are pronounced /ɒn/.

전치사는 /ɒn/으로 발음되고, 부사와 형용사는 /ɒn/으로 발음된다.

In addition to the uses shown below, **on** is used after some verbs, nouns, and adjectives in order to introduce extra information. **On** is also used in phrasal verbs such as "keep on," "cotton on," and "sign on."

on은 아래 용법 외에도 추가 정보를 나타내기 위해 일부의 동사, 명사, 형용사 뒤에 쓴다. 또한 'keep on', 'cotton on', 'sign on'과 같은 구동사에도 쓰인다.

1 PREP If someone or something is **on** a surface or object, the surface or object is immediately below them and is supporting their weight. ❑ *He is sitting beside her on the sofa.* ❑ *On top of the cupboards are vast straw baskets which Pat uses for dried flower arrangements.* **2** PREP If something is **on** a surface or object, it is stuck to it or attached to it. ❑ *I admired the peeling paint on the ceiling.* ❑ *The clock on the wall showed one minute to twelve.* ● ADV **On** is also an adverb. [ADV after v] ❑ *I know how to darn, and how to sew a button on.* **3** PREP If you put, throw, or drop something **on** a surface, you move it or drop it so that it is then supported by the surface. ❑ *He got his winter jacket from the closet and dropped it on the sofa.* **4** PREP You use **on** to say what part of your body is supporting your weight. ❑ *He continued to lie on his back and look at clouds.* ❑ *He raised himself on his elbows, squinting into the sun.* **5** PREP You use **on** to say that someone or something touches a part of a person's body. ❑ *He leaned down and kissed her lightly on the mouth.* **6** PREP If someone has a particular expression **on** their face, their face has that expression. [n PREP n] ❑ *The maid looked at him, a nervous smile on her face.* **7** ADV When you put a piece of clothing **on**, you place it over part of your body in order to wear it. If you have it **on**, you are wearing it. [ADV after v] ❑ *He put his coat on while she opened the front door.* **8** PREP You can say that you have something **on** you if you are carrying it in your pocket or in a bag. [PREP pron] ❑ *I didn't have any money on me.* **9** PREP If someone's eyes are **on** you, they are looking or staring at you. ❑ *Everyone's eyes were fixed on him.* **10** PREP If you hurt yourself on something, you accidentally hit a part of your body against it and that thing causes damage to you. ❑ *Mr. Pendle hit his head on a wall as he fell.* **11** PREP If you are **on** an area of land, you are there. ❑ *He was able to spend only a few days at a time on the island.* ❑ *You lived on the farm until you came back to America?* **12** PREP If something is situated **on** a place such as a road or coast, it forms part of it or is by the side of it. ❑ *Bergdorf Goodman has opened a men's store on Fifth Avenue.* ❑ *The hotel is on the coast.* **13** PREP If you get **on** a bus, train, or plane, you go into it in order to travel somewhere. If you are **on** it, you are traveling in it. ❑ *We waited till twelve and we finally got on the plane.* ● ADV **On** is also an adverb. [ADV after v] ❑ *He showed his ticket to the conductor and got on.* **14** PREP If there is something **on** a piece of paper, it has been written or printed there. ❑ *The writing on the back of the card was cramped but scrupulously neat.* **15** PREP If something is **on** a list, it is included in it. ❑ *I've seen your name on the list of deportees.* ❑ *The Queen now doesn't even appear on the list of the 40 richest people in Britain.* **16** PREP Books, discussions, or ideas **on** a particular subject are concerned with that subject. ❑ *They offer a free counseling service which can offer help and advice on legal matters.* ❑ *He declined to give any information on the Presidential election.* **17** PREP You use **on** to introduce the method, principle, or system which is used to do something. ❑ *...a television that we bought on credit two months ago.* ❑ *They want all groups to be treated on an equal basis.* **18** PREP If something is done **on** an instrument or a machine, it is done using that instrument or machine. ❑ *...songs that I could just sit down and play on the piano.* **19** PREP If information is, for example, **on** tape or **on** computer, that is the way that it is stored. ❑ *"I thought it was a load of rubbish." — "Right we've got that on tape."* **20** PREP If something is being broadcast, you can say that it is **on** the radio or television. ❑ *Every sporting event on television and satellite over the next seven days is listed.* ● ADJ **On** is also an adjective. [v-link ADJ] ❑ *...teenagers complaining there's nothing good on.* **21** ADJ When an activity is taking place, you can say that it is **on**. [v-link ADJ] ❑ *There's a marvelous match on at Wimbledon at the moment.* **22** ADV You use **on** in expressions such as "**have a lot on**" and "**not have very much on**" to indicate how busy someone is. [SPOKEN] ❑ *I have a lot on in the next week.* **23** PREP You use **on** to introduce an activity that someone is doing, particularly traveling. ❑ *I've always wanted to go on a cruise.* ❑ *They look happy and relaxed as they stroll in the sunshine on a shopping trip.* **24** ADV When something such as a machine or an electric light is **on**, it is functioning or in use. When you switch it **on**, it starts functioning. ❑ *The light was on and the door was open.* ❑ *The central heating's been turned off. I've turned it on again.* **25** PREP If you are **on** a committee or council, you are a member of it. ❑ *Claire and Beryl were on the organizing committee.* **26** PREP You can indicate when something happens by saying that it happens **on** a particular day or date. ❑ *This year's event will take place on June 19th, a week earlier than usual.* ❑ *I was born on Christmas day.* **27** PREP You use **on** when mentioning an event that was followed by another one. [PREP n/-ing] ❑ *She waited in her hotel to*

1 전치사 - 위에 ❑ 그는 소파에 앉은 그녀 옆에 앉아 있다. ❑ 찬장 위에는 말린 꽃을 꽂을 때 패트가 사용하는 짚으로 만든 커다란 바구니들이 놓여 있다. **2** 전치사 -에 부착되어 있는 ❑ 나는 천장에 매달려 벗겨지고 있는 페인트에 탄복하였다. ❑ 벽에 걸려 있는 시계가 12시 1분전을 가리켰다. ● 부사 위에 ❑ 나는 구멍을 꿰매고 그 위에 단추를 달 줄 안다. **3** 전치사 -위로 ❑ 그는 옷장에서 겨울 상의를 꺼내서 소파 위로 던졌다. **4** 전치사 특정 신체 부위로 체중을 받침을 나타낼 ❑ 그는 바로 누워서 계속 구름을 쳐다보았다. ❑ 그는 양 팔꿈치에 기대고 몸을 일으키며 가늘게 뜬 눈으로 태양을 보았다. **5** 전치사 (신체 부위) ❑ 그는 몸을 숙여서 그녀의 입술에 가볍게 입을 맞추었다. **6** 전치사 (얼굴) 에 ❑ 그 아가씨는 얼굴에 불안한 미소를 띤 채 그를 쳐다보았다. **7** 부사 착용하여, 입고 ❑ 그녀가 현관문을 열 때 그는 외투를 입었다. **8** 전치사 몸에 지니고 ❑ 나는 내 몸에 지닌 돈이 한 푼도 없었다. **9** 전치사 (시선이) -에게 고정된 ❑ 사람들의 눈길이 그 남자에게 고정되었다. **10** 전치사 (물건) 에 부딪쳐 ❑ 펜들 씨는 넘어지면서 머리를 벽에 부딪쳤다. **11** 전치사 (장소) ❑ 그는 그 섬에서 한 번에 며칠씩 밖에 머물 수가 없었다. ❑ 당신은 미국으로 돌아올 때까지는 그 농장에서 살았습니까? **12** 전치사 (거리나 해안) -에 ❑ 베그도르프 굿맨은 5번가에 남성복점을 개업했다. ❑ 호텔은 그 해변에 있다. **13** 전치사 탈것에 오르거나 타고 있음을 나타냄 ❑ 12시까지 기다린 후에야 마침내 우리는 그 비행기에 탔다. ● 부사 승차하여 ❑ 그는 차장에게 차표를 보여 주고 승차했다. **14** 전치사 (종이 위) 에 ❑ 카드 뒤편에 쓰인 글씨는 빽빽했지만 정성들여 깔끔하게 쓴 글씨였다. **15** 전치사 (목록이나 명단) 에 ❑ 나는 당신 이름이 송환자 명단에 포함되어 있는 것을 보았습니다. ❑ 영국 여왕은 이제 영국의 40대 갑부 명단에 들지도 않는다. **16** 전치사 -에 관하여 ❑ 그들은 법률문제에 관해 도움을 주고 조언을 해 주는 무료 상담 서비스를 제공한다. ❑ 그는 대통령 선거에 관한 어떤 정보도 제공하기를 거절했다. **17** 전치사 (방법이나 원칙) 으로 ❑ 우리가 두 달 전에 신용 카드로 샀던 텔레비전 ❑ 그들은 모든 단체가 같은 기준에 따라 대우 받기를 원한다. **18** 전치사 (기계나 악기) 로 ❑ 내가 그냥 자리에 앉아서 피아노로 연주할 수 있는 노래들 **19** 전치사 (테이프나 컴퓨터) 에 ❑ "내 생각에 그건 모두 아무 쓸모가 없었어." "맞아, 우리가 그것을 테이프에 녹음했는데." **20** 전치사 방송되어 ❑ 앞으로 7일 간 텔레비전과 위성으로 방송될 모든 스포츠 행사 이름이 적혀있다. ● 형용사 방영되고 있는 ❑ 방영되고 있는 것 중 볼 만한 것이 하나도 없다고 불평하는 십대들 **21** 형용사 진행되고 있는 ❑ 윔블던에서는 지금 멋진 경기가 진행되고 있다. **22** 부사 아주 바쁜; 별로 할 일이 없는 [구어체] ❑ 다음 주에 나는 아주 바쁘다. **23** 전치사 (여행) 을 ❑ 나는 항상 유람선 여행을 하고 싶었다. ❑ 쇼핑 여행을 하는 그들이 햇살 아래 산책하는 모습이 행복하고 편안해 보인다. **24** 부사 (전깃불 등이) 켜져 ❑ 전깃불은 켜져 있었고 문은 열려 있었다. ❑ 중앙난방 장치를 꺼 놓았다. 내가 그것을 다시 켰다. **25** 전치사 -의 일원인 ❑ 클레어와 베릴은 조직 위원회 위원이었다. **26** 전치사 (요일이나 날짜) 에 ❑ 올해 행사는 예년보다 일주일 앞당겨진, 6월 19일에 치를 예정이다. ❑ 나는 크리스마스 날에 태어났다. **27** 전치사 -할 때 ❑ 그들은 런던에서 오는 아이들이 도착할 때 그들을 맞이하기 위해서 호텔에서 기다렸다. **28** 부사 계속 ❑ 그들은 잠시 동안 말 한 마디 없이 계속 걸었다. ❑ 그 전쟁이 발발했을 때 그는 우연히

welcome her children on their arrival from London. **28** ADV You use **on** to say that someone is continuing to do something. [ADV after v] ❑ *They walked on in silence for a while.* ❑ *He happened to be in England when the war broke out and he just stayed on.* **29** ADV If you say that someone goes **on at** you, you mean that they continually criticize you, complain to you, or ask you to do something. [mainly BRIT] ❑ *She's been on at me for weeks to show her round the stables.* ❑ *He used to keep on at me about the need to win.* **30** ADV You use **on** in expressions such as **from now on** and **from then on** to indicate that something starts to happen at the time mentioned and continues to happen afterward. [*from* n ADV] ❑ *Perhaps it would be best not to see much of you from now on.* ❑ *We can expect trouble from this moment on.* **31** ADV You often use **on** after the adverbs "early," "late," "far," and their comparative forms, especially at the beginning or end of a sentence, or before a preposition. [adv ADV] ❑ *The market square is a riot of color and animation from early on in the morning.* ❑ *Later on I learned how to read music.* **32** PREP Someone who is **on** a drug takes it regularly. ❑ *She was on antibiotics for an eye infection that wouldn't go away.* **33** PREP If you live **on** a particular kind of food, you eat it. If a machine runs **on** a particular kind of power or fuel, it uses it in order to function. [v PREP n] ❑ *The caterpillars feed on a wide range of trees, shrubs and plants.* ❑ *He lived on a diet of water and tinned fish.* **34** PREP If you are **on** a particular income, that is the income that you have. ❑ *...young people who are unemployed or on low wages.* ❑ *He's on three hundred a week.* **35** PREP Taxes or profits that are obtained from something are referred to as taxes or profits **on** it. [n PREP n] ❑ *...a general strike to protest a tax on food and medicine last week.* **36** PREP When you buy something or pay for something, you spend money **on** it. [PREP n/-ing] ❑ *I resolved not to waste money on a hotel.* ❑ *He spent more on feeding the dog than he spent on feeding himself.* **37** PREP When you spend time or energy **on** a particular activity, you spend time or energy doing it. [PREP n/-ing] ❑ *People complain about how children spend so much time on computer games.* ❑ *You all know why I am here. So I won't waste time on preliminaries.* **38** PHRASE If you say that something is **not on** or is **just not on**, you mean that it is unacceptable or impossible. [mainly BRIT, INFORMAL] ❑ *We shouldn't use the police in that way. It's just not on.* **39** PHRASE If you say that something happens **on and on**, you mean that it continues to happen for a very long time. ❑ *...designers, builders, fitters – the list goes on and on.* ❑ *Lobell drove on and on through the dense and blowing snow.* **40** **on behalf of** →see **behalf. on and off** →see **off. and so on** →see **so. on top of** →see **top**

잉글랜드에 있었고 그 후로도 그냥 계속 그곳에 머물렀다. **29** 부사 계속 귀찮게 하며, 계속 잔소리를 하며 [주로 영국영어] ❑ 그녀는 수 주일 동안이나 그 마구간을 보여 달라고 계속 나를 귀찮게 했다. ❑ 그는 나에게 이겨야 할 필요성에 대해 계속 잔소리를 하곤 했다. **30** 부사 계속 ❑ 아마도 이제부터는 계속 너를 자주 만나지 않는 것이 최상일 것 같다. ❑ 지금부터 계속 어려움이 있을 것 같다. **31** 부사 early, late 등과 같은 부사 뒤에 쓰임 ❑ 시장 광장에는 아침 일찍부터 다채로운 색깔과 생기가 있다. ❑ 그 후로 나는 악보 읽는 법을 배웠다. **32** 전치사 (꾸준히) 복용하는 ❑ 그녀는 잘 치유되지 않는 눈병 때문에 꾸준히 항생제를 복용했다. **33** 전치사 ~을 먹고, ~을 써서 ❑ 그 애벌레들은 다양한 종류의 나무, 관목, 초목을 먹고 산다. ❑ 그는 물과 생선 통조림을 먹고 살았다. **34** 전치사 ~을 버는, ~을 받는 ❑ 직장이 없거나 저임금을 받는 젊은이들 ❑ 그는 일주일에 3백 파운드를 번다. **35** 전치사 ~에 붙는 ❑ 식품과 의료에 붙는 세금에 반대하기 위해 지난주에 열린 총파업 **36** 전치사 (용도) 에 ❑ 나는 호텔비로 돈을 낭비하지 않기로 결심했다. ❑ 그는 자신이 먹는 것보다 그 개를 먹이는 것에 돈을 더 많이 쓴다. **37** 전치사 (활동) 에 ❑ 사람들은 아이들이 컴퓨터 게임에 얼마나 많은 시간을 낭비하는지에 대해 불평한다. ❑ 너희들 모두 내가 왜 여기 왔는지 알고 있을 테니, 서론에 시간을 낭비하지는 않겠다. **38** 구 용납되지 않는, 불가능한 [주로 영국영어, 비격식체] ❑ 우리는 경찰력을 그런 식으로 사용해서는 안 된다. 그것은 용납될 수 없다. **39** 구 계속되는 ❑ 설계자들, 건축업자들, 조립공들 등으로 그 명단은 계속 이어진다. ❑ 로벨은 심하게 휘몰아치는 눈보라를 뚫고 계속 운전했다.

once ♦♦♦ /wʌns/ **1** ADV If something happens **once**, it happens one time only. [ADV with v] ❑ *I met Wilma once, briefly.* ❑ *Since that evening I haven't once slept through the night.* ● PRON **Once** is also a pronoun. [*the/this* PRON] ❑ *"Have they been to visit you yet?" — "Just the once, yeah."* **2** ADV You use **once** with "a" and words like "day," "week," and "month" to indicate that something happens regularly, one time in each day, week, or month. [ADV *a* n] ❑ *Lung cells die and are replaced about once a week.* **3** ADV If something was **once** true, it was true at some time in the past, but is no longer true. ❑ *The culture minister once ran a theater.* ❑ *I lived there once myself, before I got married.* **4** ADV If someone **once** did something, they did it at some time in the past. [ADV with v] ❑ *I once went camping at Lake Darling with a friend.* ❑ *We once walked across London at two in the morning.* **5** CONJ If something happens **once** another thing has happened, it happens immediately afterward. ❑ *The decision had taken about 10 seconds once he'd read a market research study.* **6** PHRASE If something happens **all at once**, it happens suddenly, often when you are not expecting it to happen. ❑ *All at once there was someone knocking on the door.* **7** PHRASE If you do something **at once**, you do it immediately. ❑ *I have to go, I really must, at once.* ❑ *Remove from the heat, add the parsley, toss, and serve at once.* **8** PHRASE If a number of different things happen **at once** or **all at once**, they all happen at the same time. ❑ *You can't be doing two things at once.* **9** PHRASE **For once** is used to emphasize that something happens on this particular occasion, especially if it has never happened before, and may never happen again. [EMPHASIS] ❑ *For once, Dad is not complaining.* **10** PHRASE If something happens **once again** or **once more**, it happens again. ❑ *Amy picked up the hairbrush and smoothed her hair once more.* **11** PHRASE If something happens **once and for all**, it happens completely or finally. [EMPHASIS] ❑ *We have to resolve this matter once and for all.* **12** PHRASE If something happens **once in a while**, it happens sometimes, but not very often. ❑ *Your body, like any other machine, needs a full service once in a while.* **13** PHRASE If you have done something **once or twice**, you have done it a few times, but not very often. ❑ *I popped my head round the door once or twice.* ❑ *Once or twice she had caught a flash of interest in William's eyes.*

1 부사 한번 ❑ 나는 윌마를 한 번 잠시 만났었다. ❑ 그날 저녁 이후로 나는 밤새 한숨도 자지 못했다. ● 대명사 한 번 ❑ "그 사람들이 벌써 너를 만나러 갔었니?" "응, 단 한 번." **2** 부사 ~에 한 번씩 ❑ 폐 세포는 일주일에 한 번씩 죽고 재생된다. **3** 부사 한 때 ❑ 그 문화부 장관은 한 때 극장을 운영했다. ❑ 나는 결혼하기 전에 한때 그곳에 실제 살았다. **4** 부사 예전에 ❑ 나는 예전에 한 친구와 함께 달링 호수로 캠핑을 하러 갔다. ❑ 우리는 예전에 새벽 2시에 런던을 이쪽 끝에서 저쪽 끝까지 걸어가 보았다. **5** 접속사 일단 ~하자 ❑ 일단 그가 시장 조사 연구서를 읽고 나자, 그 결정을 하는 데는 약 10초가 걸렸었다. **6** 구 갑자기 ❑ 갑자기 누군가가 문을 두드렸다. **7** 구 즉시 ❑ 나는 가야 해, 정말로, 그것도 즉시. ❑ 불에서 내려서 파슬리를 넣고 살살 뒤집은 후 즉시 상에 올리세요. **8** 구 동시에 ❑ 동시에 두 가지를 할 수는 없다. **9** 구 이번 한 번만 [강조] ❑ 이번 한 번만, 아빠가 뭐라고 하지 않으실 거야. **10** 구 다시 한 번 ❑ 에이미는 머리 솔을 집어 들어 머리를 다시 한 번 빗었다. **11** 구 확실히 [강조] ❑ 우리는 이 문제를 확실히 매듭지어야 한다. **12** 구 가끔씩 ❑ 다른 기계처럼, 당신의 몸도 가끔씩 전체적인 정기 검진이 필요하다. **13** 구 어쩌다 한 번씩, 가끔씩 ❑ 나는 가끔씩 문 밖으로 머리를 내밀어 보았다. ❑ 어쩌다 한 번씩 그녀는 윌리엄의 두 눈에서 번득이는 관심의 눈길을 느꼈었다.

one ♦♦♦ /wʌn/ (**ones**) **1** NUM **One** is the number 1. ❑ *They had three sons and one daughter.* ❑ *...one thousand years ago.* **2** ADJ If you say that someone or something is the **one** person or thing of a particular kind, you are emphasizing that they are the only person or thing of that kind. [EMPHASIS] [det ADJ] ❑ *They had alienated the one man who knew the business.* **3** DET **One** can be used instead of "a" to emphasize the following noun. [EMPHASIS] ❑ *There is one thing I would like to know – What is it about Tim that you find so irresistible?* **4** DET You can use **one** instead of "a" to emphasize the following adjective or expression. [INFORMAL, EMPHASIS] ❑ *If we ever get married we'll have one terrific wedding.* **5** DET You can use **one** to refer to the first of two or more things that you are comparing. ❑ *Prices vary from one shop to another.* ● ADJ **One** is also an adjective. [det ADJ] ❑ *We ask why peace should have an apparent chance in the one territory and not the other.* ● PRON **One** is also a pronoun. ❑ *The twins were dressed differently and one was thinner than the other.* **6** PRON You can use **one** or **ones** instead of a noun when it is clear what type of thing or person you are referring to and you are describing them or giving more information about them. ❑ *They are selling their house to move to a smaller one.* **7** PRON You use **ones** to refer to people in general. ❑ *We are the only ones who know.* **8** PRON You can use **one** instead of a noun group when you have just mentioned something and you want to describe it or give more information about it. [PRON *of* n, PRON *that*] ❑ *The issue of land reform was one that dominated Hungary's parliamentary elections.* **9** DET You can use **one** when you

1 수사 1, 하나 ❑ 그들은 아들 셋과 딸 하나가 있었다. ❑ 천 년 전에 **2** 형용사 단 하나 [강조] ❑ 그들은 그 사업에 대해 알고 있던 단 한 사람과 소원해져 있었다. **3** 한정사 하나의 [강조] ❑ 내가 알고 싶은 것이 하나 있어. 무엇 때문에 네가 팀한테 그렇게 맥을 못 추는 건데? **4** 한정사 그야말로 [비격식체, 강조] ❑ 우리가 혹시라도 결혼을 한다면 그야말로 멋진 결혼식을 할 거야. **5** 한정사 (비교 시) 한 쪽 ❑ 가격은 가게마다 천차만별이다. ● 형용사 한 쪽의 ❑ 우리는 왜 한쪽 지역에서는 평화 정착의 가능성이 분명히 있어 보이고 다른 지역에서는 그렇지 않은지 묻고 있다. ● 대명사 (둘 중의) 하나 ❑ 그 쌍둥이는 옷을 다르게 입고 있었는데 둘 중 하나가 더 말랐었다. **6** 대명사 그것; 그 사람 ❑ 그들은 더 작은 집으로 이사 가려고 집을 내놓은 상태이다. **7** 대명사 사람들 ❑ 우리가 알고 있는 유일한 사람들이다. **8** 대명사 ~한 것 ❑ 토지 개혁 문제는 헝가리의 예비 선거를 좌지우지하는 것이었다. **9** 한정사 어떤 ❑ "대학 학위로는 충분하지 않습니다."라고 어떤 우등생이 말했다. ● 대명사 어떤 사람 ❑ 그들 중 몇 사람들은 아무것도 먹지 못했다. 어떤 사람은 물조차도 마시지 못했다. **10** 수량사 하나

a b c d e f g h i j k l m n o p q r s t u v w x y z

have been talking or writing about a group of people or things and you want to say something about a particular member of the group. ❑ *"A college degree isn't enough," said one honors student.* ● PRON **One** is also a pronoun. ❑ *Some of them couldn't eat a thing. One couldn't even drink.* ⑩ QUANT You use **one** in expressions such as **"one of the biggest airports"** or **"one of the most experienced players"** to indicate that something or someone is bigger or more experienced than most other things or people of the same kind. [QUANT of adj-superl] ❑ *Subaru is one of the smallest Japanese car makers.* ⑪ DET You can use **one** when referring to a time in the past or in the future. For example, if you say that you did something **one day**, you mean that you did it on a day in the past. ❑ *How would you like to have dinner one night, just you and me?* **one day** →see **day** ⑫ PRON You use **one** to make statements about people in general which also apply to themselves. **One** can be used as the subject or object of a sentence. [FORMAL] ❑ *If one looks at the longer run, a lot of positive things are happening.* ❑ *Where does one go from there?*

One or **you** is used when making statements that are true of any individual person. **One** is more formal than **you**. ❑ *I suppose one can't blame him... A crisis can make you stop and take a look at your life.* **People** is used to talk about everyone in general, or about a particular group. ❑ *...the amount of bread people buy... Don't go on about it. People may get embarrassed.*

---

⑬ PHRASE You can use **for one** to emphasize that a particular person is definitely reacting or behaving in a particular way, even if other people are not. [EMPHASIS] ❑ *I, for one, hope you don't get the job.* ⑭ PHRASE You can use expressions such as **a hundred and one**, **a thousand and one**, and **a million and one** to emphasize that you are talking about a large number of things or people. [EMPHASIS] ❑ *There are a hundred and one ways in which you can raise money.* ⑮ PHRASE You can use **in one** to indicate that something is a single unit, but is made up of several different parts or has several different functions. ❑ *...a love story and an adventure all in one.* ⑯ PHRASE You use **one after the other** or **one after another** to say that actions or events happen with very little time between them. ❑ *My three guitars broke one after the other.* ⑰ PHRASE **The one and only** can be used in front of the name of an actor, singer, or other famous person when they are being introduced on a show. ❑ *...one of the greatest ever rock performers, the one and only Tina Turner.* ⑱ PHRASE You can use **one by one** to indicate that people do things or that things happen in sequence, not all at the same time. ❑ *We went into the room one by one.* ⑲ PHRASE You use **one or other** to refer to one or more things or people in a group, when it does not matter which particular one or ones are thought of or chosen. ❑ *One or other of the two women was wrong.* ⑳ PHRASE **One or two** means a few. ❑ *We may make one or two changes.* ❑ *I've also sold one or two to an American publisher.* ㉑ PHRASE If you try to get **one up on** someone, you try to gain an advantage over them. ❑ *...the competitive kind who will see this as the opportunity to be one up on you.* ㉒ **one another** →see **another**. **one thing after another** →see **another**. **of one mind** →see **mind**. **in one piece** →see **piece**

one-off (**one-offs**) ❶ N-COUNT You can refer to something as a **one-off** when it is made or happens only once. [mainly BRIT] ❑ *Our survey revealed that these allergies were mainly one-offs.* ❷ ADJ A **one-off** thing is made or happens only once. [mainly BRIT] [ADJ n] ❑ *...one-off cash benefits.*

on|er|ous /ɒnərəs, ounər-, BRIT ɑːnərəs/ ADJ If you describe a task as **onerous**, you dislike having to do it because you find it difficult or unpleasant. [FORMAL] ❑ *...parents who have had the onerous task of bringing up a very difficult child.*

one's ♦♢♢ /wʌnz/ ❶ DET Speakers and writers use **one's** to indicate that something belongs or relates to people in general, or to themselves in particular. [FORMAL] ❑ *...a feeling of responsibility for the welfare of others in one's community.* ❷ **One's** can be used as a spoken form of "one is" or "one has," especially when "has" is an auxiliary verb. ❑ *No one's going to hurt you. No one. Not any more.* →see **one**

one|self /wʌnself/

Oneself is a third person singular reflexive pronoun.

---

❶ PRON-REFL A speaker or writer uses **oneself** as the object of a verb or preposition in a clause where "oneself" meaning "me" or "any person in general" refers to the same person as the subject of the verb. [FORMAL] ❑ *One must apply oneself to the present and keep one's eyes firmly fixed on one's future goals.* ❷ PRON-REFL **Oneself** can be used as the object of a verb or preposition, when "one" is not present but is understood to be the subject of the verb. [FORMAL] ❑ *The historic feeling of the town makes it a pleasant place to base oneself for summer vacations.*

one-sided ❶ ADJ If you say that an activity or relationship is **one-sided**, you think that one of the people or groups involved does much more than the other or is much stronger than the other. ❑ *The negotiating was completely one-sided.* ❷ ADJ If you describe someone as **one-sided**, you are critical of what they say or do because you think it shows that they have considered only one side of an issue or event. [DISAPPROVAL] ❑ *The organization still believes the government is being one sided.*

one-time also **onetime** ADJ **One-time** is used to describe something such as a job, position, or role which someone used to have, or something which happened in the past. [JOURNALISM] [ADJ n] ❑ *The legislative body had voted to oust the country's one-time rulers.*

one-to-one ❶ ADJ In a **one-to-one** relationship, one person deals directly with only one other person. [ADJ n] ❑ *...one-to-one training.* ● ADV **One-to-one** is

---

❑ 스바루는 가장 작은 규모의 일본 자동차 회사들 중 하나이다. ⑪ 한정사 (미래나 과거의) 어느 ❑ 언제 한번 저녁 식사 할까요? 당신과 나 둘만. ⑫ 대명사 사람들 [격식체] ❑ 사람들이 더 긴 안목으로 사물을 본다면, 긍정적인 일들이 많이 생길 것이다. ❑ 사람들이 그 곳에서 어디로 갑니까?

---
one이나 you는 개인에게 해당되는 진술을 할 때 쓴다. one이 you 보다 더 격식적이다. ❑ 나는 사람들이 그를 비난할 수 없다고 생각한다... 위기는 사람들을 멈추어 서서 자신의 인생을 한번 살펴보게 할 수 있다. people은 일반적으로 모든 사람 또는 특정한 집단을 말할 때 쓴다. ❑ ...사람들이 사는 빵의 양... 그것 좀 그만 얘기하세요. 사람들이 난처해지겠어요.

---

⑬ 구 -야 말로 [강조] ❑ 나야 말로 내가 그 일을 안 했으면 해. ⑭ 구 수백의; 수천의; 수백만의 [강조] ❑ 당신이 모금할 수 있는 방법은 수백 가지가 있다. ⑮ 구 하나로 ❑ 연애 소설과 모험담이 모두 하나로 된 것 ⑯ 구 차례로 ❑ 내 기타 세 대가 차례로 부서졌다. ⑰ 구 그 유명한 ❑ 가장 위대한 록 음악가 중 한 명인 그 유명한 티나 터너 ⑱ 구 하나씩 ❑ 우리는 한 명씩 그 방으로 들어갔다. ⑲ 구 누구든 ❑ 그 두 여자들 중 누구든 한 명은 틀렸다. ⑳ 구 한두 가지의, 조금 ❑ 우리는 한두 가지쯤 변화를 일으킬 것이다. ❑ 나는 또한 한 미국 출판업자에게 한두 권을 팔았다. ㉑ 구 -보다 유리한 ❑ 이것을 당신보다 유리해질 기회로 여길 경쟁심 강한 부류의 사람들

❶ 가산명사 일회성의 일 [주로 영국영어] ❑ 우리의 조사에 의하면 이런 알레르기는 주로 일회성으로 나타났다. ❷ 형용사 일회성의 [주로 영국영어] ❑ 일회성 현금 혜택

형용사 힘든 [격식체] ❑ 아주 까다로운 아이를 키우는 힘든 일을 하고 있는 부모들

❶ 한정사 사람들의 [격식체] ❑ 한 사회에서 사람들이 느끼는 타인의 복지에 대한 책임감 ❷ one is의 축약형, one has의 축약형 ❑ 아무도 너를 해치지 않을 거야. 누구도. 더 이상은.

---
oneself는 3인칭 단수 재귀 대명사이다.

---

❶ 재귀대명사 자기 자신 [격식체] ❑ 누구든지 현재에 전념하면서 두 눈은 자신의 미래 목표를 확고하게 응시해야 한다. ❷ 재귀대명사 사람들 [격식체] ❑ 그 도시가 주는 역사적인 느낌 때문에 그 곳에서 사람들이 여름휴가를 보낼 곳으로 정하기에 좋은 장소이다.

❶ 형용사 일방적인 ❑ 그 협상은 완전히 일방적이었다. ❷ 형용사 편파적인 [탐탁잖음] ❑ 그 협회는 아직도 정부가 편파적이라고 믿고 있다.

형용사 예전의 [언론] ❑ 입법부는 예전에 그 나라의 통치자였던 사람들을 축출하기 위해 투표를 했었다.

❶ 형용사 일대일 ❑ 일대일 교습 ● 부사 일대일로 ❑ 그녀는 사람들과 일대일로 얘기하고 싶어 할 것이다.

also an adverb. [ADV after v] ❏ *She would like to talk to people one-to-one.* ❷ ADJ If there is a **one-to-one** match between two sets of things, each member of one set matches a member of the other set. [ADJ n] ❏ *In English, there is not a consistent one-to-one match between each written symbol and each distinct spoken sound.*

one-way ❶ ADJ In **one-way** streets or traffic systems, vehicles can only travel along in one direction. [ADJ n] ❏ *...Gotham's maze of no-thoroughfares and one-way streets.* ❷ ADJ **One-way** describes trips which go to just one place, rather than to that place and then back again. ❏ *The trailers will be rented for one-way trips.* ❸ ADJ A **one-way** ticket or fare is for a trip from one place to another, but not back again. [mainly AM] ❏ *...a one-way ticket from New York to Los Angeles.* ● ADV **One-way** is also an adverb. [BRIT usually **single**] [ADV after v] ❏ *Unrestricted fares will be increased as much as $80 one-way.*

on|going /ɒnɡoʊɪŋ/ ADJ An **ongoing** situation has been happening for quite a long time and seems likely to continue for some time in the future. ❏ *There is an ongoing debate on the issue.*

on|ion /ʌnyən/ (onions) N-VAR An **onion** is a round vegetable with a light brown skin that grows underground. It has many white layers on its inside which have a strong, sharp smell and taste. ❏ *You grind the onion and the raw cranberries together.* →see **spice**

on|line /ɒnlaɪn/ also **on-line** ❶ ADJ If a company goes **online**, its services become available on the Internet. [BUSINESS, COMPUTING] ❏ *...the first bank to go online.* ❏ *...an online shopping center.* ❷ ADJ If you are **online**, your computer is connected to the Internet. Compare **offline**. [COMPUTING] ❏ *You can chat to other people who are online.* ● ADV **Online** is also an adverb. [ADV after v] ❏ *...the cool stuff you find online.* →see **line**

on|looker /ɒnlʊkər/ (onlookers) N-COUNT An **onlooker** is someone who watches an event take place but does not take part in it. ❏ *A handful of onlookers stand in the field watching.*

only ♦♦♦ /oʊnli/

> In written English, **only** is usually placed immediately before the word it qualifies. In spoken English, however, you can use stress to indicate what **only** qualifies, so its position is not so important.

❶ ADV You use **only** to indicate the one thing that is true, appropriate, or necessary in a particular situation, in contrast to all the other things that are not true, appropriate, or necessary. ❏ *Only the President could authorize the use of the atomic bomb.* ❏ *A business can only be built and expanded on a sound financial base.* ❷ ADV You use **only** to introduce the thing which must happen before the thing mentioned in the main part of the sentence can happen. [ADV cl/prep] ❏ *The lawyer is paid only if he wins.* ❏ *The Bank of England insists that it will cut interest rates only when it is ready.* ❸ ADJ If you talk about the **only** person or thing involved in a particular situation, you mean there are no others involved in it. [det ADJ] ❏ *She was the only woman in Shell's legal department.* ❹ ADJ An **only** child is a child who has no brothers or sisters. [ADJ n] ❏ *The actor, an only child, grew up in north London.*

> When **only** is used as an adverb, its position in the sentence depends on the word or phrase it applies to. If **only** applies to the subject of a clause, you put it in front of the subject. ❏ *Only strong characters can make such decisions.* Otherwise, you normally put it in front of the verb, after the first auxiliary, or after the verb **be**. ❏ *I only want my son back, that is all... He had only agreed to see me because we had met before... I was only able to wash four times in 66 days.* However, some people think it is more correct to put **only** directly in front of the word or phrase it applies to. This is the best position if you want to be quite clear or emphatic. ❏ *It applies only to passengers carrying British passports... She'd done it only because it was necessary.* For extra emphasis, you can put **only** after the word or phrase it applies to. ❏ *The event will be for women only... I'll say this once and once only.*

❺ ADV You use **only** to indicate that something is no more important, interesting, or difficult, for example, than you say it is, especially when you want to correct a wrong idea that someone may get or has already got. ❏ *At the moment it is only a theory.* ❏ *"I'm only a sergeant," said Clements.* ❻ ADV You use **only** to emphasize how small an amount is or how short a length of time is. [EMPHASIS] [ADV n/adv] ❏ *Child car seats only cost about £10 a week to hire.* ❏ *...spacecraft guidance systems weighing only a few grams.* ❼ ADV You use **only** to emphasize that you are talking about a small part of an amount or group, not the whole of it. [EMPHASIS] [ADV n] ❏ *These are only a few of the possibilities.* ❽ ADV **Only** is used after "can" or "could" to emphasize that it is impossible to do anything except the rather inadequate or limited action that is mentioned. [EMPHASIS] [modal ADV inf] ❏ *For a moment I could say nothing. I could only stand and look.* ❾ ADV You can use **only** in the expressions **I only wish** or **I only hope** in order to emphasize what you are hoping or wishing. [EMPHASIS] ❏ *I only wish he were here now that things are getting better for me.* ❿ CONJ **Only** can be used to add a comment which slightly changes or limits what you have just said. [INFORMAL] ❏ *It's just as dramatic as a film, only it's real.* ❏ *It's a bit like my house, only nicer.* ⓫ CONJ **Only** can be used after a clause with "would" to indicate why something is not done. [SPOKEN] ❏ *I'd invite you to come with me, only it's such a long way.* ⓬ ADV You can use **only** before an infinitive to introduce an event which

❷ 형용사 일대일 대응의 ❏ 영어에서는, 각 철자와 각각의 개별 소리가 일관되게 일대일로 대응하지는 않는다.

❶ 형용사 일방통행의 ❏ 빠져나갈 가도도 없고 일방통행로로 되어 있는 고담의 미로 ❷ 형용사 편도의 ❏ 트레일러는 편도 여행용으로 대여할 것이다. ❸ 형용사 편도의 [주로 미국영어] ❏ 뉴욕에서 로스앤젤레스까지의 편도 차표 ● 부사 편도로 [영국영어 대개 **single**] ❏ 무제한 요금의 편도의 경우 80달러나 오를 것이다.

형용사 진행 중인 ❏ 그 문제에 대해서 논쟁이 진행 중이다.

가산명사 또는 불가산명사 양파 ❏ 양파와 생 크랜베리를 함께 가세요.

❶ 형용사 온라인의, 인터넷을 이용한 [경제, 컴퓨터] ❏ 온라인망을 이용하는 첫 은행 ❏ 인터넷 쇼핑센터 ❷ 형용사 (인터넷에) 접속된 [컴퓨터] ❏ 너는 인터넷에 접속된 다른 사람들과 채팅할 수 있다. ● 부사 인터넷을 이용해서 ❏ 인터넷을 이용해서 찾을 수 있는 멋진 것

가산명사 구경꾼 ❏ 소수의 구경꾼들이 경기장에 서서 구경을 하고 있다.

문어체 영어에서 only는 대개 수식하는 단어 앞에 쓴다. 그러나 구어체 영어에서는 only가 수식하는 부분을 나타내기 위해 강세를 이용할 수 있기 때문에 위치가 중요하지 않다.

❶ 부사 오직 ❏ 오직 대통령만이 핵폭탄 사용을 승인할 수 있었다. ❏ 회사는 든든한 재정 기반 위에서만 세울 수 있고 확장할 수 있다. ❷ 부사 오로지 -만 ❏ 그 변호사는 승소할 때만 수임료를 받는다. ❏ 잉글랜드 은행은 오로지 준비가 되었을 때만 금리를 삭감할 것이라고 주장한다. ❸ 형용사 유일한 ❏ 그녀가 쉘의 법무 부서에서는 유일한 여성이었다. ❹ 형용사 외동의 ❏ 외동아들이었던 그 배우는 런던 북부에서 자랐다.

only가 부사로 쓰일 때 문장에서의 위치는 only가 수식하는 단어나 구에 따라서 달라진다. only가 절의 주어를 수식하면 주어 앞에 둔다. ❏ 강한 성격의 소유자들만이 그런 결정을 내릴 수 있다. 그 외에는, only를 대개 동사 앞, 첫 조동사 뒤, be 동사 뒤에 둔다. ❏ 나는 내 아들이 돌아오기만을 원하며, 그게 전부입니다... 그는 우리가 전에 만난 적이 있기 때문에 나를 보는 데 동의했을 뿐이었다... 나는 66일 동안 네 번만 씻을 수 있었다. 그러나, 일부 사람들은 only를 수식하는 단어나 구 바로 앞에 두는 것이 더 올바르다고 생각한다. 아주 분명하게 하거나 강조를 원하는 경우에는 이것이 가장 좋은 위치이다. ❏ 그것은 영국 여권을 소지한 승객들에게만 적용된다... 그녀는 단지 필요했기 때문에 그것을 했었다. 특별히 강조가 더 필요하면 only를 수식하는 단어나 구 뒤에 둘 수도 있다. ❏ 그 행사는 여성들만을 위한 것이다... 나는 이 말을 딱 한번만 하겠다.

❺ 부사 단지 -일 뿐 ❏ 현 시점에선 그것은 단지 이론일 뿐이다. ❏ "나는 단지 하사관일 뿐입니다."라고 클레멘츠가 말했다. ❻ 부사 -에 불과하여 [강조] ❏ 아동용 카 시트를 빌리는 비용이 일주당 10파운드에 불과하다. ❏ 무게가 단지 몇 그램에 불과한 우주선 유도 장치 ❼ 부사 겨우 [강조] ❏ 이것은 가능성이 겨우 약간 있을 뿐이다. ❏ 이것들은 그저 몇 가지 가능성의 일부일 뿐이다. ❽ 부사 그저 -만 [강조] ❏ 잠시 동안 나는 아무 말도 할 수 없었다. 나는 그저 서서 바라볼 수밖에 없었다. ❾ 부사 -이기만 하더라면 ❏ 이제 내게 상황이 좋아지는 지금 당신이 여기 있기만 하다면 얼마나 좋을까. ❿ 접속사 단, 다만 [비격식체] ❏ 그것이 영화만큼이나 무척 극적이긴 하다. 단 이것은 사실이다. ❏ 그것은 우리 집이랑 솜 비슷해, 다만 좀 더 좋을 뿐이지. ⓫ 접속사 -만 아니라면, -하지 않았다면 [구어체] ❏ 그렇게 먼 거리만 아니라면 당신을 나와 같이 가자고 초대할 텐데. ⓬ 부사 결국 -할 뿐인 ❏ 라일에 대사관에 연락해 보았으나, 결국 휴가 회의 중이라는 말만 들었을 뿐이다. ⓭ 부사 정말 [강조] ❏ 그녀에게 당신이 지원하려 한다는 것을 알리는 것이 정말 공평한

happens immediately after one you have just mentioned, and which is rather surprising or unfortunate. [ADV to-inf] ❑ *Ryle tried the Embassy, only to be told that Hugh was in a meeting.* 13 ADV You can use **only** to emphasize how appropriate a certain course of action or type of behavior is. [EMPHASIS] ❑ *It's only fair to let her know that you intend to apply.* 14 ADV You can use **only** in front of a verb to indicate that the result of something is unfortunate or undesirable and is likely to make the situation worse rather than better. [ADV before v] ❑ *The embargo would only hurt innocent civilians.* 15 PHRASE If you say you **only have to** or **have only to** do one thing in order to achieve or prove a second thing, you are emphasizing how easily the second thing can be achieved or proved. [EMPHASIS] ❑ *Any time you want a babysitter, dear, you only have to ask.* 16 PHRASE You can say that something has **only just** happened when you want to emphasize that it happened a very short time ago. [EMPHASIS] ❑ *I've only just arrived.* 17 PHRASE You use **only just** to emphasize that something is true, but by such a small degree that it is almost not true at all. [EMPHASIS] ❑ *For centuries farmers there have only just managed to survive.* ❑ *I am old enough to remember the Blitz, but only just.* 18 PHRASE You can use **only too** to emphasize that something is true or exists to a much greater extent than you would expect or like. [EMPHASIS] ❑ *I know only too well that plans can easily go wrong.* 19 PHRASE You can say that you are **only too** happy to do something to emphasize how willing you are to do it. [EMPHASIS] ❑ *I'll be only too pleased to help them out with any queries.* 20 **if only** →see **if.** **not only** →see **not.** **the one and only** →see **one**

일이다. 14 부사 단지 ~할 뿐 ❑ 통상 금지 조치는 단지 무고한 민간인들에게 고통만 줄 것이다. 15 구 ~하기만 하면 된다 [강조] ❑ 여보, 당신이 아이 돌보는 사람이 필요하면, 부탁만 하면 돼요. 16 구 방금 [강조] ❑ 나는 방금 도착했다. 17 구 간신히, 겨우 [강조] ❑ 수 세기 동안 농부들은 그곳에서 간신히 연명만 했다. ❑ 나는 블리츠 작전을 기억할 정도로 나이가 들었지만, 겨우 조금 기억할 뿐이다. 18 구 너무나 [강조] ❑ 나는 계획이 쉽게 잘못 될 수 있다는 것을 너무나 잘 알고 있다. 19 구 그저 [강조] ❑ 나는 어떤 문제에 관한 것이라도 그들을 그저 기쁜 마음으로 도와주겠다.

Thesaurus	*only*의 참조어
ADJ.	alone, individual, single, solitary, unique 3

o.n.o. In advertisements, **o.n.o.** is used after a price to indicate that the person who is selling something is willing to accept slightly less money than the sum they have mentioned. **o.n.o.** is a written abbreviation for "or near offer." [BRIT] ❑ *Good condition, spare spool plus instructions £70 o.n.o.*

또는 그에 가까운 값으로, ~ 내외 [영국영어] ❑ 상태 양호, 여분의 스풀과 사용설명서를 포함해서 70파운드 내외.

on-screen also **onscreen** 1 ADJ **On-screen** means appearing on the screen of a television, movie theater, or computer. [ADJ n] ❑ *Read the on-screen lyrics and sing along.* 2 ADJ **On-screen** means relating to the roles played by film or television actors, in contrast with their real lives. [ADJ n] ❑ *...her first onscreen kiss.* ● ADV **On-screen** is also an adverb. [ADV with cl] ❑ *He was immensely attractive to women, onscreen and offscreen.*

1 형용사 화면에 나오는 ❑ 화면에 나오는 가사를 보면서 노래를 따라 부르세요. 2 형용사 극 중의 ❑ 그녀의 극 중 첫 키스 ● 부사 극 중에서 ❑ 그는 극 중에서나 실생활에서나 여자들에게 굉장히 인기가 있었다.

on|set /ɒnsɛt/ N-SING **The onset of** something is the beginning of it, used especially to refer to something unpleasant. ❑ *Most of the passes have been closed with the onset of winter.*

단수명사 시작, 개시 ❑ 대부분의 고갯길들이 겨울이 시작되면서 폐쇄되었다.

on|shore /ɒnʃɔr/ ADJ **Onshore** means happening on or near land, rather than at sea. ❑ *...Western Europe's biggest onshore oilfield.* ● ADV **Onshore** is also an adverb. [ADV after v] ❑ *They missed the ferry and remained onshore.*

형용사 내륙의 ❑ 서유럽에서 가장 규모가 큰 내륙 유전 ● 부사 육지에 ❑ 그들은 배를 놓쳐서 육지에 남아 있었다.

on|slaught /ɒnslɔt/ (**onslaughts**) 1 N-COUNT An **onslaught** on someone or something is a very violent, forceful attack against them. ❑ *The attackers launched another vicious onslaught on their victim.* 2 N-COUNT If you refer to an **onslaught of** something, you mean that there is a large amount of it, often so that it is very difficult to deal with. ❑ *...the constant onslaught of ads on American TV.*

1 가산명사 맹공격 ❑ 그 습격자들은 희생자들에게 또 다른 악의적인 맹공격을 시작했다. 2 가산명사 집중 공세 ❑ 미국 텔레비전 광고의 끊임없는 집중 공세

onto ♦◇◇ /ɒntu/

> The spelling **on to** is also used.

> 철자 on to도 쓴다.

> In addition to the uses shown below, **onto** is used in phrasal verbs such as "hold onto" and "latch onto."

> onto는 아래 용법 외에도 'hold onto', 'latch onto'와 같은 구동사에 쓰인다.

1 PREP If something moves or is put **onto** an object or surface, it is then on that object or surface. ❑ *I took my bags inside, lowered myself onto the bed and switched on the TV.* 2 PREP You can sometimes use **onto** to mention the place or area that someone moves into. ❑ *The players emerged onto the field.* ❑ *...when the photographer sets off onto the moors.* 3 PREP You can use **onto** to introduce the place toward which a light or someone's look is directed. ❑ *...the metal part of the door onto which the sun had been shining.* ❑ *The colors rotated round on a disc and were reflected onto the wall behind.* 4 PREP You can use **onto** to introduce a place that you would immediately come to after leaving another place that you have just mentioned, because they are next to each other. [V PREP n] ❑ *The door opened onto a lighted hallway.* 5 PREP When you change the position of your body, you use **onto** to introduce the part your body which is now supporting you. ❑ *As he stepped backwards she fell onto her knees, then onto her face.* ❑ *Puffing a little, Mabel shifted her weight onto her feet.* 6 PREP When you get **onto** a bus, train, or plane, you enter it in order to travel somewhere. ❑ *As he got on to the plane, he asked me how I was feeling.* 7 PREP **Onto** is used after verbs such as "hold," "hang," and "cling" to indicate what someone is holding firmly or where something is being held firmly. ❑ *The reflector is held onto the sides of the spacecraft with a frame.* 8 PREP If people who are talking get **onto** a different subject, they begin talking about it. ❑ *Let's get on to more important matters.* 9 PREP You can sometimes use **onto** to indicate that something or someone becomes included as a part of a list or system. ❑ *The Macedonian question had failed to get on to the agenda.* ❑ *The pill itself has changed a lot since it first came onto the market.* 10 PREP If someone **is onto** something, they are about to discover something important. [INFORMAL] [*be* PREP n] ❑ *He leaned across the table and whispered to me, "I'm really onto something."* 11 PREP If someone **is onto** you, they have discovered that you are doing something illegal or wrong. [INFORMAL] [*be* PREP n] ❑ *I had told people what he had been doing, so now the police were onto him.*

1 전치사 ~ 위로 ❑ 나는 내 가방을 안쪽 편에 두고, 침대 위로 몸을 눕힌 후 텔레비전을 켰다. 2 전치사 ~ 쪽으로 ❑ 선수들은 운동장으로 나왔다. ❑ 그 사진사가 광야로 출발할 때 3 전치사 ~ 쪽으로 ❑ 햇빛을 계속 받고 있는 그 문의 금속 부분 ❑ 디스크 위의 여러 가지 색깔들이 회전하면서 뒤에 있는 벽면에 반사되었다. 4 전치사 ~ 쪽으로 ❑ 그 문이 불 켜진 복도 쪽으로 열렸다. 5 전치사 ~ 위로 ❑ 그가 뒷걸음질을 치자 그녀는 무릎을 꿇으면서 앞으로 고꾸라졌다. ❑ 숨을 좀 헐떡이면서, 마벨은 몸의 무게 중심을 두 발 위로 옮겼다. 6 전치사 (탈것) 에로 ❑ 그가 비행기에 타면서 나에게 기분이 어떠냐고 물었다. 7 전치사 ~에 ❑ 우주선 측면에 반사기가 틀에 끼워져 단단히 붙어 있다. 8 전치사 ~에 대해서 ❑ 더 중요한 사안에 대해서 얘기해 보자. 9 전치사 ~에 ❑ 마케도니아 문제는 의제에 포함되지 못했었다. ❑ 그 알약이 처음 시판된 이후로 여러 번 바뀌었다. 10 전치사 발견하려고 하다 [비격식체] ❑ 그는 식탁 너머로 내게 몸을 숙이며 속삭였다. "내가 정말로 뭔가 대단한 걸 발견할 것 같애." 11 전치사 이상한 낌새를 알아채다 [비격식체] ❑ 내가 사람들에게 그가 해 왔던 일을 말했기 때문에 이제는 경찰이 그에게서 이상한 낌새를 알아챘다.

onus /oʊnəs/ N-SING If you say that **the onus** is **on** someone **to** do something, you mean it is their duty or responsibility to do it. [FORMAL] ❑ *The onus is on the shopkeeper to provide goods which live up to the quality of their description.*

단수명사 의무, 책임 [격식체] ❑ 설명서에 제시된 품질에 부응하는 물건을 제공하는 것이 소매상의 의무이다.

on|ward /ɒnwərd/ also onwards

In American and British English, **onward** is an adjective. In American English and sometimes in formal British English, **onward** may also be an adverb. In British English and sometimes in American English, **onwards** is an adverb.

1 ADJ **Onward** means moving forward or continuing a journey. ❑ *British Airways have two flights a day to Bangkok, and there are onward flights to Phnom Penh.* ● ADV **Onward** is also an adverb. [ADV after v] ❑ *The bus continued onward.* **2** ADJ **Onward** means developing, progressing, or becoming more important over a period of time. ❑ *...the onward march of progress in the British aircraft industry.* ● ADV **Onward** is also an adverb. [ADV after v] ❑ *From here, it has been onward and upward all the way.* **3** ADV If something happens from a particular time **onward** or **onwards**, it begins to happen at that time and continues to happen afterward. [from n ADV] ❑ *From the turn of the century onward, she shared the life of the aborigines.*

oops /ups, ʊps/ EXCLAM You say "**oops**" to indicate that there has been a slight accident or mistake, or to apologize to someone for it. [INFORMAL, FEELINGS] ❑ *Today they're saying, "Oops, we made a mistake."*

ooze /uz/ (**oozes, oozing, oozed**) **1** V-T/V-I When a thick or sticky liquid **oozes** from something or when something **oozes** it, the liquid flows slowly and in small quantities. ❑ *He saw there was a big hole in the back of the man's head; blood was still oozing from it.* ❑ *The lava will just ooze gently out of the crater.* **2** V-T/V-I If you say that someone or something **oozes** a quality or characteristic, or **oozes** with it, you mean that they show it very strongly. ❑ *The Elizabethan house oozes charm.*

opaque /oʊpeɪk/ **1** ADJ If an object or substance is **opaque**, you cannot see through it. ❑ *You can always use opaque glass if you need to block a street view.* **2** ADJ If you say that something is **opaque**, you mean that it is difficult to understand. ❑ *...the opaque language of the inspector's reports.*

op. cit. /ɒp sɪt/ In reference books, **op. cit.** is used after an author's name to refer to a book of theirs which has already been mentioned. [FORMAL] ❑ *...quoted in Iyer, op. cit., p. 332.*

OPEC /oʊpɛk/ N-PROPER **OPEC** is an organization of countries that produce oil. It tries to develop a common policy and system of prices. **OPEC** is an abbreviation for "Organization of Petroleum-Exporting Countries." ❑ *Each member of OPEC would seek to maximize its own production.*

open ♦♦♦ /oʊpən/ (**opens, opening, opened**) **1** V-T/V-I If you **open** something such as a door, window, or lid, or if it **opens**, its position is changed so that it no longer covers a hole or gap. ❑ *He opened the window and looked out.* ● ADJ **Open** is also an adjective. ❑ *...an open window.* **2** V-T If you **open** something such as a bottle, box, parcel, or envelope, you move, remove, or cut part of it so you can take out what is inside. ❑ *The Inspector opened the packet of cigarettes.* ● ADJ **Open** is also an adjective. ❑ *...an open bottle of milk.* ● PHRASAL VERB **Open up** means the same as **open**. ❑ *He opened up a cage and lifted out a 6ft python.* **3** V-T/V-I If you **open** something such as a book, an umbrella, or your hand, or if it **opens**, the different parts of it move away from each other so that the inside of it can be seen. ❑ *He opened the heavy Bible.* ❑ *The flower opens to reveal a Queen Bee.* ● ADJ **Open** is also an adjective. ❑ *Without warning, Bardo smacked his fist into his open hand.* ● PHRASAL VERB **Open out** means the same as **open**. ❑ *Keith took a map from the dashboard and opened it out on his knees.* **4** V-T If you **open** a computer file, you give the computer an instruction to display it on the screen. [COMPUTING] ❑ *Double click on the icon to open the file.*

Note that you do not use **open** as a verb or adjective to talk about electrical devices. If someone causes an electrical device to work by pressing a switch, you say that they **put** it **on**, **switch** it **on**, or **turn** it **on**. ❑ *It's too easy just to switch on the television.* If the device is already working, you say that it is **on**. ❑ *The answering machine is on... He cannot sleep with the light on.*

5 V-T/V-I When you **open** your eyes or your eyes **open**, you move your eyelids upward, for example when you wake up, so that you can see. ❑ *When I opened my eyes I saw a man with an axe standing at the end of my bed.* ● ADJ **Open** is also an adjective. ❑ *As soon as he saw that her eyes were open he sat up.* **6** V-T If you **open** your arms, you stretch them wide apart in front of you, usually in order to put them around someone. ❑ *She opened her arms and gave me a big hug.* **7** ADJ If you describe a person or their character as **open**, you mean they are honest and do not want or try to hide anything or to deceive anyone. ❑ *He had always been open with her and she always felt she would know if he lied.* ● **open|ness** N-UNCOUNT ❑ *...a relationship based on honesty and openness.* **8** ADJ If you describe a situation, attitude, or way of behaving as **open**, you mean it is not kept hidden or secret. [ADJ n] ❑ *The action is an open violation of the Vienna Convention.* ● **open|ness** N-UNCOUNT ❑ *...the new climate of political openness.* **9** ADJ If you are **open to** suggestions or ideas, you are ready and willing to consider or accept them. [v-link ADJ to n] ❑ *They are open to suggestions on how working conditions might be improved.* **10** ADJ If you say that a system, person, or idea is **open to** something such as abuse or criticism, you mean they might receive abuse or criticism because of their qualities, effects, or actions. [v-link ADJ to n] ❑ *The system, though well-meaning, is open to abuse.* **11** ADJ If you say that a fact or question is **open to** debate, interpretation, or discussion, you mean that people are uncertain whether it is true, what it means, or what the answer is. ❑ *The truth of the facts produced may be open to doubt.* **12** V-T/V-I If people **open** something such as a blocked road or a border, or if it **opens**, people can then pass along it or through it. ❑ *The rebels have opened the road from Monrovia to the Ivory Coast.* ● ADJ

미국영어와 영국영어에서 onward는 형용사이다. 미국영어와 가끔 격식체 영국영어에서 onward may also be an 부사가 될 수도 있다. 영국영어와 가끔 미국영어에서 onwards는 부사이다.

1 형용사 앞으로 나아가는, 계속 이어서 가는 ❑ 영국항공은 방콕으로 하루에 두 번 운행하며 프놈펜으로의 연장 운행편도 있다. ● 부사 앞으로, 계속 이어서 ❑ 버스가 계속해서 앞으로 나아갔다. **2** 형용사 향상되는, 나아가는 ❑ 영국 항공기 산업의 진보 행진 ● 부사 향상되어 ❑ 여기서부터 그것이 줄곧 앞으로 또 위로만 발달해 왔다. **3** 부사 계속해서 ❑ 세기가 바뀐 이래로 계속해서, 그녀는 원주민들과 함께 살았다.

감탄사 저런; 이런; 미안 [비격식체, 감정 개입] ❑ 요즘엔 사람들이 "이런, 우리가 실수했네."라고 말한다.

1 타동사/자동사 스며 나오다, 조금씩 흘러나오다; 스며 나오게 하다, 조금씩 흘리다 ❑ 그가 보니 그 남자의 뒤통수에 큰 구멍이 뚫려 있었고 거기서 아직도 피가 배어 나오고 있었다. ❑ 용암은 분화구에서 조금씩 서서히 흘러나오기만 할 것이다. **2** 타동사/자동사 (어떤 특성이) 흘러넘치다, 줄줄 흐르다 ❑ 그 엘리자베스 풍의 저택은 매력이 흘러넘친다.

1 형용사 불투명한 ❑ 거리가 보이는 것을 차단할 필요가 있으면 언제나 불투명 유리를 사용할 수 있다. **2** 형용사 불투명한 ❑ 조사관의 보고서에 담긴 불분명한 표현

앞서 언급한 책 [격식체] ❑ 앞에서 언급한 아이어의 책 332쪽에 인용된

고유명사 석유 수출국 기구 ❑ 각 석유 수출국 기구 회원국들은 자국의 석유 생산 극대화를 추구할 것이다.

1 타동사/자동사 열다; 열리다 ❑ 그는 창문을 열고 밖을 내다보았다. ● 형용사 열린 ❑ 열린 창문 **2** 타동사 열어젖히다, 개봉하다 ❑ 검사관이 담뱃갑을 열어젖혔다. ● 형용사 열어젖힌, 개봉한 ❑ 개봉한 우유병 ● 구동사 열어젖히다, 개봉하다 ❑ 그가 우리를 열어젖히고 길이가 6피트에 이르는 비단뱀을 들어올려 꺼냈다. **3** 타동사/자동사 펴다; 펴지다 ❑ 그가 육중한 성경을 펼쳤다. ❑ 꽃이 피면 여왕벌이 모습을 드러낸다. ● 형용사 펼쳐진 ❑ 아무런 경고도 없이 바르도가 한쪽 주먹을 쫙 편 다른 한 손에 대고 세게 쳤다. ● 구동사 펴다; 펴지다, 피다 ❑ 키스가 계기반에서 지도를 가져와 무릎 위에 놓고 펼쳤다. **4** 타동사 열다 [컴퓨터] ❑ 아이콘을 더블 클릭해서 그 파일을 여세요.

전기 기구에 대해 말할 때는 open을 동사나 형용사로 쓰지 않는다는 점을 유의하라. 누가 스위치를 눌러 전기 기구가 작동하도록 하면, 그가 전기 기구를 put on, switch on, turn on한다고 말한다. ❑ 텔레비전을 켜기만 하는 것은 너무나 쉬운 일이다. 전기 기구가 이미 작동 중이면, 그것이 on이라고 한다. ● 자동 응답기가 켜져 있다... 그는 불이 켜져 있으면 잠을 못 잔다.

5 타동사/자동사 (눈을) 뜨다 ❑ 눈을 떴을 때 나는 도끼를 든 남자가 내 침대 발치에서 있는 것을 보았다. ● 형용사 (눈을) 뜬 ❑ 그녀가 두 눈을 뜬 것을 보자마자 그는 일어나 앉았다. **6** 타동사 벌리다 ❑ 그녀가 두 팔을 벌리고 나를 꽉 껴안았다. **7** 형용사 솔직한 ❑ 그는 늘 그녀에게 솔직했었고 그녀는 그가 거짓말을 한다면 자신이 알아챌 수 있을 거라고 항상 느꼈다. ● 솔직함 불가산명사 ❑ 정직과 솔직함에 기반을 둔 관계 **8** 형용사 공공연한, 개방적인 ❑ 그 조치는 비엔나 협약을 공공연히 위반하는 것이다. ● 공개, 개방 불가산명사 ❑ 정치적 개방이라는 새로운 풍토 **9** 형용사 -에 대해 수용적인, -에 대해 열려 있는 ❑ 그들은 근무 조건 개선을 위한 제안에 대해 수용적이다. **10** 형용사 -을 받기 쉬운 ❑ 그 시스템의 의도는 좋지만 오용되기 쉽다. **11** 형용사 여지가 있는 ❑ 제시된 사실들의 진실성에 대해서는 의심의 여지가 있을 수 있다. **12** 타동사/자동사 뚫다; 뚫리다 ❑ 반군이 먼로비아에서 아이보리 코스트로 가는 길을 뚫었다. ● 형용사 소통된 ❑ 우리가 배속되었던 연대 전체가 맡은 임무는 단지 그 간선 도로가 계속 소통되게 하는 것이었다. ● 구동사 뚫다; 뚫리다 ❑ 오늘 구조대원이 길을 뚫자, 몇몇 작은 마을들이 폐허가 되다시피 한 것이 분명해졌다. **13** 자동사 (-으로) 통하다 ❑ 복도를 지나자 연기 자욱한 낮은 방이 나왔다. ● 구동사

A

Open is also an adjective. ❑ *We were part of an entire regiment that had nothing else to do but to keep that highway open.* ● PHRASAL VERB **Open up** means the same as **open.** ❑ *As rescue workers opened up roads today, it became apparent that some small towns were totally devastated.* **12** V-I If a place **opens into** another, larger place, you can move from one directly into the other. ❑ *The corridor opened into a low smoky room.* ● PHRASAL VERB **Open out** means the same as **open.** ❑ *...narrow streets opening out into charming squares.* **13** ADJ An **open** area is a large area that does not have many buildings or trees in it. ❑ *Officers will also continue their search of nearby open ground.* **13** ADJ An **open** structure or object is not covered or enclosed. [ADJ n] ❑ *Don't leave a child alone in a room with an open fire.* **15** V-T If you **open** your shirt or coat, you undo the buttons or pull down the zipper. ❑ *I opened my coat and let him see the belt.* ● ADJ **Open** is also an adjective. [ADJ n, v-link ADJ] ❑ *The top can be worn buttoned up or open over a T-shirt.* **17** V-T/V-I When a store, office, or public building **opens** or **is opened,** its doors are unlocked and the public can go in. ❑ *Banks closed on Friday afternoon and did not open again until Monday morning.* ❑ *...a gang of three who'd apparently been lying in wait for him to open the shop.* ● ADJ **Open** is also an adjective. ❑ *His shop is open Monday through Friday, 9am to 6pm.* **18** V-T/V-I When a public building, factory, or company **opens** or when someone **opens** it, it starts operating for the first time. ❑ *The original station opened in 1754.* ❑ *The complex opens to the public tomorrow.* ● ADJ **Open** is also an adjective. [v-link ADJ] ❑ *...any operating subsidy required to keep the pits open.* ● **open|ing** (**openings**) N-COUNT ❑ *He was there, though, for the official opening.* **19** V-T/V-I If something such as a meeting or series of talks **opens,** or if someone **opens** it, it begins. ❑ *...an emergency session of the Russian Parliament due to open later this morning.* ● **open|ing** N-SING ❑ *...a communique issued at the opening of the talks.* **20** V-T/V-I If an event such as a meeting or discussion **opens with** a particular activity, that activity is the first thing that happens or is dealt with. You can also say that someone such as a speaker or singer **opens by** doing a particular thing. ❑ *The service opened with a hymn.* ❑ *I opened by saying, "Honey, you look sensational."* **21** V-I On the stock exchange, the price at which currencies, shares, or commodities **opens** is their value at the start of that day's trading. [BUSINESS] ❑ *Gold declined $2 in Zurich to open at 385.50.* **22** V-I When a movie, play, or other public event **opens,** it begins to be shown, be performed, or take place for a limited period of time. ❑ *A photographic exhibition opens at the Royal College of Art on Wednesday.* ● **open|ing** N-SING [the N of n] ❑ *He is due to attend the opening of the Asian Games on Saturday.* **23** V-T If you **open** an account with a bank or a commercial organization, you begin to use their services. ❑ *He tried to open an account at the branch of his bank nearest to his workplace.* **24** ADJ If an opportunity or choice **is open** to you, you are able to do a particular thing if you choose to. [v-link ADJ to n] ❑ *There are a wide range of career opportunities open to young people.* **25** V-T/V-I To **open** opportunities or possibilities means the same as to **open** them **up.** ❑ *The chief of naval operations wants to open opportunities for women in the Navy.* **26** ADJ You can use **open** to describe something that anyone is allowed to take part in or accept. ❑ *It's an open meeting, everybody's invited.* ❑ *...an open invitation.* **27** ADJ If something such as an offer or job is **open,** it is available for someone to accept or apply for. [v-link ADJ] ❑ *The offer will remain open until further notice.* →see also **opening 6** **28** PHRASE If you do something **in the open,** you do it out of doors rather than in a house or other building. ❑ *Many are sleeping in the open because they have no shelter.* **29** PHRASE If an attitude or situation is **in the open** or **out in the open,** people know about it and it is no longer kept secret. ❑ *The medical service had advised us to keep it a secret, but we wanted it in the open.* **30** PHRASE If something is **wide open,** it is open to its full extent. ❑ *The child had left the inner door wide open.* **31** PHRASE If you say that a competition, race, or election is **wide open,** you mean that anyone could win it, because there is no competitor who seems to be much better than the others. ❑ *The competition has been thrown wide open by the absence of the world champion.* **32 with open arms** →see **arm. to keep your eyes open** →see **eye. with your eyes open** →see **eye. to open your eyes** →see **eye. to open fire** →see **fire. to open your heart** →see **heart. the heavens open** →see **heaven. an open mind** →see **mind. to open your mind** →see **mind. to keep your options open** →see **option**

Thesaurus	open의 참조어
v.	crack, reveal; (ant.) close, hide **1**
	extend, stretch **3** **6**
ADJ.	friendly, honest, outgoing; (ant.) deceptive, dishonest **7**

▶**open up** **1** →see **open 2, 12** **2** PHRASAL VERB If a place, economy, or area of interest **opens up,** or if someone **opens** it **up,** more people can go there or become involved in it. ❑ *As the market opens up, I think people are going to be able to spend more money on consumer goods.* ❑ *He said he wanted to see how Albania was opening up to the world.* **3** PHRASAL VERB If something **opens up** opportunities or possibilities, or if they **open up,** they are created. ❑ *It was also felt that the collapse of the system opened up new possibilities.* **4** PHRASAL VERB When you **open up** a building, you unlock and open the door so that people can get in. ❑ *Three armed men were waiting when the postmaster and his wife arrived to open up the shop.* **5** PHRASAL VERB If someone **opens up,** they start to say exactly what they think or feel. ❑ *Lorna found that people were willing to open up to her.*

open-air also **open air** **1** ADJ An **open-air** place or event is outside rather than in a building. ❑ *...an open air concert in brilliant sunshine.* **2** N-SING If you are **in the open air,** you are outside rather than in a building. ❑ *We sleep out under the stars, and eat our meals in the open air.*

open-door also **open door** ADJ If a country or organization has an **open-door** policy toward people or goods, it allows them to come there freely, without any restrictions. [ADJ n] ❑ *...reformers who have advocated an open door economic policy.* ● N-SING **Open door** is also a noun. ❑ *...an open door to further foreign investment.*

(-으로) 통하다 ❑ 매혹적인 광장들로 통하는 좁은 도로들 **14** 형용사 탁 트인 ❑ 경관들은 또한 계속해서 근처 공터를 수색할 것이다. **13** 형용사 덮개가 없는, 가리지 않은 ❑ 뚜껑가를 가려 놓지 않은 난로가 놓여 있는 방에 아이 혼자 두지 마세요. **16** 타동사 단추를 풀다; 지퍼를 내리다 ❑ 나는 외투의 단추를 풀고 그에게 허리띠를 보여 줬다. ● 형용사 단추를 푼; 지퍼를 내린 ❑ 그 상의는 단추를 다 채워 입거나 티셔츠 위에 단추를 풀고 덧입을 수 있다. **17** 타동사/자동사 열다; 열리다 ❑ 은행은 금요일 오후에 문을 닫아 월요일 아침까지는 다시 열지 않았다. ❑ 그가 가게 문을 열기를 기다리며 분명히 잠복하고 있었던 삼인조 폭력배들 ● 형용사 열려 있는, 영업 중인 ❑ 그의 가게는 월요일부터 금요일까지, 오전 9시부터 오후 6시까지 영업한다. **18** 타동사/자동사 최초의 억은 1754년에 문을 열었다. ❑ 그 단지는 내일 일반인들에게 문을 연다. ● 형용사 열려 있는, 운영 중인 ❑ 그 탄갱들을 계속 운영하기 위해 요구한 모든 운영 보조금 ● 개업, 개장 가산명사 ❑ 그러나 그는 공식 개장을 위해 그곳에 가 있었다. **19** 타동사/자동사 개회하다; 개회되다 ❑ 오늘 오전 늦게 개회될 예정인 러시아 국회의 임시회기 ● 개회 단수명사 ❑ 회담 개회와 함께 발표된 공식 선언문 **20** 타동사/자동사 (-하는 것으로) 시작하다 ❑ 예배는 찬송가를 부르는 것으로 시작했다. ❑ 나는 "여보, 당신 눈부셔."라는 말로 시작했다. **21** 자동사 개장하다 [경제] ❑ 취리히에서 금 시세가 2달러 하락하여 385.50포인트에서 개장했다. **22** 자동사 개막하다 ❑ 왕립 예술 대학에서 수요일에 사진전을 개막한다. ● 개막, 개막식 단수명사 ❑ 그는 토요일에 아시안 게임 개막식에 참가할 예정이다. **23** 타동사 개설하다 ❑ 그는 거래 은행 지점 중 직장에서 가장 가까운 곳에 구좌를 개설하려고 했다. **24** 형용사 -에게 열려 있다 ❑ 젊은이들에게 다양한 진로를 택할 수 있는 기회가 열려 있다. **25** 타동사/자동사 (기회나 가능성을) 열어 주다 ❑ 해군 작전 지휘관은 해군 내 여성들에게 기회를 열어 주기를 원한다. **26** 형용사 일반인에 공개된, 개방된 ❑ 그것은 공개회의로 누구나 참석할 수 있다. ❑ 누구에게나 개방된 초대 **27** 형용사 수락할 수 있는; 공석인 ❑ 추후 공지가 있기 전까지는 그 제안을 수락할 수 있다. **28** 구 옥외에서, 야외에서 ❑ 많은 사람들이 집이 없어서 야외에서 잠을 자고 있다. **29** 구 공개된 ❑ 의료 시설에서는 우리에게 그 사실을 비밀로 할 것을 권했지만 우리는 공개하기를 원했다. **30** 구 활짝 열린 ❑ 그 아이가 안쪽 문을 활짝 열어 두었었다. **31** 구 뚜렷한 우승 후보가 없는 ❑ 세계 챔피언의 불참으로 그 경기는 뚜렷한 우승 후보가 없는 상태가 되었다.

2 구동사 개방되다; 개방하다 ❑ 시장이 개방되면서, 사람들이 더 많은 돈을 소비재에 쓸 수 있을 것이다. ❑ 그는 알바니아가 어떻게 세계에 문호를 개방하게 될 것인지 보고 싶다고 말했다. **3** 구동사 창출하다; 창출되다 ❑ 체제 붕괴가 새로운 가능성을 창출하는 것으로도 느껴졌다. **4** 구동사 문을 열다 ❑ 우체국장과 그의 부인이 도착해서 우체국 문을 열려고 할 때 무장한 세 남자가 기다리고 있었다. **5** 구동사 마음을 열다, 터놓고 말하다 ❑ 로나는 사람들이 자신에게는 기꺼이 마음을 연다는 것을 깨달았다.

1 형용사 야외의, 노천의 ❑ 눈부신 햇살 아래 펼쳐지는 야외 공연 **2** 단수명사 야외 ❑ 우리는 별빛 아래서 잠을 청하고 야외에서 식사를 한다.

형용사 문호 개방의 ❑ 문호 개방 경제 정책을 주장해 온 개혁가들 ● 단수명사 문호 개방 ❑ 더 많은 외국인 투자에 대한 문호 개방

open-ended ADJ When people begin an **open-ended** discussion or activity, they do not start with any intention of achieving a particular decision or result. ☐ ...an open-ended commitment to the security of the Gulf.

형용사 제한 없는, 지속적으로 수정 가능한 ☐ 걸프만의 안전에 대한, 지속적으로 수정 가능한 공약

open|ing ◆◇◇ /ˈoʊpənɪŋ/ (openings) **1** ADJ The **opening** event, item, day, or week in a series is the first one. [ADJ n] ☐ They returned to take part in the season's opening game. **2** N-COUNT The **opening of** something such as a book, play, or concert is the first part of it. ☐ The opening of the scene depicts Akhnaten and his family in a moment of intimacy. **3** N-COUNT An **opening** is a hole or empty space through which things or people can pass. ☐ He squeezed through a narrow opening in the fence. **4** N-COUNT An **opening** in a forest is a small area where there are no trees or bushes. [mainly AM; BRIT usually **clearing**] ☐ I glanced down at the beach as we passed an opening in the trees. **5** N-COUNT An **opening** is a good opportunity to do something, for example to show people how good you are. ☐ Her capabilities were always there; all she needed was an opening to show them. **6** N-COUNT An **opening** is a job that is available. ☐ We don't have any openings now, but we'll call you if something comes up. **7** →see also **open**

1 형용사 처음의 ☐ 그들은 그 시즌의 개막 경기에 참가하기 위해 돌아왔다. **2** 가산명사 시두 ☐ 그 장면의 서두에서는 서로 친밀하던 시기의 아크나텐과 그의 가족이 그려진다. **3** 가산명사 구멍 ☐ 그는 울타리에 난 좁은 구멍을 간신히 뚫고 나아갔다. **4** 가산명사 숲 속의 빈터 [주로 미국영어; 영국영어 대개 clearing] ☐ 우리가 숲 속 빈터를 지날 때 나는 바닷가를 흘끗 내려다보았다. **5** 가산명사 좋은 기회 ☐ 그녀는 항상 능력이 있었다. 단지 그것을 드러낼 좋은 기회가 필요할 뿐이었다. **6** 가산명사 빈 자리 ☐ 지금은 빈 자리가 없습니다만 결원이 생기면 연락드리겠습니다.

N. cut, door, gap, slot, space, window **3**
clearing **4**

open|ing hours N-PLURAL **Opening hours** are the times during which a shop, bank, library, or bar is open for business. ☐ Opening hours are 9.30am-5.45pm, Mon-Fri.

복수명사 영업시간 ☐ 영업시간은 월요일부터 금요일까지, 오전 9시 30분부터 오후 5시 45분까지입니다.

open|ly /ˈoʊpənli/ ADV If you do something **openly**, you do it without hiding any facts or hiding your feelings. ☐ The Bundesbank has openly criticized the German Government.

부사 공개적으로 ☐ 독일 연방 은행이 독일 정부를 공개적으로 비난했다.

open mar|ket N-SING Goods that are bought and sold on **the open market** are advertised and sold to anyone who wants to buy them. [BUSINESS] ☐ The Central Bank is authorized to sell government bonds on the open market.

단수명사 공개 시장 [경제] ☐ 중앙은행이 공개 시장에서 국채를 판매하도록 승인받았다.

open-minded ADJ If you describe someone as **open-minded**, you approve of them because they are willing to listen to and consider other people's ideas and suggestions. [APPROVAL] ☐ He was very open-minded about other people's work. ● **open-mindedness** N-UNCOUNT ☐ He was praised for his enthusiasm and his open-mindedness.

형용사 편견이 없는, 도량이 넓은 [마음에 듦] ☐ 그는 다른 사람들의 직업에 대해서 편견이 전혀 없었다. ● 편견 없음, 도량이 넓음 불가산명사 ☐ 그는 열정과 넓은 도량으로 칭찬받았다.

open-plan ADJ An **open-plan** building, office, or room has no internal walls dividing it into smaller areas. ☐ The firm's top managers share the same open-plan office.

형용사 칸막이가 없는 ☐ 그 회사의 최고 경영자들은 칸막이 없는 사무실을 함께 쓴다.

Open Uni|ver|sity N-PROPER In Britain, **the Open University** is a university that offers degree courses using radio, television, and the Internet, for students who want to study part-time or mainly at home. ☐ She was holding down a job she was enjoying and studying at the Open University.

고유명사 방송대학 ☐ 그녀는 자신이 즐기는 일자리를 계속 유지하면서 방송대학에서 공부를 하고 있었다.

op|era ◆◇◇ /ˈɒpərə, ˈɒprə/ (operas) N-VAR An **opera** is a play with music in which all the words are sung. ☐ ...a one-act opera about contemporary women in America. ☐ ...an opera singer. →see also **soap opera** →see **music**

가산명사 또는 불가산명사 오페라, 가극 ☐ 미국의 현대 여성들에 대한 1막짜리 오페라 ☐ 오페라 가수

op|er|ate ◆◆◇ /ˈɒpəreɪt/ (operates, operating, operated) **1** V-T/V-I If you **operate** a business or organization, you work to keep it running properly. If a business or organization **operates**, it carries out its work. ☐ Until his death in 1986 Greenwood owned and operated an enormous pear orchard. ☐ ...allowing commercial banks to operate in the country. ● **op|era|tion** /ˌɒpəˈreɪʃ°n/ N-UNCOUNT ☐ Company finance is to provide funds for the everyday operation of the business. **2** V-I The way that something **operates** is the way that it works or has a particular effect. ☐ Ceiling and wall lights can operate independently. ☐ How do accounting records operate? ● **op|era|tion** N-UNCOUNT ☐ Why is it the case that taking part-time work is made so difficult by the operation of the benefit system? **3** V-T/V-I When you **operate** a machine or device, or when it **operates**, you make it work. ☐ A massive rock fall trapped the men as they operated a tunnelling machine. ● **op|era|tion** N-UNCOUNT ☐ ...over 1,000 dials monitoring every aspect of the operation of the aeroplane. **4** V-I When surgeons **operate on** a patient in a hospital, they cut open a patient's body in order to remove, replace, or repair a diseased or damaged part. ☐ The surgeon who operated on the King released new details of his injuries.

1 타동사/자동사 운영하다; 영업하다 ☐ 1986년 사망하기까지 그린우드는 거대한 배 과수원을 소유하고 있으면서 이를 운영했다. ☐ 상업적인 은행이 그 나라에서 영업할 수 있도록 허용하는 ● 운영 불가산명사 ☐ 기업 재정이란 일상적인 사업 운영을 위한 자금을 조달하는 것이다. **2** 자동사 작용하다, 영향을 미치다 ☐ 천장과 벽의 조명은 따로 작용할 수 있다. ● 작용, 영향 불가산명사 ☐ 정부 보조금 제도 영향으로 시간제 일을 찾기 아주 어려워졌다는데 왜 그렇습니까? **3** 타동사/자동사 조작하다, 운전하다; 작동하다 ☐ 육중한 바위가 떨어져서 터널 뚫는 장비를 조작하던 사람들이 갇혔다. ● 조작, 작동 불가산명사 ☐ 비행기 작동의 모든 측면을 감시하는 천 개가 넘는 눈금판 **4** 자동사 수술하다 ☐ 왕의 수술을 집도한 외과 의사가 왕의 부상에 대한 새로운 사항을 자세히 공개했다.

V. function, perform, run, work; (ant.) break down, fail **2**

N. operate **a business/company**, schools operate **1**
forces operate **1** **2**
V. **be allowed to** operate, **continue to** operate **1** **2** **4**

op|er|at|ic /ˌɒpəˈrætɪk/ ADJ **Operatic** means relating to opera. ☐ ...the local amateur operatic society.

형용사 오페라의, 가극의 ☐ 지역 아마추어 오페라단

a
b
c
d
e
f
g
h
i
j
k
l
m
n
o
p
q
r
s
t
u
v
w
x
y
z

op|er|at|ing /ɒpəreɪtɪŋ/ ADJ **Operating** profits and costs are the money that a company earns and spends in carrying out its ordinary trading activities, in contrast to such things as interest and investment. [BUSINESS] [ADJ n] □ *The group made operating profits of £8om before interest.*

형용사 영업의, 경영의 [경제] □ 그 그룹은 이자를 공제하지 않은 상태에서 8천만 파운드의 영업 이익을 냈다.

op|er|at|ing room (operating rooms) N-COUNT An **operating room** is a special room in a hospital where surgeons carry out medical operations. [BRIT **operating theatre**]

가산명사 수술실 [영국영어 operating theatre]

op|er|at|ing sys|tem (operating systems) N-COUNT The **operating system** of a computer is its most basic program, which it needs in order to function and run other programs. [COMPUTING] □ *...Microsoft's Windows NT operating system.*

가산명사 (컴퓨터) 운영 체제 [컴퓨터] □ 마이크로소프트에서 만든 윈도우 엔티 운영 체제

op|er|at|ing thea|tre (operating theatres) N-COUNT An **operating theatre** is the same as an **operating room**. [BRIT]

가산명사 수술실 [영국영어]

Word Link

oper ≈ work : cooperate, opera, operation

---

op|era|tion ♦♦♦ /ɒpəreɪʃⁿ/ (operations) **1** N-COUNT An **operation** is a highly organized activity that involves many people doing different things. □ *The rescue operation began on Friday afternoon.* □ *The soldiers were engaged in a military operation close to the Ugandan border.* **2** N-COUNT A business or company can be referred to as an **operation**. [BUSINESS] □ *Thorn's electronics operation employs around 5,000 people.* **3** N-COUNT When a patient has an **operation**, a surgeon cuts open their body in order to remove, replace, or repair a diseased or damaged part. □ *Charles was at the clinic recovering from an operation on his arm.* **4** N-UNCOUNT If a system is **in operation**, it is being used. □ *Until the rail links are in operation, passengers can only travel through the tunnel by coach.* **5** N-UNCOUNT If a machine or device is **in operation**, it is working. □ *There are three ski lifts in operation.* **6** PHRASE When a rule, system, or plan **comes into operation** or you **put** it **into operation**, you begin to use it. □ *The Financial Services Act came into operation four years ago.*

1 가산명사 작전 □ 구출 작전은 금요일 오후에 시작되었다. □ 그 병사들은 우간다 접경 인근에서 있던 군사 작전에 투입되어 있었다. **2** 가산명사 회사, 사업체 [경제] □ 쏜의 전자 회사는 대략 5천 명을 채용한다. **3** 가산명사 수술 □ 찰스는 진료소에서 팔 수술을 받고 회복 중이었다. **4** 불가산명사 실시, 시행 □ 철로 연결편이 운행될 때까지는 승객들은 버스를 타야만 터널을 통과할 수 있다. **5** 불가산명사 작동, 운행 □ 세 대의 스키 리프트가 운행 중이다. **6** 구 시행되다, 실시되다; 시행하다, 실시하다 □ 금융서비스법은 4년 전에 시행되었다.

Word Partnership operation의 연어

N.	**relief** operation, **rescue** operation **1**
ADJ.	**covert** operation, **massive** operation, **military** operation, **undercover** operation **1**
	major operation, **successful** operation **1**-**3**
	emergency operation **1** **3**
V.	**carry out an** operation, **perform an** operation, **plan an** operation **1** **3**

---

op|era|tion|al /ɒpəreɪʃənᵊl/ **1** ADJ A machine or piece of equipment that is **operational** is in use or is ready for use. □ *The whole system will be fully operational by December 1995.* **2** ADJ **Operational** factors or problems relate to the working of a system, device, or plan. □ *The nuclear industry was required to prove that every operational and safety aspect had been fully researched.* ● **op|era|tion|al|ly** ADV □ *An all-female political section would have been operationally ineffective.*

1 형용사 운용 중인, 운용 가능한 □ 시스템 전체가 1995년 12월이면 완전히 운용 가능할 것이다. **2** 형용사 운영상의 □ 그 원자력 산업은 모든 운영 및 안전상의 문제를 충분히 조사했음을 증명해야 했다. ● 운영상으로 부사 □ 모두 여성으로만 이루어진 정치 분과라면 운영상 비효율적이었을 것이다.

op|era|tive /ɒpərətɪv, -əreɪtɪv/ (operatives) **1** ADJ A system or service that is **operative** is working or having an effect. [FORMAL] □ *The commercial telephone service was no longer operative.* **2** N-COUNT An **operative** is a worker, especially one who does work with their hands. [FORMAL] □ *In an automated car plant there is not a human operative to be seen.* **3** N-COUNT An **operative** is someone who works for a government agency such as the intelligence service. [mainly AM] □ *Naturally the CIA wants to protect its operatives.* **4** PHRASE If you describe a word as **the operative word**, you want to draw attention to it because you think it is important or exactly true in a particular situation. □ *As long as the operative word is "greed," you can't count on people keeping the costs down.*

1 형용사 작동하는, 효과가 있는 [격식체] □ 일반 전화 서비스가 더 이상 작동하지 않았다. **2** 가산명사 직공 [격식체] □ 자동화된 자동차 공장에서는 사람이 정교한 일을 하는 것을 찾아볼 수 없다. **3** 가산명사 첩보원, 공작원 [주로 미국영어] □ 당연히 미 중앙 정보국은 자기 측 공작원을 보호하기를 원한다. **4** 구 중요한 단어 □ '탐욕'이 중요한 단어인 이상, 사람들이 비용을 낮게 유지하리라고 믿을 수는 없다.

op|era|tor ♦♦◇ /ɒpəreɪtər/ (operators) **1** N-COUNT An **operator** is a person who connects telephone calls at a telephone exchange or in a place such as an office or hotel. □ *He dialed the operator and put in a call for Rome.* **2** N-COUNT An **operator** is a person who is employed to operate or control a machine. □ *...computer operators.* **3** N-COUNT An **operator** is a person or a company that runs a business. [BUSINESS] □ *...'Tele-Communications,' the nation's largest cable TV operator.* **4** N-COUNT If you call someone a smooth or shrewd **operator**, you mean that they are skillful at achieving what they want, often in a slightly dishonest way. [INFORMAL] □ *He was a smart operator. Don't underestimate him.*

1 가산명사 전화 교환원 □ 그는 전화 교환원에게 전화를 걸어 로마로 통화를 하였다. **2** 가산명사 조작자, 기사 □ 컴퓨터 기사 **3** 가산명사 운영자 [경제] □ 이 나라 최대 케이블 텔레비전 운영사인 텔러커뮤니케이션스 **4** 가산명사 재간꾼, 꾀자가 [비격식체] □ 그는 재간꾼이었어. 그를 얕보지 말아.

opin|ion ♦♦◇ /əpɪnyən/ (opinions) **1** N-COUNT Your **opinion** about something is what you think or believe about it. □ *I wasn't asking for your opinion, Dick.* □ *He held the opinion that a government should think before introducing a tax.* **2** N-SING Your **opinion** of someone is your judgment of their character or ability. □ *That improved Mrs. Goole's already favorable opinion of him.* **3** N-UNCOUNT You can refer to the beliefs or views that people have as **opinion**. □ *Some, I suppose, might even be in positions to influence opinion.* **4** N-COUNT An **opinion** from an expert is the advice or judgment that they give you in the subject that they know a lot about. □ *Even if you have had a regular physical check-up recently, you should still seek a medical opinion.* **5** →see also **public opinion, second opinion** **6** PHRASE You add expressions such as "in my opinion" or "in their opinion" to a statement in order to indicate that it is what you or someone else thinks, and is not necessarily a fact. □ *The book is, in Henry's opinion, the best book on the subject.* **7** PHRASE If someone is **of the opinion that** something is the case, that is

1 가산명사 의견, 견해 □ 네 의견을 물어본 게 아니잖은. 딕. □ 그는 정부가 세금을 도입하기에 앞서 숙고를 해야 한다는 의견을 가지고 있었다. **2** 단수명사 평가 □ 그것 때문에 이미 그를 괜찮은 사람이라고 생각하던 그의 그에 대한 평가가 더욱 좋아졌다. **3** 불가산명사 여론 □ 나는 일부 사람들이 심지어 여론을 좌우하는 지위에 있을 수 있다는 생각이 들어. **4** 가산명사 (전문가의) 의견 □ 네가 최근에 정기적으로 건강 진단을 받아 왔다고 해도 의사의 의견을 들어 볼 필요가 있어. **6** 구 내 생각에는; '그들이 보기에는 □ 헨리 생각에는 그 책이 이 주제에 대한 가장 좋은 책이다. **7** 구 -라고 믿는 [격식체] □ 프랭크는 1934번 요트가 이겼어야 했다고 믿는다.

what they believe. [FORMAL] ❏ *Frank is of the opinion that the 1934 yacht should have won.*

Thesaurus	*opinion*의 참조어
N.	belief, estimation, feeling, judgment, thought, viewpoint ▯ ▯

Word Partnership	*opinion*의 연어
V.	express an opinion, give an opinion, share an opinion ▯ ▯
	ask for an opinion ▯ ▯ ▯
ADJ.	favorable opinion ▯
	expert opinion, legal opinion, majority opinion, medical opinion ▯

opin|ion poll (**opinion polls**) N-COUNT An **opinion poll** involves asking people's opinions on a particular subject, especially one concerning politics. ❏ *Nearly three-quarters of people questioned in an opinion poll agreed with the government's decision.*

opi|um /ˈoʊpiəm/ N-UNCOUNT **Opium** is a powerful drug made from the seeds of a type of poppy. Opium is used in medicines that relieve pain or help someone sleep.

op|po|nent ♦◇◇ /əˈpoʊnənt/ (**opponents**) ▯ N-COUNT A politician's **opponents** are other politicians who belong to a different party or who have different aims or policies. ❏ *...Mr. Kennedy's opponent in the leadership contest.* ▯ N-COUNT In a sports contest, your **opponent** is the person who is playing against you. ❏ *Norris twice knocked down his opponent in the early rounds of the fight.* ▯ N-COUNT The **opponents of** an idea or policy do not agree with it and do not want it to be carried out. ❏ *...opponents of the spread of nuclear weapons.* →see **chess**

op|por|tun|ist /ˌɒpərˈtuːnɪst, BRIT ˌɒpəˈtjuːnɪst/ (**opportunists**) ADJ If you describe someone as **opportunist**, you are critical of them because they take advantage of any situation in order to gain money or power, without considering whether their actions are right or wrong. [DISAPPROVAL] ❏ *...corrupt and opportunist politicians.* ● N-COUNT An **opportunist** is someone who is opportunist. ❏ *Like most successful politicians, Sinclair was an opportunist.*

op|por|tun|is|tic /ˌɒpərtuˈnɪstɪk, BRIT ˌɒpəˈtjuːnɪstɪk/ ADJ If you describe someone's behavior as **opportunistic**, you are critical of them because they take advantage of situations in order to gain money or power, without thinking about whether their actions are right or wrong. [DISAPPROVAL] ❏ *Many of the party's members joined only for opportunistic reasons.*

op|por|tu|nity ♦♦◇ /ˌɒpərˈtuːnɪti, BRIT ˌɒpəˈtjuːnɪti/ (**opportunities**) N-VAR An **opportunity** is a situation in which it is possible for you to do something that you want to do. ❏ *I had an opportunity to go to New York and study.* ❏ *...equal opportunities in employment.*

Word Partnership	*opportunity*의 연어
ADJ.	economic opportunity, educational opportunity, equal opportunity, golden opportunity, great opportunity, lost opportunity, rare opportunity, unique opportunity
N.	business opportunity, employment opportunity, investment opportunity
V.	have an opportunity, miss an opportunity, see an opportunity, seize an opportunity, opportunity to speak, take advantage of an opportunity

op|pose ♦◇◇ /əˈpoʊz/ (**opposes, opposing, opposed**) V-T If you **oppose** someone or **oppose** their plans or ideas, you disagree with what they want to do and try to prevent them from doing it. ❏ *Mr. Taylor was not bitter towards those who had opposed him.*

op|posed ♦◇◇ /əˈpoʊzd/ ▯ ADJ If you **are opposed to** something, you disagree with it or disapprove of it. [v-link ADJ to n/-ing] ❏ *I am utterly opposed to any form of terrorism.* ▯ ADJ You say that two ideas or systems are **opposed** when they are opposite to each other or very different from each other. ❏ *...people with policies almost diametrically opposed to his own.* ▯ PHRASE You use **as opposed to** when you want to make it clear that you are talking about one particular thing and not something else. ❏ *We ate in the restaurant, as opposed to the bistro.*

op|pos|ing /əˈpoʊzɪŋ/ ▯ ADJ **Opposing** ideas or tendencies are totally different from each other. [ADJ n] ❏ *I have a friend who has the opposing view and felt that the war was immoral.* ▯ ADJ **Opposing** groups of people disagree about something or are in competition with one another. [ADJ n] ❏ *The Georgian leader said in a radio address that he still favored dialogue between the opposing sides.*

op|po|site ♦◇◇ /ˈɒpəzɪt/ (**opposites**) ▯ PREP If one thing is **opposite** another, it is on the other side of a space from it. ❏ *Jennie had sat opposite her at breakfast.* ● ADV **Opposite** is also an adverb. ❏ *He looked up at the buildings opposite, but could see no open window.* ▯ ADJ The **opposite** side or part of something is the side or part that is furthest away from you. [ADJ n] ❏ *...the opposite corner of the room.* ▯ ADJ **Opposite** is used to describe things of the same kind which are completely different in a particular way. For example, north and south are opposite directions, and winning and losing are opposite results in a game. ❏ *All the cars driving in the opposite direction had their headlights on.* ▯ N-COUNT The

가산명사 여론 조사 ❏ 한 여론 조사에 응한 사람들 중 거의 4분의 3이 정부 결정에 동의했다.

불가산명사 아편

▯ 가산명사 적수, 상대 ❏ 지도자 경선에서 케네디 씨의 적수 ▯ 가산명사 상대 선수 ❏ 노리스는 권투 시합 초반에 상대 선수를 두 번 녹다운시켰다. ▯ 가산명사 반대 세력, 반대자들 ❏ 핵무기 확산에 반대하는 세력

형용사 기회주의자인 [탐탁잖음] ❏ 부패한 기회주의자 정치인들 ● 가산명사 기회주의자 ❏ 대부분의 성공한 정치인들과 마찬가지로 싱클레어도 기회주의자였다.

형용사 기회주의적인 [탐탁잖음] ❏ 그 당의 당원들 중 많은 수가 단지 기회주의적인 이유에서 입당했다.

가산명사 또는 불가산명사 기회 ❏ 내겐 뉴욕에 가서 공부할 기회가 한 번 있었다. ❏ 고용 기회의 평등

타동사 반대하다, 저지하다 ❏ 테일러 씨는 자기에게 반대한 사람들에 대해 분개하지 않았다.

▯ 형용사 반대하다, 인정하지 않다 ❏ 난 어떤 형식의 폭력주의든지 전적으로 반대한다. ▯ 형용사 반대되는 ❏ 그 자신의 정책과 거의 정반대되는 정책을 가진 사람들 ▯ 구 -와는 대조적으로 ❏ 우리는 그 작은 음식점에서와는 대조적으로 그 식당에서는 식사를 했다.

▯ 형용사 대립되는 ❏ 대립되는 견해를 가진 친구가 하나 있는데 그는 그 전쟁이 부도덕하다고 생각했다. ▯ 형용사 반대하는, 경쟁하는 ❏ 그루지야 공화국의 지도자는 라디오 연설에서 자신은 여전히 반대 측과 대화를 하고 싶다고 밝혔다.

▯ 전치사 -의 맞은편에 ❏ 제니는 아침 식사 때 그녀의 맞은편에 앉아 있었다. ● 부사 맞은편에서 ❏ 그는 맞은편에서 그 건물들을 올려다봤지만 열려 있는 창문이라곤 없었다. ▯ 형용사 저 멀리 떨어진 ❏ 방의 저쪽 구석 ▯ 형용사 정반대의 ❏ 반대 방향에서 주행해 오는 모든 차량이 전조등을 켜고 있었다. ▯ 가산명사 정반대 ❏ 리터는 아주 복잡한 남자였지만 마리우스는 정반대여서 단순한 농부였다. ❏ 글쎄, 그가 뭐라 말하건 속으로 생각하는 건 정반대가 틀림없다니까.

A

opposite of someone or something is the person or thing that is most different from them. ❑ *Ritter was a very complex man but Marius was the opposite, a simple farmer.* ❑ *Well, whatever he says you can bet he's thinking the opposite.*

B

Word Partnership	*opposite*의 연어
ADJ.	**directly** opposite 🔳
	exactly (the) opposite, **precisely (the)** opposite,
	quite the opposite 🔳 🔳 🔳
	complete opposite, **exact** opposite 🔳 🔳
N.	opposite **corner**, opposite **end**, opposite **side** 🔳
	opposite **direction**, opposite **effect** 🔳
PREP.	**the** opposite **of** *someone/something* 🔳

E

op|po|site sex N-SING If you are talking about men and refer to **the opposite sex**, you mean women. If you are talking about women and refer to **the opposite sex**, you mean men. ❑ *Body language can also be used to attract members of the opposite sex.*

단수명사 이성 ❑ 신체 언어 역시 이성의 관심을 끄는 데 쓰일 수 있다.

F

op|po|si|tion ♦♦◇ /ɒpəzɪʃ°n/ (**oppositions**) 🔳 N-UNCOUNT **Opposition** is strong, angry, or violent disagreement and disapproval. ❑ *The government is facing a new wave of opposition in the form of a student strike.* 🔳 N-COUNT-COLL **The opposition** is the political parties or groups that are opposed to a government. ❑ *The main opposition parties boycotted the election, saying it would not be conducted fairly.* 🔳 N-COUNT-COLL In a country's parliament or legislature, **the opposition** refers to the politicians or political parties than form part of the parliament or legislature, but are not the government. ❑ *...the Leader of the Opposition.* 🔳 N-SING-COLL **The opposition** is the person or team you are competing against in a sports event. ❑ *Poland provide the opposition for the Scots' last warm-up match at home.*

🔳 불가산명사 항의, 반대 ❑ 정부가 학생 파업이라는 형태의 새로운 항의의 물결에 직면하고 있다. 🔳 가산명사·집합 야당 ❑ 주요 야당들이 선거가 공정하게 실시되지 않을 것이라며 선거를 거부했다. 🔳 가산명사·집합 야당 ❑ 야당 지도자 🔳 단수명사·집합 상대 선수, 상대 팀 ❑ 스코틀랜드가 본국에서 벌이는 마지막 연습 경기에 폴란드가 상대 팀으로 나온다.

J

op|press /əpres/ (**oppresses**, **oppressing**, **oppressed**) V-T To **oppress** people means to treat them cruelly, or to prevent them from having the same opportunities, freedom, and benefits as others. ❑ *These people often are oppressed by the governments of the countries they find themselves in.*

자동사 억압하다 ❑ 이 사람들은 흔히 자신들이 머무르게 되는 나라들의 정부로부터 억압을 받는다.

K

op|pressed /əprest/ ADJ People who are **oppressed** are treated cruelly or are prevented from having the same opportunities, freedom, and benefits as others. ❑ *Before they took power, they felt oppressed by the white English speakers who controlled things.* ● N-PLURAL **The oppressed** are people who are oppressed. ❑ *...a sense of community with the poor and oppressed.*

형용사 억압받는 ❑ 그들이 정권을 잡기 전에는 그들은 모든 것을 지배하던, 영어를 말하는 백인들에게 억압을 받는다고 느꼈다. ● 복수명사 억압받는 사람들, 피억압자들 ❑ 가난하고 억압받는 사람들에 대한 공동체 의식

M

op|pres|sion /əpreʃ°n/ N-UNCOUNT **Oppression** is the cruel or unfair treatment of a group of people. ❑ *...an attempt to escape political oppression.*

불가산명사 억압 ❑ 정치적 억압에서 벗어나려는 시도

op|pres|sive /əpresɪv/ 🔳 ADJ If you describe a society, its laws, or customs as **oppressive**, you think they treat people cruelly and unfairly. ❑ *The new laws will be just as oppressive as those they replace.* 🔳 ADJ If you describe the weather or the atmosphere in a room as **oppressive**, you mean that it is unpleasantly hot and damp. ❑ *The oppressive afternoon heat had quite tired him out.* 🔳 ADJ An **oppressive** situation makes you feel depressed and uncomfortable. ❑ *...the oppressive sadness that weighed upon him like a physical pain.*

🔳 형용사 억압적인, 가혹한 ❑ 새로운 법규들도 이런 법규들만큼이나 억압적일 것이다. 🔳 형용사 후텁지근한 ❑ 후텁지근한 오후의 더위 때문에 그는 꽤 지쳐 있었다. 🔳 형용사 견디기 힘든, 숨 막힐 듯한 ❑ 마치 육체적인 고통처럼 그를 짓누르는 견디기 힘든 슬픔

O

opt ♦◇◇ /ɒpt/ (**opts**, **opting**, **opted**) V-T/V-I If you **opt for** something, or **opt to** do something, you choose it or decide to do it in preference to anything else. ❑ *Depending on your circumstances you may wish to opt for one method or the other.*

타동사/자동사 선택하다, 고르다 ❑ 당신이 처한 상황에 따라 이 둘 중 한 가지 방식을 선택하고 싶어 할 것이다.

P

▶**opt out** PHRASAL VERB If you **opt out of** something, you choose to be no longer involved in it. ❑ *... powers for hospitals to opt out of health authority control.*

구동사 손을 떼다, 관여하지 않기로 하다 ❑ 병원이 보건 당국의 통제에서 손을 뗄 수 있는 힘

Q

op|tic /ɒptɪk/ ADJ **Optic** means relating to the eyes or to sight. [ADJ n] ❑ *The reason for this is that the optic nerve is a part of the brain.* →see **eye**

형용사 눈의, 시력의 ❑ 이렇게 되는 까닭은 시신경이 뇌의 일부분이기 때문이다.

R

op|ti|cal /ɒptɪk°l/ ADJ **Optical** devices, processes, and effects involve or relate to vision, light, or images. ❑ *...optical telescopes.*

형용사 시각의, 광학의, 영상의 ❑ 광학 현미경

op|ti|cian /ɒptɪʃ°n/ (**opticians**) 🔳 N-COUNT An **optician** is someone whose job involves testing people's sight, and making or selling glasses and contact lenses. ❑ *...a qualified optician.* 🔳 N-COUNT An **optician** or an **optician's** is a store where you can have your eyes tested and buy glasses and contact lenses. ❑ *Some may need specialist treatment at the optician's.*

🔳 가산명사 검안사, 안경 제작자, 안경 판매상 ❑ 자격을 갖춘 검안사 🔳 가산명사 안경점 ❑ 어떤 사람들은 안경점에서 전문가의 조치를 받아야 할지도 모른다.

T

op|ti|mal /ɒptɪm°l/ →see **optimum**

Word Link	*optim* ≈ *the best* : *optimum, optimism, optimize*

U

op|ti|mism /ɒptɪmɪzəm/ N-UNCOUNT **Optimism** is the feeling of being hopeful about the future or about the success of something in particular. ❑ *The Indian Prime Minister has expressed optimism about India's future relations with the U.S.*

불가산명사 낙관, 낙천주의 ❑ 인도 수상이 인도와 미국과의 향후 관계에 대해 낙관을 표명했다.

V

op|ti|mist /ɒptɪmɪst/ (**optimists**) N-COUNT An **optimist** is someone who is hopeful about the future. ❑ *He has the upbeat manner of an eternal optimist.*

가산명사 낙천주의자 ❑ 그는 영원한 낙천주의자로의 쾌활한 태도를 지니고 있다.

W

op|ti|mis|tic ♦◇◇ /ɒptɪmɪstɪk/ ADJ Someone who is **optimistic** is hopeful about the future or the success of something in particular. ❑ *The President says she is optimistic that an agreement can be worked out soon.* ● **op|ti|mis|ti|cal|ly** ADV [ADV with v] ❑ *Both sides have spoken optimistically about the talks.*

형용사 낙관하는 ❑ 대통령은 협정이 곧 성립될 것으로 낙관한다고 말한다. ● 낙관적으로 부사 ❑ 양측 모두 그 회담에 대해 낙관적으로 말해 왔다.

X

op|ti|mize /ɒptɪmaɪz/ (**optimizes**, **optimizing**, **optimized**) [BRIT also **optimise**] V-T To **optimize** a plan, system, or machine means to arrange or design it so that it operates as smoothly and efficiently as possible. [FORMAL] ❑ *The new systems have been optimized for running Microsoft Windows.*

[영국영어 optimise] 타동사 가장 적합하게 하다 [격식체] ❑ 새 시스템은 마이크로소프트 윈도우를 실행하기에 가장 적합하게 되어 있다.

Y

op|ti|mum /ɒptɪməm/ or **optimal** ADJ The **optimum** or **optimal** level or state of something is the best level or state that it could achieve. [FORMAL] ❑ *Aim to do some physical activity three times a week for optimum health.*

형용사 최적의 [격식체] ❑ 최적의 건강을 위해서는 일주일에 세 번째 얼마간의 신체적 활동을 하도록 목표로 삼으세요.

Z

Word Link
opt ≈ choosing : ad**opt**, **opt**ion, **opt**ional

op|tion ♦♦◇ /ɒpʃⁿn/ (options) **1** N-COUNT An **option** is something that you can choose to do in preference to one or more alternatives. ❑ *He's argued from the start that America and its allies are putting too much emphasis on the military option.* **2** N-SING If you have the **option** of doing something, you can choose whether to do it or not. ❑ *Criminals are given the option of going to jail or facing public humiliation.* **3** N-COUNT In business, an **option** is an agreement or contract that gives someone the right to buy or sell something such as property or shares at a future date. [BUSINESS] ❑ *Each bank has granted the other an option on 19.9% of its shares.* **4** N-COUNT An **option** is one of a number of subjects which a student can choose to study as a part of his or her course. ❑ *Several options are offered for the student's senior year.* **5** PHRASE If you **keep** your **options open** or **leave** your **options open**, you delay making a decision about something. ❑ *I am keeping my options open. I have not made a decision on either matter.* **6** PHRASE If you take the **soft option**, you do the thing that is easiest or least likely to cause trouble in a particular situation. [mainly BRIT] ❑ *The job of chairman can no longer be regarded as a convenient soft option.*

Thesaurus
option의 참조어

N. alternative, choice, opportunity, preference, selection **1** **2**

Word Partnership
option의 연어

ADJ. **available** option, **best** option, **other** option, **viable** option **1** **2**
V. **have an/the** option **1** **2**
choose an option **1** **4**
option **to buy/purchase**, **exercise an** option **3**

op|tion|al /ɒpʃənⁿl/ ADJ If something is **optional**, you can choose whether or not you do it or have it. ❑ *Sex education is a sensitive area for some parents, and thus it should remain optional.*

opu|lent /ɒpyələnt/ ADJ **Opulent** things or places look grand and expensive. [FORMAL] ❑ *...an opulent office on Wimpole Street in London's West End.* • **opu|lence** N-UNCOUNT ❑ *...the elegant opulence of the German embassy.*

or ♦♦♦ /ər, STRONG ɔːr/ **1** CONJ You use **or** to link two or more alternatives. ❑ *"Tea or coffee?" John asked.* ❑ *He said he would try to write or call as soon as he reached the Canary Islands.* **2** CONJ You use **or** to give another alternative, when the first alternative is introduced by "either" or "whether." ❑ *Items like bread, milk, and meat were either unavailable or could be obtained only on the black market.* ❑ *Either you can talk to him, or I will.*

> You do not use **or** after **neither**. You use **nor** instead. ❑ *He speaks neither English nor German.*

3 CONJ You use **or** between two numbers to indicate that you are giving an approximate amount. ❑ *Everyone benefited from limiting their intake of tea to just three or four cups a day.* ❑ *When I was nine or ten someone explained to me that when you are grown up you have to work.* **4** CONJ You use **or** to introduce a comment which corrects or modifies what you have just said. ❑ *The man was a fool, he thought, or at least incompetent.* **5** CONJ If you say that someone should do something **or** something unpleasant will happen, you are warning them that if they do not do it, the unpleasant thing will happen. ❑ *She had to have the operation, or she would die.* **6** CONJ You use **or** to introduce something which is evidence for the truth of a statement you have just made. ❑ *He must have thought Jane was worth it or he wouldn't have wasted time on her, I suppose.* **7** PHRASE You use **or no** or **or not** to emphasize that a particular thing makes no difference to what is going to happen. [EMPHASIS] ❑ *Chairman or no, if I want to stop the project, I can.* **8** PHRASE You use **or no** between two occurrences of the same noun in order to say that whether something is true or not makes no difference to a situation. ❑ *The next day, rain or no rain, it was business as usual.* **9 or else** →see **else**. **or other** →see **other**. **or so** →see **so**. **or something** →see **something**

oral /ɔːrəl/ (orals) **1** ADJ **Oral** communication is spoken rather than written. ❑ *...the written and oral traditions of ancient cultures.* • **oral|ly** ADV [ADV after v] ❑ *...their ability to present ideas orally and in writing.* **2** N-COUNT An **oral** is an examination, especially in a foreign language, that is spoken rather than written. ❑ *I spoke privately to the candidate after the oral.* **3** ADJ You use **oral** to indicate that something is done with a person's mouth or relates to a person's mouth. ❑ *...good oral hygiene.* • **oral|ly** ADV ❑ *...antibiotic tablets taken orally.*

or|ange ♦♦◇ /ɒrɪndʒ, BRIT ɒrɪndʒ/ (oranges) **1** COLOR Something that is **orange** is of a color between red and yellow. ❑ *...men in bright orange uniforms.* **2** N-VAR An **orange** is a round juicy fruit with a thick, orange colored skin. ❑ *...orange trees.* **3** N-UNCOUNT **Orange** is a drink that is made from or tastes of oranges. ❑ *...vodka and orange.* →see **rainbow**

ora|tory /ɒrətɔːri, BRIT ɒrətəri/ (oratories) **1** N-UNCOUNT **Oratory** is the art of making formal speeches which strongly affect people's feelings and beliefs. [FORMAL] ❑ *He displayed determination as well as powerful oratory.* **2** N-COUNT An **oratory** is a room or building where Christians go to pray. ❑ *The wedding will be at the Brompton Oratory next month.*

---

1 가산명사 선택 ❑ 그는 처음부터 미국과 미국의 동맹국들이 군사적인 선택에 지나치게 큰 비중을 두고 있다고 주장해 왔다. **2** 단수명사 선택권 ❑ 범죄자들에게 복역을 할 것인지 공개적인 모욕을 당할 것인지를 결정하는 선택권이 주어진다. **3** 가산명사 옵션 [경제] ❑ 각 은행이 타 은행에게 자사 주가의 19.9퍼센트에 옵션을 부여했다. **4** 가산명사 선택 과목 ❑ 상급 학년이 되면 선택 과목이 몇 과목 개설된다. **5** 구 결정을 보류하다 ❑ 난 결정을 보류하고 있어. 어느 쪽 문제에 대해서도 결정을 안 내렸어. **6** 구 안전한 선택 [주로 영국영어] ❑ 의장직은 더 이상 편리하고 안전한 선택으로 간주될 수 없다.

형용사 선택의 ❑ 성교육은 일부 부모들에게는 민감한 부분이므로 선택 사항으로 남아 있어야 한다.

형용사 으리으리한 [격식체] ❑ 런던 웨스트엔드의 윔폴 가에 위치한 으리으리한 사무실 ● 으리으리함 불가산명사 ❑ 고상하고 으리으리한 독일 대사관

1 접속사 또는, 아니면, -이거나 ❑ "차, 아니면 커피?" 하고 존이 물었다. ❑ 그는 카나리아 제도에 도착하는 즉시 편지를 쓰거나 전화를 하도록 하겠다고 말했다. **2** 접속사 -이거나 또는, -아니면 ❑ 빵, 우유, 육류 같은 품목은 구할 수 없거나 암시장에서만 손에 넣을 수 있었다. ❑ 네가 그에게 말해도 좋고, 아니면 내가 할게.

neither 뒤에는 or를 쓰지 않고 nor를 쓴다. ❑ 그는 영어도 독일어도 하지 못한다.

3 접속사 -내지는 ❑ 차 섭취량을 하루에 석 잔 내지는 넉 잔으로 제한하니 모두에게 이익이었다. ❑ 내가 아홉 살 내지 열 살이었을 때 누군가가 성인이 되면 일을 해야 한다는 걸 내게 설명해 주었다. **4** 접속사 아니, -라기보다는 차라리 ❑ 그 남자는 바보, 아니 적어도 무능하다고 그는 생각했다. **5** 접속사 그렇지 않으면 ❑ 그녀는 수술을 받아야만 했다. 그렇지 않으면 죽을 것이었다. **6** 접속사 다시 말하면 ❑ 그는 제인에게 그럴 만한 가치가 있다고, 다시 말하면 자신이 그녀에게 시간을 낭비한 것이 아니라고 생각했음에 틀림없어. **7** 구 -이든 아니든 [강조] ❑ 내가 의장이든 아니든 그 계획을 중단하고 싶으면 난 그만둘 수 있어. **8** 구 -이든 아니든 ❑ 그 다음 날, 비가 오든 안 오든, 사정은 달라진 게 없었다.

1 형용사 구두의, 구술의 ❑ 기록 및 구전으로 전해 온 고대 문화의 전통 ● 구두로, 구술로 부사 ❑ 그들이 의견을 말과 글로 제시하는 능력 **2** 가산명사 구술시험 ❑ 나는 구술시험 이후에 지원자에게 비공식적으로 이야기했다. **3** 형용사 구강의 ❑ 양호한 구강 위생 ● 구강으로, 입으로 부사 ❑ 정제형의 경구 항생제

1 색채의 주황색의 ❑ 선명한 주황색 제복을 입은 남자들 **2** 가산명사 또는 불가산명사 오렌지 ❑ 오렌지 나무들 **3** 불가산명사 오렌지 주스 ❑ 보드카와 오렌지 주스

1 불가산명사 웅변, 웅변술 [격식체] ❑ 그는 힘찬 웅변과 함께 굳은 의지를 보여 줬다. **2** 가산명사 기도실, 예배당 ❑ 결혼식은 내달 브롬프턴 예배당에서 거행될 것이다.

or|bit /ɔ́rbɪt/ (orbits, orbiting, orbited) **1** N-COUNT An **orbit** is the curved path in space that is followed by an object going around and around a planet, moon, or star. [also in/into N] □ *Mars and Earth have orbits which change with time.* **2** V-T If something such as a satellite **orbits** a planet, moon, or sun, it moves around it in a continuous, curving path. □ *In 1957 the Soviet Union launched the first satellite to orbit the earth.* →see **satellite, solar system**

1 가산명사 궤도 □ 화성과 지구의 궤도는 시간에 따라 변한다. **2** 타동사 선회하다, 궤도를 돌다 □ 1957년에 구소련이 지구 궤도를 돌 최초의 인공위성을 쏘아 올렸다.

or|chard /ɔ́rtʃərd/ (orchards) N-COUNT An **orchard** is an area of land on which fruit trees are grown.

가산명사 과수원

or|ches|tra /ɔ́rkɪstrə/ (orchestras) **1** N-COUNT An **orchestra** is a large group of musicians who play a variety of different instruments together. Orchestras usually play classical music. □ *...the Royal Liverpool Philharmonic Orchestra.* →see also **symphony orchestra 2** N-SING **The orchestra** or **the orchestra seats** in a theater or concert hall are the seats on the first floor directly in front of the stage. [mainly AM; BRIT usually **stalls**] □ *With the balcony blocked off, patrons filled most of the orchestra seats.* →see Word Web: **orchestra**

1 가산명사 오케스트라, 관현악단 □ 왕립 리버풀 필하모니 오케스트라 **2** 단수명사 무대 바로 앞 좌석 [주로 미국영어; 영국영어 대개 stalls] □ 2층 특별석이 봉쇄되었으므로, 후원자들이 무대 바로 앞 좌석의 대부분을 차지했다.

or|ches|tral /ɔrkɛ́strəl/ ADJ **Orchestral** means relating to an orchestra and the music it plays. [ADJ n] □ *...an orchestral concert.*

형용사 오케스트라의, 관현악의 □ 오케스트라 연주회

or|ches|trate /ɔ́rkɪstreɪt/ (orchestrates, orchestrating, orchestrated) V-T If you say that someone **orchestrates** an event or situation, you mean that they carefully organize it in a way that will produce the result that they want. □ *The colonel was able to orchestrate a rebellion from inside an army jail.* ● **or|ches|tra|tion** N-UNCOUNT □ *...his skillful orchestration of latent nationalist feeling.*

타동사 조직하다 □ 그 대령은 교도소 내부에서 반란을 조직할 수 있었다. ● 조직 불가산명사 □ 그가 잠재된 민족주의적 감정을 능숙하게 조직함

or|ches|tra|tion /ɔ̀rkɪstreɪ́ʃən/ (orchestrations) N-COUNT An **orchestration** is a piece of music that has been rewritten so that it can be played by an orchestra. □ *Mahler's own imaginative orchestration was heard in the same concert.*

가산명사 관현악 편곡 □ 말러가 직접 편곡한 상상력 넘치는 관현악곡이 같은 연주회에서 연주되었다.

or|chid /ɔ́rkɪd/ (orchids) N-COUNT **Orchids** are plants with brightly colored, unusually shaped flowers.

가산명사 난초

or|dain /ɔrdeɪ́n/ (ordains, ordaining, ordained) **1** V-T When someone **is ordained**, they are made a member of the clergy in a religious ceremony. □ *He was ordained a Catholic priest in 1982.* □ *Women have been ordained for many years in the Church of Scotland.* **2** V-T If some authority or power **ordains** something, they decide that it should happen or be in existence. [FORMAL] □ *Nehru ordained that socialism should rule.* □ *His rule was ordained by heaven.*

1 타동사 성직자로 임명되다 □ 그는 1982년에 천주교 사제로 서품을 받았다. □ 스코틀랜드 국교회에서는 여성들이 수년간 서품을 받아 왔다. **2** 타동사 제정하다, 정하다 [격식체] □ 네루는 사회주의가 지배해야 한다고 제정했다. □ 그의 통치는 하늘의 뜻에 의해 정해졌다.

or|deal /ɔrdíl/ (ordeals) N-COUNT If you describe an experience or situation as an **ordeal**, you think it is difficult and unpleasant. □ *...the painful ordeal of the last eight months.*

가산명사 시련 □ 지난 8개월간의 고통스러운 시련

---

order

① SUBORDINATING CONJUNCTION USES
② COMMANDS AND REQUESTS
③ ARRANGEMENTS, SITUATIONS, AND GROUPINGS

---

① **or|der** ♦♦◇ /ɔ́rdər/ **1** PHRASE If you do something **in order to** achieve a particular thing or **in order that** something can happen, you do it because you want to achieve that thing. □ *Most schools are extremely unwilling to cut down on staff in order to cut costs.* **2** PHRASE If someone must be in a particular situation **in order to** achieve something they want, they cannot achieve that thing if they are not in that situation. □ *We need to get rid of the idea that we must be liked all the time in order to be worthwhile.* **3** PHRASE If something must happen **in order for** something else to happen, the second thing cannot happen if the first thing does not happen. □ *In order for their computers to trace a person's records, they need both the name and address of the individual.*

1 구 -할 목적으로, -하기 위해서 □ 대부분의 학교들은 경비 절감을 위해 직원 수를 줄이는 것을 몹시 꺼린다. **2** 구 -하려면, -하기 위해서는 □ 우리가 가치 있는 사람이 되려면 항상 사랑받아야만 한다는 그 생각을 버려야 해. **3** 구 -가 ...하려면, -가 ... 하기 위해서는 □ 그들이 컴퓨터로 개인 기록을 추적하기 위해서는 각 개인의 이름과 주소가 필요하다.

② **or|der** ♦♦♦ /ɔ́rdər/ (orders, ordering, ordered) →Please look at category **12** to see if the expression you are looking for is shown under another headword. **1** V-T If a person in authority **orders** someone **to** do something, they tell them to do it. □ *Williams ordered him to leave.* **2** V-T If someone in authority **orders** something, they give instructions that it should be done. □ *The President has ordered a full investigation.* **3** N-COUNT If someone in authority gives you an **order**, they tell you to do something. □ *The activists were shot when they refused to obey an order to halt.* □ *As darkness fell, Clinton gave orders for his men to rest.* **4** N-COUNT A court **order** is a legal instruction stating that something must be done. □ *She has decided not to appeal against a court order banning her from keeping*

1 타동사 명령하다 □ 윌리엄스가 그에게 떠나라고 명령했다. **2** 타동사 지시하다 □ 대통령이 전면 조사를 지시했다. **3** 가산명사 지시, 명령 □ 운동가들이 정지 명령을 따르지 않자 사격이 가해졌다. □ 어둠이 내리자, 클린턴은 직원들에게 휴식하라고 명령을 내렸다. **4** 가산명사 (법원의) 명령 □ 그녀는 동물을 기르지 못하게 한 법원 명령에 항소하지 않기로 결정했다. **5** 타동사/자동사 주문하다 □ 아타나스는 새우 칵테일 요리와 샐러드를 주문했다. □ 여자 종업원이 와서 물었다. "주문하시겠어요?" **6** 가산명사

Word Web   orchestra

The modern **symphony orchestra** usually has from 60 to 100 **musicians**. The largest group of musicians are in the **string** section. It gives the orchestra its rich, flowing sound. String **instruments** include **violins, violas, cellos,** and usually **double basses**. Flutes, oboes, clarinets, and bassoons make up the woodwind section. The **brass** section is usually quite small. Too much of this sound could overwhelm the more delicate strings. Brass **instruments** include the French horn, **trumpet, trombone** and tuba. The size of the **percussion** section depends on the **composition** being performed. However, there is almost always a timpani player.

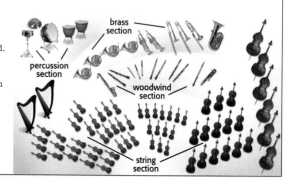

brass section

percussion section

woodwind section

string section

animals. ⑤ V-T/V-I When you **order** something that you are going to pay for, you ask for it to be brought to you, sent to you, or obtained for you. ❑ *Atanas ordered a shrimp cocktail and a salad.* ❑ *The waitress appeared. "Are you ready to order?"* ⑥ N-COUNT An **order** is a request for something to be brought, made, or obtained for you in return for money. ❑ *British Rail are going to place an order for a hundred and eighty-eight trains.* ⑦ N-COUNT Someone's **order** is what they have asked to be brought, made, or obtained for them in return for money. ❑ *The waiter returned with their order and Graham signed the bill.* ⑧ →see also **mail order, postal order, standing order** ⑨ PHRASE Something that is **on order** at a store or factory has been asked for but has not yet been supplied. ❑ *The airlines still have 2,500 new aeroplanes on order.* ⑩ PHRASE If you do something **to order**, you do it whenever you are asked to do it. ❑ *She now makes wonderful dried flower arrangements to order.* ⑪ PHRASE If you are **under orders** to do something, you have been told to do it by someone in authority. [BRIT also **order about**] ❑ *I am under orders not to discuss his mission or his location with anyone.* ⑫ **a tall order** →see **tall**

▶**order around** PHRASAL VERB If you say that someone **is ordering** you **around** or **is ordering** you **about**, you mean they are telling you what to do as if they have authority over you, and you dislike this. ❑ *When we're out he gets really bossy and starts ordering me around.*

Thesaurus	*order*의 참조어
v.	charge, command, direct, tell ② ❶
	buy, request ② ❺
N.	command, direction, instruction ② ❸ ❹

❸ **or|der** ♦♦◇ /ɔ́rdər/ (orders, ordering, ordered) →Please look at category ⑮ to see if the expression you are looking for is shown under another headword. ❶ N-UNCOUNT If a set of things are arranged or done **in a particular order**, they are arranged or done so one thing follows another, often according to a particular factor such as importance. [also *a* N, usu with supp, oft in/into N] ❑ *Write down (in order of priority) the qualities you'd like to have.* ❑ *Music shops should arrange their recordings in simple alphabetical order, rather than by category.* ❷ N-UNCOUNT **Order** is the situation that exists when everything is in the correct or expected place, or happens at the correct or expected time. ❑ *The wish to impose order upon confusion is a kind of intellectual instinct.* ❸ N-UNCOUNT **Order** is the situation that exists when people obey the law and do not fight or riot. ❑ *Troops were sent to the islands to restore order last November.* ❹ N-SING When people talk about a particular **order**, they mean the way society is organized at a particular time. ❑ *The end of the Cold War has produced the prospect of a new world order based on international co-operation.* ❺ V-T The way that something **is ordered** is the way that it is organized and structured. ❑ *...a society which is ordered by hierarchy.* ❑ *We know the French order things differently.* ❻ N-COUNT A religious **order** is a group of monks or nuns who live according to a particular set of rules. ❑ *...the Benedictine order of monks.* ❼ →see also **law and order** ❽ PHRASE If you put or keep something **in order**, you make sure that it is tidy or properly organized. ❑ *Now he has a chance to put his life back in order.* ❾ PHRASE If you think something is **in order**, you think it should happen or be provided. ❑ *Reforms are clearly in order.* ❿ PHRASE You use **in the order of** or **of the order of** when mentioning an approximate figure. ❑ *They borrowed something in the order of £10 million.* ⓫ PHRASE If something is **in good order**, it is in good condition. ❑ *The vessel's safety equipment was not in good order.* ⓬ PHRASE A machine or device that is **in working order** is functioning properly and is not broken. ❑ *Only half of the spacecraft's six science instruments are still in working order.* ⓭ PHRASE A machine or device that is **out of order** is broken and does not work. ❑ *Their phone's out of order.* ⓮ PHRASE If you say that someone or their behavior is **out of order**, you mean that their behavior is unacceptable or unfair. [INFORMAL] ❑ *You don't think the paper's a bit out of order in publishing it?* ⓯ to **put** your **house in order** →see **house. order of magnitude** →see **magnitude**

or|der book (order books) N-COUNT When you talk about the state of a company's **order book** or **order books**, you are talking about how many orders for their goods the company has. [mainly BRIT, BUSINESS] ❑ *He has a full order book for his boat-building yard on the Thames.*

or|der|ly /ɔ́rdərli/ ❶ ADJ If something is done in an **orderly** fashion or manner, it is done in a well-organized and controlled way. ❑ *The organizers guided them in orderly fashion out of the building.* ❷ ADJ Something that is **orderly** is neat or arranged in a neat way. ❑ *It's a beautiful, clean, and orderly city.* ● **or|der|li|ness** N-UNCOUNT ❑ *A balance is achieved in the painting between orderliness and unpredictability.*

or|di|nance /ɔ́rdᵊnəns/ (ordinances) N-COUNT An **ordinance** is an official rule or order. [FORMAL] ❑ *...ordinances that restrict building development.*

or|di|nar|i|ly /ɔ́rdᵊnɛ́rɪli, BRIT ɔ́:ᵈdɪnərəli/ ADV If you say what is **ordinarily** the case, you are saying what is normally the case. ❑ *The streets would ordinarily have been full of people. There was no one.*

or|di|nary ♦◇◇ /ɔ́rdᵊnɛri, BRIT ɔ́:ᵈdɪnri/ ❶ ADJ **Ordinary** people or things are normal and not special or different in any way. ❑ *I strongly suspect that most ordinary people would agree with me.* ❑ *It has 25 calories less than ordinary ice cream.* ❷ PHRASE Something that is **out of the ordinary** is unusual or different. ❑ *The boy's knowledge was out of the ordinary.*

Thesaurus	*ordinary*의 참조어
ADJ.	common, everyday, normal, regular, standard, typical, usual; (ant.) abnormal, unusual ❶

주문 ❻ 영국 국영 철도가 객차 188량을 주문할 것이다. ❼ 가산명사 주문품 ❼ 종업원이 그들이 주문한 음식을 가지고 돌아왔고 그레이엄이 계산서에 서명을 했다. ❾ 구 주문되어 있는 ❿ 항공사들은 아직도 신형 항공기 2천 5백 대를 주문해 놓은 상태이다. ❿ 구 주문을 받아서 ❑ 그녀는 이제 주문을 받아 말린 꽃으로 근사한 꽃 장식을 만든다. ⓫ 구 명령을 받고 [영국영어 order about] ❑ 나는 그의 임무나 소재에 관해 어느 누구와도 이야기하지 말라는 명령을 받았다.

구동사 마구 부리다, 이래라저래라 하다 ❑ 함께 외출을 하면 그는 확실히 상관 행세를 하며 나한테 이래라저래라 하기 시작해.

❶ 불가산명사 순서 ❑ 당신이 갖추고 싶은 자질을 (우선순위대로) 적으세요. ❑ 음반 판매점에서는 음반을 장르별보다는 단순히 알파벳순으로 배열하는 것이 좋다. ❷ 불가산명사 질서 ❑ 혼란 속에 질서를 부여하려는 소망은 일종의 지적 본능이다. ❸ 불가산명사 치안 ❑ 지난 11월에 치안 회복을 위해 그 섬들에 군대가 파견되었다. ❹ 단수명사 질서 ❑ 냉전 종식은 국제 협력에 기반한 새로운 세계 질서에 대한 기대를 불러일으켰다. ❺ 타동사 질서가 잡히다, 정돈되다 ❑ ...위계질서에 의해 정돈된 사회 ❑ 우리는 프랑스 인들이 사물을 다르게 정리한다는 것을 압니다. ❻ 가산명사 회, 교단 ❑ 베네딕트 수도회의 수도사들 ❼ 구 정돈된, 정리된 ❑ 이제 그가 자신의 삶을 다시 반듯이 정리할 기회가 왔다. ❾ 구 차례가 된 ❑ 확실히 개혁이 일어날 차례가 되었다. ❿ 구 정도의 ❑ 그들은 대략 천만 파운드 정도 되는 돈을 빌렸다. ⓫ 구 상태가 양호한 ❑ 그 선박의 안전 설비는 상태가 양호하지 않았다. ⓬ 구 쓸 만한, 제대로 작동하는 ❑ 우주선 내의 과학 기기 여섯 개 중 절반만이 아직 쓸 만하다. ⓭ 구 고장이 난 ❑ 그 사람들의 전화가 고장이 났어. ⓮ 구 부적절한 [비격식체] ❑ 발표하기에는 그 논문이 약간 부적절한 것 같지 않아요?

가산명사 주문 대장 [주로 영국영어, 경제] ❑ 그의 주문 대장은 템스 강변에 위치한 그 소유의 조선소에서 받은 주문으로 가득 차 있다.

❶ 형용사 질서 정연한 ❑ 주최자들이 질서 정연하게 그들을 빌딩 밖으로 안내했다. ❷ 형용사 정돈된 ❑ 그 도시는 아름답고 청결하고 정돈된 곳이다. ● 정연함 불가산명사 ❑ 그 그림은 정연함과 의외성이 균형을 이루고 있다.

가산명사 법령, 조례 [격식체] ❑ 건물 개발을 제한하는 법령들

부사 평상시에, 보통 ❑ 평상시에는 사람들로 거리가 넘쳐 났었는데, 아무도 없었다.

❶ 형용사 평범한, 보통의 ❑ 대부분의 평범한 사람들은 내 의견에 동의할 거라고 확신한다. ❑ 그것은 칼로리 함유량이 보통 아이스크림보다 25칼로리가 적다. ❷ 구 예외적인, 남다른 ❑ 그 소년의 지식은 남달랐다.

a
b
c
d
e
f
g
h
i
j
k
l
m
n
o
p
q
r
s
t
u
v
w
x
y
z

Word Partnership　　*ordinary*의 연어

| N. | ordinary **Americans**, ordinary **circumstances**, ordinary **citizens**, ordinary **day**, ordinary **expenses**, ordinary **folk**, ordinary **life**, ordinary **people**, ordinary **person** ◼ |
| PREP. | **out of the** ordinary ◻ |

or|di|nary shares N-PLURAL **Ordinary shares** are shares in a company that are owned by people who have a right to vote at the company's meetings and to receive part of the company's profits after the holders of preference shares have been paid. Compare **preference shares**. [BRIT, BUSINESS; AM **common stock**]

or|di|na|tion /ɔːrdˈeɪʃⁿn/ (**ordinations**) N-VAR When someone's **ordination** takes place, they are made a member of the clergy. ◻ ...*supporters of the ordination of women.*

ore /ɔːr/ (**ores**) N-MASS **Ore** is rock or earth from which metal can be obtained. ◻ ...*a huge iron ore mine.* →see **metal**

or|gan /ˈɔːrgən/ (**organs**) ◼ N-COUNT An **organ** is a part of your body that has a particular purpose or function, for example your heart or lungs. ◻ ...*damage to the muscles and internal organs.* ◻ ...*the reproductive organs.* ◻ N-COUNT An **organ** is a large musical instrument with pipes of different lengths through which air is forced. It has keys and pedals rather like a piano. ◻ ...*the church organ.* ◻ N-COUNT You refer to a newspaper or organization as **the organ of** the government or another group when it is used by them as a means of giving information or getting things done. ◻ ...*according to the People's Daily, the official organ of the Chinese communist party.* →see **donor**, **keyboard**, **nervous system**

or|gan|ic /ɔːrˈɡænɪk/ ◼ ADJ **Organic** methods of farming and gardening use only natural animal and plant products to help the plants or animals grow and be healthy, rather than using chemicals. ◻ *Organic farming is expanding everywhere.* ● **or|gan|ic|al|ly** ADV ◻ ...*organically grown vegetables.*

Food that is produced without chemicals is called **organic** or **natural** food. Organic food was once sold only in special shops known as **health food stores** at high prices. These days some of these foods and other low-impact products are sold in ordinary supermarkets.

◻ ADJ **Organic** substances are of the sort produced by or found in living things. ◻ *Incorporating organic material into chalky soils will reduce the alkalinity.* ◻ ADJ **Organic** change or development happens gradually and naturally rather than suddenly. [FORMAL] ◻ ...*to manage the company and supervise its organic growth.*

or|gani|sa|tion /ˌɔːrɡənaɪˈzeɪʃⁿn/ →see **organization**

or|gani|sa|tion|al /ˌɔːrɡənaɪˈzeɪʃⁿnᵊl/ →see **organizational**

or|gan|ise /ˈɔːrɡənaɪz/ →see **organize**

or|gan|ism /ˈɔːrɡənɪzəm/ (**organisms**) N-COUNT An **organism** is an animal or plant, especially one that is so small that you cannot see it without using a microscope. ◻ *Not all chemicals normally present in living organisms are harmless.*

or|gan|ist /ˈɔːrɡənɪst/ (**organists**) N-COUNT An **organist** is someone who plays the organ.

or|gani|za|tion ♦♦◇ /ˌɔːrɡənaɪˈzeɪʃⁿn/ (**organizations**) [BRIT also **organisation**] ◼ N-COUNT An **organization** is an official group of people, for example a political party, a business, a charity, or a club. ◻ *Most of these specialized schools are provided by voluntary organizations.* ◻ N-UNCOUNT The **organization** of an event or activity involves making all the necessary arrangements for it. ◻ ...*the exceptional attention to detail that goes into the organization of this event.* ◻ N-UNCOUNT The **organization** of something is the way in which its different parts are arranged or relate to each other. ◻ *I am aware that the organization of the book leaves something to be desired.*

or|gani|za|tion|al /ˌɔːrɡənaɪˈzeɪʃⁿnᵊl/ [BRIT also **organisational**] ◼ ADJ **Organizational** abilities and methods relate to the way that work, activities, or events are planned and arranged. [ADJ n] ◻ *Evelyn's excellent organizational skills were soon spotted by her employers.* ◻ ADJ **Organizational** means relating to the structure of an organization. [ADJ n] ◻ *The police now recognize that big organizational changes are needed.* ◻ ADJ **Organizational** means relating to organizations, rather than individuals. [ADJ n] ◻ *This problem needs to be dealt with at an organizational level.*

or|gan|ize ♦♦◇ /ˈɔːrɡənaɪz/ (**organizes, organizing, organized**) [BRIT also **organise**] ◼ V-T If you **organize** an event or activity, you make sure that the necessary arrangements are made. ◻ *In the end, we all decided to organize a concert for Easter.* ◻ ...*a two-day meeting organized by the United Nations.* ◻ V-T If you **organize** something that someone wants or needs, you make sure that it is provided. ◻ *I will organize transport.* ◻ V-T If you **organize** a set of things, you arrange them in an ordered way or give them a structure. ◻ *He began to organize his materials.* ◻ *She took a hasty cup of coffee and tried to organize her scattered thoughts.* ◻ V-T If you **organize** yourself, you plan your work and activities in an ordered, efficient way. ◻ ...*changing the way you organize yourself.* ◻ *Go right ahead, I'm sure you don't need me to organize you.*

Thesaurus　　*organize*의 참조어

| V. | coordinate, plan, set up ◼ ◻ |
| | arrange, line up, straighten out ◻ |

복수명사 보통주 [영국영어, 경제; 미국영어 common stock]

가산명사 또는 불가산명사 성직 임명, 서품 ◻ 여성의 성직자 임명을 지지하는 사람들

물질명사 광석 ◻ 거대한 철광석 광산

◼ 가산명사 장기, 기관 ◻ 근육 및 내부 장기 손상 ◻ 생식 기관 ◻ 가산명사 파이프 오르간 ◻ 교회 파이프 오르간 ◻ 가산명사 기관지; 기관 ◻ 중국 공산당의 공식 기관인 인민일보에 따르면

◼ 형용사 유기의 ◻ 유기농법은 모든 곳으로 확대되고 있다. ● 유기 재배로 부사 ◻ 유기 재배한 채소들

화학비료를 사용하지 않고 생산한 식품을 'organic(유기농)' 또는 'natural(자연) 식품'이라고 한다. 유기농 식품은 한때는 health food store(건강식품점)이라고 하는 특별한 상점에서만 고가에 팔렸다. 요즘은 일반 슈퍼마켓에서도 일부 유기농 식품과 인체와 환경에 영향이 적은 생산물을 판다.

◻ 형용사 유기체의 ◻ 유기 물질을 백악질 토양에 혼합시키면 토양의 알칼리도를 낮출 수 있다. ◻ 형용사 점진적인 [격식체] ◻ 회사를 경영하고 회사의 점진적인 성장을 감독하기 위해

가산명사 유기체 ◻ 살아 있는 유기체에 정상적으로 존재하는 화학 물질이 모두 무해한 것은 아니다.

가산명사 오르간 연주자

[영국영어 organisation] ◼ 가산명사 단체 ◻ 특수학교들의 대부분은 자원 봉사 단체들의 지원을 받는다. ◻ 불가산명사 조직 ◻ 이번 행사 조직의 세부 사항에 대한 각별한 관심 ◻ 불가산명사 구성, 편성 ◻ 나는 그 책의 구성에 고칠 부분이 있다는 것을 알고 있다.

[영국영어 organisational] ◼ 형용사 조직상의, 조직하는 ◻ 에블린의 뛰어난 조직 능력이 곧 고용주의 눈에 띄었다. ◻ 형용사 구조적인 ◻ 경찰은 이제 대대적인 구조적 변화가 필요하다는 것을 인식하고 있다. ◻ 형용사 단체의, 조직의 ◻ 이 문제는 단체 차원에서 다루어져야 한다.

[영국영어 organise] ◼ 타동사 조직하다 ◻ 결국, 우리 모두는 부활절 콘서트를 조직하기로 결정했다. ◻ 유엔이 조직한 이틀간의 회담 ◻ 타동사 준비하다, 마련하다 ◻ 교통편은 내가 준비할게. ◻ 타동사 정리하다 ◻ 그는 자신의 자료들을 정리하기 시작했다. ◻ 그녀는 급히 커피 한 잔을 마시며 산만한 생각들을 정리하려고 했다. ◻ 타동사 체계화하다 ◻ 일을 체계화하는 방법을 바꾸기 ◻ 어서 하세요. 틀림없이 저 없이도 체계적으로 준비하실 수 있을 거에요.

or|ga|nized ♦♦♢ /ɔ́rgənaɪzd/ [BRIT also **organised**] **1** ADJ An **organized** activity or group involves a number of people doing something together in a structured way, rather than doing it by themselves. [ADJ n] ❑ ...organized groups of art thieves. ❑ ...organized religion. **2** ADJ Someone who is **organized** plans their work and activities efficiently. ❑ These people are very efficient, very organized and excellent time managers.

or|ga|niz|er ♦♢♢ /ɔ́rgənaɪzər/ (**organizers**) [BRIT also **organiser**] N-COUNT The **organizer** of an event or activity is the person who makes sure that the necessary arrangements are made. ❑ He became an organizer for the Democratic Party. →see also **personal organizer**

or|gasm /ɔ́rgæzəm/ (**orgasms**) N-VAR An **orgasm** is the moment of greatest pleasure and excitement in sexual activity. ❑ ...the ability to reach orgasm.

or|gy /ɔ́rdʒi/ (**orgies**) N-COUNT An **orgy** is a party in which people behave in a very uncontrolled way, especially one involving sexual activity. ❑ It was reminiscent of a scene from a Roman orgy.

ori|en|tal /ɔ̀riént°l/ (**orientals**) ADJ **Oriental** means coming from or associated with eastern Asia, especially China and Japan. ❑ There were Oriental carpets on the floors.

ori|en|tat|ed /ɔ́riənteɪtɪd/ →see **oriented**

ori|en|ta|tion /ɔ̀riəntéɪʃ°n/ (**orientations**) **1** N-VAR If you talk about the **orientation** of an organization or country, you are talking about the kinds of aims and interests it has. ❑ ...a marketing orientation. ❑ To a society which has lost its orientation he has much to offer. **2** N-VAR Someone's **orientation** is their basic beliefs or preferences. ❑ ...legislation that would have made discrimination on the basis of sexual orientation illegal. **3** N-UNCOUNT **Orientation** is basic information or training that is given to people starting a new job, school, or course. ❑ They give their new employees a day or two of perfunctory orientation. **4** N-COUNT The **orientation** of a structure or object is the direction it faces. ❑ Farnese had the orientation of the church changed so that the front would face a square.

ori|ent|ed /ɔ́riəntɪd/

The form **orientated** is also used.

ADJ If someone **is oriented toward** or **oriented to** a particular thing or person, they are mainly concerned with that thing or person. [v-link ADJ toward/to n] ❑ It seems almost inevitable that North African economies will still be primarily oriented towards Europe.

ori|gin ♦♦♢ /ɔ́rɪdʒɪn, BRIT ɒ́rɪdʒɪn/ (**origins**) **1** N-COUNT You can refer to the beginning, cause, or source of something as its **origin** or **origins**. [usu with poss, also in/of N] ❑ ...theories about the origin of life. ❑ Their medical problems are basically physical in origin. **2** N-COUNT When you talk about a person's **origin** or **origins**, you are referring to the country, race, or social class of their parents or ancestors. [usu poss N, also of/in N] ❑ Thomas has not forgotten his humble origins. ❑ ...people of Asian origin.

Word Partnership   origin의 연어

N.	origin **of life**, **point of** origin, origin **of the universe** **1** **country of** origin, **family of** origin **2**
ADJ.	**unknown** origin **1** **2** **ethnic** origin, **Hispanic** origin, **national** origin **2**

origi|nal ♦♦♢ /ərɪ́dʒɪn°l/ (**originals**) **1** ADJ You use **original** when referring to something that existed at the beginning of a process or activity, or the characteristics that something had when it began or was made. [det ADJ] ❑ The original plan was to hold an indefinite stoppage. **2** N-COUNT If something such as a document, a work of art, or a piece of writing is an **original**, it is not a copy or a later version. ❑ When you have filled in the questionnaire, copy it and send the original to your employer. **3** ADJ An **original** document or work of art is not a copy. ❑ ...an original movie poster. **4** ADJ An **original** piece of writing or music was written recently and has not been published or performed before. ❑ ...with catchy original songs by Richard Warner. **5** ADJ If you describe someone or their work as **original**, you mean that they are very imaginative and have new ideas. [APPROVAL] ❑ It is one of the most original works of imagination in the language. ● **origi|nal|ity** /ərɪ̀dʒɪnǽlɪti/ N-UNCOUNT ❑ He was capable of writing things of startling originality.

Thesaurus   original의 참조어

ADJ.	early, first, initial **1** **2** authentic, genuine **3** creative, unique **5**
N.	master; (ant.) copy **2**

origi|nal|ly ♦♢♢ /ərɪ́dʒɪn°li/ ADV When you say what happened or was the case **originally**, you are saying what happened or was the case when something began or came into existence, often to contrast it with what happened later. ❑ The plane has been kept in service far longer than originally intended.

origi|nate /ərɪ́dʒɪneɪt/ (**originates**, **originating**, **originated**) V-T/V-I When something **originates** or when someone **originates** it, it begins to happen or exist. [FORMAL] ❑ The disease originated in Africa. ❑ All carbohydrates originate from plants.

[영국영어 organised] **1** 형용사 조직화된, 체계적인 ❑ 조직화된 미술품 절도단 ❑ 조직적인 종교 **2** 형용사 체계적인 ❑ 이 사람들은 매우 효율적이고, 매우 체계적이며 시간 관리가 뛰어나다.

[영국영어 organiser] 가산명사 조직책, 주최자 ❑ 그가 민주당의 조직책이 되었다.

가산명사 또는 불가산명사 오르가슴, 성적 흥분의 절정 ❑ 오르가슴에 도달하는 능력

가산명사 질펀한 잔치, 진탕 마시고 놀기 ❑ 그것은 로마 시대의 질펀한 주연을 생각나게 하는 장면이었다.

형용사 동양의, 동양의 ❑ 바닥에는 동양풍의 카펫들이 깔려 있었다.

1 가산명사 또는 불가산명사 방침, 방향 ❑ 마케팅 방침 ❑ 나아갈 방향을 잃은 사회에 그가 제시할 것은 많다. **2** 가산명사 또는 불가산명사 성향 ❑ 성적 성향에 근거한 차별을 위법으로 만들 수 있었던 입법안 **3** 불가산명사 오리엔테이션 ❑ 그들은 신입 사원들에게 하루나 이틀 동안의 형식적인 오리엔테이션을 열어 준다. **4** 가산명사 방향 ❑ 파르네세가 교회의 정면이 광장을 바라보도록 교회의 방향을 바꾸게 했다.

orientated도 쓴다.

형용사 -위주의 ❑ 북아프리카 경제가 근본적으로는 여전히 유럽 위주의 경제가 될 것은 거의 불가피한 것 같다.

1 가산명사 기원, 원인, 출처 ❑ 생명의 기원에 대한 이론들 ❑ 그들의 의학적 문제는 원인을 봤을 때 근본적으로는 육체적인 것이다. **2** 가산명사 가문, 혈통, 근본 ❑ 토머스는 자신이 비천한 가문 출신이라는 것을 잊지 않았다. ❑ 아시아 혈통의 사람들

1 형용사 원래의 ❑ 원래의 계획은 파업을 무기한으로 지속하는 것이었다. **2** 가산명사 원본 ❑ 설문지 작성을 마치시면, 복사 후 원본을 여러분의 고용주에게 보내십시오. **3** 형용사 원본의 ❑ 영화 포스터 원화 **4** 형용사 원작의, 원곡의 ❑ 원래 리처드 워너가 부른 호소력 있는 노래들로 **5** 형용사 독창적인 [마음에 듦] ❑ 그것은 그 언어로 상상의 세계를 표현한 가장 독창적인 작품 중 하나이다. ● 독창성 불가산명사 ❑ 그는 놀랍도록 독창적인 작품을 쓸 능력이 있었다.

부사 최초에, 원래 ❑ 그 비행기는 원래 의도했던 것보다 훨씬 오랫동안 운행 중이다.

타동사/자동사 비롯되다, 생기다, 시작하다 [격식체] ❑ 그 질병은 아프리카에서 비롯되었다. ❑ 모든 탄수화물은 식물에서 생긴다.

a b c d e f g h i j k l m n o p q r s t u v w x y z

A

or|na|ment /ɔrnəmənt/ (**ornaments**) **1** N-COUNT An **ornament** is an attractive object that you display in your home or in your garden. □ *...a shelf containing a few photographs and ornaments.* **2** N-UNCOUNT Decorations and patterns on a building or a piece of furniture can be referred to as **ornament**. [FORMAL] □ *...walls of glass overlaid with ornament.*

1 가산명사 장식품 □ 사진 몇 장과 장식품들이 얹힌 선반 **2** 불가산명사 문양, 무늬 [격식체] □ 문양을 덧씌운 유리벽

B

or|na|men|tal /ɔrnəmentʰl/ ADJ Something that is **ornamental** is attractive and decorative. □ *...ornamental plaster mouldings.*

형용사 장식용의 □ 장식용 석고 조형물

C

or|nate /ɔrneɪt/ ADJ An **ornate** building, piece of furniture, or object is decorated with complicated patterns or shapes. □ *...an ornate iron staircase.*

형용사 장식이 화려한 □ 장식이 화려한 철제 계단

D

or|phan /ɔrfən/ (**orphans, orphaned**) **1** N-COUNT An **orphan** is a child whose parents are dead. □ *...a young orphan girl brought up by peasants.* **2** V-T PASSIVE If a child **is orphaned**, their parents die, or their remaining parent dies. [no cont] □ *...a fifteen-year-old boy left orphaned by the recent disaster.*

1 가산명사 고아 □ 농부들이 키운 어린 고아 소녀 **2** 수동 타동사 고아가 되다, 부모를 잃다 □ 최근 재해로 인해 고아가 된 15세 소년

E

or|phan|age /ɔrfənɪdʒ/ (**orphanages**) N-COUNT An **orphanage** is a place where orphans live and are cared for.

가산명사 고아원

F

ortho|dox /ɔrθədɒks/

철자 Orthodox도 **2**와 **3** 의미로 쓴다.

The spelling **Orthodox** is also used for meaning **2** and **3**.

1 ADJ **Orthodox** beliefs, methods, or systems are ones which are accepted or used by most people. □ *Many of these ideas are now being incorporated into orthodox medical treatment.* **2** ADJ If you describe someone as **orthodox**, you mean that they hold the older and more traditional ideas of their religion or party. □ *...Orthodox Jews.* **3** ADJ The **Orthodox** churches are Christian churches in Eastern Europe which separated from the western church in the eleventh century. □ *...the Greek Orthodox Church.*

1 형용사 정통의 □ 이러한 생각들 중 많은 것들이 현재 정통 의술에 접목되고 있다. **2** 형용사 정통의 □ 정통 유대교도들 **3** 형용사 그리스 정교회의 □ 그리스 정교회

G

ortho|doxy /ɔrθədɒksi/ (**orthodoxies**) **1** N-VAR An **orthodoxy** is an accepted view about something. □ *These ideas rapidly became the new orthodoxy in linguistics.* **2** N-UNCOUNT The old, traditional beliefs of a religion, political party, or philosophy can be referred to as **orthodoxy**. □ *A conflict between Nat's religious orthodoxy and Rube's belief that his mission is to make money.*

1 가산명사 또는 불가산명사 정설 □ 이 사상들은 언어학에서 급속히 새로운 정설로 받아들여졌다. **2** 불가산명사 정통 □ 냇의 종교적 정통과 자신의 사명은 돈을 버는 것이라는 루브의 믿음 사이의 갈등

H

I

os|ten|ta|tious /ɒstenteɪʃəs/ **1** ADJ If you describe something as **ostentatious**, you disapprove of it because it is expensive and is intended to impress people. [FORMAL, DISAPPROVAL] □ *...his house, which, however elaborate, is less ostentatious than the preserves of other Dallas tycoons.* **2** ADJ If you describe someone as **ostentatious**, you disapprove of them because they want to impress people with their wealth or importance. [FORMAL, DISAPPROVAL] □ *Obviously he had plenty of money and was generous in its use without being ostentatious.* ● **os|ten|ta|tious|ly** ADV □ *Her servants were similarly, if less ostentatiously attired.* **3** ADJ You can describe an action or behavior as **ostentatious** when it is done in an exaggerated way to attract people's attention. □ *His wife was fairly quiet but she is not an ostentatious person anyway.* ● **os|ten|ta|tious|ly** ADV □ *Harry stopped under a street lamp and ostentatiously began inspecting the contents of his bag.*

1 형용사 지나치게 화려한, 허식이 지나친 [격식체, 탐탁찮음] □ 공들여 지었지만, 달라스의 다른 재계 거물들의 저택에 비해 덜 화려한 그의 집 **2** 형용사 과시하는 [격식체, 탐탁찮음] □ 분명히 그는 많은 돈을 갖고 있었는데 돈 씀씀이가 과시하지 않으면서도 후했다. ● 과시하듯 부사 □ 그녀의 하인들도 덜 과시적이긴 했지만 비슷하게 옷을 입고 있었다. **3** 형용사 허세 부리는 □ 그의 아내는 말수가 상당히 적었지만 어쨌든 그녀가 허세를 부리는 인물은 아니다. ● 보란 듯이, 허세 부리며 부사 □ 해리는 가로등 아래 멈춰서 보란 듯이 자기 가방의 내용물을 살피기 시작했다.

J

K

L

M

N

O

os|tra|cize /ɒstrəsaɪz/ (**ostracizes, ostracizing, ostracized**) [BRIT also **ostracise**] V-T If someone **is ostracized**, people deliberately behave in an unfriendly way toward them and do not allow them to take part in any of their social activities. [FORMAL] [usu passive] □ *She claims she's being ostracized by some members of her local community.*

[영국영어 ostracise] 타동사 배척당하다 [격식체] □ 그녀는 자신이 지역 사회의 몇몇 사람들에게 배척당해 왔다고 주장한다.

P

os|trich /ɔstrɪtʃ, BRIT ɒstrɪtʃ/ (**ostriches**) N-COUNT An **ostrich** is a very large African bird that cannot fly.

가산명사 타조

oth|er ♦♦♦ /ʌðər/ (**others**)

Q

When **other** follows the determiner **an**, it is written as one word: see **another**.

한정사 an뒤에 other가 오면 한 단어 another로 쓴다. another참조.

R

1 ADJ You use **other** to refer to an additional thing or person of the same type as one that has been mentioned or is known about. [det ADJ, ADJ n] □ *They were just like any other young couple.* ● PRON **Other** is also a pronoun. □ *Four crewmen were killed, one other was injured.* **2** ADJ You use **other** to indicate that a thing or person is not the one already mentioned, but a different one. [det ADJ, ADJ n] □ *The authorities insist that the discussions must not be linked to any other issue.* □ *He would have to accept it; there was no other way.* ● PRON **Other** is also a pronoun. □ *This issue, more than any other, has divided her cabinet.* **3** ADJ You use **the other** to refer to the second of two things or people when the identity of the first is already known or understood, or has already been mentioned. [det ADJ] □ *The Captain was at the other end of the room.* □ *You deliberately went in the other direction.* ● PRON-SING **The other** is also a pronoun. [the PRON] □ *Almost everybody had a cigarette in one hand and a martini in the other.* **4** ADJ You use **other** at the end of a list or a group of examples, to refer generally to people or things like the ones just mentioned. [det ADJ, ADJ n] □ *Queensway Quay will incorporate shops, restaurants and other amenities.* ● PRON **Other** is also a pronoun. □ *Descartes received his stimulus from the new physics and astronomy of Copernicus, Galileo, and others.* **5** ADJ You use **the other** to refer to the rest of the people or things in a group, when you are talking about one particular person or thing. [det ADJ] □ *When the other pupils were taken to an exhibition, he was left behind.* ● PRON **The others** is also a pronoun. [the PRON] □ *Aubrey's on his way here, with the others.* **6** ADJ **Other** people are people in general, as opposed to yourself or a person you have already mentioned. [ADJ n] □ *The suffering of other people appals me.* ● PRON-PLURAL **Others** means the same as **other people**. □ *His humor depended on contempt for others.*

1 형용사 다른 □ 그들은 다른 젊은 연인들과 똑같았다. ● 대명사 다른 사람; 다른 것 □ 승무원 넷이 살해당했고, 다른 한 사람은 부상을 당했다. **2** 형용사 다른 □ 당국은 그 토의가 다른 사안은 어떤 것과도 연결되어서는 안 된다고 주장한다. □ 그는 그것을 인정해야 하게 되었다. 다른 방도가 없으니까. ● 대명사 다른 것 □ 다른 무엇보다도, 이 사안에 대해서는 그녀의 내각에서 의견이 갈렸다. **3** 형용사 다른 하나의 □ 그 선장은 그 방 다른 한쪽 끝에 있었다. □ 너는 고의로 다른 방향으로 갔다. ● 단수대명사 다른 하나 □ 거의 모든 사람이 한 손에는 담배를, 다른 손에는 마티니를 들고 있었다. **4** 형용사 기타의, 다른 □ 퀸즈웨이 키 회사가 상점과 음식점, 기타 편의 시설들을 합병할 것이다. ● 대명사 그 외 다른 사람, 그 외 다른 것 □ 데카르트는 코페르니쿠스와 갈릴레오 그리고 그 외 다른 사람들의 새로운 물리학과 천문학에서 자극을 받았다. **5** 형용사 나머지의 □ 나머지 학생들이 전시장으로 인도되었을 때, 그는 혼자 뒤에 남겨졌다. ● 대명사 나머지 □ 오브리는 나머지 사람들과 여기 오고 있는 중이야. **6** 형용사 다른 □ 다른 사람들이 고생하는 것을 보니 섬뜩해진다. ● 복수대명사 다른 사람들 □ 그의 유머는 다른 사람들에 대한 경멸에 기반을 두고 있다.

S

T

U

V

W

X

Do not confuse **other** and **another**. You use **other** to refer to more than one type of person or thing. □ *Other boys were arriving now.* When you are talking about two people or things and have already referred to one of them, you refer to the second one as **the other** or **the other one**. When you are talking about several people or things and have already referred to one or more of

Y

other와 another를 혼동하지 않도록 하라. other는 세 종류 이상의 사람이나 사물을 지칭할 때에 쓴다. □ 이제 다른 소년들이 도착하고 있었다. 두 명의 사람이나 두 가지 사물에 대해 얘기하면서 그 중 한 사람이나 한 가지를 이미 언급한 뒤, 두 번째

Z

them, you usually refer to the remaining ones as **the others. Another** person or thing means one more person or thing of the same kind. It is usually followed by a singular count noun, "one," "few," or a number larger than one. ❑ *Rick's got another camera... She had a drink and then another one... I waited another few minutes... They raised another $15,000.*

사람이나 사물을 가리킬 때는 the other 또는 the other one이라고 지칭한다. 여러 사람이나 사물에 대해 얘기하면서 그 중 하나를 이미 언급했을 때, 나머지 사람들이나 사물은 보통 the others라고 지칭한다. another를 쓰면 동일한 유형의 사람이나 사물을 하나 더 가리킴을 나타낸다. another는 보통 단수 가산명사, one, few, 또는 하나보다 많은 수와 함께 쓰인다. ❑ 릭에게는 카메라가 하나 더 있다...그녀는 한 잔을 마시고 나서 한 잔을 더 했다. 나는 몇 분을 더 기다렸다... 그들은 또 다른 15,000달러를 모았다.

7 ADJ You use **other** in informal expressions of time such as **the other day, the other evening,** or **the other week** to refer to a day, evening, or week in the recent past. [the ADJ n] ❑ *I rang her the other day and she said she'd like to come round.* **8** PHRASE You use expressions like **among other** things or **among others** to indicate that there are several more facts, things, or people like the one or ones mentioned, but that you do not intend to mention them all. [VAGUENESS] ❑ *He moved to England in 1980 where, among other things, he worked as a journalist.* ❑ *His travels took him to Dublin, among other places.* **9** PHRASE If something happens, for example, **every other day** or **every other month**, there is a day or month when it does not happen between each day or month when it happens. ❑ *Their food is adequate. It includes meat at least every other day, vegetables and fruit.* **10** PHRASE You use **every other** to emphasize that you are referring to all the rest of the people or things in a group. [EMPHASIS] ❑ *The same will apply in every other country.* **11** PHRASE You use **nothing other than** and **no other than** when you are going to mention a course of action, decision, or description and emphasize that it is the only one possible in the situation. [EMPHASIS] ❑ *Nothing other than an immediate custodial sentence could be justified.* ❑ *The rebels would not be happy with anything other than the complete removal of the current regime.* **12** PHRASE You use **or other** in expressions like **somehow or other** and **someone or other** to indicate that you cannot or do not want to be more precise about the information that you are giving. [VAGUENESS] ❑ *I was going to have him called away from the house on some pretext or other.* ❑ *The Foundation is holding a dinner in honour of something or other.* **13** PHRASE You use **other than** after a negative statement to say that the person, item, or thing that follows is the only exception to the statement. ❑ *She makes no reference to any feminist work other than her own.* **14 each other** →see **each. one after the other** →see **one. one or other** →see **one. this, that and the other** →see **this. in other words** →see **word**

7 형용사 요전의, 얼마 전의 ❑ 내가 요 며칠 전에 그녀에게 전화를 걸었는데 그녀가 오고 싶다고 말했다. **8** 구 특기할 것은, 무엇보다도 [짐작투] ❑ 그는 1980년에 잉글랜드로 이사했는데, 특기할 만한 것은 그곳에서 기자로 근무했다. **9** 구 하루 걸러, ❑ 그들의 음식은 적절하다. 적어도 하루 걸러 고기와, 채소와 과일이 들어간다. **10** 구 그 외의 모든 [강조] ❑ 그 외 모든 국가에게도 똑같은 사항이 적용될 것이다. **11** 구 다름 아닌 [강조] ❑ 다름 아닌 즉결 구류 판결만이 정당화될 수 있을 것이다. ❑ 반군들은 다름 아닌 현 정권의 전면적인 퇴진 외에는 만족하지 않을 것이다. **12** 구 또는 다른, 누군가가 [짐작투] ❑ 나는 이런저런 구실로 그를 그 집 밖으로 나오게 할 작정이었다. ❑ 그 재단이 무언가를 축하하기 위해 만찬을 열고 있다. **13** 구 ~ 외에는 ❑ 그녀는 자신의 작품 외에는 어떠한 페미니스트적인 작품도 언급하지 않는다.

Word Link　*wise ≈ in the direction or manner of: clockwise, likewise, otherwise*

other|wise ♦♦◇◇ /ˈʌðərwaɪz/ **1** ADV You use **otherwise** after stating a situation or fact, in order to say what the result or consequence would be if this situation or fact was not the case. [ADV with cl] ❑ *Make a note of the questions you want to ask. You will invariably forget some of them otherwise.* ❑ *I'm lucky that I'm interested in school work, otherwise I'd go mad.* **2** ADV You use **otherwise** before stating the general condition or quality of something, when you are also mentioning an exception to this general condition or quality. [ADV group] ❑ *The decorations for the games have lent a splash of color to an otherwise drab city.* **3** ADV You use **otherwise** to refer in a general way to actions or situations that are very different from, or the opposite to, your main statement. [WRITTEN] [ADV with v] ❑ *Take approximately 60mg up to four times a day, unless advised otherwise by a doctor.* ❑ *There is no way anything would ever happen between us, and believe me I've tried to convince myself otherwise.* **4** ADV You use **otherwise** to indicate that other ways of doing something are possible in addition to the way already mentioned. [ADV before v] ❑ *The studio could punish its players by keeping them out of work, and otherwise controlling their lives.* **5** PHRASE You use **or otherwise** or **and otherwise** to mention something that is not the thing just referred to or is the opposite of that thing. ❑ *It was for the police to assess the validity or otherwise of the evidence.*

1 부사 그렇지 않으면 ❑ 질문 사항을 적어 두세요. 그렇지 않으면 항상 몇 가지는 잊게 마련이죠. ❑ 운 좋게 나는 학교 공부에 흥미가 있는데, 그렇지 않으면 아마 미쳐버릴 거야. **2** 부사 보통은 ❑ 그 대회를 위한 장식이 보통은 우중충한 도시에 한 줄기 색채감을 주었다. **3** 부사 달리 [문어체] ❑ 만약 의사의 다른 지시가 없다면 약 60밀리그램씩 하루 최대 4번 복용하세요. ❑ 우리 둘 사이에 뭔가 일어날 일은 전혀 없어, 그러면 나는 계속 나 자신을 달리 납득시키려 애써 왔다는 사실을 믿어 줘. **4** 부사 그 외에 별도로 ❑ 스튜디오가 배우들에게 일을 주지 않음으로써 처벌할 수 있고 그 외에 별도로 그들의 생활을 통제할 수도 있다. **5** 구 또는 ~ 그 반대, 또는 그 외의 것 ❑ 그것은 경찰이 그 증거가 타당한지 아닌지를 평가하는 것이었다.

OTT /ˌoʊ tiː ˈtiː/ ADJ If you describe something as **OTT**, you mean that it is exaggerated and extreme. **OTT** is an abbreviation for "over the top." [BRIT, INFORMAL] ❑ *...an OTT comedy cabaret revue.*

형용사 도가 지나친, 과장된 [영국영어, 비격식체] ❑ 과장된 카바레 코미디

ouch /aʊtʃ/ EXCLAM "**Ouch!**" is used in writing to represent the noise that people make when they suddenly feel pain. ❑ *She was barefoot and stones dug into her feet. "Ouch, ouch," she cried.*

감탄사 아야 ❑ 그녀는 맨발이었기 때문에 돌멩이가 발에 박혔다. 그녀는 "아야, 아야," 하며 울먹였다.

ought ♦◇◇ /ɔːt/

Ought to is a phrasal modal verb. It is used with the base form of a verb. The negative form of **ought to** is **ought not to**, which is sometimes shortened to **oughtn't to** in spoken English.

ought to은 구 조동사이며 동사 원형과 함께 쓴다. ought to의 부정형은 ought not to인데, 구어체 영어에서 가끔 oughtn't to로 축약된다.

1 PHRASE You use **ought to** to mean that it is morally right to do a particular thing or that it is morally right for a particular situation to exist, especially when giving or asking for advice or opinions. ❑ *Mark, you've got a good wife. You ought to take care of her.* ❑ *The people who already own a bit of money or land ought to have a voice in saying where it goes.* **2** PHRASE You use **ought to** when saying that you think it is a good idea and important for you or someone else to do a particular thing, especially when giving or asking for advice or opinions. ❑ *You don't have to be alone with him and I don't think you ought to be.* ❑ *You ought to ask a lawyer's advice.* **3** PHRASE You use **ought to** to indicate that you expect something to be true or to happen. You use **ought to have** to indicate that you expect something to have happened already. ❑ *"This ought to be fun," he told Alex, eyes gleaming.* **4** PHRASE You use **ought to** to indicate that you think that something should be the case, but might not be. ❑ *By rights the Social Democrats ought to be the favorites in the election. But nothing looks less certain.* **5** PHRASE You use **ought to** to indicate that you think that something has happened

1 구 ~해야 한다 ❑ 마크, 자네 아내는 좋은 사람이야. 자네는 그녀를 잘 돌봐야 해. ❑ 약간의 돈이나 토지를 이미 소유하고 있는 사람들은 그것이 어디에 쓰일지 자신의 의견을 나타내야 한다. **2** 구 ~하는 것이 좋다 ❑ 너는 그와 단둘이 있을 필요가 없고 네가 그와 단둘이 있는 것이 좋다고도 생각지 않아. ❑ 네가 변호사의 조언을 구하는 것이 좋을 텐데. **3** 구 ~일 것이다; ~했을 것이다 ❑ "이건 재미있을 거야." 하고 그가 눈을 반짝이며 알렉스에게 말했다. **4** 구 ~어야 할 것이다 ❑ 정당성을 본다면 사회 민주당 후보가 그 선거에서 가장 유력한 후보자들이어야 할 것이다. 그러나 그보다 더 불확실한 것은 없어 보인다. **5** 구 ~했을 것이다 [짐작투] ❑ 그는 좀 전에 그 집에 도착했을 것이다. **6** 구 ~했어야 했다 ❑ 원칙적으론 그 시스템이 작동했어야 했다. **7** 구 ~었어야 했다 ❑ 나는

a b c d e f g h i j k l m n o p q r s t u v w x y z

because of what you know about the situation, but you are not certain. [VAGUENESS] ❑ *He ought to have reached the house some time ago.* **6** PHRASE You use **ought to have** with a past participle to indicate that something was expected to happen or be the case, but it did not happen or was not the case. ❑ *Basically the system ought to have worked.* **7** PHRASE You use **ought to have** with a past participle to indicate that although it was best or correct for someone to do something in the past, they did not actually do it. ❑ *I realize I ought to have told you about it.* ❑ *I ought not to have asked you a thing like that. I'm sorry.* **8** PHRASE You use **ought to** when politely telling someone that you must do something, for example that you must leave. [POLITENESS] ❑ *I really ought to be getting back now.*

oughtn't /ɔːtᵊnt/ **Oughtn't** is a spoken form of "ought not."

ounce /aʊns/ (**ounces**) **1** N-COUNT An **ounce** is a unit of weight used in the U.S. and Britain. There are sixteen ounces in a pound and one ounce is equal to 28.35 grams. ❑ *...four ounces of sugar.* **2** N-SING You can refer to a very small amount of something, such as a quality or characteristic, as an **ounce**. ❑ *If only my father had possessed an ounce of business sense.*

our ♦♦♦ /aʊər/

> **Our** is the first person plural possessive determiner.

1 DET You use **our** to indicate that something belongs or relates both to yourself and to one or more other people. ❑ *We're expecting our first baby.* **2** DET A speaker or writer sometimes uses **our** to indicate that something belongs or relates to people in general. ❑ *We are all entirely responsible for our actions, and for our reactions.*

ours /aʊərz/

> **Ours** is the first person plural possessive pronoun.

PRON-POSS You use **ours** to refer to something that belongs or relates both to yourself and to one or more other people. ❑ *There are few strangers in a town like ours.*

our|selves ♦♢♢ /aʊərsɛlvz/

> **Ourselves** is the first person plural reflexive pronoun.

1 PRON-REFL You use **ourselves** to refer to yourself and one or more other people as a group. [V PRON, prep PRON] ❑ *We sat round the fire to keep ourselves warm.* **2** PRON-REFL A speaker or writer sometimes uses **ourselves** to refer to people in general. **Ourselves** is used as the object of a verb or preposition when the subject refers to the same people. [V PRON, prep PRON] ❑ *We all know that when we exert ourselves our heart rate increases.* **3** PRON-REFL-EMPH You use **ourselves** to emphasize a first person plural subject. In more formal English, **ourselves** is sometimes used instead of "us" as the object of a verb or preposition, for emphasis. [EMPHASIS] ❑ *Others are feeling just the way we ourselves would feel in the same situation.* **4** PRON-REFL-EMPH If you say something such as "We did it **ourselves**," you are indicating that the people you are referring to did it, rather than anyone else. ❑ *We villagers built that ourselves, we had no help from anyone.*

oust /aʊst/ (**ousts, ousting, ousted**) V-T If someone **is ousted** from a position of power, job, or place, you force them to leave it. [JOURNALISM] ❑ *The leaders have been ousted from power by nationalists.* ❑ *Last week they tried to oust him in a parliamentary vote of no confidence.* ● **oust|ing** N-UNCOUNT ❑ *The ousting of his predecessor was one of the most dramatic coups the business world had seen in years.*

> **out**
>
> ① ADVERB USES
> ② ADJECTIVE AND ADVERB USES
> ③ VERB USE
> ④ PREPOSITION USES

① out ♦♦♦ /aʊt/

> **Out** is often used with verbs of movement, such as "walk" and "pull," and also in phrasal verbs such as "give out" and "run out."

1 ADV When something is in a particular place and you take it **out**, you remove it from that place. [ADV after v] ❑ *I like the pop you get when you pull out a cork.* ❑ *He took out his notebook and flipped the pages.* **2** ADV You can use **out** to indicate that you are talking about the situation outside, rather than inside buildings. [ADV after v] ❑ *It's hot out - very hot, very humid.* **3** ADV If you are **out**, you are not at home or not at your usual place of work. ❑ *I tried to get in touch with you yesterday evening, but I think you were out.* **4** ADV If you say that someone is **out** in a particular place, you mean that they are in a different place, usually one far away. [ADV adv/prep] ❑ *The police tell me they've finished their investigations out there.* **5** ADV When the sea or tide goes **out**, the sea moves away from the shore. ❑ *The tide was out and they walked among the rock pools.* **6** ADV If you are **out** a particular amount of money, you have that amount less than you should or than you did. [mainly AM] [ADV n] ❑ *Me and my friends are out ten thousand dollars, with nothing to show for it!*

② out ♦♦♦ /aʊt/ **1** ADJ If a light or fire is **out** or goes **out**, it is no longer shining or burning. [v-link ADJ] ❑ *All the lights were out in the house.* **2** ADJ If flowers are **out**, their petals have opened. [v-link ADJ] ❑ *Well, the daffodils are out in the gardens and they're always a beautiful show.* ● ADV **Out** is also an adverb. [ADV after v] ❑ *I usually put it in my diary when I see the wild flowers coming out.* **3** ADJ If something such as a book or CD is **out**, it is available for people to buy. [v-link

---

그 일에 대해 너에게 말했어야 했다고 생각한다. ❑ 그런 일을 당신에게 부탁하지 말았어야 했어요. 미안합니다. **8** 구 -해야 합니다 [공손체] ❑ 이제 정말 돌아가야 합니다.

ought not의 구어 표현

1 가산명사 온스 ❑ 설탕 4온스 **2** 단수명사 소량, 조금 ❑ 아버지께서 사업가적인 감각을 조금이라도 갖고 계셨더라면 좋을 텐데.

---

our는 1인칭 복수 소유 한정사이다.

1 한정사 우리의 ❑ 우리는 우리의 첫 아기를 출산할 예정입니다. **2** 한정사 우리의 ❑ 우리 모두는 우리의 행동과 반응에 대해 전적으로 책임이 있다.

---

ours는 1인칭 복수 소유 대명사이다.

소유대명사 우리의 것 ❑ 우리 마을과 같은 곳에는 낯선 사람들이 거의 없다.

---

ourselves는 1인칭 복수 재귀 대명사이다.

1 재귀대명사 우리 자신 ❑ 우리는 몸을 따뜻하게 하기 위해 불가에 둘러앉았다. **2** 재귀대명사 우리들 ❑ 우리가 애를 쓰면 심장 박동률이 증가한다는 사실을 우리 모두 알고 있다. **3** 강조 재귀대명사 우리 자신 [강조] ❑ 다른 사람들도 동일한 상황에서 우리 자신이 느낄 법한 바로 그런 식으로 느끼고 있다. **4** 강조 재귀대명사 직접 ❑ 마을 사람인 우리가 직접 그것을 지었고, 아무에게서도 도움을 받지 않았다.

타동사 축출되다, 쫓겨나다 [언론] ❑ 그 지도자들은 민족주의자들에 의해 권좌에서 축출되었다. ❑ 지난주 그들은 의회에서 불신임투표를 통해 그를 축출하려고 시도했다. ● 추출, 해임 불가산명사 ❑ 그의 선임자가 해임된 것은 수년간 재계에서 있었던 가장 극적인 사건들 중 하나였다.

---

out은 종종 'walk', 'pull'과 같은 이동 동사와 함께 쓰며 'give out', 'run out'과 같은 구동사에도 쓰인다.

1 부사 밖으로 ❑ 나는 네가 코르크를 뽑을 때 들리는 뻥 하는 소리가 좋아. ❑ 그는 공책을 꺼내서 책장을 획획 넘겼다. **2** 부사 밖에, 바깥에 ❑ 밖은 더위. 너무 덥고 아주 습해. **3** 부사 외출하여 ❑ 나는 어제 저녁 당신에게 연락하려고 애썼는데, 외출 중이셨나 봐요. **4** 부사 다른 곳에 ❑ 경찰은 내게 다른 곳에서는 조사를 마쳤다고 말했다. **5** 부사 바다 쪽으로 ❑ 바닷물이 빠지고 있었고 그들은 바위틈 웅덩이들 사이를 따라 걸었다. **6** 부사 겨우 [주로 미국영어] ❑ 나와 내 친구들은 겨우 만 달러밖에 없다. 내세울 것도 없는 금액이다.

---

1 형용사 꺼진 ❑ 그 집의 불빛이 전부 꺼져 있었다. **2** 형용사 (꽃이) 핀 ❑ 자, 정원에 수선화가 피어 있는데 그 모습은 항상 아름다운 장관이야. ● 부사 피어 ❑ 나는 야생화가 피는 것을 보면, 나는 대개 그것을 일기장에 적어 둬. **3** 형용사 (시장에) 나온, 출시된 ❑ 영국 최고의 히트 곡 40곡 커버버전. 지금 판매 중. ● 부사

ADJ] ❑ ...*cover versions of 40 British Number Ones – out now.* ● ADV Out is also an adverb. [ADV after v] ❑ *The French edition came out in early 1992.* ◳ ADJ In a game or sport, if someone is **out**, they can no longer take part either because they are unable to or because they have been defeated. [v-link ADJ] ◳ ADJ In baseball, a player is **out** if they do not reach a base safely. When three players on a team are out in an inning, then the team is **out**. ◳ ADJ If you say that a proposal or suggestion is **out**, you mean that it is unacceptable. [v-link ADJ] ❑ *That's right out, I'm afraid.* ◳ ADJ If you say that a particular thing is **out**, you mean that it is no longer fashionable at the present time. [v-link ADJ] ❑ *Romance is making a comeback. Reality is out.* ◳ ADJ If you say that a calculation or measurement is **out**, you mean that it is incorrect. [v-link ADJ, oft amount ADJ] ❑ *When the two ends of the tunnel met in the middle they were only a few inches out.* ◳ ADJ If someone is **out** to do something, they intend to do it. [INFORMAL] [v-link ADJ to-inf] ❑ *Most companies these days are just out to make a quick profit.*

③ **out** /aʊt/ (**outs, outing, outed**) V-T If a group of people **out** a public figure or famous person, they reveal that person's homosexuality against their wishes. ❑ *The New York gay action group "Queer Nation" recently outed an American Congressman.* ● **out|ing** N-UNCOUNT ❑ *The gay and lesbian rights group, Stonewall, sees outing as completely unhelpful.*

④ **out** ♦♦♦

> **Out of** is used with verbs of movement, such as "walk" and "pull," and also in phrasal verbs such as "do out of" and "grow out of." In American English and informal British English, **out** is often used instead of **out of**.

◳ PHRASE If you go **out of** a place, you leave it. ❑ *She let him out of the house.* ◳ PHRASE If you take something **out of** the container or place where it has been, you remove it so that it is no longer there. ❑ *I always took my key out of my bag and put it in my pocket.* ◳ PHRASE If you look or shout **out of** a window, you look or shout away from the room where you are toward the outside. ❑ *He went on staring out of the window.* ◳ PHRASE If you are **out of** the sun, the rain, or the wind, you are sheltered from it. ❑ *People can keep out of the sun to avoid skin cancer.* ◳ PHRASE If someone or something gets **out of** a situation, especially an unpleasant one, they are then no longer in it. If they keep **out of** it, they do not start being in it. ❑ *In the past army troops have relied heavily on air support to get them out of trouble.* ❑ *The economy is starting to climb out of recession.* ◳ PHRASE You can use **out of** to say that someone leaves an institution. ❑ *That is precisely what I came out of college thinking I was supposed to do.* ◳ PHRASE If you are **out of** range of something, you are beyond the limits of that range. ❑ *Shaun was in the bedroom, out of earshot, watching television.* ◳ PHRASE You use **out of** to say what feeling or reason causes someone to do something. For example, if you do something **out of** pity, you do it because you pity someone. ❑ *He took up office out of a sense of duty.* ◳ PHRASE If you get something such as information or work **out of** someone, you manage to make them give it to you, usually when they are unwilling to give it. ❑ *"Where is she being held prisoner?" I asked. "Did you get it out of him?"* ◳ PHRASE If you get pleasure or an advantage **out of** something, you get it as a result of being involved with that thing or making use of it. ❑ *We all had a lot of fun out of him.* ◳ PHRASE If you are **out of** something, you no longer have any of it. ❑ *I can't find the sugar – and we're out of milk.* ◳ PHRASE If something is made **out of** a particular material, it consists of that material because it has been formed or constructed from it. ❑ *Would you advise people to make a building out of wood or stone?* ◳ PHRASE You use **out of** to indicate what proportion of a group of things something is true of. For example, if something is true of one **out of** five things, it is true of one fifth of all things of that kind. ❑ *Two out of five thought the business would be sold privately on their retirement or death.*

out|age /aʊtɪdʒ/ (**outages**) N-COUNT An **outage** is a period of time when the electricity supply to a building or area is interrupted, for example because of damage to the cables. [AM; BRIT **power cut**] ❑ *A windstorm in Washington is causing power outages throughout the region.*

out|back /aʊtbæk/ N-SING The parts of Australia that are far away from towns are referred to as **the outback**. ❑ *Are there many people living in the outback?*

out|bid /aʊtbɪd/ (**outbids, outbidding**)

> The form **outbid** is used in the present tense and is the past tense and past participle.

V-T If you **outbid** someone, you offer more money than they do for something that you both want to buy. ❑ *The Museum has antagonized rivals by outbidding them for the world's greatest art treasures.*

out|bound /aʊtbaʊnd/ ADJ An **outbound** flight is one that is leaving or about to leave a particular place. ❑ *Airport officials say at least 20 outbound flights were delayed.*

out box (**out boxes**) also **out-box** N-COUNT An **out box** is a shallow container used in offices to put letters and documents in when they have been dealt with and are ready to be sent somewhere else. [AM; BRIT **out tray**] ❑ *He signed his name and placed the letter in his out box.*

out|break /aʊtbreɪk/ (**outbreaks**) N-COUNT If there is an **outbreak of** something unpleasant, such as violence or a disease, it suddenly starts to happen. ❑ *The four-day festival ended a day early after an outbreak of violence involving hundreds of youths.* ❑ *...the outbreak of war in the Middle East.*

(시장에) 나와 ❑ 불어판은 1992년 초에 출판되었다. ◳ 형용사 제외된 ◳ 형용사 아웃된 ◳ 형용사 기각된 ❑ 유감이지만 그건 완전 사절이야. ◳ 형용사 구식의 ❑ 로맨스가 다시 유행하고 있어. 현실주의가 유행이 지났어. ◳ 형용사 벗어난, 틀린 ❑ 양쪽 끝에서 파 들어가기 시작한 터널이 중간 지점에서 만났을 때 단지 몇 인치 정도만 벗어났다. ◳ 형용사 애쓰는 [비격식체] ❑ 요즘 대부분의 기업들은 단기 수익을 내는 데만 애를 쓴다.

타동사 동성연애자라고 폭로하다 ❑ 뉴욕 동성애자 행동 단체 '퀴어 네이션'은 최근 한 미국 하원 의원을 동성애자라고 폭로했다. ● 동성애자임이 밝혀짐 불가산명사 ❑ 남녀 동성애자 권리 단체인 스톤월은 동성애자라고 밝히는 것이 전혀 도움이 되지 않는다고 본다.

> out은 'walk', 'pull'과 같은 이동 동사와 함께 쓰며 'do out of', 'grow out of'와 같은 구동사에도 쓰인다. 미국영어와 비격식체 영국영어에서 out은 종종 out of 대신 쓰인다.

◳ 구 –의 밖으로 ❑ 그녀는 그를 집 밖으로 내보내 주었다. ◳ 구 –에서 꺼내어 ❑ 나는 항상 가방에서 열쇠를 꺼내어 주머니 속에 넣는다. ◳ 구 –을 통해 밖을 ❑ 그는 계속 창밖을 응시했다. ◳ 구 –을 피해 ❑ 사람들은 햇빛을 피함으로써 피부암을 막을 수 있다. ◳ 구 –으로부터 벗어나 ❑ 과거엔 육군이 곤경에서 벗어나기 위해 공중 엄호에 많이 의존했다. ❑ 경제가 불경기에서 벗어나기 시작한다. ◳ 구 –을 나와서 ❑ 정확히 그것이 내가 대학을 나와서 해야 한다고 생각했던 것이다. ◳ 구 –의 범위를 넘어서 ❑ 숀은 불러도 들리지 않는 침실에서 텔레비전을 보고 있었다. ◳ 구 –때문에 ❑ 그는 의무감 때문에 공직을 맡았다. ◳ 구 –으로부터 얻어 내어 ❑ "그녀가 죄수로 잡혀 있는 곳이 어디입니까?"라고 나는 물어보았다. "그로부터 그걸 알아냈습니까?" ◳ 구 –로 인해, –으로부터 ❑ 우리 모두는 그 덕분에 매우 재미있었다. ◳ 구 –이 떨어진 ❑ 설탕을 찾을 수 없고 우유는 떨어졌다. ◳ 구 –으로 ❑ 사람들에게 나무 또는 돌로 건물을 지으라고 조언해 주시겠습니까? ◳ 구 –중에서 ❑ 다섯 명 중에서 두 명은 자신들의 은퇴나 사망 시 사업체가 개인에게 매각될 것이라고 생각했다.

가산명사 정전 [미국영어; 영국영어 power cut] ❑ 워싱턴에 몰아친 폭풍으로 인해 그 지역 전체에 정전 사태가 벌어지고 있다.

단수명사 (호주의) 오지 ❑ 오지에 사람들이 많이 살고 있나요?

> outbid는 동사의 현재, 과거, 과거 분사로 쓴다.

타동사 –보다 비싸게 값을 부르다 ❑ 그 박물관은 세계적으로 위대한 보물급 예술 작품에 대해 경쟁 박물관들보다 비싸게 값을 불러 그들의 반감을 사고 있다.

형용사 시외로 향하는; 외국행의 ❑ 공항 관계자들은 적어도 20대의 외국행 여객기가 연착되었다고 말한다.

가산명사 우편물 발송함 [미국영어; 영국영어 out tray] ❑ 그는 서명을 하고 우편물 발송함에 그 편지를 넣었다.

가산명사 발발 ❑ 나흘간의 축제는 수백 명의 젊은이들이 연루된 폭력 사태가 발발한 후 하루 일찍 끝났다. ❑ 중동 지역에서의 전쟁 발발

a b c d e f g h i j k l m n o p q r s t u v w x y z

out|burst /ˈaʊtbɜrst/ (**outbursts**) ◼ N-COUNT An **outburst** of an emotion, especially anger, is a sudden strong expression of that emotion. ❑ ...a spontaneous outburst of cheers and applause. ◼ N-COUNT An **outburst** of violent activity is a sudden period of this activity. ❑ Five people were reported killed today in a fresh outburst of violence.

◼ 가산명사 (감정의) 폭발 ❑ 자연스럽게 터져 나온 환호와 박수 ◼ 가산명사 돌발 ❑ 오늘 또 다시 돌발한 폭력 사태로 5명이 목숨을 잃었다는 보도가 있었다.

out|cast /ˈaʊtkæst/ (**outcasts**) N-COUNT An **outcast** is someone who is not accepted by a group of people or by society. ❑ He had always been an outcast, unwanted and alone.

가산명사 버림받은 자, 따돌림 받는 사람 ❑ 그는 항상 따돌림을 받고, 원하는 사람도 없이 외로이 살았다.

out|come ♦◇◇ /ˈaʊtkʌm/ (**outcomes**) N-COUNT The **outcome** of an activity, process, or situation is the situation that exists at the end of it. ❑ Mr. Singh said he was pleased with the outcome. ❑ It's too early to know the outcome of her illness.

가산명사 결과 ❑ 싱 씨는 결과에 만족한다고 말했다. ❑ 그녀의 질병에 대한 결과를 알기에는 아직 시기상조이다.

out|cry /ˈaʊtkraɪ/ (**outcries**) N-VAR An **outcry** is a reaction of strong disapproval and anger shown by the public or media about a recent event. ❑ The killing caused an international outcry.

가산명사 또는 불가산명사 격렬한 항의, 외침 ❑ 그 피살 사건은 국제 사회의 격렬한 항의를 불러일으켰다.

out|dat|ed /ˌaʊtˈdeɪtɪd/ ADJ If you describe something as **outdated**, you mean that you think it is old-fashioned and no longer useful or relevant to modern life. ❑ ...outdated and inefficient factories. ❑ ...outdated attitudes.

형용사 시대에 뒤진, 낡은 ❑ 낡고 비효율적인 공장들 ❑ 시대에 뒤진 사고방식

out|do /ˌaʊtˈdu/ (**outdoes, outdoing, outdid, outdone**) ◼ V-T If you **outdo** someone, you are a lot more successful than they are at a particular activity. ❑ It was important for me to outdo them, to feel better than they were. ◼ PHRASE You use **not to be outdone** to introduce an action which someone takes in response to a previous action. ❑ She wore a lovely tiara but the groom, not to be outdone, had on a very smart embroidered waistcoat.

◼ 타동사 능가하다 ❑ 나에게는 그들을 능가하고 그들보다 내가 더 낫다고 생각하는 것이 중요했다. ◼ 구 -에 못지않게, -에 지지 않도록 ❑ 그녀도 아름다운 머리 장식을 썼지만 신랑도 이에 못지않게 매우 맵시 있게 수놓은 조끼를 입고 있었다.

out|door /ˈaʊtdɔr/ ADJ **Outdoor** activities or things happen or are used outside and not in a building. [ADJ n] ❑ If you enjoy outdoor activities, this is the trip for you.

형용사 야외의, 옥외의 ❑ 당신이 야외 활동을 즐긴다면, 이것은 당신을 위한 여행입니다.

out|doors /ˌaʊtˈdɔrz/ ◼ ADV If something happens **outdoors**, it happens outside in the fresh air rather than in a building. ❑ It was warm enough to be outdoors all afternoon. ◼ N-SING You refer to **the outdoors** when talking about work or leisure activities which take place outside away from buildings. ❑ I'm a lover of the outdoors.

◼ 부사 야외에서, 옥외에서 ❑ 오후 내내 야외에 있어도 좋을 만큼 포근했다. ◼ 단수명사 야외 활동 ❑ 난 야외 활동이 너무 좋아.

out|er /ˈaʊtər/ ADJ The **outer** parts of something are the parts which contain or enclose the other parts, and which are furthest from the center. [ADJ n] ❑ He heard a voice in the outer room.

형용사 바깥쪽의 ❑ 그는 바깥쪽 방에서 목소리를 들었다.

out|er space N-UNCOUNT **Outer space** is the area outside the earth's atmosphere where the other planets and stars are situated. ❑ In 1957, the Soviets launched Sputnik 1 into outer space. →see **satellite**

불가산명사 우주, 지구 대기권 밖 ❑ 1957년, 구소련은 스푸트니크 1호를 지구 대기권 밖으로 쏘아 올렸다.

out|fit /ˈaʊtfɪt/ (**outfits**) ◼ N-COUNT An **outfit** is a set of clothes. ❑ She was wearing an outfit she'd bought the previous day. ◼ N-COUNT You can refer to an organization as an **outfit**. ❑ He works for a private security outfit.

◼ 가산명사 (한 벌의) 의상 ❑ 그녀는 전날 구매한 의상을 입고 있었다. ◼ 가산명사 조직 ❑ 그는 사설 보안 업체에 다닌다.

out|flow /ˈaʊtfloʊ/ (**outflows**) N-COUNT When there is an **outflow of** money or people, a large amount of money or people move from one place to another. ❑ There was a net outflow of about £650m in short-term capital.

가산명사 유출 ❑ 단기 자금 6억 5천만 파운드 가량의 순 유출이 있었다.

out|going /ˈaʊtɡoʊɪŋ/ ◼ ADJ You use **outgoing** to describe a person in charge of something who is soon going to leave that position. [ADJ n] ❑ ...the outgoing director of the Edinburgh International Festival. ◼ ADJ **Outgoing** things such as planes, mail, and passengers are leaving or being sent somewhere. [ADJ n] ❑ All outgoing flights were grounded. ◼ ADJ Someone who is **outgoing** is very friendly and likes meeting and talking to people. ❑ She's very outgoing.

◼ 형용사 퇴임하는, 나가는 ❑ 퇴임하는 에든버러 국제 페스티벌의 책임자 ◼ 형용사 출발하는; 발송되는 ❑ 모든 출발 여객기들이 이륙하지 못했다. ◼ 형용사 사교적인, 외향적인 ❑ 그녀는 매우 사교적이다.

out|go|ings /ˈaʊtɡoʊɪŋz/ N-PLURAL Your **outgoings** are the regular amounts of money which you have to spend every week or every month, for example in order to pay your rent or bills. [BRIT; AM **outlay, expenses**] ❑ She suggests you first assess your income and outgoings.

복수명사 (정기적인) 지출 [영국영어; 미국영어 outlay, expenses] ❑ 그녀는 당신이 당신의 수입과 지출을 먼저 산정해야 한다고 제안합니다.

out|grow /ˌaʊtˈɡroʊ/ (**outgrows, outgrowing, outgrew, outgrown**) ◼ V-T If a child **outgrows** a piece of clothing, they grow bigger, so that it no longer fits them. ❑ She outgrew her clothes so rapidly that Patsy was always having to buy new ones. ◼ V-T If you **outgrow** a particular way of behaving or thinking, you change and become more mature, so that you no longer behave or think in that way. ❑ The girl may or may not outgrow her interest in fashion.

◼ 타동사 자라서 -을 못 입게 되다 ❑ 그녀가 너무 빨리 자라 옷을 못 입게 되어서 팻시는 항상 새 옷을 사야만 했었다. ◼ 타동사 (성장하여) -을 벗어나다, -을 안 하게 되다 ❑ 그 소녀가 자라면 유행에 대한 관심이 없어질 수도 있고 여전히 있을 수도 있다.

out|ing /ˈaʊtɪŋ/ (**outings**) N-COUNT An **outing** is a short enjoyable trip, usually with a group of people, away from your home, school, or place of work. ❑ One evening, she made a rare outing to the local discotheque. ❑ →see also **out 3**

◼ 가산명사 나들이, 소풍 ❑ 어느 날 저녁, 그녀는 동네 디스코텍으로 좀처럼 가지 않는 나들이를 갔다.

out|law /ˈaʊtlɔ/ (**outlaws, outlawing, outlawed**) ◼ V-T When something is **outlawed**, it is made illegal. ❑ In 1975 gambling was outlawed. ❑ The German government has outlawed some fascist groups. ◼ N-COUNT An **outlaw** is a criminal who is hiding from the authorities. [OLD-FASHIONED] ❑ Jesse was an outlaw, a bandit, a criminal.

◼ 타동사 법으로 금지되다 ❑ 1975년에 도박은 법으로 금지되었다. ❑ 독일 정부는 일부 파시스트 단체들을 불법화시켰다. ◼ 가산명사 무법자, 도망 다니는 범죄자 [구식어] ❑ 제시는 무법자에다 노상강도에 범죄자였다.

out|lay /ˈaʊtleɪ/ (**outlays**) N-VAR **Outlay** is the amount of money that you have to spend in order to buy something or start a project. ❑ Apart from the capital outlay of buying the machine, dishwashers can actually save you money.

가산명사 또는 불가산명사 지출, 경비 ❑ 기계 구입에 드는 지출은 별도로 하고, 식기 세척기를 사용하면 실제로 돈을 절약할 수 있습니다.

out|let /ˈaʊtlɛt, -lɪt/ (**outlets**) ◼ N-COUNT An **outlet** is a store or organization which sells the goods made by a particular manufacturer. ❑ ...the largest retail outlet in the city. ◼ N-COUNT An **outlet** or an **outlet store** is a place which sells slightly damaged or outdated goods from a particular manufacturer, or goods that it made in greater quantities than needed. ❑ ...the factory outlet store in Belmont. ◼ N-COUNT If someone has an **outlet for** their feelings or ideas, they have a means of expressing and releasing them. ❑ Her father had found an outlet for his ambition in his work. ◼ N-COUNT An **outlet** is a hole or pipe through which liquid or air can flow away. ❑ ...a warm air outlet. ◼ N-COUNT An **outlet** is a place, usually in a wall, where you can connect electrical devices to the electricity supply. [mainly AM; BRIT usually **socket**] ❑ Just plug it into any electric outlet.

◼ 가산명사 직판점 ❑ 그 도시에서 가장 큰 소매 직판점 ◼ 가산명사 아웃렛, 할인점 ❑ 벨몬트에 있는 공장 직영 할인점 ◼ 가산명사 표현 수단, 배출구 ❑ 그녀의 아버지는 자신의 일에 대한 야망을 표현할 수단을 찾았던 것이다. ◼ 가산명사 배출구 ❑ 더운 공기 배출구 ◼ 가산명사 콘센트 [주로 미국영어; 영국영어 대개 socket] ❑ 전기 콘센트에 그것을 꽂기만 하세요.

out|line ♦◇◇ /aʊtlaɪn/ (**outlines, outlining, outlined**) **1** V-T If you **outline** an idea or a plan, you explain it in a general way. ❑ *The mayor outlined his plan to clean up the town's image.* **2** N-COUNT An **outline** is a general explanation or description of something. [also in n] ❑ *Following is an outline of the survey findings.* **3** V-T PASSIVE You say that an object **is outlined** when you can see its general shape because there is light behind it. ❑ *The Ritz was outlined against the lights up there.* **4** N-COUNT The **outline** of something is its general shape, especially when it cannot be clearly seen. ❑ *He could see only the hazy outline of the goalposts.*

1 타동사 개요를 말하다 ❑ 시장은 도시 이미지 정화에 관해 자기가 세운 계획의 개요를 설명했다. **2** 가산명사 개요 ❑ 다음은 이번 조사 결과의 개요입니다. **3** 수동 타동사 윤곽이 드러나다 ❑ 저 위쪽에 불빛을 배경으로 리츠 호텔의 윤곽이 드러났다. **4** 가산명사 윤곽 ❑ 그는 골대의 어렴풋한 윤곽만을 볼 수 있었다.

Word Partnership	outline의 연어
V.	write an outline **1** **2**
N.	chapter outline, outline a paper, outline a plan **2**
ADJ.	broad outline, detailed outline, general outline **2** **4**

out|live /aʊtlɪv/ (**outlives, outliving, outlived**) V-T If one person **outlives** another, they are still alive after the second person has died. If one thing **outlives** another thing, the first thing continues to exist after the second has disappeared or been replaced. ❑ *I'm sure Rose will outlive many of us.*

타동사 -보다 오래 살다, -보다 오래 남다 ❑ 내가 확신하건대 로즈가 우리들 대부분보다 오래 살 거야.

out|look /aʊtlʊk/ (**outlooks**) **1** N-COUNT Your **outlook** is your general attitude toward life. [usu sing, with supp, also in n] ❑ *I adopted a positive outlook on life.* **2** N-SING The **outlook** for something is what people think will happen in relation to it. ❑ *The economic outlook is one of rising unemployment.*

1 가산명사 관(觀), 견해 ❑ 나는 긍정적인 인생관을 선택했다. **2** 단수명사 전망 ❑ 그 경제 전망은 실업 증가를 말한다.

out|ly|ing /aʊtlaɪɪŋ/ ADJ **Outlying** places are far away from the main cities of a country. [ADJ n] ❑ *Tourists can visit outlying areas like the Napa Valley Wine Country.*

형용사 외곽의 ❑ 관광객들은 '나파 밸리 와인 컨트리' 같은 외곽 지역을 방문할 수 있다.

out|num|ber /aʊtnʌmbər/ (**outnumbers, outnumbering, outnumbered**) V-T If one group of people or things **outnumbers** another, the first group has more people or things in it than the second group. ❑ *...a town where men outnumber women four to one.*

타동사 -보다 수가 많다 ❑ 남녀 비율이 4대 1로 남자가 많은 마을

out of →see **out**

out of date also **out-of-date** ADJ Something that is **out of date** is old-fashioned and no longer useful. ❑ *Think how rapidly medical knowledge has gone out of date in recent years.*

형용사 구식의, 쓸모없게 된 ❑ 최근 들어 의학 지식이 얼마나 빨리 구식이 되는지 생각해 보세요.

out of touch **1** ADJ Someone who is **out of touch with** a situation is not aware of recent changes in it. [v-link ADJ, oft ADJ with n] ❑ *Washington politicians are out of touch with the American people.* **2** ADJ If you are **out of touch** with someone, you have not been in contact with them recently and are not familiar with their present situation. [v-link ADJ, oft ADJ with n] ❑ *James wasn't invited. We've been out of touch for years. But I did invite Caleb.*

1 형용사 (사정을) 모르는, 유리된 ❑ 워싱턴의 정치인들은 미국 국민들이 무엇을 바라고 있는지 모른다. **2** 형용사 왕래가 끊긴 ❑ 제임스는 초대받지 않았다. 그는 우리와 수년간 연락을 하지 않고 지낸다. 그러나 칼렙은 정말 초대했었다.

out of work ADJ Someone who is **out of work** does not have a job. ❑ *...a town where half the men are usually out of work.*

형용사 직장이 없는, 실직한 ❑ 보통 남자 절반이 실직자인 마을

out|pa|tient /aʊtpeɪʃənt/ (**outpatients**) also **out-patient** N-COUNT An **outpatient** is someone who receives treatment at a hospital but does not spend the night there. ❑ *...the outpatient clinic.* →see **hospital**

가산명사 외래 환자 ❑ 외래 환자 진료소

out|place|ment /aʊtpleɪsmənt/ N-UNCOUNT An **outplacement** agency gives advice to managers and other professional people who have recently become unemployed, and helps them find new jobs. [BUSINESS] ❑ *...an outplacement firm in Denver.*

불가산명사 전직 알선 [경제] ❑ 덴버에 위치한 전직 알선 회사

out|post /aʊtpoʊst/ (**outposts**) N-COUNT An **outpost** is a small group of buildings used for trading or military purposes, either in a distant part of your own country or in a foreign country. ❑ *...a remote mountain outpost, linked to the outside world by the poorest of roads.*

가산명사 전초 기지, 재외 기지 ❑ 열악한 도로를 지나야만 외부 세계와 통할 수 있는 외딴 산악 지대의 전초 기지

out|put ♦◇◇ /aʊtpʊt/ (**outputs**) **1** N-VAR **Output** is used to refer to the amount of something that a person or thing produces. ❑ *Government statistics show the largest drop in industrial output for ten years.* **2** N-VAR The **output** of a computer or word processor is the information that it displays on a screen or prints on paper as a result of a particular program. ❑ *You run the software, you look at the output, you make modifications.*

1 가산명사 또는 불가산명사 생산량 ❑ 정부 통계 자료에 따르면 십 년 동안 산업 생산량이 가장 큰 폭으로 떨어졌음을 알 수 있다. **2** 가산명사 또는 불가산명사 출력된 정보 ❑ 그 소프트웨어를 가동시켜 출력 정보를 보고 난 후, 수정을 해 봐.

out|rage (**outrages, outraging, outraged**)

The verb is pronounced /aʊtreɪdʒ/. The noun is pronounced /aʊtreɪdʒ/.

동사는 /aʊtreɪdʒ/로 발음되고, 명사는 /aʊtreɪdʒ/로 발음된다.

1 V-T If you **are outraged** by something, it makes you extremely shocked and angry. ❑ *Many people have been outraged by some of the things that have been said.* ● **out|raged** ADJ ❑ *He is truly outraged about what's happened to him.* **2** N-UNCOUNT **Outrage** is an intense feeling of anger and shock. ❑ *The decision provoked outrage from women and human rights groups.* **3** N-COUNT You can refer to an act or event which you find very shocking as an **outrage**. ❑ *The latest outrage was to have been a co-ordinated gun and bomb attack on the station.*

1 타동사 분노하다 ❑ 많은 사람들이 발표된 일부 사항에 대해 분노하고 있다. ● 분개한 형용사 ❑ 그는 자신에게 일어난 일에 대해 정말로 분개하고 있다. **2** 불가산명사 격분 ❑ 그 결정에 여성 및 인권 단체들이 격분했다. **3** 가산명사 충격적인 일 ❑ 최근의 충격적인 사건으로 역에서 총과 폭탄을 함께 사용한 공격이 있었다.

out|ra|geous /aʊtreɪdʒəs/ ADJ If you describe something as **outrageous**, you are emphasizing that it is unacceptable or very shocking. [EMPHASIS] ❑ *I must apologize for my outrageous behaviour.* ● **out|ra|geous|ly** ADV ❑ *...outrageously expensive skin care items.*

형용사 가당찮은, 충격적인 [강조] ❑ 가당찮은 제 행동에 대해 사과해야겠어요. ● 가당찮게, 터무니없이 부사 ❑ 터무니없이 비싼 피부 관리 제품들

out|right

The adjective is pronounced /aʊtraɪt/. The adverb is pronounced /aʊtraɪt/.

형용사는 /aʊtraɪt/으로 발음되고, 부사는 /aʊtraɪt/으로 발음된다.

1 ADJ You use **outright** to describe behavior and actions that are open and direct, rather than indirect. [ADJ n] ❑ *Kawaguchi finally resorted to an outright lie.* ● ADV **Outright** is also an adverb. [ADV after v] ❑ *Why are you so mysterious? Why don't you tell me outright?* **2** ADJ **Outright** means complete and total. [ADJ n] ❑ *She*

1 형용사 노골적인; 솔직한 ❑ 가와구치는 결국 노골적으로 거짓말을 했다. ● 부사 노골적으로; 솔직하게 ❑ 넌 왜 그리 비밀이 많니? 내게 솔직하게 말해 주면 안돼? **2** 형용사 완전한 ❑ 그녀는 완전한

a b c d e f g h i j k l m n o p q r s t u v w x y z

A

had failed to win an outright victory. ● ADV **Outright** is also an adverb. [ADV after v] ❑ *The peace plan wasn't rejected outright.* ● PHRASE If someone **is killed outright,** they die immediately, for example in an accident.

승리를 거두지 못했다. ● 부사 완전히 ❑ 그 평화안이 완전히 거부되지는 않았다. ● 구 즉사하다

B

out|sell /aʊtsel/ (outsells, outselling, outsold) V-T If one product **outsells** another product, the first product is sold more quickly or in larger quantities than the second. [BUSINESS] ❑ *The team's products easily outsell those of other American baseball clubs overseas.*

타동사 -보다 많이 판매되다 [경제] ❑ 그 팀의 상품이 다른 미국 야구 클럽의 상품보다 해외에서 단연히 많이 팔린다.

C

out|set /aʊtset/ PHRASE If something happens **at the outset** of an event, process, or period of time, it happens at the beginning of it. If something happens **from the outset** it happens from the beginning and continues to happen. ❑ *Decide at the outset what kind of learning programme you want to follow.*

구 처음에; 처음부터 ❑ 어떤 학습 프로그램을 선택할 것인지를 처음부터 결정하세요.

D

out|side ♦♦♦ /aʊtsaɪd/ (outsides)

> The form **outside of** can also be used as a preposition. This form is more usual in American English.

outside of도 전치사로 쓸 수 있다. 미국영어에서는 이 형태를 더 많이 쓴다.

E

1 N-COUNT The **outside** of something is the part which surrounds or encloses the rest of it. ❑ *...the outside of the building.* ● ADJ **Outside** is also an adjective. [ADJ n] ❑ *...high up on the outside wall.* **2** ADV If you are **outside,** you are not inside a building but are quite close to it. ❑ *I stepped outside and pulled up my collar against the cold mist.* ❑ *Outside, the light was fading rapidly.* ● PREP **Outside** is also a preposition. ❑ *The victim was outside a shop when he was attacked.* ● ADJ **Outside** is also an adjective. [ADJ n] ❑ *...the outside temperature.* **3** PREP If you are **outside** a room, you are not in it but are in the passage or area next to it. ❑ *She'd sent him outside the classroom.* ● ADV **Outside** is also an adverb. ❑ *They heard voices coming from outside in the corridor.* **4** ADJ When you talk about the **outside** world, you are referring to things that happen or exist in places other than your own home or community. [ADJ n] ❑ *...a side of Morris's character she hid carefully from the outside world.* ● ADV **Outside** is also an adverb. [ADV after v] ❑ *The scheme was good for the prisoners because it brought them outside into the community.* **5** PREP People or things **outside** a country, town, or region are not in it. [n/-ed PREP n] ❑ *...an old castle outside Budapest.* ● N-SING **Outside** is also a noun. [the N] ❑ *Peace cannot be imposed from the outside by the United States or anyone else.* **6** ADJ On a road with two-way traffic, the **outside** lanes are the ones which are closest to the median strip. [BRIT] [ADJ n] ❑ *It was travelling in the outside lane at 78mph.* **7** ADJ **Outside** people or organizations are not part of a particular organization or group. [ADJ n] ❑ *The company now makes much greater use of outside consultants.* ● PREP **Outside** is also a preposition. ❑ *He is hoping to recruit a chairman from outside the company.* **8** PREP **Outside** a particular institution or field of activity means in other fields of activity or in general life. ❑ *...the largest merger ever to take place outside the oil industry.* **9** PREP Something that is **outside** a particular range of things is not included within it. ❑ *She is a beautiful boat, but way, way outside my price range.* **10** PREP Something that happens **outside** a particular period of time happens at a different time from the one mentioned. ❑ *They are open outside normal daily banking hours.*

1 가산명사 바깥쪽, 외부 ❑ 건물의 바깥쪽 ● 형용사 바깥쪽의 ❑ 바깥쪽 벽 위로 높게 **2** 부사 밖으로, 바깥에 ❑ 나는 발걸음을 옮겨 밖으로 나왔고 차가운 안개에 옷깃을 세웠다. ❑ 바깥의 빛이 순식간에 어두워지고 있었다. ● 전치사 -의 바깥쪽에 ❑ 그 희생자는 공격을 당할 당시 상점 바깥쪽에 있었다. ● 형용사 외부의 ❑ 외부 온도 **3** 전치사 밖의 ❑ 그녀는 그를 교실 밖으로 내보냈었다. ● 부사 밖에서 ❑ 그들은 방 밖 복도에서 여러 사람의 목소리를 들었다. **4** 형용사 외부의, 국외의 ❑ 모리스가 외부 사람들에게 조심스럽게 감춰 온 자기 성격의 한 단면 ● 부사 밖으로 ❑ 그 계획은 그 수감자들에게는 제격이었다. 왜냐하면 이를 통해 그들은 지역 사회와 교류를 할 수 있게 되었기 때문이다. **5** 전치사 외곽에 ● 부다페스트 외곽에 위치한 오래된 성 ● 단수명사 외부 ❑ 평화는 미국이나 다른 누군가가 외부에서 강요할 수 없다. **6** 형용사 안쪽의, 중앙 분리대 쪽의 [영국영어] ❑ 그것은 시속 78마일의 속도로 바깥 차선을 달리고 있었다. **7** 형용사 외부의 ❑ 회사는 이제 사외 고문들을 더욱 더 최대한 활용하고 있다. ● 전치사 외부에서 ❑ 그는 회사 외부에서 회장을 영입하기를 바란다. **8** 전치사 외부의 ❑ 정유 산업계 외부에서 일어난 최대의 합병 **9** 전치사 범위를 넘어서, 벗어나 ❑ 그것은 멋진 보트지만, 내가 생각한 가격대를 훨씬 벗어나 있다. **10** 전치사 이외의 ❑ 그들은 보통 은행 업무 시간 이외 시간에 영업을 한다.

Thesaurus   outside의 참조어

ADJ.	exterior, outdoor; (ant.) interior, inside **1**
PREP.	beyond, near; (ant.) inside **3 5**

Word Partnership   outside의 연어

N.	the outside **of a building 1** outside **a building,** outside **a car,** outside **a room,** outside **a store 2 3** outside **interests,** the outside **world 4** outside **a city/town,** outside **a country 5** outside **sources 7**
ADJ.	**cold** outside, **dark** outside **2**
V.	**gather** outside, **go** outside, **park** outside, **sit** outside, **stand** outside, **step** outside, **wait** outside **2 3**

---

out|sid|er /aʊtsaɪdər/ (outsiders) **1** N-COUNT An **outsider** is someone who does not belong to a particular group or organization. ❑ *The most likely outcome may be to subcontract much of the work to an outsider.* **2** N-COUNT An **outsider** is someone who is not accepted by a particular group, or who feels that they do not belong in it. ❑ *Malone, a cop, felt as much an outsider as any of them.* **3** N-COUNT In a competition, an **outsider** is a competitor who is unlikely to win. ❑ *He was an outsider in the race to be the new UN Secretary-General.*

1 가산명사 제삼자, 외부인 ❑ 가장 유력한 결론은 제삼자에게 그 작업의 대부분을 하청 주는 것이다. **2** 가산명사 이방인 ❑ 경찰관인 멀론은 그들 중 누구 못지않게 자신도 이방인이라고 느꼈다. **3** 가산명사 승산이 없는 선수 ❑ 그는 신임 유엔 사무총장이 되기 위한 경쟁에서 승산이 없는 쪽이었다.

out|skirts /aʊtskɜrts/ N-PLURAL The **outskirts** of a city or town are the parts of it that are farthest away from its center. ❑ *Hours later we reached the outskirts of New York.*

복수명사 교외 ❑ 몇 시간 후에 우리는 뉴욕 교외에 다다랐다.

out|source /aʊtsɔrs/ (outsources, outsourcing, outsourced) V-T/V-I If a company **outsources** work or things, it pays workers from outside the company to do the work or supply the things. [BUSINESS] ❑ *Increasingly, corporate clients are seeking to outsource the management of their facilities.* ● out|sourc|ing N-UNCOUNT ❑ *The difficulties of outsourcing have been compounded by the increasing resistance of trade unions.*

타동사/자동사 외부에 위탁하다, 외부 자원을 활용하다, 아웃소싱을 주다 [경제] ❑ 기업 고객들이 점점 더 자신들의 시설 경영을 외부에 위탁하는 방법을 모색한다. ● 아웃소싱, 외부 위탁 불가산명사 ❑ 아웃소싱의 어려움은 커져 가는 노조 저항 문제도 가중되고 있다.

out|spo|ken /aʊtspoʊkən/ ADJ Someone who is **outspoken** gives their opinions about things openly and honestly, even if they are likely to shock or offend people. ❑ *Some church leaders have been outspoken in their support for political reform in Kenya.* ● out|spo|ken|ness N-UNCOUNT ❑ *His outspokenness has ensured that he has at least one senior enemy within the BBC hierarchy.*

형용사 거리낌 없는 ❑ 일부 교회 지도자들은 케냐의 정치 개혁에 대한 자신들의 지지를 거리낌 없이 표출하고 있다. ● 거리낌 없음 불가산명사 ❑ 거리낌 없는 행동으로 그는 비비시 방송국에서 서열상 상급자 중 적어도 한 명을 적으로 만든 것이 확실했다.

out|stand|ing ♦◇◇ /aʊtstændɪŋ/ **1** ADJ If you describe someone or something as **outstanding**, you think that they are very remarkable and impressive. ❑ *Derartu is an outstanding athlete and deserved to win.* **2** ADJ Money that is **outstanding** has not yet been paid and is still owed to someone. ❑ *The total debt outstanding is $70 billion.* **3** ADJ **Outstanding** issues or problems have not yet been resolved. ❑ *We still have some outstanding issues to resolve before we'll have a treaty that is ready to sign.* **4** ADJ **Outstanding** means very important or obvious. ❑ *The company is an outstanding example of a small business that grew into a big one.*

1 형용사 우수한, 뛰어난 ❑ 데라투는 우수한 선수이며 우승할 만하다. **2** 형용사 미지급의 ❑ 미지급된 부채 총액이 700억 달러이다. **3** 형용사 미해결의 ❑ 우리는 협약에 서명하기 전에 아직도 몇 가지 해결해야 할 과제가 있다. **4** 형용사 두드러지는, 눈에 띄는 ❑ 그 회사는 작은 사업체를 크게 키운 두드러진 사례이다.

out|stand|ing|ly /aʊtstændɪŋli/ ADV You use **outstandingly** to emphasize how good, or occasionally how bad, something is. [EMPHASIS] [ADV adj/adv] ❑ *Salzburg is an outstandingly beautiful place to visit.*

부사 너무나 [강조] ❑ 잘츠부르크는 방문하기에 너무나 아름다운 곳이다.

out|stretched /aʊtstrɛtʃt/ ADJ If a part of the body of a person or animal is **outstretched**, it is stretched out as far as possible. ❑ *She was staring into the fire muttering, and holding her arms outstretched to warm her hands.*

형용사 쭉 뻗친 ❑ 그녀는 뭔가를 중얼거리며 벽난로를 물끄러미 바라보면서, 팔을 쭉 뻗어 손에 불을 쬐고 있었다.

out|strip /aʊtstrɪp/ (**outstrips, outstripping, outstripped**) V-T If one thing **outstrips** another, the first thing becomes larger in amount, or more successful or important, than the second thing. ❑ *In 1989 and 1990 demand outstripped supply, and prices went up by more than a third.*

타동사 능가하다 ❑ 1989년과 1990년에 수요가 공급을 능가했고, 가격이 1/3 이상 올랐다.

out tray (**out trays**) also **out-tray** N-COUNT An **out tray** is a shallow container used in offices to put letters and documents in when they have been dealt with and are ready to be sent somewhere else. Compare **in tray**. [mainly BRIT; AM usually **out box**] ❑ *...the letter which was still lying in my out tray.*

가산명사 발송 서류함, 기결함 [주로 영국영어; 미국영어 대개 out box] ❑ 내 발송 서류함에 아직도 놓여 있는 편지

out|ward /aʊtwərd/

The form **outwards** can also be used for meanings **4** and **5**.

outwards도 **4**와 **5** 의미에 쓸 수 있다.

1 ADJ An **outward** journey is a journey that you make away from a place that you are intending to return to later. [ADJ n] ❑ *Tickets must be bought seven days in advance, with outward and return journey dates specified.* **2** ADJ The **outward** feelings, qualities, or attitudes of someone or something are the ones they appear to have rather than the ones that they actually have. [ADJ n] ❑ *In spite of my outward calm I was very shaken.* **3** ADJ The **outward** features of something are the ones that you can see from the outside. [ADJ n] ❑ *Mark was lying unconscious but with no outward sign of injury.* **4** ADV If something moves or faces **outward**, it moves or faces away from the place you are in or the place you are talking about. [ADV after v] ❑ *The top door opened outward.* **5** ADV If you say that a person or a group of people, such as a government, looks **outward**, you mean that they turn their attention to another group that they are interested in or would like greater involvement with. [ADV after v] ❑ *Other poor countries looked outward, strengthening their ties to the economic superpowers.*

1 형용사 밖으로 향하는 ❑ 왕복 여행 날짜가 명기된 표를 7일 앞서서 구매하셔야 합니다. **2** 형용사 외견상의 ❑ 나는 외견상으로 침착했지만 속으로는 매우 떨렸다. **3** 형용사 외형의 ❑ 마크는 의식을 잃고 누워 있었으나 외상은 없었다. **4** 부사 밖을 향한 ❑ 그 윗문은 바깥쪽으로 열렸다. **5** 부사 밖으로 ❑ 다른 빈곤한 나라들은 밖으로 시선을 돌려 경제 강국들과 유대를 강화했다.

out|ward|ly /aʊtwərdli/ ADV You use **outwardly** to indicate the feelings or qualities that a person or situation may appear to have, rather than the ones that they actually have. ❑ *They may feel tired and though outwardly calm, can be irritable.*

부사 겉으로 보기에는 ❑ 그들이 겉으로 보기에는 조용해도 지쳐 있고 쉽게 짜증을 낼 수도 있다.

out|weigh /aʊtweɪ/ (**outweighs, outweighing, outweighed**) V-T If one thing **outweighs** another, the first thing is of greater importance, benefit, or significance than the second thing. [FORMAL] ❑ *The advantages of this deal largely outweigh the disadvantages.*

타동사 ~보다 중요하다, ~보다 더 가치 있다 [격식체] ❑ 이 거래를 하면 손해보다 이득이 훨씬 더 많다.

out|wit /aʊtwɪt/ (**outwits, outwitting, outwitted**) V-T If you **outwit** someone, you use your intelligence or a clever trick to defeat them or to gain an advantage over them. ❑ *To win the presidency he had first to outwit his rivals within the Socialist Party.*

타동사 (술수나 꾀를 써서) 따돌리다, 앞지르다 ❑ 그가 대통령이 되기 위해서는, 우선 사회당 내 맞수들을 따돌려야 했다.

oval /oʊvᵊl/ (**ovals**) ADJ **Oval** things have a shape that is like a circle but is wider in one direction than the other. ❑ *...the small oval framed picture of a little boy.* ● N-COUNT **Oval** is also a noun. ❑ *Using 2 spoons, mould the cheese into small balls or ovals.* →see **circle**

형용사 타원형의 ❑ 작은 타원형 액자에 들어 있는 어린 남자 아이의 그림 ● 가산명사 타원 ❑ 숟가락 2개를 이용해서 치즈를 작은 공 모양이나 타원 모양으로 빚으세요.

ova|ry /oʊvəri/ (**ovaries**) N-COUNT A woman's **ovaries** are the two organs in her body that produce eggs. ❑ *...women who have had their ovaries removed.*

가산명사 난소 ❑ 난소 제거 수술을 받은 여성들

ova|tion /oʊveɪʃᵊn/ (**ovations**) N-COUNT An **ovation** is a large amount of applause from an audience for a particular performer or speaker. [FORMAL] ❑ *They became civic heroes and received a tumultuous ovation on their appearance in New York City.*

가산명사 박수갈채 [격식체] ❑ 그들은 시민의 영웅이 되었고, 뉴욕에 나타났을 때 우레와 같은 박수갈채를 받았다.

oven /ʌvᵊn/ (**ovens**) N-COUNT An **oven** is a device for cooking that is like a box with a door. You heat it and cook food inside it. ❑ *Put the onions and ginger in the oven and let them roast for thirty minutes.*

가산명사 오븐 ❑ 양파와 생강을 오븐에 넣고 30분 동안 구우세요.

over
① POSITION AND MOVEMENT
② AMOUNTS AND OCCURRENCES
③ OTHER USES

① **over** ♦♦♦ /oʊvər/

In addition to the uses shown below, **over** is used after some verbs, nouns, and adjectives in order to introduce extra information. **Over** is also used in phrasal verbs such as "hand over" and "glaze over."

over는 아래 용법 외에도 추가 정보를 나타내기 위해 일부의 동사, 명사, 형용사 뒤에 쓴다. 또한 'hand over', 'glaze over'와 같은 구동사에도 쓰인다.

1 PREP If one thing is **over** another thing or is moving **over** it, the first thing is directly above the second, either resting on it, or with a space between them. ❑ *He looked at himself in the mirror over the table.* ● ADV **Over** is also an adverb. [ADV after v] ❑ *...planes flying over every 10 or 15 minutes.* **2** PREP If one thing is **over** another thing, it is supported by it and its ends are hanging down on each side of it. ❑ *A grey mackintosh was folded over her arm.* **3** PREP If one thing is **over** another thing, it covers part or all of it. ❑ *Mix the ingredients and pour over the mushrooms.* ❑ *He was wearing a light-gray suit over a shirt.* ● ADV **Over** is also an adverb. [ADV after v] ❑ *Heat this syrup and pour it over.* **4** PREP If you lean **over** an

1 전치사 위에, 위로 ❑ 그는 탁자 위에 있는 거울에 비친 자신을 바라보았다. ● 부사 위에, 위로 ❑ 10분이나 15분마다 머리 위로 날아가는 비행기 **2** 전치사 위에 ❑ 그녀는 회색 레인코트를 접어서 팔에 걸치고 있었다. **3** 전치사 위에 ❑ 내용물을 섞어 버섯 위에 부으세요. ❑ 그는 셔츠 위에 연회색 정장을 입고 있었다. ● 부사 위에 ❑ 이 시럽을 데워서 위에 부으세요. **4** 전치사 ~ 위로, ~ 너머로 ❑ 그들은 멈춰 서서 문 너머로 내다봤다. ● 부사 ~ 위로, ~ 너머로

a b c d e f g h i j k l m n o p q r s t u v w x y z

object, you bend your body so that the top part of it is above the object. [v PREP n] ❑ *They stopped to lean over a gate.* ● ADV **Over** is also an adverb. [ADV after v] ❑ *Sam leant over to open the door of the car.* **5** PREP If you look **over** or talk **over** an object, you look or talk across the top of it. ❑ *I went and stood beside him, looking over his shoulder.* **6** PREP If a window has a view **over** an area of land or water, you can see the land or water through the window. [n PREP n, v PREP n] ❑ *...a light and airy bar with a wonderful view over the River Amstel.* **7** PREP If someone or something goes **over** a barrier, obstacle, or boundary, they get to the other side of it by going across it, or across the top of it. [v PREP n] ❑ *I stepped over a broken piece of wood.* ❑ *Nearly one million people crossed over the river into Moldavia.* ● ADV **Over** is also an adverb. [ADV after v] ❑ *I climbed over into the back seat.* **8** PREP If someone or something moves **over** an area or surface, they move across it, from one side to the other. ❑ *She ran swiftly over the lawn to the gate.* **9** PREP If something is on the opposite side of a road or river, you can say that it is **over** the road or river. ❑ *...a fashionable neighborhood, just over the river from Manhattan.* **10** ADV If you go **over** to a place, you go to that place. ❑ *I got out the car and drove over to Dervaig.* **11** ADV You can use **over** to indicate a particular position or place a short distance away from someone or something. ❑ *He noticed Rolfe standing silently over by the window.* ❑ *John reached over and took Joanna's hand.* **12** ADV You use **over** to say that someone or something falls toward or onto the ground, often suddenly or violently. [ADV after v] ❑ *If he drinks more than two glasses of wine he falls over.* ❑ *He was knocked over by a bus and broke his leg.* **13** ADV If something rolls **over** or is turned **over**, its position changes so that the part that was facing upward is now facing downward. [ADV after v] ❑ *His car rolled over after a tyre was punctured.*

Over and **above** are both used to talk about position and height. If something is higher than something else and the two things are imagined as being positioned along a vertical line, you can use either **above** or **over**. ❑ *He opened a cupboard above the sink... She leaned forward until her face was over the basin.* However, if something is higher than something else but the two things are regarded as being wide or horizontal rather than tall or vertical, you have to use **above**. ❑ *The trees rose above the row of houses.* **Above** and **over** are both used to talk about measurements, for example, when you are talking about a point that is higher than another point on a scale. ❑ *Any money earned over that level is taxed....everybody above five feet eight inches in height.* You use **over** to say that a distance or period of time is longer than the one mentioned. ❑ *...a height of over twelve thousand feet... Our relationship lasted for over a year.* **Above** and **over** are also both used to talk about people's rank or importance. You use **above** to talk about people who are more important and in a higher position than other people. ❑ *...behaving as if she was in a position above the other staff.* If someone is **over** you, they give orders or instructions to you. ❑ *...an officer in authority over him.*

---

14 PHRASE **All over** a place means in every part of it. ❑ *...doctors who work all over the country.* **15** PHRASE **Over here** means near you, or in the country you are in. ❑ *Why don't you come over here tomorrow evening.* **16** PHRASE **Over there** means in a place a short distance away from you, or in another country. ❑ *The café is just across the road over there.*

② **over** ♦♦♦ /ˈoʊvər/ **1** PREP If something is **over** a particular amount, measurement, or age, it is more than that amount, measurement, or age. [PREP amount] ❑ *They say that tobacco will kill over 4 million people worldwide this year.* ❑ *His family have accumulated property worth well over $1 million.* ● ADV **Over** is also an adverb. [amount and ADV] ❑ *...people aged 65 and over.* **2** PHRASE **Over and above** an amount, especially a normal amount, means more than that amount or in addition to it. ❑ *Expenditure on education has gone up by seven point eight per cent over and above inflation.* **3** ADV If you say that you have some food or money **over**, you mean that it remains after you have used all that you need. ❑ *Larsons pay me well enough, but there's not much over for luxuries when there's two of you to live on it.* **4** ADV If you do something **over**, you do it again or start doing it again from the beginning. [AM] [ADV after v] ❑ *She said if she had the chance to do it over, she would have hired a press secretary.* **5** PHRASE If you say that something happened **twice over**, **three times over** and so on, you are stating the number of times that it happened and emphasizing that it happened more than once. [EMPHASIS] ❑ *James had to have everything spelled out twice over for him.* **6** PHRASE If you do something **over again**, you do it again or start doing it again from the beginning. ❑ *If I could live my life over again, I would do things exactly the same way.* **7** PHRASE If you say that something is happening **all over again**, you are emphasizing that it is happening again, and you are suggesting that it is tiring, boring, or unpleasant. [EMPHASIS] ❑ *The whole process started all over again.* **8** PHRASE If you say that something happened **over and over** or **over and over again**, you are emphasizing that it happened many times. [EMPHASIS] ❑ *He plays the same songs over and over.*

③ **over** ♦♦♦ /ˈoʊvər/ **1** ADJ If an activity is **over** or **all over**, it is completely finished. [v-link ADJ] ❑ *Warplanes that have landed recently will be kept until the war is over.* ❑ *I am glad it's all over.* **2** PREP If you are **over** an illness or an experience, it has finished and you have recovered from its effects. ❑ *I'm glad that you're over the flu.* **3** PREP If you have control or influence **over** someone or something, you are able to control them or influence them. [n PREP n] ❑ *He's never had any influence over her.* **4** PREP You use **over** to indicate what a disagreement or feeling relates to or is caused by. [n PREP n, v PREP n] ❑ *...concern over recent events*

❑ 샘은 차 문을 열려고 몸을 숙였다. **5** 전치사 너머로 ❑ 나는 그의 옆으로 가 서서 그의 어깨 너머로 내다보았다. **6** 전치사 -의 경치가 보이는, -이 내다보이는 ❑ 암스텔 강의 멋진 경치가 보이는 밝고 바람이 잘 통하는 바 **7** 전치사 넘어, 건너 ❑ 나는 부러진 나무 조각 위로 넘었다. ❑ 백만 명에 가까운 사람들이 강을 건너 몰다비아로 갔다. ● 부사 넘어, 건너 ❑ 나는 뒷좌석으로 넘어갔다. **8** 전치사 위로 ❑ 그녀는 잔디밭 위를 빨리 달려서 문 쪽으로 갔다. **9** 전치사 건너 ❑ 맨해튼에서 강 바로 건너에 있는 부자 동네 **10** 부사 -로 ❑ 나는 차를 꺼내서 더베이그로 달려갔다. **11** 부사 바로 가까이 ❑ 그는 롤페가 창문 바로 옆에 조용히 서 있다는 것을 알아차렸다. ❑ 존은 손을 내밀어 가까이 있는 조애나의 손을 잡았다. **12** 부사 곤두박질치듯 ❑ 그는 포도주 두 잔 이상을 마시면 픽 쓰러진다. ❑ 그는 버스에 치여 다리가 부러졌다. **13** 부사 거꾸로, 뒤집어져 ❑ 타이어에 펑크가 나서 그의 차가 뒤집혔다.

---

over와 above는 둘 다 위치와 높이를 말할 때 쓴다. 어떤 것이 다른 것보다 높이 있고, 그 두 사물이 수직선상에 위치한 것으로 추정할 때에는 above나 over 어느 것이든 쓸 수 있다. ❑ 그는 싱크대 위의 찬장을 열었다... 그녀는 얼굴이 세면기 위까지 가도록 상체를 굽혔다. 그러나 어떤 것이 다른 것보다 높이 있기는 하지만, 그 두 사물을 그 높이나 수직선상의 관점에서가 아니라 그 너비나 수평선상의 관점에서 생각할 때에는 above를 써야 한다. ❑ 늘어선 집들로 위로 나무들이 솟아올라 있었다. above와 over는 둘 다 측정 단위로, 예를 들어 눈금상의 한 점이 다른 점보다 높은 것을 얘기할 때와 같은 경우에 쓰인다. ❑ 그 수준 이상으로 번 돈은 모두 과세된다....키가 5피트 8인치 이상인 모든 사람. 거리 또는 시간이 언급된 거리 또는 시간보다 길다고 말할 때는 over를 쓴다. ❑ ...일만 이천 피트가 넘는 높이... 우리 관계는 1년 이상 지속되었다. above와 over는 둘 다 사람의 지위나 중요도를 얘기할 때에도 쓴다. above는 다른 사람보다 더 중요하고 높은 지위에 있는 사람을 얘기할 때 쓴다. ❑ ...그녀가 다른 직원들보다 높은 지위에 있는 것처럼 행동하는. 누가 당신보다 'over'에 있다는 것은, 그 사람이 당신에게 명령과 지시를 하는 위치에 있다는 뜻이다. ❑ ...그의 상급자

---

14 구 전 ❑ 전국 방방곡곡에서 일하는 의사들 **15** 구 여기; 이 나라 ❑ 내일 저녁 여기로 오세요. **16** 구 거기, 저기; 그 나라 ❑ 그 카페는 길 건너 바로 저기이다.

1 전치사 -이상의 ❑ 담배가 올해 전 세계에서 4백만 명 이상의 목숨을 앗아갈 것이라고 말한다. ❑ 그의 가족은 족히 백만 파운드가 넘는 재산을 모았다. ● 부사 - 이상 ❑ 65세 이상인 사람 **2** 구 -에 더하여, -이상으로 ❑ 교육 관련 지출이 통화 팽창률보다 7.8퍼센트 높아졌다. **3** 부사 넘치게, 쓰고도 남게 ❑ 나는 라슨스에서 충분히 많은 월급을 받고 있지만, 두 사람이 그것만 갖고 살면서 사치를 부릴 여유는 많지 않다. **4** 부사 처음부터 다시 [미국영어] ❑ 그녀는 만일 그것을 처음부터 다시 할 기회가 있다면, 언론 담당 비서를 고용했을 것이라고 말했다. **5** 구 구 번씩이나; 세 번씩이나 [강조] ❑ 제임스를 그를 위해서 모든 것을 두 번씩이나 한 자 한 자 읽어야만 했었다. **6** 구 처음부터 다시 ❑ 내가 인생을 처음부터 다시 살 수 있다고 해도, 나는 정확하게 똑같은 방식으로 할 것이다. **7** 구 처음부터 다시 [강조] ❑ 전 과정이 처음부터 또 다시 시작됐다. **8** 구 반복해서, 거듭해서 [강조] ❑ 그는 똑같은 노래만 반복해서 튼다.

1 형용사 끝난 ❑ 그곳에 착륙한 군용기들은 전쟁이 끝날 때까지 보류될 것이다. ❑ 그게 끝나서 난 기뻐. **2** 전치사 다 나은, 다 극복한 ❑ 독감이 다 나았다니 기쁘구나. **3** 전치사 -에게 (영향을 끼치다) , -를 (통제하다) ❑ 그는 여태껏 그녀에게 영향을 끼친 적이 전혀 없다. **4** 전치사 -에 대한 ❑ 최근 미얀마에서 일어난 사태에 대한 우려 ❑ 몇몇 공항과 항구의 직원들이 급여에 대해 항의하기 시작하고 있다. **5** 전치사 -에,

in Burma. □ *Staff at some air and sea ports are beginning to protest over pay.* ⑤ PREP If something happens **over** a particular period of time or **over** something such as a meal, it happens during that time or during the meal. □ *The number of attacks on the capital had gone down over the past week.* ⑥ PREP You use **over** to indicate that you give or receive information using a telephone, radio, or other piece of electrical equipment. □ *I'm not prepared to discuss this over the telephone.* □ *The head of state addressed the nation over the radio.* ⑦ PHRASE The presenter of a radio or television program says "**over to** someone" to indicate the person who will speak next. □ *With the rest of the sports news, over to Colin Maitland.* ⑧ CONVENTION When people such as the police or the army are using a radio to communicate, they say "**Over**" to indicate that they have finished speaking and are waiting for a reply. [FORMULAE]

-를 하는 동안 □ 지난주에는 수도에 대한 공격 횟수가 줄어들었다. ⑥ 전치사 -로, -를 통해 □ 나는 이 문제를 전화로 논의할 준비가 아직 안 되어 있다. □ 국가 원수가 라디오를 통해 국민들에게 연설하였다. ⑦ 구 -가 친해 드리겠습니다 (텔레비전 등에서 사회자가 하는 말) □ 나머지 스포츠 뉴스는 콜린 메이트랜드 기자가 전해 드리겠습니다. ⑧ 관용 표현 이상 (무선 통신 용어) [의례적인 표현]

Thesaurus   over의 참조어

PREP.	above, beyond, higher than; *(ant.)* below, under ① ⑤
V.	completed, concluded, done with, ended, finished ③ ⑦

---

over|all ♦♦◇ (**overalls**)

The adjective and adverb are pronounced /ouvərɔl/. The noun is pronounced /ouvərɔl/.

형용사와 부사는 /ouvərɔl/로 발음되고, 명사는 /ouvərɔl/로 발음된다.

① ADJ You use **overall** to indicate that you are talking about a situation in general or about the whole of something. [ADJ n] □ *...the overall rise in unemployment.* ● ADV **Overall** is also an adverb. [ADV with cl] □ *Overall I was disappointed.* ② N-PLURAL **Overalls** are pants that are attached to a piece of cloth which covers your chest and which has straps going over your shoulders. [AM; BRIT **dungarees**] [also *a pair of* N] □ *An elderly man dressed in faded overalls took the witness stand.* ③ N-PLURAL **Overalls** consist of a single piece of clothing that combines pants and a jacket. You wear overalls over your clothes in order to protect them while you are working. [also *a pair of* N] □ *...workers in blue overalls.*

① 형용사 전반적인 □ 전반적인 실업 증가 ● 부사 전반적으로 □ 전반적으로 나는 실망했다. ② 복수명사 멜빵바지 [미국영어; 영국영어 dungarees] □ 빛바랜 멜빵바지를 입은 나이가 지긋한 남자가 증인석에 섰다. ③ 복수명사 오버롤 (상의와 바지가 붙어 있는 작업복), 작업복 □ 파란색 오버롤을 입은 노동자

over|awe /ouvərɔ/ (**overawes, overawing, overawed**) V-T If you **are overawed by** something or someone, you are very impressed by them and a little afraid of them. [usu passive] □ *Don't be overawed by people in authority, however important they are.*

타동사 위압당하다 □ 얼마나 중요한 사람이든 간에 권위를 지닌 사람들에게 위압당하지 마세요.

over|board /ouvərbɔrd/ ① ADV If you fall **overboard**, you fall over the side of a boat into the water. [ADV after v] □ *His sailing instructor fell overboard and drowned during a lesson.* ② PHRASE If you say that someone **goes overboard**, you mean that they do something to a greater extent than is necessary or reasonable. [INFORMAL] □ *Women sometimes damage their skin by going overboard with abrasive cleansers.*

① 부사 물속으로, 배 밖으로 □ 그에게 항해술을 가르치던 강사가 수업 도중 배에서 떨어져 익사했다. ② 구 과도하게 하다 [비격식체] □ 여자들은 가끔 연마 클렌저를 과도하게 사용하여 피부를 상하게 하기도 한다.

over|came /ouvərkeɪm/ **Overcame** is the past tense of **overcome**.

overcome의 과거

over|ca|pac|ity /ouvərkəpæsɪti/ N-UNCOUNT If there is **overcapacity** in a particular industry or area, more goods are produced than are needed, and the industry is therefore less profitable than it could be. [BUSINESS] □ *There is huge overcapacity in the world car industry.*

불가산명사 생산 과잉 [경제] □ 세계 자동차 업계엔 생산 과잉이 엄청나다.

over|charge /ouvərtʃɑrdʒ/ (**overcharges, overcharging, overcharged**) V-T If someone **overcharges** you, they charge you too much for their goods or services. □ *If you feel a taxi driver has overcharged you, say so.*

타동사 바가지 씌우다 □ 만약 택시 기사가 너한테 바가지를 씌웠다고 생각되면, 그렇게 말해.

over|coat /ouvərkout/ (**overcoats**) N-COUNT An **overcoat** is a thick warm coat that you wear in winter.

가산명사 외투

over|come ♦◇◇ /ouvərkʌm/ (**overcomes, overcoming, overcame**)

The form **overcome** is used in the present tense and is also the past participle.

overcome은 현재 및 과거 분사로 쓴다.

① V-T If you **overcome** a problem or a feeling, you successfully deal with it and control it. □ *Molly had fought and overcome her fear of flying.* ② V-T If you **are overcome by** a feeling of event, it is so strong or has such a strong effect that you cannot think clearly. □ *The night before the test I was overcome by fear and despair.* ③ V-T If you **are overcome by** smoke or a poisonous gas, you become very ill or die from breathing it in. [usu passive] □ *The residents were trying to escape from the fire but were overcome by smoke.*

① 타동사 극복하다 □ 몰리는 열심히 노력해서 비행 공포증을 극복했다. ② 타동사 압도당하다 □ 시험 보기 전날 밤 나는 두려움과 자포자기의 심정에 압도당했다. ③ 타동사 질식되다 □ 주민들은 화재 때 대피하려고 했지만 연기에 질식되었다.

Word Partnership   overcome의 연어

ADJ.	**difficult to** overcome, **hard to** overcome ①
N.	overcome **difficulties**, overcome **a fear**, overcome **an obstacle/problem**, overcome **opposition** ① overcome **by emotion**, overcome **by fear** ②

---

over|crowd|ed /ouvərkraudɪd/ ADJ An **overcrowded** place has too many things or people in it. □ *...a windswept, overcrowded, unattractive beach.*

형용사 혼잡한 □ 바람이 많이 불고, 혼잡하며, 볼 것도 없는 해변

over|crowd|ing /ouvərkraudɪŋ/ N-UNCOUNT If there is a problem of **overcrowding**, there are more people living in a place than it was designed for. □ *Students were protesting at overcrowding in the university hostels.*

불가산명사 과잉수용 □ 학생들은 대학교 기숙사에 수용 인원이 너무 많다고 항의하고 있었다.

over|do /ouvərdu/ (**overdoes, overdoing, overdid, overdone**) ① V-T If someone **overdoes** something, they behave in an exaggerated or extreme way. □ *...a recognition by the U.S. central bank that it may have overdone its tightening when it pushed rates up to 6 per cent.* ② V-T If you **overdo** an activity, you try to do more than you can physically manage. □ *It is important never to overdo new exercises.*

① 타동사 과도하게 하다 □ 수치를 6퍼센트로 올리려고 하면서 과도한 긴축을 강행했을 수도 있다고 미국 중앙은행이 시인한 ② 타동사 무리하다 □ 새로 운동을 시작할 때는 절대로 무리하지 않는 것이 중요하다.

over|dose /ouvərdous/ (**overdoses, overdosing, overdosed**) ① N-COUNT If someone takes an **overdose** of a drug, they take more of it than is safe. □ *Each year, one in 100 girls aged 15-19 takes an overdose.* ② V-I If someone **overdoses on** a drug, they take more of it than is safe. □ *He'd overdosed on heroin.* ③ N-COUNT You

① 가산명사 약물 남용, 과잉 투여 □ 매년 15세에서 19세 사이의 소녀 백 명 중 한명은 약물을 남용한다. ② 자동사 과잉 투여하다 □ 그는 헤로인을 과잉 투여했다. ③ 가산명사 과다 □ 햇볕, 바다, 모래, 염소에

A
can refer to too much of something, especially something harmful, as an **overdose**. ❏ *An overdose of sun, sea, sand and chlorine can give lighter hair a green tinge.* ◾ V-I You can say that someone **overdoses on** something if they do or have too much of it. ❏ *The city, he concluded, had overdosed on design.*

과다하게 노출되면 밝은 색의 모발이 녹색을 띠게 될 수도 있습니다. ◾ 자동사 과도하게 하다 ❏ 그 도시는 과도하게 디자인됐다고 그는 결론지었다.

B
over|draft /ˈoʊvərdræft/ (**overdrafts**) N-COUNT If you have an **overdraft**, you have spent more money than you have in your bank account, and so you are in debt to the bank. ❏ *Her bank warned that unless she repaid the overdraft she could face legal action.*

가산명사 초과 인출 ❏ 그녀가 이용하는 은행은 그녀가 초과 인출한 돈을 상환하지 않으면 법적 절차를 밟겠다고 경고했다.

C
over|drawn /ˌoʊvərˈdrɔn/ ADJ If you are **overdrawn** or if your bank account is **overdrawn**, you have spent more money than you have in your account, and so you are in debt to the bank. ❏ *Nick's bank sent him a letter saying he was £100 overdrawn.*

형용사 초과 인출하다 ❏ 닉이 이용하는 은행은 닉이 100파운드를 초과 인출했다는 편지를 그에게 보냈다.

D

E
over|due /ˌoʊvərˈdu/ ◾ ADJ If you say that a change or an event is **overdue**, you mean that you think it should have happened before now. ❏ *This debate is long overdue.* ◾ ADJ **Overdue** sums of money have not been paid, even though it is later than the date on which they should have been paid. ❏ *Teachers have joined a strike aimed at forcing the government to pay overdue salaries and allowances.* ◾ ADJ An **overdue** library book has not been returned to the library, even though the date on which it should have been returned has passed. ❏ *...a library book now weeks overdue.*

◾ 형용사 기한이 지난, 만시지탄의 감을 주는 ❏ 이 논쟁은 이미 오래전에 있어야 했다. ◾ 형용사 연체된, 체불된 ❏ 교사들은 체불된 급여와 수당 지불을 정부에 요구하기 위한 목적의 파업에 참가했다. ◾ 형용사 연체된 ❏ 이제 몇 주째 연체된 도서관 책

F

G
over|eat /ˌoʊvərˈit/ (**overeats**, **overeating**, **overate**, **overeaten**) V-I If you say that someone **overeats**, you mean they eat more than they need to or more than is healthy. ❏ *If you tend to overeat because of depression, first take steps to recognize the source of your sadness.*

자동사 과식하다, 너무 많이 먹다 ❏ 우울증 때문에 과식하는 경향이 있으시다면, 우선 슬픔의 원인을 인식하는 단계를 밟으세요.

H
over|es|ti|mate (**overestimates**, **overestimating**, **overestimated**)

The verb is pronounced /ˌoʊvərˈɛstɪmeɪt/. The noun is pronounced /ˌoʊvərˈɛstɪmɪt/.

동사는 /ˌoʊvərˈɛstɪmeɪt/ 으로 발음되고, 명사는 /ˌoʊvərˈɛstɪmɪt/ 으로 발음된다.

I

J
◾ V-T/V-I If you say that someone **overestimates** something, you mean that they think it is greater in amount or importance than it really is. ❏ *He was overestimating their desire for peace.* ◾ N-COUNT **Overestimate** is also a noun. ❏ *Average earnings in the South East were about £59,000, although that may be an overestimate.* ◾ V-T If you say that something **cannot be overestimated**, you are emphasizing that you think it is very important. [EMPHASIS] [with brd-neg] ❏ *The importance of the media in communicating anti-drug messages cannot be overestimated.* ◾ V-T If you **overestimate** someone, you think that they have more of a skill or quality than they really have. ❏ *I think you overestimate me, Fred.*

◾ 타동사/자동사 과대평가하다, 좀 많이 어림잡다 ❏ 그는 평화를 갈구하는 그들의 욕구를 과대평가하고 있었다. ◾ 가산명사 과대평가, 과다 추산 ❏ 좀 많이 어림잡은 건지도 모르겠지만 동남부의 평균 소득은 59,000파운드 정도였다. ◾ 타동사 아무리 강조해도 지나치지 않다 [강조] ❏ 마약 반대 메시지를 전달하는 데 있어서 대중 매체가 갖는 중요성은 아무리 강조해도 지나치지 않는다. ◾ 타동사 과대평가하다 ❏ 프레드, 넌 나를 과대평가하고 있는 것 같아.

K

L
over|flow (**overflows**, **overflowing**, **overflowed**)

The verb is pronounced /ˌoʊvərˈfloʊ/. The noun is pronounced /ˈoʊvərfloʊ/.

동사는 /ˌoʊvərˈfloʊ/ 로 발음되고, 명사는 /ˈoʊvərfloʊ/ 로 발음된다.

M

N
◾ V-T/V-I If a liquid or a river **overflows**, it flows over the edges of the container or place it is in. [no passive] ❏ *Pour in some of the syrup, but not all of it, as it will probably overflow.* ◾ V-I If a place or container is **overflowing** with people or things, it is too full of them. [usu cont] ❏ *Schreiber addressed an auditorium overflowing with journalists.* ◾ N-COUNT The **overflow** is the extra people or things that something cannot contain or deal with because it is not large enough. ❏ *Tents have been set up next to hospitals to handle the overflow.* ◾ PHRASE If a place or container is filled **to overflowing**, it is so full of people or things that no more can fit in. ❏ *The kitchen garden was full to overflowing with fresh vegetables.*

◾ 타동사/자동사 넘치다 ❏ 시럽을 조금 붓되 넘칠 수 있으니까 전부 다 붓지는 말아라. ◾ 자동사 넘쳐 나다 ❏ 슈라이버는 기자들로 강당에서 연설을 했다. ◾ 가산명사 넘쳐남 ❏ 넘쳐 나는 사람들을 수용하기 위해서 병원 옆에 텐트를 몇 개 세웠다. ◾ 구 넘치도록 가득한 ❏ 채마밭에 신선한 야채들이 넘쳐 나도록 가득했다.

O

P
over|grown /ˌoʊvərˈɡroʊn/ ◾ ADJ If a garden or other place is **overgrown**, it is covered with a lot of unruly plants because it has not been cared for. ❏ *We hurried on until we reached a courtyard overgrown with weeds.* ◾ ADJ If you describe an adult as an **overgrown** child, you mean that their behavior and attitudes are like those of a child, and that you dislike this. [DISAPPROVAL] [ADJ n] ❏ *...a bunch of overgrown kids.*

◾ 형용사 (풀이) 무성한, (작물이) 웃자란 ❏ 잡초가 무성한 안뜰에 도착할 때까지 우리는 서둘러 갔다. ◾ 형용사 철없는 [탐탁잖음] ❏ 철없는 아이들

Q

R
over|hang (**overhangs**, **overhanging**, **overhung**)

The verb is pronounced /ˌoʊvərˈhæŋ/. The noun is pronounced /ˈoʊvərhæŋ/.

동사는 /ˌoʊvərˈhæŋ/ 으로 발음되고, 명사는 /ˈoʊvərhæŋ/ 으로 발음된다.

S
◾ V-T If one thing **overhangs** another, it sticks out over and above it. ❏ *Part of the rock wall overhung the path at one point.* ◾ N-COUNT An **overhang** is the part of something that sticks out over and above something else. ❏ *A sharp overhang of rock gave them cover.*

◾ 타동사 - 위로 비죽 튀어나오다 ❏ 오솔길 한 지점 위로 바위가 비죽 튀어나와 있었다. ◾ 가산명사 처마 같은 것 ❏ 처마처럼 불쑥 튀어나온 바위가 그들에게 피할 곳을 제공해 주고 있다.

T
over|haul (**overhauls**, **overhauling**, **overhauled**)

The verb is pronounced /ˌoʊvərˈhɔl/. The noun is pronounced /ˈoʊvərhɔl/.

동사는 /ˌoʊvərˈhɔl/ 로 발음되고, 명사는 /ˈoʊvərhɔl/ 로 발음된다.

U
◾ V-T If a piece of equipment is **overhauled**, it is cleaned, checked thoroughly, and repaired if necessary. [usu passive] ❏ *They had ensured the plumbing was overhauled a year ago.* ● N-COUNT **Overhaul** is also a noun. ❏ *...the overhaul of a cruiser.* ◾ V-T If you **overhaul** a system or method, you examine it carefully and make many changes in it in order to improve it. ❏ *...proposals to overhaul bank regulations.* ● N-COUNT **Overhaul** is also a noun. ❏ *The study says there must be a complete overhaul of air traffic control systems.*

◾ 타동사 정비하다 ❏ 그들은 일 년 전에 분명히 그 상수도관을 정비하도록 했었다. ● 가산명사 정비 ❏ 순양함 정비 ◾ 타동사 재정비하다 ❏ 은행 규정을 재정비하자는 제안 ● 가산명사 재정비 ❏ 그 연구에서는 항공 교통 통제 시스템이 전면적으로 재정비돼야 한다고 지적했다.

V

W
over|head

The adjective is pronounced /ˈoʊvərhɛd/. The adverb is pronounced /ˌoʊvərˈhɛd/.

형용사는 /ˈoʊvərhɛd/ 로 발음되고, 부사는 /ˌoʊvərˈhɛd/ 로 발음된다.

X

Y
◾ ADJ You use **overhead** to indicate that something is above you or above the place that you are talking about. [ADJ n] ❏ *She turned on the overhead light and looked around the little room.* ● ADV **Overhead** is also an adverb. ❏ *...planes passing overhead.* ◾ N-UNCOUNT The **overhead** of a business is its regular and essential expenses, such as salaries, rent, electricity, and telephone bills. [BUSINESS; BRIT **overheads**] ❏ *Private insurers spend 27 cents of every dollar on overhead.*

◾ 형용사 머리 위의 ❏ 그녀는 머리 위에 있는 전등을 켜고 작은 방을 둘러보았다. ● 부사 머리 위로 ❏ 머리 위로 지나가는 비행기들 ◾ 불가산명사 일반 경비 [경제; 영국영어 overheads] ❏ 보험 회사들은 지출의 매 1달러 중 27센트를 일반 경비로 쓴다.

Z

over|head pro|jec|tor (**overhead projectors**) N-COUNT An **overhead projector** is a machine that has a light inside it and makes the writing or pictures on a sheet of plastic appear on a screen or wall. The abbreviation **OHP** is also used.

가산명사 오버헤드 프로젝터

over|hear /ouvərhɪər/ (**overhears, overhearing, overheard**) V-T If you **overhear** someone, you hear what they are saying when they are not talking to you and they do not know that you are listening. ☐ *I overheard two doctors discussing my case.*

타동사 우연히 듣다 ☐ 나는 의사 두 명이 내 병에 대해 이야기를 하는 것을 우연히 들었다.

over|heat /ouvərhit/ (**overheats, overheating, overheated**) **1** V-T/V-I If something **overheats** or if you **overheat** it, it becomes hotter than is necessary or desirable. ☐ *The engine was overheating and the car was not handling well.* • **over|heat|ed** ADJ ☐ *…that stuffy, overheated apartment.* **2** V-T/V-I If a country's economy **overheats** or if conditions **overheat** it, it grows so rapidly that inflation and interest rates rise very quickly. [BUSINESS] ☐ *The private sector is increasing its spending so sharply that the economy is overheating.* • **over|heat|ed** ADJ ☐ *…the disastrous consequences of an overheated market.*

1 타동사/자동사 과열되다; 과열시키다 ☐ 엔진은 과열되어 있었고 차는 말을 잘 듣지 않았다. • 과열된 형용사 ☐ 숨 막힐 것 같이 후덥지근한 아파트 **2** 타동사/자동사 과열되다 [경제] ☐ 민간 부문 지출의 급격한 신장으로 경기가 과열되고 있다. • 과열된 형용사 ☐ 시장 과열의 결과 초래된 재앙

over|heat|ed /ouvərhitɪd/ ADJ Someone who is **overheated** is very angry about something. ☐ *I think the reaction has been a little overheated.*

형용사 화가 많이 난, 격앙된 ☐ 상당히 격앙된 반응이 있어 온 것 같다.

over|hung /ouvərhʌŋ/ **Overhung** is the past tense and past participle of **overhang**.

overhang의 과거, 과거 분사

over|joyed /ouvərdʒɔɪd/ ADJ If you are **overjoyed**, you are extremely pleased about something. [v-link ADJ, oft ADJ to-inf, ADJ at n] ☐ *Shelley was overjoyed to see me.*

형용사 매우 기쁜 ☐ 셜리는 나를 보고서 기뻐서 어쩔 줄 몰라 했다.

over|land /ouvərlænd/ ADJ An **overland** journey is made across land rather than by ship or airplane. [ADJ n] ☐ *…an overland journey through Iraq, Turkey, Iran, and Pakistan.* • ADV **Overland** is also an adverb. [ADV after v] ☐ *They're traveling to Baghdad overland.*

형용사 육로의 ☐ 이라크, 터키, 이란, 파키스탄을 두루 다 거친 육로 여행 • 부사 육로로 ☐ 그들은 바그다드까지 육로로 여행하고 있다.

over|lap (**overlaps, overlapping, overlapped**)

The verb is pronounced /ouvərlæp/. The noun is pronounced /ouvərlæp/.

동사는 /ouvərlæp/으로 발음되고, 명사는 /ouvərlæp/으로 발음된다.

1 V-RECIP If one thing **overlaps** another, or if you **overlap** them, a part of the first thing occupies the same area as a part of the other thing. You can also say that two things **overlap**. ☐ *When the bag is folded flat, the bag bottom overlaps one side of the bag.* ☐ *Overlap the slices carefully so there are no gaps.* **2** V-RECIP If one idea or activity **overlaps** another, or **overlaps** with another, they involve some of the same subjects, people, or periods of time. ☐ *Christian holy week overlaps with the beginning of the Jewish holiday of Passover.* ☐ *The needs of patients invariably overlap.* • N-VAR **Overlap** is also a noun. ☐ *…the overlap between civil and military technology.*

1 상호동사 겹쳐지다; 겹치게 하다 ☐ 그 가방을 평평하게 접으면, 가방 바닥이 가방 한 면과 겹쳐진다. ☐ 얇게 썬 조각들을 틈이 생기지 않도록 조심스레 겹쳐 놓으세요. **2** 상호동사 일치하다, 겹치다 ☐ 기독교의 수난 주간은 유대교 유월절의 시작과 겹친다. ☐ 환자들의 요구는 거의 언제나 똑같았다. • 가산명사 또는 불가산명사 겹침, 일치 ☐ 민간 기술과 군사 기술의 일치

over|leaf /ouvərlif/ ADV **Overleaf** is used in books and magazines to say that something is on the other side of the page you are reading. ☐ *Answer the questionnaire overleaf.*

부사 뒷면에 ☐ 뒷면에 있는 설문지를 작성해 주세요.

over|load (**overloads, overloading, overloaded**)

The verb is pronounced /ouvərloud/. The noun is pronounced /ouvərloud/.

동사는 /ouvərloud/로 발음되고, 명사는 /ouvərloud/로 발음된다.

1 V-T If you **overload** something such as a vehicle, you put more things or people into it than it was designed to carry. ☐ *Don't overload the boat or it will sink.* • **over|load|ed** ADJ ☐ *Some trains were so overloaded that their suspension collapsed.* **2** V-T To **overload** someone **with** work, problems, or information means to give them more work, problems, or information than they can cope with. ☐ *…an effective method that will not overload staff with yet more paperwork.* • N-UNCOUNT **Overload** is also a noun. ☐ *57 percent complained of work overload.* • **over|load|ed** ADJ ☐ *The bar waiter was already overloaded with orders.* **3** V-T If you **overload** an electrical system, you cause too much electricity to flow through it, and so damage it. ☐ *Never overload an electrical socket.*

1 타동사 짐을 너무 많이 싣다, 사람을 너무 많이 태우다 ☐ 보트에 사람을 너무 많이 태우지 마세요. 안 그러면 가라앉을 거예요. • 짐을 너무 많이 실은, 사람을 너무 많이 태운 형용사 ☐ 몇몇 기차는 사람을 너무 많이 태워서 완충 장치가 나갔다. **2** 타동사 과중한 부담을 지우다 ☐ 직원들에게 더 많은 문서 업무 부담을 지우지 않게 할 효과적인 방법 • 불가산명사 과중한 부담 ☐ 57퍼센트가 과중한 업무 부담에 대해 불평했다. • 과중한 부담을 진 형용사 ☐ 바 웨이터는 너무 밀려든 주문으로 이미 정신이 없었다. **3** 타동사 과부하하다 ☐ 전기 소켓에 절대로 과부하를 걸지 마세요.

over|look /ouvərlʊk/ (**overlooks, overlooking, overlooked**) **1** V-T If a building or window **overlooks** a place, you can see the place clearly from the building or window. ☐ *Pretty and comfortable rooms overlook a flower-filled garden.* **2** V-T If you **overlook** a fact or problem, you do not notice it, or do not realize how important it is. ☐ *We overlook all sorts of warning signals about our own health.* **3** V-T If you **overlook** someone's faults or bad behavior, you forgive them and take no action. ☐ *…satisfying relationships that enable them to overlook each other's faults.*

1 타동사 내려다보이다 ☐ 예쁘고 편안한 방들은 꽃이 가득한 정원을 내다보고 있다. **2** 타동사 간과하다, 그냥 지나치다 ☐ 우리는 우리 자신의 건강에 대한 모든 종류의 위험 신호들을 그냥 간과해 버린다. **3** 타동사 눈감아 주다 ☐ 서로의 결점도 눈감아 줄 수 있는 만족스런 관계

over|ly /ouvərli/ ADV **Overly** means more than is normal, necessary, or reasonable. [ADV adj/adv/-ed] ☐ *Employers may become overly cautious about taking on new staff.*

부사 지나치게, 필요 이상의 ☐ 고용주들이 새 직원을 들이는 것에 지나치게 신중해지는 경우도 있다.

over|night ◆◇◇ /ouvərnaɪt/ **1** ADV If something happens **overnight**, it happens throughout the night or at some point during the night. [ADV after v] ☐ *The decision was reached overnight.* • ADJ **Overnight** is also an adjective. [ADJ n] ☐ *Travel and overnight accommodation are included.* **2** ADV You can say that something happens **overnight** when it happens very quickly and unexpectedly. [ADV after v] ☐ *The rules are not going to change overnight.* • ADJ **Overnight** is also an adjective. [ADJ n] ☐ *In 1970 he became an overnight success in America.* **3** ADJ **Overnight** bags or clothes are ones that you take when you go and stay somewhere for one or two nights. [ADJ n] ☐ *He realized he'd left his overnight bag at Mary's house.*

1 부사 밤새; 밤에 ☐ 그 결정은 밤에 내려졌다. • 형용사 밤을 새는 ☐ 이동과 숙박이 포함되어 있습니다. **2** 부사 하룻밤 새에, 갑작스레 ☐ 그 규칙이 하룻밤 새에 바뀌지는 않을 것이다. • 형용사 하룻밤 사이의, 갑작스런 ☐ 1970년에 그는 미국에서 하룻밤 사이에 성공했다. **3** 형용사 단기 여행용의 (가방) ☐ 그는 작은 여행용 가방을 메리의 집에 두고 온 것을 깨달았다.

over|paid /ouvərpeɪd/ ADJ If you say that someone is **overpaid**, you mean that you think they are paid more than they deserve for the work they do. ☐ *…grossly overpaid corporate lawyers.*

형용사 지나치게 많은 보수를 받는 ☐ 엄청나게 많은 보수를 받는 법인 변호사들

over|pass /ouvərpæs/ (**overpasses**) N-COUNT An **overpass** is a structure which carries one road over the top of another one. [mainly AM; BRIT usually **flyover**] ☐ *…a $16 million highway overpass over Route 1.*

가산명사 고가 도로 [주로 미국영어; 영국영어 대개 flyover] ☐ 1번 도로 위로 나 있는 1,600만 불짜리 고속 고가 도로

over|pow|er /oʊvərpaʊər/ (overpowers, overpowering, overpowered) ■ V-T If you **overpower** someone, you manage to take hold of and keep hold of them, although they struggle a lot. ❑ *It took ten guardsmen to overpower him.* ■ V-T If a feeling **overpowers** you, it suddenly affects you very strongly. ❑ *A sudden dizziness overpowered him.* ■ V-T In a sports match, when one team or player **overpowers** the other, they play much better than them and beat them easily. ❑ *Britain's tennis No 1 yesterday overpowered American Brian Garrow 7-6, 6-3.* ■ V-T If something such as a color or flavor **overpowers** another color or flavor, it is so strong that it makes the second one less noticeable. ❑ *A delicate wine will be overpowered by strong food.*

■ 타동사 제압하다 ❑ 그를 제압하는 데 열 명의 근위병이 필요했다. ■ 타동사 압도하다, 강하게 밀려오다 ❑ 그는 갑자기 현기증이 밀려왔다. ■ 타동사 제압하다, ❑ 영국 테니스 일인자는 어제 미국의 브라이언 개로우를 7-6, 6-3으로 제압했다. ■ 타동사 압도하다 ❑ 맛이 강한 음식에는 섬세한 와인의 풍미가 살아나지 못할 수도 있다.

over|pow|er|ing /oʊvərpaʊərɪŋ/ ■ ADJ An **overpowering** feeling is so strong that you cannot resist it. ❑ *The desire for revenge can be overpowering.* ■ ADJ An **overpowering** smell or sound is so strong that you cannot smell or hear anything else. ❑ *There was an overpowering smell of alcohol.* ■ ADJ An **overpowering** person makes other people feel uncomfortable because they have such a strong personality. ❑ *Mrs. Winter was large and somewhat overpowering.*

■ 형용사 강렬한, 억제할 수 없는 ❑ 복수의 욕구는 저항할 수 없을 정도로 강렬할 수도 있다. ■ 형용사 (냄새나 소리가) 강렬한 ❑ 알코올 냄새가 진동했다. ■ 형용사 위압적인 ❑ 윈터 여사는 체구가 컸고 좀 위압적이었다.

over|priced /oʊvərpraɪst/ ADJ If you say that something is **overpriced**, you mean that you think it costs much more than it should. ❑ *I went and had an overpriced cup of coffee in the hotel cafeteria.*

형용사 터무니없이 비싼 ❑ 나는 호텔 카페테리아에 가서 터무니없이 비싼 커피를 한 잔 마셨다.

over|ran /oʊvərræn/ Overran is the past tense of **overrun**.

overrun의 과거

over|rate /oʊvərreɪt/ (overrates, overrating, overrated) also **over-rate** V-T If you say that something or someone **is overrated**, you mean that people have a higher opinion of them than they deserve. ❑ *More men are finding out that the joys of work have been overrated.* ● **over|rat|ed** ADJ ❑ *Life in the wild is vastly overrated.*

타동사 과대평가하다 ❑ 일하는 기쁨이 과대평가되어 왔었다는 것을 더 많은 사람들이 깨닫고 있다. ● 과대평가된 형용사 ❑ 자연 속에서의 삶은 엄청나게 과대평가되어 있다.

over|react /oʊvərriækt/ (overreacts, overreacting, overreacted) also **over-react** V-I If you say that someone **overreacts to** something, you mean that they have and show more of an emotion than is necessary or appropriate. ❑ *I overreact to anything sad.*

자동사 과민 반응을 보이다 ❑ 나는 뭔든 슬픈 일에는 과민 반응을 하게 된다.

over|ride (overrides, overriding, overrode, overridden)

> The spelling **over-ride** is also used. The verb is pronounced /oʊvəraɪd/. The noun is pronounced /oʊvəraɪd/.

> 철자 over-ride도 쓴다. 동사는 /oʊvəraɪd /, 명사는 /oʊvəraɪd /로 발음된다.

■ V-T If one thing in a situation **overrides** other things, it is more important than them. ❑ *The welfare of a child should always override the wishes of its parents.* ■ V-T If someone in authority **overrides** a person or their decisions, they cancel their decisions. ❑ *The president vetoed the bill, and the Senate failed by a single vote to override his veto.* ■ N-COUNT An **override** is an attempt to cancel someone's decisions by using your authority over them or by gaining more votes than them in an election or contest. [AM] ❑ *The bill now goes to the House where an override vote is expected to fail.*

■ 타동사 더 중요하다, 우선하다 ❑ 아이들의 행복이 항상 부모들의 바람보다 항상 우선해야 한다. ■ 타동사 무효화하다 ❑ 대통령이 그 법안에 대해 거부권을 행사했는데, 상원에서는 한 표 차로 대통령의 거부권 무효화에 실패했다. ■ 가산명사 무효화 [미국영어] ❑ 그 법안은 지금 의회에 상정되어 있는데 의회에서의 무효투표는 부결될 것으로 보인다.

over|rid|ing /oʊvərraɪdɪŋ/ ADJ In a particular situation, the **overriding** factor is the one that is the most important. ❑ *My overriding concern is to raise the standards of state education.*

형용사 제일 중요한 ❑ 저의 최우선의 관심사는 국가 교육 수준을 향상시키는 것입니다.

over|rule /oʊvərrul/ (overrules, overruling, overruled) V-T If someone in authority **overrules** a person or their decision, they officially decide that the decision is incorrect or not valid. ❑ *In 1991, the Court of Appeal overruled this decision.*

타동사 기각하다 ❑ 1991년에 고등 법원은 이 결정을 기각했다.

over|run /oʊvərrʌn/ (overruns, overrunning, overran) ■ V-T If an army or an armed force **overruns** a place, area, or country, it succeeds in occupying it very quickly. ❑ *A group of rebels overran the port area and most of the northern suburbs.* ■ ADJ If you say that a place is **overrun with** things that you consider undesirable, you mean that there are a large number of them there. [v-link ADJ, usu ADJ with/by n] ❑ *The Hotel has been ordered to close because it is overrun by mice and rats.* ■ V-T/V-I If an event or meeting **overruns** by, for example, ten minutes, it continues for ten minutes longer than it was intended to. ❑ *Tuesday's lunch overran by three-quarters of an hour.* ■ V-T/V-I If costs **overrun**, they are higher than was planned or expected. [BUSINESS] ❑ *We should stop the nonsense of taxpayers trying to finance joint weapons whose costs always overrun hugely.* ❑ *Costs overran the budget by about 30%.* ● N-COUNT **Overrun** is also a noun. ❑ *He was stunned to discover cost overruns of at least $1 billion.*

■ 타동사 신속히 장악하다 ❑ 한 무리의 반군이 항구 지역과 북부 교외 지역 대부분을 신속하게 장악했다. ■ 형용사 득실거리는, 들끓는 ❑ 그 호텔은 쥐가 득실거려 폐쇄 명령을 받았다. ■ 타동사/자동사 예정보다 길어지다 ❑ 화요일의 점심은 예정보다 45분 길어졌다. ■ 타동사/자동사 초과하다 [경제] ❑ 비용을 예산보다 약 30퍼센트 정도 초과했다. ● 가산명사 초과 ❑ 그는 비용이 최소 10억 불이나 초과된 것을 보고 기절할 뻔했다.

over|seas ♦◊◊ /oʊvərsiz/ ■ ADJ You use **overseas** to describe things that involve or are in foreign countries, usually across a sea or an ocean. [ADJ n] ❑ *He has returned to South Africa from his long overseas trip.* ● ADV **Overseas** is also an adverb. ❑ *If you're staying for more than three months or working overseas, a full 10-year passport is required.* ■ ADJ An **overseas** student or visitor comes from a foreign country, usually across a sea or an ocean. [ADJ n] ❑ *Every year nine million overseas visitors come to London.*

■ 형용사 해외의 ❑ 그는 오랜 해외여행을 마치고 남아프리카 공화국으로 돌아왔다. ● 부사 해외로, 해외에서 ❑ 당신이 해외에서 3개월 이상 체류하거나 일하시려면, 10년 기한의 여권이 필요합니다. ■ 형용사 외국에서 온 ❑ 매년 9백만 명의 외국 방문객이 런던에 온다.

over|see /oʊvərsi/ (oversees, overseeing, oversaw, overseen) V-T If someone in authority **oversees** a job or an activity, they make sure that it is done properly. ❑ *Use a surveyor or architect to oversee and inspect the different stages of the work.*

타동사 감독하다 ❑ 조사관이나 건축가를 시켜서 작업의 각각 다른 단계들을 감독하고 감찰하세요.

over|shad|ow /oʊvərʃædoʊ/ (overshadows, overshadowing, overshadowed) ■ V-T If an unpleasant event or feeling **overshadows** something, it makes it less happy or enjoyable. ❑ *Fears for the President's safety could overshadow his peace-making mission.* ■ V-T If you **are overshadowed by** a person or thing, you are less successful, important, or impressive than they are. [usu passive] ❑ *Hester is overshadowed by her younger and more attractive sister.* ■ V-T If one building, tree, or large structure **overshadows** another, it stands near it, is much taller than it, and casts a shadow over it. ❑ *She said stations should be in the open, near housing, not overshadowed by trees or walls.*

■ 타동사 그늘을 드리우다 ❑ 대통령의 신변 안전에 대한 우려가 대통령의 평화 구현 임무에 그늘을 드리울 수도 있다. ■ 타동사 빛을 잃다 ❑ 헤스터는 더 매력적인 여동생 때문에 빛을 잃는다. ■ 타동사 그늘지게 하다 ❑ 그녀는, 정류장은 주택가와 가깝고 나무나 담 때문에 그늘이 지지 않는 트인 곳에 위치해야 한다고 말했다.

over|sight /oʊvərsaɪt/ (oversights) N-COUNT If there has been an **oversight**, someone has forgotten to do something which they should have done. ❑ *William was angered and embarrassed by his oversight.*

가산명사 깜빡 잊고 안 함 ❑ 윌리엄은 그의 실수에 화가 나고 난처했다.

over|spend (overspends, overspending, overspent)

> The verb is pronounced /ˌoʊvərˈspɛnd/. The noun is pronounced /ˈoʊvərspɛnd/.

> 동사는 /ˌoʊvərˈspɛnd/로 발음되고, 명사는 /ˈoʊvərspɛnd/로 발음된다.

1 V-I If you **overspend**, you spend more money than you can afford to. ❑ Don't overspend on your home and expect to get the money back when you sell. ❑ I overspent by £1 on your shopping so I'm afraid you owe me. **2** N-COUNT If an organization or business has an **overspend**, it spends more money than was planned or allowed in its budget. [BRIT, BUSINESS; AM **overrun**] ❑ Efforts are under way to avoid a £800,000 overspend.

1 자동사 지나치게 돈을 쓰다 ❑ 집에 지나치게 돈을 들이고는, 집을 팔 때 그 돈을 다 받을 거라고 기대하지 마세요.. ❑ 내가 너의 물건을 사는 데 1파운드를 더 썼거든. 그래서 네가 그 돈을 나한테 줘야 할 것 같은데. **2** 가산명사 초과 지출 [영국영어, 경제; 미국영어 overrun] ❑ 80만 파운드의 초과 지출을 피하기 위한 노력이 진행 중이다.

over|state /ˌoʊvərˈsteɪt/ (overstates, overstating, overstated) V-T If you say that someone **is overstating** something, you mean they are describing it in a way that makes it seem more important or serious than it really is. ❑ The authors no doubt overstated their case with a view to catching the public's attention.

타동사 과장하다 ❑ 그 작가들이 대중의 관심을 끌려고 그들의 사건을 과장한 것이 틀림없었다.

overt /oʊˈvɜrt/ ADJ An **overt** action or attitude is done or shown in an open and obvious way. ❑ Although there is no overt hostility, black and white students do not mix much. ● **overt|ly** ADV ❑ He's written a few overtly political lyrics over the years.

형용사 공공연한, 명백한 ❑ 공공연한 적대 행위는 없지만 흑백 학생들은 같이 잘 안 어울린다. ● 공공연히, 명백하게 부사 ❑ 그는 몇 해 동안 공공연히 정치적인 시를 여러 편 썼다.

over|take /ˌoʊvərˈteɪk/ (overtakes, overtaking, overtook, overtaken) **1** V-T If someone or something **overtakes** a competitor, they become more successful than them. ❑ Lung cancer has now overtaken breast cancer as a cause of death for women in the U.S. **2** V-T If a feeling **overtakes** you, it affects you very strongly. [LITERARY] ❑ Something like panic overtook me in a flood. **3** V-T/V-I If you **overtake** a vehicle or a person that is ahead of you and moving in the same direction, you pass them. [mainly BRIT; AM usually **pass**] ❑ When he eventually overtook the last truck he pulled over to the inside lane.

1 타동사 앞지르다 ❑ 지금 미국에서 여성 사망 원인 중 폐암이 차지하는 비율이 유방암을 앞질렀다. **2** 타동사 사로잡다 [문예체] ❑ 공포심 같은 게 물밀듯이 밀려와 나를 사로잡았다. **3** 타동사/자동사 추월하다 [주로 영국영어; 미국영어 대개 pass] ❑ 그는 마침내 마지막 트럭을 추월하고는 바깥쪽 차선으로 가서 차를 세웠다.

over|throw (overthrows, overthrowing, overthrew, overthrown)

> The verb is pronounced /ˌoʊvərˈθroʊ/. The noun is pronounced /ˈoʊvərθroʊ/.

> 동사는 /ˌoʊvərˈθroʊ/로 발음되고, 명사는 /ˈoʊvərθroʊ/로 발음된다.

V-T When a government or leader **is overthrown**, they are removed from power by force. ❑ That government was overthrown in a military coup three years ago. ● N-SING **Overthrow** is also a noun. ❑ They were charged with plotting the overthrow of the state.

타동사 타도되다, 축출되다, 전복되다 ❑ 그 정부는 삼 년 전에 군사 쿠데타로 전복되었다. ● 단수명사 타도, 축출, 전복 ❑ 그들은 국가 전복 음모를 꾸민 혐의로 기소되었다.

over|time /ˈoʊvərtaɪm/ **1** N-UNCOUNT **Overtime** is time that you spend doing your job in addition to your normal working hours. ❑ He would work overtime, without pay, to finish a job.

1 불가산명사 초과 근무 ❑ 그는 일을 마치기 위해 수당을 안 받고 초과 근무를 할 것이다.

> A salaried worker is paid for a standard number of hours each month. When he or she works **overtime**, instead of additional money the worker is allowed to take time off from the job to compensate for the extra time worked. This is called **comp time** in the US, and **time off in lieu** in the UK.

> 봉급을 받는 근로자는 매달 표준 근무시간에 준해 급료를 받는다. overtime(초과 근무)를 하면 근로자는 돈을 더 받는 대신 그 시간에 해당하는 시간만큼 일을 하지 않아도 되는데 이를 미국에서는 comp time, 영국에서는 time off in lieu라고 한다.

2 PHRASE If you say that someone **is working overtime** to do something, you mean that they are using a lot of energy, effort, or enthusiasm trying to do it. [INFORMAL] ❑ We had to battle very hard and our defense worked overtime to keep us in the game.

2 구 열정적으로 일하다 [비격식체] ❑ 우리는 정말 열심히 싸워야 했고 우리 수비수들은 경기를 지켜 내려고 열심히 뛰었다.

over|tone /ˈoʊvərtoʊn/ (overtones) N-COUNT If something has **overtones of** a particular thing or quality, it suggests that thing or quality but does not openly express it. ❑ The strike has taken on overtones of a civil rights campaign.

가산명사 함축 ❑ 그 파업은 인권 운동의 성격도 함축하고 있다.

over|took /ˌoʊvərˈtʊk/ **Overtook** is the past tense of **overtake**.

overtake의 과거

over|ture /ˈoʊvərtʃər, -tʃʊər/ (overtures) N-COUNT; N-IN-NAMES An **overture** is a piece of music, often one that is the introduction to an opera or play. ❑ ...Wagner's Mastersingers Overture.

가산명사; 이름명사 서곡 ❑ 바그너의 마스터싱어스 서곡

over|turn /ˌoʊvərˈtɜrn/ (overturns, overturning, overturned) **1** V-T/V-I If something **overturns** or if you **overturn** it, it turns upside down or on its side. ❑ The lorry veered out of control, overturned and smashed into a wall. ❑ Alex jumped up so violently that he overturned his glass of sherry. **2** V-T If someone in authority **overturns** a legal decision, they officially decide that that decision is incorrect or not valid. ❑ When the Russian parliament overturned his decision, he backed down. **3** V-T To **overturn** a government or system means to remove it or destroy it. ❑ He accused his opponents of wanting to overturn the government.

1 타동사/자동사 뒤집히다; 뒤집다 ❑ 그 트럭이 갑자기 중심을 잃고 뒤집히면서 담을 들이받았다. ❑ 알렉스가 너무 거칠게 벌떡 일어서는 바람에 셰리주 잔이 엎어졌다. **2** 타동사 번복하다, 뒤엎다 ❑ 러시아 의회가 그의 결정을 기각했을 때, 그는 자기주장을 굽혔다. **3** 타동사 전복시키다 ❑ 그는 자기 반대자들이 정부 전복을 원하고 있다고 비난했다.

over|view /ˈoʊvərvyu/ (overviews) N-COUNT An **overview of** a situation is a general understanding or description of it as a whole. ❑ The central section of the book is a historical overview of drug use.

가산명사 개관, 개요 ❑ 이 책의 중심 부분은 마약 사용에 대한 역사적 개관이다.

over|weight /ˌoʊvərˈweɪt/ ADJ Someone who is **overweight** weighs more than is considered healthy or attractive. ❑ Being even moderately overweight increases your risk of developing high blood pressure. →see fat, diet

형용사 과체중의 ❑ 약간의 과체중도 고혈압을 유발할 위험을 증가시킨다.

over|whelm /ˌoʊvərˈwɛlm/ (overwhelms, overwhelming, overwhelmed) **1** V-T If you **are overwhelmed by** a feeling or event, it affects you very strongly, and you do not know how to deal with it. ❑ He was overwhelmed by a longing for times past. ● **over|whelmed** ADJ ❑ Sightseers may be a little overwhelmed by the crowds and noise. **2** V-T If a group of people **overwhelm** a place or another group, they gain complete control or victory over them. ❑ It was clear that one massive Allied offensive would overwhelm the weakened enemy.

1 타동사 -에서 헤어나지 못하다, -에 어쩔 줄 모르다 ❑ 그는 지난 시절에 대한 그리움에 빠져 있었다. ● 어쩔 줄 몰라 하는, 당황하는 형용사 ❑ 유람객들이 너무 많은 사람들과 소음에 당황할 수 있다. **2** 타동사 제압하다 ❑ 연합군의 대대적인 공세 한 번이면 약해진 적군을 제압할 수 있다는 것은 자명했다.

over|whelm|ing ♦◇◇ /ˌoʊvərˈwɛlmɪŋ/ **1** ADJ If something is **overwhelming**, it affects you very strongly, and you do not know how to deal with it. ❑ The task won't feel so overwhelming if you break it down into small, easy-to-accomplish steps. ● **over|whelm|ing|ly** ADV ❑ ...the overwhelmingly strange medieval city of Fès. **2** ADJ You can use **overwhelming** to emphasize that an amount or quantity is much greater than other amounts or quantities. [EMPHASIS] ❑ The overwhelming majority of small businesses go broke within the first twenty-four months.

1 형용사 난감한 ❑ 하기 쉽게 여러 작은 단계로 나눠 보면 그 과제가 그렇게 난감하게 느껴지지는 않을 거야. ● 난감할 정도로 부사 ❑ 난감할 정도로 이상한 중세 도시 페스 **2** 형용사 압도적인 [강조] ❑ 소규모 사업체의 압도적 다수가 창업 후 첫 24개월 안에 파산한다. ● 압도적으로 부사 ❑ 하원이 살인범에 대한 사형 재도입 요청을 압도적인 표차로 거부했다.

● **over|whelm|ing|ly** ADV ❏ *The House of Commons has overwhelmingly rejected calls to bring back the death penalty for murder.*

Word Partnership overwhelming의 연어

N. overwhelming **desire**, overwhelming **response**, overwhelming **responsibility** ❶ ❷
overwhelming **approval**, overwhelming **force**, overwhelming **majority**, overwhelming **odds**, overwhelming **support**, overwhelming **victory** ❷

---

over|work /oʊvərwɜrk/ (**overworks, overworking, overworked**) V-T/V-I If you **overwork** or if someone **overworks** you, you work too hard, and are likely to become very tired or ill. ❏ *He's overworking and has got a lot on his mind.* ● N-UNCOUNT **Overwork** is also a noun. ❏ *He died of a heart attack brought on by overwork.* ● **over|worked** ADJ ❏ *...an overworked doctor.*

타동사/자동사 과로하다; 혹사시키다 ❏ 그는 과로를 하고 있고 많은 심적 부담을 지고 있다. ● 불가산명사 과로 ❏ 그는 과로로 인한 심장 마비로 사망했다. ● 혹사당하는 형용사 ❏ 혹사당하는 의사

over|worked /oʊvərwɜrkt/ ADJ If you describe a word, expression, or idea as **overworked**, you mean it has been used so often that it no longer has much effect or meaning. ❏ *"Ecological" has become one of the most overworked adjectives among manufacturers of garden supplies.*

형용사 식상한 ❏ '생태적'이란 말은 정원용 물품 생산자들 사이에서는 가장 식상한 형용사 중 하나가 되었다.

ovu|late /ɒvyəleɪt, oʊv-/ (**ovulates, ovulating, ovulated**) V-I When a woman or female animal **ovulates**, an egg is produced from one of her ovaries. ❏ *Some girls may first ovulate even before they menstruate.* ● **ovu|la|tion** /ɒvyəleɪʃʰn, oʊv-/ N-UNCOUNT ❏ *By noticing these changes, the woman can tell when ovulation is about to occur.*

자동사 배란하다 ❏ 어떤 여자 애들은 생리 전에 첫 배란을 하는 경우도 있다. ● 배란 불가산명사 ❏ 이런 변화들을 눈여겨봄으로써, 여자는 언제 배란이 시작되는지 알 수 있다.

ow /aʊ/ EXCLAM "Ow!" is used in writing to represent the noise that people make when they suddenly feel pain. ❏ *Ow! Don't do that!*

감탄사 아야 ❏ 아야! 그렇게 하지 마.

owe ♦♢♢ /oʊ/ (**owes, owing, owed**) ❶ V-T/V-I If you **owe** money **to** someone, they have lent it to you and you have not yet paid it back. You can also say that the money **is owing**. ❏ *The company owes money to more than 60 banks.* ❏ *Blake already owed him nearly £50.* ❷ V-T If someone or something **owes** a particular quality or their success **to** a person or thing, they only have it because of that person or thing. [no passive] ❏ *I always suspected she owed her first job to her friendship with Roger.* ❏ *He owed his survival to his strength as a swimmer.* ❸ V-T If you say that you **owe** a great deal **to** someone or something, you mean that they have helped you or influenced you a lot, and you feel very grateful to them. ❏ *As a professional composer I owe much to Radio 3.* ❹ V-T If you say that something **owes** a great deal to a person or thing, you mean that it exists, is successful, or has its particular form mainly because of them. ❏ *The island's present economy owes a good deal to whisky distilling.* ❺ V-T If you say that you **owe** someone gratitude, respect, or loyalty, you mean that they deserve it from you. [FORMAL] ❏ *Perhaps we owe these people more respect.* ❏ *I owe you an apology. You must have found my attitude very annoying.* ❻ V-T If you say that you **owe it to** someone to do something, you mean that you should do that thing because they deserve it. [no passive] ❏ *I can't go. I owe it to him to stay.* ❏ *You owe it to yourself to get some professional help.* ❼ PHRASE You use **owing to** when you are introducing the reason for something. ❏ *Owing to staff shortages, there was no restaurant car on the train.*

❶ 타동사/자동사 빚을 지다, 부채가 있다 ❏ 그 회사는 60개가 넘는 은행에 부채가 있다 ❏ 블레이크는 이미 그에게 거의 50파운드의 빚이 있었다. ❷ 타동사 덕분이다 ❏ 나는 항상 그녀가 첫 직장을 얻은 것은 로저와의 친분 덕분이 아닌가라고 생각했다. ❏ 그가 살아남은 것은 뛰어난 수영 실력 덕분이었다. ❸ 타동사 신세를 지다 ❏ 전문 작곡가인 나는 라디오 3의 신세를 많이 지고 있다. ❹ 타동사 - 덕분이다 ❏ 그 섬의 현 경제는 위스키 제조 덕을 크게 보고 있다. ❺ 타동사 -을 표해야 한다 [격식체] ❏ 아마 우리가 이 사람들을 더 존중해야 마땅할 것이다. ❏ 너한테 사과할 게 있어. 넌 아마 내 태도에 화가 많이 났었겠지. ❻ 타동사 -해야 하다 ❏ 난 갈 수 없어. 그에 대한 도리상 여기 있어야 해. ❏ 넌 전문가의 도움을 좀 받아야 될 것 같아. ❼ 구 -때문에 ❏ 직원이 부족해서 그 기차에는 식당차가 없었다.

Word Partnership owe의 연어

N. owe **money** ❶
owe **a great deal to** *someone* ❸
owe *someone* **an apology** ❺

---

owl /aʊl/ (**owls**) N-COUNT An **owl** is a bird with a flat face, large eyes, and a small sharp beak. Most owls obtain their food by hunting small animals at night.

가산명사 올빼미

own ♦♦♦ /oʊn/ (**owns, owning, owned**) ❶ ADJ You use **own** to indicate that something belongs to a particular person or thing. [poss ADJ] ❏ *My wife decided I should have my own shop.* ❏ *He could no longer trust his own judgement.* ● PRON **Own** is also a pronoun. [poss PRON] ❏ *He saw the Major's face a few inches from his own.* ❷ ADJ You use **own** to indicate that something is used by, or is characteristic of, only one person, thing, or group. [poss ADJ] ❏ *Jennifer insisted on her own room.* ❏ *Each nation has its own peculiarities when it comes to doing business.* ● PRON **Own** is also a pronoun. [poss PRON] ❏ *This young lady has a sense of style that is very much her own.* ❸ ADJ You use **own** to indicate that someone does something without any help from other people. [poss ADJ] ❏ *They enjoy making their own decisions.* ● PRON **Own** is also a pronoun. [poss PRON] ❏ *There's no career structure, you have to create your own.* ❹ V-T If you **own** something, it is your property. ❏ *His father owns a local pub.* ❺ PHRASE If you have something you can **call** your **own**, it belongs only to you, rather than being controlled by or shared with someone else. ❏ *I would like a place I could call my own.* ❻ PHRASE If someone or something **comes into** their **own**, they become very successful or start to perform very well because the circumstances are right. ❏ *The goalkeeper came into his own with a series of brilliant saves.* ❼ PHRASE If you **get** your **own back** on someone, you have your revenge on them because of something bad that they have done to you. [mainly BRIT, INFORMAL] ❏ *Renshaw reveals 20 bizarre ways in which women have got their own back on former loved ones.* ❽ PHRASE If you say that someone has a particular thing **of** their **own**, you mean that that thing belongs or relates to them, rather than to other people. ❏ *He set out in search of ideas for starting a company of his own.* ❾ PHRASE If someone or something has a particular quality or characteristic **of** their **own**, that quality or characteristic is especially theirs, rather than being shared by other things or people of that type. ❏ *The cries of the seagulls gave this part of the harbour a fascinating character all of its own.* ❿ PHRASE When you are **on** your **own**, you are alone. ❏ *He lives on his own.* ❏ *I felt quite lonely last year*

❶ 형용사 자기 자신의 ❏ 내가 내 가게를 가져야 한다고 아내가 결정했다. ❏ 그는 더 이상 자기 자신의 판단력을 신뢰할 수 없었다. ● 대명사 자기 자신의 것 ❏ 바로 메이저 수상의 얼굴이 그의 코앞에 있었다. ❷ 형용사 자기만의 ❏ 제니퍼는 자기 방을 갖게 해 달라고 졸랐다. ❏ 각 나라는 사업을 할 때 자기만의 특색이 있다. ❸ 대명사 자기만의 것 ❏ 이 아가씨는 자기 자신만의 스타일 감각을 가지고 있다. ❸ 형용사 스스로 하는 ❏ 그들은 스스로 결정하기를 좋아한다. ● 대명사 스스로 하는 것 ❏ 경력을 쌓아 가는 데 틀이 따로 없으니까, 네가 알아서 만들어 가야 돼. ❹ 타동사 소유하다 ❏ 그의 아버지는 지역에 술집을 하나 갖고 계신다. ❺ 구 자신만의 것으로 삼다 ❏ 나는 나만을 위한 장소를 원한다. ❻ 구 진가를 발휘하다 ❏ 그 골키퍼는 계속해서 멋지게 골을 막아 내면서 진가를 발휘했다. ❼ 구 복수하다 [주로 영국영어, 비격식체] ❏ 렌쇼는 여자들이 전 애인에게 복수하는 20가지 엽기적인 방법을 공개한다. ❽ 구 자신만의 ❏ 그는 자기 회사를 시작하기 위해 아이디어를 찾는 데 착수했다. ❾ 구 -만의 독특한 ❏ 갈매기 울음소리가 이 항구만의 독특한 정취를 만들어 내고 있었다. ❿ 구 혼자 ❏ 그는 혼자 산다. ❏ 작년에 나 혼자였을 때 나는 상당히 외로웠다. ⓫ 구 혼자서 ❏ 나는 혼자서 일할 때 가장 잘 한다.

being on my own. **11** PHRASE If you do something **on** your **own**, you do it without any help from other people. ❑ *I work best on my own.* **12** to **hold** your **own** →see **hold**

Thesaurus   own의 참조어

| ADJ. | individual, personal, private **1** **2** |
| V. | have, possess **4** |

▶**own up** PHRASAL VERB If you **own up** to something wrong that you have done, you admit that you did it. ❑ *The headmaster is waiting for someone to own up.*

own brand (**own brands**) N-COUNT **Own brands** are products which have the trademark or label of the store which sells them, especially a supermarket chain. They are normally cheaper than other popular brands. [BUSINESS] ❑ *This range is substantially cheaper than any of the other own brands available.*

own|er ♦♦◇ /ˈoʊnər/ (**owners**) N-COUNT The **owner** of something is the person to whom it belongs. ❑ *The owner of the store was sweeping his floor when I walked in.*

own|er|ship ♦◇◇ /ˈoʊnərʃɪp/ N-UNCOUNT **Ownership** of something is the state of owning it. ❑ *On January 23rd, America decided to relax its rules on the foreign ownership of its airlines.* ❑ *...the growth of home ownership in Britain.*

own la|bel (**own labels**) N-COUNT **Own label** is the same as **own brand**. [BUSINESS] ❑ *People will trade down to own labels which are cheaper.*

ox /ɒks/ (**oxen**) /ˈɒksən/ N-COUNT An **ox** is a bull that has been castrated. Oxen are used in some countries for pulling vehicles or carrying things.

oxy|gen /ˈɒksɪdʒən/ N-UNCOUNT **Oxygen** is a colorless gas that exists in large quantities in the air. All plants and animals need oxygen in order to live. ❑ *The human brain needs to be without oxygen for only four minutes before permanent damage occurs.* →see **earth**, **respiratory**

oys|ter /ˈɔɪstər/ (**oysters**) **1** N-COUNT An **oyster** is a large flat shellfish. Some oysters can be eaten and others produce valuable objects called pearls. ❑ *He had two dozen oysters and enjoyed every one of them.* **2** PHRASE If you say that **the world is** someone's **oyster**, you mean that they can do anything or go anywhere that they want to. ❑ *You're young, you've got a lot of opportunity. The world is your oyster.*

oz **Oz** is a written abbreviation for **ounce**. ❑ *Whisk 25g (1 oz) of butter into the sauce.*

ozone /ˈoʊzoʊn/ N-UNCOUNT **Ozone** is a colorless gas which is a form of oxygen. There is a layer of ozone high above the earth's surface. ❑ *What they find could provide clues to what might happen worldwide if ozone depletion continues.*

ozone-friendly ADJ **Ozone-friendly** chemicals, products, or technology do not cause harm to the ozone layer. ❑ *...ozone-friendly chemicals for fridges and air conditioners.*

ozone lay|er N-SING The **ozone layer** is the part of the Earth's atmosphere that has the most ozone in it. The ozone layer protects living things from the harmful radiation of the sun. ❑ *...the hole in the ozone layer.*

구동사 자백하다, 인정하다 ❑ 교장은 누군가가 자백하기를 기다리고 있다.

가산명사 자사 상표 제품 [경제] ❑ 이 레인지는 시중에 있는 다른 자사 상표 제품보다 상당히 더 싸다.

가산명사 주인 ❑ 그 가게 주인은 내가 들어갔을 때 바닥을 쓸고 있었다.

불가산명사 소유, 소유권 ❑ 1월 23일에 미국은 외국인의 항공사 소유권에 관한 규정을 완화하기로 결정했다. ❑ 영국에서의 주택 소유의 증가

가산명사 자사 상표 제품 [경제] ❑ 사람들은 더 값이 싼 자사 상표 제품을 고를 것이다.

가산명사 (거세한) 수소, 황소

불가산명사 산소 ❑ 4분 동안만 산소 공급이 되지 않아도 인간의 두뇌는 영구 손상을 입는다.

1 가산명사 굴 ❑ 그는 굴 24개를 하나하나 아주 맛있게 먹었다. **2** 구 원하는 것은 무엇이든 할 수 있다 ❑ 자네는 젊고 기회도 많이 있잖아. 자넨 원하는 것은 무엇이든 할 수 있어.

온스의 약어 ❑ 버터 25그램(1온스)을 소스에 넣고 휘저으세요.

불가산명사 오존 ❑ 그들의 발견은 만약 오존층 파괴가 계속된다면 전 세계적으로 어떤 일이 발생할지에 대한 단서를 제공할 수도 있다.

형용사 오존 친화적인 ❑ 냉장고나 에어컨에 쓰일 오존 친화적인 화학 물질

단수명사 오존층 ❑ 오존층에 난 구멍

Pp

P, p /piː/ (P's, p's) N-VAR P is the sixteenth letter of the English alphabet.

PA /piː eɪ/ (PAs) **1** N-COUNT A **PA** is the same as a **personal assistant**. [BUSINESS] **2** N-COUNT If you refer to the **PA** or the **PA system** in a place, you are referring to the public address system. [usu the N in sing] ❑ *A voice came booming over the PA.*

p.a. **p.a.** is a written abbreviation for **per annum**. ❑ *...dentists with an average net income of £48,000 p.a.*

pace ♦◇◇ /peɪs/ (paces, pacing, paced) **1** N-SING The **pace** of something is the speed at which it happens or is done. [usu with supp] ❑ *Many people were not satisfied with the pace of change.* ❑ *They could not stand the pace or the workload.* **2** N-SING Your **pace** is the speed at which you walk. [usu with supp] ❑ *He moved at a brisk pace down the rue St Antoine.* **3** N-COUNT A **pace** is the distance that you move when you take one step. [usu with supp] ❑ *He'd only gone a few paces before he stopped again.* **4** V-T/V-I If you **pace** a small area, you keep walking up and down it, because you are anxious or impatient. ❑ *As they waited, Kravis paced the room nervously.* ❑ *He found John pacing around the flat, unable to sleep.* **5** V-T If you **pace yourself** when doing something, you do it at a steady rate. ❑ *It was a tough race and I had to pace myself.* **6** PHRASE If something **keeps pace with** something else that is changing, it changes quickly in response to it. ❑ *Farmers are angry because the rise fails to keep pace with inflation.* **7** PHRASE If you **keep pace with** someone who is walking or running, you succeed in going as fast as them, so that you remain close to them. ❑ *With four laps to go, he kept pace with the leaders.* **8** PHRASE If you do something **at** your **own pace**, you do it at a speed that is comfortable for you. ❑ *The computer will give students the opportunity to learn at their own pace.* **9 at a snail's pace →see snail**

Word Partnership	*pace*의 연어
N.	pace **of change** 1
ADJ.	brisk pace, fast pace, record pace, slow pace 1 2
V.	pick up the pace, set a pace 1 2
	keep pace with *something* 6
	keep pace with *someone* 7

pacifier /pæsɪfaɪər/ (pacifiers) N-COUNT A **pacifier** is a rubber or plastic object that you give to a baby to suck so that he or she feels comforted. [AM; BRIT **dummy**]

pacifism /pæsɪfɪzəm/ N-UNCOUNT **Pacifism** is the belief that war and violence are always wrong. ❑ *...a leading exponent of pacifism.*

pacifist /pæsɪfɪst/ (pacifists) **1** N-COUNT A **pacifist** is someone who believes that violence is wrong and refuses to take part in wars. ❑ *Many protesters insist they are pacifists, opposed to war in all forms.* **2** ADJ If someone has **pacifist** views, they believe that war and violence are always wrong. ❑ *...his mother's pacifist ideals.*

pack ♦♦◇ /pæk/ (packs, packing, packed) **1** V-T/V-I When you **pack** a bag, you put clothes and other things into it, because you are leaving a place or going on vacation. ❑ *When I was 17, I packed my bags and left home.* ❑ *I began to pack a few things for the journey.* ● **packing** N-UNCOUNT ❑ *She left Frances to finish her packing.* **2** V-T When people **pack** things, for example in a factory, they put them into containers or boxes so that they can be transported and sold. ❑ *They offered me a job packing goods in a warehouse.* ❑ *Machines now exist to pack olives in jars.* ● **packing** N-UNCOUNT ❑ *The shipping and packing costs are passed along in the item price.* **3** V-T/V-I If people or things **pack into** a place or if they **pack** a place, there are so many of them that the place is full. ❑ *Hundreds of thousands of people packed into the mosque.* **4** N-COUNT A **pack of** things is a collection of them that is sold or given together in a box or bag. ❑ *The club will send a free information pack.* ❑ *...a pack of cigarettes.* **5** N-COUNT You can refer to a group of people who go around together as a **pack**, especially when it is a large group that you feel threatened by. ❑ *He thus avoided a pack of journalists eager to question him.* **6** N-COUNT A **pack of** wolves or dogs is a group of them that hunt together. ❑ *...a pack of stray dogs.* **7** N-COUNT A **pack of** playing cards is a complete set of playing cards. [mainly BRIT; AM usually **deck**] ❑ *...a pack of cards.* **8 →see also packed, packing 9** PHRASE If you say that an account is **a pack of lies**, you mean that it is completely untrue. ❑ *You told me a pack of lies.* **10** PHRASE If you **send** someone **packing**, you make them go away. [INFORMAL] ❑ *I decided I wanted to live alone and I sent him packing.*

가산명사 또는 불가산명사 영어 알파벳의 열여섯 번째 글자

1 가산명사 개인 비서 [경제] **2** 가산명사 방송 시스템, 확성 장치 ❑ 방송 시스템에서 사람의 목소리가 터져 나왔다.

매년, 연간 ❑ 연간 평균 순수입이 48,000파운드인 치과 의사들

1 단수명사 속도 ❑ 많은 사람들이 변화의 속도에 만족하지 못했다. ❑ 그들은 작업의 속도나 양을 견디지 못했다. **2** 단수명사 걷는 속도 ❑ 그는 성 앙투안 거리를 따라 빨리 걸어갔다. **3** 가산명사 걸음 ❑ 그는 채 몇 걸음도 안 가서 다시 멈췄다. **4** 타동사/자동사 서성거리다 ❑ 그들이 기다리는 동안 크래비스는 방 안에서 불안하게 서성거렸다. ❑ 그는 존이 잠을 못 자고 아파트 안을 서성거리는 것을 보게 되었다. **5** 타동사 속도를 조절하다 ❑ 힘든 경주여서 나는 속도를 조절해야 했다. **6** 구 속도를 맞추다 ❑ 농부들은 가격 인상이 물가 인상률과 보폭을 못 맞추기 때문에 화가 났다. **7** 구 보조를 맞추다 ❑ 네 바퀴가 남은 상태에서 그는 계속 선두 그룹을 유지했다. **8** 구 편한 속도로 ❑ 컴퓨터를 통해 학생들은 자신들에게 편한 속도로 공부할 수 있을 것이다.

가산명사 고무젖꼭지 [미국영어; 영국영어 dummy]

불가산명사 평화주의 ❑ 주도적인 평화주의 옹호자

1 가산명사 평화주의자 ❑ 많은 시위자들이 스스로가 모든 전쟁을 반대하는 평화주의자라고 주장했다. **2** 형용사 평화주의적인 ❑ 그의 어머니의 평화주의적 이상

1 타동사/자동사 싸다 ❑ 나는 열일곱 살 때 짐을 싸 들고 집을 나왔다. ❑ 나는 그 여행을 위해 짐 몇 가지를 싸기 시작했다. ● 짐 꾸리기 불가산명사 ❑ 프랜시스가 짐을 마저 꾸릴 수 있도록 그녀는 자리를 비워 줬다. **2** 타동사 포장하다 ❑ 그들은 창고에서 상품 포장하는 일을 나에게 제안했다. ❑ 이제는 올리브를 병에 넣어 포장하는 기계들이 있다. ● 포장 불가산명사 ❑ 포장 및 배송 비용이 제품 가격에 반영된다. **3** 타동사/자동사 가득 채우다 ❑ 수십만 명이 모스크를 가득 채웠다. **4** 가산명사 다발, 묶음 ❑ 클럽에서 무료 안내 패키지를 보낼 것이다. ❑ 담배 한 갑 **5** 가산명사 패거리 ❑ 그는 그렇게 그에게 질문을 하려고 안달인 기자 무리를 피했다. **6** 가산명사 무리 ❑ 주인 없는 개 한 무리 **7** 가산명사 (카드) 벌 [주로 영국영어; 미국영어 대개 deck] ❑ 카드 한 벌 **8** ● 구 거짓말투성이 ❑ 너는 나에게 온통 거짓말만 했어. **10** 구 내쫓다 [비격식체] ❑ 나는 혼자 살기로 결심했고 그래서 그를 내쫓았다.

pack|age ◆◆◇ /pǽkɪdʒ/ (packages, packaging, packaged) **1** N-COUNT A **package** is something wrapped in paper, in a bag or large envelope, or in a box, usually so that it can be sent to someone by mail. ❑ *I tore open the package.* **2** N-COUNT A **package** is a small container in which a quantity of something is sold. Packages are either small boxes made of thin cardboard, or bags or envelopes made of paper or plastic. [mainly AM; BRIT usually **packet**] ❑ *...a package of doughnuts.* **3** N-COUNT A **package** is a set of proposals that are made by a government or organization and which must be accepted or rejected as a group. ❑ *The government has announced a package of measures to help the British film industry.* **4** V-T When a product **is packaged**, it is put into containers to be sold. [usu passive] ❑ *The beans are then ground and packaged for sale as ground coffee.* **5** V-T If something **is packaged** in a particular way, it is presented or advertised in that way in order to make it seem attractive or interesting. [usu passive] ❑ *A city is like any product, it has to be packaged properly to be attractive to the consumer.* **6** N-COUNT A **package** tour, or in British English a **package** holiday, is a vacation arranged by a travel agency in which your travel and your accommodations are booked for you. ❑ *...package tours to Egypt.*

Thesaurus	*package*의 참조어
N.	batch, bundle, container, parcel **1**

---

1 가산명사 소포, 꾸러미 ❑ 나는 소포를 뜯었다. **2** 가산명사 포장 용기, 상자 [주로 미국영어; 영국영어 대개 packet] ❑ 도넛 한 상자 **3** 가산명사 종합 정책, 일련의 정책 ❑ 정부가 영국 영화 산업을 지원하기 위한 일련의 정책을 발표했다. **4** 타동사 포장되다 ❑ 그 다음 원두를 갈고 포장해서 분말 커피로 판매한다. **5** 타동사 포장되다 ❑ 도시란 상품과 똑같다. 소비자를 끌기 위해서는 제대로 포장을 해야 한다. **6** 가산명사 패키지 ❑ 이집트 패키지 관광

pack|ag|ing /pǽkɪdʒɪŋ/ N-UNCOUNT **Packaging** is the container or covering that something is sold in. ❑ *It is selling very well, in part because the packaging is so attractive.*

불가산명사 포장 ❑ 이것은 아주 잘 팔리는데, 포장이 정말 예뻐서는 것도 그것이 잘 팔리는 이유 중의 하나이다.

packed /pækt/ **1** ADJ A place that is **packed** is very crowded. ❑ *The place is packed at lunchtime.* ❑ *...a packed meeting at Westminster.* **2** ADJ Something that is **packed with** things contains a very large number of them. [v-link ADJ with n] ❑ *The Encyclopedia is packed with clear illustrations and over 250 recipes.*

1 형용사 가득 찬 ❑ 그곳은 점심시간에는 사람들로 가득 찬다. ❑ 웨스트민스터에서 열린 발 디딜 틈 없는 모임 **2** 형용사 ~으로 꽉 찬 ❑ 그 백과사전에는 명료한 그림과 250개 이상의 조리법이 꽉 차 있다.

pack|et /pǽkɪt/ (packets) **1** N-COUNT A **packet** is a small container in which a quantity of something is sold. Packets are either small boxes made of thin cardboard, or bags or envelopes made of paper or plastic. ❑ *...sugar packets.* ● N-COUNT A **packet of** something is an amount of it contained in a packet. [AM usually **pack, package**] ❑ *They also buy a packet of aspirin, just in case.* **2** N-COUNT A **packet** is a small flat package. ❑ *...to send letters and packets abroad.* **3** →see also **pay packet, wage packet**

1 가산명사 작은 통, 봉지 **2** 설탕 봉지 ● 가산명사 한 통, 한 봉지 [미국영어 대개 pack, package] ❑ 만약을 대비해 아스피린 한 통도 샀다. **2** 가산명사 소형 소포 ❑ 편지와 소형 소포를 해외로 보내는 것

pack|ing /pǽkɪŋ/ N-UNCOUNT **Packing** is the paper, plastic, or other material which is put around things that are being sent somewhere. ❑ *My fingers shook as I pulled the packing from the box.* →see also **pack**

불가산명사 패킹 ❑ 상자에서 패킹을 꺼내는 데 손가락이 떨렸다.

pact ◆◇◇ /pækt/ (pacts) N-COUNT A **pact** is a formal agreement between two or more people, organizations, or governments to do a particular thing or to help each other. ❑ *Last month he signed a new non-aggression pact with Germany.*

가산명사 조약 ❑ 지난달 그는 독일과 새로운 불가침 조약을 체결했다.

pad /pæd/ (pads, padding, padded) **1** N-COUNT A **pad** is a fairly thick, flat piece of material such as cloth or rubber. Pads are used, for example, to clean things, to protect things, or to change their shape. ❑ *He withdrew the needle and placed a pad of cotton-wool over the spot.* ❑ *...a scouring pad.* **2** N-COUNT A **pad of** paper is a number of pieces of paper which are fixed together along the top or the side, so that each piece can be torn off when it has been used. ❑ *She wrote on a pad of paper.* ❑ *Have a pad and pencil ready and jot down some of your thoughts.* **3** V-T/V-I When someone **pads** somewhere, they walk there with steps that are fairly quick, light, and quiet. ❑ *Freddy speaks very quietly and pads around in soft velvet slippers.* ❑ *...a dog padding through the streets.* **4** N-COUNT A **pad** is a platform or an area of flat, hard ground where helicopters take off and land or rockets are launched. ❑ *...a little round helicopter pad.* **5** N-COUNT The **pads** of a person's fingers and toes or of an animal's feet are the soft, fleshy parts of them. ❑ *Tap your cheeks all over with the pads of your fingers.* **6** V-T If you **pad** something, you put something soft in it or over it in order to make it less hard, to protect it, or to give it a different shape. ❑ *Pad the back of a car seat with a pillow.* ● **pad|ded** ADJ ❑ *...a padded jacket.* **7** →see also **padding** →see **skateboarding**

1 가산명사 패드 ❑ 그는 바늘을 빼내고 그 자리에 탈지면을 댔다. ❑ 냄비 닦이용 패드 **2** 가산명사 묶음 ❑ 그녀는 묶음 종이 위에다 글을 썼다. ❑ 종이 한 묶음과 연필을 준비하고 자신의 생각을 몇 가지 적으세요. **3** 타동사/자동사 조용히 걷다 ❑ 프레디는 말을 매우 조용히 하며 부드러운 벨벳 슬리퍼를 신고 조용히 돌아다닌다. ❑ 거리를 조용히 돌아다니는 개 한 마리 **4** 가산명사 이착륙장; 발사대 ❑ 작은 원형 헬리콥터 이착륙장 **5** 가산명사 (손가락 등의) 끝, (동물의) 발바닥 ❑ 손가락 끝으로 볼 전체를 가볍게 두드리세요. **6** 타동사 덧대다, 메우다 ❑ 자동차 의자의 뒷면에 베개를 덧대세요. ● 덧댄, 솜을 넣은 형용사 ❑ 솜을 넣은 재킷

▸**pad out** PHRASAL VERB If you **pad out** a piece of writing or a speech **with** unnecessary words or pieces of information, you include them in it to make it longer and hide the fact that you do not have very much to say. ❑ *The reviewer padded out his review with a lengthy biography of the author.*

구동사 내용을 부풀리다, 군더더기를 붙이다 ❑ 평론가는 저자에 대한 장황한 설명을 넣어서 서평의 내용을 부풀렸다.

pad|ding /pǽdɪŋ/ N-UNCOUNT **Padding** is soft material which is put on something or inside it in order to make it less hard, to protect it, or to give it a different shape. ❑ *...the foam rubber padding on the headphones.* ❑ *Players must wear padding to protect them from injury.*

불가산명사 충전물, 완충제 ❑ 헤드폰의 기포 고무 충전물 ❑ 선수들은 부상을 방지하기 위해 보호구를 착용해야 한다.

pad|dle /pǽdl/ (paddles, paddling, paddled) **1** N-COUNT A **paddle** is a short pole with a wide flat part at one end or at both ends. You hold it in your hands and use it as an oar to move a small boat through water. ❑ *We might be able to push ourselves across with the paddle.* **2** V-T/V-I If you **paddle** a boat, you move it through water using a paddle. ❑ *...the skills you will use to paddle the canoe.* **3** V-I If you **paddle**, you walk or stand in shallow water, for example at the edge of the sea, for pleasure. ❑ *Wear sandals when you paddle.* ● N-SING **Paddle** is also a noun. ❑ *Ruth enjoyed her paddle.*

1 가산명사 노 ❑ 노를 저어서 건너편으로 갈 수 있을지도 모른다. **2** 타동사/자동사 노를 젓다 ❑ 카누를 젓기 위해 사용하는 기술들 **3** 자동사 (얕은 물에서) 물장난을 하다 ❑ 물장난을 할 때는 샌들을 신으세요. ● 단수명사 물장난 ❑ 루스는 물장난이 즐거웠다.

pad|dock /pǽdək/ (paddocks) N-COUNT A **paddock** is a small field where horses are kept. ❑ *The family kept horses in the paddock in front of the house.*

가산명사 방목장 ❑ 가족은 말들을 집 앞의 작은 방목장 안에 두었다.

pad|dy /pǽdi/ (paddies) N-COUNT A **paddy** or a **paddy field** is a field that is kept flooded with water and is used for growing rice. ❑ *...the paddy fields of China.*

가산명사 논 ❑ 중국의 논

pad|lock /pǽdlɒk/ (padlocks, padlocking, padlocked) **1** N-COUNT A **padlock** is a lock which is used for fastening two things together. It consists of a block of

1 가산명사 맹꽁이 자물쇠 ❑ 그들은 그의 아파트 문에 맹꽁이 자물쇠를 달았다. **2** 타동사 맹꽁이 자물쇠로

metal with a U-shaped bar attached to it. One end of the bar is released by turning a key in the lock. ❑ *They had put a padlock on the door of his flat.* ❷ V-T If you **padlock** something, you lock it or fasten it to something else using a padlock. ❑ *Eddie parked his cycle against a lamp post and padlocked it.*

참그다 ❑ 에디는 자전거를 가로등에 대고 맹꽁이 자물쇠로 잠갔다.

pae|dia|tri|cian /pi̱diətrɪ̱ʃ°n/ →see pediatrician

pae|di|at|rics /pi̱diæ̱trɪks/ →see pediatrics

pae|do|phile /pi̱dəfaɪl/ →see pedophile

pae|do|philia /pi̱dəfi̱liə/ →see pedophilia

pa|gan /pe̱ɪgən/ (**pagans**) ❶ ADJ **Pagan** beliefs and activities do not belong to any of the main religions of the world and take nature and a belief in many gods as a basis. They are older, or are believed to be older, than other religions. ❑ *The Christian church has adapted many pagan ideas over the centuries.* ❷ N-COUNT In former times, **pagans** were people who did not believe in Christianity and who many Christians considered to be inferior people. ❑ *The pagans used torchlight parades and bonfires to celebrate important events.*

❶ 형용사 이교도의; (주요 종교 외) 토속신앙의 ❑ 기독교는 수세기에 걸쳐 토속신앙의 많은 개념들을 수용했다. ❷ 가산명사 이교도 ❑ 토속 신앙인 ❑ 토속 신앙을 믿는 사람들은 횃불 행렬과 화톳불을 이용하여 중요한 행사를 기념했다.

page ♦♦♦ /pe̱ɪdʒ/ (**pages, paging, paged**) ❶ N-COUNT A **page** is one side of one of the pieces of paper in a book, magazine, or newspaper. Each page usually has a number printed at the top or bottom. ❑ *Where's your book? Take it out and turn to page 4.* ❑ *...the front page of the Guardian.* ❷ N-COUNT The **pages** of a book, magazine, or newspaper are the pieces of paper it consists of. ❑ *He turned the pages of his notebook.* ❸ N-COUNT You can refer to an important event or period of time as a **page** of history. [LITERARY] ❑ *...a new page in the country's political history.* ❹ V-T If someone who is in a public place **is paged**, they receive a message, often over a speaker, telling them that someone is trying to contact them. ❑ *He was paged repeatedly as the flight was boarding.* ❺ N-COUNT A **page** is a young person who takes messages or does small jobs for members of the United States Congress or state legislatures. [AM] →see printing

❶ 가산명사 쪽, 면, 페이지 ❑ 책 어디 있어요? 꺼내서 4페이지를 펴세요. ❷ 가산명사 장 ❑ 그는 자기 노트의 책장을 넘겼다. ❸ 가산명사 장(章) [문예체] ❑ 국가 정치사의 새로운 장 ❹ 타동사 호출을 받다 ❑ 비행기의 탑승이 진행되는 도중에 그는 계속 호출을 받았다. ❺ 가산명사 의원 수행원 [미국영어]

pag|eant /pæ̱dʒənt/ (**pageants**) ❶ N-COUNT A **pageant** is a colorful public procession, show, or ceremony. Pageants are usually held out of doors and often celebrate events or people from history. ❑ *...a historical pageant of Scottish kings and queens.* ❷ N-COUNT A **pageant** or a **beauty pageant** is a competition in which young women are judged to decide which one is the most beautiful. ❑ *...the Miss Universe beauty pageant.*

❶ 가산명사 행렬; 야외극 ❑ 스코틀랜드 역사 속의 왕과 여왕들이 등장하는 야외극 ❷ 가산명사 미인 대회 ❑ 미스 유니버스 대회

pag|er /pe̱ɪdʒər/ (**pagers**) N-COUNT A **pager** is a small electronic device which you can carry around with you and which gives you a number or a message when someone is trying to contact you. [mainly BRIT; AM usually **beeper**] ❑ *Scores of messages on his pager have not been answered.*

가산명사 호출기 [주로 영국영어; 미국영어 대개 beeper] ❑ 그의 호출기에 수없이 메시지를 남겼는데 응답이 없다.

paid /pe̱ɪd/ ❶ **Paid** is the past tense and past participle of **pay**. ❷ ADJ **Paid** workers, or people who do **paid** work, receive money for the work that they do. [ADJ n] ❑ *Apart from a small team of paid staff, the organization consists of unpaid volunteers.* ❸ ADJ If you are given **paid** vacation, you get your wages or salary even though you are not at work. [ADJ n] ❑ *He agreed to hire her at slightly over minimum wage with two weeks paid vacation.* ❹ ADJ If you are well **paid**, you receive a lot of money for the work that you do. If you are badly **paid**, you do not receive much money. [adv ADJ] ❑ *...a well-paid accountant.* ❑ *Travel and tourism employees in the UK are among the worst paid in the developed world.*

❶ pay의 과거 및 과거 분사 ❷ 형용사 유급의 ❑ 그 기구는 소규모의 유급 직원들을 제외하고는 무급 봉사자들로 구성되어 있다. ❸ 형용사 유급의 ❑ 그는 그녀를 2주간의 유급 휴가와 최저 임금보다 약간 높은 월급을 주고 채용하기로 동의했다. ❹ 형용사 보수를 받는 ❑ 좋은 보수를 받는 회계사 ❑ 영국의 여행 및 관광 업계 종사자들은 선진국들 가운데에서 보수를 가장 적게 받는 사람들에 속한다.

pain ♦♦◇ /pe̱ɪn/ (**pains, pained**) ❶ N-VAR **Pain** is the feeling of great discomfort you have, for example when you have been hurt or when you are ill. ❑ *...back pain.* ❑ *To help ease the pain, heat can be applied to the area with a hot water bottle.* ❑ *I felt a sharp pain in my lower back.* ● PHRASE If you are **in pain**, you feel pain in a part of your body, because you are injured or ill. ❑ *She was writhing in pain, bathed in perspiration.* ❷ N-UNCOUNT **Pain** is the feeling of unhappiness that you have when something unpleasant or upsetting happens. ❑ *...grey eyes that seemed filled with pain.* ❸ V-T If a fact or idea **pains** you, it makes you feel upset and disappointed. [no cont] ❑ *This public acknowledgment of Ted's disability pained my mother.* ❹ PHRASE In informal English, if you call someone or something **a pain** or **a pain in the neck**, you mean that they are very annoying or irritating. Expressions such as **a pain in the ass** in American English, or **a pain in the arse** and **a pain in the backside** in British English, are also used, but most people consider them offensive. [INFORMAL, DISAPPROVAL] ❑ *Getting rid of unwanted applications from your PC can be a real pain.* ❺ PHRASE If you **take pains to** do something or **go to great pains to** do something, you try hard to do it, because you think it is important to do it. ❑ *Social workers went to great pains to acknowledge men's domestic rights.*

❶ 가산명사 또는 불가산명사 통증 ❑ 요통 ❑ 통증을 완화하기 위해 온수통을 써서 환부에 열을 가할 수도 있다. ❑ 허리 아래에 쑤시는 듯한 통증을 느꼈다. ● 구 고통스러워하는, 아파하는 ❑ 그녀는 땀에 젖은 채 아파서 몸부림치고 있었다. ❷ 불가산명사 고뇌, 수심 ❑ 수심이 가득해 보이는 회색 눈 ❸ 타동사 괴롭히다 ❑ 테드의 장애에 대한 이런 공개적 인정은 우리 어머니를 괴롭혔다. ❹ 구 왕짜증 나는 일 [비격식체, 탐탁찮음] ❑ 컴퓨터에서 불필요한 응용 프로그램을 지우는 일은 왕짜증 나는 일이 될 수도 있다. ❺ 구 애쓰다 ❑ 사회복지사들은 남성의 가사권을 인정하기 위해 무진 애썼다.

Thesaurus	*pain*의 참조어	
N.	ache, agony, discomfort ❶	
	anguish, distress, heartache, suffering ❷	
V.	bother, distress, grieve, hurt, upset, wound ❸	

pained /pe̱ɪnd/ ADJ If you have a **pained** expression or look, you look upset, worried, or slightly annoyed. ❑ *Tesla put on a pained look, as though the subject was too delicate to be spoken about.*

형용사 괴로운, 고통스러운 ❑ 말을 하기에는 너무 민감한 주제라는 듯이 테슬라가 괴로운 표정을 지었다.

pain|ful ♦◇◇ /pe̱ɪnfəl/ ❶ ADJ If a part of your body is **painful**, it hurts because it is injured or because there is something wrong with it. ❑ *Her glands were swollen and painful.* ● **pain|ful|ly** ADV [ADV with v] ❑ *His tooth had started to throb painfully again.* ❷ ADJ If something such as an illness, injury, or operation is **painful**, it causes you a lot of physical pain. ❑ *...a painful back injury.* ● **pain|ful|ly** ADV [ADV with v] ❑ *...cracking his head painfully against the cupboard.* ❸ ADJ Situations, memories, or experiences that are **painful** are difficult and unpleasant to deal with, and often make you feel sad and upset. ❑ *Remarks like that brought back painful memories.* ❑ *...the painful transition to democracy.*

❶ 형용사 아픈 ❑ 그녀의 내분비선들이 붓고 아팠다. ● 아프게 부사 ❑ 그의 이빨이 다시 욱신거리기 시작했다. ❷ 형용사 고통스러운 ❑ 고통스러운 허리 부상 ● 고통스럽게 부사 ❑ 그가 찬장에 머리를 고통스러울 정도로 세게 부딪치며 ❸ 형용사 괴로운, 고통스러운 ❑ 그런 말 때문에 괴로운 기억이 되살아났다. ❑ 민주주의로의 고통스러운 전환 ● 괴롭게 부사 ❑ 그가 힘들게 끊은 그들의 오랜 관계

• **pain|ful|ly** ADV [ADV with v] ❑ ...*their old relationship, which he had painfully broken off.*

pain|ful|ly /peɪnfəli/ ADV You use **painfully** to emphasize a quality or situation that is undesirable. [EMPHASIS] [ADV adv/adj] ❑ *Things are moving painfully slowly.* ❑ *...a painfully shy young man.* →see also **painful**

pain|killer /peɪnkɪlər/ (**painkillers**) N-COUNT A **painkiller** is a drug which reduces or stops physical pain.

pain|less /peɪnləs/ **1** ADJ If something such as a treatment is **painless** it causes no physical pain. ❑ *Acupuncture treatment is gentle, painless, and, invariably, most relaxing.* ❑ *The operation itself is a brief, painless procedure.* • **pain|less|ly** ADV [ADV with v] ❑ *...a technique to eliminate unwanted facial hair quickly and painlessly.* **2** ADJ If a process or activity is **painless**, there are no difficulties involved, and you do not have to make a great effort or suffer in any way. ❑ *House-hunting is in fact relatively painless in this region.* • **pain|less|ly** ADV [ADV with v] ❑ *...a game for children which painlessly teaches essential pre-reading skills.*

pains|taking /peɪnzteɪkɪŋ, peɪnsteɪ-/ ADJ A **painstaking** search, examination, or investigation is done extremely carefully and thoroughly. ❑ *Forensic experts carried out a painstaking search of the debris.* • **pains|taking|ly** ADV ❑ *Broken bones were painstakingly pieced together and reshaped.*

paint ♦♦◇ /peɪnt/ (**paints, painting, painted**) **1** N-MASS **Paint** is a colored liquid that you put onto a surface with a brush in order to protect the surface or to make it look nice, or that you use to produce a picture. ❑ *...a pot of red paint.* ❑ *They saw some large letters in white paint.* **2** N-SING On a wall or object, **the paint** is the covering of dried paint on it. ❑ *The paint was peeling on the window frames.* **3** V-T/V-I If you **paint** a wall or an object, you cover it with paint. ❑ *They started to mend the woodwork and paint the walls.* ❑ *I made a guitar and painted it red.* **4** V-T/V-I If you **paint** something or **paint** a picture of it, you produce a picture of it using paint. ❑ *He is painting a huge volcano.* ❑ *Why do people paint pictures?* **5** V-T When you **paint** a design or message on a surface, you put it on the surface using paint. ❑ *...a machine for painting white lines down roads.* ❑ *They went around painting rude slogans on cars.* **6** V-T If you **paint** a grim or vivid picture of something, you give a description of it that is grim or vivid. ❑ *The report paints a grim picture of life there.* **7** →see also **painting, gloss paint, oil paint**

paint|brush /peɪntbrʌʃ/ (**paintbrushes**) also **paint brush, paint-brush** N-COUNT A **paintbrush** is a brush which you use for painting. →see **painting**

paint|er /peɪntər/ (**painters**) **1** N-COUNT A **painter** is an artist who paints pictures. ❑ *...the 18th-century portrait painter George Romney.* **2** N-COUNT A **painter** is someone who paints walls, doors, and some other parts of buildings as their job. ❑ *...the son of a painter and decorator.*

paint|ing ♦♦◇ /peɪntɪŋ/ (**paintings**) **1** N-COUNT A **painting** is a picture which someone has painted. ❑ *...a large oil-painting of Queen Victoria.* **2** N-UNCOUNT **Painting** is the activity of painting pictures. ❑ *...two hobbies she really enjoyed, painting and gardening.* **3** N-UNCOUNT **Painting** is the activity of painting doors, walls, and some other parts of buildings. ❑ *...painting and decorating.* →see Word Web: **painting**

pair ♦♦◇ /peər/ (**pairs, pairing, paired**) **1** N-COUNT A **pair of** things are two things of the same size and shape that are used together or are both part of something, for example shoes, earrings, or parts of the body. ❑ *...a pair of socks.* ❑ *...earrings which cost $142.50 per pair.* **2** N-COUNT Some objects that have two main parts of the same size and shape are referred to as a **pair**, for example a

부사 지나치게, 괴로울 정도로 [강조] ❑ 일이 지나치게 천천히 진행되고 있다. ❑ 지나치게 내성적인 청년

가산명사 진통제

1 형용사 아프지 않은, 통증이 없는 ❑ 침술은 부드럽고 아프지 않으며 거의 언제나 긴장을 푸는 데 아주 좋다. ❑ 수술 자체는 간단하고 통증이 없는 절차이다. ● 아프지 않게 부사 ❑ 불필요한 얼굴 털을 빨리 그리고 통증 없이 제거하는 기술 **2** 형용사 힘들지 않은 ❑ 이 지역에서 집을 구하는 것은 그다지 힘든 일이 아니다. ● 힘들지 않게 부사 ❑ 아이들에게 수월하게 읽기 진 능력을 길러 주는 게임

형용사 면밀한 ❑ 과학 수사 전문가들이 잔해를 면밀히 살폈다. ● 면밀하게 부사 ❑ 부러진 뼈들을 면밀히 조립하고 모양을 바로 잡았다.

1 물질명사 페인트 ❑ 빨간 페인트 한 통 ❑ 그들은 흰 페인트로 칠한 큰 글자 몇 개를 봤다. **2** 단수명사 페인트칠 ❑ 창틀의 페인트칠이 벗겨지고 있었다. **3** 타동사/자동사 페인트칠하다 ❑ 그들은 목조 부분을 손보고 벽에 페인트를 칠하기 시작했다. ❑ 나는 기타를 만들어 붉은색으로 칠했다. **4** 타동사/자동사 (그림감으로) 그리다 ❑ 그는 큰 화산을 그리고 있다. ❑ 사람들은 왜 그림을 그리지? **5** 타동사 페인트칠하다 ❑ 길에 흰 선을 긋는 기계 ❑ 그들은 돌아다니며 차에 저속한 문구들을 페인트로 그렸다. **6** 타동사 그리다, 묘사하다 ❑ 보고서는 그곳에서의 암울한 생활을 그리고 있다.

가산명사 화필

1 가산명사 화가 ❑ 18세기 초상화가 조지 롬니 **2** 가산명사 페인트공 ❑ 페인트공이며 내부 수리 전문가인 사람의 아들

1 가산명사 그림 ❑ 빅토리아 여왕을 그린 대형 유화 **2** 불가산명사 그리기 ❑ 그녀가 정말 즐겼던 두 가지 취미인 그림 그리기와 원예 **3** 불가산명사 도장(塗裝) ❑ 도장과 장식

1 가산명사 쌍, 짝 ❑ 양말 한 켤레 ❑ 한 쌍에 142.50달러인 귀걸이 **2** 가산명사 벌 ❑ 낡은 청바지 한 벌 **3** 단수명사 두 사람 ❑ 두 명의 십 대 소녀가 담배를 피우고 있었다. ❑ 그 부부는 그들의 3년 된 결혼 생활이 '어려운 시기'를 겪고 있다고 인정했다. **4** 타동사

pair of pants or **a pair of scissors**. ❏ *...a pair of faded jeans.* ❸ N-SING You can refer to two people as a **pair** when they are standing or walking together or when they have some kind of relationship with each other. ❏ *A pair of teenage boys were smoking cigarettes.* ❏ *The pair admitted that their three-year-old marriage was going through "a difficult time."* ❹ V-T If one thing **is paired with** another, it is put with it or considered with it. [usu passive] ❏ *The trainees will then be paired with experienced managers.* ❺ →see also **au pair**

> The noun **pair** can take either a singular verb or a plural verb, depending on whether it refers to one thing seen as a unit or a collection of two things or people. ❏ *A good, supportive and protective pair of sneakers is essential... The pair are still friends and attend functions together.*

Thesaurus   *pair*의 참조어

N.   combination, couple, duo, match, two ❶ ❸

V.   combine, join, match up, put together, team ❹

pa|jam|as /pədʒɑməz/ →see **pyjamas**

> The spelling **pyjamas** is used in British English. The forms **pajama** and **pyjama** are used as modifiers.

N-PLURAL A pair of **pajamas** consists of loose pants and a loose jacket that people wear in bed. [also a pair of N] ❏ *I don't want to get out of my pajamas in the morning.*

pal /pæl/ (**pals**) N-COUNT Your **pals** are your friends. [INFORMAL, OLD-FASHIONED] ❏ *Stockdale traveled with his pals to watch the final.*

pal|ace ◆◇◇ /pælɪs/ (**palaces**) ❶ N-COUNT A **palace** is a very large impressive house, especially one which is the official home of a king, queen, or president. ❏ *...Buckingham Palace.* ❷ N-SING When the members of a royal palace make an announcement through an official spokesperson, they can be referred to as **the Palace**. ❏ *"We couldn't possibly comment," is the Palace's response to all questions about the family's private life.*

pal|at|able /pælətəb³l/ ❶ ADJ If you describe food or drink as **palatable**, you mean that it tastes pleasant. [FORMAL] ❏ *...flavorings and preservatives, designed to make the food look more palatable.* ❷ ADJ If you describe something such as an idea or method as **palatable**, you mean that people are willing to accept it. ❏ *...a palatable way of sacking staff.*

pal|ate /pælɪt/ (**palates**) ❶ N-COUNT Your **palate** is the top part of the inside of your mouth. ❷ N-COUNT You can refer to someone's **palate** as a way of talking about their ability to judge good food or drink. ❏ *...fresh pasta sauces to tempt more demanding palates.*

pale ◆◇◇ /peɪl/ (**paler, palest, pales, paling, paled**) ❶ ADJ If something is **pale**, it is very light in color or almost white. ❏ *Migrating birds filled the pale sky.* ❏ *As we age, our skin becomes paler.* • COMB in COLOR **Pale** is also a combining form. ❏ *...a pale blue sailor dress.* ❷ ADJ If someone looks **pale**, their face looks a lighter color than usual, usually because they are ill, frightened, or shocked. ❏ *She looked pale and tired.* ❸ V-I If one thing **pales** in comparison with another, it is made to seem much less important, serious, or good by it. ❏ *When someone you love has a life-threatening illness, everything else pales in comparison.*

pal|ette /pælɪt/ (**palettes**) ❶ N-COUNT A **palette** is a flat piece of wood or plastic on which an artist mixes paints. ❏ *The painter's right hand holds the brush, the left the palette.* ❷ N-COUNT You can refer to the range of colors that are used by a particular artist or group of artists as their **palette**. ❏ *David Fincher paints from a palette consisting almost exclusively of gray and mud brown.* →see **painting**

palm /pɑm/ (**palms**) ❶ N-COUNT A **palm** or a **palm tree** is a tree that grows in hot countries. It has long leaves growing at the top, and no branches. ❏ *...golden sands and swaying palms.* ❷ N-COUNT The **palm of** your hand is the inside part. ❏ *Dornberg slapped the table with the palm of his hand.* ❸ PHRASE If you have someone or something **in the palm of** your hand, you have control over them. ❏ *Johnson thought he had the board of directors in the palm of his hand.* →see **desert, hand**

palm|top /pɑmtɒp/ (**palmtops**) N-COUNT A **palmtop** is a small computer that you can hold in your hand. [COMPUTING]

pal|pable /pælpəb³l/ ADJ You describe something as **palpable** when it is obvious or intense and easily noticed. ❏ *The tension between Amy and Jim is palpable.* • **pal|pably** /pælpəbli/ ADV [ADV with cl/group] ❏ *The scene was palpably intense to watch.*

pal|try /pɔltri/ ADJ A **paltry** amount of money or of something else is one that you consider to be very small. ❏ *...a paltry fine of £150.*

pam|per /pæmpər/ (**pampers, pampering, pampered**) V-T If you **pamper** someone, you make them feel comfortable by doing things for them or giving them expensive or luxurious things, sometimes in a way which has a bad effect on their character. ❏ *Why don't you let your mother pamper you for a while?* ❏ *Pamper yourself with our luxury gifts.* • **pam|pered** ADJ ❏ *...today's pampered superstars.*

pam|phlet /pæmflɪt/ (**pamphlets**) N-COUNT A **pamphlet** is a very thin book, with a paper cover, which gives information about something. ❏ *...a pamphlet about smoking.*

pan ◆◇◇ /pæn/ (**pans, panning, panned**) ❶ N-COUNT A **pan** is a round metal container with a long handle, which is used for cooking things in, usually on top of a stove. ❏ *Heat the butter and oil in a large pan.* ❷ V-T If something such as a movie or a book **is panned** by journalists, they say it is very bad. [INFORMAL] [usu passive] ❏ *His first high-budget movie, called "Brain Donors," was panned by the*

짝지어지다 ❏ 그런 뒤 견습생들을 경험 많은 관리자들과 짝을 지어 줄 것이다.

> 명사 pair는 하나의 단위로 간주되는 하나의 사물을 가리키느냐 또는 두 가지나 두 사람의 모둠을 가리키느냐에 따라 단수형 또는 복수형 동사를 취할 수 있다. ❏ 품질이 좋고, 체중을 잘 받쳐 주며, 보호력이 있는 운동화 한 켤레가 필수적이다... 그 쌍의 남녀는 여전히 친구 사이이며 사교 모임 같은 곳에 함께 다닌다.

철자 pyjamas는 영국영어에서 쓴다. pajama와 pyjama는 수식어구로 쓴다.

복수명사 잠옷 ❏ 나는 아침에 잠옷을 벗기가 싫다.

가산명사 친구 [비격식체, 구식어] ❏ 스톡데일은 결승전을 보기 위해 친구들과 차를 타고 갔다.

❶ 가산명사 궁, 궁전 ❏ 버킹엄궁 ❷ 단수명사 궁궐 측 ❏ "어떠한 답변도 할 수 없습니다."라는 말이 왕가의 사생활에 관한 모든 질문에 대해 궁궐 측이 보이는 반응이다.

❶ 형용사 맛이 있는, 입에 맞는 [격식체] ❏ 음식을 좀 더 먹음직스럽게 보이게 하기 위해 쓰는 향신료와 방부제 ❷ 형용사 용인되는, 입에 맞는 ❏ 입에 맞는 직원 해고 방식

❶ 가산명사 구개, 입천장 ❷ 가산명사 미각 ❏ 보다 까다로운 미각의 소유자들을 유혹하기 위한 신선한 파스타 소스

❶ 형용사 창백한 ❏ 이동하는 철새들이 창백한 하늘을 메웠다. ❏ 나이가 들수록 피부는 창백해진다. ● 복합형-색채어 옅은 ❏ 옅은 파란색의 세일러복 ❷ 형용사 창백한 ❏ 그는 창백하고 지쳐 보였다. ❸ 자동사 무색해지다, 하찮아지다 ❏ 사랑하는 사람이 치명적인 병에 걸려 있을 땐 다른 모든 것이 하찮아진다.

❶ 가산명사 팔레트 ❏ 화가의 오른손이 붓을 들고 있고 왼손은 팔레트를 들고 있다. ❷ 가산명사 (특정 화가가 쓰는) 색채 ❏ 데이비드 핀처는 거의 전적으로 회색과 옅은 갈색으로 이루어진 색채로 영화를 만든다.

❶ 가산명사 야자수 ❏ 황금 모래사장과 하늘거리는 야자수 ❷ 가산명사 손바닥 ❏ 돈버그는 손바닥으로 탁자를 내리쳤다. ❸ 구 손아귀 안에 ❏ 존슨은 자신이 이사회를 손아귀 안에 쥐고 있다고 생각했다.

가산명사 팜탑 컴퓨터, 휴대용 컴퓨터 [컴퓨터]

형용사 뚜렷한, 선명한 ❏ 에이미와 짐 사이의 긴장감이 뚜렷이 느껴진다. ● 뚜렷하게 부사 ❏ 그 장면은 보기만 해도 긴장감이 넘쳐흘렀다.

형용사 하찮은, 얼마 안 되는 ❏ 150파운드라는 얼마 안 되는 벌금

타동사 호강을 시키다, 응석을 다 받아 주다 ❏ 가서 네 엄마에게 응석이나 부리지 그래? ❏ 저희가 드리는 고급 선물로 호사를 누리세요. ● 응석꾸러기의 형용사 ❏ 응석꾸러기가 되어 버린 오늘의 슈퍼스타들

가산명사 소책자, 팸플릿 ❏ 흡연에 관한 소책자

❶ 가산명사 팬, 납작한 냄비 ❏ 버터와 기름을 큰 팬에 데우세요. ❷ 타동사 혹평을 받다 [비격식체] ❏ '브레인 도너스'라고 불린 그의 첫 번째 대규모 예산 영화가 비평가들로부터 혹평을 받았다. ❸ 타동사/자동사 패닝하다; (카메라가) 훑어 나가다 ❏ 카메라가 선수

No **saucepan** or **frying pan** is perfect. **Copper pans** conduct heat extremely well. This makes them a popular choice for stovetop cooking. However, copper also reacts with the acid in some foods and wines. For this reason, the best copper pans have a thin layer of **tin** covering the copper. **Cast iron** pans are very heavy and **heat up** slowly. But once hot, they stay hot for a long time. Some people like **stainless steel** pans because they heat up quickly and don't react with chemicals in food. However, the bottom of a stainless pan may not heat up evenly.

critics. ﹇ v-T/v-I If you **pan** a movie or television camera or if it **pans** somewhere, it moves slowly around so that a wide area is filmed. ❑ *The camera panned along the line of players.* ❑ *A television camera panned the stadium.* →see Word Web: **pan**

진영을 죽 훑었다. ❑ 텔레비전 카메라가 경기장을 한 바퀴 훑었다.

pana|cea /pænəsiə/ (**panaceas**) N-COUNT If you say that something is not a **panacea** for a particular set of problems, you mean that it will not solve all those problems. ❑ *Trade is not a panacea for the world's economic or social ills.*

가산명사 만병통치약 ❑ 무역이 세계의 경제적 혹은 사회적 부조리에 대한 만병통치약이 아니다.

pa|nache /pənæʃ/ N-UNCOUNT If you do something **with panache**, you do it in a confident, stylish, and elegant way. ❑ *The BBC Symphony Orchestra played with great panache.*

불가산명사 기품 ❑ 비비시 교향악단은 굉장히 격조 있게 연주를 했다.

pan|cake /pænkeɪk/ (**pancakes**) N-COUNT A **pancake** is a thin, flat, circular piece of cooked batter made from milk, flour, and eggs. In America, pancakes are usually eaten for breakfast, with butter and maple syrup. Pancakes can also be rolled up or folded and eaten hot with a sweet or savory filling inside.

가산명사 팬케이크

pan|da /pændə/ (**pandas**) N-COUNT A **panda** or a **giant panda** is a large animal rather like a bear, which has black and white fur and lives in the bamboo forests of China. →see **zoo**

가산명사 판다

pan|der /pændər/ (**panders, pandering, pandered**) v-I If you **pander to** someone or **to** their wishes, you do everything that they want, often to get some advantage for yourself. [DISAPPROVAL] ❑ *He has offended the party's traditional base by pandering to the rich and the middle classes.*

자동사 -에 영합하다 [탐탁찮음] ❑ 그는 부유층과 중산층에게 영합함으로써 정당의 기존 지지층을 기분 상하게 했다.

p & p also **p and p** You use **p & p** as a written abbreviation for "postage and packing," when stating the cost of packing goods and sending them through the mail to a customer. [BRIT, BUSINESS] ❑ *They also publish an excellent cookery book called "The Flavours Of Gujarat" (£12.95, plus £2.25 p & p).*

배송료 [영국영어, 경제] ❑ 그들은 '구자랏의 맛'이라는 뛰어난 요리책도 펴낸다. (12.95파운드, 배송료 2.25파운드 별도)

pane /peɪn/ (**panes**) N-COUNT A **pane** of glass is a flat sheet of glass in a window or door. ❑ *I watch my reflection in a pane of glass.*

가산명사 창유리 ❑ 나는 유리창에 비친 내 모습을 본다.

pan|el ◆◇◇ /pæn³l/ (**panels**) ﹇ N-COUNT-COLL A **panel** is a small group of people who are chosen to do something, for example to discuss something in public or to make a decision. ❑ *He assembled a panel of scholars to advise him.* ❑ *All the writers on the panel agreed Quinn's book should be singled out for special praise.* ﹈ N-COUNT A **panel** is a flat rectangular piece of wood or other material that forms part of a larger object such as a door. ❑ *...the frosted glass panel set in the center of the door.* ﹊ N-COUNT A control **panel** or instrument **panel** is a board or surface which contains switches and controls to operate a machine or piece of equipment. [n N] ❑ *The equipment was extremely sophisticated and was monitored from a central control-panel.*

﹇ 가산명사-집합 위원단, 패널 ❑ 그는 자문을 구하기 위해 학자들로 이루어진 패널을 구성했다. ❑ 심사 위원단의 모든 작가들이 퀸의 책에 특별상을 수여하는 것에 모두 동의했다. ﹈ 가산명사 판자, 패널 ❑ 문 한가운데 설치된 불투명 유리 패널 ﹊ 가산명사 배전반 ❑ 그 장비는 굉장히 복잡했고 중앙 통제 배전반에서 관리를 했다.

pan|eled /pæn³ld/ [BRIT, sometimes AM **panelled**] ﹇ ADJ A **paneled** room has decorative wooden panels covering its walls. ❑ *...their cozy paneled den.* ● COMB in ADJ **-paneled** combines with nouns to form adjectives that describe the way a room or wall is decorated or the way a door or window is made. ❑ *...an elegant wood-paneled library.* ﹈ ADJ A **paneled** wall, door, or window does not have a flat surface but has square or rectangular areas set into its surface. ❑ *...an oil landscape on the paneled wall.*

[영국영어, 미국영어 가끔 panelled] ﹇ 형용사 패널로 장식된 ❑ 그들의 패널로 장식된 포근한 사실(私室) ● 복합형-형용사 -로 장식된 ❑ 우아하게 나무 패널로 장식된 서재 ﹈ 형용사 패널로 된 ❑ 패널로 된 벽에 걸린 유화 풍경화

pang /pæŋ/ (**pangs**) N-COUNT A **pang** is a sudden strong feeling or emotion, for example of sadness or pain. ❑ *For a moment she felt a pang of guilt about the way she was treating him.*

가산명사 기둥 ❑ 잠깐 그녀는 자신이 그를 대하는 태도에 양심의 기책을 느꼈다.

pan|han|dler /pænhændlər/ (**panhandlers**) N-COUNT A **panhandler** is a person who stops people in the street and asks them for food or money. [mainly AM, INFORMAL; BRIT usually **beggar**]

가산명사 거지 [주로 미국영어, 비격식체; 영국영어 대개 beggar]

pan|ic ◆◇◇ /pænɪk/ (**panics, panicking, panicked**) ﹇ N-VAR **Panic** is a very strong feeling of anxiety or fear, which makes you act without thinking carefully. ❑ *An earthquake has hit the capital, causing damage to buildings and panic among the population.* ﹈ N-UNCOUNT **Panic** or **a panic** is a situation in which people are affected by a strong feeling of anxiety. [also a N] ❑ *There was a moment of panic in Britain as it became clear just how vulnerable the nation was.* ❑ *I'm in a panic about getting everything done in time.* ﹊ v-T/v-I If you **panic** or if someone **panics** you, you suddenly feel anxious or afraid, and act quickly and without thinking carefully. ❑ *Guests panicked and screamed when the bomb exploded.* ❑ *The unexpected and sudden memory briefly panicked her.*

﹇ 가산명사 또는 불가산명사 공황 ❑ 지진이 수도를 강타해서 건물에 피해를 입히고 주민들을 공황 상태에 빠뜨렸다. ﹈ 불가산명사 공황 상태 ❑ 영국이 얼마나 공격에 취약한지가 분명해지자 국민들이 한 순간 공황 상태에 빠졌다. ❑ 모든 것을 제 시간에 마치지 못할까봐 너무나 두렵다. ﹊ 타동사/자동사 공황에 빠지다; 공황에 빠뜨리다 ❑ 폭탄이 터지자 손님들이 공황에 빠져 비명을 질렀다. ❑ 예상치 못했던 갑작스러운 기억 때문에 그녀는 잠깐 공황에 빠졌다.

   N.   agitation, alarm, dread, fear, fright; (ant.) calm ﹇
   V.   alarm, fear, terrify, unnerve; (ant.) relax ﹊

pano|ra|ma /pænərɑːmə, -ræmə/ (**panoramas**) ﹇ N-COUNT A **panorama** is a view in which you can see a long way over a wide area of land, usually because you are on high ground. ❑ *Horton looked out over a panorama of fertile valleys and gentle hills.* ﹈ N-COUNT A **panorama** is a broad view of a state of affairs or of a constantly changing series of events. ❑ *The play presents a panorama of the history of communism.*

﹇ 가산명사 전경 ❑ 호턴은 비옥한 계곡과 완만한 구릉들로 이루어진 전경을 바라봤다. ﹈ 가산명사 조망, 개관 ❑ 연극은 공산주의의 역사를 조망한다.

panoramic /pænərǽmɪk/ ADJ If you have a **panoramic** view, you can see a long way over a wide area. ❑ *The terrain's high points provide a panoramic view of Los Angeles.*

형용사 조망하는 ❑ 그 지역의 고지에서는 로스앤젤레스를 조망할 수 있다.

pant /pænt/ (**pants, panting, panted**) V-I If you **pant**, you breathe quickly and loudly with your mouth open, because you have been doing something energetic. ❑ *She climbed rapidly until she was panting with the effort.* →see also **pants**

자동사 헐떡거리다 ❑ 그녀는 용을 쓰느라 숨을 헐떡거리게 될 때까지 빠른 속도로 올라갔다.

panties /pǽntiz/ N-PLURAL **Panties** are short, close-fitting underpants worn by women or girls. [mainly AM; BRIT usually **pants, knickers**] ❑ *...a pair of white panties.*

복수명사 팬티 [주로 미국영어; 영국영어 대개 pants, knickers] ❑ 흰색 팬티 한 벌

┌───┐
│ **Word Link**   mim ≈ copying : mimic, mime, pantomime │
└───┘

pantomime /pǽntəmaɪm/ (**pantomimes**) 1 N-COUNT A **pantomime** is a funny musical play for children. Pantomimes are usually based on fairy tales and are performed at Christmas. [BRIT] 2 N-SING If you say that a situation or a person's behavior is a **pantomime**, you mean that it is silly or exaggerated and that there is something false about it. [mainly BRIT] ❑ *They were made welcome with the usual pantomime of exaggerated smiles and gestures.*

1 가산명사 팬터마임 [영국영어]. 2 단수명사 가식 [주로 영국영어] ❑ 그들은 으레 그랬던 것처럼 과장된 웃음과 몸짓으로 포장된 가식적인 환영을 받았다.

pants /pænts/ 1 N-PLURAL **Pants** are a piece of underwear which have two holes to put your legs through and elastic around the top to hold them up around your waist or hips. [BRIT; AM usually **underpants**] [also *a pair of N*] ❑ *I wash and dry myself and put on my bra and pants.* 2 N-PLURAL **Pants** are a piece of clothing that covers the lower part of your body and each leg. [AM; BRIT **trousers**] [also *a pair of N*] ❑ *She described him as wearing brown corduroy pants and a white cotton shirt.* →see **clothing**

1 복수명사 팬티 [영국영어; 미국영어 대개 underpants] ❑ 나는 몸을 씻고 닦은 후 브래지어와 팬티를 입는다. 2 복수명사 바지 [미국영어; 영국영어 trousers] ❑ 그녀의 묘사에 의하면 그는 갈색 코듀로이 바지와 하얀 면 남방을 입고 있었다.

pantsuit /pǽntsut/ (**pantsuits**) or **pants suit** N-COUNT A **pantsuit** is women's clothing consisting of a pair of pants and a jacket which are made from the same material. [AM; BRIT **trouser suit**] ❑ *Today she wore a red pantsuit that fit real well.*

가산명사 여성 정장 한 벌 [미국영어; 영국영어 trouser suit] ❑ 오늘 그녀는 몸에 아주 잘 맞는 붉은색 정장을 입었다.

pantyhose /pǽntihoʊz/ also **panty hose** N-PLURAL **Pantyhose** are a piece of clothing worn by women and girls. They are usually made of nylon and cover the hips, legs and feet. [mainly AM; BRIT usually **tights**] [also *a pair of N*] ❑ *She told him her pantyhose were slipping.*

복수명사 팬티스타킹 [주로 미국영어; 영국영어 대개 tights] ❑ 그녀는 팬티스타킹이 흘러내린다고 그에게 말했다.

papa /pɑ́pə, BRIT pəpɑ́ː/ (**papas**) N-FAMILY Some people refer to or address their father as **papa**. [OLD-FASHIONED] ❑ *He was so much older than me, older even than my papa.*

친족명사 아빠 [구식어] ❑ 그는 나보다 나이가 훨씬 많았다. 심지어는 우리 아빠보다 나이가 많았다.

papal /péɪpᵊl/ ADJ **Papal** is used to describe things relating to the Pope. [ADJ n] ❑ *...the doctrine of papal infallibility.*

형용사 교황의 ❑ 교황 무결점 교리

paper ♦♦♦ /péɪpər/ (**papers, papering, papered**) 1 N-UNCOUNT **Paper** is a material that you write on or wrap things with. The pages of this book are made of paper. ❑ *He wrote his name down on a piece of paper for me.* ❑ *...a paper bag.* 2 N-COUNT A **paper** is a newspaper. ❑ *I might get a paper in the village.* 3 N-COUNT You can refer to newspapers in general as **the paper** or **the papers**. ❑ *You can't believe everything you read in the paper.* 4 N-PLURAL Your **papers** are sheets of paper with writing or information on them, which you might keep in a safe place at home. ❑ *After her death, her papers – including unpublished articles and correspondence – were deposited at the library.* 5 N-PLURAL Your **papers** are official documents, for example your passport or identity card, which prove who you are or which give you official permission to do something. ❑ *A young Moroccan stopped by police refused to show his papers.* 6 N-COUNT A **paper** is a long, formal piece of writing about an academic subject. ❑ *He just published a paper in the journal Nature analyzing the fires.* 7 N-COUNT A **paper** is an essay written by a student. [mainly AM] ❑ *...the ten common errors that appear most frequently in student papers.* 8 N-COUNT A **paper** is a part of a written examination in which you answer a number of questions in a particular period of time. ❑ *She imagined herself looking at her test paper and filling in the answers easily.* ❑ *She finished the exam paper.* 9 N-COUNT A **paper** prepared by a government or a committee is a report on a question they have been considering or a set of proposals for changes in the law. ❑ *...a new government paper on European policy.* 10 ADJ **Paper** agreements, qualifications, or profits are ones that are stated by official documents to exist, although they may not really be effective or useful. [ADJ n] ❑ *They expressed deep mistrust of the paper promises.* 11 V-T If you **paper** a wall, you put wallpaper on it. ❑ *We papered all four bedrooms.* ❑ *We have papered this bedroom in softest grey.* 12 PHRASE If you put your thoughts down **on paper**, you write them down. ❑ *It is important to get something down on paper.* 13 PHRASE If something seems to be the case **on paper**, it seems to be the case from what you read or hear about it, but it may not really be the case. ❑ *On paper, their country is a multi-party democracy.* →see Word Web: **paper**

1 불가산명사 종이 ❑ 그는 자기 이름을 종이에 적어 내게 줬다. 2 가산명사 신문 ❑ 마을에서 신문을 구할지도 모르겠다. 3 가산명사 신문 ❑ 신문에서 읽는 모든 것을 믿을 수는 없다. 4 복수명사 서류, 문서 ❑ 그녀가 죽은 뒤 출판되지 않은 글과 서신 등의 문서들은 도서관에 맡겨졌다. 5 복수명사 신분증, 서류 ❑ 경찰이 검문한 젊은 모로코 인이 자신의 신분증을 보여 주기를 거부했다. 6 가산명사 논문 ❑ 그는 네이처 지에 그 화재들을 분석한 논문을 최근에 실었다. 7 가산명사 페이퍼, 과제 [주로 미국영어] ❑ 학생들의 과제에 가장 흔히 나타나는 열 가지 오류 8 가산명사 시험지 ❑ 그녀는 시험지를 보면서 쉽게 답을 적어 가는 자신을 상상했다. ❑ 그녀는 시험을 마쳤다. 9 가산명사 보고서 ❑ 유럽 정책에 관한 정부의 새 보고서 10 형용사 지면의 ❑ 그들은 그 서면 약속들에 대해 깊은 불신을 표명했다. 11 타동사 도배하다, 벽지를 바르다 ❑ 우리는 침실 네 개 모두에 벽지를 발랐다. ❑ 우리는 이 침실에 가장 옅은 회색 벽지를 발랐다. 12 구 종이에 ❑ 뭔가를 종이에 적는 것이 중요하다. 13 구 서류상으로는, 액면 상으로는 ❑ 서류상으로는 그들의 나라는 복수 정당을 갖춘 민주 국가이다.

┌──┐
│ **Word Partnership**   paper의 연어   │
│   │
│ ADJ.   **blank** paper, **brown** paper, **colored** paper 1 │
│   **daily** paper 2   │
│ V.   **fold** paper 1   │
│   **read the** paper 2 3   │
│   **present a** paper, **publish a** paper 6 │
│   **draft a** paper, **write a** paper 6 7 │
│ N.   **morning** paper 2   │
│   **research** paper 6 7   │
└──┘

Word Web   paper

Around 3000 BC, Egyptians began using the papyrus plant to produce **paper**. They cut the stems of the plant into thin slices and pressed them into **sheets**. A very different Chinese technique developed about the same time. It more closely resembles today's manufacturing process. Chinese paper makers cooked **fiber** made of tree bark. Then they pressed it into molds and let it dry. Around 200 BC, a third technique developed in the Middle East. Craftsmen started using animal skins to make parchment. Today, paper manufacturing destroys millions of trees every year. This has led to recycling programs and paperless offices.

paper|back /ˈpeɪpərbæk/ (**paperbacks**) N-COUNT A **paperback** is a book with a thin cardboard or paper cover. Compare **hardback**. [also in N] ❑ She said she would buy the book when it comes out in paperback.

가산명사 페이퍼백, 보급판 ❑ 그녀는 책이 보급판으로 나오면 그때 사겠다고 했다.

pa|per clip (**paper clips**) also **paper-clip, paperclip** N-COUNT A **paper clip** is a small piece of bent wire that is used to fasten papers together. →see **office**

가산명사 종이 클립

paper|work /ˈpeɪpərwɜrk/ N-UNCOUNT **Paperwork** is the routine part of a job which involves writing or dealing with letters, reports, and records. ❑ At every stage in the production there will be paperwork – forms to fill in, permissions to obtain, letters to write.

불가산명사 서류 작업, 문서 업무 ❑ 제작의 모든 단계에는 관련 서류 작업이 있다. 양식 작성, 허가 받기, 편지 쓰기 등.

Pap smear (**Pap smears**) also **Pap test** N-COUNT A **Pap smear** is a medical test in which cells are taken from a woman's cervix and analyzed to see if any cancer cells are present. [AM; BRIT **smear**]

가산명사 도말 표본 검사 (자궁암 검사법의 일종) [미국영어; 영국영어 smear]

par /pɑr/ ⬛ PHRASE If you say that two people or things are **on a par with** each other, you mean that they are equally good or bad, or equally important. ❑ Parts of Glasgow are on a par with the worst areas of London and Liverpool for burglaries. ⬛ N-UNCOUNT In golf, **par** is the number of strokes that a good player should take to get the ball into a hole or into all the holes on a particular golf course. [N with num, under/over N] ❑ He was five under par after the first round. ⬛ PHRASE If you say that someone or something is **below par** or **under par**, you are disappointed in them because they are below the standard you expected. ❑ Duffy's primitive guitar playing is well below par. ❑ A teacher's job is relatively safe, even if they perform under par in the classroom. ⬛ PHRASE If you say that someone or something is not **up to par**, you are disappointed in them because they are below the standard you expected. ❑ It's a constant struggle to try to keep them up to par. ⬛ PHRASE If you **feel below par** or **under par**, you feel tired and unable to perform as well as you normally do. ❑ After the birth of her baby she felt generally under par.

⬛ 구 비슷한 ❑ 빈털털이 범죄에 있어서는 글래스고 일부 지역들이 런던이나 리버풀 최악의 지역들과 비슷하다. ⬛ 불가산명사 (골프) 파 ❑ 그는 첫 라운드를 5언더 파로 마쳤다. ⬛ 구 평균 미달인 ❑ 더피의 초보적인 기타 연주는 평균에 훨씬 못 미친다. ❑ 교사라는 직업은 교실에서 평균 미달의 실력을 보여도 비교적 안전하다. ⬛ 구 기대에 부응하는 ❑ 그들이 계속 기대에 부응하게 하려면 끊임없이 애를 써야 한다. ⬛ 구 몸이 안 좋은 ❑ 아기를 출산한 후 그녀는 대개 몸이 좋지 않았다.

para|ble /ˈpærəbəl/ (**parables**) N-COUNT A **parable** is a short story, which is told in order to make a moral or religious point, like those in the Bible. ❑ ... the parable of the Good Samaritan.

가산명사 우화 ❑ 친절한 사마리아 사람에 대한 우화

para|chute /ˈpærəʃut/ (**parachutes, parachuting, parachuted**) ⬛ N-COUNT A **parachute** is a device which enables a person to jump from an aircraft and float safely to the ground. It consists of a large piece of thin cloth attached to your body by strings. [also by N] ❑ They fell 41,000 ft. before opening their parachutes. ⬛ V-T/V-I When a person **parachutes** or someone **parachutes** them somewhere, they jump from an aircraft using a parachute. ❑ He was a courier for the Polish underground and parachuted into Warsaw. ⬛ V-T To **parachute** something somewhere means to drop it somewhere by parachute. ❑ Planes parachuted food, clothing, blankets, medicine, and water into the rugged mountainous border region. →see **fly**

⬛ 가산명사 낙하산 ❑ 그들은 낙하산을 펴기 전에 41,000피트를 낙하했다. ⬛ 타동사/자동사 낙하산을 타다; 낙하산으로 낙하시키다 ❑ 그는 폴란드 지하 조직의 밀사였는데 낙하산을 타고 바르샤바로 들어갔다. ⬛ 타동사 낙하산으로 투하하다 ❑ 비행기들은 험난한 국경 산악 지역으로 음식, 옷, 이불, 의약품, 물을 낙하산으로 투하했다.

pa|rade /pəˈreɪd/ (**parades, parading, paraded**) ⬛ N-COUNT A **parade** is a procession of people or vehicles moving through a public place in order to celebrate an important day or event. ❑ A military parade marched slowly and solemnly down Pennsylvania Avenue. ⬛ V-I When people **parade** somewhere, they walk together in a formal group or a line, usually with other people watching them. ❑ More than four thousand soldiers, sailors and airmen paraded down the Champs Elysees. ⬛ N-VAR **Parade** is a formal occasion when soldiers stand in lines to be seen by an officer or important person, or march in a group. [oft on N] ❑ He had them on parade at six o'clock in the morning. ⬛ V-T If prisoners **are paraded** through the streets of a town or on television, they are shown to the public, usually in order to make the people who are holding them seem more powerful or important. [usu passive] ❑ Five leading fighter pilots have been captured and paraded before the media. ⬛ V-T If you say that someone **parades** a person, you mean that they show that person to others only in order to gain some advantage for themselves. [usu passive] ❑ Every day in this election campaign children have been paraded alongside the party leaders to publicize the latest issue. ⬛ V-T If people **parade** something, they show it in public so that it can be admired. ❑ Valentino is keen to see celebrities parading his clothes at big occasions. ⬛ V-T/V-I If you say that something **parades as** or **is paraded as** a good or important thing, you mean that some people say that it is good or important but you think it probably is not. ❑ The Chancellor will be able to parade his cut in interest rates as a small victory.

⬛ 가산명사 행렬, 퍼레이드 ❑ 군대 행렬이 펜실베이니아 가를 따라 천천히 엄숙하게 행진을 했다. ⬛ 자동사 행진하다 ❑ 4천 명 이상의 육군, 해군, 공군들이 샹젤리제를 따라 행진했다. ⬛ 가산명사 또는 불가산명사 사열 ❑ 그는 아침 6시에 그들을 사열시켰다. ⬛ 타동사 (구경거리로) 전시되다 ❑ 다섯 명의 주요 전투기 조종사들이 생포되어 언론 앞에 전시되었다. ⬛ 타동사 (이용할 목적으로) 내동댕이치다 ❑ 선거전을 치르는 동안 매일 최근의 사안을 공론화하기 위해 정당 지도자들 옆에 아이들이 대동되었다. ⬛ 타동사 과시하다 ❑ 발렌티노는 큰 행사 때 연예인들이 자기가 만든 옷을 과시하는 것을 몹시 보고 싶어 한다. ⬛ 타동사/자동사 ∼으로 광고되다 ❑ 재무 장관은 자기가 시행한 금리 인하를 하나의 작은 승리로 광고할 수 있을 것이다.

para|digm /ˈpærədaɪm/ (**paradigms**) N-VAR A **paradigm** is a model for something which explains it or shows how it can be produced. [FORMAL] ❑ ...a new paradigm of production.

가산명사 또는 불가산명사 패러다임 [격식체] ❑ 새로운 생산 패러다임

para|dise /ˈpærədaɪs/ (**paradises**) ⬛ N-PROPER According to some religions, **paradise** is a wonderful place where people go after they die, if they have led good lives. ❑ The Koran describes paradise as a place containing a garden of delight. ⬛ N-VAR You can refer to a place or situation that seems beautiful or perfect as **paradise** or **a paradise**. ❑ ...one of the world's great natural paradises.

⬛ 고유명사 천국 ❑ 코란은 천국을 기쁨의 정원이 있는 곳으로 묘사한다. ⬛ 가산명사 또는 불가산명사 낙원 ❑ 세상에서 가장 위대한 자연 낙원 중 한 곳

A

B

para|dox /pǽrədɒks/ (**paradoxes**) ■ N-COUNT You describe a situation as a **paradox** when it involves two or more facts or qualities which seem to contradict each other. ❑ *The paradox is that the region's most dynamic economies have the most primitive financial systems.* ❑ *The paradox of exercise is that while using a lot of energy it seems to generate more.* ❷ N-VAR A **paradox** is a statement in which it seems that if one part of it is true, the other part of it cannot be true. ❑ *The story contains many levels of paradox.*

가산명사 역설 ❑ 그 지역에서 경제가 가장 활발한 곳들이 가장 원시적인 금융 시스템을 갖추고 있다는 것은 역설적이다. ❑ 많은 에너지를 사용하면서도 더 많은 에너지를 생산해내는 것처럼 보이는 게 신체 운동의 역설이다. ❷ 가산명사 또는 불가산명사 모순 ❑ 그 이야기는 여러 층위에서 모순된다.

C

para|doxi|cal /pǽrədɒ́ksɪk'l/ ADJ If something is **paradoxical**, it involves two facts or qualities which seem to contradict each other. ❑ *Some sedatives produce the paradoxical effect of making the person more anxious.* ● **para|doxi|cal|ly** /pǽrədɒ́ksɪkli/ ADV ❑ *Paradoxically, the less you have to do the more you may resent the work that does come your way.*

형용사 역설적인 ❑ 일부 안정제들은 먹은 사람을 더욱 불안하게 만드는 역설적인 효과를 낳는다.
● 역설적으로 부사 ❑ 역설적이게도 해야 할 일이 적을수록 실제로 닥쳐오는 일을 더 싫어할 수도 있다.

D

par|af|fin /pǽrəfɪn/ ■ N-UNCOUNT **Paraffin** is a strong-smelling liquid which is used as a fuel in heaters, lamps, and engines. [mainly BRIT; AM **kerosene**] ❑ *...a paraffin lamp.* ❷ N-UNCOUNT **Paraffin** or in British English **paraffin wax**, is a white wax obtained from petrol or coal. It is used to make candles and in beauty treatments.

■ 불가산명사 등유 [주로 영국영어; 미국영어 kerosene] ❑ 등유 등잔 ❷ 불가산명사 파라핀

E

F

para|gon /pǽrəgɒn/ (**paragons**) N-COUNT If you refer to someone as a **paragon**, you mean that they are perfect or have a lot of a good quality. ❑ *We don't expect candidates to be paragons of virtue.* ❑ *...a paragon of neatness, efficiency, and reliability.*

가산명사 모범, 귀감 ❑ 우리는 후보들이 덕의 귀감이길 기대하는 것은 아니다. ❑ 단정함, 효율성, 신뢰의 귀감

G

para|graph /pǽrəgræf/ (**paragraphs**) N-COUNT A **paragraph** is a section of a piece of writing. A paragraph always begins on a new line and contains at least one sentence. ❑ *The length of a paragraph depends on the information it conveys.*

가산명사 단락 ❑ 단락의 길이는 그것이 전달하는 정보에 달려 있다.

H

par|al|lel /pǽrəlɛl/ (**parallels, paralleling, paralleled**) [BRIT **parallelling, parallelled**] ■ N-COUNT If something has a **parallel**, it is similar to something else, but exists or happens in a different place or at a different time. If it has **no parallel** or is **without parallel**, it is not similar to anything else. ❑ *Readers familiar with English history will find a vague parallel to the suppression of the monasteries.* ❑ *It's an ecological disaster with no parallel anywhere else in the world.* ❷ N-COUNT If there are **parallels** between two things, they are similar in some ways. ❑ *Detailed study of folk music from a variety of countries reveals many close parallels.* ❑ *There are significant parallels with the 1980s.* ❸ V-T If one thing **parallels** another, they happen at the same time or are similar, and often seem to be connected. ❑ *Often there are emotional reasons paralleling the financial ones.* ❑ *His remarks paralleled those of the president.* ❹ ADJ **Parallel** events or situations happen at the same time as one another, or are similar to one another. ❑ *...parallel talks between the two countries' Foreign Ministers.* ❑ *Their instincts do not always run parallel with ours.* ❺ ADJ If two lines, two objects, or two lines of movement are **parallel**, they are the same distance apart along their whole length. ❑ *...seventy-two ships, drawn up in two parallel lines.* ❑ *Farthing Lane's just above the High Street and parallel with it.*

[영국영어 parallelling, parallelled] ■ 가산명사 대등한 것; 필적하는 것 ❑ 영국사를 아는 독자들은 수도원의 억압과 막연하게 비슷한 것을 발견할 것이다. ❑ 그것은 세상 어느 곳에서도 비슷한 예를 찾아볼 수 없는 생태적 재앙이다. ❷ 가산명사 유사성 ❑ 여러 나라의 민속 음악을 자세히 연구하면 많은 유사성이 드러난다. ❑ 1980년대와 여러 가지 중대한 유사성이 있다. ❸ 타동사 동시에 발생하다, 병행하다; 유사하다 ❑ 대개 경제적인 이유와 병행하는 감정적인 이유도 있다. ❑ 그의 발언은 대통령의 발언과 유사했다. ❹ 형용사 동시의; 유사한 ❑ 두 나라의 외무 장관들 사이에 동시에 이루어지는 대화 ❑ 그들의 본능이 항상 우리의 것과 유사한 것은 아니다. ❺ 형용사 평행한 ❑ 두 줄로 평행하게 세워 놓은 72척의 배 ❑ 파딩 레인은 하이 스트리트 바로 위에 있으며 그 도로와 평행하게 달린다.

I

J

K

L

M

N.   analogy, correlation, resemblance, similarity ■ ❷

N

O

pa|raly|sis /pərǽləsɪs/ ■ N-UNCOUNT **Paralysis** is the loss of the ability to move and feel in all or part of your body. ❑ *...paralysis of the leg.* ❷ N-UNCOUNT **Paralysis** is the state of being unable to act or function properly. ❑ *The paralysis of the leadership leaves the army without its supreme command.*

■ 불가산명사 마비 ❑ 다리의 마비 ❷ 불가산명사 마비 ❑ 지도부의 마비 때문에 군대의 최고 지휘 체계가 사라졌다.

P

para|lyze /pǽrəlaɪz/ (**paralyzes, paralyzing, paralyzed**) [BRIT **paralyse**] ■ V-T If someone is **paralyzed** by an accident or an illness, they have no feeling in their body, or in part of their body, and are unable to move. ❑ *She is paralyzed from the waist down.* ● **para|lyzed** ADJ ❑ *A guy with paralyzed legs is not supposed to ride horses.* ❷ V-T If a person, place, or organization **is paralyzed by** something, they become unable to act or function properly. ❑ *The city has been virtually paralyzed by sudden snowstorms.* ❑ *She was paralyzed by fear and love.* ● **para|lyzed** ADJ ❑ *He sat in his chair, paralyzed with dread.*

[영국영어 paralyse] ■ 타동사 마비되다 ❑ 그녀는 하반신이 마비되었다. ● 마비된 형용사 ❑ 다리가 마비된 사람은 말을 타서는 안 된다. ❷ 타동사 마비되다 ❑ 갑작스러운 폭설로 도시가 사실상 마비되었다. ❑ 그녀는 두려움과 사랑 때문에 마비되었다. ● 마비된 형용사 ❑ 그는 두려움에 마비된 채 의자에 앉아 있었다.

Q

R

para|med|ic /pǽrəmɛ́dɪk, BRIT pǽrəmedɪk/ (**paramedics**) N-COUNT A **paramedic** is a person whose training is similar to that of a nurse and who helps to do medical work. ❑ *We intend to have a paramedic on every ambulance within the next three years.*

가산명사 응급 구조대원, 준의료 활동 종사자 ❑ 우리는 앞으로 3년 이내에 모든 구급차에 응급 구조 대원을 한 명씩 태울 것이다.

S

T

pa|ram|eter /pərǽmɪtər/ (**parameters**) N-COUNT **Parameters** are factors or limits which affect the way that something can be done or made. [FORMAL] ❑ *...some of the parameters that determine the taste of a wine.*

가산명사 범위; 요인 [격식체] ❑ 와인의 맛을 결정하는 요인들 일부

U

para|mili|tary /pǽrəmɪ́lɪteri, BRIT pǽrəmilɪtri/ (**paramilitaries**) ■ ADJ A **paramilitary** organization is organized like an army and performs either civil or military functions in a country. [ADJ n] ❑ *Searches by the army and paramilitary forces have continued today.* ● N-COUNT **Paramilitaries** are members of a paramilitary organization. ❑ *Paramilitaries and army recruits patrolled the village.* ❷ ADJ A **paramilitary** organization is an illegal group that is organized like an army. [ADJ n] ❑ *...a law which said that all paramilitary groups must be disarmed.* ● N-COUNT **Paramilitaries** are members of an illegal paramilitary organization. ❑ *Paramilitaries were blamed for the shooting.*

■ 형용사 준군사 조직 ❑ 군대와 준군사 조직의 수색이 오늘도 이어졌다. ● 가산명사 준군사 조직 대원들 ❑ 준군사 조직 대원들과 육군 신병들이 마을을 순찰했다. ❷ 형용사 민병대의 ❑ 모든 민병대의 무장 해제를 요구한 법 ● 가산명사 민병대원들 ❑ 민병대원들이 발포 사건의 범인으로 지목되었다.

V

W

para|mount /pǽrəmaunt/ ADJ Something that is **paramount** or of **paramount** importance is more important than anything else. ❑ *The child's welfare must be seen as paramount.*

형용사 최고의, 최우선하는 ❑ 아이의 안녕을 가장 중요하게 여겨야 한다.

X

Y

para|noia /pǽrənɔ́ɪə/ ■ N-UNCOUNT If you say that someone suffers from **paranoia**, you think that they are too suspicious and afraid of other people. ❑ *The mood is one of paranoia and expectation of war.* ❷ N-UNCOUNT In psychology, if someone suffers from **paranoia**, they wrongly believe that other people are

■ 불가산명사 피해망상증 ❑ 전체적으로 피해망상증에 빠져 전쟁을 예상하는 분위기이다. ❷ 불가산명사 편집증

Z

trying to harm them, or believe themselves to be much more important than they really are.

para|noid /pǽrənɔɪd/ (**paranoids**) **1** ADJ If you say that someone is **paranoid**, you mean that they are extremely suspicious and afraid of other people. ❑ *I'm not going to get paranoid about it.* ❑ *...a paranoid politician who saw enemies all around him.* **2** ADJ Someone who is **paranoid** suffers from the mental illness of paranoia. ❑ *...paranoid delusions.* ● N-COUNT A **paranoid** is someone who is paranoid. ❑ *...these sad, deluded, paranoids.*

■ 형용사 편집증적인 ❑ 그것 때문에 편집증적이 되지는 않을 것이다. ❑ 주변 모든 사람을 적으로 보는 편집증적인 정치인 ❷ 형용사 편집증의 ❑ 편집증에 의한 망상 ● 가산명사 편집증 환자 ❑ 이 불쌍하고 미혹된 편집증 환자들

para|pher|na|lia /pærəfərnéɪlyə, -fəneɪl-/ N-UNCOUNT You can refer to a large number of objects that someone has with them or that are connected with a particular activity as **paraphernalia**. ❑ *...a large courtyard full of builders' paraphernalia.*

불가산명사 장비 ❑ 건축업자들의 장비가 가득 있는 큰 마당

para|phrase /pǽrəfreɪz/ (**paraphrases, paraphrasing, paraphrased**) **1** V-T/V-I If you **paraphrase** someone or **paraphrase** something that they have said or written, you express what they have said or written in a different way. ❑ *Parents, to paraphrase Philip Larkin, can seriously damage your health.* ❑ *Baxter paraphrased the contents of the press release.* **2** N-COUNT A **paraphrase** of something written or spoken is the same thing expressed in a different way. ❑ *The last two clauses were an exact quote rather than a paraphrase of Mr. Forth's remarks.*

■ 타동사/자동사 약간 바꿔서 인용하다; 부연 설명하다 ❑ 필립 라킨의 말을 약간 바꿔서 인용하자면 부모들이 당신의 건강을 심하게 해칠 수도 있다. ❑ 백스터는 언론 보도 자료의 내용을 약간 바꿔서 전달했다. ❷ 가산명사 약간 바꿔 표현한 것, 페러프레이즈 ❑ 마지막 두 절은 포스 씨의 말을 조금도 바꾸지 않고 그대로 인용한 것이었다.

para|plegic /pærəplíːdʒɪk/ (**paraplegics**) N-COUNT A **paraplegic** is someone who cannot move the lower half of their body, for example because of an injury to their spine. ❑ *Theoretically, such equipment could help paraplegics regain movement.* ● ADJ **Paraplegic** is also an adjective. ❑ *A passenger was injured so badly he will be paraplegic for the rest of his life.*

가산명사 하반신불수 환자 ❑ 이론적으로, 그와 같은 장비는 하반신불수 환자들이 움직임을 회복하도록 도울 수 있다. ● 형용사 하반신불수의 ❑ 승객 한 명이 여생을 하반신불수로 살게 될 정도로 심하게 부상당했다.

para|site /pǽrəsaɪt/ (**parasites**) **1** N-COUNT A **parasite** is a small animal or plant that lives on or inside a larger animal or plant, and gets its food from it. ❑ *Kangaroos harbor a vast range of parasites.* **2** N-COUNT If you disapprove of someone because you think that they get money or other things from other people but do not do anything in return, you can call them a **parasite**. [DISAPPROVAL] ❑ *...a parasite, who produced nothing but lived on the work of others.*

■ 가산명사 기생 동물; 기생 식물; 기생충 ❑ 캥거루의 몸속에는 매우 다양한 종류의 기생충들이 산다. ❷ 가산명사 기생충 같은 인간 [탐탁찮음] ❑ 아무것도 생산하지 않으면서 남들이 하는 일에 의지하여 사는 기생충 같은 인간

para|sit|ic /pærəsítɪk/ also **parasitical** **1** ADJ **Parasitic** diseases are caused by parasites. ❑ *Will global warming mean the spread of tropical parasitic diseases?* **2** ADJ **Parasitic** animals and plants live on or inside larger animals or plants and get their food from them. ❑ *...tiny parasitic insects.* **3** ADJ If you describe a person or organization as **parasitic**, you mean that they get money or other things from people without doing anything in return. [DISAPPROVAL] ❑ *...a parasitic new middle class of consultants and experts.*

■ 형용사 기생충에 의한 ❑ 지구 온난화가 열대성 기생충 질병의 만연이라는 결과를 낳을 것인가? ❷ 형용사 기생하는 ❑ 작은 기생 곤충들 ❸ 형용사 (비유적) 기생하는 [탐탁찮음] ❑ 컨설턴트와 전문가들로 이루어진 새로운 기생적 중산 계층

para|troop|er /pǽrətruːpər/ (**paratroopers**) N-COUNT **Paratroopers** are soldiers who are trained to be dropped by parachute into battle or into enemy territory.

가산명사 낙하산 부대

par|cel /páːrsəl/ (**parcels**) **1** N-COUNT A **parcel** is something wrapped in paper, in a bag or large envelope, or in a box, usually so that it can be sent to someone by mail. [mainly BRIT; AM usually **package**] ❑ *...parcels of food and clothing.* **2** PHRASE If you say that something is **part and parcel** of something else, you are emphasizing that it is involved or included in it. [EMPHASIS] ❑ *Payment was part and parcel of carrying on insurance business within the UK.*

■ 가산명사 소포 [주로 영국영어; 미국영어 대개 package] ❑ 음식과 옷이 담긴 소포 ❷ 구 중요한 부분 [강조] ❑ 배상은 영국 내에서 보험 사업을 해 나가는 데 있어 중요한 부분이었다.

parched /páːrtʃt/ **1** ADJ If something, especially the ground or a plant, is **parched**, it is very dry, because there has been no rain. ❑ *The clouds gathered and showers poured down upon the parched earth.* **2** ADJ If your mouth, throat, or lips are **parched**, they are unpleasantly dry. ❑ *Her throat was parched, and she was exhausted from all the walking.* **3** ADJ If you say that you are **parched**, you mean that you are very thirsty. [INFORMAL] [v-link ADJ] ❑ *When I told them I was parched, they went and got me a bottle of mineral water.*

■ 형용사 (가뭄에) 바싹 마른 ❑ 구름이 모여들더니 바싹 마른 땅 위에 소나기가 쏟아져 내렸다. ❷ 형용사 바싹 마른 ❑ 그녀는 목이 바싹 말랐고, 걸어 다니느라 녹초가 되었다. ❸ 형용사 매우 목마른 [비격식체] ❑ 내가 그들에게 몹시 목이 마르다고 말하자, 그들이 가서 생수 한 병을 가져다줬다.

Word Link   don ≈ giving : **don**ate, **don**or, par**don**

---

par|don /páːrdⁿn/ (**pardons, pardoning, pardoned**) **1** CONVENTION You say "**Pardon?**" or "**I beg your pardon?**" or, in American English, "**Pardon me?**" when you want someone to repeat what they have just said because you have not heard or understood it. [SPOKEN, FORMULAE] ❑ *"Will you let me open it?" — "Pardon?" — "Can I open it?"* **2** CONVENTION People say "**I beg your pardon?**" when they are surprised or offended by something that someone has just said. [SPOKEN, FEELINGS] ❑ *"Would you get undressed, please?" — "I beg your pardon?" — "Will you get undressed?"* **3** CONVENTION You say "**I beg your pardon**" or "**I do beg your pardon**" as a way of apologizing for accidentally doing something wrong, such as disturbing someone or making a mistake. [SPOKEN, FORMULAE] ❑ *I was impolite and I do beg your pardon.* **4** CONVENTION Some people say "**Pardon me**" instead of "Excuse me" when they want to politely get someone's attention or interrupt them. [mainly BRIT, SPOKEN, FORMULAE] [AM usually **excuse me**] ❑ *Pardon me, are you finished, madam?* **5** V-T If someone who has been found guilty of a crime **is pardoned**, they are officially allowed to go free and are not punished. [usu passive] ❑ *Hundreds of political prisoners were pardoned and released.* ● N-COUNT **Pardon** is also a noun. ❑ *They lobbied the government on his behalf and he was granted a presidential pardon.*

■ 관용 표현 다시 한 번 말씀해 주십시오 [구어체, 의례적인 표현] ❑ "제가 그것을 열어도 될까요?" "다시 한 번 말씀해 주시겠어요?" "제가 그걸 열어도 되겠느냐고요?" ❷ 관용 표현 뭐라고요? [구어체, 감정 개입] ❑ "옷을 벗어 주시겠습니까?" "뭐라고요?" "옷을 벗어 주시겠어요?" ❸ 관용 표현 죄송합니다 [구어체, 의례적인 표현] ❑ 제가 무례했어요. 정말 죄송합니다. ❹ 관용 표현 실례합니다 [주로 영국영어, 구어체, 의례적인 표현] [미국영어 대개 excuse me] ❑ 실례합니다만, 다 드셨습니까, 사모님? ❺ 타동사 사면되다 ❑ 수백 명의 정치 사범이 사면되어 풀려났다. ● 가산명사 사면, 특사 ❑ 그들이 그를 대신하여 정부에 로비를 벌였고 그는 대통령 특사를 받았다.

pare /péər/ (**pares, paring, pared**) **1** V-T When you **pare** something, or **pare** part of it **off** or **away**, you cut off its skin or its outer layer. ❑ *Pare the brown skin from the meat with a very sharp knife.* ❑ *He took out a slab of cheese, pared off a slice and ate it hastily.* **2** V-T If you **pare** something **down** or **back**, or if you **pare** it, you reduce it. ❑ *The number of Ministries has been pared down by a third.* ❑ *The luxury tax won't really do much to pare down the budget deficit.*

■ 타동사 껍질을 벗기다 ❑ 아주 잘 드는 칼로 고기에서 김색 껍데기를 벗겨 내세요. ❑ 그는 치즈 한 판을 꺼내 얇게 한 조각 베어 내서 허겁지겁 먹었다. ❷ 타동사 절감하다, 줄이다 ❑ 부처 수가 3분의 1만큼 줄어들었다. ❑ 예산 적자를 줄이는 데 사치세가 실제로 크게 도움이 되지는 않을 것이다.

par|ent ♦♦♦ /péərənt, pǽr-/ (**parents**) **1** N-COUNT Your **parents** are your mother and father. ❑ *Children need their parents.* ❑ *This is where a lot of parents go wrong.* →see also **single parent** **2** ADJ An organization's **parent** organization is

■ 가산명사 부모 ❑ 아이들은 부모가 필요하다. ❑ 이 부분이 많은 부모들이 길을 잘못 드는 지점이다. ❷ 형용사 모체가 되는 ❑ 모회사를 포함한 각 단위가

the organization that created it and usually still controls it. [ADJ n] ❏ *Each unit including the parent company has its own, local management.* →see **child**

자체적인 지역 경영진을 두고 있다.

pa|ren|tal /pərˈentᵊl/ ADJ **Parental** is used to describe something that relates to parents in general, or to one or both of the parents of a particular child. ❏ *Medical treatment was sometimes given to children without parental consent.*

형용사 부모의 ❏ 때때로 아이들에게 부모의 동의 없이 치료가 행해졌다.

pa|ren|tal leave N-UNCOUNT **Parental leave** is time away from work, usually without pay, that parents are allowed in order to care for their children. [BUSINESS] ❏ *Parents are entitled to 13 weeks' parental leave to be taken during the first five years of a child's life.*

불가산명사 육아 휴가 [경제] ❏ 부모들은 아이가 태어난 후 처음 5년 동안에 13주의 육아 휴가를 받을 권리가 있다.

pa|ren|thesis /pərˈenθəsɪs/ (**parentheses**) /pərˈenθəsiz/ **1** N-COUNT **Parentheses** are a pair of curved marks that you put around words or numbers to indicate that they are additional, separate, or less important. (This sentence is in parentheses.) [usu pl] **2** PHRASE You say "**in parenthesis**" to indicate that you are about to add something before going back to the main topic. ❏ *In parenthesis, I'd say that there were two aspects to writing you must never lose sight of.*

1 가산명사 괄호 **2** 구 덧붙여 말하면 ❏ 덧붙여서, 글쓰기에는 결코 놓쳐서는 안 되는 두 가지 측면이 있다고 말하고 싶어요.

par|ent|hood /pˈeərənthʊd, pær-/ N-UNCOUNT **Parenthood** is the state of being a parent. ❏ *She may feel unready for the responsibilities of parenthood.*

불가산명사 부모로서의 신분 ❏ 그녀는 부모로서의 책임에 대해 미비하다고 느낄지도 모른다.

par|ent|ing /pˈeərəntɪŋ, pær-/ N-UNCOUNT **Parenting** is the activity of bringing up and taking care of your child. ❏ *Parenting is not fully valued by society.*

불가산명사 육아, 양육 ❏ 양육의 가치를 사회가 충분히 인정해 주지 않는다.

par|ish /pˈærɪʃ/ (**parishes**) **1** N-COUNT A **parish** is a village or part of a town which has its own church and priest. ❏ *...the parish of St Mark's, Lakenham.* ❏ *Parish priests have referred to it in their sermons.* **2** N-COUNT A **parish** is a small country area in England which has its own elected council. ❏ *...elected representatives, such as County and Parish Councillors.*

1 가산명사 교구 ❏ 레이켄엄 세인트 마크 교구 ❏ 교구 목사들이 설교 중에 그것을 언급해 왔다. **2** 가산명사 행정 교구 ❏ 주나 행정 교구 의원 같은 선출직 대의원

par|ity /pˈærɪti/ N-UNCOUNT If there is **parity** between two things, they are equal. [FORMAL] ❏ *Women have yet to achieve wage or occupational parity in many fields.*

불가산명사 동등; 등가 [격식체] ❏ 여성들은 아직도 많은 분야에서 임금이나 직업의 동등성을 달성해야 한다.

park ♦♦◇ /pˈɑrk/ (**parks, parking, parked**) **1** N-COUNT A **park** is a public area of land with grass and trees, usually in a town, where people go in order to relax and enjoy themselves. ❏ *...Regent's Park.* ❏ *...a brisk walk with the dog around the park.* **2** V-T/V-I When you **park** a vehicle or **park** somewhere, you drive the vehicle into a position where it can stay for a period of time, and leave it there. ❏ *Greenfield turned into the next side street and parked.* ❏ *He found a place to park the car.* **3** N-COUNT You can refer to a place where a particular activity is carried out as a **park**. [supp n] ❏ *...a science and technology park.* **4** →see also **ballpark, car park, national park**
→see Word Web: **park**

1 가산명사 공원 ❏ 리전트 공원 ❏ 개를 데리고 공원을 한 바퀴 활기차게 산책 **2** 타동사/자동사 주차하다 ❏ 그린필드는 다음 골목으로 들어가서 주차를 했다. ❏ 그는 주차할 곳을 발견했다. **3** 가산명사 (특정한 활동을 위한) 단지 ❏ 과학 기술 단지

> Note that you do not use the word "parking" to refer to a place where cars are parked. Instead, you talk about a **parking lot** in American English and a **car park** in British English. **Parking** is used only to refer to the action of parking your car, or to the state of being parked. ❏ *...a "No Parking" sign.*

> 자동차를 주차해 두는 장소를 가리킬 때는 parking이란 말을 쓰지 않음을 유의하라. 그 대신에 미국 영어에서는 parking lot이라 하고 영국 영어에서는 car park이라고 한다. parking은 자동차를 주차하는 행위나 주차된 상태를 가리킬 때만 쓴다. ❏ *...'주차 금지' 표지판*

park|ing /pˈɑrkɪŋ/ **1** N-UNCOUNT **Parking** is the action of moving a vehicle into a place in a garage or by the side of the road where it can be left. ❏ *In many towns parking is allowed only on one side of the street.* **2** N-UNCOUNT **Parking** is space for parking a vehicle in. ❏ *Cars allowed, but parking is limited.*

1 불가산명사 주차 ❏ 많은 도시에서 도로의 한쪽 면에만 주차가 허용된다. **2** 불가산명사 주차 공간 ❏ 차를 가져올 순 있지만, 주차 공간이 한정되어 있습니다.

park|ing gar|age (**parking garages**) N-COUNT A **parking garage** is a building where people can leave their cars. [AM; BRIT **car park, multi-storey car park**] ❏ *...a multi-level parking garage.*

가산명사 주차 건물 [미국영어; 영국영어 car park, multi-storey car park] ❏ 다층 주차 건물

park|ing lot (**parking lots**) N-COUNT A **parking lot** is an area of ground where people can leave their cars. [AM; BRIT **car park**] ❏ *A block up the street I found a parking lot.*

가산명사 주차장 [미국영어; 영국영어 car park] ❏ 그 거리로부터 한 블록 위쪽에서 주차장을 찾았다.

park|ing me|ter (**parking meters**) N-COUNT A **parking meter** is a device which you have to put money into when you park in a parking space.

가산명사 주차 요금 계산기

par|lia|ment ♦♦◇ /pˈɑrləmənt/ (**parliaments**) also **Parliament** **1** N-COUNT; N-PROPER The **parliament** of some countries, for example Britain, is the group of people who make or change its laws, and decide what policies the country should follow. ❏ *The Bangladesh Parliament today (Monday) approved the policy, but it has not yet become law.* →see also **Houses of Parliament, Member of Parliament** →see **parliament** **2** N-COUNT A particular **parliament** is a particular period of time in which a parliament is doing its work, between two elections or between two periods of holiday. ❏ *The legislation is expected to be passed in the next parliament.*

1 가산명사; 고유명사 의회, 국회 ❏ 방글라데시 의회는 오늘 (월요일) 그 정책을 승인했지만, 아직 법률이 된 것은 아니다. **2** 가산명사 회기 ❏ 그 법안은 다음 회기 중에 통과될 전망이다.

Word Web park

In 1858, Central Park* became the first planned urban **park** in the United States. At first only a few wealthy families lived close enough to enjoy it. Today over 20 million visitors of all ages and backgrounds use the park for **recreation** each year. Children love the many **playgrounds**, the **carousel**, and the petting **zoo**. Families spread blankets on the grass for **picnics**. Couples row around the lake in rented rowboats. Seniors **stroll** through the **gardens**. Players fill the **tennis courts** and **baseball diamonds** all summer. **Cyclists** and **runners** use Central Park Drive* when it's closed to car traffic on weekends.

Central Park: an 843-acre park in New York City.
Central Park Drive: a road in Central Park.

A B C D E F G H I J K L M N O P Q R S T U V W X Y Z

par|lia|men|ta|ry ◆◇◇ /pɑrləmɛntəri/ ADJ **Parliamentary** is used to describe things that are connected with a parliament or with Members of Parliament. [ADJ n] ❑ *He used his influence to make sure she was not selected as a parliamentary candidate.*

형용사 의회의; 국회의원의 ❑ 그는 그녀가 의회의원 후보로 선정되지 않도록 분명히 하기 위해 자신의 영향력을 사용했다.

par|lor /pɑrlər/ (**parlors**) [BRIT **parlour**] N-COUNT **Parlor** is used in the names of some types of stores which provide a service, rather than selling things. [n N] ❑ *...a funeral parlor.*

[영국영어 parlour] 가산명사 (특정 업종의) 가게 ❑ 장의사

pa|ro|chial /pəroʊkiəl/ ADJ If you describe someone as **parochial**, you are critical of them because you think they are too concerned with their own affairs and should be thinking about more important things. [DISAPPROVAL] ❑ *When her brother arrives home on a visit from Hong Kong, he sneers at her parochial existence.*

형용사 편협한 [탐탁찮음] ❑ 그녀의 오빠가 홍콩에서 집에 다니러 오면, 오빠는 그녀의 편협한 생활을 비웃는다.

paro|dy /pærədi/ (**parodies, parodying, parodied**) 1 N-VAR A **parody** is a humorous piece of writing, drama, or music which imitates the style of a well-known person or represents a familiar situation in an exaggerated way. ❑ *"The Scarlet Capsule" was a parody of the popular 1959 TV series "The Quatermass Experiment."* 2 V-T When someone **parodies** a particular work, thing, or person, they imitate it in an amusing or exaggerated way. ❑ *...a sketch parodying the views of Jean-Marie Le Pen.*

1 가산명사 또는 불가산명사 패러디 ❑ '주홍 캡슐'은 1959년의 유명한 텔레비전 연속극 '쿼터매스 실험'의 패러디였다. 2 타동사 패러디하다 ❑ 장 마리 르펭의 견해를 패러디한 그림

pa|role /pəroʊl/ (**paroles, paroling, paroled**) 1 N-UNCOUNT If a prisoner is given **parole**, he or she is released before the official end of their prison sentence and has to promise to behave well. ❑ *Although sentenced to life, he will become eligible for parole after serving 10 years.* ● PHRASE If a prisoner is **on parole**, he or she is released before the official end of their prison sentence and will not be sent back to prison if their behavior is good. 2 V-T If a prisoner **is paroled**, he or she is given parole. [usu passive] ❑ *He faces at most 12 years in prison and could be paroled after eight years.*

1 불가산명사 가석방 ❑ 그가 종신형을 선고받았지만, 10년간 복역하면 가석방을 받을 수 있는 자격이 될 것이다. ● 구 가석방되어 ❑ 2 타동사 가석방시키다 ❑ 그는 많아야 12년 형을 살 것이고 8년이 지나면 가석방될 수도 있다.

par|rot /pærət/ (**parrots, parroting, parroted**) 1 N-COUNT A **parrot** is a tropical bird with a curved beak and brightly-colored or gray feathers. Parrots can be kept as pets. Some parrots are able to copy what people say. 2 V-T If you disapprove of the fact that someone is just repeating what someone else has said, often without really understanding it, you can say that they **are parroting** it. [DISAPPROVAL] ❑ *Generations of students have learnt to parrot the standard explanations.*

1 가산명사 앵무새 2 타동사 앵무새처럼 되뇌다 [탐탁찮음] ❑ 여러 세대에 걸쳐 학생들은 모범적인 해석을 앵무새처럼 되뇌도록 배워 왔다.

pars|ley /pɑrsli, BRIT pɑːsli/ N-UNCOUNT **Parsley** is a small plant with curly leaves that are used for flavoring or decorating savory food. ❑ *...parsley sauce.*

불가산명사 파슬리 ❑ 파슬리 소스

pars|nip /pɑrsnɪp/ (**parsnips**) N-COUNT A **parsnip** is a long cream-colored root vegetable.

가산명사 서양 방풍나물, 파스닙

---

part

① NOUN USES, QUANTIFIER USES, AND PHRASES
② VERB USES

Word Link   *par ≈ equal : compare, disparate, part*

① **part** ◆◆◆ /pɑrt/ (**parts**) →Please look at category 15 to see if the expression you are looking for is shown under another headword. 1 N-COUNT A **part** of something is one of the pieces, sections, or elements that it consists of. ❑ *I like that part of Cape Town.* 2 N-COUNT A **part** for a machine or vehicle is one of the smaller pieces that is used to make it. ❑ *...spare parts for military equipment.* 3 QUANT **Part** of something is some of it. [QUANT of sing-n/n-uncount] ❑ *It was a very severe accident and he lost part of his foot.* ❑ *Woodhead spent part of his childhood in Rhodesia.* 4 ADV If you say that something is **part** one thing, **part** another, you mean that it is to some extent the first thing and to some extent the second thing. ❑ *The television producer today has to be part news person, part educator.* 5 N-COUNT You can use **part** when you are talking about the proportions of substances in a mixture. For example, if you are told to use five **parts** water to one **part** paint, the mixture should contain five times as much water as paint. ❑ *Use turpentine and linseed oil, three parts to two.* 6 N-COUNT A **part** in a play or movie is one of the roles in it which an actor or actress can perform. ❑ *Alf Sjoberg offered her a large part in the play he was directing.* 7 N-SING Your **part** in something that happens is your involvement in it. [poss N in n] ❑ *If only he could conceal his part in the accident.* 8 N-UNCOUNT If something or someone is **part of** a group or organization, they belong to it or are included in it. [also a N, N of n] ❑ *...voting on whether to remain part of the Union or become independent.* 9 N-COUNT The **part** in someone's hair is the line running from the front to the back of their head where their hair lies in different directions. [AM; BRIT **parting**] ❑ *The straight white part in her ebony hair seemed to divide the back of her head in half.* 10 PHRASE If something or someone **plays** a large or important **part in** an event or situation, they are very involved in it and have an important effect on what happens. ❑ *These days work plays an important part in a single woman's life.* 11 PHRASE If you **take part in** an activity, you do it together with other people. ❑ *Thousands of students have taken part in demonstrations.* 12 PHRASE When you are describing people's thoughts or actions, you can say **for** her **part** or **for** my **part**, for example, to introduce what a particular person thinks or does. [FORMAL] ❑ *For my part, I feel elated and close to tears.* 13 PHRASE If you talk about a feeling or action **on** someone's **part**, you are referring to something that they feel or do. ❑ *...techniques on their part to keep us from knowing exactly what's going on.* ❑ *There is no need for any further instructions on my part.* 14 PHRASE You use **in part** to indicate that something exists or happens to some extent but not completely. [FORMAL] ❑ *The levels of blood glucose depend in part on what you eat and when you eat.* 15 **part and parcel** →see **parcel**

1 가산명사 일부, 부분 ❑ 나는 케이프타운의 그 부분이 맘에 든다. 2 가산명사 부품 ❑ 군용 장비의 예비 부품 3 수량사 일부의 ❑ 그것은 매우 심한 사고였고 그는 한 쪽 발 일부를 잃었다. ❑ 우드헤드는 유년 시절 일부를 로디지아에서 보냈다. 4 부사 어느 정도 ❑ 오늘날의 텔레비전 연출자는 어느 정도는 기자여야 하고 또 어느 정도는 교육자여야 한다. 5 가산명사 비율 ❑ 테레빈유와 아마인유를 3대 2의 비율로 쓰세요. 6 가산명사 (배우의) 역 ❑ 앨프 쇼버그는 그녀에게 자신이 연출하고 있던 연극의 큰 역을 가르고 있는 것처럼 보였다. 7 단수명사 -에의 관여 ❑ 만약 그가 그 사고에 관여한 것을 숨길 수만 있다면 8 불가산명사 -의 일원 ❑ 연합의 일원으로 남을 것인가 아니면 독립할 것인가에 대한 투표 9 가산명사 가르마 [미국영어; 영국영어 parting] ❑ 그녀의 흑단색 머리카락 속에 있는 일직선의 흰 가르마가 뒷머리를 반으로 가르고 있는 것처럼 보였다. 10 구 -한 역할을 하다 ❑ 요즘에는 일이 독신 여성의 삶에서 중요한 역할을 한다. 11 구 참가하다 ❑ 수천 명의 학생들이 시위에 참가해 왔다. 12 구 -로서는, -의 경우 [격식체] ❑ 나로서는, 너무 기뻐서 거의 눈물이 날 지경이다. 13 구 -의 입장에서 [격식체] ❑ 그들 입장에서 우리로 하여금 정확히 무슨 일이 벌어지고 있는지 알 수 없도록 하는 수법들 ❑ 내 입장에서는 더 이상의 지시가 필요 없다. 14 구 부분적으로 [격식체] ❑ 혈당 수치는 부분적으로 무엇을 먹고 언제 먹는가에 달려 있다.

② **part** ◆◇◇ /pɑrt/ (**parts, parting, parted**) 1 V-T/V-I If things that are next to each other **part** or if you **part** them, they move in opposite directions, so that

1 타동사/자동사 벌어지다; 갈라놓다 ❑ 깊은 숨을 들이쉬려는 것처럼 그녀의 입술이 벌어졌다. 2 타동사

a b c d e f g h i j k l m n o p q r s t u v w x y z

A
there is a space between them. ❑ *Her lips parted as if she were about to take a deep breath.* ❷ V-T If you **part** your hair in the middle or at one side, you make it lie in two different directions so that there is a straight line running from the front of your head to the back. ❑ *Picking up a brush, Joanna parted her hair.*

B
❸ V-RECIP When two people **part**, or if one person **parts from** another, they leave each other. [FORMAL] ❑ *He gave me the envelope and we parted.* ❹ V-RECIP If you **are parted from** someone you love, you are prevented from being with them. ❑ *I don't believe Lotte and I will ever be parted.* ❺ →see also **parting**

가르마 타다 ❑ 조안나는 빗을 들고서 자기 머리에 가르마를 탔다. ❸ 상호동사 헤어지다 [격식체] ❑ 그가 내게 그 봉투를 주었고 우리는 헤어졌다. ❹ 상호동사 -와 헤어지다 ❑ 로테와 내가 헤어지는 일이 있을 거라고는 생각하지 않는다.

C

D
Thesaurus   part의 참조어

N.   component, fraction, half, ingredient, piece, portion, section; (ant.) entirety, whole ① ❶
       role, share ① ❼

E
V.   separate, split, tear ② ❶

▶**part with** PHRASAL VERB If you **part with** something that is valuable or that you would prefer to keep, you give it or sell it to someone else. ❑ *Buyers might require further assurances before parting with their cash.*

구동사 내주다 ❑ 구매자들이 현금을 내주기 전에 더 확실한 보증을 요구할 수도 있다.

F

G
par|tial /pɑʃ⁰l/ ❶ ADJ You use **partial** to refer to something that is not complete or whole. ❑ *He managed to reach a partial agreement with both republics.* ❑ *...a partial ban on the use of cars in the city.* ❷ ADJ If you are **partial to** something, you like it. [v-link ADJ to n/-ing] ❑ *He's partial to sporty women with blue eyes.* ❑ *Mollie confesses she is rather partial to pink.* ❸ ADJ Someone who is **partial** supports a particular person or thing, for example in a competition or dispute, instead of being completely fair. [v-link ADJ] ❑ *I might be accused of being partial.*

❶ 형용사 부분적인; 불완전한 ❑ 그는 그럭저럭 양국 모두와 부분적인 합의에 도달했다. ❑ 시내에서의 자동차 사용에 대한 부분적 금지 ❷ 형용사 -을 좋아하는 ❑ 그는 푸른 눈의 발랄한 여자들을 좋아한다. ❑ 몰리는 분홍색을 상당히 좋아한다고 털어놓는다. ❸ 형용사 불공평한, 편파적인 ❑ 나는 편파적이라는 비난을 받을지도 모른다.

H

I
par|tial|ly /pɑʃəli/ ADV If something happens or exists **partially**, it happens or exists to some extent, but not completely. [ADV with cl/group] ❑ *Lisa is deaf in one ear and partially blind.*

부사 부분적으로, 약간 ❑ 리사는 한쪽 귀가 안 들리고 눈도 약간 안 보인다.

J
par|tici|pant /pɑrtɪsɪpənt/ (participants) N-COUNT The **participants** in an activity are the people who take part in it. ❑ *40 of the course participants are offered employment with the company.*

가산명사 관여자, 참가자 ❑ 본 과정 참가자 중 40명에게는 회사 측에서 일자리를 제공합니다.

K
par|tici|pate ♦◇◇ /pɑrtɪsɪpeɪt/ (participates, participating, participated) V-I If you **participate** in an activity, you take part in it. ❑ *They expected him to participate in the ceremony.* ❑ *Over half the population of this country participate in sport.* ● **par|tici|pa|tion** /pɑrtɪsɪpeɪʃ⁰n/ N-UNCOUNT ❑ *...participation in religious activities.*

자동사 참가하다, 관여하다 ❑ 그들은 그가 식에 참가할 것으로 기대했다. ❑ 이 나라 인구 절반 이상이 스포츠를 즐긴다. ● 참가, 참여 불가산명사 ❑ 종교 활동 참여

L

M
Thesaurus   participate의 참조어

V.   cooperate, join in, perform, share; (ant.) observe

N
par|ti|ci|ple /pɑrtɪsɪp⁰l/ (participles) N-COUNT In grammar, a **participle** is a form of a verb that can be used in compound tenses of the verb. There are two participles in English: the past participle, which usually ends in "-ed," and the present participle, which ends in "-ing."

가산명사 분사

O

Word Link   cle ≈ small : article, cubicle, particle

P
par|ti|cle /pɑrtɪk⁰l/ (particles) ❶ N-COUNT A **particle of** something is a very small piece or amount of it. ❑ *...a particle of hot metal.* ❑ *There is a particle of truth in his statement.* ❷ N-COUNT In physics, a **particle** is a piece of matter smaller than an atom, for example an electron or a proton. [TECHNICAL] ❑ *...the sub-atomic particles that make up matter.* →see **lightning**

❶ 가산명사 극히 작은 조각 ❑ 아주 작은 뜨거운 금속 조각 ❑ 그의 진술에는 진실이 아주 조금 들어 있다. ❷ 가산명사 소립자 [과학 기술] ❑ 물질을 형성하는 원자보다 작은 소립자들

Q

R
par|ticu|lar ♦♦◇ /pɑrtɪkyələr/ ❶ ADJ You use **particular** to emphasize that you are talking about one thing or one kind of thing rather than other similar ones. [EMPHASIS] [ADJ n] ❑ *I remembered a particular story about a postman who was a murderer.* ❑ *I have to know exactly why it is I'm doing a particular job.* ❷ ADJ If a person or thing has a **particular** quality or possession, it is distinct and belongs only to them. [ADJ n] ❑ *I have a particular responsibility to ensure I make the right decision.* ❸ ADJ You can use **particular** to emphasize that something is greater or more intense than usual. [EMPHASIS] [ADJ n] ❑ *Particular emphasis will be placed on oral language training.* ❹ ADJ If you say that someone is **particular**, you mean that they choose things and do things very carefully, and are not easily satisfied. ❑ *Ted was very particular about the colors he used.* ❺ →see also **particulars** ❻ PHRASE You use **in particular** to indicate that what you are saying applies especially to one thing or person. ❑ *The situation in Ethiopia in particular is worrying.* ❑ *Why should he notice her car in particular?*

❶ 형용사 특정한, 어떤 [강조] ❑ 나는 살인을 저지른 우체부에 대한 어떤 이야기를 기억해 냈다. ❑ 내가 특정한 일을 하고 있는 이유가 뭔지 정확하게 알아야겠다. ❷ 형용사 특별한, 특유의 ❑ 내게는 확실하게 옳은 결정을 내려야 하는 특별한 책임이 있다. ❸ 형용사 특별한 [강조] ❑ 회화 훈련에 특별히 역점을 둘 것입니다. ❹ 형용사 꼼꼼한, 까다로운 ❑ 테드는 색채 사용에 있어 대단히 까다로웠다. ❻ 구 특히, 각별히 ❑ 특히 에티오피아의 사정이 염려스럽다. ❑ 왜 그가 각별히 그녀의 차를 알아봐야 한단 말인가?

S

T

U

V
Thesaurus   particular의 참조어

ADJ.   distinct, precise, specific; (ant.) general ❶ ❷
        demanding, fussy; (ant.) easygoing ❹

W

X
par|ticu|lar|ly ♦♦◇ /pɑrtɪkyələrli/ ❶ ADV You use **particularly** to indicate that what you are saying applies especially to one thing or situation. [ADV with cl/group] ❑ *Keep your office space looking good, particularly your desk.* ❑ *More local employment will be created, particularly in service industries.* ❷ ADV **Particularly** means more than usual or more than other things. [EMPHASIS] [ADV with cl/group] ❑ *Progress has been particularly disappointing.*

❶ 부사 특히, 각별히 ❑ 당신의 사무 공간, 특히 책상을 보기 좋게 관리하세요. ❑ 특히 서비스 산업에서, 더 많은 지역 고용이 창출될 것이다. ❷ 부사 특별히, 유난히 [강조] ❑ 경과가 유난히 실망스러웠다.

Y

Z
par|ticu|lars /pɑrtɪkyələz/ N-PLURAL The **particulars** of something or someone are facts or details about them which are written down and kept as a record. ❑ *You will find all the particulars in Chapter 9.*

복수명사 상세한 내용 ❑ 모든 상세한 내용은 9장에 있습니다.

part|ing /pɑrtɪŋ/ (partings) **1** N-VAR **Parting** is the act of leaving a particular person or place. A **parting** is an occasion when this happens. ❏ *Parting from any one of you for even a short time is hard.* **2** ADJ Your **parting** words or actions are the things that you say or do as you are leaving a place or person. [ADJ n] ❏ *Her parting words left him feeling empty and alone.* **3** N-COUNT The **parting** in someone's hair is the line running from the front to the back of their head where their hair lies in different directions. [BRIT; AM **part**] ❏ *The hair was thick and cut short with a side parting.*

par|ti|san /pɑrtɪzən, BRIT pɑːtɪzæn/ (partisans) **1** ADJ Someone who is **partisan** strongly supports a particular person or cause, often without thinking carefully about the matter. ❏ *He is clearly too partisan to be a referee.* **2** N-COUNT **Partisans** are ordinary people, rather than soldiers, who join together to fight enemy soldiers who are occupying their country. ❏ *He was rescued by some Italian partisans.*

par|ti|tion /pɑrtɪʃ°n/ (partitions, partitioning, partitioned) **1** N-COUNT A **partition** is a wall or screen that separates one part of a room or vehicle from another. ❏ *...new offices divided only by glass partitions.* **2** V-T If you **partition** a room, you separate one part of it from another by means of a partition. ❏ *Bedrooms have again been created by partitioning a single larger room.* **3** V-T If a country **is partitioned**, it is divided into two or more independent countries. ❏ *Korea was partitioned in 1945.* ❏ *Britain was accused of trying to partition the country "because of historic enmity."* ● N-UNCOUNT **Partition** is also a noun. ❏ *...fighting which followed the partition of India.*

part|ly ◆◇◇ /pɑrtli/ ADV You use **partly** to indicate that something happens or exists to some extent, but not completely. [ADV with cl/group] ❏ *It's partly my fault.* ❏ *I have not worried so much this year, partly because I have had other things to think about.*

part|ner ◆◆◇ /pɑrtnər/ (partners, partnering, partnered) **1** N-COUNT Your **partner** is the person you are married to or are having a romantic or sexual relationship with. ❏ *Wanting other friends doesn't mean you don't love your partner.* **2** N-COUNT Your **partner** is the person you are doing something with, for example dancing with or playing with in a game against two other people. ❏ *...to dance with a partner.* ❏ *My partner for the event was the marvelous American player.* **3** N-COUNT The **partners** in a firm or business are the people who share the ownership of it. [BUSINESS] ❏ *He's a partner in a Chicago law firm.* **4** N-COUNT The **partner** of a country or organization is another country or organization with which they work or do business. ❏ *Spain has been one of Cuba's major trading partners.* **5** V-T If you **partner** someone, you are their partner in a game or in a dance. ❏ *He had partnered the famous Russian ballerina.* ❏ *He will be partnered by Ian Baker, the defending champion.*

part|ner|ship ◆◇◇ /pɑrtnərʃɪp/ (partnerships) N-VAR **Partnership** or a **partnership** is a relationship in which two or more people, organizations, or countries work together as partners. ❏ *...the partnership between Germany's banks and its businesses.*

part-time

| The adverb is also spelled **part time**. |

ADJ If someone is a **part-time** worker or has a **part-time** job, they work for only part of each day or week. ❏ *Many businesses are cutting back by employing lower-paid part-time workers.* ❏ *Part-time work is generally hard to find.* ● ADV **Part-time** is also an adverb. [ADV after v] ❏ *I want to work part-time.*

par|ty ◆◆◆ /pɑrti/ (parties, partying, partied) **1** N-COUNT A **party** is a political organization whose members have similar aims and beliefs. Usually the organization tries to get its members elected to the government of a country. ❏ *...a member of the Labour party.* ❏ *...opposition parties.* **2** N-COUNT A **party** is a social event, often in someone's home, at which people enjoy themselves doing things such as eating, drinking, dancing, talking, or playing games. ❏ *The couple met at a party.* ❏ *We threw a huge birthday party.* **3** V-I If you **party**, you enjoy yourself doing things such as going out to parties, drinking, dancing, and talking to people. ❏ *They come to eat and drink, to swim, to party. Sometimes they never go to bed.* **4** N-COUNT A **party** of people is a group of people who are doing something together, for example traveling together. ❏ *They became separated from their party.* ❏ *...a party of sightseers.* →see also **search party** **5** N-COUNT One of the people involved in a legal agreement or dispute can be referred to as a particular **party**. [LEGAL] ❏ *It has to be proved that they are the guilty party.* ❏ *...he was the injured party.* **6** PHRASE Someone who **is a party to** or **is party to** an action or agreement is involved in it, and therefore partly responsible for it. ❏ *Crook had resigned his post rather than be party to such treachery.*

Word Partnership   party의 연어

V.	**form** a party, **join** a party, **vote for** a party **1** **attend/go to** a party, **have/host/throw** a party, **invite** *someone* **to** a party **2**
N.	party **officials**, **opposition** party, party **platform 1** **birthday** party, **victory** party **2** **wedding** party **4**
ADJ.	**governing** party, **political** party **1** **responsible** party **5**

---

pass ◆◆◆ /pɑs, pæs/ (passes, passing, passed) **1** V-T/V-I To **pass** someone or something means to go past them without stopping. ❏ *As she passed the library door, the telephone began to ring.* ❏ *Jane stood aside to let her pass.* **2** V-I When someone or something **passes** in a particular direction, they move in that

---

1 가산명사 또는 불가산명사 헤어짐, 이별 ❏ 여러분 중의 누구와 잠시 동안이라도 헤어지는 것은 힘든 일입니다. **2** 형용사 작별의 ❏ 그녀가 떠나면서 남긴 말은 그에게 공허하고 고독한 기분을 느끼게 했다. **3** 가산명사 가르마 [영국영어; 미국영어 part] ❏ 머리는 숱이 많고 짧게 깎은 데다 옆 가르마를 타고 있었다.

1 형용사 당파심이 강한 ❏ 분명 그는 중재인이 되기에는 지나치게 당파심이 강하다. **2** 가산명사 빨치산 ❏ 그는 이탈리아 빨치산 몇 명에게 구조되었다.

1 가산명사 칸막이 ❏ 유리 칸막이로만 구획된 새 사무실 **2** 타동사 칸막이로 분할하다 ❏ 더 큰 방 하나를 다시 칸막이로 분할하여 침실 몇 개를 만들었다. **3** 타동사 분할되다 ❏ 한국은 1945년에 분할되었다. ❏ 영국은 '역사적인 증오 때문에' 그 나라를 분할하려 한다는 비난을 받았다. ● 불가산명사 분할 ❏ 인도 분할에 뒤따른 전투

부사 부분적으로 ❏ 그것은 부분적으로 내 잘못이다. ❏ 부분적인 이유이지만 내가 생각해야 할 다른 일들이 있었기 때문에, 올해에는 그렇게 많이 걱정하지 않았다.

1 가산명사 배우자 ❏ 다른 친구를 갖고 싶어 하는 것이 배우자를 사랑하지 않는다는 걸 의미하지는 않는다. **2** 가산명사 (댄스 등의) 상대; 파트너 ❏ 상대와 춤을 추는 것 그 시합에서 내 파트너는 훌륭한 미국 선수였다. **3** 가산명사 공동 대표; 동업자 [경제] ❏ 그는 시카고 법률 회사의 공동 대표이다. **4** 가산명사 상대국; 상대 회사 ❏ 스페인은 지금까지 쿠바의 주요 교역 상대국 중 하나였다. **5** 타동사 -의 상대가 되다, -의 파트너가 되다 ❏ 그는 유명한 러시아 발레리나의 상대 무용수였다. ❏ 그는 현 챔피언인 이안 베이커의 파트너가 될 것이다.

가산명사 또는 불가산명사 협력 관계 ❏ 독일의 은행과 기업 간 협력 관계

| 부사는 대개 철자가 part time이다. |

형용사 파트타임의, 비상근의 ❏ 많은 기업들이 급료가 낮은 비상근직을 고용함으로써 경비를 절감하고 있다. ❏ 일반적으로 파트타임 일자리는 찾기 힘들다. ● 부사 파트타임으로 ❏ 나는 파트타임으로 일하고 싶다.

1 가산명사 정당 ❏ 노동당원 ❏ 야당 **2** 가산명사 파티 ❏ 그 한 쌍은 파티에서 만났다. ❏ 우리는 성대한 생일 파티를 열었다. **3** 자동사 파티를 열다, 파티에서 즐겁게 놀다 ❏ 그들은 와서 먹고 마시며, 헤엄치고, 파티를 벌인다. 가끔은 잠도 자지 않는다. **4** 가산명사 일행, -단 ❏ 그들은 일행들로부터 떨어졌다. ❏ 관광단 **5** 가산명사 (계약 등의) 한쪽 편 [법률] ❏ 그들이 죄를 범한 당사자라는 것이 입증되어야 한다. ❏ 그는 부상자 측이었다. **6** 구 -에 가담하다 ❏ 크룩은 그와 같은 반역 행위에 가담하지 않고 자리에서 물러났다.

1 타동사/자동사 통과하다, 지나가다 ❏ 그녀가 서재 문을 통과할 때, 전화가 울리기 시작했다. ❏ 제인은 그녀가 지나가도록 비켜섰다. **2** 자동사 움직이다, 나아가다 ❏ 그는 출입구를 통해 비(B) 방향으로

direction. ❑ *He passed through the doorway into Ward B.* ❑ *He passed down the tunnel.* **3** V-T/V-I If something such as a road or pipe **passes** along a particular route, it goes along that route. ❑ *After going over the Col de Vars, the route passes through St-Paul-sur-Ubaye.* **4** V-T If you **pass** something through, over, or around something else, you move or push it through, over, or around that thing. ❑ *She passed the needle through the rough cloth, back and forth.* ❑ *"I don't understand,"* the Inspector mumbled, passing a hand through his hair. **5** V-T If you **pass** something **to** someone, you take it in your hand and give it to them. ❑ *Ken passed the books to Sergeant Parrott.* **6** V-T/V-I If something **passes** or **is passed from** one person to another, the second person then has it instead of the first. ❑ *His mother's small estate had passed to him after her death.* ❑ *These powers were eventually passed to municipalities.* **7** V-T If you **pass** information **to** someone, you give it to them because it concerns them. ❑ *Officials failed to pass vital information to their superiors.* ● PHRASAL VERB **Pass on** means the same as **pass.** ❑ *I do not know what to do with the information if I cannot pass it on.* ❑ *From time to time he passed on confidential information.* **8** V-T/V-I If you **pass** the ball to someone on your team in a game such as football, basketball, hockey, or rugby, you kick, hit, or throw it to them. ❑ *Your partner should then pass the ball back to you.* ● N-COUNT **Pass** is also a noun. ❑ *Hirst rolled a short pass to Merson.* **9** V-I When a period of time **passes,** it happens and finishes. ❑ *He couldn't imagine why he had let so much time pass without contacting her.* ❑ *As the years passed he felt trapped by certain realities of marriage.* **10** V-T If you **pass** a period of time in a particular way, you spend it in that way. ❑ *The children passed the time playing in the streets.* **11** V-I If you **pass through** a stage of development or a period of time, you experience it. ❑ *The country was passing through a grave crisis.* **12** V-T If an amount **passes** a particular total or level, it becomes greater than that total or level. ❑ *They became the first company in their field to pass the £2 billion turn-over mark.* **13** V-T/V-I If someone or something **passes** a test, they are considered to be of an acceptable standard. ❑ *Kevin has just passed his driving test.* ❑ *...new drugs which have passed early tests to show that they are safe.* **14** N-COUNT A **pass** in an examination, test, or course is a successful result in it. ❑ *He's been allowed to re-take the exam, and he's going to get a pass.* **15** V-T If someone in authority **passes** a person or thing, they declare that they are of an acceptable standard or have reached an acceptable standard. ❑ *Several popular beaches were found unfit for bathing although the government passed them last year.* **16** V-T When people in authority **pass** a new law or a proposal, they formally agree to it or approve it. ❑ *The Estonian parliament has passed a resolution declaring the republic fully independent.* **17** V-T When a judge **passes** sentence on someone, he or she says what their punishment will be. ❑ *Passing sentence, the judge said it all had the appearance of a con trick.* **18** V-T If you **pass** comment or **pass** a comment, you say something. ❑ *I don't really know so I could not pass comment on that.* **19** V-I If someone or something **passes for** or **passes as** something that they are not, they are accepted as that thing or mistaken for that thing. ❑ *Children's toy guns now look so realistic that they can often pass for the real thing.* ❑ *It is doubtful whether Ted, even with his fluent French, passed for one of the locals.* **20** N-COUNT A **pass** is a document that allows you to do something. ❑ *I got myself a pass into the barracks.* **21** N-COUNT; N-IN-NAMES A **pass** is a narrow path or route between mountains. ❑ *The monastery is in a remote mountain pass.* **22** →see also **passing** **23** to **pass the buck** →see **buck.** to **pass judgment** →see **judgment**

Do not confuse **pass** and **spend.** If you do something while you are waiting for something else, you can say you do it to "**pass** the time." ❑ *He had brought along a book to pass the time.* You can say that time **has passed** in order to show that a period of time has finished. ❑ *The first few days passed... The time seems to have passed so quickly.* If you **spend** a period of time doing something or **spend** time in a place, you do that thing or stay in that place for all of the time you are talking about. ❑ *I spent three days cleaning our flat....a hotel where we could spend the night.*

▶**pass away** PHRASAL VERB You can say that someone **passed away** to mean that they died, if you want to avoid using the word "die" because you think it might upset or offend people. ❑ *He unfortunately passed away last year.*

▶**pass off** PHRASAL VERB If an event **passes off** without any trouble, it happens and ends without any trouble. ❑ *The main demonstration passed off peacefully.*

▶**pass off as** PHRASAL VERB If you **pass** something **off as** another thing, you convince people that it is that other thing. ❑ *He passed himself off as a senior psychologist.* ❑ *I've tried to pass off my accent as a convent school accent.*

▶**pass on** **1** PHRASAL VERB If you **pass** something **on to** someone, you give it to them so that they have it instead of you. ❑ *The Queen is passing the money on to a selection of her favorite charities.* ❑ *The late Earl passed on much of his fortune to his daughter.* **2** →see also **pass 7**

▶**pass out** **1** PHRASAL VERB If you **pass out,** you faint or collapse. ❑ *He felt sick and dizzy and then passed out.* **2** PHRASAL VERB When a police, army, navy, or air force cadet **passes out,** he or she completes his or her training. [BRIT] ❑ *He passed out in November 1924 and was posted to No 24 Squadron.*

▶**pass over** **1** PHRASAL VERB If someone **is passed over for** a job or position, they do not get the job or position and someone younger or less experienced is chosen instead. ❑ *She claimed she was repeatedly passed over for promotion while less experienced white male colleagues were given postings.* **2** PHRASAL VERB If you **pass over** a topic in a conversation or speech, you do not talk about it. ❑ *He largely passed over the government's record.*

이동했다. ❑ 그는 터널을 내려갔다. **3** 타동사/자동사 이어지다 ❑ 그 노선은 콜드바르를 넘어간 다음 생폴 쉬르 우바이를 통과한다. **4** 타동사 움직이다, 통과시키다 ❑ 그녀는 거칠거칠한 천의 이쪽저쪽으로 바늘을 움직이며 바느질을 했다. ❑ "이해할 수가 없어."라고 형사가 손으로 머리를 빗어 넘기며 중얼거렸다. **5** 타동사 건네주다 ❑ 켄은 그 책들을 패럿 병장에게 건네주었다. **6** 타동사/자동사 넘어가다, 양도되다 ❑ 그의 어머니가 돌아가신 후 얼마 안 되는 유산이 그에게 넘어갔었다. ❑ 이런 권한들이 결국 자치 단체들에게 넘어갔다. **7** 타동사 전달하다 ❑ 관리들이 상관에게 중요한 정보를 전달하는 것을 게을리 했다. ● 구동사 전달하다 ❑ 만약 그 정보를 전달할 수 없다면 그걸 가지고 어떻게 해야 할지 모르겠다. ❑ 이따금씩 그는 그 사람에게 기밀 정보를 전달했다. **8** 타동사/자동사 패스하다 ❑ 그 다음 당신의 파트너가 다시 당신에게 공을 패스해야 합니다. ● 가산명사 패스 ❑ 허스트가 머슨에게 짧은 패스를 보냈다. **9** 자동사 지나다, 경과하다 ❑ 그는 왜 그토록 오랜 시간을 그녀와 연락하지 않고 놓아두었는지 알 수가 없었다. ❑ 세월이 지나면서 그는 결혼의 어떤 현실에 갇힌 듯한 기분을 느꼈다. **10** 타동사 (시간을) 보내다 ❑ 그 아이들은 길거리에서 시간을 보냈다. **11** 자동사 겪다, 경험하다 ❑ 그 나라는 중대한 위기를 겪고 있었다. **12** 타동사 (액수나 양이) 넘어서다 ❑ 그들은 해당 분야에서 2십억 달러 매상고를 넘어선 최초의 회사가 되었다. **13** 타동사/자동사 통과하다, 합격하다 ❑ 케빈은 막 운전 시험에 합격했다. ❑ 안전성을 보여 주기 위한 초기 테스트들을 통과한 신약들 **14** 가산명사 합격 ❑ 그는 시험을 다시 칠 수 있도록 허락을 받았고, 합격할 것이다. **15** 타동사 통과시키다 ❑ 유명한 해변 및 군데가 지난해 정부에 의해 통과되었음에도 불구하고 수영하기에 부적합한 것으로 밝혀졌다. **16** 타동사 통과시키다 ❑ 에스토니아 의회가 공화국의 전면 독립을 선포하는 결의안을 통과시켰다. **17** 타동사 (판결을) 내리다, 선고하다 ❑ 판결을 내리면서, 판사는 이 모든 것이 신용 사기의 양상을 띤다고 말했다. **18** 타동사 말하다 ❑ 나는 잘 모르겠고 따라서 그것에 대해 뭐라 말할 수가 없다. **19** 자동사 ~으로 여겨지다, ~으로 오인되다 ❑ 요새 아이들의 장난감 총은 대단히 실감나서 실물로 오인될 때가 많다. ❑ 테드가 프랑스 어 실력이 유창하긴 하지만 지역 주민으로 통했을지 의심스럽다. **20** 가산명사 허가증, 통행증; 승차권 ❑ 나는 막사로 들어갈 수 있는 통행증을 얻었다. **21** 가산명사; 이름명사 산길 ❑ 그 수도원은 외딴 산길 속에 있다.

pass와 spend를 혼동하지 않도록 하라. 무엇을 기다리면서 다른 무엇을 하면, 시간을 보내기(pass the time) 위해 그것을 한다고 말할 수 있다. ❑ 그는 시간을 보내려고 책을 한 권 가져왔었다. 일정 기간의 시간이 끝났음을 나타내기 위해서는 시간이 has passed라고 말할 수 있다. ❑ 처음 며칠이 지났다... 시간이 너무도 빨리 지나간 것 같다. 무엇을 하면서 일정 기간의 시간을 spend하거나 어떤 장소에서 시간을 spend하면, 언급하고 있는 그 시간 동안 내내 그것을 하거나 그 장소에 머무는 것이다. ❑ 나는 내 집을 청소하면서 3일을 보냈다....우리가 그날 밤을 보낼 수 있었던 호텔.

구동사 죽다 ❑ 그는 불행히도 작년에 죽었다.

구동사 행해지다, 처리되다 ❑ 주요 시위는 평화적으로 처리됐다.

구동사 ~을 ...로 속여 넘기다 ❑ 그는 중진 심리학자로 행세했다. ❑ 나는 내 말투가 수녀원 부속학교 학생처럼 들리게 하려고 해 왔다.

1 구동사 넘겨주다, 양도하다 ❑ 여왕은 그 돈을 자신이 좋아하는 엄선된 자선 단체들에 넘겨주고 있다. ❑ 작고한 백작은 딸에게 재산의 대부분을 물려주었다.

1 구동사 기절하다, 의식을 잃다 ❑ 그는 메스껍고 현기증이 났으며 그런 다음 기절했다. **2** 구동사 사관학교를 졸업하다 [영국영어] ❑ 그는 1924년 11월에 사관학교를 졸업하고 제 24기병대대에 배치되었다.

1 구동사 (일자리나 직위를) 부당하게 놓치다 ❑ 그녀는 자기보다 경험이 적은 백인 남자 동료들은 직위를 받는 데 반해 자신은 계속해서 승진의 기회를 놓쳤다고 주장했다. **2** 구동사 언급하지 않다 ❑ 그는 정부 측 기록을 대부분 언급하지 않았다.

▶**pass up** PHRASAL VERB If you **pass up** a chance or an opportunity, you do not take advantage of it. ❑ *The official urged the government not to pass up the opportunity that has now presented itself.*

pas|sage ♦♦♦ /pǽsɪdʒ/ (**passages**) **1** N-COUNT A **passage** is a long narrow space with walls or fences on both sides, which connects one place or room with another. ❑ *Harry stepped into the passage and closed the door behind him.* **2** N-COUNT A **passage** in a book, speech, or piece of music is a section of it that you are considering separately from the rest. ❑ *He reads a passage from Milton.* ❑ *...the passage in which Blake spoke of the world of imagination.* **3** N-COUNT A **passage** is a long narrow hole or tube in your body, which air or liquid can pass along. ❑ *...cells that line the air passages.* **4** N-COUNT A **passage through** a crowd of people or things is an empty space that allows you to move through them. ❑ *He cleared a passage for himself through the crammed streets.* **5** N-UNCOUNT The **passage** of someone or something is their movement from one place to another. ❑ *Germany had not requested Franco's consent for the passage of troops through Spain.* **6** N-UNCOUNT The **passage** of someone or something is their progress from one situation or one stage in their development to another. ❑ *...to ease their passage to a market economy.* **7** N-SING The **passage of** a period of time is its passing. ❑ *...an asset that increases in value with the passage of time* **8** N-COUNT A **passage** is a journey by ship. ❑ *We'd arrived the day before after a 10-hour passage from Swansea.* **9** N-UNCOUNT If you are granted **passage** through a country or area of land, you are given permission to go through it. ❑ *Mr. Thomas would be given safe passage to and from Jaffna.*

passage|way /pǽsɪdʒweɪ/ (**passageways**) N-COUNT A **passageway** is a long narrow space with walls or fences on both sides, which connects one place or room with another. ❑ *Outside, in the passageway, I could hear people moving about.*

pas|sen|ger ♦♦♦ /pǽsɪndʒər/ (**passengers**) **1** N-COUNT A **passenger** in a vehicle such as a bus, boat, or plane is a person who is traveling in it, but who is not driving it or working on it. ❑ *Mr. Fullemann was a passenger in the car when it crashed.* →see **client 2** ADJ **Passenger** is used to describe something that is designed for passengers, rather than for drivers or goods. [ADJ n] ❑ *I sat in the passenger seat.* →see **fly, train**

passer-by (**passers-by**) also **passerby** N-COUNT A **passer-by** is a person who is walking past someone or something. ❑ *A passer-by described what he saw moments after the car bomb had exploded.*

pass|ing /pǽsɪŋ, pǽs-/ **1** ADJ A **passing** fashion, activity, or feeling lasts for only a short period of time and is not worth taking very seriously. [ADJ n] ❑ *Hamnett does not believe environmental concern is a passing fad.* **2** N-SING The **passing** of something such as a time or system is the fact of its coming to an end. ❑ *It was an historic day, yet its passing was not marked by the slightest excitement.* **3** N-SING You can refer to someone's death as their **passing**, if you want to avoid using the word "death" because you think it might upset or offend people. ❑ *His passing will be mourned by many people.* **4** N-SING The **passing of** a period of time is the fact or process of its going by. ❑ *The passing of time brought a sense of emptiness.* **5** ADJ A **passing** mention or reference is brief and is made while you are talking or writing about something else. [ADJ n] ❑ *It was just a passing comment, he didn't go on about it.* **6** →see also **pass 7** PHRASE If you mention something **in passing**, you mention it briefly while you are talking or writing about something else. ❑ *In passing, it should be noted that...*

pas|sion ♦♦♦ /pǽʃ°n/ (**passions**) **1** N-UNCOUNT **Passion** is strong feelings toward someone. [also N in pl] ❑ *...my passion for a dark-haired, slender boy named James.* ❑ *...the expression of love and passion.* **2** N-UNCOUNT **Passion** is a very strong feeling about something or a strong belief in something. [also N in pl] ❑ *He spoke with great passion.* **3** N-COUNT If you have a **passion for** something, you have a very strong interest in it and like it very much. ❑ *She had a passion for gardening.*

Thesaurus		*passion*의 참조어
N.	affection, desire, love, lust **1**	
	enthusiasm, interest **2** **3**	

pas|sion|ate /pǽʃənɪt/ **1** ADJ A **passionate** person has very strong feelings about something or a strong belief in something. ❑ *...his passionate commitment to peace.* ❑ *He is very passionate about the project.* ● **pas|sion|ate|ly** ADV ❑ *I am passionately opposed to the death penalty.* **2** ADJ A **passionate** person has strong romantic or sexual feelings and expresses them in their behavior. ❑ *...a beautiful, passionate woman of twenty-six.* ● **pas|sion|ate|ly** ADV ❑ *He was passionately in love with her.*

pas|sive /pǽsɪv/ **1** ADJ If you describe someone as **passive**, you mean that they do not take action but instead let things happen to them. [DISAPPROVAL] ❑ *His passive attitude made things easier for me.* ● **pas|sive|ly** ADV ❑ *He sat there passively, content to wait for his father to make the opening move.* **2** ADJ A **passive** activity involves watching, looking at, or listening to things rather than doing things. [ADJ n] ❑ *They want less passive ways of filling their time* **3** ADJ **Passive** resistance involves showing opposition to the people in power in your country by not cooperating with them and protesting in nonviolent ways. [ADJ n] ❑ *They made it clear that they would only exercise passive resistance in the event of a military takeover.* **4** N-SING In grammar, **the passive** or **the passive voice** is formed using "be" and the past participle of a verb. The subject of a passive clause does not perform the action expressed by the verb but is affected by it. For example, in "He's been murdered," the verb is in the passive. Compare **active**.

구동사 (기회 등을) 놓치다 ❑ 그 관계자는 지금 스스로 모습을 드러낸 기회를 놓치지 말라고 정부에 촉구했다.

1 가산명사 통로 ❑ 해리는 통로로 들어서서 등 뒤로 문을 닫았다. **2** 가산명사 (책 등의) 한 부분 ❑ 그는 밀턴의 책 중 한 부분을 읽는다. ❑ 블레이크가 상상의 세계에 대해 이야기한 부분 **3** 가산명사 (체내의) 관, 통로 ❑ 기도를 싸고 있는 세포들 **4** 가산명사 (인과 속의) 지나갈 공간, 길 ❑ 그는 인파가 가득 메운 거리를 뚫고 나아갔다. **5** 불가산명사 이동 ❑ 독일은 스페인을 거쳐 병력을 이동하는 것에 대해 프랑코의 승낙을 요청하지 않았다. **6** 불가산명사 이행, 진행 ❑ 시장 경제로의 이행을 늦추기 위해 **7** 단수명사 (시간의) 경과 ❑ 시간이 경과할수록 가치가 증가하는 자산 **8** 가산명사 항해 ❑ 우리는 그 전날 스완지에서 10시간 동안 항해한 끝에 도착했다. **9** 불가산명사 통행 허가 ❑ 토머스 씨는 자프나를 안전하게 드나들 수 있도록 허가를 받을 것이다.

가산명사 통로, 복도 ❑ 바깥 통로에서 사람들이 다니는 소리를 들을 수 있었다.

1 가산명사 승객 ❑ 풀레만 씨는 충돌 당시 그 차의 승객이었다. **2** 형용사 승객용의 ❑ 나는 승객용 좌석에 앉았다.

가산명사 지나가는 사람, 행인 ❑ 한 행인이 차량 폭탄이 터지고 난 얼마 후에 목격한 내용을 묘사했다.

1 형용사 일시적인, 스쳐 가는 ❑ 햄넷은 환경에 대한 관심이 일시적인 유행이라고 생각하지 않는다. **2** 단수명사 경과, 지나감 ❑ 그 날은 역사적인 날이었지만, 전혀 특별한 감동도 없이 지나가 버렸다. **3** 단수명사 죽음 ❑ 많은 사람들이 그의 죽음을 애도할 것이다. **4** 단수명사 -의 경과 ❑ 시간의 경과는 공허함을 불러일으켰다. **5** 형용사 지나가는 (말) ❑ 그것은 그저 지나가는 말이었고, 그가 그것에 대해 계속 이야기하지는 않았다. **6** 구 -하는 김에 ❑ 얘기하는 김에 말인데, 주의해야 할 점은...

1 불가산명사 정욕 ❑ 제임스라는 짙은 색 머리의 늘씬한 남자에에 대한 나의 정욕 ❑ 사랑과 정욕의 표현 **2** 불가산명사 열정 ❑ 그는 매우 열정적으로 이야기했다. **3** 가산명사 -에 대한 열중 ❑ 그녀는 정원 가꾸기에 열중했다.

1 형용사 열렬한, 열의에 찬 ❑ 평화에 대한 그의 열렬한 헌신 ❑ 그는 그 계획에 대해 매우 열의에 차 있다. ● 열렬히 부사 ❑ 나는 사형에 열렬히 반대한다. **2** 형용사 정열적인 ❑ 아름답고 정열적인 스물여섯 살의 여자 ● 정열적으로 부사 ❑ 그는 그녀를 정열적으로 사랑했다.

1 형용사 수동적인 [탐탁찮음] ❑ 그의 수동적인 태도로 내 사정이 수월해졌다. ● 수동적으로 부사 ❑ 그는 거기에 수동적으로 앉아서, 아버지가 먼저 시작하기를 느긋이 기다렸다. **2** 형용사 활동적이지 않은, 수동적인 ❑ 그들은 시간을 보다 활동적으로 보낼 수 있는 방법을 원한다. **3** 형용사 소극적인, 비폭력의 ❑ 그들은 군사 쿠데타가 일어날 경우 소극적인 저항만을 실행할 것임을 분명히 밝혔다. **4** 단수명사 수동태

a
b
c
d
e
f
g
h
i
j
k
l
m
n
o
p
q
r
s
t
u
v
w
x
y
z

A B C D E F G H I J K L M N O **P** Q R S T U V W X Y Z

pass|port /pæspɔrt/ (passports) N-COUNT Your **passport** is an official document containing your name, photograph, and personal details, which you need to show when you enter or leave a country. ❑ *You should take your passport with you when changing money.*

가산명사 여권 ❑ 환전할 때 여권을 가져와야 한다.

pass|word /pæswɜrd/ (passwords) N-COUNT A **password** is a secret word or phrase that you must know in order to be allowed to enter a place such as a military base, or to be allowed to use a computer system. ❑ *Advance and give the password.* →see **Internet**

가산명사 암호 ❑ 앞으로 나와 암호를 대세요.

past ♦♦♦ /pæst/ (pasts)

In addition to the uses shown below, **past** is used in the phrasal verb "run past."

past는 아래 용법 외에도 구동사 'run past'에 쓰인다.

1 N-SING **The past** is the time before the present, and the things that have happened. ❑ *In the past, about a third of the babies born to women with diabetes were lost.* ● PHRASE If you accuse someone of **living in the past**, you mean that they think too much about the past or believe that things are the same as they were in the past. [DISAPPROVAL] ❑ *What was the point in living in the past, thinking about what had or had not happened?* **2** N-COUNT Your **past** consists of all the things that you have done or that have happened to you. ❑ *...revelations about his past.* **3** ADJ **Past** events and things happened or existed before the present time. [ADJ n] ❑ *I knew from past experience that alternative therapies could help.* ❑ *...a return to the turbulence of past centuries.* **4** ADJ You use **past** to talk about a period of time that has just finished. For example, if you talk about the **past five years**, you mean the period of five years that has just finished. [det ADJ n] ❑ *Most shops have remained closed for the past three days.* **5** PREP You use **past** when you are stating a time which is thirty minutes or less after a particular hour. For example, if it is **twenty past** six, it is twenty minutes after six o'clock. [num PREP num] ❑ *It's ten past eleven.* ● ADV **Past** is also an adverb. [num ADV] ❑ *I have my lunch at half past.* **6** PREP If it is **past** a particular time, it is later than that time. ❑ *It was past midnight.* **7** PREP If you go **past** someone or something, you go near them and keep moving, so that they are then behind you. ❑ *I dashed past him and out of the door.* ❑ *A steady procession of people filed past the coffin.* ● ADV **Past** is also an adverb. ❑ *An ambulance drove past.* **8** PREP If you look or point **past** a person or thing, you look or point at something behind them. [v PREP n] ❑ *She stared past Christine at the bed.* **9** PREP If something is **past** a place, it is on the other side of it. [v-link PREP n] ❑ *Go north on I-15 to the exit just past Barstow.* **10** PREP If someone or something is **past** a particular point or stage, they are no longer at that point or stage. ❑ *He was well past retirement age.* →see **history**

1 단수명사 과거 ❑ 과거에는, 당뇨병이 있는 여자들에게서 난 아기들 중 3분의 1이 죽었다. ● 구 과거 속에 사는 [탐탁찮음] ❑ 과거에 일어났거나, 일어나지 않았던 일들을 생각하며 과거 속에 사는 것이 무슨 의미가 있었나? **2** 가산명사 과거의, 이력의 ❑ 그의 과거를 폭로함 **3** 형용사 지나간, 과거의 ❑ 나는 대체 요법이 도움이 될 수 있다는 것을 과거의 경험을 통해 알고 있었다. ❑ 혼란스러웠던 지난 세기들로의 회귀 **4** 형용사 방금 지난 ❑ 지난 3일간 대부분의 상점이 계속 문을 닫았다. **5** 전치사 (시각) -을 지나 ❑ 11시 10분이다. ● 부사 지나서 ❑ 나는 30분에 점심을 먹는다. **6** 전치사 -을 지나 ❑ 자정이 지난 시각이었다. **7** 전치사 -을 지나 ❑ 나는 그를 지나 문밖으로 달려 나갔다. ❑ 사람들의 행렬이 꾸준히 이어지며 관을 지나갔다. **8** 전치사 -의 너머로 ❑ 그녀는 크리스틴 너머로 침대를 응시했다. **9** 전치사 -의 건너편에 ❑ I-15번 도로를 타고 북쪽으로 바스토우를 바로 지난 다음 출구에서 나가세요. **10** 전치사 -을 지나 ❑ 그는 퇴직할 나이를 훨씬 넘겼다.

pas|ta /pɑstə, BRIT pæstə/ (pastas) N-MASS **Pasta** is a type of food made from a mixture of flour, eggs, and water that is formed into different shapes and then boiled. Spaghetti, macaroni, and noodles are types of pasta.

물질명사 파스타

Pasta comes in dozens of shapes and sizes but generally the same recipe is used: water, flour, and sometimes eggs or other flavors. Pasta is cooked in boiling water. Some of the most popular types of pasta are **spaghetti** (long, thin pasta noodles); **macaroni** (short tubes of pasta, often eaten with a cheese sauce) and **lasagne** (flat sheets of pasta, eaten in a dish made of layers of lasagne and meat sauce).

pasta(파스타)에는 수십 가지의 모양과 크기가 있지만, 만드는 방법은 대개 같아서 물과 밀가루 그리고 가끔 계란이나 다른 향료가 쓰인다. 파스타는 끓는 물에 조리한다. 가장 흔한 형태의 파스타로는 spaghetti(스파게티: 길고 가는 파스타 국수), macaroni(마카로니: 짧은 관 모양의 파스타로 흔히 치즈 소스와 함께 먹는다), lasagna(라자냐: 납작한 종이 모양의 파스타로 여러 겹의 라자냐와 고기 소스로 요리를 만들어 먹는다)가 있다.

paste /peɪst/ (pastes, pasting, pasted) **1** N-MASS **Paste** is a soft, wet, sticky mixture of a substance and a liquid, which can be spread easily. Some types of paste are used to stick things together. ❑ *He then sticks it back together with flour paste.* ❑ *Blend a little milk with the custard powder to form a paste.* **2** N-MASS **Paste** is a soft smooth mixture of crushed meat, fruit, or vegetables. You can, for example, spread it onto bread or use it in cooking. ❑ *...tomato paste.* **3** V-T If you **paste** something on a surface, you put glue or paste on it and stick it on the surface. ❑ *...pasting labels on bottles.*

1 물질명사 풀; 반죽 ❑ 그런 다음 그는 밀가루 풀로 그것을 다시 붙였다. ❑ 커스터드 분말과 우유 약간을 섞어서 반죽을 만드세요. **2** 물질명사 페이스트 (고기, 야채 등의 반죽) ❑ 토마토 페이스트 **3** 타동사 풀로 붙이다 ❑ 병에 라벨을 풀로 붙이는 일

pas|tel /pæstəl, BRIT pæstəl/ (pastels) ADJ **Pastel** colors are pale rather than dark or bright. [ADJ n, ADJ color] ❑ *...delicate pastel shades.* ❑ *...pastel pink, blue, peach, and green.* ● N-COUNT **Pastel** is also a noun. ❑ *The lobby is decorated in pastels.*

형용사 파스텔풍의 ❑ 은은한 파스텔풍의 색조 ❑ 파스텔풍의 분홍, 파랑, 복숭아색과 초록색 ● 가산명사 파스텔풍의 색조 ❑ 로비는 파스텔 색조로 장식되어 있다.

pas|time /pæstaɪm/ (pastimes) N-COUNT A **pastime** is something that you do in your spare time because you enjoy it or are interested in it. ❑ *His favorite pastime is golf.*

가산명사 여가 활동, 소일거리 ❑ 그가 좋아하는 여가 활동은 골프이다.

pas|to|ral /pæstərəl, pæstɔr-/ **1** ADJ The **pastoral** duties of a priest or other religious leader involve looking after the people he or she has responsibility for, especially by helping them with their personal problems. [ADJ n] ❑ *...the pastoral care of the sick.* **2** ADJ If a school offers **pastoral** care, it is concerned with the personal needs and problems of its students, particularly to help with their schoolwork. [mainly BRIT] [ADJ n] ❑ *A few schools now offer counseling sessions; all have some system of pastoral care.* **3** ADJ A **pastoral** place, atmosphere, or idea is characteristic of peaceful country life and scenery. [ADJ n] ❑ *...a tranquil pastoral scene.*

1 형용사 목회의 ❑ 목회 활동으로 병자들을 보살핌 **2** 형용사 생활 지도 [주로 영국영어] ❑ 현재 몇몇 학교들이 상담을 제공한다. 이 학교들은 모두 일종의 생활 지도 체계를 갖추고 있다. **3** 형용사 목가적인 ❑ 평화로운 목가적 광경

pas|try /peɪstri/ (pastries) **1** N-UNCOUNT **Pastry** is a food made from flour, fat, and water that is mixed together, rolled flat, and baked in the oven. It is used, for example, for making pies. **2** N-COUNT A **pastry** is a small cake made with sweet pastry. ❑ *...a wide range of cakes and pastries.*

1 불가산명사 가루반죽 **2** 가산명사 (가루반죽으로 만든) 빵과자 ❑ 다양한 종류의 케이크와 빵과자

pas|ture /pæstʃər/ (pastures) N-VAR **Pasture** is land with grass growing on it for farm animals to eat. ❑ *The cows are out now, grazing in the pasture.*

가산명사 또는 불가산명사 목장, 목초지 ❑ 소들은 지금 밖에 나가 목초지에서 풀을 뜯고 있다.

pat /pæt/ (pats, patting, patted) **1** V-T If you **pat** something or someone, you tap them lightly, usually with your hand held flat. ❑ *Don't you worry about any of*

1 타동사 가볍게 치다, 토닥이다 ❑ "이 일은 아무 걱정하지 마." 그녀가 내 무릎을 토닥이며 말했다.

this," she said patting me on the knee. ❑ *The landlady patted her hair nervously.* ● N-COUNT **Pat** is also a noun. ❑ *He gave her an encouraging pat on the shoulder.* ❷ N-COUNT A **pat of** butter or something else that is soft is a small lump of it. ❑ *Terreano put a pat of butter on his plate.* ❸ PHRASE If you give someone a **pat on the back** or if you **pat** them **on the back**, you show them that you think they have done well and deserve to be praised. [APPROVAL] ❑ *The players deserve a pat on the back.*

patch /pætʃ/ (patches, patching, patched) ❶ N-COUNT A **patch** on a surface is a part of it which is different in appearance from the area around it. ❑ *...the bald patch on the top of his head.* ❑ *There was a small patch of blue in the grey clouds.* ❷ N-COUNT A **patch of** land is a small area of land where a particular plant or crop grows. ❑ *...a patch of land covered in forest.* ❑ *...the little vegetable patch in her backyard.* ❸ N-COUNT A **patch** is a piece of material which you use to cover a hole in something. ❑ *...jackets with patches on the elbows.* ❹ N-COUNT A **patch** is a small piece of material which you wear to cover an injured eye. ❑ *She went to the hospital and found him lying down with a patch over his eye.* ❺ V-T If you **patch** something that has a hole in it, you mend it by fastening a patch over the hole. ❑ *He and Walker patched the barn roof.* ❑ *One of the mechanics took off the damaged tyre, and took it back to the station to be patched.* ❻ N-COUNT A **patch** is a piece of computer program code written as a temporary solution for dealing with a virus in computer software and distributed by the makers of the original program. [COMPUTING] ❑ *Older machines will need a software patch to be loaded to correct the date.* ❼ PHRASE If you have or go through a **bad patch** or a **rough patch**, you have a lot of problems for a time. [mainly BRIT] ❑ *His marriage was going through a bad patch.*

▶**patch up** ❶ PHRASAL VERB-RECIP If you **patch up** a quarrel or relationship, you try to be friendly again and not to quarrel anymore. ❑ *She has gone on holiday with her husband to try to patch up their marriage.* ❑ *France patched things up with New Zealand.* ❷ PHRASAL VERB If you **patch up** something which is damaged, you mend it or patch it. ❑ *We can patch up those holes.* ❸ PHRASAL VERB If doctors **patch** someone **up** or **patch** their wounds **up**, they treat their injuries. ❑ *...the medical staff who patched her up after the accident.*

patch|work /pætʃwɜrk/ ADJ A **patchwork** quilt, cushion, or piece of clothing is made by sewing together small pieces of material of different colors or patterns. [ADJ n] ❑ *...beds covered in patchwork quilts.* ● N-UNCOUNT **Patchwork** is also a noun. ❑ *For centuries, quilting and patchwork have been popular needlecrafts.*

patchy /pætʃi/ ❶ ADJ A **patchy** substance or color exists in some places but not in others, or is thick in some places and thin in others. ❑ *Thick patchy fog and irresponsible driving were to blame.* ❑ *Bottle tans can make your legs, arms and face look a patchy orange color.* ❷ ADJ If something is **patchy**, it is not completely reliable or satisfactory because it is not always good. ❑ *The evidence is patchy.*

pâté /pɑteɪ, BRIT pæteɪ/ (pâtés) N-MASS **Pâté** is a soft mixture of meat, fish, or vegetables with various flavorings, and is eaten cold. ❑ *...smoked-salmon pâté.*

pa|tent /pætⁿnt, BRIT peɪtⁿnt/ (patents, patenting, patented) ❶ N-COUNT A **patent** is an official right to be the only person or company allowed to make or sell a new product for a certain period of time. ❑ *P&G applied for a patent on its cookies.* ❑ *He held a number of patents for his many innovations.* ❷ V-T If you **patent** something, you obtain a patent for it. ❑ *He patented the idea that the atom could be split.* ❑ *The invention has been patented by the university.* ❸ ADJ You use **patent** to describe something, especially something bad, in order to indicate in an emphatic way that you think its nature or existence is clear and obvious. [EMPHASIS] ❑ *This was patent nonsense.* ● **pa|tent|ly** ADV ❑ *He made his displeasure patently obvious.*

pa|ter|nal /pətɜrnⁿl/ ❶ ADJ **Paternal** is used to describe feelings or actions which are typical of those of a kind father toward his child. ❑ *...paternal love for his children.* ❷ ADJ A **paternal** relative is one that is related through a person's father rather than their mother. [ADJ n] ❑ *...my paternal grandparents.*

pa|ter|nity leave /pətɜrniti liv/ N-UNCOUNT If a man has **paternity leave**, his employer allows him some time off work because his child has just been born. [BUSINESS] ❑ *Paternity leave is rare and, where it does exist, it's unlikely to be for any longer than two weeks.*

path ◆◇◇ /pæθ/ (paths) ❶ N-COUNT A **path** is a long strip of ground which people walk along to get from one place to another. ❑ *We followed the path along the clifftops.* ❑ *Feet had worn a path in the rock.* ❷ N-COUNT Your **path** is the space ahead of you as you move along. ❑ *A group of reporters blocked his path.* ❸ N-COUNT The **path** of something is the line which it moves along in a particular direction. [with poss] ❑ *He stepped without looking into the path of a reversing car.* ❑ *...people who live near airports or under the flight path of airplanes.* ❹ N-COUNT A **path** that you take is a particular course of action or way of achieving something. ❑ *The opposition appear to have chosen the path of cooperation rather than confrontation.*

pa|thet|ic /pəθɛtɪk/ ❶ ADJ If you describe a person or animal as **pathetic**, you mean that they are sad and weak or helpless, and they make you feel very sorry for them. ❑ *a pathetic little dog with a curly tail.* ❑ *The small group of onlookers presented a pathetic sight.* ● **pa|theti|cal|ly** /pəθɛtɪkli/ ADV ❑ *She was pathetically thin.* ❷ ADJ If you describe someone or something as **pathetic**, you mean that they make you feel impatient or angry, often because they are weak and very good. [DISAPPROVAL] ❑ *What pathetic excuses.* ❑ *Don't be so pathetic.* ● **pa|theti|cal|ly** ADV [ADV adj] ❑ *Five women in a group of 18 people is a pathetically small number.*

❑ 여주인이 신경질적으로 자기 머리카락을 만지작거렸다. ● 가산명사 가볍게 두드리기 ❑ 그는 그녀를 격려하며 가볍게 어깨를 두드려 주었다. ❷ 가산명사 (버터 등의) 작은 덩이 ❑ 테라아노는 자기 접시 위에 버터 한 덩이를 놓았다. ❸ 구 격려; (등을 두드리며) 격려하다 [마음에 듦] ❑ 그 선수들은 격려를 받을 만하다.

❶ 가산명사 일부분 ❑ 그의 정수리 쪽에 머리가 벗어진 부분 ❑ 회색 구름 사이로 파란색이 조금 보였다. ❷ 가산명사 밭뙈기, 땅뙈기 ❑ 숲으로 덮여 있는 땅뙈기 ❑ 그녀의 집 뒤뜰에 있는 작은 남새밭 ❸ 가산명사 (헝겊 등의) 조각 ❑ 팔꿈치에 헝겊 조각을 덧댄 재킷 ❹ 가산명사 안대 ❑ 그녀가 병원에 가니 그가 한쪽 눈에 안대를 하고 누워 있었다. ❺ 타동사 때우다, 짜깁기하다 ❑ 그와 워커는 헛간 지붕을 때웠다. ❑ 정비사 중 한 명이 손상된 타이어를 빼서, 때우기 위해 정비소로 다시 가져갔다. ❻ 가산명사 (컴퓨터) 패치 [컴퓨터] ❑ 구형 컴퓨터는 날짜를 바로잡기 위해 소프트웨어 패치를 설치해야 할 것이다. ❼ 구 난국, 고초 [주로 영국영어] ❑ 그의 결혼 생활은 난국을 겪고 있었다.

❶ 상호 구동사 수습하다 ❑ 그녀는 부부 관계를 수습하기 위해 남편과 함께 휴가를 떠났다. ❑ 프랑스는 뉴질랜드와의 관계를 수습했다. ❷ 구동사 수선하다, 때우다 ❑ 우리가 그 구멍들을 때울 수 있다. ❸ 구동사 치료하다 ❑ 사고 후 그녀를 치료한 의료진

형용사 패치워크 식의, 조각보 깁기 식의 패치워크식 누비이불을 씌운 침대 ● 불가산명사 패치워크 ❑ 수세기 동안, 퀼팅과 패치워크는 대중적인 바느질 기술이었다.

❶ 형용사 (두께나 색이) 고르지 않은 ❑ 군데군데 짙은 안개와 무책임한 운전이 문제였다. ❑ 병에 든 선탠 크림을 사용하면 다리나 팔, 얼굴 등이 얼룩덜룩하게 오렌지색이 될 수도 있습니다. ❷ 형용사 (질이 고르지 않아) 신빙성이 떨어지는 ❑ 그 증거는 신빙성이 떨어진다.

물질명사 파테 (육류나 생선을 야채와 같아 섞은 것) ❑ 훈제 연어 파테

❶ 가산명사 특허, 특허권 ❑ 피앤지는 자사 쿠키에 대해 특허를 출원했다. ❑ 그는 많은 혁신 기술에 대해 다수의 특허를 가지고 있었다. ❷ 타동사 특허를 얻다 ❑ 그는 원자를 쪼갤 수 있다는 학설에 대해 특허를 얻었다. ❑ 대학이 그 발명에 대한 특허를 획득했다. ❸ 형용사 명백한, 빤한 [강조] ❑ 이것은 명백한 엉터리였다. ● 명백히 부사 ❑ 그는 불쾌함을 명백하게 드러냈다.

❶ 형용사 아버지로서의 ❑ 자식들에 대한 부성애 ❷ 형용사 아버지 쪽의, 부계의 ❑ 내 아버지 쪽 조부모

불가산명사 아내의 출산 시에 남편이 받는 휴가 [경제] ❑ 남편이 받는 출산 휴가는 흔치 않고, 그런 것이 실제로 있는 곳에서도 기간이 2주 이상 될 가능성은 없다.

❶ 가산명사 (좁은) 길, 오솔길 ❑ 우리는 절벽 꼭대기의 오솔길을 따라갔다. ❑ 인적 때문에 바위에 길이 새겨졌다. ❷ 가산명사 길, 진로 ❑ 한 무리의 기자들이 그의 길을 막았다. ❸ 가산명사 행로, 이동 방향 ❑ 그가 후진하는 차를 보지 못하고 그 뒤로 걸어 들어갔다. ❑ 공항 근처 혹은 비행기 운항로 아래에 사는 사람들 ❹ 가산명사 노선, 방침 ❑ 야당은 대립보다는 협조하는 방침을 선택한 것 같다.

❶ 형용사 불쌍한, 측은한 ❑ 꼬리가 말린 작고 불쌍한 개 ❑ 적은 수의 구경꾼들은 초라한 광경을 연출했다. ● 불쌍하게 부사 ❑ 그녀는 측은할 정도로 말랐었다. ❷ 형용사 형편없는; 어처구니없는 [탐탁찮음] ❑ 그런 어처구니없는 변명을 ❑ 그렇게 형편없게 굴지 마. ● 형편없게; 어처구니없게 부사 ❑ 18명의 집단에서 여자가 5명밖에 없다는 것은 어처구니없게 적은 것이다.

patho|logi|cal /pæθəlɒdʒɪkᵊl/ ADJ You describe a person or their behavior as **pathological** when they behave in an extreme and unacceptable way, and have very powerful feelings which they cannot control. ☐ He experiences chronic, almost pathological jealousy. ☐ He's a pathological liar. 2 ADJ **Pathological** means relating to pathology or illness. [MEDICAL] ☐ ...pathological conditions in animals.

1 형용사 병적인 ☐ 그는 만성적인, 거의 병적인 질투심을 느낀다. ☐ 그는 병적인 거짓말쟁이다.
2 형용사 병리상의, 병리학적 [의학] ☐ 동물의 병리학적 상태

pa|thol|o|gist /pəθɒlədʒɪst/ (pathologists) N-COUNT A **pathologist** is someone who studies or investigates diseases and illnesses, and examines dead bodies in order to find out the cause of death.

가산명사 병리학자

pa|thol|o|gy /pəθɒlədʒi/ N-UNCOUNT **Pathology** is the study of the way diseases and illnesses develop. [MEDICAL]

불가산명사 병리학 [의학]

pa|thos /peɪθɒs/ N-UNCOUNT **Pathos** is a quality in a situation, movie, or play that makes people feel sadness and pity. ☐ ...the pathos of man's isolation.

불가산명사 페이소스, 비애 ☐ 인간 고독의 페이소스

path|way /pæθweɪ/ (pathways) 1 N-COUNT A **pathway** is a path which you can walk along or a route which you can take. ☐ Richard was coming up the pathway. 2 N-COUNT A **pathway** is a particular course of action or a way of achieving something. ☐ Diplomacy will smooth your pathway to success.

1 가산명사 길 ☐ 리처드는 길을 올라오고 있었다.
2 가산명사 길 ☐ 인간관계가 성공에 이르는 길을 더 수월하게 해 줄 것이다.

pa|tience /peɪʃᵊns/ 1 N-UNCOUNT If you have **patience**, you are able to stay calm and not get annoyed, for example when something takes a long time, or when someone is not doing what you want them to do. ☐ He doesn't have the patience to wait. 2 PHRASE If someone **tries** your **patience** or **tests** your **patience**, they annoy you so much that it is very difficult for you to stay calm. ☐ He tended to stutter whenever he spoke to her. It undermined her confidence in him and tried her patience.

1 불가산명사 참을성, 인내 ☐ 그에게는 기다릴 만한 참을성이 없다. 2 구 인내심을 시험하다 ☐ 그는 그녀에게 이야기를 할 때마다 말을 더듬는 경향이 있었다. 그 때문에 그에 대한 그녀의 신뢰가 약해졌고 인내심이 시험당하는 것 같았다.

pa|tient ♦♦◇ /peɪʃᵊnt/ (patients) 1 N-COUNT A **patient** is a person who is receiving medical treatment from a doctor or hospital. A **patient** is also someone who is registered with a particular doctor. ☐ The earlier the treatment is given, the better the patient's chances. ☐ She was tough but wonderful with her patients. →see **client** 2 ADJ If you are **patient**, you stay calm and do not get annoyed, for example when something takes a long time, or when someone is not doing what you want them to do. ☐ Please be patient – your cheque will arrive. ● **pa|tient|ly** ADV [ADV with v] ☐ She waited patiently for Frances to finish. →see **diagnosis, illness**

1 가산명사 환자 ☐ 치료가 일찍 시작될수록 환자의 회복 가능성이 높아진다. ☐ 그녀는 엄격했지만 환자들과 관계는 아주 좋았다. 2 형용사 참을성 있는, 인내심이 있는 ☐ 잠시만 기다려 주세요. 수표가 곧 도착할 것입니다. ● 참을성 있게 부사 ☐ 그녀는 프랜시스가 일을 마칠 때까지 참을성 있게 기다렸다.

pa|tio /pætioʊ/ (patios) N-COUNT A **patio** is an area of flat blocks of stone or concrete next to a house, where people can sit and relax or eat.

가산명사 테라스

pat|ri|ot /peɪtriət/ (patriots) N-COUNT Someone who is a **patriot** loves their country and feels very loyal toward it. ☐ They were staunch British patriots and had portraits of the Queen in their flat.

가산명사 애국자 ☐ 그들은 영국의 확고한 애국자들이었으며 아파트에 여왕의 초상화를 두고 있었다.

Word Link   otic ≈ affecting, causing : erotic, neurotic, patriotic

---

pat|ri|ot|ic /peɪtriɒtɪk/ ADJ Someone who is **patriotic** loves their country and feels very loyal toward it. ☐ Woosnam is fiercely patriotic.

형용사 애국적인 ☐ 우스남은 열렬한 애국자이다.

Word Link   ism ≈ action or state : communism, optimism, patriotism

---

pat|ri|ot|ism /peɪtriətɪzəm/ N-UNCOUNT **Patriotism** is love for your country and loyalty toward it. ☐ He was a country boy who had joined the army out of a sense of patriotism and adventure.

불가산명사 애국심 ☐ 그는 애국심과 모험심 때문에 육군에 지원한 시골 청년이었다.

pa|trol /pətroʊl/ (patrols, patrolling, patrolled) 1 V-T When soldiers, police, or guards **patrol** an area or building, they move around it in order to make sure that there is no trouble there. ☐ Prison officers continued to patrol the grounds within the jail. ● N-COUNT **Patrol** is also a noun. ☐ He failed to return from a patrol. 2 PHRASE Soldiers, police, or guards who are **on patrol** are patrolling an area. ☐ The army is now on patrol in Srinagar and a curfew has been imposed. 3 N-COUNT A **patrol** is a group of soldiers or vehicles that are patrolling an area. ☐ Guerrillas attacked a patrol with hand grenades.

1 타동사 순찰하다 ☐ 교도관들은 교도소 구내를 계속 순찰했다. ● 가산명사 순찰 ☐ 그는 순찰에서 돌아오지 못했다. 2 구 순찰 중인 ☐ 군대는 지금 스리나가르를 순찰하고 있으며 통행금지가 발효되었다. 3 가산명사 순찰대 ☐ 게릴라들이 수류탄으로 순찰대를 공격했다.

pa|tron /peɪtrən/ (patrons) 1 N-COUNT A **patron** is a person who supports and gives money to artists, writers, or musicians. ☐ Catherine the Great was a patron of the arts and sciences. 2 N-COUNT The **patron** of a charity, group, or campaign is an important person who allows his or her name to be used for publicity. ☐ Fiona and Alastair have become patrons of the National Missing Person's Helpline. 3 N-COUNT The **patrons** of a place such as a bar or hotel are its customers. [FORMAL] ☐ Few patrons of a high-priced hotel can be led to expect anything other than luxury service.

1 가산명사 후원자 ☐ 캐서린 대제는 예술과 학문의 후원자였다. 2 가산명사 후원자 ☐ 피오나와 알라스테어는 전국 실종자 전화 서비스의 후원자가 되었다. 3 가산명사 고객 [격식체] ☐ 비싼 호텔의 고객들 중 최상의 서비스보다 못한 것을 기대하는 사람은 별로 없다.

pat|ron|age /peɪtrənɪdʒ, pæt-/ N-UNCOUNT **Patronage** is the support and money given by someone to a person or a group such as a charity. ☐ ...government patronage of the arts in Europe.

불가산명사 후원 ☐ 유럽 정부들의 예술 후원

pat|ron|ize /peɪtrənaɪz, BRIT pætrənaɪz/ (patronizes, patronizing, patronized) [BRIT also **patronise**] 1 V-T If someone **patronizes** you, they speak or behave toward you in a way which seems friendly, but which shows that they think they are superior to you in some way. [DISAPPROVAL] ☐ Don't you patronize me! 2 V-T Someone who **patronizes** artists, writers, or musicians supports them and gives them money. [FORMAL] ☐ The Japanese Imperial family patronizes the Japanese Art Association. 3 V-T If someone **patronizes** a place such as a bar or hotel, they are one of its customers. [FORMAL] ☐ The ladies of Berne liked to patronize the Palace for tea and little cakes.

[영국영어 patronise] 1 타동사 은근히 무시하다, 깔보는 태도로 대하다 [탐탁잖음] ☐ 사람을 그런 식으로 은근히 무시하지 마! 2 타동사 후원하다 [격식체] ☐ 일본 황실이 일본 예술 협회를 후원한다. 3 타동사 –의 고객이 되다 [격식체] ☐ 베른의 아가씨들은 팰리스에 들러 차와 케이크를 먹는 것을 좋아했다.

pat|ron|iz|ing /peɪtrənaɪzɪŋ, BRIT pætrənaɪzɪŋ/ [BRIT also **patronising**] ADJ If someone is **patronizing**, they speak or behave towards you in a way that seems friendly, but which shows that they think they are superior to you. [DISAPPROVAL] ☐ The tone of the interview was unnecessarily patronizing.

[영국영어 patronising] 형용사 은근히 깔보는 [탐탁잖음] ☐ 인터뷰에서 어투가 기분 나쁘게 은근히 깔보는 투였다.

pat|ter /pǽtər/ (patters, pattering, pattered) **1** V-I If something **patters** on a surface, it hits it quickly several times, making quiet, tapping sounds. ❑ *Rain pattered gently outside, dripping on to the roof from the pines.* **2** N-SING A **patter** is a series of quick, quiet, tapping sounds. ❑ *...the patter of the driving rain on the roof.* **3** N-SING Someone's **patter** is a series of things that they say quickly and easily, usually in order to entertain people or to persuade them to buy or do something. ❑ *Fran began her automatic patter about how Jon had been unavoidably detained.*

pat|tern ◆◇◇ /pǽtərn/ (patterns) **1** N-COUNT A **pattern** is the repeated or regular way in which something happens or is done. ❑ *All three attacks followed the same pattern.* **2** N-COUNT A **pattern** is an arrangement of lines or shapes, especially a design in which the same shape is repeated at regular intervals over a surface. ❑ *...a golden robe embroidered with red and purple thread stitched into a pattern of flames.* **3** N-COUNT A **pattern** is a diagram or shape that you can use as a guide when you are making something such as a model or a piece of clothing. ❑ *...cutting out a pattern for trousers.* ❑ *Send for our free patterns to knit yourself.*
→see **quilt**

Word Partnership	pattern의 연어
ADJ.	**familiar** pattern, **normal** pattern, **typical** pattern **1**
	different pattern, **same** pattern, **similar** pattern **1** **2**
V.	**change** a pattern, **fit** a pattern, **see** a pattern **1**
	follow a pattern **1**-**3**

pat|terned /pǽtərnd/ **1** ADJ Something that is **patterned** is covered with a pattern or design. ❑ *...a plain carpet with a patterned border.* **2** V-T PASSIVE If something new **is patterned on** something else that already exists, it is deliberately made so that it has similar features. [mainly AM] ❑ *New York City announced a 10-point policy patterned on the federal bill of rights for taxpayers.*

pause ◆◇◇ /pɔz/ (pauses, pausing, paused) **1** V-I If you **pause** while you are doing something, you stop for a short period and then continue. ❑ *"It's rather embarrassing," he began, and paused.* ❑ *He talked for two hours without pausing for breath.* **2** N-COUNT A **pause** is a short period when you stop doing something before continuing. ❑ *After a pause Alex said sharply: "I'm sorry if I've upset you."*

Word Partnership	pause의 연어
ADJ.	**awkward** pause, **brief** pause, **long** pause, **short** pause, **slight** pause **2**

pave /peɪv/ (paves, paving, paved) V-T If a road or an area of ground **has been paved**, it has been covered with flat blocks of stone or concrete, so that it is suitable for walking or driving on. [usu passive] ❑ *The avenue had never been paved, and deep mud made it impassable in winter.*

pave|ment /peɪvmənt/ (pavements) **1** N-COUNT The **pavement** is the hard surface of a road. [AM] ❑ *The tires of Lenny's bike hissed over the wet pavement.* **2** N-COUNT A **pavement** is a path with a hard surface, usually by the side of a road. [BRIT; AM **sidewalk**] ❑ *He was hurrying along the pavement.*

pa|vil|ion /pəvɪljən/ (pavilions) **1** N-COUNT A **pavilion** is a large temporary structure such as a tent, which is used at outdoor public events. ❑ *...heading across the beautiful green lawn towards the International Pavilion.* **2** N-COUNT A **pavilion** is a building on the edge of a sports field where players can change their clothes and wash. [BRIT] ❑ *...the cricket pavilion.*

paw /pɔ/ (paws, pawing, pawed) **1** N-COUNT The **paws** of an animal such as a cat, dog, or bear are its feet, which have claws for gripping things and soft pads for walking on. ❑ *The kitten was black with white front paws and a white splotch on her chest.* **2** V-T/V-I If an animal **paws** something or **paws** at it, it draws its foot over it or down it. ❑ *Madigan's horse pawed the ground.* **3** V-T/V-I If one person **paws** another or **paws** at them, they touch or stroke them in a way that the other person finds offensive. [DISAPPROVAL] ❑ *Stop pawing me, Giles!*

pawn /pɔn/ (pawns, pawning, pawned) **1** V-T If you **pawn** something that you own, you leave it with a pawnbroker, who gives you money for it and who can sell it if you do not pay back the money before a certain time. ❑ *He is contemplating pawning his watch.* **2** N-COUNT In chess, a **pawn** is the smallest and least valuable playing piece. Each player has eight pawns at the start of the game. **3** N-COUNT If you say that someone is using you as a **pawn**, you mean that they are using you for their own advantage. ❑ *It looks as though he is being used as a political pawn by the President.*
→see **chess**

pawn|broker /pɔnbroʊkər/ (pawnbrokers) N-COUNT A **pawnbroker** is a person who lends people money. People give the pawnbroker something they own, which can be sold if they do not pay back the money before a certain time.

pay ◆◆◆ /peɪ/ (pays, paying, paid) **1** V-T/V-I When you **pay** an amount of money to someone, you give it to them because you are buying something from them or because you owe it to them. When you **pay** something such as a bill or a debt, you pay the amount that you owe. ❑ *Owners who have already paid for repairs will be reimbursed.* ❑ *The wealthier may have to pay a little more in taxes.* **2** V-T When you **are paid**, you get your wages or salary from your employer. ❑ *The lawyer was paid a huge salary.* ❑ *I get paid monthly.* **3** N-UNCOUNT Your **pay** is the

1 자동사 후드득거리다 ❑ 밖에 비가 후드득거리더니, 소나무에서 지붕 위로 빗방울 떨어지는 소리가 들렸다. **2** 단수명사 후드득거림 ❑ 몰아치는 비가 지붕 위로 후드득거리는 소리 **3** 단수명사 기침없이 쏟아 놓는 말, 청산유수 ❑ 존이 어떻게 어쩔 수 없이 늦게 되었는지에 대해 프랜이 따발총 같이 말을 쏟아 놓기 시작했다.

1 가산명사 양식, 패턴 ❑ 세 공격 모두 같은 양식을 따랐다. **2** 가산명사 무늬, 모양 ❑ 빨강과 보라색 실로 불꽃 모양의 수를 놓은 황금색 가운 **3** 가산명사 본 ❑ 바지의 본을 오려 내기 ❑ 옷을 직접 짤 수 있도록 저희가 무료로 드리는 본을 주문하세요.

1 형용사 무늬가 있는 ❑ 테두리에만 무늬가 있는 민무늬 카펫 **2** 수동 타동사 본뜨다 [주로 미국영어] ❑ 뉴욕 시는 납세자를 위한 연방 권리 장전을 본뜬 열 가지 정책을 발표했다.

1 자동사 잠깐 멈추다 ❑ "사실 좀 창피해"라고 그가 말을 꺼내고는 잠깐 멈추었다. ❑ 그는 숨조차 쉬지 않고 두 시간 동안 이야기를 했다. **2** 가산명사 휴지, 일시적 정지 ❑ 잠깐의 침묵 뒤에 알렉스가 갑자기 말했다 "기분 상하게 했다면 미안해."

타동사 포장되다 ❑ 그 길은 포장된 적이 없으며 겨울에는 깊은 진흙탕 때문에 통행이 불가능했다.

1 가산명사 포장도로 [미국영어] ❑ 레니가 탄 자전거의 타이어가 젖은 포장도로를 지나가며 쐐 하는 소리를 냈다. **2** 가산명사 인도 [영국영어; 미국영어 sidewalk] ❑ 그는 인도를 따라 서둘러 가고 있었다.

1 가산명사 대형 천막, 임시 구조물 ❑ 아름다운 푸른 잔디밭을 건너 국제관 천막으로 가면서 **2** 가산명사 선수용 탈의실 [영국영어] ❑ 크리켓 선수용 탈의실

1 가산명사 (동물의) 발 ❑ 고양이 새끼는 검정색이었는데 앞발은 하얗고 가슴엔 큼직한 흰 반점이 있었다. **2** 타동사/자동사 (발로) 긁다 ❑ 마디간의 말이 땅을 발로 긁었다. **3** 타동사/자동사 기분 나쁘게 더듬다, 함부로 만지다 [탐탁잖음] ❑ 내 몸 그만 더듬어, 자일스!

1 타동사 전당포에 잡히다 ❑ 그는 시계를 전당포에 맡길까 생각 중이다. **2** 가산명사 (장기) 졸 **3** 가산명사 (비유적) 졸 ❑ 대통령이 그를 쓰다 버릴 졸로 보는 것 같다.

가산명사 전당포 주인

1 타동사/자동사 지불하다 ❑ 수리비를 이미 낸 주인들은 보상을 받을 것이다. ❑ 돈이 많을수록 세금을 조금 더 내야 할지도 모른다. **2** 타동사 보수를 받다 ❑ 그 변호사는 엄청난 보수를 받았다. ❑ 나는 매달 월급을 받는다. **3** 불가산명사 보수 ❑ 보수와 업무 조건에 대한 그들의 불만

money that you get from your employer as wages or salary. ❑ ...*their complaints about their pay and conditions.*

> When used as a noun, **pay** is a general word which you can use to refer to the money you get from your employer for doing your job. Professional people and office workers receive a **salary**, which is paid monthly. However, when talking about someone's salary, you usually give the annual figure. ❑ *I'm paid a salary of $15,000 a year.* Manual workers are paid **wages**, or **a wage**. The plural is more common than the singular, especially when you are talking about the actual cash that someone receives. ❑ *Every week he handed all his wages in cash to his wife.* Wages are usually paid, and quoted, as an hourly or a weekly sum. ❑ ...*a starting wage of five dollars an hour.* Your **income** consists of all the money you receive from all sources, including your pay.

❹ V-T If you **are paid to** do something, someone gives you some money so that you will help them or perform some service for them. ❑ *Students were paid substantial sums of money to do nothing all day but lie in bed.* ❺ V-I If a government or organization makes someone **pay for** something, it makes them responsible for providing the money for it, for example by increasing prices or taxes. ❑ ...*a legally binding international treaty that establishes who must pay for environmental damage.* ❻ V-T/V-I If a job, deal, or investment **pays** a particular amount, it brings you that amount of money. ❑ *I'm stuck in jobs that don't pay very well.* ❼ V-I If a job, deal, or investment **pays**, it brings you a profit or earns you some money. ❑ *There are some agencies now specialising in helping older people to find jobs which pay.* ❽ V-T When you **pay** money **into** a bank account, you put the money in the account. ❑ *He paid £20 into his savings account.* ❾ V-T/V-I If a course of action **pays**, it results in some advantage or benefit for you. ❑ *It pays to invest in protective clothing.* ❿ V-T/V-I If you **pay for** something that you do or have, you suffer as a result of it. ❑ *Britain was to pay dearly for its lack of resolve.* ❑ *Why should I pay the penalty for somebody else's mistake?* ⓫ V-T You use **pay** with some nouns, for example in the expressions **pay a visit** and **pay attention**, to indicate that something is given or done. ❑ *Do pay us a visit next time you're in Birmingham.* ❑ *He felt a heavy bump, but paid no attention to it.* ⓬ →see also **paid, sick pay** ⓭ PHRASE If something that you buy or invest in **pays for itself** after a period of time, the money you gain from it, or save because you have it, is greater than the amount you originally spent or invested. ❑ ...*investments in energy efficiency that would pay for themselves within five years.* ⓮ **to pay dividends** →see **dividend. to pay through the nose** →see **nose**

> Do not confuse **pay** and **buy**. If you **pay** someone, **pay** them money, or **pay for** something, you give someone money for something they are selling to you. ❑ *I paid the taxi driver... I need some money to pay the window cleaner... Some people are forced to pay for their own medicines.* If you **pay** a bill or debt, you pay the amount of money that is owed. ❑ *He paid his bill and left... We were paying $50 for a single room.* If you **buy** something, you obtain it by paying money for it. ❑ *Gary's bought a bicycle.*

Thesaurus   pay의 참조어

V.   clear, remit, settle ❶
N.   compensation, salary, wage ❸

▶**pay back** ❶ PHRASAL VERB If you **pay back** some money that you have borrowed or taken from someone, you give them an equal sum of money at a later time. ❑ *He burst into tears, begging her to forgive him and swearing to pay back everything he had stolen.* ❷ PHRASAL VERB If you **pay** someone **back for** doing something unpleasant to you, you take your revenge on them or make them suffer for what they did. ❑ *Some day I'll pay you back for this!*

▶**pay off** ❶ PHRASAL VERB If you **pay off** a debt, you give someone all the money that you owe them. ❑ *It would take him the rest of his life to pay off that loan.* ❷ PHRASAL VERB If an action **pays off**, it is successful or profitable after a period of time. ❑ *Sandra was determined to become a doctor and her persistence paid off.* ❸ →see also **payoff**

▶**pay out** ❶ PHRASAL VERB If you **pay out** money, usually a large amount, you spend it on something. ❑ *The insurance industry will pay out about $7.3 billion for damage caused by Hurricane Andrew.* ❷ →see also **payout**

▶**pay up** PHRASAL VERB If you **pay up**, you give someone the money that you owe them or that they are entitled to, even though you would prefer not to give it. ❑ *We claimed a refund from the association, but they would not pay up.*

pay|able /peɪəbᵊl/ ❶ ADJ If an amount of money is **payable**, it has to be paid or it can be paid. [v-link ADJ, oft ADJ on/to n] ❑ *Purchase tax was not payable on goods for export.* ❷ ADJ If a check or money order is made **payable to** you, it has your name written on it to indicate that you are the person who will receive the money. [v n ADJ, n ADJ, ADJ to n] ❑ *Write, enclosing a cheque made payable to Cobuild Limited.*

pay|back /peɪbæk/ (**paybacks**) also **pay-back** ❶ N-COUNT You can use **payback** to refer to the profit or benefit that you obtain from something that you have spent money, time, or effort on. [mainly AM] ❑ *There is a substantial payback in terms of employee and union relations.* ❷ ADJ The **payback** period of a loan is the time in which you are required or allowed to pay it back. [ADJ n] ❑ *The payback period can be as short as seven years.* ❸ PHRASE **Payback time** is when someone has to take the consequences of what they have done in the past. You can use this expression to talk about good or bad consequences. ❑ *This was payback time. I've proved once and for all I can become champion.*

pay|check /peɪtʃek/ (**paychecks**) [BRIT **paycheque**] N-COUNT Your **paycheck** is a piece of paper that your employer gives you as your wages or salary, and which

---

pay는 명사로 쓰면, 자기가 일을 한 것에 대해 고용주로부터 받는 돈을 가리킬 때 쓸 수 있는 일반적인 말이다. 전문직과 사무직 종사자들은 매달 지급되는 salary를 받는다. 그러나, 누구의 salary를 말할 때에는 대개 연봉을 말한다. ❑ 나는 일년에 15,000달러의 연봉을 받는다. 육체노동자는 wages 또는 a wage를 받는다. 특히 실제로 받는 현금을 말할 때는 단수보다 복수가 더 일반적이다. ❑ 매주 그는 현금으로 된 자기 임금 전부를 자기 아내에게 주었다. 임금은 대개 시급 또는 주급으로 지불하고 매긴다. ❑ ...시간당 5달러의 초임. income은 급료를 포함해서 모든 소득원으로부터 받는 총액으로 구성된다.

❹ 타동사 돈을 받다 ❑ 학생들은 하루 종일 아무 일도 안하고 그냥 침대에 누워 있기만 하는 일로 상당한 양의 돈을 받았다. ❺ 자동사 대가를 치르다 ❑ 환경 훼손에 대한 대가를 누가 처리야 하는지를 규정하는 법적 구속력을 갖는 국제 조약 ❻ 타동사/자동사 ...의 돈을 안겨 주다 ❑ 우리는 그다지 많은 돈을 주지 않는 일자리에 묶여 있다. ❼ 자동사 돈이 되다 ❑ 이제는 나이든 사람들이 돈이 되는 일자리를 찾을 수 있도록 전문적으로 도와주는 기관들이 몇 개 있다. ❽ 타동사 입금하다 ❑ 그는 예금 통장에 20파운드를 입금했다. ❾ 타동사/자동사 이득이 되다 ❑ 보호용 의복에 투자하면 도움이 된다. ❿ 타동사/자동사 대가를 치르다 ❑ 결단력 부족으로 영국은 훗날 큰 대가를 치르게 되었다. ❑ 남의 실수에 대한 대가를 왜 내가 치러야 하는가? ⓫ 타동사 -하다; 방문하다 ❑ 다음에 버밍엄에 오실 때 꼭 들러 주세요. ❑ 그는 뭔가 둔탁한 것을 느꼈으나 신경 쓰지 않았다. ⓭ 구 흑자를 낳다, 이익이 되다 ❑ 5년 안에 이익을 가져다 줄 에너지 효율성에 대한 투자

pay와 buy를 혼동하지 않도록 하라. 누구에게 pay하면, 그에게 돈을 pay하는 것이고, 무엇에 대해 pay for하면, 당신에게 파는 물건 값으로 누구에게 돈을 지불하는 것이다. ❑ 나는 택시 기사에게 돈을 지불했다...나는 창문 닦는 사람에게 돈이 좀 필요하다... 어떤 사람들은 자신의 건강 보험료를 직접 내야만 한다. pay a bill(고지서) or debt(빚)이라고 하면 당신이 지불하거나 갚아야 할 액수의 돈을 주는 것이다. ❑ 그는 자기 계산서대로 계산을 하고 떠났다... 우리는 일인용 방 하나에 50달러를 내고 있었다. 무엇을 buy하면, 그것에 대해 돈을 지불하고 그것을 얻는 것이다. ❑ 개리는 자전거를 샀다.

❶ 구동사 갚다 ❑ 그는 울음을 터뜨리며 그녀에게 용서를 빌고 훔친 모든 것을 갚겠다고 약속했다. ❷ 구동사 갚다, 복수하다 ❑ 이것을 언젠가는 내게 갚아 주겠어!

❶ 구동사 다 갚다 ❑ 그가 그 대출금을 다 갚으려면 평생이 걸릴 것이다. ❷ 구동사 결실을 맺다 ❑ 산드라는 의사가 되겠다는 결심을 했으며 노력이 결국 결실을 맺었다.

❶ 구동사 지불하다 ❑ 태풍 앤드류 때문에 생긴 피해로 보험 업계가 보상금 약 73억 달러를 지불할 것이다.

구동사 (마지못해) 지불하다 ❑ 우리는 협회에 환불을 요청했지만 그들은 돈을 주려 하지 않았다.

❶ 형용사 내야 하는; 낼 수 있는 ❑ 수출품에 대한 구매세는 낼 필요가 없었다. ❷ 형용사 -를 수취인으로 하는 ❑ 편지를 써서 코빌드 사를 수취인으로 하는 수표를 동봉해서 보내세요.

❶ 가산명사 수익, 이익 [주로 미국영어] ❑ 직원 및 노조 관계 면에서 상당한 이익이 있다. ❷ 형용사 상환의 ❑ 상환 기간은 최소한 7년이다. ❸ 구 응분의 대가를 받는 순간 ❑ 모든 것이 결실을 맺는 순간이었다. 나는 내가 챔피언이 될 수 있다는 것을 완전히 증명했다.

[영국영어] paycheque 가산명사 급여 수표; 급여 ❑ 그들은 급여 없이 약 2주간 일했다.

you can then cash at a bank. You can also use **paycheck** as a way of referring to your wages or salary. ❑ *They've worked for about two weeks without a paycheck.*

pay day (**pay days**) also payday N-UNCOUNT **Pay day** is the day of the week or month on which you receive your wages or salary. [also N in pl] ❑ *Until next payday, I was literally without any money.*

불가산명사 월급날 ❑ 그 다음 월급날까지 나는 정말 돈이 한 푼도 없었다.

PAYE /pi eɪ waɪ iː/ N-UNCOUNT In Britain, **PAYE** is a system of paying income tax in which your employer pays your tax directly to the government, and then takes this amount from your salary or wages. **PAYE** is an abbreviation for "pay as you earn." [BUSINESS]

불가산명사 영국에서 고용주가 근로자의 세금을 대신 낸 후 나중에 임금에서 차감하는 제도 [경제]

payee /peɪiː/ (**payees**) N-COUNT The **payee** of a check or similar document is the person who should receive the money. [FORMAL] ❑ *On the check, write the name of the payee and then sign your name.*

가산명사 수취인 [격식체] ❑ 수표에 수취인의 이름을 쓴 다음에 본인의 이름을 서명하세요.

pay en|velope (**pay envelopes**) N-COUNT Your **pay envelope** is the envelope containing your wages, which your employer gives you. [AM; BRIT **pay packet**] ❑ *When Howard opened her pay envelope and found the same bonus she got the year before, she complained directly to her bosses.*

가산명사 월급봉투 [미국영어; 영국영어 pay packet] ❑ 하워드는 월급봉투를 열어 보고 전년도와 같은 보너스를 받았다는 것을 알고는 상관들에게 직접 불만을 말했다.

pay|er /peɪər/ (**payers**) N-COUNT You can refer to someone as a **payer** if they pay a particular kind of bill or fee. For example, a mortgage **payer** is someone who pays a mortgage. [usu with supp, oft n N] ❑ *Lower interest rates pleased millions of mortgage payers.* →see also **taxpayer** ② N-COUNT A **good payer** pays you quickly or pays you a lot of money. A **bad payer** takes a long time to pay you, or does not pay you very much. ❑ *Small businesses, hit hard by the recession, blame the government, banks, and late payers.*

① 가산명사 지불인 ❑ 금리 인하는 주택담보 대출자 수백만 명을 기쁘게 했다. ② 가산명사 성실 납부자; 불량 납부자 ❑ 불황의 피해를 심하게 본 소규모 사업체들은 정부, 은행, 그리고 불량 납부자들을 탓한다.

pay|ment ♦♢◇ /peɪmənt/ (**payments**) ① N-COUNT A **payment** is an amount of money that is paid to someone, or the act of paying this money. ❑ *Thousands of its customers are in arrears with loans and mortgage payments.* ② N-UNCOUNT **Payment** is the act of paying money to someone or of being paid. ❑ *He had sought to obtain payment of a sum which he had claimed was owed to him.* ③ →see also **balance of payments, down payment**

① 가산명사 상환금; 상환 ❑ 수천 명의 고객이 대출 및 주택담보 대출 상환금을 체납한 상태이다. ② 불가산명사 지불 ❑ 그는 자기가 받아야 한다고 주장한 액수를 받기 위해 노력했다.

Word Partnership	payment의 연어
V.	**accept** payment, **make a** payment, **receive** payment ①
ADJ.	**late** payment, **minimum** payment, **monthly** payment ①
N.	payment **in cash**, payment **by check**, **mortgage** payment ①
	payment **date** ① ②
	payment **method**, payment **plan** ②

pay|off /peɪɔf/ (**payoffs**) also pay-off ① N-COUNT The **payoff from** an action is the advantage or benefit that you get from it. ❑ *If such materials became generally available to the optics industry the payoffs from such a breakthrough would be enormous.* ② N-COUNT A **payoff** is a payment which is made to someone, often secretly or illegally, so that they will not cause trouble. ❑ *Soldiers in both countries supplement their incomes with payoffs from drugs exporters.* ③ N-COUNT A **payoff** is a large payment made to someone by their employer when the person has been forced to leave their job. ❑ *The ousted chairman received a £1.5 million payoff from the loss-making oil company.*

① 가산명사 이득 ❑ 그러한 재료가 광학 업계에 일반적으로 보급된다면 그러한 혁신으로 얻은 이득은 어마어마할 것이다. ② 가산명사 뇌물 ❑ 두 나라의 군인 모두 마약 수출상들이 주는 뇌물로 수입을 보충한다. ③ 가산명사 명예 퇴직금 ❑ 적자를 낳는 석유 회사로부터 쫓겨난 회장은 150만 파운드의 명예 퇴직금을 받았다.

pay|out /peɪaʊt/ (**payouts**) also pay-out N-COUNT A **payout** is a sum of money, especially a large one, that is paid to someone, for example by an insurance company or as a prize. ❑ *...long delays in receiving insurance payouts.* →see **lottery**

가산명사 배상금, 배당금 ❑ 보험 배상금을 받는 데 시간이 길게 지연되는 사례들

pay pack|et (**pay packets**) ① N-COUNT Your **pay packet** is the envelope containing your wages, which your employer gives you at the end of every week. [BRIT; AM **pay envelope**] ❑ *...the checked blouse she bought with her first pay packet for 19 shillings and sixpence.* ② N-COUNT You can refer to someone's wages or salary as their **pay packet**. [BRIT; AM **paycheck, pay**] ❑ *Over those 16 years, his pay packet has increased beyond all reckoning.*

① 가산명사 주급 봉투 [영국영어; 미국영어 pay envelope] ❑ 그녀가 최초의 주급 봉투로 19실링 6펜스를 주고 산 체크무늬 블라우스 ② 가산명사 보수, 급료 [영국영어; 미국영어 paycheck, pay] ❑ 그 16년 사이에 그의 보수는 상상할 수 없을 정도로 증가했다.

pay-per-view N-UNCOUNT **Pay-per-view** is a cable or satellite television system in which you have to pay a fee if you want to watch a particular program. ❑ *The match appeared on pay-per-view television.*

불가산명사 페이퍼뷰 (프로그램당 시청료) ❑ 그 경기는 페이퍼뷰 채널에 방영되었다.

pay|phone /peɪfoʊn/ (**payphones**) also pay phone N-COUNT A **payphone** is a telephone which you need to put coins or a card in before you can make a call. Payphones are usually in public places.

가산명사 공중전화

pay|roll /peɪroʊl/ (**payrolls**) N-COUNT The people **on the payroll** of a company or an organization are the people who work for it and are paid by it. [BUSINESS] ❑ *They had 87,000 employees on the payroll.*

가산명사 급료 지급 명부 [경제] ❑ 그들은 급료 지급 명부상으로 87,000명의 직원을 두고 있었다.

pay|slip /peɪslɪp/ (**payslips**) also pay slip N-COUNT A **payslip** is the same as a **paystub**. [BRIT]

가산명사 급료 명세표 [영국영어]

pay|stub /peɪstʌb/ (**paystubs**) also pay stub N-COUNT A **paystub** is a piece of paper given to an employee when he or she is paid, which states how much money has been earned and how much has been taken from that sum for things such as tax. [AM; BRIT **payslip**]

가산명사 급료 명세표 [미국영어; 영국영어 payslip]

PC /piː siː/ (**PCs**) ① N-COUNT A **PC** is a computer that is used by one person at a time in a business, a school, or at home. **PC** is an abbreviation for **personal computer**. ❑ *The price of a PC has fallen by an average of 25% a year since 1982.* ② ADJ If you say that someone is **PC**, you mean that they are extremely careful not to offend or upset any group of people in society who have a disadvantage. **PC** is an abbreviation for "politically correct." ❑ *Certainly, when you're with a group of guys and you're talking about women, you're not PC.* ③ N-COUNT; N-TITLE In Britain, a **PC** is a male police officer of the lowest rank. **PC** is an abbreviation for "police constable." ❑ *The PCs took her to the local station.*

① 가산명사 개인용 컴퓨터 ❑ 개인용 컴퓨터의 가격은 1982년 이후 매년 평균 25퍼센트 정도 하락했다. ② 형용사 차별적이 아닌 ❑ 남자들하고 같이 있으면서 여자들에 대해서 이야기한다면 분명히 비차별적이 될 수는 없다. ③ 가산명사; 경정명사 순경 ❑ 순경들이 그녀를 지역 경찰서로 데리고 갔다.

pd pd is a written abbreviation for **paid**. It is written on a bill to indicate that it has been paid.

지불 완료

PDA /pi di eɪ/ (PDAs) N-COUNT A **PDA** is a handheld computer, used mainly for storing and accessing personal information such as addresses, telephone numbers, and memos. PDA is an abbreviation for "personal digital assistant." ❑ *A typical PDA can function as a mobile phone, fax sender, and personal organizer.*

가산명사 개인용 휴대 정보 단말기 ❑ 일반적으로 휴대용 단말기는 휴대 전화, 팩스 송신기, 개인 수첩 등의 기능을 갖추고 있다.

pea /pi/ (peas) N-COUNT **Peas** are round green seeds which grow in long thin cases and are eaten as a vegetable.

가산명사 완두콩

peace ♦♦♦ /pis/ ❶ N-UNCOUNT If countries or groups involved in a war or violent conflict are discussing **peace**, they are talking to each other in order to try to end the conflict. ❑ *Peace talks involving other rebel leaders and government representatives broke up without agreement last week, but are due to resume shortly.* ❑ *Leaders of some rival factions signed a peace agreement last week.* ❷ N-UNCOUNT If there is **peace** in a country or in the world, there are no wars or violent conflicts going on. ❑ *The President spoke of a shared commitment to world peace and economic development.* ❸ N-UNCOUNT If you disapprove of weapons, especially nuclear weapons, you can use **peace** to refer to campaigns and other activities intended to reduce their numbers or stop their use. ❑ *...two peace campaigners accused of causing damage to an F1-11 nuclear bomber.* ❹ N-UNCOUNT If you have **peace**, you are not being disturbed, and you are in calm, quiet surroundings. ❑ *All I want is to have some peace and quiet and spend a couple of nice days with my grandchildren.* ❺ N-UNCOUNT If you have a feeling of **peace**, you feel contented and calm and not at all worried. You can also say that you are **at peace**. ❑ *I had a wonderful feeling of peace and serenity when I saw my husband.* ❑ *The peace of the Lord be always with you.* ❻ N-UNCOUNT If there is **peace** among a group of people, they live or work together in a friendly way and do not quarrel. You can also say that people live or work **in peace with** each other. ❑ *...a period of relative peace in the country's industrial relations.* ❼ PHRASE If someone in authority, such as the army or the police, **keeps the peace**, they make sure that people behave and do not fight or quarrel with each other. ❑ *...the first UN contingent assigned to help keep the peace in Cambodia.* ❽ PHRASE If something gives you **peace of mind**, it stops you from worrying about a particular problem or difficulty. ❑ *The main appeal these bonds hold for individual investors is the safety and peace of mind they offer.*

❶ 불가산명사 평화 ❑ 지난주 반군 지도자와 정부 대표 사이의 평화회담이 합의 결렬되었으나 곧 재개될 예정이다. ❑ 일부 경쟁 분파 지도자들이 지난주에 평화협정에 서명했다. ❷ 불가산명사 평화 ❑ 대통령은 세계 평화와 경제 발전을 위한 공동의 헌신에 대해 이야기했다. ❸ 불가산명사 평화 ❑ 에프1-11 핵폭격기를 손괴한 혐의를 받는 두 명의 평화 운동가 ❹ 불가산명사 평안 ❑ 내가 원하는 것은 다만 조용하고 평안한 가운데 손주들과 며칠이라도 즐겁게 지내는 것이다. ❺ 불가산명사 평온, 평화; 평온한 ❑ 남편을 보자 내 마음이 매우 평온한고 차분해졌다. ❑ 주님의 평화가 항상 그대와 함께 하기를 ❻ 불가산명사 화목; -와 관계가 화목한 ❑ 국가 내 기업 간의 관계가 비교적 화목했던 시기 ❼ 구 평화를 유지하다 ❑ 캄보디아 내 평화 유지를 위해 파견된 최초의 유엔 부대 ❽ 구 마음의 평화 ❑ 개인 투자자에게 이 채권이 가지는 가장 큰 매력은 안정성과 마음의 평화이다.

peaceful ♦♦◇ /pisfəl/ ❶ ADJ **Peaceful** activities and situations do not involve war. ❑ *He has attempted to find a peaceful solution to the Ossetian conflict.* ● **peace|ful|ly** ADV [ADV with v] ❑ *The U.S. military expects the matter to be resolved peacefully.* ❷ ADJ **Peaceful** occasions happen without violence or serious disorder. ❑ *The farmers staged a noisy but peaceful protest outside the headquarters of the organization.* ● **peace|ful|ly** ADV [ADV with v] ❑ *Ten thousand people are reported to have taken part in the protest which passed off peacefully.* ❸ ADJ **Peaceful** people are not violent and try to avoid quarreling or fighting with other people. ❑ *...warriors who killed or enslaved the peaceful farmers.* ● **peace|ful|ly** ADV [ADV with v] ❑ *They've been living and working peacefully with members of various ethnic groups.* ❹ ADJ A **peaceful** place or time is quiet, calm, and free from disturbance. ❑ *...a peaceful Georgian house in the heart of Dorset.* ● **peace|ful|ly** ADV [ADV after v] ❑ *Except for traffic noise the night passed peacefully.*

❶ 형용사 평화적인 ❑ 그는 오세티아 분쟁에 대한 평화적인 해결책을 찾으려고 시도해 왔다. ● 평화적으로 부사 ❑ 미군은 그 사태가 평화적으로 해결되기를 기대한다. ❷ 형용사 평화적인 ❑ 농부들은 기구 본부 밖에서 소란스럽지만 평화적인 시위를 벌였다. ● 평화적으로 부사 ❑ 평화적으로 끝난 그 시위에 천 명이 참가한 것으로 보도되었다. ❸ 형용사 평화로운 ❑ 평화로운 농부들을 살해하거나 노예로 만든 전사들 ● 평화롭게 부사 ❑ 그들은 다양한 인종 집단과 평화롭게 공존하며 함께 일해 왔다. ❹ 형용사 평온한 ❑ 도싯의 중심에 위치한 평온한 조지 왕조풍의 집 ● 평온하게 부사 ❑ 차량의 소음을 제외하면 그 날 저녁은 평온하게 지나갔다.

Thesaurus   peaceful의 참조어

ADJ.   calm, friendly, gentle, harmonious, placid, quiet, tranquil; *(ant.)* hostile, warring ❸ ❹

---

peace|ful|ly /pisfəli/ ADV If you say that someone died **peacefully**, you mean that they suffered no pain or violence when they died. [ADV after v] ❑ *He died peacefully on 10th December after a short illness.* →see also **peaceful**

부사 편안히 ❑ 그는 잠깐 투병 생활을 하다가 12월 10일에 편안히 숨을 거두었다.

peach /pitʃ/ (peaches) ❶ N-COUNT A **peach** is a soft, round, slightly furry fruit with sweet yellow flesh and pinky-orange skin. Peaches grow in warm countries. ❷ COLOR Something that is **peach** is pale pinky-orange in color. ❑ *...a peach silk blouse.*

❶ 가산명사 복숭아 ❷ 색채어 복숭아색 ❑ 복숭아색 비단 블라우스

peak ♦◇◇ /pik/ (peaks, peaking, peaked) ❶ N-COUNT The **peak** of a process or an activity is the point at which it is at its strongest, most successful, or most fully developed. ❑ *The party's membership has fallen from a peak of fifty-thousand after the Second World War.* ❑ *...a flourishing career that was at its peak at the time of his death.* ❷ V-I When something **peaks**, it reaches its highest value or its highest level. ❑ *Temperatures have peaked at over thirty degrees Celsius.* ❸ ADJ The **peak** level or value of something is its highest level or value. [ADJ n] ❑ *Today's price is 59% lower than the peak level of $1.5 million.* ❹ ADJ **Peak** times are the times when there is most demand for something or most use of something. [ADJ n] ❑ *It's always crowded at peak times.* ❺ N-COUNT A **peak** is a mountain or the top of a mountain. ❑ *...the snow-covered peaks.* ❻ N-COUNT The **peak** of a cap is the part at the front that sticks out above your eyes. ❑ *The man touched the peak of his cap.*

❶ 가산명사 최고점, 정점, 절정 ❑ 정당의 당원 수는 2차 대전 이후 5만 명에 달했던 최고점에서 떨어져 왔다. ❑ 그의 사망 당시 절정에 달해 있던 한창 화려했던 경력 ❷ 자동사 최고점에 달하다, 절정에 이르다 ❑ 기온이 최고 섭씨 30도를 넘었다. ❸ 형용사 최고의 ❑ 오늘의 가격은 150만 달러의 최고가보다 59퍼센트 하락한 것이다. ❹ 형용사 피크, 한창 ❑ 한창 때는 항상 붐빈다. ❺ 가산명사 산꼭대기, 봉우리 ❑ 눈 덮인 봉우리들 ❻ 가산명사 챙 ❑ 그 남자가 모자의 챙을 만졌다.

peak time N-UNCOUNT Programs which are broadcast at **peak time** are broadcast when the greatest number of people are watching television or listening to the radio. [mainly BRIT; AM usually **prime time**] ❑ *The news programme goes out four times a week at peak time.*

불가산명사 황금 시간대 [주로 영국영어; 미국영어 대개 prime time] ❑ 그 뉴스 프로그램은 일주일에 네 번 황금 시간대에 방영된다.

peal /pil/ (peals, pealing, pealed) ❶ V-I When bells **peal**, they ring one after another, making a musical sound. ❑ *Church bells pealed at the stroke of midnight.* ● N-COUNT **Peal** is also a noun. ❑ *...the great peal of the Abbey bells.* ❷ N-COUNT A **peal of** laughter or thunder consists of a long, loud series of sounds. ❑ *I heard a peal of merry laughter.*

❶ 자동사 (종이) 울리다 ❑ 밤 12시를 기해 교회 종소리가 울려 퍼졌다. ● 가산명사 종소리 ❑ 대수도원의 큰 종소리 ❷ 가산명사 (웃음이) 터지는 소리, (천둥이) 울리는 소리 ❑ 즐거운 웃음소리가 터지는 것이 들렸다.

pea|nut /pinʌt, -nət/ (peanuts) N-COUNT **Peanuts** are small nuts that grow under the ground. Peanuts are often eaten as a snack, especially roasted and salted. ❑ *...a packet of peanuts.* →see Word Web: **peanut**

가산명사 땅콩 ❑ 땅콩 한 봉지

Word Web   peanut

The **peanut** is not actually a **nut**. It is a legume and grows under the ground. Peanuts originated in South America about 3,500 years ago. Explorers took them to Africa. Later, African slaves introduced the peanut into North America. At first only poor people ate them. However, by 1900 they had become a popular **snack**. You could buy roasted peanuts on city streets and at baseball games and circuses. Some scientists believe that roasted peanuts cause more **allergic** reactions than boiled peanuts. George Washington Carver, an African-American scientist, found 325 different uses for peanuts—including peanut butter.

In the early 20th century, African-American scientist George Washington Carver ground **peanuts** into a smooth paste. This food, called **peanut butter** is used to make sandwiches. Peanut butter and jelly sandwiches are a popular food with American children.

20세기 초에 아프리카계 미국인 과학자 조지 워싱턴 카버가 peanuts(땅콩)을 갈아 부드러운 반죽으로 만들었다. peanut butter(땅콩 버터)라고 하는 이 식품은 샌드위치를 만들 때 쓰인다. 땅콩 버터와 잼을 넣은 샌드위치는 미국 어린이들에게 인기있는 음식이다.

pear /pɛər/ (**pears**) N-COUNT A **pear** is a sweet, juicy fruit which is narrow near its stalk, and wider and rounded at the bottom. Pears have white flesh and thin green or yellow skin.

가산명사 배

pearl /pɜrl/ (**pearls**) **1** N-COUNT A **pearl** is a hard round object which is shiny and creamy white in color. Pearls grow inside the shell of an oyster and are used for making expensive jewelry. ❑ *She wore a string of pearls at her throat.* **2** ADJ **Pearl** is used to describe something which looks like a pearl. ❑ *...tiny pearl buttons.*

1 가산명사 진주 ❑ 그녀는 목에 진주 목걸이를 하고 있었다. **2** 형용사 진주의 ❑ 작은 진주 모양 단추

peas|ant /pɛznt/ (**peasants**) N-COUNT A **peasant** is a poor person of low social status who works on the land; used of people who live in countries where farming is still a common way of life. ❑ *...the peasants in the Peruvian highlands.*

가산명사 농부, 소작농 ❑ 페루 고산 지대의 농민들

peat /pit/ N-UNCOUNT **Peat** is decaying plant material which is found under the ground in some cool, wet regions. Peat can be added to soil to help plants grow, or can be burned on fires instead of coal. ❑ *...a peat fire.* →see **wetland**

불가산명사 토탄 ❑ 토탄 불

peb|ble /pɛbᵊl/ (**pebbles**) N-COUNT A **pebble** is a small, smooth, round stone which is found on beaches and at the bottom of rivers. →see **beach**

가산명사 조약돌

peck /pɛk/ (**pecks, pecking, pecked**) **1** V-T/V-I If a bird **pecks at** something or **pecks** something, it moves its beak forward quickly and bites at it. ❑ *It was winter and the sparrows were pecking at whatever they could find.* ❑ *Chickens pecked in the dust.* ❑ *It pecked his leg.* **2** V-T If you **peck** someone **on** the cheek, you give them a quick, light kiss. ❑ *Elizabeth walked up to him and pecked him on the cheek.* ● N-COUNT **Peck** is also a noun. ❑ *He gave me a little peck on the cheek.*

1 타동사/자동사 쪼다, 쪼아 먹다 ❑ 겨울이었고 참새들은 닥치는 대로 쪼아 먹고 있었다. ❑ 닭들이 땅속을 쪼아 대고 있었다. ❑ 그게 그의 다리를 쪼았다. **2** 타동사 가볍게 입을 맞추다 ❑ 엘리자베스는 그에게 다가가 볼에 가볍게 입을 맞추었다. ● 가산명사 가벼운 입맞춤 ❑ 그가 내 볼에 가볍게 입을 맞추었다.

pe|cu|liar /pɪkyulyər/ **1** ADJ If you describe someone or something as **peculiar**, you think that they are strange or unusual, sometimes in an unpleasant way. ❑ *Mr. Kennet has a rather peculiar sense of humor.* ● **pe|cu|liar|ly** ADV ❑ *His face had become peculiarly expressionless.* **2** ADJ If something is **peculiar to** a particular thing, person, or situation, it belongs or relates only to that thing, person, or situation. ❑ *Punks, soldiers, hippies, and Sumo wrestlers all have distinct hair styles, peculiar to their group.* ● **pe|cu|liar|ly** ADV ❑ *But cricket, surely, is so peculiarly English that the continentals will never catch on.*

1 형용사 특이한 ❑ 케넷 씨는 약간 특이한 유머 감각을 가지고 있다. ● 특이하게 부사 ❑ 그의 얼굴이 특이하게 무표정한 모습으로 변했다. **2** 형용사 특유한, 독특한 ❑ 펑크족, 군인, 히피족, 스모 선수 모두 자신들 집단 특유의 독특한 머리 스타일을 한다. ● 특유하게 부사 ❑ 그러나 크리켓은 분명히 너무나도 독특하게 영국적이어서 대륙에서는 절대로 인기를 얻지 못 할 것이다.

pe|cu|li|ar|ity /pɪkyuliæriti/ (**peculiarities**) **1** N-COUNT A **peculiarity** that someone or something has is a strange or unusual characteristic or habit. ❑ *Joe's other peculiarity was that he was constantly munching hard candy.* **2** N-COUNT A **peculiarity** is a characteristic or quality which belongs or relates only to one person or thing. ❑ *...a strange peculiarity of the Soviet system.*

1 가산명사 특이함 ❑ 조의 또 다른 별난 점은 항상 딱딱한 사탕을 아작아작 깨먹는 것이다. **2** 가산명사 특성, 독특함 ❑ 소련 제도의 별난 특성

pe|cu|ni|ary /pɪkyunieri, BRIT pɪkyuːnɪəri/ ADJ **Pecuniary** means concerning or involving money. [FORMAL] ❑ *She denies obtaining a pecuniary advantage by deception.*

형용사 금전의 [격식체] ❑ 그녀는 사기를 통해 금전적 이득을 얻었다는 것을 부인한다.

peda|gogi|cal /pɛdəgɒdʒɪkᵊl/ ADJ **Pedagogical** means concerning the methods and theory of teaching. [FORMAL] [ADJ n] ❑ *With a teacher like Mr. Innes, the pedagogical method used in the classroom was by no means standardized.*

형용사 교육학의 [격식체] ❑ 이네스 씨와 같은 교사의 경우 교실에서 사용하는 교수법은 절대로 표준화된 것이 아니었다.

ped|al /pɛdᵊl/ (**pedals, pedaling, pedaled**) [BRIT, sometimes AM **pedalling, pedalled**] **1** N-COUNT The **pedals** on a bicycle are the two parts that you push with your feet in order to make the bicycle move. **2** V-T/V-I When you **pedal** a bicycle, you push the pedals around with your feet to make it move. ❑ *She climbed on her bike with a feeling of pride and pedaled the five miles home.* **3** N-COUNT A **pedal** in a car or on a machine is a lever that you press with your foot in order to control the car or machine. ❑ *...the brake or accelerator pedals.* →see **bicycle**

[영국영어, 미국영어 가끔 pedalling, pedalled] **1** 가산명사 페달 **2** 타동사/자동사 페달을 밟다 ❑ 그녀는 자부심을 느낀 채 자전거에 올라 앉아 5마일 동안 페달을 저어 집으로 갔다. **3** 가산명사 페달 ❑ 브레이크 혹은 가속 페달

pe|dan|tic /pɪdæntɪk/ ADJ If you think someone is **pedantic**, you mean that they are too concerned with unimportant details or traditional rules, especially in connection with academic subjects. [DISAPPROVAL] ❑ *His lecture was so pedantic and uninteresting.*

형용사 현학적인 [탐탁찮음] ❑ 그의 강의는 너무 현학적이고 지루했다.

ped|dle /pɛdᵊl/ (**peddles, peddling, peddled**) **1** V-T Someone who **peddles** things goes from place to place trying to sell them. [OLD-FASHIONED] ❑ *His attempts to peddle his paintings around London's tiny gallery scene proved unsuccessful.* **2** V-T Someone who **peddles** drugs sells illegal drugs. ❑ *When a drug pusher offered the Los Angeles youngster $100 to peddle drugs, Jack refused.* ● **ped|dling** N-UNCOUNT ❑ *The war against drug peddling is all about cash.* **3** V-T If someone **peddles** an idea or a piece of information, they try very hard to get people to accept it. [DISAPPROVAL] ❑ *They even set up their own news agency to peddle anti-isolationist propaganda.*

1 타동사 행상하다 [구식어] ❑ 그가 자기 그림을 런던의 작은 화랑가에서 팔아 보려던 시도는 소득을 거두지 못했다. **2** 타동사 밀매하다 ❑ 마약 밀매꾼이 로스앤젤레스 젊은이인 잭에게 100달러를 제안하여 마약을 팔아 줄 것을 요청하자 잭은 거절했다. ● 밀매 불가산명사 ❑ 마약 밀매에 대한 전쟁은 모두 돈과 관계된다. **3** 타동사 설득시키다, 강요하다 [탐탁찮음] ❑ 반고립주의 선전 내용을 유포하기 위해 그들은 심지어 자체적인 뉴스 기관을 세웠다.

ped|es|tal /pɛdɪstᵊl/ (**pedestals**) **1** N-COUNT A **pedestal** is the base on which something such as a statue stands. ❑ *...a larger than life sized bronze statue on a*

1 가산명사 받침대 ❑ 화강암 받침대에 올려진 실물보다 더 큰 청동 조상 **2** 가산명사 받침대 위에;

granite **pedestal**. **2** N-COUNT If you put someone **on a pedestal**, you admire them very much and think that they cannot be criticized. If someone is knocked **off** a **pedestal** they are no longer admired. ◻ *Since childhood, I put my own parents on a pedestal. I felt they could do no wrong.*

받침대 아래로 ◻ 어렸을 적부터 나는 우리 부모님을 우러러봤다. 내 생각에 그분들은 항상 옳았다.

Word Link | an, ian ≈ one of, relating to : Christian, pedestrian, vegan

pe|des|trian /pɪdɛstriən/ (**pedestrians**) **1** N-COUNT A **pedestrian** is a person who is walking, especially in a town or city, rather than traveling in a vehicle. ◻ *Ingrid was a walker, even in Los Angeles, where a pedestrian is a rare spectacle.* **2** ADJ If you describe something as **pedestrian**, you mean that it is ordinary and not at all interesting. [DISAPPROVAL] ◻ *His style is so pedestrian that the book becomes a real bore.*

1 가산명사 보행자 ◻ 잉그리드는 보행자를 거의 찾아볼 수 없는 로스앤젤레스에서조차 걸어 다녔다. **2** 형용사 단조로운, 평이한 [탐탁잖음] ◻ 그의 문체는 너무 단조로워서 책이 정말 지루해졌다.

Word Link | ician ≈ person who works at : musician, pediatrician, physician

pe|dia|tri|cian /pidiətrɪʃᵊn/ (**pediatricians**) [BRIT **paediatrician**] N-COUNT A **pediatrician** is a doctor who specializes in treating children.

[영국영어 paediatrician] 가산명사 소아과 의사

pe|di|at|rics /pidiætrɪks/

The spelling **paediatrics** is used in British English. The form **pediatric** is used as a modifier.

철자 paediatrics는 영국영어에서 쓴다. pediatric은 수식어구로 쓴다.

N-UNCOUNT **Pediatrics** is the area of medicine that is concerned with the treatment of children. ◻ *She voiced a desire for a career in pediatrics.*

불가산명사 소아과 ◻ 그녀는 소아과 쪽으로 진료를 정하고 싶다고 얘기했다.

pedi|gree /pɛdɪgri/ (**pedigrees**) **1** N-COUNT If a dog, cat, or other animal has a **pedigree**, its ancestors are known and recorded. An animal is considered to have a good pedigree when all its known ancestors are of the same type. ◻ *60 per cent of dogs and ten per cent of cats have pedigrees.* **2** ADJ A **pedigree** animal is descended from animals which have all been of a particular type, and is therefore considered to be of good quality. ◻ *...a pedigree dog.* **3** N-COUNT Someone's **pedigree** is their background or their ancestors. ◻ *Hammer's business pedigree almost guaranteed him the acquaintance of U.S. presidents.*

1 가산명사 혈통서 ◻ 개의 60퍼센트, 그리고 고양이의 10퍼센트는 혈통서를 가지고 있다. **2** 형용사 순종 ◻ 순종 개 **3** 가산명사 혈통, 배경 ◻ 해머는 사업적인 배경 덕분에 미국 대통령을 만나는 것이 매우 쉬웠다.

pe|do|phile /pidəfaɪl/ (**pedophiles**) [BRIT **paedophile**] N-COUNT A **pedophile** is a person, usually a man, who is sexually attracted to children.

[영국영어 paedophile] 가산명사 소아애자

pe|do|philia /pidəfɪliə/ [BRIT **paedophilia**] N-UNCOUNT **Pedophilia** is sexual activity with children or the condition of being sexually attracted to children. ◻ *...allegations of his pedophilia.* ◻ *He addressed the clinical aspects of pedophilia and abuse.*

[영국영어 paedophilia] 불가산명사 소아애 ◻ 그의 소아애에 대한 혐의 ◻ 그는 소아애와 학대의 병리학적인 측면을 따졌다.

peek /pik/ (**peeks, peeking, peeked**) V-I If you **peek at** something or someone, you take a quick look at them, often secretly. ◻ *On two occasions she had peeked at him through a crack in the wall.* ● N-COUNT **Peek** is also a noun. ◻ *American firms have been paying outrageous fees for a peek at the technical data.*

자동사 엿보다, 훔쳐보다 ◻ 그녀는 벽 사이의 틈으로 그를 엿본 적이 두 번 있다. ● 가산명사 엿봄, 훔쳐봄 ◻ 미국 회사들은 기술 자료를 살짝 엿보기 위해 황당한 금액을 지불해 왔다.

peel /pil/ (**peels, peeling, peeled**) **1** N-UNCOUNT The **peel** of a fruit such as a lemon or an apple is its skin. ◻ *...grated lemon peel.* ● N-COUNT You can also refer to a **peel**. [AM] ◻ *...a banana peel.* **2** V-T When you **peel** fruit or vegetables, you remove their skins. ◻ *She sat down in the kitchen and began peeling potatoes.* **3** V-T/V-I If you **peel off** something that has been sticking to a surface or if it **peels off**, it comes away from the surface. ◻ *One of the kids was peeling plaster off the wall.* ◻ *It took me two days to peel off the labels.* ◻ *Paint was peeling off the walls.* **4** V-I If a surface **is peeling**, the paint on it is coming away. [usu cont] ◻ *Its once-elegant white pillars are peeling.*

1 불가산명사 껍질 ◻ 레몬 껍질을 간 것 ● 가산명사 껍질 [미국영어] ◻ 바나나 껍질 **2** 타동사 껍질을 벗기다 ◻ 그녀는 부엌에 앉아 감자 껍질을 벗기기 시작했다. **3** 타동사/자동사 벗기다; 벗겨지다 ◻ 아이 중 하나가 벽의 회반죽을 벗기고 있었다. ◻ 그 라벨을 벗기는 데 이틀이 걸렸다. ◻ 벽의 페인트칠이 벗겨지고 있었다. **4** 자동사 페인트가 벗겨지다 ◻ 한때는 우아했던 흰색 기둥의 페인트가 벗겨지고 있다.

peep /pip/ (**peeps, peeping, peeped**) **1** V-I If you **peep**, or **peep at** something, you take a quick look at it, often secretly and quietly. ◻ *Children came to peep at him round the doorway.* ● N-SING **Peep** is also a noun. [a n] ◻ *"Fourteen minutes," Chris said, taking a peep at his watch.* **2** V-I If something **peeps** out from behind or under something, a small part of it is visible or becomes visible. ◻ *Purple and yellow flowers peeped up between rocks.*

1 자동사 엿보다, 훔쳐보다 ◻ 아이들은 그를 엿보기 위해 문간으로 왔다. ● 단수명사 엿봄, 훔쳐봄 ◻ '14분'이라고 크리스가 시계를 훔쳐보며 말했다. **2** 자동사 살짝 보이다 ◻ 바위 사이로 보라색과 노란색 꽃들이 살짝 보였다.

peer ♦◇◇ /pɪər/ (**peers, peering, peered**) **1** V-I If you **peer at** something, you look at it very hard, usually because it is difficult to see clearly. ◻ *I had been peering at a computer print-out that made no sense at all.* **2** N-COUNT In Britain, a **peer** is a member of the nobility who has or had the right to vote in the House of Lords. ◻ *Lord Swan was made a life peer in 1981.* **3** N-COUNT Your **peers** are the people who are the same age as you or who have the same status as you. ◻ *His engaging personality made him popular with his peers.*

1 자동사 뚫어지게 보다, 유심히 보다 ◻ 나는 도저히 의미를 알 수 없는 컴퓨터 인쇄물을 뚫어지게 바라보고 있었다. **2** 가산명사 귀족 ◻ 스완 경은 1981년에 일대(一代) 귀족이 되었다. **3** 가산명사 또래, 동료 ◻ 그는 매력적인 성격 때문에 동료들 사이에 인기가 있었다.

peer|age /pɪərɪdʒ/ (**peerages**) **1** N-COUNT If someone has a **peerage**, they have the rank of a peer. ◻ *The Prime Minister offered him a peerage.* **2** N-SING The peers of a particular country are referred to as **the peerage**. ◻ *...members of the peerage.*

1 가산명사 작위 ◻ 수상은 그에게 작위를 주겠다고 제안했다. **2** 단수명사 귀족 계급 ◻ 귀족 계급의 성원들

peg ♦◇◇ /pɛg/ (**pegs, pegging, pegged**) **1** N-COUNT A **peg** is a small device which you use to fasten clothes to a clothes line. [mainly BRIT; AM usually **clothespin**] **2** N-COUNT A **peg** is a small piece of wood or metal that is used for fastening something to something else. ◻ *He builds furniture using wooden pegs instead of nails.* **3** N-COUNT A **peg** is a small hook or knob that is attached to a wall or door and is used for hanging things on. ◻ *His work jacket hung on the peg in the kitchen.* **4** V-T If you **peg** something somewhere or **peg** it **down**, you fix it there with pegs. ◻ *Peg down netting over the top to keep out leaves.* ◻ *...a tent pegged to the ground nearby for the kids.* **5** V-T If a price or amount of something is **pegged at** a particular level, it is fixed at that level. ◻ *Its currency is pegged to the dollar.* ◻ *The Bank wants to peg rates at 9%.*

1 가산명사 빨래집게 [주로 영국영어; 미국영어 대개 clothespin] ◻ 빨래집게 (나무나 금속의) 못, 쐐기 ◻ 그는 못 대신 나무못을 이용하여 가구를 만든다. **3** 가산명사 걸이못 ◻ 그의 작업복이 부엌의 걸이못에 걸려 있었다. **4** 타동사 못 같은 것으로 고정하다 ◻ 나뭇잎이 안 들어가도록 위에다 그물을 쳐서 고정하세요. ◻ 아이들을 위해 가까운 땅에 세워 놓은 텐트 **5** 타동사 고정되다 ◻ 통화는 달러에 고정되어 있다. ◻ 중앙은행은 금리를 9퍼센트로 고정하고 싶어 한다.

pel|let /pɛlɪt/ (**pellets**) N-COUNT A **pellet** is a small ball of paper, mud, lead, or other material. ◻ *He was shot in the head with an air gun pellet.*

가산명사 총알 (같은 것), 탄알 ◻ 그는 공기총탄을 머리에 맞았다.

pelt /pɛlt/ (**pelts, pelting, pelted**) **1** N-COUNT The **pelt** of an animal is its skin, which can be used to make clothing or rugs. ◻ *...a bed covered with beaver pelts.* **2** V-T If you **pelt** someone **with** things, you throw things at them. ◻ *Some of the*

1 가산명사 가죽 ◻ 비버 가죽을 씌운 침대 **2** 타동사 -에게 ...을 던지다 ◻ 젊은 남자 몇 명이 서로에게 눈덩이를 던지기 시작했다. **3** 자동사 마구 퍼붓다

younger men began to pelt one another with snowballs. ■ V-I If the rain **is pelting down**, or if **it is pelting with** rain, it is raining very hard. [INFORMAL] [usu cont] ❑ *The rain now was pelting down.* ❑ *It's pelting with rain.*

[비격식체] ❑ 이제 비가 마구 퍼붓고 있었다. ❑ 비가 마구 퍼붓고 있다.

pel|vic /pɛlvɪk/ ADJ **Pelvic** means near or relating to your pelvis. [ADJ n] ❑ *...an inflammation of the pelvic region.*

형용사 골반의 ❑ 골반 부위의 염증

pel|vis /pɛlvɪs/ (**pelvises**) N-COUNT Your **pelvis** is the wide, curved group of bones at the level of your hips.

가산명사 골반

pen ♦◇◇ /pɛn/ (**pens, penning, penned**) ■ N-COUNT A **pen** is a long thin object which you use to write in ink. **felt-tip pen** →see **felt-tip** ② V-T If someone **pens** a letter, article, or book, they write it. [FORMAL] ❑ *I really intended to pen this letter to you early this morning.* ③ N-COUNT A **pen** is also a small area with a fence around it in which farm animals are kept for a short time. ❑ *...a holding pen for sheep.* ④ V-T If people or animals **are penned** somewhere or **are penned up**, they are forced to remain in a very small area. [usu passive] ❑ *...to drive the cattle back to the house so they could be milked and penned for the night.* ❑ *The goats are penned in and fodder has to be cut and carried each day.*
→see **drawing, office**

■ 가산명사 펜 ② 타동사 쓰다 [격식체] ❑ 나는 정말 이 편지를 오늘 아침 일찍 네게 쓰려고 했었다. ③ 가산명사 우리 ④ 양을 가둬 두는 우리 ④ 타동사 간히다 ❑ 밤새 젖을 짜고 우리에 가둘 수 있도록 소들을 다시 집으로 몰고 가는 것 ❑ 염소들을 우리에 가두고 매일 꼴을 베다 날라야 한다.

Thesaurus	pen의 참조어
N.	cage, enclosure ③
V.	cage, enclose, shut in ④

pe|nal /pin³l/ ADJ **Penal** means relating to the punishment of criminals. ❑ *...director-general of penal affairs at the justice ministry.*

형용사 교정의 ❑ 법무부에서 교정 업무를 담당하는 국장

pe|nal|ize /pinəlaɪz/ (**penalizes, penalizing, penalized**) [BRIT also **penalise**] V-T If a person or group **is penalized** for something, they are made to suffer in some way because of it. [usu passive] ❑ *Some of the players may, on occasion, break the rules and be penalized.*

[영국영어 penalise] 타동사 처벌을 받다 ❑ 일부 선수들이 규칙을 어기고 처벌을 받을 수도 있다.

pen|al|ty ♦◇◇ /pɛn³lti/ (**penalties**) ■ N-COUNT A **penalty** is a punishment that someone is given for doing something which is against a law or rule. ❑ *One of those arrested could face the death penalty.* ② N-COUNT In sports such as soccer, rugby, and hockey, a **penalty** is an opportunity to score a goal, which is given to the attacking team if the defending team breaks a rule near their own goal. ❑ *Referee Michael Reed had no hesitation in awarding a penalty.* ③ N-COUNT The **penalty** that you pay for something you have done is something unpleasant that you experience as a result. ❑ *Why should I pay the penalty for somebody else's mistake?*

■ 가산명사 처벌 ❑ 체포된 자 중 하나는 사형 선고를 받을 수도 있다. ② 가산명사 페널티 ❑ 심판 마이클 리드는 페널티를 부르는 데 어떠한 주저함도 없었다. ③ 가산명사 죄값, 대가 ❑ 다른 사람이 저지른 실수에 대해 내가 왜 대가를 치러야 하지?

pence /pɛns/ →see **penny**

pen|chant /pɛntʃɒnt/ N-SING If someone has a **penchant for** something, they have a special liking for it or a tendency to do it. [FORMAL] ❑ *...a stylish woman with a penchant for dark glasses.*

단수명사 -에 대한 기호, -에 대한 선호 [격식체] ❑ 짙은 색 안경을 선호하는 멋쟁이 여자

pen|cil /pɛns³l/ (**pencils**) N-COUNT A **pencil** is an object that you write or draw with. It consists of a thin piece of wood with a rod of a black or colored substance through the middle. If you write or draw something **in pencil**, you do it using a pencil. [also *in* N] ❑ *I found a pencil and some blank paper in her desk.* →see **drawing, office**

가산명사 연필 ❑ 나는 그녀의 책상에서 연필과 백지 몇 장을 찾았다.

Word Link	pend ≈ hanging : de**pend**, **pend**ant, **pend**ing

pen|dant /pɛndənt/ (**pendants**) N-COUNT A **pendant** is an ornament on a chain that you wear around your neck. →see **jewelry**

가산명사 펜던트

pend|ing /pɛndɪŋ/ ■ ADJ If something such as a legal procedure is **pending**, it is waiting to be dealt with or settled. [FORMAL] ❑ *The cause of death was listed as pending.* ❑ *In 1989, the court had 600 pending cases.* ② PREP If something is done **pending** a future event, it is done until that event happens. [FORMAL] ❑ *Mendoza is here pending his request for political asylum.* ③ ADJ Something that is **pending** is going to happen soon. [FORMAL] ❑ *A growing number of customers have been inquiring about the pending price rises.*

■ 형용사 미정의, 계류 중인 [격식체] ❑ 사인(死因)은 아직 미정이었다. ❑ 1989년에 법원에 계류 중인 사건은 6백 건이었다. ② 전치사 -할 때까지 [격식체] ❑ 멘도자는 정치적 망명 신청에 대한 결정이 날 때까지 이곳에 있다. ③ 형용사 임박한 [격식체] ❑ 점점 많은 손님들이 임박한 가격 인상에 대해 문의를 해 왔다.

pen|du|lum /pɛndʒələm/ (**pendulums**) ■ N-COUNT The **pendulum** of a clock is a rod with a weight at the end which swings from side to side in order to make the clock work. ② N-SING You can use the idea of a **pendulum** and the way it swings regularly as a way of talking about regular changes in a situation or in people's opinions. ❑ *The political pendulum has swung in favor of the liberals.*

■ 가산명사 진자, 추 ② 단수명사 (변화의) 추 ❑ 정치적 추가 자유당에게 유리한 쪽으로 기울었다.

pen|etrate /pɛnɪtreɪt/ (**penetrates, penetrating, penetrated**) ■ V-T If something or someone **penetrates** a physical object or an area, they succeed in getting into it or passing through it. ❑ *X-rays can penetrate many objects.* ● **pen|etra|tion** /pɛnɪtreɪʃ³n/ (**penetrations**) N-UNCOUNT [also N *in* pl] ❑ *The exterior walls are three to three and a half feet thick to prevent penetration by bombs.* ② V-T If someone **penetrates** an organization, a group, or a profession, they succeed in entering it although it is difficult to do so. ❑ *...the continuing failure of women to penetrate the higher levels of engineering.* ③ V-T If someone **penetrates** an enemy group or a rival organization, they succeed in joining it in order to get information or cause trouble. ❑ *The CIA had requested our help to penetrate a drugs ring operating out of Munich.* ● **pen|etra|tion** N-UNCOUNT ❑ *...the successful penetration by the KGB of the French intelligence service.* ④ V-T If a company or country **penetrates** a market or area, they succeed in selling their products there. [BUSINESS] ❑ *There have been around 15 attempts from outside France to penetrate the market.* ● **pen|etra|tion** N-UNCOUNT ❑ *...import penetration across a broad range of heavy industries.*

■ 타동사 꿰뚫다, 통과하다 ❑ 엑스레이는 많은 물질을 통과할 수 있다. ● 관통 불가산명사 ❑ 폭탄의 관통을 막을 수 있도록 외벽은 3에서 3.5피트 두께로 되어 있다. ② 타동사 돌파하다 ❑ 여성들이 계속 공학 분야의 고급 단계로 돌파해 들어가지 못하는 것 ③ 타동사 잠입하다, 침투하다 ❑ 뮌헨 밖에서 활동하고 있는 마약 조직에 잠입하기 위해 시아이에이(CIA)가 우리의 도움을 요청했었다. ● 잠입, 침투 불가산명사 ❑ 케이지비의 성공적인 프랑스 정보국 잠입 ④ 타동사 침투하다 [경제] ❑ 프랑스 외부에서 시장에 침투하기 위한 시도가 약 열다섯 번 있었다. ● 침투 불가산명사 ❑ 다양한 중공업 분야에 걸친 수입 침투

pen|etrat|ing /pɛnɪtreɪtɪŋ/ ■ ADJ A **penetrating** sound is loud and usually high-pitched. ❑ *Mary heard the penetrating bell of an ambulance.* ② ADJ If someone

■ 형용사 날카로운 ❑ 메리는 구급차의 날카로운 사이렌 소리를 들었다. ② 형용사 예리한, 꿰뚫어 보는

gives you a **penetrating** look, it makes you think that they know what you are thinking. ❑ *He gazed at me with a sharp, penetrating look that made my heart pound.*

둔한 ❑ 그는 심장을 두근거리게 하는 날카롭고 예리한 눈초리로 나를 바라봤다.

pen|guin /pɛŋgwɪn/ (penguins) N-COUNT A **penguin** is a type of large black and white sea bird found mainly in the Antarctic. Penguins cannot fly but use their short wings for swimming.

가산명사 펭귄

peni|cil|lin /pɛnɪsɪlɪn/ N-UNCOUNT **Penicillin** is a drug that kills bacteria and is used to treat infections.

불가산명사 페니실린

pen|in|su|la /pənɪnsələ, -nɪnsyə-/ (peninsulas) N-COUNT A **peninsula** is a long narrow piece of land which sticks out from a larger piece of land and is almost completely surrounded by water. ❑ *...the political situation in the Korean peninsula.*

가산명사 반도 ❑ 한반도의 정치적 상황

pe|nis /pinɪs/ (penises) N-COUNT A man's **penis** is the part of his body that he uses when urinating and when having sex.

가산명사 음경

pen|ni|less /pɛnɪlɪs/ ADJ Someone who is **penniless** has hardly any money at all. ❑ *They'd soon be penniless and homeless if she couldn't find suitable work.*

형용사 무일푼의 ❑ 만약 그녀가 적절한 일자리를 찾지 못한다면 그들은 곧 돈도 집도 없는 신세가 될 것이다.

pen|ny ◆◇◇ /pɛni/ (pennies, pence)

The form **pence** is used for the plural of meaning **1**.

pence은 **1** 의미의 복수로 쓰인다.

1 N-COUNT A **penny** is one cent, or a coin worth one cent. [AM, INFORMAL] ❑ *Unleaded gasoline rose more than a penny a gallon.* **2** N-COUNT In Britain, a **penny** is one hundredth of a pound, or a coin worth this amount of money. ❑ *Cider also goes up by a penny a pint while sparkling wine will cost another eight pence a bottle.* **3** N-COUNT A **penny** is a British coin used before 1971 that was worth one twelfth of a shilling. **4** N-SING If you say, for example, that you do not have **a penny**, or that something does not cost **a penny**, you are emphasizing that you do not have any money at all, or that something did not cost you any money at all. [EMPHASIS] ❑ *From the day you arrive at my house, you need not spend a single penny.*

1 가산명사 1센트 [미국영어, 비격식체] ❑ 무연 휘발유 가격이 갤런당 1센트 이상 올랐다. **2** 가산명사 1페니 ❑ 사과주 가격도 파인트 당 1페니 이상 오르고 탄산 포도주는 병당 8페니가 더 오른다. **3** 가산명사 1페니(1/12 실링)짜리 동전 **4** 단수명사 한 푼 [강조] ❑ 우리 집에 도착하는 그 날부터 너는 단 한 푼도 쓸 필요가 없다.

pen|ny shares N-PLURAL **Penny shares** are shares that are offered for sale at a very low price. [BUSINESS]

복수명사 저가주 [경제]

pen|sion ◆◇◇ /pɛnʃ°n/ (pensions, pensioning, pensioned) N-COUNT Someone who has a **pension** receives a regular sum of money from the state or from a former employer because they have retired or because they are widowed or disabled. ❑ *...struggling by on a pension.*

가산명사 연금 ❑ 연금으로 연명하는

▶**pension off** PHRASAL VERB If someone **is pensioned off**, they are made to retire from work and are given a pension. ❑ *Many successful women do not want to be pensioned off at 60.*

구동사 퇴직하여 연금을 받다 ❑ 많은 성공한 여성들은 예순 살에 퇴직해서 연금이나 받고 싶어 하지 않는다.

pen|sion|able /pɛnʃənəb°l/ ADJ **Pensionable** means relating to someone's right to receive a pension. [ADJ n] ❑ *...civil servants who were nearing pensionable age.*

형용사 연금을 받을 수 있는 ❑ 연금 수령 연령이 다 되어 가는 공무원들

pen|sion|er /pɛnʃənər/ (pensioners) N-COUNT A **pensioner** is someone who receives a pension, especially a pension paid by the state to retired people. ❑ *Five years from now there will be more pensioners than children.*

가산명사 연금 수령자 ❑ 오늘로부터 5년 뒤에는 아이들 수보다 연금 수령자 수가 더 많을 것이다.

pen|sion plan (pension plans) N-COUNT A **pension plan** is an arrangement to receive a pension from an organization such as an insurance company or a former employer in return for making regular payments to them over a number of years. [BUSINESS] ❑ *I would have been much wiser to start my own pension plan when I was younger.*

가산명사 연금 제도 [경제] ❑ 더 젊었을 때 연금에 가입하는 것이 훨씬 현명한 일이었는데.

pen|sion scheme (pension schemes) N-COUNT A **pension scheme** is the same as a **pension plan**. [mainly BRIT, BUSINESS] ❑ *His company has the best pension scheme in the industry.*

가산명사 연금 제도 [주로 영국영어, 경제] ❑ 그의 회사는 업계에서 가장 좋은 연금 제도를 두고 있다.

Pen|ta|gon N-PROPER The **Pentagon** is the main building of the U.S. Defense Department, in Washington D.C. The U.S. Defense Department is often referred to as **the Pentagon**. ❑ *...a news conference at the Pentagon.*

고유명사 미국방성 ❑ 미국방성에서 가진 기자 회견

pent|house /pɛnthaʊs/ (penthouses) N-COUNT A **penthouse** or a **penthouse** apartment or suite is a luxurious apartment or set of rooms at the top of a tall building. ❑ *...her swish Manhattan penthouse.*

가산명사 펜트하우스 ❑ 그녀의 멋진 맨해튼 펜트하우스

pent-up /pɛnt ʌp/ ADJ **Pent-up** emotions, energies, or forces have been held back and not expressed, used, or released. ❑ *He still had a lot of pent-up anger to release.*

형용사 억눌린 ❑ 그에겐 아직도 표출해야 할 억눌린 분노가 많이 있었다.

pe|nul|ti|mate /pɪnʌltɪmɪt/ ADJ The **penultimate** thing in a series of things is the last but one. [FORMAL] [det ADJ] ❑ *...on the penultimate day of the Asian Games.*

형용사 끝에서 두 번째의 [격식체] ❑ 아시안 게임이 끝나기 전날에

peo|ple ◆◆◆ /pip°l/ (peoples, peopling, peopled) **1** N-PLURAL **People** are men, women, and children. **People** is normally used as the plural of **person**, instead of "persons." ❑ *Millions of people have lost their homes.* ❑ *...the people of Angola.* **2** N-PLURAL **The people** is sometimes used to refer to ordinary men and women, in contrast to the government or the upper classes. ❑ *...the will of the people.* **3** N-COUNT-COLL A **people** is all the men, women, and children of a particular country or race. ❑ *...the native peoples of Central and South America.* **4** V-T If a place or country **is peopled by** a particular group of people, that group of people live there. [usu passive] ❑ *It was peopled by a fiercely independent race of peace-loving Buddhists.*

1 복수명사 사람들 ❑ 수백만 명이 집을 잃었다. ❑ 앙골라 사람들 **2** 복수명사 일반 국민 ❑ 일반 국민의 뜻 **3** 가산명사-집합 국민, 주민 ❑ 중앙 및 남아메리카의 원주민들 **4** 타동사 ~한 사람들이 거주하다 ❑ 그곳의 주민들은 자립심이 굉장히 강한 평화주의자인 불교도들이다.

pep|per ◆◇◇ /pɛpər/ (peppers, peppering, peppered) **1** N-UNCOUNT **Pepper** is a hot-tasting spice which is used to flavor food. ❑ *Season with salt and pepper.* **2** N-COUNT A **pepper**, or in American English a **bell pepper**, is a hollow green, red, or yellow vegetable with seeds inside it. ❑ *...2 red or green peppers, sliced.* **3** V-T If something **is peppered with** small objects, a lot of those objects hit it. [usu passive] ❑ *He was wounded in both legs and severely peppered with shrapnel.* →see **spice**

1 불가산명사 후추 ❑ 소금과 후추로 간을 맞추세요. **2** 가산명사 피망 ❑ 채 썬 빨간색이나 파란색 피망 두 개 **3** 타동사 ~에 여러 군데를 맞다 ❑ 그는 두 다리 모두를 다치고 폭탄 파편이 온몸에 박혔다.

pep|per|mint /pɛpərmɪnt/ (peppermints) **1** N-UNCOUNT **Peppermint** is a strong, sharp flavoring that is obtained from the peppermint plant or that is made artificially. **2** N-COUNT A **peppermint** is a peppermint-flavored piece of candy.

1 불가산명사 박하 **2** 가산명사 박하사탕

pep talk /pɛp tɔk/ (**pep talks**) also pep-talk N-COUNT A **pep talk** is a speech which is intended to encourage someone to make more effort or feel more confident. [INFORMAL] ❑ *Powell and Cheney spent the day giving pep talks to the troops.*

가산명사 격려 연설 [비격식체] ❑ 파월과 체이니는 병사들에게 격려 연설을 하며 하루를 보냈다.

per ♦♦◇ /pər, STRONG pɜr/ PREP You use **per** to express rates and ratios. For example, if something costs $50 **per** year, you must pay $50 each year for it. If a vehicle is traveling at 40 miles **per** hour, it travels 40 miles each hour. [amount PREP n] ❑ *...$6 per week for lunch.* **per head** →see **head**

전치사 -당, -마다 ❑ 주당 6달러의 점심 식대

per an|num /pər ænəm/ ADV A particular amount **per annum** means that amount each year. [amount ADV] ❑ *...a fee of $35 per annum.*

부사 연간, 해마다 ❑ 연간 35달러의 요금

per cap|i|ta /pər kæpɪtə/ ADJ The **per capita** amount of something is the total amount of it in a country or area divided by the number of people in that country or area. [ADJ n] ❑ *They have the world's largest per capita income.* ● ADV **Per capita** is also an adverb. [n ADV] ❑ *Ethiopia has almost the lowest oil consumption per capita in the world.*

형용사 1인당의 ❑ 그들은 1인당 수입이 세계에서 가장 높다. ● 부사 1인당 ❑ 에티오피아는 1인당 석유 소비량이 거의 세계 최저 수준이다.

Word Link   per ≈ through, thoroughly : perceive, perfect, permit
---

per|ceive /pərsiv/ (**perceives, perceiving, perceived**) **1** V-T If you **perceive** something, you see, notice, or realize it, especially when it is not obvious. ❑ *A key task is to get pupils to perceive for themselves the relationship between success and effort.* **2** V-T If you **perceive** someone or something **as** doing or being a particular thing, it is your opinion that they do this thing or that they are that thing. ❑ *Stress is widely perceived as contributing to coronary heart disease.*

1 타동사 지각하다, 감지하다 ❑ 핵심적인 임무는 학생들로 하여금 성공과 노력의 관계를 스스로 알아차리게 하는 것이다. **2** 타동사 (-로 ...으로) 인식하다 ❑ 스트레스는 관상동맥질환을 유발하는 요인으로 널리 인식된다.

per|cent ♦♦♦ /pərsɛnt/ (**percent**) N-COUNT You use **percent** to talk about amounts. For example, if an amount is 10 percent (10%) of a larger amount, it is equal to 10 hundredths of the larger amount. ❑ *Sixteen percent of children live in poverty in this country.* ❑ *Sales of new homes fell by 1.4 percent in August.* ● ADJ **Percent** is also an adjective. [ADJ n] ❑ *...a 15 percent increase in border patrols.* ● ADV **Percent** is also an adverb. [BRIT usually, AM sometimes **per cent**] [ADV with v] ❑ *He predicted sales will fall 2 percent to 6 percent in the second quarter.*

가산명사 퍼센트 ❑ 이 나라에서는 아이들 중 16퍼센트가 가난하게 산다. ● 신규 주택 매매가 8월에 1.4퍼센트 떨어졌다. ● 형용사 -퍼센트의 ❑ 국경 순찰 병력 15퍼센트 증가 ● 부사 -퍼센트로 [대개 영국영어, 미국영어 가끔 per cent] ❑ 그는 2/4분기에 매상 고가 2퍼센트 내지 6퍼센트 떨어질 것으로 예측했다.

per|cent|age ♦◇◇ /pərsɛntɪdʒ/ (**percentages**) N-COUNT A **percentage** is a fraction of an amount expressed as a particular number of hundredths of that amount. ❑ *Only a few vegetable-origin foods have such a high percentage of protein.*

가산명사 백분율; 비율 ❑ 일부의 야채 식품만이 그만큼 높은 비율의 단백질을 함유하고 있다.

per|cep|tion /pərsɛpʃⁿn/ (**perceptions**) **1** N-COUNT Your **perception of** something is the way that you think about it or the impression you have of it. ❑ *He is interested in how our perceptions of death affect the way we live.* **2** N-UNCOUNT Someone who has **perception** realizes or notices things that are not obvious. ❑ *It did not require a great deal of perception to realize the interview was over.* **3** N-COUNT **Perception** is the recognition of things using your senses, especially the sense of sight. ❑ *...the revolution in human perception brought about by the invention of photography in the late 1830s.*

1 가산명사 인식 ❑ 그는 죽음에 대한 인식이 살아가는 방식에 어떻게 영향을 미치는가에 흥미를 가지고 있다. **2** 불가산명사 통찰력 ❑ 인터뷰가 끝났다는 것을 깨닫는데 대단한 통찰력이 필요한 것은 아니었다. **3** 가산명사 지각 ❑ 1830년대 후반 사진의 발명으로 말미암아 일어난 인간 지각의 혁명

per|cep|tive /pərsɛptɪv/ ADJ If you describe a person or their remarks or thoughts as **perceptive**, you think that they are good at noticing or realizing things, especially things that are not obvious. [APPROVAL] ❑ *He was one of the most perceptive U.S. political commentators.*

형용사 통찰력이 있는 [마음에 듦] ❑ 그는 가장 통찰력 있는 미국 정치 논평가 중 한 명이었다.

perch /pɜrtʃ/ (**perches, perching, perched**)

The form **perch** is used for both the singular and plural in meaning **6**.

perch는 **6** 의미의 단수 및 복수로 쓰인다.

1 V-T/V-I If you **perch on** something, you sit down lightly on the very edge or tip of it. ❑ *He lit a cigarette and perched on the corner of the desk.* **2** V-I To **perch** somewhere means to be on the top or edge of something. ❑ *...the vast slums that perch precariously on top of the hills around which the city was built.* **3** V-T If you **perch** something **on** something else, you put or balance it on the top or edge of that thing. ❑ *The use of steel and concrete has allowed the builders to perch a light concrete dome on eight slender columns.* **4** V-I When a bird **perches on** something such as a branch or a wall, it lands on it and stands there. ❑ *A blackbird flew down and perched on the parapet outside his window.* **5** N-COUNT A **perch** is a short rod for a bird to stand on. ❑ *A small, yellow bird in a cage sat on its perch outside the house.* **6** N-COUNT A **perch** is an edible fish. There are several kinds of perch.

1 타동사/자동사 걸터앉다 ❑ 그는 담배에 불을 붙이고 책상 모서리에 걸터앉았다. **2** 자동사 (꼭대기나 모서리에) 자리 잡다 ❑ 주위에 도시가 세워진 언덕 꼭대기에 불안하게 자리 잡은 광대한 빈민굴 **3** 타동사 (꼭대기나 모서리에) 얹어 놓다 ❑ 철강과 콘크리트 사용으로 건설업자들은 어딜 개의 가느다란 기둥 위에 둥근 콘크리트 지붕을 얹을 수 있게 되었다. **4** 자동사 (새가 횃대 등에) 앉다 ❑ 검정 새 한 마리가 날아와서 그의 창문 밖 난간에 앉았다. **5** 가산명사 횃대 ❑ 새장 속 작은 노란 새 한 마리가 집 밖 횃대에 앉아 있었다. **6** 가산명사 농어류의 식용 담수어

per|cus|sion /pərkʌʃⁿn/ N-UNCOUNT **Percussion** instruments are musical instruments that you hit, such as drums. ❑ *...a large orchestra, with a vast percussion section.* →see **drum, orchestra**

불가산명사 타악기 ❑ 방대한 타악기 부를 거느린 대형 관현악단

per diem /pɜr diəm, pər/ N-SING A **per diem** is an amount of money that someone is given to cover their daily expenses while they are working. [mainly AM] ❑ *He received a per diem allowance to cover his travel expenses.*

단수명사 일비(日費) [주로 미국영어] ❑ 그는 여비를 충당할 일비를 받았다.

Word Link   enn ≈ year : centennial, millennium, perennial
---

per|en|nial /pərɛniəl/ (**perennials**) **1** ADJ You use **perennial** to describe situations or states that keep occurring or which seem to exist all the time; used especially to describe problems or difficulties. ❑ *...the perennial urban problems of drugs and homelessness.* **2** ADJ A **perennial** plant lives for several years and has flowers each year. ❑ *...a perennial herb with greenish-yellow flowers.* ● N-COUNT **Perennial** is also a noun. ❑ *...a low-growing perennial.* →see **plant**

1 형용사 끊이지 않는, 계속되는 ❑ 마약과 노숙자 등의 끊이지 않는 도시 문제 **2** 형용사 다년생의 ❑ 녹색이 감도는 노란 꽃이 피는 다년생 허브 ● 가산명사 다년생 식물 ❑ 키 작은 다년생 식물

per|fect ♦♦◇ (**perfects, perfecting, perfected**)

The adjective is pronounced /pɜrfɪkt/. The verb is pronounced /pərfɛkt/.

형용사는 /pɜrfɪkt/로 발음되고, 동사는 /pərfɛkt/ 로 발음된다.

a b c d e f g h i j k l m n o p q r s t u v w x y z

A

1 ADJ Something that is **perfect** is as good as it could possibly be. ❑ *He spoke perfect English.* ❑ *Nobody is perfect.* **2** ADJ If you say that something is **perfect for** a particular person, thing, or activity, you are emphasizing that it is very suitable for them or for that activity. [EMPHASIS] ❑ *Carpet tiles are perfect for kitchens because they're easy to take up and wash.* **3** ADJ If an object or surface is **perfect**, it does not have any marks on it, or does not have any lumps, hollows, or cracks in it. ❑ *Use only clean, Grade A, perfect eggs.* **4** ADJ You can use **perfect** to give emphasis to the noun following it. [EMPHASIS] [ADJ n] ❑ *She was a perfect fool.* ❑ *Some people are always coming up to perfect strangers and asking them what they do.* **5** V-T If you **perfect** something, you improve it so that it becomes as good as it can possibly be. ❑ *We perfected a hand-signal system so that he could keep me informed of hazards.* ❑ *I removed the fibroid tumors, using the techniques that I have perfected.*

B

C

D

E

Thesaurus	*perfect*의 참조어
ADJ.	flawless, ideal; *(ant.)* defective, faulty **1**-**3**
	complete **3**

F

per|fec|tion /pərfɛkʃn/ **1** N-UNCOUNT **Perfection** is the quality of being as good as it is possible for something of a particular kind to be. ❑ *His quest for perfection is relentless.* **2** N-UNCOUNT **The perfection of** something such as a skill, system, or product involves making it as good as it could possibly be. ❑ *Madame Clicquot is credited with the perfection of this technique.*

G

per|fec|tion|ist /pərfɛkʃənɪst/ (**perfectionists**) N-COUNT Someone who is a **perfectionist** refuses to do or accept anything that is not as good as it could possibly be. ❑ *He was such a perfectionist that he published only those results that satisfied him completely.*

H

I

per|fect|ly ♦♢♢ /pɜrfɪktli/ **1** ADV You can use **perfectly** to emphasize an adjective or adverb, especially when you think the person you are talking to might doubt what you are saying. [EMPHASIS] [ADV adj/adv] ❑ *There's no reason why you can't have a perfectly normal child.* ❑ *You know perfectly well what happened.* **2** ADV If something is done **perfectly**, it is done so well that it could not possibly be done better. [ADV with v] ❑ *This ambitious adaptation perfectly captures the spirit of Kurt Vonnegut's acclaimed novel.*

J

K

per|form ♦♦♢ /pərfɔrm/ (**performs, performing, performed**) **1** V-T When you **perform** a task or action, especially a complicated one, you do it. ❑ *We're looking for people of all ages who have performed outstanding acts of bravery, kindness or courage.* ❑ *His council had had to perform miracles on a tiny budget.* **2** V-T If something **performs** a particular function, it has that function. ❑ *A complex engine has many separate components, each performing a different function.* **3** V-T/V-I If you **perform** a play, a piece of music, or a dance, you do it in front of an audience. ❑ *Gardiner has pursued relentlessly high standards in performing classical music.* ❑ *This play was first performed in 411 BC.* **4** V-I If someone or something **performs well**, they work well or achieve a good result. If they **perform badly**, they work badly or achieve a poor result. ❑ *He had not performed well in his exams.* ❑ *England performed so well against France at Wembley.*

L

M

N

O

Word Partnership	*perform*의 연어
N.	perform **miracles**, perform **tasks** **1**
ADJ.	**able to** perform **1** **2** **3**
V.	**continue to** perform **1** **3**
ADV.	perform **well** **1** **3** **4**

P

Word Link	*ance* ≈ *quality, state : bal*ance, *perform*ance, *resist*ance

Q

per|for|mance ♦♦♢ /pərfɔrməns/ (**performances**) **1** N-COUNT A **performance** involves entertaining an audience by doing something such as singing, dancing, or acting. ❑ *Inside the theater, they were giving a performance of Bizet's Carmen.* ❑ *...her performance as the betrayed Medea.* **2** N-VAR Someone's or something's **performance** is how successful they are or how well they do something. ❑ *That study looked at the performance of 18 surgeons.* ❑ *The poor performance has been blamed on the recession and cheaper sports car imports.* **3** N-SING **The performance of** a task is the fact or action of doing it. ❑ *He devoted in excess of seventy hours a week to the performance of his duties.* →see **concert, theater**

R

S

T

U

Word Partnership	*performance*의 연어
ADJ.	**live** performance **1**
	good performance, **poor** performance, **strong** performance **1**-**3**
	academic performance, **economic** performance,
	sexual performance **2**
N.	performance **appraisal**, **company** performance,
	job performance **2**

V

W

X

performance-related pay N-UNCOUNT **Performance-related pay** is a rate of pay which is based on how well someone does their job. [BUSINESS] ❑ *Teachers will fight Ministers' plans to introduce performance-related pay in schools.*

Y

per|form|er /pərfɔrmər/ (**performers**) **1** N-COUNT A **performer** is a person who acts, sings, or does other entertainment in front of audiences. ❑ *A performer in*

Z

---

1 형용사 완벽한 ❑ 그는 완벽한 영어를 구사하였다. ❑ 그 누구도 완벽하지 않다. **2** 형용사 안성맞춤인, 이상적인 [강조] ❑ 카펫 타일은 걸어서 세탁하기 쉽기 때문에 주방에 이상적입니다. **3** 형용사 흠이 전혀 없는 ❑ 깨끗한 에이(A) 등급의 흠이 전혀 없는 계란만 사용하세요. **4** 형용사 완전한; 지독한 [강조] ❑ 그녀는 지독한 바보였다. ❑ 어떤 사람들은 항상 전혀 모르는 사람에게 다가가서 무슨 일을 하냐고 물어본다. **5** 타동사 완전하게 개선하다 ❑ 그가 나에게 위험 요소를 계속 알려 줄 수 있도록 우리는 수신호 체계를 완전하게 개선했다. ❑ 나는 내가 완전하게 개량한 기술을 사용하여 그 유섬유종을 제거했다.

1 불가산명사 완전, 완벽 ❑ 그의 완벽 추구는 끈질기다. **2** 불가산명사 완성 ❑ 끌리꿔 여사는 이 기법을 완성한 사람으로 인정받고 있다.

가산명사 완벽주의자 ❑ 그는 스스로가 완전히 만족하는 결과만을 발표할 정도로 철저한 완벽주의자였다.

1 부사 완전히, 아주 [강조] ❑ 당신이 완전히 정상적인 아이를 갖지 못할 이유가 없어요. ❑ 무슨 일이 일어났는지 당신은 아주 잘 알고 있습니다. **2** 부사 더할 나위 없이 ❑ 이 야심적인 각색은 많은 찬사를 받은 커트 보니거트 소설의 정신을 더할 나위 없이 잘 포착하고 있다.

1 타동사 행하다, 수행하다 ❑ 우리는 모든 연령 대에 걸쳐 뛰어나게 용감하거나 친절한 일을 수행해 온 분들을 찾고 있습니다. ❑ 그의 지방 의회는 아주 적은 예산을 가지고 기적을 일으켜야만 했었다. **2** 타동사 수행하다 ❑ 복합 기관은 여러 개의 독립적인 부분으로 되어 있는데, 각 부분이 각기 다른 기능을 수행한다. **3** 타동사/자동사 공연하다; 연주하다 ❑ 가디너는 고전음악을 연주하는 데 있어서 끊임없이 높은 수준을 추구해 왔다. ❑ 이 연극은 기원전 411년에 초연되었다. **4** 자동사 잘하다; 잘 못하다 ❑ 그는 시험을 잘 못 봤었다. ❑ 잉글랜드는 웸블리 구장에서 프랑스를 상대로 아주 훌륭한 경기를 펼쳤다.

1 가산명사 공연; 연기 ❑ 극장 안에서는 비제의 카르멘 공연을 하고 있었다. ❑ 배반당한 메데아로 분한 그녀의 연기 **2** 가산명사 또는 불가산명사 성적, 적은 ❑ 그 조사에서는 외과 의사 18명의 성과를 살펴보았다. ❑ 성과가 빈약한 것은 경기 후퇴와 저렴한 스포츠카 수입 탓으로 돌려졌다. **3** 단수명사 수행, 이행 ❑ 그는 자신의 임무 수행에 주당 70시간 이상을 쏟아 부었다.

불가산명사 성과급 [경제] ❑ 교사들은 학교에 성과급을 도입하려는 각료들의 계획에 맞서 싸울 것이다.

1 가산명사 연기자; 연주자 ❑ 야회복을 입은 한 연주자가 바이올린으로 고전 음악 발췌곡들을

evening dress plays classical selections on the violin. ◨ N-COUNT You can use **performer** when describing someone or something in a way that indicates how well they do a particular thing. ❑ *Until 1987, Canada's industry had been the star performer.*

연주한다. ◨ 가산명사 (어떤 일을 잘) 하는 사람 ❑ 1987년까지는, 캐나다의 산업이 뛰어난 활약을 보여 왔었다.

per|fume /pɜːrfjuːm, pərfjuːm/ (**perfumes, perfuming, perfumed**) ◧ N-MASS **Perfume** is a pleasant-smelling liquid which women put on their skin to make themselves smell nice. ❑ *The hall smelled of her mother's perfume.* ❑ *...a bottle of perfume.* ◨ N-MASS **Perfume** is the ingredient that is added to some products to make them smell nice. ❑ *...a delicate white soap without perfume.* ◪ V-T If something is used to **perfume** a product, it is added to the product to make it smell nice. ❑ *The oil is used to flavor and perfume soaps, foam baths, and scents.*

◧ 물질명사 향수 ❑ 홀에서는 그녀 어머니의 향수 냄새가 났다. ❑ 향수 한 병 ◨ 물질명사 향료 ❑ 향료가 들어 있지 않은 은은한 흰색 비누 ◪ 타동사 -에 향을 내다 ❑ 그 기름은 비누와 거품 입욕제, 향수 등에 향을 내는 데 쓰인다.

per|haps ◆◆◆ /pərhæps, præps/ ◧ ADV You use **perhaps** to express uncertainty, for example, when you do not know that something is definitely true, or when you are mentioning something that may possibly happen in the future in the way you describe. [VAGUENESS] [ADV with cl/group] ❑ *Millson regarded her thoughtfully. Perhaps she was right.* ❑ *In the end they lose millions, perhaps billions.* ❑ *Perhaps, in time, the message will get through.* ◨ ADV You use **perhaps** in opinions and remarks to make them appear less definite or more polite. [VAGUENESS] [ADV with cl/group] ❑ *Perhaps the most important lesson to be learned is that you simply cannot please everyone.* ❑ *His very last paintings are perhaps the most puzzling.* ◪ ADV You use **perhaps** when you are making suggestions or giving advice. **Perhaps** is also used in formal English to introduce requests. [POLITENESS] [ADV with cl] ❑ *Perhaps I may be permitted a few suggestions.* ❑ *Well, perhaps you'll come and see us at our place?*

◧ 부사 어쩌면 [짐작투] ❑ 밀슨은 그녀를 주의 깊게 응시했다. 어쩌면 그녀가 옳을지도 몰랐다. ❑ 결국 그들은 수백만, 어쩌면 수십억의 손해를 봤다. ◨ 부사 ❑ 어쩌면, 전깃이 때맞춰 도착할지도 모른다. ◨ 부사 아마 [짐작투] ❑ 아마도 깨달아야 할 가장 중요한 교훈은 당신이 그저 모든 사람을 기쁘게 할 수는 없다는 사실일 것입니다. ❑ 그의 가장 최근 그림들이 아마도 가장 어려운 작품들일 것이다. ◪ 부사 제안이나 조언, 요청 등에 쓰이는 표현 [공손체] ❑ 몇 가지 제안을 해도 괜찮을까요. ❑ 글쎄, 네가 우리가 있는 곳으로 와서 보는 게 어떨까?

per|il /pɛrɪl/ (**perils**) N-VAR **Perils** are great dangers. [FORMAL] ❑ *...the perils of the sea.* ❑ *In spite of great peril, I have survived.*

가산명사 또는 불가산명사 위험 [격식체] ❑ 바다의 위험 ❑ 엄청난 위험에도 불구하고, 나는 목숨을 부지해 왔다.

per|il|ous /pɛrɪləs/ ADJ Something that is **perilous** is very dangerous. [LITERARY] ❑ *...a perilous journey across the war-zone.* ❑ *The road grew even steeper and more perilous.* ● **per|il|ous|ly** ADV ❑ *The track snaked perilously upwards.*

형용사 매우 위험한 [문예체] ❑ 교전 지대를 가로지르는 위험한 여정 ❑ 길이 더욱 더 가파르고 위험해져 갔다. ● 위험하게 부사 ❑ 그 길은 위쪽으로 꾸불꾸불 위험하게 나 있다.

Word Link	meter ≈ measuring : kilometer, meter, perimeter

Word Link	peri ≈ around : perimeter, periodic, periphery

pe|rim|eter /pərɪmɪtər/ (**perimeters**) N-COUNT The **perimeter** of an area of land is the whole of its outer edge or boundary. ❑ *...the perimeter of the airport.* →see **area**

가산명사 둘레, 주위 ❑ 공항 주위

pe|ri|od ◆◆◇ /pɪəriəd/ (**periods**) ◧ N-COUNT A **period** is a length of time. [usu with supp] ❑ *This crisis might last for a long period of time.* ❑ *...a period of a few months.* ◨ N-COUNT A **period** in the life of a person, organization, or society is a length of time which is remembered for a particular situation or activity. ❑ *...a period of economic good health and expansion.* ❑ *He went through a period of wanting to be accepted.* ◪ N-COUNT A particular length of time in history is sometimes called a **period.** For example, you can talk about **the Victorian period** or **the Elizabethan period** in Britain. ❑ *...the Roman period.* ❑ *No reference to their existence appears in any literature of the period.* ◫ ADJ **Period** costumes, furniture, and instruments were made at an earlier time in history, or look as if they were made then. [ADJ n] ❑ *...dressed in full period costume.* ◬ N-COUNT Exercise, training, or study **periods** are lengths of time that are set aside for exercise, training, or study. ❑ *They accompanied him during his exercise periods.* ◧ N-COUNT When a woman has a **period,** she bleeds from her womb. This usually happens once a month, unless she is pregnant. ❑ *Can you get pregnant if you have sex during your period?* ◨ N-COUNT A **period** is the punctuation mark (.) which you use at the end of a sentence when it is not a question or an exclamation. [AM; BRIT **full stop**]

◧ 가산명사 기간 ❑ 이 위기가 오랜 기간 동안 지속될 수도 있다. ❑ 몇 달 동안의 기간 ◨ 가산명사 (특정한) 시기 ❑ 경제적 번영과 팽창의 시기 ❑ 그는 받아들여지기를 바라는 시기를 겪었다. ◪ 가산명사 시대 ❑ 로마 시대 ❑ 그 시대의 어떤 문헌에도 그들의 존재에 대한 언급이 나타나 있지 않다. ◫ 형용사 (역사상 특정한) 시대의 ❑ 역사상 한 시대의 의상을 완전히 갖춰 입고 ◬ 가산명사 (특정한 일을 위한) 시간 ❑ 그들은 그가 운동을 하는 시간 동안에 그와 함께 했다. ◧ 가산명사 월경, 생리 ❑ 생리 기간 동안 성관계를 갖고도 임신할 수 있나요? ◨ 가산명사 마침표 [미국영어; 영국영어 full stop]

Thesaurus	period의 참조어
N.	age, epoch, era, term, time ◧-◪

pe|ri|od|ic /pɪəriɒdɪk/ ADJ **Periodic** events or situations happen occasionally, at fairly regular intervals. ❑ *Periodic checks are taken to ensure that high standards are maintained.*

형용사 주기적인 ❑ 높은 수준 유지를 보장하기 위해 주기적인 점검이 이루어진다.

pe|ri|od|ical /pɪəriɒdɪkəl/ (**periodicals**) ◧ N-COUNT **Periodicals** are magazines, especially serious or academic ones, that are published at regular intervals. ❑ *The walls would be lined with books and periodicals.* ◨ ADJ **Periodical** events or situations happen occasionally, at fairly regular intervals. ❑ *She made periodical visits to her dentist.* ● **pe|ri|od|ical|ly** /pɪəriɒdɪkli/ ADV [ADV with v] ❑ *Meetings are held periodically to monitor progress on the case.* →see **library**

◧ 가산명사 정기 간행물, 잡지 ❑ 모든 벽에는 책과 정기 간행물이 나란히 세워져 있곤 했다. ◨ 형용사 주기적인 ❑ 그녀는 주기적으로 치과 주치의를 찾아갔다. ● 주기적으로 부사 ❑ 사건의 추이를 점검하기 위해 회의가 주기적으로 열린다.

pe|riph|er|al /pərɪfərəl/ (**peripherals**) ◧ ADJ A **peripheral** activity or issue is one which is not very important compared with other activities or issues. ❑ *Companies are increasingly keen to contract out peripheral activities like training.* ❑ *...peripheral and boring information.* ◨ ADJ **Peripheral** areas of land are ones which are on the edge of a larger area. ❑ *...urban development in the outer peripheral areas of large towns.* ◪ N-COUNT **Peripherals** are devices that can be attached to computers. [COMPUTING] ❑ *...peripherals to expand the use of our computers.*

◧ 형용사 주변적인, 그다지 중요하지 않은 ❑ 회사들은 점점 훈련 같은 주변적인 활동들을 하청으로 내주는 데 열을 쏟고 있다. ❑ 그다지 중요하지 않고 따분한 소식 ◨ 형용사 주변의 ❑ 대도시 주변의 내도시 외곽 지역에서의 도시 개발 ◪ 가산명사 (컴퓨터) 주변 장치 [컴퓨터] ❑ 컴퓨터의 쓰임새를 확장하는 주변 장치들

pe|riph|ery /pərɪfəri/ (**peripheries**) N-COUNT If something is on the **periphery** of an area, place, or thing, it is on the edge of it. [FORMAL] ❑ *Geographically, the UK is on the periphery of Europe, while Paris is at the heart of the continent.*

가산명사 주변, 언저리 [격식체] ❑ 지리적으로, 파리가 유럽 대륙의 한가운데 있는 데 반해, 영국은 대륙 언저리에 있다.

per|ish /pɛrɪʃ/ (**perishes, perishing, perished**) **1** V-I If people or animals **perish**, they die as a result of very harsh conditions or as the result of an accident. [WRITTEN] ❏ *Most of the butterflies perish in the first frosts of autumn.* **2** V-I If a substance or material **perishes**, it starts to fall to pieces and becomes useless. [mainly BRIT] ❏ *Obviously the plaster's just perished and all fallen off.*

1 자동사 죽다, 비명횡사하다 [문어체] ❏ 대부분의 나비들은 가을의 첫 서리에 죽는다. **2** 자동사 못 쓰게 되다 [주로 영국영어] ❏ 분명히 알 수 있듯이 그 회반죽은 최근에 못쓰게 되어 모두 떨어져 나왔다.

per|jury /pɜrdʒəri/ N-UNCOUNT If someone who is giving evidence in a court of law commits **perjury**, they lie. [LEGAL] ❏ *This witness has committed perjury and no reliance can be placed on her evidence.*

불가산명사 위증 [법률] ❏ 이 증인은 위증을 해 왔기에 그녀의 증언을 전혀 신뢰할 수 없습니다.

perk /pɜrk/ (**perks, perking, perked**) N-COUNT **Perks** are special benefits that are given to people who have a particular job or belong to a particular group. ❏ *...a company car, private medical insurance and other perks.*

가산명사 특전 ❏ 회사 차량, 개인 의료 보험과 여타의 특전

▶**perk up 1** PHRASAL VERB If something **perks** you **up** or if you **perk up**, you become cheerful and lively, after feeling tired, bored, or depressed. ❏ *He perks up and jokes with them.* **2** PHRASAL VERB If you **perk** something **up**, you make it more interesting. ❏ *To make the bland taste more interesting, the locals began perking it up with local produce.* **3** PHRASAL VERB If sales, prices, or economies **perk up**, or if something **perks** them **up**, they begin to increase or improve. [JOURNALISM] ❏ *House prices could perk up during the autumn.*

1 구동사 기운 나게 하다; 활기를 되찾다 ❏ 그는 활기를 되찾고 그들과 농담을 한다. **2** 구동사 ~을 더 흥미롭게 하다 ❏ 그 순한 맛을 더 흥미롭게 만들기 위해, 지방 사람들은 거기에 지방 고유 산물을 첨가하기 시작했다. **3** 구동사 증가하다, 나아지다; 증가시키다, 개선하다 [언론] ❏ 가을 동안 집값이 오를지도 모른다.

perm /pɜrm/ (**perms, perming, permed**) **1** N-COUNT If you have a **perm**, your hair is curled and treated with chemicals so that it stays curly for several months. ❏ *...a middle-aged lady with a perm.* **2** V-T When a hairstylist **perms** someone's hair, they curl it and treat it with chemicals so that it stays curly for several months. ❏ *She had her hair permed.*

1 가산명사 파마 ❏ 파마머리를 한 중년 부인 **2** 타동사 파마하다 ❏ 그녀는 머리를 파마했다.

per|ma|nent ♦◇◇ /pɜrmənənt/ (**permanents**) **1** ADJ Something that is **permanent** lasts forever. ❏ *Heavy drinking can cause permanent damage to the brain.* ❏ *...a permanent solution to the problem.* ● **per|ma|nent|ly** ADV ❏ *His reason had been permanently affected by what he had witnessed.* ● **per|ma|nence** N-UNCOUNT ❏ *Anything which threatens the permanence of the treaty is a threat to stability and to peace.* **2** ADJ You use **permanent** to describe situations or states that keep occurring or which seem to exist all the time; used especially to describe problems or difficulties. ❏ *...a permanent state of tension.* ❏ *They feel under permanent threat.* ● **per|ma|nent|ly** ADV ❏ *...the heavy, permanently locked gate.* **3** ADJ A **permanent** employee is one who is employed for an unlimited length of time. [ADJ n] ❏ *At the end of the probationary period you will become a permanent employee.* ● **per|ma|nent|ly** ADV V ❏ *...permanently employed registered dockers.* **4** ADJ Your **permanent** home or your **permanent** address is the one at which you spend most of your time or the one that you return to after having stayed in other places. [ADJ n] ❏ *York Cottage was as near to a permanent home as the children knew.* **5** N-COUNT A **permanent** is a treatment where a hairstylist curls your hair and treats it with a chemical so that it stays curly for several months. [AM; BRIT **perm**] ❏ *Her hair had had a permanent, but had grown out.*

1 형용사 영구적인 ❏ 과음은 뇌에 영구적인 손상을 일으킬 수 있다. ❏ 그 문제에 대한 영구적인 해법 ● 영구적으로 부사 ❏ 자신이 목격했던 것에 의해 그의 이성이 영구적으로 영향을 받아 왔었다. ● 영구, 영속 불가산명사 ❏ 그 조약의 영속을 위협하는 것은 그 무엇이든 안정과 평화를 위협하는 것이다. **2** 형용사 지속적인 ❏ 지속적인 긴장 상태 ❏ 그들은 지속적인 위협을 받고 있다고 느낀다. ● 지속적으로 부사 ❏ 계속 잠겨 있는 무거운 문 **3** 형용사 정규직의 ❏ 수습 기간이 끝나면 정규 직원이 될 것입니다. ● 정규적으로 부사 ❏ 정규 직원으로 등록된 부두 노동자 **4** 형용사 항구적인 ❏ 요크 코티지는 아이들이 아는 항구적인 집이나 다름없었다. **5** 가산명사 파마 [미국영어; 영국영어 perm] ❏ 그녀의 머리는 파마를 했었지만, 머리가 길어서 파마기가 풀려져 버렸다.

<table>
<tr><td colspan="2">**Thesaurus**   permanent의 참조어</td></tr>
<tr><td>ADJ.</td><td>continual, irreversible, lasting; (ant.) fleeting, temporary **1** **2**</td></tr>
</table>

per|me|ate /pɜrmieɪt/ (**permeates, permeating, permeated**) **1** V-T/V-I If an idea, feeling, or attitude **permeates** a system or **permeates** society, it affects every part of it or is present throughout it. ❏ *Bias against women permeates every level of the judicial system.* **2** V-T/V-I If something **permeates** a place, it spreads throughout it. ❏ *The smell of roast beef permeated the air.*

1 타동사/자동사 퍼지다, 스며들다; 충만하다 ❏ 여성에 대한 편견이 사법 체계 전반에 걸쳐 퍼져 있다. **2** 타동사/자동사 퍼지다 ❏ 쇠고기 굽는 냄새가 공기 중에 퍼졌다.

per|mis|sible /pərmɪsəbəl/ ADJ If something is **permissible**, it is considered to be acceptable because it does not break any laws or rules. ❏ *Religious practices are permissible under the Constitution.*

형용사 허용되는 ❏ 종교 의식은 헌법하에서 허용된다.

per|mis|sion ♦◇◇ /pərmɪʃən/ N-UNCOUNT If someone who has authority over you gives you **permission to** do something, they say that they will allow you to do it. ❏ *He asked permission to leave the room.* ❏ *They cannot leave the country without permission.*

불가산명사 허가 ❏ 그는 그 방을 떠나도 좋다는 허가를 구했다. ❏ 그들은 허가 없이는 나라를 떠날 수 없다.

<table>
<tr><td colspan="2">**Word Partnership**   permission의 연어</td></tr>
<tr><td>V.</td><td>ask (for) permission, get permission, permission to leave, need permission, obtain permission, receive permission, request permission, seek permission</td></tr>
<tr><td>ADJ.</td><td>special permission, written permission</td></tr>
</table>

per|mis|sive /pərmɪsɪv/ ADJ A **permissive** person, society, or way of behaving allows or tolerates things which other people disapprove of. ❏ *The call for law and order replaced the "permissive tolerance" of the 1960s.* ● **per|mis|sive|ness** N-UNCOUNT ❏ *Permissiveness and democracy go together.*

형용사 관대한, 너그러운 ❏ 법과 질서에 대한 요구가 1960년대의 '너그러운 관용'을 대체했다. ● 관대함 불가산명사 ❏ 관대함과 민주주의는 공존하는 것이다.

<table>
<tr><td colspan="2">**Word Link**   per ≈ through, thoroughly : perceive, perfect, permit</td></tr>
</table>

per|mit ♦◇◇ (**permits, permitting, permitted**)

The verb is pronounced /pərmɪt/. The noun is pronounced /pɜrmɪt/.

동사는 /pərmɪt/으로 발음되고, 명사는 /pɜrmɪt/으로 발음된다.

1 V-T If someone **permits** something, they allow it to happen. If they **permit** you **to** do something, they allow you to do it. [FORMAL] ❏ *He can let the court's decision stand and permit the execution.* ❏ *The guards permitted me to bring my camera and tape recorder.* **2** N-COUNT A **permit** is an official document which says that you may do something. For example you usually need a **permit** to work in a foreign country. ❏ *The majority of foreign nationals working here have work permits.* **3** V-T/V-I If a situation **permits** something, it makes it possible for that thing

1 타동사 허락하다, 허가하다 [격식체] ❏ 그는 법정 판결을 확정하고 사형 집행을 허가할 수 있다. ❏ 내가 카메라와 녹음기를 가져오는 것을 경비원들이 허락했다. **2** 가산명사 면허증, 허가증 ❏ 이곳에서 일하는 외국인들 대부분은 노동 허가증을 가지고 있다. **3** 타동사/자동사 ~을 가능케 하다 [격식체] ❏ 날씨가 괜찮으면, 점심시간에 산책하러 나가도록 해 보세요.

to exist, happen, or be done or it provides the opportunity for it. [FORMAL] ❏ *Try to go out for a walk at lunchtime, if the weather permits.* ❏ *This method of cooking also permits heat to penetrate evenly from both sides.*

❏ 이 요리법은 열이 양쪽에 고르게 퍼지도록 해 주기도 한다.

Thesaurus   permit의 참조어

v.   allow, authorize, let; *(ant.)* ban, forbid, prohibit **1** **3**

N.   consent, permission; *(ant.)* ban **2**

---

per|ni|cious /pərnɪ́ʃəs/ ADJ If you describe something as **pernicious**, you mean that it is very harmful. [FORMAL] ❏ *I did what I could, but her mother's influence was pernicious.*

형용사 유해한, 치명적인 [격식체] ❏ 나는 할 수 있는 일을 했지만, 그녀 어머니의 영향력은 치명적이었다.

per|pe|trate /pɜ́ːrpɪtreɪt/ (**perpetrates, perpetrating, perpetrated**) V-T If someone **perpetrates** a crime or any other immoral or harmful act, they do it. [FORMAL] ❏ *A high proportion of crime in any country is perpetrated by young males in their teens and twenties.* ● **per|pe|tra|tor** (**perpetrators**) N-COUNT ❏ *The perpetrator of the crime not have to be traced before you can claim compensation.*

타동사 저지르다, 자행하다 [격식체] ❏ 어느 나라에서나 위법 행위의 많은 부분은 10대나 20대의 젊은 남자들에 의해 저질러진다. ● 범죄자 가산명사 ❏ 당신이 배상을 요구할 수 있게 되기 전에는 그 범행을 저지른 사람을 추적하지 않아도 된다.

per|pet|ual /pərpɛ́tʃuəl/ **1** ADJ A **perpetual** feeling, state, or quality is one that never ends or changes. ❏ *...the creation of a perpetual union.* ● **per|pet|ual|ly** ADV ❏ *They were all perpetually starving.* **2** ADJ A **perpetual** act, situation, or state is one that happens again and again and so seems never to end. ❏ *I thought her perpetual complaints were going to prove too much for me.* ● **per|pet|ual|ly** ADV ❏ *He perpetually interferes in political affairs.*

1 형용사 영구적인, 영속하는 ❏ 영구적인 연합 창설 ● 영구적으로 부사 ❏ 그들은 모두 영구적으로 굶주리고 있었다. **2** 형용사 부단한, 끊임없는 ❏ 나는 그녀의 끊임없는 불평이 견딜 수 없게 될 거라고 생각했다. ● 끊임없이 부사 ❏ 그는 정치적인 일에 끊임없이 간섭한다.

per|petu|ate /pərpɛ́tʃueɪt/ (**perpetuates, perpetuating, perpetuated**) V-T If someone or something **perpetuates** a situation, system, or belief, especially a bad one, they cause it to continue. ❏ *We must not perpetuate the religious divisions of the past.*

타동사 영속시키다, 영구화하다 ❏ 우리는 과거의 종교적 분열을 영속시켜서는 안 된다.

per|plexed /pərplɛ́kst/ ADJ If you are **perplexed**, you feel confused and slightly worried by something because you do not understand it. ❏ *She is perplexed about what to do for her daughter.*

형용사 당혹스러워 하는, 당황한 ❏ 그녀는 딸을 위해 무엇을 해야 할지 당혹스럽다.

per se /pɜr seɪ, pər/ ADV **Per se** means "by itself" or "in itself," and is used when you are talking about the qualities of one thing considered on its own, rather than in connection with other things. ❏ *The authors' argument is not with the free market per se but with the western society in which it works.*

부사 그 자체로서, 본질적으로 ❏ 저자의 주장은 자유 시장 그 자체에 대한 것이 아니라 자유 시장이 작동하는 서구 사회에 대한 것이다.

per|se|cute /pɜ́ːrsɪkyut/ (**persecutes, persecuting, persecuted**) V-T If someone **is persecuted**, they are treated cruelly and unfairly, often because of their race or beliefs. ❏ *Mr. Weaver and his family have been persecuted by the authorities for their beliefs.* ❏ *They began by brutally persecuting the Catholic Church.*

타동사 박해를 받다 ❏ 위버 씨와 그의 가족들은 그들이 가진 신념 때문에 당국으로부터 박해를 받아 왔다. ❏ 그들은 우선 가톨릭 교회를 모질게 박해하는 것부터 시작했다.

per|se|cu|tion /pɜ̀ːrsɪkyúʃⁿ/ (**persecutions**) N-UNCOUNT **Persecution** is cruel and unfair treatment of a person or group, especially because of their religious or political beliefs, or their race. [also N in pl] ❏ *...the persecution of minorities.* ❏ *...victims of political persecution.*

불가산명사 박해 ❏ 소수 민족에 대한 박해 ❏ 정치적 박해의 희생자들

per|sever|ance /pɜ̀ːrsɪvíərəns/ N-UNCOUNT **Perseverance** is the quality of continuing with something even though it is difficult. ❏ *I'm delighted for Diego. He has never stopped trying and showed great perseverance.*

불가산명사 불굴, 끈기 ❏ 나는 디에고 때문에 아주 기쁘다. 그는 절대로 노력을 멈추지 않으며 굉장한 끈기를 보여 주었다.

per|se|vere /pɜ̀ːrsɪvíər/ (**perseveres, persevering, persevered**) V-I If you **persevere with** something, you keep trying to do it and do not give up, even though it is difficult. ❏ *This ability to persevere despite obstacles and setbacks is the quality people most admire in others.* ❏ *...a school with a reputation for persevering with difficult and disruptive children.*

자동사 견디어 내다, 굴하지 않고 해내다 ❏ 방해와 좌절에도 불구하고 견디어 내는 이런 능력은 사람들이 다른 사람들에게서 발견할 때 매우 칭찬하는 자질이다. ❏ 다루기 힘들고 문제를 일으키는 아이들을 포기하지 않고 교육하는 것으로 유명한 한 학교

per|sist /pərsɪ́st/ (**persists, persisting, persisted**) **1** V-I If something undesirable **persists**, it continues to exist. ❏ *Contact your doctor if the cough persists.* **2** V-T/V-I If you **persist in** doing something, you continue to do it, even though it is difficult or other people are against it. ❏ *Why does Britain persist in running down its defense forces?* ❏ *He urged the United States to persist with its efforts to bring about peace.*

1 자동사 존속하다 ❏ 기침이 계속 나면 의사에게 문의하세요. **2** 타동사/자동사 고집하다, 계속하다 ❏ 왜 영국은 계속해서 고집스럽게 방위력을 삭감하는 걸까? ❏ 그는 미국에 평화를 이룩하기 위한 노력을 계속할 것을 촉구했다.

per|sis|tence /pərsɪ́stəns/ **1** N-UNCOUNT If you have **persistence**, you continue to do something even though it is difficult or other people are against it. ❏ *Skill comes only with practice, patience, and persistence.* **2** N-UNCOUNT **The persistence** of something, especially something bad, is the fact of its continuing to exist for a long time. ❏ *...an expression of concern at the persistence of inflation and high interest rates.*

1 불가산명사 끈기; 고집 ❏ 숙련된 솜씨는 연습과 인내, 끈기가 있어야만 얻을 수 있다. **2** 불가산명사 지속 ❏ 지속적인 인플레이션과 고금리에 대해 우려를 표함

per|sis|tent /pərsɪ́stənt/ **1** ADJ Something that is **persistent** continues to exist or happen for a long time; used especially about bad or undesirable states or situations. ❏ *Her position as national leader has been weakened by persistent fears of another coup attempt.* ❏ *His cough grew more persistent until it never stopped.* **2** ADJ Someone who is **persistent** continues trying to do something, even though it is difficult or other people are against it. ❏ *...a persistent critic of the government's transport policies.*

1 형용사 지속되는, 끊임없는 ❏ 그녀의 국가 지도자로서의 지위가 또 다른 쿠데타 시도에 대한 끊임없는 두려움 때문에 약화되어 왔다. ❏ 그의 기침은 더 지속적이 되더니 급기야는 쉼 없이 계속되는 지경이 되었다. **2** 형용사 끈덕진, 고집 있는 ❏ 정부의 운송 정책을 끈덕지게 비난하는 어떤 사람

per|sis|tent|ly /pərsɪ́stəntli/ **1** ADV If something happens **persistently**, it happens again and again or for a long time. ❏ *The allegations have been persistently denied by ministers.* **2** ADV If someone does something **persistently**, they do it with determination even though it is difficult or other people are against it. [ADV with v] ❏ *Rachel gently but persistently imposed her will upon Douglas.*

1 부사 지속적으로, 계속 ❏ 그와 같은 주장을 각료들은 계속 부인해 왔다. **2** 부사 끈덕지게, 고집스럽게 ❏ 레이첼은 부드럽지만 고집스럽게 자신의 뜻을 더글러스에게 강요했다.

per|son ♦♦♦ /pɜ́ːrsⁿn/ (**people, persons**)

The usual word for "more than one person" is **people**. The form **persons** is used as the plural in formal or legal language.

‘한 사람 이상’의 의미로는 people을 쓴다. persons는 격식체 또는 법률어에서 복수로 쓴다.

1 N-COUNT A **person** is a man, woman, or child. ❏ *At least one person died and several others were injured.* ❏ *They were both lovely, friendly people.* **2** N-PLURAL **Persons** is used as the plural of **person** in formal, legal, and technical writing. ❏ *...removal of the right of accused persons to remain silent.* **3** N-COUNT If you talk about someone **as a person**, you are considering them from the point of view

1 가산명사 사람 ❏ 최소한 한 사람이 사망하고 다른 몇 사람이 부상을 입었다. ❏ 그들은 둘 다 사랑스럽고 상냥한 사람들이었다. **2** 복수명사 사람들 ❏ 피고들에 대한 묵비권 박탈 **3** 가산명사 있는 그대로 ❏ 이제 나는 그를 있는 그대로 대할 시간이 많이 있다. **4** 구

of their real nature. ❑ *I've a lot of time for him as a person now.* **4** PHRASE If you do something **in person**, you do it yourself rather than letting someone else do it for you. ❑ *You must collect the mail in person and take along some form of identification.* **5** PHRASE If you meet, hear, or see someone **in person**, you are in the same place as them, rather than, for example, speaking to them on the telephone, writing to them, or seeing them on television. ❑ *It was the first time she had seen him in person.* **6** N-COUNT Your **person** is your body. [FORMAL] ❑ *The suspect had refused to give any details of his identity and had carried no documents on his person.* **7** N-COUNT In grammar, we use the term **first person** when referring to "I" and "we," **second person** when referring to "you," and **third person** when referring to "he," "she," "it," "they," and all other noun groups. **Person** is also used like this when referring to the verb forms that go with these pronouns and noun groups.

per|so|na /pərsoʊnə/ (**personas** or **personae** /pərsoʊnaɪ/) N-COUNT Someone's **persona** is the aspect of their character or nature that they present to other people, perhaps in contrast to their real character or nature. [FORMAL] ❑ *The contradictions between her private life and the public persona are not always fully explored.*

per|son|al ♦♦◊ /pɜrsən°l/ **1** ADJ A **personal** opinion, quality, or thing belongs or relates to one particular person rather than to other people. [ADJ n] ❑ *He learned this lesson the hard way – from his own personal experience.* ❑ *That's my personal opinion.* **2** ADJ If you give something your **personal** care or attention, you deal with it yourself rather than letting someone else deal with it. ❑ *...a business that requires a great deal of personal contact.* ❑ *...a personal letter from the President's secretary.* **3** ADJ **Personal** matters relate to your feelings, relationships, and health. ❑ *...teaching young people about marriage and personal relationships.* ❑ *You never allow personal problems to affect your performance.* **4** ADJ **Personal** comments refer to someone's appearance or character in an offensive way. ❑ *Newspapers resorted to personal abuse.* **5** ADJ **Personal** care involves looking after your body and appearance. [ADJ n] ❑ *...the new breed of men who take as much time and trouble over personal hygiene as the women in their lives.* **6** ADJ A **personal** relationship is one that is not connected with your job or public life. ❑ *He was a great and valued personal friend whom I've known for many many years.*

per|son|al as|sis|tant (**personal assistants**) N-COUNT A **personal assistant** is a person who does office work and administrative work for someone. The abbreviation **PA** is also used. [BUSINESS] ❑ *She was a hard-pressed personal assistant to a frenetic company chairman.*

per|son|al com|put|er (**personal computers**) N-COUNT A **personal computer** is a computer that is used by one person at a time in a business, a school, or at home. The abbreviation **PC** is also used.

per|son|al digi|tal as|sis|tant (**personal digital assistants**) N-COUNT A **personal digital assistant** is a handheld computer, used mainly for storing and accessing personal information such as addresses, telephone numbers, and memos. The abbreviation **PDA** is also used. ❑ *...devices such as mobile phones and personal digital assistants*

per|son|al|ity ♦◊◊ /pɜrsənælɪti/ (**personalities**) **1** N-VAR Your **personality** is your whole character and nature. ❑ *She has such a kind, friendly personality.* ❑ *The contest was as much about personalities as it was about politics.* **2** N-VAR If someone has **personality** or **is a personality**, they have a strong and lively character. ❑ *...a woman of great personality.* **3** N-COUNT You can refer to a famous person, especially in entertainment, broadcasting, or sports, as a **personality**. ❑ *...the radio and television personality, Jimmy Saville.*

Word Partnership	personality의 연어
ADJ.	**strong** personality, **unique** personality **1** **2**
N.	personality **trait** **1**
	radio personality, **television/TV** personality **3**

per|son|al|ly ♦◊◊ /pɜrsənəli/ **1** ADV You use **personally** to emphasize that you are giving your own opinion. [EMPHASIS] [ADV with cl] ❑ *Personally I think it's a waste of time.* ❑ *You can disagree about them, and I personally do, but they are great ideas that have made people think.* **2** ADV If you do something **personally**, you do it yourself rather than letting someone else do it. [ADV with v] ❑ *The minister is returning to Paris to answer the allegations personally.* ❑ *When the great man arrived, the club's manager personally escorted him upstairs.* **3** ADV If you meet or know someone **personally**, you meet or know them in real life, rather than knowing about them or knowing their work. [ADV with v] ❑ *He did not know them personally, but he was familiar with their reputation.* **4** ADV You can use **personally** to say that something refers to an individual person rather than to other people. ❑ *To a far greater degree than other leaders, he was personally responsible for all that the people had suffered under his rule.* **5** ADV You can use **personally** to show that you are talking about someone's private life rather than their professional or public life. ❑ *This has taken a great toll on me personally and professionally.* **6** PHRASE If you **take** someone's remarks **personally**, you are upset because you think that they are criticizing you in particular. ❑ *I take everything too personally.*

per|son|al or|gan|iz|er (**personal organizers**) [BRIT also **personal organiser**] N-COUNT A **personal organizer** is a book containing personal or business information, which you can add pages to or remove pages from to keep the information up to date. Small computers with a similar function are also called **personal organizers**.

per|son|al ste|reo (**personal stereos**) N-COUNT A **personal stereo** is a small cassette or CD player with very light headphones, which people carry around so that they can listen to music while doing something else.

몸소, 직접 ❑ 네가 직접 우편물을 받으러 가야 하고 무엇이든 신분을 증명할 수 있는 것을 가지고 가야 한다. **5** 구 직접, 실물로 ❑ 그녀가 그를 직접 보기는 그때가 처음이었다. **6** 가산명사 몸, 신체 [격식체] ❑ 그 용의자는 자기 신원에 대한 자세한 내용을 일체 밝히지 않으려 했고 어떤 기록도 몸에 지니고 있지 않았다. **7** 가산명사 인칭

가산명사 외양, 겉모습 [격식체] ❑ 그녀의 사생활과 공적인 겉모습 사이의 모순이 항상 충분히 탐구되는 것은 아니다.

1 형용사 개인의 ❑ 그는 이 교훈을 어렵게 얻었다. 직접 개인적인 경험을 통해서. ❑ 그것은 제 개인적인 의견입니다. **2** 형용사 본인 스스로의, 직접의 ❑ 직접적인 접촉을 많이 요하는 사업 ❑ 대통령 비서의 친서 **3** 형용사 개인적인 ❑ 젊은이들에게 결혼과 대인 관계에 대해 가르치는 일 ❑ 당신은 절대로 개인적인 문제들이 업무에 영향을 미치도록 놔두지 않습니다. **4** 형용사 인신공격적인 ❑ 신문들이 인신공격을 했다. **5** 형용사 신체의; 외모의 ❑ 생활 속에서 개인위생에 여성들만큼 많은 시간과 노력을 들이는 새로운 유형의 남성 **6** 형용사 사적인 ❑ 그는 내가 아주 오랫동안 사적으로 알고 지내온 아주 귀중한 친구이다.

가산명사 개인 비서 [경제] ❑ 그녀는 어떤 정신없이 바쁜 기업 회장의 죽어나는 개인 비서였다.

가산명사 개인용 컴퓨터

가산명사 피디에이 ❑ 휴대 전화나 피디에이 같은 기기들

1 가산명사 또는 불가산명사 성격, 인격 ❑ 그녀는 성격이 대단히 친절하고 상냥하다. ❑ 그 경연은 정치는 물론 인격에 관한 것이기도 했다. **2** 가산명사 또는 불가산명사 개성 ❑ 대단히 개성 있는 여자 **3** 가산명사 명사 ❑ 라디오와 텔레비전을 통해 유명한 지미 새빌

1 부사 개인적으로는 [강조] ❑ 나 개인적으로는 그 일이 시간 낭비라고 생각한다. ❑ 당신이 그것들에 대해 의견이 다를 수도 있고, 나도 개인적으로 그렇지만, 그것들은 사람들로 하여금 생각을 하게 만들어 준 위대한 사상들이다. **2** 부사 몸소, 직접 ❑ 장관이 여러 가지 혐의에 직접 답하기 위해 파리로 돌아가고 있다. ❑ 그 위인이 도착했을 때, 클럽 지배인이 몸소 그를 위층으로 안내했다. **3** 부사 직접적으로 ❑ 그는 그들을 직접적으로 알지는 못했지만, 그들의 명성은 익히 알고 있었다. **4** 부사 개인적으로 ❑ 민중이 그의 통치하에서 겪었던 그 모든 것에 대해 다른 지도자들보다 훨씬 더 큰 책임이 그 개인에게 있었다. **5** 부사 개인적으로 ❑ 이 일로 나는 개인적으로 직업상으로 큰 대가를 치러 왔다. **6** 구 ~을 기분 나쁘게 받아들이다 ❑ 나는 모든 것을 너무 기분 나쁘게 받아들인다.

[영국영어 personal organiser] 가산명사 개인용 수첩

가산명사 휴대용 음향기기

per|soni|fi|ca|tion /pərsɒnɪfɪkeɪʃ³n/ (**personifications**) N-SING If you say that someone is **the personification of** a particular thing or quality, you mean that they are a perfect example of that thing or that they have a lot of that quality. ❑ *Janis Joplin was the personification of the '60s female rock singer.*

단수명사 전형, 화신 ❑ 재니스 조플린은 60년대 여성 록 가수의 전형이었다.

per|soni|fy /pərsɒnɪfaɪ/ (**personifies, personifying, personified**) V-T If you say that someone **personifies** a particular thing or quality, you mean that they seem to be a perfect example of that thing, or to have that quality to a very large degree. ❑ *She seemed to personify goodness and nobility.*

타동사 –의 화신이 되다 ❑ 그녀는 선량함과 고결함의 화신인 것 같았다.

per|son|nel ♦♢♢ /pɜrsənel/ **1** N-PLURAL The **personnel** of an organization are the people who work for it. ❑ *Since 1954 Japan has never dispatched military personnel abroad.* ❑ *There has been very little renewal of personnel in higher education.* **2** N-UNCOUNT **Personnel** is the department in a large company or organization that deals with employees, keeps their records, and helps with any problems they might have. [BUSINESS] ❑ *Her first job was in personnel.*

1 복수명사 전 직원, 인원 ❑ 1954년 이래로 일본은 군 병력을 해외로 파병한 적이 없다. ❑ 고등 교육계에서는 인적 쇄신이 거의 이루어지지 않았다. **2** 불가산명사 인사과 [경제] ❑ 그녀의 첫 번째 일자리는 인사과였다.

per|spec|tive ♦♢♢ /pərspektɪv/ (**perspectives**) **1** N-COUNT A particular **perspective** is a particular way of thinking about something, especially one that is influenced by your beliefs or experiences. ❑ *He says the death of his father 18 months ago has given him a new perspective on life.* ❑ *...two different perspectives on the nature of adolescent development.* **2** PHRASE If you get something **in perspective** or **into perspective**, you judge its real importance by considering it in relation to everything else. If you get something **out of perspective**, you fail to judge its real importance in relation to everything else. ❑ *Remember to keep things in perspective.* ❑ *I let things get out of perspective.*

1 가산명사 시각, 견해 ❑ 그는 18개월 전에 겪은 아버지의 죽음으로 인해 인생에 대해 새로운 시각을 갖게 되었다고 말한다. ❑ 청소년기 발달의 특징에 대한 두 가지의 다른 견해 **2** 구 균형 잡힌 시각으로; 균형을 잃은 시각으로 ❑ 잊지 말고 사태를 계속 균형 잡힌 시각으로 보다. ❑ 내가 사태를 보는 시각의 균형을 잃었다.

Thesaurus　　*perspective*의 참조어

N.　　attitude, outlook, viewpoint **1**

---

per|spi|ra|tion /pɜrspɪreɪʃ³n/ N-UNCOUNT **Perspiration** is the liquid which comes out on the surface of your skin when you are hot or frightened. [FORMAL] ❑ *His hands were wet with perspiration.* →see **sweat**

불가산명사 땀 [격식체] ❑ 그의 양손은 땀으로 축축했다.

Word Link　　suad, suas ≈ urging: dissuade, persuade, persuasive

---

per|suade ♦♢♢ /pərsweɪd/ (**persuades, persuading, persuaded**) **1** V-T If you **persuade** someone **to** do something, you cause them to do it by giving them good reasons for doing it. ❑ *My husband persuaded me to come.* ❑ *We're trying to persuade manufacturers to sell them here.* **2** V-T If something **persuades** someone **to** take a particular course of action, it causes them to take that course of action because it is a good reason for doing so. ❑ *The Conservative Party's victory in April's general election persuaded him to run for President again.* **3** V-T If you **persuade** someone that something is true, you say things that eventually make them believe that it is true. ❑ *I've persuaded Mrs. Tennant that it's time she retired.* ❑ *We had managed to persuade them that it was worth working with us.*

1 타동사 설득하다 ❑ 남편이 나를 설득해서 오게 했다. ❑ 우리는 생산자들을 설득해서 그 상품들을 여기서 팔게 하려고 노력하고 있습니다. **2** 타동사 –하게 하다 ❑ 4월 총선거에서 보수당이 승리함으로써 그가 다시 한 번 대통령 후보로 출마하게 되었다. **3** 타동사 설득하다; 납득시키다 ❑ 나는 테넌트 여사에게 이제 은퇴할 시기라고 설득해 왔다. ❑ 우리는 우리와 함께 일할 만한 가치가 있다는 것을 가까스로 그들에게 납득시켰었다.

Thesaurus　　*persuade*의 참조어

V.　　cajole, convince, influence, sway, talk into, win over; (ant.) discourage, dissuade **1 3**

Word Partnership　　*persuade*의 연어

V.　　**attempt to** persuade, **be able to** persuade, **fail to** persuade, **try to** persuade **1 3**

---

per|sua|sion /pərsweɪʒ³n/ (**persuasions**) **1** N-UNCOUNT **Persuasion** is the act of persuading someone to do something or to believe that something is true. ❑ *Only after much persuasion from Ellis had she agreed to hold a show at all.* **2** N-COUNT If you are **of** a particular **persuasion**, you have a particular belief or set of beliefs. [FORMAL] ❑ *It is a national movement and has within it people of all political persuasions.*

1 불가산명사 설득 ❑ 엘리스가 열심히 설득을 한 다음에야 그녀는 어쨌든 쇼를 여는 것을 승낙했다. **2** 가산명사 신조, 신념 [격식체] ❑ 그것은 전국적 운동이며 그 안에는 다양한 정치적 신조를 가진 사람들이 망라되어 있다.

per|sua|sive /pərsweɪsɪv/ ADJ Someone or something that is **persuasive** is likely to persuade a person to believe or do a particular thing. ❑ *What do you think were some of the more persuasive arguments on the other side?* ❑ *I can be very persuasive when I want to be.* ● **per|sua|sive|ly** ADV [ADV with v] ❑ *...a trained lawyer who can present arguments persuasively.*

형용사 설득력 있는 ❑ 다른 한편으로 더 설득력 있는 논거로는 어떤 것이 있었다고 생각하십니까? ❑ 나는 내가 원할 때는 아주 설득을 잘 할 수 있다. ● 설득력 있게 부사 ❑ 설득력 있게 논거를 제시할 수 있는 훈련된 변호사

per|tain /pərteɪn/ (**pertains, pertaining, pertained**) V-I If one thing **pertains to** another, it relates, belongs, or applies to it. [FORMAL] ❑ *...matters pertaining to naval district defense.*

자동사 속하다, 관계되다 [격식체] ❑ 해군 방위대에 관련된 문제들

per|ti|nent /pɜrt³nənt/ ADJ Something that is **pertinent** is relevant to a particular subject. [FORMAL] ❑ *She had asked some pertinent questions.* ❑ *Pertinent information will be forwarded to the appropriate party.*

형용사 관련된 [격식체] ❑ 그녀는 관련된 질문 몇 가지를 했었다. ❑ 관련 정보가 당사자에게 전달될 것이다.

per|vade /pərveɪd/ (**pervades, pervading, pervaded**) V-T If something **pervades** a place or thing, it is a noticeable feature throughout it. [FORMAL] ❑ *The smell of sawdust and glue pervaded the factory.*

타동사 널리 퍼지다, 가득 차다 [격식체] ❑ 톱밥과 접착제 냄새가 공장에 가득 찼다.

per|va|sive /pərveɪsɪv/ ADJ Something, especially something bad, that is **pervasive** is present or felt throughout a place or thing. [FORMAL] ❑ *...the pervasive influence of the army in national life.*

형용사 널리 미치는 [격식체] ❑ 국민 생활에 널리 미치는 군대의 영향

per|verse /pərvɜrs/ ADJ Someone who is **perverse** deliberately does things that are unreasonable or that result in harm for themselves. [DISAPPROVAL] ❑ *It would be perverse to stop this healthy trend.* ❑ *Psychotherapists often take a perverse delight in criticizing other psychotherapists.* ● **per|verse|ly** ADV ❑ *She was perversely pleased to be causing trouble.*

형용사 뒤틀린, 비뚤어진 [탐탁잖음] ❑ 이런 건전한 추세를 막으려 하는 것은 비뚤어진 일일 터이다. ❑ 심리 치료사들은 종종 다른 심리 치료사들을 욕하는 것에서 뒤틀린 즐거움을 얻는다. ● 비뚤어져 부사 ❑ 그녀는 비뚤어져서 문제를 일으키며 즐거워했다.

a
b
c
d
e
f
g
h
i
j
k
l
m
n
o
p
q
r
s
t
u
v
w
x
y
z

per|ver|sion /pərvɜrʒ³n, -ʃ³n/ (perversions) **1** N-VAR You can refer to a sexual desire or action that you consider to be abnormal and unacceptable as a **perversion**. [DISAPPROVAL] ❑ *The book had a firm position as the authority on sexual perversions.* **2** N-VAR A **perversion of** something is a form of it that is bad or wrong, or the changing of it into this form. [DISAPPROVAL] ❑ *What monstrous perversion of the human spirit leads a sniper to open fire on a bus carrying children?*

1 가산명사 또는 불가산명사 성적 도착 [탐탁찮음] ❑ 그 책은 성적 도착에 대한 권위서로서 확고부동한 위치를 차지하고 있었다. **2** 가산명사 또는 불가산명사 타락; 타락한 상태 [탐탁찮음] ❑ 인간의 정신이 어떻게 어처구니없이 타락했기에 저격수로 하여금 아이들을 실어 나르는 버스에 총질을 해대게 만드는 것일까?

per|vert (perverts, perverting, perverted)

The verb is pronounced /pərvɜrt/. The noun is pronounced /pɜrvɜrt/.

동사는 /pərvɜrt/으로 발음되고, 명사는 /pɜrvɜrt/으로 발음된다.

1 V-T If you **pervert** something such as a process or society, you interfere with it so that it is not as good as it used to be or as it should be. [FORMAL, DISAPPROVAL] ❑ *Any reform will destroy and pervert our constitution.* **2** N-COUNT If you say that someone is a **pervert**, you mean that you consider their behavior, especially their sexual behavior, to be immoral or unacceptable. [DISAPPROVAL] ❑ *I hope the police track down these perverts and charge them with rape.*

1 타동사 (바른길에서) 벗어나게 하다 [격식체, 탐탁찮음] ❑ 어떠한 개혁도 우리의 헌법을 파괴하고 잘못된 길로 이끌 것이다. **2** 가산명사 성도착자 [탐탁찮음] ❑ 나는 경찰이 이 성도착자들을 추적해서 강간 혐의로 기소하기를 바란다.

per|vert|ed /pərvɜrtɪd/ **1** ADJ If you say that someone is **perverted**, you mean that you consider their behavior, especially their sexual behavior, to be immoral or unacceptable. [DISAPPROVAL] ❑ *You've been protecting sick and perverted men.* **2** ADJ You can use **perverted** to describe actions or ideas which you think are wrong, unnatural, or harmful. [DISAPPROVAL] ❑ *...a perverted form of knowledge.*

1 형용사 도착적인, 변태의 [탐탁찮음] ❑ 당신은 병적이고 도착적인 사람들을 보호해 왔던 겁니다. **2** 형용사 잘못된, 비뚤어진 [탐탁찮음] ❑ 잘못된 형태의 지식

pes|si|mism /pɛsɪmɪzəm/ N-UNCOUNT **Pessimism** is the belief that bad things are going to happen. ❑ *...universal pessimism about the economy.*

불가산명사 비관론, 염세주의 ❑ 경제에 대한 보편적인 비관론

pes|si|mist /pɛsɪmɪst/ (pessimists) N-COUNT A **pessimist** is someone who thinks that bad things are going to happen. ❑ *I'm a natural pessimist; I usually expect the worst.*

가산명사 비관론자, 염세주의자 ❑ 나는 타고난 염세주의자로 보통 최악의 상태를 예상한다.

pes|si|mis|tic /pɛsɪmɪstɪk/ ADJ Someone who is **pessimistic** thinks that bad things are going to happen. ❑ *Not everyone is so pessimistic about the future.* ❑ *Hardy has often been criticised for an excessively pessimistic view of life.*

형용사 비관적인, 염세적인 ❑ 모든 사람이 미래에 대해 그처럼 비관적인 것은 아니다. ❑ 하디는 극도로 염세적인 인생관 때문에 종종 비난을 받아 왔다.

pest /pɛst/ (pests) **1** N-COUNT **Pests** are insects or small animals which damage crops or food supplies. ❑ *...crops which are resistant to some of the major insect pests and diseases.* ❑ *Each year ten percent of the crop is lost to a pest called corn rootworm.* **2** N-COUNT You can describe someone, especially a child, as a **pest** if they keep bothering you. [INFORMAL, DISAPPROVAL] ❑ *He climbed on the table, pulled my hair, and was generally a pest.* →see **farm**

1 가산명사 해충 ❑ 몇 가지 주요 병충해에 저항력이 있는 농작물 ❑ 매년 농작물의 10퍼센트가 옥수수 뿌리벌레라는 해충에 손실을 입는다. **2** 가산명사 골칫덩이 [비격식체, 탐탁찮음] ❑ 그 아이는 탁자에 기어 올라가고, 내 머리를 잡아당기고, 여러 모로 골칫덩이였다.

pes|ter /pɛstər/ (pesters, pestering, pestered) V-T If you say that someone is **pestering** you, you mean that they keep asking you to do something, or keep talking to you, and you find this annoying. [DISAPPROVAL] ❑ *I thought she'd stop pestering me, but it only seemed to make her worse.* ❑ *I know he gets fed up with people pestering him for money.*

타동사 성가시게 굴다, 괴롭히다 [탐탁찮음] ❑ 나는 그녀가 나를 괴롭히는 것을 그만두리라고 생각했지만, 그것이 그녀를 악화시키기만 한 것 같았다. ❑ 사람들이 돈을 달라고 귀찮게 하는 것에 그가 넌더리를 낸다는 것을 나는 알고 있다.

Word Link   cide ≈ killing : genocide, homicide, pesticide

---

pes|ti|cide /pɛstɪsaɪd/ (pesticides) N-MASS **Pesticides** are chemicals which farmers put on their crops to kill harmful insects. →see **pollution**

물질명사 농약

pet ♦◇◇ /pɛt/ (pets, petting, petted) **1** N-COUNT A **pet** is an animal that you keep in your home to give you company and pleasure. ❑ *It is plainly cruel to keep turtles as pets.* ❑ *...a bachelor living alone in a flat with his pet dog.* **2** ADJ Someone's **pet** theory, project, or subject is one that they particularly support or like. ❑ *He would not stand by and let his pet project be killed off.* **3** V-T If you **pet** a person or animal, you touch them in an affectionate way. ❑ *The policeman reached down and petted the wolfhound.* →see Word Web: **pet**

1 가산명사 애완동물 ❑ 바다거북을 애완동물로 기르는 건 명백히 잔인한 일이다. ❑ 애완견과 함께 아파트에서 혼자 살고 있는 독신 남자 **2** 형용사 특별히 아끼는 ❑ 그는 가만히 서서 자신이 아끼는 계획이 무산되도록 내버려 두지는 않을 것이다. **3** 타동사 쓰다듬다, 애무하다 ❑ 그 경찰관은 손을 아래로 뻗어 울프하운드를 쓰다듬었다.

pet|al /pɛt³l/ (petals) N-COUNT The **petals** of a flower are the thin colored or white parts which together form the flower. ❑ *...bowls of dried rose petals.*

가산명사 꽃잎 ❑ 말린 장미 꽃잎 여러 그릇

pe|ter /pitər/ (peters, petering, petered)

▶ **peter out** PHRASAL VERB If something **peters out**, it gradually comes to an end. ❑ *The six-month strike seemed to be petering out.*

구동사 점차 소멸하다 ❑ 여섯 달 동안의 파업이 점차 끝나 가는 듯이 보였다.

pe|tite /pətit/ ADJ If you describe a woman as **petite**, you are politely saying that she is small and is not fat. ❑ *Though small, the woman wasn't quite petite – certainly not from the waist up.*

형용사 (몸집이) 아담한 ❑ 그 여자는 작긴 하지만 아담한 편은 아니었다. 분명히 허리 위쪽으로는.

pe|ti|tion /pətɪʃ³n/ (petitions, petitioning, petitioned) **1** N-COUNT A **petition** is a document signed by a lot of people which asks a government or other

1 가산명사 탄원서, 진정서 ❑ 사람들의 입장이 매우 강경해서 우리는 얼마 전 정부에 4,500명의 서명이

Word Web   pet

Americans love **pets**. They own more than 51 million **dogs**, 56 million **cats**, 45 million **birds**, 75 million small **mammals** and **reptiles**, and millions of **fish**. Recent studies have shown that adult pet owners are healthier overall than those who don't have companion animals. One study (Katcher, 1982) suggests that owning a pet lowers blood pressure. The 2001 German Socio-Economic Panel Survey found that pet owners made fewer doctor visits than others in the group. And a study in the *American Journal of Cardiology* found that male dog owners were less likely to die within a year after a heart attack than people who didn't own dogs.

official group to do a particular thing. □ *People feel so strongly that we recently presented the government with a petition signed by 4,500 people.* ▣ N-COUNT A **petition** is a formal request made to a court of law for some legal action to be taken. [LEGAL] □ *His lawyers filed a petition for all charges to be dropped.* ▣ V-T/V-I If you **petition** someone in authority, you make a formal request to them. [FORMAL] □ *...couples petitioning for divorce.* □ *All the attempts to petition the Congress had failed.*

담긴 탄원서를 제출했다. ▣ 가산명사 청원 [법률] □ 그의 변호사들이 모든 고발 건의 취하를 요청하는 청원을 냈다. ▣ 타동사/자동사 청원하다, 신청하다 [격식체] □ 이혼 신청을 낸 부부들 □ 의회에 청원하려는 모든 시도들이 실패로 돌아갔다.

pet|ri|fied /pɛtrɪfaɪd/ ▣ ADJ If you are **petrified**, you are extremely frightened, perhaps so frightened that you cannot think or move. □ *I've always been petrified of being alone.* ▣ ADJ A **petrified** plant or animal has died and has gradually turned into stone. [ADJ n] □ *...a block of petrified wood.*

▣ 형용사 몹시 두려운, (무서워서) 얼어붙은 □ 나는 항상 혼자 있는 것이 몹시 두려웠다. ▣ 형용사 손아서 돌이 된, 석화(石化)된 □ 굳어서 돌이 된 나무토막

pet|rol /pɛtrəl/ N-UNCOUNT **Petrol** is a liquid which is used as a fuel for motor vehicles. [BRIT; AM **gas, gasoline**]

불가산명사 휘발유 [영국영어; 미국영어 gas, gasoline]

pe|tro|leum /pətroʊliəm/ N-UNCOUNT **Petroleum** is oil which is found under the surface of the earth or under the sea bed. Gasoline and paraffin are obtained from petroleum. →see **energy, oil**

불가산명사 석유

pet|rol sta|tion (**petrol stations**) N-COUNT A **petrol station** is a garage by the side of the road where gasoline is sold and put into vehicles. [BRIT; AM **gas station**]

가산명사 주유소 [영국영어; 미국영어 gas station]

pet|ty /pɛti/ (**pettier, pettiest**) ▣ ADJ You can use **petty** to describe things such as problems, rules, or arguments which you think are unimportant or relate to unimportant things. [DISAPPROVAL] □ *He was miserable all the time and rows would start over petty things.* □ *...endless rules and petty regulations.* ▣ ADJ If you describe someone's behavior as **petty**, you mean that they care too much about small, unimportant things and perhaps that they are unnecessarily unkind. [DISAPPROVAL] □ *He was petty-minded and obsessed with detail.* ● **pet|ti|ness** N-UNCOUNT □ *Never had she met such spite and pettiness.* ▣ ADJ **Petty** is used of people or actions that are less important, serious, or great than others. [ADJ n] □ *...petty crime, such as handbag-snatching and minor break-ins.*

▣ 형용사 사소한 [탐탁찮음] □ 그는 항상 비참했고 사소한 일을 놓고 말다툼이 벌어지곤 했다. □ 끝없는 규칙들과 사소한 규정들 ▣ 형용사 마음이 좁은, 쩨쩨한 [탐탁찮음] □ 그는 마음이 좁고 사소한 부분에 집착했다. ● 쩨쩨함 불가산명사 □ 그녀는 그와 같이 심술궂고 쩨쩨한 일을 당해 본 적이 없었다. ▣ 형용사 사소한 □ 핸드백 날치기나 좀도둑질 같은 사소한 범죄

pet|ty cash N-UNCOUNT **Petty cash** is money that is kept in the office of a company, for making small payments in cash when necessary. [BUSINESS] □ *After having her expense claims overruled, she took the money from petty cash.*

불가산명사 소액 지급 준비금 [경제] □ 그녀는 자신이 낸 비용 지급 요구가 각하된 다음, 소액 지급 준비금에서 돈을 가져갔다.

petu|lant /pɛtʃələnt/ ADJ Someone who is **petulant** is unreasonably angry and upset in a childish way. □ *His critics say he's just being silly and petulant.*

형용사 성마른 □ 그를 비난하는 사람들은 그가 그저 어리석고 성마르게 굴고 있을 뿐이라고 말한다.

pew /pyu/ (**pews**) N-COUNT A **pew** is a long wooden seat with a back, which people sit on in church. □ *Claire sat in the front pew.*

가산명사 (교회의) 신도석 □ 클레어는 신도석 맨 앞줄에 앉았다.

pew|ter /pyutər/ N-UNCOUNT **Pewter** is a grey metal which is made by mixing tin and lead. Pewter was often used in former times to make ornaments or containers for eating and drinking. □ *...pewter plates.*

불가산명사 백랍 □ 백랍 접시

phan|tom /fæntəm/ (**phantoms**) ▣ N-COUNT A **phantom** is a ghost. □ *They vanished down the stairs like two phantoms.* ▣ ADJ You use **phantom** to describe something which you experience but which is not real. [ADJ n] □ *...phantom pregnancies.* ▣ ADJ **Phantom** is used to describe business organizations, agreements, or goods which do not really exist, but which someone pretends do exist in order to cheat people. [ADJ n] □ *A phantom trading scheme at a Wall Street investment bank went unnoticed for three years.*

▣ 가산명사 유령 □ 그들 2명은 유령처럼 층계 아래로 사라졌다. ▣ 형용사 상상의 □ 상상 임신 ▣ 형용사 유령 같은, 실체가 없는 □ 월가의 한 투자 은행에서 유령 주식 거래 음모가 3년 동안 발각되지 않고 진행되었다.

pha|raoh /fɛəroʊ, færoʊ, feɪ-/ (**pharaohs**) N-COUNT; N-PROPER A **pharaoh** was a king of ancient Egypt. □ *...Rameses II, Pharaoh of All Egypt.*

가산명사; 고유명사 파라오, 고대 이집트의 왕 □ 전 이집트의 파라오, 람세스 2세

Word Link

*pharma ≈ drug : pharma**ceutical**, pharma**cist**, pharma**cy***

phar|ma|ceu|ti|cal /fɑrməsutɪkəl/ (**pharmaceuticals**) ▣ ADJ **Pharmaceutical** means connected with the industrial production of medicines. [ADJ n] □ *...a Swiss pharmaceutical company.* ▣ N-PLURAL **Pharmaceuticals** are medicines. □ *Antibiotics were of no use, neither were other pharmaceuticals.*

▣ 형용사 제약의 □ 한 스위스 제약 회사 ▣ 복수명사 약 □ 항생제는 소용이 없었고, 다른 약도 마찬가지였다.

phar|ma|cist /fɑrməsɪst/ (**pharmacists**) ▣ N-COUNT A **pharmacist** is a person who is qualified to prepare and sell medicines. □ *Ask your pharmacist for advice.* ▣ N-COUNT A **pharmacist** or a **pharmacist's** is a store in which drugs and medicines are sold by a pharmacist. [mainly BRIT; AM usually **pharmacy**] □ *...a pharmacist's counter.*

▣ 가산명사 약사 □ 약사에게 조언을 구하세요. ▣ 가산명사 약국 [주로 영국영어; 미국영어 대개 pharmacy] □ 약국 판매대

phar|ma|cy /fɑrməsi/ (**pharmacies**) ▣ N-COUNT A **pharmacy** is a store or a department in a store where medicines are sold or given out. □ *Pick up the medicine from the pharmacy.* ▣ N-UNCOUNT **Pharmacy** is the job or the science of preparing medicines. □ *He spent four years studying pharmacy.*

▣ 가산명사 약국 □ 약국에서 약을 받아 가세요. ▣ 불가산명사 제약업; 약학 □ 그는 약학을 공부하며 4년을 보냈다.

In American English, the usual way of referring to a store where medicines are sold is a **drugstore**. □ *She went into a drugstore and bought some aspirin.* **Pharmacy** refers specifically to a part of the drugstore where you get prescription medicines. Pharmacies are often located in stores that mainly sell other merchandise, such as food supermarkets and discount centers. In Britain, the nearest equivalent of a drugstore is a **chemist's**.

미국 영어에서는 약을 파는 상점을 흔히 drugstore라고 한다. □ 그녀는 약국에 들어가서 아스피린을 좀 샀다. pharmacy는 약국에서 특별히 처방약을 사는 곳을 지칭한다. pharmacy는 흔히 식료품 슈퍼마켓이나 할인점과 같이 주로 다른 상품을 파는 상점 안에 있다. 영국에서 drugstore와 가장 비슷한 것은 chemist's이다.

phase ◆◇◇ /feɪz/ (**phases, phasing, phased**) ▣ N-COUNT A **phase** is a particular stage in a process or in the gradual development of something. □ *This autumn, 6000 residents will participate in the first phase of the project.* □ *The crisis is entering a crucial, critical phase.* ▣ V-T If an action or change **is phased over** a period of time, it is done in stages. [usu passive] □ *The redundancies will be phased over two years.*

▣ 가산명사 단계, 국면 □ 올 가을, 6천 명의 거주자들이 그 계획의 첫 번째 단계에 참여할 것이다. □ 위기가 결정적이고 중대한 국면에 접어들고 있다. ▣ 타동사 단계적으로 실행되다 □ 정리해고는 2년에 걸쳐 단계적으로 이루어질 것이다.

Thesaurus

phase의 참조어

N.   chapter, period, point, stage, time ▣

▶phase in PHRASAL VERB If a new way of doing something **is phased in**, it is introduced gradually. ❑ *The Health Secretary told Parliament that the reforms would be phased in over three years.*

구동사 단계적으로 도입되다 ❑ 개혁은 3년간에 걸쳐 단계적으로 도입될 것이라고 보건부 장관이 의회에 말했다.

▶phase out PHRASAL VERB If something **is phased out**, people gradually stop using it. ❑ *They said the present system of military conscription should be phased out.*

구동사 단계적으로 폐지되다 ❑ 그들은 현재의 징병 제도가 단계적으로 폐지되어야 한다고 말했다.

Ph.D. /ˌpiː eɪtʃ ˈdiː/ (**Ph.D.s**) also PhD **1** N-COUNT A **Ph.D.** is a degree awarded to people who have done advanced research into a particular subject. **Ph.D.** is an abbreviation for "Doctor of Philosophy." ❑ *He is more highly educated, with a Ph.D. in Chemistry.* **2 Ph.D.** is written after someone's name to indicate that they have a Ph.D. ❑ *...R.D. Combes, Ph.D.*

1 가산명사 박사 학위 ❑ 그는 더 많은 고등 교육을 받았고, 화학 박사 학위를 가지고 있다. **2** 박사 (학위 소지자) ❑ 알 디 콤스 박사

pheas|ant /ˈfɛzᵊnt/ (**pheasants**)

Pheasant can also be used as the plural form.

pheasant도 복수형으로 쓰일 수 있다.

N-COUNT A **pheasant** is a bird with a long tail. Pheasants are often shot as a sport and then eaten. ● N-UNCOUNT **Pheasant** is the flesh of this bird eaten as food. ❑ *...roast pheasant.*

가산명사 꿩 ● 불가산명사 꿩고기 ❑ 구운 꿩고기

phe|nom|enal /fɪˈnɒmɪnᵊl/ ADJ Something that is **phenomenal** is so great or good that it is very unusual indeed. [EMPHASIS] ❑ *Exports of Australian wine are growing at a phenomenal rate.* ● **phe|nom|enal|ly** ADV ❑ *Scots-born Annie, 37, has recently re-launched her phenomenally successful singing career.*

형용사 경이적인, 굉장한 [강조] ❑ 호주산 와인 수출이 경이적인 속도로 증가하고 있다. ● 굉장히 부사 ❑ 스코틀랜드 태생으로 서른일곱 살인 애니는 최근 들어 굉장히 성공적인 가수 활동을 재개했다.

phe|nom|enon /fɪˈnɒmɪnɒn, BRIT fɪˈnɒmɪnən/ (**phenomena**) N-COUNT A **phenomenon** is something that is observed to happen or exist. [FORMAL] ❑ *...scientific explanations of natural phenomena.*

가산명사 현상 [격식체] ❑ 자연현상에 대한 과학적 설명

phi|loso|pher /fɪˈlɒsəfər/ (**philosophers**) **1** N-COUNT A **philosopher** is a person who studies or writes about philosophy. ❑ *...the Greek philosopher Plato.* **2** N-COUNT If you refer to someone as a **philosopher**, you mean that they think deeply and seriously about life and other basic matters. ❑ *Cus was something of a philosopher.* →see **philosophy**

1 가산명사 철학자 ❑ 그리스 철학자 플라톤 **2** 가산명사 현자, 철학자 ❑ 커스는 일종의 철학자 같은 사람이었다.

philo|sophi|cal /ˌfɪləˈsɒfɪkᵊl/ **1** ADJ **Philosophical** means concerned with or relating to philosophy. ❑ *He was more accustomed to cocktail party chatter than to political or philosophical discussions.* ● **philo|sophi|cal|ly** /ˌfɪləˈsɒfɪkli/ ADV ❑ *Wiggins says he's not a coward, but that he's philosophically opposed to war.* **2** ADJ Someone who is **philosophical** does not get upset when disappointing or disturbing things happen. [APPROVAL] ❑ *Lewis has grown philosophical about life.* ● **philo|sophi|cal|ly** ADV [ADV after v] ❑ *She says philosophically: "It could have been far worse."*

1 형용사 철학의, 철학적인 ❑ 그는 정치적이거나 철학적인 토론보다는 칵테일 파티에서 지껄이는 수다에 더 익숙했다. ● 철학적으로 부사 ❑ 자신은 겁쟁이가 아니지만, 철학적으로 전쟁에 반대한다고 위긴스는 말한다. **2** 형용사 달관한 [마음에 둠] ❑ 루이스는 삶에 달관해 갔다. ● 달관하여 부사 ❑ 그녀는 달관한 듯이 말한다. "더 나빠질 수도 있었지."

phi|loso|phy ♦♢♢ /fɪˈlɒsəfi/ (**philosophies**) **1** N-UNCOUNT **Philosophy** is the study or creation of theories about basic things such as the nature of existence, knowledge, and thought, or about how people should live. ❑ *He studied philosophy and psychology at Cambridge.* **2** N-COUNT A **philosophy** is a particular set of ideas that a philosopher has. ❑ *...the philosophies of Socrates, Plato, and Aristotle.* **3** N-COUNT A **philosophy** is a particular theory that someone has about how to live or how to deal with a particular situation. ❑ *The best philosophy is to change your food habits to a low-sugar diet.* →see Word Web: **philosophy**

1 불가산명사 철학 ❑ 그는 케임브리지에서 철학과 심리학을 공부했다. **2** 가산명사 철학 ❑ 소크라테스와 플라톤, 그리고 아리스토텔레스 철학 **3** 가산명사 인생철학, 처세법 ❑ 최선의 방법은 식습관을 저당분 식이 요법으로 바꾸는 것이다.

Thesaurus   *philosophy*의 참조어

N.   attitude, outlook, reasoning **3**

---

pho|bia /ˈfoʊbiə/ (**phobias**) N-COUNT A **phobia** is a very strong irrational fear or hatred of something. ❑ *The man had a phobia about flying.*

가산명사 공포증, 병적인 공포 ❑ 남자는 비행 공포증이 있었다.

phone ♦♦♢ /ˈfoʊn/ (**phones, phoning, phoned**) **1** N-SING The **phone** is an electrical system that you use to talk to someone else in another place, by dialing a number on a piece of equipment and speaking into it. [usu the N, also by N] ❑ *"I didn't tell you over the phone," she said. "I didn't know who might be listening."* ❑ *She looked forward to talking to her daughter by phone.* **2** N-COUNT The **phone** is the piece of equipment that you use when you dial someone's phone number and talk to them. ❑ *Two minutes later the phone rang.* →see also **cellular phone** **3** N-SING If you say that someone picks up or puts down **the phone**, you mean that they lift or replace the receiver. ❑ *She picked up the phone, and began to dial Maurice Campbell's number.* **4** V-T/V-I When you **phone** someone, you dial their phone number and speak to them by phone. ❑ *He'd phoned Laura to see if she was*

1 단수명사 전화 ❑ "전화상으로는 당신에게 이야기하지 않았어요. 누가 듣고 있을지도 모르잖아요." 그녀가 말했다. ❑ 그녀는 딸과 통화하기를 간절히 기다렸다. **2** 가산명사 전화기 ❑ 2분 후에 전화가 울렸다. **3** 단수명사 수화기 ❑ 그녀는 수화기를 들고 모리스 캠벨의 전화번호를 누르기 시작했다. **4** 타동사/자동사 전화하다 ❑ 그는 로라가 좀 나아졌는지 보려고 전화를 걸었다. **5** 구 통화 중인 ❑ 그녀는 항상 전화를 해서 내가 무엇을 하는지 알고 싶어 한다.

Word Web   philosophy

Philosophy helps us **understand** ourselves and the purpose of our lives. **Philosophers** have studied the same **issues** for thousands of years. The Chinese philosopher Confucius* wrote about personal and **political morals**. He taught that people should love others and honor their parents. They should do what is right, not what is best for themselves. He thought that a ruler who had to use force had already failed as a ruler. The Greek philosopher Plato* wrote about politics and science. Later, Aristotle* outlined a system of **logic** and **reasoning**. He wanted to be absolutely sure what is true and what isn't.

Confucius (551-479 BC)
Plato (427-347 BC)
Aristotle (384-322 BC)

Plato

Aristotle

Confucius

better. **5** PHRASE If you say that someone is **on the phone**, you mean that they are speaking to someone else by phone. ❑ *She's always on the phone, wanting to know what I've been up to.*
→see **office**

▶**phone in** **1** PHRASAL VERB If you **phone in** to a radio or television show, you telephone the show in order to give your opinion on a matter that the show has raised. ❑ *Listeners have been invited to phone in to pick the winner.* **2** PHRASAL VERB If you **phone in** to a place, you make a telephone call to that place. ❑ *He has phoned in to say he is thinking over his options.* **3** PHRASAL VERB If you **phone in** an order for something, you place the order by telephone. ❑ *Just phone in your order three or more days prior to departure.* **4** PHRASE If you **phone in sick**, you telephone your workplace to say that you will not come to work because you are ill. ❑ *On Monday I was still upset and I phoned in sick to work.*

▶**phone up** PHRASAL VERB When you **phone** someone **up**, you dial their phone number and speak to them by phone. ❑ *Phone him up and tell him to come and have dinner with you one night.*

phone book (**phone books**) N-COUNT A **phone book** is a book that contains an alphabetical list of the names, addresses, and telephone numbers of the people and businesses in a town or area.

phone booth (**phone booths**) **1** N-COUNT A **phone booth** is a place in a station, hotel, or other public building where there is a public telephone. **2** N-COUNT A **phone booth** is a small shelter in the street in which there is a public telephone. [AM; BRIT **phone box**]

phone box (**phone boxes**) N-COUNT A **phone box** is the same as a **phone booth** [BRIT]

phone call (**phone calls**) N-COUNT If you make a **phone call**, you dial someone's phone number and speak to them by phone. ❑ *Wait there for a minute. I have to make a phone call.*

phone|card /foʊnkɑrd/ (**phonecards**) also **phone card** N-COUNT A **phonecard** is a plastic card that you can use instead of money to pay for telephone calls in some public telephones.

phone-in (**phone-ins**) N-COUNT A **phone-in** is a program on radio or television in which people telephone with questions or opinions and their calls are broadcast. [mainly BRIT; AM usually **call-in**] ❑ *She took part in a BBC radio phone-in programme.*

pho|ney /foʊni/ also **phony** ADJ If you describe something as **phoney**, you disapprove of it because it is false rather than genuine. [INFORMAL, DISAPPROVAL] ❑ *He'd telephoned with some phoney excuse she didn't believe for a minute.* ❑ *He didn't really have that moustache. It was phoney.*

phos|phate /fɒsfeɪt/ (**phosphates**) N-MASS A **phosphate** is a chemical compound that contains phosphorus. Phosphates are often used in fertilizers.

pho|to ♦♦♦ /foʊtoʊ/ (**photos**) N-COUNT A **photo** is the same as a **photograph**. ❑ *We must take a photo!* →see **photography**

photo|copi|er /foʊtəkɒpiər/ (**photocopiers**) N-COUNT A **photocopier** is a machine which quickly copies documents onto paper by photographing them. →see **copy**

photo|copy /foʊtəkɒpi/ (**photocopies, photocopying, photocopied**) **1** N-COUNT A **photocopy** is a copy of a document made using a photocopier. ❑ *He was shown a photocopy of the certificate.* **2** V-T If you **photocopy** a document, you make a copy of it using a photocopier. ❑ *Staff photocopied the cheque before cashing it.*

photo|graph ♦♦◊ /foʊtəɡræf/ (**photographs, photographing, photographed**) **1** N-COUNT A **photograph** is a picture that is made using a camera. ❑ *He wants to take some photographs of the house.* **2** V-T When you **photograph** someone or something, you use a camera to obtain a picture of them. ❑ *She photographed the children.* ❑ *I hate being photographed.*

pho|tog|ra|pher ♦♦◊ /fətɒɡrəfər/ (**photographers**) N-COUNT A **photographer** is someone who takes photographs as a job or hobby. ❑ *...a professional photographer.* ❑ *...a keen amateur photographer.* →see **photography**

photo|graph|ic /foʊtəɡræfɪk/ **1** ADJ **Photographic** means connected with photographs or photography. ❑ *...photographic equipment.* **2** ADJ If you have a **photographic memory**, you are able to remember things in great detail after you have seen them. ❑ *He had a photographic memory for maps.*

pho|tog|ra|phy /fətɒɡrəfi/ N-UNCOUNT **Photography** is the skill, job, or process of producing photographs. ❑ *Photography is one of her hobbies.*
→see Word Web: **photography**

phras|al verb /freɪzəl vɜrb/ (**phrasal verbs**) N-COUNT A **phrasal verb** is a combination of a verb and an adverb or preposition, for example "shut up" or "look after," which together have a particular meaning.

phrase ♦◊◊ /freɪz/ (**phrases, phrasing, phrased**) **1** N-COUNT A **phrase** is a short group of words that people often use as a way of saying something. The meaning of a phrase is often not obvious from the meaning of the individual words in it. ❑ *He used a phrase I hate: "You have to be cruel to be kind."* **2** N-COUNT A **phrase** is a small group of words which forms a unit, either on its own or within a sentence. ❑ *A writer spends many hours going over and over a scene – changing a phrase here, a word there.* **3** V-T If you **phrase** something in a particular way, you express it in words in that way. ❑ *I would have phrased it quite differently.* ❑ *The speech was carefully phrased.* **4** PHRASE If someone has a particular **turn of phrase**, they have a particular way of expressing themselves in words. ❑ *...Schwarzkopf's distinctive turn of phrase.* **to coin a phrase** →see **coin**

1 구동사 방송국에 전화하다 ❑ 청취자들이 전화를 걸어 승자를 고를 수 있도록 해 왔다. **2** 구동사 전화하다 ❑ 그가 전화를 걸어 여러 대안을 두고 생각 중이라고 말했다. **3** 구동사 전화로 주문을 하다 ❑ 출발 전에 3일 이상 여유를 두고 전화로 주문하시면 됩니다. **4** 구 전화로 병가를 내다 ❑ 월요일까지도 마음이 심란하여 나는 아파서 출근 못 한다고 전화를 했다.

구동사 ~에게 전화를 걸다 ❑ 그에게 전화해서 언제 한번 밤에 놀러 와 너랑 같이 저녁 먹자고 해.

가산명사 전화번호부

1 가산명사 공중전화실 **2** 가산명사 공중전화실 [미국영어; 영국영어 phone box]

가산명사 공중전화실 [영국영어]

가산명사 전화 ❑ 잠깐만 거기서 기다리세요. 전화 한 통 해야 돼요.

가산명사 전화 카드

가산명사 청취자 전화 참여 프로그램, 시청자 전화 참여 프로그램 [주로 영국영어; 미국영어 대개 call-in] ❑ 그녀는 비비시 라디오 청취자 전화 참여 프로그램에 참가했다.

형용사 가짜의, 허위의 [비격식체, 탐탁찮음] ❑ 그가 전화해서 거짓 변명을 늘어놓았지만 그녀는 하나도 믿지 않았다. ❑ 사실 그 콧수염은 그 사람 게 아니었어. 가짜였다고.

물질명사 인산, 인산비료

가산명사 사진 ❑ 우리 사진 찍어야 해요!

가산명사 복사기

1 가산명사 복사본 ❑ 그에게 증명서 복사본을 보여 주었다. **2** 타동사 사진 복사기로 복사하다 ❑ 직원이 수표를 현금으로 바꾸기 전에 사진 복사기로 복사를 했다.

1 가산명사 사진 ❑ 그는 집 사진을 몇 장 찍고 싶어 한다. **2** 타동사 사진을 찍다 ❑ 그녀는 아이들의 사진을 찍었다. ❑ 나는 사진 찍는 것을 싫어한다.

가산명사 사진기사, 사진작가 ❑ 전문 사진작가 ❑ 열렬한 아마추어 사진작가

1 형용사 사진의 ❑ 사진 장비 **2** 형용사 사진처럼 정확한 ❑ 그는 지도를 사진처럼 정확히 기억했다.

불가산명사 사진 ❑ 사진은 그녀의 취미 중의 하나이다.

가산명사 구동사

1 가산명사 경구, 명언 ❑ 그는 내가 싫어하는 경구를 사용했다. "상대방을 위해 모질게 굴어야 할 때도 있다." **2** 가산명사 구 ❑ 작가는 여기 저기 구문과 단어를 바꿔 가며 한 장면을 여러 번 검토하는 데 많은 시간을 보낸다. **3** 타동사 표현하다, 말로 바꾸다 ❑ 나라면 아주 다르게 표현했을 거야. ❑ 말을 신중하게 골라 쓴 연설이었다. **4** 구 어투, 말씨 ❑ 슈바르츠코프의 독특한 어투

a
b
c
d
e
f
g
h
i
j
k
l
m
n
o
p
q
r
s
t
u
v
w
x
y
z

Word Web — photography

It's easy to **take** a **picture** with a digital **camera**. You just look through the viewfinder and push the **shutter button**. But professional **photographers** need to produce high quality **photos**. So their job is more difficult. First they decide on the correct **film** for the job and **load** the camera. Then they check the **lighting** and carefully **focus** the camera. They usually take several **shots**, one after another. Then it's time to **develop** the film and make **prints**. Sometimes a photographer will **crop** a photo or **enlarge** it to create a more striking **image**.

Word Link — physi ≈ of nature : physics, physical, physician

physi|cal ♦♦◇ /fízɪkᵊl/ (physicals) **1** ADJ **Physical** qualities, actions, or things are connected with a person's body, rather than with their mind. ❑ ...*the physical and mental problems caused by the illness.* ❑ *Physical activity promotes good health.* ● **physi|cal|ly** ADV ❑ *You may be physically and mentally exhausted after a long flight.* **2** ADJ **Physical** things are real things that can be touched and seen, rather than ideas or spoken words. ❑ *Physical and ideological barriers had come down in Eastern Europe.* ❑ ...*physical evidence to support the story.* ● **physi|cal|ly** ADV ❑ ...*physically cut off from every other country.* **3** ADJ **Physical** means relating to the structure, size, or shape of something that can be touched and seen. [ADJ n] ❑ ...*the physical characteristics of the terrain.* **4** ADJ **Physical** means connected with physics or the laws of physics. [ADJ n] ❑ ...*the physical laws of combustion and thermodynamics.* **5** ADJ Someone who is **physical** touches people a lot, either in an affectionate way or in a rough way. ❑ *We decided that in the game we would be physical and aggressive.* **6** ADJ **Physical** is used in expressions such as **physical love** and **physical relationships** to refer to sexual relationships between people. [ADJ n] ❑ *It had been years since they had shared any meaningful form of physical relationship.* **7** N-COUNT A **physical** is a medical examination, done in order to see if someone is fit and well enough to do a particular job or to join the army. ❑ *Bob failed his physical.*

Thesaurus — physical의 참조어

ADJ.   bodily, earthly, mortal; (ant.) mental **1**
     concrete, natural, real, solid, tangible, visible; (ant.) intangible, theoretical **2**

Word Link — ician ≈ person who works at : musician, pediatrician, physician

phy|si|cian /fɪzɪ́ʃᵊn/ (physicians) N-COUNT In formal American English or old-fashioned British English, a **physician** is a doctor. ❑ ...*Queen Victoria's personal physician.* →see **diagnosis, hospital, medicine**

physi|cist /fɪ́zɪsɪst/ (physicists) N-COUNT A **physicist** is a person who does research connected with physics or who studies physics. ❑ ...*a nuclear physicist.*

Word Link — ics ≈ system, knowledge : economics, electronics, physics

phys|ics /fɪ́zɪks/ N-UNCOUNT **Physics** is the scientific study of forces such as heat, light, sound, pressure, gravity, and electricity, and the way that they affect objects. ❑ ...*the laws of physics.*

physi|ol|ogy /fɪziɒ́lədʒi/ **1** N-UNCOUNT **Physiology** is the scientific study of how people's and animals' bodies function, and of how plants function. ❑ ...*the Nobel Prize for Medicine and Physiology.* **2** N-UNCOUNT The **physiology** of a human or animal's body or of a plant is the way that it functions. ❑ ...*the physiology of respiration.* ● **physio|logi|cal** /fɪziəlɒ́dʒɪkᵊl/ ADJ ❑ ...*the physiological effects of stress.*

physio|thera|pist /fɪ̀ziouθérəpɪst/ (physiotherapists) N-COUNT A **physiotherapist** is a person who treats people using physiotherapy.

physio|thera|py /fɪ̀ziouθérəpi/ N-UNCOUNT **Physiotherapy** is medical treatment for problems of the joints, muscles, or nerves, which involves doing exercises or having part of your body massaged or warmed. ❑ *He'll need intensive physiotherapy.*

phy|sique /fɪzíːk/ (physiques) N-COUNT Someone's **physique** is the shape and size of their body. ❑ *He has the physique and energy of a man half his age.*

pia|nist /piǽnɪst, píːənɪst, BRIT piːǽnɪst/ (pianists) N-COUNT A **pianist** is a person who plays the piano. ❑ *She was an accomplished pianist, a superb swimmer and a gifted artist.*

pi|ano /piǽnou, pyǽnou/ (pianos) N-VAR A **piano** is a large musical instrument with a row of black and white keys. When you press these keys with your fingers, little hammers hit wire strings inside the piano which vibrate to produce musical notes. ❑ *I taught myself how to play the piano.* ❑ *He started piano lessons at the age of 7.* →see **keyboard, music**

pick ♦♦◇ /pík/ (picks, picking, picked) **1** V-T If you **pick** a particular person or thing, you choose that one. ❑ *Mr. Nowell had picked ten people to interview for six sales jobs in London.* **2** N-SING You can refer to the best things or people in a

---

1 형용사 육체의, 신체의 ❑ 질병으로 인한 육체적 정신적 문제들 ❑ 신체 활동은 건강을 증진시킨다. ● 육체적으로, 신체적으로 부사 ❑ 당신은 장거리 비행 후에 육체적 정신적으로 많이 지칠지도 모른다. **2** 형용사 물리적인, 물질적인 ❑ 동유럽에서 물리적 이념적 장벽이 무너졌다. ❑ 이야기를 뒷받침할 수 있는 물증 ● 물리적으로, 물질적으로 부사 ❑ 다른 모든 국가로부터 물리적으로 떨어진 **3** 형용사 물리적인 ❑ 지형의 물리적인 특징 **4** 형용사 물리학의, 물리의 ❑ 연소와 열역학에 관한 물리학 법칙 **5** 형용사 신체 접촉이 많은 ❑ 우리는 게임 중에 몸을 많이 부딪치고 공격적으로 나가기로 했다. **6** 형용사 육체적인, 성적인 ❑ 그들이 의미심장한 육체적 관계를 나눈 지 몇 년이 지난 상태였다. **7** 가산명사 신체검사 ❑ 밥은 신체검사에서 탈락하였다.

가산명사 의사 ❑ 빅토리아 여왕의 주치의

가산명사 물리학자 ❑ 핵물리학자

불가산명사 물리학 ❑ 물리학 법칙

1 불가산명사 생리학 ❑ 의학 및 생리학 부문 노벨상 **2** 불가산명사 생리, 생리 기능 ❑ 호흡작용 ● 생리적인, 생리학의 형용사 ❑ 스트레스의 생리적 영향

가산명사 물리 치료사

불가산명사 물리 치료 ❑ 그는 물리 치료를 집중적으로 받아야 할 것이다.

가산명사 체격 ❑ 그는 체격과 힘이 자기 나이 반밖에 안 되는 남자와 같다.

가산명사 피아니스트 ❑ 그녀는 피아노를 잘 치고 수영 실력도 뛰어나며 미술에도 재능이 있었다.

가산명사 또는 불가산명사 피아노 ❑ 나는 피아노를 독학으로 배웠다. ❑ 그는 7살에 피아노 레슨을 시작했다.

1 타동사 고르다 ❑ 노웰 씨가 런던 영업 사원 6명을 뽑기 위해 면접 대상으로 10명을 골랐다. **2** 단수명사 최고의 것; 최고의 사람 ❑ 여기 이 소년들은 국내

particular group as **the pick of** that group. ❑ *The boys here are the pick of the under-15 cricketers in the country.* ❸ V-T When you **pick** flowers, fruit, or leaves, you break them off the plant or tree and collect them. ❑ *She used to pick flowers in the Cromwell Road.* ❹ V-T If you **pick** something from a place, you remove it from there with your fingers or your hand. ❑ *He picked the napkin from his lap and placed it alongside his plate.* ❺ V-T If you **pick** your **nose** or **teeth**, you remove substances from inside your nose or between your teeth. ❑ *Edgar, don't pick your nose, dear.* ❻ V-T If you **pick** a fight or quarrel **with** someone, you deliberately cause one. ❑ *He picked a fight with a waiter and landed in jail.* ❼ V-T If someone such as a thief **picks** a lock, they open it without a key, for example by using a piece of wire. ❑ *He picked each lock deftly, and rifled the papers within each drawer.* ❽ N-COUNT A **pick** is the same as a **pickax**. ❾ PHRASE If you are told to **take** your **pick**, you can choose any one that you like from a group of things. ❑ *Accountants can take their pick of company cars.* ❿ to **pick holes in** something →see hole. to **pick** someone's **pocket** →see pocket

Thesaurus	*pick*의 참조어
v.	choose, decide on, elect, select ❶ collect, gather, harvest, pull ❸

▶**pick on** PHRASAL VERB If someone **picks on** you, they repeatedly criticize you unfairly or treat you unkindly. [INFORMAL] ❑ *Bullies pick on younger children.*

▶**pick out** ❶ PHRASAL VERB If you **pick out** someone or something, you recognize them when it is difficult to see them, for example because they are among a large group. ❑ *The detective-constable picked out the words with difficulty.* ❷ PHRASAL VERB If you **pick out** someone or something, you choose them from a group of people or things. ❑ *I have been picked out to represent the whole team.*

▶**pick up** ❶ PHRASAL VERB When you **pick** something **up**, you lift it up. ❑ *He picked his cap up from the floor and stuck it back on his head.* ❷ PHRASAL VERB When you **pick yourself up** after you have fallen or been knocked down, you stand up rather slowly. ❑ *Anthony picked himself up and set off along the track.* ❸ PHRASAL VERB When you **pick up** someone or something that is waiting to be collected, you go to the place where they are and take them away, often in a car. ❑ *She was going over to her parents' house to pick up some clean clothes for Owen.* ❹ PHRASAL VERB If someone **is picked up** by the police, they are arrested and taken to a police station. ❑ *Rawlings had been picked up by police at his office.* ❺ PHRASAL VERB If you **pick up** something such as a skill or an idea, you acquire it without effort over a period of time. [INFORMAL] ❑ *Where did you pick up your English?* ❻ PHRASAL VERB If you **pick up** an illness, you get it from somewhere or something. ❑ *They've picked up a really nasty infection from something they've eaten.* ❼ PHRASAL VERB If a piece of equipment, for example a radio or a microphone, **picks up** a signal or sound, it receives it or detects it. ❑ *We can pick up Italian television.* ❽ PHRASAL VERB If you **pick up** something, such as a feature or a pattern, you discover or identify it. ❑ *Consumers in Europe are slow to pick up trends in the use of information technology.* ❾ PHRASAL VERB If someone **picks up** a point or topic that has already been mentioned, or if they **pick up on** it, they refer to it or develop it. ❑ *Can I just pick up that gentleman's point?* ❿ PHRASAL VERB If trade or the economy of a country **picks up**, it improves. ❑ *Industrial production is beginning to pick up.* ⓫ →see also **pick-up** ⓬ PHRASE When a vehicle **picks up** **speed**, it begins to move more quickly. ❑ *Brian started the engine and pulled away slowly, but picked up speed once he entered Oakwood Drive.*

pick|ax /pɪkæks/ (pickaxes) [BRIT, sometimes AM pickaxe] N-COUNT A **pickax** is a large tool consisting of a curved, pointed piece of metal with a long handle joined to the middle. Pickaxes are used for breaking up rocks or the ground.

pick|et /pɪkɪt/ (pickets, picketing, picketed) ❶ V-T/V-I When a group of people, usually labor union members, **picket** a place of work, they stand outside it in order to protest about something, to prevent people from going in, or to persuade the workers to join a strike. ❑ *The miners went on strike and picketed the power stations.* ● N-COUNT **Picket** is also a noun. ❑ *...forty demonstrators who have set up a twenty-four-hour picket.* ❷ N-COUNT **Pickets** are people who are picketing a place of work. ❑ *The strikers agreed to remove their pickets and hold talks with the government.*

pick|et line (picket lines) N-COUNT A **picket line** is a group of pickets outside a place of work. ❑ *No one tried to cross the picket lines.*

pick|le /pɪkᵊl/ (pickles, pickling, pickled) ❶ N-PLURAL **Pickles** are vegetables or fruit, sometimes cut into pieces, which have been kept in vinegar or salt water for a long time so that they have a strong, sharp taste. ❑ *...a bowl of sliced pickles in lemon juice.* ❷ N-MASS **Pickle** is a cold spicy sauce with pieces of vegetables and fruit in it. ❑ *...jars of pickle.* ❸ V-T When you **pickle** food, you keep it in vinegar or salt water so that it does not go bad and it develops a strong, sharp taste. ❑ *Select your favorite fruit or veg and pickle them while they are still fresh.*

pick|led /pɪkᵊld/ ADJ **Pickled** food, such as vegetables, fruit, and fish, has been kept in vinegar or salt water to preserve it. ❑ *...a jar of pickled fruit.*

pick|pocket /pɪkpɒkɪt/ (pickpockets) N-COUNT A **pickpocket** is a person who steals things from people's pockets or bags in public places. ❑ *Beware of pickpockets, especially when making a purchase.*

pick-up ◆◇◇ (pick-ups) also pickup ❶ N-COUNT A **pick-up** or a **pick-up truck** is a small truck with low sides that can be easily loaded and unloaded. ❷ N-SING A **pick-up in** trade or **in** a country's economy is an improvement in it. ❑ *...a pick-up in the housing market.* ❸ N-COUNT A **pick-up** takes place when someone picks

---

열다섯 살 이하 크리켓 선수 중 최고의 선수들이다. ❸ 타동사 깎다, 따다 ❑ 그녀는 크롬웰 로드에서 꽃을 꺾곤 했다. ❹ 타동사 집다, 들다 ❑ 그는 무릎에 있는 냅킨을 집어 접시 옆에 놓았다. ❺ 타동사 후비다, 쑤시다 ❑ 에드가, 코 좀 후비지 마세요. ❻ 타동사 ~에게 싸움을 걸다 ❑ 그는 웨이터에게 싸움을 걸어 감방 신세를 지게 되었다. ❼ 타동사 (몰래) 자물쇠를 따다 ❑ 그는 능숙한 솜씨로 하나하나 자물쇠를 따고 모든 서랍의 서류를 샅샅이 뒤졌다. ❽ 가산명사 곡괭이 ❾ 구 고르다 ❑ 회계사들은 회사차를 골라 탈 수 있다.

구동사 괴롭히다 [비격식체] ❑ 불량배들이 어린아이들을 괴롭힌다.

❶ 구동사 구별해 내다, 알아보다 ❑ 형사가 단어들을 겨우 알아볼 수 있었다. ❷ 구동사 뽑다 ❑ 팀 전체를 대표하는 사람으로 내가 뽑혔다.

❶ 구동사 집어 올리다, 들다 ❑ 그는 바닥에서 모자를 집어 올려 다시 머리에 눌러 썼다. ❷ 구동사 몸을 일으키다 ❑ 안토니가 몸을 일으켜 트랙을 따라 달리기 시작했다. ❸ 구동사 가지러 가다, 데리러 가다 ❑ 그녀는 오웬이 입을 깨끗한 옷을 가지러 부모님 집에 가던 중이었다. ❹ 구동사 연행되다 ❑ 롤링스가 자신의 사무실에서 경찰에 연행된 후였다. ❺ 구동사 익히다, 습득하다 [비격식체] ❑ 영어는 어디서 배웠어요? ❻ 구동사 걸리다 ❑ 그들은 음식을 잘못 먹어서 정말 지독한 전염병에 걸렸다. ❼ 구동사 수신하다, 포착하다 ❑ 우리는 이탈리아 텔레비전 전파를 잡을 수 있다. ❽ 구동사 발견하다, 파악하다 ❑ 유럽 소비자들은 정보 기술사용 유행 파악에 느리다. ❾ 구동사 언급하다 ❑ 제가 신사 분께서 언급하신 점에 대해 제가 잠깐 말씀드려도 될까요? ❿ 구동사 개선되다, 호전되다 ❑ 산업 생산이 호전되기 시작하고 있다. ⓬ 구 속력을 내다 ❑ 브라이언은 시동 걸고 차를 뺄 때에는 천천히 했지만, 일단 오크우드 드라이브에 들어서자 속력을 냈다.

[영국영어, 미국영어 가끔 pickaxe] 가산명사 곡괭이

❶ 타동사/자동사 피켓 농성을 벌이다 ❑ 광부들이 파업에 돌입해 발전소 근처에서 피켓 농성을 벌였다. ● 가산명사 피켓 농성 ❑ 24시간 피켓 농성에 돌입한 시위자 40명 ❷ 가산명사 피켓 농성 시위자 ❑ 파업자들이 피켓 농성을 철회하고 정부와 협상하기로 합의했다.

가산명사 피켓 농성 대열 ❑ 아무도 피켓 농성 대열을 뚫고 지나가려 하지 않았다.

❶ 복수명사 피클 ❑ 잘라서 레몬즙에 절인 피클 한 그릇 ❷ 물질명사 피클 소스 ❑ 여러 병의 피클 소스 ❸ 타동사 식초나 소금물에 절이다, 피클을 만들다 ❑ 가장 좋아하는 과일이나 야채를 고른 후 싱싱할 때 식초에 절이세요.

형용사 식초나 소금물에 절인 음식 ❑ 과일 피클 한 병

가산명사 소매치기 ❑ 특히 물건을 구입할 때 소매치기를 조심하세요.

❶ 가산명사 픽업트럭, 소형 트럭 ❷ 단수명사 호전 ❑ 주택 시장 호전 ❸ 가산명사 태우기; 싣기 ❑ 회사가 대부분의 도시에 집합 장소를 두고 있었다.

A

up a person or thing that is waiting to be collected. ❏ *The company had pick-up points in most cities.*

pic|nic /pɪ́knɪk/ (**picnics, picnicking, picnicked**) **1** N-COUNT When people have a **picnic**, they eat a meal out of doors, usually in a field or a forest, or at the beach. ❏ *We're going on a picnic tomorrow.* **2** V-I When people **picnic** somewhere, they have a picnic. ❏ *Afterwards, we picnicked on the riverbank.* →see **park**

B

pic|to|rial /pɪktɔ́riəl/ ADJ **Pictorial** means using or relating to pictures. ❏ *...a pictorial history of the Special Air Service.*

C

Word Link   pict ≈ painting : **depict, picture, picturesque**

pic|ture ♦♦◇ /pɪ́ktʃər/ (**pictures, picturing, pictured**) **1** N-COUNT A **picture** consists of lines and shapes which are drawn, painted, or printed on a surface and show a person, thing, or scene. ❏ *...drawing a small picture with colored chalks.* **2** N-COUNT A **picture** is a photograph. ❏ *The tourists have nothing to do but take pictures of each other.* **3** N-COUNT Television **pictures** are the scenes which you see on a television screen. ❏ *...heartrending television pictures of human suffering.* **4** V-T To **be pictured** somewhere, for example in a newspaper or magazine, means to appear in a photograph or picture. [usu passive] ❏ *The golfer is pictured on many of the front pages, kissing his trophy as he holds it aloft.* ❏ *...a woman who claimed she had been pictured dancing with a celebrity in Stringfellows nightclub.* **5** N-COUNT You can refer to a movie as a **picture**. ❏ *...a director of epic action pictures.* **6** N-PLURAL If you go to **the pictures**, you go to a movie theater to see a movie. [BRIT; AM **the movies**] ❏ *We're going to the pictures tonight.* **7** N-COUNT If you have a **picture** of something in your mind, you have a clear idea or memory of it in your mind as if you were actually seeing it. ❏ *We are just trying to get our picture of the whole afternoon straight.* **8** V-T If you **picture** something in your mind, you think of it and have such a clear memory or idea of it that you seem to be able to see it. ❏ *He pictured her with long black braided hair.* ❏ *He pictured Claire sitting out in the car, waiting for him.* **9** N-COUNT A **picture** of something is a description of it or an indication of what it is like. ❏ *I'll try and give you a better picture of what the boys do.* **10** N-SING When you refer to the **picture** in a particular place, you are referring to the situation there. ❏ *It's a similar picture across the border in Ethiopia.* **11** PHRASE If you **put** someone **in the picture**, you tell them about a situation which they need to know about. ❏ *Has Inspector Fayard put you in the picture?* →see **photography**

Thesaurus   *picture*의 참조어

N.   drawing, illustration, image, painting **1**
      photograph **2**
V.   envision, imagine, visualize **8**

Word Partnership   *picture*의 연어

ADJ. **pretty as a** picture **1**
      mental picture **6**
      clear picture **6** **8**
      accurate picture, **complete** picture, **different** picture,
      larger picture, **overall** picture, **vivid** picture, **whole** picture **6**-**9**
      the big picture **8**

pic|tur|esque /pɪ̀ktʃərɛ́sk/ ADJ A **picturesque** place is attractive and interesting, and has no ugly modern buildings. ❏ *Alte, in the hills northwest of Loule, is the Algarve's most picturesque village.* ● N-SING You can refer to picturesque things as **the picturesque**. ❏ *...lovers of the picturesque.*

pie /paɪ/ (**pies**) **1** N-VAR A **pie** consists of fruit, meat or vegetables baked in pastry. ❏ *...a slice of apple pie.* **2** to **eat humble pie** →see **humble** →see **dessert**

piece ♦♦◇ /piːs/ (**pieces, piecing, pieced**) **1** N-COUNT A **piece of** something is an amount of it that has been broken off, torn off, or cut off. ❏ *...a piece of cake.* ❏ *Cut the ham into pieces.* **2** N-COUNT A **piece** of an object is one of the individual parts or sections which it is made of, especially a part that can be removed. ❏ *...assembling objects out of standard pieces.* **3** N-COUNT A **piece of** land is an area of land. ❏ *People struggle to get the best piece of land.* **4** N-COUNT You can use **piece of** with many uncount nouns to refer to an individual thing of a particular kind. For example, you can refer to some advice as a **piece of advice**. ❏ *When I produced this piece of work, my lecturers were very critical.* ❏ *...an interesting piece of information.* **5** N-COUNT You can refer to an article in a newspaper or magazine, some music written by someone, a broadcast, or a play as a **piece**. ❏ *I disagree with Andrew Russell over his piece on British Rail.* ❏ *...a vaguely familiar orchestral piece.* **6** N-COUNT You can refer to a work of art as a **piece**. [FORMAL] ❏ *Each piece is unique, an exquisite painting of a real person, done on ivory.* **7** N-COUNT You can refer to specific coins as **pieces**. For example, a 10 cent **piece** is a coin that is worth 10 cents. ❏ *...lots of 10 cent, 20 cent and 50 cent pieces.* **8** N-COUNT The **pieces** which you use when you play a board game such as chess are the specially made objects which you move around on the board. ❏ *How many pieces does each player have in backgammon?* **9** PHRASE If you **give** someone **a piece of** your **mind**, you tell them very clearly that you think they have behaved badly. [INFORMAL] ❏ *How very thoughtless. I'll give him a piece of my mind.* **10** PHRASE If someone or something is still in **one piece** after a dangerous journey or experience, they are safe and not damaged or hurt. ❏ *...providing that my brother gets back alive and in one piece from his mission.* **11** PHRASE You use **to pieces** in expressions such as "smash to pieces," or "take something to pieces," when you are describing how something is broken or comes apart so that it is in separate pieces.

D

E

F

G

H

I

J

K

L

M

N

O

P

Q

R

S

T

U

V

W

X

Y

Z

1 가산명사 소풍, 야외에서의 간단한 식사 ❏ 우리 내일 소풍 가. **2** 자동사 소풍 하다, 야외에서 식사하다 ❏ 나중에 우리는 강둑에서 밥을 먹었어요.

형용사 그림의 ❏ 사진으로 보는 영국 공군특수부대의 역사

1 가산명사 그림 ❏ 색깔 분필로 작은 그림을 그리기 **2** 가산명사 사진 ❏ 여행객들은 서로 사진 찍어 주는 일밖에 할 일이 없다. **3** 가산명사 장면 ❏ 인간의 고통을 담은 가슴 아픈 텔레비전 장면들 **4** 타동사 사진이나 그림에 등장하다 ❏ 그 골퍼가 높이 든 트로피에 키스하는 장면이 여러 신문의 전면 사진에 등장한다. ❏ 스트링펠로스 나이트클럽에서 자신이 유명인사와 함께 춤추는 모습이 사진에 찍혔다고 주장하던 여성 **5** 가산명사 영화 ❏ 장편 액션 영화감독 **6** 복수명사 영화 관람 [영국영어; 미국영어 the movies] ❏ 우리 오늘 밤 영화 보러 갈 거야. **7** 가산명사 영상, 기억 ❏ 우리는 단지 그날 오후 일을 제대로 기억하려는 것뿐이다. **8** 타동사 상상하다, 마음속에 그리다 ❏ 그는 길고 검은 머리를 땋아 내린 그녀의 모습을 그려 보았다. ❏ 그는 클레어가 차에 앉아 그를 기다리는 모습을 상상해 보았다. **9** 가산명사 묘사 ❏ 제가 그 남자 아이들이 하는 일을 더 잘 설명해 볼게요. **10** 단수명사 상황 ❏ 국경을 넘어 에티오피아에서도 상황은 비슷하다. **11** 구 상황 설명을 하다 ❏ 파야르 수사관이 당신에게 상황 설명을 했나요?

형용사 그림 같은 ❏ 로우레이 서북쪽 구릉지대에 위치한 알테는 알가르베에서 가장 그림 같은 마을이다. ● 단수명사 그림 같은 것 ❏ 그림 같은 것을 좋아하는 사람들

1 가산명사 또는 불가산명사 파이 ❏ 사과 파이 한 조각

1 가산명사 조각 ❏ 케이크 한 조각 ❏ 햄을 조각조각 자르세요. **2** 가산명사 부품, 부분 ❏ 표준 부품으로 물건을 조립하기 **3** 가산명사 조각 ❏ 사람들이 가장 좋은 땅을 얻기 위해 몸부림친다. **4** 가산명사 샌 없는 명사의 개별성을 부여할 때 사용 ❏ 제가 이 연구를 발표할 때 교수님들께서 많이 비판하셨어요. **5** 가산명사 기사 하나나 음악 한 곡을 말할 때 사용 ❏ 저는 영국 철도에 관해 앤드류 러셀이 쓴 글과 생각이 다릅니다. ❏ 어렴풋이 들어 본 듯한 관현악곡 **6** 가산명사 작품 [격식체] ❏ 각각의 작품은 상아에 실제 인물을 정교하게 그린 독특한 작품이다. **7** 가산명사 동전 ❏ 수많은 10센트, 20센트, 50센트짜리 동전들 **8** 가산명사 말 ❏ 백개먼을 할 때 한 사람당 말이 몇 개씩이죠? **9** 구 솔직한 심정; 싫은 소리 [비격식체] ❏ 이렇게 생각이 없을 수가. 내가 그 사람한테 솔직히 말해야겠어. **10** 구 틈 없이, 무사히 ❏ 오빠가 임무를 마치고 무사히 살아서 돌아온다면 **11** 구 산산조각 **12** 구 신경 쇠약이 되다, 자포자기하다 [비격식체] ❏ 그녀는 강한 여자다. 하지만 아니가 죽었을 때엔 거의 제정신이 아니었다.

12 PHRASE If you **go to pieces**, you are so upset or nervous that you lose control of yourself and cannot do what you should do. [INFORMAL] ❑ *She's a strong woman, but she nearly went to pieces when Arnie died.* **13** **a piece of the action** →see action. **bits and pieces** →see bit →see chess

N.   bit, fragment, part, portion, section, segment; (ant.) whole **1 2 3**
arrangement, article, creation, production, work **5 6**

▶**piece together** **1** PHRASAL VERB If you **piece together** the truth about something, you gradually discover it. ❑ *They've pieced together his movements for the last few days before his death.* ❑ *In the following days, Francis was able to piece together what had happened.* **2** PHRASAL VERB If you **piece** something **together**, you gradually make it by joining several things or parts together. ❑ *This process is akin to piecing together a jigsaw puzzle.*

piece|meal /pismil/ ADJ If you describe a change or process as **piecemeal**, you disapprove of it because it happens gradually, usually at irregular intervals, and is probably not satisfactory. [DISAPPROVAL] ❑ *Instead of the government's piecemeal approach, what is needed is a radical shake-up of 16-19 education.* ● ADV **Piecemeal** is also an adverb. [ADV after v] ❑ *The government plans to sell the railways piecemeal to the private sector.*

pie chart (pie charts) N-COUNT A **pie chart** is a circle divided into sections to show the relative proportions of a set of things.

pier /pɪər/ (piers) N-COUNT A **pier** is a platform sticking out into water, usually the sea, which people walk along or use when getting onto or off boats. ❑ *...Brighton Pier.*

pierce /pɪərs/ (pierces, piercing, pierced) **1** V-T If a sharp object **pierces** something, or if you **pierce** something **with** a sharp object, the object goes into it and makes a hole in it. ❑ *One bullet pierced the left side of his chest.* **2** V-T If you have your ears or some other part of your body **pierced**, you have a small hole made through them so that you can wear a piece of jewelry in them. ❑ *I'm having my ears pierced on Saturday.*

pierc|ing /pɪərsɪŋ/ **1** ADJ A **piercing** sound or voice is high-pitched and very sharp and clear in an unpleasant way. ❑ *A piercing scream split the air.* **2** ADJ If someone has **piercing** eyes or a **piercing** stare, they seem to look at you very intensely. [WRITTEN] ❑ *...his sandy blond hair and piercing blue eyes.* **3** ADJ A **piercing** wind makes you feel very cold. ❑ *Warm clothing is recommended as the wind can be piercing.*

piety /paɪɪti/ N-UNCOUNT **Piety** is strong religious belief, or behavior that is religious or morally correct. ❑ *Although only sporadically exposed to the teachings of the Church, her piety was marked from a very young age.*

pig /pɪg/ (pigs) **1** N-COUNT A **pig** is a pink or black animal with short legs and not much hair on its skin. Pigs are often kept on farms for their meat, which is called pork, ham, or bacon. ❑ *...the grunting of the pigs.* →see also **guinea pig** **2** N-COUNT If you call someone a **pig**, you think that they are unpleasant in some way, especially that they are greedy or unkind. [INFORMAL, DISAPPROVAL] ❑ *These guys destroyed the company. They're all a bunch of greedy pigs.* **3** PHRASE If you say "**pigs might fly**" after someone has said that something might happen, you are emphasizing that you think it is very unlikely. [HUMOROUS, INFORMAL, EMPHASIS] ❑ *"There's a chance he won't get involved in this, of course."* — *"And pigs might fly."* →see **meat**

pi|geon /pɪdʒɪn/ (pigeons) N-COUNT A **pigeon** is a bird, usually gray in color, which has a fat body. Pigeons often live in cities and towns.

pigeon|hole /pɪdʒɪnhoʊl/ (pigeonholes, pigeonholing, pigeonholed) also **pigeon-hole** **1** N-COUNT A **pigeonhole** is one of the sections in a frame on a wall where letters and messages can be left for someone, or one of the sections in a writing desk where you can keep documents. **2** V-T To **pigeonhole** someone or something means to decide that they belong to a particular class or category, often without considering all their qualities or characteristics. ❑ *He felt they had pigeonholed him.*

pig|ment /pɪgmənt/ (pigments) N-MASS A **pigment** is a substance that gives something a particular color. [FORMAL] ❑ *The Romans used natural pigments on their fabrics and walls.*

pike /paɪk/

> The plural can be either **pike** or **pikes.**

N-VAR A **pike** is a large fish that lives in rivers and lakes and eats other fish. ● N-UNCOUNT **Pike** is this fish eaten as food. ❑ *...a mousse of pike.*

pile ◆◇◇ /paɪl/ (piles, piling, piled) **1** N-COUNT A **pile of** things is a mass of them that is high in the middle and has sloping sides. ❑ *...a pile of sand.* ❑ *...a little pile of crumbs.* **2** N-COUNT A **pile of** things is a quantity of things that have been put neatly somewhere so that each thing is on top of the one below. ❑ *...a pile of boxes.* ❑ *We sat in Sam's study, among the piles of books.*

> A **pile** of things can be tidy or untidy. ❑ *...a neat pile of clothes.* A **heap** is usually untidy, and often has the shape of a hill or mound. ❑ *Now, the house is a heap of rubble.* A **stack** is usually tidy, and often consists of flat objects placed directly on top of each other. ❑ *...a neat stack of dishes.*

1 구동사 아귀를 맞추다, 종합하다 ❑ 그들은 그가 죽기 전 며칠 동안의 행적을 아귀를 맞추어 왔다. ❑ 다음 며칠 동안 프란시스는 그간 일어났던 일들을 서서히 밝혀 낼 수 있었다. **2** 구동사 아귀를 맞추다 ❑ 이 과정은 조각 그림을 맞추는 것과 비슷하다.

형용사 단편적인, 조금씩의 [탐탁잖음] ❑ 정부의 단편적인 접근 대신에 현재 필요한 것은 16-19세 교육의 급진적인 개편이다. ● 부사 단편적으로, 조금씩 ❑ 정부는 철도를 조금씩 민영화하려고 계획하고 있다.

가산명사 파이 차트, 원형 도표

가산명사 부두 잔창 ❑ 브라이튼 부두

1 타동사 구멍을 뚫다 ❑ 총알 하나가 그의 가슴 왼쪽을 관통했다. **2** 타동사 피어싱을 하다, 뚫다 ❑ 나 이번 주 토요일에 귀 뚫을 거예요.

1 형용사 귀청을 찢는 듯한 ❑ 귀청을 찢는 듯한 비명 소리가 허공을 갈랐다. **2** 형용사 날카로운, 예리한 [문어체] ❑ 그의 금모래빛 머리와 날카로운 푸른 눈 **3** 형용사 살을 에는 듯한 ❑ 살을 에는 듯한 바람이 불 수 있으므로 따뜻한 옷을 가져가는 것이 좋다.

불가산명사 신앙심, 경건함 ❑ 비록 가끔씩만 교회의 가르침을 받기는 했지만 그녀의 신앙심은 어릴 때부터 눈에 띄었다.

1 가산명사 돼지 ❑ 돼지가 꿀꿀거리는 소리 **2** 가산명사 돼지 같은 인간 [비격식체, 탐탁잖음] ❑ 이 사람들이 회사를 말췄어. 모두 탐욕스러운 돼지 같은 인간들이야. **3** 구 기의 불가능한 일임을 강조하는 말 [해학체, 비격식체, 강조] ❑ "물론 그가 이 일에 관계하지 않을 수도 있지." "천지개벽을 하면 또 모르지."

가산명사 비둘기

1 가산명사 여러 칸으로 이뤄진 물건의 한 칸 **2** 타동사 아무 곳에나 분류해 넣다 ❑ 그는 그들이 자기를 아무 곳에나 집어넣었다고 생각했다.

물질명사 색소 [격식체] ❑ 로마인들은 옷감과 벽에 천연색소를 사용했다.

복수는 pike 또는 pikes이다.

가산명사 또는 불가산명사 창꼬치 ● 불가산명사 창꼬치 무스

1 가산명사 더미 ❑ 모래 더미 ❑ 작은 빵 부스러기 더미 **2** 가산명사 쌓아올린 더미 ❑ 쌓아올린 박스 더미 ❑ 우리는 샘의 서재에서 여기저기 쌓아 놓은 책 사이에 앉았다.

물건의 pile은 정리되어 있을 수도 있고, 그렇지 않을 수도 있다. ❑ ...단정하게 포개어 놓은 옷. heap은 대개 정돈되어 있지 않은 상태로 수북이 쌓여 있는 것이다. ❑ 이제, 그 집은 파편 더미다. stack은 보통 정돈되어 있고, 흔히 납작한 물체들을 층층이 위로 쌓아 올린 것이다. ❑ ... 가지런히 포개져 있는 접시들

3 V-T If you **pile** things somewhere, you put them there so that they form a pile. ❑ *He was piling clothes into the suitcase.* **4** V-T If something **is piled with** things, it is covered or filled with piles of things. [usu passive] ❑ *Tables were piled high with local produce.* **5** V-I If a group of people **pile into** or **out of** a vehicle, they all get into it or out of it in a disorganized way. ❑ *They all piled into Jerrold's car.* **6** N-COUNT **Piles** are wooden, concrete, or metal posts which are pushed into the ground and on which buildings or bridges are built. Piles are often used in very wet areas so that the buildings do not flood. ❑ *...settlements of wooden houses, set on piles along the shore.* **7** N-PLURAL **Piles** are painful swellings that can appear in the veins inside a person's anus. ❑ *I have now been told that I have piles, so I want a remedy for this.* **8** N-SING The **pile** of a carpet or of a fabric such as velvet is its soft surface. It consists of a lot of little threads standing on end. ❑ *...the carpet's thick pile.* **9** PHRASE Someone who is **at the bottom of the pile** is low down in society or low down in an organization. Someone who is **at the top of the pile** is high up in society or high up in an organization. [INFORMAL] ❑ *These staff are fed up with being at the bottom of the pile when it comes to pay.*

Thesaurus
pile의 참조어

N.	accumulation, collection, heap, quantity, stack **1 2**
V.	assemble, collect, heap, stack **3**

▶**pile up 1** PHRASAL VERB If you **pile up** a quantity of things or if they **pile up**, they gradually form a pile. ❑ *Bulldozers piled up huge mounds of dirt.* **2** PHRASAL VERB If you **pile up** work, problems, or losses or if they **pile up**, you get more and more of them. ❑ *Problems were piling up at work.*

pil|grim /pɪlgrɪm/ (**pilgrims**) N-COUNT **Pilgrims** are people who make a journey to a holy place for a religious reason. ❑ *This is where pilgrims to the abbey would pay their first devotions.*

pil|grim|age /pɪlgrɪmɪdʒ/ (**pilgrimages**) **1** N-COUNT If you make a **pilgrimage** to a holy place, you go there for a religious reason. ❑ *...the pilgrimage to Mecca.* **2** N-COUNT A **pilgrimage** is a journey that someone makes to a place that is very important to them. ❑ *...a private pilgrimage to family graves.*

pill ♦♢♢ /pɪl/ (**pills**) **1** N-COUNT **Pills** are small solid round masses of medicine or vitamins that you swallow without chewing. ❑ *Why do I have to take all these pills?* **2** N-SING If a woman is **on the pill**, she takes a special pill that prevents her from becoming pregnant. ❑ *She had been on the pill for three years.* **3** PHRASE If a person or group has to accept a failure or an unpleasant piece of news, you can say that it was a **bitter pill** or a **bitter pill to swallow**. ❑ *You're too old to be given a job. That's a bitter pill to swallow.* **4** PHRASE If someone does something to **sweeten the pill** or **sugar the pill**, they do it to make some unpleasant news or an unpleasant measure more acceptable. ❑ *A few words of praise help to sweeten the pill of criticism.*

pil|lar /pɪlər/ (**pillars**) **1** N-COUNT A **pillar** is a tall solid structure, which is usually used to support part of a building. ❑ *...the pillars supporting the roof.* **2** N-COUNT If something is the **pillar of** a system or agreement, it is the most important part of it or what makes it strong and successful. ❑ *The pillar of her economic policy was keeping tight control over money supply.* **3** N-COUNT If you describe someone as a **pillar** of society or as a **pillar** of the community, you approve of them because they play an important and active part in society or in the community. [APPROVAL] ❑ *My father had been a pillar of the community.*

pil|low /pɪloʊ/ (**pillows**) N-COUNT A **pillow** is a rectangular cushion which you rest your head on when you are in bed. →see **sleep**

pi|lot ♦♢♢ /paɪlət/ (**pilots, piloting, piloted**) **1** N-COUNT A **pilot** is a person who is trained to fly an aircraft. ❑ *He spent seventeen years as an airline pilot.* **2** N-COUNT A **pilot** is a person who steers a ship through a difficult stretch of water, for example the entrance to a harbor. ❑ *It seemed that the pilot had another ship to take up the river that evening.* **3** V-T If someone **pilots** an aircraft or ship, they act as its pilot. ❑ *He piloted his own plane part of the way to Washington.* **4** N-COUNT A **pilot** plan or a **pilot** project is one which is used to test an idea before deciding whether to introduce it on a larger scale. ❑ *The plan is to launch a pilot program next summer.* **5** V-T If a government or organization **pilots** a program or project, they test it, before deciding whether to introduce it on a larger scale. ❑ *The trust is looking for 50 schools to pilot a programme aimed at teenage pupils preparing for work.* **6** V-T If a government official **pilots** a new law or bill through a legislature, he or she makes sure that it is introduced successfully. ❑ *We are now piloting through Parliament, as promised, the most comprehensive strategy in a generation to tackle youth crime.*

pimp /pɪmp/ (**pimps, pimping, pimped**) **1** N-COUNT A **pimp** is a man who gets clients for prostitutes and takes a large part of the money the prostitutes earn. **2** V-T Someone who **pimps** gets clients for prostitutes and takes a large part of the money the prostitutes earn. ❑ *He stole, lied, deceived, and pimped his way out of poverty.*

pin ♦♢♢ /pɪn/ (**pins, pinning, pinned**) **1** N-COUNT **Pins** are very small thin pointed pieces of metal. They are used in sewing to fasten pieces of material together until they have been sewn. ❑ *...needles and pins.* **2** V-T If you **pin** something **on** or **to** something, you attach it with a pin, a safety pin or a thumbtack. ❑ *They pinned a notice to the door.* ❑ *Everyone was supposed to dance with the bride and pin money on her dress.* **3** V-T If someone **pins** you to something, they press you against a surface so that you cannot move. ❑ *I pinned him against the wall.* ❑ *I'd try to get away and he'd pin me down, saying he would kill me.* **4** N-COUNT A **pin** is any long narrow piece of metal or wood that is not sharp, especially one that is used to fasten two things together. ❑ *...the 18-inch steel pin holding his left*

---

3 타동사 쌓다 ❑ 그는 여행 가방에 옷을 쌓아 넣고 있었다. **4** 타동사 ~가 쌓여 있다 ❑ 탁자들마다 지역 농산물이 높이 쌓여 있다. **5** 자동사 우르르 타다; 우르르 내리다 ❑ 그들 모두 제롤드의 차에 우르르 탔다. **6** 가산명사 말뚝, 파일 ❑ 해안을 따라 박은 파일 위에 지은 나무집 **7** 복수명사 치질, 치핵 ❑ 나는 치질이라는 진단을 받고 치료법을 찾고 있다. **8** 단수명사 카펫이나 벨벳과 같은 천의 짧고 부드러운 털 ❑ 카펫의 두꺼운 털 **9** 구 하위의, 하급의; 상위의, 상급의 [비격식체] ❑ 여기 직원들은 급료 수준이 밑바닥에 속한다는 사실에 질려 있다.

1 구동사 쌓아올리다; 쌓이다 ❑ 불도저가 거대한 흙더미를 쌓아올렸다. **2** 구동사 쌓아 가다; 쌓이다 ❑ 직장에서 문제가 쌓이고 있었다.

가산명사 순례자 ❑ 이곳은 대성당으로 향하는 순례자들이 처음으로 기도를 드리던 곳이다.

1 가산명사 순례 ❑ 메카 순례 **2** 가산명사 (중요한) 여행, 여정 ❑ 가족 무덤으로의 개인적인 여정

1 가산명사 알약 ❑ 왜 내가 이 알약을 다 먹어야 하죠? **2** 단수명사 피임약을 복용 중인 ❑ 그녀는 3년 동안 피임약을 복용했다. **3** 구 싫지만 어쩔 수 없는 일 ❑ 당신은 직장을 구하기엔 나이가 너무 많아요. 어쩔 수 없는 현실이죠. **4** 구 싫은 것을 그나마 좋아 보이게 만들다 ❑ 칭찬 몇 마디를 섞으면 비판을 포장하는 데 도움이 될 것이다.

1 가산명사 기둥 ❑ 지붕을 떠받치고 있는 기둥 **2** 가산명사 핵심, 기둥 ❑ 그녀의 경제 정책의 핵심은 통화 공급량의 철저한 통제 유지였다. **3** 가산명사 중심적인 인물, 기둥 [마음에 듦] ❑ 우리 아버지는 지역 사회의 기둥이었다.

가산명사 베개

1 가산명사 파일럿, 조종사 ❑ 그는 비행기 조종사로 17년 근무했다. **2** 가산명사 도선사, 수로 안내인 ❑ 그날 저녁 도선사가 강 상류로 조종해야 할 배가 하나 더 있는 것처럼 보였다. **3** 타동사 조종하다 ❑ 그는 워싱턴으로 가는 길 중간에 자기 비행기를 조종했다. **4** 가산명사 시범 계획, 시험작 ❑ 내년 여름 시범 프로그램을 시작할 계획이다. **5** 타동사 시범운영을 하다, 테스트하다 ❑ 그 기금은 취업을 준비하는 10대 학생을 대상으로 프로그램을 시범 운영할 학교 50곳을 물색 중이다. **6** 타동사 추진하다 ❑ 우리는 약속한 대로 지난 30년 이래 가장 포괄적인 청소년 범죄 퇴치 전략을 현재 의회에서 추진 중이다.

1 가산명사 포주, 뚜쟁이 **2** 타동사 포주 노릇을 하다 ❑ 그는 절도, 거짓말, 사기, 포주 노릇을 통해 가난에서 벗어났다.

1 가산명사 핀 ❑ 바늘과 핀 **2** 타동사 (핀 등으로) 꽂다, 고정하다 ❑ 그들이 문에 공지 사항을 꽂아 놓았다. ❑ 모든 사람들이 신부와 춤을 추고 신부의 드레스에 돈을 꽂아 주기로 되어 있었다. **3** 타동사 밀어붙이다, 몰아세우다 ❑ 내가 그를 벽으로 밀어붙였다. ❑ 나는 도망가려 하고 그는 나를 죽이겠다며 바닥으로 밀어붙이곤 했다. **4** 가산명사 고정 핀 ❑ 그의 왼쪽 다리를 연결시키고 있는 18인치 철제 고정 핀 **5** 타동사 잘못을 ~에게 돌리다; 책임을 ~에게 지우다 ❑ 그들이 우리에게 잘못을 돌리려 하

leg together. **5** V-T If someone tries to **pin** something **on** you or to **pin the blame on** you, they say, often unfairly, that you were responsible for something bad or illegal. ❏ *They're trying to pin it on us.* **6** V-T If you **pin** your hopes **on** something or **pin** your faith **on** something, you hope very much that it will produce the result you want. ❏ *The Democrats are pinning their hopes on the next election.* **7** N-COUNT A **pin** is something worn on your clothing, for example as jewelry, which is fastened with a pointed piece of metal. [AM] ❏ *...necklaces, bracelets, and pins.* **8** →see also **drawing pin, jewelry, safety pin**

있어요. **6** 타동사 -에 희망을 걸다; -을 믿다 ❏ 민주당원들은 다음 선거에 희망을 걸고 있다. **7** 가산명사 장식 핀, 브로치 [미국영어] ❏ 목걸이와 팔찌, 브로치

▶**pin down** **1** PHRASAL VERB If you try to **pin** something **down**, you try to discover exactly what, where, or when it is. ❏ *It has taken until now to pin down its exact location.* ❏ *I can only pin it down to between 1936 and 1942.* **2** PHRASAL VERB If you **pin** someone **down**, you force them to make a decision or to tell you what their decision is, when they have been trying to avoid doing this. ❏ *She couldn't pin him down to a date.*

1 구동사 정확히 밝히다, 포집어 내다 ❏ 지금까지 계속 그것의 정확한 위치를 찾고 있었다. ❏ 1936년과 1942년 사이의 일이라는 것까지 밖에 추정 못하겠네요. **2** 구동사 강요하다, 놓아세우다 ❏ 그녀는 데이트하자고 그에게 강요할 수 없었다.

PIN /pɪn/ N-SING Someone's **PIN** or **PIN number** is a secret number which they can use, for example, with a bank card to withdraw money from a cash machine or ATM. PIN is an abbreviation for "personal identification number." [oft N n] ❏ *To use the service you'll need a PIN number.*

단수명사 비밀 번호 ❏ 서비스를 사용하려면 비밀 번호가 필요할 것이다.

pina|fore /pɪnəfɔr/ (pinafores) N-COUNT A **pinafore** or a **pinafore dress** is a sleeveless dress. It is worn over a blouse or sweater. [mainly BRIT; AM usually **jumper**]

가산명사 소매 없는 원피스 [주로 영국영어; 미국영어 대개 jumper]

pin|cer /pɪnsər/ (pincers) **1** N-PLURAL **Pincers** consist of two pieces of metal that are hinged in the middle. They are used as a tool for gripping things or for pulling things out. [also *a pair of* N] ❏ *His surgical instruments were a knife and a pair of pincers.* **2** N-COUNT The **pincers** of an animal such as a crab or a lobster are its front claws.

1 복수명사 못뽑이, 족집게 ❏ 그의 수술 도구는 칼과 족집게였다. **2** 가산명사 집게발

pinch /pɪntʃ/ (pinches, pinching, pinched) **1** V-T If you **pinch** a part of someone's body, you take a piece of their skin between your thumb and first finger and give it a short squeeze. ❏ *She pinched his arm as hard as she could.* ● N-COUNT **Pinch** is also a noun. ❏ *She gave him a little pinch.* **2** N-COUNT A **pinch of** an ingredient such as salt is the amount of it that you can hold between your thumb and your first finger. ❏ *Put all the ingredients, including a pinch of salt, into a food processor.* to **take** something **with a pinch of salt** →see **salt** **3** V-T To **pinch** something, especially something of little value, means to steal it. [INFORMAL] ❏ *Do you remember when I pinched your glasses?* **4** PHRASE If a person or company **is feeling the pinch**, they do not have as much money as they used to, and so they cannot buy the things they would like to buy. ❏ *Consumers are spending less and traders are feeling the pinch.*

1 타동사 꼬집다 ❏ 그녀가 그의 팔을 최대한 세게 꼬집었다. ● 가산명사 꼬집기 ❏ 그녀가 그를 살짝 꼬집었다. **2** 가산명사 약간 ❏ 푸드 프로세스에 모든 재료와 소금을 조금 집어넣으세요. **3** 타동사 훔치다 [비격식체] ❏ 내가 네 안경 훔쳤던 거 기억나? **4** 구 쪼들리다 ❏ 소비자들이 지출을 줄이고 있으며 상인들은 돈에 쪼들리고 있다.

pine /paɪn/ (pines, pining, pined) **1** N-VAR A **pine tree** or a **pine** is a tall tree which has very thin, sharp leaves and a fresh smell. Pine trees have leaves all year round. ❏ *...high mountains covered in pine trees.* ● N-UNCOUNT **Pine** is the wood of this tree. ❏ *...a big pine table.* **2** V-I If you **pine for** someone who has died or gone away, you want them to be with you very much and feel sad because they are not there. ❏ *She'd be sitting at home pining for her lost husband.* **3** V-I If you **pine for** something, you want it very much, especially when it is unlikely that you will be able to have it. ❏ *I pine for the countryside.*

1 가산명사 또는 불가산명사 소나무 ❏ 소나무로 뒤덮인 높은 산들 ● 불가산명사 소나무 재목 ❏ 큰 소나무 탁자 **2** 자동사 애타게 그리워하다 ❏ 그녀는 죽은 남편을 애타게 그리며 집에 앉아 있곤 했다. **3** 자동사 간절히 바라다 ❏ 시골이 너무나 그립다.

pine|apple /paɪnæpᵊl/ (pineapples) N-VAR A **pineapple** is a large oval fruit that grows in hot countries. It is sweet, juicy, and yellow inside. It has a thick brownish skin.

가산명사 또는 불가산명사 파인애플

pink ♦◇◇ /pɪŋk/ (pinker, pinkest, pinks) **1** COLOR **Pink** is the color between red and white. ❏ *...pink lipstick.* ❏ *...white flowers edged in pink.* **2** COLOR If you **go pink**, your face turns a slightly redder color than usual because you are embarrassed or angry, or because you are doing something energetic. ❏ *She went pink again as she remembered her mistake.* **3** ADJ **Pink** is used to refer to things relating to or connected with homosexuals. ❏ *I think business now realises that they've got to be more aware of the so-called "pink pound."*

1 색채어 분홍색, 핑크색 ❏ 분홍색 립스틱 ❏ 가장자리가 분홍색인 하얀 꽃 **2** 색채어 얼굴이 빨개지다 ❏ 자신의 실수를 기억하자 그녀의 얼굴이 다시 빨개졌다. **3** 형용사 동성애의 ❏ 기업이 이제 동성애자들이 쓰는 돈에 좀 더 민감해져야 할 필요성을 깨닫고 있다고 나는 생각한다.

pin|na|cle /pɪnəkᵊl/ (pinnacles) **1** N-COUNT A **pinnacle** is a pointed piece of stone or rock that is high above the ground. ❏ *A walker broke his arms, legs, and pelvis yesterday when he plunged 80ft from a rocky pinnacle.* **2** N-COUNT If someone reaches **the pinnacle of** their career or **the pinnacle of** a particular area of life, they are at the highest point of it. ❏ *John Major has reached the pinnacle of British politics.*

1 가산명사 산봉우리 ❏ 어제 등반객 한 명이 바위 봉우리에서 80피트 추락해 팔과 다리, 골반뼈가 부러졌다. **2** 가산명사 정상, 절정 ❏ 존 메이저가 영국 정계의 정상에 올랐다.

pin|point /pɪnpɔɪnt/ (pinpoints, pinpointing, pinpointed) **1** V-T If you **pinpoint** the cause of something, you discover or explain the cause exactly. ❏ *It was almost impossible to pinpoint the cause of death.* ❏ *...if you can pinpoint exactly what the anger is about.* **2** V-T If you **pinpoint** something or its position, you discover or show exactly where it is. ❏ *I could pinpoint his precise location on a map.*

1 타동사 딱 집어내다, 정확히 규명하다 ❏ 정확한 사인 규명이 거의 불가능하다. ❏ 뭐 때문에 화가 나는지 정확히 집어 낼 수 있다면 **2** 타동사 정확한 위치를 집어내다 ❏ 나는 그의 위치를 지도상에서 정확히 집어낼 수 있었다.

pin|stripe /pɪnstraɪp/ (pinstripes) also **pin-stripe** N-COUNT **Pinstripes** are very narrow vertical stripes found on certain types of clothing. Businessmen's suits often have pinstripes. ❏ *He wore an expensive, dark blue pinstripe suit.*

가산명사 가는 세로줄 무늬 ❏ 그는 가는 세로줄 무늬의 값비싼 남색 정장을 입고 있었다.

pint /paɪnt/ (pints) N-COUNT A **pint** is a unit of measurement for liquids. In America, it is equal to 473 cubic centimeters or one eighth of an American gallon. In Britain, it is equal to 568 cubic centimeters or one eighth of an imperial gallon. ❏ *...a pint of milk.*

가산명사 파인트 ❏ 우유 1파인트

pin-up (pin-ups) also **pinup** N-COUNT A **pin-up** is an attractive man or woman who appears on posters, often wearing very few clothes. ❏ *...pin-up boys.*

가산명사 핀업 (포스터의 미남 미녀) ❏ 꽃미남

pio|neer /paɪənɪər/ (pioneers, pioneering, pioneered) **1** N-COUNT Someone who is referred to as a **pioneer** in a particular area of activity is one of the first people to be involved in it and develop it. ❏ *...one of the leading pioneers of British photo journalism.* **2** V-T Someone who **pioneers** a new activity, invention, or process is one of the first people to do it. ❏ *...Professor Alec Jeffreys, who invented and pioneered DNA tests.* **3** N-COUNT **Pioneers** are people who leave their own

1 가산명사 선구자 ❏ 영국 보도 사진의 주요 선구자 중 한 명 **2** 타동사 개척하다 ❏ 디엔에이 검사를 개발하고 개척한 알렉 제프리스 교수 **3** 가산명사 개척자 ❏ 이제는 사람이 살지 않는 초기 유럽 개척자들의 정착촌

A

country or the place where they were living, and go and live in a place that has not been lived in before. ❑ *...abandoned settlements of early European pioneers.*

B

pio|neer|ing /paɪəniərɪŋ/ ADJ **Pioneering** work or a **pioneering** individual does something that has not been done before, for example by developing or using new methods or techniques. ❑ *The school has won awards for its pioneering work with the community.*

형용사 선구적인, 선도적인 ❑ 그 학교는 지역 사회와 선구적인 노력을 펼친 것으로 상을 여러 번 받았다.

C

pi|ous /paɪəs/ ADJ Someone who is **pious** is very religious and moral. ❑ *He was brought up by pious female relatives.* ● **pi|ous|ly** ADV [ADV with v] ❑ *Conti kneeled and crossed himself piously.*

형용사 독실한, 경건한 ❑ 그는 독실한 여자 친척들 밑에서 자랐다. ● 독실하게, 경건하게 부사 ❑ 콘티는 무릎을 꿇고 경건하게 성호를 그었다.

D

pip /pɪp/ (pips, pipping, pipped) **1** N-COUNT **Pips** are the small hard seeds in a fruit such as an apple, orange, or pear. [BRIT] ❑ *Slice 6 juicy oranges, removing all the pips.* **2** V-T If someone **is pipped to** something such as a prize or an award, they are defeated by only a small amount. [BRIT, INFORMAL] ❑ *It's still possible for the losers to be pipped by West Germany for a semi-final place.*

1 가산명사 씨 [영국영어] ❑ 즙이 많은 오렌지 여섯 개를 잘라 씨를 모두 제거하세요. **2** 타동사 근소한 차이로 지다 [영국영어, 비격식체] ❑ 패자들이 결승 진출을 두고 서독과 싸워 근소한 차이로 질 수도 있다.

E

F

pipe ◆◇◇ /paɪp/ (pipes, piping, piped) **1** N-COUNT A **pipe** is a long, round, hollow object, usually made of metal or plastic, through which a liquid or gas can flow. ❑ *The liquid can't escape into the air, because it's inside a pipe.* **2** N-COUNT A **pipe** is an object which is used for smoking tobacco. You put the tobacco into the cup-shaped part at the end of the pipe, light it, and breathe in the smoke through a narrow tube. ❑ *Do you smoke a pipe?* **3** N-COUNT A **pipe** is a simple musical instrument in the shape of a tube with holes in it. You play a pipe by blowing into it while covering and uncovering the holes with your fingers. **4** N-COUNT An **organ pipe** is one of the long hollow tubes in which air vibrates and produces a musical note. **5** V-T If liquid or gas **is piped** somewhere, it is transferred from one place to another through a pipe. ❑ *The heated gas is piped through a coil surrounded by water.* ❑ *The Communists brought electricity to his village and piped in drinking water from the reservoir.* **6** →see also **piping** →see **plumbing**

1 가산명사 파이프, 관 ❑ 액체가 파이프 안에 있기 때문에 공기 중으로 빠져 나갈 수 없다. **2** 가산명사 파이프 담배, 담뱃대 ❑ 파이프 담배 피우세요? **3** 가산명사 피리 **4** 가산명사 파이프 오르간의 음관 **5** 타동사 파이프로 전달되다 ❑ 가열된 기체가 물에 둘러싸인 동그란 모양의 파이프를 통해 전달된다. ❑ 공산주의자들이 그가 사는 마을에 전기가 들어오게 했으며 저수지로부터 파이프를 설치해 식수도 끌어왔다.

G

H

I

pipe|line /paɪplaɪn/ (pipelines) **1** N-COUNT A **pipeline** is a large pipe which is used for carrying oil or gas over a long distance, often underground. ❑ *A consortium plans to build a natural-gas pipeline from Russia to supply eastern Germany.* **2** PHRASE If something is **in the pipeline**, it has already been planned or begun. ❑ *Already in the pipeline is a 2.9 per cent pay increase for teachers.* →see **oil**

1 가산명사 파이프라인, 수송관 ❑ 한 컨소시엄에서는 동독에 공급할 천연가스 파이프라인을 러시아로부터 건설할 계획이다. **2** 구 계획된, 진행 중인 ❑ 이미 계획된 사항으로 교사 봉급의 2.9퍼센트 인상이 있다.

J

K

pip|ing /paɪpɪŋ/ N-UNCOUNT **Piping** is metal, plastic, or another substance made in the shape of a pipe or tube. ❑ *...rolls of bright yellow plastic piping.*

불가산명사 관 ❑ 돌돌 말아 놓은 밝은 노랑색 플라스틱 관

pi|ra|cy /paɪrəsi/ **1** N-UNCOUNT **Piracy** is robbery at sea carried out by pirates. ❑ *Seven of the fishermen have been formally charged with piracy.* **2** N-UNCOUNT You can refer to the illegal copying of things such as videotapes and computer programs as **piracy**. ❑ *...protection against piracy of books, films, and other intellectual property.*

1 불가산명사 해적행위 ❑ 어민 중 일곱 명이 해적 행위 혐의로 정식으로 기소됐다. **2** 불가산명사 불법 복제, 저작권 침해 ❑ 책, 영화를 비롯한 지적 재산에 대한 저작권 침해 예방

L

M

pi|rate /paɪrɪt/ (pirates, pirating, pirated) **1** N-COUNT **Pirates** are sailors who attack other ships and steal property from them. ❑ *In the nineteenth century, pirates roamed the seas.* **2** V-T Someone who **pirates** videotapes, cassettes, books, or computer programs copies and sells them when they have no right to do so. ❑ *A school technician pirated anything from video nasties to computer games.* **3** ADJ A **pirate** version of something is an illegal copy of it. [ADJ n] ❑ *Pirate copies of the video are already said to be in Britain.*

1 가산명사 해적 ❑ 19세기에는 바다에 해적들이 돌아다녔다. **2** 타동사 불법 복제하다 ❑ 한 학교 기술자가 공포영화 비디오에서 게임에 이르기까지 여러 가지를 불법 복제했다. **3** 형용사 해적판의, 불법 복제된 ❑ 그 비디오의 해적판이 이미 영국에서 판매되고 있다고 한다.

N

O

P

piss /pɪs/ (pisses, pissing, pissed) **1** V-I To **piss** means to urinate. [INFORMAL, VULGAR] ❑ *A man pissed against a wall.* **2** V-I If **it is pissing with** rain, it is raining very hard. [usu cont] ● PHRASAL VERB **Piss down** means the same as **piss**. [BRIT, INFORMAL, VULGAR] ❑ *It was pissing down out there.* **3** PHRASE If you **take the piss out of** someone, you tease them and make fun of them. [BRIT, INFORMAL, VULGAR] ❑ *All you did was take the piss out of him because he came from a Public School.*

1 자동사 오줌 싸다 [비격식체, 비속어] ❑ 한 남자가 벽에 대고 오줌을 쌌다. **2** 자동사 비가 억수같이 쏟아지다 ● 구동사 비가 억수같이 쏟아지다 [영국영어, 비격식체, 비속어] ❑ 밖에 비가 억수같이 쏟아지고 있었다. **3** 구 놀리다, 조롱하다 [영국영어, 비격식체, 비속어] ❑ 네가 한 일이라곤 사립학교 출신이라는 이유로 그를 조롱한 것뿐이다.

Q

▶ **piss off** **1** PHRASAL VERB If someone or something **pisses** you **off**, they annoy you. [INFORMAL, VULGAR] ❑ *It pisses me off when they start moaning about going to war.* ● **pissed off** ADJ ❑ *I was really pissed off.* **2** PHRASAL VERB If someone tells a person to **piss off**, they are telling the person in a rude way to go away. [INFORMAL, VULGAR] [V P]

1 구동사 화나게 하다, 돌게 만들다 [비격식체, 비속어] ❑ 그들이 전쟁 시작에 대해 불평하기 시작하면 나는 돌겠다. ● 화난 형용사 ❑ 나는 정말 화가 났다. **2** 구동사 꺼지다, 사라지다 [비격식체, 비속어]

R

S

pissed /pɪst/ **1** ADJ If you say that someone is **pissed**, you mean that they are annoyed. [AM, INFORMAL, VULGAR] [v-link ADJ, oft ADJ at n] ❑ *You know Molly's pissed at you.* **2** ADJ Someone who is **pissed** is drunk. [BRIT, INFORMAL, VULGAR] ❑ *He was just lying there completely pissed.*

1 형용사 열 받는, 화난 [미국영어, 비격식체, 비속어] ❑ 너도 몰리가 너한테 열 받은 거 알지. **2** 형용사 술에 취한 [영국영어, 비격식체, 비속어] ❑ 그가 술에 엄청 취해 거기 누워 있었다.

T

piste /pist/ (pistes) N-COUNT A **piste** is a track of firm snow for skiing on. ❑ *...confident skiers who want to move off the piste.*

가산명사 피스트 (탄탄하게 다져진 활강 코스) ❑ 피스트를 벗어나 달리고 싶은 자신만만한 스키어들

U

pis|tol /pɪstəl/ (pistols) N-COUNT A **pistol** is a small gun.

가산명사 권총

pis|ton /pɪstən/ (pistons) N-COUNT A **piston** is a cylinder or metal disk that is part of an engine. Pistons slide up and down inside tubes and cause various parts of the engine to move.

가산명사 피스톤

V

W

X

Y

Z

pit ◆◇◇ /pɪt/ (pits, pitting, pitted) **1** N-COUNT A **pit** is a coal mine. ❑ *It was a better community then, when all the pits were working.* **2** N-COUNT A **pit** is a large hole that is dug in the ground. ❑ *Eric lost his footing and began to slide into the pit.* **3** N-COUNT A **gravel pit** or **clay pit** is a very large hole that is left where gravel or clay has been dug from the ground. ❑ *This area of former farmland was worked as a gravel pit until 1964.* **4** V-T If two opposing things or people **are pitted against** one another, they are in conflict. [usu passive] ❑ *You will be pitted against two, three, or four people who are every bit as good as you are.* **5** N-PLURAL In auto racing, **the pits** are the areas at the side of the track where drivers stop to get more fuel and to repair their cars during races. ❑ *He moved quickly into the pits and climbed rapidly out of the car.* **6** N-COUNT A **pit** is the large hard seed of a fruit or vegetable. [AM] ❑ *...cherry pits.* **7** →see also **pitted** **8** PHRASE If you **pit your wits against** someone, you compete with them in a test of knowledge or intelligence. ❑ *I'd like to manage at the very highest level and pit my wits against the*

1 가산명사 탄광, 갱 ❑ 모든 탄광이 돌아가고 있었을 당시에는 더 좋은 고장이었다. **2** 가산명사 구덩이 ❑ 에릭은 발을 헛디뎌 구덩이 속으로 미끄러지기 시작했다. **3** 가산명사 자갈 채취장; 흙 채취장 ❑ 전에 농지였던 이곳은 1964년까지 자갈 채취장으로 사용됐었다. **4** 타동사 ~와 싸우다, ~와 맞붙다 ❑ 당신은 모든 면에서 당신과 실력이 맞먹는 둘, 셋, 혹은 네 사람과 싸우게 될 것이다. **5** 복수명사 피트 (자동차 경주에서 급유나 수리를 하는 곳) ❑ 그는 재빨리 피트로 가서 급히 차 밖으로 나왔다. **6** 가산명사 (크고 딱딱한) 씨 [미국영어] ❑ 체리 씨 **8** 구 ~와 지혜를 겨루다 ❑ 나는 최고 수준에서 해나가며 최상의 사람들과 지혜를 겨루고 싶다. **9** 구 가슴이 답답하다 ❑ 나는 이상하게도 가슴이 답답했다.

best. **9** PHRASE If you have a feeling **in the pit of** your **stomach**, you have a tight or sick feeling in your stomach, usually because you are afraid or anxious. ❑ *I had a funny feeling in the pit of my stomach.* →see **fruit**

pitch ♦♦♦ /pɪtʃ/ (**pitches, pitching, pitched**) **1** V-T If you **pitch** something somewhere, you throw it with quite a lot of force, usually aiming it carefully. ❑ *Simon pitched the empty bottle into the lake.* **2** V-T/V-I To **pitch** somewhere means to fall forwards suddenly and with a lot of force. ❑ *The movement took him by surprise, and he pitched forward.* ❑ *Alan staggered sideways, pitched head-first over the low wall and fell into the lake.* **3** V-T If someone **is pitched into** a new situation, they are suddenly forced into it. ❑ *They were being pitched into a new adventure in which they would have to fight the whole world.* **4** V-T In the game of baseball or rounders, when you **pitch** the ball, you throw it to the batter for them to hit it. ❑ *We passed long, hot afternoons pitching a baseball.* **5** N-UNCOUNT The **pitch** of a sound is how high or low it is. ❑ *He raised his voice to an even higher pitch.* **6** V-T If a sound **is pitched at** a particular level, it is produced at the level indicated. [usu passive] ❑ *His cry is pitched at a level that makes it impossible to ignore.* ❑ *His voice was pitched high, the words muffled by his crying.* →see also **high-pitched** **7** V-T If something **is pitched at** a particular level or degree of difficulty, it is set at that level. ❑ *Whilst this is very important material I think it's probably pitched at rather too high a level for our purposes.* **8** N-SING If something such as a feeling or a situation rises to a high **pitch**, it rises to a high level. ❑ *I feel very sorry for the competitors who have all worked themselves up to a very high pitch for this first day.* **9** N-COUNT A **pitch** is an area of ground that is marked out and used for playing a game such as soccer, cricket, or hockey. [BRIT; AM **field**] ❑ *There was a swimming-pool, cricket pitches, playing fields.* **10** PHRASE If someone **makes a pitch for** something, they try to persuade people to do or buy it. ❑ *The President speaks in New York today, making another pitch for his economic program.* →see also **sales pitch**

▶**pitch for** PHRASAL VERB If someone is **pitching for** something, they are trying to persuade other people to give it to them. ❑ *It was middle-class votes they were pitching for.*

▶**pitch in** PHRASAL VERB If you **pitch in**, you join in and help with an activity. [INFORMAL] ❑ *The agency says international relief agencies also have pitched in.*

pitch|er /pɪtʃər/ (**pitchers**) **1** N-COUNT A **pitcher** is a cylindrical container with a handle and is used for holding and pouring liquids. [mainly AM] ❑ *...a pitcher of iced water.* **2** N-COUNT In baseball, the **pitcher** is the person who throws the ball to the batter, who tries to hit it.

pit|fall /pɪtfɔl/ (**pitfalls**) N-COUNT The **pitfalls** involved in a particular activity or situation are the things that may go wrong or may cause problems. ❑ *The pitfalls of working abroad are numerous.*

piti|ful /pɪtɪfəl/ **1** ADJ Someone or something that is **pitiful** is so sad, weak, or small that you feel pity for them. ❑ *He sounded both pitiful and eager to get what he wanted.* ● **piti|fully** ADV ❑ *His legs were pitifully thin compared to the rest of his bulk.* **2** ADJ If you describe something as **pitiful**, you mean that it is completely inadequate. [DISAPPROVAL] ❑ *The choice is pitiful and the quality of some of the products is very low.* ● **piti|fully** ADV ❑ *State help for the mentally handicapped is pitifully inadequate.*

pit|ted /pɪtɪd/ **1** ADJ **Pitted** fruits have had their pits removed. [ADJ n] ❑ *...green and black pitted olives.* **2** ADJ If the surface of something is **pitted**, it is covered with a lot of small, shallow holes. ❑ *Everywhere building facades are pitted with shell and bullet holes.*

pity /pɪti/ (**pities, pitying, pitied**) **1** N-UNCOUNT If you feel **pity for** someone, you feel very sorry for them. ❑ *He felt a sudden tender pity for her.* →see also **self-pity** **2** V-T If you **pity** someone, you feel very sorry for them. ❑ *I don't know whether to hate or pity him.* **3** N-SING If you say that it is **a pity** that something is the case, you mean that you feel disappointment or regret about it. [FEELINGS] ❑ *It is a great pity that all pupils in the city cannot have the same chances.* ❑ *Pity you haven't got your car, isn't it.* **4** N-UNCOUNT If someone shows **pity**, they do not harm or punish someone they have power over. ❑ *Non-communist forces have some pity towards people here.* **5** PHRASE If you **take pity on** someone, you feel sorry for them and help them. ❑ *No woman had ever felt the need to take pity on him before.*

piv|ot /pɪvət/ (**pivots, pivoting, pivoted**) **1** N-COUNT The **pivot** in a situation is the most important thing which everything else is based on or arranged around. ❑ *Forming the pivot of the exhibition is a large group of watercolors.* **2** V-T/V-I If something **pivots**, it balances or turns on a central point. ❑ *The boat pivoted on its central axis and pointed straight at the harbor entrance.* ❑ *She pivots gracefully on the stage.* **3** N-COUNT A **pivot** is the pin or the central point on which something balances or turns. ❑ *The pedal had sheared off at the pivot.*

piv|ot|al /pɪvətəl/ ADJ A **pivotal** role, point, or figure in something is one that is very important and affects the success of that thing. ❑ *The Court of Appeal has a pivotal role in the English legal system.*

pix|el /pɪksəl/ (**pixels**) N-COUNT A **pixel** is the smallest area on a computer screen which can be given a separate color by the computer. [COMPUTING] ❑ *...a display screen that measures one million pixels.* →see **television**

piz|za /pitsə/ (**pizzas**) N-VAR A **pizza** is a flat, round piece of dough covered with tomatoes, cheese, and other savory food, and then baked in an oven. ❑ *...the last piece of pizza.*

pkg. N-VAR **Pkg.** is a written abbreviation for **package**.

plac|ard /plækɑrd, -kərd/ (**placards**) N-COUNT A **placard** is a large notice that is carried in a march or displayed in a public place. ❑ *The protesters sang songs and waved placards.*

pla|cate /pleɪkeɪt, BRIT pləkeɪt/ (**placates, placating, placated**) V-T If you **placate** someone, you do or say something to make them stop feeling angry. [FORMAL] ❑ *He smiled, and made a gesture intended to placate me.*

1 타동사 던지다 ❑ 사이면이 호수로 빈 병을 던졌다. **2** 타동사/자동사 쓰러지다 ❑ 갑작스러운 움직임에 그가 앞으로 팍 하고 쓰러졌다. ❑ 앨런이 옆으로 비틀거리다 낮은 벽 위로 고꾸라지더니 호수에 빠졌다. **3** 타동사 ~에 내던져지다 ❑ 그들은 전 세계와 싸워야 하게 될 새로운 모험에 내던져지고 있었다. **4** 타동사 던지다 ❑ 우리는 야구공을 던지며 길고 더운 오후를 보냈다. **5** 불가산명사 소리의 높낮이, 음조 ❑ 그는 목소리를 훨씬 더 높였다. **6** 타동사 -한 정도의 소리가 나다 ❑ 그의 울음소리가 그냥 지나치기 불가능할 정도로 컸었다. ❑ 그의 목소리는 높았으며 울음소리 때문에 말을 알아듣기가 힘들었다. **7** 타동사 -한 수준으로 설정되다, ~수준에 맞춰지다 ❑ 이것이 매우 중요한 자료이긴 하지만 우리 목적에 비해 지나치게 높은 수준에 맞춰진 것 같아요. **8** 단수명사 수준 ❑ 나는 오늘 첫 날 매우 높은 기량을 발휘해 주신 참가자 모두에게 정말 미안한 마음입니다. **9** 가산명사 경기장 [영국영어; 미국영어 field] ❑ 수영장 하나와, 크리켓 경기장 몇 개, 운동장 몇 개가 있었다. **10** 구 선전하다 ❑ 대통령이 오늘 뉴욕 연설에서 현 정부의 경제 계획을 또 다시 선전한다.

구동사 얻으려고 노력하다 ❑ 그들이 얻으려고 노력한 것은 중산층의 표였다.

구동사 참여해서 돕다 [비격식체] ❑ 그 기구는 국제 구호 단체들 역시 참여해서 도왔다고 말한다.

1 가산명사 주전자, 피처 [주로 미국영어] ❑ 얼음물 한 주전자 **2** 가산명사 투수

가산명사 함정 ❑ 해외 취업의 함정은 셀 수 없이 많다.

1 형용사 딱한, 측은한 ❑ 그는 딱해 보이면서도 자신이 원하는 것을 얻고자 몹시 열심인 것 같았다. ● 딱하게도 부사 ❑ 그의 두 다리는 튼튼한 신체의 다른 부위에 비해 딱하게도 가늘었다. **2** 형용사 한심한 [탐탁찮음] ❑ 그 선택은 한심하고 일부 상품의 질은 아주 저조하다. ● 한심하게 부사 ❑ 정신 지체 장애인에 대한 국가 지원이 한심할 정도로 부실하다.

1 형용사 씨를 뺀 ❑ 씨를 뺀 녹색과 검은색의 올리브 열매 **2** 형용사 구멍이 숭숭한, 읽은 ❑ 건물 전면에 모두 포탄과 총알구멍이 숭숭 나 있다.

1 불가산명사 연민 ❑ 그는 갑자기 그녀에게 약간의 연민을 느꼈다. **2** 타동사 동정하다 ❑ 그를 미워해야 할지 동정해야 할지 모르겠다. **3** 단수명사 애석한 일 [감정 개입] ❑ 그 도시의 모든 학생들이 동등한 기회를 가질 수 없다니 대단히 애석한 일이다. ❑ 네가 차가 없으니 애석한 일이야, 그렇지 않아? **4** 불가산명사 동정심 ❑ 비공산주의자 군대가 이곳 사람들에게 약간의 동정심을 가지고 있다. **5** 구 ~을 불쌍히 여겨 도와주다 ❑ 어떤 여자도 그전까지는 그를 불쌍히 여겨 도와줘야 할 필요를 느낀 적이 없었다.

1 가산명사 주축 ❑ 전시회의 주축을 이루는 것은 대규모의 수채화 작품들이다. **2** 타동사/자동사 균형을 잡다; (~을 축으로) 회전하다 ❑ 그 선박은 중심축을 중심으로 균형을 잡고 곧장 항구 어귀로 향했다. ❑ 그녀는 무대 위에서 우아하게 회전한다. **3** 가산명사 축; 회전축 ❑ 발판의 회전축에서 벗어나 있었다.

형용사 중추적인 ❑ 항소 법원이 잉글랜드의 법제에서 중추적인 역할을 한다.

가산명사 화소, 픽셀 [컴퓨터] ❑ 해상도가 백만 화소인 디스플레이 스크린

가산명사 또는 불가산명사 피자 ❑ 마지막 남은 피자 한 조각

가산명사 또는 불가산명사 package의 생략형

가산명사 플래카드 ❑ 시위자들이 노래를 부르며 플래카드를 흔들었다.

타동사 달래다, 진정시키다 [격식체] ❑ 그가 미소를 짓고는 나를 달래려는 듯한 몸짓을 했다.

place ♦♦♦ /pleɪs/ (**places, placing, placed**) **1** N-COUNT A **place** is any point, building, area, town, or country. □ ...*a list of museums and places of interest.* □ *We're going to a place called Mont-St-Jean.* □ *The pain is always in the same place.* **2** N-COUNT You can use **the place** to refer to the point, building, area, town, or country that you have already mentioned. □ *Except for the remarkably tidy kitchen, the place was a mess.* **3** N-COUNT You can refer to somewhere that provides a service, such as a hotel, restaurant, or institution, as a particular kind of **place**. □ *He found a bed-and-breakfast place.* □ *My wife and I discovered some superb places to eat.* **4** PHRASE When something **takes place**, it happens, especially in a controlled or organized way. □ *The discussion took place in a famous villa on the lake's shore.* □ *She wanted Hugh's wedding to take place quickly.* **5** N-SING **Place** can be used after "any," "no," "some," or "every" to mean "anywhere," "nowhere," "somewhere," or "everywhere." [mainly AM, INFORMAL] □ *The poor guy obviously didn't have any place to go for Easter.* **6** ADV If you go **places**, you visit pleasant or interesting places. [mainly AM] [ADV after v] □ *I don't have money to go places.* **7** N-COUNT You can refer to the position where something belongs, or where it is supposed to be, as its **place**. □ *He returned the album to its place on the shelf.* **8** N-COUNT A **place** is a seat or position that is available for someone to occupy. □ *He walked back to the table and sat at the nearest of two empty places.*

You can use **place** or, more often, **seat** to refer to somewhere where someone can sit. □ *The women looked around for a place to sit... There was only one seat free on the train.* More generally, you can refer to a **space** which someone or something can occupy. □ *He was clearing a space for her to lie down.* You do not use **place** as an uncount noun to refer to an open or empty area. You should use **room** or **space** instead. **Room** is more likely to be used when you are talking about space inside an enclosed area. □ *There's not enough room in the bathroom for both of us... Leave plenty of space between you and the car in front.*

9 N-COUNT Someone's or something's **place** in a society, system, or situation is their position in relation to other people or things. □ *They want to see more women take their place higher up the corporate or professional ladder.* **10** N-COUNT Your **place** in a race or competition is your position in relation to the other competitors. If you are in first place, you are ahead of all the other competitors. □ *Jane's goals helped Britain win third place in the Barcelona games.* **11** N-COUNT If you get a **place** on a team, on a committee, or in a course of study, for example, you are accepted as a member of the team or committee or as a student in the course. □ *Derek had lost his first-string place on the team.* □ *They should be in residential care but there are no places available.* **12** N-SING A good **place to** do something in a situation or activity is a good time or stage at which to do it. □ *It seemed an appropriate place to end somehow.* **13** N-COUNT Your **place** is the house or apartment where you live. [INFORMAL] □ *Let's all go back to my place!* **14** N-COUNT Your **place** in a book or speech is the point you have reached in reading the book or making the speech. □ ...*her finger marking her place in the book.* **15** N-COUNT If you say how many decimal **places** there are in a number, you are saying how many numbers there are to the right of the decimal point. □ *A pocket calculator only works to eight decimal places.* **16** V-T If you **place** something somewhere, you put it in a particular position, especially in a careful, firm, or deliberate way. □ *Brand folded it in his handkerchief and placed it in the inside pocket of his jacket.* **17** V-T To **place** a person or thing in a particular state means to cause them to be in it. □ *Widespread protests have placed the President under serious pressure.* □ *The crisis could well place the relationship at risk.* **18** V-T You can use **place** instead of "put" or "lay" in certain expressions where the meaning is carried by the following noun. For example, if you **place emphasis** on something, you emphasize it, and if you **place the blame on** someone, you blame them. □ *He placed great emphasis on the importance of family life and ties.* □ *She seemed to be placing most of the blame on her mother.* **19** V-T If you **place** someone or something in a particular class or group, you label or judge them in that way. □ *The authorities have placed the drug in Class A, the same category as heroin and cocaine.* **20** V-T If a competitor **is placed** first, second, or last, for example, that is their position at the end of a race or competition. In American English, **be placed** often means "finish in second position." [usu passive] □ *I had been placed 2nd and 3rd a few times but had never won.* **21** V-T If you **place an order for** a product or **for** a meal, you ask for it to be sent or brought to you. □ *It is a good idea to place your order well in advance as delivery can often take months rather than weeks.* **22** V-T If you **place an advertisement in** a newspaper, you arrange for the advertisement to appear in the newspaper. □ *They placed an advertisement in the local paper for a secretary.* **23** V-T If you **place a bet**, you bet money on something. □ *For this race, though, he had already placed a bet on one of the horses.* **24** V-T If an agency or organization **places** someone, it finds them a job or somewhere to live. □ *In 1861, they managed to place fourteen women in paid positions in the colonies.* **25** PHRASE If something is happening **all over the place**, it is happening in many different places. □ *Businesses are closing down all over the place.* **26** PHRASE If things are **all over the place**, they are spread over a very large area, usually in a disorganized way. □ *Our fingerprints are probably all over the place.* **27** PHRASE If you **change places with** another person, you start being in their situation or role, and they start being in yours. □ *With his door key in his hand, knowing Millie and the kids awaited him, he wouldn't change places with anyone.* **28** PHRASE If you have been trying to understand something puzzling and then everything **falls into place** or **clicks into place**, you suddenly understand how different pieces of information are connected and everything becomes clearer. □ *When the reasons behind the decision were explained, of course, it all fell into place.* **29** PHRASE If things **fall into place**, events happen naturally to produce a situation you want. □ *Once the decision was made, things fell into place rapidly.* **30** PHRASE If you say that someone **is going places**, you mean that they are showing a lot of talent or ability and are likely to become very successful. □ *You always knew Barbara was going places, she was different.* **31** PHRASE People **in high places** are people who

1 가산명사 곳, 장소 □ 박물관 및 명소의 목록 □ 우리는 몽생장이라는 곳으로 가고 있어. □ 통증이 항상 같은 곳에서 느껴져. **2** 단수명사 그곳, 거기 □ 눈에 띄게 깔끔한 주방을 빼고는 그곳은 엉망진창이었다. **3** 가산명사 곳, 장소 □ 그는 숙박과 조식을 제공하는 곳을 발견했다. □ 내 아내와 나는 기막힌 식당들을 찾아냈다. **4** 구 일어나다, 거행되다 □ 그 토론은 호숫가에 있는 유명한 저택에서 이루어졌다. □ 그녀는 휴의 결혼식이 빨리 거행되기를 바랐다. **5** 단수명사 어디 [주로 미국영어, 비격식체] □ 그 불쌍한 녀석은 분명히 부활절에 갈 곳이 없었다. **6** 부사 유흥지 [주로 미국영어] □ 난 놀러 다닐 돈이 없다. **7** 가산명사 제자리, 있어야 할 곳 □ 그는 앨범을 선반 제자리에 다시 꽂아놓았다. **8** 가산명사 자리, 좌석 □ 그는 탁자 쪽으로 다시 걸어와서 빈 자리 두 개 중 가까운 곳에 앉았다.

사람이 앉을 수 있는 장소를 가리킬 때는 place, 또는 더 흔히는 seat을 쓴다. □ 그 여자는 앉을 자리를 찾으려고 둘러보았다... 기차에는 빈 자리가 하나밖에 없었다. 더 일반적으로는, 사람 또는 사물이 차지할 수 있는 장소를 가리켜 space라고 할 수 있다. □ 그는 그녀가 누울 자리를 치우고 있었다. place를 틔어 있거나 비어 있는 공간을 의미하는 불가산 명사로는 사용하지 않고, 그 대신에 room이나 space를 사용해야 한다. room은 둘러싸인 영역 내에 있는 공간을 말할 때 더 흔히 쓰인다. □ 욕실에는 우리 둘이 들어갈 수 있는 공간이 없다... 당신과 앞 차 사이에 충분한 공간을 두시오.

9 가산명사 지위, 신분 □ 그들은 직장에서나 전문 분야에서 더 많은 여성들이 보다 높은 지위를 차지하기를 원한다. **10** 가산명사 순위 □ 제인이 넣은 골로 영국이 바르셀로나 경기에서 3등을 차지했다. **11** 가산명사 자리, 자격 □ 데릭은 팀에서 일군 자격을 잃은 상태였다. □ 그들은 시설에 머무르며 보살핌을 받아야 마땅한데 빈 자리가 없다. **12** 단수명사 기회 □ 아무튼 끝장을 낼만한 적당한 기회 같았다. **13** 가산명사 집, 거주지 [비격식체] □ 모두들 다시 우리 집으로 가자! **14** 가산명사 (읽고 있던) 대목 □ 그녀가 손가락으로 책에서 읽던 대목을 표시하며 **15** 가산명사 소수점 아래 자리 □ 휴대용 계산기에서는 소수점 아래 여덟 자리까지만 계산된다. **16** 타동사 놓다, 두다 □ 브랜드는 그것을 손수건에 싸서 재킷 안쪽 주머니에 넣었다. **17** 타동사 ~하게 하다 □ 광범위한 시위 때문에 대통령이 심각한 압력을 받고 있다. □ 그 위기로 인해 관계가 쉽게 위태로워질 수 있다. **18** 타동사 두다 □ 그는 가족생활과 유대의 중요성을 무척 강조했다. □ 그녀는 자신의 어머니에게 대부분의 죄를 씌우고 있는 것 같았다. **19** 타동사 등급을 매기다, 평가하다 □ 당국은 그 약물을 헤로인 및 코카인과 같은 종류인 에이급으로 등급을 정했다. **20** 타동사 (경기에서) ~등을 하다 □ 나는 2등과 3등은 몇 번 했지만 우승한 적은 없었다. **21** 타동사 주문하다 □ 배달이 몇 주가 아니라 몇 달씩 걸릴 수도 있으니 충분히 시간을 두고 미리 주문을 한다는 것은 좋은 생각이다. **22** 타동사 광고를 내다 □ 그들은 비서를 뽑는다는 광고를 냈다. **23** 타동사 내기를 걸다 □ 그렇지만 이 경주를 위해 그가 이미 그 말들 중 한 마리에 내기를 걸고 난 후였다. **24** 타동사 일자리를 알선하다; 살 곳을 찾아 주다 □ 1861년에 그들은 간신히 식민지에서 여자 14명에게 유급 일자리를 구해 주었다. **25** 구 도처에 널려 있는 □ 우리 지문이 도처에 널려 있을 것이다. **27** 구 입장을 바꾸다, 위치를 바꾸다 □ 밀리와 아이들이 자기를 기다리고 있다는 것을 아는 그는 손에 문 열쇠를 쥔 채로 누구와도 위치를 바꾸려 들지 않았다. **28** 구 앞뒤가 들어맞다 □ 결정 이면에 있는 이유를 듣고 나니 물론 앞뒤가 모두 들어맞았다. **29** 구 제자리를 찾다 □ 일단 결정이 내려졌기 때문에, 모든 게 빠르게 제자리를 찾았다. **30** 구 성공할 것이다 □ 바바라가 성공할 것이라는 것을 너는 언제나 알고 있었잖아. 그녀는 남달랐어. **31** 구 고위층에 속한 □ 그는 고위층 친구들이 있었다. **26** 구 제자리에 있는; 제자리를 벗어난 □ 제프가 서둘러 자기를 제자리로 다시 밀어 넣었다. **33** 구 시행 중인 □ 유사한 법령이 웨일스에서 이미 시행 중이다. **34** 구 ~ 대신에 □ 로렌스 위터스가 불행히도 병이 난 존 트레드웰을 대신해서 우리를 방문했다. **35** 구 곳곳에 □ 그때까지도 길가를 따라 쌓인 눈이 곳곳에서 5 내지 6피트 높이나 되었다. **36** 구 ~의 처지에 있다면 □ 내가 그의 처지에 있다면 나 그것에 저항할 수 없었을 텐데. **37** 구 처음에 □ 처음에 무슨 일로 워싱턴에 오게 되었니? **38** 구 첫 번째로, 우선; 두 번째로, 그 다음으로 □ 우선, 자넨 늙은 게 아닐세,

have powerful and influential positions in a government, society, or organization. □ *He had friends in high places.* ㉜ PHRASE If something is in place, it is in its correct or usual position. If it is out of place, it is not in its correct or usual position. □ *Geoff hastily pushed the drawer back into place.* ㉝ PHRASE If something such as a law, a policy, or an administrative structure is in place, it is working or able to be used. □ *Similar legislation is already in place in Wales.* ㉞ PHRASE If one thing or person is used or does something in place of another, they replace the other thing or person. □ *Laurence Waters visited us in place of John Trethewy who was unfortunately ill.* ㉟ PHRASE If something has particular characteristics or features in places, it has them at several points within an area. □ *Even now the snow along the roadside was five or six feet deep in places.* ㊱ PHRASE If you say what you would have done in someone else's place, you say what you would have done if you had been in their situation and had been experiencing what they were experiencing. □ *In her place I wouldn't have been able to resist it.* ㊲ PHRASE You say in the first place when you are talking about the beginning of a situation or about the situation as it was before a series of events. □ *What brought you to Washington in the first place?* ㊳ PHRASE You say in the first place and in the second place to introduce the first and second in a series of points or reasons. In the first place can also be used to emphasize a very important point or reason. □ *In the first place you are not old, Norman. And in the second place, you are a very strong and appealing man.* ㊴ PHRASE If you say that it is not your place to do something, you mean that it is not right or appropriate for you to do it, or that it is not your responsibility to do it. □ *He says that it is not his place to comment on government commitment to further funds.* ㊵ PHRASE If someone or something seems out of place in a particular situation, they do not seem to belong there or to be suitable for that situation. □ *I felt out of place in my suit and tie.* ㊶ PHRASE If you place one thing above, before, or over another, you think that the first thing is more important than the second and you show this in your behavior. □ *He continued to place security above all other objectives.* ㊷ PHRASE If you put someone in their place, you show them that they are less important or clever than they think they are. □ *In a few words she had not only put him in his place but delivered a precise and damning assessment of his movie.* ㊸ PHRASE If you say that someone should be shown their place or be kept in their place, you are saying, often in a humorous way, that they should be made aware of their low status. □ *...an uppity publican who needs to be shown his place.* ㊹ PHRASE If one thing takes second place to another, it is considered to be less important and is given less attention than the other thing. □ *My personal life has had to take second place to my career.* ㊺ PHRASE If one thing or person takes the place of another or takes another's place, they replace the other thing or person. □ *Optimism was gradually taking the place of pessimism.* →see zero

place|ment /pleɪsmənt/ (placements) ◾ N-UNCOUNT The placement of something or someone is the act of putting them in a particular place or position. □ *The treatment involves the placement of twenty-two electrodes in the inner ear.* ◼ N-COUNT If someone who is training gets a placement, they get a job for a period of time which is intended to give them experience in the work they are training for. □ *He spent a year studying Japanese in Tokyo, followed by a six-month work placement with the Japanese government.* ◾ N-UNCOUNT The placement of someone in a job, home, or school is the act or process of finding them a job, home, or school. □ *The children were waiting for placement in a foster care home.*

plac|id /plæsɪd/ ◾ ADJ A placid person or animal is calm and does not easily become excited, angry, or upset. □ *She was a placid child who rarely cried.* ◼ ADJ A placid place, area of water, or life is calm and peaceful. □ *...the placid waters of Lake Erie.*

pla|gia|rism /pleɪdʒərɪzəm/ N-UNCOUNT Plagiarism is the practice of using or copying someone else's idea or work and pretending that you thought of it or created it. □ *Now he's in real trouble. He's accused of plagiarism.*

> Writing a paper entirely or partly composed of the words of others without giving them credit for their work is called **plagiarism**. It is a punishable offense at American colleges and universities where students will be asked to leave. Professional writers who are caught cheating in this way may lose their jobs.

pla|gia|rize /pleɪdʒəraɪz/ (plagiarizes, plagiarizing, plagiarized) [BRIT also plagiarise] V-T If someone plagiarizes another person's idea or work, they use it or copy it and pretend that they thought of it or created it. □ *He has pointed out that moderates are plagiarizing his ideas in hopes of wooing voters.*

plague /pleɪg/ (plagues, plaguing, plagued) ◾ N-UNCOUNT Plague or the plague is a very infectious disease which usually results in death. The patient has a severe fever and swellings on his or her body. [also the N] □ *...a fresh outbreak of plague.* ◼ N-COUNT A plague of unpleasant things is a large number of them that arrive or happen at the same time. □ *The city is under threat from a plague of rats.* ◾ V-T If you are plagued by unpleasant things, they continually cause you a lot of trouble or suffering. □ *She was plagued by weakness, fatigue, and dizziness.*

plaice /pleɪs/

> Plaice is both the singular and the plural form.

N-VAR Plaice are a type of flat sea fish. ● N-UNCOUNT Plaice is this fish eaten as food. □ *...a fillet of plaice with sautéed rice and vegetables.*

plain ♦◇◇ /pleɪn/ (plainer, plainest, plains) ◾ ADJ A plain object, surface, or fabric is entirely in one color and has no pattern, design, or writing on it. □ *In general, a plain carpet makes a room look bigger.* □ *He placed the paper in a plain*

노면. 두 번째로 자넨 아주 강하고 매력적인 남자일세. ㉝ 구 -할 자리가 아니다, -하는 것이 적절하지 않다 □ 그는 추가 기금에 대한 정부 결정을 자신이 논평하는 것은 적절하지 못하다고 말한다. ㊵ 구 어울리지 않다 □ 정장을 입고 넥타이를 맨 나는 어울리지 않는다는 느낌이 들었다. ㊶ 구 -보다 중요시하다, -보다 우선시하다 □ 그는 계속해서 보안을 다른 모든 목표보다 우선시했다. ㊷ 구 자기 분수를 알게 해 주다 □ 몇 마디 말로 그녀는 그가 자기 분수를 알도록 해 주었을 뿐 아니라 그의 영화에 대해 정확하고 지독한 평가도 내렸다. ㊸ 구 주제넘을 알게 해 주다 □ 자신의 주제를 알게 해 줄 필요가 있는 주제넘은 정치인 □ 내 사생활은 내 일보다 덜 중요하다고 간주되어야만 했다. ㊺ 구 -을 대신하다 □ 낙관주의가 차츰 비관주의를 대신하고 있었다.

◾ 불가산명사 배치 □ 치료에는 내이에 22개의 전극을 배치하는 것이 포함된다. ◼ 가산명사 수습직 □ 그는 도쿄에서 일본어를 공부하면서 한 해를 보낸 후에 일본 정부에서 6개월간 수습 직원으로 일했다. ◾ 불가산명사 소개, 알선 □ 그 아이들은 수양 가정에 소개 받기를 기다리고 있었다.

◾ 형용사 차분한 □ 그녀는 거의 우는 법이 없는 차분한 아이였다. ◼ 형용사 산잔한 □ 잔잔한 이리 호

불가산명사 표절 행위 □ 이제 그가 정말 난처하게 되었어. 표절 행위로 고소당했거든.

> 다른 사람이 쓴 글의 전부 또는 일부를 인용 표시 없이 논문에 쓰는 것을 plagiarism(표절)이라고 한다. 미국 대학에서 이것은 처벌 대상이 되는 위반 행위이며, 학생이 학교를 그만 두게 할 수도 있다. 전문적으로 글을 쓰는 사람들은 표절 행위가 드러날 경우 직장을 잃을 수도 있다.

[영국영어 plagiarise] 타동사 표절하다, 도용하다 □ 그는 온건파들이 유권자의 환심을 얻고자 자신의 아이디어를 도용하고 있다고 지적했다.

◾ 불가산명사 페스트, 흑사병 □ 페스트의 새로운 발병 ◼ 가산명사 (해충 등의) 많은 수 □ 도시가 수많은 쥐떼의 위협을 받고 있다. ◾ 타동사 시달리다 □ 그녀는 허약함과 피로, 그리고 어지럼증에 시달렸다.

> plaice은 단수형 및 복수형이다.

가산명사 또는 불가산명사 가자미류 ● 불가산명사 가자미, 넙치 □ 짝 볶은 밥과 야채를 곁들인 가자미 필레 요리

◾ 형용사 무늬가 없는, 단색의 □ 대개 무늬가 없는 카펫을 깔면 방이 더 커 보인다. □ 그는 서류를 단색 봉투에 넣었다. ◼ 형용사 소박한 □ 브론웬의 드레스는

envelope. **2** ADJ Something that is **plain** is very simple in style. ❑ *Bronwen's dress was plain but it hung well on her.* ● **plain|ly** ADV [ADV -ed] ❑ *He was very tall and plainly dressed.* **3** ADJ If a fact, situation, or statement is **plain**, it is easy to recognize or understand. ❑ *It was plain to him that I was having a nervous breakdown.* **4** ADJ If you describe someone as **plain**, you think they look ordinary and not at all beautiful. ❑ *...a shy, rather plain girl with a pale complexion.* **5** N-COUNT A **plain** is a large flat area of land with very few trees on it. ❑ *Once there were 70 million buffalo on the plains.* **6** PHRASE If a police officer is **in plain clothes**, he or she is wearing ordinary clothes instead of a police uniform. ❑ *Three officers in plain clothes told me to get out of the car.* **plain sailing** →see **sailing**

소박했지만 그녀에게 잘 어울렸다. ● 소박하게 부사 ❑ 그는 무척 키가 컸고 옷을 소박하게 입고 있었다. **3** 형용사 알기 쉬운, 명백한 ❑ 그는 내가 신경 쇠약에 시달리고 있는 것을 쉽게 알아보았다. **4** 형용사 평범한, 예쁘지 않은 ❑ 부끄럼을 타는 창백한 안색의 다소 평범하게 생긴 소녀 **5** 가산명사 평원 ❑ 한때 그 평원에는 7천만 마리의 들소가 살았다. **6** 구 사복 차림의 ❑ 사복 차림의 경관 세 명이 나에게 차에서 내리라고 지시했다.

plain|ly /pleɪnli/ **1** ADV You use **plainly** to indicate that you believe something is obviously true, often when you are trying to convince someone else that it is true. [EMPHASIS] [ADV with cl, not last in cl] ❑ *The judge's conclusion was plainly wrong.* ❑ *Plainly, a more objective method of description must be adopted.* **2** ADV You use **plainly** to indicate that something is easily seen, noticed, or recognized. ❑ *He was plainly annoyed.* ❑ *I could plainly see him turning his head to the right and left.* →see also **plain**

1 부사 명백히, 분명히 [강조] ❑ 판사의 판정은 명백히 잘못된 것이었다. ❑ 분명히, 좀 더 객관적으로 기술할 수 있는 방법을 채택해야만 한다. **2** 부사 노골적으로, 확실히 ❑ 그는 노골적으로 짜증을 내고 있었다. ❑ 난 그가 고개를 좌우로 돌리는 것을 확실히 볼 수 있었다.

plain|tiff /pleɪntɪf/ (**plaintiffs**) N-COUNT A **plaintiff** is a person who brings a legal case against someone in a court of law. ❑ *The lead plaintiff of the lawsuit is the University of California.* →see **trial**

가산명사 원고, 고소인 ❑ 그 소송의 대표 원고는 캘리포니아 대학이다.

plain|tive /pleɪntɪv/ ADJ A **plaintive** sound or voice sounds sad. [LITERARY] ❑ *They lay on the firm sands, listening to the plaintive cry of the seagulls.*

형용사 구슬픈 [문예체] ❑ 그들은 단단한 모래 위에 드러누워서 갈매기들의 구슬픈 울음소리를 듣고 있었다.

plait /pleɪt, BRIT plæt/ (**plaits, plaiting, plaited**) **1** V-T If you **plait** three or more lengths of hair, rope, or other material together, you twist them over and under each other to make one thick length. [mainly BRIT; AM usually **braid**] ❑ *Joanna parted her hair, and then began to plait it into two thick braids.* **2** N-COUNT A **plait** is a length of hair that has been plaited [mainly BRIT; AM usually **braid**] ❑ *...a plain girl with plaits.*

1 타동사 땋다 [주로 영국영어; 미국영어 대개 braid] ❑ 조애너는 머리 가르마를 탄 후에 두툼하게 양 갈래로 땋기 시작했다. **2** 가산명사 땋은 머리 [주로 영국영어; 미국영어 대개 braid] ❑ 땋은 머리를 한 평범한 소녀

plan ♦♦♦ /plæn/ (**plans, planning, planned**) **1** N-COUNT A **plan** is a method of achieving something that you have worked out in detail beforehand. [usu with supp, also *according to N*] ❑ *The three leaders had worked out a peace plan.* ❑ *He maintains that everything is going according to plan.* **2** V-T/V-I If you **plan** what you are going to do, you decide in detail what you are going to do, and you intend to do it. ❑ *If you plan what you're going to eat, you reduce your chances of overeating.* ❑ *He planned to leave Baghdad on Monday.* **3** N-PLURAL If you have **plans**, you are intending to do a particular thing. ❑ *"I'm sorry," she said. "I have plans for tonight."* **4** V-T When you **plan** something that you are going to make, build, or create, you decide what the main parts of it will be and do a drawing of how it should be made. ❑ *It is no use trying to plan an 18-hole golf course on a 120-acre site if you have to ruin the environment to do it.* **5** N-COUNT A **plan of** something that is going to be built or made is a detailed diagram or drawing of it. ❑ *...when you have drawn a plan of the garden.* **6** →see also **planning**

1 가산명사 계획 ❑ 지도자들 세 명이 평화 계획을 수립했다. ❑ 그는 모든 것이 계획에 따라 진행되고 있다고 주장한다. **2** 타동사/자동사 계획을 세우다, 계획하다 ❑ 무얼 먹을 것인지 계획을 세우면 과식할 가능성이 줄어든다. ❑ 그는 월요일에 바그다드를 떠나려고 계획했다. **3** 복수명사 계획 ❑ "미안하지만," 그녀가 말했다. "전 오늘 밤에 계획이 있어요." **4** 타동사 설계하다 ❑ 그 과정에서 어쩔 수 없이 환경을 해치게 된다면 120에이커의 부지에 18홀을 갖춘 골프장을 설계하려 해 봐야 소용없는 일이다. **5** 가산명사 설계도 ❑ 네가 정원 설계도를 다 그렸을 때

▶**plan on** PHRASAL VERB If you **plan on** doing something, you intend to do it. ❑ *They were planning on getting married.*

구동사 -할 작정이다 ❑ 그들은 결혼할 작정이었다.

plane ♦♦◇ /pleɪn/ (**planes, planing, planed**) **1** N-COUNT A **plane** is a vehicle with wings and one or more engines, which can fly through the air. ❑ *He had plenty of time to catch his plane.* ❑ *Her mother was killed in a plane crash.* **2** N-COUNT A **plane** is a flat, level surface which may be sloping at a particular angle. ❑ *...a building with angled planes.* **3** N-SING If a number of points are in the same **plane**, one line or one flat surface could pass through them all. ❑ *All the planets orbit the Sun in roughly the same plane, round its equator.* **4** N-COUNT A **plane** is a tool that has a flat bottom with a sharp blade in it. You move the plane over a piece of wood in order to remove thin pieces of its surface. **5** V-T If you **plane** a piece of wood, you make it smaller or smoother by using a plane. ❑ *She watches him plane the surface of a walnut board.* **6** N-COUNT A **plane** or a **plane tree** is a large tree with broad leaves which often grows in towns and cities.

1 가산명사 비행기 ❑ 그는 비행기를 탈 시간이 충분히 있었다. ❑ 그녀의 어머니는 비행기 사고로 사망했다. **2** 가산명사 면, 평면 ❑ 각진 평면으로 이루어진 건물 **3** 단수명사 평면 ❑ 모든 행성들이 얼추 동일한 평면에서 태양 적도 주위에서 태양을 선회한다. **4** 가산명사 대패 **5** 타동사 대패질하다 ❑ 그녀는 그가 호두나무 판자의 표면을 대패질하는 것을 지켜보았다. **6** 가산명사 플라타너스

plan|et ◆◇◇ /plǽnɪt/ (**planets**) N-COUNT A **planet** is a large, round object in space that moves around a star. The Earth is a planet. ❑ *The picture shows six of the nine planets in the solar system.* →see **galaxy**, **satellite**, **solar system**

가산명사 행성 ❑ 그 사진에서는 태양계의 아홉 개 행성 중 여섯 개가 보인다.

plan|etary /plǽnɪteri, BRIT plǽnɪtri/ ADJ **Planetary** means relating to or belonging to planets. [ADJ n] ❑ *Within our own galaxy there are probably tens of thousands of planetary systems.*

형용사 행성의 ❑ 우리가 속한 은하계 안에는 아마도 수만 개의 행성계가 있을 것이다.

plank /plǽŋk/ (**planks**) ■ N-COUNT A **plank** is a long, flat, rectangular piece of wood. ❑ *It was very strong, made of three solid planks of wood.* ◻ N-COUNT The main **plank** of a particular group or political party is the main principle on which it bases its policy, or its main aim. [JOURNALISM] ❑ *The Saudi authorities have made agricultural development a central plank of policy to make the country less dependent on imports.*

■ 가산명사 널빤지 ❑ 그것은 단단한 나무 널빤지 세 개로 만든 것이라 아주 튼튼했다. ◻ 가산명사 강령 [언론] ❑ 사우디아라비아 당국은 자국의 수입 의존도를 줄이기 위해 농업 발전을 정책의 중심 강령으로 채택했다.

plan|ner /plǽnər/ (**planners**) N-COUNT **Planners** are people whose job is to make decisions about what is going to be done in the future. For example, town planners decide how land should be used and what new buildings should be built. ❑ *a panel that includes city planners, art experts and historians.*

가산명사 계획가, 설계사 ❑ 도시 계획가들과 미술 전문가들, 역사학자들로 구성된 패널

plan|ning ◆◇◇ /plǽnɪŋ/ ■ N-UNCOUNT **Planning** is the process of deciding in detail how to do something before you actually start to do it. ❑ *The trip needs careful planning.* →see also **family planning** ◻ N-UNCOUNT **Planning** is control by the local government of the way that land is used in an area and of what new buildings are built there. ❑ *...a masterpiece of 18th-century town planning.*

■ 불가산명사 계획 수립 ❑ 그 여행은 조심스럽게 계획을 세울 필요가 있어. ◻ 불가산명사 계획 ❑ 18세기 도시 계획학의 걸작

plant ◆◆◆ /plɑnt, plǽnt/ (**plants, planting, planted**) ■ N-COUNT A **plant** is a living thing that grows in the earth and has a stem, leaves, and roots. ❑ *Water each plant as often as required.* ◻ V-T When you **plant** a seed, plant, or young tree, you put it into the ground so that it will grow there. ❑ *He says he plans to plant fruit trees and vegetables.* ● **planting** N-UNCOUNT ❑ *Extensive flooding in the country has delayed planting and many crops are still under water.* ◼ V-T When someone **plants** land **with** a particular type of plant or crop, they put plants, seeds, or young trees into the land to grow them there. ❑ *They plan to plant the area with grass and trees.* ❑ *Recently much of their energy has gone into planting a large vegetable garden.* ◻ N-COUNT A **plant** is a factory or a place where power is produced. ❑ *...Ford's British car assembly plants.* ◻ N-UNCOUNT **Plant** is large machinery that is used in industrial processes. ❑ *Firms may start to invest in plant and equipment abroad where costs may be lower.* ◻ V-T If you **plant** something somewhere, you put it there firmly. ❑ *She planted her feet wide and bent her knees slightly.* ◻ V-T To **plant** something such as a bomb means to hide it somewhere so that it explodes or works there. ❑ *So far no one has admitted planting the bomb.* ◻ V-T If something such as a weapon or drugs **is planted** on someone, it is put among their possessions or in their house so that they will be wrongly accused of a crime. [oft passive] ❑ *He always protested his innocence and claimed that the drugs had been planted to incriminate him.* ◻ V-T If an organization **plants** someone somewhere, they send that person there so that they can get information or watch someone secretly. ❑ *Journalists informed police who planted an undercover detective to trap Smith.* →see **earth**, **farm**, **food**, **fruit**, **tree** →see Word Web: **plant**

■ 가산명사 식물 ❑ 필요할 때마다 모든 식물에 물을 주세요. ◻ 타동사 (씨를) 뿌리다, 심다 ❑ 그는 과수와 채소를 심을 계획이라고 말한다. ● 파종 불가산명사 ❑ 그 지방에서는 엄청난 홍수로 파종이 늦어지고 있고 많은 농작물이 여전히 물속에 잠겨 있다. ◼ 타동사 심다, 가꾸다 ❑ 그들은 그 지역에 잔디와 나무를 심을 계획이다. ❑ 최근에 그들은 큰 채소밭을 가꾸는 데 많은 노력을 쏟아 왔다. ◻ 가산명사 공장, 발전소 ❑ 포드 사의 영국 내 자동차 조립 공장들 ◻ 불가산명사 공장 설비 ❑ 기업들이 경비를 낮출 수 있는 해외에서 공장 설비 및 장비에 투자하기 시작할지도 모른다. ◻ 타동사 단단히 놓다 ❑ 그녀는 두 발을 벌려 단단히 딛고 서서 무릎을 약간 구부렸다. ◻ 타동사 몰래 장치하다 ❑ 지금까지 그 누구도 그 폭탄을 장치했다고 인정하지 않았다. ◻ 타동사 (혐의를 씌우기 위해 물건을) 몰래 두다 ❑ 그는 항상 자신의 결백을 항변했고 그 마약은 자신에게 죄를 뒤집어씌우려고 누군가가 고의로 놓아둔 것이었다고 주장했다. ◻ 타동사 첩자를 심다 ❑ 언론인들이 누가 스미스를 함정에 빠뜨리기 위해 위장한 형사를 심는지를 경찰에 알려 줬다.

plan|ta|tion /plæntéɪʃn/ (**plantations**) ■ N-COUNT A **plantation** is a large piece of land, especially in a tropical country, where crops such as rubber, coffee, tea, or sugar are grown. ❑ *...banana plantations in Costa Rica.* ◻ N-COUNT A **plantation** is a large number of trees that have been planted together. ❑ *...a plantation of almond trees.*

■ 가산명사 (특히 열대 지역의) 재배 농장 ❑ 코스타리카에 있는 바나나 재배 농장 ◻ 가산명사 인공림 ❑ 아몬드 나무 인공림

plaque /plǽk/ (**plaques**) ■ N-COUNT A **plaque** is a flat piece of metal or stone with writing on it which is fixed to a wall or other structure to remind people of an important person or event. ❑ *After touring the hospital, Her Majesty unveiled a commemorative plaque.* ◻ N-UNCOUNT **Plaque** is a substance containing bacteria that forms on the surface of your teeth. ❑ *Deposits of plaque build up between the tooth and the gum.* →see **teeth**

■ 가산명사 명판 ❑ 병원을 돌아보신 후 여왕께서 기념 명판에 씌워진 덮개를 벗기셨다. ◻ 불가산명사 플라크, 치석 ❑ 플라크 덩어리는 치아와 잇몸 사이에 생긴다.

plas|ma /plǽzmə/ N-UNCOUNT **Plasma** is the clear liquid part of blood which contains the blood cells.

불가산명사 혈장

plas|ter /plǽstər/ (**plasters, plastering, plastered**) ■ N-UNCOUNT **Plaster** is a smooth paste made of sand, lime, and water which gets hard when it dries. Plaster is used to cover walls and ceilings and is also used to make sculptures. ❑ *There were huge cracks in the plaster, and the green shutters were faded.* ◻ V-T If you **plaster** a wall or ceiling, you cover it with a layer of plaster. ❑ *The ceiling he had just plastered fell in and knocked him off his ladder.* ◻ V-T If you **plaster** a surface or a place **with** posters or pictures, you stick a lot of them all over it. ❑ *He has plastered the city with posters proclaiming his qualifications and experience.* ◻ V-T If you **plaster yourself in** some kind of sticky substance, you cover yourself in it. ❑ *She gets sunburnt even when she plasters herself from head to toe in Factor 7 sun lotion.*

■ 불가산명사 회반죽 ❑ 회반죽을 칠한 벽에 커다란 금이 가 있었고 초록색 덧문은 색이 바래 있었다. ◻ 타동사 회반죽을 칠하다 ❑ 그가 방금 회반죽을 칠한 천장이 내려앉는 바람에 그가 사다리에서 떨어졌다. ◻ 타동사 더덕더덕 붙이다 ❑ 그는 온 도시에 자신의 자격과 경험을 알리는 포스터를 더덕더덕 붙였다. ◻ 타동사 더덕더덕 바르다 ❑ 그녀는 차단 지수 7인 자외선 차단 로션을 머리끝부터 발끝까지 더덕더덕 발라도 햇볕에 탄다. ◻ 가산명사 반창고, 밴드 [영국영어; 미국영어 대개 Band-Aid] ◻ 구 깁스를 한

Word Web　　plant

There are over 300,000 **species** in the **plant kingdom**. They vary from microscopic **algae** to giant redwood **trees**. However, they share one characteristic—they all use photosynthesis to manufacture food. Various plants exhibit three different types of **life cycles**. An **annual** plant grows, flowers, and then dies in one growing **season**. Examples of annuals are tomatoes and marigolds. Biennial plants, such as carrots, require two years to complete their life cycle and produce **seeds**. **Perennial** plants come back every year after remaining **dormant** over the winter. Perennials include **oak** trees, **roses**, and **daisies**.

a b c d e f g h i j k l m n o p q r s t u v w x y z

5 N-COUNT A **plaster** is a strip of sticky material used for covering small cuts or sores on your body. [BRIT; AM usually **Band-Aid**] **6** →see also **plastered** **7** PHRASE If you have a leg or arm **in plaster**, you have a cover made of plaster of Paris around your leg or arm, in order to protect a broken bone and allow it to mend. [mainly BRIT; AM **in a cast**] □ *Carney's foot has been in plaster since mid-April.*

[주로 영국영어; 미국영어 in a cast] □ 카니는 4월 중순 이후로 발에 깁스를 하고 있다.

plas|tered /plǽstərd/ **1** ADJ If something is **plastered to** a surface, it is sticking to the surface. [v-link ADJ prep/adv] □ *His hair was plastered down to his scalp by the rain.* **2** ADJ If something or someone is **plastered with** a sticky substance, they are covered with it. [v-link ADJ, usu ADJ with/in n] □ *My hands, boots, and trousers were plastered with mud.* **3** ADJ If a story or photograph is **plastered all over** the front page of a newspaper, it is given a lot of space on the page and made very noticeable. [v-link ADJ prep/adv] □ *His picture was plastered all over the newspapers on the weekend.*

1 형용사 ~에 달라붙은 □ 그의 머리카락이 비에 젖어 머리에 착 달라붙어 있었다. **2** 형용사 ~가 더덕더덕 발린 □ 내 두 손과 장화, 그리고 바지에 진흙이 덕지덕지 발려 있었다. **3** 형용사 (신문을) 장식한 □ 그의 사진이 주말 동안 온 신문을 장식했다.

plas|tic ♦◇◇ /plǽstɪk/ (plastics) **1** N-MASS **Plastic** is a material which is produced from oil by a chemical process and which is used to make many objects. It is light in weight and does not break easily. □ *...a wooden crate, sheltered from wetness by sheets of plastic.* □ *A lot of the plastics that carmakers are using cannot be recycled.* **2** ADJ If you describe something as **plastic**, you mean that you think it looks or tastes unnatural or not real. [DISAPPROVAL] □ *You wanted proper home-cooked meals, you said you had enough plastic hotel food and airline food.* **3** N-UNCOUNT If you use **plastic** or **plastic money** to pay for something, you pay for it with a credit card instead of using cash. [INFORMAL] □ *Using plastic to pay for an order is simplicity itself.* **4** ADJ Something that is **plastic** is soft and can easily be made into different shapes. □ *You can also enjoy mud packs with the natural mud, smooth, gray, soft, and plastic as butter.* →see **oil**

1 물질명사 플라스틱, 합성수지 □ 플라스틱 판을 덧대 물에 젖지 않게 만든 나무 상자 □ 자동차 제조 회사들이 사용하고 있는 많은 플라스틱은 재활용할수 없다. **2** 형용사 인공적인, 진짜가 아닌 [탐탁찮음] □ 너는 집에서 만든 진짜 음식을 원했다. 겉만 그럴듯한 호텔 음식과 기내식을 먹을 만큼 먹었다고 네가 그랬어. **3** 불가산명사 신용 카드 [비격식체] □ 주문할 때 신용 카드로 지불하면 정말 간단하다. **4** 형용사 가소성의, 모양을 마음대로 만들 수 있는 □ 매끄럽고, 회색빛에, 부드럽고, 버터처럼 마음대로 모양을 만들 수도 있는 천연 진흙으로 진흙 팩도 즐기실 수 있습니다.

plas|tic sur|gery N-UNCOUNT **Plastic surgery** is the practice of performing operations to repair or replace skin which has been damaged, or to improve people's appearance. □ *She even had plastic surgery to change the shape of her nose.*

불가산명사 성형 수술 □ 그녀는 코 모양을 바꾸려고 성형 수술까지 받았다.

plas|tic wrap N-UNCOUNT **Plastic wrap** is a thin, clear, stretchy plastic which you use to cover food to keep it fresh. [AM; BRIT **clingfilm**]

불가산명사 랩, 비닐 랩 [미국영어; 영국영어 clingfilm]

plate ♦♦◇ /pleɪt/ (plates) **1** N-COUNT A **plate** is a round or oval flat dish that is used to hold food. □ *Anita pushed her plate away; she had eaten virtually nothing.* ● N-COUNT A **plate of** food is the amount of food on the plate. □ *...a huge plate of bacon and eggs.* **2** N-COUNT A **plate** is a flat piece of metal, especially on machinery or a building. □ *...a recess covered by a brass plate.* **3** N-COUNT A **plate** is a small, flat piece of metal with someone's name written on it, which you usually find beside the front door of an office or house. □ *An age-worn brass plate by the front door announced: L. L. Herring & Sons Ltd., Numismatists, Since 1789.* **4** N-PLURAL On a road vehicle, the **plates** are the panels at the front and back which display the license number in the United States, and the registration number in Britain. □ *...dusty-looking cars with New Jersey plates.* →see also **number plate, license plate** **5** N-COUNT A **plate** in a book is a picture or photograph which takes up a whole page and is usually printed on better quality paper than the rest of the book. □ *Fermor's book has 55 color plates.* **6** PHRASE If you **have enough on** your **plate** or **have a lot on** your **plate**, you have a lot of work to do or a lot of things to deal with. □ *We have enough on our plate. There is plenty of work to be done on what we have.* **7** PHRASE If you say that someone has things **handed to** them **on a plate**, you disapprove of them because they get good things easily. [mainly BRIT, DISAPPROVAL] □ *Even the presidency was handed to him on a plate.*

1 가산명사 접시 □ 애니타가 자기 접시를 밀어냈다. 그녀는 사실상 아무것도 먹지 않았다. ● 가산명사 한 접시 (분량) □ 엄청나게 많은 베이컨과 달걀 한 접시 **2** 가산명사 금속판 □ 동판으로 가려진 우묵한 곳 **3** 가산명사 문패, 표찰 □ 정문 옆의 오래된 놋쇠 문패에는 '엘 엘 헤링 앤 선스 유한 회사, 화폐 연구가들, 1789년 설립'이라고 쓰여 있었다. **4** 복수명사 자동차 번호판 □ 뉴저지 번호판을 단, 먼지를 뒤집어쓴 것처럼 보이는 자동차들 **5** 가산명사 별쇄 삽화 □ 퍼모의 책에는 55쪽의 별쇄 삽화가 들어 있다. **6** 구 할 일이 많다 □ 우리는 할 일이 많아. 우린 할 일이 넘쳐 난다니까. **7** 구 쉽게 얻은 [주로 영국영어, 탐탁찮음] □ 대통령직조차도 그는 쉽게 얻어 냈다.

pla|teau /plǽtoʊ, BRIT plǽtəʊ/

The plural can be either **plateaus** or **plateaux**.

복수는 plateaus 또는 plateaux이다.

1 N-COUNT A **plateau** is a large area of high and fairly flat land. □ *A broad valley opened up leading to a high, flat plateau of cultivated land.* **2** N-COUNT If you say that an activity or process has reached a **plateau**, you mean that it has reached a stage where there is no further change or development. □ *The U.S. heroin market now appears to have reached a plateau.*

1 가산명사 고원 □ 널찍한 골짜기는 높고 평평한 고원의 경작지로 이어졌다. **2** 가산명사 정체기, 안정기 □ 미국의 헤로인 시장은 이제 정체기에 이른 것 같다.

-plated /-pleɪtɪd/ COMB in ADJ Something made of metal that is **plated** is covered with a thin layer of another type of metal such as gold and silver. □ *...a gold-plated watch.*

복합형-형용사 도금한 □ 금도금 손목시계

plat|form ♦◇◇ /plǽtfɔːrm/ (platforms) **1** N-COUNT A **platform** is a flat raised structure, usually made of wood, which people stand on when they make speeches or give a performance. □ *Nick finished what he was saying and jumped down from the platform.* **2** N-COUNT A **platform** is a flat raised structure or area, usually one which something can stand on or land on. □ *Some of these flood shelters are on raised platforms, which have allowed government helicopters to land amid the continuing floods.* **3** N-COUNT A **platform** is a structure built for people to work and live on when drilling for oil or gas at sea, or when extracting it. □ *The platform began to produce oil in 1994.* **4** N-COUNT A **platform** in a train or subway station is the area beside the tracks where you wait for or get off a train. □ *The train was about to leave and I was not even on the platform.* **5** N-COUNT The **platform** of a political party is what they say they will do if they are elected. □ *The party has announced a platform of political and economic reforms as it campaigns for the country's first multiparty elections next month.* **6** N-COUNT If someone has a **platform**, they have an opportunity to tell people what they think or want. □ *The demonstration provided a platform for a broad cross section of speakers.* →see **skateboarding**

1 가산명사 연단, 단상 □ 닉은 하던 말을 마치고 연단에서 뛰어내려 왔다. **2** 가산명사 단 □ 이러한 홍수 대피용 시설들 중 일부는 높게 쌓은 단 위에 위치하고 있어서 정부의 헬리콥터가 계속되는 홍수 속에서도 착륙할 수 있었다. **3** 가산명사 석유 굴착 플랫폼, 가스 굴착 플랫폼 □ 그 석유 굴착 플랫폼은 1994년에 석유를 생산하기 시작했다. **4** 가산명사 승강장, 플랫폼 □ 기차가 막 떠나려 했지만 난 승강장에도 닿지 못했다. **5** 가산명사 (정당의) 기본 방침, 강령 □ 그 당은 다음 달에 국가 최초의 복수 정당이 치를 선거를 위한 선거 운동을 하면서 정치 및 경제 개혁이라는 기본 방침을 발표했다. **6** 가산명사 연설 기회 □ 그 시위는 사회 각층의 연사들에게 연설할 기회를 마련해 주었다.

Thesaurus	*platform*의 참조어
N.	floor, podium, table **1**
	agenda, objective, policy, principle, program, promise **5**

plat|i|num /plætɪnəm, plætnəm/ N-UNCOUNT **Platinum** is a very valuable, silvery-gray metal. It is often used for making jewelry.

불가산명사 백금

plat|i|tude /plætɪtud, BRIT plætɪtyuːd/ (platitudes) N-COUNT A **platitude** is a statement which is considered meaningless and boring because it has been made many times before in similar situations. [DISAPPROVAL] ❏ *Why couldn't he, for once, say something vital and original instead of just spouting the same old platitudes?*

가산명사 진부한 문장, 상투적인 말 [탐탁찮음] ❏ 그는 어째서, 늘 하던 상투적인 말을 쏟아 내지만 말고, 한 번만이라도 중요하고 독창적인 말을 할 수 없었을까?

pla|ton|ic /plətɒnɪk/ ADJ **Platonic** relationships or feelings of affection do not involve sex. ❏ *She values the platonic friendship she has had with Chris for ten years.*

형용사 정신적인 ❏ 그녀는 크리스와 10년 동안 나눠 온 정신적인 우정을 소중히 여긴다.

plat|ter /plætər/ (platters) N-COUNT A **platter** is a large flat plate used for serving food. [mainly AM] ❏ *The food was being served on silver platters.* ● N-COUNT A **platter of** food is the amount of food on a platter.

가산명사 (상차림용) 큰 접시 [주로 미국영어] ❏ 음식은 커다란 차림용 은 접시에 담겨 나오고 있었다. ● 가산명사 큰 접시 (분량)

plau|si|ble /plɔːzəbəl/ ❶ ADJ An explanation or statement that is **plausible** seems likely to be true or valid. ❏ *A more plausible explanation would seem to be that people are fed up with the Conservative government.* ● **plau|si|bly** /plɔːzɪbli/ ADV [ADV with v] ❏ *Having bluffed his way in without paying, he could not plausibly demand his money back.* ● **plau|si|bil|ity** /plɔːzɪbɪliti/ N-UNCOUNT ❏ *...the plausibility of the theory.* ❷ ADJ If you say that someone is **plausible**, you mean that they seem to be telling the truth and to be sincere and honest. ❏ *All I can say is that he was so plausible it wasn't just me that he conned.*

❶ 형용사 그럴듯한 ❏ 사람들이 보수적인 정부에 진저리가 났다는 것이 좀 더 그럴듯한 설명이 될 것 같다. ● 그럴듯하게 부사 ❏ 그는 돈을 내지 않고 속이고 들어왔기 때문에, 그는 돈을 돌려 달라고 그럴듯하게 요구할 수 없었다. ● 그럴듯함 불가산명사 ❏ 그 이론의 그럴듯함 ❷ 형용사 그럴듯하게 말하는, 말주변이 좋은 ❏ 오직 내가 할 수 있는 말은 그가 말하는 게 너무나 그럴듯해서 그에게 속은 사람이 나뿐이 아니었다는 것이다.

play ♦♦♦ /pleɪ/ (plays, playing, played) ❶ V-I When children, animals, or perhaps adults **play**, they spend time doing enjoyable things, such as using toys and taking part in games. ❏ *...invite the children round to play.* ❏ *They played in the little garden.* ● N-UNCOUNT **Play** is also a noun. ❏ *...a few hours of play until the baby-sitter takes them off to bed.* ❷ V-RECIP When you **play** a sport, game, or match, you take part in it. ❏ *While the twins played cards, Francis sat reading.* ❏ *I used to play basketball.* ● N-UNCOUNT **Play** is also a noun. ❏ *Both sides adopted the Continental style of play.* ❸ V-T/V-I When one person or team **plays** another or **plays against** them, they compete against them in a sport or game. ❏ *Northern Ireland will play Latvia.* ● N-UNCOUNT **Play** is also a noun. ❏ *Fischer won after 5 hours and 41 minutes of play.* ❹ V-T If you **play** a joke or a trick on someone, you deceive them or give them a surprise in a way that you think is funny, but that often causes problems for them or annoys them. ❏ *Someone had played a trick on her, stretched a piece of string at the top of those steps.* ❺ V-I If you **play with** an object or with your hair, you keep moving it or touching it with your fingers, perhaps because you are bored or nervous. ❏ *She stared at the floor, idly playing with the strap of her handbag.* ❻ N-COUNT A **play** is a piece of writing which is performed in a theater, on the radio, or on television. ❏ *It's my favorite Shakespeare play.* ❼ V-T If an actor **plays** a role or character in a play or movie, he or she performs the part of that character. ❏ *...Dr. Jekyll and Mr. Hyde, in which he played Hyde.* ❽ V-LINK You can use **play** to describe how someone behaves, when they are deliberately behaving in a certain way or like a certain type of person. For example, to **play the innocent**, means to pretend to be innocent, and to **play deaf** means to pretend not to hear something. ❏ *Hill tried to play the peacemaker.* ❏ *She was just playing the devoted mother.* ❾ V-T You can describe how someone deals with a situation by saying that they **play it** in a certain way. For example, if someone **plays it cool**, they keep calm and do not show much emotion, and if someone **plays it straight**, they behave in an honest and direct way. ❏ *Investors are playing it cautious, and they're playing it smart.* ❿ V-T/V-I If you **play** a musical instrument or **play** a tune on a musical instrument, or if a musical instrument **plays**, music is produced from it. ❏ *Nina had been playing the piano.* ❏ *He played for me.* ⓫ V-T/V-I If you **play** a record, a CD, or a tape, you put it into a machine and sound is produced. If a record, CD, or tape **is playing**, sound is being produced from it. ❏ *She played her records too loudly.* ❏ *There is classical music playing in the background.* ⓬ V-T/V-I If a musician or group of musicians **plays** or **plays** a concert, they perform music for people to listen or dance to. ❏ *A band was playing.* ⓭ PHRASE When something **comes into play** or **is brought into play**, it begins to be used or to have an effect. ❏ *The real existence of a military option will come into play.* ⓮ PHRASE If something or someone **plays a part** or **plays a role** in a situation, they are involved in it and have an effect on it. ❏ *They played a part in the life of their community.* ❏ *The UN would play a major role in monitoring a ceasefire.* ⓯ to **play the fool** →see **fool**. to **play to the gallery** →see **gallery**. to **play hard to get** →see **hard**. to **play havoc** →see **havoc**. to **play host** →see **host**. to **play safe** →see **safe**. to **play truant** →see **truant** →see **DVD, lottery**

❶ 자동사 놀다, 장난하다 ❏ 근처 아이들을 놀러 오라고 초대하다 ❏ 그들은 자그마한 정원에서 놀았다. ● 불가산명사 놀이, 장난 ❏ 아기 봐 주는 사람이 아기들을 잠자리에 들게 하기 전까지 몇 시간 동안 놀기 ❷ 상호동사 (게임, 경기 등을) 하다 ❏ 쌍둥이가 카드 게임을 하는 동안, 프랜시스는 앉아서 책을 읽고 있었다. ❏ 나는 예전에 야구를 했었다. ● 불가산명사 게임, 경기 ❏ 양측 모두 유럽 대륙 방식의 경기를 채택했다. ❸ 타동사/자동사 -와 시합하다 ❏ 북아일랜드가 라트비아와 시합할 것이다. ● 불가산명사 시합 ❏ 5시간 41분 동안의 시합 후에 피셔가 이겼다. ❹ 타동사 (농담 등을) 걸다; (속임수를) 쓰다 ❏ 누군가가 그 계단 꼭대기에서 끈 한 가닥을 늘어뜨리며 그녀에게 장난을 쳤다. ❺ 자동사 -을 만지작거리다 ❏ 그녀는 바닥을 빤히 내려다보며 하릴없이 자신의 손가방 끈을 만지작거리고 있었다. ❻ 가산명사 희곡, 각본 ❏ 그것이 내가 가장 좋아하는 셰익스피어 희곡이야. ❼ 타동사 (- 을) 연기하나 ❏ 그가 하이드 역을 연기했던 '지킬 박사와 하이드' 공연 ❽ 연결동사 -인 체하다 ❏ 힐은 애써 중재인인 체했다. ❏ 그녀는 그저 헌신적인 어머니인 척할 뿐이었다. ❾ 타동사 대처하다 ❏ 투자자들은 신중하게 그리고 영리하게 대처하고 있다. ❿ 타동사/자동사 (악기나 곡을) 연주하다; 연주되다 ❏ 니나는 피아노를 연주하고 있는 중이었다. ❏ 그는 날 위해 연주를 했다. ⓫ 타동사/자동사 (테이프 등을) 틀다; 음악이 나오다 ❏ 그녀는 음반을 너무 크게 틀었다. ❏ 배경 음악으로 고전 음악이 나오고 있다. ⓬ 타동사/자동사 연주하다 ❏ 악단이 연주하고 있었다. ⓭ 구 시행되기 시작하다, 활동하기 시작하다 ❏ 군사적 선택이 실질적으로 시행될 것이다. ⓮ 구 영향을 끼치다, 역할을 하다 ❏ 그들은 자신들이 속한 지역 사회의 생활에 영향을 끼쳤다. ❏ 유엔이 휴전 감시에 있어 주요 역할을 할 것이다.

▶**play around** ❶ PHRASAL VERB If you **play around**, you behave in a silly way to amuse yourself or other people. [INFORMAL] ❏ *Stop playing around and eat!* ❏ *There was no doubt he was serious, it wasn't just playing around.* ❷ PHRASAL VERB If you **play around with** a problem or an arrangement of objects, you try different ways of organizing it in order to find the best solution or arrangement. [INFORMAL] ❏ *I can play around with the pictures in all sorts of ways to make them more eye-catching.*

❶ 구동사 바보같이 굴다 [비격식체] ❏ 바보같이 굴지 말고 먹기나 해! ❏ 그가 진지하다는 긴 의심의 여지가 없었으니 그게 그냥 바보같이 구는 건 아니었을 거야. ❷ 구동사 온갖 궁리를 하다, 곰곰이 생각하다 [비격식체] ❏ 나는 그 사진들이 사람들의 눈길을 더 많이 끌 온갖 방법들을 궁리해 볼 수 있다.

▶**play at** ❶ PHRASAL VERB If you say that someone **is playing at** something, you disapprove of the fact that they are doing it casually and not very seriously. [DISAPPROVAL] [no passive] ❏ *We were still playing at war – dropping leaflets instead of bombs.* ❷ PHRASAL VERB If someone, especially a child, **plays at** being someone or doing something, they pretend to be that person or do that thing as a game. [no passive] ❏ *Ed played at being a pirate.* ❸ PHRASAL VERB If you do not know what someone **is playing at**, you do not understand what they are doing or what they are trying to achieve. [INFORMAL] ❏ *She began to wonder what he was playing at.*

❶ 구동사 장난삼아 하다 [탐탁찮음] ❏ 우리는 폭탄 대신 전단을 뿌려 대며 여전히 장난삼아 전쟁을 하고 있었다. ❷ 구동사 놀이를 하다 ❏ 에드는 해적 놀이를 했다. ❸ 구동사 -을 하다, -을 하려 하다 [비격식체] ❏ 그녀는 그가 뭘 하려는 건지 궁금해지기 시작했다.

▶**play back** PHRASAL VERB When you **play back** a tape or film, you listen to the sounds or watch the pictures after recording them. ❏ *He bought an answering machine that plays back his messages when he calls.* ❏ *Ted might benefit from hearing his own voice recorded and played back.*

구동사 (소리나 영화를) 재생하나 ❏ 그는 자기가 전화를 걸면 녹음된 메시지를 재생해 주는 자동 응답 전화기를 샀다. ❏ 테드가 자신의 목소리를 녹음해서 재생해 들으면 도움이 될 수도 있다.

a b c d e f g h i j k l m n o p q r s t u v w x y z

▶**play down** PHRASAL VERB If you **play down** something, you try to make people believe that it is not particularly important. ❏ *Western diplomats have played down the significance of the reports.* ❏ *Foreign exchange traders played down recent speculation about a currency devaluation.*

구동사 경시하다 ❏ 서방측 외교관들은 그 보고서의 중요성을 경시해 왔다. ❏ 외환 거래자들은 화폐 평가 절하에 대한 최근의 추측을 경시했다.

▶**play on** PHRASAL VERB If you **play on** someone's fears, weaknesses, or faults, you deliberately use them in order to persuade that person to do something, or to achieve what you want. ❏ *...an election campaign which plays on the population's fear of change.*

구동사 이용하다 ❏ 국민들의 변화에 대한 두려움을 이용하는 선거 운동

▶**play up** PHRASAL VERB If you **play up** something, you emphasize it and try to make people believe that it is important. ❏ *The media played up the prospects for a settlement.*

구동사 강조하다 ❏ 대중 매체가 타협의 가능성을 강조했다.

play|er ◆◆◇ /pleɪər/ (**players**) **1** N-COUNT A **player** in a sport or game is a person who takes part, either as a job or for fun. ❏ *...his greatness as a player.* ❏ *She was a good golfer and tennis player.* **2** N-COUNT You can use **player** to refer to a musician. For example, a **piano player** is someone who plays the piano. ❏ *...a professional trumpet player.* **3** N-COUNT If a person, country, or organization is a **player in** something, they are involved in it and important in it. ❏ *Big business has become a major player in the art market.* **4** →see also **CD player, record player** →see **basketball, chess, football, soccer, theater**

1 가산명사 선수, 경기자 ❏ 선수로서의 그의 탁월함 ❏ 그녀는 훌륭한 골프 선수이자 테니스 선수였다. **2** 가산명사 연주자 **3** 가산명사 주요 역할자 ❏ 대기업이 미술품 거래에 있어서 주요한 역할을 하는 존재가 되었다.

play|ful /pleɪfəl/ **1** ADJ A **playful** gesture or person is friendly or humorous. ❏ *...a playful kiss on the tip of his nose.* ❏ *...a playful fight.* ● **play|ful|ly** ADV ❏ *She pushed him away playfully.* ● **play|ful|ness** N-UNCOUNT ❏ *...the child's natural playfulness.* **2** ADJ A **playful** animal is lively and cheerful. ❏ *...a playful puppy.*

1 형용사 명랑한; 장난스런 ❏ 그의 코 끝에 하는 장난스런 키스 ❏ 장난 같은 싸움 ● 명랑하게 부사 ❏ 그녀는 그를 장난스레 밀어냈다. ● 명랑함, 장난스러움 불가산명사 ❏ 아이의 꾸밈없는 명랑함 **2** 형용사 팔팔한, 활발한 ❏ 활발한 강아지

play|ground /pleɪgraʊnd/ (**playgrounds**) N-COUNT A **playground** is a piece of land, at school or in a public area, where children can play. ❏ *...a seven-year-old boy playing in a school playground.* →see **park**

가산명사 운동장 ❏ 학교 운동장에서 놀고 있는 일곱 살 난 소년

play|group /pleɪgrup/ (**playgroups**) also **play group** N-COUNT A **playgroup** is an informal school for very young children, where they learn things by playing. [also prep N]

가산명사 유아 놀이방

play|ing card (**playing cards**) N-COUNT **Playing cards** are thin pieces of cardboard with numbers or pictures printed on them, which are used to play various games. ❏ *...a pack of playing cards.*

가산명사 (놀이용) 카드 ❏ 카드 한 벌

play|ing field (**playing fields**) **1** N-COUNT A **playing field** is a large area of grass where people play sports. ❏ *...the playing fields of the girls' Grammar School.* **2** PHRASE You talk about **a level playing field** to mean a situation that is fair, because no competitor or opponent in it has an advantage over another. ❏ *American businessmen ask for a level playing field when they compete with foreign companies.*

1 가산명사 경기장, 운동장 ❏ 여학교의 운동장 **2** 구 공정성 ❏ 미국인 사업가들은 외국 업체와 경쟁할 때 공정성을 요구한다.

play|list /pleɪlɪst/ (**playlists, playlisting, playlisted**) **1** N-COUNT A **playlist** is a list of songs, albums, and artists that a radio station broadcasts. ❏ *Radio 1's playlist is dominated by top-selling youth-orientated groups.* **2** V-T If a song, album, or artist **is playlisted**, it is put on a radio station's playlist. ❏ *We've playlisted many artists like Beth Orton who got picked up down the line by others.*

1 가산명사 방송 내용 목록 ❏ '라디오 1'의 방송 내용 목록에는 가장 인기 있는 젊은이 취향의 그룹이 주류를 이룬다. **2** 타동사 방송 예정 녹음 목록에 오르다 ❏ 우리는 전적으로 다른 사람들에 의해 추천된 베쓰 오튼 같은 많은 음악가들의 곡을 방송 예정 녹음 목록에 올렸다.

play|off /pleɪɔf, BRIT pleɪɒf (**playoffs**) also **play-off** **1** N-COUNT A **playoff** is an extra game which is played to decide the winner of a sports competition when two or more people have the same score. ❏ *Nick Faldo was beaten by Peter Baker in a play-off.* **2** N-COUNT You use **playoffs** to refer to a series of games which are played to decide the winner of a championship. ❏ *The winner of the American League East race will face the powerful Oakland A's in the playoffs this weekend.*

1 가산명사 연장전, 재시합 ❏ 닉 팔도는 연장전에서 피터 베이커에게 졌다. **2** 가산명사 우승 결정전 시리즈, 플레이오프 ❏ 아메리칸리그 동부 지구 우승자는 강력한 '오클랜드 에이스'와 이번 주말에 있을 플레이오프에서 대전하게 됩니다.

play park (**play parks**) N-COUNT A **play park** is a children's playground. [mainly BRIT] ❏ *The development includes tennis courts and a children's play park.*

가산명사 놀이터 [주로 영국영어] ❏ 테니스 코트와 어린이 놀이터가 개발에 포함되어 있다.

play|wright /pleɪraɪt/ (**playwrights**) N-COUNT A **playwright** is a person who writes plays.

가산명사 극작가

pla|za /plɑzə, plæzə, BRIT plɑːzə/ (**plazas**) **1** N-COUNT A **plaza** is an open square in a city. ❏ *Across the busy plaza, vendors sell hot dogs and croissant sandwiches.* **2** N-COUNT A **plaza** is a group of stores or buildings that are joined together or share common areas. [AM] ❏ *...a small store on the main plaza in Chamula.*

1 가산명사 광장 ❏ 분주한 광장 전역에서 노점상들이 핫도그와 크로와상 샌드위치를 판다. **2** 가산명사 쇼핑센터 [미국영어] ❏ 챠뮬라의 주요 쇼핑센터에 위치한 작은 상점

plc /pi ɛl si/ (**plcs**) also **PLC** N-COUNT In Britain, **plc** means a company whose shares can be bought by the public and is usually used after the name of a company. **plc** is an abbreviation for **public limited company**. Compare **Ltd**. [BUSINESS] ❏ *...British Telecommunications plc.*

가산명사 (영국) 주식회사 [경제] ❏ 브리티시 텔레커뮤니케이션 주식회사

plea /pli/ (**pleas**) **1** N-COUNT A **plea** is an appeal or request for something, made in an intense or emotional way. [JOURNALISM] ❏ *Mr. Nicholas made his emotional plea for help in solving the killing.* **2** N-COUNT In a court of law, a person's **plea** is the answer that they give when they have been charged with a crime, saying whether or not they are guilty of that crime. ❏ *The judge questioned him about his guilty plea.* ❏ *We will enter a plea of not guilty.* **3** N-COUNT A **plea** is a reason which is given, to a court of law or to other people, as an excuse for doing something or for not doing something. ❏ *Phillips murdered his wife, but got off on a plea of insanity.*

1 가산명사 간청, 탄원 [언론] ❏ 니콜라스 씨는 그 살인 사건을 해결하도록 도와 달라고 간절히 탄원했다. **2** 가산명사 답변, 항변 ❏ 판사는 그에게 유죄 답변에 대해 심문했다. ❏ 우리는 무죄라고 항변할 것이다. **3** 가산명사 구실 ❏ 필립스는 아내를 살해했지만 정신 이상이라는 구실로 처벌을 면했다.

plead /plid/ (**pleads, pleading, pleaded**) **1** V-T/V-I If you **plead with** someone to do something, you ask them in an intense, emotional way to do it. ❏ *The lady pleaded with her daughter to come back home.* ❏ *He was kneeling on the floor pleading for mercy.* **2** V-I When someone charged with a crime **pleads guilty** or **not guilty** in a court of law, they officially state that they are guilty or not guilty of the crime. ❏ *Morris had pleaded guilty to robbery.* **3** V-T If you **plead the case** or **cause** of someone or something, you speak out in their support or defense. ❏ *He appeared before the Committee to plead his case.* **4** V-T If you **plead** a particular thing as the reason for doing or not doing something, you give it as your excuse. ❏ *Mr. Giles pleads ignorance as his excuse.* →see **trial**

1 타동사/자동사 간청하다 ❏ 그 부인은 딸에게 집으로 돌아오라고 간청했다. ❏ 그는 바닥에 무릎을 꿇고 용서를 빌었다. **2** 자동사 유죄를 인정하다; 무죄를 주장하다 ❏ 모리스가 강도 행위에 대해 유죄를 인정했었다. **3** 타동사 변호하다, 변론하다 ❏ 그는 자신을 변호하기 위해 위원회에 출두했다. **4** 타동사 이유로 내세우다, 변명하다 ❏ 자일즈 씨는 무지를 이유로 내세웠다.

plead|ing /plídɪŋ/ (**pleadings**) **1** ADJ A **pleading** expression or gesture shows someone that you want something very much. ❑ ...*his pleading eyes.* ❑ ...*the pleading expression on her face.* **2** N-UNCOUNT **Pleading** is asking someone for something you want very much, in an intense or emotional way. [also N in pl] ❑ *He simply ignored Sid's pleading.*

1 형용사 간절한 ❑ 그의 간절한 눈빛 ❑ 그녀의 얼굴에 나타난 간절한 표정 **2** 불가산명사 간청, 탄원 ❑ 그는 시드의 간청을 간단히 묵살했다.

pleas|ant ◆◇◇ /plɛ́zᵊnt/ (**pleasanter**, **pleasantest**) **1** ADJ Something that is **pleasant** is nice, enjoyable, or attractive. ❑ *I've got a pleasant little apartment.* ● **pleas|ant|ly** ADV ❑ *We talked pleasantly of old times.* **2** ADJ Someone who is **pleasant** is friendly and likeable. ❑ *The woman had a pleasant face.*

1 형용사 멋진, 즐거운 ❑ 난 멋진 조그마한 아파트가 있어. ● 즐겁게 부사 ❑ 우리는 즐겁게 지난 일들을 이야기했다. **2** 형용사 호감 가는, 상냥한 ❑ 그 여자는 호감이 가는 얼굴이었다.

Thesaurus   pleasant의 참조어

ADJ.   agreeable, cheerful, delightful, likable, friendly, nice;
        (ant.) unpleasant **2**

---

please ◆◆◇ /plíz/ (**pleases**, **pleasing**, **pleased**) **1** ADV You say **please** when you are politely asking or inviting someone to do something. [POLITENESS] [ADV with cl] ❑ *Can you help us please?* ❑ *Please come in.* ❑ *Can we have the bill please?* **2** ADV You say **please** when you are accepting something politely. [FORMULAE] ❑ *"Tea?" — "Yes, please."* **3** CONVENTION You can say **please** to indicate that you want someone to stop doing something or stop speaking. You would say this if, for example, what they are doing or saying makes you angry or upset. [FEELINGS] ❑ *Please, Mary, this is all so unnecessary.* **4** CONVENTION You can say **please** in order to attract someone's attention politely. Children in particular say "**please**" to attract the attention of a teacher or other adult. [mainly BRIT, POLITENESS] ❑ *Please, Miss Smith, a moment.* **5** V-T/V-I If someone or something **pleases** you, they make you feel happy and satisfied. ❑ *More than anything, I want to please you.* ❑ *It pleased him to talk to her.* **6** PHRASE You use **please** in expressions such as **as she pleases**, **whatever you please**, and **anything he pleases** to indicate that someone can do or have whatever they want. ❑ *Women should be free to dress and act as they please.* ❑ *He does whatever he pleases.*

1 부사 부탁이나 초대할 때 공손한 뜻을 더함. [공손체] ❑ 저희를 좀 도와주실 수 있나요? ❑ 들어오세요. ❑ 계산서 주시겠어요? **2** 부사 그리세요 공손하게 수락할 때 씀. [의례적인 표현] ❑ "차 드릴까요?" "네, 주세요." **3** 관용 표현 제발 [감정 개입] ❑ 제발, 메리, 이런 건 전혀 필요 없다니까. **4** 관용 표현 저 공손히 부르는 말 [주로 영국영어, 공손체] ❑ 저, 스미스 양, 잠시만요. **5** 타동사/자동사 기쁘게 하다, 즐겁게 하다 ❑ 그 무엇보다도, 난 널 기쁘게 해 주고 싶어. ❑ 그녀와 이야기를 해서 그는 기뻤다. **6** 구 원하는 대로, 하고 싶은 대로 ❑ 여성들은 원하는 대로 자유롭게 옷을 입고 행동해야 한다. ❑ 그는 뭐든 내키는 대로 한다.

pleased ◆◇◇ /plízd/ **1** ADJ If you are **pleased** about something or satisfied with something. ❑ *Felicity seemed pleased at the suggestion.* ❑ *I think he's going to be pleased that we identified the real problems.* **2** ADJ If you say you will be **pleased to** do something, you are saying in a polite way that you are willing to do it. [POLITENESS] [v-link ADJ to-inf] ❑ *We will be pleased to answer any questions you may have.* **3** ADJ You can tell someone that you are **pleased with** something they have done in order to express your approval. [FEELINGS] [v-link ADJ, usu ADJ prep/that/to-inf] ❑ *I'm pleased with the way things have been going.* ❑ *I am very pleased about the result.* ❑ *We are pleased that the problems have been resolved.* **4** ADJ When you are about to give someone some news which you know will please them, you can say that you are **pleased to** tell them the news or that they will be **pleased to** hear it. [v-link ADJ to-inf] ❑ *I'm pleased to say that he is now doing well.* **5** ADJ In official letters, people often say they will be **pleased to** do something, as a polite way of introducing what they are going to do or inviting people to do something. [POLITENESS] [v-link ADJ to-inf] ❑ *We will be pleased to delete the charge from the original invoice.* **6** PHRASE If someone seems very satisfied with something they have done, you can say that they are **pleased with themselves**, especially if you think they are more satisfied than they should be. ❑ *"I dare say Sophie was glad to see you," he said, pleased with himself again for having remembered her name.* **7** CONVENTION You can say "**Pleased to meet you**" as a polite way of greeting someone who you are meeting for the first time. [FORMULAE]

1 형용사 기쁜, 만족스러운 ❑ 펠리시티는 그 제안에 기뻐하는 것 같았다. ❑ 그는 우리가 진짜 문제가 되는 것들을 밝혀낸 것에 만족해할 거야. **2** 형용사 기꺼이 [공손체] ❑ 혹시 질문이 있으시면 기꺼이 답해 드리겠습니다. **3** 형용사 만족스러운, 기쁜 [감정 개입] ❑ 저는 지금까지의 상황에 만족합니다. ❑ 저는 그 결과에 대단히 만족합니다. ❑ 우리는 그 문제들이 해결되어서 기쁩니다. **4** 형용사 기쁜 ❑ 그가 지금 잘 지내고 있다고 말하게 되어서 기뻐. **5** 형용사 감사하는 [공손체] ❑ 청구서 원본에서 청구 금액을 삭제해 주시면 감사하겠습니다. **6** 구 (지나치게) 뿌듯해 하는 ❑ "내가 보기엔 소피가 널 보고 기뻐했다니까."라고 그가 말하면서, 자기가 그녀의 이름을 기억하고 있다는 사실에 다시 한 번 뿌듯해했다. **7** 관용 표현 뵙게 되어 반갑습니다 [의례적인 표현]

pleas|ing /plízɪŋ/ ADJ Something that is **pleasing** gives you pleasure and satisfaction. ❑ *This area of France has a pleasing climate in August.* ❑ *Such a view is pleasing.* ● **pleas|ing|ly** ADV ❑ *The interior design is pleasingly simple.*

형용사 유쾌하게 하는, 기분 좋게 하는 ❑ 8월이 되면 프랑스의 이곳은 날씨가 상쾌하다. ❑ 그런 장관을 보면 기분이 좋아진다. ● 산뜻하게, 기분 좋게 부사 ❑ 실내장식 디자인이 군더더기 없이 산뜻하다.

pleas|ur|able /plɛ́ʒᵊrᵊbᵊl/ ADJ **Pleasurable** experiences or sensations are pleasant and enjoyable. ❑ *The most pleasurable experience of the evening was the wonderful fireworks display.*

형용사 즐거운 ❑ 그날 저녁 가장 즐거운 경험은 멋진 불꽃놀이였다.

pleas|ure ◆◆◇ /plɛ́ʒᵊr/ (**pleasures**) **1** N-UNCOUNT If something gives you **pleasure**, you get a feeling of happiness, satisfaction, or enjoyment from it. ❑ *Watching sport gave him great pleasure.* ❑ *Everybody takes pleasure in eating.* **2** N-UNCOUNT **Pleasure** is the activity of enjoying yourself, especially rather than working or doing what you have a duty to do. ❑ *He mixed business and pleasure in a perfect and dynamic way.* **3** N-COUNT A **pleasure** is an activity, experience or aspect of something that you find very enjoyable or satisfying. ❑ *Watching TV is our only pleasure.* ❑ *...the pleasure of seeing a smiling face.* **4** CONVENTION If you meet someone for the first time, you can say, as a way of being polite, that it is **a pleasure to meet** them. You can also ask for **the pleasure of** someone's **company** as a polite and formal way of inviting them somewhere. [POLITENESS] ❑ *"A pleasure to meet you, sir," he said.* **5** CONVENTION You can say "**It's a pleasure**" or "**My pleasure**" as a polite way of replying to someone who has just thanked you for doing something. [FORMULAE] ❑ *"Thanks very much anyhow." — "It's a pleasure."*

1 불가산명사 기쁨, 즐거움 ❑ 스포츠 관람이 그에겐 큰 기쁨이었다. ❑ 누구나 음식 먹는 걸 즐긴다. **2** 불가산명사 즐거운 일, 오락 ❑ 그는 일과 오락을 역동적이고 완벽하게 잘 조화시켰다. **3** 가산명사 오락거리, 위안 ❑ 텔레비전 시청이 우리의 유일한 오락거리이다. ❑ 웃는 얼굴을 보는 데서 받는 위안 **4** 관용 표현 기쁨 [공손체] ❑ "뵙게 되어 기쁩니다, 선생님."라고 그가 말했다. **5** 관용 표현 별말씀을 다 하십니다 [의례적인 표현] ❑ "어쨌든 정말 감사합니다." "별말씀을 다 하세요."

Word Partnership   pleasure의 연어

ADJ.   **sexual** pleasure **1**
        great pleasure, **intense** pleasure, **simple** pleasure **1** **3**

---

pleat /plít/ (**pleats**) N-COUNT A **pleat** in a piece of clothing is a permanent fold that is made in the cloth by folding one part over the other and sewing across the top end of the fold. ❑ *Her skirt hangs in perfect wide pleats.*

가산명사 주름 ❑ 그녀의 스커트는 폭넓은 주름이 완벽하게 잡힌 채로 걸려 있다.

a b c d e f g h i j k l m n o p q r s t u v w x y z

pleat|ed /plítɪd/ ADJ A **pleated** piece of clothing has pleats in it. ❑ ...*a short white pleated skirt.*

형용사 주름이 잡힌 ❑ 짧은 흰색 주름치마

pledge ♦♢♢ /plɛdʒ/ (**pledges, pledging, pledged**) **1** N-COUNT When someone makes a **pledge**, they make a serious promise that they will do something. ❑ *The meeting ended with a pledge to step up cooperation between the six states of the region.* **2** V-T When someone **pledges to** do something, they promise in a serious way to do it. When they **pledge** something, they promise to give it. ❑ *The Communists have pledged to support the opposition's motion.* ❑ *Philip pledges support and offers to help in any way that he can.* **3** V-T If you **pledge** a sum of money to an organization or activity, you promise to pay that amount of money to it at a particular time or over a particular period. ❑ *The French President is pledging $150 million in French aid next year.* ● N-COUNT **Pledge** is also a noun. ❑ ...*a pledge of forty two million dollars a month.* **4** V-T If you **pledge yourself to** something, you commit yourself to following a particular course of action or to supporting a particular person, group, or idea. ❑ *The President pledged himself to increase taxes for the rich but not the middle classes.* **5** V-T If you **pledge** something such as a valuable possession or a sum of money, you leave it with someone as a guarantee that you will repay money that you have borrowed. ❑ *He asked her to pledge the house as security for a loan.*

1 가산명사 서약, 맹세 ❑ 그 회담은 이 지역 6개국의 협력 강화 서약과 함께 끝났다. **2** 타동사 서약하다, 맹세하다 ❑ 공산당원들은 야당의 제의를 지지하겠다고 서약했다. ❑ 필립은 지지를 맹세하고 그가 할 수 있는 어떠한 방법을 통해서라도 돕겠다고 제안한다. **3** 타동사 (돈을 내겠다고) 약속하다 ❑ 프랑스 대통령은 내년에 원조금으로 1억 5천만 달러를 내겠다고 약속하고 있다. ● 가산명사 기부 약속 ❑ 매달 4천 2백만 달러를 내겠다는 기부 약속 **4** 타동사 공약하다 ❑ 대통령은 중산층이 아닌 부유층의 세금을 올릴 것을 공약했다. **5** 타동사 저당 잡히다 ❑ 그는 그녀에게 대부금에 대한 담보로 그 집을 저당 잡힐 것을 요구했다.

Thesaurus   pledge의 참조어

N.   agreement, covenant, guarantee, promise **1**
V.   commit, contract, guarantee, promise, swear, vow **2 4**

Word Link   plen ≈ full : *plentiful, plenty, replenish*

---

plen|ti|ful /plɛntɪfəl/ ADJ Things that are **plentiful** exist in such large amounts or numbers that there is enough for people's wants or needs. ❑ *Fish are plentiful in the lake.*

형용사 풍부한 ❑ 그 호수에는 물고기들이 가득하다.

plen|ty ♦♢♢ /plɛnti/ QUANT If there is **plenty of** something, there is a large amount of it. If there are **plenty of** things, there are many of them. **Plenty** is used especially to indicate that there is enough of something, or more than you need. [QUANT of n-uncount/pl-n] ❑ *There was still plenty of time to take Jill out for pizza.* ❑ *Most businesses face plenty of competition.* ● PRON **Plenty** is also a pronoun. ❑ *I don't believe in long interviews. Fifteen minutes is plenty.*

수량사 많은, 충분한 ❑ 아직 질을 데리고 나가 피자를 사줄 시간이 많이 있었다. ❑ 대부분의 사업체가 많은 경쟁에 부딪힌다. ● 대명사 충분함 ❑ 나는 긴 면접이 좋다고 생각하지 않아. 15분이면 충분해.

Thesaurus   plenty의 참조어

QUANT.   abundance, capacity, quantity; *(ant.)* scarcity

---

pletho|ra /plɛθərə/ N-SING A **plethora of** something is a large amount of it, especially an amount of it that is greater than you need, want, or can cope with. [FORMAL] ❑ *A plethora of new operators will be allowed to enter the market.*

단수명사 과다, 과잉 [격식체] ❑ 과다한 수의 신규 사업자들이 시장에 진출할 수 있게 될 것이다.

pli|able /plaɪəbᵊl/ ADJ If something is **pliable**, you can bend it easily without cracking or breaking it. ❑ *As your baby grows bigger, his bones become less pliable.*

형용사 유연한 ❑ 아기가 성장할수록, 아기의 뼈대가 유연성을 잃어 간다.

pli|ers /plaɪərz/ N-PLURAL **Pliers** are a tool with two handles at one end and two hard, flat, metal parts at the other. **Pliers** are used for holding or pulling out things such as nails, or for bending or cutting wire. [also *a pair of N*]

복수명사 펜치

plight /plaɪt/ (**plights**) N-COUNT If you refer to someone's **plight**, you mean that they are in a difficult or distressing situation that is full of problems. ❑ ...*the worsening plight of Third World countries plagued by debts, economic dependency, corruption and militarism.*

가산명사 곤경 ❑ 부채와 경제적 의존, 부패와 군부 지배에 시달리는 제3세계 국가의 악화되는 곤경

Thesaurus   plight의 참조어

N.   difficulty, problem, situation

---

plod /plɒd/ (**plods, plodding, plodded**) **1** V-I If someone **plods**, they walk slowly and heavily. ❑ *Crowds of French and British families plodded around in yellow plastic macs.* **2** V-I If you say that someone **plods on** or **plods along** with a job, you mean that the job is taking a long time. ❑ *He is plodding on with negotiations.*

1 자동사 터벅터벅 걷다 ❑ 프랑스 및 영국 가족들로 이루어진 군중이 노란 비닐 비옷을 입고 주위를 터벅터벅 걸어 다녔다. **2** 자동사 시간을 상당히 들이다 ❑ 그는 협상에 시간을 상당히 들이고 있다.

plot ♦♢♢ /plɒt/ (**plots, plotting, plotted**) **1** N-COUNT A **plot** is a secret plan by a group of people to do something that is illegal or wrong, usually against a person or a government. ❑ *Security forces have uncovered a plot to overthrow the government.* **2** V-T/V-I If people **plot to** do something or **plot** something that is illegal or wrong, they plan secretly to do it. ❑ *Prosecutors in the trial allege the defendants plotted to overthrow the government.* ❑ *The military were plotting a coup.* **3** V-T When people **plot** a strategy or a course of action, they carefully plan each step of it. ❑ *Yesterday's meeting was intended to plot a survival strategy for the party.* **4** N-VAR The **plot** of a movie, novel, or play is the connected series of events which make up the story. ❑ *He began to tell me the plot of his new book.* **5** N-COUNT A **plot** of land is a small piece of land, especially one that has been measured or marked out for a special purpose, such as building houses or growing vegetables. ❑ *I thought that I'd buy myself a small plot of land and build a house on it.* **6** V-T When someone **plots** something on a graph, they mark certain points on it and then join the points up. ❑ *So we form the cumulative distribution in the usual way and plot about eight points on the graph.* **7** V-T When someone **plots** the position or course of a plane or ship, they mark it on a map using instruments to obtain accurate information. ❑ *We were trying to plot the course of the submarine.* **8** V-T If someone **plots** the progress or development of something, they make a diagram or a plan which shows how it has developed in order to give some indication of how it will develop in the future. ❑ *They used a computer to plot the movements of everyone in the police station on December 24, 1990.*

1 가산명사 음모 ❑ 보안군이 정부를 전복시키려는 음모를 적발해 냈다. **2** 타동사/자동사 음모하다, 획책하다 ❑ 검찰 측은 재판에서 피고들이 정부 전복을 음모했다고 주장한다. ❑ 군부가 쿠데타를 획책하고 있었다. **3** 타동사 구상하다 ❑ 어제 회담은 그 정당의 생존 전략을 구상하기 위해 열린 것이었다. **4** 가산명사 또는 불가산명사 줄거리 ❑ 그가 내게 자기 새 책의 줄거리를 이야기하기 시작했다. **5** 가산명사 자그마한 부지, 소구획지 ❑ 나는 자그마한 부지를 하나 사서 그 위에 집을 지을까 하고 생각했다. **6** 타동사 (도표 등에) 표시하다 ❑ 그래서 우리는 누적 분포도를 평소의 방법대로 작성한 후 약 여덟 개의 점을 도표에 표시해 연결한다. **7** 타동사 지도에 표시하다 ❑ 우리는 그 잠수함의 진로를 지도에 표시하기 위해 노력하고 있었다. **8** 타동사 도표로 그리다 ❑ 그들이 컴퓨터를 이용해서 1990년 12월 24일 그 경찰서에 있었던 모든 사람들의 이동 상황을 도표로 그려 냈다.

plough /plaʊ/ →see **plow**

plow /plaʊ/ (**plows, plowing, plowed**) [BRIT **plough**] **1** N-COUNT A **plow** is a large farming tool with sharp blades which is pulled across the soil to turn it over, usually before seeds are planted. ❑ *There are new tractors and new plows in the machinery lot.* →see also **snowplow** **2** V-T When someone **plows** an area of land, they turn over the soil using a plow. ❑ *They were no longer using mules and horses to plow their fields.*

▶**plow back** PHRASAL VERB If profits **are plowed back into** a business, they are used to increase the size of the business or to improve it. [BUSINESS] [usu passive] ❑ *...cash profits that are quickly plowed back into the market.*

ploy /plɔɪ/ (**ploys**) N-COUNT A **ploy** is a way of behaving that someone plans carefully and secretly in order to gain an advantage for themselves. ❑ *Christmas should be a time of excitement and wonder, not a cynical marketing ploy.*

pls **Pls** is a written abbreviation for **please**. ❑ *Have you moved yet? Pls advise address, phone no.*

pluck /plʌk/ (**plucks, plucking, plucked**) **1** V-T If you **pluck** a fruit, flower, or leaf, you take it between your fingers and pull it in order to remove it from its stalk where it is growing. [WRITTEN] ❑ *I plucked a lemon from the tree.* **2** V-T If you **pluck** something from somewhere, you take it between your fingers and pull it sharply from where it is. [WRITTEN] ❑ *He plucked the cigarette from his mouth and tossed it out into the street.* ❑ *He plucked the baby out of my arms.* **3** V-T If you **pluck** a guitar or other musical instrument, you pull the strings with your fingers and let them go, so that they make a sound. ❑ *Nell was plucking a harp.* **4** V-T If you **pluck** a chicken or other dead bird, you pull its feathers out to prepare it for cooking. ❑ *She looked relaxed as she plucked a chicken.* **5** V-T If a woman **plucks** her **eyebrows**, she pulls out some of the hairs using tweezers. ❑ *You've plucked your eyebrows at last!* **6** PHRASE If you **pluck up the courage** to do something that you feel nervous about, you make an effort to be brave enough to do it. ❑ *It took me about two hours to pluck up courage to call.*

plug /plʌg/ (**plugs, plugging, plugged**) **1** N-COUNT A **plug** on a piece of electrical equipment is a small plastic object with two or three metal pins which fit into the holes of an electric outlet and connects the equipment to the electricity supply. ❑ *I used to go round and take every plug out at night.* **2** N-COUNT A **plug** is an electric outlet. [INFORMAL] ❑ *Then Bob spotted the problem - the plug in the wall hadn't been switched on.* **3** N-COUNT A **plug** is a thick, circular piece of rubber or plastic that you use to block the hole in a bath or sink when it is filled with water. ❑ *She put the plug in the sink and filled it with cold water.* **4** N-COUNT A **plug** is a small, round piece of wood, plastic, or wax which is used to block holes. ❑ *A plug had been inserted in the drill hole.* **5** V-T If you **plug** a hole, you block it with something. ❑ *Crews are working to plug a major oil leak.* **6** V-T If someone **plugs** a commercial product, especially a book or a movie, they praise it in order to encourage people to buy it or see it because they have an interest in it doing well. ❑ *We did not want people on the show who are purely interested in plugging a book or film.* ● N-COUNT **Plug** is also a noun. ❑ *Let's do this show tonight and it'll be a great plug, a great promotion.* **7** PHRASE If someone in a position of power **pulls the plug on** a project or **on** someone's activities, they use their power to stop them from continuing. ❑ *The banks have the power to pull the plug on the project.*

▶**plug in** or **plug into** PHRASAL VERB If you **plug** a piece of electrical equipment **into** an electricity supply or if you **plug** it **in**, you push its plug into an electric outlet so that it can work. ❑ *They plugged in their tape-recorders.* ❑ *I filled the kettle while she was talking and plugged it in.* **2** PHRASAL VERB If you **plug** one piece of electrical equipment **into** another or if you **plug** it **in**, you make it work by connecting the two. ❑ *They plugged their guitars into amplifiers.* **3** PHRASAL VERB If one piece of electrical equipment **plugs in** or **plugs into** another piece of electrical equipment, it works by being connected by an electrical cord or lead to an electricity supply or to the other piece of equipment. ❑ *A CD-I deck looks like a video recorder and plugs into the home television and stereo system.* ❑ *They plug into a laptop, desktop, or handheld computer.* **4** PHRASAL VERB If you **plug** something **into** a hole, you push it into the hole. ❑ *Her instructor plugged live bullets into the gun's chamber.* **5** →see also **plug-in**

plug-and-play ADJ **Plug-and-play** is used to describe computer equipment, for example a printer, that is ready to use immediately when you connect it to a computer. [COMPUTING] [ADJ n] ❑ *... a plug-and-play USB camera.*

plug-in (**plug-ins**) **1** ADJ A **plug-in** machine is a piece of electrical equipment that is operated by being connected to an electricity supply or to another piece of electrical equipment by means of a plug. [ADJ n] ❑ *...a plug-in radio.* **2** N-COUNT A **plug-in** is something such as a piece of software that can be added to a computer system to give extra features or functions. [COMPUTING] ❑ *...a plug-in memory card.*

plum /plʌm/ (**plums**) **1** N-COUNT A **plum** is a small, sweet fruit with a smooth purple, red or yellow skin and a pit in the middle. **2** COLOR Something that is **plum** or **plum-colored** is a dark reddish- purple color. ❑ *...plum-colored silk.*

plumb|er /plʌmər/ (**plumbers**) N-COUNT A **plumber** is a person whose job is to connect and repair things such as water and drainage pipes, bathtubs, and toilets.

plumb|ing /plʌmɪŋ/ **1** N-UNCOUNT The **plumbing** in a building consists of the water and drainage pipes, bathtubs, and toilets in it. ❑ *The electrics and the plumbing were sound but everything else had to be cleaned up.* **2** N-UNCOUNT **Plumbing** is the work of connecting and repairing things such as water and drainage pipes, baths, and toilets. ❑ *She learned the rudiments of brick-laying, wiring, and plumbing.*
→see Word Web: **plumbing**

[영국영어 **plough**] **1** 가산명사 쟁기 ❑ 새로 나온 트랙터와 쟁기들이 기계 창고에 있다. **2** 타동사 갈다, 경작하다 ❑ 그들은 더 이상 노새나 말을 이용해서 경작지를 갈지 않고 있었다.

구동사 (수익이) 재투자되다 [경제] ❑ 시장으로 신속히 재투자되는 현금 수익

가산명사 계략 ❑ 크리스마스는 신나고 경이로운 시간이 되어야지 냉소적인 상업적 계략을 위한 때가 되어서는 안 된다.

please의 축약형 표기 ❑ 벌써 이사 갔어? 주소와 전화번호 좀 알려줘.

1 타동사 따다, 잡아 뜯다 [문어체] ❑ 나는 나무에서 레몬 한 개를 땄다. **2** 타동사 꽉 잡아 빼서 밖으로 톡 내던지다 [문어체] ❑ 그는 물고 있던 담배를 꽉 잡아 빼서 밖으로 톡 내던졌다. ❑ 그가 내 품에서 아기를 낚아채 갔다. **3** 타동사 (악기를) 뜯다 ❑ 넬은 하프를 뜯고 있었다. **4** 타동사 (털을) 뽑다 ❑ 그녀는 닭털을 뽑을 때 느긋해 보였다. **5** 타동사 눈썹을 뽑다 ❑ 너 결국 눈썹을 뽑았구나! **6** 구 용기를 내다 ❑ 내가 용기를 내어 전화 걸기까지는 약 2시간이 걸렸다.

1 가산명사 플러그 ❑ 나는 밤이면 이리저리 돌아다니며 모든 플러그를 뽑곤 했다. **2** 가산명사 콘센트 [비격식체] ❑ 그리고 나서 밥은 문제점을 발견해 냈다. 바로 벽에 있는 콘센트가 켜지지 않았던 것이었다. **3** 가산명사 마개 ❑ 그녀는 마개로 싱크대를 막고 찬물을 채웠다. **4** 가산명사 마개 ❑ 드릴 구멍 안에 마개가 꽂혀 있었다. **5** 타동사 막다 ❑ 승무원들이 기름이 가장 많이 누출되는 곳을 막기 위해 애쓰고 있다. **6** 타동사 선전하다, 칭찬하다 ❑ 우리는 책이나 영화를 선전하는 데만 관심 있는 사람들이 그 쇼에 출연하는 것을 원하지 않았다. ● 가산명사 선전, 시선 끌기 ❑ 오늘 밤 이 쇼를 공연하자. 이건 엄청난 선전이고 광장한 홍보가 될 거야. **7** 구 ~을 중단시키다 ❑ 은행들은 그 계획을 중단시킬 권한을 가지고 있다.

1 구동사 (전원 등에) 연결하다 ❑ 그들은 테이프 녹음기를 콘센트에 연결했다. ❑ 그녀가 말하면서 주전자를 콘센트에 연결하는 동안 나는 주전자를 채웠다. **2** 구동사 연결하다 ❑ 그들은 기타에 증폭기를 연결했다. **3** 구동사 ~와 연결되다 ❑ 시디 원 플레이어는 비디오 녹음기처럼 보이는데 가정용 텔레비전과 스테레오 시스템에 연결된다. ❑ 그것들은 노트북 컴퓨터와 탁상용 컴퓨터 또는 포켓용 컴퓨터에 연결된다. **4** 구동사 ~에 밀어 넣다 ❑ 그녀의 교관이 약실에 실탄을 장전했다.

형용사 플러그 앤 플레이식의 [컴퓨터] ❑ 플러그 앤 플레이식의 범용 직렬 버스 카메라

1 형용사 플러그 접속식의 ❑ 플러그 접속식의 라디오 **2** 가산명사 플러그인 [컴퓨터] ❑ 플러그인 메모리카드

1 가산명사 서양 자두 **2** 색채어 짙은 자색의 ❑ 짙은 자색 비단

가산명사 배관공

1 불가산명사 배관 ❑ 전기 설비와 배관은 상태가 양호했지만 그 외에는 모두 깨끗이 치워야 했다. **2** 불가산명사 배관 작업 ❑ 그녀는 벽돌공사, 배선공사 및 배관 작업의 기초를 배웠다.

Word Web   plumbing

Babylonian* homes of 4,000 years ago had **bathrooms** where people bathed themselves with **water**. The waste water **drained** off through a hole in the floor. At about the same time, the Minoans* in Crete* invented the **flush toilet**. It used rain water held in cisterns. The early Egyptians discovered how to make **pipes** out of clay and **basins** out of **copper**. Some homes in ancient Greece contained latrines that drained into a sewer beneath the street. The Romans were the first to use **lead** for **plumbing** purposes. The word "plumbing" comes from *plumbus*, the Latin word for "lead."

Babylonian: from the ancient city of Babylon.
Minoans (3000 BC – 1100 BC): people who lived on Crete.
Crete: an island in the eastern Mediterranean Sea.

plume /plum/ (**plumes**) ◼ N-COUNT A **plume** of smoke, dust, fire, or water is a large quantity of it that rises into the air in a column. ❑ *The rising plume of black smoke could be seen all over Kabul.* ◼ N-COUNT A **plume** is a large, soft bird's feather. ❑ *...broad straw hats decorated with ostrich plumes.*

plum|met /plʌmɪt/ (**plummets, plummeting, plummeted**) V-I If an amount, rate, or price **plummets**, it decreases quickly by a large amount. [JOURNALISM] ❑ *In Tokyo share prices have plummeted for the sixth successive day.* ❑ *The Prime Minister's popularity has plummeted to an all-time low in recent weeks.*

plump /plʌmp/ (**plumper, plumpest, plumps, plumping, plumped**) ◼ ADJ You can describe someone or something as **plump** to indicate that they are rather fat or rounded. ❑ *Maria was a pretty little thing, small and plump with a mass of curly hair.* ❑ *He pushed a plump little hand towards me.* →see **fat** ◼ V-T If you **plump** a pillow or cushion, you shake it and hit it gently so that it goes back into a rounded shape. ❑ *She panics when people pop in unexpectedly, rushing round plumping cushions.* ● PHRASAL VERB **Plump up** means the same as **plump**. ❑ *"You need to rest," she told him reassuringly as she moved to plump up his pillows.*

plun|der /plʌndər/ (**plunders, plundering, plundered**) V-T If someone **plunders** a place or **plunders** things **from** a place, they steal things from it. [LITERARY] ❑ *He plundered the palaces and ransacked the treasuries.* ❑ *She faces charges of helping to plunder her country's treasury of billions of dollars.* ● N-UNCOUNT **Plunder** is also a noun. ❑ *...a guerrilla group infamous for torture and plunder.*

plunge ◆◇◇ /plʌndʒ/ (**plunges, plunging, plunged**) ◼ V-I If something or someone **plunges** in a particular direction, especially into water, they fall, rush, or throw themselves in that direction. ❑ *At least 50 people died when a bus plunged into a river.* ● N-COUNT **Plunge** is also a noun. ❑ *...a plunge into cold water.* ◼ V-T If you **plunge** an object **into** something, you push it quickly or violently into it. ❑ *A soldier plunged a bayonet into his body.* ❑ *She plunged her face into a bowl of cold water.* ◼ V-T/V-I If a person or thing **is plunged into** a particular state or situation, or if they **plunge into** it, they are suddenly in that state or situation. ❑ *The government's political and economic reforms threaten to plunge the country into chaos.* ❑ *Eddy finds himself plunged into a world of brutal violence.* ● N-COUNT **Plunge** is also a noun. ❑ *That peace often looked like a brief truce before the next plunge into war.* ◼ V-T/V-I If you **plunge into** an activity or **are plunged into** it, you suddenly get very involved in it. ❑ *The two men plunged into discussion.* ❑ *The prince should be plunged into work.* ● N-COUNT **Plunge** is also a noun. ❑ *His sudden plunge into the field of international diplomacy is a major surprise.* ◼ V-T/V-I If an amount or rate **plunges**, it decreases quickly and suddenly. ❑ *His weight began to plunge.* ❑ *The Pound plunged to a new low on the foreign exchange markets yesterday.* ● N-COUNT **Plunge** is also a noun. ❑ *Japan's banks are in trouble because of bad loans and the stock market plunge.* ◼ PHRASE If you **take the plunge**, you decide to do something that you consider difficult or risky. ❑ *If you have been thinking about buying shares, now could be the time to take the plunge.*

plu|ral /plʊərəl/ (**plurals**) ◼ ADJ The **plural** form of a word is the form that is used when referring to more than one person or thing. ❑ *"Data" is the Latin plural form of "datum."* ◼ N-COUNT The **plural** of a noun is the form of it that is used to refer to more than one person or thing. ❑ *What is the plural of "person"?*

plu|ral|ism /plʊərəlɪzəm/ N-UNCOUNT If there is **pluralism** within a society, it has many different groups and political parties. [FORMAL] ❑ *...as the country shifts towards political pluralism.*

plus ◆◆◇ /plʌs/ (**pluses** or **plusses**) ◼ CONJ You say **plus** to show that one number or quantity is being added to another. ❑ *...$5 for a small locker, plus a $3 deposit;.* ◼ ADJ **Plus** before a number or quantity means that the number or quantity is greater than zero. [ADJ amount] ❑ *The aircraft was subjected to temperatures of minus 65 degrees and plus 120 degrees.* ◼ CONJ You can use **plus** when mentioning an additional item or fact. [INFORMAL] ❑ *There's easily enough room for two adults and three children, plus a dog in the boot.* ◼ ADJ You use **plus** after a number or quantity to indicate that the actual number or quantity is greater than the one mentioned. [amount ADJ] ❑ *There are only 35 staff to serve 30,000-plus customers.* ◼ Teachers use **plus** in grading work in schools and colleges. "B plus" is a better grade than "B," but it is not as good as "A." ◼ N-COUNT A **plus** is an advantage or benefit. [INFORMAL] ❑ *Well-known figures would be a big plus for the new board.*

plush /plʌʃ/ (**plusher, plushest**) ADJ If you describe something as **plush**, you mean that it is very comfortable and expensive. ❑ *...a plush, four-storey, Georgian house in Mayfair.*

◼ 가산명사 (연기 등의) 기둥 ❑ 솟아오르는 검은 연기 기둥은 카불 전역에서 볼 수 있었다. ◼ 가산명사 깃털 ❑ 타조 깃털로 장식한 챙 넓은 밀짚모자

자동사 폭락하다 [언론] ❑ 도쿄 주가가 6일 연속 폭락했다. ❑ 수상의 인기가 최근 몇 주 동안 사상 최저로 폭락했다.

◼ 형용사 포동포동한, 토실토실한 ❑ 마리아는 아주 귀여운 계집애로, 자그마하고 포동포동하며 술 많은 곱슬머리였다. ❑ 그가 나에게 포동포동한 작은 손을 내밀었다. ◼ 타동사 불룩하게 만들다 ❑ 그녀는 사람들이 갑자기 들어와 쿠션을 불룩하게 만들며 설쳐대면 겁을 집어 먹는다. ● 구동사 불룩하게 만들다 ❑ 그녀가 그의 베개를 불룩하게 만들어 주면서 "좀 쉬어요."라고 그에게 위안조로 말했다.

타동사 약탈하다 [문예체] ❑ 그는 궁궐들을 약탈하고 보물들을 탈취했다. ❑ 그녀는 수십억 달러에 이르는 자국의 국보 약탈을 도왔다는 혐의를 받고 있다. ● 불가산명사 약탈 ❑ 고문과 약탈로 악명 높은 게릴라 단체

◼ 자동사 추락하다, 뛰어들다 ❑ 버스가 강으로 추락해 적어도 50명이 사망했다. ● 가산명사 뛰어듦 ❑ 찬물로 뛰어듦 ◼ 타동사 찌르다, 쑤시다 ❑ 한 병사가 그의 몸을 총검으로 찔렀다. ❑ 그녀는 찬물이 든 그릇에 얼굴을 처넣었다. ◼ 타동사/자동사 (한 상태에) 빠뜨리다; (한 상태에) 빠지다 ❑ 정부의 정치 및 경제 개혁으로 인해 나라가 혼란에 빠질 우려가 있다. ❑ 에디는 자신이 무지막지한 폭력의 세계에 빠져 있다는 것을 깨닫고 있다. ● 가산명사 빠짐 ❑ 종종 그 평화는 다시 전쟁에 빠지기 전 잠시 동안 찾아오는 휴전 같았다. ◼ 타동사/자동사 느닷없이 –하다 ❑ 그 두 남자는 느닷없이 토의에 빠져들었다. ❑ 왕자는 느닷없이 일을 해야 할 것이다. ● 가산명사 갑자기 뛰어듦 ❑ 국제 외교에 그가 갑자기 뛰어든 것은 매우 놀라운 일이다. ◼ 타동사/자동사 갑자기 떨어지다 ❑ 그의 몸무게가 갑자기 줄기 시작했다. ❑ 파운드화 시세가 어제 외환 시장에서 다시 한 번 최저치로 하락했다. ● 가산명사 폭락 ❑ 일본의 은행들은 부실 채권과 주가 폭락으로 곤경에 빠져 있다. ◼ 구 과감히 하다 ❑ 주식 구매를 생각해 오고 있었다면, 지금이 과감히 실행에 옮길 때이다.

◼ 형용사 복수의 ❑ 'data'는 'datum'의 라틴어 복수형이다. ◼ 가산명사 복수형 ❑ 'person'의 복수형은 뭐지?

불가산명사 다원주의 [격식체] ❑ 그 나라가 정치적 다원주의로 변환할 때

◼ 접속사 플러스, 추가로 ❑ 작은 사물함 하나에 5달러, 추가로 예치금 3달러 ◼ 형용사 플러스의, 영보다 큰 ❑ 그 항공기는 마이너스 65도와 플러스 120도를 견디게 되어 있었다. ◼ 접속사 이외에, 게다가 [비격식체] ❑ 어른 두 명과 어린이 세 명이 가볍게 들어갈 정도로 공간이 넉넉하고, 게다가 짐칸에 개 한 마리도 실을 수 있다. ◼ 형용사 이 –이 넘는 ❑ 3만 명이 넘는 손님들을 시중들기 위한 직원이 고작 35명이다. ◼ 플러스 (성적) ◼ 가산명사 이익 [비격식체] ❑ 유명한 인사를 기용하면 새 이사진에 큰 이익이 될 것이다.

형용사 호화스런, 편한 ❑ 메이페어에 위치한 조지 왕조풍의 호화스런 4층짜리 저택

plu|to|nium /pluˈtoʊniəm/ N-UNCOUNT **Plutonium** is a radioactive element used especially in nuclear weapons and as a fuel in nuclear power stations.

ply /plaɪ/ (**plies, plying, plied**) ◆ V-T If you **ply** someone **with** food or drink, you keep giving them more of it. ❑ *Elsie, who had been told that Maria wasn't well, plied her with food.* ◆ V-T If you **ply** someone **with** questions, you keep asking them questions. ❑ *Giovanni plied him with questions and comments with the deliberate intention of prolonging his stay.*

ply|wood /ˈplaɪwʊd/ N-UNCOUNT **Plywood** is wood that consists of thin layers of wood stuck together. ❑ *...a sheet of plywood.*

PM ◆◇◇ /piˈɛm/ (**PMs**) N-COUNT The **PM** is an abbreviation for the **Prime Minister**. [BRIT, INFORMAL] ❑ *The reform will help meet the PM's pledge to make life better for the poorest families.* →see **government**

p.m. /piˈɛm/ also **pm** ADV **p.m.** is used after a number to show that you are referring to a particular time between 12 noon and 12 midnight. Compare **a.m.** [num ADV] ❑ *The spa is open from 7:00 am to 9:00 pm every day of the year.*

pneu|mo|nia /nʊˈmoʊnyə, -ˈmoʊniə/ N-UNCOUNT **Pneumonia** is a serious disease which affects your lungs and makes it difficult for you to breathe. ❑ *She nearly died of pneumonia.*

poach /poʊtʃ/ (**poaches, poaching, poached**) ◆ V-T/V-I If someone **poaches** fish, animals, or birds, they illegally catch them on someone else's property. ❑ *Many national parks set up to provide a refuge for wildlife are regularly invaded by people poaching game.* ● **poach|er** (**poachers**) N-COUNT ❑ *Security cameras have been installed to guard against poachers.* ● **poaching** N-UNCOUNT ❑ *The poaching of elephants for their tusks could start to decline soon.* ◆ V-T If an organization **poaches** members or customers **from** another organization, they secretly or dishonestly persuade them to join them or become their customers. ❑ *The company authorized its staff to poach customers and instigate dirty tricks against the opposition.* ● **poaching** N-UNCOUNT ❑ *The union was accused of poaching.* ◆ V-T If someone **poaches** an idea, they dishonestly or illegally use the idea. ❑ *The opposition parties have complained that the government has poached many of their ideas.* ◆ V-T If you **poach** food such as fish, you cook it gently in boiling water, milk, or other liquid. ❑ *Poach the chicken until just cooked.* ❑ *...a pear poached in red wine.* ● **poaching** N-UNCOUNT ❑ *You will need a pot of broth for poaching.*

PO Box /piˈoʊ bɒks/ also **P.O. Box** **PO Box** is used before a number as a kind of address. The Post Office keeps letters addressed to the PO Box until they are collected by the person who has paid for the service. ❑ *Send your order and a check to PO Box 2855, Sunnyvale 94087.*

pock|et ◆◇◇ /ˈpɒkɪt/ (**pockets, pocketing, pocketed**) ◆ N-COUNT A **pocket** is a kind of small bag which forms part of a piece of clothing, and which is used for carrying small things such as money or a handkerchief. ❑ *He took his flashlight from his jacket pocket and switched it on.* ◆ N-COUNT You can use **pocket** in a lot of different ways to refer to money that people have, get, or spend. For example, if someone gives or pays a lot of money, you can say that they **dig deep into** their **pocket**. If you approve of something because it is very cheap to buy, you can say that it **suits people's pockets**. ❑ *When you come to choosing a dining table, it really is worth digging deep into your pocket for the best you can afford.* ❑ *...ladies' fashions to suit all shapes, sizes and pockets.* ◆ ADJ You use **pocket** to describe something that is small enough to fit into a pocket, often something that is a smaller version of a larger item. [ADJ n] ❑ *...a pocket calculator.* ◆ N-COUNT A **pocket of** something is a small area where something is happening, or a small area which has a particular quality, and which is different from the other areas around it. ❑ *Trapped in a pocket of air, they had only 40 minutes before the tide flooded the chamber.* ◆ V-T If someone who is in possession of something valuable such as a sum of money **pockets** it, they steal it or take it for themselves, even though it does not belong to them. ❑ *Dishonest importers would be able to pocket the VAT collected from customers.* ◆ V-T If you say that someone **pockets** something such as a prize or sum of money, you mean that they win or obtain it, often without needing to make much effort or in a way that seems unfair. [JOURNALISM] ❑ *He pocketed more money from this tournament than in his entire three years as a professional.* ◆ V-T If someone **pockets** something, they put it in their pocket, for example because they want to steal it or hide it. ❑ *Anthony snatched his letters and pocketed them.* ◆ PHRASE If you are **out of pocket**, you have less money than you should have or than you intended, for example because you have spent too much or because of a mistake. ❑ *They were well out of pocket – they had spent far more in Hollywood than he had earned.* ◆ PHRASE If someone **picks** your **pocket**, they steal something from your pocket, usually without you noticing. ❑ *They were more in danger of having their pockets picked than being shot at.*

Word Partnership	*pocket*의 연어
N.	**back** pocket, **hip** pocket, **jacket** pocket, **pants** pocket, **shirt** pocket ◆

pocket|book /ˈpɒkɪtbʊk/ (**pocketbooks**) ◆ N-COUNT A **pocketbook** is a small bag which a woman uses to carry things such as her money and keys in when she goes out. [AM; BRIT **handbag, bag**] ◆ N-COUNT A **pocketbook** is a small flat folded case, usually made of leather or plastic, where you can keep banknotes and credit cards. [mainly AM; BRIT usually **wallet**]

pock|et mon|ey also **pocket-money** N-UNCOUNT **Pocket money** is money which children are given by their parents, usually every week. [mainly BRIT; AM usually **allowance**] ❑ *We agreed to give her £6 a week pocket money.*

불가산명사 플루토늄

■ 타동사 퍼 주다 ❑ 마리아의 건강이 좋지 않다는 소식을 접했던 엘시는 그녀에게 먹을 것을 퍼 주었다. ◻ 타동사 퍼붓다 ❑ 지오반니는 일부러 그를 더 오래 있게 하려고 그에게 질문과 논평을 퍼부었다.

불가산명사 합판 ❑ 합판 한 장

가산명사 수상 [영국영어, 비격식체] ❑ 그 개혁은 저소득층들이 더 나은 생활을 할 수 있게 하겠다는 수상의 공약을 실현시키는 데 기여할 것이다.

부사 오후 ❑ 그 온천은 연중무휴로 오전 7시부터 오후 9시까지 연다.

불가산명사 폐렴 ❑ 그녀는 폐렴으로 하마터면 죽을 뻔했다.

■ 타동사/자동사 밀렵하다 ❑ 야생 동물들을 보호하기 위해 설립된 많은 국립공원에 밀렵꾼들이 주기적으로 침범하고 있다. ● 밀렵꾼 가산명사 ❑ 밀렵꾼을 감시하기 위한 보안 카메라가 설치되어 있다. ● 밀렵 행위 불가산명사 ❑ 코끼리 상아를 갖기 위한 밀렵 행위는 곧 줄어들기 시작할 수 있었다. ◻ 타동사 빼내다 ❑ 그 회사는 직원들이 상대 회사를 상대로 고객들을 빼내고 추잡한 속임수를 쓰는 걸 허락했다. ● 인력 빼내기 불가산명사 ❑ 그 조합은 인력을 빼낸다고 비난을 받았다. ◻ 타동사 도용하다 ❑ 야당들은 자신들의 수많은 아이디어를 정부가 도용했다고 불만을 토로했다. ◻ 타동사 익히다; 데치다 ❑ 닭을 살짝만 익히세요. ❑ 적포도주에 넣어 익힌 배 ● 익힘; 데침 불가산명사 ❑ 익히려면 국물 한 냄비가 필요할 것입니다.

사서함 ❑ 주문서와 수표를 서니베일 94087의 사서함 2855로 보내십시오.

■ 가산명사 주머니 ❑ 그는 재킷 주머니에서 손전등을 꺼내어 스위치를 켰다. ◻ 가산명사 자금, 주머니 사정; 거금을 들이다; 사람들의 주머니 사정에 알맞다 ❑ 식탁을 고르게 되려든 정말이지 형편이 닿는 대로 거금을 들일 가치가 있다. ◻ 모양과 크기, 그리고 주머니 사정까지 고려한 숙녀복 패션 ◻ 형용사 포켓형의 ❑ 포켓형 계산기 ◻ 가산명사 (주변과는 다른) 작은 지역 ❑ 겨우 숨쉴 수 있는 작은 공간에 갇힌 그들에게는 조수가 방으로 밀려들어 오기까지 겨우 40분만 남아 있었다. ◻ 타동사 착복하다 ❑ 부정직한 수입업자들이라면 고객들에게서 받는 부가 가치세를 착복할 수도 있을 것이다. ◻ 타동사 손에 넣다 [언론] ❑ 그는 직업 선수로서 3년 동안 번 돈보다 이번 토너먼트에서 더 많은 돈을 손에 넣었다. ◻ 타동사 주머니 속에 감추다, 주머니 속에 집어넣다 ❑ 안토니는 그의 편지들을 낚아채서 주머니 속에 감추었다. ◻ 구 주머니 사정이 안 좋은 ❑ 그들은 주머니 사정이 안 좋았다. 그가 버는 것보다 훨씬 많은 돈을 할리우드에서 써 버렸기 때문이다. ◻ 구 소매치기하다 ❑ 그들은 총에 맞는 위험보다는 소매치기 당할 위험이 더 컸다.

■ 가산명사 핸드백 [미국영어; 영국영어 handbag, bag] ◻ 가산명사 지갑 [주로 미국영어; 영국영어 대개 wallet]

불가산명사 용돈 [주로 영국영어; 미국영어 대개 allowance] ❑ 우리는 그 애에게 1주일에 한 번씩 용돈으로 6파운드를 주기로 했다.

a b c d e f g h i j k l m n o p q r s t u v w x y z

pod /pɒd/ (**pods**) N-COUNT A **pod** is a seed container that grows on plants such as peas or beans. ❑ ...*fresh peas in the pod.*

가산명사 꼬투리 ❑ 꼬투리 속에 들어 있는 싱싱한 완두콩

po|dium /poʊdiəm/ (**podiums**) N-COUNT A **podium** is a small platform on which someone stands in order to give a lecture or conduct an orchestra. ❑ *Unsteadily he mounted the podium, adjusted the microphone, coughed and went completely blank.*

가산명사 연단 ❑ 불안하게 연단에 올라선 그는 마이크를 조정하고 기침을 하더니 완전히 멍해졌다.

poem ♦♢♢ /poʊəm/ (**poems**) N-COUNT A **poem** is a piece of writing in which the words are chosen for their beauty and sound and are carefully arranged, often in short lines which rhyme. ❑ ...*a book of love poems.*

가산명사 시 ❑ 연애시가 담긴 시집

poet ♦♢♢ /poʊɪt/ (**poets**) N-COUNT A **poet** is a person who writes poems. ❑ *He was a painter and poet.*

가산명사 시인 ❑ 그는 화가이자 시인이었다.

po|et|ic /poʊɛtɪk/ **1** ADJ Something that is **poetic** is very beautiful and expresses emotions in a sensitive or moving way. ❑ *Nikolai Demidenko gave an exciting yet poetic performance.* **2** ADJ **Poetic** means relating to poetry. ❑ *There's a very rich poetic tradition in Gaelic.*

1 형용사 시적인 ❑ 니콜라이 데미덴코는 신나면서도 시적인 연주를 선보였다. **2** 형용사 시의 ❑ 게일 어에는 시적 전통이 아주 풍부하다.

po|et|ry ♦♢♢ /poʊɪtri/ **1** N-UNCOUNT Poems, considered as a form of literature, are referred to as **poetry**. ❑ ...*Russian poetry.* ❑ *Lawrence Durrell wrote a great deal of poetry.* **2** N-UNCOUNT You can describe something very beautiful as **poetry**. ❑ *His music is purer poetry than a poem in words.*

1 불가산명사 시 ❑ 러시아의 시 ❑ 로런스 듀렐은 수많은 시를 썼다. **2** 불가산명사 한 편의 시와 같은 것 ❑ 그의 음악은 글로 된 한 편의 시보다 더 순수한 시 같다.

poign|ant /pɔɪnyənt/ ADJ Something that is **poignant** affects you deeply and makes you feel sadness or regret. ❑ ...*a poignant combination of beautiful surroundings and tragic history.* ❑ ...*a poignant love story.*

형용사 가슴을 에는, 가슴에 사무치는 ❑ 주위의 아름다운 풍경과 이에 담긴 역사적 비극의 가슴을 에는 조합 ❑ 가슴에 사무치는 사랑 이야기

point ♦♦♦ /pɔɪnt/ (**points, pointing, pointed**) **1** N-COUNT You use **point** to refer to something that someone has said or written. ❑ *We disagree with every point Mr. Blunkett makes.* ❑ *Dave Hill's article makes the right point about the Taylor Report.* **2** N-SING If you say that someone **has a point**, or if you **take** their **point**, you mean that you accept that what they have said is important and should be considered. ❑ *"If he'd already killed once, surely he'd have killed Sarah?" She had a point there.* **3** N-SING **The point** of what you are saying or discussing is the most important part that provides a reason or explanation for the rest. ❑ *"Did I ask you to talk to me?" — "That's not the point."* **4** N-SING If you ask what **the point of** something is, or say that there is **no point in** it, you are indicating that a particular action has no purpose or would not be useful. ❑ *What was the point of thinking about him?* **5** N-COUNT A **point** is a detail, aspect, or quality of something or someone. ❑ *Many of the points in the report are correct.* ❑ *The most interesting point about the village was its religion.* **6** N-COUNT A **point** is a particular place or position where something happens. ❑ *As a mark of respect the emperor met him at a point several weeks' march from the capital.* **7** N-SING You use **point** to refer to a particular time, or to a particular stage in the development of something. ❑ *We're all going to die at some point.* ❑ *It got to the point where he had to leave.* **8** N-COUNT The **point** of something such as a pin, needle, or knife is the thin, sharp end of it. ❑ *Put the tomatoes into a bowl and stab each one with the point of a knife.* **9** In spoken English, you use **point** to refer to the dot or mark in a decimal number that separates the whole numbers from the fractions. ❑ *This is FM stereo one oh three point seven.* **10** N-COUNT In some sports, competitions, and games, a **point** is one of the single marks that are added together to give the total score. ❑ *They lost the 1977 World Cup final to Australia by a single point.* **11** N-COUNT The **points of the compass** are directions such as North, South, East, and West. ❑ *Sightseers arrived from all points of the compass.* **12** N-PLURAL On a railroad track, the **points** are the levers and rails at a place where two tracks join or separate. The points enable a train to move from one track to another. [BRIT; AM **switches**] ❑ ...*the rattle of the wheels across the points.* **13** N-COUNT A **point** is an electric outlet. [BRIT] ❑ ...*too far away from the nearest electrical point.* **14** V-I If you **point at** a person or thing, you hold out your finger toward them in order to make someone notice them. ❑ *I pointed at the boy sitting nearest me.* ❑ *He pointed at me with the stem of his pipe.* **15** V-T If you **point** something **at** someone, you aim the tip or end of it toward them. ❑ *David Khan pointed his finger at Mary.* **16** V-I If something **points to** a place or **points** in a particular direction, it shows where that place is or it faces in that direction. ❑ *An arrow pointed to the toilets.* ❑ *He controlled the car until it was pointing forwards again.* **17** V-I If something **points to** a particular situation, it suggests that the situation exists or is likely to occur. ❑ *Earlier reports pointed to pupils working harder, more continuously, and with enthusiasm.* **18** V-I If you **point to** something that has happened or that is happening, you are using it as proof that a particular situation exists. ❑ *George Fodor points to other weaknesses in the way the campaign has progressed.* **19** →see also **pointed, breaking point, focal point, point of sale, point of view, sticking point, vantage point** **20** PHRASE If you say that something is **beside the point**, you mean that it is not relevant to the subject that you are discussing. ❑ *Brian didn't like it, but that was beside the point.* **21** PHRASE When someone **comes to the point** or **gets to the point**, they start talking about the thing that is most important to them. ❑ *He came to the point at once. "You did a splendid job on this case."* **22** PHRASE If you **make** your **point** or **prove** your **point**, you prove that something is true, either by arguing about it or by your actions or behavior. ❑ *I think you've made your point, dear.* ❑ *Dr. David McCleland, of Boston University, studied one-hundred people, aged eighteen to sixty, to prove the point.* **23** PHRASE If you **make a point of** doing something, you do it in a very deliberate or obvious way. ❑ *She made a point of spending as much time as possible away from Osborne House.* **24** PHRASE If you are **on the point of** doing something, you are about to do it. ❑ *He was on the point of saying something when the phone rang.* **25** PHRASE Something that is **to the point** is relevant to the subject that you are discussing, or expressed neatly without wasting words or time. ❑ *The description which he had been given was brief and to the point.* **26** PHRASE If you say that something is true **up to a point**, you mean that it is partly but not completely true. ❑ *"Was she good?" — "Mmm. Up to a point."* **27** in

1 가산명사 지적 ❑ 우리는 블런케트 씨의 모든 지적에 반대한다. ❑ 데이브 힐의 논문은 테일러 리포트에 대해 타당한 지적을 하고 있다. **2** 단수명사 일리가 있다, 취지를 이해하다 ❑ "그가 전에 살인을 한 적이 있다면, 확실히 그가 사라를 죽였겠지?"라고 그녀가 일리 있는 말을 했다. **3** 단수명사 핵심 ❑ "누가 너더러 말해 달랬니?" "그게 핵심이 아니잖아." **4** 단수명사 소용; 무익 ❑ 그를 생각한다고 해서 무슨 소용이 있었니? **5** 가산명사 사항 ❑ 보고서에 나온 많은 사항들이 옳다. ❑ 그 마을에 대한 가장 흥미로운 사항은 마을 사람들의 종교였다. **6** 가산명사 지점 ❑ 존경의 증표로서 황제는 수도에서부터 수주 간 행군을 해야 가 닿는 지점까지 그들 마주 나갔다. **7** 단수명사 시점 ❑ 우리는 모두 어느 시점에서는 죽는다. ❑ 그가 떠나야만 하는 시점에 이르렀다. **8** 가산명사 (뾰족한) 끝 ❑ 사발에 토마토를 넣고 칼끝으로 하나하나 찌르세요. **9** 소수점 ❑ 여기는 에프엠 스테레오 103.7입니다. **10** 가산명사 점수 ❑ 그들은 1977년 월드컵 결승전에서 호주에 단 한 점 차이로 졌다. **11** 가산명사 나침반의 32방위 ❑ 관광객들이 도처에서 몰려왔다. **12** 복수명사 전철기, 선로 바꿈틀 [영국영어; 미국영어 **switches**] ❑ 전철기 저쪽에서 들려오는 덜컹거리는 바퀴 소리 **13** 가산명사 콘센트 [영국영어] ❑ 가장 가까운 전기 콘센트도 너무 멀리 떨어진 **14** 자동사 가리키다 ❑ 나는 나와 가장 가까이 앉아 있는 소년을 가리켰다. ❑ 그는 담뱃대의 대를 가리켰다. **15** 타동사 가리키다 ❑ 데이비드 칸이 손가락으로 메리를 가리켰다. **16** 자동사 -쪽으로 향해 있다 ❑ 화살표가 화장실 쪽을 가리키고 있었다. ❑ 그는 그 자동차가 다시 앞쪽으로 향하도록 조정했다. **17** 자동사 -을 언급하다 ❑ 이전 보고서들은 열정을 가지고 더 꾸준히, 더 열심히 공부하는 학생들에 대해 언급했다. **18** 자동사 -을 지적하다 ❑ 조지 포더는 그 캠페인 진행 방식에 내재된 다른 취약점들을 지적한다. **20** 구 상관없다, 요점을 벗어난 ❑ 브라이언은 그것을 좋아하지 않았으나, 그건 상관없는 일이었다. **21** 구 요점을 말하다 ❑ 그는 즉시 요점을 말했다. "너는 이 일을 아주 멋지게 해냈어." **22** 구 주장을 입증하다 ❑ 애야, 나는 네가 네 주장을 입증했다고 생각해. ❑ 보스턴대학교의 데이비드 맥클레랜드 박사는 그 주장을 입증하기 위해 열여덟 살에서 예순 살에 해당하는 백 명의 사람을 대상으로 연구했다. **23** 구 꼭 -하다 ❑ 그녀는 꼭 오스본 하우스에서 벗어나 가능한 한 많은 시간을 보냈다. **24** 구 -하려고 막 할 때 ❑ 그는 막 무언가를 말하려는 참에 전화벨이 울렸다. **25** 구 적절한 ❑ 그가 들었던 설명은 간결했고 적절했다. **26** 구 어느 정도까지는 ❑ "그녀가 친절했어요?" "음. 어느 정도는."

point of fact →see fact. to **point the finger at** someone →see finger. a sore point →see sore

---

▶**point out** 🔳 PHRASAL VERB If you **point out** an object or place, you make people look at it or show them where it is. ❑ *They kept standing up to take pictures and point things out to each other.* 🔲 PHRASAL VERB If you **point out** a fact or mistake, you tell someone about it or draw their attention to it. ❑ *I should point out that these estimates cover just the hospital expenditures.*

🔳 구동사 가리키다 ❑ 그들은 계속 서서 사진을 찍고 서로에게 이것저것을 가리켜 보였다. 🔲 구동사 지적하다 ❑ 이 견해는 병원 지출에만 해당된다는 것을 지적해야겠습니다.

point-blank 🔳 ADV If you say something **point-blank**, you say it very directly or rudely, without explaining or apologizing. [ADV after v] ❑ *The army apparently refused point-blank to do what was required of them.* ● ADJ **Point-blank** is also an adjective. [ADJ n] ❑ *...a point-blank refusal.* 🔲 ADV If someone or something is shot **point-blank**, they are shot when the gun is touching them or extremely close to them. [ADV after v] ❑ *He put a gun through the open window of the car and fired point-blank at Bernadette.* ● ADJ **Point-blank** is also an adjective. [ADJ n] ❑ *He had been shot at point-blank range in the back of the head.*

🔳 부사 단도직입적으로 ❑ 군대가 자신들에게 요구된 일을 단도직입적으로 거부한 것이 분명해 보였다. ● 형용사 단도직입적인 ❑ 단도직입적인 거절 🔲 부사 아주 가까이에서, 직사 거리에서 ❑ 그는 열린 차창으로 총을 대고 아주 가까이에서 버나데트를 저격했다. ● 형용사 아주 가까운, 직사 거리의 ❑ 그는 바로 머리 뒤쪽에서 총을 맞은 것이었다.

point|ed /pɔɪntɪd/ 🔳 ADJ Something that is **pointed** has a point at one end. ❑ *...a pointed roof.* 🔲 ADJ **Pointed** comments or behavior express criticism in a clear and direct way. ❑ *I couldn't help notice the pointed remarks slung in my direction.* ● **point|ed|ly** ADV ❑ *They were pointedly absent from the news conference.*

🔳 형용사 뾰족한 ❑ 뾰족한 지붕 🔲 형용사 드러내 놓고 하는, 노골적인 ❑ 드러내 놓고 나더러 들으라고 한 발언인데 내가 눈치 못 챌 수 없지. ● 드러내 놓고, 노골적으로 부사 ❑ 그들은 드러내 놓고 기자 회견에 불참했다.

point|er /pɔɪntər/ (**pointers**) 🔳 N-COUNT A **pointer** is a piece of advice or information which helps you to understand a situation or to find a way of making progress. ❑ *I hope at least my daughter was able to offer you some useful pointers.* 🔲 N-COUNT A **pointer to** something suggests that it exists or gives an idea of what it is like. [mainly BRIT] ❑ *His victory in the first race here on Tuesday was a timely pointer to his chance of remaining unbeaten.* 🔳 N-COUNT A **pointer** is a long stick that is used to point at something such as a large chart or diagram when explaining something to people. ❑ *She tapped on the world map with her pointer.* 🔳 N-COUNT The **pointer** on a measuring instrument is the long, thin piece of metal that points to the numbers. ❑ *A series of levers joined to a pointer shows pressure on a dial.*

🔳 가산명사 조언, 정보 ❑ 난 적어도 내 딸이 자네에게 유용한 조언을 제공할 수 있었을 것이라고 생각한다. 🔲 가산명사 암시 [주로 영국영어] ❑ 화요일 이곳 첫 번째 경주에서 그가 승리한 것은 그가 계속 승리할 것이라는 가능성에 대한 시기적절한 암시였다. 🔳 가산명사 지시봉 ❑ 그녀는 지침봉으로 세계 지도를 톡톡 두드렸다. 🔳 가산명사 지침(針), 바늘 ❑ 지침으로 연결된 일련의 레버들이 눈금판에서 압력을 나타낸다.

point|less /pɔɪntlɪs/ ADJ If you say that something is **pointless**, you are criticizing it because it has no sense or purpose. [DISAPPROVAL] ❑ *Violence is always pointless.* ❑ *Without an audience the performance is pointless.* ● **point|less|ly** ADV ❑ *Chemicals were pointlessly poisoning the soil.*

형용사 무의미한; 무익한 [탐탁찮음] ❑ 폭력은 백해무익한 짓이다. ❑ 관객이 없는 공연은 무의미하다. ● 무의미하게, 무익하게 부사 ❑ 화학 물질이 무익하게 토양을 오염시키고 있었다.

point of sale (**points of sale**) 🔳 N-COUNT The **point of sale** is the place in a store where a product is passed from the seller to the customer. The abbreviation **POS** is also used. [BUSINESS] ❑ *Demand-chain management captures information on consumer behavior at the point of sale and feeds it up the supply chain.* 🔲 N-UNCOUNT **Point-of-sale** is used to describe things which occur or are located or used at the place where you buy something. The abbreviation **POS** is also used. [BUSINESS] [usu N n] ❑ *Introduction of electronic point-of-sale systems is improving efficiency.*

🔳 가산명사 매장 [경제] ❑ 수요체계 관리는 매장에서의 소비자 행동에 대한 정보를 입수하고 공급체계에 그 정보를 제공한다. 🔲 불가산명사 판매 관리 [경제] ❑ 전자 판매시점 관리 시스템의 도입으로 능률이 향상되고 있다.

point of view ♦◇◇ (**points of view**) 🔳 N-COUNT You can refer to the opinions or attitudes that you have about something as your **point of view**. ❑ *Thanks for your point of view, John.* 🔲 N-COUNT If you consider something **from** a particular **point of view**, you are using one aspect of a situation in order to judge that situation. ❑ *Do you think that, from the point of view of results, this exercise was worth the cost?* →see history

🔳 가산명사 의견, 견해 ❑ 의견 감사해요, 존. 🔲 가산명사 관점, 견지 ❑ 결과라는 관점에서 볼 때, 이 연습이 비용을 들일만한 가치가 있었다고 생각하십니까?

poise /pɔɪz/ N-UNCOUNT If someone has **poise**, they are calm, dignified, and self-controlled. ❑ *What amazed him even more than her appearance was her poise.*

불가산명사 침착한 태도, 평정 ❑ 그녀의 외모보다 훨씬 너 그를 놀라게 한 것은 그녀의 침착한 태도였다.

poised /pɔɪzd/ 🔳 ADJ If a part of your body is **poised**, it is completely still but ready to move at any moment. ❑ *He studied the keyboard carefully, one finger poised.* 🔲 ADJ If someone is **poised to** do something, they are ready to take action at any moment. [v-link ADJ, usu ADJ to-inf, ADJ for n] ❑ *Britain was poised to fly medical staff to the country at short notice.* 🔳 ADJ If you are **poised**, you are calm, dignified, and self-controlled. ❑ *She was self-assured, poised, almost self-satisfied.*

🔳 형용사 자세를 취한 ❑ 그는 한 손가락은 움직일 자세를 취한 채로 신중하게 자판을 살펴보았다. 🔲 형용사 ~할 준비가 되어 있는 ❑ 영국은 당장 그 나라에 항공편으로 의료진을 보낼 준비가 되어 있었다. 🔳 형용사 침착한 ❑ 그녀는 확신감에 찼고, 침착했으며, 거의 자만하고 있는 것 같기도 했다.

poi|son /pɔɪzᵊn/ (**poisons, poisoning, poisoned**) 🔳 N-MASS **Poison** is a substance that harms or kills people or animals if they swallow it or absorb it. ❑ *Poison from the fish causes paralysis, swelling, and nausea.* 🔲 V-T If someone **poisons** another person, they kill the person or make them ill by giving them poison. ❑ *The rumors that she had poisoned him could never be proved.* ● **poi|son|ing** N-UNCOUNT ❑ *She was sentenced to twenty years' imprisonment for poisoning and attempted murder.* 🔳 V-T If you **are poisoned by** a substance, it makes you very ill and sometimes kills you. ❑ *Employees were taken to hospital yesterday after being poisoned by fumes.* ● **poi|son|ing** N-UNCOUNT ❑ *...acute alcohol poisoning.* 🔳 V-T If someone **poisons** a food, drink, or weapon, they add poison to it so that it can be used to kill someone. ❑ *If I was your wife I would poison your coffee.* 🔳 V-T To **poison** water, air, or land means to damage it with harmful substances such as chemicals. ❑ *...the textile and fibre industries that taint the air, poison the water, and use vast amounts of natural resources.* ❑ *The land has been completely poisoned by chemicals.* 🔳 V-T Something that **poisons** a good situation or relationship spoils it or destroys it. ❑ *The whole atmosphere has really been poisoned.*

🔳 물질명사 독 ❑ 그 물고기의 독은 마비 증상과 피부 부종, 메스꺼움을 유발시킨다. 🔲 타동사 독살하다 ❑ 그녀가 그를 독살했다는 소문은 결코 입증될 수 없었다. ● 독살 불가산명사 ❑ 그녀는 독살 미수로 20년 형을 선고 받았다. 🔳 타동사 중독되다 ❑ 종업원들이 어제 가스 중독으로 병원에 실려 갔다. ● 중독 불가산명사 ❑ 급성 알코올 중독 🔳 타동사 독을 넣다 ❑ 내가 당신의 아내라면 당신의 커피에 독을 넣을 텐데. 🔳 타동사 오염시키다 ❑ 공기와 수질을 오염시키고 막대한 천연자원을 소비하는 직물 및 섬유 산업 ❑ 그 땅은 화학 물질로 인해 완전히 오염되어 있다. 🔳 타동사 망치다 ❑ 전체적인 분위기가 진짜 엉망이 되어 버렸다.

poi|son|ous /pɔɪzᵊnəs/ 🔳 ADJ Something that is **poisonous** will kill you or make you ill if you swallow or absorb it. ❑ *All parts of the yew tree are poisonous,*

🔳 형용사 독이 있는, 유독한 ❑ 주목은 열매를 포함해서 모든 부분에 독이 있다. 🔲 형용사 독을 가진

including the berries. **2** ADJ An animal that is **poisonous** produces a poison that will kill you or make you ill if the animal bites you. □ *There are hundreds of poisonous spiders and snakes.* **3** ADJ If you describe something as **poisonous**, you mean that it is extremely unpleasant and likely to spoil or destroy a good relationship or situation. □ *...poisonous comments.* □ *...lying awake half the night tormented by poisonous suspicions.*

□ 독거미와 독사가 수백 마리 있다. **3** 형용사 해로운 □ 해로운 논평 □ 유해한 의심으로 괴로워하며 거의 뜬눈으로 밤을 지새우며 누워 있는

poison pill (poison pills) N-COUNT A **poison pill** refers to what some companies do to reduce their value in order to prevent themselves being taken over by another company. [BUSINESS] □ *Some believe this level of compensation is essentially a poison pill to put off any rival bidders.*

가산명사 기업매수 방어책 [경제] □ 일부 사람들은 이 정도의 배상은 경쟁 입찰업체들의 의지를 꺾기 위해 반드시 필요한 기업매수 방어책이라고 믿고 있다.

poke /poʊk/ (pokes, poking, poked) **1** V-T If you **poke** someone or something, you quickly push them with your finger or with a sharp object. □ *Lindy poked him in the ribs.* ● N-COUNT **Poke** is also a noun. □ *John smiled at them and gave Richard a playful poke.* **2** V-T If you **poke** one thing **into** another, you push the first thing into the second thing. □ *He poked his finger into the hole.* **3** V-I If something **pokes out of** or **through** another thing, you can see part of it appearing from behind or underneath the other thing. □ *He saw the dog's twitching nose poke out of the basket.* **4** V-T/V-I If you **poke** your head through an opening or if it **pokes** through an opening, you push it through, often so that you can see something more easily. □ *Julie tapped on my door and poked her head in.* **5** to **poke fun** at →see **fun**. to **poke** your **nose into** →see **nose**

1 타동사 쿡 찌르다 □ 린디가 그의 옆구리를 쿡 찔렀다. ● 가산명사 찌름 □ 존은 그들을 보고 웃으며 장난스럽게 리처드를 쿡 찔렀다. **2** 타동사 ~안에 집어넣다, 손으로 쿡 찌르다 □ 그가 그 구멍 안에 손가락을 집어넣었다. **3** 자동사 ~에서 비죽이 내밀다 □ 그는 그 개의 벌름거리는 코가 바구니 밖으로 비죽이 나와 있는 것을 보았다. **4** 타동사/자동사 들이밀다 □ 줄리가 내 방문을 톡톡 두드리더니 머리를 들이밀었다.

poker /poʊkər/ (pokers) **1** N-UNCOUNT **Poker** is a card game that people usually play in order to win money. □ *Lon and I play in the same weekly poker game.* **2** N-COUNT A **poker** is a metal bar which you use to move coal or wood in a fire in order to make it burn better. □ *Niigata stirred the wood with a poker, put another log on.*

1 불가산명사 포커 □ 론과 나는 매주 같은 포커 게임을 한다. **2** 가산명사 부지깽이 □ 니가타는 부지깽이로 장작들을 헤집고 또 다른 통나무를 얹었다.

polar /poʊlər/ **1** ADJ **Polar** means near the North and South Poles. [ADJ n] □ *...the rigors of life in the polar regions.* □ *There was a period of excessive warmth which melted some of the polar ice.* **2** ADJ **Polar** is used to describe things which are completely opposite in character, quality, or type. [FORMAL] [ADJ n] □ *The nomads' lifestyle was the polar opposite of collectivization.*

1 형용사 극지방의 □ 극지방에서의 혹독한 삶 □ 극지방의 얼음 일부를 녹인 몹시 더운 시대가 있었다. **2** 형용사 정반대의 (격식체) □ 유목민들의 생활양식은 집단주의 양식과는 완전히 정반대였다.

polarize /poʊləraɪz/ (polarizes, polarizing, polarized) [BRIT also **polarise**] V-T/V-I If something **polarizes** people or if something **polarizes**, two separate groups are formed with opposite opinions or positions. □ *Missile deployment did much to further polarize opinion in Britain.* □ *As the car rental industry polarizes, business will go to the bigger companies.* ● **polarization** /poʊlərɪzeɪʃn/ N-UNCOUNT □ *There is increasing polarization between blacks and whites in the U.S.*

[영국영어 polarise] 타동사/자동사 양극화시키다; 양극화되다 □ 미사일 개발이 영국 내 의견을 한층 더 양극화시키는 데 큰 역할을 하였다. □ 자동차 렌탈 산업이 양극화될수록, 규모가 큰 회사들이 업계를 장악하게 될 것이다. ● 양극화 불가산명사 □ 미국에서 흑백 간의 양극화 현상이 커지고 있다.

pole ♦♢♢ /poʊl/ (poles) **1** N-COUNT A **pole** is a long thin piece of wood or metal, used especially for supporting things. □ *The truck crashed into a telegraph pole.* **2** N-COUNT The earth's **poles** are the two opposite ends of its axis, its most northern and southern points. □ *For six months of the year, there is hardly any light at the poles.* **3** N-COUNT The two **poles** of a range of qualities, opinions, or beliefs are the completely opposite qualities, opinions, or beliefs at either end of the range. □ *The two politicians represent opposite poles of the political spectrum.* **4** PHRASE If you say that two people or things are **poles apart**, you mean that they have completely different beliefs, opinions, or qualities. [EMPHASIS] □ *It should make for an intriguing evening because, in some ways, the two composers are poles apart.* →see **magnet**

1 가산명사 막대기, 지지대 □ 그 트럭은 전봇대와 충돌했다. **2** 가산명사 극지, (지구의) 극 □ 극지에서는 1년 중 6개월 동안, 빛을 거의 볼 수 없다. **3** 가산명사 양극단 □ 그 두 정치인은 다양한 정치적 신념의 양극단을 대표한다. **4** 구 정반대인 [강조] □ 여러 면으로 볼 때, 그 두 작곡가들의 성향이 정반대이므로 흥미로운 저녁이 될 것이다.

polemic /pəlemɪk/ (polemics) N-VAR A **polemic** is a very strong written or spoken attack on, or defense of, a particular belief or opinion. □ *...a polemic against the danger of secret societies.*

가산명사 또는 불가산명사 강한 논박, 심한 비판 □ 비밀 결사들의 위험에 대한 강한 논박

Word Link

poli ≈ city: metropolis, police, policy

police ♦♦♦ /pəlis/ (polices, policing, policed) **1** N-SING-COLL The **police** are the official organization that is responsible for making sure that people obey the law. □ *The police are also looking for a second car.* □ *Police say they have arrested twenty people following the disturbances.* **2** N-PLURAL **Police** are men and women who are members of the official organization that is responsible for making sure that people obey the law. □ *More than one hundred police have ringed the area.* **3** V-T If the police or military forces police an area or event, they make sure that law and order is preserved in that area or at that event. □ *...the tiny UN observer force whose job it is to police the border.* →see also **secret police** **4** V-T If a person or group in authority **polices** a law or an area of public life, they make sure that what is done is fair and legal. □ *...Imro, the self-regulatory body that polices the investment management business.*

1 단수명사-집합 경찰 □ 경찰은 또한 제 2의 차량도 찾고 있다. □ 경찰은 소요 사태 후 20명을 체포했다고 말한다. **2** 복수명사 경찰관 □ 백 명이 넘는 경찰관들이 그 지역을 에워쌌다. **3** 타동사 치안을 유지하다 □ 국경 지대 치안유지 업무를 맡은 소수의 유엔 감시군 **4** 타동사 관할하다 □ 투자 관리 업무를 관할하는 자치 규율 조직인 임로

police force (police forces) N-COUNT A **police force** is the police organization in a particular country or area. □ *...the South Wales police force.*

가산명사 경찰력 □ 사우스 웨일스 경찰력

policeman ♦♢♢ /pəlismən/ (policemen) N-COUNT A **policeman** is a man who is a member of the police force.

가산명사 (남자) 경찰관

police officer ♦♢♢ (police officers) N-COUNT A **police officer** is a member of the police force. □ *...a meeting of senior police officers.*

가산명사 경찰관 □ 고위급 경찰관 회동

police station (police stations) N-COUNT A **police station** is the local office of a police force in a particular area. □ *Two police officers arrested him and took him to Kensington police station.*

가산명사 경찰서 □ 경찰관 두 명이 그를 체포해서 켄싱턴 경찰서로 연행했다.

policewoman /pəliswʊmən/ (policewomen) N-COUNT A **policewoman** is a woman who is a member of the police force.

가산명사 (여자) 경찰관

policy ♦♦♦ /pɒlɪsi/ (policies) **1** N-VAR A **policy** is a set of ideas or plans that is used as a basis for making decisions, especially in politics, economics, or business. □ *...plans which include changes in foreign policy and economic reforms.* **2** N-COUNT An official organization's **policy** on a particular issue or towards a country is their attitude and actions regarding that issue or country. □ *...the organization's future policy towards South Africa.* □ *...the government's policy on*

1 가산명사 또는 불가산명사 정책 □ 외교 정책과 경제 개혁의 변화를 담고 있는 계획안 **2** 가산명사 방침 □ 남아프리카 공화국에 대한 그 기구의 향후 방침 □ 본국 송환에 대한 정부 방침 가산명사 보험 증권 [경제] □ 가계 및 자동차 보험 증권의 자세한 사항을 읽으시기를 권해 드립니다.

repatriation. **3** N-COUNT An insurance **policy** is a document which shows the agreement that you have made with an insurance company. [BUSINESS] ❏ *You are advised to read the small print of household and motor insurance policies.*

Word Partnership	*policy*의 연어
ADJ.	**domestic** policy, **economic** policy, **educational** policy, **foreign** policy, **new** policy, **official** policy, **public** policy **1**
N.	policy **analyst**, **defense** policy, **energy** policy, **immigration** policy **1**
	policy **change** (or **change** of policy), policy **objectives**, policy **shift** **1** **2**
	administration policy, **government** policy **2**
	insurance policy **3**

policy|holder /pɒlɪsihoʊldər/ (**policyholders**) also **policy-holder** N-COUNT A **policyholder** is a person who has an insurance policy with an insurance company. [BUSINESS] ❏ *The first 10 per cent of legal fees will be paid by the policy-holder.*

po|lio /poʊlioʊ/ N-UNCOUNT **Polio** is a serious infectious disease which often makes people unable to use their legs. ❏ *Gladys was crippled by polio at the age of 3.* →see **hospital**

pol|ish /pɒlɪʃ/ (**polishes, polishing, polished**) **1** N-MASS **Polish** is a substance that you put on the surface of an object in order to clean it, protect it, and make it shine. ❏ *The still air smelt faintly of furniture polish.* **2** V-T If you **polish** something, you put polish on it or rub it with a cloth to make it shine. ❏ *Each morning he shaved and polished his shoes.* ● N-SING **Polish** is also a noun. ❏ *He gave his counter a polish with a soft duster.* ● **pol|ished** ADJ ❏ *...a highly polished floor.* **3** N-UNCOUNT If you say that a performance or piece of work has **polish**, you mean that it is of a very high standard. [APPROVAL] ❏ *The opera lacks the polish of his later work.* **4** V-T If you **polish** your technique, performance, or skill at doing something, you work on improving it. ❏ *They just need to polish their technique.* ● PHRASAL VERB **Polish up** means the same as **polish**. ❏ *Polish up your writing skills on a one-week professional course.* **5** →see also **polished**

pol|ished /pɒlɪʃt/ **1** ADJ Someone who is **polished** shows confidence and knows how to behave socially. [APPROVAL] ❏ *He is polished, charming, articulate, and an excellent negotiator.* **2** ADJ If you describe a performance, ability, or skill as **polished**, you mean that it is of a very high standard. [APPROVAL] ❏ *It was simply a very polished performance.* **3** →see also **polish**

po|lite /pəlaɪt/ (**politer, politest**) ADJ Someone who is **polite** has good manners and behaves in a way that is socially correct and not rude to other people. ❏ *Everyone around him was trying to be polite, but you could tell they were all bored.* ❏ *Gately, a quiet and very polite young man, made a favorable impression.* ● **po|lite|ly** ADV ❏ *"Your home is beautiful," I said politely.* ● **po|lite|ness** N-UNCOUNT ❏ *She listened to him, but only out of politeness.*

Thesaurus	*polite*의 참조어
ADJ.	considerate, courteous, gracious, respectful; *(ant.)* brash, impolite, rude

po|liti|cal ♦♦♦ /pəlɪtɪkᵊl/ **1** ADJ **Political** means relating to the way power is achieved and used in a country or society. ❏ *All other political parties there have been completely banned.* ❏ *The Canadian government is facing another political crisis.* ● **po|liti|cal|ly** /pəlɪtɪkli/ ADV ❏ *They do not believe the killings were politically motivated.* **2** ADJ Someone who is **political** is interested or involved in politics and holds strong beliefs about it. ❏ *Oh I'm not political, I take no interest in politics.* →see **empire**, **philosophy**

po|liti|cal asy|lum N-UNCOUNT **Political asylum** is the right to live in a foreign country and is given by the government of that country to people who have to leave their own country for political reasons. ❏ *...a university teacher who is seeking political asylum in Britain.*

po|liti|cal econo|my N-UNCOUNT **Political economy** is the study of the way in which a government influences or organizes a nation's wealth.

po|liti|cal|ly cor|rect ADJ If you say that someone is **politically correct**, you mean that they are extremely careful not to offend or upset any group of people in society who have a disadvantage, or who have been treated differently because of their sex, race, or disability. ❏ *...environmentalists and politically correct liberals.* ● **The politically correct** are people who are politically correct. *[the N]* ❏ *...the hypocrisy of the politically correct.*

po|liti|cian ♦♦♦ /pɒlɪtɪʃᵊn/ (**politicians**) N-COUNT A **politician** is a person whose job is in politics, especially a member of the government. ❏ *They have arrested a number of leading opposition politicians.*

poli|tics ♦♦♦ /pɒlɪtɪks/ **1** N-PLURAL **Politics** are the actions or activities concerned with achieving and using power in a country or society. The verb that follows **politics** may be either singular or plural. ❏ *The key question in British politics was how long the prime minister could survive* ❏ *He quickly involved himself in local politics.* **2** N-PLURAL Your **politics** are your beliefs about how a country ought to be governed. ❏ *My politics are well to the left of center.* **3** N-UNCOUNT **Politics** is the study of the ways in which countries are governed. ❏ *He began studying politics and medieval history.* **4** N-PLURAL **Politics** can be used to talk about the ways that power is shared in an organization and the ways it is affected by personal relationships between people who work together. The verb that follows **politics** may be either singular or plural. ❏ *You need to understand how office politics influence the working environment.*

가산명사 보험 계약자 [경제] ❏ 법적 수수료의 최초 10퍼센트는 보험 계약자가 지불하게 될 것입니다.

불가산명사 소아마비 ❏ 글래디스는 세 살 때 소아마비를 앓아 다리를 절게 되었다.

1 물질명사 광택제 ❏ 바람 한 점 없는 대기에서 희미하게 가구 광택제 냄새가 났다. **2** 타동사 닦다, 윤을 내다 ❏ 매일 아침 그는 면도를 하고 구두를 닦았다. ● 단수명사 윤 ❏ 그는 부드러운 걸레로 카운터에 윤을 냈다 ● 윤이 나는 형용사 ❏ 반들반들 윤이 나는 바닥 **3** 불가산명사 세련 [마음에 듦] ❏ 그 오페라에는 그의 후기 작품에서 볼 수 있는 세련미가 결여되어 있다. **4** 타동사 연마하다 ❏ 그들은 그저 자신들의 기술을 연마할 필요가 있다. ● 구동사 연마하다 ❏ 일주일간의 전문가 과정에서 당신의 작문 솜씨를 연마하십시오.

1 형용사 세련된 [마음에 듦] ❏ 그는 세련되고 매력적이며 논리 정연할 뿐 아니라 탁월한 협상가이다. **2** 형용사 수준 높은 [마음에 듦] ❏ 그것은 매우 수준 높은 공연이었다.

형용사 공손한, 예의 바른 ❏ 그를 둘러싼 모든 사람이 예의 바르게 행동하려 노력하고 있었지만, 그들 모두 따분해 하고 있다는 것을 알 수 있었다. ● 말수 적고 아주 공손한 청년 ❏ 그는 좋은 인상을 주었다. ● 공손하게 부사 ❏ "집이 아름답군요."라고 나는 공손히 말했다. ● 공손함 불가산명사 ❏ 그녀는 그의 말에 경청했으나 단지 예의상 그런 것뿐이었다.

1 형용사 정치적인 ❏ 그곳의 다른 모든 정당은 전면 금지되었다. ❏ 캐나다 정부는 또 다른 정치적 위기에 직면해 있다. ● 정치적으로 부사 ❏ 그들은 그 살해 사건들이 정치적인 동기를 띠고 있다고 생각하지 않는다. **2** 형용사 정치에 관심이 있는, 정치 활동을 하는 ❏ 아, 난 정치에 관심 없어. 정치엔 흥미도 없다고.

불가산명사 정치적 망명 ❏ 영국에 정치적 망명을 요청하고 있는 대학 선생

불가산명사 정치 경제학

형용사 (성, 인종, 장애인들에) 정치적으로 정당한 ❏ 환경주의자들과 정치적으로 정당한 진보주의자들 ● 복수명사 정치적으로 정당한 사람들 ❏ 정치적으로 정당한 사람들의 위선

가산명사 정치인 ❏ 그들은 지도급 야당 정치인 여러 명을 체포했다.

1 복수명사 정치 ❏ 영국 정치의 핵심 문제는 총리가 얼마나 오래 살아남느냐 하는 것이었다. ❏ 그는 재빨리 지역 정치에 참여했다. **2** 복수명사 정치적 성향 ❏ 내 정치적 성향은 중도 좌파이다. **3** 불가산명사 정치학 ❏ 그는 정치학과 중세사를 공부하기 시작했다. **4** 복수명사 역학 관계 ❏ 당신은 사내의 역학 관계가 작업 환경에 어떻게 영향을 끼치는지 알 필요가 있다.

a
b
c
d
e
f
g
h
i
j
k
l
m
n
o
p
q
r
s
t
u
v
w
x
y
z

poll ♦♦◇ /poʊl/ (**polls, polling, polled**) ◻ N-COUNT A **poll** is a survey in which people are asked their opinions about something, usually in order to find out how popular something is or what people intend to do in the future. ◻ *Polls show that the European treaty has gained support in Denmark.* ◻ *We are doing a weekly poll on the president, and clearly his popularity has declined.* →see also **opinion poll** ◻ V-T If you **are polled on** something, you are asked what you think about it as part of a survey. [usu passive] ◻ *More than 18,000 people were polled.* ◻ *Audiences were going to be polled on which of three pieces of contemporary music they liked best.* ◻ N-PLURAL **The polls** means an election for a country's government, or the place where people go to vote in an election. ◻ *In 1945, Winston Churchill was defeated at the polls.* ◻ *Voters are due to go to the polls on Sunday to elect a new president.* ◻ V-T If a political party or a candidate **polls** a particular number or percentage of votes, they get that number or percentage of votes in an election. ◻ *It was a disappointing result for the Greens who polled three percent.* ◻ →see also **polling**

pol|len /ˈpɒlən/ (**pollens**) N-MASS **Pollen** is a fine powder produced by flowers. It fertilizes other flowers of the same species so that they produce seeds.

poll|ing /ˈpoʊlɪŋ/ N-UNCOUNT **Polling** is the act of voting in an election. ◻ *There has been a busy start to polling in today's local elections.* →see **election, vote**

pol|lu|tant /pəˈluːtªnt/ (**pollutants**) N-VAR **Pollutants** are substances that pollute the environment, especially gases from vehicles and poisonous chemicals produced as waste by industrial processes. ◻ *Industrial pollutants are responsible for a sizable proportion of all cancers.*

pol|lute /pəˈluːt/ (**pollutes, polluting, polluted**) V-T To **pollute** water, air, or land means to make it dirty and dangerous to live in or to use, especially with poisonous chemicals or sewage. ◻ *Heavy industry pollutes our rivers with noxious chemicals.* ● **pol|lut|ed** ADJ ◻ *The police have warned the city's inhabitants not to bathe in the polluted river.*

pol|lu|tion ♦♦◇ /pəˈluːʃªn/ ◻ N-UNCOUNT **Pollution** is the process of polluting water, air, or land, especially with poisonous chemicals. ◻ *The fine was for the company's pollution of the air near its plants.* ◻ N-UNCOUNT **Pollution** is poisonous or dirty substances that are polluting the water, air, or land somewhere. ◻ *The level of pollution in the river was falling.* →see **factory** →see Word Web: **pollution**

polo /ˈpoʊloʊ/ N-UNCOUNT **Polo** is a game played between two teams of players. The players ride horses and use wooden hammers with long handles to hit a ball.

poly|es|ter /ˈpɒliestər, BRIT ˌpɒliestɑːʳ/ (**polyesters**) N-MASS **Polyester** is a type of artificial cloth used especially to make clothes. ◻ *...a green polyester shirt.*

poly|eth|yl|ene /ˌpɒliˈeθɪliːn/ N-UNCOUNT **Polyethylene** is a type of plastic made into thin sheets or bags and used especially to keep food fresh or to keep things dry. [mainly AM; BRIT usually **polythene**]

poly|sty|rene /ˌpɒliˈstaɪriːn/ N-UNCOUNT **Polystyrene** is a very light plastic substance used to make containers or to keep things warm, cool, or protected from damage. ◻ *...polystyrene cups.*

poly|thene /ˈpɒliθiːn/ N-UNCOUNT **Polythene** is a type of plastic made into thin sheets or bags and used especially to keep food fresh or to keep things dry. [mainly BRIT; AM usually **polyethylene**] ◻ *Simply put them into a polythene bag and store them in the freezer for a day.*

pomp /pɒmp/ N-UNCOUNT **Pomp** is the use of a lot of ceremony, fine clothes, and decorations, especially on a special occasion. ◻ *...the pomp and splendor of the English aristocracy.*

pom|pos|ity /pɒmˈpɒsɪti/ N-UNCOUNT **Pomposity** means speaking or behaving in a very serious manner which shows that you think you are more important than you really are. [DISAPPROVAL] ◻ *Einstein was a scientist who hated pomposity and disliked being called a genius.*

pomp|ous /ˈpɒmpəs/ ◻ ADJ If you describe someone as **pompous**, you mean that they behave or speak in a very serious way because they think they are more important than they really are. [DISAPPROVAL] ◻ *He was somewhat pompous and had a high opinion of his own capabilities.* ● **pomp|ous|ly** ADV ◻ *Robin told me firmly and pompously that he had an important business appointment.* ◻ ADJ A **pompous** building or ceremony is very grand and elaborate. ◻ *The service was grand without being pompous.*

pond /pɒnd/ (**ponds**) ◻ N-COUNT A **pond** is a small area of water that is smaller than a lake. Ponds are often made artificially. ◻ *She chose a bench beside the duck pond and sat down.* ◻ N-SING People sometimes refer to the Atlantic Ocean as **the pond**. [MAINLY JOURNALISM] ◻ *Tourist numbers from across the pond have dropped dramatically.*

◻ 가산명사 여론 조사 ◻ 여론 조사에 의하면 덴마크에서는 유럽 조약에 대한 지지도가 올라가고 있다. ◻ 우리는 매주 대통령에 관해서 여론 조사를 하고 있는데, 확실히 그의 지지도는 하락했다. ◻ 타동사 여론 조사에 응하다, 설문에 응하다 ◻ 1만 8천 명이 넘는 사람들이 여론 조사에 응했다. ◻ 청중들에게 세 곡의 현대 음악 중 어떤 것이 가장 좋은지를 물을 예정이었다. ◻ 복수명사 선거; 투표소 ◻ 1945년에 윈스턴 처칠은 선거에서 졌다. ◻ 투표자들은 일요일에 새 대통령을 뽑기 위해서 투표소로 갈 예정이다. ◻ 타동사 득표하다 ◻ 3퍼센트밖에 득표하지 못했다는 것은 녹색당으로서는 실망스러운 결과였다.

물질명사 꽃가루

불가산명사 선거 ◻ 오늘 있었던 지방 선거는 아주 바쁘게 시작했다.

가산명사 또는 불가산명사 오염 물질 ◻ 산업 오염 물질이 모든 암 발생 원인에 대해 상당한 비중을 차지한다.

타동사 오염시키다 ◻ 중공업은 유해 화학 물질로 우리의 강을 오염시킨다. ● 오염된 형용사 ◻ 경찰은 그 도시 주민들에게 오염된 강에서 목욕하지 말라고 경고했다.

◻ 불가산명사 오염 ◻ 그 벌금은 그 회사가 공장 근처의 대기를 오염시킨 데 대한 것이었다. ◻ 불가산명사 오염 물질 ◻ 그 강의 오염 물질 수치가 떨어지고 있었다.

불가산명사 폴로 (운동 경기)

물질명사 폴리에스터 ◻ 녹색 폴리에스터 셔츠

불가산명사 폴리에틸렌 [주로 미국영어; 영국영어 대개 polythene]

불가산명사 폴리스티렌 ◻ 폴리스티렌 컵

불가산명사 폴리에틸렌 [주로 영국영어; 미국영어 대개 polyethylene] ◻ 그것들을 그냥 폴리에틸렌 봉지에 넣어 냉동실에 하루 정도 보관하세요.

불가산명사 장려(행렬), 장엄함 ◻ 영국 귀족 사회의 인상적인 장엄함

불가산명사 거드름 [탐탁찮음] ◻ 아인슈타인은 거드름을 혐오하고 천재라고 불리는 것을 싫어했던 과학자였다.

◻ 형용사 거만한, 거드름 피우는 [탐탁찮음] ◻ 그는 약간 거드름을 피웠고 자신의 능력을 과대평가하고 있었다. ● 거만하게 부사 ◻ 로빈은 중요한 사업상의 약속이 있다고 거만하고도 단호하게 내게 말했다. ◻ 형용사 으리으리한 ◻ 그 교회 의식은 으리으리하지 않으면서 장엄했다.

◻ 가산명사 연못 ◻ 그녀는 오리 연못 옆에 있는 벤치에 가서 앉았다. ◻ 단수명사 대서양 [주로 언론] ◻ 대서양 너머에서 오는 관광객의 수가 급격히 떨어졌다.

Word Web   pollution

Pollution affects all aspects of the **environment**. **Airborne emissions** from industrial plants and vehicle **exhaust** cause air pollution. When these smoky **emissions** combine with fog, the result is **smog**. Airborne pollutants can travel long distances. **Acid rain** caused by factories in the Midwest falls on states to the east. There it damages trees and kills fish in lakes. Chemical waste from factories, **sewage**, and **garbage** have polluted the water and land in many areas. The overuse of **pesticides** and **fertilizers** have added to the problem. These chemicals accumulate in the soil and poison the earth.

pon|der /pɒndər/ (**ponders, pondering, pondered**) V-T/V-I If you **ponder** something, you think about it carefully. ❑ *I found myself constantly pondering the question: "How could anyone do these things?"* ❑ *The Prime Minister pondered on when to go to the polls.*

타동사/자동사 깊이 생각하다 ❑'어떻게 사람이 이렇게 할 수 있지?'라는 물음을 나는 계속 곰곰이 생각하고 있었다. ❑ 총리는 언제 선거를 해야 할지 깊이 생각하고 있었다.

pon|der|ous /pɒndərəs/ ADJ **Ponderous** writing or speech is very serious, uses more words than necessary, and is rather dull. [DISAPPROVAL] ❑ *He had a dense, ponderous style.* ● **pon|der|ous|ly** ADV [ADV with v] ❑ *...the rather ponderously titled "Recommendation for National Reconciliation and Salvation."*

형용사 장황한 [탐탁찮음] ❑ 그의 문체는 복잡하고 장황하다. ● 장황하게 부사 ❑ 약간 장황하게 붙여진 제목 "민족 화해와 구원을 위한 제언"

pony /poʊni/ (**ponies**) N-COUNT A **pony** is a type of small horse.

가산명사 조랑말

pony|tail /poʊniteɪl/ (**ponytails**) also **pony-tail** N-COUNT A **ponytail** is a hairstyle in which someone's hair is tied up at the back of the head and hangs down like a tail. ❑ *Her long, fine hair was swept back in a ponytail.*

가산명사 뒤로 하나로 묶은 머리 ❑ 그녀는 길고 고운 머리카락을 뒤로 빗어 넘겨 하나로 묶고 있었다.

poo|dle /pud³l/ (**poodles**) N-COUNT A **poodle** is a type of dog with thick curly hair.

가산명사 푸들 (개)

pool ◆◇◇ /pul/ (**pools, pooling, pooled**) ❶ N-COUNT A **pool** is the same as a **swimming pool**. ❑ *...a heated indoor pool.* ❷ N-COUNT A **pool** is a fairly small area of still water. ❑ *The pool had dried up and was full of broken reeds.* ❸ N-COUNT A **pool** of liquid or light is a small area of it on the ground or on a surface. ❑ *She was found lying in a pool of blood.* ❑ *It was raining quietly and steadily and there were little pools of water on the gravel drive.* ❹ N-COUNT A **pool** of people, money, or things is a quantity or number of them that is available for an organization or group to use. ❑ *The available pool of healthy manpower was not as large as military officials had expected.* →see also **carpool** ❺ V-T If a group of people or organizations **pool** their money, knowledge, or equipment, they share it or put it together so that it can be used for a particular purpose. ❑ *We pooled ideas and information.*

❶ 가산명사 수영장 ❑ 난방이 되는 실내 수영장 ❷ 가산명사 웅덩이, 연못 ❑ 그 연못은 다 말라 있었고 고사리와 갈대가 무성했다. ❸ 가산명사 (액체 등이) 흥건한 곳 ❑ 그녀는 피가 흥건하게 고인 가운데 누워 있는 채로 발견됐다. ❑ 비가 조용히 계속 내리고 있어서, 자갈길 진입로에 물이 흥건한 곳이 몇 군데 있었다. ❹ 가산명사 동원 가능 인력, 동원 가능 자금 ❑ 동원 가능한 건강한 인력이 장교들이 기대했던 것만큼 많지 않았다. ❺ 타동사 (돈 등을) 공유하다, 갹출하다 ❑ 우리는 아이디어와 정보를 함께 모았다.

poor ◆◆◇ /pʊər/ (**poorer, poorest**) ❶ ADJ Someone who is **poor** has very little money and few possessions. ❑ *The reason our schools cannot afford better teachers is because people here are poor.* ● N-PLURAL **The poor** are people who are poor. ❑ *Even the poor have their pride.* ❷ ADJ The people in a **poor** country or area have very little money and few possessions. ❑ *Many countries in the Third World are as poor as they have ever been.* ❸ ADJ You use **poor** to express your sympathy for someone. [FEELINGS] [ADJ n] ❑ *I feel sorry for that poor child.* ❑ *It was way too much for the poor guy to overcome.* ❹ ADJ If you describe something as **poor**, you mean that it is of a low quality or standard or that it is in bad condition. ❑ *...the poor state of the economy.* ❑ *The gap between the best and poorest childcare provision in the European Union has widened.* ● **poor|ly** ADV ❑ *Some are living in poorly built dormitories, even in tents.* ❺ ADJ If you describe an amount, rate, or number as **poor**, you mean that it is less than expected or less than is considered reasonable. ❑ *...poor wages and working conditions.* ● **poor|ly** ADV ❑ *During the first week, the evening meetings were poorly attended.* ❻ ADJ You use **poor** to describe someone who is not very skillful in a particular activity. ❑ *He was a poor actor.* ● **poor|ly** ADV [ADV after v] ❑ *Cheetahs breed very poorly in captivity.* ❼ ADJ If something is **poor in** a particular quality or substance, it contains very little of the quality or substance. [v-link ADJ in n] ❑ *Fats and sugar are very rich in energy but poor in vitamins and minerals.*

❶ 형용사 가난한 ❑ 우리 학교가 더 수준 높은 교사를 초빙하지 못하는 이유는 여기 사람들이 가난하기 때문이다. ● 복수명사 가난한 사람들 ❑ 가난한 사람일지라도 자존심이 있는 법이다. ❷ 형용사 가난한 ❑ 제3 세계의 많은 국가들은 예나 지금이나 여전히 가난하다. ❸ 형용사 불쌍한 [감정 개입] ❑ 나는 저 불쌍한 아이가 안쓰럽다. ❑ 그건 그 불쌍한 청년이 극복하기에는 너무 벅찼다. ❹ 형용사 형편없는, 열악한 ❑ 형편없는 경제 상태 ❑ 유럽 연합 내 가장 훌륭한 육아 혜택과 가장 열악한 혜택 사이의 격차가 더 넓어졌다. ● 형편없이 부사 ❑ 몇몇은 형편없이 지어진 기숙사에 살거나 심지어는 텐트에서 살고 있다. ❺ 형용사 형편없는 ❑ 형편없는 급여와 근무 조건 ● 형편없이 부사 ❑ 첫 주 동안, 저녁 모임의 참석률은 형편없었다. ❻ 형용사 어설픈, 잘 못하는 ❑ 그는 어설픈 배우였다. ● 잘 못하여 부사 ❑ 치타는 갇혀 있으면 번식을 거의 못한다. ❼ 형용사 -이 거의 없는 ❑ 지방과 설탕이 열량은 풍부하지만 비타민과 미네랄은 거의 없다.

poor|ly /pʊərli/ ADJ If someone is **poorly**, they are ill. [mainly BRIT, INFORMAL; AM **sick**] ❑ *I've just phoned Julie and she's still poorly.* →see also **poor**

형용사 아픈 [주로 영국영어, 비격식체; 미국영어 sick] ❑ 방금 전에 줄리에게 전화를 걸었는데 아직도 아프대.

pop ◆◇◇ /pɒp/ (**pops, popping, popped**) ❶ N-UNCOUNT **Pop** is modern music that usually has a strong rhythm and uses electronic equipment. ❑ *...the perfect combination of Caribbean rhythms, European pop, and American soul.* ❑ *...a life-size poster of a pop star.* ❷ N-UNCOUNT You can refer to carbonated drinks such as cola as **pop**. [BRIT, INFORMAL; AM usually **soda pop**, **soda**] ❑ *He still visits the village shop for buns and fizzy pop.* ❸ N-COUNT; SOUND **Pop** is used to represent a short sharp sound, for example the sound made by bursting a balloon or by pulling a cork out of a bottle. ❑ *Each corn kernel will make a loud pop when cooked.* ❹ V-I If something **pops**, it makes a short sharp sound. ❑ *He untwisted the wire off the champagne bottle, and the cork popped and shot to the ceiling.* ❺ V-I If your eyes **pop**, you look very surprised or excited when you see something. [INFORMAL] ❑ *My eyes popped at the sight of the rich variety of food on show.* ❻ V-T If you **pop** something somewhere, you put it there quickly. [INFORMAL] ❑ *Marianne got a couple of mugs from the dresser and popped a teabag into each of them.* ❼ V-I If you **pop** somewhere, you go there for a short time. [BRIT, INFORMAL] ❑ *He does pop down to the pub, but he seldom stays longer than an hour.* ❽ N-FAMILY Some people call their father **pop**. [mainly AM, INFORMAL; BRIT usually **dad**] ❑ *I looked at Pop and he had big tears in his eyes.* ❾ to **pop the question** →see **question**

❶ 불가산명사 팝 (음악) ❑ 카리브 식 리듬, 유럽 팝, 미국 소울 음악의 완벽한 조화 ❑ 한 팝 스타의 실물 크기 포스터 ❷ 불가산명사 탄산음료 [영국영어, 비격식체; 미국영어 대개 soda pop, soda] ❑ 그는 빵이나 탄산음료를 사기 위해 아직도 그 마을 가게에 들른다. ❸ 가산명사; 소리 펑 (소리) , 뻥 ❑ 옥수수 알갱이가 익으면 펑 하는 요란한 소리를 낼 것이다. ❹ 자동사 펑 하는 소리를 내다 ❑ 그가 샴페인 병의 철사를 풀자, 쿠르크 마개가 펑 소리를 내며 천장까지 튀어 올랐다. ❺ 자동사 (눈이) 휘둥그레지다 [비격식체] ❑ 나는 엄청나게 다양한 음식이 차려져 있는 것을 보고 두 눈이 휘둥그레졌다. ❻ 타동사 빨리 집어넣다 [비격식체] ❑ 매리앤은 머그잔 두 개를 화장대에서 꺼내서 각 잔에 티백을 하나씩 톡톡 집어넣었다. ❼ 자동사 잠깐 들르다 [영국영어, 비격식체] ❑ 그는 그 술집에 잠깐 들르기는 하지만, 한 시간 이상 머무를 때는 거의 없다. ❽ 친족명사 아빠 [주로 미국영어, 비격식체; 영국영어 대개 dad] ❑ 아빠를 쳐다보았더니 아빠 두 눈에 눈물이 가득 고여 있었다.

▶ **pop up** PHRASAL VERB If someone or something **pops up**, they appear in a place or situation unexpectedly. [INFORMAL] ❑ *She was startled when Lisa popped up at the door all smiles.*

구동사 불쑥 나타나다 [비격식체] ❑ 리사가 한껏 웃으면서 문 앞에 불쑥 나타나서 그녀는 깜짝 놀랐다.

POP /pi oʊ pi/ (**POPs**) N-COUNT A **POP** is equipment that gives access to the Internet. POP is an abbreviation for "point of presence." [COMPUTING]

가산명사 팝 (서비스 제공자의 위치) [컴퓨터]

pop|corn /pɒpkɔrn/ N-UNCOUNT **Popcorn** is a snack which consists of grains of corn that have been heated until they have burst and become large and light.

불가산명사 팝콘

pope /poʊp/ (**popes**) N-COUNT **The Pope** is the head of the Roman Catholic Church. [usu the N; N-TITLE] ❑ *The highlight of the Pope's visit will be his message to the people.*

가산명사 교황 ❑ 교황 방문의 하이라이트는 교황이 사람들에게 전하는 메시지가 될 것이다.

pop|py /pɒpi/ (**poppies**) N-COUNT A **poppy** is a plant with a large, delicate flower, usually red in color. The drug opium is obtained from one type of poppy. ❑ *...a field of poppies.*

가산명사 양귀비 ❑ 양귀비 밭

Pop|si|cle /pɒpsɪk³l/ (**Popsicles**) N-COUNT A **Popsicle** is a piece of flavored ice on a stick. [AM, TRADEMARK; BRIT **ice lolly**]

가산명사 아이스 바 [미국영어, 상표; 영국영어 ice lolly]

a b c d e f g h i j k l m n o p q r s t u v w x y z

Word Link

popul ≈ people : *populace, popular, population*

popu|lace /pɒpyələs/ N-UNCOUNT The **populace** of a country is its people. [FORMAL] ❑ *...a large proportion of the populace.*

불가산명사 국민 [격식체] ❑ 국민 대다수

popu|lar ♦♦◇ /pɒpyələr/ **1** ADJ Something that is **popular** is enjoyed or liked by a lot of people. ❑ *Chocolate sauce is always popular with youngsters.* ● **popu|lar|ity** /pɒpyəlæriti/ N-UNCOUNT ❑ *...the growing popularity of Australian wines among consumers.* **2** ADJ Someone who is **popular** is liked by most people, or by most people in a particular group. ❑ *He remained the most popular politician in France.* ● **popu|lar|ity** N-UNCOUNT ❑ *It is his popularity with ordinary people that sets him apart.* **3** ADJ **Popular** newspapers, television programs, or forms of art are aimed at ordinary people and not at experts or intellectuals. [ADJ n] ❑ *Once again the popular press in Britain has been rife with stories about their marriage.* ❑ *...one of the classics of modern popular music.* **4** ADJ **Popular** ideas, feelings, or attitudes are approved of or held by most people. ❑ *Contrary to popular belief, the oil companies can't control the price of crude.* ❑ *The military government has been unable to win popular support.* ● **popu|lar|ity** N-UNCOUNT ❑ *Over time, though, Watson's views gained in popularity.* **5** ADJ **Popular** is used to describe political activities which involve the ordinary people of a country, and not just members of political parties. [ADJ n] ❑ *The late President Ferdinand Marcos was overthrown by a popular uprising in 1986.*

1 형용사 인기 있는 ❑ 초콜릿 소스는 어린이들에게 항상 인기 인기가 있다. ● 인기 불가산명사 소비자들 사이에서 증가하고 있는 호주산 포도주의 인기 **2** 형용사 인기 있는 ❑ 그는 프랑스에서 가장 인기 있는 정치가로 남아 있다. ● 인기 불가산명사 ❑ 그는 보통 사람들 사이에서 인기가 있는 점이 다르다. **3** 형용사 대중적인 ❑ 다시 한 번 영국의 대중적인 신문에 그들의 결혼 생활 관련 기사들이 잔뜩 실리고 있다. ❑ 현대 대중음악의 고전적 작품 중 하나 **4** 형용사 일반적인, 대중적인 ❑ 일반 통념과는 달리, 석유 회사들이 원유 가격을 통제할 수는 없다. ❑ 그 군사 정부는 일반 대중의 지지를 얻을 수 없었다. ● 대중적 지지 불가산명사 ❑ 그럼에도 불구하고, 시간이 흐르면서 왓슨의 견해는 대중적인 지지를 받게 되었다. **5** 형용사 전 국민적인 ❑ 페르디난드 마르코스 전 대통령은 1986년에 전 국민적 봉기로 축출되었다.

Word Partnership popular의 연어

| N. | popular **culture**, popular **magazine**, popular **movie**, popular **music**, popular **novel**, popular **restaurant**, popular **show**, popular **song** **1** **3** |
| ADV. | **extremely**, **increasingly** popular, **more** popular, **most** popular, **wildly** popular **1** **2** **4** |

popu|lar|ize /pɒpyələraɪz/ (**popularizes, popularizing, popularized**) [BRIT also **popularise**] V-T To **popularize** something means to make a lot of people interested in it and able to enjoy it. ❑ *Irving Brokaw, who had studied figure skating in Europe, returned to the U.S. and popularized the new sport.* ● **popu|lari|za|tion** /pɒpyələrɪzeɪʃ°n/ N-UNCOUNT ❑ *...the popularization of sport through television.*

[영국영어 popularise] 타동사 대중화하다 ❑ 유럽에서 피겨 스케이팅을 배운 어빙 브로코는 미국으로 돌아가서 이 새로운 스포츠를 대중화시켰다. ● 대중화 불가산명사 ❑ 텔레비전을 통한 스포츠의 대중화

popu|lar|ly /pɒpyələrli/ **1** ADV If something or someone is **popularly** known as something, most people call them that, although it is not their official name or title. [ADV with -ed] ❑ *...the Mesozoic era, more popularly known as the age of dinosaurs.* ❑ *...an infection popularly called mad cow disease.* **2** ADV If something is **popularly** believed or supposed to be the case, most people believe or suppose it to be the case, although it may not be true. [ADV -ed] ❑ *Schizophrenia is not a "split mind" as is popularly believed.* **3** ADV A **popularly elected** leader or government has been elected by a majority of the people in a country. [ADV -ed] ❑ *Walesa was Poland's first popularly elected President.*

1 부사 흔히 (알려진), 일반적으로 ❑ 공룡의 시대로 더 흔히 알려져 있는 중생대 ❑ 광우병이라고 흔히 불리는 전염병 **2** 부사 통념대로, 흔히 생각하듯 ❑ 정신 분열증은 흔히 생각하듯 '정신이 분열된 것'이 아니다. **3** 부사 국민 대다수의 지지를 받고 선출된 ❑ 바웬사는 폴란드에서 처음으로 국민 대다수의 지지를 받고 선출된 대통령이었다.

popu|late /pɒpyəleɪt/ (**populates, populating, populated**) **1** V-T If an area **is populated** by certain people or animals, those people or animals live there, often in large numbers. ❑ *Before all this the island was populated by Native American Arawaks.* ● **popu|lat|ed** ADJ [adv ADJ] ❑ *The southeast is the most densely populated area.* **2** V-T To **populate** an area means to cause people to live there. ❑ *Successive regimes annexed the region and populated it with lowland people.*

1 타동사 거주하다, 서식하다 ❑ 이런 모든 일이 있기 전에, 이 섬에는 아메리카 원주민 아라와크 족이 거주하고 있었다. ● 거주하는, 서식하는 형용사 ❑ 동남부 지역은 인구 밀도가 가장 높은 곳이다. **2** 타동사 거주시키다 ❑ 다음 정권들은 그 지역을 병합했고 로랜드 사람들을 그곳에 거주하게 했다.

popu|la|tion ♦♦◇ /pɒpyəleɪʃ°n/ (**populations**) **1** N-COUNT The **population** of a country or area is all the people who live in it. ❑ *Bangladesh now has a population of about 110 million.* ❑ *...the annual rate of population growth.* **2** N-COUNT If you refer to a particular type of **population** in a country or area, you are referring to all the people or animals of that type there. [FORMAL] ❑ *...75.6 per cent of the male population over sixteen.* ❑ *...areas with a large black population.*
→see Word Web: **population**

1 가산명사 인구 ❑ 방글라데시의 인구는 지금 1억 1천만 명 정도이다. ❑ 연 인구 증가율 **2** 가산명사 (특정 유형의) 인구, (특정) 개체 수 [격식체] ❑ 16세 이상 남자의 75.6 퍼센트 ❑ 흑인이 많이 살고 있는 지역들

porce|lain /pɔrsəlɪn, pɔrslɪn/ N-UNCOUNT **Porcelain** is a hard, shiny substance made by heating clay. It is used to make delicate cups, plates, and ornaments. ❑ *There were lilies everywhere in tall white porcelain vases.* →see **pottery**

불가산명사 자기 ❑ 긴 백자 화병에 꽂힌 백합들이 도처에 있었다.

porch /pɔrtʃ/ (**porches**) **1** N-COUNT A **porch** is a sheltered area at the entrance to a building. It has a roof and sometimes has walls. ❑ *She huddled inside the porch as she rang the bell.* **2** N-COUNT A **porch** is a raised platform built along the outside wall of a house and often covered with a roof. [AM; BRIT usually **veranda**] ❑ *He was standing on the porch, waving as we drove away.*

1 가산명사 현관 ❑ 그녀는 현관으로 바짝 다가가 종을 울렸다. **2** 가산명사 베란다 [미국영어; 영국영어 대개 veranda] ❑ 그는 우리가 차를 몰고 떠날 때 베란다에 서서 손을 흔들었다.

pore /pɔr/ (**pores, poring, pored**) **1** N-COUNT Your **pores** are the tiny holes in your skin. ❑ *The size of your pores is determined by the amount of oil they produce.* **2** V-I If you **pore over** or **through** information, you look at it and study it very carefully. ❑ *We spent hours poring over travel brochures.*

1 가산명사 모공 ❑ 모공의 크기는 그것이 얼마나 많은 피지를 분비하는냐에 따라 결정된다. **2** 자동사 탐구하다, 자세히 살펴보다 ❑ 우리는 몇 시간 동안 여행안내 책자를 자세히 살펴보았다.

Word Web population

In 1987 the world's **population** was 5 billion. By the year 2000, it had climbed to 6 billion. Demographers predict that the total will top 9 billion by the year 2050. Improvements in medicine, sanitation, and nutrition have caused a decline in **death rates**. At the same time, there has been no overall decrease in **birth rates**. In a few countries, like Japan, the birth rate has dropped dramatically. As Japan's population ages, its workforce shrinks. India has the opposite problem. With its population **trend**, it has more young people wanting to join the workforce than there are jobs available.

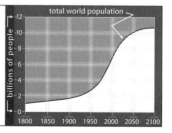

total world population

pork /pɔrk/ N-UNCOUNT **Pork** is meat from a pig, usually fresh and not smoked or salted. ❑ *...fried pork chops.* →see **meat**

불가산명사 돼지고기 ❑ 볶은 돼지갈비

porn /pɔrn/ N-UNCOUNT **Porn** is the same as **pornography**. [INFORMAL] ❑ *...a porn cinema.*

불가산명사 포르노 [비격식체] ❑ 포르노 영화관

por|no|graph|ic /pɔrnəgræfɪk/ ADJ **Pornographic** materials such as movies, videos, and magazines are designed to cause sexual excitement by showing naked people or referring to sexual acts. [DISAPPROVAL] ❑ *I found out he'd been watching pornographic videos.*

형용사 포르노의 [탐탁잖음] ❑ 나는 그가 그 동안 포르노 비디오를 봐 왔다는 것을 알게 되었다.

por|nog|ra|phy /pɔrnɒgrəfi/ N-UNCOUNT **Pornography** refers to books, magazines, and movies that are designed to cause sexual excitement by showing naked people or referring to sexual acts. [DISAPPROVAL] ❑ *China's leading newspaper has called for a new campaign against pornography in China.*

불가산명사 포르노그래피, 음란물 [탐탁잖음] ❑ 중국의 주요 일간지가 중국 내 음란물 추방을 위한 새로운 캠페인 실시를 요구했다.

po|rous /pɔrəs/ ADJ Something that is **porous** has many small holes in it, which water and air can pass through. ❑ *The local limestone is so porous that all the rainwater immediately sinks below ground.* →see **pottery**

형용사 작은 구멍이 많은, 투과성의 ❑ 그 지방의 석회암은 작은 구멍이 많아서 비가 내리면 빗물이 땅으로 바로 다 흡수된다.

por|ridge /pɔrɪdʒ, BRIT pɒrɪdʒ/ N-UNCOUNT **Porridge** is a thick sticky food made from oats cooked in water or milk and eaten hot, especially for breakfast. [mainly BRIT; AM usually **oatmeal**]

불가산명사 포리지 (죽) [주로 영국영어; 미국영어 대개 oatmeal]

port ◆◇◇ /pɔrt/ (**ports**) **1** N-COUNT A **port** is a town by the sea or on a river, which has a harbor. ❑ *...the Mediterranean port of Marseilles.* **2** N-COUNT A **port** is a harbor area where ships load and unload goods or passengers. ❑ *...the bridges which link the port area to the city center.* **3** N-COUNT A **port** on a computer is a place where you can attach another piece of equipment, for example a printer. [COMPUTING] ❑ *The devices, attached to a PC through standard ports, print bar codes onto envelopes.* **4** ADJ In sailing, the **port** side of a ship is the left side when you are on it and facing towards the front. [TECHNICAL] ❑ *Her official number is carved on the port side of the forecabin.* ● N-UNCOUNT **Port** is also a noun. ❑ *USS Ogden turned to port.* **5** N-UNCOUNT **Port** is a type of strong, sweet red wine. ❑ *He asked for a glass of port after dinner.* →see **ship**

1 가산명사 항구 도시 ❑ 지중해 항구 도시 마르세유 **2** 가산명사 항구 ❑ 항구 지역과 시내를 잇는 다리 **3** 가산명사 (컴퓨터) 포트 [컴퓨터] ❑ 기본 포트로 피시(PC)에 연결된 그 장치들이 봉투에 바코드를 인쇄한다. **4** 형용사 좌현의 [과학 기술] ❑ 그 배의 공식 번호가 앞쪽 선실의 좌현에 새겨져 있다. ● 불가산명사 좌현 ❑ 미 해군 소속 오그덴호가 좌현 쪽으로 방향을 틀었다. **5** 불가산명사 포트 와인 ❑ 그는 저녁을 먹고 나서 포트 한 잔을 부탁했다.

port|able /pɔrtəb°l/ (**portables**) **1** ADJ A **portable** machine or device is designed to be easily carried or moved. ❑ *There was a little portable television switched on behind the bar.* **2** N-COUNT A **portable** is something such as a television, radio, or computer which can be easily carried or moved. ❑ *We bought a portable for the bedroom.*

1 형용사 휴대용의, 이동하기 쉬운 ❑ 그 술집의 카운터 뒤편에 작은 휴대용 텔레비전이 켜져 있었다. **2** 가산명사 휴대 가능한 물건, 이동이 용이한 물건 ❑ 우리는 침실에서 쓰려고 휴대용을 샀다.

por|tal /pɔrt°l/ (**portals**) N-COUNT On the Internet, a **portal** is a website that consists of links to other sites. [COMPUTING] ❑ *The site acts as a portal for thousands of online dealers.*

가산명사 포털사이트 [컴퓨터] ❑ 그 사이트는 수천 명의 온라인 딜러에게 포털사이트 역할을 한다.

por|ter /pɔrtər/ (**porters**) **1** N-COUNT A **porter** is a person whose job is to carry things, for example people's luggage at a train station or in a hotel. ❑ *Our taxi pulls up at Old Delhi station and a porter sprints to the door.* **2** N-COUNT In a hospital, a **porter** is someone whose job is to move patients from place to place. [BRIT; AM **orderly**] ❑ *... a 17-year-old porter at the local psychiatric hospital.* **3** N-COUNT A **porter** is a person whose job is to be in charge of the entrance of a building such as a hotel. [BRIT; AM **doorman**] ❑ *I asked the hotel porter for directions.*

1 가산명사 짐꾼, 운반꾼 ❑ 우리가 탄 택시가 구 델리 역에 서자, 짐꾼 한 명이 문 쪽으로 즉각 뛰어왔다. **2** 가산명사 (병원의) 환자 이동 도우미 [영국영어; 미국영어 orderly] ❑ 지방 정신 병원에서 일하는 17세의 환자 이동 도우미 **3** 가산명사 (호텔 등의) 도어맨 [영국영어; 미국영어 doorman] ❑ 나는 호텔 도어맨에게 길을 물었다.

port|fo|lio /pɔrtfoʊlioʊ/ (**portfolios**) **1** N-COUNT A **portfolio** is a set of pictures by someone, or photographs of examples of their work, which they use when entering competitions or applying for work. ❑ *After dinner that evening, Edith showed them a portfolio of her own political cartoons.* **2** N-COUNT In finance, a **portfolio** is the combination of shares or other investments that a particular person or company has. [BUSINESS] ❑ *...Roger Early, a portfolio manager at Federated Investors Corp.* **3** N-COUNT In politics, a **portfolio** is a minister's responsibility for a particular area of a government's activities. ❑ *He has held the defense portfolio since the first free elections in 1990.* **4** N-COUNT A company's **portfolio** of products or designs is their range of products or designs. [BUSINESS] ❑ *The company has continued to invest heavily in a strong portfolio of products.*

1 가산명사 포트폴리오, 작품집 ❑ 그날 저녁 식사 후, 에디스는 자신이 그린 정치 만화 포트폴리오를 그들에게 보여 주었다. **2** 가산명사 유가 증권, 유가 증권 일람표 [경제] ❑ 투자자 연방사의 유가 증권 관리자인 로저 얼리 **3** 가산명사 장관직 ❑ 그는 1900년의 첫 자유선거 이후 국방 장관직을 맡아 왔다. **4** 가산명사 (제품이나 디자인의) 다양성 [경제] ❑ 그 회사는 다양한 제품을 개발하는 데에 지속적으로 많은 투자를 해 왔다.

por|tion /pɔrʃ°n/ (**portions**) **1** N-COUNT A **portion of** something is a part of it. ❑ *Damage was confined to a small portion of the castle.* ❑ *I have spent a fairly considerable portion of my life here.* **2** N-COUNT A **portion** is the amount of food that is given to one person at a meal. ❑ *Desserts can be substituted by a portion of fresh fruit.* ❑ *The portions were generous.*

1 가산명사 부분 ❑ 손실은 그 성의 작은 부분에 한정되었다. ❑ 나는 여기서 내 인생의 상당 부분을 보냈다. **2** 가산명사 1인분 ❑ 디저트 대신 신선한 과일 1인분이 나갈 수도 있습니다. ❑ 1인분치고는 양이 많았다.

por|trait ◆◇◇ /pɔrtrɪt, -treɪt/ (**portraits**) N-COUNT A **portrait** is a painting, drawing, or photograph of a particular person. ❑ *Lucian Freud has been asked to paint a portrait of the Queen.* →see **painting**

가산명사 초상화 ❑ 루시안 프로이드는 여왕의 초상화를 그려 달라는 요청을 받았다.

por|tray /pɔrtreɪ/ (**portrays**, **portraying**, **portrayed**) **1** V-T When an actor or actress **portrays** someone, he or she plays that person in a play or movie. ❑ *In 1975 he portrayed the king in a Los Angeles revival of "Camelot."* **2** V-T When a writer or artist **portrays** something, he or she writes a description or produces a painting of it. ❑ *...this northern novelist, who accurately portrays provincial domestic life.* **3** V-T If a movie, book, or television program **portrays** someone in a certain way, it represents them in that way. ❑ *...complaints about the way women are portrayed in adverts.*

1 타동사 －의 역을 맡다 ❑ 1975년에 그는 '캐밀롯' 로스앤젤레스 재공연에서 왕 역할을 맡았다. **2** 타동사 묘사하다, 그려 내다 ❑ 지방의 가정생활을 정확하게 묘사한 북부 지방의 이 소설가 **3** 타동사 묘사하다 ❑ 광고에서 여성들을 묘사하는 방식에 대한 불만들

por|tray|al /pɔrtreɪəl/ (**portrayals**) **1** N-COUNT An actor's **portrayal of** a character in a play or movie is the way that he or she plays the character. ❑ *Mr. Ying is well-known for his portrayal of a prison guard in the film "The Last Emperor".* **2** N-COUNT An artist's **portrayal of** something is a drawing, painting, or photograph of it. ❑ *...a moving portrayal of St John the Evangelist by Simone Martini.*

1 가산명사 (특정 인물을 그려 대는) 연기 ❑ 잉은 영화 '마지막 황제'에서 간수 역으로 널리 알려져 있다. **2** 가산명사 그림, 사진 ❑ 시몬 마티니가 그린 복음서 저자 성 요한의 가슴 뭉클한 그림 **3** 가산명사 묘사 ❑ 영국 사회에 대한 리의 묘사 **4** 가산명사 기술, 묘사

A

3 N-COUNT The **portrayal of** something in a book or movie is the act of describing it or showing it. ❑ ...*Leigh's portrayal of English society.* **4** N-COUNT The **portrayal** of something in a book, movie, or program is the way that it is made to appear. ❑ *The media persists in its portrayal of us as muggers, dope sellers, and gangsters.*

언론은 우리를 강도, 마약 밀매꾼, 조직 폭력배로 묘사하기를 고집한다.

B

POS /piː oʊ ɛs/ The **POS** is the place in a store where a product is passed from the seller to the customer. **POS** is an abbreviation for "point of sale." [BUSINESS] ❑ ...*a POS system that doubles as a stock and sales control system.*

상점 카운터 [경제] ❑ 재고 및 판매 관리 시스템 기능도 하는 상점 카운터 업무 처리 시스템

C

pose ♦♢♢ /poʊz/ (**poses, posing, posed**) **1** V-T If something **poses** a problem or a danger, it is the cause of that problem or danger. ❑ *This could pose a threat to jobs in the coal industry.* **2** V-T If you **pose** a question, you ask it. If you **pose** an issue that needs considering, you mention the issue. [FORMAL] ❑ *When I finally posed the question, "Why?" he merely shrugged.* **3** V-I If you **pose as** someone, you pretend to be that person in order to deceive people. ❑ *The team posed as drug dealers to trap the ringleaders.* **4** V-I If you **pose for** a photograph or painting, you stay in a particular position so that someone can photograph you or paint you. ❑ *Before going into their meeting the six foreign ministers posed for photographs.* **5** N-COUNT A **pose** is a particular way that you stand, sit, or lie, for example when you are being photographed or painted. ❑ *We have had several preliminary sittings in various poses.*

D

1 타동사 (문제나 위험을) 야기하다 ❑ 이것은 석탄 산업의 일자리에 위협을 줄 수도 있다. **2** 타동사 (질문 등을) 던지다 [격식체] ❑ 내가 마침내 그 질문을 던졌을 때, 그는 "왜?"라고 하면서 그냥 어깨를 으쓱거렸다. **3** 자동사 -로 가장하다 ❑ 그 팀은 두목을 잡기 위해 마약 딜러로 가장했다. **4** 자동사 포즈를 취하다 ❑ 회담에 들어가기 전에 여섯 명의 외무 장관들은 사진을 찍기 위해 포즈를 취했다. **5** 가산명사 포즈, 자세 ❑ 우리는 화가에게 다양한 포즈로 준비 자세를 여러 번 취해 보았다.

E

posh /pɒʃ/ (**posher, poshest**) **1** ADJ If you describe something as **posh**, you mean that it is elegant, fashionable, and expensive. [INFORMAL] ❑ *Celebrating a promotion, I took her to a posh hotel for a cocktail.* ❑ ...*a posh car.* **2** ADJ If you describe a person as **posh**, you mean that they belong to or behave as if they belong to the upper classes. [INFORMAL] ❑ *I wouldn't have thought she had such posh friends.*

F

1 형용사 호화로운 [비격식체] ❑ 승진을 축하하기 위해서, 칵테일 한 잔 사 주러 나는 그녀를 고급 호텔로 데리고 갔다. ❑ 호화스러운 차 **2** 형용사 상류 사회에 속한 [비격식체] ❑ 그녀에게 그런 상류층 친구들이 있다고는 생각하지 못했을 것이다.

G

po|si|tion ♦♦♦ /pəzɪʃⁿn/ (**positions, positioning, positioned**) **1** N-COUNT The **position** of someone or something is the place where they are in relation to other things. ❑ *The ship was identified, and its name and position were reported to the coastguard.* **2** N-COUNT When someone or something is in a particular **position**, they are sitting, lying, or arranged in that way. ❑ *It is crucial that the upper back and neck are held in an erect position to give support for the head.* ❑ *Mr. Dambar had raised himself to a sitting position.* **3** V-T If you **position** something somewhere, you put it there carefully, so that it is in the right place or position. ❑ *Position the cursor where you want the new margins to begin.* **4** N-COUNT Your **position** in society is the role and the importance that you have in it. ❑ *Adjustment to their changing role and position in society can be painful for some elderly people.* **5** N-COUNT A **position** in a company or organization is a job. [FORMAL] ❑ *He left a career in teaching to take up a position with the Arts Council.* **6** N-COUNT Your **position** in a race or competition is how well you did in relation to the other competitors or how well you are doing. ❑ *By the ninth hour the car was running in eighth position.* **7** N-COUNT You can describe your situation at a particular time by saying that you are in a particular **position**. ❑ *He's going to be in a very difficult position indeed if things go badly for him.* ❑ *Companies should be made to reveal more about their financial position.* **8** N-COUNT Your **position on** a particular matter is your attitude toward it or your opinion of it. [FORMAL] ❑ *He could be depended on to take a moderate position on most of the key issues.* **9** N-SING If you are **in a position** to do something, you are able to do it. If you are **in no position** to do something, you are unable to do it. ❑ *I am not in a position to comment.* **10** PHRASE If someone or something is **in position**, they are in their correct or usual place or arrangement. ❑ *28,000 U.S. troops are moving into position.* →see **navigation**

H

I

J

K

L

M

N

O

1 가산명사 위치 ❑ 그 배는 정체가 확인되어서, 배의 이름과 위치가 해안 경비대에 보고 되었다. **2** 가산명사 자세 ❑ 머리를 떠받치기 위해서는 등의 윗부분과 목을 꼿꼿이 세운 자세로 유지하는 것이 중요하다. ❑ 댐바 씨는 몸을 일으켜 앉았다. **3** 타동사 두다, 놓다 ❑ 새로운 여백을 시작하고 싶은 곳에 커서를 갖다 놓으세요. **4** 가산명사 지위 ❑ 연로하신 분들에게는 사회 내에서 자신들의 변화하는 역할과 지위에 적응하는 것이 고통스러울 수도 있다. **5** 가산명사 직책 [격식체] ❑ 그는 예술 위원회의 직책을 맡기 위해 교단을 떠났다. **6** 가산명사 등위 ❑ 9시간째가 되자 그 차는 8위를 달리고 있었다. **7** 가산명사 처지, 상황 ❑ 만약 사정이 그에게 불리하게 전개된다면 그는 아주 곤란한 처지에 놓이게 될 것이다. ❑ 회사들이 그들의 재정 상태를 더 많이 공개하도록 만들어야 한다. **8** 가산명사 태도, 견해 [격식체] ❑ 그가 대부분의 중요한 사안에 대해 온건한 태도를 취하리라고 믿어도 될 것이다. **9** 단수명사 -할 수 있는 입장인; -할 입장이 아닌 ❑ 내가 뭐라고 언급할 입장이 아니다. **10** 구 제 위치에 ❑ 2만 8천 명의 미군들이 제 위치로 이동하고 있다.

P

Word Partnership position의 연어

ADJ.	
better position	**1**-**7**
fetal position	**2**
(un)comfortable position	**2** **7**
difficult position, **financial** position	**7**
official position	**8**

Q

R

posi|tive ♦♦♢ /pɒzɪtɪv/ **1** ADJ If you are **positive about** things, you are hopeful and confident, and think of the good aspects of a situation rather than the bad ones. ❑ *Be positive about your future and get on with living a normal life.* ❑ *Her husband became much more positive and was soon back in full-time employment.* ● **posi|tive|ly** ADV [ADV after v] ❑ *You really must try to start thinking positively.* **2** ADJ A **positive** fact, situation, or experience is pleasant and helpful to you in some way. ❑ *The parting from his sister had a positive effect on John.* ● N-SING The **positive** in a situation is the good and pleasant aspects of it. [the N] ❑ *He prefers to focus on the positive.* **3** ADJ If you make a **positive** decision or take **positive** action, you do something definite in order to deal with a task or problem. ❑ *There are positive changes that should be implemented in the rearing of animals.* **4** ADJ A **positive** response to something indicates agreement, approval, or encouragement. ❑ *There's been a positive response to the UN Secretary-General's recent peace efforts.* ● **posi|tive|ly** ADV [ADV after v] ❑ *He responded positively and accepted the fee of £1000 I had offered.* **5** ADJ If you are **positive** about something, you are completely sure about it. [v-link ADJ] ❑ *"Judith's never late. You sure she said eight?" — "Positive."* **6** ADJ **Positive** evidence gives definite proof of the truth or identity of something. [ADJ n] ❑ *There was no positive evidence that any birth defects had arisen as a result of Vitamin A intake.* ● **posi|tive|ly** ADV [ADV with v] ❑ *He has positively identified the body as that of his wife.* **7** ADJ If a medical or scientific test is **positive**, it shows that something has happened or is present. ❑ *If the test is positive, a course of antibiotics may be prescribed.* **HIV positive** →see **HIV** **8** ADJ A **positive** number is greater than zero. [ADJ n] ❑ *It's really a simple numbers game with negative and positive numbers.* →see **lightning, magnet**

S

T

U

V

W

X

Y

Z

1 형용사 희망적인, 낙관적인 ❑ 너의 미래에 대해 낙관적으로 생각하고 평소대로 살아. ❑ 그녀의 남편은 훨씬 더 낙관적이 되었고 곧 정규직으로 돌아왔다. ● 희망적으로, 낙관적으로 부사 ❑ 너는 낙관적으로 생각하도록 정말 노력해야 돼. **2** 형용사 긍정적인 ❑ 존이 자신의 누나와 헤어진 것은 존에게 긍정적인 영향을 끼쳤다. ● 단수명사 긍정적 측면 ❑ 그는 긍정적인 측면에 초점을 맞추는 것을 선호한다. **3** 형용사 분명한 ❑ 동물을 사육하는 데 적용되어야 할 분명한 변화들이 있다. **4** 형용사 긍정적인 ❑ 유엔 사무총장이 최근에 했던 평화 구현을 위한 노력에 대해 긍정적인 반응이 있었다. ● 긍정적으로 부사 ❑ 그는 내가 제시했던 1,000 파운드라는 수임료에 대해 긍정적인 반응을 보이며 수락하는 ❑ "주디스는 늦은 적이 없어. 주디스가 8시라고 한 것 확실해?" "확실해." **6** 형용사 명확한 ❑ 비타민 에이 복용 때문에 선천적인 장애가 발생한다는 명확한 증거는 없었다. ● 명확하게 부사 ❑ 그는 그 사체가 자기 부인이라는 것을 명확하게 확인했다. **7** 형용사 양성의 ❑ 그 시험 결과가 양성이면, 항생제 복용이 처방될 것입니다. **8** 형용사 양수의 ❑ 그건 음수와 양수로 이루어진 정말로 단순한 숫자 놀이이다.

posi|tive dis|crimi|na|tion N-UNCOUNT **Positive discrimination** means making sure that people such as women, members of smaller racial groups, and disabled people get a fair share of the opportunities available. [BRIT; AM **affirmative action**] ❑ *Mr. Singh wanted to reserve places for low-caste Indians within the country's public sector, as a form of positive discrimination.*

불가산명사 사회적 약자 우대 정책 [영국영어; 미국영어 affirmative action] ❑ 싱 씨는 사회적 약자 우대 정책의 일환으로, 국가 공직에 하위 신분의 인도인들을 위한 자리를 확보해 주기를 원했다.

posi|tive|ly /pɒzɪtɪvli/ ■ ADV You use **positively** to emphasize that you really mean what you are saying. [EMPHASIS] [ADV adj-superl] ❑ *This is positively the last chance for the industry to establish such a system.* ❷ ADV You use **positively** to emphasize that something really is the case, although it may sound surprising or extreme. [EMPHASIS] ❑ *Mike's changed since he came back – he seems positively cheerful.*

■ 부사 정말로 [강조] ❑ 이것은 그 업계가 그런 시스템을 구축하기 위한 정말 마지막 기회이다. ❷ 부사 정말로 [강조] ❑ 마이크는 다시 돌아온 후로 많이 바뀌었다. 정말 명랑해 보인다.

pos|sess /pəzes/ (**possesses, possessing, possessed**) V-T If you **possess** something, you have it or own it. [no passive] ❑ *He was then arrested and charged with possessing an offensive weapon.*

타동사 소유하다 ❑ 그 후 그는 체포되었고 공격성 무기 소지죄로 기소되었다.

pos|ses|sion /pəzeʃ³n/ (**possessions**) ■ N-UNCOUNT If you are **in possession of** something, you have it, because you have obtained it or because it belongs to you. [FORMAL] ❑ *Those documents are now in the possession of the Guardian.* ❑ *He was also charged with illegal possession of firearms.* ❷ N-COUNT Your **possessions** are the things that you own or have with you at a particular time. ❑ *People had lost their homes and all their possessions.*

■ 불가산명사 소유 [격식체] ❑ 그 서류들은 지금 가디언 지가 소유하고 있다. ❑ 그는 불법화기 소지죄로도 기소되었다. ❷ 가산명사 소유물, 재산 ❑ 사람들은 집과 전 재산을 잃은 상태였다.

Word Partnership possession의 연어

N. **cocaine** possession, **drug** possession, possession **of a firearm**, possession **of illegal drugs**, **marijuana** possession, possession **of property**, **weapons** possession ■

---

pos|ses|sive /pəzesɪv/ (**possessives**) ■ ADJ Someone who is **possessive about** another person wants all that person's love and attention. ❑ *Danny could be very jealous and possessive about me.* ● **pos|ses|sive|ness** N-UNCOUNT ❑ *I've ruined every relationship with my possessiveness.* ❷ ADJ Someone who is **possessive about** things that they own does not like other people to use them. ❑ *People were very possessive about their coupons.* ❸ ADJ In grammar, a **possessive determiner** or **possessive adjective** is a word such as "my" or "his" which shows who or what something belongs to or is connected with. The **possessive** form of a name or noun has 's added to it, as in "Jenny's" or "cat's." [ADJ n]

■ 형용사 (다른 사람을) 소유하려고 하는 ❑ 대니가 질투심이 아주 많고 나를 소유하려고 하는 것일 수도 있다. ● 소유욕 불가산명사 ❑ 나는 내 소유욕 때문에 모든 관계를 망쳤다. ❷ 형용사 소유욕이 강한 ❑ 사람들은 자신들의 쿠폰에 대해 강한 소유욕을 보였다. ❸ 형용사 소유를 나타내는, 소유격의

pos|si|bil|ity ◆◇ /pɒsɪbɪlɪti/ (**possibilities**) ■ N-COUNT If you say there is a **possibility that** something is the case or **that** something will happen, you mean that it might be the case or it might happen. ❑ *We were not in the least worried about the possibility that sweets could rot the teeth.* ❷ N-COUNT A **possibility** is one of several different things that could be done. ❑ *There were several possibilities open to each manufacturer.*

■ 가산명사 가능성 ❑ 우리는 사탕이 충치를 유발할 수도 있다는 가능성에 대해 조금도 걱정하지 않았다. ❷ 가산명사 가능성 ❑ 각 제조사들에게 열린 가능성이 몇 가지가 있었다.

> Note that you do not use **possibility** in sentences like "I had the possibility to do it." The words you need are **opportunity** or **chance**. **Opportunity** is more formal. ❑ *Later Donald had the opportunity of driving the car... The people of Northern Ireland would have the chance to shape their own future.*

> possibility를 "I had the possibility to do it." 과 같은 문장으로는 쓰지 않음을 유의하라. 여기서 필요한 단어는 opportunity나 chance인데, opportunity가 더 격식적이다. ❑ 나중에 도널드는 그 차를 운전할 기회가 있었다... 북아일랜드 사람들은 그들 자신의 미래를 구체화할 기회가 있을 것이다.

Word Link ible ≈ able to be : audible, flexible, possible

pos|sible ◆◆◆ /pɒsɪb³l/ (**possibles**) ■ ADJ If it is **possible** to do something, it can be done. ❑ *If it is possible to find out where your brother is, we shall.* ❑ *Everything is possible if we want it enough.* ❷ ADJ A **possible** event is one that might happen. ❑ *He referred the matter to the Attorney General for possible action against several newspapers.* ❑ *One possible solution, if all else fails, is to take legal action.* ❸ ADJ If you say that it is **possible that** something is true or correct, you mean that although you do not know whether it is true or correct, you accept that it might be. [VAGUENESS] [v-link ADJ, oft it v-link ADJ that] ❑ *It is possible that there's an explanation for all this.* ❹ ADJ If you do something **as soon as possible**, you do it as soon as you can. If you get **as much as possible** of something, you get as much of it as you can. [as adv/pron as ADJ] ❑ *Please make your decision as soon as possible.* ❑ *Mrs. Pollard decided to learn as much as possible about the People's Republic of China.* ❺ ADJ You use **possible** with superlative adjectives to emphasize that something has more or less of a quality than anything else of its kind. [EMPHASIS] [adj-superl ADJ, adj-superl n ADJ] ❑ *They have joined the job market at the worst possible time.* ❑ *We expressed in the clearest possible way our disappointment, hurt, and anger.* ❻ ADJ If you describe someone as, for example, a **possible** Prime Minister, you mean that they may become Prime Minister. [ADJ n] ❑ *Government sources are now openly speculating about a possible successor for Dr. Lawrence.* ● N-COUNT **Possible** is also a noun. ❑ *Kennedy, who divorced wife Joan in 1982, was tipped as a presidential possible.* ❼ N-SING **The possible** is everything that can be done in a situation. ❑ *He is a democrat with the skill, nerve, and ingenuity to push the limits of the possible.*

■ 형용사 실현 가능한, ~할 수 있는 ❑ 너의 형이 어디 있는지 찾을 수만 있다면, 우리는 그를 찾을 것이다. ❑ 우리가 간절히 원한다면 모든 것은 가능하다. ❷ 형용사 가능한, 있을 수 있는 ❑ 그는 몇몇 신문사에 대해 가능한 조치를 취하도록 법무 장관에게 그 사건을 의뢰했다. ❑ 다른 모든 것이 실패한다면, 한 가지 가능한 해결책은 법적 절차를 밟는 것이다. ❸ 형용사 ~일 수도 있는 [짐작투] ❑ 이 모든 것을 해명할 수 있는 것이 있을 수도 있다. ❹ 형용사 가능한 한, 될 수 있는 대로 ❑ 최대한 빨리 결정을 내려 주세요. ❑ 폴라드 여사는 중화 인민 공화국에 대해 가능한 한 많이 공부를 하기로 결심했다. ❺ 형용사 가장 ~한 [강조] ❑ 그들은 가장 최악의 시기에 인력 시장에 참여했다. ❑ 우리는 할 수 있는 가장 분명한 방식으로 우리의 실망과 상처와 분노를 표했다. ❻ 형용사 후보의 ❑ 정부 관계 당국은 이제 로렌스 박사의 후계자 후보에 대해 공개적으로 검토하고 있다. ● 가산명사 후보자 ❑ 1982년에 부인 조안과 이혼한 케네디가 대통령 후보 중 하나로 예상되고 있었다. ❼ 단수명사 가능한 일 ❑ 그는 노련하고 대담하며 가능성의 한계를 확장시킬 수 있는 재주를 지닌 민주주의자이다.

Thesaurus possible의 참조어

ADJ. feasible, likely; (ant.) impossible, unlikely ■ ❷

---

pos|si|bly ◆◆◇ /pɒsɪbli/ ■ ADV You use **possibly** to indicate that you are not sure whether something is true or might happen. [VAGUENESS] ❑ *Exercise will not only lower blood pressure but possibly protect against heart attacks.* ❑ *They were smartly but casually dressed; possibly students.* ❷ ADV You use **possibly** to emphasize that you are surprised, puzzled, or shocked by something that you have seen or heard. [EMPHASIS] [ADV before v] ❑ *It was the most unexpected piece of news one could possibly imagine.* ❸ ADV You use **possibly** to emphasize that someone has

■ 부사 아마도 [짐작투] ❑ 운동은 혈압을 낮출 뿐만 아니라 아마 심장 마비를 방지하기도 할 것이다. ❑ 그들은 말쑥하지만 캐주얼하게 옷을 입고 있었다. 아마도 학생들인 것 같았다. ❷ 부사 아무리 해도, 도저히 (놀람, 충격 등을 강조하기 위해 쓰는 말) [강조] ❑ 그것은 그 누구도 도저히 상상할 수 없었던 전혀 예기치 못한 소식이었다. ❸ 부사 한껏, 가능한 모든 걸

tried their hardest to do something, or has done it as well as they can. [EMPHASIS] [ADV before v] ❑ *They've done everything they can possibly think of.* ◆ ADV You use **possibly** to emphasize that something definitely cannot happen or definitely cannot be done. [EMPHASIS] [with brd-neg, ADV before v] ❑ *No I really can't possibly answer that!*

기울여 [강조] ❑ 그들은 생각해 낼 수 있는 모든 것을 다 해 보아 왔다. ◆ 부사 절대로 [강조] ❑ 아니, 나는 정말 절대로 그 문제에 대답할 수 없어.

---

post

① LETTERS, PARCELS, AND INFORMATION
② JOBS AND PLACES
③ POLES

---

① **post** ♦♦◇ /poʊst/ (**posts, posting, posted**) ■ V-T If you **post** notices, signs, or other pieces of information somewhere, you fix them to a wall or board so that everyone can see them. ❑ *Officials began posting warning notices.* ● PHRASAL VERB **Post up** means the same as **post**. ❑ *He has posted a sign up that says "No Fishing."* ② V-T If you **post** information on the Internet, you make the information available to other people on the Internet. [COMPUTING] ❑ *A consultation paper has been posted on the Internet inviting input from Net users.* ③ PHRASE If you **keep** someone **posted**, you keep giving them the latest information about a situation that they are interested in. ❑ *Keep me posted on your progress.* ④ N-SING **The post** is the public service or system by which letters and packages are collected and delivered. [mainly BRIT; AM usually **mail**] [the N, also by N] ❑ *You'll receive your book through the post.* ❑ *The winner will be notified by post.* ⑤ N-UNCOUNT You can use **post** to refer to letters and packages that are delivered to you. [mainly BRIT; AM usually **mail**] ❑ *He flipped through the post without opening any of it.* ⑥ N-UNCOUNT **Post** is used to refer to an occasion when letters or packages are delivered. For example, **first post** on a particular day is the first time that things are delivered. [mainly BRIT] ❑ *Entries must arrive by first post next Wednesday.* ⑦ V-T If you **post** a letter or package, you send it to someone by putting it in a mailbox or by taking it to a post office. [mainly BRIT] ❑ *If I write a letter, would you post it for me?* ❑ *I'm posting you a cheque tonight.* ● PHRASAL VERB **Post off** means the same as **post**. [AM usually **mail**] ❑ *He'd left me to pack up the mail and post it off.*

■ 타동사 붙이다, 게시하다 ❑ 공무원들은 경고 안내문을 게시하기 시작했다. ● 구동사 붙이다, 게시하다 ❑ 그는 '낚시 금지'라는 표지를 붙였다. ② 타동사 (인터넷에 글을) 올리다 [컴퓨터] ❑ 인터넷을 사용하는 사람들의 의견을 묻는 의뢰서가 인터넷에 올라와 있다. ③ 구 -에게 계속 알려 주다 ❑ 너의 진행 상황을 계속 알려 줘. ④ 단수명사 우편 [주로 영국영어; 미국영어 대개 mail] ❑ 귀하는 책을 우편으로 받아 보시게 될 것입니다. ❑ 당첨자는 우편을 통해 통보될 것입니다. ⑤ 불가산명사 우편물 [주로 영국영어; 미국영어 대개 mail] ❑ 그는 우편물들을 하나도 열어 보시는 않고 그냥 훑어 넘겨보았다. ⑥ 불가산명사 우편배달; 첫 배달 [주로 영국영어] ❑ 참가자 명단이 다음 주 수요일 첫 배달 시간 때까지 도착해야 한다. ⑦ 타동사 (편지나 소포를) 부치다 [주로 영국영어] ❑ 내가 편지 쓰면, 네가 좀 부쳐 줄래? ❑ 오늘 밤에 네게 우편으로 수표를 부칠게. ● 구동사 부치다 [미국영어 대개 mail] ❑ 그는 그 우편물을 포장해서 부치는 것을 나에게 맡겼다.

② **post** ♦♦◇ /poʊst/ (**posts, posting, posted**) ■ N-COUNT A **post** in a company or organization is a job or official position in it, usually one that involves responsibility. [FORMAL] ❑ *She had earlier resigned her post as President Menem's assistant.* ② V-T If you **are posted** somewhere, you are sent there by the organization that you work for and usually work there for several years. [usu passive] ❑ *After training she was posted to Brixton.* ③ V-T If a soldier, guard, or other person **is posted** somewhere, they are told to stand there, in order to supervise an activity or guard a place. ❑ *Police have now been posted outside all temples.* ❑ *British Rail had to post a signalman at the entrance to the tunnel.* ④ →see also **posting**

■ 가산명사 자리, 직위 [격식체] ❑ 그녀는 그보다 일찍 메넴 대통령 보좌 역 자리를 사임했었다. ② 타동사 발령나다, 배치되다 ❑ 연수 후에 그녀는 브릭스턴으로 발령이 났다. ③ 타동사 배치되다 ❑ 지금 경찰이 모든 사원 밖에 배치되어 있다. ❑ 영국 철도는 터널 입구에 신호원을 배치해야만 했다.

③ **post** /poʊst/ (**posts**) ■ N-COUNT A **post** is a strong upright pole made of wood or metal that is fixed into the ground. ❑ *The device is fixed to a post.* ② N-COUNT A **post** is the same as a **goalpost**. ❑ *Jenkins missed a penalty, hitting the post in the 13th minute.* ③ N-SING On a horse-racing track, **the post** is a pole which marks the finishing point.

■ 가산명사 기둥 ❑ 그 장치는 기둥에 고정되어 있다. ② 가산명사 골대 ❑ 젠킨스는 경기 13분에 골대를 맞힘으로써, 페널티 킥의 득점 기회를 놓쳤다. ③ 단수명사 (경마에서의) 결승 푯말

post|age /poʊstɪdʒ/ N-UNCOUNT **Postage** is the money that you pay for sending letters and packages by mail. ❑ *All prices include postage and packing.*

불가산명사 우편료 ❑ 모든 가격에는 우편료와 포장료가 포함되어 있습니다.

post|al /poʊstᵊl/ ■ ADJ **Postal** is used to describe things or people connected with the public service of carrying letters and packages from one place to another. [ADJ n] ❑ *Compensation for lost or damaged mail will be handled by the postal service.* ② ADJ **Postal** is used to describe activities that involve sending things by mail. [mainly BRIT] [ADJ n] ❑ *Unions would elect their leadership by secret postal ballot.*

■ 형용사 우편의 ❑ 분실 또는 파손 우편물에 대한 배상은 우체국에서 처리될 것입니다. ② 형용사 우편의 [주로 영국영어] ❑ 노동조합은 우편을 통한 비밀 투표를 이용하여 지도부를 선출할 것이다.

postal or|der (**postal orders**) N-COUNT A **postal order** is a piece of paper representing a sum of money which you can buy at a post office and send to someone as a way of sending them money by mail. [BRIT; AM **money order**]

가산명사 우편환 [영국영어; 미국영어 money order]

post|box /poʊstbɒks/ (**postboxes**) also post box N-COUNT A **postbox** is a metal box in a public place, where you put letters and small parcels to be collected. They are then sorted and delivered. Compare **letterbox**. [BRIT; AM **mailbox**]

가산명사 우편함 [영국영어; 미국영어 mailbox]

post|card /poʊstkɑrd/ (**postcards**) also post card N-COUNT A **postcard** is a piece of thin card, often with a picture on one side, which you can write on and mail to people without using an envelope.

가산명사 우편엽서

post|code /poʊstkoʊd/ (**postcodes**) also post code N-COUNT Your **postcode** is a short sequence of numbers and letters at the end of your address, which helps the post office to sort the mail. [BRIT; AM **zip code**] ❑ *The first part of each London postcode represents a district.*

가산명사 우편 번호 [영국영어; 미국영어 zip code] ❑ 모든 런던 우편 번호의 첫 글자는 해당 지역을 의미한다.

post|dated /poʊstdeɪtɪd/ ADJ On a **postdated** check, the date is a later one than the date when the check was actually written. You write a postdated check to allow a period of time before the money is taken from your account.

형용사 (수표에) 실제 날짜보다 늦춰 적은

post|er /poʊstər/ (**posters**) N-COUNT A **poster** is a large notice or picture that you stick on a wall or board, often in order to advertise something. ❑ *I had seen the poster for the jazz festival in Monterey.* →see **advertising**

가산명사 포스터 ❑ 나는 몬터레이에서 열리는 재즈 페스티벌 포스터를 보았었다.

post|er child (**poster children**) or poster boy or poster girl ■ N-COUNT If someone is a **poster child** for a particular cause, characteristic, or activity, they are seen as a very good or typical example of it. [mainly AM] ❑ *Zidane has become the poster child for a whole generation of French-born youths of North African extraction.* ② N-COUNT A **poster child** is a young man or woman who appears on an advertising poster. [mainly AM] ❑ *She went out with a famous hockey player, an actor, and a Calvin Klein poster boy.*

■ 가산명사 표상 [주로 미국영어] ❑ 지단은 북아프리카 혈통을 갖고 프랑스에서 태어난 모든 젊은 세대에게 표상이 되었다. ② 가산명사 광고 포스터에 나오는 인물 [주로 미국영어] ❑ 그녀는 유명한 하키 선수나, 배우, 그리고 캘빈 클라인 광고 모델과 사귀었다.

pos|ter|i|ty /pɒstɛrɪti/ N-UNCOUNT You can refer to everyone who will be alive in the future as **posterity**. [FORMAL] ❑ *A photographer recorded the scene on video for posterity.*

불가산명사 후세 [격식체] ❑ 한 사진작가가 후세를 위해 그 광경을 비디오에 담았다.

Word Link	*post ≈ after* : *post*graduate, *post*pone, *post*script

post|grad|u|ate /poʊstgrædʒuɪt/ (postgraduates) also **post-graduate**
■ N-COUNT A **postgraduate** or a **postgraduate student** is a student with a first degree from a university who is studying or doing research at a more advanced level. [BRIT; AM **graduate student**] ■ ADJ **Postgraduate** study or research is done by a student who has a first degree and is studying or doing research at a more advanced level. [BRIT; AM **graduate**] [ADJ n] ❑ *...postgraduate courses.*

■ 가산명사 대학원, 대학원생 [영국영어; 미국영어 graduate student] ■ 형용사 대학원의 [영국영어; 미국영어 graduate] ❑ 대학원 과정

post|ing /poʊstɪŋ/ (postings) ■ N-COUNT If a member of an armed force gets a **posting** to a particular place, they are sent to live and work there for a period. ❑ *...awaiting his posting to a field ambulance corps in early 1941.* ■ N-COUNT If you get a **posting** to a different town or country, your employers send you to work there, usually for several years. [mainly BRIT; AM usually **assignment**] ❑ *He was rewarded with a posting to New York.* →see also **post** ■ N-COUNT A **posting** is a message that is placed on the Internet, for example on a bulletin board or website, for everyone to read. [COMPUTING] ❑ *Postings on the Internet can be accessed from anywhere in the world.*

■ 가산명사 배치 ❑ 그가 1942년 초에 야전 병원 부대로 배치되기를 기다리면서 ■ 가산명사 발령 [주로 영국영어; 미국영어 대개 assignment] ❑ 포상으로 그는 뉴욕으로 발령이 났다. ■ 가산명사 인터넷에 올린 글 [컴퓨터] ❑ 인터넷에 올린 글은 세계 어느 곳에서도 읽을 수 있다.

post|man /poʊstmən/ (postmen) N-COUNT A **postman** is a man whose job is to collect and deliver letters and packages that are sent by mail. [mainly BRIT; AM usually **mailman**]

가산명사 집배원 [주로 영국영어; 미국영어 대개 mailman]

post|mor|tem /poʊstmɔrtəm/ (postmortems) also **post-mortem, post mortem** ■ N-COUNT A **postmortem** is a medical examination of a dead person's body in order to find out how they died. ❑ *A postmortem was carried out to establish the cause of death.* ■ N-COUNT A **postmortem** is an examination of something that has recently happened, especially something that has failed or gone wrong. ❑ *The postmortem on the presidential campaign is under way.*

■ 가산명사 부검, 검시 ❑ 사망 원인을 밝히기 위해 부검이 실시되었다. ■ 가산명사 사후 검토 ❑ 대통령 선거 운동에 대한 사후 검토가 진행 중이다.

post office (post offices) ■ N-SING **The Post Office** is the national organization that is responsible for postal services. ❑ *The Post Office confirmed that up to fifteen thousand jobs could be lost.* ■ N-COUNT A **post office** is a building where you can buy stamps, mail letters and packages, and use other services provided by the national postal service. ❑ *She rushed to get to the post office before it closed.*

■ 단수명사 체신청 ❑ 체신청은 최대 1만 5천 개의 일자리가 없어질 수도 있다는 것을 확인했다. ■ 가산명사 우체국 ❑ 그녀는 우체국이 문을 닫기 전에 그곳에 닿기 위해 달려갔다.

post office box (post office boxes) N-COUNT A **post office box** is a numbered box in a post office where a person's mail is kept for them until they come to collect it.

가산명사 사서함

post|pone /poʊstpoʊn, poʊspoʊn/ (postpones, postponing, postponed) V-T If you **postpone** an event, you delay it or arrange for it to take place at a later time than was originally planned. ❑ *He decided to postpone the expedition until the following day.*

타동사 연기하다, 미루다 ❑ 그는 그 탐험을 다음 날로 미루기로 결정하였다.

If you **cancel** or **call off** an arrangement or an appointment, you stop it from happening. ❑ *His failing health forced him to cancel the meeting... The European Community has threatened to call off peace talks.* If you **postpone** or **put off** an arrangement or an appointment, you make another arrangement for it to happen at a later time. ❑ *Elections have been postponed until next year... The Senate put off a vote on the nomination for one week.* If you **delay** something that has been arranged, you make it happen later than planned. ❑ *Space agency managers decided to delay the launch of the space shuttle.* If something **delays** you or **holds** you **up**, you start or finish what you are doing later than you planned. ❑ *He was delayed in traffic... Delivery of equipment had been held up by delays and disputes.*

합의나 약속을 cancel 또는 call off하면, 그것이 일어나지 않도록 하는 것이다. ❑ 그는 건강이 나빠져서 회의를 취소해야 했다... 유럽 공동체가 평화 협상을 취소하겠다고 협박해 왔다. 어떤 조치나 약속을 연기(postpone 또는 put off)하면, 그것이 더 뒤의 어느 시기에 일어날 수 있도록 새로운 약속을 하는 것이다. ❑ 선거가 내년으로 연기되었다... 상원은 지명 투표를 일주일 동안 연기했다. 이미 약속된 것을 delay하면, 그것이 계획했던 것보다 나중에 일어나도록 하는 것이다. ❑ 우주항공 센터 관리자들이 우주선 발사를 연기하기로 결정했다. 무슨 일이 당신을 delay하거나 당신을 hold up하면, 일의 시작이나 마무리를 계획보다 늦게 하는 것이다. ❑ 그 사람은 차가 막혀서 늦었다... 장비 배달이 일정 연기와 의견 충돌 때문에 지연되었었다.

---

post|pone|ment /poʊstpoʊnmənt, poʊspoʊn-/ (postponements) N-VAR The **postponement** of an event is the act of delaying it or arranging for it to take place at a later time than originally planned. ❑ *The postponement was due to a dispute over where the talks should be held.*

가산명사 또는 불가산명사 연기 ❑ 회담을 어디에서 개최할 것인가에 관한 논쟁 때문에 연기되었다.

post|script /poʊstskrɪpt/ (postscripts) ■ N-COUNT A **postscript** is something written at the end of a letter after you have signed your name. You usually write "PS" in front of it. ❑ *A brief, hand-written postscript lay beneath his signature.* ■ N-COUNT A **postscript** is an addition to a finished story, account, or statement, which gives further information. ❑ *I should like to add a postscript to your obituary for John Cage.*

■ 가산명사 추신 ❑ 그의 서명 밑에 간단하게 직접 손으로 쓴 추신이 있었다. ■ 가산명사 덧붙이는 말 ❑ 존 케이지에 대한 부고 내용에 제가 몇 마디 덧붙이고 싶습니다.

pos|tu|late /pɒstʃəleɪt/ (postulates, postulating, postulated) V-T If you **postulate** something, you suggest it as the basis for a theory, argument, or calculation, or assume that it is the basis. [FORMAL] ❑ *He dismissed arguments postulating differing standards for human rights in different cultures and regions.*

타동사 가정하다 [격식체] ❑ 그는 문화와 지역에 따라 서로 다른 인권 기준을 가정하는 주장들을 묵살했다.

pos|ture /pɒstʃər/ (postures, posturing, postured) ■ N-VAR Your **posture** is the position in which you stand or sit. ❑ *You can make your stomach look flatter instantly by improving your posture.* ❑ *Exercise, fresh air, and good posture are all helpful.* ■ N-COUNT A **posture** is an attitude that you have toward something. [FORMAL] ❑ *The military machine is ready to change its defensive posture to one prepared for action.* ■ V-I You can say that someone **is posturing** when you disapprove of their behavior because you think they are trying to give a particular impression in order to deceive people. [FORMAL, DISAPPROVAL] [usu cont] ❑ *She says the President may just be posturing.*

■ 가산명사 또는 불가산명사 자세 ❑ 자세를 개선함으로써 당신의 배를 더 날씬하게 보이게 할 수 있습니다. ❑ 운동, 맑은 공기, 좋은 자세는 모두 도움이 된다. ■ 가산명사 태도, 자세 [격식체] ❑ 그 군사 조직은 방어적 태도에서 작전 준비 완료로 바꿀 준비가 되어 있다. ■ 자동사 가식을 부리다 [격식체, 탐탁찮음] ❑ 그녀는 대통령이 그냥 가식을 부리고 있는 것일 수도 있다고 말한다.

A

post|war /poʊstwɔr/ also **post-war** ADJ **Postwar** is used to describe things that happened, existed, or were made in the period immediately after a war, especially the Second World War, 1939-45. ❏ *Anesthetics and bottle feeding were popular in the early postwar years.*

형용사 전후(戰後)의 ❏ 전후 초기 몇 년 동안은 마취제 사용과 우유 수유가 일반적이었다.

B

pot ◆◇◇ /pɒt/ (**pots**) **1** N-COUNT A **pot** is a deep round container used for cooking stews, soups, and other food. ❏ *...metal cooking pots.* ● N-COUNT A **pot of** stew, soup, or other food is an amount of it contained in a pot. ❏ *He was stirring a pot of soup.* **2** N-COUNT You can use **pot** to refer to a teapot or coffeepot. ❏ *There's tea in the pot.* ● N-COUNT A **pot of** tea or coffee is an amount of it contained in a pot. ❏ *He spilt a pot of coffee.* **3** N-COUNT A **pot** is a cylindrical container for jam, paint, or some other thick liquid. ❏ *Hundreds of jam pots lined her scrubbed shelves.* ● N-COUNT A **pot of** jam, paint, or some other thick liquid is an amount of it contained in a pot. ❏ *...a pot of red paint.* **4** N-UNCOUNT **Pot** is sometimes used to refer to the drugs cannabis and marijuana. [INFORMAL] ❏ *I started smoking pot when I was about eleven.* **5** →see also **melting pot**

1 가산명사 냄비 ❏ 요리용 쇠 냄비들 ● 가산명사 (국, 찌개 등) 한 냄비 ❏ 그는 수프 한 냄비를 젓고 있었다. **2** 가산명사 찻주전자 ❏ 찻주전자 안에 차가 들어 있다. ● 가산명사 (차나 커피) 한 주전자 ❏ 그가 커피 한 주전자를 엎질렀다. **3** 가산명사 단지, 통 ❏ 그녀가 닦아 놓은 선반에 잼통 수백 개가 줄지어 놓여 있었다. ● 가산명사 (잼이나 페인트 등) 한 통 ❏ 붉은색 페인트 한 통 **4** 불가산명사 대마초 [비격식체] ❏ 나는 열한 살 때 대마초를 피우기 시작했다.

C

D

E

po|ta|to ◆◇◇ /pəteɪtoʊ/ (**potatoes**) **1** N-VAR **Potatoes** are quite round vegetables with brown or red skins and white insides. They grow under the ground. **2** PHRASE You can refer to a difficult subject that people disagree on as a **hot potato**. ❏ *...a political hot potato such as abortion.*

1 가산명사 또는 불가산명사 감자 **2** 구 뜨거운 감자 ❏ 낙태 같은 정치적으로 뜨거운 감자

F

po|ta|to chip (**potato chips**) **1** N-COUNT **Potato chips** are very thin slices of potato that have been fried until they are hard, dry, and crisp. [AM; BRIT **crisps**] **2** N-COUNT **Potato chips** are long, thin pieces of potato fried in oil or fat and eaten hot, usually with a meal. [BRIT; AM **French fries**] [usu pl]

1 가산명사 감자 칩 [미국영어; 영국영어 crisps] **2** 가산명사 감자튀김, 프렌치프라이 [영국영어; 미국영어 french fries]

G

po|ten|cy /poʊtənsi/ **1** N-UNCOUNT **Potency** is the power and influence that a person, action, or idea has to affect or change people's lives, feelings, or beliefs. ❏ *All their songs have a lingering potency.* **2** N-UNCOUNT The **potency** of a drug, poison, or other chemical is its strength. ❏ *Sunscreen can lose its potency if left over winter in the bathroom cabinet.*

1 불가산명사 힘, 세력 ❏ 그들의 노래는 모두 오랫동안 기억에 남는 힘이 있다. **2** 불가산명사 효능 ❏ 선크림을 겨우내 욕실 수납장에 내버려 두면 약효가 사라질 수도 있다.

H

I

po|tent /poʊtənt/ ADJ Something that is **potent** is very effective and powerful. ❏ *Their most potent weapon was the Exocet missile.*

형용사 위력적인 ❏ 그들의 가장 위력적인 무기는 엑조세 미사일이었다.

J

po|ten|tial ◆◆◇ /pətenʃəl/ **1** ADJ You use **potential** to say that someone or something is capable of developing into the particular kind of person or thing mentioned. [ADJ n] ❏ *The firm has identified 60 potential customers at home and abroad.* ❏ *We are aware of the potential problems and have taken every precaution.* ● **po|ten|tial|ly** ADV [ADV with cl/group] ❏ *Clearly this is a potentially dangerous situation.* **2** N-UNCOUNT If you say that someone or something has **potential**, you mean that they have the necessary abilities or qualities to become successful or useful in the future. ❏ *The boy has great potential.* ❏ *The school strives to treat pupils as individuals and to help each one to achieve their full potential.* **3** N-UNCOUNT If you say that someone or something has **potential for** doing a particular thing, you mean that it is possible they may do it. If there is the **potential for** something, it may happen. ❏ *John seemed as horrified as I about his potential for violence.* ❏ *The meeting has the potential to be a watershed event.*

1 형용사 잠재적인, 가능한 ❏ 그 회사는 국내외에서 60명의 잠재적 고객의 신원을 파악했다. ❏ 우리는 잠재적인 문제들을 인식하고 있고 모든 예방 조치를 해 놓았다. ● 잠재적으로 부사 ❏ 확실히 이건 잠재적으로 위험한 상황이다. **2** 불가산명사 잠재력 ❏ 그 소년은 엄청난 잠재력을 가지고 있다. ❏ 그 학교는 학생들을 인격체로 다루고 개개인이 잠재력을 최대한 발휘할 수 있도록 도우려고 애를 쓴다. **3** 가산명사 잠재성 ❏ 존은 자신의 잠재된 폭력성에 대해서 나만큼 놀란 것 같았다. ❏ 이 회동은 사건의 분수령이 될 잠재성이 있다.

K

L

M

po|tion /poʊʃən/ (**potions**) N-COUNT A **potion** is a drink that contains medicine, poison, or something that is supposed to have magic powers. ❏ *...a magic potion that will make Siegfried forget Brunnhilde and fall in love with Gutrune.*

가산명사 (마법의) 물약 ❏ 지크프리트가 브륀힐데를 잊고 구트룬과 사랑에 빠지게 만들 마법의 물약

N

pot|ter /pɒtər/ (**potters, pottering, pottered**)

▶**potter around** or **potter about** PHRASAL VERB If you **potter around** or **potter about**, you do pleasant but unimportant things, without hurrying. [BRIT; AM **putter around**] ❏ *I was perfectly happy just pottering around doing up my flat.*

구동사 소일하다 [영국영어; 미국영어 putter around] ❏ 나는 소일 삼아 내 아파트를 손보면서 지극히 행복했다.

O

P

pot|tery /pɒtəri/ (**potteries**) **1** N-UNCOUNT You can use **pottery** to refer to pots, dishes, and other objects which are made from clay and then baked in an oven until they are hard. ❏ *...a fine range of pottery.* **2** N-UNCOUNT You can use **pottery** to refer to the hard clay that some pots, dishes, and other objects are made of. ❏ *Some bowls were made of pottery and wood.* **3** N-UNCOUNT **Pottery** is the craft or activity of making objects out of clay. ❏ *In 1935 he went to study pottery at Burslem School of Art.* **4** N-COUNT A **pottery** is a factory or other place where pottery is made. ❏ *...the many galleries and potteries which sell pieces by local artists.* →see Word Web: **pottery**

1 불가산명사 도기 ❏ 훌륭한 도기 세트 **2** 불가산명사 점토 ❏ 어떤 사발은 점토와 나무로 만들어져 있었다. **3** 불가산명사 도기 제조(법) ❏ 1935년에 그는 도기 제조법을 공부하기 위해 부슬렘 미술 학교에 갔다. **4** 가산명사 도기 제조소 ❏ 지역 예술가들의 작품을 파는 많은 화랑과 도기 제조소

Q

R

pot|ty /pɒti/ (**potties**) N-COUNT A **potty** is a deep bowl which a small child uses instead of a toilet.

가산명사 소아용 변기

S

pouch /paʊtʃ/ (**pouches**) **1** N-COUNT A **pouch** is a flexible container like a small bag. ❏ *Hugh took out his pipe and dug it into a pouch of tobacco.* **2** N-COUNT The **pouch** of an animal such as a kangaroo or a koala bear is the pocket of skin on its stomach in which its baby grows. ❏ *...a kangaroo, with its baby in its pouch.*

1 가산명사 쌈지, 주머니 ❏ 휴는 곰방대를 꺼내서 담배쌈지 안에 쑤셔 넣었다. **2** 가산명사 (아기) 주머니 ❏ 주머니 속에 새끼를 안고 있는 캥거루

T

U

Word Web · pottery

There are three basic types of **pottery**. Earthenware **dishes** are made from **clay** and **fired** at a relatively low temperature. They are **porous** and require a **glaze** in order to hold water. Potters first created earthenware objects about 15,000 years ago. Stoneware pieces are heavier and are fired at a higher temperature. They are impermeable even without a glaze. **Porcelain ceramics** are more fragile. They have thin walls and are **translucent**. Stoneware and porcelain are not as old as earthenware. They appeared about 2,000 years ago when the Chinese started building high-temperature kilns. Another name for porcelain is **china**.

V

W

X

Y

Z

poul|try /ˈpoʊltri/ N-PLURAL You can refer to chickens, ducks, and other birds that are kept for their eggs and meat as **poultry**. ❏ *... a poultry farm.* ● N-UNCOUNT Meat from these birds is also referred to as **poultry**. ❏ *The menu features roast meats and poultry.* →see **meat**

pounce /paʊns/ (**pounces, pouncing, pounced**) ◆ V-I If someone **pounces on** you, they come up toward you suddenly and take hold of you. ❏ *He pounced on the photographer, beat him up and smashed his camera.* ◆ V-I If someone **pounces on** something such as a mistake, they quickly draw attention to it, usually in order to gain an advantage for themselves or to prove that they are right. ❏ *The Democrats were ready to pounce on any Republican failings or mistakes.* ◆ V-I When an animal or bird **pounces on** something, it jumps on it and holds it, in order to kill it. ❏ *...like a tiger pouncing on its prey.*

pound ◆◆◆ /paʊnd/ (**pounds, pounding, pounded**) ◆ N-COUNT A **pound** is a unit of weight used mainly in America, Britain and other countries where English is spoken. One pound is equal to 0.454 kilograms. A **pound** of something is a quantity of it that weighs one pound. ❏ *Her weight was under ninety pounds.* →see **weight** ◆ N-COUNT The **pound** is the unit of money which is used in Britain. It is represented by the symbol £. One British pound is divided into a hundred pence. Some other countries, for example Egypt, also have a unit of money called a **pound**. ❏ *Beer cost three pounds a bottle.* ❏ *...multi-million pound profits.* ◆ N-SING The **pound** is used to refer to the British currency system, and sometimes to the currency systems of other countries which use pounds. ❏ *The pound is expected to continue to increase against most other currencies.* ◆ N-COUNT A **pound** is a place where dogs and cats found wandering in the street are taken and kept until they are claimed by their owners. ❏ *...cages at the local pound.* ◆ N-COUNT A **pound** is a place where cars that have been parked illegally are taken by the police and kept until they have been claimed by their owners. ❏ *The car remained in the police pound for a month.* ◆ V-T/V-I If you **pound** something or **pound on** it, you hit it with great force, usually loudly and repeatedly. ❏ *He pounded the table with his fist.* ❏ *Somebody began pounding on the front door.* ◆ V-T If you **pound** something, you crush it into a paste or a powder or into very small pieces. ❏ *She pounded the maize grains.* ◆ V-I If your heart **is pounding**, it is beating with an unusually strong and fast rhythm, usually because you are afraid. ❏ *I'm sweating, my heart is pounding. I can't breathe.*

pour ◆◇◇ /pɔr/ (**pours, pouring, poured**) ◆ V-T If you **pour** a liquid or other substance, you make it flow steadily out of a container by holding the container at an angle. ❏ *Pour a pool of sauce on two plates and arrange the meat neatly.* ❏ *Francis poured a generous measure of the whisky into a fresh glass.* ◆ V-T If you **pour** someone a drink, you put some of the drink in a cup or glass so that they can drink it. ❏ *He got up and poured himself another drink.* ❏ *She asked Tillie to pour her a cup of coffee.* ◆ V-I When a liquid or other substance **pours** somewhere, for example through a hole, it flows quickly and in large quantities. ❏ *Blood was pouring from his broken nose.* ❏ *Tears poured down both our faces.* ◆ V-I When it rains very heavily, you can say that **it is pouring**. [usu cont] ❏ *It has been pouring with rain all week.* ❏ *The rain was pouring down.* ◆ V-I If people **pour** into or out of a place, they go there quickly and in large numbers. ❏ *Any day now, the Northern forces may pour across the new border.* ❏ *At six p.m. large groups poured from the numerous offices.* ◆ V-I If something such as information **pours** into a place, a lot of it is obtained or given. ❏ *Martin, 78, died yesterday. Tributes poured in from around the globe.* ◆ to **pour cold water on** something →see **water**

<table>
<tr><td colspan="2">**Word Partnership**   pour의 연어</td></tr>
<tr><td>N.</td><td>pour **a liquid**, pour **a mixture**, pour **water** ◆
pour **coffee**, pour **a drink** ◆</td></tr>
</table>

▶ **pour out** ◆ PHRASAL VERB If you **pour out** a drink, you put some of it in a cup or glass. ❏ *Larry was pouring out four glasses of champagne.* ◆ PHRASAL VERB If you **pour out** your thoughts, feelings, or experiences, you tell someone all about them. ❏ *I poured my thoughts out on paper in an attempt to rationalize my feelings.*

pout /paʊt/ (**pouts, pouting, pouted**) V-I If someone **pouts**, they stick out their lips, usually in order to show that they are annoyed or to make themselves sexually attractive. ❏ *Like one of the kids, he whined and pouted when he did not get what he wanted.* ● N-COUNT **Pout** is also a noun. ❏ *She shot me a reproachful pout.*

pov|er|ty ◆◆◇ /ˈpɒvərti/ ◆ N-UNCOUNT **Poverty** is the state of being extremely poor. ❏ *According to World Bank figures, 41 per cent of Brazilians live in absolute poverty.* ◆ N-SING You can use **poverty** to refer to any situation in which there is not enough of something or its quality is poor. [FORMAL] [also no det, N of n] ❏ *Britain has suffered from a poverty of ambition.*

pov|er|ty trap (**poverty traps**) N-COUNT If someone is in a **poverty trap**, they are very poor but cannot improve their income because the money they get from the government decreases as the money they earn increases. ❏ *Many elderly people are caught in the poverty trap.*

pow|der /ˈpaʊdər/ (**powders, powdering, powdered**) ◆ N-MASS **Powder** consists of many tiny particles of a solid substance. ❏ *Put a small amount of the powder into a container and mix with water.* ❏ *...cocoa powder.* ◆ V-T If a woman **powders** her face or some other part of her body, she puts face powder or talcum powder on it. ❏ *She powdered her face and applied her lipstick and rouge.* →see **makeup**

pow|dered /ˈpaʊdərd/ ADJ A **powdered** substance is one which is in the form of a powder although it can come in a different form. ❏ *There are only two tins of powdered milk left.*

복수명사 가금류 ❏ 가금류 농장 ● 불가산명사 가금고기 ❏ 메뉴에는 특별히 여러 가지 구운 육류와 가금고기가 있다.

◆ 자동사 달려들다, 덮치다 ❏ 그는 사진사에게 달려들어 그를 흠씬 두들겨 패고 카메라를 박살 냈다. ◆ 자동사 꼬투리를 잡다 ❏ 민주당은 공화당이 실패하거나 실수하는 즉시 꼬투리를 잡고 늘어질 기세였다. ◆ 자동사 덮치다 ❏ 사냥감을 덮치는 호랑이처럼

◆ 가산명사 파운드 ❏ 그의 몸무게는 90파운드 미만이었다. ◆ 가산명사 파운드 ❏ 맥주는 병당 3파운드였다. ❏ 수백만 파운드에 달하는 수익 ◆ 단수명사 파운드화 ❏ 파운드화가 다른 화폐에 비해 계속 상승할 전망이다. ◆ 가산명사 동물 보호소 ❏ 지역 동물 보호소의 우리들 ◆ 가산명사 견인 차량 보관소 ❏ 그 자동차는 경찰 견인 차량 보관소에 한 달동안 계속 그대로 있었다. ◆ 타동사/자동사 세게 치다, 마구 두드리다 ❏ 그는 주먹으로 탁자를 세게 쳤다. ❏ 누군가가 현관문을 쿵쿵 두드리기 시작했다. ◆ 타동사 으깨다, 빻다 ❏ 그녀는 옥수수 알갱이들을 빻았다. ◆ 자동사 두근거리다 ❏ 땀이 나고 심장이 두근거려 숨을 쉴 수가 없어.

◆ 타동사 붓다 ❏ 소스를 접시 바닥에 고르게 부은 다음 고기를 정갈하게 올리세요. ❏ 프랜시스는 새 잔에 위스키를 넉넉히 부었다. ◆ 타동사 붓다, 따르다 ❏ 그는 일어서서 마실 술을 한 잔 더 부었다. ❏ 그녀는 틸리에게 커피를 한 잔 따라 달라고 했다. ◆ 자동사 쏟아지다 ❏ 그의 부러진 코에서 코피가 쏟아지고 있었다. ❏ 우리 두 사람 다 눈물이 쏟아져 얼굴을 적셨다. ◆ 자동사 폭우가 쏟아지다 ❏ 일주일 내내 폭우가 쏟아지고 있다. ❏ 비가 쏟아지고 있었다. ◆ 자동사 몰려오다, 쏟아져 들어오다; 쏟아져 나가다 ❏ 조만간 북군이 새 국경 너머로 쏟아져 들어올지도 모른다. ❏ 저녁 6시가 되자 사람들이 떼를 지어 수많은 사무실들에서 쏟아져 나왔다. ◆ 자동사 밀려들다, 쏟아지다 ❏ 마틴은 78세를 일기로 어제 사망했다. 전 세계에서 조문(弔文)이 밀려들었다.

◆ 구동사 따르다 ❏ 래리는 샴페인 네 잔을 따르고 있었다. ◆ 구동사 쏟아 붓다 ❏ 나는 내 감정을 정리해 보기 위해 생각들을 종이 위에 쏟아 부었다.

자동사 삐죽거리다 ❏ 아이처럼 자신이 원하는 것을 얻지 못할 때 그는 투덜대고 입을 삐죽거렸다. ● 가산명사 삐죽거림 ❏ 그녀는 원망스럽다는 듯이 내게 입을 삐죽거렸다.

◆ 불가산명사 빈곤 ❏ 세계은행의 수치에 의하면 브라질 국민의 41퍼센트가 절대 빈곤 상태로 생활한다. ◆ 단수명사 빈곤, 결핍 [격식체] ❏ 영국은 야망의 빈곤에 허덕여 왔다.

가산명사 빈곤의 올가미 ❏ 많은 노년층 인구가 빈곤의 올가미에 걸려 있다.

◆ 물질명사 가루 ❏ 소량의 가루를 통에 넣고 물과 섞으세요. ❏ 코코아 분말 ◆ 타동사 분을 바르다 ❏ 그녀는 얼굴에 분을 바르고 립스틱과 볼연지를 발랐다.

형용사 분말 형태의 ❏ 분유가 두 통밖에 안 남았다.

a b c d e f g h i j k l m n o p q r s t u v w x y z

pow|er ♦♦♦ /paʊər/ (powers, powering, powered) **1** N-UNCOUNT If someone has **power**, they have a lot of control over people and activities. ❑ *In a democracy, power must be divided.* **2** N-UNCOUNT Your **power to** do something is your ability to do it. ❑ *Human societies have the power to solve the problems confronting them.* ❑ *Fathers have the power to dominate children and young people.* **3** N-UNCOUNT If it is **in** or **within** your **power to** do something, you are able to do it or you have the resources to deal with it. ❑ *Your debt situation is only temporary, and it is within your power to resolve it.* **4** N-UNCOUNT If someone in authority has the **power** to do something, they have the legal right to do it. [also N in pl, oft the N to-inf] ❑ *The police have the power of arrest.* **5** N-UNCOUNT If people take **power** or come to **power**, they take charge of a country's affairs. If a group of people are **in power**, they are in charge of a country's affairs. ❑ *In 1964 Labour came into power.* ❑ *He first assumed power in 1970.* **6** N-COUNT You can use **power** to refer to a country that is very rich or important, or has strong military forces. ❑ *In Western eyes, Iraq is a major power in an area of great strategic importance.* ❑ *He first assumed power in 1970.* **7** N-UNCOUNT The **power** of something is the ability that it has to move or affect things. ❑ *The Roadrunner had better power, better tyres, and better brakes.* **8** N-UNCOUNT **Power** is energy, especially electricity, that is obtained in large quantities from a fuel source and used to operate lights, heating, and machinery. ❑ *Nuclear power is cleaner than coal.* ❑ *Power has been restored to most parts that were hit last night by high winds.* **9** V-T The device or fuel that **powers** a machine provides the energy that the machine needs in order to work. ❑ *The "flywheel" battery, it is said, could power an electric car for 600 miles on a single charge.* **10** ADJ **Power** tools are operated by electricity. [ADJ n] ❑ *...large power tools, such as chainsaws.* →see **electricity, energy**

Thesaurus   power의 참조어

N.   authority, control **1**
        energy, force, potency, strength **7**

Word Partnership   power의 연어

ADJ.   **divine** power, **political** power **1**
       real power **1** **2**
       tremendous power **1** **2** **7**
       absolute power, power **hungry** **1** **5**
       economic power **1** **6**
       electric(al) power, **nuclear** power, **solar** power **8**
V.   **exercise** power, **wield** power **1** **4** **5**
       come into power, **hold** power, **maintain** power, **remain in** power,
       restore to power, **rise to** power, **seize** power, **share** power,
       take power, **transfer** power **5**

▶**power up** PHRASAL VERB When you **power up** something such as a computer or a machine, you connect it to a power supply and switch it on. ❑ *He comes in the next morning, powers up the computer, and that infective diskette is in the drive.*

pow|er bro|ker (power brokers) N-COUNT A **power broker** is someone who has a lot of influence, especially in politics, and uses it to help other people gain power. ❑ *Jackson had been a major power-broker in the 1988 Presidential elections.*

pow|er cut (power cuts) N-COUNT A **power cut** is a period of time when the electricity supply to a particular building or area is stopped, sometimes deliberately. [BRIT; AM **outage**]

pow|er|ful ♦♦◇ /paʊərfəl/ **1** ADJ A **powerful** person or organization is able to control or influence people and events. ❑ *You're a powerful man – people will listen to you.* ❑ *...Russia and India, two large, powerful countries.* **2** ADJ You say that someone's body is **powerful** when it is physically strong. ❑ *Hans flexed his powerful muscles.* ● **pow|er|ful|ly** ADV [ADV with v] ❑ *He is described as a strong, powerfully-built man of 60.* **3** ADJ A **powerful** machine or substance is effective because it is very strong. ❑ *The more powerful the car the more difficult it is to handle.* ❑ *...powerful computer systems.* ● **pow|er|ful|ly** ADV [ADV adj] ❑ *Crack is a much cheaper, smokable form of cocaine which is powerfully addictive.* **4** ADJ A **powerful** smell is very strong. ❑ *There was a powerful smell of stale beer.* ● **pow|er|ful|ly** ADV [ADV after v] ❑ *The railway station smelt powerfully of cats and drains.* **5** ADJ A **powerful** voice is loud and can be heard from a long way away. ❑ *At that moment Mrs. Jones's powerful voice interrupted them, announcing a visitor.* **6** ADJ You describe a piece of writing, speech, or work of art as **powerful** when it has a strong effect on people's feelings or beliefs. ❑ *...Bleasdale's powerful 11-part drama about a corrupt city leader.* ● **pow|er|ful|ly** ADV ❑ *It's a play – painful, funny and powerfully acted.*

pow|er|less /paʊrlɪs/ **1** ADJ Someone who is **powerless** is unable to control or influence events. ❑ *If you don't have money, you're powerless.* ● **pow|er|less|ness** N-UNCOUNT ❑ *If we can't bring our problems under control, feelings of powerlessness and despair often ensue.* **2** ADJ If you are **powerless to** do something, you are completely unable to do it. [ADJ to-inf] ❑ *People are being murdered every day and I am powerless to stop it.*

pow|er line (power lines) N-COUNT A **power line** is a cable, especially above ground, along which electricity is passed to an area or building.

pow|er plant (power plants) N-COUNT A **power plant** is the same as a **power station**.

power-sharing also **power sharing** N-UNCOUNT **Power-sharing** is a political arrangement in which different or opposing groups all take part in government together. ❑ *They agreed a power-sharing arrangement, but it collapsed after five months.*

---

1 불가산명사 권력 ❑ 민주 국가에서는 권력이 분리되어야 한다. **2** 불가산명사 힘 ❑ 인간 사회는 대면하게 되는 문제들을 해결할 수 있는 힘을 지니고 있다. ❑ 아버지들은 자녀와 젊은 사람들을 지배할 수 있는 힘을 가지고 있다. **3** 불가산명사 능력 ❑ 당신 채무 상황은 일시적인 것에 불과하고 당신 능력으로 그것을 해결할 수 있다. **4** 불가산명사 권한 ❑ 경찰에겐 체포 권한이 있다. **5** 불가산명사 정권; 정권을 잡음 ❑ 1964년에 노동당이 정권을 잡았다. ❑ 그는 1970년에 처음 정권을 잡았다. **6** 가산명사 강대국, 힘 있는 나라 ❑ 서방의 시각에서 볼 때 이라크는 전략적으로 매우 중요한 지역에 있는 주요 국가이다. **7** 불가산명사 힘 ❑ 로드러너는 힘, 타이어, 브레이크 등에 있어 모두 우월했다. **8** 불가산명사 에너지, 전력 ❑ 핵에너지가 석탄에서 얻는 에너지보다 깨끗하다. ❑ 어젯밤 강풍에 맞은 대부분의 지역에 전력 공급이 재개되었다. **9** 타동사 동력을 공급하다 ❑ 사람들 말에 의하면 플라이휠 건전지를 단 한 번 충전하면 전기 자동차가 600마일을 달릴 수 있다고 한다. **10** 형용사 전력으로 작동하는 ❑ 전기 원형톱과 같은 대형 전동 공구

구동사 전원을 켜다 ❑ 그가 다음 날 아침 들어와서 컴퓨터를 켜는데 바이러스에 감염된 그 디스켓이 드라이브 안에 있었다.

가산명사 킹 메이커, 유력 인사 ❑ 잭슨은 1988년 대통령 선거 때 중요한 킹 메이커였다.

가산명사 정전 [영국영어; 미국영어 outage]

1 형용사 영향력 있는 ❑ 당신은 영향력 있는 사람입니다. 사람들은 당신의 말에 귀를 기울일 것입니다. ❑ 러시아와 인도라는 두 개의 강대국 **2** 형용사 건강한, 탄탄한 ❑ 한스는 자신의 탄탄한 근육을 과시했다. ● 건강하게 부사 ❑ 그는 힘세고 건강하게 생긴 60세 남자로 묘사된다. **3** 형용사 강력한 ❑ 차가 강력할수록 다루기도 힘들다. ❑ 강력한 컴퓨터 시스템 ● 강력하게 부사 ❑ 크랙은 훨씬 더 저렴하고 중독성이 매우 강한 것으로 흡연이 가능한 코카인의 한 형태이다. **4** 형용사 강한 ❑ 퀴퀴한 맥주 냄새가 강하게 풍겼다. ● 강하게 부사 ❑ 기차역에서는 고양이와 하수구 냄새가 강하게 풍겼다. **5** 형용사 큰 ❑ 그 순간 존스 부인의 큰 목소리가 끼어들더니 손님이 찾아왔다고 알렸다. **6** 형용사 강력한 ❑ 타락한 도시 지도자에 관한 블리스데일의 강력한 11부작 드라마 ● 강력하게 부사 ❑ 연극이야. 고통스럽고 웃기고 연기가 강력했다.

1 형용사 무력한 ❑ 네게 돈이 없으면 무력해. ❑ 무력감 불가산명사 ❑ 자신의 문제를 다스리지 못하면 흔히 무력감과 절망감이 뒤따른다. **2** 형용사 무력한 ❑ 사람들이 매일 살해당하고 있는데 내겐 그것을 막을 힘이 없다.

가산명사 송전선

가산명사 발전소

불가산명사 권력 공조 ❑ 그들은 권력 공조를 하기로 합의했으나 5개월 만에 무산되었다.

pow|er sta|tion (**power stations**) N-COUNT A **power station** is a place where electricity is produced. →see **electricity**

가산명사 발전소

pow|er steer|ing N-UNCOUNT In a vehicle, **power steering** is a system for steering which uses power from the engine so that it is easier for the driver to steer the vehicle.

불가산명사 파워 스티어링

pp ♦◇◇ **1** **pp** is written before a person's name at the bottom of a formal or business letter in order to indicate that they have signed the letter on behalf of the person whose name appears before theirs. [BUSINESS] ❑ *...J.R. Adams, pp D. Philips.* **2** **pp.** is the plural of "p." and means "pages." [WRITTEN] ❑ *See chapter 6, pp. 137-41.*

1 대리인 [경제] ❑ 더 필립스의 대리인 제이 알 아담스
2 페이지 [문어체] ❑ 6장 137-41페이지 참조

PR /pi ɑr/ N-UNCOUNT **PR** is an abbreviation for **public relations**. [BUSINESS] ❑ *It will be good PR.*

불가산명사 홍보 [경제] ❑ 좋은 홍보가 될 것이다.

prac|ti|ca|ble /prǽktɪkəbᵊl/ ADJ If a task, plan, or idea is **practicable**, people are able to carry it out. [FORMAL] ❑ *It is not reasonably practicable to offer her the original job back.*

형용사 실행 가능한 [격식체] ❑ 그녀에게 원래 자리를 다시 제안하는 것은 실행 타당한 방법이 아니다.

prac|ti|cal ♦◇◇ /prǽktɪkᵊl/ (**practicals**) **1** ADJ The **practical** aspects of something involve real situations and events, rather than just ideas and theories. ❑ *We can offer you practical suggestions on how to increase the fibre in your daily diet.* **2** ADJ You describe people as **practical** when they make sensible decisions and deal effectively with problems. [APPROVAL] ❑ *You were always so practical, Maria.* ❑ *How could she be so practical when he'd just told her something so shattering?* **3** ADJ **Practical** ideas and methods are likely to be effective or successful in a real situation. ❑ *Although the causes of cancer are being uncovered, we do not yet have any practical way to prevent it.* **4** ADJ You can describe clothes and things in your house as **practical** when they are suitable for a particular purpose rather than just being fashionable or attractive. ❑ *Our clothes are lightweight, fashionable, practical for holidays.* **5** N-COUNT A **practical** is an examination or a lesson in which you make things or do experiments rather than simply writing answers to questions. [mainly BRIT] ❑ *I have never done anything so badly as yesterday's physics practical.*

1 형용사 실용적인 ❑ 매일 식사에서 섬유질의 섭취를 늘릴 수 있는 실용적인 조언을 제공할 수 있습니다. **2** 형용사 현실적인, 분별 있는 [마음에 듦] ❑ 당신은 항상 그렇게 현실적이었지, 마리아. ❑ 그가 방금 그녀에게 그렇게 심한 말을 했는데도 어떻게 그녀는 그렇게 분별 있게 처신할 수 있지? **3** 형용사 실질적인 ❑ 비록 암의 원인이 이제 드러나기 시작했으나, 우리에게는 아직 그것을 막을 실질적인 방도가 없다. **4** 형용사 실용적인 ❑ 저희 옷은 가볍고 유행에 뒤지지 않으며 휴가 때 입을 수 있을 정도로 실용적입니다. **5** 가산명사 실기 시험, 실습 [주로 영국영어] ❑ 내가 여태까지 어제 치른 물리 실기 시험보다 더 못한 것은 없을 거야.

Thesaurus
*practical*의 참조어

ADJ. businesslike, pragmatic, reasonable, sensible, systematic; *(ant.)* impractical **2** **3**

---

prac|ti|cal|ity /prǽktɪkǽlɪti/ (**practicalities**) N-VAR The **practicalities of** a situation are the practical aspects of it, as opposed to its theoretical aspects. ❑ *Decisions about your children should be based on the practicalities of everyday life.*

가산명사 또는 불가산명사 실질적인 측면 ❑ 자녀들에 대한 판단은 일상생활의 실질적인 측면에 근거를 두어야 한다.

prac|ti|cal|ly /prǽktɪkli/ **1** ADV **Practically** means almost, but not completely or exactly. [ADV with group/cl] ❑ *He'd known the old man practically all his life.* **2** ADV You use **practically** to describe something which involves real actions or events rather than ideas or theories. [ADV adj/-ed] ❑ *The course is more practically based than the Masters degree.*

1 부사 사실상 ❑ 그는 그 노인을 사실상 평생 동안 알고 지내 왔었다. **2** 부사 실용적으로, 실천적으로 ❑ 그 과정은 석사 학위보다 더 실용적인 것에 기반을 둔다.

prac|tice /prǽktɪs/ (**practices, practicing, practiced**) [BRIT **practise** for meanings **7**, **8**, **9** and **10**] **1** N-COUNT You can refer to something that people do regularly as a **practice**. ❑ *Some firms have reached agreements to cut workers' pay below the level set in their contract, a practice that is illegal in Germany.* **2** N-VAR **Practice** means doing something regularly in order to be able to do it better. A **practice** is one of these periods of doing something. ❑ *She was taking all three of her daughters to basketball practice every day.* ❑ *...the hard practice necessary to develop from a learner to an accomplished musician.* **3** N-UNCOUNT The work done by doctors and lawyers is referred to as the **practice** of medicine and law. People's religious activities are referred to as the **practice** of a religion. ❑ *...maintaining or improving his skills in the practice of internal medicine.* ❑ *I eventually realized I had to change my attitude toward medical practice.* **4** N-COUNT A doctor's or lawyer's **practice** is his or her business, often shared with other doctors or lawyers. ❑ *The new doctor's practice was miles away from where I lived.* **5** PHRASE What happens **in practice** is what actually happens, in contrast to what is supposed to happen. ❑ *...the difference between foreign policy as presented to the public and foreign policy in actual practice.* **6** PHRASE If you **put** a belief or method **into practice**, you behave or act in accordance with it. ❑ *Now that he is back, the prime minister has another chance to put his new ideas into practice.* **7** V-T/V-I If you **practice** something, you keep doing it regularly in order to be able to do it better. ❑ *She practiced the piano in the grade school basement.* →see also **practiced** **8** V-T When people **practice** something such as a custom, craft, or religion, they take part in the activities associated with it. ❑ *Her parents had yearned to be free to practice their religion.* ❑ *He was brought up in a family which practiced traditional Judaism.* ● **prac|tic|ing** ADJ [ADJ n] ❑ *And he was more or less a practicing Moslem throughout his life.* **9** V-T If something cruel is regularly done to people, you can say that it is **practiced** on them. [usu passive] ❑ *Female circumcision is practiced on 2 million girls a year.* **10** V-T/V-I Someone who **practices** medicine or law works as a doctor or a lawyer. ❑ *He doesn't practice medicine for the money.* ❑ *...the obligations of my license to practice as a lawyer.*

[의미 **7**, **8**, **9**, **10**은 영국영어로 practise] **1** 가산명사 관행 ❑ 일부 회사들은 계약서에 지정된 수준 이하로 근로자의 급여를 삭감하기로 협의했는데 이러한 관행은 독일에서는 불법이다. **2** 가산명사 또는 불가산명사 연습 ❑ 그녀는 딸 셋을 모두 매일 농구 연습을 시키러 데리고 다녔다. ❑ 초보자에서 뛰어난 음악가로 발전하기 위해 필요한 강도 높은 연습 **3** 불가산명사 (의사, 변호사 등의) 업무; (종교) 의식 ❑ 그가 내과 업무를 보기 위한 실력을 유지하거나 향상시키는 것 ❑ 의사 업무에 관한 나의 태도를 바꿔야 한다는 것을 나는 결국 깨달았다. **4** 가산명사 (의사, 변호사 등의) 사업체 ❑ 그 의사가 새로 개업한 곳은 내가 사는 곳으로부터 수마일 떨어진 곳이었다. **5** 구 실제로 ❑ 대중에게 선전되는 대외 정책과 실제로 행해지는 대외 정책 사이의 차이 **6** 구 실천에 옮기다 ❑ 그가 돌아왔으니 수상은 이제 자신의 새로운 생각을 다시 실행할 수 있는 기회를 얻었다. **7** 타동사/자동사 연습하다 ❑ 그녀는 초등학교 지하실에서 피아노를 연습했다. **8** 타동사 실천하다, 관례대로 행하다 ❑ 그녀의 부모는 자신들의 종교 생활을 자유롭게 할 수 있기를 염원했었다. ❑ 그는 전통 유대교를 믿었던 가정에서 성장했다. ● 실천하는 형용사 ❑ 그리고 그는 평생, 정도의 차이는 있었지만, 꾸준히 종교 생활을 한 회교도였다. **9** 타동사 자행하다 ● 음핵 할례가 매년 2백만 명의 여자 아이들에게 자행된다. **10** 타동사/자동사 (의사나 변호사가) 개업 중이다 ❑ 그는 돈 때문에 의사 노릇을 하는 것은 아니다. ❑ 변호사로 활동하기 위한 내 자격증의 의무 조항들

Thesaurus
*practice*의 참조어

N. custom, habit, method, procedure, system, way **1**
exercise, rehearsal, training, workout **2**

Word Partnership
*practice*의 연어

PREP. **after** practice, **during** practice **2**
ADJ. **clinical** practice, **legal** practice, **medical** practice, **private** practice **3**

A

prac|ticed /prǽktɪst/ [BRIT **practised**] ADJ Someone who is **practiced at** doing something is good at it because they have had experience and have developed their skill at it. ❑ *Once you are practiced at this sort of relaxation you will feel quite refreshed afterwards.*

[영국영어 practised] 형용사 숙달된 ❑ 긴장을 푸는 이런 방식에 숙달이 되면, 하고 난 뒤에 기분이 상당히 상쾌해질 것이다.

B

prac|ti|tion|er /prǽktɪʃənər/ (practitioners) N-COUNT Doctors are sometimes referred to as **practitioners** or **medical practitioners**. →see also GP [FORMAL]

가산명사 의사, 개업의 [격식체]

C

prag|mat|ic /prægmǽtɪk/ ADJ A **pragmatic** way of dealing with something is based on practical considerations, rather than theoretical ones. A **pragmatic** person deals with things in a practical way. ❑ *Robin took a pragmatic look at her situation.* ● **prag|mati|cal|ly** /prægmǽtɪkli/ ADV ❑ *"I can't ever see us doing anything else," states Brian pragmatically.*

형용사 실용주의적인 ❑ 로빈은 자신의 처지를 실용주의적인 눈으로 한번 바라봤다. ● 실용주의적으로 부사 ❑ "우리가 다른 것을 하는 것은 상상하기 어려운데."라고 브라이언이 실용주의자처럼 이야기했다.

D

prag|ma|tism /prǽgmətɪzəm/ N-UNCOUNT **Pragmatism** means thinking of or dealing with problems in a practical way, rather than by using theory or abstract principles. [FORMAL] ❑ *She had a reputation for clear thinking and pragmatism.* ● **prag|ma|tist** (pragmatists) N-COUNT ❑ *He is a political pragmatist, not an idealist.*

불가산명사 실용주의 [격식체] ❑ 그녀는 사고가 분명하며 실용주의적이기로 정평이 나 있었다. ● 실용주의자 가산명사 ❑ 그는 이상주의자가 아닌 정치적 실용주의자이다.

E

F

prai|rie /prɛəri/ (prairies) N-VAR A **prairie** is a large area of flat, grassy land in North America. Prairies have very few trees. →see **grassland**

가산명사 또는 불가산명사 대초원

G

praise ♦◇◇ /prɛɪz/ (praises, praising, praised) **1** V-T If you **praise** someone or something, you express approval for their achievements or qualities. ❑ *The American president praised Turkey for its courage.* ❑ *Many others praised Sanford for taking a strong stand.* **2** N-UNCOUNT **Praise** is what you say or write about someone when you are praising them. ❑ *All the ladies are full of praise for the staff and service they received.* ❑ *I have nothing but praise for the police.*

1 타동사 칭찬하다 ❑ 미국 대통령은 터키의 용기를 칭찬했다. ❑ 다른 많은 이들은 샌퍼드가 강한 소신을 보였다고 칭찬했다. **2** 불가산명사 칭찬 ❑ 모든 여성들은 그 직원들과 받은 서비스에 대해 칭찬 일색이다. ❑ 나는 경찰에 대해 칭찬밖에 할 말이 없다.

H

I

Thesaurus	praise의 참조어
N.	applause, compliment, congratulations; (ant.) criticism, insult **2**

J

pram /prǽm/ (prams) N-COUNT A **pram** is a small vehicle in which a baby can lie as it is pushed along. [BRIT; AM usually **baby carriage**]

가산명사 유모차 [영국영어; 미국영어 대개 baby carriage]

K

prank /prǽŋk/ (pranks) N-COUNT A **prank** is a childish trick. [OLD-FASHIONED] ❑ *Their pranks are amusing at times.*

가산명사 장난 [구식어] ❑ 그들의 장난은 때로는 재미있다.

L

prawn /prɔ́n/ (prawns) N-COUNT A **prawn** is a shellfish which is like a shrimp but is larger. [BRIT]

가산명사 왕새우, 대하 [영국영어]

M

pray /prɛɪ/ (prays, praying, prayed) **1** V-T/V-I When people **pray**, they speak to God in order to give thanks or to ask for his help. ❑ *He spent his time in prison praying and studying.* ❑ *Now all we have to do is help ourselves and to pray to God.* **2** V-T/V-I When someone is hoping very much that something will happen, you can say that they **are praying** that it will happen. [usu cont] ❑ *I'm just praying that somebody in Congress will do something before it's too late.* →see **religion**

1 타동사/자동사 기도하다 ❑ 그는 감옥에서 기도하고 공부하며 시간을 보냈다. ❑ 이제 우리가 해야 할 일은 스스로를 도우며 신에게 기도하는 것뿐이다. **2** 타동사/자동사 빌다 ❑ 너무 늦기 전에 의회에서 누군가가 어떻게 해 주기를 빌 뿐이다.

N

prayer /prɛər/ (prayers) **1** N-UNCOUNT **Prayer** is the activity of speaking to God. ❑ *They had joined a religious order and dedicated their lives to prayer and good works.* **2** N-COUNT A **prayer** is the words a person says when they speak to God. ❑ *They should take a little time and say a prayer for the people on both sides.* **3** N-COUNT You can refer to a strong hope that you have as your **prayer**. ❑ *This drug could be the answer to our prayers.* **4** N-PLURAL A short religious service at which people gather to pray can be referred to as **prayers**. ❑ *He promised that the boy would be back at school in time for evening prayers.*

1 불가산명사 기도 ❑ 그들은 한 종교 단체에 가입하여 일생을 기도와 선행에 바쳤다. **2** 가산명사 기도 ❑ 그들은 시간을 조금 내서 양쪽 사람들을 위해 기도를 해야 한다. **3** 가산명사 염원 ❑ 이 약이 우리의 염원에 대한 대답이 될 수도 있다. **4** 복수명사 기도식 ❑ 그는 소년이 저녁 기도 시간에 맞춰 학교에서 돌아오도록 하겠다고 약속했다.

O

P

preach /prítʃ/ (preaches, preaching, preached) **1** V-T/V-I When a member of the clergy **preaches** a sermon, he or she gives a talk on a religious or moral subject during a religious service. ❑ *At High Mass the priest preached a sermon on the devil.* ❑ *The bishop preached to a crowd of several hundred local people.* **2** V-T/V-I When people **preach** a belief or a course of action, they try to persuade other people to accept the belief or to take the course of action. ❑ *The Prime Minister said he was trying to preach peace and tolerance to his people.* ❑ *Health experts are now preaching that even a little exercise is far better than none at all.* **3** V-I If someone gives you advice in a very serious, boring way, you can say that they **are preaching at** you. [DISAPPROVAL] ❑ *"Don't preach at me," he shouted.*

1 타동사/자동사 설교하다 ❑ 대미사 때 신부는 악마에 대한 설교를 했다. ❑ 주교는 지역 주민 수백 명 앞에서 설교를 했다. **2** 타동사/자동사 설파하다 ❑ 수상은 국민에게 평화와 관용을 설파하려고 한다고 말했다. ❑ 보건 전문가들은 이제 운동을 아예 안 하는 것보다는 조금이라도 하는 것이 훨씬 낫다고 설파한다. **3** 자동사 설교하려 들다 [탐탁잖음] ❑ "나한테 설교하려 들지 마."라고 그가 소리쳤다.

Q

R

S

preach|er /prítʃər/ (preachers) N-COUNT A **preacher** is a person, usually a member of the clergy, who preaches sermons as part of a church service.

가산명사 설교자

T

pre|cari|ous /prɪkɛəriəs/ **1** ADJ If your situation is **precarious**, you are not in complete control of events and might fail in what you are doing at any moment. ❑ *Our financial situation had become precarious.* ● **pre|cari|ous|ly** ADV ❑ *We lived precariously. I suppose I wanted to squeeze as much pleasure from each day as I possibly could.* **2** ADJ Something that is **precarious** is not securely held in place and seems likely to fall or collapse at any moment. ❑ *They looked rather comical as they crawled up precarious ladders.* ● **pre|cari|ous|ly** ADV ❑ *One of my grocery bags was still precariously perched on the car bumper.*

1 형용사 위태로운 ❑ 우리의 재정 사정은 위태롭게 된 상태였다. ● 위태롭게 부사 ❑ 우리는 위태롭게 살았다. 아무래도 매일매일 최대한 많은 즐거움을 짜내려고 했던 것 같다. **2** 형용사 불안정한 ❑ 불안정한 사다리를 기어오르는 그들의 모습은 약간 우스꽝스러웠다. ● 불안정하게 부사 ❑ 내가 가져온 식료품 봉투 중 하나가 아직도 차 범퍼 위에 불안정하게 얹혀 있었다.

U

V

W

Word Link	pre ≈ before : precaution, precede, predict

X

pre|cau|tion /prɪkɔ́ʃn/ (precautions) N-COUNT A **precaution** is an action that is intended to prevent something dangerous or unpleasant from happening. ❑ *Could he not, just as a precaution, move to a place of safety?*

가산명사 예방 조치 ❑ 그냥 예방 조치 차원에서 그가 안전한 곳으로 이사를 가면 안 될까?

Y

pre|cede /prɪsíd/ (precedes, preceding, preceded) **1** V-T/V-I If one event or period of time **precedes** another, it happens before it. [FORMAL] ❑ *Intensive negotiations between the main parties preceded the vote.* ❑ *The earthquake was preceded by a loud roar and lasted 20 seconds.* **2** V-T If you **precede** someone somewhere, you go in front of them. [FORMAL] ❑ *He gestured to Alice to precede them from the room.*

1 타동사/자동사 선행하다 [격식체] ❑ 투표에 앞서 주요 양당 간에 치열한 협상이 있었다. ❑ 지진 발발 직전에 크게 흔들리는 소리가 났으며 지진은 약 20초간 계속되었다. **2** 타동사 앞서다 [격식체] ❑ 그는 앨리스에게 먼저 방을 앞서 나가라고 손짓했다.

Z

3 V-T/V-I A sentence, paragraph, or chapter that **precedes** another one comes just before it. ❑ *Look at the information that precedes the paragraph in question.*

타동사/자동사 바로 앞에 나오다 ❑ 문제되는 단락 바로 앞에 나오는 정보를 한번 보세요.

prec|edence /prɛsɪdəns/ N-UNCOUNT If one thing takes **precedence over** another, it is regarded as more important than the other thing. ❑ *Have as much fun as possible at college, but don't let it take precedence over work.*

불가산명사 우선순위 ❑ 대학에서 최대한 재미를 봐도 되지만 학업보다 그것에 우선순위를 두지는 마세요.

prec|edent /prɛsɪdənt/ (**precedents**) N-VAR If there is a **precedent for** an action or event, it has happened before, and this can be regarded as an argument for doing it again. [FORMAL] ❑ *The trial could set an important precedent for dealing with large numbers of similar cases.*

가산명사 또는 불가산명사 선례 [격식체] ❑ 그 재판은 많은 비슷한 사건을 다루는 데 있어 중요한 선례가 될 수도 있다.

pre|cept /prisɛpt/ (**precepts**) N-COUNT A **precept** is a general rule that helps you to decide how you should behave in particular circumstances. [FORMAL] ❑ *...an electoral process based on the central precept that all men are born equal regardless of race or color.*

가산명사 교훈, 계율 [격식체] ❑ 모든 사람은 인종이나 피부색에 상관없이 평등하게 태어났다는 중심 계율에 기반을 둔 선거 절차

pre|cinct /prisɪŋkt/ (**precincts**) **1** N-COUNT A **precinct** is a part of a city or town which has its own police force. [AM] ❑ *The shooting occurred in the 34th Precinct.* **2** N-COUNT A shopping **precinct** is an area in the center of a city or town in which cars are not allowed. [BRIT] ❑ *The center was a pedestrian precinct with a bandstand in the middle.*

1 가산명사 경찰 자치 구역 [미국영어] ❑ 총격은 34번 경찰 자치 구역에서 발생했다. **2** 가산명사 차 없는 거리 [영국영어] ❑ 센터는 중앙에 야외 음악당이 설치된 보행자 전용 구역이었다.

pre|cious /prɛʃəs/ **1** ADJ If you say that something such as a resource is **precious**, you mean that it is valuable and should not be wasted or used badly. ❑ *After four months in foreign parts, every hour at home was precious.* ❑ *A family break allows you to spend precious time together.* **2** ADJ **Precious** objects and materials are worth a lot of money because they are rare. ❑ *...jewellery and precious objects belonging to her mother.* **3** ADJ If something is **precious** to you, you regard it as important and do not want to lose it. ❑ *Her family's support is particularly precious to Josie.*

1 형용사 소중한 ❑ 외국에서 4개월을 보낸 터라 집에서 보내는 모든 시간이 소중했다. ❑ 가족 휴가는 소중한 시간을 같이 보낼 수 있게 해 준다. **2** 형용사 귀중한 ❑ 그녀 어머니 소유의 보석과 귀중품들 **3** 형용사 소중한 ❑ 조시에게는 가족의 원조가 특히 중요하다.

pre|cipi|tate (**precipitates, precipitating, precipitated**)

> The verb is pronounced /prɪsɪpɪteɪt/. The adjective is pronounced /prɪsɪpɪtɪt/.

동사는 /prɪsɪpəteɪt /으로 발음되고, 형용사는 /prɪsɪpɪtɪt /으로 발음된다.

1 V-T If something **precipitates** an event or situation, usually a bad one, it causes it to happen suddenly or sooner than normal. [FORMAL] ❑ *The killings in Vilnius have precipitated the worst crisis yet.* **2** ADJ A **precipitate** action or decision happens or is made more quickly or suddenly than most people think is sensible. [FORMAL] ❑ *I don't think we should make precipitate decisions.*

1 타동사 촉발시키다 [격식체] ❑ 빌니우스에서의 살해 사건들이 지금까지 있었던 위기 중 최악의 위기를 촉발시켰다. **2** 형용사 성급한 [격식체] ❑ 성급한 판단을 하면 안 될 것 같아.

pré|cis /preɪsi, BRIT preɪsi/

> The form **précis** is both the singular and the plural form. It is pronounced /preɪsiz/ when it is the plural.

précis는 단수형 및 복수형이다. 복수일 경우에는 /preɪsiz /로 발음된다.

N-COUNT A **précis** is a short written or spoken account of something, which gives the important points but not the details. [FORMAL] [oft N of n] ❑ *A nine-page précis of the manuscript was sent to the Australian magazine New Idea.*

가산명사 요약본 [격식체] ❑ 9페이지짜리 요약본이 뉴아이디어라는 호주 잡지사에 보냈다.

pre|cise /prisaɪs/ **1** ADJ You use **precise** to emphasize that you are referring to an exact thing, rather than something vague. [EMPHASIS] [ADJ n] ❑ *I can remember the precise moment when my daughter came to see me and her new baby brother in hospital.* ❑ *The precise location of the wreck was discovered in 1988.* **2** ADJ Something that is **precise** is exact and accurate in all its details. ❑ *They speak very precise English.*

1 형용사 정확한 [강조] ❑ 내 딸이 나와 새로 태어난 남동생을 보기 위해 병원에 온 정확한 순간을 기억할 수 있다. ❑ 잔해의 정확한 위치는 1988년에 발견되었다. **2** 형용사 정확한 ❑ 그들은 매우 정확한 영어를 구사한다.

pre|cise|ly ◆◇◇ /prisaɪsli/ **1** ADV **Precisely** means accurately and exactly. ❑ *Nobody knows precisely how many people are still living in the camp.* ❑ *The first bell rang at precisely 10:29 a.m.* **2** ADV You can use **precisely** to emphasize that a reason or fact is the only important one there is, or that it is obvious. [EMPHASIS] [ADV with cl/group] ❑ *Children come to zoos precisely to see captive animals.* **3** ADV You can say "**precisely**" to confirm in an emphatic way that what someone has just said is true. [EMPHASIS] [as reply] ❑ *"So, you're trying to put trained, responsible people in every place where you think they might be able to help?"* — *"Precisely."*

1 부사 정확히 ❑ 정확히 얼마나 많은 사람들이 아직도 그 캠프에 살고 있는지는 아무도 모른다. ❑ 첫 번째 벨은 정확히 오전 10시 29분에 울렸다. **2** 부사 바로 [강조] ❑ 아이들은 바로 우리에 갇힌 동물들을 보기 위해 동물원에 온다. **3** 부사 바로 그것이다 [강조] ❑ "그러니 숙련되고 책임감 있는 사람들을 도움이 될 만한 모든 곳에 두자는 것이 자네의 의도인가?" "바로 그거야."

pre|ci|sion /prisɪʒⁿn/ N-UNCOUNT If you do something **with precision**, you do it exactly as it should be done. ❑ *The choir sang with precision.*

불가산명사 정확성 ❑ 합창단은 정확하게 노래를 불렀다.

pre|clude /priklud/ (**precludes, precluding, precluded**) **1** V-T If something **precludes** an event or action, it prevents the event or action from happening. [FORMAL] ❑ *At 84, John feels his age precludes too much travel.* **2** V-T If something **precludes** you **from** doing something or going somewhere, it prevents you from doing it or going there. [FORMAL] ❑ *A constitutional amendment precludes any president from serving more than two terms.*

1 타동사 방지하다 [격식체] ❑ 84세인 존은 나이 때문에 너무 많은 여행을 못한다고 생각한다. **2** 타동사 막다, 방지하다 [격식체] ❑ 헌법 개정안은 어떤 대통령도 세 번 이상은 연임하지 못하도록 하고 있다.

pre|co|cious /prikoʊʃəs/ ADJ A **precocious** child is very clever, mature, or good at something, often in a way that you usually only expect to find in an adult. ❑ *Margaret was always a precocious child.* ❑ *She burst on to the world tennis scene as a precocious 14-year old.*

형용사 조숙한 ❑ 마거릿은 항상 조숙한 아이였어. ❑ 그녀는 조숙한 14세 소녀로서 세계 테니스 무대에 뛰어들었다.

pre|con|cep|tion /prikənsɛpⁿn/ (**preconceptions**) N-COUNT Your **preconceptions** about something are beliefs formed about it before you have enough information or experience. ❑ *Did you have any preconceptions about the sort of people who did computing?*

가산명사 선입견 ❑ 컴퓨터를 하는 사람들에 대한 어떠한 선입견이라도 가지고 있었나요?

pre|con|di|tion /prikəndɪʃⁿn/ (**preconditions**) N-COUNT If one thing is a **precondition for** another, it must happen or be done before the second thing can happen or exist. [FORMAL] ❑ *They have been demanding the release of three of their colleagues from prison as a precondition for further negotiation.*

가산명사 전제 조건 [격식체] ❑ 그들은 추가 협상에 대한 전제 조건으로 동료 세 명을 감옥에서 석방하라고 요구하고 있다.

pre|cur|sor /prikɜrsər/ (**precursors**) N-COUNT A **precursor** of something is a similar thing that happened or existed before it, often something which led to the existence or development of that thing. ❑ *He said that the deal should not be seen as a precursor to a merger.*

가산명사 선구자, 사전 단계 ❑ 그는 그 계약을 합병에 대한 사전 단계로 인식하지 말라고 했다.

A

preda|tor /prɛdətər/ (**predators**) ■ N-COUNT A **predator** is an animal that kills and eats other animals. ❑ *With no natural predators on the island, the herd increased rapidly.* ■ N-COUNT People sometimes refer to predatory people or organizations as **predators**. ❑ *Rumors of a takeover by Hanson are probably far-fetched, but the company is worried about other predators.* →see **food, shark**

B

preda|tory /prɛdətɔːri, BRIT prɛdətri/ ■ ADJ **Predatory** animals live by killing other animals for food. ❑ *...predatory birds like the eagle.* ■ ADJ **Predatory** people or organizations are eager to gain something out of someone else's weakness or suffering. ❑ *People will not set up new businesses while they are frightened by the predatory behavior of the banks.*

C

pre|de|ces|sor /prɛdɪsɛsər, BRIT priːdɪsesəʳ/ (**predecessors**) ■ N-COUNT Your **predecessor** is the person who had your job before you. ❑ *He maintained that he learned everything he knew from his predecessor Kenneth Sisam.* ■ N-COUNT The **predecessor** of an object or machine is the object or machine that came before it in a sequence or process of development. ❑ *Although the car is some 40mm shorter than its predecessor, its boot is 20 per cent larger.*

D

E

pre|dica|ment /prɪdɪkəmənt/ (**predicaments**) N-COUNT If you are in a **predicament**, you are in an unpleasant situation that is difficult to get out of. ❑ *Hank explained our predicament.*

F

| Word Link | *dict ≈ speaking : contradict, dictate, predict* |

G

| Word Link | *pre ≈ before : precaution, precede, predict* |

H

pre|dict ◆◇◇ /prɪdɪkt/ (**predicts, predicting, predicted**) V-T If you **predict** an event, you say that it will happen. ❑ *The latest opinion polls are predicting a very close contest.* ❑ *He predicted that my hair would grow back "in no time."* →see **forecast**

I

pre|dict|able /prɪdɪktəbˀl/ ADJ If you say that an event is **predictable**, you mean that it is obvious in advance that it will happen. ❑ *This was a predictable reaction, given the bitter hostility between the two countries.* ● **pre|dict|ably** ADV ❑ *His article is, predictably, a scathing attack on capitalism.* ● **pre|dict|abil|ity** /prɪdɪktəbɪlɪti/ N-UNCOUNT ❑ *Your mother values the predictability of your Sunday calls.*

J

K

pre|dic|tion /prɪdɪkʃˀn/ (**predictions**) N-VAR If you make a **prediction** about something, you say what you think will happen. ❑ *He was unwilling to make a prediction for the coming year: "It's hard to tell which of our books are going to sell."* ❑ *Predictions that the recession will be short are small comfort to those already affected.* →see **science**

L

M

pre|dis|pose /prɪdɪspoʊz/ (**predisposes, predisposing, predisposed**) ■ V-T If something **predisposes** you to behave in a particular way, it makes it likely that you will think or behave in that way. [FORMAL] ❑ *They take pains to hire people whose personalities predispose them to serve customers well.* ● **pre|dis|posed** ADJ [v-link ADJ, usu ADJ to-inf, ADJ to n] ❑ *...people who are predisposed to violent crime.* ■ V-T If something **predisposes** you to a disease or illness, it makes it likely that you will suffer from that disease or illness. [FORMAL] ❑ *...a gene that predisposes people to alcoholism.* ● **pre|dis|posed** ADJ [v-link ADJ, usu ADJ to n] ❑ *Some people are genetically predisposed to diabetes.*

N

O

P

pre|dis|po|si|tion /prɪdɪspəzɪʃˀn/ (**predispositions**) ■ N-COUNT If you have a **predisposition to** behave in a particular way, you tend to behave like that because of the kind of person that you are or the attitudes that you have. [FORMAL] ❑ *There is a thin dividing line between educating the public and creating a predisposition to panic.* ■ N-COUNT If you have a **predisposition to** a disease or illness, it is likely that you will suffer from that disease or illness. [FORMAL] ❑ *...a genetic predisposition to lung cancer.*

Q

R

| Word Link | *dom, domin ≈ rule, master : dominate, domain, predominant* |

S

pre|domi|nant /prɪdɒmɪnənt/ ADJ If something is **predominant**, it is more important or noticeable than anything else in a set of people or things. ❑ *Amanda's predominant emotion was that of confusion.*

T

pre|domi|nant|ly /prɪdɒmɪnɪtli/ ADV You use **predominantly** to indicate which feature or quality is most noticeable in a situation. ❑ *The landscape has remained predominantly rural in appearance.*

U

pre|domi|nate /prɪdɒmɪneɪt/ (**predominates, predominating, predominated**) ■ V-I If one type of person or thing **predominates** in a group, there is more of that type of person or thing in the group than of any other. ❑ *In older age groups women predominate because men tend to die younger.* ■ V-I When a feature or quality **predominates**, it is the most important or noticeable one in a situation. [FORMAL] ❑ *He wants to create a society where Islamic principles predominate.*

V

W

pre|emi|nent /priːɛmɪnənt/ [BRIT, sometimes AM **pre-eminent**] ADJ If someone or something is **preeminent** in a group, they are more important, powerful, or capable than other people or things in the group. [FORMAL] ❑ *...some of the preeminent names in baseball.* ● **pre|emi|nence** /priːɛmɪnəns/ N-UNCOUNT ❑ *Europe was poised to reassert its traditional preeminence in Western art.*

X

Y

pre|empt /priːɛmpt/ (**preempts, preempting, preempted**) [BRIT, sometimes AM **pre-empt**] V-T If you **preempt** an action, you prevent it from happening by doing something which makes it unnecessary or impossible. ❑ *The law would preempt stronger local rules.* ❑ *"The survival of the fittest," a slogan that virtually preempted all debate.*

Z

가산명사 포식자, 육식 동물 ❑ 섬에 천연 포식자가 없는 상태에서 그 무리는 급격히 수가 늘어났다. ② 가산명사 약탈자 ❑ 한슨의 경영권 인수에 대한 소문은 근거 없는 것일 가능성이 높으나 회사는 다른 기업 사냥꾼들을 우려하고 있다.

■ 형용사 포식하는, 육식의 ❑ 독수리와 같은 맹금 ② 형용사 약탈하는 ❑ 은행들의 약탈적인 행태를 두려워하는 한 사람들은 새로운 사업을 시작하려고 하지 않을 것이다.

■ 가산명사 전임자 ❑ 그는 자신이 아는 모든 것을 선임자인 케네스 시삼으로부터 배웠다고 주장했다. ② 가산명사 이전 모델 ❑ 비록 그 차가 이전 모델보다 약 40밀리미터 짧지만 트렁크는 20퍼센트 더 크다.

가산명사 곤경 ② 행크가 우리의 곤경을 설명했다.

타동사 예측하다 ❑ 최근의 여론 조사는 박빙의 대결을 예측하고 있다. ❑ 그는 내 머리가 아주 빨리 다시 자라날 것이라고 예측했다.

형용사 예상할 수 있는 ❑ 두 나라 사이의 강한 적대감을 생각하면 이는 예상할 수 있는 반응이다. ● 예상되는 대로 부사 ❑ 예상되는 대로 그의 글은 자본주의에 대한 통렬한 비판이다. ● 예측 가능성 불가산명사 ❑ 네 어머니는 예상대로 네가 일요일에 방문하는 것을 소중하게 여기신다.

가산명사 또는 불가산명사 예측 ❑ 그는 다음 해에 대해 예측하기를 꺼려했다. 즉 "내년에 우리의 책 중 어떤 것이 잘 팔릴지는 알 수 없습니다." ❑ 불황이 짧으리라는 예상은 이미 타격을 받은 사람들에게는 별로 큰 위안이 못 된다.

■ 타동사 -할 소지를 심어 주다, -하는 경향을 갖게 하다 [격식체] ❑ 그들은 성격상 고객을 잘 대할 것 같은 사람들을 고용하기 위해 애를 쓴다. ● -하는 성향이 있는 형용사 ❑ 폭력 범죄를 저지를 성향이 강한 사람들 ② 타동사 (질병의) 소인이 되다 [격식체] ❑ 알코올 중독 소인이 되는 유전자 ● 소인이 있는 형용사 ❑ 어떤 사람들은 유전적으로 당뇨병 소인을 갖고 태어난다.

■ 가산명사 성향 [격식체] ❑ 대중을 교육하는 것과 공황 상태의 성향을 유발하는 것은 종이 한 장 차이다. ② 가산명사 소인(素人) [격식체] ❑ 폐암의 유전적 소인

형용사 우세한, 주된 ❑ 아만다의 주된 감정 상태는 혼란스러움이었다.

부사 우세하게, 주로 ❑ 그 풍경은 외관상으로는 전원적인 모습이 여전히 우세하다.

■ 자동사 우세하다 [격식체] ❑ 보다 고연령의 집단에서는 남성들이 더 빨리 죽는 경향이 있기 때문에 여성들이 우세하다 ② 자동사 우위를 점하다 [격식체] ❑ 그는 회교도 원리가 우위를 점하는 사회를 만들고 싶어 한다.

[영국영어, 미국영어 가끔 pre-eminent] 형용사 출중한 [격식체] ❑ 야구계의 출중한 인물들 중 몇 명 ● 출중함 불가산명사 ❑ 유럽은 서구 미술의 전통적으로 자랑했던 출중함을 다시 쟁취할 준비가 되어 있었다.

[영국영어, 미국영어 가끔 pre-empt] 타동사 선제하다, 사전에 차단하다 ❑ 그 법은 보다 강력한 지방법을 선제할 것이다. ❑ '적자생존의 법칙,' 모든 토론을 사실상 사전에 차단하는 문구

pre|emp|tive /priˈɛmptɪv/ [BRIT, sometimes AM **pre-emptive**] ADJ A preemptive attack or strike is intended to weaken or damage an enemy or opponent, for example by destroying their weapons before they can do any harm. ❑ *A preemptive strike against a sovereign nation raises moral and legal issues.*

pref|ace /ˈprɛfɪs/ (**prefaces, prefacing, prefaced**) ■ N-COUNT A **preface** is an introduction at the beginning of a book, which explains what the book is about or why it was written. ❑ *...the preface to Kelman's novel.* ◻ V-T If you **preface** an action or speech **with** something else, you do or say this other thing first. ❑ *I will preface what I am going to say with a few lines from Shakespeare.*

pre|fer ♦♢◇ /prɪˈfɜr/ (**prefers, preferring, preferred**) V-T If you **prefer** someone or something, you like that person or thing better than another, and so you are more likely to choose them if there is a choice. [no cont] ❑ *Does he prefer a particular sort of music?* ❑ *I became a teacher because I preferred books and people to politics.* ❑ *I prefer to think of peace not war.* ❑ *I would prefer him to be with us next season.*

> Note that **prefer** can often sound rather formal in ordinary conversation. Verbal expressions such as **like...better** and **would rather** are used more frequently. For example, instead of saying "I prefer football to tennis," you can say "**I like football better than tennis,**" instead of "I'd prefer an apple," you can say "**I'd rather have an apple,**" and instead of "I'd prefer to walk," you can say "**I'd rather walk.**"

pref|er|able /ˈprɛfrəbªl/ ADJ If you say that one thing is **preferable to** another, you mean that it is more desirable or suitable. ❑ *A big earthquake a long way off is preferable to a smaller one nearby.* ❑ *The hazards of the theater seemed preferable to joining the family paint business.* ● **pref|er|ably** /ˈprɛfrəbli/ ADV ❑ *Do something creative or take exercise, preferably in the fresh air.*

pref|er|ence /ˈprɛfərəns/ (**preferences**) ■ N-VAR If you have a **preference for** something, you would like to have or do that thing rather than something else. ❑ *The Bill will allow parents the right to express a preference for the school their child attends.* ◻ N-UNCOUNT If you **give preference** to someone with a particular qualification or feature, you choose them rather than someone else. ❑ *The Pentagon has said it will give preference to companies with which it can do business electronically.*

pref|er|ence shares N-PLURAL **Preference shares** are the same as **preferred stock.** →see also **ordinary shares** [BRIT, BUSINESS]

pref|er|en|tial /ˌprɛfəˈrɛnʃ°l/ ADJ If you get **preferential** treatment, you are treated better than other people and therefore have an advantage over them. ❑ *Despite her status, the Duchess will not be given preferential treatment.*

pre|ferred stock N-UNCOUNT **Preferred stock** is the shares in a company that are owned by people who have the right to receive part of the company's profits before the holders of common stock. They also have the right to have their capital repaid if the company fails and has to close. Compare **common stock.** →see also **common stock** [AM, BUSINESS; BRIT **preference shares**]

Word Link
fix ≈ fastening : fixture, prefix, suffix

pre|fix /ˈprifɪks/ (**prefixes**) ■ N-COUNT A **prefix** is a letter or group of letters, for example "un-" or "multi-," which is added to the beginning of a word in order to form a different word. For example, the prefix "un-" is added to "happy" to form "unhappy." Compare **affix** and **suffix.** ◻ N-COUNT A **prefix** is one or more numbers or letters added to the beginning of a code number to indicate, for example, what area something belongs to. ❑ *To telephone from the U.S. use the prefix 011 33 before the numbers given here.*

preg|nan|cy ♦♢◇ /ˈprɛgnənsi/ (**pregnancies**) N-VAR **Pregnancy** is the condition of being pregnant or the period of time during which a female is pregnant. ❑ *It would be wiser to cut out all alcohol during pregnancy.*

preg|nant ♦♢◇ /ˈprɛgnənt/ ■ ADJ If a woman or female animal is **pregnant,** she has a baby or babies developing in her body. ❑ *Lena got pregnant and married.* ◻ ADJ A **pregnant** silence or moment has a special meaning which is not obvious but which people are aware of. [ADJ n, v-link ADJ with n] ❑ *There was a long, pregnant silence, which Mrs. Madrigal punctuated by reaching for the check.*

Word Partnership
pregnant의 연어

N.	pregnant **with a baby/child,** pregnant **mother,** pregnant **wife,** pregnant **woman** ■
v.	be pregnant, become pregnant, get pregnant ■

pre|heat /priˈhit/ (**preheats, preheating, preheated**) V-T If you **preheat** an oven, you switch it on and allow it to reach a certain temperature before you put food inside it. ❑ *Preheat the oven to 400 degrees.*

pre|his|tor|ic /ˌprihɪˈstɔrɪk, BRIT priːhɪsˈtɒrɪk/ ADJ **Prehistoric** people and things existed at a time before information was written down. ❑ *...the famous prehistoric cave paintings of Lascaux.*

preju|dice /ˈprɛdʒədɪs/ (**prejudices, prejudicing, prejudiced**) ■ N-VAR **Prejudice** is an unreasonable dislike of a particular group of people or things, or a preference for one group of people or things over another. ❑ *There was a deep-rooted racial prejudice long before the two countries became rivals and went to war.* ❑ *There is widespread prejudice against workers over 45.* ◻ V-T If you **prejudice** someone or something, you influence them so that they are unfair in some way. ❑ *I think your South American youth has prejudiced you.* ❑ *The report was held back for fear of prejudicing his trial.* ◼ V-T If someone **prejudices** another person's

---

[영국영어, 미국영어 가끔 pre-emptive] 형용사 선제하는 ❑ 주권 국가에 대한 선제공격은 도덕적 그리고 법적 문제를 야기한다.

■ 가산명사 서문 ❑ 켈만 소설의 서문 ◻ 타동사 서두를 시작하다 ❑ 셰익스피어 작품에 나오는 구절을 몇 개 인용하는 것으로 제가 드릴 말씀을 시작하겠습니다.

타동사 선호하다, 더 좋아하다 ❑ 그는 특정 종류의 음악을 선호하는가? ❑ 나는 정치보다 책과 사람을 더 좋아하기 때문에 교사가 되었다. ❑ 나는 전쟁보다는 평화에 대해 생각하는 게 더 좋다. ❑ 나는 그가 다음 시즌에 우리와 함께 했으면 좋겠다.

> prefer는 일상 대화에서는 흔히 약간 격식적으로 들릴 수 있음을 유의하라. like...better와 would rather와 같은 표현이 더 자주 쓰인다. 예를 들면, "I prefer football to tennis." 대신에 "I like football better than tennis."라고 하고, "I'd prefer an apple." 대신에 "I'd rather have an apple."이라고 하며, "I'd prefer to walk." 대신에 "I'd rather walk."라고 한다.

형용사 더 나은 ❑ 근처의 작은 지진보다 멀리서 일어나는 큰 지진이 더 낫다. ❑ 연극계의 험난함이 가족의 페인트 사업에 동참하는 것보다 나아 보였다. ● 부사로는, 가급적 ❑ 창조적인 일을 하거나 운동을 하세요. 가급적 공기가 신선한 곳에서.

■ 가산명사 또는 불가산명사 선호 ❑ 그 법안은 부모에게 자녀가 다닐 학교에 대한 선호도를 표명할 수 있는 권리를 허용할 것이다. ◻ 불가산명사 우선권을 주다, 선취권을 주다 ❑ 전자 상거래를 할 수 있는 회사들에게 선취권을 주겠다고 국방성은 밝혔다.

복수명사 우선주 [영국영어, 경제]

형용사 우대받는, 특혜의 ❑ 신분에도 불구하고 공작 부인에게 특혜를 주지 않을 것이다.

불가산명사 우선주 [미국영어, 경제; 영국영어 preference shares]

■ 가산명사 접두사 ◻ 가산명사 부가 번호, 부가 약호 ❑ 미국에서 전화하려면 아래 번호 앞에 부가 번호 011 33을 붙이세요.

가산명사 또는 불가산명사 임신 ❑ 임신 기간 중에는 완전히 금주하는 것이 보다 현명할 것이다.

■ 형용사 임신한 ❑ 레나는 임신하고 결혼을 했다. ◻ 형용사 의미심장한 ❑ 길고 의미심장한 침묵을 마드리갈 부인이 계산서를 향해 팔을 내뻗으면서 깼다.

타동사 예열하다 ❑ 오븐을 400도로 예열하세요.

형용사 선사 시대의 ❑ 유명한 라스코의 선사 시대 동굴 벽화

■ 가산명사 또는 불가산명사 편견, 선입관 ❑ 두 나라가 적이 되고 전쟁을 벌이기 오래전부터 뿌리 깊은 인종적 편견이 있었다. ❑ 45세 이상의 근로자에 대해 선입관이 널리 퍼져 있다. ◻ 타동사 편견을 가지게 하다 ❑ 네가 남아메리카에서 보낸 젊은 시절이 네게 편견을 심은 것 같다. ❑ 그의 재판에 대해 편견을 초래할까 봐 보고서는 발표되지 않았다. ◼ 타동사 악영향을 끼치다 [격식체] ❑ 그녀의 연구에는 대학의

situation, they do something which makes it worse than it should be. [FORMAL] ❑ *Her study was not in any way intended to prejudice the future development of the college.*

향후 발전에 어떤 식으로도 악영향을 끼치겠다는 의도가 없었다.

| **Thesaurus** | *prejudice*의 참조어 |

N. bias, bigotry, disapproval, intolerance; (ant.) tolerance ◼

---

preju|diced /prɛdʒədɪst/ ADJ A person who is **prejudiced** against someone has an unreasonable dislike of them. A person who is **prejudiced** in favor of someone has an unreasonable preference for them. ❑ *Some landlords and landladies are racially prejudiced.*

형용사 편견을 가진 ❑ 일부 집주인들은 인종적인 편견을 가지고 있다.

pre|lim|i|nary /prɪlɪmɪnɛri, BRIT prɪlɪmɪnri/ (preliminaries) ◼ ADJ **Preliminary** activities or discussions take place at the beginning of an event, often as a form of preparation. ❑ *Preliminary results show the Republican party with 11 percent of the vote.* ◢ N-COUNT A **preliminary** is something that you do at the beginning of an activity, often as a form of preparation. ❑ *You all know why I am here. So I won't waste time on preliminaries.*

◼ 형용사 사전의, 예비의 ❑ 예비 선거 결과에 의하면 공화당이 전체 표의 11퍼센트를 차지하고 있다. ◢ 가산명사 예비 행위, 사전 준비 ❑ 제가 여기 와 있는 이유는 모두 아시겠죠. 그러니 서두는 짧게 하겠습니다.

prel|ude /prɛljud, preɪlud, BRIT prɛlyu:d/ (preludes) N-COUNT You can describe an event as a **prelude to** a more important event when it happens before it and acts as an introduction to it. ❑ *Most unions see privatization as an inevitable prelude to job losses.*

가산명사 전주곡 ❑ 많은 노조가 민영화를 일자리 감축의 피할 수 없는 전주곡이라고 여긴다.

pre|ma|ture /primətʃʊər, BRIT prɛmətʃʊər/ ◼ ADJ Something that is **premature** happens earlier than usual or earlier than people expect. ❑ *Accidents are still the number one cause of premature death for Americans.* ❑ *His career was brought to a premature end by a succession of knee injuries.* ● **pre|ma|ture|ly** ADV ❑ *The war and the years in the harsh mountains had prematurely aged him.* ◢ ADJ You can say that something is **premature** when it happens too early and is therefore inappropriate. ❑ *It now seems their optimism was premature.* ● **pre|ma|ture|ly** ADV ❑ *Holmgren is careful not to celebrate prematurely.* ◣ ADJ A **premature** baby is one that was born before the date when it was expected to be born. ❑ *Even very young premature babies respond to their mother's presence.* ● **pre|ma|ture|ly** ADV [ADV after v] ❑ *Danny was born prematurely, weighing only 3lb 3oz.*

◼ 형용사 때 이른, 조기의 ❑ 미국인들에겐 사고가 여전히 조기 사망의 가장 큰 원인이다. ❑ 그의 선수 생활은 연속된 무릎 부상으로 너무 일찍 좌절되었다. ● 때 이르게, 조기에 부사 ❑ 전쟁과 험한 산속 생활로 인하여 그는 조로해 있었다. ◢ 형용사 때 이른, 시기상조의 ❑ 지금 보면 그들의 낙관은 시기상조였다. ● 시기상조의 부사 ❑ 홈그렌은 지나치게 빨리 축배를 들지 않도록 조심하고 있다. ◣ 형용사 조산한 ❑ 매우 빨리 조산한 아기들조차 엄마가 있나 없나에 반응을 보인다. ● 조산하여 부사 ❑ 대니는 조산아로 태어났는데 체중이 3파운드 3온스로

prem|ier ♦◇◇ /prɪmiər, BRIT prɛmiər/ (premiers) ◼ N-COUNT The leader of the government of a country is sometimes referred to as the country's **premier**. ❑ *...Australian premier Paul Keating.* ◢ ADJ **Premier** is used to describe something that is considered to be the best or most important thing of a particular type. [ADJ n] ❑ *...the country's premier opera company.*

◼ 가산명사 수상 ❑ 호주 수상 폴 키팅 ◢ 형용사 최고의 ❑ 국내 최고의 오페라 극단

prem|iere /prɪmiər, prɪmyɛər, BRIT prɛmiɛər/ (premieres, premiering, premiered) ◼ N-COUNT The **premiere** of a new play or movie is the first public performance of it. ❑ *Four astronauts visited for last week's premiere of the movie Space Station.* ◢ V-T/V-I When a movie or show **premieres** or **is premiered**, it is shown to an audience for the first time. ❑ *The documentary premiered at the Jerusalem Film Festival.*

◼ 가산명사 개봉 시사회, 초연 ❑ 네 명의 우주 조종사가 지난주 스페이스 스테이션이라는 영화의 개봉 시사회에 참석했다. ◢ 타동사/자동사 개봉되다, 초연되다 ❑ 그 다큐멘터리는 예루살렘 영화제에서 최초 개봉되었다.

prem|ier|ship /prɪmiərʃɪp, BRIT prɛmiəʃɪp/ N-SING The **premiership** of a leader of a government is the period of time during which they are the leader. ❑ *...the final years of Margaret Thatcher's premiership.*

단수명사 수상 임기 ❑ 마거릿 대처 수상의 임기 말년

prem|ise /prɛmɪs/ (premises)

The spelling **premiss** is also used in British English for meaning ◢.

철자 premiss도 영국영어에서 ◢ 의미로 쓴다.

◼ N-PLURAL The **premises** of a business or an institution are all the buildings and land that it occupies in one place. ❑ *There is a kitchen on the premises.* ◢ N-COUNT A **premise** is something that you suppose is true and that you use as a basis for developing an idea. [FORMAL] ❑ *The premise is that schools will work harder to improve if they must compete.*

◼ 복수명사 구내 ❑ 구내에 부엌이 있다. ◢ 가산명사 기본 전제 [격식체] ❑ 경쟁을 해야 한다면 학교들이 발전을 하기 위해 보다 노력할 것이라는 것이 기본 전제이다.

pre|mi|um ♦◇◇ /primiəm/ (premiums) ◼ N-COUNT A **premium** is a sum of money that you pay regularly to an insurance company for an insurance policy. ❑ *It is too early to say whether insurance premiums will be affected.* ◢ N-COUNT A **premium** is a sum of money that you have to pay for something in addition to the normal cost. ❑ *Even if customers want "solutions," most are not willing to pay a premium for them.* ◣ ADJ **Premium** goods are of a higher than usual quality and are often expensive. [ADJ n] ❑ *At the premium end of the market, business is booming.* ◤ PHRASE If something is **at a premium**, it is wanted or needed, but is difficult to get or achieve. ❑ *If space is at a premium, choose adaptable furniture that won't fill the room.* ◥ PHRASE If you buy or sell something **at a premium**, you buy or sell it at a higher price than usual, for example because it is in short supply. ❑ *He eventually sold the shares back to the bank at a premium.*

◼ 가산명사 보험료 ❑ 보험료가 영향을 받을지를 이야기하기에는 시기가 너무 이르다. ◢ 가산명사 할증료 ❑ 고객들이 '해결책'을 원하더라도 대부분은 그에 대한 할증료를 낼 의사가 없다. ◣ 형용사 고급의 ❑ 시장의 다른 한쪽 끝 고급품 시장에서는 사업이 호황이다. ◤ 구 귀한, 품귀의 ❑ 만약 공간이 부족하다면 방을 채우지 않고 배치할 수 있는 가구를 고르세요. ◥ 구 프리미엄을 붙여 ❑ 그는 결국 주식을 은행에 프리미엄을 붙여 되팔았다.

premo|ni|tion /primənɪʃⁿn, BRIT prɛmənɪʃⁿn/ (premonitions) N-COUNT If you have a **premonition**, you have a feeling that something is going to happen, often something unpleasant. ❑ *He had an unshakable premonition that he would die.*

가산명사 (불길한) 예감 ❑ 그는 자신이 죽을 것이라는 예감을 떨칠 수가 없었다.

pre|na|tal /prineɪt³l/ ADJ **Prenatal** is used to describe things relating to the medical care of women during pregnancy. ❑ *I'd met her briefly in a prenatal class.*

형용사 출산 전의 ❑ 나는 그를 태교 교실에서 잠시 만났다.

pre|oc|cu|pa|tion /priɒkyəpeɪʃⁿn/ (preoccupations) ◼ N-COUNT If you have a **preoccupation with** something or someone, you keep thinking about them because they are important to you. ❑ *Karouzos's poetry shows a profound preoccupation with the Orthodox Church.* ◢ N-UNCOUNT **Preoccupation** is a state of mind in which you think about something so much that you do not consider other things to be important. ❑ *The arrest of Senator Pinochet has created a climate of preoccupation among our citizens.*

◼ 가산명사 -에 대한 심취, -에 대한 몰두 ❑ 카루조스의 시는 정교회에 대한 깊은 심취를 드러낸다. ◢ 불가산명사 깊은 우려, 신경을 많이 씀 ❑ 피노체트 상원 의원의 체포로 시민들이 깊이 우려하는 분위기이다.

pre|oc|cu|pied /priɒkyəpaɪd/ ADJ If you are **preoccupied**, you are thinking a lot about something or someone, and so you hardly notice other things. ❑ *Tom Banbury was preoccupied with the missing Shepherd child and did not want to devote time to the new murder.*

형용사 마음이 빼앗긴 ❑ 톰 밴베리는 '양치는 소년'이라 불리는 실종된 아이에게 마음이 뺏긴 상태여서 새로운 살인 사건에 시간을 들이고 싶지 않았다.

pre|oc|cu|py /priɒkyəpaɪ/ (**preoccupies, preoccupying, preoccupied**) V-T If something **is preoccupying** you, you are thinking about it a lot. ❑ *Crime and the fear of crime preoccupy the community.*

타동사 생각을 사로잡다 ❑ 범죄와 범죄에 대한 두려움이 주민들의 생각을 사로잡고 있다.

pre|paid /pripeɪd/ also **pre-paid** ADJ **Prepaid** items are paid for in advance, before the time when you would normally pay for them. ❑ *Return the enclosed Donation Form today in the prepaid envelope provided.*

형용사 선불된 ❑ 동봉된 기부 서류를 같이 있는 요금 선납 봉투에 넣어서 오늘 반송해 주세요.

prepa|ra|tion ♦◇◇ /prɛpəreɪʃᵊn/ (**preparations**) 1 N-UNCOUNT **Preparation** is the process of getting something ready for use or for a particular purpose or making arrangements for something. ❑ *Rub the surface of the wood in preparation for the varnish.* ❑ *Few things distracted the Pastor from the preparation of his weekly sermons.* 2 N-PLURAL **Preparations** are all the arrangements that are made for a future event. ❑ *The United States is making preparations for a large-scale airlift of 1,200 American citizens.* 3 N-COUNT A **preparation** is a mixture that has been prepared for use as food, medicine, or a cosmetic. ❑ *...anti-ageing creams and sensitive-skin preparations.*

1 불가산명사 준비 ❑ 유약 처리에 대한 준비로 나무의 표면을 문지르세요. ❑ 목사가 매주 하는 설교 준비로 다른 것에는 관심을 돌리지 않았다. 2 복수명사 준비 ❑ 미국은 미국인 1,200명에 대한 대규모 공수를 위해 준비를 하고 있다. 3 가산명사 조제, 용액, 사전에 준비된 것 ❑ 노화 방지 크림과 민감한 피부를 위한 조제 화장품

pre|para|tory /prɪpærətɔri, prɛpərə-, BRIT prɪpærətri/ ADJ **Preparatory** actions are done before doing something else as a form of preparation or as an introduction. ❑ *At least a year's preparatory work will be necessary before building can start.*

형용사 준비의 ❑ 건축을 시작할 수 있기 전에 최소한 일 년의 준비 작업이 필요하다.

pre|pare ♦♦◇ /prɪpɛər/ (**prepares, preparing, prepared**) 1 V-T If you **prepare** something, you make it ready for something that is going to happen. ❑ *Two technicians were preparing a videotape recording of last week's programme.* ❑ *On average each report requires 1,000 hours to prepare.* 2 V-T/V-I If you **prepare for** an event or action that will happen soon, you get yourself ready for it or make the necessary arrangements. ❑ *The Party leadership is using management consultants to help prepare for the next election.* ❑ *He had to go back to his hotel and prepare to catch a train for New York.* 3 V-T When you **prepare** food, you get it ready to be eaten, for example by cooking it. ❑ *She made her way to the kitchen, hoping to find someone preparing dinner.*

1 타동사 준비하다 ❑ 두 명의 기술자가 지난주 프로그램의 비디오테이프 녹화물을 준비하고 있었다. ❑ 평균적으로 각 보고서는 준비하는 데 1,000시간이 필요하다. 2 타동사/자동사 준비하다 ❑ 당 지도부는 다음 선거에 대비하기 위해 경영 컨설턴트를 이용하고 있다. ❑ 그는 호텔에 돌아가 뉴욕으로 가는 기차를 타기 위한 채비를 해야 했다. 3 타동사 준비하다 ❑ 그녀는 누군가가 저녁을 준비하고 있기를 바라며 부엌으로 향했다.

Thesaurus *prepare*의 참조어

V. arrange, plan, ready 1
fix, make 3

Word Partnership *prepare*의 연어

N. prepare **a list**, prepare **a plan**, prepare **a report** 1
prepare **for battle/war**, prepare **for the future**,
prepare **for the worst** 2
prepare **dinner**, prepare **food**, prepare **a meal** 3

pre|pared ♦♦◇ /prɪpɛərd/ 1 ADJ If you are **prepared to** do something, you are willing to do it if necessary. [v-link ADJ to-inf] ❑ *Are you prepared to take industrial action?* 2 ADJ If you are **prepared for** something that you think is going to happen, you are ready for it. [v-link ADJ for n] ❑ *Police are prepared for large numbers of demonstrators.* 3 ADJ You can describe something as **prepared** when it has been done or made beforehand, so that it is ready when it is needed. [ADJ n] ❑ *He ended his prepared statement by thanking the police.*

1 형용사 각오가 된 ❑ 노동 쟁의를 할 각오가 되어 있습니까? 2 형용사 -에 대비하는 ❑ 경찰은 시위자가 많을 것에 대비하고 있다. 3 형용사 사전에 준비된 ❑ 그는 경찰에게 감사를 표함으로써 준비된 발언을 마쳤다.

Word Link *pos ≈ placing : **depos**it, **prepos**ition, **repos**itory*

prepo|si|tion /prɛpəzɪʃᵊn/ (**prepositions**) N-COUNT A **preposition** is a word such as "by," "for," "into," or "with" which usually has a noun group as its object. ❑ *There is nothing in the rules of grammar to suggest that ending a sentence with a preposition is wrong.*

가산명사 전치사 ❑ 문장을 전치사로 끝내는 것이 올바르지 않다는 것을 시사하는 문법 규칙은 전혀 없다.

pre|pos|ter|ous /prɪpɒstᵊrəs, -trəs/ ADJ If you describe something as **preposterous**, you mean that it is extremely unreasonable and foolish. [DISAPPROVAL] ❑ *The whole idea was preposterous.* ● **pre|pos|ter|ous|ly** ADV ❑ *Some prices are preposterously high.*

형용사 터무니없는 [탐탁찮음] ❑ 생각 자체가 터무니없는 것이었다. ● 터무니없이 부사 ❑ 일부 가격은 터무니없이 높다.

prep school /prɛp skul/ (**prep schools**) 1 N-VAR In Britain, a **prep school** is a private school where children are educated until the age of 11 or 13. 2 N-VAR In the United States, a **prep school** is a private school for students who intend to go to college after they leave. ❑ *...an exclusive prep school in Washington.*

1 가산명사 또는 불가산명사 사립 초등학교 (영국) 2 가산명사 또는 불가산명사 사립 고등학교 (미국) ❑ 워싱턴에 있는 비싼 사립 고등학교

pre|requi|site /prirɛkwɪzɪt/ (**prerequisites**) N-COUNT If one thing is a **prerequisite for** another, it must happen or exist before the other thing is possible. ❑ *Good self-esteem is a prerequisite for a happy life.*

가산명사 필수 조건 ❑ 훌륭한 자긍심은 행복한 삶을 위해 반드시 필요하다.

pre|roga|tive /prɪrɒgətɪv/ (**prerogatives**) N-COUNT If something is the **prerogative** of a particular person or group, it is a privilege or a power that only they have. [FORMAL] ❑ *Constitutional changes are exclusively the prerogative of the parliament.*

가산명사 특권 [격식체] ❑ 헌법 개정은 전적으로 의회의 특권이다.

pre|scribe /prɪskraɪb/ (**prescribes, prescribing, prescribed**) 1 V-T If a doctor **prescribes** medicine or treatment for you, he or she tells you what medicine or treatment to have. ❑ *Our doctor diagnosed a throat infection and prescribed antibiotics and junior aspirin.* ❑ *She took twice the prescribed dose of sleeping tablets.* 2 V-T If a person or set of laws or rules **prescribes** an action or duty, they state that it must be carried out. [FORMAL] ❑ *...article II of the constitution, which prescribes the method of electing a president.*

1 타동사 처방하다 ❑ 우리 의사가 후두염이라고 진단하고 항생제와 어린이용 아스피린을 처방했다. ❑ 그녀는 처방된 약의 두 배나 되는 수면제를 먹었다. 2 타동사 규정하다, 지시하다 [격식체] ❑ 대통령 선출 방식을 규정한 헌법 제2조

pre|scrip|tion /prɪskrɪpʃᵊn/ (**prescriptions**) 1 N-COUNT A **prescription** is the piece of paper on which your doctor writes an order for medicine and which you give to a pharmacist to get the medicine. ❑ *The new drug will not require a physician's prescription.* 2 N-COUNT A **prescription** is a medicine which a doctor

1 가산명사 처방전 ❑ 그 새 약은 의사의 처방전이 필요 없을 것입니다. 2 가산명사 처방약 ❑ 애커먼이 준 처방약을 먹고서도 잠이 오지 않는다. ● 구 처방전이 있어야만 3 가산명사 처리 방안, 처방 ❑ 아일랜드

has told you to take. ❏ *I'm not sleeping even with the prescription Ackerman gave me.* ● PHRASE If a medicine is available **by** or **on prescription**, you can only get it from a pharmacist if a doctor gives you a prescription for it. ❸ N-COUNT A **prescription** is a proposal or a plan which gives ideas about how to solve a problem or improve a situation. ❏ *There's not much difference in the economic prescriptions of Ireland's two main political parties.*

양대 정당의 경제 처방에는 별 큰 차이가 없다.

pres|ence ♦♦◇ /prɛzᵊns/ (presences) ❶ N-SING Someone's **presence** in a place is the fact that they are there. ❏ *They argued that his presence in the village could only stir up trouble.* ❷ N-UNCOUNT If you say that someone has **presence**, you mean that they impress people by their appearance and manner. [APPROVAL] ❏ *They do not seem to have the vast, authoritative presence of those great men.* ❸ N-COUNT A **presence** is a person or creature that you cannot see, but that you are aware of. [LITERARY] ❏ *She started to be affected by the ghostly presence she could feel in the house.* ❹ N-SING If a country has a military **presence** in another country, it has some of its armed forces there. ❏ *The Philippine government wants the U.S. to maintain a military presence in Southeast Asia.* ❺ N-UNCOUNT If you refer to the **presence** of a substance in another thing, you mean that it is in that thing. ❏ *The somewhat acid flavor is caused by the presence of lactic acid.* ❻ PHRASE If you are **in** someone's **presence**, you are in the same place as that person, and are close enough to them to be seen or heard. ❏ *The talks took place in the presence of a diplomatic observer.*

❶ 단수명사 있음 ❏ 그들은 그가 그 마을에 있어 봤자 불화를 일으킬 뿐이라고 주장했다. ❷ 불가산명사 풍채 [마음에 듦] ❏ 그들은 위대한 사람들처럼 비상하고 권위 있는 풍채를 가진 것 같지 않다. ❸ 가산명사 존재 [문예체] ❏ 그녀는 집 안에서 느껴지는 유령의 존재에 영향을 받기 시작했다. ❹ 단수명사 (군대의) 주둔 ❏ 필리핀 정부는 미국이 동남아시아에 군대를 계속 주둔시키기를 원한다. ❺ 불가산명사 (어떤 성분이) 들어 있음 ❏ 다소 신맛이 나는 것은 젖산이 들어 있기 때문이다. ❻ 구 -의 면전에서, -가 있는 데서 ❏ 회담은 외교 담당 참관인들이 보는 앞에서 개최되었다.

---

present

① EXISTING OR HAPPENING NOW
② BEING SOMEWHERE
③ GIFT
④ VERB USES

---

① **pres|ent** ♦♦◇ /prɛzᵊnt/ ❶ ADJ You use **present** to describe things and people that exist now, rather than those that existed in the past or those that may exist in the future. [ADJ n] ❏ *He has brought much of the present crisis on himself.* ❏ *...the government's present economic difficulties.* ❷ N-SING **The present** is the period of time that we are in now and the things that are happening now. ❏ *...his struggle to reconcile the past with the present.* ❏ *...continuing right up to the present.* ❸ PHRASE A situation that exists **at present** exists now, although it may change. ❏ *There is no way at present of predicting which individuals will develop the disease.* ❹ PHRASE **The present day** is the period of history that we are in now. ❏ *...Western European art from the period of Giotto to the present day.* ❺ PHRASE Something that exists or will be done **for the present** exists now or will continue for a while, although the situation may change later. ❏ *The ministers had expressed the unanimous view that sanctions should remain in place for the present.*

❶ 형용사 현재의 ❏ 그는 현재 위기의 많은 부분을 자초했다. ❏ 정부가 현재 처한 경제적 곤경 ❷ 단수명사 현재, 오늘날 ❏ 과거와 현재를 융화시키기 위한 그의 고투 ❏ 바로 오늘날까지 지속되면서 ❸ 구 현재로서는 ❏ 현재로서는 어떤 사람들이 그 병에 걸릴지 예측할 방법이 없다. ❹ 구 현재, 오늘날 ❏ 조토가 활동하던 시기부터 오늘날까지의 서유럽 미술 ❺ 구 현재로서는, 당분간 ❏ 각료들은 만장일치로 제재 규약을 당분간 그대로 두어야 한다는 견해를 표명했었다.

② **pres|ent** ♦♦◇ /prɛzᵊnt/ ❶ ADJ If someone is **present at** an event, they are there. [v-link ADJ, oft ADJ at n] ❏ *The president was not present at the meeting.* ❏ *Nearly 85 percent of men are present at the birth of their children.* ❷ ADJ If something, especially a substance or disease, is **present in** something else, it exists within that thing. [v-link ADJ, oft ADJ in n] ❏ *This special form of vitamin D is naturally present in breast milk.*

❶ 형용사 -에 있는, -에 참석한 ❏ 대통령은 그 회의에 참석하지 않았다. ❏ 남자들 중 거의 85퍼센트가 자식이 태어날 때 자리를 지킨다. ❷ 형용사 -에 들어 있는 ❏ 모유에는 이 특수한 형태의 비타민 디(D)가 원래부터 들어 있다.

③ **pres|ent** (presents) /prɛzᵊnt/ N-COUNT A **present** is something that you give to someone, for example at Christmas or when you visit them. ❏ *The carpet was a wedding present from the Prime Minister.* ❏ *I bought a birthday present for my mother.*

가산명사 선물 ❏ 그 양탄자는 수상이 준 결혼 선물이었다. ❏ 나는 어머니께 생일 선물을 사 드렸다.

④ **pres|ent** ♦♦◇ /prɪzɛnt/ (presents, presenting, presented) ❶ V-T If you **present** someone **with** something such as a prize or document, or if you **present** it to them, you formally give it to them. ❏ *The mayor presented him with a gold medal at an official city reception.* ❏ *Prince Michael of Kent presented the prizes.* ● **pres|en|ta|tion** N-UNCOUNT ❏ *Then came the presentation of the awards by the Queen Mother.* ❷ V-T If something **presents** a difficulty, challenge, or opportunity, it causes it or provides it. ❏ *This presents a problem for many financial consumers.* ❏ *The future is going to be one that presents many challenges.* ❸ V-T If an opportunity or problem **presents itself**, it occurs, often when you do not expect it. ❏ *Their colleagues insulted them whenever the opportunity presented itself.* ❹ V-T When you **present** information, you give it to people in a formal way. ❏ *We spend the time collating and presenting the information in a variety of chart forms.* ❏ *We presented three options to the unions for discussion.* ● **pres|en|ta|tion** (presentations) N-VAR ❏ *...in his first presentation of the theory to the Berlin Academy.* ❏ *...a fair presentation of the facts to a jury.* ❺ V-T If you **present** someone or something in a particular way, you describe them in that way. ❏ *The government has presented these changes as major reforms.* ❻ V-T The way you **present yourself** is the way you speak and act when meeting new people. ❏ *...all those tricks which would help him to present himself in a more confident way in public.* ❼ V-T If someone or something **presents** a particular appearance or image, that is how they appear or try to appear. ❏ *The small group of onlookers presented a pathetic sight.* ❏ *But some feel in presenting a more professional image the party risks losing its radical edge and its individuality.* ❽ V-T If you **present yourself** somewhere, you officially arrive there, for example for an appointment. ❏ *Get word to him right away that he's to present himself at the castle by tomorrow afternoon.* ❾ V-T If someone **presents** a programme on television or radio, they introduce each item in it. [mainly BRIT; AM usually host, introduce] ❏ *She presents a monthly magazine program on the BBC.* ❿ V-T When someone **presents** something such as a production of a play or an exhibition, they organize it. ❏ *The Lyric Theatre is presenting a new production of "Over the Bridge".* ⓫ V-T If you **present** someone **to** someone else, often an important person, you formally introduce them. ❏ *Fox stepped forward, welcomed him in Malay, and presented him to Jack.*

❶ 타동사 주다, 증정하다 ❏ 시장이 시 공식 환영회에서 그에게 금메달을 증정했다. ❏ 마이클 왕자가 시상을 했다. ● 수여 (-를 불가산명사 ❏ 그런 다음 황태후의 시상이 이어졌다. ❷ 타동사 (문제 따위를) 일으키다 ❏ 이것은 많은 금융 소비자들에게 문제를 일으킨다. ❏ 미래는 많은 도전을 안겨 주는 시대가 될 것이다. ❸ 타동사 일어나다, 나타나다 ❏ 동료들은 기회가 날 때마다 그들을 모욕했다. ❹ 타동사 발표하다, 제시하다 ❏ 우리는 다양한 도표 형태로 정보를 조합하며 발표하며 그 시간을 보낸다. ❏ 우리는 대화를 위해 노조 측에 세 가지 선택을 제시했다. ● 발표, 제시 가산명사 또는 불가산명사 ❏ 그가 베를린 학회에서 최초로 발표한 그 이론에서 ❏ 배심원에게 진상을 잘 알림 ❺ 타동사 설명하다 ❏ 정부는 이런 변화들을 주요한 개혁으로 설명해 왔다. ❻ 타동사 스스로를 드러내다 ❏ 대중 앞에 스스로를 보다 자신 있는 모습으로 드러내도록 도와줄 그런 모든 수법들 ❼ 타동사 (-한 모습을) 만들어 내다, 연출하다 ❏ 소수의 구경꾼 무리가 처량한 광경을 연출하고 있었다. ❏ 하지만 몇몇 사람들은 그 정당이 보다 전문적인 인상을 만들어 내기 위해 자신들이 가진 급진성과 개성을 상실할 위험을 무릅쓰고 있다고 느낀다. ❽ 타동사 나타나다, 출두하다 ❏ 내일 오후까지 성에 출두해야 한다고 그에게 즉시 말을 전하세요. ❾ 타동사 진행하다 [주로 영국영어; 미국영어 대개 host, introduce] ❏ 그녀는 비비시에서 한 달에 한 번 하는 매거진 프로그램을 진행한다. ❿ 타동사 상연하다, (전시회 등을) 열다 ❏ 리릭 시어터는 새 작품 '오버 더 브리지'를 상연 중이다. ⓫ 타동사 소개하다 ❏ 폭스는 앞으로 걸어 나와 말레이 말로 그를 환영한 다음 잭에게 소개했다.

Word Partnership   *present*의 연어

N. present **century**, present **circumstances**, present **location**,
present **position**, present **situation**, present **time** ① ■
present **a check** ④ ■
present **a challenge**, present **a danger**, present **an opportunity**,
present **a problem**, present **a threat** ④ ■
present **an argument**, present **evidence**, present **a plan** ④ ■

pres|en|ta|tion /prɪzɛnteɪʃ°n, BRIT prɛz³nteɪʃ°n/ (presentations) ■ N-UNCOUNT **Presentation** is the appearance of something, which someone has worked to create. ❑ *We serve traditional French food cooked in a lighter way, keeping the presentation simple.* ■ N-COUNT A **presentation** is a formal event at which someone is given a prize or award. ❑ *...after receiving his award at a presentation in London yesterday.* ■ N-COUNT When someone gives a **presentation**, they give a formal talk, often in order to sell something or get support for a proposal. ❑ *James Watson, Philip Mayo and I gave a slide and video presentation.* ■ →see also **present**

■ 불가산명사 외관, 겉모습 ❑ 우리는 더 손쉬운 방식으로 요리하고 외관을 간소화한 프랑스 전통 음식을 제공합니다. ■ 가산명사 수여식, 시상식 ❑ 그가 어제 런던에서 있었던 한 시상식에서 상을 받은 다음 ■ 가산명사 발표 ❑ 제임스 왓슨, 필립 메이오와 나는 슬라이드와 비디오를 이용한 발표를 했다.

present-day also present day ADJ **Present-day** things, situations, and people exist at the time in history we are now in. [ADJ n] ❑ *Even by present-day standards these were large aircraft.* ❑ *...a huge area of northern India, stretching from present-day Afghanistan to Bengal.*

형용사 현대의, 오늘날의 ❑ 오늘날의 기준에 비추어 보아도 이들은 대형 항공기였다. ❑ 오늘날의 아프가니스탄에서 벵골까지 뻗어 있는 인도 북부의 광대한 지역

pre|sent|er /prɪzɛntər/ (presenters) N-COUNT A radio or television **presenter** is a person who introduces the items in a particular program. [mainly BRIT; AM usually **host**, **anchor**] ❑ *Most people think being a television presenter is exciting.*

가산명사 진행자 [주로 영국영어; 미국영어 대개 host, anchor] ❑ 대부분의 사람들은 텔레비전 진행자가 되는 것이 신나는 일이라고 생각한다.

pres|ent|ly /prɛz°ntli/ ■ ADV If you say that something is **presently** happening, you mean that it is happening now. ❑ *She is presently developing a number of projects.* ❑ *The island is presently uninhabited.* ■ ADV You use **presently** to indicate that something happened quite a short time after the time or event that you have just mentioned. [WRITTEN] [ADV with cl] ❑ *He was shown to a small office. Presently, a young woman in a white coat came in.*

■ 부사 현재 ❑ 그녀는 현재 다수의 사업 계획을 진전시키고 있다. ❑ 그 섬에는 현재 사람이 살지 않는다. ■ 부사 이내, 곧 [문어체] ❑ 그는 어떤 작은 사무실로 안내되었다. 이내, 흰색 외투를 입은 젊은 여자 한 명이 들어왔다.

pre|serva|tive /prɪzɜrvətɪv/ (preservatives) N-MASS A **preservative** is a chemical that prevents things from decaying. Some preservatives are added to food, and others are used to treat wood or metal. ❑ *Nitrates are used as preservatives in food manufacture.* →see **salt**

물질명사 방부제 ❑ 질산염은 식품 제조 공정에서 방부제로 사용된다.

Word Link   serv ≈ keeping : con*serv*e, ob*serv*e, pre*serv*e

Word Link   ation ≈ state of : educ*ation*, elev*ation*, preserv*ation*

pre|serve ♦♢♢ /prɪzɜrv/ (preserves, preserving, preserved) ■ V-T If you **preserve** a situation or condition, you make sure that it remains as it is, and does not change or end. ❑ *We will do everything to preserve peace.* ● pres|er|va|tion /prɛzərveɪʃ°n/ N-UNCOUNT ❑ *...the preservation of the status quo.* ■ V-T If you **preserve** something, you take action to save it or protect it from damage or decay. ❑ *We need to preserve the forest.* ● pres|er|va|tion N-UNCOUNT ❑ *...the preservation of buildings of architectural or historic interest.* ■ V-T If you **preserve** food, you treat it in order to prevent it from decaying so that you can store it for a long time. ❑ *I like to make puree, using only enough sugar to preserve the plums.* ■ N-PLURAL **Preserves** are foods such as jam that are made by cooking fruit with a large amount of sugar so that they can be stored for a long time. ❑ *She decided to make peach preserves for Christmas gifts.* ■ N-COUNT If you say that a job or activity is the **preserve of** a particular person or group of people, you mean that they are the only ones who take part in it. ❑ *The making and conduct of foreign policy is largely the preserve of the president.* →see **can**

■ 타동사 유지하다 ❑ 우리는 평화를 유지하기 위해 무슨 일이든 다 할 것이다. ● 유지 불가산명사 ❑ 현상 유지 ■ 타동사 보존하다 ❑ 우리는 숲을 보존해야 한다. ● 보존 불가산명사 ❑ 건축적 혹은 역사적으로 중요한 건물들의 보존 ■ 타동사 저장 식품으로 만들다 ❑ 나는 자두가 변질되지 않을 만큼의 설탕만을 사용해서 퓨레 만드는 걸 좋아한다. ■ 복수명사 설탕 조림 ❑ 그녀는 크리스마스 선물로 복숭아 설탕 조림을 만들기로 마음먹었다. ■ 가산명사 (특정인 또는 특정 집단만의) 고유 영역 ❑ 외교 정책을 수립하고 지휘하는 일은 대체로 대통령의 고유 영역이다.

Word Link   sid ≈ sitting : pre*sid*e, pre*sid*ent, re*sid*e

pre|side /prɪzaɪd/ (presides, presiding, presided) V-I If you **preside over** a meeting or an event, you are in charge. ❑ *The PM returned to Downing Street to preside over a meeting of his inner Cabinet.*

자동사 (회의 또는 행사 등을) 주재하다 ❑ 수상은 다우닝 가로 돌아와서 최고 각료 회의를 주재했다.

presi|den|cy ♦♢♢ /prɛzɪdənsi/ (presidencies) N-COUNT The **presidency** of a country or organization is the position of being the president or the period of time during which someone is president. ❑ *Britain will support him as a candidate for the presidency of the organisation.*

가산명사 대통령 직위; 대통령 임기, 의장직; 의장 임기 ❑ 영국은 그 기구의 의장 후보로 그를 지지할 것이다.

presi|dent ♦♦♦ /prɛzɪdənt/ (presidents) ■ N-TITLE; N-COUNT The **president** of a country that has no king or queen is the person who is the head of state of that country. [oft the N; N-VOC] ❑ *...President Mubarak.* ■ N-COUNT The **president** of an organization is the person who has the highest position in it. ❑ *...Alexandre de Merode, the president of the medical commission.* →see **election**

■ 경칭명사; 가산명사 대통령 ❑ 무바라크 대통령 ■ 가산명사 의장, 위원장 ❑ 의료 위원회 위원장 알렉상드르 드 메로드

presi|den|tial ♦♦♢ /prɛzɪdɛnʃ°l/ ADJ **Presidential** activities or things relate or belong to a president. [ADJ n] ❑ *...campaigning for Peru's presidential election.* →see **election**

형용사 대통령의; 의장의 ❑ 페루 대통령 선거 운동

press ♦♦♦ /prɛs/ (presses, pressing, pressed) ■ V-T If you **press** something somewhere, you push it firmly against something else. ❑ *He pressed his back against the chair.* ■ V-T If you **press** a button or switch, you push it with your finger in order to make a machine or device work. ❑ *Drago pressed a button and the door closed.* ● N-COUNT **Press** is also a noun. ❑ *...a TV which rises from a table at the press of a button.* ■ V-T/V-I If you **press** something or **press down on** it, you push hard against it with your foot or hand. ❑ *The engine stalled. He pressed the accelerator hard.* ■ V-I If you **press for** something, you try hard to persuade someone to give it to you or to agree to it. ❑ *Police might now press for changes in*

■ 타동사 밀다, 밀어붙이다 ❑ 그는 등으로 문을 밀었다. ■ 타동사 누르다 ❑ 드라고가 버튼을 누르자 문이 닫혔다. ● 가산명사 누름 ❑ 버튼을 누르면 탁자에서 튀어 올라오는 텔레비전 ■ 타동사/자동사 누르다; 밟다 ❑ 엔진이 멈췄다. 그는 가속 페달을 세게 밟았다. ■ 자동사 ... 을 위해 압력을 가하다 ❑ 경찰은 이제 법률 개정을 위해 압력을 가할지도 모른다. ■ 타동사 압박하다, 요구하다 ❑ 산별 노조들이 확고한 태도를 취하라고 그를 압박하고 있다. ❑ 킹 씨는

a b c d e f g h i j k l m n o p q r s t u v w x y z

A

the law. ◼ V-T If you **press** someone, you try hard to persuade them to do something. ❑ *Trade unions are pressing him to stand firm.* ❑ *Mr. King seems certain to be pressed for further details.* ◼ V-T If someone **presses** their claim, demand, or point, they state it in a very forceful way. ❑ *The protest campaign has used mass strikes and demonstrations to press its demands.* ◼ V-T If you **press** something **on** someone, you give it to them and insist that they take it. ❑ *All I had was money, which I pressed on her reluctant mother.* ◼ V-T If you **press** clothes, you iron them in order to get rid of the creases. ❑ *Vera pressed his shirt.* ❑ *There's a couple of dresses to be pressed.* ◼ N-SING-COLL Newspapers are referred to as **the press.** [the N] ❑ *Today the British press is full of articles on India's new prime minister.* ❑ *...freedom of the Press.* ◼ N-SING-COLL Journalists are referred to as **the press.** ❑ *Christie looked relaxed and calm as he faced the press afterwards.* ◼ N-COUNT A **press** or a **printing press** is a machine used for printing things such as books and newspapers. ◼ →see also **pressed, pressing** ◼ PHRASE If someone or something **gets a bad press**, they are criticized, especially in the newspapers, on television, or on radio. If they **get a good press** or **get good press**, they are praised. ❑ *...the bad press that career women consistently get in this country.* ◼ PHRASE If you **press charges against** someone, you make an official accusation against them which has to be decided in a court of law. ❑ *I could have pressed charges against him.* ◼ PHRASE When a newspaper or magazine **goes to press**, it starts being printed. ❑ *We check prices at the time of going to press.* →see **newspaper**

B
C
D
E
F
G

Word Partnership   press의 연어

N.	press **a button, at the** press **of a button** ◼
	press **accounts,** press **coverage, freedom of the** press,
	press **reports** ◼ ◼
	press **charges** ◼

H
I

분명히 더 상세한 내용을 대라는 압력을 받을 것 같다. ◼ 타동사 역설하다, 주장하다 ❑ 그 저항 운동에서는 요구 사항을 주장하기 위해 대규모 파업과 데모 등의 방법을 써 왔었다. ◼ 타동사 떠안기다, 억지로 쥐어 주다 ❑ 내가 가진 것은 돈뿐이었기에, 내키지 않아 하는 그녀의 어머니에게 억지로 쥐어 주었다. ◼ 타동사 다림질하다 ❑ 베라가 그의 셔츠를 다림질했다. ❑ 다림질 할 드레스가 두 벌 있다. ◼ 단수명사-집합 신문; 언론 ❑ 오늘 자 영국 신문들에는 인도의 신임 수상에 대한 기사가 가득 실린다. ❑ 언론의 자유 ◼ 단수명사-집합 기자 ❑ 나중에 기자들을 대할 때 크리스티는 편안하고 침착해 보였다. ◼ 가산명사 인쇄기 ◼ 구 (언론 또는 방송에서) 부정적 평가를 받다; 긍정적 평가를 받다 ❑ 이 나라에서 직업여성들에게 끊임없이 쏟아지는 언론의 부정적 평가 ◼ 구 -을 고발하다 ❑ 내가 그를 고발할 수도 있었을 것이다. ◼ 구 인쇄에 들어가다 ❑ 인쇄에 들어가는 시간에 우리는 가격을 점검한다.

J

press con|fer|ence (press conferences) N-COUNT A **press conference** is a meeting held by a famous or important person in which they answer journalists' questions. ❑ *She gave her reaction to his release at a press conference.*

가산명사 기자 회견 ❑ 그녀는 그가 기자 회견에서 한 발표에 대해 반응을 보였다.

K

pressed /prɛst/ ADJ If you say that you are **pressed for** time or **pressed for** money, you mean that you do not have enough time or money at the moment. [v-link ADJ, usu ADJ for n] ❑ *Are you pressed for time, Mr. Bayliss? If not, I suggest we have lunch.* →see also **hard-pressed**

형용사 - 때문에 압박을 받는, -가 부족한 ❑ 시간이 없으십니까, 베일리스 씨? 그렇지 않으면, 점심 식사라도 같이 하시죠.

L

press|ing /prɛsɪŋ/ ◼ ADJ A **pressing** problem, need, or issue has to be dealt with immediately. ❑ *It is one of the most pressing problems facing this country.* ◼ →see also **press**

◼ 형용사 절박한, 긴급한 ❑ 그것은 이 나라가 직면한 가장 긴급한 문제들 중 하나이다.

M

press of|fic|er (press officers) N-COUNT A **press officer** is a person who is employed by an organization to give information about that organization to the press. ❑ *...the Press Officer of the Bavarian Government.*

가산명사 공보 담당관 ❑ 바이에른 정부의 공보 담당관

N

press re|lease (press releases) N-COUNT A **press release** is a written statement about a matter of public interest which is given to the press by an organization concerned with the matter. ❑ *The next day, Fox issued a press release saying the show had sold out in 24 hours.*

가산명사 보도 자료 ❑ 다음 날, 폭스는 그 공연의 표가 24시간 만에 매진되었다는 보도 자료를 내놓았다.

O

press sec|re|tary (press secretaries) N-COUNT A government's or political leader's **press secretary** is someone who is employed by them to give information to the press. ❑ *The Prime Minister's official press secretary told reporters that a majority of one would be a sufficient mandate.*

가산명사 공보 담당 비서 ❑ 수상의 공식 공보 담당 비서가 기자들에게 한 표 차이의 투표 결과로 신임을 받은 것으로 보기에 충분하리라고 말했다.

P

press-up (press-ups) N-COUNT **Press-ups** are exercises to strengthen your arms and chest muscles. They are done by lying with your face toward the floor and pushing with your hands to raise your body until your arms are straight. [BRIT; AM **push-ups**] ❑ *He made me do 30 press-ups.*

가산명사 팔 굽혀 펴기 [영국영어; 미국영어 push-ups] ❑ 그는 나에게 팔 굽혀 펴기 30회를 하도록 했다.

Q

pres|sure ♦♦♦ /prɛʃər/ (pressures, pressuring, pressured) ◼ N-UNCOUNT **Pressure** is force that you produce when you press hard on something. ❑ *She kicked at the door with her foot, and the pressure was enough to open it.* ❑ *The pressure of his fingers had relaxed.* ◼ N-UNCOUNT The **pressure** in a place or container is the force produced by the quantity of gas or liquid in that place or container. [also N in pl] ❑ *The window in the cockpit had blown in and the pressure dropped dramatically.* ◼ N-UNCOUNT If there is **pressure on** a person, someone is trying to persuade or force them to do something. [also N in pl] ❑ *He may have put pressure on her to agree.* ❑ *Its government is under pressure from the European Commission.* ◼ N-UNCOUNT If you are experiencing **pressure**, you feel that you must do a lot of tasks or make a lot of decisions in very little time, or that people expect a lot from you. [also N in pl] ❑ *Can you work under pressure?* ❑ *Even if I had the talent to play tennis I couldn't stand the pressure.* ◼ V-T If you **pressure** someone **to** do something, you try forcefully to persuade them to do it. ❑ *He will never pressure you to get married.* ❑ *The Government should not be pressured into making hasty decisions.* ● **pressured** ADJ ❑ *You're likely to feel anxious and pressured.* ◼ →see also **blood pressure** →see **flight, forecast, weather**

R
S
T
U
V

◼ 불가산명사 압력 ❑ 그녀는 문을 발로 찼고, 그 압력은 문을 열기에 충분했다. ❑ 그의 손가락 압력이 느슨해졌다. ◼ 불가산명사 기압; 수압 ❑ 조종석 창문이 바람에 열리자 기압이 급격히 떨어졌다. ◼ 불가산명사 압박 ❑ 그가 그녀에게 동의하라고 압박을 가했을지도 모른다. ❑ 그 나라 정부는 유럽 연합 의회로부터 압박을 받고 있다. ◼ 불가산명사 압박감 ❑ 당신은 압박감을 받으며 일할 수 있습니까? ❑ 설사 내가 테니스에 재능이 있다 하더라도 그와 같은 압박감은 견딜 수 없을 것이다. ◼ 타동사 압력을 가하다 ❑ 그는 너에게 결혼하라는 압력을 결코 가하지 않을 것이다. ❑ 정부는 성급한 결정을 내려서는 안 된다. ● 압력을 받는 형용사 ❑ 내가 걱정스럽고 압력을 받는 기분이 들 수 있다.

W

pres|sure group (pressure groups) N-COUNT A **pressure group** is an organized group of people who are trying to persuade a government or other authority to do something, for example to change a law. ❑ *...the environmental pressure group Greenpeace.*

가산명사 압력 단체 ❑ 환경 압력 단체 그린피스

X

pres|sur|ize /prɛʃəraɪz/ (pressurizes, pressurizing, pressurized) [BRIT also **pressurise**] V-T If you are **pressurized into** doing something, you are forcefully persuaded to do it. ❑ *Do not be pressurized into making your decision immediately.*

[영국영어 pressurise] 타동사 압력 때문에 -하게 되다 ❑ 압력 때문에 즉각 결정을 내려지는 않도록 하세요.

Y

pres|sur|ized /prɛʃəraɪzd/ [BRIT also **pressurised**] ADJ In a **pressurized** container or area, the pressure inside is different from the pressure outside. ❑ *Certain types of foods are also dispensed in pressurized canisters.*

[영국영어 pressurised] 형용사 압력을 받는 ❑ 어떤 유형의 음식들은 압력통에 담겨 나오기도 한다.

Z

pres|tige /prɛstiʒ, -stidʒ/ ■ N-UNCOUNT If a person, a country, or an organization has **prestige**, they are admired and respected because of the position they hold or the things they have achieved. ❑ ...*efforts to build up the prestige of the United Nations.* ❑ *It was his responsibility for foreign affairs that gained him international prestige.* ■ ADJ **Prestige** is used to describe products, places, or activities which people admire because they are associated with being rich or having a high social position. [ADJ n] ❑ ...*such prestige cars as Cadillac, Mercedes, Porsche and Jaguar.*

■ 불가산명사 위신, 명성 ❑ 유엔의 위신을 쌓아 올리기 위한 노력 ❑ 그에게 국제적 명성을 가져다 준 것은 외교 문제에 대한 그의 책무였다. ■ 형용사 명문의, 고급의 ❑ 캐딜락, 메르세데스, 포르쉐, 재규어 같은 고급 자동차들

pres|tig|ious /prɛstidʒəs, -stidʒəs/ ADJ A **prestigious** institution, job, or activity is respected and admired by people. ❑ *It's one of the best equipped and most prestigious schools in the country.*

형용사 명망 있는, 존경받는 ❑ 그것은 그 나라에서 가장 설비가 잘 갖추어지고 명성이 높은 학교들 중 한 곳이다.

pre|sum|ably ♦♢♢ /prɪzuːməbli, BRIT prɪzyuːməbli/ ADV If you say that something is **presumably** the case, you mean that you think it is very likely to be the case, although you are not certain. [VAGUENESS] ❑ *The spear is presumably the murder weapon.*

부사 아마 [짐작투] ❑ 그 창이 아마 그 살인에 쓰인 무기일 것이다.

| **Word Link** | *sume ≈ taking : as**sume**, con**sume**, pre**sume*** |

pre|sume /prɪzuːm, BRIT prɪzyuːm/ (presumes, presuming, presumed) ■ V-T If you **presume that** something is the case, you think that it is the case, although you are not certain. ❑ *I presume you're here on business.* ❑ *"Had he been home all week?" — "I presume so."* ■ V-T If you say that someone **presumes to** do something, you mean that they do it even though they have no right to do it. [FORMAL] ❑ *They're resentful that outsiders presume to meddle in their affairs.* ■ V-T If an idea, theory, or plan **presumes** certain facts, it regards them as true so that they can be used as a basis for further ideas and theories. [FORMAL] ❑ *The legal definition of "know" often presumes mental control.*

■ 타동사 짐작하다, 추측하다 ❑ 사업차 이곳에 오신 것 같군요. ❑ "그가 한 주 내내 집에 있었니?" "그런 것 같아." ■ 타동사 주제넘게 -하다 [격식체] ❑ 그들은 외부인들이 주제넘게 자기들 일에 참견하는 것을 기분 나쁘게 생각한다. ■ 타동사 가정하다 [격식체] ❑ '안다'는 것의 법적 정의는 흔히 정신적 통제력을 가정한다.

| **Word Link** | *sumpt ≈ taking : as**sumpt**ion, con**sumpt**ion, pre**sumpt**ion* |

pre|sump|tion /prɪzʌmpʃⁿn/ (presumptions) N-COUNT A **presumption** is something that is accepted as true but is not certain to be true. ❑ ...*the presumption that a defendant is innocent until proved guilty.*

가산명사 가정 ❑ 유죄임이 밝혀질 때까지는 피고가 무죄라는 가정

pre|sump|tu|ous /prɪzʌmptʃuəs/ ADJ If you describe someone or their behavior as **presumptuous**, you disapprove of them because they are doing something that they have no right or authority to do. [DISAPPROVAL] ❑ *It would be presumptuous to judge what the outcome will be.*

형용사 주제넘은, 건방진 [탐탁찮음] ❑ 결과가 어떨지 판단하는 것은 주제넘은 일일 것이다.

pretax /priːtæks/ also **pre-tax** ADJ **Pretax** profits or losses are the total profits or losses made by a company before tax has been taken away. [BUSINESS] [ADJ n] ❑ *They announced a fall in pretax profits.* ● ADV **Pretax** is also an adverb. [ADV after v] ❑ *Last year it made £2.5m pre-tax.*

형용사 세전의 [경제] ❑ 그들은 세전 수익이 하락했다고 발표했다. ● 부사 세전에 ❑ 작년에 그 회사는 세전 수익으로 2백 5십만 파운드를 벌어들였다.

pre|tence /priːtɛns, prɪtɛns/ →see **pretense**

pre|tend /prɪtɛnd/ (pretends, pretending, pretended) ■ V-T If you **pretend that** something is the case, you act in a way that is intended to make people believe that it is the case, although in fact it is not. ❑ *I pretend that things are really okay when they're not.* ❑ *Sometimes the boy pretended to be asleep.* ■ V-T If children or adults **pretend that** they are doing something, they imagine that they are doing it, for example as part of a game. ❑ *She can sunbathe and pretend she's in Spain.* ■ V-T If you do not **pretend that** something is the case, you do not claim that it is the case. [with neg] ❑ *We do not pretend that the past six years have been without problems for us.*

■ 타동사 -인 체하다 ❑ 사실 그렇지 않았지만 나는 사정이 정말 괜찮은 체했다. ❑ 때때로 그 소년은 잠든 체했다. ■ 타동사 -라고 가상하다 ❑ 그녀는 일광욕을 하며 자기가 스페인에 있다고 가상할 수 있다. ■ 타동사 주장하다 ❑ 지난 육 년 간 우리에게 아무런 문제가 없었던 것처럼 가장하지 않는다.

pre|tense /priːtɛns, prɪtɛns, BRIT prɪtɛns/ (pretenses) [BRIT **pretence**] ■ N-VAR A **pretense** is an action or way of behaving that is intended to make people believe something that is not true. ❑ *He goes to the library and makes a pretense of reading some Dickens.* ❑ *The pretense that truckers could never seriously compete for railroad business has been shattered.* ■ PHRASE If you do something **under false pretenses**, you do it when people do not know the truth about you and your intentions. ❑ *This interview was conducted under false pretenses.*

[영국영어 pretence] ■ 가산명사 또는 불가산명사 시늉, 위장 ❑ 그는 도서관에 가서 디킨스의 소설을 좀 읽는 시늉을 한다. ❑ 트럭 운송업자들이 철도 사업을 놓고 진지하게 경쟁할 리 없으리라는 위장은 이미 다 들통이 났다. ■ 구 거짓 구실로 ❑ 이 인터뷰는 거짓 구실로 이루어졌다.

pre|ten|sion /prɪtɛnʃⁿn/ (pretensions) ■ N-VAR If you say that someone has **pretensions**, you disapprove of them because they claim or pretend that they are more important than they really are. [DISAPPROVAL] ❑ *Her wide-eyed innocence soon exposes the pretensions of the art world.* ■ N-UNCOUNT If someone has **pretensions to** something, they claim to be or do that thing. [also N in pl, N to n/-ing, N to-inf] ❑ *The city has unrealistic pretensions to world-class status.*

■ 가산명사 또는 불가산명사 허세, 허풍 [탐탁찮음] ❑ 그녀의 때 묻지 않은 천진함이 이내 미술계의 허세를 폭로한다. ■ 불가산명사 주장 ❑ 그 도시는 자기들이 세계 정상의 위치에 있다는 비현실적인 주장을 한다. 형용사 허풍스러운, 허세 부리는 [탐탁찮음] ❑ 그의 대답은 말도 안 되는 허세투성이였다.

pre|ten|tious /prɪtɛnʃəs/ ADJ If you say that someone or something is **pretentious**, you mean that they try to seem important or significant, but you do not think that they are. [DISAPPROVAL] ❑ *His response was full of pretentious nonsense.*

pre|text /priːtɛkst/ (pretexts) N-COUNT A **pretext** is a reason which you pretend has caused you to do something. ❑ *They wanted a pretext for subduing the region by force.*

가산명사 구실, 핑계 ❑ 그들은 그 지역을 무력 정복하려는 것에 대한 구실을 원했다.

pret|ty ♦♦♢ /prɪti/ (prettier, prettiest) ■ ADJ If you describe someone, especially a girl, as **pretty**, you mean that they look nice and are attractive in a delicate way. ❑ *She's a very charming and very pretty girl.* ● **pret|ti|ly** /prɪtɪli/ ADV ❑ *She smiled again, prettily.* ■ ADJ A place or a thing that is **pretty** is attractive and pleasant, in a charming but not particularly unusual way. ❑ *Whitstable is still a very pretty little town.* ● **pret|ti|ly** ADV ❑ *The living-room was prettily decorated.* ■ ADV You can use **pretty** before an adjective or adverb to mean "quite" or "rather." [INFORMAL] [ADV adj/adv] ❑ *I had a pretty good idea what she was going to do.*

■ 형용사 예쁜, 귀여운 ❑ 그녀는 아주 매력적이고 매우 예쁜 소녀이다. ● 예쁘게 부사 ❑ 그녀는 다시 예쁘게 미소 지었다. ■ 형용사 멋진 ❑ 휫스터블은 여전히 아주 멋진 작은 도시이다. ● 멋지게 부사 ❑ 거실은 멋지게 꾸며져 있었다. ■ 부사 꽤, 상당히 [비격식체] ❑ 나는 그녀가 무슨 일을 하려는지 어지간히 알 것 같았다.

When you are describing someone's appearance, you generally use **pretty** and **beautiful** to describe women, girls, and babies. **Beautiful** is a much stronger word than **pretty**. The equivalent word for a man is **handsome**.

무엇의 price는 판매자가 구매자에게 지불하도록 요구하는 돈의 액수이다. ❑ 상자에 표시된 가격은 5달러였다. 서비스나 이용하기 위해 돈을

Good-looking and **attractive** can be used to describe people of either sex. **Pretty** can also be used to modify adjectives and adverbs but is less strong than **very**. In this sense, **pretty** is informal.

Thesaurus — pretty의 참조어

ADJ. beautiful, cute, lovely **1**
attractive, charming, pleasant **2**

---

pre|vail /prɪveɪl/ (prevails, prevailing, prevailed) **1** V-I If a proposal, principle, or opinion **prevails**, it gains influence or is accepted, often after a struggle or argument. □ *We hope that common sense would prevail.* □ *Rick still believes that justice will prevail.* **2** V-I If a situation, attitude, or custom **prevails** in a particular place at a particular time, it is normal or most common in that place at that time. □ *A similar situation prevails in America.* □ *...the confusion which had prevailed at the time of the revolution.* **3** V-I If one side in a battle, contest, or dispute **prevails**, it wins. □ *He appears to have the votes he needs to prevail.*

preva|lent /prevələnt/ ADJ A condition, practice, or belief that is **prevalent** is common. □ *This condition is more prevalent in women than in men.* □ *Smoking is becoming increasingly prevalent among younger women.* ● **preva|lence** N-UNCOUNT □ *...the prevalence of asthma in Britain and western Europe.*

pre|vent ♦♦◇ /prɪvent/ (prevents, preventing, prevented) **1** V-T To **prevent** something means to ensure that it does not happen. □ *These methods prevent pregnancy.* □ *Further treatment will prevent cancer from developing.* ● **pre|ven|tion** N-UNCOUNT □ *...the prevention of heart disease.* **2** V-T To **prevent** someone from doing something means to make it impossible for them to do it. □ *He said this would prevent companies from creating new jobs.* □ *Its nationals may be prevented from leaving the country.*

Thesaurus — prevent의 참조어

V. avoid, hold off, stop **1**

Word Partnership — prevent의 연어

N. prevent **attacks**, prevent **cancer**, prevent **damage**, prevent **disease**, prevent **infection**, prevent **injuries**, prevent **loss**, prevent **pregnancy**, prevent **problems**, prevent **violence**, prevent **war** **1**

---

pre|ven|ta|tive /prɪventətɪv/ ADJ **Preventative** means the same as **preventive**. [ADJ n]

pre|ven|tive /prɪventɪv/ ADJ **Preventive** actions are intended to help prevent things such as disease or crime. □ *Too much is spent on expensive curative medicine and too little on preventive medicine.*

pre|view /priːvjuː/ (previews) N-COUNT A **preview** is an opportunity to see something such as a movie, exhibition, or invention before it is open or available to the public. □ *He had gone to see the preview of a play.*

pre|vi|ous ♦♦◇ /priːviəs/ **1** ADJ A **previous** event or thing is one that happened or existed before the one that you are talking about. [ADJ n] □ *She has a teenage daughter from a previous marriage.* **2** ADJ You refer to the period of time or the thing immediately before the one that you are talking about as the **previous** one. [det ADJ] □ *It was a surprisingly dry day after the rain of the previous week.*

pre|vi|ous|ly ♦♦◇ /priːviəsli/ **1** ADV **Previously** means at some time before the period that you are talking about. □ *Guyana's railways were previously owned by private companies.* □ *The contract was awarded to a previously unknown company.* **2** ADV You can use **previously** to say how much earlier one event was than another event. [n ADV] □ *He had first entered the House 12 years previously.*

pre|war /priːwɔːr/ also **pre-war** ADJ **Prewar** is used to describe things that happened, existed, or were made in the period immediately before a war, especially the Second World War, 1939-45. □ *...Poland's prewar leader.*

prey /preɪ/ (preys, preying, preyed) **1** N-UNCOUNT-COLL A creature's **prey** are the creatures that it hunts and eats in order to live. □ *Electric rays stun their prey with huge electrical discharges.* **2** V-I A creature that **preys on** other creatures lives by catching and eating them. □ *The effect was to disrupt the food chain, starving many animals and those that preyed on them.* **3** N-UNCOUNT You can refer to the people who someone tries to harm or trick as their **prey**. □ *Police officers lie in wait for the gangs who stalk their prey at night.* **4** V-I If someone **preys on** other people, especially people who are unable to protect themselves, they take advantage of them or harm them in some way. [DISAPPROVAL] □ *Pam had never learned that there were men who preyed on young runaways.* **5** V-I If something **preys on** your mind, you cannot stop thinking and worrying about it. □ *It was a misunderstanding. Herr Kettner was unwise and it preyed on his conscience.* →see shark

price ♦♦♦ /praɪs/ (prices, pricing, priced) **1** N-COUNT The **price** of something is the amount of money that you have to pay in order to buy it. [usu with supp, also n N] □ *...a sharp increase in the price of petrol.* □ *They expected house prices to rise.* **2** N-SING The **price** that you pay for something that you want is an unpleasant thing that you have to do or suffer in order to get it. □ *Slovenia will have to pay a high price for independence.* □ *There may be a price to pay for such relentless activity, perhaps ill health or even divorce.* **3** V-T If something **is priced at** a particular amount, the price is set at that amount. □ *The shares are expected to be priced at*

지불하는 사물에 대해 말할 때에는, 대개 price보다는 charge나 fee를 쓴다. □ 전화 예약에는 1달러의 수수료가 있다....미지불된 400달러의 자료료. 무엇의 cost는 그것에 대해 실제 지불하거나 지불할 금액이다. □ 그 방을 현대화하는 데 든 총비용은 800달러밖에 안 되었다. cost의 주석도 보라.

1 자동사 우세하다, 승리하다 □ 우리는 상식이 우세하기를 바란다. □ 릭은 여전히 정의가 승리하리라고 믿는다. **2** 자동사 흔하다, 유행하다 □ 비슷한 상황이 미국에서는 흔히 있다. □ 혁명기에 흔히 있었던 혼란 **3** 자동사 이기다 □ 그는 이기기 위해 필요한 투표수를 확보한 것으로 보인다.

형용사 흔한, 널리 퍼진 □ 이 같은 상태는 여성들보다 남성들에게 더 흔하다. □ 흡연이 더 어린 여성들 사이에서 점점 더 흔해지고 있다. ● 널리 퍼짐, 유행 불가산명사 □ 영국과 서유럽에서의 천식의 유행

1 타동사 방지하다 □ 이러한 방법들은 임신을 방지한다. □ 치료를 더 받으면 암이 진행되는 것을 방지할 수 있을 겁니다. ● 방지, 예방 불가산명사 □ 심장 질환 예방 **2** 타동사 -하는 것을 막다 □ 그는 이것이 회사들의 새로운 일자리 창출을 막을 것이라고 말했다. □ 그 나라 국민들은 출국이 금지될 수도 있다.

형용사 예방의, 방지하는

형용사 예방의, 방지하는 □ 사람들은 치료약에 너무 많은 돈을 쓰고 예방약에는 너무 적은 돈을 쓴다.

가산명사 시사회, 시연회 □ 그는 어떤 연극의 시사회를 보러 갔었다.

1 형용사 이전의 □ 그녀에게는 이전 결혼에서 얻은 십 대인 딸이 하나 있다. **2** 형용사 바로 전의 □ 그 전주에 쏟아진 비 이후에 찾아온 놀랄 정도로 건조한 날이었다.

1 부사 이전에 □ 가이아나의 철도는 이전에는 민간 기업의 소유였다. □ 그 계약은 이전에 무명이었던 회사에게 주어졌다. **2** 부사 - 앞서, - 전에 □ 그가 의회에 처음 몸을 담은 것은 그보다 12년 전이었다.

형용사 전쟁 이전의 □ 폴란드의 전전(戰前) 지도자

1 불가산명사-집합 먹이 □ 시끈가오리는 강한 전기를 방전해서 먹이를 기절시킨다. **2** 자동사 -을 잡아먹고 살다 □ 그 결과 먹이 사슬이 교란되어 많은 동물들과 그것들을 먹이로 하는 동물들이 굶어 죽게 되었다. **3** 불가산명사 희생자, 제물 □ 경찰관들이 야간에 희생자에게 접근하는 갱들을 기다리며 잠복해 있다. **4** 자동사 이용해 먹다, 착취하다 [탐탁찮음] □ 팸은 어린 가출자들을 이용해 먹는 사람들이 있다는 사실을 들은 적이 없었다. **5** 자동사 (자꾸 떠올라) 괴롭히다 □ 그것은 오해였다. 케트너 씨는 어리석었고 그 일이 그의 양심을 괴롭혔다.

1 가산명사 가격 □ 기름값의 급격한 인상 □ 그들은 주택 가격이 오를 것으로 예상했다. **2** 단수명사 대가 □ 슬로베니아는 독립에 대해 비싼 대가를 치러야 할 것이다. □ 그와 같은 가차 없는 행동에는 대가가 따를 것이다. 어쩌면 건강 악화나 심지어는 이혼까지도 있을 수 있다. **3** 타동사 -로 가격이 책정되다 □ 그 주식들은 330펜스 정도에 가격이 책정될 것으로 예상된다. □ 분석가들은 디지털 사가 신제품 가격을 비교 가능한

about 330p. ❑ *Analysts predict that Digital will price the new line at less than half the cost of comparable IBM mainframes.* ● **pric**|**ing** N-UNCOUNT ❑ *It's hard to maintain competitive pricing.* ◳ →see also **retail price index, selling price.** ◳ PHRASE If you want something **at any price**, you are determined to get it, even if unpleasant things happen as a result. ❑ *If they wanted a deal at any price, they would have to face the consequences.* ◳ PHRASE If you can buy something that you want **at a price**, it is for sale, but it is extremely expensive. ❑ *Most goods are available, but at a price.* ◳ PHRASE If you get something that you want **at a price**, you get it but something unpleasant happens as a result. ❑ *Fame comes at a price.* ◳ to **price yourself out of the market** →see **market**

> The **price** of something is the amount of money that the seller is asking people to pay in order to buy them. ❑ *The price marked on the box was $5.* When you are referring to services, or to things that you pay to use, you usually talk about a **charge** or a **fee**, rather than a **price**. ❑ *There is a one dollar handling charge for telephone reservations....$400 in unpaid consulting fees.* The **cost** of something is the amount of money that you actually pay, or would pay, for it. ❑ *The total cost of modernizing the room came to just $800.* See also note at **cost.**

price|**less** /praɪslɪs/ ◳ ADJ If you say that something is **priceless**, you are emphasizing that it is worth a very large amount of money. [EMPHASIS] ❑ *They are priceless, unique and irreplaceable.* ◳ ADJ If you say that something is **priceless**, you approve of it because it is extremely useful. [APPROVAL] ❑ *They are a priceless record of a brief period in British history.*

price tag (**price tags**) also **price-tag** ◳ N-COUNT If something has a **price tag** of a particular amount, that is the amount that you must pay in order to buy it. [WRITTEN] ❑ *The monorail can be completed at the price tag of $1.7 billion.* ◳ N-COUNT In a store, the **price tag** on an article for sale is a small piece of card or paper which is attached to the article and which has the price written on it.

price war (**price wars**) N-COUNT If competing companies are involved in a **price war**, they each try to gain an advantage by lowering their prices as much as possible in order to sell more of their products and damage their competitors financially. [BUSINESS] ❑ *Their loss was partly due to a vicious price war between manufacturers that has cut margins to the bone.*

pricey /praɪsi/ (**pricier, priciest**) also **pricy** ADJ If you say that something is **pricey**, you mean that it is expensive. [INFORMAL] ❑ *Medical insurance is very pricey.*

prick /prɪk/ (**pricks, pricking, pricked**) ◳ V-T If you **prick** something or **prick** holes in it, you make small holes in it with a sharp object such as a pin. ❑ *Prick the potatoes and rub the skins with salt.* ◳ V-T If something sharp **pricks** you or if you **prick yourself with** something sharp, it sticks into you or presses your skin and causes you pain. ❑ *She had just pricked her finger with the needle.* ◳ N-COUNT A **prick** is a small, sharp pain that you get when something pricks you. ❑ *At the same time she felt a prick on her neck.*

prick|**ly** /prɪkəli/ ◳ ADJ Something that is **prickly** feels rough and uncomfortable, as if it has a lot of prickles. ❑ *The bunk mattress was hard, the blankets prickly and slightly damp.* ◳ ADJ Someone who is **prickly** loses their temper or gets upset very easily. ❑ *You know how prickly she is.* ◳ ADJ A **prickly** issue or subject is one that is rather complicated and difficult to discuss or resolve. ❑ *The issue is likely to prove a prickly one.*

pricy /praɪsi/ →see **pricey**

pride ♦◇◇ /praɪd/ (**prides, priding, prided**) ◳ N-UNCOUNT **Pride** is a feeling of satisfaction which you have because you or people close to you have done something good or possess something good. ❑ *...the sense of pride in a job well done.* ❑ *We take pride in offering you the highest standards.* ◳ N-UNCOUNT **Pride** is a sense of the respect that other people have for you, and that you have for yourself. ❑ *Davis had to salvage his pride.* ◳ N-UNCOUNT Someone's **pride** is the feeling that they have that they are better or more important than other people. [DISAPPROVAL] ❑ *His pride may still be his downfall.* ◳ V-T If you **pride** yourself **on** a quality or skill that you have, you are very proud of it. ❑ *Smith prides himself on being able to organize his own life.*

Word Partnership	pride의 연어
V.	take pride in *something* ◳
	feel pride ◳ ◳ ◳
N.	sense of pride, source of pride ◳-◳

priest ♦◇◇ /prist/ (**priests**) ◳ N-COUNT A **priest** is a member of the Christian clergy in the Catholic, Anglican, or Orthodox church. ❑ *He had trained to be a Catholic priest.* ◳ N-COUNT In many non-Christian religions a **priest** is a man who has particular duties and responsibilities in a place where people worship. ❑ *...a New Age priest or priestess.*

priest|**ess** /pristɪs/ (**priestesses**) N-COUNT A **priestess** is a woman in a non-Christian religion who has particular duties and responsibilities in a place where people worship. ❑ *...the priestess of the temple.*

priest|**hood** /pristhʊd/ ◳ N-UNCOUNT **Priesthood** is the position of being a priest or the period of time during which someone is a priest. ❑ *...the early rites*

아이비엠 사 본체 가격의 절반 이하로 매길 것으로 예측한다. ● 가격 책정 불가산명사 ❑ 계속해서 경쟁력 있는 가격을 책정하기는 어렵다. ◳ 구 어떠한 대가를 치르더라도 ❑ 만약 그들이 어떠한 대가를 치르더라도 협정을 원한다면, 그 결과를 직시해야만 할 것이다. ◳ 구 대단히 비싸게 ❑ 대부분의 상품들은 구입이 가능하지만, 가격이 대단히 비싸다. ◳ 구 대가를 치르고 ❑ 명성은 대가를 치러야만 얻을 수 있다.

> 무엇의 price는 판매자가 사람들에게 그것을 사려면 지불하도록 하는 금액이다. ❑ 상자에 표시된 가격은 5달러이다. 이용하기 위해 돈을 지불하는 서비스나 사물을 지칭할 때에는, 대개 price 보다는 charge 또는 fee를 쓴다. ❑ 전화 예약에는 1달러의 수수료가 있다....지불하지 않은 자문료 400달러. 무엇의 cost는 그것에 대해 실제 지불하거나 지불할 금액이다. ❑ 그 방을 현대화하는 데 든 총비용은 800달러밖에 안되었다. cost의 주석도 보시오.

◳ 형용사 대단히 값진 [강조] ❑ 그것들은 대단히 값지고 독특하며 다른 것과 바꿀 수 없다. ◳ 형용사 대단히 귀중한 [마음에 듦] ❑ 그것들은 영국 역사상 짧은 한 시기에 대한 대단히 귀중한 기록이다.

◳ 가산명사 가격, 비용 [문어체] ❑ 그 모노레일은 17억 달러의 비용을 들여야 완공될 수 있다. ◳ 가산명사 가격표

가산명사 가격 할인 경쟁 [경제] ❑ 그들의 손실은 부분적으로는 이문을 극도로 감축해 온 제조사들 간의 치열한 가격 할인 경쟁에 기인한 것이었다.

형용사 비싼 [비격식체] ❑ 의료 보험은 매우 비싸다.

◳ 타동사 살짝 찔러 작은 구멍을 내다 ❑ 감자를 살짝살짝 찔러 작은 구멍을 낸 다음 껍질을 소금으로 문지르세요. ◳ 타동사 찌르다 ❑ 그녀는 막 바늘에 손가락을 찔린 참이었다. ◳ 가산명사 동증, 따끔함 ❑ 동시에 그녀는 목에 찌르는 듯한 통증을 느꼈다.

◳ 형용사 따끔거리는 ❑ 침대 매트리스는 딱딱했고, 담요는 따끔거리고 약간 축축했다. ◳ 형용사 팩 하고 화를 잘 내는 ❑ 그녀가 얼마나 팩 하고 화를 잘 내는지 알잖아. ◳ 형용사 성가신, 골치 아픈 ❑ 그 문제가 골치 아픈 것이 될 것 같다.

◳ 불가산명사 자부심, 자랑스러움 ❑ 잘 해 낸 일에 대한 자부심 ❑ 우리는 여러분께 최고의 수준을 제공해 드리는 것을 자랑스럽게 생각합니다. ◳ 불가산명사 자존심 ❑ 데이비스는 자신의 자존심을 회복해야 했다. ◳ 불가산명사 자만심, 오만 [탐탁찮음] ❑ 그의 자만심이 여전히 그가 몰락하는 원인이 될 수 있다. ◳ 타동사 ~을 자랑스러워하다 ❑ 스미스는 자신의 인생을 체계적으로 조직할 수 있음을 자랑스러워한다.

◳ 가산명사 사제 ❑ 그는 천주교 사제 교육을 받았었다. ◳ 가산명사 성직자 ❑ 뉴 에이지 남녀 성직자들

가산명사 여자 사제, 여성 성직자 ❑ 그 신전의 여자 사제

◳ 불가산명사 성직자의 지위; 성직자로서 보낸 기간 ❑ 성직자가 되기 위한 초기 의례 ◳ 단수명사 (집합적)

a b c d e f g h i j k l m n o p q r s t u v w x y z

A

of priesthood. **2** N-SING **The priesthood** is all the members of the Christian clergy, especially in a particular Church. ❏ *Should the General Synod vote women into the priesthood?*

성직자 **2** 전체 종교 회의에서 여성들을 성직자로 선출해야 할까?

B

prim /prɪm/ ADJ If you describe someone as **prim**, you disapprove of them because they behave too correctly and are too easily shocked by anything vulgar. [DISAPPROVAL] ❏ *We tend to imagine that the Victorians were very prim and proper.* ● **prim|ly** ADV [ADV with v] ❏ *We sat primly at either end of a long settee.*

형용사 딱딱한, 근엄한 [탐탁잖음] ❏ 우리는 빅토리아 시대의 사람들이 매우 근엄하고 점잖았다고 생각하는 경향이 있다. ● 딱딱하게, 근엄하게 부사 ❏ 우리는 기다란 의자 양 끝에 딱딱하게 앉아 있었다.

C

pri|mal /ˈpraɪml/ ADJ **Primal** is used to describe something that relates to the origins of things or that is very basic. [FORMAL] ❏ *Jealousy is a primal emotion.*

형용사 근원적인 [격식체] ❏ 질투는 원시적인 감정이다.

D

pri|mar|i|ly /praɪˈmɛərɪli, BRIT ˈpraɪmərɪli/ ADV You use **primarily** to say what is mainly true in a particular situation. ❏ *...a book aimed primarily at high-energy physicists.* ❏ *Public order is primarily an urban problem.*

부사 주로 ❏ 주로 고 에너지 물리학자들을 겨냥한 책 ❏ 공공 치안은 주로 도시 문제이다.

E

Word Link   *prim ≈ first : primary, primate, prime*

F

pri|ma|ry ♦◇◇ /ˈpraɪməri, -mɛri, BRIT ˈpraɪməri/ (**primaries**) **1** ADJ You use **primary** to describe something that is very important. [FORMAL] [ADJ n] ❏ *That's the primary reason the company's share price has held up so well.* ❏ *His misunderstanding of language was the primary cause of his other problems.* **2** ADJ **Primary** education is given to students between the ages of 5 and 11. [mainly BRIT; AM **elementary**] [ADJ n] ❏ *Britain did not introduce compulsory primary education until 1880.* ❏ *Ninety-nine per cent of primary pupils now have hands-on experience of computers.* **3** ADJ **Primary** is used to describe something that occurs first. [ADJ n] ❏ *It is not the primary tumor that kills, but secondary growths elsewhere in the body.* **4** N-COUNT A **primary** or a **primary election** is an election in an American state in which people vote for someone to become a candidate for a political office. Compare **general election.** ❏ *...the 1968 New Hampshire primary.*

1 형용사 중요한 [격식체] ❏ 그것이 그 회사 주가가 그렇게 잘 버텨 온 중요한 이유이다. ❏ 말을 오해하는 것이 그가 가진 다른 문제들의 중요한 원인이다. **2** 형용사 초등 교육의 [주로 영국영어; 미국영어 elementary] ❏ 영국은 1880년이 되어서야 초등 의무 교육을 도입했다. ❏ 현재 초등학생의 99 퍼센트가 컴퓨터를 실제로 조작해 본 경험이 있다. **3** 형용사 첫째의, 일차적인 ❏ 사람을 죽게 하는 것은 1차 종양이 아니라, 채내 다른 부위에 생기는 2차 종양이다. **4** 가산명사 예비 선거 ❏ 1968년의 뉴햄프셔 예비 선거

G

H

I

J

pri|ma|ry school (**primary schools**) N-VAR A **primary school** is a school for children between the ages of 5 and 11. [mainly BRIT; AM usually **elementary school**] ❏ *...eight-to nine-year-olds in their third year at primary school.*

가산명사 또는 불가산명사 초등학교 [주로 영국영어; 미국영어 대개 elementary school] ❏ 초등학교 3학년인 여덟, 아홉 살짜리 아이들

pri|mate /ˈpraɪmət/ (**primates**)

The pronunciation /ˈpraɪmeɪt/ is also used for meaning **2**.

2의 의미일 때는 발음이 /ˈpraɪmeɪt /으로도 된다.

K

1 N-COUNT A **primate** is a member of the group of mammals which includes humans, monkeys, and apes. ❏ *The woolly spider monkey is the largest primate in the Americas.* **2** N-COUNT **The Primate of** a particular country or region is the most important priest in that country or region. ❏ *...the Roman Catholic Primate of All Ireland.*
→see Word Web: **primate**

1 가산명사 영장류 (동물) ❏ 털이 많은 거미원숭이는 아메리카 대륙에서 가장 큰 영장류이다. **2** 가산명사 대주교 ❏ 전(全) 아일랜드 로마 가톨릭 대주교

L

M

prime ♦◇◇ /praɪm/ (**primes, priming, primed**) **1** ADJ You use **prime** to describe something that is most important in a situation. [ADJ n] ❏ *Political stability, meanwhile, will be a prime concern.* ❏ *It could be a prime target for guerrilla attack.* **2** ADJ You use **prime** to describe something that is of the best possible quality. [ADJ n] ❏ *It was one of the City's prime sites, giving a clear view of the Stock Exchange and the Bank of England.* **3** ADJ You use **prime** to describe an example of a particular kind of thing that is absolutely typical. [ADJ n] ❏ *The prime example is Macy's, once the undisputed king of California retailers.* **4** N-UNCOUNT If someone or something is **in their prime**, they are at the stage in their existence when they are at their strongest, most active, or most successful. ❏ *We've had a series of athletes trying to come back well past their prime.* **5** V-T If you **prime** someone **to** do something, you prepare them to do it, for example by giving them information about it beforehand. ❏ *Claire wished she'd primed Sarah beforehand.* ❏ *Marianne had not known until Arnold primed her for her duties that she was to be the sole female.*

1 형용사 가장 중요한 ❏ 그러는 동안, 정치적 안정이 가장 중요한 관심사가 될 것이다. ❏ 그것은 게릴라 공격의 가장 중요한 표적이 될지도 모른다. **2** 형용사 최고의 ❏ 그곳은 그 시에서 가장 좋은 터 중 하나로, 증권 거래소와 영국 중앙은행이 한눈에 들어왔다. **3** 형용사 전형적인 ❏ 전형적인 예는, 한때 의심할 바 없는 캘리포니아 소매업계의 제왕이었던 메이시스 백화점이다. **4** 불가산명사 전성기 ❏ 아마도 나는 지금 전성기에 접어들고 있는 것 같다. ❏ 전성기를 한참 지난 뒤에 재기를 시도하는 육상 선수들이 계속 있어 왔다. **5** 타동사 귀띔을 해 주다, 준비시키다 ❏ 클레어는 미리 사라에게 귀띔을 해 주었다면 좋았을 텐데 하고 생각했다. ❏ 메리앤은 아놀드로부터 자신의 임무에 대한 귀띔을 받기 전까지 자신이 유일한 여자가 되리라는 사실을 알지 못했다.

N

O

P

Q

Prime Min|is|ter ♦♦♦ (**Prime Ministers**) N-COUNT The leader of the government in some countries is called **the Prime Minister.** [usu the N; N-TITLE; N-VOC] ❏ *...the former Prime Minister of Pakistan, Miss Benazir Bhutto.* →see **government**

가산명사 수상 ❏ 파키스탄의 전 수상 베나지르 부토

R

prime rate (**prime rates**) N-COUNT A bank's **prime rate** is the lowest rate of interest which it charges at a particular time and which is offered only to certain customers. [BUSINESS] ❏ *At least one bank cut its prime rate today.*

가산명사 우대 금리 [경제] ❏ 최소한 한 개 은행이 오늘 우대 금리를 낮췄다.

S

prime time also **primetime** N-UNCOUNT **Prime time** television or radio programs are broadcast when the greatest number of people are watching television or listening to the radio, usually in the evenings. ❏ *...a prime-time television show.*

불가산명사 황금 시간대 ❏ 황금 시간대 텔레비전 프로그램

T

primi|tive /ˈprɪmɪtɪv/ **1** ADJ **Primitive** means belonging to a society in which people live in a very simple way, usually without industries or a writing

1 형용사 원시적인 ❏ 원시 사회에 대한 연구 **2** 형용사 원시 생물의 ❏ 원시 고래 ❏ 원시 인류는 위험한

U

V

Word Web   primate

The classification **primate** includes **monkeys, apes,** and **humans.** Scientists have shown that humans and the other primates share some surprising similarities. We used to believe that only humans favor one hand over the other. However, researchers carefully observed a group of 66 **chimpanzees.** They found that chimps are also right-handed and left-handed. Other researchers have learned that chimpanzee groups have different cultures. In 1972 a female **gorilla** named Koko began to learn sign language from a college student. Today Koko understands about 2,000 words and can sign about 500 of them. She makes up sentences using three to six words.

W

X

Y

Z

system. □ ...*studies of primitive societies.* ◳ ADJ **Primitive** means belonging to a very early period in the development of an animal or plant. □ ...*primitive whales.* □ *Primitive humans needed to be able to react like this to escape from dangerous animals.* ◳ ADJ If you describe something as **primitive**, you mean that it is very simple in style or very old-fashioned. □ *The conditions are primitive by any standards.*

prim|rose /prɪmrouz/ (**primroses**) N-VAR A **primrose** is a wild plant which has pale yellow flowers in the spring.

prince ♦♦◇ /prɪns/ (**princes**) ◳ N-TITLE; N-COUNT A **prince** is a male member of a royal family, especially the son of the king or queen of a country. □ ...*Prince Edward and other royal guests.* ◳ N-TITLE; N-COUNT A **prince** is the male royal ruler of a small country or state. □ *He was speaking without the prince's authority.*

prin|cess ♦♦◇ /prɪnsɪs, -sɛs, BRIT prɪnsɪz/ (**princesses**) N-TITLE; N-COUNT A **princess** is a female member of a royal family, usually the daughter of a king or queen or the wife of a prince. □ *Princess Anne topped the guest list.*

prin|ci|pal ♦◇◇ /prɪnsɪp^əl/ (**principals**) ◳ ADJ **Principal** means first in order of importance. [ADJ n] □ *The principal reason for my change of mind is this.* □ ...*the country's principal source of foreign exchange earnings.* ◳ N-COUNT The **principal** of a school, or in Britain the **principal** of a college, is the person in charge of the school or college. □ *Donald King is the principal of Dartmouth High School.* →see **bank, interest rate**

prin|ci|pal|ly /prɪnsɪpli/ ADV **Principally** means more than anything else. [ADV with cl/group] □ *This is principally because the major export markets are slowing.*

prin|ci|ple ♦♦◇ /prɪnsɪp^əl/ (**principles**) ◳ N-VAR A **principle** is a general belief that you have about the way you should behave, which influences your behavior. □ *Buck never allowed himself to be bullied into doing anything that went against his principles.* □ *It's not just a matter of principle.* ◳ N-COUNT The **principles of** a particular theory or philosophy are its basic rules or laws. □ ...*a violation of the basic principles of Marxism.* ◳ N-COUNT Scientific **principles** are general scientific laws which explain how something happens or works. □ *These people lack all understanding of scientific principles.* ◳ PHRASE If you agree with something in **principle**, you agree in general terms to the idea of it, although you do not yet know the details or know if it will be possible. □ *I agree with it in principle but I doubt if it will happen in practice.* ◳ PHRASE If something is possible in **principle**, there is no known reason why it should not happen, even though it has not happened before. □ *Even assuming this to be in principle possible, it will not be achieved soon.* ◳ PHRASE If you refuse to do something **on principle**, you refuse to do it because of a particular belief that you have. □ *He would vote against it on principle.*

prin|ci|pled /prɪnsɪp^əld/ ADJ If you describe someone as **principled**, you approve of them because they have strong moral principles. [APPROVAL] □ *She was a strong, principled woman.*

print ♦♦◇ /prɪnt/ (**prints, printing, printed**) ◳ V-T If someone **prints** something such as a book or newspaper, they produce it in large quantities using a machine. □ *He started to print his own posters to distribute abroad.* □ *Our brochure is printed on environmentally-friendly paper.* ● PHRASAL VERB In American English, **print up** means the same as **print**. □ *Community workers here are printing up pamphlets for peace demonstrations.* ● **printing** N-UNCOUNT [oft N n] □ *His brother ran a printing and publishing company.* ◳ V-T If a newspaper or magazine **prints** a piece of writing, it includes it or publishes it. □ *We can only print letters which are accompanied by the writer's name and address.* ◳ V-T If numbers, letters, or designs **are printed on** a surface, they are put on it in ink or dye using a machine. You can also say that a surface **is printed with** numbers, letters, or designs. □ ...*the number printed on the receipt.* □ *The company has for some time printed its phone number on its products.* ◳ N-COUNT A **print** is a piece of clothing or material with a pattern printed on it. You can also refer to the pattern itself as a **print**. □ *Her mother wore one of her dark summer prints.* □ *In this living room we've mixed glorious floral prints.* ◳ V-T When you **print** a photograph, you produce it from a negative. □ *Printing a black-and-white negative on to color paper produces a similar monochrome effect.* ◳ N-COUNT A **print** is a photograph from a film that has been developed. □ ...*black and white prints of Margaret and Jean as children.* ◳ N-COUNT A **print** is one of a number of copies of a particular picture. It can be either a photograph, something such as a painting, or a picture made by an artist who puts ink on a prepared surface and presses it against paper. □ ...*12 original copper plates engraved by William Hogarth for his famous series of prints.* ◳ N-UNCOUNT **Print** is used to refer to letters and numbers as they appear on the pages of a book, newspaper, or printed document. □ ...*columns of tiny print.* ◳ ADJ The **print** media consists of newspapers and magazines, but not television or radio. [ADJ n] □ *I have been convinced that the print media are more accurate and more reliable than television.* ◳ V-T If you **print** words, you write in letters that are not joined together and that look like the letters in a book or newspaper. □ *Print your name and address on a postcard and send it to us.* ◳ N-COUNT You can refer to a mark left by someone's foot as a **print**. □ *He crawled from print to print, sniffing at the earth, following the scent left in the tracks.* ◳ N-COUNT You can refer to invisible marks left by someone's fingers as their **prints**. □ *Fresh prints of both girls were found in the flat.* ◳ →see also **printing** ◳ PHRASE If you appear in **print**, or get **into print**, what you say or write is published in a book, newspaper, or magazine. □ *Many of these poets appeared in print only long after their deaths.* ◳ PHRASE The **small print** or the **fine print** of something such as an advertisement or a contract consists of the technical details and legal conditions, which are often printed in much smaller letters than the rest of the text. □ *I'm looking at the small print; I don't want to sign anything that I shouldn't sign.*

동물들에게서 달아나기 위해 이처럼 반응할 수 있어야 했다. ◳ 형용사 단순한, 투박한 □ 그 조건들은 어떤 기준에 비추어 보더라도 소박하다.

가산명사 또는 불가산명사 앵초

◳ 경칭명사; 가산명사 왕자 □ 에드워드 왕자와 다른 왕족 내빈들 ◳ 경칭명사; 가산명사 (작은 나라의) 군주 □ 그는 군주로서의 권위 없이 이야기를 하고 있었다.

경칭명사; 가산명사 공주 □ 앤 공주가 내빈 명단 맨 위에 올라 있었다.

◳ 형용사 주된, 가장 중요한 □ 내가 마음을 바꾼 가장 중요한 이유는 이것이다. □ 그 나라의 주된 대외 교역 수입원 ◳ 가산명사 교장; 학장 □ 도널드 킹은 다트머스 고등학교 교장이다.

부사 주로, 무엇보다도 □ 이는 무엇보다도 주요 수출 시장이 둔화되고 있기 때문이다.

◳ 가산명사 또는 불가산명사 원칙 □ 벅은 절대로 위협에 굴복해 자신의 원칙에 반하는 일을 하지 않았다. □ 그것은 단순히 원칙의 문제가 아니다. ◳ 가산명사 원리 □ 마르크시즘의 기본 원리에 대한 위반 ◳ 가산명사 원리 □ 이 사람들은 과학적 원리에 대한 이해가 전혀 부족하다. ◳ 구 원칙적으로 □ 나는 원칙적으로 그것에 동의하지만 실제로 그것이 성사될지는 미심쩍다. ◳ 구 원칙적으로 □ 이것이 원칙적으로 가능하다고 추정하더라도, 그것이 빠른 시일 내에 성사되지는 않을 것이다. ◳ 구 원칙에 따라 □ 그는 원칙에 따라 그것에 반대표를 던질 것이었다.

형용사 절조가 있는 [마음에 듦] □ 그녀는 강인하고 절조가 있는 여자였다.

◳ 타동사 인쇄하다 □ 그는 해외에 배포하기 위해 자신의 포스터를 인쇄하기 시작했다. □ 저희 책자는 환경 친화적 용지로 제작됩니다. ● 구동사 인쇄하다 □ 이곳의 지역 운동가들이 평화 시위를 위한 선전물을 인쇄하고 있습니다. ● 인쇄 불가산명사 □ 그의 형은 인쇄 출판 회사를 운영했다. ◳ 타동사 게재하다 □ 우리는 보낸 사람의 이름과 주소가 적혀 있는 편지들만 게재할 수 있습니다. ◳ 타동사 찍히다, 인쇄되다 □ 영수증에 찍힌 숫자 □ 그 회사는 한동안 제품에 자사 전화번호를 찍어 넣어 왔다. ◳ 가산명사 날염 옷감; 날염 무늬 □ 그녀의 어머니는 짙은 색의 여름용 무늬옷 중 하나를 입고 있었다. □ 이 거실에는 화려한 여러 가지 꽃무늬들을 섞어서 꾸며 보았습니다. ◳ 타동사 인화하다 □ 흑백 원판을 컬러 인화지에 인화하면 비슷한 단색 효과가 나옵니다. ◳ 가산명사 (인화된) 사진 □ 마거릿과 진의 어린 시절 흑백 사진들 ◳ 가산명사 판화 □ 윌리엄 호가스가 그의 유명한 판화 연작을 위해 판 12개의 동판 원본 ◳ 불가산명사 인쇄된 글자, 활자 □ 작은 활자로 인쇄된 칼럼들 ◳ 형용사 인쇄 매체의 □ 나는 인쇄 매체가 텔레비전보다 더 정확하고 믿을 만하다고 확신해 왔다. ◳ 타동사 활자체로 쓰다 □ 우편엽서에 이름과 주소를 활자체로 적어서 저희에게 보내 주세요. ◳ 가산명사 발자국 □ 그 개는 발자국 하나하나를 따라가며 땅에 코를 대고 킁킁거리면서 지나간 길에 남겨진 냄새를 좇아갔다. ◳ 가산명사 지문 □ 최근에 생긴 듯한 두 소녀의 지문이 그 아파트에서 발견되었다. ◳ 구 활자화되어 □ 이 시인들 중 많은 사람의 작품이 그들이 죽고 나서 오랜 후에야 출간되었다. ◳ 구 (계약서 등의) 작은 글자 부분 □ 나는 작은 글자로 된 부분을 보고 있어. 서명하지 말아야 할 것에 서명하고 싶지 않거든.

a
b
c
d
e
f
g
h
i
j
k
l
m
n
o
p
q
r
s
t
u
v
w
x
y
z

▶print out PHRASAL VERB If a computer or a machine attached to a computer **prints** something **out**, it produces a copy of it on paper. □ *You measure yourself, enter measurements and the computer will print out the pattern.* →see also **printout** →see **photography**

구동사 인쇄하다 (컴퓨터), 출력하다 □ 자신의 치수를 재서 입력하면 컴퓨터가 견본을 인쇄 출력할 것이다.

print|er /prɪntər/ (**printers**) **1** N-COUNT A **printer** is a machine that can be connected to a computer in order to make copies on paper of documents or other information held by the computer. →see also **laser printer 2** N-COUNT A **printer** is a person or company whose job is printing things such as books. □ *The manuscript had already been sent off to the printers.* →see **office, printing**

1 가산명사 프린터 **2** 가산명사 인쇄업자, 인쇄소 □ 원고는 이미 인쇄소에 보내진 상태였다.

print|ing /prɪntɪŋ/ (**printings**) N-COUNT If copies of a book are printed and published on a number of different occasions, you can refer to each of these occasions as a **printing**. □ *The American edition of "Cloud Street" is already in its third printing.* →see also **print** →see Word Web: **printing**

가산명사 -쇄 □ '클라우드 스트리트'의 미국판은 이미 3쇄에 들어가 있다.

print|out /prɪntaʊt/ (**printouts**) also **print-out** N-COUNT A **printout** is a piece of paper on which information from a computer or similar device has been printed. □ *...a computer printout of various financial projections.*

가산명사 인쇄 출력한 문서 □ 여러 가지 재무 계획을 컴퓨터로 인쇄 출력한 문서

pri|or ♦◇◇ /praɪər/ **1** ADJ You use **prior** to indicate that something has already happened, or must happen, before another event takes place. [ADJ n] □ *He claimed he had no prior knowledge of the protest.* □ *The Constitution requires the president to seek the prior approval of Congress for military action.* **2** ADJ A **prior** claim or duty is more important than other claims or duties and needs to be dealt with first. [ADJ n] □ *The firm I wanted to use had prior commitments.* **3** PHRASE If something happens **prior to** a particular time or event, it happens before that time or event. [FORMAL] □ *In the car industry, the August sales will involve a build up of stocks prior to this date.*

1 형용사 사전의, 앞의 □ 그는 그 시위에 대한 사전 지식이 없었다고 주장했다. □ 헌법은 군사 행동에 대해 의회의 사전 동의를 구할 것을 대통령에게 요구한다. **2** 형용사 (-보다) 중요한, 우선적인 □ 내가 이용하려 싶었던 업체는 먼저 예약된 다른 일들이 있었다. **3** 구 -보다 전에 [격식체] □ 자동차 업계에서는, 8월 판매를 위해 이 날짜 이전에 재고의 축적이 필요할 것이다.

Word Partnership	prior의 연어
N.	prior **approval**, prior **experience**, prior **knowledge**, prior **notice**, prior **year** **1** prior **commitment** **2**

pri|or|itize /praɪɒrɪtaɪz, BRIT praɪɒrɪtaɪz/ (**prioritizes, prioritizing, prioritized**) [BRIT also **prioritise**] **1** V-T If you **prioritize** something, you treat it as more important than other things. □ *The government is prioritizing the service sector, rather than investing in industry and production.* **2** V-T If you **prioritize** the tasks that you have to do, you decide which are the most important and do them first. □ *Make lists of what to do and prioritize your tasks.*

[영국영어 prioritise] **1** 타동사 우선시하다 □ 정부는 산업과 생산에 투자하기보다 서비스 분야를 우선시하고 있다. **2** 타동사 우선순위를 매기다 □ 해야 할 일의 목록을 만들어서 당신의 과업에 우선순위를 매기시오.

pri|or|ity ♦◇◇ /praɪɒrɪti/ (**priorities**) **1** N-COUNT If something is a **priority**, it is the most important thing you have to do or deal with, or must be done or dealt with before everything else you have to do. □ *Being a parent is her first priority.* □ *The government's priority is to build more power plants.* **2** PHRASE If you **give priority to** something or someone, you treat them as more important than anything or anyone else. □ *Women are more likely to give priority to child care and education policies.* **3** PHRASE If something **takes priority** or **has priority over** other things, it is regarded as being more important than them and is dealt with first. □ *The fight against inflation took priority over measures to combat the deepening recession.*

1 가산명사 급선무, 우선 사항 □ 아이를 갖는 것이 그녀의 최고 급선무였다. □ 정부의 급선무는 발전소를 더 짓는 것이다. **2** 구 -을 우선시하다 □ 여성들은 육아와 교육 정책을 우선시할 가능성이 더 크다. **3** 구 -보다 우선시되다 □ 심화되는 경기 침체에 맞서 싸우기 위한 조치보다 인플레이션에 맞선 투쟁이 우선시되었다.

prise /praɪz/ →see **prize**

pris|on ♦♦◇ /prɪzᵊn/ (**prisons**) N-VAR A **prison** is a building where criminals are kept as punishment or where people accused of a crime are kept before their trial. □ *The prison's inmates are being kept in their cells.*

가산명사 또는 불가산명사 교도소 □ 교도소 재소자들은 감방 안에 갇혀 있다.

Word Partnership	prison의 연어
N.	**life in** prison, prison **officials**, prison **population**, prison **reform**, prison **sentence**, prison **time**
V.	**die in** prison, **escape from** prison, **face** prison, **go to** prison, **release** *someone* **from** prison, **send** *someone* **to** prison, **serve/spend time in** prison

pris|on|er ♦♦◇ /prɪzənər/ (**prisoners**) **1** N-COUNT A **prisoner** is a person who is kept in a prison as a punishment for a crime that they have committed. □ *The committee is concerned about the large number of prisoners sharing cells.* **2** N-COUNT A **prisoner** is a person who has been captured by an enemy, for example in war. [also hold/take n N] □ *...wartime hostages and concentration-camp prisoners.* →see **war**

1 가산명사 죄수 □ 위원회는 감방을 함께 쓰는 죄수들의 숫자가 많은 것에 대해 염려하고 있다. **2** 가산명사 포로 □ 전시 인질들과 수용소 포로들

Word Web   printing

Before the invention of **printing**, scribes wrote **documents** by hand. The earliest **printers** were the Chinese. They used pieces of wood with rows of **characters** carved into them. Later, they started using **movable type** made of baked clay. They created full **pages** by lining up rows of type. A German named Gutenberg expanded on the idea of movable type. He produced the first metal type. He also introduced the printing press. The idea came from the centuries-old wine press. In the 1500s, printed advertisements first appeared in the form of handbills. The earliest newspapers were **published** in the 1600s.

pris|tine /ˈprɪstin, prɪsˈtin/ ADJ **Pristine** things are extremely clean or new. [FORMAL] ❑ *Now the house is in pristine condition.*

pri|va|cy /ˈpraɪvəsi, BRIT ˈprɪvəsi/ N-UNCOUNT If you have **privacy**, you are in a place or situation which allows you to do things without other people seeing you or disturbing you. ❑ *He greatly resented the publication of this book, which he saw as an embarrassing invasion of his privacy.* ❑ *Thatched pavilions provide shady retreats for relaxing and reading in privacy.*

pri|vate ♦♦◇ /ˈpraɪvɪt/ (**privates**) **1** ADJ **Private** industries and services are owned or controlled by an individual person or a commercial company, rather than by the government or an official organization. [BUSINESS] ❑ *...a joint venture with private industry.* ❑ *Bupa runs private hospitals in Britain.* ● **pri|vate|ly** ADV [ADV with v] ❑ *No other European country has so much state ownership and so few privately owned businesses.* **2** ADJ **Private** individuals are acting only for themselves, and are not representing any group, company, or organization. [ADJ n] ❑ *...the law's insistence that private citizens are not permitted to have weapons.* ❑ *The King was on a private visit to enable him to pray at the tombs of his ancestors.* **3** ADJ Your **private** things belong only to you, or may only be used by you. ❑ *They want more State control over private property.* **4** ADJ **Private** places or gatherings may be attended only by a particular group of people, rather than by the general public. ❑ *673 private golf clubs took part in a recent study.* ❑ *The door is marked "Private."* **5** ADJ **Private** meetings, discussions, and other activities involve only a small number of people, and very little information about them is given to other people. ❑ *Don't bug private conversations, and don't buy papers that reprint them.* ● **pri|vate|ly** ADV ❑ *Few senior figures have issued any public statements but privately the resignation's been welcomed.* **6** ADJ Your **private life** is that part of your life that is concerned with your personal relationships and activities, rather than with your work or business. ❑ *I've always kept my private and professional life separate.* **7** ADJ Your **private** thoughts or feelings are ones that you do not talk about to other people. ❑ *We all felt as if we were intruding on his private grief.* ● **pri|vate|ly** ADV ❑ *Privately, she worries about whether she's really good enough.* **8** ADJ If you describe a place as **private**, or as somewhere where you can be **private**, you mean that it is a quiet place and you can be alone there without being disturbed. ❑ *It was the only reasonably private place they could find.* **9** ADJ If you describe someone as a **private** person, you mean that they are very quiet by nature and do not reveal their thoughts and feelings to other people. ❑ *Gould was an intensely private individual.* **10** N-COUNT; N-TITLE A **private** is a soldier of the lowest rank in an army or the marines. ❑ *He was a private in the U.S. Army.* **11** →see also **privately** **12** PHRASE If you do something **in private**, you do it without other people being present, often because it is something that you want to keep secret. ❑ *Some of what we're talking about might better be discussed in private.*

pri|vate en|ter|prise N-UNCOUNT **Private enterprise** is industry and business which is owned by individual people or commercial companies, and not by the government or an official organization. [BUSINESS] ❑ *...the government's plans to sell state companies to private enterprise.*

pri|vate|ly /ˈpraɪvɪtli/ ADV If you buy or sell something **privately**, you buy it from or sell it to another person directly, rather than in a store or through a business. [ADV after v] ❑ *The whole process makes buying a car privately as painless as buying from a garage.* →see also **private**

pri|vate school (**private schools**) N-VAR A **private school** is a school which is not supported financially by the government and which parents have to pay for their children to go to. ❑ *He attended Eton, the most exclusive private school in Britain.*

pri|vate sec|tor N-SING The **private sector** is the part of a country's economy which consists of industries and commercial companies that are not owned or controlled by the government. [BUSINESS] ❑ *...small firms in the private sector.*

pri|vat|ize ♦◇◇ /ˈpraɪvətaɪz/ (**privatizes, privatizing, privatized**) [BRIT also **privatise**] V-T If a company, industry, or service that is owned by the state **is privatized**, the government sells it and makes it a private company. [BUSINESS] ❑ *The water boards are about to be privatized.* ❑ *...a pledge to privatize the rail and coal industries.* ● **pri|vati|za|tion** /ˌpraɪvətaɪˈzeɪʃⁿn/ (**privatizations**) N-VAR ❑ *...the privatization of British Rail.*

privi|lege /ˈprɪvɪlɪdʒ, ˈprɪvlɪdʒ/ (**privileges**) **1** N-COUNT A **privilege** is a special right or advantage that only one person or group has. ❑ *The Russian Federation has issued a decree abolishing special privileges for government officials.* **2** N-UNCOUNT If you talk about **privilege**, you are talking about the power and advantage that only a small group of people have, usually because of their wealth or their high social class. ❑ *Pironi was the son of privilege and wealth, and it showed.* **3** N-SING You can use **privilege** in expressions such as **be a privilege** or **have the privilege** when you want to show your appreciation of someone or something or to show your respect. ❑ *It must be a privilege to know such a man.*

Word Partnership	*privilege*의 연어
ADJ.	**special** privilege **1**
N.	**attorney-client** privilege, **executive** privilege **1**
	power and privilege **2**

privi|leged /ˈprɪvɪlɪdʒd, ˈprɪvlɪdʒd/ **1** ADJ Someone who is **privileged** has an advantage or opportunity that most other people do not have, often because

형용사 아주 깨끗한; 완전 새것인 [격식체] ❑ 현재 그 집은 완전 새 집 상태이다.

불가산명사 사적 자유; 사생활 ❑ 그는 이 책의 출판에 몹시 분개했는데, 그것을 자신의 사생활에 대한 심각한 침해로 보았기 때문이다. ❑ 초가지붕을 인 정자들이 방해받지 않고 편안히 쉬면서 독서를 할 수 있는 그늘진 휴식처를 제공합니다.

1 형용사 사설의, 민간의 [경제] ❑ 민간 산업체와의 공동 벤처 사업 ❑ 부파는 영국에서 사설 병원을 운영한다. ● 사설로 부사 ❑ 그 정도로 국유 사업체는 많으면서 사유 산업체가 적은 유럽 국가는 그 나라밖에 없었다. **2** 형용사 개인으로서의 ❑ 민간인들의 무기 소지를 금한다는 그 법의 주장 ❑ 왕은 조상들의 묘소에서 기도를 올릴 수 있도록 개인 자격으로 방문 중이었다. **3** 형용사 사유의 ❑ 그들은 사유 재산에 대한 국가의 더 많은 통제를 원한다. **4** 형용사 일반인의 접근이 불허된, 회원제의 ❑ 673곳의 회원제 골프장이 최근의 연구에 참여했다. ❑ 그 문에는 '일반인 출입 금지'라는 표시가 붙어 있다. **5** 형용사 비공개의 ❑ 비공개 대화를 도청하지 말고, 그 도청한 내용을 기사화한 신문들을 사지 마세요. ● 비공개로 부사 ❑ 공식적인 논평을 낸 원로 인사들은 별로 없었지만, 비공개적으로 그 사임은 기쁘게 받아들여졌다. **6** 형용사 사적인 ❑ 나는 항상 사생활과 직업 생활을 분리해 왔다. **7** 형용사 자기 혼자만의, 은밀한 ❑ 우리 모두 우리가 그의 은밀한 슬픔에 간섭하고 있는 것처럼 느껴졌다. ● 혼자서만, 은밀히 부사 ❑ 그녀는 혼자 속으로 자신이 정말 충분히 유능한지 걱정한다. **8** 형용사 조용한, 방해받지 않는 ❑ 그곳이 그들이 찾을 수 있는 비교적 방해받지 않을 유일한 장소였다. **9** 형용사 마음을 잘 드러내지 않는 ❑ 굴드는 마음을 정말 잘 안 드러내는 사람이었다. **10** 가산명사; 경칭명사 이등병 ❑ 그는 미 육군 이등병이었다. **12** 구 내밀히, 비공개로 ❑ 우리가 이야기하고 있는 것 중 일부는 내밀히 의논하는 편이 나을 것이다.

불가산명사 민간 기업 [경제] ❑ 공기업을 민간 기업에 팔려는 정부의 계획

부사 개인적으로 ❑ 그 전 과정은 개인적인 차량 구입을 자동차 정비소에서 사는 것만큼이나 쉽게 해 준다.

가산명사 또는 불가산명사 사립학교 ❑ 그는 영국에서 가장 들어가기 어려운 사립학교인 이튼에 다녔다.

단수명사 민간 부문 [경제] ❑ 민간 부문의 소규모 회사들

[영국영어 privatise] 타동사 민영화되다 [경제] ❑ 수자원 관리국들이 민영화될 예정이다. ❑ 철도 및 석탄 산업을 민영화하겠다는 약속 ● 민영화 가산명사 또는 불가산명사 ❑ 영국 철도의 민영화

1 가산명사 특권 ❑ 러시아연방은 정부 관리들에 대한 특전을 철폐하는 법령을 공표했다. **2** 불가산명사 특혜, 특권 ❑ 피로니는 부유한 특권층 아들이었고 그런 티가 났다. **3** 단수명사 영광 ❑ 그런 남자를 알면 영광스럽겠다.

1 형용사 특혜 ❑ 그들은 대체로 굉장히 부유하고 특혜 받은 엘리트 집단이었다. ● 복수명사 특혜를 누리는

of their wealth or high social class. ❑ *They were, by and large, a very wealthy, privileged elite.* ● N-PLURAL **The privileged** are people who are privileged. ❑ *They are only interested in preserving the power of the privileged and the well off.* ❷ ADJ **Privileged** information is known by only a small group of people, who are not legally required to give it to anyone else. ❑ *The data is privileged information, not to be shared with the general public.*

자들, 특권층 ❑ 그들은 넉넉하고 특혜받은 자들의 권력을 유지하는 데에만 관심이 있다. ❷ 형용사 내외비의 ❑ 이 자료는 대외비 정보이며 일반 대중에게 공개해서는 안 된다.

prize ♦♦◇ /praɪz/ (prizes, prizing, prized)

The spelling **prise** is also used in British English for meaning ❺.

철자 prise도 영국영어에서 ❺ 의미로 쓴다.

❶ N-COUNT A **prize** is money or something valuable that is given to someone who has the best results in a competition or game, or as a reward for doing good work. ❑ *You must claim your prize by telephoning our claims line.* ❑ *He was awarded the Nobel Prize for Physics in 1985.* ❷ ADJ You use **prize** to describe things that are of such good quality that they win prizes or deserve to win prizes. [ADJ n] ❑ *...a prize bull.* ❸ N-COUNT You can refer to someone or something as a **prize** when people consider them to be of great value or importance. ❑ *With no lands of his own, he was no great matrimonial prize.* ❹ V-T Something that **is prized** is wanted and admired because it is considered to be very valuable or very good quality. [usu passive] ❑ *Military figures made out of lead are prized by collectors.* ❺ V-T If you **prize** something **open** or **prize** it away from a surface, you force it to open or force it to come away from the surface. [mainly BRIT; AM usually **pry**] ❑ *He tried to prize the dog's mouth open.* ❑ *I prized off the metal rim surrounding one of the dials.*

❶ 가산명사 상 ❑ 청구 서비스에 전화를 걸어 상을 받아야 한다. ❑ 그는 1985년에 노벨 물리학상을 받았다. ❷ 형용사 뛰어난, 훌륭한 ❑ 훌륭한 황소 ❸ 가산명사 가치 있는 것, 훌륭한 것 ❑ 자기 땅을 가지지 않은 그는 그다지 훌륭한 신랑감은 아니었다. ❹ 타동사 귀하게 여겨지다 ❑ 납으로 만든 군사 인형을 수집가들은 귀하게 여긴다. ❺ 타동사 비틀어 열다 [주로 영국영어; 미국영어 대개 pry] ❑ 그는 개의 입을 비틀어 열려고 했다. ❑ 나는 다이얼을 둘러싸고 있는 금속 테를 비틀어서 떼어냈다.

Word Partnership	prize의 연어
ADJ.	**first** prize, **grand** prize, **top** prize ❶
V.	**award** a prize, **claim** a prize, **receive** a prize, **share** a prize, **win** a prize ❶

pro /proʊ/ (pros) ❶ N-COUNT A **pro** is a professional. [INFORMAL] ❑ *In the professional theater, there is a tremendous need to prove that you're a pro.* ❷ ADJ A **pro** player is a professional athlete. You can also use **pro** to refer to sports that are played by professional athletes. [AM] [ADJ n] ❑ *...a former college and pro basketball player.* ❸ PREP If you are **pro** a particular course of action or belief, you agree with it or support it. ❑ *They're still very pro the Communist party.* ❹ PHRASE The **pros and cons** of something are its advantages and disadvantages, which you consider carefully so that you can make a sensible decision. ❑ *Motherhood has both its pros and cons.*

❶ 가산명사 프로 [비격식체] ❑ 전문 연극계에서는 자신이 프로라는 것을 보여줘야 할 엄청난 필요성이 있다. ❷ 형용사 프로의, 프로인 [미국영어] ❑ 전에는 대학의 그리고 현재는 프로인 농구선수 ❸ 전치사 찬성하는 ❑ 그들은 아직도 공산당을 열렬히 지지하고 있다. ❹ 구 장단점 ❑ 어머니가 된다는 것에는 장단점이 있다.

Word Link	pro ≈ in front, before : proactive, proceed, produce

pro|ac|tive /proʊˈæktɪv/ ADJ **Proactive** actions are intended to cause changes, rather than just reacting to change. ❑ *In order to survive the competition a company should be proactive not reactive.*

형용사 먼저 행동하는 ❑ 경쟁에서 살아남기 위해서는 회사가 반응을 하기보다는 먼저 행동을 취해야 한다.

prob|abil|ity /prɒbəˈbɪlɪti/ (probabilities) ❶ N-VAR The **probability of** something happening is how likely it is to happen, sometimes expressed as a fraction or a percentage. ❑ *Without a transfusion, the victim's probability of dying was 100%.* ❑ *The probabilities of crime or victimization are higher with some situations than with others.* ❷ N-VAR You say that there is a **probability that** something will happen when it is likely to happen. [VAGUENESS] ❑ *If you've owned property for several years, the probability is that values have increased.* ❑ *Formal talks are still said to be a possibility, not a probability.* ❸ PHRASE If you say that something will happen **in all probability**, you mean that you think it is very likely to happen. [VAGUENESS] ❑ *The Republicans had better get used to the fact that in all probability, they are going to lose.*

❶ 가산명사 또는 불가산명사 확률 ❑ 수혈 없이는 피해자의 사망 확률은 100퍼센트였다. ❑ 범죄 혹은 피해자를 낳을 확률은 일부 상황이 다른 상황에 비해 더 높다. ❷ 가산명사 또는 불가산명사 개연성, 가망 [짐작투] ❑ 몇 년간 부동산을 소유했다면 가치가 상승했을 개연성이 크다. ❑ 공식 대화는 아직 개연성이 아닌 가능성의 단계이다. ❸ 구 십중팔구는 [짐작투] ❑ 공화당은 그들이 십중팔구 질 것이라는 사실에 적응을 해야 할 것이다.

prob|able /prɒbəb^əl/ ❶ ADJ If you say that something is **probable**, you mean that it is likely to be true or likely to happen. [VAGUENESS] ❑ *It is probable that the medication will suppress the symptom without treating the condition.* ❷ ADJ You can use **probable** to describe a role or function that someone or something is likely to have. [ADJ n] ❑ *The Socialists united behind their probable presidential candidate, Michel Rocard.*

❶ 형용사 가능성이 높은 [짐작투] ❑ 그 약이 질환을 치료하지 않고 증상만 억제할 가능성이 높다. ❷ 형용사 유력한 ❑ 사회당원들이 그들의 유력한 대통령 후보인 미셸 로카르드 뒤에서 결집했다.

prob|ably ♦♦♦ /prɒbəbli/ ❶ ADV If you say that something is **probably** the case, you think that it is likely to be the case, although you are not sure. [VAGUENESS] [ADV with cl/group] ❑ *The White House probably won't make this plan public until July.* ❑ *Van Gogh is probably the best-known painter in the world.* ❷ ADV You can use **probably** when you want to make your opinion sound less forceful or definite, so that you do not offend people. [VAGUENESS] [ADV with cl/group] ❑ *What would he think of their story. He'd probably think she and Lenny were both crazy!*

❶ 부사 아마도 [짐작투] ❑ 백악관은 이 계획을 7월까지는 아마도 공표하지 않을 것이다. ❑ 반 고흐는 아마도 세상에서 가장 유명한 화가일 것이다. ❷ 부사 아마 [짐작투] ❑ 그는 그들의 이야기를 어떻게 생각할까. 그는 아마 그녀와 레니 둘 다 미쳤다고 생각하겠지!

pro|ba|tion /proʊˈbeɪʃ^ən, BRIT prəˈbeɪʃ^ən/ ❶ N-UNCOUNT **Probation** is a period of time during which a person who has committed a crime has to obey the law and be supervised by a probation officer, rather than being sent to prison. ❑ *A young woman admitted three theft charges and was put on probation for two years.* ❷ N-UNCOUNT **Probation** is a period of time during which someone is judging your character and ability while you work, in order to see if you are suitable for that type of work. ❑ *Employee appointment to the Council will be subject to a term of probation of 6 months.*

❶ 불가산명사 집행 유예 ❑ 젊은 여자가 세 건의 절도 혐의를 인정하고 집행 유예 2년을 선고받았다. ❷ 불가산명사 수습 기간 ❑ 6개월의 수습 기간을 거쳐야 위원회 직원으로 임명된다.

pro|ba|tion of|fic|er (probation officers) N-COUNT A **probation officer** is a person whose job is to supervise and help people who have committed crimes and been put on probation.

가산명사 보호관찰관

probe /proʊb/ (probes, probing, probed) ❶ V-T/V-I If you **probe into** something, you ask questions or try to discover facts about it. ❑ *The more they*

❶ 타동사/자동사 조사하다 ❑ 그들이 그의 배경을 조사해 들어갈수록 그들의 의심은 더욱 커져갈 것이다.

probed into his background, the more inflamed their suspicions would become. ❑ *For three years, I have probed for understanding.* ● N-COUNT **Probe** is also a noun. ❑ *...a federal grand-jury probe into corruption within the FDA.* **2** V-I If a doctor or dentist **probes**, he or she uses a long instrument to examine part of a patient's body. ❑ *The surgeon would pick up his instruments, probe, repair and stitch up again.* ❑ *Dr. Amid probed around the sensitive area.* **3** N-COUNT A **probe** is a long thin instrument that doctors and dentists use to examine parts of the body. ❑ *...a fibre-optic probe.* **4** V-T/V-I If you **probe** a place, you search in it in order to find someone or something that you are looking for. ❑ *A flashlight beam probed the underbrush only yards away from their hiding place.*

prob|lem ♦♦♦ /prɒbləm/ (**problems**) **1** N-COUNT A **problem** is a situation that is unsatisfactory and causes difficulties for people. ❑ *...the economic problems of the inner city.* ❑ *I do not have a simple solution to the drug problem.* **2** N-COUNT A **problem** is a puzzle that requires logical thought or mathematics to solve it. ❑ *With mathematical problems, you can save time by approximating.*

Thesaurus	*problem*의 참조어
N.	complication, difficulty, hitch **1**
	puzzle, question, riddle **2**

prob|lem|at|ic /prɒbləmætɪk/ ADJ Something that is **problematic** involves problems and difficulties. ❑ *Some places are more problematic than others for women traveling alone.*

pro|cedur|al /prəsidʒərəl/ ADJ **Procedural** means involving a formal procedure. [FORMAL] ❑ *A Spanish judge rejected the suit on procedural grounds.*

pro|cedure ♦♦◇ /prəsidʒər/ (**procedures**) N-VAR A **procedure** is a way of doing something, especially the usual or correct way. ❑ *A biopsy is usually a minor surgical procedure.* ❑ *Police insist that Michael did not follow the correct procedure in applying for a visa.*

Word Partnership	*procedure*의 연어
ADJ.	**simple** procedure, **standard (operating)** procedure, **surgical** procedure
V.	**follow** a procedure, **perform** a procedure, **use** a procedure

Word Link	*pro ≈ in front, before : proactive, proceed, produce*

pro|ceed ♦◇◇ (**proceeds, proceeding, proceeded**)

The verb is pronounced /prəsi:d/. The plural noun in meaning **4** is pronounced /prousi:dz/.

1 V-T If you **proceed to** do something, you do it, often after doing something else first. ❑ *He proceeded to tell me of my birth.* **2** V-I If you **proceed with** a course of action, you continue with it. [FORMAL] ❑ *The group proceeded with a march they knew would lead to bloodshed.* **3** V-I If an activity, process, or event **proceeds**, it goes on and does not stop. ❑ *The ideas were not new. Their development had proceeded steadily since the war.* **4** N-PLURAL The **proceeds** of an event or activity are the money that has been obtained from it. ❑ *The proceeds of the concert went to charity.*

pro|ceed|ing /prəsidɪŋ/ (**proceedings**) **1** N-COUNT Legal **proceedings** are legal action taken against someone. [FORMAL] ❑ *...criminal proceedings against the former prime minister.* **2** N-COUNT The **proceedings** are an organized series of events that take place in a particular place. [FORMAL] ❑ *The proceedings of the enquiry will take place in private.* **3** N-PLURAL You can refer to a written record of the discussions at a meeting or conference as **the proceedings**. ❑ *The Department of Transport is to publish the conference proceedings.*

pro|cess ♦♦♦ /prɒsɛs, BRIT prouses/ (**processes, processing, processed**) **1** N-COUNT A **process** is a series of actions which are carried out in order to achieve a particular result. ❑ *There was total agreement to start the peace process as soon as possible.* ❑ *They decided to spread the building process over three years.* **2** N-COUNT A **process** is a series of things which happen naturally and result in a biological or chemical change. ❑ *It occurs in elderly men, apparently as part of the ageing process.* **3** V-T When raw materials or foods **are processed**, they are prepared in factories before they are used or sold. ❑ *...fish which are processed by the best methods: from freezing to canning and smoking.* ❑ *The material will be processed into plastic pellets.* ● N-COUNT **Process** is also a noun. ❑ *...the cost of re-engineering the production process.* ● **pro|cess|ing** N-UNCOUNT [usu with supp] ❑ *America sent cotton to England for processing.* **4** V-T When people **process** information, they put it through a system or into a computer in order to deal with it. ❑ *...facilities to process the data, and the right to publish the results.* ● **pro|cess|ing** N-UNCOUNT ❑ *...data processing.* →see also **word processing** **5** V-T When people **are processed** by officials, their case is dealt with in stages and they pass from one stage of the process to the next. [usu passive] ❑ *Patients took more than two hours to be processed through the department.* **6** PHRASE If you are **in the process of** doing something, you have started to do it and are still doing it. ❑ *The administration is in the process of drawing up a peace plan.* **7** PHRASE If you are doing something and you do something else **in the process**, you do the second thing as part of doing the first thing. ❑ *You have to let us struggle for ourselves, even if we must die in the process.*

❑ 3년간 나는 이해를 얻기 위해 탐색했다. ● 가산명사 조사 ❑ 식품의약청 내의 비리에 관한 연방 대배심 조사 **2** 자동사 (의사가 탐침으로) 검사하다 ❑ 외과의사는 도구를 집어 들어 검사한 다음 고치고 다시 꿰맬 것이다. ❑ 아미드 의사가 환부를 검사했다. **3** 가산명사 탐침(探針) ❑ 광섬유 탐침 **4** 타동사/자동사 탐사하다 ❑ 전등 불빛이 그들이 숨은 곳으로부터 단지 몇 야드 떨어진 덤불을 탐사했다.

1 가산명사 문제 ❑ 도심 빈곤 지역의 경제적 문제 ❑ 내가 마약 문제에 대해 간단한 해결책을 가지고 있지는 않다. **2** 가산명사 문제 ❑ 수리적인 문제의 경우 근삿값을 사용하여 시간을 절약할 수 있다.

형용사 문제가 있는 ❑ 혼자 여행하는 여성에게 일부 지역은 다른 지역에 비해 더 다니기 어렵다.

형용사 절차상의 [격식체] ❑ 스페인 판사가 절차상의 이유로 소송을 기각했다.

가산명사 또는 불가산명사 절차 ❑ 조직검사는 대개 작은 수술 절차이다. ❑ 경찰은 마이클이 비자를 신청하면서 올바른 절차를 따르지 않았다고 주장한다.

동사는 /prəsi:d/로 발음된다. **4** 의미의 복수 명사일 때는 /prousi:dz/로 발음된다.

1 타동사 (이어서 ~을) 하다 ❑ 그는 이어서 내 탄생에 대한 이야기를 하기 시작했다. **2** 자동사 계속 진행하다 [격식체] ❑ 그 단체는 결국 유혈 사태로 이어질 것을 알면서도 행진을 계속하였다. **3** 자동사 계속되다 ❑ 그 개념들은 새로운 것이 아니었다. 그것들은 전쟁 이후 꾸준히 계속해서 개발되어 온 것이었다. **4** 복수명사 수익금 ❑ 콘서트의 수익금은 자선 단체에 기부되었다.

1 가산명사 소송 절차 [격식체] ❑ 전 총리에 대한 형사 소송 절차 **2** 가산명사 정식 절차 [격식체] ❑ 그 조사에 대한 정식 절차는 비공개로 진행될 것이다. **3** 복수명사 의사록 ❑ 교통부는 회의 의사록을 출판할 것이다.

1 가산명사 절차 ❑ 평화 수립 절차를 최대한 빨리 시작하자는 전적인 합의가 있었다. ❑ 그들은 건설 절차를 3년에 걸쳐 분산하기로 결정했다. **2** 가산명사 과정 ❑ 그것은 남성 노년층에서 발생하는데 노화 과정의 일부인 것 같다. **3** 타동사 처리되다, 가공되다 ❑ 냉동에서 통조림 보관과 훈제에 이르기까지 최선의 방식으로 처리되는 생선 ❑ 그 재료는 플라스틱 알갱이로 가공될 것이다. ● 가산명사 처리 과정, 공정 ❑ 생산 공정을 재설계하는 데 드는 비용 ● 처리, 가공 불가산명사 ❑ 미국은 처리를 위해 목화를 영국에 보냈다. **4** 타동사 처리하다 ❑ 자료를 처리할 시설과 결과를 출판할 수 있는 권리 ● 처리 불가산명사 ❑ 정보처리 **5** 타동사 처리되다 ❑ 그 부서에서 환자를 처리하는 데 두 시간이 넘게 소요되었다. **6** 구 ~하는 중인 ❑ 행정부가 평화안을 짜는 중이다. **7** 구 도중에 ❑ 설령 우리가 그 과정 중에 죽는다 하더라도 우리가 스스로를 위해서 투쟁하도록 놔둬야 한다.

a b c d e f g h i j k l m n o p q r s t u v w x y z

Word Partnership *process*의 연어

ADJ.	**difficult** process, **political** process 🔟
	gradual process, **normal** process 🔟 🔢
	complicated process, **long** process, **slow** process,
	whole process 🔟 🔢
N.	**application** process, **approval** process, **decision** process,
	learning process, **planning** process 🔟
	process **information** 🔢
V.	**participate in** a process 🔟
	begin a process, **complete** a process, **control** a process,
	describe a process, **start** a process 🔟 🔢

pro|ces|sion /prəsɛʃᵊn/ (**processions**) N-COUNT A **procession** is a group of people who are walking, riding, or driving in a line as part of a public event. ❏ ...*a funeral procession.*

가산명사 행렬 ❏ 장례 행렬

pro|ces|sor /prɒsɛsər, BRIT prəʊsesəʳ/ (**processors**) 🔟 N-COUNT A **processor** is the part of a computer that interprets commands and performs the processes the user has requested. →see also **word processor** [COMPUTING] 🔢 N-COUNT A **processor** is someone or something which carries out a process. ❏ *The frozen-food industry could be supplied entirely by growers and processors outside the country.*

🔟 가산명사 처리 장치 [컴퓨터] 🔢 가산명사 가공업자; 처리기 ❏ 냉동식품 업체는 외국에 있는 생산자와 가공업자로부터 전적으로 공급을 받을 수도 있다.

pro|claim /proʊkleɪm/ (**proclaims, proclaiming, proclaimed**) 🔟 V-T If people **proclaim** something, they formally make it known to the public. ❏ *The Boers rebelled against British rule, proclaiming their independence on 30 December 1880.* ❏ *Britain proudly proclaims that it is a nation of animal lovers.* 🔢 V-T If you **proclaim** something, you state it in an emphatic way. ❏ *"I think we have been heard today,"* he proclaimed.*

🔟 타동사 선언하다 ❏ 보어 인들은 영국의 지배에 저항하며 1880년 12월 30일에 독립을 선언했다. ❏ 영국은 동물 애호가들의 국가임을 자랑스럽게 선언한다. 🔢 타동사 선언하다 ❏ 오늘 "우리의 목소리가 들렸을 것입니다." 그가 선언했다.

proc|la|ma|tion /prɒkləmeɪʃᵊn/ (**proclamations**) N-COUNT A **proclamation** is a public announcement about something important, often about something of national importance. ❏ *The proclamation of independence was broadcast over the radio.*

가산명사 선언 ❏ 독립 선언은 라디오를 통해 방송되었다.

pro|cure /prəkyʊər/ (**procures, procuring, procured**) V-T If you **procure** something, especially something that is difficult to get, you obtain it. [FORMAL] ❏ *It remained very difficult to procure food, fuel and other daily necessities.*

타동사 조달하다, 구하다 [격식체] ❏ 음식, 연료, 기타 생필품을 구하기가 여전히 매우 어려웠다.

pro|cure|ment /prəkyʊərmənt/ **Procurement** is the act of obtaining something such as supplies for an army or other organization. [FORMAL] ❏ *Russia was cutting procurement of new weapons "by about 80 percent," he said.*

불가산명사 조달 [격식체] ❏ 러시아가 새로운 무기의 조달을 '80 퍼센트' 줄일 것이라고 그는 말했다.

prod /prɒd/ (**prods, prodding, prodded**) 🔟 V-T/V-I If you **prod** someone or something, you give them a quick push with your finger or with a pointed object. ❏ *He prodded Murray with the shotgun.* ❏ *Prod the windowsills to check for signs of rot.* ● N-COUNT **Prod** is also a noun. ❏ *He gave the donkey a mighty prod in the backside.* 🔢 V-T If you **prod** someone **into** doing something, you remind or persuade them to do it. ❏ *The report was a shock tactic to prod the Government into spending more on the Health Service.*

🔟 타동사/자동사 (살짝) 찌르다 ❏ 그가 산탄총으로 머레이를 쿡 찔렀다. ❏ 혹시 부식 흔적이 있는지 확인하려면 창턱을 찔러 보아라. ● 가산명사 찌름 ❏ 그는 나귀의 등을 세게 찔렀다. 🔢 타동사 -하도록 상기시키다; -을 하라고 촉구하다 ❏ 그 보고서는 정부가 보건부에 더 많은 돈을 쓰도록 촉구하기 위한 쇼크 요법이었다.

pro|di|gious /prədɪdʒəs/ ADJ Something that is **prodigious** is very large or impressive. [LITERARY] ❏ *This business generates cash in prodigious amounts.* ● **pro|di|gious|ly** ADV ❏ *She ate prodigiously.*

형용사 엄청난 [문예체] ❏ 이 사업은 엄청난 양의 현금을 번다. ● 엄청나게 부사 ❏ 그녀는 엄청나게 먹었다.

prodigy /prɒdɪdʒi/ (**prodigies**) N-COUNT A **prodigy** is someone young who has a great natural ability for something such as music, mathematics, or sports. ❏ *The Russian tennis prodigy is well on the way to becoming the youngest world champion of all time.*

가산명사 신동 ❏ 이 러시아 테니스 신동은 역대 최연소 세계 챔피언이 될 가능성이 매우 높다.

Word Link pro ≈ in front, before : *proactive, proceed, produce*

pro|duce ◆◆◆ (**produces, producing, produced**)

The verb is pronounced /prədus/. The noun is pronounced /prɒdus/ or /proʊdus/.

동사는 /prədus/로, 명사는 /prɒdus/ 또는 /proʊdus/로 발음된다.

🔟 V-T To **produce** something means to cause it to happen. ❏ *The drug is known to produce side-effects in women.* 🔢 V-T If you **produce** something, you make or create it. ❏ *The company produced circuitry for communications systems.* 🔟 V-T When things or people **produce** something, it comes from them or slowly forms from them, especially as the result of a biological or chemical process. ❏ *These plants are then pollinated and allowed to mature and produce seed.* 🔢 V-T If you **produce** evidence or an argument, you show it or explain it to people in order to make them agree with you. ❏ *They challenged him to produce evidence to support his allegations.* 🔟 V-T If you **produce** an object from somewhere, you show it or bring it out so that it can be seen. ❏ *To hire a car you must produce a passport and a current driving licence.* 🔢 V-T If someone **produces** something such as a movie, a magazine, or a CD, they organize it and decide how it should be done. ❏ *He has produced his own sports magazine called Yes Sport.* 🔟 N-UNCOUNT **Produce** is food or other things that are grown in large quantities to be sold. ❏ *We manage to get most of our produce in Britain.*

🔟 타동사 낳다, 초래하다 ❏ 그 약은 여성들에게 부작용을 낳는 것으로 알려져 있다. 🔢 타동사 생산하다 ❏ 그 회사는 통신 시스템용 회로를 생산했다. 🔟 타동사 생성하다 ❏ 그런 뒤 이 식물들에 수분을 하고 이들이 성장하여 씨가 생성될 수 있도록 한다. 🔢 타동사 제시하다 ❏ 그들은 그에게 그의 주장을 뒷받침할 증거를 제시하라고 반박했다. 🔟 타동사 제시하다 ❏ 차를 빌리기 위해서는 여권과 유효한 운전면허증을 제시해야 한다. 🔢 타동사 제작하다 ❏ 그는 예스 스포트라는 자신만의 스포츠 잡지를 제작했다. 🔟 불가산명사 농산물 ❏ 우리는 그럭저럭 대부분의 농산물을 영국에서 구한다.

pro|duc|er ◆◆◇ /prədusər, BRIT prədyuːsəʳ/ (**producers**) 🔟 N-COUNT A **producer** is a person whose job is to produce plays, movies, programs, or CDs. ❏ *Vanya Kewley is a freelance film producer.* 🔢 N-COUNT A **producer** of a food or material is a company or country that grows or manufactures a large amount of it. ❏ ...*Saudi Arabia, the world's leading oil producer.*

🔟 가산명사 제작자 ❏ 바냐 큘리는 프리랜스 영화 제작자이다. 🔢 가산명사 생산자 ❏ 세계 주요 석유 생산국인 사우디아라비아

prod|uct ◆◆◆ /prɒdʌkt/ (**products**) 🔟 N-COUNT A **product** is something that is produced and sold in large quantities, often as a result of a manufacturing process. ❏ *Try to get the best product at the lowest price.* 🔢 N-COUNT If you say that

🔟 가산명사 생산물, 제품 ❏ 가장 좋은 제품을 가장 낮은 가격에 구해 보도록 하세요. 🔢 가산명사 -의 산물 ❏ 우리는 모두 시대의 산물이다.

someone or something is a **product of** a situation or process, you mean that the situation or process has had a significant effect in making them what they are. ❑ *We are all products of our time.* →see **advertising**, **industry**, **inventor**

pro|duc|tion ♦♦◇ /prədʌkʃⁿn/ (**productions**) **1** N-UNCOUNT **Production** is the process of manufacturing or growing something in large quantities. ❑ *That model won't go into production before late 1990.* **2** N-UNCOUNT **Production** is the amount of goods manufactured or grown by a company or country. ❑ *We needed to increase the volume of production.* **3** N-UNCOUNT The **production of** something is its creation as the result of a natural process. ❑ *These proteins stimulate the production of blood cells.* **4** N-UNCOUNT **Production** is the process of organizing and preparing a play, movie, program, or CD, in order to present it to the public. ❑ *She is head of the production company.* **5** N-COUNT A **production** is a play, opera, or other show that is performed in a theater. ❑ *...a critically acclaimed production of Othello.* **6** PHRASE When you can do something **on production of** or **on the production of** documents, you need to show someone those documents in order to be able to do that thing. ❑ *Entry to the show is free to members on production of their membership cards.* →see **theater**

불가산명사 생산 ❑ 그 모델은 1990년 후반이나 되어야 생산에 들어갈 것이다. **2** 불가산명사 생산량 ❑ 우리는 생산량의 규모를 증가시킬 필요가 있었다. **3** 불가산명사 -의 생성 ❑ 이 단백질들은 혈구의 생성을 촉진한다. **4** 불가산명사 제작 ❑ 그녀는 그 제작 회사의 대표이다. **5** 가산명사 작품 ❑ 평단의 찬사를 받은 작품인 오셀로 **6** 구 -을 제시하여 ❑ 회원 카드를 제시하면 공연 입장은 회원들에게 무료이다.

pro|duc|tion line (**production lines**) N-COUNT A **production line** is an arrangement of machines in a factory where the products pass from machine to machine until they are finished. ❑ *Honda added a production line this year, hoping to boost domestic sales.*

가산명사 생산 라인 ❑ 국내 판매 촉진을 희망하며 혼다가 올해 생산 라인 하나를 추가했다.

pro|duc|tive /prədʌktɪv/ **1** ADJ Someone or something that is **productive** produces or does a lot for the amount of resources used. ❑ *Training makes workers highly productive.* ❑ *More productive farmers have been able to provide cheaper food.* **2** ADJ If you say that a relationship between people is **productive**, you mean that a lot of good or useful things happen as a result of it. ❑ *He was hopeful that the next round of talks would also be productive.*

1 형용사 생산적인 ❑ 훈련을 통해 근로자의 생산성을 크게 높일 수 있다. ❑ 더 생산적인 농부들은 더 저렴한 식량을 공급할 수 있었다. **2** 형용사 생산적인 ❑ 그는 다음번의 대화 또한 생산적일 것이라고 기대했다.

pro|duc|tiv|ity /prɒdʌktɪvɪti/ N-UNCOUNT **Productivity** is the rate at which goods are produced. ❑ *The third-quarter results reflect continued improvements in productivity.*

불가산명사 생산성 ❑ 삼 분기의 결과는 생산성의 계속적인 향상을 반영하고 있다.

prod|uct line (**product lines**) N-COUNT A **product line** is a group of related products produced by one manufacturer, for example products that are intended to be used for similar purposes or to be sold in similar types of stores. [BUSINESS] ❑ *A well-known UK supermarket launches more than 1,000 new product lines each year.*

가산명사 제품 계열 [경제] ❑ 한 유명한 영국 슈퍼마켓은 매년 새로운 제품 계열을 1,000가지 이상 내놓는다.

prod|uct place|ment (**product placements**) N-VAR **Product placement** is a form of advertising in which a company has its product placed where it can be clearly seen during a movie or television program. [BUSINESS] ❑ *It was the first movie to feature onscreen product placement for its own merchandise.*

가산명사 또는 불가산명사 작품 속 광고 [경제] ❑ 그것은 그 자체의 상품을 위해 영화 속 광고를 시행한 최초의 영화였다.

pro|fess /prəfɛs/ (**professes**, **professing**, **professed**) **1** V-T If you **profess to** do or have something, you claim that you do it or have it, often when you do not. [FORMAL] ❑ *She professed to hate her nickname.* ❑ *Why do organizations profess that they care?* **2** V-T If you **profess** a feeling, opinion, or belief, you express it. [FORMAL] ❑ *He professed to be content with the arrangement.* ❑ *Bacher professed himself pleased with the Indian tour.*

1 타동사 (보통 거짓된 것을) 단언하다 [격식체] ❑ 그녀는 말로는 자기 별명이 싫다고 했다. ❑ 왜 조직들이 말로는 관심 있는 척을 하는가? **2** 타동사 고백하다, 표명하다 [격식체] ❑ 그녀는 그 결정에 만족한다고 했다. ❑ 배처는 인도 관광이 마음에 들었다고 했다.

pro|fes|sion ♦◇◇ /prəfɛʃⁿn/ (**professions**) **1** N-COUNT A **profession** is a type of job that requires advanced education or training. [also by N] ❑ *Harper was a teacher by profession.* **2** N-COUNT-COLL You can use **profession** to refer to all the people who have the same profession. ❑ *The attitude of the medical profession is very much more liberal now.*

1 가산명사 (전문적인) 직업 ❑ 하퍼는 직업이 교사였다. **2** 가산명사-집합 일게 의료 업계의 태도가 이제 훨씬 개방적이다.

pro|fes|sion|al ♦♦◇ /prəfɛʃənⁿl/ (**professionals**) **1** ADJ **Professional** means relating to a person's work, especially work that requires special training. [ADJ n] ❑ *His professional career started at Liverpool University.* ● **pro|fes|sion|al|ly** ADV ❑ *...a professionally-qualified architect.* **2** ADJ **Professional** people have jobs that require advanced education or training. [ADJ n] ❑ *...highly qualified professional people like doctors and engineers.* ● N-COUNT **Professional** is also a noun. ❑ *My father wanted me to become a professional and have more stability.* **3** ADJ You use **professional** to describe people who do a particular thing to earn money rather than as a hobby. ❑ *This has been my worst time for injuries since I started as a professional footballer.* ● N-COUNT **Professional** is also a noun. ❑ *He had been a professional since March 1985.* ● **pro|fes|sion|al|ly** ADV [ADV after v] ❑ *By age 16 he was playing professionally with bands in Greenwich Village.* **4** ADJ **Professional** sports are played for money rather than as a hobby. [ADJ n] ❑ *...an art student who had played professional football for a short time.* **5** ADJ If you say that something that someone does or produces is **professional**, you approve of it because you think that it is of a very high standard. [APPROVAL] ❑ *They run it with a truly professional but personal touch.* ● N-COUNT **Professional** is also a noun. ❑ *...a dedicated professional who worked harmoniously with the cast and crew.* ● **pro|fes|sion|al|ly** ADV [ADV with v] ❑ *These tickets have been produced very professionally.*

1 형용사 직업의 ❑ 그는 직장 생활을 리버풀 대학에서 시작했다. ● 직업적으로 부사 ❑ 직업상의 자격을 갖춘 건축가 **2** 형용사 전문가의 ❑ 의사나 공학자처럼 고도의 자격을 갖춘 전문가들 ● 가산명사 전문가 ❑ 아버지께서는 내가 전문가가 되어 보다 안정성을 누리기를 바랐다. **3** 형용사 직업적인, 프로의 ❑ 내가 프로 축구 선수가 된 이후 올해가 가장 부상을 많이 당한 때이다. ● 가산명사 프로, 직업인 ❑ 그는 1985년 3월부터 프로로 뛰고 있었다. ● 프로로서, 직업인으로서 부사 ❑ 열여섯 살이 되었을 때 그는 그리니치 마을에서 직업적인 음악가로 밴드들과 활동하고 있었다. **4** 형용사 프로 ❑ 잠시 동안 프로 축구를 한 미술 학도 **5** 형용사 전문적인 [마음에 듦] ❑ 그들은 진정 전문적이면서도 사적인 면을 가미하여 그것을 운영한다. ● 가산명사 전문가 ❑ 배우 및 제작진과 조화롭게 일한 헌신적인 전문가 ● 전문적으로 부사 ❑ 이 표들은 매우 전문적으로 만들어졌다.

pro|fes|sion|al|ism /prəfɛʃənⁿlɪzəm/ N-UNCOUNT **Professionalism** in a job is a combination of skill and high standards. [APPROVAL] ❑ *American companies pride themselves on their professionalism.*

불가산명사 전문성 [마음에 듦] ❑ 미국 회사들은 자신들의 전문성에 자부심을 갖는다.

pro|fes|sor ♦♦◇ /prəfɛsər/ (**professors**) **1** N-COUNT; N-TITLE; N-VOC A **professor** in an American or Canadian university or college is a teacher of the highest rank. ❑ *Robert Dunn is a professor of economics at George Washington University.* **2** N-TITLE; N-COUNT; N-VOC A **professor** in a British university is the most senior teacher in a department. ❑ *...Professor Cameron.* →see **graduation**

1 가산명사; 경칭명사; 호격명사 교수 ❑ 로버트 던은 조지 워싱턴 대학 경제학 교수이다. **2** 경칭명사; 가산명사; 호격명사 교수 ❑ 카메론 교수

prof|fer /prɒfər/ (**proffers**, **proffering**, **proffered**) **1** V-T If you **proffer** something to someone, you hold it toward them so that they can take it or touch

1 타동사 내밀다, 내놓다 [격식체] ❑ 그는 일어서서 담배가 가득 든 은상자를 내놓았다. **2** 타동사 내놓다,

A
it. [FORMAL] ❑ *He rose and proffered a silver box full of cigarettes.* ◻ v-т If you **proffer** something such as advice to someone, you offer it to them. [FORMAL] ❑ *The army has not yet proffered an explanation of how and why the accident happened.*

제시하다 [격식체] ❑ 육군은 그 사고가 어떻게 그리고 왜 발생했는지에 대한 설명을 아직 내놓지 않았다.

B
pro|fi|cien|cy /prəfɪʃ°nsi/ N-UNCOUNT If you show **proficiency in** something, you show ability or skill at it. ❑ *Evidence of basic proficiency in English is part of the admission requirement.*

불가산명사 능숙도 ❑ 입시 요건에는 기본적인 영어 능숙도에 대한 증빙이 포함된다.

C
pro|fi|cient /prəfɪʃ°nt/ ADJ If you are **proficient in** something, you can do it well. ❑ *A great number of Egyptians are proficient in foreign languages.*

형용사 능숙한 ❑ 많은 이집트인들이 외국어에 능통하다.

D
pro|file ♦◇◇ /prəʊfaɪl/ (**profiles**) ◼ N-COUNT Your **profile** is the outline of your face as it is seen when someone is looking at you from the side. ❑ *His handsome profile was turned away from us.* ◻ N-UNCOUNT If you see someone **in profile**, you see them from the side. ❑ *This picture shows the girl in profile.* ◼ N-COUNT A **profile of** someone is a short article or program in which their life and character are described. ❑ *A Washington newspaper published comparative profiles of the candidates' wives.* ◼ PHRASE If someone has a **high profile**, people notice them and what they do. If you **keep a low profile**, you avoid doing things that will make people notice you. ❑ *...a move that would give Egypt a much higher profile in the upcoming peace talks.* →see also **high-profile**

◼ 가산명사 (얼굴의) 윤곽, 옆모습 ❑ 그의 잘 생긴 옆모습이 우리 반대 방향을 보고 있었다. ◻ 불가산명사 옆모습으로 ❑ 이 사진에는 소녀의 옆모습이 보인다. ◼ 가산명사 프로필, 신상 명세 ❑ 한 워싱턴 신문이 후보 부인들을 비교하는 프로필을 게재했다. ◼ 구 사람들 눈에 잘 띔; 사람들 눈에 잘 안 띔 ❑ 다가올 평화 협상에서 이집트를 훨씬 더 두드러져 보이게 할 움직임

F
prof|it ♦♦◇ /prɒfɪt/ (**profits, profiting, profited**) ◼ N-VAR A **profit** is an amount of money that you gain when you are paid more for something than it cost you to make, get, or do it. ❑ *The bank made pre-tax profits of £3.5 million.* ❑ *You can improve your chances of profit by sensible planning.* ◻ v-I If you **profit from** something, you earn a profit from it. ❑ *No one was profiting inordinately from the war effort.* ❑ *He has profited by selling his holdings to other investors.* ◼ v-т/v-I If you **profit from** something, or it **profits** you, you gain some advantage or benefit from it. [FORMAL] ❑ *Jennifer wasn't yet totally convinced that she'd profit from a more relaxed lifestyle.* ❑ *So far the French alliance had profited the rebels little.* →see **company**

◼ 가산명사 또는 불가산명사 이익 ❑ 그 은행은 세전 3백5십만 파운드의 이익을 거두었다. ❑ 합리적인 계획을 통해 이익을 거둘 확률을 높일 수 있다. ◻ 자동사 이익을 거두다 ❑ 아무도 전쟁과 관련하여 폭리를 취하고 있지는 않았다. ❑ 그는 자기 지분을 다른 투자자에게 팔아서 이익을 남겼다. ◼ 타동사/자동사 이득을 보다; 이익을 주다 [격식체] ❑ 제니퍼는 보다 느긋한 삶을 통해 이득을 보리라는 것을 아직 전적으로 확신하지 못하고 있었다. ❑ 아직까지 프랑스와의 연합을 통해 반군이 이득을 본 것이 별로 없었다.

Word Partnership   *profit*의 연어

N.	**decline in** profit, profit **and loss**, profit **margin**, **operating** profit, profit **sharing** ◼
V.	**make a** profit, **maximize** profit, **post a** profit, **report a** profit, **turn a** profit ◼

L
prof|it|able /prɒfɪtəb°l/ ◼ ADJ A **profitable** organization or practice makes a profit. ❑ *Drug manufacturing is the most profitable business in America.* ● **prof|it|ably** /prɒfɪtəbli/ ADV [ADV with v] ❑ *The 28 French stores are trading profitably.* ● **prof|it|abil|ity** /prɒfɪtəbɪlɪti/ N-UNCOUNT ❑ *Changes were made in operating methods in an effort to increase profitability.* ◻ ADJ Something that is **profitable** results in some benefit for you. ❑ *...close collaboration with industry which leads to a profitable exchange of personnel and ideas.* ● **prof|it|ably** ADV [ADV with v] ❑ *In fact he could scarcely have spent his time more profitably.*

◼ 형용사 이익을 내는 ❑ 제약업이 미국에서 가장 많은 이익을 내는 사업이다. ● 이익을 내며 부사 ❑ 28개의 그 프랑스 가게들은 이익을 남기며 장사를 하고 있다. ● 수익성 불가산명사 ❑ 수익성을 높이기 위해 운영 방식에 변화가 가해졌다. ◻ 형용사 유익한 ❑ 인원과 아이디어의 유익한 교환으로 이어지는 산업계와의 긴밀한 연계 ● 유익하게 부사 ❑ 사실 그가 그보다 더 시간을 알차게 보내기는 어려웠을 것이다.

O
prof|it|eer|ing /prɒfɪtɪərɪŋ/ N-UNCOUNT **Profiteering** involves making large profits by charging high prices for goods that are hard to get. [BUSINESS, DISAPPROVAL] ❑ *There's been a wave of profiteering and corruption.*

불가산명사 부당 이득 행위, 폭리 취득 행위 [경제, 탐탁잖음] ❑ 부당 이득 행위와 부패가 급증하고 있다.

profit-making ADJ A **profit-making** business or organization makes a profit. [BUSINESS] ❑ *He wants to set up a profit-making company, owned mostly by the university.* →see also **nonprofit-making**

형용사 영리를 위한 [경제] ❑ 그는 대학이 대부분을 소유하는 영리 목적의 회사를 세우고 싶어 한다.

Q
prof|it mar|gin (**profit margins**) N-COUNT A **profit margin** is the difference between the selling price of a product and the cost of producing and marketing it. [BUSINESS] ❑ *The group had a net profit margin of 30% last year.*

가산명사 이윤 폭 [경제] ❑ 그 그룹은 작년의 순 이윤 폭이 30퍼센트였다.

R
profit-sharing N-UNCOUNT **Profit-sharing** is a system by which all the people who work in a company have a share in its profits. [BUSINESS] ❑ *...the bank's profit-sharing scheme.*

불가산명사 이익 분배 [경제] ❑ 은행의 이익 분배 계획

profit-taking N-UNCOUNT **Profit-taking** is the selling of stocks and shares at a profit after their value has risen or just before their value falls. [BUSINESS] ❑ *The market was held down by profit-taking in the banking sector yesterday.*

불가산명사 차익 거래 [경제] ❑ 주식 시장은 어제 금융 부문의 차익 거래로 인하여 보합세를 보였다.

T
pro|found /prəfaʊnd/ (**profounder, profoundest**) ◼ ADJ You use **profound** to emphasize that something is very great or intense. [EMPHASIS] ❑ *...discoveries which had a profound effect on many areas of medicine.* ❑ *...profound disagreement.* ● **pro|found|ly** ADV ❑ *This has profoundly affected my life.* ◻ ADJ A **profound** idea, work, or person shows great intellectual depth and understanding. ❑ *This is a book full of profound, original and challenging insights.*

◼ 형용사 지대한 [강조] ❑ 의학의 많은 분야에 지대한 영향을 끼친 발견들 ❑ 엄청난 불화 ● 지대하게 부사 ❑ 이것은 나의 인생에 지대한 영향을 끼쳤다. ◻ 형용사 심오한 ❑ 이 책은 심오하고 독창적이며 만만잖은 통찰력을 지니고 있다.

V
pro|fuse /prəfyus/ ◼ ADJ **Profuse** sweating, bleeding, or vomiting is sweating, bleeding, or vomiting large amounts. ❑ *...a remedy that produces profuse sweating.* ● **pro|fuse|ly** ADV [ADV after v] ❑ *He was bleeding profusely.* ◻ ADJ If you offer **profuse** apologies or thanks, you apologize or thank someone a lot. ❑ *Then the policeman recognized me, breaking into profuse apologies.* ● **pro|fuse|ly** ADV [ADV after v] ❑ *They were very grateful to be put right and thanked me profusely.*

◼ 형용사 다량의, 심한 ❑ 땀을 다량으로 흘리게 하는 요법 ● 다량으로, 심하게 부사 ❑ 그는 피를 심하게 흘리고 있었다. ◻ 형용사 심심한 (사과, 감사) ❑ 그 때 경찰이 나를 알아보고 거듭 심심한 사과를 표했다. ● 심심히, 깊이 부사 ❑ 그들은 틀린 부분을 바로잡아 준 것을 매우 고마워했고 나에게 심심한 감사를 표했다.

X
prog|no|sis /prɒgnəʊsɪs/ (**prognoses**) /prɒgnəʊsiz/ N-COUNT A **prognosis** is an estimate of the future of someone or something, especially about whether a patient will recover from an illness. [FORMAL] ❑ *The hospital physiotherapist's prognosis was that Laurence might walk within 12 months.*

가산명사 (병의) 예후 [격식체] ❑ 병원 물리 치료사의 예후로는 로렌스가 12개월 안에 걸을지도 모른다는 것이었다.

Word Link   *gram* ≈ *writing : diagram, program, telegram*

Z
pro|gram ♦♦◇ /prəʊgræm, -grəm/ (**programs, programming, programmed**) [BRIT **programme** for meanings ◼, ◻ and ◼] ◼ N-COUNT A **program** of actions or events is a series of actions or events that are planned to be done. ❑ *The nation's*

[의미 ◼, ◻, ◼은 영국영어로 programme] ◼ 가산명사 프로그램 ❑ 10대들을 위한 전국 최대의 훈련 및 교육 프로그램 ◻ 가산명사 프로그램 ❑ 전국 방송 텔레비전

largest training and education program for teenagers. **2** N-COUNT A television or radio **program** is something that is broadcast on television or radio. ❑ *...a network television program.* **3** N-COUNT A theater or concert **program** is a small book or sheet of paper which gives information about the play or concert you are attending. ❑ *When you go to concerts, read the program notes, which are always written by knowledgeable people.* **4** V-T When you **program** a machine or system, you set its controls so that it will work in a particular way. ❑ *Parents can program the machine not to turn on at certain times.* **5** N-COUNT A **program** is a set of instructions that a computer follows in order to perform a particular task. [COMPUTING] ❑ *The chances of an error occurring in a computer program increase with the size of the program.* **6** V-T When you **program** a computer, you give it a set of instructions to make it able to perform a particular task. [COMPUTING] ❑ *He programmed his computer to compare the 1431 possible combinations of pairs in this population.* ❑ *...45 million people, about half of whom can program their own computers.* ● **pro|gram|ming** N-UNCOUNT ❑ *...programming skills.* →see **radio**

프로그램 **3** 가산명사 프로그램 ❑ 콘서트에 갈 때는 프로그램 해설을 읽으세요. 그 해설들은 항상 그 공연에 대해 잘 아는 사람들이 씁니다. **4** 타동사 조작하다 ❑ 그 기계가 특정 시간에는 켜지지 않도록 부모들이 기계를 조작할 수 있다. **5** 가산명사 (컴퓨터의) 프로그램 [컴퓨터] ❑ 컴퓨터 프로그램에서 에러가 발생할 확률은 프로그램의 크기에 비례하여 커진다. **6** 타동사 프로그램을 넣다, 프로그램을 짜다 [컴퓨터] ❑ 그는 이 인구 집단에서 1,431개 쌍의 가능한 조합을 비교하기 위해서 자신의 컴퓨터에 프로그램을 넣었다. ❑ 이 중 절반이 자신의 컴퓨터에 프로그램을 짤 수 있는 4천 5백만 명의 사람들 ● 프로그래밍 불가산명사 ❑ 프로그래밍 기술

Word Partnership   program의 연어

N.	**computer** program, **software** program **5**
	program **a computer 6**
V.	**create** a program, **expand** a program, **implement** a program,
	launch a program, **run** a program **1** **5**

pro|gramme ♦♦♦ /prˈoʊgræm/ →see **program**

pro|gram|mer /prˈoʊgræmər/ (**programmers**) N-COUNT A computer **programmer** is a person whose job involves writing programs for computers. [COMPUTING]

가산명사 프로그래머 [컴퓨터]

pro|gress ♦♦◇ (**progresses, progressing, progressed**)

The noun is pronounced /prˈɒgrɛs/. The verb is pronounced /prəgrˈɛs/.

명사는 /prˈɒgrɛs/로 발음되고, 동사는 /prəgrˈɛs/로 발음된다.

1 N-UNCOUNT **Progress** is the process of gradually improving or getting nearer to achieving or completing something. ❑ *The medical community continues to make progress in the fight against cancer.* **2** N-SING **The progress of** a situation or action is the way in which it develops. ❑ *The Chancellor is reported to have been delighted with the progress of the first day's talks.* **3** V-I To **progress** means to move over a period of time to a stronger, more advanced, or more desirable state. ❑ *He will visit once a fortnight to see how his new staff are progressing.* **4** V-I If events **progress**, they continue to happen gradually over a period of time. ❑ *As the evening progressed, sadness turned to rage.* **5** PHRASE If something is **in progress**, it has started and is still continuing. ❑ *The game was already in progress when we took our seats.*

1 불가산명사 진보 ❑ 의료계는 암과의 싸움에서 계속 진보를 보이고 있다. **2** 단수명사 진척, 진행 ❑ 재무장관이 첫 날 대화의 진행에 대해 매우 만족한 것으로 보도되었다. **3** 자동사 진전되다 ❑ 그는 새 직원들이 얼마나 진전을 보이는지 보기 위해 2주에 한 번씩 방문할 것이다. **4** 자동사 진행되다 ❑ 밤이 깊어지면서 슬픔이 분노로 바뀌었다. **5** 구 진행 중인 ❑ 우리가 자리를 잡았을 때 경기는 이미 진행 중이었다.

pro|gres|sion /prəgrˈɛʃˀn/ (**progressions**) N-COUNT A **progression** is a gradual development from one state to another. ❑ *Both drugs slow the progression of HIV, but neither cures the disease.*

가산명사 진행 ❑ 두 약 모두 에이즈 바이러스의 진행을 늦추지만 둘 다 병을 치료하지는 못한다.

pro|gres|sive /prəgrˈɛsɪv/ (**progressives**) **1** ADJ Someone who is **progressive** or has **progressive** ideas has modern ideas about how things should be done, rather than traditional ones. ❑ *...a progressive businessman who had voted for Roosevelt in 1932 and 1936.* ❑ *Willan was able to point to the progressive changes he had already introduced.* ● N-COUNT A **progressive** is someone who is progressive. ❑ *The Republicans were deeply split between progressives and conservatives.* **2** ADJ A **progressive** change happens gradually over a period of time. ❑ *One prominent symptom of the disease is progressive loss of memory.* ● **pro|gres|sive|ly** ADV ❑ *Her symptoms became progressively worse.*

1 형용사 진보적인 ❑ 1932년과 1936년에 루즈벨트에게 투표했던 진보적 사업가 ❑ 윌란은 자신이 이미 도입한 진보적 변화들을 짚어 보일 수 있었다. ● 가산명사 진보주의자 ❑ 공화당이 진보주의자와 보수주의자로 깊이 분열되어 있었다. **2** 형용사 점진적인 ❑ 그 병의 두드러진 증상 하나는 기억의 점진적인 상실이다. ● 점진적으로 부사 ❑ 그녀의 병세는 점차 악화되었다.

pro|hib|it /prˈoʊhɪbɪt, BRIT prəhˈɪbɪt/ (**prohibits, prohibiting, prohibited**) V-T If a law or someone in authority **prohibits** something, they forbid it or make it illegal. [FORMAL] ❑ *...a law that prohibits tobacco advertising in newspapers and magazines.* ❑ *Fishing is prohibited.* ● **pro|hi|bi|tion** N-UNCOUNT ❑ *The Air Force and the Navy retain and codify their prohibition of women on air combat missions.*

타동사 금지하다 [격식체] ❑ 신문과 잡지에서 담배 광고를 금지하는 법 ❑ 어로 활동은 금지되어 있다. ● 금지 불가산명사 ❑ 공군과 해군은 공중전 임무에 여성의 참여 금지를 존속시키고 그것을 법제화했다.

pro|hi|bi|tion /prˌoʊhɪbˈɪʃˀn/ (**prohibitions**) N-COUNT A **prohibition** is a law or rule forbidding something. ❑ *...a prohibition on discrimination.* →see also **prohibit**

가산명사 금지법, 금지 규칙 ❑ 차별 금지법

pro|hibi|tive /prˈoʊhɪbɪtɪv, BRIT prəhˈɪbɪtɪv/ ADJ If the cost of something is **prohibitive**, it is so high that many people cannot afford it. [FORMAL] ❑ *The cost of private treatment can be prohibitive.* ● **pro|hibi|tive|ly** ADV [ADV adj] ❑ *Meat and butter were prohibitively expensive.*

형용사 엄청나게 비싼, 살 수 없을 정도인 [격식체] ❑ 비보험 치료비용이 엄청나게 비쌀 수 있다. ● 엄청나게 비싸게, 살 수 없을 정도로 부사 ❑ 고기와 버터는 엄청나게 비쌌다.

proj|ect ♦♦◇ (**projects, projecting, projected**)

The noun is pronounced /prˈɒdʒɛkt/. The verb is pronounced /prədʒˈɛkt/.

명사는 /prˈɒdʒɛkt/로 발음되고, 동사는 /prədʒˈɛkt/로 발음된다.

1 N-COUNT A **project** is a task that requires a lot of time and effort. ❑ *Money will also go into local development projects in Vietnam.* ❑ *...an international science project.* **2** N-COUNT A **project** is a detailed study of a subject by a student. ❑ *Students complete projects for a personal tutor, working at home at their own pace.* **3** V-T If something **is projected**, it is planned or expected. ❑ *Africa's mid-1993 population is projected to more than double by 2025.* ❑ *The government had been projecting a 5% consumer price increase for the entire year.* **4** V-T If you **project** someone or something in a particular way, you try to make people see them in that way. If you **project** a particular feeling or quality, you show it in your behavior. ❑ *Bradley projects a natural warmth and sincerity.* ❑ *He just hasn't been able to project himself as the strong leader.* **5** V-T If you **project** a film or picture **onto** a screen or wall, you make it appear there. ❑ *The team tried projecting the maps with two different projectors onto the same screen.* **6** V-I If something **projects**, it sticks out above or beyond a surface or edge. [FORMAL] ❑ *...the remains of a war-time defence which projected out from the shore.*

1 가산명사 사업 계획, 프로젝트 ❑ 베트남의 지역 개발 사업에도 자금이 투입될 것이다. ❑ 국제 과학 프로젝트 **2** 가산명사 과제 ❑ 학생들은 집에서 자기에게 맞는 속도로 공부하면서 개인 지도 교사에게 제출할 과제를 완성한다. **3** 타동사 예측되다 ❑ 1993년 중반의 아프리카 인구가 2025년이 되면 갑절 이상 증가할 것으로 예측된다. ❑ 정부는 그 해 전체에 대해 5퍼센트의 소비자 물가 인상을 전망하고 있었다. **4** 타동사 인식시키다; 발산하다 ❑ 브래들리는 자연스러운 따뜻함과 진솔함을 발산한다. ❑ 그는 그저 사람들에게 자신을 강한 지도자로 인식시키지 못하고 있다. **5** 타동사 투영하다, 비추다 ❑ 그 팀은 두 지도들을 두 대의 다른 영사기로 동일한 화면에 투영시켜 봤다. **6** 자동사 튀어나오다 [격식체] ❑ 해안에서 툭 튀어나와 있는 전시 방어 시설의 잔해

A
B
C
D
E
F
G
H
I
J
K
L
M
N
O
P
Q
R
S
T
U
V
W
X
Y
Z

pro|jec|tion /prədʒɛkʃⁿn/ (**projections**) ■ N-COUNT A **projection** is an estimate of a future amount. ❑ ...the company's projection of 11 million visitors for the first year. ■ N-UNCOUNT The **projection** of a film or picture is the act of projecting it onto a screen or wall. ❑ They took me into a projection room to see a picture.

pro|jec|tor /prədʒɛktər/ (**projectors**) N-COUNT A **projector** is a machine that projects films or slides onto a screen or wall. ❑ ...a 35-millimeter slide projector. →see also **overhead projector**

pro|lif|er|ate /prəlɪfəreɪt/ (**proliferates, proliferating, proliferated**) V-I If things **proliferate**, they increase in number very quickly. [FORMAL] ❑ Computerized data bases are proliferating fast. ● **pro|lif|era|tion** /prəlɪfəreɪʃⁿn/ N-UNCOUNT ❑ ...the proliferation of nuclear weapons.

pro|lif|ic /prəlɪfɪk/ ■ ADJ A **prolific** writer, artist, or composer produces a large number of works. ❑ She is a prolific writer of novels and short stories. ■ ADJ An animal, person, or plant that is **prolific** produces a large number of babies, young plants, or fruit. ❑ They are prolific breeders, with many hens laying up to six eggs.

pro|logue /proʊlɒg, BRIT proʊlɒg/ (**prologues**) N-COUNT A **prologue** is a speech or section of text that introduces a play or book. ❑ The prologue to the novel is written in the form of a newspaper account.

pro|long /prəlɒŋ, BRIT prəlɒŋ/ (**prolongs, prolonging, prolonged**) V-T To **prolong** something means to make it last longer. ❑ Mr. Chesler said foreign military aid was prolonging the war.

pro|longed /prəlɒŋd, BRIT prəlɒŋd/ ADJ A **prolonged** event or situation continues for a long time, or for longer than expected. ❑ ...a prolonged period of low interest rates.

promi|nence /prɒmɪnəns/ N-UNCOUNT If someone or something is in a position of **prominence**, they are well-known and important. ❑ He came to prominence during the World Cup in Italy.

promi|nent ♦♢♢ /prɒmɪnənt/ ■ ADJ Someone who is **prominent** is important. ❑ ...a prominent member of the Law Society. ■ ADJ Something that is **prominent** is very noticeable or is an important part of something else. ❑ Here the window plays a prominent part in the design. ● **promi|nent|ly** ADV [ADV with v] ❑ Trade will figure prominently in the second day of talks in Washington.

pro|mis|cu|ous /prəmɪskyuəs/ ADJ Someone who is **promiscuous** has sex with many different people. [DISAPPROVAL] ❑ She is perceived as vain, spoilt, and promiscuous. ● **promis|cu|ity** /prɒmɪskyuɪti/ N-UNCOUNT ❑ He has recently urged more tolerance of sexual promiscuity.

prom|ise ♦♦♢ /prɒmɪs/ (**promises, promising, promised**) ■ V-T/V-I If you **promise that** you will do something, you say to someone that you will definitely do it. ❑ The post office has promised to resume first class mail delivery to the area on Friday. ❑ He had promised that the rich and privileged would no longer get preferential treatment. ❑ Promise me you will not waste your time. ■ V-T If you **promise** someone something, you tell them that you will definitely give it to them or make sure that they have it. ❑ In 1920 the great powers promised them an independent state. ■ N-COUNT A **promise** is a statement which you make to a person in which you say that you will definitely do something or give them something. ❑ If you make a promise, you should keep it. ■ V-T If a situation or event **promises** to have a particular quality or **to** be a particular thing, it shows signs that it will have that quality or be that thing. ❑ While it will be fun, the seminar also promises to be most instructive. ■ N-UNCOUNT If someone or something shows **promise**, they seem likely to be very good or successful. ❑ The boy first showed promise as an athlete in grade school.

prom|is|ing /prɒmɪsɪŋ/ ADJ Someone or something that is **promising** seems likely to be very good or successful. ❑ A school has honoured one of its brightest and most promising former pupils.

prom|is|sory note /prɒmɪsəri noʊt, BRIT prɒmɪsəri noʊt/ (**promissory notes**) N-COUNT A **promissory note** is a written promise to pay a specific sum of money to a particular person. [mainly AM, BUSINESS] ❑ ...a $36.4 million, five-year promissory note.

■ 가산명사 예측 ❑ 첫 해에 천백만 명의 방문객이 있으리라는 회사의 예측 ■ 불가산명사 영사(映寫), 투영 ❑ 그들은 영화를 보도록 나를 영사실에 데리고 갔다.

가산명사 프로젝터, 영사기 ❑ 35밀리 슬라이드 프로젝터

자동사 급증하다, 확산되다 [격식체] ❑ 전산화된 데이터베이스가 급속히 확산되고 있다. ● 급증, 확산 불가산명사 ❑ 핵무기의 확산

■ 형용사 다작의 ❑ 그녀는 소설과 단편을 쓰는 다작을 하는 작가이다. ■ 형용사 다산의 ❑ 그들은 다산을 하며 많은 암탉의 경우 알을 여섯 개까지 낳는다.

가산명사 머리말, 도입 부분 ❑ 소설의 도입부는 신문 기사의 형태로 쓰였다.

타동사 연장하다 ❑ 체슬러 씨는 외국의 군사 원조가 전쟁을 연장시키고 있다고 했다.

형용사 장기화된 ❑ 장기화된 저금리 시대

불가산명사 저명 ❑ 그는 이태리에서 벌어진 월드컵에서 유명해졌다.

■ 형용사 저명한 ❑ 법률 학회의 저명한 회원 ■ 형용사 두드러진, 중요한 ❑ 여기서 창문이 그 디자인에서 중요한 역할을 한다. ● 중요하게 부사 ❑ 워싱턴에서 개최되는 회담 둘째 날에는 무역이 중요한 부분이 될 것이다.

형용사 성관계가 문란한 [탐탁찮음] ❑ 그녀는 허영심이 많고 버릇없고 성적으로 문란하다고 여겨진다. ● 문란함 불가산명사 ❑ 그는 최근 성적 문란함에 대해 보다 많은 관용을 촉구했다.

■ 타동사/자동사 약속하다 ❑ 우체국은 그 지역에 대한 1종 우편물 배달을 금요일에 재개하기로 약속했다. ❑ 그는 부유한 특권층이 더 이상 특별대우를 받지는 않을 것이라고 약속했다. ❑ 당신 시간을 허비하지 않겠다고 약속해 주세요. ■ 타동사 (주겠다고) 약속하다 ❑ 1920년에 강대국들은 그들에게 독립 국가를 약속했다. ■ 가산명사 약속 ❑ 약속을 했다면 지켜야 한다. ■ 타동사 징조가 보이다 ❑ 그 세미나는 재미도 있겠지만 매우 유익할 것 같다. ■ 불가산명사 가능성, 유망함 ❑ 그 소년은 초등학교 때 선수로서의 가능성을 처음 보였다.

형용사 가능성이 있는, 유망한 ❑ 학교가 가장 총명하고 유망한 졸업생 중 한 명에게 우등상을 주었다.

가산명사 약속 어음 [주로 미국영어, 경제] ❑ 3,640만 달러짜리 5년 만기 약속 어음

Word Link	*mot ≈ moving : mo*tion, *mo*tivate, *pro*mote

pro|mote ♦♦◇ /prəmoʊt/ (promotes, promoting, promoted) **1** V-T If people **promote** something, they help or encourage it to happen, increase, or spread. ❑ *You don't have to sacrifice environmental protection to promote economic growth.* ● **pro|mo|tion** N-UNCOUNT ❑ *The government has pledged to give the promotion of democracy higher priority.* **2** V-T If a firm **promotes** a product, it tries to increase the sales or popularity of that product. ❑ *Paul Weller has announced a full British tour to promote his second solo album.* **3** V-T If someone **is promoted**, they are given a more important job or rank in the organization that they work for. [usu passive] ❑ *I was promoted to editor and then editorial director.* **4** V-T If a team that competes in a league **is promoted**, it starts competing in a higher division in the next season because it was one of the most successful teams in the lower division. [BRIT] [usu passive] ❑ *Woodford Green won the Second Division title and are promoted to the First Division.* ● **pro|mo|tion** N-UNCOUNT ❑ *Fans of Leeds United football club have been celebrating their team's promotion to the first division.* →see **concert**

1 타동사 촉진하다 ❑ 경제 성장을 촉진하기 위해 환경 보호를 희생할 필요는 없다. ● 촉진 불가산명사 ❑ 민주주의 촉진에 더 많은 우선권을 두겠다고 정부는 약속했다. **2** 타동사 홍보하다, 판촉을 벌이다 ❑ 폴 웰러가 자신의 두 번째 솔로 앨범을 홍보하기 위한 영국 전역 순회공연을 발표했다. **3** 타동사 승진되다 ❑ 나는 편집장, 그 다음에는 편집이사로 승진했다. **4** 타동사 (상급 리그로) 승격되다 [영국영어] ❑ 우드포드 그린은 2부 리그에서 우승하여 1부 리그로 승격된다. ● 승격 불가산명사 ❑ 리즈 유나이티드 축구팀의 팬들은 자신들의 팀이 1부 리그로 승격된 것을 축하하고 있다.

Word Partnership	*promote*의 연어
N.	promote **competition**, promote **democracy**, promote **development**, promote **education**, promote **growth**, promote **health**, promote **peace**, promote **stability**, promote **trade**, promote **understanding 1**
	promote **a product 2**

---

pro|mot|er /prəmoʊtər/ (promoters) **1** N-COUNT A **promoter** is a person who helps organize and finance an event, especially a sports event. ❑ *...one of the top boxing promoters in Britain.* **2** N-COUNT The **promoter of** a cause or idea tries to make it become popular. ❑ *Aaron Copland was always the most energetic promoter of American music.*

1 가산명사 프로모터 ❑ 영국 내 최고의 복싱 프로모터 중 한 명 **2** 가산명사 후원자 ❑ 애런 코플랜드는 항상 미국 음악의 가장 열정적인 후원자였다.

pro|mo|tion ♦♦◇ /prəmoʊʃⁿn/ (promotions) **1** N-VAR If you are given **promotion** or a **promotion** in your job, you are given a more important job or rank in the organization that you work for. ❑ *Consider changing jobs or trying for promotion.* **2** N-VAR A **promotion** is an attempt to make a product or event popular or successful, especially by advertising. [BUSINESS] ❑ *During 1984, Remington spent a lot of money on advertising and promotion.* →see also **promote**

1 가산명사 또는 불가산명사 승진 ❑ 직장을 바꾸든지 승진을 노리는 것을 고려해 보세요. **2** 가산명사 또는 불가산명사 홍보, 판촉 [경제] ❑ 1984년에 레밍턴은 광고와 홍보에 많은 돈을 썼다.

pro|mo|tion|al /prəmoʊʃən³l/ ADJ **Promotional** material, events, or ideas are designed to increase the sales of a product or service. ❑ *"Jeans," according to one company's promotional material, "are designed and made to be worn hard."*

형용사 홍보의 ❑ 한 회사의 홍보 자료에 의하면 "청바지는 험하게 입도록 디자인되고 만들어진다."

prompt ♦◇◇ /prɒmpt/ (prompts, prompting, prompted) **1** V-T To **prompt** someone **to** do something means to make them decide to do it. ❑ *Japan's recession has prompted consumers to cut back on buying cars.* **2** V-T If you **prompt** someone when they stop speaking, you encourage or help them to continue. If you **prompt** an actor, you tell them what their next line is when they have forgotten what comes next. ❑ *"You wouldn't have wanted to bring those people to justice anyway, would you?" Brand prompted him.* **3** ADJ A **prompt** action is done without any delay. ❑ *It is not too late, but prompt action is needed.* **4** ADJ If you are **prompt** to do something, you do it without delay or you are not late. [v-link ADJ] ❑ *You have been so prompt in carrying out all these commissions.*

1 타동사 (~하도록) 자극하다 ❑ 일본의 불경기는 소비자들로 하여금 차를 사는 것을 자제하게 만들었다. **2** 타동사 말을 계속하게 만들다; 대사를 알려주다 ❑ "어쨌든 당신은 그 사람들을 법정에 세우려 한 게 아니었잖아요?"라며 브랜드는 그의 말을 유도했다. **3** 형용사 즉각적인 ❑ 너무 늦지는 않았지만 즉각적인 행동이 필요하다. **4** 형용사 신속한 ❑ 이 모든 의뢰 사항을 매우 신속히 처리해 주셨습니다.

prompt|ing /prɒmptɪŋ/ (promptings) N-UNCOUNT If you respond to **prompting**, you do what someone encourages or reminds you to do. [also N in pl] ❑ *New York needed little prompting from their coach Bill Parcells.*

불가산명사 격려; 재촉 ❑ 뉴욕은 자신들의 코치인 빌 파셀스로부터 별다른 재촉을 받을 필요가 없었다.

prompt|ly /prɒmptli/ **1** ADV If you do something **promptly**, you do it immediately. [ADV with v] ❑ *Sister Francesca entered the chapel, took her seat, and promptly fell asleep.* **2** ADV If you do something **promptly at** a particular time, you do it at exactly that time. ❑ *Promptly at a quarter past seven, we left the hotel.*

1 부사 즉시 ❑ 프란체스카 수녀는 성당에 들어가 자리를 잡고 곧 잠이 들었다. **2** 부사 정각에 ❑ 7시 15분 정각에 우리는 호텔을 떠났다.

prone /proʊn/ **1** ADJ To be **prone** to something, usually something bad, means to have a tendency to be affected by it or to do it. [v-link ADJ, ADJ to n, ADJ to-inf] ❑ *For all her experience as a television reporter, she was still prone to camera nerves.* ● COMB in ADJ **-prone** combines with nouns to make adjectives that describe people who are frequently affected by something bad. ❑ *...the most injury-prone rider on the circuit.* **2** ADJ If you are lying **prone**, you are lying on your front. [FORMAL] [ADJ after v, ADJ n] ❑ *Bob slid from his chair and lay prone on the floor.*

1 형용사 ~의 경향이 있는, 자주 ~하는 ❑ 텔레비전 리포터로서의 숱한 경험에도 불구하고 그녀는 아직도 카메라 앞에 서면 긴장을 잘 했다. ● 복합형-형용사 ~의 경향이 있는, 잘 ~하는 ❑ 경주 중에 가장 부상을 잘 당하는 기수 **2** 형용사 엎드린 [격식체] ❑ 밥은 의자에서 미끄러져 내려와 바닥에 엎드렸다.

pro|noun /proʊnaʊn/ (pronouns) N-COUNT A **pronoun** is a word that you use to refer to someone or something when you do not need to use a noun, often because the person or thing has been mentioned earlier. Examples are "it," "she," "something," and "myself."

가산명사 대명사

Word Link	*nounce ≈ reporting : an*nounce, *de*nounce, *pro*nounce

pro|nounce /prənaʊns/ (pronounces, pronouncing, pronounced) **1** V-T To **pronounce** a word means to say it using particular sounds. ❑ *Have I pronounced your name correctly?* **2** V-T If you **pronounce** something to be true, you state that it is the case. [FORMAL] ❑ *A specialist has now pronounced him fully fit.* →see **trial**

1 타동사 발음하다 ❑ 제가 당신의 이름을 제대로 발음했나요? **2** 타동사 선언하다 [격식체] ❑ 전문의가 그는 이제 완전히 건강하다고 선언했다.

pro|nounced /prənaʊnst/ ADJ Something that is **pronounced** is very noticeable. ❑ *Most of the art exhibitions have a pronounced Scottish theme.*

형용사 뚜렷한 ❑ 미술 전시 작품 대부분이 뚜렷이 스코틀랜드적 주제를 보인다.

pro|nounce|ment /prənaʊnsmənt/ (pronouncements) N-COUNT
Pronouncements are public or official statements on an important subject.
❑ ...the President's latest pronouncements about the protection of minorities.

가산명사 선언 ❑ 소수 인종의 보호에 관한 대통령의 최근 선언

pro|nun|cia|tion /prənʌnsieɪʃən/ (pronunciations) N-VAR The **pronunciation** of a word or language is the way in which it is pronounced. ❑ She gave the word its French pronunciation.

가산명사 또는 불가산명사 발음 ❑ 그녀는 그 단어를 원래 프랑스식대로 발음했다.

proof ♦◇◇ /pruf/ (proofs) **1** N-VAR **Proof** is a fact, argument, or piece of evidence which shows that something is definitely true or definitely exists. ❑ You have to have proof of residence in the state of Texas, such as a Texas ID card. ❑ This is not necessarily proof that he is wrong. **2** ADJ **Proof** is used after a number of degrees or a percentage, when indicating the strength of a strong alcoholic drink such as whiskey. [amount ADJ] ❑ ...a glass of Wild Turkey bourbon: 101 degrees proof.

1 가산명사 또는 불가산명사 증거 ❑ 텍사스 신분증 같은 텍사스 주민이라는 증거가 있어야 한다. ❑ 이것이 반드시 그가 틀리다는 증거는 아니다. **2** 형용사 (알코올) 도수의, 프루프의 ❑ 알코올 도수가 101도인 와일드 터키 버번 위스키 한 잔

Word Partnership	proof의 연어
ADJ.	**convincing** proof, **final** proof, **living** proof, proof **positive** **1**
V.	**have** proof, **need** proof, **offer** proof, **provide** proof, **require** proof, **show** proof **1**

-proof /-pruf/ (-proofs, -proofing, -proofed) **1** COMB in ADJ **-proof** combines with nouns and verbs to form adjectives which indicate that something cannot be damaged or badly affected by the thing or action mentioned. ❑ ...a bomb-proof aircraft. ❑ In a large microwave-proof dish, melt butter for 20 seconds. **2** **-proof** combines with nouns to form verbs which refer to protecting something against being damaged or badly affected by the thing mentioned. ❑ ...home energy efficiency grants towards the cost of draught-proofing your home. **3** →see also **bullet-proof**, **waterproof**

1 복합형-형용사 -을 견디어 내는 ❑ 폭탄에도 끄떡없는 비행기 ❑ 전자레인지 사용이 가능한 큰 접시에 버터를 20초간 녹이세요. **2** -을 견디어 내게 하다 ❑ 집의 외풍 방지 비용을 보조해 주는 가정 에너지 효율성 보조금

prop /prɒp/ (props, propping, propped) **1** V-T If you **prop** an object **on** or **against** something, you support it by putting something underneath it or by resting it somewhere. ❑ He rocked back in the chair and propped his feet on the desk. ● PHRASAL VERB **Prop up** means the same as **prop**. ❑ Sam slouched back and propped his elbows up on the bench behind him. **2** N-COUNT A **prop** is a stick or other object that you use to support something. ❑ Using the table as a prop, he dragged himself to his feet. **3** N-COUNT To be a **prop** for a system, institution, or person means to be the main thing that keeps them strong or helps them survive. ❑ The army is one of the main props of the government. **4** N-COUNT The **props** in a play or movie are all the objects or pieces of furniture that are used in it. ❑ ...the backdrop and props for a stage show.

1 타동사 기대다, 받치다 ❑ 그는 의자를 뒤로 젖히고 발을 책상에 기댔다. ● 구동사 기대다, 받치다 ❑ 샘은 몸을 뒤로 비스듬히 젖히고 팔꿈치를 뒤의 벤치에 대고 기댔다. **2** 가산명사 받침대 ❑ 그는 탁자를 받침대 삼아 힘겹게 일어섰다. **3** 가산명사 지주(支柱) ❑ 군대는 정부의 주요 지주 중 하나이다. **4** 가산명사 소품 ❑ 무대 공연의 배경 및 소품

▶prop up **1** PHRASAL VERB To **prop up** something means to support it or help it to survive. ❑ Investments in the U.S. money market have propped up the American dollar. **2** →see **prop** 1

1 구동사 지지하다, 뒷받침하다 ❑ 미국 금융 시장에 대한 투자가 미국 달러의 버팀목이 되어 주었다.

propa|gan|da /prɒpəgændə/ N-UNCOUNT **Propaganda** is information, often inaccurate information, which a political organization publishes or broadcasts in order to influence people. [DISAPPROVAL] ❑ The Front adopted an aggressive propaganda campaign against its rivals.

불가산명사 정치 선전 [탐탁찮음] ❑ 그 전선은 경쟁자에 대한 공격적인 정치 선전 운동을 개시하기로 했다.

propa|gate /prɒpəgeɪt/ (propagates, propagating, propagated) **1** V-T If people **propagate** an idea or piece of information, they spread it and try to make people believe it or support it. [FORMAL] ❑ They propagated political doctrines which promised to tear apart the fabric of British society. ● propa|ga|tion /prɒpəgeɪʃən/ N-UNCOUNT ❑ These two countries must work together towards the propagation of true Buddhism. **2** V-T If you **propagate** plants, you grow more of them from the original ones. [TECHNICAL] ❑ The easiest way to propagate a vine is to take hardwood cuttings.

1 타동사 유포하다 [격식체] ❑ 영국 사회의 근간을 허물수도 있는 정치적 이념들을 그들은 유포했다. ● 유포 불가산명사 ❑ 이 두 나라는 진정한 불교의 전파를 위해 협력해야 한다. **2** 타동사 번식시키다 [과학 기술] ❑ 넝쿨을 번식시키는 가장 좋은 방법은 단단한 경목 접지를 이용하는 것이다.

Word Link	pel ≈ driving, forcing : compel, expel, propel

pro|pel /prəpɛl/ (propels, propelling, propelled) V-T To **propel** something in a particular direction means to cause it to move in that direction. ❑ The tiny rocket is attached to the spacecraft and is designed to propel it toward Mars. ● COMB in ADJ **-propelled** combines with nouns to form adjectives which indicate how something, especially a weapon, is propelled. ❑ ...rocket-propelled grenades.

타동사 나아가게 하다, 밀쳐 올리다 ❑ 이 작은 로켓은 우주선에 부착되어 그것이 화성까지 날아가게 하도록 설계되어 있다. ● 복합형-형용사 -으로 추진되는 ❑ 로켓 추진 소화탄

pro|pel|ler /prəpɛlər/ (propellers) N-COUNT A **propeller** is a device with blades which is attached to a boat or aircraft. The engine makes the propeller spin around and causes the boat or aircraft to move. ❑ ...a fixed three-bladed propeller. →see **flight**

가산명사 프로펠러 ❑ 날 세 개짜리 고정식 프로펠러

pro|pen|sity /prəpɛnsɪti/ (propensities) N-COUNT A **propensity to** do something or a **propensity for** something is a natural tendency that you have to behave in a particular way. [FORMAL] ❑ Mr. Bint has a propensity to put off decisions to the last minute.

가산명사 경향, 성벽 [격식체] ❑ 빈트 씨는 마지막 순간까지 결정을 미루는 경향이 있다.

prop|er ♦◇◇ /prɒpər/ **1** ADJ You use **proper** to describe things that you consider to be real and satisfactory rather than inadequate in some way. [ADJ n] ❑ Two out of five people lack a proper job. **2** ADJ The **proper** thing is the one that is correct or most suitable. [ADJ n] ❑ The Supreme Court will ensure that the proper procedures have been followed. **3** ADJ If you say that a way of behaving is **proper**, you mean that it is considered socially acceptable and right. ❑ In those days it was not thought entirely proper for a woman to be on the stage. **4** ADJ You can add **proper** after a word to indicate that you are referring to the central and most important part of a place, event, or object and want to distinguish it from other things which are not regarded as being important or central to it. [n ADJ] ❑ A distinction must be made between archeology proper and science-based archeology.

1 형용사 적당한 ❑ 다섯 사람 중 두 사람이 적당한 일자리가 없다. **2** 형용사 적절한 ❑ 적절한 조처를 따라 왔음을 대법원이 보증할 것이다. **3** 형용사 온당한; 예의 바른 ❑ 그 시절에는 여성이 무대 위에 서는 것이 완전히 온당한 일로 여겨지지 않았다. **4** 형용사 본래의, 엄격한 의미의 ❑ 엄격한 의미의 고고학과 과학에 근거한 고고학 사이에 구분이 지어져야 한다.

a

prop|er|ly ♦◇◇ /prɒpərli/ ■ ADV If something is done **properly**, it is done in a correct and satisfactory way. ❑ *You're too thin. You're not eating properly.* ■ ADV If someone behaves **properly**, they behave in a way that is considered acceptable and not rude. [ADV after v] ❑ *He's a spoilt brat and it's about time he learnt to behave properly.*

■ 부사 적절히 ❑ 너는 너무 말랐어. 넌 제대로 먹지를 않아. ■ 부사 예의 바르게 ❑ 그는 버릇없는 개구쟁이고 이제는 예의 바르게 행동하는 법을 배울 때가 되었다.

b

prop|er noun (**proper nouns**) also **proper name** N-COUNT A **proper noun** is the name of a particular person, place, organization, or thing. Proper nouns begin with a capital letter. Examples are "Margaret," "London," and "the United Nations." Compare **common noun**.

가산명사 고유 명사

c

prop|er|ty ♦◇◇ /prɒpərti/ (**properties**) ■ N-UNCOUNT Someone's **property** is all the things that belong to them or something that belongs to them. [FORMAL] ❑ *Richard could easily destroy her personal property to punish her for walking out on him.* ■ N-VAR A **property** is a building and the land belonging to it. [FORMAL] ❑ *Cecil inherited a family property near Stamford.* ■ N-COUNT The **properties** of a substance or object are the ways in which it behaves in particular conditions. ❑ *A radio signal has both electrical and magnetic properties.* →see **element**

d

■ 불가산명사 재산 [격식체] ❑ 리처드는 자신을 버린 그녀를 벌하기 위해 그녀를 쉽게 파산시킬 수 있었다. ■ 가산명사 또는 불가산명사 부동산; 대지 [격식체] ❑ 세실은 스탬퍼드 인근의 가족 소유지를 상속받았다. ■ 가산명사 성질, 특성 ❑ 무선 신호는 전기적 특성과 자기적 특성을 모두 가지고 있다.

e

proph|ecy /prɒfɪsi/ (**prophecies**) N-VAR A **prophecy** is a statement in which someone says they strongly believe that a particular thing will happen. ❑ *The youth, too, fulfilled the prophecy.*

가산명사 또는 불가산명사 예언 ❑ 그 젊은이 역시 예언을 만족시켰다.

f

proph|esy /prɒfɪsaɪ/ (**prophesies, prophesying, prophesied**) V-T If you **prophesy** that something will happen, you say that you strongly believe that it will happen. ❑ *He prophesied that within five years his opponent would either be dead or in prison.*

타동사 예언하다 ❑ 그는 5년 안에 자신의 적이 죽거나 감옥에 갇힐 것이라고 예언했다.

g

proph|et /prɒfɪt/ (**prophets**) N-COUNT A **prophet** is a person who is believed to be chosen by God to say the things that God wants to tell people. ❑ *...the sacred name of the Holy Prophet of Islam.*

가산명사 예언자 ❑ 성스러운 이슬람 예언자의 신성한 이름

h

pro|phet|ic /prəfɛtɪk/ ADJ If something was **prophetic**, it described or suggested something that did actually happen later. ❑ *This ominous warning soon proved prophetic.*

형용사 예언적인; 실현된 ❑ 이 불길한 경고는 머지않아 현실이 되었다.

i

pro|po|nent /prəpoʊnənt/ (**proponents**) N-COUNT If you are a **proponent of** a particular idea or course of action, you actively support it. [FORMAL] ❑ *Halsey was identified as a leading proponent of the values of progressive education.*

가산명사 옹호자 [격식체] ❑ 핼시는 진보적 교육의 유용성에 대한 주도적 옹호자로 여겨졌다.

j

pro|por|tion ♦◇◇ /prəpɔrʃⁿn/ (**proportions**) ■ N-COUNT A **proportion of** a group or an amount is a part of it. [FORMAL] ❑ *A large proportion of the dolphins in that area will eventually die.* ■ N-COUNT The **proportion of** one kind of person or thing in a group is the number of people or things of that kind compared to the total number of people or things in the group. ❑ *The proportion of women in the profession had risen to 17.3%.* ■ N-COUNT The **proportion of** one amount to another is the relationship between the two amounts in terms of how much there is of each thing. ❑ *Women's bodies tend to have a higher proportion of fat to water.* ■ N-PLURAL If you refer to the **proportions** of something, you are referring to its size, usually when this is extremely large. [WRITTEN] ❑ *In the tropics plants grow to huge proportions.* ■ PHRASE If one thing increases or decreases **in proportion to** another thing, it increases or decreases to the same degree as that thing. ❑ *The pressure in the cylinders would go up in proportion to the boiler pressure.* ■ PHRASE If something is small or large **in proportion to** something else, it is small or large when compared with that thing. ❑ *Children tend to have relatively larger heads than adults in proportion to the rest of their body.* ■ PHRASE If you say that something is **out of all proportion to** something else, you think that it is far greater or more serious than it should be. ❑ *The punishment was out of all proportion to the crime.* →see **ratio**

k

■ 가산명사 부분 [격식체] ❑ 그 지역에 있는 돌고래 중 다수가 결국 죽을 것이다. ■ 가산명사 비율 ❑ 그 직종 내 여성 비율이 17.3퍼센트까지 상승했다. ■ 가산명사 비율 ❑ 여성의 몸은 물보다 지방 비율을 더 높은 경향이 있다. ■ 복수명사 크기, 규모 [문어체] ❑ 열대 지방에서는 초목이 거대한 크기로 자란다. ■ 구 -에 비례하여; 실린더 내의 압력이 보일러 압력에 비례하여 상승할 것이다. ■ 구 -에 비해 ❑ 아이들은 성인보다 다른 신체 부위에 비해 머리가 상대적으로 큰 경향이 있다. ■ 구 -에 비해 지나친, -에 균형이 안 맞는 ❑ 죄에 비추어 볼 때 처벌이 지나치게 무거웠다.

l

m

	Word Partnership	proportion의 연어
N.	proportion **of the population** ■	
	proportion **of adults/children/men/women** ■ ■	
	sense **of** proportion ■	
ADJ.	**large** proportion, **significant** proportion,	
	small proportion ■ ■	
	greater proportion, **higher** proportion, **larger** proportion ■	
	in direct proportion ■ ■	

n

o

pro|por|tion|al /prəpɔrʃⁿn°l/ ADJ If one amount is **proportional to** another, the two amounts increase and decrease at the same rate so there is always the same relationship between them. [FORMAL] ❑ *Loss of weight is directly proportional to the rate at which the disease is progressing.*

p

형용사 -에 비례하는 [격식체] ❑ 체중 감소는 병이 진행되는 속도에 정비례한다.

q

pro|por|tion|al rep|re|sen|ta|tion N-UNCOUNT **Proportional representation** is a system of voting in which each political party is represented in a legislature or parliament in proportion to the number of people who vote for it in an election.

불가산명사 비례 대표제

r

pro|por|tion|ate /prəpɔrʃənɪt/ ADJ **Proportionate** means the same as **proportional**. ❑ *Republics will have voting rights proportionate to the size of their economies.* ● **pro|por|tion|ate|ly** ADV ❑ *We have significantly increased the number of people in education but the size of the classes hasn't changed proportionately.*

s

형용사 비례하는 ❑ 공화국들은 각자의 경제 규모에 비례하는 투표권을 갖게 될 것이다. ● 비례하여 부사 ❑ 교육받는 사람들의 숫자는 크게 증가해 왔지만 학급 규모는 그에 맞추어 변하지 않았다.

t

pro|pos|al ♦◇◇ /prəpoʊzⁿl/ (**proposals**) ■ N-COUNT A **proposal** is a plan or an idea, often a formal or written one, which is suggested for people to think about and decide upon. ❑ *The President is to put forward new proposals for resolving the country's constitutional crisis.* ❑ *...the government's proposals to abolish free health care.* ■ N-COUNT A **proposal** is the act of asking someone to marry you. ❑ *After a three-weekend courtship, Pamela accepted Randolph's proposal of marriage.*

u

■ 가산명사 계획, 안 ❑ 대통령이 국가의 헌법적 위기를 해결하기 위한 새로운 계획들을 내놓을 예정이다. ❑ 무료 의료 서비스를 폐지하는 정부의 안 ■ 가산명사 청혼 ❑ 3주에 걸친 구혼 끝에, 파멜라는 랜돌프의 청혼을 받아들였다.

v

w

x

y

z

Word Partnership   proposal의 연어

ADJ.	new proposal, original proposal **1**
V.	adopt a proposal, approve a proposal, support a proposal, vote on a proposal **1**
	accept a proposal, make a proposal, reject a proposal **1** **2**
N.	budget proposal, peace proposal **1**
	marriage proposal **2**

pro|pose ♦♦◇ /prəpóʊz/ (proposes, proposing, proposed) **1** V-T If you **propose** something such as a plan or an idea, you suggest it for people to think about and decide upon. ❑ *Britain is about to propose changes to some institutions.* **2** V-T If you **propose** to do something, you intend to do it. ❑ *It's still far from clear what action the government proposes to take over the affair.* **3** V-T If you **propose** a motion for debate, or a candidate for election, you begin the debate or the election procedure by formally stating your support for that motion or candidate. ❑ *He has proposed a resolution limiting the role of U.S. troops.* **4** V-I If you **propose to** someone, or **propose marriage to** them, you ask them to marry you. ❑ *He proposed to his girlfriend over a public-address system.*

1 타동사 제안하다 ❑ 영국은 몇몇 제도에 대한 변경을 제안할 참이다. **2** 타동사 꾀하다, 기도하다 ❑ 정부가 그 일을 인수하기 위해 어떤 조처를 꾀하는지는 아직 전혀 분명하지 않다. **3** 타동사 (안건 등을) 제출하다; (후보를) 추천하다 ❑ 그는 미군의 역할을 제한하는 결의안을 제출했다. **4** 자동사 청혼하다 ❑ 그는 확성기를 통해 여자 친구에게 청혼했다.

Word Partnership   propose의 연어

N.	propose changes, propose legislation, propose a plan, propose a solution, propose a tax, propose a theory, propose a toast **1** **2**
	propose marriage **4**

propo|si|tion /prɒpəzɪ́ʃ°n/ (propositions) **1** N-COUNT If you describe something such as a task or an activity as, for example, a difficult **proposition** or an attractive **proposition**, you mean that it is difficult or pleasant to do. ❑ *Making easy money has always been an attractive proposition.* **2** N-COUNT A **proposition** is a statement or an idea which people can consider or discuss to decide whether it is true. [FORMAL] ❑ *The proposition that democracies do not fight each other is based on a tiny historical sample.* **3** N-COUNT In the United States, a **proposition** is a question or statement about an issue of public policy which appears on a voting paper so that people can vote for or against it. ❑ *Vote Yes on Proposition 136, but No on Propositions 129, 133 and 134.* **4** N-COUNT A **proposition** is an offer or a suggestion that someone makes to you, usually concerning some work or business that you might be able to do together. ❑ *You came to see me at my office the other day with a business proposition.*

1 가산명사 일, 문제 ❑ 쉽게 돈 벌기는 항상 매력적인 일이었다. **2** 가산명사 진술, 주장 [격식체] ❑ 민주국가들은 서로 싸우지 않는다는 주장은 아주 작은 역사적 본보기 하나에 근거를 두고 있다. **3** 가산명사 (주민 투표에 회부된) 제안 ❑ 136번 제안에는 찬성투표를 하고, 129번과 133번, 134번에는 반대 투표를 하세요. **4** 가산명사 제안 ❑ 일전에 당신이 사업 제안 한 가지를 들고 내 사무실로 나를 만나러 왔어요.

pro|pri|etary /prəpráɪətəri, BRIT prəpráɪətri/ ADJ **Proprietary** substances or products are sold under a trade name. [FORMAL] [ADJ n] ❑ *...some proprietary brands of dog food.*

형용사 전매 상표가 붙은, 독점 재산의 [격식체] ❑ 개먹이 전매 상표 몇 가지

pro|pri|etor /prəpráɪətər/ (proprietors) N-COUNT The **proprietor** of a hotel, store, newspaper, or other business is the person who owns it. [FORMAL] ❑ *...the proprietor of a local restaurant.*

가산명사 소유주, 경영자 [격식체] ❑ 한 현지 음식점 소유주

pro|pri|etress /prəpráɪətrɪs/ (proprietresses) N-COUNT The **proprietress** of a hotel, store, or business is the woman who owns it. [FORMAL] ❑ *The proprietress was alone in the bar.*

가산명사 여성 소유주 [격식체] ❑ 여주인은 바에 혼자 있었다.

pro ra|ta /proʊ réɪtə, BRIT proʊ rɑ́ːtə/ also **pro-rata** ADV If something is distributed **pro rata**, it is distributed in proportion to the amount or size of something. [FORMAL] [ADV after v] ❑ *All part-timers should be paid the same, pro rata, as full-timers doing the same job.* ● ADJ **Pro rata** is also an adjective. [ADJ n] ❑ *They are paid their salaries and are entitled to fringe benefits on a pro-rata basis.*

부사 비례하여 [격식체] ❑ 모든 비상근 근무자들은 같은 일을 하는 상근 근무자들에 비례하여 동일한 임금을 받아야 한다. ● 형용사 비례하는 ❑ 그들은 봉급을 받고 비례에 기초하여 부수적인 혜택을 받게 됩니다.

pro|sa|ic /proʊzéɪɪk/ ADJ Something that is **prosaic** is dull and uninteresting. [FORMAL] ❑ *His instructor offered a more prosaic explanation for the surge in interest.*

형용사 단조로운, 따분한 [격식체] ❑ 그의 교사는 그와 같은 관심의 급증에 대해 더 단조로운 해석을 내놓았다.

prose /proʊz/ N-UNCOUNT **Prose** is ordinary written language, in contrast to poetry. ❑ *Shute's prose is stark and chillingly unsentimental.*

불가산명사 산문 ❑ 슈트의 산문은 경직되어 있고 냉담하게 감정이 배제되어 있다.

pros|ecute /prɒ́sɪkyut/ (prosecutes, prosecuting, prosecuted) **1** V-T/V-I If the authorities **prosecute** someone, they charge them with a crime and put them on trial. ❑ *The police have decided not to prosecute because the evidence is not strong enough.* ❑ *Photographs taken by roadside cameras will soon be enough to prosecute drivers for speeding.* **2** V-T/V-I When a lawyer **prosecutes** a case, he or she tries to prove that the person who is on trial is guilty. ❑ *The attorney who will prosecute the case says he cannot reveal how much money is involved.*

1 타동사/자동사 고소하다, 고발하다 ❑ 증거가 불충분해서 경찰은 고발하지 않기로 결정했다. ❑ 노변의 카메라에 찍힌 사진들이 곧 운전자들을 과속으로 고발하기에 충분할 만큼 될 것이다. **2** 타동사/자동사 기소하다 ❑ 그 사건을 기소할 검사는 얼마만큼의 돈이 연루되어 있는지 밝힐 수 없다고 말한다.

pros|ecu|tion ♦◇◇ /prɒ̀sɪkyúːʃ°n/ (prosecutions) **1** N-VAR **Prosecution** is the action of charging someone with a crime and putting them on trial. ❑ *Yesterday the head of government called for the prosecution of those responsible for the deaths.* **2** N-SING The lawyers who try to prove that a person on trial is guilty are called **the prosecution.** ❑ *The star witness for the prosecution took the stand.*

1 가산명사 또는 불가산명사 기소, 고소 ❑ 어제 정부 수반이 그 죽음들에 책임이 있는 사람들을 기소할 것을 요구했다. **2** 단수명사 기소자 측, 검찰 당국 ❑ 검찰 측의 가장 중요한 증인이 증언대에 섰다.

pros|ecu|tor /prɒ́sɪkyutər/ (prosecutors) N-COUNT In some countries, a **prosecutor** is a lawyer or official who brings charges against someone or tries to prove in a trial that they are guilty.

가산명사 검사

pros|pect ♦◇◇ (prospects, prospecting, prospected) /prɒ́spɛkt/ **1** N-VAR If there is some **prospect of** something happening, there is a possibility that it will happen. ❑ *Unfortunately, there is little prospect of seeing these big questions answered.* ❑ *The prospects for peace in the country's eight-year civil war are becoming brighter.* **2** N-SING A particular **prospect** is something that you expect or know is going to happen. ❑ *There was a mixed reaction to the prospect of having new neighbors.* **3** N-PLURAL Someone's **prospects** are their chances of being

1 가산명사 또는 불가산명사 가망 ❑ 유감스럽게도, 이러한 커다란 질문들에 대한 대답이 돌아오는 것을 보게 될 가망은 별로 없다. ❑ 그 나라의 8년에 걸친 내전 속에 평화가 찾아 올 가망이 더욱 밝아지고 있다. **2** 단수명사 예상 ❑ 새 이웃이 생기게 될 예상을 두고 반응이 엇갈렸다. **3** 복수명사 (성공의) 가망, 전망 ❑ 나는 경력 상의 전망을 더 낮게 하기 위해 외국에서

successful, especially in their career. ❑ *I chose to work abroad to improve my career prospects.* ◳ V-I When people **prospect for** oil, gold, or some other valuable substance, they look for it in the ground or under the sea. ❑ *He had prospected for minerals everywhere from the Gobi Desert to the Transvaal.*

일하는 것을 택했다. ◳ 자동사 시굴하다, 답사하다 ❑ 그는 고비 사막에서 트란스발에 이르기까지 모든 곳에서 광물 시굴을 했었다.

Word Partnership	*prospect*의 연어
N.	prospect **for/of** for peace, prospect **for/of** war ◳
V.	prospect **of being** *something*, prospect **of having** *something* ◳

pro|spec|tive /prəspɛktɪv, BRIT prəspɛktɪv/ ◳ ADJ You use **prospective** to describe someone who wants to be the thing mentioned or who is likely to be the thing mentioned. [ADJ n] ❑ *The story should act as a warning to other prospective buyers.* ◲ ADJ You use **prospective** to describe something that is likely to happen soon. [ADJ n] ❑ *The terms of the prospective deal are most clearly spelt out in the Financial Times.*

◳ 형용사 예상되는 ❑ 그 이야기가 다른 예상 구매자들에게 틀림없이 일종의 경고로 작용할 것이다. ◲ 형용사 곧 있을 ❑ 곧 있을 협정의 조건들은 파이낸셜 타임스에 가장 똑똑히 설명되어 있다.

pro|spec|tus /prəspɛktəs, BRIT prəspɛktəs/ (**prospectuses**) N-COUNT A **prospectus** is a detailed document produced by a company, college, or school, which gives details about it. ❑ *...a prospectus for a new share issue.*

가산명사 안내 책자 ❑ 신주 발행 안내 책자

pros|per /prɒspər/ (**prospers, prospering, prospered**) V-I If people or businesses **prosper**, they are successful and do well. [FORMAL] ❑ *The high street banks continue to prosper.*

자동사 번영하다, 번창하다 [격식체] ❑ 중심가 은행들은 계속해서 번창한다.

pros|per|ity /prɒspɛrɪti/ N-UNCOUNT **Prosperity** is a condition in which a person or community is doing well financially. ❑ *...a new era of peace and prosperity.*

불가산명사 번영, 번창 ❑ 평화와 번영의 새 시대

pros|per|ous /prɒspərəs/ ADJ **Prosperous** people, places, and economies are rich and successful. [FORMAL] ❑ *...the youngest son of a relatively prosperous British family.*

형용사 성공한, 번창한 [격식체] ❑ 비교적 부유한 영국인 집안의 막내아들

pros|ti|tute /prɒstɪtut, BRIT prɒstɪtyuːt/ (**prostitutes**) N-COUNT A **prostitute** is a person, usually a woman, who has sex with men in exchange for money. ❑ *He admitted last week he paid for sex with a prostitute.*

가산명사 매춘부 ❑ 그는 지난주에 돈을 주고 매춘부와 성관계를 했다고 인정했다.

pros|ti|tu|tion /prɒstɪtuʃ°n, BRIT prɒstɪtyuːʃ°n/ N-UNCOUNT **Prostitution** means having sex with people in exchange for money. ❑ *She eventually drifts into prostitution.*

불가산명사 매춘 ❑ 그녀는 결국 매춘에 빠져든다.

Word Link	*agon ≈ struggling : agonize, agony, protagonist*

pro|tago|nist /prɒtægənɪst, BRIT prətægənɪst/ (**protagonists**) ◳ N-COUNT Someone who is a **protagonist of** an idea or movement is a supporter of it. [FORMAL] ❑ *He was one of the most active protagonists of British membership of the EEC.* ◲ N-COUNT A **protagonist** in a play, novel, or real event is one of the main people in it. [FORMAL] ❑ *...the protagonist of J. D. Salinger's novel "The Catcher in the Rye".*

◳ 가산명사 주창자, 지지자 [격식체] ❑ 그는 영국의 유럽 경제 공동체 가입을 가장 의욕적으로 지지하는 사람들 중 하나였다. ◲ 가산명사 주인공 [격식체] ❑ 제이 디 샐린저의 소설 "호밀밭의 파수꾼" 속 주인공

pro|tect ♦♦◇ /prətɛkt/ (**protects, protecting, protected**) ◳ V-T To **protect** someone or something means to prevent them from being harmed or damaged. ❑ *So, what can women do to protect themselves from heart disease?* ❑ *A long thin wool coat and a purple headscarf protected her against the wind.* ◲ V-T If an insurance policy **protects** you **against** an event such as death, injury, fire, or theft, the insurance company will give you or your family money if that event happens. ❑ *Many manufacturers have policies to protect themselves against blackmailers.* →see **hero**

◳ 타동사 보호하다, 지키다 ❑ 그러면, 여성들이 심장 질환으로부터 스스로를 지키기 위해 무엇을 할 수 있을까? ❑ 길고 얇은 울 코트와 보라색 스카프가 그녀를 바람으로부터 보호해 주었다. ◲ 타동사 (보험) 보상을 보장하다 ❑ 많은 생산자들은 공갈 협박에 대한 피해 보상을 보장하는 보험을 들고 있다.

Word Partnership	*protect*의 연어
N.	protect **against attacks**, protect **children**, protect **citizens**, **duty** to protect, **efforts** to protect, protect **the environment**, **laws** protect, protect **people**, protect **privacy**, protect **women**, protect **workers** ◳
	protect **property** ◳ ◲
ADJ.	**designed** to protect, **necessary** to protect, **supposed** to protect ◳ ◲

pro|tec|tion ♦♦◇ /prətɛkʃ°n/ (**protections**) ◳ N-VAR To give or be **protection** against something unpleasant means to prevent people or things from being harmed or damaged by it. ❑ *Such a diet is widely believed to offer protection against a number of cancers.* ❑ *It is clear that the primary duty of parents is to provide protection for our children.* ◲ N-UNCOUNT If an insurance policy gives you **protection against** an event such as death, injury, fire, or theft, the insurance company will give you or your family money if that event happens. [oft N against n] ❑ *Insurance can be purchased to provide protection against such risks.* ◳ N-UNCOUNT If a government has a policy of **protection**, it helps its own industries by putting a tax on imported goods or by restricting imports in some other way. [BUSINESS] ❑ *Over the same period trade protection has increased in the rich countries.*

◳ 가산명사 또는 불가산명사 보호 ❑ 그와 같은 식습관은 여러 종류의 암을 막아 주는 것으로 널리 믿어진다. ◲ 불가산명사 피해 보상 보장 ❑ 그와 같은 위험에 의한 피해 보상을 보장해 주는 보험 상품을 구입할 수 있다. ◳ 불가산명사 보호무역 [경제] ❑ 같은 기간 동안 부유한 국가들에서는 무역 보호가 증가해 왔다.

pro|tec|tion|ism /prətɛkʃənɪzəm/ N-UNCOUNT **Protectionism** is the policy some countries have of helping their own industries by putting a tax on imported goods or by restricting imports in some other way. [BUSINESS] ❑ *The aim of the current round of talks is to promote free trade and to avert the threat of increasing protectionism.*

불가산명사 보호 무역주의 [경제] ❑ 현재 진행되고 있는 회담의 목표는 자유 무역을 장려하고 점증하는 보호 무역주의의 위협을 피하는 것이다.

pro|tec|tion|ist /prətɛkʃənɪst/ (**protectionists**) ◳ N-COUNT A **protectionist** is someone who agrees with and supports protectionism. [BUSINESS] ❑ *Trade frictions between the two countries had been caused by trade protectionists.* ◲ ADJ **Protectionist** policies, measures, and laws are meant to stop or reduce

◳ 가산명사 보호 무역론자 [경제] ❑ 양국 간의 무역 마찰은 보호 무역론자들에 의해 야기되어 왔다. ◲ 형용사 보호 무역주의의 [경제] ❑ 가트 회원국들은 세계 무역에 있어서 돈이 많이 들고 비효율적인 보호

imports. [BUSINESS] ❑ *GATT member countries have largely agreed to replace expensive and inefficient protectionist policies with a competitive free market system for world trade.*

무역 정책들을 자유 경쟁에 의한 자유 시장 체제로 대체하는 것에 대체로 동의해 왔다.

pro|tec|tive /prətɛktɪv/ **1** ADJ **Protective** means designed or intended to protect something or someone from harm. ❑ *Protective gloves reduce the absorption of chemicals through the skin.* **2** ADJ If someone is **protective toward** you, they look after you and show a strong desire to keep you safe. ❑ *He is very protective towards his mother.*

1 형용사 보호용의 ❑ 보호용 장갑은 피부를 통한 화학 약품의 흡수를 줄여준다. **2** 형용사 보호하는 ❑ 그는 어머니를 보호하려는 마음이 아주 크다.

pro|tec|tor /prətɛktər/ (**protectors**) **1** N-COUNT If you refer to someone as your **protector**, you mean that they protect you from being harmed. ❑ *Many mothers see their son as a potential protector and provider.* **2** N-COUNT A **protector** is a device that protects someone or something from physical harm. ❑ *He was the only National League umpire to wear an outside chest protector.*

1 가산명사 보호자 ❑ 많은 어머니들은 아들을 잠재적인 보호자 겸 부양자로 여긴다. **2** 가산명사 보호대, 보호구 ❑ 그는 내셔널 리그에서 유일하게 외부 가슴 보호대를 착용하는 심판이었다.

pro|té|gé /proʊtɪʒeɪ, BRIT prɒtɪʒeɪ/ (**protégés**)

> The spelling **protégée** is often used when referring to a woman.

철자 protégée는 종종 여성을 지칭할 때 쓴다.

N-COUNT The **protégé** of an older and more experienced person is a young person who is helped and guided by them over a period of time. ❑ *He had been a protégé of Captain James.*

가산명사 피보호자; 부하 ❑ 그는 제임스 대위의 부하였었다.

pro|tein ♦♢♢ /proʊtiːn/ (**proteins**) N-MASS **Protein** is a substance found in food and drink such as meat, eggs, and milk. You need protein in order to grow and be healthy. ❑ *Fish was a major source of protein for the working man.* →see **calories**, **diet**

물질명사 단백질 ❑ 생선이 그 노동자에게는 단백질의 주 급원이었다.

pro|test ♦♦♢ /proʊtɛst/ (**protests**, **protesting**, **protested**)

> The verb is usually pronounced /prətɛst/. The noun, and sometimes the verb, is pronounced /proʊtɛst/.

동사는 보통 /prətɛst/로, 명사는, 가끔은 동사도, /proʊtɛst/로 발음된다.

1 V-T/V-I If you **protest** something, you say or show publicly that you object to it. In British English, you usually say that you **protest against** it or **about** it. ❑ *They were protesting soaring prices.* ❑ *Groups of women took to the streets to protest against the arrests.* **2** N-VAR A **protest** is the act of saying or showing publicly that you object to something. ❑ *The opposition now seems too weak to stage any serious protests against the government.* ❑ *The unions called a two-hour strike in protest at the railway authority's announcement.* **3** V-T If you **protest** that something is the case, you insist that it is the case, when other people think that it may not be. ❑ *When we tried to protest that Mo was beaten up they didn't believe us.* ❑ *"I never said any of that to her," he protested.*

1 타동사/자동사 항의하다, 이의를 제기하다 ❑ 그들은 치솟는 물가에 대해 항의하는 중이었다. ❑ 여러 무리의 여자들이 거리에 나서서 그 사람들을 체포한 것에 항의했다. **2** 가산명사 또는 불가산명사 항의, 이의 ❑ 현재 야당은 정부에 심각하게 이의를 제기하기에는 너무 약한 것처럼 보인다. ❑ 철도 당국의 발표에 노조는 두 시간 동안의 항의 파업을 실시했다. **3** 타동사 주장하다, 단언하다 ❑ 모가 구타를 당했다고 우리가 주장하려 할 때 그들은 우리를 믿지 않았다. ❑ "나는 절대 그녀에게 그런 얘기를 하지 않았어."라고 그가 주장했다.

	Word Partnership	protest의 연어
N.	**workers** protest **1**	
	protest **demonstrations**, protest **groups**, protest **march**, protest **rally** **2**	
ADJ.	**anti-war** protest, **anti-government** protest, **organized** protest, **peaceful** protest, **political** protest **2**	

Prot|es|tant /prɒtɪstənt/ (**Protestants**) **1** N-COUNT A **Protestant** is a Christian who belongs to the branch of the Christian church which separated from the Catholic church in the sixteenth century. **2** ADJ **Protestant** means relating to Protestants or their churches. ❑ *Most Protestant churches now have women ministers.*

1 가산명사 신교도 **2** 형용사 신교의, 신교도의 ❑ 대부분의 신교 교회에는 이제 여자 목사들이 있다.

pro|test|er /prətɛstər/ (**protesters**) also **protestor** N-COUNT **Protesters** are people who protest publicly about an issue. ❑ *The protesters say the government is corrupt and inefficient.*

가산명사 항의자, 시위자 ❑ 시위자들은 정부가 부패하고 무능하다고 말한다.

pro|to|col /proʊtəkɒl, BRIT proʊtəkɒl/ (**protocols**) **1** N-VAR **Protocol** is a system of rules about the correct way to act in formal situations. ❑ *He has become something of a stickler for the finer observances of royal protocol.* **2** N-COUNT A **protocol** is a set of rules for exchanging information between computers. [COMPUTING] ❑ *...a computer protocol which could communicate across different languages.* **3** N-COUNT A **protocol** is a written record of a treaty or agreement that has been made by two or more countries. [FORMAL] ❑ *...the Montreal Protocol to phase out use and production of CFCs.* **4** N-COUNT A **protocol** is a plan for a course of medical treatment, or a plan for a scientific experiment. [AM, FORMAL] ❑ *...the detoxification protocol.*

1 가산명사 또는 불가산명사 의례, 의전 ❑ 그는 왕실 의전을 더욱 꼼꼼히 준수해야 한다고 까다롭게 따지는 사람이 되었다. **2** 가산명사 (컴퓨터) 통신 규약, 프로토콜 [컴퓨터] ❑ 서로 다른 언어들 사이에 소통이 가능한 컴퓨터 프로토콜 **3** 가산명사 의정서 [격식체] ❑ 프레온 가스의 생산과 사용을 단계적으로 억제하기로 한 몬트리올 의정서 **4** 가산명사 (과학 실험 등의) 계획안 [미국영어, 격식체] ❑ 해독 계획안

pro|to|type /proʊtətaɪp/ (**prototypes**) N-COUNT A **prototype** is a new type of machine or device which is not yet ready to be made in large numbers and sold. ❑ *Chris Retzler has built a prototype of a machine called the wave rotor.*

가산명사 시제품 ❑ 크리스 레츨러는 '웨이브 로터'라고 불리는 장치의 시제품을 만들어 냈다.

pro|tract|ed /proʊtræktɪd, BRIT prətræktɪd/ ADJ Something, usually something unpleasant, that is **protracted** lasts a long time, especially longer than usual or longer than you hoped. [FORMAL] ❑ *However, after protracted negotiations Ogden got the deal he wanted.* ❑ *...a protracted civil war.*

형용사 오래 끄는 [격식체] ❑ 그러나, 오랫동안 계속된 협상 끝에 오그덴은 원하던 것을 얻어 냈다. ❑ 오래 끄는 내전

pro|trude /proʊtruːd, prə-, BRIT prətruːd/ (**protrudes**, **protruding**, **protruded**) V-I If something **protrudes from** somewhere, it sticks out. [FORMAL] ❑ *...a huge round mass of smooth rock protruding from the water.*

자동사 불쑥 튀어나오다, 돌출하다 [격식체] ❑ 물에서 불쑥 튀어 나온 거대한, 매끈매끈하고 둥근 돌덩어리

proud ♦♦♢ /praʊd/ (**prouder**, **proudest**) **1** ADJ If you feel **proud**, you feel pleased about something good that you possess or have done, or about something good that a person close to you has done. ❑ *I felt proud of his efforts.* ❑ *They are proud that she is doing well at school.* ● **proud|ly** ADV [ADV with v] ❑ *"That's the first part finished," he said proudly.* **2** ADJ Your **proudest** moments or achievements are the ones that you are most proud of. [ADJ n, usu ADJ-superl] ❑ *This must have been one of the proudest moments of his busy and hard working life.* **3** ADJ Someone who is **proud** has respect for themselves and does not want to lose the respect that other people have for them. ❑ *He was too proud to ask his family for help and support.* **4** ADJ Someone who is **proud** feels that they are better or more important than other people. [DISAPPROVAL] ❑ *She was said to be proud and arrogant.*

1 형용사 자랑스러운 ❑ 나는 그가 들인 노력이 자랑스러웠다. ❑ 그들은 그녀가 학교에서 잘 해 내고 있어서 자랑스럽다. ● 자랑스럽게 부사 ❑ "그것이 완성된 첫 번째 부분입니다."라고 그가 자랑스럽게 말했다. **2** 형용사 가장 자랑스러운 ❑ 이는 그의 분주하고 근면한 직장 생활에서 가장 자랑스러운 순간 중 하나였음에 틀림없다. **3** 형용사 자존심이 있는 ❑ 그는 식구들에게 도움과 원조를 청하기에는 너무 자존심이 세다. **4** 형용사 거만한 [탐탁찮음] ❑ 사람들은 그녀가 거만하고 건방지다고 말했다.

prove ♦♦♦ /pr**u**v/ (proves, proving, proved, proven)

The forms **proved** and **proven** can both be used as a past participle.

proved와 proven 모두 과거 분사로 쓸 수 있다.

1 V-LINK If something **proves to** be true or **to** have a particular quality, it becomes clear after a period of time that it is true or has that quality. □ *We have been accused of exaggerating before, but unfortunately all our reports proved to be true.* □ *In the past this process of transition has often proven difficult.* **2** V-T If you **prove that** something is true, you show by means of argument or evidence that it is definitely true. □ *You brought this charge. You prove it! I have nothing to say.* □ *The results prove that regulation of the salmon farming industry is inadequate.* □ *That made me hopping mad and determined to prove him wrong.* **3** V-T If you **prove yourself** to have a certain good quality, you show by your actions that you have it. □ *Margaret proved herself to be a good mother.* □ *As a composer he proved himself adept at large dramatic forms.* →see **science**

1 연결동사 밝혀지다, 드러나다 □ 우리는 예전에 과장한다는 비난을 받아 왔지만, 유감스럽게도 우리의 모든 보고가 사실인 것으로 밝혀졌다. □ 과거에는 흔히 이와 같은 변화 과정이 어려운 것으로 밝혀지곤 했다. **2** 타동사 증명하다, 입증하다 □ 네가 이런 혐의를 제기했어. 네가 그것을 입증해! 나는 아무것도 할 말이 없어. □ 그 결과에 의해 연어 양식 산업의 단속이 부적절하다는 것이 입증된다. □ 그 때문에 나는 화가 나서 펄펄 뛰었으며 그가 틀리다는 것을 증명하겠다고 결심하게 되었다. **3** 타동사 (자신이 ~임을) 입증하다 □ 마거릿은 자신이 좋은 엄마라는 것을 입증했다. □ 작곡가로서 그는 자신이 규모가 큰 극적 형식에 뛰어남을 입증했다.

Word Partnership   prove의 연어

ADJ.	prove **(to be) difficult**, prove **helpful**, prove **useful**, prove **worthy** **1**
	difficult to prove, **hard to** prove **2**
V.	**have to** prove, **try to** prove **2**
	able to prove **2** **3**
	have *something* to prove **3**

Word Link   verb ≈ word : pro**verb**, **verb**al, **verb**atim

prov|erb /pr**ɒ**vɜrb/ (proverbs) N-COUNT A **proverb** is a short sentence that people often quote, which gives advice or tells you something about life. □ *An old Arab proverb says, "The enemy of my enemy is my friend."*

가산명사 속담, 격언 □ 오랜 아랍 격언은 이렇게 말한다. "적의 적은 나의 친구이다."

pro|ver|bial /prəv**ɜ**rbiəl/ ADJ You use **proverbial** to show that you know the way you are describing something is one that is often used or is part of a popular saying. [ADJ n] □ *The limousine sped off down the road in the proverbial cloud of dust.*

형용사 속담 투의, 흔히 말하는 □ 그 리무진은 속도를 내어 흔히 말하듯 먼저 구름 사이로 도로를 달려 내려갔다.

pro|vide ♦♦♦ /prəv**aɪ**d/ (provides, providing, provided) **1** V-T If you **provide** something that someone needs or wants, or if you **provide** them **with** it, you give it to them or make it available to them. □ *I'll be glad to provide a copy of this.* □ *They would not provide any details.* **2** V-T If a law or agreement **provides that** something will happen, it states that it will happen. [FORMAL] □ *The treaty provides that, by the end of the century, the United States must have removed its bases.* **3** →see also **provided, providing**

1 타동사 제공하다, 공급하다 □ 이것의 사본을 제공할 수 있다면 기쁠 것이다. □ 그들은 상세한 내용을 알려 주지 않으려 했다. **2** 타동사 규정하다 [격식체] □ 그 조약은 이번 세기말까지 미국이 기지 이전을 완료하도록 규정하고 있다.

▶**provide for** **1** PHRASAL VERB If you **provide for** someone, you support them financially and make sure that they have the things that they need. □ *Elaine wouldn't let him provide for her.* **2** PHRASAL VERB If you **provide for** something that might happen or that might need to be done, you make arrangements to deal with it. □ *James had provided for just such an emergency.*

1 구동사 부양하다 □ 일레인은 그가 자신을 부양하도록 내버려 두려 하지 않았다. **2** 구동사 대비하다 □ 제임스는 바로 그와 같은 비상사태를 대비해 왔다.

pro|vid|ed /prəv**aɪ**dɪd/ CONJ If you say that something will happen **provided** or **provided that** something else happens, you mean that the first thing will happen only if the second thing also happens. □ *The other banks are going to be very eager to help, provided that they see that he has a specific plan.*

접속사 ~을 조건으로, 만약 ~이면 □ 그가 구체적인 계획을 갖고 있는 것을 안다면, 다른 은행들이 몹시 도우려 할 것이다.

provi|dence /pr**ɒ**vɪdəns/ N-UNCOUNT **Providence** is God, or a force which is believed by some people to arrange the things that happen to us. [LITERARY] □ *These women regard his death as an act of providence.*

불가산명사 신; 섭리 [문예체] □ 이 여자들은 그의 죽음을 섭리로 여긴다.

pro|vid|ing /prəv**aɪ**dɪŋ/ CONJ If you say that something will happen **providing** or **providing that** something else happens, you mean that the first thing will happen only if the second thing also happens. □ *I do believe in people being able to do what they want to do, providing they're not hurting someone else.*

접속사 ~을 조건으로, 만약 ~이면 □ 나는 사람들이 다른 이들을 해치지 않는 한에서 하고 싶은 일을 할 수 있다고 믿는다.

prov|ince ♦♦◇ /pr**ɒ**vɪns/ (provinces) **1** N-COUNT A **province** is a large section of a country which has its own administration. □ *The Algarve, Portugal's southernmost province, has become one of the most popular destinations for British holidaymakers.* **2** N-PLURAL The **provinces** are all the parts of a country except the part where the capital is situated. □ *The government plans to transfer some 30,000 government jobs from Paris to the provinces.* **3** N-SING If you say that a subject or activity is a particular person's **province**, you mean that this person has a special interest in it, a special knowledge of it, or a special responsibility for it. □ *Industrial research is the province of the Department of Trade and Industry.*

1 가산명사 지방, 지역 □ 포르투갈 최남단 지방인 알가르베는 영국 휴가객들에게 가장 인기 있는 행선지 중 하나가 되었다. **2** 복수명사 지방, 지역 □ 정부는 3만여 개의 공무원 일자리를 파리에서 지방으로 옮기는 것을 계획하고 있다. **3** 단수명사 분야, 직분 □ 산업 조사는 통상부 소관이다.

pro|vin|cial /prəv**ɪ**nʃ°l/ **1** ADJ **Provincial** means connected with the parts of a country away from the capital city. [ADJ n] □ *Jeremy Styles, 34, was the house manager for a provincial theater for ten years.* **2** ADJ If you describe someone or something as **provincial**, you disapprove of them because you think that they are old-fashioned and boring. [DISAPPROVAL] □ *He decided to revamp the company's provincial image.*

1 형용사 지방의, 시골의 □ 서른네 살의 제러미 스타일스는 십 년간 한 시골 극장의 지배인이었다. **2** 형용사 낡아빠진, 촌스러운 [탐탁찮음] □ 그는 그 회사의 낡아빠진 이미지를 쇄신하기로 결정했다.

pro|vi|sion ♦♦◇ /prəv**ɪ**ʒ°n/ (provisions) **1** N-UNCOUNT The **provision of** something is the act of giving it or making it available to people who need or want it. [also a N, with supp, oft N of n] □ *The department is responsible for the provision of residential care services.* **2** N-VAR If you make **provision for** something that might happen or that might need to be done, you make arrangements to deal with it. □ *Mr. King asked if it had ever occurred to her to make provision for her own pension.* **3** N-UNCOUNT If you make **provision for** someone, you support them financially and make sure that they have the things that they need. [also N in pl, N for n] □ *Special provision should be made for children.* **4** N-COUNT A **provision** in a law or an agreement is an arrangement which is included in it. □ *He backed a provision that would allow judges to delay granting a divorce decree in some cases.*

1 불가산명사 공급, 제공 □ 그 부처는 주거 보호 서비스 제공에 대하여 책임이 있다. **2** 가산명사 또는 불가산명사 대비 □ 킹 씨는 그녀에게 스스로의 연금에 대비할 생각이 떠오른 적이 있었는지 물었다. **3** 불가산명사 부양 □ 아이들을 특별히 부양해야 한다. **4** 가산명사 규정, 조항 □ 그는 어떤 경우에는 재판관들이 이혼 선고를 연기할 수 있도록 허용하는 조항을 지지했다.

pro|vi|sion|al /prəvɪʒənˀl/ ADJ You use **provisional** to describe something that has been arranged or appointed for the present, but may be changed in the future. □ ...the possibility of setting up a provisional coalition government. □ If you have never held a driving licence before, you should apply for a provisional licence. ● **pro|vi|sion|al|ly** ADV [ADV with v] □ The European Community then provisionally agreed to increase the quotas.

형용사 임시의, 잠정적인 □ 임시 연립 정부를 세울 가능성 □ 만약 이전에 면허를 가져 본 적이 없으시다면, 임시 면허를 신청하셔야 합니다. ● 임시로, 잠정적으로 부사 □ 유럽 공동체는 그런 다음 분담액을 늘리는 데 잠정 합의했다.

provo|ca|tion /prɒvəkeɪʃən/ (**provocations**) N-VAR If you describe a person's action as **provocation** or a **provocation**, you mean that it is a reason for someone else to react angrily, violently, or emotionally. □ He denies murder on the grounds of provocation.

가산명사 또는 불가산명사 도발, 자극 □ 그는 도발 때문에 살인을 저지른 것이 아니라고 말한다.

pro|voca|tive /prəvɒkətɪv/ ■ ADJ If you describe something as **provocative**, you mean that it is intended to make people react angrily or argue against it. □ He has made a string of outspoken and sometimes provocative speeches in recent years. ■ ADJ If you describe someone's clothing or behavior as **provocative**, you mean that it is intended to make someone feel sexual desire. □ Some adolescents might be more sexually mature and provocative than others.

■ 형용사 도발적인, 성나게 하는 □ 근년에 그는 일련의 거리낌 없고 때로는 도발적인 연설을 해 왔다. ② 형용사 (성적으로) 도발적인 □ 어떤 청소년들은 또래보다 더 성적으로 성숙하고 도발적일 수 있다.

pro|voke ♦◇◇ /prəvoʊk/ (**provokes, provoking, provoked**) ■ V-T If you **provoke** someone, you deliberately annoy them and try to make them behave aggressively. □ He started beating me when I was about fifteen but I didn't do anything to provoke him. ② V-T If something **provokes** a reaction, it causes it. □ His election success has provoked a shocked reaction.

■ 타동사 성나게 하다, 자극하다 □ 그는 내가 열다섯 살쯤일 무렵 나를 구타하기 시작했지만 나는 그를 자극하는 어떤 일도 하지 않았다. ② 타동사 유발하다, 야기하다 □ 선거에서의 그의 승리는 충격에 휩싸인 반응을 유발했다.

prow|ess /praʊɪs/ N-UNCOUNT Someone's **prowess** is their great skill at doing something. [FORMAL] □ He's always bragging about his prowess as a cricketer.

불가산명사 훌륭한 솜씨 [격식체] □ 그는 항상 자신의 뛰어난 크리켓 실력을 자랑한다.

prowl /praʊl/ (**prowls, prowling, prowled**) V-I If an animal or a person **prowls around**, they move around quietly, for example when they are hunting. □ He prowled around the room, not sure what he was looking for or even why he was there.

자동사 배회하다 □ 그는 자신이 무엇을 찾고 있는지, 심지어 자기가 왜 거기 있는지도 확실히 모르는 채 그 방을 배회했다.

Word Link proxim ≈ near : ap**proxim**ate, ap**proxim**ation, **proxim**ity

---

prox|im|ity /prɒksɪmɪti/ N-UNCOUNT **Proximity to** a place or person is nearness to that place or person. [FORMAL] □ Part of the attraction is Darwin's proximity to Asia. □ He became aware of the proximity of the Afghans.

불가산명사 근접, 가까움 [격식체] □ 매력적인 점 하나는 다윈이 아시아에 가깝다는 것이다. □ 그는 아프가니스탄 인들이 가까이에 있음을 알아차렸다.

proxy /prɒksi/ N-UNCOUNT If you do something **by proxy**, you arrange for someone else to do it for you. □ Those not attending the meeting may vote by proxy.

불가산명사 대리인 □ 회의에 참석하지 못하는 사람들은 대리인을 통해 투표할 수 있습니다.

prude /prud/ (**prudes**) N-COUNT If you call someone a **prude**, you mean that they are too easily shocked by things relating to sex.. [DISAPPROVAL] □ Caroline was very much a prude. She wouldn't let me see her naked.

가산명사 내숭 떠는 사람, 숙녀연하는 사람 [탐탁찮음] □ 캐롤라인은 아주 내숭 덩어리였다. 자기가 벌거벗은 걸 나에게 보지도 못하게 했다.

pru|dence /prud°ns/ N-UNCOUNT **Prudence** is care and good sense that someone shows when making a decision or taking action. [FORMAL] □ Western businessmen are showing remarkable prudence in investing in the region.

불가산명사 신중함, 세심함 [격식체] □ 서구 사업가들은 그 지역에 투자하는 데 있어 대단한 신중함을 보이고 있다.

pru|dent /prud°nt/ ADJ Someone who is **prudent** is sensible and careful. □ It is clearly prudent to take all precautions. ● **pru|dent|ly** ADV □ I believe it is essential that we act prudently.

형용사 신중한, 세심한 □ 모든 예방책을 강구하는 것이 분명히 신중한 태도일 것이다. ● 신중하게 부사 □ 신중하게 행동하는 것이 필수적이라고 생각한다.

prune /prun/ (**prunes, pruning, pruned**) ■ N-COUNT A **prune** is a dried plum. ② V-T/V-I When you **prune** a tree or bush, you cut off some of the branches so that it will grow better the next year. □ You have to prune a bush if you want fruit. ● PHRASAL VERB **Prune back** means the same as **prune**. □ Apples, pears and cherries can be pruned back when they've lost their leaves. ③ V-T If you **prune** something, you cut out all the parts that you do not need. □ Firms are cutting investment and pruning their product ranges. ● PHRASAL VERB **Prune back** means the same as **prune**. □ The company has pruned back its workforce by 20,000 since 1989.

■ 가산명사 말린 자두 ② 타동사/자동사 가지치기하다 □ 열매를 얻고자 한다면 관목의 가지를 쳐 주어야 한다. ● 구동사 가지치기하다 □ 사과, 배, 벚나무는 잎이 떨어지고 난 다음 가지치기를 할 수 있다. ③ 타동사 불필요한 부분을 제거하다 □ 회사들은 투자를 축소하고 생산품 범위에서 불필요한 부분을 제거하고 있다. ● 구동사 불필요한 부분을 제거하다 □ 그 회사는 1989년 이래로 불필요한 인력 2만 명을 감축해 왔다.

pry /praɪ/ (**pries, prying, pried**) ■ V-I If someone **pries**, they try to find out about someone else's private affairs, or look at their personal possessions. □ We do not want people prying into our affairs. □ Imelda might think she was prying. ② V-T If you **pry** something **open** or **pry** it away from a surface, you force it open or away from a surface. □ They pried open a sticky can of blue paint. □ I pried the top off a can of chilli.

■ 자동사 꼬치꼬치 캐다 □ 사람들이 우리 일을 꼬치꼬치 파고드는 걸 원치 않는다. □ 이멜다는 자신이 꼬치꼬치 캐묻고 있다고 생각했을지도 모른다. ② 타동사 비집어 열다 □ 그들은 들러붙은 파란색 페인트 통을 비집어 열었다. □ 나는 칠리 깡통 뚜껑을 비집어 열었다.

PS /piː ɛs/ also **P.S.** You write **PS** to introduce something that you add at the end of a letter after you have signed it. □ PS. Please show your friends this letter and the enclosed leaflet.

추신 □ 추신, 친구들에게 이 편지와 동봉된 전단을 보여 주세요.

pseudo|nym /sudənɪm, BRIT syuːdənɪm/ (**pseudonyms**) N-COUNT A **pseudonym** is a name which someone, usually a writer, uses instead of his or her real name. □ Both plays were published under the pseudonym of Philip Dayre.

가산명사 필명 □ 두 편의 희곡 모두 필립 데이어라는 필명으로 출판되었다.

Word Link psych ≈ mind : **psych**e, **psych**iatrist, **psych**ic

---

psy|che /saɪki/ (**psyches**) N-COUNT In psychology, your **psyche** is your mind and your deepest feelings and attitudes. [TECHNICAL] □ His exploration of the myth brings insight into the American psyche.

가산명사 정신세계, 마음 [과학 기술] □ 그의 신화 탐구는 미국인의 정신세계에 대한 통찰을 제시한다.

psyche|del|ic /saɪkədɛlɪk/ ■ ADJ **Psychedelic** means relating to drugs such as LSD which have a strong effect on your mind, often making you see things that are not there. □ ...his first real, full-blown psychedelic experience. ② ADJ **Psychedelic** art has bright colors and strange patterns. □ ...psychedelic patterns.

■ 형용사 환각제의; 환각제를 사용한 □ 그의 맨 첫 본격적 실제 환각제 사용 경험 ② 형용사 사이키델릭한 (색채 등이 환각 상태를 연상시키는) □ 사이키델릭한 무늬

psy|chi|at|ric /saɪkiætrɪk/ ■ ADJ **Psychiatric** means relating to psychiatry. [ADJ n] □ We finally insisted that he seek psychiatric help. ② ADJ **Psychiatric** means involving mental illness. [ADJ n] □ About 4% of the prison population have chronic psychiatric illnesses.

■ 형용사 정신 의학의 □ 우리는 마침내 그가 정신 의학적 도움을 구해야 한다고 주장했다. ② 형용사 정신병의 □ 교도소 수감자 중 약 4퍼센트가 만성적인 정신 질환을 앓는다.

psy|chia|trist /sɪkaɪətrɪst, BRIT saɪkaɪətrɪst/ (**psychiatrists**) N-COUNT A **psychiatrist** is a doctor who treats people suffering from mental illness.

가산명사 정신과 의사

psy|chia|try /sɪkaɪətri, BRIT saɪkaɪətri/ N-UNCOUNT **Psychiatry** is the branch of medicine concerned with the treatment of mental illness.

불가산명사 정신 의학

> **Word Link**   psych ≈ mind : psyche, psychiatrist, psychic

psy|chic /saɪkɪk/ (**psychics**) **■** ADJ If you believe that someone is **psychic** or has **psychic** powers, you believe that they have strange mental powers, such as being able to read the minds of other people or to see into the future. ❑ Trevor helped police by using his psychic powers. ● N-COUNT A **psychic** is someone who seems to be psychic. ❑ ...her latest role as a psychic who can foretell the future. **②** ADJ **Psychic** means relating to ghosts and the spirits of the dead. ❑ He declared his total disbelief in psychic phenomena.

■ 형용사 심령력을 가진; 심령력의 ❑ 트레버는 심령력을 사용해서 경찰을 도왔다. ● 가산명사 심령력을 가진 사람 ❑ 그녀가 최근에 맡은 미래를 예언할 수 있는 심령술자 역할 **②** 형용사 심령의 ❑ 그는 심령 현상을 전적으로 믿지 않는다고 밝혔다.

psycho|analy|sis /saɪkoʊənælɪsɪs/ N-UNCOUNT **Psychoanalysis** is the treatment of someone who has mental problems by asking them about their feelings and their past in order to try to discover what may be causing their condition.

불가산명사 정신 분석

psycho|ana|lyst /saɪkoʊænⁿlɪst/ (**psychoanalysts**) N-COUNT A **psychoanalyst** is someone who treats people who have mental problems using psychoanalysis.

가산명사 정신 분석가

psycho|logi|cal ♦◇◇ /saɪkəlɒdʒɪkᵊl/ **■** ADJ **Psychological** means concerned with a person's mind and thoughts. ❑ John received constant physical and psychological abuse from his father. ● **psycho|logi|cal|ly** /saɪkəlɒdʒɪkli/ ADV ❑ It was very important psychologically for us to succeed. **②** ADJ **Psychological** means relating to psychology. [ADJ n] ❑ ...psychological testing. →see **myth**

■ 형용사 정신적인, 심리적인 ❑ 존은 아버지로부터 끊임없이 신체적 및 정신적 학대를 받았다. ● 정신적으로, 심리적으로 부사 ❑ 우리에게는 성공하는 것이 심리적으로 매우 중요했다. **②** 형용사 심리적인 ❑ 심리학적 실험

psy|cholo|gist /saɪkɒlədʒɪst/ (**psychologists**) N-COUNT A **psychologist** is a person who studies the human mind and tries to explain why people behave in the way that they do.

가산명사 심리학자

psy|chol|ogy /saɪkɒlədʒi/ **■** N-UNCOUNT **Psychology** is the scientific study of the human mind and the reasons for people's behavior. ❑ ...Professor of Psychology at Bedford College. **②** N-UNCOUNT The **psychology of** a person is the kind of mind that they have, which makes them think or behave in the way that they do. ❑ ...a fascination with the psychology of murderers.

■ 불가산명사 심리학 ❑ 베드퍼드 대학 심리학 교수 **②** 불가산명사 심리 (상태) ❑ 살인자들의 심리에 마음을 빼앗김

psycho|path /saɪkəpæθ/ (**psychopaths**) N-COUNT A **psychopath** is someone who has serious mental problems and who may act in a violent way without feeling sorry for what they have done. ❑ She was abducted by a dangerous psychopath.

가산명사 정신병자 ❑ 그녀는 위험한 정신병자에게 유괴되었다.

psy|cho|sis /saɪkoʊsɪs/ (**psychoses**) N-VAR **Psychosis** is mental illness of a severe kind which can make people lose contact with reality. [MEDICAL] ❑ He may have some kind of neurosis or psychosis later in life.

가산명사 또는 불가산명사 정신병, 정신 이상 [의학] ❑ 그는 만년에 어떤 종류의 신경증이나 정신 질환을 앓을 수도 있다.

psycho|thera|pist /saɪkoʊθerəpɪst/ (**psychotherapists**) N-COUNT A **psychotherapist** is a person who treats people who are mentally ill using psychotherapy.

가산명사 정신 요법 의사, 심리 치료사

psycho|thera|py /saɪkoʊθerəpi/ N-UNCOUNT **Psychotherapy** is the use of psychological methods in treating people who are mentally ill, rather than using physical methods such as drugs or surgery. ❑ For milder depressions, certain forms of psychotherapy do work well.

불가산명사 정신 요법, 심리 요법 ❑ 정도가 더 가벼운 우울증에는, 특정 형태의 정신 요법이 정말 잘 듣는다.

psy|chot|ic /saɪkɒtɪk/ (**psychotics**) ADJ Someone who is **psychotic** has a type of severe mental illness. [MEDICAL] ❑ The man, who police believe is psychotic, is thought to be responsible for eight attacks.

형용사 정신 이상의 [의학] ❑ 경찰이 정신 이상자로 생각하고 있는 그 남자는 여덟 번의 폭행을 저지른 것으로 여겨진다.

PTO /pi ti oʊ/ also P.T.O. **PTO** is a written abbreviation for "please turn over." You write it at the bottom of a page to indicate that there is more writing on the other side.

뒷면에 계속

pub ♦◇◇ /pʌb/ (**pubs**) N-COUNT A **pub** is a building where people can have drinks, especially alcoholic drinks, and talk to their friends. Many pubs also serve food. [mainly BRIT] ❑ He was in the pub until closing time. →see **bar**

가산명사 술집 [주로 영국영어] ❑ 그는 폐점 시간까지 술집에 있었다.

> During **happy hour** customers in pubs, bars and cafés can buy alcoholic drinks more cheaply than usual. This practice was introduced by owners and managers to entice people into their bars. Happy hour is usually during the late afternoon or early evening, the exact time being chosen by the bar; strangely, it quite often lasts more than an hour.

> happy hour(해피 아워)에는 술집이나 카페 같은 데서 술을 보통 때보다 싸게 살 수 있다. 이것은 주인이나 지배인들이 손님을 끌기 위해 도입한 전략이다. 해피 아워는 보통 늦은 오후나 이른 저녁 시간대이다. 그 정확한 시간은 업소마다 다른데, 이름과 다르게 대개는 흔히 한 시간이 넘는다.

pu|ber|ty /pyubɜrti/ N-UNCOUNT **Puberty** is the stage in someone's life when their body starts to become physically mature. ❑ Margaret had reached the age of puberty.

불가산명사 사춘기 ❑ 마거릿은 사춘기에 이르러 있었다.

pub|lic ♦♦♦ /pʌblɪk/ **■** N-SING-COLL You can refer to people in general, or to all the people in a particular country or community, as **the public**. ❑ Lauderdale House is now open to the public. ❑ Pure alcohol is not for sale to the general public. **②** N-SING-COLL You can refer to a set of people in a country who share a common interest, activity, or characteristic as a particular kind of **public**. ❑ Market research showed that 93% of the viewing public wanted a hit film channel. **③** ADJ **Public** means relating to all the people in a country or community. [ADJ n] ❑ The President is attempting to drum up public support for his economic program. **④** ADJ **Public** means relating to the government or state, or things that are done for the people by the state. [ADJ n] ❑ The social services account for a substantial part of public spending. ● **pub|lic|ly** ADV [ADV -ed] ❑ ...publicly funded legal services. **⑤** ADJ **Public** buildings and services are provided for everyone to use. [ADJ n] ❑ ...the New York Public Library. ❑ The new museum must be accessible by public transport. **⑥** ADJ A **public** place is one where people can go about freely and where you can easily be seen and heard. ❑ ...the heavily congested public areas of international airports. **⑦** ADJ If someone is a **public figure** or in **public life**, many people know who they are because they are often mentioned in newspapers and on television. [ADJ n] ❑ The Archbishop of Canterbury yesterday hit out at public figures who commit adultery. **⑧** ADJ **Public** is used to describe statements, actions,

■ 단수명사-집합 일반인, 대중 ❑ 로더데일 하우스는 현재 일반인에게 개방된다. ❑ 순수 알코올은 일반 대중에게는 팔지 않는다. **②** 단수명사-집합 (특정한) 사람들 ❑ 시장 조사에 의하면 시청자들의 93퍼센트가 인기 영화 채널을 원했다. **③** 형용사 공중의, 대중의 ❑ 대통령은 자신의 경제 계획에 대한 대중적 지지를 모아 내려고 시도하고 있다. **④** 형용사 공적인, 공무의 ❑ 사회 복지 사업은 공적 지출의 상당 부분을 차지한다. ● 공적으로 부사 ❑ 공적 자금이 들어간 법률 서비스 **⑤** 형용사 공공의 ❑ 뉴욕 공공 도서관 ❑ 새 박물관은 대중교통으로 접근이 용이해야 한다. **⑥** 형용사 공공의 (장소) ❑ 국제공항의 심하게 붐비는 공공 구역 **⑦** 형용사 유명한, 저명한 ❑ 캔터베리 대주교는 어제 간통을 저지른 유명 인사들을 맹렬히 공격했다. **⑧** 형용사 국가유산위원회는 해답을 찾기 위해 공개 심리를 시행해 왔다. ❑ 그 논평은 그 주제에 대한 그 정부 부처의 첫 번째 자세한 공개 발언이었다. ● 공개적으로 부사 ❑ 그는 절대 그 일에 대해 공개적으로 이야기하지 않았다. **⑨** 형용사

and events that are made or done in such a way that any member of the public can see them or be aware of them. [ADJ n] ❑ *The National Heritage Committee has conducted a public inquiry to find the answer.* ❑ *The comments were the ministry's first detailed public statement on the subject.* ● **pub**|**lic**|**ly** ADV ❑ *He never spoke publicly about the affair.* ⑤ ADJ If a fact is made **public** or becomes **public**, it becomes known to everyone rather than being kept secret. [V-link ADJ] ❑ *Blair wants any new evidence on IRA pub bombs made public.* ⑩ PHRASE If a company **goes public**, it starts selling its shares on the stock exchange. [BUSINESS] ❑ *In 1951 AC went public, having achieved an average annual profit of more than £50,000.* ⑪ PHRASE If you say or do something **in public**, you say or do it when a group of people are present. ❑ *By-laws are to make it illegal to smoke in public.* →see **library**

널리 알려진 ❑ 블레어는 뭔든 반영(反映) 지하 조직의 술집 폭파 사건에 대한 새로운 증거가 있으면 그것을 널리 알리길 원한다. ⑩ 구 (회사가) 주식을 공개하다 [경제] ❑ 에이시(AC)는 5만 파운드 이상의 평균 연간 수익을 달성하고 나서 1951년에 주식을 공개했다. ⑪ 구 공공연히, 사람들 앞에서 ❑ 내규에 의해 공공장소에서 흡연하는 것이 불법화될 예정이다.

pub|**li**|**ca**|**tion** ◆◇◇ /pʌblɪkeɪʃⁿn/ (publications) ① N-UNCOUNT The **publication** of a book or magazine is the act of printing it and sending it to stores to be sold. ❑ *The guide is being translated into several languages for publication near Christmas.* ② N-COUNT A **publication** is a book or magazine that has been published. ❑ *They have started legal proceedings against two publications which spoke of an affair.* ③ N-UNCOUNT The **publication of** something such as information is the act of making it known to the public, for example by informing journalists or by publishing a government document. ❑ *A spokesman said: "We have no comment regarding the publication of these photographs."*

① 불가산명사 출판, 간행 ❑ 그 안내서는 크리스마스 무렵 출판하기 위해 몇 개 국어로 번역되고 있다. ② 가산명사 출판물 ❑ 그들은 불륜 관계에 대해 쓴 출판물 두 권에 대한 법적 조처에 착수했다. ③ 불가산명사 발표, 공표 ❑ 한 대변인이 말했다. "이 사진들을 발표하는 것과 관련해서는 드릴 말씀이 없습니다."

pub|**lic com**|**pa**|**ny** (public companies) N-COUNT A **public company** is a company whose shares can be bought by the general public. [BUSINESS]

가산명사 주식 공모 회사 [경제]

pub|**li**|**cist** /pʌblɪsɪst/ (publicists) N-COUNT A **publicist** is a person whose job involves getting publicity for people, events, or things such as movies or books. ❑ *...Derek Taylor, the Beatles' former publicist.*

가산명사 홍보 담당자 ❑ 비틀스의 전 홍보 담당자였던 데릭 테일러

pub|**lic**|**i**|**ty** ◆◇◇ /pʌblɪsɪti/ ① N-UNCOUNT **Publicity** is information or actions that are intended to attract the public's attention to someone or something. ❑ *Much advance publicity was given to the talks.* ❑ *...government publicity campaigns.* ② N-UNCOUNT When the news media and the public show a lot of interest in something, you can say that it is receiving **publicity**.. ❑ *The case has generated enormous publicity in Brazil.*

① 불가산명사 홍보, 광고 ❑ 회담에 대한 사전 홍보가 많이 이루어졌다. ❑ 정부의 공보 활동 ② 불가산명사 (언론의) 주목 ❑ 그 사건은 브라질에서 대단한 주목을 받았다.

Word Partnership	publicity의 연어
V.	**generate** publicity ① ②
	get publicity, **receive** publicity, publicity **surrounding** *someone/something* ②
ADJ.	**bad** publicity, **negative** publicity ②

pub|**li**|**cize** /pʌblɪsaɪz/ (publicizes, publicizing, publicized) [BRIT also **publicise**] V-T If you **publicize** a fact or event, you make it widely known to the public. ❑ *The author appeared on television to publicize her latest book.* ❑ *He never publicized his plans.*

[영국영어 publicise] 타동사 홍보하다; 공표하다 ❑ 작가가 최신간 저서 홍보를 위해 텔레비전에 출연했다. ❑ 그는 자신의 계획을 공표하지 않았다.

pub|**lic lim**|**it**|**ed com**|**pa**|**ny** (public limited companies) N-COUNT A **public limited company** is the same as a **public company**. The abbreviation **plc** is used after such companies' names. [BUSINESS]

가산명사 주식 공모 회사 [경제]

pub|**lic opin**|**ion** N-UNCOUNT **Public opinion** is the opinion or attitude of the public regarding a particular matter. ❑ *He mobilized public opinion all over the world against hydrogen-bomb tests.*

불가산명사 이론 ❑ 그는 전 세계적으로 수소 폭탄 실험 반대 여론을 동원했다.

pub|**lic re**|**la**|**tions** ① N-UNCOUNT **Public relations** is the part of an organization's work that is concerned with obtaining the public's approval for what it does. The abbreviation **PR** is often used. [BUSINESS] ❑ *The move was good public relations.* ② N-PLURAL You can refer to the opinion that the public has of an organization as **public relations**. ❑ *Limiting casualties is important for public relations.*

① 불가산명사 홍보 활동 [경제] ❑ 그와 같은 조처는 좋은 홍보 활동이었다. ② 복수명사 (조직에 대한) 대중의 평판 ❑ 사상자 수를 억제하는 것은 대중의 평판에 중요하다.

pub|**lic school** (public schools) ① N-VAR In the United States, Australia, and many other countries, a **public school** is a school that is supported financially by the government and usually provides free education. ❑ *...Milwaukee's public school system.* ② N-VAR In Britain, a **public school** is a private school that provides secondary education which parents have to pay for. The students often live at the school during the school term. ❑ *He was headmaster of a public school in the West of England.*

① 가산명사 또는 불가산명사 공립학교 ❑ 밀위키의 공립학교 체계 ② 가산명사 또는 불가산명사 (영국) 사립학교 ❑ 그는 잉글랜드 서부에 있는 사립학교 교장이었다.

pub|**lic sec**|**tor** N-SING The **public sector** is the part of a country's economy which is controlled or supported financially by the government. [BUSINESS] ❑ *...Carlos Menem's policy of reducing the public sector and opening up the economy to free-market forces.*

단수명사 공공 부문 [경제] ❑ 공공 부문을 축소하고 자유 시장 세력에 경제를 개방하는 카를로스 메넴의 정책

pub|**lic ser**|**vice** (public services) ① N-COUNT A **public service** is something such as health care, transportation, or the removal of waste which is organized by the government or an official body in order to benefit all the people in a particular society or community. ❑ *The money is used by local authorities to pay for public services.* ② N-COUNT You use **public service** to refer to activities and jobs which are provided or paid for by a government, especially through the civil service. [oft N n] ❑ *...a distinguished career in public service.* ③ N-UNCOUNT **Public service** activities and types of work are concerned with helping people and providing them with what they need, rather than making a profit. ❑ *...the notion of public service and obligation which has been under such attack.*

① 가산명사 공익사업 ❑ 그 돈은 지방 당국의 공익사업에 쓰인다. ② 불가산명사 공무, 공직 ❑ 공직에서의 탁월한 경력 ③ 불가산명사 사회봉사 ❑ 그처럼 공격받아 온 사회봉사와 공적 책무 개념

pub|**lic util**|**i**|**ty** (public utilities) N-COUNT **Public utilities** are services provided by the government or state, such as the supply of electricity and gas, or the train network. ❑ *Officials said water supplies and other public utilities in the capital were badly affected.*

가산명사 공공사업 ❑ 상수도 사업과 여타 공공사업들이 심각하게 영향을 받았다고 관계자들은 말했다.

pub|lish ♦♦◇ /pʌblɪʃ/ (**publishes**, **publishing**, **published**) **1** v-т When a company **publishes** a book or magazine, it prints copies of it, which are sent to stores to be sold. ❑ *They publish reference books.* **2** v-т When the people in charge of a newspaper or magazine **publish** a piece of writing or a photograph, they print it in their newspaper or magazine. ❑ *The ban was imposed after the magazine published an article satirizing the government.* **3** v-т If someone **publishes** a book or an article that they have written, they arrange to have it published. ❑ *John Lennon found time to publish two books of his humorous prose.* **4** v-т If you **publish** information or an opinion, you make it known to the public by having it printed in a newspaper, magazine, or official document. ❑ *The demonstrators called on the government to publish a list of registered voters.* →see **laboratory**, **printing**

pub|lish|er ♦◇◇ /pʌblɪʃər/ (**publishers**) N-COUNT A **publisher** is a person or a company that publishes books, newspapers, or magazines. ❑ *The publishers planned to produce the journal on a weekly basis.*

pub|lish|ing ♦◇◇ /pʌblɪʃɪŋ/ N-UNCOUNT **Publishing** is the profession of publishing books. ❑ *I had a very high-powered job in publishing.* →see **newspaper**

pub|lish|ing house (**publishing houses**) N-COUNT A **publishing house** is a company which publishes books.

pud|ding /pʊdɪŋ/ (**puddings**) **1** N-VAR A **pudding** is a cooked sweet food made with flour, fat, and eggs, and usually served hot. ❑ *...a cherry sponge pudding with warm custard.* **2** N-VAR Some people refer to the sweet course of a meal as the **pudding**. [BRIT] ❑ *...a menu featuring canapes, a starter, a main course and a pudding.* →see **dessert**

pud|dle /pʌdəl/ (**puddles**) N-COUNT A **puddle** is a small, shallow pool of liquid that has spread on the ground. ❑ *The road was shiny with puddles, but the rain was at an end.*

puff /pʌf/ (**puffs**, **puffing**, **puffed**) **1** v-ı If someone **puffs at** a cigarette, cigar, or pipe, they smoke it. ❑ *He lit a cigar and puffed at it twice.* ● N-COUNT **Puff** is also a noun. ❑ *She was taking quick puffs at her cigarette like a beginner.* **2** v-т/v-ı If you **puff** smoke or moisture from your mouth or if it **puffs** from your mouth, you breathe it out. ❑ *Richard lit another cigarette and puffed smoke towards the ceiling.* ● PHRASAL VERB **Puff out** means the same as **puff**. ❑ *He drew heavily on his cigarette and puffed out a cloud of smoke.* **3** v-т If an engine, chimney, or boiler **puffs** smoke or steam, clouds of smoke or steam come out of it. ❑ *As I completed my 26th lap the Porsche puffed blue smoke.* ● N-COUNT A **puff of** something such as air or smoke is a small amount of it that is blown out from somewhere. ❑ *Wind caught the sudden puff of dust and blew it inland.* **5** v-ı If you **are puffing**, you are breathing loudly and quickly with your mouth open because you are out of breath after a lot of physical effort. [usu cont] ❑ *I know nothing about boxing, but I could see he was unfit, because he was puffing.*

pull ♦♦◇ /pʊl/ (**pulls**, **pulling**, **pulled**) **1** v-т/v-ı When you **pull** something, you hold it firmly and use force in order to move it toward you or away from its previous position. ❑ *They have pulled out patients' teeth unnecessarily.* ❑ *Erica was solemn, pulling at her blonde curls.* ❑ *I helped pull him out of the water.* ❑ *Someone pulled her hair.* ● N-COUNT **Pull** is also a noun. ❑ *The feather must be removed with a straight, firm pull.* **2** v-т When you **pull** an object from a bag, pocket, or cabinet, you put your hand in and bring the object out. ❑ *Jack pulled the slip of paper from his shirt pocket.* **3** v-т When a vehicle, animal, or person **pulls** a cart or piece of machinery, they are attached to it or hold it, so that it moves along behind them when they move forward. ❑ *This is early-20th-century rural Sussex, when horses still pulled the plough.* **4** v-т/v-ı If you **pull yourself** or **pull** a part of your body in a particular direction, you move your body or a part of your body with effort or force. ❑ *Hughes pulled himself slowly to his feet.* ❑ *He pulled his arms out of the sleeves.* **5** v-ı When a driver or vehicle **pulls to** a stop or a halt, the vehicle stops. ❑ *He pulled to a stop behind a pickup truck.* **6** v-ı In a race or contest, if you **pull ahead of** or **pull away from** an opponent, you gradually increase the amount by which you are ahead of them. ❑ *He pulled away, extending his lead to 15 seconds.* **7** v-т If you **pull** something **apart**, you break or divide it into small pieces, often in order to put them back together again in a different way. ❑ *If I wanted to improve the car significantly I would have to pull it apart and start again.* **8** v-т To **pull** crowds, viewers, or voters means to attract them. [INFORMAL] ❑ *The organisers have to employ performers to pull a crowd.* ● PHRASAL VERB **Pull in** means the same as **pull**. ❑ *They provided a far better news service and pulled in many more viewers.* **9** N-COUNT A **pull** is a strong physical force which causes things to move in a particular direction. ❑ *...the pull of gravity.* **10** to **pull a face** →see **face**. to **pull** someone's **leg** →see **leg**. to **pull strings** →see **string**. to **pull** your **weight** →see **weight**

Thesaurus		*pull*의 참조어
v.	drag, haul, lug, tow; *(ant.)* push **1 3 4**	
	attract, draw, lure; *(ant.)* repel **8**	

▶**pull away** **1** PHRASAL VERB When a vehicle or driver **pulls away**, the vehicle starts moving forward. ❑ *I stood in the driveway and watched him back out and pull away.* **2** PHRASAL VERB If you **pull away from** someone that you have had close links with, you deliberately become less close to them. ❑ *Other daughters, faced with their mother's emotional hunger, pull away.*

▶**pull back** **1** PHRASAL VERB If someone **pulls back from** an action, they decide not to do it or continue with it, because it could have bad consequences. ❑ *They will plead with him to pull back from confrontation.* **2** PHRASAL VERB If troops **pull back** or if their leader **pulls** them **back**, they go some or all of the way back

1 타동사 출판하다, 발행하다 ❑ 그들은 참고 서적을 출판한다. **2** 타동사 게재하다 ❑ 그 잡지가 정부를 비꼬는 기사를 게재한 후 그와 같은 금지 조처가 내려졌다. **3** 타동사 출간하다 ❑ 존 레논은 자신의 익살스러운 산문을 담은 책 두 권을 출간할 시간을 얻었다. **4** 타동사 (안에 게재를 통해) 발표하다 ❑ 시위자들은 등록된 유권자들의 명단을 발표할 것을 정부에 요구했다.

가산명사 출판인; 출판사 ❑ 출판업자들은 그 잡지를 주간지로 제작할 계획이었다.

불가산명사 출판업 ❑ 나는 출판업에서 아주 영향력이 큰 지위를 가지고 있었다.

가산명사 출판사

1 가산명사 또는 불가산명사 푸딩 ❑ 따뜻한 커스터드를 곁들인 체리 스펀지 푸딩 **2** 가산명사 또는 불가산명사 디저트 [영국영어] ❑ 카나페와 스타터, 주요리와 디저트로 이루어진 메뉴

가산명사 웅덩이 ❑ 그 길은 곳곳에 물이 고여 반짝거렸지만 비는 그쳐 있었다.

1 자동사 (담배를) 피우다, 빨다 ❑ 그는 시가에 불을 붙이고 두 모금 빨았다. ● 가산명사 (담배) 한 모금 ❑ 그녀는 초심자처럼 담배를 빠르게 몇 모금 빨았다. **2** 타동사/자동사 내뿜다; 뿜어 나오다 ❑ 리처드는 담배를 한 대 더 불을 붙이더니 천장을 향해 연기를 내뿜었다. ● 구동사 내뿜다; 뿜어 나오다 ❑ 그는 담배를 깊이 빨아들이더니 구름 같은 연기를 뿜어냈다. **3** 타동사 뿜어내다 ❑ 내가 26번째 바퀴를 다 돌았을 때 포르쉐 자동차가 푸른색 연기를 내뿜었다. **4** 가산명사 (연기, 먼지 등이) 날림 ❑ 바람이 갑자기 휙 먼지를 날려 올려 내륙으로 몰고 갔다. **5** 자동사 헐떡거리다 ❑ 나는 권투에 대해 아무것도 모르지만, 그가 문제가 있다는 것은 알 수 있었다. 그가 숨을 헐떡거리고 있었으니까.

1 타동사/자동사 당기다, 끌다 ❑ 그들은 불필요하게 환자들의 이를 뽑아 왔다. ❑ 에리카는 곱슬곱슬한 금발머리를 잡아당기며 심각하게 있었다. ❑ 내가 그를 물 밖으로 끌어내는 것을 도왔다. ❑ 누군가가 그녀의 머리를 잡아당겼다. ● 가산명사 잡아당기기, 끌기 ❑ 똑바로 세게 잡아당겨서 깃털을 제거하셔야 합니다. **2** 타동사 꺼내다 ❑ 잭은 그 종잇조각을 셔츠 주머니에서 꺼냈다. **3** 타동사 끌다 ❑ 여기는 20세기 초 시골 서섹스로, 아직까지 말이 쟁기를 끌던 시절이었다. **4** 타동사/자동사 (힘이) 몸을 움직이다 ❑ 휴스는 천천히 몸을 움직여 일어났다. ❑ 그는 힘들여 팔을 소매 밖으로 빼냈다. **5** 자동사 차량을 세우다; (차량이) 멈춰 서다 ❑ 그는 픽업 트럭 뒤에 차를 세웠다. **6** 자동사 격차를 벌리다 ❑ 그는 15초 차로 앞서 나가며 격차를 벌렸다. **7** 타동사 분해하다 ❑ 만약 내가 그 차를 상당 정도 개량하길 원한다면 분해한 다음 다시 시작해야 할 것이다. **8** 타동사 끌어 모으다 [비격식체] ❑ 주최 측은 사람들을 끌어 모으기 위해 연예인을 고용해야 한다. ● 구동사 끌어 모으다 ❑ 그들은 훨씬 더 나은 뉴스 서비스를 제공하여 더 많은 시청자들을 끌어 모았다. **9** 가산명사 당기는 힘 ❑ 중력의 당기는 힘

1 구동사 (차 등이 앞으로) 나아가다 ❑ 나는 진입로에 서서 그가 차를 후진시켰다가 앞으로 나아가는 것을 지켜보았다. **2** 구동사 멀리하다, 거리를 두다 ❑ 다른 딸들은 어머니의 정서적 굶주림에 직면하자 거리를 둔다.

1 구동사 그만두다 ❑ 그들은 대결을 그만두라고 그에게 간청할 것이다. **2** 구동사 철수하다; 철수시키다 ❑ 그들은 그 도시 주위의 포병 진지에서 철수하라는 요청을 받았다.

a
b
c
d
e
f
g
h
i
j
k
l
m
n
o
p
q
r
s
t
u
v
w
x
y
z

to their own territory. ❑ *They were asked to pull back from their artillery positions around the city.*

▶**pull down** PHRASAL VERB To **pull down** a building or statue means to deliberately destroy it. ❑ *They'd pulled the registry office down which then left an open space.*

▶**pull in 1** PHRASAL VERB When a vehicle or driver **pulls in** somewhere, the vehicle stops there. ❑ *He pulled in at the side of the road.* **2** →see **pull 8**

▶**pull into** PHRASAL VERB When a vehicle or driver **pulls into** a place, the vehicle moves into the place and stops there. ❑ *He pulled into the driveway in front of her garage.*

▶**pull off 1** PHRASAL VERB If you **pull off** something very difficult, you succeed in achieving it. ❑ *The National League for Democracy pulled off a landslide victory.* **2** PHRASAL VERB If a vehicle or driver **pulls off** the road, the vehicle stops by the side of the road. ❑ *I pulled off the road at a small village pub.*

▶**pull out 1** PHRASAL VERB When a vehicle or driver **pulls out**, the vehicle moves out into the road or nearer the center of the road. ❑ *She pulled out into the street.* **2** PHRASAL VERB If you **pull out of** an agreement, a contest, or an organization, you withdraw from it. ❑ *The World Bank should pull out of the project.* ❑ *France was going to pull out of NATO.* **3** PHRASAL VERB If troops **pull out of** a place or if their leader **pulls them out**, they leave it. ❑ *The militia in Lebanon has agreed to pull out of Beirut.* ❑ *Economic sanctions will be lifted once two-thirds of their forces have pulled out.* **4** PHRASAL VERB If a country **pulls out of** recession or if someone **pulls it out**, it begins to recover from it. ❑ *Sterling has been hit by the economy's failure to pull out of recession.*

▶**pull over 1** PHRASAL VERB When a vehicle or driver **pulls over**, the vehicle moves closer to the side of the road and stops there. ❑ *He noticed a man behind him in a blue Ford gesticulating to pull over.* **2** →see also **pullover**

▶**pull through** PHRASAL VERB If someone with a serious illness or someone in a very difficult situation **pulls through**, they recover. ❑ *Everyone was very concerned whether he would pull through or not.* ❑ *It is only our determination to fight that has pulled us through.*

▶**pull together 1** PHRASAL VERB If people **pull together**, they help each other or work together in order to deal with a difficult situation. ❑ *The nation was urged to pull together to avoid a slide into complete chaos.* **2** PHRASAL VERB If you are upset or depressed and someone tells you to **pull yourself together**, they are telling you to control your feelings and behave calmly again. ❑ *Pull yourself together, you stupid woman!*

▶**pull up 1** PHRASAL VERB When a vehicle or driver **pulls up**, the vehicle slows down and stops. ❑ *The cab pulled up and the driver jumped out.* **2** PHRASAL VERB If you **pull up** a chair, you move it closer to something or someone and sit on it. ❑ *He pulled up a chair behind her and put his chin on her shoulder.*

pull|over /pʊloʊvər/ (pullovers) N-COUNT A **pullover** is a piece of woollen clothing that covers the upper part of your body and your arms. You put it on by pulling it over your head.

pulp /pʌlp/ (pulps, pulping, pulped) **1** N-SING If an object is pressed into a **pulp**, it is crushed or beaten until it is soft, smooth, and wet. ❑ *The olives are crushed to a pulp by stone rollers.* **2** N-SING In fruit or vegetables, **the pulp** is the soft part inside the skin. ❑ *Make maximum use of the whole fruit, including the pulp which is high in fibre.* **3** N-UNCOUNT Wood **pulp** is material made from crushed wood. It is used to make paper. **4** ADJ People refer to stories or novels as **pulp** fiction when they consider them to be of poor quality and intentionally shocking or sensational. [ADJ n] ❑ *...lurid '50s pulp novels.* **5** V-T If paper, vegetables, or fruit **are pulped**, they are crushed into a smooth, wet paste. [usu passive] ❑ *Onions can be boiled and pulped to a puree.* **6** V-T If money or documents **are pulped**, they are destroyed. This is done to stop the money being used or to stop the documents being seen by the public. [usu passive] ❑ *25 million pounds worth of five pound notes have been pulped because the designers made a mistake.* **7** PHRASE If someone **is beaten to a pulp** or **beaten to pulp**, they are hit repeatedly until they are very badly injured. ❑ *I tried to talk myself out of a fight and got beaten to a pulp instead by three other boys.*

pul|pit /pʊlpɪt, pʌl-/ (pulpits) N-COUNT A **pulpit** is a small raised platform with a rail or barrier around it in a church, where a member of the clergy stands to speak. ❑ *The time came for the sermon and he ascended the pulpit steps.*

pul|sate /pʌlseɪt, BRIT pʌlseɪt/ (pulsates, pulsating, pulsated) V-I If something **pulsates**, it beats, moves in and out, or shakes with strong, regular movements. ❑ *The Pole Star appears to be changing rapidly from a star that pulsates into one that is stable.*

pulse /pʌls/ (pulses, pulsing, pulsed) **1** N-COUNT Your **pulse** is the regular beating of blood through your body, which you can feel when you touch particular parts of your body, especially your wrist. ❑ *Mahoney's pulse was racing, and he felt confused.* **2** N-COUNT In music, a **pulse** is a regular beat, which is often produced by a drum. ❑ *...the repetitive pulse of the music.* **3** N-COUNT A **pulse of** electrical current, light, or heat is a temporary increase in its level. ❑ *The switch works by passing a pulse of current between the tip and the surface.* **4** N-SING If you refer to **the pulse of** a group in society, you mean the ideas, opinions, or feelings they have at a particular time. ❑ *The White House insists that the president is in touch with the pulse of the black community.* **5** V-I If something **pulses**, it moves, appears, or makes a sound with a strong regular rhythm. ❑ *His temples pulsed a little, threatening a headache.* **6** N-PLURAL Some seeds which can be cooked and eaten are called **pulses**, for example peas, beans, and lentils.

구동사 허물다 ❑ 그들은 등기소를 허물었고 그 후 그 자리에는 공터가 남았다.

1 구동사 차를 세우다; (차가) 멈추다 ❑ 그는 도로변에 차를 세웠다.

구동사 차를 몰고 들어가서 세우다; (차가) 들어가서 멈추다 ❑ 그는 그녀의 차고 앞 진입로에 들어가서 차를 세웠다.

1 구동사 달성하다, 획득하다 ❑ 민족민주동맹이 압도적인 승리를 얻어 냈다. **2** 구동사 차를 길가에 대다; (차가) 멈추다 ❑ 나는 작은 동네 술집 앞 길가에 차를 댔다.

1 구동사 차를 몰아 도로에 진입하다; (차가) 도로에 진입하다 ❑ 그녀는 차를 몰아 도로에 들어섰다. **2** 구동사 -에서 손을 떼다 ❑ 세계은행은 그 사업에서 손을 떼야 한다. ❑ 프랑스는 나토에서 손을 뗄 예정이었다. **3** 구동사 -에서 철수하다; -에서 철수시키다 ❑ 레바논 민병대는 베이루트에서 철수하기로 동의했다. ❑ 그들의 병력 중 3분의 2가 철수를 완료하면 경제 제재가 해제될 것이다. **4** 구동사 (경기 침체에서) 벗어나다; 벗어나게 하다 ❑ 경제가 경기 침체에서 벗어나지 못함에 따라 영국 파운드화가 타격을 입어 왔다.

1 구동사 차를 길가에 대다; (차가) 길가에 붙어 서다 ❑ 그는 자기 뒤에 파란색 포드 자동차를 탄 사람이 차를 길가에 대라고 손짓하는 것을 알아차렸다.

구동사 회복하다, 완쾌하다 ❑ 그가 완쾌할지 아닐지 모두 몹시 걱정스러워 했다. ❑ 우리를 회복시킨 것은 다만 싸우고자 하는 우리의 결의뿐이었다.

1 구동사 협력하여 일하다 ❑ 국민들에게 전면적인 대혼란으로 빠져드는 것을 막을 수 있도록 힘을 한데 모을 것을 촉구했다. **2** 구동사 정신을 차리다 ❑ 정신 차려, 이 바보 같은 여자야!

1 구동사 차를 멈추다; (차가) 멎다 ❑ 택시가 멎고 운전사가 뛰쳐나왔다. **2** 구동사 (의자를) 끌어당겨 앉다 ❑ 그는 그녀 뒤에 의자를 끌어당겨 앉아서 그녀의 어깨에 턱을 얹었다.

가산명사 풀오버 (앞트임이 없는 윗도리), 스웨터

1 단수명사 걸쭉한 물질, 짓이겨진 것 ❑ 올리브는 돌 압착기에 갈려 걸쭉하게 된다. **2** 단수명사 과육 ❑ 섬유질이 풍부한 과육을 포함해서 과일 전체를 최대한 다 먹도록 하세요. **3** 불가산명사 펄프 **4** 형용사 선정적이고 통속적인 ❑ 50년대의 야한 통속 소설들 **5** 타동사 걸쭉하게 되다 ❑ 양파는 삶으면 걸쭉하니 퓌레가 된다. **6** 타동사 (지폐 등이) 폐기되다 ❑ 2천 5백만 파운드어치의 5파운드짜리 지폐가 도안가의 실수 때문에 폐기되었다. **7** 구 곤죽이 되도록 맞다, 죽도록 두들겨 맞다 ❑ 나는 말을 잘해서 싸우지 않으려 했지만 그러기는커녕 세 명의 다른 사내아이들에게 죽도록 두들겨 맞았다.

가산명사 설교단 ❑ 설교 시간이 되어서 그가 설교단의 계단을 올라갔다.

자동사 고동치다, 두근거리다, 진동하다 ❑ 북극성은 별빛이 섬멸하다가 안정된 빛으로 급속히 바뀌는 것처럼 보인다.

1 가산명사 맥박 ❑ 마호니는 맥박이 빠르게 뛰고 혼란스러웠다. **2** 가산명사 (음악) 박자 ❑ 그 음악의 반복적인 박자 **3** 가산명사 (음향 등의) 파동 ❑ 스위치는 그 끝과 표면 사이에 전류를 통과시킴으로써 작동한다. **4** 단수명사 (특정 집단의) 동향, 견해 ❑ 백악관은 대통령이 흑인 사회의 동향을 파악하고 있다고 주장한다. **5** 자동사 진동하다, 펄떡거리다 ❑ 그의 관자놀이가 두통을 예고하며 조금씩 씰룩거렸다. **6** 복수명사 콩, 콩류

pump ♦♢♢ /pʌmp/ (pumps, pumping, pumped) **1** N-COUNT A **pump** is a machine or device that is used to force a liquid or gas to flow in a particular direction. ❑ ...pumps that circulate the fuel around in the engine. ❑ There was no water in the building, just a pump in the courtyard. **2** V-T/V-I To **pump** a liquid or gas in a particular direction means to force it to flow in that direction using a pump. ❑ It's not enough to get rid of raw sewage by pumping it out to sea. ❑ The money raised will be used to dig bore holes to pump water into the dried-up lake. **3** N-COUNT A fuel or gas **pump** is a machine with a tube attached to it that you use to fill a car with gasoline. ❑ The average price for all grades of gas at the pump was at $1.35 a gallon. **4** V-T If someone **has** their stomach **pumped**, doctors remove the contents of their stomach, for example because they have swallowed poison or drugs. [usu passive] ❑ One woman was rushed to the emergency room to have her stomach pumped.

▶ **pump out** PHRASAL VERB To **pump out** something means to produce or supply it continually and in large amounts. ❑ Japanese companies have been pumping out plenty of innovative products.

▶ **pump up** PHRASAL VERB If you **pump up** something such as a tire, you fill it with air using a pump. ❑ Pump all the tires up.

pump|kin /pʌmpkɪn/ (**pumpkins**) N-VAR A **pumpkin** is a large, round, orange vegetable with a thick skin. ❑ Quarter the pumpkin and remove the seeds.

pun /pʌn/ (**puns**) N-COUNT A **pun** is a clever and amusing use of a word or phrase with two meanings, or of words with the same sound but different meanings. For example, if someone says "The peasants are revolting," this is a pun because it can be interpreted as meaning either that the peasants are fighting against authority, or that they are disgusting. ❑ He spoke of a hatchet job, which may be a pun on some senator's name.

punch ♦♢♢ /pʌntʃ/ (**punches, punching, punched**) **1** V-T If you **punch** someone or something, you hit them hard with your fist. ❑ After punching him on the chin she wound up hitting him over the head. ● PHRASAL VERB In American English, **punch out** means the same as **punch**. ❑ "I almost lost my job today." — "What happened?" — "Oh, I punched out this guy." ● N-COUNT **Punch** is also a noun. ❑ He was hurting Johansson with body punches in the fourth round. **2** V-T If you **punch** something such as the buttons on a keyboard, you touch them in order to store information on a machine such as a computer or to give the machine a command to do something. ❑ Mrs. Baylor strode to the elevator and punched the button. **3** V-T If you **punch** holes in something, you make holes in it by pushing or pressing it with something sharp. ❑ I took a ballpoint pen and punched a hole in the carton. **4** N-COUNT A **punch** is a tool that you use for making holes in something. ❑ Make two holes with a hole punch. **5** N-UNCOUNT If you say that something has **punch**, you mean that it has force or effectiveness. ❑ My nervousness made me deliver the vital points of my address without sufficient punch. **6** N-MASS **Punch** is a drink made from wine or spirits mixed with things such as sugar, lemons, and spices. ❑ ...a bowl of punch.

Word Partnership	punch의 연어
V.	pack a punch, throw a punch **1**
N.	punch a button **2**
	punch a hole in *something* **3**

▶ **punch in** PHRASAL VERB If you **punch in** a number on a machine or **punch** numbers **into** it, you push the machine's buttons or keys in order to give it a command to do something. ❑ You can bank by phone in the U.S., punching in account numbers on the phone.

punc|tual /pʌŋktʃuəl/ ADJ If you are **punctual**, you do something or arrive somewhere at the right time and are not late. ❑ He's always very punctual. I'll see if he's here yet. ● **punc|tu|al|ly** ADV ❑ My guest arrived punctually.

punc|tu|ate /pʌŋktʃueɪt/ (**punctuates, punctuating, punctuated**) V-T If an activity or situation **is punctuated by** particular things, it is interrupted by them at intervals. [WRITTEN] [usu passive] ❑ The game was punctuated by a series of injuries.

punc|tua|tion /pʌŋktʃueɪʃ°n/ **1** N-UNCOUNT **Punctuation** is the use of symbols such as periods, commas, or question marks to divide written words into sentences and clauses. ❑ He was known for his poor grammar and punctuation. **2** N-UNCOUNT **Punctuation** is the symbols that you use to divide written words into sentences and clauses. ❑ Jessica had rapidly scanned the lines, none of which boasted a capital letter or any punctuation.

punc|tua|tion mark (**punctuation marks**) N-COUNT A **punctuation mark** is a symbol such as a period, comma, or question mark that you use to divide written words into sentences and clauses.

punc|ture /pʌŋktʃər/ (**punctures, puncturing, punctured**) **1** N-COUNT A **puncture** is a small hole in a car tire or bicycle tire that has been made by a sharp object. ❑ Somebody helped me to mend the puncture. **2** N-COUNT A **puncture** is a small hole in someone's skin that has been made by or with a sharp object. ❑ An instrument called a trocar makes a puncture in the abdominal wall. **3** V-T If a sharp object **punctures** something, it makes a hole in it. ❑ The bullet punctured the skull. **4** V-T/V-I If a car tire or bicycle tire **punctures** or if something **punctures** it, a hole is made in the tire. ❑ His bike's rear tire punctured.

pun|dit /pʌndɪt/ (**pundits**) N-COUNT A **pundit** is a person who knows a lot about a subject and is often asked to give information or opinions about it to the public. ❑ ...a well known political pundit.

pun|gent /pʌndʒ°nt/ ADJ Something that is **pungent** has a strong, sharp smell or taste which is often so strong that it is unpleasant. ❑ The more herbs you use, the more pungent the sauce will be.

1 가산명사 펌프 ❑ 엔진에 연료를 순환시키는 펌프들 ❑ 그 건물 내에는 물이 없고, 안마당에 펌프가 있을 뿐이었다. **2** 타동사/자동사 (펌프질로) 흘려보내다 ❑ 정화 처리되지 않은 하수를 바다로 퍼 내보내는 것으로는 충분하지 않다. ❑ 모금된 돈은 말라 버린 호수에 대기 위해 펌프로 뿜어 올릴 물을 찾아 땅 속을 시추하는 데 쓰일 것이다. **3** 가산명사 주유기 ❑ 주유기에 있는 모든 등급의 휘발유 평균 가격은 갤런당 1.35달러였다. **4** 타동사 위세척을 하다 ❑ 한 여자가 위세척을 위해 급히 응급실로 실려 왔다.

구동사 (다량으로) 쏟아 내다, 쏟아 있다 ❑ 일본 기업들은 수많은 혁신적인 상품들을 계속 쏟아 내 왔다.

구동사 펌프로 공기를 넣다 ❑ 모든 타이어에 공기를 주입하세요.

가산명사 또는 불가산명사 호박 ❑ 호박을 4등분 하고 씨를 제거하세요.

가산명사 (동음이의어를 이용한) 말장난 ❑ 그는 손도끼 작업에 대해 이야기했는데, 그것은 어떤 상원 의원의 이름에 대한 동음이의어 말장난일 수도 있다.

1 타동사 주먹으로 치다 ❑ 그녀가 그의 턱에 주먹을 날린 다음 그의 머리를 쳐서 끝장을 냈다. ● 구동사 주먹으로 치다 ❑ "나 오늘 실직할 뻔했어." "무슨 일로?" "아, 내가 이 녀석을 주먹으로 쳤거든." ● 가산명사 주먹질, 펀치 ❑ 그는 4회전에서 몸통을 치면서 요한슨에게 고통을 주고 있었다. **2** 타동사 (컴퓨터 자판의 키 등을) 두들기다, 누르다 ❑ 베일러 부인은 엘리베이터로 성큼성큼 걸어가서 버튼을 눌렀다. **3** 타동사 구멍을 뚫다 ❑ 나는 볼펜을 가지고 우유 곽에 구멍을 뚫었다. **4** 가산명사 천공기, 펀치 ❑ 펀치로 구멍을 두 개 뚫으세요. **5** 불가산명사 박력, 위기 ❑ 나는 초조해서 연설의 핵심 부분들을 충분히 활기 있게 전달하지 못했다. **6** 물질명사 펀치 (술과 향료를 섞어 만든 음료) ❑ 펀치 한 그릇

구동사 (숫자를) 누르다 ❑ 미국에서는 전화로 계좌 번호를 눌러 은행 업무를 볼 수 있다.

형용사 시간을 지키는, 늦지 않는 ❑ 그는 항상 시간을 잘 지켜. 그가 와 있나 볼게. ● 시간을 맞추어, 정시에 부사 ❑ 손님들이 정시에 도착했다.

타동사 (간간이) 중단되다 [문어체] ❑ 게임이 잇단 부상으로 간간이 중단되었다.

1 불가산명사 구두법 ❑ 그는 문법과 구두법이 서투른 것으로 유명했다. **2** 불가산명사 구두점 ❑ 제시카는 재빨리 그 문장들을 훑어보았는데, 거기에는 대문자나 구두점이 전혀 눈에 띄지 않았다.

가산명사 구두점

1 가산명사 (타이어) 펑크 ❑ 어떤 사람이 내 펑크 수리를 도와주었다. **2** 가산명사 (뾰족한 것에 찔린) 구멍 ❑ 투관침이라고 불리는 기구는 위벽에 구멍을 낸다. **3** 타동사 구멍을 내다 ❑ 총알이 두개골을 꿰뚫어 구멍을 냈다. **4** 타동사/자동사 (타이어가) 펑크 나다; 펑크를 내다 ❑ 그의 자전거 뒷바퀴가 펑크 났다.

가산명사 전문가, 권위자 ❑ 널리 알려진 정치 문제 전문가

형용사 자극적인, 맛이 강한, 톡 쏘는 ❑ 허브를 많이 넣을수록 소스 맛이 더 강해진다.

a b c d e f g h i j k l m n o p q r s t u v w x y z

pun|ish /pʌnɪʃ/ (punishes, punishing, punished) **1** V-T To **punish** someone means to make them suffer in some way because they have done something wrong. ❑ *I don't believe that George ever had to punish the children.* ❑ *According to present law, the authorities can only punish smugglers with small fines.* **2** V-T To **punish** a crime means to punish anyone who commits that crime. ❑ *The government voted to punish corruption in sport with up to four years in jail.*

pun|ish|ing /pʌnɪʃɪŋ/ ADJ A **punishing** schedule, activity, or experience requires a lot of physical effort and makes you very tired or weak. ❑ *He claimed his punishing work schedule had made him resort to taking the drug.*

pun|ish|ment /pʌnɪʃmənt/ (punishments) **1** N-UNCOUNT **Punishment** is the act of punishing someone or of being punished. ❑ *...a group which campaigns against the physical punishment of children.* **2** N-VAR A **punishment** is a particular way of punishing someone. ❑ *The government is proposing tougher punishments for officials convicted of corruption.* **3** N-UNCOUNT You can use **punishment** to refer to severe physical treatment of any kind. ❑ *Don't expect these boots to take the punishment that gardening will give them.* **4** →see also **capital punishment**, **corporal punishment**

pu|ni|tive /pyuːnɪtɪv/ ADJ **Punitive** actions are intended to punish people. [FORMAL] ❑ *...a punitive bombing raid.*

punk /pʌŋk/ (punks) **1** N-UNCOUNT **Punk** or **punk rock** is rock music that is played in a fast, loud, and aggressive way and is often a protest against conventional attitudes and behavior. Punk rock was particularly popular in the late 1970s. ❑ *I was never really into punk.* **2** N-COUNT A **punk** or a **punk rocker** is a young person who likes punk music and dresses in a very noticeable and unconventional way, for example by having brightly colored hair and wearing metal chains. ❑ *In the 1970s, punks wore safety pins through their cheeks.*

punt|er /pʌntər/ (punters) **1** N-COUNT A **punter** is a person who bets money, especially on horse races. [BRIT, INFORMAL] ❑ *Punters are expected to gamble £70m on the Grand National.* **2** N-COUNT People sometimes refer to their customers or clients as **punters**. [mainly BRIT, INFORMAL] ❑ *Business has been slow -- only two punters in two hours.*

pup /pʌp/ (pups) **1** N-COUNT A **pup** is a young dog. ❑ *I'll get you an Alsatian pup for Christmas.* **2** N-COUNT The young of some other animals, for example seals, are called **pups**. ❑ *Two thousand grey seal pups are born there every autumn.*

pu|pil ◆◇◇ /pyuːpɪl/ (pupils) **1** N-COUNT The **pupils** of a school are the children who go to it. ❑ *Over a third of those now at secondary school in Wales attend schools with over 1,000 pupils.* **2** N-COUNT A **pupil** of a painter, musician, or other expert is someone who studies under that expert and learns his or her skills. ❑ *After his education, Goldschmidt became a pupil of the composer Franz Schreker.* **3** N-COUNT The **pupils** of your eyes are the small, round, black holes in the center of them. ❑ *The sick man's pupils were dilated.* →see also **eye**

pup|pet /pʌpɪt/ (puppets) **1** N-COUNT A **puppet** is a doll that you can move, either by pulling strings which are attached to it or by putting your hand inside its body and moving your fingers. **2** N-COUNT You can refer to a person or country as a **puppet** when you mean that their actions are controlled by a more powerful person or government, even though they may appear to be independent. [DISAPPROVAL] ❑ *When the invasion occurred he seized power and ruled the country as a puppet of the occupiers.*

pup|py /pʌpi/ (puppies) N-COUNT A **puppy** is a young dog. ❑ *One Sunday he began trying to teach the two puppies to walk on a leash.*

pur|chase ◆◆◇ /pɜːrtʃɪs/ (purchases, purchasing, purchased) **1** V-T When you **purchase** something, you buy it. [FORMAL] ❑ *He purchased a ticket and went up on the top deck.* ● **pur|chas|er** (purchasers) N-COUNT ❑ *The broker will get 5% if he finds a purchaser.* **2** N-UNCOUNT The **purchase** of something is the act of buying it. [FORMAL] ❑ *This week he is to visit China to discuss the purchase of military supplies.* →see also **hire purchase** **3** N-COUNT A **purchase** is something that you buy. [FORMAL] ❑ *She opened the tie box and looked at her purchase. It was silk, with maroon stripes.*

pur|chas|ing pow|er **1** N-UNCOUNT The **purchasing power** of a currency is the amount of goods or services that you can buy with it. [BUSINESS] ❑ *The real purchasing power of the rouble has plummeted.* **2** N-UNCOUNT The **purchasing power** of a person or group of people is the amount of goods or services that they can afford to buy. [BUSINESS] ❑ *Stores have been smartening up their window displays to match the new found purchasing power of their customers.*

pure ◆◇◇ /pyʊər/ (purer, purest) **1** ADJ A **pure** substance is not mixed with anything else. ❑ *...a carton of pure orange juice.* **2** ADJ Something that is **pure** is clean and does not contain any harmful substances. ❑ *In remote regions, the air is pure and the crops are free of poisonous insecticides.* ● **pu|ri|ty** N-UNCOUNT [with poss] ❑ *They worried about the purity of tap water.* **3** ADJ If you describe something such as a color, a sound, or a type of light as **pure**, you mean that it is very clear and represents a perfect example of its type. ❑ *These flowers bring to the garden a whole family of blue colors with the occasional pure white.* ● **pu|ri|ty** N-UNCOUNT ❑ *The soaring purity of her voice conjured up the frozen bleakness of the Far North.* **4** ADJ **Pure** science or **pure** research is concerned only with theory and not with how this theory can be used in practical ways. [ADJ n] ❑ *Physics isn't just about pure science with no immediate applications.* **5** ADJ **Pure** means complete and total. [EMPHASIS] ❑ *The old man turned to give her a look of pure surprise.* →see **science**

pu|ree /pyʊreɪ, -riː/ (purees, pureeing, pureed) also **purée** **1** N-VAR **Puree** is food which has been crushed or beaten so that it forms a thick, smooth liquid. ❑ *...a can of tomato puree.* **2** V-T If you **puree** food, you make it into a puree. ❑ *In a blender, puree the fruit with the orange juice.*

1 타동사 처벌하다, 벌주다 ❑ 나는 조지가 그 아이들에게 벌을 주어야 했다는 것을 믿을 수가 없다. ❑ 현행법에 따르면, 당국은 밀수업자들에게 소액의 벌금만 물릴 수 있을 뿐이다. **2** 타동사 처벌하다 ❑ 정부는 스포츠 계 부정에 대해 최대 4년까지 징역형을 내릴 수 있도록 투표를 했다.

형용사 매우 힘든, 지치게 하는 ❑ 그는 자신의 매우 힘든 작업 일정 때문에 마약에 손을 대게 되었다고 주장했다.

1 불가산명사 처벌, 형벌 ❑ 아동 체벌 반대 운동을 하는 모임 **2** 가산명사 또는 불가산명사 징계 ❑ 정부는 부정부패 사범 공무원들에 대해 더욱 엄한 징계를 제안하고 있다. **3** 불가산명사 학대, 혹사 ❑ 이 부츠가 정원을 가꾸는 그런 거친 일을 감당할 것이라 생각하지 마세요.

형용사 처벌의, 보복의 [격식체] ❑ 보복 폭격

1 불가산명사 펑크 록 ❑ 나는 결코 펑크 록을 좋아하지 않았다. **2** 가산명사 펑크족 ❑ 1970년대에 펑크족들은 볼에 안전핀을 꽂고 다녔다.

1 가산명사 (경마) 도박꾼 [영국영어, 비격식체] ❑ 도박꾼들이 그랜드 내셔널에서 7천만 파운드의 돈을 걸 것으로 예상된다. **2** 가산명사 고객, 손님 [주로 영국영어, 비격식체] ❑ 계속 장사가 잘 안 된다. 두 시간 동안 손님이 딱 두 명뿐이다.

1 가산명사 강아지 ❑ 성탄절에 세퍼드 강아지 한 마리 사 줄게. **2** 가산명사 새끼 ❑ 2천 마리의 회색 물개 새끼들이 매년 가을 저기에서 태어난다.

1 가산명사 학생 ❑ 웨일스의 현 중학생 중 3분의 1 이상이 1,000명 이상의 재학생이 있는 학교에 다닌다. **2** 가산명사 제자, 문하생 ❑ 골드슈미트는 학업을 마치고 작곡가인 프란츠 슈레커의 문하생이 되었다. **3** 가산명사 동공, 눈동자 ❑ 환자의 동공이 확대되어 있었다.

1 가산명사 꼭두각시, 인형극용 인형 **2** 가산명사 꼭두각시, 앞잡이 [탐탁찮음] ❑ 침략 전쟁이 발발하자 그는 권력을 잡고 정복자의 꼭두각시로서 나라를 다스렸다.

가산명사 강아지 ❑ 어느 일요일에 그는 강아지 두 마리에게 끈에 매인 채 걷는 것을 가르치려 들기 시작했다.

1 타동사 구매하다 [격식체] ❑ 그는 표를 사서 맨 위층으로 올라갔다. ● 구매자 가산명사 ❑ 중개인이 구매자를 구하면 5퍼센트를 가질 것이다. **2** 불가산명사 구매, 구입 [격식체] ❑ 이번 주에 그는 군수 물자 구매 상담을 위해 중국을 방문한다. **3** 가산명사 구입품, 산 물건 [격식체] ❑ 그녀는 넥타이 상자를 열고 자기가 산 물건을 보았다. 그것은 적갈색 줄무늬가 있는 실크였다.

1 불가산명사 (화폐의) 구매력 [경제] ❑ 루블화의 실제 구매력이 폭락했다. **2** 불가산명사 (사람의) 구매력 [경제] ❑ 자기 고객들의 새로 찾은 구매력에 부응하기 위해 상점들이 윈도우 진열을 말쑥하게 단장하고 있다.

1 형용사 순수한, 다른 게 섞이지 않은 ❑ 순 오렌지 주스 한 통 **2** 형용사 깨끗한, 청정한 ❑ 외딴 지역에서는, 공기가 맑고 곡물에는 독성 살충제를 뿌리지 않는다. ● 깨끗함, 순도 불가산명사 ❑ 그들은 수돗물이 깨끗한지 걱정이었다. **3** 형용사 순수한, 완벽한 ❑ 이 꽃들은 가끔씩 나타나는 순백색과 더불어 정원에 다양한 푸르름을 선사한다. ● 순수함, 완벽함 불가산명사 ❑ 그녀 목소리의 완벽한 고음은 북극 지방 동토의 황량한 기분을 자아내었다. **4** 형용사 순수한, 이론적인 ❑ 물리학이 즉각 응용되지 않는 순수 학문에 관한 것만은 아니다. **5** 형용사 완전한, 전적인 [강조] ❑ 그 노인은 완전히 놀란 표정으로 그녀를 돌아보았다. →see **science**

1 가산명사 또는 불가산명사 퓌레 ❑ 토마토 퓌레 통조림 하나 **2** 타동사 퓌레로 만들다 ❑ 혼합기에 넣고 그 과일을 오렌지 주스와 섞어 퓌레로 만드세요.

pure|ly /pyʊərli/ **1** ADV You use **purely** to emphasize that the thing you are mentioning is the most important feature or that it is the only thing which should be considered. [EMPHASIS] [ADV with cl/group] ❑ *It is a racing machine, designed purely for speed.* **2** PHRASE You use **purely and simply** to emphasize that the thing you are mentioning is the only thing involved. [EMPHASIS] ❑ *If Arthur was attracted here by the prospects of therapy, John came down purely and simply to make money.*

purge /pɜrdʒ/ (**purges, purging, purged**) **1** V-T To **purge** an organization **of** its unacceptable members means to remove them from it. You can also talk about **purging** people **from** an organization. ❑ *The leadership voted to purge the party of "hostile and anti-party elements."* ❑ *He recently purged the armed forces, sending hundreds of officers into retirement.* ● N-COUNT **Purge** is also a noun. ❑ *The army have called for a more thorough purge of people associated with the late President.* **2** V-T If you **purge** something **of** undesirable things, you get rid of them. ❑ *He closed his eyes and lay still, trying to purge his mind of anxiety.*

pu|ri|fy /pyʊərɪfaɪ/ (**purifies, purifying, purified**) V-T If you **purify** a substance, you make it pure by removing any harmful, dirty, or inferior substances from it. ❑ *I take wheat and yeast tablets daily to purify the blood.* ● **pu|ri|fi|ca|tion** /pyʊərɪfɪkeɪʃ³n/ N-UNCOUNT ❑ *...a water purification plant.*

pur|ist /pyʊərɪst/ (**purists**) **1** N-COUNT A **purist** is a person who wants something to be totally correct or unchanged, especially something they know a lot about. ❑ *The new edition of the dictionary carries 7000 additions to the language, which purists say is under threat.* **2** ADJ **Purist** attitudes are the kind of attitudes that purists have. ❑ *Britain wanted a "more purist" approach.*

pu|ri|tan /pyʊərɪt³n/ (**puritans**) **1** N-COUNT You describe someone as a **puritan** when they live according to strict moral or religious principles, especially when they disapprove of physical pleasures. [DISAPPROVAL] ❑ *Bykov had forgotten that Malinin was something of a puritan.* **2** ADJ **Puritan** attitudes are based on strict moral or religious principles and often involve disapproval of physical pleasures. [DISAPPROVAL] ❑ *Paul was someone who certainly had a puritan streak in him.*

pu|ri|tani|cal /pyʊərɪtænɪk³l/ ADJ If you describe someone as **puritanical**, you mean that they have very strict moral principles, and often try to make other people behave in a more moral way. [DISAPPROVAL] ❑ *He has a puritanical attitude towards sex.*

pu|ri|ty /pyʊərɪti/ →see **pure**

pur|ple ♦♢♢ /pɜrp³l/ (**purples**) COLOR Something that is **purple** is of a reddish-blue color. ❑ *She wore purple and green silk.*

pur|port /pərpɔrt/ (**purports, purporting, purported**) V-T If you say that someone or something **purports** to do or be a particular thing, you mean that they claim to do or be that thing, although you may not always believe that claim. [FORMAL] ❑ *...a book that purports to tell the whole truth.*

pur|pose ♦♦♢ /pɜrpəs/ (**purposes**) **1** N-COUNT The **purpose** of something is the reason for which it is made or done. ❑ *The purpose of the occasion was to raise money for medical supplies.* ❑ *...the use of nuclear energy for military purposes.* **2** N-COUNT Your **purpose** is the thing that you want to achieve. ❑ *They might well be prepared to do you harm in order to achieve their purpose.* **3** N-UNCOUNT **Purpose** is the feeling of having a definite aim and of being determined to achieve it. ❑ *The teachers are enthusiastic and have a sense of purpose.* **4** PHRASE If you do something **on purpose**, you do it intentionally. ❑ *Was it an accident or did David do it on purpose?*

Word Partnership	purpose의 연어
V.	serve a purpose **1**
	accomplish a purpose, achieve a purpose **2**
ADJ.	main purpose, original purpose, primary purpose, real purpose,
	sole purpose **1**-**3**

purpose-built ADJ A **purpose-built** building has been specially designed and built for a particular use. [mainly BRIT; AM usually **custom-built**] ❑ *The company has recently moved into a new purpose-built factory.*

pur|pose|ful /pɜrpəsfəl/ ADJ If someone is **purposeful**, they show that they have a definite aim and a strong desire to achieve it. ❑ *She had a purposeful air, and it became evident that this was not a casual visit.* ● **pur|pose|ful|ly** ADV ❑ *He strode purposefully towards the barn.*

purr /pɜr/ (**purrs, purring, purred**) **1** V-I When a cat **purrs**, it makes a low vibrating sound with its throat because it is contented. ❑ *The plump ginger kitten had settled comfortably in her arms and was purring enthusiastically.* **2** V-I When the engine of a machine such as a car **purrs**, it is working and making a quiet, continuous, vibrating sound. ❑ *Both boats purred out of the cave mouth and into open water.* ● N-SING **Purr** is also a noun. ❑ *Carmela heard the purr of a motor-cycle coming up the drive.*

purse /pɜrs/ (**purses, pursing, pursed**) **1** N-COUNT A **purse** is a small bag that women carry. [AM; BRIT **bag, handbag**] ❑ *She looked at me and then reached in her purse for cigarettes.* **2** N-COUNT A **purse** is a very small bag that people, especially women, keep their money in. [mainly BRIT; AM usually **change purse**] ❑ *She searched for her purse in her handbag.* **3** N-SING **Purse** is used to refer to the total amount of money that a country, family, or group has. ❑ *The money could simply go into the public purse, helping to lower taxes.* **4** V-T If you **purse** your lips, you move them into a small, rounded shape, usually because you disapprove of something or when you are thinking. ❑ *She pursed her lips in disapproval.*

1 부사 전적으로, 순전히 [강조] ❑ 이것은 전적으로 속도를 내도록 고안된 경주용 자동차이다. **2** 구 오로지, 순전히 [강조] ❑ 아서는 치료 가능성 때문에 이곳에 끌렸지만, 존은 순전히 돈을 벌기 위해 왔다.

1 타동사 숙청하다, 제거하다 ❑ 지도부는 당에서 '적대적이고 당 반대파인 분자들'을 숙청할 것을 제안했다. ❑ 그는 최근에 군부에 대한 숙청에 들어가 수백 명의 장교들을 퇴역시켰다. ● 가산명사 숙청, 제거 ❑ 군부는 사망한 대통령과 관련된 사람들에 대해 더 철저한 숙청을 요구해 왔다. **2** 타동사 없애다 ❑ 그는 눈을 감고 가만히 누워 마음속에서 근심을 몰아내려고 했다.

타동사 정화하다 ❑ 나는 피를 맑게 하려고 매일 밀과 효모 정제를 먹는다. ● 명사 정화 불가산명사 ❑ 수질 정화 식물

1 가산명사 순수주의자 ❑ 그 사전의 개정판에는 그 언어에 새로 추가된 어휘 7,000개가 포함되어 있는데, 순수주의자들은 이 언어가 위험을 받고 있다고 말한다. **2** 형용사 순수주의의 ❑ 영국은 '더 순수주의적'인 접근 방법을 원했다.

1 가산명사 청교도 [탐탁찮음] ❑ 바이코프는 말리닌이 상당한 청교도라는 것을 잊었었다. **2** 형용사 청교도적인 [탐탁찮음] ❑ 폴은 분명히 청교도적인 데가 있는 사람이었다.

형용사 청교도적인, 엄격한 [탐탁찮음] ❑ 그는 섹스에 대해 청교도적인 태도를 갖고 있다.

색채어 자주색 ❑ 그녀는 자주색과 녹색 비단옷을 입고 있었다.

타동사 (표면상으로) 내세우다 [격식체] ❑ 모든 진실을 다 말하겠다고 내세우는 책

1 가산명사 목적 ❑ 그 행사의 목적은 의료 물자용 자금을 모으기 위한 것이다. ❑ 군사 목적을 위한 원자력의 사용 **2** 가산명사 목적 ❑ 그들은 자기들의 목적을 달성하기 위해 기꺼이 너에게 해를 끼치려고 할지도 모른다. **3** 불가산명사 목적의식 ❑ 선생님들은 열정적이고 목적의식을 가지고 있다. **4** 구 의도적으로, 고의로 ❑ 그것이 우연이었니, 아니면 데이비드가 고의로 했니?

형용사 특별한 목적을 위해 세워진 [주로 영국영어; 미국영어 대개 custom-built] ❑ 그 회사는 최근 특별한 목적으로 지은 새 공장으로 이전했다.

형용사 목적의식이 있는, 결의가 강한 ❑ 그녀는 분명히 목적하는 바가 있어 보였고 이것이 평범한 방문이 아니라는 것이 분명해졌다. ● 목적을 가지고, 결의에 차서 부사 ❑ 그는 결의에 차서 헛간 쪽으로 성큼성큼 걸어갔다.

1 자동사 가르랑거리다 (고양이가 기분 좋을 때 내는 소리) ❑ 토실토실한 황갈색 아기 고양이가 그녀의 팔에 편안히 안겨서 열심히 가르랑거렸다. **2** 자동사 (엔진이 낮게) 부르릉거리다 ❑ 보트 두 대가 다 낮은 소리로 부르릉거리며 동굴 입구를 벗어나 넓은 바다로 나왔다. ● 단수명사 (엔진의) 부르릉거리는 소리 ❑ 카멜라는 오토바이가 부르릉거리며 집 앞 진입로를 올라오는 소리를 들었다.

1 가산명사 손가방, 핸드백 [미국영어; 영국영어 bag, handbag] ❑ 그녀는 나를 보고는 핸드백 속에서 담배를 찾았다. **2** 가산명사 지갑 [주로 영국영어; 미국영어 대개 change purse] ❑ 그녀는 지갑을 찾아 핸드백 속을 뒤졌다. **3** 단수명사 재정, 재산 ❑ 그 돈은 오로지 공공 재원에 귀속되어 세금을 낮추는 데 도움이 될 것이다. **4** 타동사 (입술을) 오므리다 ❑ 그녀는 불만스러운 입술을 삐죽거렸다.

pur|sue ◆◇◇ /pərsu:/ (pursues, pursuing, pursued) ■ V-T If you **pursue** an activity, interest, or plan, you carry it out or follow it. [FORMAL] ❏ *He said Japan would continue to pursue the policies laid down at the London summit.* ■ V-T If you **pursue** a particular aim or result, you make efforts to achieve it, often over a long period of time. [FORMAL] ❏ *The implication seems to be that it is impossible to pursue economic reform and democracy simultaneously.* ■ V-T If you **pursue** a particular topic, you try to find out more about it by asking questions. [FORMAL] ❏ *If your original request is denied, don't be afraid to pursue the matter.* ■ V-T If you **pursue** a person, vehicle, or animal, you follow them, usually in order to catch them. [FORMAL] ❏ *She pursued the man who had stolen a woman's bag.*

pur|su|er /pərsuːər, BRIT pəˈsyuːəʳ/ (pursuers) N-COUNT Your **pursuers** are the people who are chasing or searching for you. [FORMAL] ❏ *They had shaken off their pursuers.*

pur|suit /pərsuːt, BRIT pəˈsyuːt/ (pursuits) ■ N-UNCOUNT Your **pursuit of** something is your attempts at achieving it. If you do something **in pursuit of** a particular result, you do it in order to achieve that result. ❏ *...a young man whose relentless pursuit of excellence is conducted with single-minded determination.* ■ N-UNCOUNT The **pursuit of** an activity, interest, or plan consists of all the things that you do when you are carrying it out. ❏ *The vigorous pursuit of policies is no guarantee of success.* ■ N-UNCOUNT Someone who is **in pursuit of** a person, vehicle, or animal is chasing them. ❏ *...a police officer who drove a patrol car at more than 120mph in pursuit of a motor cycle.* ■ N-COUNT Your **pursuits** are your activities, usually activities that you enjoy when you are not working. ❏ *They both love outdoor pursuits.*

pur|vey|or /pərveɪər/ (purveyors) N-COUNT A **purveyor of** goods or services is a person or company that provides them. [FORMAL] ❏ *...purveyors of gourmet foods.*

push ◆◆◇ /pʊʃ/ (pushes, pushing, pushed) ■ V-T/V-I When you **push** something, you use force to make it move away from you or away from its previous position. ❏ *The woman pushed back her chair and stood up.* ❏ *They pushed him into the car.* ❏ *...a pregnant woman pushing a stroller.* • N-COUNT **Push** is also a noun. ❏ *He gave me a sharp push.* ■ V-T/V-I If you **push through** things that are blocking your way or **push** your **way through** them, you use force in order to move past them. ❏ *I pushed through the crowds and on to the escalator.* ❏ *Dix pushed forward carrying a glass.* ■ V-I If an army **pushes into** a country or area that it is attacking or invading, it moves further into it. ❏ *One detachment pushed into the eastern suburbs towards the airfield.* • N-COUNT **Push** is also a noun. ❏ *All that was needed was one final push, and the enemy would be vanquished once and for all.* ■ V-T To **push** a value or amount **up** or **down** means to cause it to increase or decrease. ❏ *Any shortage could push up grain prices.* ❏ *The government had done everything it could to push down inflation.* ■ V-T If someone or something **pushes** an idea or project in a particular direction, they cause it to develop or progress in a particular way. ❏ *China would use its influence to help push forward the peace process.* ■ V-T If you **push** someone to do something or **push** them into doing it, you encourage or force them to do it. ❏ *She thanks her parents for keeping her in school and pushing her to study.* ❏ *James did not push her into stealing the money.* • N-COUNT **Push** is also a noun. ❏ *We need a push to take the first step.* ■ V-I If you **push for** something, you try very hard to achieve it or to persuade someone to do it. ❏ *Britain's health experts are pushing for a ban on all cigarette advertising.* • N-COUNT **Push** is also a noun. ❏ *In its push for economic growth it has ignored projects that would improve living standards.* ■ V-T If someone **pushes** an idea, a point, or a product, they try in a forceful way to convince people to accept it or buy it. ❏ *Ministers will push the case for opening the plant.* ■ V-T When someone **pushes** drugs, they sell them illegally. [INFORMAL] ❏ *She was sent for trial yesterday accused of pushing drugs.* ⑩ →see also **pushed** ⑪ if **push comes to shove** →see **shove**

Thesaurus   push의 참조어

v.   drive, force, move, propel, shove, thrust; (ant.) pull ■ ■
      encourage, force, persuade, pressure, urge ■ ■ ■

Word Partnership   push의 연어

N.   push **a button**, at the push of a button, push **a door** ■
      push **prices**, push **rates** ■
      push **an agenda**, push **legislation** ■
      push **drugs** ■

▶**push ahead** or **push forward** PHRASAL VERB If you **push ahead** or **push forward with** something, you make progress with it. ❏ *The government intends to push ahead with its reform programme.*

▶**push in** PHRASAL VERB When someone **pushes in**, they unfairly join a line in front of other people who have been waiting longer. [DISAPPROVAL] ❏ *Nina pushed in next to Liddie.*

▶**push on** PHRASAL VERB When you **push on**, you continue with a journey or task. ❏ *Although the journey was a long and lonely one, Tumalo pushed on.*

▶**push over** PHRASAL VERB If you **push** someone or something **over**, you push them so that they fall onto the ground. ❏ *We have had trouble with people damaging hedges, uprooting trees, and pushing over walls.*

▶**push through** PHRASAL VERB If someone **pushes through** a law, they succeed in getting it accepted although some people oppose it. ❏ *The vote will enable the Prime Minister to push through tough policies.*

push|chair /pʊʃtʃeər/ (pushchairs) N-COUNT A **pushchair** is a small chair on wheels, in which a baby or small child can sit and be wheeled around. [BRIT; AM **stroller**]

■ 타동사 수행하다, 실행하다 [격식체] ❏ 그는 일본이 런던 정상 회의에서 공언된 정책을 계속해서 실행해 나갈 것이라고 말했다. ■ 타동사 추구하다 [격식체] ❏ 함축된 의미는 경제 개혁과 민주주의를 동시에 추구하는 것은 불가능하다는 것 같다. ■ 타동사 인구하다, 천착하다 [격식체] ❏ 당신의 원래 요구가 거부당하더라도, 두려워 말고 그것을 계속 천착하세요. ■ 타동사 추적하다 [격식체] ❏ 그녀는 어떤 여자의 가방을 훔친 남자를 추적했다.

가산명사 추적자 [격식체] ❏ 그들은 추적자들을 따돌린 참이다.

■ 불가산명사 _에 대한 추구; _을 추구하여 ❏ 번치 않는 열정으로 우수성을 추구하는 ... ■ 불가산명사 _의 수행 ❏ 정책을 열심히 수행하는 것이 성공을 보장하지는 않는다. ■ 불가산명사 _을 추적하는 ❏ 오토바이를 뒤쫓아 경찰차를 시속 120마일 이상으로 달렸던 경찰관 ■ 가산명사 취미 활동 ❏ 그들은 둘 다 야외 활동을 아주 좋아한다.

가산명사 공급 업자, 공급 회사 [격식체] ❏ 고급 식품 공급 업자

■ 타동사/자동사 밀다 ❏ 그 여자는 의자를 뒤로 밀고 일어섰다. ❏ 그들은 그를 차 안으로 밀어 넣었다. ❏ 유모차를 밀고 가는 임산부 • 가산명사 밀기 ❏ 그는 나를 세게 밀쳤다. ■ 타동사/자동사 밀치다 ❏ 나는 인파를 밀치고 에스컬레이터에 탔다. ❏ 딕스는 잔을 들고 앞으로 밀치고 나갔다. ■ 자동사 밀고 들어가다, 진격하다 ❏ 한 파견대가 비행장을 향해 동쪽 교외로 진격하면서 ... • 가산명사 진격 ❏ 이제 마지막 한 번만 진격하면 되었다. 그러면 적은 완전히 격파될 것이었다. ■ 타동사 밀어 올리다, 증가시키다; 억누르다, 감소시키다 ❏ 곡물의 조금만 부족해도 가격이 올라갈 것이다. ❏ 정부는 인플레를 억제하기 위해 할 수 있는 모든 것을 했었다. ■ 타동사 밀어붙이다 ❏ 중국은 평화 협상의 추진을 돕기 위해 영향력을 행사할 것이다. ■ 타동사 다그치다, 몰아붙이다; 독려하다 ❏ 그녀는 학교를 그만두지 않고 공부를 하도록 독려해 주신 부모님께 감사한다. ❏ 제임스가 그녀에게 돈을 훔치도록 몰아붙이지 않았다. • 가산명사 분발 ❏ 우리는 첫 발을 내딛기 위해 분발할 필요가 있다. ■ 자동사 ... 을 위해 분투하다 ❏ 영국의 건강 전문가들은 모든 담배 광고 금지를 위해 분투하고 있다. • 가산명사 분투 ❏ 국가가 경제 성장을 위해 분투하면서 생활수준을 향상시킬 계획들은 무시해 왔다. ■ 타동사 밀다 ❏ 장관들이 그 공장을 가동하기 위한 그 건을 밀어붙일 것이다. ■ 타동사 (마약을) 밀매하다 [비격식체] ❏ 그녀는 마약 밀매 혐의로 어제 재판에 회부되었다.

구동사 밀고 나아가다, 추진하다 ❏ 정부는 개혁 프로그램을 추진해 나가려고 한다.

구동사 끼어들다 [탐탁찮음] ❏ 니나가 리디 옆으로 끼어들었다.

구동사 계속하다 ❏ 길고 외로운 여행이었지만 투말로는 계속해 나아갔다.

구동사 떠밀어 넘어뜨리다 ❏ 우리는 사람들이 생울타리를 망가뜨리고, 나무를 뽑고, 담을 넘어뜨리고 해서 계속 골치를 썩어 왔다.

구동사 관철시키다 ❏ 그 투표는 수상이 강력한 정책을 관철시키도록 해 줄 것이다.

가산명사 유모차 [영국영어; 미국영어 stroller]

pushed /puʃt/ ADJ If you are **pushed for** something such as time or money, you do not have enough of it. [BRIT, INFORMAL; AM **pressed for**] [v-link ADJ, usu ADJ for n] ❑ *He's going to be a bit pushed for money.*

push·er /puʃər/ (**pushers**) N-COUNT A **pusher** is a person who sells illegal drugs. [INFORMAL] ❑ *His father accused him of acting as a carrier for some drug pushers.*

push-up (**push-ups**) N-COUNT **Push-ups** are exercises to strengthen your arms and chest muscles. They are done by lying with your face towards the floor and pushing with your hands to raise your body until your arms are straight. [AM; BRIT **press-ups**] ❑ *He did push-ups after games.*

pussy /pusi/ (**pussies**) N-COUNT **Pussy** is a child's word for a cat.

put ♦♦♦ /put/ (**puts, putting**)

> The form **put** is used in the present tense and is the past tense and past participle.

> **Put** is used in a large number of expressions which are explained under other words in this dictionary. For example, the expression **to put someone in the picture** is explained at **picture**.

1 V-T When you **put** something in a particular place or position, you move it into that place or position. ❑ *Leaphorn put the photograph on the desk.* ❑ *She hesitated, then put her hand on Grace's arm.* **2** V-T If you **put** someone somewhere, you cause them to go there and to stay there for a period of time. ❑ *Rather than put him in the hospital, she had been caring for him at home.* **3** V-T To **put** someone or something in a particular state or situation means to cause them to be in that state or situation. ❑ *This is going to put them out of business.* ❑ *He was putting himself at risk.* **4** V-T To **put** something **on** people or things means to cause them to have it, or to cause them to be affected by it. ❑ *The ruling will put extra pressure on health authorities to change working practices and shorten hours.* ❑ *Be aware of the terrible strain it can put on a child when you expect the best reports.* **5** V-T If you **put** your trust, faith, or confidence in someone or something, you trust them or have faith or confidence in them. ❑ *He had decided long ago that he would put his trust in socialism when the time came.* **6** V-T If you **put** time, strength, or energy **into** an activity, you use it in doing that activity. ❑ *We're not saying that activists should put all their effort and time into party politics.* **7** V-T If you **put** money **into** a business or project, you invest money in it. ❑ *Investors should consider putting some money into an annuity.* **8** V-T When you **put** an idea or remark in a particular way, you express it in that way. You can use expressions like **to put it simply** and **to put it bluntly** before saying something when you want to explain how you are going to express it. ❑ *I had already met Pete a couple of times through – how should I put it – friends in low places.* ❑ *He admitted the security forces might have made some mistakes, as he put it.* **9** V-T When you **put a question to** someone, you ask them the question. ❑ *Is this fair? Well, I put that question today to Craig Gillen.* **10** V-T If you **put** a case, opinion, or proposal, you explain it and list the reasons why you support or believe it. ❑ *He always put his point of view with clarity and with courage.* ❑ *He put the case to the Saudi Foreign Minister.* **11** V-T If you **put** something **at** a particular value or **in** a particular category, you consider that it has that value or that it belongs in that category. ❑ *I would put her age at about 50 or so.* ❑ *All the more technically advanced countries put a high value on science.* **12** V-T If you **put** written information somewhere, you write, type, or print it there. ❑ *Mary's family were so pleased that they put an announcement in the local paper to thank them.* ❑ *I think what I put in that book is now pretty much the agenda for this country.* **13** PHRASE If you **put it to** someone **that** something is true, you suggest that it is true, especially when you think that they will be unwilling to admit this. ❑ *But I put it to you that they're useless.* **14** PHRASE If you say that something is bigger or better than several other things **put together**, you mean that it is bigger or has more good qualities than all of those other things if they are added together. ❑ *London has more pubs and clubs than the rest of the country put together.*

▶ **put across** or **put over** PHRASAL VERB When you **put** something **across** or **put** it **over**, you succeed in describing or explaining it to someone. ❑ *He has taken out a half-page advertisement in his local paper to put his point across.*

▶ **put aside** PHRASAL VERB If you **put** something **aside**, you keep it to be dealt with or used at a later time. ❑ *Encourage children to put aside some of their pocket-money to buy Christmas presents.*

▶ **put away** PHRASAL VERB If you **put** something **away**, you put it into the place where it is normally kept when it is not being used, for example in a drawer. ❑ *She finished putting the milk away and turned around.* ❑ *"Yes, Mom," replied Cheryl as she slowly put away her doll.*

▶ **put back** PHRASAL VERB To **put** something **back** means to delay it or arrange for it to happen later than you previously planned. [mainly BRIT] ❑ *There are always new projects which seem to put the reunion back further.*

▶ **put down** **1** PHRASAL VERB If you **put** something **down** somewhere, you write or type it there. ❑ *Never put anything down on paper which might be used in evidence against you at a later date.* ❑ *We've put down on our staff development plan for this year that we would like some technology courses.* **2** PHRASAL VERB If you **put down** some money, you pay part of the price of something, and will pay the rest later. ❑ *He bought an investment property for $100,000 and put down $20,000.* **3** PHRASAL VERB When soldiers, police, or the government **put down** a riot or rebellion, they stop it by using force. ❑ *Soldiers went in to put down a rebellion.* **4** PHRASAL VERB When an animal **is put down**, it is killed because it is dangerous or very ill. [mainly BRIT] ❑ *Magistrates ordered his dog Samson to be put down immediately.*

▶ **put down to** PHRASAL VERB If you **put** something **down to** a particular thing, you believe that it is caused by that thing. ❑ *You may be a sceptic and put it down to life's inequalities.*

형용사 -에 쪼들리는 [영국영어, 비격식체; 미국영어 pressed for] ❑ 그는 돈에 좀 쪼들릴 것이다.

가산명사 밀매상 [비격식체] ❑ 그의 아버지는 그를 마약 밀매상들의 운반책 역을 했다고 비난했다.

가산명사 팔 굽혀 펴기 [미국영어; 영국영어 press-ups] ❑ 그는 경기 후 팔 굽혀 펴기를 했다.

가산명사 (유아어) 고양이

put은 동사의 현재, 과거, 과거 분사로 쓴다.

이 사전에서 put이 포함된 많은 표현들이 다른 표제어에서 설명된다. 예를 들어, to put someone in the picture는 picture에서 설명된다.

1 타동사 놓다, 두다 ❑ 립호른은 사진을 책상 위에 놓았다. ❑ 그녀는 주저하더니 자기 손을 그레이스의 팔에 올려놓았다. **2** 타동사 (사람을 -에) 있게 하다 ❑ 그녀는 그를 병원에 입원시키는 대신에 집에서 계속 돌보고 있었다. **3** 타동사 (어떤 상태로) 놓이게 하다 ❑ 이것 때문에 그들은 사업이 망할 것이다. ❑ 그는 자신을 위험에 처하게 하고 있었다. **4** 타동사 -에게 -을 가하다 ❑ 그 판결은 근로 관행을 바꾸고 근무 시간을 단축하도록 보건 당국에 추가로 압박을 가할 것이다. ❑ 아이들이 최고의 성적을 받기를 기대하는 것이 그들에게 끔찍한 부담을 줄 수 있다는 것을 생각하세요. **5** 타동사 -을 신뢰하다 ❑ 그는 때가 되면 사회주의를 신봉할 것이라고 오래전에 결심한 상태였다. **6** 타동사 -에 시간을 들이다; -에 힘을 쏟다 ❑ 우리는 활동가들이 모든 시간과 노력을 정당 정책에 쏟아 부어야 한다고 말하는 게 아니다. **7** 타동사 -에 투자하다 ❑ 투자자들은 일부 자금을 연금에 투자할 것을 고려해 보아야 한다. **8** 타동사 표현하다 ❑ 간단히 말하면, 단도직입적으로 말해서 ❑ 나는 이미 피트를 두어 번 만났는데, 어떻게 말해야 할까, 밑바닥 친구들을 통해서였다. ❑ 그 표현에 따르면, 보안대가 실수를 저질렀을지도 모른다고 그가 인정했다. **9** 타동사 -에게 질문하다 ❑ 이게 공정한가요? 글쎄요, 그 질문을 오늘은 크레이그 질런에게 드리고 싶군요. **10** 타동사 (의견 등을) 제시하다, 설명하다 ❑ 그는 항상 자기 견해를 명확하고 용기 있게 제시한다. ❑ 그는 사우디아라비아 외무장관에게 상황을 설명했다. **11** 타동사 -을 ...으로 보다; -에 두다 ❑ 나는 그녀의 나이를 대략 50세 정도로 본다. ❑ 기술적으로 더 발달한 국가들은 모두 과학에 높은 가치를 둔다. **12** 타동사 적어 넣다 ❑ 메리의 가족은 아주 기뻐서 지역 신문에 그들에게 감사하는 광고를 내었다. ❑ 나는 내가 그 책에 쓴 내용이 거의 지금 이 나라가 다루어야 할 의제라고 생각한다. **13** 구 -라고 말하다 ❑ 하지만 난 그것들이 쓸모없다고 말씀드리고 싶은데요. **14** 구 다 합친, 통합한 ❑ 런던에는 전국 다른 지역에 있는 것을 모두 합친 것보다 더 많은 술집과 클럽이 있다.

구동사 이해시키다 ❑ 그는 자기의 요점을 이해시키기 위해 지역 신문에 난 반면짜리 광고 하나를 뽑아냈다.

구동사 따로 남겨 두다, 제쳐놓다 ❑ 아이들에게 성탄절 선물을 살 수 있도록 용돈의 일부를 따로 남겨 두도록 장려하세요.

구동사 치워 두다 ❑ 그녀는 우유를 치워 두고 돌아섰다. ❑ "알았어요, 엄마."라고 체릴이 인형을 천천히 한쪽으로 치우면서 대답했다.

구동사 늦추다, 연기하다 [주로 영국영어] ❑ 재회를 뒤로 더 늦추게 만드는 것 같은 새로운 계획들이 항상 있다.

1 구동사 기입하다, 적다 ❑ 나중에 당신에게 불리한 증거로 사용될 수 있는 것은 절대 종이에 적지 마세요. ❑ 우리는 올해 직원 연수 계획에 몇 가지 기술 연수 과정을 원한다고 기입했다. **2** 구동사 계약금으로 지불하다 ❑ 그는 10만 달러짜리 부동산 투자를 했는데 2만 달러를 계약금으로 지불했다. **3** 구동사 진압하다 ❑ 군인들이 반란을 진압하기 위해 개입했다. **4** 구동사 (위험한 동물을) 도살하다 [주로 영국영어] ❑ 법정은 그의 개 삼손을 즉각 도살하라는 명령을 내렸다.

구동사 -의 탓으로 돌리다 ❑ 당신이 회의론자이고 만사가 인생이 불공평하기 때문이라고 생각할지도 모른다.

a b c d e f g h i j k l m n o p q r s t u v w x y z

▶**put forward** PHRASAL VERB If you **put forward** a plan, proposal, or name, you suggest that it should be considered for a particular purpose or job. ❑ *He has put forward new peace proposals.*

구동사 제시하다, 내세우다 ❑ 그는 새로운 평화안을 제시했다.

▶**put in** ▮ PHRASAL VERB If you **put in** an amount of time or effort doing something, you spend that time or effort doing it. ❑ *Wade was going to be paid a salary, instead of by the hour, whether he put in forty hours or not.* ❑ *They've put in time and effort to keep the strike going.* ▮ PHRASAL VERB If you **put in** a request or **put in for** something, you formally request or apply for that thing. ❑ *I also put in a request for some overtime.* ▮ PHRASAL VERB If you **put in** a remark, you interrupt someone or add to what they have said with the remark. ❑ *"He was a lawyer before that," Mary Ann put in.*

▮ 구동사 (시간이나 노력을) 들이다 ❑ 웨이드는 40시간을 일하든 그렇지 않든 시급이 아니라 월급을 받기로 되어 있었다. ❑ 그들은 파업이 계속될 수 있도록 시간과 노력을 들여왔다. ▮ 구동사 요청하다, 신청하다 ❑ 나는 초과 근무도 좀 요청했다. ▮ 구동사 참견하다 ❑ "그는 그전에 변호사였어요."라고 메리 앤이 참견했다.

▶**put off** ▮ PHRASAL VERB If you **put** something **off**, you delay doing it. ❑ *Women who put off having a baby often make the best mothers.* ▮ PHRASAL VERB If you **put** someone **off**, you make them wait for something that they want. ❑ *The old priest tried to put them off, saying that the hour was late.* ▮ PHRASAL VERB If something **puts** you **off** something, it makes you dislike it, or decide not to do or have it. ❑ *The high divorce figures don't seem to be putting people off marriage.* ❑ *His personal habits put them off.* ▮ PHRASAL VERB If someone or something **puts** you **off**, they take your attention from what you are trying to do and make it more difficult for you to do it. ❑ *She asked me to be serious – said it put her off if I laughed.*

▮ 구동사 미루다 ❑ 아기 갖기를 미루는 여자들이 흔히 최고의 엄마가 된다. ▮ 구동사 기다리게 만들다 ❑ 나이든 사제는 시간이 늦었다고 하면서 그들을 기다리게 하려고 했다. ▮ 구동사 -을 싫어하게 하다, -을 외면하게 만들다 ❑ 이혼율이 높은 게 사람들이 결혼을 외면하게 만들지는 않는 것 같다. ❑ 그의 개인적인 버릇이 그들을 멀어지게 했다. ▮ 구동사 방해하다 ❑ 그녀는 내게 진지하게 하라고 하면서, 내가 웃으면 집중할 수가 없다고 말했다.

▶**put on** ▮ PHRASAL VERB When you **put on** clothing or make-up, you place it on your body in order to wear it. ❑ *She put on her coat and went out.* ❑ *Maximo put on a pair of glasses.* ▮ PHRASAL VERB When people **put on** a show, exhibition, or service, they perform it or organize it. ❑ *The band are hoping to put on a UK show before the end of the year.* ❑ *British Airways is putting on an extra flight to London tomorrow.* ▮ PHRASAL VERB If someone **puts on** weight, they become heavier. ❑ *I can eat what I want but I never put on weight.* ▮ PHRASAL VERB If you **put on** a piece of equipment or a device, you make it start working, for example by pressing a switch or turning a knob. ❑ *I put the radio on.* ▮ PHRASAL VERB If you **put a** record, tape, or CD **on**, you place it in a record, tape, or CD player and listen to it. ❑ *She poured them drinks, and put a record on loud.*

▮ 구동사 입다; 쓰다; 신다; (화장을) 하다 ❑ 그녀는 코트를 입고 밖으로 나갔다. ❑ 맥시모는 안경을 썼다. ▮ 구동사 (공연 등을) 하다, 무대에 올리다; (서비스를) 제공하다 ❑ 그 밴드는 올해가 가기 전에 영국 공연을 희망하고 있다. ❑ 영국 항공은 내일 런던 행 편수를 추가로 늘린다. ▮ 구동사 (체중이) 늘다, (살이) 찌다 ❑ 나는 원하는 것을 다 먹어도 절대 살이 찌지 않는다. ▮ 구동사 (장치를) 켜다 ❑ 나는 라디오를 켰다. ▮ 구동사 (시디 등을) 틀다 ❑ 그녀는 그들에게 술을 부어 주고 레코드를 크게 틀었다.

▶**put out** ▮ PHRASAL VERB If you **put out** an announcement or story, you make it known to a lot of people. ❑ *The French news agency put out a statement from the Trade Minister.* ▮ PHRASAL VERB If you **put out** a fire, candle, or cigarette, you make it stop burning. ❑ *Firemen tried to free the injured and put out the blaze.* ▮ PHRASAL VERB If you **put out** an electric light, you make it stop shining by pressing a switch. ❑ *He crossed to the bedside table and put out the light.* ▮ PHRASAL VERB If you **put out** things that will be needed, you place them somewhere ready to be used. ❑ *Paula had put out her luggage for the coach.* ▮ PHRASAL VERB If you **put out** your **hand**, you move it forward, away from your body. ❑ *He put out his hand to Alfred.* ▮ PHRASAL VERB If you **put** someone **out**, you cause them trouble because they have to do something for you. ❑ *It is a very sociable diet to follow because you don't have to put anyone out.* ▮ →see also **put out**

▮ 구동사 (발표 등을) 내보내다 ❑ 프랑스 통신사는 통상 장관의 발표를 내보냈다. ▮ 구동사 (불을) 끄다 ❑ 소방대원들은 부상자들을 구하고 화재를 진압하려고 애썼다. ▮ 구동사 (전등을) 끄다 ❑ 그는 침대 옆 탁자로 건너가서 전등을 껐다. ▮ 구동사 준비해 두다 ❑ 폴라는 버스에 싣기 위해 짐을 내놓았다. ▮ 구동사 손을 내밀다 ❑ 그는 알프레드에게 손을 내밀었다. ▮ 구동사 -을 귀찮게 하다 ❑ 그것은 다른 사람을 귀찮게 할 필요가 없기 때문에 아주 사교적인 식습관이다.

▶**put over** →see **put across**

▶**put through** ▮ PHRASAL VERB When someone **puts through** someone who is making a telephone call, they make the connection that allows the telephone call to take place. ❑ *The operator will put you through.* ▮ PHRASAL VERB If someone **puts** you **through** an unpleasant experience, they make you experience it. ❑ *She wouldn't want to put them through the ordeal of a huge ceremony.*

▮ 구동사 전화에 연결하다 ❑ 교환원이 연결해 드릴 겁니다. ▮ 구동사 -을 겪게 만들다 ❑ 그녀는 그들이 거대한 예식에 참석하는 고충을 겪게 하고 싶지 않을 것이다.

▶**put together** ▮ PHRASAL VERB If you **put** something **together**, you join its different parts to each other so that it can be used. ❑ *He took it apart brick by brick, and put it back together again.* ▮ PHRASAL VERB If you **put together** a group of people or things, you form them into a team or collection. ❑ *It will be able to put together a governing coalition.* ▮ PHRASAL VERB If you **put together** an agreement, plan, or product, you design and create it. ❑ *We wouldn't have time to put together an agreement.* ❑ *Reports speak of Berlin putting together an aid package for Moscow.* →see also **put 14**

▮ 구동사 조립하다 ❑ 그는 그것을 하나하나 분해한 다음 다시 조립했다. ▮ 구동사 모으다, 구성하다 ❑ 그러한 통치 연합체를 구성할 수 있을 것이다. ▮ 구동사 계획하다, 만들어 내다 ❑ 우리는 합의를 도출해 낼 시간이 없을 것이다. ❑ 보고서에 의하면 독일이 러시아를 위한 종합 구호 정책을 계획하고 있다고 한다.

▶**put up** ▮ PHRASAL VERB If people **put up** a wall, building, tent, or other structure, they construct it so that it is upright. ❑ *Protesters have been putting up barricades across a number of major intersections.* ▮ PHRASAL VERB If you **put up** a poster or notice, you fix it to a wall or board. ❑ *They're putting new street signs up.* ▮ PHRASAL VERB To **put up** resistance to something means to resist it. ❑ *In the end the Kurds surrendered without putting up any resistance.* ❑ *He'd put up a real fight to keep you there.* ▮ PHRASAL VERB If you **put up** money for something, you provide the money that is needed to pay for it. ❑ *The state agreed to put up $69,000 to start his company.* ▮ PHRASAL VERB To **put up** the price of something means to cause it to increase. ❑ *Their friends suggested they should put up their prices.* ▮ PHRASAL VERB If a person or hotel **puts** you **up** or if you **put up** somewhere, you stay there for one or more nights. ❑ *I wanted to know if she could put me up for a few days.* ❑ *Hundreds of junior civil servants have to be put up in hotel rooms and temporary hostels.* ▮ PHRASAL VERB If a political party **puts up** a candidate in an election or if the candidate **puts up**, the candidate takes part in the election. ❑ *The new party is putting up 15 candidates for 22 seats.*

▮ 구동사 세우다, 설치하다 ❑ 시위대가 상당수의 주요 교차로에 바리케이드를 설치하고 있다. ▮ 구동사 게시하다 ❑ 새로운 거리 표지판이 붙여지고 있다. ▮ 구동사 (저항 등을) 하다 ❑ 결국 쿠르드 인들은 아무런 저항도 하지 못하고 항복했다. ❑ 그는 너를 그 자리에 두기 위해 한바탕 싸움을 할 것이다. ▮ 구동사 (돈을) 내다 ❑ 주 정부는 그의 회사를 설립하는 데 6만 9천 달러를 내기로 합의했다. ▮ 구동사 (값을) 올리다 ❑ 그들의 친구들은 값을 올릴 것을 제의했다. ▮ 구동사 재워 주다, 묵다 ❑ 나는 그녀가 나를 며칠 재워 줄 수 있는지 알고 싶었다. ❑ 수백 명의 하급 공무원들이 호텔 방과 임시 호스텔에 묵어야만 한다. ▮ 구동사 출마시키다; 출마하다 ❑ 새 정당은 22개 의석에 15명의 후보를 출마시키고 있다.

▶**put up with** PHRASAL VERB If you **put up with** something, you tolerate or accept it, even though you find it unpleasant or unsatisfactory. ❑ *They had put up with behavior from their son which they would not have tolerated from anyone else.*

구동사 -을 참다 ❑ 그들은 다른 사람의 행동이었으면 참지 못했을 텐데 자기들 아들의 행동은 참았었다.

put out ADJ If you feel **put out**, you feel rather annoyed or upset. [v-link ADJ] ❑ *I did not blame him for feeling put out.*

형용사 화난 ❑ 나는 그가 화내는 것을 탓하지 않았다.

putt /pʌt/ (**putts, putting, putted**) ▮ N-COUNT A **putt** is a stroke in golf that you make when the ball has reached the green in an attempt to get the ball in the hole. ❑ *...a 5-foot putt.* ▮ V-I In golf, when you **putt** the ball, you hit a putt. ❑ *Turner, however, putted superbly, twice holing from 40 feet.*

▮ 가산명사 (골프) 퍼트 ❑ 5피트 거리의 퍼트 ▮ 자동사 퍼트하다 ❑ 그러나 터너는 멋지게 퍼트를 해서 40피트 거리에서 공을 두 번째로 홀에 넣었다.

puz|zle /pʌzᵊl/ (puzzles) ◼ v-т If something **puzzles** you, you do not understand it and feel confused. ❑ *My sister puzzles me and causes me anxiety.* ● **puz|zling** ADJ ❑ *His letter poses a number of puzzling questions.* ◾ v-ı If you **puzzle over** something, you try hard to think of the answer to it or the explanation for it. ❑ *In rehearsing Shakespeare, I puzzle over the complexities of his verse and prose.* ◾ N-COUNT A **puzzle** is a question, game, or toy which you have to think about carefully in order to answer it correctly or put it together properly. [oft supp N] ❑ *...a word puzzle.* →see also **crossword** ◾ N-SING You can describe a person or thing that is hard to understand as **a puzzle.** [*a* N] ❑ *Data from Voyager II has presented astronomers with a puzzle about why our outermost planet exists.*

puz|zled /pʌzᵊld/ ADJ Someone who is **puzzled** is confused because they do not understand something. ❑ *Critics remain puzzled by the British election results.*

PVC /pi vi si/ N-UNCOUNT **PVC** is a plastic material that is used for many purposes, for example to make clothing or shoes or to cover chairs. **PVC** is an abbreviation for "polyvinyl chloride."

py|ja|mas /pɪdʒɑməz/ →see **pajamas**

pyra|mid /pɪrəmɪd/ (pyramids) ◼ N-COUNT **Pyramids** are ancient stone buildings with four triangular sloping sides. The most famous pyramids are those built in ancient Egypt to contain the bodies of their kings and queens. ❑ *We set off to see the Pyramids and Sphinx.* ◾ N-COUNT A **pyramid** is a shape, object, or pile of things with a flat base and sloping triangular sides that meet at a point. ❑ *On a plate in front of him was piled a pyramid of flat white biscuits.* ◾ N-COUNT You can describe something as a **pyramid** when it is organized so that there are fewer people at each level as you go towards the top. ❑ *Traditionally, the Brahmins, or the priestly class, are set at the top of the social pyramid.* →see **volume**

pyra|mid sell|ing N-UNCOUNT **Pyramid selling** is a method of selling in which one person buys a supply of a particular product direct from the manufacturer and then sells it to a number of other people at an increased price. These people sell it on to others in a similar way, but eventually the final buyers are only able to sell the product for less than they paid for it. [BUSINESS] ❑ *If the scheme appears to be a pyramid selling scam, have nothing to do with it.*

py|thon /paɪθɒn, -θən/ (pythons) N-COUNT A **python** is a large snake that kills animals by squeezing them with its body.

◼ 타동사 곤혹스럽게 하다 ❑ 내 누이는 나를 곤혹스럽게 만들고 걱정을 끼친다. ● 곤혹하게 하는 형용사 ❑ 그의 편지는 많은 곤혹스런 질문들을 제기하고 있다. ◾ 자동사 ~을 두고 머리를 짜다, ~을 두고 머리를 싸매다 ❑ 셰익스피어 작품을 리허설 할 때, 나는 그의 운문과 산문의 복잡함에 머리를 싸맸다. ◾ 가산명사 수수께끼, 알아맞히기 게임; 퍼즐 [주로 보충어 N] ❑ 단어 알아맞히기 ◾ 단수명사 이해하기 어려운 사람; 골칫거리 ❑ 보이저 2호로부터 온 자료는 천문학자들에게 왜 지구에서 가장 먼 행성이 존재하는지에 대한 난제를 세공했다.

형용사 어리둥절한, 혼란스러운 ❑ 비평가들은 영국의 선거 결과에 계속 어리둥절해 하고 있다.

불가산명사 플라스틱 물질, polyvinyl chloride의 약자

◼ 가산명사 피라미드 ❑ 우리는 피라미드와 스핑크스를 보러 떠났다. ◾ 가산명사 피라미드 모양의 것 ❑ 그의 앞에 놓인 접시에 납작하고 하얀 비스킷이 피라미드처럼 쌓여 있었다. ◾ 가산명사 피라미드 조직 ❑ 전통적으로 브라민, 즉 승려 계급이 사회 피라미드 조직의 맨 위에 있다.

불가산명사 다단계 판매, 피라미드식 판매 [경제] ❑ 그 계획이 다단계 판매 사기처럼 보이면 그것에 관여하지 마세요.

가산명사 비단뱀

Qq

Q, q /kyu/ (Q's, q's) N-VAR Q is the seventeenth letter of the English alphabet.

가산명사 또는 불가산명사 영어 알파벳의 열일곱 번째 글자

Q & A /kyu ən eɪ/ or **Q and A** N-UNCOUNT Q & A is a situation in which a person or group of people asks questions and another person or group of people answers them. Q & A is short for "question and answer." ❑ About 10 years ago, I went to a Q & A session with a prominent politician.

불가산명사 질의응답 ❑ 한 10년 전쯤, 나는 어느 저명한 정치인이 자리한 질의응답 시간에 참석하였다.

quad|ru|ple /kwɒdrupᵊl/ (quadruples, quadrupling, quadrupled) **1** V-T/V-I If someone **quadruples** an amount or if it **quadruples**, it becomes four times bigger. ❑ China seeks to quadruple its income in twenty years. **2** PREDET If one amount is **quadruple** another amount, it is four times bigger. [PREDET det n] ❑ Fifty-nine percent of its residents have attended graduate school – quadruple the national average. **3** ADJ You use **quadruple** to indicate that something has four parts or happens four times. [ADJ n] ❑ The quadruple murder has replaced property prices as the sole topic of interest.

1 타동사/자동사 네 배로 늘리다 ❑ 중국은 20년 후에는 소득을 네 배로 늘리고자 한다. **2** 전치 한정사 네 배의 ❑ 주민의 59퍼센트가 대학원에 다녔다. 이는 전국 평균의 네 배에 달하는 수치이다. **3** 형용사 네 부분으로 이루어진; 네 차례의 ❑ 네 건의 살인 사건이 부동산 가격을 제치고 유일한 관심사로 떠올랐다.

quaint /kweɪnt/ (quainter, quaintest) ADJ Something that is **quaint** is attractive because it is unusual and rather old-fashioned. ❑ ...a small, quaint town with narrow streets and traditional half-timbered houses.

형용사 예스러운 ❑ 좁은 거리와 전통적인 반목조 가옥들이 있는 조그마한 예스러운 마을

quake /kweɪk/ (quakes, quaking, quaked) **1** N-COUNT A **quake** is the same as an **earthquake**. ❑ The quake destroyed mud buildings in many remote villages. **2** V-I If you **quake**, you shake, usually because you are very afraid. ❑ I just stood there quaking with fear. **3** PHRASE If you **are quaking in** your **boots** or **quaking in** your **shoes**, you feel very nervous or afraid, and may be feeling slightly weak as a result. ❑ If you stand up straight, you'll give an impression of self-confidence, even if you're quaking in your boots.

1 가산명사 지진 ❑ 많은 외딴 마을에서 토옥들이 지진에 파괴되었다. **2** 자동사 (두려워서 몸을) 떨다 ❑ 나는 그저 두려움에 몸을 떨며 거기에 서 있었다. **3** 구 오금이 저리다 ❑ 비록 오금이 저릴지라도 똑바로 서 있기만 하면 자신감이 있어 보인다는 인상을 줄 것이다.

quali|fi|ca|tion /kwɒlɪfɪkeɪʃᵊn/ (qualifications) **1** N-COUNT Your **qualifications** are the examinations that you have passed. ❑ Lucy Thomson, 16, wants to study theater but needs more qualifications. **2** N-UNCOUNT **Qualification** is the act of passing the examinations you need to work in a particular profession. ❑ Following qualification, he worked as a social worker. **3** N-COUNT The **qualifications** you need for an activity or task are the qualities and skills that you need to be able to do it. ❑ Responsibility and reliability are necessary qualifications, as well as a friendly and outgoing personality. **4** N-VAR A **qualification** is a detail or explanation that you add to a statement to make it less strong or less general. ❑ The empirical evidence considered here is subject to many qualifications.

1 가산명사 자격 ❑ 열여섯 살의 루시 톰슨은 연극을 전공하고 싶어 하지만 자격이 모자란다. **2** 불가산명사 자격 취득 ❑ 자격 취득 후 그는 사회 복지사로 일했다. **3** 가산명사 자질, 자격 ❑ 친절하고 외향적인 성격뿐만 아니라 책임감과 신뢰감도 필요한 자질이다. **4** 가산명사 또는 불가산명사 단서(但書), 조건 ❑ 현재 고려 중인 경험적인 증거에는 많은 단서가 붙어야 한다.

Thesaurus
qualification의 참조어

N.   capability, proficiency, skill **3**
       condition **4**

Word Partnership
qualification의 연어

N.   qualification **for a job, standards for** qualification **3**
ADJ.   **necessary** qualification **3**
PREP.   **without** qualification **3 4**

---

quali|fied ◆◇◇ /kwɒlɪfaɪd/ **1** ADJ Someone who is **qualified** has passed the examinations that they need to pass in order to work in a particular profession. ❑ Demand has far outstripped supply of qualified teachers. **2** ADJ If you give someone or something **qualified** support or approval, your support or approval is not total because you have some doubts. [ADJ n] ❑ The government has in the past given qualified support to the idea of tightening the legislation. **3** PHRASE If you describe something as a **qualified success**, you mean that it is only partly successful. ❑ Even as a humanitarian mission it has been only a qualified success.

1 형용사 자격을 갖춘 ❑ 자격을 갖춘 교사에 대한 수요가 공급을 훨씬 앞질렀다. **2** 형용사 부분적인, 제한적인 ❑ 과거에 정부는 법률을 강화하는 방안에 대해 제한적인 지지를 해 왔다. **3** 구 절반의 성공 ❑ 단순히 인도적 차원의 파견이라고 여긴다 해도 그것은 절반의 성공만을 거두었다.

quali|fi|er /kwɒlɪfaɪər/ (qualifiers) **1** N-COUNT A **qualifier** is an early round or match in some competitions. The players or teams who are successful are able to continue to the next round or to the main competition. ❑ Last week Wales lost 5-1 to Romania in a World Cup qualifier. **2** →see also qualify

1 가산명사 예선전 ❑ 웨일스는 지난주에 열린 월드컵 예선전에서 루마니아에 5대 1로 패했다.

quali|fy ◆◇◇ /kwɒlɪfaɪ/ (qualifies, qualifying, qualified) **1** V-T When someone **qualifies**, they pass the examinations that they need to be able to work in a particular profession. ❑ But when I'd qualified and started teaching it was a different story. **2** V-T/V-I If you **qualify** for something or if something **qualifies** you for it, you have the right to do it or have it. ❑ To qualify for maternity leave you must have worked for the same employer for two years. ❑ The basic course does not qualify you to practise as a therapist. **3** V-T/V-I To **qualify as** something or to **be qualified as** something means to have all the features that are needed to be that thing. ❑ 13 percent of American households qualify as poor, says Mr. Mishel. **4** V-I If you **qualify**

1 타동사 (시험을 통과하여) 자격을 취득하다 ❑ 하지만 내가 교사 자격을 딴 후 실제로 가르치는 일을 시작했을 때는 사정이 달랐다. **2** 타동사/자동사 자격이 있다; 자격을 갖게 하다 ❑ 출산 휴가를 받을 자격을 갖기 위해서는 2년 이상 근무해야 한다. ❑ 기초 과정을 수강한다고 치료사로 활동할 수 있는 자격이 주어지지는 않는다. **3** 타동사/자동사 자격을 갖추다 ❑ 미국 전체 가구의 13퍼센트가 빈곤층에 든다고 미셸 씨는 말한다. **4** 자동사 예선을 통과하다 ❑ 화요일에

in a competition, you are successful in one part of it and go on to the next stage. ❏ *Nottingham Forest qualified for the final by beating Tranmere on Tuesday.* ● **qualifier** (**qualifiers**) N-COUNT ❏ *Kenya's Robert Kibe was the fastest qualifier for the 800 meters final.* ⑤ V-T If you **qualify** a statement, you make it less strong or less general by adding a detail or explanation to it. ❏ *I would qualify that by putting it into context.* ⑥ →see also **qualified**

노팅엄 포레스트가 트랜미어를 꺾고 결승에 진출했다. ● 예선 통과자 가산명사 ❏ 케냐의 로버트 키브가 가장 빠른 기록으로 800미터 결승에 진출했다. ⑤ 타동사 (진술 등을) 수정하다, 조건을 달다 ❏ 전후 사정과 함께 다시 말씀을 드리겠습니다.

<table>
<tr><td colspan="2">**Word Partnership**   *qualify*의 연어</td></tr>
<tr><td>PREP.</td><td>qualify **as** *something* ⑤
qualify **for** *something* ②</td></tr>
<tr><td>V.</td><td>**chance to** qualify, **fail to** qualify ①-⑤</td></tr>
</table>

qualitative /kwɒlɪteɪtɪv, BRIT -tət-/ ADJ **Qualitative** means relating to the nature or standard of something, rather than to its quantity. [FORMAL] ❏ *There are qualitative differences in the way children of different ages and adults think.*

형용사 질적 (연구)의, 질적인 [격식체] ❏ 다양한 연령대의 아이들과 성인들의 사고방식 간에는 질적인 차이가 있다.

quality ♦♦♢ /kwɒlɪti/ (**qualities**) ① N-UNCOUNT The **quality** of something is how good or bad it is. ❏ *Everyone can greatly improve the quality of life.* ② N-UNCOUNT Something of **quality** is of a high standard. ❏ *...a college of quality.* ③ N-COUNT Someone's **qualities** are the good characteristics that they have which are part of their nature. ❏ *Sometimes you wonder where your kids get their good qualities.* ④ N-COUNT You can describe a particular characteristic of a person or thing as a **quality**. ❏ *...a childlike quality.*

① 불가산명사 질(質) ❏ 모든 사람이 삶의 질을 크게 향상시킬 수 있다. ② 불가산명사 좋은 품질, 우수함 ❏ 우수 대학 ③ 가산명사 (좋은) 성품 ❏ 이따금씩 여러분들은 자녀들이 훌륭한 성품을 어디서 얻은까 궁금해 하시지요. ④ 가산명사 성격, 특징 ❏ 어린애 같은 성격

<table>
<tr><td colspan="2">**Thesaurus**   *quality*의 참조어</td></tr>
<tr><td>N.</td><td>class, kind, position, rank, virtue, worth ①
aspect, attribute, characteristic, feature, trait ④</td></tr>
</table>

<table>
<tr><td colspan="2">**Word Partnership**   *quality*의 연어</td></tr>
<tr><td>N.</td><td>**air** quality, quality **of life**, quality **of service**, **water** quality, quality **of work** ①</td></tr>
<tr><td>ADJ.</td><td>**best/better/good** quality, **high/higher** quality, **low** quality, **poor** quality, **top** quality ① ②</td></tr>
</table>

quality control N-UNCOUNT In an organization that produces goods or provides services, **quality control** is the activity of checking that the goods or services are of an acceptable standard. [BUSINESS] ❏ *Mismanagement in the rail industry led to negligence. There was no quality control anywhere.*

불가산명사 품질 관리 [경제] ❏ 철도 업계의 관리 소홀이 업무 태만을 초래했다. 품질 관리라고는 어디에서도 찾아볼 수가 없었다.

quality time N-UNCOUNT If people spend **quality time** together, they spend a period of time relaxing or doing things that they both enjoy, and not worrying about work or other responsibilities. [APPROVAL] ❏ *Today I can spend quality time with my family for a change.*

불가산명사 즐거운 시간 [마음에 듦] ❏ 오늘은 가족들과 단란한 시간을 보내며 기분 전환 좀 할 수 있겠다.

qualm /kwɑm/ (**qualms**) N-COUNT If you have no **qualms** about doing something, you are not worried that it may be wrong in some way. ❏ *I have no qualms about recommending the same approach to other doctors.*

가산명사 거리낌 ❏ 나는 아무 거리낌 없이 다른 의사들에게도 같은 방법을 추천한다.

<table>
<tr><td colspan="2">**Word Link**   quant ≈ how much : *quantify*, *quantitative*, *quantity*</td></tr>
</table>

quantify /kwɒntɪfaɪ/ (**quantifies**, **quantifying**, **quantified**) V-T If you try to **quantify** something, you try to calculate how much of it there is. [usu with brd-neg] ❏ *It is difficult to quantify an exact figure as firms are reluctant to declare their losses.*

타동사 양을 말하다, 양을 재다 ❏ 기업은 손실을 공개하기를 꺼리므로, 손실의 정확한 수치를 말하기 어렵다.

quantitative /kwɒntɪteɪtɪv, BRIT -tət-/ ADJ **Quantitative** means relating to different sizes or amounts of things. [FORMAL] ❏ *...the advantages of quantitative and qualitative research.*

형용사 양적인, 양에 관한 [격식체] ❏ 정량(定量) 및 정성(定性)적 연구의 이점

quantity ♦♢♢ /kwɒntɪti/ (**quantities**) ① N-VAR A **quantity** is an amount that you can measure or count. ❏ *...a small quantity of water.* ② N-UNCOUNT Things that are produced or available in **quantity** are produced or available in large amounts. ❏ *After some initial problems, acetone was successfully produced in quantity.* ③ N-UNCOUNT You can use **quantity** to refer to the amount of something that there is, especially when you want to contrast it with its quality. ❏ *...the less discerning drinker who prefers quantity to quality.* ④ PHRASE If you say that someone or something is an **unknown quantity**, you mean that not much is known about what they are like or how they will behave. ❏ *She had known Max for some years now, but he was still pretty much an unknown quantity.* →see **mathematics**

① 가산명사 또는 불가산명사 양 ❏ 적은 양의 물 ② 불가산명사 다량 ❏ 초기에 약간의 문제가 있은 뒤로, 아세톤을 다량으로 생산하는 데 성공하였다. ③ 불가산명사 양 ❏ 질보다 양을 선호하는 분별력이 떨어지는 음주가 ④ 구 알 수 없는 것, 알 수 없는 사람 ❏ 그녀가 맥스를 알게 된 지 이제 여러 해 되었지만, 여전히 그는 거의 알 수 없는 사람이었다.

quantity surveyor (**quantity surveyors**) N-COUNT A **quantity surveyor** is a person who calculates the cost and amount of materials and workers needed for a job such as building a house or a road. [BRIT] ❏ *Architects, engineers, and quantity surveyors have set the cost at $7 million.*

가산명사 (건축) 견적사(見積士) [영국영어] ❏ 건축가, 기술자 그리고 견적사들이 비용을 7백만 달러로 책정하였다.

quantum /kwɒntəm/ ① ADJ In physics, **quantum** theory and **quantum** mechanics are concerned with the behavior of atomic particles. [ADJ n] ❏ *Both quantum mechanics and chaos theory suggest a world constantly in flux.* ② ADJ A **quantum leap** or **quantum jump** in something is a very great and sudden increase in its size, amount, or quality. [ADJ n] ❏ *A vaccine which can halt this suffering represents a quantum leap in healthcare in this country.*

① 형용사 (물리) 양자(量子 f)의 ❏ 양자 역학과 카오스 이론 둘 다 세상은 끊임없이 변화함을 시사한다. ② 형용사 비약적인 발전, 약진(躍進)의 ❏ 이러한 고통을 멈추게 하는 백신은 이 나라 의료계의 비약적인 발전을 보여 준다.

quarantine /kwɒrəntin, BRIT kwɒr-/ (**quarantines**, **quarantining**, **quarantined**) ① N-UNCOUNT If a person or animal is **in quarantine**, they are being kept separate from other people or animals for a set period of time, usually because they have or may have a disease. ❏ *She was sent home to Oxford and put in quarantine.* ② V-T If people or animals **are quarantined**, they are stopped from having contact with other people or animals. If a place **is**

① 불가산명사 격리 ❏ 그녀는 격리되어 옥스퍼드에 있는 집으로 보내졌다. ② 타동사 격리되다 ❏ 개는 국내로 들어오기 전에 6개월 동안 격리시켜 놓아야 한다.

a b c d e f g h i j k l m n o p q r s t u v w x y z

quarantined, people and animals are prevented from entering or leaving it. [usu passive] ❑ *Dogs have to be quarantined for six months before they'll let them in.* →see **illness**

quar|rel /ˈkwɒrəl, BRIT ˈkwɒri-/ (**quarrels, quarrelling, quarrelled**) [AM **quarreling, quarreled**] ◼ N-COUNT A **quarrel** is an angry argument between two or more friends or family members. ❑ *I had a terrible quarrel with my other brothers.* ◻ N-COUNT **Quarrels** between countries or groups of people are disagreements, which may be diplomatic or include fighting. [JOURNALISM] ❑ *New Zealand's quarrel with France over the Rainbow Warrior incident was formally ended.* ◼ V-RECIP When two or more people **quarrel**, they have an angry argument. ❑ *At one point we quarrelled, over something silly.* ◼ N-SING If you say that you have no **quarrel** with someone or something, you mean that you do not disagree with them. ❑ *We have no quarrel with the people of Spain or of any other country.*

quar|ry /ˈkwɒri, BRIT ˈkwɒri/ (**quarries, quarrying, quarried**) ◼ N-COUNT A **quarry** is an area that is dug out from a piece of land or the side of a mountain in order to get stone or minerals. ❑ *...an old limestone quarry.* ◻ V-T When stone or minerals **are quarried** or when an area **is quarried** for them, they are removed from the area by digging, drilling, or using explosives. ❑ *The large limestone caves are also quarried for cement.*

Word Link   quart ≈ four : *quart, quarter, quartet*

---

quart /ˈkwɔrt/ (**quarts**) N-COUNT A **quart** is a unit of volume that is equal to two pints. ❑ *Pick up a quart of milk or a loaf of bread.*

quar|ter ◆◆◇ /ˈkwɔrtər/ (**quarters, quartering, quartered**) ◼ FRACTION A **quarter** is one of four equal parts of something. ❑ *A quarter of the residents are over 55 years old.* ❑ *Prices have fallen by a quarter since January.* ● PREDET **Quarter** is also a predeterminer. ❑ *The largest asteroid is Ceres, which is about a quarter the size of the moon.* ● ADJ **Quarter** is also an adjective. [ADJ n] ❑ *...the past quarter century.* ◻ N-COUNT A **quarter** is a fixed period of three months. Companies often divide their financial year into four quarters. ❑ *The group said results for the third quarter are due on October 29.* ◼ N-UNCOUNT When you are telling the time, you use **quarter** to talk about the fifteen minutes before or after an hour. For example, 8.15 is a **quarter past** eight, and 8.45 is a **quarter to** nine. In American English, you can also say that 8.15 is a **quarter after** eight and 8.45 is a **quarter of** nine. [also a n] ❑ *It was a quarter to six.* ◼ V-T If you **quarter** something such as a fruit or a vegetable, you cut it into four roughly equal parts. ❑ *Chop the mushrooms and quarter the tomatoes.* ◼ V-T If the number or size of something **is quartered**, it is reduced to about a quarter of its previous number or size. [usu passive] ❑ *The doses I suggested for adults could be halved or quartered.* ◼ N-COUNT A **quarter** is an American or Canadian coin that is worth 25 cents. ❑ *I dropped a quarter into the slot of the pay phone.* ◼ N-COUNT A particular **quarter** of a town is a part of the town where a particular group of people traditionally live or work. ❑ *We wandered through the Chinese quarter.* ◼ PHRASE If you do something **at close quarters**, you do it very near to a particular person or thing. ❑ *You can watch aircraft take off or land at close quarters.*

Word Partnership   quarter의 연어

N.	**quarter (of a) century**, **quarter (of a) pound** ◼
ADJ.	**first/fourth/second/third** quarter ◻
PREP.	**for the** quarter, **in the** quarter ◻
	quarter **after**, quarter **of**, quarter **past**, quarter **to** ◼

---

quarter-final (**quarter-finals**) [AM **quarterfinal**] N-COUNT A **quarter-final** is one of the four matches in a competition which decides which four players or teams will compete in the semi-final. ❑ *The very least I'm looking for at Wimbledon is to reach the quarter-finals.*

quar|ter|ly /ˈkwɔrtərli/ (**quarterlies**) ◼ ADJ A **quarterly** event happens four times a year, at intervals of three months. ❑ *...the latest Bank of Japan quarterly survey of 5,000 companies.* ● ADV **Quarterly** is also an adverb. [ADV after v] ❑ *It makes no difference whether dividends are paid quarterly or annually.* ◻ N-COUNT A **quarterly** is a magazine that is published four times a year, at intervals of three months. ❑ *The quarterly had been a forum for sound academic debate.*

quar|tet /ˈkwɔrtɛt/ (**quartets**) ◼ N-COUNT-COLL A **quartet** is a group of four people who play musical instruments or sing together. ❑ *...a string quartet.* ◻ N-COUNT A **quartet** is a piece of music for four instruments or four singers. ❑ *The String Quartet No 1 is an early work, composed in California in 1941.*

quartz /ˈkwɔrts/ N-UNCOUNT **Quartz** is a mineral in the form of a hard, shiny crystal. It is used in making electronic equipment and very accurate watches and clocks. ❑ *...a quartz crystal.*

quash /ˈkwɒʃ/ (**quashes, quashing, quashed**) ◼ V-T If a court or someone in authority **quashes** a decision or judgment, they officially reject it. ❑ *The Appeal Court has quashed the convictions of all eleven people.* ◻ V-T If someone **quashes** rumors, they say or do something to demonstrate that the rumors are not true. ❑ *Graham attempted to quash rumors of growing discontent in the dressing room.* ◼ V-T To **quash** a rebellion or protest means to stop it, often in a violent way. ❑ *Troops were displaying an obvious reluctance to get involved in quashing demonstrations.*

quay /ˈki/ (**quays**) N-COUNT A **quay** is a long platform beside the sea or a river where boats can be tied up and loaded or unloaded. ❑ *Jack and Stephen were waiting for them on the quay.*

[미국영어 quarreling, quarreled] ◼ 가산명사 말다툼 ❑ 나는 형제들과 심한 말다툼을 했다. ◻ 가산명사 불화 [언론] ❑ 레인보우 워리어 사건을 둘러싼 뉴질랜드와 프랑스 사이의 불화가 공식적으로는 종식되었다. ◼ 상호동사 말다툼하다 ❑ 우리는 한때 하찮은 것을 두고 말다툼을 하였다. ◼ 단수명사 불평, 불만 ❑ 우리는 스페인 사람들에게든 다른 어떤 나라 사람들에게든 아무런 불만이 없다.

◼ 가산명사 채석장 ❑ 예전의 석회암 채석장 ◻ 타동사 채석하다 ❑ 대형 석회 동굴들에서는 시멘트 원료 채석 작업도 진행된다.

가산명사 쿼트 (약 1리터) ❑ 우유 1쿼트나 빵 한 줄 좀 사오세요.

◼ 분수 4분의 1 ❑ 주민들의 4분의 1이 55세 이상이다. ❑ 1월 이후로 물가가 25퍼센트 떨어졌다. ● 전치 한정사 -의 4분의 1 ❑ 가장 큰 소행성은 케레스로, 크기는 달의 4분의 1 정도이다. ● 형용사 4분의 1의 ❑ 지난 사반세기 ◻ 가산명사 1분기 (3개월) ❑ 그 기업은 3분기 실적을 10월 29일에 발표하겠다고 밝혔다. ◼ 불가산명사 15분 ❑ 6시 15분 전이었다. ◼ 타동사 4등분하다 ❑ 버섯은 다지고 토마토는 4등분 하세요. ◼ 타동사 4분의 1로 줄이다 ❑ 제가 제시한 성인 복용량을 반이나 4분의 1로 줄여도 좋습니다. ◼ 가산명사 1쿼터짜리 동전 (25센트) ❑ 나는 공중전화의 동전 투입구에 1쿼터짜리 동전 한 개를 넣었다. ◼ 가산명사 (특정) 지구 ❑ 우리는 중국인 거주지 구석구석을 돌아다녔다. ◼ 구 아주 가까이에서 ❑ 당신은 비행기의 이착륙을 코앞에서 볼 수 있습니다.

[미국영어 quarterfinal] 가산명사 준준결승, 8강 ❑ 나는 윔블던 대회에서 최소한 8강전까지는 진출할 것으로 예상하고 있습니다.

◼ 형용사 연 4회의, 분기별의 ❑ 5천 개 기업을 대상으로 한 최근 일본 중앙은행의 분기별 조사 ● 부사 분기별로 ❑ 배당금은 분기별로 지급하든 연도별로 지급하든 상관없습니다. ◻ 가산명사 계간지 ❑ 그 계간지는 건전한 학술 토론의 장이었었다.

◼ 가산명사·집합 사중주단, 사중창단 ❑ 현악 사중주단 ◻ 가산명사 4중주곡, 4중창곡 ❑ 현악4중주 제1번은 초기작으로 1941년 캘리포니아에서 작곡되었다.

불가산명사 석영 ❑ 수정 결정체

◼ 타동사 (판결 등을) 기각하다 ❑ 상소심 법원이 열한 명 전원의 유죄 평결을 기각했다. ◻ 타동사 (소문을) 잠재우다, 불식시키다 ❑ 그레이엄은 분장실에서 불만이 커지고 있다는 소문을 불식시키려고 했다. ◼ 타동사 (반란 등을) 진압하다 ❑ 군인들은 시위 진압에 연루되기를 꺼린다는 의사를 분명히 드러내고 있었다.

가산명사 부두, 선창 ❑ 잭과 스티븐은 부두에서 그들을 기다리고 있었다.

queen ♦♦♦ /kwin/ (queens) **1** N-TITLE; N-COUNT A **queen** is a woman who rules a country as its monarch. ❑ ...Queen Victoria. **2** N-TITLE; N-COUNT A **queen** is a woman who is married to a king. ❑ The king and queen had fled. **3** N-COUNT If you refer to a woman as **the queen of** a particular activity, you mean that she is well-known for being very good at it. ❑ ...the queen of crime writing. **4** N-COUNT In chess, the **queen** is the most powerful piece. It can be moved in any direction. ❑ Chris will either have to take his queen's knight and lose his own knight, or he'll lose a rook. **5** N-COUNT A **queen** is a playing card with a picture of a queen on it. ❑ ...the queen of spades. **6** N-COUNT A **queen** or a **queen bee** is a large female bee which can lay eggs. ❑ Glass hives offer a close-up view of the bees at work, with the queen bee in each hive marked by a white dot. →see **chess**

queer /kwɪər/ (queerer, queerest, queers) **1** ADJ Something that is **queer** is strange. [OLD-FASHIONED] ❑ If you ask me, there's something a bit queer going on. **2** N-COUNT People sometimes call homosexual men **queers**. [INFORMAL, OFFENSIVE] ● ADJ **Queer** is also an adjective. ❑ But most queer men led a double life. They constantly moved between at least two worlds.

quell /kwɛl/ (quells, quelling, quelled) **1** V-T To **quell** opposition or violent behavior means to stop it. ❑ Troops eventually quelled the unrest. **2** V-T If you **quell** an unpleasant feeling such as fear or anger, you stop yourself or other people from having that feeling. ❑ The Information Minister is trying to quell fears of a looming oil crisis.

quench /kwɛntʃ/ (quenches, quenching, quenched) V-T If someone who is thirsty **quenches** their **thirst**, they lose their thirst by having a drink. ❑ He stopped to quench his thirst at a stream.

que∣ry /kwɪəri/ (queries, querying, queried) **1** N-COUNT A **query** is a question, especially one that you ask an organization, publication, or expert. ❑ If you have any queries about this insurance, please contact Travel Insurance Services Limited. **2** V-T If you **query** something, you check it by asking about it because you are not sure if it is correct. ❑ It's got a number you can ring to query your bill. **3** V-T To **query** means to ask a question. ❑ "Is there something else?" Ryle queried as Helen stopped speaking.

quest /kwɛst/ (quests) N-COUNT A **quest** is a long and difficult search for something. [LITERARY] ❑ My quest for a better bank continues. ● PHRASE If you go **in quest of** something, you try to find or obtain it.

ques∣tion ♦♦♦ /kwɛstʃⁿn/ (questions, questioning, questioned) **1** N-COUNT A **question** is something that you say or write in order to ask a person about something. ❑ They asked a great many questions about England. **2** V-T If you **question** someone, you ask them a lot of questions about something. ❑ This led the therapist to question Jim about his parents and their marriage. ● **question∣ing** N-UNCOUNT ❑ The police have detained thirty-two people for questioning. **3** V-T If you **question** something, you have or express doubts about whether it is true, reasonable, or worthwhile. ❑ It never occurs to them to question the doctor's decisions. **4** N-SING If you say that there is some **question** about something, you mean that there is doubt or uncertainty about it. If something is **in question** or has been **called into question**, doubt or uncertainty has been expressed about it. [with supp, also prep N] ❑ There's no question about their success. **5** N-COUNT A **question** is a problem, matter, or point which needs to be considered. ❑ But the whole question of aid is a tricky political one. **6** N-COUNT The **questions** in an examination are the problems which are set in order to test your knowledge or ability. ❑ That question did come up in the examination. **7** →see also **questioning** **8** PHRASE The person, thing, or time **in question** is one which you have just been talking about or which is relevant. ❑ Add up all the income you've received over the period in question. **9** PHRASE If you say that something is **out of the question**, you are emphasizing that it is completely impossible or unacceptable. [EMPHASIS] ❑ For the homeless, private medical care is simply out of the question. **10** PHRASE If you **pop the question**, you ask someone to marry you. [INFORMAL, JOURNALISM] ❑ Stuart got serious quickly and popped the question six months later. **11** PHRASE If you say **there is no question of** something happening, you are emphasizing that it is not going to happen. [EMPHASIS] ❑ There is no question of the tax-payer picking up the bill for the party.

Thesaurus   question의 참조어

N.	query **1**
V.	ask, inquire; (ant.) answer **2**
	doubt **3**

Word Partnership   question의 연어

V.	**answer** a question, **ask** a question, **pose a** question, **raise a** question **1**
N.	**answer/response to a** question **1**
ADJ.	**difficult** question, **good** question, **important** question **1**

---

ques∣tion∣able /kwɛstʃənəbᵊl/ ADJ If you say that something is **questionable**, you mean that it is not completely honest, reasonable, or acceptable. [FORMAL] ❑ He has been dogged by allegations of questionable business practices.

Thesaurus   questionable의 참조어

ADJ.	doubtful, dubious, problematic, uncertain

---

1 경칭명사; 가산명사 여왕 ❑ 빅토리아 여왕 **2** 경칭명사; 가산명사 왕비 ❑ 왕과 왕비는 피신했다. **3** 가산명사 ~의 여왕, ~의 대가 (인 여자) ❑ 범죄소설의 여왕 **4** 가산명사 (체스) 퀸 ❑ 크리스는 자기가 가진 여왕의 기사를 잡고 자기 기사를 내주거나, 아니면 자신의 루크를 잃을 수밖에 없을 것이다. **5** 가산명사 (카드) 퀸 ❑ 스페이드 퀸 **6** 가산명사 여왕벌 ❑ 유리로 된 벌집은 각각 흰 점으로 표시된 벌집에 있는 여왕벌과 함께 벌들이 일하는 모습을 자세히 볼 수 있게 해 준다.

1 형용사 기이한, 이상한 [구식어] ❑ 내 생각엔 뭔가 이상한 일이 벌어지고 있는 것 같아. **2** 가산명사 호모, (남자) 동성애자 [비격식체, 모욕어] ● 형용사 호모의, (남성) 동성애의 ❑ 그러나 호모들 대부분은 이중생활을 했다. 그들은 최소한 두 개의 세계를 끊임없이 넘나들었다.

1 타동사 진압하다 ❑ 군인들이 마침내 소요 사태를 진압했다. **2** 타동사 억누르다, 잠재우다 ❑ 정보부 장관은 석유 파동이 있을지도 모른다는 우려를 잠재우려 하고 있다.

타동사 (갈증을) 해소하다 ❑ 그는 목을 축이기 위해 냇가에 멈춰 섰다.

1 가산명사 문의 ❑ 이 보험에 관해 문의하실 사항은 '트래블 인슈어런스 서비스'로 연락 주시길 바랍니다. **2** 타동사 문의하다 ❑ 청구서에 문의할 수 있는 전화번호가 기재되어 있습니다. **3** 타동사 묻다 ❑ "다른 것도 있니?"라고 라일은 헬렌이 말을 멈추자 물었다.

가산명사 탐색, 탐구 [문예체] ❑ 보다 좋은 은행을 탐색하기 위한 내 노력은 계속될 것이다. ● 구 ~을 찾아

1 가산명사 질문 ❑ 그들은 영국에 대해 굉장히 많은 질문을 했다. **2** 타동사 질문하다, 심문하다 ❑ 이를 계기로 임상 치료사는 짐에게 부모님과 그들의 결혼 생활에 관해 물어보게 되었다. ● 질문 불가산명사 ❑ 경찰은 심문을 위해 32명을 구금하였다. **3** 타동사 의심하다, 의혹을 제기하다 ❑ 그들은 의사의 결정에 이의를 제기할 생각을 전혀 못하고 있다. **4** 단수명사 의심 ❑ 그들의 성공에 관해서는 의심의 여지가 없다. **5** 가산명사 문제 ❑ 하지만 원조라는 문제 자체가 정치적으로 미묘한 사안이다. **6** 가산명사 문제 ❑ 그 문제가 시험에 정말 출제되었다. **8** 구 문제의, 해당되는 ❑ 해당 기간 동안 얻은 소득을 모두 합산하세요. **9** 구 생각조차 할 수 없는, 불가능한 [강조] ❑ 노숙자들에게 사설 병원 진료는 그저 꿈도 꿀 수 없는 일이다. **10** 구 청혼하다 [비격식체, 언론] ❑ 스튜어트는 이내 진지하게 사귀기 시작해서 6개월 후에 청혼했다. **11** 구 일어날 가능성도 없는, 생각조차 할 수 없는 [강조] ❑ 정당의 경비를 납세자가 부담한다는 것은 생각조차 할 수 없다.

형용사 의심스러운, 수상쩍은 [격식체] ❑ 그에게는 수상쩍은 사업 행위를 한다는 의혹이 늘 따라다녔다.

a b c d e f g h i j k l m n o p q r s t u v w x y z

ques|tion|ing /kw<u>e</u>stʃənɪŋ/ ADJ If someone has a **questioning** expression on their face, they look as if they want to know the answer to a question. [WRITTEN] [ADJ n] □ *He raised a questioning eyebrow.* →see also **question**

형용사 의아해하는 [문어체] □ 그는 의아하다는 듯이 눈썹을 치켜올렸다.

ques|tion mark (question marks) ■ N-COUNT A **question mark** is the punctuation mark ? which is used in writing at the end of a question. □ *Who invented the question mark?* ② N-COUNT If there is doubt or uncertainty about something, you can say that there is a **question mark over** it. □ *There are bound to be question marks over his future.*

■ 가산명사 물음표 □ 물음표는 누가 만들었을까? ② 가산명사 미지수, 불확실성 □ 필시 그의 장래가 불확실할 것이다.

ques|tion|naire /kw<u>e</u>stʃən<u>eə</u>r/ (questionnaires) N-COUNT A **questionnaire** is a written list of questions which are answered by a lot of people in order to provide information for a report or a survey. □ *Headteachers will be asked to fill in a questionnaire.* →see **census**

가산명사 설문지 □ 교장 선생님들은 설문지 작성을 요청받을 것이다.

queue /kj<u>u</u>/ (queues, queuing, queued)

<hr>

Queueing can also be used as the continuous form.

queueing도 진행형으로 쓰일 수 있다.

<hr>

■ N-COUNT A **queue** is a line of people or vehicles that are waiting for something. [mainly BRIT; AM usually **line**] □ *I watched as he got a tray and joined the queue.* ② N-COUNT If you say that there is a **queue** of people who want to do or have something, you mean that a lot of people are waiting for an opportunity to do it or have it. [mainly BRIT; AM usually **line**] □ *Manchester United would be at the front of a queue of potential buyers.* ③ V-I When people **queue**, they stand in a line waiting for something. [mainly BRIT] □ *I had to queue for quite a while.* • PHRASAL VERB **Queue up** means the same as **queue**. [AM usually **line up**] □ *A mob of journalists are queuing up at the gate to photograph him.* ④ N-COUNT A **queue** is a list of computer tasks which will be done in order. [COMPUTING] □ *Your print job has already been sent from your PC to the network print queue.* ⑤ V-T To **queue** a number of computer tasks means to arrange them to be done in order. [COMPUTING]

■ 가산명사 (차례를 기다리는) 줄 [주로 영국영어; 미국영어 대개 line] □ 나는 그가 쟁반을 하나 집어 들고 줄을 서는 것을 지켜봤다. ② 가산명사 행렬 [주로 영국영어; 미국영어 대개 line] □ 맨체스터 유나이티드가 구매 가능성이 있는 팀 중에서 가장 앞서 있을 것이다. ③ 자동사 줄을 서다 [주로 영국영어] □ 나는 꽤 오랫동안 줄을 서야 했다. • 구동사 줄을 서다 [미국영어 대개 line up] □ 그의 사진을 찍기 위해 많은 기자들이 정문 앞에 줄을 서 있다. ④ 가산명사 (컴퓨터) 작업 대기열 [컴퓨터] □ 인쇄할 서류는 피시에서 네트워크 프린트 작업 대기열로 이미 전송되었습니다. ⑤ 타동사 (컴퓨터) 작업 대기열로 보내다 [컴퓨터]

quib|ble /kw<u>ɪ</u>b^əl/ (quibbles, quibbling, quibbled) ■ V-RECIP When people **quibble over** a small matter, they argue about it even though it is not important. □ *Council members spent the day quibbling over the final wording of the resolution.* ② N-COUNT A **quibble** is a small and unimportant complaint about something. □ *These are minor quibbles.*

■ 상호동사 사소한 다툼을 벌이다, 옥신각신하다 □ 의원들은 결의안의 최종 문구를 두고 하루 종일 옥신각신했다. ② 가산명사 (사소한) 불만 □ 이건 사소한 불만거리들이다.

quick ♦♦♦ /kw<u>ɪ</u>k/ (quicker, quickest) ■ ADJ Someone or something that is **quick** moves or does things with great speed. □ *You'll have to be quick. The flight leaves in about three hours.* • **quick|ly** ADV [ADV with v] □ *Cussane worked quickly and methodically.* • **quick|ness** N-UNCOUNT □ *...the natural quickness of his mind.* ② ADV **Quicker** is sometimes used to mean "at a greater speed," and **quickest** to mean "at the greatest speed." **Quick** is sometimes used to mean "with great speed." Some people consider this to be non-standard. [INFORMAL] [ADV after v] □ *Warm the sugar slightly first to make it dissolve quicker.* ③ ADJ Something that is **quick** takes or lasts only a short time. □ *He took one last quick look about the room.* • **quick|ly** ADV [ADV with v] □ *You can become fitter quite quickly and easily.* ④ ADJ **Quick** means happening without delay or with very little delay. □ *Officials played down any hope for a quick end to the bloodshed.* • **quick|ly** ADV [ADV with v] □ *We need to get it back as quickly as possible.* ⑤ ADV **Quick** is sometimes used to mean "with very little delay." [INFORMAL] [ADV after v] □ *I got away as quick as I could.* ⑥ ADJ If you are **quick to** do something, you do not hesitate to do it. [v-link ADJ, usu ADJ to-inf] □ *Mark says the ideas are Katie's own, and is quick to praise her talent.* ⑦ ADJ If someone has a **quick** temper, they are easily made angry. [ADJ n] □ *He readily admitted to the interviewer that he had a quick temper, with a tendency toward violence.* ⑧ **quick as a flash** →see **flash**

■ 형용사 빠른 □ 빨리 움직여야 할 걸. 비행기가 약 세 시간 뒤에 떠나거든. • 빨리 부사 □ 쿠세인은 일을 신속하고 질서 정연하게 했다. • 빠름, 민첩함 불가산명사 □ 그의 천부적인 빠른 사고력 ② 부사 더 빨리; 가장 빨리 [비격식체] □ 설탕을 더 빨리 녹이려면 살짝 열을 가하세요. ③ 형용사 재빠른, 신속한 □ 그는 방을 마지막으로 한번 재빨리 둘러봤다. • 빨리 부사 □ 당신은 비교적 빨리 그리고 쉽게 건강해질 수 있다. ④ 형용사 조속한, 재빠른 □ 정부 당국자들은 유혈 사태가 조속히 종결될 가망은 없다는 듯한 태도를 취했다. • 빨리 부사 □ 우리는 그것을 최대한 빨리 되찾아야 할 필요가 있다. ⑤ 부사 곧바로, 지체 없이 [비격식체] □ 나는 최대한 빨리 도망쳤다. ⑥ 형용사 주저하지 않는 □ 마크는 그 생각들이 케이티의 것이라며 선뜻 그녀의 재능을 칭찬한다. ⑦ 형용사 성깔 있는, 급한, 불같은, 성미가 급한 □ 그는 인터뷰를 하면서 자신이 성미가 급하고 폭력적인 성향이 있다고 서슴없이 인정했다.

<hr>

Thesaurus   *quick*의 참조어

ADJ.   brisk, fast, rapid, speedy, swift; (ant.) slow ■

<hr>

Word Partnership   *quick*의 연어

N.   quick **glance**, quick **kiss**, quick **look**, quick **question**, quick **smile** ③
       quick **action**, quick **profit**, quick **response**, quick **start**, quick **thinking** ④
V.   **think** quick ⑤

<hr>

quick|en /kw<u>ɪ</u>kən/ (quickens, quickening, quickened) V-T/V-I If something **quickens** or if you **quicken** it, it becomes faster or moves at a greater speed. □ *Ainslie's pulse quickened in alarm.*

타동사/자동사 빠르게 하다; 빨라지다 □ 에인슬리는 놀라서 맥박이 빨라졌다.

quick fix (quick fixes) N-COUNT If you refer to a **quick fix** to a problem, you mean a way of solving a problem that is easy but temporary or inadequate. [DISAPPROVAL] □ *Any tax measures enacted now as a quick fix would only be reversed in a few years when the economy picks up.*

가산명사 임시방편, 미봉책 [탐탁찮음] □ 당장 미봉책으로 제정된 조세 법령들은 몇 년 뒤 경기가 호전되면 철회될 것이다.

quid /kw<u>ɪ</u>d/

<hr>

Quid is both the singular and the plural form.

quid은 단수형 및 복수형이다.

<hr>

N-COUNT A **quid** is a pound in money. [BRIT, INFORMAL] □ *It cost him five hundred quid.*

가산명사 1파운드 [영국영어, 비격식체] □ 그것을 사느라 그는 500파운드를 썼다.

qui|et ♦♦♦ /kw<u>aɪ</u>ɪt/ (quieter, quietest, quiets, quieting, quieted) ■ ADJ Someone or something that is **quiet** makes only a small amount of noise. □ *Tania kept the children reasonably quiet and contented.* • **qui|et|ly** ADV [ADV with v] □ "*This is goodbye, isn't it?*" *she said quietly.* • **qui|et|ness** N-UNCOUNT □ *...the smoothness and quietness of the flight.* ② ADJ If a place is **quiet**, there is very little noise there. □ *She was received in a small, quiet office.* • **qui|et|ness** N-UNCOUNT □ *I miss the quietness of the countryside.* ③ ADJ If a place, situation, or time is **quiet**, there is no excitement, activity, or trouble. □ *...a quiet rural backwater.* • **qui|et|ly** ADV [ADV

■ 형용사 조용한 □ 타니아는 아이들을 적당히 얌전하고 만족해 하도록 하였다. • 조용하게 부사 □ "이젠 안녕이지, 그렇지?"라고 그녀는 조용히 말했다. • 고요, 정적 불가산명사 □ 편안하고 조용한 비행 ② 형용사 조용한 □ 그녀는 작고 조용한 사무실로 안내되었다. • 조용함 불가산명사 □ 난 조용한 시골이 그립다. ③ 형용사 조용한, 한적한 □ 한적한 벽촌 • 조용히, 한적하게 부사 □ 그러나 그는 가장 소중한

with v] ❑ *His most prized time, though, will be spent quietly on his farm in Karklaaf, Durban.* ● **qui|et|ness** N-UNCOUNT ❑ *I do very much appreciate the quietness and privacy here.* **4** N-UNCOUNT **Quiet** is silence. ❑ *He called for quiet and announced that the next song was in our honor.* **5** ADJ If you are **quiet**, you are not saying anything. [v-link ADJ] ❑ *I told them to be quiet and go to sleep.* ● **qui|et|ly** ADV [ADV with v] ❑ *Amy stood quietly in the doorway watching him.* **6** ADJ A **quiet** person behaves in a calm way and is not easily made angry or upset. ❑ *He's a nice quiet man.* **7** V-T/V-I If someone or something **quiets** or if you **quiet** them, they become less noisy, less active, or silent. [mainly AM; BRIT usually **quieten**] ❑ *The wind dropped and the sea quieted.* **8** V-T To **quiet** tears or complaints means to persuade people that there is no good reason for them. [mainly AM; BRIT usually **quieten**] ❑ *Supporters of the Constitution had to quiet fears that aristocrats plotted to steal the fruits of the Revolution.* **9** PHRASE If you **keep quiet about** something or you **keep something quiet**, you do not say anything about it. ❑ *I told her to keep quiet about it.* **10** PHRASE If something is done **on the quiet**, it is done secretly or in such a way that people do not notice it. ❑ *She'd promised to give him driving lessons, on the quiet, when no one could see.*

Thesaurus	*quiet*의 참조어
ADJ.	low, placid, silent, soft; (*ant.*) loud **1**
	calm, serene, tranquil; (*ant.*) busy **2 3 6**
N.	calm, hush, lull **4**
V.	calm, hush, soothe; (*ant.*) agitate, excite, stir up **7**

Word Partnership	*quiet*의 연어
ADV.	**real** quiet, **relatively** quiet, **too** quiet, **very** quiet **1**-**3 5**
V.	**be** quiet, **keep** quiet **1 5**
N.	**peace and** quiet, quiet **neighborhood/street**, quiet **place/ spot 2 3**
	quiet **day/evening/night**, quiet **life 3**

qui|et|en /kwaɪɪtⁿn/ (**quietens**, **quietening**, **quietened**) **1** V-T/V-I If you **quieten** someone or something, or if they **quieten**, you make them become less noisy, less active, or silent. [mainly BRIT; AM usually **quiet**] ❑ *She tried to quieten her breathing.* **2** V-T To **quieten** fears or complaints means to persuade people that there is no good reason for them. [mainly BRIT; AM usually **quiet**] ❑ *Russian intelligence will take a long time to quieten the paranoia of the West.*

quilt /kwɪlt/ (**quilts**) N-COUNT A **quilt** is a thin cover filled with feathers or some other warm, soft material, which you put over your blankets when you are in bed. ❑ *...an old patchwork quilt.*
→see Word Web: **quilt**

quip /kwɪp/ (**quips**) N-COUNT A **quip** is a remark that is intended be amusing or clever. [WRITTEN] ❑ *The commentators make endless quips about the female players' appearance.*

quirk /kwɜrk/ (**quirks**) **1** N-COUNT A **quirk** is something unusual or interesting that happens by chance. ❑ *By a tantalizing quirk of fate, the pair have been drawn to meet in the first round of the championship.* **2** N-COUNT A **quirk** is a habit or aspect of a person's character which is odd or unusual. ❑ *Brown was always fascinated by the quirks and foibles of people in everyday situations.*

quirky /kwɜrki/ (**quirkier**, **quirkiest**) ADJ Something or someone that is **quirky** is rather odd or unpredictable in their appearance, character, or behavior. ❑ *We've developed a reputation for being quite quirky and original.* ● **quirki|ness** N-UNCOUNT ❑ *You will probably notice an element of quirkiness in his behavior.*

quit /kwɪt/ (**quits**, **quitting**)

The form **quit** is used in the present tense and is the past tense and past participle.

1 V-T/V-I If you **quit** your job, you choose to leave it. [INFORMAL] ❑ *He quit his job as an office boy in Athens.* **2** V-T If you **quit** an activity or **quit** doing something, you stop doing it. [mainly AM] ❑ *A nicotine spray can help smokers quit the habit without putting on weight.* **3** V-T If you **quit** a place, you leave it completely and do not go back to it. ❑ *Science fiction writers have long dreamt that humans might one day quit the earth to colonize other planets.* **4** PHRASE If you say that you are going to **call it quits**, you mean that you have decided to stop doing something or being involved in something. ❑ *They raised $630,000 through listener donations, and then called it quits.*

If you **quit** your job or school, it means that you leave by choice. If you are **laid off** (from work) or **expelled** (from school), it was not your choice. A boss can **fire** an employee for poor performance. The boss may **resign** his position if he is found guilty of wrongdoing.

Thesaurus	*quit*의 참조어
V.	resign, vacate **1**
	break off, cease, discontinue **2**
	abandon, leave **3**

시간을 더반의 카를라프에 있는 자기 농장에서 조용히 보낼 것이다. ● 조용함, 고요함 불가산명사 ❑ 나는 이곳이 조용하고 남의 눈에 띄지 않아 정말 좋다. **4** 불가산명사 침묵, 잠잠 ❑ 그는 조용히 해 달라고 하면서 우리를 위해 다음 곡을 부르겠다고 말했다. **5** 형용사 조용한, 잠자코 있는 ❑ 나는 그들에게 조용히 하고 자라고 했다. ● 조용히 부사 ❑ 에이미는 그를 바라보며 조용히 문간에 서 있었다. **6** 형용사 차분한, 조용한 ❑ 그는 착하고 차분한 사람이다. **7** 타동사/자동사 조용해지다, 잠잠해지다, 조용히 시키다 [주로 미국영어; 영국영어 대개 quieten] ❑ 바람이 가라앉고 바다도 잠잠해졌다. **8** 타동사 무마시키다, 잠재우다 [주로 미국영어; 영국영어 대개 quieten] ❑ 헌법 옹호자들은 귀족들이 혁명의 성과를 가로채려 한다는 우려를 잠재워야만 했다. **9** 구 함구하라, 입을 다물라 ❑ 나는 그녀에게 그것에 관해 함구하라고 했다. **10** 구 몰래, 비밀리에 ❑ 그녀는 그에게 남들이 볼 수 없을 때 몰래 운전 연습을 시켜 주겠다고 약속했다.

1 타동사/자동사 조용히 시키다; 조용해지다 [주로 영국영어; 미국영어 대개 quiet] ❑ 그녀는 숨을 고르려고 애썼다. **2** 타동사 (공포 등을) 가라앉히다 [주로 영국영어; 미국영어 대개 quiet] ❑ 러시아 정보 기관이 서방 세계의 불신을 가라앉히는 데는 오랜 세월이 걸릴 것이다.

가산명사 누비이불 ❑ 낡은 조각보 이불

가산명사 재치 있는 말, 너스레 [문어체] ❑ 해설자들은 여자 선수들의 외모를 가지고 끊임없이 너스레를 늘어놓는다.

1 가산명사 기변(奇變), 운명의 장난 ❑ 얄궂은 운명의 장난으로, 그 두 사람은 선수권 대회 1회전에서 맞붙게 되었다. **2** 가산명사 기벽(奇癖), 기이한 버릇 ❑ 브라운은 항상 사람들이 일상을 살아가며 드러내는 기벽과 결점에 매료되었다.

형용사 기이한, 평범하지 않은 ❑ 우리는 상당히 특이하고 독창적이라는 평판을 얻었다. ● 별스러움 불가산명사 ❑ 아마 그의 행동에 별난 구석이 있다는 걸 눈치 채게 될 거예요.

quit은 동사의 현재, 과거, 과거 분사로 쓴다.

1 타동사/자동사 그만두다 [비격식체] ❑ 그는 아테네에서 하던 사환 일을 그만두었다. **2** 타동사 포기하다, 중단하다 [주로 미국영어] ❑ 니코틴 스프레이를 사용하면 흡연자가 체중이 늘지 않으면서도 담배를 끊을 수 있다. **3** 타동사 떠나다 ❑ 공상 과학 소설가들은 인류가 언젠가는 지구를 떠나 다른 행성에 식민지를 건설할 수 있으리라고 오랫동안 꿈꿔 왔다. **4** 구 그만두기로 하다 ❑ 그들은 청취자들로부터 63만 달러의 기부금을 모은 뒤 그만두기로 했다.

직장이나 학교를 quit(그만두다)한다는 것은 스스로 선택해서 떠나는 것을 의미한다. (직장에서) laid off(해고되거나) (학교에서) expelled(퇴학 당하는) 것은 선택에 의한 것이 아니다. 사장은 직원이 실적이 나쁘면 fire(해고하다) 할 수 있다. 사장은 불법 행위를 한 것으로 유죄 판결이 나면 자리를 resign(사임하다) 하기도 한다.

a b c d e f g h i j k l m n o p q r s t u v w x y z

Word Web quilt

The Hmong* tribes are famous for their colorful **quilts**. Many people think of a quilt as a bed covering. However, these **textiles** feature pictures that tell stories about the people who made them. A favorite story shows how the Hmong fled from China to southeast Asia in the early 1800s. The story sometimes shows the quiltmaker's arrival in a new country. The seamstress **sews** small pieces of colorful **fabric** together to make the **design**. The needlework is very elaborate. It includes cross-stitching, **embroidery**, and appliqué. A common border **pattern** is a design that represents mountains—the Hmong's original home.

Hmong: a group of people who live in the mountains of China, Vietnam, Laos, and Thailand.

quite ♦♦♦ /kwaɪt/ **1** ADV You use **quite** to indicate that something is the case to a fairly great extent. **Quite** is less emphatic than "very" and "extremely." [VAGUENESS] ❑ *I felt quite bitter about it at the time.* ❑ *Well, actually it requires quite a bit of work and research.* **2** ADV You use **quite** to emphasize what you are saying. [EMPHASIS] ❑ *It is quite clear that we were firing in self defence.* **3** ADV You use **quite** after a negative to make what you are saying weaker or less definite. [VAGUENESS] ❑ *Something here is not quite right.* **4** PREDET You use **quite** in front of a noun group to emphasize that a person or thing is very impressive or unusual. [APPROVAL] [PREDET *a* n] ❑ *"Oh, he's quite a character," Sean replied.* **5** ADV You can say "**quite**" to express your agreement with someone. [SPOKEN, FORMULAE] [ADV as reply] ❑ *"And if you buy the record it's your choice isn't it." — "Quite."*

You can use **quite** in front of **a** or **an** when it is followed by an adjective plus noun. For example, you can say "**It's quite an old car.**" Note that, in sentences like these, **quite** comes in front of the indefinite article. You cannot say, for example, "It's a quite old car." You can also say "**The car is quite old.**" This sentence is slightly formal in American English; most speakers would say "**The car is pretty old.**" **Quite** can be used to modify adjectives and adverbs, and is stronger than **fairly**. **Quite** may suggest that something has more of a quality than expected. ❑ *Nobody here's ever heard of it but it is actually quite common.*

Thesaurus quite의 참조어

ADV.	entirely, extremely, wholly **1**

quiver /kwɪvər/ (quivers, quivering, quivered) **1** V-I If something **quivers**, it shakes with very small movements. ❑ *Her bottom lip quivered and big tears rolled down her cheeks.* **2** V-I If you say that someone or their voice **is quivering with** an emotion such as rage or excitement, you mean that they are strongly affected by this emotion and show it in their appearance or voice. ❑ *Cooper arrived, quivering with rage.* ● N-COUNT **Quiver** is also a noun. ❑ *I recognized it instantly and felt a quiver of panic.*

quiz /kwɪz/ (quizzes, quizzing, quizzed) **1** N-COUNT A **quiz** is a game or competition in which someone tests your knowledge by asking you questions. ❑ *We'll have a quiz at the end of the show.* **2** V-T If you **are quizzed** by someone about something, they ask you questions about it. ❑ *He was quizzed about his income, debts, and eligibility for state benefits.*

quota /kwoʊtə/ (quotas) **1** N-COUNT A **quota** is the limited number or quantity of something which is officially allowed. ❑ *The quota of four tickets per person had been reduced to two.* **2** N-COUNT A **quota** is a fixed maximum or minimum proportion of people from a particular group who are allowed to do something, such as come and live in a country or work for the government. ❑ *The bill would force employers to adopt a quota system when recruiting workers.* **3** N-COUNT Someone's **quota of** something is their expected or deserved share of it. ❑ *They have the usual quota of human weaknesses, no doubt.*

quotation /kwoʊteɪʃᵊn/ (quotations) **1** N-COUNT A **quotation** is a sentence or phrase taken from a book, poem, or play, which is repeated by someone else. ❑ *He illustrated his argument with quotations from Pasternak.* **2** N-COUNT When someone gives you a **quotation**, they tell you how much they will charge to do a particular piece of work. ❑ *Get several written quotations and check exactly what's included in the cost.* **3** N-COUNT A company's **quotation** on the stock exchange is its registration on the stock exchange, which enables its shares to be officially listed and traded. [BUSINESS] ❑ *an American-dominated investment manager with a quotation on the London stock market.*

quotation mark (quotation marks) N-COUNT **Quotation marks** are punctuation marks that are used in writing to show where speech or a quotation begins and ends. They are usually written or printed as "..." or, in Britain, '...'. ❑ *Make sure you have quotation marks at both the beginning and the end of quotes.*

quote ♦♦◇ /kwoʊt/ (quotes, quoting, quoted) **1** V-T/V-I If you **quote** someone as saying something, you repeat what they have written or said. ❑ *He quoted Mr Polay as saying that peace negotiations were already underway.* **2** N-COUNT A **quote from** a book, poem, play, or speech is a passage or phrase from it. ❑ *The paper starts its editorial comment with a quote from an unnamed member of the Cabinet.* **3** V-T If you **quote** something such as a law or a fact, you state it because it supports what you are saying. ❑ *Mr Meacher quoted statistics saying that the standard of living of the poorest people had fallen.* **4** V-T If someone **quotes** a price for doing something, they say how much money they would charge you for a service they are offering or a for a job that you want them to do. ❑ *A travel agent quoted her £160 for a flight from Bristol to Palma.* **5** N-COUNT A **quote for** a piece of work is

1 부사 꽤, 상당히 [짐작투] ❑ 나는 당시 그 일에 관해 꽤 씁쓸했다. ❑ 글쎄, 사실 그건 상당한 일과 연구를 요한다. **2** 부사 상당히, 아주 [강조] ❑ 우리가 정당방위 차원에서 발포했다는 것은 아주 명백하다. **3** 부사 좀, 약간 [짐작투] ❑ 여기 뭔가가 좀 석연찮아. **4** 전치 한정사 상당한, 대단한 [마음에 듦] ❑ "아, 그는 꽤나 독특한 인물이야." 숀이 대답했다. **5** 부사 그렇지, 그래 [구어체, 의례적인 표현] ❑ "그리고 네가 그 음반을 산다면, 그것은 네 선택 아니겠니?" "그야 그렇지."

quite는 'quite + a/an + 형용사 + 명사'의 순서로 쓸 수 있다. 이런 문장에서는 quite가 부정관사 앞에 온다는 점을 유의하라. 예를 들어, "It's a quite old car."라고는 할 수 없다. "The car is quite old."라고 할 수는 있다. 이 문장은 미국영어에서는 약간 격식체이다. 대부분의 사람들은 "The car is pretty old."라고 말할 것이다. quite는 형용사와 부사를 수식하기 위해 쓸 수 있으며, fairly 보다 더 강하다. quite는 어떤 것이 어떤 특질을 기대보다 더 많이 지니고 있음을 시사할 수 있다. ❑ 여기 있는 사람 아무도 그것에 대해 들어 본 적이 없지만 그것은 실제로 아주 흔하다.

1 자동사 떨다, 떨리다 ❑ 그녀의 아랫입술이 떨리며 커다란 눈물방울이 볼을 타고 흘러내렸다. **2** 자동사 봄을 떨다 ❑ 쿠퍼가 도착했을 때 그는 분노에 온몸을 떨고 있었다. ● 가산명사 떨림, 전율 ❑ 나는 즉시 그것을 알아보고 공포에 몸을 떨었다.

1 가산명사 퀴즈 ❑ 프로그램 끝 무렵에 퀴즈가 나갑니다. **2** 타동사 질문을 받다 ❑ 그는 소득, 부채 그리고 연금 수령 적격 여부에 대해 질문을 받았다.

1 가산명사 쿼터, 한도량 ❑ 일 인당 티켓 할당량이 넉 장에서 두 장으로 줄어들어 있었다. **2** 가산명사 쿼터, 할당제, 할당 의원 ❑ 이번 법안으로 고용주가 직원을 채용할 때 할당제 적용이 의무화될 것이다. **3** 가산명사 몫 ❑ 그들도 틀림없이 누구에게나 있는 인간적인 약점이 있지.

1 가산명사 인용, 인용문 ❑ 그는 파스테르나크의 말을 인용해 가며 자신의 주장을 폈다. **2** 가산명사 견적, 견적서 ❑ 견적서를 몇 장 받아서 비용 내역을 꼼꼼히 살펴보세요. **3** 가산명사 상장(上場) [경제] ❑ 런던 증시에 상장된 미국의 주도 투자사

가산명사 따옴표 ❑ 인용구의 처음 부분과 끝 부분에는 꼭 인용 부호를 달도록 하세요.

1 타동사/자동사 인용하다 ❑ 그는 평화 협상이 이미 진행 중이라는 폴레이 씨의 말을 인용했다. **2** 가산명사 인용, 인용구 ❑ 그 신문은 이름을 밝히지 않은 한 각료의 말을 사설의 첫 문장에 인용했다. **3** 타동사 인용하다 ❑ 그는 미처 빈곤층의 생활수준이 더 낮아졌음을 보여 주는 통계 수치를 인용했다. **4** 타동사 견적을 뽑다, 가격을 부르다 ❑ 한 여행사는 그녀에게 브리스톨 발 팔마 항공료로 160파운드를 제시했다. **5** 가산명사 견적, 견적서 ❑ 수리가 필요한 경우엔 항상 견적서를 받으세요. **6** 수동 타동사 시가를 매기다 [경제] ❑ 어제 홍콩에서 거래 초 금값이

the price that someone says they will charge you to do the work. ❑ *Always get a written quote for any repairs needed.* **6** V-T PASSIVE If a company's shares, a substance, or a currency **is quoted** at a particular price, that is its current market price. [BUSINESS] ❑ *In early trading in Hong Kong yesterday, gold was quoted at $368.20 an ounce.* **7** N-PLURAL **Quotes** are the same as **quotation marks**. [INFORMAL] ❑ *The word "remembered" is in quotes.*

1온스당 미화 368.20달러로 매겨졌다. **7** 복수명사 따옴표, 인용 부호 [비격식체] ❑ '기억했다'라는 단어는 인용 부호가 붙어 있다.

Quran /kɔrɑn, -ræn, kʊ-/ also **Koran, Qur'an** N-PROPER **The Quran** is the holy book on which the religion of Islam is based. ❑ *Still a devout Muslim, Lindh reads the Quran and prays every day.*

고유명사 코란 ❑ 여전히 독실한 회교도인 린드는 매일 코란을 읽고 기도를 한다.

QWERTY /kwɜrti/ also **Qwerty, qwerty** ADJ A **QWERTY** keyboard on a typewriter or computer is the standard English language keyboard, on which the top line of keys begins with the letters q, w, e, r, t, and y. [ADJ n] ❑ *You can enter text on the QWERTY keyboard or simply write on the screen.*

형용사 쿼티 자판의, 표준 키보드의 ❑ 일반 자판으로 본문을 입력하거나 그냥 화면에 글을 쓰셔도 됩니다.

Rr

R, r /ɑr/ (R's, r's) N-VAR **R** is the eighteenth letter of the English alphabet.

가산명사 또는 불가산명사 영어 알파벳의 열여덟 번째 글자

rab|bi /ræbaɪ/ (**rabbis**) N-COUNT; N-TITLE A **rabbi** is a Jewish religious leader, usually one who is in charge of a synagogue, one who is qualified to teach Judaism, or one who is an expert on Jewish law.

가산명사; 경칭명사 랍비, 유대교 지도자, 유대교 율법 학자

rab|bit /ræbɪt/ (**rabbits**) N-COUNT A **rabbit** is a small furry animal with long ears. Rabbits are sometimes kept as pets, or live wild in holes in the ground.

가산명사 토끼

rab|ble /ræb³l/ N-SING A **rabble** is a crowd of noisy people who seem likely to cause trouble. ❏ He seems to attract a rabble of supporters more loyal to the man than to the cause.

단수명사 오합지졸 ❏ 그에게는 대의보다 사람을 보고 따르는 오합지졸로 구성된 지지자들만 몰리는 것처럼 보인다.

ra|bies /reɪbiz/ N-UNCOUNT **Rabies** is a serious disease which causes people and animals to go mad and die. Rabies is particularly common in dogs.

불가산명사 광견병, 공수병

race ♦♦♦ /reɪs/ (**races, racing, raced**) ◨ N-COUNT A **race** is a competition to see who is the fastest, for example in running, swimming, or driving. ❏ The women's race was won by the only American in the field, Patti Sue Plumer. ◪ V-T/V-I If you **race**, you take part in a race. ❏ In the 10 years I raced in Europe, 30 drivers were killed. ◳ N-PLURAL **The races** are a series of horse races that are held in a particular place on a particular day. People go to watch and to bet on which horse will win. ❏ The high point of this trip was a day at the races. ◴ N-COUNT A **race** is a situation in which people or organizations compete with each other for power or control. ❏ The race for the White House begins in earnest today. →see also **rat race** ◵ N-VAR A **race** is one of the major groups which human beings can be divided into according to their physical features, such as the color of their skin. ❏ The College welcomes students of all races, faiths, and nationalities. →see also **human race, race relations** ◶ V-I If you **race** somewhere, you go there as quickly as possible. ❏ He raced across town to the State House building. ◷ V-I If something **races** toward a particular state or position, it moves very fast towards that state or position. ❏ Do they realize we are racing towards complete economic collapse? ◸ V-T If you **race** a vehicle or animal, you prepare it for races and make it take part in races. ❏ He still raced sports cars as often as he could. ◹ V-I If your mind **races**, or if thoughts **race** through your mind, you think very fast about something, especially when you are in a difficult or dangerous situation. ❏ I made sure I sounded calm but my mind was racing. ◺ V-I If your heart **races**, it beats very quickly because you are excited or afraid. ❏ Her heart raced uncontrollably. ◻—see also **racing** ◼ PHRASE You describe a situation as a **race against time** when you have to work very fast in order to do something before a particular time, or before another thing happens. ❏ An air force spokesman said the rescue operation was a race against time.

◨ 가산명사 경주 ❏ 여자 부문 경주의 우승은 출전 선수 중 유일한 미국인인 패티 수 플러머가 차지했다. ◪ 타동사/자동사 경주하다 ❏ 내가 유럽에서 경주에 참가한 10년 동안, 레이서 30명이 목숨을 잃었다. ◳ 복수명사 경마 ❏ 이번 여행의 하이라이트는 경마장에서 보낸 날이었다. ◴ 가산명사 경쟁 ❏ 백악관을 차지하기 위한 경쟁이 오늘 본격적으로 시작된다. ◵ 가산명사 또는 불가산명사 인종 ❏ 본 대학은 인종과 종교, 국적에 상관없이 모든 학생들을 환영한다. ◶ 자동사 질주하다 ❏ 그는 시내를 가로질러 주 의회 의사당으로 최대한 빨리 달려갔다. ◷ 자동사 치닫다 ❏ 우리가 완전 경제 붕괴로 치닫고 있음을 그들이 알고 있을까? ◸ 타동사 경주에 내보내다 ❏ 그는 여전히 할 수 있을 때마다 스포츠카 경주에 나갔다. ◹ 자동사 (머리가) 빠르게 돌아가다 ❏ 내가 말을 침착하게 하려고 신경 쓰는 와중에도 내 머리는 빠르게 돌아가고 있었다. ◺ 자동사 (심장이) 빨리 뛰다 ❏ 그녀의 심장이 걷잡을 수 없을 정도로 빠르게 뛰었다. ◼ 구 시간과의 싸움 ❏ 구조 작업은 시간과의 싸움이었다고 한 공군 대변인이 말했다.

race|course /reɪskɔrs/ (**racecourses**) also **race course** N-COUNT A **racecourse** is a track on which horses race. [mainly BRIT; AM usually **racetrack**]

가산명사 경마장의 경주로 [주로 영국영어; 미국영어 대개 racetrack]

race|horse /reɪshɔrs/ (**racehorses**) N-COUNT A **racehorse** is a horse that is trained to run in races.

가산명사 경주마

rac|er /reɪsər/ (**racers**) ◨ N-COUNT A **racer** is a person or animal that takes part in races. ❏ Tim Powell is a former champion powerboat racer. ◪ N-COUNT A **racer** is a vehicle such as a car or bicycle that is designed to be used in races and therefore travels fast. ❏ ...everything from small boats to ocean racers.

◨ 가산명사 주자; 경주마 ❏ 팀 파월은 전 모터보트 경주 챔피언이다. ◪ 가산명사 레이서, 경주용 차량 ❏ 작은 배에서 경주용 요트에 이르기까지 모든 종류의 선박

race re|la|tions N-PLURAL **Race relations** are the ways in which people of different races living together in the same community behave toward one another. ❏ ...a breakdown in race relations.

복수명사 인종 간의 관계 ❏ 인종 간의 관계 와해

race|track /reɪstræk/ (**racetracks**) also **race track** ◨ N-COUNT A **racetrack** is a track on which horses race. [AM; BRIT **racecourse**] ❏ ...the Breeders' Cup, run Oct. 26 at Arlington racetrack near Chicago. ◪ N-COUNT A **racetrack** is a track for races, for example car or bicycle races. ❏ ...the sound of cars roaring around a racetrack.

◨ 가산명사 경마장 경주로 [미국영어; 영국영어 racecourse] ❏ 10월 26일 시카고 근처 알링턴 경마장에서 열린 브리더스컵 ◪ 가산명사 (자동차 등의) 경주로 ❏ 경주로를 따라 포효하는 자동차 소리

ra|cial ♦♦◇ /reɪʃ³l/ ADJ **Racial** describes things relating to people's race. ❏ ...the protection of national and racial minorities. ● **ra|cial|ly** ADV ❏ We are both children of racially mixed marriages.

형용사 인종의 ❏ 소수 민족 및 소수 인종 보호 ● 인종적으로 부사 ❏ 우리는 둘 다 서로 인종간 결혼을 하신 부모님 밑에서 태어났다.

Word Partnership	racial의 연어
N.	racial **differences**, racial **discrimination**, racial **diversity**, racial **equality**, racial **groups**, racial **minorities**, racial **prejudice**, racial **tensions**

rac|ing ♦◇◇ /reɪsɪŋ/ N-UNCOUNT **Racing** refers to races between animals, especially horses, or between vehicles. ❏ Mr. Honda was himself a keen racing driver in his younger days.

불가산명사 경주 ❏ 혼다 씨 자신도 젊은 시절 열성적인 자동차 경주 선수였다.

rac|ism /reɪsɪzəm/ N-UNCOUNT **Racism** is the belief that people of some races are inferior to others, and the behavior which is the result of this belief. ❑ *There is a feeling among some black people that the level of racism is declining.*

불가산명사 인종 차별주의 ❑ 일부 흑인들은 인종 차별주의 정도가 약해지고 있다는 느낌을 받고 있다.

rac|ist /reɪsɪst/ (**racists**) ADJ If you describe people, things, or behavior as **racist**, you mean that they are influenced by the belief that some people are inferior because they belong to a particular race. [DISAPPROVAL] ❑ *You have to acknowledge that we live in a racist society.* ● N-COUNT A **racist** is someone who is racist. ❑ *He has a hard core of support among white racists.*

형용사 인종 차별주의의 [탐탁찮음] ❑ 당신은 우리가 인종 차별주의적인 사회에서 살고 있음을 인정해야 한다. ● 가산명사 인종 차별주의자 ❑ 그는 백인 인종 차별주의자 사이에서 확고한 지지를 받고 있다.

rack /ræk/ (**racks, racking, racked**)

> The spelling **wrack** is also used for meanings 2 and 3 and mainly in old-fashioned or American English.

철자 wrack도 주로 구식이나 미국영어에서 2와 3 의미로 쓰인다.

■ N-COUNT A **rack** is a frame or shelf, usually with bars or hooks, that is used for holding things or for hanging things on. ❑ *A luggage rack, which fits over the spare wheel, is a sensible option.* 2 V-T If someone **is racked by** something such as illness or anxiety, it causes them great suffering or pain. [usu passive] ❑ *His already infirm body was racked by high fever* 3 PHRASE If you **rack** your **brains**, you try very hard to think of something. ❑ *She began to rack her brains to remember what had happened at the nursing home.*

■ 가산명사 걸이, 선반 ❑ 비상 바퀴 위에 거는 화물용 선반은 현명한 선택 사양이다. 2 타동사 —로 고통스러워하다 ❑ 가뜩이나 몸이 약한 그가 고열에 시달렸다. 3 구 골똘히 생각하다 ❑ 그녀는 양로원에서 있었던 일을 기억하려고 골똘히 생각하기 시작했다.

▶**rack up** PHRASAL VERB If a business **racks up** profits, losses, or sales, it makes a lot of them. If a sportsman, sportswoman, or team **racks up** wins, they win a lot of matches or races. [no passive] ❑ *Lower rates mean that firms are more likely to rack up profits in the coming months.*

구동사 올리다, 달성하다 ❑ 금리가 내려가면 기업들이 향후 몇 개월간 수익을 올릴 가능성이 커진다.

rack|et /rækɪt/ (**rackets**)

> The spelling **racquet** is also used for meaning 3.

철자 racquet도 3 의미로 쓴다.

■ N-SING A **racket** is a loud unpleasant noise. ❑ *He makes such a racket I'm afraid he disturbs the neighbors.* 2 N-COUNT You can refer to an illegal activity used to make money as a **racket**. [INFORMAL] ❑ *I'm sure he'll admit he was in the drugs racket in the end.* 3 N-COUNT A **racket** is an oval-shaped bat with strings across it. Rackets are used in tennis, squash, and badminton. ❑ *Tennis rackets and balls are provided.*

■ 단수명사 소음, 소란 ❑ 그가 너무 시끄럽게 구는 바람에 이웃에 방해가 되지 않을까 걱정이다. 2 가산명사 부정한 돈벌이, 불법 거래 [비격식체] ❑ 결국 그가 불법 마약 거래 사실을 시인할 것으로 나는 확신한다. 3 가산명사 라켓 ❑ 테니스 라켓과 공이 제공된다.

rack|et|eer|ing /rækɪtɪərɪŋ/ N-UNCOUNT **Racketeering** is making money from illegal activities such as threatening people or selling worthless, immoral, or illegal goods or services. ❑ *Edwards was indicted on racketeering charges but never convicted.*

불가산명사 사기, 공갈 ❑ 에드워즈는 사기 혐의로 기소되었어도 한 번도 유죄 판결을 받은 적은 없었다.

racy /reɪsi/ (**racier, raciest**) ADJ **Racy** writing or behavior is lively, amusing, and slightly shocking. ❑ *He listened to David Bright's racy stories about life in the navy.*

형용사 아슬아슬한, 흥미진진한 ❑ 그는 데이비드 브라이트가 해 주는 흥미진진한 해군 시절 이야기를 귀 기울여 들었다.

Word Link | rad ≈ ray : radar, radiant, radiate

---

ra|dar /reɪdɑr/ (**radars**) N-VAR **Radar** is a way of discovering the position or speed of objects such as aircraft or ships when they cannot be seen, by using radio signals. ❑ *...a ship's radar screen.* →see **forecast**

가산명사 또는 불가산명사 레이더 ❑ 함선의 레이더 화면

ra|di|ance /reɪdiəns/ ■ N-UNCOUNT **Radiance** is great happiness which shows in someone's face and makes them look very attractive. [also a N] ❑ *She has the vigour and radiance of someone young enough to be her grand-daughter.* 2 N-UNCOUNT **Radiance** is a glowing light shining from something. [also a N] ❑ *The dim bulb of the bedside lamp cast a soft radiance over his face.*

■ 불가산명사 (얼굴의) 광채, 화색 ❑ 그녀는 손녀뻘 되는 젊은이의 원기와 화색을 지니고 있다. 2 불가산명사 광채, 빛 ❑ 침대맡에 놓인 희미한 전구가 그의 얼굴에 부드러운 빛을 비췄다.

ra|di|ant /reɪdiənt/ ■ ADJ Someone who is **radiant** is so happy that their happiness shows in their face. ❑ *On her wedding day the bride looked truly radiant.* 2 ADJ Something that is **radiant** glows brightly. ❑ *The evening sun warms the old red brick wall to a radiant glow.*

■ 형용사 환한 얼굴의 ❑ 결혼식 날 신부의 얼굴이 정말 환해 보였다. 2 형용사 밝게 빛나는 ❑ 따사로운 석양 햇살을 받은 붉은색 벽돌이 밝게 빛난다.

ra|di|ate /reɪdieɪt/ (**radiates, radiating, radiated**) ■ V-I If things **radiate** out **from** a place, they form a pattern that is like lines drawn from the center of a circle to various points on its edge. ❑ *Many kinds of woodland can be seen on the various walks which radiate from the Heritage Centre.* 2 V-T/V-I If you **radiate** an emotion or quality or if it **radiates from** you, people can see it very clearly in your face and in your behavior. ❑ *She radiates happiness and health.* 3 V-T If something **radiates** heat or light, heat or light comes from it. ❑ *The metal plate behind my head radiated heat like a cooker's hotplate.*

■ 자동사 사방으로 뻗다 ❑ 헤리티지 센터에서 사방으로 뻗어 있는 산책로로서 다양한 종류의 숲을 볼 수 있다. 2 타동사/자동사 발산하다 ❑ 그녀의 모습은 행복하고 건강한 기색이 역력하다 3 타동사 발산하다, 방출하다 ❑ 내 머리 뒤에 있는 철판이 요리용 철판처럼 열을 뿜어냈다.

ra|dia|tion /reɪdieɪʃ°n/ ■ N-UNCOUNT **Radiation** consists of very small particles of a radioactive substance. Large amounts of radiation can cause illness and death. ❑ *They suffer from health problems and fear the long term effects of radiation.* 2 N-UNCOUNT **Radiation** is energy, especially heat, that comes from a particular source. ❑ *The $617 million satellite will study energy radiation from the most violent stars in the universe.* →see **cancer, greenhouse effect, wave**

■ 불가산명사 방사능 ❑ 그들은 여러 질환을 앓고 있으며 방사능의 장기적인 영향을 두려워하고 있다. 2 불가산명사 복사 에너지 ❑ 6억 1,700만 달러짜리 그 인공위성은 우주에서 가장 활발한 활동을 하는 별들에서 나오는 복사 에너지를 관찰할 것이다.

Word Partnership | radiation의 연어

N.	radiation **levels**, radiation **therapy/treatment** ■
	radiation **damage**, **effects** of radiation, **exposure to** radiation ■ 2
ADJ.	**nuclear** radiation ■ 2

---

ra|dia|tor /reɪdieɪtər/ (**radiators**) ■ N-COUNT A **radiator** is a hollow metal device, usually connected by pipes to a central heating system, that is used to heat a room. 2 N-COUNT The **radiator** in a car is the part of the engine which is filled with water in order to cool the engine.

■ 가산명사 라디에이터, 방열기 2 가산명사 (자동차) 냉각 장치

radi|cal ◆◇◇ /rædɪk°l/ (**radicals**) ■ ADJ **Radical** changes and differences are very important and great in degree. ❑ *The country needs a period of calm without more surges of radical change.* ● **radi|cal|ly** /rædɪkli/ ADV ❑ *...two large groups of people with radically different beliefs and cultures.* 2 ADJ **Radical** people believe that there should be great changes in society and try to bring about these changes.

■ 형용사 극단적인 ❑ 그 나라가 필요한 것은 더 이상의 극단적인 변화가 아닌 평온한 시기이다. ● 극단적으로 부사 ❑ ...극단적으로 다른 믿음과 문화를 가진 사람들로 구성된 커다란 두 집단 2 형용사 급진적인, 과격한 ❑ 진행을 방해하겠다는 좌파 과격

❑ ...threats by left-wing **radical** groups to disrupt the proceedings. ● N-COUNT A **radical** is someone who has radical views. ❑ Vanessa and I had been student radicals together at Berkeley from 1965 to 1967.

ra|dii /ˈreɪdiaɪ/ **Radii** is the plural of **radius**.

ra|dio ◆◆◇ /ˈreɪdioʊ/ (**radios, radioing, radioed**) **1** N-UNCOUNT **Radio** is the broadcasting of programs for the public to listen to, by sending out signals from a transmitter. ❑ The last 12 months have been difficult ones for local radio. **2** N-SING You can refer to the programs broadcast by radio stations as the **radio**. ❑ A lot of people tend to listen to the radio in the mornings. **3** N-COUNT A **radio** is the piece of equipment that you use in order to listen to radio programs. ❑ He sat down in the armchair and turned on the radio. **4** N-UNCOUNT **Radio** is a system of sending sound over a distance by transmitting electrical signals. ❑ They are in twice daily radio contact with the rebel leader. **5** N-COUNT A **radio** is a piece of equipment that is used for sending and receiving messages. ❑ Judge Bruce Laughland praised the courage of the young constable, who managed to raise the alarm on his radio. **6** V-T/V-I If you **radio** someone, you send a message to them by radio. ❑ The officer radioed for advice. →see **wave** →see Word Web: **radio**

radio|ac|tive /ˌreɪdioʊˈæktɪv/ ADJ Something that is **radioactive** contains a substance that produces energy in the form of powerful and harmful rays. ❑ The government has been storing radioactive waste at Fernald for 50 years. ● **radio|ac|tiv|ity** /ˌreɪdioʊækˈtɪvɪti/ N-UNCOUNT ❑ ...the storage and disposal of solid waste which is contaminated with low levels of radioactivity.

ra|dius /ˈreɪdiəs/ (**radii**) /ˈreɪdiaɪ/ **1** N-SING The **radius** around a particular point is the distance from it in any direction. ❑ Nigel has searched for work in a ten-mile radius around his home. **2** N-COUNT The **radius** of a circle is the distance from its center to its outside edge. ❑ He indicated a semicircle with a radius of about thirty miles. →see **area**

RAF /ˌɑr eɪ ˈɛf, ræf/ N-PROPER The **RAF** is the air force of the United Kingdom. **RAF** is an abbreviation for "Royal Air Force." ❑ An RAF helicopter rescued the men after the boat began taking in water.

raf|fle /ˈræfᵊl/ (**raffles, raffling, raffled**) **1** N-COUNT A **raffle** is a competition in which you buy tickets with numbers on them. Afterward some numbers are chosen, and if your ticket has one of these numbers on it, you win a prize. ❑ Any more raffle tickets? Twenty-five pence each or five for a pound. **2** V-T If someone **raffles** something, they give it as a prize in a raffle. ❑ During each show we will be raffling a fabulous prize.

raft /ræft/ (**rafts**) **1** N-COUNT A **raft** is a floating platform made from large pieces of wood or other materials tied together. ❑ ...a river trip on bamboo rafts through dense rainforest. **2** N-COUNT A **raft** is a small rubber or plastic boat that you blow air into to make it float. ❑ The crew spent two days and nights in their raft.

raft|er /ˈræftər/ (**rafters**) N-COUNT **Rafters** are the sloping pieces of wood that support a roof. ❑ From the rafters of the thatched roofs hung strings of dried onions and garlic.

rag /ræg/ (**rags**) **1** N-VAR A **rag** is a piece of old cloth which you can use to clean or wipe things. ❑ He was wiping his hands on an oily rag. **2** N-PLURAL **Rags** are old torn clothes. ❑ There were men, women and small children, some dressed in rags. **3** N-COUNT People refer to a newspaper as a **rag** when they have a poor opinion of it. [INFORMAL, DISAPPROVAL] ❑ "This man Tom works for a local rag," he said.

rage ◆◇◇ /reɪdʒ/ (**rages, raging, raged**) **1** N-VAR **Rage** is strong anger that is difficult to control. ❑ He was red-cheeked with rage. **2** V-I You say that something powerful or unpleasant **rages** when it continues with great force or violence. ❑ Train services were halted as the fire raged for more than four hours. **3** V-T/V-I If you **rage** about something, you speak or think very angrily about it. ❑ Monroe was on the phone, raging about her mistreatment by the brothers. ❑ Inside, Frannie was raging. **4** N-UNCOUNT You can refer to the strong anger that someone feels in a particular situation as a particular **rage**, especially when this results in violent or aggressive behavior. ❑ Cabin crews are reporting up to nine cases of air rage a week. →see also **road rage 5** →see also **raging**

Thesaurus	rage의 참조어
N.	anger, frenzy, tantrum **1 4**
V.	fume, scream, yell **3**

Word Web   radio

Radio originally provided **communication** between ships at sea. Ships could also contact **stations** on the land. In 1912, the *Titanic* sank in the North Atlantic with over 2,000 people on board. However, a radio call to a nearby ship helped save a third of the passengers. What we call a radio is actually a **receiver**. The **waves** it receives come from a **transmitter**. Radio is an important source of **entertainment**. AM radio carries all kinds of radio **programs**. However, **listeners** often prefer musical programs on the FM waveband or from **satellites** because the sound quality is better.

단체들의 위험 ● 가산명사 과격론자, 급진파 ❑ 나와 바네사는 1965년부터 1967년까지 버클리대 급진파 운동권 학생으로 함께 활동했다.

radius의 복수형

1 불가산명사 라디오 방송 ❑ 지난 열두 달은 지방 라디오 방송에 있어 힘겨운 시기였다. **2** 단수명사 라디오 프로그램 ❑ 많은 사람들이 아침에는 라디오를 듣는 경향이 있다. **3** 가산명사 라디오 ❑ 그는 안락의자에 앉아 라디오를 틀었다. **4** 불가산명사 무선 전신, 무전 ❑ 그들은 반군 지도자와 하루 두 번 무전으로 연락한다. **5** 가산명사 무선 전신기, 무전기 ❑ 브루스 래프랜드 판사가 무전기로 응케 경보를 울린 젊은 순경의 용기를 칭찬했다. **6** 타동사/자동사 무전으로 연락하다 ❑ 장교가 무전으로 조언을 청했다.

형용사 방사능의, 방사성의 ❑ 정부가 50년 동안 퍼날드에 방사성 폐기물을 저장해 왔다. ● 방사능, 방사성 불가산명사 ❑ 강도가 약한 방사능에 오염된 고형 폐기물의 저장 및 처리

1 단수명사 반경 ❑ 나이젤은 집 주위 반경 10마일 내에서 일거리를 찾아 헤맸다. **2** 가산명사 반지름, 반경 ❑ 그가 반경 30마일 정도 되는 반원을 가리켰다.

고유명사 영국 공군 ❑ 배에 물이 들어오기 시작한 후 영국 공군 헬리콥터가 선원들을 구조했다.

1 가산명사 추첨식 복권 ❑ 추첨식 복권 더 드릴까요? 한 장에 25펜스, 1파운드에 다섯 장입니다. **2** 타동사 추첨을 통해 주다 ❑ 프로그램마다 추첨을 통해 멋진 상품을 드립니다.

1 가산명사 뗏목 ❑ 대나무 뗏목을 타고 울창한 밀림 속으로 강을 따라 가는 여행 **2** 가산명사 고무보트 ❑ 선원들은 이틀 밤낮을 고무보트에서 보냈다.

가산명사 서까래 ❑ 이엉으로 덮인 지붕 서까래에 말린 양파와 마늘을 엮은 줄이 매달려 있었다.

1 가산명사 또는 불가산명사 걸레, 형겊 ❑ 그가 기름투성이 형겊에 손을 닦고 있었다. **2** 복수명사 누더기 ❑ 남자, 여자, 어린 아이들이 있었고 몇몇은 누더기 차림이었다. **3** 가산명사 신문을 경멸적으로 이르는 말 [비격식체, 탐탁찮음] ❑ "이 톰이라는 작자는 형편없는 지방 신문사에서 일해."라고 그가 말했다.

1 가산명사 또는 불가산명사 분노 ❑ 그는 분노로 얼굴이 붉게 달아올랐다. **2** 자동사 맹위를 떨치다 ❑ 네 시간 이상 화재가 맹렬히 계속되면서 열차 운행이 중단되었다. **3** 타동사/자동사 격노하다 ❑ 먼로는 오빠들이 그녀를 홀대한 것에 대해 분통을 터뜨리며 통화를 하고 있었다. ❑ 안에서는 프래니가 노발대발하고 있었다. **4** 불가산명사 (특정한 상황에서) 폭력 사태 ❑ 승무원들에 따르면 기내 폭력 사태가 일주일에 9건까지 빚어진다고 한다.

rag|ged /rǽgɪd/ ❶ ADJ Someone who is **ragged** looks messy and is wearing clothes that are old and torn. ❏ *The five survivors eventually reached safety, ragged, half-starved and exhausted.* ❷ ADJ **Ragged** clothes are old and torn. ❏ *...an elderly, bearded man in ragged clothes.* ❸ ADJ You can say that something is **ragged** when it is rough or uneven. ❏ *O'Brien formed the men into a ragged line.*

rag|ing /réɪdʒɪŋ/ ❶ ADJ **Raging** water moves very forcefully and violently. [ADJ n] ❏ *The field trip involved crossing a raging torrent.* ❷ ADJ **Raging** fire is very hot and fierce. [ADJ n] ❏ *As he came closer he saw a gigantic wall of raging flame before him.* ❸ ADJ **Raging** is used to describe things, especially bad things, that are very intense. [ADJ n] ❏ *If raging inflation returns, then interest rates will shoot up.* ❹ →see also **rage**

raid ◆◇◇ /réɪd/ (**raids, raiding, raided**) ❶ V-T When soldiers **raid** a place, they make a sudden armed attack against it, with the aim of causing damage rather than occupying any of the enemy's land. ❏ *The guerrillas raided banks and destroyed a police barracks and an electricity substation.* ● N-COUNT **Raid** is also a noun. ❏ *The rebels attempted a surprise raid on a military camp.* →see also **air raid** ❷ V-T If the police **raid** a building, they enter it suddenly and by force in order to look for dangerous criminals or for evidence of something illegal, such as drugs or weapons. ❏ *Fraud squad officers raided the firm's offices.* ● N-COUNT **Raid** is also a noun. ❏ *They were arrested early this morning after a raid on a house by thirty armed police.* ❸ V-T If someone **raids** a building or place, they enter it by force in order to steal something. [BRIT] ❏ *A 19-year-old man has been found guilty of raiding a bank.* ● N-COUNT **Raid** is also a noun. ❏ *...an armed raid on a small Post Office.*

raid|er /réɪdər/ (**raiders**) ❶ N-COUNT **Raiders** are people who enter a building or place by force in order to steal something. [BRIT] ❏ *The raiders escaped with cash and jewellery.* ❷ →see also **corporate raider**

rail ◆◇◇ /réɪl/ (**rails**) ❶ N-COUNT A **rail** is a horizontal bar attached to posts or fixed around the edge of something as a fence or support. ❏ *They had to walk across an emergency footbridge, holding onto a rope that served as a rail.* ❷ N-COUNT A **rail** is a horizontal bar that you hang things on. ❏ *This pair of curtains will fit a rail up to 7ft 6in wide.* ❸ N-COUNT **Rails** are the steel bars which trains run on. ❏ *The train left the rails but somehow forced its way back onto the line.* ❹ N-UNCOUNT If you travel or send something **by rail**, you travel or send it on a train. ❏ *The president traveled by rail to his home town.* ❺ PHRASE If something is **back on the rails**, it is beginning to be successful again after a period when it almost failed. [JOURNALISM] ❏ *They are keen to get the negotiating process back on the rails.* ❻ PHRASE If someone **goes off the rails**, they start to behave in a way that other people think is unacceptable or very strange, for example they start taking drugs or breaking the law. ❏ *They've got to do something about these children because clearly they've gone off the rails.* →see **train, transportation**

rail|ing /réɪlɪŋ/ (**railings**) N-COUNT A fence made from metal bars is called a **railing** or **railings**. ❏ *He walked out on to the balcony where he rested his arms on the railing.*

rail|road /réɪlroʊd/ (**railroads, railroading, railroaded**) ❶ N-COUNT A **railroad** is a route between two places along which trains travel on steel rails. [AM; BRIT **railway**] ❏ *...railroad tracks that led to nowhere.* ❷ N-COUNT A **railroad** is a company or organization that operates railroad routes. [AM; BRIT **railway**] ❏ *The Chicago and Northwestern Railroad wouldn't go along with that arrangement and said it would shut down completely.* ❸ V-T If you **railroad** someone **into** doing something, you make them do it although they do not really want to, by hurrying them and putting pressure on them. ❏ *He more or less railroaded the rest of Europe into recognising the new "independent" states.*

rail|way ◆◇◇ /réɪlweɪ/ (**railways**) ❶ N-COUNT A **railway** is the system and network of tracks that trains travel on. [mainly AM] ❷ N-COUNT A **railway** is a route between two places along which trains travel on steel rails. [mainly BRIT; AM usually **railroad**] ❏ *The road ran beside a railway.* ❸ N-COUNT A **railway** is a company or organization that operates railroad routes. [BRIT; AM **railroad**] ❏ *...the state-owned French railway.* →see **train**

rain ◆◆◇ /réɪn/ (**rains, raining, rained**) ❶ N-UNCOUNT **Rain** is water that falls from the clouds in small drops. [also the N] ❏ *I hope you didn't get soaked standing out in the rain.* ❷ N-PLURAL In countries where rain only falls in certain seasons, this rain is referred to as **the rains**. ❏ *...the spring, when the rains came.* ❸ V-I When rain falls, you can say that **it is raining**. ❏ *It was raining hard, and she hadn't an umbrella.* ❹ V-T/V-I If someone **rains** blows, kicks, or bombs **on** a person or place, the person or place is attacked by many blows, kicks, or bombs. You can also say that blows, kicks, or bombs **rain on** a person or place. ❏ *The police, raining blows on rioters and spectators alike, cleared the park.* ● PHRASAL VERB **Rain down** means the same as **rain**. ❏ *Fighter aircraft rained down high explosives.* →see **disaster, storm, water**

Thesaurus　　　　rain의 참조어

N.　　drizzle, shower, sleet ❶

---

rain|bow /réɪnboʊ/ (**rainbows**) N-COUNT A **rainbow** is an arch of different colors that you can sometimes see in the sky when it is raining. ❏ *...silk and satin in every shade of the rainbow.*
→see Word Web: **rainbow**

rain check PHRASE If you say you will take a **rain check** on an offer or suggestion, you mean that you do not want to accept it now, but you might accept it at another time. ❏ *I was planning to ask you in for a brandy, but if you want to take a rain check, that's fine.*

---

❶ 형용사 남루한 차림의 ❏ 생존자 다섯 명이 마침내 안전한 곳에 닿았을 때 그들은 남루한 옷차림에 지칠 대로 지쳐 거의 굶어 죽어 가는 상태였다. ❷ 형용사 해어진, 누더기너덜한 ❏ 해어진 옷을 입고 턱수염을 한 노인 ❸ 형용사 울퉁불퉁한, 들쭉날쭉한 ❏ 오브라이언이 부하들을 대충 들쭉날쭉 줄을 세웠다.

❶ 형용사 맹렬한, 세찬 ❏ 야외 활동에 세찬 급류 횡단도 포함되어 있었다. ❷ 형용사 활활 타오르는 ❏ 그가 가까이 다가서자 눈앞에 활활 타오르는 거대한 불길이 나타났다. ❸ 형용사 극심한 ❏ 인플레가 다시 극심해지면, 금리가 치솟을 것이다.

❶ 타동사 습격하다 ❏ 게릴라들이 은행을 습격하고 경찰 막사 하나와 변전소가 있는 곳을 파괴했다. ● 가산명사 습격 ❏ 반군이 군 막사에 대한 기습 공격을 시도했다. ❷ 타동사 불시에 덮치다, 불시 단속하다 ❏ 사기 단속반 경찰들이 그 회사 사무실을 불시에 덮쳤다. ● 가산명사 불시 단속 ❏ 오늘 새벽 무장 경찰 30명이 한 집을 불시 단속한 후 그들이 체포되었다. ❸ 타동사 침입하다 [영국영어] ❏ 19세 청년이 은행 침입으로 유죄 판결을 받았다. ● 가산명사 침입 ❏ 작은 우체국에 무장 괴한 침입

❶ 가산명사 침입자, 강도 [영국영어] ❏ 강도들은 현금과 보석을 가지고 달아났다.

❶ 가산명사 난간 ❏ 그들은 난간 역할을 하는 줄을 잡고 비상 인도교를 건너가야 했다. ❷ 가산명사 가로대 ❏ 이 한 쌍의 커튼은 폭이 7피트 6인치 가로대에까지 사용 가능하다. ❸ 가산명사 철도 ❏ 기차가 철도를 벗어났지만 어떻게 해서 다시 궤도에 올랐다. ❹ 불가산명사 철도로, 기차로 ❏ 대통령이 고향까지 기차로 여행했다. ❺ 구 다시 정상 궤도에 오른 [언론] ❏ 그들은 협상 과정을 다시 정상 궤도에 올리는 데 열중하고 있다. ❻ 구 탈선하다 ❏ 그들은 이들이 분명 탈선한 아이들이므로 이 아이들에 대해 뭔가 조치를 취해야 한다.

가산명사 난간 ❏ 그는 발코니로 나가 난간 위에 팔을 얹었다.

❶ 가산명사 철도, 선로 [미국영어; 영국영어 railway] ❏ 갈 곳을 잃은 철로 ❷ 가산명사 철도 회사 [미국영어; 영국영어 railway] ❏ 시카고 노스웨스트 철도는 그 협상안을 수용하지 않을 것이며 운행을 완전 중단하겠다고 말했다. ❸ 타동사 다그치다 ❏ 그는 신생 '독립국'들을 인정하게끔 나머지 유럽 국가들을 다소 다그쳤다.

❶ 가산명사 철도 [주로 미국영어] ❷ 가산명사 선로 [주로 영국영어; 미국영어 대개 railroad] ❏ 도로가 선로 옆을 따라 나 있었다. ❸ 가산명사 철도 회사 [영국영어; 미국영어 railroad] ❏ 프랑스 국영 철도 회사

❶ 불가산명사 비 ❏ 나는 네가 비를 맞아서 흠뻑 젖지 않았기를 바래. ❷ 복수명사 우기 ❏ 봄, 그리고 찾아온 우기 ❸ 자동사 비가 오다 ❏ 비가 많이 내리고 있었고 그녀는 우산이 없었다. ❹ 타동사/자동사 퍼붓다 ❏ 경찰이 폭도와 일반인을 가리지 않고 연신 구타하며 사람들을 공원에서 해산시켰다. ● 구동사 퍼붓다 ❏ 전투기가 고성능 폭약을 퍼부었다.

가산명사 무지개 ❏ 무지개의 다양한 색깔로 나온 실크와 공단

구 다음번으로 미루다 ❏ 우리 집에서 브랜디 한 잔 마시자고 물어보려고 했는데, 네가 다음으로 미루고 싶으면 그래도 돼.

a b c d e f g h i j k l m n o p q r s t u v w x y z

Word Web   rainbow

Sunlight contains all of the colors. When a **ray** of sunlight passes through a prism, it splits into separate colors. This is also what happens when light passes through the drops of water in the air. The light is refracted, and we see a **rainbow**. The colors of the rainbow are **red**, **orange**, **yellow**, **green**, **blue**, indigo, and **violet**. One tradition says that there is a pot of gold at the end of the rainbow. Other myths say that the rainbow is a bridge between Earth and the land of the gods.

rain|coat /reɪnkoʊt/ (**raincoats**) N-COUNT A **raincoat** is a waterproof coat.
→see **clothing**

rain|drop /reɪndrɒp/ (**raindrops**) N-COUNT A **raindrop** is a single drop of rain.

rain|fall /reɪnfɔl/ (**rainfalls**) N-UNCOUNT **Rainfall** is the amount of rain that falls in a place during a particular period. ❑ *There have been four years of below average rainfall.* →see **erosion, storm**

rain|for|est /reɪnfɒrɪst, BRIT reɪnfɒrɪst/ (**rainforests**) [AM also **rain forest**] N-VAR A **rainforest** is a thick forest of tall trees which is found in tropical areas where there is a lot of rain. ❑ *...the destruction of the Amazon rainforest.*

rainy /reɪni/ (**rainier, rainiest**) ADJ During a **rainy** day, season, or period it rains a lot. ❑ *The rainy season in the Andes normally starts in December.*

raise ◆◆◆ /reɪz/ (**raises, raising, raised**) **1** V-T If you **raise** something, you move it so that it is in a higher position. ❑ *He raised his hand to wave.* ❑ *Milton raised the glass to his lips.* **2** V-T If you **raise** a flag, you display it by moving it up a pole or into a high place where it can be seen. ❑ *They had raised the white flag in surrender.* **3** V-T If you **raise yourself**, you lift your body so that you are standing up straight, or so that you are no longer lying flat. ❑ *He raised himself into a sitting position.* **4** V-T If you **raise** the rate or level of something, you increase it. ❑ *The Republic of Ireland is expected to raise interest rates.* **5** V-T To **raise** the standard of something means to improve it. ❑ *...a new drive to raise standards of literacy in Britain's schools.* **6** V-T If you **raise** your **voice**, you speak more loudly, usually because you are angry. ❑ *Don't you raise your voice to me, Henry Rollins!* **7** N-COUNT A **raise** is an increase in your wages or salary. [AM; BRIT **rise**] ❑ *Within two months Kelly got a raise.* **8** V-T If you **raise** money for a charity or an institution, you ask people for money which you collect on its behalf. ❑ *...events held to raise money for Help the Aged.* **9** V-T If a person or company **raises** money that they need, they manage to get it, for example by selling their property or by borrowing. ❑ *They raised the money to buy the house and two hundred acres of grounds.* **10** V-T If an event **raises** a particular emotion or question, it makes people feel the emotion or consider the question. ❑ *The agreement has raised hopes that the war may end soon.* **11** V-T If you **raise** a subject, an objection, or a question, you mention it or bring it to someone's attention. ❑ *He had been consulted and had raised no objections.* **12** V-T Someone who **raises** a child takes care of it until it is grown up. ❑ *My mother was an amazing woman. She raised four of us kids virtually singlehandedly.* **13** V-T If someone **raises** a particular type of animal or crop, they breed that type of animal or grow that type of crop. ❑ *He raises 2,000 acres of wheat and hay.* **14 to raise the alarm** →see **alarm. to raise** your **eyebrows** →see **eyebrow. to raise a finger** →see **finger**

You should be careful not to confuse the verbs **raise** and **rise. Raise** is a transitive verb and usually followed by an object, whereas **rise** is an intransitive verb and not followed by an object. **Rise** can also not be used in the passive. ❑ *...the government's decision to raise prices... The number of dead is likely to rise.* Both **raise** and **rise** can be used as nouns with meaning pay increase. **Raise** is used in American English, and **rise** is used in British English. ❑ *Millions of Americans get a pay raise today....a rise of at least 12 percent.*

Thesaurus   raise의 참조어

V.   elevate, hold up, lift; *(ant.)* lower **1**
N.   addition, hike, increase **7**

Word Partnership   raise의 연어

N.   raise *your* hand **1**
   raise fares, raise interest rates, raise the level of *something*, raise prices, raise taxes **4**
   raise your voice **6**
   pay raise **7**
   raise money **8 9**
   raise capital/revenue **9**
   raise doubts, raise eyebrows, raise hopes **10**
   raise concerns, raise an issue, raise questions **10 11**
   raise objections **11**
   raise a children/family/kids **12**
   raise crops **13**

rai|sin /reɪzⁿn/ (**raisins**) N-COUNT **Raisins** are dried grapes. ❑ *For breakfast I have porridge made with water, to which I add raisins.*

가산명사 우의, 레인코트

가산명사 빗방울

불가산명사 강우량 ❑ 지금까지 4년 연속 강우량이 평균치를 밑돌고 있다.

[미국영어 rain forest] 가산명사 또는 불가산명사 열대 우림 ❑ 아마존 열대 우림 파괴

형용사 비가 많이 오는 ❑ 안데스 산맥의 우기는 보통 12월에 시작된다.

1 타동사 올리다, 들어 올리다 ❑ 그는 손을 들어 흔들었다. ❑ 밀턴이 잔을 들어 올려 입술에 갖다 댔다. **2** 타동사 들어 올리다, 게양하다 ❑ 그들은 항복의 표시로 백기를 들어 올렸다. **3** 타동사 몸을 일으키다 ❑ 그가 몸을 일으켜 앉았다. **4** 타동사 올리다, 인상하다 ❑ 아일랜드 공화국이 금리 인상을 단행할 것으로 예상된다. **5** 타동사 올리다, 향상시키다 ❑ 영국 학생들의 읽기 및 쓰기 능력 수준을 높이기 위한 새로운 운동 **6** 타동사 목소리를 높이다 ❑ 헨리 롤린스, 내 앞에서 목소리 높이지 마! **7** 가산명사 임금 인상 [미국영어; 영국영어 rise] ❑ 켈리는 두 달도 못 돼 봉급을 올려 받았다. **8** 타동사 모금하다 ❑ '노인 구호' 기금 조성을 위해 열린 행사들 **9** 타동사 마련하다, 조달하다 ❑ 그들은 집과 땅 200에이커를 살 돈을 마련했다. **10** 타동사 일으키다, 자아내다, 제기하다 ❑ 이번 합의는 전쟁이 곧 끝날 수도 있다는 희망을 불러일으켰다. **11** 타동사 제기하다 ❑ 의견을 물었을 때 그는 아무런 반대도 하지 않았었다. **12** 타동사 키우다 ❑ 우리 어머니는 놀라운 분이셨다. 어머니는 우리 네 명의 자식을 사실상 혼잣손으로 키우셨다. **13** 타동사 사육하다; 재배하다 ❑ 그의 2천 에이커에 달하는 밀과 건초를 재배한다.

동사 raise와 rise를 혼동하지 않도록 주의해야 한다. raise는 타동사이며 대개 목적어가 뒤에 오는 반면, rise는 자동사이며 목적어가 따라 오지 않는다. rise는 또한 수동태로도 쓸 수 없다. ❑ ...물가를 인상하려는 정부의 결정... 사망자의 수가 늘어날 것 같다. raise와 rise는 모두 임금 인상을 의미하는 명사로 쓸 수 있다. raise는 미국 영어에서, rise는 영국 영어에서 쓰인다. ❑ 수백만 미국인들의 임금이 오늘 인상된다.... 적어도 12퍼센트의 임금 인상

가산명사 건포도 ❑ 나는 아침 식사로 물을 넣어 만든 포리지에 건포도를 곁들여 먹는다.

rake /reɪk/ (**rakes, raking, raked**) **1** N-COUNT A **rake** is a garden tool consisting of a row of metal or wooden teeth attached to a long handle. You can use a rake to make the earth smooth and level before you put plants in, or to gather leaves together. **2** V-T If you **rake** a surface, you move a rake across it in order to make it smooth and level. □ *Rake the soil, press the seed into it, then cover it lightly.* **3** V-T If you **rake** leaves or ashes, you move them somewhere using a rake or a similar tool. □ *I watched the men rake leaves into heaps.*

▶**rake in** PHRASAL VERB If you say that someone **is raking in** money, you mean that they are making a lot of money very easily, more easily than you think they should. [INFORMAL] □ *The privatization allowed companies to rake in huge profits.*

rake-off (**rake-offs**) N-COUNT If someone who has helped to arrange a business deal takes or gets a **rake-off**, they illegally or unfairly take a share of the profits. [INFORMAL] □ *Hall takes a rake-off, individually negotiated, often amounting to tens of thousands of pounds on most project deals.*

rally ♦◇◇ /ˈræli/ (**rallies, rallying, rallied**) **1** N-COUNT A **rally** is a large public meeting that is held in order to show support for something such as a political party. □ *About three thousand people held a rally to mark international human rights day.* **2** V-T/V-I When people **rally to** something or when something **rallies** them, they unite to support it. □ *Her cabinet colleagues have continued to rally to her support.* **3** V-I When someone or something **rallies**, they begin to recover or improve after having been weak. □ *He rallied enough to thank his doctors.* ● N-COUNT **Rally** is also a noun. □ *After a brief rally the shares returned to 126p.* **4** N-COUNT A **rally** is a competition in which vehicles are driven over public roads. □ *Carlos Sainz of Spain has won the New Zealand Motor Rally.* **5** N-COUNT A **rally** in tennis, badminton, or squash is a continuous series of shots that the players exchange without stopping. [BRIT also **rally round**] □ *...a long rally.*

Word Partnership	*rally*의 연어
ADJ.	**political** rally **1**
N.	**campaign** rally, **protest** rally **1**
	rally **in support of** *someone/something* **2**
	prices/stocks rally **3**

▶**rally around** PHRASAL VERB When people **rally around** or **rally round**, they work as a group in order to support someone or something at a difficult time. □ *So many people have rallied round to help the family.*

ram /ræm/ (**rams, ramming, rammed**) **1** V-T If a vehicle **rams** something such as another vehicle, it crashes into it with a lot of force, usually deliberately. □ *The thieves fled, ramming the policeman's car.* **2** V-T If you **ram** something somewhere, you push it there with great force. □ *He rammed the key into the lock and kicked the front door open.* **3** N-COUNT A **ram** is an adult male sheep. **4** PHRASE If something **rams home** a message or a point, it makes it clear in a way that is very forceful and that people are likely to listen to. □ *The report by Marks & Spencer's chairman will ram this point home.* **5** to **ram** something **down** someone's **throat** →see **throat**

RAM /ræm/ N-UNCOUNT **RAM** is the part of a computer in which information is stored while you are using it. **RAM** is an abbreviation for "Random Access Memory." [COMPUTING] □ *...an IBM PC with hard disk drive and 256k RAM minimum. 512k RAM is recommended and 640k RAM is preferred.*

ram|ble /ˈræmbᵊl/ (**rambles, rambling, rambled**) **1** N-COUNT A **ramble** is a long walk in the countryside. □ *...an hour's ramble through the woods.* **2** V-I If you **ramble**, you go on a long walk in the countryside. □ *...freedom to ramble across the moors.* **3** V-I If you say that a person **rambles** in their speech or writing, you mean they do not make much sense because they keep going off the subject in a confused way. □ *Sometimes she spoke sensibly; sometimes she rambled.*

rami|fi|ca|tion /ˌræmɪfɪˈkeɪʃᵊn/ (**ramifications**) N-COUNT The **ramifications** of a decision, plan, or event are all its consequences and effects, especially ones which are not obvious at first. □ *The book analyses the social and political ramifications of AIDS for the gay community.*

ramp /ræmp/ (**ramps**) N-COUNT A **ramp** is a sloping surface between two places that are at different levels. □ *Lillian was coming down the ramp from the museum.* →see **skateboarding, traffic**

ram|page (**rampages, rampaging, rampaged**)

Pronounced /ræmˈpeɪdʒ/ for meaning **1**, and /ˈræmpeɪdʒ/ for meaning **2**.

1 V-I When people or animals **rampage** through a place, they rush about there in a wild or violent way, causing damage or destruction. □ *Hundreds of youths rampaged through the town, shop windows were smashed and cars overturned.* **2** PHRASE If people go **on the rampage**, they rush about in a wild or violent way, causing damage or destruction. □ *The prisoners went on the rampage destroying everything in their way.*

ram|pant /ˈræmpənt/ ADJ If you describe something bad, such as a crime or disease, as **rampant**, you mean that it is very common and is increasing in an uncontrolled way. □ *Inflation is rampant and industry in decline.*

ram|shack|le /ˈræmʃækᵊl/ **1** ADJ A **ramshackle** building is badly made or in bad condition, and looks as if it is likely to fall down. □ *They entered the shop, which was a curious ramshackle building.* **2** ADJ A **ramshackle** system, union, or collection of things has been put together without much thought and is not likely to work very well. □ *They joined with a ramshackle alliance of other rebels.*

---

1 가산명사 갈퀴, 써레 **2** 타동사 써레질을 하다 □ 땅에 쓰레질을 하고 써를 눌러 심은 다음에 흙을 가볍게 덮어 주세요. **3** 타동사 (갈퀴로) 긁어모으다 □ 나는 남자들이 나뭇잎을 수북이 긁어모으는 모습을 지켜보았다.

구동사 (돈을) 긁어 들이다 [비격식체] □ 민영화로 기업들이 엄청난 수익을 긁어 들일 수 있었다.

가산명사 (부정한 수법에 의한) 몫, 리베이트 [비격식체] □ 홀은 대부분의 프로젝트 계약에서 개별 협상하에 종종 수만 파운드에 달하는 리베이트를 받았다.

1 가산명사 대회, 집회 □ 대략 3천 명의 사람들이 국제 인권의 날을 기념하기 위해 집회를 열었다. **2** 타동사/자동사 뒤받치다; 단결시키다 □ 그녀의 내각 동료들은 계속 단결해서 그녀를 지지해 왔다. **3** 자동사 회복하다; 반등하다 □ 그는 의사들에게 감사의 말을 전할 수 있을 정도로 회복했다. ● 가산명사 회복; 반등 □ 일시적 반등 후 주가가 다시 126포인트가 되었다. **4** 가산명사 랠리 (자동차 경주) □ 스페인의 카를로스 사인즈가 뉴질랜드 모터랠리에서 우승을 차지했다. **5** 가산명사 (테니스 등의) 랠리 [영국영어 rally round] □ 오래 계속된 랠리

구동사 (도우려) 한데 모이다 □ 상당히 많은 사람들이 이 가족을 돕기 위해 한데 모여들었다.

1 타동사 치다, 충돌하다 □ 도둑들이 경찰차를 치고 달아났다. **2** 타동사 쑤셔 넣다, 밀어 넣다 □ 그는 자물쇠에 열쇠를 쑤셔 넣고 현관문을 발로 차서 열었다. **3** 가산명사 숫양 **4** 구 강조하다 □ 막스 앤 스펜서 회장의 보고서는 이 점을 강조할 것이다.

불가산명사 (컴퓨터) 램 [컴퓨터] □ 하드디스크와 최저 256킬로 램을 갖춘 아이비엠 피시. 512킬로 램 추천, 640킬로 램 인기.

1 가산명사 (시골길) 산책 □ 한 시간 동안의 숲 속 산책 **2** 자동사 산책하다, 산책하러 □ 황야를 거닐 수 있는 자유 **3** 자동사 두서없이 말하다; 두서없이 쓰다 □ 그녀는 조리 있게 말할 때도 있고 두서없이 말할 때도 있다.

가산명사 파장, 영향 □ 책은 에이즈가 동성연애자 사회에 미치는 사회적 정치적 파장을 분석하고 있다.

가산명사 경사로, 램프 □ 릴리안이 박물관 경사로를 내려오고 있었다.

1의 의미일 때는 /ræmˈpeɪdʒ/로, **2**의 의미일 때는 /ˈræmpeɪdʒ/로 발음된다.

1 자동사 미친 듯이 날뛰다, 휩쓸고 지나가다 □ 수백 명의 젊은이들이 마을을 휩쓸고 지나갔다. 상점 창문이 부서지고 자동차는 전복되었다. **2** 구 미쳐 날뛰다, 휩쓸고 지나가는 □ 재소자들이 갇히는 것은 모두 파괴하며 미친 듯이 날뛰었다.

형용사 만연한, 걷잡을 수 없는 □ 인플레는 걷잡을 수 없으며 산업은 쇠퇴하고 있다.

1 형용사 쓰러질 듯한 □ 그들은 가게로 들어갔다. 금방 쓰러질 듯 기이한 건물이었다. **2** 형용사 엉성한, 아무렇게나 만든 □ 그들은 다른 반군들로 구성된 오합지졸과 행동을 같이했다.

a b c d e f g h i j k l m n o p q r s t u v w x y z

A

ran /ræn/ Ran is the past tense of **run**.

run의 과거

ranch /ræntʃ/ (**ranches**) N-COUNT A **ranch** is a large farm used for raising animals, especially cattle, horses, or sheep. ❑ He lives on a cattle ranch in Australia.

가산명사 대목장 ❑ 그는 호주에 있는 한 소 목장에서 산다.

B

R & D /ɑr ən di/ also **R and D** N-UNCOUNT **R&D** refers to the research and development work or department within a large company or organization. **R&D** is an abbreviation for "Research and Development." ❑ Businesses need to train their workers better, and spend more on R&D.

불가산명사 연구 개발, 연구 개발부 ❑ 기업들은 직원 교육을 강화하고 연구 개발에 지출을 늘릴 필요가 있다.

C

ran|dom /rændəm/ ▸ ADJ A **random** sample or method is one in which all the people or things involved have an equal chance of being chosen. ❑ The survey used a random sample of two thousand people across England and Wales. ● **ran|dom|ly** ADV [ADV with v] ❑ ...interviews with a randomly selected sample of thirty girls aged between 13 and 18. ▸ ADJ If you describe events as **random**, you mean that they do not seem to follow a definite plan or pattern. ❑ ...random violence against innocent victims. ● **ran|dom|ly** ADV [ADV with v] ❑ ...drinks and magazines left scattered randomly around. ▸ PHRASE If you choose people or things **at random**, you do not use any particular method, so they all have an equal chance of being chosen. ❑ We received several answers, and we picked one at random. ▸ PHRASE If something happens **at random**, it happens without a definite plan or pattern. ❑ Three people were killed by shots fired at random from a minibus.

❶ 형용사 무작위의, 임의의 ❑ 설문 조사는 잉글랜드와 웨일스 전역에서 2천 명을 무작위로 추출한 표본 집단을 대상으로 실시되었다. ● 무작위로 부사 ❑ 13세에서 18세 사이의 여학생 30명을 무작위로 표본 추출해야 한 인터뷰 ❷ 형용사 닥치는 대로의, 되는 대로의 ❑ 무고한 사람들을 상대로 닥치는 대로 행사한 폭력 ● 닥치는 대로, 아무렇게나 부사 ❑ 여기저기 아무렇게나 흩어져 있는 술과 잡지 ❸ 구 무작위로, 임의로 ❑ 우리는 몇 가지 답변을 받았고 그 중에서 무작위로 하나를 뽑았다. ❹ 구 닥치는 대로, 되는 대로 ❑ 소형 버스에서 마구잡이로 쏜 총에 맞아 세 명이 목숨을 잃었다.

D

E

F

G

rang /ræŋ/ Rang is the past tense of **ring**.

ring의 과거

range ♦♦◇ /reɪndʒ/ (**ranges, ranging, ranged**) ❶ N-COUNT A **range of** things is a number of different things of the same general kind. ❑ A wide range of colors and patterns are available. ❷ N-COUNT A **range** is the complete group that is included between two points on a scale of measurement or quality. ❑ The average age range is between 35 and 55. ❸ N-COUNT The **range** of something is the maximum area in which it can reach things or detect things. ❑ The 120mm mortar has a range of 18,000 yards. ❹ V-I If things **range between** two points or **range from** one point **to** another, they vary within these points on a scale of measurement or quality. ❑ They range in price from $3 to $15. ❑ ...offering merchandise ranging from the everyday to the esoteric. ❺ N-COUNT A **range** of mountains or hills is a line of them. ❑ ...the massive mountain ranges to the north. ❻ N-COUNT A rifle **range** or a shooting **range** is a place where people can practice shooting at targets. ❑ It reminds me of my days on the rifle range preparing for duty in Vietnam. ❼ N-COUNT A **range** or **kitchen range** is an old-fashioned metal stove. [BRIT] ❽ N-COUNT A **range** or **kitchen range** is a large metal device for cooking food using gas or electricity. A range consists of a broiler, an oven, and some gas or electric burners. [AM; BRIT usually **cooker**] ❾ N-COUNT A **free-range** ❿ PHRASE If something is **in range** or **within range**, it is near enough to be reached or detected. If it is **out of range**, it is too far away to be reached or detected. ❑ Cars are driven through the mess, splashing everyone in range. ⓫ PHRASE If you see or hit something **at close range** or **from close range**, you are very close to it when you see it or hit it. If you do something **at a range of** half a mile, for example, you are half a mile away from it when you do it. ❑ He was shot in the head at close range. →see **graph**

❶ 가산명사 범위 ❑ 다양한 색상과 문양을 폭넓게 선택할 수 있다. ❷ 가산명사 범위, ~ 대 ❑ 평균 연령대는 35세에서 55세 사이다. ❸ 가산명사 사정거리 ❑ 120밀리미터 박격포의 사정거리는 1만8천 야드이다. ❹ 자동사 범위가 ~이다, ~에 이르다 ❑ 이들의 가격대는 3~15달러이다. ❑ 생활용품에서부터 은밀한 물품에 이르기까지 모든 상품 제공 ❺ 가산명사 산맥, 산줄기 ❑ 북으로 펼쳐지는 거대한 산맥 ❻ 가산명사 사격장 ❑ 그러고 보니 베트남 참전을 준비하며 사격장에서 보낸 나날들이 떠오른다. ❼ 가산명사 취사용 화덕 [영국영어] ❽ 가산명사 (조리용) 레인지 [미국영어; 영국영어 대개 cooker] ❿ 구 사정거리 내의, 닿을 수 있는; 사정거리 밖의, 닿을 수 없는 ❑ 차가 진창을 지나가면서 주변 사람들 모두에게 흙탕물을 튀긴다. ⓫ 구 바로 가까이에; ~의 거리에서 ❑ 그는 바로 가까이에서 쏜 총에 머리를 맞았다.

H

I

J

K

L

M

N

O

P

Q

R

rang|er /reɪndʒər/ (**rangers**) N-COUNT A **ranger** is a person whose job is to take care of a forest or large park. ❑ Bill Justice is a park ranger at the Carlsbad Caverns National Park.

가산명사 (공원 등의) 관리인, 감시원 ❑ 빌 저스티스는 칼스배드 동굴 국립공원의 공원 경비원이다.

S

rank ♦♦◇ /ræŋk/ (**ranks, ranking, ranked**) ❶ N-VAR Someone's **rank** is the position or grade that they have in an organization. ❑ He eventually rose to the rank of captain. ❷ N-VAR Someone's **rank** is the social class, especially the high social class, that they belong to. [FORMAL] ❑ He must be treated as a hostage of high rank, not as a common prisoner. ❸ V-T/V-I If an official organization **ranks** someone or something 1st, 5th, or 50th, for example, they calculate that the person or thing has that position on a scale. You can also say that someone or something **ranks** 1st, 5th, or 50th, for example. ❑ The report ranks the UK 20th out of 22 advanced nations. ❑ ...the only British woman to be ranked in the top 50 of the women's world rankings. ❹ V-T/V-I If you say that someone or something **ranks** high or low on a scale, you are saying how good or important you think they are. ❑ His prices rank high among those of other contemporary photographers. ❑ Investors ranked South Korea high among Asian nations. ❑ St Petersburg's night life ranks as more exciting than the capital's. ❺ N-PLURAL The **ranks** of a group or organization are the people who belong to it. ❑ There were some misgivings within the ranks of the media too. ❻ N-PLURAL The **ranks** are the ordinary members of an organization, especially of the armed forces. ❑ Most store managers have worked their way up through the ranks. ❼ N-COUNT A **rank of** people or things is a row of them. ❑ Ranks of police in riot gear stood nervously by. ❽ N-COUNT A **taxi rank** is a place on a city street where taxis park when they are available. [mainly BRIT; AM **stand**] ❑ The man led the way to the taxi rank. ❾ PHRASE If you say that a member of a group or organization **breaks ranks**, you mean that they disobey the instructions of their group or organization. ❑ Britain appears unlikely to break ranks with other members of the European Union. ❿ PHRASE If you say that the members of a group **close ranks**, you mean that they are supporting each other only because their group is being criticized. ❑ Institutions tend to close ranks when a member has been accused of misconduct.

❶ 가산명사 또는 불가산명사 계급, 지위 ❑ 그는 결국 대위 계급까지 올라갔다. ❷ 가산명사 또는 불가산명사 계층 [격식체] ❑ 그는 일반 포로가 아니라 고위층 인질 대우를 해야 한다. ❸ 타동사/자동사 순위를 매기다 ❑ 보고서에 따르면 영국은 선진국 22개국 가운데 20위이다. ❑ 여성 세계 랭킹 상위 50위 안에 든 유일한 영국 여성 ❹ 타동사/자동사 위치하다; 평가하다 ❑ 그의 작품 가격은 현대 사진작가 중에서도 높은 축에 속한다. ❑ 투자자들은 아시아 국가 중 한국을 높이 평가한다. ❑ 세인트 피터스버그의 야간 문화는 수도의 야간 문화보다 더 흥미진진하다고 꼽힌다. ❺ 복수명사 구성원 ❑ 언론계 종사자에게도 어느 정도 우려가 있었다. ❻ 복수명사 일반 직원; 사병 ❑ 대부분의 상점 지배인들은 일반 점원에서 시작해 경력을 쌓아 온 사람들이다. ❼ 가산명사 줄, 열 ❑ 전투 경찰대가 긴장된 상태로 줄을 지어 대기하고 있었다. ❽ 가산명사 (택시) 승강장 [주로 영국영어; 미국영어 stand] ❑ 남자가 택시 승강장으로 길을 안내했다. ❾ 구 이탈하다, 따르지 않다 ❑ 영국이 유럽 연합의 기타 회원국과 다른 노선을 취할 가능성이 적어 보인다. ❿ 구 결속을 굳히다 ❑ 구성원이 비행으로 비난받을 때 그 단체의 결속력이 높아지는 경향이 있다.

T

U

V

W

X

Y

Z

a b c d e f g h i j k l m n o p q r s t u v w x y z

<table>
<tr><td colspan="2">Thesaurus   rank의 참조어</td></tr>
<tr><td>N.</td><td>class, grade, position, status ▮ ▮</td></tr>
<tr><td>V.</td><td>assign, place ▮</td></tr>
</table>

<table>
<tr><td colspan="2">Word Partnership   rank의 연어</td></tr>
<tr><td>ADJ.</td><td>high rank, top rank ▮ ▮</td></tr>
<tr><td>ADV.</td><td>rank above, rank below ▮
rank high ▮</td></tr>
</table>

rank and file N-SING The **rank and file** are the ordinary members of an organization or the ordinary workers in a company, as opposed to its leaders or managers. [JOURNALISM] ❏ *There was widespread support for him among the rank and file.*

ran|sack /rǽnsæk/ (ransacks, ransacking, ransacked) V-T If people **ransack** a building, they damage things in it or make it very messy, often because they are looking for something in a quick and careless way. ❏ *Demonstrators ransacked and burned the house where he was staying.*

ran|som /rǽnsəm/ (ransoms, ransoming, ransomed) ▮ N-VAR A **ransom** is the money that has to be paid to someone so that they will set free a person they have kidnapped. ❏ *Her kidnapper successfully extorted a £17,000 ransom for her release.* ▮ V-T If you **ransom** someone who has been kidnapped, you pay the money to set them free. ❏ *The same system was used for ransoming or exchanging captives.* ▮ PHRASE If a kidnapper **is holding** a person **for ransom** in American English, or **is holding** someone **to ransom** or **holding** them **ransom** in British English, they keep that person prisoner until they are given what they want ❏ *He is charged with kidnapping a businessman last year and holding him for ransom.* ▮ PHRASE If you say that someone **is holding** you **for ransom** in American English, or **holding** you **to ransom** in British English, you mean that they are using their power to try to force you to do something which you do not want to do. [DISAPPROVAL] ❏ *Unison and the other unions have the power to hold the Government to ransom; as do the British Medical Association and other professional bodies.*

rant /rænt/ (rants, ranting, ranted) V-T/V-I If you say that someone **rants**, you mean that they talk loudly or angrily, and exaggerate or say foolish things. ❏ *As the boss began to rant, I stood up and went out.* ❏ *Even their three dogs got bored and fell asleep as he ranted on.* ● N-COUNT Rant is also a noun. ❏ *Part I is a rant against organized religion.* ● **rant|ing** (rantings) N-VAR ❏ *He had been listening to Goldstone's rantings all night.*

rap /ræp/ (raps, rapping, rapped) ▮ N-UNCOUNT **Rap** is a type of music in which the words are not sung but are spoken in a rapid, rhythmic way. ❏ *Her favorite music was by Run DMC, a rap group.* ▮ V-I Someone who **raps** performs rap music. ❏ *...the unexpected pleasure of hearing the Kids not only rap but even sing.* ▮ N-COUNT A **rap** is a piece of music performed in rap style, or the words that are used in it. ❏ *Every member contributes to the rap, singing either solo or as part of a rap chorus.* ▮ V-T/V-I If you **rap on** something or **rap** at it, you hit it with a series of quick blows. ❏ *Mary Ann turned and rapped on Simon's door.* ❏ *...rapping the glass with the knuckles of his right hand.* ● N-COUNT Rap is also a noun. ❏ *There was a sharp rap on the door.* ▮ N-COUNT A **rap** is an act of criticizing or blaming someone. [JOURNALISM] ❏ *Paul Ringer faces a rap after playing for Penarth on Boxing Day.* ▮ V-T If you **rap** someone **for** something, you criticize or blame them for it. [JOURNALISM] ❏ *Water industry chiefs were rapped yesterday for failing their customers.* ▮ PHRASE If someone in authority **raps** your **knuckles** or **raps** you **on the knuckles**, they criticize you or blame you for doing something they think is wrong. [JOURNALISM] ❏ *I joined the workers on strike and was rapped over the knuckles.*

rape ♦◇◇ /reɪp/ (rapes, raping, raped) ▮ V-T If someone **is raped**, they are forced to have sex, usually by violence or threats of violence. ❏ *A young woman was brutally raped in her own home.* ▮ N-VAR **Rape** is the crime of forcing someone to have sex. ❏ *Almost ninety per cent of all rapes and violent assaults went unreported.* ▮ N-COUNT **Rape** is a plant with yellow flowers which is grown as a crop. Its seeds are crushed to make cooking oil. [AM; BRIT **oilseed rape**]

rap|id ♦♦◇ /rǽpɪd/ ▮ ADJ A **rapid** change is one that happens very quickly. ❏ *...the country's rapid economic growth in the 1980's.* ● **rap|id|ly** ADV ❏ *...countries with rapidly growing populations.* ❏ *Try to rip it apart as rapidly as possible.* ● **ra|pid|ity** /rəpɪ́dɪti/ N-UNCOUNT ❏ *...the rapidity with which the weather can change.* ▮ ADJ A **rapid** movement is one that is very fast. ❏ *He walked at a rapid pace along Charles Street.* ● **rap|id|ly** ADV [ADV with v] ❏ *He was moving rapidly around the room.* ● **ra|pid|ity** N-UNCOUNT ❏ *The water rushed through the holes with great rapidity.*

<table>
<tr><td colspan="2">Thesaurus   rapid의 참조어</td></tr>
<tr><td>ADJ.</td><td>fast, speedy, swift; (ant.) slow ▮ ▮</td></tr>
</table>

<table>
<tr><td colspan="2">Word Partnership   rapid의 연어</td></tr>
<tr><td>N.</td><td>rapid change, rapid decline, rapid development, rapid expansion,
rapid growth, rapid increase, rapid progress ▮
rapid pace, rapid pulse ▮</td></tr>
</table>

rap|ids /rǽpɪdz/ N-PLURAL **Rapids** are a section of a river where the water moves very fast, often over rocks. ❏ *His canoe was there, on the river below the rapids.*

rap|ist /reɪpɪst/ (rapists) N-COUNT A **rapist** is a man who has raped someone. ❏ *The convicted murderer and rapist is scheduled to be executed next Friday.*

단수명사 평사원늘 [언론] ❏ 그는 평사원늘 사이에서 폭넓은 지지를 받고 있었다.

타동사 뒤지다, 들쑤시다 ❏ 시위자들이 그가 머물고 있던 집을 뒤지고 불태웠다.

▮ 가산명사 또는 불가산명사 몸값 ❏ 납치범이 그녀를 풀어 주는 대가로 17만 5천 파운드를 뜯어내는 데 성공했다. ▮ 타동사 몸값을 치르고 되찾다 ❏ 똑같은 시스템이 인질을 교환하거나 몸값을 주고 되찾는 데도 사용됐다. ▮ 구 -을 인질로 잡고 몸값을 요구하다 ❏ 그는 작년 사업가 한 명을 납치한 후 몸값을 요구한 혐의를 받고 있다. ▮ 구 압력을 넣다 [탐탁잖음] ❏ 유니슨을 비롯한 기타 노조들도 영국 의료 협회나 다른 전문가 단체들처럼 정부에 압력을 넣을 수 있는 힘이 있다.

타동사/자동사 고함치다, 떠들어 대다 ❏ 사장이 고함치기 시작하자 나는 일어서서 나와 버렸다. ❏ 그가 계속 떠들어 대자 그들의 개 세 마리조차 지루한지 잠이 들어 버렸다. ● 가산명사 고함, 외침 ❏ 1부는 조직화된 종교에 대한 비판이다. ● 고함 소리, 떠드는 소리 가산명사 또는 불가산명사 ❏ 그는 밤새도록 골드스톤이 떠들어 대는 소리를 들은 터였다.

▮ 불가산명사 랩 ❏ 그녀는 랩 그룹 '달려라 디엠시'의 음악을 가장 좋아했다. ▮ 자동사 랩을 하다 ❏ 키즈의 랩뿐만이 아니라 노래까지 듣는 예상외의 즐거움 ▮ 가산명사 랩 ❏ 솔로로 부르거나 랩 코러스에서 한 몫 담당하면서 모든 멤버들이 랩에 참여한다. ▮ 타동사/자동사 (연속해서) 두드리다 ❏ 메리 앤이 돌아서서 사이먼의 문을 똑똑 두드렸다. ❏ 오른손 손가락 마디로 유리잔을 톡톡 두드리며 ● 가산명사 두드림 ❏ 문을 두드리는 소리가 날카롭게 들렸다. ▮ 가산명사 비난, 혹평 ❏ 폴 링거가 크리스마스 다음 날 페나스 대표 선수로 출전한 후 비난에 직면해 있다. ▮ 타동사 비난하다, 혹평하다 [언론] ❏ 생수 업계 사장들이 소비자들의 기대에 미치지 못했다는 이유로 어제 비난받았다. ▮ 구 질책하다 [언론] ❏ 나는 파업 중인 노동자들과 합류했다가 질책을 받았다.

▮ 타동사 강간하다 ❏ 젊은 여성이 자신의 집에서 잔인하게 강간당했다. ▮ 가산명사 또는 불가산명사 강간 ❏ 강간과 폭행의 거의 90퍼센트가 신고되지 않고 넘어갔다. ▮ 가산명사 유채, 평지 [미국영어; 영국영어 oilseed rape]

▮ 형용사 신속한 ❏ 1980년대에 그 나라가 이룬 신속한 경제 성장 ● 빠르게 부사 ❏ 인구가 빠르게 늘어나는 국가들 ❏ 그것을 될 수 있는 한 빨리 찢어 버리도록 하세요. ● 빠름 불가산명사 ❏ 날씨가 변할 수 있는 속도 ▮ 형용사 빠른 ❏ 그는 찰스 가를 따라 빠른 속도로 걸었다. ● 빠르게 부사 ❏ 그는 방 여기저기를 빠르게 움직이고 있었다. ● 속도 불가산명사 ❏ 물이 아주 빠른 속도로 구멍을 빠져나갔다.

복수명사 여울, 급류 ❏ 그의 카누는 급류 아래쪽 강 위에 있었다.

가산명사 강간범 ❏ 유죄 판결을 받은 그 강간 살인범은 다음 주 금요일 처형될 예정이다.

rap|per /ræpər/ (rappers) N-COUNT A **rapper** is a person who performs rap music. ❑ *The British pop charts have been dominated by rappers like MC Hammer in recent months.*

가산명사 래퍼 ❑ 최근 몇 달간 영국 대중음악 순위는 엠시 해머 같은 래퍼가 휩쓸었다.

rap|port /ræpɔr/ N-SING If two people or groups have a **rapport**, they have a good relationship in which they are able to understand each other's ideas or feelings very well. [also no det, oft N with/between n] ❑ *He said he wanted "to establish a rapport with the Indian people."*

단수명사 우호 관계, 친선 관계 ❑ 그는 '인도 사람들과 친선 관계를 맺고' 싶다고 밝혔다.

rap|ture /ræptʃər/ N-UNCOUNT **Rapture** is a feeling of extreme happiness or pleasure. [LITERARY] ❑ *The film was shown to gasps of rapture at the Democratic Convention.* ❑ *His speech was received with rapture by his supporters.*

불가산명사 황홀함, 광희(狂喜) [문예체] ❑ 민주당 전당 대회에서 영화가 상영되자 황홀한 탄성이 터져 나왔다. ❑ 그의 연설에 지지자들이 광희에 찬 반응을 보였다.

rap|tur|ous /ræptʃərəs/ ADJ A **rapturous** feeling or reaction is one of extreme happiness or enthusiasm. [JOURNALISM] ❑ *The students gave him a rapturous welcome.*

형용사 광희에 찬, 열광적인 [언론] ❑ 학생들이 그를 열광적으로 환영해 주었다.

rare ♦♢♢ /rɛər/ (rarer, rarest) **1** ADJ Something that is **rare** is not common and is therefore interesting or valuable. ❑ *...the black-necked crane, one of the rarest species in the world.* **2** ADJ An event or situation that is **rare** does not occur very often. ❑ *...on those rare occasions when he did eat alone.* **3** ADJ You use **rare** to emphasize an extremely good or remarkable quality. [EMPHASIS] [ADJ n] ❑ *Ferris has a rare ability to record her observations on paper.* **4** ADJ Meat that is **rare** is cooked very lightly so that the inside is still red. ❑ *Thick tuna steaks are eaten rare, like beef.*

1 형용사 희귀한, 진귀한 ❑ 세계에서 가장 희귀한 종 중의 하나인 검은목두루미 **2** 형용사 드문 ❑ 그가 진짜 혼자 식사를 하는 드문 경우에 **3** 형용사 드문, 훌륭한 [강조] ❑ 페리스는 관찰한 바를 기록하는 드문 능력을 지녔다. **4** 형용사 살짝 익힌 ❑ 두꺼운 참치 스테이크는 쇠고기처럼 살짝 익혀 먹는다.

Thesaurus	*rare*의 참조어
ADJ.	incomparable, unique; (*ant.*) commonplace, ordinary **1**
	uncommon, unusual; (*ant.*) common, frequent **2**
	raw **4**

rare|ly ♦♢♢ /rɛərli/ ADV If something **rarely** happens, it does not happen very often. ❑ *They battled against other Indian tribes, but rarely fought with the whites.*

부사 드물게, 좀처럼 -하지 않는 ❑ 그들은 다른 인디언 부족들과는 싸웠지만 백인들과 싸우는 경우는 거의 없었다.

rar|ity /rɛəriti/ (rarities) **1** N-COUNT If someone or something is a **rarity**, they are interesting or valuable because they are so unusual. [JOURNALISM] ❑ *Sontag has always been that rarity, a glamorous intellectual.* **2** N-UNCOUNT The **rarity** of something is the fact that it is very uncommon. ❑ *It was a real prize due to its rarity and good condition.*

1 가산명사 진기한 사람; 진기한 것 [언론] ❑ 손탁은 매력적인 지식인으로서 언제나 진기한 인물이었다. **2** 가산명사 희귀성 ❑ 그것은 그 희귀성이나 좋은 보존 상태로 보아 진정한 횡재였다.

rash /ræʃ/ (rashes) **1** ADJ If someone is **rash** or does **rash** things, they act without thinking carefully first, and therefore make mistakes or behave foolishly. ❑ *It would be rash to rely on such evidence.* ● **rash|ly** ADV ❑ *I made quite a lot of money, but I rashly gave most of it away.* **2** N-COUNT A **rash** is an area of red spots that appears on your skin when you are ill or have a bad reaction to something that you have eaten or touched. ❑ *He may break out in a rash when he eats these nuts.* **3** N-SING If you talk about a **rash of** events or things, you mean a large number of unpleasant events or undesirable things, which have happened or appeared within a short period of time. ❑ *...one of the few major airlines left untouched by the industry's rash of takeovers.*

1 형용사 경솔한, 성급한 ❑ 그런 증거에 의존한다면 경솔한 일일 것이다. ● 경솔하게, 성급하게 부사 ❑ 나는 돈을 많이 벌었지만 대부분 경솔하게 써 버렸다. **2** 가산명사 발진, 발진 ❑ 그가 이 같은 견과류를 먹으면 몸에 발진이 생길 수 있다. **3** 단수명사 (비유적) 홍역 ❑ 업계에 불어 닥친 기업 인수 홍역을 비켜 간 몇 안 되는 주요 항공사 중 하나

rasp /ræsp/ (rasps, rasping, rasped) **1** V-T/V-I If someone **rasps**, their voice or breathing is harsh and unpleasant to listen to. ❑ *"Where've you put it?" he rasped.* ● N-SING **Rasp** is also a noun. ❑ *He was still laughing when he heard the rasp of Rennie's voice.* **2** V-T/V-I If something **rasps**, it makes a harsh, unpleasant sound as it rubs against something hard or rough. ❑ *Sabres rasped from scabbards and the horsemen spurred forward.* ● N-SING **Rasp** is also a noun. ❑ *...the rasp of something being drawn across the sand.*

1 타동사/자동사 쉰 목소리로 말하다 ❑ "어디에 놔뒀어?" 그가 쉰 목소리로 말했다. ● 단수명사 쉰 목소리 ❑ 레니의 쉰 목소리가 들릴 때까지도 그는 웃고 있었다. **2** 타동사/자동사 쇳소리를 내다, 귀에 거슬리는 소리를 내다 ❑ 칼이 쇳소리를 내며 칼집에서 뽑히고 기수들이 박차를 가하며 달려 나갔다. ● 단수명사 쇳소리, 귀에 거슬리는 소리 ❑ 무언가가 모래 위에 끌리며 내는, 귀에 거슬리는 소리

rasp|ber|ry /ræzbɛri, BRIT rɑːzbri/ (raspberries) N-COUNT **Raspberries** are small, soft, red fruit that grow on bushes.

가산명사 산딸기

rat /ræt/ (rats, ratting, ratted) **1** N-COUNT A **rat** is an animal which has a long tail and looks like a large mouse. ❑ *This was demonstrated in a laboratory experiment with rats.* **2** N-COUNT If you call someone a **rat**, you mean that you are angry with them or dislike them, often because they have cheated you or betrayed you. [INFORMAL, DISAPPROVAL] ❑ *What did you do with the gun you took from that little rat Turner?* **3** V-I If someone **rats on** you, they tell someone in authority about things that you have done, especially bad things. [INFORMAL] ❑ *They were accused of encouraging children to rat on their parents.* **4** V-I If someone **rats on** an agreement, they do not do what they said they would do. [INFORMAL] ❑ *She claims he ratted on their divorce settlement.* **5** PHRASE If you **smell a rat**, you begin to suspect or realize that something is wrong in a particular situation, for example that someone is trying to deceive you or harm you. ❑ *If I don't send a picture, he'll smell a rat.*

1 가산명사 쥐 ❑ 이는 실험실에서 쥐를 대상으로 한 실험을 통해 입증되었다. **2** 가산명사 배신자, 쥐새끼 같은 놈 [비격식체, 탐탁찮음] ❑ 그 주목할만한 쥐새끼 같은 놈 터너한테 받은 총은 어떻게 한 거야? **3** 자동사 밀고하다, 배반하다 [비격식체] ❑ 그들은 아이들이 부모를 밀고하도록 부추겼다는 혐의를 받았다. **4** 자동사 어기다, 위반하다 [비격식체] ❑ 그녀는 그가 이혼 합의 사항을 어겼다고 주장한다. **5** 구 킁새를 채다 ❑ 내가 사진을 보내지 않으면 그가 킁새를 챌 거야.

rate ♦♦♦ /reɪt/ (rates, rating, rated) **1** N-COUNT The **rate** at which something happens is the speed with which it happens. ❑ *The rate at which hair grows can be agonizingly slow.* **2** N-COUNT The **rate** at which something happens is the number of times it happens over a period of time. ❑ *New diet books appear at a rate of nearly one a week.* **3** N-COUNT A **rate** is the amount of money that is charged for goods or services. ❑ *A special weekend rate is available from mid-November.* →see also exchange rate **4** N-COUNT The **rate** of taxation or interest is the amount of tax or interest that needs to be paid. It is expressed as a percentage of the amount that is earned, gained as profit, or borrowed. [BUSINESS] ❑ *The government insisted that it would not be panicked into interest rate cuts.* **5** V-T/V-I If you **rate** someone or something as good or bad, you consider them to be good or bad. You can also say that someone or something **rates** as good or bad. [no cont] ❑ *Of all the men in the survey, they rate themselves the least fun-loving and the most responsible.* ❑ *Most rated it a hit.* ❑ *We rate him as one of the best.*

1 가산명사 속도 ❑ 머리카락이 자라는 속도가 괴로울 정도로 느릴 수 있다. **2** 가산명사 빈도 ❑ 거의 일주일에 한 권으로 새로운 다이어트 책이 나온다. **3** 가산명사 요금, 특별 요금 ❑ 주말 특별 요금은 3월 중순부터 적용된다. **4** 가산명사 비율, 율 [경제] ❑ 정부가 당황한 나머지 성급히 금리를 인하하는 일은 없을 것이라고 강조했다. **5** 타동사/자동사 평가하다, 간주하다 ❑ 그들은 조사 대상 남성 전체 중에서 자신들이 재미 추구 면에서는 최하, 책임감 면에서는 최고라고 평가했다. ❑ 대부분 그를 히트작으로 평가했다. ❑ 우리는 그를 최고 중 한 명으로 생각한다. **6** 타동사 높이 평가하다 [주로 영국영어, 비격식체] ❑ 다른 구단에서 관심을 보여 주고 저를 높이 평가해 주는 것 같아 기분이 좋아요. **7** 수동 타동사 평가되다

⑥ v-T If you **rate** someone or something, you think that they are good. [mainly BRIT, INFORMAL] ❏ *It's flattering to know that other clubs have shown interest and seem to rate me.* **⑦** v-T PASSIVE If someone or something **is rated** at a particular position or rank, they are calculated or considered to be in that position on a list. [no cont] ❏ *He is generally rated Italy's No. 3 industrialist.* **⑧** v-T If you say that someone or something **rates** a particular reaction, you mean that this is the reaction you consider to be appropriate. [no cont] ❏ *This is so extraordinary, it rates a medal and a phone call from the President.* **⑨** →see also **rating** **⑩** PHRASE You use **at any rate** to indicate that what you have just said might be incorrect or unclear in some way, and that you are now being more precise. ❏ *His friends liked her – well, most of them at any rate.* **⑪** PHRASE If you say that **at this rate** something bad or extreme will happen, you mean that it will happen if things continue to develop as they have been doing. ❏ *At this rate they'd be lucky to get home before eight-thirty or nine.* →see **interest rate**, **motion**

❏ 그는 보통 이탈리아 기업가 중 3인자로 꼽힌다. **⑧** 타동사 -을 받을 만하다 ❏ 이는 참으로 이례적인 일이다. 대통령으로부터 메달과 전화를 받을 만하다. **⑩** 구 어쨌든, 좌우간에 ❏ 그의 친구들은 그녀를 좋아했다. 어쨌든 그들 대부분은 그랬단 이야기이다. **⑪** 구 이대로 나가면, 이대로라면 ❏ 이대로 나가면 그들이 8시 반이나 9시 전에 귀가할 수만 있어도 다행일 것이다.

Word Partnership   rate의 연어

N.	**rate of change** **①** **birth** rate, **crime** rate, **dropout** rate, **heart** rate, **pulse** rate, **survival** rate, **unemployment** rate **②** **interest** rate **④**
ADJ.	**average** rate, **slow** rate, **steady** rate **①** **②** **high** rate, **low** rate **①-④**

rate of re|turn (rates of return) N-COUNT The **rate of return** on an investment is the amount of profit it makes, often shown as a percentage of the original investment. [BUSINESS] ❏ *High rates of return can be earned on these investments.*

가산명사 수익률 [경제] ❏ 이 같은 투자를 통해 높은 수익률을 거둘 수 있다.

ra|ther ♦♦♦ /ˈræðər/ **①** PHRASE You use **rather than** when you are contrasting two things or situations. **Rather than** introduces the thing or situation that is not true or that you do not want. ❏ *The problem was psychological rather than physiological.* ● CONJ **Rather** is also a conjunction. ❏ *She made students think for themselves, rather than telling them what to think.* **②** ADV You use **rather** when you are correcting something that you have just said, especially when you are describing a particular situation after saying what it is not. [ADV with cl/group] ❏ *Twenty million years ago, Idaho was not the arid place it is now. Rather, it was warm and damp, populated by dense primordial forest.* **③** PHRASE If you say that you **would rather** do something or you'd **rather** do it, you mean that you would prefer to do it. If you say that you **would rather not** do something, you mean that you do not want to do it. ❏ *If it's all the same to you, I'd rather work at home.* ❏ *Kids would rather play than study.* **④** ADV You use **rather** to indicate that something is true to a fairly great extent, especially when you are talking about something unpleasant or undesirable. ❏ *I grew up in rather unusual circumstances.* ❏ *I'm afraid it's rather a long story.* **⑤** ADV You use **rather** before verbs that introduce your thoughts and feelings, in order to express your opinion politely, especially when a different opinion has been expressed. [POLITENESS] [ADV before v] ❏ *I rather think he was telling the truth.*

① 구 -보다 ❏ 문제는 생리적인 것이라기보다 심리적인 것이었다. ● 접속사 -라기보다 오히려 ❏ 그녀는 학생들에게 무엇을 생각하라고 지시하기보다 스스로 생각하게끔 한다. **②** 부사 더 정확히 말하자면 ❏ 2천만 년 전 아이다호는 지금처럼 건조한 지역이 아니었다. 더 정확히 말하자면, 원시 밀림으로 뒤덮인 따뜻하고 습한 곳이었다. **③** 구 차라리 -하고 싶다; 별로 -하고 싶지 않다 ❏ 당신만 상관없다면, 집에서 일하고 싶어요. ❏ 아이들은 공부보다 놀려고 할 것이다. **④** 부사 다소, 꽤 ❏ 나는 다소 특이한 환경에서 살았다. ❏ 다소 긴 이야기가 될 것 같아요. **⑤** 부사 상대방과 다른 의견을 공손하게 표현하기 위해 동사 앞에 사용 [공손체] ❏ 제 생각에는 그가 진실을 말했던 것 같아요.

rati|fi|ca|tion /ˌrætɪfɪˈkeɪʃən/ (ratifications) N-VAR The **ratification** of a treaty or written agreement is the process of ratifying it. ❏ *We welcome this development and we look forward to early ratification by China of the treaty.*

가산명사 또는 불가산명사 비준, 승인 ❏ 우리는 이 개발안을 환영하며 그 조약에 대한 중국 측의 조속한 비준을 기대한다.

rati|fy /ˈrætɪfaɪ/ (ratifies, ratifying, ratified) v-T When national leaders or organizations **ratify** a treaty or written agreement, they make it official by giving their formal approval to it, usually by signing it or voting for it. ❏ *The parliaments of Australia and Indonesia have yet to ratify the treaty.*

타동사 비준하다, 승인하다 ❏ 아직 호주 의회와 인도네시아 의회가 그 조약을 비준해야 한다.

rat|ing ♦♦◇◇ /ˈreɪtɪŋ/ (ratings) **①** N-COUNT A **rating** of something is a score or measurement of how good or popular it is. ❏ *New public opinion polls show the president's approval rating at its lowest point since he took office.* →see also **credit rating** **②** N-PLURAL The **ratings** are the statistics published each week which show how popular each television programme is. ❏ *CBS's ratings again showed huge improvement over the previous year.*

① 가산명사 등급, 평가 ❏ 새로운 국민 여론 조사에 의하면 대통령에 대한 지지율이 취임한 이래 가장 낮은 것으로 나타난다. **②** 복수명사 시청률 ❏ 시비에스의 시청률이 작년에 비하여 다시 한 번 월등히 높아졌다.

Word Partnership   rating의 연어

N.	**approval** rating **①**
ADJ.	**high** rating, **low** rating, **poor** rating, **top** rating **①** **②**

ra|tio /ˈreɪʃoʊ, -ʃioʊ, BRIT ˈreɪʃioʊ/ (ratios) N-COUNT A **ratio** is a relationship between two things when it is expressed in numbers or amounts. For example, if there are ten boys and thirty girls in a room, the ratio of boys to girls is 1:3, or one to three. ❏ *The adult to child ratio is 1 to 6.* →see Word Web: **ratio**

가산명사 비율 ❏ 성인 대 아동의 비율이 1대 6이다.

ra|tion /ˈræʃən/ (rations, rationing, rationed) **①** N-COUNT When there is not enough of something, your **ration** of it is the amount that you are allowed to have. ❏ *The meat ration was down to one pound per person per week.* **②** v-T When something **is rationed** by a person or government, you are only allowed to have a limited amount of it, usually because there is not enough of it. ❏ *Staples such as bread, rice, and tea are already being rationed.* ❏ *The City Council of Moscow has decided that it will begin rationing bread, butter, and meat.* **③** N-PLURAL **Rations** are the food which is given to people who do not have enough food or to soldiers. ❏ *Aid officials said that the first emergency food rations of wheat and oil were handed out here last month.* **④** N-COUNT Your **ration of** something is the amount of it that you normally have. ❏ *...after consuming his ration of junk food and two cigarettes.* **⑤** →see also **rationing**

① 가산명사 배급량 ❏ 고기 배급량이 일주일에 한 사람당 1파운드씩으로 내려갔다. **②** 타동사 배급제가 되다, 제한되다 ❏ 빵이나 쌀, 차와 같은 주식이 이미 할당되고 있다. ❏ 모스크바의 시의회는 빵과 버터와 고기를 배급제로 하기로 결정했다. **③** 복수명사 배급 식량 ❏ 구호품 담당 관리들은 밀과 기름 같은 일차 비상 구호 배급 식량이 지난달에 여기에서 배포되었다고 말했다. **④** 가산명사 일정량 ❏ 그가 자신의 일정량인 인스턴트식품과 두 갑의 담배를 다 소비한 후에

Word Web ratio

The golden **ratio** is a phrase invented by the ancient Greeks. It refers to a specific mathematical **proportion**—1:1.618. **Mathematicians** named this number "Phi" in honor of the sculptor Phidias*. He frequently used this ratio in his sculptures. Architects and artists find this proportion attractive. The floor plan of the Parthenon is 1.618 times as **long** as it is **wide**. Drawing a **rectangle** around the face of Da Vinci's* "Mona Lisa"* results in the same ratio. The golden ratio is even found in the comparison of the **width** and the **length** of an egg.

Phidias (490-430 BC): a Greek sculptor.
Leonardo da Vinci (1452-1519): an Italian artist.
"Mona Lisa": a famous painting of a woman.

Word Link ratio ≈ reasoning : ir*ratio*nal, *ratio*nal, *ratio*nale

ra|tion|al /ræʃənªl/ **1** ADJ **Rational** decisions and thoughts are based on reason rather than on emotion. ❑ *He's asking you to look at both sides of the case and come to a rational decision.* ● **ra|tion|al|ly** ADV ❑ *It can be very hard to think rationally when you're feeling so vulnerable and alone.* ● **ra|tion|al|ity** /ræʃənæliti/ N-UNCOUNT ❑ *We live in an era of rationality.* **2** ADJ A **rational** person is someone who is sensible and is able to make decisions based on intelligent thinking rather than on emotion. ❑ *Did he come across as a sane rational person?*

Word Partnership rational의 연어

N.	rational **approach**, rational **choice**, rational **decision**, rational **explanation** **1**
	rational **human being**, rational **person** **2**

ra|tion|ale /ræʃənal, -næl/ (**rationales**) N-COUNT The **rationale** for a course of action, practice, or belief is the set of reasons on which it is based. [FORMAL] ❑ *However, the rationale for such initiatives is not, of course, solely economic.*

ra|tion|al|ist /ræʃənªlɪst/ (**rationalists**) **1** ADJ If you describe someone as **rationalist**, you mean that their beliefs are based on reason and logic rather than emotion or religion. ❑ *White was both visionary and rationalist.* **2** N-COUNT If you describe someone as a **rationalist**, you mean that they base their life on rationalist beliefs. ❑ *...the rationalists and scientists of the nineteenth century.*

ra|tion|al|ize /ræʃənªlaɪz/ (**rationalizes, rationalizing, rationalized**) [BRIT also **rationalise**] **1** V-T If you try to **rationalize** attitudes or actions that are difficult to accept, you think of reasons to justify or explain them. ❑ *He further rationalized his activity by convincing himself that he was actually promoting peace.* **2** V-T When a company, system, or industry **is rationalized**, it is made more efficient, usually by getting rid of staff and equipment that are not essential. [mainly BRIT, BUSINESS] [usu passive] ❑ *The network of 366 local offices is being rationalized to leave the company with 150 to 200 larger branch offices.* ● **ra|tion|ali|za|tion** N-UNCOUNT ❑ *...the rationalization of the textile industry.*

ra|tion|ing /ræʃənɪŋ/ N-UNCOUNT **Rationing** is the system of limiting the amount of food, water, gasoline, or other necessary substances that each person is allowed to have or buy when there is not enough of them. ❑ *The municipal authorities here are preparing for food rationing.*

rat race N-SING If you talk about getting out of **the rat race**, you mean leaving a job or way of life in which people compete aggressively with each other to be successful. ❑ *I had to get out of the rat race and take a look at the real world again.*

rat|tle /ræt̬ªl/ (**rattles, rattling, rattled**) **1** V-T/V-I When something **rattles** or when you **rattle** it, it makes short sharp knocking sounds because it is being shaken or it keeps hitting against something hard. ❑ *She slams the kitchen door so hard I hear dishes rattle.* ● N-COUNT **Rattle** is also a noun. ❑ *There was a rattle of rifle-fire.* **2** N-COUNT A **rattle** is a baby's toy with loose bits inside which make a noise when the baby shakes it. **3** V-T If something or someone **rattles** you, they make you nervous. ❑ *Officials are not normally rattled by any reporter's question.* ● **rat|tled** ADJ ❑ *He swore in Spanish, another indication that he was rattled.*

rau|cous /rɔkəs/ ADJ A **raucous** sound is loud, harsh, and rather unpleasant. ❑ *They heard a bottle being smashed, then more raucous laughter.* ● **rau|cous|ly** ADV ❑ *They laughed together raucously.*

rav|age /rævɪdʒ/ (**ravages, ravaging, ravaged**) V-T A town, country, or economy that **has been ravaged** is one that has been damaged so much that it is almost completely destroyed. [usu passive] ❑ *For two decades the country has been ravaged by civil war and foreign intervention.*

rav|ages /rævɪdʒɪz/ N-PLURAL The **ravages** of time, war, or the weather are the damaging effects that they have. ❑ *...the ravages of two world wars.*

rave /reɪv/ (**raves, raving, raved**) **1** V-T/V-I If someone **raves**, they talk in an excited and uncontrolled way. ❑ *She cried and raved for weeks, and people did not know what to do.* **2** V-T/V-I If you **rave about** something, you speak or write about it with great enthusiasm. ❑ *Rachel raved about the new foods she ate while she was there.* **3** N-COUNT A **rave** is a big event at which young people dance to

1 형용사 합리적인, 이성적인 ❑ 그는 너에게 그 상황의 양면을 다 본 후에 합리적인 결정을 하라고 요청하고 있다. ● 합리적으로, 이성적으로 부사 ❑ 당신이 마음이 몹시 약해지고 외로울 때는 이성적으로 생각하는 것이 매우 힘들 수도 있다. ● 합리성 불가산명사 ❑ 우리는 합리성의 시대에 살고 있다. **2** 형용사 이성적인 ❑ 그 사람을 정신 멀쩡한 이성적인 사람으로 생각했니?

가산명사 이유, 근거 [격식체] ❑ 그러나 물론, 그런 발의의 이유가 경제적인 것만은 아니다.

1 형용사 이성적인, 합리적인 ❑ 화이트는 예견력도 있고 합리적이기도 했다. **2** 가산명사 이성주의자, 합리주의자 ❑ 19세기의 이성주의자들과 과학자들

[영국영어 rationalise] **1** 타동사 합리화하다 ❑ 그는 자신이 사실은 평화를 촉진시키는 거라고 스스로를 확신시키면서 자기 행동을 더욱 합리화했다. **2** 타동사 경영합리화가 이뤄지다 [주로 영국영어, 경제] ❑ 경영 합리화를 통해 회사의 366개 지방 사무실 조직망을 150개에서 200개 정도의 더 큰 지점들로 조정하는 중이다. ● 경영 합리화, 경영 효율화 불가산명사 ❑ 섬유 업계의 경영 합리화

불가산명사 배급제 ❑ 이 곳의 시 당국은 식량 배급제를 준비하고 있다.

단수명사 극심한 경쟁 ❑ 나는 극심한 경쟁에서 벗어나서 진정한 세상을 다시 한 번 맛봐야 만 했다.

1 타동사/자동사 달그락거리다 ❑ 그녀가 부엌문을 아주 세게 닫아서 그릇이 달그락거리는 소리가 들린다. ● 가산명사 달그락거리는 소리, 따각거리는 소리 ❑ 따닥 하고 소총을 발사하는 소리가 들렸다. **2** 가산명사 딸랑이 **3** 타동사 당황하게 만들다 ❑ 관리들은 어떤 기자의 질문에도 보통 당황하지 않는다. ● 당황한 형용사 ❑ 그가 스페인 어로 맹세했는데, 이것은 그가 당황했다는 또 다른 증거였다.

형용사 (소리가) 요란한 ❑ 그들은 병이 깨지는 소리와 뒤이어 더 요란한 웃음소리를 들었다. ● 요란하게 부사 ❑ 그들은 다 함께 요란하게 웃어댔다.

타동사 참화를 입다, 유린당하다 ❑ 20년 동안 그 나라는 내란과 외세의 내정 간섭으로 유린당해 왔다.

복수명사 유린, 참화 ❑ 두 차례에 걸친 세계 대전의 참화

1 타동사/자동사 (미친 듯이) 마구 지껄이다, 절규하다 ❑ 그녀가 몇 주일 동안이나 울부짖으며 절규했지만, 사람들은 어쩔 바를 몰랐다. **2** 타동사/자동사 정신없이 설명하다; 극찬하다 ❑ 레이첼은 그곳에 머무는 동안 먹었던 음식에 대해서 극찬을 했다.

electronic music in a large building or in the open air. Raves are often associated with illegal drugs. [mainly BRIT] ❑ ...an all-night rave at Castle Donington. **4** →see also **raving**

ra|ven /ˈreɪvᵊn/ (ravens) N-COUNT A **raven** is a large bird with shiny black feathers and a deep harsh call.

❸ 가산명사 떠들썩한 파티 [주로 영국영어] ❑ 캐슬 도닝턴에서 밤새도록 열린 떠들썩한 파티

가산명사 갈가마귀

ra|vine /rəˈvin/ (ravines) N-COUNT A **ravine** is a very deep narrow valley with steep sides. ❑ The bus is said to have overturned and fallen into a ravine.

가산명사 협곡 ❑ 그 버스가 전복되어 협곡으로 떨어졌다고 한다.

rav|ing /ˈreɪvɪŋ/ **1** ADJ You use **raving** to describe someone who you think is completely mad. [INFORMAL] ❑ Malcolm looked at her as if she were a raving lunatic. ● ADV **Raving** is also an adverb. [ADV adj] ❑ I'm afraid Jean-Paul has gone raving mad. **2** →see also **rave**

❶ 형용사 정신 나간 [비격식체] ❑ 말콤은 마치 그녀가 정신 나간 미치광이인 것처럼 그녀를 바라보았다. ● 부사 완전히 미쳐서 ❑ 장폴이 완전히 정신이 나간 것 같다.

raw ♦♢♢ /rɔ/ (rawer, rawest) **1** ADJ **Raw** materials or substances are in their natural state before being processed or used in manufacturing. ❑ We import raw materials and energy and export mainly industrial products. **2** ADJ **Raw** food is food that is eaten uncooked, that has not yet been cooked, or that has not been cooked enough. ❑ ...a popular dish made of raw fish. **3** ADJ If a part of your body is **raw**, it is red and painful, perhaps because the skin has come off or has been burned. ❑ ...the drag of the rope against the raw flesh of my shoulders. **4** ADJ **Raw** emotions are strong basic feelings or responses which are not weakened by other influences. ❑ Her grief was still raw and he did not know how to help her. **5** ADJ If you describe something as **raw**, you mean that it is simple, powerful, and real. ❑ ...the raw power of instinct. **6** ADJ **Raw** data is information that has not yet been sorted, analyzed, or prepared for use. ❑ Analyses were conducted on the raw data. **7** ADJ If you describe someone in a new job as **raw**, or as a **raw** recruit, you mean that they lack experience in that job. ❑ ...replacing experienced men with raw recruits. **8** ADJ **Raw** weather feels unpleasantly cold. ❑ ...a raw December morning. **9** ADJ **Raw** sewage is sewage that has not been treated to make it cleaner. [ADJ n] ❑ ...contamination of bathing water by raw sewage.

❶ 형용사 가공하지 않은 ❑ 우리는 원자재와 에너지를 수입하고 주로 공산품을 수출한다. ❷ 형용사 날것의 ❑ 생선회로 만든 인기 있는 음식 ❸ 형용사 살갗이 벗겨진 ❑ 살갗이 벗겨진 내 어깨 위로 밧줄을 끌어당김 ❹ 형용사 원초적인, 날것 그대로의 ❑ 그녀의 슬픔이 아직 임청난 상태이지 그는 어떻게 그녀를 도와줄 지 몰랐다. ❺ 형용사 생짜의, 진정한 ❑ 진정한 본능의 힘 ❻ 형용사 (자료가) 처리되지 않은 ❑ 처리되지 않은 데이터를 가지고 분석했다. ❼ 형용사 경험 없는, 미숙한 ❑ 경험 많은 일꾼들을 미숙한 신참들로 대체함 ❽ 형용사 으슬으슬한, 으스스한 ❑ 으스스한 12월의 어느 아침 ❾ 형용사 (하수가) 정화 처리되지 않은 ❑ 정화 처리 되지 않은 하수로 인한 목욕물의 오염

Thesaurus
raw의 참조어

ADJ.   natural **1**
      fresh, uncooked; (ant.) cooked **2**
      scraped, skinned **3**

---

ray ♦♢♢ /reɪ/ (rays) **1** N-COUNT **Rays** of light are narrow beams of light. ❑ The sun's rays can penetrate water up to 10 feet. →see also **X-ray 2** N-COUNT A **ray of** hope, comfort, or other positive quality is a small amount of it that you welcome because it makes a bad situation seem less bad. ❑ They could provide a ray of hope amid the general business and economic gloom. →see **rainbow**

❶ 가산명사 광선 ❑ 태양 광선은 수중 10피트까지 통과할 수 있다. ❷ 가산명사 (희망 등의) 서광, 빛 ❑ 그것들은 전반적인 경기 침체 속에서도 한 줄기 희망의 서광을 비춰 줄 수 있었다.

ra|zor /ˈreɪzər/ (razors) N-COUNT A **razor** is a tool that people use for shaving. ❑ ...a plastic disposable razor.

가산명사 면도기 ❑ 일회용 플라스틱 면도기

Rd.

The spelling **Rd** is also used, especially in British English.

Rd. is a written abbreviation for **road**. It is used especially in addresses and on maps or signs. ❑ Chicago Botanic Garden, 1000 Lake-Cook Rd., Glencoe.

철자 Rd도 특히 영국영어에서 쓰인다.

로드 (거리 이름) ❑ 글렌코우, 1000 레이크 쿡 로드, 시카고 식물원

re /ri/ You use **re** in business letters, faxes, or other documents to introduce a subject or item which you are going to discuss or refer to in detail. ❑ Dear Mrs. Cox, Re: Household Insurance. We note from our files that we have not yet received your renewal instructions.

(업무용 서신 등의 제목 앞에) -건, -에 관하여, 제목 ❑ 콕스 여사님께, 가게 보험 건. 저희 서류철을 보니 귀하의 갱신 서류가 아직 들어와 있지 않습니다.

-'re /ər/ -'re is the usual spoken form of "are." It is added to the end of the pronoun or noun which is the subject of the verb. For example, "they are" can be shortened to "they're".

are의 줄임말

reach ♦♦♦ /ritʃ/ (reaches, reaching, reached) **1** V-T When someone or something **reaches** a place, they arrive there. ❑ He did not stop until he reached the door. **2** V-T If someone or something has **reached** a certain stage, level, or amount, they are at that stage, level, or amount. ❑ The process of political change in South Africa has reached the stage where it is irreversible. **3** V-I If you **reach** somewhere, you move your arm and hand to take or touch something. ❑ Judy reached into her handbag and handed me a small printed leaflet. **4** V-T If you can **reach** something, you are able to touch it by stretching out your arm or leg. ❑ Can you reach your toes with your fingertips?

❶ 타동사 도착하다 ❑ 그는 그 문에 도착해서야 비로소 멈춰 섰다. ❷ 타동사 도달하다 ❑ 남아프리카의 정치 변화 추이가 돌이킬 수 없는 단계에 도달했다. ❸ 자동사 손을 뻗다 ❑ 주디가 핸드백에 손을 넣어 인쇄된 작은 전단 한 장을 내게 건네주었다. ❹ 타동사 닿다 ❑ 너는 손끝이 발가락에 닿니?

You use both **reach** and **arrive** to talk about coming to a particular place. **Reach** is always followed by a noun or pronoun referring to a place, and you can use it to emphasize the effort required to get there. ❑ To reach the capital might not be easy. You can use **arrive** to emphasize being in a place rather than traveling to it. ❑ When I arrived in England I was exhausted. **Arrive at** and **reach** can also be used to say that someone eventually makes a decision or finds the answer to something. ❑ It took hours to arrive at a decision... They were unable to reach a decision.

특정한 장소에 도착하는 것을 얘기할 때는 reach와 arrive를 둘 다 쓸 수 있다. reach는 항상 뒤에 장소를 지정하는 명사나 대명사가 나온다. reach는 거기에 도달하는 데 소요되는 노력을 강조하기 위해 쓸 수 있다. ❑ 그 수도에 도달하는 것이 쉽지 않을 수도 있다. arrive는 어떤 장소까지 가는 과정보다 거기에 가 있는 것을 강조할 때 쓴다. ❑ 내가 영국에 도착했을 때에는 기진맥진한 상태였다. arrive at과 reach는 누가 마침내 어떤 결정을 내리게 되었거나 무엇에 대한 답을 찾게 되었을 때에도 쓸 수 있다. ❑ 결정을 내리는 데 몇 시간이나 걸렸다... 그들은 결정에 이를 수 없었다.

---

5 V-T If you try to **reach** someone, you try to contact them, usually by telephone. ❑ Has the doctor told you how to reach him or her in emergencies? **6** V-T/V-I If something **reaches** a place, point, or level, it extends as far as that place, point, or level. ❑ ...a nightshirt which reached to his knees. **7** V-T When people **reach** an agreement or a decision, they succeed in achieving it. ❑ A meeting of agriculture ministers in Luxembourg today has so far failed to reach agreement over farm subsidies. **8** N-UNCOUNT Someone's or something's **reach** is the distance or limit to which they can stretch, extend, or travel. ❑ Isabelle placed a wine cup on the table within his reach. **9** N-UNCOUNT If a place or thing is within **reach**, it is

❺ 타동사 연락하다 ❑ 의사가 비상시 자기와 연락할 수 있는 방법을 네게 말해 주었니? ❻ 타동사/자동사 이르다, 닿다 ❑ 무릎까지 이르는 그의 잠옷 ❼ 타동사 도달하다, 이르다 ❑ 오늘 룩셈부르크에서 열린 농림부 장관 회의에서 농업 지원금에 대한 합의에 아직 도달하지 못했다. ❽ 불가산명사 손이 닿을 수 있는 곳 ❑ 이사벨은 그의 손이 닿을 수 있는 탁자 위에 포도주 잔을 두었다. ❾ 불가산명사 입수 가능성; 갈 수 있는 거리 ❑ 그곳은 베이오를 포함한 여러 노르만

a b c d e f g h i j k l m n o p q r s t u v w x y z

possible to have it or get to it. If it is out of **reach**, it is not possible to have it or get to it. □ *It is located within reach of many important Norman towns, including Bayeux.*

도시에서 갈 수 있는 거리 내에 위치하고 있다.

Thesaurus   reach의 참조어

V.	arrive, enter, get in **1**
	extend to, hold out, stretch **4**
	call, contact **5**
	arrive, succeed **7**

Word Partnership   reach의 연어

N.	reach **a destination 1**
	reach **a goal**, reach *one's* **potential 2**
	reach **(an) agreement**, reach **a compromise**, reach **a conclusion**, reach **a consensus**, reach **a decision 7**

---

re|act ♦◇◇ /riˈækt/ (**reacts, reacting, reacted**) **1** V-I When you **react to** something that has happened to you, you behave in a particular way because of it. □ *They reacted violently to the news.* **2** V-I If you **react against** someone's way of behaving, you deliberately behave in a different way because you do not like the way they behave. □ *My father never saved and perhaps I reacted against that.* **3** V-I If you **react to** a substance such as a drug, or **to** something you have touched, you are affected unpleasantly or made ill by it. □ *Someone allergic to milk is likely to react to cheese.* **4** V-RECIP When one chemical substance **reacts with** another, or when two chemical substances **react**, they combine chemically to form another substance. □ *Calcium reacts with water but less violently than sodium and potassium do.*

1 자동사 반응을 보이다 □ 그들은 그 뉴스에 대해 격렬한 반응을 보였다. **2** 자동사 -에 대한 반작용을 보이다, -에 반발하다 □ 우리 아버지께서는 전혀 저축을 하지 않으셨는데 내가 그것에 반발을 한 것 같다. **3** 자동사 (약물 등에) 반응하다 □ 우유에 알레르기가 있는 사람은 치즈에도 같은 반응을 일으킬 가능성이 있다. **4** 상호동사 (화학 물질이 서로) 반응하다 □ 칼슘은 물과 반응하지만 나트륨과 칼륨 사이의 반응보다는 덜하다.

Word Partnership   react의 연어

ADJ.	**slow to** react **1**
N.	react **to news**, react **to a situation 1**
ADV.	**how to** react, react **positively 1**

re|ac|tion ♦♦◇ /riˈækʃⁿn/ (**reactions**) **1** N-VAR Your **reaction** to something that has happened or something that you have experienced is what you feel, say, or do because of it. □ *Reaction to the visit is mixed.* **2** N-COUNT A **reaction against** something is a way of behaving or doing something that is deliberately different from what has been done before. □ *All new fashion starts out as a reaction against existing convention.* **3** N-SING If there is a **reaction against** something, it becomes unpopular. [also no det, N *against* n] □ *Premature moves in this respect might well provoke a reaction against the reform.* **4** N-PLURAL Your **reactions** are your ability to move quickly in response to something, for example when you are in danger. □ *The sport requires very fast reactions.* **5** N-UNCOUNT **Reaction** is the belief that the political or social system of your country should not change. [DISAPPROVAL] □ *Thus, he aided reaction and thwarted progress.* **6** N-COUNT A chemical **reaction** is a process in which two substances combine together chemically to form another substance. □ *Ozone is produced by the reaction between oxygen and ultra-violet light.* **7** N-COUNT If you have a **reaction to** a substance such as a drug, or **to** something you have touched, you are affected unpleasantly or made ill by it. □ *Every year, 5000 people have life-threatening reactions to anesthetics.*
→see **motion**

1 가산명사 또는 불가산명사 반응 □ 그 방문에 대한 반응은 다양하다. **2** 가산명사 반작용 □ 모든 새로운 유행은 기존 관습에 대한 반작용으로서 시작된다. **3** 단수명사 -에 대한 반발 □ 이런 점에서 때 이른 움직임은 당연히 개혁에 대한 반발을 불러일으킬 것이다. **4** 복수명사 반응력 □ 스포츠는 매우 빠른 반응력을 요구한다. **5** 불가산명사 (사회 제도 등의) 보수성 [탐탁찮음] □ 그래서, 그는 보수를 옹호하고 진보를 반대했다. **6** 가산명사 (화학적) 반응 □ 오존은 산소와 자외선의 반응으로 생성된다. **7** 가산명사 (부정적인) 반응 □ 매년 5천 명의 사람들이 마취제로 생명이 위태로운 반응을 일으킨다.

Word Partnership   reaction의 연어

ADJ.	**mixed** reaction, **negative** reaction, **positive** reaction **1**
	emotional reaction, **initial** reaction **1**–**3**
	chemical reaction **6**
	allergic reaction **7**

re|ac|tion|ary /riˈækʃəneri, BRIT riˈækʃⁿnri/ (**reactionaries**) ADJ A **reactionary** person or group tries to prevent changes in the political or social system of their country. [DISAPPROVAL] □ *It grew ever more clear to everyone that the Minister was too reactionary, too blinkered.* ● N-COUNT A **reactionary** is someone with reactionary views. □ *Critics viewed him as a reactionary, even a monarchist.*

형용사 보수적인 [탐탁찮음] □ 누가 보아도 그 장관이 너무나 보수적이고 편협했다는 것이 점점 더 분명해졌다. ● 가산명사 보수주의자 □ 비평가들은 그를 보수주의자로, 심지어 군주제주의자로 보았다.

re|ac|tor /riˈæktər/ (**reactors**) N-COUNT A **reactor** is the same as a **nuclear reactor**.

가산명사 원자로

read ♦♦♦ (**reads, reading**)

> The form **read** is pronounced /riːd/ when it is the present tense, and /rɛd/ when it is the past tense and past participle.

read는 현재일 때는 /riːd/로 발음되고, 과거 또는 과거 분사일 때는 /rɛd/로 발음된다.

1 V-T/V-I When you **read** something such as a book or article, you look at and understand the words that are written there. □ *Have you read this book?* □ *I read about it in the paper.* □ *She spends her days reading and watching television.* ● N-SING **Read** is also a noun. □ *I settled down to have a good read.* **2** V-T/V-I When you **read** a piece of writing to someone, you say the words aloud. □ *Jay reads poetry so beautifully.* □ *I like it when she reads to us.* **3** V-T/V-I People who can **read** have the ability to look at and understand written words. □ *He couldn't read or write.* **4** V-T If you can **read** music, you have the ability to look at and understand the symbols that are used in written music to represent musical sounds. □ *Later on I learned how to read music.* **5** V-T When a computer **reads** a file or a document, it takes information from a disk or tape. [COMPUTING] □ *How can I read a Microsoft Excel file on a computer that only has Works installed?* **6** V-T You can use

1 타동사/자동사 읽다 □ 이 책 읽어 봤니? □ 나는 그것에 대한 것을 신문에서 읽었다. □ 그녀는 책을 읽고 텔레비전을 보며 나날을 보낸다. ● 단수명사 독서 □ 나는 독서를 편안히 하기 위해서 자리를 잡고 앉았다. **2** 타동사/자동사 소리 내어 읽다, 낭독하다 □ 제이는 시를 너무나 아름답게 낭송한다. □ 그녀가 우리에게 책을 읽어 줄 때가 나는 좋다. **3** 타동사/자동사 읽고 이해하다, 읽다 □ 그는 글을 읽을 줄도 쓸 줄도 몰랐다. **4** 타동사 (악보) 읽다 □ 나는 나중에 악보 읽는 법을 배웠다. **5** 타동사 (컴퓨터의 정보를) 읽다 [컴퓨터] □ 웍스만 설치되어 있는 컴퓨터에서 어떻게 마이크로소프트의 엑셀

read when saying what is written on something or in something. For example, if a notice **reads** "Entrance," the word "Entrance" is written on it. [no cont] ☐ *The sign on the bus read "Private: Not In Service."* ☑ V-I If you refer to how a piece of writing **reads**, you are referring to its style. ☐ *The book reads like a ballad.* ☑ N-COUNT If you say that a book or magazine is a good **read**, you mean that it is very enjoyable to read. [adj n] ☐ *Ben Okri's latest novel is a good read.* ☑ V-T If something **is read** in a particular way, it is understood or interpreted in that way. ☐ *The play is being widely read as an allegory of imperialist conquest.* ☑ V-T If you **read** someone's mind or thoughts, you know exactly what they are thinking without them telling you. ☐ *From behind her, as if he could read her thoughts, Benny said, "You're free to go any time you like, Madame."* ☑ V-T If you can **read** someone or you can **read** their gestures, you can understand what they are thinking or feeling by the way they behave or the things they say. ☐ *If you have to work in a team you must learn to read people.* ☑ V-T When you **read** a measuring device, you look at it to see what the figure or measurement on it is. ☐ *It is essential that you are able to read a thermometer* ☑ V-T If a measuring device **reads** a particular amount, it shows that amount. ☐ *The thermometer read 105 degrees Fahrenheit.* ☑ →see also **reading**

Word Partnership   *read*의 연어

V.	like to read, want to read ☑ ☑
	listen to *someone* read ☑
	learn (how) to read ☑
N.	read a book/magazine/(news)paper, read a sentence, read a sign,
	read a statement ☑ ☑
	read a verdict ☑
	ability to read ☑

▶**read into** PHRASAL VERB If you **read** a meaning **into** something, you think it is there although it may not actually be there. ☐ *The addict often misinterprets the signals coming to him, reading disapproval into people's reactions to him even where it does not exist.*

▶**read out** PHRASAL VERB If you **read out** a piece of writing, you say it aloud. ☐ *He's obliged to take his turn at reading out the announcements.*

▶**read up on** PHRASAL VERB If you **read up on** a subject, you read a lot about it so that you become informed about it. ☐ *I've read up on the dangers of all these drugs.*

read|able /rídəbªl/ ☑ ADJ If you say that a book or article is **readable**, you mean that it is enjoyable and easy to read. ☐ *This is an impeccably researched and very readable book.* ☑ ADJ A piece of writing that is **readable** is written or printed clearly and can be read easily. ☐ *My secretary worked long hours translating my almost illegible writing into a typewritten and readable script.*

read|er ♦♦◊ /rídər/ (**readers**) ☑ N-COUNT The **readers** of a newspaper, magazine, or book are the people who read it. ☐ *These texts give the reader an insight into the Chinese mind.* ☐ *The Sun's success is simple: we give our readers what they want.* ☑ N-COUNT A **reader** is a person who reads, especially one who reads for pleasure. ☐ *Thanks to that job I became an avid reader.*

read|er|ship /rídərʃɪp/ (**readerships**) N-COUNT The **readership** of a book, newspaper, or magazine is the number or type of people who read it. ☐ *Its readership has grown to over 15,000 subscribers.*

read|ily /rédɪli/ ☑ ADV If you do something **readily**, you do it in a way which shows that you are very willing to do it. [ADV with v] ☐ *I asked her if she would allow me to interview her, and she readily agreed.* ☑ ADV You also use **readily** to say that something can be done or obtained quickly and easily. For example, if you say that something can be readily understood, you mean that people can understand it quickly and easily. ☐ *The components are readily available in hardware shops.*

Word Partnership   *readily*의 연어

V.	readily accept, readily admit, readily agree ☑ ☑
ADV.	readily apparent ☑ ☑
ADJ.	*be* readily available, make readily available ☑

---

readi|ness /rédɪnɪs/ ☑ N-UNCOUNT If someone is very willing to do something, you can talk about their **readiness to** do it. ☐ *...their readiness to co-operate with the new U.S. envoy.* ☑ N-UNCOUNT If you do something **in readiness for** a future event, you do it so that you are prepared for that event. ☐ *Security tightened in the capital in readiness for the president's arrival.*

read|ing ♦♦◊ /rídɪŋ/ (**readings**) ☑ N-UNCOUNT **Reading** is the activity of reading books. ☐ *I have always loved reading.* ☑ N-COUNT A **reading** is an event at which poetry or extracts from books are read to an audience. ☐ *...a poetry reading.* ☑ N-COUNT Your **reading** of a word, text, or situation is the way in which you understand or interpret it. ☐ *My reading of her character makes me feel that she was too responsible a person to do those things.* ☑ N-COUNT The **reading** on a measuring device is the figure or measurement that it shows. ☐ *The gauge must be giving a faulty reading.*

re|adjust /ríadʒʌst/ (**readjusts, readjusting, readjusted**) ☑ V-I When you **readjust to** a new situation, usually one you have been in before, you adapt to it. ☐ *I can understand why astronauts find it difficult to readjust to life on earth.* ☑ V-T If you **readjust** the level of something, your attitude to something, or the way

---

파일을 읽을 수 있겠습니까? ☑ 타동사 쓰여 있다 ☐ 버스에 '회사용: 일반승객 탑승 불가'라고 쓰여 있다. ☑ 자동사 - 스타일로 쓰여 있다 ☐ 그 책은 민요처럼 쓰여 있다. ☑ 가산명사 읽을거리 ☐ 벤 오크리의 최근 소설은 재미있는 읽을거리이다. ☑ 타동사 해석되다 ☐ 그 연극은 제국주의 정복에 대한 우화로 널리 해석되고 있다. ☑ 타동사 (마음을) 읽다 ☐ 마치 그녀의 생각을 읽기라도 한 듯이, 그녀 뒤에서 베니가 말했다. "원하신다면 언제라도 자유롭게 갈 수 있습니다, 부인." ☑ 타동사 (생각 등을) 읽다 ☐ 팀으로 일을 해야 한다면 사람들의 생각을 읽는 법을 배우어야 한다. ☑ 타동사 (기기나 숫자를) 읽다 ☐ 온도계를 읽을 줄 아는 것이 필수적이다. ☑ 타동사 (수치를) 나타내다 ☐ 온도계가 화씨 105도를 나타내고 있었다.

구동사 의미를 잘못 이해하다 ☐ 그 중독자는 실제로 그렇지 않은데도 불구하고 사람들이 그에게 하는 행동이 자신에 대한 비난이라고 이해하며, 그에게 보내는 상대방의 신호를 종종 잘못 해석한다.

구동사 크게 읽다, 낭독하다 ☐ 그는 그 선언문을 교대로 낭독해야만 한다.

구동사 충분히 연구하다 ☐ 나는 이 약물들의 위험성에 대하여 충분히 연구했다.

☑ 형용사 잘 읽히는 ☐ 이 책은 연구 내용도 완벽하면서도 아주 잘 읽힌다. ☑ 형용사 읽을 수 있는, 알아 볼 수 있는 ☐ 내 비서가 거의 읽기 힘든 필체의 내 글을 타이프로 쳐서 읽을 수 있는 원고로 바꾸느라 오랜 시간 동안 작업했다.

☑ 가산명사 독자 ☐ 이 내용들은 독자에게 중국인의 기질을 간파할 수 있게 해준다. ☐ 선(Sun) 지의 성공은 간단하다. 우리는 독자들에게 그들이 원하는 것을 준다. ☑ 가산명사 독서가 ☐ 그 직업 덕분에 나는 열렬한 독서가가 되었다.

가산명사 독자 수; 독자층 ☐ 그것의 독자 수는 구독자가 15,000 명이 넘을 정도로 증가했다.

☑ 부사 선뜻 ☐ 나는 그녀에게 인터뷰해도 되겠냐고 물어보았고, 그녀는 선뜻 승낙했다. ☑ 부사 쉽게 ☐ 그 부품은 하드웨어 판매점에서 쉽게 살 수 있다.

☑ 불가산명사 기꺼이 하려는 자세 ☐ 새 미국 대표에 기꺼이 협력하려는 그들의 자세 ☑ 불가산명사 대비 ☐ 대통령 도착에 대비하여 수도 경비가 강화되었다.

☑ 불가산명사 독서 ☐ 나는 늘 독서를 좋아했다. ☑ 가산명사 낭독, 낭송 ☑ 가산명사 판단, 해석 ☐ 그녀의 성격을 내가 판단해 보건대, 그녀는 책임감이 너무나 강해서 그런 일을 할 수 없었던 것 같다. ☑ 가산명사 (측정 기구의) 수치 ☐ 그 계기판의 수치가 잘못된 게 분명하다.

☑ 자동사 다시 적응하다 ☐ 나는 우주 비행사들이 지구에서의 생활에 다시 적응하기가 왜 어려운 지를 이해할 수 있다. ☑ 타동사 재조정하다 ☐ 결국 너는 너의 기대치를 재조정해야 한다. ☑ 타동사 다시

you do something, you change it to make it more effective or appropriate. ❑ *In the end you have to readjust your expectations.* ◳ V-T If you **readjust** something such as a piece of clothing or a mechanical device, you correct or alter its position or setting. ❑ *Readjust your watch. You are now on Moscow time.*

조정하다, 다시 맞추다 ❑ 시계를 다시 맞춰라. 이제 모스크바 시간이다.

re|ad|just|ment /riːədʒʌstmənt/ (**readjustments**) N-VAR **Readjustment** is the process of adapting to a new situation, usually one that you have been in before. ❑ *The next few weeks will be a period of readjustment, and will probably not be easy.*

가산명사 또는 불가산명사 재적응❑ 다음 몇 주동안은 재적응 기간이 될 것인데, 아마 쉽지 않을 것이다.

ready ♦♦◇ /rɛdi/ (**readier, readiest, readies, readying, readied**) ◳ ADJ If someone is **ready**, they are properly prepared for something. If something is **ready**, it has been properly prepared and is now able to be used. [v-link ADJ, oft ADJ for n, ADJ to-inf] ❑ *It took her a long time to get ready for church.* ❑ *Are you ready to board, Mr. Daly?* ◳ ADJ If you are **ready for** something or **ready to** do something, you have enough experience to do it or you are old enough and sensible enough to do it. [v-link ADJ, usu ADJ for n, ADJ to-inf] ❑ *She says she's not ready for marriage.* ◳ ADJ If you are **ready to** do something, you are willing to do it. [v-link ADJ to-inf] ❑ *They were ready to die for their beliefs.* ◳ ADJ If you are **ready for** something, you need it or want it. [v-link ADJ for n] ❑ *I don't know about you, but I'm ready for bed.* ◳ ADJ To be **ready to** do something means to be about to do it or likely to do it. [v-link ADJ to-inf] ❑ *She looked ready to cry.* ◳ ADJ You use **ready** to describe things that are able to be used very quickly and easily. [ADJ n] ❑ *I didn't have a ready answer for this dilemma.* ◳ ADJ **Ready** money is in the form of bills and coins rather than checks or credit cards, and so it can be used immediately. [ADJ n] ❑ *I'm afraid I don't have enough ready cash, but I'll call a colleague from another store.* ◳ V-T When you **ready** something, you prepare it for a particular purpose. [FORMAL] ❑ *John's soldiers were readying themselves for the final assault.*

◳ 형용사 준비된 ❑ 그녀가 교회 갈 준비를 하는 데 오랜 시간이 걸렸다. ❑ 달리 씨, 탑승 준비가 되셨습니까? ◳ 형용사 -할 때가 된 ❑ 그녀는 아직 결혼할 때가 안 되었다고 말한다. ◳ 형용사 기꺼이 -하는 ❑ 그들은 자신의 믿음을 위해서는 기꺼이 죽을 각오가 되어 있었다. ◳ 형용사 -이 필요한; -하고 싶은 ❑ 너는 어떨지 모르겠지만, 나는 자고 싶다. ◳ 형용사 막 -하려는 ❑ 그녀는 금방이라도 울 것 같았다. ◳ 형용사 즉시 사용할 수 있는, 즉각적인 ❑ 나는 이런 난제에 대해 즉각적인 답을 갖고 있지 않았다. ◳ 형용사 즉시 사용할 수 있는 ❑ 내가 즉시 쓸 수 있는 현금은 없지만, 지금 다른 상점에 있는 동료를 부를 게요. ◳ 타동사 채비를 하다, 준비를 갖추다 [격식체] ❑ 존의 부대원들은 최후의 돌격을 위해 채비를 하고 있었다.

Word Partnership ready의 연어

N.	ready **for** bed, ready **for** dinner ◳
ADV.	**always** ready, **not quite** ready, **not** ready **yet** ◳-◳
V.	**get** ready ◳
	ready **to begin**, ready **to fight**, ready **to go/leave**, ready **to play**, ready **to start** ◳-◳
	ready **to burst** ◳

---

ready-made ◳ ADJ If something that you buy is **ready-made**, you can use it immediately, because the work you would normally have to do has already been done. ❑ *We rely quite a bit on ready-made meals – they are so convenient.* ◳ ADJ **Ready-made** means extremely convenient or useful for a particular purpose. ❑ *Those wishing to study urban development have a ready-made example on their doorstep.*

◳ 형용사 이미 만들어 놓은, 기성품의 ❑ 우리는 이미 조리되어 있는 식사에 상당히 많이 의지한다. 왜냐하면 너무나 편리하니까. ◳ 형용사 아주 유용한 ❑ 도시 개발을 연구하고자 하는 사람들은 그들 가까운 곳에 아주 유용한 예를 가지고 있다.

re|affirm /riːəfɜːrm/ (**reaffirms, reaffirming, reaffirmed**) V-T If you **reaffirm** something, you state it again clearly and firmly. [FORMAL] ❑ *He reaffirmed his commitment to the country's economic reform programme.*

타동사 재확인하다, 다시 분명히 말하다 [격식체] ❑ 그는 국가 경제 개혁 프로그램에 대한 약속을 재차 확인했다.

real ♦♦♦ /riːl/ ◳ ADJ Something that is **real** actually exists and is not imagined, invented, or theoretical. ❑ *No, it wasn't a dream. It was real.* ◳ ADJ If something is **real to** someone, they experience it as though it really exists or happens, even though it does not. ❑ *Whitechild's life becomes increasingly real to the reader.* ◳ ADJ A material or object that is **real** is natural or functioning, and not artificial or an imitation. ❑ *...the smell of real leather.* ◳ ADJ You can use **real** to describe someone or something that has all the characteristics or qualities that such a person or thing typically has. [ADJ n] ❑ *...his first real girlfriend.* ◳ ADJ You can use **real** to describe something that is the true or original thing of its kind, in contrast to one that someone wants you to believe is true. [ADJ n] ❑ *This was the real reason for her call.* ◳ ADJ You can use **real** to describe something that is the most important or typical part of a thing. [ADJ n] ❑ *When he talks, he only gives glimpses of his real self.* ◳ ADJ You can use **real** when you are talking about a situation or feeling to emphasize that it exists and is important or serious. [EMPHASIS] ❑ *Global warming is a real problem.* ❑ *The prospect of civil war is very real.* ◳ ADJ You can use **real** to emphasize a quality that is genuine and sincere. [EMPHASIS] ❑ *You've been drifting from job to job without any real commitment.* ◳ ADJ You can use **real** before nouns to emphasize your description of something or someone. [mainly SPOKEN, EMPHASIS] [ADJ n] ❑ *"You must think I'm a real idiot."* ◳ ADJ The **real** cost or value of something is its cost or value after other amounts have been added or subtracted and when factors such as the level of inflation have been considered. [ADJ n] ❑ *...the real cost of borrowing.* ● PHRASE You can also talk about the cost or value of something **in real terms.** ❑ *In real terms the cost of driving is cheaper than a decade ago.* ◳ ADV You can use **real** to emphasize an adjective or adverb. [AM, INFORMAL, EMPHASIS] [ADV adj/adv] ❑ *He is finding prison life "real tough".* ◳ PHRASE If you say that someone does something **for real**, you mean that they actually do it and do not just pretend to do it. ❑ *I have gone to premieres in my dreams but I never thought I'd do it for real.*

◳ 형용사 진짜의, 실제의 ❑ 아니야, 그건 꿈이 아니었어. 실제였어. ◳ 형용사 현실 같은 ❑ 화이트차일드의 인생이 독자에게 점차 현실 같아진다. ◳ 형용사 진짜의 ❑ 진짜 가죽 냄새 ◳ 형용사 진정한 ❑ 그의 진정한 첫 여자 친구. ◳ 형용사 진짜의 ❑ 이것이 그녀가 전화한 진짜 이유였다. ◳ 형용사 진짜의 ❑ 그는 말을 할 때, 자신의 진짜 모습을 조금씩만 보여줄 뿐이다. ◳ 형용사 정말 중요한, 정말 심각한 [강조] ❑ 지구 온난화는 정말 심각한 문제이다. ❑ 내란의 가능성이 진짜 심각하다. ◳ 형용사 진정한 [강조] ❑ 너는 진정으로 열심히 하지 않고 이 일 저 일 떠돌고 있다. ◳ 형용사 진짜의 [주로 구어체, 강조] ❑ 넌 내가 진짜 멍청이라고 생각하는 모양이구나. ◳ 형용사 실질적인 ❑ 실질적인 차용 경비 ● 구 실질적으로 보면 ❑ 실질적으로 보면 차량 유지비가 10년 전보다 더 적게 든다. ◳ 부사 정말로 [미국영어, 비격식체, 강조] ❑ 그는 감옥 생활이 정말 힘들다는 것을 깨닫고 있다. ◳ 구 실제로 ❑ 나는 꿈에 영화 시사회에 가 본 적은 여러 번 있지만 내가 실제로 그러리라고는 전혀 생각하지 못했다.

Do not confuse **real** and **actual**. You use **real** to describe things that exist rather than being imagined or theoretical. ❑ *Robert squealed in mock terror, then in real pain.* You use **actual** to emphasize that what you are referring to is real or genuine, for example, the **actual** cost of something is what it costs rather than what you expect it to cost. You can also use **actual** to contrast different aspects of something, for example, the time taken to prepare for something and to do something. ❑ *The actual boat trip takes about forty-five minutes.*

pass와 spend를 혼동하지 않도록 하라. 무엇을 기다리면서 다른 무엇을 하면, 시간을 보내기(pass the time) 위해 그것을 한다고 말할 수 있다. ❑ 그는 시간을 보내려고 책을 한 권 가져왔다. 일정 기간의 시간이 끝났음을 나타내기 위해서는 시간이 has passed라고 말할 수 있다. ❑ 처음 며칠이 지나갔다... 시간이 너무도 빨리 지나간 것 같다. 무엇을 하면서 일정 기간의 시간을 spend하거나 어떤 장소에서 시간을 spend하면, 언급하고 있는 그 시간 동안 내내 그것을 하거나 그 장소에 머무는 것이다. ❑ 나는 내 집을 청소하면서 3일을 보냈다....우리가 그날 밤을 보낼 수 있었던 호텔.

real es|tate ☐ N-UNCOUNT **Real estate** is property in the form of land and buildings, rather than personal possessions. [mainly AM] ☐ *By investing in real estate, he was one of the richest men in the United States.* ☐ N-UNCOUNT **Real estate** businesses or **real estate** agents sell houses, buildings, and land. [AM; BRIT **estate agency, estate agents**] ☐ *...the real estate agent who sold you your house.*

☐ 불가산명사 부동산 [주로 미국영어] ☐ 부동산에 투자함으로써, 그는 미국에서 가장 부유한 사람들 중 하나가 되었다. ☐ 불가산명사 부동산 [미국영어; 영국영어 estate agency, estate agents] ☐ 당시 집을 팔아 주었던 부동산 중개인

re|al|ise /ríəlaɪz/ →see **realize**

re|al|ism /ríəlɪzəm/ ☐ N-UNCOUNT When people show **realism** in their behavior, they recognize and accept the true nature of a situation and try to deal with it in a practical way. [APPROVAL] ☐ *It was time now to show more political realism.* ☐ N-UNCOUNT If things and people are presented with **realism** in paintings, stories, or movies, they are presented in a way that is like real life. [APPROVAL] ☐ *Greene's stories had an edge of realism that made it easy to forget they were fiction.*

☐ 불가산명사 현실주의 [마음에 듦] ☐ 이제 좀 더 정치적인 현실주의를 보여 줄 때가 되었다. ☐ 불가산명사 (문화, 예술) 사실주의, 리얼리즘 [마음에 듦] ☐ 그린의 소설은 그것이 허구임을 쉽게 잊게 할 정도로 날카로운 사실주의를 보여 주었다.

re|al|ist /ríəlɪst/ (**realists**) ☐ N-COUNT A **realist** is someone who recognizes and accepts the true nature of a situation and tries to deal with it in a practical way. [APPROVAL] ☐ *I see myself not as a cynic but as a realist.* ☐ ADJ A **realist** painter or writer is one who represents things and people in a way that is like real life. [ADJ n] ☐ *...perhaps the foremost realist painter of our times.*

☐ 가산명사 현실주의자 [마음에 듦] ☐ 나는 나 자신을 냉소주의자가 아니라 현실주의자로 생각한다. ☐ 형용사 사실주의의 ☐ 아마도 우리 시대의 가장 뛰어난 사실주의 화가

re|al|is|tic /ríəlɪstɪk/ ☐ ADJ If you are **realistic** about a situation, you recognize and accept its true nature and try to deal with it in a practical way. ☐ *Police have to be realistic about violent crime.* ● **re|al|is|ti|cal|ly** ADV ☐ *As an adult, you can assess the situation realistically.* ☐ ADJ Something such as a goal or target that is **realistic** is one which you can sensibly expect to achieve. ☐ *A more realistic figure is eleven million.* ☐ ADJ You say that a painting, story, or movie is **realistic** when the people and things in it are like people and things in real life. ☐ *...Steven Spielberg's realistic war film Saving Private Ryan.* ● **re|al|is|ti|cal|ly** ADV ☐ *The film starts off realistically and then develops into a ridiculous fantasy.* →see **fantasy**

☐ 형용사 현실적인 ☐ 경찰은 폭력 범죄에 대해서 현실적으로 대처해야 한다. ● 현실적으로 부사 ☐ 당신은 성인이므로 그 상황을 현실적으로 평가할 수 있다. ☐ 형용사 현실적인, 현실적으로 가능한 ☐ 더 현실적인 수치는 천백만이다. ☐ 형용사 사실적인 ☐ 스티븐 스필버그의 사실주의 전쟁 영화 '라이언 일병 구하기' ● 사실적으로 부사 ☐ 그 영화는 사실적으로 시작하다가 우스꽝스러운 공상으로 전개되어 간다.

Word Partnership	*realistic*의 연어
V.	**be** realistic ☐
ADV.	**more** realistic, **very** realistic ☐-☐
N.	realistic **assessment**, realistic **expectations**, realistic **view** ☐ ☐
	realistic **goals** ☐

re|al|is|ti|cal|ly /ríəlɪstɪkli/ ADV You use **realistically** when you want to emphasize that what you are saying is true, even though you would prefer it not to be true. [EMPHASIS] [ADV with cl] ☐ *Realistically, there is never one right answer.* →see also **realistic**

부사 사실 [강조] ☐ 사실, 정답이 결코 하나일 수는 없다.

Word Link	real ≈ actual : *reality*, *realize*, *really*

re|al|ity ♦♦◇ /riǽlɪti/ (**realities**) ☐ N-UNCOUNT You use **reality** to refer to real things or the real nature of things rather than imagined, invented, or theoretical ideas. ☐ *Fiction and reality were increasingly blurred.* →see also **virtual reality** ☐ N-COUNT The **reality of** a situation is the truth about it, especially when it is unpleasant or difficult to deal with. ☐ *...the harsh reality of top international competition.* ☐ N-SING You say that something has become a **reality** when it actually exists or is actually happening. ☐ *...the whole procedure that made this book become a reality.* ☐ PHRASE You can use **in reality** to introduce a statement about the real nature of something, when it contrasts with something incorrect that has just been described. ☐ *He came across as streetwise, but in reality he was not.* →see **fantasy**

☐ 불가산명사 사실 ☐ 허구와 사실의 구분이 점점 모호해졌다. ☐ 가산명사 현실 ☐ 치열한 국제 경쟁의 가혹한 현실 ☐ 단수명사 사실, 실물 ☐ 이 책이 실물이 되기까지의 전 과정 ☐ 구 사실은 ☐ 그는 도시 물정에 밝은 사람으로 통했지만, 사실은 그렇지 못했다.

Word Partnership	*reality*의 연어
ADJ.	**virtual** reality ☐
V.	**distort** reality ☐
	become a reality ☐
N.	reality **of life**, reality **of war** ☐
PREP.	**in** reality ☐

re|al|ity TV N-UNCOUNT **Reality TV** is a type of television programming which aims to show how ordinary people behave in everyday life, or in situations, often created by the program makers, which are intended to represent everyday life. ☐ *'Storm Warning' is really just typical voyeuristic reality TV.*

불가산명사 리얼리티 텔레비전 프로 (일반인의 일상 생활을 보여 주는 프로그램) ☐ '스톰 워닝'은 전형적인 엿보기 취향의 텔레비전 프로일 뿐이다.

re|al|iz|able /ríəlaɪzəbəl/ [BRIT also **realisable**] ☐ ADJ If your hopes or aims are **realizable**, there is a possibility that the things that you want to happen will happen. [FORMAL] ☐ *...the reasonless assumption that one's dreams and desires were realizable.* ☐ ADJ **Realizable** wealth is money that can be easily obtained by selling something. [FORMAL] ☐ *In many cases this realizable wealth is not realized during the lifetime of the home owner.*

[영국영어 realisable] ☐ 형용사 실현 가능한 [격식체] ☐ 개인의 꿈과 소망이 실현 가능하다는 불합리한 가정 ☐ 형용사 현금화할 수 있는 [격식체] ☐ 많은 경우 집 주인이 살아 있는 동안은 이런 현금화할 수 있는 재산이 현금화되지는 않는다.

re|al|ize ♦♦◇ /ríəlaɪz/ (**realizes, realizing, realized**) [BRIT also **realise**] ☐ V-T/V-I If you **realize** that something is true, you become aware of that fact or understand it. ☐ *As soon as we realized something was wrong, we moved the children away.* ☐ *People don't realize how serious this recession has actually been.* ● **re|al|iza|tion** /ríəlaɪzéɪʃən/ (**realizations**) N-VAR ☐ *There is now a growing realization that things cannot go on like this for much longer.* ☐ V-T If your hopes, desires, or fears **are realized**, the things that you hope for, desire, or fear actually happen. [usu passive] ☐ *All his worst fears were realized.* ● **re|al|iza|tion** N-UNCOUNT ☐ *In Kravis's venomous tone he recognized the realization of his worst fears.* ☐ V-T When someone **realizes** a design or an idea, they make or organize something based on that design or idea. [FORMAL] ☐ *I knew the technique that I*

[영국영어 realise] ☐ 타동사/자동사 깨닫다 ☐ 뭔가가 잘못되었다고 깨닫자마자, 우리는 아이들을 멀리 이동시켰다. ☐ 사람들은 이번 불경기가 실제로 얼마나 심각한지를 깨닫지 못하고 있다. ● 깨달음, 인식 가산명사 또는 불가산명사 ☐ 이제 이런 식으로 일이 계속 진행될 수 없다는 인식이 점점 커지고 있다. ☐ 타동사 실현되다, 현실이 되다 ☐ 그가 가장 두려워했던 것들이 모두 현실이 되었다. ● 실현, 현실이 됨 불가산명사 ☐ 크라비스의 악의에 찬 목소리에서 그는 자신이 가장 두려워했던 것이 현실이 되었음을 느꼈다. ☐ 타동사 구현하다 [격식체] ☐ 내가

would have to create in order to realize that structure. ◢ V-T If someone or something **realizes** their potential, they do everything they are capable of doing, because they have been given the opportunity to do so. ◻ *The support systems to enable women to realize their potential at work are seriously inadequate.* ◻ V-T If something **realizes** a particular amount of money when it is sold, that amount of money is paid for it. [FORMAL] ◻ *A selection of correspondence from P G Wodehouse realized 1,232 pounds.* ● re|ali|za|tion N-VAR ...*a total cash realization of about $23 million.*

그 구조물을 구현하기 위해서 개발해 내야 할 기술을 나는 알고 있었다. ◢ 타동사 이루다, 실현하다 ◻ 여성들이 직장에서 자신의 잠재력을 실현할 수 있도록 도와주는 지원 체제가 아주 불충분하다. ◻ 타동사 -에 팔리다, -을 벌다 [격식체] ◻ 피 지 워드하우스에게서 온 서간집이 1,232파운드에 팔렸다. ● (제물 등의) 취득 가산명사 또는 불가산명사 ◻ 총 약 이천삼백만 달러의 현금 취득

Thesaurus   *realize*의 참조어

v.	pick up, see, understand ◻

Word Partnership   *realize*의 연어

ADV.	**suddenly** realize ◻
	finally realize, **fully** realize ◻ ◢
V.	**come to** realize, **make** *someone* realize ◻
	begin to realize, **fail to** realize ◻ ◢
N.	realize **a dream** ◻
	realize **your potential** ◢

---

real life N-UNCOUNT If something happens **in real life**, it actually happens and is not just in a story or in someone's imagination. ◻ *In real life men like Richard Gere don't marry street girls.* ● ADJ **Real life** is also an adjective. [ADJ n] ◻ ...*a real-life horror story.*

불가산명사 현실, 실생활 ◻ 실생활에서는 리처드 기어 같은 남자들이 창녀와 결혼하지는 않는다. ● 형용사 실생활에서의 ◻ 실생활에서의 공포 이야기

re|al|lo|cate /riæləkeɪt/ (reallocates, reallocating, reallocated) V-T When organizations **reallocate** money or resources, they decide to change the way they spend the money or use the resources. ◻ ...*a cost-cutting program to reallocate people and resources within the company.*

타동사 전용(轉用)하다 ◻ 사내에서 인력과 자원을 전용하는 비용 절감 프로그램

Word Link   real ≈ actual : reality, realize, really

---

re|al|ly ♦♦♦ /riəli/ ◻ ADV You can use **really** to emphasize a statement. [SPOKEN, EMPHASIS] ◻ *I'm very sorry. I really am.* ◻ ADV You can use **really** to emphasize an adjective or adverb. [EMPHASIS] [ADV adj/adv] ◻ *It was really good.* ◻ ADV You use **really** when you are discussing the real facts about something, in contrast to the ones someone wants you to believe. ◻ *My father didn't really love her.* ◢ ADV People use **really** in questions and negative statements when they want you to answer "no." [EMPHASIS] [ADV before v] ◻ *Do you really think he would be that stupid?* ◻ ADV If you refer to a time when something **really** begins to happen, you are emphasizing that it starts to happen at that time to a much greater extent and much more seriously than before. [EMPHASIS] [ADV before v] ◻ *That's when the pressure really started.* ◻ ADV People sometimes use **really** to slightly reduce the force of a negative statement. [SPOKEN, VAGUENESS] ◻ *I'm not really surprised.* ◻ CONVENTION You can say **really** to express surprise or disbelief at what someone has said. [SPOKEN, FEELINGS] ◻ *"We discovered it was totally the wrong decision." — "Really?"*

◻ 부사 정말로 [구어체, 강조] ◻ 미안해. 정말로. ◻ 부사 정말 [강조] ◻ 그것은 정말 좋았다. ◻ 부사 실제로 ◻ 우리 아버지는 그녀를 실제로 사랑하지는 않았다. ◢ 부사 진짜 [강조] ◻ 그가 그 정도로 멍청할 거라고 진짜 생각하는 거니? ◻ 부사 정말로 [강조] ◻ 그 때가 압박감이 정말로 시작되었던 때야. ◻ 부사 별로 [구어체, 짐작투] ◻ 난 별로 안 놀랐어. ◻ 관용 표현 정말 [구어체, 감정 개입] ◻ "우린 그것이 완전히 잘못된 결정이었다는 걸 알았어." "정말?"

Note that **really** and **actually** are both used to emphasize statements. You use **really** in conversation to emphasize something that you are saying. ◻ *I really think he's sick.* Note that when **really** is used in a negative sentence, its position in relation to the verb affects the meaning. For instance, if you say 'I really don't like Richard,' with **really** in front of the verb, you are emphasizing how much you dislike Richard. However, if you say 'I don't really like Richard,' with **really** coming after the negative, you are still saying that you dislike Richard, but the feeling is not particularly strong. When you use **really** in front of an adjective or adverb, it has a similar meaning to **very**. ◻ *This is really serious.* **Actually** is used to emphasize what is true or genuine in a situation, often when this is surprising, or a contrast with what has just been said. ◻ *All the characters in the novel actually existed... He actually began to cry.* It can also be used to be precise or to correct someone. ◻ *No one was actually drunk... We couldn't actually see the garden.*

really와 actually는 둘 다 진술을 강조하기 위해 쓴다는 점을 유의하라. really는 대화에서 말하고 있는 것을 강조할 때 쓴다. ◻ 나는 그가 정말 아프다고 생각한다. really를 부정문에 쓰면, 동사와 관련된 really의 위치가 의미에 영향을 미친다는 점을 유의하라. 예를 들면, really를 동사 앞에 써서 "I really don't like Richard."라고 하면, 리처드를 아주 싫어한다는 점을 강조하는 것이다. 그러나, really를 부정어 뒤에 써서 "I don't really like Richard."라고 하면, 여전히 리처드를 싫어한다는 뜻이지만 그 감정이 특별히 강하지는 않다. really를 형용사 또는 부사 앞에 쓰면 'very'와 비슷한 뜻을 갖는다. ◻ 이건 정말 심각하다. actually는 어떤 상황에서 진실이거나 진짜인 것을 강조하기 위해 쓰이는데, 흔히 이런 것이 놀랍거나 막 언급한 내용과 대조를 이룰 때 쓴다. ◻ 그 소설의 모든 등장인물들은 실제로 존재했다... 그가 실제로 울기 시작했다. actually는 또한 정확하게 말하거나 다른 사람의 말을 정정해 줄 때도 쓴다. ◻ 정말 아무도 취하지 않았다... 우리는 정원을 정말 볼 수가 없었다.

---

realm /rɛlm/ (realms) ◻ N-COUNT You can use **realm** to refer to any area of activity, interest, or thought. [FORMAL] ◻ ...*the realm of politics.* ◻ N-COUNT A **realm** is a country that has a king or queen. [FORMAL] ◻ *Defence of the realm is crucial.*

◻ 가산명사 분야 [격식체] ◻ 정치학 분야 ◻ 가산명사 왕국 [격식체] ◻ 왕국을 지키는 것은 아주 중요하다.

real prop|er|ty N-UNCOUNT **Real property** is property in the form of land and buildings, rather than personal possessions. [AM] ◻ ...*the owner or tenant of a piece of real property.*

불가산명사 부동산 [미국영어] ◻ 부동산 한 곳의 소유주 혹은 임차인

real-time ADJ **Real-time** processing is a type of computer programming or data processing in which the information received is processed by the computer almost immediately. [COMPUTING] [ADJ n] ◻ ...*real-time language translations.*

형용사 실시간의 [컴퓨터] ◻ 실시간 언어 번역

Real|tor /riəltər, -tɔr/ (Realtors) also realtor N-COUNT A **Realtor** is a person whose job is to sell houses, buildings, and land, and who is a member of the National Association of Realtors. [AM, TRADEMARK; BRIT **estate agent**] ◻ *When the Realtor showed us this house, we knew we wanted it right way.*

가산명사 부동산 공인 중개사 (전국 부동산업자 협회 회원) [미국영어, 상표; 영국영어 **estate agent**] ◻ 부동산 중개업자가 이 집을 우리에게 보여 주었을 때, 우리는 이 집을 사고 싶은 생각이 바로 들었다.

real world N-SING If you talk about **the real world**, you are referring to the world and life in general, in contrast to a particular person's own life, experience, and ideas, which may seem untypical and unrealistic. ❑ *When they eventually leave the school they will be totally ill-equipped to deal with the real world.*

reap /rip/ (**reaps, reaping, reaped**) V-T If you **reap** the benefits or the rewards of something, you enjoy the good things that happen as a result of it. ❑ *You'll soon begin to reap the benefits of being fitter.*

re|appear /riːəpɪər/ (**reappears, reappearing, reappeared**) V-I When people or things **reappear**, they return again after they have been away or out of sight for some time. ❑ *Thirty seconds later she reappeared and beckoned them forward.*

re|appear|ance /riːəpɪərəns/ (**reappearances**) N-COUNT The **reappearance** of someone or something is their return after they have been away or out of sight for some time. ❑ *His sudden reappearance must have been a shock.*

rear /rɪər/ (**rears, rearing, reared**) ◆◇◇ ◼ N-SING The **rear** of something such as a building or vehicle is the back part of it. ❑ *He settled back in the rear of the taxi.* ● ADJ **Rear** is also an adjective. [ADJ n] ❑ *Manufacturers have been obliged to fit rear seat belts in all new cars.* ◻ N-SING If you are at the **rear** of a moving line of people, you are the last person in it. [FORMAL] ❑ *Musicians played at the front and rear of the procession.* ◼ V-T If you **rear** children, you take care of them until they are old enough to take care of themselves. ❑ *She reared sixteen children, six her own and ten her husband's.* ◼ V-T If you **rear** a young animal, you keep and look after it until it is old enough to be used for work or food, or until it can look after itself. [mainly BRIT; AM usually **raise**] ❑ *She spends a lot of time rearing animals.* ◼ V-I When a horse **rears**, it moves the front part of its body upward, so that its front legs are high in the air and it is standing on its back legs. ❑ *The horse reared and threw off its rider.* ◼ PHRASE If a person or vehicle **is bringing up the rear**, they are the last person or vehicle in a moving line of them. ❑ *...police motorcyclists bringing up the rear of the procession.*

re|arrange /riːəreɪndʒ/ (**rearranges, rearranging, rearranged**) ◼ V-T If you **rearrange** things, you change the way in which they are organized or ordered. ❑ *When she returned, she found Malcolm had rearranged all her furniture.* ◻ V-T If you **rearrange** a meeting or an appointment, you arrange for it to take place at a different time to that originally intended. ❑ *You may cancel or rearrange the appointment.*

re|arrange|ment /riːəreɪndʒmənt/ (**rearrangements**) N-VAR A **rearrangement** is a change in the way that something is arranged or organized. ❑ *...a rearrangement of the job structure.*

rear-view mirror (**rear-view mirrors**) also **rearview mirror** N-COUNT Inside a car, the **rear-view mirror** is the mirror that enables you to see the traffic behind when you are driving.

rea|son ◆◆◆ /riːzən/ (**reasons, reasoning, reasoned**) ◼ N-COUNT The **reason for** something is a fact or situation which explains why it happens or what causes it to happen. ❑ *There is a reason for every important thing that happens.* ◻ N-UNCOUNT If you say that you have **reason to** believe something or **to** have a particular emotion, you mean that you have evidence for your belief or there is a definite cause of your feeling. ❑ *They had reason to believe there could be trouble.* ◼ N-UNCOUNT The ability that people have to think and to make sensible judgments can be referred to as **reason**. ❑ *...a conflict between emotion and reason.* ◼ V-T If you **reason that** something is true, you decide that it is true after thinking carefully about all the facts. ❑ *I reasoned that changing my diet would lower my cholesterol level.* →see also **reasoned, reasoning** ◼ PHRASE If one thing happens **by reason of** another, it happens because of it. [FORMAL] ❑ *The boss retains enormous influence by reason of his position.* ◼ PHRASE If you try to make someone **listen to reason**, you try to persuade them to listen to sensible arguments and be influenced by them. ❑ *The company's top executives had refused to listen to reason.* ◼ PHRASE If you say that something happened or was done **for no reason, for no good reason,** or **for no reason at all,** you mean that there was no obvious reason why it happened or was done. ❑ *The guards, he said, would punch them for no reason.* ◼ PHRASE If you say that you will do anything **within reason,** you mean that you will do anything that is fair or reasonable and not too extreme. ❑ *I will take any job that comes along, within reason.* ◼ to **see reason** →see **see. it stands to reason** →see **stand**

Thesaurus   reason의 참조어

N.   argument, defense, excuse, explanation ◼
     analysis, comprehension, intellect, logic ◼

Word Partnership   reason의 연어

ADJ.   **main** reason, **major** reason, **obvious** reason, **only** reason, **primary** reason, **real** reason, **same** reason, **simple** reason ◼
     compelling reason, **good** reason, **sufficient** reason ◼ ◻

▸**reason with** PHRASAL VERB If you try to **reason with** someone, you try to persuade them to do or accept something by using sensible arguments. ❑ *I have watched parents trying to reason with their children and have never seen it work.*

rea|son|able ◆◇◇ /riːzənəbəl/ ◼ ADJ If you think that someone is fair and sensible you can say that they are **reasonable**. ❑ *He's a reasonable sort of chap.* ● **rea|son|ably** /riːzənəbli/ ADV ❑ *"I'm sorry, Andrew," she said reasonably.* ● **rea|son|able|ness** N-UNCOUNT ❑ *"I can understand how you feel," Desmond said with great reasonableness.* ◻ ADJ If you say that a decision or action is **reasonable**,

---

단수명사 현실 세계 ❑ 마침내 그들이 학교를 떠날 때는 현실 세계에 대처할 아무런 준비도 되어 있지 않을 것이다.

타동사 수확하다, 누리다 ❑ 당신은 곧 더 건강해진 것의 혜택을 누리기 시작할 것이다.

자동사 다시 나타나다 ❑ 30초 후에 그녀가 다시 나타나서 그들에게 오라고 손짓했다.

가산명사 재출현 ❑ 그의 갑작스러운 재출현은 분명 충격이었을 것이다.

◼ 단수명사 뒤쪽 ❑ 그는 택시 뒷좌석에 편히 앉았다. ● 형용사 뒤쪽의 ❑ 자동차 회사가 모든 신차에 뒷좌석 벨트를 장착시키도록 되어 있다. ◻ 단수명사 맨 뒤 [격식체] ❑ 연주가들이 그 행렬의 맨 앞과 맨 뒤에서 연주를 했다. ◼ 타동사 기르다, 키우다 ❑ 그녀는 자신의 여섯 자녀와 남편의 10명의 자녀, 모두 16명의 자녀를 키웠다. ◼ 타동사 (동물을) 기르다 [주로 영국영어; 미국영어 대개 raise] ❑ 그녀는 동물들을 기르는 데 많은 시간을 보낸다. ◼ 자동사 (말 등이) 뒷다리로만 서다, 앞다리를 들어 올리다 ❑ 그 말이 앞다리를 들어 올리며 기수를 떨어뜨려 버렸다. ◼ 구 맨 뒤에 오다 ❑ 그 행렬 맨 뒤에 오고 있는 오토바이를 탄 경찰들

◼ 타동사 재배열하다 ❑ 그녀가 돌아왔을 때, 말콤이 그녀의 가구를 모두 재배열해 놓았었다. ◻ 타동사 재조정하다 ❑ 그 약속을 취소하거나 재조정할 수 있다.

가산명사 또는 불가산명사 재조정 ❑ 직업 구조의 재조정

가산명사 (자동차의) 뒷거울, 백미러

◼ 가산명사 이유 ❑ 모든 중요한 일에는 일어날 만한 이유가 있다. ◻ 불가산명사 까닭, 이유 ❑ 그들이 문제가 있을 수 있다고 믿을 만한 까닭이 있었다. ◼ 불가산명사 이성 ❑ 감정과 이성 간의 갈등 ◼ 타동사 (논리적으로) 판단하다 ❑ 나는 식습관을 바꾸면 내 콜레스테롤 수치를 낮출 수 있을 것이라고 판단했다. ◼ 구 -을 이유로, -로 인하여 [격식체] ❑ 그 사장은 자신의 직위를 이유로 엄청난 영향력을 계속 행사한다. ◼ 구 이성의 소리에 귀 기울이다, 합당하게 여기고 바꾸다 ❑ 회사의 최고 경영자들이 이성의 소리에 귀 기울이기를 거부한 상태였다. ◼ 구 이유 없이, 아무런 이유 없이 ❑ 경비원들이 이유 없이 그들을 주먹으로 칠 거라고 그는 말했다. ◼ 구 합당한 정도인, 너무 지나치지 않은 ❑ 합당하기만 한 일이라면 앞으로 생기는 어떤 일이라도 할 것이다.

구동사 알아듣게 이야기하다, 이치를 따져 설득하다 ❑ 나는 부모들이 자식들에게 알아듣게 이야기하려고 애쓰는 것을 봐 왔지만, 성공하는 부모를 결코 보지 못했다.

◼ 형용사 도리를 아는 ❑ 그는 도리를 아는 편인 사람이다. ● 도리에 맞게 부사 "미안해, 앤드류."라고 그녀가 도리에 맞게 말했다. ● 도리에 맞음 불가산명사 ❑ "당신이 어떤 느낌일지 이해할 수 있어요."라고 데스몬드가 아주 도리에 맞게 말했다. ◻ 형용사

you mean that it is fair and sensible. ❏ ...*a perfectly reasonable decision.* ③ ADJ If you say that an expectation or explanation is **reasonable**, you mean that there are good reasons why it may be correct. ❏ *It seems reasonable to expect rapid urban growth.* ● **rea|son|ably** ADV [ADV with v] ❏ *You can reasonably expect your goods to arrive within six to eight weeks.* ④ ADJ If you say that the price of something is **reasonable**, you mean that it is fair and not too high. ❏ *You get an interesting meal for a reasonable price.* ● **rea|son|ably** ADV [ADV with v] ❏ *...reasonably priced accommodation.* ⑤ ADJ You can use **reasonable** to describe something that is fairly good, but not very good. ❏ *The boy answered him in reasonable French.* ● **rea|son|ably** ADV [ADV adj/adv] ❏ *I can dance reasonably well.* ⑥ ADJ A **reasonable** amount of something is a fairly large amount of it. ❏ *They will need a reasonable amount of desk area and good light.* ● **rea|son|ably** ADV [ADV adj/adv] ❏ *From now on events moved reasonably quickly.*

타당한 ❏ 매우 타당한 결정 ③ 형용사 일리가 있는 ❏ 도시가 빠르게 성장할 것이라고 예상하는 것은 일리가 있는 것 같다. ● 당연히, 타당하게 부사 ❏ 당신은 당연히 6주에서 8주 내에 당신의 상품이 도착할 것이라고 예상할 수 있다. ④ 형용사 적당한, 적정한 ❏ 당신은 적당한 가격으로 맛있는 음식을 먹는다. ● 적절하게 부사 ❏ 적절하게 가격이 책정된 숙박 시설 ⑤ 형용사 꽤 괜찮은, 꽤 괜찮은 ❏ 그 소년은 꽤 잘하는 불어로 그에게 대답했다. ● 꽤 부사 ❏ 나는 춤을 꽤 잘 출 수 있다. ⑥ 형용사 상당한 ❏ 그들은 책상을 놓을 상당한 넓이의 공간과 밝은 조명이 필요할 것이다. ● 상당히 부사 ❏ 이제부터는 행사가 상당히 빨리 진행되었다.

Thesaurus
*reasonable*의 참조어

ADJ.	
rational	①-③
acceptable, fair, sensible; (ant.) unreasonable	②
likely, probable, right	③
fair, inexpensive	④

Word Partnership
*reasonable*의 연어

N.
reasonable **person** ①
reasonable **expectation**, reasonable **explanation** ③
reasonable **cost**, reasonable **price**, reasonable **rates** ④
reasonable **amount** ④ ⑥
reasonable **chance**, reasonable **time** ⑤

rea|soned /ríz°nd/ ADJ A **reasoned** discussion or argument is based on sensible reasons, rather than on an appeal to people's emotions. [APPROVAL] ❏ *Abortion is an issue which produces a lot of sound and fury, but little reasoned argument.*

형용사 이성에 의거한 [마음에 듦] ❏ 낙태는 화나서 떠드는 소리들만 낳을 뿐 이성에 의거한 논쟁은 거의 없는 사안이다.

rea|son|ing /rízənɪŋ/ (reasonings) N-VAR **Reasoning** is the process by which you reach a conclusion after thinking about all the facts. ❏ *...the reasoning behind the decision.* →see **philosophy**

가산명사 또는 불가산명사 추론 과정 ❏ 그 결정 이면의 추론 과정

re|as|sert /ríəsɜ́rt/ (reasserts, reasserting, reasserted) ① V-T If you **reassert** your control or authority, you make it clear that you are still in a position of power, or you strengthen the power that you had. ❏ *...the government's continuing effort to reassert its control in the region.* ② V-T If something such as an idea or habit **reasserts itself**, it becomes noticeable again. ❏ *His sense of humor was beginning to reassert itself.*

① 타동사 거듭 주장하다 ❏ 그 지역 내의 지배권을 거듭 주장하려는 정부 측의 계속되는 노력 ② 타동사 (아이디어 등이) 다시 발휘되다 ❏ 그의 유머 감각이 다시 발휘되기 시작하고 있었다.

re|as|sess /ríəsɛ́s/ (reassesses, reassessing, reassessed) V-T If you **reassess** something, you think about it and decide whether you need to change your opinion about it. ❏ *I will reassess the situation when I get home.*

타동사 재평가하다 ❏ 내가 집에 돌아가면 그 상황을 재평가해 볼 것이다.

re|as|sess|ment /ríəsɛ́smənt/ (reassessments) N-VAR If you make a **reassessment** of something, you think about it and decide whether you need to change your opinion about it. ❏ *Forty, more than any other birthday seems to mark the moment when we make a reassessment of ourselves.*

가산명사 또는 불가산명사 재평가 ❏ 다른 어떤 생일 때보다도 마흔이 되면 우리가 스스로를 재평가하게 되는 것 같다.

re|as|sur|ance /ríəʃʊ́ərəns/ (reassurances) ① N-UNCOUNT **reassurance**, they are very worried and need someone to help them stop worrying by saying kind or helpful things. ❏ *She needed reassurance that she belonged somewhere.* ② N-COUNT **Reassurances** are things that you say to help people stop worrying about something. ❏ *...reassurances that pesticides are not harmful.*

① 불가산명사 안심, 안도감 ❏ 그녀는 자신이 어딘가에 소속되어 있다는 안도감이 필요했다. ② 가산명사 안심시키는 말 ❏ 살충제가 해롭지 않다고 안심시키는 말

re|as|sure /ríəʃʊ́ər/ (reassures, reassuring, reassured) V-T If you **reassure** someone, you say or do things to make them stop worrying about something. ❏ *I tried to reassure her, "Don't worry about it. We won't let it happen again."*

타동사 안심시키다 ❏ 나는 그녀를 안심시키려고 노력했다. "걱정하지 마, 다시는 그런 일이 없을 거야."

Word Partnership
*reassure*의 연어

N.
reassure **citizens**, reassure **customers**, reassure **investors**, reassure **the public**

V.
seek to reassure, **try to** reassure

re|as|sured /ríəʃʊ́ərd/ ADJ If you feel **reassured**, you feel less worried about something, usually because you have received help or advice. ❏ *I feel much more reassured when I've been for a health check.*

형용사 안심하는 ❏ 건강 검진을 받고 나니 나는 훨씬 더 안심이 된다.

re|as|sur|ing /ríəʃʊ́ərɪŋ/ ADJ If you find someone's words or actions **reassuring**, they make you feel less worried about something. ❏ *It was reassuring to hear John's familiar voice.* ● **re|as|sur|ing|ly** ADV ❏ *"It's okay now," he said reassuringly.*

형용사 안심시키는 ❏ 존의 귀에 익은 목소리를 들으니 안심이 되었다. ● 안심시키듯 부사 ❏ "이제 괜찮아요."라며 그는 안심시키듯 말했다.

re|bate /ríbeɪt/ (rebates) N-COUNT A **rebate** is an amount of money which is returned to you after you have paid for goods or services or after you have paid tax or rent. ❏ *...a tax rebate.*

가산명사 (지불액의 일부) 환불 ❏ 세금 환불

re|bel ◆◇◇ (rebels, rebelling, rebelled)

The noun is pronounced /rɛ́bəl/. The verb is pronounced /rɪbɛ́l/.

명사는 /rɛ́bəl/로 발음되고, 동사는 /rɪbɛ́l/로 발음된다.

① N-COUNT **Rebels** are people who are fighting against their own country's army in order to change the political system there. ❏ *...fighting between rebels and government forces.* ② N-COUNT Politicians who oppose some of their own party's policies can be referred to as **rebels**. ❏ *The rebels want another 1% cut in interest rates.* ③ V-I If politicians **rebel** against one of their own party's policies, they show that they oppose it. ❏ *More than forty Conservative MPs rebelled against*

① 가산명사 반역자, 반란군 ❏ 반군과 정부군 간의 싸움 ② 가산명사 (소속 정당의 정책에) 반대 의견을 가진 정치인, 반대파 ❏ 그 반대파들은 금리를 1퍼센트 더 내리기를 원한다. ③ 자동사 (소속 정당 정책에) 반대하다 ❏ 40명 이상의 보수당 의원들이 정부 측에 반대하여 그 법안에 반대표를 던졌다. ④ 가산명사

the government and voted against the bill. **4** N-COUNT You can say that someone is a **rebel** if you think that they behave differently from other people and have rejected the values of society or of their parents. ❑ *She had been a rebel at school.* **5** V-I When someone **rebels**, they start to behave differently from other people and reject the values of society or of their parents. ❑ *The child who rebels is unlikely to be overlooked.*

re|bel|lion /rɪbɛljən/ (rebellions) **1** N-VAR A **rebellion** is a violent organized action by a large group of people who are trying to change their country's political system. ❑ *The British soon put down the rebellion.* **2** N-VAR A situation in which politicians show their opposition to their own party's policies can be referred to as a **rebellion**. ❑ *On Tuesday night, on the Budget vote, there was a Labour rebellion when some left-wing MPs voted against the Chancellor's tax cuts.*

re|bel|lious /rɪbɛljəs/ **1** ADJ If you think someone behaves in an unacceptable way and does not do what they are told, you can say they are **rebellious**. ❑ *...a rebellious teenager.* ● re|bel|lious|ness N-UNCOUNT ❑ *...the normal rebelliousness of youth.* **2** ADJ A **rebellious** group of people is a group involved in taking violent action against the rulers of their own country, usually in order to change the system of government there. [ADJ n] ❑ *The rebellious officers, having seized the radio station, broadcast the news of the overthrow of the monarchy.*

re|birth /rib3rθ/ N-UNCOUNT You can refer to a change that leads to a new period of growth and improvement in something as its **rebirth**. ❑ *...the rebirth of democracy in Latin America.*

re|bound /rɪbaʊnd/ (rebounds, rebounding, rebounded) **1** V-I If something **rebounds** from a solid surface, it bounces or springs back from it. ❑ *His shot in the 21st minute of the game rebounded from a post.* **2** V-I If an action or situation **rebounds on** you, it has an unpleasant effect on you, especially when this effect was intended for someone else. ❑ *Mia realised her trick had rebounded on her.*

re|brand /ribrænd/ (rebrands, rebranding, rebranded) V-T To **rebrand** a product or organization means to present it to the public in a new way, for example by changing its name or appearance. [BUSINESS] ❑ *There are plans to rebrand many Texas stores.*

re|brand|ing /ribrændɪŋ/ N-UNCOUNT **Rebranding** is the process of giving a product or an organization a new image, in order to make it more attractive or successful. [BUSINESS] ❑ *A complete rebranding of the school is expected within two years.*

re|buff /rɪbʌf/ (rebuffs, rebuffing, rebuffed) V-T If you **rebuff** someone or **rebuff** a suggestion that they make, you refuse to do what they suggest. ❑ *His proposals have already been rebuffed by the Prime Minister.* ● N-VAR **Rebuff** is also a noun. ❑ *The results of the poll dealt a humiliating rebuff to Mr. Jones.*

re|build /ribɪld/ (rebuilds, rebuilding, rebuilt) **1** V-T When people **rebuild** something such as a building or a city, they build it again after it has been damaged or destroyed. ❑ *They say they will stay to rebuild their homes rather than retreat to refugee camps.* **2** V-T When people **rebuild** something such as an institution, a system, or an aspect of their lives, they take action to bring it back to its previous condition. ❑ *The President's message was that everyone would have to work hard together to rebuild the economy.*

re|buke /rɪbyuk/ (rebukes, rebuking, rebuked) V-T If you **rebuke** someone, you speak severely to them because they have said or done something that you do not approve of. [FORMAL] ❑ *The president rebuked the House and Senate for not passing those bills within 100 days.* ● N-VAR **Rebuke** is also a noun. ❑ *UN member countries delivered a strong rebuke to both countries for persisting with nuclear testing programs.*

re|call ♦♦◇ (recalls, recalling, recalled)

The verb is pronounced /rɪkɔl/. The noun is pronounced /rikɔl/.

1 V-T/V-I When you **recall** something, you remember it and tell others about it. ❑ *Henderson recalled that he first met Pollard during a business trip to Washington.* ❑ *His mother later recalled: "He used to stay up until two o'clock in the morning playing these war games."* **2** N-UNCOUNT **Recall** is the ability to remember something that has happened in the past or the act of remembering it. ❑ *He had a good memory, and total recall of her spoken words.* **3** V-T If you **are recalled** to your home, country, or the place where you work, you are ordered to return there. ❑ *Spain has recalled its Ambassador after a row over refugees seeking asylum at the embassy.* ● N-SING **Recall** is also a noun. ❑ *The recall of ambassador Alan Green is a public signal of America's concern.* **4** V-T If a company **recalls** a product, it asks the stores or the people who have bought that product to return it because there is something wrong with it. ❑ *The company said it was recalling one of its drugs and had stopped selling two others.*

re|cap /rikæp/ (recaps, recapping, recapped) V-T/V-I You can say that you are going to **recap** when you want to draw people's attention to the fact that you are going to repeat the main points of an explanation, argument, or description, as a summary of it. ❑ *To recap briefly, an agreement negotiated to cut the budget deficit in the coming year was rejected 10 days ago.* ● N-SING **Recap** is also a noun. ❑ *Each report starts with a summary of the last month, a recap of how we did versus our projections, and a rundown on the significant events of the period.*

re|capi|tal|ize /rikæpɪtᵊlaɪz/ (recapitalizes, recapitalizing, recapitalized) V-T/V-I If a company **recapitalizes**, it changes the way it manages its financial affairs, for example by borrowing money or reissuing shares. [AM, BUSINESS] ❑ *Mr. Warnock resigned as the company abandoned a plan to recapitalize.* ● re|capi|tali|za|tion /rikæpɪtᵊlizeɪʃᵊn/ (recapitalizations) N-COUNT ❑ *A substantial thrust of the effort of management is to explore a recapitalization of the company.*

별종 ❑ 그녀는 학교에서 별종이었다. **5** 자동사 (사회적 가치 등에) 반항하다 ❑ 반항하는 아이를 너그럽게 봐주기는 힘들다.

1 가산명사 또는 불가산명사 반란, 모반 ❑ 영국인들은 곧 그 반란을 진압했다. **2** 가산명사 또는 불가산명사 (소속당 정책에 대한) 반대 ❑ 화요일 밤, 예산안 표결에서 좌파 의원 몇 명이 재무 장관의 세금 삭감안에 대해 반대표를 던져서 노동당 내 정책 반대 사태가 발생했다.

1 형용사 반항하는, 반항적인 ❑ 반항적인 10대 ● 반항심 불가산명사 ❑ 젊은이들의 정상적인 반항심 **2** 형용사 반란의 ❑ 반란군 장교들은 라디오 방송국을 점령한 후 군주제가 전복되었다는 소식을 방송했다.

불가산명사 부활 ❑ 라틴 아메리카 지역의 민주주의 부활

1 자동사 (공 등이) 되튀다 ❑ 그가 게임 시작 21분에 던진 공이 기둥을 맞고 되튀어 나왔다. **2** 자동사 (결과 등이) 되돌아오다 ❑ 미아는 자신의 계략이 다시 자신에게로 되돌아왔음을 깨달았다.

타동사 (브랜드를) 새롭게 선보이다 [경제] ❑ 많은 텍사스 상점들을 새롭게 선보이려는 계획들이 있다.

불가산명사 (브랜드의) 이미지 쇄신 [경제] ❑ 2년 내에 학교 이미지를 완전히 새롭게 바꿀 예정이다.

타동사 거절하다, 퇴짜 놓다 ❑ 그의 제안은 이미 수상에게 퇴짜를 맞았다. ● 가산명사 또는 불가산명사 퇴짜 ❑ 여론 조사 결과 존스 씨는 모욕적인 퇴짜를 맞았다.

1 타동사 재건하다 ❑ 그들은 피난민 수용소로 들어가기 보다는 남아서 자신들의 집을 재건하겠다고 말한다. **2** 타동사 재건하다 ❑ 대통령의 교서 내용은 모든 사람들이 경제를 재건하기 위해 다같이 힘써야 할 것이라는 것이었다.

타동사 질책하다 [격식체] ❑ 대통령은 100일 내에 그 법안들을 통과시키지 못한 것에 대해 하원과 상원을 질책했다. ● 가산명사 또는 불가산명사 질책 ❑ 유엔 회원국들은 핵실험을 고집하는 두 나라를 강하게 질책했다.

동사는 /rɪkɔl /로 발음되고, 명사는 /rikɔl /로 발음된다.

1 타동사/자동사 기억해 내다 ❑ 헨더슨은 워싱턴에 출장 갔을 때 폴라드를 처음 만났던 것을 기억해 냈다. ❑ 나중에 그의 어머니는 기억해 내셨다. "그 아이는 이런 전쟁놀이를 하느라 새벽 두 시까지 있곤 했지." **2** 불가산명사 기억력 ❑ 그는 기억력이 좋아서 그녀가 말했던 한마디 한마디를 모두 기억했다. **3** 타동사 소환하다 ❑ 스페인은 그 대사관에서 보호를 요청하는 난민들을 둘러싼 소동이 있은 후 대사를 소환했다. ● 단수명사 소환 ❑ 앨런 그린 대사의 소환은 미국의 대외적으로 우려를 나타내는 신호이다. **4** 타동사 회수하다, 리콜하다 ❑ 그 회사는 판매했던 약 중 한 가지는 회수하고 있고, 나머지 두 가지는 판매를 중단시켰다고 말했다.

타동사/자동사 요약하다, 개괄하다 ❑ 간략하게 요약하면, 차기 연도 예산 적자 감소를 위해 협상된 동의안은 열흘 전에 거부되었다. ● 단수명사 개괄 ❑ 모든 보고서는 지난날의 요약, 예측 대비 실적 개괄, 그리고 그 기간 중의 중대 행사 개요로 시작한다.

타동사/자동사 자기 자본을 확충하다 [미국영어, 경제] ❑ 워녹 씨는 회사가 자기 자본을 확충하려던 계획을 포기함에 따라 사임했다. ● 자기 자본 확충 가산명사 ❑ 경영 노력의 실질적인 추진력은 기업의 자기 자본 확충을 강구하는 것이다.

a b c d e f g h i j k l m n o p q r s t u v w x y z

A

re|ca|pitu|late /rɪkəpɪtʃəleɪt/ (recapitulates, recapitulating, recapitulated) v-T/v-I You can say that you are going to **recapitulate** the main points of an explanation, argument, or description when you want to draw attention to the fact that you are going to repeat the most important points as a summary. ❏ *Let's just recapitulate the essential points.* ● **re|ca|pitu|la|tion** /rɪkəpɪtʃəleɪʃ³n/ N-SING ❏ *Chapter 9 provides a valuable recapitulation of the material already presented.*

타동사/자동사 요약하다 ❏ 핵심 사항을 한 번 요약해 봅시다. ● 요약 단수명사 ❏ 9장은 앞서 제시한 내용에 대한 유익한 요약을 담고 있다.

B

re|cap|ture /rɪkæptʃər/ (recaptures, recapturing, recaptured) ❶ v-T When soldiers **recapture** an area of land or a place, they gain control of it again from an opposing army who had taken it from them. ❏ *They said the bodies were found when rebels recaptured the area.* ● N-SING **Recapture** is also a noun. ❏ *...an offensive to be launched for the recapture of the city.* ❷ v-T When people **recapture** something that they have lost to a competitor, they get it back again. ❏ *I do genuinely believe that he would be the best possibility to recapture the center vote and also the youngsters' vote in the forthcoming election.* ❸ v-T To **recapture** a person or animal which has escaped from somewhere means to catch them again. ❏ *Police have recaptured Alan Lord, who escaped from a police cell in Bolton.* ● N-SING **Recapture** is also a noun. ❏ *...the recapture of a renegade police chief in Panama.*

❶ 타동사 탈환하다 ❏ 그들은 반군이 그 지역을 탈환했을 때 그 시신들이 발견되었다고 말했다. ● 단수명사 탈환 ❏ 그 도시 탈환을 위해 개시될 공격 ❷ 타동사 되찾다 ❏ 나는 그가 이번 선거에서 온건파의 표뿐 아니라 젊은이들의 표까지 되찾는, 당선 가능성이 가장 높은 사람이라고 진심으로 믿는다. ❸ 타동사 다시 체포하다 ❏ 경찰이 볼튼의 경찰서 유치장을 탈출한 앨런 로드를 다시 체포했다. ● 단수명사 다시 체포함 ❏ 변절한 경찰서장을 파나마에서 다시 체포함

C

D

E

re|cede /rɪsid/ (recedes, receding, receded) ❶ v-I If something **recedes** from you, it moves away. ❏ *Luke's footsteps receded into the night.* ❏ *As she receded he waved goodbye.* ❷ v-I When something such as a quality, problem, or illness **recedes**, it becomes weaker, smaller, or less intense. ❏ *Just as I started to think that I was never going to get well, the illness began to recede.* ❸ v-I If a man's hair starts to **recede**, it no longer grows on the front of his head. ❏ *...a youngish man with dark hair just beginning to recede.*

❶ 자동사 멀어지다, 물러나다 ❏ 루크의 발소리가 밤의 어둠 속으로 멀어져 갔다. ❏ 그녀가 멀어질 때 그는 잘 가라며 손을 흔들었다. ❷ 자동사 약해지다 ❏ 내가 절대 회복하지 못할 것이라는 생각이 들자마자 병이 약화되기 시작했다. ❸ 자동사 이마가 벗어지다 ❏ 이제 막 이마가 벗어지기 시작하는 검은 머리카락의 아직 젊은 남자

F

G

H

re|ceipt /rɪsit/ (receipts) ❶ N-COUNT A **receipt** is a piece of paper that you get from someone as proof that they have received money or goods from you. In British English a **receipt** is a piece of paper that you get in a store when you buy something, but in American English the more usual term for this is **sales slip**. ❏ *I wrote her a receipt for the money.* ❷ N-PLURAL **Receipts** are the amount of money received during a particular period, for example by a store or theater. ❏ *He was tallying the day's receipts.* ❸ N-UNCOUNT The **receipt** of something is the act of receiving it. [FORMAL] ❏ *Goods should be supplied within 28 days after the receipt of your order.* ❹ PHRASE If you are **in receipt of** something, you have received it or you receive it regularly. [FORMAL] ❏ *We are taking action, having been in receipt of a letter from him.*

❶ 가산명사 수령증, 영수증 ❏ 나는 그녀에게 그 돈을 받았다는 수령증을 써 주었다. ❷ 복수명사 수령액 ❏ 그는 그날의 수령액을 합산하고 있었다. ❸ 불가산명사 받음, 수취 [격식체] ❏ 물품은 주문을 받은 후 28일 내에 배달됩니다. ❹ 구 (정기적으로) 받는 [격식체] ❏ 우리는 그에게 정기적으로 편지를 받으면서 조치를 취하고 있다.

I

J

K

re|ceive ♦♦♦ /rɪsiv/ (receives, receiving, received) ❶ v-T When you **receive** something, you get it after someone gives it to you or sends it to you. ❏ *They will receive their awards at a ceremony in Stockholm.* ❷ v-T You can use **receive** to say that certain kinds of things happen to someone. For example if they are injured, you can say that they **received** an injury. ❏ *He received more of the blame than anyone when the plan failed to work.* ❸ v-T When you **receive** a visitor or a guest, you greet them. ❏ *The following evening the duchess was again receiving guests.* ❹ v-T If you say that something **is received** in a particular way, you mean that people react to it in that way. [usu passive] ❏ *The resolution had been received with great disappointment within the PLO.* ❺ v-T When a radio or television **receives** signals that are being transmitted, it picks them up and converts them into sound or pictures. ❏ *The reception was a little faint but clear enough for him to receive the signal.* ❻ PHRASE If you **are on the receiving end** or **at the receiving end** of something unpleasant, you are the person that it happens to. ❏ *You saw hate in their eyes and you were on the receiving end of that hate.*

❶ 타동사 받다 ❏ 그들은 스톡홀름에서 열릴 시상식에서 상을 받게 될 것이다. ❷ 타동사 받다, 입다 ❏ 그는 그 계획이 실패했을 때 누구보다 더 많은 비난을 받았다. ❸ 타동사 맞이하다 ❏ 다음 날 저녁 공작 부인은 다시 손님을 맞이하고 있었다. ❹ 타동사 받아들여지다, 이해되다 ❏ 그 결의안은 팔레스타인 해방 기구 내에서 대단히 실망스러운 것으로 받아들여졌다. ❺ 타동사 수신하다 ❏ 수신율이 약간 미미했지만 그가 신호를 받을 수 있을 만큼은 선명했다. ❻ 구 (언짢은 일의) 대상이 되다 ❏ 네가 그들의 눈에서 증오를 보았고 그 증오의 대상이 되었다.

L

M

N

O

┌───┐
│ **Thesaurus**   receive의 참조어   │
│   │
│   v.   accept, collect, get, take; (ant.) give, present ❶ │
│   entertain, take in, welcome ❸   │
└───┘

P

Q

R

re|ceiv|er /rɪsivər/ (receivers) ❶ N-COUNT A telephone's **receiver** is the part that you hold near to your ear and speak into. ❏ *She picked up the receiver and started to dial.* ❷ N-COUNT A **receiver** is the part of a radio or television that picks up signals and converts them into sound or pictures. ❏ *Auto-tuning VHF receivers are now common in cars.* ❸ N-COUNT The **receiver** is someone who is appointed by a court of law to manage the affairs of a business, usually when it is facing financial failure. [BUSINESS] [usu the N] ❏ *Between July and September, a total of 1,059 firms called in the receiver.* →see **radio**, **television**, **tennis**

❶ 가산명사 수화기 ❏ 그녀가 수화기를 집어 들고 번호를 누르기 시작했다. ❷ 가산명사 수신기, 수상기 ❏ 자동 조정 초단파 수신기가 이제는 차량에도 흔히 탑재된다. ❸ 가산명사 재산 관리인 [경제] ❏ 7월에서 9월 사이에 모두 1,059개 업체가 재산 관리인을 불러들였다.

S

T

re|ceiv|er|ship /rɪsivərʃɪp/ (receiverships) N-VAR If a company goes **into receivership**, it faces financial failure and the administration of its business is handled by the receiver. [BUSINESS] ❏ *The company has now gone into receivership with debts of several million.*

가산명사 또는 불가산명사 법정 재산 관리 [경제] ❏ 그 회사는 수백만의 부채를 안고 이제 법정 재산 관리에 들어갔다.

U

re|cent ♦♦♦ /ris³nt/ ADJ A **recent** event or period of time happened only a short while ago. ❏ *In the most recent attack one man was shot dead and two others were wounded.*

형용사 최근의 ❏ 가장 최근 있었던 습격에서는 한 남자가 총에 맞아 숨지고 다른 두 사람은 부상을 당했다.

V

re|cent|ly ♦♦◇ /ris³ntli/ ADV If you have done something **recently** or if something happened **recently**, it happened only a short time ago. ❏ *The bank recently opened a branch in Germany.*

부사 최근에 ❏ 그 은행은 최근에 독일에 지점을 열었다.

W

re|cep|tion /rɪsɛpʃ³n/ (receptions) ❶ N-COUNT A **reception** is a formal party which is given to welcome someone or to celebrate a special event. ❏ *At the reception they served smoked salmon.* ❷ N-SING The **reception** in a hotel is the desk or office that books rooms for people and answers their questions. [the N, oft at N n, also at N] ❏ *Have him bring a car round to the reception.* ❸ N-SING The **reception** in an office or hospital is the place where people's appointments and questions are dealt with. [mainly BRIT] [the N, oft N n, also at N] ❏ *Wait at reception for me.* ❹ N-COUNT If someone or something has a particular kind of **reception**, that is the way that people react to them. ❏ *Mr. Mandela was given a tumultuous reception in Washington.* ❺ N-UNCOUNT If you get good **reception** from your radio or

❶ 가산명사 환영회, 리셉션 ❏ 리셉션에서는 훈제 연어가 나왔다. ❷ 단수명사 (호텔의) 프런트 ❏ 그에게 프런트 쪽으로 차를 몰고 오라고 하세요. ❸ 단수명사 접수처 [주로 영국영어] ❏ 접수처에서 기다려 주세요. ❹ 가산명사 대접 ❏ 만델라 씨는 워싱턴에서 요란한 대접을 받았다. ❺ 불가산명사 수신 상태, 수신율 ❏ 빈약한 라디오 수신 상태

X

Y

Z

television, the sound or picture is clear because the signal is strong. If the **reception** is poor, the sound or picture is unclear because the signal is weak. ❑ ...*poor radio reception.* →see **wedding**

re|cep|tion|ist /rɪsɛpʃənɪst/ (**receptionists**) ◼ N-COUNT In an office or hospital, the **receptionist** is the person whose job is to answer the telephone, arrange appointments, and deal with people when they first arrive. ◼ N-COUNT In a hotel, the **receptionist** is the person whose job is to book rooms for people and answer their questions.

re|cep|tive /rɪsɛptɪv/ ◼ ADJ Someone who is **receptive to** new ideas or suggestions is prepared to consider them or accept them. ❑ *The voters had seemed receptive to his ideas.* ◼ ADJ If someone who is ill is **receptive to** treatment, they start to get better when they are given treatment. [v-link ADJ to n] ❑ *For those patients who are not receptive to treatment, the chance for improvement is small.*

re|cess /rɪsɛs, riːsɛs/ (**recesses, recessing, recessed**) ◼ N-COUNT A **recess** is a break between the periods of work of an official body such as a committee, a court of law, or a government. [also in/from n] ❑ *The conference broke for a recess, but the 10-minute break stretched to two hours.* ◼ V-I When formal meetings or court cases **recess**, they stop temporarily. [FORMAL] ❑ *The hearings have now recessed for dinner.* ◼ N-COUNT In a room, a **recess** is part of a wall which is built further back than the rest of the wall. Recesses are often used as a place to put furniture such as shelves. ❑ *...a discreet recess next to a fireplace.* ◼ N-COUNT The **recesses of** something or somewhere are the parts of it which are hard to see because light does not reach them or they are hidden from view. ❑ *He emerged from the dark recesses of the garage.* ◼ N-COUNT If you refer to the **recesses of** someone's mind or soul, you are referring to thoughts or feelings they have which are hidden or difficult to describe. ❑ *There was something in the darker recesses of his unconscious that was troubling him.*

re|ces|sion ♦♦◇ /rɪsɛʃ⁰n/ (**recessions**) N-VAR A **recession** is a period when the economy of a country is doing badly, for example because industry is producing less and more people are becoming unemployed. ❑ *The oil price increases sent Europe into deep recession.*

reci|pe /rɛsɪpi/ (**recipes**) ◼ N-COUNT A **recipe** is a list of ingredients and a set of instructions that tell you how to cook something. ❑ *...a traditional recipe for oatmeal biscuits.* ◼ N-SING If you say that something is **a recipe for** a particular situation, you mean that it is likely to result in that situation. ❑ *Large-scale inflation is a recipe for disaster.*

re|cipi|ent /rɪsɪpiənt/ (**recipients**) N-COUNT The **recipient** of something is the person who receives it. [FORMAL] ❑ *...the largest recipient of American foreign aid.* →see **donor**

re|cip|ro|cal /rɪsɪprək⁰l/ ADJ A **reciprocal** action or agreement involves two people or groups who do the same thing to each other or agree to help each another in a similar way. [FORMAL] ❑ *They expected a reciprocal gesture before more hostages could be freed.*

re|cip|ro|cate /rɪsɪprəkeɪt/ (**reciprocates, reciprocating, reciprocated**) V-T/V-I If your feelings or actions toward someone **are reciprocated**, the other person feels or behaves in the same way toward you as you have felt or behaved toward them. ❑ *I would like to think the way I treat people is reciprocated.*

re|cit|al /rɪsaɪt⁰l/ (**recitals**) N-COUNT A **recital** is a performance of music or poetry, usually given by one person. ❑ *...a solo recital by the harpsichordist Maggie Cole.*

re|cite /rɪsaɪt/ (**recites, reciting, recited**) ◼ V-T When someone **recites** a poem or other piece of writing, they say it aloud after they have learned it. ❑ *They recited poetry to one another.* ◼ V-T If you **recite** something such as a list, you say it aloud. ❑ *All he could do was recite a list of Government failings.*

reck|less /rɛkləs/ ADJ If you say that someone is **reckless**, you mean that they act in a way which shows that they do not care about danger or the effect their behavior will have on other people. ❑ *He is charged with causing death by reckless driving.* ● **reck|less|ly** ADV ❑ *He was leaning recklessly out of the unshuttered window.* ● **reck|less|ness** N-UNCOUNT ❑ *He felt a surge of recklessness.*

reck|on ♦♦◇ /rɛkən/ (**reckons, reckoning, reckoned**) ◼ V-T If you **reckon** that something is true, you think that it is true. [INFORMAL] ❑ *Toni reckoned that it must be about three o'clock.* ◼ V-T If something **is reckoned** to be a particular figure, it is calculated to be roughly that amount. [usu passive] ❑ *The market's revised threshold is now reckoned to be 22,000-22,500 on the Nikkei index.*

▶**reckon with** ◼ PHRASAL VERB If you say that you had not **reckoned with** something, you mean that you had not expected it and so were not prepared for it. [with brd-neg] ❑ *Giles had not reckoned with the strength of Sally's feelings for him.* ◼ PHRASE If you say that there is someone or something **to be reckoned with**, you mean that they must be dealt with and it will be difficult. ❑ *This act was a signal to his victim's friends that he was someone to be reckoned with.*

reck|on|ing /rɛkənɪŋ/ (**reckonings**) N-VAR Someone's **reckoning** is a calculation they make about something, especially a calculation that is not very exact. ❑ *By my reckoning we were seven or eight kilometers from Borj Mechaab.*

re|claim /rɪkleɪm/ (**reclaims, reclaiming, reclaimed**) ◼ V-T If you **reclaim** something that you have lost or that has been taken away from you, you succeed in getting it back. ❑ *In 1986, they got the right to reclaim South African citizenship.* ◼ V-T If you **reclaim** an amount of money, for example tax that you have paid, you claim it back. ❑ *There are an estimated eight million people currently thought to be eligible to reclaim income tax.* ◼ V-T When people **reclaim** land, they make it suitable for a purpose such as farming or building, for example by draining it or by building a barrier against the sea. ❑ *The Netherlands has been reclaiming farmland from water.* ◼ V-T If a piece of land that was used for farming or building **is reclaimed by** a desert, forest, or the sea, it turns back into desert,

---

◼ 가산명사 접수계원 ◼ 가산명사 접수계원, 프런트 직원

◼ 형용사 수용적인 ❑ 유권자들이 그의 의견에 수용적이었던 것 같았다. ◼ 형용사 (치료가) 잘 듣는 ❑ 치료가 잘 듣지 않는 환자들의 경우는 호전 가능성이 적다.

◼ 가산명사 휴식 ❑ 회담이 휴식을 위해 중단되었는데 10분간의 휴식이 두 시간으로 늘어났다. ◼ 자동사 휴회, 휴정 [격식체] ❑ 공판이 저녁 식사를 위해 방금 휴회했다. ◼ 가산명사 벽감, 벽의 옴폭 들어간 곳 ❑ 벽난로 옆, 눈에 잘 뜨이지 않는 벽의 옴폭 들어간 부분 ◼ 가산명사 구석진 곳, 잘 보이지 않는 부분 ❑ 그가 차고의 어두운 구석에서 나타났다. ◼ 가산명사 (마음속) 깊은 곳 ❑ 더욱 알 수 없는 그의 무의식 깊은 곳에서 무언가가 그를 괴롭히고 있었다.

가산명사 또는 불가산명사 경기 침체, 불경기 ❑ 유가 상승으로 유럽은 극심한 경기 침체에 빠졌다.

◼ 가산명사 요리법, 조리법 ❑ 전통적인 오트밀 비스킷 만드는 법 ◼ 단수명사 -의 원인 ❑ 대규모 인플레이션은 대재난의 원인이 된다.

가산명사 수령인, 수혜자 [격식체] ❑ 미국 대외 원조의 최대 수혜자

형용사 호혜적인, 상호간의 [격식체] ❑ 그들은 인질이 더 풀려나기 전에 호혜적인 제스처를 기대했다.

타동사/자동사 -에 보답하다, -을 서로 주고 받다 ❑ 내가 사람들을 대하는 대로 그대로 내게 돌아온다고 생각하고 싶다.

가산명사 독주회, 낭송회 ❑ 하프시코드 연주자 매기 콜의 독주회

◼ 타동사 암송하다 ❑ 그들은 서로에게 시를 암송해 주었다. ◼ 타동사 큰 소리로 늘어놓다 ❑ 그가 할 수 있는 일이라고는 정부의 실책을 큰 소리로 늘어놓는 것뿐이었다.

형용사 무모한, 난폭한 ❑ 그는 난폭 운전으로 사람을 죽게 한 혐의를 받고 있다. ● 무모하게 부사 ❑ 그는 무모하게도 덧문이 달리지 않은 창밖으로 몸을 내밀고 있었다. ● 무모함, 난폭함 불가산명사 ❑ 그는 욱하는 마음이 치미는 것을 느꼈다.

◼ 타동사 생각하다 [비격식체] ❑ 토니는 분명히 3시쯤 되었을 거라고 생각했다. ◼ 타동사 -쯤으로 계산되다 ❑ 주식 시작의 수정된 기준점이 현재 니케이 지수 22,000에서 22,500쯤으로 계산된다.

◼ 구동사 -을 고려에 넣다 ❑ 자일스는 자신에 대한 샐리의 감정이 얼마나 강력한지를 고려하지 않았었다. ◼ 구 청산해야 할, 처리해야 할 ❑ 이 행동은 그의 피해자의 친구들에게 그가 청산되어야 할 사람이라는 것을 알려 주는 신호였다.

가산명사 또는 불가산명사 추산 ❑ 내 추산으로는 우리가 보르즈 메카부에서 7 내지 8킬로미터 거리에 있었다.

◼ 타동사 되찾다 ❑ 1986년에 그들은 남아프리카 시민권을 되찾을 권리를 부여 받았다. ◼ 타동사 돌려받다 ❑ 현재 대략 8백만 명이 소득세를 돌려받을 자격이 있다고 여겨진다. ◼ 타동사 개간하다, 매립하다 ❑ 네덜란드는 바다를 경작지로 매립해 오고 있다. ◼ 타동사 -로 되돌아가다 ❑ 다이아몬드가 많이 나는 그 마을들은 점차 다시 사막화 되어가고 있다.

a b c d e f g h i j k l m n o p q r s t u v w x y z

forest, or sea. [usu passive] ❑ *The diamond towns are gradually being reclaimed by the desert.*

Word Link

clin ≈ leaning : decline, incline, recline

re|cline /rɪklaɪn/ (reclines, reclining, reclined) **1** V-I If you **recline on** something, you sit or lie on it with the upper part of your body supported at an angle. ❑ *She proceeded to recline on a chaise longue.* **2** V-T/V-I When a seat **reclines** or when you **recline** it, you lower the back so that it is more comfortable to sit in. ❑ *Air France first-class seats recline almost like beds.* ❑ *Ramesh had reclined his seat and was lying back smoking.*

1 자동사 비스듬히 앉다, 비스듬히 눕다 ❑ 그녀는 이어서 등받이가 뒤로 젖혀지는 긴 의자에 비스듬히 앉았다. **2** 타동사/자동사 (등받이가) 뒤로 젖혀지다; (등받이를) 뒤로 젖히다 에어프랑스의 일등석은 거의 침대처럼 등받이가 뒤로 젖혀진다. ❑ 라메쉬는 의자를 뒤로 젖히고 비스듬히 누워 담배를 피고 있었다.

re|cluse /rɪklus, BRIT rɪkluːs/ (recluses) N-COUNT A **recluse** is a person who lives alone and deliberately avoids other people. ❑ *His widow became a virtual recluse for the remainder of her life.*

가산명사 은둔자 ❑ 그의 미망인은 여생을 사실상 은둔자로 지냈다.

re|clu|sive /rɪklusɪv/ ADJ A **reclusive** person or animal lives alone and deliberately avoids the company of others. ❑ *A reclusive millionaire left his luxury home to the housekeeper he had hardly spoken to for 21 years.*

형용사 은둔한 ❑ 은둔한 백만장자가 자신의 호화로운 집을 21년 동안 말 한마디 나누지 않다시피 한 가정부에게 남겼다.

rec|og|ni|tion ♦◇◇ /rɛkəgnɪʃⁿn/ **1** N-UNCOUNT **Recognition** is the act of recognizing someone or identifying something when you see it. ❑ *He searched for a sign of recognition on her face, but there was none.* **2** N-UNCOUNT **Recognition of** something is an understanding and acceptance of it. ❑ *The CBI welcomed the Chancellor's recognition of the recession and hoped for a reduction in interest rates.* **3** N-UNCOUNT When a government gives diplomatic **recognition** to another country, they officially accept that its status is valid. ❑ *His government did not receive full recognition by Britain until July.* **4** N-UNCOUNT When a person receives **recognition** for the things that they have done, people acknowledge the value or skill of their work. ❑ *At last, her father's work has received popular recognition.* **5** PHRASE If something is done **in recognition of** someone's achievements, it is done as a way of showing official appreciation of them. ❑ *Brazil is about to normalize its diplomatic relations with South Africa in recognition of the steps taken to end apartheid.*

1 불가산명사 알아봄, 인식 ❑ 그는 그녀가 혹시 자신을 알아보는지 그녀의 얼굴을 살폈으나 전혀 그런 기미가 없었다. **2** 불가산명사 인지, 인정 영국 산업 연맹은 재무 장관이 경기 불황을 인정한 사실을 환영하며 금리 인하를 희망했다. **3** 불가산명사 승인, 인가 ❑ 그가 이끄는 정부는 7월까지 영국으로부터 정식 승인을 받지 못했다. **4** 불가산명사 인정, 알아줌 ❑ 결국 그녀의 아버지가 한 일이 대중의 인정을 받았다. **5** 구 ∼을 인정하여, ∼의 답으로 ❑ 브라질은 남아프리카 공화국이 인종 차별 정책 종식을 인정하여 남아프리카 공화국과 외교 관계를 정상화하려 하고 있다.

Word Partnership

recognition의 연어

V.	**deserve** recognition, **receive** recognition **2**-**4**
ADJ.	**formal** recognition, **full** recognition **3**
	special recognition **4**

rec|og|niz|able /rɛkəgnaɪzəbⁿl/ [BRIT also **recognisable**] ADJ If something can be easily recognized or identified, you can say that it is easily **recognizable**. ❑ *The vault was opened and the body found to be well preserved, his features easily recognizable.*

[영국영어 recognisable] 형용사 알아볼 수 있는 ❑ 지하 무덤을 여니 시체가 잘 보존되어 있고 그의 이목구비도 쉽게 알아볼 수 있었다.

rec|og|nize ♦♦◇ /rɛkəgnaɪz/ (recognizes, recognizing, recognized) [BRIT also **recognise**] **1** V-T If you **recognize** someone or something, you know who that person is or what that thing is. [no cont] ❑ *The receptionist recognized him at once.* **2** V-T If someone says that they **recognize** something, they acknowledge that it exists or that it is true. [no cont] ❑ *I recognize my own shortcomings.* **3** V-T If people or organizations **recognize** something as valid, they officially accept it or approve of it. ❑ *Most doctors appear to recognize homeopathy as a legitimate form of medicine.* ❑ *France is on the point of recognizing the independence of the Baltic States.* **4** V-T When people **recognize** the work that someone has done, they show their appreciation of it, often by giving that person an award of some kind. ❑ *The RAF recognized him as an outstandingly able engineer.*

[영국영어 recognise] **1** 타동사 알아보다 ❑ 접수계원이 한눈에 그를 알아봤다. **2** 타동사 인지하다, 인정하다 ❑ 내 단점을 알고 있습니다. **3** 타동사 승인하다, 인가하다 ❑ 대부분의 의사들이 동종 요법을 합법적인 치료 방식으로 승인하는 것 같다. ❑ 프랑스가 바야흐로 발트 제국의 독립을 승인하려 한다. **4** 타동사 인정하다, 표창하다 ❑ 영국 공군은 그가 뛰어나게 유능한 기술자라고 인정했다.

Thesaurus

recognize의 참조어

V.	acknowledge, identify, know, notice; *(ant.)* ignore **1**
	accept, believe, understand **2** **3**

re|coil (recoils, recoiling, recoiled)

The verb is pronounced /rɪkɔɪl/. The noun is pronounced /rikɔɪl/.

동사는 /rɪkɔɪl/로 발음되고, 명사는 /rikɔɪl/로 발음된다.

1 V-I If something makes you **recoil**, you move your body quickly away from it because it frightens, offends, or hurts you. ❑ *For a moment I thought he was going to kiss me. I recoiled in horror.* ● N-UNCOUNT **Recoil** is also a noun. ❑ *...his small body jerking in recoil from the volume of his shouting.* **2** V-I If you **recoil from** doing something or **recoil at** the idea of something, you refuse to do it or accept it because you dislike it so much. ❑ *People used to recoil from the idea of getting into debt.*

1 자동사 뒷걸음치다, 움찔하다 ❑ 나는 일순간 그가 내게 키스하려 한다고 생각했으나 두려움에 뒷걸음쳤다. ● 불가산명사 뒷걸음질, 움찔함 ❑ 자신이 외친 소리가 너무 커서 갑자스레 움찔하는 그의 작은 체구 **2** 자동사 진저리치다, 끔찍하게 여기다 ❑ 사람들이 예전에는 빚을 진다는 생각을 끔찍하게 여겼다.

rec|ol|lect /rɛkəlɛkt/ (recollects, recollecting, recollected) V-T If you **recollect** something, you remember it. ❑ *Ramona spoke with warmth when she recollected the doctor who used to be at the county hospital.*

타동사 회상하다 ❑ 라모나는 예전에 카운티 병원에 있던 그 의사를 회상할 때면 따뜻한 마음이 되어 이야기를 했다.

rec|ol|lec|tion /rɛkəlɛkʃⁿn/ (recollections) N-VAR If you have a **recollection** of something, you remember it. ❑ *Pat has vivid recollections of the trip, and remembers some of the frightening aspects I had forgotten.*

가산명사 또는 불가산명사 회상, 기억 ❑ 팻은 그 여행을 생생하게 회상하며 내가 잊어버린 무서웠던 일들도 얼마간 기억하고 있다.

rec|om|mend ♦♦◇ /rɛkəmɛnd/ (recommends, recommending, recommended) **1** V-T If someone **recommends** a person or thing to you, they suggest that you would find that person or thing good or useful. ❑ *I have just spent a holiday there and would recommend it to anyone.* ❑ *"You're a good worker, boy," he told him. "I'll recommend you for a promotion."* ● **rec|om|mend|ed** ADJ ❑ *Though ten years old, this book is highly recommended.* **2** V-T If you **recommend** that something is done, you suggest that it should be done. ❑ *The judge recommended that he serve 20 years in prison.* ❑ *We strongly recommend reporting the incident to the police.* **3** V-T If something or someone has a particular quality to **recommend** them, that

1 타동사 추천하다 ❑ 그곳에서 휴가를 보내고 방금 왔는데 누구에게든 그곳을 추천할까 해. ❑ "여보게, 자넨 일을 잘하네."라고 그가 그에게 말했다. "자네가 승진하도록 내 추천함세." ● 추천받은, 권장되는 형용사 ❑ 10년이나 되었지만 이 책은 많이 추천된다. **2** 타동사 권고하다, 충고하다 ❑ 판사는 그를 20년 동안 복역시켜야 한다고 권고했다. ❑ 경찰에 그 사건을 신고할 것을 강력히 권고합니다. **3** 타동사 권장하다 ❑ 라노블리스 음식점은 권장할 만한 점이 많다.

quality makes them attractive or gives them an advantage over similar things or people. ❑ *La Noblesse restaurant has much to recommend it.*

Thesaurus recommend의 참조어

V. endorse, put forward, suggest **1**
advise, urge **2**

Word Partnership recommend의 연어

N. **doctors** recommend, **experts** recommend **1** **2**
recommend **changes** **2**

ADV. **highly** recommend **1**-**3**

---

rec|om|men|da|tion ♦◇◇ /rɛkəmɛndeɪʃ°n/ (**recommendations**) **1** N-VAR The **recommendations** of a person or a committee are their suggestions or advice on what is the best thing to do. ❑ *The committee's recommendations are unlikely to be made public.* **2** N-VAR A **recommendation** of something is the suggestion that someone should have or use it because it is good. ❑ *The best way of finding a solicitor is through personal recommendation.*

rec|om|pense /rɛkəmpɛns/ (**recompenses, recompensing, recompensed**) **1** N-UNCOUNT If you are given something, usually money, **in recompense**, you are given it as a reward or because you have suffered. [FORMAL] ❑ *He demands no financial recompense for his troubles.* **2** V-T If you **recompense** someone **for** their efforts or their loss, you give them something, usually money, as a payment or reward. [FORMAL] ❑ *The fees offered by the NHS do not recompense dental surgeons for their professional time.*

rec|on|cile /rɛkənsaɪl/ (**reconciles, reconciling, reconciled**) **1** V-T If you **reconcile** two beliefs, facts, or demands that seem to be opposed or completely different, you find a way in which they can both be true or both be successful. ❑ *It's difficult to reconcile the demands of my job and the desire to be a good father.* **2** V-RECIP-PASSIVE If two people **are reconciled with** someone, you become friendly with them again after a quarrel or disagreement. ❑ *He never believed he and Susan would be reconciled.* **3** V-T If you **reconcile** two people, you make them become friends again after a quarrel or disagreement. ❑ *...my attempt to reconcile him with Toby.* **4** V-T If you **reconcile yourself to** an unpleasant situation, you accept it, although it does not make you happy to do so. ❑ *She had reconciled herself to never seeing him again.* ● **rec|on|ciled** ADJ [v-link ADJ to n/-ing] ❑ *She felt, if not grateful for her own lot, at least a little more reconciled to it.*

rec|on|cilia|tion /rɛkənsɪlieɪʃ°n/ (**reconciliations**) **1** N-VAR **Reconciliation** between two people or countries who have quarrelled is the process of their becoming friends again. A **reconciliation** is an instance of this. ❑ *...an appeal for reconciliation between Catholics and Protestants.* **2** N-SING The **reconciliation** of two beliefs, facts, or demands that seem to be opposed is the process of finding a way in which they can both be true or both be successful. ❑ *...the ideal of democracy based upon a reconciliation of the values of equality and liberty.*

re|con|nais|sance /rɪkɒnɪsəns/ N-UNCOUNT **Reconnaissance** is the activity of obtaining military information about a place by sending soldiers or planes there, or by the use of satellites. ❑ *The helicopter was returning from a reconnaissance mission.*

re|con|sid|er /rikənsɪdər/ (**reconsiders, reconsidering, reconsidered**) V-T/V-I If you **reconsider** a decision or opinion, you think about it and try to decide whether it should be changed. ❑ *We want you to reconsider your decision to resign from the board.*

re|con|struct /rikənstrʌkt/ (**reconstructs, reconstructing, reconstructed**) **1** V-T If you **reconstruct** something that has been destroyed or badly damaged, you build it and make it work again. ❑ *The government must reconstruct the shattered economy.* **2** V-T To **reconstruct** a system or policy means to change it so that it works in a different way. ❑ *She actually wanted to reconstruct the state and transform society.* **3** V-T If you **reconstruct** an event that happened in the past, you try to get a complete understanding of it by combining a lot of small pieces of information. ❑ *He began to reconstruct the events of 21 December 1988, when flight 103 disappeared.*

re|con|struc|tion /rikənstrʌkʃ°n/ (**reconstructions**) **1** N-UNCOUNT **Reconstruction** is the process of making a country normal again after a war, for example by making the economy stronger and by replacing buildings that have been damaged. ❑ *...America's part in the post-war reconstruction of Germany.* **2** N-UNCOUNT The **reconstruction** of a building, structure, or road is the activity of building it again, because it has been damaged. ❑ *Work began on the reconstruction of the road.* **3** N-COUNT The **reconstruction** of a crime or event is when people try to understand or show exactly what happened, often by acting it out. ❑ *Mrs. Kerr was too upset to take part in a reconstruction of her ordeal.*

re|con|vene /rikənvin/ (**reconvenes, reconvening, reconvened**) V-I If a legislature, court, or conference **reconvenes** or if someone **reconvenes** it, it meets again after a break. ❑ *The conference might reconvene after its opening session.*

rec|ord ♦♦♦ (**records, recording, recorded**)

The noun is pronounced /rɛkərd/. The verb is pronounced /rɪkɔrd/.

1 N-COUNT If you keep a **record of** something, you keep a written account or photographs of it so that it can be referred to later. ❑ *Keep a record of all the payments.* ❑ *There's no record of any marriage or children.* **2** V-T If you **record** a piece of information or an event, you write it down, photograph it, or put it into a computer so that in the future people can refer to it. ❑ *Her letters record the*

1 가산명사 또는 불가산명사 권고, 충고 ❑ 위원회의 권고안은 발표되지 않을 것 같다. **2** 가산명사 또는 불가산명사 추천, 소개 ❑ 사무 변호사를 찾는 가장 좋은 방법은 개인적으로 추천을 받는 것이다.

1 불가산명사 보상 [격식체] ❑ 그는 자신이 겪은 애로 사항에 대해 어떤 재정적인 보상도 요구하지 않는다. **2** 타동사 보답하다, 보상하다 [격식체] ❑ 국민 건강 보험이 제시하는 수고비는 치과 의사들이 전문직 종사자로서 들이는 시간에 대한 보상이 되지 못한다.

1 타동사 조화시키다, 양립시키다 ❑ 직업적으로 내게 요구되는 사항과 좋은 아버지가 되고자 하는 욕구를 조화시키기란 어렵다. **2** 상호동사-수동 화해하다 ❑ 그는 자신과 수잔이 화해할 것이라고 전혀 믿지 않았다. **3** 타동사 화해시키다 ❑ 그와 토비를 화해시키려는 나의 시도 **4** 타동사 감수하게 하다 ❑ 그녀는 그를 다시 볼 수 없다는 사실을 감수했다. ● 감수하는 형용사 ❑ 그녀는 자기 운명에 감사하는 게 아니라, 최소한 조금 더 그것을 감수하는 것이라고 느꼈다.

1 가산명사 또는 불가산명사 화해, 조정 ❑ 구교도와 신교도의 화해를 간청함 **2** 단수명사 조화, 양립 ❑ 평등과 자유라는 가치의 조화에 기반을 둔 이상적인 민주주의

불가산명사 정찰 ❑ 헬리콥터가 정찰 임무를 마치고 돌아오고 있었다.

타동사/자동사 재고하다 ❑ 우리는 당신이 위원회에서 사임하려는 결정을 재고해 주셨으면 합니다.

1 타동사 재건하다 ❑ 정부는 엉망이 된 경제를 재건해야만 한다. **2** 타동사 개조하다 ❑ 사실 그녀는 국가를 개조하고 사회를 변혁하고 싶어 했다. **3** 타동사 재구성하다 ❑ 그는 103편 비행기가 사라졌던 1988년 12월 21일의 사건들을 재구성해 보기 시작했다.

1 불가산명사 재건 ❑ 전후 독일 재건에 있어서의 미국의 역할 **2** 불가산명사 복구 ❑ 도로 복구 작업이 시작되었다. **3** 가산명사 재구성, 재현 ❑ 커 부인은 너무 혼란스러워서 자신이 겪은 고통스러운 체험을 재현하는 데 참여할 수 없었다.

자동사 재소집하다; 재소집되다 ❑ 그 회의는 첫 회기를 마친 후에 재소집될지도 모른다.

명사는 /rɛkərd /로 발음되고, 동사는 /rɪkɔrd /로 발음된다.

1 가산명사 기록 ❑ 모든 지불 건의 기록을 보존하세요. ❑ 결혼이나 자녀에 대한 기록은 없다. **2** 타동사 기록하다 ❑ 그녀의 편지에는 중국에 주재하는 외교관의 가정 및 사회생활에 대한 상세한 내용이 기록되어 있다. **3** 타동사 녹음하다, 녹화하다

domestic and social details of diplomatic life in China. **3** V-T If you **record** something such as a speech or performance, you put it on tape or film so that it can be heard or seen again later. ❑ *There is nothing to stop viewers recording the films on videotape.* **4** V-T If a musician or performer **records** a piece of music or a television or radio show, they perform it so that it can be put onto CD, tape, or film. ❑ *It took the musicians two and a half days to record their soundtrack for the film.* **5** N-COUNT A **record** is a round, flat piece of black plastic on which sound, especially music, is stored, and which can be played on a record player. You can also refer to the music stored on this piece of plastic as a **record**. ❑ *This is one of my favorite records.* **6** V-T If a dial or other measuring device **records** a certain measurement or value, it shows that measurement or value. ❑ *The test records the electrical activity of the brain.* **7** N-COUNT A **record** is the best result that has ever been achieved in a particular sport or activity, for example the fastest time, the furthest distance, or the greatest number of victories. ❑ *Roger Kingdom set the world record of 12.92 seconds.* **8** ADJ You use **record** to say that something is higher, lower, better, or worse than has ever been achieved before. [ADJ n] ❑ *Profits were at record levels.* **9** N-COUNT Someone's **record** is the facts that are known about their achievements or character. ❑ *His record reveals a tough streak.* **10** N-COUNT If someone has a criminal **record**, it is officially known that they have committed crimes in the past. ❑ *...a heroin addict with a criminal record going back 15 years.* **11** →see also **recording, track record** **12** PHRASE If you say that what you are going to say next is **for the record**, you mean that you are saying it publicly and officially and you want it to be written down and remembered. ❑ *We're willing to state for the record that it has enormous value.* **13** PHRASE If you give some information **for the record**, you give it in case people might find it useful at a later time, although it is not a very important part of what you are talking about. ❑ *For the record, most Moscow girls leave school at about 18.* **14** PHRASE If something that you say is **off the record**, you do not intend it to be considered as official, or published with your name attached to it. ❑ *May I speak off the record?* **15** PHRASE If you are **on record as** saying something, you have said it publicly and officially and it has been written down. ❑ *The Chancellor is on record as saying that the increase in unemployment is "a price worth paying" to keep inflation down.* **16** PHRASE If you keep information **on record**, you write it down or store it in a computer so that it can be used later. ❑ *The practice is to keep on record any analysis of samples.* →see **diary, history**

Word Partnership   record의 연어

N.   record **a song** **4**
    record **album**, record **company**, hit record, record **producer**, record **store** **5**
    world record **7**
    record **high**, record **low**, record **temperatures**, record **time** **8**
    record **earnings**, record **numbers** **8**
    criminal record **10**
V.   **break a** record, **set a** record **7** **8**

---

re|cord|er /rɪkɔrdər/ (**recorders**) **1** N-COUNT You can refer to a cassette recorder, a tape recorder, or a video recorder as a **recorder**. ❑ *Rodney put the recorder on the desk top and pushed the play button.* →see also **tape recorder, video recorder** **2** N-VAR A **recorder** is a wooden or plastic musical instrument in the shape of a pipe. You play the recorder by blowing into the top of it and covering and uncovering the holes with your fingers. **3** N-COUNT A **recorder** is a machine or instrument that keeps a record of something, for example in an experiment or on a vehicle. ❑ *Data recorders also pin-point mechanical faults rapidly, reducing repair times.*

re|cord|ing ♦◇◇ /rɪkɔrdɪŋ/ (**recordings**) **1** N-COUNT A **recording of** something is a record, CD, tape, or video of it. ❑ *...a video recording of a police interview.* **2** N-UNCOUNT **Recording** is the process of making records, CDs, tapes, or videos. ❑ *...the recording industry.*

re|cord play|er (**record players**) also **record-player** N-COUNT A **record player** is a machine on which you can play a record in order to listen to the music or other sounds on it.

re|count (**recounts, recounting, recounted**)

The verb is pronounced /rɪkaʊnt/. The noun is pronounced /rikaʊnt/.

1 V-T If you **recount** a story or event, you tell or describe it to people. [FORMAL] ❑ *He then recounted the story of the interview for his first job.* **2** N-COUNT A **recount** is a second count of votes in an election when the result is very close. ❑ *She wanted a recount. She couldn't believe that I had got more votes than her.*

re|coup /rɪkup/ (**recoups, recouping, recouped**) V-T If you **recoup** a sum of money that you have spent or lost, you get it back. ❑ *Insurance companies are trying to recoup their losses by increasing premiums.*

re|course /rɪkɔrs/ N-UNCOUNT If you achieve something without **recourse to** a particular course of action, you succeed without carrying out that action. To have **recourse to** a particular course of action means to have to do that action in order to achieve something. [FORMAL] ❑ *It enabled its members to settle their differences without recourse to war.*

re|cov|er ♦◇◇ /rɪkʌvər/ (**recovers, recovering, recovered**) **1** V-I When you **recover from** an illness or an injury, you become well again. ❑ *He is recovering from a knee injury.*

❑ 시청자들이 영화를 비디오테이프에 녹화하는 것을 막을 수 있는 방법은 없다. **4** 타동사 녹음하다, 녹화하다 ❑ 음악가들이 그 영화의 사운드트랙을 녹음하는 데 이틀하고도 한나절이 걸렸다. **5** 가산명사 음반, 레코드 ❑ 이것은 내가 아주 좋아하는 음반들 중 하나이다. **6** 타동사 표시하다, 보여 주다 ❑ 그 검사는 뇌의 전기 활동을 보여 준다. **7** 가산명사 최고 기록 ❑ 로저 킹덤이 12.92초로 세계 최고 기록을 세웠다. **8** 형용사 기록적인 ❑ 수익이 기록적인 수준이었다. **9** 가산명사 경력, 신상 기록 ❑ 그의 신상 기록을 보면 그가 거친 데가 있음을 알 수 있다. **10** 가산명사 전과 ❑ 15년 전부터 전과가 있는 헤로인 중독자 **12** 구 공식적으로, 공개적으로 분명히 ❑ 우리는 공식적으로 그것이 막대한 가치가 있다고 기꺼이 주장하겠습니다. **13** 구 참고로 ❑ 참고로, 모스크바 소녀들 대부분은 열여덟 살쯤 되면 학교를 마친다. **14** 구 비공개를 조건으로 ❑ 비공개 조건으로 말해도 될까요? **15** 구 공식 기록에 의하면 ❑ 공식 기록에 의하면 재무 장관이, 실직 증가가 인플레이션을 계속 억제하기 위해 '치를 가치가 있는 대가'라고 말한 것으로 되어 있다. **16** 구 기록하는 ❑ 관례적으로는 모든 견본 분석 내용을 컴퓨터에 계속 기록하는 것이다.

1 가산명사 녹음기, 녹화기 ❑ 로드니는 녹음기를 책상 위에 놓고 재생 버튼을 눌렀다. **2** 가산명사 또는 불가산명사 (악기) 리코더 **3** 가산명사 기록기 ❑ 자료 기록기들 역시 기계적인 결함의 위치를 정확하게 잡아내어 수리 시간을 단축시킨다.

1 가산명사 녹음한 것, 녹화한 것 ❑ 경찰 취재를 비디오로 녹화한 것 **2** 불가산명사 녹음, 녹화 ❑ 음반 산업

가산명사 축음기, 전축

동사는 /rɪkaʊnt/로 발음되고, 명사는 /rikaʊnt/로 발음된다.

1 타동사 이야기하다, 상술하다 [격식체] ❑ 그는 그리고 나서 자신이 첫 직장에 들어갈 때의 취업 면접 이야기를 했다. **2** 가산명사 재개표, 재검표 ❑ 그녀는 재개표를 원했다. 그녀는 내가 자기보다 더 많은 표를 얻었다는 사실을 믿을 수가 없었던 것이다.

타동사 만회하다, 벌충하다 ❑ 보험 회사들은 보험료를 인상해서 자신들의 손실을 벌충하려 애쓰고 있다.

불가산명사 의지, 의뢰 [격식체] ❑ 그것을 통해 소속 회원국들이 전쟁에 의지하지 않고 서로 간의 의견 차이를 조정할 수 있었다.

1 자동사 (건강을) 회복하다 ❑ 그는 무릎 부상에서 회복 중이야.

Recover is a fairly formal word. In conversation, you usually say that someone **gets better**. ❑ *Qualified nurses help patients get better more quickly.*

recover는 상당히 격식적인 말이다. 대화에서는 대개 누가 get better한다고 말한다. ❑ 자격 있는 간호사는 환자가 더 빨리 낫도록 돕는다.

2 V-I If you **recover from** an unhappy or unpleasant experience, you stop being upset by it. ❑ *...a tragedy from which he never fully recovered.* **3** V-I If something **recovers from** a period of weakness or difficulty, it improves or gets stronger again. ❑ *He recovered from a 4-2 deficit to reach the quarter-finals.* **4** V-T If you **recover** something that has been lost or stolen, you find it or get it back. ❑ *Police raided five houses in south-east London and recovered stolen goods.* **5** V-T If you **recover** a mental or physical state, it comes back again. For example, if you **recover** consciousness, you become conscious again. ❑ *She had a severe attack of asthma and it took an hour to recover her breath.* **6** V-T If you **recover** money that you have spent, invested, or lent to someone, you get the same amount back. ❑ *Legal action is being taken to try to recover the money.*

2 자동사 정상을 되찾다, 극복하다 ❑ 그가 결코 극복하지 못한 비극적인 사건 **3** 자동사 만회하다 ❑ 그는 ´4대 2라는 열세를 만회하여 준준결승전에 진출했다. **4** 타동사 찾아내다, 되찾다 ❑ 경찰이 런던 동남부에 위치한 다섯 가구를 불시 단속하여 도난품을 찾아냈다. **5** 타동사 회복하다 ❑ 그녀는 천식으로 한차례 심한 발작을 했고 한 시간이 지나서야 숨을 가다듬었다. **6** 타동사 되찾다, 만회하다 ❑ 그 돈을 되찾기 위한 노력으로 법적 대응을 취하고 있다.

Thesaurus
recover의 참조어

v.   recuperate **1**
      get over *something* **2**
      get *something* back, reclaim **4**-**6**

re|cov|ery ◆◇◇ /rɪkʌvəri/ (**recoveries**) **1** N-VAR If a sick person makes a **recovery**, he or she becomes well again. ❑ *He made a remarkable recovery from a shin injury.* **2** N-VAR When there is a **recovery** in a country's economy, it improves. ❑ *Interest-rate cuts have failed to bring about economic recovery.* **3** N-UNCOUNT You talk about the **recovery of** something when you get it back after it has been lost or stolen. ❑ *A substantial reward is being offered for the recovery of a painting by Turner.* **4** N-UNCOUNT You talk about the **recovery of** someone's physical or mental state when they return to this state. ❑ *...the abrupt loss and recovery of consciousness.* **5** PHRASE If someone is **in recovery**, they are being given a course of treatment to help them recover from something such as a drug habit or mental illness. ❑ *...Carole, a compulsive pot smoker and alcoholic in recovery.*

1 가산명사 또는 불가산명사 (건강) 회복 ❑ 그는 정강이뼈 부상에서 놀라운 회복을 보였다. **2** 가산명사 또는 불가산명사 (경기) 회복 ❑ 금리 인하가 경기 회복을 가져오지는 못했다. **3** 불가산명사 되찾음, 회수 ❑ 터너의 그림을 되찾기 위해 상당한 현상금이 걸려 있다. **4** 불가산명사 (의식 등의) 회복 ❑ 갑작스레 의식을 잃었다가 회복함 **5** 구 치료 중인 ❑ 치료 중인 상습적인 마리화나 흡연가이자 알코올 중독자인 캐롤

Word Link
creat ≈ making : creation, creature, recreate

re|cre|ate /rikrieɪt/ (**recreates, recreating, recreated**) V-T If you **recreate** something, you succeed in making it exist or seem to exist in a different time or place to its original time or place. ❑ *I am trying to recreate family life far from home.*

타동사 재현하다 ❑ 난 고국에서 멀리 떠나 가정생활을 재현하려고 노력 중이야.

rec|rea|tion (**recreations**)

Pronounced /rɛkrieɪʃⁿn/ for meaning **1**. Pronounced /rikrieɪʃⁿn/ and hyphenated re|crea|tion for meaning **2**.

1의 의미일 때는 /rɛkrieɪʃⁿn/으로 발음되고, **2**의 의미일 때는 /rikrieɪʃⁿn/으로 발음되며, re|cre|altion으로 분철된다.

1 N-VAR **Recreation** consists of things that you do in your spare time to relax. ❑ *Saturday afternoon is for recreation and outings.* **2** N-COUNT A **recreation of** something is the process of making it exist or seem to exist again in a different time or place. ❑ *They are seeking to build a faithful recreation of the original Elizabethan theater.* →see **park**

1 가산명사 또는 불가산명사 기분 전환, 휴양 ❑ 토요일 오후는 기분 전환과 소풍을 위한 시간이다. **2** 가산명사 재현 ❑ 그들은 엘리자베스 시대 극장의 원형(原形)을 정확히 재현하기 위해 애쓰고 있다.

rec|rea|tion|al /rɛkrieɪʃənˀl/ ADJ **Recreational** means relating to things people do in their spare time to relax. ❑ *...parks and other recreational facilities.*

형용사 휴양의 ❑ 공원과 그 외 휴양 시설들

rec|rea|tion|al drug (**recreational drugs**) N-COUNT **Recreational drugs** are drugs that people take occasionally for enjoyment, especially when they are spending time socially with other people. ❑ *Society largely turns a blind eye to recreational drug use.*

가산명사 기분 전환용 마약 ❑ 사회에서는 대개 기분 전환용 마약 사용을 못 본 체한다.

re|crimi|na|tion /rɪkrɪmɪneɪʃⁿn/ (**recriminations**) N-UNCOUNT **Recriminations** are accusations that two people or groups make about each other. [also N in pl] ❑ *The bitter rows and recriminations have finally ended the relationship.*

불가산명사 맞비난 ❑ 심한 언쟁을 벌이고 서로 비난을 해 대다가 마침내 그 관계가 끝났다.

re|cruit ◆◇◇ /rɪkrut/ (**recruits, recruiting, recruited**) **1** V-T If you **recruit** people for an organization, you select them and persuade them to join it or work for it. ❑ *The police are trying to recruit more black and Asian officers.* ❑ *She set up her stand to recruit students to the Anarchist Association.* ● **re|cruit|ing** N-UNCOUNT ❑ *A bomb exploded at an army recruiting office.* **2** N-COUNT A **recruit** is a person who has recently joined an organization or an army. ❑ *...a new recruit to the LA Police Department.*

1 타동사 모집하다, 가입시키다 ❑ 경찰은 흑인 및 아시아 인 경관을 더 많이 모집하려고 노력 중이다. ❑ 그녀는 무정부주의자 연합에 학생들을 가입시키려고 자리를 벌였다. ● 모집, 모병 불가산명사 ❑ 육군 모병 사무소가 폭탄이 터졌다. **2** 가산명사 신입 요원, 신병 ❑ 엘에이 경찰청의 신참 형사

re|cruit|ment /rɪkrutmənt/ N-UNCOUNT The **recruitment** of workers, soldiers, or members is the act or process of selecting them for an organization or army and persuading them to join. ❑ *...the examination system for the recruitment of civil servants.*

불가산명사 신규 모집, 신병 모집 ❑ 공무원 신규 모집을 위한 시험 제도

Word Link
rect ≈ right, straight : correct, rectangle, rectify

rec|tan|gle /rɛktæŋgˀl/ (**rectangles**) N-COUNT A **rectangle** is a four-sided shape whose corners are all ninety degree angles. Each side of a rectangle is the same length as the one opposite to it. →see **ratio**, **volume**

가산명사 직사각형

rec|tan|gu|lar /rɛktæŋgyələr/ ADJ Something that is **rectangular** is shaped like a rectangle. ❑ *...a rectangular table.*

형용사 직사각형의, 장방형의 ❑ 직사각형의 탁자

rec|ti|fy /rɛktɪfaɪ/ (**rectifies, rectifying, rectified**) V-T If you **rectify** something that is wrong, you change it so that it becomes correct or satisfactory. ❑ *Only an act of Congress could rectify the situation.*

타동사 바로잡다, 고치다 ❑ 국회 제정법만이 그 상황을 바로잡을 수 있었다.

re|cu|per|ate /rɪkupəreɪt/ (**recuperates, recuperating, recuperated**) V-I When you **recuperate**, you recover your health or strength after you have been ill or injured. ❑ *I went away to the country to recuperate.* ● **re|cu|pera|tion** /rɪkupəreɪʃⁿn/ N-UNCOUNT ❑ *Leonard was very pleased with his powers of recuperation.*

자동사 건강을 회복하다 ❑ 나는 건강을 회복하기 위해 시골로 갔다. ● 회복 불가산명사 ❑ 레너드는 그의 회복력에 무척 만족했다.

a
b
c
d
e
f
g
h
i
j
k
l
m
n
o
p
q
r
s
t
u
v
w
x
y
z

re|cur /rɪkɜr/ (recurs, recurring, recurred) V-I If something **recurs**, it happens more than once. □ ...a theme that was to recur frequently in his work.

자동사 재발하다, 반복되다 □ 그의 작품에서 빈번하게 반복되곤 된 주제

re|cur|rence /rɪkɜrəns, BRIT rɪkʌrəns/ (recurrences) N-VAR If there is a **recurrence of** something, it happens again. □ Police are out in force to prevent a recurrence of the violence.

가산명사 또는 불가산명사 반복, 재발 □ 경찰이 폭력 사태 재발을 방지하기 위해 대대적으로 나와 있다.

re|cur|rent /rɪkɜrənt, BRIT rɪkʌrənt/ ADJ A **recurrent** event or feeling happens or is experienced more than once. □ Race is a recurrent theme in the work.

형용사 반복되는 □ 인종은 그 작품에서 반복되는 주제이다.

re|cy|cle /risaɪkəl/ (recycles, recycling, recycled) V-T If you **recycle** things that have already been used, such as bottles or sheets of paper, you process them so that they can be used again. □ The objective would be to recycle 98 per cent of domestic waste. ● **re|cy|cling** N-UNCOUNT □ ...a recycling scheme.

타동사 재활용하다 □ 목표는 일반 가정 쓰레기의 98퍼센트를 재활용하는 일이 될 것이었다. ● 재활용 불가산명사 □ 재활용 계획

> Recycling has become so common in North America that many communities have special procedures for sorting and collecting the trash. Glass, metal, paper and plastic can be separated and used again. In some places, residents must pay a fine if they do not recycle.

> 북미에서는 recycling(재활용)이 아주 일상적인 일이 되어서 많은 지역 사회가 쓰레기를 분류하고 모으는 특별한 절차를 마련해 두고 있다. 유리, 금속, 종이, 플라스틱은 분리하여 다시 사용할 수 있다. 어떤 지역에서는 주민이 재활용을 하지 않으면 벌금을 내야 한다.

red ♦♦♦ /rɛd/ (reds, redder, reddest) **1** COLOR Something that is **red** is the color of blood or fire. □ ...a bunch of red roses. **2** ADJ If you say that someone's face is **red**, you mean that it is redder than its normal color, because they are embarrassed, angry, or out of breath. □ With a bright red face I was forced to admit that I had no real idea. **3** ADJ You describe someone's hair as **red** when it is between red and brown in color. □ ...a girl with red hair. **4** N-MASS You can refer to red wine as **red**. □ The spicy flavors in these dishes call for reds rather than whites. **5** PHRASE If a person or company is **in the red** or if their bank account is **in the red**, they have spent more money than they have in their account and therefore they owe money to the bank. □ The theatre is £500,000 in the red. **6** PHRASE If you **see red**, you suddenly become very angry. □ I didn't mean to break his nose. I just saw red. →see **rainbow**

1 색채어 빨간, 붉은 □ 빨간 장미 한 다발 **2** 형용사 붉어진, 빨개진 □ 나는 새빨개진 얼굴로 내게는 진정한 아이디어가 없다는 것을 인정할 수밖에 없었다. **3** 형용사 적갈색의, 빨간 □ 빨간 머리의 소녀 **4** 물질명사 적포도주 □ 매콤한 맛이 나는 이 음식들에는 백포도주보다는 적포도주가 제격이다. **5** 구 적자의, 빚지고 있는 □ 그 극장은 5십만 파운드를 빚지고 있다. **6** 구 격노하다 □ 그의 코뼈를 부러뜨릴 의도는 없었어. 난 그저 격노했던 것뿐이라구.

red card (red cards) N-COUNT In soccer or rugby, if a player is shown the **red card**, the referee holds up a red card to indicate that the player must leave the field for breaking the rules. □ He was shown a red card for a rough tackle.

가산명사 레드카드, 퇴장 명령 카드 □ 그는 과격한 태클로 레드카드를 받았다.

red|dish /rɛdɪʃ/ ADJ **Reddish** means slightly red in color. □ He had reddish brown hair.

형용사 불그스레한, 붉은빛을 띤 □ 그는 머리카락이 불그스레한 갈색이었다.

re|deem /rɪdim/ (redeems, redeeming, redeemed) **1** V-T/V-I If you **redeem yourself** or your reputation, you do something that makes people have a good opinion of you again after you have behaved or performed badly. □ He had realized the mistake he had made and wanted to redeem himself. **2** V-T/V-I When something **redeems** an unpleasant thing or situation, it prevents it from being completely bad. □ Work is the way that people seek to redeem their lives from futility. **3** V-T If you **redeem** a debt or money that you have promised to someone, you pay money that you owe or that you promised to pay. [FORMAL] □ The amount required to redeem the mortgage was £358,587. **4** V-T In religions such as Christianity, to **redeem** someone means to save them by freeing them from sin and evil. □ ...a new female spiritual force to redeem the world.

1 타동사/자동사 (명예를) 회복하다 □ 그는 자신이 저지른 실수를 깨닫고 나서 만회하고 싶었다. **2** 타동사/자동사 (부족한 것을) 메우다 □ 일은 사람들이 삶의 무의미함을 메우기 위해 찾는 방식이다. **3** 타동사 상환하다 [격식체] □ 융자금을 상환하기 위해 필요한 금액은 358,587파운드였다. **4** 타동사 구원하다 □ 이 세상을 구원할 새로운 여성 영적 지도자

re|deem|able /rɪdiməbəl/ ADJ If something is **redeemable**, it can be exchanged for a particular sum of money or for goods worth a particular sum. □ Their full catalogue costs £5, redeemable against a first order.

형용사 상환할 수 있는, 되찾을 수 있는 □ 전체 물품 목록은 5달러이며, 첫 구매 시 되돌려 드립니다.

re|demp|tion /rɪdɛmpʃən/ (redemptions) **1** N-VAR **Redemption** is the act of redeeming something or of being redeemed by something. [FORMAL] □ He craves redemption for his sins. □ ...redemption of the loan. **2** PHRASE If you say that someone or something is **beyond redemption**, you mean that they are so bad it is unlikely that anything can be done to improve them. □ No man is beyond redemption.

1 가산명사 또는 불가산명사 구원; 상환 [격식체] □ 그는 자신의 죄를 구원받기를 열망한다. □ 대출금 상환 **2** 구 구제할 수 없는, 개선의 여지가 없는 □ 구제할 수 없는 사람은 아무도 없다.

re|devel|op|ment /ridɪvɛləpmənt/ N-UNCOUNT When **redevelopment** takes place, the buildings in one area of a town are knocked down and new ones are built in their place. □ It is understood that the group's intention is to clear the site for redevelopment.

불가산명사 재개발 □ 그 단체의 의도는 재개발을 위해 그 부지를 정리하는 것이라고 여겨진다.

red-hot **1** ADJ **Red-hot** metal or rock has been heated to such a high temperature that it has turned red. □ ...red-hot iron. **2** ADJ A **red-hot** object is too hot to be touched safely. □ In the main rooms red-hot radiators were left exposed. **3** ADJ **Red-hot** is used to describe a person or thing that is very popular, especially someone who is very good at what they do or something that is new and exciting. [JOURNALISM] □ Some traders are already stacking the red-hot book on their shelves.

1 형용사 시뻘겋게 단 □ 시뻘겋게 단 쇠 **2** 형용사 매우 뜨거운 □ 주요 방들에는 매우 뜨거운 라디에이터가 밖으로 드러나 있었다. **3** 형용사 아주 인기 있는, 최신의 [언론] □ 일부 상인들은 벌써 최신 도서를 선반에 쌓아 놓고 있다.

re|di|rect /ridɪrɛkt, -daɪ-/ (redirects, redirecting, redirected) **1** V-T If you **redirect** your energy, resources, or ability, you begin doing something different or trying to achieve something different. □ Controls were used to redistribute or redirect resources. **2** V-T If you **redirect** someone or something, you change their course or destination. □ She redirected them to the men's department.

1 타동사 다른 목적으로 사용하다, 전용(轉用)하다 □ 관리 감독을 통해 자원을 재분배하거나 전용했다. **2** 타동사 -의 방향을 수정하다 □ 그녀는 그들이 방향을 바꿔 남성복 매장으로 가게 했다.

re|dis|tribute /ridɪstrɪbyut/ (redistributes, redistributing, redistributed) V-T If something such as money or property **is redistributed**, it is shared among people or organizations in a different way from the way that it was previously shared. □ Wealth was redistributed more equitably among society. ● **re|dis|tri|bu|tion** /ridɪstrɪbyuʃən/ N-UNCOUNT □ One of a government's primary duties is to achieve some redistribution of income so that the better off can help to keep the worse off out of poverty.

타동사 재분배하다 □ 부가 사회 전반에 걸쳐 좀 더 공정하게 재분배되었다. ● 재분배 불가산명사 □ 정부의 기본적 의무 가운데 하나는 소득 재분배의 달성이고, 그래서 좀 더 잘 사는 사람들의 도움으로 못 사는 사람들이 빈곤에 빠지지 않게 하는 것이다.

re|dress /rɪdrɛs/ (redresses, redressing, redressed)

> The noun is also pronounced /ridrɛs/ in American English.

> 미국 영어에서 명사는 /ridrɛs/로도 발음된다.

1 V-T If you **redress** something such as a wrong or a complaint, you do something to correct it or to improve things for the person who has been badly treated. [FORMAL] □ More and more victims turn to litigation to redress wrongs

1 타동사 시정하다, 바로잡다 [격식체] □ 점점 더 많은 희생자들이 자신들이 당한 부당 행위들을 바로잡기 위해 소송에 의지한다. **2** 타동사 바로잡다 [격식체]

done to them. **2** V-T If you **redress** the balance or the imbalance between two things that have become unfair or unequal, you make them fair and equal again. [FORMAL] ❑ *So we're trying to redress the balance and to give teachers a sense that both spoken and written language are equally important.* **3** N-UNCOUNT **Redress** is money that someone pays you because they have caused you harm or loss. [FORMAL] ❑ *They are continuing their legal battle to seek some redress from the government.*

❑ 그리하여 우리는 균형을 바로잡고 교사들에게 구어와 문어가 둘 다 똑같이 중요하다는 의식을 심어 주려고 노력하고 있다. **3** 불가산명사 보상금 [격식체] ❑ 그들은 정부로부터 보상금을 받고자 계속해서 법적 투쟁을 하고 있다.

red tape N-UNCOUNT You refer to official rules and procedures as **red tape** when they seem unnecessary and cause delay. [DISAPPROVAL] ❑ *The little money that was available was tied up in bureaucratic red tape.*

불가산명사 (불필요한) 요식 [탐탁잖음] ❑ 쓸 수 있는 그 적은 돈도 관료주의적 요식에 묶여 있었다.

re|duce ♦♦◇ /rɪdus, BRIT rɪdyuːs/ (**reduces, reducing, reduced**) **1** V-T If you **reduce** something, you make it smaller in size or amount, or less in degree. ❑ *It reduces the risks of heart disease.* **2** V-T If someone **is reduced to** a weaker or inferior state, they become weaker or inferior as a result of something that happens to them. [usu passive] ❑ *They were reduced to extreme poverty.* **3** V-T If you say that someone **is reduced to** doing something, you mean that they have to do it, although it is unpleasant or embarrassing. [usu passive] ❑ *He was reduced to begging for a living.* **4** V-T If something is changed to a different or less complicated form, you can say that it **is reduced to** that form. [usu passive] ❑ *All the buildings in the town have been reduced to rubble.* **5** V-T/V-I If you **reduce** liquid when you are cooking, or if it **reduces**, it is boiled in order to make it less in quantity and thicker. ❑ *Boil the liquid in a small saucepan to reduce it by half.* **6** PHRASE If someone or something **reduces** you **to tears**, they make you feel so unhappy that you cry. ❑ *The attentions of the media reduced her to tears.* →see **mineral**

1 타동사 줄이다 ❑ 그것이 심장병의 발병 위험을 줄인다. **2** 타동사 (좋지 않은 상황에) 처하다, 빠지다 ❑ 그들은 극심한 가난에 빠지게 되었다. **3** 타동사 -하는 처지가 되다, -해야만 하게 되다 ❑ 그는 빌어먹고 사는 처지가 되었다. **4** 타동사 (형태 등이 바뀌어) -가 되다 ❑ 그 마을의 모든 건물이 잔해가 되어 버렸다. **5** 타동사/자동사 졸이다; 졸아들다 ❑ 그 국물을 작은 냄비에 담고 반쯤 졸아들 때까지 끓이세요. **6** 구 울리다 ❑ 언론의 관심이 그녀를 울렸다.

Thesaurus   reduce의 참조어

  v.   cut back, decrease, lessen, lower; (*ant.*) increase **1**

Word Partnership   reduce의 연어

  N.   reduce **anxiety**, reduce **costs**, reduce **crime**, reduce **debt**, reduce **pain**, reduce **spending**, reduce **stress**, reduce **taxes**, reduce **violence**, reduce **waste** **1**
  ADV.   **greatly** reduce, **substantially** reduce **1**
  v.   **help** reduce, **plan to** reduce, **try to** reduce **1**

re|duc|tion ♦◇◇ /rɪdʌkʃ°n/ (**reductions**) **1** N-COUNT When there is a **reduction** in something, it is made smaller. ❑ *...a future reduction in UK interest rates.* **2** N-UNCOUNT **Reduction** is the act of making something smaller in size or amount, or less in degree. ❑ *...a new strategic arms reduction agreement.*

1 가산명사 인하, 감소 ❑ 장차 있을 영국의 금리 인하 **2** 불가산명사 인하, 감소 ❑ 새로운 전략적 무기 감축 협정

Word Partnership   reduction의 연어

  N.   **budget** reduction, **cost** reduction, **debt** reduction, **deficit** reduction, **noise** reduction, **rate** reduction, **risk** reduction, **tax** reduction **2**

re|dun|dan|cy /rɪdʌndənsi/ (**redundancies**) **1** N-COUNT When there are **redundancies**, an organization tells some of its employees to leave because their jobs are no longer necessary or because the organization can no longer afford to pay them. [BRIT, BUSINESS; AM **dismissals, layoffs**] ❑ *The ministry has said it hopes to avoid compulsory redundancies.* **2** N-UNCOUNT **Redundancy** means being made redundant. [BUSINESS] ❑ *Thousands of bank employees are facing redundancy as their employers cut costs.*

1 가산명사 정리 해고 [영국영어, 경제; 미국영어 dismissals, layoffs] ❑ 주무 부처에서 강제 정리 해고는 피하고 싶다고 말했다. **2** 불가산명사 정리 해고 [경제] ❑ 고용주가 비용을 삭감함에 따라 은행 직원 수천 명이 정리 해고에 직면하고 있다.

re|dun|dant /rɪdʌndənt/ **1** ADJ If you are made **redundant**, your employer tells you to leave because your job is no longer necessary or because your employer cannot afford to keep paying you. [BRIT, BUSINESS; AM **be dismissed**] ❑ *My husband was made redundant late last year.* **2** ADJ Something that is **redundant** is no longer needed because its job is being done by something else or because its job is no longer necessary or useful. ❑ *Changes in technology may mean that once-valued skills are now redundant.*

1 형용사 정리 해고되는 [영국영어, 경제; 미국영어 be dismissed] ❑ 내 남편은 작년 말에 정리 해고당했다. **2** 형용사 불필요해진 ❑ 과학 기술에 있어서의 변화란 한때 가치 있다고 여겨지던 기술들이 이제는 불필요해진다는 뜻일 수도 있다.

reed /rid/ (**reeds**) **1** N-COUNT **Reeds** are tall plants that grow in large groups in shallow water or on ground that is always wet and soft. They have strong, hollow stems that can be used for making things such as mats or baskets. **2** N-COUNT A **reed** is a small piece of cane or metal inserted into the mouthpiece of a woodwind instrument. The reed vibrates when you blow through it and makes a sound.

1 가산명사 갈대 **2** 가산명사 리드, (관악기의) 혀

reef /rif/ (**reefs**) N-COUNT A **reef** is a long line of rocks or sand, the top of which is just above or just below the surface of the sea. ❑ *An unspoilt coral reef encloses the bay.*

가산명사 암초 ❑ 손상되지 않은 산호초가 그 만을 둘러싸고 있다.

reek /rik/ (**reeks, reeking, reeked**) **1** V-I To **reek of** something, usually something unpleasant, means to smell very strongly of it. ❑ *Your breath reeks of stale cigar smoke.* ● N-SING **Reek** is also a noun. ❑ *He smelt the reek of whisky.* **2** V-I If you say that something **reeks of** unpleasant things such as cinema film, magnetic tape, feelings, or practices, you disapprove of it because it gives a strong impression that it involves those ideas, feelings, or practices. [DISAPPROVAL] ❑ *The whole thing reeks of hypocrisy.*

1 자동사 악취를 풍기다 ❑ 당신 입에서 엽궐련을 피운 퀴퀴한 악취가 나요. ● 단수명사 악취 ❑ 그는 위스키 악취를 맡았다. **2** 자동사 (불쾌한) 기미가 보이다, 냄새가 나다 [탐탁잖음] ❑ 이 모든 것에서 위선의 냄새가 나.

reel ♦◇◇ /ril/ (**reels, reeling, reeled**) **1** N-COUNT A **reel** is a cylindrical object around which you wrap something such as cinema film, magnetic tape, fishing line, or cotton thread. [mainly BRIT; AM usually **spool**] ❑ *...a 30m reel of cable.* **2** V-I If someone **reels**, they move about in an unsteady way as if they are going to fall. ❑ *He was reeling a little. He must be very drunk.* **3** V-I If you **are reeling**

1 가산명사 릴, 실패 [주로 영국영어; 미국영어 대개 spool] ❑ 30미터짜리 케이블 릴 **2** 자동사 비틀거리다, 휘청거리다 ❑ 그가 약간 비틀거리고 있었다. 분명히 무척 취한 것 같았다. **3** 자동사 크게 동요하다 ❑ 나는 아직도 그것을 들은 충격으로 진정이 안 된다.

A

from a shock, you are feeling extremely surprised or upset because of it. [usu cont] ❑ *I'm still reeling from the shock of hearing of it.* ◳ V-I If you say that your brain or your mind **is reeling**, you mean that you are very confused because you have too many things to think about. ❑ *His mind reeled at the question.*

자동사 혼란스럽다 ❑ 그 질문에 그는 마음이 혼란스러웠다.

B

▶**reel off** PHRASAL VERB If you **reel off** information, you repeat it from memory quickly and easily. ❑ *She reeled off the titles of a dozen or so of the novels.*

구동사 술술 늘어놓다 ❑ 그녀는 십여 개쯤 되는 소설 제목을 술술 늘어놓았다.

C

re|elect /riːɪlɛkt/ (**reelects**, **reelecting**, **reelected**) [BRIT, sometimes AM **re-elect**] V-T When someone such as a politician or an official who has been elected **is reelected**, they win another election and are therefore able to continue in their position as, for example, president, or an official in an organization. ❑ *He needs 51 percent to be reelected.* ● **re-election** /riːɪlɛkʃᵊn/ N-UNCOUNT ❑ *He is heavily favored to win reelection.*

[영국영어, 미국영어 가끔 re-elect] 타동사 재선되다 ❑ 그가 재선되려면 51퍼센트를 득표해야 한다. ● 재선 불가산명사 ❑ 그는 재선될 만큼 대단한 지지를 받고 있다.

D

re|examine /riːɪgzæmɪn/ (**reexamines**, **reexamining**, **reexamined**) [BRIT, sometimes AM **re-examine**] V-T If a person or group of people **reexamines** their ideas, beliefs, or attitudes, they think about them carefully because they are no longer sure if they are correct. ❑ *The marriage will cause Drew to reexamine his life.* ● **re|examination** /riːɪgzæmɪneɪʃᵊn/ (**reexaminations**) N-VAR ❑ *The issue has led to a reexamination of censorship rules.*

[영국영어, 미국영어 가끔 re-examine] 타동사 재검토하다 ❑ 그 결혼으로 드루는 자신의 삶을 재검토하게 될 것이다. ● 재검토 가산명사 또는 불가산명사 ❑ 그 문제를 계기로 검열 규정의 재검토가 이루어졌다.

E

F

ref /rɛf/ (**refs**) ◳ **Ref.** is an abbreviation for **reference**. It is written in front of a code at the top of business letters and documents. The code refers to a file where all the letters and documents about the same matter are kept. [BUSINESS] ❑ *Our Ref: JAH/JW.* ◲ N-COUNT The **ref** in a sports game, such as football, soccer, or boxing, is the same as the **referee**. [INFORMAL] ❑ *The ref gave a penalty and Platini scored.*

◳ 참조 번호 [경제] ❑ 우리 참조 번호는 제이에이에이취/제이더블유입니다. ◲ 가산명사 심판 [비격식체] ❑ 심판이 페널티를 주었고 플라티니가 득점을 올렸다.

G

H

re|fer ♦♦◇ /rɪfɜː/ (**refers**, **referring**, **referred**) ◳ V-I If you **refer to** a particular subject or person, you talk about them or mention them. ❑ *In his speech, he referred to a recent trip to Canada.* ◲ V-I If you **refer to** someone or something **as** a particular thing, you use a particular word, expression, or name to mention or describe them. ❑ *Marcia had referred to him as a dear friend.* ◳ V-I If a word **refers to** a particular thing, situation, or idea, it describes it in some way. ❑ *The term electronics refers to electrically-induced action.* ◴ V-T If a person who is ill **is referred to** a hospital or a specialist, they are sent there by a doctor in order to be treated. [usu passive] ❑ *She was referred to the hospital by a neighborhood clinic.* ◵ V-T If you **refer** a task or a problem **to** a person or an organization, you formally tell them about it, so that they can deal with it. ❑ *He could refer the matter to the high court.* ◶ V-T If you **refer** someone **to** a person or organization, you send them there for the help they need. ❑ *Now and then I referred a client to him.* ◷ V-I If you **refer to** a book or other source of information, you look at it in order to find something out. ❑ *He referred briefly to his notebook.* ◸ V-T If you **refer** someone **to** a source of information, you tell them the place where they will find the information which they need or which you think will interest them. ❑ *Mr. Bryan also referred me to a book by the American journalist Anthony Scaduto.*

I

J

K

L

M

◳ 자동사 언급하다 ❑ 그는 자신의 연설에서 최근의 캐나다 여행을 언급했다. ◲ 자동사 부르다 ❑ 마시아는 그를 소중한 친구라고 불렀다. ◳ 자동사 나타내다, 가리키다 ❑ 전자 공학이라는 용어는 전기적으로 유도되는 작용을 가리킨다. ◴ 타동사 ❑ 그녀는 이웃 진료소에 의해 그 병원에 보내졌다. ◵ 타동사 의뢰하다 ❑ 그는 그 문제를 고등 법원에 의뢰할 수도 있다. ◶ 타동사 도움을 받도록 보내다 ❑ 이따금 나는 고객을 그에게 보내 도움을 받게 했다. ◷ 타동사 참고하다, 참조하다 ❑ 그는 잠깐 자기 공책을 참고했다. ◸ 타동사 참고하라고 하다 ❑ 브라이언 씨도 나에게 미국인 언론인인 앤터니 스카두토가 쓴 책을 참고하라고 했다.

N

ref|eree /rɛfəriː/ (**referees**, **refereeing**, **refereed**) ◳ N-COUNT The **referee** is the official who controls a sports event such as a football game or a boxing match. ◲ V-I When someone **referees** a sports event or contest, they act as referee. ❑ *Vautrot has refereed in two World Cups.* ◳ N-COUNT A **referee** is a person who gives you a reference, for example when you are applying for a job. [mainly BRIT; AM **reference**] ❑ *You will be expected to give the names of two referees and to have a full medical examination.* →see **basketball**, **football**, **tennis**

O

◳ 가산명사 심판 ◲ 자동사 심판을 보다 ❑ 보트로는 두 번의 월드컵 경기에서 심판을 봤다. ◳ 가산명사 신원 보증인 [주로 영국영어; 미국영어 reference] ❑ 신원 보증인 두 명의 이름을 제시하고 정식 건강 검진을 받으세요.

P

ref|er|ence ♦♦◇ /rɛfərəns/ (**references**) ◳ N-VAR **Reference to** someone or something is the act of talking about them or mentioning them. A **reference** is a particular example of this. ❑ *He made no reference to any agreement.* ◲ N-UNCOUNT **Reference** is the act of consulting someone or something in order to get information or advice. ❑ *Please keep this sheet in a safe place for reference.* ◳ ADJ **Reference** books are ones that you look at when you need specific information or facts about a subject. [ADJ n] ❑ *...a useful reference work for teachers.* ◴ N-COUNT A **reference** is a word, phrase, or idea which comes from something such as a book, poem, or play and which you use when making a point about something. ❑ *...a reference from the Quran.* ◵ N-COUNT A **reference** is something such as a number or a name that tells you where you can obtain the information you want. ❑ *Make a note of the reference number shown on the form.* ◶ N-COUNT A **reference** is a letter that is written by someone who knows you and which describes your character and abilities. When you apply for a job, an employer might ask for **references**. ❑ *The firm offered to give her a reference.* ◷ N-COUNT A **reference** is a person who gives you a reference, for example when you are applying for a job. [mainly AM; BRIT usually **referee**] ❑ *The official at the American Embassy asked me for two references.* ◸ PHRASE You use **with reference to** or **in reference to** in order to indicate what something relates to. ❑ *I am writing with reference to your article on salaries for scientists.* ◹ →see also **cross-reference**

Q

R

S

T

U

◳ 가산명사 또는 불가산명사 언급 ❑ 그는 어떤 협약도 언급하지 않았다. ◲ 불가산명사 참고, 참조 ❑ 나중에 참고할 수 있도록 이 서류를 안전한 곳에 보관하세요. ◳ 형용사 참고용의 ❑ 교사에게 유용한 참고 작품 ◴ 가산명사 인용구, 인용문 ❑ 코란에서 따온 인용문 ◵ 가산명사 참조 기호 ❑ 그 서식에 나타난 참조 번호를 기록하세요. ◶ 가산명사 추천서, 신원 증명서 ❑ 그 회사가 그녀에게 추천서를 써 주겠다고 했다. ◷ 가산명사 신원 보증인 [주로 미국영어; 영국영어 대개 referee] ❑ 미국 대사관 직원이 나에게 신원 보증인 두 사람을 요구했다. ◸ 구 -에 관하여 ❑ 나는 당신이 과학자들의 급여에 관해 쓴 기사와 관련해서 글을 쓰고 있는 중이다.

V

Word Partnership	*reference의 연어*	
ADJ.	**clear** reference, **specific** reference ◳ ◴	
	quick reference ◲	
N.	reference **books**, reference, **materials** ◳	
	reference **number** ◵	

W

X

ref|er|en|dum ♦◇◇ /rɛfərɛndəm/ (**referendums** or **referenda**) /rɛfərɛndə/ N-COUNT If a country holds a **referendum** on a particular policy, they ask the people to vote on the policy and show whether or not they agree with it. ❑ *Estonia said today it too plans to hold a referendum on independence.*

가산명사 국민 투표 ❑ 에스토니아도 오늘 독립에 대해 국민 투표를 실시할 계획이라고 말했다.

Y

re|fer|ral /rɪfɜːrəl/ (**referrals**) N-VAR **Referral** is the act of officially sending someone to a person or authority that is qualified to deal with them. A **referral** is an instance of this. ❑ *Legal Aid can often provide referral to other types of agencies.*

가산명사 또는 불가산명사 소개, 위탁 ❑ 리걸 에이드가 흔히 다른 종류의 기관에 위탁을 할 수도 있다.

Z

re|fill (refills, refilling, refilled)

> The verb is pronounced /rɪfɪl/. The noun is pronounced /riːfɪl/.

동사는 /rɪfɪl/로 발음되고, 명사는 /riːfɪl/로 발음된다.

1 V-T If you **refill** something, you fill it again after it has been emptied. ❑ *I refilled our wine glasses.* ● N-COUNT **Refill** is also a noun. [INFORMAL] ❑ *Max held out his cup for a refill.* **2** N-COUNT A **refill** of a particular product, such as soap powder, is a quantity of that product sold in a cheaper container than the one it is usually sold in. You use a refill to fill the more permanent container when it is empty. ❑ *Refill packs are cheaper and lighter.*

1 타동사 다시 채우다 ❑ 나는 우리 와인 잔에 와인을 다시 채웠다. ● 가산명사 다시 채움 [비격식체] ❑ 맥스가 더 달라고 자기 컵을 내밀었다. **2** 가산명사 리필제품 ❑ 리필 팩이 더 싸고 더 가볍다.

re|fi|nance /riːfaɪnæns, rɪfaɪnæns/ (refinances, refinancing, refinanced) V-T/V-I If a person or a company **refinances** a debt or if they **refinance**, they borrow money in order to pay the debt. [BUSINESS] ❑ *A loan was arranged to refinance existing debt.*

타동사/자동사 차환하다 [경제] ❑ 기존 부채를 상환하기 위한 융자가 주선되었다.

re|fine /rɪfaɪn/ (refines, refining, refined) **1** V-T When a substance **is refined**, it is made pure by having all other substances removed from it. [usu passive] ❑ *Oil is refined to remove naturally occurring impurities.* ● **re|fin|ing** N-UNCOUNT ❑ *...oil refining.* **2** V-T If something such as a process, theory, or machine **is refined**, it is improved by having small changes made to it. [usu passive] ❑ *Surgical techniques are constantly being refined.* →see **industry, sugar**

1 타동사 정제되다 ❑ 자연 발생적인 불순물을 제거하기 위해 석유를 정제한다. ● 정제 불가산명사 ❑ 석유 정유 **2** 타동사 개선되다, 개량되다 ❑ 수술 기법이 계속해서 개선되고 있다.

re|fined /rɪfaɪnd/ **1** ADJ A **refined** substance has been made pure by having other substances removed from it. ❑ *...refined sugar.* **2** ADJ If you say that someone is **refined**, you mean that they are very polite and have good manners and good taste. ❑ *...refined and well-dressed ladies.* **3** ADJ If you describe a machine or a process as **refined**, you mean that it has been carefully developed and is therefore very efficient or elegant. ❑ *This technique is becoming more refined and more acceptable all the time.*

1 형용사 정제된 ❑ 정제당 **2** 형용사 세련된, 교양 있는 ❑ 세련되고 잘 차려입은 숙녀들 **3** 형용사 정교한, 우아한 ❑ 이 기법은 끊임없이 더욱 정교해지고 더욱 만족스러워지고 있다.

re|fine|ment /rɪfaɪnmənt/ (refinements) **1** N-VAR **Refinements** are small changes or additions that you make to something in order to improve it. **Refinement** is the process of making refinements. ❑ *Older cars inevitably lack the latest safety refinements.* **2** N-UNCOUNT **Refinement** is politeness and good manners.

1 가산명사 또는 불가산명사 개량 장치; 공들임 ❑ 오래된 차량은 어쩔 수 없이 최신형처럼 공들인 안전장치가 부족하다. **2** 불가산명사 우아함, 정중함

re|fin|ery /rɪfaɪnəri/ (refineries) N-COUNT A **refinery** is a factory where a substance such as oil or sugar is refined. ❑ *...an oil refinery.* →see **mineral, oil**

가산명사 정제소 ❑ 정유 공장

re|fit (refits, refitting, refitted)

> The verb is pronounced /riːfɪt/. The noun is pronounced /riːfɪt/.

동사는 /riːfɪt/으로 발음되고, 명사는 /riːfɪt/으로 발음된다.

V-T When a ship **is refitted**, it is repaired or is given new parts, equipment, or furniture. [usu passive] ❑ *During the war, Navy ships were refitted here.* ● N-COUNT **Refit** is also a noun. ❑ *The ship finished an extensive refit last year.*

타동사 (배가) 수리되다, 개장(改裝)되다 ❑ 전쟁 중에 해군 함정은 이곳에서 수리를 받았다. ● 가산명사 (배의) 수리, 개장(改裝) ❑ 그 선박은 지난해 대대적인 수리를 마쳤다.

Word Link ｜ re ≈ back, again : reflect, refresh, restate

re|flect ♦♦◇ /rɪflɛkt/ (reflects, reflecting, reflected) **1** V-T If something **reflects** an attitude or situation, it shows that the attitude or situation exists or it shows what it is like. ❑ *A newspaper report seems to have reflected the view of most MPs.* **2** V-T/V-I When light, heat, or other rays **reflect** off a surface or when a surface **reflects** them, they are sent back from the surface and do not pass through it. ❑ *The sun reflected off the snow-covered mountains.* **3** V-T When something **is reflected** in a mirror or in water, you can see its image in the mirror or in the water. [usu passive] ❑ *His image seemed to be reflected many times in the mirror.* **4** V-I When you **reflect on** something, you think deeply about it. ❑ *We should all give ourselves time to reflect.* **5** V-T You can use **reflect** to indicate that a particular thought occurs to someone. ❑ *Things were very much changed since before the war, he reflected.* **6** V-I If an action or situation **reflects** in a particular way **on** someone or something, it gives people a good or bad impression of them. ❑ *The affair hardly reflected well on the British.* →see **echo**

1 타동사 반영하다 ❑ 한 신문 기사가 의회의원들 대부분의 견해를 반영하고 있는 듯하다. **2** 타동사/자동사 반사되다; 반사하다 ❑ 태양이 눈 덮인 산에 비춰 반사되었다. **3** 타동사 비치다 ❑ 그의 모습이 거울에 여러 번 비치는 것 같았다. **4** 자동사 깊이 생각하다, 숙고하다 ❑ 우리 모두 깊이 생각할 시간을 가져야 한다. **5** 타동사 떠올리다 ❑ 전쟁 발발 전과는 달리 상황이 상당히 많이 변했음을 그는 떠올렸다. **6** 자동사 인상을 주다 ❑ 그 사건은 영국인들에 대해 별로 좋은 인상을 주지 못했다.

re|flec|tion /rɪflɛkʃən/ (reflections) **1** N-COUNT A **reflection** is an image that you can see in a mirror or in glass or water. ❑ *Meg stared at her reflection in the bedroom mirror.* **2** N-UNCOUNT **Reflection** is the process by which light and heat are sent back from a surface and do not pass through it. ❑ *...the reflection of a beam of light off a mirror.* **3** N-COUNT If you say that something is a **reflection of** a particular person's attitude or **of** a situation, you mean that it is caused by that attitude or situation and therefore reveals something about it. ❑ *Inhibition in adulthood seems to be very clearly a reflection of a person's experiences as a child.* **4** N-SING If something is a **reflection** or a **sad reflection on** a person or thing, it gives a bad impression of them. ❑ *Infection with head lice is no reflection on personal hygiene.* **5** N-UNCOUNT **Reflection** is careful thought about a particular subject. Your **reflections** are your thoughts about a particular subject. [also N in pl] ❑ *After days of reflection she decided to write back.* ● PHRASE If someone admits or accepts something **on reflection**, they admit or accept it after having thought carefully about it. →see **echo**

1 가산명사 비친 모습, 영상 ❑ 멕은 침실 거울에 비친 자신의 모습을 응시했다. **2** 불가산명사 반사 ❑ 거울에서 반사되어 나오는 빛줄기 **3** 가산명사 반영 ❑ 성인기의 억압은 개인이 아동기 때 경험한 것을 매우 분명히 반영해 주는 것 같다. **4** 단수명사 흠, 불명예 ❑ 머리에 이가 옮은 것이 개인위생에 흠이 되는 것은 아니다. **5** 불가산명사 깊이 생각함, 숙고; (숙고한 후의) 의견 ❑ 며칠 동안의 숙고 끝에 그녀는 답장하기로 결심했다. ● 구 곰곰이 생각한 후에

re|flec|tive /rɪflɛktɪv/ **1** ADJ If you are **reflective**, you are thinking deeply about something. [WRITTEN] ❑ *I walked on in a reflective mood to the car, thinking about the poor honeymooners.* **2** ADJ If something is **reflective of** a particular situation or attitude, it is typical of that situation or attitude, or is a consequence of it. [v-link ADJ of n] ❑ *The German government's support of the U.S. is not entirely reflective of German public opinion.* **3** ADJ A **reflective** surface or material sends back light or heat. [FORMAL] ❑ *Avoid pans with a shiny, reflective base as the heat will be reflected back.*

1 형용사 생각에 잠긴 [문어체] ❑ 나는 가엾은 신혼부부들을 떠올리며, 생각에 잠겨서 차 쪽으로 걸어 나갔다. **2** 형용사 반영하는 ❑ 미국에 대한 독일 정부의 지지가 독일 여론을 전적으로 반영하는 것은 아니다. **3** 형용사 반사하는 [격식체] ❑ 바닥이 광택이 나고 빛을 반사하는 팬은 열을 다시 반사하니 사용하지 마세요.

Word Link ｜ flex ≈ bending : flex, flexible, reflex

re|flex /riːflɛks/ (reflexes) **1** N-COUNT A **reflex** or a **reflex action** is something that you do automatically and without thinking, as a habit or as a reaction to

1 가산명사 습관적인 행동 ❑ 윌시는 자신의 주머니를 더듬었는데 이는 담배를 피던 시절의 습관적인

A

something. ❏ *Walsh fumbled in his pocket, a reflex from his smoking days.* ❷ N-COUNT A **reflex** or a **reflex action** is a normal, uncontrollable reaction of your body to something that you feel, see, or experience. ❏ *...tests for reflexes, like tapping the knee or the heel with a rubber hammer.* ❸ N-PLURAL Your **reflexes** are your ability to react quickly with your body when something unexpected happens, for example when you are involved in sports or when you are driving a car. ❏ *It takes great skill, cool nerves, and the reflexes of an athlete.*

B

re|form ♦♦◇ /rɪfɔrm/ (reforms, reforming, reformed) ❶ N-VAR **Reform** consists of changes and improvements to a law, social system, or institution. A **reform** is an instance of such a change or improvement. ❏ *The party embarked on a programme of economic reform.* ❷ V-T If someone **reforms** something such as a law, social system, or institution, they change or improve it. ❏ *...his plans to reform the country's economy.* ❸ V-T/V-I When someone **reforms** or when something **reforms** them, they stop doing things that society does not approve of, such as breaking the law or drinking too much alcohol. ❏ *When his court case was coming up, James promised to reform.* ● re|formed ADJ ❏ *...a reformed alcoholic.*

C

D

E

H

re|form|er /rɪfɔrmər/ (reformers) N-COUNT A **reformer** is someone who tries to change and improve something such as a law or a social system. ❏ *How could he be a reformer and a defender of established interests at the same time?*

I

re|frain /rɪfreɪn/ (refrains, refraining, refrained) ❶ V-I If you **refrain from** doing something, you deliberately do not do it. ❏ *Mrs. Hardie refrained from making any comment.* ❷ N-COUNT A **refrain** is a short, simple part of a song, which is repeated many times. ❏ *...a refrain from an old song.* ❸ N-COUNT A **refrain** is a comment or saying that people often repeat. ❏ *Rosa's constant refrain is that she doesn't have a life.*

J

K

re|fresh /rɪfreʃ/ (refreshes, refreshing, refreshed) ❶ V-T If something **refreshes** you when you have become hot, tired, or thirsty, it makes you feel cooler or more energetic. ❏ *The lotion cools and refreshes the skin.* ● re|freshed ADJ ❏ *He awoke feeling completely refreshed.* ❷ V-T If you **refresh** something old or dull, you make it as good as it was when it was new. ❏ *Many view these meetings as an occasion to share ideas and refresh friendship.* ❸ V-T If someone **refreshes** your memory, they tell you something that you had forgotten. ❏ *He walked on the opposite side of the street to refresh his memory of the building.* ❹ V-T If you **refresh** a web page, you click a button in order to get the most recent version of the page. [COMPUTING] ❏ *The "reload" button on your web browser is what you click in order to refresh the site and get the most current version.*

L

M

re|fresh|er course (refresher courses) N-COUNT A **refresher course** is a training course in which people improve their knowledge or skills and learn about new developments that are related to the job that they do.

N

re|fresh|ing /rɪfreʃɪŋ/ ❶ ADJ You say that something is **refreshing** when it is pleasantly different from what you are used to. ❏ *It's refreshing to hear somebody speaking common sense.* ● re|fresh|ing|ly ADV ❏ *He was refreshingly honest.* ❷ ADJ A **refreshing** bath or drink makes you feel energetic or cool again after you have been tired or hot. ❏ *Herbs have been used for centuries to make refreshing drinks.*

O

P

re|fresh|ment /rɪfreʃmənt/ (refreshments) ❶ N-PLURAL **Refreshments** are drinks and small amounts of food that are provided, for example, during a meeting or a journey. ❏ *Lunch and refreshments will be provided.* ❷ N-UNCOUNT You can refer to food and drink as **refreshment**. [FORMAL] ❏ *May I offer you some refreshment?*

Q

R

re|frig|er|ate /rɪfrɪdʒəreɪt/ (refrigerates, refrigerating, refrigerated) V-T If you **refrigerate** food, you make it cold by putting it in a refrigerator, usually in order to preserve it. ❏ *Refrigerate the dough overnight.*

S

re|frig|era|tor /rɪfrɪdʒəreɪtər/ (refrigerators) N-COUNT A **refrigerator** is a large container which is kept cool inside, usually by electricity, so that the food and drink in it stays fresh.
→see Word Web: refrigerator

T

re|fuel /rifyuəl/ (refuels, refueling, refueled) [BRIT, sometimes AM **refuelling**, **refuelled**] V-T/V-I When an aircraft or other vehicle **refuels** or when someone

U

V

Word Web   refrigerator

W

Refrigerators and **freezers** cool and freeze food, but how do they work? A gas passes through coils inside the walls of the refrigerator or freezer. As it does so, it absorbs heat and **chills** the interior. Then a pump compresses the gas, which raises its **temperature**. It pushes the gas through coils on the outside of the refrigerator. There it expands and becomes a liquid. At the same time, it gives off heat into the surrounding air. The liquid then flows through a valve into a low pressure area. There it becomes a gas again. Then the cycle repeats itself.

X

Y

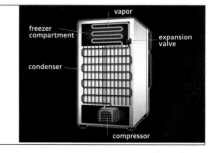

Z

행동이었다. ❷ 가산명사 반사 작용 ❏ 고무망치로 무릎이나 발뒤꿈치를 두드리는 등의 반사 작용 검사 ❸ 복수명사 반사 신경, 재빨리 반응하는 능력 ❏ 그것은 운동선수의 굉장한 기술과 담대함, 그리고 반사 신경을 요구한다.

❶ 가산명사 또는 불가산명사 개혁 ❏ 그 정당은 경제 개혁 프로그램에 착수했다. ❷ 타동사 개혁하다 ❏ 국가 경제를 개혁하려는 그의 계획 ❸ 타동사/자동사 교화시키다; 교화되다 ❏ 자신의 법정 소송 사건이 언급되자, 제임스는 교화되기로 약속했다. ● 교화된 형용사 ❏ 교화된 알코올 중독자

가산명사 개혁가 ❏ 어떻게 그가 동시에 개혁가이자 기득권의 수호자일 수가 있는가?

❶ 자동사 자제하다 ❏ 하디 부인은 어떠한 논평을 하는 것도 자제했다. ❷ 가산명사 후렴 ❏ 옛 노래의 후렴 ❸ 가산명사 흔히 반복되는 말 ❏ 로사가 끊임없이 반복하는 말은 자기에겐 삶이 없다는 것이다.

❶ 타동사 개운하게 하다, 원기를 회복시키다 ❏ 그 로션을 피부에 바르면 시원하고 개운한 느낌이 든다. ● 상쾌한 형용사 ❏ 그는 깨어났을 때 기분이 아주 상쾌했다. ❷ 타동사 새롭게 하다 ❏ 많은 사람들은 이런 모임들을 의견을 나누고 우정을 새롭게 다지는 기회라고 여긴다. ❸ 타동사 (기억을) 되살리다 ❏ 그는 그 건물에 대한 기억을 되살리기 위해 길 반대편으로 걸었다. ❹ 타동사 (웹페이지를) 새로 고치다 [컴퓨터] ❏ 사이트를 새로 고쳐서 최신 페이지를 보이고자 할 때는 웹브라우저의 '새로 고침' 버튼을 누르세요.

가산명사 재교육 과정

❶ 형용사 참신한 ❏ 누군가가 상식을 말하는 것을 들으니 참신했다. ● 참신하게 부사 ❏ 그는 참신하게도 정직했다. ❷ 형용사 기운을 돋우는, 상쾌한 ❏ 허브는 수세기 동안 기운을 돋우는 음료를 만드는 데 쓰이고 있다.

❶ 복수명사 다과, 간단한 먹을거리 ❏ 점심 식사와 다과가 제공됩니다. ❷ 불가산명사 다과 [격식체] ❏ 다과 좀 드시겠어요?

타동사 냉장 보관하다 ❏ 가루반죽을 밤새 냉장 보관하세요.

가산명사 냉장고

[영국영어, 미국영어 가끔 refuelling, refuelled] 타동사/자동사 연료를 보충받다; 연료를 보충하다

refuels it, it is filled with more fuel so that it can continue its journey. ❑ *His plane stopped in France to refuel.* ● **re·fu·el·ing** N-UNCOUNT ❑ *...nighttime refueling of vehicles.*

❑ 그가 탄 비행기가 연료를 보충하기 위해 프랑스에 기착했다. ● 연료 보충 불가산명사 ❑ 차량의 야간 연료 보충

ref·uge /rɛfyudʒ/ (refuges) **1** N-UNCOUNT If you take **refuge** somewhere, you try to protect yourself from physical harm by going there. ❑ *They took refuge in a bomb shelter.* **2** N-COUNT A **refuge** is a place where you go for safety and protection, for example from violence or from bad weather. ❑ *Eventually Suzanne fled to a refuge for battered women.* **3** N-UNCOUNT If you take **refuge in** a particular way of behaving or thinking, you try to protect yourself from unhappiness or unpleasantness by behaving or thinking in that way. ❑ *All too often, they get bored, and seek refuge in drink and drugs.*

1 불가산명사 피난, 피신 ❑ 그들은 방공호로 피신했다. **2** 가산명사 보호소, 피신처 ❑ 결국 수잰은 매 맞는 여성들을 위한 보호소로 피했다. **3** 불가산명사 위안 ❑ 그들은 너무 자주 따분해하며 술과 마약에서 위안을 구한다.

ref·u·gee ♦♦◇ /rɛfyudʒi/ (refugees) N-COUNT **Refugees** are people who have been forced to leave their homes or their country, either because there is a war there or because of their political or religious beliefs. ❑ *...a political refugee from Cameroon.*

가산명사 난민, 망명자 ❑ 카메룬에서 온 정치적 망명자

re·fund (refunds, refunding, refunded)

The noun is pronounced /riˈfʌnd/. The verb is pronounced /rɪˈfʌnd/.

명사는 /riˈfʌnd /로 발음되고, 동사는 /rɪˈfʌnd /로 발음된다.

1 N-COUNT A **refund** is a sum of money which is returned to you, for example because you have paid too much or because you have returned goods to a store. ❑ *Face it - you'll just have to take those cowboy boots back and ask for a refund.* **2** V-T If someone **refunds** your money, they return it to you, for example because you have paid too much or because you have returned goods to a store. ❑ *We guarantee to refund your money if you're not delighted with your purchase.*

1 가산명사 환불 ❑ 현실을 직시하세요. 당신은 그냥 그 카우보이 장화를 돌려주고 환불해 달라고 해야 하는 거예요. **2** 타동사 환불하다 ❑ 구매하신 물품이 맘에 안 드신다면 환불을 보장합니다.

Thesaurus *refund의 참조어*

| N. | payment, reimbursement **1** |
| V. | give back, pay back, reimburse **2** |

---

re·fund·able /rɪˈfʌndəbəl/ ADJ A **refundable** payment will be paid back to you in certain circumstances. ❑ *A refundable deposit is payable on arrival.*

형용사 반환 가능한 ❑ 반환 가능한 예치금은 도착하는 대로 지불해 드립니다.

re·fur·bish /rɪˈfɜrbɪʃ/ (refurbishes, refurbishing, refurbished) V-T To **refurbish** a building or room means to clean it and decorate it and make it more attractive or better equipped. ❑ *We have spent money on refurbishing the offices.*

타동사 개장(改裝)하다, 새로 꾸미다 ❑ 우리는 비용을 들여 사무실을 개장했다.

re·fus·al /rɪˈfyuzəl/ (refusals) **1** N-VAR Someone's **refusal to** do something is the fact of them showing or saying that they will not do it, allow it, or accept it. ❑ *Her country suffered through her refusal to accept change.* **2** PHRASE If someone has **first refusal** on something that is being sold or offered, they have the right to decide whether or not to buy it or take it before it is offered to anyone else. ❑ *A tenant may have a right of first refusal if a property is offered for sale.*

1 가산명사 또는 불가산명사 거부, 거절 ❑ 그녀의 국가는 그녀가 변화를 거부함으로써 어려움을 겪었다. **2** 구 제1선매권 ❑ 부동산이 매물로 나오면 세입자가 제1선매권을 가질 수 있다.

re·fuse ♦♦◇ (refuses, refusing, refused)

The verb is pronounced /rɪˈfyuz/. The noun is pronounced /rɛfyus/ and is hyphenated ref·use.

동사는 /rɪˈfyuz /로 발음되고, 명사는 /rɛfyus /로 발음되고, ref·use로 분철된다.

1 V-T/V-I If you **refuse** to do something, you deliberately do not do it, or you say firmly that you will not do it. ❑ *He refused to comment after the trial.* **2** V-T If someone **refuses** you something, they do not give it to you or do not allow you to have it. ❑ *The United States has refused him a visa.* **3** V-T If you **refuse** something that is offered to you, you do not accept it. ❑ *The patient has the right to refuse treatment.* **4** N-UNCOUNT **Refuse** consists of the trash and all the things that are not wanted in a house, store, or factory, and that are regularly thrown away; used mainly in official language. ❑ *The District Council made a weekly collection of refuse.*

1 타동사/자동사 거절하다 ❑ 그는 재판 후 논평하기를 거절했다. **2** 타동사 거부하다 ❑ 미국은 그에게 비자 발급을 거부했다. **3** 타동사 거부하다 ❑ 환자는 치료를 거부할 권리가 있다. **4** 불가산명사 쓰레기 ❑ 그 지방 자치구가 일주일 단위로 쓰레기를 수집했다.

Do not confuse **refuse** and **deny**. If you **refuse** to do something, you deliberately do not do it, or you say firmly that you will not do it. ❑ *...people who refuse to change their opinions... He refused to condemn them.* You can **refuse** something that someone offers you. ❑ *The patient has the right to refuse treatment.* If someone does not allow you to have what you ask for, or to do something you have asked to do, you can say that they **refuse** you. ❑ *He can run to Dad for money if I refuse him.* If you **deny** something, you say that it is not true. ❑ *The allegation was denied by government spokesmen.* If someone **denies** you something, they do not allow you to have it. ❑ *I never denied her anything.*

refuse와 deny를 혼동하지 않도록 하라. 무엇을 하는 것을 refuse하면, 의도적으로 그것을 하지 않거나 그것을 하지 않겠다고 확고하게 말하는 것이다. ❑ ...자기의 의견을 바꾸기를 거부하는 사람들... 그는 그들을 비난하기를 거부했다. 누가 당신에게 제공하는 것을 refuse할 수도 있다. ❑ 환자는 치료를 거부할 권리가 있다. 누가 당신이 요청하는 것을 갖도록 허락하지 않거나, 하겠다고 요청하는 것을 하도록 허락하지 않으면, 그 사람이 당신을 refuse한다고 말할 수 있다. ❑ 내가 그에게 거절하면 그는 아빠에게 돈을 얻으러 달려갈 수 있다. 무엇을 deny하면, 그것이 사실이 아니라고 말하는 것이다. ❑ 그 주장은 정부 대변인들에 의해 부인되었다. 누가 당신에게 무엇을 deny하면, 당신이 그것을 갖도록 허락하지 않는 것이다. ❑ 나는 결코 그녀에게 어떤 것도 거절하지 않았다.

Thesaurus *refuse의 참조어*

| V. | decline, reject, turn down; (ant.) accept **1** **3** |
| N. | garbage, rubbish, trash **4** |

Word Partnership *refuse의 연어*

V.	refuse **to answer**, refuse **to cooperate**, refuse **to go**, refuse **to participate**, refuse **to pay** **1**
	refuse **to allow**, refuse **to give** **1** **2**
	refuse **to accept** **1** **3**

---

re·fute /rɪˈfyut/ (refutes, refuting, refuted) **1** V-T If you **refute** an argument, accusation, or theory, you prove that it is wrong or untrue. [FORMAL] ❑ *It was the kind of rumor that it is impossible to refute.* **2** V-T If you **refute** an argument or accusation, you say that it is not true. [FORMAL] ❑ *Isabelle is quick to refute any suggestion of intellectual snobbery.*

1 타동사 반박하다 [격식체] ❑ 그것은 반박이 불가능한 그런 종류의 소문이었다. **2** 타동사 이의를 제기하다 [격식체] ❑ 이사벨은 지적인 속물근성이 조금이라도 언급될까 봐 재빠르게 이의를 제기한다.

re·gain /rɪˈɡeɪn/ (regains, regaining, regained) V-T If you **regain** something that you have lost, you get it back again. ❑ *Troops have regained control of the city.*

타동사 되찾다 ❑ 군대는 그 도시를 다시 장악했다.

re|gal /ˈriːgᵊl/ ADJ If you describe something as **regal**, you mean that it is suitable for a king or queen, because it is very impressive or beautiful. ❑ *He sat with such regal dignity.*

형용사 왕다운, 왕에 걸맞은 ❑ 그는 가히 왕에 걸맞은 위엄을 갖추고 앉아 있었다.

re|gard ◆◇◇ /rɪˈgɑːrd/ (regards, regarding, regarded) **1** V-T If you **regard** someone or something **as** being a particular thing or **as** having a particular quality, you believe that they are that thing or have that quality. ❑ *He was regarded as the most successful Chancellor of modern times.* **2** V-T If you **regard** something or someone **with** a feeling such as dislike or respect, you have that feeling about them. ❑ *He regarded drug dealers with loathing.* **3** N-UNCOUNT If you have **regard for** someone or something, you respect them and care about them. If you hold someone in high **regard**, you have a lot of respect for them. ❑ *I have a very high regard for him and what he has achieved.* **4** N-PLURAL **Regards** are greetings. You use **regards** in expressions such as **best regards** and **with kind regards** as a way of expressing friendly feelings toward someone, especially in a letter. [FORMULAE] ❑ *Give my regards to your family.* **5** PHRASE You can use **as regards** to indicate the subject that is being talked or written about. ❑ *As regards the war, Haig believed in victory at any price.* **6** PHRASE You can use **with regard to** or **in regard to** to indicate the subject that is being talked or written about. ❑ *The department is reviewing its policy with regard to immunization.*

1 타동사 여기다, 간주하다 ❑ 그는 현시대의 가장 성공한 재무 장관으로 여겨졌다. **2** 타동사 (-한 감정으로) 대하다, 보다 ❑ 그는 마약 판매상들을 혐오스럽다고 여겼다. **3** 불가산명사 존경, 배려 ❑ 나는 그와 그가 이룬 업적을 매우 존경한다. **4** 복수명사 안부; 안녕히 계십시오 (편지 끝맺음 인사) [의례적인 표현] ❑ 가족들께 안부 전해 주세요. **5** 구 -에 대해 ❑ 그 전쟁에 대해 헤이그는 어떠한 희생을 치러서라도 승리한다고 믿었다. **6** 구 -에 관하여 ❑ 그 부서는 면역 조치에 관한 자체 정책을 검토 중이다.

Word Partnership   *regard의 연어*

PREP.	regard **as** **1**
	regard **with** **2**
	regard **for** **3**
	in/with regard to, **with/without** regard **6**

---

re|gard|ing /rɪˈgɑːrdɪŋ/ PREP You can use **regarding** to indicate the subject that is being talked or written about. ❑ *He refused to divulge any information regarding the man's whereabouts.*

전치사 -에 관하여 ❑ 그는 그 남자의 행방에 대해 어떤 정보도 발설하기를 거부했다.

re|gard|less /rɪˈgɑːrdlɪs/ **1** PHRASE If something happens **regardless of** something else, it is not affected or influenced at all by that other thing. ❑ *It takes in anybody regardless of religion, color, or creed.* **2** ADV If you say that someone did something **regardless**, you mean that they did it even though there were problems or factors that could have stopped them, or perhaps should have stopped them. [ADV after v] ❑ *Despite her recent surgery she has been carrying on regardless.*

1 구 -에 관계없이 ❑ 그곳은 종교, 피부색, 신념에 관계없이 누구나 받아들인다. **2** 부사 개의치 않고 ❑ 최근에 수술을 받았음에도 그녀는 개의치 않고 일을 계속 해 나가고 있다.

re|gen|er|ate /rɪˈdʒɛnəreɪt/ (regenerates, regenerating, regenerated) **1** V-T To **regenerate** something means to develop and improve it to make it more active, successful, or important, especially after a period when it has been getting worse. ❑ *The government will continue to try to regenerate inner city areas.* ● **re|gen|era|tion** /rɪˌdʒɛnəreɪˈʃᵊn/ N-UNCOUNT ❑ *...the physical and economic regeneration of the area.* **2** V-T/V-I If organs or tissues **regenerate** or if something **regenerates** them, they heal and grow again after they have been damaged. ❑ *Nerve cells have limited ability to regenerate if destroyed.* ● **re|gen|era|tion** N-UNCOUNT ❑ *Vitamin B assists in red-blood-cell regeneration.*

1 타동사 재건하다, 재생하다 ❑ 정부는 도시 저소득층 지역을 재건하기 위해 계속 노력할 것이다. ● 재건, 쇄신 불가산명사 ❑ 그 지역의 물질적·경제적 재건 **2** 타동사/자동사 재생되다; 재생시키다 ❑ 신경 세포는 손상 시 재생 능력이 제한되어 있다. ● 재생 불가산명사 ❑ 비타민 비(B)는 적혈구 재생에 도움이 된다.

reg|gae /ˈrɛgeɪ/ N-UNCOUNT **Reggae** is a kind of West Indian popular music with a very strong beat. ❑ *Many people will remember Bob Marley for providing them with their first taste of reggae music.*

불가산명사 레게 ❑ 많은 사람들은 밥 말리를 레게 음악이 무엇인지 처음 알게 해 준 사람으로 기억할 것이다.

re|gime ◆◇◇ /rəˈʒiːm, reɪ-/ (regimes) **1** N-COUNT If you refer to a government or system of running a country as a **regime**, you are critical of it because you think it is not democratic and uses unacceptable methods. [DISAPPROVAL] ❑ *...the collapse of the Fascist regime at the end of the war.* **2** N-COUNT A **regime** is the way that something such as an institution, company, or economy is run, especially when it involves tough or severe action. ❑ *The authorities moved him to the less rigid regime of an open prison.* **3** N-COUNT A **regime** is a set of rules about food, exercise, or beauty that some people follow in order to stay healthy or attractive. ❑ *He has a new fitness regime to strengthen his back.*

1 가산명사 정권 [탐탁찮음] ❑ 전쟁 종식에 따른 파시스트 정권의 몰락 **2** 가산명사 체제 ❑ 당국은 그를 관리 체제가 덜 엄격한 개방 교도소로 이송했다. **3** 가산명사 수칙 ❑ 그는 허리를 강화시키기 위한 새로운 건강 수칙을 가지고 있다.

regi|ment /ˈrɛdʒɪmənt/ (regiments) **1** N-COUNT A **regiment** is a large group of soldiers that is commanded by a colonel. **2** N-COUNT A **regiment of** people is a large number of them. ❑ *...robust food, good enough to satisfy a regiment of hungry customers.*

1 가산명사 연대 **2** 가산명사 수많은 ❑ 허기에 지친 수많은 손님들을 충분히 만족시킬 수 있는 맛있는 음식

regi|men|tal /ˌrɛdʒɪˈmɛntᵊl/ ADJ **Regimental** means belonging to a particular regiment. [ADJ n] ❑ *Mills was regimental colonel.*

형용사 연대의 ❑ 밀스는 연대장이었다.

re|gion ◆◆◇ /ˈriːdʒᵊn/ (regions) **1** N-COUNT A **region** is a large area of land that is different from other areas of land, for example because it is one of the different parts of a country with its own customs and characteristics, or because it has a particular geographical feature. ❑ *...Barcelona, capital of the autonomous region of Catalonia.* **2** N-PLURAL **The regions** are the parts of a country that are not the capital city and its surrounding area. [BRIT] ❑ *...London and the regions.* **3** N-COUNT You can refer to a part of your body as a **region**. ❑ *...the pelvic region.* **4** PHRASE You say **in the region of** to indicate that an amount that you are stating is approximate. [VAGUENESS] ❑ *The scheme will cost in the region of six million dollars.*

1 가산명사 지역 ❑ 카탈로니아 자치 지역의 수도인 바르셀로나 **2** 복수명사 지방 [영국영어] ❑ 런던과 지방 **3** 가산명사 (신체) 부위 ❑ 골반부 **4** 구 약 [짐작투] ❑ 그 계획에는 6백만 달러 정도가 소요될 것이다.

re|gion|al ◆◆◇ /ˈriːdʒᵊnᵊl/ ADJ **Regional** is used to describe things which relate to a particular area of a country or of the world. ❑ *...the autonomous regional government of Andalucia.*

형용사 지역의, 지방의 ❑ 자치 지역 정부인 안달루시아

reg|is|ter ◆◆◇ /ˈrɛdʒɪstər/ (registers, registering, registered) **1** N-COUNT A **register** is an official list or record of people or things. ❑ *...registers of births, deaths and marriages.* **2** V-T/V-I If you **register** to do something, you put your name on an official list, in order to be able to do that thing or to receive a service. ❑ *Have you come to register at the school?* ❑ *Thousands lined up to register to vote.* **3** V-T If you **register** something, such as the name of a person who has just died or information about something you own, you have these facts

1 가산명사 등록부, 기록부 ❑ 출생, 사망, 결혼 기록부 **2** 타동사/자동사 등록하다 ❑ 학교에 등록하러 오셨습니까? 선거인 명부에 등록하기 위해 수천 명이 줄을 섰다. **3** 타동사 신고하다, 신고하다 ❑ 일본에서 차량 등록은 소유자가 주차 공간을 확보해야만 가능하다. **4** 타동사/자동사 (저울 등에) 나타나다 ❑ 그것은 정교한 엑스레이 장비에만 나타날 것이다.

recorded on an official list. ❑ *In order to register a car in Japan, the owner must have somewhere to park it.* 4 V-T/V-I When something **registers on** a scale or measuring instrument, it shows on the scale or instrument. ❑ *It will only register on sophisticated X-ray equipment.* 5 V-T If you **register** your feelings or opinions about something, you do something that makes them clear to other people. ❑ *Voters wish to register their dissatisfaction with the ruling party.* 6 V-I If a feeling **registers on** someone's face, their expression shows clearly that they have that feeling. ❑ *Surprise again registered on Rodney's face.* 7 V-T/V-I If a piece of information does not **register** or if you do not **register** it, you do not really pay attention to it, and so you do not remember it or react to it. ❑ *It wasn't that she couldn't hear me, it was just that what I said sometimes didn't register in her brain.* 8 →see also **cash register**

5 타동사 (감정 등을) 나타내다 ❑ 유권자들은 여당에 대한 자신들의 불만을 나타내기를 바란다. 6 자동사 (감정이) 확연히 드러나다 ❑ 놀라운 표정이 다시 한 번 로드니의 얼굴에 확연히 드러났다. 7 타동사/자동사 마음에 새겨지다; 명심하다 ❑ 그녀가 내 말을 들을 수 없었던 것이 아니라, 내가 한 말이 때때로 그녀 머릿속에 새겨지지 않았을 뿐이야.

Word Partnership *register*의 연어

N. **voters** register 1
V. register **to vote** 2

reg|is|trar /rɛ̲dʒɪstrɑr, BRIT re̲dʒɪstrɑːʳ/ (**registrars**) 1 N-COUNT In Britain, a **registrar** is a person whose job is to keep official records, especially of births, marriages, and deaths. 2 N-COUNT A **registrar** is an administrative official in a college or university who is responsible for student records.

1 가산명사 기록원, 등기관 2 가산명사 학적 담당자

reg|is|tra|tion /rɛ̲dʒɪstreɪʃᵊn/ (**registrations**) N-UNCOUNT The **registration** of something such as a person's name or the details of an event is the recording of it in an official list. ❑ *They have campaigned strongly for compulsory registration of dogs.*

불가산명사 등록 ❑ 그들은 애완견 의무 등록 운동을 강력히 펴 오고 있다.

reg|is|tra|tion num|ber (**registration numbers**) N-COUNT The **registration number** or the **registration** of a car or other road vehicle is the series of letters and numbers that are shown at the front and back of it. [BRIT; AM **license number**] ❑ *Another driver managed to get the registration number of the car.*

가산명사 (차량의) 등록 번호 [영국영어; 미국영어 license number] ❑ 또 다른 운전자가 그 차의 등록 번호를 용케 알아냈다.

reg|is|try /rɛ̲dʒɪstri/ (**registries**) N-COUNT A **registry** is a collection of all the official records relating to something, or the place where they are kept. ❑ *There is no international registry of stolen art.*

가산명사 기록, 등기; 등록소 ❑ 도난 미술품에 대한 국제 등록소가 없다.

re|gress /rɪgrɛ̲s/ (**regresses, regressing, regressed**) V-I When people or things **regress**, they return to an earlier and less advanced stage of development. [FORMAL] ❑ *If your child regresses to babyish behavior, all you know for certain is that the child is under stress.* ● **re|gres|sion** /rɪgrɛ̲ʃᵊn/ (**regressions**) N-VAR ❑ *Calderdale accepts that this can cause regression in a pupil's learning process.*

자동사 퇴보하다, 퇴행하다 [격식체] ❑ 만약 여러분의 아이가 유아기 행동으로 퇴행한다면 분명히 아셔야 할 사실은 아이가 스트레스를 받고 있다는 것입니다. ● 퇴행, 퇴보 가산명사 또는 불가산명사 ❑ 칼더데일은 이것이 학생의 학습 과정에 퇴행을 초래할 수 있다는 것을 인정한다.

re|gret ♦◇◇ /rɪgrɛ̲t/ (**regrets, regretting, regretted**) 1 V-T If you **regret** something that you have done, you wish that you had not done it. ❑ *I simply gave in to him, and I've regretted it ever since.* ❑ *Ellis seemed to be regretting that he had asked the question.* 2 N-VAR **Regret** is a feeling of sadness or disappointment, which is caused by something that has happened or something that you have done or not done. ❑ *Lillee said he had no regrets about retiring.* 3 V-T You can say that you **regret** something as a polite way of saying that you are sorry about it. You use expressions such as **I regret to say** or **I regret to inform you** to show that you are sorry about something. [POLITENESS] ❑ *"I very much regret the injuries he sustained," he said.* ❑ *I regret that the United States has added its voice to such protests.*

1 타동사 후회하다 ❑ 나는 간단히 그에게 굴복했는데 그 후로 내내 후회하고 있다. ❑ 엘리스는 그 질문을 한 것에 대해 후회하고 있는 것 같았다. 2 가산명사 또는 불가산명사 후회 ❑ 릴리는 퇴직에 대해 전혀 후회하지 않는다고 말했다. 3 타동사 유감스럽게 생각하다; 유감스럽지만 -입니다 [공손체] ❑ "그분이 부상을 입은 것을 매우 유감스럽게 생각합니다."라고 그가 말했다. ❑ 나는 미국이 그런 항변에 가담한 것에 대해 유감스럽게 생각한다.

Word Partnership *regret*의 연어

V. **come to** regret 1
express regret 2
N. regret **a decision** 1
regret **a loss** 3

re|gret|table /rɪgrɛ̲təbᵊl/ ADJ You describe something as **regrettable** when you think that it is bad and that it should not happen or have happened. [FORMAL, FEELINGS] ❑ *The army said it had started an investigation into what it described as a regrettable incident.* ● **re|gret|tably** ADV ❑ *Regrettably we could find no sign of the man and the search was terminated.*

형용사 유감스러운 [격식체, 감정 개입] ❑ 육군은 스스로 유감스럽다고 말한 사건에 대해 조사를 착수했다고 발표했다. ● 유감스럽게 부사 ❑ 유감스럽게도 우리는 그 남자의 흔적을 찾을 수 없었고 수색은 종결되었다.

re|group /rigru̲p/ (**regroups, regrouping, regrouped**) V-T/V-I When people, especially soldiers, **regroup**, or when someone **regroups** them, they form an organized group again, in order to continue fighting. ❑ *Now the rebel army has regrouped and reorganized.*

타동사/자동사 재편성되다; 재편성하다 ❑ 반군은 이제 재편성되고 재조직되었다.

regu|lar ♦♦◇ /rɛ̲gyələr/ (**regulars**) 1 ADJ **Regular** events have equal amounts of time between them, so that they happen, for example, at the same time each day or each week. ❑ *Take regular exercise.* ❑ *We're going to be meeting there on a regular basis.* ● **regu|lar|ly** ADV [ADV with v] ❑ *He also writes regularly for "International Management" magazine.* ● **regu|lar|ity** /rɛ̲gyʊlæ̲rɪti/ N-UNCOUNT ❑ *The overdraft arrangements had been generous because of the regularity of the half-yearly payments.* 2 ADJ **Regular** events happen often. ❑ *Although it may look unpleasant, this condition is harmless, and usually clears up with regular shampooing.* ● **regu|lar|ly** ADV [ADV with v] ❑ *Fox, badger, weasel, and stoat are regularly seen here.* ● **regu|lar|ity** N-UNCOUNT ❑ *Closures and job losses are again being announced with monotonous regularity.* 3 ADJ If you are, for example, a **regular** customer at a store or a **regular** visitor to a place, you go there often. [ADJ n] ❑ *She has become a regular visitor to Houghton Hall.* 4 N-COUNT The **regulars** at a place or in a team are the people who often go to the place or are often in the team. ❑ *Regulars at his local pub have set up a fund to help out.* 5 ADJ You use **regular** when referring to the thing, person, time, or place that is usually used by someone. For example, someone's **regular** place is the place where they usually sit. [det ADJ n] ❑ *The man shook his hand and then sat at his regular table near the windows.* 6 ADJ A **regular**

1 형용사 규칙적인, 정기적인 ❑ 규칙적으로 운동을 하세요. ❑ 우리는 그곳에서 정기적으로 만날 것이다. ● 규칙적으로, 정기적으로 부사 ❑ 그는 또한 정기적으로 '인터내셔널 매니지먼트' 잡지에 기고한다. ● 규칙성 불가산명사 ❑ 초과 인출 제도는 관대해서 규칙적으로 연 2회 상환하게 되어 있었다. 2 형용사 자주 일어나는 ❑ 이러한 증상은 불쾌해 보이겠지만, 인체에 무해하며 자주 머리를 감으면 대개의 경우에는 깨끗해집니다. ● 자주 부사 ❑ 이곳에서는 여우와 오소리, 그리고 족제비와 담비가 자주 보인다. ● 주기적임 불가산명사 ❑ 직장 폐쇄와 실직이 또 다시 일상적인 주기로 발표되고 있다. 3 형용사 단골의 ❑ 그녀는 하우톤 홀의 단골손님이 되었다. 4 가산명사 단골 ❑ 그의 지역 술집 단골들이 그를 돕고자 자금을 조성했다. 5 형용사 평소의 ❑ 그 남자는 그와 악수를 하고 나서 평소에 앉는 창가 쪽 의자에 앉았다. 6 형용사 규칙적인 ❑ 매우 규칙적인 박자 ● 규칙적으로 부사 ❑ 규칙적으로 호흡하는 것을

rhythm consists of a series of sounds or movements with equal periods of time between them. □ *...a very regular beat.* ● **regu|lar|ly** ADV [ADV with v] □ *Remember to breathe regularly.* ● **regu|lar|ity** N-UNCOUNT □ *Experimenters have succeeded in controlling the rate and regularity of the heartbeat.* ▨ ADJ **Regular** is used to mean "normal." [mainly AM] [ADJ n] □ *The product looks and burns like a regular cigarette.* ▩ ADJ In some restaurants, a **regular** drink or quantity of food is of medium size. [mainly AM] [ADJ n] □ *...a cheeseburger and regular fries.* ▪ ADJ A **regular** pattern or arrangement consists of a series of things with equal spaces between them. □ *...strange small rounded sandy hillocks, that look as if they've been scattered in a regular pattern on the ground.* ▫ ADJ If something has a **regular** shape, both halves are the same and it has straight edges or a smooth outline. □ *...some regular rounded shape.* ● **regu|lar|ity** N-UNCOUNT □ *...the chessboard regularity of their fields.* ⬛ ADJ In grammar, a **regular** verb, noun, or adjective inflects in the same way as most verbs, nouns, or adjectives in the language.

명심하세요. ● 규칙성 불가산명사 □ 실험자들은 심장 박동률의 횟수와 규칙성을 조절하는 데 성공했다. ▨ 형용사 보통의 [주로 미국영어] □ 그 제품은 생김새나 타는 것이 보통 담배같다. ▩ 형용사 중간 크기의 [주로 미국영어] □ 치즈버거 하나와 중간 크기의 감자튀김 ▪ 형용사 일정하게 반복되는 □ 땅 위에 일정한 모양으로 흩어 놓은 것처럼 보이는 작은 둥근 모양의 이상한 모래 언덕들 ▫ 형용사 규칙적인 모양을 한, 둥변 등거의 □ 어떤 규칙적인 모양을 띤 기하학적 형태 ● 규칙적인 모양을 함 불가산명사 □ 서양장기판같이 규칙적인 모양을 한 그들의 경작지 ⬛ 형용사 규칙적인

Word Partnership regular의 연어

N.   regular **basis**, regular **checkups**, regular **exercise**, regular
     meetings, regular **schedule**, regular **visits** ▣ ▤
     regular **customer**, regular **visitor** ▥
     regular **guy**, regular **hours**, regular **mail**, regular **season** ▨
     regular **verbs** ⬛

regu|late /rɛɡyəleɪt/ (**regulates, regulating, regulated**) V-T To **regulate** an activity or process means to control it, especially by means of rules. □ *The powers of the European Commission to regulate competition are increasing.*

타동사 규제하다 □ 경쟁을 규제하는 유럽 위원회의 힘이 증가하고 있다.

regu|la|tion ♦◇◇ /rɛɡyəleɪʃⁿn/ (**regulations**) ▣ N-COUNT **Regulations** are rules made by a government or other authority in order to control the way something is done or the way people behave. □ *The European Union has proposed new regulations to control the hours worked by its employees.* ▤ N-UNCOUNT **Regulation** is the controlling of an activity or process, usually by means of rules. □ *Some in the market now want government regulation in order to reduce costs.* →see **factory**

▣ 가산명사 규정 □ 유럽 연합은 자체 직원들의 근무 시간을 관리하기 위해 새 규정을 제안했다. ▤ 불가산명사 규제 □ 시장 일각에서는 이제 비용 절감을 위해 정부 규제를 원하고 있다.

Word Partnership regulation의 연어

ADJ.   **new** regulation ▣
     federal regulation, **financial** regulation, **strict** regulation ▣ ▤
N.   **banking** regulation, **government** regulation,
     industry regulation ▣ ▤

regu|la|tor ♦◇◇ /rɛɡyəleɪtər/ (**regulators**) N-COUNT A **regulator** is a person or organization appointed by a government to regulate an area of activity such as banking or industry. □ *An independent regulator will be appointed to ensure fair competition.* ● **regu|la|tory** /rɛɡyələtɔːri, BRIT rɛɡyʊleɪtəri/ ADJ [ADJ n] □ *...the UK's financial regulatory system.*

가산명사 규제자, 규제 기관 □ 공정한 경쟁을 보장하기 위해 독립된 규제 기관이 정해질 것이다. ● 규제하는 형용사 □ 영국의 금융 규제 제도

re|hab /riːhæb/ N-UNCOUNT **Rehab** is the process of helping someone to lead a normal life again after they have been ill, or when they have had a drug or alcohol problem. **Rehab** is short for **rehabilitation**. [INFORMAL] □ *...a hospital rehab program.*

불가산명사 갱생, 재활 (rehabilitation의 축약형) [비격식체] □ 병원 내 재활 프로그램

re|ha|bili|tate /riːhəbɪlɪteɪt/ (**rehabilitates, rehabilitating, rehabilitated**) V-T To **rehabilitate** someone who has been ill or in prison means to help them to live a normal life again. To **rehabilitate** someone who has a drug or alcohol problem means to help them stop using drugs or alcohol. □ *Considerable efforts have been made to rehabilitate patients who have suffered in this way.* ● **re|ha|bili|ta|tion** /riːhəbɪlɪteɪʃⁿn/ N-UNCOUNT □ *A number of other techniques are now being used by psychologists in the rehabilitation of young offenders.*

타동사 재활시키다, 갱생시키다 □ 이러한 고생을 하는 환자들을 재활시키도록 상당한 노력이 기울여졌다. ● 재활, 갱생 불가산명사 □ 요즘에는 심리학자들이 미성년 범법자들의 갱생을 위해 다른 수많은 기술들을 사용하고 있다.

re|hears|al /rɪhɜːrsⁿl/ (**rehearsals**) ▣ N-VAR A **rehearsal** of a play, dance, or piece of music is a practice of it in preparation for a performance. □ *The band was scheduled to begin rehearsals for a concert tour.* →see also **dress rehearsal** ▤ N-COUNT You can describe an event or object which is a preparation for a more important event or object as a **rehearsal for** it. □ *Daydreams may seem to be rehearsals for real-life situations, but we know they are not.*

▣ 가산명사 또는 불가산명사 예행연습, 리허설 □ 그 악단은 콘서트 순회공연을 위한 예행연습을 시작할 예정이었다. ▤ 가산명사 시연 □ 공상이 실제 상황에 대한 시연인 것처럼 보일 수도 있으나, 우리는 그렇지 않다는 것을 알고 있다.

re|hearse /rɪhɜːrs/ (**rehearses, rehearsing, rehearsed**) ▣ V-T/V-I When people **rehearse** a play, dance, or piece of music, they practice it in order to prepare for a performance. □ *In his version, a group of actors are rehearsing a play about Joan of Arc.* □ *Tens of thousands of people have been rehearsing for the opening ceremony in the workers' stadium.* ▤ V-T If you **rehearse** something that you are going to say or do, you silently practice it by imagining that you are saying or doing it. □ *Anticipate any tough questions and rehearse your answers.* →see **memory**

▣ 타동사/자동사 예행연습하다 □ 일단의 배우들이 그가 각색한 잔 다르크에 관한 연극을 예행연습하고 있다. □ 수만 명의 사람들이 근로자 경기장에서 개막식 예행연습을 해 오고 있다. ▤ 타동사 (속으로) 연습하다 □ 곤란할 만한 어떤 질문이든 예상을 해 보고 답할 수 있도록 연습하세요.

reign /reɪn/ (**reigns, reigning, reigned**) ▣ V-I If you say, for example, that silence **reigns** in a place or confusion **reigns** in a situation, you mean that the place is silent or the situation is confused. [WRITTEN] □ *Last night confusion reigned about how the debate, which continues today, would end.* ▤ V-I When a king or queen **reigns**, he or she rules a country. □ *...Henry II, who reigned from 1154 to 1189.* ● N-COUNT **Reign** is also a noun. □ *...Queen Victoria's reign.*

▣ 자동사 가득하다 [문어체] □ 지난밤에는 오늘도 계속되고 있는 이 논쟁이 어떻게 끝날 것인가에 대해 온통 혼란스러웠다. ▤ 자동사 통치하다 □ 1154년에서 1189년까지 통치한 헨리 2세 ● 가산명사 통치 □ 빅토리아 여왕의 통치

re|im|burse /riːɪmbɜːrs/ (**reimburses, reimbursing, reimbursed**) V-T If you **reimburse** someone for something, you pay them back the money that they have spent or lost because of it. [FORMAL] □ *I'll be happy to reimburse you for any expenses you might have incurred.*

타동사 배상하다 [격식체] □ 당신이 지불한 모든 비용을 기꺼이 배상해 드리겠습니다.

re|im|burse|ment /riːɪmbɜːrsmənt/ (**reimbursements**) N-VAR If you receive **reimbursement for** money that you have spent, you get your money back, for

가산명사 또는 불가산명사 배상 [격식체] □ 그녀는 의료비 및 기타 비용에 대한 배상을 요구하고 있다.

example because the money should have been paid by someone else. [FORMAL] ❑ *She is demanding reimbursement for medical and other expenses.*

rein /reɪn/ (**reins, reining, reined**) **1** N-PLURAL **Reins** are the thin leather straps attached around a horse's neck which are used to control the horse. ❑ *Cord held the reins while the stallion tugged and snorted.* **2** N-PLURAL Journalists sometimes use the expression **the reins** or **the reins of power** to refer to the control of a country or organization. ❑ *He indicated he was determined to see the party keep a hold on the reins of power.* **3** PHRASE If you **give free rein to** someone, you give them a lot of freedom to do what they want. ❑ *The government continued to believe it should give free rein to the private sector in transport.* **4** PHRASE If you **keep a tight rein on** someone, you control them firmly. ❑ *Her parents had kept her on a tight rein with their narrow and inflexible views.*

▶**rein back** PHRASAL VERB To **rein back** something such as spending means to control it strictly. ❑ *He promised that between now and the end of the year the government would try to rein back inflation.*

▶**rein in** PHRASAL VERB To **rein in** something means to control it. ❑ *His administration's economic policy would focus on reining in inflation and reducing the budget deficit.*

re|incar|na|tion /riːɪŋkɑːrneɪʃᵊn/ (**reincarnations**) **1** N-UNCOUNT If you believe in **reincarnation**, you believe that you will be reincarnated after you die. ❑ *Many African tribes believe in reincarnation.* **2** N-COUNT A **reincarnation** is a person or animal whose body is believed to contain the spirit of a dead person. ❑ *Another little girl, believed to be the reincarnation of her grandmother, was obsessed with sewing.*

rein|deer /reɪndɪər/

> **Reindeer** is both the singular and the plural form.

N-COUNT A **reindeer** is a deer with large horns called antlers that lives in northern areas of Europe, Asia, and America. ❑ *... a herd of reindeer.*

re|inforce /riːɪnfɔːrs/ (**reinforces, reinforcing, reinforced**) **1** V-T If something **reinforces** a feeling, situation, or process, it makes it stronger or more intense. ❑ *A stronger European Parliament would, they fear, only reinforce the power of the larger countries.* **2** V-T If something **reinforces** an idea or point of view, it provides more evidence or support for it. ❑ *The delegation hopes to reinforce the idea that human rights are not purely internal matters.* **3** V-T To **reinforce** an object means to make it stronger or harder. ❑ *Eventually, they had to reinforce the walls with exterior beams.* **4** V-T To **reinforce** an army or a police force means to make it stronger by increasing its size or providing it with more weapons. To **reinforce** a position or place means to make it stronger by sending more soldiers or weapons. ❑ *Both sides have been reinforcing their positions after yesterday's fierce fighting.*

Word Partnership   reinforce의 연어

N.   reinforce **behaviors** **1**
     reinforce **a belief**, reinforce **a message**, reinforce **a stereotype** **2**

---

re|inforce|ment /riːɪnfɔːrsmənt/ (**reinforcements**) **1** N-PLURAL **Reinforcements** are soldiers or police officers who are sent to join an army or group of police in order to make it stronger. ❑ *Mr. Vlok promised new measures to protect residents, including the despatch of police and troop reinforcements.* **2** N-VAR The **reinforcement** of something is the process of making it stronger. ❑ *I am sure that this meeting will contribute to the reinforcement of peace and security all over the world.*

re|instate /riːɪnsteɪt/ (**reinstates, reinstating, reinstated**) **1** V-T If you **reinstate** someone, you give them back a job or position which had been taken away from them. ❑ *The governor is said to have agreed to reinstate five senior workers who were dismissed.* **2** V-T To **reinstate** a law, facility, or practice means to start having it again. ❑ *She says the public response was a factor in the decision to reinstate the grant.*

re|instate|ment /riːɪnsteɪtmənt/ **1** N-UNCOUNT **Reinstatement** is the act of giving someone back a job or position which has been taken away from them. ❑ *Parents campaigned in vain for her reinstatement.* **2** N-UNCOUNT The **reinstatement** of a law, facility, or practice is the act of causing it to exist again. ❑ *He welcomed the reinstatement of the 10 per cent bank base rate.*

re|it|er|ate /riːɪtəreɪt/ (**reiterates, reiterating, reiterated**) V-T If you **reiterate** something, you say it again, usually in order to emphasize it. [FORMAL, JOURNALISM] ❑ *He reiterated his opposition to the creation of a central bank.*

re|ject ♦♦◇ (**rejects, rejecting, rejected**)

> The verb is pronounced /rɪdʒekt/. The noun is pronounced /riːdʒekt/.

1 V-T If you **reject** something such as a proposal, a request, or an offer, you do not accept it or you do not agree to it. ❑ *The British government is expected to reject the idea of state subsidy for a new high speed railway.* ● **re|jec|tion** /rɪdʒekʃᵊn/ (**rejections**) N-VAR ❑ *The rejection of such initiatives by no means indicates that voters are unconcerned about the environment.* **2** V-T If you **reject** a belief or a political system, you refuse to believe in it or to live by its rules. ❑ *...the children of Eastern European immigrants who had rejected their parents' political and religious beliefs.* ● **re|jec|tion** N-VAR ❑ *His rejection of our values is far more complete than that of D. H. Lawrence.* **3** V-T If someone **is rejected** for a job or course of study, it is not offered to them. ❑ *One of my most able students was rejected by another university.*

---

1 복수명사 고삐 ❑ 종마가 콧김을 내뿜으며 버티는 동안 코드가 고삐를 잡고 있었다. **2** 복수명사 (비유적) 고삐, 통제권 ❑ 그는 그 정당이 정권을 계속 쥐는 것을 보기로 결심했음을 내비쳤다. **3** 구 -에게 자율권을 주다 ❑ 정부는 계속 운송 분야는 민간 기업에게 자율권을 주어야 한다고 믿었다. **4** 구 -을 엄격히 통제하다, -에 대해 고삐를 바짝 쥐다 ❑ 그녀의 부모는 자신들의 편협하고 융통성 없는 시각으로 그녀를 엄격히 통제했다.

구동사 엄격히 통제하다 ❑ 그는 그 순간부터 연말까지 정부가 인플레이션을 엄격히 통제할 것이라고 약속했다.

구동사 통제하다 ❑ 그의 행정부 경제 정책은 인플레이션을 통제하고 예산 적자를 줄이는 데 중점을 둘 것이다.

1 불가산명사 환생 ❑ 많은 아프리카 부족들은 환생을 믿는다. **2** 가산명사 화신 ❑ 할머니의 화신으로 여겨지는 또 다른 작은 소녀는 바느질에 푹 빠져 있었다.

reindeer은 단수형 및 복수형이다.

가산명사 순록 ❑ 순록 무리

1 타동사 강화하다 ❑ 더 강력해진 유럽 의회는 강대국들의 권한만 강화할 것이라고 그들은 우려한다. **2** 타동사 힘을 더하다, 보강하다 ❑ 대표단은 인권이 국내 문제만이 아니라는 인식에 힘을 더하기를 바란다. **3** 타동사 보강하다 ❑ 결국 그들은 외부에 기둥을 세워 벽을 보강해야만 했다. **4** 타동사 보강하다, 증원하다 ❑ 양측 모두 어제 격렬한 전투가 있은 후에 진지를 보강하고 있다.

1 복수명사 증원 병력 ❑ 블록 씨는 주민들의 신변 안전을 위해 경찰 및 군 증원 병력을 포함한 새로운 조치들을 약속했다. **2** 가산명사 또는 불가산명사 강화, 보강 ❑ 나는 이번 회담이 전 세계의 평화와 안보를 강화하는 데 기여할 것이라고 확신한다.

1 타동사 복직시키다 ❑ 주지사가 해고된 고참 근로자 다섯 명의 복직에 동의했다고 한다. **2** 타동사 부활시키다, 원상태로 되돌리다 ❑ 그녀는 여론이 보조금을 부활시키는 결정 요소 중 하나였다고 말한다.

1 불가산명사 복직 ❑ 부모들이 그녀의 복직을 위해 캠페인을 벌였으나 허사였다. **2** 불가산명사 부활 ❑ 그는 10퍼센트의 은행 기준 금리의 부활을 반겼다.

타동사 재차 말하다 [격식체, 언론] ❑ 그는 중앙은행 창설에 대한 자신의 반대 입장을 재차 표명했다.

동사는 /rɪdʒekt/로 발음되고, 명사는 /riːdʒekt/로 발음된다.

1 타동사 거절하다 ❑ 영국 정부는 새 고속 철도를 위한 정부 보조금 안을 거절할 것으로 예상된다. ● 거절 가산명사 또는 불가산명사 ❑ 그러한 발의안의 부결이 결코 유권자들이 환경에 관심이 없다는 것을 의미하지는 않는다. **2** 타동사 거부하다 ❑ 부모들의 정치적·종교적 신념을 거부했던 동유럽 이민자들의 자녀들 ● 거부 가산명사 또는 불가산명사 ❑ 그가 우리들의 가치관을 거부한 것은 디 에이치 로렌스가 거부했던 것보다 훨씬 더 철저하다. **3** 타동사 불합격되다 ❑ 가장 유능한 내 제자들 중 한 명이 또

● re|jec|tion N-COUNT ❑ *Be prepared for lots of rejections before you land a job.* ◢ V-T If someone **rejects** another person who expects affection from them, they are cold and unfriendly toward them. ❑ *...people who had been rejected by their lovers.* ● re|jec|tion N-VAR ❑ *These feelings of rejection and hurt remain.* ● re|jec|tion N-VAR ❑ If a person's body **rejects** something such as a new heart that has been transplanted into it, it tries to attack and destroy it. ❑ *It was feared his body was rejecting a kidney he received in a transplant four years ago.* ● re|jec|tion N-VAR ❑ *...a special drug which stops rejection of transplanted organs.* ◳ N-COUNT A **reject** is a product that has not been accepted for use or sale, because there is something wrong with it. ❑ *The check shirt is a reject - too small.*

다른 대학교에 불합격되었다. ● 불합격 가산명사 ❑ 일자리를 갖게 되기 전에 여러 번 불합격을 당할 각오를 하세요. ◢ 타동사 퇴짜 놓다 ❑ 애인에게 퇴짜를 맞았던 사람들 ● 퇴짜 가산명사 또는 불가산명사 ❑ 퇴짜 맞고 상처받은 이런 감정은 계속 남는다. ◳ 타동사 거부 반응을 보이다 ❑ 그의 몸이 4년 전 이식한 신장에 대해 거부 반응을 보이지 않을까 우려되었다. ● 거부 반응 가산명사 또는 불가산명사 ❑ 이식 장기의 거부 반응을 중단시키는 특수한 약 ◳ 가산명사 불량품 ❑ 그 체크무늬 셔츠는 불량품이야. 너무 작아.

Thesaurus   reject의 참조어

v.   decline, refuse, turn down; *(ant.)* accept ❶ ❸

Word Partnership   reject의 연어

v.   **vote to** reject ❶
N.   reject **an offer**, reject **a plan**, reject **a proposal**, **voters** reject ❶
reject **an idea** ❶ ❷
reject **an application** ❸

---

re|joice /rɪdʒɔɪs/ (**rejoices, rejoicing, rejoiced**) V-T/V-I If you **rejoice**, you are very pleased about something and you show it in your behavior. ❑ *Garbo plays the Queen, rejoicing in the love she has found in Antonio.* ● re|joic|ing N-UNCOUNT ❑ *There was general rejoicing at the news.*

타동사/자동사 크게 기뻐하다 ❑ 가르보가 안토니오와 사랑에 빠져 기뻐하는 여왕 역을 연기한다. ● 기쁨 불가산명사 ❑ 사람들은 대체로 그 소식에 기뻐했다.

re|ju|ve|nate /rɪdʒuvəneɪt/ (**rejuvenates, rejuvenating, rejuvenated**) ❶ V-T If something **rejuvenates** you, it makes you feel or look young again. ❑ *Shelley was advised that the Italian climate would rejuvenate him.* ❷ V-T If you **rejuvenate** an organization or system, you make it more lively and more efficient, for example by introducing new ideas. ❑ *The government pushed through schemes to rejuvenate the inner cities.*

❶ 타동사 활력을 주다 ❑ 설리는 이탈리아 기후가 그에게 활력을 줄 것이라는 조언을 들었다. ❷ 타동사 활성화하다 ❑ 정부는 도심 저소득 지역의 활성화 방안을 관철시켰다.

re|kin|dle /rikɪndᵊl/ (**rekindles, rekindling, rekindled**) ❶ V-T If something **rekindles** an interest, feeling, or thought that you used to have, it makes you think about it or feel about it again. ❑ *Ben Brantley's article on Sir Ian McKellen rekindled many memories.* ❷ V-T If something **rekindles** an unpleasant situation, it makes the unpleasant situation happen again. ❑ *There are fears that the series could rekindle animosity between the two countries.*

❶ 타동사 되살아나게 하다 ❑ 이안 멕켈런 경에 대한 벤 브랜틀리의 기사는 많은 기억들을 되살아나게 했다. ❷ 타동사 다시 불을 붙이다 ❑ 그 시리즈가 두 국가 간의 적개심에 다시 불을 붙일 수 있다는 우려가 있다.

re|lapse /rɪlæps/ (**relapses, relapsing, relapsed**)

The noun can be pronounced /rɪlæps/ or /rilæps/.

명사는 /rɪlæps/ 또는 /rilæps/로 발음된다.

❶ V-I If you say that someone **relapses into** a way of behaving that is undesirable, you mean that they start to behave in that way again. ❑ *"I wish I did," said Phil Jordan, relapsing into his usual gloom.* ● N-COUNT **Relapse** is also a noun. ❑ *...a relapse into the nationalism of the nineteenth century.* ❷ V-I If a sick person **relapses**, their health suddenly gets worse after it had been improving. ❑ *In 90 per cent of cases the patient will relapse within six months.* ● N-VAR **Relapse** is also a noun. ❑ *The treatment is usually given to women with a high risk of relapse after surgery.*

❶ 자동사 (바람직하지 못한 상태로) 되돌아가다 ❑ "내가 한다면 좋을 텐데."라고 필 조던이 여느 때처럼 다시 침울해지면서 말했다. ● 가산명사 되돌아감 ❑ 19세기 민족주의로 되돌아감 ❷ 자동사 (병이) 재발하다 ❑ 환자의 90퍼센트가 6개월 안에 병이 재발한다. ● 가산명사 또는 불가산명사 (병의) 재발, 다시 악화됨 ❑ 그 치료는 대개 수술 후 재발 위험이 높은 여성들이 받는다.

re|late ♦♢♢ /rɪleɪt/ (**relates, relating, related**) ❶ V-I If something **relates to** a particular subject, it concerns that subject. ❑ *Other recommendations relate to the details of how such data is stored.* ❷ V-RECIP The way that two things **relate**, or the way that one thing **relates to** another, is the sort of connection that exists between them. ❑ *Cornell University offers a course that investigates how language relates to particular cultural codes.* ❑ *Many Christians today feel the need to relate their experience to that of the Hindu, the Buddhist, and the Muslim.* ❸ V-RECIP If you can **relate to** someone, you can understand how they feel or behave so that you are able to communicate with them or deal with them easily. ❑ *He is unable to relate to other people.*

❶ 자동사 -와 관련이 있다, -와 관계되다 ❑ 다른 권고안들은 이런 자료를 어떻게 저장하는가에 대한 세부 정보에 관계된 것이다. ❷ 상호동사 관련되다, 관련짓다 ❑ 코넬대학교는 언어가 특정한 문화적 코드와 어떻게 관련되어 있는가를 연구하는 과정을 개설하고 있다. ❑ 오늘날 많은 기독교인들은 그들의 종교적 체험을 힌두교도와 불교도 그리고 회교도의 종교적 체험과 관련지어야 한다고 느낀다. ❸ 상호동사 공감하다, 이해하다 ❑ 그는 다른 사람들을 이해하지 못한다.

re|lat|ed ♦♢♢ /rɪleɪtɪd/ ❶ ADJ If two or more things are **related**, there is a connection between them. ❑ *The philosophical problems of chance and of free will are closely related.* ❷ ADJ People who are **related** belong to the same family. [v-link ADJ, oft ADJ to n] ❑ *...people in countries like Bangladesh who have been able to show they are related to a spouse or parent living in Britain.* ❸ ADJ If you say that different types of things, such as languages, are **related**, you mean that they developed from the same language. ❑ *He recognized that Sanskrit, the language of India, was related very closely to Latin, Greek, and the Germanic and Celtic languages.*

❶ 형용사 관련된 ❑ 우연과 자유 의지에 대한 철학적 문제들은 서로 밀접한 연관이 있다. ❷ 형용사 친족인 ❑ 영국에 사는 배우자나 부모와 친족관계임을 증명할 수 있는 방글라데시와 같은 나라의 사람들 ❸ 형용사 동족의 ❑ 그는 인도어인 산스크리트 어가 라틴 어, 그리스 어, 게르만 어, 켈트 어와 매우 가까운 동족어라는 사실을 인정했다.

-related /-rɪleɪtɪd/ COMB in ADJ **-related** combines with nouns to form adjectives with the meaning "connected with the thing referred to by the noun." ❑ *More than 50 arrests were made, mostly for drug-related offenses.*

복합형-형용사 -와 관련된 ❑ 50명 이상이 체포되었는데 대부분이 마약 관련 범죄 때문이었다.

re|la|tion ♦♦♢ /rɪleɪʃᵊn/ (**relations**) ❶ N-COUNT **Relations** between people, groups, or countries are contacts between them and the way in which they behave toward each other. ❑ *Greece has established full diplomatic relations with Israel.* →see also **industrial relations, public relations, race relations** ❷ N-COUNT If you talk about the **relation of** one thing **to** another, you are talking about the ways in which they are connected. ❑ *It is a question of the relation of ethics to economics.* ❸ N-COUNT Your **relations** are the members of your family. ❑ *...visits to friends and relations.* ◢ PHRASE You can talk about something **in relation to** something else when you want to compare the size, condition, or position of the two things. ❑ *The money he'd been ordered to pay was minimal in relation to his salary.* ❺ PHRASE If something is said or done **in relation to** a subject, it is said or done in connection with that subject. ❑ *...a question which has been asked many times in relation to Irish affairs.*

❶ 가산명사 관계 ❑ 그리스는 이스라엘과 완전한 외교 관계를 수립했다. ❷ 가산명사 관계 ❑ 그것은 윤리와 경제와의 관계에 대한 문제이다. ❸ 가산명사 친척 ❑ 친구와 친척 방문 ◢ 구 -에 비하여 ❑ 그가 지불하도록 지시받았던 금액은 그의 급여에 비하면 극히 적은 액수였다. ❺ 구 -와 관련하여 ❑ 아일랜드 정세와 관련하여 수차례 제기되었던 한 가지 질문

Word Partnership *relation*의 연어

V.	**bear a** relation ②
PREP.	relation **between** *someone/something* **and** *someone/something* ①
	relation **of** *something* **to** *something* ②
	in relation **to** *something* ④ ⑤

re|la|tion|ship ♦♦♦ /rɪˈleɪʃ°nʃɪp/ (relationships) ① N-COUNT The **relationship** between two people or groups is the way in which they feel and behave towards each other. ❑ ...*the friendly relationship between France and Britain.* ② N-COUNT A **relationship** is a close friendship between two people, especially one involving romantic or sexual feelings. ❑ *We had been together for two years, but both of us felt the relationship wasn't really going anywhere.* ③ N-COUNT The **relationship** between two things is the way in which they are connected. ❑ *A number of small-scale studies have already indicated that there is a relationship between diet and cancer.*

① 가산명사 관계 ❑ 프랑스와 영국 간의 우호 관계 ② 가산명사 (이성) 관계 ❑ 우리는 2년 동안 함께 지냈으나, 우리 둘 다 관계가 진척되고 있다는 느낌은 없었다. ③ 가산명사 연관, 관련 ❑ 수많은 소규모 연구들이 이미 밝혀낸 바에 따르면 식습관과 암은 관련이 있다.

Word Partnership *relationship*의 연어

ADJ.	**professional** relationship, **working** relationship ①
	abusive relationship, **good** relationship, **healthy** relationship, **loving** relationship ① ②
	close relationship, **intimate** relationship ①-③
	romantic relationship, **sexual** relationship ②
V.	**develop a** relationship, **end a** relationship, **have a** relationship, **maintain a** relationship ① ②
	establish a relationship ①-③

rela|tive ♦♦♢ /ˈrelətɪv/ (relatives) ① N-COUNT Your **relatives** are the members of your family. ❑ *Get a relative to look after the children.* ② ADJ You use **relative** to say that something is true to a certain degree, especially when compared with other things of the same kind. [ADJ n] ❑ *The fighting resumed after a period of relative calm.* ③ ADJ You use **relative** when you are comparing the quality or size of two things. [ADJ n] ❑ *They chatted about the relative merits of London and Paris as places to live.* ④ PHRASE **Relative to** something means with reference to it or in comparison with it. ❑ *Japanese interest rates rose relative to America's.* ⑤ ADJ If you say that something is **relative**, you mean that it needs to be considered and judged in relation to other things. ❑ *Fitness is relative; one must always ask "Fit for what?"* ⑥ N-COUNT If one animal, plant, language, or invention is a **relative of** another, they have both developed from the same type of animal, plant, language, or invention. ❑ *The pheasant is a close relative of the Guinea hen.*

① 가산명사 친척 ❑ 그 아이들을 돌볼 친척을 데려오세요. ② 형용사 비교적인, 상대적인 ❑ 전투는 조용한 소강상태가 있은 후에 재개되었다. ③ 형용사 상대적인 ❑ 그들은 주거 지역으로서 런던과 파리의 상대적인 장점들에 대해 한담을 나누었다. ④ 구 ~에 비해 ❑ 일본 금리가 미국 금리에 비해 상승했다. ⑤ 형용사 상대적인 ❑ 적합성이란 상대적인 것이다. 언제나 '무엇에 적합한가?'라고 물어야 한다. ⑥ 가산명사 계통이 같은 것 ❑ 그 꿩은 뿔닭 암컷과 계통상 밀접하다.

Word Partnership *relative*의 연어

ADJ.	**close** relative, **distant** relative ①
N.	**friend and** relative ①
	relative **calm**, relative **ease**, relative **safety**, relative **stability** ②

rela|tive clause (relative clauses) N-COUNT In grammar, a **relative clause** is a subordinate clause which specifies or gives information about a person or thing. Relative clauses come after a noun or pronoun and, in English, often begin with a relative pronoun such as "who," "which," or "that."

가산명사 (문법) 관계절

rela|tive|ly ♦♦♢ /ˈrelətɪvli/ ADV **Relatively** means to a certain degree, especially when compared with other things of the same kind. [ADV adj/adv] ❑ *The sums needed are relatively small.*

부사 상대적으로, 비교적 ❑ 필요한 금액이 비교적 적다.

re|launch /riˈlɔːntʃ/ (relaunches, relaunching, relaunched) V-T To **relaunch** something such as a company, a product, or a program means to start it again or to produce it in a different way. ❑ *He is hoping to relaunch his film career with a remake of the 1971 British thriller.* ● N-COUNT **Relaunch** is also a noun. ❑ *Football kit relaunches are simply a way of boosting sales.*

타동사 다시 시작하다, 재개하다 ❑ 그는 1971년도 영국 스릴러 영화의 리메이크를 통해 자신의 영화 인생을 다시 시작하기를 희망하고 있다. ● 가산명사 재개시, 재발매 ❑ 축구 장비 재발매는 단순히 판매를 늘리려는 방안이다.

Word Link *lax ≈ allowing, loosening : lax, laxative, relax*

re|lax ♦♦♢ /rɪˈlæks/ (relaxes, relaxing, relaxed) ① V-T/V-I If you **relax** or if something **relaxes** you, you feel more calm and less worried or tense. ❑ *I ought to relax and stop worrying about it.* ② V-T/V-I When a part of your body **relaxes**, or when you **relax** it, it becomes less stiff or firm. ❑ *Massage is used to relax muscles, relieve stress and improve the circulation.* ③ V-T If you **relax** your grip or hold on something, you hold it less tightly than before. ❑ *He gradually relaxed his grip on the arms of the chair.* ④ V-T/V-I If you **relax** a rule or your control over something, or if it **relaxes**, it becomes less firm or strong. ❑ *Rules governing student conduct relaxed somewhat in recent years.* ⑤ →see also **relaxed**, **relaxing** →see muscle

① 타동사/자동사 긴장을 풀어 주다; 긴장을 풀다 ❑ 긴장을 풀고 그 일에 대해 그만 걱정해야겠어. ② 타동사/자동사 이완시키다; 이완되다 ❑ 마사지는 근육을 이완시키고, 스트레스를 경감시키며 혈액 순환을 더욱 원활하게 한다. ③ 타동사 느슨하게 하다 ❑ 의자 팔걸이를 움켜잡은 그의 손에서 서서히 힘이 빠졌다. ④ 타동사/자동사 완화하다; 완화되다 ❑ 학생들의 품행에 관한 규율이 최근 몇 년 동안 다소 완화되었다.

Thesaurus *relax*의 참조어

V.	calm down, rest, *take it* easy, unwind ①
	ease up, loosen ③

Word Partnership *relax*의 연어

V.	**sit back and** relax ①
	begin to relax, **try to** relax ① ②
N.	**time to** relax ①
	relax *your* **body**, **muscles** relax ②

re|lax|ation /riːlækseɪʃ°n/ ■ N-UNCOUNT **Relaxation** is a way of spending time in which you rest and feel comfortable. ❑ *You should be able to find the odd moment for relaxation.* ❷ N-UNCOUNT If there is **relaxation** of a rule or control, it is made less firm or strong. ❑ *The relaxation of travel restrictions means they are free to travel and work.*

■ 불가산명사 기분 전환 ❑ 짬을 내서 기분 전환을 할 수 있어야 한다. ❷ 불가산명사 완화 ❑ 여행 규제 완화는 그들이 자유롭게 여행하고 일할 수 있다는 것을 의미한다.

re|laxed /riːlækst/ ■ ADJ If you are **relaxed**, you are calm and not worried or tense. ❑ *As soon as I had made the final decision, I felt a lot more relaxed.* ❷ ADJ If a place or situation is **relaxed**, it is calm and peaceful. ❑ *The atmosphere at lunch was relaxed.*

■ 형용사 느긋한 ❑ 최종 결정을 내리자마자 나는 훨씬 더 느긋해짐을 느꼈다. ❷ 형용사 차분한 ❑ 점심 때 분위기가 차분했다.

re|lax|ing /riːlæksɪŋ/ ADJ Something that is **relaxing** is pleasant and helps you to relax. ❑ *I find cooking very relaxing.*

형용사 편한 ❑ 나는 요리하는 게 아주 편하다.

re|lay (relays, relaying, relayed)

The noun is pronounced /riːleɪ/. The verb is pronounced /riːleɪ/.

명사는 /riːleɪ/로 발음되고, 동사는 /riːleɪ/로 발음된다.

■ N-COUNT A **relay** or a **relay race** is a race between two or more teams, for example teams of runners or swimmers. Each member of the team runs or swims one section of the race. ❑ *Britain's prospects of beating the United States in the relay looked poor.* ❷ V-T To **relay** television or radio signals means to send them or broadcast them. ❑ *The satellite will be used mainly to relay television programmes.* ❸ V-T If you **relay** something that has been said to you, you repeat it to another person. [FORMAL] ❑ *She relayed the message, then frowned.*

■ 가산명사 계주, 릴레이 경주 ❑ 계주에서 영국이 미국을 이길 가능성은 밝지 않았다. ❷ 타동사 중계하다 ❑ 그 위성은 주로 텔레비전 프로그램을 중계하는 데 사용될 것이다. ❸ 타동사 (들은 이야기를) 전달하다 [격식체] ❑ 그녀는 그 메시지를 전달하고 나서 얼굴을 찌푸렸다.

re|lease ♦♦♦ /riːliːs/ (releases, releasing, released) ■ V-T If a person or animal **is released** from somewhere where they have been locked up or cared for, they are set free or allowed to go. [usu passive] ❑ *He was released from custody the next day.* ❷ N-COUNT When someone is released, you refer to their **release**. [with supp] ❑ *He called for the immediate release of all political prisoners.* ❸ V-T If someone or something **releases** you **from** a duty, task, or feeling, they free you from it. [FORMAL] ❑ *Divorce releases both the husband and wife from all marital obligations to each other.* ● N-UNCOUNT **Release** is also a noun. [also a N, oft N from N] ❑ *Our therapeutic style offers release from stored tensions, traumas and grief.* ❹ V-T To **release** feelings or abilities means to allow them to be expressed. ❑ *Becoming your own person releases your creativity.* ● N-UNCOUNT **Release** is also a noun. ❑ *She felt the sudden sweet release of her own tears.* ❺ V-T If someone in authority **releases** something such as a document or information, they make it available. ❑ *They're not releasing any more details yet.* ● N-COUNT **Release** is also a noun. ❑ *Action had been taken to speed up the release of cheques.* ❻ V-T If you **release** someone or something, you stop holding them. [FORMAL] ❑ *He stopped and faced her, releasing her wrist.* ❼ V-T If something **releases** gas, heat, or a substance, it causes it to leave its container or the substance that it was part of and enter the surrounding atmosphere or area. ❑ *...a weapon which releases toxic nerve gas.* ● N-COUNT **Release** is also a noun. ❑ *Under the agreement, releases of cancer-causing chemicals will be cut by about 80 per cent.* ❽ V-T When an entertainer or company **releases** a new CD, video, or movie, it becomes available so that people can buy it or see it. ❑ *He is releasing an album of love songs.* ❾ N-COUNT A new **release** is a new CD, video, or movie that has just become available for people to buy or see. ❑ *Of the new releases that are out there now, which do you think are really good?* ❿ →see also **press release**

■ 타동사 석방되다, 풀러나다 ❑ 그는 그 다음날 유치장에서 풀려났다. ❷ 가산명사 석방 ❑ 그는 모든 정치범들의 즉각적인 석방을 요구했다. ❸ 타동사 벗어나게 하다, 면하게 하다 [격식체] ❑ 이혼을 통해 남편과 아내는 서로에 대한 부부로서의 모든 의무를 벗게 된다. ● 불가산명사 벗어남, 해방 ❑ 우리의 치료 방식은 누적된 긴장과 정신적 충격 그리고 깊은 슬픔으로부터 벗어날 수 있게 해 드립니다. ❹ 타동사 드러내다, 표출하다 ❑ 자기 자신다워지는 것은 자신의 창의성을 표출하는 것이다. ● 불가산명사 드러냄, 표출 ❑ 그녀는 갑자기 눈물이 쏟아지면서 후련한 기분이 들었다. ❺ 타동사 공개하다, 발표하다 ❑ 그들은 아직 더 구체적인 내용을 공개하고 있지 않다. ● 가산명사 공개, 발행 ❑ 수표 발행을 앞당기기 위한 조치가 취해졌다. ❻ 타동사 놓아 주다 [격식체] ❑ 그는 멈춰 서서 그녀를 마주 보며 손목을 놓아 주었다. ❼ 타동사 방출하다 ❑ 신경 독가스를 방출하는 무기 ● 가산명사 방출 ❑ 그 협정에 따라 발암 화학 물질의 방출이 약 80퍼센트만큼 줄어들 것이다. ❽ 타동사 발매하다, 출시하다 ❑ 그는 사랑의 노래를 담은 앨범을 한 장 내려고 한다. ❾ 가산명사 발매품, 출시품 ❑ 지금 나와 있는 새 발매품 중에 어떤 것이 정말 좋다고 생각하니?

Thesaurus	release의 참조어
v.	clear, excuse, free; (ant.) detain, imprison ■
N.	acquittal, liberation; (ant.) detention, imprisonment ❷

rel|egate /religeɪt/ (relegates, relegating, relegated) ■ V-T If you **relegate** someone or something **to** a less important position, you give them this position. ❑ *Might it not be better to relegate the King to a purely ceremonial function?* ❷ V-T If a sports team that competes in a league **is relegated**, it has to compete in a lower division in the next competition, because it was one of the least successful teams in the higher division. [BRIT] [usu passive] ❑ *If Leigh lose, they'll be relegated.* ● **rel|ega|tion** /religeɪʃ°n/ N-UNCOUNT ❑ *Relegation to the Third Division would prove catastrophic.*

■ 타동사 격하시키다, 좌천시키다 ❑ 국왕을 단순히 관례적인 역할만 하도록 격하시키는 것이 더 낫지 않을까? ❷ 타동사 (하위 그룹으로) 격하되다 [영국영어] ❑ 리가 패배할 경우엔, 그들은 하위 그룹으로 격하될 것이다. ● 좌천, 격하 불가산명사 ❑ 3부 리그로 격하되면 파멸을 몰고 올 것이다.

re|lent /riːlent/ (relents, relenting, relented) V-I If you **relent**, you allow someone to do something that you had previously refused to allow them to do. ❑ *Finally his mother relented and gave permission for her youngest son to marry.*

자동사 마음이 누그러지다 ❑ 결국 어머니가 마음이 누그러져서 막내아들의 결혼을 허락했다.

re|lent|less /riːlentlɪs/ ■ ADJ Something bad that is **relentless** never stops or never becomes less intense. ❑ *The pressure now was relentless.* ● **re|lent|less|ly** ADV ❑ *The sun is beating down relentlessly.* ❷ ADJ Someone who is **relentless** is determined to do something and refuses to give up, even if what they are doing is unpleasant or cruel. ❑ *Relentless in his pursuit of quality, his technical ability was remarkable.* ● **re|lent|less|ly** ADV ❑ *She always questioned me relentlessly.*

■ 형용사 가차없는, 무자비한 ❑ 억압이 이제 가차없었다. ● 가차없이 부사 ❑ 햇살이 가차없이 내리쬐고 있다. ❷ 형용사 끈질긴 ❑ 끈질기게 품질을 추구하는 그의 기술적 능력은 주목할 만했다. ● 끈질기게 부사 ❑ 그녀는 항상 끈질기게 내게 질문을 했다.

rel|evance /reləv°ns/ N-UNCOUNT Something's **relevance to** a situation or person is its importance or significance in that situation or to that person. ❑ *Politicians' private lives have no relevance to their public roles.*

불가산명사 관련성, 관련 ❑ 정치인들의 사생활은 공인으로서의 역할과는 관련이 없다.

rel|evant /reləv°nt/ ADJ Something that is **relevant to** a situation or person is important or significant in that situation or to that person. ❑ *Is socialism still relevant to people's lives?*

형용사 관련된 ❑ 사회주의가 아직도 사람들의 삶과 관련이 있습니까?

re|li|able ♦◇◇ /riːlaɪəb°l/ ■ ADJ People or things that are **reliable** can be trusted to work well or to behave in the way that you want them to. ❑ *She was efficient and reliable.* ● **re|li|ably** /riːlaɪəbli/ ADV ❑ *It's been working reliably for years.* ● **re|li|abil|ity** /riːlaɪəbɪlɪti/ N-UNCOUNT ❑ *He's not at all worried about his car's reliability.* ❷ ADJ Information that is **reliable** or that is from a **reliable** source is very likely to be correct. ❑ *There is no reliable information about civilian casualties.* ● **re|li|ably** ADV ❑ *Sonia, we are reliably informed, loves her family very much.*

■ 형용사 신뢰할 수 있는, 믿을 만한 ❑ 그녀는 실력 있고 신뢰할 수 있는 인물이었다. ● 믿음직하게, 견실하게 부사 ❑ 그것은 수년 동안 견실하게 작동하고 있다. ● 신뢰도 불가산명사 ❑ 그는 자기 차의 신뢰도에 대해 전혀 걱정하지 않는다. ❷ 형용사 확실한, 믿을 만한 ❑ 민간인 희생에 대해서는 확실한 정보가 없다. ● 확실히 부사 ❑ 소냐가 자기 가족을 매우 사랑한다는

• re|li|abil|ity N-UNCOUNT ❏ *Both questioned the reliability of recent opinion polls.*

것을 우리는 확실히 듣고 있다. ● 신빙성 불가산명사 ❏ 양측 모두 최근 여론 조사의 신빙성을 문제 삼았다.

Word Partnership	reliable의 연어
N.	reliable **service** ◼
	reliable **data**, reliable **information**, reliable **source** ◻
ADV.	**highly** reliable, **less/more/most** reliable, **usually** reliable, **very** reliable ◼ ◻

re|li|ance /rɪlaɪəns/ N-UNCOUNT A person's or thing's **reliance on** something is the fact that they need it and often cannot live or work without it. ❏ *...the country's increasing reliance on foreign aid.*

불가산명사 의존 ❏ 그 국가의 해외 원조에 대한 의존도 증가

re|li|ant /rɪlaɪənt/ ADJ A person or thing that is **reliant on** something needs it and often cannot live or work without it. [v-link ADJ on/upon n] ❏ *These people are not wholly reliant on Western charity.*

형용사 의존하는 ❏ 이 사람들은 서방 세계의 구호품에 전적으로 의존하고 있지는 않다.

rel|ic /rɛlɪk/ (relics) ◼ N-COUNT If you refer to something or someone as a **relic of** an earlier period, you mean that they belonged to that period but have survived into the present. ❏ *Germany's asylum law is a relic of an era in European history which has passed.* ◻ N-COUNT A **relic** is something which was made or used a long time ago and which is kept for its historical significance. ❏ *...a museum of war relics.*

◼ 가산명사 유물 ❏ 독일의 망명법은 유럽 역사상 지난 시대의 유물이다. ◻ 가산명사 유물 ❏ 전쟁 유물 박물관

re|lief ♦♦◇ /rɪliːf/ (reliefs) ◼ N-UNCOUNT If you feel a sense of **relief**, you feel happy because something unpleasant has not happened or is no longer happening. [also a N] ❏ *I breathed a sigh of relief.* ◻ N-UNCOUNT If something provides **relief from** pain or distress, it stops the pain or distress. ❏ *...a self-help programme which can give lasting relief from the torment of hay fever.* ◼ N-UNCOUNT **Relief** is money, food, or clothing that is provided for people who are very poor, or who have been affected by war or a natural disaster. ❏ *Relief agencies are stepping up efforts to provide food, shelter, and agricultural equipment.* ◼ N-COUNT A **relief** worker is someone who does your work when you go home, or who is employed to do it instead of you when you are sick. ❏ *No relief drivers were available.*

◼ 불가산명사 안도 ❏ 나는 안도의 한숨을 쉬었다. ◻ 불가산명사 (고통 등을) 덜어 줌 ❏ 건초열의 고통을 지속적으로 덜어 줄 수 있는 자활 프로그램 ◼ 불가산명사 구호 물품 ❏ 구호 단체들은 식량, 수용 시설, 농기계를 제공하기 위한 노력을 배가하고 있다. ◼ 가산명사 대리인, 교체자 ❏ 대리 운전기사를 구할 수 없었다.

Word Partnership	relief의 연어
V.	express relief ◼
	feel relief, seek relief ◼ ◻
	bring relief, get relief, provide relief ◼-◼
	supply relief ◻ ◼
N.	sense of relief, sigh of relief ◼
	pain relief, relief from symptoms, relief from tension ◻
	disaster relief, emergency relief ◼

re|lieve /rɪliːv/ (relieves, relieving, relieved) ◼ V-T If something **relieves** an unpleasant feeling or situation, it makes it less unpleasant or causes it to disappear completely. ❏ *Drugs can relieve much of the pain.* ◻ V-T If someone or something **relieves** you of an unpleasant feeling or difficult task, they take it from you. ❏ *A part-time bookkeeper will relieve you of the burden of chasing unpaid invoices.* ◼ V-T If you **relieve** someone, you take their place and continue to do the job or duty that they have been doing. ❏ *At seven o'clock the night nurse came in to relieve her.* ◼ V-T If someone **is relieved of** their duties or **is relieved of** their post, they are told that they are no longer required to continue in their job. [FORMAL] [usu passive] ❏ *The officer involved was relieved of his duties because he had violated strict guidelines.*

◼ 타동사 (고통 등을) 경감시키다, 없애다 ❏ 진통제는 통증을 상당 부분 경감시켜 줄 수 있다. ◻ 타동사 덜어 주다 ❏ 파트타임으로 일하는 부기계원이 미지불된 송장을 추적하는 당신의 일을 덜어 줄 것이다. ◼ 타동사 교대하다 ❏ 7시에 야간 근무 간호사가 그녀와 교대하러 왔다. ◼ 타동사 해임되다 [격식체] ❏ 엄격한 지침을 어겼기 때문에 연루된 그 장교는 보직에서 해임됐다.

re|lieved /rɪliːvd/ ADJ If you are **relieved**, you feel happy because something unpleasant has not happened or is no longer happening. ❏ *We are all relieved to be back home.*

형용사 안심하는 ❏ 우리 모두가 집으로 돌아와서 안심이다.

re|li|gion ♦♦◇ /rɪlɪdʒən/ (religions) ◼ N-UNCOUNT **Religion** is belief in a god or gods and the activities that are connected with this belief, such as praying or worshiping in a building such as a church or temple. ❏ *...his understanding of Indian philosophy and religion.* ◻ N-COUNT A **religion** is a particular system of belief in a god or gods and the activities that are connected with this system. ❏ *...the Christian religion.*
→see Word Web: religion

◼ 불가산명사 종교 ❏ 인도 철학과 종교에 대한 그의 이해 ◻ 가산명사 종교, -교 ❏ 기독교

re|li|gious ♦♦◇ /rɪlɪdʒəs/ ◼ ADJ You use **religious** to describe things that are connected with religion or with one particular religion. [ADJ n] ❏ *Religious*

◼ 형용사 종교의 ❏ 이제 종교 단체들은 상당히 공개적으로 만날 수 있게 되었다. ◻ 형용사 독실한,

Word Web religion

Today the world's population is about 33% **Christian**, 21% **Islamic**, 16% **agnostic**, and 14% **Hindu**. Christians believe in one **god**, but they also **pray** to his son, Jesus Christ. Followers of **Islam** believe in a single god, Allah, and follow the teachings of the prophet Muhammad. Their **divine scripture** is the Koran. They also honor parts of the **Jewish** and **Christian Bible**. Hinduism recognizes a single **deity** along with other **gods** and **goddesses**. **Buddhism** developed after Hinduism in India and does not include a god figure. All religions seem to share one traditional **belief**—the idea of treating others the way we wish to be treated.

 Buddhism
 Christianity
 Judaism
  Hinduism

a b c d e f g h i j k l m n o p q r s t u v w x y z

groups are now able to meet quite openly. **2** ADJ Someone who is **religious** has a strong belief in a god or gods. ❑ *They are both very religious and felt it was a gift from God.*

신앙심이 깊은 ❑ 그들은 둘 다 신앙심이 아주 깊었고 그것이 하나님이 주신 선물이라고 생각했다.

re|lin|quish /rɪlɪŋkwɪʃ/ (relinquishes, relinquishing, relinquished) V-T If you **relinquish** something such as power or control, you give it up. [FORMAL] ❑ *He does not intend to relinquish power.*

타동사 포기하다 [격식체] ❑ 그는 권력을 포기할 의사가 없다.

rel|ish /rɛlɪʃ/ (relishes, relishing, relished) V-T If you **relish** something, you get a lot of enjoyment from it. ❑ *I relish the challenge of doing jobs that others turn down.* ● N-UNCOUNT **Relish** is also a noun. ❑ *The three men ate with relish.*

타동사 즐기다 ❑ 나는 다른 사람들이 거부하는 일에 도전하는 것을 좋아한다. ● 불가산명사 즐거움 ❑ 그 세 남자는 아주 즐겁게 먹었다.

re|live /riːlɪv/ (relives, reliving, relived) V-T If you **relive** something that has happened to you in the past, you remember it and imagine that you are experiencing it again. ❑ *There is no point in reliving the past.*

타동사 회상하다 ❑ 과거를 회상해 봤자 의미가 없다.

re|lo|cate /riːloʊkeɪt, BRIT riːloʊkeɪt/ (relocates, relocating, relocated) V-T/V-I If people or businesses **relocate** or if someone **relocates** them, they move to a different place. ❑ *If the company was to relocate, most employees would move.* ● **re|lo|ca|tion** /riːloʊkeɪʃ°n/ (relocations) N-UNCOUNT ❑ *The company says the cost of relocation will be negligible.*

타동사/자동사 이전시키다; 이전하다 ❑ 회사가 이전하게 되면 대부분의 직원들이 이사를 할 것이다. ● 이동, 이전 불가산명사 ❑ 그 회사는 이전 비용이 아주 적게 들 것이라고 말한다.

re|lo|ca|tion ex|penses N-PLURAL **Relocation expenses** are a sum of money that a company pays to someone who moves to a new area in order to work for the company. The money is to help them pay for moving their belongings. [BUSINESS] ❑ *Relocation expenses were paid to encourage senior staff to move to the region.*

복수명사 이전 비용 [경제] ❑ 상급 직원들이 그 지역으로 이사하는 것을 장려하기 위해 이전 비용이 지급됐다.

re|luc|tant ◆◇◇ /rɪlʌktənt/ ADJ If you are **reluctant to** do something, you are unwilling to do it and hesitate before doing it, or do it slowly and without enthusiasm. ❑ *Mr. Spero was reluctant to ask for help.* ● **re|luc|tant|ly** ADV [ADV with v] ❑ *We have reluctantly agreed to let him go.* ● **re|luc|tance** N-UNCOUNT ❑ *Ministers have shown extreme reluctance to explain their position to the media.*

형용사 주저하는, 꺼리는 ❑ 스페로 씨는 도움을 요청하기를 꺼렸다. ● 마지못해 부사 ❑ 우리는 마지못해 그를 보내는 것에 동의했다. ● 꺼림 불가산명사 ❑ 장관들은 언론에 자기들의 결정 사항을 설명하는 것을 극히 꺼렸다.

Thesaurus *reluctant*의 참조어

ADJ. hesitant, unwilling; *(ant.)* eager, willing

rely ◆◇◇ /rɪlaɪ/ (relies, relying, relied) **1** V-I If you **rely on** someone or something, you need them and depend on them in order to live or work properly. ❑ *They relied heavily on the advice of their professional advisers.* **2** V-I If you can **rely on** someone to work well or to behave as you want them to, you can trust them to do this. ❑ *I know I can rely on you to sort it out.*

1 자동사 의존하다 ❑ 그들은 전문 상담자의 조언에 전적으로 의존했다. **2** 자동사 믿고 맡기다 ❑ 너한테 이것을 정리하도록 믿고 맡겨도 되겠지.

re|main ◆◆◆ /rɪmeɪn/ (remains, remaining, remained) **1** V-LINK If someone or something **remains** in a particular state or condition, they stay in that state or condition and do not change. ❑ *The three men remained silent.* ❑ *The government remained in control.* **2** V-I If you **remain** in a place, you stay there and do not move away. ❑ *They have asked the residents to remain in their homes.* **3** V-I You can say that something **remains** when it still exists. ❑ *The wider problem remains.* **4** V-LINK If something **remains to be** done, it has not yet been done and still needs to be done. ❑ *Major questions remain to be answered about his work.* **5** N-PLURAL The **remains of** something are the parts of it that are left after most of it has been taken away or destroyed. ❑ *They were tidying up the remains of their picnic.* **6** N-PLURAL The **remains** of a person or animal are the parts of their body that are left after they have died, sometimes after they have been dead for a long time. ❑ *The unrecognizable remains of a man had been found.* **7** →see also **remaining**

1 연결동사 계속 -인 채로 있다 ❑ 그 세 남자는 계속 조용히 있었다. ❑ 정부는 계속 통제권을 가지고 있었다. **2** 자동사 남다 ❑ 그들은 주민들에게 집에 남아 있으라고 요청했다. **3** 자동사 남아 있다 ❑ 더 광범위한 문제가 남아 있다. **4** 연결동사 여전히 -한 상태로 있다 ❑ 그의 일에 관한 주요 질문들이 아직도 미답변 상태에 있다. **5** 복수명사 잔해, 흔적 ❑ 그들은 소풍을 마친 후 자리를 정리하고 있었다. **6** 복수명사 유골 ❑ 신원을 확인할 수 없는 남자의 유골이 발견되었다.

Thesaurus *remain*의 참조어

V. last, linger, stay; *(ant.)* depart, leave **1** **2**

re|main|der /rɪmeɪndər/ QUANT The **remainder of** a group are the things or people that still remain after the other things or people have gone or have been dealt with. [QUANT of def-n] ❑ *He gulped down the remainder of his coffee.* ● PRON **Remainder** is also a pronoun. ❑ *Only 5.9 per cent of the area is now covered in trees. Most of the remainder is farmland.*

수량사 나머지 ❑ 그는 남은 커피를 꿀꺽 마셔 버렸다. ● 대명사 나머지 ❑ 지금은 그 지역의 5.9퍼센트만이 숲이다. 나머지의 대부분은 농지이다.

re|main|ing ◆◇◇ /rɪmeɪnɪŋ/ **1** ADJ The **remaining** things or people out of a group are the things or people that still exist, are still present, or have not yet been dealt with. [ADJ n] ❑ *The three parties will meet next month to work out remaining differences.* **2** →see also **remain**

1 형용사 남아 있는, 그대로 있는 ❑ 그 세 정당은 다음 달에 여전히 남아 있는 정견 차를 해결하기 위해 모임을 가질 것이다.

re|mand /rɪmænd/ (remands, remanding, remanded) **1** V-T If a person who is accused of a crime **is remanded** in custody or on bail, they are told to return to the court at a later date, when their trial will take place. [usu passive] ❑ *Carter was remanded in custody for seven days.* **2** N-UNCOUNT **Remand** is used to refer to the process of remanding someone in custody or on bail, or to the period of time until their trial begins. ❑ *The remand hearing is often over in three minutes.*

1 타동사 재구류되다, 불구속 입건되다 ❑ 카터는 7일간 재구류되었다. **2** 불가산명사 재구류 ❑ 재구류 심리는 보통 30분 내에 끝난다.

re|mark ◆◇◇ /rɪmɑrk/ (remarks, remarking, remarked) **1** V-T/V-I If you **remark** that something is the case, you say that it is the case. ❑ *I remarked that I would go shopping that afternoon.* ❑ *On several occasions she had remarked on the boy's improvement.* **2** N-COUNT If you make a **remark** about something, you say something about it. ❑ *She has made outspoken remarks about the legalization of cannabis in Britain.*

1 타동사/자동사 말하다 ❑ 나는 그날 오후에 쇼핑하러 갈 거라고 말했다. ❑ 그녀는 여러 차례 그 아이의 성적 향상에 대해 언급했다. **2** 가산명사 언급 ❑ 그녀는 영국에서 대마초를 합법화하는 것에 대해 공개적으로 언급해 왔다.

If you **remark on** something, or make a **remark** about it, you say what you think or what you have noticed, often in a casual way. ❑ *Visitors remark on how well the children look... General Sutton's remarks about the conflict.* If you **comment** on a situation, or make a **comment** about it, you give your opinion on it. ❑ *Mr.*

무엇에 대해 remark한다고 하면, 생각하는 바나 인지한 바를 흔히 가볍게 말하는 것이다. ❑ 방문객들은 그 아이들이 얼마나 좋아 보이는지에 대해 말한다... 그 분쟁에 대한 서튼

Cook has not commented on these reports... I was wondering whether you had any comments. If you **mention** something, you say it, but only briefly, especially when you have not talked about it before. ❑ *He mentioned that he might go to New York.*

Word Partnership		*remark의 연어*
ADJ.	**casual** remark 2	
V.	**hear a** remark, **make a** remark 2	

장군의 발언. 어떤 상황에 대해서 comment하거나 make a comment하면, 그것에 대한 의견을 말하는 것이다. ❑ 쿡 씨는 이 보고서들에 대해 논평을 하지 않았다... 나는 논평할 것이 있는지 궁금해 하던 참이었습니다. 특히 이전에 무엇에 대해 이야기한 적이 없으면서 그것을 mention하면, 그것에 대해 간략하게 얘기하는 것이다. ❑ 그는 뉴욕에 갈지도 모른다고 언급했다.

re|mark|able ♦◇◇ /rɪmɑrkəbʲl/ ADJ Someone or something that is **remarkable** is unusual or special in a way that makes people notice them and be surprised or impressed. ❑ *He was a remarkable man.* ● **re|mark|ably** /rɪmɑrkəbli/ ADV ❑ *The Scottish labor market has been remarkably successful in absorbing the increase in the number of graduates.*

형용사 남다른, 주목할 만한 ❑ 그는 남다른 사람이었다. ● 눈에 띄게, 놀랄 만큼 부사 ❑ 스코틀랜드 노동 시장은 늘어나는 대학 졸업생을 놀랄 만큼 성공적으로 흡수해 왔다.

re|match /rɪmætʃ/ (**rematches**) **1** N-COUNT A **rematch** is a second game that is played between two people or teams, for example because their first match was a draw or because there was a dispute about some aspect of it. [mainly BRIT] ❑ *Duff said he would be demanding a rematch.* **2** N-COUNT A **rematch** is a second game or contest between two people or teams who have already faced each other. [mainly AM; BRIT usually **return match**] ❑ *Stanford will face UCLA in a rematch.*

1 가산명사 재시합 [주로 영국영어] ❑ 더프는 재시합을 요구할 것이라고 말했다. **2** 가산명사 다시 맞붙게 되는 경기 [주로 미국영어; 영국영어 대개 return match] ❑ 스탠퍼드는 유시엘에이와 다시 맞붙게 될 것이다.

re|me|dial /rɪmidiəl/ **1** ADJ **Remedial** education is intended to improve a person's ability to read, write, or do mathematics, especially when they find these things difficult. ❑ *...children who required special remedial education.* **2** ADJ **Remedial** action is intended to correct something that has been done wrong or that has not been successful. [FORMAL] ❑ *Some authorities are now having to take remedial action.*

1 형용사 보충의 ❑ 특수 보충 교육이 필요한 아이들 **2** 형용사 개선하는 [격식체] ❑ 몇몇 관료들은 지금 개선책을 취해야 한다.

rem|edy /remədi/ (**remedies, remedying, remedied**) **1** N-COUNT A **remedy** is a successful way of dealing with a problem. ❑ *The remedy lies in the hands of the government.* **2** N-COUNT A **remedy** is something that is intended to cure you when you are ill or in pain. ❑ *There are many different kinds of natural remedies to help overcome winter infections.* **3** V-T If you **remedy** something that is wrong or harmful, you correct it or improve it. ❑ *A great deal has been done internally to remedy the situation.*

1 가산명사 해결책 ❑ 해결책은 정부 손안에 있다. **2** 가산명사 치료 ❑ 겨울철 전염병의 치료를 돕는 다양한 종류의 자연 치료법이 있다. **3** 타동사 개선하다, 교정하다 ❑ 내부적으로 그 사태를 개선하기 위해서 상당히 많은 조치를 취해 왔다.

re|mem|ber ♦♦♦ /rɪmɛmbər/ (**remembers, remembering, remembered**) **1** V-T/V-I If you **remember** people or events from the past, you still have an idea of them in your mind and you are able to think about them. ❑ *You wouldn't remember me. I was in another group.* ❑ *I remembered that we had drunk the last of the coffee the week before.* **2** V-T If you **remember** that something is the case, you become aware of it again after a time when you did not think about it. ❑ *She remembered that she was going to the club that evening.* **3** V-T/V-I If you cannot **remember** something, you are not able to bring it back into your mind when you make an effort to do so. [usu with brd-neg] ❑ *If you can't remember your number, write it in code in a diary.* ❑ *I can't remember what I said.* **4** V-T If you **remember to** do something, you do it when you intend to. ❑ *Please remember to enclose a stamped addressed envelope when writing.* **5** V-T You tell someone to **remember that** something is the case when you want to emphasize its importance. It may be something that they already know about or a new piece of information. [EMPHASIS] ❑ *It is important to remember that each person reacts differently.*
→see **memory**

1 타동사/자동사 기억하다 ❑ 넌 날 기억 못하겠다. 나는 다른 그룹에 있었어. ❑ 우리가 그 전주에 마지막 남은 커피를 마셨던 것을 나는 기억하고 있었다. **2** 타동사 생각나다 ❑ 그녀는 그날 저녁에 클럽에 갈 것이 생각났다. **3** 타동사/자동사 기억하다 ❑ 번호를 기억할 수 없다면, 암호로 수첩에 적어 놓으세요. ❑ 내가 뭐라고 했는지 기억이 안 나. **4** 타동사 잊지 않다 ❑ 편지 쓸 때 회송용 봉투를 동봉하는 것을 잊지 마세요. **5** 타동사 명심하다 [강조] ❑ 사람마다 다르게 반응한다는 것을 명심하는 것이 중요하다.

Do not confuse **remember** and **remind**. If you **remember** something, you are able to bring it back into your mind. ❑ *He remembers everything that happened... I could not remember her name.* If you **remember** to do something, you do what you are meant to do without forgetting or needing to be told to do it. ❑ *He remembered to turn the gas off... Remember to put all your tools away.* If someone **reminds** you of someone or something, they make you think about that person or thing. ❑ *He reminds me of Maurice Fitzgerald... The pink dress reminds me of when I was a chauffeur in New York.* You cannot use 'remember' in this way. You can use **remember** with the 'to' infinitive or the '-ing' form of the verb, but note that they have different meanings. If you **remember to** do something, you do it when you intend to. ❑ *He remembered to buy his wife chocolates.* If you **remember** doing something, you are thinking back to the past. ❑ *I remember reading the newspaper aloud to my father at five.*

remember와 remind를 혼동하지 않도록 하라. 무엇을 remember하면, 그것을 마음속에 다시 떠올릴 수 있다. ❑ 그는 일어난 모든 일을 기억한다... 나는 그녀의 이름을 기억할 수 없었다. 무엇을 할 것을 remember하면, 잊어버리지 않고 할 일을 하거나 또는 하라는 말을 들을 필요가 없이 할 일을 하는 것을 기억했다... 잊지 말고 연장을 모두 치우시오. 어떤 사람이 당신에게 누구나 무엇에 대해 remind한다면, 그 사람이 당신에게 누구 또는 무엇에 대한 생각이 나도록 하는 것이다. ❑ 그는 내게 모리스 피체제럴드를 생각나게 한다... 그 분홍색 드레스는 내가 뉴욕에서 운전기사였던 시절을 생각나게 한다. remember는 이런 식으로 쓰지 못한다. remember는 to 부정사나 동사의 -ing 형태와 함께 쓸 수 있지만 의미가 다름을 유의하라. 무엇을 할 것을 remember하면, 그것을 하기로 한 때에 하는 것이다. ❑ 그는 아내에게 초콜릿을 사줄 것을 기억했다. 무엇을 한 것을 remember하면, 과거를 생각하는 것이다. ❑ 나는 다섯 살 때 아버지께 신문을 크게 읽어 주던 것을 기억한다.

Thesaurus		*remember의 참조어*
V.	look back, recall, think back; *(ant.)* forget 1 3	

Word Partnership		*remember의 연어*
ADJ.	**easy to** remember, **important to** remember 1 2 4 5	
ADV.	remember **exactly, still** remember 1 3	
	always remember 1 4 5	
CONJ.	remember **what,** remember **when,** remember **where,** remember **why** 1-3	

re|mem|brance /rɪmɛmbrəns/ N-UNCOUNT If you do something **in remembrance** of a dead person, you do it as a way of showing that you want to remember them and that you respect them. [FORMAL] ❑ *They wore black in remembrance of those who had died.*

불가산명사 추도, 애도 [격식체] ❑ 그들은 고인들을 애도하여 검은색 옷을 입었다.

re|mind ♦◇◇ /rɪmaɪnd/ (**reminds, reminding, reminded**) **1** V-T If someone **reminds** you of a fact or event that you already know about, they say

1 타동사 상기시키다 ❑ 그래서 그녀는 팀을 반갑게 맞이했고 팀에게 그들이 마지막으로 만났던 때의

something which makes you think about it. ❏ *So she simply welcomed Tim and reminded him of the last time they had met.* **②** V-T You use **remind** in expressions such as **Let me remind you that** and **May I remind you that** to introduce a piece of information that you want to emphasize. It may be something that the hearer already knows about or a new piece of information. Sometimes these expressions can sound unfriendly. [SPOKEN, EMPHASIS] ❏ *"Let me remind you," said Marianne, "that Manchester is also my home town."* **③** V-T If someone **reminds** you **to** do a particular thing, they say something which makes you remember to do it. ❏ *Can you remind me to buy a bottle of Martini?* **④** V-T If you say that someone or something **reminds** you **of** another person or thing, you mean that they are similar to the other person or thing and that they make you think about them. ❏ *She reminds me of the wife of the pilot who used to work for you.*

얘기를 꺼냈다. **②** 타동사 생각나게 하다; 다시 한 번 알려 주다 [구어체, 강조] ❏ "다시 한 번 알려 드릴게요." 마리안이 말을 이었다. "맨체스터도 제 고향이에요." **③** 타동사 잊지 않게 알려 주다 ❏ 마티니 한 병 사는 것 잊지 말라고 내게 알려 주겠니? **④** 타동사 -을 보면…가 생각나다 ❏ 그녀를 보면 나는 전에 당신 밑에서 일했던 비행기 조종사의 부인이 생각난다.

> Do not confuse **remind** and **remember**. If someone **reminds** you **of** someone or something, they make you think about that person or thing. ❏ *He reminds me of Maurice Fitzgerald... The pink dress reminds me of when I was a chauffeur in New York.* If you **remember** something, you are able to bring it back into your mind. ❏ *He remembers everything that happened... I could not remember her name.* If you **remember** to do something, you do what you are meant to do without forgetting or needing to be told to do it. ❏ *He remembered to turn the gas off... Remember to put all your tools away.*

> remind와 remember를 혼동하지 않도록 하라. 어떤 사람이 당신에게 누구나 무엇에 대해 remind한다면, 그 사람이 당신에게 누구 또는 무엇에 대한 생각이 나도록 하는 것이다. ❏ 그는 내게 모리스 피처제럴드를 생각나게 한다... 그 분홍색 드레스는 내가 뉴욕에서 운전기사였던 시절을 생각나게 한다. 무엇을 remember하면, 그것을 마음속에 다시 떠올릴 수 있다. ❏ 그는 일어난 모든 것을 remember한다... 나는 그녀의 이름을 기억할 수 없었다. 무엇을 할 것을 remember하면, 잊어버리지 않고 할 일을 하거나 또는 하라는 말을 들을 필요가 없이 할 일을 하는 것이다. ❏ 그는 가스를 잠그는 것을 기억했다... 잊지 말고 연장을 모두 치우시오.

Word Partnership   remind의 연어

PREP.	remind *someone* of *something* **①**
	remind *you* of *someone/something* **④**
V.	**let me** remind **you, may I** remind **you ②**

---

re|mind|er /rɪmaɪndər/ (**reminders**) **①** N-COUNT Something that serves as a **reminder of** another thing makes you think about the other thing. [WRITTEN] ❏ *The British are about to be given a sharp reminder of what fighting abroad really means.* **②** N-COUNT A **reminder** is a letter or note that is sent to tell you that you have not done something such as pay a bill or return library books. [mainly BRIT] ❏ *...the final reminder for the gas bill.*

① 가산명사 깨닫게 하는 계기 [문어체] ❏ 영국인들에게 남의 땅에서 싸운다는 것이 진정 무엇을 의미하는지 절실히 깨닫게 하는 계기가 될 것이다. **②** 가산명사 독촉장 [주로 영국영어] ❏ 가스 요금 납부 최후 독촉장

rem|i|nisce /reminɪs/ (**reminisces, reminiscing, reminisced**) V-I If you **reminisce** about something from your past, you write or talk about it, often with pleasure. [FORMAL] ❏ *I don't like reminiscing because it makes me feel old.*

자동사 추억에 잠기다 [격식체] ❏ 나는 내 자신이 늙어진다는 생각이 들기 때문에 추억에 잠기는 것이 싫다.

rem|i|nis|cence /reminɪsəns/ (**reminiscences**) N-VAR Someone's **reminiscences** are things that they remember from the past, and which they talk or write about. **Reminiscence** is the process of remembering these things and talking or writing about them. [FORMAL] ❏ *Here I am boring you with my reminiscences.*

가산명사 또는 불가산명사 추억; 회상 [격식체] ❏ 여기서 내 과거에 대한 이야기로 당신을 지루하게 했군요.

rem|i|nis|cent /reminɪsənt/ ADJ If you say that one thing is **reminiscent of** another, you mean that it reminds you of it. [FORMAL] [v-link ADJ of n] ❏ *The decor was reminiscent of a municipal arts-and-leisure center.*

형용사 연상하게 하는 [격식체] ❏ 그 실내 장식은 시립 예술 레저센터를 연상하게 했다.

re|mis|sion /rɪmɪʃⁿn/ (**remissions**) **①** N-VAR If someone who has had a serious disease such as cancer is **in remission** or if the disease is **in remission**, the disease has been controlled so that they are not as ill as they were. ❏ *Brain scans have confirmed that the disease is in remission.* **②** N-UNCOUNT If someone in prison gets **remission**, their prison sentence is reduced, usually because they have behaved well. [BRIT] ❏ *With remission for good behavior, she could be freed in a year.*

① 가산명사 또는 불가산명사 (병의) 진정, 소강 ❏ 뇌를 정밀 검사 해 본 결과, 그 병이 일단 가라앉은 상태라는 것이 확인됐다. **②** 불가산명사 감형 [영국영어] ❏ 모범 수감 생활로 감형을 받아, 그녀는 일 년 있으면 석방될 수 있을 것이다.

re|mit (**remits, remitting, remitted**) /rɪmɪt/ **①** V-T If you **remit** money to someone, you send it to them. [FORMAL] ❏ *Many immigrants regularly remit money to their families.* **②** N-COUNT Someone's **remit** is the area of activity which they are expected to deal with, or which they have authority to deal with. [BRIT] ❏ *That issue is not within the remit of the working group.*

① 타동사 송금하다 [격식체] ❏ 많은 이민자들은 가족들에게 정기적으로 송금을 한다. **②** 가산명사 소관 [영국영어] ❏ 그 문제는 그 조사단의 소관이 아니다.

re|mit|tance /rɪmɪtⁿns/ (**remittances**) N-VAR A **remittance** is a sum of money that you send to someone. [FORMAL] ❏ *Please enclose your remittance, making cheques payable to Thames Valley Technology.*

가산명사 또는 불가산명사 송금액 [격식체] ❏ 템즈 밸리 테크놀로지 명의로 수표를 작성하셔서 귀하의 송금액을 동봉하세요.

rem|nant /remnənt/ (**remnants**) N-COUNT The **remnants of** something are small parts of it that are left over when the main part has disappeared or been destroyed. ❏ *Beneath the present church were remnants of Roman flooring.*

가산명사 잔재 ❏ 현재 그 교회의 바닥에는 로마 시대 바닥재의 잔재가 깔려 있었다.

re|morse /rɪmɔrs/ N-UNCOUNT **Remorse** is a strong feeling of sadness and regret about something wrong that you have done. ❏ *He was full of remorse and asked Beatrice what he could do to make amends.*

불가산명사 죄책감, 회한 ❏ 그는 죄책감으로 가득 차서 베아트리체에게 어떻게 보상해야 할지 물어보았다.

re|mote ◆◇◇ /rɪmoʊt/ (**remoter, remotest**) **①** ADJ **Remote** areas are far away from cities and places where most people live, and are therefore difficult to get to. ❏ *Landslides have cut off many villages in remote areas.* **②** ADJ The **remote** past or **remote** future is a time that is many years distant from the present. ❏ *Slabs of rock had slipped sideways in the remote past, and formed this hole.* **③** ADJ If something is **remote from** a particular subject or area of experience, it is not relevant to it because it is very different. ❏ *This government depends on the wishes of a few who are remote from the people.* **④** ADJ If you say that there is a **remote** possibility or chance that something will happen, you are emphasizing that there is only a very small chance that it will happen. [EMPHASIS] ❏ *I use a sunscreen whenever there is even a remote possibility that I will be in the sun.* **⑤** ADJ If you describe someone as **remote**, you mean that they behave as if they do not want to be friendly or closely involved with other people. ❏ *She looked so beautiful, and at the same time so remote.*

① 형용사 외진 ❏ 산사태로 인해 외진 곳에 사는 많은 마을들이 고립되었다. **②** 형용사 먼 ❏ 먼 옛날에 석판들이 옆으로 미끄러져 떨어지면서 이 구멍이 생겼다. **③** 형용사 동떨어진 ❏ 이 정부는 일반 대중들과는 동떨어져 있는 소수 사람들의 희망에만 의지하고 있다. **④** 형용사 (가능성이) 희박한 [강조] ❏ 나는 아주 희박하게라도 내가 햇볕에 노출될 가능성이 있을 때는 언제나 자외선 차단 크림을 바른다. **⑤** 형용사 쌀쌀맞은 ❏ 그녀는 정말 아름다워 보였고 동시에 아주 쌀쌀맞아 보였다.

re|mote ac|cess N-UNCOUNT **Remote access** is a system which allows you to gain access to a particular computer or network using a separate computer. [COMPUTING] ❏ *The diploma course would offer remote access to course materials via the Internet's world wide web.*

불가산명사 원격 접속 [컴퓨터] ❏ 그 수료 과정에서는 인터넷의 웹 사이트를 통해 교과 내용의 원격 접속을 제공할 것입니다.

re|mote con|trol (remote controls) **1** N-UNCOUNT **Remote control** is a system of controlling a machine or a vehicle from a distance by using radio or electronic signals. ❑ *The bomb was detonated by remote control.* **2** N-COUNT The **remote control** for a television or video recorder is the device that you use to control the machine from a distance, by pressing the buttons on it. ❑ *Richard picked up the remote control and turned on the television.*

■ 불가산명사 원격 조종 ❑ 그 폭탄은 원격 조종으로 터뜨렸다. ② 가산명사 리모컨 ❑ 리처드는 리모컨을 들어 텔레비전을 켰다.

re|mote|ly /rɪmoʊtli/ **1** ADV You use **remotely** with a negative statement to emphasize the statement. [EMPHASIS] ❑ *We had never seen anything remotely like it before.* **2** ADV If someone or something is **remotely** placed or situated, they are a long way from other people or places. [ADV -ed] ❑ *...the remotely situated, five bedroom house.*

■ 부사 진의 [강조] ❑ 우리는 예전에는 그런 것을 진혀 본 적이 없었다. ② 부사 멀리 ❑ 멀리 떨어진 곳에 있는 침실 다섯 개짜리 주택

re|mov|al /rɪmuːvəl/ (removals) **1** N-UNCOUNT The **removal** of something is the act of removing it. ❑ *What they expected to be the removal of a small lump turned out to be major surgery.* **2** N-VAR **Removal** is the process of transporting furniture or equipment from one building to another. [mainly BRIT; AM **moving**] ❑ *Home removals are best done in cool weather.*

■ 불가산명사 제거 ❑ 그들이 작은 혹 제거 정도로 예상했던 것이 결국은 대수술이 되었다. ② 가산명사 또는 불가산명사 이사 [주로 영국영어; 미국영어 moving] ❑ 가정집 이사는 시원할 때 하는 것이 가장 좋다.

re|move ♦♦♢ /rɪmuːv/ (removes, removing, removed) **1** V-T If you **remove** something from a place, you take it away. [WRITTEN] ❑ *As soon as the cake is done, remove it from the oven.* **2** V-T If you **remove** clothing, you take it off. [WRITTEN] ❑ *He removed his jacket.* **3** V-T If you **remove** a stain from something, you make the stain disappear by treating it with a chemical or by washing it. ❑ *This treatment removes the most stubborn stains.* **4** V-T If people **remove** someone **from** power or **from** something such as a committee, they stop them being in power or being a member of the committee. ❑ *The student senate voted to remove Fuller from office.* **5** V-T If you **remove** an obstacle, a restriction, or a problem, you get rid of it. ❑ *The agreement removes the last serious obstacle to the signing of the arms treaty.*

■ 타동사 옮기다, 지우다 [문어체] ❑ 케이크가 다 되는 대로 오븐에서 꺼내세요. ② 타동사 벗다 [문어체] ❑ 그는 재킷을 벗었다. ③ 타동사 (얼룩 등을) 빼다 ❑ 이 처리를 하면 대부분의 찌든 때는 빠집니다. ④ 타동사 (권좌에서) 몰아내다, (모임 등에서) 축출하다 ❑ 학생회가 풀러를 학생회에서 축출하기 위해서 투표를 했다. ⑤ 타동사 제거하다 ❑ 이 합의로 군축 조약 서명에 마지막 중대 걸림돌이던 것이 제거된다.

> ### Thesaurus   remove의 참조어
>
> v.   take away, take out **1**
>   take off, undress **2**

re|moved /rɪmuːvd/ ADJ If you say that an idea or situation is far **removed from** something, you mean that it is very different from it. [v-link adv ADJ from n] ❑ *He found it hard to concentrate on conversation so far removed from his present preoccupations.*

형용사 동떨어진 ❑ 그는 자신의 현재 관심사와 너무 동떨어진 대화에는 집중하기 어렵다는 것을 깨달았다.

re|mu|ner|ate /rɪmyuːnəreɪt/ (remunerates, remunerating, remunerated) V-T If you **are remunerated** for work that you do, you are paid for it. [FORMAL] [usu passive] ❑ *You will be remunerated and so will your staff.*

타동사 보수를 받다 [격식체] ❑ 당신과 당신 직원들 역시 보수를 받게 될 것입니다.

re|mu|nera|tion /rɪmyuːnəreɪʃən/ (remunerations) N-VAR Someone's **remuneration** is the amount of money that they are paid for the work that they do. [FORMAL] ❑ *...the continuing marked increase in the remuneration of the company's directors.*

가산명사 또는 불가산명사 보수 [격식체] ❑ 그 회사 이사들이 받는 보수가 눈에 띄게 지속적으로 증가함

re|nais|sance /renɪsɒns, BRIT rɪneɪsɒns/ **1** N-PROPER **The Renaissance** was the period in Europe, especially Italy, in the 14th, 15th, and 16th centuries, when there was a new interest in art, literature, science, and learning. ❑ *...the Renaissance masterpieces in London's galleries.* **2** N-SING If something experiences a **renaissance**, it becomes popular or successful again after a time when people were not interested in it. ❑ *Popular art is experiencing a renaissance.*

■ 고유명사 르네상스 ❑ 런던 미술관에 있는 르네상스 시대의 걸작들 ② 단수명사 부흥 ❑ 대중 예술이 지금 부흥을 맞고 있다.

ren|der /rendər/ (renders, rendering, rendered) V-T You can use **render** with an adjective that describes a particular state to say that someone or something is changed into that state. For example, if someone or something makes a thing harmless, you can say that they **render** it harmless. ❑ *It contained so many errors as to render it worthless.*

타동사 ...되게 만들다 ❑ 그것에는 그것 자체를 쓸모없게 만들 정도로 너무나 많은 오류가 있었다.

ren|dez|vous /rɒndeɪvuː/ (rendezvousing, rendezvoused)

> The form **rendezvous** is pronounced /rɒndeɪvuːz/ when it is the plural of the noun or the third person singular of the verb.

1 N-COUNT A **rendezvous** is a meeting, often a secret one, that you have arranged with someone for a particular time and place. ❑ *I had almost decided to keep my rendezvous with Tony.* **2** N-COUNT A **rendezvous** is the place where you have arranged to meet someone, often secretly. ❑ *Their rendezvous would be the Penta Hotel at Heathrow Airport.* **3** V-RECIP If you **rendezvous with** someone or if the two of you **rendezvous**, you meet them at a time and place that you have arranged. ❑ *The plan was to rendezvous with him on Sunday afternoon.*

형태 rendezvous는 명사의 복수형이거나 동사의 3인칭 단수형일 때는 /rɒndeɪvuːz/로 발음된다.

■ 가산명사 (은밀한) 만남 ❑ 나는 토니와의 만남을 계속하기로 거의 결심했었다. ② 가산명사 만나는 장소 ❑ 그들이 만날 장소는 히드로 공항에 있는 펜타 호텔이 될 것이다. ③ 상호동사 만나다 ❑ 그 계획은 일요일 오후에 그를 만나는 것이었다.

ren|egade /renɪgeɪd/ (renegades) N-COUNT A **renegade** is a person who abandons the religious, political, or philosophical beliefs that he or she used to have, and accepts opposing or different beliefs. ❑ *On the other hand, many Jungian psychologists call Hillman a renegade, heretic, or not a Jungian at all.*

가산명사 변절자 ❑ 반면에, 많은 칼 융학파 심리학자들은 힐맨을 변절자나 이단아로 부르거나 칼 융학파가 전혀 아니라고 했다.

ren|ege /rɪnɪg, BRIT rɪniːg/ (reneges, reneging, reneged) V-I If someone **reneges on** a promise or an agreement, they do not do what they have promised or agreed to do. ❑ *He reneged on a promise to leave his wife.*

자동사 (합의 등을) 저버리다 ❑ 그는 부인과 헤어지겠다는 약속을 저버렸다.

re|new ♦♢♢ /rɪnuː, BRIT rɪnjuː/ (renews, renewing, renewed) **1** V-T If you **renew** an activity, you start it again. ❑ *He renewed his attack on government policy towards Europe.* **2** V-RECIP If you **renew** a relationship **with** someone, you start it again after you have not seen them or have not been friendly with them for some time. ❑ *When the two men met again after the war they renewed their friendship.* **3** V-T When you **renew** something such as a license or a contract, you extend the period of time for which it is valid. ❑ *Larry's landlord threatened not to renew his lease.* **4** V-T You can say that something **is renewed** when it grows again or is

■ 타동사 재개하다 ❑ 그는 정부의 대유럽 정책에 대한 공격을 재개했다. ② 상호동사 (관계를) 회복하다 ❑ 그 두 남자가 전쟁이 끝난 후에 만났을 때, 그들은 우정을 회복하였다. ③ 타동사 갱신하다, 연장하다 ❑ 래리의 집주인은 임대 계약을 갱신해 주지 않겠다고 으름장을 놓았다. ④ 타동사 재생되다 ❑ 세포들이 지속적으로 재생됨으로써 자연의 회복 과정은 느리지만 꾸준히 일어난다.

replaced after it has been destroyed or lost. [usu passive] ❑ *Nature's repair process is slow and steady, with cells being constantly renewed.*

Thesaurus　　　renew의 참조어

v.　　continue, resume, revive ❶ ❷

---

re|new|able /rɪnuːəbəl, BRIT rɪnjuːəbəl/ ❶ ADJ **Renewable** resources are natural ones such as wind, water, and sunlight which are always available. ❑ *...renewable energy sources.* ❷ ADJ If a contract or agreement is **renewable**, it can be extended when it reaches the end of a fixed period of time. ❑ *A formal contract is signed which is renewable annually.*

❶ 형용사 재생 가능한 ❑ 재생 가능한 에너지원 ❷ 형용사 연장 가능한 ❑ 해마다 다시 연장할 수 있는 정식 계약이 체결되었다.

re|new|al /rɪnuːəl, BRIT rɪnjuːəl/ (**renewals**) ❶ N-SING If there is a **renewal of** an activity or a situation, it starts again. ❑ *They will discuss the possible renewal of diplomatic relations.* ❷ N-VAR The **renewal** of a document such as a license or a contract is an official increase in the period of time for which it remains valid. ❑ *His contract came up for renewal.* ❸ N-UNCOUNT **Renewal** of something lost, dead, or destroyed is the process of it growing again or being replaced. ❑ *...a political lobbyist concentrating on urban renewal and regeneration.*

❶ 단수명사 재개 ❑ 그들은 외교 관계 재개 가능성에 대해 논의할 것이다. ❷ 가산명사 또는 불가산명사 갱신, 연장 ❑ 그의 계약 갱신 기일이 다가왔다. ❸ 불가산명사 재생, 재개발 ❑ 도시의 재개발과 재건에 힘쓰고 있는 한 정치 로비스트

re|nounce /rɪnaʊns/ (**renounces, renouncing, renounced**) V-T If you **renounce** a belief or a way of behaving, you decide and declare publicly that you no longer have that belief or will no longer behave in that way. ❑ *After a period of imprisonment she renounced terrorism.*

타동사 포기를 공표하다 ❑ 수감 생활을 마친 후, 그녀는 폭력주의를 포기한다고 공표했다.

Word Link　　　nov ≈ new : innovate, novel, renovate

---

reno|vate /rɛnəveɪt/ (**renovates, renovating, renovated**) V-T If someone **renovates** an old building, they repair and improve it and get it back into good condition. ❑ *The couple spent thousands renovating the house.* ● **reno|va|tion** /rɛnəveɪʃən/ (**renovations**) N-VAR ❑ *...a property which will need extensive renovation.*

타동사 수리하다 ❑ 그 부부는 그 집을 수리하는 데 수천을 들였다. ● 수리 가산명사 또는 불가산명사 ❑ 대대적인 수리를 필요로 하는 집

re|nown /rɪnaʊn/ N-UNCOUNT A person **of renown** is well known, usually because they do or have done something good. ❑ *She used to be a singer of some renown.*

불가산명사 명성 ❑ 그녀는 한때 제법 유명한 가수였다.

re|nowned /rɪnaʊnd/ ADJ A person or place that is **renowned for** something, usually something good, is well known because of it. ❑ *The area is renowned for its Romanesque churches.*

형용사 잘 알려진 ❑ 그 지역은 로마네스크 양식의 교회들로 잘 알려져 있다.

rent ♦◇◇ /rɛnt/ (**rents, renting, rented**) ❶ V-T If you **rent** something, you regularly pay its owner a sum of money in order to be able to have it and use it yourself. ❑ *She rents a house with three other girls.* ❷ V-T If you **rent** something **to** someone, you let them have it and use it in exchange for a sum of money which they pay you regularly. ❑ *She rented rooms to university students.* ● PHRASAL VERB **Rent out** means the same as **rent.** ❑ *Last summer Brian Williams rented out his house and went camping.* ❸ N-VAR **Rent** is the amount of money that you pay regularly to use a house, apartment, or piece of land. ❑ *She worked to pay the rent while I went to college.* ❹ PHRASE If something is **for rent**, it is available for you to hire. [mainly AM; BRIT usually **for hire**] ❑ *Helmets will be available for rent at all Vail Resort ski areas.*

❶ 타동사 빌리다, 임차하다 ❑ 그녀는 세 명의 다른 여자들과 함께 집 하나를 임차해서 살고 있다. ❷ 타동사 빌려 주다, 임대하다 ❑ 그녀는 대학생들에게 방을 임대해 주었다. ● 구동사 빌려 주다, 임대하다 ❑ 작년 여름에 브라이언 윌리엄스는 자신의 집을 임대하고 캠핑을 떠났다. ❸ 가산명사 또는 불가산명사 집세, 임차료 ❑ 내가 대학에 다닐 때 그녀는 집세를 벌기 위해 일을 했다. ❹ 구 빌릴 수 있는, 임차할 수 있는 [주로 미국영어; 영국영어 대개 for hire] ❑ 베일 리조트 스키장 어디에서든 헬멧을 빌리실 수 있을 겁니다.

Do not confuse **rent, hire,** and **let.** If you make a series of payments to use something for a long time, you say that you **rent** it. ❑ *...the apartment he had rented... He rented a TV.* You can say that you **rent** or **rent out** a house or room to someone when they pay you money to live there. ❑ *We rented our house to a college professor.* In British English, it is more common to say that you **let** it. ❑ *They were letting a room to a school teacher.* Americans also use **rent** when you pay a sum of money to use something for a short time. ❑ *He rented a car for the weekend.* In British English, if you pay a sum of money to use something for a short time, you usually say that you **hire** it. ❑ *He was unable to hire another car.*

rent, hire, let을 혼동하지 않도록 하라. 장기간 어떤 것을 사용하기 위해 연속적으로 돈을 지불한다면, 그것을 rent한다고 표현한다. ❑ *...그가 세 낸 아파트... 그는 텔레비전을 빌렸다.* 집이나 방을, 돈을 지불하고 거기서 살고자하는 사람에게 rent하거나 rent out한다고 쓸 수 있다. ❑ 우리는 대학 교수에게 집을 세놓았다. 영국 영어에서는 이럴 때 let을 쓰는 것이 더 일반적이다. ❑ 그들은 학교 교사에게 방을 세 놓고 있었다.미국인들은 단기간 무엇을 사용하기 위해 돈을 지불할 때도 rent를 쓴다. ❑ 그는 주말 동안 차를 빌렸다. 영국 영어에서는 단기간 무엇을 사용하기 위해 돈을 지불할 때는, 대개 hire를 사용한다. ❑ 그는 차를 한 대 더 빌릴 수가 없었다.

---

rent|al /rɛntəl/ (**rentals**) ❶ N-UNCOUNT The **rental** of something such as a car or piece of equipment is the activity or process of renting it. [also N in pl, with supp] ❑ *We can organize car rental from Chicago O'Hare Airport.* ❷ N-COUNT The **rental** is the amount of money that you pay when you rent something such as a car, property, or piece of equipment. ❑ *It has been let at an annual rental of £393,000.* ❸ ADJ You use **rental** to describe things that are connected with the renting out of goods, properties, and services. [ADJ n] ❑ *A friend drove her to Oxford, where she picked up a rental car.*

❶ 불가산명사 임대 ❑ 우리는 시카고 오헤어 공항에서 차를 임대해 드리고 있습니다. ❷ 가산명사 임차료 ❑ 그 집은 연 임대료가 39만 3천 파운드였다. ❸ 형용사 빌린, 임차한 ❑ 한 친구가 그녀를 옥스퍼드까지 데려다 주었고, 그녀는 거기서 렌터카를 빌렸다.

re|or|gan|ize /riɔrgənaɪz/ (**reorganizes, reorganizing, reorganized**) [BRIT also **reorganise**] V-T/V-I To **reorganize** something means to change the way in which it is organized, arranged, or done. ❑ *It is the mother who is expected to reorganize her busy schedule.* ❑ *Four thousand troops have been reorganized into a fighting force.* ● **re|or|gan|iza|tion** /riɔrgənɪzeɪʃən/ (**reorganizations**) N-VAR ❑ *...the reorganization of the legal system.*

[영국영어 reorganise] 타동사/자동사 재편성하다 ❑ 그녀의 바쁜 스케줄을 재편성해 줄 것으로 예상되는 사람은 바로 그녀의 어머니이다. ❑ 4천 명의 군인들이 전투 부대로 재편성되었다. ● 개편, 재편 가산명사 또는 불가산명사 ❑ 법률 제도 개편

rep /rɛp/ (**reps**) ❶ N-COUNT A **rep** is a person whose job is to sell a company's products or services, especially by traveling around and visiting other companies. **Rep** is short for **representative**. ❑ *I'd been working as a sales rep for a photographic company.* ❷ N-COUNT A **rep** is a person who acts as a representative for a group of people, usually a group of people who work together. ❑ *Contact the health and safety rep at your union.*

❶ 가산명사 외판원 ❑ 나는 사진 관련 회사의 외판원으로 일하고 있었다. ❷ 가산명사 대표자 ❑ 당신이 속해 있는 노동조합의 건강 안전 담당자와 연락해 보세요.

re|paid /rɪpeɪd/ **Repaid** is the past tense and past participle of **repay**.

re|pair ♦♢♢ /rɪpeər/ (**repairs, repairing, repaired**) **1** V-T If you **repair** something that has been damaged or is not working properly, you mend it. ❑ *Goldsmith has repaired the roof to ensure the house is wind-proof.* ● **re|pair|er** (**repairers**) N-COUNT ❑ ...*services provided by builders, plumbers, and TV repairers.* **2** V-T If you **repair** a relationship or someone's reputation after it has been damaged, you do something to improve it. ❑ *The government continued to try to repair the damage caused by the minister's interview.* **3** N-VAR A **repair** is something that you do to mend a machine, building, piece of clothing, or other thing that has been damaged or is not working properly. ❑ *Many women know how to carry out repairs on their cars.*

1 타동사 고치다, 수리하다 ❑ 골드스미스는 바람이 불어도 집이 끄떡없도록 지붕을 수리했다. ● 수리공 가산명사 ❑ 건축가, 배관공, 텔레비전 수리공이 제공하는 서비스 **2** 타동사 (관계나 명성을) 회복하다 ❑ 정부는 그 장관이 했던 인터뷰로 인해 입은 체면 손상을 회복하려고 계속 노력했다. **3** 가산명사 또는 불가산명사 수리 ❑ 많은 여자들이 자기 차를 수리할 줄 안다.

Word Partnership   repair의 연어

N.   repair **a chimney**, repair **equipment**, repair **parts**, repair **a roof 1**
     repair **damage 1 2**
     repair **a relationship 2**
     auto repair, **car** repair, **home** repair, **road** repair, repair **service**, repair **shop 3**

---

re|pat|ri|ate /ripeɪtrieɪt, BRIT riːpætrieɪt/ (**repatriates, repatriating, repatriated**) V-T If a country **repatriates** someone, it sends them back to their home country. ❑ *It was not the policy of the government to repatriate genuine refugees.* ● **re|pat|ri|a|tion** /ripeɪtrieɪʃ°n, BRIT riːpætrieɪʃ°n/ (**repatriations**) N-VAR ❑ *Today they begin the forced repatriation of Vietnamese boat people.*

타동사 본국으로 송환하다 ❑ 진성 난민들을 본국으로 송환하는 것이 정부 정책은 아니었다. ● 본국 송환 가산명사 또는 불가산명사 ❑ 그들은 오늘 베트남 보트 피플을 본국으로 강제 송환하기 시작했다.

re|pay /rɪpeɪ/ (**repays, repaying, repaid**) **1** V-T If you **repay** a loan or a debt, you pay back the money that you owe to the person who you borrowed or took it from. ❑ *He advanced funds of his own to his company, which was unable to repay him.* **2** V-T If you **repay** a favor that someone did for you, you do something for them in return. ❑ *It was very kind. I don't know how I can ever repay you.*

1 타동사 (빚을) 갚다 ❑ 그는 자기 개인 돈을 회사에 선불해 주었지만, 회사는 그 돈을 갚을 수 없었다. **2** 타동사 (은혜를) 갚다 ❑ 정말 고맙습니다. 어떻게 이 은혜를 갚아야 될지 모르겠습니다.

re|pay|able /rɪpeɪəb°l/ ADJ A loan that is **repayable** within a certain period of time must be paid back within that time. [mainly BRIT; AM usually **payable**] ❑ *The loan is repayable over twenty years.*

형용사 (특정 기간 내에) 상환해야 할 [주로 영국영어; 미국영어 대개 payable] ❑ 그 대출은 20년 상환이다.

re|pay|ment /rɪpeɪmənt/ (**repayments**) **1** N-COUNT **Repayments** are amounts of money which you pay at regular intervals to a person or organization in order to repay a debt. ❑ *They were unable to meet their mortgage repayments.* **2** N-UNCOUNT The **repayment of** money is the act or process of paying it back to the person you owe it to. ❑ *He failed to meet last Friday's deadline for repayment of a £114m loan.*

1 가산명사 상환금 ❑ 그들은 주택 융자 상환금을 낼 수 없었다. **2** 불가산명사 상환 ❑ 그는 지난 금요일인 1억 1,400만 파운드 대출금의 상환 기한을 지키지 못했다.

re|peal /rɪpil/ (**repeals, repealing, repealed**) V-T If the government **repeals** a law, it officially ends it, so that it is no longer valid. ❑ *The government has just repealed the law segregating public facilities.* ● N-UNCOUNT **Repeal** is also a noun. ❑ *Next year will be the 60th anniversary of the repeal of Prohibition.*

타동사 (법안을) 폐지하다 ❑ 정부는 공공시설에서의 인종 차별법을 지금 막 폐지했다. ● 불가산명사 (법안) 폐지 ❑ 내년은 금주법 폐지 60주년이 될 것이다.

re|peat ♦♦♢ /rɪpit/ (**repeats, repeating, repeated**) **1** V-T If you **repeat** something, you say or write it again. You can say **I repeat** to show that you feel strongly about what you are repeating. ❑ *He repeated that he had been mis-quoted.* ❑ *The Libyan leader Colonel Gadaffi repeated his call for the release of hostages.* **2** V-T If you **repeat** something that someone else has said or written, you say or write the same thing, or tell it to another person. ❑ *She had an irritating habit of repeating everything I said to her.* ❑ *I trust you not to repeat that to anyone else.* **3** V-T If you **repeat yourself**, you say something which you have said before, usually by mistake. ❑ *He spoke well to begin with, but then started rambling and repeating himself.* **4** V-T/V-I If you **repeat** an action, you do it again. ❑ *The next day I repeated the procedure.* **5** V-T If an event or series of events **repeats itself**, it happens again. ❑ *The UN will have to work hard to stop history repeating itself.* **6** N-COUNT If there is a **repeat of** an event, usually an undesirable event, it happens again. ❑ *There were fears that there might be a repeat of last year's campaign of strikes.* **7** ADJ If a company gets **repeat** business or **repeat** customers, people who have bought their goods or services before buy them again. [BUSINESS] [ADJ n] ❑ *Nearly 60% of our bookings come from repeat business and personal recommendation.* **8** N-COUNT A **repeat** is a television or radio program that has been broadcast before. ❑ *There's nothing except sport and repeats on TV.*

1 타동사 반복하다 ❑ 그는 자신이 한 말이 잘못 인용되었다고 반복해서 말했다. ❑ 리비아 지도자 가다피 대령은 반복해서 인질 석방을 요구했다. **2** 타동사 따라 하다; (다른 사람에게) 그대로 전하다 ❑ 그녀는 내가 말하는 모든 것을 따라 하는 짜증나는 버릇이 있었다. ❑ 난 네가 그 말을 다른 사람에게 퍼뜨리지 않으리라 믿어. **3** 타동사 중언부언하다 ❑ 그는 처음에는 말을 곧잘 하더니 나중에는 두서없이 중언부언하기 시작했다. **4** 타동사/자동사 다시 하다 ❑ 그 다음 날 나는 그 과정을 다시 했다. **5** 타동사 반복되다 ❑ 유엔은 이런 역사가 반복되지 않도록 열심히 노력해야 할 것이다. **6** 가산명사 재발하다 ❑ 작년의 파업 운동이 재발할지도 모른다는 우려가 있었다. **7** 형용사 재구매의 [경제] ❑ 예약의 약 60퍼센트가 재구매자와 개인적인 추천에 의해 이루어진다. **8** 가산명사 재방송 ❑ 텔레비전에서는 스포츠와 재방송만 하고 있다.

Thesaurus   repeat의 참조어

V.   reiterate, restate **1 2**
N.   encore **8**

---

re|peat|ed /rɪpitɪd/ ADJ **Repeated** actions or events are ones which happen many times. [ADJ n] ❑ *Mr. Lawssi apparently did not return the money, despite repeated reminders.*

형용사 거듭된 ❑ 로시 씨는 거듭된 독촉장에도 아랑곳하지 않고 돈을 되돌려 주지 않은 것 같았다.

re|peat|ed|ly /rɪpitɪdli/ ADV If you do something **repeatedly**, you do it many times. [ADV with v] ❑ *Both men have repeatedly denied the allegations.*

부사 거듭해서 ❑ 그 남자들은 둘 다 그 혐의를 거듭 부인했다.

re|pel /rɪpɛl/ (**repels, repelling, repelled**) **1** V-T When an army **repels** an attack, they successfully fight and drive back soldiers from another army who have attacked them. [FORMAL] ❑ *They have fifty thousand troops along the border ready to repel any attack.* **2** V-T If something **repels** you, you find it horrible and disgusting. [no cont] ❑ ...*a violent excitement that frightened and repelled her.* ● **re|pelled** ADJ ❑ *She was very striking but in some way I felt repelled.*
→see **magnet**

1 타동사 격퇴하다 [격식체] ❑ 그들은 어떠한 공격도 격퇴할 준비가 되어 있는 5만의 병력을 국경 지역에 배치하고 있다. **2** 타동사 섬뜩하게 하다 ❑ 그녀를 섬뜩하고 겁에 질리게 만든 격렬한 흥분 상태 ● 섬뜩하게 하는 형용사 ❑ 그녀는 아주 인상적이었지만 나는 어떤 면에서는 섬뜩했다.

re|pel|lent /rɪpɛlənt/ (**repellents**)

The spelling **repellant** is also used for meaning 2.

철자 repellant도 2 의미로 쓰인다.

1 ADJ If you think that something is horrible and disgusting you can say that it is **repellent**. [FORMAL] ❑ ...a very large, very repellent toad. 2 N-MASS Insect **repellent** is a product containing chemicals that you spray into the air or on your body in order to keep insects away. ❑ ...mosquito repellent.

1 형용사 섬뜩한 [격식체] ❑ 아주 크고 아주 섬뜩하게 생긴 두꺼비 2 물질명사 (벌레) 퇴치제, 방충제 ❑ 모기 퇴치제

re|pent /rɪpɛnt/ (**repents, repenting, repented**) V-I If you **repent**, you show or say that you are sorry for something wrong you have done. ❑ Those who refuse to repent, he said, will be punished.

자동사 뉘우치다, 회개하다 ❑ 회개하기를 거부하는 자는 벌을 받을 것이라고 그가 말했다.

re|pent|ance /rɪpɛntəns/ N-UNCOUNT If you show **repentance** for something wrong that you have done, you make it clear that you are sorry for doing it. ❑ They showed no repentance during their trial.

불가산명사 반성, 회개 ❑ 그들은 재판을 받는 동안 반성의 기미를 전혀 보이지 않았다.

re|pent|ant /rɪpɛntənt/ ADJ Someone who is **repentant** shows or says that they are sorry for something wrong they have done. ❑ He was feeling guilty and depressed, repentant and scared.

형용사 뉘우치는, 반성하는 ❑ 그는 죄책감을 느껴 기가 죽은 채로 반성하고 있었고 겁에 질려 있었다.

rep|er|toire /rɛpərtwɑr/ (**repertoires**) N-COUNT A performer's **repertoire** is all the plays or pieces of music that he or she has learned and can perform. ❑ Meredith D'Ambrosio has thousands of songs in her repertoire.

가산명사 레퍼토리 ❑ 메레디스 담브로시오는 수천 곡의 레퍼토리를 가지고 있다.

rep|er|tory /rɛpərtɔri, BRIT rɛpəˈtri/ N-UNCOUNT A **repertory** company is a group of actors and actresses who perform a small number of plays for just a few weeks at a time. They work in a **repertory** theater. [usu N n] ❑ ...a well-known repertory company in Boston.

불가산명사 레퍼토리 (극단) ❑ 보스턴에 있는 잘 알려진 레퍼토리 극단

rep|eti|tion /rɛpɪtɪʃən/ (**repetitions**) 1 N-VAR If there is a **repetition of** an event, usually an undesirable event, it happens again. ❑ Today the city government has taken measures to prevent a repetition of last year's confrontation. 2 N-VAR **Repetition** means using the same words again. ❑ He could also have cut out much of the repetition and thus saved many pages.

1 가산명사 또는 불가산명사 반복 ❑ 오늘 시 정부는 작년의 대결 상황이 반복되는 것을 막기 위한 대책을 세웠다. 2 가산명사 또는 불가산명사 반복 ❑ 그는 또한 반복된 부분을 많이 삭제해서 종이 여러 장을 절약할 수 있었다.

rep|eti|tive /rɪpɛtɪtɪv/ 1 ADJ Something that is **repetitive** involves actions or elements that are repeated many times and is therefore boring. [DISAPPROVAL] ❑ ...factory workers who do repetitive jobs. 2 ADJ **Repetitive** movements or sounds are repeated many times. ❑ This technique is particularly successful where problems occur as the result of repetitive movements.

1 형용사 반복되는 [탐탁찮음] ❑ 단순 반복 작업을 하는 공장 노동자들 2 형용사 반복적인 ❑ 이 기술은 반복적인 움직임의 결과로 생기는 문제를 해결하는 것에 특히 성공적이다.

re|place ♦♦◊ /rɪpleɪs/ (**replaces, replacing, replaced**) 1 V-T If one thing or person **replaces** another, the first is used or acts instead of the second. ❑ The council tax replaces the poll tax next April. ❑ ...the lawyer who replaced Robert as chairman of the company. 2 V-T If you **replace** one thing or person **with** another, you put something or someone else in their place to do their job. ❑ I clean all out the grease and replace it with oil so it works better in very low temperatures. 3 V-T If you **replace** something that is broken, damaged, or lost, you get a new one to use instead. ❑ The shower that we put in a few years back has broken and we cannot afford to replace it. 4 V-T If you **replace** something, you put it back where it was before. ❑ Replace the caps on the bottles.

1 타동사 대신하다, 대체하다 ❑ 내년 4월에 지방세가 주민세를 대체한다. ❑ 로버트 대신 그 회사 사장이 된 변호사 2 타동사 대체하다 ❑ 나는 아주 낮은 기온에서 더 잘 작동하도록 수지를 다 닦아 낸 대신 기름을 넣었다. 3 타동사 교체하다 ❑ 몇 년 전에 설치한 샤워기가 고장이 났지만 우리는 그것을 교체할 형편이 안 된다. 4 타동사 다시 제자리에 놓다 ❑ 병뚜껑을 다시 닫으세요.

re|place|ment ♦◊◊ /rɪpleɪsmənt/ (**replacements**) 1 N-UNCOUNT If you refer to the **replacement** of one thing by another, you mean that the second thing takes the place of the first. [with supp] ❑ ...the replacement of damaged or lost books. 2 N-COUNT Someone who takes someone else's place in an organization, government, or team can be referred to as their **replacement**. ❑ Taylor has nominated Adams as his replacement.

1 불가산명사 교체 ❑ 파손되거나 분실된 책을 교체함 2 가산명사 후임자 ❑ 테일러는 자기 후임자로 애덤스를 지명했다.

re|play (**replays, replaying, replayed**)

The verb is pronounced /riːpleɪ/. The noun is pronounced /riːpleɪ/.

동사는 /riːpleɪ/로 발음되고, 명사는 /riːpleɪ/로 발음된다.

1 V-T If a game or match between two sports teams **is replayed**, the two teams play it again, because neither team won the first time, or because the game was stopped because of bad weather. [usu passive] ❑ Drawn matches were replayed three or four days later. ● N-COUNT You can refer to a game that is replayed as a **replay**. ❑ If there has to be a replay we are confident of victory. 2 V-T If you **replay** something that you have recorded on film or tape, you play it again in order to watch it or listen to it. ❑ He stopped the machine and replayed the message. ● N-COUNT **Replay** is also a noun. ❑ I watched a slow-motion videotape replay of his fall. 3 V-T If you **replay** an event in your mind, you think about it again and again. ❑ She spends her nights lying in bed, replaying the fire in her mind.

1 타동사 재경기를 갖다 ❑ 무승부가 난 경기들은 사나흘 후에 재경기를 가졌다. ● 가산명사 재경기 ❑ 재경기를 갖게 된다면 우리는 이길 자신이 있다. 2 타동사 재생하다 ❑ 그는 응답기를 멈추고 나서 그 메시지를 재생했다. ● 가산명사 재생 ❑ 나는 그가 넘어지는 장면을 담은 비디오테이프의 느린 동작 재생 화면을 보았다. 3 타동사 회상하다 ❑ 그는 밤새도록 침대에 누워 그 불꽃을 회상했다.

Word Link   *plen* ≈ *full* : *plentiful, plenty, replenish*

re|plen|ish /rɪplɛnɪʃ/ (**replenishes, replenishing, replenished**) V-T If you **replenish** something, you make it full or complete again. [FORMAL] ❑ Three hundred thousand tons of cereals are needed to replenish stocks.

타동사 보충하다, 새로 보급하다 [격식체] ❑ 비축량을 다시 채우려면 30만 톤의 곡물이 필요하다.

rep|li|ca /rɛplɪkə/ (**replicas**) N-COUNT A **replica of** something such as a statue, building, or weapon is an accurate copy of it. ❑ ...a human-sized replica of the Statue of Liberty.

가산명사 복제품 ❑ 사람 크기의 자유의 여신상 복제품

re|ply ♦♦◊ /rɪplaɪ/ (**replies, replying, replied**) 1 V-T/V-I When you **reply to** something that someone has said or written to you, you say or write an answer to them. ❑ "That's a nice dress," said Michael. "Thanks," she replied solemnly. ❑ He replied that this was absolutely impossible. 2 N-COUNT A **reply** is something that you say or write when you answer someone or answer a letter or advertisement. [oft N to/from n, also in N] ❑ I called out a challenge, but there was no reply. ❑ He said in reply that the question was unfair. 3 V-I If you **reply** to something such as an attack **with** violence or **with** another action, you do something in response. ❑ During a number of violent incidents farmers threw eggs and empty bottles at police, who replied with tear gas.

1 타동사/자동사 대답하다 ❑ "멋진 드레스인데."라고 마이클이 말하자 "고마워."라고 그녀가 근엄하게 대답했다. ❑ 그는 이건 절대로 불가능한 일이라고 대답했다. 2 가산명사 대답 ❑ 내가 도전을 제기하는데 아무런 대답이 없었다. ❑ 그는 그 질문이 부당하다고 대답했다. 3 자동사 응수하다 ❑ 수차례의 폭력 사건에서 농민들은 달걀과 빈 병을 경찰에게 던졌고, 경찰은 최루탄으로 응수했다.

Thesaurus — reply의 참조어

v. acknowledge, answer, respond, return ◫1
n. acknowledgement, answer, response ◫2

Word Partnership — reply의 연어

n. reply **card**, reply **envelope**, reply **form** ◫2
v. **make a** reply, **receive a** reply ◫2

re|port ♦♦♦ /rɪpɔ́rt/ (reports, reporting, reported) ◫1 V-T If you **report** something that has happened, you tell people about it. ❑ I reported the theft to the police. ❑ The officials also reported that two more ships were apparently heading for Malta. ❑ "He seems to be all right now," reported a relieved Taylor. ❑ She reported him missing the next day. ◫2 V-I If you **report on** an event or subject, you tell people about it, because it is your job or duty to do so. ❑ Many journalists based outside of Sudan have been refused visas to enter the country to report on political affairs. ◫3 N-COUNT A **report** is a news article or broadcast which gives information about something that has just happened. ❑ According to a report in London's Independent newspaper, he still has control over the remaining shares. ◫4 N-COUNT A **report** is an official document which a group of people issue after investigating a situation or event. ❑ The education committee will today publish its report on the supply of teachers for the 1990's. ◫5 N-COUNT If you give someone a **report** on something, you tell them what has been happening. ❑ She came back to give us a progress report on how the project is going. ◫6 N-COUNT If you say that there are **reports** that something has happened, you mean that some people say it has happened but you have no direct evidence of it. [VAGUENESS] ❑ There are unconfirmed reports that two people have been shot in the neighboring town of Lalitpur. ◫7 V-T If someone **reports** you to a person in authority, they tell that person about something wrong that you have done. ❑ His ex-wife reported him to police a few days later. ◫8 V-I If you **report to** a person or place, you go to that person or place and say that you are ready to start work or say that you are present. ❑ Mr. Ashwell has to surrender his passport and report to the police every five days. ◫9 V-I If you say that one employee **reports** to another, you mean that the first employee is told what to do by the second one and is responsible to them. [FORMAL] [no cont] ❑ He reported to a section chief, who reported to a division chief, and so on up the line. ◫10 →see also **reporting**

Thesaurus — report의 참조어

v. broadcast, cover, narrate, publish ◫1 ◫2
appear, arrive, show up ◫8
n. announcement, communication, release, story ◫3 ◫4

re|port card (report cards) ◫1 N-COUNT A **report card** is an official written account of how well or how badly a student has done during the term or year that has just finished. [AM; BRIT **report**] ❑ The only time I got their attention was when I brought home straight A's on my report card. ◫2 N-COUNT A **report card** is a report on how well a person, organization, or country has been doing recently. [AM, JOURNALISM] ❑ The President today issued his final report card on the state of the economy.

re|port|ed|ly /rɪpɔ́rtɪdli/ ADV If you say that something is **reportedly** true, you mean that someone has said that it is true, but you have no direct evidence of it. [FORMAL, VAGUENESS] ❑ More than two hundred people have reportedly been killed in the past week's fighting.

re|port|er ♦♦◇ /rɪpɔ́rtər/ (reporters) N-COUNT A **reporter** is someone who writes news articles or who broadcasts news reports. ❑ ...a TV reporter.

re|port|ing ♦♦◇ /rɪpɔ́rtɪŋ/ N-UNCOUNT **Reporting** is the presenting of news in newspapers, on radio, and on television. ❑ This newspaper has achieved a reputation for honest and impartial political reporting.

Word Link — pos ≈ placing : deposit, preposition, repository

re|posi|tory /rɪpɒ́zɪtɔri, BRIT rɪpɒ́zɪtri/ (repositories) N-COUNT A **repository** is a place where something is kept safely. [FORMAL] ❑ A church in Moscow became a repository for police files.

re|pos|sess /ríːpəzés/ (repossesses, repossessing, repossessed) V-T If your car or house **is repossessed**, the people who supplied it take it back because they are still owed money for it. [usu passive] ❑ His car was repossessed by the company.

re|pos|ses|sion /ríːpəzéʃən/ (repossessions) N-VAR The **repossession** of someone's house is the act of repossessing it. ❑ ...the problem of home repossessions.

rep|re|sent ♦♦◇ /rɛprɪzɛ́nt/ (represents, representing, represented) ◫1 V-T If someone such as a lawyer or a politician **represents** a person or group of people, they act on behalf of that person or group. ❑ ...the politicians we elect to represent us. ◫2 V-T If you **represent** a person or group at an official event, you go there on their behalf. ❑ The general secretary may represent the president at official ceremonies. ◫3 V-T If you **represent** your country or city in a competition or sports event, you take part in it on behalf of the country or city where you live. ❑ My only aim is to represent Britain at the Olympics. ◫4 V-T PASSIVE If a group of people or things **is** well **represented** in a particular activity or in a particular place, a lot of them can be found there. ❑ Women are already well represented in the area of TV drama. ◫5 V-T If a sign or symbol **represents** something, it is accepted as meaning that thing. [no cont] ❑ ...a black dot in the middle of the circle is supposed to represent the source of the radiation. ◫6 V-T To **represent** an idea or quality means

◫1 타동사 보고하다, 신고하다 ❑ 나는 그 절도 사건을 경찰에 신고했다. ❑ 그 관리들은 배 두 척이 더 몰타로 향하고 있는 것 같다고 보고했다. ❑ "그는 이제 괜찮아 보여."라고 안도한 테일러가 말했다. ❑ 다음날 그녀는 그가 실종되었다고 신고했다. ◫2 자동사 보도하다 ❑ 수단 외곽에 본부를 둔 많은 언론인들이 정치 사건들을 보도하기 위해 그 나라로 들어가려 했으나 입국 비자 발급을 거부당했다. ◫3 가산명사 보도 ❑ 런던 인디펜던트 지의 보도에 따르면 그는 여전히 잔여 주식에 대한 권한을 갖고 있다고 한다. ◫4 가산명사 보고서 ❑ 교육 위원회는 오늘 1990년대 교원 수급에 대한 보고서를 발표할 것이다. ◫5 가산명사 보고 ❑ 그녀는 그 프로젝트 진행 상황을 우리에게 보고하기 위해서 돌아왔다. ◫6 가산명사 소문 [짐작투] ❑ 랄릿푸르 인근 마을에서 두 사람이 총에 맞았다는 확인되지 않은 소문이 있다. ◫7 타동사 고발하다 ❑ 그의 전처가 며칠 후에 그를 경찰에 고발했다. ◫8 자동사 (상황 등을) 보고하다 ❑ 애쉬웰 씨는 자신의 여권을 내주어야 했고 5일에 한 번씩 자신의 소재를 경찰에 신고해야 했다. ◫9 자동사 보고하다 [격식체] ❑ 그는 과장에게 보고했고, 과장은 부장에게 보고했고, 이런 식으로 계속 보고 라인을 따라 올라갔다.

◫1 가산명사 성적표 [미국영어; 영국영어 report] ❑ 내가 그들의 관심을 받은 유일한 때는 내가 전체 에이의 성적표를 집으로 가져왔을 때뿐이었다. ◫2 가산명사 성과표, 성적표 [미국영어, 언론] ❑ 대통령은 오늘 국가 경제에 대한 최종 성과표를 발표했다.

부사 소문에 의하면 [격식체, 짐작투] ❑ 소문에 의하면 지난주에 있었던 전투에서 이백 명도 넘는 사람들이 죽었다고 한다.

가산명사 기자 ❑ 텔레비전 기자

불가산명사 보도 ❑ 그 신문은 정직하고 공정한 정치 보도로 정평을 받고 있다.

가산명사 보관소 [격식체] ❑ 모스크바에 있는 한 교회는 경찰 관련 문서의 보관소가 되었다.

타동사 (담보물을 미지불물로) 회수당하다 ❑ 그는 차를 회사에 회수당했다.

가산명사 또는 불가산명사 회수 ❑ 주택 회수 문제

◫1 타동사 대표하다 ❑ 우리를 대표하도록 우리가 선출하는 정치인들 ◫2 타동사 대신하다 ❑ 공식 행사에서 사무총장이 회장을 대신할 수도 있다. ◫3 타동사 대표 선수로 출전하다 ❑ 나의 유일한 목표는 영국 대표 선수로 올림픽에 출전하는 것이다. ◫4 수동 타동사 쉽게 만나 볼 수 있다 ❑ 텔레비전 드라마 부문에는 여자들이 이미 자주 등장한다. ◫5 타동사 의미하다, 나타내다 ❑ 원 중앙에 있는 검은 점은 방사능 물질의 근원을 의미하도록 되어 있다. ◫6 타동사 구현하다 ❑ 우리는 네가 영국 경마가 필요로 하는 모든 기술을 구현할 수 있다는 것을 믿는다. ◫7 타동사 묘사하다 ❑ 대중지는 그를 환경 전문가로 묘사하는 경향이 있다.

A

to be a symbol or an expression of that idea or quality. [no cont, no passive]
❏ *We believe you represent everything British racing needs.* **7** V-T If you **represent** a person or thing **as** a particular thing, you describe them as being that thing. ❏ *The popular press tends to represent him as an environmental guru.*

B

rep|re|sen|ta|tion /ˌrɛprɪzɛnˈteɪʃⁿn/ (**representations**) **1** N-UNCOUNT If a group or person has **representation** in a legislature or on a committee, someone in the legislature or on the committee supports them and makes decisions on their behalf. ❏ *Puerto Ricans are U.S. citizens but they have no representation in Congress.* →see also **proportional representation** **2** N-COUNT You can describe a picture, model, or statue of a person or thing as a **representation of** them. [FORMAL] ❏ *...a lifelike representation of Christ.*

C

1 불가산명사 대표 ❏ 푸에르토리코 인들은 미국 시민이지만 의회 내에 그들의 이익을 대변할 대표자가 없다. **2** 가산명사 표현한 것, 구현물 [격식체] ❏ 실물 같은 그리스도 조각상

D

rep|re|senta|tive ♦♦◇ /ˌrɛprɪˈzɛntətɪv/ (**representatives**) **1** N-COUNT A **representative** is a person who has been chosen to act or make decisions on behalf of another person or a group of people. ❏ *...trade union representatives.* **2** N-COUNT A **representative** is a person whose job is to sell a company's products or services, especially by traveling around and visiting other companies. [FORMAL] ❏ *She had a stressful job as a sales representative.* **3** ADJ A **representative** group consists of a small number of people who have been chosen to make decisions on behalf of a larger group. [ADJ n] ❏ *The new head of state should be chosen by an 87 member representative council.* **4** ADJ Someone who is typical of the group to which they belong can be described as **representative**. ❏ *He was in no way representative of dog-trainers in general.* **5** N-COUNT In the United States, a **representative** is a member of the House of Representatives, the less powerful of the two parts of Congress. ❏ *...a Republican representative from Wyoming.* **6** →see also **House of Representatives**

E

F

G

1 가산명사 대표자 ❏ 산별 노조 대표자들 **2** 가산명사 외판원 [격식체] ❏ 그는 외판원이라는 스트레스 쌓이는 일을 하고 있었다. **3** 형용사 대표 ❏ 새 국가 원수는 87명으로 구성된 대표자 회의에서 선출되어야 한다. **4** 형용사 전형적인 ❏ 그는 일반적인 개 조련사의 전형과는 거리가 멀었다. **5** 가산명사 하원 의원 ❏ 와이오밍 출신의 공화당 하원 의원

H

re|press /rɪˈprɛs/ (**represses, repressing, repressed**) **1** V-T If you **repress** a feeling, you make a deliberate effort not to show or have this feeling. ❏ *It is anger that is repressed that leads to violence and loss of control.* **2** V-T If you **repress** a smile, sigh, or moan, you try hard not to smile, sigh, or moan. ❏ *He repressed a smile.* **3** V-T If a section of society is **repressed**, their freedom is restricted by the people who have authority over them. [DISAPPROVAL] ❏ *...a UN resolution banning him from repressing his people.*

I

1 타동사 (감정을) 억누르다 ❏ 폭력을 휘두르거나 자제력을 잃도록 만드는 것은 바로 억눌려 있는 분노이다. **2** 타동사 (웃음 등을) 억지로 참다 ❏ 그는 미소를 짓고 싶은 걸 억지로 참았다. **3** 타동사 억압하다 ❏ 그가 국민들을 억압하는 것을 금지하기로 한 유엔의 결의안

J

re|pressed /rɪˈprɛst/ ADJ A **repressed** person is someone who does not allow themselves to have natural feelings and desires, especially sexual ones. ❏ *Some have charged that the Puritans were sexually repressed.*

K

형용사 억압된 ❏ 어떤 사람들은 청교도인들이 성적으로 억압되어 있었다고 비난해 왔다.

re|pres|sion /rɪˈprɛʃⁿn/ (**repressions**) **1** N-UNCOUNT **Repression** is the use of force to restrict and control a society or other group of people. [DISAPPROVAL] ❏ *...a society conditioned by violence and repression.* **2** N-UNCOUNT **Repression** of feelings, especially sexual ones, is a person's unwillingness to allow themselves to have natural feelings and desires. ❏ *Much of the anger he's felt during his life has stemmed from the repression of his feelings about men.*

L

M

1 불가산명사 압제, 억압 [탐탁잖음] ❏ 폭력과 억압에 길들여진 사회 **2** 불가산명사 억제 ❏ 그가 일생 동안 느낀 분노의 대부분은 남자에 대한 자신의 감정을 억제하는 것에서 비롯되었다.

N

re|pres|sive /rɪˈprɛsɪv/ ADJ A **repressive** government is one that restricts people's freedom and controls them by using force. [DISAPPROVAL] ❏ *The military regime in power was unpopular and repressive.*

형용사 억압하는 [탐탁잖음] ❏ 권력을 쥔 그 군사 정권은 국민들로부터 외면을 받는 억압적인 정권이었다.

O

re|prieve /rɪˈpriːv/ (**reprieves, reprieving, reprieved**) **1** V-T If someone who has been sentenced in a court **is reprieved**, their punishment is officially delayed or canceled. [usu passive, no cont] ❏ *Fourteen people, waiting to be hanged for the murder of a former prime minister, have been reprieved.* ● N-VAR **Reprieve** is also a noun ❏ *A man awaiting death by lethal injection has been saved by a last minute reprieve.* **2** N-COUNT A **reprieve** is a delay before a very unpleasant or difficult situation which may or may not take place. ❏ *It looked as though the college would have to shut, but this week it was given a reprieve.*

P

1 타동사 집행 유예를 받다 ❏ 전 수상 살해죄로 교수형 집행을 기다리던 14명이 집행 유예를 받았다. ● 가산명사 또는 불가산명사 집행 유예 ❏ 독극물 주입을 통한 사형을 기다리던 남자가 마지막 순간에 집행 유예로 형 집행을 면했다. **2** 가산명사 유예 결정 ❏ 그 대학이 문을 닫아야 할 것처럼 보였지만, 이번 주에 그 유예 결정을 받았다.

Q

rep|ri|mand /ˈrɛprɪmænd/ (**reprimands, reprimanding, reprimanded**) V-T If someone **is reprimanded**, they are spoken to angrily or seriously for doing something wrong, usually by a person in authority. [FORMAL] ❏ *He was reprimanded by a teacher for talking in the corridor.* ● N-VAR **Reprimand** is also a noun. ❏ *He has been fined five thousand pounds and given a severe reprimand.*

타동사 야단맞다, 질책받다 [격식체] ❏ 그는 복도에서 떠든다고 선생님께 크게 야단맞았다. ● 가산명사 또는 불가산명사 질책 ❏ 그는 5만 파운드 벌금형을 받았고 호된 질책을 받았다.

R

re|print (**reprints, reprinting, reprinted**)

The verb is pronounced /ˌriːˈprɪnt/. The noun is pronounced /ˈriːprɪnt/.

동사는 /ˌriːˈprɪnt/로 발음되고, 명사는 /ˈriːprɪnt/로 발음된다.

S

1 V-T If a book **is reprinted**, further copies of it are printed when all the other ones have been sold. [usu passive] ❏ *It remained an exceptionally rare book until it was reprinted in 1918.* **2** N-COUNT A **reprint** is a process in which new copies of a book or article are printed because all the other ones have been sold. ❏ *Demand picked up and a reprint was required last November.* **3** N-COUNT A **reprint** is a new copy of a book or article, printed because all the other ones have been sold or because minor changes have been made to the original. ❏ *...a reprint of a 1962 novel.*

T

1 타동사 (책의) 재판이 발행되다 ❏ 그 책은 1918년에 재판을 찍을 때까지 예외적인 희귀서로 남아 있었다. **2** 가산명사 (책의) 재판 ❏ 수요가 증가해서 작년 11월에 재판을 찍어야 했다. **3** 가산명사 재판(再版) 수정판 ❏ 1962년판 소설의 수정판

U

re|pris|al /rɪˈpraɪzⁿl/ (**reprisals**) N-VAR If you do something to a person in reprisal, you hurt or punish them because they have done something violent or unpleasant to you. ❏ *There were fears that some of the Western hostages might be killed in reprisal.*

V

가산명사 또는 불가산명사 보복 ❏ 서방의 인질 중 몇 명이 보복으로 살해될 수도 있다는 우려가 있었다.

W

re|proach /rɪˈproʊtʃ/ (**reproaches, reproaching, reproached**) **1** V-T If you **reproach** someone, you say or show that you are disappointed, upset, or angry because they have done something wrong. ❏ *She is quick to reproach anyone who doesn't live up to her own high standards.* **2** N-VAR If you look at or speak to someone with **reproach**, you show or say that you are disappointed, upset, or angry because they have done something wrong. ❏ *He looked at her with reproach.* **3** V-T If you **reproach yourself**, you think with regret about something you have done wrong. ❏ *You've no reason to reproach yourself, no reason to feel shame.*

X

Y

1 타동사 비난하다, 책망하다 ❏ 그녀는 자신의 높은 수준에 맞추지 않는 사람은 누구든 쉽게 비난한다. **2** 가산명사 또는 불가산명사 비난, 책망 ❏ 그는 그녀를 책망하는 눈길로 쳐다보았다. **3** 타동사 자책하다 ❏ 자책할 이유도 없고, 부끄러워할 이유도 없어.

Z

re|pro|duce /ˌriːprəˈduːs, BRIT ˌriːprəˈdjuːs/ (**reproduces, reproducing, reproduced**) **1** V-T If you try to **reproduce** something, you try to copy it. ❏ *The effect has proved hard to reproduce.* **2** V-T If you **reproduce** a picture, speech, or a piece of

1 타동사 복제하다 ❏ 그 효과는 복제하기 어려운 것으로 밝혀졌다. **2** 타동사 (글 등을) 복사하다, 다시 싣다 ❏ 이 글을 다시 실을 수 있게 허락해 주셔서

writing, you make a photograph or printed copy of it. ❑ *We are grateful to you for permission to reproduce this article.* ❸ V-T If you **reproduce** an action or an achievement, you repeat it. ❑ *If we can reproduce the form we have shown in the last couple of months we will be successful.* ❹ V-T/V-I When people, animals, or plants **reproduce**, they produce young. ❑ *...a society where women are defined by their ability to reproduce.* ● re|pro|duc|tion /riprədʌkʃ°n/ N-UNCOUNT ❑ *Treatments using assisted reproduction techniques jumped 30 percent* →see **flower**

re|pro|duc|tion /riprədʌkʃ°n/ (reproductions) N-COUNT A **reproduction** is a copy of something such as a piece of furniture or a work of art. ❑ *...a reproduction of a popular religious painting.* →see also **reproduce**

re|pro|duc|tive /riprədʌktɪv/ ADJ **Reproductive** processes and organs are concerned with the reproduction of living things. ❑ *...the female reproductive system.*

rep|tile /reptaɪl, -tɪl, BRIT reptaɪl/ (reptiles) N-COUNT **Reptiles** are a group of cold-blooded animals which lay eggs and have skins covered with small hard plates called scales. Snakes, lizards, and crocodiles are reptiles. →see **pet**

re|pub|lic ♦♦◇ /rɪpʌblɪk/ (republics) N-COUNT A **republic** is a country where power is held by the people or the representatives that they elect. Republics have presidents who are elected, rather than kings or queens. ❑ *In 1918, Austria became a republic.* ❑ *...the Baltic republics.*

re|pub|li|can ♦♦◇ /rɪpʌblɪkən/ (republicans) ❶ ADJ **Republican** means relating to a republic. In **republican** systems of government, power is held by the people or the representatives that they elect. ❑ *...the nations that had adopted the republican form of government.* ❷ ADJ In the United States, if someone is **Republican**, they belong to or support the Republican Party. ❑ *Lower taxes made Republican voters happier with their party.* ● N-COUNT A **Republican** is someone who supports or belongs to the Republican Party. ❑ *What made you decide to become a Republican, as opposed to a Democrat?*

re|pu|di|ate /rɪpyudieɪt/ (repudiates, repudiating, repudiated) V-T If you **repudiate** something or someone, you show that you strongly disagree with them and do not want to be connected with them in any way. [FORMAL or WRITTEN] ❑ *Leaders urged people to turn out in large numbers to repudiate the violence.* ● re|pu|dia|tion /rɪpyudieɪʃ°n/ (repudiations) N-VAR ❑ *He believes his public repudiation of the conference decision will enhance his standing as a leader.*

re|pul|sive /rɪpʌlsɪv/ ADJ If you describe something or someone as **repulsive**, you mean that they are horrible and disgusting and you want to avoid them. ❑ *...repulsive fat white slugs.*

repu|table /repyətəb°l/ ADJ A **reputable** company or person is reliable and can be trusted. ❑ *You are well advised to buy your car through a reputable dealer.*

Word Link put ≈ thinking : *computer, dispute, reputation*

repu|ta|tion ♦♦◇ /repyəteɪʃ°n/ (reputations) ❶ N-COUNT To have a **reputation** for something means to be known or remembered for it. ❑ *Alice Munro has a reputation for being a very depressing writer.* ❷ N-COUNT Something's or someone's **reputation** is the opinion that people have about how good they are. If they have a good reputation, people think they are good. ❑ *This college has a good academic reputation.* ❸ PHRASE If you know someone **by reputation**, you have never met them but you have heard of their reputation. ❑ *She was by reputation a good organizer.*

Word Partnership *reputation*의 연어

ADJ.	**bad** reputation, **good** reputation ❶ ❷
V.	**acquire** a reputation, **build** a reputation, **damage** *someone's* reputation, **earn** a reputation, **establish** a reputation, **gain** a reputation, **have** a reputation, **ruin** *someone's* reputation, **tarnish** *someone's* reputation ❶ ❷

---

re|put|ed /rɪpyutɪd/ V-T PASSIVE If you say that something **is reputed to** be true, you mean that people say it is true, but you do not know if it is definitely true. [FORMAL, VAGUENESS] ❑ *...the monster, which is reputed to live in the deep dark water of a Scottish loch.* ● re|put|ed|ly /rɪpyutɪdli/ ADV ❑ *He reputedly earns two million dollars a year.*

re|quest ♦♦◇ /rɪkwɛst/ (requests, requesting, requested) ❶ V-T If you **request** something, you ask for it politely or formally. [FORMAL] ❑ *Mr. Dennis said he had requested access to a telephone.* ❷ V-T If you **request** someone **to** do something, you politely or formally ask them to do it. [FORMAL] ❑ *Students are requested to park at the rear of the Department.* ❸ N-COUNT If you make a **request**, you politely or formally ask someone to do something. ❑ *France had agreed to his request for political asylum.* ❹ PHRASE If you do something **at** someone's **request**, you do it because they have asked you to. ❑ *The evacuation is being organized at the request of the United Nations Secretary General.* ❺ PHRASE If something is given or done **on request**, it is given or done whenever you ask for it. ❑ *Leaflets giving details are available on request.*

Word Partnership *request*의 연어

N.	**request** aid, **request** a hearing, **request** information, **request** permission, **request** a response ❶
V.	**agree to** a request, **consider** a request, **deny** a request, **grant** a request, **make** a request, **refuse** a request, **reject** a request, **respond to** a request, **send** a request, **submit** a request ❸

감사합니다. ❸ 타동사 재현하다 ❑ 우리가 지난 몇 달 동안 보여 준 그 자세를 재현할 수 있다면, 우리는 성공할 것이다. ❹ 타동사/자동사 자식을 낳다, 번식하다 ❑ 여자를 출산 능력으로 규정하는 사회 ●번식 불가산명사 ❑ 인공 수정과 같은 기술을 이용한 치료가 30퍼센트나 급증했다.

가산명사 복제품 ❑ 유명한 종교화의 복제품

형용사 생식의 ❑ 여성 생식 체계

가산명사 파충류

가산명사 공화국 ❑ 오스트리아는 1918년에 공화국이 되었다. ❑ 발트 해 공화국

❶ 형용사 공화국의 ❑ 공화제 정부를 도입했던 나라들 ❷ 형용사 공화당의, 공화당을 지지하는 ❑ 세금 인하로 공화당을 지지하는 사람들이 자기들 지지 정당에 더 만족하게 되었다. ● 가산명사 공화당원 ❑ 무엇 때문에 민주당원이 아닌, 공화당원이 되기로 결심하셨습니까?

타동사 반대하다 [격식체 또는 문어체] ❑ 지도자들이 사람들에게 그 폭력 반대 시위에 대규모로 참가하라고 촉구했다. ● 반대 가산명사 또는 불가산명사 ❑ 그는 그 회의의 결정을 공개적으로 반대하는 것이 지도자로서의 자신의 입지를 공고하게 해 줄 것이라고 믿는다.

형용사 혐오스러운 ❑ 혐오스러울 정도로 살찐 하얀 민달팽이들

형용사 평판 있는 ❑ 차는 평판 있는 판매상에게서 구입해야 후환이 없을 것이다.

❶ 가산명사 정평 ❑ 앨리스 먼로는 굉장히 우울한 작가라고 정평이 나 있다. ❷ 가산명사 평판 ❑ 이 대학은 학문적으로 좋은 평판을 받는다. ❸ 구 명성이 나서, 평판을 듣고 ❑ 그녀는 좋은 기획자라고 명성이 나 있었다.

수동 타동사 ―라고 알려져 있다 [격식체, 짐작투] ❑ 어느 스코틀랜드 호수의 어둡고 깊은 물속에 존재한다고 전해지는 그 괴물● 알려져 있기로, 평판에 의하면 부사 ❑ 소문에 의하면 그는 일년에 2백만 달러를 번다.

❶ 타동사 요청하다 [격식체] ❑ 데니스 씨는 전화 사용을 요청했다고 말했다. ❷ 타동사 요청하다 [격식체] ❑ 학생들은 학과의 후면에 주차하도록 권장된다. ❸ 가산명사 요청 ❑ 프랑스가 그의 정치 망명 요구를 수락한 상태였다. ❹ 구 ―의 요청에 따라 ❑ 대피는 유엔 사무총장의 요청에 따라 준비되고 있다. ❺ 구 요청이 있으면 ❑ 요청할 경우 내용을 담은 책자를 보내 드립니다.

a b c d e f g h i j k l m n o p q r s t u v w x y z

A

re|quire ♦♦◇ /rɪkwaɪər/ (**requires, requiring, required**) **1** V-T If you **require** something or if something **is required**, you need it or it is necessary. [FORMAL] ❑ *If you require further information, you should consult the registrar.* ❑ *This isn't the kind of crisis that requires us to drop everything else.* **2** V-T If a law or rule **requires** you to do something, you have to do it. [FORMAL] ❑ *The rules also require employers to provide safety training.* ❑ *At least 35 manufacturers have flouted a law requiring prompt reporting of such malfunctions.*

B

re|quire|ment ♦◇◇ /rɪkwaɪərmənt/ (**requirements**) **1** N-COUNT A **requirement** is a quality or qualification that you must have in order to be allowed to do something or to be suitable for something. ❑ *Its products met all legal requirements.* **2** N-COUNT Your **requirements** are the things that you need. [FORMAL] ❑ *Variations of this programme can be arranged to suit your requirements.*

C

1 타동사 ~을 필요로 하다; ~이 필요하다 [격식체] ❑ 더 많은 정보가 필요하시면 총무과에 문의하세요. ❑ 우리가 다른 모든 것에서 손을 떼야 할 정도로 이것이 심각한 위기는 아니다. **2** 타동사 요구하다 [격식체] ❑ 또한 규정에 따르면 고용주들은 안전 교육을 해야 한다. ❑ 최소한 35개의 제조사가 그러한 고장은 즉각 보고해야 한다는 법을 지키지 않았다.

1 가산명사 요구 사항 ❑ 제품들은 모든 법적 기준들에 부합했다. **2** 가산명사 필요 [격식체] ❑ 필요에 따라 프로그램을 조정할 수 있습니다.

D

Word Partnership   requirement의 연어

ADJ.	**legal** requirement, **minimum** requirement **1**
V.	**meet** a requirement **1**

E

F

requi|site /rɛkwɪzɪt/ (**requisites**) **1** ADJ You can use **requisite** to indicate that something is necessary for a particular purpose. [FORMAL] ❑ *She filled in the requisite paperwork.* **2** N-COUNT A **requisite** is something which is necessary for a particular purpose. [FORMAL] ❑ *An understanding of accounting techniques is a major requisite for the work of the analysts.*

G

1 형용사 필요한 [격식체] ❑ 그녀는 필요한 서류들을 작성했다. **2** 가산명사 필요조건 [격식체] ❑ 분석가들의 작업을 위해서는 회계 기술에 대한 이해가 반드시 요구된다.

re|sale /riseɪl/ N-UNCOUNT The **resale** price of something that you own is the amount of money that you would get if you sold it. ❑ *...a well-maintained used car with a good resale value.*

불가산명사 되팔기, 전매(轉買) ❑ 유지가 잘 되고 되팔기 가격이 양호한 중고차

H

re|sched|ule /riʃkedʒul, -dʒuəl, BRIT riːʃedyuːl/ (**reschedules, rescheduling, rescheduled**) **1** V-T If someone **reschedules** an event, they change the time at which it is supposed to happen. ❑ *Since I'll be away, I'd like to reschedule the meeting.* **2** V-T To **reschedule** a debt means to arrange for the person, organization, or country that owes money to pay it back over a longer period because they are in financial difficulty. ❑ *...companies that have gone bust or had to reschedule their debts.*

1 타동사 재조정하다, 일정을 다시 잡다 ❑ 제가 이곳에 없을 것이므로 회의 일정을 재조정하고 싶습니다. **2** 타동사 채무 연장을 하다 ❑ 파산했거나 채무 연장을 해야 했던 회사들

I

J

res|cue ♦◇◇ /rɛskyu/ (**rescues, rescuing, rescued**) **1** V-T If you **rescue** someone, you get them out of a dangerous or unpleasant situation. ❑ *Helicopters rescued nearly 20 people from the roof of the burning building.* ● **res|cu|er** (**rescuers**) N-COUNT ❑ *It took rescuers 90 minutes to reach the trapped men.* **2** N-UNCOUNT **Rescue** is help which gets someone out of a dangerous or unpleasant situation. ❑ *A big rescue operation has been launched for a trawler missing in the English Channel.* **3** N-COUNT A **rescue** is an attempt to save someone from a dangerous or unpleasant situation. ❑ *A major air-sea rescue is under way.* **4** PHRASE If you **go to** someone's **rescue** or **come to** their **rescue**, you help them when they are in danger or difficulty. ❑ *The 23-year-old's screams alerted a passerby who went to her rescue.*

K

L

1 타동사 구조하다 ❑ 헬리콥터로 불타는 건물의 옥상에서 거의 20명을 구조했다. ● 구조대원 가산명사 ❑ 구조대원들이 갇힌 남자들에게까지 도달하는 데 90분이 소요되었다. **2** 불가산명사 구조 ❑ 영국 해협에서 실종된 트롤선 때문에 대규모 구조 작업이 펼쳐지고 있다. **3** 가산명사 구조 ❑ 대규모 해공 구조 작업이 진행 중이다. **4** 구 구조하러 가다; 구조하러 오다 ❑ 지나가던 사람이 그 23세 된 아가씨의 비명을 듣고 구조하러 갔다.

M

N

Word Partnership   rescue의 연어

N.	rescue **a hostage**, rescue **miners**, rescue **people**, **police** rescue, **volunteers** rescue, rescue **wildlife** **1**
	rescue **attempt**, rescue **crews**, rescue **effort**, rescue **mission**, rescue **operation**, rescue **teams**, rescue **workers** **2**

O

P

Q

re|search ♦♦♦ /rɪsɜrtʃ, riːsɜrtʃ/ (**researches, researching, researched**) **1** N-UNCOUNT **Research** is work that involves studying something and trying to discover facts about it. [also N in pl] ❑ *65 percent of the 1987 budget went for nuclear weapons research and production.* **2** V-T If you **research** something, you try to discover facts about it. ❑ *She spent two years in South Florida researching and filming her documentary.* ● **re|search|er** (**researchers**) N-COUNT ❑ *He chose to join the company as a market researcher.* →see **hospital, inventor, laboratory, medicine, science, zoo**

R

1 불가산명사 연구 ❑ 1987년 예산의 65퍼센트가 핵무기 연구와 생산에 투입되었다. **2** 타동사 연구하다 ❑ 그녀는 자신의 다큐멘터리를 연구하고 촬영하며 2년을 남부 플로리다에서 보냈다. ● 연구원 가산명사 ❑ 그는 시장 조사원으로서 그 회사에 취직하기로 했다.

S

Word Partnership   research의 연어

ADJ.	**biological** research, **clinical** research, **current** research, **experimental** research, **medical** research, **recent** research, **scientific** research **1**
N.	**animal** research, **cancer** research, research **and development**, research **facility**, research **findings**, **laboratory** research, research **methods**, research **paper**, research **project**, research **report**, research **results**, research **scientist** **1**

T

U

V

re|sell /risel/ (**resells, reselling, resold**) V-T/V-I If you **resell** something that you have bought, you sell it again. ❑ *Shopkeepers buy them in bulk and resell them for £150 each.*

타동사/자동사 전매(轉賣)하다, 되팔기하다 ❑ 가게 주인들은 그것을 도매금으로 구매하여 각각 150파운드에 전매한다.

W

re|sem|blance /rɪzɛmbləns/ (**resemblances**) N-VAR If there is a **resemblance** between two people or things, they are similar to each other. ❑ *There was a remarkable resemblance between him and Pete.*

가산명사 또는 불가산명사 유사성 ❑ 그와 피트 사이에는 놀라운 유사성이 있었다.

X

re|sem|ble /rɪzɛmbəl/ (**resembles, resembling, resembled**) V-T If one thing or person **resembles** another, they are similar to each other. [no cont] ❑ *Some of the commercially produced venison resembles beef in flavor.*

타동사 닮다, 비슷하다 ❑ 상업적으로 사육된 사슴고기의 일부는 쇠고기와 맛이 비슷하다.

Y

re|sent /rɪzɛnt/ (**resents, resenting, resented**) V-T If you **resent** someone or something, you feel bitter and angry about them. ❑ *She resents her mother for being so tough on her.*

타동사 억울하게 생각하다, 분해하다, 삐치다 ❑ 그녀는 엄마가 자신에게 그렇게 매정하게 대한 것에 대해 원망하였다.

Z

re|sent|ful /rɪzɛntfəl/ ADJ If you are **resentful**, you feel resentment. ❑ *At first I felt very resentful and angry about losing my job.*

re|sent|ment /rɪzɛntmənt/ (resentments) N-UNCOUNT **Resentment** is bitterness and anger that someone feels about something. [also N in pl] ❑ *She expressed resentment at being interviewed by a social worker.*

res|er|va|tion /rɛzərveɪʃn/ (reservations) **1** N-VAR If you have **reservations about** something, you are not sure that it is entirely good or right. ❑ *I told him my main reservation about his film was the ending.* **2** N-COUNT If you make a **reservation**, you arrange for something such as a table in a restaurant or a room in a hotel to be kept for you. ❑ *He went to the desk to enquire and make a reservation.* **3** N-COUNT A **reservation** is an area of land that is kept separate for a particular group of people to live in. ❑ *...a Native American who grew up on a reservation...* →see **hotel**

re|serve ♦♦◇ /rɪzɜrv/ (reserves, reserving, reserved) **1** V-T If something **is reserved for** a particular person or purpose, it is kept specially for that person or purpose. [usu passive] ❑ *A double room with a balcony overlooking the sea had been reserved for him.* **2** V-T If you **reserve** something such as a table, ticket, or magazine, you arrange for it to be kept specially for you, rather than sold or given to someone else. ❑ *I'll reserve a table for five.* **3** N-COUNT A **reserve** is a supply of something that is available for use when it is needed. ❑ *The Gulf has 65 per cent of the world's oil reserves.* **4** N-COUNT A nature **reserve** is an area of land where the animals, birds, and plants are officially protected. ❑ *Marine biologists are calling for Cardigan Bay to be created a marine nature reserve to protect the dolphins.* **5** N-UNCOUNT If someone shows **reserve**, they keep their feelings hidden. ❑ *I do hope that you'll overcome your reserve and let me know.* **6** PHRASE If you have something **in reserve**, you have it available for use when it is needed. ❑ *He poked around the top of his cupboard for the bottle of whisky that he kept in reserve.* **7** to **reserve judgment** →see **judgment**. to **reserve the right** →see **right**

Thesaurus   reserve의 참조어

V.   hold, save, set aside **1** **2**

N.   stock, store, supply **3**

---

re|served /rɪzɜrvd/ **1** ADJ Someone who is **reserved** keeps their feelings hidden. ❑ *He was unemotional, quite quiet, and reserved.* **2** ADJ A table in a restaurant or a seat in a theater that is **reserved** is being kept for someone rather than given or sold to anyone else. ❑ *Seats, or sometimes entire tables, were reserved.*

re|serve price (reserve prices) N-COUNT A **reserve price** is the lowest price which is acceptable to the owner of property being auctioned or sold. [BRIT, BUSINESS] ❑ *Some 90 percent of the items fetched their reserve price or more.*

res|er|voir /rɛzərvwɑr/ (reservoirs) **1** N-COUNT A **reservoir** is a lake that is used for storing water before it is supplied to people. **2** N-COUNT A **reservoir of** something is a large quantity of it that is available for use when needed. ❑ *...the huge oil reservoir beneath the Kuwaiti desert.* →see **dam**

Word Link   sid ≈ sitting : preside, president, reside

---

re|side /rɪzaɪd/ (resides, residing, resided) **1** V-I If someone **resides** somewhere, they live there or are staying there. [FORMAL] ❑ *Margaret resides with her invalid mother in a London suburb.* **2** V-I If a quality **resides in** something, the thing has that quality. [FORMAL] [no cont] ❑ *Happiness does not reside in strength or money.*

resi|dence /rɛzɪdəns/ (residences) **1** N-COUNT A **residence** is a house where people live. [FORMAL] ❑ *The house is currently run as a country house hotel, but could easily convert back into a private residence.* **2** N-UNCOUNT Your place of **residence** is the place where you live. [FORMAL] ❑ *There were significant differences among women based on age, place of residence and educational levels.* **3** N-UNCOUNT Someone's **residence** in a particular place is the fact that they live there or that they are officially allowed to live there. ❑ *They had entered the country and had applied for permanent residence.* **4** →see also **residence hall** **5** PHRASE If someone is **in residence** in a particular place, they are living there. ❑ *Windsor is open to visitors when the Royal Family is not in residence.*

resi|dence hall (residence halls) N-COUNT **Residence halls** are buildings with rooms or apartments, usually built by universities or colleges, in which students live during the term. [AM; BRIT **hall of residence**] ❑ *A freshman adviser lives in each residence hall.*

Word Link   ent ≈ one who does, has : dependent, resident, superintendent

---

resi|dent ♦♦◇ /rɛzɪdənt/ (residents) **1** N-COUNT The **residents** of a house or area are the people who live there. ❑ *The Archbishop called upon the government to build more low cost homes for local residents.* **2** ADJ Someone who is **resident in** a country or a town lives there. [v-link ADJ, usu ADJ in n] ❑ *He moved to Belgium in 1990 to live with his son, who had been resident in Brussels since 1967.* **3** N-COUNT A **resident** or a **resident** doctor is a doctor who is receiving a period of specialized training in a hospital after completing his or her internship. [AM] **4** ADJ A **resident** doctor or teacher lives in the place where he or she works. [BRIT] ❑ *The morning after your arrival, you meet with the resident physician for a private consultation.* →see **hospital**

형용사 억울한, 분한 ❑ 처음에 나는 일자리를 잃은 것이 매우 억울하고 화가 났었다.

불가산명사 억울함, 분함 ❑ 사회 복지사로부터 인터뷰를 당한 것이 그녀는 억울하다고 했다.

1 가산명사 또는 불가산명사 판단이 안 서는 점 ❑ 그의 영화에 대해 내가 제일 판단이 안 서는 부분이 결말 부분이라고 그에게 얘기했다. **2** 가산명사 예약 ❑ 그는 예약에 대해 알아보고 예약을 하기 위해 안내 데스크로 갔다. **3** 가산명사 (특정 집단의) 보호 구역 ❑ 보호 구역에서 성장한 아메리카 원주민

1 타동사 떼어 두다 ❑ 바다가 보이는 발코니가 있는 2인실이 그를 위해 별도로 준비되어 있었다. **2** 타동사 예약하다 ❑ 다섯 명을 위해 테이블을 예약하겠다. **3** 가산명사 비축물 ❑ 페르시아 만 지역이 세계 석유 매장량의 65퍼센트를 보유하고 있다. **4** 가산명사 (동식물) 보호 구역 ❑ 해양 생물학자들이 돌고래를 보호하기 위해 카디간 만을 해양 보호 구역으로 지정할 것을 요청하고 있다. **5** 불가산명사 마음을 숨김, 주저함 ❑ 주저하지 말고 저에게 이야기해 주면 좋겠네요. **6** 구 비축용으로 ❑ 그는 비축해 둔 위스키 병을 찾기 위해 찬장 맨 윗부분을 뒤졌다.

1 형용사 속마음을 드러내지 않는 ❑ 그는 냉정하고 상당히 조용했으며 속마음을 잘 드러내지 않았다. **2** 형용사 예약된 ❑ 좌석, 때로는 모든 테이블이 예약이 되었다.

가산명사 최저 경매 가격, 최저가 [영국영어, 경제] ❑ 물품의 90퍼센트 정도가 최저 경매 가격 이상에 팔렸다.

1 가산명사 저수지 **2** 가산명사 비축량, 보유량 ❑ 쿠웨이트 사막 밑에 있는 엄청난 석유 매장량

1 자동사 거주하다 [격식체] ❑ 마가렛은 거동을 못하는 어머니와 함께 런던의 교외에 거주한다. **2** 자동사 존재하다, 있다 [격식체] ❑ 행복은 힘이나 돈에 있지 않다.

1 가산명사 주거지 [격식체] ❑ 그 집은 현재 시골 호텔로 운영되고 있지만 쉬이 개인 주거지로 다시 전환할 수 있다. **2** 불가산명사 거주지 [격식체] ❑ 나이, 거주지, 교육 수준 등에 따라 여성들 사이에 상당한 차이가 존재했다. **3** 불가산명사 거주 ❑ 그들은 그 나라에 입국하여 영주권을 신청한 상태였다. **5** 구 거주하고 있는 ❑ 윈저 궁은 왕족이 거주하고 있지 않을 때는 방문객에게 개방한다.

가산명사 기숙사 [미국영어; 영국영어 hall of residence] ❑ 신입생 지도교수가 각 기숙사마다 기거한다.

1 가산명사 주민 ❑ 지역 주민들을 위해 보다 많은 저가 주택을 지으라고 대주교가 정부 측에 요청했다. **2** 형용사 거주하고 있는 ❑ 1967년 이후 브뤼셀에서 거주하고 있는 아들과 살기 위해 그는 1990년에 벨기에로 이사 갔다. **3** 가산명사 레지던트, 수련의 [미국영어] **4** 형용사 일하는 곳에서 거주하는 [영국영어] ❑ 도착한 다음 날 아침에 개별 상담을 위해 그곳에서 거주하는 의사와 만납니다.

a b c d e f g h i j k l m n o p q r s t u v w x y z

resi|den|tial /rɛzɪdɛnʃəl/ ■ ADJ A **residential** area contains houses rather than offices or factories. ❑ *He was born in Kensington, West London, then a smart residential area of large terrace houses.* ■ ADJ A **residential** institution is one where people live while they are studying there or being cared for there. ❑ *Training involves a two-year residential course.*

re|sid|ual /rɪzɪdʒuəl/ ADJ **Residual** is used to describe what remains of something when most of it has gone. ❑ *...residual radiation from nuclear weapons testing.*

resi|due /rɛzɪduː, -dyuː/ (residues) N-COUNT A **residue** of something is a small amount that remains after most of it has gone. ❑ *Always using the same shampoo means that a residue can build up on the hair.*

re|sign ◆◇◇ /rɪzaɪn/ (resigns, resigning, resigned) ■ V-T/V-I If you **resign** from a job or position, you formally announce that you are leaving it. ❑ *A hospital administrator has resigned over claims he lied to get the job.* ■ V-T If you **resign yourself to** an unpleasant situation or fact, you accept it because you realize that you cannot change it. ❑ *Pat and I resigned ourselves to yet another summer without a boat.* ■ →see also **resigned**

Do not confuse **resign** and **retire**. If someone **resigns** from their job, they leave it after saying that they do not want to do it any more. ❑ *He hasn't decided whether he will resign.* You can **resign** from your job at any age, and perhaps start another job soon afterwards. When someone **retires**, they leave their job and stop working, often because they have reached the age when they can get a pension. ❑ *He had been planning for some time to retire at around age 60.* When professional athletes stop playing sport as their job, you can also say that they **retire**, even if they are fairly young ❑ *A heart attack at the age of 36 forced him to retire from tennis.*

Thesaurus resign의 참조어
v. leave, quit, step down ■

res|ig|na|tion ◆◇◇ /rɛzɪgneɪʃən/ (resignations) ■ N-VAR Your **resignation** is a formal statement of your intention to leave a job or position. ❑ *Mr. Morgan has offered his resignation and it has been accepted.* ■ N-UNCOUNT **Resignation** is the acceptance of an unpleasant situation or fact because you realize that you cannot change it. ❑ *He sighed with profound resignation.*

re|signed /rɪzaɪnd/ ADJ If you are **resigned to** an unpleasant situation or fact, you accept it without complaining because you realize that you cannot change it. ❑ *He is resigned to the noise, the mess, the constant upheaval.*

re|sili|ent /rɪzɪlyənt/ ■ ADJ Something that is **resilient** is strong and not easily damaged by being hit, stretched, or squeezed. ❑ *...an armchair of some resilient plastic material.* ● **re|sili|ence** N-UNCOUNT [also a N] ❑ *Do you feel that your muscles do not have the strength and resilience that they should have?* ■ ADJ People and things that are **resilient** are able to recover easily and quickly from unpleasant or damaging events. ❑ *When the U.S. stock market collapsed in October 1987, the Japanese stock market was the most resilient.* ● **re|sili|ence** N-UNCOUNT [also a N] ❑ *...the resilience of human beings to fight after they've been attacked.*

res|in /rɛzɪn/ (resins) ■ N-MASS **Resin** is a sticky substance that is produced by some trees. ❑ *...a tropical tree which is bled regularly for its resin.* ■ N-MASS **Resin** is a substance that is produced chemically and used to make plastics. ❑ *The plastic resin is used in a wide range of products, including electrical wire insulation.*

re|sist ◆◇◇ /rɪzɪst/ (resists, resisting, resisted) ■ V-T If you **resist** something such as a change, you refuse to accept it and try to prevent it. ❑ *She says she will resist a single European currency being imposed.* ■ V-T/V-I If you **resist** someone or **resist** an attack by them, you fight back against them. ❑ *The man was shot outside his house as he tried to resist arrest.* ■ V-T If you **resist** doing something, or **resist** the temptation to do it, you stop yourself from doing it although you would like to do it. [oft with neg] ❑ *Students should resist the temptation to focus on exams alone.* ■ V-T If someone or something **resists** damage of some kind, they are not damaged. ❑ *...bodies trained and toughened to resist the cold.*

Word Link ance ≈ quality, state : balance, performance, resistance

re|sist|ance ◆◇◇ /rɪzɪstəns/ (resistances) ■ N-UNCOUNT **Resistance** to something such as a change or a new idea is a refusal to accept it. ❑ *The U.S. wants big cuts in European agricultural export subsidies, but this is meeting resistance.* ■ N-UNCOUNT **Resistance** to an attack consists of fighting back against the people who have attacked you. ❑ *A BBC correspondent in Colombo says the troops are encountering stiff resistance.* ■ N-UNCOUNT The **resistance** of your body to germs or diseases is its power to remain unharmed or unaffected by them. ❑ *This disease is surprisingly difficult to catch as most people have a natural resistance to it.* ■ N-UNCOUNT Wind or air **resistance** is a force which slows down a moving object or vehicle. ❑ *The design of the bicycle has managed to reduce the effects of wind resistance and drag.* ■ N-VAR In electrical engineering or physics, **resistance** is the ability of a substance or an electrical circuit to stop the flow of an electrical current through it. ❑ *Superconductors, materials that lose all their electrical resistance, conduct electricity faster than ordinary materials.* →see **flight**

re|sist|ant /rɪzɪstənt/ ■ ADJ Someone who is **resistant to** something is opposed to it and wants to prevent it. ❑ *Some people are very resistant to the idea of exercise.* ■ ADJ If something is **resistant to** a particular thing, it is not harmed by it. ❑ *...how to improve plants to make them more resistant to disease.*

■ 형용사 주거의 ❑ 그는 당시 큰 연립 주택들로 이루어진 깔끔한 주거 지역이 있던 런던의 서부 켄싱턴에서 태어났다. ■ 형용사 숙식을 함께 하는 ❑ 교육에는 2년 동안 숙식을 함께 하는 교육 과정이 포함되어 있다.

형용사 찌꺼기의 ❑ 핵무기 실험 찌꺼기인 방사능

가산명사 찌꺼기 ❑ 항상 같은 샴푸를 사용하면 그 찌꺼기가 머리카락에 축적된다.

■ 타동사/자동사 사직하다, 사인하다 ❑ 한 병원 행정 직원이 그 자리를 얻기 위해 거짓말을 했다는 혐의 때문에 사직했다. ■ 타동사 (체념하며) 받아들이다 ❑ 팻과 나는 보트 없이 또 한 번 여름을 보내야 한다는 사실을 받아들였다.

resign과 retire를 혼동하지 않도록 하라. 누가 자기 직장을 사직하면(resign), 그 사람은 더 이상 그 일을 하고 싶지 않다고 말한 다음 그 직장을 그만두는 것이다. ❑ 그는 사임할지 결정하지 않았다. 어떤 나이에도 직장에서 resign할 수 있으며, 아마도 그 뒤에 곧 새로운 일을 시작하게 될 것이다. 누가 은퇴(retire)하면, 그 사람은 흔히 연금을 받을 수 있는 나이에 이르렀기 때문에 직장을 그만두고 일을 하지 않는 것이다. ❑ 그 사람은 60살 경에 은퇴하기로 마음먹은 지 꽤 된 상태였다. 전문 운동선수가 직업으로 하는 운동을 그만두면, 그 사람이 상당히 젊더라도 retire한다고 말할 수 있다. ❑ 그는 36살의 나이에 심장마비에 걸려서 테니스에서 은퇴할 수밖에 없었다.

■ 가산명사 또는 불가산명사 사표 ❑ 모건 씨는 사표를 냈고 그것은 수리되었다. ■ 불가산명사 받아들임, 체념 ❑ 그는 깊이 체념하며 한숨을 내쉬었다.

형용사 (체념하며) 받아들이는 ❑ 그는 소음, 지저분함, 잦은 변화 등을 어쩔 수 없다고 받아들인다.

■ 형용사 탄력 있는 ❑ 약간 탄력 있는 비닐 소재로 만든 안락의자 ● 탄력 불가산명사 ❑ 당신의 근육에 제대로 된 힘과 탄력이 없다고 생각하십니까? ■ 형용사 회복력이 강한 ❑ 미국의 주식 시장이 1987년 10월에 붕괴됐을 때 일본의 주식 시장이 가장 회복이 빨랐다. ● 회복력 불가산명사 ❑ 공격을 당한 후 싸울 수 있는 인간의 회복력

■ 물질명사 수지 ❑ 나뭇진을 뽑으려 주기적으로 흠을 내는 열대 나무 ■ 물질명사 합성수지 ❑ 플라스틱 수지는 전선 절연체 등을 포함한 다양한 종류의 제품에 사용된다.

■ 타동사 거부하다 ❑ 그녀는 단일 유럽 통화 부과를 거부할 것이라고 한다. ■ 타동사/자동사 저항하다 ❑ 그 남자는 체포에 저항하다 자신의 집 밖에서 총에 맞았다. ■ 타동사 거부하다 ❑ 학생들은 시험에만 집중하려는 유혹을 거부해야 한다. ■ 타동사 저항하다 ❑ 추위에 저항하게끔 훈련되고 강화된 몸

■ 불가산명사 저항 ❑ 미국은 유럽의 농산물 수출 지원에 대한 대규모 삭감을 원하지만 이는 상당한 저항을 받고 있다. ■ 불가산명사 저항 ❑ 콜롬보의 비비시 통신원에 따르면 군대가 강력한 저항에 부딪히고 있다고 한다. ■ 불가산명사 저항력 ❑ 대부분의 사람들이 그에 대한 타고난 저항력이 있기 때문에 그 병은 매우 걸리기 어렵다. ■ 불가산명사 저항 ❑ 자전거의 설계를 통해 바람의 저항과 항력을 줄일 수 있었다. ■ 가산명사 또는 불가산명사 저항 ❑ 모든 전기 저항을 받지 않는 재료인 초전도체는 일반 재료보다 전기를 빨리 전달한다.

■ 형용사 저항하는 ❑ 어떤 사람들은 운동의 개념 자체에 완강히 저항한다. ■ 형용사 저항력이 있는 ❑ 식물을 병에 대한 면역력을 높이도록 개량하는 방법

re|skill /ɾiːskɪl/ (reskills, reskilling, reskilled) V-T/V-I If you **reskill**, or if someone **reskills** you, you learn new skills, so that you can do a different job or do your old job in a different way. [BUSINESS] ❏ We needed to reskill our workforce to cope with massive technological change. ● **re|skill|ing** N-UNCOUNT ❏ Everyone knows that lifelong learning and reskilling are important.

reso|lute /ɾɛzəluːt/ ADJ If you describe someone as **resolute**, you approve of them because they are very determined not to change their mind or not to give up a course of action. [FORMAL] ❏ Voters perceive him as a resolute and resolute international leader. ● **reso|lute|ly** ADV ❏ He resolutely refused to speak English unless forced to.

reso|lu|tion ♦♦◇ /ɾɛzəluːʃən/ (resolutions) **1** N-COUNT A **resolution** is a formal decision made at a meeting by means of a vote. ❏ He replied that the UN had passed two major resolutions calling for a complete withdrawal. **2** N-COUNT If you make a **resolution**, you decide to try very hard to do something. ❏ They made a resolution to lose all the weight gained during the Christmas period. **3** N-UNCOUNT **Resolution** is determination to do something or not do something. ❏ "I think I'll try a hypnotist," I said with sudden resolution. **4** N-SING The **resolution** of a problem or difficulty is the final solving of it. [FORMAL] ❏ ...the successful resolution of a dispute involving UN inspectors in Baghdad.

re|solve ♦♦◇ /ɾɪzɒlv/ (resolves, resolving, resolved) **1** V-T To **resolve** a problem, argument, or difficulty means to find a solution to it. [FORMAL] ❏ We must find a way to resolve these problems before it's too late. **2** V-T If you **resolve** to do something, you make a firm decision to do it. [FORMAL] ❏ She resolved to report the matter to the hospital's nursing manager. **3** N-VAR **Resolve** is determination to do what you have decided to do. [FORMAL] ❏ So you're saying this will strengthen the American public's resolve to go to war if necessary?

re|solved /ɾɪzɒlvd/ ADJ If you are **resolved to** do something, you are determined to do it. [FORMAL] [v-link ADJ to-inf] ❏ Most folk with property to lose were resolved to defend it.

reso|nance /ɾɛzənəns/ (resonances) **1** N-VAR If something has a **resonance** for someone, it has a special meaning or is particularly important to them. ❏ The ideas of order, security, family, religion, and country had the same resonance for them as for Michael. **2** N-UNCOUNT If a sound has **resonance**, it is deep, clear, and strong. ❏ His voice had lost its resonance; it was tense and strained.

reso|nant /ɾɛzənənt/ ADJ A sound that is **resonant** is deep and strong. ❏ His voice sounded oddly resonant in the empty room.

reso|nate /ɾɛzəneɪt/ (resonates, resonating, resonated) **1** V-I If something **resonates**, it vibrates and produces a deep, strong sound. ❏ The bass guitar began to thump so loudly that it resonated in my head. **2** V-I You say that something **resonates** when it has a special meaning or when it is particularly important to someone. ❏ What are the issues resonating with voters?

re|sort ♦♦◇ /ɾɪzɔːrt/ (resorts, resorting, resorted) **1** V-I If you **resort to** a course of action that you do not really approve of, you adopt it because you cannot see any other way of achieving what you want. ❏ His punishing work schedule had made him resort to drugs. **2** N-UNCOUNT If you achieve something without **resort** to a particular course of action, you succeed without carrying out that action. To have **resort** to a particular course of action means to have to do that action in order to achieve something. ❏ Congress has a responsibility to ensure that all peaceful options are exhausted before we resort to war. **3** PHRASE If you do something **as a last resort**, you do it because you can find no other way of getting out of a difficult situation or of solving a problem. ❏ Nuclear weapons should be used only as a last resort. **4** N-COUNT A **resort** is a place where a lot of people spend their vacation. ❏ The ski resorts are expanding to meet the growing number of skiers that come here.

re|sound|ing /ɾɪzaʊndɪŋ/ **1** ADJ A **resounding** sound is loud and clear. ❏ There was a resounding slap as Andrew struck him violently across the face. **2** ADJ You can refer to a very great success as a **resounding** success. [EMPHASIS] ❏ The good weather helped to make the occasion a resounding success.

re|source ♦♦◇ /ɾiːsɔːrs, BRIT ɾɪzɔːrs/ (resources) **1** N-COUNT The **resources** of an organization or person are the materials, money, and other things that they have and can use in order to function properly. ❏ Some families don't have the resources to feed themselves properly. **2** N-COUNT A country's **resources** are the things that it has and can use to increase its wealth, such as coal, oil, or land. ❏ ...resources like coal, tungsten, oil, and copper.

re|sourced /ɾiːsɔːrst, BRIT ɾɪzɔːrst/ ADJ If an organization is **resourced**, it has all the things, such as money and materials, that it needs to function properly. [BRIT] ❏ We are not yet fully resourced in Northern Ireland.

re|source|ful /ɾɪzɔːrsfəl/ ADJ Someone who is **resourceful** is good at finding ways of dealing with problems. ❏ He was amazingly inventive and resourceful, and played a major role in my career. ● **re|source|ful|ness** N-UNCOUNT ❏ Because of his adventures, he is a person of far greater experience and resourcefulness.

re|spect ♦♦◇ /ɾɪspɛkt/ (respects, respecting, respected) **1** V-T If you **respect** someone, you have a good opinion of their character or ideas. ❏ I want him to respect me as a career woman. **2** N-UNCOUNT If you have **respect for** someone, you have a good opinion of them. ❏ I have tremendous respect for Dean. →see also **self-respect 3** V-T If you **respect** someone's wishes, rights, or customs, you avoid doing things that they would dislike or regard as wrong. ❏ Finally, trying to respect her wishes, I said I'd leave. **4** N-UNCOUNT If you show **respect for** someone's wishes, rights, or customs, you avoid doing anything they would dislike or regard as wrong. ❏ They will campaign for the return of traditional lands and respect for aboriginal rights and customs. **5** V-T If you **respect** a law or moral principle, you agree not to break it. ❏ It is about time tour operators respected the law and their own

code of conduct. ● N-UNCOUNT **Respect** is also a noun. ❑ ...respect for the law and the rejection of the use of violence. ◻ PHRASE You can say **with respect** when you are politely disagreeing with someone or criticizing them. [POLITENESS] ❑ With respect, I hardly think that's the point. ◻ PHRASE If you **pay** your **respects to** someone, you go to see them or speak to them. You usually do this to be polite, and not necessarily because you want to do it. [FORMAL] ❑ Carl had asked him to visit the hospital and to pay his respects to Francis. ◻ PHRASE You use expressions like **in this respect** and **in many respects** to indicate that what you are saying applies to the feature you have just mentioned or to many features of something. ❑ The children are not unintelligent – in fact, they seem quite normal in this respect. ◻ PHRASE You use **with respect to** to say what something relates to. In British English, you can also say **in respect of**. [FORMAL] ❑ Parents often have little choice with respect to the way their child is medically treated. →see also **respected**

봅니다. ◻ 구 안부를 묻다 [격식체] ❑ 칼은 그에게 병원을 방문해서 프란시스를 문병하라고 요청했었다. ◻ 구 이런 면에서; 여러 면에서 ❑ 그 아이들은 지능이 부족하지 않다. 사실 이런 면에서는 매우 정상으로 보인다. ◻ 구 ~과 관련하여 [격식체] ❑ 부모들은 아이가 치료를 받는 것과 관련하여 별다른 선택권이 없다.

Thesaurus
respect의 참조어

V.	admire, esteem ◻
N.	consideration, courtesy, esteem; (ant.) disrespect ◻

Word Partnership
respect의 연어

V.	**deserve** respect, **earn** respect, **gain** respect ◻
	lack respect **for** someone/something,
	show respect **for** someone/something,
	treat someone/something **with** respect ◻ ◻ ◻
N.	**lack of** respect ◻ ◻ ◻
	respect someone's **privacy**, respect someone's **rights**,
	respect someone's **wishes** ◻ ◻
	respect **the law** ◻

---

re|spect|able /rɪspɛktəbᵊl/ ◻ ADJ Someone or something that is **respectable** is approved of by society and considered to be morally correct. ❑ He came from a perfectly respectable middle-class family. ● **re|spect|abil|ity** /rɪspɛktəbɪlɪti/ N-UNCOUNT ❑ If she divorced Tony, she would lose the respectability she had as Mrs. Tony Tatterton. ◻ ADJ You can say that something is **respectable** when you mean that it is good enough or acceptable. ❑ ...investments that offer respectable and highly attractive rates of return.

◻ 형용사 훌륭한, 존경할 만한 ❑ 그는 아주 훌륭한 중산층 가문 출신이다. ● 훌륭함, 신망 불가산명사 ❑ 만약 그녀가 토니와 이혼한다면 그녀는 토니 태터턴 부인으로서 누리던 신망을 잃게 될 것이다. ◻ 형용사 아주 괜찮은 ❑ 아주 괜찮고 매우 매력적인 수익률을 제공하는 투자

re|spect|ed /rɪspɛktɪd/ ADJ Someone or something that is **respected** is admired and considered important by many people. ❑ He is highly respected for his novels and plays as well as his translations of American novels.

형용사 존경을 받는 ❑ 그는 미국 소설 번역뿐 아니라 자기가 쓴 희곡으로도 많은 존경을 받는다.

re|spect|ful /rɪspɛktfəl/ ADJ If you are **respectful**, you show respect for someone. ❑ The children in our family are always respectful to their elders. ● **re|spect|ful|ly** ADV ❑ "You are an artist," she said respectfully.

형용사 공손한 ❑ 우리 집안의 아이들은 어른들에게 항상 공손하다. ● 공손히 부사 ❑ "당신은 예술가입니다."라고 그녀가 공손히 말했다.

re|spec|tive /rɪspɛktɪv/ ADJ **Respective** means relating or belonging separately to the individual people you have just mentioned. [ADJ n, usu poss ADJ pl-n] ❑ Steve and I were at very different stages in our respective careers.

형용사 각기의 ❑ 스티브와 나는 각자의 일에서 아주 다른 단계에 도달해 있었다.

re|spec|tive|ly /rɪspɛktɪvli/ ADV **Respectively** means in the same order as the items that you have just mentioned. [ADV with cl/group] ❑ Their sons, Ben and Jonathan, were three and six respectively.

부사 각각 ❑ 그들의 아들들 벤과 조나단은 각각 세 살과 여섯 살이었다.

Word Link
spir ≈ breath : aspire, inspire, respiratory

---

res|pira|tory /rɛspərətɔri, BRIT rɛspərətri/ ADJ **Respiratory** means relating to breathing. [MEDICAL] [ADJ n] ❑ ...people with severe respiratory problems. →see Word Web: **respiratory system**

형용사 호흡의 [의학] ❑ 심한 호흡 장애를 가진 사람들

res|pite /rɛspɪt/ ◻ N-SING A **respite** is a short period of rest from something unpleasant. [FORMAL] [also no det, oft N from n] ❑ It was some weeks now since they had had any respite from shellfire. ◻ N-SING A **respite** is a short delay before a very unpleasant or difficult situation which may or may not take place. [FORMAL] [also no det] ❑ Devaluation would only give the economy a brief respite.

◻ 단수명사 일시 중지 [격식체] ❑ 일시적으로나마 포화가 중단된 지 이제 몇 주가 지난 후였다. ◻ 단수명사 휴식, 여유 [격식체] ❑ 평가 저하는 경제에 잠깐의 여유만을 줄 것이다.

re|spond ♦♦◇ /rɪspɒnd/ (**responds, responding, responded**) ◻ V-T/V-I When you **respond** to something that is done or said, you react to it by doing or saying something yourself. ❑ They are likely to respond positively to the President's request for aid. ❑ The army responded with gunfire and tear gas. ◻ V-I When you **respond to** a need, crisis, or challenge, you take the necessary or appropriate action. ❑ This modest group size allows our teachers to respond to the needs of each

◻ 타동사/자동사 반응하다, 응답하다 ❑ 그들은 대통령의 원조 요청에 긍정적으로 반응할 가능성이 높다. ❑ 군대는 총격과 최루탄으로 대응했다. ◻ 자동사 대응하다 ❑ 이렇게 집단의 크기가 작은 덕분에 교사들이 각 학생의 요구에 대응할 수 있다. ◻ 자동사 반응을 보이다 ❑ 그가 이제는 호전이 되었고

Word Web
respiratory system

Respiration moves **air** in and out of the **lungs**. Air comes in through the **nose** or mouth. Then it travels down the **windpipe** and into the **lungs**. In the lungs **oxygen** absorbs into the bloodstream. Blood carries oxygen to the heart and other organs. The lungs also remove **carbon dioxide** from the blood. This gas is then **exhaled** through the mouth. During **inhalation** the **diaphragm** moves downward and the lungs fill with air. During exhalation the diaphragm relaxes and air flows out. Adult humans **breathe** about six liters of air each minute.

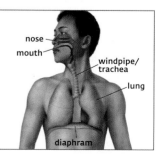

nose
mouth
windpipe/
trachea
lung
diaphram

student. **3** V-I If a patient or their injury or illness **is responding to** treatment, the treatment is working and they are getting better. ❑ *I'm pleased to say that he is now doing well and responding to treatment.*

치료에도 반응을 보이고 있다고 말씀드릴 수 있어서 기쁩니다.

re|sponse ♦♦◇ /rɪspɒns/ (**responses**) N-COUNT Your **response** to an event or to something that is said is your reply or reaction to it. [oft N to/from n, also in N] ❑ *There has been no response to his remarks from the government.*

가산명사 반응, 대답 ❑ 그의 발언에 대해 정부로부터 아직까지 아무런 반응이 없다.

Word Partnership   *response*의 연어

ADJ.	**correct** response, **enthusiastic** response, **immediate** response, **negative/positive** response, **overwhelming** response, **quick** response, **written** response

---

re|sponse time (**response times**) N-COUNT **Response time** is the time taken for a computer to do something after you have given an instruction. [COMPUTING] ❑ *The only flaw is the slightly slow response times when you press the buttons.*

가산명사 응답 시간 [컴퓨터] ❑ 유일한 단점은 버튼을 누른 후 걸리는 응답 시간이 약간 느리다는 것이다.

re|spon|sibil|ity ♦♦◇ /rɪspɒnsɪbɪlɪti/ (**responsibilities**) **1** N-UNCOUNT If you have **responsibility** for something or someone, or if they are your **responsibility**, it is your job or duty to deal with them and to make decisions relating to them. ❑ *Each manager had responsibility for just under 600 properties.* **2** N-UNCOUNT If you accept **responsibility for** something that has happened, you agree that you were to blame for it or you caused it. ❑ *No one admitted responsibility for the attacks.* **3** N-PLURAL Your **responsibilities** are the duties that you have because of your job or position. ❑ *I am told that he handled his responsibilities as a counselor in a highly intelligent and caring fashion.* **4** N-UNCOUNT If someone is given **responsibility**, they are given the right or opportunity to make important decisions or to take action without having to get permission from anyone else. ❑ *She would have loved to have a better-paying job with more responsibility.* **5** N-SING If you think that you have a **responsibility to** do something, you feel that you ought to do it because it is morally right to do it. ❑ *The court feels it has a responsibility to ensure that customers are not misled.* **6** N-SING If you think that you have a **responsibility to** someone, you feel that it is your duty to take action that will protect their interests. ❑ *She had decided that as a doctor she had a responsibility to her fellow creatures.*

1 불가산명사 책임 ❑ 각 관리자는 거의 600건에 달하는 부동산을 책임지고 있었다. **2** 불가산명사 책임 ❑ 아무도 그 공격들에 대해 책임을 인정하지 않았다. **3** 복수명사 책무 ❑ 그가 고문으로서의 책무를 매우 현명하고 성실하게 수행했다고 나는 들었다. **4** 불가산명사 책임 ❑ 그녀는 책임이 더 크고 급여가 더 많은 직장을 원했을 것이다. **5** 단수명사 책임 ❑ 법원은 본인들에게 소비자가 현혹되지 않도록 조치를 취해야 할 책임이 있다고 생각한다. **6** 단수명사 ~에 대한 책임 ❑ 그녀는 자신이 의사이므로 동료 인간에 대한 책임이 있다고 생각했었다.

Word Partnership   *responsibility*의 연어

V.	**assume** responsibility, **bear** responsibility, **share** responsibility, **take** responsibility **1**–**4**
	have (a) responsibility **1** **4**–**6**
	accept responsibility, **claim** responsibility **2**
	be given responsibility **4**
ADJ.	**financial** responsibility, **personal** responsibility **1**–**4**
	moral responsibility **5**

---

re|spon|sible ♦♦◇ /rɪspɒnsɪbəl/ **1** ADJ If someone or something is **responsible for** a particular event or situation, they are the cause of it or they can be blamed for it. [v-link ADJ, usu ADJ for n/-ing] ❑ *He still felt responsible for her death.* **2** ADJ If you are **responsible for** something, it is your job or duty to deal with it and make decisions relating to it. [v-link ADJ, usu ADJ for n/-ing] ❑ *...the minister responsible for the environment.* **3** ADJ If you are **responsible to** a person or group, they have authority over you and you have to report to them about what you do. [v-link ADJ to n] ❑ *I'm responsible to my board of directors.* **4** ADJ **Responsible** people behave properly and sensibly, without needing to be supervised. ❑ *He feels that the media should be more responsible in what they report.* ● **re|spon|sibly** ADV [ADV with v] ❑ *He urged everyone to act responsibly.* **5** ADJ **Responsible** jobs involve making important decisions or carrying out important tasks. [ADJ n] ❑ *I work in a government office. It's a responsible position, I suppose, but not very exciting.*

1 형용사 책임이 있는 ❑ 그는 여전히 그녀의 죽음에 대해 책임이 있다고 생각했다. **2** 형용사 담당하는 ❑ 환경을 담당하는 장관 ~의 관할 아래 있는 ❑ 나는 이사회의 관할 아래에 있다. **4** 형용사 책임감 있는 ❑ 그는 언론이 보도 내용에 대해 좀 더 책임감을 가질 필요가 있다고 생각한다. ● 책임감 있게 부사 ❑ 그는 모든 사람들에게 책임감 있게 행동하라고 촉구했다. **5** 형용사 책임이 무거운 ❑ 나는 정부에서 일한다. 책임이 무거운 일인 것 같기는 하지만 그다지 재미있는 일은 아니다.

re|spon|sive /rɪspɒnsɪv/ **1** ADJ A **responsive** person is quick to react to people or to show emotions such as pleasure and affection. ❑ *Harriet was an easy, responsive little girl.* ● **re|spon|sive|ness** N-UNCOUNT ❑ *This condition decreases sexual desire and responsiveness.* **2** ADJ If someone or something is **responsive**, they react quickly and favorably. ❑ *With an election coming soon, your MP should be very responsive to your request.* ● **re|spon|sive|ness** N-UNCOUNT ❑ *Such responsiveness to public pressure is extraordinary.*

1 형용사 쉽게 넘어가는 ❑ 해리엇은 헤프고 쉽게 넘어가는 작은 여자 애였다. ● 반응 불가산명사 ❑ 이 질환은 성적 욕구와 반응을 저하시킨다. **2** 형용사 빠른 반응을 보이는 ❑ 선거가 곧 다가오므로 의회의원은 당신의 요청에 아주 빨리 대처를 해 줄 겁니다. ● 빠른 대응 불가산명사 ❑ 대중의 압력에 그렇게 빨리 대응하는 것은 이례적이다.

---

rest

① QUANTIFIER USES
② VERB AND NOUN USES

---

① **rest** ♦♦◇ /rest/ **1** QUANT The **rest** is used to refer to all the parts of something or all the things in a group that remain or that you have not already mentioned. [QUANT of def-n] ❑ *It was an experience I will treasure for the rest of my life.* ● PRON **Rest** is also a pronoun. ❑ *Only 55 per cent of the raw material is canned. The rest is thrown away, or fed to cows.* **2** PHRASE You can add **and the rest** or **all the rest of** it to the end of a statement or list when you want to refer in a vague way to other things that are associated with the ones you have already mentioned. [SPOKEN, VAGUENESS] ❑ *...a man with nice clothes, a Range Rover and the rest.*

1 수량사 나머지 ❑ 그것은 내가 여생 동안 소중히 간직할 경험이었다. ● 대명사 나머지 ❑ 원재료의 55퍼센트만이 통조림으로 만들어진다. 나머지는 버려지거나 소의 사료로 쓰인다. **2** 구 기타 등등 [구어체, 짐작투] ❑ 좋은 옷에, 레인지 로버 자동차에, 기타 등등을 갖춘 남자

If you are talking about an uncountable noun, for example "food," the verb following **rest** is singular. ❑ *The rest of the food was delicious.* If you are talking about a countable noun, such as "boys," the verb is plural. ❑ *The rest of the boys were delighted.*

예를 들어, 'food'와 같이 셀 수 없는 것을 말할 때, rest 다음에 오는 동사는 단수를 쓴다. ❑ 나머지 음식은 맛이 있었다. 'boys'와 같이 셀 수 있는 것을 말할 때, rest 다음에 오는 동사는 복수를 쓴다. ❑ 나머지 소년들은 기뻤다.

a
b
c
d
e
f
g
h
i
j
k
l
m
n
o
p
q
r
s
t
u
v
w
x
y
z

Thesaurus   rest의 참조어

v.   lie down, relax ② ■ ■

② **rest** ♦♦◇ /rɛst/ (rests, resting, rested) →Please look at category ⑭ to see if the expression you are looking for is shown under another headword. **1** V-T/V-I If you **rest** or if you **rest** your body, you do not do anything active for a time. ❑ *He's tired and exhausted, and has been advised to rest for two weeks.* **2** N-VAR If you get some **rest** or have a **rest**, you do not do anything active for a time. ❑ *"You're worn out, Laura," he said. "Go home and get some rest."* **3** V-I If something such as a theory or someone's success **rests on** a particular thing, it depends on that thing. [FORMAL] ❑ *Such a view rests on a number of incorrect assumptions.* **4** V-I If authority, a responsibility, or a decision **rests with** you, you have that authority or responsibility, or you are the one who will make that decision. [FORMAL] ❑ *The final decision rested with the President.* **5** V-T If you **rest** something somewhere, you put it there so that its weight is supported. ❑ *He rested his arms on the back of the chair.* **6** V-T/V-I If something **is resting** somewhere, or if you **are resting** it there, it is in a position where its weight is supported. ❑ *His head was resting on her shoulder.* **7** V-I If you **rest** on or against someone or something, you lean on them so that they support the weight of your body. ❑ *He rested on his pickaxe for a while.* **8** N-COUNT A **rest** is an object that is used to support something, especially your head, arms, or feet. ❑ *When you are sitting, keep your elbow on the arm rest.* **9** V-I If your eyes **rest on** a particular person or object, you look directly at them, rather than somewhere else. [WRITTEN] ❑ *As she spoke, her eyes rested on her husband's face.* **10** →see also **rested** **11** PHRASE When an object that has been moving **comes to rest**, it finally stops. [FORMAL] ❑ *The plane had plowed a path through a patch of forest before coming to rest in a field.* **12** PHRASE If someone refuses to **let** a subject **rest**, they refuse to stop talking about it, especially after they have been talking about it for a long time. ❑ *I am not prepared to let this matter rest.* **13** PHRASE To **put** someone's **mind at rest** or **set** their **mind at rest** means to tell them something that stops them from worrying. ❑ *A brain scan last Friday finally set his mind at rest.* **14 rest assured** →see **assured**. **to rest on** your **laurels** →see **laurel** →see **motion, sleep**

1 타동사/자동사 쉬다; ~을 쉬게 하다 ❑ 그는 피곤하고 지쳐서 2주간 휴식을 취하라는 권고를 받았다. **2** 가산명사 또는 불가산명사 휴식 ❑ "당신은 지쳤어, 로라. 집에 가서 좀 쉬어."라고 그가 말했다. **3** 자동사 ~에 달려 있다, ~에 의존하다 [격식체] ❑ 그런 견해는 상당수 부정확한 억측에 근거한다. **4** 자동사 달려 있다 [격식체] ❑ 최종 결정은 대통령에게 달려 있었다. **5** 타동사 놓다 ❑ 그는 의자 등에 팔을 얹었다. **6** 타동사/자동사 ~에 놓여 있다, ~에 놓다 ❑ 그의 머리는 그녀의 어깨 위에 얹혀 있었다. **7** 자동사 기대다 ❑ 그는 잠시 곡괭이에 몸을 기댔다. **8** 가산명사 받침 ❑ 앉아 있을 때는 팔꿈치를 팔 받침대에 얹으세요. **9** 자동사 ~을 주시하다, (눈길이) 머물다 [문어체] ❑ 그녀는 말을 하면서 눈길은 계속 남편의 얼굴을 주시했다. **11** 구 멈춰 서다 [격식체] ❑ 비행기는 나무를 깔아뭉개며 숲을 뚫고 나가 마침내 들판에 멈춰 섰다. **12** 구 ~에 대한 이야기를 그만두다 ❑ 나는 이 사안에 대해 조용히 할 의향이 없다. **13** 구 안심시키다 ❑ 마침내 지난 금요일에 한 뇌 촬영이 그를 안심할 수 있게 해 주었다.

rest area (rest areas) N-COUNT A **rest area** is a place beside a highway where you can buy gas and other things, or have a meal. [mainly AM; BRIT **services**] ❑ *...a freeway rest area in Texas Canyon.*

가산명사 고속도로 휴게소 [주로 미국영어; 영국영어 services] ❑ 텍사스 캐넌의 고속도로 휴게소

Word Link   re ≈ back, again : reflect, refresh, restate

re|state /riːsteɪt/ (restates, restating, restated) V-T If you **restate** something, you say it again in words or writing, usually in a slightly different way. [FORMAL] ❑ *He continued throughout to restate his opposition to violence.*

타동사 고쳐 말하다 [격식체] ❑ 그는 줄곧 계속해서 말을 고쳐 가며 폭력에 대한 반대 입장을 밝혔다.

res|tau|rant ♦♦◇ /rɛstərənt, -tərɑnt, -trɑnt, BRIT rɛstərɒnt/ (restaurants) N-COUNT A **restaurant** is a place where you can eat a meal and pay for it. In restaurants your food is usually served to you at your table by a waiter or waitress. ❑ *They ate in an Italian restaurant in Forth Street.* →see **café, city** →see Word Web: **restaurant**

가산명사 식당 ❑ 그들은 4번가에 있는 이탈리아 식당에서 식사를 했다.

The **salad bar** is a popular feature of American restaurants, and allows the customer to choose what kind of and how much salad to eat for a set price. Salad bars may offer bread, soup, or dessert as well.

salad bar(샐러드 바)는 미국 식당에 흔히 있으며 손님이 일정 가격에 샐러드의 종류와 양을 선택할 수 있다. 샐러드 바에서 빵, 스프, 디저트를 제공하는 경우도 있다.

rest|ed /rɛstɪd/ ADJ If you feel **rested**, you feel more energetic because you have just had a rest. [v-link ADJ] ❑ *He looked tanned and well rested after his vacation.*

형용사 휴식을 취해 다시 생기가 도는, 잘 쉰 ❑ 휴가를 보내고 온 그는 그을린 피부에 푹 잘 쉰 것처럼 보였다.

rest|less /rɛstlɪs/ **1** ADJ If you are **restless**, you are bored, impatient, or dissatisfied, and you want to do something else. ❑ *By 1982, she was restless and needed a new impetus for her talent.* ● **rest|less|ness** N-UNCOUNT ❑ *From the audience came increasing sounds of restlessness.* **2** ADJ If someone is **restless**, they keep moving around because they find it difficult to keep still. ❑ *My father seemed very restless and excited.* ● **rest|less|ness** N-UNCOUNT ❑ *Karen complained of hyperactivity and restlessness.* ● **rest|less|ly** ADV ❑ *He paced up and down restlessly, trying to put his thoughts in order.*

1 형용사 답답한 ❑ 1982년이 되자 그녀는 답답했고 자신의 재능을 표출할 새로운 자극제가 필요했다. ● 답답함 불가산명사 ❑ 관중석으로부터 답답해하는 듯한 소리가 점점 많이 들려왔다. **2** 형용사 안절부절못하는 ❑ 우리 아버지는 안절부절못하며 매우 흥분하신 것 같았다. ● 안절부절못함 불가산명사 ❑ 카렌은 마음이 불안하고 안절부절못하겠다고 호소했다. ● 안절부절못하겠다는 듯이 부사 ❑ 그는 안절부절못하겠다는 듯이 왔다 갔다 하며 생각을 정리하려고 애썼다.

re|stock /riːstɒk/ (restocks, restocking, restocked) V-T/V-I If you **restock** something such as a shelf, refrigerator, or store, you fill it with food or other goods to replace what you have used or sold. ❑ *I have to restock the freezer.*

타동사/자동사 (물건을) 다시 채우다 ❑ 냉장고에 물건을 다시 사서 넣어야 한다.

Word Web   restaurant

There are over 900,000 **restaurants** in the United States. These include traditional sit-down eateries as well as **coffee shops, cafeterias,** and **takeout** places. Here are some more key statistics. Forty percent of American adults have worked in a restaurant at some point in their lives. Only the government employs more people than the food service business. The restaurant industry has more minority **managers** than any other industry. In 2005, the average **tip** received by a **waiter** or **waitress** was 18%. The average **meal** cost $31.51. The most popular **cuisine** was Italian (31% preferred it), followed by Asian (25%).

re|store ◆◇◇ /rɪstɔːr/ (restores, restoring, restored) **1** V-T To **restore** a situation or practice means to cause it to exist again. ❑ *The army has recently been brought in to restore order.* ● **res|to|ra|tion** /ˌrɛstəreɪʃⁿn/ N-UNCOUNT ❑ *His visit is expected to lead to the restoration of diplomatic relations.* **2** V-T To **restore** someone or something **to** a previous condition means to cause them to be in that condition once again. ❑ *We will restore her to health but it may take time.* ● **res|to|ra|tion** N-UNCOUNT ❑ *I owe the restoration of my hearing to this remarkable new technique.* **3** V-T When someone **restores** something such as an old building, painting, or piece of furniture, they repair and clean it, so that it looks like it did when it was new. ❑ *...experts who specialize in examining and restoring ancient parchments.* ● **res|to|ra|tion** (restorations) N-VAR ❑ *I specialized in the restoration of old houses.* **4** V-T If something that was lost or stolen **is restored to** its owner, it is returned to them. [FORMAL] [usu passive] ❑ *The following day their horses and goods were restored to them.*

re|strain /rɪstreɪn/ (restrains, restraining, restrained) **1** V-T If you **restrain** someone, you stop them from doing what they intended or wanted to do, usually by using your physical strength. ❑ *Wally gripped my arm, partly to restrain me and partly to reassure me.* **2** V-T If you **restrain** an emotion or you **restrain yourself from** doing something, you prevent yourself from showing that emotion or doing what you wanted or intended to do. ❑ *She was unable to restrain her desperate anger.* **3** V-T To **restrain** something that is growing or increasing means to prevent it from getting too large. ❑ *The radical 500-day plan was very clear on how it intended to try to restrain inflation.*

re|strained /rɪstreɪnd/ **1** ADJ Someone who is **restrained** is very calm and unemotional. ❑ *In the circumstances he felt he'd been very restrained.* **2** ADJ If you describe someone's clothes or the decorations in a house as **restrained**, you mean that you like them because they are simple and not too brightly-colored. [APPROVAL] ❑ *Her black suit was restrained and expensive.*

re|straint /rɪstreɪnt/ (restraints) **1** N-VAR **Restraints** are rules or conditions that limit or restrict someone or something. ❑ *The Prime Minister is calling for new restraints on trade unions.* **2** N-UNCOUNT **Restraint** is calm, controlled, and unemotional behavior. ❑ *They behaved with more restraint than I'd expected.*

re|strict /rɪstrɪkt/ (restricts, restricting, restricted) **1** V-T If you **restrict** something, you put a limit on it in order to reduce it or prevent it becoming too great. ❑ *There is talk of raising the admission requirements to restrict the number of students on campus.* ● **re|stric|tion** /rɪstrɪkʃⁿn/ N-UNCOUNT ❑ *Since the costs of science were rising faster than inflation, some restriction on funding was necessary.* **2** V-T To **restrict** the movement or actions of someone or something means to prevent them from moving or acting freely. ❑ *The government imprisoned dissidents, forbade travel, and restricted the press.* ● **re|stric|tion** N-UNCOUNT ❑ *...the justification for this restriction of individual liberty.* **3** V-T If you **restrict** someone or their activities **to** one thing, they can only do, have, or deal with that thing. If you **restrict** them **to** one place, they cannot go anywhere else. ❑ *For the first two weeks patients are restricted to the grounds.* **4** V-T If you **restrict** something **to** a particular group, only that group can do it or have it. If you **restrict** something **to** a particular place, it is allowed only in that place. ❑ *Ministers had decided to restrict university entry to about 30 per cent of a declining school-leaving population.*

re|strict|ed /rɪstrɪktɪd/ **1** ADJ Something that is **restricted** is quite small or limited. ❑ *...the monotony of a heavily restricted diet.* **2** ADJ If something is **restricted to** a particular group, only members of that group have it. If it is **restricted to** a particular place, it exists only in that place. [v-link ADJ *to* n] ❑ *Discipline problems are by no means restricted to children in families dependent on benefits.* **3** ADJ A **restricted** area is one that only people with special permission can enter. ❑ *...a highly restricted area close to the old Khodinka airfield.*

re|stric|tion ◆◇◇ /rɪstrɪkʃⁿn/ (restrictions) **1** N-COUNT A **restriction** is an official rule that limits what you can do or that limits the amount or size of something. ❑ *...the lifting of restrictions on political parties and the news media.* **2** N-COUNT You can refer to anything that limits what you can do as a **restriction**. ❑ *His parents are trying to make up to him for the restrictions of urban living.* **3** →see also restrict

re|stric|tive /rɪstrɪktɪv/ ADJ Something that is **restrictive** prevents people from doing what they want to do, or from moving freely. ❑ *Britain is to adopt a more restrictive policy on arms sales.*

re|stric|tive prac|tice (restrictive practices) N-COUNT **Restrictive practices** are ways in which people involved in an industry, trade, or profession protect their own interests, rather than having a system which is fair to the public, employers, and other workers. [BRIT, BUSINESS] ❑ *The Act was introduced to end restrictive practices in the docks.*

rest|room /rɛstrʊm, -rʊm/ (restrooms) also **rest room** N-COUNT In a restaurant, theater, or other public place, a **restroom** is a room with a toilet for customers to use. [AM; BRIT usually **toilet**]

re|struc|ture /rɪstrʌktʃər/ (restructures, restructuring, restructured) V-T To **restructure** an organization or system means to change the way it is organized, usually in order to make it work more effectively. ❑ *The President called on educators and politicians to help him restructure American education.* ● **re|struc|tur|ing** (restructurings) N-VAR ❑ *Pirelli, the Italian tyre company, is to lay off 1,520 workers as part of a restructuring.*

re|sult ◆◆◆ /rɪzʌlt/ (results, resulting, resulted) **1** N-COUNT A **result** is something that happens or exists because of something else that has happened. ❑ *Compensation is available for people who have developed asthma as a direct result of their work.* **2** V-I If something **results in** a particular situation or event, it causes that situation or event to happen. ❑ *Fifty per cent of road accidents*

---

1 타동사 회복하다, 복구하다 ❑ 질서 회복을 위해 군대가 다시 동원되었다. ● 회복, 복구 불가산명사 ❑ 그의 방문이 외교 관계 회복으로 이어질 전망이다. **2** 타동사 회복시키다 ❑ 우리가 그녀의 건강을 회복시킬 것이나 시간이 조금 걸릴 수도 있다. ● 회복 불가산명사 ❑ 나의 청력 회복은 이 놀라운 신기술 덕분이다. **3** 타동사 복원하다 ❑ 고대 양피지를 검토하고 복원하는 일을 전문으로 하는 전문가들 ● 복원 가산명사 또는 불가산명사 ❑ 나는 옛날 집들의 복원을 전문으로 했다. **4** 타동사 (원래 주인에게) 되돌아가다 [격식체] ❑ 다음 날 그들의 말과 물건들은 다시 그들에게 돌아왔다.

1 타동사 제지하다 ❑ 한편으로는 나를 제지하기 위해 또 한편으로는 나를 안심시키기 위해 월리가 나의 팔을 잡았다. **2** 타동사 억누르다, 억제하다 ❑ 그녀는 자신의 지독한 분노를 억누를 수가 없었다. **3** 타동사 억제하다 ❑ 그 급진적인 500일 작전에서는 물가 인상을 어떻게 억제하려고 하는가가 아주 명확했다.

1 형용사 자제하는 ❑ 상황을 고려하면 그는 자신이 굉장히 자제했다고 생각했다. **2** 형용사 수수한 [마음에 듦] ❑ 그녀의 검은 정장은 수수하면서도 비쌌다.

1 가산명사 또는 불가산명사 규제 ❑ 수상은 산별 노조에 대한 새로운 규제를 요청하고 있다. **2** 불가산명사 자제 ❑ 그들은 내가 예상했던 것보다 더 자제력 있게 행동했다.

1 타동사 제한하다 ❑ 캠퍼스 내의 학생 수를 제한할 수 있도록 입학 요건을 강화하자는 말이 있다. ● 제한 불가산명사 ❑ 학문에 드는 비용이 물가 인상률보다 빠르게 상승하고 있었기 때문에 자금 지원에 대한 약간의 제한이 필요했다. **2** 타동사 통제하다 ❑ 정부는 반체제 인사를 구속하고 여행을 금지했으며 언론을 통제했다. ● 통제 불가산명사 ❑ 개인 자유에 대한 이러한 통제의 정당화 **3** 타동사 구속하다, 속박하다 ❑ 첫 2주 동안 환자들은 구내를 벗어날 수 없다. **4** 타동사 제한하다 ❑ 각료들은 점점 줄어드는 졸업생 수의 약 30퍼센트 이내로 대학 진학생을 제한하기로 결정한 상태였다.

1 형용사 제한된 ❑ 심하게 제한된 식사의 단조로움 **2** 형용사 제한된 ❑ 훈육 문제가 정부 보조금을 받는 집안의 아이들에게만 국한된 것은 절대로 아니다. **3** 형용사 출입이 제한된 ❑ 구 코딘카 비행장 근처의 출입이 엄격히 제한된 구역

1 가산명사 규제 ❑ 정당과 언론 매체에 대한 규제 해제 **2** 가산명사 제약, 한계점 ❑ 그의 부모는 그에게 도시 생활의 한계점들을 보상해 주려 하고 있다.

형용사 제한적인 ❑ 영국은 무기 판매에 대해 보다 제한적인 정책을 채택할 것이다.

가산명사 제한적 관행 [영국영어, 경제] ❑ 그 법령은 부두 노동자들의 제한적 관행을 종식시키기 위해 도입되었다.

가산명사 화장실 [미국영어; 영국영어 대개 toilet]

타동사 구조 조정하다 ❑ 대통령은 자신이 미국의 교육 체제를 구조 조정하는 것을 도와 달라고 교육자와 정치인들에게 요청했다. ● 구조 조정 가산명사 또는 불가산명사 ❑ 이탈리아의 타이어 회사인 피렐리는 구조 조정의 일환으로 노동자 1,520명을 정리 해고할 예정이다.

1 가산명사 결과 ❑ 업무의 직접적인 결과로 천식에 걸린 사람들은 보상을 받을 수 있다. **2** 자동사 결과 -한 결과가 되다, -을 초래하다 ❑ 도로 교통사고의 50퍼센트가 머리 부상을 초래한다. **3** 자동사 기인하다 ❑ 많은 머리카락 문제는 먹는 음식에서 기인한다.

result in head injuries. **3** V-I If something **results from** a particular event or action, it is caused by that event or action. ❑ *Many hair problems result from what you eat.* **4** N-COUNT A **result** is the situation that exists at the end of a contest. ❑ *The final election results will be announced on Friday.* **5** N-COUNT A **result** is the number that you get when you do a calculation. ❑ *They found their computers producing different results from exactly the same calculation.* **6** N-COUNT Your **results** are the marks or grades that you get for examinations you have taken. [mainly BRIT; AM usually **scores**] ❑ *Kate's exam results were excellent.*

4 가산명사 결과 ❑ 최종 투표 결과는 금요일에 발표될 것이다. **5** 가산명사 결과 ❑ 그들의 컴퓨터가 완전히 동일한 계산에서 다른 결과를 내는 것을 발견했다. **6** 가산명사 결과, 성적 [주로 영국영어; 미국영어 대개 scores] ❑ 케이트의 시험 성적은 훌륭했다.

Thesaurus   result의 참조어

N.	by-product, consequence **1**
V.	come about, produce, turn out **2**

---

re|sult|ant /rɪzʌ́ltənt/ ADJ **Resultant** means caused by the event just mentioned. [FORMAL] [ADJ n] ❑ *At least a quarter of a million people have died in the fighting and the resultant famines.*

형용사 그에 따른, 그 결과로 생긴 [격식체] ❑ 최소한 25만 명이 전쟁과 그 결과로 생긴 기근으로 죽었다.

re|sume ◆◇◇ /rɪzúm, BRIT rɪzjúːm/ (**resumes, resuming, resumed**) **1** V-T/V-I If you **resume** an activity or if it **resumes**, it begins again. [FORMAL] ❑ *After the war he resumed his duties at Emmanuel College.* ● **re|sump|tion** /rɪzʌ́mpʃən/ N-UNCOUNT ❑ *It is premature to speculate about the resumption of negotiations.* **2** V-T If you **resume** your seat or position, you return to the seat or position you were in before you moved. [FORMAL] ❑ *"I changed my mind," Blanche said, resuming her seat.*

1 타동사/자동사 재개하다 [격식체] ❑ 전쟁 후에 그는 엠마뉴엘 대학에서 자신의 업무를 재개했다. ● 재개 불가산명사 ❑ 협상 재개에 대해 추측하기에는 아직 이르다. **2** 타동사 (제 위치로) 돌아오다 [격식체] ❑ "마음을 바꿨어."라고 블랑쉬가 제자리에 다시 앉으며 말했다.

ré|su|mé /rézʊmeɪ, BRIT rezjúmeɪ/ (**résumés**) also **resumé** **1** N-COUNT A **résumé** is a short account, either spoken or written, of something that has happened or that someone has said or written. ❑ *I will leave with you a résumé of his most recent speech.* **2** N-COUNT Your **résumé** is a brief account of your personal details, your education, and the jobs you have had. You are often asked to send a résumé when you are applying for a job. [mainly AM; BRIT usually **curriculum vitae**]

1 가산명사 요약 ❑ 그가 가장 최근에 한 연설의 요약본을 당신게 한 부 드리겠습니다. **2** 가산명사 이력서 [주로 미국영어; 영국영어 대개 curriculum vitae]

re|sur|gence /rɪsɜ́rdʒəns/ N-SING If there is a **resurgence of** an attitude or activity, it reappears and grows. [FORMAL] [also no det, oft N of n] ❑ *Police say drugs traffickers are behind the resurgence of violence.*

단수명사 부활, 재개 [격식체] ❑ 폭력 사건의 부활 배후에는 마약 밀매업자들이 있다고 경찰은 말한다.

re|sur|rect /rézərekt/ (**resurrects, resurrecting, resurrected**) V-T If you **resurrect** something, you cause it to exist again after it had disappeared or ended. ❑ *Attempts to resurrect the ceasefire have already failed once.* ● **res|ur|rec|tion** /rézərékʃən/ N-UNCOUNT ❑ *This is a resurrection of an old story from the mid-70s.*

타동사 부활시키다, 소생시키다 ❑ 정전 협정을 부활시키는 시도는 이미 한 번 실패했다. ● 부활 불가산명사 ❑ 이건 70년대 중반의 흔한 이야기를 부활시킨 것이다.

re|sus|ci|tate /rɪsʌ́sɪteɪt/ (**resuscitates, resuscitating, resuscitated**) **1** V-T If you **resuscitate** someone who has stopped breathing, you cause them to start breathing again. ❑ *A policeman and then a paramedic tried to resuscitate her.* ● **re|sus|ci|ta|tion** /rɪsʌ̀sɪteɪʃən/ N-UNCOUNT ❑ *They must even now be rushing her to the hospital for resuscitation and treatment.* **2** V-T If you **resuscitate** something, you cause it to become active or successful again. ❑ *He has submitted a bid to resuscitate the weekly magazine, which closed in April with losses of £1million a year.* ● **re|sus|ci|ta|tion** N-UNCOUNT ❑ *The economy needs vigorous resuscitation.*

1 타동사 (심폐 소생술로) 소생시키다 ❑ 경찰관, 그 다음엔 응급 구조 요원이 그녀를 소생시키려고 애를 썼다. ● 소생 불가산명사 ❑ 지금도 그들은 그녀를 소생시키고 치료하기 위해 병원으로 달리고 있을 것이다. **2** 타동사 소생시키다, 부활시키다 ❑ 그는 연간 백만 파운드의 손실을 내고 4월에 문을 닫은 그 주간지를 소생시키기 위해 입찰가를 제출했다. ● 소생 불가산명사 ❑ 경제는 강력한 소생술이 필요하다.

re|tail ◆◇◇ /ríteɪl/ (**retails, retailing, retailed**) **1** N-UNCOUNT **Retail** is the activity of selling goods direct to the public, usually in small quantities. Compare **wholesale**. [BUSINESS] ❑ *Retail stores usually count on the Christmas season to make up to half of their annual profits.* **2** ADV If something is sold **retail**, it is sold in ordinary stores direct to the public. [BUSINESS] [ADV after v] ❑ *We sell wholesale to several state-owned chains that sell retail to the public.* **3** V-I If an item in a store **retails at** or **for** a particular price, it is on sale at that price. [BUSINESS] ❑ *It originally retailed at £23.50.* →see also **retailing**

1 불가산명사 소매 [경제] ❑ 소매점들은 연간 매출의 절반까지를 크리스마스 기간에 의존한다. **2** 부사 소매로 [경제] ❑ 우리는 일반인들에게 소매가로 판매하는 여러 개의 국영 체인점에 도매로 물건을 판매한다. **3** 자동사 (어떤 가격에) 팔리다 [경제] ❑ 그것은 원래 23.50파운드에 팔렸다.

re|tail|er /ríteɪlər/ (**retailers**) N-COUNT A **retailer** is a person or business that sells goods to the public. [BUSINESS] ❑ *Furniture and carpet retailers are among those reporting the sharpest annual decline in sales.*

가산명사 소매상 [경제] ❑ 가구 및 카펫 소매상들이 가장 심한 연간 매출 하락을 보고한 집단 중 하나이다.

re|tail|ing /ríteɪlɪŋ/ N-UNCOUNT **Retailing** is the activity of selling goods direct to the public, usually in small quantities. Compare **wholesaling**. [BUSINESS] ❑ *She spent fourteen years in retailing.*

불가산명사 소매 [경제] ❑ 그녀는 소매업에 종사하며 14년을 보냈다.

re|tail park (**retail parks**) N-COUNT A **retail park** is a large specially built area, usually at the edge of a town or city, where there are a lot of large stores and sometimes other facilities such as movie theaters and restaurants.

가산명사 쇼핑몰

re|tail price in|dex N-PROPER The **retail price index** is a list of the prices of typical goods which shows how much the cost of living changes from one month to the next. [BRIT, BUSINESS; AM **cost-of-living index**] ❑ *The retail price index for September, to be released on Friday, is expected to show inflation edging up to about 10.8 per cent.*

고유명사 소매 물가 지수 [영국영어, 경제; 미국영어 cost-of-living index] ❑ 금요일에 발표될 9월 소매 물가 지수에서 물가 인상률이 거의 10.8퍼센트에 육박하는 것으로 드러날 전망이다.

re|tain ◆◇◇ /rɪtéɪn/ (**retains, retaining, retained**) V-T To **retain** something means to continue to have that thing. [FORMAL] ❑ *The interior of the shop still retains a nineteenth-century atmosphere.*

타동사 유지하다, 보유하다 [격식체] ❑ 가게들의 내부는 아직도 19세기 분위기를 지니고 있다.

Thesaurus   retain의 참조어

V.	hold, keep, maintain, remember, save; *(ant.)* give up, lose

---

re|tain|er /rɪtéɪnər/ (**retainers**) N-COUNT A **retainer** is a fee that you pay to someone in order to make sure that they will be available to do work for you if you need them to. ❑ *I'll need a five-hundred-dollar retainer.*

가산명사 (변호사 등의) 선임료 ❑ 500달러의 선임료가 필요할 겁니다.

re|tali|ate /rɪtǽlieɪt/ (**retaliates, retaliating, retaliated**) V-I If you **retaliate** when someone harms or annoys you, you do something which harms or annoys them in return. ❑ *I was sorely tempted to retaliate.* ❑ *Christie retaliated by sending his friend a long letter detailing Carl's utter incompetence.* ● **re|talia|tion** /rɪtæ̀lieɪʃən/

자동사 보복하다, 앙갚음하다 ❑ 나는 보복하고 싶은 마음이 간절했다. ❑ 크리스티는 그의 친구에게 칼의 절대적인 무능함을 소상히 밝히는 긴 편지를 써서 보복했다. ● 보복, 앙갚음 불가산명사 ❑ 경찰은 그

N-UNCOUNT ❑ *Police said they believed the attack was in retaliation for the death of the drug trafficker.*

마약 밀매업자의 죽음에 대한 보복으로 그 공격이 이루어졌을 것이라고 했다.

re|ten|tion /rɪtenʃ°n/ N-UNCOUNT The **retention of** something is the keeping of it. [FORMAL] ❑ *The Citizens' Forum supported special powers for Quebec but also argued for the retention of a strong central government.*

불가산명사 유지, 보유 [격식체] ❑ 시민 포럼은 퀘벡의 특수 권한을 지지하면서도 또한 강력한 중앙 정부 유지도 주장했다.

re|think /riːθɪŋk/ (rethinks, rethinking, rethought) ❶ V-T If you **rethink** something such as a problem, a plan, or a policy, you think about it again and change it. ❑ *Both major political parties are having to rethink their policies.* ❷ N-SING If you have a **rethink** of a problem, a plan, or a policy, you think about it again and change it. [JOURNALISM] ❑ *There must be a rethink of government policy towards this vulnerable group.*

❶ 타동사 재고하다 ❑ 두 주요 정당은 자신들의 정책을 재고해야 하는 상황에 처해 있다. ❷ 단수명사 재고 [언론] ❑ 이 취약한 집단에 대한 정부 정책의 재고가 있어야 한다.

reti|cent /retɪsənt/ ADJ Someone who is **reticent** does not tell people about things. ❑ *She is so reticent about her achievements.* ● reti|cence N-UNCOUNT ❑ *Pearl didn't mind his reticence; in fact she liked it.*

형용사 과묵한 ❑ 그녀는 자신의 업적에 대해 매우 과묵하다. ● 과묵함 불가산명사 ❑ 펄은 그의 과묵함이 싫지 않았다. 사실 그것이 좋았다.

reti|na /retɪnə/ (retinas) N-COUNT Your **retina** is the area at the back of your eye. It receives the image that you see and then sends the image to your brain. ❑ *Bruno had to have eye surgery on a torn retina two years ago.* →see **eye**

가산명사 망막 ❑ 브루노는 2년 전에 망막이 찢어져 눈 수술을 받아야 했다.

re|tire ♦♢♢ /rɪtaɪər/ (retires, retiring, retired) ❶ V-I When older people **retire**, they leave their job and usually stop working completely. ❑ *At the age when most people retire, he is ready to face a new career.* ❷ V-I When an athlete **retires from** their sport, they stop playing in competitions. When they **retire from** a race or a game, they stop competing in it. ❑ *I have decided to retire from Formula One racing at the end of the season.* ❸ V-I When a jury in a court of law **retires**, the members of it leave the court in order to decide whether someone is guilty or innocent. ❑ *The jury will retire to consider its verdict today.* ❹ →see also **retired**

❶ 자동사 은퇴하다 ❑ 대부분의 사람들이 은퇴하는 나이에 그는 새로운 일을 시작할 준비가 되어 있다. ❷ 자동사 은퇴하다; 물러나다 ❑ 나는 이번 시즌이 끝날 때 포뮬러원 경주에서 은퇴하기로 결정했다. ❸ 자동사 (배심원들이 평결을 토의하기 위해) 물러나다 ❑ 배심원들이 오늘 물러가서 평결을 토의할 것이다.

> Do not confuse **retire** and **resign**. When someone **retires**, they leave their job and stop working, often because they have reached the age when they can get a pension. ❑ *He had been planning for some time to retire at around age 60.* When professional sportsmen and women stop playing sport as their job, you can also say that they **retire**, even if they are fairly young. ❑ *A heart attack at the age of 36 forced him to retire from tennis.* If someone **resigns** from their job, they leave it after saying that they do not want to do it any more. ❑ *He hasn't decided whether he will resign.* You can **resign** from your job at any age, and perhaps start another job soon afterwards.

retire와 resign을 혼동하지 않도록 하라. 누가 은퇴(retire)하면, 그 사람은 흔히 연금을 받을 수 있는 나이에 이르렀기 때문에 직장을 그만두고 일을 하지 않는 것이다. ❑ 그는 60살 경에 은퇴하기로 마음먹은 지 꽤 된 상태였다. 전문 운동선수가 직업으로 하는 운동을 그만두면, 그 사람이 상당히 젊더라도 retire한다고 말할 수 있다. ❑ 그는 36살의 나이에 심장마비에 걸려서 테니스에서 은퇴할 수밖에 없었다. 누가 자기 직장을 사직하면(resign), 그 사람은 더 이상 그 일을 하고 싶지 않다고 말한 다음 그 직장을 그만두는 것이다. ❑ 그는 사임할지 결정하지 않았다. 어떤 나이에도 직장에서 resign할 수 있으며, 아마도 그 뒤에 곧 새로운 일을 시작하게 될 것이다.

Thesaurus   *retire*의 참조어

v.   finish, leave, stop, quit ❶

re|tired /rɪtaɪərd/ ❶ ADJ A **retired** person is an older person who has left his or her job and usually stopped working completely. ❑ *...a seventy-three-year-old retired teacher from Florida.* ❷ →see also **retire**

❶ 형용사 은퇴한 ❑ 교직을 은퇴한 플로리다 출신의 73세 된 사람

re|tire|ment ♦♢♢ /rɪtaɪərmənt/ (retirements) ❶ N-VAR **Retirement** is the time when a worker retires. ❑ *The proportion of the population who are over retirement age has grown tremendously in the past few years.* ❷ N-UNCOUNT A person's **retirement** is the period in their life after they have retired. ❑ *"Growing Older" considered the needs of the elderly for financial support during retirement.*

❶ 가산명사 또는 불가산명사 정년 ❑ 정년을 넘어선 인구의 비율이 지난 몇 년 사이에 엄청나게 증가했다. ❷ 불가산명사 정년 이후, 은퇴 생활 ❑ '그로잉 올더'는 정년 이후 노년층에게 필요한 재정적 지원을 고려했다.

re|tort /rɪtɔrt/ (retorts, retorting, retorted) V-T To **retort** means to reply angrily to someone. [WRITTEN] ❑ *Was he afraid, he was asked. "Afraid of what?" he retorted.* ● N-COUNT **Retort** is also a noun. ❑ *His sharp retort clearly made an impact.*

타동사 되받아치다; 말대꾸하다 [문어체] ❑ 그는 두렵느냐는 질문을 받았다. "뭐가 두려워?"하고 그가 되받아쳤다. ● 가산명사 반박, 말대꾸 ❑ 그의 매서운 반박이 분명히 영향을 미쳤다.

re|trace /riːtreɪs/ (retraces, retracing, retraced) V-T If you **retrace** your steps or **retrace** your way, you return to the place you started from by going back along the same route. ❑ *He retraced his steps to the spot where he'd left the case.*

타동사 되짚어가다 ❑ 그는 온 길을 되짚어서 상자를 놓아두었던 자리로 갔다.

re|tract /rɪtrækt/ (retracts, retracting, retracted) ❶ V-T/V-I If you **retract** something that you have said or written, you say that you did not mean it. [FORMAL] ❑ *Mr. Smith hurriedly sought to retract the statement, but it had just been broadcast on national radio.* ● re|trac|tion /rɪtrækʃ°n/ (retractions) N-COUNT ❑ *Miss Pearce said she expected an unqualified retraction of his comments within twenty four hours.* ❷ V-T/V-I When a part of a machine or a part of a person's body **retracts** or **is retracted**, it moves inward or becomes shorter. [FORMAL] ❑ *Torn muscles retract, and lose strength, structure, and tightness.*

❶ 타동사/자동사 취소하다, 철회하다 [격식체] ❑ 스미스 씨가 서둘러 성명을 철회하려고 했지만, 막 라디오를 통해 전국에 방송된 상태였다. ● 취소, 철회 가산명사 ❑ 피어스 양은 24시간 안에 그의 논평의 무조건적인 철회를 기대한다고 말했다. ❷ 타동사/자동사 수축하다; 수축시키다 [격식체] ❑ 찢어진 근육은 수축하며, 힘과 구조와 단단함을 잃는다.

re|train /riːtreɪn/ (retrains, retraining, retrained) V-T/V-I If you **retrain**, or if someone **retrains** you, you learn new skills, especially in order to get a new job. ❑ *Look at what you can do to retrain for a job which will make you happier.* ● re|train|ing N-UNCOUNT ❑ *...measures such as the retraining of the workforce at their place of work.*

타동사/자동사 재교육받다; 재교육하다 ❑ 당신 자신을 더 행복하게 만들어 줄 일자리를 얻을 수 있도록 재교육을 받기 위해 당신이 무엇을 할 수 있는지 보세요. ● 재교육 불가산명사 ❑ 작업 현장에서의 노동력 재교육 같은 조처들

re|treat ♦♢♢ /rɪtriːt/ (retreats, retreating, retreated) ❶ V-I If you **retreat**, you move away from something or someone. ❑ *"I've already got a job," I said quickly, and retreated from the room.* ❷ V-I When an army **retreats**, it moves away from enemy forces in order to avoid fighting them. ❑ *The French, suddenly outnumbered, were forced to retreat.* ● N-COUNT **Retreat** is also a noun. ❑ *In June 1942, the British 8th Army was in full retreat.* ❸ V-I If you **retreat from** something such as a plan or a way of life, you give it up, usually in order to do something safer or less extreme. ❑ *I believe people should live in houses that allow them to retreat from the harsh realities of life.* ● N-VAR **Retreat** is also a noun. ❑ *The President's remarks appear to signal that there will be no retreat from his position.* ❹ N-COUNT A **retreat** is a quiet, isolated place that you go to in order to rest or to do things in private. ❑ *He spent yesterday hidden away in his country retreat.*

❶ 자동사 물러나다 ❑ "나는 이미 직장이 있어요."라고 나는 급하게 말한 다음 방에서 물러났다. ❷ 자동사 후퇴하다, 퇴각하다 ❑ 프랑스군은 갑자기 수적으로 열세에 몰려 퇴각할 수밖에 없었다. ● 가산명사 또는 불가산명사 후퇴, 퇴각 ❑ 1942년 6월, 영국 제8군단은 전면 퇴각 중이었다. ❸ 자동사 그만두다, 손을 떼다 ❑ 인생의 모진 현실에서 벗어날 수 있도록 해 주는 집에서 사람들이 살아야 한다고 생각한다. ● 가산명사 또는 불가산명사 그만두기, 물러남 ❑ 대통령의 말은 자리에서 물러나는 일이 없으리라고 신호하는 것처럼 보인다. ❹ 가산명사 은신처, 은둔지 ❑ 그는 어제 하루를 시골의 은둔지에 숨어서 보냈다.

re|trench /rɪtrentʃ/ (retrenches, retrenching, retrenched) V-I If a person or organization **retrenches**, they spend less money. [FORMAL] ❑ *Shortly afterwards, cuts in defence spending forced the aerospace industry to retrench.*

자동사 비용을 절감하다 [격식체] ❑ 얼마 후, 방위비 지출 삭감으로 인해 항공업계는 비용을 절감해야 했다.

retribution 1164

ret|ri|bu|tion /rɛtrɪbyuʃ°n/ N-UNCOUNT **Retribution** is punishment for a crime, especially punishment which is carried out by someone other than the official authorities. [FORMAL] ❑ He didn't want any further involvement for fear of retribution.

불가산명사 보복; 징벌 [격식체] ❑ 그는 보복이 두려워 더 이상 개입하기를 원치 않았다.

re|triev|al /rɪtriv°l/ ■ N-UNCOUNT The **retrieval** of information from a computer is the process of getting it back. ❑...electronic storage and retrieval systems. ② N-UNCOUNT The **retrieval** of something is the process of getting it back from a particular place, especially from a place where it should not be. ❑ Its real purpose is the launching and retrieval of small aeroplanes in flight.

■ 불가산명사 검색 ❑ 전자 저장 및 검색 시스템 ② 불가산명사 회수 ❑ 그것의 진짜 용도는 소형 비행기를 발진시키고 비행 중인 것들을 회수하는 것이다.

re|trieve /rɪtriv/ (retrieves, retrieving, retrieved) ■ V-T If you **retrieve** something, you get it back from the place where you left it. ❑ The men were trying to retrieve weapons left when the army abandoned the island. ② V-T If you manage to **retrieve** a situation, you succeed in bringing it back into a more acceptable state. ❑ He, the one man who could retrieve that situation, might receive the call. ③ V-T To **retrieve** information from a computer or from your memory means to get it back. ❑ Computers can instantly retrieve millions of information bits.

■ 타동사 회수하다 ❑ 그 사람들은 군대가 그 섬을 떠날 때 남기고 간 무기를 회수하려 애쓰고 있었다. ② 타동사 만회하다 ❑ 그 상황을 만회할 수 있는 유일한 사람인 그가 전화를 받을지도 모른다. ③ 타동사 검색하다; 가져오다 ❑ 컴퓨터는 즉각 수백만 비트의 정보를 검색할 수 있다.

ret|ro /rɛtroʊ/ ADJ **Retro** clothes, music, and objects are based on the styles of the past. [JOURNALISM] ❑...clothes shops where original versions of many of today's retro looks can be found for a fraction of the price.

형용사 복고풍의 [언론] ❑ 오늘날의 많은 복고풍 패션의 원형들을 아주 싼 가격에 구할 수 있는 옷가게들

ret|ro|spect /rɛtrəspɛkt/ PHRASE When you consider something in retrospect, you think about it afterward, and often have a different opinion about it from the one that you had at the time. ❑ In retrospect, I wish that I had thought about alternative courses of action.

구 되돌아보면 ❑ 되돌아보면, 내가 다른 행동 방식에 대해 생각했었더라면 좋았을 텐데.

retro|spec|tive /rɛtrəspɛktɪv/ (retrospectives) ■ N-COUNT A **retrospective** is an exhibition or showing of work done by an artist over many years, rather than his or her most recent work. ❑...a retrospective of the films of Judy Garland. ② ADJ **Retrospective** feelings or opinions concern things that happened in the past. ❑ Afterwards, retrospective fear of the responsibility would make her feel almost faint. ● retro|spec|tive|ly ADV ❑ Retrospectively, it seems as if they probably were negligent. ③ ADJ **Retrospective** laws or legal actions take effect from a date before the date when they are officially approved. ❑ Bankers are quick to condemn retrospective tax legislation. ● retro|spec|tive|ly ADV [ADV with v] ❑...a decree which retrospectively changes the electoral law under which last year's national elections were held.

■ 가산명사 회고전 ❑ 주디 갈랜드 출연 영화 회고전 ② 형용사 회고적인, 회상의 ❑ 그 후, 책임을 회고해 보면 그녀는 아찔할 정도로 두려워진다. ● 돌이켜 보면 부사 ❑ 돌이켜 보면, 그들이 아마 부주의했던 것 같다. ③ 형용사 소급 적용되는 ❑ 금융인들은 잽싸게 조세 소급 입법을 비난하고 나섰다. ● 소급하여 부사 ❑ 지난해 전국 선거에 적용되었던 선거법을 소급 개정한다는 포고

re|turn ♦♦♦ /rɪtɜrn/ (returns, returning, returned) ■ V-I When you **return to** a place, you go back there after you have been away. ❑ There are unconfirmed reports that Aziz will return to Moscow within hours. ② N-SING Your **return** is your arrival back at a place where you had been before. ❑ Ryle explained the reason for his sudden return to London. ③ V-T If you **return** something that you have borrowed or taken, you give it back or put it back. ❑ I enjoyed the book and said so when I returned it. ● N-SING **Return** is also a noun. ❑ Efforts are being made to arrange for the return of stolen treasures. ④ V-T If you **return** something somewhere, you put it back where it was. ❑ He returned the notebook to his jacket. ⑤ V-T If you **return** someone's action, you do the same thing to them as they have just done to you. If you **return** someone's feeling, you feel the same way toward them as they feel toward you. ❑ Back at the station the Chief Inspector returned the call. ⑥ V-I If a feeling or situation **returns**, it comes back or happens again after a period when it was not present. ❑ Official reports in Algeria suggest that calm is returning to the country. ● N-SING **Return** is also a noun. ❑ It was like the return of his youth. ⑦ V-I If you **return to** a state that you were in before, you start being in that state again. ❑ Life has improved and returned to normal. ● N-SING **Return** is also a noun. ❑ He made an uneventful return to normal health. ⑧ V-I If you **return to** a subject that you have mentioned before, you begin talking about it again. ❑ The power of the Church is one theme all these writers return to. ⑨ V-I If you **return to** an activity that you were doing before, you start doing it again. ❑ At that stage he will be 52, young enough to return to politics if he wishes to do so. ● N-SING **Return** is also a noun. ❑ He has not ruled out the shock possibility of a return to football. ⑩ V-T When a judge or jury **returns** a verdict, they announce whether they think the person on trial is guilty or not. ❑ They returned a verdict of not guilty. ⑪ ADJ A **return** ticket is a ticket for a trip from one place to another and then back again. [mainly BRIT] ❑ He bought a return ticket and boarded the next train for home. ● N-COUNT **Return** is also a noun. [AM usually **round trip**] ❑ BA and Air France charge more than £400 for a return to Nice. ⑫ ADJ The **return** trip or journey is the part of a journey that takes you back to where you started from. [ADJ n] ❑ Buy an extra ticket for the return trip. ⑬ N-COUNT The **return on** an investment is the profit that you get from it. [BUSINESS] ❑ Profits have picked up this year but the return on capital remains tiny. ⑭ PHRASE If you do something **in return for** what someone else has done for you, you do it because they did that thing for you. ❑ You pay regular premiums and in return the insurance company will pay out a lump sum. ⑮ to **return fire** →see **fire**
→see library

■ 자동사 돌아가다, 귀환하다 ❑ 아지즈가 수 시간 내에 모스크바로 돌아갈 것이라는 미확인 보도가 있다. ② 단수명사 돌아옴, 귀환 ❑ 라일은 갑자기 런던으로 돌아온 이유를 설명했다. ③ 타동사 돌려주다 ❑ 나는 그 책을 재미있게 읽었고 그것을 돌려줄 때 그렇게 말했다. ● 단수명사 반환 ❑ 도난당한 귀중품의 반환을 조율하기 위해 노력하고 있는 중이다. ④ 타동사 (제자리에) 다시 갖다 놓다 ❑ 그는 공책을 자신의 재킷 있는 데 다시 갖다 놓았다. ⑤ 타동사 (상대가 한 대로) 되돌려 주다, 화답하다 ❑ 경찰서에서는 그 경감이 화답 전화를 걸었다. ⑥ 자동사 다시 찾아오다, 다시 일어나다 ❑ 알제리 공식 보고서는 그 나라에 평온이 다시 찾아오고 있음을 시사한다. ● 단수명사 다시 찾아옴 ❑ 그것은 그의 젊음이 다시 찾아온 것과 같았다. ⑦ 자동사 (이전의 상태로) 되돌아가다, 회복되다 ❑ 생활이 나아져서 정상으로 되돌아갔다. ● 단수명사 되돌아감, 회복 ❑ 그는 별일 없이 정상적인 건강 상태로 회복되었다. ⑧ 자동사 다시 이야기하다 ❑ 교회의 권력은 이 모든 작가들이 거듭 다루는 한 가지 주제이다. ⑨ 자동사 다시 하다, 재개하다 ❑ 그 시기에 그는 쉰두 살이 될 것인데, 그것은 원한다면 다시 정치를 할 수 있을 만큼 젊은 나이이다. ● 단수명사 재개 ❑ 그는 축구를 다시 시작할 충격적인 가능성을 배제하지 않고 있다. ⑩ 타동사 (평결을) 내리다 ❑ 그들은 무죄 평결을 내렸다. ⑪ 형용사 왕복의 [주로 영국영어] ❑ 그는 왕복표를 한 장 사서 집으로 가는 다음 열차에 올랐다. ● 가산명사 왕복표 [미국영어 대개 round trip] ❑ 영국항공과 에어프랑스의 니스 왕복 항공권은 4백 파운드가 넘는다. ⑫ 형용사 돌아오는 ❑ 돌아올 때를 위해 여분의 표를 한 장 사세요. ⑬ 가산명사 수익 [경제] ❑ 올해의 이윤은 높았지만 자본 수익은 여전히 낮다. ⑭ 구 ~의 답례로, ~에 대해 ❑ 정기적으로 보험료를 납부하시면 그에 대해 보험사가 목돈을 지불할 것입니다.

Thesaurus return의 참조어

N. arrival, homecoming; (ant.) departure ②
V. come again, come back, go back, reappear ①
     give back, pay back; (ant.) keep ③

Word Partnership return의 연어

N. return a (phone) call ⑤
     return to work ⑨
     return trip ⑫
     return on an investment, rate of return ⑬
V. decide to return, plan to return, want to return ① ③-⑤ ⑨

re|uni|fi|ca|tion /riyunɪfɪkeɪʃ³n/ N-UNCOUNT The **reunification** of a country or city that has been divided into two or more parts for some time is the joining of it together again. [with supp] ❑ ...the reunification of East and West Beirut in 1991.

불가산명사 재통일 ❑ 1991년 동베이루트와 서베이루트의 재통일

re|union /riyuniən/ (**reunions**) **1** N-COUNT A **reunion** is a party attended by members of the same family, school, or other group who have not seen each other for a long time. ❑ The Association holds an annual reunion. **2** N-VAR A **reunion** is a meeting between people who have been separated for some time. ❑ The children weren't allowed to see her for nearly a week. It was a very emotional reunion.

1 가산명사 친목회 ❑ 그 협회는 매년 한 번씩 친목회를 연다. **2** 가산명사 또는 불가산명사 재회 ❑ 그 아이들은 일주일 가까이 그녀를 볼 수 없었다. 그것은 아주 감동적인 재회였다.

re|unite /riyunaɪt/ (**reunites, reuniting, reunited**) **1** V-T If people **are reunited**, or if they **reunite**, they meet each other again after they have been separated for some time. ❑ She and her youngest son were finally allowed to be reunited with their family. **2** V-T/V-I If a divided organization or country **is reunited**, or if it **reunites**, it becomes one united organization or country again. ❑ As of this evening, Germany is reunited. In Berlin they're celebrating. ❑ His first job will be to reunite the army.

1 타동사 재회하다 ❑ 그녀와 막내아들은 마침내 가족과의 재회가 허용되었다. **2** 타동사/자동사 재통합하다 ❑ 오늘 저녁을 기해, 독일이 재통일되었습니다. 베를린에서는 사람들이 경축을 하고 있습니다. ❑ 그의 첫 번째 임무는 육군을 재통합하는 일이 될 것이다.

re|value /rivælyu/ (**revalues, revaluing, revalued**) **1** V-T When a country **revalues** its currency, it increases the currency's value so that it can buy more foreign currency than before. ❑ Countries enjoying surpluses will be under no pressure to revalue their currencies. **2** V-T To **revalue** something means to increase the amount that you calculate it is worth so that its value stays roughly the same in comparison with other things, even if there is inflation. ❑ It is now usual to revalue property assets on a more regular basis.

1 타동사 평가 절상하다 ❑ 흑자를 누리고 있는 나라들은 통화 평가 절상 압력을 받지 않을 것이다. **2** 타동사 재평가하다 ❑ 현재는 부동산을 보다 정기적으로 재평가하는 일이 흔히 있다.

re|vamp /rivæmp/ (**revamps, revamping, revamped**) V-T If someone **revamps** something, they make changes to it in order to try and improve it. ❑ All Italy's political parties have accepted that it is time to revamp the system. ● N-SING **Revamp** is also a noun. ❑ The revamp includes replacing the old navy uniform with a crisp blue and white cotton outfit.

타동사 개혁하다, 개조하다 ❑ 이탈리아의 모든 정당들이 이제 제도를 개혁할 때가 되었음을 인정했다. ● 단수명사 개혁, 개편 ❑ 그 개편에는 낡은 해군 제복을 빳빳한 청색과 백색의 면 재질 제복으로 교체하는 것이 포함된다.

re|veal ♦♦◇ /rivil/ (**reveals, revealing, revealed**) **1** V-T To **reveal** something means to make people aware of it. ❑ She has refused to reveal the whereabouts of her daughter. ❑ A survey of the British diet has revealed that a growing number of people are overweight. **2** V-T If you **reveal** something that has been out of sight, you uncover it so that people can see it. ❑ In the principal room, a grey carpet was removed to reveal the original pine floor.

1 타동사 드러내다, 밝히다 ❑ 그녀는 딸의 소재를 밝히기를 거부해 왔다. ❑ 영국인의 식생활에 대한 한 조사에 따르면 과체중인 사람들이 늘어나고 있다. **2** 타동사 드러내다, 폭로하다 ❑ 주실에는 회색 양탄자가 걷히고 원래의 소나무 바닥이 드러나 있었다.

re|veal|ing /rivilɪŋ/ ADJ A **revealing** statement, account, or action tells you something that you did not know, especially about the person doing it or making it. ❑ ...a revealing interview.

형용사 폭로적인 ❑ 폭로성 인터뷰

rev|el /rɛv³l/ (**revels, reveling, reveled**) [BRIT, sometimes AM **revelling, revelled**] V-I If you **revel in** a situation or experience, you enjoy it very much. ❑ Annie was smiling and laughing, clearly reveling in the attention.

[영국영어, 미국영어 가끔 revelling, revelled] 자동사 한껏 즐기다 ❑ 애니는 미소 짓고 웃으면서, 분명히 그런 관심을 한껏 즐기고 있었다.

rev|ela|tion /rɛvəleɪʃ³n/ (**revelations**) **1** N-COUNT A **revelation** is a surprising or interesting fact that is made known to people. ❑ ...the seemingly everlasting revelations about his private life. **2** N-VAR The **revelation of** something is the act of making it known. ❑ ...following the revelation of his affair with a former secretary. **3** N-SING If you say that something you experienced was **a revelation**, you are saying that it was very surprising or very good. ❑ Degas's work had been a revelation to her.

1 가산명사 폭로되는 것, 뜻밖의 사실 ❑ 그의 사생활에 대해 끝이 없을 것처럼 계속 드러나는 사실들 **2** 가산명사 또는 불가산명사 폭로, 누설 ❑ 그의 이전 비서와의 불륜 관계에 대한 폭로에 이어 **3** 단수명사 계시 ❑ 드가의 작품은 그녀에게는 일종의 계시였다.

re|venge /rivɛndʒ/ (**revenges, revenging, revenged**) **1** N-UNCOUNT **Revenge** involves hurting or punishing someone who has hurt or harmed you. ❑ The attackers were said to be taking revenge on the 14-year-old, claiming he was a school bully. **2** V-T If you **revenge** yourself on someone who has hurt you, you hurt them in return. [WRITTEN] ❑ The Sunday Mercury accused her of trying to revenge herself on her former lover.

1 불가산명사 보복, 복수 ❑ 가해자들은 그 열네 살짜리 아이가 학교 불량배라고 주장하며 그 아이에게 보복을 하는 중이었다고 말한 것으로 알려져 있다. **2** 타동사 보복하다, 복수하다 [문어체] ❑ '선데이 머큐리'지는 그녀가 예전 애인에게 복수하려 했다고 비난했다.

rev|enue ♦♦◇ /rɛvənyu/ (**revenues**) N-UNCOUNT **Revenue** is money that a company, organization, or government receives from people. [BUSINESS] [also N in pl, usu with supp] ❑ ...a boom year at the cinema, with record advertising revenue and the highest ticket sales since 1980. →see also **Inland Revenue, IRS**

불가산명사 세입, 수입 [경제] ❑ 기록적인 광고 수입과 1980년 이래로 가장 높은 티켓 매상고를 기록한, 영화계로서는 급성장한 한 해

re|ver|ber|ate /rivɜrbəreɪt/ (**reverberates, reverberating, reverberated**) **1** V-I When a loud sound **reverberates** through a place, it echoes through it. ❑ Day in and day out, the flat crack of the tank guns reverberates through the little Bavarian town. **2** V-I You can say that an event or idea **reverberates** when it has a powerful effect which lasts a long time. ❑ The controversy surrounding the take-over yesterday continued to reverberate around the television industry.

1 자동사 울리다, 울려 퍼지다 ❑ 날이면 날마다, 단조로운 탱크 포 소리가 그 작은 바바리아 도시에 울려 퍼졌다. **2** 자동사 반향을 불러일으키다 ❑ 경영권 인수를 둘러싼 논란이 어제 계속 텔레비전 업계에서 반향을 불러일으켰다.

Word Link   vere ≈ fear, awe : irre**vere**nt, re**vere**, re**vere**nce

re|vere /rɪvɪər/ (**reveres, revering, revered**) V-T If you **revere** someone or something, you respect and admire them greatly. [FORMAL] ❑ The Chinese revered corn as a gift from heaven. ● re**|vered** ADJ ❑ ...some of the country's most revered institutions.

타동사 존경하다, 숭배하다 [격식체] ❑ 그 중국인은 옥수수를 하늘이 내린 선물이라고 숭배했다. ● 존경받는 형용사 ❑ 그 나라에서 가장 존경받는 기관 중 몇몇

rev|er|ence /rɛvərəns/ N-UNCOUNT **Reverence for** someone or something is a feeling of great respect for them. [FORMAL] ❑ We stand together now in mutual support and in reverence for the dead.

불가산명사 존경, 숭배 [격식체] ❑ 우리는 이제 서로 의지하고 돌아가신 분들께 경의를 표하며 함께 서 있습니다.

Rev|er|end /rɛvərənd/ N-TITLE **Reverend** is a title used before the name or rank of an officially appointed religious leader. The abbreviation **Rev** or **Revd** is also used. ❑ The service was led by the Reverend Jim Simons.

경칭명사 목사, 성직자 ❑ 예배는 짐 시몬스 목사가 집전하였다.

re|ver|sal /rɪvɜrs³l/ (**reversals**) **1** N-COUNT A **reversal of** a process, policy, or trend is a complete change in it. ❑ The Financial Times says the move represents a complete reversal of previous U.S. policy. **2** N-COUNT When there is a role **reversal** or a **reversal of** roles, two people or groups exchange their positions or functions. ❑ When children end up taking care of their parents, it is a strange role reversal indeed.

1 가산명사 역전, 반전 ❑ 파이낸셜 타임즈는 그 조처가 이전의 미국 정책의 일대 전환을 의미한다고 말한다. **2** 가산명사 (역할의) 전환 ❑ 결국 자녀들이 부모를 돌보게 되면, 그것은 실로 묘한 역할 전환이다.

re|verse ♦♢♢ /rɪvɜːrs/ (**reverses, reversing, reversed**) **1** V-T When someone or something **reverses** a decision, policy, or trend, they change it to the opposite decision, policy, or trend. ◻ *They have made it clear they will not reverse the decision to increase prices.* **2** V-T If you **reverse** the order of a set of things, you arrange them in the opposite order, so that the first thing comes last. ◻ *Because the normal word order is reversed in passive sentences, they are sometimes hard to follow.* **3** V-T If you **reverse** the positions or functions of two things, you change them so that each thing has the position or function that the other one had. ◻ *He reversed the position of the two stamps.* **4** V-T/V-I When a car **reverses** or when you **reverse** it, the car is driven backward. [mainly BRIT; AM usually **back up**] ◻ *Another car reversed out of the drive.* **5** N-UNCOUNT If your car is **in reverse**, you have changed gear so that you can drive it backward. ◻ *He lurched the car in reverse along the road to the access road.* **6** ADJ **Reverse** means opposite to what you expect or to what has just been described. ◻ *The wrong attitude will have exactly the reverse effect.* **7** N-SING If you say that one thing is **the reverse** of another, you are emphasizing that the first thing is the complete opposite of the second thing. ◻ *There is absolutely no evidence at all that spectators want longer cricket matches. Quite the reverse.* **8** N-SING **The reverse** or **the reverse side** of a flat object which has two sides is the less important or the other side. ◻ *Cheques should be made payable to Country Living and your address written on the reverse.* **9** PHRASE If something happens **in reverse** or goes **into reverse**, things happen in the opposite way to what usually happens or to what has been happening. ◻ *Amis tells the story in reverse, from the moment the man dies.* **10** PHRASE If you **reverse the charges** when you make a telephone call, the person who you are phoning pays the cost of the call and not you. [BRIT; AM **call collect**] ◻ *From abroad call 0705 471234 and reverse the charges.*

Word Link   *vert ≈ turning : con*vert, in*vert, re*vert

re|vert /rɪvɜːrt/ (**reverts, reverting, reverted**) **1** V-I When people or things **revert to** a previous state, system, or type of behavior, they go back to it. ◻ *Jackson said her boss became increasingly depressed and reverted to smoking heavily.* **2** V-I When someone **reverts to** a previous topic, they start talking or thinking about it again. [WRITTEN] ◻ *In the car she reverted to the subject uppermost in her mind. "You know, I really believe what Gran told you."* **3** V-I If property, rights, or money **revert to** someone, they become that person's again after someone else has had them for a period of time. [LEGAL] ◻ *When the lease ends, the property reverts to the freeholder.*

re|view ♦♦♢ /rɪvjuː/ (**reviews, reviewing, reviewed**) **1** N-COUNT A **review of** a situation or system is its formal examination by people in authority. This is usually done in order to see whether it can be improved or corrected. [oft N of n, also prep N] ◻ *The president ordered a review of U.S. economic aid to Jordan.* **2** V-T If you **review** a situation or system, you consider it carefully to see what is wrong with it or how it could be improved. ◻ *The Prime Minister reviewed the situation with his Cabinet yesterday.* **3** N-COUNT A **review** is a report in the media in which someone gives their opinion of something such as a new book or movie. ◻ *We've never had a good review in the music press.* **4** V-T If someone **reviews** something such as a new book or movie, they write a report or give a talk on television or radio in which they express their opinion of it. ◻ *Richard Coles reviews all of the latest video releases.* **5** V-T/V-I When you **review for** an examination, you read things again and make notes in order to be prepared for the examination. [AM] ◻ *Reviewing for exams gives you a chance to bring together all the individual parts of the course.* ● N-COUNT **Review** is also a noun. [BRIT **revise**] ◻ *If you have to cover twelve chapters in American history, begin by planning on three two-hour reviews with four chapters per session.*

Thesaurus   review의 참조어

N.	analysis, study **1**
V.	prepare, read, study **5**

Word Partnership   review의 연어

N.	review **a case**, review **evidence**, **performance** review **2**
	book review, **film/movie** review, **restaurant** review **3 4**
	review **questions 5**

re|view|er /rɪvjuːər/ (**reviewers**) N-COUNT A **reviewer** is a person who reviews new books, movies, television programs, CDs, plays, or concerts. ◻ *...the reviewer for the Times Literary Supplement.*

re|vise /rɪvaɪz/ (**revises, revising, revised**) **1** V-T If you **revise** the way you think about something, you adjust your thoughts, usually in order to make them better or more suited to how things are. ◻ *With time he fairly soon came to revise his opinion of the profession.* **2** V-T If you **revise** a price, amount, or estimate, you change it to make it more fair, realistic, or accurate. ◻ *They realized that some of their prices were higher than their competitors' and revised prices accordingly.* **3** V-T When you **revise** an article, a book, a law, or a piece of music, you change it in order to improve it, make it more modern, or make it more suitable for a particular purpose. ◻ *Three editors handled the work of revising the articles for publication.* **4** V-I When you **revise for** an examination, you read things again and make notes in order to be prepared for it. [BRIT; AM **review**] ◻ *I have to revise for maths.*

re|vi|sion /rɪvɪʒ°n/ (**revisions**) **1** N-VAR To make a **revision of** something that is written or something that has been decided means to make changes to it in order to improve it, make it more modern, or make it more suitable for a particular purpose. ◻ *The phase of writing that is actually most important is revision.*

---

1 타동사 뒤집다, 반대로 하다 ◻ 그들은 가격을 올리기로 한 결정을 뒤집지 않을 것임을 분명히 해 왔다. **2** 타동사 (순서를) 거꾸로 하다 ◻ 수동태 문장에서는 일반적인 어순이 거꾸로 되어 있기 때문에, 때때로 이해하기 어렵다. **3** 타동사 바꾸어 놓다, 전환하다 ◻ 그는 두 도장의 위치를 바꿔 놓았다. **4** 타동사/자동사 후진하다; 후진시키다 [주로 영국영어; 미국영어 대개 back up] ◻ 또 다른 차 한 대가 후진을 해서 진입로를 빠져 나오고 있었다. **5** 불가산명사 후진 기어 ◻ 그는 바퀴 자국을 따라 진입로까지 차를 후진시켜 덜컹거리며 나아갔다. **6** 형용사 반대의, 거꾸로의 ◻ 잘못된 자세는 정반대의 결과를 낳을 것이다. **7** 단수명사 역, 반대 ◻ 더 오래 끄는 크리켓 경기를 관중들이 원한다는 증거는 절대로 없다. 사실은 그 반대이다. **8** 단수명사 이면, 뒷면 ◻ 지불 대상을 '컨트리 리빙'이라고 쓴 수표 뒷면에 고객님의 주소를 적어 주세요. **9** 구 거꾸로 ◻ 에이미스는 그 이야기를 거꾸로, 남자가 죽는 순간부터 이야기한다. **10** 구 통화 요금을 수신인 부담으로 하다 [영국영어; 미국영어 call collect] ◻ 해외에서는 0705 471234로 전화하시고 통화 요금은 수신인 부담으로 하세요.

1 자동사 (본래의 상태로) 되돌아가다 ◻ 잭슨은 자기 상사가 점점 더 우울해져서 다시 담배를 많이 피게 되었다고 말했다. **2** 자동사 (원래 하던 얘기로) 되돌아가다 [문어체] ◻ 차 안에서 그녀는 가장 마음에 두고 있던 주제로 되돌아갔다. "있지, 나는 할머니가 너에게 말한 걸 진짜로 믿어." **3** 자동사 (∼의 소유로) 되돌아가다 [법률] ◻ 계약 기간이 끝나면, 그 부동산은 자유 부동산 보유자에게 되돌아간다.

1 가산명사 검토 ◻ 대통령이 미국의 대요르단 경제 원조에 대한 검토를 명령했다. **2** 타동사 검토하다 ◻ 어제 수상이 내각과 함께 그 사태를 검토했다. **3** 가산명사 (언론의) 논평 ◻ 우리는 음악 전문 잡지에서 좋은 평을 받아 본 적이 없다. **4** 타동사 논평하다 ◻ 리처드 콜스는 최근에 새로 나온 모든 비디오에 대해 논평을 한다. **5** 타동사/자동사 복습하다 [미국영어] ◻ 시험을 대비한 복습은 여러분에게 수업 중에 들은 개별적인 부분들을 종합할 수 있는 기회를 준다. ● 가산명사 복습 [영국영어] revise ◻ 미국사 과목에서 12장을 봐야 한다면, 두 시간을 한 차례로 잡고 4장씩 세 차례에 걸쳐 복습하는 계획을 세우는 것으로 시작하세요.

가산명사 논평가 ◻ 타임스 지 문학 증보판의 서평가

1 타동사 (생각을) 바꾸다 ◻ 시간이 흐르자 그는 금방 그 직업에 대한 생각을 바꾸게 되었다. **2** 타동사 조정하다, 수정하다 ◻ 그들은 자사 가격 일부가 경쟁사보다 높다는 것을 깨닫고 그에 따라 가격을 조정했다. **3** 타동사 교정하다, 수정하다 ◻ 3명의 편집자가 출판을 위해 글을 교정하는 작업을 맡아 했다. **4** 자동사 복습하다 [영국영어; 미국영어 review] ◻ 나는 수학 복습을 해야 해.

1 가산명사 또는 불가산명사 교정, 수정 ◻ 글쓰기에서 실질적으로 가장 중요한 단계는 수정이다. **2** 불가산명사 복습 [영국영어; 미국영어 review] ◻ 어떤 여자 아이들은 집에서 복습하기를 더 좋아한다.

2 N-UNCOUNT When people who are studying do **revision**, they read things again and make notes in order to prepare for an examination. [BRIT; AM review] ❏ *Some girls prefer to do their revision at home.*

re·vis·it /riːvɪzɪt/ (revisits, revisiting, revisited) V-T If you **revisit** a place, you return there for a visit after you have been away for a long time, often after the place has changed a lot. ❏ *In the summer, when we returned to Canada, we revisited this lake at dawn.*

Word Link	vita ≈ life : *revitalize*, *vital*, *vitality*

re·vi·tal·ize /riːvaɪtəlaɪz/ (revitalizes, revitalizing, revitalized) [BRIT also revitalise] V-T To **revitalize** something that has lost its activity or its health means to make it active or healthy again. ❏ *This hair conditioner is excellent for revitalizing dry, lifeless hair.*

Word Link	viv ≈ living : *revival*, *survive*, *vivacious*

re·viv·al /riːvaɪvəl/ (revivals) **1** N-COUNT When there is a **revival of** something, it becomes active or popular again. ❏ *This return to realism has produced a revival of interest in a number of artists.* **2** N-COUNT A **revival** is a new production of a play, an opera, or a ballet. ❏ *...John Clement's revival of Chekhov's "The Seagull."* **3** N-UNCOUNT A **revival** meeting is a public religious event that is intended to make people more interested in Christianity. ❏ *He toured South Africa organizing revival meetings.*

re·vive /riːvaɪv/ (revives, reviving, revived) **1** V-T/V-I When something such as the economy, a business, a trend, or a feeling **is revived** or when it **revives**, it becomes active, popular, or successful again. ❏ *...an attempt to revive the British economy.* **2** V-T When someone **revives** a play, opera, or ballet, they present a new production of it. ❏ *The Gaiety is reviving John B. Kean's comedy "The Man from Clare."* **3** V-T/V-I If you manage to **revive** someone who has fainted or if they **revive**, they become conscious again. ❏ *She and a neighbor tried in vain to revive him.*

re·voke /riːvoʊk/ (revokes, revoking, revoked) V-T When people in authority **revoke** something such as a license, a law, or an agreement, they cancel it. [FORMAL] ❏ *The government revoked her husband's license to operate migrant labor crews.*

re·volt /riːvoʊlt/ (revolts, revolting, revolted) **1** N-VAR A **revolt** is an illegal and often violent attempt by a group of people to change their country's political system. ❏ *It was undeniably a revolt by ordinary people against their leaders.* **2** V-I When people **revolt**, they make an illegal and often violent attempt to change their country's political system. ❏ *In 1375 the townspeople revolted.* **3** N-VAR A **revolt** by a person or group against someone or something is a refusal to accept the authority of that person or thing. ❏ *The prime minister is facing a revolt by Conservative party activists over his refusal to hold a referendum.* **4** V-I When people **revolt against** someone or something, they reject the authority of that person or reject that thing. ❏ *The prime minister only reacted when three of his senior cabinet colleagues revolted and resigned in protest on Friday night.*

re·volt·ing /riːvoʊltɪŋ/ ADJ If you say that something or someone is **revolting**, you mean you think they are horrible and disgusting. ❏ *The smell in the cell was revolting.*

revo·lu·tion ♦◇◇ /revəluːʃən, BRIT revəluːʃᵊn/ (revolutions) **1** N-COUNT A **revolution** is a successful attempt by a large group of people to change the political system of their country by force. ❏ *The period since the revolution has been one of political turmoil.* **2** N-COUNT A **revolution** in a particular area of human activity is an important change in that area. ❏ *The nineteenth century witnessed a revolution in ship design and propulsion.*

revo·lu·tion·ary ♦◇◇ /revəluːʃəneri/ (revolutionaries) **1** ADJ **Revolutionary** activities, organizations, or people have the aim of causing a political revolution. ❏ *Do you know anything about the revolutionary movement?* **2** N-COUNT A **revolutionary** is a person who tries to cause a revolution or who takes an active part in one. ❏ *The revolutionaries laid down their arms and its leaders went into voluntary exile.* **3** ADJ **Revolutionary** ideas and developments involve great changes in the way that something is done or made. ❏ *Invented in 1951, the rotary engine is a revolutionary concept in internal combustion.*

revo·lu·tion·ize /revəluːʃənaɪz/ (revolutionizes, revolutionizing, revolutionized) [BRIT also revolutionise] V-T When something **revolutionizes** an activity, it causes great changes in the way that it is done. ❏ *Over the past forty years plastics have revolutionized the way we live.*

re·volve /riːvɒlv/ (revolves, revolving, revolved) **1** V-I If you say that one thing **revolves around** another thing, you mean that the second thing is the main feature or focus of the first thing. ❏ *Since childhood, her life has revolved around tennis.* **2** V-I If a discussion or conversation **revolves around** a particular topic, it is mainly about that topic. ❏ *The debate revolves around specific accounting techniques.* **3** V-I If one object **revolves around** another object, the first object turns in a circle around the second object. ❏ *The satellite revolves around the Earth once every hundred minutes.* **4** V-T/V-I When something **revolves** or when you **revolve** it, it moves or turns in a circle around a central point or line. ❏ *Overhead, the fan revolved slowly.*

re·volv·er /riːvɒlvər/ (revolvers) N-COUNT A **revolver** is a kind of hand gun. Its bullets are kept in a revolving cylinder in the gun.

re·vue /riːvjuː/ (revues) N-COUNT A **revue** is a theatrical performance consisting of songs, dances, and jokes about recent events.

re·vul·sion /riːvʌlʃən/ N-UNCOUNT Someone's **revulsion** at something is the strong feeling of disgust or disapproval they have toward it. ❏ *...their revulsion at the act of desecration.*

타동사 다시 찾아가다 ❏ 여름에 캐나다로 돌아왔을 때, 우리는 새벽녘에 이 호수를 다시 찾았다.

[영국영어 revitalise] 타동사 새로운 활력을 주다, 소생시키다 ❏ 이 헤어컨디셔너는 건조하고 생기를 잃은 모발에 아주 좋습니다.

1 가산명사 되살아남, 부활 ❏ 이와 같이 리얼리즘으로 회귀함에 따라 많은 예술가들에 대한 관심이 되살아나고 있다. **2** 가산명사 리바이벌, 재상연 ❏ 체홉의 '갈매기'를 존 클레멘트가 리바이벌한 작품 **3** 불가산명사 부흥 ❏ 그는 남아프리카를 돌며 부흥 집회를 조직했다.

1 타동사/자동사 되살리다; 되살아나다 ❏ 영국 경제를 되살리려는 시도 **2** 타동사 리바이벌하다, 재상연하다 ❏ 게이어티 극장에서는 존 B. 킨의 희극 '클레어에서 온 사나이'를 다시 무대에 올리고 있다. **3** 타동사/자동사 소생시키다; 의식을 되찾다 ❏ 그녀와 한 이웃 사람이 그를 소생시키려 애썼으나 허사였다.

타동사 취소하다, 철회하다 [격식체] ❏ 정부는 그녀의 남편이 받았던 이주노동자 관리 인가를 취소했다.

1 가산명사 또는 불가산명사 반란, 반역 ❏ 그것은 분명히 지도자에 대한 일반 대중의 반란이었다. **2** 자동사 반란을 일으키다 ❏ 1375년에 마을 사람들이 반란을 일으켰다. **3** 가산명사 또는 불가산명사 반항, 거역 ❏ 수상은 국민 투표 실시를 거부한 것을 두고 보수당 활동가들의 반항에 직면해 있다. **4** 자동사 반항하다, 거역하다 ❏ 수상은 금요일 밤 중진 각료 3명이 거역하여 항의하는 뜻으로 사임했을 때에야 반응을 보였다.

형용사 역겨운, 혐오스러운 ❏ 그 방은 냄새가 역했다.

1 가산명사 혁명 ❏ 혁명 이후의 시대는 정치적 혼란의 시대였다. **2** 가산명사 혁명적 변화, 변혁 ❏ 19세기에 이르러 선박 설계와 추진 기관 분야에서 혁명이 일어났다.

1 형용사 혁명의 ❏ 혁명 운동에 대해 아는 것이 있어요? **2** 가산명사 혁명가 ❏ 혁명가들은 무기를 내려놓았고 지도자들은 자진해서 망명했다. **3** 형용사 혁명적인 ❏ 1951년에 발명된 회전 엔진은 내연 기관계의 혁명적인 발상이다.

[영국영어 revolutionise] 타동사 혁신시키다, 혁명적으로 바꾸다 ❏ 지난 40년 동안 플라스틱은 우리의 생활 방식을 혁명적으로 변화시켜 왔다.

1 자동사 ∼에 집중하다, ∼을 중심에 두다 ❏ 어릴 적부터, 그녀의 삶 중심에는 테니스가 있어 왔다. **2** 자동사 ∼을 중심으로 이루어지다 ❏ 토론은 특정한 회계 기술 중심으로 이루어진다. **3** 자동사 ∼의 주위를 회전하다 ❏ 그 위성은 백 분에 한 바퀴씩 지구 둘레를 돈다. **4** 타동사/자동사 회전하다; 돌리다 ❏ 머리 위에서 선풍기가 천천히 돌았다.

가산명사 리볼버, 회전식 연발 권총

가산명사 레뷔, 시사 풍자극

불가산명사 역겨움, 혐오감 ❏ 신성 모독 행위에 대한 그들의 강한 불쾌감

a b c d e f g h i j k l m n o p q **r** s t u v w x y z

A

re|ward ♦◇◇ /rɪwɔ̱rd/ (**rewards**, **rewarding**, **rewarded**) **1** N-COUNT A **reward** is something that you are given, for example because you have behaved well, worked hard, or provided a service to the community. □ *A bonus of up to 5 per cent can be added to a pupil's final exam marks as a reward for good spelling, punctuation and grammar.* **2** N-COUNT A **reward** is a sum of money offered to anyone who can give information about lost or stolen property or about someone who is wanted by the police. □ *The firm last night offered a £10,000 reward for information leading to the conviction of the killer.* **3** V-T If you do something and **are rewarded** with a particular benefit, you receive that benefit as a result of doing that thing. □ *Make the extra effort to impress the buyer and you will be rewarded with a quicker sale at a better price.* **4** N-COUNT The **rewards** of something are the benefits that you receive as a result of doing or having that thing. □ *The company is only just starting to reap the rewards of long-term investments.*

1 가산명사 상 □ 철자법과 구두법, 문법을 잘 지킨 것에 대한 상으로 최고 5퍼센트의 가산점이 학생의 기말 시험 평점에 추가될 수 있다. **2** 가산명사 현상금, 보상금 □ 그 회사는 지난밤 그 살인범의 유죄를 증명할 정보에 대해 10,000파운드의 현상금을 내걸었다. **3** 타동사 보답을 받다 □ 구매자에게 감명을 주기 위해 특별한 노력을 기울이면 더 빨리 더 좋은 값에 파는 것으로 보답을 받을 것이다. **4** 가산명사 보상, 보답 □ 그 회사는 이제 겨우 장기 투자에 대한 보상을 받기 시작하는 중이다.

Thesaurus reward의 참조어

N. bonus, prize; (*ant.*) punishment **1**

Word Partnership reward의 연어

N. reward **for good behavior**, **risk and** reward **1**
reward **for information** **2**
V. **give** *someone* a reward, **offer a** reward **1** **2**

---

re|ward|ing /rɪwɔ̱rdɪŋ/ ADJ An experience or action that is **rewarding** gives you satisfaction or brings you benefits. □ *...a career which she found stimulating and rewarding.*

형용사 보람 있는, 득이 되는 □ 그녀가 고무적이고 보람 있다고 느낀 직장 생활

re|wind /riːwaɪnd/ (**rewinds**, **rewinding**, **rewound**) V-T/V-I When the tape in a video or tape recorder **rewinds** or when you **rewind** it, the tape goes backwards so that you can play it again. Compare **fast forward**. □ *Waddington rewound the tape and played the message again.*

타동사/자동사 되감기다; 되감다 □ 와딩턴은 테이프를 되감아서 그 메시지를 다시 틀었다.

re|work /riːwɜ̱rk/ (**reworks**, **reworking**, **reworked**) V-T If you **rework** something such as an idea or a piece of writing, you reorganize it and make changes to it in order to improve it or bring it up to date. □ *See if you can rework your schedule and come up with practical ways to reduce the number of hours you're on call.*

타동사 고치다, 조정하다 □ 일정을 조정해서 대기하는 시간을 줄일 수 있는 실질적인 방안을 찾아보세요.

re|write /riːraɪt/ (**rewrites**, **rewriting**, **rewrote**, **rewritten**) **1** V-T If someone **rewrites** a piece of writing such as a book, an article, or a law, they write it in a different way in order to improve it. □ *Following this critique, students rewrite their papers and submit them for final evaluation.* **2** V-T If you accuse a government of **rewriting** history, you are criticizing them for selecting and presenting particular historical events in a way that suits their own purposes. [DISAPPROVAL] □ *We have always been an independent people, no matter how they rewrite history.*

1 타동사 고쳐 쓰다 □ 이 비평에 따라, 학생들이 과제물을 고쳐 쓴 다음 최종 평가를 위해 제출한다. **2** 타동사 고쳐 쓰다, 왜곡하다 [탐탁찮음] □ 그들이 어떻게 역사를 왜곡하든, 우리는 항상 독립된 민족이었다.

rheto|ric /re̱tərɪk/ **1** N-UNCOUNT If you refer to speech or writing as **rhetoric**, you disapprove of it because it is intended to convince and impress people but may not be sincere or honest. [DISAPPROVAL] □ *The change is largely cosmetic, a matter of acceptable political rhetoric rather than social reality.* **2** N-UNCOUNT **Rhetoric** is the skill or art of using language effectively. [FORMAL] □ *...the noble institutions of political life, such as political rhetoric, public office, and public service.*

1 불가산명사 수사, 미사여구 [탐탁찮음] □ 그 변화는 대부분 표면적인 것으로, 사회적 진실보다는 수용 가능한 정치적 수사의 문제이다. **2** 불가산명사 수사, 수사학 [격식체] □ 정치적 수사와 관공서, 공무 등과 같은 정치 생활의 고상한 제도들

rhe|tori|cal /rɪtɔ̱rɪkᵊl, BRIT rɪtɒrɪkᵊl/ **1** ADJ A **rhetorical** question is one which is asked in order to make a statement rather than to get an answer. □ *He grimaced slightly, obviously expecting no answer to his rhetorical question.* ● **rhe|tori|cal|ly** /rɪtɔ̱rɪkli, BRIT rɪtɒrɪkli/ ADV [ADV with v] □ *"Do these kids know how lucky they are?" Jackson asked rhetorically.* **2** ADJ **Rhetorical** language is intended to be grand and impressive. [FORMAL] □ *These arguments may have been used as a rhetorical device to argue for a perpetuation of a United Nations role.* ● **rhe|tori|cal|ly** ADV □ *Suddenly, the narrator speaks in his most rhetorically elevated mode.*

1 형용사 수사적인 □ 그가 살짝 얼굴을 찡그렸다. 분명 자신이 던진 수사적인 질문에 대해 답을 기대하지 않았던 것이다. ● 수사적으로 부사 □ "이 아이들은 자기들이 얼마나 운이 좋은지 알까?" 잭슨이 수사적으로 물었다. **2** 형용사 수사적인, 거창한 [격식체] □ 이 논거들은 유엔 역할의 영속화를 주장하기 위한 수사적 장치로 쓰였을지도 모른다. ● 수사적으로, 거창하게 부사 □ 갑자기, 해설자가 자신이 구사할 수 있는 가장 거창한 방식으로 이야기한다.

rhi|no /ra̱ɪnoʊ/ (**rhinos**) N-COUNT A **rhino** is the same as a **rhinoceros**. [INFORMAL]

가산명사 코뿔소 [비격식체]

rhi|noc|er|os /raɪnɒ̱sərəs/ (**rhinoceroses**) N-COUNT A **rhinoceros** is a large Asian or African animal with thick gray skin and a horn, or two horns, on its nose.

가산명사 코뿔소

rhyme /ra̱ɪm/ (**rhymes**, **rhyming**, **rhymed**) **1** V-RECIP If one word **rhymes with** another or if two words **rhyme**, they have a very similar sound. Words that rhyme with each other are often used in poems. □ *June always rhymes with moon in old love songs.* □ *...the sort of people who give their children names that rhyme: Donnie, Ronnie, Connie.* **2** V-I If a poem or song **rhymes**, the lines end with words that have very similar sounds. □ *In his efforts to make it rhyme he seems to have chosen the first word that comes into his head.* **3** N-COUNT A **rhyme** is a word which rhymes with another word, or a set of lines which rhyme. □ *The one rhyme for passion is fashion.* **4** N-COUNT A **rhyme** is a short poem which has rhyming words at the ends of its lines. □ *He was teaching Helen a little rhyme.* **5** N-UNCOUNT **Rhyme** is the use of rhyming words as a technique in poetry. If something is written **in rhyme**, it is written as a poem in which the lines rhyme. □ *The plays are in rhyme.*

1 상호동사 운이 맞다 □ 6월(June)은 옛사랑 노래에서 언제나 달(moon)과 운을 맞춰 쓰인다. □ 도니, 로니, 코니 하는 식으로 자녀들에게 운을 맞춰 이름을 지어 주는 그런 사람들 **2** 자동사 (시나 노래가) 운이 맞다 □ 그는 운을 맞추려고 노력하면서 머리에 떠오르는 첫 번째 단어를 선택했던 것으로 보인다. **3** 가산명사 (다른 단어와) 운이 맞는 단어; 서로 운이 맞는 시행 □ passion과 운이 맞는 단어 하나는 fashion이다. **4** 가산명사 운문, 시 □ 그는 헬렌에게 짧은 시 한 편을 가르치고 있었다. **5** 불가산명사 압운 □ 그 희곡들은 압운으로 쓰였다.

rhythm ♦◇◇ /rɪ̱ðəm/ (**rhythms**) **1** N-VAR A **rhythm** is a regular series of sounds or movements. □ *His music of that period fused the rhythms of jazz with classical forms.* **2** N-COUNT A **rhythm** is a regular pattern of changes, for example changes in your body, in the seasons, or in the tides. □ *Begin to listen to your own body rhythms.* →see **drum**

1 가산명사 또는 불가산명사 리듬 □ 그 시기 그의 음악은 재즈 리듬과 클래식 음악 형식을 융합했다. **2** 가산명사 리듬 □ 자신의 신체 리듬에 귀 기울이기 시작하세요.

rhyth|mic /rɪ̱ðmɪk/ or **rhyth+mi+cal** /rɪ̱ðmɪkᵊl/ ADJ A **rhythmic** movement or sound is repeated at regular intervals, forming a regular pattern or beat. □ *Good*

형용사 리드미컬한 □ 좋은 호흡은 느리고 리드미컬하며 깊다. ● 리드미컬하게 부사 □ 그녀는

breathing is slow, rhythmic and deep. ● **rhyth|mi|cal|ly** /rɪðmɪkli/ ADV [ADV after v] ❏ *She stood, swaying her hips, moving rhythmically.*

rib /rɪb/ (**ribs**) ■ N-COUNT Your **ribs** are the 12 pairs of curved bones that surround your chest. ❏ *Her heart was thumping against her ribs.* ■ N-COUNT A **rib of** meat such as beef or pork is a piece that has been cut to include one of the animal's ribs. ❏ *...a rib of beef.*

rib|bon /rɪbən/ (**ribbons**) ■ N-VAR A **ribbon** is a long, narrow piece of cloth that you use for tying things together or as a decoration. ❏ *She had tied back her hair with a peach satin ribbon.* ■ N-COUNT A typewriter or printer **ribbon** is a long, narrow piece of cloth containing ink and is used in a typewriter or printer.

rice ♦◇◇ /raɪs/ (**rices**) N-MASS **Rice** consists of white or brown grains taken from a cereal plant. You cook rice and usually eat it with meat or vegetables. ❏ *...a meal consisting of chicken, rice, and vegetables.* →see **grain** →see Word Web: **rice**

rich ♦♦◇ /rɪtʃ/ (**richer, richest, riches**) ■ ADJ A **rich** person has a lot of money or valuable possessions. ❏ *You're going to be a very rich man.* ● N-PLURAL The **rich** are rich people. ❏ *This is a system in which the rich are cared for and the poor are left to suffer.* ■ N-PLURAL **Riches** are valuable possessions or large amounts of money. ❏ *An Olympic gold medal can lead to untold riches for an athlete.* ■ ADJ A **rich** country has a strong economy and produces a lot of wealth, so many people who live there have a high standard of living. ❏ *There is hunger in many parts of the world, even in rich countries.* ■ N-PLURAL If you talk about the earth's **riches**, you are referring to things that exist naturally in large quantities and that are useful and valuable, for example minerals, wood, and oil. ❏ *...Russia's vast natural riches.* ■ ADJ If something is **rich in** a useful or valuable substance or is a **rich source of** it, it contains a lot of it. [v-link ADJ in n, ADJ n] ❏ *Liver and kidney are particularly rich in vitamin A.* ■ ADJ **Rich** food contains a lot of fat or oil. ❏ *Additional cream would make it too rich.* ● **rich|ness** N-UNCOUNT ❏ *A squeeze of fresh lime juice cuts the richness of the avocado.* ■ ADJ **Rich** soil contains large amounts of substances that make it good for growing crops or flowers in. ❏ *Farmers grow rice in the rich soil.* ■ ADJ A **rich** deposit of a mineral or other substance is a large amount of it. ❏ *...the country's rich deposits of the metal, lithium.* ● **rich|ness** N-UNCOUNT ❏ *...the richness of Tibet's mineral deposits.* ■ ADJ If you say that something is a **rich** vein or source of something such as humor, ideas, or information, you mean that it can provide a lot of that thing. [ADJ n] ❏ *The director discovered a rich vein of sentimentality.* ■ ADJ **Rich** smells are strong and very pleasant. **Rich** colors and sounds are deep and very pleasant. ❏ *...a rich and luxuriously perfumed bath essence.* ● **rich|ness** N-UNCOUNT ❏ *His musicals were infused with richness of color and visual detail.* ■ ADJ A **rich** life or history is one that is interesting because it is full of different events and activities. ❏ *A rich and varied cultural life is essential for this couple.* ● **rich|ness** N-UNCOUNT ❏ *It all adds to the richness of human life.* ■ ADJ A **rich** collection or mixture contains a wide and interesting variety of different things. ❏ *Visitors can view a rich and colorful array of aquatic plants and animals.* ● **rich|ness** N-UNCOUNT ❏ *...a huge country, containing a richness of culture and diversity of landscape.*

Thesaurus
        *rich*의 참조어

ADJ.	affluent, wealthy; (ant.) poor ■

Word Partnership
        *rich*의 연어

ADJ.	rich **and beautiful**, rich **and famous**, rich **and powerful** ■
V.	**become** rich, **get** rich **(quick)** ■
N.	rich **kids**, rich **man/people**, rich **and poor** ■
	rich **country/nation** ■
	rich **in natural resources** ■
	rich **diet**, rich **food** ■
	rich **color** ■
	rich **culture**, rich **heritage**, rich **history**, rich **tradition** ■

---

rich|ly /rɪtʃli/ ■ ADV If something is **richly** colored, flavored, or perfumed, it has a pleasantly strong color, flavor, or perfume. ❏ *...Renaissance masterpieces, so richly colored and lustrous.* ■ ADV If something is **richly** decorated, patterned, or furnished, it has a lot of elaborate and beautiful decoration, patterns, or furniture. ❏ *Coffee steamed in the richly decorated silver pot.* ■ ADV If you say that someone **richly** deserves an award, success, or victory, you approve of what they have done and feel very strongly that they deserve it. [FEELINGS] ❏ *He achieved the success he so richly deserved.* ■ ADV If you are **richly** rewarded for doing something, you get something very valuable or pleasant in return for doing it. ❏ *It is a difficult book to read, but it richly rewards the effort.*

Word Web   rice

An ancient Chinese myth says that an animal gave humans the gift of **rice**. Once a large flood destroyed all the crops. When the people returned from the hills, they saw a dog. It had bunches of rice **seeds** in its tail. They planted this new **grain** and were never hungry again. In many Asian countries the words for rice and **food** are identical. Rice has many non-food uses. It is the main ingredient in some kinds of laundry **starch**. The Japanese make a liquor called saké from it. And in Thailand, rice **straw** is made into hats and shoes.

서서 엉덩이를 살살 흔들며 리드미컬하게 움직이고 있었다.

■ 가산명사 늑골, 갈빗대 ❏ 그녀의 심장이 갈비뼈가 터지도록 쿵쾅쿵쾅 뛰었다. ■ 가산명사 갈비 ❏ 쇠갈비 한 대

■ 가산명사 또는 불가산명사 리본, 띠 ❏ 그녀는 복숭앗빛 공단 리본으로 머리를 다시 묶고 있었다. ■ 가산명사 (타자기나 프린터의) 리본

물질명사 쌀; 밥 ❏ 닭고기와 밥, 야채로 구성된 식사

■ 형용사 부자의, 부유한 ❏ 너는 큰 부자가 될 거야. ● 복수명사 부자 ❏ 이것은 부자들은 보살펴 주고 가난한 사람들은 고생하도록 내버려 두는 제도이다. ■ 복수명사 부, 재산 ❏ 올림픽 금메달을 따면 운동선수는 막대한 부를 이룰 수 있다. ■ 형용사 부국의, 부유한 ❏ 세상의 많은 곳에, 심지어 부유한 나라들에도 굶주림은 존재한다. ■ 복수명사 풍부한 자원 ❏ 러시아의 막대한 천연자원 ■ 형용사 ~이 많은, ~이 풍부한 ❏ 간과 신장은 특히 비타민 에이(A)가 풍부하다. ■ 형용사 기름진 ❏ 크림을 더 첨가하면 너무 기름질지도 모른다. ● 기름짐 불가산명사 ❏ 신선한 라임 즙을 한 번 짜 넣으면 아보카도의 기름기를 줄여 준다. ■ 형용사 비옥한 ❏ 농부들은 비옥한 토양에 벼를 재배한다. ■ 형용사 풍부한 ❏ 그 나라의 풍부한 철과 리튬 매장량 ● 풍부 불가산명사 ❏ 티베트의 풍부한 광물 매장량 ■ 형용사 풍부한 ❏ 그 감독은 풍부한 감상벽을 발견했다. ■ 형용사 짙은; 낭랑한 ❏ 짙고 풍부한 향기가 나는 목욕용 에센스 ● 짙음; 깊이 불가산명사 ❏ 그의 뮤지컬에는 다양한 색채와 상세한 시각적 요소가 풍부하게 배어 있었다. ■ 형용사 풍성한 ❏ 풍성하고 다채로운 문화생활이 이 부부에게는 필수적이다. ■ 형용사 풍성한 불가산명사 ❏ 그 모두가 인간 생활의 풍성함을 더해 줍니다. ■ 형용사 다양하게 갖춘 ❏ 방문객들은 다양하고 다채로운 수생 동식물을 볼 수 있다. ● 다양함 불가산명사 ❏ 다양한 문화와 가지각색의 풍경을 담고 있는 거대한 나라

■ 부사 진하게, 진하게 ❏ 아주 선명하게 채색된 번쩍거리는 르네상스 시대의 걸작들 ■ 부사 화려하게 ❏ 화려하게 장식된 은주전자 속에서 커피가 김을 뿜고 있었다. ■ 부사 마땅히 [감정 개입] ❏ 그는 마땅히 차지할 만한 성공을 이루었다. ■ 부사 값지게 ❏ 그 책은 읽기 힘든 책이지만, 노력에 값진 보상을 해 준다.

a b c d e f g h i j k l m n o p q r s t u v w x y z

rick|ety /ˈrɪkɪti/ ADJ A **rickety** structure or piece of furniture is not very strong or well made, and seems likely to collapse or break. □ *Mona climbed the rickety wooden stairway.*

형용사 허약한; 망가질 듯한 □ 모나는 부서질 듯한 계단을 올라갔다.

rid ◆◇◇ /rɪd/ (**rids, ridding**)

The form **rid** is used in the present tense and is the past tense and past participle of the verb.

rid는 동사의 현재, 과거, 과거 분사로 쓰인다.

1 PHRASE When you **get rid of** something that you do not want or do not like, you take action so that you no longer have it or suffer from it. □ *The owner needs to get rid of the car for financial reasons.* **2** PHRASE If you **get rid of** someone who is causing problems for you or who you do not like, you do something to prevent them affecting you anymore, for example by making them leave. □ *He believed that his manager wanted to get rid of him for personal reasons.* **3** V-T If you **rid** a place or person **of** something undesirable or unwanted, you succeed in removing it completely from that place or person. □ *The proposals are an attempt to rid the country of political corruption.* **4** V-T If you **rid yourself of** something you do not want, you take action so that you no longer have it or are no longer affected by it. □ *Why couldn't he ever rid himself of those thoughts, those worries?* **5** ADJ If you **are rid of** someone or something that you do not want or that caused problems for you, they are no longer with you or causing problems for you. [v-link ADJ of n] □ *The family had sought a way to be rid of her and the problems she had caused them.*

1 구 -을 없애다; -을 처분하다 □ 차주가 재정적인 이유로 차를 처분해야 한다. **2** 구 제거하다 □ 그는 부장이 사적인 이유로 자신을 제거하고 싶어 한다고 믿었다. **3** 타동사 -에서 ...을 제거하다 □ 그 제안은 그 나라에서 정치적 부패를 일소하기 위한 시도이다. **4** 타동사 -을 없애다 □ 그는 왜 그런 생각과 걱정들을 떨쳐 없애지 못했을까? **5** 형용사 -을 벗어나다 □ 그 가족은 그녀와 그녀가 그들에게 일으켰던 문제들에서 벗어날 수 있는 길을 모색해 왔다.

rid|den /ˈrɪdən/ **Ridden** is the past participle of **ride**.

ride의 과거 분사

-ridden /-rɪdən/ COMB in ADJ **-ridden** combines with nouns to form adjectives that describe something as having a lot of a particular undesirable thing or quality, or suffering very much because of it. □ *...the debt-ridden economies of Latin America.*

복합형-형용사 -에 지배된; -에 고통 받는 □ 빚에 쪼들리는 라틴 아메리카 경제

rid|dle /ˈrɪdəl/ (**riddles, riddling, riddled**) **1** N-COUNT A **riddle** is a puzzle or joke in which you ask a question that seems to be nonsense but which has a clever or amusing answer. □ *All comers to the Sphinx were asked a riddle, and failure to solve it meant death.* **2** N-COUNT You can describe something as a **riddle** if people have been trying to understand or explain it but have not been able to. □ *Scientists claimed yesterday to have solved the riddle of the birth of the Universe.* **3** V-T If someone **riddles** something **with** bullets or bullet holes, they fire a lot of bullets into it. □ *Unknown attackers riddled two homes with gunfire.*

1 가산명사 수수께끼 □ 스핑크스에게 온 사람들은 모두 수수께끼 질문을 받았고, 그것을 풀지 못하는 것은 죽음을 의미했다. **2** 가산명사 수수께끼, 난제 □ 어제 과학자들이 우주 탄생의 난제를 풀었노라고 주장했다. **3** 타동사 (총알로) 벌집을 만들다 □ 신원 미상의 습격자들이 총을 마구 쏘아 집 두 채를 벌집으로 만들었다.

rid|dled /ˈrɪdəld/ **1** ADJ If something is **riddled with** bullets or bullet holes, it is full of bullet holes. □ *The bodies of four people were found riddled with bullets.* **2** ADJ If something is **riddled with** undesirable qualities or features, it is full of them. [v-link ADJ with n] □ *They were the principal shareholders in a bank riddled with corruption.*

1 형용사 (총에 맞아) 벌집이 된 □ 네 구의 시신은 총에 맞아 벌집이 된 채 발견되었다. **2** 형용사 -투성이인 □ 그들은 부패투성이인 어떤 은행의 대주주였다.

ride ◆◆◇ /raɪd/ (**rides, riding, rode, ridden**) **1** V-T/V-I When you **ride** a horse, you sit on it and control its movements. □ *I saw a girl riding a horse.* **2** V-T/V-I When you **ride** a bicycle or a motorcycle, you sit on it, control it, and travel along on it. □ *Riding a bike is great exercise.* □ *Two men riding on motorcycles opened fire on him.* **3** V-I When you **ride in** a vehicle such as a car, you travel in it. □ *He prefers travelling on the Tube to riding in a limousine.* **4** N-COUNT A **ride** is a trip on a horse or bicycle, or in a vehicle. □ *She took some friends for a ride in the family car.* **5** N-COUNT In an amusement park, a **ride** is a large machine that people ride on for fun. □ *...roller coasters or other thrill rides at amusement parks.* **6** V-I If you say that one thing **is riding on** another, you mean that the first thing depends on the second thing. [oft cont] □ *Billions of dollars are riding on the outcome of the election.* **7** →see also **riding**

1 타동사/자동사 (말을) 타다 □ 나는 한 소녀가 말을 타는 것을 보았다. □ 너 말 탈 줄 아니? **2** 타동사/자동사 (탈것을) 타다 □ 자전거 타기는 굉장한 운동이다. □ 오토바이를 탄 2명의 남자가 그에게 총을 쏘았다. **3** 자동사 타다 □ 그는 리무진을 타는 것보다 지하철로 이동하는 것을 더 좋아한다. **4** 가산명사 타기, 드라이브 □ 그녀는 가족 자동차에 친구들을 몇 명 태우고 드라이브를 시켜 주었다. **5** 가산명사 (유원지의) 놀이 기구 □ 유원지의 롤러코스터나 다른 스릴 넘치는 놀이 기구들 **6** 자동사 -에 달려 있다 □ 수십억 달러가 선거 결과에 달려 있다.

When you want to say that someone is controlling a horse, bicycle, or motorbike, you can use **ride** as a transitive verb, with the object coming immediately after it. □ *Whether you ride a motorbike, scooter or moped, get yourself properly trained.* However, if you want to say that someone is a passenger in a vehicle, **ride** must be followed by a preposition. □ *I was riding on the back of a friend's bicycle... We are still letting our children ride in the front seat of our cars.* If **ride** is used without an object, a preposition, or any other phrase that specifies the context, it usually refers to the activity of riding a horse. □ *"Do you ride?" — "No, I've never been on a horse."*

누가 말, 자전거, 오토바이를 탄다고 말하고 싶으면, 목적어가 바로 뒤에 오게 해서 ride를 타동사로 쓸 수 있다. □ 너 말 탈 줄 아니? 오토바이, 스쿠터, 모페드 중 어떤 것을 타더라도 적절하게 훈련을 받도록 하시오. 그러나, 누가 차량의 승객이라고 말하고 싶으면, ride 뒤에는 전치사가 와야 한다. □ 나는 친구의 자전거 뒤에 타고 있었다... 우리는 아직도 아이들을 우리 차 앞좌석에 타도록 내버려둔다. 목적어나 전치사, 또는 문맥을 밝히는 다른 구가 없이 쓰이면, ride는 대개 말을 타는 행위를 가리킨다. □ "승마를 하십니까?" — "아니오, 저는 말을 타 본 적이 없습니다."

8 PHRASE If you say that someone faces **a rough ride**, you mean that things are going to be difficult for them because people will criticize them a lot or treat them badly. [INFORMAL] □ *The Chancellor could face a rough ride unless the plan works.* **9** PHRASE If you say that someone **has been taken for a ride**, you mean that they have been deceived or cheated. [INFORMAL] □ *You've been taken for a ride. Why did you give him five thousand dollars?*

8 구 험한 꼴 [비격식체] □ 그 계획이 먹히지 않으면 재무 장관은 험한 꼴을 당할지도 모른다. **9** 구 속다; 이용당하다 [비격식체] □ 넌 이용당한 거야. 왜 그 사람한테 5천 달러를 줬어?

Word Partnership	*ride의 연어*	
V.	give *someone* a ride, go for a ride, offer *someone* a ride **4**	
N.	bus/car/subway/train ride, ride home **4**	
ADJ.	long ride, scenic ride, short ride, smooth ride **4 5**	

▶**ride out** PHRASAL VERB If someone **rides out** a storm or a crisis, they manage to survive a difficult period without suffering serious harm. □ *The ruling party think they can ride out the political storm.*

구동사 견디 내다 □ 여당은 정치적 격변을 견뎌 낼 수 있다고 생각한다.

rid|er ◆◆◇ /ˈraɪdər/ (**riders**) N-COUNT A **rider** is someone who rides a horse, a bicycle, or a motorcycle as a hobby or job. You can also refer to someone who is riding a horse, a bicycle, or a motorcycle as a rider. □ *She is a very good and experienced rider.*

가산명사 기수; 타는 사람 □ 그녀는 아주 경험이 많고 뛰어난 기수이다.

ridge /rɪdʒ/ (**ridges**) **1** N-COUNT A **ridge** is a long, narrow piece of raised land. ❑ *...a high road along a mountain ridge.* **2** N-COUNT A **ridge** is a raised line on a flat surface. ❑ *...the bony ridge of the eye socket.*

1 가산명사 등성이 ❑ 산등성이를 따라 높이 난 길 **2** 가산명사 융기선, 길쭉하게 돋은 선 ❑ 안와골의 융기선

Word Link	
	rid, ris ≈ laughing : deride, derision, ridicule

ridi|cule /rɪdɪkyul/ (**ridicules, ridiculing, ridiculed**) **1** V-T If you **ridicule** someone or **ridicule** their ideas or beliefs, you make fun of them in an unkind way. ❑ *I admired her all the more for allowing them to ridicule her and never striking back.* **2** N-UNCOUNT If someone or something is an object of **ridicule** or is held up to **ridicule**, someone makes fun of them in an unkind way. ❑ *As a heavy child, she became the object of ridicule from classmates.*

1 다동사 비웃다, 조롱하다 ❑ 그들이 자신을 비웃도록 내버려 두고 결코 반박하지 않는 것 때문에 나는 더더욱 그녀에게 감탄했다. **2** 불가산명사 비웃음, 조롱 ❑ 몸무게가 많이 나가는 아이였던 그녀는 급우들의 놀림감이 되었다.

Thesaurus	ridicule의 참조어
v.	humiliate, mimic, mock; (ant.) praise **1**

ri|dicu|lous /rɪdɪkyələs/ ADJ If you say that something or someone is **ridiculous**, you mean that they are very foolish. ❑ *It is ridiculous to suggest we are having a romance.*

형용사 웃기는, 터무니없는 ❑ 우리가 연애를 하고 있다는 듯이 말하는 것은 웃기는 일이다.

ri|dicu|lous|ly /rɪdɪkyələsli/ ADV You use **ridiculously** to emphasize the fact that you think something is unreasonable or very surprising. [EMPHASIS] ❑ *Dena bought rolls of silk that seemed ridiculously cheap.*

부사 말도 안 되게; 엄청나게 [강조] ❑ 데나는 엄청나게 싼 것 같아 보이는 비단 두루마리를 여러 개 샀다.

rid|ing /raɪdɪŋ/ N-UNCOUNT **Riding** is the activity or sport of riding horses. ❑ *The next morning we went riding again.*

불가산명사 승마 ❑ 다음날 아침 우리는 다시 승마하러 갔다.

rife /raɪf/ ADJ If you say that something, usually something bad, is **rife** in a place or that the place is **rife with** it, you mean that it is very common. [v-link ADJ, oft ADJ with n] ❑ *Speculation is rife that he will be sacked.*

형용사 만연한 ❑ 그가 해고되리라는 추측이 만연하다.

ri|fle /raɪfəl/ (**rifles, rifling, rifled**) **1** N-COUNT A **rifle** is a gun with a long barrel. ❑ *They shot him at point blank range with an automatic rifle.* **2** V-T/V-I If you **rifle through** things or **rifle** them, you make a quick search among them in order to find something or steal something. ❑ *I discovered my husband rifling through the filing cabinet.*

1 가산명사 소총 ❑ 그들은 자동소총으로 직사 거리에서 그를 쏘았다. **2** 타동사/자동사 샅샅이 뒤지다 ❑ 나는 내 남편이 서류 캐비닛을 샅샅이 뒤지고 있는 것을 발견했다.

rift /rɪft/ (**rifts**) **1** N-COUNT A **rift** between people or countries is a serious quarrel or disagreement that stops them having a good relationship. ❑ *The interview reflected a growing rift between the President and the government.* **2** N-COUNT A **rift** is a split that appears in something solid, especially in the ground. ❑ *The earth convulsed uncontrollably, a rift opened suddenly and, with a horrid sucking sound, swallowed the entire pool.*

1 가산명사 불화 ❑ 그 대담은 대통령과 정부 사이에 불화가 점점 더 커지고 있음을 보여 주었다. **2** 가산명사 갈라진 틈 ❑ 땅이 마구 흔들리다가 갑자기 쩍 갈라지더니 그 틈 속으로 무시무시한 소리와 함께 수영장 물이 통째로 다 빨려 들어가버렸다.

rig /rɪg/ (**rigs, rigging, rigged**) **1** V-T If someone **rigs** an election, a job appointment, or a game, they dishonestly arrange it to get the result they want or to give someone an unfair advantage. ❑ *She accused her opponents of rigging the vote.* **2** N-COUNT A **rig** is a large structure that is used for looking for oil or gas and for taking it out of the ground or the sea bed. ❑ *...a supply vessel for gas rigs in the North Sea.* →see oil

1 타동사 ―에서 부정을 저지르다, 조작하다 ❑ 그녀는 상대를 선거 부정을 저지른 혐의로 고발했다. **2** 가산명사 유정 굴착 장치 ❑ 북해의 가스정 굴착 장치 보급선

rig|ging /rɪgɪŋ/ **1** N-UNCOUNT Vote or ballot **rigging** is the act of dishonestly organizing an election to get a particular result. [usu supp N] ❑ *She was accused of corruption, of vote rigging on a massive scale.* **2** N-UNCOUNT On a ship, the **rigging** is the ropes which support the ship's masts and sails. ❑ *...the howling of the wind in the rigging.*

1 불가산명사 부정 (행위), 조작 ❑ 그녀는 부패와 대규모 선거 부정 혐의로 고발되었다. **2** 불가산명사 삭구 ❑ 삭구를 스치며 바람이 윙윙거리는 소리

right	
①	CORRECT, APPROPRIATE, OR ACCEPTABLE
②	DIRECTION AND POLITICAL GROUPINGS
③	ENTITLEMENT
④	DISCOURSE USES
⑤	USED FOR EMPHASIS

① **right** ♦♦♦ /raɪt/ (**rights, righting, righted**) →Please look at category **15** to see if the expression you are looking for is shown under another headword. **1** ADJ If something is **right**, it is correct and agrees with the facts. ❑ *That's absolutely right.* ❑ *Clocks never told the right time.* ● ADV **Right** is also an adverb. [ADV after v] ❑ *He guessed right about some things.* **2** ADJ If you do something in the **right** way or in the **right** place, you do it as or where it should be done or was planned to be done. ❑ *Walking, done in the right way, is a form of aerobic exercise.* ❑ *They have computerized systems to ensure delivery of the right pizza to the right place.* ● ADV **Right** is also an adverb. [ADV after v] ❑ *To make sure I did everything right, I bought a fat instruction book.* **3** ADJ If you say that someone is seen in **all the right** places or knows **all the right** people, you mean that they go to places which are socially acceptable or know people who are socially acceptable. ❑ *He was always to be seen in the right places.* **4** ADJ If someone is **right about** something, they are correct in what they say or think about it. ❑ *Ron has been right about the result of every General Election but one.* **5** ADJ If something such as a choice, action, or decision is the **right** one, it is the best or most suitable one. ❑ *She'd made the right choice in leaving New York.* **6** ADJ If something is **not right**, there is something unsatisfactory about the situation or thing that you are talking about. [v-link ADJ, with brd-neg] ❑ *Ratatouille doesn't taste right with any other oil.* **7** ADJ If you think that someone was **right to** do something, you think that there were good moral reasons why they did it. [v-link ADJ, usu ADJ to-inf] ❑ *You were right to do what you did, under the circumstances.* **8** ADJ **Right** is used to refer to activities or actions that are considered to be morally good and acceptable. [v-link ADJ, oft with brd-neg] ❑ *It's not right, leaving her like this.* ● N-UNCOUNT **Right** is also a noun. ❑ *At least he knew right from wrong.* ● **right|ness** N-UNCOUNT ❑ *Many people have very strong opinions about the rightness or wrongness of abortion.* **9** V-T If

1 형용사 옳은, 올바른 ❑ 그것은 전적으로 옳다. ❑ 시계들이 결코 시간을 가리키지 않았다. ● 부사 옳게, 바르게 ❑ 그는 몇 가지 일에 대해 옳게 추측했다. **2** 형용사 바른, 적절한 ❑ 제대로 하면, 걷기는 유산소 운동의 한 형태가 된다. ❑ 그들은 피자가 제 곳에 제대로 배달되는 것을 보장하는 전산화 시스템을 갖추고 있다. ● 부사 바르게, 제대로 ❑ 모든 일을 제대로 했는지 확인하기 위해, 두꺼운 설명서를 한 권 샀다. **3** 형용사 건전한 ❑ 그는 언제나 건전한 장소에서 모습을 볼 수 있었다. **4** 형용사 옳은, 맞는 ❑ 론은 지금까지 한 번 빼고는 총선거 결과를 모두 맞혔다. **5** 형용사 최선의 ❑ 그녀가 뉴욕을 떠난 것은 최선의 선택이었다. **6** 형용사 만족스러운 ❑ 래터튜이는 다른 기름을 쓰면 어떤 걸 넣어도 제 맛이 나지 않는다. **7** 형용사 합당한 ❑ 그런 상황에서 네가 그렇게 한 것은 합당했다. **8** 형용사 올바른 ❑ 이렇게 그녀를 떠나는 것은 옳지 않다. ● 불가산명사 올바름 ❑ 적어도 그는 옳고 그름은 구분했다. ● 정당함 불가산명사 ❑ 많은 사람들이 낙태의 정당성 혹은 부당성에 대해 아주 확고한 견해를 가지고 있다. **9** 타동사 바로잡다; 원상을 회복하다 ❑ 그들은 경제를 바로잡는 일의 긴급성을 인식하고 있다. **10** 타동사 보상하다 ❑ 우리가 과거의 잘못을 보상하는 데 진전이 있었다. **11** 타동사 (넘어진 것을) 다시 세우다; 바로 서다 ❑ 그는 요트를 다시 세워 경주를 계속했다. **12** 형용사 같의, 표면의 ❑ 여분의 천을 잘라 내고

a b c d e f g h i j k l m n o p q r s t u v w x y z

you **right** something or if it **rights itself**, it returns to its normal or correct state, after being in an undesirable state. ❑ *They recognise the urgency of righting the economy.* ⑩ V-T If you **right** a wrong, you do something to make up for a mistake or something bad that you did in the past. ❑ *We've made progress in righting the wrongs of the past.* ⑪ V-T If you **right** something that has fallen or rolled over, or if it **rights itself**, it returns to its normal upright position. ❑ *He righted the yacht and continued the race.* ⑫ ADJ The **right** side of a material is the side that is intended to be seen and that faces outward when it is made into something. [ADJ n] ❑ *Trim off excess fabric and turn the right side out.* ⑬ PHRASE If you say that things **are going right**, you mean that your life or a situation is developing as you intended or expected and you are pleased with it. ❑ *I can't think of anything in my life that's going right.* ⑭ PHRASE If you **put** something **right**, you correct something that was wrong or that was causing problems. ❑ *We've discovered what's gone wrong and are going to put it right.* ⑮ **heart in the right place** →see **heart. it serves** you **right** →see **serve**

② **right** ♦♦♦ /raɪt/

The spelling **Right** is also used for meaning ❸.

❶ N-SING The **right** is one of two opposite directions, sides, or positions. If you are facing north and you turn to the right, you will be facing east. In the word "to," the "o" is to the right of the "t." ❑ *Ahead of you on the right will be a lovely garden.* ● ADV **Right** is also an adverb. [ADV after v] ❑ *Turn right into the street.* ❷ ADJ Your **right** arm, leg, or ear, for example, is the one which is on the right side of your body. Your **right** shoe or glove is the one which is intended to be worn on your right foot or hand. [ADJ n] ❑ *She shattered her right leg in a fall.* ❸ N-SING-COLL You can refer to people who support the political ideals of capitalism and conservatism as **the right**. They are often contrasted with **the left**, who support the political ideals of socialism. ❑ *The Tory Right despise him.*

Thesaurus	*right*의 참조어
ADJ.	appropriate, correct, just, true; (ant.) unjust, wrong ① ❶
	conservative, right-wing; (ant.) left, liberal ② ❸

③ **right** ♦♦♦ /raɪt/ (**rights**) ❶ N-PLURAL Your **rights** are what you are morally or legally entitled to do or to have. ❑ *They don't know their rights.* ❷ N-SING If you have a **right to** do or to have something, you are morally or legally entitled to do it or to have it. ❑ *...a woman's right to choose.* ❸ N-PLURAL If someone has the **rights to** a story or book, they are legally allowed to publish it or reproduce it in another form, and nobody else can do so without their permission. ❑ *An agent bought the rights to his life.* ❹ PHRASE If something is not the case but you think that it should be, you can say that **by rights** it should be the case. ❑ *She did work which by rights should be done by someone else.* ❺ PHRASE If someone is a successful or respected person in their **own right**, they are successful or respected because of their own efforts and talents rather than those of the people they are closely connected with. ❑ *Although now a celebrity in her own right, actress Lynn Redgrave knows the difficulties of living in the shadow of her famous older sister.* ❻ PHRASE If you say that you **reserve the right to** do something, you mean that you will do it if you feel that it is necessary. ❑ *He reserved the right to change his mind.* ❼ PHRASE If you say that someone is **within** their **rights to** do something, you mean that they are morally or legally entitled to do it. ❑ *You were quite within your rights to refuse to co-operate with him.*

④ **right** ♦♦♦ /raɪt/ ❶ ADV You use **right** in order to attract someone's attention or to indicate that you have dealt with one thing so you can go on to another. [SPOKEN] [ADV cl] ❑ *Right, I'll be back in a minute.* ❷ CONVENTION You can use **right** to check whether what you have just said is correct. [SPOKEN] ❑ *They have a small plane, right?* ❸ ADV You can say "**right**" to show that you are listening to what someone is saying and that you accept it or understand it. [SPOKEN] [ADV as reply] ❑ *"Your children may well come away speaking with a bit of a broad country accent" — "Right." — "because they're mixing with country children."* ❹ →see also **all right**

⑤ **right** ♦♦♦ /raɪt/ ❶ ADV You can use **right** to emphasize the precise place, position, or time of something. [EMPHASIS] [ADV adv/prep] ❑ *The back of a car appeared right in front of him.* ❷ ADV You can use **right** to emphasize how far something moves or extends or how long it continues. [EMPHASIS] [ADV prep/adv] ❑ *...the highway that runs through the Indian zone right to the army positions.* ❸ ADV You can use **right** to emphasize that an action or state is complete. [EMPHASIS] [ADV adv/prep] ❑ *The candle had burned right down.* ❹ ADV If you say that something happened **right after** a particular time or event or **right before** it, you mean that it happened immediately after or before it. [EMPHASIS] [ADV prep/adv] ❑ *All of a sudden, right after the summer, Mother gets married.* ❺ ADV If you say **I'll be right there** or **I'll be right back**, you mean that you will get to a place or get back to it in a very short time. [EMPHASIS] [ADV adv] ❑ *I'm going to get some water. I'll be right back.* ❻ PHRASE If you do something **right away** or **right off**, you do it immediately. [INFORMAL, EMPHASIS] ❑ *He wants to see you right away.* ❼ PHRASE You can use **right now** to emphasize that you are referring to the present moment. [INFORMAL, EMPHASIS] ❑ *Right now I'm feeling very excited.*

right an|gle (**right angles**) also **right-angle** ❶ N-COUNT A **right angle** is an angle of ninety degrees. A square has four right angles. ❷ PHRASE If two things are **at right angles**, they are situated so that they form an angle of ninety degrees where they touch each other. You can also say that one thing is **at right angles** to another. ❑ *...two lasers at right angles.*

right-click (**right-clicks, right-clicking, right-clicked**) V-I To **right-click** or to **right-click on** something means to press the right-hand button on a computer mouse. [COMPUTING] ❑ *All you have to do is right-click on the desktop and select New Folder.*

겉면이 밖으로 오게 뒤집으세요. ⑬ 구 잘 되어 가다 ❑ 내 삶에서 잘 되어 가는 것이라고는 아무것도 생각해 낼 수가 없다. ⑭ 구 바로잡다 ❑ 무엇이 잘못되었는지 알아냈고 그 문제를 바로잡을 것이다.

철자 Right도 ❸ 의미로 쓴다.

❶ 단수명사 오른쪽 ❑ 여러분의 전방 오른쪽에 아름다운 정원이 있을 겁니다. ● 부사 오른쪽으로 ❑ 우회전해서 차도로 들어가세요. ❷ 형용사 오른쪽의 ❑ 그녀는 떨어져서 오른쪽 다리가 으스러졌다. ❸ 단수명사-집합 우파, 우익 ❑ 토리당 우파는 그를 경멸한다.

❶ 복수명사 권리 ❑ 그들은 자신들의 권리를 모른다. ❷ 단수명사 권리 ❑ 여성의 선택권 ❸ 복수명사 판권 ❑ 한 대행사가 그의 전기에 대한 판권을 샀다. ❹ 구 원칙대로라면 ❑ 원칙대로라면 다른 사람이 했어야 할 일을 그녀가 했다. ❺ 구 본인 자신도 ❑ 지금은 본인 자신도 유명인이지만, 여배우 린 레드그레이브는 유명한 언니의 그늘에서 살아가는 것의 어려움을 알고 있다. ❻ 구 필요하면 -할 수 있다 ❑ 그는 필요하면 마음을 고쳐먹을 수 있었다. ❼ 구 -할 권리가 있는, 마땅히 -할 수 있는 ❑ 그와 협력하는 것을 거절한 것은 마땅히 네가 할 수 있는 일이었다.

❶ 부사 자; 그럼 [구어체] ❑ 그럼, 금방 돌아올게. ❷ 관용 표현 그렇지? [구어체] ❑ 그들은 작은 비행기를 가지고 있어, 그렇지? ❸ 부사 맞아, 그래 [구어체] ❑ "네 아이들이 순 시골 사투리를 약간 섞어 가며 말하게 된 것도 당연해." "맞죠." "개들이 시골 아이들과 어울렸으니까."

❶ 부사 바로 [강조] ❑ 바로 그의 앞에 어떤 차의 뒷부분이 나타났다. ❷ 부사 줄곧, 쭉 [강조] ❑ 인디언 구역을 지나 육군 기지까지 쭉 뻗어 있는 고속도로 ❸ 부사 완전히 [강조] ❑ 초가 완전히 다 타 버린 상태였다. ❹ 부사 직후에; 직전에 [강조] ❑ 여름이 끝나면 우리 어머니가 갑작스레 결혼을 하실 것이다. ❺ 부사 금방, 곧바로 [강조] ❑ 물 좀 가져와야겠다. 금방 올게. ❻ 구 즉시, 당장 [비격식체, 강조] ❑ 그가 지금 당장 당신을 만나고 싶어 해요. ❼ 구 바로 지금 [비격식체, 강조] ❑ 바로 지금 저는 매우 들뜬 기분이에요.

❶ 가산명사 직각 ❷ 구 직각으로 ❑ 직각으로 교차한 레이저 두 개

자동사 마우스의 오른쪽 버튼을 클릭하다 [컴퓨터] ❑ 노트북 마우스의 오른쪽 버튼을 클릭하고 새 폴더를 선택하기만 하면 된다.

right|eous /ˈraɪtʃəs/ ADJ If you think that someone behaves or lives in a way that is morally good, you can say that they are **righteous**. People sometimes use **righteous** to express their disapproval when they think someone is only behaving in this way so that others will admire or support them. [FORMAL] ❑ *Aren't you afraid of being seen as a righteous crusader?*

형용사 도덕적인, 올바른; 도덕군자인 척하는 [격식체] ❑ 도덕군자인 척하는 운동가로 비춰질까 봐 두렵지 않습니까?

right|ful /ˈraɪtfəl/ ADJ If you say that someone or something has returned to its **rightful** place or position, they have returned to the place or position that you think they should have. [ADJ n] ❑ *The Baltics' own democratic traditions would help them to regain their rightful place in Europe.* ● **right|ful|ly** ADV [ADV group] ❑ *Jealousy is the feeling that someone else has something that rightfully belongs to you.*

형용사 걸맞은, 마땅히 있어야 할 ❑ 발트 해 3국의 민주적 전통이 그들이 유럽에서 정당한 입지를 되찾는 데 힘이 될 것이다. ● 부사 마땅히, 당연한 ❑ 질투란 당연히 당신의 소유물이어야 할 무언가를 다른 사람이 가졌을 때 느끼는 감정이다.

right-hand ADJ If something is on the **right-hand** side of something, it is positioned on the right of it. [ADJ n] ❑ *...a church on the right-hand side of the road.*

형용사 오른쪽의, 오른편의 ❑ 길 오른편에 있는 교회

right-handed ADJ Someone who is **right-handed** uses their right hand rather than their left hand for activities such as writing and sports, and for picking things up. ● ADV **Right-handed** is also an adverb. [ADV after v] ❑ *I batted left-handed and bowled right-handed.*

형용사 오른손잡이의 ● 부사 오른손으로 ❑ 나는 공을 칠 때는 왼손잡이고, 던질 때는 오른손잡이다.

right-hand man (**right-hand men**) N-COUNT Someone's **right-hand man** is the person who acts as their chief assistant and helps and supports them a lot in their work. ❑ *He is Rupert Murdoch's right-hand man at News International.*

가산명사 오른팔 같은 사람, 심복 ❑ 그는 뉴스인터내셔널에서 루퍼트 머독의 오른팔 같은 존재이다.

rights is|sue (**rights issues**) N-COUNT A **rights issue** is when a company offers shares at a reduced price to people who already have shares in the company. [BUSINESS] ❑ *Last year's rights issue bolstered Pearson's financial position.*

가산명사 신주 인수권 [경제] ❑ 지난해 신주 인수권 덕에 피어슨의 재정 상태가 좋아졌다.

right tri|an|gle (**right triangles**) N-COUNT A **right triangle** has one angle that is a right angle. [AM; BRIT **right-angled triangle**]

가산명사 직각 삼각형 [미국영어; 영국영어 right-angled triangle]

right-wing ◆◇◇

The spelling **right wing** is also used for meaning ②.

철자 right wing도 ② 의미로 쓴다.

1 ADJ A **right-wing** person or group has conservative or capitalist views. ❑ *...a right-wing government.* 2 N-SING The **right wing** of a political party consists of the members who have the most conservative or the most capitalist views. ❑ *...the right wing of the Conservative Party.*

1 형용사 우익의, 우파의 ❑ 우파 정부 2 단수명사 우익, 보수파 ❑ 보수당 내 우익

right-winger (**right-wingers**) N-COUNT If you think someone has views which are more right-wing than most other members of their party, you can say they are a **right-winger**. ❑ *Across Europe hard-line right-wingers are gaining power.*

가산명사 보수파 ❑ 유럽 전역에서 강경 보수파가 힘을 얻고 있다.

rig|id /ˈrɪdʒɪd/ 1 ADJ Laws, rules, or systems that are **rigid** cannot be changed or varied, and are therefore considered to be rather severe. [DISAPPROVAL] ❑ *Several colleges in our study have rigid rules about student conduct.* ● **ri|gid|ity** /rɪˈdʒɪdɪti/ N-UNCOUNT ❑ *...the rigidity of government policy.* ● **rig|id|ly** ADV [ADV with v] ❑ *The caste system was so rigidly enforced that non-Hindus were not even allowed inside a Hindu house.* 2 ADJ If you disapprove of someone because you think that they are not willing to change their way of thinking or behaving, you can describe them as **rigid**. [DISAPPROVAL] ❑ *She was a fairly rigid person who had strong religious views.* 3 ADJ A **rigid** substance or object is stiff and does not bend, stretch, or twist easily. ❑ *...rigid plastic containers.* ● **ri|gid|ity** N-UNCOUNT ❑ *...the strength and rigidity of glass.*

1 형용사 엄격한, 경직된 [탐탁찮음] ❑ 우리 연구에서 다룬 몇몇 대학들은 학생 품행에 대해 엄격한 규정을 두고 있다. ● 엄격함, 경직함 ● 엄격하게, 융통성 없이 부사 ❑ 카스트 제도가 워낙 엄격히 시행되었기 때문에 비힌두교 신자는 힌두교 신자의 집 안에 들어갈 수조차 없었다. 2 형용사 융통성 없는, 완고한 [탐탁찮음] ❑ 그녀는 종교적 견해가 확고한, 꽤 완고한 사람이었다. 3 형용사 단단한, 빳빳한 ❑ 단단한 플라스틱 용기 ● 단단함, 경도 불가산명사 ❑ 유리의 강도와 경도

rig|or /ˈrɪɡər/ (**rigors**) [BRIT **rigour**] 1 N-PLURAL If you refer to **the rigors of** an activity or job, you mean the difficult, demanding, or unpleasant things that are associated with it. ❑ *They're accustomed to the rigors of army life.* 2 N-UNCOUNT If something is done with **rigor**, it is done in a strict, thorough way. ❑ *The prince had performed his social duties with professional rigor.*

[영국영어 rigour] 1 복수명사 고초, 고됨 ❑ 그들은 고된 군 생활에 익숙해져 있다. 2 불가산명사 엄격함 ❑ 왕자는 전문가다운 엄격한 자세로 사회적인 의무를 수행했었다.

rig|or|ous /ˈrɪɡərəs/ 1 ADJ A test, system, or procedure that is **rigorous** is very thorough and strict. ❑ *The selection process is based on rigorous tests of competence and experience.* ● **rig|or|ous|ly** ADV ❑ *...rigorously conducted research.* 2 ADJ If someone is **rigorous** in the way that they do something, they are very careful and thorough. ❑ *He is rigorous in his control of expenditure.*

1 형용사 엄격한, 철저한 ❑ 선발 과정은 능력과 경험에 대한 엄격한 테스트에 기반을 둔다. ● 엄격하게, 철저하게 부사 ❑ 엄격하게 진행된 연구 2 형용사 철저한 ❑ 그는 지출 관리에 철저하다.

rim /rɪm/ (**rims**) 1 N-COUNT The **rim** of a container such as a cup or glass is the edge that goes all the way around the top. ❑ *She looked at him over the rim of her glass.* 2 N-COUNT The **rim** of a circular object is its outside edge. ❑ *...a round mirror with white metal rim.*

1 가산명사 가장자리 ❑ 그녀는 컵 가장자리 너머로 그를 바라봤다. 2 가산명사 테두리 ❑ 하얀 금속 테두리의 동그란 거울

rind /raɪnd/ (**rinds**) 1 N-VAR The **rind** of a fruit such as a lemon or orange is its thick outer skin. ❑ *...grated lemon rind.* 2 N-VAR The **rind** of cheese or bacon is the hard outer edge which you do not usually eat. ❑ *Discard the bacon rind and cut each rasher in half.*

1 가산명사 또는 불가산명사 (오렌지 등의) 껍질 ❑ 레몬 껍질을 갈아 놓은 것 2 가산명사 또는 불가산명사 (치즈 등의) 딱딱한 껍질 ❑ 베이컨의 딱딱한 부분을 버리고 부드러운 부분을 각각 반으로 자르세요.

---

ring

① TELEPHONING OR MAKING A SOUND
② SHAPES AND GROUPS

① **ring** ◆◆◇ /rɪŋ/ (**rings, ringing, rang, rung**)→Please look at category ⑧ to see if the expression you are looking for is shown under another headword. 1 V-I When a telephone **rings**, it makes a sound to let you know that someone is phoning you. ❑ *As soon as he got home, the phone rang.* ● N-COUNT **Ring** is also a noun. ❑ *After at least eight rings, an ancient-sounding maid answered the phone.* ● **ring|ing** N-UNCOUNT ❑ *She was jolted out of her sleep by the ringing of the telephone.* 2 V-T/V-I When you **ring** someone, you telephone them. [mainly BRIT] ❑ *He rang me at my mother's.* ❑ *I would ring when I got back to the hotel.* ● PHRASAL VERB **Ring up** means the same as **ring**. [AM usually **call**] ❑ *You can ring us up anytime.* ❑ *John rang up and invited himself over for dinner.* 3 V-T/V-I When you **ring** a bell or when a bell **rings**, it makes a sound. ❑ *He heard the school bell ring.* ● N-COUNT **Ring** is also a noun. ❑ *There was a ring at the bell.* ● **ring|ing** N-UNCOUNT ❑ *...the ringing of church bells.* 4 V-I If you say that a place **is ringing with** sound, usually

1 자동사 전화벨이 울리다 ❑ 그가 집에 오자마자 전화벨이 울렸다. ● 가산명사 전화벨 ❑ 전화벨이 여덟 번쯤 울리고 나서, 나이 지긋한 목소리의 가정부가 전화를 받았다. ● 전화벨 소리 불가산명사 ❑ 그녀는 전화벨 소리에 자다가 벌떡 깼다. 2 타동사/자동사 전화하다 [주로 영국영어] ❑ 그는 우리 어머니 집으로 나에게 전화를 했다. ❑ 나는 호텔로 돌아와서 전화를 하곤 했다. ● 구동사 전화하다 [미국영어 대개 call] ❑ 언제든지 전화하셔도 됩니다. ❑ 존이 전화해서 저녁 먹고 오겠다는 말을 했다. 3 타동사/자동사 종을 울리다 ❑ 그는 학교 종이 울리는 소리를 들었다. ● 가산명사 울림 ❑ 종이 울렸다. ● 울리는 소리 불가산명사 ❑ 교회 종이 울리는 소리 4 자동사 울려 퍼지다 [문예체]

pleasant sound, you mean that the place is completely filled with that sound. [LITERARY] ❑ *The whole place was ringing with music.* ◻ N-SING You can use **ring** to describe a quality that something such as a statement, discussion, or argument seems to have. For example, if an argument **has a familiar ring**, it seems familiar. ❑ *His proud boast of leading "the party of low taxation" has a hollow ring.* ◻ PHRASE If you **give** someone **a ring**, you phone them. [mainly BRIT, INFORMAL; AM usually **call**] ❑ *We'll give him a ring as soon as we get back.* ◻ PHRASE If a statement **rings true**, it seems to be true or genuine. If it **rings hollow**, it does not seem to be true or genuine. ❑ *Joanna's denial rang true.* ◻ →see also **ringing**. **to ring a bell** →see **bell**

▶**ring back** PHRASAL VERB If you **ring** someone **back**, you phone them either because they phoned you earlier and you were not there or because you did not finish an earlier telephone conversation. [mainly BRIT; AM usually **call back**] [no passive] ❑ *Tell her I'll ring back in a few minutes.*

▶**ring in** PHRASAL VERB If you **ring in**, you phone a place, such as the place where you work. [mainly BRIT; AM usually **call in**] ❑ *Cecil wasn't there, having rung in to say he was taking the day off.*

▶**ring off** PHRASAL VERB When you **ring off**, you put down the receiver at the end of a telephone call. [mainly BRIT; AM usually **hang up**] ❑ *She had rung off before he could press her for an answer.*

▶**ring round** or **ring around** PHRASAL VERB If you **ring round** or **ring around**, you phone several people, usually when you are trying to organize something or to find some information. [mainly BRIT; AM usually **call around**] ❑ *She'd ring around and get back to me.*

▶**ring up** ◻ →see **ring 2** ◻ PHRASAL VERB If a store clerk **rings up** a sale on a cash register, he or she presses the keys in order to record the amount that is being spent. ❑ *She was ringing up her sale on an ancient cash register.* ◻ PHRASAL VERB If a company **rings up** an amount of money, usually a large amount of money, it makes that amount of money in sales or profits. ❑ *The advertising agency rang up 1.4 billion dollars in yearly sales.*

②**ring** ◆◇◇ /rɪŋ/ (**rings, ringing, ringed**) ◻ N-COUNT A **ring** is a small circle of metal or other substance that you wear on your finger as jewelry. ❑ *...a gold wedding ring.* ◻ N-COUNT An object or substance that is in the shape of a circle can be described as a **ring**. ❑ *Frank took a large ring of keys from his pocket.* ◻ N-COUNT A group of people or things arranged in a circle can be described as a **ring**. ❑ *They then formed a ring around the square.* ◻ N-COUNT At a boxing or wrestling match or a circus, the **ring** is the place where the contest or performance takes place. It consists of an enclosed space with seats round it. ❑ *He will never again be allowed inside a British boxing ring.* ◻ N-COUNT You can refer to an organized group of people who are involved in an illegal activity as a **ring**. ❑ *Police are investigating the suspected drug ring at the school.* ◻ N-COUNT A gas or electric ring is one of the small flat areas on top of a stove which heat up and which you use for cooking. [mainly BRIT; AM usually **burner**] ◻ V-T If a building or place **is ringed with** or **by** something, it is surrounded by it. [usu passive] ❑ *The areas are sealed off and ringed by troops.* →see **circle, jewelry**

ring bind|er (**ring binders**) N-COUNT A **ring binder** is a file with hard covers, which you can insert pages into. The pages are held in by metal rings on a bar attached to the inside of the file. →see **office**

ring|ing /rɪŋɪŋ/ ◻ ADJ A **ringing** sound is loud and can be heard very clearly. [ADJ n] ❑ *He hit the metal steps with a ringing crash.* ◻ ADJ A **ringing** statement or declaration is one that is made forcefully and is intended to make a powerful impression. [ADJ n] ❑ *...the party's 14th Congress, which gave a ringing endorsement to capitalist-style economic reforms.*

ring tone (**ring tones**) N-COUNT The **ring tone** is the sound made by a telephone, especially a cell phone, when it rings. ❑ *They offer 70 hours' standby time, 2hr 50min talk time, and 15 ring tones.*

rink /rɪŋk/ (**rinks**) N-COUNT A **rink** is a large area covered with ice where people go to ice-skate, or a large area of concrete where people go to roller-skate. ❑ *The other skaters were ordered off the rink.*

rinse /rɪns/ (**rinses, rinsing, rinsed**) ◻ V-T When you **rinse** something, you wash it in clean water in order to remove dirt or soap from it. ❑ *It's important to rinse the rice to remove the starch.* ● N-COUNT **Rinse** is also a noun. ❑ *Clean skin means plenty of lather followed by a rinse with water.* ◻ V-T If you **rinse** your mouth, you wash it by filling your mouth with water or with a liquid that kills germs, then spitting it out. ❑ *Use a toothbrush on your tongue as well, and rinse your mouth frequently.* ● PHRASAL VERB **Rinse out** means the same as **rinse**. ❑ *After her meal she invariably rinsed out her mouth.* ● N-MASS **Rinse** is also a noun. ❑ *...mouth rinses with fluoride.*

riot ◆◇◇ /raɪət/ (**riots, rioting, rioted**) ◻ N-COUNT When there is a **riot**, a crowd of people behave violently in a public place, for example they fight, throw stones, or damage buildings and vehicles. ❑ *Twelve inmates have been killed during a riot at the prison.* ◻ V-I If people **riot**, they behave violently in a public place. ❑ *Last year 600 inmates rioted, starting fires and building barricades.* ● **ri|ot|er** (**rioters**) N-COUNT ❑ *The militia dispersed the rioters.* ● **ri|ot|ing** N-UNCOUNT ❑ *At least fifteen people are now known to have died in three days of rioting.* ◻ N-SING If you say that there is **a riot of** something such as color, you mean that there is a large amount of various types of it. [APPROVAL] ❑ *It would be a riot of color, of poppies and irises and flowers of every kind.* ◻ PHRASE If someone in authority **reads** you **the riot act**, they tell you that you will be punished unless you start behaving properly. ❑ *I'm glad you read the riot act to Billy. He's still a kid and still needs to be told what to do.* ◻ PHRASE If people **run riot**, they behave in a wild and uncontrolled manner. ❑ *Rampaging prisoners ran riot through Strangeways jail.*

◻ 주변에 온통 음악 소리가 울려 퍼지고 있었다. ◻ 단수명사 울림, (들리는) 느낌 ◻ '저과세 당' 지도자라는 그의 자신에 찬 발언이 공허하게 들린다. ◻ 구 -에게 전화하다 [주로 영국영어, 비격식체; 미국영어 대개 call] ◻ 우리는 돌아오자마자 그에게 전화할 것이다. ◻ 구 진실 같다; 공허하게 느껴지다 ◻ 조애너가 부인하는 게 정말 같았다.

구동사 다시 전화하다 [주로 영국영어; 미국영어 대개 call back] ◻ 그녀한테 몇 분 있다가 내가 다시 전화한다고 전해 줘.

구동사 -로 전화하다 [주로 영국영어; 미국영어 대개 call in] ◻ 시슬은 하루 쉬겠다고 전화를 하고 거기 나오지 않았다.

구동사 전화를 끊다 [주로 영국영어; 미국영어 대개 hang up] ◻ 그가 답을 요구하기도 전에 그녀가 전화를 끊어 버렸다.

구동사 여러 사람에게 전화를 돌리다 [주로 영국영어; 미국영어 대개 call around] ◻ 그녀는 여러 사람에게 전화를 돌린 후 나한테 다시 전화를 하곤 했다.

◻ 구동사 금전 등록기에 금액을 입력하다 ◻ 그녀가 구식 금전 등록기에 물건 금액을 입력하고 있었다. ◻ 구동사 수익을 올리다 ◻ 그 광고 대행사는 14억 달러에 달하는 연간 매출을 올렸다.

◻ 가산명사 반지 ◻ 금으로 된 결혼반지 ◻ 가산명사 고리 ◻ 프랭크가 주머니에서 커다란 열쇠고리를 꺼냈다. ◻ 가산명사 빙 둘러선 모양 ◻ 그리고 나서 그들은 광장에 빙 둘러섰다. ◻ 가산명사 경기장, 링 ◻ 그는 다시는 복싱 선수로서 영국 링 위에 서지 못할 것이다. ◻ 가산명사 일당 ◻ 경찰이 마약 밀매 혐의를 받고 있는 학내 집단을 조사 중이다. ◻ 가산명사 버너, 점화구 [주로 영국영어; 미국영어 대개 burner] ◻ 타동사 -로 둘러싸이다 ◻ 이 지역들은 봉쇄된 상태로 군인들에게 둘러싸여 있다.

가산명사 링바인더

◻ 형용사 울리는, 울려 퍼지는 ◻ 그가 철 계단을 밟자 쿵 하는 소리가 울려 퍼졌다. ◻ 형용사 강력한, 단호한 ◻ 자본주의에 입각한 경제 개혁에 강력한 지지 의사를 표명한 열네 번째 당 대회

가산명사 벨 소리 ◻ 그들은 통화 대기 시간 70시간, 통화 시간 2시간 50분, 벨 소리 15개를 제공한다.

가산명사 스케이트장; 롤러스케이트장 ◻ 나머지 사람들은 스케이트장에서 나오라는 지시를 받았다.

◻ 타동사 헹구다, 씻어 내다 ◻ 쌀을 씻어서 녹말가루를 없애 주는 것이 중요하다. ● 가산명사 헹구기, 씻어 내기 ◻ 깨끗한 피부를 위해 비누 거품을 많이 낸 후 물로 헹궈 준다. ◻ 타동사 입을 헹구다 ◻ 혀에도 칫솔질을 하고 입을 자주 헹궈 주세요. ● 구동사 입을 헹구다 ◻ 식사 후 그녀는 꼭 입을 헹궜다. ● 불질명사 입안을 헹굼; 입 안 세척제 ◻ 불소가 든 입안 세척제

◻ 가산명사 폭동 ◻ 교도소 폭동 기간 동안 수감자 12명이 살해됐다. ◻ 자동사 폭동을 일으키다, 난동을 부리다 ◻ 지난해 수감자 600명이 불을 지르고 바리케이드를 치면서 폭동을 일으켰다. ● 폭도 가산명사 ◻ 민병대가 폭도들을 해산시켰다. ● 폭동, 소요 사태 불가산명사 ◻ 3일간의 소요 사태 동안 최소한 15명이 사망한 것으로 알려져 있다. ◻ 단수명사 가지각색의, 다채로운 [마음에 듦] ◻ 양귀비, 붓꽃을 비롯한 모든 종류의 꽃들이 가지각색으로 만발할 것이다. ◻ 구 단단히 혼을 내다 ◻ 빌리를 단단히 혼을 낸다니 기뻐요. 걔가 아직도 어려서 어떻게 해야 하는지 가르쳐 줘야 하거든요. ◻ 구 날뛰다 ◻ 광포한 수감자들이 스트레인지웨이스 감옥 속에서 미친 듯이 날뛰었다. ◻ 구 거칠게 자라다

6 PHRASE If something such as your imagination **runs riot**, it is not limited or controlled, and produces ideas that are new or exciting, rather than sensible. ❏ *She dressed strictly for comfort and economy, but let her imagination run riot with costume jewelry.*

❏ 그녀는 옷의 편안함과 경제성을 엄격히 따져 입지만 의복 장신구로 거침없는 상상력을 발휘한다.

rip /rɪp/ (**rips, ripping, ripped**) **1** V-T/V-I When something **rips** or when you **rip** it, you tear it forcefully with your hands or with a tool such as a knife. ❏ *I felt the banner rip as we were pushed in opposite directions.* **2** N-COUNT A **rip** is a long cut or split in something made of cloth or paper. ❏ *Looking at the rip in her new dress, she flew into a rage.* **3** V-T If you **rip** something **away**, you remove it quickly and forcefully. ❏ *He ripped away a wire that led to the alarm button.* **4** V-I If something **rips** into someone or something or **rips** through them, it enters that person or thing so quickly and forcefully that it often goes completely through them. ❏ *A volley of bullets ripped into the facing wall.* **5** PHRASE If you **let rip**, you do something forcefully and without trying to control yourself. [INFORMAL] ❏ *Turn the guitars up full and let rip.*

1 타동사/자동사 찢어지다; 찢다 ❏ 우리가 반대 방향으로 밀릴 때 현수막이 찢어지는 것이 느껴졌다. **2** 가산명사 찢어진 부분 ❏ 새 드레스가 찢어진 것을 보고 그녀는 벌컥 화를 냈다. **3** 타동사 확 뜯어내다 ❏ 그는 비상 버튼에 연결된 전선을 확 뜯어 버렸다. **4** 자동사 뚫고 지나가다, 뚫고 지나가다 ❏ 총알이 일제히 발사돼 맞은편 벽을 뚫고 들어갔다. **5** 구 발산하다 [비격식체] ❏ 전자 기타를 최대한 크게 틀고 마음껏 연주하세요.

▶**rip off** PHRASAL VERB If someone **rips** you **off**, they cheat you by charging you too much money for something or by selling you something that is broken or damaged. [INFORMAL] ❏ *Ticket touts ripped off soccer fans to the tune of £138,000 in the FA Cup Final.*
→see also **rip-off**

구동사 바가지 씌우다 [비격식체] ❏ 암표 장사들이 축구 팬들에게 에프에이컵 결승전 표를 팔면서 138,000파운드에 달하는 바가지를 씌웠다.

▶**rip up** PHRASAL VERB If you **rip** something **up**, you tear it into small pieces. ❏ *If we wrote I think he would rip up the letter.*

구동사 갈기갈기 찢다 ❏ 내 생각에 우리가 편지를 쓰면 그가 다 찢어 버릴 것 같아.

ripe /raɪp/ (**riper, ripest**) **1** ADJ **Ripe** fruit or grain is fully grown and ready to eat. ❏ *Always choose firm, but ripe fruit.* **2** ADJ If a situation is **ripe for** a particular development or event, you mean that development or event is likely to happen soon. [v-link ADJ for n/-ing] ❏ *A hospital consultant said conditions were ripe for an outbreak of cholera and typhoid.* **3** PHRASE If someone lives to a **ripe old age**, they live until they are very old. ❏ *He lived to the ripe old age of 95.*

1 형용사 익은 ❏ 항상 단단하고 잘 익은 과일을 선택하세요. **2** 형용사 분위기가 무르익은, 알맞은 ❏ 병원의 고문인 전문의가 현재 콜레라와 장티푸스가 발병하기 딱 좋은 조건이라고 밝혔다. **3** 구 노년, 만년 ❏ 그는 95세까지 장수했다.

rip|en /raɪpən/ (**ripens, ripening, ripened**) V-T/V-I When crops **ripen** or when the sun **ripens** them, they become ripe. ❏ *I'm waiting for the apples to ripen.*

타동사/자동사 익다; 익게 하다 ❏ 나는 사과가 익기를 기다리고 있다.

rip-off (**rip-offs**) N-COUNT If you say that something that you bought was a **rip-off**, you mean that you were charged too much money or that it was of very poor quality. [INFORMAL] ❏ *The service charge is a rip-off, but I'm willing to pay if I'm guaranteed a seat.*
guaranteed a seat.

가산명사 바가지 쓴 것 [비격식체] ❏ 바가지요금이긴 하지만 확실히 자리만 하나 구할 수 있다면 돈을 지불할 의향이 있다.

rip|ple /rɪpəl/ (**ripples, rippling, rippled**) **1** N-COUNT **Ripples** are little waves on the surface of water caused by the wind or by something moving in or on the water. ❏ *Gleaming ripples cut the lake's surface.* **2** V-T/V-I When the surface of an area of water **ripples** or when something **ripples** it, a number of little waves appear on it. ❏ *You throw a pebble in a pool and it ripples.* **3** V-I If something such as a feeling **ripples** over someone's body, it moves across it or through it. [LITERARY] ❏ *A chill shiver rippled over his skin.* **4** N-COUNT If an event causes **ripples**, its effects gradually spread, causing several other events to happen one after the other. ❏ *The ripples of Europe's currency crisis continue to be felt in most of the member states.*

1 가산명사 잔물결 ❏ 호수 표면에 잔잔한 물결이 반짝였다. **2** 타동사/자동사 잔물결이 일다; 잔물결을 일으키다 ❏ 연못에 조약돌을 던지면 잔물결이 인다. **3** 자동사 퍼지다 [문예체] ❏ 온 몸에 한기가 퍼졌다. **4** 가산명사 여파, 파문 ❏ 대부분의 회원국들에서 유럽 통화 위기의 여파가 계속 감지되고 있다.

rise ♦♦♦ /raɪz/ (**rises, rising, rose, risen**) **1** V-I If something **rises**, it moves upward. ❏ *Wilson's ice-cold eyes watched the smoke rise from his cigarette.* ● PHRASAL VERB **Rise up** means the same as **rise**. ❏ *Spray rose up from the surface of the water.* **2** V-I When you **rise**, you stand up. [FORMAL] ❏ *Luther rose slowly from the chair.* ● PHRASAL VERB **Rise up** means the same as **rise**. ❏ *The only thing I wanted was to rise up from the table and leave this house.* **3** V-I When you **rise**, you get out of bed. [FORMAL] ❏ *Tony had risen early and gone to the cottage to work.* **4** V-I When the sun or moon **rises**, it appears in the sky. ❏ *He wanted to be over the line of the ridge before the sun had risen.* **5** V-I You can say that something **rises** when it appears as a large tall shape. [LITERARY] ❏ *The building rose before him, tall and stately.* ● PHRASAL VERB **Rise up** means the same as **rise**. ❏ *The White Mountains rose up before me.* **6** V-I If the level of something such as the water in a river **rises**, it becomes higher. ❏ *The waters continue to rise as more than 1,000 people are evacuated.* **7** V-I If land **rises**, it slopes upward. ❏ *He looked up the slope of land that rose from the house.* **8** V-T/V-I If an amount **rises**, it increases. ❏ *Interest rates rise from 4% to 5%.* ❏ *Tourist trips of all kinds in Britain rose by 10.5% between 1977 and 1987.* **9** N-COUNT A **rise in** the amount of something is an increase in it. ❏ *...the prospect of another rise in interest rates.* **10** N-COUNT A **rise** is an increase in your wages or your salary. [BRIT; AM **raise**] ❏ *He will get a pay rise of nearly £4,000.* **11** N-SING The **rise of** a movement or activity is an increase in its popularity or influence. ❏ *The rise of racism in America is a serious concern.* **12** V-I If the wind **rises**, it becomes stronger. ❏ *The wind was still rising, approaching a force nine gale.* **13** V-I If a sound **rises** or if someone's voice **rises**, it becomes louder or higher. ❏ *"Bernard?" Her voice rose hysterically.* **14** V-I When the people in a country **rise**, they try to defeat the government or army that is controlling them. ❏ *The National Convention has promised armed support to any people who wish to rise against armed oppression.* ● PHRASAL VERB **Rise up** means the same as **rise**. ❏ *He warned that if the government moved against them the people would rise up.* **15** V-I If someone **rises to** a higher position or status, they become more important, successful, or powerful. ❏ *She is a strong woman who has risen to the top of a deeply sexist organization.* ● PHRASAL VERB **Rise up** means the same as **rise**. ❏ *I started with Hoover 26 years ago in sales and rose up through the ranks.* **16** N-SING The **rise** of someone is the process by which they become more important, successful, or powerful. ❏ *Haig's rise was fuelled by an all-consuming sense of patriotic duty.* **17** PHRASE If something **gives rise to** an event or situation, it causes that event or situation to happen. ❏ *Low levels of choline in the body can give rise to*

1 자동사 오르다, 올라가다 ❏ 윌슨은 얼음처럼 차가운 눈으로 담배에서 연기가 피어오르는 모습을 지켜봤다. ● 구동사 오르다, 올라가다 ❏ 수면에서 물안개가 피어올랐다. **2** 자동사 일어서다 [격식체] ❏ 루터가 의자에서 천천히 일어섰다. ● 구동사 일어서다 ❏ 내가 유일하게 하고 싶은 것은 식탁에서 일어나 이 집을 떠나는 것이었다. **3** 자동사 일어나다 [격식체] ❏ 토니는 일찍 일어나 오두막으로 일하러 가고 있었다. **4** 자동사 뜨다, 떠오르다 ❏ 그는 해가 뜨기 전에 산등성이를 넘고 싶었다. **5** 자동사 우뚝 솟아오르다 [문예체] ❏ 높고 웅장한 빌딩이 그의 앞에 우뚝 솟아 있었다. ● 구동사 우뚝 솟아오르다 ❏ 눈앞에 화이트 마운틴이 우뚝 솟아 있었다. **6** 자동사 높아지다, 상승하다 ❏ 천 명이 넘는 사람들이 대피하는 동안 수위가 계속 높아지고 있다. **7** 자동사 오르막이 되다 ❏ 그는 집에서 올라가는 오르막길을 올려다보았다. **8** 타동사/자동사 증가하다 ❏ 금리가 4퍼센트에서 5퍼센트로 오른다. ❏ 영국의 총 관광객 수가 1977년에서 1987년 사이 10.5퍼센트 늘었다. **9** 가산명사 증가 ❏ 금리 추가 인상 전망 **10** 가산명사 급여 인상 [영국영어; 미국영어 raise] ❏ 그는 급여가 4천 파운드 가까이 인상될 것이다. **11** 단수명사 부상, 확산 ❏ 미국의 인종주의 확산은 심각한 문제이다. **12** 자동사 일다, 세지다 ❏ 바람이 계속 세지면서 강도 9의 강풍에 가까워졌다. **13** 자동사 높아지다 ❏ "버나드?"라고 그녀의 목소리가 신경질적으로 높아졌다. **14** 자동사 봉기하다 ❏ 무장 압제에 맞서 싸울 의향이 있는 사람은 누구든 군사적으로 지원하겠다고 약속했다. ● 구동사 봉기하다, 들고일어나다 ❏ 정부가 자기네에 반하는 행동을 취하면 민중 봉기가 있을 것이라고 경고했다. **15** 자동사 출세하다, 승진하다 ❏ 그녀는 지극히 남녀 차별적인 조직에서 최고의 자리에까지 오른 강인한 여성이다. ● 구동사 출세하다, 승진하다 ❏ 나는 26년 전 후버에서 영업 사원으로 시작해 꾸준히 승진했다. **16** 단수명사 부상, 출세 ❏ 헤이그의 부상은 활활 타오르는 애국심에 힘입은 바 컸다. **17** 구

A

high blood-pressure. 18 to **rise to the challenge** →see **challenge**. to **rise to the occasion** →see **occasion**

초래하다 ❑ 인체 내 콜린 수치가 낮으면 고혈압이 생길 수 있다.

B

> You should be careful not to confuse the verbs **rise** and **raise**. Rise is an intransitive verb and cannot be followed by an object, whereas **raise** is a transitive verb and is usually followed by an object. Rise can also not be used in the passive. ❑ *The number of dead is likely to rise....the government's decision to raise prices.* Both **raise** and **rise** can be used as nouns with meaning pay increase. **Raise** is used in American English, and **rise** is used in British English. ❑ *Millions of Americans get a pay raise today....a rise of at least 12 per cent.*

동사 rise 와 raise를 혼동하지 않도록 주의해야 한다. rise는 자동사이며 목적어가 따라 오지 않는 반면, raise는 타동사이며 대개 목적어가 뒤에 온다. rise는 또한 수동태로도 쓸 수 없다. ❑ 사망자의 수가 늘어날 것 같다....물가를 인상하려는 정부의 결정. raise 와 rise는 모두 임금 인상을 의미하는 명사로 쓸 수 있다. raise는 미국 영어에서, rise는 영국 영어에서 쓰인다. ❑ 수백만 미국인들의 임금이 오늘 인상된다....적어도 12퍼센트의 임금 인상.

C

D

▶**rise above** PHRASAL VERB If you **rise above** a difficulty or problem, you manage not to let it affect you. ❑ *It tells the story of an aspiring young man's attempt to rise above the squalor of the street.*

구동사 극복하다 ❑ 이는 야심에 찬 젊은이가 누추한 거리 생활을 극복하려는 시도를 담은 이야기이다.

E

▶**rise up** →see **rise 1, 2, 5, 14, 15**

F

risk ♦♦◇ /rɪsk/ (risks, risking, risked) 1 N-VAR If there is a **risk of** something unpleasant, there is a possibility that it will happen. ❑ *There is a small risk of brain damage from the procedure.* 2 N-COUNT If something that you do is a **risk**, it might have unpleasant or undesirable results. ❑ *You're taking a big risk showing this to Kravis.* 3 N-COUNT If you say that something or someone is a **risk**, you mean they are likely to cause harm. ❑ *It's being overfat that constitutes a health risk.* 4 N-COUNT If you are considered a good **risk**, a bank or store thinks that it is safe to lend you money or let you have goods without paying for them at the time. ❑ *Before providing the cash, they will have to decide whether you are a good or bad risk.* 5 V-T If you **risk** something unpleasant, you do something which might result in that thing happening or affecting you. ❑ *Those who fail to register risk severe penalties.* 6 V-T If you **risk** doing something, you do it, even though you know that it might have undesirable consequences. ❑ *The skipper was not willing to risk taking his ship through the straits until he could see where he was going.* 7 V-T If you **risk** your life or something else important, you behave in a way that might result in it being lost or harmed. ❑ *She risked her own life to help a disabled woman.* 8 PHRASE To be **at risk** means to be in a situation where something unpleasant might happen. ❑ *Up to 25,000 jobs are still at risk.* 9 PHRASE If you do something **at the risk of** something unpleasant happening, you do it even though you know that the unpleasant thing might happen again a result. ❑ *At the risk of being repetitive, I will say again that statistics are only a guide.* 10 PHRASE If you tell someone that they are doing something at their **own risk**, you are warning them that, if they are harmed, it will be their own responsibility. ❑ *Those who wish to come here will do so at their own risk.* 11 PHRASE If you **run the risk of** doing or experiencing something undesirable, you do something knowing that the undesirable thing might happen as a result. ❑ *The officers had run the risk of being dismissed.*

1 가산명사 또는 불가산명사 위험, 위험성 ❑ 시술로 두뇌 손상을 입을 위험이 조금 있다. 2 가산명사 위험, 모험 ❑ 네가 이것을 크라비스에게 보여 주는 건 큰 모험을 하는 거야. 3 가산명사 위험 분자, 위험 요인 ❑ 건강상 위험 요인이 되는 것은 지나친 비만이다. 4 가산명사 상환 가능성 ❑ 돈을 빌려 주기 전에 그들은 당신의 상환 가능성이 좋은지 안 좋은지 판단해야 할 것이다. 5 타동사 ~할 위험이 있다 ❑ 등록을 못한 사람들은 엄중한 처벌을 받을 위험이 있다. 6 타동사 위험을 무릅쓰고 하다 ❑ 선장은 배가 나아가는 방향을 눈으로 확인할 수 있을 때까지 위험 속으로 배를 몰고 가는 위험을 무릅쓰고 싶지 않았다. 7 타동사 걸다 ❑ 그녀는 자신의 목숨을 걸고 한 장애인 여성을 도왔다. 8 구 위험한 상태에 있는 ❑ 자그마치 2만 5천 명의 사람들이 아직도 직장을 잃을 위기에 처해 있다. 9 구 ~을 무릅쓰고 ❑ 같은 말을 반복하는 무례를 무릅쓰고, 통계만이 유일한 지표라고 다시 한 번 말씀드리겠습니다. 10 구 자신이 책임지고 ❑ 여기 오고 싶은 사람은 그렇게 하세요. 단, 모든 책임은 자신이 져야 합니다. 11 구 위험을 무릅쓰다 ❑ 그 장교들은 해임당할 위험을 무릅썼다.

G

H

I

J

K

L

M

N

Thesaurus	risk의 참조어
N.	danger, gamble, hazard; (ant.) safety 2 3
V.	chance, endanger, gamble, jeopardize 5 7

O

risk man|age|ment N-UNCOUNT **Risk management** is the skill or job of deciding what the risks are in a particular situation and taking action to prevent or reduce them. ❑ *Good risk management and higher sales can both boost profits.*

불가산명사 위험 관리 ❑ 우수한 위험 관리와 매출 향상 둘 다 이윤을 높일 수 있다.

P

risky /rɪski/ (riskier, riskiest) ADJ If an activity or action is **risky**, it is dangerous or likely to fail. ❑ *Investing in airlines is a very risky business.*

형용사 위험한, 모험적인 ❑ 항공사 투자는 매우 위험한 사업이다.

Q

rite /raɪt/ (rites) N-COUNT A **rite** is a traditional ceremony that is carried out by a particular group or within a particular society. ❑ *Most traditional societies have transition rites at puberty.*

가산명사 의식, 의례 ❑ 대부분의 전통 사회에서는 사춘기에 통과 의례를 치른다.

R

ritu|al /rɪtʃuəl/ (rituals) 1 N-VAR A **ritual** is a religious service or other ceremony which involves a series of actions performed in a fixed order. ❑ *This is the most ancient, and holiest of the Shinto rituals.* 2 ADJ **Ritual** activities happen as part of a ritual or tradition. [ADJ n] ❑ *...fastings and ritual dancing.* 3 N-VAR A **ritual** is a way of behaving or a series of actions which people regularly carry out in a particular situation, because it is their custom to do so. ❑ *The whole Italian culture revolves around the ritual of eating.* 4 ADJ You can describe something as a **ritual** action when it is done in exactly the same way whenever a particular situation occurs. [ADJ n] ❑ *I realized that here the conventions required me to make the ritual noises.* →see **myth**

1 가산명사 또는 불가산명사 (종교적인) 의식 ❑ 이는 일본 신도 의식 중 가장 역사가 깊고 성스러운 의식이다. 2 형용사 의식의 ❑ 의식을 위한 춤 3 가산명사 또는 불가산명사 관습, 습관, 특정한 상황에 꼭 하는 일 ❑ 이탈리아 문화 전체가 식생활 문화를 중심으로 돌아간다. 4 형용사 의례적인 ❑ 나는 여기서 사회 관습상 의례적인 소리를 내야 한다는 것을 깨달았다.

S

ri|val ♦♦◇ /raɪvªl/ (rivals, rivaling, rivaled) [BRIT **rivalling, rivalled**] 1 N-COUNT Your **rival** is a person, business, or organization who you are competing or fighting against in the same area or for the same things. ❑ *The world champion finished more than two seconds ahead of his nearest rival.* 2 N-COUNT If you say that someone or something has **no rivals** or is **without rival**, you mean that it is best of its type. ❑ *The area is famous for its wonderfully fragrant wine which has no rivals in the Rhone.* 3 V-T If you say that one thing **rivals** another, you mean that they are both of the same standard or quality. ❑ *Cassette recorders cannot rival the sound quality of CDs.*

[영국영어 rivalling, rivalled] 1 가산명사 경쟁 상대 ❑ 세계 챔피언은 2위 선수보다 2초 이상 먼저 결승선을 통과했다. 2 가산명사 맞수, 필적할 만한 상대 ❑ 그 지역은 론에서 타의 추종을 불허하는 향이 훌륭한 와인으로 유명하다. 3 타동사 필적하다, 맞먹다 ❑ 카세트 녹음기는 시디 음질을 따라잡을 수 없다.

T

U

V

ri|val|ry /raɪvªlri/ (rivalries) N-VAR **Rivalry** is competition or fighting between people, businesses, or organizations who are in the same area or want the same things. ❑ *The rivalry between the Inkatha and the ANC has resulted in violence in the black townships.*

가산명사 또는 불가산명사 경쟁, 대항 ❑ 잉카타와 아프리카 민족 동맹 사이의 적대적인 관계 때문에 흑인 마을에 폭력 사태가 벌어졌다.

W

X

riv|er ♦♦◇ /rɪvər/ (rivers) N-COUNT A **river** is a large amount of fresh water flowing continuously in a long line across the land. ❑ *...a chemical works on the banks of the river.*
→see Picture Dictionary: **river**

가산명사 강 ❑ 강둑 위의 화학 공장

Y

Z

Picture Dictionary river spring lake stream gorge valley river delta ocean

river|side /rɪvərsaɪd/ N-SING The **riverside** is the area of land by the banks of a river. ❑ *They walked back along the riverside.*

riv|et /rɪvɪt/ (**rivets, riveting, riveted**) V-T If you **are riveted** by something, it fascinates you and holds your interest completely. ❑ *As a child I remember being riveted by my grandfather's appearance.* ❑ *He was riveted to the John Wayne movie.*

riv|et|ing /rɪvɪtɪŋ/ ADJ If you describe something as **riveting**, you mean that it is extremely interesting and exciting, and that it holds your attention completely. ❑ *...Jeffrey Wolf's riveting new novel.*

roach /roʊtʃ/ (**roaches**) N-COUNT A **roach** is the same as a **cockroach**. [mainly AM] ❑ *He found his brother in a seedy, roach-infested apartment.*

road ♦♦♦ /roʊd/ (**roads**) **1** N-COUNT A **road** is a long piece of hard ground which is built between two places so that people can drive or ride easily from one place to the other. [oft in names, also by N] ❑ *There was very little traffic on the roads.* ❑ *We just go straight up the Bristol Road.* **2** N-COUNT The **road to** a particular result is the means of achieving it or the process of achieving it. ❑ *We are bound to see some ups and downs along the road to recovery.* **3** PHRASE If you say that someone is **on the road to** something, you mean that they are likely to achieve it. ❑ *The government took another step on the road to political reform.* **4** the end of the road →see end
→see traffic

road rage N-UNCOUNT **Road rage** is anger or violent behavior caused by someone else's bad driving or the stress of being in heavy traffic. ❑ *Two women were being hunted by police after a road rage attack on a male motorist.*

road|side /roʊdsaɪd/ (**roadsides**) N-COUNT The **roadside** is the area at the edge of a road. ❑ *Bob was forced to leave the car at the roadside and run for help.*

road|works /roʊdwɜrks/ N-PLURAL **Roadworks** are repairs or other work being done on a road. ❑ *The traffic was stationary due to three sets of roadworks in less than a mile.*

roam /roʊm/ (**roams, roaming, roamed**) V-T/V-I If you **roam** an area or **roam around** it, you wander or travel around it without having a particular purpose. ❑ *Barefoot children roamed the streets.* ❑ *I spent a couple of years roaming around the countryside, sleeping rough.*

roam|ing /roʊmɪŋ/ N-UNCOUNT **Roaming** refers to the service provided by a cellphone company which makes it possible for you to use your cellphone when you travel. ❑ *International Roaming is your digital mobile phone's passport to travel but the cost of calls is high.*

roar /rɔr/ (**roars, roaring, roared**) **1** V-I If something, usually a vehicle, **roars** somewhere, it goes there very fast, making a loud noise. [WRITTEN] ❑ *A police car roared past.* **2** V-I If something **roars**, it makes a very loud noise. [WRITTEN] ❑ *The engine roared, and the vehicle leapt forward.* ● N-COUNT **Roar** is also a noun. ❑ *...the roar of traffic.* **3** V-I If someone **roars with** laughter, they laugh in a very noisy way. ❑ *Max threw back his head and roared with laughter.* ● N-COUNT **Roar** is also a noun. ❑ *There were roars of laughter as he stood up.* **4** V-T/V-I If someone **roars**, they shout something in a very loud voice. [WRITTEN] ❑ *"I'll kill you for that," he roared.* ❑ *During the playing of the national anthem the crowd roared and whistled.* ● N-COUNT **Roar** is also a noun. ❑ *There was a roar of approval.* **5** V-I When a lion **roars**, it makes the loud sound that lions typically make. ❑ *The lion roared once, and sprang.* ● N-COUNT **Roar** is also a noun. ❑ *...the roar of lions in the distance.*

roar|ing /rɔrɪŋ/ **1** ADJ A **roaring** fire has large flames and is sending out a lot of heat. [ADJ n] ❑ *...nighttime beach parties, with a roaring fire.* **2** ADJ If something is

단수명사 강변 ❑ 그들은 강변을 따라 되돌아 걸었다.

타동사 사로잡히다 ❑ 어린 시절 내가 할아버지 모습에 사로잡혔던 기억이 난다. ❑ 그는 존 웨인의 영화에 사로잡혔다.

형용사 눈을 뗄 수 없는, 마음을 사로잡는 ❑ 제프리 울프의 마음을 사로잡는 신작 소설

가산명사 바퀴벌레 [주로 미국영어] ❑ 그는 지저분하고 바퀴벌레가 들끓는 아파트에서 형을 발견했다.

1 가산명사 길, 도로 ❑ 도로에 차가 거의 없었다. ❑ 우리는 브리스톨 로드를 곧장 올라가기만 하면 돼. **2** 가산명사 방법, 과정 ❑ 우리는 회복하는 과정에 어느 정도 우여곡절을 겪게 될 것이다. **3** 구 -로 이르는 길에서 ❑ 정부는 정치 개혁에 이르는 길에서 한 걸음 더 나아갔다.

불가산명사 도로상에서 분통을 터뜨리는 일 ❑ 여자 두 명이 횟김에 남성 운전자를 친 후 경찰의 추격을 받고 있었다.

가산명사 길가, 노변 ❑ 밥은 차를 길가에 세워 놓고 도와줄 사람을 찾으러 달려갈 수밖에 없었다.

복수명사 도로 공사 ❑ 1마일 이내의 도로 세 곳에서 공사가 진행 중이어서 교통 정체가 빚어졌다.

타동사/자동사 배회하다, 돌아다니다 ❑ 맨발인 아이들이 거리를 배회했다. ❑ 나는 두어 해 동안 시골을 돌아다니며 한뎃잠을 잤다.

불가산명사 로밍 서비스 ❑ 해외 로밍 서비스는 여행 시 휴대 전화의 디지털 여권과 같지만 전화 요금이 비싸다.

1 자동사 굉음을 내며 가다 [문어체] ❑ 경찰차가 굉음을 내며 지나갔다. **2** 자동사 굉음을 내다 [문어체] ❑ 엔진이 굉음을 내더니 차가 앞으로 잽싸게 튀어 나갔다. ● 가산명사 굉음 ❑ 시끄러운 자동차 소리 **3** 자동사 큰 소리로 웃다, 박장대소를 하다 ❑ 맥스가 고개를 뒤로 젖히고 큰 소리로 웃었다. ● 가산명사 큰 웃음소리 ❑ 그가 일어서자 웃음소리가 왁자지껄 터져 나왔다. **4** 타동사/자동사 소리를 지르다, 으르렁거리다 [문어체] ❑ "그렇게 한 널 죽여 버리겠어."라고 그가 악을 쓰며 말했다. ❑ 국가가 연주되는 동안 군중들이 함성을 지르고 휘파람을 불었다. ● 가산명사 외침, 함성 ❑ 찬성의 외침이 터져 나왔다. **5** 자동사 으르렁거리다 ❑ 사자가 한번 으르렁거리더니 뛰어올랐다. ● 가산명사 포효, 으르렁거리는 소리 ❑ 멀리서 사자들이 포효하는 소리

1 형용사 활활 타오르는 ❑ 밤에 해변에서 활활 타오르는 모닥불과 함께 하는 파티 **2** 형용사

a **roaring** success, it is very successful indeed. [ADJ n] ❑ *The government's first effort to privatize a company has been a roaring success.* ❸ →see also **roar**

roast /rou̇st/ (**roasts, roasting, roasted**) ❶ V-T When you **roast** meat or other food, you cook it by dry heat in an oven or over a fire. ❑ *I personally would rather roast a chicken whole.* ❷ ADJ **Roast** meat has been cooked by roasting. [ADJ n] ❑ *They serve the most delicious roast beef.* ❸ N-COUNT A **roast** is a piece of meat that is cooked by roasting. ❑ *Come into the kitchen. I've got to put the roast in.* →see **cook**

rob /rɒb/ (**robs, robbing, robbed**) ❶ V-T If someone **is robbed**, they have money or property stolen from them. ❑ *Mrs. Yacoub was robbed of her £3,000 designer watch at her West London home.* ❷ V-T If someone **is robbed of** something that they deserve, have, or need, it is taken away from them. ❑ *When Miles Davis died last September, jazz was robbed of its most distinctive voice.*

> Do not confuse **rob** and **steal**. If someone **robs** someone or somewhere, they take something, often violently, from that person or place without asking and without intending to give it back. ❑ *They planned to rob an old widow… They joined forces to rob a factory.* You can also say that someone **robs** you of something when referring to what has been taken. ❑ *The two men were robbed of more than $700.* If someone **steals** something, for example, money or a car, they take it without asking and without intending to give it back. ❑ *My car was stolen on Friday evening.* Note that you cannot say that someone **steals** someone.

rob|ber /rɒbər/ (**robbers**) N-COUNT A **robber** is someone who steals money or property from a bank, store, or vehicle, often by using force or threats. ❑ *Armed robbers broke into a jeweler's through a hole in the wall.*

> Anyone who steals can be called a **thief**. A **robber** often uses violence or the threat of violence to steal things from places such as banks or businesses. A **burglar** breaks into houses or other buildings and steals things.

rob|bery /rɒbəri/ (**robberies**) N-VAR **Robbery** is the crime of stealing money or property from a bank, store, or vehicle, often by using force or threats. ❑ *The gang members committed dozens of armed robberies over the past year.*

robe /roub/ (**robes**) ❶ N-COUNT A **robe** is a loose piece of clothing which covers all of your body and reaches the ground. You can describe someone as wearing a **robe** or as wearing **robes**. [FORMAL] ❑ *Pope John Paul II knelt in his white robes before the simple altar.* ❷ N-COUNT A **robe** is a piece of clothing, usually made of toweling, which people wear in the house, especially when they have just gotten up or taken a bath. ❑ *Ryle put on a robe and went down to the kitchen.*

ro|bot /roubɒt, -bət, BRIT roubɒt/ (**robots**) N-COUNT A **robot** is a machine which is programmed to move and perform certain tasks automatically. ❑ *…very light-weight robots that we could send to the moon for planetary exploration.* →see **mass production**

ro|bust /roubʌst, roubʌst/ ❶ ADJ Someone or something that is **robust** is very strong or healthy. ❑ *More women than men go to the doctor. Perhaps men are more robust or worry less?* ❷ ADJ **Robust** views or opinions are strongly held and forcefully expressed. ❑ *A British Foreign Office minister has made a robust defence of the agreement.*

rock ♦♦◇ /rɒk/ (**rocks, rocking, rocked**) ❶ N-UNCOUNT **Rock** is the hard substance which the Earth is made of. ❑ *The hills above the valley are bare rock.* ❷ N-COUNT A **rock** is a large piece of rock that sticks up out of the ground or the sea, or that has broken away from a mountain or a cliff. ❑ *She sat cross-legged on the rock.* ❸ N-COUNT A **rock** is a piece of rock that is small enough for you to pick up. ❑ *She bent down, picked up a rock and threw it into the trees.* ❹ V-T/V-I When something **rocks** or when you **rock** it, it moves slowly and regularly backward and forward or from side to side. ❑ *His body rocked from side to side with the train.* ❺ V-T/V-I If an explosion or an earthquake **rocks** a building or an area, it causes the building or area to shake. [JOURNALISM] ❑ *Three people were injured yesterday when an explosion rocked one of Britain's best known film studios.* ❻ V-T If an event or a piece of news **rocks** a group or society, it shocks them or makes them feel less secure. [JOURNALISM] ❑ *His death rocked the fashion business.* ❼ N-UNCOUNT **Rock** is loud music with a strong beat that is usually played and sung by a small group of people using instruments such as electric guitars and drums. ❑ *…a rock concert.* ❽ N-UNCOUNT **Rock** is candy that is made in long, hard sticks and is often sold in towns by the sea in Britain. [BRIT] ❑ *…a stick of rock.* →see **concert, crystal, earth, fossil**

rock and roll also **rock'n'roll** N-UNCOUNT **Rock and roll** is a kind of popular music developed in the 1950s which has a strong beat and is played on electrical instruments. ❑ *…Elvis Presley – the King of Rock and Roll.*

rock bot|tom also **rock-bottom** ❶ N-UNCOUNT If something has reached **rock bottom**, it is at such a low level that it cannot go any lower. ❑ *Morale in the armed forces was at rock bottom.* ❷ ADJ A **rock-bottom** price or level is a very low one, mainly in advertisements. [APPROVAL] ❑ *What they do offer is a good product at a rock-bottom price.*

rock|et ♦◇◇ /rɒkɪt/ (**rockets, rocketing, rocketed**) ❶ N-COUNT A **rocket** is a space vehicle that is shaped like a long tube. ❑ *…the Apollo 12 rocket that took astronauts to the moon.* ❷ N-COUNT A **rocket** is a missile containing explosive that is powered by gas. ❑ *There has been a renewed rocket attack on the capital.*

대성공의 ❑ 기업 민영화를 위한 정부의 첫 시도는 대성공이었다. ❸ →see also **roar**

❶ 타동사 (오븐 등에) 굽다 ❑ 나 같으면 닭을 통째로 굽겠다. ❷ 형용사 구운 ❑ 그들은 가장 맛있는 쇠고기구이를 판다. ❸ 가산명사 고기구이, 로스트 ❑ 부엌으로 오세요. 오븐에 로스트 감을 넣어야 해요. →see **cook**

❶ 타동사 도둑맞다 ❑ 야쿱 여사는 웨스트 런던 집에서 3천 파운드짜리 고가 시계를 도둑맞았다. ❷ 타동사 빼앗기다 ❑ 지난 9월 마일스 데이비스의 사망으로 재즈계는 가장 특색 있는 목소리를 잃었다.

> rob과 steal을 혼동하지 않도록 하라. 어떤 사람이 누구를 또는 어디를 rob하면, 그 사람이 누구 또는 어디로부터 요청하거나 되돌려 줄 의사가 없이 흔히 폭력을 써서 무엇을 가져가는 것이다. ❑ 그들은 한 나이든 미망인에게 강도짓을 하려고 계획했다… 그들은 공장을 털려고 힘을 합쳤다. 빼앗긴 것을 나타내려 할 때는 someone robs you of something이라고 할 수도 있다. ❑ 그 두 남자는 700 달러 이상을 강탈당했다. 어떤 사람이 무엇을, 예를 들어 돈이나 자동차를 steal하면, 그것을 요청하지 않거나 되돌려 줄 의사가 없이 가져가는 것이다. ❑ 내 자동차는 금요일 저녁에 도둑맞았다. 누가 누구를 steal 한다고 말할 수는 없음을 유의하라.

가산명사 강도, 도둑 ❑ 무장 강도가 벽에 난 구멍을 통해 보석상 안으로 침입했다.

> 물건을 훔치는 사람은 누구든 thief이라고 부를 수 있다. robber는 흔히 은행이나 사무실 같은 장소에서 물건을 훔치기 위해 폭력을 사용하거나, 폭력을 사용하겠다고 위협한다. burglar는 집이나 여타 건물에 침입하여 물건을 훔친다.

가산명사 또는 불가산명사 강도 (범행) ❑ 그 폭력단원들은 지난 한 해 동안 수십 건의 무장 강도 범행을 저질렀다.

❶ 가산명사 가운, 예복 [격식체] ❑ 교황 요한 바오로 2세가 흰색 예복을 입고 소박한 제단 앞에서 무릎을 꿇었다. ❷ 가산명사 가운, 목욕 가운 ❑ 라일이 가운을 입고 부엌으로 내려갔다.

가산명사 로봇 ❑ 행성 탐험을 위해 달로 보낼 수 있는 매우 가벼운 로봇

❶ 형용사 건장한, 튼튼한 ❑ 남자보다 여자가 병원에 많이 간다. 남자가 더 튼튼하고 걱정을 덜 해서 그럴까? ❷ 형용사 확고한 ❑ 영국 외무부 장관이 그 협약에 대한 확고한 지지 의사를 표명했다.

❶ 불가산명사 암석 ❑ 계곡 위 언덕은 벌거벗은 암석 덩이다. ❷ 가산명사 바위 ❑ 그녀가 바위 위에 다리를 꼬고 앉았다. ❸ 가산명사 돌, 돌멩이 ❑ 그녀가 허리를 굽혀 돌 하나를 주워 숲 속으로 던졌다. ❹ 타동사/자동사 흔들리다, 흔들다 ❑ 그의 몸이 기차와 함께 이리저리 흔들렸다. ❺ 타동사/자동사 흔들다 [언론] ❑ 어제 영국에서 가장 유명한 영화 제작사 중 한 곳의 폭발에 흔들리면서 3명이 부상당했다. ❻ 타동사 동요시키다, 뒤흔들어 놓다 [언론] ❑ 그의 죽음이 의류 산업을 뒤흔들어 놓았다. ❼ 불가산명사 록음악 ❑ 록 콘서트 ❽ 불가산명사 막대 사탕 [영국영어] ❑ 막대 사탕 하나

불가산명사 로큰롤 ❑ 로큰롤의 황제 엘비스 프레슬리

❶ 불가산명사 최저, 밑바닥 ❑ 군대 사기가 밑바닥까지 떨어져 있었다. ❷ 형용사 최저의 [마음에 듦] ❑ 그들은 정말 최저가에 양질의 상품을 제공한다.

❶ 가산명사 로켓 ❑ 우주 비행사를 달로 싣고 간 아폴로 12호 로켓 ❷ 가산명사 로켓 미사일 ❑ 수도에 로켓 미사일 공격이 재개되었다. ❸ 가산명사 불꽃, 신호탄 ❹ 자동사 치솟다 [언론] ❑ 신선한 식품이 귀한

⒊ N-COUNT A **rocket** is a firework that quickly goes high into the air and then explodes. **⒋** V-I If things such as prices or social problems **rocket**, they increase very quickly and suddenly. [JOURNALISM] ❑ *Fresh food is so scarce that prices have rocketed.* **⒌** V-I If something such as a vehicle **rockets** somewhere, it moves there very quickly. ❑ *A train rocketed by, shaking the walls of the row houses.*

rocky /ˈrɒki/ (**rockier, rockiest**) **⒈** ADJ A **rocky** place is covered with rocks or consists of large areas of rock and has nothing growing on it. ❑ *The paths are often very rocky so strong boots are advisable.* **⒉** ADJ A **rocky** situation or relationship is unstable and full of difficulties. ❑ *They had gone through some rocky times together when Ann was first married.*

rod /rɒd/ (**rods**) N-COUNT A **rod** is a long, thin metal or wooden bar. ❑ *...a 15-foot thick roof that was reinforced with steel rods.*

rode /roʊd/ **Rode** is the past tense of **ride**.

rodent /ˈroʊdənt/ (**rodents**) N-COUNT **Rodents** are small mammals which have sharp front teeth. Rats, mice, and squirrels are rodents.

rodeo /ˈroʊdioʊ, roʊˈdeɪoʊ/ (**rodeos**) N-COUNT In the United States, a **rodeo** is a public entertainment event in which cowboys show different skills, including riding wild horses and catching cattle with ropes.

rogue /roʊg/ (**rogues**) **⒈** N-COUNT A **rogue** is a man who behaves in a dishonest or criminal way. ❑ *Mr. Ward wasn't a rogue at all.* **⒉** N-COUNT If a man behaves in a way that you do not approve of but you still like him, you can refer to him as a **rogue**. [FEELINGS] ❑ *...Falstaff, the loveable rogue.* **⒊** ADJ A **rogue** element is someone or something that behaves differently from others of its kind, often causing damage. [ADJ n] ❑ *Computer systems throughout the country are being affected by a series of mysterious rogue programs, known as viruses.*

role ♦♦♦ /roʊl/ (**roles**) **⒈** N-COUNT If you have a **role** in a situation or in society, you have a particular position and function in it. ❑ *Until now scientists had very little clear evidence about the drug's role in preventing more serious effects of infection.* **⒉** N-COUNT A **role** is one of the characters that an actor or singer can play in a movie, play, or opera. ❑ *She has just landed the lead role in The Young Vic's latest production.*

Word Partnership		*role*의 연어
N.	leadership role, role **reversal** ⒈	
	lead role ⒈ ⒉	
ADJ.	**active** role, **key** role, **parental** role, **positive** role, **significant** role, **traditional** role, **vital** role ⒈	
V.	**leading** role, **major** role ⒈ ⒉	
	play a role, **take on** a role ⒈ ⒉	

role model (**role models**) N-COUNT A **role model** is someone you admire and try to imitate. ❑ *Five out of the ten top role models for British teenagers are black.*

roll ♦♦◊ /roʊl/ (**rolls, rolling, rolled**) **⒈** V-T/V-I When something **rolls** or when you **roll** it, it moves along a surface, turning over many times. ❑ *The ball rolled into the net.* **⒉** V-I If you **roll** somewhere, you move on a surface while lying down, turning your body over and over, so that you are sometimes on your back, sometimes on your side, and sometimes on your front. ❑ *When I was a little kid I rolled down a hill and broke my leg.* **⒊** V-I When vehicles **roll** along, they move slowly. ❑ *The lorry quietly rolled forward and demolished all the old wooden fencing.* **⒋** V-I If a machine **rolls**, it is operating. ❑ *He slipped and fell on an airplane gangway as the cameras rolled.* **⒌** V-I If drops of liquid **roll** down a surface, they move quickly down it. ❑ *She looked at Ginny and tears rolled down her cheeks.* **⒍** V-T If you **roll** something flexible **into** a cylinder or a ball, you form it into a cylinder or a ball by wrapping it several times around itself or by shaping it between your hands. ❑ *He took off his sweater, rolled it into a pillow and lay down on the grass.* ● PHRASAL VERB **Roll up** means the same as **roll**. ❑ *Stein rolled up the paper bag with the money inside.* **⒎** N-COUNT A **roll** of paper, plastic, cloth, or wire is a long piece of it that has been wrapped many times around itself or around a tube. ❑ *The photographers had already shot a dozen rolls of film.* **⒏** V-T If you **roll up** something such as a car window or a blind, you cause it to move upward by turning a handle. If you **roll** it **down**, you cause it to move downward by turning a handle. ❑ *In mid-afternoon, shopkeepers began to roll down their shutters.* **⒐** V-T/V-I If you **roll** your eyes or if your eyes **roll**, they move around and upward. People sometimes roll their eyes when they are frightened, bored, or annoyed. [WRITTEN] ❑ *People may roll their eyes and talk about overprotective, interfering grandmothers.* **⒑** N-COUNT A **roll** is a small piece of bread that is round or long and is made to be eaten by one person. Rolls can be eaten plain, with butter, or with a filling. ❑ *He sipped at his coffee and spread butter and marmalade on a roll.* **⒒** N-COUNT A **roll** of drums is a long, low, fairly loud sound made by drums. ❑ *As the town clock struck two, they heard the roll of drums.* **⒓** N-COUNT A **roll** is an official list of people's names. ❑ *Pro-democracy activists say a new electoral roll should be drawn up.* **⒔** →see also **rolling, rock and roll ⒕** PHRASE If something is several things **rolled into one**, it combines the main features or qualities of those things. ❑ *This is our kitchen, sitting and dining room all rolled into one.* **⒖** **heads will roll** →see **head**

▶**roll back** PHRASAL VERB To **roll back** prices, taxes, or benefits means to reduce them. [mainly AM] ❑ *One provision of the law was to roll back taxes to the 1975 level.*

▶**roll in** PHRASAL VERB If something such as money **is rolling in**, it is appearing or being received in large quantities. [INFORMAL] ❑ *Don't forget, I have always kept the money rolling in.*

▶**roll up** ⒈ PHRASAL VERB If you **roll up** your sleeves or pant legs, you fold the ends back several times, making them shorter. ❑ *The jacket was too big for him so*

까닭에 가격이 치솟았다. **⒌** 자동사 돌진하다 ❑ 기차가 빠르게 지나가자 연립 주택 벽이 흔들렸다.

⒈ 형용사 바위투성이의 ❑ 길 중간 중간 바위가 많기 때문에 튼튼한 부츠를 신는 것이 좋다. **⒉** 형용사 불안정한, 힘든 ❑ 앤이 처음 결혼했을 때는 그들이 힘든 시기를 함께 견디 낸 후였다.

가산명사 막대기, 봉 ❑ 강철봉으로 보강된 15피트 두께의 지붕

ride의 과거

가산명사 설치 동물

가산명사 로데오 (카우보이들이 기술을 겨루는 행사)

⒈ 가산명사 악한, 악당 ❑ 와드 씨는 전혀 나쁜 사람이 아니었다. **⒉** 가산명사 귀여운 악당 [감정 개입] ❑ 귀여운 악당 폴스타프 **⒊** 형용사 불순한, 불량한 ❑ 전국 컴퓨터 시스템이 바이러스로 알려진 정체를 알 수 없는 일련의 불량 프로그램으로 인해 피해를 입고 있다.

⒈ 가산명사 역할 ❑ 그 당시까지 과학자들은 감염의 더 큰 피해를 예방하는 데 그 약이 어떤 역할을 하는지에 대한 명확한 증거가 거의 없었다. **⒉** 가산명사 배역 ❑ 그녀는 얼마 전 '영 빅' 최신작의 주인공 역으로 낙찰되었다.

가산명사 역할 모델, 우상 ❑ 영국 청소년들 사이에서 가장 인기 있는 우상 10명 중 5명이 흑인이다.

⒈ 타동사/자동사 구르다; 굴리다 ❑ 공이 네트 안으로 굴러 들어갔다. **⒉** 자동사 구르다 ❑ 나는 어린 시절 언덕 아래로 굴러서 다리가 부러진 적이 있다. **⒊** 자동사 굴러가다, 천천히 나아가다 ❑ 화물 트럭이 조용히 그리고 천천히 앞으로 굴러가면서 오래된 나무 담장을 전부 허물었다. **⒋** 자동사 돌아가다 ❑ 카메라가 돌아가는 가운데 그가 비행기 트랩에서 발을 헛디뎌 넘어졌다. **⒌** 자동사 굴러 떨어지다, 흘러내리다 ❑ 그녀가 지니를 바라보는데, 눈물이 두 뺨에 흘러내렸다. **⒍** 타동사 말아 만들다, 동그랗게 말다 ❑ 그는 스웨터를 벗은 후 돌돌 말아서 베개로 만든 다음 잔디 위에 누웠다. ● 구동사 돌돌 말다, 동그랗게 말다 ❑ 스타인은 안에 돈이 든 종이봉투를 돌돌 말았다. **⒎** 가산명사 두루마리, 돌돌 말이 놓은 것 ❑ 사진작가들이 이미 필름 12통을 찍은 상태였다. **⒏** 타동사 말아 올리다; 롤을 내리다 ❑ 한낮에 가게 주인들이 셔터를 내리기 시작했다. **⒐** 타동사/자동사 (눈동자를) 굴리다; (눈을) 부라리다 [문어체] ❑ 사람들이 눈을 부라리며 과보호에 간섭이 심한 할머니들에 대해 이야기할지도 모른다. **⒑** 가산명사 롤빵 ❑ 그는 커피를 마시면서 롤빵에 버터와 마멀레이드를 발랐다. **⒒** 가산명사 연달아 크게 울리는 북소리 ❑ 마을 시계가 2시를 알릴 때 그들은 북소리를 들었다. **⒓** 가산명사 명부 ❑ 민주주의 운동가들이 선거인 명부를 새로 작성해야 한다고 주장한다. **⒕** 구 하나로 합친 ❑ 여기가 우리 집 부엌, 거실, 식당을 전부 하나로 합쳐 놓은 곳이다.

구동사 내리다, 줄이다 [주로 미국영어] ❑ 법률 조항 중 하나가 1975년 수준으로 세금을 삭감하는 것이었다.

구동사 많이 모이다, 굴러 들어오다 [비격식체] ❑ 잊지 마세요. 난 항상 돈이 굴러 들어오게 했어요.

⒈ 구동사 걷어붙이다, 걷어 올리다 ❑ 그는 재킷이 너무 커서 소매를 걷어 올렸다. **⒉** 구동사 모여들다

he rolled up the cuffs. **2** PHRASAL VERB If people **roll up** somewhere, they arrive there, especially in large numbers, to see something interesting. [INFORMAL] ❏ *Roll up, roll up, come and join The Greatest Show on Earth.* **3** →see also **roll 6**

[비격식체] ❏ 모이세요, 모이세요. 와서 '지상에서 가장 훌륭한 쇼'에 참여하세요.

roll|er /roʊlər/ (rollers) **1** N-COUNT A **roller** is a cylinder that turns around in a machine or device. **2** N-COUNT **Rollers** are hollow tubes that women roll their hair round in order to make it curly. ❏ *James's mother gets up every morning and puts her hair in rollers.*

1 가산명사 롤러 **2** 가산명사 헤어롤 ❏ 제임스의 엄마는 매일 아침 일어나면 헤어롤로 머리를 만다.

Roll|er|blade /roʊlərbleɪd/ (Rollerblades) N-COUNT **Rollerblades** are a type of roller skates with a single line of wheels along the bottom. [TRADEMARK] ● **roll|er|blad|ing** N-UNCOUNT ❏ *Rollerblading is great for all ages.*

가산명사 롤러블레이드 [상표] ● 롤러블레이드 타기 불가산명사 ❏ 롤러블레이드는 나이에 상관없이 탈 수 있다.

roll|er-coast|er (roller-coasters) also **rollercoaster** **1** N-COUNT A **roller-coaster** is a small railroad at an amusement park that goes up and down steep slopes fast and that people ride on for pleasure or excitement. ❏ *It's great to go on the roller coaster five times and not be sick.* **2** N-COUNT If you say that someone or something is on a **roller-coaster**, you mean that they go through many sudden or extreme changes in a short time. [JOURNALISM] ❏ *I've been on an emotional roller-coaster since I've been here.*

1 가산명사 롤러코스터 ❏ 롤러코스터를 다섯 번이나 타고도 멀미가 나지 않아 좋다. **2** 가산명사 단기간의 심한 변화 [언론] ❏ 여기에 온 후로 나는 기분이 하루에도 몇 번씩 변했다.

roll|er-skate (roller-skates, roller-skating, roller-skated) **1** N-COUNT **Roller-skates** are shoes with four small wheels on the bottom. ❏ *A boy of about ten came up on roller-skates.* **2** V-I If you **roller-skate**, you move over a flat surface wearing roller-skates. ❏ *On the day of the accident, my son Gary was roller-skating outside our house.*

1 가산명사 롤러스케이트 ❏ 열 살 정도 되는 남자 아이가 롤러스케이트를 신고 다가왔다. **2** 자동사 롤러스케이트를 타다 ❏ 사고 당일 우리 아들 게리는 집 밖에서 롤러스케이트를 타고 있었다.

roll|ing /roʊlɪŋ/ ADJ **Rolling** hills are small hills with gentle slopes that extend a long way into the distance. [ADJ n] ❏ *...the rolling countryside of south western France.*

형용사 완만하게 펼쳐지는 ❏ 구릉이 완만하게 펼쳐지는 프랑스 서남부의 시골 지역

ROM /rɒm/ N-UNCOUNT **ROM** is the permanent part of a computer's memory. The information stored there can be read but not changed. **ROM** is an abbreviation for "read-only memory." [COMPUTING] ❏ *It's got 32 megabytes of ROM and 64 megabytes of RAM.* →see also **CD-ROM**

불가산명사 [컴퓨터] 롬 [컴퓨터] ❏ 이 제품은 32메가짜리 롬과 64메가짜리 램을 갖추고 있다.

Ro|man ♦◇◇ /roʊmən/ (Romans) **1** ADJ **Roman** means related to or connected with ancient Rome and its empire. ● N-COUNT A **Roman** was a citizen of ancient Rome or its empire. ❏ *When they conquered Britain, the Romans brought this custom with them.* **2** ADJ **Roman** means related to or connected with modern Rome. ❏ *...a Roman hotel room.* ● N-COUNT A **Roman** is someone who lives in or comes from Rome. ❏ *...soccer-mad Romans.*

1 형용사 고대 로마의 ❏ 로마 제국의 멸망 ● 가산명사 로마 시민 ❏ 로마인들이 영국을 정복하면서 이 같은 관습이 영국에 유입되었다. **2** 형용사 로마의 ❏ 로마에 있는 호텔 방 ● 가산명사 로마인 ❏ 열성 축구 팬인 로마인들

Ro|man Catho|lic (Roman Catholics) **1** ADJ The **Roman Catholic** Church is the same as the **Catholic** Church. ❏ *...a Roman Catholic priest.* **2** N-COUNT A **Roman Catholic** is the same as a **Catholic**. ❏ *Like her, Maria was a Roman Catholic.*

1 형용사 천주교의, 가톨릭 교회의 ❏ 가톨릭 신부 **2** 가산명사 천주교도, 가톨릭교도 ❏ 그녀와 마찬가지로 마리아도 천주교도였다.

ro|mance /roʊmæns, roʊmæns/ (romances) **1** N-COUNT A **romance** is a relationship between two people who are in love with each other but who are not married to each other. ❏ *After a whirlwind romance the couple announced their engagement in July.* **2** N-UNCOUNT **Romance** refers to the actions and feelings of people who are in love, especially behavior which is very caring or affectionate. ❏ *He still finds time for romance by cooking candlelit dinners for his girlfriend.* **3** N-UNCOUNT You can refer to the pleasure and excitement of doing something new or exciting as **romance**. ❏ *We want to recreate the romance and excitement that used to be part of rail journeys.* **4** N-COUNT A **romance** is a novel or movie about a love affair. ❏ *Her taste in fiction was for chunky historical romances.* →see **love**

1 가산명사 연애, 로맨스 ❏ 이 커플은 불꽃 같은 연애 끝에 7월 약혼을 정식으로 밝혔다. **2** 불가산명사 애정 표현; 연애 감정 ❏ 그는 아직도 시간을 내어, 여자 친구를 위해 촛불을 켜고 하는 저녁 식사를 준비하면서 자신의 애정을 표현한다. **3** 불가산명사 설렘 ❏ 우리는 기차 여행의 일부였던 설렘과 흥분을 재현하고 싶다. **4** 가산명사 연애 소설; 멜로 영화 ❏ 그녀의 취향에 맞는 소설은 두꺼운 역사 로맨스였다.

Ro|man nu|mer|al /roʊmən numərəl, BRIT roʊmən nyuːmərəl/ (Roman numerals) N-COUNT **Roman numerals** are the letters used by the ancient Romans to represent numbers, for example I, IV, VIII, and XL, which represent 1, 4, 8, and 40. Roman numerals are still sometimes used today. [usu pl] →see Picture Dictionary: **Roman numerals**

가산명사 로마 숫자

ro|man|tic ♦◇◇ /roʊmæntɪk/ (romantics) **1** ADJ Someone who is **romantic** or does **romantic** things says and does things that make their wife, husband, girlfriend, or boyfriend feel special and loved. ❏ *When we're together, all he talks about is business. I wish he were more romantic.* **2** ADJ **Romantic** means connected with sexual love. [ADJ n] ❏ *He was not interested in a romantic relationship with Ingrid.* ● **ro|man|ti|cal|ly** ADV ❏ *We are not romantically involved.* **3** ADJ A **romantic** play, movie, or story describes or represents a love affair. [ADJ n] ❏ *It is a lovely*

1 형용사 낭만적인 ❏ 함께 있을 때 그가 말하는 것이라곤 사업 이야기뿐이다. 그가 좀 더 낭만적이었으면 좋겠다. **2** 형용사 연애의, 육체관계의 ❏ 그는 잉그리드와 연애하는 것에 관심이 없었다. ● 연애하며, 육체관계를 가지며 부사 ❏ 우리는 서로 사귀는 사이가 아니다. **3** 형용사 사랑 이야기를 담은 ❏ 이는 사랑스러운 로맨틱 코미디로 충분히 볼 만한

Picture Dictionary   Roman numerals

I	1	XI	11	XXI	21	XL	40
II	2	XII	12	XXII	22	L	50
III	3	XIII	13	XXIII	23	LX	60
IV	4	XIV	14	XXIV	24	LXX	70
V	5	XV	15	XXV	25	LXXX	80
VI	6	XVI	16	XXVI	26	XC	90
VII	7	XVII	17	XXVII	27	C	100
VIII	8	XVIII	18	XXVIII	28	D	500
IX	9	XIX	19	XXIX	29	M	1000
X	10	XX	20	XXX	30	MMVII	2007

A B C D E F G H I J K L M N O P Q R S T U V W X Y Z

romantic comedy, well worth seeing. ◳ ADJ If you say that someone has a **romantic** view or idea of something, you are critical of them because their view of it is unrealistic and they think that thing is better or more exciting than it really is. [DISAPPROVAL] ◻ *He has a romantic view of rural society.* ● N-COUNT A **romantic** is a person who has romantic views. ◻ *You're a hopeless romantic.* ◳ ADJ Something that is **romantic** is beautiful in a way that strongly affects your feelings. ◻ *Scaliff House is one of the most romantic ruins in Scotland* ● ro|man|ti|cal|ly ADV ◻ *...the romantically named, but very muddy, Cave of the Wild Horses.* →see love

romp /rɒmp/ (**romps**, **romping**, **romped**) ◲ V-I Journalists use **romp** in expressions like **romp home**, **romp in**, or **romp to victory**, to say that a person or horse has won a race or competition very easily. ◻ *Mr. Foster romped home with 141 votes.* ◳ V-I When children or animals **romp**, they play noisily and happily. ◻ *Dogs and little children romped happily in the garden.*

roof ◆◇◇ /ruːf/ (**roofs**)

> The plural can be pronounced /ruːfs/ or /ruːvz/.

◲ N-COUNT The **roof** of a building is the covering on top of it that protects the people and things inside from the weather. ◻ *...a small stone cottage with a red slate roof.* ◳ N-COUNT The **roof** of a car or other vehicle is the top part of it, which protects passengers or goods from the weather. ◻ *The car rolled onto its roof, trapping him.* ◴ N-COUNT The **roof of** your mouth is the highest part of the inside of your mouth. ◻ *She clicked her tongue against the roof of her mouth.* ◵ PHRASE If the level of something such as the price of a product or the rate of inflation **goes through the roof**, it suddenly increases very rapidly indeed. [INFORMAL] ◻ *Prices for Korean art have gone through the roof.* ◶ PHRASE If you **hit the roof** or **go through the roof**, you become very angry indeed, and usually show your anger by shouting at someone. [INFORMAL] ◻ *Sergeant Long will hit the roof when I tell him you've gone off.* ◷ PHRASE If a number of things or people are **under one roof** or **under the same roof**, they are in the same building. ◻ *The firms intend to open either together under one roof or alongside each other in shopping malls.*

Word Partnership	*roof*의 연어
N.	roof **of a building/house**, **metal** roof, **rain on a** roof, **slate** roof, **tin** roof ◲
V.	roof **collapses**, roof **leaks**, **repair a** roof ◲

rookie /rʊki/ (**rookies**) ◲ N-COUNT A **rookie** is someone who has just started doing a job and does not have much experience, especially someone who has just joined the army or police force. [mainly AM, INFORMAL] ◻ *I don't want to have another rookie to train.* ◳ N-COUNT A **rookie** is a person who has been competing in a professional sport for less than a year. [AM] ◻ *...the oldest rookie on the European Tour.*

room ◆◆◆ /ruːm, rʊm/ (**rooms**, **rooming**, **roomed**) ◲ N-COUNT A **room** is one of the separate sections or parts of the inside of a building. Rooms have their own walls, ceilings, floors, and doors, and are usually used for particular activities. You can refer to all the people who are in a room as **the room**. ◻ *A minute later he excused himself and left the room.* ◻ *The largest conference room could seat 5,000 people.* ◳ N-COUNT If you talk about your **room**, you are referring to the room that you alone use, especially your bedroom at home or your office at work. ◻ *If you're running upstairs, go to my room and bring down my sweater, please.* ◴ N-COUNT A **room** is a bedroom in a hotel. ◻ *Toni booked a room in an hotel not far from Arzfeld.* ◵ V-I If you **room with** someone, you share a rented room, apartment, or house with them, for example when you are a student. [AM] ◻ *I had roomed with him in New Haven when we were both at Yale Law School.* ◶ N-UNCOUNT If there is **room** somewhere, there is enough empty space there for people or things to be fitted in, or for people to move freely or do what they want to. ◻ *There is usually room to accommodate up to 80 visitors.* ◷ N-UNCOUNT If there is **room for** a particular kind of behavior or action, people are able to behave in that way or to take that action. ◻ *The intensity of the work left little room for personal grief or anxiety.* ◸ →see also **chat room, dining room, drawing room, emergency room, restroom**

> You should use **room** or **space** to refer to an open or empty area. You do not use **place** as an uncount noun in this sense. **Room** is more likely to be used when you are talking about space inside an enclosed area. ◻ *There's not enough room in the bathroom for both of us... Leave plenty of space between you and the car in front.*

room|mate /ruːmmeɪt, rʊm-/ (**roommates**) also **room-mate** ◲ N-COUNT Your **roommate** is the person you share a room, apartment, or house with, for example when you are at college. [AM] ◻ *Derek and I are close; we were roommates for two years.* ◳ N-COUNT Your **roommate** is the person you share a rented room with, for example when you are at a university. [BRIT]

room ser|vice N-UNCOUNT **Room service** is a service in a hotel by which meals or drinks are provided for guests in their rooms. ◻ *The hotel did not normally provide room service.* →see **hotel**

roomy /ruːmi/ (**roomier**, **roomiest**) ADJ If you describe a place as **roomy**, you mean that you like it because it is large inside and you can move around freely and comfortably. [APPROVAL] ◻ *The car is roomy and a good choice for anyone who needs to carry equipment.*

roost /ruːst/ (**roosts**, **roosting**, **roosted**) ◲ N-COUNT A **roost** is a place where birds or bats rest or sleep. ◻ *Something disturbed the bird on its roost.* ◳ V-I When birds or bats **roost** somewhere, they rest or sleep there. ◻ *The peacocks roost in nearby shrubs.* ◴ PHRASE If bad or wrong things that someone has done in the

---

가치가 있다. ◳ 형용사 비현실적인, 몽상적인 [탐탁잖음] ◻ 그는 농촌 사회에 대해 비현실적인 견해를 갖고 있다. ● 가산명사 몽상가, 공상가 ◻ 당신은 구제 불능 몽상가야. ◵ 형용사 아름다운 ◻ 시클리프 하우스는 스코틀랜드 지역에서 가장 아름다운 유적 중의 하나이다. ● 아름답게 부사 ◻ 이름이 아름답긴 하지만 상당히 애매한 '야생마 동굴'

◲ 자동사 쉽게 이기다, 낙승하다 ◻ 포스터 씨가 141표를 얻어 낙승했다. ◳ 자동사 뛰논다 ◻ 개와 어린 아이들이 정원에서 즐겁게 뛰놀았다.

복수는 /ruːfs/ 또는 /ruːvz/로 발음할 수 있다.

◲ 가산명사 지붕 ◻ 빨간 슬레이트 지붕의 자그마한 석조 주택 ◳ 가산명사 (자동차의) 지붕 ◻ 그 자동차가 굴러 뒤집어져서, 그 차 속에 갇혀 버렸다. ◴ 가산명사 (입) 천장 ◻ 그녀는 입천장에 대고 혀를 찼다. ◵ 구 (가격 등이) 급격히 치솟다 [비격식체] ◻ 한국 미술품 가격이 급격히 치솟았다. ◶ 구 (화가 나서) 길길이 뛰다 [비격식체] ◻ 네가 가버렸다고 말하면 통 병장이 길길이 뛸 거야. ◷ 구 한 지붕 아래 ◻ 그 회사들은 한 지붕 아래서 같이 개업을 하거나, 쇼핑몰에서 나란히 개업을 하려고 한다.

◲ 가산명사 신참 [주로 미국영어, 비격식체] ◻ 나는 신참을 한 명 더 훈련시키고 싶지는 않다. ◳ 가산명사 (프로 팀의) 신인 선수 [미국영어] ◻ 유러피언 투어에서 가장 나이든 신인 선수

◲ 가산명사 방 ◻ 잠시 후 그는 양해를 구하고 그 방을 떠났다. ◻ 가장 넓은 회의실은 5천 명을 수용할 수 있었다. ◳ 가산명사 방 ◻ 2층에 올라갈 거면, 내 방에 가서 내 스웨터 좀 가지고 내려와 주세요. ◴ 가산명사 방, 객실 ◻ 토니는 아즈펠트에서 멀지 않은 곳에 호텔방 하나를 예약했다. ◵ 자동사 룸메이트이다, 방이나 집을 함께 쓴다 [미국영어] ◻ 우리가 둘 다 예일 법대를 다닐 때 나는 뉴 헤이븐에서 그와 룸메이트였다. ◶ 불가산명사 공간 ◻ 보통은 손님을 80명까지 수용할 수 있는 공간이 있다. ◷ 불가산명사 여지 ◻ 그 작업의 강도는 개인적으로 슬퍼하거나 걱정할 여지를 주지 않았다.

틔어 있거나 비어 있는 공간을 가리킬 때에는 room이나 space를 써야 한다. 이런 의미의 불가산 명사로는 place를 쓰지 않는다. room은 둘러싸인 영역 내에 있는 공간을 말할 때 더 흔히 쓰인다. ◻ 욕실에는 우리 둘이 들어 갈 만한 공간이 없다... 당신과 앞 차 사이에 충분한 공간을 두시오.

◲ 가산명사 룸메이트, 동숙자 [미국영어] ◻ 데렉과 나는 친하다. 왜냐하면 우리는 2년 동안이나 룸메이트였으니까. ◳ 가산명사 룸메이트 [영국영어]

불가산명사 (호텔의) 룸 서비스 ◻ 그 호텔은 일반적으로 룸 서비스를 제공하지 않았다.

형용사 공간이 넓은, 널찍한 [마음에 듦] ◻ 그 차는 공간이 넓어서 장비를 가지고 다닐 필요가 있는 사람이라면 누구에게든 잘 맞는 것이다.

◲ 가산명사 (새들의) 보금자리, 홰 ◻ 뭔가가 홰에 앉아 있던 새를 불안하게 했다. ◳ 자동사 (새 등이) 앉아 쉬다, 자다 ◻ 공작들은 근처 관목 숲에서 잠을 잔다. ◴ 구 자업자득이다 ◻ 정치적 타협은 자업자득이다.

a
b
c
d
e
f
g
h
i
j
k
l
m
n
o
p
q
r
s
t
u
v
w
x
y
z

past **have come home to roost**, or if their **chickens have come home to roost**, they are now experiencing the unpleasant effects of these actions. □ *Appeasement has come home to roost.* ■ PHRASE If you say that someone **rules the roost** in a particular place, you mean that they have control and authority over the people there. [INFORMAL] □ *Today the country's nationalists rule the roost and hand out the jobs.*

■ 구 쥐고 흔들다, 좌지우지 하다 [비격식체]
□ 요즘에는 그 나라의 국수주의자들이 쥐고 흔들며 일자리를 나눠 준다.

roost|er /rúːstər/ (**roosters**) N-COUNT A **rooster** is an adult male chicken. [AM; BRIT **cock**]

가산명사 수탉 [미국영어; 영국영어 cock]

root ◆◇◇ /rúːt/ (**roots, rooting, rooted**) ■ N-COUNT The **roots** of a plant are the parts of it that grow under the ground. □ *...the twisted roots of an apple tree.* ■ V-T/V-I If you **root** a plant or cutting or if it **roots**, roots form on the bottom of its stem and it starts to grow. □ *Most plants will root in about six to eight weeks.* ■ ADJ **Root** vegetables or **root** crops are grown for their roots which are large and can be eaten. [ADJ n] □ *...root crops such as carrots and potatoes.* ■ N-COUNT The **root** of a hair or tooth is the part of it that is underneath the skin. □ *...decay around the roots of teeth.* ■ N-PLURAL You can refer to the place or culture that a person or their family comes from as their **roots**. □ *I am proud of my Brazilian roots.* ■ N-COUNT You can refer to the cause of a problem or of an unpleasant situation as **the root of** it or **the roots of** it. □ *We got to the root of the problem.* ■ V-I If you **root through** or in something, you search for something by moving other things around. □ *She rooted through the bag, found what she wanted, and headed toward the door.* ■ →see also **rooted, grassroots, square root** ■ PHRASE If someone **puts down roots**, they make a place their home, for example by taking part in activities there or by making a lot of friends there. □ *When they got to Montana, they put down roots and built a life.* ■ PHRASE If an idea, belief, or custom **takes root**, it becomes established among a group of people. □ *Time would be needed for democracy to take root.*

■ 가산명사 뿌리 □ 사과나무의 뒤틀린 뿌리
■ 타동사/자동사 뿌리가 나다 □ 대부분의 식물들은 약 6주에서 8주 내에 뿌리가 난다. ■ 형용사 뿌리의, 뿌리를 먹는 □ 당근이나 감자와 같은 뿌리채소
■ 가산명사 (치아 등의) 뿌리 □ 치근 주변의 충치
■ 복수명사 근본, 뿌리 □ 나는 나의 뿌리가 브라질인 것이 자랑스럽다. ■ 가산명사 (문제의) 근원, 핵심 □ 우리는 그 문제의 근원에 봉착했다. ■ 자동사 뒤지다 □ 그녀는 가방을 뒤져서 자신이 찾던 것을 꺼낸 후, 문 쪽으로 갔다. ■ 구 뿌리를 내리다, 정착하다 □ 그들은 몬태나에 도착해서 뿌리를 내리고 삶을 설계했다. ■ 구 (관습 등이) 정착되다 □ 민주주의가 정착하려면 시간이 필요할 것이다.

→see Word Web: rope

Word Partnership   root의 연어

N.	**tree root** ■
	root **cause of** *something*, root **of a problem** ■
V.	**take root** ■

▶**root out** ■ PHRASAL VERB If you **root out** a person, you find them and force them from the place they are in, usually in order to punish them. □ *The generals want to root out traitors.* ■ PHRASAL VERB If you **root out** a problem or an unpleasant situation, you find out who or what is the cause of it and put an end to it. □ *There would be a major drive to root out corruption.*

■ 구동사 뿌리 뽑다 □ 그 장군들은 반역자들을 뿌리 뽑아야 한다. ■ 구동사 (문제점을) 근절하다 □ 부정부패를 근절하기 위한 대대적인 운동이 있을 것이다.

root|ed /rúːtɪd/ ■ ADJ If you say that one thing is **rooted in** another, you mean that it is strongly influenced by it or has developed from it. [v-link ADJ in n] □ *The crisis is rooted in deep rivalries between the two groups.* ■ ADJ If someone has deeply **rooted** opinions or feelings, they believe or feel something extremely strongly and are unlikely to change. □ *Racism is a deeply rooted prejudice which has existed for thousands of years.* ■ PHRASE If you are **rooted to the spot**, you are unable to move because you are very frightened or shocked. □ *We just stopped there, rooted to the spot.*

■ 형용사 -에 뿌리를 둔 □ 그 위기 상황은 두 집단 간에 깊이 박혀 있는 경쟁의식에 뿌리를 두고 있다.
■ 형용사 깊은 □ 인종 차별주의는 수천 년 동안 존재해 온 깊이 뿌리박힌 편견이다. ■ 구 (무서워서) 얼어붙다 □ 우리는 그냥 그 자리에서 꼼짝도 못하고 얼어붙어 버렸다.

rope /róʊp/ (**ropes, roping, roped**) ■ N-VAR A **rope** is a thick cord or wire that is made by twisting together several thinner cords or wires. Ropes are used for jobs such as pulling cars, tying up boats, or tying things together. □ *He tied the rope around his waist.* ■ V-T If you **rope** one thing **to** another, you tie the two things together with a rope. □ *I roped myself to the chimney.* ■ PHRASE If you **give someone enough rope to hang themselves**, you give them the freedom to do a job in their own way because you hope that their attempts will fail and that they will look foolish. □ *The King has merely given the politicians enough rope to hang themselves.* ■ PHRASE If you **are learning the ropes**, you are learning how a particular task or job is done. [INFORMAL] □ *He tried hiring more salesmen to push his radio products, but they took too much time to learn the ropes.* ■ PHRASE If you **know the ropes**, you know how a particular job or task should be done. [INFORMAL] □ *The moment she got to know the ropes, there was no stopping her.* ■ PHRASE If you describe a payment as **money for old rope**, you are emphasizing that it is earned very easily, for very little effort. [BRIT, INFORMAL, EMPHASIS] □ *So far as he was concerned, it was a nice, safe office job, money for old rope.* ■ PHRASE If you **show** someone **the ropes**, you show them how to do a particular job or task. [INFORMAL] □ *We had a patrol out on the border, breaking in some young soldiers, showing them the ropes.*
→see Word Web: rope

■ 가산명사 또는 불가산명사 밧줄 □ 그는 자기 허리에 밧줄을 묶었다. ■ 타동사 밧줄로 묶다 □ 나는 밧줄로 굴뚝에 내 몸을 묶었다. ■ 구 (혼 좀 더 뽀려 하도록) 제멋대로 하도록 내버려 두다 □ 왕은 어디 한 번 혼 좀 나 봐라 하는 심정으로 정치인들이 제멋대로 하도록 내버려 두었다. ■ 구 일에 익숙해지다, 요령을 터득하다 [비격식체] □ 그는 더 많은 영업 사원을 고용해서 자신의 무선 제품을 팔려고 했지만, 그 사람들이 일에 익숙해지는 데 너무나 많은 시간이 걸렸다. ■ 구 요령을 안다 [비격식체] □ 그녀가 요령을 알게 된 순간, 그녀는 아무도 못 말리게 되었다. ■ 구 쉽게 번 돈 [영국영어, 비격식체, 강조] □ 그가 생각할 때는, 그것이 사무실에서 일하며 쉽게 돈을 벌 수 있는 안정된 일이었다. ■ 구 업무 수행 요령을 가르쳐 주다 [비격식체] □ 우리는 경계 지대에 순찰병 배치해서, 젊은 신병들을 일에 익숙해지게 만들고 그들에게 업무 수행 요령을 가르쳐 주었다.

Word Web   rope

Rope consists of a number of **threads, strands,** or **fiber**. A machine twists the strands around one another in such a way that they won't **unravel**. Natural materials like hemp and synthetic ones like **nylon** are used. Rope has played a central role in the history of humanity. The Egyptians used it to help build the pyramids. The ships Columbus* discovered America with required rope to raise the sails. Early mountain climbers used thick **cords** to reach high peaks. Using rope always involves making **knots**. The square knot and clove hitch are two of the most common knots.

Christopher Columbus (1451-1506): an Italian explorer.

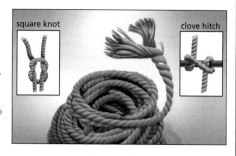

square knot

clove hitch

▶**rope in** PHRASAL VERB If you say that you **were roped in to** do a particular task, you mean that someone persuaded you to help them do that task. [INFORMAL] ❑ *Visitors were roped in for potato picking and harvesting.*

rose ◆◇◇ /roʊz/ (roses) **1** Rose is the past tense of **rise**. **2** N-COUNT A **rose** is a flower, often with a pleasant smell, which grows on a bush with stems that have sharp points called thorns on them. ❑ *She bent to pick a red rose.* **3** N-COUNT A **rose** is bush that roses grow on. ❑ *Prune rambling roses when the flowers have faded.* **4** COLOR Something that is **rose** is reddish-pink in color. [LITERARY] ❑ *...the rose and violet hues of a twilight sky.* **5** PHRASE If you say that a situation is not **a bed of roses**, you mean that it is not as pleasant as it seems, and that there are some unpleasant aspects to it. ❑ *We all knew that life was unlikely to be a bed of roses back in England.* →see **plant**

rosé /roʊzeɪ/ , BRIT roʊzeɪ/ (rosés) N-MASS **Rosé** is wine which is pink in color. ❑ *The vast majority of wines produced in this area are reds or rosé.*

ro|sette /roʊzɛt/ (rosettes) N-COUNT A **rosette** is a large circular decoration made from colored ribbons which is given as a prize in a competition, or, especially in Britain, is worn to show support for a political party or sports team. ❑ *I saw her father with his rosette on, canvassing for the Conservatives.*

ros|ter /rɒstər/ (rosters) **1** N-COUNT A **roster** is a list which gives details of the order in which different people have to do a particular job. ❑ *The next day he put himself first on the new roster for domestic chores.* **2** N-COUNT A **roster** is a list, especially of the people who work for a particular organization or are available to do a particular job. It can also be a list of the athletes who are available for a particular team, especially in American English. ❑ *The Amateur Softball Association's roster of umpires has declined to 57,000.*

rosy /roʊzi/ (rosier, rosiest) **1** ADJ If you say that someone has a **rosy** face, you mean that they have pink cheeks and look very healthy. ❑ *Bethan's round, rosy face seemed hardly to have aged at all.* **2** ADJ If you say that a situation looks **rosy** or that the picture looks **rosy**, you mean that the situation seems likely to be good or successful. ❑ *The job prospects for those graduating in engineering are far less rosy now than they used to be.*

rot /rɒt/ (rots, rotting, rotted) **1** V-T/V-I When food, wood, or another substance **rots**, or when something **rots** it, it becomes softer and is gradually destroyed. ❑ *If we don't unload it soon, the grain will start rotting in the silos.* **2** N-UNCOUNT If there is **rot** in something, especially something that is made of wood, parts of it have decayed and fallen apart. ❑ *Investigations had revealed extensive rot in the beams under the ground floor.* **3** N-SING You can use **the rot** to refer to the way something gradually gets worse. For example, if you are talking about the time when **the rot set in**, you are talking about the time when a situation began to get steadily worse and worse. ❑ *In many schools, the rot is beginning to set in. Standards are falling all the time.* **4** V-I If you say that someone is being left to **rot** in a particular place, especially in a prison, you mean that they are being left there and their physical and mental condition is being allowed to get worse and worse. ❑ *Most governments simply leave the long-term jobless to rot on the dole.*

rota /roʊtə/ (rotas) N-COUNT A **rota** is a list which gives details of the order in which different people have to do a particular job. [mainly BRIT] ❑ *I suggest that you work out a careful rota which will make it clear who tidies the room on which day.*

Word Link	rot ≈ turning : rotary, rotate, rotation

ro|ta|ry /roʊtəri/ **1** ADJ **Rotary** means turning or able to turn around a fixed point. [ADJ n] ❑ *...turning linear into rotary motion.* **2** ADJ **Rotary** is used in the names of some machines that have parts that turn around a fixed point. [ADJ n] ❑ *...a rotary engine.*

ro|tate /roʊteɪt/, BRIT roʊteɪt/ (rotates, rotating, rotated) **1** V-T/V-I When something **rotates** or when you **rotate** it, it turns with a circular movement. ❑ *The earth rotates around the sun.* **2** V-T/V-I If people or things **rotate**, or if someone **rotates** them, they take it in turns to do a particular job or serve a particular purpose. ❑ *The members of the club can rotate and one person can do all the preparation for the evening.* →see **moon**

ro|ta|tion /roʊteɪʃ°n/ (rotations) **1** N-VAR **Rotation** is circular movement. A **rotation** is the movement of something through one complete circle. ❑ *...the daily rotation of the earth upon its axis.* **2** N-UNCOUNT The **rotation** of a group of things or people is the fact of them taking turns to do a particular job or serve a particular purpose. If people do something **in rotation**, they take turns to do it. ❑ *He grew a different crop on the same field five years in a row, what researchers call crop rotation.*

rot|ten /rɒt°n/ **1** ADJ If food, wood, or another substance is **rotten**, it has decayed and can no longer be used. ❑ *The smell outside this building is overwhelming – like rotten eggs.* **2** ADJ If you describe something as **rotten**, you think it is very unpleasant or of very poor quality. [INFORMAL] ❑ *I personally think it's a rotten idea.* **3** ADJ If you feel **rotten**, you feel bad, either because you are ill or because you are sorry about something. [INFORMAL] ❑ *I had glandular fever and spent that year feeling rotten.*

rough ◆◇◇ /rʌf/ (rougher, roughest, roughs, roughing, roughed) **1** ADJ If a surface is **rough**, it is uneven and not smooth. ❑ *His hands were rough and calloused, from years of karate practice.* ● **rough|ness** N-UNCOUNT ❑ *She rested her cheek against the roughness of his jacket.* **2** ADJ If people or their actions are **rough** when they use too much force and not enough care or gentleness. ❑ *Rugby's a rough game at the best of times.* ● **rough|ly** ADV ❑ *They roughly pushed her forward.* ● **rough|ness** N-UNCOUNT ❑ *He regretted his roughness.* **3** ADJ A **rough**

1 rise의 과거 **2** 가산명사 장미 ❑그녀가 붉은 장미를 꺾기 위해서 몸을 굽혔다. **3** 가산명사 장미 넝쿨 ❑ 장미꽃이 지고 나면, 마구 뻗어 나가는 덩굴을 가지치기 하세요. **4** 색채어 장밋빛의 [문예체] ❑ 황혼이 지는 하늘에 번지는 장밋빛과 보랏빛 색조 **5** 관용표현 ❑ 영국으로 되돌아간 생활이 안락한 생활은 아닌 것이라는 것을 우리 모두 알고 있었다.

물질명사 로제 (행크빛 포도주) ❑ 이 지역에서 생산하는 포도주는 거의 대부분이 적포도주 또는 로제이다.

가산명사 리본 모양의 장식; 리본 모양의 장식 ❑나는 그녀의 아버지가 리본 모양 장식을 달고서, 보수당 선거 운동을 하고 있는 것을 봤다.

1 가산명사 근무 당번 표 ❑ 다음날 그는 새 집안일 당번 표에 자기 자신을 제 1 순위로 적어 놓았다. **2** 가산명사 명부, 등록부 ❑아마추어 소프트볼 협회의 감독들 명단이 57,000명으로 줄어들었다.

1 형용사 혈색이 좋은 ❑베단의 둥글고 혈색 좋은 얼굴은 전혀 나이가 든 것 같지 않았다. **2** 형용사 희망적인, 장밋빛의 ❑공학을 전공한 졸업생들의 취업 전망은 예전보다 훨씬 덜 희망적이다.

1 타동사/자동사 썩다, 부패하다 ❑우리가 빨리 그 곡식을 처리하지 않으면, 저장고에서 썩기 시작할 것이다. **2** 불가산명사 썩음, 부식 ❑조사단은 1층 아랫부분의 기둥이 대대적으로 썩어 있음을 밝혀냈었다. **3** 단수명사 악화 ❑많은 학교들에서 상황이 점점 더 악화되기 시작하고 있다. 규범이 계속 무너지고 있다. **4** 자동사 (천체적, 정신적으로) 쇠약해지다, 썩어 나가다 ❑대부분의 정부들이 장기 실업자들을 실업 수당에 의지한 채 타락해 가도록 내버려 둔다.

가산명사 근무 당번 표 [주로 영국영어] ❑누가 어느 요일에 방 청소를 해야 할지를 명확하게 할 수 있도록, 당번 표를 잘 짜 보세요.

1 형용사 회전하는 ❑ 직선 운동에서 회전 운동으로 바꾸는 **2** 형용사 (기계 등이) 회전식의 ❑ 회전식 엔진

1 타동사/자동사 회전하다; 회전시키다 ❑지구는 태양 주위를 회전한다. **2** 타동사/자동사 교대하다; 교대시키다 ❑그 클럽 회원들은 교대할 수 있어서 한 사람이 그 날 저녁 준비를 모두 맡아 할 수 있다.

1 가산명사 또는 불가산명사 회전 ❑지구 축을 중심으로 한 지구의 자전 **2** 불가산명사 교대, 윤번; 교대로 ❑그는 같은 밭에 5년 동안 잇달아 다른 작물을 재배하는데, 그것을 연구자들은 윤작이라고 부른다.

1 형용사 썩은 ❑이 건물 바깥에는 냄새가 엄청나다. 마치 썩은 달걀 냄새 같다. **2** 형용사 아무짝에도 못쓸 [비격식체] ❑나는 개인적으로 그것은 아무짝에도 못쓸 아이디어라고 생각한다. **3** 형용사 몸이 아픈, 기분이 안 좋은 [비격식체] ❑나는 선열로 그 해를 앓으면서 보냈다.

1 형용사 거칠거칠한, 꺼끌꺼끌한 ❑수년간의 가라데 연습으로, 그는 손이 거칠고 못이 박혀 있었다. ● 거칠거칠함, 꺼끌꺼끌함 불가산명사 ❑그녀는 그의 거칠거칠한 재킷에 볼을 기댔다. **2** 형용사 (행동 등이) 거친 ❑ 럭비는 아무리 살살 한다 해도 거친 경기이다. ● 거칠게 부사 ❑그들은 거칠게 그녀를 앞으로 밀었다. ● 거친 행동 불가산명사 ❑그는 자신의 거칠었던

A

area, city, school, or other place is unpleasant and dangerous because there is a lot of violence or crime there. ❑ *It was quite a rough part of our town.* ❹ ADJ If you say that someone has had a **rough** time, you mean that they have had some difficult or unpleasant experiences. ❑ *All women have a rough time in our society.* ❺ ADJ If you feel **rough**, you feel ill. [BRIT, INFORMAL] [v-link ADJ] ❑ *The virus won't go away and the lad is still feeling a bit rough.* ❻ ADJ A **rough** calculation or guess is approximately correct, but not exact. ❑ *We were only able to make a rough estimate of how much fuel would be required.* ● **rough|ly** ADV [ADV with cl/group] ❑ *Gambling and tourism pay roughly half the entire state budget.* ❼ ADJ If you give someone a **rough** idea, description, or drawing of something, you indicate only the most important features, without much detail. ❑ *I've got a rough idea of what he looks like.* ● **rough|ly** ADV ❑ *He knew roughly what was about to be said.* ❽ ADJ You can say that something is **rough** when it is not neat and well made. ❑ *The bench had a rough wooden table in front of it.* ● **rough|ly** ADV [ADV with v] ❑ *Roughly chop the tomatoes and add them to the casserole.* ❾ ADJ If the sea or the weather at sea is **rough**, the weather is windy or stormy and there are very big waves. ❑ *A fishing vessel and a cargo ship collided in rough seas.* ❿ ADV When people sleep or live **rough**, they sleep out of doors, usually because they have no home. [BRIT] [ADV after v] ❑ *It makes me so sad when I see young people begging or sleeping rough on the streets.* ⓫ **rough justice** →see **justice**

Thesaurus		*rough*의 참조어
ADJ.		coarse, harsh; (*ant.*) smooth ❶
		approximate, vague; (*ant.*) exact ❻ ❼

rou|lette /ruːlet/ N-UNCOUNT **Roulette** is a gambling game in which a ball is dropped onto a wheel with numbered holes in it while the wheel is spinning around. The players bet on which hole the ball will be in when the wheel stops spinning. ❑ *I had been playing roulette at the casino.*

round
① PREPOSITION AND ADVERB USES
② NOUN USES
③ ADJECTIVE USES
④ VERB USES

① round ♦♦◇ /raʊnd/

Round is an adverb and preposition that has the same meanings as "around." **Round** is often used with verbs of movement, such as "walk" and "drive," and also in phrasal verbs such as "get round" and "hand round." **Round** is commoner in British English than American English, and it is slightly more informal.

→Please look at category ⓯ to see if the expression you are looking for is shown under another headword. ❶ PREP To be positioned **round** a place or object means to surround it or be on all sides of it. To move **round** a place means to go along its edge, back to the point where you started. ❑ *They were sitting round the kitchen table.* ❑ *All round us was desert.* ● ADV **Round** is also an adverb. [ADV after v] ❑ *Visibility was good all round.* ❷ PREP If you move **round** a corner or obstacle, you move to the other side of it. If you look **round** a corner or obstacle, you look to see what is on the other side. ❑ *Suddenly a car came round a corner on the opposite side.* ❸ PREP You use **round** to say that something happens in or relates to different parts of a place, or is near a place. ❑ *He happens to own half the land round here.* ❑ *I think he has earned the respect of leaders all round the world.* ● ADV **Round** is also an adverb. ❑ *Shirley found someone to show them round.* ❹ ADV If a wheel or object spins **round**, it turns on its axis. [ADV after v] ❑ *When you push a lever all the wheels go round.* ❺ ADV If you turn **round**, you turn so that you are facing or going in the opposite direction. [ADV after v] ❑ *She paused, but did not turn round.* ❻ ADV If you move things **round**, you move them so they are in different places. [ADV after v] ❑ *He will be glad to refurnish where possible, change things round and redecorate.* ❼ ADV If you hand or pass something **round**, it is passed from person to person in a group. [ADV after v] ❑ *John handed round the plate of sandwiches.* ● PREP **Round** is also a preposition. ❑ *They started handing the microphone out round the girls at the front.* ❽ ADV If you go **round** to someone's house, you visit them. [ADV after v] ❑ *I think we should go round and tell Kevin to turn his music down.* ● PREP **Round** is also a preposition in nonstandard English. ❑ *I went round my wife's house.* ❾ ADV You use **round** in informal expressions such as **sit round** or **hang round** when you are saying that someone is spending time in a place and is not doing anything very important. [ADV after v] ❑ *As we sat round chatting, I began to think I'd made a mistake.* ● PREP **Round** is also a preposition. ❑ *She would spend the day hanging round street corners.* ❿ PREP If something is built or based **round** a particular idea, that idea is the basis for it. ❑ *... a design built round an existing American engine.* ⓫ PREP If you get **round** a problem or difficulty, you find a way of dealing with it. ❑ *Don't just immediately give up but think about ways round a problem.* ⓬ ADV If you win someone **round**, or if they come **round**, they change their mind about something and start agreeing with you. [ADV after v] ❑ *He did his best to talk me round, but I wouldn't speak to him.* ⓭ ADV You use **round** in expressions such as **this time round** or **to come round** when you are describing something that has happened before or things that happen regularly. ❑ *In the past, the elections have been marked by hundreds of murders, but this time round the violence has been much more limited.* ⓮ PREP You can use **round** to give the measurement of the outside of something that is shaped like a circle or a cylinder. ❑ *I'm about two inches larger round the waist.* ● ADV **Round** is also an adverb. ❑ *It's six feet high and five feet round.* ⓯ ADV You use **round** in front of

---

행동을 후회했다. ❸ 형용사 위험한, 험악한 ❑ 그 곳은 우리 마을에서 꽤 위험한 지역이었다. ❹ 형용사 힘든 ❑ 우리 사회에서 모든 여성들은 힘들게 살고 있다. ❺ 형용사 아픈 [영국영어, 비격식체] ❑ 바이러스가 쉽게 치료되지 않아서 아직도 그 소년은 많이 아프다. ❻ 형용사 대략의, 대충의 ❑ 우리는 얼마만큼의 연료가 필요할지를 대충 계산할 수밖에 없었다. ● 대략 부사 ❑ 도박과 관광으로 얻는 수입이 그 주 전체 수입의 대략 절반을 차지한다. ❼ 형용사 전체적인, 대충의 ❑ 나는 그가 어떻게 생겼는지 대충으로 알고 있다. ● 대충 부사 ❑ 그는 무슨 말을 듣게 될 지 대충 알고 있었다. ❽ 형용사 대충 만든 ❑ 그 벤치 앞에는 대충 만든 나무 탁자가 있었다. ● 대충 부사 ❑ 토마토를 대충 썰어서 찜 요리에 넣으세요. ❾ 형용사 (바다가) 험한 ❑ 험난한 바다에서 어선과 화물선이 서로 충돌했다. ❿ 부사 한데서, 집 밖에서 [영국영어] ❑ 젊은이들이 구걸하거나 거리에서 노숙하는 것을 보면 나는 너무나 슬퍼진다.

불가산명사 룰렛 게임 ❑ 나는 카지노에서 룰렛 게임을 하고 있었었다.

round는 'around'와 같은 의미를 갖는 부사, 전치사이다. round는 종종 'walk', 'drive'와 같은 이동 동사와 함께 쓰며 'get round', 'hand round'와 같은 구동사에도 쓰인다. round는 미국영어보다 영국영어에서 더 많이 쓰며 조금 더 비격식적이다.

❶ 전치사 – 주위에, -에 빙 둘러 ❑ 그들은 부엌 식탁에 빙 둘러 앉아 있었다. ❑ 우리 주위는 모두 사막이었다. ● 부사 주변에, 주위에 ❑ 시계(視界)가 사방에 훤했다. ❷ 전치사 -을 돌아서 ❑ 갑자기 자동차 한 대가 반대편에서 모퉁이를 돌아 나왔다. ❸ 전치사 – 전역의, 여기저기의; – 근처의 ❑ 그가 마침 이 근처 땅의 절반을 소유하고 있다. ❑ 나는 그가 전 세계 지도자들의 존경을 받고 있다고 생각한다. ● 부사 여기저기 ❑ 셜리가 그들을 여기저기 안내해 줄 사람을 찾았다. ❹ 부사 회전하여, 빙 돌아 ❑ 레버를 밀면 바퀴가 모두 돌아간다. ❺ 부사 돌아서서 ❑ 그녀가 잠시 멈췄지만 돌아서지는 않았다. ❻ 부사 다른 곳으로 돌려, 이리저리 ❑ 가구를 가능한 대로 재배치하고, 물건들을 돌려놓기도 하고, 장식을 다시 하게 되면, 그가 기뻐할 것이다. ● 전치사 -에게 돌아가며 ❑ 그들은 마이크를 앞자리에 있는 소녀들에게 돌아가며 건네주기 시작했다. ❽ 부사 다른 곳으로 가서 ❑ 내 생각에는 우리가 케빈 집으로 가서 음악 소리 좀 줄여달라고 말해야겠다. ● 전치사 -로 ❑ 나는 내 아내의 집으로 갔다. ❾ 부사 빈둥대며, 빈둥거리는 ❑ 우리가 잡담을 하며 빈둥거릴 때, 나는 내가 실수를 했다는 생각이 들기 시작했다. ● 전치사 -에서 빈둥거리며 ❑ 그녀는 길거리 이 구석 저 구석에서 빈둥대며 하루를 보내곤 했다. ❿ 전치사 -을 중심으로 ❑ 기존의 미국식 엔진을 중심으로 설계된 디자인 ⓫ 전치사 -을 극복하여 ❑ 곧방 포기하지 말고 문제를 해결할 방법을 생각해 보세요. ⓬ 부사 (생각 등을) 바꾸어 ❑ 그가 내 마음을 바꾸려 애를 썼지만, 나는 그와 말하지 않을 거다. ⓭ 부사 (기간이) 다시 돌아와서; 이번에는; 다시 돌아오다 ● 옛날에는 선거철이 수백 건의 살인으로 얼룩졌었는데, 이번에는 폭력 행위가 훨씬 더 제한되었다. ⓮ 전치사 – 둘레에 ❑ 나는 허리둘레가 약 2인치 정도 더 크다. ● 부사 둘레가 -인 ❑ 그것은 높이가 6 피트에 둘레가 5피트다. ⓯ 부사 대략 [짐작투] ❑ 나는 대략 밤 11시쯤에 잔다. ⓰ 구 약 [짐작투] ❑ 약 백오십만 명 정도가 사망했다. ⓱ 구 하나도 빠짐없이 모두, 속속들이 [주로 영국영어, 강조] ❑ 그가 진정으로 삶을 속속들이 훨씬 더 쉬워지도록 만들어야만 한다. ⓲ 구 일년 내내 ❑ 이런 식물들 중 많은 것들이 상록수라서, 일년 내내 볼 수 있다.

times or amounts to indicate that they are approximate. [VAGUENESS] [ADV amount] ❑ *I go to bed round 11:00 at night.* 16 PHRASE In spoken English, **round about** means approximately. [VAGUENESS] ❑ *Round about one and a half million people died.* 17 PHRASE You say **all round** to emphasize that something affects all parts of a situation or all members of a group. [mainly BRIT, EMPHASIS] ❑ *It ought to make life much easier all round.* 18 PHRASE If something happens **all year round**, it happens throughout the year. ❑ *Many of these plants are evergreen, so you can enjoy them all year round.* 19 **round the corner** →see **corner. the other way round** →see **way**

② **round** ♦♦◇ /raʊnd/ (rounds) 1 N-COUNT A **round of** events is a series of related events, especially one which comes after or before a similar series of events. ❑ *It was agreed that another round of preliminary talks would be held in Peking.* 2 N-COUNT In sports, a **round** is a series of games in a competition. The winners of these games go on to play in the next round, and so on, until only one player or team is left. ❑ *...in the third round of the Pilkington Cup.* 3 N-COUNT In a boxing or wrestling match, a **round** is one of the periods during which the boxers or wrestlers fight. ❑ *He was declared the victor in the 11th round.* 4 N-COUNT A **round** of golf is one game, usually including 18 holes. ❑ *...two rounds of golf.* 5 N-COUNT If you do your **rounds** or your **round**, you make a series of visits to different places or people, for example as part of your job. ❑ *The consultants still did their morning rounds.* 6 N-COUNT If you buy a **round** of drinks, you buy a drink for each member of the group of people that you are with. ❑ *They sat on the clubhouse terrace, downing a round of drinks.* 7 N-COUNT A **round** of ammunition is the bullet or bullets released when a gun is fired. ❑ *...firing 1650 rounds of ammunition during a period of ten minutes.* 8 N-COUNT If there is a **round** of applause, everyone claps their hands to welcome someone or to show that they have enjoyed something. ❑ *Sue got a sympathetic round of applause.* 9 PHRASE If you **make the rounds** or **do the rounds**, you visit a series of different places. ❑ *After school, I had picked up Nick and Ted and made the rounds of the dry cleaner and the grocery store.*

③ **round** /raʊnd/ (rounder, roundest) 1 ADJ Something that is **round** is shaped like a circle or ball. ❑ *She had small feet and hands and a flat, round face.* 2 ADJ A **round** number is a multiple of 10, 100, 1000, and so on. Round numbers are used instead of precise ones to give the general idea of a quantity or proportion. [ADJ n] ❑ *I asked how much silver could be bought for a million dollars, which seemed a suitably round number.*

④ **round** /raʊnd/ (rounds, rounding, rounded) 1 V-T If you **round** a place or obstacle, you move in a curve past the edge or corner of it. ❑ *The house disappeared from sight as we rounded a corner.* 2 V-T If you **round** an amount **up** or **down**, or if you **round** it **off**, you change it to the nearest whole number or nearest multiple of 10, 100, 1000 and so on. ❑ *We needed to do decimals to round up and round down numbers.* ❑ *The fraction was then multiplied by 100 and rounded to the nearest half or whole number.* 3 →see also **rounded**

▶ **round on** PHRASAL VERB If someone **rounds on** you, they criticize you fiercely and attack you with aggressive words. ❑ *The Conservative Party rounded angrily on him for damaging the Government.*

▶ **round up** 1 PHRASAL VERB If the police or army **round up** a number of people, they arrest or capture them. ❑ *The police rounded up a number of suspects.* 2 PHRASAL VERB If you **round up** animals or things, you gather them together. ❑ *He had sought work as a cowboy, rounding up cattle.* 3 →see also **round 2, roundup**

round|about /raʊndəbaʊt/ (roundabouts) 1 ADJ If you go somewhere by a **roundabout** route, you do not go there by the shortest and quickest route. ❑ *He left today on a roundabout route for Jordan and is also due soon in Egypt.* 2 ADJ If you do or say something in a **roundabout** way, you do not do or say it in a simple, clear, and direct way. ❑ *We made a bit of a fuss in a roundabout way.* 3 N-COUNT A **roundabout** is a circular structure in the road at a place where several roads meet. You drive around it until you come to the road that you want. [BRIT; AM **traffic circle**] ❑ *After taking the wrong exit at a roundabout, I phone the restaurant for directions.* 4 N-COUNT A **roundabout** at an amusement park is a large, circular mechanical device with seats, often in the shape of animals or cars, on which children sit and go around and around. [BRIT; AM **merry-go-round, carousel**] 5 N-COUNT A **roundabout** in a park or school play area is a circular platform that children sit or stand on. People push the platform to make it spin around. [BRIT; AM **merry-go-round**] 6 **round about** →see **round**

round|ed /raʊndɪd/ 1 ADJ Something that is **rounded** is curved in shape, without any points or sharp edges. ❑ *...a low rounded hill.* 2 ADJ You describe something or someone as **rounded** or **well-rounded** when you are expressing approval of them because they have a personality which is fully developed in all aspects. [APPROVAL] ❑ *...his carefully organized narrative, full of rounded, believable, and interesting characters.*

round trip (round trips) 1 N-COUNT If you make a **round trip**, you travel to a place and then back again. ❑ *The train operates the 2,400-mile round trip once a week.* 2 ADJ A **round-trip** ticket is a ticket for a train, bus, or plane that allows you to travel to a particular place and then back again. [AM; BRIT **return**] [ADJ n] ❑ *Mexicana Airlines has announced cheaper round-trip tickets between Los Angeles and cities it serves in Mexico.*

round|up /raʊndʌp/ (roundups) also **round-up** N-COUNT In journalism, especially television and radio, a **roundup** of news is a summary of the main events that have happened. ❑ *First, we have this roundup of the day's news.*

rouse /raʊz/ (rouses, rousing, roused) 1 V-T/V-I If someone **rouses** you when you are sleeping or if you **rouse**, you wake up. [LITERARY] ❑ *Hilton roused him at eight-thirty by rapping on the door.* 2 V-T If you **rouse yourself**, you stop being inactive and start doing something. ❑ *She seemed to be unable to rouse herself to do anything.* 3 V-T If something or someone **rouses** you, they make you very

1 가산명사 (연속되는 일들의) 한 차례 ❑ 또 한 차례의 예비회담을 베이징에서 여는 것이 합의되었다. 2 가산명사 (경기의) 회전 ❑ 필킹턴컵 경기의 3회전에서 3 가산명사 (경기의) 라운드 ❑ 11라운드 때 그가 우승자로 발표되었다. 4 가산명사 (골프) 한 경기 ❑ 골프 두 경기 5 가산명사 회진, 순회 ❑ 전문의들은 여전히 오전 회진을 돌았다. 6 가산명사 술을 시작 한 잔씩 돌림 ❑ 그들은 클럽 테라스에 앉아 술을 한 잔씩 돌리며 들이키고 있었다. 7 가산명사 (총알) 한 발 ❑ 10분 동안 1,650발을 사격함 8 가산명사 (박수) 한 바탕 ❑ 수는 사람들이 공감하며 일제히 보내 주는 박수를 받았다. 9 구 차례로 들르다 ❑ 방과 후에 나는 닉과 테드를 데리러 갔다가 세탁소와 식료품점을 차례로 들렀다.

1 형용사 둥근 ❑ 그녀는 손과 발이 작고, 얼굴은 납작하고 둥글었다. 2 형용사 우수리 없는, 어림수의 ❑ 나는 백만 달러로 은을 얼마나 살 수 있는지 물었는데, 그 정도 액수면 적절한 어림수일 것 같았다.

1 타동사 돌아가다 ❑ 우리가 모퉁이를 돌자 그 집이 시야에서 사라졌다. 2 타동사 (수의 나머지를) 반올림하다 ❑ 우리는 반올림을 하기 위해서 십진법으로 계산할 필요가 있었다. ❑ 그런 다음 그 분수에 100을 곱해서 가장 가까운 반수나 정수로 나머지를 정리했다.

구동사 질타하다 ❑ 보수당이 국정을 엉망으로 만든 것에 대해 그를 심하게 질타했다.

1 구동사 체포하다 ❑ 경찰이 많은 용의자들을 체포했다. 2 구동사 (동물을) 모으다 ❑ 그는 소몰이하는 목동 자리를 찾았었다.

1 형용사 (길이) 우회하는 ❑ 그는 오늘 우회 도로를 이용해서 요르단으로 떠나서 곧 이집트에 도착할 예정이다. 2 형용사 (말 등이) 우회적인 ❑ 우리는 우회적으로 약간 법석을 떨었다. 3 가산명사 로터리 [영국영어; 미국영어 traffic circle] ❑ 로터리에서 잘못 빠져나와서, 나는 방향을 묻기 위해 그 음식점에 전화를 한다. 4 가산명사 회전목마 [영국영어; 미국영어 merry-go-round, carousel] 5 가산명사 회전목마 [영국영어; 미국영어 merry-go-round]

1 형용사 둥근 ❑ 낮고 둥근 언덕 2 형용사 (성격이) 모나지 않은, 원만한 [마음에 듦] ❑ 아주 조리 있게 말하며, 원만하며, 신뢰할 수 있고 흥미를 끄는 그의 성격

1 가산명사 왕복 여행 ❑ 그 기차는 일주일에 한 번씩 왕복 2,400마일을 운행한다. 2 형용사 왕복의 [미국영어; 영국영어 return] ❑ 멕시코 항공사는 로스앤젤레스와 그들이 운항하고 있는 멕시코의 여러 도시들 간에 더 저렴한 왕복 항공권 판매를 발표했다.

가산명사 (주요 뉴스의) 요약, 간추린 소식 ❑ 먼저, 오늘의 주요 뉴스를 요약해 드리겠습니다.

1 타동사/자동사 깨우다; (잠을) 깨다 [문예체] ❑ 8시 30분에 힐튼은 문을 두드려서 그를 깨웠다. 2 타동사 기운을 차리다 ❑ 그녀는 무슨 일을 할 만큼 기운을 차리지 못하는 것 같았다. 3 타동사 (감정을) 자극하다, 흥분시키다 ❑ 그가 다른 누구보다도 더 그

emotional or excited. ❏ *He did more to rouse the crowd there than anybody else.*
● **rous|ing** ADJ ❏ *...a rousing speech to the convention in support of the president.* ◆ V-T
If something **rouses** a feeling in you, it causes you to have that feeling. ❏ *It roused a feeling of rebellion in him.* →see **dream**

rout /raʊt/ (**routs, routing, routed**) V-T If an army, sports team, or other group **routs** its opponents, it defeats them completely and easily. ❏ *...the Battle of Hastings at which the Norman army routed the English opposition.* ● N-COUNT **Rout** is also a noun. ❏ *One after another the Italian bases in the desert fell as the retreat turned into a rout.*

route ♦♦◇ /ruːt, -aʊt/ (**routes, routing, routed**) ◼ N-COUNT A **route** is a way from one place to another. ❏ *...the most direct route to the town center.* ◻ N-COUNT A bus, air, or shipping **route** is the way between two places along which buses, planes, or ships travel regularly. ❏ *...the main shipping routes to Japan.* ◼ N-IN-NAMES In the United States, **Route** is used in front of a number in the names of main roads between major cities. ❏ *From San Francisco take the freeway to the Broadway-Webster exit on Route 580.* ◆ N-COUNT Your **route** is the series of visits you make to different people or places, as part of your job. [mainly AM; BRIT usually **round, rounds**] ❏ *He began cracking open big blue tins of butter cookies and feeding the dogs on his route.* ◻ N-COUNT You can refer to a way of achieving something as a **route**. ❏ *Researchers are trying to get at the same information through an indirect route.* ◼ V-T If vehicles, goods, or passengers **are routed** in a particular direction, they are made to travel in that direction. [usu passive] ❏ *Trains are taking a lot of freight that used to be routed via trucks.* ◻ PHRASE **En route to** a place means on the way to that place. **En route** is sometimes spelled **on route** in nonstandard English. ❏ *They have arrived in London en route to the United States.* ◼ PHRASE Journalists sometimes use **en route** when they are mentioning an event that happened as part of a longer process or before another event. ❏ *The German set three tournament records and equalled two others en route to grabbing golf's richest prize.*

Thesaurus   route의 참조어

N.   path, road, trail ◼ ◻

Word Partnership   route 의 연어

N.	**escape** route, **parade** route ◼
ADJ.	**scenic** route ◼
	main route ◼ ◻
	alternative route ◼ ◻ ◼
	different route, **direct** route ◼ ◼

---

rou|tine ♦◇◇ /ruːtiːn/ (**routines**) ◼ N-VAR A **routine** is the usual series of things that you do at a particular time. A **routine** is also the practice of regularly doing things in a fixed order. ❏ *The players had to change their daily routine and lifestyle.* ◻ ADJ You use **routine** to describe activities that are done as a normal part of a job or process. ❏ *...a series of routine medical tests including X-rays and blood tests.* ◼ ADJ A **routine** situation, action, or event is one which seems completely ordinary, rather than interesting, exciting, or different. [DISAPPROVAL] ❏ *So many days are routine and uninteresting, especially in winter.* ◆ N-VAR You use **routine** to refer to a way of life that is uninteresting and ordinary, or hardly ever changes. [DISAPPROVAL] ❏ *...the mundane routine of her life.* ◼ N-COUNT A **routine** is a computer program, or part of a program, that performs a specific function. [COMPUTING] ❏ *... an installation routine.* ◼ N-COUNT A **routine** is a short sequence of jokes, remarks, actions, or movements that forms part of a longer performance. ❏ *...an athletic dance routine.*

Word Partnership   routine의 연어

N.	**exercise** routine, **morning** routine, **work** routine ◼
	routine **maintenance**, routine **tests** ◻
	routine **day** ◼
	comedy routine, **dance** routine ◼
ADJ.	**daily** routine, **normal** routine, **regular** routine, **usual** routine ◼ ◻

---

rou|tine|ly /ruːtiːnli/ ◼ ADV If something is **routinely** done, it is done as a normal part of a job or process. ❏ *Vitamin K is routinely given in the first week of life to prevent bleeding.* ◻ ADV If something happens **routinely**, it happens repeatedly and is not surprising, unnatural, or new. [ADV with v] ❏ *Any outside criticism is routinely dismissed as interference.*

rov|ing /roʊvɪŋ/ ADJ You use **roving** to describe a person who travels around, rather than staying in a fixed place. [ADJ n] ❏ *He is to join the BBC to cover the Olympic Games in Barcelona next month as a roving reporter.*

---

row

① ARRANGEMENT OR SEQUENCE
② MAKING A BOAT MOVE
③ DISAGREEMENT OR NOISE

---

① **row** ♦◇◇ /roʊ/ (**rows**) ◼ N-COUNT A **row of** things or people is a number of them arranged in a line. ❏ *...a row of pretty little cottages.* ◻ N-IN-NAMES **Row** is sometimes used in the names of streets. ❏ *...the house at 236 Larch Row.* ◼ →see also **death row** ◆ PHRASE If something happens several times **in a row**, it happens that number of times without a break. If something happens several

---

곳에 모인 군중들을 흥분시켰다. ● 힘찬 형용사 □ 전당 대회에서 현 대통령을 지지하는 힘찬 연설 ◼ 타동사 (감정을) 자아내다 □ 그것이 그에게 반발심을 들게 했다.

타동사 완패시키다 □ 노르만군이 영국군을 완패시켰던 헤이스팅스 전투 ● 가산명사 참패 □ 후퇴가 참패로 바뀌면서 사막에 세웠던 이탈리아의 기지들이 하나씩 무너졌다.

◼ 가산명사 길 □ 도심지로 가는 가장 가까운 길 ◻ 가산명사 노선 □ 일본행 주요 선박 노선 ◼ 이름명사 도로 □ 샌프란시스코에서 올 때는 고속도로를 타다가 브로드웨이-웹스터 간 나들목에서 빠져 580번 도로를 타세요. ◆ 가산명사 순회; 메타 [주로 미국영어; 영국영어 대개 round, rounds] □ 그는 순찰하는 길에 버터 쿠키가 들어 있는 큰 파란색 양철통을 열어서 개들을 먹이기 시작했다. ◼ 가산명사 경로, 방법 □ 연구자들은 똑같은 정보를 간접적인 경로로 입수하려고 애쓰고 있다. ◼ 타동사 운송되다 □ 과거에는 트럭으로 운송되던 많은 화물을 이제는 기차가 실어 나르고 있다. ◼ 구 -로 가는 길에 □ 그들은 미국으로 가는 길에 런던에 도착했다. ◼ 구 (주요 사건) 전에 □ 독일 팀은 골프 경기 최고의 상금을 거머쥐기 전에 이미 세 개의 토너먼트 기록과 또 다른 두 기록에 버금가는 기록을 세웠다.

◼ 가산명사 또는 불가산명사 일상적인 일, 틀에 박힌 일 □ 그 선수들은 그들의 일과와 생활 방식을 바꾸어야 했다. ◻ 형용사 일상적인, 정기적인 □ 엑스레이와 혈액 검사를 포함하는 일련의 정기 검진 ◼ 형용사 판에 박힌, 따분한 [탐탁찮음] □ 특히 겨울에는 하루하루가 따분하고 재미없다. ◆ 가산명사 또는 불가산명사 틀에 박힌 생활 [탐탁찮음] □ 단조로운 그녀의 틀에 박힌 생활 ◼ 가산명사 루틴, (컴퓨터) 일련의 작업 [컴퓨터] □ 일련의 설치 작업 ◼ 가산명사 (공연의 일부인) 전체 순서 □ 스포츠 댄스 순서

◼ 부사 정례적으로 □ 출혈을 막기 위해서 정례적으로 생후 일주일 내에 비타민 케이(K)를 투여한다. ◻ 부사 으레 □ 외부의 비평은 으레 간섭으로 치부된다.

형용사 순회하는, 상주하지 않는 □ 그는 순회 기자로서 바르셀로나 올림픽을 취재하기 위해 다음 달에 비비시와 합류할 것이다.

◼ 가산명사 줄, 열 □ 줄지어 선 작고 예쁜 시골집들 ◻ 이름명사 로우 (거리 이름) □ 라치 로우 236번지에 있는 집 ◼ 구 연속해서 □ 그들은 5연승을 했다.

days **in a row**, it happens on each of those days. ❑ *They have won five championships in a row.*

② **row** /roʊ/ (**rows, rowing, rowed**) V-T/V-I When you **row**, you sit in a boat and make it move through the water by using oars. If you **row** someone somewhere, you take them there in a boat, using oars. ❑ *He rowed as quickly as he could to the shore.* ❑ *The boatman refused to row him back.* ● N-COUNT **Row** is also a noun. ❑ *I took Daniel for a row.* →see also **rowing**

③ **row** ◆◇◇ /raʊ/ (**rows, rowing, rowed**) ❶ N-COUNT A **row** is a serious disagreement between people or organizations. [BRIT, INFORMAL] ❑ *This is likely to provoke a further row about the bank's role in the affair.* ❷ V-RECIP If two people **row** or if one person **rows with** another, they have a noisy argument. [BRIT, INFORMAL] ❑ *They rowed all the time and thought it couldn't be good for the baby.* ❸ N-SING If you say that someone is making a **row**, you mean that they are making a loud, unpleasant noise. [BRIT, INFORMAL] ❑ *"Whatever is that row?" she demanded. "Pop festival," he answered.*

row|dy /raʊdi/ (**rowdier, rowdiest**) ADJ When people are **rowdy**, they are noisy, rough, and likely to cause trouble. ❑ *He has complained to the police about rowdy neighbors.*

row house /roʊ haʊs/ (**row houses**) also **rowhouse** N-COUNT A **row house** is one of a row of similar houses that are joined together by both of their side walls. [AM; BRIT **terraced house**] ❑ *...a city block of row houses.*

row|ing /roʊɪŋ/ N-UNCOUNT **Rowing** is a sport in which people or teams race against each other in boats with oars. ❑ *...competitions in rowing, swimming and water skiing.*

roy|al ◆◆◇ /rɔɪəl/ (**royals**) ❶ ADJ **Royal** is used to indicate that something is connected with a king, queen, or emperor, or their family. A **royal** person is a king, queen, or emperor, or a member of their family. ❑ *...an invitation to a royal garden party.* ❷ ADJ **Royal** is used in the names of institutions or organizations that are officially appointed or supported by a member of a royal family. [ADJ n] ❑ *...the Royal Academy of Music.* ❸ N-COUNT Members of the royal family are sometimes referred to as **royals**. [INFORMAL] ❑ *The royals have always been patrons of charities pulling in large donations.*

roy|al|ist /rɔɪəlɪst/ (**royalists**) N-COUNT A **royalist** is someone who supports their country's royal family or who believes that their country should have a king or queen. ❑ *He was hated by the royalists and mistrusted by the communists.*

roy|al|ty /rɔɪəlti/ (**royalties**) ❶ N-UNCOUNT The members of royal families are sometimes referred to as **royalty**. ❑ *Royalty and government leaders from all around the world are gathering in Japan.* ❷ N-PLURAL **Royalties** are payments made to authors and musicians when their work is sold or performed. They usually receive a fixed percentage of the profits from these sales or performances. ❑ *I lived on about £3,000 a year from the royalties from my book.* ❸ N-COUNT Payments made to someone whose invention, idea, or property is used by a commercial company can be referred to as **royalties**. ❑ *The royalties enabled the inventor to re-establish himself in business.*

RSI /ɑr ɛs aɪ/ N-UNCOUNT People who suffer from **RSI** have pain in their hands and arms as a result of repeating similar movements over a long period of time, usually as part of their job. **RSI** is an abbreviation for "repetitive strain injury." ❑ *The women developed painful RSI because of poor working conditions.*

RSVP /ɑr ɛs viː piː/ also **R.S.V.P.** **RSVP** is an abbreviation for "répondez s'il vous plaît," which means "please reply." It is written on the bottom of a card inviting you to a party or special occasion. [FORMAL]

> When **RSVP** appears on an invitation, the sender needs to know whether or not the guest will come to the event. The guest should answer in plenty of time so the host can make plans. If the note **BYOB** also appears, it means the host wants the guest to "Bring Your Own Bottle" if they wish to drink alcoholic drinks.

rub /rʌb/ (**rubs, rubbing, rubbed**) ❶ V-T/V-I If you **rub** a part of your body or if you **rub** at it, you move your hand or fingers backward and forward over it while pressing firmly. ❑ *He rubbed his arms and stiff legs.* ❷ V-T/V-I If you **rub against** a surface or **rub** a part of your body **against** a surface, you move it backward and forward while pressing it against the surface. ❑ *A cat was rubbing against my leg.* ❸ V-T/V-I If you **rub** an object or a surface, you move a cloth backward and forward over it in order to clean or dry it. ❑ *She took off her glasses and rubbed them hard.* ❹ V-T If you **rub** a substance **into** a surface or **rub** something such as dirt **from** a surface, you spread it over the surface or remove it from the surface using your hand or something such as a cloth. ❑ *He rubbed oil into my back.* ❺ V-T/V-I If you **rub** two things **together** or if they **rub together**, they move backward and forward, pressing against each other. ❑ *He rubbed his hands together a few times.* ❻ V-I If something you are wearing or holding **rubs**, it makes you sore because it keeps moving backward and forward against your skin. ❑ *It should be comfortable against the skin without rubbing, chafing, or cutting into anything.* ❼ N-COUNT A massage can be referred to as a **rub**. ❑ *She sometimes asks if I want a back rub.* ❽ PHRASE If you **rub shoulders with** famous people, you meet them and talk to them. You can also say that you **rub elbows with** someone, especially in American English. ❑ *He regularly rubbed shoulders with the likes of Elizabeth Taylor and Kylie Minogue.* ❾ PHRASE If you **rub** someone **the wrong way** in American English, or **rub** someone **up the wrong way** in British English, you offend or annoy them without intending to. [INFORMAL] ❑ *What are you going to get out of him if you rub him up the wrong way?* ❿ to **rub** someone's **nose** in it →see **nose**

타동사/자동사 노 젓다 ❑ 그는 할 수 있는 한 가장 빨리 해안 쪽으로 노를 저었다. ❑ 그 뱃사공은 다시 배를 저어 그를 데려오기를 거부했다. ● 가산명사 노 젓기, 보트타기 ❑ 나는 다니엘을 보트 태워 주러 갔다.

❶ 가산명사 언쟁 [영국영어, 비격식체] ❑ 이것이 그 사건에서의 은행의 역할에 대해 더 큰 언쟁을 야기할 가능성이 있다. ❷ 상호동사 말다툼하다, 언쟁을 받아다 [영국영어, 비격식체] ❑ 그들은 항상 말다툼을 했고 그것이 아기에게 좋지 않을 것이라고 생각했다. ❸ 단수명사 소동 [영국영어, 비격식체] ❑ "웬 소동이지?"라고 그녀가 물었다. "팝 페스티벌이야." 그가 대답했다.

형용사 시끄러운 ❑ 그는 시끄러운 이웃들에 대해서 경찰에게 불평했다.

가산명사 연립 주택 [미국영어; 영국영어 terraced house] ❑ 도시의 연립 주택 구역

불가산명사 조정(漕艇) ❑ 조정, 수영, 수상 스키 대회

❶ 형용사 왕실의 ❑ 왕실 가든파티에의 초대 ❷ 형용사 왕립의 ❑ 왕립 음악원 ❸ 가산명사 왕족 [비격식체] ❑ 왕족은 옛날부터 항상 거액의 기부금을 끌어 모으는 자선 단체의 후원자이다.

가산명사 왕정주의자 ❑ 그는 왕정주의자들로부터는 미움을 받았고 공산주의자들에게서는 불신을 받았다.

❶ 불가산명사 왕족 ❑ 전 세계의 왕족과 정부 지도자들이 일본에 모여들고 있다. ❷ 복수명사 로열티, 저작권 사용료, 인세 ❑ 나는 매년 3천 파운드 정도의 인세로 생활했다. ❸ 가산명사 특허권 사용료 ❑ 그 발명가는 특허권 사용료를 받아 발명하는 일을 계속할 수 있었다.

불가산명사 (단순 반복 작업에 의한) 근육통 ❑ 열악한 근무 환경 때문에 그 여자들이 근육통을 앓고 있었다.

답변 바랍니다 (초대장) [격식체]

> 초대장에 RSVP가 있는 것은 초청자가 손님이 행사에 올 것인지 여부를 알 필요가 있는 경우이다. 초대를 받은 사람은 초청자가 계획을 세울 수 있도록 충분히 시간을 두고 답을 해주어야 한다. 또 초대장에 BYOB라는 말이 있으면 초대를 받은 사람이 술을 마시고 싶으면 '자기가 마실 술을 가져오라'는 뜻이다.

❶ 타동사/자동사 주무르다, 문지르다 ❑ 그는 자신의 팔과 뻣뻣해진 다리를 주물렀다. ❷ 타동사/자동사 비비다 ❑ 고양이 한 마리가 내 다리에 대고 몸을 비비고 있었다. ❸ 타동사/자동사 닦다 ❑ 그녀가 안경을 벗어서 열심히 닦았다. ❹ 타동사 문질러 바르다; 문질러 닦다 ❑ 그가 내 등에 오일을 발라 주었다. ❺ 타동사/자동사 서로 비벼 대다 ❑ 그가 두 손을 몇 번 비벼 댔다. ❻ 자동사 피부가 벗겨지다 ❑ 그 무엇에도 피부가 벗겨지거나, 쓸리거나, 베이는 일이 없어 피부에 편안할 것이다. ❼ 가산명사 안마 ❑ 내가 등에 안마를 받고 싶어 하는지 그녀는 가끔 묻는다. ❽ 구 (유명인과) 어울리다 ❑ 그는 정기적으로 엘리자베스 테일러와 카일리 미노그와 같은 유명인과 어울렸다. ❾ 구 비위를 건드리다 [비격식체] ❑ 네가 그 사람 비위를 건드리면, 그에게서 뭘 얻어 낼 수 있겠니?

Word Partnership   *rub*의 연어

PREP.	rub **against** 2
	rub **off**, rub **with** 3
ADV.	rub **together** 5

▶**rub out** PHRASAL VERB If you **rub out** something that you have written on paper or a board, you remove it using a rubber or eraser. ❏ *She began rubbing out the pencilled marks in the margin.*

구동사 지워 버리다 ❏ 그녀가 가장자리에 연필로 쓴 것들을 지우기 시작했다.

rub|ber /rʌbər/ (**rubbers**) **1** N-UNCOUNT **Rubber** is a strong, waterproof, elastic substance made from the juice of a tropical tree or produced chemically. It is used for making tires, boots, and other products. ❏ *...the smell of burning rubber.* **2** N-COUNT A **rubber** is a condom. [AM, INFORMAL] ❏ *Alma asked Ennis to use rubbers because she dreaded another pregnancy.* **3** N-COUNT A **rubber** is a small piece of rubber or other material that is used to remove mistakes that you have made while writing, drawing, or typing. [BRIT; AM **eraser**]

1 불가산명사 고무 ❏ 고무 타는 냄새 **2** 가산명사 콘돔 [미국영어, 비격식체] ❏ 알마는 또 다시 임신하는 것이 두려우니 콘돔을 쓰자고 에니스에게 말했다. **3** 가산명사 지우개 [영국영어; 미국영어 eraser]

rub|ber band (**rubber bands**) N-COUNT A **rubber band** is a thin circle of very elastic rubber. You put it around things such as papers in order to keep them together. →see **office**

가산명사 고무줄

rub|ber stamp (**rubber stamps, rubber stamping, rubber stamped**) also **rubber-stamp** **1** N-COUNT A **rubber stamp** is a small device with a name, date, or symbol on it. You press it onto an ink pad and then on to a document in order to show that the document has been officially dealt with. ❏ *In Post Offices, virtually every document that's passed across the counter is stamped with a rubber stamp.* **2** V-T When someone in authority **rubber-stamps** a decision, plan, or law, they agree to it without thinking about it much. ❏ *Parliament's job is to rubber-stamp his decisions.*

1 가산명사 고무도장 ❏ 우체국에서는 실질적으로 창구를 넘어 온 모든 서류에 고무도장으로 도장을 찍는다. **2** 타동사 충분한 고려 없이 승인해 주다 ❏ 의회가 하는 일은 그가 한 결정들을 별 고려 없이 그저 승인만 해 주는 것이다.

rub|bish /rʌbɪʃ/ (**rubbishes, rubbishing, rubbished**) **1** N-UNCOUNT **Rubbish** consists of unwanted things or waste material such as used paper, empty cans and bottles, and waste food. [mainly BRIT; AM usually **garbage, trash**] ❏ *...unwanted household rubbish.* **2** N-UNCOUNT If you think that something is of very poor quality, you can say that it is **rubbish**. [mainly BRIT, INFORMAL] ❏ *He described her book as absolute rubbish.* **3** ADJ If you think that someone is not very good at something, you can say that they are **rubbish** at it. [BRIT, INFORMAL] [v-link ADJ, usu ADJ at n] ❏ *He was rubbish at his job.* **4** V-T If you **rubbish** a person, their ideas or their work, you say they are of little value. [BRIT, INFORMAL; AM **trash**] ❏ *Five whole pages of script were devoted to rubbishing her political opponents.*

1 불가산명사 쓰레기 [주로 영국영어; 미국영어 대개 garbage, trash] ❏ 필요 없는 가정용 쓰레기 **2** 불가산명사 (품질이) 형편없는 것, 쓰레기 같은 것 [주로 영국영어, 비격식체] ❏ 그는 그녀의 책을 형편없는 쓰레기로 묘사했다. **3** 형용사 엉망인 [영국영어, 비격식체] ❏ 그는 자신의 일을 엉망으로 했다. **4** 타동사 무시하다 [영국영어, 비격식체; 미국영어 trash] ❏ 대본의 다섯 페이지 전체가 그녀의 정적(政敵)들을 무시하는 내용으로 채워져 있었다.

In British English, **rubbish** is the word most commonly used to refer to waste material that is thrown away. In American English, the words **garbage** and **trash** are more usual. ❏ *...the smell of rotting garbage... She threw the bottle into the trash.* Garbage and **trash** are sometimes used in British English, but only informally and metaphorically. ❏ *I don't have to listen to this garbage... The book was trash.*

영국 영어에서는 버리는 쓰레기를 가리킬 때 rubbish가 가장 흔히 쓰인다. 미국 영어에서는 garbage와 trash가 더 흔히 쓰인다. ❏ ...쓰레기 썩는 냄새... 그녀는 그 병을 쓰레기 속에 던져 넣었다. 때로는 영국 영어에서 garbage와 trash가 쓰이기도 하지만, 비격식체나 은유적으로만 쓴다. ❏ 난 이런 쓰레기 같은 이야기를 들을 필요가 없다... 그 책은 허섭스레기였다.

rub|ble /rʌbəl/ **1** N-UNCOUNT When a building is destroyed, the pieces of brick, stone, or other materials that remain are referred to as **rubble**. ❏ *Thousands of bodies are still buried under the rubble.* **2** N-UNCOUNT **Rubble** is used to refer to the small pieces of bricks and stones that are used as a bottom layer on which to build roads, paths, or houses. ❏ *Brick rubble is useful as the base for paths and patios.*

1 불가산명사 건물 잔해 ❏ 수천 구의 시신이 아직도 건물 잔해 속에 묻혀 있다. **2** 불가산명사 잡석, 자갈 ❏ 벽돌 조각은 길이나 테라스의 토대를 만드는 데 유용하다.

ruby /rubi/ (**rubies**) **1** N-COUNT A **ruby** is a dark red jewel. ❏ *...a ruby and diamond ring.* **2** COLOR Something that is **ruby** is dark red in color. ❏ *...a glass of ruby-red Cabernet Sauvignon.*

1 가산명사 루비 (보석) ❏ 루비와 다이아몬드가 박힌 반지 **2** 색채어 검붉은 색, 루비빛 ❏ 검붉은 카베르네 소비뇽 한 잔

ruck|sack /rʌksæk/ (**rucksacks**) N-COUNT A **rucksack** is a bag with straps that go over your shoulders, so that you can carry things on your back, for example when you are walking or climbing. [BRIT; AM usually **knapsack, pack, backpack**]

가산명사 배낭 [영국영어; 미국영어 대개 knapsack, pack, backpack]

rud|der /rʌdər/ (**rudders**) **1** N-COUNT A **rudder** is a device for steering a boat. It consists of a vertical piece of wood or metal at the back of the boat. **2** N-COUNT An airplane's **rudder** is a vertical piece of metal at the back which is used to make the plane turn to the right or to the left.

1 가산명사 (배의) 키 **2** 가산명사 (비행기의) 방향타

rud|dy /rʌdi/ (**ruddier, ruddiest**) ADJ If you describe someone's face as **ruddy**, you mean that their face is a reddish color, usually because they are healthy or have been working hard, or because they are angry or embarrassed. ❏ *He had a naturally ruddy complexion, even more flushed now from dancing.*

형용사 (안색이) 불그스레한 ❏ 그는 본래 안색이 불그스레한데, 지금은 춤을 춘 뒤라 훨씬 더 붉어졌다.

rude /rud/ (**ruder, rudest**) **1** ADJ When people are **rude**, they act in an impolite way toward other people or say impolite things about them. ❏ *He's rude to her friends and obsessively jealous.* ● **rude|ly** ADV ❏ *I could not understand why she felt compelled to behave so rudely to a friend.* ● **rude|ness** N-UNCOUNT ❏ *Mother is cross at Caleb's rudeness, but I can forgive it.* **2** ADJ **Rude** is used to describe words and behavior that are likely to embarrass or offend people, because they relate to sex or to body functions. [mainly BRIT; AM usually **vulgar**] ❏ *Fred keeps cracking rude jokes with the guests.* **3** ADJ If someone receives a **rude** shock, something unpleasant happens unexpectedly. [ADJ n] ❏ *It will come as a rude shock when their salary or income-tax refund cannot be cashed.* ● **rude|ly** ADV [ADV with v] ❏ *People were awakened rudely by a siren just outside their window.* **4** **rude awakening** →see **awakening**

1 형용사 무례한 ❏ 그는 그녀의 친구들에게 무례하고 지나치게 시기심이 많다. ● 무례하게 부사 ❏ 그녀가 왜 친구에게 굳이 그렇게 무례하게 구는지 나는 이해할 수 없었다. ● 무례함 불가산명사 ❏ 어머니께서는 칼렙의 무례함을 언짢아하시지만, 나는 그것을 용서할 수 있다. **2** 형용사 낯 뜨거운 [주로 영국영어; 미국영어 대개 vulgar] ❏ 프레드는 계속 손님들에게 낯 뜨거운 농담을 한다. **3** 형용사 예기치 못한 ❏ 월급이나 소득세 환불분을 현금으로 찾지 못하면 그들에게 예기치 못한 충격일 것이다. ● 별안간 부사 ❏ 사람들이 바로 창 밖에서 나는 사이렌 소리에 별안간 잠에서 깼다.

Thesaurus   *rude*의 참조어

| ADJ. | impolite, vulgar; *(ant.)* polite 1 2 |

ru|di|men|ta|ry /ruːdɪmɛntəri, -tri/ 1 ADJ **Rudimentary** things are very basic or simple and are therefore unsatisfactory. [FORMAL] ❏ *The earth surface of the courtyard extended into a kind of rudimentary kitchen.* 2 ADJ **Rudimentary** knowledge includes only the simplest and most basic facts. [FORMAL] ❏ *He had only a rudimentary knowledge of French.*

ruf|fle /rʌfᵊl/ (ruffles, ruffling, ruffled) 1 V-T If you **ruffle** someone's hair, you move your hand backward and forward through it as a way of showing your affection toward them. ❏ *"Don't let that get you down," he said ruffling Ben's dark curls.* 2 V-T When the wind **ruffles** something such as the surface of the sea, it causes it to move gently in a wave-like motion. [LITERARY] ❏ *The evening breeze ruffled the pond.* 3 V-T If something **ruffles** someone, it causes them to panic and lose their confidence or to become angry or upset. ❏ *I could tell that my refusal to allow him to ruffle me infuriated him.* 4 V-T/V-I If a bird **ruffles** its feathers or if its feathers **ruffle**, they stand out on its body, for example when it is cleaning itself or when it is frightened. ❏ *Tame birds, when approached, will stretch out their necks and ruffle their neck feathering.* 5 N-COUNT **Ruffles** are folds of cloth at the neck or the ends of the arms of a piece of clothing, or are sometimes sewn on things as a decoration. ❏ *...a white blouse with ruffles at the neck and cuffs.* 6 PHRASE To **ruffle** someone's **feathers** means to cause them to become very angry, nervous, or upset. ❏ *His direct, often abrasive approach will doubtless ruffle a few feathers.*

ruf|fled /rʌfᵊld/ ADJ Something that is **ruffled** is no longer smooth or neat. ❏ *Her short hair was oddly ruffled and then flattened around her head.*

rug /rʌg/ (rugs) 1 N-COUNT A **rug** is a piece of thick material that you put on a floor. It is like a carpet but covers a smaller area. ❏ *A Persian rug covered the hardwood floors.* 2 N-COUNT A **rug** is a small blanket which you use to cover your shoulders or your knees to keep them warm. [mainly BRIT] ❏ *The old lady was seated in her chair at the window, a rug over her knees.* 3 PHRASE If someone **pulls the rug from under** a person or thing or **pulls the rug from under** someone's **feet**, they stop giving their help or support. ❏ *If the banks opt to pull the rug from under the ill-fated project, it will go into liquidation.* to **sweep** something **under the rug** →see **sweep**

rug|by ◆◇◇ /rʌgbi/ N-UNCOUNT **Rugby** or rugby football is a game played by two teams using an oval ball. Players try to score points by carrying the ball to their opponents' end of the field, or by kicking it over a bar fixed between two posts.

rug|ged /rʌgɪd/ 1 ADJ A **rugged** area of land is uneven and covered with rocks, with few trees or plants. [LITERARY] ❏ *We left the rough track and bumped our way over a rugged mountainous terrain.* 2 ADJ If you describe a man as **rugged**, you mean that he has strong, masculine features. [LITERARY, APPROVAL] ❏ *A look of pure disbelief crossed Shankly's rugged face.* 3 ADJ If you describe someone's character as **rugged**, you mean that they are strong and determined, and have the ability to cope with difficult situations. [APPROVAL] ❏ *Rugged individualism forged America's frontier society.* 4 ADJ A **rugged** piece of equipment is strong and is designed to last a long time, even if it is treated roughly. ❏ *The camera combines rugged reliability with unequalled optical performance and speed.*

ruin ◆◇◇ /ruːɪn/ (ruins, ruining, ruined) 1 V-T To **ruin** something means to severely harm, damage, or spoil it. ❏ *My wife was ruining her health through worry.* 2 V-T To **ruin** someone means to cause them to no longer have any money. ❏ *She accused him of ruining her financially with his taste for the high life.* 3 N-UNCOUNT **Ruin** is the state of no longer having any money. ❏ *The farmers say recent inflation has driven them to the brink of ruin.* 4 N-UNCOUNT **Ruin** is the state of being severely damaged or spoiled, or the process of reaching this state. ❏ *The vineyards were falling into ruin.* 5 N-PLURAL **The ruins of** something are the parts of it that remain after it has been severely damaged or weakened. ❏ *The new Turkish republic he helped to build emerged from the ruins of a great empire.* 6 N-COUNT **The ruins** of a building are the parts of it that remain after the rest has fallen down or been destroyed. ❏ *One dead child was found in the ruins almost two hours after the explosion.* 7 →see also **ruined** 8 PHRASE If something is **in ruins**, it is completely spoiled. ❏ *Its heavily-subsidized economy is in ruins.* 9 PHRASE If a building or place is **in ruins**, most of it has been destroyed and only parts of it remain. ❏ *The abbey was in ruins.*

Thesaurus	ruin의 참조어
v.	destroy, smash, wreck 1

ruined /ruːɪnd/ ADJ A **ruined** building or place has been very badly damaged or has gradually fallen down because no one has taken care of it. [ADJ n] ❏ *...a ruined church.*

rule ◆◆◆ /ruːl/ (rules, ruling, ruled) 1 N-COUNT **Rules** are instructions that tell you what you are allowed to do and what you are not allowed to do. ❏ *...a thirty-two-page pamphlet explaining the rules of basketball.* 2 N-COUNT A **rule** is a statement telling people what they should do in order to achieve success or a benefit of some kind. ❏ *An important rule is to drink plenty of water during any flight.* 3 N-COUNT The **rules of** something such as a language or a science are statements that describe the way that things usually happen in a particular situation. ❏ *...according to the rules of quantum theory.* 4 N-SING If something is **the rule**, it is the normal state of affairs. ❏ *However, for many Americans today, weekend work has unfortunately become the rule rather than the exception.* 5 V-T/V-I The person or group that **rules** a country controls its affairs. ❏ *For four centuries, he says, foreigners have ruled Angola.* ❏ *He ruled for eight months.* ● N-UNCOUNT **Rule** is also a noun. ❏ *...demands for an end to one-party rule.* 6 V-T If something **rules** your life, it influences or restricts your actions in a way that is not good for you. ❏ *Scientists have always been aware of how fear can rule our lives and make us ill.* 7 V-T/V-I When someone in authority **rules** that something is true or should

1 형용사 아주 기본적인 [격식체] ❏ 안뜰의 홈이랑은 기본적인 설비만 갖춘 부엌으로 연결되어 있었다. 2 형용사 초보적인, 기초적인 [격식체] ❏ 그는 불어에 대해 초보적인 지식만 가지고 있었다.

1 타동사 (애정 표시로 상대방의 머리를) 헝클어 놓다 ❏ "그것 때문에 실망하지 마세요." 그가 벤의 갈색 곱슬머리를 헝클어 놓으며 말했다. 2 타동사 잔물결을 일으키다 [문예체] ❏ 부드러운 저녁 바람이 연못에 잔물결을 일으켰다. 3 타동사 화나게 만들다, (마음을) 뒤흔들다 ❏ 그가 어떻게 하든 내가 꿈쩍 않고 마음이 흔들리지 않으면 그가 몹시 화를 낼 것임을 나는 알 수 있었다. 4 타동사/자동사 (깃털을) 곤두세우다 ❏ 길들여진 새는 뭔가가 다가오면, 예를 들게 털을 뽑으면서 목 깃털을 곤두세운다. 5 가산명사 (옷의) 주름 장식 ❏ 목과 손목에 주름 장식이 있는 흰색 블라우스 6 구 화나게 만들다 ❏ 그의 직접적이고도 흔히 거슬리는 태도가 분명히 여러 사람을 화나게 만들 것이다.

형용사 헝클어진 ❏ 그녀의 짧은 머리카락이 이상하게 헝클어지더니, 머리에 납작하게 붙어 버렸다.

1 가산명사 깔개, 작은 카펫 ❏ 페르시아산 깔개가 딱딱한 나무 바닥에 깔려 있었다. 2 가산명사 무릎 덮게 [주로 영국영어] ❏ 그 노부인은 무릎 덮개를 덮은 채 창가에서 의자에 앉아 있었다. 3 구 원조를 중지하다 ❏ 만약 그 은행들이 그 불운한 프로젝트에 주던 원조를 중지하기로 결정하면, 그 프로젝트는 청산될 것이다.

불가산명사 럭비

1 형용사 바위투성이의 [문예체] ❏ 우리는 험한 산길을 벗어나서 바위투성이의 산간 지역을 덜컹거리며 지나갔다. 2 형용사 다부진, 강인한 [문예체, 마음에 듦] ❏ 백 퍼센트 불신하는 표정이 샨클리의 다부진 얼굴을 스쳐 지나갔다. 3 형용사 굳건한 [마음에 듦] ❏ 굳건한 개인주의 정신이 미국의 서부 개척민 사회를 만들었다. 4 형용사 견고한 ❏ 그 사진기는 견고한 내구성과 다양한 광학 기능 및 속도 기능을 겸비하고 있다.

1 타동사 망치다 ❏ 내 아내는 지나친 걱정 때문에 건강을 망치고 있었다. 2 타동사 파산시키다 ❏ 그녀는 그의 상류 생활 취향 때문에 자신이 파산했다고 그를 비난했다. 3 불가산명사 파산 ❏ 농부들은 최근의 인플레이션 때문에 자신들이 파산 직전에 있다고 말한다. 4 불가산명사 폐허, 황폐화 ❏ 그 포도밭은 완전히 폐허가 되어 가고 있었다. 5 복수명사 유적 ❏ 그가 재건을 도왔던 새로운 터키 공화국이 위대한 제국의 유적으로부터 모습을 드러냈다. 6 가산명사 잔해 ❏ 그 폭발이 있은 지 거의 두 시간 만에 잔해 속에서 어린이 시신 한 구를 발견했다. 8 구 완전히 무너진 ❏ 정부 보조금에 지나치게 의존하던 그 국가의 경제는 완전히 무너졌다. 9 구 거의 폐허가 된 ❏ 그 사원은 거의 폐허가 되어 있었다.

형용사 폐허가 된 ❏ 폐허가 된 교회

1 가산명사 규칙 ❏ 농구 규칙을 설명하는 32쪽짜리 책자 2 가산명사 주의 사항 ❏ 중요한 주의 사항 한 가지는 어떤 경우든 비행 중에 물을 많이 마시라는 것이다. 3 가산명사 법칙 ❏ 양자학 이론의 법칙에 의하면 4 단수명사 관례 ❏ 그러나, 불행하게도 주말에 일하는 것이 오늘날 많은 미국인들에게 예외적이라기보다는 관례가 되고 있다. 5 타동사/자동사 통치하다 ❏ 4세기 동안 이방인들이 앙골라를 통치해 왔다고 그는 말한다. ❏ 그는 8개월간 통치했다. ● 불가산명사 통치 ❏ 일당 독재의 종식에 대한 요구 6 타동사 지배하다 ❏ 과학자들은 공포심이 어떻게 우리의 삶을 지배하고, 또 우리를 병들게 하는지 늘 알고 있었다. 7 타동사/자동사 판결하다 [격식체] ❏ 법정은 의회에서 통과된 법률이 여전히 유효하다고 판결했다. ❏ 이스라엘 법정이 아직 그 사건에 대해 판결을 내리지 않았다. 8 타동사 (자로)

happen, they state that they have officially decided that it is true or should happen. [FORMAL] ❑ *The court ruled that laws passed by the assembly remained valid.* ❑ *The Israeli court has not yet ruled on the case.* ⑧ V-T If you **rule** a straight line, you draw it using something that has a straight edge. ❑ *...a ruled grid of horizontal and vertical lines.* ⑨ →see also **golden rule**, **ground rule**, **ruling** ⑩ PHRASE If you say that something happens **as a rule**, you mean that it usually happens. ❑ *As a rule, however, such attacks have been aimed at causing damage rather than taking life.* ⑪ PHRASE If someone in authority **bends the rules** or **stretches the rules**, they do something even though it is against the rules. ❑ *There happens to be a particular urgency in this case, and it would help if you could bend the rules.* ⑫ PHRASE A **rule of thumb** is a rule or principle that you follow which is not based on exact calculations, but rather on experience. ❑ *A good rule of thumb is that a broker must generate sales of ten times his salary if his employer is to make a profit.* ⑬ PHRASE If workers **work to rule**, they protest by working according to the rules of their job without doing any extra work or taking any new decisions. [BRIT] ❑ *Nurses are continuing to work to rule.*

줄을 긋다 ❑ 가로와 세로로 줄을 그은 빙고판 ⑩ 일반적으로 ❑ 그러나, 일반적으로, 그런 공격의 목적은 인명살상보다는 손상을 입히기 위한 것이다. ⑪ 구 규칙을 융통성 있게 적용시키다 ❑ 이런 경우에는 마침 특정한 비상사태가 발생한 것이니 규칙을 융통성 있게 적용시킬 수 있다면 도움이 될 것이다. ⑫ 구 경험에서 얻은 법칙 ❑ 경험상 볼 때, 고용주가 이윤을 내려면 중개인은 자기 월급의 10배에 달하는 실적을 올려야 한다. ⑬ 구 준법 투쟁을 하다 [영국영어] ❑ 간호사들이 준법 투쟁을 계속하고 있다.

Thesaurus *rule*의 참조어

N.	guideline, law, standard ① ②
	authority, leadership ⑤
V.	command, dictate, govern ⑤ ⑥

Word Partnership *rule*의 연어

V.	break a rule, change a rule, follow a rule ①
N.	exception to a rule ①-④
	majority rule, minority rule ⑤
	courts rule, judges rule ⑦
	rule of thumb ⑫
PREP.	against a rule, under a rule ①
	rule over *something* ⑤

▶**rule out** ① PHRASAL VERB If you **rule out** a course of action, an idea, or a solution, you decide that it is impossible or unsuitable. ❑ *The Prime Minister is believed to have ruled out cuts in child benefit or pensions.* ② PHRASAL VERB If something **rules out** a situation, it prevents it from happening or from being possible. ❑ *A serious car accident in 1986 ruled out a permanent future for him in farming.*

① 구동사 (불가능하다고) 배제하다 ❑ 수상이 육아 수당이나 연금에 대한 삭감안을 배제시켰었다고 사람들은 믿고 있다. ② 구동사 불가능하게 만들다 ❑ 1986년에 일어난 심각한 교통사고로 그는 영원히 농장 일을 할 수 없게 되었다.

rul|er /rúlər/ (**rulers**) ① N-COUNT The **ruler** of a country is the person who rules the country. ❑ *The former military ruler of Lesotho has been placed under house arrest.* ② N-COUNT A **ruler** is a long flat piece of wood, metal, or plastic with straight edges marked in or inches or centimeters. Rulers are used to measure things and to draw straight lines. ❑ *...a twelve inch ruler.*

① 가산명사 통치자 ❑ 레소토의 전 군부 통치자가 가택 연금에 처해졌다. ② 가산명사 자 ❑ 12인치짜리 자

rul|ing ♦◇◇ /rúlɪŋ/ (**rulings**) ① ADJ The **ruling** group of people in a country or organization is the group that controls its affairs. [ADJ n] ❑ *...the Mexican voters' growing dissatisfaction with the ruling party.* ② N-COUNT A **ruling** is an official decision made by a judge or court. ❑ *Goodwin tried to have the court ruling overturned.* ③ ADJ Someone's **ruling** passion or emotion is the feeling they have most strongly, which influences their actions. [ADJ n] ❑ *Even my love of literary fame, my ruling passion, never soured my temper.*

① 형용사 통치하는, 지배하는 ❑ 집권당에 대한 멕시코 유권자들의 점증하는 불만 ② 가산명사 판결 ❑ 굿윈은 법원 판결이 번복되게 하려고 노력했다. ③ 형용사 주된, 우세한 ❑ 내가 가진 주된 열정인 문학적 명성에 대한 사랑도 내 성격을 비뚤어지게 하지 않았다.

rum /rʌm/ (**rums**) N-MASS **Rum** is an alcoholic drink made from sugar. ❑ *...a bottle of rum.*

물질명사 럼주 ❑ 럼주 한 병

rum|ble /rʌmbᵊl/ (**rumbles, rumbling, rumbled**) ① N-COUNT A **rumble** is a low continuous noise. ❑ *The silence of the night was punctuated by the distant rumble of traffic.* ② V-I If a vehicle **rumbles**, it moves slowly forward while making a low continuous noise. ❑ *A bus rumbled along the road.* ③ V-I If something **rumbles**, it makes a low, continuous noise. ❑ *The sky, swollen like a black bladder, rumbled and crackled.* ④ V-I If your stomach **rumbles**, it makes a vibrating noise, usually because you are hungry. ❑ *Her stomach rumbled. She hadn't eaten any breakfast.* ⑤ V-T If someone **is rumbled**, the truth about them or something they were trying to hide is discovered. [BRIT, INFORMAL] [usu passive] ❑ *When his fraud was rumbled he had just £20.17 in the bank.*

① 가산명사 우르릉거리는 소리, 덜컹거리는 소리 ❑ 멀리서 들려오는 차들의 우르릉거리는 소리가 간간이 밤의 정적을 깨뜨렸다. ② 자동사 (자동차 등이) 덜컹거리며 가다 ❑ 버스 한 대가 그 길을 따라 덜컹거리며 달렸다. ③ 자동사 우르릉거리다 ❑ 검은 고무공처럼 부풀어 오른 하늘에서 우르릉거리고 우지직 하는 소리가 났다. ④ 자동사 꼬르륵 소리를 내다 ❑ 그녀의 배에서 꼬르륵 소리가 났다. 그녀는 아침을 전혀 먹지 않은 상태였다. ⑤ 타동사 간파당하다, 들통 나다 [영국영어, 비격식체] ❑ 사기 행위가 들통 났을 때 그는 은행에 고작 20.17파운드밖에 없었다.

▶**rumble on** PHRASAL VERB If you say that something such as an argument **rumbles on**, you mean that it continues for a long time after it should have been settled. [BRIT, JOURNALISM] ❑ *And still the row rumbles on over who is to blame for the steadily surging crime statistics.*

구동사 (다툼 등으로) 계속 시끄럽다 [영국영어, 언론] ❑ 그리고 꾸준히 증가하는 범죄 통계치에 대해 누가 책임을 져야 하는지에 대한 언쟁으로 여전히 시끄럽다.

rum|bling /rʌmblɪŋ/ (**rumblings**) ① N-COUNT A **rumbling** is a low continuous noise. ❑ *...the rumbling of an empty stomach.* ② N-COUNT **Rumblings** are signs that a bad situation is developing or that people are becoming annoyed or unhappy. ❑ *Even Bayldon had become aware that there were rumblings of discontent within the ranks.*

① 가산명사 덜컹거리는 소리, 우르르거리는 소리, 꼬르륵 소리 ❑ 빈속에서 나는 꼬르륵 소리 ② 가산명사 (불길한) 조짐, (불만을 품은) 웅성거림 ❑ 심지어 베일든마저도 사원들이 불만으로 웅성거린다는 것을 알게 되었다.

rum|mage /rʌmɪdʒ/ (**rummages, rummaging, rummaged**) V-I If you **rummage** through something, you search for something you want by moving things around in a careless or hurried way. ❑ *They rummage through piles of second-hand clothes for something that fits.* ● N-SING **Rummage** is also a noun. ❑ *A brief rummage will provide several pairs of gloves.* ● PHRASAL VERB **Rummage about** and **rummage around** mean the same as **rummage**. ❑ *I opened the fridge and rummaged about.*

자동사 뒤적거리다 ❑ 그들은 몸에 맞는 것을 찾아 헌 옷 더미를 뒤적거린다. ● 단수명사 뒤적거리기 ❑ 잠깐 뒤적거려 보면 장갑 몇 켤레를 구할 수 있을 것이다. ● 구동사 뒤적거리다 ❑ 나는 냉장고를 열고 뒤적거렸다.

a

People trying to raise funds for charity, for a school (for example, to buy a computer), or for a church (to repair the roof, perhaps) may come up with the idea of holding a **rummage sale** (or **jumble sale** in the UK) in the school or church hall. Items such as clothing, toys, books, and household goods are donated by people who no longer need them, and shoppers come along in the hope of finding a second-hand bargain.

자선 단체나 학교(예를 들어, 컴퓨터를 사기 위해서) 또는 교회(예컨대, 지붕 수리가 필요하다든지 해서) 등에서 자금을 마련할 필요가 있을 때 학교나 교회 홀에서 rummage sale(자선바자: 영국에서는 jumble sale)이라고 함을 열 수가 있다. 사람들이 자기에게 더 이상 필요하지 않은 옷, 장난감, 책, 가정용품 등을 기증하고, 구매자들은 싼 값에 알뜰하게 중고품을 사러 온다.

ru|mor ◆◇◇ /rúmər/ (**rumors**) [BRIT **rumour**] N-VAR A **rumor** is a story or piece of information that may or may not be true, but that people are talking about. ❑ *U.S. officials are discounting rumors of a coup.*

[영국영어 rumour] 가산명사 또는 불가산명사 소문, 풍설 ❑ 미국 관계자들은 쿠데타 소문을 대수롭지 않게 생각하고 있다.

Word Partnership	*rumor*의 연어
ADJ.	**false** rumor
V.	**hear** a rumor, **spread** a rumor, **start** a rumor

ru|mored /rúmərd/ [BRIT **rumoured**] V-T PASSIVE If something **is rumored to** be the case, people are suggesting that it is the case, but they do not know for certain. ❑ *The company is rumored to be a takeover target.*

[영국영어 rumoured] 수동 타동사 ~라는 소문이 나다 ❑ 그 회사가 인수 대상이라는 소문이 있다.

rump /rʌmp/ (**rumps**) ■ N-COUNT An animal's **rump** is its rear end. ❑ *The cows' rumps were marked with their owner's initials and a number.* ◻ N-UNCOUNT **Rump** or **rump steak** is meat cut from the rear end of a cow. ❑ *...a kilo of rump.* ◻ N-SING The **rump of** a group, organization, or country consists of the members who remain in it after the rest have left. [mainly BRIT] ❑ *The rump of the party does in fact still have considerable assets.*

■ 가산명사 (짐승 등의) 엉덩이 ❑ 그 소들의 엉덩이에는 주인의 이름 약어와 숫자가 찍혀 있었다. ◻ 불가산명사 엉덩잇살 ◻ 우둔살 1킬로그램 ◻ 단수명사 잔류파, 잔당 [주로 영국영어] ❑ 그 정당의 잔류파들이 사실상 아직 상당한 자산을 보유하고 있다.

run ◆◆◆ /rʌn/ (**runs, running, ran**)

The form **run** is used in the present tense and is also the past participle of the verb.

run은 동사의 현재 및 과거 분사로 쓰인다.

→Please look at category 55 to see if the expression you are looking for is shown under another headword. ■ V-T/V-I When you **run**, you move more quickly than when you walk, for example because you are in a hurry to get somewhere, or for exercise. ❑ *I excused myself and ran back to the telephone.* ❑ *He ran the last block to the White House with two cases of gear.* ● N-COUNT **Run** is also a noun. ❑ *After a six-mile run, Jackie returns home for a substantial breakfast.* ◻ V-T/V-I When someone **runs** in a race, they run in competition with other people. ❑ *...when I was running in the New York Marathon.* ◻ V-T/V-I When a horse **runs** in a race or when its owner **runs** it, it competes in a race. ❑ *He was overruled by the owner, Peter Bolton, who insisted on Cool Ground running in the Gold Cup.* ◻ V-I If you say that something long, such as a road, **runs** in a particular direction, you are describing its course or position. You can also say that something **runs** the length or width of something else. ❑ *...the sun-dappled trail which ran through the beech woods.* ◻ V-T If you **run** a wire or tube somewhere, you fix it or pull it from, to, or across a particular place. ❑ *Our host ran a long extension cord out from the house and set up a screen and a projector.* ◻ V-T If you **run** your hand or an object **through** something, you move your hand or the object through it. ❑ *He laughed and ran his fingers through his hair.* ◻ V-T If you **run** something through a machine, process, or series of tests, you make it go through the machine, process, or tests. ❑ *They have gathered the best statistics they can find and run them through their own computers.* ◻ V-I If someone **runs for** office in an election, they take part as a candidate. ❑ *It was only last February that he announced he would run for president.* ❑ *It is no easy job to run against John Glenn, Ohio's Democratic senator.* ◻ N-SING A **run for** office is an attempt to be elected to office. [mainly AM; BRIT usually **bid**] [N for n] ❑ *He was already preparing his run for the presidency.* ◻ V-T If you **run** something such as a business or an activity, you are in charge of it or you organize it. ❑ *His stepfather ran a prosperous paint business.* ❑ *...a well-run, profitable organization.* ◻ V-I If you talk about how a system, an organization, or someone's life is **running**, you are saying how well it is operating or progressing. [usu cont] ❑ *Officials in charge of the camps say the system is now running extremely smoothly.* ◻ V-T/V-I If you **run** an experiment, computer program, or other process, or start it **running**, you start it and let it continue. ❑ *He ran a lot of tests and it turned out I had an infection called mycoplasma.* ◻ V-T/V-I When you **run** a cassette or videotape or when it **runs**, it moves through the machine as the machine operates. ❑ *Leaphorn pushed the play button again, ran the tape, pushed stop, pushed rewind.* ◻ V-T/V-I When a machine **is running** or when you **are running** it, it is switched on and is working. [usu cont] ❑ *We told him to wait out front with the engine running.* ◻ V-I A machine or equipment that **runs on** or **off** a particular source of energy functions using that source of energy. ❑ *Black cabs run on diesel.* ◻ V-T If you **run** a car or a piece of equipment, you have it and use it. [mainly BRIT] ❑ *I ran a 1960 Rover 100 from 1977 until 1983.* ◻ V-I When you say that vehicles such as trains and buses **run** from one place to another, you mean they regularly travel along that route. ❑ *A shuttle bus runs frequently between the Inn and the Country Club.* ◻ V-T If you **run** someone somewhere in a car, you drive them there. [INFORMAL] ❑ *Could you run me up to Baltimore?* ◻ V-I If you **run** over or down to a place that is quite near, you drive there. [INFORMAL] ❑ *I'll run over to Short Mountain and check on Mrs. Adams.* ◻ N-COUNT A **run** is a trip somewhere. ❑ *...doing the morning school run.* ◻ V-I If a liquid **runs** in a particular direction, it flows in that direction. ❑ *Tears were running down her cheeks.* ◻ V-T If you **run** water, or if you **run** a faucet or a bath, you cause water to flow from a faucet. ❑ *She went to the sink and ran water into her empty glass.* ◻ V-I If a faucet or a bath **is running**, water is coming out of a faucet. [only cont] ❑ *The kitchen sink had been stopped up and the faucet left running, so water spilled over onto the floor.* ◻ V-I If your nose **is running**, liquid is flowing out of it, usually because you have a cold. [usu cont] ❑ *Timothy was crying, mostly from exhaustion, and his nose was running.* ◻ V-I If a surface **is running with** a liquid, that liquid is flowing down

[영국영어 rumoured] 수동 타동사 ~라는 소문이 나다 ❑ 그 회사가 인수 대상이라는 소문이 있다.

■ 타동사/자동사 달리다, 뛰다 ❑ 나는 양해를 구하고 다시 전화기로 달려갔다. ❑ 그는 백악관까지 마지막 블록을 장비가 든 상자 두 개를 들고 뛰어서 갔다. ● 가산명사 달리기 ❑ 달리기를 6마일 한 후, 재키는 풍성한 아침 식사를 하기 위해 집으로 돌아온다. ◻ 타동사/자동사 (경주에서) 달리다 ❑ 내가 뉴욕 마라톤 대회에 출전하고 있을 때 ◻ 타동사/자동사 (말이 경주에 나가) 달리다, (말을 경주에서) 달리게 하다 ❑ 그는 골드컵 경주에서 '쿨 그라운드'가 뛸 것을 고집한 마주 피터 볼턴에게 퇴짜를 맞았다. ◻ 자동사 (긴 등이) 나 있다, 뻗어 있다 ❑ 너도밤나무 숲 사이로 나 있던, 햇빛이 스며 비치던 오솔길 ◻ 타동사 (전선 등을) 연결하다, 끌어오다 ❑ 주인이 집에서 전선을 길게 연결해서 끌어 와 스크린과 영사기를 설치했다. ◻ 타동사 (사이로) 지나가게 하다 ❑ 그는 웃으며 손가락으로 머리를 빗어 넘겼다. ◻ 타동사 (기계 등으로) 처리하다 ❑ 그들은 구할 수 있는 최고의 통계 자료를 수집해서 자체 컴퓨터를 통해 처리했다. ◻ 자동사 입후보하다 ❑ 그가 대통령 입후보를 선언한 것이 고작 지난 2월이었다. ❑ 오하이오 민주당 상원 의원 존 글렌에 맞서 후보로 나서는 것은 쉬운 일이 아니다. ◻ 단수명사 입후보 [주로 미국영어; 영국영어 대개 bid] ❑ 그는 이미 대통령 입후보를 준비하고 있었다. ◻ 타동사 경영하다, 운영하다 ❑ 그의 의붓아버지는 번창한 페인트 사업체를 경영했다. ❑ 잘 운영되며 수익성 있는 조직 ◻ 자동사 굴러가다, 작동하다 ❑ 수용소 감독을 맡고 있는 관리들은 현재 시스템이 아주 순조롭게 굴러가고 있다고 말한다. ◻ 타동사/자동사 (장비 등을) 돌리다 ❑ 그가 많은 검사를 했고, 나는 미코플라스마라는 미생물에 감염되었음이 판명되었다. ◻ 타동사(테이프를) 틀다 ❑ 리폰은 다시 재생 버튼을 눌러 테이프를 틀었다가, 정지 버튼을 누른 다음, 되감기 버튼을 눌렀다. ◻ 타동사/자동사 작동하다; 작동시키다 ❑ 우리는 그에게 나가 시동을 걸고 기다리라고 했다. ◻ 자동사 ~을 동력원으로 하여 작동하다 ❑ 전통적인 택시는 디젤유를 쓴다. ◻ 타동사 (차량 등을) 굴리다 [주로 영국영어] ❑ 나는 1977년부터 1983년까지 1960년형 로버100을 타고 다녔다. ◻ 자동사 운행하다 ❑ 순환 버스 한 대가 여관과 컨트리클럽 사이를 자주 운행한다. ◻ 타동사 (차로) 데려다 주다 [비격식체] ❑ 저를 볼티모어까지 차로 데려다 주시겠어요? ◻ 자동사 차로 보고 가다 [비격식체] ❑ 차를 몰고 쇼트 마운틴으로 가서 애덤스 부인을 살펴보겠다. ◻ 가산명사 짧은 이동 ❑ 아침에 학교에 등교하면서 ◻ 자동사 흐르다 ❑ 그녀의 두 뺨에 눈물이 타고 흘러내리고 있었다. ◻ 타동사 (수도를) 틀다 ❑ 그녀는 개수대로 가서 물을 틀어 빈 잔에 받았다. ◻ 자동사 (수도에서) 물이 나오고 있다[흐르다] ❑ 무엇 개수대 구멍이 막혀 있는 수도꼭지를 틀어 놓은 채로 내버려 둬서, 물이 바닥으로 흘러 넘쳤다. ◻ 자동사 (콧물을) 흘리다 ❑ 티머시는 주로 기진맥진한 탓에 울고 있었고, 코에서 콧물이 흘러내리고 있었다. ◻ 자동사 ~가 흘러내리다 ❑ 한 시간 후 그는 완전히 온몸에 땀이 줄줄 흐르고 있는 걸 깨달았다. ◻ 자동사 (잉크 등이) 번지다 ❑ 종이가

b
c
d
e
f
g
h
i
j
k
l
m
n
o
p
q
r
s
t
u
v
w
x
y
z

it. [usu cont] ❑ *After an hour he realized he was completely running with sweat.* 25 V-I If the dye in some cloth or the ink on some paper **runs**, it comes off or spreads when the cloth or paper gets wet. ❑ *The ink had run on the wet paper.* 27 V-I If a feeling **runs through** your body or a thought **runs through** your mind, you experience it or think it quickly. ❑ *She felt a surge of excitement run through her.* 28 V-I If a feeling or noise **runs through** a group of people, it spreads among them. ❑ *A buzz of excitement ran through the crowd.* 29 V-I If a theme or feature **runs through** something such as someone's actions or writing, it is present in all of it. ❑ *Another thread running through this series is the role of doctors in the treatment of the mentally ill.* 30 V-T/V-I When newspapers or magazines **run** a particular item or story or if it **runs**, it is published or printed. ❑ *The New Orleans Times-Picayune ran a series of four scathing editorials entitled "The Choice of Our Lives."* 31 V-I If an amount **is running** at a particular level, it is at that level. ❑ *Today's RPI figure shows inflation running at 10.9 per cent.* 32 V-I If a play, event, or legal contract **runs** for a particular period of time, it lasts for that period of time. ❑ *It pleased critics but ran for only three years in the West End.* ❑ *The contract was to run from 1992 to 2020.* 33 V-I If someone or something **is running** late, they have taken more time than had been planned. If they **are running** to time or ahead of time, they have taken the time planned or less than the time planned. [usu cont] ❑ *Tell her I'll call her back later, I'm running late again.* 34 V-T If you **are running** a temperature or a fever, you have a high temperature because you are ill. ❑ *The little girl is running a fever and she needs help.* 35 N-COUNT A **run** of a play or television program is the period of time during which performances are given or programs are shown. ❑ *The show will transfer to the West End on October 9, after a month's run in Birmingham.* 36 N-COUNT A **run** of successes or failures is a series of successes or failures. ❑ *The England skipper is haunted by a run of low scores.* 37 N-COUNT A **run** of a product is the amount that a company or factory decides to produce at one time. ❑ *Wayne plans to increase the print run to 1,000.* 38 N-COUNT In baseball or cricket, a **run** is a score of one, which is made by players running between marked places on the field after hitting the ball. ❑ *At 20 he became the youngest player to score 2,000 runs in a season.* 39 N-SING If someone gives you the **run of** a place, they give you permission to go where you like in it and use it as you wish. ❑ *He had the run of the house and the pool.* 40 N-SING If there is a **run on** something, a lot of people want to buy it or get it at the same time. ❑ *A run on sterling has killed off hopes of a rate cut.* 41 N-COUNT A ski **run** or bobsled **run** is a course or route that has been designed for skiing or for riding in a bobsled. ❑ *...an avalanche on Britain's highest ski run.* 42 →see also **running** 43 PHRASE If something happens **against the run of** play or **against the run of** events, it is different from what is generally happening in a game or situation. [BRIT] ❑ *The decisive goal arrived against the run of play.* 44 PHRASE If you **run** someone **close**, **run** them **a close second**, or **run a close second**, you almost beat them in a race or competition. ❑ *The Under-21 team has defeated Wales and Scotland this season, and ran England very close.* 45 PHRASE If a river or well **runs dry**, it no longer has any water in it. If an oil well **runs dry**, it no longer produces any oil. ❑ *Streams had run dry for the first time in memory.* 46 PHRASE If a source of information or money **runs dry**, no more information or money can be obtained from it. ❑ *Three days into production, the kitty had run dry.* 47 PHRASE If a characteristic **runs in** someone's **family**, it often occurs in members of that family, in different generations. ❑ *The insanity which ran in his family haunted him.* 48 PHRASE If you **make a run for it** or if you **run for it**, you run away in order to escape from someone or something. ❑ *A helicopter hovered overhead as one of the gang made a run for it.* 49 PHRASE If people's feelings **are running high**, they are very angry, concerned, or excited. ❑ *Feelings there have been running high in the wake of last week's killing.* 50 PHRASE If you talk about what will happen **in the long run**, you are saying that you think will happen over a long period of time in the future. If you talk about what will happen **in the short run**, you are saying what you think will happen in the near future. ❑ *Sometimes expensive drugs or other treatments can be economical in the long run.* 51 PHRASE If you say that someone could **give** someone else **a run for** their **money**, you mean you think they are almost as good as the other person. ❑ *...a youngster who even now could give Meryl Streep a run for her money.* 52 PHRASE If someone is **on the run**, they are trying to escape or hide from someone such as the police or an enemy. ❑ *Fifteen-year-old Danny is on the run from a local authority home.* 53 PHRASE If someone is **on the run**, they are being severely defeated in a contest or competition. ❑ *I knew I had him on the run.* 54 PHRASE If you **are running short of** something or **running low on** something, you do not have much of it left. If a supply of something **is running short** or **running low**, there is not much of it left. ❑ *Government forces are running short of ammunition and fuel.* 55 to **run deep** →see deep. to **run an errand** →see errand. to **run the gauntlet** →see gauntlet. to **run riot** →see riot. to **run a risk** →see risk. to **run to seed** →see seed. to **run wild** →see wild

Thesaurus	run의 참조어

v. dash, jog, sprint 1
    follow, go 4
    administer, conduct, manage 10

▶**run across** PHRASAL VERB If you **run across** someone or something, you meet them or find them unexpectedly. ❑ *We ran across some old friends in the village.*

▶**run away** 1 PHRASAL VERB If you **run away** from a place, you leave it because you are unhappy there. ❑ *I ran away from home when I was sixteen.* ❑ *After his beating Colin ran away and hasn't been heard of since.* 2 PHRASE VERB-RECIP If you **run away** with someone, you secretly go away with them in order to live with them or marry them. ❑ *She ran away with a man called McTavish last year.* 3 PHRASAL VERB If you **run away from** something unpleasant or new, you try

젖어서 잉크가 번져 있었다. 27 자동사 (생각 등이) 스쳐 가다 ❑ 그녀는 갑자기 엄청난 흥분이 온몸을 훑고 지나가는 것 같았다. 28 자동사 퍼지다 ❑ 사람들 사이로 흥분하며 웅성거리는 소리가 퍼졌다. 29 자동사 관통하다 ❑ 이 시리즈를 관통하는 또 다른 맥락은 정신 질환자들 치료에 있어서의 의사들의 역할이다. 30 타동사/자동사 게재되다; 게재되다 ❑ '뉴올리언스 타임스 피카윤' 지는 '우리 삶의 선택'이라는 제목으로 통렬한 논설 4편을 시리즈로 게재했다. 31 자동사 (수량이) 달하다 ❑ 금일 소매 물가 지수는 물가 상승률이 10.9퍼센트에 달하고 있음을 보여 준다. 32 자동사 지속되다 ❑ 그 공연은 평론가들을 기쁘게 했지만 웨스트엔드에서 삼 년밖에 가지 못했다. ❑ 그 계약은 1992년부터 2020년까지 지속될 예정이었다. 33 자동사 (시간적으로) ~하다 ❑ 그녀에게 내가 다시 전화하겠다고 말하세요. 나 또 늦어지고 있어요. 34 타동사 (열이) 나다 ❑ 그 작은 여자 아이는 열이 나서 도움이 필요하다. 35 가산명사 (장기) 공연, 방영 ❑ 그 공연은 한 달간의 버밍엄 공연을 마친 후, 10월 9일에 웨스트엔드로 장소를 옮길 것이다. 36 단수명사 연속 ❑ 잉글랜드 팀 주장 선수는 계속된 저조한 성적에 시달린다. 37 가산명사 산출량 ❑ 웨인은 인쇄 부수를 천 부로 늘릴 계획이다. 38 가산명사 득점, 1점 ❑ 그는 20세 때 한 시즌에 2천 득점을 기록한 최연소 선수가 되었다. 39 단수명사 출입 및 사용의 자유 ❑ 그는 자유롭게 그 집과 풀장을 드나들며 사용할 수 있었다. 40 단수명사 큰 수요 ❑ 영국 파운드화 수요가 크게 몰려 환율 인하의 희망이 사그라졌다. 41 가산명사 (스키) 슬로프, (봅슬레이) 코스 ❑ 영국에서 가장 높은 스키 슬로프에서 일어난 눈사태 42 구 이례적으로 [영국영어] ❑ 이례적으로 결정 골이 터졌다. 44 구 바짝 따라붙다, 거의 맞먹다 ❑ 21세 이하 팀이 이번 시즌에 웨일스와 스코틀랜드 팀을 물리치고 잉글랜드 팀을 바짝 따라잡았다. 45 구 마르다, 말라붙다 ❑ 기억하기로는 처음으로 시냇물이 말라붙었다. 46 구 고갈되다 ❑ 생산 돌입 사흘 만에 공동 출자금이 고갈되었다. 47 구 유전되다 ❑ 그의 가문에 유전되어 내려오는 정신병에 대한 두려움이 그를 계속 괴롭혔다. 48 구 급히 달아나다 ❑ 일당 중 한 명이 급히 달아날 때 헬리콥터가 머리 위를 맴돌았다. 49 구 격앙되다 ❑ 지난주의 살상으로 말미암아 그 지역의 감정은 계속 매우 격앙된 상태이다. 50 구 장기적으로; 단기적으로 보면 ❑ 때로는 비싼 약이나 여타 치료법이 장기적으로 보면 경제적일 수도 있다. 51 구 ~에 거의 맞먹다 ❑ 이제는 심지어 메릴 스트립에 거의 맞먹을 수도 있는 한 젊은이 52 구 도망 중인 ❑ 열다섯 살인 대니는 지방 당국에서 운영하는 복지원으로부터 도망 중이다. 53 구 대패하다 ❑ 내가 그를 대패시켰다는 것을 알고 있었다. 54 구 다 떨어져 가다 ❑ 정부군은 탄약과 연료가 다 떨어져 간다.

구동사 마주치다, 우연히 만나다 ❑ 우리는 그 마을에서 우연히 옛 친구 몇 명을 만났다.

1 구동사 달아나다; 가출하다 ❑ 나는 열여섯 살 때 가출했다. ❑ 콜린은 그에게 맞은 후 달아나서 그 이후로 계속 소식이 없다. 2 상호 구동사 사랑의 도피를 하다 ❑ 그녀는 작년에 맥타비시라는 남자와 몰래 달아났다. 3 구동사 회피하다 ❑ 그들은 그 문제가 저절로 사라지기를 바라면서 회피한다.

to avoid dealing with it or thinking about it. ❑ *They run away from the problem, hoping it will disappear of its own accord.* **4** →see also **runaway**

▶**run away with** PHRASAL VERB If you let your imagination or your emotions **run away with** you, you fail to control them and cannot think sensibly. ❑ *You're letting your imagination run away with you.*

구동사 자제력을 잃게 하다 ❑ 너는 마구 상상의 나래를 펴는구나.

▶**run by** PHRASAL VERB If you **run** something **by** someone, you tell them about it or mention it, to see if they think it is a good idea, or can understand it. ❑ *I'm definitely interested, but I'll have to run it by Larry Estes.*

구동사 _에게 의견을 묻다 ❑ 나는 확실히 관심이 있지만, 래리 이스티스에게 의견을 물어봐야겠다.

▶**run down** **1** PHRASAL VERB If you **run** people or things **down**, you criticize them strongly. ❑ *I'm always running myself down.* **2** PHRASAL VERB If a vehicle or its driver **runs** someone **down**, the vehicle hits them and injures them. ❑ *Lozano claimed that motorcycle driver Clement Lloyd was trying to run him down.* **3** PHRASAL VERB If a machine or device **runs down**, it gradually loses power or works more slowly. ❑ *The batteries are running down.* **4** PHRASAL VERB If people **run down** an industry or an organization, they deliberately reduce its size or the amount of work that it does. [mainly BRIT] ❑ *The government is cynically running down Sweden's welfare system.* **5** PHRASAL VERB If someone **runs down** an amount of something, they reduce it or allow it to decrease. [mainly BRIT] ❑ *But the survey also revealed firms were running down stocks instead of making new products.* **6** →see also **run-down**

1 구동사 헐뜯다, 욕하다 ❑ 나는 언제나 나 자신을 헐뜯는다. **2** 구동사 (차로) 치다 ❑ 로사노는 오토바이 운전자인 클레먼트 로이드가 자신을 치려 했다고 주장했다. **3** 구동사 (기능 등이) 다하다 ❑ 전지가 다 떨어져 가고 있다. **4** 구동사 (규모 등을) 축소하다 [주로 영국영어] ❑ 정부는 편의주의적으로 스웨덴 복지 제도 규모를 축소하고 있다. **5** 구동사 줄이다 [주로 영국영어] ❑ 그러나 그 조사를 통해 기업들이 신상품을 만드는 대신 주식을 줄이고 있다는 사실도 또한 드러났다.

▶**run into** **1** PHRASAL VERB If you **run into** problems or difficulties, you unexpectedly begin to experience them. ❑ *Wang agreed to sell IBM Systems last year after it ran into financial problems.* **2** PHRASAL VERB If you **run into** someone, you meet them unexpectedly. ❑ *He ran into Krettner in the corridor a few minutes later.* **3** PHRASAL VERB If a vehicle **runs into** something, it accidentally hits it. ❑ *The driver failed to negotiate a bend and ran into a tree.* **4** PHRASAL VERB You use **run into** when indicating that the cost or amount of something is very great. ❑ *He said companies should face punitive civil penalties running into millions of pounds.*

1 구동사 (곤란 등에) 빠지다 ❑ 왕은 작년에 아이비엠 시스템스가 재정난에 빠진 후 그것을 매각하는 데 동의했다. **2** 구동사 마주치다, 우연히 만나다 ❑ 그는 몇 분 후 복도에서 크레트너와 마주쳤다. **3** 구동사 들이받다 ❑ 운전자가 굽은 길을 잘 빠져나가지 못하고 나무를 들이받았다. **4** 구동사 (금액 등이) 달하다 ❑ 그는 기업들이 수백만 파운드에 달하는 징벌적 민사 제재금 규모를 당해야 한다고 말했다.

▶**run off** **1** PHRASAL VERB-RECIP If you **run off** with someone, you secretly go away with them in order to live with them or marry them. ❑ *The last thing I'm going to do is run off with somebody's husband.* **2** PHRASAL VERB If you **run off** copies of a piece of writing, you produce them using a machine. ❑ *If you want to run off a copy sometime today, you're welcome to.*

1 상호 구동사 사랑의 도피를 하다 ❑ 내가 절대로 하지 않을 일은 다른 사람의 남편과 몰래 달아나는 것이다. **2** 구동사 (기계로 문서를) 뽑다, 인쇄하다 ❑ 오늘 언제 한 부 뽑고 싶으시다면, 얼마든지 그렇게 하세요.

▶**run out** **1** PHRASAL VERB If you **run out of** something, you have no more of it left. ❑ *They have run out of ideas.* ❑ *We're running out of time.* to **run out of steam** →see **steam** **2** PHRASAL VERB If something **runs out**, it becomes used up so that there is no more left. ❑ *Conditions are getting worse and supplies are running out.* **3** PHRASAL VERB When a legal document **runs out**, it stops being valid. ❑ *When the lease ran out the family moved to Campigny.*

1 구동사 다 떨어지다 ❑ 그들은 아이디어가 바닥이 나 버렸다. ❑ 우리는 시간이 없다. **2** 구동사 바닥나다, 다 떨어지다 ❑ 상황이 더 나빠지고 있고 비축 물자는 다 떨어져 간다. **3** 구동사 만기가 되다, 만료되다 ❑ 임차 기간이 만료되자 그 가족은 캉피니로 옮겨 갔다.

▶**run over** PHRASAL VERB If a vehicle or its driver **runs** a person or animal **over**, it knocks them down or drives over them. ❑ *You can always run him over and make it look like an accident.*

구동사 (차로) 치다 ❑ 당신은 언제든 그를 차로 치고서 사고처럼 보이게 할 수 있다.

▶**run through** **1** PHRASAL VERB If you **run through** a list of items, you read or mention all the items quickly. ❑ *I ran through the options with him.* **2** PHRASAL VERB If you **run through** a performance or a series of actions, you practice it. ❑ *Doug stood still while I ran through the handover procedure.*

1 구동사 훑어보다 ❑ 나는 그와 함께 옵션을 훑어보았다. **2** 구동사 연습하다 ❑ 더그는 내가 전달식 절차를 연습해 보는 동안 가만히 서 있었다.

▶**run up** **1** PHRASAL VERB If someone **runs up** bills or debts, they acquire them by buying a lot of things or borrowing money. ❑ *She managed to run up a credit card debt of $60,000.* **2** →see also **run-up**

1 구동사 (빚 등을) 늘리다 ❑ 그녀는 재주도 좋게 카드 빚을 6만 달러나 졌다.

▶**run up against** PHRASAL VERB If you **run up against** problems, you suddenly begin to experience them. ❑ *I ran up against the problem of getting taken seriously long before I became a writer.*

구동사 -에 부딪치다, -에 봉착하다 ❑ 나는 작가가 되기 오래 전에 사람들이 나를 대단하게 여기는 문제에 부딪혔다.

run|away /rʌnəweɪ/ (**runaways**) **1** ADJ You use **runaway** to describe a situation in which something increases or develops very quickly and cannot be controlled. [ADJ n] ❑ *Our Grand Sale in June was a runaway success.* **2** N-COUNT A **runaway** is someone, especially a child, who leaves home without telling anyone or without permission. ❑ *...a teenage runaway.* **3** ADJ A **runaway** vehicle or animal is moving forward quickly, and its driver or rider has lost control of it. [ADJ n] ❑ *The runaway car careered into a bench, hitting an elderly couple.*

1 형용사 정신없이 늘어나는, 무섭게 치솟는 ❑ 우리의 6월 대바겐세일은 정신을 못 차릴 정도로 대성공이었다. **2** 가산명사 가출 청소년 ❑ 십 대 가출 청소년 **3** 형용사 제어력을 잃은; 고삐 풀린 ❑ 제어력을 잃은 그 자동차가 한 벤치로 돌진하여 노부부를 치었다.

run-down

The spelling **rundown** is also used. The adjective is pronounced /rʌn daʊn/. The noun is pronounced /rʌn daʊn/.

철자 rundown도 쓴다. 형용사는 /rʌn daʊn/, 명사는 /rʌn daʊn/로 발음된다.

1 ADJ If someone is **run-down**, they are tired or slightly ill. [INFORMAL] ❑ *When 23-year-old Marilyn Brown started to feel run-down last December, it never occurred to her that she could have tuberculosis.* **2** ADJ A **run-down** building or area is in very poor condition. ❑ *They have put substantial funds into rebuilding one of the most run-down areas in Scotland.* **3** ADJ A **run-down** place of business is not as active as it used to be or does not have many customers. ❑ *...a run-down slate quarry.* **4** N-SING If you give someone a **run-down of** a group of things or a **run-down on** something, you give them details about it. [INFORMAL] ❑ *Here's a rundown of the options.*

1 형용사 몹시 피곤한, 몸 상태가 좋지 않은 [비격식체] ❑ 지난 12월, 스물세 살 된 마릴린 브라운이 몸이 좋지 않다고 느끼기 시작했을 때, 그녀는 자기가 결핵에 걸렸을 수도 있다는 생각은 결코 하지 못했다. **2** 형용사 황폐한 ❑ 그들은 스코틀랜드에서 가장 황폐한 지역 중 한 곳을 재건하는 데 상당한 자금을 투입했다. **3** 형용사 쇠퇴한, 퇴락한 ❑ 퇴락한 슬레이트 채석장 **4** 단수명사 설명 [비격식체] ❑ 옵션에 대한 설명이 여기 있습니다.

rung /rʌŋ/ (**rungs**) **1** Rung is the past participle of **ring**. **2** N-COUNT The **rungs** on a ladder are the wooden or metal bars that form the steps. ❑ *I swung myself onto the ladder and felt for the next rung.* **3** N-COUNT If you reach a particular **rung** in your career, in an organization, or in a process, you reach that level in it. ❑ *I first worked with him in 1971 when we were both on the lowest rung of our careers.*

1 ring의 과거 분사 **2** 가산명사 (사다리의) 가로대, 단 ❑ 나는 몸을 흔들어 사다리에 올라서서 다음 단을 더듬어 찾았다. **3** 가산명사 단계, 지위 ❑ 우리 둘 다 각자의 이력상에서 가장 낮은 단계에 있었던 1971년에 나는 처음 그와 함께 일했다.

run-in (**run-ins**) N-COUNT A **run-in** is an argument or quarrel with someone. [INFORMAL] ❑ *I had a monumental run-in with him a couple of years ago.*

가산명사 싸움, 언쟁 [비격식체] ❑ 나는 2년 전에 그와 엄청나게 심한 언쟁을 벌였다.

run|ner ◆◇◇ /rʌnər/ (**runners**) **1** N-COUNT A **runner** is a person who runs, especially for sport or pleasure. ❑ *...a marathon runner.* **2** N-COUNT The **runners** in a horse race are the horses taking part. ❑ *There are 18 runners in the top race of the day.* **3** N-COUNT A drug **runner** or gun **runner** is someone who illegally takes

1 가산명사 달리는 사람, 주자 ❑ 마라톤 주자 **2** 가산명사 경주마 ❑ 오늘의 최상급 경주에는 열여덟 필의 경주마가 출전한다. **3** 가산명사 밀수업자 ❑ 흉악한 총기 밀수업자 일당 **4** 가산명사 전설부위금

A
B
C
D
E
F
G
H
I
J
K
L
M
N
O
P
Q
R
S
T
U
V
W
X
Y
Z

drugs or guns into a country. ❑ *...a gang of evil gun runners.* **4** N-COUNT Someone who is a **runner** for a particular person or company is employed to take messages, collect money, or do other small tasks for them. ❑ *...a bookie's runner.* **5** N-COUNT **Runners** are thin strips of wood or metal underneath something which help it to move smoothly. ❑ *...the runners of his sled.* →see **park**

runner-up (runners-up) N-COUNT A **runner-up** is someone who has finished in second place in a race or competition. ❑ *The ten runners-up will receive a case of wine.*

run|ning ♦♦◇ /rʌnɪŋ/ **1** N-UNCOUNT **Running** is the activity of moving fast on foot, especially as a sport. ❑ *We chose to do cross-country running.* **2** N-SING The **running of** something such as a business is the managing or organizing of it. ❑ *...the committee in charge of the day-to-day running of the party.* **3** ADJ You use **running** to describe things that continue or keep occurring over a period of time. [ADJ n] ❑ *He also began a running feud with Dean Acheson.* **4** ADJ A **running** total is a total which changes because numbers keep being added to it as something progresses. [ADJ n] ❑ *He kept a running tally of who had called him, who had visited, who had sent flowers.* **5** ADV You can use **running** when indicating that something keeps happening. For example, if something has happened every day for three days, you can say that it has happened for the third day **running** or for three days **running**. [n ADV] ❑ *He said drought had led to severe crop failure for the second year running.* **6** ADJ **Running** water is water that is flowing rather than standing still. [ADJ n] ❑ *The forest was filled with the sound of running water.* **7** ADJ If a house has **running** water, water is supplied to the house through pipes and faucets. [ADJ n] ❑ *...a house without electricity or running water in a tiny African village.* **8** PHRASE If someone is **in the running for** something, they have a good chance of winning or obtaining it. If they are **out of the running for** something, they have no chance of winning or obtaining it. ❑ *Until this week he appeared to have ruled himself out of the running because of his age.* **9** PHRASE If something such as a system or place is **up and running**, it is operating normally. ❑ *We're trying to get the medical facilities up and running again.*

run|ning costs N-PLURAL The **running costs** of a business are the amount of money that is regularly spent on things such as salaries, heating, lighting, and rent. [BUSINESS] ❑ *It was enough to cover their taxes and running costs.*

run|ning mate (running mates) N-COUNT In an election campaign, a candidate's **running mate** is the person that they have chosen to help them in the election. If the candidate wins, the running mate will become the second most important person after the winner. [mainly AM] ❑ *...Clinton's selection of Al Gore as his running mate.*

run|ny /rʌni/ (runnier, runniest) **1** ADJ Something that is **runny** is more liquid than usual or than was intended. ❑ *Warm the honey until it becomes runny.* **2** ADJ If someone has a **runny** nose or **runny** eyes, liquid is flowing from their nose or eyes. ❑ *Symptoms are streaming eyes, a runny nose, headache, and a cough.*

run time (run times) N-COUNT **Run time** is the time during which a computer program is running. [COMPUTING] ❑ *With run time for most applications lasting days or weeks, the queue fills up quickly.*

run-up (run-ups) N-SING The **run-up to** an event is the period of time just before it. [mainly BRIT] ❑ *The company believes the products will sell well in the run-up to Christmas.*

run|way /rʌnweɪ/ (runways) N-COUNT At an airport, the **runway** is the long strip of ground with a hard surface which an airplane takes off or lands on. ❑ *The plane started taxiing down the runway.*

rup|ture /rʌptʃər/ (ruptures, rupturing, ruptured) **1** N-COUNT A **rupture** is a severe injury in which an internal part of your body tears or bursts open, especially the part between the bowels and the abdomen. ❑ *He died of an abdominal infection caused by a rupture of his stomach.* **2** V-T/V-I If a person or animal **ruptures** a part of their body or if it **ruptures**, it tears or bursts open. ❑ *His stomach might rupture from all the acid.* ❑ *Whilst playing badminton, I ruptured my Achilles tendon.* **3** V-T If you **rupture yourself**, you rupture a part of your body, usually because you have lifted something heavy. ❑ *He ruptured himself playing football.* **4** V-T/V-I If an object **ruptures** or if something **ruptures** it, it bursts open. ❑ *Certain truck gasoline tanks can rupture and burn in a collision.* **5** N-COUNT If there is a **rupture** between people, relations between them get much worse or end completely. ❑ *The incidents have not yet caused a major rupture in the political ties between countries.* **6** V-T If someone or something **ruptures** relations between people, they damage them, causing them to become worse or to end. ❑ *Brutal clashes in Berlin between squatters and police yesterday ruptured the city's governing coalition between Social Democrats and Greens.*

ru|ral ♦♦◇ /rʊərəl/ **1** ADJ **Rural** places are far away from large towns or cities. ❑ *These plants have a tendency to grow in the more rural areas.* **2** ADJ **Rural** means having features which are typical of areas that are far away from large towns or cities. [ADJ n] ❑ *...the old rural way of life.*

ruse /ruːz, rʊs, BRIT ruːz/ (ruses) N-COUNT A **ruse** is an action or plan which is intended to deceive someone. [FORMAL] ❑ *It is now clear that this was a ruse to divide them.*

rush ♦♦◇ /rʌʃ/ (rushes, rushing, rushed) **1** V-T/V-I If you **rush** somewhere, you go there quickly. ❑ *A schoolgirl rushed into a burning flat to save a man's life.* ❑ *I've got to rush. Got a meeting in a few minutes.* **2** V-T If people **rush to** do something, they do it as soon as they can, because they are very eager to do it. ❑ *Russian banks rushed to buy as many dollars as they could.* **3** N-SING A **rush** is a situation in which you need to go somewhere or do something very quickly. ❑ *The men left in a rush.* **4** N-SING If there is a **rush for** something, many people suddenly try to get it or do it. ❑ *Record stores are expecting a huge rush for the single.* **5** N-SING The **rush** is a period of time when many people go somewhere or do something. ❑ *The shop's opening coincided with the Christmas rush.* **6** V-T/V-I If you **rush** something, you do it in a hurry, often too quickly and without much care. ❑ *You can't rush a search.*

❑ 마권업자의 잠심부름꾼 **5** 가산명사 (스케이트 등의) 활주부 ❑ 그의 썰매의 활주부

가산명사 차점자; 입상자 ❑ 입상자 열 분은 와인 한 상자를 받게 됩니다.

1 불가산명사 달리기, 경주 ❑ 우리는 크로스컨트리 경주를 하기로 결정했다. **2** 단수명사 운영, 경영 ❑ 그 당의 나날의 운영을 맡고 있는 위원회 **3** 형용사 지속적인, 계속되는 ❑ 그는 또 딘 애치슨과의 지속적인 싸움을 시작했다. **4** 형용사 누계의 ❑ 그는 누가 전화를 했고, 누가 방문했으며, 누가 꽃을 보냈는지에 대해 일일이 누계를 내며 기록했다. **5** 부사 잇달아, 계속해서 ❑ 그는 가뭄으로 인해 2년 연속 극심한 흉년이 들었다고 말했다. **6** 형용사 흐르는 ❑ 숲에는 흐르는 물소리가 가득 했다. **7** 형용사 수돗물의 ❑ 작은 아프리카 마을의 전기도 수돗물도 공급되지 않는 집 **8** 구 승산이 있는; 승산이 없는 ❑ 이번 주까지 그는 나이 때문에 자신은 승산이 없다고 판단을 내렸던 것처럼 보였다. **9** 구 정상 가동 중인 ❑ 우리는 의료 시설이 다시 정상 가동되도록 하기 위해 노력하고 있다.

복수명사 운영비 [경제] ❑ 그것은 그들의 세금과 운영비를 대기에 충분했다.

가산명사 러닝메이트, 동반 출마자 [주로 미국영어] ❑ 앨 고어를 부통령 후보로 택한 클린턴의 선택

1 형용사 액체 같은; 묽은 ❑ 액체처럼 될 때까지 꿀을 데우세요. **2** 형용사 콧물이 흐르는; 눈물이 흐르는 ❑ 증상으로는 심한 눈물, 콧물, 두통과 기침이 난다.

가산명사 (컴퓨터) 실행 시간 [컴퓨터] ❑ 대부분의 응용 프로그램 실행 시간이 며칠 혹은 몇 주까지 계속되어, 작업 대기열이 금방 가득 찬다.

단수명사 - 직전 기간 [주로 영국영어] ❑ 회사는 그 제품이 크리스마스 직전 기간에 잘 팔릴 것이라고 믿고 있다.

가산명사 활주로 ❑ 비행기가 활주로를 내닫기 시작했다.

1 가산명사 파열 ❑ 그는 장 파열에 의한 복부 감염으로 죽었다. **2** 타동사/자동사 파열시키다; 파열되다 ❑ 그 모든 위산 때문에 그의 위가 파열될 수도 있다. ❑ 나는 배드민턴을 치다가 아킬레스건이 파열됐다. **3** 타동사 근육이 파열되다 ❑ 그는 축구를 하다가 근육이 파열됐다. **4** 타동사/자동사 터뜨리다; 터지다 ❑ 충돌 시 특정 화물차의 휘발유 탱크가 터져서 불이 날 수도 있다. **5** 가산명사 불화, 사이가 틀어짐 ❑ 그 사건은 아직 국가 간의 정치적 유대에 큰 불화를 일으키지 않았다. **6** 타동사 (관계를) 손상시키다 ❑ 어제 베를린에서 일어난 불법 거주자들과 경찰 간의 격렬한 충돌로 그 도시 내의 사민당과 녹색당의 연정이 삐걱거리게 되었다.

1 형용사 시골의, 지방의 ❑ 이 식물들은 비교적 시골 지역에서 자라는 경향이 있다. **2** 형용사 시골풍의, 전원의 ❑ 오래된 시골풍의 생활 방식

가산명사 책략, 계략 [격식체] ❑ 이는 그들을 갈라놓기 위한 계략이었음이 이제 분명하다.

1 타동사/자동사 서둘러 가다 ❑ 한 여학생이 어떤 남자의 생명을 구하기 위해 불타오르는 아파트로 뛰어들었다. ❑ 빨리 가야 돼. 몇 분 뒤에 회의가 있어. **2** 타동사 서둘러 -하다 ❑ 러시아 은행들은 서둘러 달러를 최대한 많이 사들였다. **3** 단수명사 서두름 ❑ 그 남자들은 서둘러 떠났다. **4** 단수명사 쇄도, 붐빔 ❑ 음반 가게들은 그 싱글 앨범을 찾는 사람들이 몰려들 것으로 기대하고 있다. **5** 단수명사 성수기 ❑ 그 상점의 개장은 크리스마스 성수기와 맞아떨어졌다. **6** 타동사/자동사 급히 해치우다 ❑ 조사를 급하게 해치워서는 안 된다. ● 급하게 해치운 형용사 ❑ 그

● **rushed** ADJ ❏ *The report had all the hallmarks of a rushed job.* **7** V-T If you **rush** someone or something to a place, you take them there quickly. ❏ *They had rushed him to a hospital for a life-saving operation.* **8** V-T/V-I If you **rush into** something or **are rushed into** it, you do it without thinking about it for long enough. ❏ *He will not rush into any decisions.* ❏ *They had rushed in without adequate appreciation of the task.* ● **rushed** ADJ ❏ *At no time did I feel rushed or under pressure.* **9** V-T/V-I If you **rush** something or someone, you move quickly and forcefully at them, often in order to attack them. ❏ *They rushed the entrance and forced their way in.* **10** V-I If air or liquid **rushes** somewhere, it flows there suddenly and quickly. ❏ *Water rushes out of huge tunnels.* ● N-COUNT **Rush** is also a noun. ❏ *A rush of air on my face woke me.* **11** N-COUNT If you experience a **rush of** a feeling, you suddenly experience it very strongly. ❏ *A rush of pure affection swept over him.*

보고서는 온통 급하게 해치운 흔적이 가득했다. **7** 타동사 급히 내려가다 ❏ 그들은 구멍 수술을 위해 그를 병원으로 급히 데려갔다. **8** 타동사/자동사 성급히 덤비다 ❏ 그는 어떤 결정도 성급히 내리려 하지 않을 것이다. ❏ 그들은 그 임무를 적절히 평가하지도 않은 채 성급히 덤벼들었다. ● 성급히 떠밀린 형용사 ❏ 나는 한 순간도 성급히 떠밀리거나 압력을 받고 있다는 느낌이 들지 않았다. **9** 타동사/자동사 -을 향해 돌진하다 ❏ 그들은 입구를 향해 돌진하여 억지로 헤치고 들어갔다. **10** 자동사 급속히 흐르다 ❏ 거대한 터널에서 물이 급속히 흘러나왔다. ● 가산명사 급속한 흐름 ❏ 얼굴에 한 줄기 세찬 바람이 불어 나는 잠에서 깨어났다. **11** 가산명사 (감정의) 복받침 ❏ 북받쳐 오르는 순수한 애정이 그를 휩쌌다.

<table>
<tr><th colspan="2">Word Partnership</th><th>rush의 연어</th></tr>
<tr><td>ADJ.</td><td colspan="2">**mad** rush **3** **4**
sudden rush **3** **4** **10** **11**</td></tr>
<tr><td>N.</td><td colspan="2">**evening** rush, **morning** rush **5**
rush **to judgment** **6**
rush **of air**, rush **of water** **10**</td></tr>
</table>

rush hour (**rush hours**) also **rush-hour** N-COUNT The **rush hour** is one of the periods of the day when most people are traveling to or from work. [also at/during N] ❏ *During the evening rush hour it was often solid with vehicles.*

가산명사 러시아워, 교통 혼잡 시간 ❏ 저녁의 교통 혼잡 시간 동안 그곳은 흔히 차로 꽉 찼다.

rust /rʌst/ (**rusts, rusting, rusted**) **1** N-UNCOUNT **Rust** is a brown substance that forms on iron or steel, for example when it comes into contact with water. ❏ *...a decaying tractor, red with rust.* **2** V-I When a metal object **rusts**, it becomes covered in rust and often loses its strength. ❏ *Copper nails are better than iron nails because the iron rusts.* **3** COLOR **Rust** is sometimes used to describe things that are reddish-brown in color. ❏ *...rust and gold leaves from the maples.*

1 불가산명사 녹 ❏ 녹이 벌겋게 손 채, 부식되고 있는 트랙터 **2** 자동사 녹슬다, 부식하다 ❏ 쇠는 녹이 슬기 때문에 쇠못보다 구리못이 더 낫다. **3** 색채어 적갈색 ❏ 단풍나무에서 떨어진 적갈색과 황금색의 나뭇잎들

rus|tic /rʌstɪk/ ADJ You can use **rustic** to describe things or people that you approve of because they are simple or unsophisticated in a way that is typical of the countryside. [APPROVAL] ❏ *...the rustic charm of a country lifestyle.*

형용사 소박한 [마음에 듦] ❏ 시골 생활양식의 소박한 매력

rus|tle /rʌsᵊl/ (**rustles, rustling, rustled**) V-T/V-I When something thin and dry **rustles** or when you **rustle** it, it makes soft sounds as it moves. ❏ *The leaves rustled in the wind.* ❏ *She rustled her papers impatiently.* ● N-COUNT **Rustle** is also a noun. ❏ *She sat perfectly still, without even a rustle of her frilled petticoats.* ● **rus|tling** (**rustlings**) N-VAR ❏ *We were all terrified by a rustling sound coming from beneath one of the seats.*

타동사/자동사 바스락거리다; 바스락거리게 하다 ❏ 바람에 나뭇잎들이 바스락거렸다. ❏ 그녀는 조급하게 서류를 바스락거렸다. ● 가산명사 바스락거리는 소리 ❏ 그녀는 주름진 페티코트를 바스락거리는 소리조차 한 번 내지 않고 더할 나위 없이 조용히 앉아 있었다. ● 바스락거리는 소리 가산명사 또는 불가산명사 ❏ 한 좌석 밑에서 나오는 바스락 소리에 우리는 모두 겁이 났다.

▶**rustle up** PHRASAL VERB If you **rustle up** something to eat or drink, you make or prepare it quickly, with very little planning. ❏ *Let's see if somebody can rustle up a cup of coffee.*

구동사 서둘러 만들다, 서둘러 준비하다 ❏ 누가 커피 한 잔 후다닥 만들 수 있는지 봅시다.

rusty /rʌsti/ (**rustier, rustiest**) **1** ADJ A **rusty** metal object such as a car or a machine is covered with rust, which is a brown substance that forms on iron or steel when it comes into contact with water. ❏ *...a rusty iron gate.* **2** ADJ If a skill that you have or your knowledge of something is **rusty**, it is not as good as it used to be, because you have not used it for a long time. ❏ *You may be a little rusty, but past experience and teaching skills won't have been lost.*

1 형용사 녹슨 ❏ 녹슨 철문 **2** 형용사 (솜씨 등이) 녹슨, 이전만 못한 ❏ 당신은 약간 솜씨가 무디어질 수도 있지만, 과거의 경험과 교수 기술은 잃어버리지 않을 것이다.

rut /rʌt/ (**ruts**) **1** N-COUNT If you say that someone is **in a rut**, you disapprove of the fact that they have become fixed in their way of thinking and doing things, and find it difficult to change. You can also say that someone's life or career is **in a rut**. [DISAPPROVAL] ❏ *I don't like being in a rut – I like to keep moving on.* **2** N-COUNT A **rut** is a deep, narrow mark made in the ground by the wheels of a vehicle. ❏ *Our driver slowed up as we approached the ruts in the road.*

1 가산명사 (고정된) 판 [탐탁찮음] ❏ 나는 판에 박히는 것이 싫다. 계속 움직이는 것이 좋다. **2** 가산명사 바퀴 자국 ❏ 도로에 있는 바퀴 자국에 가까이 다가가자 우리 운전사가 속도를 낮췄다.

ruth|less /ruːθlɪs/ **1** ADJ If you say that someone is **ruthless**, you mean that you disapprove of them because they are very harsh or cruel, and will do anything that is necessary to achieve what they want. [DISAPPROVAL] ❏ *The President was ruthless in dealing with any hint of internal political dissent.* ● **ruth|less|ly** ADV [ADV with v] ❏ *The Party has ruthlessly crushed any sign of organized opposition.* ● **ruth|less|ness** N-UNCOUNT ❏ *...a powerful political figure with a reputation for ruthlessness.* **2** ADJ A **ruthless** action or activity is done forcefully and thoroughly, without much concern for its effects on other people. ❏ *Her lawyers have been ruthless in thrashing out a divorce settlement.* ● **ruth|less|ly** ADV ❏ *Ghislaine showed signs of turning into the ruthlessly efficient woman her father wanted her to be.* ● **ruth|less|ness** N-UNCOUNT ❏ *...a woman with a brain and business acumen and a certain healthy ruthlessness.*

1 형용사 무자비한 [탐탁찮음] ❏ 그 대통령은 내부적으로 정치적 반대 낌새가 조금이라도 있으면 무자비하게 다루었다. ● 무자비하게 부사 ❏ 그 정당은 어떤 조직적인 반대의 조짐도 무자비하게 분쇄해 왔다. ● 무자비함 불가산명사 ❏ 무자비하다는 평판을 받는 한 유력 정치 인사 **2** 형용사 인정사정없는, 가차없는 ❏ 그녀의 변호사들은 이혼 문제를 해결하기 위해 가차없이 행동해 왔다. ● 단호하게, 가차없이 부사 ❏ 기슬렌은 아버지가 원했던 대로 단호하게 유능한 여성이 될 조짐이 보였다. ● 가차없음 불가산명사 ❏ 두뇌와 사업적 수완, 그리고 어떤 사리에 맞게 딱 부러지는 성격을 갖춘 여자

RV /ɑːr viː/ (**RVs**) N-COUNT An **RV** is a van which is equipped with such things as beds and cooking equipment, so that people can live in it, usually while they are on vacation. **RV** is an abbreviation for "recreational vehicle." [mainly AM; BRIT usually **camper, camper van**] ❏ *...a group of RVs pulled over on the side of the highway.*

가산명사 레저용 차량 [주로 미국영어; 영국영어 대개 camper, camper van] ❏ 한 무리의 레저용 차량들이 고속도로 가에 차를 세웠다.

rye /raɪ/ **1** N-UNCOUNT **Rye** is a cereal grown in cold countries. Its grains can be used to make flour, bread, or other foods. ❏ *One of the first crops that I grew when we came here was rye.* **2** N-UNCOUNT **Rye** is bread made from rye. [AM] ❏ *I was eating ham and Swiss cheese on rye.*

1 불가산명사 호밀 ❏ 우리가 이곳에 왔을 때 내가 처음 기른 작물 중 하나가 호밀이었다. **2** 불가산명사 호밀빵 [미국영어] ❏ 나는 햄과 스위스 치즈를 얹은 호밀빵을 먹고 있었다.

a b c d e f g h i j k l m n o p q r s t u v w x y z

Ss

S, s /ɛs/ (**S's, s's**) N-VAR **S** is the nineteenth letter of the English alphabet.

Sab|bath /sæbəθ/ N-PROPER **The Sabbath** is the day of the week when members of some religious groups do not work. The Jewish Sabbath is on Saturday and the Christian Sabbath is on Sunday. ❑ ...a deeply religious man who will not discuss politics on the Sabbath.

sab|bati|cal /səbætɪkᵊl/ (**sabbaticals**) N-COUNT A **sabbatical** is a period of time during which someone such as a university teacher can leave their ordinary work and travel or study. [also on N] ❑ He took a year's sabbatical from the Foreign Office.

sabo|tage /sæbətɑʒ/ (**sabotages, sabotaging, sabotaged**) ◼ V-T If a machine, railroad line, or bridge **is sabotaged**, it is deliberately damaged or destroyed, for example in a war or as a protest. [usu passive] ❑ The main pipeline supplying water was sabotaged by rebels. ● N-UNCOUNT **Sabotage** is also a noun. ❑ The bombing was a spectacular act of sabotage. ◼ V-T If someone **sabotages** a plan or a meeting, they deliberately prevent it from being successful. ❑ He accused the opposition of doing everything they could to sabotage the election.

sa|chet /sæʃeɪ, BRIT sæʃeɪ/ (**sachets**) ◼ N-COUNT A **sachet** is a small soft bag containing a perfumed powder or other substance placed in drawers to give clothing a pleasant smell. ❑ ...a lilac sachet. ◼ N-COUNT A **sachet** is a small closed plastic or paper bag containing a small quantity of something. [BRIT] ❑ ...individual sachets of instant coffee.

sack ◇◇◇ /sæk/ (**sacks, sacking, sacked**) ◼ N-COUNT A **sack** is a large bag made of rough woven material. Sacks are used to carry or store things such as vegetables or coal. ❑ ...a sack of potatoes. ◼ V-T If your employers **sack** you, they tell you that you can no longer work for them because you have done something that they did not like or because your work was not good enough. [INFORMAL] ❑ Earlier today the Prime Minister sacked 18 government officials for corruption. ● N-SING **Sack** is also a noun. ❑ People who make mistakes can be given the sack the same day.

sack|ing /sækɪŋ/ (**sackings**) ◼ N-UNCOUNT **Sacking** is rough woven material that is used to make sacks. ❑ ...a piece of sacking. ◼ N-COUNT A **sacking** is when an employer tells a worker to leave their job. [INFORMAL] ❑ ...the sacking of twenty-three thousand miners.

sa|cred /seɪkrɪd/ ◼ ADJ Something that is **sacred** is believed to be holy and to have a special connection with God. ❑ The owl is sacred for many Californian Indians. ◼ ADJ Something connected with religion or used in religious ceremonies is described as **sacred**. [ADJ n] ❑ ...sacred art. ◼ ADJ You can describe something as **sacred** when it is regarded as too important to be changed or interfered with. ❑ My memories are sacred.

sac|ri|fice ◆◇◇ /sækrɪfaɪs/ (**sacrifices, sacrificing, sacrificed**) ◼ V-T To **sacrifice** an animal or person means to kill them in a special religious ceremony as an offering to a god. ❑ The priest sacrificed a chicken. ● N-COUNT **Sacrifice** is also a noun. ❑ ...animal sacrifices to the gods. ◼ V-T If you **sacrifice** something that is valuable or important, you give it up, usually to obtain something else for yourself or for other people. ❑ She sacrificed family life to her career. ❑ Kitty Aldridge has sacrificed all for her first film. ● N-VAR **Sacrifice** is also a noun. ❑ She made many sacrifices to get Anita a good education.

sac|ri|fi|cial /sækrɪfɪʃᵊl/ ADJ **Sacrificial** means connected with or used in a sacrifice. [ADJ n] ❑ ...the sacrificial altar.

sad ◆◆◇ /sæd/ (**sadder, saddest**) ◼ ADJ If you are **sad**, you feel unhappy, usually because something has happened that you do not like. ❑ The relationship had been important to me and its loss left me feeling sad and empty. ❑ I'm sad that Julie's marriage is on the verge of splitting up. ● **sad|ly** ADV ❑ ...a gallant man who will be sadly missed by all his comrades. ● **sad|ness** N-UNCOUNT ❑ It is with a mixture of sadness and joy that I say farewell. ◼ ADJ **Sad** stories and **sad** news make you feel sad. ❑ ...a desperately humorous, impossibly sad novel. ◼ ADJ A **sad** event or situation is unfortunate or undesirable. ❑ It's a sad truth that children are the biggest victims of passive smoking. ● **sad|ly** ADV ❑ Sadly, bamboo plants die after flowering. ◼ ADJ If you describe someone as **sad**, you do not have any respect for them and think their behavior or ideas are ridiculous. [INFORMAL, DISAPPROVAL] ❑ ...sad old bikers and youngsters who think that Jim Morrison is God. →see **cry**

Thesaurus	sad의 참조어
ADJ.	depressed, down, gloomy, unhappy; (ant.) cheerful, happy ◼
	miserable, tragic, unhappy ◼

가산명사 또는 불가산명사 영어 알파벳의 열아홉 번째 글자

고유명사 안식일 ❑ 안식일에는 정치 문제를 논하지 않으려 하는 독실한 신앙인

가산명사 안식 휴가 ❑ 그는 외무부로부터 1년간의 안식 휴가를 얻었다.

◼ 타동사 (시위 등으로 고의로) 파괴되다 ❑ 반란군들이 물을 공급하는 주요 송수관을 고의적으로 파괴했다. ● 불가산명사 사보타주, (고의적) 파괴 행위 ❑ 그 폭격 공격은 엄청난 파괴 행위였다. ◼ 타동사 고의적으로 방해하다 ❑ 그는 야당이 선거를 고의적으로 방해할 수 있는 온갖 짓을 하고 있다고 비난했다.

◼ 가산명사 향주머니 [미국영어] ❑ 라일락 향이 나는 향주머니 ◼ 가산명사 작은 봉지 [영국영어] ❑ 인스턴트커피가 들어 있는 개별 포장 봉지

◼ 가산명사 부대 ❑ 감자 한 부대 ◼ 타동사 해고하다, 자르다 [비격식체] ❑ 총리가 오늘 일찍 공직자 18명을 부패 행위를 이유로 해고했다. ● 단수명사 해고 ❑ 실수를 하는 사람들은 그날로 해고를 통보 받을 수 있다.

◼ 불가산명사 (부대를 만드는) 거친 천 ❑ 거친 천 조각 ◼ 가산명사 해고함 [비격식체] ❑ 2만 3천 명의 광부를 해고함

◼ 형용사 성스러운 ❑ 부엉이는 많은 캘리포니아 인디언들에게 성스러운 존재이다. ◼ 형용사 종교적인 ❑ 종교 미술 ◼ 형용사 신성한 ❑ 내 추억은 신성한 것이야.

◼ 타동사 제물로 바치다 ❑ 그 사제는 닭을 제물로 바쳤다. ● 가산명사 제물 ❑ 신께 바치는 짐승 제물들 ◼ 타동사 포기하다, 희생하다 ❑ 그녀는 직장 생활을 위해서 가정생활을 포기했다. ❑ 키티 알드리지는 자신의 첫 영화를 위해서 모든 것을 희생했다. ● 가산명사 또는 불가산명사 희생 ❑ 그녀는 애니타에게 좋은 교육을 시키기 위해서 많은 희생을 했다.

형용사 제물의 ❑ 제단

◼ 형용사 슬픈, 애석한 ❑ 그 관계가 나에게는 중요했었고, 그래서 그 관계가 끝났을 때 나는 슬프고 허전했다. ❑ 줄리의 결혼 생활이 파탄날 위기라니 애석하다. ● 슬프게, 애석해 하며 부사 ❑ 그의 동료들이 모두 애석해 하며 보고 싶어 할 씩씩한 남자 ● 슬픔 불가산명사 ❑ 작별인사를 할 때면 나는 슬프면서도 즐겁다. ◼ 형용사 슬픈 ❑ 몹시 웃기면서도 너무나 슬픈 소설 ◼ 형용사 애처로운, 유감스러운 ❑ 간접흡연의 가장 큰 피해자가 아이들이라는 것은 유감스러운 사실이다. ● 애처롭게도 부사 ❑ 애처롭게도, 대나무는 꽃을 피우고 나면 죽는다. ◼ 형용사 한심한 [비격식체, 탐탁찮음] ❑ 짐 모리슨이 신이라고 여기는 한심한 폭주족과 젊은이들

Word Partnership	*sad*의 연어
V.	**feel** sad, **look** sad, **seem** sad ◼
ADV.	**kind of** sad, **a little** sad, **really** sad, **so** sad, **too** sad, **very** sad ◼-◼
N.	sad **news**, sad **story** ◼
	sad **day**, sad **eyes**, sad **face**, sad **fact**, sad **truth** ◼

sad|den /sǽd²n/ (**saddens, saddened**) V-T If something **saddens** you, it makes you feel sad. [no cont] □ *The cruelty in the world saddens me incredibly.* ● **sad|dened** ADJ [v-link ADJ] □ *He was disappointed and saddened that legal argument had stopped the trial.*

타동사 슬프게 하다 □ 이 세상의 잔인함이 나를 너무나 슬프게 한다. ● 슬픈 형용사 □ 그는 법적 논쟁 때문에 재판이 중지되었던 것에 대해 실망하고 슬퍼했다.

sad|dle /sǽd²l/ (**saddles, saddling, saddled**) ◼ N-COUNT A **saddle** is a leather seat that you put on the back of an animal so that you can ride the animal. ◼ V-T/V-I If you **saddle** a horse, you put a saddle on it so that you can ride it. □ *Why don't we saddle a couple of horses and go for a ride?* ● PHRASAL VERB **Saddle up** means the same as **saddle**. □ *I want to be gone from here as soon as we can saddle up.* ◼ N-COUNT A **saddle** is a seat on a bicycle or motorcycle. →see **horse**

◼ 가산명사 (말) 안장 ◼ 타동사/자동사 안장을 얹다 □ 말 두 마리에 안장을 얹고서 우리 한번 타 보는 게 어때? ● 구동사 안장을 얹다 □ 나는 우리가 안장만 얹으면 바로 여기에서 떠나 버리고 싶다. ◼ 가산명사 (자전거 등의) 안장

sad|ism /séɪdɪzəm/ N-UNCOUNT **Sadism** is a type of behavior in which a person obtains pleasure from hurting other people and making them suffer physically or mentally. □ *Psychoanalysts tend to regard both sadism and masochism as arising from childhood deprivation.* ● **sad|ist** /séɪdɪst/ (**sadists**) N-COUNT □ *The man was a sadist who tortured animals and people.*

불가산명사 사디즘, 가학적 변태 성욕 □ 정신 분석학자들은 사디즘과 마조히즘이 모두 어린 시절의 애정 결핍에서 비롯된다고 생각하는 편이다. ● 사디스트 가산명사 □ 그 남자는 동물과 사람을 고문했던 사디스트였다.

sa|dis|tic /sədɪ́stɪk/ ADJ A **sadistic** person obtains pleasure from hurting other people and making them suffer physically or mentally. □ *The prisoners rioted against mistreatment by sadistic guards and a starvation diet.*

형용사 가학적인 □ 죄수들은 가학적인 간수들의 학대와 굶겨 죽일 정도의 식사 때문에 반란을 일으켰다.

s.a.e. /ɛ́s eɪ íː/ (**s.a.e.s**) N-COUNT An **s.a.e.** is an envelope on which you have stuck a stamp and written your own name and address. You send it to an organization so that they can reply to you in it. **s.a.e.** is an abbreviation for "stamped addressed envelope" or "self addressed envelope." [BRIT; AM **SASE**] □ *Send an s.a.e. for a free information pack.*

가산명사 회신용 봉투 [영국영어; 미국영어 SASE] □ 회신용 봉투를 보내 주시면 무료 정보집을 보내 드립니다.

sa|fa|ri /səfɑ́ːri/ (**safaris**) N-COUNT A **safari** is a trip to observe or hunt wild animals, especially in East Africa. [also *on* N] □ *He'd like to go on safari to photograph snakes and tigers.*

가산명사 사파리, (아프리카의) 사냥 여행 □ 그는 뱀과 호랑이 사진을 찍을 수 있도록 사파리 여행을 가고 싶어 한다.

safe ♦♢♢ /séɪf/ (**safer, safest**) ◼ ADJ Something that is **safe** does not cause physical harm or danger. □ *Officials arrived to assess whether it is safe to bring emergency food supplies into the city.* □ *Most foods that we eat are safe for birds.* ◼ ADJ If a person or thing is **safe from** something, they cannot be harmed or damaged by it. [v-link ADJ, usu ADJ *from* n] □ *They are safe from the violence that threatened them.* ◼ ADJ If you are **safe**, you have not been harmed, or you are not in danger of being harmed. [v-link ADJ] □ *Where is Sophy? Is she safe?* ● **safe|ly** ADV [ADV with v] □ *All 140 guests were brought out of the building safely by firemen.* ◼ ADJ A **safe** place is one where it is unlikely that any harm, damage, or unpleasant things will happen to the people or things that are there. □ *The continuing tension has prompted more than half the inhabitants of the refugee camp to flee to safer areas.* ● **safe|ly** ADV [ADV after v] □ *The banker keeps the money tucked safely under his bed.* ◼ ADJ If people or things have a **safe** journey, they reach their destination without harm, damage, or unpleasant things happening to them. [ADJ n] □ *"I'm heading back to Ireland again for another weekend." — "Have a safe journey."* ● **safe|ly** ADV □ *The space shuttle returned safely today from a 10-day mission.* ◼ ADJ If you are at a **safe** distance from something or someone, you are far enough away from them to avoid any danger, harm, or unpleasant effects. [ADJ n] □ *I shall conceal myself at a safe distance from the battlefield.* ◼ ADJ If something you have or expect to obtain is **safe**, you cannot lose it or be prevented from having it. □ *We as consumers need to feel confident that our jobs are safe before we will spend spare cash.* ◼ ADJ A **safe** course of action is one in which there is very little risk of loss or failure. □ *Electricity shares are still a safe investment.* ● **safe|ly** ADV □ *We reveal only as much information as we can safely risk at a given time.* ◼ ADJ If **it is safe to** say or assume something, you can say it with very little risk of being wrong. □ *I think it is safe to say that very few students expend the effort to do quality work in school.* ● **safe|ly** ADV [ADV before v] □ *I think you can safely say she will not be appearing in another of my films.* ◼ N-COUNT A **safe** is a strong metal cabinet with special locks, in which you keep money, jewelry, or other valuable things. □ *The files are now in a safe to which only he has the key.* ◼ →see also **safely** ◼ PHRASE If you say that a person or thing is **in safe hands**, or is **safe in** someone's **hands**, you mean that they are being taken care of by a reliable person and will not be harmed. □ *I had a huge responsibility to ensure these packets remained in safe hands.* ◼ PHRASE If you **play safe** or **play it safe**, you do not take any risks. □ *If you want to play safe, cut down on the amount of salt you eat.* ◼ PHRASE If you say you are doing something **to be on the safe side**, you mean that you are doing it in case something undesirable happens, even though this may be unnecessary. □ *You might still want to go for an X-ray, however, just to be on the safe side.* ◼ PHRASE If you say **it's better to be safe than sorry**," you are advising someone to take action in order to avoid possible unpleasant consequences later, even if this seems unnecessary. □ *Don't be afraid to have this checked by a doctor – better safe than sorry!* ◼ PHRASE You say that someone is **safe and sound** when they are still alive or unharmed after being in danger. □ *All I'm hoping for is that wherever Trevor is he will come home safe and sound.*

◼ 형용사 안전한 □ 그 도시로 비상식량 보급품을 들여와도 안전한지를 조사하기 위해서 점검관이 도착했다. □ 우리가 먹는 대부분의 음식은 새들에게도 안전하다. ◼ 형용사 안전한 □ 그들은 자신들을 위협했던 그 폭력 사태로부터 이제는 안전하다. ◼ 형용사 안전한 □ 소피는 어디 있습니까? 그녀는 안전한 겁니까? ● 안전하게 부사 □ 소방관들이 140명의 손님들을 모두 안전하게 그 건물에서 데리고 나왔다. ◼ 형용사 안전한 □ 계속되는 긴장 상태로 인해 난민 수용소에 머물고 있던 사람들 절반 이상이 더 안전한 지역으로 도피해야 했다. ● 안전하게 부사 □ 그 은행원은 그 돈을 자신의 침대 밑에 안전하게 넣어 둔다. ◼ 형용사 무사한 □ "나는 아일랜드로 다시 돌아가서 일주일을 더 지내련다 해." "무사히 잘 다녀와라." ● 무사히 부사 □ 우주 왕복선이 10일간의 임무를 마치고 오늘 무사히 귀환했다. ◼ 형용사 안전한 □ 나는 전장으로부터 안전하게 떨어진 곳에 숨어 있을 것이다. ◼ 형용사 안정된 □ 우리는 소비자로서 여분의 돈을 쓰기 전에 우리의 직장이 안정적이라는 것을 확신할 필요가 있다. ◼ 형용사 안전한 □ 전기 관련 주식이 아직은 안전한 투자이다. ● 안전하게 부사 □ 우리는 주어진 시간에 안전하게 위험을 감수할 수 있는 만큼의 정보만 유출시킨다. ◼ 형용사 무방한 □ 나는 학교에서 질 높은 공부를 위해 노력을 경주하는 학생이 극히 드물다고 말해도 무방하다고 생각한다. ● 무방하게 부사 □ 다음에도 그녀가 내 영화에 나오지 않을 것이라고 말씀하셔도 무방하리라고 봅니다. ◼ 가산명사 금고 □ 그 서류들은 지금 그만이 열쇠를 가지고 있는 금고 안에 있다. ◼ 구 안전한 곳에 □ 나는 이 돈다발들을 안전한 곳에 잘 보관해야 할 무거운 책임을 지고 있었다. ◼ 구 안전하게 하다 □ 당신이 안전을 꾀하려 한다면, 섭취하는 소금의 양을 줄이세요. ◼ 구 만약을 대비해서 □ 그러나 당신은 만약을 대비해서 여전히 엑스레이를 찍으러 가고 싶을지도 모른다. ◼ 구 나중에 후회하는 것보다 안전한 것이 더 낫다 □ 의사에게 이에 대한 검진받는 것을 두려워하지 마세요. 나중에 후회하는 것보다는 안전한 것이 더 나으니까. ◼ 구 무사히 □ 내가 지금 바라는 것은 오직 트레버가 어디에 있든지 무사히 집에만 돌아오는 것이다.

Word Partnership	*safe*의 연어
N.	**children/kids** are safe, safe **at home** ◼
	safe **environment**, safe **neighborhood**, safe **place**, safe **streets** ◼
	safe **bet**, safe **investment**, safe **operation** ◼
ADV.	**perfectly** safe, **relatively** safe ◼

safe de·pos·it box (**safe deposit boxes**) N-COUNT A **safe deposit box** is a small box, usually kept in a special room in a bank, in which you can store valuable objects. 가산명사 (은행의) 귀중품 금고

safe·guard /seɪfgɑrd/ (**safeguards, safeguarding, safeguarded**) ■ V-T To **safeguard** something or someone means to protect them from being harmed, lost, or badly treated. [FORMAL] ❏ *They will press for international action to safeguard the ozone layer.* ■ N-COUNT A **safeguard** is a law, rule, or measure intended to prevent someone or something from being harmed. ❏ *As an additional safeguard against weeds you can always use an underlay of heavy duty polythene.* ■ 타동사 보호하다 [격식체] ❏ 그들은 오존층을 보호하기 위한 국제적인 조치를 요구할 것이다. ■ 가산명사 안전 조치 ❏ 잡초를 방지할 수 있는 추가 안전 조치로서, 항상 질긴 폴리에틸렌 깔판을 사용하면 된다.

safe ha·ven (**safe havens**) ■ N-COUNT If part of a country is declared a **safe haven**, people who need to escape from a dangerous situation such as a war can go there and be protected. ❏ *Countries overwhelmed by the human tide of refugees want safe havens set up at once.* ■ N-UNCOUNT If a country provides **safe haven** for people from another country who have been in danger, it allows them to stay there under its official protection. [AM] ❏ *Some Democrats support granting the Haitians temporary safe haven in the U.S.* ■ N-COUNT A **safe haven** is a place, a situation, or an activity which provides people with an opportunity to escape from things that they find unpleasant or worrying. ❏ *...the idea of the family as a safe haven from the brutal outside world.* ■ 가산명사 안전한 피신처 ❏ 피난민들의 물결에 놀란 국가들이 안전한 피신처가 즉시 마련되기를 원하고 있다. ■ 불가산명사 은신처 [미국영어] ❏ 몇몇 민주당 의원들은 아이티 사람들에게 미국 내에 임시 은신처를 마련해 주는 것을 지지한다. ■ 가산명사 피신처 ❏ 냉엄한 바깥세상으로부터 피신처로서의 가정이라는 개념

safe·ly /seɪfli/ ■ ADV If something is done **safely**, it is done in a way that makes it unlikely that anyone will be harmed. ❏ *The waste is safely locked away until it is no longer radioactive.* ❏ *"Drive safely," he said and waved goodbye.* ■ ADV You also use **safely** to say that there is no risk of a situation being changed. ❏ *Once events are safely in the past, this idea seems to become less alarming.* ■ →see also **safe** ■ 부사 안전하게 ❏ 그 폐기물에 방사능 물질이 더 이상 없을 때까지 안전하게 격리해 둔다. ❏ "운전 조심해."라며 그가 손을 흔들며 인사했다. ■ 부사 확실히 ❏ 일단 사건들이 확실히 끝났다면, 이 생각은 덜 염려스러울 것 같다.

safe sex also **safer sex** N-UNCOUNT **Safe sex** is sexual activity in which people protect themselves against the risk of AIDS and other diseases, usually by using condoms. ❏ *You must practice safe sex and know your partner well.* 불가산명사 안전한 성행위 ❏ 당신은 안전한 성행위를 해야 하며 상대를 잘 알아야 한다.

safe·ty ♦♦◇ /seɪfti/ ■ N-UNCOUNT **Safety** is the state of being safe from harm or danger. ❏ *The report goes on to make a number of recommendations to improve safety on aircraft.* ■ N-UNCOUNT If you reach **safety**, you reach a place where you are safe from danger. ❏ *He stumbled through smoke and fumes given off from her burning sofa to pull her to safety.* ❏ *Guests ran for safety as the device went off in a ground-floor men's toilet.* ■ N-SING If you are concerned about the **safety** of something, you are concerned that it might be harmful or dangerous. ❏ *...consumers are showing growing concern about the safety of the food they buy.* ■ N-SING If you are concerned for someone's **safety**, you are concerned that they might be in danger. ❏ *There is grave concern for the safety of witnesses.* ■ ADJ **Safety** features or measures are intended to make something less dangerous. [ADJ n] ❏ *The built-in safety device compensates for a fall in water pressure.* ■ 불가산명사 안전성 ❏ 그 보고서는 비행기에 대한 안전성을 향상시키기 위한 많은 제안을 하고 있다. ■ 불가산명사 안전한 곳 ❏ 그는 그녀를 안전한 곳으로 끌어내기 위해 불붙은 소파에서 나오는 연기와 화염을 뚫고 비틀거리며 들어왔다. ❏ 1층 남자 화장실에서 그 장치가 폭발하자, 손님들은 안전한 곳을 찾아 뛰어갔다. ■ 단수명사 안전성 ❏ 소비자들은 자신들이 구매하는 음식물의 안전성에 대해 점점 더 우려를 나타내고 있다. ■ 단수명사 안전 ❏ 증인들의 안전에 대해 심각한 우려가 있다. ■ 형용사 안전의 ❏ 부착되어 있는 안전장치가 수압의 낙차를 보정해 준다.

Word Partnership	safety의 연어
V.	**improve** safety, **provide** safety ■
	ensure safety ■ ■ ■
	fear for *someone's* safety ■
N.	**child** safety, **fire** safety, **health and** safety, **highway/traffic** safety, safety **measures, public** safety, safety **regulations,** safety **standards, workplace** safety ■
	safety **concerns, food** safety ■
	safety **device,** safety **equipment** ■

safe·ty belt (**safety belts**) also **safety-belt** N-COUNT A **safety belt** is a strap attached to a seat in a car or airplane. You fasten it around your body and it stops you being thrown forward if there is an accident. ❏ *Please return to your seats and fasten your safety belts.* 가산명사 안전벨트 ❏ 좌석으로 돌아가서 안전벨트를 매 주시기 바랍니다.

safe·ty net (**safety nets**) ■ N-COUNT A **safety net** is something that you can rely on to help you if you get into a difficult situation. ❏ *Welfare is the only real safety net for low-income workers.* ■ N-COUNT In a circus, a **safety net** is a large net that is placed below performers on a high wire or trapeze in order to catch them and prevent them being injured if they fall off. ■ 가산명사 안전망 ❏ 생활 보조금이야말로 저소득 노동자들에게는 실질적인 안전망이다. ■ 가산명사 (서커스의) 안전망

safe·ty of·fi·cer (**safety officers**) N-COUNT The **safety officer** in a company or an organization is the person who is responsible for the safety of the people who work or visit there. ❏ *Organisers had consulted widely with police, stewards, and safety officers to ensure tight security.* 가산명사 안전 담당관 ❏ 주최 측은 삼엄한 경비를 위해서 경찰, 진행 요원, 안전 담당관들과 함께 광범위하게 상의했다.

safe·ty pin (**safety pins**) N-COUNT A **safety pin** is a bent metal pin used for fastening things together. The point of the pin has a cover so that when the pin is closed it cannot hurt anyone. ❏ *...trousers which were held together with safety pins.* 가산명사 안전핀 ❏ 안전핀으로 고정되어 있던 바지

sag /sæg/ (**sags, sagging, sagged**) V-I When something **sags**, it hangs down loosely or sinks downward in the middle. ❏ *The shirt's cuffs won't sag and lose their shape after washing.* 자동사 처지다, 늘어지다 ❏ 그 셔츠는 세탁한 후에도 소매 단이 늘어지거나 변형되지 않을 것이다.

saga /sɑgə/ (**sagas**) ■ N-COUNT A **saga** is a long story, account, or sequence of events. ❏ *...a 600 page saga about 18th century slavery.* ■ N-COUNT A **saga** is a long story composed in medieval times in Norway or Iceland. ❏ *...a Nordic saga of giants and trolls.* ■ 가산명사 긴 이야기, 대하소설 ❏ 18세기 노예 제도에 관한 600페이지 분량의 대하소설 ■ 가산명사 (중세의) 무용담 ❏ 거인들과 못생긴 난쟁이들이 나오는 북유럽의 무용담

sage /seɪdʒ/ N-UNCOUNT **Sage** is an herb, used in cooking. 불가산명사 (식물) 세이지

said /sed/ **Said** is the past tense and past participle of **say**. say의 과거, 과거 분사

sail ♦◇◇ /seɪl/ (**sails, sailing, sailed**) ■ N-COUNT **Sails** are large pieces of material attached to the mast of a ship. The wind blows against the sails and pushes the ship along. ❏ *The white sails billow with the breezes they catch.* ■ V-I You say a ship **sails** when it moves over the sea. ❏ *The trawler had sailed from the port of* ■ 가산명사 돛 ❏ 흰 돛이 불어오는 미풍에 나부낀다. ■ 자동사 항해하다, 출항하다 ❏ 그 저인망 어선은 제이브르그 항구에서 출항했다. ■ 타동사/자동사 항해하다 ❏ 나는 작은 배에 몸을 싣고 전 세계를

Zeebrugge. ❸ V-T/V-I If you **sail** a boat or if a boat **sails**, it moves across water using its sails. ❑ *I shall get myself a little boat and sail her around the world.* ◄ →see also **sailing** ❺ PHRASE When a ship **sets sail**, it leaves a port. ❑ *He loaded his vessel with another cargo and set sail.*

▶**sail through** PHRASAL VERB If someone or something **sails through** a difficult situation or experience, they deal with it easily and successfully. ❑ *While she sailed through her maths exams, he struggled.*

sail|ing /seɪlɪŋ/ (**sailings**) ❶ N-UNCOUNT **Sailing** is the activity or sport of sailing boats. ❑ *There was swimming and sailing down on the lake.* ❷ N-COUNT **Sailings** are trips made by a ship carrying passengers. ❑ *Ferry companies are providing extra sailings from Calais.* ❸ PHRASE If you say that a task was not all **plain sailing**, you mean that it was not very easy. ❑ *Pregnancy wasn't all plain sailing and once again there were problems.*

sail|or /seɪlər/ (**sailors**) N-COUNT A **sailor** is someone who works on a ship or sails a boat. ❑ *...sailors, marines, and Coast Guard personnel.*

saint ♦♢♢ /seɪnt/ (**saints**)

> The title is usually pronounced /sənt/.

❶ N-COUNT; N-TITLE A **saint** is someone who has died and been officially recognized and honored by the Christian church because his or her life was a perfect example of the way Christians should live. ❑ *Every parish was named after a saint.* ❷ N-COUNT If you refer to a living person as a **saint**, you mean that they are extremely kind, patient, and unselfish. [APPROVAL] ❑ *My girlfriend Geraldine must be a bit of a saint to put up with me.*

saint|ly /seɪntli/ ADJ A **saintly** person behaves in a very good or very holy way. [APPROVAL] ❑ *She has been saintly in her self-restraint.*

sake ♦♦♢ /seɪk/ (**sakes**) ❶ PHRASE If you do something **for the sake of** something, you do it for that purpose or in order to achieve that result. You can also say that you do it **for** something's **sake**. ❑ *Let's assume for the sake of argument that we manage to build a satisfactory database.* ❑ *For the sake of historical accuracy, please permit us to state the true facts.* ❷ PHRASE If you do something **for** its **own sake**, you do it because you want to, or because you enjoy it, and not for any other reason. You can also talk about, for example, **art for art's sake** or **sport for sport's sake**. ❑ *Economic change for its own sake did not appeal to him.* ❸ PHRASE When you do something **for** someone's **sake**, you do it in order to help them or make them happy. ❑ *I trust you to do a good job for Stan's sake.* ❹ PHRASE Some people use expressions such as **for God's sake, for heaven's sake, for goodness sake,** or **for Pete's sake** in order to express annoyance or impatience, or to add force to a question or request. The expressions "for God's sake" and "for Christ's sake" could cause offense. [INFORMAL, FEELINGS] ❑ *For goodness sake, why didn't you ring me?*

sal|ad /sæləd/ (**salads**) N-VAR A **salad** is a mixture of raw foods such as lettuce, cucumber, and tomatoes. It is often served with other food as part of a meal. ❑ *...a salad of tomato, onion and cucumber.*

sal|aried /sælərid/ ADJ **Salaried** people receive a salary from their job. [BUSINESS] ❑ *...salaried employees.*

sal|ary ♦♦♢ /sæləri/ (**salaries**) N-VAR A **salary** is the money that someone earns each month or year from their employer. [BUSINESS] ❑ *...the lawyer was paid a huge salary.*
→see salt

> Professional people and office workers receive a **salary**, which is paid monthly. However, when talking about someone's salary, you usually give the annual figure. ❑ *I'm paid a salary of $29,000 a year.* **Pay** is a general noun which you can use to refer to the money you get from your employer for doing your job. Manual workers are paid **wages**, or **a wage**. The plural is more common than the singular, especially when you are talking about the actual cash that someone receives. ❑ *Every week he handed all his wages in cash to his wife.* Wages are usually paid, and quoted, as an hourly or a weekly sum. ❑ *...a starting wage of five dollars an hour.* Your **income** consists of all the money you receive from all sources, including your pay.

sale ♦♦♦ /seɪl/ (**sales**) ❶ N-SING The **sale** of goods is the act of selling them for money. ❑ *Efforts were made to limit the sale of alcohol.* ❑ *...a proposed arms sale to Saudi Arabia.* ❷ N-PLURAL The **sales** of a product are the quantity of it that is sold. ❑ *The newspaper has sales of 1.72 million.* ❑ *...the huge Christmas sales of computer games.* ❸ N-PLURAL The part of a company that deals with **sales** deals with selling the company's products. ❑ *Until 1983 he worked in sales and marketing.* ❹ N-COUNT A **sale** is an occasion when a store sells things at less than their normal price. ❑ *...a pair of jeans bought half-price in a sale.* ❺ N-COUNT A **sale** is an event when goods are sold to the person who offers the highest price. ❑ *The Old Master was bought by London dealers at the Christie's sale.* ❻ PHRASE If something is **for sale**, it is being offered to people to buy. ❑ *The yacht is for sale at a price of 1.7 million dollars.* ❼ PHRASE Products that are **on sale** can be bought in stores. [mainly BRIT] ❑ *English textbooks and dictionaries are on sale everywhere.* ❽ PHRASE If products in a store are **on sale**, they can be bought for less than their normal price. [AM] ❑ *He bought a sports jacket on sale at Gowings Men's Store.* ❾ PHRASE If a property or company is **up for sale**, its owner is trying to sell it. ❑ *The castle has been put up for sale.*

sales clerk (**sales clerks**) also **salesclerk** N-COUNT A **sales clerk** is a person who works in a store selling things to customers and helping them to find what they want. [AM; BRIT **shop assistant**]

항해할 것이다. ❺구 운항하다 ❑ 그는 대형 선박에 화물을 더 싣고 출항했다.

구동사 수월하게 해내다 ❑ 그녀는 수학 시험을 수월하게 치른 반면에, 그는 어려워했다.

❶ 불가산명사 보트 타기, 요트 타기 ❑ 호수에서는 수영도 요트도 탔다. ❷ 가산명사 배 여행 ❑ 페리 회사들은 칼레에서 떠나는 선박 여행 특별 상품을 내놓고 있다. ❸구 쉬운 일 ❑ 임신은 쉬운 일이 아니었고 또 다시 여러 문제점들이 생겼다.

가산명사 선원 ❑ 선원과, 해병과 해안 경비대원들

> 이 칭호는 대개 /sənt/로 발음된다.

❶ 가산명사; 경칭명사 성인(聖人) ❑ 모든 교구는 성인의 이름을 따서 지어졌다. ❷ 가산명사 성자와 같은 사람 [마음에 듦] ❑ 나 같은 사람을 참아 내는 것을 보면 내 여자 친구 제럴딘은 성자 같은 사람임이 분명하다.

형용사 성자 같은 [마음에 듦] ❑ 그녀는 자제심이 성자 같았다.

❶구 ～을 위하여 ❑ 논의를 하기 위해서, 우리가 간신히 만족스러운 데이터베이스를 구축한다고 생각해 봅시다. ❑ 역사의 정확성을 기하기 위해서, 우리가 진실을 기술할 수 있도록 허가해 주시기 바랍니다. ❷구 그 자체로; 예술을 위한 예술, 스포츠를 위한 스포츠 ❑ 경제 개혁 그 자체는 그의 마음에 와 닿지 않았다. ❸구 ～을 위하여 ❑ 나는 네가 스탠을 위해서 잘 하리라 믿어. ❹구 제발, 맙소사 [비격식체, 감정 개입] ❑ 맙소사, 왜 내게 전화하지 않았니?

가산명사 또는 불가산명사 샐러드 ❑ 토마토, 양파, 오이를 넣은 샐러드

형용사 봉급을 받는 [경제] ❑ 봉급 받는 직원들

가산명사 또는 불가산명사 봉급 [경제] ❑ 그 변호사는 엄청난 봉급을 받았다.

> 전문직과 사무직 종사자들은 매달 지급되는 월급(salary)을 받는다. 그러나, 누구의 봉급을 말할 때에는 대개 연봉을 말한다. ❑ 나는 일년에 29,000달러의 연봉을 받는다. pay는 명사로 쓰면, 자기 일을 한 것에 대해 고용주로부터 받은 돈을 지칭할 때 쓸 수 있는 일반적인 말이다. 노동자는 wages 또는 a wage를 받는다. 특히 실제로 받는 현금을 말할 때는 단수보다 복수가 더 일반적이다. ❑ 매주 그는 임금 전부를 자기 부인에게 주었다. 임금은 대개 시급 또는 주급으로 지불하고 매긴다. ❑ ...시간당 5달러의 초임. 수입(income)은 급료를 포함해서 모든 소득원으로부터 받는 총액으로 이루어진다.

❶ 단수명사 판매 ❑ 술 판매를 제한하기 위한 여러 가지 노력이 이뤄졌다. ❑ 사우디아라비아에 제기된 무기 판매 ❷ 복수명사 판매량 ❑ 그 신문은 판매 부수가 177만 부이다. ❑ 크리스마스 시기의 엄청난 컴퓨터 게임 판매량 ❸ 복수명사 영업 ❑ 1983년까지 그는 영업부에서 일했다. ❹ 가산명사 인기 판매, 세일 ❑ 세일 때 반 가격으로 산 면바지 ❺ 가산명사 경매 ❑ 그 저장의 작품은 크리스티 경매에서 런던 딜러에게 팔렸다. ❻구 팔려고 내놓은 ❑ 그 요트는 170만 달러의 판매가로 나와 있다. ❼구 ～로 영국영어] ❑ 영어 교과서와 사전은 어느 곳에서나 살 수 있다. ❽구 할인하는 [미국영어] ❑ 그는 고윙스 남성복 매장에서 스포츠 재킷을 할인해서 샀다. ❾구 팔려고 내놓은 ❑ 그 성은 팔려고 내놓았다.

가산명사 판매 사원 [미국영어; 영국영어 shop assistant]

sales force (**sales forces**) also **salesforce** N-COUNT A company's **sales force** is all the people that work for that company selling its products. [BUSINESS] ❏ *His sales force is signing up schools at the rate of 25 a day.*

가산명사 영업부 직원들 [경제] ❏ 그의 영업부 직원들은 하루에 25개의 학교가 구매 동의서에 서명하도록 권유하고 있다.

sales|man /séɪlzmən/ (**salesmen**) N-COUNT A **salesman** is a man whose job is to sell things, especially directly to stores or other businesses on behalf of a company. ❏ *...an insurance salesman.* [BUSINESS]

가산명사 영업 사원 ❏ 보험 영업 사원 [경제]

sales|person /séɪlzpɜrsᵊn/ (**salespeople** or **salespersons**) N-COUNT A **salesperson** is a person who sells things, either in a store or directly to customers on behalf of a company. [BUSINESS] ❏ *They will usually send a salesperson out to measure your bathroom.*

가산명사 영업 사원, 판매원 [경제] ❏ 그들은 보통 당신의 목욕탕 크기를 알아보기 위해 영업 사원을 내보낼 것이다.

sales pitch (**sales pitches**) N-COUNT A salesperson's **sales pitch** is what they say in order to persuade someone to buy something from them. ❏ *His sales pitch was smooth and convincing.* [BUSINESS]

가산명사 구매 권유 ❏ 그의 구매 권유는 능수능란하고 확신에 차 있었다. [경제]

sales|room /séɪlzrum/ (**salesrooms**) **1** N-COUNT A **salesroom** is the same as a **showroom.** [AM] **2** N-COUNT A **salesroom** is a place where things are sold by auction. [AM; BRIT **saleroom**] ❏ *Whether buying from dealer or salesroom, certain features of drawings should always be considered.*

1 가산명사 상품 전시장 [미국영어] **2** 가산명사 경매장 [미국영어; 영국영어 saleroom] ❏ 딜러에게 사든 경매장에서 사든 간에, 그림을 살 때는 몇 가지 요소들을 항상 고려해야 한다.

sales slip (**sales slips**) N-COUNT A **sales slip** is a piece of paper that you are given when you buy something in a store, which shows when you bought it and how much you paid. [AM; BRIT **receipt**]

가산명사 영수증 [미국영어; 영국영어 receipt]

sales tax (**sales taxes**) N-VAR The **sales tax** on things that you buy is the amount of money that you pay to the local or state government or, in Britain, to the national government. [BUSINESS] ❏ *The state's unpopular sales tax on snacks has ended.*

가산명사 또는 불가산명사 판매세 [경제] ❏ 주에서 스낵에 대해 매기던, 사람들이 싫어하던 판매세가 없어졌다.

sales|wom|an /séɪlzwʊmən/ (**saleswomen**) N-COUNT A **saleswoman** is a woman who sells things, either in a store or directly to customers on behalf of a company. ❏ *...an insurance saleswoman.*

가산명사 여성 판매원, 여성 영업 사원 [경제] ❏ 여성 보험 영업 사원

sa|li|ent /séɪliənt, séɪljənt/ ADJ The **salient** points or facts of a situation are the most important ones. [FORMAL] ❏ *He read the salient facts quickly.*

형용사 핵심적인 [격식체] ❏ 그는 핵심 사항을 빨리 읽었다.

sa|li|va /səláɪvə/ N-UNCOUNT **Saliva** is the watery liquid that forms in your mouth and helps you to chew and digest food. ❏ *He noticed a lot of saliva settling in his mouth.*

불가산명사 침 ❏ 그는 입 속에 침이 많이 고이는 것을 알아차렸다.

salm|on /sǽmən/

Salmon is both the singular and the plural form.

salmon은 단수형 및 복수형이다.

N-COUNT A **salmon** is a large silver-colored fish. ● N-UNCOUNT **Salmon** is the orangey-pink flesh of this fish which is eaten as food. It is often smoked and eaten raw. ❏ *He gave them a splendid lunch of smoked salmon.*

가산명사 연어 ● 불가산명사 연어살 ❏ 그는 그들에게 멋진 훈제 연어 점심 식사를 대접했다.

sa|lon /səlɑ́n, BRIT sǽlɒn / (**salons**) N-COUNT A **salon** is a place where people have their hair cut or colored, or have beauty treatments. ❏ *...a new hair salon.*

가산명사 미용실 ❏ 새로 개업한 미용실

sa|loon /səlún/ (**saloons**) **1** N-COUNT A **saloon** is a place where alcoholic drinks are sold and drunk. [AM] ❏ *In the saloon, he drank whisky and let his eyes become accustomed to the dimness.* **2** N-COUNT A **saloon** or a **saloon car** is a car with seats for four or more people, a fixed roof, and a trunk that is separated from the rear seats. [BRIT; AM **sedan**]

1 가산명사 술집 [미국영어] ❏ 그 술집에서 그는 위스키를 마시며 어두컴컴한 실내에 시야가 적응되어 갔다. **2** 가산명사 세단형 승용차 [영국영어; 미국영어 sedan]

salt ♦♢♢ /sɔ́lt/ (**salts, salting, salted**) **1** N-UNCOUNT **Salt** is a strong-tasting substance, in the form of white powder or crystals, which is used to improve the flavor of food or to preserve it. Salt occurs naturally in sea water. ❏ *Season lightly with salt and pepper.* **2** V-T When you **salt** food, you add salt to it. ❏ *Salt the stock to your taste and leave it simmering very gently.* ● **salt|ed** ADJ ❏ *Put a pan of salted water on to boil.* **3** N-COUNT **Salts** are substances that are formed when an acid reacts with an alkali. ❏ *The rock is rich in mineral salts.* **4** PHRASE If you **take** something **with a pinch of salt**, you do not believe that it is completely accurate or true. ❏ *You have to take these findings with a pinch of salt because respondents tend to give the answers they feel they should.* **5** PHRASE If you say, for example, that any doctor **worth** his or her **salt** would do something, you mean that any doctor who was good at his or her job or who deserved respect would do it. ❏ *No golf teacher worth his salt would ever recommend that you grip the club tightly.* →see **crystal**, **sweat**
→see Word Web: **salt**

1 불가산명사 소금 ❏ 소금과 후추로 간을 조금 하세요. **2** 타동사 소금을 넣다 ❏ 입맛에 맞게 육수에 소금을 넣고 뭉근히 끓도록 놓아 두세요. ● 소금을 넣은 형용사 ❏ 냄비에 소금물을 넣고 끓도록 불 위에 올려 두세요. **3** 가산명사 염(鹽) ❏ 이 암석은 무기산염이 풍부하다 **4** 구 에누리해서 듣다, 감안을 해서 받아들이다 ❏ 응답자들은 씨야 되리라고 생각되는 대답을 쓰는 경향이 있으므로 감안을 해서 이 결과들을 받아들여야 한다. **5** 구 제값을 하는 ❏ 제값을 하는 골프 교사라면 클럽을 꽉 쥐라고 권하지는 않을 것이다.

Word Partnership   *salt*의 연어

N.	salt air, salt and pepper, pinch of salt, teaspoon of salt **1**
V.	add salt, season with salt, sprinkle salt, taste salt **1**

salty /sɔ́lti/ (**saltier, saltiest**) ADJ Something that is **salty** contains salt or tastes of salt. ❏ *...salty foods such as ham and bacon.* →see **taste**

형용사 (맛이) 짠 ❏ 햄이나 베이컨 같은 짠 음식

Word Web   salt

Since prehistoric times, **salt** has been used for a **seasoning**, a **preservative**, and even **money**. A book about salt published in China around 2700 BC describes methods of producing salt that are strikingly similar to current methods. The ancient Greeks exchanged salt for slaves, giving rise to the expression, "not worth his salt." Roman soldiers received *salarium argentum* (salt money), which is the source of the English word *salary*. And salt has altered the course of history. For example, the salt tax was one major cause of the French Revolution.

sa|lute /səlut/ (salutes, saluting, saluted) **1** V-T/V-I If you **salute** someone, you greet them or show your respect with a formal sign. Soldiers usually salute officers by raising their right hand so that their fingers touch their forehead. ❑ *One of the company stepped out and saluted the General.* ● N-COUNT **Salute** is also a noun. [also in N] ❑ *He gave his salute and left.* **2** V-T To **salute** a person or their achievements means to publicly show or state your admiration for them. ❑ *I salute Governor Castle for the leadership role that he is taking.*

sal|vage /sælvɪdʒ/ (salvages, salvaging, salvaged) **1** V-T If something **is salvaged**, someone manages to save it, for example from a ship that has sunk, or from a building that has been damaged. [usu passive] ❑ *The team's first task was to decide what equipment could be salvaged.* **2** N-UNCOUNT **Salvage** is the act of salvaging things from somewhere such as a damaged ship or building. ❑ *The salvage operation went on.* **3** N-UNCOUNT The **salvage** from somewhere such as a damaged ship or building is the things that are saved from it. ❑ *They climbed up on the rock with their salvage.* **4** V-T If you manage to **salvage** a difficult situation, you manage to get something useful from it so that it is not a complete failure. ❑ *Officials tried to salvage the situation.* **5** V-T If you **salvage** something such as your pride or your reputation, you manage to keep it even though it seems likely you will lose it, or you get it back it after losing it. ❑ *We definitely wanted to salvage some pride for British tennis.*

sal|va|tion /sælveɪʃⁿn/ **1** N-UNCOUNT In Christianity, **salvation** is the fact that Christ has saved a person from evil. ❑ *The church's message of salvation has changed the lives of many.* **2** N-UNCOUNT The **salvation** of someone or something is the act of saving them from harm, destruction, or an unpleasant situation. ❑ *...those whose marriages are beyond salvation.* **3** N-SING If someone or something is your **salvation**, they are responsible for saving you from harm, destruction, or an unpleasant situation. ❑ *The country's salvation lies in forcing through democratic reforms.*

same ♦♦♦ /seɪm/ **1** ADJ If two or more things, actions, or qualities are the **same**, or if one is the **same as** another, they are very like each other in some way. [the ADJ, oft ADJ as n/-ing] ❑ *The houses were all the same – square, close to the street, needing paint.* ❑ *People with the same experience in the job should be paid the same.* **2** PHRASE If something is happening **the same as** something else, the two things are happening in a way that is similar or exactly the same. ❑ *I mean, it's a relationship, the same as a marriage is a relationship.* **3** ADJ You use **same** to indicate that you are referring to only one place, time, or thing, and not to different ones. [the ADJ, oft ADJ n as n, adj n that] ❑ *Bernard works at the same institution as Arlette.* ❑ *It's impossible to get everybody together at the same time.* **4** ADJ Something that is still **the same** has not changed in any way. [the ADJ] ❑ *Taking ingredients from the same source means the beers stay the same.* **5** PRON You use **the same** to refer to something that has previously been mentioned or suggested. [the PRON] ❑ *We made the decision which was right for us. Other parents must do the same.* ❑ *In the United States small specialised bookshops survive quite well. The same applies to small publishers.* ● ADJ **Same** is also an adjective. [the ADJ] ❑ *He's so effective. I admire Ginny for pretty much the same reason.* **6** CONVENTION You say "**same here**" in order to suggest that you feel the same way about something as the person who has just spoken to you, or that you have done the same thing. [INFORMAL, SPOKEN, FORMULAE] ❑ *"Nice to meet you," said Michael. "Same here," said Mary Ann.* **7** CONVENTION You say "**same to you**" in response to someone who wishes you well with something. [INFORMAL, SPOKEN, FORMULAE] ❑ *"Have a nice Easter." — "And the same to you Bridie."* **8** PHRASE You say "**same again**" when you want to order another drink of the same kind as the one you have just had. [INFORMAL, SPOKEN] ❑ *Give Roger another pint, Imogen, and I'll have the same again.* **9** PHRASE You can say **all the same** or **just the same** to introduce a statement which indicates that a situation or your opinion has not changed, in spite of what has happened or what has just been said. ❑ *I arranged to pay him the dollars when he got there, a purely private arrangement. All the same, it was illegal.* **10** PHRASE If you say "**It's all the same to me**," you mean that you do not care which of several things happens or is chosen. [mainly SPOKEN] ❑ *Whether I've got a moustache or not it's all the same to me.* **11** **at the same time** →see **time**

Thesaurus	same의 참조어
ADJ.	alike, equal, identical; *(ant.)* different **1**
	constant, unchanged; *(ant.)* different **4**

sam|ple ♦◇◇ /sæmpⁿl/ (samples, sampling, sampled) **1** N-COUNT A **sample** of a substance or product is a small quantity of it that shows you what it is like. ❑ *You'll receive samples of paint, curtains and upholstery.* ❑ *We're giving away 2000 free samples.* **2** N-COUNT A **sample** of a substance is a small amount of it that is examined and analyzed scientifically. ❑ *They took samples of my blood.* **3** N-COUNT A **sample** of people or things is a number of them chosen out of a larger group and then used in tests or used to provide information about the whole group. ❑ *We based our analysis on a random sample of more than 200 males.* **4** V-T If you **sample** food or drink, you taste a small amount of it in order to find out if you like it. ❑ *We sampled a selection of different bottled waters.* **5** V-T If you **sample** a place or situation, you experience it for a short time in order to find out about it. ❑ *...the chance to sample a different way of life.* →see **laboratory**

Thesaurus	sample의 참조어
N.	bit, piece, portion, specimen **1** **2**
V.	experience, taste, try **4** **5**

1 타동사/자동사 경례하다 ❑ 일행 중 한 명이 열에서 나와 장군에게 경례했다. ● 가산명사 경례 ❑ 그는 경례를 하고 떠났다. **2** 타동사 경의를 표하다 ❑ 나는 캐슬 주지사가 맡고 있는 지도자 역할에 대해서 경의를 표한다.

1 타동사 인양되다, 구조되다 ❑ 그 팀의 첫 번째 임무는 어떤 장비를 인양할 수 있을까를 결정하는 것이었다. **2** 불가산명사 인양, 구조 ❑ 인양 작업이 계속되었다. **3** 불가산명사 인양물, 구조된 물건 ❑ 그들은 배에서 건진 물건들을 가지고 바위 위로 기어 올라갔다. **4** 타동사 (상황을) 수습하다 ❑ 관계자들이 상황을 수습하려고 애를 썼다. **5** 타동사 (자존심 등을) 지키다, (자존심 등을) 되찾다 ❑ 우리는 분명히 영국 테니스의 자존심을 지키고 싶어 했다.

1 불가산명사 (기독교의) 구원 ❑ 교회의 구원의 메시지가 많은 사람의 삶을 바꾸어 놓았다. **2** 불가산명사 구원, 구제 ❑ 결혼 생활이 구제될 수 있는 단계를 벗어난 사람들 **3** 단수명사 구원자 ❑ 그 나라를 구하는 길은 민주개혁을 밀고 나가는 것에 있다.

1 형용사 똑같은, 동일한 ❑ 그 집들은 구역이나, 도로에 가까운 것, 페인트칠을 해야 하는 것하며, 아주 똑같았다. **2** 구 ~인 것처럼 ❑ 내 말은, 결혼도 두 사람의 관계인 것처럼, 이것도 그런 관계라는 말이다. **3** 형용사 같은 ❑ 버나드는 알렛과 같은 연구소에서 일한다. ❑ 모든 사람을 같은 시간에 다 모이게 하는 것은 불가능하다. **4** 형용사 똑같은, 변함없는 ❑ 똑같은 곳에서 재료를 구한다는 것은 맥주 맛이 똑같다는 것을 의미한다. **5** 대명사 마찬가지 ❑ 우리는 우리에게 맞는 결정을 했다. 다른 부모들도 마찬가지로 해야 한다. ❑ 미국에서는 소규모의 전문 서점들이 잘 유지되고 있다. 이것은 소규모 출판사들도 마찬가지이다. ● 형용사 마찬가지의 ❑ 그는 매우 유능하다. 나는 지니도 거의 마찬가지 이유로 존경한다. **6** 관용 표현 나도 마찬가지야 [비격식체, 구어체, 의례적인 표현] ❑ "만나서 반가워요."라고 마이클이 말했다. "저도요."라고 메리 앤이 말했다. **7** 관용 표현 당신도요 [비격식체, 구어체, 의례적인 표현] ❑ "부활절 잘 보내세요." "브리디, 당신도요." **8** 구 같은 것으로 [비격식체, 구어체] ❑ 이모젠, 로저에게 한 잔 더 주고 나도 같은 걸로 주세요. **9** 구 여전히, 그래도 ❑ 나는 그가 그곳에 도착하면 그 돈을 주려고 순전히 개인적인 계획으로 준비해 두었다. 여전히, 그것도 불법이었지만. **10** 구 나에게는 상관없다 [주로 구어체] ❑ 내가 콧수염을 기르든 말든, 나는 상관없다.

1 가산명사 견본 ❑ 당신은 페인트, 커튼, 소파 덮개 견본품을 받을 것이다. ❑ 우리는 2천 개의 무료 견본품을 배포할 것이다. **2** 가산명사 시료, (분석용) 샘플 ❑ 그들은 내 혈액 시료를 가져갔다. **3** 가산명사 표본 ❑ 우리는 200명 이상의 남성을 무작위 표본 추출하여 분석했다. **4** 타동사 맛보다 ❑ 우리는 선택된 각종 물을 조금씩 맛보았다. **5** 타동사 잠시 시도해 보다 ❑ 다른 생활 방식을 잠시 시도해 볼 기회

sanc|tion ♦♦◇ /sǽŋkʃⁿn/ (sanctions, sanctioning, sanctioned) **1** V-T If someone in authority **sanctions** an action or practice, they officially approve of it and allow it to be done. ❑ *He may now be ready to sanction the use of force.* ● N-UNCOUNT **Sanction** is also a noun. ❑ *The king could not enact laws without the sanction of Parliament.* **2** N-PLURAL **Sanctions** are measures taken by countries to restrict trade and official contact with a country that has broken international law. ❑ *The continued abuse of human rights has now led the United States to impose sanctions against the regime.*

1 타동사 승인하다, 재가하다 ❑ 그는 이제 무력 사용을 승인하려고 하는 것 같다. ● 불가산명사 승인, 재가 ❑ 왕은 의회의 승인 없이는 법을 시행할 수 없었다. **2** 복수명사 (국제법상의) 제재 ❑ 계속되는 인권 침해 사례 때문에 미국은 이제 그 정권에 대해서 제재를 가하게 되었다.

	Word Partnership	sanction의 연어
ADJ.	**legal** sanction, **official** sanction **2**	
PREP.	sanction **against**, **without** sanction **1**	
V.	**impose** a sanction, **lift** a sanction **1**	

sanc|tity /sǽŋktɪti/ N-UNCOUNT If you talk about **the sanctity of** something, you mean that it is very important and must be treated with respect. ❑ *...the sanctity of human life.*

불가산명사 신성함 ❑ 인간 생명의 신성함

sanc|tu|ary /sǽŋktʃuɛri, BRIT sǽŋktʃuəri/ (sanctuaries) **1** N-COUNT A **sanctuary** is a place where people who are in danger from other people can go to be safe. ❑ *His church became a sanctuary for thousands of people who fled the civil war.* **2** N-UNCOUNT **Sanctuary** is the safety provided in a sanctuary. ❑ *Some of them have sought sanctuary in the church.* **3** N-COUNT A **sanctuary** is a place where birds or animals are protected and allowed to live freely. ❑ *...a bird sanctuary.*

1 가산명사 성역, 피신처 ❑ 그의 교회는 내란을 피해 도망 나온 수천 명에게 피신처가 되었다. **2** 불가산명사 보호 ❑ 그들 중 몇 명은 교회에 보호를 요청했다. **3** 가산명사 동물 보호 구역 ❑ 조류 보호 구역

sand ♦◇◇ /sǽnd/ (sands, sanding, sanded) **1** N-UNCOUNT **Sand** is a substance that looks like powder, and consists of extremely small pieces of stone. Some deserts and many beaches are made up of sand. ❑ *They all walked barefoot across the damp sand to the water's edge.* **2** N-PLURAL **Sands** are a large area of sand, for example a beach. ❑ *...miles of golden sands.* **3** V-T If you **sand** a wood or metal surface, you rub sandpaper over it in order to make it smooth or clean. ❑ *Sand the surface softly and carefully.* ● PHRASAL VERB **Sand down** means the same as **sand**. ❑ *I was going to sand down the chairs and repaint them.* →see **beach, desert, erosion**

1 불가산명사 모래 ❑ 그들은 모두 맨발로 촉촉한 모래밭을 가로질러 물가까지 걸어갔다. **2** 복수명사 모래밭 ❑ 수마일에 걸친 황금 모래밭 **3** 타동사 사포로 문지르다 ❑ 사포로 표면을 부드럽게 살살 문지르세요. ● 구동사 사포로 문지르다 ❑ 나는 그 의자들을 사포로 문질러서 다시 칠할 생각이었다.

san|dal /sǽndⁿl/ (sandals) N-COUNT **Sandals** are light shoes that you wear in warm weather, which have straps instead of a solid part over the top of your foot. ❑ *...a pair of old sandals.*

가산명사 샌들 ❑ 낡은 샌들 한 켤레

S & L /ɛs ən ɛl/ (S & Ls) N-COUNT **S & L** is an abbreviation for **savings and loan**. [BUSINESS]

가산명사 저축과 융자 [경제]

sand|paper /sǽndpeɪpər/ N-UNCOUNT **Sandpaper** is strong paper that has a coating of sand on it. It is used for rubbing wood or metal surfaces to make them smoother. ❑ *...a piece of sandpaper.*

불가산명사 사포 ❑ 사포 한 장

sand|stone /sǽndstoʊn/ N-MASS **Sandstone** is a type of rock which contains a lot of sand. It is often used for building houses and walls. ❑ *...the reddish sandstone walls.*

물질명사 (지질) 사암 ❑ 붉은 색조의 사암으로 만든 담

sand|wich /sǽnwɪtʃ, sǽnd-/ (sandwiches, sandwiching, sandwiched) **1** N-COUNT A **sandwich** usually consists of two slices of bread with a layer of food such as cheese or meat between them. ❑ *...a ham sandwich.* **2** V-T If you **sandwich** two things **together** with something else, you put that other thing between them. If you **sandwich** one thing between two other things, you put it between them. ❑ *Carefully split the sponge ring, then sandwich the two halves together with whipped cream.* →see **meal**

1 가산명사 샌드위치 ❑ 햄 샌드위치 **2** 타동사 사이에 끼우다 ❑ 둥근 스펀지케이크를 반으로 잘 자른 다음, 거품을 낸 크림을 그 사이에 넣으세요.

sand|wich course (sandwich courses) N-COUNT A **sandwich course** is an educational course in which you have periods of study between periods of being at work. [BRIT] ❑ *...students on sandwich courses.*

가산명사 샌드위치 과정 (현장 실습이 포함된 교육 과정) [영국영어] ❑ 샌드위치 과정을 듣고 있는 학생들

sandy /sǽndi/ (sandier, sandiest) ADJ A **sandy** area is covered with sand. ❑ *...long, sandy beaches.*

형용사 모래의 ❑ 긴 모래 해변

	Word Link	san ≈ health : in**san**e, **san**e, **san**itation

sane /seɪn/ (saner, sanest) **1** ADJ Someone who is **sane** is able to think and behave normally and reasonably, and is not mentally ill. ❑ *He seemed perfectly sane.* **2** ADJ If you refer to a **sane** person, action, or system, you mean one that you think is reasonable and sensible. ❑ *No sane person wishes to see conflict or casualties.*

1 형용사 제 정신의 ❑ 그는 완전히 제 정신인 것 같았다. **2** 형용사 분별 있는 ❑ 분별 있는 사람은 아무도 갈등이나 재해를 겪고 싶어 하지 않는다.

sang /sǽŋ/ **Sang** is the past tense of **sing**.

sing의 과거

sani|tary /sǽnɪteri, BRIT sǽnɪtri/ **1** ADJ **Sanitary** means concerned with keeping things clean and healthy, especially by providing a sewage system and a clean water supply. [ADJ n] ❑ *Sanitary conditions are appalling.* **2** ADJ If you say that a place is not **sanitary**, you mean that it is not very clean. ❑ *It's not the most sanitary place one could swim.*

1 형용사 위생의 ❑ 위생 상태가 형편없다. **2** 형용사 위생적인 ❑ 이곳이 수영하기에 가장 위생적인 장소는 아니다.

sani|tary nap|kin (sanitary napkins) N-COUNT A **sanitary napkin** is a pad of thick soft material which women wear to absorb the blood during their periods. [AM; BRIT **sanitary towel**]

가산명사 생리대 [미국영어; 영국영어 sanitary towel]

sani|tary tow|el (sanitary towels) N-COUNT A **sanitary towel** is the same as a **sanitary napkin**. [BRIT]

가산명사 생리대 [영국영어]

sani|ta|tion /sǽnɪteɪʃⁿn/ N-UNCOUNT **Sanitation** is the process of keeping places clean and healthy, especially by providing a sewage system and a clean water supply. ❑ *...the hazards of contaminated water and poor sanitation.*

불가산명사 하수 처리; 공중위생 ❑ 오염된 물과 미비한 하수 처리의 위험성

san|ity /sǽnɪti/ N-UNCOUNT A person's **sanity** is their ability to think and behave normally and reasonably. ❑ *He and his wife finally had to move from their apartment just to preserve their sanity.*

불가산명사 제정신 ❑ 마침내 그와 그의 아내는 제정신을 지키기 위해서 아파트에서 이사를 해야 했다.

sank /sǽŋk/ **Sank** is the past tense of **sink**.

sink의 과거

sap /sæp/ (**saps**, **sapping**, **sapped**) **1** V-T If something **saps** your strength or confidence, it gradually weakens or destroys it. ❑ *I was afraid the sickness had sapped my strength.* **2** N-UNCOUNT **Sap** is the watery liquid in plants and trees. ❑ *The leaves, bark, and sap are also common ingredients of local herbal remedies.*

■ 타동사 (기력 등을) 빼다 ❑ 그 병 때문에 내 기력이 약해졌던 것 같아 두려웠다. **2** 불가산명사 (나무의) 수액 ❑ 나뭇잎, 나무껍질, 수액도 그 지방 약초 치료제의 일반적인 재료이다.

sap|phire /sæfaɪər/ (**sapphires**) **1** N-VAR A **sapphire** is a precious stone which is blue in color. ❑ *...a sapphire engagement ring.* **2** COLOR Something that is **sapphire** is bright blue in color. [LITERARY] ❑ *...white snow and sapphire skies.*

1 가산명사 또는 불가산명사 사파이어 ❑ 사파이어 약혼반지 **2** 색채어 사파이어색, 파란색 [문예체] ❑ 하얀 눈과 파란 하늘

sar|casm /sɑrkæzəm/ N-UNCOUNT **Sarcasm** is speech or writing which actually means the opposite of what it seems to say. Sarcasm is usually intended to mock or insult someone. ❑ *"I hope I didn't get you out of your shower," Philpott said with thinly veiled sarcasm.*

불가산명사 비꼼, 빈정댐 ❑ "나 때문에 샤워를 못했던 것은 아니기를 바래요."라며 필포트가 은근히 비꼬며 말했다.

sar|cas|tic /sɑrkæstɪk/ ADJ Someone who is **sarcastic** says or does the opposite of what they really mean in order to mock or insult someone. ❑ *She poked fun at people's shortcomings with sarcastic remarks.* ● **sar|cas|ti|cal|ly** /sɑrkæstɪkli/ ADV ❑ *"What a surprise!" Caroline murmured sarcastically.*

형용사 비꼬는 ❑ 그녀는 비꼬는 말로 사람들의 결점에 대해 농담을 했다. ● 비꼬면서 부사 ❑ "웬일이야!" 하며 캐롤라인이 비꼬면서 중얼거렸다.

sar|dine /sɑrdin/ (**sardines**) N-COUNT **Sardines** are a kind of small sea fish, often eaten as food. ❑ *They opened a tin of sardines.*

가산명사 정어리 ❑ 그들은 정어리 통조림 하나를 땄다.

sar|don|ic /sɑrdɒnɪk/ ADJ If you describe someone as **sardonic**, you mean their attitude to people or things is humorous but rather critical. ❑ *He was a big, sardonic man, who intimidated even the most self-confident students.*

형용사 냉소적인 ❑ 그는 가장 자신감 넘치는 학생들조차도 겁먹게 하는 체구가 큰 냉소적인 사람이었다.

SASE /ɛs eɪ ɛs i/ (**SASEs**) N-SING An **SASE** is an envelope on which you have stuck a stamp and written your own name and address. You send it to a person or organization so that they can reply to you in it. **SASE** is an abbreviation for "self-addressed stamped envelope." [AM; BRIT **s.a.e.**]

단수명사 회신용 봉투 [미국영어; 영국영어 s.a.e.]

sash /sæʃ/ (**sashes**) N-COUNT A **sash** is a long piece of cloth which people wear around their waist or over one shoulder, especially with formal or official clothes. ❑ *She wore a white dress with a thin blue sash.*

가산명사 (어깨 등에 두르는) 장식띠 ❑ 그녀는 흰 드레스를 입고 얇은 푸른색 장식띠를 두르고 있었다.

sas|sy /sæsi/ ADJ If an older person describes a younger person as **sassy**, they mean that they are disrespectful in a lively, confident way. [AM, INFORMAL] ❑ *Are you that sassy with your parents, young lady?*

형용사 버릇없는 [미국영어, 비격식체] ❑ 이봐, 아가씨, 아가씨는 부모님께도 그렇게 버릇없이 구나?

sat /sæt/ **Sat** is the past tense and past participle of **sit**.

sit의 과거 및 과거 분사

SAT /ɛs eɪ ti/ (**SATs**) N-PROPER The **SAT** is an examination which is usually taken by students who wish to enter a college or university. **SAT** is an abbreviation for "Scholastic Aptitude Test." [AM] ❑ *The average SAT score among this year's freshman class is 1,200.*

고유명사 대학 진학 적성 검사 [미국영어] ❑ 올 신입생의 대학 수학 적성 시험 평균 점수는 1,200점이었다.

Sat. **Sat.** is a written abbreviation for **Saturday**.

토

Satan /seɪtⁿn/ N-PROPER In the Christian religion, **Satan** is the Devil, a powerful evil being who is the chief opponent of God.

고유명사 사탄, 악마

sa|tan|ic /sətænɪk, seɪ-/ ADJ Something that is **satanic** is considered to be caused by or influenced by Satan. ❑ *...satanic cults.*

형용사 악마의 ❑ 악마 숭배 집단들

sat|el|lite ♦◇◇ /sætⁿlaɪt/ (**satellites**) **1** N-COUNT A **satellite** is an object which has been sent into space in order to collect information or to be part of a communications system. Satellites move continually around the earth or around another planet. [also by N] ❑ *The rocket launched two communications satellites.* **2** ADJ **Satellite** television is broadcast using a satellite. [ADJ n] ❑ *They have four satellite channels.* **3** N-COUNT A **satellite** is a natural object in space that moves round a planet or star. ❑ *...the satellites of Jupiter.* **4** N-COUNT You can refer to a country, area, or organization as a **satellite** when it is controlled by or depends on a larger and more powerful one. ❑ *...China's satellite territories.* →see **forecast, navigation, radio, television** →see Word Web: **satellite**

1 가산명사 인공위성, 위성 ❑ 그 로켓이 두 개의 통신 위성을 쏘아 올렸다. **2** 형용사 위성의 ❑ 그들은 네 개의 위성 방송 채널이 있다. **3** 가산명사 위성 ❑ 목성의 위성들 **4** 가산명사 위성 국가, 위성 지역 ❑ 중국의 위성 지역들

sat|el|lite dish (**satellite dishes**) N-COUNT A **satellite dish** is a piece of equipment which people need to have on their house in order to receive satellite television.

가산명사 위성 방송 수신용 안테나

sat|in /sætⁿn, BRIT sætɪn/ (**satins**) **1** N-MASS **Satin** is a smooth, shiny kind of cloth, usually made from silk. ❑ *...a peach satin ribbon.* **2** ADJ If something such as a paint, wax, or cosmetic gives something a **satin** finish, it reflects light to some extent but is not very shiny. [ADJ n] ❑ *The final stage of waxing left it with a satin sheen.*

1 물질명사 공단 ❑ 복숭아색 공단 리본 **2** 형용사 매끄러운 ❑ 그것을 와스칠로 마무리하니 매끄러운 광택이 났다.

sat|ire /sætaɪər/ (**satires**) **1** N-UNCOUNT **Satire** is the use of humor or exaggeration in order to show how foolish or wicked some people's behavior or ideas are. ❑ *The commercial side of the Christmas season is an easy target for satire.* **2** N-COUNT A **satire** is a play, movie, or novel in which humor or exaggeration is used to criticize something. ❑ *...a sharp satire on the American political process.*

1 불가산명사 풍자 ❑ 크리스마스의 상업적인 측면은 풍자의 쉬운 표적이 되고 있다. **2** 가산명사 풍자극 ❑ 미국 정치판에 대한 날카로운 풍자극

Word Web   satellite

The **moon** is the earth's best-known **satellite**. However, humans began **launching** other objects into **space** starting in 1957. That's when the first artificial satellite, Sputnik, began to **orbit** the earth. Today, hundreds of satellites circle the **planet**. The largest of these is the International **Space Station**. It completes an orbit about every 90 minutes and sometimes can be seen from the earth. Others, such as the Hubbell Telescope, help us learn more about **outer space**. The NOAA 12 monitors the earth's climate. Most TV weather forecasts feature images taken from satellites. Today, many TV programs are also broadcast by satellite.

sa|tiri|cal /sətɪrɪkəl/ ADJ A **satirical** drawing, piece of writing, or comedy show is one in which humor or exaggeration is used to criticize something. ❑ ...a satirical novel about London life in the late 80s.

형용사 풍자적인 ❑ 1980년대 후반의 런던 생활상에 대한 풍자 소설

sat|is|fac|tion /sætɪsfækʃən/ ■ N-UNCOUNT **Satisfaction** is the pleasure that you feel when you do something or get something that you wanted or needed to do or get. ❑ She felt a small glow of satisfaction. ❑ Both sides expressed satisfaction with the progress so far. ② N-UNCOUNT If you get **satisfaction** from someone, you get money or an apology from them because you have been treated badly. ❑ If you can't get any satisfaction, complain to the park owner. ③ PHRASE If you do something **to** someone's **satisfaction**, they are happy with the way that you have done it. ❑ She never could seem to do anything right or to his satisfaction.

■ 불가산명사 만족 ❑ 그녀는 작은 만족감을 느꼈다. ❑ 지금까지의 진행 상황에 대해 양측이 모두 만족감을 표시했다. ② 불가산명사 보상, 사과 ❑ 만약 아무런 보상을 못 받으면, 그 공원 소유주에게 항의하세요. ③ 구 -의 마음에 들도록, -가 만족스럽도록 ❑ 그녀는 일을 제대로 하거나 그의 마음에 들도록 하는 적이 없는 것 같다.

sat|is|fac|tory /sætɪsfæktəri/ ADJ Something that is **satisfactory** is acceptable to you or fulfills a particular need or purpose. ❑ I never got a satisfactory answer.

형용사 만족스러운 ❑ 나는 만족스러운 답을 전혀 듣지 못했다.

sat|is|fied ♦◇◇ /sætɪsfaɪd/ ■ ADJ If you are **satisfied with** something, you are happy because you have gotten what you wanted or needed. ❑ We are not satisfied with these results. ② ADJ If you are **satisfied that** something is true or has been done properly, you are convinced about this after checking it. [v-link ADJ, oft ADJ that] ❑ People must be satisfied that the treatment is safe.

■ 형용사 만족하는 ❑ 우리는 이런 결과에 만족하지 않는다. ② 형용사 납득하는 ❑ 사람들이 그 치료법이 안전하다고 납득해야 한다.

Word Link   sat, satis ≈ enough : dissatisfaction, insatiable, satisfy

---

sat|is|fy /sætɪsfaɪ/ (**satisfies, satisfying, satisfied**) ■ V-T If someone or something **satisfies** you, they give you enough of what you want or need to make you pleased or contented. ❑ The pace of change has not been quick enough to satisfy everyone. ② V-T To **satisfy** someone that something is true or has been done properly means to convince them by giving them more information or by showing them what has been done. ❑ He has to satisfy the environmental lobby that real progress will be made to cut emissions. ③ V-T If you **satisfy** the requirements for something, you are good enough or have the right qualities to fulfill these requirements. ❑ The Executive Committee recommends that the procedures should satisfy certain basic requirements.

■ 타동사 만족시키다 ❑ 변화의 속도가 모든 사람을 만족시킬 만큼 그렇게 빠르지 않았다. ② 타동사 납득시키다 ❑ 그는 배출 가스를 줄이기 위한 실질적인 조치가 취해질 것임을 환경 단체에게 납득시켜야 한다. ③ 타동사 충족시키다 ❑ 집행 위원회는 그 운영 절차가 특정 기본 요건들을 충족시키기를 권고하고 있다.

Word Partnership   satisfy의 연어

| N. | satisfy **an appetite**, satisfy **critics**, satisfy *someone's* **curiosity**, satisfy **demands**, satisfy **a desire** ■ |
| | satisfy **a need** ■ ③ |

---

sat|is|fy|ing /sætɪsfaɪɪŋ/ ADJ Something that is **satisfying** makes you feel happy, especially because you feel you have achieved something. ❑ I found wood carving satisfying.

형용사 만족감을 주는 ❑ 나는 목각이 만족감을 주는 일임을 알게 되었다.

satu|rate /sætʃəreɪt/ (**saturates, saturating, saturated**) ■ V-T If people or things **saturate** a place or object, they fill it completely so that no more can be added. ❑ In the last days before the vote, both sides are saturating the airwaves. ② V-T If someone or something **is saturated**, they become extremely wet. ❑ If the filter has been saturated with motor oil, it should be discarded and replaced.

■ 타동사 잔뜩 채우다, 포화 상태를 만들다 ❑ 투표가 시작되기 전 며칠 동안은, 양측이 모두 방송 프로를 다 채울 것이다. ② 타동사 흠뻑 젖다 ❑ 필터가 모터 기름으로 절어 있다면, 그것을 제거하고 교체해야 한다.

satu|ra|tion /sætʃəreɪʃən/ ■ N-UNCOUNT **Saturation** is the process or state that occurs when a place or thing is filled completely with people or things, so that no more can be added. ❑ Japanese car makers have been equally blind to the saturation of their markets at home and abroad. ② ADJ **Saturation** is used to describe a campaign or activity that is carried out very thoroughly, so that nothing is missed. [ADJ n] ❑ The concept of saturation marketing makes perfect sense.

■ 불가산명사 포화 상태 ❑ 일본 자동차 제조사들이 하나같이 자신들의 국내외 자동차 시장이 포화 상태임을 외면해 왔다. ② 형용사 철두철미한 ❑ 철두철미한 마케팅이라는 발상은 정말 일리가 있다.

Sat|ur|day ♦♦♦ /sætərdeɪ, -di/ (**Saturdays**) N-VAR **Saturday** is the day after Friday and before Sunday. ❑ She had a call from him on Saturday morning at the studio. ❑ Every Saturday dad made a beautiful pea and ham soup.

가산명사 또는 불가산명사 토요일 ❑ 그녀는 토요일 아침에 스튜디오에서 그의 전화를 받았다. ❑ 토요일마다 아빠는 콩과 햄을 넣은 맛있는 수프를 만드셨다.

sauce ♦◇◇ /sɔs/ (**sauces**) N-MASS A **sauce** is a thick liquid which is served with other food. ❑ ...pasta cooked in a sauce of garlic, tomatoes, and cheese.

물질명사 소스 ❑ 마늘, 토마토, 치즈를 넣은 소스를 넣은 파스타 요리

sauce|pan /sɔspæn, BRIT sɔːspən/ (**saucepans**) N-COUNT A **saucepan** is a deep metal cooking pot, usually with a long handle and a lid. ❑ Place the potatoes and turnips in a large saucepan, cover with cold water and bring to the boil. →see **pan**

가산명사 (긴 손잡이가 있는) 냄비 ❑ 감자와 순무를 큰 냄비에 넣고 찬물을 부은 다음 끓이세요.

sau|cer /sɔsər/ (**saucers**) N-COUNT A **saucer** is a small curved plate on which you stand a cup. ❑ Rae's coffee cup clattered against the saucer as she picked it up.

가산명사 (컵의) 받침 접시 ❑ 레이가 커피잔을 들자, 그 잔이 받침 접시에 부딪쳐서 달가닥거렸다.

saucy /sɔsi/ (**saucier, sauciest**) ADJ Someone or something that is **saucy** refers to sex in a light-hearted, amusing way. ❑ ...a saucy joke.

형용사 음탕한, 짓궂은 ❑ 음담패설

sau|na /sɔnə/ (**saunas**) ■ N-COUNT If you have a **sauna**, you sit or lie in a room that is so hot that it makes you sweat. People have saunas in order to relax and to clean their skin thoroughly. ❑ Every month I have a sauna. ② N-COUNT A **sauna** is a room or building where you can have a sauna. ❑ The hotel has a sauna, solarium and heated indoor swimming pool.

■ 가산명사 사우나 ❑ 매달 나는 사우나를 한다. ② 가산명사 사우나실 ❑ 그 호텔에는 사우나실, 일광욕실, 온수 실내 수영장이 있다.

saun|ter /sɔntər/ (**saunters, sauntering, sauntered**) V-I If you **saunter** somewhere, you walk there in a slow, casual way. ❑ We watched our fellow students saunter into the building.

자동사 천천히 걷다 ❑ 우리는 친구들이 그 건물 안으로 천천히 걸어 들어가는 것을 보았다.

sau|sage /sɔsɪdʒ, BRIT sɒsɪdʒ/ (**sausages**) N-VAR A **sausage** consists of minced meat, usually pork, mixed with other ingredients and is contained in a tube made of skin or a similar material. ❑ ...sausages and fries.

가산명사 또는 불가산명사 소시지 ❑ 소시지와 감자튀김

sau|te /sɔteɪ, BRIT sɒteɪ/ (**saute, sauting, sauted**) V-T When you **saute** food, you fry it quickly in hot oil or butter. ❑ Saute the chicken until golden brown.

타동사 살짝 튀기다 ❑ 닭이 황갈색이 될 때까지 살짝 튀기세요.

sav|age /sævɪdʒ/ (**savages, savaging, savaged**) ■ ADJ Someone or something that is **savage** is extremely cruel, violent, and uncontrolled. ❑ This was a savage attack on a defenceless young girl. ❑ ...the savage wave of violence that swept the country in November 1987. ● **sav|age|ly** ADV ❑ He was savagely beaten. ② N-COUNT If you

■ 형용사 야만적인 ❑ 이것은 무방비한 어린 소녀에게 가한 야만적인 폭행이었다. ❑ 1987년 11월에 전국을 휩쓸었던 야만적인 폭동 사태 ● 야만적으로, 잔인하게 부사 ❑ 그는 잔인하게 맞았다. ② 가산명사 야만인

refer to people as **savages**, you dislike them because you think that they do not have an advanced society and are violent. [DISAPPROVAL] ❑ ...*their conviction that the area was a frozen desert peopled with uncouth savages.* ❸ V-T If someone **is savaged** by a dog or other animal, the animal attacks them violently. [usu passive] ❑ *The animal turned on him and he was savaged to death.*

sav|age|ry /ˈsævɪdʒri/ N-UNCOUNT **Savagery** is extremely cruel and violent behavior. ❑ ...*the sheer savagery of war.*

save ♦♦◇ /seɪv/ (**saves**, **saving**, **saved**) ❶ V-T If you **save** someone or something, you help them to avoid harm or to escape from a dangerous or unpleasant situation. ❑ ...*an austerity program designed to save the country's failing economy.* ❑ *The meeting is an attempt to mobilize nations to save children from death by disease and malnutrition.* ❷ V-I If you **save**, you gradually collect money by spending less than you get, usually in order to buy something that you want. ❑ *The majority of people intend to save, but find that by the end of the month there is nothing left.* ❑ *Tim and Barbara are now saving for a house in the suburbs.* ● PHRASAL VERB **Save up** means the same as **save**. ❑ *Julie wanted to put some of her money aside for holidays or save up for something special.* ❸ V-T If you **save** something such as time or money, you prevent the loss or waste of it. ❑ *It saves time in the kitchen to have things you use a lot within reach.* ❑ *I'll try to save him the expense of a flight from Perth.* ❹ V-T If you **save** something, you keep it because it will be needed later. ❑ *Drain the beans thoroughly and save the stock for soup.* ❺ V-T If someone or something **saves** you **from** an unpleasant action or experience, they change the situation so that you do not have to do it or experience it. ❑ *The scanner will reduce the need for exploratory operations which will save risk and pain for patients.* ❑ *She was hoping that something might save her from having to make a decision.* ❻ V-I If you **save** data in a computer, you give the computer an instruction to store the data on a tape or disk. [COMPUTING] ❑ *Try to get into the habit of saving your work regularly.* ❼ V-T/V-I If a goalkeeper **saves**, or **saves** a shot, they succeed in preventing the ball from going into the net. ❑ *He saved one shot when the ball hit him on the head.* ● N-COUNT **Save** is also a noun. ❑ *Spurs could have had several goals but for some brilliant saves from John Hallworth.* ❽ to **save the day** →see **day**. to **save face** →see **face**

Thesaurus		save의 참조어
v.		defend, protect, rescue ❶
		conserve, economize, hoard; (ant.) waste ❷ ❸ ❹

▶save up →see save 2

sav|er /seɪvər/ (**savers**) N-COUNT A **saver** is a person who regularly saves money, especially by paying it into a bank account or a building society. ❑ *Low interest rates are bad news for savers, who have seen their income halved over the last year.*

sav|ing ♦◇◇ /seɪvɪŋ/ (**savings**) ❶ N-COUNT A **saving** is a reduction in the amount of time or money that is used or needed. ❑ *Fill in the form below and you will be making a saving of £6.60 on a one-year subscription.* ❷ N-PLURAL Your **savings** are the money that you have saved, especially in a bank or a building society. ❑ *Her savings were in the Post Office Savings Bank.*

sav|ings and loan N-SING A **savings and loan** association is a business where people save money to earn interest, and which lends money to savers to buy houses. Compare **building society**. [mainly AM, BUSINESS]

sav|ior /seɪvyər/ (**saviors**) [BRIT **saviour**] N-COUNT A **savior** is a person who saves someone or something from danger, ruin, or defeat. ❑ ...*the savior of his country.*

sa|vor /seɪvər/ (**savors**, **savoring**, **savored**) [BRIT **savour**] ❶ V-T If you **savor** an experience, you enjoy it as much as you can. ❑ *She savored her newfound freedom.* ❷ V-T If you **savor** food or drink, you eat or drink it slowly in order to taste its full flavor and to enjoy it properly. ❑ *Just relax, eat slowly and savor the full flavor of your food.*

sa|vory /seɪvəri/ (**savories**) [BRIT **savoury**] ❶ ADJ **Savory** food has a salty or spicy flavor rather than a sweet one. ❑ ...*all sorts of sweet and savory breads.* ❷ N-COUNT **Savories** are small items of savory food that are usually eaten as a snack, for example with alcoholic drinks at a party or before a meal. [BRIT]

saw /sɔ/ (**saws**, **sawing**, **sawed**, **sawn**) ❶ **Saw** is the past tense of **see**. ❷ N-COUNT A **saw** is a tool for cutting wood, which has a blade with sharp teeth along one edge. Some saws are pushed backward and forward by hand, and others are powered by electricity. ❸ V-T/V-I If you **saw** something, you cut it with a saw. ❑ *He escaped by sawing through the bars of his cell.*

saw|dust /sɔdʌst/ N-UNCOUNT **Sawdust** is dust and very small pieces of wood which are produced when you saw wood. ❑ ...*a layer of sawdust.*

sawn /sɔn/ **Sawn** is the past participle of **saw**.

sax /sæks/ (**saxes**) N-COUNT A **sax** is the same as a **saxophone**. [INFORMAL]

saxo|phone /sæksəfoʊn/ (**saxophones**) N-VAR A **saxophone** is a musical instrument in the shape of a curved metal tube with a narrower part that you blow into and keys that you press.

sax|opho|nist /sæksəfoʊnɪst, BRIT sæksɒfənɪst/ (**saxophonists**) N-COUNT A **saxophonist** is someone who plays the saxophone.

say ♦♦♦ /seɪ/ (**says** /sɛz/, **saying**, **said** /sɛd/) ❶ V-T When you **say** something, you speak words. ❑ *"I'm sorry," he said.* ❑ *She said they were very impressed.* ❑ *Forty-one people are said to have been seriously hurt.* ❑ *I packed and said goodbye to Charlie.* ❷ V-T You use **say** in expressions such as **I would just like to say** to introduce what you are actually saying, or to indicate that you are expressing an opinion or admitting a fact. If you state that you **can't say** something or you **wouldn't say** something, you are indicating in a polite or indirect way that it is not the case. ❑ *I would just like to say that this is the most hypocritical thing I have*

[탐탁찮음] ❑ 그 지역이 거친 야만인들로 가득 찬 동토의 불모지라는 그들의 확신 ❸ 타동사 (짐승에게) 공격당하다 ❑ 그리고 나서 그 짐승이 그에게 달려들었고 그는 무참하게 물려 죽었다.

불가산명사 만행 ❑ 전쟁의 엄청난 만행

❶ 타동사 구하다 ❑ 그 나라의 추락하는 경제를 구하기 위해 고안된 긴축 프로그램 ❑ 그 모임은 질병과 영양실조로 죽어 가는 아이들을 구하기 위해 국가들을 동원하려는 의도이다. ❷ 자동사 돈을 모으다, 저축하다 ❑ 대다수 사람들이 돈을 모으려고 하지만, 월말이 되면 한 푼도 남지 않는다는 것을 알게 된다. ❑ 팀과 바바라는 현재 교외에 집을 사려고 돈을 모으고 있는 중이다 ● 구동사 저축하다 ❑ 줄리는 휴가를 위해서 돈을 조금 떼어 놓거나 특별한 일이 생길 때를 대비해서 저축하고 싶어 했다. ❸ 타동사 절약하다 ❑ 부엌에 자주 사용하는 물건들을 손 닿는 곳에 두면 시간을 절약하게 된다. ❑ 나는 그가 버스에서 오는 비행기 값을 절약할 수 있도록 해 볼 것이다. ❹ 타동사 보관해 두다 ❑ 콩에서 물을 완전히 따라 내어 수프 끓일 육수로 보관해 두세요. ❺ 타동사 면해 주다 ❑ 단층 촬영기는 탐색적 수술을 해야 할 필요를 줄여 줌으로써 환자들이 겪을 사고 발생 위험이나 통증을 면하게 해줄 것이다. ❑ 그녀는 혹시라도 어떤 일이 일어나서 자신의 결정을 내려야만 하는 상황을 면하게 해 주기를 바라고 있었다. ❻ 타동사 저장하다 [컴퓨터] ❑ 규칙적으로 작업한 내용을 저장하는 습관을 들이도록 하세요. ❼ 타동사/자동사 (골키퍼가) 득점을 막아 내다, 선방하다 ❑ 공이 그의 머리에 맞아서 그가 슛을 막아 냈다. ● 가산명사 선방 ❑ 존 홀워스의 몇 차례 멋진 선방이 없었더라면, 스퍼스 팀이 몇 점을 올렸을 것이다.

가산명사 꼬박꼬박 저축을 하는 사람, 저축인 ❑ 저금리는 저축인들에게는 나쁜 소식인데, 그들은 작년 한 해 동안 수입이 절반으로 줄어들었다.

❶ 가산명사 절약 ❑ 아래 양식에 기입하시면 일 년 구독료를 6.60파운드 절약하게 될 것입니다. ❷ 복수명사 예금 ❑ 그녀의 예금은 우체국 저축에 들어 있었다.

단수명사 저축 대부 [주로 미국영어, 경제]

[영국영어 saviour] 가산명사 구세주, 구원자 ❑ 그의 조국의 구세주

[영국영어 savour] ❶ 타동사 만끽하다 ❑ 그녀는 새로 찾은 자유를 만끽했다. ❷ 타동사 음미하다 ❑ 여유를 갖고 음식을 천천히 먹으면서 충분히 음미해 보세요.

[영국영어 savoury] ❶ 형용사 짭짤한 ❑ 달콤하고 짭짤한 온갖 종류의 빵 ❷ 가산명사 짭짤한 스낵 [영국영어]

see의 과거 ❷ 가산명사 톱 ❸ 타동사/자동사 톱으로 켜다 ❑ 그는 감방 창살을 톱으로 자른 후 탈출했다.

불가산명사 톱밥 ❑ 톱밥 켜

saw의 과거 분사

가산명사 색소폰 [비격식체]

가산명사 또는 불가산명사 색소폰

가산명사 색소폰 연주자

❶ 타동사 말하다 ❑ "미안해요."라고 그가 말했다. ❑ 그녀는 그들이 깊은 인상을 받았다고 말했다. ❑ 41명이 중상을 입었냐고 전해진다. ❑ 나는 짐을 꾸린 후 찰리에게 작별 인사를 고했다. ❷ 타동사 말하다; ~라고 말하다; ~은 아닌 것 같군요 ❑ 저는 이것이 제가 지금껏 들은 이야기 중 가장 위선적이라고 말하고 싶습니다. ❑ 나 또한 그 일로 인해 다소 충격을 받았다고 말하고 싶군요. ❸ 타동사

ever heard in my life. ❑ *I must say that rather shocked me, too.* **3** V-T You can mention the contents of a piece of writing by mentioning what it **says** or what someone **says** in it. ❑ *The report says there is widespread and routine torture of political prisoners in the country.* ❑ *You can't have one without the other, as the song says.* **4** V-T If you **say** something **to yourself**, you think it. ❑ *Perhaps I'm still dreaming, I said to myself.* **5** N-SING If you have a **say** in something, you have the right to give your opinion and influence decisions relating to it. [usu a N, also more/some N] ❑ *You can get married at sixteen, and yet you haven't got a say in the running of the country.* **6** V-T You indicate the information given by something such as a clock, dial, or map by mentioning what it **says**. ❑ *The clock said four minutes past eleven.* **7** V-T If something **says** something **about** a person, situation, or thing, it gives important information about them. ❑ *I think that says a lot about how well Seles is playing.* **8** V-T If something **says** a lot **for** a person or thing, it shows that this person or thing is very good or has a lot of good qualities. ❑ *That the Escort is still the nation's bestselling car in 1992 says a lot for the power of Ford's marketing people.* **9** V-T You use **say** in expressions such as **I'll say that for them** and **you can say this for them** after or before you mention a good quality that someone has, usually when you think they do not have many good qualities. ❑ *He's usually smartly-dressed, I'll say that for him.* **10** V-T You can use **say** when you want to discuss something that might possibly happen or be true. [only imper] ❑ *Say you lived in Boston, Massachusetts, and dug straight down through the center of the Earth, what country would you come out nearest to?* **11** You can use **say** or **let's say** when you mention something as an example. ❑ *To see the problem here more clearly, let's look at a different biological system, say, an acorn.*

Note that, with the verb **say**, if you want to mention the person who is being addressed, you should use the preposition **to**. "What did she say you?" is wrong. "**What did she say to you?**" is correct. The verb **tell**, however, is usually followed by a direct object indicating the person who is being addressed. ❑ *He told Alison he was suffering from leukemia... What did she tell you?* "What did she tell to you?" is wrong. **Say** is the most general verb for reporting the words that someone speaks. **Tell** is used to report information that is given to someone. ❑ *The manufacturer told me that the product did not contain corn.* **Tell** can also be used with a "to" infinitive to report an order or instruction. ❑ *My mother told me to shut up and eat my dinner.*

---

12 PHRASE If you say that something **says it all**, you mean that it shows you very clearly the truth about a situation or someone's feelings. ❑ *This is my third visit in a week, which says it all.* **13** CONVENTION You can use "**You don't say**" to express surprise at what someone has told you. People often use this expression to indicate that in fact they are not surprised. [FEELINGS] ❑ *"I'm a writer." — "You don't say. What kind of book are you writing?"* **14** PHRASE If you say there is a lot **to be said for** something, you mean you think it has a lot of good qualities or aspects. ❑ *There's a lot to be said for being based in the country.* **15** PHRASE If someone asks **what you have to say for yourself**, they are asking what excuse you have for what you have done. ❑ *"Well," she said eventually, "what have you to say for yourself?"* **16** PHRASE If something **goes without saying**, it is obvious. ❑ *It goes without saying that if someone has lung problems they should not smoke.* **17** PHRASE When one of the people or groups involved in a discussion **has** their **say**, they give their opinion. ❑ *Voters were finally having their say today.* **18** CONVENTION You use "**I wouldn't say no**" to indicate that you would like something, especially something that has just been offered to you. [INFORMAL, FORMULAE] ❑ *I wouldn't say no to a drink.* **19** PHRASE You use "**that is to say**" or "**that's to say**" to indicate that you are about to express the same idea more clearly or precisely. [FORMAL] ❑ *We're basically talking about an independent state in the territories that were occupied in 1967, that is to say, in the West Bank and Gaza.* **20** CONVENTION You can use "**You can say that again**" to express strong agreement with what someone has just said. [INFORMAL, EMPHASIS] ❑ *"You are in enough trouble already." — "You can say that again," sighed Richard.*

Thesaurus   *say*의 참조어

v.   announce, communicate, declare, speak **1**

---

saying /seɪɪŋ/ (**sayings**) N-COUNT A **saying** is a sentence that people often say and that gives advice or information about human life and experience. ❑ *We also realize the truth of that old saying: Charity begins at home.*

scab /skæb/ (**scabs**) N-COUNT A **scab** is a hard, dry covering that forms over the surface of a wound. ❑ *The area can be very painful until scabs form after about ten days.*

scaffold /skæfəld, -oʊld/ (**scaffolds**) **1** N-COUNT A **scaffold** was a raised platform on which criminals were hanged or had their heads cut off. ❑ *Ascending the shaky ladder to the scaffold, More addressed the executioner.* **2** N-COUNT A **scaffold** is a temporary raised platform on which workers stand to paint, repair, or build high parts of a building. ❑ *They were standing on top of a giant scaffold.*

scaffolding /skæfəldɪŋ/ N-UNCOUNT **Scaffolding** consists of poles and boards made into a temporary framework that is used by workers when they are painting, repairing, or building high parts of a building, usually outside. ❑ *Workers have erected scaffolding around the base of the tower below the roadway.*

Word Link   cal, caul ≈ hot, heat : cauldron, calorie, scald

---

scald /skɔld/ (**scalds, scalding, scalded**) **1** V-T If you **scald yourself**, you burn yourself with very hot liquid or steam. ❑ *A patient jumped into a bath being*

쓰여 있다, 나와 있다 ❑ 그 국가에서 정치범들에 대한 고문이 일상적이며 만연하다고 그 보고서에 씌어 있다. ❑ 그 노래에 나와 있는 것처럼 다른 하나 없이는 나머지 하나를 가질 수 없다. **4** 타동사 (속으로) 생각하다, 혼잣말하다 ❑ 아마도 난 여전히 꿈을 꾸고 있는 것이라고 속으로 생각했다. **5** 단수명사 발언권 ❑ 열여섯 살이 되면 결혼을 할 수 있는데 국가 운영에 대한 발언권은 가질 수 없다. **6** 타동사 (시계 등이) 가리키다 ❑ 그 시계는 11시 4분을 가리키고 있었다. **7** 타동사 알려 주다 ❑ 나는 셀레스가 얼마나 훌륭하게 경기를 하고 있는지에 관해 그것이 많은 것을 알려 준다고 생각한다. **8** 타동사 (좋은 점을) 보여 주다 ❑ 에스코트가 1992년에도 여전히 이 나라에서 가장 많이 판매되고 있다는 사실은 포드 사 판매 직원들의 역량을 잘 보여 준다. **9** 타동사 말하다; 그들에 대해서 그렇게만 말하겠다; 그들에 대해서 이렇게는 말할 수 있겠다 ❑ 그는 대개 말쑥하게 차려입는다고, 그에 대해서는 그렇게만 말하겠다. **10** 타동사 가정하다 ❑ 네가 매사추세츠 주의 보스턴에 산다고 가정할 때 지구 중심을 지나 곧바로 파내려 간다면, 어느 나라 쪽으로 가장 가깝게 빠져나오겠니? **11** 예컨대 ❑ 여기서 이 문제를 더욱 명확히 보기 위해서 다른 생물 조직, 예컨대 도토리에 대해 한번 살펴봅시다.

동사 say에서 말을 듣는 사람을 언급하고 싶으면, 전치사 to를 써야 한다는 점을 유념하시오. 'What did she say you?'는 틀렸고, 'What did she say to you?'가 맞다. 그러나, 동사 tell은 대개 말을 듣는 사람을 나타내는 직접 목적어가 뒤에 온다. ❑ 그는 자기가 백혈병을 앓고 있다고 앨리스에게 말했다... 그녀가 당신에게 뭐라고 말했죠? 'What did she tell to you?'는 틀렸다. say는 누가 하는 말을 전달하는데 쓰는 가장 일반적인 동사다. tell은 주어진 정보를 제공할 때 쓴다. ❑ 제조업자는 내게 그 생산품에는 옥수수가 들어있지 않다고 말했다. tell은 명령이나 지시를 전달하기 위해 'to' 부정사와 함께 쓸 수 있다. ❑ 우리 어머니가 내게 그만 떠들고 저녁을 먹으라고 하셨다.

---

12 구 모든 것을 말해 주다 ❑ 이번이 내가 한 주 동안에 세 번째 방문하는 것인데, 이것이 모든 걸 말해 준다. **13** 관용 표현 그러시군요 [감정 개입] ❑ "저는 작가입니다." "그러시군요. 어떤 종류의 책을 쓰고 계십니까?" **14** 구 ~에 대해 말해야 할 ❑ 그 나라에 주안하는 것에 대해 말할 말이 많다. **15** 구 ~에 대해 하고 싶은 변명 ❑ "음, 네가 하고 싶은 변명이 뭐냐?"라고 이윽고 그녀가 말했다. **16** 구 말할 나위도 없다 ❑ 폐에 문제가 있다면 담배를 피우지 말아야 한다는 것은 말할 나위도 없다. **17** 구 목소리를 내다 ❑ 유권자들이 마침내 오늘 자신들의 목소리를 내고 있었다. **18** 관용 표현 마다할 리가 없다 [비격식체, 의례적인 표현] ❑ 난 한 잔 하는 걸 마다할 리가 없지. **19** 구 즉 [격식체] ❑ 우리는 근본적으로 1967년에 점령당한 영토, 즉 서안과 가자 지역에 관해서 말하고 있는 것입니다. **20** 관용 표현 바로 그거야, 정말 그래 [비격식체, 강조] ❑ "넌 이미 큰 문제에 빠져 있어." "정말 그래."라고 리처드가 한숨을 지으며 말했다.

가산명사 격언, 속담 ❑ 우리는 또한 '자선은 집에서부터 시작한다'라는 예전부터 내려오는 격언의 진리를 깨닫고 있다.

가산명사 (상처의) 딱지 ❑ 약 10일 후 딱지가 생기게 될 때까지는 그 부위가 매우 아플 것입니다.

1 가산명사 교수대 ❑ 교수대를 향해 흔들리는 사다리를 올라가며, 모어는 사형 집행인에게 말을 걸었다. **2** 가산명사 (건축) 비계 ❑ 그들은 거대한 비계 상단에 서 있었다.

불가산명사 (건축 현장의) 비계 ❑ 인부들은 철길 아래쪽의 탑 기반 근처에 비계를 세웠다.

1 타동사 (뜨거운 것에) 데다 ❑ 환자 한 명이 의료진 중 한 사람이 준비 중인 욕조에 풍덩 들어갔다가 몸을

prepared by a member of staff and scalded herself. **2** N-COUNT A **scald** is a burn caused by very hot liquid or steam. ❏ *Scalds, burns, and poisoning can all be life-threatening.*

Word Link	scal, scala ≈ ladder, stairs : e*scal*ate, e*scala*tor, *scal*e

scale ♦♦◇ /skeɪl/ (**scales, scaling, scaled**) **1** N-SING If you refer to the **scale** of something, you are referring to its size or extent, especially when it is very big. ❏ *However, he underestimates the scale of the problem.* ❏ *The breakdown of law and order could result in killing on a massive scale.* →see also **full-scale, large-scale, small-scale 2** N-COUNT A **scale** is a set of levels or numbers which are used in a particular system of measuring things or are used when comparing things. ❏ *...an earthquake measuring five-point-five on the Richter scale.* ❏ *The patient rates the therapies on a scale of zero to ten.* →see also **timescale 3** N-COUNT A **pay scale** or **scale of** fees is a list that shows how much someone should be paid, depending, for example, on their age or what work they do. ❏ *...those on the high end of the pay scale.* **4** N-COUNT The **scale** of a map, plan, or model is the relationship between the size of something in the map, plan, or model and its size in the real world. ❏ *The map, on a scale of 1:10,000, shows over 5,000 individual paths.* →see also **full-scale, large-scale 5** ADJ A **scale** model or **scale** replica of a building or object is a model of it which is smaller than the real thing but has all the same parts and features. [ADJ n] ❏ *Franklin made his mother an intricately detailed scale model of the house.* **6** N-COUNT In music, a **scale** is a fixed sequence of musical notes, each one higher than the next, which begins at a particular note. ❏ *...the scale of C major.* **7** N-COUNT The **scales** of a fish or reptile are the small, flat pieces of hard skin that cover its body. ❏ *Remove any excess scales from the fish skin.* **8** N-PLURAL **Scales** are a piece of equipment used for weighing things, for example for weighing amounts of food that you need in order to make a particular meal. [also *a pair of N*] ❏ *a pair of kitchen scales.* **9** V-T If you **scale** something such as a mountain or a wall, you climb up it or over it. [WRITTEN] ❏ *...Rebecca Stephens, the first British woman to scale Everest.* **10** PHRASE If something is **out of scale with** the things near it, it is too big or too small in relation to them. ❏ *...the tower surmounted by its enormous golden statue of the Virgin, utterly out of scale with the building.* **11** PHRASE If the different parts of a map, drawing, or model are **to scale**, they are the right size in relation to each other. ❏ *...a miniature garden, with little pagodas and bridges all to scale.* →see **graph**

▶**scale down** PHRASAL VERB If you **scale down** something, you make it smaller in size, amount, or extent than it used to be. ❏ *One Peking factory has had to scale down its workforce from six hundred to only six.*

▶**scale up** PHRASAL VERB If you **scale up** something, you make it greater in size, amount, or extent than it used to be. ❏ *Simply scaling up a size 10 garment often leads to disaster.*

scalp /skælp/ (**scalps, scalping, scalped**) **1** N-COUNT Your **scalp** is the skin under the hair on your head. ❏ *He smoothed his hair back over his scalp.* **2** V-T If someone **scalps** tickets, they sell them outside a sports stadium or theater, usually for more than their original value. [AM; BRIT **tout**] ❏ *He was trying to pick up some cash scalping tickets.* →see **hair**

scal|pel /skælpᵊl/ (**scalpels**) N-COUNT A **scalpel** is a knife with a short, thin, sharp blade. Scalpels are used by surgeons during operations.

scal|per /skælpər/ (**scalpers**) N-COUNT A **scalper** is someone who sells tickets outside a sports stadium or theater, usually for more than their original value. [AM; BRIT **tout**] ❏ *Another scalper said he'd charge $1000 for a $125 ticket.*

scam /skæm/ (**scams**) N-COUNT A **scam** is an illegal trick, usually with the purpose of getting money from people or avoiding paying tax. [INFORMAL] ❏ *They believed they were participating in an insurance scam, not a murder.*

scam|per /skæmpər/ (**scampers, scampering, scampered**) V-I When people or small animals **scamper** somewhere, they move there quickly with small, light steps. ❏ *Children scampered off the yellow school bus and into the playground.*

scan /skæn/ (**scans, scanning, scanned**) **1** V-T When you **scan** written material, you look through it quickly in order to find important or interesting information. ❏ *She scanned the advertisement pages of the newspapers.* ● N-SING **Scan** is also a noun. ❏ *I just had a quick scan through your book again.* **2** V-T When you **scan** a place or group of people, you look at it carefully, usually because you are looking for something or someone. [no passive] ❏ *The officer scanned the room.* ❏ *She was nervous and kept scanning the crowd for Paul.* **3** V-T If people **scan** something such as luggage, they examine it using a machine that can show or find things inside it that cannot be seen from the outside. ❏ *Their approach is to scan every checked-in bag with a bomb detector.* **4** V-T If a computer disk **is scanned**, a program on the computer checks the disk to make sure that it does not contain a virus. [COMPUTING] ❏ *Not all ISPs are equipped to scan for viruses.* **5** V-T If a picture or document **is scanned** into a computer, a machine passes a beam of light over it to make a copy of it in the computer. [COMPUTING] [usu passive] ❏ *The entire paper contents of all libraries will eventually be scanned into computers.* **6** V-T If a radar or sonar machine **scans** an area, it examines or searches it by sending radar or sonar beams over it. ❏ *The ship's radar scanned the sea ahead.* **7** N-COUNT A **scan** is a medical test in which a machine sends a beam of X-rays over a part of your body in order to check that it is healthy. ❏ *A brain scan revealed the blood clot.*

scan|dal ♦◇◇ /skændᵊl/ (**scandals**) **1** N-COUNT A **scandal** is a situation or event that is thought to be shocking and immoral and that everyone knows about. ❏ *...a financial scandal.* **2** N-UNCOUNT **Scandal** is talk about the shocking and immoral aspects of someone's behavior or something that has happened. ❏ *He loved gossip and scandal.*

scan|dal|ous /skændᵊləs/ **1** ADJ **Scandalous** behavior or activity is considered immoral and shocking. ❏ *They would be sacked for criminal or scandalous behavior.*

대었다. **2** 가산명사 (뜨거운 것에) 뎀 ❏ 뜨거운 것에 데는 것, 불에 데는 것 그리고 중독이 모두 생명을 위태롭게 할 수 있다.

1 단수명사 규모 ❏ 그러나, 그는 그 문제의 규모를 과소평가한다. ❏ 치안 붕괴는 대규모 살상을 불러올 수 있다. **2** 가산명사 스케일, 등급, 단계 ❏ 리히터 지진계로 5.5를 기록한 지진 ❏ 그 환자는 치료법을 0에서 10단계까지 등급을 매긴다. **3** 가산명사 등급 ❏ 급여 등급의 최상위에 있는 사람들 **4** 가산명사 축척 ❏ 일만분의 일 축척으로 그려진 그 지도는 5천 개가 넘는 길을 하나하나 나타내고 있다. **5** 형용사 축소 모형의 ❏ 프랭클린은 어머니께 정교하고 자세한 그 집의 축소 모델을 만들어 드렸다. **6** 가산명사 음계 ❏ 시장조 음계 **7** 가산명사 비늘 ❏ 생선에서 과다한 비늘은 다 벗겨 내세요. **8** 복수명사 저울 ❏ 주방용 저울 한 쌍 **9** 타동사 오르다 [문어체] ❏ 에베레스트에 오른 최초의 영국 여성, 레베카 스티븐스 **10** 구 균형이 안 맞는 ❏ 그 건물과는 전적으로 균형이 안 맞는 거대한 성모 마리아 금조각상을 올려놓은 탑 **11** 구 일정한 비율로, 비율을 맞춰 ❏ 작은 탑들과 다리들을 일정한 비율로 맞춰 배치한 축소 모형 정원

구동사 축소하다 ❏ 베이징 내 한 공장이 인력을 600명에서 겨우 6명으로 축소했다.

구동사 확대하다 ❏ 치수가 10인 옷을 단순히 넓히기만 하면 흔히 아무 짝에도 쓸모없게 된다.

1 가산명사 두피 ❏ 그는 두피 위로 머리카락을 단정히 넘겼다. **2** 타동사 암표 장사를 하다 [미국영어; 영국영어 tout] ❏ 그는 암표 장사를 하면서 현금을 좀 모으려고 애쓰고 있었다.

가산명사 외과용 메스

가산명사 암표상 [미국영어; 영국영어 tout] ❏ 또 다른 암표상은 125달러짜리 입장권을 1,000달러에 팔 수도 있다고 말했다.

가산명사 신용 사기 [비격식체] ❏ 그들은 자신들이 살인 사건이 아니라 보험 사기 사건에 관여하고 있다고 믿었다.

자동사 깡충거리다 ❏ 어린이들이 노란 학교 버스에서 깡충거리며 뛰어내려 운동장으로 달려갔다.

1 타동사 훑어보다 ❏ 그녀는 신문 광고면을 훑어보았다. ● 단수명사 훑어보기 ❏ 나는 단지 네 책을 다시 훑어보았을 뿐이야. **2** 타동사 자세히 살펴보다 ❏ 그 경관은 그 방을 자세히 살펴보았다. ❏ 그녀는 안절부절못하며 폴을 찾기 위해 사람들을 자세히 살펴보았다. **3** 타동사 정밀 검사하다 ❏ 그들의 방식은 수속을 마친 모든 가방을 폭발물 탐지기로 정밀 검사하는 것이다. **4** 타동사 바이러스 검사를 받다 [컴퓨터] ❏ 모든 인터넷 서비스 공급자가 바이러스 검사 장비를 갖추고 있는 것은 아니다. **5** 타동사 스캐너로 읽히다 [컴퓨터] ❏ 모든 도서관의 종이에 적힌 내용이 결국에는 모두 스캐너로 읽혀 컴퓨터에 입력될 것이다. **6** 타동사 (레이더 등으로) 탐지하다 ❏ 그 선박의 레이더가 앞에 펼쳐진 바다를 탐지했다. **7** 가산명사 (의학) 스캔, 정밀 촬영 ❏ 뇌 정밀 촬영 결과 응고된 피가 발견되었다.

1 가산명사 부정 사건, 독직 사건, 스캔들 ❏ 금융 스캔들 **2** 불가산명사 스캔들, 추문 ❏ 그는 가십이나 스캔들을 좋아했다.

1 형용사 불명예스러운, 추한 ❏ 그들은 범법 행위나 불명예스러운 행동으로 인해 해고될 것이다.

scan|dal|ous|ly ADV [ADV with v] ❏ *He asked only that Ingrid stop behaving so scandalously.* ◾ ADJ **Scandalous** stories or remarks are concerned with the immoral and shocking aspects of someone's behavior or something that has happened. ❏ *Newspaper columns were full of scandalous tales.*

● 불명예스럽게, 추하게 부사 ❏ 그는 잉그리드가 아주 추하게 행동하는 것을 그만두었는지에 대해서만 물어보았다. ◾ 형용사 추문에 얽힌 ❏ 신문 칼럼들은 온통 추문에 얽힌 이야기들로 가득 찼다.

scan|dal sheet (scandal sheets) N-COUNT You can refer to newspapers and magazines which print mainly stories about sex and crime as **scandal sheets**. [AM; BRIT **gutter press**] ❏ *What if someone sells the story to the scandal sheets?*

가산명사 가십 신문 [미국영어; 영국영어 gutter press] ❏ 누군가 가십 신문에 그 이야기를 팔면 어떻게 되지?

scan|ner /skǽnər/ (scanners) ◼ N-COUNT A **scanner** is a machine which is used to examine, identify, or record things, for example by using a beam of light, sound, or X-rays. ❏ *...brain scanners.* ◾ N-COUNT A **scanner** is a piece of computer equipment that you use for copying a picture or document into a computer. [COMPUTING] ❏ *...a color printer and scanner.* →see **laser**

◼ 가산명사 (의학) 스캐너 ❏ 뇌 스캐너 ◾ 가산명사 (컴퓨터) 스캐너 [컴퓨터] ❏ 컬러 프린터와 스캐너

scant /skǽnt/ ADJ You use **scant** to indicate that there is very little of something or not as much of something as there should be. ❏ *She began to berate the police for paying scant attention to the theft from her car.*

형용사 부족한, 빈약한 ❏ 그녀는 자신의 차에서 일어난 도난 사건에 대해 관심이 부족하다는 이유로 경찰을 비난하기 시작했다.

scape|goat /skéipgout/ (scapegoats, scapegoating, scapegoated) ◼ N-COUNT If you say that someone is made a **scapegoat for** something bad that has happened, you mean that people blame them and may punish them for it although it may not be their fault. ❏ *I don't think I deserve to be messed about and made the scapegoat for a couple of bad results.* ◾ V-T To **scapegoat** someone means to blame them publicly for something bad that has happened, even though it was not their fault. ❏ *...a climate where ethnic minorities are continually scapegoated for the lack of jobs and housing problems.*

◼ 가산명사 희생양 ❏ 내가 몇 가지 나쁜 결과 때문에 비난을 받고 희생양이 되어야 한다는 것에는 생각지 않는다. ◾ 타동사 희생양으로 삼다, 책임을 전가하다 ❏ 일자리 부족과 주택난에 대해 소수 민족들이 끊임없이 희생양이 되는 상황

scar /skɑr/ (scars, scarring, scarred) ◼ N-COUNT A **scar** is a mark on the skin which is left after a wound has healed. ❏ *He had a scar on his forehead.* ◾ V-T If your skin **is scarred**, it is badly marked as a result of a wound. [usu passive] ❏ *He was scarred for life during a pub fight.* ◾ V-T If a surface **is scarred**, it is damaged and there are ugly marks on it. [usu passive] ❏ *The arena was scarred by deep muddy ruts.* ◾ N-COUNT If an unpleasant physical or emotional experience leaves a **scar** on someone, it has a permanent effect on their mind. ❏ *The early years of fear and the hostility left a deep scar on the young boy.* ◾ V-T If an unpleasant physical or emotional experience **scars** you, it has a permanent effect on your mind. ❏ *This is something that's going to scar him forever.*

◼ 가산명사 흉터 ❏ 그는 이마에 흉터가 있었다. ◾ 타동사 흉터가 남다 ❏ 그는 한 술집에서 한 싸움으로 평생 흉터가 남게 되었다. ◾ 타동사 자국이 생기다 ❏ 그 투기장에는 진흙에 깊은 바퀴 자국이 생겼다. ◾ 가산명사 (마음의) 상처, 상흔 ❏ 유년 시절에 겪은 공포와 적개심으로 그 어린 소년은 마음에 깊은 상처를 받았다. ◾ 타동사 (마음의) 상처를 주다 ❏ 이것 때문에 그는 영원히 마음의 상처를 입게 될 것이다.

scarce /skɛərs/ (scarcer, scarcest) ◼ ADJ If something is **scarce**, there is not enough of it. ❏ *Food was scarce and expensive.* ❏ *Jobs are becoming increasingly scarce.* ◾ PHRASE If you **make yourself scarce**, you quickly leave the place you are in, usually in order to avoid a difficult or embarrassing situation. [INFORMAL] ❏ *It probably would be a good idea if you made yourself scarce.*

◼ 형용사 부족한 ❏ 음식이 부족했고 비쌌다. ❏ 일자리가 더욱더 부족해지고 있다. ◾ 구 슬쩍 빠져나가다 [비격식체] ❏ 슬쩍 빠져나간다면 아마도 그것이 좋은 생각일 것이다.

scarce|ly /skɛərsli/ ◼ ADV You use **scarcely** to emphasize that something is only just true or only just the case. [EMPHASIS] ❏ *He could scarcely breathe.* ❏ *I scarcely knew him.* ◾ ADV You can use **scarcely** to say that something is not true or is not the case, in a humorous or critical way. ❏ *It can scarcely be coincidence.* ◾ ADV If you say **scarcely had** one thing happened when something else happened, you mean that the first event was followed immediately by the second. [ADV before v] ❏ *Scarcely had they left the university campus before soldiers armed with bayonets and rifles charged into the students.*

◼ 부사 가까스로, 거의 – 않는 [강조] ❏ 그는 가까스로 숨을 쉴 수 있었다. ❏ 나는 그를 거의 알지 못했다. ◾ 부사 결코 –이 아닌 ❏ 그것은 결코 우연일 리가 없다. ◾ 부사 –하자마자 ❏ 그들이 대학 캠퍼스를 떠나자마자 총검과 소총을 든 군인들이 학생들을 향해 돌진했다.

scar|city /skɛərsiti/ (scarcities) N-VAR If there is a **scarcity of** something, there is not enough of it for the people who need it or want it. [FORMAL] ❏ *...an ever increasing scarcity of water.*

가산명사 또는 불가산명사 부족, 결핍 [격식체] ❏ 계속 증가하는 물 부족 사태

scare /skɛər/ (scares, scaring, scared) ◼ V-T If something **scares** you, it frightens or worries you. ❏ *You're scaring me.* ❏ *The prospect of failure scares me rigid.* ● PHRASE If you want to emphasize that something scares you a lot, you can say that it **scares the hell out of** you or **scares the life out of** you. [INFORMAL, EMPHASIS] ◾ N-SING If a sudden unpleasant experience gives you a **scare**, it frightens you. ❏ *Don't you realize what a scare you've given us all?* ◾ N-COUNT A **scare** is a situation in which many people are afraid or worried because they think something dangerous is happening which will affect them all. ❏ *She has been recovering from her health scare late last year.* ◾ N-COUNT A bomb **scare** or a security **scare** is a situation in which there is believed to be a bomb in a place. ❏ *Despite many recent bomb scares, no one has yet been hurt.* ◾ →see also **scared**

◼ 타동사 겁주다 ❏ 네가 나에게 겁을 주고 있잖아. ❏ 실패할 걸 생각하면 너무 겁이 난다. ● 구 혼비백산하게 만들다 [비격식체, 강조] ◾ 단수명사 겁 ❏ 네가 우리 모두를 얼마나 겁나게 했는지 모르겠니? ◾ 가산명사 공포 ❏ 그녀는 작년 말에 겪었던 건강 공포에서 회복되고 있다. ◾ 가산명사 소동 ❏ 최근 많은 폭발물 소동이 있었지만, 다친 사람은 아직 없다.

▶**scare away** →see **scare off** ◼

▶**scare off** ◼ PHRASAL VERB If you **scare off** or **scare away** a person or animal, you frighten them so that they go away. ❏ *...an alarm to scare off an attacker.* ◾ PHRASAL VERB If you **scare** someone **off**, you accidentally make them unwilling to become involved with you. ❏ *I don't think that revealing your past to your boyfriend scared him off.*

◼ 구동사 겁주어 쫓아 버리다 ❏ 공격자를 겁먹고 달아나게 만드는 경보기 ◾ 구동사 꺼리게 만들다 ❏ 나는 네가 과거를 털어놓는다고 해서 남자 친구가 널 꺼릴 것이라고 생각하지 않아.

scare|crow /skɛərkrou/ (scarecrows) N-COUNT A **scarecrow** is an object in the shape of a person, which is put in a field where crops are growing in order to frighten birds away.

가산명사 허수아비

scared /skɛərd/ ◼ ADJ If you are **scared of** someone or something, you are frightened of them. ❏ *I'm certainly not scared of him.* ❏ *I was too scared to move.* ◾ ADJ If you are **scared that** something unpleasant might happen, you are nervous and worried because you think that it might happen. ❏ *I was scared that I might be sick.*

◼ 형용사 겁먹은, 무서워하는 ❏ 나는 그에게 겁을 먹은 것은 분명히 아냐. ❏ 나는 너무 겁이 나서 움직일 수가 없었다. ◾ 형용사 걱정스러운 ❏ 나는 몸이 아픈 건 아닌가 하고 걱정스러웠다.

scare|monger|ing /skɛərmʌŋgərɪŋ, -mɒŋ-/ N-UNCOUNT If one person or group accuses another person or group of **scaremongering**, they accuse them of deliberately spreading worrying stories to try and frighten people. ❏ *The Government yesterday accused Greenpeace of scaremongering.*

불가산명사 세상을 소란스럽게 하는 사람, 유언비어를 퍼뜨리는 사람 ❏ 정부는 어제 그린피스가 유언비어를 퍼뜨리는 존재라고 비난했다.

scarf /skɑrf/ (scarfs or scarves) N-COUNT A **scarf** is a piece of cloth that you wear around your neck or head, usually to keep yourself warm. ❏ *He reached up to loosen the scarf around his neck.*

가산명사 스카프 ❏ 그는 손을 뻗어 목에 두른 스카프를 느슨하게 했다.

A B C D E F G H I J K L M N O P Q R S T U V W X Y Z

scar|let /skɑrlɪt/ (**scarlets**) COLOR Something that is **scarlet** is bright red. ❑ ...her scarlet lipstick.

scarves /skɑrvz/ Scarves is a plural of **scarf**.

scary /skɛəri/ (**scarier, scariest**) ADJ Something that is **scary** is rather frightening. [INFORMAL] ❑ I think prison is going to be a scary thing for Harry. ❑ There's something very scary about him.

scath|ing /skeɪðɪŋ/ ADJ If you say that someone is being **scathing** about something, you mean that they are being very critical of it. ❑ The society has been particularly scathing about the planning record of West Somerset District Council.

scat|ter /skætər/ (**scatters, scattering, scattered**) ■ V-T If you **scatter** things over an area, you throw or drop them so that they spread all over the area. ❑ She tore the rose apart and scattered the petals over the grave. ❑ They've been scattering toys everywhere. ■ V-T/V-I If a group of people **scatter** or if you **scatter** them, they suddenly separate and move in different directions. ❑ After dinner, everyone scattered. ■ →see also **scattered, scattering**

scat|tered /skætərd/ ■ ADJ **Scattered** things are spread over an area in an untidy or irregular way. [ADJ n, v-link ADJ prep/adv] ❑ He picked up the scattered toys. ❑ Tomorrow there will be a few scattered showers. ■ ADJ If something is **scattered with** a lot of small things, they are spread all over it. [v-link ADJ with n] ❑ Every surface is scattered with photographs.

scat|ter|ing /skætərɪŋ/ (**scatterings**) N-COUNT A **scattering of** things or people is a small number of them spread over an area. ❑ ...the scattering of houses east of the village.

scav|enge /skævɪndʒ/ (**scavenges, scavenging, scavenged**) V-I If people or animals **scavenge for** things, they collect them by searching among waste or unwanted objects. ❑ Many are orphans, their parents killed as they scavenged for food. ❑ Children scavenge through garbage. ● **scav|en|ger** (**scavengers**) N-COUNT ❑ ...scavengers such as rats.

sce|nario /sɪnɛərioʊ, BRIT sɪnɑːrioʊ/ (**scenarios**) N-COUNT If you talk about a likely or possible **scenario**, you are talking about the way in which a situation may develop. ❑ ...the nightmare scenario of a divided and irrelevant Royal Family.

scene ♦♦◇ /siːn/ (**scenes**) ■ N-COUNT A **scene** in a play, movie, or book is part of it in which a series of events happen in the same place. ❑ ...the opening scene of "A Christmas Carol." ❑ ...Act I, scene 1. ■ N-COUNT You refer to a place as a **scene** when you are describing its appearance and indicating what impression it makes on you. ❑ It's a scene of complete devastation. ❑ Thick black smoke billowed over the scene. ■ N-COUNT You can describe an event that you see, or that is broadcast or shown in a picture, as a **scene** of a particular kind. ❑ There were emotional scenes as the refugees enjoyed their first breath of freedom. ❑ Television broadcasters were warned to exercise caution over depicting scenes of violence. ■ N-COUNT The **scene** of an event is the place where it happened. ❑ The area has been the scene of fierce fighting for three months. ❑ ...traces left at the scene of a crime. ■ N-SING You can refer to an area of activity as a particular type of **scene**. ❑ Sandman's experimentation has made him something of a cult figure on the local music scene. ■ N-COUNT If you make a **scene**, you embarrass people by publicly showing your anger about something. ❑ I'm sorry I made such a scene. ■ PHRASE If something is done **behind the scenes**, it is done secretly rather than publicly. ❑ But behind the scenes Mr. Cain will be working quietly to try to get a deal done. ■ PHRASE If you refer to what happens **behind the scenes**, you are referring to what happens during the making of a movie, play, or radio or television program. ❑ It's an exciting opportunity to learn what goes on behind the scenes. ■ PHRASE If you have **a change of scene**, you go somewhere different after being in a particular place for a long time. ❑ What you need is a change of scene. Why not go on a cruise? ■ PHRASE Something that **sets the scene for** a particular event creates the conditions in which the event is likely to happen. ❑ Farmers mounted a "commando operation" to open up the lake's sluice gate and drain off 40 centimeters of water, so setting the scene for disaster. ■ PHRASE When a person or thing appears **on the scene**, they come into being or become involved in something. When they disappear **from the scene**, they are no longer there or are no longer involved. ❑ He could react rather jealously when and if another child comes on the scene. →see **animation, drawing**

Word Partnership	scene의 연어
N.	**movie** scene, **sex** scene ■
	scene **of an accident, crime** scene, scene **of a murder,**
	scene **of a shooting** ■
	music scene ■
ADJ.	**final** scene, **first/opening** scene, **nude** scene ■
	political scene ■
V.	**describe** a scene ■ ■
	arrive at a scene, **leave** a scene, **rush to** a scene ■

scen|ery /siːnəri/ ■ N-UNCOUNT The **scenery** in a country area is the land, water, or plants that you can see around you. ❑ ...the island's spectacular scenery. ■ N-UNCOUNT In a theater, the **scenery** consists of the structures and painted backgrounds that show where the action in the play takes place. ❑ Instead of stagehands, the actors would move the scenery right in front of the audience.

Do not confuse **scenery, landscape, countryside**, and **nature**. With **landscape**, the emphasis is on the physical features of the land, while **scenery** includes everything you can see when you look out over an area of land. ❑ ...the landscape of steep woods and distant mountains....unattractive urban

색채어 진홍색 ❑ 그녀의 진홍색 립스틱

scarf의 복수

형용사 무서운 [비격식체] ❑ 나는 교도소가 해리에게는 무서운 곳이 될 것이라고 생각한다. ❑ 그에게는 매우 무서운 구석이 있다.

형용사 신랄한, 가혹한 ❑ 그 단체는 웨스트 서머싯 지방 자치 지역의 개발 기록에 대해 계속 유난히 신랄하다.

■ 타동사 흩뿌리다, 흩트리다 ❑ 그녀는 장미 꽃잎을 일일이 뜯은 후 그 무덤 위에 꽃잎들을 뿌렸다. ❑ 그들이 장난감을 여기저기 흩어 놓고 있다. ■ 타동사/자동사 뿔뿔이 흩어지다; 뿔뿔이 흩어지게 하다 ❑ 식사 후에, 모두 뿔뿔이 흩어졌다.

■ 형용사 흩어진, 산재적인 ❑ 그는 흩어진 장난감들을 주웠다. ❑ 내일은 소나기가 산발적으로 몇 차례 내리겠습니다. ■ 형용사 _이 흩어져 있는, _이 널려 있는 ❑ 모든 표면에 사진이 널려 있었다.

가산명사 산재해 있는 것 ❑ 마을 동쪽에 산재해 있는 가옥들

자동사 (먹을 것을 찾아) 쓰레기 더미를 뒤지다 ❑ 다수가 고아인데, 그들의 부모는 먹을 것을 찾아 쓰레기 더미를 뒤지다가 살해되었다. ❑ 아이들이 음식 쓰레기 더미를 뒤진다. ● 먹을 것을 찾아 다니는 동물 가산명사 ❑ 쥐같이 먹을 것을 찾아다니는 동물

가산명사 시나리오, 기본 ❑ 분열되고 시대와 동떨어진 왕실에 대한 악몽 같은 시나리오

■ 가산명사 장면 ❑ '크리스마스 캐럴'의 첫 장면 ❑ 1막 1장 ■ 가산명사 현장 ❑ 그곳은 철저한 파괴의 현장이다. ❑ 시커먼 연기가 그 현장 위에 자욱했다. ■ 가산명사 장면 ❑ 피난민들이 처음으로 자유를 누리는 감동적인 장면들이 있었다. ❑ 텔레비전 방송국들은 폭력 장면을 내보낼 때 주의를 기울이라는 경고를 받았다. ■ 가산명사 현장 ❑ 그 지역은 3개월 간 계속 격렬한 전투가 벌어진 현장이다. ❑ 범죄 현장에 남겨진 흔적들 ■ 단수명사 계, 분야 ❑ 샌드맨은 자신의 실험성으로 지역 음악계에서 우상과 같은 존재가 되었다. ■ 가산명사 추태, 소동 ❑ 그와 같은 추태를 보여 죄송합니다. ■ 구 비밀리에 ❑ 그러나 비밀리에 케인 씨는 거래 성사를 위해 조용히 노력하고 있을 것이다. ■ 구 무대 뒤에서 ❑ 그것은 무대 뒤에서 무슨 일이 진행되는지를 배울 수 있는, 마음을 설레게 하는 기회이다. ■ 구 환경의 변화 ❑ 네가 필요한 건 환경을 바꿔 보는 거야. 유람선을 타고 여행하는 것은 어때? ■ 구 _에 대비하다 ❑ 농부들은 그 호수의 수문을 열어 40센티미터 높이의 물을 빼내기 위한 '특공 대작전'에 착수함으로써 재앙에 대비했다. ■ 구 현장에; 현장으로부터 ❑ 만약 또 한 명의 아이가 그 현장에 나타나면 그때는 그가 약간 시샘하는 반응을 보일 것이다.

■ 불가산명사 풍경 ❑ 그 섬의 장엄한 풍경 ■ 불가산명사 무대 장치 ❑ 무대 담당자들 대신 배우들이 무대 장치를 관중 바로 앞으로 옮길 것이다.

scenery, landscape, countryside, nature를 혼동하지 마시오. scenery는 어떤 지역에서 눈에 보이는 모든 것을 포함하는 반면, landscape은 땅의 물리적 형태를 강조한다. ❑ ...가파른 숲과 먼 산으로

scenery. **Countryside** is land which is away from towns and cities. ❑ *...3,500 acres of mostly flat countryside.* **Nature** includes the landscape, the weather, animals, and plants, which are not created by man. ❑ *These creatures roamed the Earth as the finest and rarest wonders of nature.*

이루어진 지형....볼품없는 도회지 풍경. countryside는 도시에서 떨어진 지역이다. ❑ ...대부분이 평지인 3,500에이커의 전원지역. nature는 지형, 기후, 동식물을 모두 포괄한다. ❑ 이 생물체들은 가장 멋지고 가장 희귀한 자연의 경이로서 지구상을 활보했다.

3 PHRASE If you have **a change of scenery**, you go somewhere different after being in a particular place for a long time. ❑ *A change of scenery might do you the power of good.*

3 구 환경의 변화 환경에 변화를 주는 것이 너에게 도움이 될 거야.

sce|nic /síːnɪk/ ❶ ADJ A **scenic** place has attractive scenery. ❑ *This is an extremely scenic part of America.* ❷ ADJ A **scenic** route goes through attractive scenery and has nice views. ❑ *It was even marked on the map as a scenic route.*

❶ 형용사 경치가 아름다운 ❑ 이곳은 미국에서 경치가 유난히 아름다운 곳입니다. **❷** 형용사 경치 좋은 ❑ 그곳은 심지어 경치 좋은 길이라고 지도에 표시가 되어 있었다.

scent /sɛnt/ (**scents, scenting, scented**) ❶ N-COUNT The **scent** of something is the pleasant smell that it has. ❑ *Flowers are chosen for their scent as well as their look.* ❷ V-T If something **scents** a place or thing, it makes it smell pleasant. ❑ *Jasmine flowers scent the air.* ❸ N-MASS **Scent** is a liquid which women put on their necks and wrists to make themselves smell nice. ❑ *She dabbed herself with scent.* ❹ N-VAR The **scent** of a person or animal is the smell that they leave and that other people sometimes follow when looking for them. ❑ *A police dog picked up the murderer's scent.* ❺ V-T When an animal **scents** something, it becomes aware of it by smelling it. [no cont] ❑ *...dogs which scent the hidden birds.* →see **flower**

❶ 가산명사 향기 ❑ 꽃을 고를 때는 모양뿐만 아니라 향기도 중요하다. **❷** 타동사 향긋하게 하다 ❑ 재스민 꽃이 있어 공기가 향긋하다. **❸** 물질명사 향수 ❑ 그녀는 몸에 향수를 가볍게 발랐다. **❹** 가산명사 또는 불가산명사 남긴 냄새 ❑ 경찰견이 살인범이 남긴 냄새를 찾아냈다. **❺** 타동사 냄새를 맡다 ❑ 숨은 새들의 냄새를 맡는 개들

scent|ed /sɛntɪd/ ADJ **Scented** things have a pleasant smell, either naturally or because perfume has been added to them. ❑ *The white flowers are pleasantly scented.*

형용사 좋은 냄새가 나는 ❑ 그 흰 꽃은 기분 좋은 냄새가 난다.

scep|tic /skɛptɪk/ →see **skeptic**

scep|ti|cal /skɛptɪkᵊl/ →see **skeptical**

scep|ti|cism /skɛptɪsɪzəm/ →see **skepticism**

sched|ule ♦♦◇ /skɛdʒuːl, -uəl, BRIT ʃɛdjuːl/ (**schedules, scheduling, scheduled**) ❶ N-COUNT A **schedule** is a plan that gives a list of events or tasks and the times at which each one should happen or be done. ❑ *He has been forced to adjust his schedule.* ❷ N-UNCOUNT You can use **schedule** to refer to the time or way something is planned to be done. For example, if something is completed **on schedule**, it is completed at the time planned. ❑ *The jet arrived in Johannesburg two minutes ahead of schedule.* ❑ *Everything went according to schedule.* ❸ V-T If something **is scheduled** to happen at a particular time, arrangements are made for it to happen at that time. [usu passive] ❑ *The space shuttle had been scheduled to blast off at 04:38.* ❑ *A presidential election was scheduled for last December.* ❹ N-COUNT A **schedule** is a written list of things, for example a list of prices, details, or conditions. ❑ *Ticket plans and a pricing schedule will not be released until later this year.* ❺ N-COUNT A **schedule** is a list of all the times when trains, boats, buses, or aircraft are supposed to arrive at or leave a particular place. [mainly AM; BRIT usually **timetable**] ❑ *...a bus schedule.* ❻ N-COUNT In a school or college, a **schedule** is a diagram that shows the times in the week at which particular subjects are taught. [AM; BRIT usually **timetable**] ❑ *He began college with a schedule that included biology, calculus, and political science.*

❶ 가산명사 일정, 스케줄 ❑ 그는 자신의 일정을 조절하도록 강요받고 있다. **❷** 불가산명사 예정; 예정대로 ❑ 그 제트기는 예정보다 2분 빨리 요하네스버그에 도착했다. ❑ 모든 일이 예정에 맞춰 진행되었다. **❸** 타동사 예정되어 있다 ❑ 그 우주 왕복선은 오전 4시 38분에 발사되기로 예정되어 있었다. ❑ 대통령 선거가 지난 12월로 예정되어 있었다. **❹** 가산명사 일람표 ❑ 입장권 계획표와 가격 일람표가 올해 말이나 되어서 공개될 것이다. **❺** 가산명사 운행 시각표 [주로 미국영어; 영국영어 대개 timetable] ❑ 버스 운행 시각표 **❻** 가산명사 수업 시간표 [미국영어; 영국영어 대개 timetable] ❑ 그의 대학 생활 첫 시간표에는 생물학과 미적분학, 그리고 정치학이 들어 있었다.

Word Partnership   schedule의 연어

ADJ.	**busy** schedule, **hectic** schedule ❶
	regular schedule ❶ ❺
N.	**change** of schedule, schedule **of events**, **payment** schedule,
	playoff schedule, **work** schedule ❶ ❹
	bus schedule, **train** schedule ❺
PREP.	**according to** schedule, **ahead of** schedule, **behind** schedule,
	on schedule ❷

scheme ♦♦◇ /skiːm/ (**schemes, scheming, schemed**) ❶ N-COUNT A **scheme** is someone's plan for achieving something, especially something that will bring them some benefit. ❑ *...a quick money-making scheme to get us through the summer.* ❑ *They would first have to work out some scheme for getting the treasure out.* ❷ V-I If you say that people **are scheming**, you mean that they are making secret plans in order to gain something for themselves. [DISAPPROVAL] [oft cont] ❑ *Everyone's always scheming and plotting.* ❑ *The bride's family were scheming to prevent a wedding.* ❸ N-COUNT A **scheme** is a plan or arrangement involving many people which is made by a government or other organization. [mainly BRIT; AM **program**] ❑ *...schemes to help combat unemployment.* ❑ *...a private pension scheme.* ❹ PHRASE When people talk about **the scheme of things** or **the grand scheme of things** , they are referring to the way that everything in the world seems to be organized. ❑ *We realize that we are infinitely small within the scheme of things.*

❶ 가산명사 계획 ❑ 우리가 여름을 나기 위해 단기간에 돈을 벌 수 있는 계획 ❑ 그들은 그 보물을 꺼낼 수 있는 어떤 계획을 먼저 강구해야 할 것이다. **❷** 자동사 (비밀스런) 계획을 세우다 [탐탁잖음] ❑ 누구나 항상 계획을 세우고 음모를 꾸민다. ❑ 신부의 가족들은 결혼식을 저지할 계획을 세우고 있었다. **❸** 가산명사 시책 [주로 영국영어; 미국영어 program] ❑ 실업 타개에 도움이 되는 시책 ❑ 개인연금 시책 **❹** 구 조직 세계 ❑ 우리는 우리가 세상이라는 거대한 체계 속에서 지극히 작은 존재임을 깨닫는다.

Thesaurus   scheme의 참조어

N.	design, plan, strategy ❶

schizo|phre|nia /skɪtsəfriːniə/ N-UNCOUNT **Schizophrenia** is a serious mental illness. People who suffer from it are unable to relate their thoughts and feelings to what is happening around them and often withdraw from society.

불가산명사 정신 분열증

schizo|phren|ic /skɪtsəfrɛnɪk/ (**schizophrenics**) N-COUNT A **schizophrenic** is a person who is suffering from schizophrenia. ❑ *He was diagnosed as a paranoid schizophrenic.* ● ADJ **Schizophrenic** is also an adjective. ❑ *...a schizophrenic patient.*

가산명사 정신 분열증 환자 ❑ 그는 편집증적 정신 분열증 환자라는 진단을 받았다. ● 형용사 정신 분열증의 ❑ 정신 분열증 환자

Word Link   schol ≈ school : *schol*ar, *schol*arship, *schol*astic

schol|ar /skɒlər/ (scholars) N-COUNT A **scholar** is a person who studies an academic subject and knows a lot about it. [FORMAL] ❑ *The library attracts thousands of scholars and researchers.* →see **history**

가산명사 학자 [격식체] ❑ 그 도서관에는 수천 명의 학자들과 연구자들이 모여든다.

schol|ar|ly /skɒlərli/ ■ ADJ A **scholarly** person spends a lot of time studying and knows a lot about academic subjects. ❑ *He was an intellectual, scholarly man.* ② ADJ A **scholarly** book or article contains a lot of academic information and is intended for academic readers. ❑ *...the more scholarly academic journals.* ③ ADJ **Scholarly** matters and activities involve people who do academic research. ❑ *This has been the subject of intense scholarly debate.*

■ 형용사 학구적인 ❑ 그는 지적이며, 학구적인 사람이었다. ② 형용사 학문적인, 전문적인 ❑ 더 전문적인 학술지 ③ 형용사 학술의 ❑ 이것이 학계의 격렬한 논쟁의 주제가 되어 왔다.

schol|ar|ship /skɒlərʃɪp/ (scholarships) ■ N-COUNT If you get a **scholarship** to a school or university, your studies are paid for by the school or university or by some other organization. ❑ *He got a scholarship to the Pratt Institute of Art.* ② N-UNCOUNT **Scholarship** is serious academic study and the knowledge that is obtained from it. ❑ *I want to take advantage of your lifetime of scholarship.*

■ 가산명사 장학금 ❑ 그는 프랫 미술 대학에서 공부할 수 있는 장학금을 받았다. ② 불가산명사 학식 ❑ 저는 당신이 일생 동안 이룬 학식을 이용하고 싶습니다.

scho|las|tic /skəlæstɪk/ ADJ Your **scholastic** achievement or ability is your academic achievement or ability while you are at school. [FORMAL] [ADJ n] ❑ *...the values which encouraged her scholastic achievement.*

형용사 학문적인 [격식체] ❑ 그녀의 학문적 업적을 고취시켰던 가치

school ◆◆◆ /skul/ (schools, schooling, schooled) ■ N-VAR A **school** is a place where children are educated. You usually refer to this place as **school** when you are talking about the time that children spend there and the activities that they do there. ❑ *...a boy who was in my class at school.* ❑ *Even the good students say homework is what they most dislike about school.* ❑ *...a school built in the Sixties.*

■ 가산명사 또는 불가산명사 학교 ❑ 나와 학교에서 같은 반에 있었던 한 소년 ❑ 심지어 모범생들도 학교에서 가장 싫은 것이 숙제라고 말한다. ❑ 1960년대에 지어진 학교

> In public education in the United States, most schools are **co-educational** or **coed**, that is they allow both male and female students to enroll. Schools that are not coed are usually private schools.

> 미국의 공교육에서는 대부분의 학교가 co-educational(남녀 공학) 또는 coed인에게는 남녀 학생이 같이 다닌다. 남녀 공학이 아닌 학교는 대개 사립학교이다.

② N-COUNT-COLL A **school** is the students or staff at a school. ❑ *Deirdre, the whole school's going to hate you.* ③ N-COUNT; N-IN-NAMES A privately-run place where a particular skill or subject is taught can be referred to as a **school**. ❑ *...a riding school and equestrian center near Chepstow.* ④ N-VAR; N-IN-NAMES A university, college, or university department specializing in a particular type of subject can be referred to as a **school**. ❑ *...a lecturer in the school of veterinary medicine at the University of Pennsylvania.* ⑤ N-UNCOUNT **School** is used to refer to college. [AM] ❑ *Moving rapidly through school, he graduated Phi Beta Kappa from the University of Kentucky at age 18.* ⑥ N-COUNT-COLL A particular **school of** writers, artists, or thinkers is a group of them whose work, opinions, or theories are similar. [usu with supp] ❑ *...the Chicago school of economists.* ⑦ V-T If you **school** someone **in** something, you train or educate them to have a certain skill, type of behavior, or way of thinking. [WRITTEN] ❑ *Many mothers schooled their daughters in the myth of female inferiority.* ⑧ →see also **schooling, boarding school, grade school, graduate school, grammar school, high school, junior school, nursery school, prep school, primary school, private school, public school, state school**

② 가산명사-집합 전교 학생 및 교직원 ❑ 데어드레이, 학교의 모든 사람들이 너를 싫어할 거야. ③ 가산명사; 이름명사 학원 ❑ 쳅스토우 인근의 승마 학원과 기마 센터 ④ 가산명사 또는 불가산명사; 이름명사 학부 ❑ 펜실베이니아대학교의 수의학 학부 강사 ⑤ 불가산명사 대학 [미국영어] ❑ 학점을 조기 이수하면서, 그는 18세의 나이로 켄터키 대학을 우수한 성적으로 졸업했다. ⑥ 가산명사-집합 학파 ❑ 시카고 경제학자들 ⑦ 타동사 교육하다, 가르치다 [문어체] ❑ 많은 엄마들이 딸에게 여성은 열등하다는 통념을 갖도록 교육시켰다.

school board (school boards) N-COUNT-COLL A **school board** is a committee in charge of education in a particular city or area, or in a particular school, especially in the United States. [AM] ❑ *Colonel Richard Nelson served on the school board until this year.*

가산명사-집합 교육 위원회 [미국영어] ❑ 리처드 넬슨 대령은 올해까지 교육 위원회에서 근무를 했다.

school|boy /skulbɔɪ/ (schoolboys) N-COUNT A **schoolboy** is a boy who goes to school. ❑ *...a group of ten-year-old schoolboys.*

가산명사 남학생 ❑ 한 무리의 열 살짜리 남학생들

school|child /skultʃaɪld/ (schoolchildren) N-COUNT **Schoolchildren** are children who go to school. ❑ *Last year I had an audience of schoolchildren and they laughed at everything.*

가산명사 어린 학생들 ❑ 지난해 나는 어린 학생들을 대상으로 강의를 했는데 그들은 무슨 얘기를 해도 웃었다.

school|days /skuldeɪz/ also school days N-PLURAL Your **schooldays** are the period of your life when you were at school. ❑ *He was happily married to a girl he had known since his schooldays.*

복수명사 학창 시절 ❑ 그는 학창 시절부터 알던 한 아가씨와 결혼을 해서 행복하게 살고 있었다.

school friend (school friends) also schoolfriend N-COUNT A **school friend** is a friend of yours who is at the same school as you, or who used to be at the same school when you were children. ❑ *I spent the evening with an old school friend.*

가산명사 동창 ❑ 나는 옛 동창과 그날 저녁 시간을 보냈다.

school|girl /skulgɜrl/ (schoolgirls) N-COUNT A **schoolgirl** is a girl who goes to school. ❑ *...half a dozen giggling schoolgirls.*

가산명사 여학생 ❑ 킥킥대며 웃는 6명의 여학생들

school|ing /skulɪŋ/ N-UNCOUNT **Schooling** is education that children receive at school. ❑ *His formal schooling continued erratically until he reached the age of eleven.*

불가산명사 학교 교육 ❑ 그의 정규 학교 교육은 그가 열한 살이 될 때까지 불규칙하게 계속되었다.

school leav|er (school leavers) N-COUNT **School leavers** are young people who have just left school, because they have completed their time there. [BRIT; AM **high school graduate**] ❑ *...the lack of job opportunities, particularly for school-leavers.*

가산명사 학교 공부를 마친 사람 [영국영어; 미국영어 high school graduate] ❑ 특히 학교 공부를 마친 사람들의 구직 기회 감소

school|teacher /skultiʃər/ (schoolteachers) N-COUNT A **schoolteacher** is a teacher in a school.

가산명사 학교 교사

Word Link   sci ≈ knowing : con*sci*ence, con*sci*ous, *sci*ence

sci|ence ◆◆◇ /saɪəns/ (sciences) ■ N-UNCOUNT **Science** is the study of the nature and behavior of natural things and the knowledge that we obtain about them. ❑ *The best discoveries in science are very simple.* ② N-COUNT A **science** is a particular branch of science such as physics, chemistry, or biology. ❑ *Physics is the best example of a science which has developed strong, abstract theories.* ③ N-COUNT A **science** is the study of some aspect of human behavior, for example sociology or anthropology. ❑ *...the modern science of psychology.* ④ →see also **social science**

■ 불가산명사 과학 ❑ 과학의 가장 훌륭한 발견들은 매우 난순하다. ② 가산명사 자연 과학, 과학 ❑ 물리학은 확고하고 추상적인 이론들을 발전시킨 자연 과학의 가장 좋은 예이다. ③ 가산명사 학문 ❑ 현대 심리학

→see Word Web: **science**

Word Web science

Science is the study of the laws that govern the natural world. It uses **research** and **experiments** to try to explain various phenomena. Scientists follow the scientific method which begins with **observation** and measurement. Then they state a **hypothesis**, which is a possible explanation for the observations and measurements. Next, scientists make a **prediction**, which is a logical **deduction** based on the hypothesis. The last step is to conduct experiments which **prove** or **disprove** the hypothesis. Scientists construct and modify **theories** based on empirical **findings**. **Pure** science deals only with theories, while **applied** science has practical applications.

sci|ence fic|tion N-UNCOUNT **Science fiction** consists of stories in books, magazines, and movies about events that take place in the future or in other parts of the universe.

불가산명사 공상 과학적 이야기

sci|en|tif|ic ♦◇◇ /saɪəntɪfɪk/ ■1 ADJ **Scientific** is used to describe things that relate to science or to a particular science. ❑ *Scientific research is widely claimed to be the source of the high standard of living in the U.S.* ❑ *...the use of animals in scientific experiments.* ● **sci|en|tifi|cal|ly** /saɪəntɪfɪkli/ ADV ❑ *...scientifically advanced countries.* ■2 ADJ If you do something in a **scientific** way, you do it carefully and thoroughly, using experiments or tests. ❑ *It's not a scientific way to test their opinions.* ● **sci|en|tifi|cal|ly** ADV ❑ *Efforts are being made to research it scientifically.*

■1 형용사 과학의, 과학적인 ❑ 과학 연구는 미국에서 높은 생활수준의 원천으로 널리 요구된다. ❑ 과학 실험에서의 동물 사용 ● 과학과 관련해서 부사 ❑ 과학 선진 국가들 ■2 형용사 과학적인, 체계적인 ❑ 그들의 의견을 테스트하는 것은 과학적인 방법이 아니다. ● 과학적으로, 체계적으로 부사 ❑ 그것을 과학적으로 연구하려는 노력이 이루어지고 있다.

sci|en|tist ♦♦◇ /saɪəntɪst/ (**scientists**) N-COUNT A **scientist** is someone who has studied science and whose job is to teach or do research in science. ❑ *Scientists say they've already collected more data than had been expected.*

가산명사 과학자 ❑ 과학자들은 그들이 이미 기대했던 것보다도 더 많은 자료를 수집했다고 말한다.

sci-fi /saɪ faɪ/ N-UNCOUNT **Sci-fi** is short for **science fiction**. [INFORMAL] ❑ *...a two-and-a-half hour sci-fi film.*

불가산명사 공상 과학적 이야기 [비격식체] ❑ 2시간 30분 길이의 공상 과학 영화

scis|sors /sɪzərz/ N-PLURAL **Scissors** are a small cutting tool with two sharp blades that are screwed together. You use scissors for cutting things such as paper and cloth. [also *a pair of* N] ❑ *He told me to get some scissors.* →see **office**

복수명사 가위 ❑ 그가 나에게 가위 좀 가져오라고 말했다.

scoff /skɒf/ (**scoffs, scoffing, scoffed**) V-I If you **scoff at** something, you speak about it in a way that shows you think it is ridiculous or inadequate. ❑ *At first I scoffed at the notion.*

자동사 비웃다 ❑ 처음엔 난 그 생각을 비웃었다.

scold /skoʊld/ (**scolds, scolding, scolded**) V-T If you **scold** someone, you speak angrily to them because they have done something wrong. [FORMAL] ❑ *If he finds out, he'll scold me.* ❑ *Later she scolded her daughter for having talked to her father like that.*

타동사 꾸짖다 [격식체] ❑ 그가 알아낸다면, 날 꾸짖을 거야. ❑ 나중에 그녀는 아빠에게 그런 식으로 말했다고 딸을 꾸짖었다.

scoop /skuːp/ (**scoops, scooping, scooped**) ■1 V-T If you **scoop** a person or thing somewhere, you put your hands or arms under or around them and quickly move them there. ❑ *Michael knelt next to her and scooped her into his arms.* ■2 V-T If you **scoop** something from a container, you remove it with something such as a spoon. ❑ *...the sound of a spoon scooping dog food out of a can.* ■3 N-COUNT A **scoop** is an object like a spoon which is used for picking up a quantity of a food such as ice cream or an ingredient such as flour. ❑ *...a small ice-cream scoop.* ■4 N-COUNT You can use **scoop** to refer to an exciting news story which is reported in one newspaper or on one television program before it appears anywhere else. ❑ *...one of the biggest scoops in the history of newspapers.*

■1 타동사 (두 손으로 푸듯이) 들어 옮기다 ❑ 마이클은 그녀 옆에 무릎을 꿇은 후 두 팔로 그녀를 덥석 안아 올렸다. ■2 타동사 퍼내다 ❑ 숟가락으로 깡통에서 개 먹이를 퍼내는 소리 ■3 가산명사 국자, 주걱 ❑ 작은 아이스크림 국자 ■4 가산명사 특종 기사 ❑ 신문 역사상 가장 큰 특종 기사 중 하나

▶**scoop up** PHRASAL VERB If you **scoop** something **up**, you put your hands or arms under it and lift it in a quick movement. ❑ *Use both hands to scoop up the leaves.*

구동사 (두 손으로 푸듯이) 들어 옮기다 ❑ 양손을 사용해서 잎들을 퍼올렸다.

scoot|er /skuːtər/ (**scooters**) ■1 N-COUNT A **scooter** is a small light motorcycle which has a low seat. ■2 N-COUNT A **scooter** is a type of child's bicycle which has two wheels joined by a wooden board and a handle on a long pole attached to the front wheel. The child stands on the board with one foot, and uses the other foot to move forward.

■1 가산명사 스쿠터, 소형 오토바이 ■2 가산명사 스쿠터, 킥보드

scope /skoʊp/ ■1 N-UNCOUNT If there is **scope for** a particular kind of behavior or activity, people have the opportunity to behave in that way or do that activity. ❑ *He believed in giving his staff scope for initiative.* ■2 N-SING The **scope of** an activity, topic, or piece of work is the whole area which it deals with or includes. ❑ *Mr. Dobson promised to widen the organization's scope of activity.*

■1 불가산명사 기회 ❑ 그는 직원들에게 주도할 수 있는 기회를 주어야 한다고 믿었다. ■2 단수명사 범위 ❑ 돕슨 씨는 조직의 활동 범위를 확대하겠다고 약속했다.

scorch /skɔrtʃ/ (**scorches, scorching, scorched**) ■1 V-T To **scorch** something means to burn it slightly. ❑ *The bomb scorched the side of the building.* ● **scorched** ADJ ❑ *...scorched black earth.* ■2 V-T/V-I If something **scorches** or **is scorched**, it becomes marked or changes color because it is affected by too much heat or by a chemical. ❑ *The leaves are inclined to scorch in hot sunshine.*

■1 타동사 그슬리다 ❑ 폭탄으로 인해 그 건물의 측면이 그슬렸다. ● 그을린 형용사 ❑ 검게 그을린 땅 ■2 타동사/자동사 그슬리다 ❑ 나뭇잎들은 뜨거운 햇빛을 받으면 그슬린다.

scorch|ing /skɔrtʃɪŋ/ ADJ **Scorching** or **scorching hot** weather or temperatures are very hot indeed. [INFORMAL, EMPHASIS] ❑ *That race was run in scorching weather.*

형용사 모든 걸 태울 듯이 더운 [비격식체, 강조] ❑ 그 경주는 모든 것을 태울 듯이 더운 날씨에 진행되었다.

> In informal English, if you want to emphasize how hot the weather is, you can say that it is **boiling** or **scorching**. In winter, if the temperature is above average, you can say that it is **mild**. In general, **hot** suggests a higher temperature than **warm**, and **warm** things are usually pleasant. ❑ *...a warm evening.*

> 격식을 차리지 않은 영어에서는, 날씨가 얼마나 더운지를 강조하고 싶으면, boiling이나 scorching을 쓴다. 겨울에 기온이 평균보다 높을 때, 날씨가 mild하다고 쓴다. 대체로, hot은 warm보다 더 기온이 높은 것을 나타내고, warm한 것은 대개 쾌적하다. ❑ ...따스한 저녁.

score ♦♦◇ /skɔr/ (**scores, scoring, scored**)

> In meaning ■9, the plural form is **score**.

> ■9 의미로 복수형은 score이다.

■1 V-T/V-I In a sport or game, if a player **scores**, or **scores** a goal or a point, they gain a goal or point. ❑ *Against which country did Ian Wright score his first international goal?* ❑ *England scored 282 in their first innings.* ■2 V-T If you **score** a particular number or amount, for example as a mark in a test, you achieve that number or amount. ❑ *Kelly had scored an average of 147 on three separate IQ*

■1 타동사/자동사 득점하다 ❑ 어느 국가를 상대로 이안 라이트가 국제 경기에서 첫 득점을 했어요? ❑ 잉글랜드가 첫회 때 282점을 득점했다. ■2 타동사 점수를 얻다 ❑ 켈리는 별도의 세 차례 지능 지수 시험에서 평균 147점을 얻었다. ■3 가산명사 득점

tests. **3** N-COUNT Someone's **score** in a game or test is a number, for example, a number of points or runs, which shows what they have achieved or what level they have reached. ❑ *The U.S. Open golf tournament was won by Ben Hogan, with a score of 287. ❑ Robin Smith made 167, the highest score by an England batsman in this form of cricket.* **4** N-COUNT The **score** in a game is the result of it or the current situation, as indicated by the number of goals, runs, or points obtained by the two teams or players. ❑ *4-1 was the final score.* ❑ *They beat the Giants by a score of 7 to 3.* **5** V-T If you **score** a success, a victory, or a hit, you are successful in what you are doing. [WRITTEN] ❑ *His abiding passion was ocean racing, at which he scored many successes.* **6** N-COUNT The **score** of a movie, play, or similar production is the music which is written or used for it. ❑ *The dance is accompanied by an original score by Henry Torgue.* **7** N-COUNT The **score** of a piece of music is the written version of it. ❑ *He recognizes enough notation to be able to follow a score.* **8** QUANT If you refer to **scores** of things or people, you are emphasizing that there are very many of them. [WRITTEN, EMPHASIS] [QUANT of pl-n] ❑ *Campaigners lit scores of bonfires in ceremonies to mark the anniversary.* **9** NUM A **score** is twenty or approximately twenty. [WRITTEN] ❑ *A score of countries may be either producing or planning to obtain chemical weapons.* **10** V-T If you **score** a surface with something sharp, you cut a line or number of lines in it. ❑ *Lightly score the surface of the steaks with a sharp cook's knife.* **11** PHRASE If you **keep score** of the number of things that are happening in a certain situation, you count them and record them. ❑ *You can keep score of your baby's movements before birth by recording them on a kick chart.* **12** PHRASE If you **know the score**, you know what the real facts of a situation are and how they affect you, even though you may not like them. [SPOKEN] ❑ *I don't feel sorry for Carl. He knew the score, he knew what he had to do and couldn't do it.* **13** PHRASE You can use **on that score** or **on this score** to refer to something that has just been mentioned, especially an area of difficulty or concern. ❑ *I became pregnant easily. At least I've had no problems on that score.* **14** PHRASE If you **settle a score** or **settle an old score with** someone, you take revenge on them for something they have done in the past. ❑ *The groups had historic scores to settle with each other.* →see **music**

score|board /skɔrbɔrd/ (**scoreboards**) N-COUNT A **scoreboard** is a large board, for example at a sports arena or stadium, which shows the score in a game or competition. ❑ *The figures flash up on the scoreboard.*

scor|er /skɔrər/ (**scorers**) **1** N-COUNT In football, hockey, and many other sports and games, a **scorer** is a player who scores a goal, runs, or points. ❑ *...David Hirst, the scorer of 11 goals this season.* **2** N-COUNT A **scorer** is an official who writes down the score of a game or competition as it is being played.

scorn /skɔrn/ (**scorns, scorning, scorned**) **1** N-UNCOUNT If you treat someone or something **with scorn**, you show contempt for them. ❑ *Researchers greeted the proposal with scorn.* **2** V-T If you **scorn** someone or something, you feel or show contempt for them. ❑ *Several leading officers have quite openly scorned the peace talks.* **3** V-T If you **scorn** something, you refuse to have it or accept it because you think it is not good enough or suitable for you. ❑ *...people who scorned traditional methods.*

scorn|ful /skɔrnfəl/ ADJ If you are **scornful of** someone or something, you show contempt for them. ❑ *He is deeply scornful of politicians.*

scotch /skɒtʃ/ (**scotches, scotching, scotched**) V-T If you **scotch** a rumor, plan, or idea, you put an end to it before it can develop any further. ❑ *They have scotched rumors that they are planning a special London show.*

Scotch /skɒtʃ/ (**Scotches**) N-MASS **Scotch** or **Scotch whisky** is whiskey made in Scotland. ❑ *...a bottle of Scotch.* ● N-COUNT A **Scotch** is a glass of Scotch. ❑ *He poured himself a Scotch.*

scot-free /skɒt fri/ ADV If you say that someone got away **scot-free**, you are emphasizing that they escaped punishment for something that you believe they should have been punished for. [EMPHASIS] [ADV after v] ❑ *Others who were guilty were being allowed to get off scot-free.*

scour /skaʊər/ (**scours, scouring, scoured**) **1** V-T If you **scour** something such as a place or a book, you make a thorough search of it to try to find what you are looking for. ❑ *Rescue crews had scoured an area of 30 square miles.* **2** V-T If you **scour** something such as a sink, floor, or pan, you clean its surface by rubbing it hard with something rough. ❑ *He decided to scour the sink.*

scourge /skɜrdʒ/ (**scourges, scourging, scourged**) **1** N-COUNT A **scourge** is something that causes a lot of trouble or suffering to a group of people. [oft N of n] ❑ *...the best chance in 20 years to end the scourge of terrorism.* **2** V-T If something **scourges** a place or group of people, it causes great pain and suffering to people. ❑ *Economic anarchy scourged the post-war world.*

scout /skaʊt/ (**scouts, scouting, scouted**) **1** N-COUNT A **scout** is someone who is sent to an area of countryside to find out the position of an enemy army. ❑ *They set off, two men out in front as scouts, two behind in case of any attack from the rear.* **2** V-T/V-I If you **scout** somewhere **for** something, you go through that area searching for it. ❑ *I wouldn't have time to scout the area for junk.* ❑ *A team of four was sent to scout for a nuclear test site.*

scowl /skaʊl/ (**scowls, scowling, scowled**) V-I When someone **scowls**, an angry or hostile expression appears on their face. ❑ *He scowled, and slammed the door behind him.* ● N-COUNT **Scowl** is also a noun. ❑ *Chris met the remark with a scowl.*

scram|ble /skræmbəl/ (**scrambles, scrambling, scrambled**) **1** V-I If you **scramble** over rocks or up a hill, you move quickly over them or up it using your hands to help you. ❑ *Tourists were scrambling over the rocks looking for the perfect camera angle.* **2** V-I If you **scramble** to a different place or position, you move there in a hurried, awkward way. ❑ *Ann threw back the covers and scrambled out of bed.* **3** V-I If a number of people **scramble for** something, they compete energetically with each other for it. ❑ *More than three million fans are expected to scramble for tickets.* ● N-COUNT **Scramble** is also a noun. ❑ *...the scramble for jobs.*

❑ 유에스 오픈 골프 대회에서 벤 호건이 287점을 득점해 승리했다. ❑ 로빈 스미스가 167점을 득점했는데 이는 영국인 타자가 이런 크리켓 방식으로 세운 최고 점수였다. **4** 가산명사 점수 ❑ 4 대 1이 최종 점수였다. ❑ 그들은 7 대 3의 점수로 자이언츠를 물리쳤다. **5** 타동사 (승리 등을) 거두다 [문어체] ❑ 그는 변함없는 열정을 바다 보트 경주에 쏟았고, 그 경주에서 많은 성공을 거두었다. **6** 가산명사 (영화 등의) 음악 ❑ 그 춤은 헨리 토규가 창작한 음악에 맞춰 춘다. **7** 가산명사 악보 ❑ 그는 악보를 따라갈 수 있을 만큼 기보법을 충분히 알고 있다. **8** 수량사 수많은 [문어체, 강조] ❑ 운동원들은 기념일을 기리기 위해 의식에서 수많은 모닥불을 피웠다. **9** 수사 이십인 [문어체] ❑ 이십여 국가들이 아마도 화학 무기를 생산하거나 보유할 계획을 하고 있을 것이다. **10** 타동사 칼집을 내다, (칼 등으로) 금을 긋다 ❑ 날카로운 주방용 칼로 스테이크 표면에 살짝 칼집을 내세요. **11** 구 (수를) 세어) 기록하다 ❑ 당신은 태동표에 아기 움직임을 적어 둠으로써 출생 전에 태아의 움직임을 기록할 수 있습니다. **12** 구 사정을 안다 [구어체] ❑ 나는 칼이 안됐다고 생각지 않아. 그는 사정을 알고 있었고, 뭘 해야 할지도, 또 그것을 하지 못하리라는 것도 알고 있었어. **13** 구 그 점에 대해서는 ❑ 나는 쉽게 임신이 되었다. 적어도 그 점에 대해서는 나는 아무 문제가 없었다. **14** 구 원한을 갚다 ❑ 그 단체들은 서로 갚아야 할 역사적인 원한이 있었다.

가산명사 점수판, 득점 게시판 ❑ 숫자가 점수판에 번쩍거리며 나타난다.

1 가산명사 득점자 ❑ 이번 시즌에 11골을 득점한 데이비드 허스트 **2** 가산명사 점수 기록원

1 불가산명사 경멸 ❑ 연구자들은 그 제안을 경멸하는 태도로 받아들였다. **2** 타동사 경멸하다 ❑ 몇몇 고위 관리들은 그 평화 회담을 상당히 공개적으로 경멸했다. **3** 타동사 (경멸하며) 거절하다, 무시하다 ❑ 전통적인 방식을 무시한 사람들

형용사 경멸하는 ❑ 그는 정치인들을 매우 경멸한다.

타동사 잠재우다, 중단시키다 ❑ 그들은 자신들이 런던에서 특별 쇼를 계획하고 있다는 풍문을 잠재웠다.

물질명사 스카치위스키 ❑ 스카치위스키 한 병 ● 가산명사 스카치위스키 한 잔 ❑ 그는 스카치위스키 한 잔을 마시려고 따랐다.

부사 처벌도 안 받고 [강조] ❑ 죄를 지은 다른 사람들은 처벌도 안 받고 풀려났다.

1 타동사 샅샅이 뒤지다 ❑ 구조대원들이 30평방마일에 이르는 지역을 샅샅이 뒤졌다. **2** 타동사 문질러 닦다 ❑ 그는 싱크대를 문질러 닦기로 마음먹었다.

1 가산명사 재앙 ❑ 테러리즘이라는 재앙을 종식할 수 있는 20년 만의 호기 **2** 타동사 재앙을 안기 구다, 극심한 고통을 주다 ❑ 경제적 혼란으로 인해 전후 세계가 극심한 고통을 받았다.

1 가산명사 정찰병 ❑ 정찰병 두 명을 앞서 보내고, 적의 후위 공격에 대비하여 두 명을 뒤에 세우고, 그들은 출발했다. **2** 타동사/자동사 찾아다니다, 정찰하다 ❑ 쓸모없는 물건을 찾아 그 지역을 돌아다닐 시간은 없을 것이다. ❑ 핵 실험 장소를 정찰하기 위해 4인으로 된 팀이 파견되었다.

자동사 얼굴을 찌푸리다 ❑ 그는 얼굴을 찌푸리고, 뒤로 문을 쾅 닫고 나갔다. ● 가산명사 찌푸린 얼굴 ❑ 크리스는 그 말을 듣고 얼굴을 찌푸렸다.

1 자동사 (재빨리) 기어오르다 ❑ 관광객들은 완벽한 카메라 앵글을 위해 바위를 재빨리 기어오르고 있었다. **2** 자동사 허둥대다 ❑ 앤은 침대 커버를 젖힌 후 허둥대며 침대에서 나왔다. **3** 자동사 쟁탈전을 벌이다 ❑ 300만 명 이상의 팬들이 입장권을 구하기 위해 쟁탈전을 벌일 것으로 예상된다. ● 가산명사 쟁탈전 ❑ 일자리를 얻기 위한 쟁탈전 **4** 타동사 (달걀을) 휘저으며 익히다, 스크램블하다 ❑ 토스트를 굽고

a b c d e f g h i j k l m n o p q r s t u v w x y z

A
B

④ V-T If you **scramble** eggs, you break them, mix them together and then heat and stir the mixture in a pan. ❑ *Make the toast and scramble the eggs.* ● **scram|bled** ADJ ❑ *...scrambled eggs and bacon.* **⑤** V-T If a device **scrambles** a radio or telephone message, it interferes with the sound so that the message can only be understood by someone with special equipment. ❑ *The latest machines scramble the messages so that the conversation cannot easily be intercepted.*

달걀을 휘저으며 익히세요. ● 휘저으며 익힌, 스크램블한 형용사 ❑ 스크램블한 계란과 베이컨 **⑤** 타동사 주파수대를 변환하다, 다른 사람이 도청하지 못하도록 전파를 의도적으로 교란시키다 [언론] ❑ 최신 기계는 메시지를 일부러 교란시키기 때문에 다른 사람이 대화 내용을 쉽게 도청할 수 없다.

scrap /skræp/ (scraps, scrapping, scrapped) **①** N-COUNT A **scrap** of something is a very small piece or amount of it. ❑ *A crumpled scrap of paper was found in her handbag.* **②** N-PLURAL **Scraps** are pieces of unwanted food which are thrown away or given to animals. ❑ *...the scraps from the Sunday dinner table.* **③** V-T If you **scrap** something, you get rid of it or cancel it. [JOURNALISM] ❑ *President Hussein called on all countries in the Middle East to scrap nuclear or chemical weapons.* **④** ADJ **Scrap** metal or paper is no longer wanted for its original purpose, but may have some other use. [ADJ n] ❑ *There's always tons of scrap paper in Dad's office.* **⑤** N-UNCOUNT **Scrap** is metal from old or damaged machinery or cars. ❑ *Thousands of tanks, artillery pieces and armored vehicles will be cut up for scrap.*

① 가산명사 조각 ❑ 그녀의 핸드백에서 구겨진 종이 조각이 발견되었다. **② 복수명사 찌꺼기, 부스러기** ❑ 일요일 저녁상에서 남은 음식 찌꺼기 **③ 타동사 폐기하다** [언론] ❑ 후세인 대통령은 중동의 모든 국가들에게 핵무기나 화학 무기를 폐기하라고 요청했다. **④ 형용사 폐품인** ❑ 아빠의 사무실에는 폐지가 항상 산더미처럼 쌓여 있다. **⑤ 불가산명사 고철** ❑ 수천 대의 탱크, 대포, 장갑 차량 등이 고철로 분해될 것이다.

C
D
E

scrap|book /skræpbʊk/ (scrapbooks) N-COUNT A **scrapbook** is a book with empty pages on which you can stick things such as pictures or newspaper articles in order to keep them. ❑ *... a large scrapbook of press clippings and photographs.*

가산명사 스크랩북 ❑ 신문 기사와 사진을 모은 큰 스크랩북

F

scrape /skreɪp/ (scrapes, scraping, scraped) **①** V-T If you **scrape** something from a surface, you remove it, especially by pulling a sharp object over the surface. ❑ *She went round the car scraping the frost off the windows.* **②** V-T/V-I If something **scrapes** against something else, or **scrapes** it, it rubs against it, making a noise or causing slight damage. ❑ *The only sound is that of knives and forks scraping against china.* ❑ *The car hurtled past us, scraping the wall and screeching to a halt.* **③** V-T If you **scrape** a part of your body, you accidentally rub it against something hard and rough, and damage it slightly. ❑ *She stumbled and fell, scraping her palms and knees.*

① 타동사 긁어내다 ❑ 그녀는 차를 한 바퀴 돌며 유리창에서 서리를 긁어내었다. **② 타동사/자동사 긁다** ❑ 칼과 포크가 그릇을 긁을 때 나는 소리밖에 들리지 않는다. ❑ 차는 우리 옆을 쏜살같이 지나며 벽을 긁고는 끽 하며 섰다. **③ 타동사 긁히다, 찰과상을 내다** ❑ 그녀는 비틀거리며 넘어져 손바닥과 무릎이 긁혔다.

G
H

▶**scrape through** PHRASAL VERB If you **scrape through** an examination, you just succeed in passing it. If you **scrape through** a competition or a vote, you just succeed in winning it. ❑ *Both my brothers have university degrees. I just scraped through a couple of A-levels.*

구동사 가까스로 합격하다; 가까스로 이기다 ❑ 우리 형은 둘 다 대학을 졸업했지만 나는 에이(A)-레벨을 두어 과목만 간신히 통과했다.

J

▶**scrape together** PHRASAL VERB If you **scrape together** an amount of money or a number of things, you succeed in obtaining it with difficulty. ❑ *They only just managed to scrape the money together.*

구동사 간신히 모으다 ❑ 그들은 그 돈을 간신히 모았다.

K

scrap|heap /skræphip/ also **scrap heap** **①** N-SING If you say that someone has been thrown on **the scrapheap**, you mean that they have been forced to leave their job by an uncaring employer and are unlikely to get other work. ❑ *Thousands of miners have been thrown on the scrapheap with no jobs and no prospects.* **②** N-SING If things such as machines or weapons are thrown on **the scrapheap**, they are thrown away because they are no longer needed. ❑ *Thousands of Europe's tanks and guns are going to the scrap heap.*

① 단수명사 쓰레기더미 ❑ 수천 명의 광부들이 일자리도 앞날도 없이 일방적으로 해고당했다. **② 단수명사 (비유적) 쓰레기 더미** ❑ 유럽에서 수천 대의 탱크와 총이 폐기 처분되다시피 했다.

L
M
N

scratch /skrætʃ/ (scratches, scratching, scratched) **①** V-T If you **scratch yourself**, you rub your fingernails against your skin because it is itching. ❑ *He scratched himself under his arm.* ❑ *The old man lifted his cardigan to scratch his side.* **②** V-T If a sharp object **scratches** someone or something, it makes small shallow cuts on their skin or surface. ❑ *The branches tore at my jacket and scratched my hands and face.* **③** N-COUNT **Scratches** on someone or something are small shallow cuts. ❑ *The seven-year-old was found crying with scratches on his face and neck.* **④** PHRASE If you do something **from scratch**, you do it without making use of anything that has been done before. ❑ *Building a home from scratch can be both exciting and challenging.* **⑤** PHRASE If you say that someone is **scratching** their **head**, you mean that they are thinking hard and trying to solve a problem or puzzle. ❑ *The Institute spends a lot of time scratching its head about how to boost American productivity.*

① 타동사 긁다 ❑ 그가 겨드랑이를 긁었다. ❑ 그 노인은 카디건을 들어 올리고 옆구리를 긁었다. **② 타동사 긁다, 할퀴다** ❑ 나뭇가지들에 나는 재킷이 잡아뜯기고 손과 얼굴이 긁혔다. **③ 가산명사 긁힌 자국** ❑ 일곱 살짜리 아이는 얼굴과 목에 긁힌 자국이 난 상태에서 울고 있는 채로 발견되었다. **④ 구 완전 처음부터, 아무도 없는 상태에서** ❑ 완전 처음부터 집을 짓는 것은 흥미진진하면서도 도전적이다. **⑤ 구 뒤통수를 긁적이며 고민하다** ❑ 연구소는 미국의 생산성을 어떻게 향상시킬까에 대해 고민하며 많은 시간을 보낸다.

O
P
Q

scratch card (scratch cards) also **scratchcard** N-COUNT A **scratch card** is a card with hidden words or symbols on it. You scratch the surface off to reveal the words or symbols and find out if you have won a prize.

가산명사 긁는 복권

R
S

scrawl /skrɔl/ (scrawls, scrawling, scrawled) **①** V-T If you **scrawl** something, you write it in a careless and messy way. ❑ *Someone had scrawled "Scum" on his car.* **②** N-VAR You can refer to writing that looks careless and messy as a **scrawl**. ❑ *The letter was handwritten, in a hasty, barely decipherable scrawl.*

① 타동사 끼적이다, 휘갈겨 쓰다 ❑ 그는 아내에게 급히 메모를 끼적였다. ❑ 누군가가 그의 차에 '인간쓰레기'라고 휘갈겨 놓았었다. **② 가산명사 또는 불가산명사 졸필, 휘갈겨 쓴 글씨** ❑ 그 편지는 서둘러 써서 거의 읽을 수 없는 졸필로 쓰여 있었다.

T

scrawny /skrɔni/ (scrawnier, scrawniest) ADJ If you describe a person or animal as **scrawny**, you mean that they look unattractive because they are so thin. [DISAPPROVAL] ❑ *...a scrawny woman with dyed black hair.*

형용사 비쩍 굶은 [탐탁잖음] ❑ 검정색으로 머리를 염색한 비쩍 굶은 여자

U

scream ◆◇◇ /skrim/ (screams, screaming, screamed) **①** V-I When someone **screams**, they make a very loud, high-pitched cry, for example because they are in pain or are very frightened. ❑ *Women were screaming; some of the houses nearest the bridge were on fire.* ● N-COUNT **Scream** is also a noun. ❑ *Hilda let out a scream.* **②** V-T If you **scream** something, you shout it in a loud, high-pitched voice. ❑ *"Brigid!" she screamed. "Get up!"*

① 자동사 비명을 지르다 ❑ 여자들이 비명을 지르고 있었다. 다리에 근접한 집 몇 채가 불타고 있었다. ● 가산명사 비명 ❑ 힐다가 비명을 질렀다. **② 타동사 소리 지르다** ❑ "브리지드!" 그녀가 소리 질렀다. "일어나!"

V
W

screech /skritʃ/ (screeches, screeching, screeched) **①** V-I If a vehicle **screeches** somewhere or if its tires **screech**, its tires make an unpleasant high-pitched noise on the road. ❑ *A black Mercedes screeched to a halt beside the helicopter.* **②** V-T/V-I When you **screech**, or **screech** something, you shout it in a loud, unpleasant, high-pitched voice. ❑ *"Get me some water, Jeremy!" I screeched.* ● N-COUNT **Screech** is also a noun. ❑ *The figure gave a screech.* **③** V-I When a bird, animal, or thing **screeches**, it makes a loud, unpleasant, high-pitched noise. ❑ *A macaw screeched at him from its perch.* ● N-COUNT **Screech** is also a noun. ❑ *He heard the screech of brakes.*

① 자동사 끼익 하는 소리를 내다 ❑ 검정색 메르세데스가 헬리콥터 옆에 끼익 하고 섰다. **② 타동사/자동사 날카로운 소리로 말하다** ❑ "물 좀 갖다 줘, 제레미!"라고 나는 날카롭게 소리를 질렀다. ● 가산명사 날카로운 고함 ❑ 그 인물이 날카롭게 외쳤다. **③ 자동사 날카로운 소리를 내다** ❑ 마코앵무새가 홰에 앉은 채 그를 향해 날카로운 소리를 냈다. ● 가산명사 날카로운 소리 ❑ 그는 브레이크가 끼익 하는 소리를 들었다.

X
Y
Z

screen ◆◇◇ /skriːn/ (**screens, screening, screened**) **1** N-COUNT A **screen** is a flat vertical surface on which pictures or words are shown. Television sets and computers have screens, and movies are shown on a screen in movie theaters. →see also **widescreen 2** N-SING You can refer to movie or television as the **screen**. [the N, also on/off N] □ *Many viewers have strong opinions about violence on the screen.* **3** V-T When a movie or a television program **is screened**, it is shown in the movie theater or broadcast on television. □ *The series is likely to be screened in January.* ● **screen|ing** (**screenings**) N-COUNT □ *The film-makers will be present at the screenings to introduce their works.* **4** N-COUNT A **screen** is a vertical panel which can be moved around. It is used to keep cold air away from part of a room, or to create a smaller area within a room. □ *They put a screen in front of me so I couldn't see what was going on.* **5** V-T If something **is screened by** another thing, it is behind it and hidden by it. [usu passive] □ *Most of the road behind the hotel was screened by a block of flats.* **6** V-I To **screen for** a disease means to examine people to make sure that they do not have it. □ *...a quick saliva test that would screen for people at risk of tooth decay.* ● **screen|ing** N-VAR □ *Britain has an enviable record on breast screening for cancer.* **7** V-T When an organization **screens** people who apply to join it, it investigates them to make sure that they are not likely to cause problems. □ *They will screen all their candidates.* **8** V-T To **screen** people or luggage means to check them using special equipment to make sure they are not carrying a weapon or a bomb. □ *The airline had not been searching unaccompanied baggage by hand, but only screening it on X-ray machines.* →see **computer, television**

screen|play /skriːnpleɪ/ (**screenplays**) N-COUNT A **screenplay** is the words to be spoken in a movie, and instructions about what will be seen in it.

screensav|er /skriːnseɪvər/ (**screensavers**) also **screen saver** N-COUNT A **screensaver** is a moving picture which appears on a computer screen when the computer is not used for a while. [COMPUTING]

screen|writer /skriːnraɪtər/ (**screenwriters**) N-COUNT A **screenwriter** is a person who writes screenplays.

screw /skruː/ (**screws, screwing, screwed**) **1** N-COUNT A **screw** is a metal object similar to a nail, with a raised spiral line around it. You turn a screw using a screwdriver so that it goes through two things, for example two pieces of wood, and fastens them together. □ *Each bracket is fixed to the wall with just four screws.* **2** V-T/V-I If you **screw** something somewhere or if it **screws** somewhere, you fix it in place by means of a screw or screws. □ *I had screwed the shelf on the wall myself.* □ *Screw down any loose floorboards.* **3** ADJ A **screw** lid or fitting is one that has a raised spiral line on the inside or outside of it, so that it can be fixed in place by twisting. [ADJ n] □ *...an ordinary jam jar with a screw lid.* **4** V-T/V-I If you **screw** something somewhere or if it **screws** somewhere, you fix it in place by twisting it around and around. □ *"Yes, I know that," Kelly said, screwing the silencer onto the pistol.* □ *Screw down the lid fairly tightly.* **5** V-T If you **screw** something such as a piece of paper into a ball, you squeeze it or twist it tightly so that it is in the shape of a ball. □ *He screwed the paper into a ball and tossed it into the fire.* **6** V-T If you **screw** your face or your eyes **into** a particular expression, you tighten the muscles of your face to form that expression, for example because you are in pain or because the light is too bright. □ *He screwed his face into an expression of mock pain.* **7** V-RECIP If someone **screws** someone else or if two people **screw**, they have sex together. [INFORMAL, VULGAR] □ *"Are you screwing her?" she said.* **8** V-T Some people use **screw** in expressions such as **screw you** or **screw that** to show that they are not concerned about someone or something or that they feel contempt for them. [INFORMAL, VULGAR, FEELINGS] [only imper] □ *Something inside me snapped. "Well, screw you then!"* **9** V-T If someone **screws** something, especially money, **out of** you, they get it from you by putting pressure on you. [mainly BRIT, INFORMAL] □ *After decades of rich nations screwing money out of poor nations, it's about time some went the other way.*

▶**screw up 1** PHRASAL VERB If you **screw up** your eyes or your face, you tighten your eye or face muscles, for example because you are in pain or because the light is too bright. □ *She had screwed up her eyes, as if she found the sunshine too bright.* □ *Close your eyes and screw them up tight.* **2** PHRASAL VERB If you **screw up** a piece of paper, you squeeze it tightly so that it becomes very creased and no longer flat, usually when you are throwing it away. □ *He would start writing to his family and would screw the letter up in frustration.* **3** PHRASAL VERB To **screw** something **up**, or to **screw up**, means to cause something to fail or be spoiled. [INFORMAL] □ *You can't open the window because it screws up the air conditioning.* □ *Get out. Haven't you screwed things up enough already!*

screw|driver /skruːdraɪvər/ (**screwdrivers**) N-COUNT A **screwdriver** is a tool that is used for turning screws. It consists of a metal rod with a flat or cross-shaped end that fits into the top of the screw.

screwed up ADJ If you say that someone is **screwed up**, you mean that they are very confused or worried, or that they have psychological problems. [INFORMAL] □ *He was really screwed up with his emotional problems.*

scrib|ble /skrɪbᵊl/ (**scribbles, scribbling, scribbled**) **1** V-T If you **scribble** something, you write it quickly and roughly. □ *She scribbled a note to tell Mom she'd gone out.* **2** V-I To **scribble** means to make meaningless marks or rough drawings using a pencil or pen. □ *When Caroline was five she scribbled on a wall.* **3** N-VAR **Scribble** is something that has been written or drawn quickly and roughly. □ *I'm sorry what I wrote was such a scribble.*

scrip /skrɪp/ (**scrips**) N-COUNT A **scrip** is a certificate which shows that an investor owns part of a share or stock. [BUSINESS] □ *The cash or scrip would be offered as part of a pro rata return of capital to shareholders.*

script ◆◇◇ /skrɪpt/ (**scripts, scripting, scripted**) **1** N-COUNT The **script** of a play, movie, or television program is the written version of it. □ *Jenny's writing a film script.* **2** V-T The person who **scripts** a movie or a radio or television play writes

───

1 가산명사 화면 **2** 단수명사 화면 □ 많은 시청자들은 화면 내의 폭력에 대해 확고한 의견을 가지고 있다. **3** 타동사 상영되다; 방영되다 □ 그 시리즈는 1월에 방영될 것 같다. ● 상영; 방영 가산명사 □ 영화 제작자들이 작품을 소개하기 위해 영화 상영 때 참석할 것이다. **4** 가산명사 칸막이, 가리개 □ 그들이 내 앞에 칸막이를 갖다 놓아서 나는 무슨 일이 일어나고 있는지 알 수가 없었다. **5** 타동사 가려지다 □ 호텔 뒤의 길 대부분이 아파트 건물에 가려져 있었다. **6** 자동사 검사하다 □ 충치의 위험이 있는 사람들을 검사하기 위한 간단한 타액 검사 ● 검사 가산명사 또는 불가산명사 □ 영국에서는 유방암 검사가 부러울 정도로 잘 실시되고 있다. **7** 타동사 심사하다 □ 그들은 모든 후보를 심사할 것이다. **8** 타동사 검사하다 □ 그 항공사는 비휴대성 화물을 손으로 뒤지지 않고 엑스-선 기계로만 검사를 해 왔다.

가산명사 영화 대본, 시나리오

가산명사 화면보호기 [컴퓨터]

가산명사 시나리오 작가

1 가산명사 나사 □ 각 까치발은 단지 세 개의 나사로만 벽에 고정된다. **2** 타동사/자동사 나사로 고정하다 □ 내가 직접 나사로 선반을 벽에 고정했었다. □ 느슨한 모든 마루청을 나사로 고정하세요. **3** 형용사 돌려 따는 □ 돌려 따는 뚜껑이 있는 평범한 잼 병 **4** 타동사/자동사 돌려서 고정하다 □ "그래, 나도 그건 알아." 소음기를 총구에 돌려 끼면서 켈리는 말했다. □ 뚜껑을 제법 세게 돌려서 조이세요. **5** 타동사 구기다 □ 그는 종이를 공 모양으로 구겨 불 속에 던져 넣었다. **6** 타동사 -한 표정으로 찡그리다 □ 그는 짐짓 아프다는 표정을 지으며 얼굴을 찡그렸다. **7** 상호동사 성교하다 [비격식체, 비속어] □ "그년하고 같이 자는 거야?"라고 그녀가 물었다. **8** 타동사 엿 먹다 [비격식체, 비속어, 감정 개입] □ 내 안에서 뭔가가 폭발했다. "그럼 엿이나 먹어라!" **9** 타동사 -을 뜯어내다 [주로 영국영어, 비격식체] □ 부유한 나라들이 가난한 국가들로부터 돈을 수십 년간 뜯어낸 뒤 이제 그 반대의 상황이 일어날 때이다.

1 구동사 -을 찡그리다 □ 그녀는 마치 햇빛이 너무 밝다는 듯이 눈을 꼭 감고 찡그렸다. □ 눈을 꼭 감고 찡그려 보세요. **2** 구동사 완전히 구기다 □ 그는 가족에게 편지를 쓰기 시작했다가 마음에 안 들어 그것을 완전히 구겨 버리곤 했다. **3** 구동사 망치다 [비격식체] □ 에어컨 가동에 문제가 생기므로 창문을 열면 안 된다. □ 나가. 이미 충분히 일을 망쳐 놓지 않았어!

가산명사 드라이버

형용사 맛이 간, 머리가 돈 [비격식체] □ 그는 감정적인 문제들로 완전히 맛이 간 상태였다.

1 타동사 끼적이다, 휘갈겨 쓰다 □ 그녀는 어머니에게 자신이 나갔다는 것을 알리기 위해 메모를 휘갈겨 썼다. **2** 자동사 낙서하다 □ 캐럴린이 다섯 살이었을 때 벽에 낙서를 했다. **3** 가산명사 또는 불가산명사 악필 □ 제가 쓴 것이 그렇게 악필이어서 죄송합니다.

가산명사 가증권 [경제] □ 현금 혹은 가증권이 주주들에게 자본 투자에 비례한 배당금의 일부로 제공될 수도 있다.

1 가산명사 대본 □ 제니는 영화 대본을 쓰고 있다. **2** 타동사 대본을 쓰다 □ 두 영화 모두의 대본을 쓰고 감독한 제임스 카메론 **3** 가산명사 또는 불가산명사

it. ❑ *...James Cameron, who scripted and directed both films.* ❸ N-VAR You can refer to a particular system of writing as a particular **script**. [usu adj N] ❑ *...a text in the Malay language but written in Arabic script.* ❹ N-VAR **Script** is handwriting in which the letters are joined together. ❑ *When you're writing in script, there are four letters of the alphabet that you can't complete in one stroke.* →see **animation**

문자 ❑ 말레이시아 어이지만 아랍어 문자로 쓰인 텍스트 ❹ 가산명사 또는 불가산명사 필기체 ❑ 필기체를 쓸 때의 획으로 끝낼 수 없는 알파벳 글자가 네 개 있다.

| Word Link | script ≈ writing : manu*script*, *scripture*, tran*script* |

scrip|ture /skrɪptʃər/ (**scriptures**) N-VAR **Scripture** or **the scriptures** refers to writings that are regarded as holy in a particular religion, for example the Bible in Christianity. ❑ *...a quote from scripture.* →see **religion**

가산명사 또는 불가산명사 경전 ❑ 경전에서 따온 구절

scroll /skroʊl/ (**scrolls, scrolling, scrolled**) ❶ N-COUNT A **scroll** is a long roll of paper or a similar material with writing on it. ❑ *Ancient scrolls were found in caves by the Dead Sea.* ❷ N-COUNT A **scroll** is a painted or carved decoration made to look like a scroll. ❑ *...a handsome suite of chairs incised with Grecian scrolls.* ❸ V-I If you **scroll** through text on a computer screen, you move the text up or down to find the information that you need. [COMPUTING] ❑ *I scrolled down to find "United States of America."*

❶ 가산명사 두루마리 ❑ 사해 옆의 동굴들에서 오래된 두루마리들이 발견되었다. ❷ 가산명사 소용돌이무늬 ❑ 고대 그리스식 소용돌이무늬가 새겨진 멋진 의자의 세트 ❸ 자동사 (컴퓨터) 스크롤하다 [컴퓨터] ❑ '미국'을 찾기 위해 아래로 스크롤했다.

scroll bar (**scroll bars**) N-COUNT On a computer screen, a **scroll bar** is a long thin box along one edge of a window, which you click on with the mouse to move the text up, down, or across the window. [COMPUTING]

가산명사 스크롤바 [컴퓨터]

scrounge /skraʊndʒ/ (**scrounges, scrounging, scrounged**) V-T If you say that someone **scrounges** something such as food or money, you disapprove of them because they get it by asking for it, rather than by buying it or earning it. [INFORMAL, DISAPPROVAL] ❑ *We managed to scrounge every piece of gear you requested.*

타동사 우려내다 [비격식체, 탐탁찮음] ❑ 당신이 요청한 모든 장비를 어떻게 여기저기서 우려냈습니다.

scrub /skrʌb/ (**scrubs, scrubbing, scrubbed**) ❶ V-T If you **scrub** something, you rub it hard in order to clean it, using a stiff brush and water. ❑ *Surgeons began to scrub their hands and arms with soap and water before operating.* ● N-SING **Scrub** is also a noun. ❑ *The walls needed a good scrub.* ❷ V-T If you **scrub** dirt or stains **off** something, you remove them by rubbing hard. ❑ *I started to scrub off the dirt.* ❸ N-UNCOUNT **Scrub** consists of low trees and bushes, especially in an area that has very little rain. ❑ *There is an area of scrub and woodland beside the railway.*

❶ 타동사 문지르다 ❑ 의사들은 수술하기 전에 손과 팔을 비누와 물로 문질러 씻었다. ● 단수명사 문지르기 ❑ 벽들을 세게 문질러 청소를 해야 했다. ❷ 타동사 문질러 닦아내다 ❑ 나는 흙을 문질러서 닦아내기 시작했다. ❸ 불가산명사 덤불, 관목 ❑ 철길 옆에 덤불과 수풀로 이루어진 지역이 있다.

scruffy /skrʌfi/ (**scruffier, scruffiest**) ADJ Someone or something that is **scruffy** is dirty and messy. ❑ *...a young man, pale, scruffy and unshaven.*

형용사 꾀죄죄한 ❑ 창백하고 꾀죄죄하고 면도를 안 한 젊은 남자

scrunch /skrʌntʃ/ (**scrunches, scrunching, scrunched**)

▶**scrunch up** PHRASAL VERB If you **scrunch** something **up**, you squeeze it or bend it so that it is no longer in its natural shape and is often crushed. ❑ *She scrunched up three pages of notes and threw them in the bin.*

구동사 구기다 ❑ 그녀는 메모지 세 장을 구긴 다음 쓰레기통에 던져 넣었다.

scru|ple /skrup³l/ (**scruples**) N-VAR **Scruples** are moral principles or beliefs that make you unwilling to do something that seems wrong. ❑ *...a man with no moral scruples.*

가산명사 또는 불가산명사 양심 ❑ 어떤 도덕적 양심도 없는 남자

scru|pu|lous /skrupyələs/ ❶ ADJ Someone who is **scrupulous** takes great care to do what is fair, honest, or morally right. [APPROVAL] ❑ *You're being very scrupulous, but to what end?* ❑ *I have been scrupulous about telling them the dangers.* ❷ ADJ **Scrupulous** means thorough, exact, and careful about details. ❑ *Both readers commend Knutson for his scrupulous attention to detail.*

❶ 형용사 양심적인 [마음에 듦] ❑ 당신은 굉장히 양심적이지만 그러면 뭐해죠? ❑ 나는 양심적으로 그들에게 계속 위험을 알려 주었다. ❷ 형용사 세심한, 꼼꼼한 ❑ 두 독자 모두 크넛슨이 세부적인 내용을 꼼꼼하게 챙긴 것에 대해 칭찬한다.

scru|ti|nize /skrutɪnaɪz/ (**scrutinizes, scrutinizing, scrutinized**) [BRIT also **scrutinise**] V-T If you **scrutinize** something, you examine it very carefully, often to find out some information from it or about it. ❑ *Her purpose was to scrutinize his features to see if he was an honest man.*

[영국영어 scrutinise] 타동사 면밀히 관찰하다, 세심히 조사하다 ❑ 그녀의 목표는 그의 생김새를 면밀히 관찰하여 그가 정직한 남자인지를 알아내는 것이었다.

scru|ti|ny /skrut³ni/ N-UNCOUNT If a person or thing is under **scrutiny**, they are being studied or observed very carefully. ❑ *His private life came under media scrutiny.*

불가산명사 면밀한 관찰, 정밀 조사 ❑ 그의 개인 생활이 언론의 면밀한 관찰을 받게 되었다.

scu|ba div|ing /skubə daɪvɪŋ/ N-UNCOUNT **Scuba diving** is the activity of swimming underwater using special breathing equipment. The equipment consists of cylinders of air which you carry on your back and which are connected to your mouth by rubber tubes. →see Picture Dictionary: scuba diving

불가산명사 스쿠버다이빙

scuf|fle /skʌf³l/ (**scuffles, scuffling, scuffled**) ❶ N-COUNT A **scuffle** is a short, disorganized fight or struggle. ❑ *Violent scuffles broke out between rival groups demonstrating for and against independence.* ❷ V-RECIP If people **scuffle**, they fight for a short time in a disorganized way. ❑ *Police scuffled with some of the protesters.*

❶ 가산명사 드잡이, 난투 ❑ 독립을 찬성 혹은 반대하는 경쟁 집단들 사이에서 폭력적인 난투가 벌어졌다. ❷ 상호동사 드잡이하다, 난투를 벌이다 ❑ 경찰이 일부 시위자들과 난투를 벌였다.

sculpt /skʌlpt/ (**sculpts, sculpting, sculpted**) ❶ V-T When an artist **sculpts** something, they carve or shape it out of a material such as stone or clay. ❑ *An artist sculpted a full-size replica of her head.* ❷ V-T If something **is sculpted**, it is made into a particular shape. ❑ *More familiar landscapes have been sculpted by surface erosion.*

❶ 타동사 조각하다 ❑ 한 미술가가 그녀의 머리를 동일한 크기로 조각했다. ❷ 타동사 조각되다, 형성되다 ❑ 보다 익숙한 경관들이 지표 풍화 작용에 의해 만들어졌다.

Picture Dictionary scuba diving

hose
wet suit
mouthpiece
diver
scuba mask
flippers
air tank
pressure gauge

sculp|tor /skʌlptər/ (**sculptors**) N-COUNT A **sculptor** is someone who creates sculptures.

가산명사 조각가

sculp|ture /skʌlptʃər/ (**sculptures**) ◼ N-VAR A **sculpture** is a work of art that is produced by carving or shaping stone, wood, clay, or other materials. ❑ *...stone sculptures of figures and animals.* ◼ N-UNCOUNT **Sculpture** is the art of creating sculptures. ❑ *Both studied sculpture.*

◼ 가산명사 또는 불가산명사 조각 ❑ 사람과 동물을 조각한 석상들 ◼ 불가산명사 조각술 ❑ 둘 다 조각을 공부했다.

scum /skʌm/ ◼ N-PLURAL If you refer to people as **scum**, you are expressing your feelings of dislike and disgust for them. [INFORMAL, DISAPPROVAL] ❑ *She never would have even spoken to scum like him when Mom was alive.* ◼ N-UNCOUNT **Scum** is a layer of a dirty or unpleasant-looking substance on the surface of a liquid. ❑ *...scum marks around the bath.*

◼ 복수명사 인간쓰레기 [비격식체, 탐탁찮음] ❑ 엄마가 살아 있을 당시에는 그녀는 그와 같은 인간쓰레기에는 말조차 걸지 않았을 것이다. ◼ 불가산명사 버캐, 더껑이 ❑ 욕조 주변의 때가 엉긴 자국들

scup|per /skʌpər/ (**scuppers, scuppering, scuppered**) V-T To **scupper** a plan or attempt means to spoil it completely. [mainly BRIT, JOURNALISM] ❑ *Any increase in the female retirement age would scupper the plans of women like Gwen Davis.*

타동사 망치다 [주로 영국영어, 언론] ❑ 여성 은퇴 연령의 증가는 그웬 데이비스 같은 여성들의 계획을 망칠 것이다.

scur|ry /skʌri, BRIT skʌri/ (**scurries, scurrying, scurried**) V-I When people or small animals **scurry** somewhere, they move there quickly and hurriedly, especially because they are frightened. [WRITTEN] ❑ *The attack began, sending residents scurrying for cover.*

자동사 허둥지둥 달리다, 허둥대다 [문어체] ❑ 공격이 개시되고 주민들은 숨을 곳을 찾아 허둥거렸다.

scut|tle /skʌtᵊl/ (**scuttles, scuttling, scuttled**) ◼ V-I When people or small animals **scuttle** somewhere, they run there with short quick steps. ❑ *Two very small children scuttled away in front of them.* ◼ V-T To **scuttle** a plan or a proposal means to make it fail or cause it to stop. ❑ *Such threats could scuttle the peace conference.*

◼ 자동사 종종걸음으로 달리다 ❑ 두 명의 아주 어린 아이들이 그들 앞을 종종 걸음으로 달려갔다. ◼ 타동사 무산시키다 ❑ 그런 위협은 평화 회담을 무산시킬 수도 있다.

sea ♦♦◇ /si/ (**seas**) ◼ N-SING The **sea** is the salty water that covers about three-quarters of the earth's surface. [the N, also by N] ❑ *Most of the kids have never seen the sea.* ◼ N-PLURAL You use **seas** when you are describing the sea at a particular time or in a particular area. [LITERARY] ❑ *He drowned after 30 minutes in the rough seas.* ◼ N-COUNT; N-IN-NAMES A **sea** is a large area of salty water that is part of an ocean or is surrounded by land. ❑ *...the North Sea.* ◼ PHRASE **At sea** means on or under the sea, far away from land. ❑ *The boats remain at sea for an average of ten days at a time.* ◼ PHRASE If you go or look out **to sea**, you go or look across the sea. ❑ *...fishermen who go to sea for two weeks at a time.*

◼ 단수명사 바다 ❑ 대부분의 아이들은 바다를 본 적이 없다. ◼ 복수명사 바다 [문어체] ❑ 그는 거친 바다에서 30분을 버티다 익사했다. ◼ 가산명사; 이름명사 바다, -해(海) ❑ 북해 ◼ 구 바다에 ❑ 그 배들은 한 번 나가면 평균 10일간 바다에서 머문다. ◼ 구 바다로 ❑ 한 번 나가면 바다에서 2주를 보내는 어부들

Word Partnership	sea의 연어
ADJ.	**calm** sea, **deep** sea ◼
N.	sea **air**, sea **coast**, **land and** sea, sea **voyage** ◼
PREP.	**above** the sea, **across** the sea, **below** the sea, **beneath** the sea, **by** sea, **from** the sea, **into** the sea, **near** the sea, **over** the sea ◼

sea|bed /sibɛd/ also **sea bed** N-SING The **seabed** is the ground under the sea. ❑ *The wreck was raised from the seabed in June 2000.*

단수명사 해저 ❑ 그 잔해를 해저에서 2000년 6월에 꺼냈다.

sea change (**sea changes**) N-COUNT A **sea change** in someone's attitudes or behavior is a complete change. ❑ *A sea change has taken place in young people's attitudes to their parents.*

가산명사 상전벽해의 변화, 완전한 변모 ❑ 젊은이들의 부모에 대한 태도가 완전히 바뀌었다.

sea|food /sifud/ N-UNCOUNT **Seafood** is shellfish such as lobsters, mussels, and crabs, and sometimes other sea creatures that you can eat. ❑ *...a seafood restaurant.*

불가산명사 해산물 ❑ 해산물 식당

sea|front /sifrʌnt/ (**seafronts**) N-COUNT The **seafront** is the part of a seaside town that is nearest to the sea. It usually consists of a road with buildings that face the sea. ❑ *They decided to meet on the seafront.*

가산명사 해안 지구, 해안 도로 ❑ 그들은 해안 지구에서 만나기로 했다.

sea|gull /sigʌl/ (**seagulls**) N-COUNT A **seagull** is a common kind of bird with white or gray feathers.

가산명사 갈매기

seal
① CLOSING
② ANIMAL

① seal ♦◇◇ /sil/ (**seals, sealing, sealed**) ◼ V-T When you **seal** an envelope, you close it by folding part of it over and sticking it down, so that it cannot be opened without being torn. ❑ *He sealed the envelope and put on a stamp.* ❑ *Write your letter and seal it in a blank envelope.* ◼ V-T If you **seal** a container or an opening, you cover it with something in order to prevent air, liquid, or other material from getting in or out. If you **seal** something **in** a container, you put it inside and then close the container tightly. ❑ *She merely filled the containers, sealed them with a cork, and pasted on labels.* ❑ *A woman picks them up and seals them in plastic bags.* ◼ N-COUNT The **seal** on a container or opening is the part where it has been sealed. ❑ *When assembling the pie, wet the edges where the two crusts join, to form a seal.* ◼ N-COUNT A **seal** is a device or a piece of material, for example in a machine, which closes an opening tightly so that air, liquid, or other substances cannot get in or out. [oft N on n] ❑ *Check seals on fridges and freezers regularly.* ◼ N-COUNT A **seal** is something such as a piece of sticky paper or wax that is fixed to a container or door and must be broken before the container or door can be opened. [oft N on n] ❑ *The seal on the box broke when it fell from its hiding-place.* ◼ N-COUNT A **seal** is a special mark or design, for example on a document, representing someone or something. It may be used to show that something is genuine or officially approved. ❑ *...a supply of note paper bearing the Presidential seal.* ◼ V-T If someone in authority **seals** an area, they stop people entering or passing through it, for example by placing barriers in the way. ❑ *The soldiers were deployed to help paramilitary police seal the border.* ● PHRASAL VERB **Seal off** means the same as **seal**. ❑ *Police and troops sealed off the area after the attack.* ◼ V-T To **seal** something means to make it definite or confirm how it is going to be. [WRITTEN] ❑ *McLaren are close to sealing a deal with Renault.* ❑ *A General Election will be held which will seal his destiny one way or the other.*
→see **can**

◼ 타동사 봉하다 ❑ 그는 봉투를 봉하고는 우표를 붙였다. ❑ 편지를 써서 빈 봉투에 넣어 봉하세요. ◼ 타동사 밀봉하다 ❑ 그녀는 단지 용기에 내용물을 채워 넣고 코르크 마개로 밀봉한 다음 라벨을 풀로 붙이는 일만 했다. ❑ 한 여자가 그것들을 주운 다음 플라스틱 봉지에 넣어 단단히 봉한다. ◼ 가산명사 봉인된 부분 ❑ 파이를 합칠 때 껍질 부분이 겹쳐지는 가장자리에 물을 해서 단단히 맞물게 하세요. ◼ 가산명사 봉입부, 밀봉 부분 ❑ 냉장고와 냉동고의 밀봉 부분을 주기적으로 확인하세요. ◼ 가산명사 봉인 ❑ 숨겨 놓은 장소에서 떨어지면서 상자의 봉인이 부서졌다. ◼ 가산명사 도장, 인장 ❑ 대통령 직인이 찍힌 메모지 한 뭉치 ◼ 타동사 봉쇄하다 ❑ 의용 경찰들이 국경을 봉쇄하는 것을 돕기 위해 군인들이 배치되었다. ● 구동사 봉쇄하다 ❑ 그 공격이 있은 후 경찰과 군인이 그 지역을 봉쇄했다. ◼ 타동사 확정하다 [문어체] ❑ 맥라렌이 르노사와 계약을 거의 확정 짓는 단계이다. ❑ 그의 운명을 양단 간에 확정 지을 총선거가 치러질 것이다.

►seal off 1 PHRASAL VERB If one object or area **is sealed off** from another, there is a physical barrier between them, so that nothing can pass between them. ❏ *Windows are usually sealed off.* 2 →see **seal** 7

1 구동사 봉쇄되다 ❏ 창문은 대개 밀봉한다.

② **seal** /siːl/ (**seals**) N-COUNT A **seal** is a large animal with a rounded body and flat legs called flippers. Seals eat fish and live in and near the sea, usually in cold parts of the world.

가산명사 바다표범

sea level also **sea-level** N-UNCOUNT **Sea level** is the average level of the sea with respect to the land. The height of mountains or other areas is calculated in relation to **sea level**. ❏ *The stadium was 2275 meters above sea level.* ❏ *The whole place is at sea level.*

불가산명사 해수면 ❏ 그 경기장은 해발 고도 2,275미터에 위치하고 있었다. ❏ 그 곳 전체가 해수면 높이에 있다.

seam /siːm/ (**seams**) 1 N-COUNT A **seam** is a line of stitches which joins two pieces of cloth together. ❏ *The skirt ripped along a seam.* 2 N-COUNT A **seam** of coal is a long, narrow layer of it underneath the ground. ❏ *The average UK coal seam is one meter thick.* 3 PHRASE If something **is coming apart at the seams** or is **falling apart at the seams**, it is no longer working properly and may soon stop working completely. ❏ *Britain's university system is in danger of falling apart at the seams.* 4 PHRASE If a place is very full, you can say that it **is bursting at the seams.** ❏ *The hotels of Warsaw, Prague and Budapest were bursting at the seams.*

1 가산명사 솔기 ❏ 치마가 솔기 부분이 죽 터져 있었다. 2 가산명사 (석탄의 맥층) 층 ❏ 영국의 석탄층은 평균 두께가 1미터이다. 3 구 와해되다 ❏ 영국의 대학 시스템이 와해될 위험에 처해 있다. 4 구 초만원이다, 터져 나갈 지경이다 ❏ 바르샤바, 프라하, 부다페스트의 호텔들은 초만원이었다.

sea|man /siːmən/ (**seamen**) N-COUNT A **seaman** is a sailor, especially one who is not an officer. ❏ *The men emigrate to work as seamen.*

가산명사 선원 ❏ 남자들은 선원 생활을 하기 위해 이민을 간다.

seam|less /siːmlɪs/ ADJ You use **seamless** to describe something that has no breaks or gaps in it or which continues without stopping. ❏ *It was a seamless procession of wonderful electronic music.* ● **seam|less|ly** ADV [ADV with v] ❏ *It's a class move, allowing new and old to blend seamlessly.*

형용사 천의무봉의, 매끄러운 ❏ 훌륭한 전자 음악 여러 곡이 매끄럽게 이어졌다. ● 부사 천의무봉으로, 매끄럽게 ❏ 옛것과 새것이 매끄럽게 섞이도록 한 훌륭한 조치이다.

search ♦♦◇ /sɜːrtʃ/ (**searches, searching, searched**) 1 V-I If you **search for** something or someone, you look carefully for them. ❏ *The Turkish security forces have started searching for the missing men.* ❏ *They searched for a spot where they could sit on the floor.* 2 V-T If you **search** a place, you look carefully for something or someone there. ❏ *Armed troops searched the hospital yesterday.* ❏ *She searched her desk for the necessary information.* 3 N-COUNT A **search** is an attempt to find something or someone by looking for them carefully. ❏ *There was no chance of him being found alive and the search was abandoned.* 4 V-T If a police officer or someone else in authority **searches** you, they look carefully to see whether you have something hidden on you. ❏ *The man took her suitcase from her and then searched her.* 5 V-I If you **search for** information on a computer, you give the computer an instruction to find that information. [COMPUTING] ❏ *You can use a directory service to search for people on the Internet.* ● N-COUNT **Search** is also a noun. ❏ *He came across this story while he was doing a computer search of local news articles.* 6 →see also **searching** 7 PHRASE If you go **in search of** something or someone, you try to find them. ❏ *Miserable, and unexpectedly lonely, she went in search of Jean-Paul.* 8 CONVENTION You say "**search me**" when someone asks you a question and you want to emphasize that you do not know the answer. [INFORMAL, EMPHASIS] ❏ *"So why did he get interested all of a sudden?" — "Search me."*

1 자동사 찾다, 살피다 ❏ 터키의 치안 유지군이 사라진 남자들이 찾기 위한 수색을 시작했다. ❏ 그들은 바닥에 앉을 수 있는 자리를 찾아 살폈다. 2 타동사 수색하다, 뒤지다 ❏ 무장 병력이 어제 병원을 수색했다. ❏ 그녀는 필요한 정보를 찾기 위해 그녀의 책상을 뒤졌다. 3 가산명사 수색 ❏ 그가 생존 상태로 발견될 가능성은 없었고 수색은 중단되었다. 4 타동사 몸을 수색하다 ❏ 남자는 그녀에게서 가방을 가져간 다음 그녀의 몸을 수색했다. 5 자동사 검색하다 [컴퓨터] ❏ 디렉터리 서비스를 이용해서 인터넷에서 사람을 검색할 수 있다. ● 가산명사 검색 ❏ 그는 지역 신문 기사를 컴퓨터로 검색하다가 이 이야기를 우연히 발견했다. 7 구 ~을 찾아 ❏ 침울한데다 예기치 않게 외로워진 그녀는 장폴을 찾아 나섰다. 8 관용 표현 낸들 아니? [비격식체, 강조] ❏ "그럼 그가 왜 갑자기 흥미를 가지게 되었지?" "낸들 알아?"

Thesaurus   *search*의 참조어

v.	hunt, inspect, look for, seek 1 2
N.	hunt, quest 3

Word Partnership   *search*의 연어

N.	search **for a job**, search **for the truth** 1
	search **an area**, search **for clues** 1 2
	search **for information** 1 5
	investigators search, **police** search, search **suspects** 4
	computer search, search **the Internet**, **online** search 5
v.	**conduct** a search 3

---

search en|gine (**search engines**) N-COUNT A **search engine** is a computer program that searches for documents containing a particular word or words on the Internet. [COMPUTING]

가산명사 검색 엔진 [컴퓨터]

search|ing /sɜːrtʃɪŋ/ ADJ A **searching** question or look is intended to discover the truth about something. ❏ *They asked her some searching questions on moral philosophy and logic.*

형용사 탐색하는 ❏ 그들은 그녀에게 도덕 철학과 논리에 대해 탐색적인 질문 몇 개를 했다.

search|light /sɜːrtʃlaɪt/ (**searchlights**) N-COUNT A **searchlight** is a large powerful light that can be turned to shine a long way in any direction. ❏ *Helicopters threw searchlights over the meadows and the lake.*

가산명사 탐조등 ❏ 헬리콥터들이 들판과 호수에 탐조등을 비췄다.

search par|ty (**search parties**) N-COUNT A **search party** is an organized group of people who are searching for someone who is missing.

가산명사 수색대

search war|rant (**search warrants**) N-COUNT A **search warrant** is a special document that gives the police permission to search a house or other building. ❏ *Officers armed with a search warrant entered the flat.*

가산명사 수색 영장 ❏ 수색 영장을 가진 경관들이 그 아파트에 들어갔다.

sear|ing /sɪərɪŋ/ 1 ADJ **Searing** is used to indicate that something such as pain or heat is very intense. [ADJ n] ❏ *She woke to feel a searing pain in her feet.* 2 ADJ A **searing** speech or piece of writing is very critical. [ADJ n] ❏ *The British civil service has long been subject to searing criticism.*

1 형용사 타는 듯한 ❏ 그녀는 발에 타는 듯한 통증을 느끼며 깨어났다. 2 형용사 혹독한 ❏ 영국의 공무원들은 오랫동안 혹독한 비판을 받아왔다.

sea|shore /siːʃɔːr/ (**seashores**) N-COUNT The **seashore** is the part of a coast where the land slopes down into the sea. ❏ *She takes inspiration from shells and stones she finds on the seashore.*

가산명사 해안 ❏ 그녀는 해안에서 발견하는 조가비와 돌들로부터 영감을 얻는다.

sea|sick /siːsɪk/ ADJ If someone is **seasick** when they are traveling in a boat, they vomit or feel sick because of the way the boat is moving. ❏ *It was quite rough at*

형용사 뱃멀미가 난 ❏ 때로는 바다가 상당히 거칠어졌고 그녀는 뱃멀미가 났다. ● 뱃멀미

A B C D E F G H I J K L M N O P Q R S T U V W X Y Z

times, and she was seasick. ● sea|sick|ness N-UNCOUNT ❑ He very prone to seasickness and already felt queasy.

불가산명사 뱃멀미 ❑ 그는 뱃멀미가 잘 났는데 벌써 속이 메슥거렸다.

sea|side /síːsaɪd/ N-SING You can refer to an area that is close to the sea, especially one where people go for their vacation, as **the seaside**. ❑ I went to spend a few days at the seaside.

단수명사 해변 ❑ 나는 해변에서 며칠을 보내러 갔다.

sea|son ◆◆◆ /síːzˀn/ (seasons, seasoning, seasoned) **1** N-COUNT The **seasons** are the main periods into which a year can be divided and which each have their own typical weather conditions. ❑ Autumn's my favorite season. ❑ ...the only region of Brazil where all four seasons are clearly defined. **2** N-COUNT You can use **season** to refer to the period during each year when a particular activity or event takes place. For example, the planting **season** is the period when a particular plant or crop is planted. ❑ ...birds arriving for the breeding season. **3** N-COUNT You can use **season** to refer to the period when a particular fruit, vegetable, or other food is ready for eating and is widely available. [n N, also in/out of N] ❑ The plum season is about to begin. **4** N-COUNT You can use **season** to refer to a fixed period during each year when a particular sport is played. ❑ ...the baseball season. **5** N-COUNT A **season** is a period in which a play or show, or a series of plays or shows, is performed in one place. ❑ ...a season of three new plays. **6** N-COUNT A **season** of movies is several of them shown as a series because they are connected in some way. ❑ ...a brief season of films in which Artaud appeared. **7** N-COUNT The vacation or holiday **season** is the time when most people take their vacation. [usu sing, usu supp N, also in/out of N] ❑ ...the peak vacation season. **8** V-T If you **season** food with salt, pepper, or spices, you add them to it in order to improve its flavor. ❑ Season the meat with salt and pepper. **9** →see also **seasoned, seasoning 10** PHRASE If a female animal is **in season**, she is in a state where she is ready to have sex. ❑ There are a few ideas around on how to treat fillies and mares in season. →see **plant**

1 가산명사 계절 ❑ 내가 제일 좋아하는 계절은 가을이다. ❑ 브라질에서 유일하게 사계절이 뚜렷한 곳 **2** 가산명사 철 ❑ 번식 철에 맞춰 도착하는 새들 **3** 가산명사 철 ❑ 자두 철이 곧 시작될 것이다. **4** 가산명사 (스포츠) 시즌 ❑ 야구 시즌 **5** 가산명사 (공연) 시즌 ❑ 새로운 연극 세 편을 공연하는 시즌 **6** 가산명사 특별 상영 기간 ❑ 단기간의 아르토 출연 영화 특별 상영 기간 **7** 가산명사 철 ❑ 휴가철의 절정 **8** 타동사 양념을 하다 ❑ 소금과 후추로 고기에 양념을 하세요. **10** 구 번식기의 ❑ 번식기의 암망아지와 암말을 어떻게 다루어야 하는지에 대해서는 몇 가지 의견들이 있다.

sea|son|al /síːzˀnˀl/ ADJ A **seasonal** factor, event, or change occurs during one particular time of the year. [ADJ n] ❑ ...blaming seasonal factors for the unemployment increase in the west. ● **sea|son|al|ly** ADV ❑ The seasonally adjusted unemployment figures show a rise of twelve-hundred.

형용사 계절적인 ❑ 서부에서의 실업 증가를 계절적인 요인 탓으로 돌림 ● 계절적으로 부사 ❑ 계절적으로 조정된 실업 수치가 1,200명의 증가를 보이고 있다.

sea|soned /síːzˀnd/ ADJ You can use **seasoned** to describe a person who has a lot of experience of something. For example, a **seasoned** traveler is a person who has traveled a lot. ❑ The author is a seasoned academic.

형용사 경험이 풍부한 ❑ 저자는 중견 학자이다.

sea|son|ing /síːzənɪŋ/ (seasonings) N-MASS **Seasoning** is salt, pepper, or other spices that are added to food to improve its flavor. ❑ Mix the meat with the onion, carrot, and some seasoning. →see **salt**

물질명사 양념 ❑ 양파, 당근, 그리고 양념을 고기와 섞으세요.

sea|son tick|et (season tickets) N-COUNT A **season ticket** is a ticket that you can use repeatedly during a certain period, without having to pay each time. You can buy **season tickets** for things such as buses, trains, regular sports events, or theater performances. ❑ We went to renew our monthly season ticket.

가산명사 정기 이용권 ❑ 우리는 월 정기 이용권을 갱신하기 위해 갔다.

seat ◆◆◇ /síːt/ (seats, seating, seated) **1** N-COUNT A **seat** is an object that you can sit on, for example a chair. ❑ Stephen returned to his seat. **2** N-COUNT The **seat** of a chair is the part that you sit on. ❑ The stool had a torn, red plastic seat. **3** V-T If you **seat yourself** somewhere, you sit down. [WRITTEN] ❑ He waved towards a chair, and seated himself at the desk. **4** V-T A building or vehicle that **seats** a particular number of people has enough seats for that number. ❑ The theater seats 570. **5** N-SING The **seat** of a piece of clothing is the part that covers your bottom. [usu sing, usu N of n] ❑ Then he got up, brushed off the seat of his jeans, and headed slowly down the slope. **6** N-COUNT When someone is elected to a legislature you can say that they, or their party, have won a **seat**. ❑ Independent candidates won the majority of seats on the local council. **7** N-COUNT If someone has a **seat** on the board of a company or on a committee, they are a member of it. ❑ He has been unsuccessful in his attempt to win a seat on the board of the company. **8** N-COUNT The **seat** of an organization, a wealthy family, or an activity is its base. ❑ Gunfire broke out early this morning around the seat of government in Lagos. **9** →see also **deep-seated 10** PHRASE If you **take a back seat**, you allow other people to have all the power and to make all the decisions. ❑ You need to take a back seat and think about both past and future. **11** PHRASE If you **take a seat**, you sit down. [FORMAL] ❑ "Take a seat," he said in a bored tone.

1 가산명사 좌석, 자리 ❑ 스티븐은 자기 자리로 돌아왔다. **2** 가산명사 앉는 부분 ❑ 등받이가 없는 그 의자는 앉는 부분이 깨진 붉은 플라스틱이었다. **3** 타동사 앉다 [문어체] ❑ 그는 의자 하나를 가리키고 자신은 책상 앞에 앉았다. **4** 타동사 수용하다 ❑ 그 극장은 570명을 수용할 수 있다. **5** 단수명사 엉덩이 부분 ❑ 그런 뒤 그는 일어서서 청바지의 엉덩이를 털고는 비탈 아래로 천천히 내려갔다. **6** 가산명사 의석 ❑ 무소속 후보들이 지방 의회 의석의 대다수를 차지했다. **7** 가산명사 자리 ❑ 회사 이사회에서 한 자리를 차지하려는 그의 시도는 여태껏 성공하지 못했다. **8** 가산명사 위치, 소재지 ❑ 라고스의 행정부가 있는 곳에서 오늘 새벽에 총격전이 벌어졌다. **10** 구 뒤로 나앉다 ❑ 너는 뒤로 나앉아서 과거와 미래 둘 다에 대해 생각할 필요가 있다. **11** 구 앉다 [격식체] ❑ "앉아."라고 그는 지겨워하는 목소리로 말했다.

Word Partnership	seat의 연어
ADJ.	back seat, empty seat, front seat **1**
	vacant seat **1 6 7**
	congressional seat **6**
N.	car seat, child seat, driver's seat, passenger seat, seat at a table, theater seat, toilet seat **1**
	seat on the board **7**

seat belt (seat belts) also **seatbelt** N-COUNT A **seat belt** is a strap attached to a seat in a car or an aircraft. You fasten it across your body in order to prevent yourself being thrown out of the seat if there is a sudden movement. ❑ The fact I was wearing a seat belt saved my life. →see **car**

가산명사 안전띠 ❑ 내가 안전띠를 매고 있어서 목숨을 건졌다.

Laws have been passed in most of the US requiring motorists and their passengers to wear **seat belts** while in a moving vehicle. For small children's safety, **car seats** especially designed with belts to fit them must be used. Those caught not using seat belts are liable for a heavy fine.

미국 대부분 지역에서 운행 중인 차량을 타고 있는 운전사와 승객은 seat belt(안전 벨트)를 매도록 하는 법률이 정해져 있다. 유아의 안전을 위해서는, 유아에게 맞도록 특별히 고안된 벨트가 달린 car seat(자동차내 유아용 의자)를 사용해야 한다. 안전 벨트를 착용하지 않다가 걸리면 무거운 벌금을 내야 한다.

seat|ing /síːtɪŋ/ **1** N-UNCOUNT You can refer to the seats in a place as the **seating**. ❑ The stadium has been fitted with seating for over eighty thousand spectators.

1 불가산명사 자리, 관중석, 객석 ❑ 그 경기장에는 8만 명이 넘는 관객들을 위한 자리가 마련되었다.

A

2 N-UNCOUNT The **seating** at a public place or a formal occasion is the arrangement of where people will sit. ❑ *She made a mental note to check the seating arrangements before the guests filed into the dining-room.*

2 불가산명사 좌석 배치 ❑ 그녀는 손님들이 식당으로 줄지어 들어가기 전에 좌석 배치를 확인해야 한다고 머릿속에 메모를 했다.

B

sea|weed /ˈsiːwiːd/ (**seaweeds**) N-MASS **Seaweed** is a plant that grows in the sea. There are many kinds of seaweed. ❑ *...seaweed washed up on a beach.*

물질명사 해초, 해조류 ❑ 해변에 올라온 해초

sec /sɛk/ (**secs**) N-COUNT If you ask someone to wait a **sec**, you are asking them to wait for a very short time. [INFORMAL] ❑ *Can you just hang on a sec?*

가산명사 잠깐 [비격식체] ❑ 잠깐 끊지 말고 기다려 주실래요?

C

sec. /sɛk/ (**secs**) **Sec.** is a written abbreviation for **second** or **seconds**. ❑ *The first woman to finish was Grete Waitz of Norway, with a time of 2 hrs. 29 min., 30 sec.*

초 ❑ 노르웨이의 그리트 웨이츠가 2시간 29분 30초의 기록으로 1등으로 들어왔다.

D

se|clud|ed /sɪˈkluːdɪd/ ADJ A **secluded** place is quiet and private. ❑ *We were tucked away in a secluded corner of the room.*

형용사 한적한, 외딴 ❑ 우리는 방의 한쪽 구석에 쿡 박혀 있었다.

E

se|clu|sion /sɪˈkluːʒ³n/ N-UNCOUNT If you are living **in seclusion**, you are in a quiet place away from other people. ❑ *She lived in seclusion with her husband on their farm in Panama.*

불가산명사 은둔 ❑ 그녀는 파나마의 농장에서 남편과 함께 은둔 생활을 했다.

F

---

second

① PART OF A MINUTE
② COMING AFTER SOMETHING ELSE
③ SENDING SOMEONE TO DO A JOB

G

① **sec|ond** ♦♦♦ /ˈsɛkənd/ (**seconds**) N-COUNT A **second** is one of the sixty parts that a minute is divided into. People often say "**a second**" or "**seconds**" when they simply mean a very short time. ❑ *For a few seconds nobody said anything.* ❑ *It only takes forty seconds.*

가산명사 초, 순간 ❑ 몇 초 동안 아무도 말을 꺼내지 않았다. ❑ 40초밖에 안 걸린다.

H

② **sec|ond** ♦♦♦ /ˈsɛkənd/ (**seconds, seconding, seconded**) →Please look at category **12** to see if the expression you are looking for is shown under another headword. **1** ORD The **second** item in a series is the one that you count as number two. ❑ *...the second day of his visit to Delhi.* ❑ *...their second child.* ❑ *...the Second World War.* **2** ORD **Second** is used before superlative adjectives to indicate that there is only one thing better or larger than the thing you are referring to. [ORD adj-superl] ❑ *The party is still the second strongest in Italy.* **3** ADV You say **second** when you want to make a second point or give a second reason for something. [ADV cl] ❑ *First, the weapons should be intended for use only in retaliation after a nuclear attack. Second, the possession of the weapons must be a temporary expedient.* **4** N-COUNT In Britain, an **upper second** is a good honors degree and a **lower second** is an average honors degree. ❑ *I then went up to Lancaster University and got an upper second.* **5** N-PLURAL If you have **seconds**, you have a second helping of food. [INFORMAL] ❑ *There's seconds if you want them.* **6** N-COUNT **Seconds** are goods that are sold cheaply in stores because they have slight faults. ❑ *These are not seconds, or unbranded goods, but first-quality products.* **7** V-T If you **second** a proposal in a meeting or debate, you formally express your agreement with it so that it can then be discussed or voted on. ❑ *...Bryan Sutton, who seconded the motion against fox hunting.* **8** V-T If you **second** what someone has said, you say that you agree with them or say the same thing yourself. ❑ *The Prime Minister seconded the call for discipline and austerity in a speech to the assembly last week.* **9** PHRASE If you experience something **at second hand**, you are told about it by other people rather than experiencing it yourself. ❑ *Most of them, after all, had not been at the battle and had only heard of the massacre at second hand.* →see also **secondhand** **10** PHRASE If you say that something is **second to none**, you are emphasizing that it is very good indeed or the best that there is. [EMPHASIS] ❑ *Our scientific research is second to none.* **11** PHRASE If you say that something is **second only to** something else, you mean that only that thing is better or greater than it. ❑ *As a major health risk hepatitis is second only to tobacco.* **12** **second nature** →see **nature. in the second place** →see **place**

I

1 서수 두 번째 ❑ 그가 델리를 방문한 둘째 날 ❑ 그들의 둘째 아이 ❑ 2차 세계 대전 **2** 서수 두 번째 ❑ 그 정당은 여전히 이탈리아에서 두 번째로 강하다 **3** 부사 둘째로 ❑ 첫째, 그 무기들은 핵 공격 이후에만 보복 공격을 위해서만 사용한다. 둘째, 그 무기들은 임시방편으로만 소유한다. **4** 가산명사 2 등급 (새 등급으로 나눈 학교 성적의 두 번째 등급. 2등급(second)은 다시 우수 2등급(upper second)과 보통 2등급(lower second)으로 나뉜다.) ❑ 나는 그런 뒤 랭커스터 대학에 진학해 우수 2등급의 성적을 받았다. **5** 복수명사 두 번째 덜어 먹는 음식, 한 차례 더 먹는 음식 [비격식체] ❑ 원하신다면 한 그릇 더 드셔도 돼요. **6** 가산명사 2급품, 2급 ❑ 이것들은 2급품이나 상표가 없는 물품이 아닌 1등급 상품이다. **7** 타동사 (회의에서) 재청하다 ❑ 여우 사냥 금지안에 재청을 표한 브라이언 서턴 **8** 타동사 찬성하다, 지지하다 ❑ 수상은 지난주 대국회 연설에서 규율과 긴축에 대한 요청을 지지했다. **9** 구 간접적으로 ❑ 사실 그들 대부분은 전쟁터에 있지 않았으며 학살에 대해 간접적으로만 전해 들었었다. **10** 구 최고의, 그 무엇에도 뒤지지 않는 [강조] ❑ 우리의 과학 연구는 최고이다. **11** 구 -에만 뒤지는, - 외에는 으뜸인 ❑ 건강에 대한 주요 위험 요인으로 간염보다 위험한 것은 담배밖에 없다.

J

K

L

M

N

O

P

Q

③ **se|cond** /sɪˈkɒnd/ (**seconds, seconding, seconded**) V-T If you **are seconded** somewhere, you are sent there temporarily by your employer in order to do special duties. [BRIT] [usu passive] ❑ *In 1937 he was seconded to the Royal Canadian Air Force in Ottawa as air armament adviser.*

타동사 임시로 배치되다 [영국영어] ❑ 1937년에 그는 공군 자문으로 오타와의 왕립 캐나다 공군에 임시로 배치되었다.

R

sec|ond|ary /ˈsɛkəndri, BRIT sɛkˈændri/ **1** ADJ If you describe something as **secondary**, you mean that it is less important than something else. ❑ *The street erupted in a huge explosion, with secondary explosions in the adjoining buildings.* ❑ *They argue that human rights considerations are now of only secondary importance.* **2** ADJ **Secondary** diseases or infections happen as a result of another disease or infection that has already happened. ❑ *These patients had been operated on for the primary cancer but there was evidence of secondary tumors.* **3** ADJ **Secondary** education is given to students between the ages of 11 or 12 and 17 or 18. ❑ *Examinations are taken after about five years of secondary education.*

S

1 형용사 2차의, 부차적인 ❑ 거리에서 커다란 폭발이 일어났고 인근 건물에서 2차 폭발이 발생했다. ❑ 그들은 인권에 대한 고려가 이제는 부차적인 사안에 불과하다고 주장한다. **2** 형용사 2차적인 (질병) ❑ 이 환자들은 원발암에 대해 수술을 받았지만 2차 종양의 증거가 있었다. **3** 형용사 중등 ❑ 중등 교육을 약 5년간 받은 후 시험을 친다.

T

sec|ond|ary school (**secondary schools**) N-VAR A **secondary school** is a school for students between the ages of 11 or 12 and 17 or 18. ❑ *She taught history at a secondary school.*

가산명사 또는 불가산명사 중등학교 ❑ 그녀는 중등학교에서 역사를 가르쳤다.

U

sec|ond best also **second-best** **1** ADJ **Second best** is used to describe something that is not as good as the best thing of its kind but is better than all the other things of that kind. ❑ *He put on his second best suit.* **2** ADJ You can use **second best** to describe something that you have to accept even though you would have preferred something else. ❑ *...a messy, second-best solution.* ● N-SING **Second best** is also a noun. ❑ *Oatmeal is a good second best.*

V

1 형용사 두 번째로 가장 좋은 ❑ 그는 두 번째로 가장 좋은 옷을 입었다. **2** 형용사 차선의 ❑ 깔끔하지 못한 차선의 해결책 ● 단수명사 차선책 ❑ 오트밀은 괜찮은 차선책이다.

W

second-class also **second class** **1** ADJ If someone treats you as a **second-class citizen**, they treat you as if you are less valuable and less important than other people. [ADJ n] ❑ *Too many airlines treat our children as second-class citizens.* **2** ADJ If you describe something as **second-class**, you mean that it is of poor quality. ❑ *I am not prepared to see children in some parts of this country having to settle for a second-class education.* **3** ADJ The **second-class** accommodations on a train or ship are the ordinary accommodations, which are cheaper and less

X

Y

1 형용사 이류의 ❑ 너무 많은 항공사들이 아이들을 이류 시민 취급한다. **2** 형용사 질 낮은, 열등한 ❑ 이 나라 일부 지역의 아이들이 질 낮은 교육을 어쩔 수 없이 받는 것을 용납하지 않겠다. **3** 형용사 이등석의 ❑ 이등석의 구석 자리에 앉아 있었다. ● 부사 이등석으로 ❑ 나는 최근에 피사에서 벤티밀리아까지 이등석을 타고

Z

comfortable than the first-class accommodations. [ADJ n] ❑ *He sat in the corner of a second-class carriage.* ❑ *Seven second-class passengers prepared to disembark.* ● ADV **Second class** is also an adverb. [ADV after v] ❑ *I recently travelled second class from Pisa to Ventimiglia.* ❑ N-UNCOUNT **Second class** is second-class accommodations on a train or ship. ❑ *"Is there any chance of a compartment to myself?" — "Not in second class."* ❑ ADJ In the United States, **second-class** postage is the type of postage that is used for sending newspapers and magazines. In Britain, **second-class** postage is the slower and cheaper type of postage. [ADJ n] ❑ *...a second-class stamp.* ● ADV **Second class** is also an adverb. [ADV after v] ❑ *They're going to send it second class.* ❑ ADJ In Britain, a **second-class** degree is a good university degree, but not as good as a first-class degree. [ADJ n] ❑ *A second-class honours degree is the minimum requirement.*

sec|ond|hand /sɛkəndhænd/ also **second-hand** ❑ ADJ **Secondhand** things are not new and have been owned by someone else. ❑ *They could afford a secondhand car, she thought.* ● ADV **Secondhand** is also an adverb. [ADV after v] ❑ *Household appliances were bought secondhand and are outdated.* ❑ ADJ A **secondhand** store sells secondhand goods. [ADJ n] ❑ *...lovingly restored old pieces bought from a secondhand store.* ❑ ADJ **Secondhand** stories, information, or opinions are those you learn about from other people rather than directly or from your own experience. ❑ *He urged the committee to discount any secondhand knowledge or hearsay.* ❑ **at second hand** →see **second 9**

② **sec|ond lan|guage** (**second languages**) N-COUNT Someone's **second language** is a language which is not their native language but which they use at work or at school. ❑ *Lucy teaches English as a second language.*

sec|ond|ly /sɛkəndli/ ADV You say **secondly** when you want to make a second point or give a second reason for something. [ADV with cl (not last in cl)] ❑ *The problems were numerous. Firstly, I didn't know exactly when I was going to America; secondly, who was going to look after Doran and Lili?*

sec|ond|ment /sɪkɒndmənt/ (**secondments**) N-VAR Someone who is **on secondment** from their normal employer has been sent somewhere else temporarily in order to do special duties. [BRIT] ❑ *We have two full-time secretaries, one of whom is on secondment from the Royal Navy.*

sec|ond opin|ion (**second opinions**) N-COUNT If you get a **second opinion**, you ask another qualified person for their opinion about something such as your health. ❑ *I would like to see a specialist for a second opinion on my doctor's diagnosis.*

second-rate ADJ If you describe something as **second-rate**, you mean that it is of poor quality. ❑ *...second-rate restaurants.*

sec|ond thought (**second thoughts**) ❑ N-SING If you do something without **a second thought**, you do it without thinking about it carefully, usually because you do not have enough time or you do not care very much. ❑ *This murderous lunatic could kill them both without a second thought.* ❑ N-PLURAL If you have **second thoughts about** a decision that you have made, you begin to doubt whether it was the best thing to do. ❑ *I had never had second thoughts about my decision to leave the company.* ❑ PHRASE You can say **on second thoughts** or **on second thought** when you suddenly change your mind about something that you are saying or something that you have decided to do. ❑ *"Wait there!" Kathryn rose. "No, on second thought, follow me."*

se|cre|cy /siːkrəsi/ N-UNCOUNT **Secrecy** is the act of keeping something secret, or the state of being kept secret. ❑ *The British government has thrown a blanket of secrecy over the details.*

se|cret ♦♦♦ /siːkrɪt/ (**secrets**) ❑ ADJ If something is **secret**, it is known about by only a small number of people, and is not told or shown to anyone else. [ADJ n, v n ADJ, v-link ADJ] ❑ *Soldiers have been training at a secret location.* →see also **top secret** ● **se|cret|ly** ADV ❑ *He wore a hidden microphone to secretly tape-record conversations.* ❑ N-COUNT A **secret** is a fact that is known by only a small number of people, and is not told to anyone else. ❑ *I think he enjoyed keeping our love a secret.* ❑ N-SING If you say that a particular way of doing things is **the secret of** achieving something, you mean that it is the best or only way to achieve it. ❑ *The secret of success is honesty and fair dealing.* ❑ N-COUNT Something's **secrets** are the things about it which have never been fully explained. ❑ *We have an opportunity now to really unlock the secrets of the universe.* ❑ PHRASE If you do something **in secret**, you do it without anyone else knowing. ❑ *Dan found out that I had been meeting my ex-boyfriend in secret.* ❑ PHRASE If you say that someone can **keep a secret**, you mean that they can be trusted not to tell other people a secret that you have told them. ❑ *Tom was utterly indiscreet, and could never keep a secret.* ❑ PHRASE If you **make no secret** of something, you tell others about it openly and clearly. ❑ *His wife made no secret of her hatred for the formal occasions.*

sec|re|tari|al /sɛkrətɛəriəl/ ADJ **Secretarial** work is the work done by a secretary in an office. [ADJ n] ❑ *I was doing temporary secretarial work.*

sec|re|tari|at /sɛkrətɛəriət/ (**secretariats**) N-COUNT A **secretariat** is a department that is responsible for the administration of an international political organization. ❑ *...the UN secretariat.*

sec|re|tary ♦♦♦ /sɛkrətri, BRIT sɛkrətɹi/ (**secretaries**) ❑ N-COUNT A **secretary** is a person who is employed to do office work, such as typing letters, answering phone calls, and arranging meetings. ❑ N-COUNT The **secretary** of an organization such as a trade union, a political party, or a club is its official manager. [BRIT] ❑ *My grandfather was secretary of the Scottish Miners' Union.* ❑ N-COUNT The **secretary** of a company is the person who has the legal duty of keeping the company's records. ❑ N-COUNT; N-TITLE **Secretary** is used in the titles of ministers and officials who are in charge of main government departments. ❑ *...the British Foreign Secretary.*

여행했다. ● 불가산명사 이등석 ❑ *"저 혼자만 쓸 수 있는 칸막이 객실이 있을까요?" "이등석에서는 안 됩니다."* ❑ 형용사 보통 우편의 ❑ 보통 우표 ● 부사 보통 우편으로 ❑ *그들은 그것을 보통 우편으로 보낼 것이다.* ❑ 형용사 이등급의 ❑ *최소한 이등급 우등 학사 학위는 받아야 한다.*

❑ 형용사 중고의 ❑ *그들이 중고차는 살 수 있겠지 하고 그녀는 생각했다.* ● 부사 중고로 ❑ *가전제품을 중고로 샀던 터라 지금은 낡았다.* ❑ 형용사 중고품을 파는 ❑ *중고품 가게에서 산, 멋지게 복구된 옛 물건들* ❑ 형용사 간접적인 ❑ *그는 위원회에게 모든 간접적인 지식이나 소문은 크게 믿지 말라고 촉구했다.*

가산명사 제 2언어 ❑ *루시는 영어를 제 2언어로 가르친다.*

부사 둘째 ❑ *여러 문제가 있었다. 첫째, 나는 내가 미국에 언제 갈지 몰랐다. 둘째, 그러면 도란과 릴리는 누가 돌볼 것인가?*

가산명사 또는 불가산명사 임시 파견 [영국영어] ❑ *우리에겐 두 명의 정식 비서가 있는데 그 중 한 명은 영국 해군에서 임시로 파견되었다.*

가산명사 2차 소견 ❑ *내 의사가 내린 진단에 대해 2차 소견을 얻을 수 있도록 전문의를 만나고 싶다.*

형용사 질 낮은, 열등한 ❑ *질 낮은 식당*

❑ 단수명사 충분한 생각 ❑ *이 광적인 살인마가 그들 둘을 별로 깊이 생각하지도 않고 죽일 수도 있다.* ❑ 복수명사 재고, 생각함 ❑ *회사를 떠나려는 나의 결정이 흔들린 적은 한 번도 없다.* ❑ 구 다시 생각해 보니 ❑ *"잠깐만!"이라고 말하며 캐서린이 일어났다. "아니, 다시 생각해 보니 나를 따라오는 게 좋겠어."*

불가산명사 비밀 ❑ *영국 정부가 그 세부 사항들은 비밀에 부쳤다.*

❑ 형용사 비밀의 ❑ *군인들이 비밀 장소에서 훈련해 왔다.* ● 비밀리에, 몰래 부사 ❑ *그는 대화를 몰래 녹취하기 위해 마이크를 몸에 숨기고 다녔다.* ❑ 가산명사 비밀 ❑ *그가 우리의 사랑을 비밀로 한 것을 좋아한 것 같다.* ❑ 단수명사 비결 ❑ *성공의 비결은 정직성과 공평한 처사이다.* ❑ 가산명사 신비 ❑ *이제 우주의 신비를 진정으로 밝힐 수 있는 기회가 우리에게 왔다.* ❑ 구 비밀리에 ❑ *댄이 이전 남자 친구를 몰래 만나 왔다는 것을 알아냈다.* ❑ 구 비밀을 지키다 ❑ *탐은 너무나 분별이 없었고 비밀을 절대로 지키지 못했다.* ❑ 구 숨기지 않다 ❑ *그의 아내는 공식적인 모임에 대한 혐오감을 숨기지 않았다.*

형용사 비서의 ❑ *나는 임시로 비서 일을 하고 있었다.*

가산명사 사무국 ❑ *유엔 사무국*

❑ 가산명사 비서 ❑ 가산명사 총무 [영국영어] ❑ *우리 할아버지는 스코틀랜드 광부 노동조합의 총무였다.* ❑ 가산명사 총무 ❑ 가산명사; 경칭명사 장관 ❑ *영국 외무 장관*

secretary-general ♦♢♢ (**secretaries-general**) also Secretary General N-COUNT The **secretary-general** of an international political organization is the person in charge of its administration. ❑ ...the United Nations Secretary-General.

가산명사 사무총장 ❑ 유엔 사무총장

Sec|re|tary of State ♦♢♢ (**Secretaries of State**) **1** N-COUNT In the United States, **the Secretary of State** is the head of the government department which deals with foreign affairs. **2** N-COUNT In Britain, **the Secretary of State** for a particular government department is the head of that department. ❑ ...the Secretary of State for Education.

1 가산명사 (미국) 국무장관 **2** 가산명사 (영국) 장관 ❑ 교육부장관

se|crete /sɪkriːt/ (**secretes, secreting, secreted**) **1** V-T If part of a plant, animal, or human **secretes** a liquid, it produces it. ❑ The sweat glands secrete water. **2** V-T If you **secrete** something somewhere, you hide it there so that nobody will find it. [LITERARY] ❑ She secreted the gun in the kitchen cabinet.

1 타동사 분비하다 ❑ 땀샘에서는 수분이 분비된다. **2** 타동사 숨기다 [문예체] ❑ 그녀는 총을 부엌 캐비닛에 숨겼다.

se|cre|tion /sɪkriːʃ°n/ (**secretions**) **1** N-UNCOUNT **Secretion** is the process by which certain liquid substances are produced by parts of plants or from the bodies of people or animals. ❑ ...the secretion of adrenaline. **2** N-PLURAL **Secretions** are liquid substances produced by parts of plants or bodies. ❑ ...gastric secretions.

• **1** 불가산명사 분비 ❑ 아드레날린 분비 **2** 복수명사 분비물 ❑ 위 분비물

se|cre|tive /siːkrətɪv, sɪkriːt-/ ADJ If you are **secretive**, you like to have secrets and to keep your knowledge, feelings, or intentions hidden. ❑ Billionaires are usually fairly secretive about the exact amount that they're worth.

형용사 숨기는, 비밀스러운 ❑ 억만장자들은 대체로 자신들의 정확한 재산 내역에 대해 상당히 비밀스럽다.

se|cret po|lice N-UNCOUNT The **secret police** is a police force in some countries that works secretly and deals with political crimes committed against the government. [also the N] ❑ ... former members of the secret police.

불가산명사 비밀경찰 요원 ❑ 전직 비밀경찰 대원들

se|cret ser|vice (**secret services**) **1** N-COUNT A country's **secret service** is a secret government department whose job is to find out enemy secrets and to prevent its own government's secrets from being discovered. ❑ ... French secret service agents. **2** N-COUNT The **secret service** is the government department in the United States which protects the president. [AM] ❑ He finished his career as head of the Secret Service team assigned to President Reagan.

1 가산명사 첩보부 ❑ 프랑스의 첩보 요원들 **2** 가산명사 (미국) 재무부 비밀 검찰국 [미국영어] ❑ 그는 레이건 대통령 경호를 담당한 비밀 검찰국장 자리에서 은퇴했다.

sect /sɛkt/ (**sects**) N-COUNT A **sect** is a group of people that has separated from a larger group and has a particular set of religious or political beliefs.

가산명사 분파, 교파

sec|tar|ian /sɛktɛəriən/ ADJ **Sectarian** means resulting from the differences between different religions. ❑ He was the fifth person to be killed in sectarian violence last week. ❑ The police said the murder was sectarian.

형용사 종파의, 파벌적인 ❑ 그는 지난주 종파 간 분쟁으로 인하여 살해된 다섯 번째 희생자가 되었다. ❑ 경찰은 살인 동기가 파벌적인 것이라고 했다.

Word Link   sect ≈ cutting : dissect, intersect, section

---

sec|tion ♦♦♢ /sɛkʃ°n/ (**sections, sectioning, sectioned**) **1** N-COUNT A **section** of something is one of the parts into which it is divided or from which it is formed. ❑ He said it was wrong to single out any section of society for Aids testing. ❑ ...the Georgetown section of Washington, D.C. →see also **cross-section** **2** V-T If something **is sectioned**, it is divided into sections. [usu passive] ❑ It holds vegetables in place while they are being peeled or sectioned. **3** N-COUNT A **section** is a diagram of something such as a building or a part of the body. It shows how the object would appear to you if it were cut from top to bottom and looked at from the side. ❑ For some buildings a vertical section is more informative than a plan.

1 가산명사 부분, 부문, 구획 ❑ 그는 사회의 한 부분을 뽑아내어 에이즈 검사를 실시하는 것은 올바르지 않다고 했다. ❑ 워싱턴의 조지타운 지구 **2** 타동사 분할되다, 구분되다 ❑ 그 기구는 야채의 껍질을 벗기거나 그것을 몇 등분으로 나눌 때 야채가 움직이지 않게 해 준다. **3** 가산명사 단면도 ❑ 일부 건물에 대해서는 수직 단면도가 설계도보다 더 많은 것을 알려 준다.

Word Partnership   section의 연어

| ADJ. | **main** section, **new** section, **special** section, **thin** section **1** |
| N. | section **of a city**, section **of a coast**, **sports** section **1** |

---

sec|tor ♦♦♢ /sɛktər/ (**sectors**) **1** N-COUNT A particular **sector** of a country's economy is the part connected with that specified type of industry. ❑ ...the nation's manufacturing sector. →see also **public sector, private sector** **2** N-COUNT A **sector** of a large group is a smaller group which is part of it. ❑ Workers who went to the Gulf came from the poorest sectors of Pakistani society. **3** N-COUNT A **sector** is an area of a city or country which is controlled by a military force. ❑ Officers were going to retake sectors of the city.

1 가산명사 분야 ❑ 국가의 제조업 분야 **2** 가산명사 계층 ❑ 페르시아 만에 진출한 근로자들은 파키스탄 사회의 가장 빈곤한 계층 출신이다. **3** 가산명사 지구(地區) ❑ 장교들은 도시의 여러 지구를 재탈환할 계획이었다.

Word Partnership   sector의 연어

| N. | **banking** sector, **business** sector, **government** sector, **growth in a** sector, **job in a** sector, **technology** sector, **telecommunications** sector **1** |

---

secu|lar /sɛkyələr/ ADJ You use **secular** to describe things that have no connection with religion. ❑ He spoke about preserving the country as a secular state.

형용사 세속적인, 비종교적인 ❑ 그는 나라를 비종교 국가로 유지하는 것에 관해 이야기했다.

se|cure ♦♦♢ /sɪkyʊər/ (**secures, securing, secured**) **1** V-T If you **secure** something that you want or need, you obtain it, often after a lot of effort. [FORMAL] ❑ Federal leaders continued their efforts to secure a ceasefire. **2** V-T If you **secure** a place, you make it safe from harm or attack. [FORMAL] ❑ Staff withdrew from the main part of the prison but secured the perimeter. **3** ADJ A **secure** place is tightly locked or well protected, so that people cannot enter it or leave it. ❑ We shall make sure our home is as secure as possible from now on. • **se|cure|ly** ADV [ADV with v] ❑ He locked the heavy door securely and kept the key in his pocket. **4** V-T If you **secure** an object, you fasten it firmly to another object. ❑ He helped her close the cases up, and then he secured the canvas straps as tight as they would go. **5** ADJ If an object is **secure**, it is fixed firmly in position. ❑ Check joints are secure and the wood is sound. • **se|cure|ly** ADV [ADV with v] ❑ Ensure that the frame is securely fixed to the ground with bolts. **6** ADJ If you describe something such as a job as **secure**, it is

1 타동사 획득하다, 손에 넣다 [격식체] ❑ 연방 지도자들은 정전을 이루어 내기 위한 노력을 계속했다. **2** 타동사 안전하게 하다, 굳게 지키다 [격식체] ❑ 요원들이 감옥의 주요 지역에서는 철수했지만 그 주변을 굳게 지켰다. **3** 형용사 굳게 닫힌; 단단히 지켜지는 ❑ 이제부터 반드시 집안속을 최대한 단단히 할 것이다. • 부사 군게, 단단히 ❑ 그는 그 무거운 문을 굳게 닫아걸고 열쇠를 주머니에 보관했다. **4** 타동사 잡아매다, 단단히 고정시키다 ❑ 그는 그녀가 상자를 닫는 것을 도운 다음, 최대한 단단히 범포 끈을 잡아맸다. **5** 형용사 단단히 고정된 ❑ 이음매가 단단하고 나무가 이상이 없는지 점검하세요. • 부사 단단히 ❑ 뼈대를 나사로 지면에 단단히 고정했는지

certain not to change or end. □ ...*trade union demands for secure wages and employment.* □ *Senior citizens long for a more predictable and secure future.* **7** ADJ A **secure** base or foundation is strong and reliable. □ *He was determined to give his family a secure and solid base.* **8** ADJ If you feel **secure**, you feel safe and happy and are not worried about life. □ *She felt secure and protected when she was with him.* **9** V-T If a loan **is secured**, the person who lends the money may take property such as a house from the person who borrows the money if they fail to repay it. [BUSINESS] [usu passive] □ *The loan is secured against your home.*

확인하세요. **6** 형용사 확실한, 안정적인 ➋ 안정된 임금과 고용에 대한 노조의 요구 □ 노인들은 보다 예측 가능하고 안정된 미래를 열망한다. **7** 형용사 튼튼한, 믿음직한 □ 그는 가족들에게 믿음직하고 견실한 기반을 마련해 주기로 마음먹었다. **8** 형용사 안심하는, 걱정 없는 □ 그녀는 그와 함께 있을 때면 안심이 되고 보호받는 기분이었다. **9** 타동사 담보를 잡다 [경제] □ 그 융자는 집을 담보로 잡는다.

Thesaurus
*secure*의 참조어

V.	catch, get, obtain; (*ant.*) lose **1**
	attach, fasten **4** **5**
ADJ.	safe, sheltered **3** **8**
	tight **5**

Word Partnership
*secure*의 연어

N.	secure a job/place/position, secure peace, secure *your* rights **1**
	secure a loan **1** **9**
	secure borders **3**
	secure future, secure jobs **6**
ADV.	less secure, more secure **3** **5** **7** **8**

se|cu|rity ♦♦♦ /sɪkyʊ͡əriti/ (**securities**) **1** N-UNCOUNT **Security** refers to all the measures that are taken to protect a place, or to ensure that only people with permission enter it or leave it. □ *They are now under a great deal of pressure to tighten their airport security.* □ *Strict security measures are in force in the capital.* **2** N-UNCOUNT A feeling of **security** is a feeling of being safe and free from worry. □ *He loves the security of a happy home life.* □ *If an alarm gives you that feeling of security, then it's worth carrying.* ● PHRASE If something gives you **a false sense of security**, it makes you believe that you are safe when you are not. **3** N-UNCOUNT If something is **security** for a loan, you promise to give that thing to the person who lends you money, if you fail to pay the money back. [BUSINESS] □ *The central bank will provide special loans, and the banks will pledge the land as security.* **4** N-PLURAL **Securities** are stocks, shares, bonds, or other certificates that you buy in order to earn regular interest from them or to sell them later for a profit. [BUSINESS] □ *National banks can package their own mortgages and underwrite them as securities.* **5** →see also **social security**

1 불가산명사 보안, 방위 □ 그들은 현재 공항 보안을 강화하라는 엄청난 압력을 받고 있다. □ 수도에서는 엄중한 보안 조처가 실시되고 있다. **2** 불가산명사 안도감, 안심 □ 그는 행복한 가정생활의 안도감을 좋아한다. □ 경보기가 있어서 안심이 된다면, 가지고 다닐 만한 가치가 있다. ● 구 근거 없는 안도감 **3** 불가산명사 담보 [경제] □ 중앙은행이 특별 차관을 제공하고, 은행들은 토지를 담보로 잡힐 것이다. **4** 복수명사 유가 증권 [경제] □ 국립 은행들은 자신들이 보유한 저당권을 유가 증권으로서 일괄 인수할 수 있다.

se|cu|rity cam|era (**security cameras**) N-COUNT A **security camera** is a video camera that records people's activities in order to detect and prevent crime.

가산명사 보안 카메라

Se|cu|rity Coun|cil ♦♦◇ N-PROPER The **Security Council** is the committee which governs the United Nations. It has permanent representatives from the United States, Russia, China, France, and the United Kingdom, and temporary representatives from some other countries.

고유명사 (유엔) 안전 보장 이사회

se|cu|rity guard (**security guards**) N-COUNT A **security guard** is someone whose job is to protect a building or to collect and deliver large amounts of money.

가산명사 경비원, 감호원

se|cu|rity risk (**security risks**) N-COUNT If you describe someone as a **security risk**, you mean that they may be a threat to the safety of a country or organization. □ *Individuals considered a security risk will have to report to immigration authorities within 30 days.*

가산명사 위험인물 □ 위험인물로 간주되는 사람들은 30일 이내에 이민국 기관에 신고해야 할 것이다.

se|dan /sɪdæn/ (**sedans**) N-COUNT A **sedan** is a car with seats for four or more people, a fixed roof, and a trunk that is separate from the part of the car that you sit in. [AM; BRIT **saloon**] →see **car**

가산명사 세단 (자동차) [미국영어; 영국영어 saloon]

se|date /sɪdeɪt/ (**sedates, sedating, sedated**) **1** ADJ If you describe someone or something as **sedate**, you mean that they are quiet and rather dignified, though perhaps a bit dull. □ *She took them to visit her sedate, elderly cousins.* □ *Her London life was sedate, almost mundane.* **2** ADJ If you move along at a **sedate** pace, you move slowly, in a controlled way. □ *We set off again at a more sedate pace.* **3** V-T If someone **is sedated**, they are given a drug to calm them or to make them sleep. □ *The patient is sedated with intravenous use of sedative drugs.*

1 형용사 차분한, 조용한 □ 그녀는 그들을 데리고 차분하고 나이가 지긋한 자신의 사촌 형제들을 찾아갔다. □ 그녀의 런던 생활은 조용했고, 거의 평범할 정도였다. **2** 형용사 느린, 조심스러운 □ 우리는 더 느린 속도로 다시 출발했다. **3** 타동사 진정제를 투여 받다 □ 그 환자는 정맥 주사로 진정제를 투여 받는다.

se|da|tion /sɪdeɪʃ³n/ N-UNCOUNT If someone is **under sedation**, they have been given medicine or drugs in order to calm them or make them sleep. □ *His mother was under sedation after the boy's body was brought back from Germany.*

불가산명사 진정 상태 투여받음 □ 그의 어머니는 아들의 시신이 독일에서 실려 온 뒤 진정제를 맞고 있었다.

seda|tive /sɛdətɪv/ (**sedatives**) N-COUNT A **sedative** is a medicine or drug that calms you or makes you sleep. □ *They use opium as a sedative, rather than as a narcotic.*

가산명사 진정제 □ 그들은 아편을 마약으로가 아니라 진정제로 사용한다.

sed|en|tary /sɛdᵊnteri, BRIT sɛdᵊntəri/ ADJ Someone who has a **sedentary** lifestyle or job sits down a lot of the time and does not do much exercise. □ *Obesity and a sedentary lifestyle have been linked with an increased risk of heart disease.*

형용사 주로 앉아 지내는, 주로 앉아서 일하는 □ 비만과 주로 앉아 지내는 생활양식이, 증가하는 심장 질환의 위험과 연관성이 있는 것으로 여겨져 왔다.

sedi|ment /sɛdɪmənt/ (**sediments**) N-VAR **Sediment** is solid material that settles at the bottom of a liquid, especially earth and pieces of rock that have been carried along and then left somewhere by water, ice, or wind. □ *Many organisms that die in the sea are soon buried by sediment.*

가산명사 또는 불가산명사 침전물, 퇴적물 □ 바다 속에서 죽는 많은 생물들은 곧 퇴적물에 묻힌다.

se|duce /sɪdus, BRIT sɪdyuːs/ (**seduces, seducing, seduced**) **1** V-T If something **seduces** you, it is so attractive that it makes you do something that you would not otherwise do. □ *The view of lake and plunging cliffs seduces visitors.* ● **se|duc|tion** /sɪdʌkʃ³n/ (**seductions**) N-VAR □ ...*the seduction of words.* **2** V-T If someone **seduces** another person, they use their charm to persuade that person to have sex with them. □ *She has set out to seduce Stephen.* ● **se|duc|tion** N-VAR □ *Her methods of seduction are subtle.*

1 타동사 꾀다, 유혹하다 □ 호수와 깎아지른 절벽이 있는 경치가 관광객들을 유혹한다. ● 유혹 가산명사 또는 불가산명사 □ 말의 유혹 **2** 타동사 유혹하다 □ 그녀는 스티븐을 유혹하는 일에 착수했다. ● 유혹 가산명사 또는 불가산명사 □ 그녀가 유혹하는 방식은 미묘하다.

A

se|duc|tive /sɪdʌktɪv/ **1** ADJ Something that is **seductive** is very attractive or makes you want to do something that you would not otherwise do. ❑ *It's a seductive argument.* ● **se|duc|tive|ly** ADV ❑ *...his seductively simple assertion.* **2** ADJ A person who is **seductive** is very attractive sexually. ❑ *...a seductive woman.* ● **se|duc|tive|ly** ADV ❑ *...looking seductively over her shoulder.*

B

see ◆◆◆ /siː/ (**sees, seeing, saw, seen**) →Please look at category **26** to see if the expression you are looking for is shown under another headword. **1** V-T/V-I When you **see** something, you notice it using your eyes. [no cont] ❑ *You can't see colors at night.* ❑ *She can see, hear, touch, smell, and taste.* **2** V-T If you **see** someone, you visit them or meet them. ❑ *I saw him yesterday.* ❑ *Mick wants to see you in his office right away.* **3** V-T If you **see** an entertainment such as a play, movie, concert, or sports game, you watch it. [no cont] ❑ *He had been to see a Semi-Final of the FA Cup.* **4** V-T/V-I If you **see** that something is true or exists, you realize by observing it that it is true or exists. [no cont] ❑ *I could see she was lonely.* ❑ *...a lot of people saw what was happening but did nothing about it.* ❑ *My taste has changed a bit over the years as you can see.* **5** V-T If you **see** what someone means or **see** why something happened, you understand what they mean or understand why it happened. [no cont, no passive] ❑ *Oh, I see what you're saying.* ❑ *I really don't see any reason for changing it.* **6** V-T If you **see** someone or something **as** a certain thing, you have the opinion that they are that thing. ❑ *She saw him as a visionary, but her father saw him as a man who couldn't make a living.* ❑ *Others saw it as a betrayal.* ❑ *As I see it, Llewelyn has three choices open to him.* **7** V-T If you **see** a particular quality in someone, you believe they have that quality. If you ask what someone **sees in** a particular person or thing, you want to know what they find attractive about that person or thing. [no cont, no passive] ❑ *Frankly, I don't know what Paul sees in her.* **8** V-T If you **see** something happening in the future, you imagine it, or predict that it will happen. [no cont] ❑ *A good idea, but can you see Taylor trying it?* **9** V-T If a period of time or a person **sees** a particular change or event, it takes place during that period of time or while that person is alive. [no passive] ❑ *Yesterday saw the resignation of the acting Interior Minister.* ❑ *He had worked with the General for three years and was sorry to see him go.* **10** V-T You can use **see** in expressions to do with finding out information. For example, if you say "**I'll see what's happening**," you mean that you intend to find out what is happening. ❑ *Let me just see what the next song is.* ❑ *Every time we asked our mother, she said, "Well, see what your father says."* **11** V-T You can use **see** to promise to try and help someone. For example, if you say "**I'll see if I can do it**," you mean that you will try to do the thing concerned. ❑ *I'll see if I can call her for you.* **12** V-T If you **see that** something is done or if you **see to it** that it is done, you make sure that it is done. ❑ *See that you take care of him.* **13** V-T If you **see** someone to a particular place, you accompany them to make sure that they get there safely, or to show politeness. ❑ *He didn't offer to see her to her car.* **14** V-T If you **see** a lot **of** someone, you often meet each other or visit each other. ❑ *We used to see quite a lot of his wife, Carolyn.* **15** V-T If you **are seeing** someone, you spend time with them socially, and are having a romantic or sexual relationship. ❑ *My husband was still seeing her and he was having an affair with her.* **16** V-T Some writers use **see** in expressions such as **we saw** and **as we have seen** to refer to something that has already been explained or described. ❑ *We saw in Chapter 16 how annual cash budgets are produced.* ❑ *Using the figures given above, it can be seen that machine A pays back the initial investment in two years.* **17** V-T **See** is used in books to indicate to readers that they should look at another part of the book, or at another book, because more information is given there. [only imper] ❑ *Surveys consistently find that men report feeling safe on the street after dark. See, for example, Hindelang and Garofalo (1978).* **18** PHRASE You can use **seeing that** or **seeing as** to introduce a reason for what you are saying. [INFORMAL, SPOKEN] ❑ *He is in the marriage bureau business, which is mildly ironic seeing that his dearest wish is to get married himself.* **19** CONVENTION You can say "**I see**" to indicate that you understand what someone is telling you. [SPOKEN, FORMULAE] ❑ *"He came home in my car." — "I see."* **20** CONVENTION People say "**I'll see**" or "**We'll see**" to indicate that they do not intend to make a decision immediately, and will decide later. ❑ *We'll see. It's a possibility.* **21** CONVENTION People say "**let me see**" or "**let's see**" when they are trying to remember something, or are trying to find something. ❑ *Let's see, they're six – no, make that five hours ahead of us.* **22** PHRASE If you try to make someone **see sense** or **see reason**, you try to make them realize that they are wrong or are being stupid. ❑ *He was hopeful that by sitting together they could both see sense and live as good neighbors.* **23** CONVENTION You can say "**you see**" when you are explaining something to someone, to encourage them to listen and understand. [SPOKEN] ❑ *Well, you see, you shouldn't really feel that way about it.* **24** CONVENTION "**See you**," "**be seeing you**," and "**see you later**" are ways of saying goodbye to someone when you expect to meet them again soon. [INFORMAL, SPOKEN, FORMULAE] ❑ *"Talk to you later." — "All right. See you love."* **25** CONVENTION You can say "**You'll see**" to someone if they do not agree with you about what you think will happen in the future, and you believe that you will be proved right. ❑ *The thrill wears off after a few years of marriage. You'll see.* **26** to have seen better days →see **day**. to be seen dead →see **dead**. as far as the eye can see →see **eye**. to see eye to eye →see **eye**. as far as I can see →see **far**. see fit →see **fit**. to see red →see **red**. wait and see →see **wait**

You use **see** to talk about things that you are aware of because a visual impression reaches your eyes. You often use **can** in this way. ❑ *I can see the fax here on the desk.* If you want to say that someone is paying attention to something they can see, you say that they **are looking at** it or **are watching** it. In general, you **look at** something that is not moving, while you **watch** something that is moving or changing. ❑ *I asked him to look at the picture above his bed... He watched Blake run down the stairs.*

---

1 형용사 유혹적인, 매력적인 **□** 그것은 매력적인 주장이다. ● 매혹적으로 부사 **□** 그의 매혹적일 만큼 간결한 단언 **2** 형용사 (성적으로) 매력적인 **□** 매력적인 여자 ● 매력적으로 부사 **□** 그녀의 어깨 너머로 매력적으로 쳐다보면서

1 타동사/자동사 보다 **□** 밤에는 색깔이 보이지 않는다. **□** 그녀는 보고 듣고 만지고 냄새를 맡고 맛볼 수 있다. **2** 타동사 만나다, 보다 **□** 어제 그를 만났다. **□** 믹이 즉시 자기 사무실에서 너를 만나고 싶어 한다. **3** 타동사 관람하, 보다 **□** 그는 축구 연맹컵 준결승전을 관전하러 가 본 적이 있었다. **4** 타동사/자동사 알다, 깨닫다 **□** 그녀가 외롭다는 걸 알 수 있었다. **□** 많은 사람들이 무슨 일이 벌어지고 있는지 알았지만 그에 대해 아무 일도 하지 않았다. **□** 네가 알 수 있듯이 세월이 지남에 따라 내 취향이 약간 바뀌었다. **5** 타동사 알다, 이해하다 **□** 아, 무슨 말인지 알겠어. **□** 그걸 바꾸는 이유를 정말이지 모르겠다. **6** 타동사 생각하다, 여기다, 보다 **□** 그녀는 그를 몽상가라고 생각했지만, 그녀의 아버지는 그를 생계를 꾸릴 수 없는 남자로 보았다. **□** 다른 사람들은 그것을 배반으로 여겼다. **□** 내가 볼 때, 루웰린에게는 세 가지 선택의 여지가 있다. **7** 타동사 -에게서 어떤 자질을 보다, 알아내다 **□** 솔직히, 폴이 그녀에게서 어떤 점을 보는지 모르겠다. **8** 타동사 상상하다, 내다보다 **□** 좋은 생각이지만, 테일러가 그 일을 시도하는 걸 상상할 수 있겠는가? **9** 타동사 (변화 등을) 보게 되다 **□** 어제 내무부 장관 서리가 사임하는 일이 일어났다. **□** 그는 3년간 장군과 함께 일했는데 그가 떠나는 것을 보게 되어 서운했다. **10** 타동사 알아보다, 살펴보다 **□** 다음 노래가 어떤 곡인지 좀 봅시다. **□** 우리가 물어볼 때마다, 어머니는 이렇게 말씀하셨다. "글쎄, 아버지께서 뭐라고 하시는지 보자." **11** 타동사 해 보다; 내가 할 수 있는지 해 볼게 **□** 너를 위해 그녀에게 전화를 걸 수 있도록 해 볼게. **12** 타동사 꼭 -하도록 하다 **□** 꼭 그를 잘 돌보세요. **13** 타동사 바래다주다, 배웅하다 **□** 그는 그녀를 차까지 바래다주겠다고 말하지 않았다. **14** 타동사 -과 만나다 **□** 우리는 그의 아내 캐롤린을 상당히 자주 만나곤 했다. **15** 타동사 만나다, 사귀다 **□** 내 남편은 여전히 그녀를 만나며 바람을 피우고 있었다. **16** 타동사 살펴보다 **□** 어떻게 연간 현금 예산이 산출되는지 16장에서 살펴보았다. **□** 위의 도표를 보면, 에이(A) 기계로는 2년 만에 최초 투자액을 환수할 수 있다는 것을 알 수 있다. **17** 타동사 참조하시오 **□** 구 -하무로, -인 것을 보면 [비격식체, 구어체] **□** 그는 결혼상담소 사업을 하는데, 그 자신의 가장 소중한 바람이 결혼하는 것임을 볼 때 약간 모순적이다. **18** 관용 표현 알았어, 그렇군 [구어체, 의례적인 표현] **□** "그는 내 차를 타고 집에 왔어." "그랬군." **20** 관용 표현 차차 두고 보자 **□** 차차 두고 보자. 그건 가능한 일이야. **21** 관용 표현 어디 보자 **□** 어디 보자, 그들이 우리보다 여섯, 아니, 다섯 시간을 앞섰군. **22** 구 잘못을 깨닫다 **□** 그는 같이 둘러앉음으로써 양쪽 모두 잘못을 깨닫고 서로 좋은 이웃으로 살 수 있기를 바랐다. **23** 관용 표현 알겠지 [구어체] **□** 저, 있잖아, 그 일에 대해 정말 그런 식으로 받아들여서는 안 돼. **24** 관용 표현 그럼 또 봐 [비격식체, 구어체, 의례적인 표현] **□** "나중에 이야기하자." "그래, 이따 봐, 자기." **25** 관용 표현 두고 봐 **□** 그런 짜릿함은 결혼 후 몇 년이 지나면 사라진다고. 두고 보세요.

---

see는 시각적 인상이 눈에 들어와서 인지하게 되는 것을 말할 때 쓴다. 이 경우에 종종 can을 쓴다. **□** 책상 위 여기에 팩스가 보인다. 누가 자기에게 보이는 것에 주의를 기울인다는 것을 말하고 싶으면, 그 사람이 그것을 are looking at 또는 그 사람이 그것을 are watching 한다고 말한다. 일반적으로, 움직이거나 변하는 것을 watch하는 반면, 움직이지 않는 것을 look at한다. **□** 나는 그에게 그의 침대 위에 있는 그림을 보라고 요청했다... 그는 블레이크가 계단 아래로 뛰어내려가는 것을 보았다.

Thesaurus	see의 참조어
v.	glimpse, look, observe, watch ■
	grasp, observe, understand ■

▶see about PHRASAL VERB When you **see about** something, you arrange for it to be done or provided. ❑ Tony announced it was time to see about lunch.

▶see off ■ PHRASAL VERB When you **see** someone **off**, you go with them to the station, airport, or port that they are leaving from, and say goodbye to them there. ❑ Ben had planned a steak dinner for himself after seeing Jackie off on her plane. ■ PHRASAL VERB If you **see off** an opponent, you defeat them. [BRIT] ❑ There is no reason why they cannot see off the Republican challenge.

▶see through PHRASAL VERB If you **see through** someone or their behavior, you realize what their intentions are, even though they are trying to hide them. ❑ I saw through your little ruse from the start. →see also **see-through**

▶see to PHRASAL VERB If you **see to** something that needs attention, you deal with it. ❑ While Franklin saw to the luggage, Sara took Eleanor home.

seed ◆◇◇ /sid/ (seeds, seeding, seeded) ■ N-VAR A **seed** is the small, hard part of a plant from which a new plant grows. ❑ ...a packet of cabbage seed. ❑ I sow the seed in pots of soil-based compost. ■ V-T If you **seed** a piece of land, you plant seeds in it. ❑ Men mowed the wide lawns and seeded them. ❑ The primroses should begin to seed themselves down the steep hillside. ■ N-PLURAL You can refer to the **seeds of** something when you want to talk about the beginning of a feeling or process that gradually develops and becomes stronger or more important. [LITERARY] ❑ He raised questions meant to plant seeds of doubts in the minds of jurors. ■ N-COUNT In sports such as tennis or badminton, a **seed** is a player who has been ranked according to his or her ability. ❑ ...Pete Sampras, Wimbledon's top seed and the world No.1. ■ V-T When a player or a team is **seeded** in a sports competition, they are ranked according to their ability. [usu passive] ❑ In the UEFA Cup the top 16 sides are seeded for the first round. ❑ He is seeded second, behind Brad Beven. ■ PHRASE If vegetable plants **go to seed** or **run to seed**, they produce flowers and seeds as well as leaves. ❑ If unused, winter radishes run to seed in spring. ■ PHRASE If you say that someone or something **has gone to seed** or **has run to seed**, you mean that they have become much less attractive, healthy, or efficient. ❑ He says the economy has gone to seed. →see **flower, fruit, plant, rice**

seed capital N-UNCOUNT **Seed capital** is an amount of money that a new company needs to pay for the costs of producing a business plan so that they can raise further capital to develop the company. [BUSINESS] ❑ I am negotiating with financiers to raise seed capital for my latest venture.

seed corn N-UNCOUNT **Seed corn** is money that businesses spend at the beginning of a project in the hope that it will eventually produce profits. [mainly BRIT, BUSINESS] ❑ The scheme offers seed corn finance with loans of up to £10,000 at only 4% interest.

seed|ling /sidlɪŋ/ (seedlings) N-COUNT A **seedling** is a young plant that has been grown from a seed.

seed mon|ey N-UNCOUNT **Seed money** is money that is given to someone to help them start a new business or project. [BUSINESS] ❑ The government will give seed money to the project.

seedy /sidi/ (seedier, seediest) ADJ If you describe a person or place as **seedy**, you disapprove of them because they look dirty and messy, or they have a bad reputation. [DISAPPROVAL] ❑ Frank ran dodgy errands for a seedy local villain. ❑ We were staying in a seedy hotel close to the red light district.

seeing-eye dog (seeing-eye dogs) also Seeing Eye dog, seeing eye dog N-COUNT A **seeing-eye dog** is a dog that has been trained to lead a blind person. [AM; BRIT **guide dog**]

seek ◆◇◇ /sik/ (seeks, seeking, sought) ■ V-T If you **seek** something such as a job or a place to live, you try to find one. [FORMAL] ❑ They have had to seek work as labourers. ❑ Four people who sought refuge in the Italian embassy have left voluntarily. ■ V-T When someone **seeks** something, they try to obtain it. [FORMAL] ❑ The prosecutors have warned they will seek the death penalty. ■ V-T If you **seek** someone's help or advice, you contact them in order to ask for it. [FORMAL] ❑ Always seek professional legal advice before entering into any agreement. ❑ On important issues, they seek a second opinion. ■ V-T If you **seek to** do something, you try to do it. [FORMAL] ❑ He also denied that he would seek to annex the country.

Word Partnership	seek의 연어
N.	seek **asylum**, seek **election**, seek **employment**, seek **shelter** ■ ■
	seek **justice**, seek **revenge** ■
	seek **advice**, seek **approval**, seek **assistance/help**, seek **counseling**, seek **permission**, seek **protection**, seek **support** ■

▶seek out PHRASAL VERB If you **seek out** someone or something or **seek** them **out**, you keep looking for them until you find them. ❑ Now is the time for local companies to seek out business opportunities in Europe.

seek|er /sikər/ (seekers) N-COUNT A **seeker** is someone who is looking for or trying to get something. ❑ I am a seeker after truth. →see also **asylum seeker**

seem ◆◆◆ /sim/ (seems, seeming, seemed) ■ V-LINK You use **seem** to say that someone or something gives the impression of having a particular quality, or of happening in the way you describe. [no cont] ❑ We heard a series of explosions.

구동사 준비하다, 채비하다 ❑ 토니는 점심 식사 준비를 할 시간이 되었다고 알렸다.

■ 구동사 배웅하다 ❑ 벤은 재키를 비행기까지 배웅한 다음 자신은 저녁 식사로 스테이크를 먹을 계획을 세웠었다. ■ 구동사 이기다, 격퇴하다 [영국영어] ❑ 그들이 공화당의 도전을 이겨 내지 못할 이유는 없다.

구동사 꿰뚫어 보다, 간파하다 ❑ 처음부터 네 비열한 계략을 간파했다.

구동사 처리하다 ❑ 프랭클린이 짐을 처리하는 동안, 사라가 엘리너를 집에 데리고 갔다.

■ 가산명사 또는 불가산명사 씨 ❑ 양배추 씨 한 묶음 ❑ 흙을 주성분으로 한 배양토를 담은 화분에 그 씨앗을 뿌렸다. ■ 타동사 ~에 씨를 뿌리다 ❑ 사람들이 넓은 잔디밭에서 잔디를 깎고 씨를 뿌렸다. ❑ 앵초꽃은 가파른 언덕 사면에서 스스로 씨를 뿌리기 시작할 것이다. ■ 복수명사 씨앗, 근원 [문예체] ❑ 그는 배심원들의 마음속에 의혹의 씨앗을 심기 위해 의도된 질문들을 했다. ■ 가산명사 (테니스 등의) 시드 선수 ❑ 윔블던 탑 시드 선수이자 세계 1위인 피트 샘프라스 ■ 타동사 시드를 배정받다 ❑ 유럽 축구연맹 컵에서는 상위 16개 팀이 1회전 시드를 배정받는다. ❑ 그는 브래드 베번 다음으로, 두 번째 시드를 배정받는다. ■ 구 꽃과 열매를 맺다 ❑ 뽑지 않고 놔두면, 겨울 무는 봄에 꽃과 열매를 맺는다. ■ 구 한창때가 지나다, 한물가다 ❑ 그는 경제가 한물갔다고 말한다.

불가산명사 초기 투입 자본 [경제] ❑ 나는 최근의 벤처 사업 초기 투입 자본을 조달하기 위해 자본가들과 협상하고 있다.

불가산명사 초기 투자금 [주로 영국영어, 경제] ❑ 그 계획은 단 4퍼센트의 금리로 최고 10,000파운드의 융자를 초기 투자금으로 제공한다.

가산명사 묘목

불가산명사 착수 자금, 종잣돈 [경제] ❑ 정부가 그 계획에 착수 자금을 댈 것이다.

형용사 지저분한, 평판이 나쁜 [탐탁찮음] ❑ 프랭크는 평판이 나쁜 동네 악당을 위해 위험한 심부름을 했다. ❑ 우리는 홍등가 가까이에 있는 지저분한 호텔에 머물고 있었다.

가산명사 맹도견 [미국영어; 영국영어 guide dog]

■ 타동사 찾다, 구하다 [격식체] ❑ 그들은 인부 일자리를 찾아야 했다. ❑ 이탈리아 대사관으로 피난했던 네 사람이 자발적으로 떠났다. ■ 타동사 얻으려고 하다 [격식체] ❑ 검찰 측에서는 사형에 처할 수 있도록 하겠다고 경고해 왔다. ■ 타동사 구하다 [격식체] ❑ 합의에 들어가기 전에 항상 전문가의 법률적 조언을 구하세요. ❑ 중요한 사안에 대해서는, 그들은 2차 소견을 구한다. ■ 타동사 ~하려고 시도하다 [격식체] ❑ 그는 그 나라의 합병을 시도하리라는 것 역시 부인했다.

구동사 ~을 열심히 찾다 ❑ 지금이 지역 기업들에게는 유럽에서 사업 기회를 찾을 때이다.

가산명사 탐구자, 추구하는 사람 ❑ 나는 진리를 탐구하는 사람이다.

■ 연결동사 ~처럼 보이다, ~인 것 같다 ❑ 우리는 일련의 폭발음을 들었다. 꽤 가까운 곳인 것 같았다. ❑ 그들을 아는 모든 사람들에게, 그들은 이상적인 한

They seemed quite close by. ❏ *To everyone who knew them, they seemed an ideal couple.* ❏ *The calming effect seemed to last for about ten minutes.* ❏ *It was a record that seemed beyond reach.* ❏ *The proposal seems designed to break opposition to the government's economic program.* ❏ *It seems that the attack this morning was very carefully planned to cause few casualties.* ❏ *It seemed as if she'd been gone forever.* ◳ V-LINK You use **seem** when you are describing your own feelings or thoughts, or describing something that has happened to you, in order to make your statement less forceful. [VAGUENESS] [no cont] ❏ *I seem to have lost all my self-confidence.* ❏ *I seem to remember giving you very precise instructions.* ◳ PHRASE If you say that you **cannot seem** or **could not seem to** do something, you mean that you have tried to do it and were unable to. ❏ *No matter how hard I try I cannot seem to catch up on all the bills.*

쌍으로 보였다. ❏ 진정 효과가 약 10분 가량 지속되는 것 같았다. ❏ 그것은 믿을 수 없을 것 같은 기록이었다. ❏ 그 제안은 정부의 경제 계획에 대한 반대를 분쇄하기 위해 계획된 것처럼 보인다. ❏ 오늘 아침의 공습은 극소수의 사상자만을 내도록 아주 면밀히 계획되었던 것 같다. ❏ 마치 그녀가 아주 가 버린 것 같았다. ◳ 연결동사 -인 것 같다 [짐작투] ❏ 나는 자신감을 모두 상실한 것 같다. ❏ 너에게 아주 세세한 지시를 했던 기억이 나는 것 같다. ◳ 구 -할 수 있을 것 같지 않다 ❏ 아무리 노력해도 그 모든 공과금을 다 감당할 수 있을 것 같지 않다.

seem|ing /síːmɪŋ/ ADJ **Seeming** means appearing to be the case, but not necessarily the case. For example, if you talk about someone's **seeming** ability to do something, you mean that they appear to be able to do it, but you are not certain. [FORMAL, VAGUENESS] [ADJ n] ❏ *Wall Street analysts have been highly critical of the company's seeming inability to control costs.*

형용사 외관상의, 겉보기의 [격식체, 짐작투] ❏ 월 스트리트 분석가들은 그 회사의 외형적인 비용 조절 능력 부족을 크게 비판해 왔다.

seem|ing|ly /síːmɪŋli/ ◳ ADV If something is **seemingly** the case, you mean that it appears to be the case, even though it may not really be so. [ADV adj/adv] ❏ *A seemingly endless line of trucks waits in vain to load up.* ◳ ADV You use **seemingly** when you want to say that something seems to be true. [VAGUENESS] ❏ *He has moved to Spain, seemingly to enjoy a slower style of life.*

◳ 부사 겉보기에는 ❏ 끝없이 이어진 것처럼 보이는 화물차들이 짐을 싣기 위해 헛되이 기다린다. ◳ 부사 -인 듯이 [짐작투] ❏ 그는 보다 느린 생활 방식을 누리기 위해서인 듯, 스페인으로 이주했다.

seen /siːn/ **Seen** is the past participle of **see**.

see의 과거 분사

seep /siːp/ (**seeps, seeping, seeped**) ◳ V-I If something such as liquid or gas **seeps** somewhere, it flows slowly and in small amounts into a place where it should not go. ❏ *Radioactive water had seeped into underground reservoirs.* ❏ *The gas is seeping out of the rocks.* ● N-COUNT **Seep** is also a noun. ❏ *...an oil seep.* ◳ V-I If something such as secret information or an unpleasant emotion **seeps** somewhere, it comes out gradually. ❏ *...the tide of racism which is sweeping Europe seeps into Britain.*

◳ 자동사 새다, 스미다 ❏ 방사능을 띤 물이 지하 저수지로 스며 들어가 있다. ● 가산명사 누출 ❏ 기름 누출 ◳ 자동사 서서히 퍼지다 ❏ 유럽을 휩쓸고 있는 인종 차별주의의 조류가 영국에 서서히 퍼져 든다.

see|saw /síːsɔː/ (**seesaws**) also **see-saw** N-COUNT A **seesaw** is a long board which is balanced on a fixed part in the middle. To play on it, a child sits on each end, and when one end goes up, the other goes down. ❏ *There was a sandpit, a seesaw, and a swing in the playground.*

가산명사 시소 ❏ 놀이터에는 모래밭과 시소, 그네가 있었다.

seethe /siːð/ (**seethes, seething, seethed**) V-I When you **are seething**, you are very angry about something but do not express your feelings about it. ❏ *She took it calmly at first but under the surface was seething.* ❏ *She put a hand on her hip, grinning derisively, while I seethed with rage.*

자동사 (속으로) 화가 끓어오르다 ❏ 그녀는 처음에는 침착하게 받아들였으나 속으로는 화가 끓어오르고 있었다. ❏ 나는 미칠 듯이 화가 치밀어 오르는데 그녀는 비웃듯이 싱글거리며 엉덩이께를 한 손으로 짚었다.

see-through ADJ **See-through** clothes are made of thin cloth, so that you can see a person's body or underwear through them. ❏ *She was wearing a white, see-through blouse, a red bra showing beneath.*

형용사 속이 비치는 ❏ 그녀는 속이 비치는 흰색 블라우스를 입고 있었고, 그 안에 입은 빨간 브래지어가 보였다.

seg|ment ◆◇◇ /ségmənt/ (**segments**) ◳ N-COUNT A **segment of** something is one part of it, considered separately from the rest. ❏ *...the poorer segments of society.* ◳ N-COUNT A **segment** of fruit such as an orange or grapefruit is one of the sections into which it is easily divided. ❏ *Peel all the fruit except the lime and separate into segments.* ◳ N-COUNT A **segment** of a circle is one of the two parts into which it is divided when you draw a straight line through it. ❏ *The other children stood around the circle, one in each segment.*

◳ 가산명사 부분 ❏ 사회의 빈곤한 층들 ◳ 가산명사 조각, (과일의) 쪽 ❏ 라임을 제외한 나머지 모든 과일의 껍질을 벗겨서 조각조각 떼어 놓으세요. ◳ 가산명사 (원의) 활꼴 ❏ 다른 아이들은 원 주위에, 각각 다른 활꼴 안에 한 명씩 섰다.

seg|re|gate /ségrɪɡeɪt/ (**segregates, segregating, segregated**) V-T To **segregate** two groups of people or things means to keep them physically apart from each other. ❏ *A large detachment of police was used to segregate the two rival camps of protesters.*

타동사 분리하다; 차별하다 ❏ 서로 맞선 두 시위 진영을 분리하기 위해 대규모의 경찰 분견대가 투입되었다.

seg|re|gat|ed /ségrɪɡeɪtɪd/ ADJ **Segregated** buildings or areas are kept for the use of one group of people who are the same race, sex, or religion, and no other group is allowed to use them. ❏ *...racially segregated schools.*

형용사 특수한 인종이나 집단에 한정된 ❏ 특정 인종의 학생들만 다니는 학교들

seg|re|ga|tion /ségrɪɡeɪʃ°n/ N-UNCOUNT **Segregation** is the official practice of keeping people apart, usually people of different sexes, races, or religions. ❏ *The Supreme Court unanimously ruled that racial segregation in schools was unconstitutional.*

불가산명사 분리, 차별 ❏ 대법원은 전원 일치로 학교에서의 인종 차별은 헌법에 위배된다는 판결을 내렸다.

seis|mic /sáɪzmɪk/ ADJ **Seismic** means caused by or relating to an earthquake. [ADJ n] ❏ *Earthquakes produce two types of seismic waves.* →see **earthquake**

형용사 지진의, 지진에 의한 ❏ 지진은 두 가지 형태의 지진파를 발생시킨다.

seize ◆◇◇ /siːz/ (**seizes, seizing, seized**) ◳ V-T If you **seize** something, you take hold of it quickly, firmly, and forcefully. ❏ *"Leigh," he said seizing my arm to hold me back.* ◳ V-T When a group of people **seize** a place or **seize** control of it, they take control of it quickly and suddenly, using force. ❏ *Troops have seized the airport and railroad terminals.* ◳ V-T If a government or other authority **seizes** someone's property, they take it from them, often by force. ❏ *Police were reported to have seized all copies of this morning's edition of the newspaper.* ◳ V-T When someone **is seized**, they are arrested or captured. ❏ *UN officials say two military observers were seized by the Khmer Rouge yesterday.* ◳ V-T When you **seize** an opportunity, you take advantage of it and do something that you want to do. ❏ *During the riots hundreds of people seized the opportunity to steal property.*

◳ 타동사 왁 붙들다 ❏ "리."라고 그가 나를 말리려고 팔을 붙들며 말했다. ◳ 타동사 점령하다, 장악하다 ❏ 군대가 공항과 철도 터미널을 점령했다. ◳ 타동사 압수하다, 몰수하다 ❏ 경찰이 그 신문의 오늘 조간판을 전부 압수했다고 보도됐다. ◳ 타동사 붙잡히다, 체포되다 ❏ 어제 군사 시찰자 두 명이 크메르 루주에게 붙잡혔다고 유엔 임원들이 말한다. ◳ 타동사 (기회를) 붙잡다, 포착하다 ❏ 폭동 중에 수백 명의 사람들이 기회를 포착하여 물건을 훔쳤다.

▶ **seize on** PHRASAL VERB If you **seize on** something or **seize upon** it, you show great interest in it, often because it is useful to you. ❏ *When the results were published, newspapers around the world seized on them as proof that global warming isn't really happening.*

구동사 -에 큰 관심을 보이다 ❏ 그 결과가 발표되었을 때, 전 세계 신문들은 그것을 지구 온난화가 실제 일어나지 않고 있다는 증거로 여기고 큰 관심을 보였다.

▶ **seize up** ◳ PHRASAL VERB If a part of your body **seizes up**, it suddenly stops working, because you have strained it or because you are getting old. ❏ *After two days' exertions, it's the arms and hands that seize up, not the legs.* ◳ PHRASAL VERB If something such as an engine **seizes up**, it stops working, because it has not been properly cared for. ❏ *She put diesel fuel, instead of petrol, into the tank causing the motor to seize up.*

◳ 구동사 (몸이) 굳다, 말을 안 듣다 ❏ 이틀 동안 힘든 작업을 하고 나니, 말을 듣지 않는 것이 다리가 아니라 팔과 손이다. ◳ 구동사 (기계 등이) 멈추다 ❏ 그녀가 연료 탱크에 가솔린 대신 디젤 연료를 넣어서 모터가 서 버렸다.

sei|zure /siːʒər/ (**seizures**) **1** N-COUNT If someone has a **seizure**, they have a sudden violent attack of an illness, especially one that affects their heart or brain. □ ...a mild cardiac seizure. **2** N-COUNT If there is a **seizure of** power or a **seizure of** an area of land, a group of people suddenly take control of the place, using force. □ ...the seizure of territory through force. **3** N-COUNT When an organization such as the police or customs service makes a **seizure of** illegal goods, they find them and take them away. □ Police have made one of the biggest seizures of heroin there's ever been in Britain.

1 가산명사 발작 □ 가벼운 심장 발작 **2** 가산명사 장악 □ 영토의 무력 장악 **3** 가산명사 압수, 몰수 □ 경찰은 영국에서 사상 최대 규모의 헤로인 압수 건을 올렸다.

sel|dom /sɛldəm/ ADV If something **seldom** happens, it happens only occasionally. □ They seldom speak. □ I've seldom felt so happy.

부사 좀처럼 ~않는 □ 그들은 좀처럼 말을 하지 않는다. □ 그렇게 행복한 적이 별로 없었다.

se|lect ♦♢♢ /sɪlɛkt/ (**selects, selecting, selected**) **1** V-T If you **select** something, you choose it from a number of things of the same kind. □ Voters are selecting candidates for both U.S. Senate seats and for 52 congressional seats. □ With a difficult tee shot, select a club which will keep you short of the trouble. **2** V-T If you **select** a file or a piece of text on a computer screen, you click on it so that it is marked in a different color, usually in order for you to give the computer an instruction relating to that file or piece of text. [COMPUTING] □ I selected a file and pressed the Delete key. **3** ADJ A **select** group is a small group of some of the best people or things of their kind. [ADJ n] □ ...a select group of French cheeses. **4** ADJ If you describe something as **select**, you mean it has many desirable features, but is available only to people who have a lot of money or who belong to a high social class. □ Christian Lacroix is throwing a very lavish and very select party.

1 타동사 뽑다, 선택하다, 고르다 □ 유권자들은 미 상원 의석과 52석의 하원 의석 두 가지 모두에 대한 후보들을 뽑고 있다. □ 까다로운 티 샷을 할 때는, 트러블을 피할 수 있는 채를 선택하세요. **2** 타동사 (마우스를 클릭하여) 선택하다 [컴퓨터] □ 나는 파일 하나를 선택한 다음 삭제 키를 눌렀다. **3** 형용사 추려 낸, 엄선한 □ 엄선한 프랑스산 치즈 모음 **4** 형용사 상류층용의, 고급의 □ 크리스티앙 라크로아가 대단히 사치스럽고 고급스러운 파티를 열고 있다.

Thesaurus	select의 참조어
V.	choose, pick out, take **1**
ADJ.	best, exclusive **3** **4**

se|lec|tion ♦♢♢ /sɪlɛkʃən/ (**selections**) **1** N-UNCOUNT **Selection** is the act of selecting one or more people or things from a group. □ ...Darwin's principles of natural selection. □ Dr. Sullivan's selection to head the Department of Health was greeted with satisfaction. **2** N-COUNT A **selection of** people or things is a set of them that have been selected from a larger group. □ ...this selection of popular songs. **3** N-COUNT The **selection of** goods in a store is the particular range of goods that it has available and from which you can choose what you want. □ It offers the widest selection of antiques of every description in a one day market.

1 불가산명사 선발, 선택 □ 다윈의 자연 도태의 원리 □ 설리번 박사의 보건부 장관 인선은 환영을 받았다. **2** 가산명사 엄선된 사람들, 엄선된 것들 □ 이 정선된 대중가요 모음집 **3** 가산명사 취급 품목 □ 그 상점은 온갖 종류의 골동품을 일일장에서 가장 폭넓게 취급한다.

se|lec|tive /sɪlɛktɪv/ **1** ADJ A **selective** process applies only to a few things or people. [ADJ n] □ Selective breeding may result in a greyhound running faster and seeing better than a wolf. ● **se|lec|tive|ly** ADV □ Within the project, trees are selectively cut on a 25-year rotation. **2** ADJ When someone is **selective**, they choose things carefully, for example the things that they buy or do. □ Sales still happen, but buyers are more selective. ● **se|lec|tive|ly** ADV [ADV with v] □ ...people on small incomes who wanted to shop selectively. **3** ADJ If you say that someone has a **selective** memory, you disapprove of the fact that they remember certain facts about something and deliberately forget others, often because it is convenient for them to do so. [DISAPPROVAL] □ We seem to have a selective memory for the best bits of the past. ● **se|lec|tive|ly** ADV [ADV with v] □ ...a tendency to remember only the pleasurable effects of the drug and selectively forget all the adverse effects.

1 형용사 선택적인 □ 선택 교배를 통해 늑대보다 더 빨리 달리고 더 앞을 잘 보는 그레이하운드를 만들어 낼 수도 있다. ● 선택적으로 부사 □ 그 사업 계획에서, 나무들이 25년 주기로 돌아가면서 선택적으로 벌체된다. **2** 형용사 신중하게 고르는 □ 여전히 세일이 벌어지지만, 소비자들은 더 신중하게 고른다. ● 신중하게 골라 부사 □ 신중하게 쇼핑을 하고 싶어 하는 저소득층 사람들 **3** 형용사 선택적인, 편의적인 [탐탁찮음] □ 우리는 과거의 가장 좋은 부분들에 대해 선택적으로 기억을 하는 것 같다. ● 선택적으로, 편의에 따라 부사 □ 마약의 좋은 효과만을 기억하고 모든 해로운 결과는 편의에 따라 잊어버리는 경향

self ♦♢♢ /sɛlf/ (**selves**) **1** N-COUNT Your **self** is your basic personality or nature, especially considered in terms of what you are really like as a person. □ You're looking more like your usual self. **2** N-COUNT A person's **self** is the essential part of their nature which makes them different from everyone and everything else. □ I want to explore and get in touch with my inner self. □ The face is the true self visible to others.

1 가산명사 자신, 자아 □ 네가 일상적인 네 자신의 모습에 더 가까워 보인다. **2** 가산명사 본성 □ 나의 내적 본성을 탐구하고 그것에 접촉하고 싶다. □ 얼굴은 다른 이들이 볼 수 있는 진정한 본성이다.

self-access ADJ In a school or college, a **self-access** centre is a place where students can choose and use books, tapes, or other materials. [BRIT] □ ...a self-access study centre.

형용사 자율 학습의 [영국영어] □ 자율 학습 센터

self-adhesive ADJ Something that is **self-adhesive** is covered on one side with a sticky substance like glue, so that it will stick to surfaces. □ ...self-adhesive labels.

형용사 접착제가 발라져 있는 □ 접착제가 발라져 있는 라벨

self-assessment N-SING In Britain, **self-assessment** refers to a system for paying tax in which people have to fill in an official form giving details of how much money they have earned in the previous year. [BUSINESS]

단수명사 자진 신고 납세 [경제]

self-assured ADJ Someone who is **self-assured** shows confidence in what they say and do because they are sure of their own abilities. □ He's a self-assured, confident negotiator.

형용사 자신 있는 □ 그는 자신감 있고 확신에 찬 교섭자이다.

self-catering N-UNCOUNT If you go on a **self-catering** holiday or you stay in **self-catering** accommodation, you stay in a place where you have to make your own meals. [BRIT] □ ...a week's self-catering in Majorca for £239.

불가산명사 식사를 직접 해 먹을 수 있는 숙소; 식사를 직접 해 먹으며 보내는 휴가 [영국영어] □ 239파운드으로 식사를 직접 해 먹을 수 있으며 일주일을 보내는 마요르카 여행

self-centered [BRIT **self-centred**] ADJ Someone who is **self-centered** is only concerned with their own wants and needs and never thinks about other people. [DISAPPROVAL] □ It's very self-centered to think that people are talking about you.

[영국영어 self-centred] 형용사 자기중심의, 자기 본위의 [탐탁찮음] □ 사람들이 너에 대해 이야기하고 있다고 생각하는 건 매우 자기중심적인 일이다.

self-confessed ADJ If you describe someone as a **self-confessed** murderer or a **self-confessed** romantic, for example, you mean that they admit openly that they are a murderer or a romantic. [ADJ n] □ The self-confessed drug addict was arrested 13 months ago.

형용사 자인하는 □ 스스로 마약 중독자라고 밝힌 그 사람은 13개월 전에 체포되었다.

self-confidence N-UNCOUNT If you have **self-confidence**, you behave confidently because you feel sure of your abilities or value. □ With the end of my love affair, I lost all the self-confidence I once had.

불가산명사 자신감 □ 연애가 끝남과 함께 나는 한때 가졌던 자신감을 모두 잃었다.

self-confident ADJ Someone who is **self-confident** behaves confidently because they feel sure of their abilities or value. □ She'd blossomed into a self-confident young woman.

형용사 자신감 있는 □ 그녀는 자신감 있는 젊은 여성이 되어 있었다.

A

self-conscious ADJ Someone who is **self-conscious** is easily embarrassed and nervous because they feel that everyone is looking at them and judging them. ❑ *I felt a bit self-conscious in my swimming costume.*

형용사 타인의 시선을 의식하는, 자의식이 강한 ❑ 수영복을 입자 다른 사람의 시선이 신경 쓰였다.

B

self-contained ◼ ADJ You can describe someone or something as **self-contained** when they are complete and separate and do not need help or resources from outside. ❑ *He seems completely self-contained and he doesn't miss you when you're not there.* ◼ ADJ **Self-contained** accommodations such as an apartment have all their own facilities, so that a person living there does not have to share rooms such as a kitchen or bathroom with other people. ❑ *Her family lives in a self-contained three-bedroom suite in the back of the main house.*

◼ 형용사 자족적인 ❑ 그는 완전히 자족하는 것처럼 보이며 네가 없어도 너를 아쉬워하지 않는다. ◼ 형용사 일체 설비가 완비된 ❑ 그녀의 가족은 본채 뒤에 있는 일체 설비가 완비된 침실 세 개짜리 스위트에서 산다.

C

D

self-control N-UNCOUNT **Self-control** is the ability to not show your feelings or not do the things that your feelings make you want to do. ❑ *His self-control, reserve, and aloofness were almost inhuman.*

불가산명사 자제력 ❑ 그의 자제력과 침착함, 초연함은 거의 초인적인 것이었다.

E

self-defense [BRIT **self-defence**] ◼ N-UNCOUNT **Self-defense** is the use of force to protect yourself against someone who is attacking you. ❑ *The women acted in self-defense after years of abuse.* ◼ N-UNCOUNT **Self-defense** is the action of protecting yourself against something bad. ❑ *Hapkido is a Korean form of self-defense.*

[영국영어 self-defence] ◼ 불가산명사 자기 방어; 정당방위 ❑ 그 여자들은 수년간의 학대를 겪은 후 정당방위를 행사했다. ◼ 불가산명사 자기 방어 ❑ 합기도는 한국 호신술의 한 형태이다.

F

self-determination N-UNCOUNT **Self-determination** is the right of a country to be independent, instead of being controlled by a foreign country, and to choose its own form of government. ❑ *...Lithuania's right to self-determination.*

불가산명사 자결(自決) ❑ 리투아니아의 자결권

G

self-employed ADJ If you are **self-employed**, you organize your own work and taxes and are paid by people for a service you provide, rather than being paid a regular salary by a person or a firm. [BUSINESS] ❑ *There are no paid holidays or sick leave if you are self-employed.* ● N-PLURAL The **self-employed** are people who are self-employed. ❑ *We want more support for the self-employed.*

형용사 자영업의 [경제] ❑ 당신이 자영업을 한다면 유급 휴가나 병가는 없다. ● 복수명사 자영업자 ❑ 우리는 자영업자에게 더 많은 지원이 주어지기를 바란다.

H

self-esteem N-UNCOUNT Your **self-esteem** is how you feel about yourself. For example, if you have low **self-esteem**, you do not like yourself, you do not think that you are a valuable person, and therefore you do not behave confidently. ❑ *Poor self-esteem is at the centre of many of the difficulties we experience in our relationships.*

불가산명사 자존심, 자부심 ❑ 우리가 관계 속에서 경험하는 많은 어려움의 중심에는 허약한 자부심이 있다.

I

J

self-evident ADJ A fact or situation that is **self-evident** is so obvious that there is no need for proof or explanation. ❑ *It is self-evident that we will never have enough resources to meet the demand.*

형용사 자명한 ❑ 우리가 수요를 충족시킬 만큼 충분한 자원을 갖지 못하리라는 것은 자명하다.

K

self-explanatory ADJ Something that is **self-explanatory** is clear and easy to understand without needing any extra information or explanation. ❑ *I hope the graphs on the following pages are self-explanatory.*

형용사 자명한, 설명이 필요 없는 ❑ 다음 페이지들에 나오는 그래프로 충분한 설명이 되리라고 봅니다.

L

self-help N-UNCOUNT **Self-help** consists of people providing support and help for each other in an informal way, rather than relying on the government, authorities, or other official organizations. ❑ *She helped her Mom set up a self-help group for parents with over-weight children.*

불가산명사 자립, 자조 ❑ 그녀는 어머니가 체중 과다 아동 부모들의 자립 모임을 만드는 것을 도왔다.

M

self-image (**self-images**) N-COUNT Your **self-image** is the set of ideas you have about your own qualities and abilities. ❑ *Children who have a positive self-image are less likely to present behavior and discipline problems.*

가산명사 자아상 ❑ 긍정적인 자아상을 가지고 있는 아이들은 행동 문제나 훈육 문제를 일으킬 가능성이 더 적다.

N

self-important ADJ If you say that someone is **self-important**, you disapprove of them because they behave as if they are more important than they really are. [DISAPPROVAL] ❑ *He was self-important, vain, and ignorant.* ● **self-importance** N-UNCOUNT ❑ *Many visitors complained of his bad manners and self-importance.*

형용사 젠체하는, 자만심이 강한 [탐탁찮음] ❑ 그는 자만심이 강하고 우쭐대는데다가 무식했다. ● 젠체함, 거만함 불가산명사 ❑ 많은 방문객들이 그의 무례함과 거만함에 대해 불평했다.

O

self-imposed ADJ A **self-imposed** restriction, task, or situation is one that you have deliberately created or accepted for yourself. ❑ *He returned home after eleven years of self-imposed exile.*

형용사 스스로 부과한, 자진해서 하는 ❑ 그는 십일 년간의 자진 유배 끝에 고국으로 돌아왔다.

P

self-indulgence (**self-indulgences**) N-VAR **Self-indulgence** is the act of allowing yourself to have or do the things that you enjoy very much. ❑ *He prayed to be saved from self-indulgence.*

가산명사 또는 불가산명사 방종, 제멋대로 삶 ❑ 그는 방종으로부터 구원받기를 기도했다.

Q

self-indulgent ADJ If you say that someone is **self-indulgent**, you mean that they allow themselves to have or do the things that they enjoy very much. ❑ *Why give publicity to this self-indulgent, adolescent oaf?*

형용사 방종한, 제멋대로 구는 ❑ 왜 이 제멋대로이며 애송이인 명청이에게 인기를 안겨 줘야 한단 말인가?

R

S

self-inflicted ADJ A **self-inflicted** wound or injury is one that you do to yourself deliberately. ❑ *He is being treated for a self-inflicted gunshot wound.*

형용사 스스로에게 가한, 자초한 ❑ 그는 본인이 자초한 총상을 치료받고 있다.

self-interest N-UNCOUNT If you accuse someone of **self-interest**, you disapprove of them because they always want to do what is best for themselves rather than for anyone else. [DISAPPROVAL] ❑ *Their current protests are motivated purely by self-interest.*

불가산명사 사리사욕, 사리 추구 [탐탁찮음] ❑ 그들이 현재 벌이고 있는 항의는 순전히 사리사욕에 기인한 것이다.

T

U

self|ish /sɛlfɪʃ/ ADJ If you say that someone is **selfish**, you mean that he or she cares only about himself or herself, and not about other people. ❑ *I think I've been very selfish. I've been mainly concerned with myself.* ● **self|ish|ly** ADV ❑ *The government's image has been tarnished because Cabinet Ministers are selfishly pursuing their own vested interests.* ● **self|ish|ness** N-UNCOUNT ❑ *The arrogance and selfishness of different interest groups never ceases to amaze me.*

형용사 이기적인 [탐탁찮음] ❑ 내가 대단히 이기적이었던 것 같다. 나는 대체로 내 자신에 대해서만 관심을 가져 왔다. ● 이기적으로 부사 ❑ 각료들이 이기적으로 자신들의 기득권을 추구하고 있기 때문에 정부의 이미지가 손상되어 왔다. ● 이기심 불가산명사 ❑ 각 이익 집단의 오만과 이기심이 끊임없이 나를 아연케 한다.

V

W

self|less /sɛlflɪs/ ADJ If you say that someone is **selfless**, you approve of them because they care about other people more than themselves. [APPROVAL] ❑ *She was a wonderful companion and her generosity to me was entirely selfless.*

형용사 이타적인, 사심 없는 [마음에 듦] ❑ 그녀는 훌륭한 동반자였으며 나에 대한 그녀의 관대함은 완전히 사심 없는 것이었다.

X

self-pity N-UNCOUNT **Self-pity** is a feeling of unhappiness that you have about yourself and your problems, especially when this is unnecessary or greatly exaggerated. [DISAPPROVAL] ❑ *I was unable to shake off my self-pity.*

불가산명사 자기 연민 [탐탁찮음] ❑ 나는 자기 연민을 떨쳐 버릴 수가 없었다.

Y

self-portrait (**self-portraits**) N-COUNT A **self-portrait** is a drawing, painting, or written description that you do of yourself.

가산명사 자화상

Z

self-regulation N-UNCOUNT **Self-regulation** is the controlling of a process or activity by the people or organizations that are involved in it rather than by an

불가산명사 자기 규제 ❑ 자기 규제가 효과를 보기에는 기업들 간의 경쟁이 지나치게 격심하다.

outside organization such as the government. ❏ *Competition between companies is too fierce for self-regulation to work.*

self-respect N-UNCOUNT **Self-respect** is a feeling of confidence and pride in your own ability and worth. ❏ *They have lost not only their jobs, but their homes, their self-respect and even their reason for living.*

불가산명사 자기 존중, 자존심 ❏ 그들은 일자리만 잃은 것이 아니라, 집과 자존심, 살아갈 이유마저도 잃어버렸다.

self-righteous ADJ If you describe someone as **self-righteous**, you disapprove of them because they are convinced that they are right in their beliefs, attitudes, and behavior and that other people are wrong. [DISAPPROVAL] ❏ *He is critical of the monks, whom he considers narrow-minded and self-righteous.* ● **self-righteousness** N-UNCOUNT ❏ *Her aggressiveness and self-righteousness caused prickles of anger at the back of her neck.*

형용사 독선적인 [탐탁잖음] ❏ 그는 그 수도사들을 비난하는데, 그가 보기에 그들은 편협하고 독선적이기 때문이다. ● 독선 불가산명사 ❏ 그녀의 호전성과 독선에 그는 화가 나서 목뒤가 쑤시는 듯이 아팠다.

self-service ADJ A **self-service** store, restaurant, or garage is one where you get things for yourself rather than being served by another person. ❏ *... a self-service cafeteria with a wide choice.*

형용사 셀프서비스의, 손님이 손수 갖다 먹는 식의 ❏ 선택의 폭이 넓은 셀프서비스식 카페테리아

> Gasoline stations in the North America offer **full-service** and **self-service**. In **self-service** gas stations, the customer pumps his own gasoline and pays the attendant. Self-serve gasoline is cheaper than gas pumped by the attendant.

> 북미의 주유소에는 full-service(풀서비스)와 self-service(셀프서비스)가 있다. 셀프서비스 주유소에서는 고객이 직접 주유하고 주유소 직원에게 돈을 낸다. 직접 주유하는 기름이 주유소 직원이 주유해 주는 기름보다 값이 싸다.

self-study N-UNCOUNT **Self-study** is study that you do on your own, without a teacher. ❏ *Individuals can enroll on self-study courses in the university's language institute.*

불가산명사 독학 ❏ 개인이 그 대학 언어 연구소의 독학 강좌에 등록할 수도 있다.

self-styled ADJ If you describe someone as a **self-styled** leader or expert, you disapprove of them because they claim to be a leader or expert but they do not actually have the right to call themselves this. [DISAPPROVAL] [ADJ n] ❏ *Two of those arrested are said to be self-styled area commanders.*

형용사 자칭하는, 자임하는 [탐탁잖음] ❏ 구속된 자들 중 두 명은 자칭 지구 사령관이라고 일컬어진다.

self-sufficiency /sɛlf səfɪʃ°nsi/ N-UNCOUNT **Self-sufficiency** is the state of being self-sufficient.

불가산명사 자급자족

self-sufficient ■ ADJ If a country or group is **self-sufficient**, it is able to produce or make everything that it needs. ❏ *This enabled the country to become self-sufficient in sugar.* ■ ADJ Someone who is **self-sufficient** is able to live happily without anyone else. ❏ *Although she had various boyfriends, Madeleine was, and remains, fiercely self-sufficient.*

■ 형용사 자급자족할 수 있는 ❏ 이로 인해 그 나라는 설탕을 자급자족할 수 있게 되었다. ② 형용사 혼자서도 잘 사는, 독립적인 ❏ 많은 남자 친구들이 있었지만, 마델레인은 과거에나 현재나 철저하게 혼자서도 행복하게 잘 산다.

sell ♦♦♦ /sɛl/ (**sells, selling, sold**) ■ V-T/V-I If you **sell** something that you own, you let someone have it in return for money. ❏ *Catlin sold the paintings to Philadelphia industrialist Joseph Harrison.* ❏ *The directors sold the business for £14.8 million.* ② V-T If a store **sells** a particular thing, it is available for people to buy there. ❏ *It sells everything from hair ribbons to oriental rugs.* ③ V-I If something **sells** for a particular price, that price is paid for it. ❏ *Unmodernized property can sell for up to 40 per cent of its modernized market value.* ④ V-I If something **sells**, it is bought by the public, usually in fairly large quantities. ❏ *Even if this album doesn't sell and the critics don't like it, we wouldn't ever change.* ⑤ V-T Something that **sells** a product makes people want to buy the product. ❏ *It is only the sensational that sells news magazines.* ⑥ V-T If you **sell** someone an idea or proposal, or **sell** someone **on** an idea, you convince them that it is a good one. ❏ *She tried to sell me the idea of buying my own paper shredder.* ❏ *She is hoping she can sell the idea to clients.* ⑦ PHRASE If someone **sells** their **body**, they have sex for money. ❏ *85 per cent said they would rather not sell their bodies for a living.* ⑧ PHRASE If you talk about someone **selling** their **soul** in order to get something, you are criticizing them for abandoning their principles. [DISAPPROVAL] ❏ *...a man who would sell his soul for political viability.*

■ 타동사/자동사 팔다 ❏ 캐틀린은 그 그림들을 필라델피아의 실업가 조셉 해리슨에게 팔았다. ❏ 이사들이 그 기업체를 1천 4백 8십만 달러에 매각했다. ② 타동사 팔다, 취급하다 ❏ 그곳에서는 머리 리본에서 동양 양탄자까지 모든 물건을 취급한다. ③ 자동사 -의 가격에 팔리다 ❏ 미개발된 땅은 개발된 상태에서의 시장 가치의 최고 40퍼센트 가격에 팔릴 수 있다. ④ 자동사 팔리다 ❏ 비록 이 음반이 팔리지 않고 평론가들이 좋아하지 않는다 해도, 우리는 결코 변하지 않을 것이다. ⑤ 타동사 -의 판매를 촉진하다 ❏ 뉴스 잡지를 팔리게 하는 것은 오로지 선정적인 것들뿐이다. ⑥ 타동사 -에게 ...을 받아들이게 하다, 납득시키다 ❏ 그녀는 나만의 종이 분쇄기를 장만할 것을 납득시키려 했다. ❏ 그녀는 그 생각을 고객들에게 납득시킬 수 있기를 바라고 있다. ⑦ 구 몸을 팔다, 매춘하다 ❏ 85퍼센트가 생계를 위해 몸을 팔지는 않겠다고 말했다. ⑧ 구 영혼을 팔다; 원칙을 저버리다 [탐탁잖음] ❏ 정치적 생존을 위해 자기 영혼이라도 팔 사람

┌─────────────────────────────────────┐
Thesaurus   *sell*의 참조어

   v.   exchange, retail; *(ant.)* buy ■ ②
└─────────────────────────────────────┘

▶**sell off** PHRASAL VERB If you **sell** something **off**, you sell it because you need the money. ❏ *The company is selling off some sites and concentrating on cutting debts.* →see also **sell-off**

구동사 팔아 치우다 ❏ 그 회사는 몇 군데 부지를 매각해서 부채를 탕감하는 데 전력을 기울이고 있다.

▶**sell on** PHRASAL VERB If you buy something and then **sell** it **on**, you sell it to someone else soon after buying it, usually in order to make a profit. ❏ *Mr. Farrier bought cars at auctions and sold them on.*

구동사 (차익을 노리고) 되팔다 ❏ 패리어 씨는 경매에서 자동차들을 산 다음 그것들을 되팔았다.

▶**sell out** ■ PHRASAL VERB If a shop **sells out** of something, it sells all its stocks of it, so that there is no longer any left for people to buy. ❏ *Hardware stores have sold out of water pumps and tarpaulins.* ② PHRASAL VERB If a performance, sports event, or other entertainment **sells out**, all the tickets for it are sold. ❏ *Football games often sell out well in advance.* ③ PHRASAL VERB When things **sell out**, all of them that are available are sold. ❏ *Sleeping bags sold out almost immediately.* ④ PHRASAL VERB If you accuse someone of **selling out**, you disapprove of the fact that they do something which used to be against their principles, or give in to an opposing group. [DISAPPROVAL] ❏ *The young in particular see him as a man who will not sell out or be debased by the compromises of politics.* ⑤ PHRASAL VERB If you **sell out**, you sell everything you have, such as your house or your business, because you need the money. ❏ *I'll have a going out of business sale. I'll sell out and move out of here.* ⑥ →see also **sell-out, sold out**

■ 구동사 죄다 팔아 치우다 ❏ 철물점들은 양수기와 방수포를 죄다 팔아 치워 버렸다. ② 구동사 매진되다 ❏ 미식축구 경기는 종종 미리 매진되곤 한다. ③ 구동사 다 팔리다 ❏ 침낭은 거의 즉시 다 팔렸다. ④ 구동사 배반하다, 원칙을 저버리다 [탐탁잖음] ❏ 특히 젊은 사람들은 그를 원칙을 저버리거나 정치적 타협으로 타락하지 않을 사람으로 본다. ⑤ 구동사 가진 것을 모두 팔아 치우다 ❏ 폐업 정리 염가 판매를 할 예정이다. 모두 팔아 치우고 여기서 떠날 것이다.

▶**sell up** PHRASAL VERB To **sell up** means the same as to **sell out**. [BRIT] ❏ *...all these farmers going out of business and having to sell up.*

구동사 가진 것을 모두 팔아 치우다 [영국영어] ❏ 사업을 접으며 가진 것을 모두 팔아 치워야 하는 이 모든 농민들

sell-by date (**sell-by dates**) ■ N-COUNT The **sell-by date** on a food container is the date by which the food should be sold or eaten before it starts to decay. [BRIT; AM **expiration date**] ❏ *...a piece of cheese four weeks past its sell-by date.* ② PHRASE If you say that someone or something is **past** their **sell-by date**, you mean they are no longer effective, interesting, or useful. [BRIT, DISAPPROVAL]

■ 가산명사 유통 기한 [영국영어; 미국영어 expiration date] ❏ 유통 기한이 4주 지난 치즈 ② 구 효용을 상실한, 쓸모가 없어진 [영국영어, 탐탁잖음] ❏ 그들은 아마 오래전에 쓸모없어진 사람들이 남아 빠진 방식을 앵무새처럼 되풀이하고 있는 것에 질렸다.

[N inflects, v-link PHR] ❑ They are tired of clapped-out formulas being regurgitated by people long past their sell-by date.

sell|er /sɛlər/ (**sellers**) **1** N-COUNT A **seller** of a type of thing is a person or company that sells that type of thing. ❑ ...a flower seller. **2** N-COUNT In a business deal, the **seller** is the person who is selling something to someone else. ❑ In theory, the buyer could ask the seller to have a test carried out. **3** N-COUNT If you describe a product as, for example, a big **seller**, you mean that large numbers of it are being sold. ❑ The gift shop's biggest seller is a photo of Nixon meeting Presley. →see also **bestseller**

1 가산명사 판매인, 장수; 판매사 ❑ 꽃 장수 **2** 가산명사 파는 쪽 사람, 판매자 ❑ 이론적으로, 구매자는 판매자에게 검사를 해 볼 것을 요청할 수 있다. **3** 가산명사 잘 팔리는 상품 ❑ 그 선물 가게에서 가장 잘 팔리는 상품은 닉슨이 프레슬리를 만나고 있는 모습이 담긴 사진이다.

seller's mar|ket N-SING When there is a **seller's market** for a particular product, there are fewer of the products for sale than people who want to buy them, so buyers have little choice and prices go up. [BUSINESS] ❑ It's a seller's market, and no one is forced to discount to remain competitive. →see also **buyer's market**

단수명사 판매자 시장 (공급이 적고 수요가 많음) [경제] ❑ 공급이 적고 수요가 많아서, 아무도 경쟁력 유지를 위해 가격 할인을 강요당하지 않는다.

sell|ing point (**selling points**) N-COUNT A **selling point** is a desirable quality or feature that something has which makes it likely that people will want to buy it. [BUSINESS] ❑ A garden is one of the biggest selling points with house-hunters.

가산명사 상품의 장점 [경제] ❑ 정원은 집을 물색하는 사람들을 끌어들이는 최대의 장점들 중 하나이다.

sell|ing price (**selling prices**) N-COUNT The **selling price** of something is the price for which it is sold. [BUSINESS] ❑ Palm said the average selling price of its devices was $183.

가산명사 판매 가격 [경제] ❑ 팜 사는 자사 장비의 평균 판매 가격이 183달러라고 말했다.

sell-off (**sell-offs**) also **selloff** N-COUNT The **sell-off** of something, for example an industry owned by the state or a company's shares, is the selling of it. [BUSINESS] ❑ The privatisation of the electricity industry – the biggest sell-off of them all.

가산명사 매각 [경제] ❑ 전력 사업의 민영화, 그 모든 것들 중 가장 큰 규모의 매각

sell-out (**sell-outs**) also **sellout** **1** N-COUNT If a play, sports event, or other entertainment is a **sell-out**, all the tickets for it are sold. ❑ Their concert there was a sell-out. **2** N-COUNT If you describe someone's behavior as a **sell-out**, you disapprove of the fact that they have done something which used to be against their principles, or given in to an opposing group. [DISAPPROVAL] ❑ For some, his decision to become a Socialist candidate at Sunday's election was simply a sell-out.

1 가산명사 매진 ❑ 그곳에서 그들의 콘서트는 매진이었다. **2** 가산명사 배반, 내통 [탐탁찮음] ❑ 어떤 이들에게는, 일요일 선거에서 그가 사회당 후보로 나서기로 결정한 것은 그저 배반 행위에 지나지 않았다.

selves /sɛlvz/ **Selves** is the plural of **self**.

self의 복수형

se|man|tics /sɪmæntɪks/

<table><tr><td>The form **semantic** is used as a modifier.</td><td>semantic은 수식어구로 쓴다.</td></tr></table>

N-UNCOUNT **Semantics** is the branch of linguistics that deals with the meanings of words and sentences.

불가산명사 의미론

sem|blance /sɛmbləns/ N-UNCOUNT If there is a **semblance of** a particular condition or quality, it appears to exist, even though this may be a false impression. [FORMAL] ❑ At least a semblance of normality has been restored to parts of the country.

불가산명사 외관, 겉보기 [격식체] ❑ 그 나라의 일부 지역들은 적어도 외관상으로는 정상적인 상태가 되찾았다.

se|men /siːmen/ N-UNCOUNT **Semen** is the liquid containing sperm that is produced by the sex organs of men and male animals.

불가산명사 정액

se|mes|ter /sɪmɛstər/ (**semesters**) N-COUNT In colleges and universities in some countries, a **semester** is one of the two main periods into which the year is divided. ❑ ...February 22nd when most of their students begin their spring semester.

가산명사 학기 ❑ 대부분의 학생들이 봄학기를 시작하는 2월 22일

semi /sɛmi, sɛmaɪ/ (**semis**) **1** N-COUNT In a sports competition, the **semis** are the semifinals. [INFORMAL] ❑ He reached the semis after beating Lendl in the quarterfinal. **2** N-COUNT A **semi** is a semidetached house. [BRIT, INFORMAL] ❑ ... a spacious semi in Surbiton.

1 가산명사 준준승 [비격식체] ❑ 그는 준준결승에서 렌들을 꺾고 준결승에 진출했다. **2** 가산명사 반단독 주택 [영국영어, 비격식체] ❑ 서비턴에 있는 널찍한 반단독 주택

Word Link	semi ≈ half : semicircle, semiconductor, semifinal

semi|cir|cle /sɛmisɜːrkəl, sɛmaɪ-/ (**semicircles**) also **semi-circle** N-COUNT A **semicircle** is one half of a circle, or something having the shape of half a circle. ❑ They sit cross-legged in a semicircle and share stories.

가산명사 반원; 반원형의 물체 ❑ 그들은 책상다리를 하고 반원형으로 둘러앉아 이야기를 나눈다.

semi|co|lon /sɛmikoʊlən/ (**semicolons**) [BRIT, sometimes AM **semi-colon**] N-COUNT A **semicolon** is the punctuation mark ; which is used in writing to separate different parts of a sentence or list or to indicate a pause.

[영국영어, 미국영어 가끔 semi-colon] 가산명사 쌍반점, 세미 콜론

semi|con|duc|tor /sɛmikəndʌktər, sɛmaɪ-/ (**semiconductors**) also **semi-conductor** N-COUNT A **semiconductor** is a substance used in electronics whose ability to conduct electricity increases with greater heat.

가산명사 반도체

semi|de|tached /sɛmidɪtætʃt, sɛmaɪ-/ also **semi-detached** ADJ A **semidetached** house is a house that is joined to another house on one side by a shared wall. [mainly BRIT] ❑ The houses were semidetached, with two stories and shared driveways. ● N-SING **Semidetached** is also a noun. ❑ I grew up in a three-bedroomed semidetached.

형용사 반단독 주택형의, 한쪽 벽이 옆집에 붙은 [주로 영국영어] ❑ 그 집들은 2층이고 진입로를 함께 쓰는 반단독 주택이었다. ● 단수명사 반단독 주택 ❑ 나는 침실 세 개짜리 반단독 주택에서 자랐다.

semi|fi|nal /sɛmifaɪnəl, sɛmaɪ-/ (**semifinals**) [BRIT, sometimes AM **semi-final**] N-COUNT A **semifinal** is one of the two games or races in a competition that are held to decide who will compete in the final. ❑ We want to go into the semifinal, no matter who the rival is. ● N-PLURAL The **semifinals** is the round of a competition in which these two games or races are held. ❑ Team USA reached the semifinals by defeating New Zealand in the second round.

[영국영어, 미국영어 가끔 semi-final] 가산명사 준결승전 ❑ 상대가 누구든 간에 우리는 준결승전에 나가고 싶다. ● 복수명사 준결승 ❑ 미국 대표팀이 2회전에서 뉴질랜드를 꺾음으로써 준결승에 진출했다.

semi|nal /sɛmɪnəl/ ADJ **Seminal** is used to describe things such as books, works, events, and experiences that have a great influence in a particular field. [FORMAL] ❑ ...author of the seminal book "Animal Liberation."

형용사 영향력이 큰 [격식체] ❑ '동물 해방'이라는 영향력 있는 책의 저자

semi|nar /sɛmɪnɑːr/ (**seminars**) **1** N-COUNT A **seminar** is a meeting where a group of people discuss a problem or topic. ❑ ...a series of half-day seminars to help businessmen get the best value from investing in information technology. **2** N-COUNT A **seminar** is a class at a college or university in which the teacher and a small group of students discuss a topic. ❑ Students are asked to prepare material in advance of each weekly seminar.

1 가산명사 세미나 ❑ 사업가들이 정보 기술 투자에서 최선의 대가를 얻어 내도록 돕기 위해 연속되는 반나절 동안 진행되는 세미나 **2** 가산명사 세미나 (수업) ❑ 학생들은 매주 세미나 수업에 앞서 자료를 준비해야 한다.

semi|skilled /sɛmɪskɪld, sɛmaɪ-/ also semi-skilled ADJ A **semiskilled** worker has some training and skills, but not enough to do specialized work. [BUSINESS]

형용사 약간 숙련된; 다소 숙련을 요하는 [경제]

Sen|ate ♦♦◇ /sɛnɪt/ (**Senates**) ◻ N-PROPER-COLL The **Senate** is the smaller and more important of the two parts of the legislature in some countries, for example the United States and Australia. ◻ *The Senate is expected to pass the bill shortly.* →see **government** ◻ N-PROPER-COLL **Senate** or the **Senate** is the governing council at some universities. ◻ *By the time I was Vice Chancellor, Senate had become a much larger and a much more democratic body.*

◻ 고유명사-집합 상원 ◻ 상원이 그 법안을 즉시 통과시킬 것으로 예상된다. ◻ 고유명사-집합 평의회, 이사회 ◻ 내가 부총장일 때쯤에 이르러서는, 평의회는 훨씬 더 크고 민주적인 조직이 되어 있었다.

| **Word Link** | *sen* ≈ *old* : *sen**ator**, *sen**ile**, *sen**ior** |

sena|tor ♦◇◇ /sɛnɪtər/ (**senators**) N-COUNT; N-TITLE A **senator** is a member of a political Senate, for example in the United States or Australia. ◻ *... Texas' first black senator.* →see **government**

가산명사; 경칭명사 상원 의원 ◻ 텍사스 주 최초의 흑인 상원 의원

send ♦♦♦ /sɛnd/ (**sends**, **sending**, **sent**) ◻ V-T When you **send** someone something, you arrange for it to be taken and delivered to them, for example by mail. ◻ *Myra Cunningham sent me a note thanking me for dinner.* ◻ *I sent a copy to the minister for transport.* ◻ V-T If you **send** someone somewhere, you tell them to go there. ◻ *Inspector Banbury came up to see her, but she sent him away.* ◻ *...the government's decision to send troops to the region.* ◻ *I suggested that he rest, and sent him for an X-ray.* ◻ V-T If you **send** someone **to** an institution such as a school or a prison, you arrange for them to stay there for a period of time. ◻ *It's his parents' choice to send him to a boarding school, rather than a convenient day school.* ◻ V-T To **send** a signal means to cause it to go to a place by means of radio waves or electricity. ◻ *The transmitters will send a signal automatically to a local base station.* ◻ V-T If something **sends** things or people in a particular direction, it causes them to move in that direction. ◻ *The explosion sent shrapnel flying through the sides of cars on the crowded highway.* ◻ *He let David go with a thrust of his wrist that sent the lad reeling.* ◻ V-T To **send** someone or something **into** a particular state means to cause them to go into or be in that state. ◻ *My attempt to fix it sent Lawrence into fits of laughter.* ◻ *...before civil war and famine sent the country plunging into anarchy.* ◻ to **send** someone **packing** →see **pack**

◻ 타동사 보내다 ◻ 마이라 커닝엄이 저녁 식사에 대해 감사하는 짧은 편지를 내게 보냈다. ◻ 나는 한 부를 교통부 장관에게 보냈다. ◻ 타동사 가게 하다, 보내다 ◻ 밴버리 형사가 그녀를 만나러 왔지만, 그녀는 그를 내쫓았다. ◻ 그 지역에 군대를 보내기로 한 정부의 결정 ◻ 그에게 쉴 것을 제안하고, 엑스선 사진을 찍으러 가게 했다. ◻ 타동사 다니게 하다, 보내다 ◻ 그를 가까운 통학 학교 대신 기숙학교에 다니게 한 것은 그 부모가 선택한 바이다. ◻ 타동사 송전하다, 보내다 ◻ 송신기들이 자동으로 지역 기지국에 신호를 보낼 것이다. ◻ 타동사 (어떤 방향으로) 움직이게 하다 ◻ 폭발로 유탄들이 붐비는 간선 도로에 있는 자동차들의 옆면을 관통했다. ◻ 그가 손목을 한번 밀어 제치며 놓아 주자 데이비드는 비틀거렸다. ◻ 타동사 - 한 상태로 되게 하다 ◻ 내가 그것을 고치려고 시도하는 것을 보고 로렌스가 폭소를 터뜨렸다. ◻ 내전과 기근 때문에 그 나라가 무정부 상태에 빠져들기 전에

| **Thesaurus** | *send*의 참조어 |

v.   issue, mail, ship, transmit; (*ant.*) receive ◻

▶**send away for** →see **send for 2**
▶**send for** ◻ PHRASAL VERB If you **send for** someone, you send them a message asking them to come and see you. ◻ *I've sent for the doctor.* ◻ PHRASAL VERB If you **send for** something, you write and ask for it to be sent to you. ◻ *Send for your free catalogue today.*

◻ 구동사 -을 부르러 사람을 보내다 ◻ 의사를 부르러 사람을 보냈다. ◻ 구동사 편지를 써서 -을 요청하다 ◻ 오늘 우편으로 무료 상품 목록을 신청하세요.

▶**send in** ◻ PHRASAL VERB If you **send in** something such as a competition entry or a letter applying for a job, you mail it to the organization concerned. ◻ *Applicants are asked to send in a CV and a covering letter.* ◻ PHRASAL VERB When a government **sends in** troops or police officers, it orders them to deal with a crisis or problem somewhere. ◻ *He has asked the government to send in troops to end the fighting.*

◻ 구동사 내다, 제출하다 ◻ 지원자들은 이력서와 자기소개서를 제출해야 합니다. ◻ 구동사 파견하다 ◻ 그는 싸움을 끝내기 위해 병력을 파견할 것을 정부에 요구해 왔다.

▶**send off** ◻ PHRASAL VERB When you **send off** a letter or package, you send it somewhere by mail. ◻ *He sent off copies to various people for them to read and make comments.* ◻ PHRASAL VERB If a soccer player **is sent off**, the referee makes them leave the field during a game, as a punishment for seriously breaking the rules. ◻ *The 30-year-old Scottish international was sent off for arguing with a linesman.*

◻ 구동사 (우편으로) 발송하다 ◻ 그는 읽고서 평을 해 달라고 여러 사람들에게 사본을 발송했다. ◻ 구동사 퇴장당하다 ◻ 국제 경기에 출전한 30세의 스코틀랜드 선수가 선심과 말다툼한 것 때문에 퇴장당했다.

▶**send off for** →see **send for 2**
▶**send out** ◻ PHRASAL VERB If you **send out** things such as letters or bills, you send them to a large number of people at the same time. ◻ *She had sent out well over four hundred invitations that afternoon.* ◻ PHRASAL VERB To **send out** a signal, sound, light, or heat means to produce it. ◻ *The crew did not send out any distress signals.*

◻ 구동사 발송하다 ◻ 그날 오후 그녀는 400장은 족히 넘는 초대장을 발송한 참이었다. ◻ 구동사 보내다; 내다 ◻ 승무원들은 조난 신호를 보내지 않았다.

▶**send out for** PHRASAL VERB If you **send out for** food, for example pizza or sandwiches, you phone and ask for it to be delivered to you. ◻ *Let's send out for a pizza and watch The Late Show.*

구동사 (전화로) 배달을 주문하다, 배달시키다 ◻ 피자 한 판 시켜서 '레이트 쇼'를 봅시다.

send|er /sɛndər/ (**senders**) N-COUNT The **sender of** a letter, package, or radio message is the person who sent it. ◻ *The sender of the best letter every week will win a cheque for £20.*

가산명사 보낸 사람, 발송인 ◻ 매주 가장 훌륭한 편지를 보내 주신 분께 20파운드짜리 수표를 드립니다.

| **Word Link** | *sen* ≈ *old* : *sen**ator**, *sen**ile**, *sen**ior** |

se|nile /siːnaɪl/ ADJ If old people become **senile**, they become confused, can no longer remember things, and are unable to take care of themselves. ● **se|nil|ity** /sɪnɪlɪti/ N-UNCOUNT ◻ *The old man was forced to resign after showing unmistakable signs of senility.*

형용사 노망든 ● 망령, 노망 불가산명사 ◻ 노인은 몇 차례 뚜렷한 치매기를 보인 후 사임할 수밖에 없었다.

sen|ior ♦♦◇ /siːnyər/ (**seniors**) ◻ ADJ The **senior** people in an organization or profession have the highest and most important jobs. [ADJ n] ◻ *...senior officials in the Israeli government.* ◻ *...the company's senior management.* ◻ ADJ If someone is **senior to** you in an organization or profession, they have a higher and more important job than you or they are considered to be superior to you because they have worked there for longer and have more experience. ◻ *The position had to be filled by an officer senior to Haig.* ● N-PLURAL Your **seniors** are the people who are senior to you. ◻ *He was described by his seniors as a model officer.* ◻ N-SING **Senior** is used when indicating how much older one person is than another. For example, if someone is ten years your **senior**, they are ten years older than you. ◻ *She became involved with a married man many years her senior.* ◻ N-COUNT

◻ 형용사 고위의, 상위의 ◻ 이스라엘 정부 고위 관리 ◻ 기업의 고위 경영진 ◻ 형용사 상위의, 상관의 ◻ 그 자리는 헤이그보다 계급이 높은 장교에게 돌아가야 했다. ● 복수명사 선배, 상관 ◻ 그는 상관들 사이에서 모범 장교로 통했다. ◻ 단수명사 나이가 더 많은 ◻ 그녀는 자기보다 나이가 훨씬 더 많은 유부남과 만나기 시작했다. ◻ 가산명사 상급생, 최고 학년 [미국영어] ◻ 대학에 진학하는 고3 학생들의 수 ◻ 형용사 (스포츠) 시니어 부문 ◻ 이는 그에게 국제 대회에서는 다섯 번째 우승, 시니어 부문에서는 세 번째 우승이 될 것이다.

a b c d e f g h i j k l m n o p q r s t u v w x y z

Seniors are students in a high school, university, or college who are the oldest and who have reached an advanced level in their studies. [AM] *...the number of high school seniors who go on to college.* ◻ ADJ If you take part in a sport at **senior** level, you take part in competitions with adults and people who have reached a high degree of achievement in that sport. [ADJ n] ◻ *This will be his fifth international championship and his third at senior level.*

sen|ior cit|i|zen (**senior citizens**) N-COUNT A **senior citizen** is an older person who has retired or receives social security benefits. ◻ *... suicide rates among senior citizens.* →see **age**

가산명사 노인, 노령자 ◻ 노인 자살률

sen|ior|ity /siːniɒriti, BRIT siːniɒriti/ N-UNCOUNT A person's **seniority** in an organization is the importance and power that they have compared with others, or the fact that they have worked there for a long time. ◻ *He has said he will fire editorial employees without regard to seniority.*

불가산명사 연공서열 ◻ 그는 연공서열에 관계없이 편집부 직원을 해고할 생각이라고 밝혔다.

Word Link   sens ≈ feeling : sensation, senseless, sensitive

---

sen|sa|tion /sɛnseɪʃn/ (**sensations**) ◻ N-COUNT A **sensation** is a physical feeling. ◻ *Floating can be a very pleasant sensation.* ◻ N-UNCOUNT **Sensation** is your ability to feel things physically, especially through your sense of touch. ◻ *The pain was so bad that she lost all sensation.* ◻ N-COUNT You can use **sensation** to refer to the general feeling or impression caused by a particular experience. ◻ *It's a funny sensation to know someone's talking about you in a language you don't understand.* ◻ N-COUNT If a person, event, or situation is a **sensation**, it causes great excitement or interest. ◻ *...the film that turned her into an overnight sensation.* ◻ N-SING If a person, event, or situation causes a **sensation**, they cause great interest or excitement. ◻ *She was just 14 when she caused a sensation at the Montreal Olympics.* →see **taste**

◻ 가산명사 감각, 느낌 ◻ 둥둥 떠다니면 매우 기분 좋은 느낌이 들 수 있다. ◻ 불가산명사 감각 ◻ 통증이 너무나 아파서 모든 감각을 잃었다. ◻ 가산명사 느낌, 기분 ◻ 누군가 내가 모르는 언어로 나에 대해 이야기하고 있을 때 묘한 기분이 든다. ◻ 가산명사 큰 관심과 인기의 대상 ◻ 그녀를 하룻밤에 스타로 만든 영화 ◻ 단수명사 돌풍, 폭발적인 반응, 센세이션 ◻ 그녀가 몬트리올 올림픽에서 돌풍을 일으킨 것은 겨우 열네 살 때였다.

sen|sa|tion|al /sɛnseɪʃənl/ ◻ ADJ A **sensational** result, event, or situation is so remarkable that it causes great excitement and interest. ◻ *The world champions suffered a sensational defeat.* ● **sen|sa|tion|al|ly** ADV ◻ *The rape trial was sensationally halted yesterday.* ◻ ADJ You can describe stories or reports as **sensational** if you disapprove of them because they present facts in a way that is intended to cause feelings of shock, anger, or excitement. [DISAPPROVAL] ◻ *...sensational tabloid newspaper reports.* ◻ ADJ You can describe something as **sensational** when you think that it is extremely good. ◻ *Her voice is sensational.* ● **sen|sa|tion|al|ly** ADV ◻ *...sensationally good food.*

◻ 형용사 화제가 되는, 선풍적인 ◻ 세계 챔피언 팀이 패배해 화제가 되었다. ● 화제를 모으며, 선풍적으로 부사 ◻ 그 강간 사건 재판이 어제 중단되면서 화제를 불러일으켰다. ◻ 형용사 선정적인 [탐탁잖음] ◻ 타블로이드 신문의 선정적인 보도 ◻ 형용사 환상적인, 매우 훌륭한 ◻ 그녀의 목소리는 환상적이다. ● 환상적으로 부사 ◻ 맛이 환상적인 음식

sense ♦♦♦ /sɛns/ (**senses, sensing, sensed**) ◻ N-COUNT Your **senses** are the physical abilities of sight, smell, hearing, touch, and taste. ◻ *She stared at him again, unable to believe the evidence of her senses.* ◻ V-T If you **sense** something, you become aware of it or you realize it, although it is not very obvious. ◻ *She probably sensed that I wasn't telling her the whole story.* ◻ *He looks about him, sensing danger.* ◻ N-SING If you have a **sense that** something is the case, you think that it is the case, although you may not have firm, clear evidence for this belief. ◻ *Suddenly you got this sense that people were drawing themselves away from each other.* ◻ N-SING If you have a **sense of** guilt or relief, for example, you feel guilty or relieved. ◻ *When your child is struggling for life, you feel this overwhelming sense of guilt.* ◻ N-SING If you have a **sense of** something such as duty or justice, you are aware of it and believe it is important. ◻ *My sense of justice was offended.* ◻ *We must keep a sense of proportion about all this.* ◻ N-SING Someone who has a **sense of** timing or style has a natural ability with regard to timing or style. You can also say that someone has a bad **sense of** timing or style. [N of n, also n] ◻ *He has an impeccable sense of timing.* ◻ *Her dress sense is appalling.* →see also **sense of humor** ◻ N-UNCOUNT **Sense** is the ability to make good judgments and to behave sensibly. ◻ *...when he was younger and had a bit more sense.* ◻ *When that doesn't work they sometimes have the sense to seek help.* →see also **common sense** ◻ N-SING If you say that there is no **sense** or little **sense in** doing something, you mean that it is not a sensible thing to do because nothing useful would be gained by doing it. ◻ *There's no sense in pretending this doesn't happen.* ◻ N-COUNT A **sense** of a word or expression is one of its possible meanings. ◻ *...a noun which has two senses.* ◻ PHRASE **Sense** is used in several expressions to indicate how true your statement is. For example, if you say that something is true **in a sense**, you mean that it is partly true, or true in one way. If you say that something is true **in a general sense**, you mean that it is true in a general way. ◻ *In a sense, both were right.* ◻ *Though his background was modest, it was in no sense deprived.* ◻ PHRASE If something **makes sense**, you can understand it. ◻ *He was sitting there saying, "Yes, the figures make sense."* ◻ PHRASE When you **make sense of** something, you succeed in understanding it. ◻ *Provided you didn't try to make sense of it, it sounded beautiful.* ◻ PHRASE If a course of action **makes sense**, it seems sensible. ◻ *It makes sense to look after yourself.* ◻ *The project should be re-appraised to see whether it made sound economic sense.* ◻ PHRASE If you say that someone **has come to** their **senses** or **has been brought to** their **senses**, you mean that they have stopped being foolish and are being sensible again. ◻ *Eventually the world will come to its senses and get rid of them.* ◻ PHRASE If you say that someone **talks sense**, you mean that what they say is sensible. ◻ *When he speaks, he talks sense.* ◻ PHRASE If you **have a sense that** something is true or **get a sense that** something is true, you think that it is true. [mainly SPOKEN] ◻ *Do you have the sense that you are loved by the public?* ◻ to **see sense** →see **see** →see **smell**

◻ 가산명사 감각, 오감 ◻ 그녀는 자신의 눈과 귀를 믿기지 않아서 그를 다시 한 번 쳐다봤다. ◻ 타동사 감지하다, 알아채다 ◻ 내가 있는 그대로 다 이야기하지 않았음을 그녀가 눈치 챘을지도 모른다. ◻ 그가 위험을 감지하며 주위를 살핀다. ◻ 단수명사 생각, 느낌 ◻ 당신은 갑자기 사람들이 서로에게서 멀어지고 있다는 생각이 들었다. ◻ 단수명사 느낌, -감 ◻ 자식이 죽음과 맞서 싸우고 있을 때 부모는 이처럼 걷잡을 수 없는 죄책감을 느낀다. ◻ 단수명사 관념, 인식 ◻ 내 정의감에 어긋난 일이었다. ◻ 우리는 이 모든 일에 대해 균형 감각을 유지해야 한다. ◻ 단수명사 -감각, -관념 ◻ 그는 시간관념이 철저하다. ◻ 그녀의 패션 감각은 끔찍하다. ◻ 불가산명사 분별, 지각, 상식 ◻ 그가 더 젊고 더 지각 있는 사람이었을 때 ◻ 그들은 그 방법이 통하지 않으면 도움을 구하는 지각 있는 행동도 가끔씩 한다. ◻ 단수명사 분별, 일리 ◻ 마치 이 일이 일어나지 않을 것처럼 가장해봐 소용없다. ◻ 가산명사 의미 ◻ 두 가지 의미를 가진 명사 ◻ 구 어느 정도, 어떤 면에서는 ◻ 어떤 면에서는 둘 다 옳았다. ◻ 그가 자란 환경이 그저 그렇긴 해도 결코 불우하지는 않았다. ◻ 구 이해되다 ◻ "네, 그 수치들이 이해가 되네요."라고 그가 거기 앉아서 말했다. ◻ 구 이해하다 ◻ 굳이 이해하려 애쓰지 않는다면 아름답게 들릴 것이다. ◻ 구 이치에 닿다, 받이 되다 ◻ 자기 자신을 돌보다니 말이 된다. ◻ 그 프로젝트는 경제적으로 타당한 프로젝트였는지 재평가 받아야 한다. ◻ 구 정신 차리다 ◻ 결국엔 세계가 이성을 찾고 그들을 제거할 것이다. ◻ 구 이치에 닿는 말을 하다 ◻ 그는 말을 하면 이치에 닿는 말을 한다. ◻ 구 -라고 생각하다 [주로 구어체] ◻ 본인이 대중의 사랑을 받는다고 생각하십니까?

Thesaurus   sense의 참조어

N.   feeling, perception ◻ ◻ ◻
V.   notice, perceive, realize ◻

| Word Link | sens ≈ feeling : sensation, senseless, sensitive |

sense|less /sɛnslɪs/ **1** ADJ If you describe an action as **senseless**, you think it is wrong because it has no purpose and produces no benefit. ❑ ...people whose lives have been destroyed by acts of senseless violence. **2** ADJ If someone is **senseless**, they are unconscious. [ADJ after v, v-link ADJ] ❑ They were knocked to the ground, beaten senseless and robbed of their wallets.

1 형용사 무의미한, 무분별한 ❑ 무분별한 폭력 행사로 삶을 파괴당한 사람들 **2** 형용사 의식을 잃은 ❑ 그들은 땅으로 내동댕이쳐져 의식을 잃을 때까지 두드려 맞고 지갑을 도둑맞았다.

sense of hu|mor [BRIT **sense of humour**] N-SING Someone who has a **sense of humor** often finds things amusing, rather than being serious all the time. ❑ She seems to have a good sense of humor.

[영국영어 sense of humour] 단수명사 유머 감각 ❑ 그녀는 유머 감각이 뛰어난 사람 같아 보인다.

sen|si|bil|ity /sɛnsɪbɪlɪti/ (**sensibilities**) **1** N-UNCOUNT Sensibility is the ability to experience deep feelings. ❑ Everything he writes demonstrates the depth of his sensibility. **2** N-VAR Someone's **sensibility** is their tendency to be influenced or offended by things. ❑ He was unable to control his sensibility.

1 불가산명사 감성 ❑ 그가 쓰는 글마다 풍부한 감수성이 돋보인다. **2** 가산명사 또는 불가산명사 감정, 감수성 ❑ 그는 자신의 감정을 통제할 수 없었다.

sen|si|ble ♦◇◇ /sɛnsɪbəl/ **1** ADJ **Sensible** actions or decisions are good because they are based on reasons rather than emotions. ❑ It might be sensible to get a solicitor. ❑ The sensible thing is to leave them alone. ● **sen|si|bly** /sɛnsɪbli/ ADV ❑ He sensibly decided to lie low for a while. **2** ADJ **Sensible** people behave in a sensible way. ❑ She was a sensible girl and did not panic. ❑ Oh come on, let's be sensible about this. **3** ADJ **Sensible** shoes or clothes are practical and strong rather than fashionable and attractive. ❑ Wear loose clothing and sensible footwear. ● **sen|si|bly** ADV ❑ They were not sensibly dressed.

1 형용사 현명한, 합리적인 ❑ 사무 변호사를 고용하는 편이 현명할지도 모른다. ❑ 그들을 그냥 내버려 두는 게 현명한 일이다. ● 현명하게, 합리적으로 부사 ❑ 그는 당분간 조용히 지내겠다는 현명한 결정을 내렸다. **2** 형용사 분별 있는, 상식적인 ❑ 그녀는 분별 있는 사람답게 당황하지 않았다. ❑ 제발 이 문제에 대해 상식적으로 접근해 봅시다. **3** 형용사 실용적인, 편하고 튼튼한 ❑ 옷을 헐렁하게 입고 편한 신발을 신으세요. ● 실용적으로, 편하게 부사 ❑ 그들은 편한 차림이 아니었다.

Take care not to confuse **sensible** and **sensitive**. You do not use **sensible** to describe someone whose feelings or emotions are strongly affected by their experiences. The word you need is **sensitive**. ❑ ...a highly sensitive artist.

sensible과 sensitive를 혼동하지 않도록 주의하시오. sensible은 그 사람의 느낌이나 감정이 자기의 경험으로 크게 영향을 받은 사람을 기술하기 위해 쓰지 않는다. 이때 쓰는 말은 sensitive이다. ❑ ...아주 감수성이 강한 예술가.

sen|si|tive ♦◇◇ /sɛnsɪtɪv/ **1** ADJ If you are **sensitive to** other people's needs, problems, or feelings, you show understanding and awareness of them. [APPROVAL] ❑ The classroom teacher must be sensitive to a child's needs. ● **sen|si|tive|ly** ADV ❑ The abuse of women needs to be treated seriously and sensitively. ● **sen|si|tiv|ity** /sɛnsɪtɪvɪti/ N-UNCOUNT [oft N for n] ❑ A good relationship involves concern and sensitivity for each other's feelings. **2** ADJ If you are **sensitive about** something, you are easily worried and offended when people talk about it. ❑ Young people are very sensitive about their appearance. ● **sen|si|tiv|ity** (**sensitivities**) N-VAR ❑ ...people who suffer extreme sensitivity about what others think. **3** ADJ A **sensitive** subject or issue needs to be dealt with carefully because it is likely to cause disagreement or make people angry or upset. ❑ Employment is a very sensitive issue. ● **sen|si|tiv|ity** N-UNCOUNT [oft N of n] ❑ Due to the obvious sensitivity of the issue he would not divulge any details. **4** ADJ **Sensitive** documents or reports contain information that needs to be kept secret and dealt with carefully. ❑ He instructed staff to shred sensitive documents. **5** ADJ Something that is **sensitive** to a physical force, substance, or treatment is easily affected by it and often harmed by it. ❑ ...a chemical which is sensitive to light. ● **sen|si|tiv|ity** N-UNCOUNT ❑ ...the sensitivity of cells to damage by chemotherapy. **6** ADJ A **sensitive** piece of scientific equipment is capable of measuring or recording very small changes. ❑ ...an extremely sensitive microscope. ● **sen|si|tiv|ity** N-UNCOUNT ❑ ...the sensitivity of the detector.

1 형용사 세심한 [마음에 듦] ❑ 일선 교사들은 학생의 필요에 세심한 배려를 보여야 한다. ● 세심하게 부사 ❑ 여성 학대 문제는 진지하고 세심하게 다루어져야 한다. ● 세심함 불가산명사 ❑ 좋은 관계라면 서로의 감정에 대해 관심을 갖고 세심하게 배려해 주는 관계다. **2** 형용사 민감한, 예민한 ❑ 젊은 사람들은 자신의 외모에 매우 민감하다. ● 민감함, 예민함 가산명사 또는 불가산명사 ❑ 다른 사람들의 생각을 지나치게 예민하게 받아들이는 사람들 **3** 형용사 민감한 ❑ 고용 문제는 매우 민감한 사안이다. ● 민감성 불가산명사 ❑ 누구나 알다시피 민감한 사안이기 때문에, 그가 자세한 내용은 발설하지 않았다. **4** 형용사 기밀의, 신중을 요하는 ❑ 그는 직원들에게 기밀문서를 분쇄하라는 지시를 내렸다. **5** 형용사 민감한 ❑ 빛에 민감한 화학물질 ● 민감성 불가산명사 ❑ 세포가 민감해서 화학 요법에 손상됨 **6** 형용사 정밀한 ❑ 초정밀 현미경 ● 정밀성 불가산명사 ❑ 탐지기의 정밀성

Thesaurus	sensitive의 참조어
ADJ.	conscious, perceptive, understanding; (ant.) insensitive **1** emotional, irritable, touchy **2**

Word Partnership	sensitive의 연어
ADV.	overly sensitive, so sensitive, too sensitive **1** **2** highly sensitive, very sensitive **1**-**6**
N.	sensitive **areas**, sensitive **issue** **3** sensitive **information**, sensitive **material** **4** **heat** sensitive, **light** sensitive, sensitive **skin** **5** sensitive **equipment** **6**

sen|sor /sɛnsər/ (**sensors**) N-COUNT A **sensor** is an instrument which reacts to certain physical conditions or impressions such as heat or light, and which is used to provide information. ❑ The latest Japanese vacuum cleaners contain sensors that detect the amount of dust and type of floor.

가산명사 감지기 ❑ 최신 일제 진공청소기는 먼지의 양과 바닥의 유형까지 탐지할 수 있는 감지기가 장착돼 있다.

sen|so|ry /sɛnsəri/ ADJ **Sensory** means relating to the physical senses. [FORMAL] [ADJ n] ❑ Almost all sensory information from the trunk and limbs passes through the spinal cord. →see **nervous system**, **smell**

형용사 감각의 [격식체] ❑ 몸통과 사지에서 입수된 거의 모든 감각 정보가 척수를 통해 전달된다.

sen|sual /sɛnʃuəl/ **1** ADJ Someone or something that is **sensual** shows or suggests a great liking for physical pleasures, especially sexual pleasures. ❑ He was a very sensual person. ❑ Clothing doesn't need to be overt to be sensual. ● **sen|su|al|ity** /sɛnʃuælɪti/ N-UNCOUNT ❑ The wave and curl of her blonde hair gave her sensuality and youth. **2** ADJ Something that is **sensual** gives pleasure to your physical senses rather than to your mind. ❑ It was an opera, very glamorous and very sensual. ● **sen|su|al|ity** N-UNCOUNT ❑ These perfumes have warmth and sensuality.

1 형용사 관능적인, 섹시한 ❑ 그는 매우 관능적인 사람이었다. ❑ 섹시한 옷이라고 해서 꼭 노출이 심할 필요는 없다. ● 관능미 불가산명사 ❑ 물결치듯 꼬불거리는 그녀의 금발 머리가 관능미와 젊음을 뿜어냈다. **2** 형용사 감각적인 ❑ 매우 화려하고 감각적인 오페라였다. ● 감각적임 불가산명사 ❑ 이 향들은 따뜻하고 감각적이다.

sen|su|ous /sɛnʃuəs/ **1** ADJ Something that is **sensuous** gives pleasure to the mind or body through the senses. ❑ The film is ravishing to look at and boasts a sensuous musical score. ● **sen|su|ous|ly** ADV ❑ She lay in the deep bath for a long time,

1 형용사 감각적인, 심미적인 ❑ 이 영화는 황홀한 영상과 마음을 울리는 음악을 자랑한다. ● 감각적으로, 심미적으로 부사 ❑ 그녀는 오랫동안 욕조에 몸을 푹

a b c d e f g h i j k l m n o p q r s t u v w x y z

enjoying its sensuously perfumed water. **2** ADJ Someone or something that is **sensuous** shows or suggests a great liking for sexual pleasure. ❑ *...his sensuous young mistress, Marie-Therese.* ❑ *...wide sensuous lips.* ● **sen|su|ous|ly** ADV ❑ *The nose was straight, the mouth sensuously wide and full.*

담그고 그윽한 향이 나는 물에서 목욕을 즐겼다. **2** 형용사 육감적인 ❑ 그의 육감적인 젊은 정부 마리 테레즈 ❑ 육감적으로 벌어진 입술 ● 육감적으로 부사 ❑ 코는 곧고 입가는 통통해 육감적으로 보였다.

sent /sɛnt/ **Sent** is the past tense and past participle of **send**.

*send*의 과거 및 과거 분사

sen|tence ♦♦◇ /sɛntəns/ (**sentences, sentencing, sentenced**) **1** N-COUNT A **sentence** is a group of words which, when they are written down, begin with a capital letter and end with a period, question mark, or exclamation mark. Most sentences contain a subject and a verb. ❑ *Here we have several sentences incorrectly joined by commas.* **2** N-VAR In a law court, a **sentence** is the punishment that a person receives after they have been found guilty of a crime. ❑ *They are already serving prison sentences for their part in the assassination.* ❑ *He was given a four-year sentence.* ❑ *The court is expected to pass sentence later today.* →see also **death sentence** **3** V-T When a judge **sentences** someone, he or she states in court what their punishment will be. ❑ *A military court sentenced him to death in his absence.* ❑ *She was sentenced to nine years in prison.* →see **trial**

1 가산명사 문장 ❑ 여기 잘못 사용된 쉼표로 연결된 문장이 몇 개 있다. **2** 가산명사 또는 불가산명사 선고, 형벌 ❑ 그들은 암살에 동조한 죄로 이미 실형을 살고 있다. ❑ 그는 징역 4년을 구형받았다. ❑ 법원이 오늘 오후 판결을 내릴 것으로 예상된다. **3** 타동사 선고하다 ❑ 군사 재판소가 부재자 재판으로 그에게 사형 선고를 내렸다. ❑ 그녀는 징역 9년을 선고받았다.

sen|ti|ment /sɛntəmənt/ (**sentiments**) **1** N-VAR A **sentiment** that people have is an attitude which is based on their thoughts and feelings. ❑ *Public sentiment rapidly turned anti-American.* ❑ *He's found growing sentiment for military action.* **2** N-COUNT A **sentiment** is an idea or feeling that someone expresses in words. ❑ *I must agree with the sentiments expressed by John Prescott.* **3** N-UNCOUNT **Sentiment** is feelings such as pity or love, especially for things in the past, and may be considered exaggerated and foolish. ❑ *Laura kept that letter out of sentiment.*

1 가산명사 또는 불가산명사 정서, 감정 ❑ 여론이 급격히 반미로 돌아섰다. **2** 가산명사 의견, 감상 ❑ 저도 존 프레스코트의 의견에 전적으로 동의합니다. **3** 불가산명사 감상 ❑ 로라는 편지를 감상적으로 되지 않도록 했다.

sen|ti|men|tal /sɛntɪmɛntᵊl/ **1** ADJ Someone or something that is **sentimental** feels or shows pity or love, sometimes to an extent that is considered exaggerated and foolish. ❑ *I'm trying not to be sentimental about the past.* ● **sen|ti|men|tal|ly** ADV ❑ *Childhood had less freedom and joy than we sentimentally attribute to it.* ● **sen|ti|men|tal|ity** /sɛntɪmɛntælɪti/ N-UNCOUNT ❑ *In this book there is no sentimentality.* **2** ADJ **Sentimental** means relating to or involving feelings such as pity or love, especially for things in the past. ❑ *Our paintings and photographs are of sentimental value only.*

1 형용사 감상적인 ❑ 나는 과거에 대한 감상적인 태도를 버리려고 하고 있다. ● 감상적으로 부사 ❑ 유년 시절이 우리가 감상적으로 생각하는 것만큼 자유롭고 즐겁지는 않았다. ● 감상적임 불가산명사 ❑ 이 책에 감상적인 대목이라곤 단 한 군데도 없다. **2** 형용사 감정상의 ❑ 우리 그림과 사진들은 감정상의 면에서만 가치가 있다.

sen|try /sɛntri/ (**sentries**) N-COUNT A **sentry** is a soldier who guards a camp or a building. ❑ *The sentry would not let her enter.*

가산명사 보초, 경비 ❑ 보초가 그녀를 들여보내 주려 하지 않았다.

sepa|rate ♦♦◇ (**separates, separating, separated**)

The adjective and noun are pronounced /sɛpərət/. The verb is pronounced /sɛpəreɪt/.

형용사와 명사는 /sɛpərət/로 발음된다. 동사는 /sɛpəreɪt/로 발음된다.

1 ADJ If one thing is **separate from** another, there is a barrier, space, or division between them, so that there are clearly two things. ❑ *Each villa has a separate sitting-room.* ❑ *They are now making plans to form their own separate party.* **2** ADJ If you refer to **separate** things, you mean several different things, rather than just one thing. ❑ *Use separate chopping boards for raw meats, cooked meats, vegetables, and salads.* ❑ *Men and women have separate exercise rooms.* **3** V-RECIP If you **separate** people or things that are together, or if they **separate**, they move apart. ❑ *Police moved in to separate the two groups.* ❑ *The pans were held in both hands and swirled around to separate gold particles from the dirt.* ❑ *The front end of the car separated from the rest of the vehicle.* **4** V-RECIP If you **separate** people or things that have been connected, or if one **separates from** another, the connection between them is ended. ❑ *They want to separate teaching from research.* ❑ *It's very possible that we may see a movement to separate the two parts of the country.* **5** V-RECIP If a couple who are married or living together **separate**, they decide to live apart. ❑ *Her parents separated when she was very young.* **6** V-T An object, obstacle, distance, or period of time which **separates** two people, groups, or things exists between them. ❑ *...the white-railed fence that separated the yard from the paddock.* ❑ *...although they had undoubtedly made progress in the six years that separated the two periods.* **7** V-T If you **separate** one idea or fact **from** another, you clearly see or show the difference between them. ❑ *It is difficult to separate legend from truth.* ❑ *...learning how to separate real problems from imaginary illnesses.* ● PHRASAL VERB **Separate out** means the same as **separate**. ❑ *How can one ever separate out the act from the attitudes that surround it?* **8** V-T A quality or factor that **separates** one thing **from** another is the reason why the two things are different from each other. ❑ *The single most important factor that separates ordinary photographs from good photographs is the lighting.* **9** V-T If a particular number of points **separate** two teams or competitors, one of them is winning or has won by that number of points. ❑ *In the end only three points separated the two teams.* **10** V-T/V-I If you **separate** a group of people or things **into** smaller elements, or if a group **separates**, it is divided into smaller elements. ❑ *The police wanted to separate them into smaller groups.* ❑ *Let's separate into smaller groups.* ● PHRASAL VERB **Separate out** means the same as **separate**. ❑ *If prepared many hours ahead, the mixture may separate out.* **11** N-PLURAL **Separates** are clothes such as skirts, pants, and shirts which cover just the top half or the bottom half of your body. ❑ *She wears coordinated separates instead of a suit.* **12** →see also **separated** **13** PHRASE When two or more people who have been together for some time **go** their **separate ways**, they go to different places or end their relationship. ❑ *Sue was 27 when she and her husband decided to go their separate ways.*

1 형용사 독립된, 개별적인 ❑ 빌라마다 거실이 별도로 있다. ❑ 그들은 현재 자신들만의 독립된 정당을 구성하기 위한 계획을 마련 중이다. **2** 형용사 각각 다른 ❑ 날고기, 익은 고기, 야채, 샐러드에 따라 각각 다른 도마를 사용하세요. ❑ 남녀 체육관이 분리되어 있다. **3** 상호동사 분리하다, 떼어 놓다; 분리되다, 떨어지다 ❑ 경찰이 개입해 두 그룹을 떼어 놓았다. ❑ 양손에 접시를 들고 소용돌이 모양으로 돌려서 흙에서 금가루를 분리했다. ❑ 차체 앞부분이 차에서 떨어져 나왔다. **4** 상호동사 분리하다, 갈라놓다; 분리되다, 갈라지다 ❑ 그들은 수업과 연구를 분리하고 싶어 한다. ❑ 그 나라를 둘로 갈라놓으려는 움직임을 보게 될 가능성이 매우 높다. **5** 상호동사 헤어지다 ❑ 부모님은 그녀가 아주 어릴 적에 헤어졌다. **6** 타동사 가르다 ❑ 방목장 마구간과 마당을 가르는 난간이 하얀 담장 ❑ 비록 이들이 그 기간을 가르는 6년 동안의 의심할 여지없이 발전을 이루기는 했지만 **7** 타동사 구별하다, 구분하다 ❑ 전설과 사실을 구분하기 어렵다. ❑ 진짜로 아픈 것과 생각으로만 아픈 것을 구별하는 법을 배우기 ● 구동사 구별하다, 구분하다 ❑ 행동 자체와 그 행동을 둘러싼 태도를 도대체 어떻게 구분할 수 있단 말인가? **8** 타동사 구분 짓다 ❑ 평범한 사진과 훌륭한 사진을 구분 짓는 가장 중요한 한 가지 요소는 조명이다. **9** 타동사 가르다, 갈라놓다 ❑ 결국 겨우 3점차로 그 두 팀의 승부가 갈렸다. **10** 타동사/자동사 나누다, 분리하다; 나뉘다, 분리되다 ❑ 경찰은 그들을 소그룹으로 나누기를 원했다. ❑ 몇 명씩 소규모로 나눕시다. ● 구동사 나누다, 분리하다; 나뉘다, 분리되다 ❑ 너무 미리 준비해 두면 섞어 놓은 재료가 따로따로 분리될 수도 있다. **11** 복수명사 스커트, 바지, 셔츠와 같이 몸 아래나 위만 덮는 옷 ❑ 그녀는 아래 위 한 벌로 된 정장보다 따로따로 사서 맞춰 입는다. **13** 구 헤어지다, 각기 제 갈 길을 가다 ❑ 그녀는 27세에 남편과 각기 제 길을 가기로 합의했다.

Thesaurus — separate의 참조어
ADJ. disconnected, divided; (ant.) attached, connected **1**
V. divide, remove, split **3** **4**

▶ **separate out** PHRASAL VERB If you **separate out** something from the other things it is with, you take it out. ❑ *The ability to separate out reusable elements from other waste is crucial.* →see also **separate 7, 10**

구동사 골라내다 ❑ 쓰레기에서 재사용 가능한 것을 골라낼 줄 아는 능력이 핵심적이다.

sep|a|rat|ed /sɛpəreɪtɪd/ ◨ ADJ Someone who is **separated** from their wife or husband lives apart from them, but is not divorced. [v-link ADJ, oft ADJ *from* n] ❏ *Most single parents are either divorced or separated.* ◪ ADJ If you are **separated** from someone, for example your family, you are not able to be with them. ❏ *The idea of being separated from him, even for a few hours, was torture.*

◨ 형용사 별거 중인 ❏ 혼자서 자식을 키우는 사람 대부분이 이혼했거나 별거 중인 사람들이다. ◪ 형용사 떨어진, 헤어진 ❏ 단 몇 시간이라도 그와 떨어져 있을 생각을 하면 너무나 괴로웠다.

sep|a|rate|ly /sɛpərɪtli/ ADV If people or things are dealt with **separately** or do something **separately**, they are dealt with or do or something at different times or places, rather than together. ❏ *Cook each vegetable separately until just tender.*

부사 따로따로, 개별적으로 ❏ 야채가 부드러워질 때까지 각각 따로따로 익히세요.

sep|a|ra|tion /sɛpəreɪʃⁿn/ (separations) N-VAR The **separation** of two or more things or groups is the fact that they are separate or become separate, and are not linked. [oft N *of/from/between* n] ❏ *He believes in the separation of the races.* ◪ N-VAR During a **separation**, people who usually live together are not together. ❏ *She wondered if Harry had been unfaithful to her during this long separation.* ◖ N-VAR If a couple who are married or living together have a **separation**, they decide to live apart. ❏ *They agreed to a trial separation.*

◨ 가산명사 또는 불가산명사 분리 ❏ 그는 인종 분리 정책 신봉자이다. ◪ 가산명사 또는 불가산명사 떨어짐, 헤어짐 ❏ 그녀는 이렇게 오래 떨어져 있는 동안 해리가 바람을 피우지는 않았나 궁금했다. ◖ 가산명사 또는 불가산명사 별거 ❏ 그들은 시험적 별거를 하기로 합의하였다.

sep|a|ra|tism /sɛpərətɪzəm/ N-UNCOUNT **Separatism** is the beliefs and activities of separatists. ❏ *... a doctrine of racial separatism.*

불가산명사 분리주의 ❏ 인종 분리주의

sep|a|rat|ist /sɛpərətɪst/ (separatists) ◨ ADJ **Separatist** organizations and activities within a country involve members of a group of people who want to establish their own separate government or are trying to do so. [ADJ n] ❏ *Spanish police say they have arrested ten people suspected of being members of the Basque separatist movement.* ◪ N-COUNT **Separatists** are people who want their own separate government or are involved in separatist activities. ❏ *The army has come under attack by separatists.*

◨ 형용사 분리주의의 ❏ 스페인 경찰이 바스크 분리주의 운동 소속으로 의심되는 사람 10명을 체포했다고 한다. ◪ 가산명사 분리주의자 ❏ 군이 분리주의자들의 공격을 받았다.

Sept. **Sept.** is a written abbreviation for **September**. ❏ *I've booked it for Thurs. Sept. 8th.*

9월 ❏ 9월 8일 목요일로 예약했습니다.

Sep|tem|ber ◆◆◇ /sɛptɛmbər/ (Septembers) N-VAR **September** is the ninth month of the year in the Western calendar. ❏ *Her son, Jerome, was born in September.* ❏ *They returned to Moscow on 22 September 1930.*

가산명사 또는 불가산명사 9월 ❏ 그녀의 아들 제롬은 9월에 태어났다. ❏ 그들은 1930년 9월 22에 모스크바로 돌아갔다.

sep|tic /sɛptɪk/ ADJ If a wound or a part of your body becomes **septic**, it becomes infected. ❏ *A flake of plaster from the ceiling fell into his eye, which became septic.*

형용사 염증이 생긴 ❏ 지붕에서 회반죽 파편이 그의 눈에 떨어져서 눈에 염증이 생겼다.

Word Link

sequ ≈ following : consequence, sequel, sequence

---

se|quel /siːkwⁿl/ (sequels) N-COUNT A book or movie which is a **sequel to** an earlier one continues the story of the earlier one. ❏ *She is currently writing a sequel to Daphne du Maurier's "Rebecca."*

가산명사 속편 ❏ 그녀는 현재 대프니 뒤 모리어의 소설 '레베카'의 속편을 집필 중이다.

se|quence /siːkwəns/ (sequences) ◨ N-COUNT A **sequence of** events or things is a number of events or things that come one after another in a particular order. ❏ *...the sequence of events which led to the murder.* ◪ N-COUNT A particular **sequence** is a particular order in which things happen or are arranged. ❏ *...the color sequence yellow, orange, purple, blue, green and white.*

◨ 가산명사 인속, 연쇄 ❏ 결국 그 살인으로 이른 일련의 사건들 ◪ 가산명사 순서, 차례 ❏ 노랑, 주황, 보라, 파랑, 초록, 하양의 색깔 순서

se|quin /siːkwɪn/ (sequins) N-COUNT **Sequins** are small, shiny disks that are sewn on clothes to decorate them. ❏ *The frocks were covered in sequins, thousands of them.*

가산명사 (옷의) 금박 장식, 반짝이 ❏ 수천 개나 되는 금박 장식이 드레스들을 덮고 있었다.

se|rene /sɪriːn/ ADJ Someone or something that is **serene** is calm and quiet. ❏ *She looked as calm and serene as she always did.* ❏ *He didn't speak much, he just smiled with that serene smile of his.* ● **se|rene|ly** ADV ❏ *We sailed serenely down the river.* ❏ *She carried on serenely sipping her gin and tonic.* ● **se|ren|ity** /sɪrɛnɪti/ N-UNCOUNT ❏ *I had a wonderful feeling of peace and serenity when I saw my husband.*

형용사 조용한, 차분한; 고요한, 평온한 ❏ 그녀는 언제나 그렇듯이 차분하고 조용해 보였다. ❏ 그는 그다지 말을 많이 하지 않았다. 다만 특유의 조용한 미소를 짓고 있을 뿐이었다. ● 조용히; 고요하게, 평온하게 부사 ❏ 우리는 평온하게 강 아래로 항해했다. ❏ 그녀는 계속해서 조용히 진토닉을 마셨다. ● 평온, 침착 불가산명사 ❏ 나는 남편을 봤을 때 평화롭고도 평온한 굉장히 좋은 기분을 느꼈다.

ser|geant /sɑːrdʒⁿnt/ (sergeants) ◨ N-COUNT; N-TITLE; N-VOC A **sergeant** is a non-commissioned officer of middle rank in the army, marines, or air force. ❏ *A sergeant with a detail of four men came into view.* ◪ N-COUNT; N-TITLE; N-VOC In American police forces, a **sergeant** is an officer with the rank immediately below a captain. In the British police force, a **sergeant** is an officer with the next to lowest rank. ❏ *The unit was staffed by 11 officers from Greater Manchester Police headed by Sergeant Bell.*

◨ 가산명사; 경칭명사; 호격명사 하사관 ❏ 하사관이 선발대 4명을 데리고 나타났다. ◪ 가산명사; 경칭명사; 호격명사 경사 ❏ 그 팀은 벨 경사가 이끄는 그레이터맨체스터 경찰 소속 경찰관 11명으로 구성되어 있었다.

ser|geant ma|jor (sergeant majors) also **sergeant-major** N-COUNT; N-TITLE; N-VOC A **sergeant major** is a noncommissioned army or marine officer of the highest rank.

가산명사; 경칭명사; 호격명사 특무 상사

se|rial /sɪəriəl/ (serials) ◨ N-COUNT A **serial** is a story which is broadcast on television or radio or is published in a magazine or newspaper in a number of parts over a period of time. ❏ *...one of BBC television's most popular serials, Eastenders.* ◪ ADJ **Serial** killings or attacks are a series of killings or attacks committed by the same person. This person is known as a **serial** killer or attacker. [ADJ n] ❏ *...serial murders.*

◨ 가산명사 연속극, 연재물 ❏ 가장 인기 있는 비비시 텔레비전 연속극 중 하나인 '이스트엔더스' ◪ 형용사 연쇄의 ❏ 연쇄 살인

se|ri|ali|za|tion /sɪəriəlaɪzeɪʃⁿn/ (serializations) [BRIT also **serialisation**] ◨ N-UNCOUNT **Serialization** is the act of serializing a book. ❏ *It was first written for serialization in a magazine.* ◪ N-COUNT A **serialization** is a story, originally written as a book, which is published or broadcast in a number of parts. ❏ *...the serialisation of Jane Austen's "Pride and Prejudice."*

[영국영어 serialisation] ◨ 불가산명사 연재 ❏ 이 작품은 처음에 잡지 연재용으로 쓰였다. ◪ 가산명사 연속극화, 연재 ❏ 제인 오스틴의 '오만과 편견'을 연속극으로 만듦

se|ri|al|ize /sɪəriəlaɪz/ (serializes, serializing, serialized) [BRIT also **serialise**] V-T If a book **is serialized**, it is broadcast on the radio or television or is published in a magazine or newspaper in a number of parts over a period of time. [usu passive] ❏ *Attention was first drawn to the book when a condensed version was serialized in "The New Yorker."*

[영국영어 serialise] 타동사 연속극으로 방영되다, 연재되다 ❏ 이 책은 축약본이 뉴요커에 연재되기 시작하면서 처음 주목받기 시작했다.

se|rial num|ber (serial numbers) ◨ N-COUNT The **serial number** of an object is a number on that object which identifies it. ❏ *...the gun's serial number.* ❏ *...your*

◨ 가산명사 일련번호 ❏ 총의 일련번호 ❏ 네 자전거의 일련번호 ◪ 가산명사 (미군의) 군번 ❏ 그는

bike's serial number. **2** N-COUNT The **serial number** of a member of the United States military forces is a number which identifies them. ❑ *He could never ever give any responses to his captor other than name, rank, serial number, and date of birth.*

남치범에게 이름, 계급, 군번, 생일을 제외하고는 전혀 아무런 대답도 할 수 없었다.

se|rial port (**serial ports**) N-COUNT A **serial port** on a computer is a place where you can connect the computer to a device such as a modem or a mouse. [COMPUTING]

가산명사 (컴퓨터) 시리얼 포트 [컴퓨터]

se|ries ♦♦◇ /sɪəriːz/

Series is both the singular and the plural form.

series는 단수형 및 복수형이다.

1 N-COUNT A **series of** things or events is a number of them that come one after the other. ❑ *...a series of meetings with students and political leaders.* **2** N-COUNT A radio or television **series** is a set of programs of a particular kind which have the same title. ❑ *...the TV series "The Trials of Life" presented by David Attenborough.*

1 가산명사 연속, 연쇄 ❑ 학생과 정치 지도자들과의 연이은 만남 **2** 가산명사 시리즈 ❑ 데이비드 아텐보로가 진행하는 텔레비전 시리즈 '생명의 시련'

se|ri|ous ♦♦♦ /sɪəriəs/ **1** ADJ **Serious** problems or situations are very bad and cause people to be worried or afraid. ❑ *Crime is an increasingly serious problem in Russian society.* ❑ *The government still face very serious difficulties.* ● **se|ri|ous|ly** ADV ❑ *If this ban was to come in it would seriously damage my business.* ● **se|ri|ous|ness** N-UNCOUNT [oft N of n] ❑ *...the seriousness of the crisis.* **2** ADJ **Serious** matters are important and deserve careful and thoughtful consideration. ❑ *I regard this as a serious matter.* ❑ *Don't laugh, boy. This is serious.* **3** ADJ When important matters are dealt with in a **serious** way, they are given careful and thoughtful consideration. ❑ *My parents never really faced up to my drug use in any serious way.* ❑ *It was a question which deserved serious consideration.* ● **se|ri|ous|ly** ADV [ADV with v] ❑ *The management will have to think seriously about their positions.* **4** ADJ **Serious** music or literature requires concentration to understand or appreciate it. [ADJ n] ❑ *...serious classical music.* **5** ADJ If someone is **serious about** something, they are sincere about what they are saying, doing, or intending to do. ❑ *You really are serious about this, aren't you?* ● **se|ri|ous|ly** ADV ❑ *Are you seriously jealous of Erica?* ● **se|ri|ous|ness** N-UNCOUNT [oft N of n] ❑ *In all seriousness, there is nothing else I can do.* **6** ADJ **Serious** people are thoughtful and quiet, and do not laugh very often. ❑ *He's quite a serious person.* ● **se|ri|ous|ly** ADV [ADV with v] ❑ *They spoke to me very seriously but politely.*

1 형용사 심각한 ❑ 범죄가 러시아 사회에서 갈수록 심각한 문제가 되고 있다. ❑ 정부는 여전히 매우 심각한 난관에 직면해 있다. ● 심각하게 부사 ❑ 이번 금지가 실시되면 나의 사업에 타격을 받을 것이다. ● 심각성 불가산명사 ❑ 위기의 심각성 **2** 형용사 중대한 ❑ 나는 이것이 중대한 문제라고 생각한다. ❑ 웃지 마. 중요한 문제라고. **3** 형용사 진지한 ❑ 부모들은 나의 약물 복용을 단 한 번도 진지하게 받아들인 적이 없다. ❑ 그것은 진지하게 고려해야 마땅한 문제였다. ● 진지하게 부사 ❑ 경영진은 그들의 위치에 대해 진지하게 생각해 봐야 할 것이다. **4** 형용사 딱딱한, 무거운 ❑ 딱딱한 클래식 음악 **5** 형용사 진심인, 진정인 ❑ 그 말 정말 진심이지. 그렇지? ● 진심으로, 진정으로 부사 ❑ 진짜 에리카가 질투나? ● 진심, 진정 불가산명사 ❑ 정말 진정으로 하는 말인데, 내가 달리 할 수 있는 것이 하나도 없어. **6** 형용사 진지한 ❑ 그는 상당히 진지한 사람이다. ● 진지하게 부사 ❑ 그들은 나에게 매우 진지하면서도 예의 바르게 말했다.

Thesaurus serious의 참조어

ADJ. crucial, important, significant; (ant.) unimportant **2**
businesslike, quiet, solemn, thoughtful; (ant.) cheerful **6**

Word Partnership serious의 연어

N. serious **accident**, serious **condition**, serious **crime**, serious **danger**, serious **harm**, serious **illness**, serious **injury**, serious **mistake**, serious **problem**, serious **threat**, serious **trouble** **1**
serious **matter**, serious **situation** **1 2**
serious **business**, serious **question** **2**
serious **consideration**, serious **doubts** **3**
serious **expression**, serious **face** **6**

ADV. **extremely** serious, **more** serious, **quite** serious, **really** serious, **very** serious **1**-**3 5 6**
deadly serious **2 5 6**

---

se|ri|ous|ly ♦♦◇ /sɪəriəsli/ **1** ADV You use **seriously** to indicate that you are not joking and that you really mean what you say. [ADV with cl] ❑ *Seriously, I only smoke in the evenings.* **2** CONVENTION You say "**seriously**" when you are surprised by what someone has said, as a way of asking them if they really mean it. [SPOKEN, FEELINGS] ❑ *"I tried to chat him up at the general store." He laughed. "Seriously?"* **3** →see also **serious** **4** PHRASE If you **take** someone or something **seriously**, you believe that they are important and deserve attention. ❑ *It's hard to take them seriously in their pretty grey uniforms.*

1 부사 정말이지 ❑ 정말이지 나는 저녁에만 담배를 피워. **2** 관용 표현 정말이야 [구어체, 감정 개입] ❑ "잡화점에서 그한테 말을 걸어 보려 했었어." 그가 웃었다. "정말이야?" **4** 구 진지하게 받아들이다, 심각하게 받아들이다 ❑ 귀여운 회색 제복 차림의 그들을 심각하게 받아들이기는 힘들다.

ser|mon /sɜːrmən/ (**sermons**) N-COUNT A **sermon** is a talk on a religious or moral subject that is given by a member of the clergy as part of a church service. ❑ *Cardinal Cormac Murphy-O'Connor will deliver the sermon on Sunday, January 13.*

가산명사 설교 ❑ 코르막 머피 오코너 추기경이 1월 13일 설교를 맡을 것이다.

ser|pent /sɜːrpənt/ (**serpents**) N-COUNT A **serpent** is a snake. [LITERARY] ❑ *...the serpent in the Garden of Eden.*

가산명사 뱀 [문예체] ❑ 에덴동산의 뱀

se|rum /sɪərəm/ (**serums**) **1** N-VAR A **serum** is a liquid that is injected into someone's blood to protect them against a poison or disease. ❑ *...painful injections of anti-cancer serum.* **2** N-UNCOUNT **Serum** is the watery, pale yellow part of blood. ❑ *The strip, which accepts blood, serum, or plasma, is inserted into the analyser.*

1 가산명사 또는 불가산명사 혈청 주사액 ❑ 아픈 혈청 항암 주사 **2** 불가산명사 혈청 ❑ 혈액, 혈청, 혈장이 들어오는 관을 분석기에 넣는다.

serv|ant ♦♦◇ /sɜːrvənt/ (**servants**) **1** N-COUNT A **servant** is someone who is employed to work at another person's home, for example as a cleaner or a gardener. ❑ *...a large Victorian family with several servants.* **2** N-COUNT You can use **servant** to refer to someone or something that provides a service for people or can be used by them. ❑ *Like any other public servants, police must respond to public demand.* →see also **civil servant**

1 가산명사 하인, 종 ❑ 하인 몇 명을 둔 빅토리아 시대의 대가족 **2** 가산명사 종사자, 종업원 ❑ 기타 다른 공무원들처럼 경찰도 국민들의 요구에 부응해야 한다.

serve ♦♦◇ /sɜːrv/ (**serves, serving, served**) **1** V-T If you **serve** your country, an organization, or a person, you do useful work for them. ❑ *It is unfair to soldiers who have served their country well for many years.* **2** V-I If you **serve** in a particular place or as a particular official, you perform official duties, especially in the armed forces, as a civil servant, or as a politician. ❑ *During the second world war he served with RAF Coastal Command.* ❑ *He also served on the National Front's national executive committee.* **3** V-T/V-I If something **serves as** a particular thing or

1 타동사 -을 위해 일하다, 봉사하다 ❑ 수년 동안 훌륭하게 나라를 지킨 군인들에게 부당한 일이다. **2** 자동사 복무하다, 근무하다 ❑ 그는 2차 세계 대전 동안 영국 공군 해안 사령부에서 복무했다. ❑ 그는 영국 국민 전선의 집행 위원회에서도 근무했다. **3** 타동사/자동사 -로 기능하다, - 목적을 충족시키다 ❑ 그녀는 자기 사무실로 쓰고 있는 앞방으로 나를

serves a particular purpose, it performs a particular function, which is often not its intended function. ❑ *She ushered me into the front room, which served as her office.* ❑ *I really do not think that an inquiry would serve any useful purpose.* ◆ V-T If something **serves** people or an area, it provides them with something that they need. ❑ *This could mean the closure of thousands of small businesses which serve the community.* ❑ *...improvements in the public water-supply system serving the Nairobi area.* ◆ V-T Something that **serves** someone's interests benefits them. ❑ *The economy should be organized to serve the interests of all the people.* ◆ V-T When you **serve** food and drink, you give people food and drink. ❑ *Serve it with French bread.* ❑ *Serve the cakes warm.* ◆ PHRASAL VERB **Serve up** means the same as **serve**. ❑ *After all, it is no use serving up TV dinners if the kids won't eat them.* ◆ V-T **Serve** is used to indicate how much food a recipe produces. For example, a recipe that **serves** six provides enough food for six people. [no cont] ❑ *Garnish with fresh herbs. Serves 4.* ◆ V-T Someone who **serves** customers in a store or a bar helps them and provides them with what they want to buy. ❑ *They wouldn't serve me in any pubs 'cos I looked too young.* ◆ V-T When the police or other officials **serve** someone **with** a legal order or **serve** an order **on** them, they give or send the legal order to them. [LEGAL] ❑ *...as immigration officers accompanied by the police tried to serve her with a deportation order.* ◆ V-T If you **serve** something such as a prison sentence or an apprenticeship, you spend a period of time doing it. ❑ *...Leo, who is currently serving a life sentence for murder.* ◆ V-T/V-I When you **serve** in games such as tennis and badminton, you throw up the ball or shuttlecock and hit it to start play. ❑ *He served 17 double faults.* ◆ N-COUNT **Serve** is also a noun. ❑ *His second serve clipped the net.* ◆ N-COUNT When you describe someone's **serve**, you are indicating how well or how fast they serve a ball or shuttlecock. ❑ *His powerful serve was too much for the defending champion.* ◆ →see also **serving** ◆ PHRASE If you say **it serves** someone **right** when something unpleasant happens to them, you mean that it is their own fault and you have no sympathy for them. [FEELINGS] ❑ *Serves her right for being so stubborn.*

▶serve up →see serve 6

Word Partnership   serve의 연어

N.	serve **a community**, serve **the public** ◆ ◆
	serve **a purpose**
	serve *someone's* **needs** ◆
	serve **cake**, serve **food** ◆

---

serv|er /sɜrvər/ (**servers**) ◆ N-COUNT In computing, a **server** is part of a computer network which does a particular task, for example storing or processing information, for all or part of the network. [COMPUTING] ◆ N-COUNT In tennis and badminton, the **server** is the player whose turn it is to hit the ball or shuttlecock to start play. ❑ *...a brilliant server and volleyer.* →see **Internet, tennis**

ser|vice ◆◆◆ /sɜrvɪs/ (**services, servicing, serviced**)

For meaning ◆, **services** is both the singular and the plural form.

→Please look at category ◆ to see if the expression you are looking for is shown under another headword. ◆ N-COUNT A **service** is something that the public needs, such as transportation, communications facilities, hospitals, or energy supplies, which is provided in a planned and organized way by the government or an official body. ❑ *The postal service has been trying to cut costs.* ❑ *We have started a campaign for better nursery and school services.* ◆ N-COUNT You can sometimes refer to an organization or private company as a particular **service** when it provides something for the public or acts on behalf of the government. ❑ *All these changes follow months of negotiations between the BBC and the Foreign Office, which provides the money for the World Service.* ◆ N-COUNT If an organization or company provides a particular **service**, they can do a particular job or a type of work for you. ❑ *The kitchen maintains a twenty-four hour service and can be contacted via Reception.* ◆ N-PLURAL **Services** are activities such as tourism, banking, and selling things which are part of a country's economy but are not concerned with producing or manufacturing goods. ❑ *Mining rose by 9.1%, manufacturing by 9.4%, and services by 4.3%.* ◆ N-UNCOUNT The level or standard of **service** provided by an organization or company is the amount or quality of the work it can do for you. ❑ *Taking risks is the only way employees can provide effective and efficient customer service.* ◆ N-COUNT A bus or train **service** is a route or regular trip that is part of a transportation system. ❑ *The local bus service is well run and extensive.* ◆ N-PLURAL Your **services** are the things that you do or the skills that you use in your job, which other people find useful and are usually willing to pay you for. ❑ *I have obtained the services of a top photographer to take our pictures.* ◆ N-UNCOUNT If you refer to someone's **service** or **services** to a particular organization or activity, you mean that they have done a lot of work for it or spent a lot of their time on it. [also N in pl, oft N to n] ❑ *You've given a lifetime of service to athletics.* ❑ *Most employees had long service with the company and were familiar with our products.* ◆ N-COUNT **The Services** are the army, the navy, the air force, and the marines. ❑ *Some of the money could be spent on persuading key specialists to stay in the Services.* ◆ N-UNCOUNT **Service** is the work done by people or equipment in the army, navy, or air force, for example during a war. ❑ *Units are being called up today for service in the Gulf.* ◆ N-UNCOUNT When you receive **service** in a restaurant, hotel, or store, an employee asks you what you want or gives you what you have ordered. ❑ *Service was attentive and the meal proceeded at a leisurely pace.* ◆ N-COUNT A **service** is a religious ceremony that takes place in a church or synagogue. [also no det] ❑ *After the hour-long service, his body was taken to a cemetery in the south of the city.* ◆ N-COUNT A **dinner service** or a **tea service** is a complete set of plates, cups, saucers, and other pieces of china. ❑ *...a 60-piece dinner service.* ◆ N-COUNT A **services** is a place beside a highway where you can buy gas and other things, or have a

---

안내했다. ❑ 나는 정말 조사가 아무런 소용도 없으리라고 생각한다. ◆ 타동사 필요한 것을 공급하다, 담당하다 ❑ 이는 지역 사회를 먹여 살리는 수천 개에 달하는 소규모 사업장의 폐쇄를 의미한다. ❑ 나이로비 지역에 대한 공공 수자원 공급 시스템 개선 ◆ 타동사 이익이 되다 ❑ 모든 사람들에게 이익이 되도록 경제를 만들어야 한다. ◆ 타동사 (음식을) 내놓다, 주다 ❑ 그 요리를 프랑스빵과 함께 내놓으세요. ❑ 케이크는 따뜻하게 해서 내놓으세요. ● 구동사 (음식을) 내놓다, 주다 ◆ 결국 아이들이 먹지 않는다면 이미 다 만들어진 요리를 사다가 차려 줘 봐야 소용이 없다. ◆ 타동사 ~인분을 만들다 ❑ 신선한 허브로 고명을 얹으세요. 4인분입니다. ◆ 타동사 시중들다, 서비스를 제공하다 ❑ 너무 어려 보인다면서 어느 술집에서도 나를 받아 주려 하지 않았다. ◆ 타동사 송달하다, 집행하다 [법률] ❑ 경찰을 동반한 출입국 관리가 그녀에 대한 국외 추방 명령을 집행하려 해서 ◆ 타동사 인한을 채우다; 징역을 살다 ❑ 현재 살인죄로 종신형을 살고 있는 레오 ◆ 자동사/타동사 (경기) 서브를 넣다 ❑ 그는 서브에서 더블폴트를 17개나 기록했다. ● 가산명사 서브 ❑ 그의 두 번째로 서브한 공이 네트에 맞았다. ◆ 가산명사 서브 ❑ 그의 서브는 전 챔피언도 감당할 수 없을 정도로 강력했다. ◆ 구 당해도 싸다 [감정 개입] ❑ 그렇게 고집을 피우니까 그런 꼴을 당하지.

◆ 가산명사 서버 (컴퓨터) [컴퓨터] ◆ 가산명사 서브하는 사람 ❑ 서브와 발리에 뛰어난 선수

◆ 의미로 services은 단수형 및 복수형이다.

◆ 가산명사 공공 서비스, 공공사업 ❑ 체신 사업은 비용 절감을 위해 노력해 왔다. ❑ 우리는 보육 및 교육 서비스 향상을 위한 캠페인을 시작했다. ◆ 가산명사 기관, 회사 ❑ 이 같은 변화는 비비시와 비비시의 '월드서비스'에 자금을 제공하는 외무부 간의 몇 달에 걸친 협상 끝에 일어나게 됐다. ◆ 가산명사 영업, 서비스 ❑ 식당은 24시간 영업하며 안내 데스크를 통해 연락이 가능하다. ◆ 복수명사 서비스 업종 ❑ 광업은 9.1퍼센트, 제조업은 9.4퍼센트, 서비스 부문은 4.3퍼센트 올랐다. ◆ 불가산명사 서비스 ❑ 위험 감수만이 직원들이 효과적이고 효율적인 고객 서비스를 제공할 수 있는 방법이다. ◆ 가산명사 운행 ❑ 지방 버스의 경우 운영도 훌륭하고 노선도 다양하다. ◆ 복수명사 용역, 일 ❑ 최고의 사진작가가 우리 사진을 찍어 주기로 했다. ◆ 불가산명사 공헌, 이바지 ❑ 귀하께서는 평생 동안 체육 발전에 힘써 주셨습니다. ❑ 대부분의 직원들은 오랫동안 회사에 이바지했으며 우리 제품에 대해 잘 알고 있었다. ◆ 가산명사 군대 ❑ 돈의 일부는 주요 전문가들이 군을 떠나지 않도록 설득하는 데 사용될 수도 있다. ◆ 불가산명사 군무 ❑ 오늘 몇몇 부대가 걸프전 수행을 위해 소집된다. ◆ 불가산명사 접대, 서비스 ❑ 손님 접대는 세심했으며 식사는 느긋하게 진행되었다. ◆ 가산명사 예배, 의식 ❑ 1시간 가량 장례식이 진행된 후 그의 시신이 도시 남부의 공동묘지로 운구 됐다. ◆ 가산명사 (식기) 한 벌, 한 세트 ❑ 60개로 구성된 정찬용 식기 세트 ◆ 가산명사 휴게소 [영국영어; 미국영어 rest area] ❑ 그들은 차를 세우고 어떻게 해서든 고속도로 휴게소 같은 곳에 가야 했다. ◆ 가산명사 (경기) 서브 넣을 차례 ❑ 그녀는 1세트에서 자신이 서브 넣을 차례에서는 단 3점만 내주었다. ◆ 형용사 직원용의, 업무용의 ❑ 나는 부엌을 통해 직원용 엘리베이터를 타고 내려갔다. ◆ 타동사 정비를 받다 ❑ 만약 당신이 정비소에서 자동차 정비를 받았더라면 ● 가산명사 정비 ❑ 그 차는 정비가 필요하다. ◆ 타동사 편의를 제공하다, 일을 보다 ❑ 현재 본사에서 400명의 직원들이 우리의 지역 및 해외 업무에 편의를 제공하고 있다. ◆ 구 도움을 주다 ❑ 저를 많이 도와주셔서 대단히 감사합니다. ◆ 구 가동되는, 사용되는; 가동되지 않는 ❑ 자금을 줄인 것은 교체

meal. [BRIT; AM **rest area**] ❑ *They had to pull up, possibly go to a motorway services or somewhere like that.* **15** N-COUNT In tennis, badminton, and some other sports, when it is your **service**, it is your turn to serve. ❑ *She conceded just three points on her service during the first set.* **16** ADJ **Service** is used to describe the parts of a building or structure that are used by the staff who clean, repair, or take care of it, and are not usually used by the public. [ADJ n] ❑ *I went out through the kitchen and down the service elevator.* **17** V-T If you have a vehicle or machine **serviced**, you arrange for someone to examine, adjust, and clean it so that it will keep working efficiently and safely. ❑ *...if you had had your car serviced at the local garage.* ● N-COUNT **Service** is also a noun. ❑ *The car needs a service.* **18** V-T If someone or something **services** an organization, a project, or a group of people, they provide it with the things that it needs in order to function properly or effectively. ❑ *There are now 400 staff at headquarters, servicing our regional and overseas work.* **19** →see also **Civil Service, community service, emergency services, in-service, National Health Service, public service, room service 20** PHRASE If you **do** someone **a service**, you do something that helps or benefits them. ❑ *You are doing me a great service, and I'm very grateful to you.* **21** PHRASE If a piece of equipment or type of vehicle is **in service**, it is being used or is able to be used. If it is **out of service**, it is not being used, usually because it is not working properly. ❑ *Cuts in funding have meant that equipment has been kept in service long after it should have been replaced.* ❑ *In 1882, London's first electric tram cars went into service.* →see **dry cleaning, economics, industry**

시한이 넘은 지 오래된 장비가 지금까지 사용됐다는 것을 뜻한다. ❑ 1882년 런던의 첫 전동차가 가동에 들어갔다.

ser|vice charge (**service charges**) N-COUNT A **service charge** is an amount that is added to your bill in a restaurant to pay for the work of the person who comes and serves you. ❑ *Most restaurants add a 10 per cent service charge to the bill.*

가산명사 봉사료, 팁 ❑ 대부분의 음식점은 10퍼센트의 봉사료를 부과한다.

ser|vice in|dus|try (**service industries**) N-COUNT A **service industry** is an industry such as banking or insurance that provides a service but does not produce anything. ❑ *Seventy-two percent of people now work in service industries.*

가산명사 서비스 산업 ❑ 72퍼센트의 사람들이 현재 서비스직에 종사한다.

ser|vice|man /sɜrvɪsmən/ (**servicemen**) N-COUNT A **serviceman** is a man who is in the army, navy, air force, or marines. ❑ *He was an American serviceman based in Vietnam during the war.*

가산명사 군인 ❑ 그는 전쟁 당시 베트남에서 미군으로 복무했다.

ser|vice pro|vid|er (**service providers**) N-COUNT A **service provider** is a company that provides a service, especially an Internet service. [COMPUTING]

가산명사 (인터넷) 서비스 제공업체 [컴퓨터]

ser|vice sta|tion (**service stations**) **1** N-COUNT A **service station** is a place that sells things for vehicles such as gas, oil, and spare parts. Service stations often sell food, drink, and other goods. **2** N-COUNT A **service station** is a place beside a highway where you can buy gas and other things, or have a meal. [BRIT; AM **rest area**]

1 가산명사 주유소 **2** 가산명사 휴게소 [영국영어; 미국영어 rest area]

serv|ing /sɜrvɪŋ/ (**servings**) **1** N-COUNT A **serving** is an amount of food that is given to one person at a meal. ❑ *Quantities will vary according to how many servings of soup you want to prepare.* **2** ADJ A **serving** spoon or dish is used for giving out food at a meal. [ADJ n] ❑ *Pile the potatoes into a warm serving dish.*

1 가산명사 1인분 ❑ 몇 인분의 수프를 준비하고 싶어하는지에 따라 양이 달라진다. **2** 형용사 음식 분배용의 ❑ 따뜻한 음식 분배용 접시에 감자를 쌓아 놓으세요.

ses|sion ◆◇◇ /sɛʃn/ (**sessions**) **1** N-COUNT A **session** is a meeting of a court, legislature, or other official group. [also in N] ❑ *...an emergency session of parliament.* ❑ *After two late night sessions, the Security Council has failed to reach agreement.* **2** N-COUNT A **session** is a period during which the meetings of a court, legislature, or other official group are regularly held. [also in N] ❑ *The parliamentary session ends on October 4th.* **3** N-COUNT A **session** of a particular activity is a period of that activity. ❑ *The two leaders emerged for a photo session.*

1 가산명사 회의 ❑ 의회 비상회의의 ❑ 두 차례의 심야 회의에도 불구하고 안전 보장 위원회가 합의 도출에 실패했다. **2** 가산명사 회기, 개회, 개정 ❑ 국회 회기가 10월 4일 끝난다. **3** 가산명사 (특정한 활동을 위한) 시간 ❑ 두 정상이 사진 촬영 시간에 모습을 드러냈다.

---
set
① NOUN USES
② VERB AND ADJECTIVE USES
---

① **set** ◆◆◆ /sɛt/ (**sets**) **1** N-COUNT A **set of** things is a number of things that belong together or that are thought of as a group. ❑ *There must be one set of laws for the whole of the country.* ❑ *The mattress and base are normally bought as a set.* ❑ *...a chess set.* **2** N-COUNT In tennis, a **set** is one of the groups of six or more games that form part of a match. ❑ *Graf was leading 5-1 in the first set.* **3** N-COUNT In mathematics, a **set** is a group of mathematical quantities that have some characteristic in common. ❑ *...the field of set theory.* **4** N-COUNT The **set** for a play, movie, or television show is the furniture and scenery that is on the stage when the play is being performed or in the studio where filming takes place. [also on/off N] ❑ *From the first moment he got on the set, he wanted to be a director too.* ❑ *He achieved fame for his stage sets for the Folies Bergères.* **5** N-COUNT A **set** is an appliance that receives television or radio signals. For example, a television **set** is a television. ❑ *Children spend so much time in front of the television set.*

1 가산명사 세트, 비슷한 성격을 가진 일련의 것들 ❑ 나라 전체에 적용되는 일련의 법이 있어야 한다. ❑ 매트리스와 매트리스 받침은 보통 세트로 판매된다. ❑ 체스 세트 **2** 가산명사 (테니스) 세트 ❑ 그래프가 첫 세트에서 5-1로 앞서고 있었다. **3** 가산명사 (수학) 집합 ❑ 집합 이론 분야 **4** 가산명사 무대 장치, 세트장 ❑ 그는 처음 세트장에 들어선 순간부터 감독도 해 보고 싶었다. ❑ 그는 '폴리 베르제르'의 무대 장치로 명성을 얻었다. **5** 가산명사 수상기, 수신기 ❑ 아이들이 텔레비전 수상기 앞에서 보내는 시간이 너무 많다.

② **set** ◆◆◆ /sɛt/ (**sets, setting**)

The form **set** is used in the present tense and is the past tense and past participle of the verb.
---

set은 동사의 현재, 과거, 과거 분사로 쓴다.

→Please look at category **23** to see if the expression you are looking for is shown under another headword. **1** V-T If you **set** something somewhere, you put it there, especially in a careful or deliberate way. ❑ *He took the case out of her hand and set it on the floor.* **2** ADJ If something is **set** in a particular place or position, it is in that place or position. [v-link ADJ prep/adv] ❑ *The castle is set in 25 acres of beautiful grounds.* **3** ADJ If something is **set into** a surface, it is fixed there and does not stick out. [v-link ADJ prep/adv] ❑ *The man unlocked a gate set in a high wall and let me through.* **4** V-T You can use **set** to say that a person or thing causes another person or thing to be in a particular condition or situation. For example, to **set** someone free means to cause them to be free, and to **set** something going means to cause it to start working. ❑ *Set the kitchen timer going.* ❑ *Dozens of people have been injured and many vehicles set on fire.* **5** V-T When

1 타동사 놓다, 두다 ❑ 그는 그녀의 손에서 상자를 빼내어 바닥에 놓았다. **2** 형용사 놓인, 위치한 ❑ 성은 25에이커의 아름다운 땅에 자리 잡고 있다. **3** 형용사 고정된 ❑ 남자가 높은 담에 나 있는 문을 열어 내가 들어갈 수 있게 해 주었다. **4** 타동사 특정한 상태가 되게 하다 ❑ 부엌용 타이머를 작동시키세요. ❑ 수십 명의 사람들이 다치고 상당수의 차량에 불이 붙었다. **5** 타동사 붙이다, 조정하다 ❑ 소리를 최대한 크게 틀어 놓으세요. **6** 타동사 정하다 ❑ 이번 회의의 의장이 내일 오후로 마감 시한을 정했다. ❑ 향후 회담이 열릴 날짜가 정해질 것이다. **7** 타동사 값을 매기다, 평가하다 ❑ 그녀는 자율성을 높이 평가한다.

you **set** a clock or control, you adjust it to a particular point or level. ❑ *Set the volume as high as possible.* ⑤ V-T If you **set** a date, price, goal, or level, you decide what it will be. ❑ *The conference chairman has set a deadline of noon tomorrow.* ❑ *A date will be set for a future meeting.* ⑦ V-T If you **set** a certain value on something, you think it has value. ❑ *She sets a high value on autonomy.* ⑧ V-T If you **set** something such as a record, an example, or a precedent, you do something that people will want to copy or try to achieve. ❑ *Legal experts said her case would not set a precedent because it was an out-of-court settlement.* ⑨ V-T If someone **sets** you a task or aim or if you **set yourself** a task or aim, you need to succeed in doing it. ❑ *I have to plan my academic work very rigidly and set myself clear objectives.* ⑩ V-T To **set** an examination means to decide what questions will be asked in it. [BRIT; AM **make up**] ❑ *He broke with the tradition of setting examinations in Latin.* ⑪ ADJ You use **set** to describe something which is fixed and cannot be changed. ❑ *A set period of fasting is supposed to bring us closer to godliness.* ⑫ ADJ A **set** book must be studied by students taking a particular course. [BRIT; AM **required**] [ADJ n] ❑ *One of the set books is Jane Austen's "Emma."* ⑬ ADJ If a play, movie, or story is **set** in a particular place or period of time, the events in it take place in that place or period. [v-link ADJ prep/adv] ❑ *The play is set in a small Midwestern town.* ⑭ ADJ If you are **set** to do something, you are ready to do it or are likely to do it. If something is **set** to happen, it is about to happen or likely to happen. [v-link ADJ to-inf] ❑ *Roberto Baggio was set to become one of the greatest players of all time.* ⑮ ADJ If you are **set** on something, you are strongly determined to do or have it. If you are **set against** something, you are strongly determined not to do or have it. [v-link ADJ on/against n/-ing] ❑ *She was set on going to an all-girls school.* ⑯ V-I When something such as jelly, melted plastic, or cement **sets**, it becomes firm or hard. ❑ *You can add ingredients to these desserts as they begin to set.* ⑰ V-I When the sun **sets**, it goes below the horizon. ❑ *They watched the sun set behind the distant dales.* ⑱ V-T To **set** a trap means to prepare it to catch someone or something. ❑ *He seemed to think I was setting some sort of trap for him.* ⑲ V-T When someone **sets** the table, they prepare it for a meal by putting plates and flatware on it. ❑ *One would shop and cook, another would set the table, and another would wash up.* ⑳ V-T If someone **sets** a poem or a piece of writing **to** music, they write music for the words to be sung to. ❑ *He has attracted much interest by setting ancient religious texts to music.* ㉑ →see also **setting** ㉒ PHRASE If someone **sets the scene** or **sets the stage for** an event to take place, they make preparations so that it can take place. ❑ *The Democratic convention has set the scene for a ferocious election campaign this autumn.* ㉓ to **set fire to** something →see **fire**. to **set foot** somewhere →see **foot**. to **set your heart on** something →see **heart**. to **set sail** →see **sail**. to **set to work** →see **work**

Thesaurus		*set*의 참조어
N.	bunch, group ①	①
	scene	① ④
V.	arrange, place ②	① ②
	decide, determine, fix ②	⑥ ⑦
ADJ.	established, fixed ②	⑪

▶**set aside** ① PHRASAL VERB If you **set** something **aside for** a special use or purpose, you keep it available for that use or purpose. ❑ *Some doctors advise setting aside a certain hour each day for worry.* ② PHRASAL VERB If you **set aside** a belief, principle, or feeling, you decide that you will not be influenced by it. ❑ *He urged the participants to set aside minor differences for the sake of achieving peace.*

▶**set back** ① PHRASAL VERB If something **sets** you **back** or **sets back** a project or plan, it causes a delay. ❑ *It has set us back in so many respects that I'm not sure how long it will take for us to catch up.* ② PHRASAL VERB If something **sets** you **back** a certain amount of money, it costs you that much money. [INFORMAL] ❑ *A bottle of imported beer will set you back $7.* ③ →see also **setback**

▶**set down** ① PHRASAL VERB If a committee or organization **sets down** rules for doing something, it decides what they should be and officially records them. ❑ *The Dublin Convention of June 1990 set down rules for deciding which EC country should deal with an asylum request.* ② PHRASAL VERB If you **set down** your thoughts or experiences, you write them all down. ❑ *Old Walter is setting down his memories of village life.*

▶**set in** PHRASAL VERB If something unpleasant **sets in**, it begins and seems likely to continue or develop. ❑ *Winter is setting in and the population is facing food and fuel shortages.*

▶**set off** ① PHRASAL VERB When you **set off**, you start a journey. ❑ *Nichols set off for his remote farmhouse in Connecticut.* ❑ *The President's envoy set off on another diplomatic trip.* ② PHRASAL VERB If something **sets off** something such as an alarm or a bomb, it makes it start working so that, for example, the alarm rings or the bomb explodes. ❑ *Any escape, once it's detected, sets off the alarm.* ❑ *Someone set off a fire extinguisher.* ③ PHRASAL VERB If something **sets off** an event or a series of events, it causes it to start happening. ❑ *The arrival of the charity van set off a minor riot as villagers scrambled for a share of the aid.*

▶**set out** ① PHRASAL VERB When you **set out**, you start a journey. ❑ *When setting out on a long walk, always wear suitable boots.* ② PHRASAL VERB If you **set out to** do something, you start trying to do it. ❑ *He has achieved what he set out to do three years ago.* ③ PHRASAL VERB If you **set things out**, you arrange or display them somewhere. ❑ *Set out the cakes attractively, using lacy doilies.* ④ PHRASAL VERB If you **set out** a number of facts, beliefs, or arguments, you explain them in writing or speech in a clear, organized way. ❑ *He has written a letter to "The Times" setting out his views.*

▶**set up** ① PHRASAL VERB If you **set** something **up**, you create or arrange it. ❑ *The two sides agreed to set up a commission to investigate claims.* ❑ *...an organization*

⑧ 타동사 (기록 같은 것을) 세우다 ❑ 법률 전문가들은 그녀의 사건이 당사자 간 합의로 끝났기 때문에 전례가 되지는 않을 것이라고 밝혔다. ⑨ 타동사 (목표 등을) 설정하다 ❑ 나는 아주 빡빡하게 학과 계획을 짜고 명확한 목표를 세워야 한다. ⑩ 타동사 문제를 내다 [영국영어; 미국영어 **make up**] ❑ 그는 라틴 어로 시험 문제를 내는 전통을 깼다. ⑪ 형용사 정해진, 고정된 ❑ 일정 기간 동안 하는 단식은 본래 종교적인 믿음을 심화시키기 위한 것이다. ⑫ 형용사 지정된 [영국영어; 미국영어 **required**] ❑ 지정서 중에 하나가 제인 오스틴의 '에마'이다. ⑬ 형용사 ~ 배경의 ❑ 연극의 배경은 중서부 지방의 작은 읍내이다. ⑭ 형용사 준비된, ~할 태세의 ❑ 로베르토 바조가 역사상 가장 훌륭한 선수 중 한 명으로 탄생하려는 순간이었다. ⑮ 형용사 단호한, 확고한 ❑ 그녀는 여학교에 갈 결심이 확고했다. ⑯ 자동사 ❑ 디저트가 굳기 시작하면 재료를 넣어도 된다. ⑰ 자동사 지다, 저물다 ❑ 그들은 멀리 골짜기 너머로 해가 지는 광경을 지켜보았다. ⑱ 타동사 놓다, 설치하다 ❑ 그는 내가 자기한테 일종의 덫을 놓고 있다고 생각하는 것 같았다. ⑲ 타동사 (상을) 차리다 ❑ 한 사람이 장을 보고 요리를 하면, 다른 사람이 상을 차리고 또 다른 사람이 설거지를 하곤 했다. ⑳ 타동사 노래로 만들다 ❑ 그는 고대 종교 경전을 노래로 만들어서 많은 관심을 모았다. ㉓ 구 사전 준비를 하다 ❑ 민주당 전당 대회에서 이번 가을 치열한 선거전의 사전 준비를 완료했다.

① 구동사 따로 마련해 두다, 따로 떼어 두다 ❑ 몇몇 의사들은 매일 얼마간 걱정하는 시간을 따로 마련하라고 조언한다. ② 구동사 치워 두다, 무시하다 ❑ 그는 참가자들에게 평화 달성을 위해 사소한 차이점은 무시하라고 촉구했다.

① 구동사 저지하다, 지연시키다 ❑ 그 일로 우리가 아주 여러 가지 점에서 뒤처졌기 때문에 따라잡는 데 얼마나 걸릴지 확실히 모르겠다. ② 구동사 비용을 물리다 [비격식체] ❑ 수입 맥주 한 병을 사는 데 7달러가 들 것이다.

① 구동사 규정하다 ❑ 1990년 6월 더블린 협약에서는 망명 신청을 처리할 유럽 공동체 회원국을 결정하는 규칙을 정했다. ② 구동사 적다, 기록하다 ❑ 올드 월터가 시골 생활의 추억을 글로 남기고 있다.

구동사 시작되다; 자리 잡기 시작하다 ❑ 겨울이 시작되면서 사람들이 식량과 연료 부족 문제에 직면하고 있다.

① 구동사 출발하다 ❑ 니콜라스가 코네티컷에 있는 자신의 외딴 농가를 향해 출발했다. ❑ 대통령 특사가 외교 사절로 또 한 차례 길을 떠났다. ② 구동사 작동시키다, 폭발시키다 ❑ 탈출의 조짐이 감지되면 경보가 울린다. ❑ 누군가가 소화기를 분사했다. ③ 구동사 일으키다 ❑ 구호물자를 실은 차량이 도착하자 마을 사람들이 제 몫을 챙기려고 다투면서 작은 소동이 빚어졌다.

① 구동사 출발하다 ❑ 오랫동안 걸어서 나설 때는 항상 알맞은 신발을 신으세요. ② 구동사 착수하다, 시작하다 ❑ 그는 3년 전에 착수한 일을 완수했다. ③ 구동사 배치하다, 진열하다 ❑ 레이스 받침을 사용해서 케이크를 보기 좋게 진열하세요. ④ 구동사 설명하다, 제시하다 ❑ 그는 타임스 지에 자신의 견해를 상술한 서한을 작성해 보냈다.

① 구동사 설치하다, 설립하다 ❑ 양측이 진상 규명을 위해 특별 위원회를 설치하기로 합의했다. ❑ 여성들의

(letter index right margin: a b c d e f g h i j k l m n o p q r s t u v w x y z)

which sets up meetings about issues of interest to women. ● **set|ting up** N-UNCOUNT ❑ *The British government announced the setting up of a special fund.* **2** PHRASAL VERB If you **set up** a temporary structure, you place it or build it somewhere. ❑ *They took to the streets, setting up roadblocks of burning tyres.* **3** PHRASAL VERB If you **set up** a device or piece of machinery, you do the things that are necessary for it to be able to start working. ❑ *Setting up the camera can be tricky.* **4** PHRASAL VERB If you **set up** somewhere or **set yourself up** somewhere, you establish yourself in a new business or new area. ❑ *...the mayor's scheme offers incentives to firms setting up in lower Manhattan.* ❑ *He worked as a dance instructor in London before setting himself up in Bucharest.* **5** PHRASAL VERB If you **set up** house or home or **set up** shop, you buy a house or business of your own and start living or working there. ❑ *They married, and set up home in Ramsgate.* **6** PHRASAL VERB If you **are set up** by someone, they make it seem that you have done something wrong when you have not. [INFORMAL] ❑ *He claimed yesterday that he had been set up after drugs were discovered at his home.* **7** →see also **set-up**

set|back /sɛtbæk/ (setbacks) also **set-back** N-COUNT A **setback** is an event that delays your progress or reverses some of the progress that you have made. [oft N for/in/to n] ❑ *The move represents a setback for the Middle East peace process.*

set|tee /sɛti/ (settees) N-COUNT A **settee** is a long comfortable seat with a back and arms, which two or more people can sit on.

set|ting /sɛtɪŋ/ (settings) **1** N-COUNT A particular **setting** is a particular place or type of surroundings where something is or takes place. ❑ *Rome is the perfect setting for romance.* **2** N-COUNT A **setting** is one of the positions to which the controls of a device such as a stove or heater can be adjusted. ❑ *You can boil the fish fillets on a high setting.*

set|tle ♦♦◇ /sɛtl/ (settles, settling, settled) **1** V-T If people **settle** an argument or problem, or if something **settles** it, they solve it, for example by making a decision about who is right or about what to do. ❑ *They agreed to try to settle their dispute by negotiation.* **2** V-T/V-I If people **settle** a legal dispute or if they **settle**, they agree to end the dispute without going to a court of law, for example by paying some money or by apologizing. ❑ *In an attempt to settle the case, Molken has agreed to pay restitution.* ❑ *She got much less than she would have done if she had settled out of court.* **3** V-T If you **settle** a bill or debt, you pay the amount that you owe. ❑ *I settled the bill for my coffee and his two glasses of wine.* **4** V-T If something **is settled**, it has all been decided and arranged. [usu passive] ❑ *As far as we're concerned, the matter is settled.* **5** V-T/V-I When people **settle** a place or in a place, or when a government **settles** them there, they start living there permanently. ❑ *Refugees settling in Britain suffer from a number of problems.* ❑ *He visited Paris and eventually settled there.* **6** V-T/V-I If you **settle yourself** somewhere or **settle** somewhere, you sit down or make yourself comfortable. ❑ *Albert settled himself on the sofa.* **7** V-T/V-I If something **settles** or if you **settle** it, it sinks slowly down and becomes still. ❑ *A black dust settled on the walls.* ❑ *Once its impurities had settled, the oil could be graded.* **8** V-I If your eyes **settle** on or **upon** something, you stop looking around and look at that thing for some time. ❑ *The man let his eyes settle upon Cross's face.* **9** V-I When birds or insects **settle on** something, they land on it from above. ❑ *Moths flew in front of it, eventually settling on the rough painted metal.* **10** →see also **settled** **11** when the dust **settles** →see **dust.** to **settle** a score →see **score**

Word Partnership	*settle*의 연어
N.	settle **differences,** settle **things** **1**
	settle **a dispute,** settle **a matter** **1** **2**
	settle **a case,** settle **a claim,** settle **a lawsuit/suit** **2**
V.	agree to settle, decide to settle **1**-**3**

▶**settle down** **1** PHRASAL VERB When someone **settles down,** they start living a quiet life in one place, especially when they get married or buy a house. ❑ *One day I'll want to settle down and have a family.* **2** PHRASAL VERB If a situation or a person that has been going through a lot of problems or changes **settles down,** they become calm. ❑ *It'd be fun, after the situation in Europe settles down, to take a trip over to France.* **3** PHRASAL VERB If you **settle down** to do something or to something, you prepare to do it and concentrate on it. ❑ *He got his coffee, came back and settled down to listen.* **4** PHRASAL VERB If you **settle down** for the night, you get ready to lie down and sleep. ❑ *They put up their tents and settled down for the night.*

▶**settle for** PHRASAL VERB If you **settle for** something, you choose or accept it, especially when it is not what you really want but there is nothing else available. ❑ *Virginia was a perfectionist. She was just not prepared to settle for anything mediocre.*

▶**settle in** PHRASAL VERB If you **settle in,** you become used to living in a new place, doing a new job, or going to a new school. ❑ *I enjoyed King Edward's School enormously once I'd settled in.*

▶**settle on** PHRASAL VERB If you **settle on** a particular thing, you choose it after considering other possible choices. ❑ *I finally settled on a Mercedes estate. It's the ideal car for me.*

▶**settle up** PHRASAL VERB When you **settle up,** you pay a bill or a debt. ❑ *Let's give him credit, and we'll settle up at the end of the evening.*

set|tled /sɛtld/ **1** ADJ If you have a **settled** way of life, you stay in one place, in one job, or with one person, rather than moving around or changing. ❑ *He decided to lead a more settled life with his partner.* **2** ADJ A **settled** situation or system stays the same all the time. ❑ *There has been a period of settled weather.*

set|tle|ment ♦♦◇ /sɛtlmənt/ (settlements) **1** N-COUNT A **settlement** is an official agreement between two sides who were involved in a conflict or

관심사를 논의하는 자리를 만드는 조직 ● 설치, 설립 불가산명사 ❑ 영국 정부가 특별 기금 설치를 발표했다. **2** 구동사 세우다, 만들다 ❑ 그들은 거리로 뛰어나가 불타는 타이어로 바리케이드를 쳤다. **3** 구동사 맞추다, 설치하다, 설정하다 ❑ 카메라를 맞추기가 까다로울 수 있다. **4** 구동사 자리 잡다 ❑ 시장이 내놓은 계획은 맨해튼 저지대에 자리 잡은 기업들을 우대를 받게 된다. ❑ 그는 부쿠레슈트에서 자리 잡기 전에 런던에서 댄스 강사로 일했다. **5** 구동사 장만하다 ❑ 그들은 결혼해서 람스게이트에 집을 장만했다. **6** 구동사 누명을 쓰다 [비격식체] ❑ 그는 자신의 집에서 마약이 발견된 후 누명을 쓰게 되었다고 어제 주장했다. **7** →참조 set-up

가산명사 방해, 역행 ❑ 그 조치는 중동 평화 수립 절차의 역행을 나타낸다.

가산명사 (등받이와 팔걸이가 있는) 긴 의자

1 가산명사 장소, 무대 ❑ 로마는 연애를 하기에 완벽한 장소이다. **2** 가산명사 (조절기 등의) 설정 ❑ 생선살을 높은 불에 맞춰 놓고 끓여도 된다.

1 타동사 해결하다 ❑ 그들은 협상을 통해 분쟁을 해결하기로 합의했다. **2** 타동사/자동사 합의를 보다 ❑ 사건에 대한 합의를 보기 위해 몰켄은 배상금을 지불하기로 동의했다. ❑ 그녀는 법정 밖에서 합의를 봤으면 받을 수 있을 것보다 훨씬 적게 받았다. **3** 타동사 계산하다, 지불하다 ❑ 나는 내 커피와 그의 와인 두 잔 값을 계산했다. **4** 타동사 결정되다 ❑ 우리에겐 그 사안은 결정된 것이다. **5** 타동사/자동사 정착하다; 정착시키다 ❑ 영국에 정착하는 난민들은 여러 가지 문제에 부닥친다. ❑ 그는 파리를 방문했고 결국 그곳에 정착했다. **6** 타동사/자동사 자리를 잡다, 편안히 앉다 ❑ 앨버트는 소파에 자리를 잡았다. **7** 타동사/자동사 가라앉다; 가라앉히다 ❑ 벽에 검은 먼지가 앉아 있었다. ❑ 불순물이 가라앉은 다음에는 기름의 등급을 정할 수 있었다. **8** 자동사 (눈이) 멎다 ❑ 남자의 눈이 크로스의 얼굴에 멎었다. **9** 자동사 (새 등이) 앉다 ❑ 나방들이 그 앞에서 날다 결국 거칠게 도색이 된 금속 위에 앉았다.

1 구동사 정착하다 ❑ 언젠가는 내가 정착해서 가정을 꾸리고 싶어질 것이다. **2** 구동사 진정되다 ❑ 유럽의 상황이 진정된 다음에 프랑스에 여행을 간다면 재미있을 것이다. **3** 구동사 본격적으로 착수하다 ❑ 그는 커피를 가지고 돌아와서 본격적으로 듣기 시작했다. **4** 구동사 잠자리에 들다 ❑ 그들은 텐트를 치고 잠자리에 들었다.

구동사 ~에 만족하다 ❑ 버지니아는 완벽주의자였다. 그녀는 어중간한 것으로는 절대로 만족하지 않았다.

구동사 적응하다 ❑ 일단 적응한 다음에는 킹 에드워드 학교가 내겐 아주 즐거웠다.

구동사 정하다 ❑ 나는 결국 메르세데스 에스테이트로 정했다. 나에게 이상적인 차이다.

구동사 계산하다, 지불하다 ❑ 그에게 맡기고 저녁이 끝날 때 계산합시다.

1 형용사 안정된 ❑ 그는 자신의 동반자와 좀 더 안정된 삶을 누리기로 결정했다. **2** 형용사 변화가 없는 ❑ 얼마 동안 날씨에 변화가 없었다.

1 가산명사 합의, 해결 ❑ 우리의 목표는 평화 합의를 달성하는 것이다. **2** 가산명사 합의 ❑ 그녀는 소송을

argument. ❑ *Our objective must be to secure a peace settlement.* ◻ N-COUNT A **settlement** is an agreement to end a disagreement or dispute without going to a court of law, for example by offering someone money. ❑ *She accepted an out-of-court settlement of £4,000.* ◻ N-UNCOUNT The **settlement of** a debt is the act of paying back money that you owe. ❑ *...ways to delay the settlement of debts.* ◻ N-COUNT A **settlement** is a place where people have come to live and have built homes. ❑ *The village is a settlement of just fifty houses.*

거치지 않고 4,000파운드를 받기로 합의했다. ◻ 불가산명사 상환, 지불 ❑ 채무의 상환을 지연할 수 있는 방법 ◻ 가산명사 정착지 ❑ 그 마을은 단 50가구가 있는 정착지이다.

set|tler /sɛtlər, setəl-/ (**settlers**) N-COUNT **Settlers** are people who go to live in a new country. ❑ *The first German village in south-western Siberia was founded a century ago by settlers from the Volga region.*

가산명사 정착민 ❑ 남서부 시베리아 최초의 독일인 마을은 볼가 지역에서 온 정착민들에 의해 1세기 전에 세워졌다.

set-top box (**set-top boxes**) N-COUNT A **set-top box** is a piece of equipment that rests on top of your television and receives digital television signals.

가산명사 셋톱박스

set-up ◆◇◇ (**set-ups**) also **setup** ◻ N-COUNT A particular **set-up** is a particular system or way of organizing something. [INFORMAL] ❑ *It appears to be an idyllic domestic set-up.* ◻ N-COUNT If you describe a situation as a **set-up**, you mean that people have planned it in order to deceive you or to make it look as if you have done something wrong. [INFORMAL] ❑ *He was asked to pick somebody up and bring them to a party, not realizing it was a setup.* ◻ N-SING The **set-up** of computer hardware or software is the process of installing it and making it ready to use. [COMPUTING] ❑ *The worst part of the set-up is the poor instruction manual.*

◻ 가산명사 구성 (방식) [비격식체] ❑ 평화로운 가정환경인 것 같다. ◻ 가산명사 계략 [비격식체] ❑ 그는 누군가를 태워서 파티에 데려오라는 요청을 받았는데, 그것이 계략인 줄을 몰랐다. ◻ 단수명사 설치 [컴퓨터] ❑ 그 설치에서 제일 힘든 것은 설치 안내서가 굉장히 부실하다는 것이다.

sev|en ◆◆◆ /sɛvən/ (**sevens**) NUM **Seven** is the number 7. ❑ *Sarah and Ella have been friends for seven years.*

수사 7 ❑ 새러와 엘라는 7년간 사귄 친구이다.

Word Link   teen ≈ plus ten, from 13-19 : eigh*teen*, seven*teen*, *teen*ager

---

sev|en|teen ◆◆◇ /sɛvəntin/ (**seventeens**) NUM **Seventeen** is the number 17. ❑ *Jenny is seventeen years old.*

수사 17, 열일곱 ❑ 제니는 열일곱 살이다.

sev|en|teenth ◆◆◇ /sɛvəntinθ/ (**seventeenths**) ◻ ORD The **seventeenth** item in a series is the one that you count as number seventeen. ❑ *She gave birth to Annabel just after her seventeenth birthday.* ◻ FRACTION A **seventeenth** is one of seventeen equal parts of something.

◻ 서수 열일곱 번째 ❑ 그녀는 열일곱 번째 생일이 막 지난 뒤에 애너벨을 낳았다. ◻ 분수 17분의 1

sev|enth ◆◆◇ /sɛvənθ/ (**sevenths**) ◻ ORD The **seventh** item in a series is the one that you count as number seven. ❑ *I was the seventh child in the family. There were 11 of us altogether.* ◻ FRACTION A **seventh** is one of seven equal parts of something. ❑ *A million people died, a seventh of the population.*

◻ 서수 일곱 번째 ❑ 나는 형제 중에 일곱 번째 아이였다. 형제는 모두 11명이었다. ◻ 분수 7분의 1 ❑ 인구의 7분의 1인 백만 명이 죽었다.

sev|en|ti|eth ◆◆◇ /sɛvəntiəθ/ (**seventieths**) ◻ ORD The **seventieth** item in a series is the one that you count as number seventy. ❑ *...the seventieth anniversary of the discovery of Tutankhamun's tomb.* ◻ FRACTION A **seventieth** is one of seventy equal parts of something.

◻ 서수 칠십 번째 ❑ 투탕카멘 무덤 발견 70주년 ◻ 분수 70분의 1

sev|en|ty ◆◆◆ /sɛvənti/ (**seventies**) ◻ NUM **Seventy** is the number 70. ❑ *Seventy people were killed.* ◻ N-PLURAL When you talk about the **seventies**, you are referring to numbers between 70 and 79. For example, if you are **in** your **seventies**, you are aged between 70 and 79. If the temperature is **in** the **seventies**, it is between 70 and 79. ❑ *I thought it was a long way to go for two people in their seventies, but Sylvia loved the idea.* ◻ N-PLURAL The **seventies** is the decade between 1970 and 1979. ❑ *In the late Seventies, things had to be new, modern, revolutionary.*

◻ 수사 70, 칠십 ❑ 70명이 사망했다. ◻ 복수명사 70대의 ❑ 나는 그곳이 70대 노인 두 명이 가기에는 먼 거리라고 생각했지만 실비아는 그 제안을 너무 좋아했다. ◻ 복수명사 70년대 ❑ 70년대 말에는 모든 것들이 새롭고 현대적이고 혁신적이어야 했다.

Word Link   sever ≈ separating : sever, several, severance

---

sev|er /sɛvər/ (**severs, severing, severed**) ◻ V-T To **sever** something means to cut completely through it or to cut it completely off. [FORMAL] ❑ *Richardson severed his right foot in a motorbike accident.* ◻ V-T If you **sever** a relationship or connection that you have with someone, you end it suddenly and completely. [FORMAL] ❑ *She severed her ties with England.*

◻ 타동사 자르다 [격식체] ❑ 리처드슨은 오토바이 사고로 오른발이 절단되었다. ◻ 타동사 끊다, 단절하다 [격식체] ❑ 그 나라는 영국과의 관계를 단절했다.

sev|er|al ◆◆◆ /sɛvrəl/ DET **Several** is used to refer to an imprecise number of people or things that is not large but is greater than two. ❑ *I had lived two doors away from this family for several years.* ❑ *Several blue plastic boxes under the window were filled with record albums.* ● QUANT **Several** is also a quantifier. [QUANT of pl-n] ❑ *Supporters are urging him to take action against the demonstrators, several of whom are members of the parliament.* ● PRON **Several** is also a pronoun. ❑ *No one drug will suit or work for everyone and sometimes several may have to be tried.*

한정사 몇몇의 ❑ 나는 몇 해 동안 이 가족과 두 집 떨어진 곳에서 살았다. ❑ 창 밑의 파란 플라스틱 상자 몇 개에 레코드판이 가득 들어 있었다. ● 수량사 몇몇의 ❑ 지지자들은 그에게 시위자들에 대해 행동을 취하라고 요구하고 있는데 그들 중 일부는 의회의 의원들이다. ● 대명사 몇몇 ❑ 약 하나가 모든 사람에게 적합하거나 효과를 내지는 못하므로 때로는 여러 가지를 시도해야 할지도 모른다.

sev|er|ance /sɛvrəns, -ərəns/ ADJ **Severance** pay is a sum of money that a company gives to its employees when it has to stop employing them. [BUSINESS] [ADJ n] ❑ *We were offered 13 weeks' severance pay.*

형용사 퇴직의 [경제] ❑ 우리는 13주치 급여에 해당하는 퇴직금을 제안 받았다.

se|vere ◆◆◇ /sɪvɪər/ (**severer, severest**) ◻ ADJ You use **severe** to indicate that something bad or undesirable is great or intense. ❑ *...a business with severe cash flow problems.* ❑ *Shortages of professional staff are very severe in some places.* ● **se|vere|ly** ADV ❑ *The UN wants to send food aid to 10 countries in Africa severely affected by the drought.* ❑ *An aircraft overshot the runway and was severely damaged.* ● **se|ver|ity** /sɪvɛrɪti/ N-UNCOUNT [usu with supp] ❑ *Several drugs are used to lessen the severity of the symptoms.* ◻ ADJ **Severe** punishments or criticisms are very strong or harsh. ❑ *This was a dreadful crime and a severe sentence is necessary.* ● **se|vere|ly** ADV [ADV with v] ❑ *...a campaign to try to change the law to punish dangerous drivers more severely.* ● **se|ver|ity** N-UNCOUNT [usu with supp] ❑ *The Bishop said he was sickened by the severity of the sentence.*

◻ 형용사 심각한 ❑ 심각한 현금 유동성 문제를 안고 있는 기업 ❑ 어떤 곳에서는 전문 일손의 부족이 매우 심각하다. ● 심각하게 부사 ❑ 유엔은 가뭄의 피해를 심각하게 입은 아프리카의 10개 국가에 원조 식량을 보내고 싶어 한다. ❑ 비행기가 활주로를 지나쳐서 심각하게 파손되었다. ● 심각한 불가산명사 ❑ 증상의 심각함을 줄이기 위해 여러 가지의 약물을 사용한다. ◻ 형용사 엄격한 ❑ 이것은 끔찍한 범죄였으며 준엄이 요구된다. ● 엄격하게 부사 ❑ 난폭 운전자들을 보다 엄격하게 처벌할 수 있도록 법을 개정하려는 운동 ● 엄격한 불가산명사 ❑ 선고의 엄격함에 질렸다고 주교는 이야기했다.

Thesaurus   severe의 참조어

ADJ.   critical, extreme, harsh, intense, tough ◻ ◻

Word Partnership *severe의 연어*

| N. | severe **consequences**, severe **depression**, severe **disease/illness**, severe **drought**, severe **flooding**, severe **injuries**, severe **pain**, severe **problem**, severe **symptoms**, severe **weather** 🔟 severe **penalty**, severe **punishment** 🔁 |
| ADV. | **less/more/most** severe, **very** severe 🔟 🔁 |

sew /soʊ/ (sews, sewing, sewed, sewn) V-T/V-I When you **sew** something such as clothes, you make them or repair them by joining pieces of cloth together by passing thread through them with a needle. ❑ *She sewed the dresses on the sewing machine.* ❑ *Anyone can sew on a button, including you.*

타동사/자동사 바느질하다 ❑ 그녀는 재봉틀로 원피스를 만들었다. ❑ 단추는 너를 포함해 아무나 달 수 있다.

sew|age /suːɪdʒ/ N-UNCOUNT **Sewage** is waste matter such as feces or dirty water from homes and factories, which flows away through sewers. ❑ *...the MPs' call for more treatment of raw sewage.* →see pollution

불가산명사 하수, 오물 ❑ 미처리 하수의 보완 처리에 대한 의회의원들의 요구

sew|er /suːər/ (sewers) N-COUNT A **sewer** is a large underground channel that carries waste matter and rain water away, usually to a place where it is treated and made harmless. ❑ *...the city's sewer system.*

가산명사 하수도 ❑ 도시의 하수도 체계

sew|ing /soʊɪŋ/ 🔟 N-UNCOUNT **Sewing** is the activity of making or mending clothes or other things using a needle and thread. ❑ *Her mother had always done all the sewing.* 🔁 N-UNCOUNT **Sewing** is clothes or other things that are being sewn. ❑ *We all got out our own sewing and sat in front of the log fire.*

🔟 불가산명사 바느질 ❑ 모든 바느질은 항상 그녀의 어머니가 했었다. 🔁 불가산명사 바느질감 ❑ 우리는 각자 바느질감을 꺼낸 다음 장작불 앞에 앉았다.

sewn /soʊn/ **Sewn** is the past participle of **sew**.

sew의 과거 분사

sex ♦♦♢ /sɛks/ (sexes, sexing, sexed) 🔟 N-COUNT The two **sexes** are the two groups, male and female, into which people and animals are divided according to the function they have in producing young. ❑ *...an entertainment star who appeals to all ages and both sexes.* →see also **opposite sex** 🔁 N-COUNT The **sex** of a person or animal is their characteristic of being either male or female. ❑ *She continually failed to gain promotion because of her sex.* ❑ *The new technique has been used to identify the sex of foetuses.* 🔢 N-UNCOUNT **Sex** is the physical activity by which people can produce young. ❑ *He was very open in his attitudes about sex.* ❑ *The entire film revolves around drugs, sex, and violence.* 🔺 PHRASE If two people **have sex**, they perform the act of sex. ❑ *Have you ever thought about having sex with someone other than your husband?*

🔟 가산명사 성별 ❑ 남녀노소 모두에게 인기가 있는 연예계 스타 🔁 가산명사 성별 ❑ 그녀는 자신의 성별 때문에 계속 승진에 실패했다. ❑ 새로운 기술이 태아의 성별을 감별하는 데 사용되고 있다. 🔢 불가산명사 성교, 섹스 ❑ 그는 섹스에 대한 태도가 굉장히 개방적이었다. ❑ 그 영화 전체가 마약, 섹스, 그리고 폭력을 중심으로 전개된다. 🔺 구 섹스하다 ❑ 혹시 당신 남편 이외의 사람과 섹스하는 것을 생각해 본 적 있나요?

sex|ism /sɛksɪzəm/ N-UNCOUNT **Sexism** is the belief that the members of one sex, usually women, are less intelligent or less capable than those of the other sex and need not be treated equally. It is also the behavior which is the result of this belief. ❑ *Groups like ours are committed to eradicating homophobia, racism, and sexism.*

불가산명사 성 차별주의 ❑ 우리 같은 단체는 동성애자 혐오, 인종 차별주의, 성 차별주의 등을 근절시키는 데 전념한다.

sex|ist /sɛksɪst/ (sexists) ADJ If you describe people or their behavior as **sexist**, you mean that they are influenced by the belief that the members of one sex, usually women, are less intelligent or less capable than those of the other sex and need not be treated equally. [DISAPPROVAL] ❑ *Old-fashioned sexist attitudes are still common.* ● N-COUNT A **sexist** is someone with sexist views or behavior. ❑ *It's got nothing to do with sexism. You know I'm not a sexist.*

형용사 성 차별적인 [탐탁찮음] ❑ 구시대적 성 차별 의식이 여전히 흔하다. ● 가산명사 성 차별주의자 ❑ 성 차별과는 아무 상관이 없어. 내가 성 차별주의자가 아닌 것은 너도 알잖아.

sex sym|bol (sex symbols) N-COUNT A **sex symbol** is a famous person, especially an actor or a singer, who is considered by many people to be sexually attractive. ❑ *...Hollywood sex symbols of the Forties.*

가산명사 섹스 심벌 ❑ 40년대의 할리우드 섹스 심벌

sex|ual ♦♦♢ /sɛkʃuəl/ 🔟 ADJ **Sexual** feelings or activities are connected with the act of sex or with people's desire for sex. ❑ *This was the first sexual relationship I had had.* ● **sex|ual|ly** ADV ❑ *...sexually transmitted diseases.* 🔁 ADJ **Sexual** means relating to the differences between male and female people. ❑ *Women's groups denounced sexual discrimination.* ● **sex|ual|ly** ADV [ADV with v] ❑ *If you're sexually harassed, you ought to do something about it.* 🔢 ADJ **Sexual** means relating to the differences between heterosexuals and homosexuals. ❑ *...couples of all sexual persuasions.* 🔺 ADJ **Sexual** means relating to the biological process by which people and animals produce young. ❑ *Girls generally reach sexual maturity two years earlier than boys.* ● **sex|ual|ly** ADV ❑ *The first organisms that reproduced sexually were free-floating plankton.*

🔟 형용사 성적인 ❑ 이번이 내가 가진 최초의 성관계였다. ● 성적으로 부사 🔁 형용사 성별의 ❑ 여성 단체들이 성 차별을 비난했다. ● 성별에 의해 부사 ❑ 성희롱을 당했다면 조치를 취해야 한다. 🔢 형용사 성지향의 ❑ 모든 성적 취향의 커플들 🔺 형용사 성적인 ❑ 여자 아이들이 남자 아이들보다 2년 빨리 성적 성숙기에 이른다. ● 성적으로 부사 ❑ 처음으로 양성 생식을 한 생물체는 부유하는 플랑크톤이었다.

sex|ual abuse N-UNCOUNT If a child or other person suffers **sexual abuse**, someone forces them to take part in sexual activity with them, often regularly over a period of time. ❑ *...victims of sexual abuse.*

불가산명사 성적 학대 ❑ 성적 학대 피해자

sex|ual har|ass|ment N-UNCOUNT **Sexual harassment** is repeated and unwelcome sexual comments, looks, or physical contact at work, usually a man's actions that offend a woman. ❑ *Sexual harassment of women workers by their bosses is believed to be widespread.*

불가산명사 성희롱 ❑ 상사에 의한 여성 직원의 성희롱은 광범위하게 행해지리라고 여겨진다.

sex|ual inter|course N-UNCOUNT **Sexual intercourse** is the physical act of sex between two people. [FORMAL] ❑ *I have never had sexual intercourse with her and that is the truth.*

불가산명사 성관계 [격식체] ❑ 나는 그 여자와 성관계를 가진 적이 없으며 그것은 진실이다.

sexu|al|ity /sɛkʃuælɪti/ 🔟 N-UNCOUNT A person's **sexuality** is their sexual feelings. ❑ *In Britain, the growing discussion of women's sexuality raised its own disquiet.* 🔁 N-UNCOUNT You can refer to a person's **sexuality** when you are talking about whether they are sexually attracted to people of the same sex or a different sex. ❑ *He believes he has been discriminated against because of his sexuality.*

🔟 불가산명사 성생활 ❑ 영국에서는 점점 늘어나는 여성의 성생활에 대한 담론이 그 자체의 불안을 야기했다. 🔁 불가산명사 성적 취향 ❑ 그는 자신의 성적 취향 때문에 차별을 받았다고 생각한다.

sexy /sɛksi/ (sexier, sexiest) ADJ You can describe people and things as **sexy** if you think they are sexually exciting or sexually attractive. ❑ *She was one of the sexiest women I had seen.*

형용사 섹시한 ❑ 그녀는 내가 본 가장 섹시한 여성 중의 한 명이다.

sh /ʃ/ also shh CONVENTION You can say "Sh!" to tell someone to be quiet. [INFORMAL, SPOKEN] ❑ *Sh! You want to listen or don't you?*

관용 표현 쉿 [비격식체, 구어체] ❑ 쉿! 듣고 싶어, 아니면 듣기 싫어?

shab|by /ʃæbi/ (shabbier, shabbiest) ADJ **Shabby** things or places look old and in bad condition. ❑ *His clothes were old and shabby.*

형용사 후줄근한 ❑ 그의 옷은 낡고 후줄근했다.

shack /ʃæk/ (**shacks**) N-COUNT A **shack** is a simple hut built from tin, wood, or other materials.

shade ◆◇◇ /ʃeɪd/ (**shades, shading, shaded**) **1** N-COUNT A **shade of** a particular color is one of its different forms. For example, emerald green and olive green are shades of green. □ *In the mornings the sky appeared a heavy shade of mottled gray.* □ *The walls were painted in two shades of green.* **2** N-UNCOUNT **Shade** is an area of darkness under or next to an object such as a tree, where sunlight does not reach. □ *Temperatures in the shade can reach forty-eight degrees celsius at this time of year.* □ *Alexis walked up the coast, and resumed his reading in the shade of an overhanging cliff.* **3** V-T If you say that a place or person **is shaded** by objects such as trees, you mean that the place or person cannot be reached, harmed, or bothered by strong sunlight because those objects are in the way. □ *...a health resort whose beaches are shaded by palm trees.* **4** V-T If you **shade** your eyes, you put your hand or an object partly in front of your face in order to prevent a bright light from shining into your eyes. □ *You can't look directly into it; you've got to shade your eyes or close them altogether.* **5** N-UNCOUNT **Shade** is darkness or shadows as they are shown in a picture. □ *...Rembrandt's skilful use of light and shade to create the atmosphere of movement.* **6** N-COUNT The **shades of** something abstract are its many, slightly different forms. □ *...the capacity to convey subtle shades of meaning.* **7** N-COUNT A **shade** is a piece of stiff cloth or heavy paper that you can pull down over a window as a covering. [AM; BRIT **blind**] □ *Nancy left the shades down and the lights off.*

shad|ow ◆◇◇ /ʃædoʊ/ (**shadows, shadowing, shadowed**) **1** N-COUNT A **shadow** is a dark shape on a surface that is made when something stands between a light and the surface. □ *An oak tree cast its shadow over a tiny round pool.* □ *Nothing would grow in the shadow of the grey wall.* **2** N-UNCOUNT **Shadow** is darkness in a place caused by something preventing light from reaching it. □ *Most of the lake was in shadow.* **3** V-T If something **shadows** a thing or place, it covers it with a shadow. □ *The hood shadowed her face.* **4** V-T If someone **shadows** you, they follow you very closely wherever you go. □ *The supporters are being shadowed by a large and highly visible body of police.* **5** ADJ A British Member of Parliament who is a member of the **shadow** cabinet or who is a **shadow** cabinet minister belongs to the main opposition party and takes a special interest in matters which are the responsibility of a particular government minister. [ADJ n] □ *...the shadow chancellor.* ● N-COUNT **Shadow** is also a noun. □ *Clarke swung at his shadow the accusation that he was "a tabloid politician".* **6** PHRASE If you say that something is true **without a shadow of a doubt** or **without a shadow of doubt**, you are emphasizing that there is no doubt at all that it is true. [EMPHASIS] □ *It was without a shadow of a doubt the best we've played.* **7** PHRASE If you live **in the shadow of** someone or **in their shadow**, their achievements and abilities are so great that you are not noticed or valued. □ *He has always lived in the shadow of his brother.*

> **Word Partnership**　　　shadow의 연어
>
> N.　　　**someone's** shadow **1**
> 　　　　shadow **of** *something* **1** **6**
> V.　　　**cast a** shadow **1** **2**
> 　　　　**live in the** shadow **7**

shad|owy /ʃædoʊi/ **1** ADJ A **shadowy** place is dark or full of shadows. □ *I watched him from a shadowy corner.* **2** ADJ A **shadowy** figure or shape is someone or something that you can hardly see because they are in a dark place. [ADJ n] □ *...a tall, shadowy figure silhouetted against the pale wall.* **3** ADJ You describe activities and people as **shadowy** when very little is known about them. □ *...the shadowy world of spies.*

shady /ʃeɪdi/ (**shadier, shadiest**) **1** ADJ You can describe a place as **shady** when you like the fact that it is sheltered from bright sunlight, for example by trees or buildings. □ *After flowering, place the pot in a shady spot in the garden.* **2** ADJ You can describe activities as **shady** when you think that they might be dishonest or illegal. You can also use **shady** to describe people who are involved in such activities. [DISAPPROVAL] □ *In the 1980s, the company was notorious for shady deals.*

shaft /ʃæft/ (**shafts**) **1** N-COUNT A **shaft** is a long vertical passage, for example for an elevator. □ *The fire began in an elevator shaft and spread to the roof.* **2** N-COUNT In a machine, a **shaft** is a rod that turns around continually in order to transfer movement in the machine. □ *...a drive shaft.* **3** N-COUNT A **shaft** is a long thin piece of wood or metal that forms part of a spear, ax, golf club, or other object. □ *...golf clubs with steel shafts.* **4** N-COUNT A **shaft** of light is a beam of light, for example sunlight shining through an opening. □ *A brilliant shaft of sunlight burst through the doorway.*

shag /ʃæg/ (**shags, shagging, shagged**) V-RECIP If someone **shags** another person, or if two people **shag**, they have sex together. [BRIT, INFORMAL, VULGAR] □ *...a documentary series about people shagging on holiday.* ● N-COUNT **Shag** is also a noun. □ *...a spy movie with car chases, a murder, a shag, and a happy ending.*

shag|gy /ʃægi/ (**shaggier, shaggiest**) ADJ **Shaggy** hair or fur is long and messy. □ *Tim, who still has longish, shaggy hair, used to turn up at official dinners in jeans and T-shirt.*

shake ◆◇◇ /ʃeɪk/ (**shakes, shaking, shook, shaken**) **1** V-T If you **shake** something, you hold it and move it quickly backward and forward or up and down. You can also **shake** a person, for example, because you are angry with them or because you want them to wake up. □ *The nurse took the thermometer, shook it, and put it under my armpit.* ● N-COUNT **Shake** is also a noun. □ *She picked up the bag of salad and gave it a shake.* **2** V-T If you **shake yourself** or your body, you make a lot of quick, small, repeated movements without moving from the place where you are. □ *As soon as he got inside, the dog shook himself.* ● N-COUNT

가산명사 판잣집

1 가산명사 색조 □ 아침에는 하늘이 얼룩덜룩한 짙은 회색을 띠었다. 두 가지 녹색 색조로 칠해져 있었다. **2** 불가산명사 그늘 □ 매년 이맘때쯤이면 그늘에서의 온도가 섭씨 48도까지 올라갈 수도 있다. □ 알렉시스는 해안선을 따라 걷다가 돌출된 절벽 아래의 그늘에서 다시 책을 읽기 시작했다. **3** 타동사 그늘지다 □ 야자수의 그늘이 드리워진 해변이 있는 건강 휴양지 **4** 타동사 손으로 가리다 □ 그것을 직접 바라봐서는 안 된다. 눈을 손으로 가리든지 아니면 완전히 감아야 한다. **5** 불가산명사 음영 □ 움직임의 분위기를 만들기 위해 명암을 능숙하게 사용한 렘브란트의 기술 **6** 가산명사 미묘한 차이 □ 의미의 미묘한 차이를 전달할 수 있는 능력 **7** 가산명사 차양 [미국영어; 영국영어 blind] □ 낸시는 차양을 쳐진 채로 그리고 빛은 꺼진 채로 놔뒀다.

1 가산명사 그림자 □ 떡갈나무가 작고 둥그런 수영장 위에 그림자를 드리웠다. □ 그 회색 벽의 그림자 아래에서는 어떤 것도 자라지 않을 것이다. **2** 불가산명사 그늘 □ 호수의 내부분은 그늘 속에 있었다. **3** 타동사 그림자를 드리우다 □ 두건이 그녀의 얼굴에 그림자를 드리웠다. **4** 타동사 그림자처럼 따라다니다 □ 지지자들 뒤를 눈에 띄게 많은 경찰이 그림자처럼 따라다니고 있다. **5** 형용사 (영국 의회) 제 1 야당의 □ 제1 야당 내각의 재무 장관 ● 가산명사 야당 내각, 야당 내각 각료 □ 클라크는 야당 내각에서 같은 자리를 가진 의원에게 그가 '선정적인 정치인'이라고 비난을 던졌다. **6** 구 일말의 의심 [강조] □ 일말의 의심할 여지도 없이 그 경기는 우리가 최고로 선전한 경기였다. **7** 구 ...의 그늘에 가려 □ 그는 항상 형의 그늘에 가려진 채 살아 왔다.

1 형용사 어두운 □ 나는 어두운 구석에서 그를 관찰했다. **2** 형용사 어슴푸레한 □ 옅은 벽을 배경으로 보이는 어슴푸레한 키 큰 사람의 옆모습 **3** 형용사 알 수 없는 □ 첩보원들의 알 수 없는 세계

1 형용사 그늘진 □ 꽃이 핀 다음에는 화분을 정원의 그늘진 곳에 두세요. **2** 형용사 수상한 [탐탁잖음] □ 1980년대에 그 회사는 수상한 거래로 악명이 높았다.

1 가산명사 수직 통로, 갱 □ 불은 엘리베이터 통로에서 시작한 다음 지붕까지 번졌다. **2** 가산명사 축 □ 구동축 **3** 가산명사 (기름하게 생긴) 자루 □ 자루가 쇠로 된 골프채 **4** 가산명사 (빛) 줄기 □ 문간으로 갑자기 한 줄기 눈부신 햇살이 쏟아져 들어왔다.

상호동사 성교하다 [영국영어, 비격식체, 비속어] □ 휴가철에 성관계를 가지는 사람들에 관한 다큐멘터리 시리즈 ● 가산명사 성교 □ 자동차 추격전, 살인, 성교, 그리고 행복한 결말을 담은 정보 영화

형용사 덥수룩한 □ 여전히 길고 덥수룩한 머리를 한 팀은 공식 만찬에 청바지와 티셔츠를 입고 나타나곤 했다.

1 타동사 흔들다 □ 간호사는 체온계를 잡고 흔든 후 내 겨드랑이에 넣었다. ● 가산명사 흔듦 □ 그녀는 샐러드 아래 봉지를 집어 들고는 한 번 흔들었다. **2** 타동사 흔들다, 털다 □ 개는 들어가자마자 몸을 흔들어서 털었다. ● 가산명사 흔듦 □ 천천히 깊이 몇 번 숨을 쉰 다음 몸을 약간 흔드세요. **3** 타동사 (고개를) 젓다 □ "더 필요한 것은?"콜럼이 물었다. 캐스린은 지친 듯 고개를 저었다. ● 가산명사 젓기

Shake is also a noun. ❑ *Take some slow, deep breaths and give your body a bit of a shake.* ❸ V-T If you **shake** your **head**, you turn it from side to side in order to say "no" or to show disbelief or sadness. ❑ *"Anything else?" Colum asked. Kathryn shook her head wearily.* ❹ N-COUNT **Shake** is also a noun. ❑ *"The elm trees are all dying," said Palmer, with a sad shake of his head.* ❹ V-I If you **are shaking**, or a part of your body **is shaking**, you are making quick, small movements that you cannot control, for example because you are cold or afraid. ❑ *He roared with laughter, shaking in his chair.* ❑ *My hand shook so much that I could hardly hold the microphone.* ❺ V-T If you **shake** your fist or an object such as a stick **at** someone, you wave it in the air in front of them because you are angry with them. ❑ *The colonel rushed up to Earle, and shaking his gun at him exclaimed in a voice quivering with passion: "Curse you!"* ❻ V-T/V-I If a force **shakes** something, or if something **shakes**, it moves from side to side or up and down with quick, small, but sometimes violent movements. ❑ *...an explosion that shook buildings several kilometers away.* ❼ V-T To **shake** something into a certain place or state means to bring it into that place or state by moving it quickly up and down or from side to side. ❑ *Small insects can be collected from nettle beds by shaking them into an upturned umbrella and tipping the contents into a jam jar.* ❽ V-I If your voice **is shaking**, you cannot control it properly and it sounds very unsteady, for example because you are nervous or angry. ❑ *His voice shaking with rage, he asked how the committee could keep such a report from the public.* ❾ V-T If an event or a piece of news **shakes** you, or **shakes** your confidence, it makes you feel upset and unable to think calmly. ❑ *There was no doubt that the news of Tandy's escape had shaken them all.* ❿ V-T If an event **shakes** a group of people or their beliefs, it causes great uncertainty and makes them question their beliefs. ❑ *It won't shake the football world if we beat Torquay.* ⓫ PHRASE If you **shake** someone's **hand** or **shake** someone **by the hand**, you shake hands with them. ❑ *I said congratulations and walked over to him and shook his hand.* ⓬ PHRASE If you **shake hands with** someone, you take their right hand in your own for a few moments, often moving it up and down slightly, when you are saying hello or goodbye to them, congratulating them, or agreeing on something. You can also say that two people **shake hands**. ❑ *He nodded greetings to Mary Ann and Michael and shook hands with Burke.*

Thesaurus   *shake*의 참조어

v.	jerk, move, ruffle, swing ❶ ❷

Word Partnership   *shake*의 연어

v.	**begin to** shake ❶-❼
n.	shake *your* head ❸
	shake *someone's* confidence ❾
	shake *someone's* hand ⓫
	shake hands (with *someone*) ⓬

▶**shake off** ❶ PHRASAL VERB If you **shake off** something that you do not want such as an illness or a bad habit, you manage to recover from it or get rid of it. ❑ *Businessmen are frantically trying to shake off the bad habits learned under six decades of a protected economy.* ❷ PHRASAL VERB If you **shake off** someone who is following you, you manage to get away from them, for example by running faster than them. ❑ *I caught him a lap later, and although I could pass him I could not shake him off.*

▶**shake up** PHRASAL VERB If someone **shakes up** something such as an organization, an institution, or a profession, they make major changes to it. ❑ *The government wanted to accelerate the reform of the institutions, to find new ways of shaking up the country.* →see also **shakeup**

shake|up /ˈʃeɪkʌp/ (**shakeups**) [BRIT **shake-up**] N-COUNT A **shakeup** is a major set of changes in an organization or a system. [JOURNALISM] ❑ *Community leaders say a complete departmental shakeup is needed.*

shaky /ˈʃeɪki/ (**shakier, shakiest**) ❶ ADJ If you describe a situation as **shaky**, you mean that it is weak or unstable, and seems unlikely to last long or be successful. ❑ *A shaky ceasefire is holding after three days of fighting between rival groups.* ❷ ADJ If your body or your voice is **shaky**, you cannot control it properly and it shakes, for example because you are ill or nervous. ❑ *We have all had a shaky hand and a dry mouth before speaking in public.*

shall ♦♦◇ /ʃəl, STRONG ʃæl/

Shall is a modal verb. It is used with the base form of a verb.

❶ MODAL You use **shall** with "I" and "we" in questions in order to make offers or suggestions, or to ask for advice. ❑ *Shall I get the keys?* ❑ *Well, shall we go?* ❑ *Let's have a nice little stroll, shall we?* ❷ MODAL You use **shall**, usually with "I" and "we," when you are referring to something that you intend to do, or when you are referring to something that you are sure will happen to you in the future. ❑ *We shall be landing in Paris in sixteen minutes, exactly on time.* ❑ *I shall know more next month, I hope.* ❸ MODAL You use **shall** with "I" or "we" during a speech or piece of writing to say what you are going to discuss or explain later. [FORMAL] ❑ *In Chapter 3, I shall describe some of the documentation that I gathered.* ❹ MODAL You use **shall** to indicate that something must happen, usually because of a rule or law. You use **shall not** to indicate that something must not happen. ❑ *The president shall hold office for five years.* ❺ MODAL You use **shall**, usually with "you," when you are telling someone that they will be able to do or have something they want. ❑ *Very well, if you want to go, go you shall.* ❻ MODAL You use **shall** with verbs such as "look forward to" and "hope" to say politely that you are looking forward to something or hoping to do something. [FORMAL, POLITENESS] ❑ *Well, we shall look forward to seeing him tomorrow.*

❑ "느릅나무가 모두 죽어 가고 있어."라고 파머는 고개를 슬프게 저으며 말했다. ❹ 자동사 떨다, 흔들다 ❑ 그는 의자에 앉아 온몸을 흔들며 박장대소를 했다. ❑ 나는 손이 너무 떨려서 마이크를 잡기가 힘들었다. ❺ 타동사 흔들다 ❑ 대령은 얼에게 급히 다가가 그에게 총을 흔들어 대며 감정이 격해 떨리는 목소리로 소리쳤다. "저주받을 놈!" ❻ 타동사/자동사 뒤흔들다; 뒤흔들리다 ❑ 수킬로 떨어진 건물도 뒤흔든 폭발 ❼ 타동사 흔들다, 떨다 ❑ 쐐기풀 밭에서 작은 벌레를 채집하려면 우산을 뒤집어 그 안으로 벌레를 털어 넣은 다음 잼 병에 내용물을 부으면 된다. ❽ 자동사 떨리다 ❑ 그는 분노에 떨리는 목소리로 위원회가 어떻게 그런 보고서를 대중에게 숨길 수 있는지 물었다. ❾ 타동사 동요시키다, 흔들다 ❑ 탠디의 도주 소식이 그들 모두를 동요시켰음이 틀림없었다. ❿ 타동사 동요시키다, 흔들다 ❑ 우리가 토쿠비를 이긴다 해도 축구계는 크게 동요하지 않을 것이다. ⓫ 구 악수하다 ❑ 나는 축하한다는 말을 한 다음 그에게 다가가 악수했다. ⓬ 구 악수하다 ❑ 그는 매리 앤과 마이클에게 고개를 끄덕여 인사한 다음 버크와 악수했다.

❶ 구동사 떨쳐 버리다 ❑ 사업가들은 60년간의 보호 경제 체제 안에서 생긴 나쁜 버릇을 떨쳐 버리기 위해 필사적으로 노력하고 있다. ❷ 구동사 따돌리다, 떨치다 ❑ 나는 나중에 그를 한 바퀴 따라잡다가 그를 앞지르기는 했지만 떨쳐 버리지는 못했다.

구동사 대대적으로 개혁하니 ❑ 정부는 기관들의 개편을 가속화하고 나라를 대대적으로 개혁할 수 있는 새로운 방식들을 찾고자 했다.

[영국영어 shake-up] 가산명사 대대적인 개혁 [언론] ❑ 지역 사회 지도자들은 대대적인 부서 개혁이 필요하다고 말한다.

❶ 형용사 불안정한 ❑ 경쟁 집단 사이에 벌어진 3일간의 전투 후에 불안정한 휴전이 유지되고 있다. ❷ 형용사 떨리는 ❑ 우리 모두 대중 앞에서 연설하기 전에 손이 떨리고 입안이 마르는 것을 경험해 봤다.

shall은 조동사이며 동사 원형과 함께 쓰인다.

❶ 법조동사 제안, 충고, 부탁 등을 나타내는 의문문에 쓰임 ❑ 열쇠를 가져올까? ❑ 그럼, 갈까? ❑ 기분 좋은 산책 좀 하는 건 어때? ❷ 법조동사 의도 혹은 확실한 예측을 나타낼 때 쓴 ❑ 우리는 16분 뒤에 예정된 시간에 맞춰 파리에 착륙할 것입니다. ❑ 다음 달에는 더 많은 것을 알게 되기를 바란다. ❸ 법조동사 앞으로 다룰 주제를 언급할 때 쓴 [격식체] ❑ 3장에서는 제가 수집한 문서 몇 건을 다룹니다. ❹ 법조동사 법규에 정해진 내용을 나타낼 때 쓴 ❑ 대통령의 임기는 5년이다. ❺ 법조동사 허락을 나타낼 때 쓴 ❑ 좋아, 가고 싶다면 가거라. ❻ 법조동사 희망 사항을 정중히 표현할 때 쓴 [격식체, 공손체] ❑ 저희는 내일 그 분을 뵙게 되길 고대하고 있습니다.

shal|low /ʃǽloʊ/ (**shallower, shallowest**) **1** ADJ A **shallow** container, hole, or area of water measures only a short distance from the top to the bottom. □ *Put the milk in a shallow dish.* **2** ADJ If you describe a person, piece of work, or idea as **shallow**, you disapprove of them because they do not show or involve any serious or careful thought. [DISAPPROVAL] □ *I think he is shallow, vain, and untrustworthy.* **3** ADJ If your breathing is **shallow**, you take only a very small amount of air into your lungs at each breath. □ *She began to hear her own taut, shallow breathing.*

■ 형용사 앝은 □ 우유를 얕은 접시에 놓으세요.
■ 형용사 천박한 [탐탁잖음] □ 나는 그가 천박하고 허영심이 강하고 믿을 수 없다고 생각한다. ■ 형용사 (호흡이) 얕은 □ 그녀는 자신의 호흡이 긴장되고 얕아지는 소리를 내는 것을 듣기 시작했다.

sham /ʃæm/ (**shams**) N-COUNT Something that is a **sham** is not real or is not really what it seems to be. [DISAPPROVAL] □ *The government's promises were exposed as a hollow sham.*

가산명사 가짜 [탐탁잖음] □ 정부의 약속은 텅 빈 거짓말이었음이 드러났다.

sham|bles /ʃǽmbᵊlz/ N-SING If a place, event, or situation is **a shambles** or is **in a shambles**, everything is in disorder. □ *The ship's interior was an utter shambles.*

단수명사 난장판 □ 배의 내부는 완전 난장판이었다.

shame ♦♦♢ /ʃeɪm/ (**shames, shaming, shamed**) **1** N-UNCOUNT **Shame** is an uncomfortable feeling that you get when you have done something wrong or embarrassing, or when someone close to you has. □ *She felt a deep sense of shame.* □ *Her father and her brothers would die of shame.* **2** N-UNCOUNT If someone brings **shame** on you, they make other people lose their respect for you. □ *I don't want to bring shame on the family name.* **3** V-T If something **shames** you, it causes you to feel shame. □ *Her son's affair had humiliated and shamed her.* **4** V-T If you **shame** someone **into** doing something, you force them to do it by making them feel ashamed not to. □ *He would not let neighbors shame him into silence.* **5** N-SING If you say that something is **a shame**, you are expressing your regret about it and indicating that you wish it had happened differently. [FEELINGS] □ *It's a crying shame that police have to put up with these mindless attacks.* **6** CONVENTION You can use **shame** in expressions such as **shame on you** and **shame on him** to indicate that someone ought to feel shame for something they have said or done. [FEELINGS] □ *He tried to deny it. Shame on him!* **7** PHRASE If someone **puts** you **to shame**, they make you feel ashamed because they do something much better than you do. □ *His playing really put me to shame.* →see **emotion**

■ 불가산명사 수치심 □ 그녀는 깊은 수치심을 느꼈다. □ 그녀의 아버지와 형제들은 죽고 싶을 정도로 수치심을 느낄 것이다. **2** 불가산명사 오명을 안기다 □ 집안의 이름에 먹칠을 하고 싶지는 않다. **3** 타동사 부끄럽게 만들다, 망신시키다 □ 아들의 불륜은 그녀를 망신시켰다. **4** 타동사 창피를 주다 □ 그가 이웃들 때문에 창피해서 입을 다물지는 않을 것이다. **5** 단수명사 딱한 일 [감정 개입] □ 경찰이 이런 어리석은 공격을 견뎌야 한다는 것은 정말 딱한 일이다. **6** 관용 표현 창피; 창피한 줄 알아라 □ 그는 창피한 줄 알아야 한다 [감정 개입] □ 그는 그것을 부인하려 했다. 창피한 줄 알아야지! **7** 구 무색하게 만들다 □ 그의 실력은 정말 나를 무색하게 만들었다.

Word Partnership *shame*의 연어

N.   **feelings of** shame, **sense of** shame **1**
V.   **experience** shame, **feel** shame **1**

shame|ful /ʃéɪmfəl/ ADJ If you describe a person's action or attitude as **shameful**, you think that it is so bad that the person ought to be ashamed. [DISAPPROVAL] □ ...*the most shameful episode in U.S. naval history.* ● **shame|ful|ly** ADV □ *At times they have been shamefully neglected.*

형용사 창피스러운 [탐탁잖음] □ 미 해군의 역사에 있어 가장 창피스러운 사건 ● 창피스럽게 부사 □ 그들은 때로 면목 없을 정도로 방치되었다.

shame|less /ʃéɪmlɪs/ ADJ If you describe someone as **shameless**, you mean that they should be ashamed of their behavior, which is unacceptable to other people. [DISAPPROVAL] □ ...*a shameless attempt to stifle democratic debate.* ● **shame|less|ly** ADV □ ...*a shamelessly lazy week-long trip.*

형용사 파렴치한, 뻔뻔한 [탐탁잖음] □ 민주적인 토론을 억누르려는 파렴치한 시도 ● 뻔뻔하게 부사 □ 뻔뻔스러울 정도로 게으르게 보낸 일주일간의 여행

sham|poo /ʃæmpú/ (**shampoos, shampooing, shampooed**) **1** N-MASS **Shampoo** is a soapy liquid that you use for washing your hair. □ ...*a bottle of shampoo.* **2** V-T When you **shampoo** your hair, you wash it using shampoo. □ *Shampoo your hair and dry it.* →see **hair**

■ 물질명사 샴푸 □ 샴푸 한 병 **2** 타동사 머리를 감다 □ 머리를 감고 말리세요.

shan't /ʃænt/ **Shan't** is the usual spoken form of "shall not."

shall not의 축약형

shape ♦♦♢ /ʃeɪp/ (**shapes, shaping, shaped**) **1** N-COUNT The **shape of** an object, a person, or an area is the appearance of their outside edges or surfaces, for example whether they are round, square, curved, or flat. [oft N of n, also in N] □ *Each mirror is made to order and can be designed to almost any shape or size.* □ ...*little pens in the shape of baseball bats.* □ ...*sofas and chairs of contrasting shapes and colors.* **2** N-COUNT You can refer to something that you can see as a **shape** if you cannot see it clearly, or if its outline is the clearest or most striking aspect of it. □ *The great grey shape of a tank rolled out of the village.* **3** N-COUNT A **shape** is a space enclosed by an outline, for example a circle, a square, or a triangle. □ ...*if you imagine a sort of a kidney shape.* **4** N-SING The **shape** of something that is planned or organized is its structure and character. □ *The last two weeks have seen a lot of talk about the future shape of Europe.* **5** V-T Someone or something that **shapes** a situation or an activity has a very great influence on the way it develops. □ *Like it or not, our families shape our lives and make us what we are.* **6** V-T If you **shape** an object, you give it a particular shape, using your hands or a tool. □ *Cut the dough in half and shape each half into a loaf.* **7** →see also **shaped** **8** PHRASE If you say, for example, that you will not accept something **in any shape or form**, or **in any way, shape or form**, you are emphasizing that you will not accept it in any circumstances. [EMPHASIS] □ *I don't condone violence in any shape or form.* **9** PHRASE If someone or something is **in shape**, or **in good shape**, they are in a good state of health or in a good condition. If they are in **bad shape**, they are in a bad state of health or in a bad condition. □ ...*the Fatburner Diet Book, a comprehensive guide to getting in shape.* □ *He was still in better shape than many young men.* **10** PHRASE If you **lick, knock,** or **whip** someone or something **into shape**, you use whatever methods are necessary to change or improve them so that they are in the condition that you want them to be in. □ *You'll have four months in which to lick the recruits into shape.* **11** PHRASE If something is **out of shape**, it is no longer in its proper or original shape, for example because it has been damaged or wrongly handled. □ *Once most wires are bent out of shape, they don't return to the original position.* **12** PHRASE If you are **out of shape**, you are unhealthy and unable to do a lot of physical activity without getting tired. □ *I weighed 245 pounds and was out of shape.* **13** PHRASE When something **takes shape**, it develops or starts to appear in such a way that it becomes fairly clear what

■ 가산명사 모양 □ 모든 거울은 주문에 따라 만들어지며 거의 모든 모양이나 크기로 맞출 수 있다. □ 야구 방망이 모양의 작은 펜 □ 대조적인 모양과 색상의 소파와 걸상 **2** 가산명사 형체 □ 회색빛 형체로만 보이는 거대한 탱크가 마을에서 굴러 나왔다. **3** 가산명사 형태 □ 신장과 비슷한 모양을 상상한다면 **4** 단수명사 형상, 모습 □ 지난 2주간 유럽의 미래 모습에 대해 많은 이야기가 오갔다. **5** 타동사 결정짓다 □ 좋든 싫든 우리의 가족이 우리의 삶을 결정짓고 우리의 현재 모습을 만든다. **6** 타동사 모양을 만들다, 빚다 □ 반죽을 반으로 자른 다음 각각을 빵 모양으로 빚으세요. **7** □ **8** 구 [강조] □ 나는 폭력은 어떤 형태든 용납하지 않는다. **9** 구 건강한; 건강하지 못한 □ 건강한 몸매 유지를 위한 종합적인 안내서인 '지방 연소 다이어트 책' □ 그는 여전히 많은 젊은 남자보다 건강이 좋았다. **10** 구 제 모습을 갖추게 하다 □ 4개월 만에 신병들을 제대로 된 군인으로 만들어야 한다. **11** 구 본래 모습을 잃은 □ 대부분의 철사는 한번 형체를 알아볼 수 없을 정도로 구부러지면 원래 모습으로 돌아오지 않는다. **12** 구 건강이 안 좋은 □ 나는 몸무게가 245파운드였고 건강이 안 좋았다. **13** 구 형태를 갖추다 □ 1912년에 여자 종목이 추가되었고 현대 올림픽 프로그램의 형태가 갖추어지기 시작했다.

its final form will be. ❑ *In 1912 women's events were added, and the modern Olympic programme began to take shape.* →see **circle**, **mathematics**

Word Partnership   *shape*의 연어

V.	**change shape** ◼
	change the shape of *something* ◢
	get in shape ◢
ADJ.	**dark shape** ◼
	(pretty) bad/good/great shape, better/worse shape, physical shape, terrible shape ◢

▶**shape up** ◼ PHRASAL VERB If something **is shaping up**, it is starting to develop or seems likely to happen. ❑ *There are also indications that a major tank battle may be shaping up for tonight.* ❑ *The accident is already shaping up as a significant environmental disaster.* ◢ PHRASAL VERB If you ask how someone or something **is shaping up**, you want to know how well they are doing in a particular situation or activity. ❑ *I did have a few worries about how Hugh and I would shape up as parents.*

shaped ◆◇◇ /ʃeɪpt/ ADJ Something that is **shaped** like a particular object or in a particular way has the shape of that object or a shape of that type. [v-link ADJ *like* n, adv ADJ] ❑ *A new perfume from Russia came in a bottle shaped like a tank.*

share ◆◆◆ /ʃeər/ (**shares, sharing, shared**) ◼ N-COUNT A company's **shares** are the many equal parts into which its ownership is divided. Shares can be bought by people as an investment. [BUSINESS] ❑ *This is why Sir Colin Marshall, British Airways' chairman, has been so keen to buy shares in US-AIR.* ◢ V-RECIP If you **share** something **with** another person, you both have it, use it, or occupy it. You can also say that two people **share** something. ❑ *...the small income he had shared with his brother from his father's estate.* ❑ *Two Americans will share this year's Nobel Prize for Medicine.* ◢ V-RECIP If you **share** a task, duty, or responsibility **with** someone, you each carry out or accept part of it. You can also say that two people **share** something. ❑ *You can find out whether they are prepared to share the cost of the flowers with you.* ◢ V-RECIP If you **share** an experience **with** someone, you have the same experience, often because you are with them at the time. You can also say that two people **share** something. ❑ *Yes, I want to share my life with you.* ◢ V-T If you **share** someone's opinion, you agree with them. [no cont] ❑ *The forum's members share his view that business can be a positive force for change in developing countries.* ◢ V-RECIP If one person or thing **shares** a quality or characteristic **with** another, they have the same quality or characteristic. You can also say that two people or things **share** something. [no cont] ❑ *La Repubblica and El Pais are politically independent newspapers which share similar characteristics with certain British newspapers.* ◢ V-T If you **share** something that you have **with** someone, you give some of it to them or let them use it. ❑ *The village tribe is friendly and they share their water supply with you.* ❑ *Scientists now have to compete for funding, and do not share information among themselves.* ◢ V-T If you **share** something personal such as a thought or a piece of news **with** someone, you tell them about it. ❑ *It can be beneficial to share your feelings with someone you trust.* ◢ N-COUNT If something is divided or distributed among a number of different people or things, each of them has, or is responsible for, a **share** of it. ❑ *Sara also pays a share of the gas, electricity and phone bills.* ◢ N-COUNT If you have or do your **share** of something, you have or do an amount that seems reasonable to you, or to other people. ❑ *Women must receive their fair share of training for good-paying jobs.* ◢ →see also **lion's share, market share, power-sharing**
→see **company**

▶**share out** PHRASAL VERB If you **share out** an amount of something, you give each person in a group an equal or fair part of it. ❑ *If you start taking the prize money off the people from the top then you could share it out a bit more equally.*

share capital N-UNCOUNT A company's **share capital** is the money that shareholders invest in order to start or expand the business. [BUSINESS] ❑ *The bank has a share capital of almost 100 million dollars.*

shareholder ◆◇◇ /ʃeərhoʊldər/ (**shareholders**) N-COUNT A **shareholder** is a person who owns shares in a company. [BUSINESS] ❑ *...a shareholders' meeting.*

shareholding /ʃeərhoʊldɪŋ/ (**shareholdings**) N-COUNT If you have a **shareholding** in a company, you own some of its shares. [BUSINESS] ❑ *She will retain her very significant shareholding in the company.*

share index (**share indices** or **share indexes**) N-COUNT A **share index** is a number that indicates the state of a stock market. It is based on the combined share prices of a set of companies. [BUSINESS] ❑ *The FT 30 share index was up 16.4 points to 1,599.6.*

share issue (**share issues**) N-COUNT When there is a **share issue**, shares in a company are made available for people to buy. [BUSINESS] ❑ *The deal will be financed by a share issue that will raise $128.9 million.*

share option (**share options**) N-COUNT A **share option** is an opportunity for the employees of a company to buy shares at a special price. [BRIT, BUSINESS; AM **stock option**] ❑ *Only a handful of firms offer share option schemes to all their employees.*

share shop (**share shops**) N-COUNT A **share shop** is a store or Internet website where members of the public can buy shares in companies. [BUSINESS]

shareware /ʃeərweər/ N-UNCOUNT **Shareware** is computer software that you can try before deciding whether or not to buy the legal right to use it. [COMPUTING] ❑ *...a shareware program.*

◼ 구동사 징조를 보이다 ❑ 오늘밤 대규모 탱크 전투가 벌어질지도 모른다는 조짐이 있다. ❑ 그 사고는 이미 심각한 환경 재앙이 될 징조를 보이고 있다. ◢ 구동사 모습을 보이다 ❑ 나와 휴가 부모로서 어떤 모습을 보일지에 대해서는 약간의 걱정이 되었다.

형용사 형태의 ❑ 어떤 러시아산 새 향수는 탱크 모양의 병에 담겨 나왔다.

◼ 가산명사 지분 [경제] ❑ 바로 이런 이유 때문에 영국 항공의 회장인 콜린 마셜 경이 미국 항공의 지분을 그렇게 간절히 매입하고자 했다. ◢ 상호동사 공유하다, 나눠 갖다 ❑ 아버지의 땅에서 얻어 그가 형과 나눠 가진 적은 수입 ❑ 두 명의 미국인이 올해의 노벨 의학상을 공동 수상할 것이다. ◢ 상호동사 공동으로 부담하다 ❑ 그들이 당신과 꽃 값을 공동으로 부담할 용의가 있는지에 대해 알아볼 수 있을 것이다. ◢ 상호동사 공유하다 ❑ 그래요, 인생을 당신과 함께 하고 싶어요. ◢ 타동사 동의하다, 의견을 같이하다 ❑ 토론회 참석자들은 사업이 개발 국가들의 변화에 긍정적인 영향을 끼칠 수 있다는 그의 의견에 동의한다. ◢ 상호동사 공유하다 ❑ 라 레푸블리카와 엘 파이스는 일부 영국 신문들과 유사한 특징을 공유하는, 정치적으로 독립된 신문들이다. ◢ 타동사 나누어 쓰다 ❑ 마을 부족은 친절하며 자신들의 물을 당신에게 나누어 준다. ❑ 과학자들은 이제 기금을 얻기 위해 경쟁해야 하며 자리끼리 정보를 나누지도 않는다. ◢ 타동사 공유하다 ❑ 자신의 감정을 믿을 수 있는 사람과 공유하는 것이 이로울 수도 있다. ◢ 가산명사 몫 ❑ 새라는 또한 가스, 전기, 통화료에서 자기 몫을 부담한다. ◢ 가산명사 몫 ❑ 여성들은 고임금 직장을 위해 자신들의 몫에 알맞은 평등한 훈련을 받아야 한다.

구동사 분배하다 ❑ 최상위 사람들의 상금을 깎기 시작하면 그들은 보다 균등하게 분배할 수 있다.

불가산명사 주식 자본금 [경제] ❑ 그 은행은 자본금이 거의 1억 달러에 달한다.

가산명사 주주 [경제] ❑ 주주 회의

가산명사 (소유) 지분 [경제] ❑ 그녀는 자신이 가지고 있는 상당량의 그 회사 지분을 보유할 것이다.

가산명사 주가 지수 [경제] ❑ 에프티 30 주가 지수는 16.4포인트 상승해 1,599.6이 되었다.

가산명사 주식 발행 [경제] ❑ 그 거래는 주식 발행을 통해 거둬들일 1억 2,890만 달러로 자금을 조달할 것이다.

가산명사 스톡옵션 [영국영어, 경제; 미국영어 stock option] ❑ 극히 일부 기업들만이 모든 직원에게 스톡옵션을 제공한다.

가산명사 증권 회사 [경제]

불가산명사 쉐어웨어 [컴퓨터] ❑ 쉐어웨어 프로그램

Word Web　　　shark

Sharks are different from other **fish**. The **skeleton** of a shark is made of **cartilage**, not bone. The flexibility of cartilage allows this **predator** to maneuver around its **prey** easily. Sharks also have several gill **slits** with no flap covering them. Its scales are also much smaller and harder than fish scales. And its teeth are special too. Sharks grow new teeth when they lose old ones. It's almost impossible to escape from a shark. Some of them can swim up to 44 miles per hour. But sharks only kill 50 to 75 people each year worldwide.

shark /ʃɑrk/

The plural is **shark** or **sharks**.

N-VAR A **shark** is a very large fish. Some sharks have very sharp teeth and may attack people.
→see Word Web: **shark**

sharp ♦♦♢ /ʃɑrp/ (sharps, sharper, sharpest) **1** ADJ A **sharp** point or edge is very thin and can cut through things very easily. A **sharp** knife, tool, or other object has a point or edge of this kind. ❑ *The other end of the twig is sharpened into a sharp point to use as a toothpick.* **2** ADJ You can describe a shape or an object as **sharp** if part of it or one end of it comes to a point or forms an angle. ❑ *His nose was thin and sharp.* **3** ADJ A **sharp** bend or turn is one that changes direction suddenly. ❑ *I was approaching a fairly sharp bend that swept downhill to the left.* ● ADV **Sharp** is also an adverb. [ADV adv] ❑ *Do not cross the bridge but turn sharp left to go down on to the towpath.* ● **sharp|ly** ADV [ADV after v] ❑ *Room number nine was at the far end of the corridor where it turned sharply to the right.* **4** ADJ If you describe someone as **sharp**, you are praising them because they are quick to notice, hear, understand, or react to things. [APPROVAL] ❑ *He is very sharp, a quick thinker and swift with repartee.* **5** ADJ If someone says something in a **sharp** way, they say it suddenly and rather firmly or angrily, for example because they are warning or criticizing you. ❑ *"Don't contradict your mother," was Charles's sharp reprimand.* ● **sharp|ly** ADV ❑ *"You've known," she said sharply, "and you didn't tell me?"* **6** ADJ A **sharp** change, movement, or feeling occurs suddenly, and is great in amount, force, or degree. ❑ *There's been a sharp rise in the rate of inflation.* ❑ *Tennis requires a lot of short sharp movements.* ● **sharp|ly** ADV ❑ *Unemployment among the over forties has risen sharply in recent years.* **7** ADJ A **sharp** difference, image, or sound is very easy to see, hear, or distinguish. ❑ *Many people make a sharp distinction between humans and other animals.* ❑ *All the footmarks are quite sharp and clear.* ● **sharp|ly** ADV ❑ *Opinions on this are sharply divided.* **8** ADJ A **sharp** taste or smell is rather strong or bitter, but is often also clear and fresh. ❑ *The apple tasted just as I remembered – sharp, sour, yet sweet.* **9** ADV **Sharp** is used after stating a particular time to show that something happens at exactly the time stated. [n ADV] ❑ *She planned to unlock the store at 8:00 sharp this morning.* **10** N-COUNT **Sharp** is used after a letter representing a musical note to show that the note should be played or sung half a tone higher. **Sharp** is often represented by the symbol ♯. ❑ *A solitary viola plucks a lonely, soft F sharp.*

Word Partnership　　sharp의 연어

ADV.	**very** sharp **1**-**8**
N.	sharp **edge**, sharp **point**, sharp **teeth 1 2**
	sharp **mind 4**
	sharp **criticism 5**
	sharp **decline**, sharp **increase**, sharp **pain 6**
	sharp **contrast 7**

sharp|en /ʃɑrpən/ (sharpens, sharpening, sharpened) **1** V-T/V-I If your senses, understanding, or skills **sharpen** or **are sharpened**, you become better at noticing things, thinking, or doing something. ❑ *Her gaze sharpened, as if she had seen something unusual.* **2** V-T If you **sharpen** an object, you make its edge very thin or you make its end pointed. ❑ *He started to sharpen his knife.*

sharp|en|er /ʃɑrpənər/ (sharpeners) N-COUNT A **sharpener** is a tool or machine used for sharpening pencils or knives. ❑ *...a pencil sharpener.*

shat /ʃæt/ **Shat** is the past tense and past participle of **shit**.

shat|ter /ʃætər/ (shatters, shattering, shattered) **1** V-T/V-I If something **shatters** or is **shattered**, it breaks into a lot of small pieces. ❑ *...safety glass that won't shatter if it's broken.* ❑ *The car shattered into a thousand burning pieces in a 200mph crash.* ● **shat|ter|ing** N-UNCOUNT ❑ *...the shattering of glass.* **2** V-T If something **shatters** your dreams, hopes, or beliefs, it completely destroys them. ❑ *A failure would shatter the hopes of many people.* **3** V-T If someone **is shattered** by an event, it shocks and upsets them very much. ❑ *He had been shattered by his son's death.* **4** →see also **shattered**

shat|tered /ʃætərd/ **1** ADJ If you are **shattered** by something, you are extremely shocked and upset about it. ❑ *It is desperately sad news and I am absolutely shattered to hear it.* **2** ADJ If you say you are **shattered**, you mean you are extremely tired and have no energy left. [BRIT, INFORMAL] ❑ *He was shattered and too tired to concentrate on schoolwork.*

shave /ʃeɪv/ (shaves, shaving, shaved) **1** V-T/V-I When a man **shaves**, he removes the hair from his face using a razor or shaver so that his face is smooth. ❑ *He took a bath and shaved before dinner.* ❑ *He had shaved his face until it was*

복수는 shark 또는 sharks이다.

가산명사 또는 불가산명사 상어

1 형용사 뾰족한, 날카로운 ❑ 작은 가지의 반대쪽 끝은 이쑤시개로 쓰기 위해 뾰족하게 만들어졌다. **2** 형용사 뾰족한 ❑ 그의 코는 가늘고 뾰족했다. **3** 형용사 (모퉁이 등이) 급한 ❑ 나는 언덕 아래 왼쪽으로 상당히 급하게 꺾이는 커브 길에 다가가고 있었다. ● 급하게 부사 ❑ 다리를 건너지 말고 급하게 왼쪽으로 꺾어서 강변로를 따라 가세요. ● 급하게 부사 ❑ 9번 방은 복도가 갑자기 오른쪽으로 꺾이는 복도 끝에 있었다. **4** 형용사 예리한 [마음에 듦] ❑ 그는 굉장히 예리하고 생각이 빨라서 재치 있는 말도 잘했다. **5** 형용사 날카로운, 통렬한 ❑ "네 어머니한테 말대꾸하지 마."라고 찰스는 날카롭게 꾸짖었다. ● 날카롭게 부사 ❑ "너는 알았는데도 나한테 이야기하지 않았단 말이야?"라고 그녀는 날카롭게 말했다. **6** 형용사 급격한, 급작스러운 ❑ 물가 상승률이 최근 급격히 증가했다. ❑ 테니스에는 짧고 급격한 동작이 많이 필요하다. ● 급격히 부사 ❑ 40대 이상의 실업률이 최근 급격히 증가했다. **7** 형용사 뚜렷한 ❑ 많은 사람들이 인간과 다른 동물들을 뚜렷하게 구분 짓는다. ❑ 모든 발자국이 상당히 뚜렷하고 선명하다. ● 뚜렷이 부사 ❑ 이에 대한 의견들은 뚜렷이 나뉜다. **8** 형용사 자극적인 ❑ 이 사과 맛은 내가 기억한 그대로였다. 즉 자극적이고 시면서도 달콤했다. **9** 부사 정각에 ❑ 그녀는 가게를 오늘 아침 8시 정각에 열 생각이었다. **10** 가산명사 올림표 ❑ 비올라 한 대가 외롭고 부드러운 올림 바를 탄주한다.

1 타동사/자동사 날카로워지다; 날카롭게 하다 ❑ 그녀의 눈빛이 뭔가 특이한 것을 본 것처럼 날카로워졌다. **2** 타동사 날카롭게 만들다 ❑ 그는 자신의 칼을 갈기 시작했다.

가산명사 가는 것 ❑ 연필깎이

shit의 과거, 과거 분사

1 타동사/자동사 산산이 부서지다, 산산조각 나다 ❑ 깨져도 산산이 부서지지 않는 안전유리 ❑ 그 자동차는 시속 200마일로 달리다 충돌하여 불에 타며 산산조각 나 버렸다. ● 산산이 부서짐 불가산명사 ❑ 유리가 산산조각 남 **2** 타동사 (희망 등을) 산산조각 내다 ❑ 실패하면 많은 사람들의 희망이 산산조각 날 것이다. **3** 타동사 엄청난 충격을 받다 ❑ 그는 아들의 죽음으로 엄청난 충격을 받았다.

1 형용사 엄청난 충격을 받은 ❑ 그것은 절망적일 정도로 슬픈 소식이며 그 소식을 듣고 나는 정말 엄청난 충격을 받았다. **2** 형용사 완전히 지친 [영국영어, 비격식체] ❑ 그는 완전히 지쳤고 학교 공부에 신경을 쓰기에는 너무 피곤했다.

1 타동사/자동사 면도하다 ❑ 그는 저녁 식사 전에 목욕을 하고 면도를 했다. ❑ 그는 얼굴이 매끈해질 때까지 면도를 한 참이었다. ● 가산명사 면도 ❑ 그는

smooth. ● N-COUNT **Shave** is also a noun. ❑ *He never seemed to need a shave.*
● **shav|ing** N-UNCOUNT ❑ *...a range of shaving products.* **2** V-T If you **shave off** part of a piece of wood or other material, you cut very thin pieces from it. ❑ *I set the log on the ground and shaved off the bark.* **3** V-T If you **shave** a small amount **off** something such as a record, cost, or price, you reduce it by that amount. ❑ *She's already shaved four seconds off the national record for the mile.* **4** →see also **shaving** **5** PHRASE If you describe a situation as **a close shave,** you mean that there was nearly an accident or a disaster but it was avoided. ❑ *I can't quite believe the close shaves I've had just recently.*

생전 면도를 할 필요가 없어져 보였다. ● 면도 불가산명사 ❑ 다양한 면도용 제품 **2** 타동사 깎다, 대패질하다 ❑ 나는 통나무를 땅바닥에 놓은 다음 나무 껍질을 깎아냈다. **3** 타동사 깎다 ❑ 그는 이미 2마일에 대한 국내 기록을 4초나 단축했다. **5** 구 아슬아슬한 순간 ❑ 내가 최근에 겪은 아슬아슬한 순간들이 잘 믿어지지 않는다.

shav|er /ʃeɪvər/ (**shavers**) N-COUNT A **shaver** is an electric device, used for shaving hair from the face and body. ❑ *...men's electric shavers.*

가산명사 면도기 ❑ 남성용 전기면도기

shav|ing /ʃeɪvɪŋ/ (**shavings**) N-COUNT **Shavings** are small very thin pieces of wood or other material which have been cut from a larger piece. ❑ *The floor was covered with shavings from his wood carvings.* →see also **shave**

가산명사 대팻밥, 깎아 낸 부스러기 ❑ 바닥은 그가 나무 조각을 하면서 떨어뜨린 나무 부스러기들로 덮여 있었다.

shawl /ʃɔl/ (**shawls**) N-COUNT A **shawl** is a large piece of woolen cloth which a woman wears over her shoulders or head, or which is wrapped around a baby to keep it warm. →see **clothing**

가산명사 숄

she ♦♦♦ /ʃɪ, STRONG ʃi/

She is a third person singular pronoun. **She** is used as the subject of a verb.

she는 3인칭 단수 대명사이다. she는 동사의 주어로 쓰인다.

1 PRON-SING You use **she** to refer to a woman, girl, or female animal who has already been mentioned or whose identity is clear. ❑ *When Ann arrived home that night, she found Brian in the house watching TV.* ❑ *She was seventeen and she had no education or employment.* **2** PRON-SING Some writers may use **she** to refer to a person who is not identified as either male or female. They do this because they wish to avoid using the pronoun "he" all the time. Some people dislike this use and prefer to use "he or she" or "they." ❑ *The student may show signs of feeling the strain of responsibility and she may give up.* **3** PRON-SING **She** is sometimes used to refer to a country or nation. ❑ *Now Britain needs new leadership if she is to play a significant role shaping Europe's future development.*

1 단수대명사 그녀 ❑ 앤이 그날 저녁 집에 도착했을 때 브라이언이 집안에서 텔레비전을 보고 있는 것을 발견했다. ❑ 그녀는 열일곱 살이었고 학교도 직장도 없었다. **2** 단수대명사 (남녀 구별 없이 가리켜) 그, 그 사람 ❑ 그 학생이 책임감을 부담스러워 하는 징조를 보이며 포기할지도 모른다. **3** 단수대명사 (국가를 지칭하여) 그 나라 ❑ 유럽의 앞날을 형성하는 데 중추적인 역할을 하려면 이제 영국은 새로운 지도력을 갖춰야 한다.

shear /ʃɪər/ (**shears, shearing, sheared, shorn**) **1** V-T To **shear** a sheep means to cut its wool off. ❑ *In the Hebrides they shear their sheep later than anywhere else.* ● **shear|ing** N-UNCOUNT ❑ *...a display of sheep shearing.* **2** N-PLURAL A pair of **shears** is a garden tool like a very large pair of scissors. Shears are used especially for cutting hedges. [also *a pair of* N] ❑ *Trim the shrubs with shears.*

1 타동사 (양의) 털을 깎다 ❑ 헤브리디스에서는 다른 어느 곳보다 양털을 늦게 깎는다. ● 털 깎기 불가산명사 ❑ 양털 깎기 시범 **2** 복수명사 큰 가위 ❑ 전정가위로 관목을 다듬으세요.

sheath /ʃiθ/ (**sheaths**) N-COUNT A **sheath** is a covering for the blade of a knife.

가산명사 칼집

shed ♦♢♢ /ʃɛd/ (**sheds, shedding**)

The form **shed** is used in the present tense and in the past tense and past participle of the verb.

shed는 동사의 현재, 과거, 과거 분사로 쓰인다.

1 N-COUNT A **shed** is a small building that is used for storing things such as garden tools. ❑ *...a garden shed.* **2** N-COUNT A **shed** is a large shelter or building, for example at a train station, port, or factory. ❑ *...a vast factory shed.* **3** V-T When a tree **sheds** its leaves, its leaves fall off in the autumn. When an animal **sheds** hair or skin, some of its hair or skin drops off. ❑ *Some of the trees were already beginning to shed their leaves.* **4** V-T To **shed** something means to get rid of it. [FORMAL] ❑ *The firm is to shed 700 jobs.* **5** V-T If a truck or lorry **sheds** its load, the goods that it is carrying accidentally fall onto the road. [mainly BRIT] ❑ *A lorry piled with scrap metal had shed its load.* **6** V-T If you **shed** tears, you cry. ❑ *They will shed a few tears at their daughter's wedding.* **7** V-T To **shed** blood means to kill people in a violent way. If someone **sheds** their blood, they are killed in a violent way, usually when they are fighting in a war. [FORMAL] ❑ *Gunmen in Ulster shed the first blood of the new year.* **8** to **shed light on** something →see **light** →see **cry**

1 가산명사 헛간 ❑ 정원 헛간 **2** 가산명사 창고 ❑ 거대한 공장 창고 **3** 타동사 (나뭇잎을) 떨어뜨리다, (털을) 갈다, (허물을) 벗다 ❑ 일부 나무들은 이미 잎을 떨어뜨리기 시작하고 있었다. **4** 타동사 없애다 [격식체] ❑ 회사는 일자리 700개를 감축할 것이다. **5** 타동사 (트럭이 짐을) 흘리다 [주로 영국영어] ❑ 고철을 가득 실은 트럭이 길에 짐을 흘렸다. **6** 타동사 흘리다 ❑ 그들은 딸의 결혼식에서 눈물을 꽤나 흘릴 것이다. **7** 타동사 피를 흘리며 죽게 만들다; 피를 흘리며 죽다 [격식체] ❑ 얼스터에서 총을 든 괴한들이 새해 들어 처음으로 피를 흘리며 죽어 갔다.

Word Partnership shed의 연어

N. storage shed **1**
shed *your* clothes, shed *your* image, shed pounds **4**
shed a tear, shed tears **6**
shed blood **7**

she'd /ʃid, ʃɪd/ **1** **She'd** is the usual spoken form of "she had," especially when "had" is an auxiliary verb. ❑ *She was scared she'd have to drop out of college.* **2** **She'd** is a spoken form of "she would." ❑ *She'd do anything for a bit of money.*

1 she had의 축약형 ❑ 그녀는 대학을 그만둬야 할까 봐 두려워했다. **2** she would의 축약형 ❑ 그녀는 약간의 돈을 위해서라면 어떤 짓이든 했다.

sheen /ʃin/ N-SING If something has a **sheen,** it has a smooth and gentle brightness on its surface. ❑ *The carpet had a silvery sheen to it.*

단수명사 광택, 윤 ❑ 그 카펫은 은빛 광택이 났다.

sheep /ʃip/

Sheep is both the singular and the plural form.

sheep은 단수형 및 복수형이다.

N-COUNT A **sheep** is a farm animal which is covered with thick curly hair called wool. Sheep are kept for their wool or for their meat. ❑ *...grassland on which a flock of sheep were grazing.* →see **meat**

가산명사 양 ❑ 한 무리의 양 떼가 풀을 뜯고 있던 초원

sheep|ish /ʃipɪʃ/ ADJ If you look **sheepish,** you look slightly embarrassed because you feel foolish or you have done something silly. ❑ *I asked him why. He looked a little sheepish when he answered.*

형용사 수줍어하는; 당황한 ❑ 그에게 이유를 물었다. 대답할 때 그는 약간 당황한 듯이 보였다.

sheer /ʃɪər/ (**sheerer, sheerest**) **1** ADJ You can use **sheer** to emphasize that a state or situation is complete and does not involve or is not mixed with anything else. [EMPHASIS] ❑ *His music is sheer delight.* ❑ *Sheer chance quite often plays an important part in sparking off an idea.* **2** ADJ A **sheer** cliff or drop is extremely steep or completely vertical. ❑ *There was a sheer drop just outside my window.* **3** ADJ **Sheer** material is very thin, light, and delicate. ❑ *...sheer black tights.*

1 형용사 순전한 [강조] ❑ 그의 음악은 순전한 기쁨이다. ❑ 아이디어가 번쩍 떠오르는 데 있어 순전히 운이 중요하게 작용하는 경우가 매우 자주 있다. **2** 형용사 깎아지른 듯한 ❑ 내 창문 바로 밖에 깎아지른 듯 가파른 비탈이 있었다. **3** 형용사 얇은 ❑ 얇은 검은색 타이츠

sheet ♦♦♢♢ /ʃiːt/ (**sheets**) **1** N-COUNT A **sheet** is a large rectangular piece of cotton or other cloth that you sleep on or cover yourself with in a bed. ❏ *Once a week, a maid changes the sheets.* **2** N-COUNT A **sheet** of paper is a rectangular piece of paper. ❏ *...a sheet of newspaper.* **3** N-COUNT You can use **sheet** to refer to a piece of paper which gives information about something. ❏ *...information sheets on each country in the world.* **4** N-COUNT A **sheet of** glass, metal, or wood is a large, flat, thin piece of it. ❏ *...a cracked sheet of glass.* ❏ *Overhead cranes were lifting giant sheets of steel.* **5** N-COUNT A **sheet of** something is a thin wide layer of it over the surface of something else. ❏ *...a sheet of ice.* **6** →see also **balance sheet, broadsheet, fact sheet, spreadsheet, worksheet** →see **paper**

1 가산명사 침대 시트 ❏ 일주일에 한 번씩 하녀가 침대 시트를 간다. **2** 가산명사 (종이) 한 장 ❏ 신문지 한 장 **3** 가산명사 (식료) 한 장 ❏ 세계 각국에 대한 정보지들 **4** 가산명사 (유리·나무 등의) 한 장 ❏ 금이 간 유리 한 장 ❏ 고가 기중기들이 거대한 철판 여러 장을 들어 올리고 있었다. **5** 가산명사 얇은 층 ❏ 얇은 얼음층

sheikh /ʃiːk, ʃeɪk, BRIT ʃeɪx/ (**sheikhs**) N-TITLE; N-COUNT A **sheikh** is a male Arab chief or ruler. ❏ *...Sheikh Khalifa.*

경칭명사; 가산명사 셰이크 (회교권의 수장) ❏ 셰이크 칼리파

shelf /ʃelf/ (**shelves**) **1** N-COUNT A **shelf** is a flat piece of wood, metal, or glass which is attached to a wall or to the sides of a cabinet. Shelves are used for keeping things on. ❏ *He took a book from the shelf.* **2** PHRASE If you buy something **off the shelf**, you buy something that is not specially made for you. ❏ *Any car you can buy off the shelf in a pastel pink has got to be saying something.*

1 가산명사 선반, 시렁; 책꽂이 ❏ 그는 책꽂이에서 책 한 권을 꺼냈다. **2** 구 기성품이어서; 곧 살 수 있어 ❏ 어떤 차든 파스텔 분홍색으로 즉시 구입하실 수 있다는 것은 대단한 겁니다.

shell ♦♢♢ /ʃel/ (**shells, shelling, shelled**) **1** N-COUNT The **shell** of a nut or egg is the hard covering which surrounds it. ❏ *They cracked the nuts and removed their shells.* ● N-UNCOUNT **Shell** is the substance that a shell is made of. ❏ *...beads made from ostrich egg shell.* **2** N-COUNT The **shell** of an animal such as a tortoise, snail, or crab is the hard protective covering that it has around its body or on its back. ❏ *...the spiral form of a snail shell.* **3** N-COUNT **Shells** are hard objects found on beaches. They are usually pink, white, or brown and are the coverings which used to surround small sea creatures. ❏ *I collect shells and interesting seaside items.* **4** V-T If you **shell** nuts, peas, shrimp, or other food, you remove their natural outer covering. ❏ *She shelled and ate a few nuts.* **5** N-COUNT If someone comes out of their **shell**, they become more friendly and interested in other people and less quiet, shy, and reserved. ❏ *Her normally shy son had come out of his shell.* **6** N-COUNT The **shell** of a building, boat, car, or other structure is the outside frame of it. ❏ *...the shells of burned buildings.* **7** N-COUNT A **shell** is a weapon consisting of a metal container filled with explosives that can be fired from a large gun over long distances. ❏ *Tanks fired shells at the house.* **8** V-T To **shell** a place means to fire explosive shells at it. ❏ *The rebels shelled the densely-populated suburbs near the port.* ● **shelling** (**shellings**) N-VAR ❏ *Out on the streets, the shelling continued.*

1 가산명사 껍데기, 껍질 ❏ 그들은 호두를 까서 껍데기를 제거했다. ● 불가산명사 껍데기 (성분) ❏ 타조 알 껍데기로 만든 구슬 **2** 가산명사 (거북 등의) 등딱지 ❏ 달팽이 등딱지 같은 나선 형태 **3** 가산명사 조개비, 조개껍데기 ❏ 나는 조개비와 바닷가의 흥미로운 물건들을 수집한다. **4** 타동사 껍데기를 벗기다 ❏ 그녀는 호두 몇 알을 까서 먹었다. **5** 가산명사 (마음의) 외피 ❏ 평소 부끄럼을 타던 그녀의 아들이 마음을 터놓았다. **6** 가산명사 외부 구조 ❏ 불탄 건물들의 외부 구조 **7** 가산명사 포탄 ❏ 탱크들이 그 집을 향해 포탄을 발사했다. **8** 타동사 포격하다 ❏ 반군이 항구 인근에 인구가 조밀한 교외 지역을 포격했다. ● 포격 가산명사 또는 불가산명사 ❏ 거리에서는 포격이 계속되었다.

▶ **shell out** PHRASAL VERB If you **shell out for** something, you spend a lot of money on it. [INFORMAL] ❏ *You won't have to shell out a fortune for it.*

구동사 -에 큰돈을 쓰다 [비격식체] ❏ 그 때문에 큰돈을 쓸 필요가 없게 될 겁니다.

she'll /ʃiːl, ʃɪl/ **She'll** is the usual spoken form of "she will." ❏ *Sharon was a wonderful lady and I know she'll be greatly missed.*

she will의 단축형 ❏ 샤론은 멋진 여자였고 난 그녀를 몹시 그리워하게 되리라는 걸 안다.

shell company (**shell companies**) N-COUNT A **shell company** is a company that another company takes over in order to use its name to gain an advantage. [BUSINESS] ❏ *The U.S. shell company was set up to mount a bid for Kingston Communications.*

가산명사 명의뿐인 회사 [경제] ❏ 그 미국 국적의 명의뿐인 회사는 킹스턴 커뮤니케이션스 사에 대한 입찰을 하기 위해 세워졌다.

shellfish /ʃelfɪʃ/

Shellfish is both the singular and the plural form.

shellfish는 단수형 및 복수형이다.

N-VAR **shellfish** are small creatures that live in the sea and have a shell. ❏ *Fish and shellfish are the specialties.*

가산명사 또는 불가산명사 조개류, 갑각류 ❏ 생선과 갑각류가 명물이다.

shell program (**shell programs**) N-COUNT A **shell program** is a basic computer program that provides a framework within which the user can develop the program to suit their own needs. [COMPUTING]

가산명사 (컴퓨터) 셸 프로그램 [컴퓨터]

shelter ♦♦♢♢ /ʃeltər/ (**shelters, sheltering, sheltered**) **1** N-COUNT A **shelter** is a small building or covered place which is made to protect people from bad weather or danger. ❏ *The city's bomb shelters were being prepared for possible air raids.* **2** N-UNCOUNT If a place provides **shelter**, it provides you with a place to stay or live, especially when you need protection from bad weather or danger. ❏ *The number of families seeking shelter rose by 17 percent.* ❏ *Although horses do not generally mind the cold, shelter from rain and wind is important.* **3** N-COUNT A **shelter** is a building where homeless people can sleep and get food. ❏ *...a shelter for homeless women.* **4** V-I If you **shelter** in a place, you stay there and are protected from bad weather or danger. ❏ *...a man sheltering in a doorway.* **5** V-T If a place or thing **is sheltered** by something, it is protected by that thing from wind and rain. [usu passive] ❏ *...a wooden house, sheltered by a low pointed roof.* **6** V-T If you **shelter** someone, usually someone who is being hunted by police or other people, you provide them with a place to stay or live. ❏ *A neighbor sheltered the boy for seven days.*

1 가산명사 대피처; 방공호 ❏ 만일의 공습에 대비해 그 도시에 방공호가 마련되고 있었다. **2** 불가산명사 (비바람을 피할) 처소, 집 ❏ 집을 구하는 가구 수가 17퍼센트 증가했다. ❏ 말은 일반적으로 추위에 아랑곳하지 않지만, 비바람을 막아 줄 처소는 중요하다. **3** 가산명사 (노숙자) 쉼터 ❏ 여성 노숙자 쉼터 **4** 자동사 기거하다, 비바람을 피하다 ❏ 남의 문간에서 기거하는 한 남자 **5** 타동사 비바람을 피하다 ❏ 낮고 뾰족한 지붕이 비바람을 막아 주는 목조 가옥 **6** 타동사 거처를 제공하다 ❏ 한 이웃이 그 소년에게 7일간 거처를 제공했다.

A
B
C
D
E
F
G
H
I
J
K
L
M
N
O
P
Q
R
S
T
U
V
W
X
Y
Z

shel|tered /ʃɛltərd/ **1** ADJ A **sheltered** place is protected from wind and rain. □ ...a shallow-sloping beach next to a sheltered bay. **2** ADJ If you say that someone has led a **sheltered** life, you mean that they have been protected from difficult or unpleasant experiences. □ Perhaps I've just led a really sheltered life. **3** ADJ **Sheltered** accommodations or work is designed for old or disabled people. It allows them to be independent but also allows them to get help when they need it. [ADJ n] □ Call the family service agencies to find out if they sponsor this kind of sheltered housing. **4** →see also **shelter**

1 형용사 비바람이 들이치지 않는 □ 비바람이 차단된 만 옆에 있는 야트막하니 경사진 해변 **2** 형용사 우환 없는, 시련 없는 □ 어쩌면 나는 정말 시련 없는 삶을 살아왔을 뿐인지도 모른다. **3** 형용사 보호 목적의, 사회적 약자를 돕기 위한 □ 가족 문제 상담소에 전화를 걸어 이런 종류의 보호 시설을 후원하는지 알아보세요.

shelve /ʃɛlv/ (**shelves, shelving, shelved**) **1** V-T If someone **shelves** a plan or project, they decide not to continue with it, either for a while or permanently. □ Atlanta has shelved plans to include golf in the 1996 Games. **2** **Shelves** is the plural of **shelf**.

1 타동사 보류하다; 묵살하다 □ 애틀랜타는 1996년 올림픽에서 골프를 포함하는 계획을 보류해 왔다. **2** shelf의 복수형

shep|herd /ʃɛpərd/ (**shepherds, shepherding, shepherded**) **1** N-COUNT A **shepherd** is a person, especially a man, whose job is to take care of sheep. **2** V-T If you **are shepherded** somewhere, someone takes you there to make sure that you arrive at the right place safely. [usu passive] □ She was shepherded by her guards up the rear ramp of the aircraft.

1 가산명사 양치기 **2** 타동사 인도되다 □ 그녀는 경호원들의 인도를 받아 항공기 뒤쪽의 이동 트랩을 올라갔다.

sher|iff /ʃɛrɪf/ (**sheriffs**) N-COUNT; N-TITLE In the United States, a **sheriff** is a person who is elected to make sure that the law is obeyed in a particular county. □ ...the local sheriff.

가산명사; 경칭명사 보안관 □ 지역 보안관

sher|ry /ʃɛri/ (**sherries**) N-MASS **Sherry** is a type of strong wine that is made in southwestern Spain. It is usually drunk before a meal. □ I poured us a glass of sherry.

물질명사 셰리주 (스페인산 백포도주) □ 내가 우리가 마실 셰리주 한 잔을 따랐다.

she's /ʃiz, ʃɪz/ **1** **She's** is the usual spoken form of "she is." □ She's an exceptionally good cook. **2** **She's** is a spoken form of "she has," especially when "has" is an auxiliary verb. □ She's been married for seven years and has two daughters.

1 she is의 축약형 □ 그녀는 아주 훌륭한 요리사이다. **2** she has의 축약형 □ 그녀는 결혼한 지 7년이 되었고 딸이 둘 있다.

shield /ʃild/ (**shields, shielding, shielded**) **1** N-COUNT Something or someone which is a **shield** against a particular danger or risk provides protection from it. □ He used his left hand as a shield against the reflecting sunlight. **2** V-T If something or someone **shields** you **from** a danger or risk, they protect you from it. □ He shielded his head from the sun with an old sack. **3** V-T If you **shield** your eyes, you put your hand above your eyes to protect them from direct sunlight. □ He squinted and shielded his eyes. **4** N-COUNT A **shield** is a large piece of metal or leather which soldiers used to carry to protect their bodies while they were fighting. □ He clanged his sword three times on his shield. **5** N-COUNT A **shield** is a sports prize or badge that is shaped like a shield. □ ...the first English team to win the European Shield. →see **army**

1 가산명사 보호물; 보호자 □ 그는 왼손으로 반사되는 햇빛을 가렸다. **2** 타동사 보호하다, 막다 □ 그는 낡은 자루를 가지고 햇빛으로부터 머리를 보호했다. **3** 타동사 (손으로 눈을) 가리다 □ 그는 눈을 가늘게 뜨고 손으로 눈을 가렸다. **4** 가산명사 방패 □ 그는 칼로 방패를 세 번 쳐서 땡그렁 소리를 냈다. **5** 가산명사 방패 꼴 우승패 □ 유러피언 우승패를 거머쥔 최초의 영국 팀

shift ♦◊◊ /ʃɪft/ (**shifts, shifting, shifted**) **1** V-T/V-I If you **shift** something or if it **shifts**, it moves slightly. □ He stopped, shifting his cane to his left hand. □ He shifted from foot to foot. **2** V-T/V-I If someone's opinion, a situation, or a policy **shifts** or is **shifted**, it changes slightly. □ Attitudes to mental illness have shifted in recent years. ● N-COUNT **Shift** is also a noun. [usu N prep] □ ...a shift in government policy. **3** V-T If someone **shifts** the responsibility or blame for something onto you, they unfairly make you responsible or make people blame you for it, instead of them. [DISAPPROVAL] □ It was a vain attempt to shift the responsibility for the murder to somebody else. **4** V-T If you **shift** gears in a car, you put the car into a different gear. [AM; BRIT **change**] □ He shifts gears and pulls away slowly. **5** N-COUNT If a group of factory workers, nurses, or other people work **shifts**, they work for a set period before being replaced by another group, so that there is always a group working. Each of these set periods is called a **shift**. You can also use **shift** to refer to a group of workers who work together on a particular shift. □ His father worked shifts in a steel mill.

1 타동사/자동사 옮기다, 이동하다; 이동되다 □ 그는 멈춰 서서 지팡이를 왼손으로 옮겨 쥐었다. □ 그는 한 발 한 발 걸음을 옮겼다. **2** 타동사/자동사 바뀌다; 바꾸다 □ 최근 들어 정신 질환에 대한 태도가 바뀌었다. ● 가산명사 변화 □ 정부 방침의 변화 **3** 타동사 전가하다 [탐탁찮음] □ 다른 누군가에게 살인에 대한 책임을 전가하려는 것은 헛된 시도였다. **4** 타동사 (기어를) 바꾸다 [미국영어; 영국영어 change] □ 그는 기어를 바꾸고 천천히 차를 출발시킨다. **5** 가산명사 교대 근무; 교대조 □ 그의 아버지는 제철소에서 교대 근무를 했다.

Word Partnership   shift의 연어

N.	shift *your* weight **1**
	shift *your* position **1** **2**
	shift *your* attention, shift in focus, policy shift,
	shift in/of power, shift in priorities **2**
	shift blame **3**
	shift gears **4**
	shift change, night shift **5**
ADJ.	dramatic shift, major shift, significant shift **2**

---

shim|mer /ʃɪmər/ (**shimmers, shimmering, shimmered**) V-I If something **shimmers**, it shines with a faint, unsteady light or has an unclear, unsteady appearance. □ The lights shimmered on the water. ● N-SING **Shimmer** is also a noun. □ ...a shimmer of starlight.

자동사 (희미하게) 반짝이다, (빛이) 어른거리다 □ 불빛들이 수면 위에 어른거렸다. ● 단수명사 희미한 빛, 어른거리는 빛 □ 희미한 별빛

shin /ʃɪn/ (**shins**) N-COUNT Your **shins** are the front parts of your legs between your knees and your ankles. □ She punched him on the nose and kicked him in the shins.

가산명사 정강이 □ 그녀는 그의 코를 주먹으로 후려갈기고 정강이를 발로 찼다.

shine /ʃaɪn/ (**shines, shining, shined, shone**) **1** V-I When the sun or a light **shines**, it gives out bright light. □ It is a mild morning and the sun is shining. **2** V-T If you shine a flashlight or other light somewhere, you point it there, so that you can see something when it is dark. □ One of the men shone a torch in his face. □ The man walked slowly towards her, shining the flashlight. **3** V-I Something that **shines** is very bright and clear because it is reflecting light. □ Her blue eyes shone and caught the light. □ ...a pair of patent shoes that shone like mirrors. **4** N-SING Something that has a **shine** is bright and clear because it is reflecting light. □ This gel gives a beautiful shine to the hair. **5** V-I Someone who **shines** at a skill or

1 자동사 빛나다 □ 화창한 아침이고 태양이 빛나고 있다. **2** 타동사 비추다 □ 그 중 한 남자가 그의 얼굴에 햇불을 비추었다. □ 그 남자는 회중전등을 비추며 그녀 쪽으로 천천히 걸어갔다. **3** 자동사 반짝이다 □ 그녀의 푸른 눈이 반짝이며 빛을 받았다. □ 거울처럼 반짝거리는 에나멜가죽 구두 한 켤레 **4** 단수명사 윤, 광택 □ 이 젤은 모발에 아름다운 윤기를 줍니다. **5** 자동사 두드러지다, 뛰어나게 잘하다 □ 너 학교 다닐 때 뛰어난 학생이었니?

activity does it extremely well. ❑ *Did you shine at school?* ⑥ →see also **shining**
→see **light bulb**

Thesaurus   *shine*의 참조어

v.   glare, gleam, illuminate, shimmer ① ③
N.   light, radiance, sheen ④

---

shin|gle /ʃɪŋgᵊl/ (shingles) ① N-UNCOUNT Shingle is a mass of small rough
pieces of stone on the shore of a sea or a river. ❑ *...a beach of sand and shingle.*
② N-UNCOUNT Shingles is a disease in which painful red spots spread in bands
over a person's body, especially around their waist.

shin|ing /ʃaɪnɪŋ/ ADJ A shining achievement or quality is a very good one which
should be greatly admired. ❑ *She is a shining example to us all.* →see also **shine**

shiny /ʃaɪni/ (shinier, shiniest) ADJ Shiny things are bright and reflect light.
❑ *Her blonde hair was shiny and clean.* →see **metal**

ship ♦♦◇ /ʃɪp/ (ships, shipping, shipped) ① N-COUNT A ship is a large boat
which carries passengers or cargo. [also by N] ❑ *Within ninety minutes the ship was
ready for departure.* ❑ *We went by ship over to America.* ② V-T If people or things are
shipped somewhere, they are sent there on a ship or by some other means of
transport. [usu passive] ❑ *Food is being shipped to drought-stricken Southern Africa.*
③ →see also **shipping**
→see Word Web: **ship**

① 불가산명사 조약돌 ❑ 모래와 조약돌이 깔린 해변
② 불가산명사 대상 포진

형용사 빛나는, 훌륭한 ❑ 그녀는 우리 모두에게 훌륭한
귀감이다.

형용사 반짝이는, 반들반들한 ❑ 그녀의 금발 머리는
윤기가 나고 깨끗했다.

① 가산명사 배, 함선 ❑ 90분 이내에 그 배는 출항
준비를 갖췄다. ❑ 우리는 배를 타고 미국에 건너갔다.
② 타동사 수송되다, 운송되다 ❑ 가뭄에 시달리는
남아프리카로 식량이 수송되고 있다.

Word Partnership   *ship*의 연어

N.   bow of a ship, captain of a ship, cargo ship, ship's crew ①
V.   board a ship, build a ship, ship docks, sink a ship ①

---

ship|ment /ʃɪpmənt/ (shipments) ① N-COUNT A shipment is an amount of a
particular kind of cargo that is sent to another country on a ship, train,
airplane, or other vehicle. ❑ *After that, food shipments to the port could begin in a
matter of weeks.* ② N-UNCOUNT The shipment of a cargo somewhere is the
sending of it there by ship, train, airplane, or some other vehicle. ❑ *Bananas
are packed before being transported to the docks for shipment overseas.*

ship|ping /ʃɪpɪŋ/ N-UNCOUNT Shipping is the transport of cargo as a business,
especially on ships. [usu with supp] ❑ *...the international shipping industry.*

ship|wreck /ʃɪprɛk/ (shipwrecks, shipwrecked) ① N-VAR If there is a
shipwreck, a ship is destroyed in an accident at sea. ❑ *He was drowned in a
shipwreck off the coast of Spain.* ② N-COUNT A shipwreck is a ship which has been
destroyed in an accident at sea. ❑ *More than 1000 shipwrecks litter the coral reef
ringing the islands.* ③ V-T PASSIVE If someone is shipwrecked, their ship is
destroyed in an accident at sea but they survive and manage to reach land.
❑ *He was shipwrecked after visiting the island.*

ship|yard /ʃɪpyɑrd/ (shipyards) N-COUNT A shipyard is a place where ships are
built and repaired.

shirt ♦◇◇ /ʃɜrt/ (shirts) ① N-COUNT A shirt is a piece of clothing that you wear
on the upper part of your body. Shirts have a collar, sleeves, and buttons down
the front. ② →see also **sweatshirt**, **T-shirt** →see **clothing**

shit /ʃɪt/ (shits, shitting, shat) ① N-UNCOUNT Some people use shit to refer to
solid waste matter from the body of a human being or animal. [INFORMAL,
VULGAR] ❑ *...a pile of dog shit.* ② V-I To shit means to get rid of solid waste matter
from the body. [INFORMAL, VULGAR] ❑ *...his memories of the yellow dog shitting on
the stairs.* ③ N-SING To have a shit means to get rid of solid waste matter from
the body. [INFORMAL, VULGAR] ❑ *Before dying he confesses that he hasn't taken a shit
in weeks.* ④ N-UNCOUNT People sometimes refer to things that they do not like
as shit. [INFORMAL, VULGAR, DISAPPROVAL] ❑ *This is a load of shit.*

shiv|er /ʃɪvər/ (shivers, shivering, shivered) V-I When you shiver, your body
shakes slightly because you are cold or frightened. ❑ *He shivered in the cold.*
● N-COUNT Shiver is also a noun. ❑ *The emptiness here sent shivers down my
spine.*

① 가산명사 선적 ❑ 그 이후엔, 그 항구로의 식량
선적은 몇 주 후면 시작할 수 있을 것이다.
② 불가산명사 수송 ❑ 바나나가 해외 수송을 위해
선착장으로 운반되기에 앞서 포장된다.

불가산명사 수송, 해운 ❑ 국제 해운업

① 가산명사 또는 불가산명사 난파, 조난 사고 ❑ 그는
스페인 근해에서 일어난 조난 사고에서 익사했다.
② 가산명사 난파선 ❑ 천 대 이상의 난파선이 그
제도를 둘러싸고 있는 산호초대에 널려 있다. ③ 수동
타동사 조난당하다 ❑ 그는 그 섬을 방문한 후 조난을
당했다.

가산명사 조선소

① 가산명사 셔츠

① 불가산명사 똥 [비격식체, 비속어] ❑ 개똥 무더기
② 자동사 똥 누다 [비격식체, 비속어] ❑ 층계에서 똥을
누고 있던 노란 개에 대한 그의 기억 ③ 단수명사 똥
(누기) [비격식체, 비속어] ❑ 죽기 전에 그는 몇 주동안
똥을 누지 않았다고 털어놓는다. ④ 불가산명사 쓰레기
같은 것, 허섭스레기 [비격식체, 비속어, 탐탁찮음]
❑ 이건 모두 허섭스레기야.

자동사 몸을 떨다 ❑ 그는 추워서 몸을 떨었다.
● 가산명사 떨림 ❑ 이곳의 공허함이 내 등골을
오싹하게 했다.

Word Partnership   *shiver*의 연어

V.   feel a shiver, shiver goes/runs down *your* spine,
something makes *you* shiver, *something* sends a shiver
down *your* spine

Word Web   ship

Large ocean-going **vessels** remain an important way of transporting people and
cargo. **Oil tankers** and **container ships** are a common sight in many **ports**. Ocean
liners serve as both transportation and hotel for tourists. Some of these **ships** are
several stories tall. The **captain** steers a cruise ship from the **bridge**, while passengers enjoy themselves on the promenade deck. Huge **warships** carry thousands of
soldiers to battlefields around the world. Aircraft carriers include a flight deck
where planes can take off and land. **Ferries, barges,** fishing **craft,** and research
boats are also an important part of the **marine** industry.

shoal /ʃoʊl/ (shoals) N-COUNT A **shoal of** fish is a large group of them swimming together. ❑ Among them swam shoals of fish.

> 가산명사 (물고기) 떼 ❑ 그들 사이에서 물고기 떼가 헤엄쳤다.

shock ♦♦◇ /ʃɒk/ (shocks, shocking, shocked) **1** N-COUNT If you have a **shock**, something suddenly happens which is unpleasant, upsetting, or very surprising. ❑ The extent of the violence came as a shock. ❑ He has never recovered from the shock of your brother's death. **2** N-UNCOUNT **Shock** is a person's emotional and physical condition when something very frightening or upsetting has happened to them. ❑ The little boy was speechless with shock. **3** N-UNCOUNT If someone is **in shock**, they are suffering from a serious physical condition in which their blood is not flowing around their body properly, for example because they have had a bad injury. ❑ He was found beaten and in shock. **4** V-T If something **shocks** you, it makes you feel very upset, because it involves death or suffering and because you had not expected it. ❑ After forty years in the police force nothing much shocks me. ● **shocked** ADJ ❑ This was a nasty attack and the woman is still very shocked. **5** V-T If someone or something **shocks** you, it upsets or offends you because you think it is vulgar or morally wrong. ❑ You can't shock me. ❑ They were easily shocked in those days. ● **shocked** ADJ ❑ Don't look so shocked. **6** N-VAR A **shock** is the force of something suddenly hitting or pulling something else. ❑ Steel barriers can bend and absorb the shock. **7** N-COUNT A **shock** is the same as an **electric shock**. **8** →see also **electric shock**

> **1** 가산명사 (심리적) 충격 ❑ 그 폭력의 정도가 충격으로 다가왔다. ❑ 그는 네 형이 죽은 충격에서 결코 회복하지 못했다. **2** 불가산명사 (정서적, 신체적) 충격 ❑ 그 어린 소년은 충격을 받아 입을 열지 못했다. **3** 불가산명사 (의학적) 쇼크 ❑ 그는 두들겨 맞아 쇼크 상태로 발견되었다. **4** 타동사 충격을 주다 ❑ 경찰대에서 40년을 보내고 나니 아무것도 나에게 큰 충격을 주지 못한다. ● 충격을 받은 형용사 ❑ 이것은 비열한 습격이었고 그 여자는 아직도 큰 충격을 받은 상태이다. **5** 타동사 충격을 주다, 경악하게 하다, 아연실색하게 하다 ❑ 네가 나를 경악하게 만들 수는 없을 걸. ❑ 그 시절 그들은 쉽게 충격을 받았다. ● 충격을 받은 형용사 ❑ 그렇게 충격받은 얼굴 하지 마세요. **6** 가산명사 또는 불가산명사 충격 ❑ 강철 방벽은 휘어지면서 충격을 흡수할 수 있다. **7** 가산명사 전기 충격

shock|ing /ʃɒkɪŋ/ **1** ADJ You can say that something is **shocking** if you think that it is very bad. [INFORMAL] ❑ The media coverage was shocking. ● **shock|ing|ly** ADV [ADV adj/adv] ❑ His memory was becoming shockingly bad. **2** ADJ You can say that something is **shocking** if you think that it is morally wrong. ❑ It is shocking that nothing was said. ● **shock|ing|ly** ADV ❑ Shockingly, this useless and dangerous surgery did not end until the 1930s. **3** →see also **shock**

> **1** 형용사 형편없는 [비격식체] ❑ 언론 보도는 형편없었다. ● 형편없이 부사 ❑ 그의 기억력은 형편없이 나빠지고 있었다. **2** 형용사 충격적인, 망측한 ❑ 아무 말도 하지 않았다는 사실이 충격적이다. ● 충격적으로 부사 ❑ 충격적이게도, 이 쓸모없고 위험한 외과 수술은 1930년대에 이르러서야 사라졌다.

shock wave (shock waves) also shockwave **1** N-COUNT A **shock wave** is an area of very high pressure moving through the air, earth, or water. It is caused by an explosion or an earthquake, or by an object traveling faster than sound. ❑ The shock waves yesterday were felt from Las Vegas to San Diego. **2** N-COUNT A **shock wave** is the effect of something surprising, such as a piece of unpleasant news, that causes strong reactions when it spreads through a place. ❑ The crime sent shock waves throughout the country. →see **sound**

> **1** 가산명사 (폭발 등에 의한) 충격파 ❑ 어제의 충격파는 라스베가스에서 샌디에이고까지 감지되었다. **2** 가산명사 (비유적) 충격의 여파 ❑ 그 범행은 전국을 충격으로 몰아넣었다.

shod|dy /ʃɒdi/ (shoddier, shoddiest) ADJ **Shoddy** work or a **shoddy** product has been done or made carelessly or badly. ❑ I'm normally quick to complain about shoddy service. ● **shod|di|ly** ADV ❑ These products are shoddily produced.

> 형용사 조잡한, 질 나쁜 ❑ 나는 보통 질 나쁜 서비스에 즉각 불만을 제기한다. ● 조잡하게, 엉망으로 부사 ❑ 이 상품들은 엉망으로 만들어졌다.

shoe ♦◇◇ /ʃuː/ (shoes) **1** N-COUNT **Shoes** are objects which you wear on your feet. They cover most of your foot and you wear them over socks or stockings. ❑ ...a pair of shoes. ❑ Low-heeled comfortable shoes are best. **2** PHRASE If you **fill** someone's **shoes** or **step into** their **shoes**, you take their place by doing the job they were doing. ❑ No one has been able to fill his shoes. **3** PHRASE If you talk about being in someone's **shoes**, you talk about what you would do or how you would feel if you were in their situation. ❑ I wouldn't want to be in his shoes. →see **clothing**

> **1** 가산명사 신, 신발 ❑ 신 한 켤레 ❑ 굽이 낮은 편한 신발이 가장 좋다. **2** 구 ~을 대신하다 ❑ 지금껏 아무도 그를 대신할 수 없었다. **3** 구 ~의 입장이 되다 ❑ 나는 그의 입장이 되고 싶지 않아.

shoe|string /ʃuːstrɪŋ/ **1** ADJ A **shoestring** budget is one where you have very little money to spend. [ADJ n] ❑ The British-produced film was made on a shoestring budget. **2** PHRASE If you do something or make something **on a shoestring**, you do it using very little money. ❑ The theater will be run on a shoestring.

> **1** 형용사 여윳돈이 거의 없는, 영세한 ❑ 그 영국 영화는 저예산으로 만들어졌다. **2** 구 저예산으로 ❑ 그 극장은 저예산으로 운영될 것이다.

shone /ʃoʊn, BRIT ʃɒn/ **Shone** is the past tense and past participle of **shine**.

> shine의 과거, 과거 분사

shook /ʃʊk/ **Shook** is the past tense of **shake**.

> shake의 과거

shoot ♦♦◇ /ʃuːt/ (shoots, shooting, shot) **1** V-T If someone **shoots** a person or an animal, they kill or injure them by firing a bullet or arrow at them. ❑ The police had orders to shoot anyone who attacked them. ❑ The man was shot dead by the police during a raid on his house. **2** V-I To **shoot** means to fire a bullet from a weapon such as a gun. ❑ He taunted armed officers by pointing to his head, as if inviting them to shoot. ❑ The police came around the corner and they started shooting at us. **3** V-I If someone or something **shoots** in a particular direction, they move in that direction quickly and suddenly. ❑ They had almost reached the boat when a figure shot past them. **4** V-T/V-I If you **shoot** something somewhere or if it **shoots** somewhere, it moves there quickly and suddenly. ❑ Masters shot a hand across the table and gripped his wrist. ❑ As soon as she got close, the old woman's hand shot out. **5** V-T If you **shoot** a look at someone, you look at them quickly and briefly, often in a way that expresses your feelings. ❑ Mary Ann shot him a rueful look. **6** V-I If someone **shoots to** fame, they become famous or successful very quickly. ❑ Alina Reyes shot to fame a few years ago with her extraordinary first novel. **7** V-T When people **shoot** a movie or **shoot** photographs, they make a movie or take photographs using a camera. ❑ He'd love to shoot his film in Cuba. ● **Shoot** is also a noun. ❑ ...a barn presently being used for a video shoot. **8** N-COUNT **Shoots** are plants that are beginning to grow, or new parts growing from a plant or tree. ❑ Prune established plants annually as new shoots appear. **9** V-I In sports such as soccer or basketball, when someone **shoots**, they try to score by kicking, throwing, or hitting the ball toward the goal. ❑ Spencer scuttled away from Young to shoot wide when he should have scored. **10** →see also **shooting, shot 11** to **shoot from the hip** →see **hip**

> **1** 타동사 ~을 총으로 쏘다 ❑ 경찰은 자신들을 공격하는 사람은 누구든 발포하라는 명령을 받아 놓고 있었다. ❑ 그 남자는 자기 집에 대한 불시 단속 중에 경찰이 쏜 총에 맞아 죽었다. **2** 자동사 (총을) 쏘다 ❑ 그는 마치 총을 쏘라는 듯이 자신의 머리를 가리키며 무장 경관에게 욕설을 퍼부었다. ❑ 경찰이 가까이로 오더니 우리를 향해 총을 쏘기 시작했다. **3** 자동사 휙 움직이다 ❑ 그들이 거의 보트에 다다랐을 때 어떤 사람 그림자가 휙 그들을 스쳐 지나갔다. **4** 타동사/자동사 불쑥 움직이게 하다; 불쑥 움직이다 ❑ 매스터스가 탁자 너머로 불쑥 손을 뻗어 그의 손목을 움켜잡았다. ❑ 그녀가 가까이 가자마자, 그 늙은 여자가 손을 불쑥 내밀었다. **5** 타동사 (어떤 표정을) 던지다 ❑ 메리 앤이 그에게 미안한 듯한 눈길을 던졌다. **6** 자동사 (명성을) 얻게 되다 ❑ 알리나 레예스는 몇 년 전 비범한 첫 소설로 일거에 유명해졌다. **7** 타동사 (사진 등을) 찍다 ❑ 그는 자신의 영화를 쿠바에서 찍고 싶어 한다. ● 가산명사 촬영 ❑ 현재 비디오 촬영에 쓰이고 있는 헛간 **8** 가산명사 새싹 ❑ 해마다 새싹이 나오면 기존의 나무들을 가지치기해 주세요. **9** 자동사 (스포츠에서) 슛하다 ❑ 꼭 득점했어야 하는 상황에서, 스펜서 영에게서 허겁지겁 벗어나더니 빗나간 슛을 했다.

Word Partnership	shoot의 연어
V.	**going to shoot, try to shoot 1 2**
	shoot **to kill 2**
N.	**orders to shoot, soldiers shoot 1 2**
	shoot **a gun, shoot missiles 2**
	shoot **a film, photo shoot 7**

▶**shoot down** ■ PHRASAL VERB If someone **shoots down** an airplane, a helicopter, or a missile, they make it fall to the ground by hitting it with a bullet or missile. ❑ *They claimed to have shot down one incoming missile.* ■ PHRASAL VERB If one person **shoots down** another, they shoot them with a gun. ❑ *He was prepared to suppress rebellion by shooting down protesters.*

▶**shoot up** PHRASAL VERB If something **shoots up**, it grows or increases very quickly. ❑ *Sales shot up by 9% last month.*

shoot|ing /ʃuːtɪŋ/ (**shootings**) ■ N-COUNT A **shooting** is an occasion when someone is killed or injured by being shot with a gun. ❑ *Two more bodies were found nearby after the shooting.* ■ N-UNCOUNT **Shooting** is hunting animals with a gun as a leisure activity. ❑ *Grouse shooting begins in August.* ■ N-UNCOUNT The **shooting** of a movie is the act of filming it. ❑ *Ingrid was busy learning her lines for the next day's shooting.*

shop ♦♦♢ /ʃɒp/ (**shops**, **shopping**, **shopped**) ■ N-COUNT A **shop** is a building or part of a building where things are sold. [mainly BRIT; AM usually **store**] ❑ *...health food shops.* ❑ *...a record shop.*

> Americans use **shop** to mean a small business that sells only one product or service, like a record shop or a shoe repair shop. **Store** is used when the business sells a variety of products. A **shopping center** or **mall** will have a department store or two, as well as several kinds of shops and stores at one location.

■ V-I When you **shop**, you go to stores or shops and buy things. ❑ *He always shopped at the Co-op.* ❑ *...some advice that's worth bearing in mind when shopping for a new carpet.* ● **shop|per** (**shoppers**) N-COUNT ❑ *...crowds of Christmas shoppers.* ■ N-COUNT You can refer to a place where a particular service is offered as a particular type of shop. ❑ *...the barber shop where Rodney sometimes had his hair cut.* ❑ *...betting shops.* ■ →see also **shopping, coffee shop** ■ PHRASE If you say that people **are talking shop**, you mean that they are talking about their work, and this is boring for other people who do not do the same work. ❑ *Although I get on well with my colleagues, if you hang around together all the time you just end up talking shop.*

	Word Partnership *shop*의 연어
N.	**antique** shop, **pet** shop, **souvenir** shop ■
	shop **owner** ■ ■
	auto shop, **barber** shop, **beauty** shop, **repair** shop ■

▶**shop around** PHRASAL VERB If you **shop around**, you go to different stores or companies in order to compare the prices and quality of goods or services before you decide to buy them. ❑ *Prices may vary so it's well worth shopping around before you buy.*

shop as|sis|tant (**shop assistants**) N-COUNT A **shop assistant** is a person who works in a store selling things to customers. [BRIT; AM **sales clerk**]

shop floor also **shop-floor, shopfloor** N-SING The **shop floor** is used to refer to all the ordinary workers in a factory or the area where they work, especially in contrast to the people who are in charge. ❑ *Cost must be controlled, not just on the shop floor but in the boardroom too.*

shop|keep|er /ʃɒpkiːpər/ (**shopkeepers**) N-COUNT A **shopkeeper** is a person who owns or manages a shop or store. [BRIT; AM usually **storekeeper**, **merchant**]

shop|lift /ʃɒplɪft/ (**shoplifts**, **shoplifting**, **shoplifted**) V-T/V-I If someone **shoplifts**, they steal goods from a store by hiding them in a bag or in their clothes. ❑ *He openly shoplifted from a supermarket.* ● **shop|lift|er** (**shoplifters**) N-COUNT ❑ *A persistent shoplifter has been banned from every Marks & Spencer store in Britain.*

shop|lift|ing /ʃɒplɪftɪŋ/ N-UNCOUNT **Shoplifting** is stealing from a store by hiding things in a bag or in your clothes. ❑ *The grocer accused her of shoplifting and demanded to look in her bag.*

shop|ping ♦♢♢ /ʃɒpɪŋ/ ■ N-UNCOUNT When you do **the shopping**, you go to the stores or shops and buy things. ❑ *I'll do the shopping this afternoon.* ■ N-UNCOUNT Your **shopping** is the things that you have bought from stores, especially food. ❑ *We put the shopping away.*

	Word Partnership *shopping*의 연어
N.	shopping **bag**, **Christmas** shopping, shopping **district**, **food** shopping, **grocery** shopping, **holiday** shopping, **online** shopping, shopping **spree** ■

shop|ping cen|ter (**shopping centers**) [BRIT **shopping centre**] N-COUNT A **shopping center** is a specially built area containing a lot of different stores. ❑ *They met in the parking lot at the new shopping center.*

shop|ping chan|nel (**shopping channels**) N-COUNT A **shopping channel** is a television channel that broadcasts programs showing products that you can phone the channel and buy.

shop|ping mall (**shopping malls**) N-COUNT A **shopping mall** is a specially built covered area containing stores and restaurants which people can walk between, and where cars are not allowed.

■ 구동사 격추하다 ❑ 그들은 날아드는 미사일 한 기를 격추했다고 주장했다. ■ 구동사 -을 총으로 쏘다 ❑ 그는 시위자들에게 발포를 해서 반란을 진압할 각오가 되어 있었다.

구동사 급성장하다 ❑ 지난달 매상이 9퍼센트 급성장했다.

■ 가산명사 총격 ❑ 그 총격 이후 인근에서 두 구의 시체가 더 발견되었다. ■ 불가산명사 (총으로 하는) 사냥 ❑ 뇌조 사냥이 8월에 시작된다. ■ 불가산명사 촬영 ❑ 잉그리드는 다음 날 촬영을 위해 대사를 외우느라 바빴다.

■ 가산명사 가게, 상점 [주로 영국영어; 미국영어 대개 store] ❑ 건강식품 상점 ❑ 레코드 가게

> 미국에서 shop은 음반 상점 또는 신발 수선점과 같이 한가지 상품이나 서비스만을 제공하는 작은 상점을 뜻한다. store는 상점에서 다양한 상품을 팔 때 사용한다. shopping center 또는 mall에는 한 장소에 여러 종류의 상점이 있을 뿐만 아니라 백화점도 한 두 개의 있다.

■ 자동사 물건을 사다, 쇼핑하다 ❑ 그는 항상 생활 협동조합에서 물건을 샀다. ❑ 새 양탄자를 살 때 명심할 만한 가치가 있는 조언 ● 쇼핑객 가산명사 ❑ 수많은 크리스마스 쇼핑객들 ■ 가산명사 (특정 서비스를 제공하는) 점포 ❑ 로드니가 이따금 머리를 잘랐던 이발소 ❑ 마권 판매장 ■ 구인 이야기만 하나 ❑ 내가 동료들과 사이좋게 지내기는 하지만, 항상 함께 어울려 있다 보면 결국 일 이야기만 하게 된다.

구동사 값을 비교하며 여기저기를 둘러보다 ❑ 가격이 차이가 날 수도 있으니 구입하시기 전에 여러 곳을 둘러보며 비교해 보는 것이 좋습니다.

가산명사 점원 [영국영어; 미국영어 sales clerk]

단수명사 노동자 ❑ 노동자 쪽에 대해서만이 아니라 경영진에 대해서도 비용을 통제해야 한다.

가산명사 가게 주인, 소매상인 [영국영어; 미국영어 대개 storekeeper, merchant]

타동사/자동사 (가게 물건을) 들치기하다, 후무리다 ❑ 그는 공공연히 슈퍼마켓에서 물건을 후무렸다. ● 들치기범 가산명사 ❑ 영국 내 막스 앤 스펜서 전 지점에서 한 끈질긴 들치기범에 대해 출입 금지 조치를 내렸다.

불가산명사 들치기 ❑ 식료품점 주인이 그녀가 들치기를 했다고 하며 가방 안을 보여 달라고 다그쳤다.

■ 불가산명사 쇼핑 ❑ 오늘 오후에 쇼핑을 할 것이다. ■ 불가산명사 쇼핑한 물건 ❑ 우리는 쇼핑한 물건들을 치워 두었다.

[영국영어 shopping centre] 가산명사 쇼핑센터 ❑ 그들은 새로 생긴 쇼핑센터 주차장에서 만났다.

가산명사 (텔레비전의) 홈쇼핑 채널

가산명사 쇼핑 몰

a b c d e f g h i j k l m n o p q r s t u v w x y z

A

shore ♦◇◇ /ʃɔːr/ (shores, shoring, shored) N-COUNT The **shores** or the **shore** of a sea, lake, or wide river is the land along the edge of it. Someone who is **on shore** is on the land rather than on a ship. [also prep N] ❑ *They walked down to the shore.* ❑ *...elephants living on the shores of Lake Kariba.*

가산명사 바닷가; (호수 등의) 기슭 ❑ 그들은 바닷가까지 걸어 내려갔다. ❑ 카리바 호안에 사는 코끼리들

B

You can use **beach**, **coast**, and **shore** to talk about the piece of land beside a stretch of water. The **shore** is the area of land along the edge of the sea, a lake, or a wide river. The **coast** is the area of land that lies alongside the sea. You may be referring just to the land close to the sea, or to a wider area that extends further inland. A **beach** is a flat area of sand or pebbles next to the sea.

물가에 펼쳐진 땅을 얘기할 때 beach, coast, shore를 쓸 수 있다. shore는 바닷가, 호숫가, 넓은 강가를 따라 있는 뭍이다. coast는 바닷가를 따라 길게 펼쳐져 있는 지역인데, 바다에 인접한 땅만을 또는 내륙으로 더 확장해서 넓은 지역을 지칭할 수 있다. beach는 바닷가의 평평한 모래 또는 자갈 지역이다.

C

▶**shore up** PHRASAL VERB If you **shore up** something that is weak or about to fail, you do something in order to strengthen it or support it. ❑ *The democracies of the West may find it hard to shore up their defences.*

구동사 지주로 받치다, 강화하다 ❑ 서구 민주주의 국가들이 방위를 강화하는 일이 어렵다는 것을 알게 될 수도 있다.

D

shore|line /ʃɔːrlaɪn/ (shorelines) N-COUNT A **shoreline** is the edge of a sea, lake, or wide river. ❑ *...the rocks along the shoreline.*

가산명사 해안선, 물가 ❑ 해안선을 따라 있는 바위들

E

shorn /ʃɔːrn/ **Shorn** is the past participle of **shear**.

shear의 과거 분사

F

---
short
---

① ADJECTIVE AND ADVERB USES
② NOUN USES

G

① short ♦♦♦ /ʃɔːrt/ (shorter, shortest) →Please look at category ⑰ to see if the expression you are looking for is shown under another headword. **1** ADJ If something is **short** or lasts for a **short** time, it does not last very long. ❑ *The announcement was made a short time ago.* ❑ *Kemp gave a short laugh.* **2** ADJ A **short** speech, letter, or book does not have many words or pages in it. ❑ *They were performing a short extract from Shakespeare's "Two Gentlemen of Verona."* **3** ADJ Someone who is **short** is not as tall as most people are. ❑ *I'm tall and thin and he's short and fat.* ❑ *...a short, elderly woman with grey hair.* **4** ADJ Something that is **short** measures only a small amount from one end to the other. ❑ *The city centre and shops are only a short distance away.* ❑ *A short flight of steps led to a grand doorway.* **5** ADJ If you are **short** of something or if it is **short**, you do not have enough of it. If you are running **short** of something or if it is running **short**, you do not have much of it left. [v-link ADJ, usu ADJ of n] ❑ *Her father's illness left the family short of money.* ❑ *Government forces are running short of ammunition and fuel.* **6** ADJ If someone or something is or stops **short** of a place, they have not quite reached it. If they are or fall **short** of an amount, they have not quite achieved it. [v-link ADJ of n] ❑ *He stopped a hundred yards short of the building.* **7** PHRASE **Short** of a particular thing means except for that thing or without actually doing that thing. ❑ *Short of gagging the children, there was not much she could do about the noise.* **8** ADV If something is **cut short** or **stops short**, it is stopped before people expect it to or before it has finished. [ADV after v] ❑ *His glittering career was cut short by a heart attack.* **9** ADJ If a name or abbreviation is **short for** another name, it is the short version of that name. [v-link ADJ for n] ❑ *Her friend Kes (short for Kesewa) was in tears.* **10** ADJ If you have a **short** temper, you get angry very easily. ❑ *...an awkward, self-conscious woman with a short temper.* **11** ADJ If you are **short** with someone, you speak briefly and rather rudely to them, because you are impatient or angry. [v-link ADJ, usu ADJ with n] ❑ *She seemed nervous or tense, and she was definitely short with me.* **12** PHRASE If a person or thing is called something **for short**, that is the short version of their name. ❑ *Opposite me was a woman called Jasminder (Jazzy for short).* **13** PHRASE If you **go short of** something, especially food, you do not have as much of it as you want or need. ❑ *Some people may manage their finances badly and therefore have to go short of essentials.* **14** PHRASE You use **in short** when you have been giving a lot of details and you want to give a conclusion or summary. ❑ *Try tennis, badminton, or windsurfing. In short, anything challenging.* **15** PHRASE If someone or something **is short on** a particular good quality, they do not have as much of it as you think they should have. [DISAPPROVAL] ❑ *The proposals were short on detail.* **16** PHRASE If someone **stops short of** doing something, they come close to doing it but do not actually do it. ❑ *He stopped short of explicitly criticizing the government.* **17** **short of breath** →see **breath. at short notice** →see **notice. to draw the short straw** →see **straw. in short supply** →see **supply. in the short term** →see **term**

1 형용사 (시간적으로) 짧은, 잠깐 ❑ 그 발표는 조금 전에 이루어졌다. ❑ 켐프가 짧게 웃었다. **2** 형용사 (분량이) 짧은 ❑ 그들은 셰익스피어 작 '베로나의 두 신사'의 짧게 발췌한 내용을 공연하고 있었다. **3** 형용사 키가 작은 ❑ 나는 키가 크고 말랐고 그는 키가 작고 뚱뚱하다. ❑ 키가 작고 머리가 희끗희끗한 나이가 지긋한 여자 **4** 형용사 (길이 등이) 짧은 ❑ 도시 중심부와 상점들은 조금 떨어져 있을 뿐이다. ❑ 짧은 층계를 오르자 웅장한 현관에 이르렀다. **5** 형용사 -이 부족한, -이 불충분한 ❑ 그녀의 아버지가 병에 걸려 가족들은 돈이 부족했다. ❑ 정부군은 탄약과 연료가 떨어져 가고 있었다. **6** 형용사 -에 못 미치는 ❑ 그는 그 건물에 100야드 못 미친 곳에서 멈췄다. **7** 구 -을 제외하고 ❑ 아이들의 재갈을 물리는 것 말고는, 떠드는 것을 놓고 그녀가 할 수 있는 일이 많지 않았다. **8** 부사 갑자기 멈추다 ❑ 그의 화려한 출세 가도는 심장 발작으로 인해 갑자기 멈추었다. **9** 형용사 -의 약칭인 ❑ 그녀의 친구 케스(케세와의 약칭)는 눈물을 흘렸다. **10** 형용사 성마른 ❑ 눈치 없고 자의식이 강하며 성마른 기질의 여자 **11** 형용사 -에게 통명스럽게 대하는 ❑ 그녀는 초조하고 긴장한 것 같았고, 확실히 내게 통명스럽게 대했다. **12** 구 요약하면, 줄여서 ❑ 내 맞은편에는 재스민더(줄여서 재지)라는 여자가 있었다. **13** 구 -이 부족하다, -없이 지내다 ❑ 몇몇 사람들은 재정 관리를 잘못해서 꼭 필요한 것들 없이 지내야 한다. **14** 구 요컨대 ❑ 테니스나 배드민턴 아니면 윈드서핑, 요컨대 무엇이든 도전적인 일을 시도해 보세요. **15** 구 -이 부족하다 [탐탁찮음] ❑ 그 안들은 상세하지 못했다. **16** 구 -까지는 하지 않다 ❑ 그는 노골적으로 정부를 비난하는 데까지는 가지 않았다.

S

Thesaurus short의 참조어

ADJ. brief, quick; (ant.) long ① **1** **2**
petite, slight, small; (ant.) tall ① **3**

U

V

② short /ʃɔːrt/ (shorts) **1** N-PLURAL **Shorts** are pants with very short legs, that people wear in hot weather or for taking part in sports. [also a pair of N] ❑ *...two women in bright cotton shorts and tee shirts.* **2** N-PLURAL **Shorts** are men's underpants with short legs. [mainly AM] [also a pair of N]

1 복수명사 반바지 ❑ 밝은 색 면직 반바지와 티셔츠를 입은 여자 두 명 **2** 복수명사 남자용 팬티 [주로 미국영어]

W

X

short|age ♦◇◇ /ʃɔːrtɪdʒ/ (shortages) N-VAR If there is a **shortage of** something, there is not enough of it. ❑ *A shortage of funds is preventing the UN from monitoring relief.* ❑ *Vietnam is suffering from food shortage.*

가산명사 또는 불가산명사 부족 ❑ 자금 부족으로 인해 유엔이 원조를 감시하지 못하고 있다. ❑ 베트남은 식량 부족으로 어려움을 겪고 있다.

Y

short-change (short-changes, short-changing, short-changed) **1** V-T If someone **short-changes** you, they do not give you enough change after you have bought something from them. ❑ *The cashier made a mistake and short-changed him.* **2** V-T If you **are short-changed**, you are treated unfairly or

1 타동사 -에게 거스름돈을 덜 주다 ❑ 출납원이 실수로 그에게 거스름돈을 덜 주었다. **2** 타동사 부당한 대우를 받다 ❑ 여성들은 사실 아직도 언론에 부당한 대우를 받고 있다.

Z

dishonestly, often because you are given less of something than you deserve. [usu passive] ❑ *Women are in fact still being short-changed in the press.*

short|coming /ʃɔ͟ːtkʌmɪŋ/ (**shortcomings**) N-COUNT Someone's or something's **shortcomings** are the faults or weaknesses which they have. ❑ *Marriages usually break down as a result of the shortcomings of both partners.*

가산명사 결점, 단점 ❑ 결혼 생활은 일반적으로 양쪽 당사자 모두의 결점의 결과로 파탄난다.

short cut (**short cuts**) also **short-cut, shortcut** ◼ N-COUNT A **short cut** is a quicker way of getting somewhere than the usual route. ❑ *I tried to take a short cut and got lost.* ◼ N-COUNT A **short cut** is a method of achieving something more quickly or more easily than if you use the usual methods. ❑ *Fame can be a shortcut to love and money.* ◼ N-COUNT On a computer, a **shortcut** is an icon on the desktop that allows you to go immediately to a program or document. [COMPUTING] ❑ *There are any number of ways to move or copy icons or create shortcuts in Windows.* ◼ N-COUNT On a computer, a **shortcut** is a keystroke or a combination of keystrokes that allows you to give commands without using the mouse. [COMPUTING] ❑ *There is a handy keyboard shortcut to save you having to mouse up to the top of the screen.*

◼ 가산명사 지름길 ❑ 나는 지름길로 가려고 하다가 길을 잃었다. ◼ 가산명사 (비유적) 지름길 ❑ 명성이 사랑과 돈을 얻는 지름길이 될 수 있다. ◼ 가산명사 (컴퓨터) 바로 가기 [컴퓨터] ❑ 윈도에서 아이콘을 이동 혹은 복사하거나 바로 가기를 만들 수 있는 방법들이 있다. ◼ 가산명사 (컴퓨터) 단축키 [컴퓨터] ❑ 스크린 맨 위로 마우스 커서를 옮기는 수고를 덜어 주는 편리한 단축키가 있다.

short|en /ʃɔ͟ːtʰn/ (**shortens, shortening, shortened**) ◼ V-T/V-I If you **shorten** an event or the length of time that something lasts, or if it **shortens**, it does not last as long as it would otherwise do or as it used to do. ❑ *Smoking can shorten your life.* ❑ *The trading day is shortened in observance of the Labor Day holiday.* ◼ V-T/V-I If you **shorten** an object or if it **shortens**, it becomes smaller in length. ❑ *Her father paid £1,000 for an operation to shorten her nose.* ◼ V-T If you **shorten** a name or other word, you change it by removing some of the letters. ❑ *Originally called Lili, she eventually shortened her name to Lee.*

◼ 타동사/자동사 짧게 하다, 단축하다; 짧아지다, 단축되다 ❑ 흡연은 수명을 단축시킬 수 있다. ❑ 노동절 휴일을 기념하여 업무일이 단축되었다. ◼ 타동사/자동사 짧게 하다, 줄이다; 짧아지다, 준다 ❑ 그녀의 아버지는 그녀의 코를 짧게 하는 수술에 1,000파운드를 지불했다. ◼ 타동사 축약하다 ❑ 원래 릴리라고 불렸던 그녀는 마침내 리로 이름을 줄였다.

short|fall /ʃɔ͟ːtfɔːl/ (**shortfalls**) N-COUNT If there is a **shortfall in** something, there is less of it than you need. ❑ *The government has refused to make up a £30,000 shortfall in funding.*

가산명사 부족분 ❑ 정부는 자금 조달 부족분 30,000파운드를 벌충하기를 거부했다.

short|hand /ʃɔ͟ːthænd/ ◼ N-UNCOUNT **Shorthand** is a quick way of writing that uses signs to represent words or syllables. Shorthand is used by secretaries and journalists to write down what someone is saying. ❑ *Ben took notes in shorthand.* ◼ N-UNCOUNT You can use **shorthand** to mean a quick or simple way of referring to something. [also a n] ❑ *Laslett uses the shorthand of "second age" for the group of younger people who are creating families.*

◼ 불가산명사 속기 ❑ 벤은 속기로 필기를 했다. ◼ 불가산명사 약칭 ❑ 라슬릿은 가족을 형성하고 있는 젊은 사람들 집단을 지칭하기 위해 '제2세대'라는 약칭을 쓴다.

short-haul ADJ **Short-haul** is used to describe things that involve transporting passengers or goods over short distances. Compare **long-haul**. [ADJ n] ❑ *Short-haul flights operate from Heathrow and Gatwick.*

형용사 단거리의 ❑ 단거리 항공편이 히드로 공항과 개트윅 공항 사이를 운항한다.

short|list /ʃɔ͟ːtlɪst/ (**shortlists, shortlisting, shortlisted**)

> The spelling **short list** is used in American English and sometimes in British English for the noun.

◼ N-COUNT If someone is on a **shortlist**, for example for a job or a prize, they are one of a small group of people who have been chosen from a larger group. The successful person is then chosen from the small group. ❑ *If you've been asked for an interview you are probably on a shortlist of no more than six.* ◼ V-T If someone or something **is shortlisted for** a job or a prize, they are put on a shortlist. [usu passive] ❑ *He was shortlisted for the Nobel Prize for literature several times.*

철자 short list은 미국영어에서 쓰이며, 가끔 영국영어에서 명사로 쓰인다.

◼ 가산명사 최종 후보자 명단, 최종 심사 대상자 ❑ 면접 요청을 받았다면 아마도 최고 여섯 명까지 뽑는 최종 심사 대상자에 들었을 것입니다. ◼ 타동사 최종 후보자 명단에 오르다 ❑ 그는 여러 번 노벨 문학상 최종 후보 명단에 올랐다.

short-lived ADJ Something that is **short-lived** does not last very long. ❑ *Any hope that the speech would end the war was short-lived.*

형용사 단명의; 덧없는 ❑ 그 연설로 전쟁이 끝나리라는 어떤 희망도 덧없는 것이었다.

short|ly ◆◇◇ /ʃɔ͟ːtli/ ADV If something happens **shortly** after or before something else, it happens not long after or before it. If something is going to happen **shortly**, it is going to happen soon. ❑ *Their trial will shortly begin.* ❑ *Shortly after moving into her apartment, she found a job.*

부사 곧 ❑ 그들의 공판이 곧 시작될 것이다. ❑ 자신의 아파트로 이사해 들어간 후 곧 그녀는 일자리를 구했다.

short-sighted also **shortsighted** ◼ ADJ If you are **short-sighted**, you cannot see things properly when they are far away, because there is something wrong with your eyes. [mainly BRIT; AM usually **near-sighted**] ❑ *Testing showed her to be very short-sighted.* ◼ ADJ If someone is **short-sighted** about something, or if their ideas are **short-sighted**, they do not make proper or careful judgments about the future. ❑ *Environmentalists fear that this is a short-sighted approach to the problem of global warming.*

◼ 형용사 근시의 [주로 영국영어; 미국영어 대개 near-sighted] ❑ 검사 결과 그녀는 심한 근시임이 드러났다. ◼ 형용사 선견지명이 없는, 근시안적인 ❑ 환경 보호론자들은 이것이 지구 온난화 문제에 대한 근시안적인 접근이라고 염려한다.

short-term ◆◇◇ ADJ **Short-term** is used to describe things that will last for a short time, or things that will have an effect soon rather than in the distant future. ❑ *Investors weren't concerned about short-term profits over the next few years.* ❑ *The company has 90 staff, almost all on short-term contracts.* →see **memory**

형용사 단기의 ❑ 투자들은 추후 몇 년간의 단기 이익에 대해 관심을 갖지 않았다. ❑ 그 회사는 90명의 직원을 두었는데, 거의 전부가 단기 계약을 한 상태이다.

shot ◆◆◇ /ʃɒ̱t/ (**shots**) ◼ **Shot** is the past tense and past participle of **shoot**. ◼ N-COUNT A **shot** is an act of firing a gun. ❑ *He had murdered Perceval at point blank range with a single shot.* ◼ N-COUNT In sports such as soccer, golf, or tennis, a **shot** is an act of kicking, hitting, or throwing the ball, especially in an attempt to score a point. ❑ *He had only one shot at goal.* ◼ N-COUNT A **shot** is a photograph or a particular sequence of shots in a movie. ❑ *I decided to try for a more natural shot of a fox peering from the bushes.* ◼ N-COUNT If you have a **shot at** something, you attempt to do it. [INFORMAL] ❑ *The heavyweight champion will be given a shot at Holyfield's world title.* ◼ N-COUNT A **shot of** a drug is an injection of it. ❑ *He administered a shot of Nembutal.* ◼ N-COUNT A **shot of** a strong alcoholic drink is a small glass of it. [AM] ❑ *...a shot of vodka.* ◼ PHRASE If you **give** something your **best shot**, you do it as well as you possibly can. [INFORMAL] ❑ *I don't expect to win. But I am going to give it my best shot.* ◼ PHRASE The person who **calls the shots** is in a position to tell others what to do. ❑ *The directors call the shots and nothing happens without their say-so.* ◼ PHRASE If

◼ shoot의 과거, 과거 분사 ◼ 가산명사 발포, 발사 ❑ 그는 직사 거리에서 단 한 발로 퍼시발을 살해했다. ◼ 가산명사 (스포츠) 슛 ❑ 그는 단한 번의 슛을 기록했다. ◼ 가산명사 사진; 영화 화면 ❑ 나는 덤불 속에서 내다보는 여우를 담은 보다 자연스런 사진을 찍어 보기로 결심했다. ◼ 가산명사 ...에 대한 시도; 도전권 [비격식체] ❑ 헤비급 챔피언은 홀리필드가 가진 세계 타이틀에 대한 도전권을 갖게 될 것이다. ◼ 가산명사 (약 한번 분의) 그는 넴뷰탈 1회분을 투여했다. ◼ 가산명사 (독한 술의) 한 잔 [미국영어] ❑ 보드카 한 잔 ◼ 구 최선을 다하다 [비격식체] ❑ 이길 것을 기대하지 않는다. 하지만 최선을 다할 것이다. ◼ 구 감독하다, 지휘하다 ❑ 이사들이 지휘를 하며 그들의 명령 없이는 아무 일도 일어나지 않는다. ◼ 구 쏜살같이, 쏜살같이 [비격식체]

you do something **like a shot**, you do it without any delay or hesitation. [INFORMAL] ❑ *I heard the key turn in the front door and I was out of bed like a shot.* ⓫ PHRASE If you describe something as **a long shot**, you mean that it is unlikely to succeed, but is worth trying. ❑ *The deal was a long shot, but Bagley had little to lose.* ⓬ PHRASE People sometimes use the expression **by a long shot** to emphasize the opinion they are giving. [EMPHASIS] ❑ *The missile-reduction treaty makes sweeping cuts, but the arms race isn't over by a long shot.* →see **photography**

❑ 나는 현관문에서 열쇠가 돌아가는 소리를 듣고 쏜살같이 침대에서 나왔다. ⓫ 구 승산 없는 일 ❑ 그 거래는 승산이 없는 일이었지만, 배글리는 잃을 것이 별로 없었다. ⓬ 구 훨씬; 결코 [강조] ❑ 미사일 감축 협정을 통해 전면적인 감축이 이루어지지만, 군비 확대 경쟁은 결코 끝나지 않았다.

Word Partnership   *shot*의 연어

V.	**fire a** shot, **hear a** shot ❷
	miss a shot ❷ ❸
	take a shot ❷-❺ ❼
	block a shot ❸ ❹
	get a shot, **give** *someone* **a** shot ❻
ADJ.	**single** shot, **warning** shot ❷
	good shot ❷ ❸ ❹
	winning shot ❸

---

shot|gun /ʃɒtgʌn/ (**shotguns**) N-COUNT A **shotgun** is a gun used for shooting birds and animals which fires a lot of small metal balls at one time.

가산명사 산탄총, 엽총

should ♦♦♦ /ʃəd, STRONG ʃʊd/

> **Should** is a modal verb. It is used with the base form of a verb.

❶ MODAL You use **should** when you are saying what would be the right thing to do or the right state for something to be in. ❑ *I should exercise more.* ❑ *He's never going to be able to forget it. And I don't think he should.* ❑ *Should our children be taught to swim at school?* ❷ MODAL You use **should** to give someone an order to do something, or to report an official order. ❑ *All visitors should register with the British Embassy.* ❸ MODAL If you say that something **should have** happened, you mean that it did not happen, but that you wish it had. If you say that something **should not have** happened, you mean that it did happen, but that you wish it had not. ❑ *I should have gone this morning but I was feeling a bit ill.* ❑ *You should have written to the area manager again.* ❹ MODAL You use **should** when you are saying that something is probably the case or will probably happen in the way you are describing. If you say that something **should have** happened by a particular time, you mean that it will probably have happened by that time. ❑ *You should have no problem with reading this language.* ❑ *The doctor said it will take six weeks and I should be fine by then.* ❺ MODAL You use **should** in questions when you are asking someone for advice, permission, or information. ❑ *Should I take out a loan?* ❑ *What should I do?* ❻ MODAL You say "**I should**," usually with the expression "if I were you," when you are giving someone advice by telling them what you would do if you were in their position. [FORMAL] ❑ *I should look out if I were you!* ❼ MODAL You use **should** in conditional clauses when you are talking about things that might happen. [FORMAL] ❑ *If you should be fired, your health and pension benefits will not be automatically cut off.* ❽ MODAL You use **should** in "that" clauses after certain verbs, nouns, and adjectives when you are talking about a future event or situation. ❑ *He raised his glass and indicated that I should do the same.* ❑ *I insisted that we should have a look at every car.* ❾ MODAL You use **should** in expressions such as **I should think** and **I should imagine** to indicate that you think something is true but you are not sure. [VAGUENESS] ❑ *I should think it's going to rain soon.* ❿ MODAL You use **should** in expressions such as **You should have seen us** and **You should have heard him** to emphasize how funny, shocking, or impressive something that you experienced was. [SPOKEN, EMPHASIS] ❑ *You should have heard him last night!*

should는 조동사이며 동사 원형과 함께 쓰인다.

❶ 법조동사 -해야 한다, -하는 것이 마땅하다 ❑ 나는 운동을 더 해야 한다. ❑ 그는 그 일을 결코 잊을 수 없을 것이다. 그리고 나는 그가 그래야 한다고 생각한다. ❑ 우리 아이들이 학교에서 수영을 배워야 할까? ❷ 법조동사 해야 한다 ❑ 모든 방문자는 영국 대사관에 등록해야 한다. ❸ 법조동사 -했어야 했는데; -하지 말았어야 했는데 ❑ 오늘 아침 갔어야 했지만 몸이 약간 좋지 않았다. ❑ 너는 지역 관리자에게 다시 편지를 썼어야 했어. ❹ 법조동사 아마 -일 것이다; 아마 -했을 것이다 ❑ 아마 너는 이 언어를 읽는 데 문제가 없을 거야. ❑ 의사는 6주가 걸릴 것이고 그때가 되면 아마 내가 괜찮아질 거라고 말했다. ❺ 법조동사 -해야 하나 ❑ 융자를 받아야 할까? ❑ 내가 뭘 해야 하지? ❻ 법조동사 (내가 너라면) -하겠다 [격식체] ❑ 내가 너라면 주의하겠어! ❼ 법조동사 if와 함께 '만일 -하면'이라는 뜻을 나타냄 [격식체] ❑ 네가 만일 해고된다 하더라도, 의료 및 연금 혜택이 자동적으로 끊기지는 않을 것이다. ❽ 법조동사 특정한 동사, 명사, 그리고 형용사 뒤의 that 절에 씀 ❑ 그는 잔을 들어 올리고 나도 똑같이 하라는 눈치를 주었다. ❑ 나는 모든 차를 봐야 한다고 주장했다. ❾ 법조동사 -일 것 같다 [짐작투] ❑ 아무래도 곧 비가 내릴 것 같다. ❿ 법조동사 -했어야 했다 (자신의 경험을 강조하는 표현) [구어체, 강조] ❑ 너도 어젯밤에 그의 얘기를 들었어야 했어!

shoul|der ♦♦◇ /ʃoʊldər/ (**shoulders, shouldering, shouldered**) ❶ N-COUNT Your **shoulders** are between your neck and the tops of your arms. ❑ *She led him to an armchair, with her arm round his shoulder.* ❷ N-PLURAL When you talk about someone's problems or responsibilities, you can say that they carry them **on** their **shoulders**. ❑ *No one suspected the anguish he carried on his shoulders.* ❸ V-T If you **shoulder** the responsibility or the blame for something, you accept it. ❑ *He has had to shoulder the responsibility of his father's mistakes.* ❹ V-T If you **shoulder** someone **aside** or if you **shoulder** your **way** somewhere, you push past people roughly using your shoulder. ❑ *The policemen rushed past him, shouldering him aside.* ❑ *She could do nothing to stop him as he shouldered his way into the house.* ❺ N-VAR A **shoulder** is a joint of meat from the upper part of the front leg of an animal. ❑ *...shoulder of lamb.* ❻ PHRASE If someone offers you **a shoulder to cry on** or is **a shoulder to cry on**, they listen sympathetically as you talk about your troubles. ❑ *Mrs. Barrantes longs to be at her daughter's side to offer her a shoulder to cry on.* ❼ PHRASE If you say that someone or something stands **head and shoulders above** other people or things, you mean that they are a lot better than them. ❑ *The two candidates stood head and shoulders above the rest.* ❽ PHRASE If two or more people stand **shoulder to shoulder**, they are standing next to each other, with their shoulders touching. ❑ *They fell into step, walking shoulder to shoulder with their heads bent against the rain.* ❾ PHRASE If people work or stand **shoulder to shoulder**, they work together in order to achieve something, or support each other. ❑ *They could fight shoulder-to-shoulder against a common enemy.* ❿ to **rub shoulders with** →see **rub** →see **body**

❶ 가산명사 어깨 ❑ 그녀는 그의 어깨에 팔을 두르고서 그를 안락의자로 데려갔다. ❷ 복수명사 (어깨에) 짊어지다 ❑ 아무도 그가 짊어진 번민을 알아챘지 못했다. ❸ 타동사 떠맡다, 짊어지다 ❑ 그는 아버지의 실수에 대한 책임을 떠맡아야 했다. ❹ 타동사 어깨로 밀다; 이에로 밀치고 나아가다 ❑ 경찰관들이 그를 어깨로 밀어 제치며 급하게 지나쳐 갔다. ❑ 그가 어깨로 밀치며 집으로 들어올 때 그녀는 그를 막기 위해 아무것도 할 수 없었다. ❺ 가산명사 또는 불가산명사 어깨살 ❑ 양 어깨살 ❻ 구 하소연할 곳 ❑ 바란테스 여사는 딸의 곁에 있으면서 하소연을 들어 주고 싶어 한다. ❼ 구 훨씬 뛰어난 ❑ 그 두 명의 후보가 나머지 후보자들보다 훨씬 뛰어났다. ❽ 구 어깨를 나란히 하여 ❑ 그들은 비를 피해 머리를 숙이고 어깨를 나란히 한 채로 보조를 맞추어 걷기 시작했다. ❾ 구 협력하여 ❑ 그들이 공동의 적에 맞서 힘을 합쳐 싸울 수 있을 것이다.

Word Partnership	*shoulder*의 연어
ADJ.	**bare** shoulder, **broken** shoulder, **left/right** shoulder ▯
N.	**head on** *someone's* shoulder ▯
	shoulder **a burden** ▮
V.	**look over** *your* shoulder, **tap** *someone* **on the** shoulder ▯
	cry on *someone's* shoulder ▮

shouldn't /ʃʊdᵊnt/ Shouldn't is the usual spoken form of "should not."

should've /ʃʊdəv/ Should've is the usual spoken form of "should have," especially when "have" is an auxiliary verb.

shout ♦♢♢ /ʃaʊt/ (shouts, shouting, shouted) V-T/V-I If you **shout**, you say something very loudly, usually because you want people a long distance away to hear you or because you are angry. ❑ *He had to shout to make himself heard above the near gale-force wind.* ❑ *"She's alive!" he shouted triumphantly.* ❑ *Andrew rushed out of the house, shouting for help.* ● N-COUNT **Shout** is also a noun. ❑ *The decision was greeted with shouts of protest from opposition MPs.*

should not의 축약형

should have의 축약형

타동사/자동사 고함치다, 소리치다 ❑ 그는 강풍급의 바람을 뚫고 목소리가 들리게 하기 위해 고함을 쳐야 했다. ❑ "그녀가 살아 있어!" 그가 의기양양하게 소리쳤다. ❑ 앤드루가 도와 달라고 소리치며 집 밖으로 뛰쳐나왔다. ● 가산명사 외침, 고함 ❑ 그 결정에 야당의원들이 항의 섞인 고함을 보냈다.

Word Partnership	*shout*의 연어
PREP.	shout **at** *someone*
V.	**hear a/**someshout, **want to** shout

▶**shout out** PHRASAL VERB If you **shout** something **out**, you say it very loudly so that people can hear you clearly. ❑ *They shouted out the names of those detained.* ❑ *I shouted out "I'm OK."*

구동사 외치나, 큰 소리로 말하다 ❑ 그들은 억류된 사람들의 이름을 큰 소리로 불렀다. ❑ 나는 "난 괜찮아."라고 외쳤다.

shove /ʃʌv/ (shoves, shoving, shoved) ▯ V-T If you **shove** someone or something, you push them with a quick, violent movement. ❑ *He shoved her out of the way.* ❑ *He's the one who shoved me.* ● N-COUNT **Shove** is also a noun. ❑ *She gave Gracie a shove towards the house.* ▮ V-T If you **shove** something somewhere, you push it there quickly and carelessly. ❑ *We shoved a copy of the newsletter beneath their door.* ▮ PHRASE If you talk about what you think will happen **if push comes to shove**, you are talking about what you think will happen if a situation becomes very bad or difficult. [INFORMAL] ❑ *If push comes to shove, if you should lose your case in the court, what will you do?*

▯ 타동사 밀치다, 떠밀다 ❑ 그는 그녀를 옆으로 밀쳐 냈다. ❑ 그가 나를 밀쳤던 사람이다. ● 가산명사 밀침, 떠밀기 ❑ 그녀는 그레이시를 집 쪽으로 떠밀었다. ▮ 타동사 밀다 ❑ 우리는 소식지 한 부를 그들의 문 밑으로 밀어 넣었다. ▮ 구 상황이 어려워지면 [비격식체] ❑ 만약 상황이 어려워지면, 법정에서 패소한다면, 어떻게 하겠는가?

Word Partnership	*shove*의 연어
ADV.	shove *someone* **down** ▯
PREP.	shove *someone* **down**, shove *someone/something*
	into *someone/something* ▯
V.	**give** *someone/something* **a** shove ▯

shov|el /ʃʌvᵊl/ (shovels, shoveling, shoveled) [BRIT, sometimes AM **shovelling, shovelled**] ▯ N-COUNT A **shovel** is a tool with a long handle that is used for lifting and moving earth, coal, or snow. ❑ *...a coal shovel.* ▮ V-T If you **shovel** earth, coal, or snow, you lift and move it with a shovel. ❑ *He has to get out and shovel snow.* ▮ V-T If you **shovel** something somewhere, you push a lot of it quickly into that place. ❑ *There was silence, except for Randall, who was obliviously shoveling food into his mouth.*

[영국영어, 미국영어 가끔 shovelling, shovelled] ▯ 가산명사 삽 ❑ 석탄 삽 ▮ 타동사 삽으로 푸다 ❑ 그가 나가서 삽으로 눈을 치워야 한다. ▮ 타동사 재빠르게 퍼 넣다 ❑ 아랑곳하지 않고 입에 음식을 퍼 넣고 있는 랜달을 제외하고는 정적이 맴돌았다.

show ♦♦♦ /ʃoʊ/ (shows, showing, showed, shown) ▯ V-T If something **shows that** a state of affairs exists, it gives information that proves it or makes it clear to people. ❑ *Research shows that a high-fibre diet may protect you from bowel cancer.* ❑ *These figures show an increase of over one million in unemployment.* ▮ V-T If a picture, chart, movie, or piece of writing **shows** something, it represents it or gives information about it. ❑ *Figure 4.1 shows the respiratory system.* ❑ *The cushions, shown left, measure 20 x 12 inches and cost $39.95.* ❑ *Much of the film shows the painter simply going about his task.* ▮ V-T If you **show** someone something, you give it to them, take them to it, or point to it, so that they can see it or know what you are referring to. ❑ *Cut out this article and show it to your bank manager.* ❑ *He showed me the flat he shares with Esther.* ▮ V-T If you **show** someone to a room or seat, you lead them there. ❑ *It was very good of you to come. Let me show you to my study.* ❑ *Milton was shown into the office.* ▮ V-T If you **show** someone how to do something, you do it yourself so that they can watch you and learn how to do it. ❑ *Claire showed us how to make a chocolate roulade.* ❑ *There are seasoned professionals who can teach you and show you what to do.* ▮ V-T/V-I If something **shows** or if you **show** it, it is visible or noticeable. ❑ *When he smiled he showed a row of strong white teeth.* ❑ *Faint glimmers of daylight were showing through the trees.* ▮ V-T/V-I If you **show** a particular attitude, quality, or feeling, or if it **shows**, you behave in a way that makes this attitude, quality, or feeling clear to other people. ❑ *She showed no interest in her children.* ❑ *Ferguson was unhappy and it showed.* ❑ *You show me respect.* ▮ V-T If something **shows** a quality or characteristic or if that quality or characteristic **shows itself**, it can be noticed or observed. ❑ *The story shows a strong narrative gift and a vivid eye for detail.* ❑ *Her popularity clearly shows no sign of waning.* ▮ N-COUNT A **show of** a feeling or quality is an attempt by someone to make it clear that they have that feeling or quality. [usu N N of n] ❑ *Miners gathered in the centre of Bucharest in a show of support for the government.* ▮ N-UNCOUNT If you say that something is **for show**, you mean that it has no real purpose and is done just to give a good impression. ❑ *The change in government is more for show than for real.* ▮ V-T If a company **shows** a profit or a loss, its accounts indicate that it has made a profit or a loss. ❑ *It is the only one of the three companies expected to show a profit for the quarter.* ▮ V-I If a person you are

▯ 타동사 보이다, 증명하다 ❑ 연구에 의하면 고섬유식이 장암을 막아 줄 수 있다는 것이 증명된다. ❑ 이 수치들은 백만 명 이상 실업이 증가했음을 보여 준다. ▮ 타동사 보이다 ❑ 그림 4.1은 호흡기 계통을 보여 준다. ❑ 왼쪽에 보이는 방석은 치수가 20 x 12인치이며 가격은 39.95달러입니다. ❑ 그 영화의 대부분은 그저 자신의 작업에 힘쓰고 있는 화가의 모습을 보여 준다. ▮ 타동사 보여 주다 ❑ 이 기사를 오려 내서 은행 간부에게 보여 주세요. ❑ 그는 에스터와 같이 쓰는 아파트를 내게 보여 주었다. ▮ 타동사 안내하다 ❑ 와 주셔서 정말 감사합니다. 제 서재로 안내해 드리지요. ❑ 밀턴은 사무실로 안내되었다. ▮ 타동사 해 보이다, 가르쳐 주나 ❑ 클레어가 우리에게 초콜릿 물라드 만드는 법을 보여 주었다. ❑ 당신을 교육하고 무슨 일을 해야 할지 가르쳐 줄 경험 많은 전문가들이 있습니다. ▮ 타동사/자동사 드러내다, 보이다 ❑ 그는 미소를 지으니 튼튼한 흰 치열이 드러났다. ❑ 나무들 사이로 희미한 햇살이 보이고 있었다. ▮ 타동사/자동사 (감정 등을) 보이다; (감정 등이) 드러나다 ❑ 그녀는 자녀들에게 전혀 관심을 보이지 않았다. ❑ 퍼거슨은 행복하지 못했고 그것이 겉으로 드러났다. ❑ 너희들은 나에게 존경을 보인다. ▮ 타동사 (두드러지게) 보이다, 두드러지다 ❑ 그 소설에서는 이야기를 풀어 가는 뛰어난 재능과 생생한 세부 묘사가 두드러진다. ❑ 확실히 그녀의 인기는 식을 기미가 보이지 않는다. ▮ 가산명사 보이기, 표시 ❑ 광부들이 정부에 대한 지지를 보이기 위해 부카레스트 중심가에 집결했다. ▮ 명사불가산 과시, 내보임 ❑ 정부 내의 변화는 실질적이기보다는 과시하기 위한 것이다. ▮ 타동사 (이익 등을) 보다 ❑ 그곳이 세 회사 중 유일하게 해당 분기에 이익을 볼 것으로 예상되는 회사이다.

a
b
c
d
e
f
g
h
i
j
k
l
m
n
o
p
q
r
s
t
u
v
w
x
y
z

expecting to meet does not **show**, they do not arrive at the place where you expect to meet them. [mainly AM] ❑ *There was always a chance he wouldn't show.* ● PHRASAL VERB **Show up** means the same as **show**. ❑ *We waited until five o'clock, but he did not show up.* 🔢 N-COUNT A television or radio **show** is a program on television or radio. ❑ *I had my own TV show.* ❑ *...a popular talk show on a Cuban radio station.* 🔢 N-COUNT A **show** in a theater is an entertainment or concert, especially one that includes different items such as music, dancing, and comedy. ❑ *How about going shopping and seeing a show in London?* 🔢 V-T If someone **shows** a film or television program, it is broadcast or appears on television or in the movie theater. ❑ *The BBC World Service Television news showed the same film clip.* 🔢 N-COUNT A **show** is a public exhibition of things, such as works of art, fashionable clothes, or things that have been entered in a competition. [also on N] ❑ *Currently, the show is in Boston.* ❑ *It plans about 30 such fashion shows this fall in department stores.* 🔢 V-T To **show** things such as works of art means to put them in an exhibition where they can be seen by the public. ❑ *50 dealers will show oils, watercolors, drawings, and prints from 1900 to 1992.* 🔢 PHRASE If you **have something to show** for your efforts, you have achieved something as a result of what you have done. ❑ *I'm nearly 31 and it's about time I had something to show for my time in my job.* 🔢 PHRASE If you say that **it just goes to show that** or **it just shows that** something is the case, you mean that what you have just said or experienced demonstrates that it is the case. ❑ *I forgot all about the ring. Which just goes to show that getting good grades in school doesn't mean you're clever.* 🔢 **to show** someone **the door** →see **door**. **to show your face** →see **face**
→see **concert, theater**

Thesaurus — show의 참조어

V.	demonstrate, display, exhibit, present; (*ant.*) hide 🔢 🔢
N.	demonstration, display, presentation; (*ant.*) hide 🔢
	act, entertainment, production, program 🔢

▶**show off** 🔢 PHRASAL VERB If you say that someone **is showing off**, you are criticizing them for trying to impress people by showing in a very obvious way what they can do or what they own. [DISAPPROVAL] ❑ *All right, there's no need to show off.* 🔢 PHRASAL VERB If you **show off** something that you have, you show it to a lot of people or make it obvious that you have it, because you are proud of it. ❑ *Naomi was showing off her engagement ring.* 🔢 →see also **show-off**

▶**show up** 🔢 PHRASAL VERB If something **shows up** or if something **shows it up**, it can be clearly seen or noticed. ❑ *You may have some strange disease that may not show up for 10 or 15 years.* ❑ *The orange tip shows up well against most backgrounds.* 🔢 PHRASAL VERB If someone or something **shows you up**, they make you feel embarrassed or ashamed of them. ❑ *He wanted to teach her a lesson for showing him up in front of Leonov.* 🔢 →see **show 12**

show busi|ness N-UNCOUNT **Show business** is the entertainment industry of movies, theater, and television. ❑ *He started his career in show business by playing the saxophone and singing.*

show|down /ʃoʊdaʊn/ (**showdowns**) also **show-down** N-COUNT A **showdown** is a big argument or conflict which is intended to settle a dispute that has lasted for a long time. ❑ *They may be pushing the Prime Minister towards a final showdown with his party.*

show|er /ʃaʊər/ (**showers, showering, showered**) 🔢 N-COUNT A **shower** is a device for washing yourself. It consists of a pipe which ends in a flat cover with a lot of holes in it so that water comes out in a spray. ❑ *She heard him turn on the shower.* 🔢 N-COUNT A **shower** is a small enclosed area containing a shower. ❑ *Do you sing in the shower?* 🔢 N-COUNT **The showers** or **the shower** in a place such as a sports center is the area containing showers. ❑ *The showers are a mess.* 🔢 N-COUNT If you have a **shower**, you wash yourself by standing under a spray of water from a shower. ❑ *I think I'll have a shower before dinner.* 🔢 V-I If you **shower**, you wash yourself by standing under a spray of water from a shower. ❑ *There wasn't time to shower or change clothes.* 🔢 N-COUNT A **shower** is a short period of rain, especially light rain. ❑ *There'll be bright or sunny spells and scattered showers this afternoon.* 🔢 N-COUNT You can refer to a lot of things that are falling as a **shower** of them. ❑ *Showers of sparks flew in all directions.* 🔢 V-T If you **are showered with** a lot of small objects or pieces, they are scattered over you. [usu passive] ❑ *They were showered with rice in the traditional manner.* 🔢 N-COUNT A **shower** is a party or celebration at which the guests bring gifts. [mainly AM] ❑ *...a baby shower.* →see **soap, wedding**

shown /ʃoʊn/ **Shown** is the past participle of **show**.

show-off (**show-offs**)

The spelling **showoff** is also used, especially in American English.

N-COUNT If you say that someone is a **show-off**, you are criticizing them for trying to impress people by showing in a very obvious way what they can do or what they own. [INFORMAL, DISAPPROVAL] ❑ *Many jet ski riders are big show-offs who stick around populated areas so everyone can see their turns and manoeuvres.*

show|piece /ʃoʊpiːs/ (**showpieces**) also **show-piece** N-COUNT A **showpiece** is something that is admired because it is the best thing of its type, especially something that is intended to be impressive. ❑ *The factory was to be a showpiece of Western investment in the East.*

show|room /ʃoʊruːm/ (**showrooms**) N-COUNT A **showroom** is a store in which goods are displayed for sale, especially goods such as cars or electrical or gas appliances. ❑ *...a car showroom.*

shrank /ʃræŋk/ **Shrank** is the past tense of **shrink**.

🔢 자동사 나타나다 [주로 미국영어] ❑ 그가 나타나지 않을 가능성이 항상 있었다. ● 구동사 나타나다 ❑ 우리가 5시까지 기다렸지만, 그는 나타나지 않았다. 🔢 가산명사 (방송) 프로그램 ❑ 나는 내가 진행하는 텔레비전 프로그램을 가지고 있었다. ❑ 쿠바 라디오 방송국의 한 인기 토크쇼 🔢 가산명사 쇼 ❑ 런던에서 쇼핑하고 쇼를 한 편 보는 건 어떨까요? 🔢 타동사 방영하다; 상영하다 ❑ 비비시 월드 서비스 텔레비전 뉴스가 같은 영상을 방영했다. 🔢 가산명사 전시회, (패션) 쇼 ❑ 현재, 그 전시회는 보스턴에서 벌어지고 있다. ❑ 그 회사는 이번 가을 여러 백화점에서 그와 같은 패션쇼를 30여 차례 계획하고 있다. 🔢 타동사 전시하다 ❑ 50명의 거래상들이 1900년부터 1992년까지의 유화, 수채화, 드로잉, 판화 작품들을 전시할 것이다. 🔢 구 -의 성과가 있다 ❑ 나는 거의 서른한 살이고 이제 내 일에 들인 시간들의 성과를 볼 때가 되었다. 🔢 구 -이라는 것이 증명되다, -임이 명백하다 ❑ 나는 그 반지에 대한 것을 전부 잊어버렸다. 이는 학교에서 성적을 잘 받는 것이 똑똑함을 의미하지 않는다는 것을 증명한다.

🔢 구동사 뽐내다 [탐탁잖음] ❑ 좋아, 뽐낼 필요는 없어. 🔢 구동사 자랑스레 보이다 ❑ 나오미는 약혼반지를 자랑스레 보여 주고 있었다.

🔢 구동사 뚜렷이 드러나다; 뚜렷이 나타내다 ❑ 당신이 10년 혹은 15년 동안 겉으로 드러나지 않는 이상한 질병을 가지고 있을 수도 있습니다. ❑ 오렌지색 끝부분은 대부분의 바탕색에 대비되어 뚜렷하게 보인다. 🔢 구동사 -을 무안하게 하다 ❑ 그는 레오노프 앞에서 자신에게 무안을 준 것에 대해 그녀를 혼내 주고 싶었다.

불가산명사 연예계 ❑ 그는 색소폰 연주와 노래로 연예계에 데뷔했다.

가산명사 결판, 막판 대결 ❑ 그들이 총리가 소속당과 최종 결판을 내리도록 떠밀고 있는 것일지도 모른다.

🔢 가산명사 샤워기 ❑ 그가 샤워기 트는 소리가 그녀에게 들렸다. 🔢 가산명사 샤워부스 ❑ 샤워부스에서 노래를 부르나요? 🔢 가산명사 샤워장 ❑ 샤워장이 엉망진창이네. 🔢 가산명사 샤워 ❑ 나 저녁 먹기 전에 샤워하려고 해. 🔢 자동사 샤워하다 ❑ 샤워를 하거나 옷을 갈아입을 시간이 없었다. 🔢 가산명사 소나기 ❑ 오늘 오후는 화창하거나 해가 나다가 간간이 소나기가 뿌리곤 하겠습니다. 🔢 가산명사 빗발침, 쇄도 ❑ 불꽃이 사방으로 튀었다. 🔢 타동사 -세례를 받다, -로 뒤덮이다 ❑ 그들은 전통에 따라 쌀 세례를 받았다. 🔢 가산명사 축하 파티 (결혼이나 출산을 기념하여 선물을 전해 주는 파티) [주로 미국영어] ❑ 출산 축하 파티

show의 과거 분사

철자 showoff도 특히 미국영어에서 쓰인다.

가산명사 자랑꾼 [비격식체, 탐탁잖음] ❑ 각종 턴과 묘기들을 한껏 뽐낼 수 있도록 꼭 사람이 많은 지역에서 제트스키를 즐기는 스키어가 많다.

가산명사 대표작 ❑ 그 공장은 서양이 동양에 투자해 만든 대표작이 될 것이었다.

가산명사 전시실, 진열실 ❑ 자동차 전시실

shrink의 과거

shrap|nel /ˈʃræpnᵊl/ N-UNCOUNT Shrapnel consists of small pieces of metal which are scattered from exploding bombs and shells. ☐ *He was hit by shrapnel from a grenade.*

불가산명사 폭탄 파편 ☐ 그가 수류탄 파편에 맞았다.

shred /ʃrɛd/ (shreds, shredding, shredded) **1** V-T If you shred something such as food or paper, you cut it or tear it into very small, narrow pieces. ☐ *They may be shredding documents.* **2** N-COUNT If you cut or tear food or paper into shreds, you cut or tear it into small, narrow pieces. ☐ *Cut the cabbage into fine long shreds.* **3** N-COUNT If there is not a shred of something, there is not even a small amount of it. ☐ *He said there was not a shred of evidence to support such remarks.* ☐ *There is not a shred of truth in the story.*

1 타동사 갈가리 찢다; 채를 썰다 ☐ 그들이 서류를 갈가리 찢고 있을지도 모른다. **2** 가산명사 갈가리 찢은 조각; 채 ☐ 양배추는 가늘게 채를 써세요. **3** 가산명사 아주 조금 ☐ 그와 같은 발언을 뒷받침할 만한 증거는 조금도 없다고 그가 말했다. ☐ 그 이야기에 진실이라곤 조금도 없다.

shrewd /ʃruːd/ (shrewder, shrewdest) ADJ A shrewd person is able to understand and judge a situation quickly and to use this understanding to their own advantage. ☐ *She's a shrewd businesswoman.*

형용사 영리한, 능수능란한 ☐ 그녀는 영리한 사업가이다.

shriek /ʃriːk/ (shrieks, shrieking, shrieked) V-I When someone shrieks, they make a short, very loud cry, for example because they are suddenly surprised, are in pain, or are laughing. ☐ *She shrieked and leapt from the bed.* ● N-COUNT Shriek is also a noun. ☐ *Sue let out a terrific shriek and leapt out of the way.*

자동사 비명을 지르다, 날카로운 소리를 내다 ☐ 그녀는 비명을 지르며 침대에서 벌떡 일어났다. ● 가산명사 비명, 날카로운 소리 ☐ 수가 날카로운 비명을 지르며 재빨리 길에서 벗어났다.

shrill /ʃrɪl/ (shriller, shrillest) ADJ A shrill sound is high-pitched and unpleasant. ☐ *Shrill cries and startled oaths flew up around us as pandemonium broke out.* ☐ *...the shrill whistle of the engine.*

형용사 날카로운, 새된 ☐ 대혼란이 빚어지면서 날카로운 비명 소리와 깜짝 놀라 내뱉는 거친 말들이 터져 나왔다. ☐ 날카로운 엔진 소리

shrimp /ʃrɪmp/

> The plural can be either **shrimp** or **shrimps**.

> 복수는 shrimp 또는 shrimps이다.

N-COUNT Shrimps are small shellfish with long tails and many legs. ☐ *Add the shrimp and cook for 30 seconds.*

가산명사 새우 ☐ 새우를 넣고 30초간 요리한다.

shrimp cock|tail (shrimp cocktails) N-VAR A shrimp cocktail is a dish that consists of shrimp, salad, and a sauce. It is usually eaten at the beginning of a meal. [mainly AM; BRIT **prawn cocktail**]

가산명사 또는 불가산명사 새우 칵테일 [주로 미국영어; 영국영어 prawn cocktail]

shrine /ʃraɪn/ (shrines) **1** N-COUNT A shrine is a place of worship which is associated with a particular holy person or object. ☐ *...the holy shrine of Mecca.* **2** N-COUNT A shrine is a place that people visit and treat with respect because it is connected with a dead person or with dead people that they want to remember. ☐ *The monument has been turned into a shrine to the dead and the missing.*

1 가산명사 성지 ☐ 신성한 성지 메카 **2** 가산명사 추모지, 제단 ☐ 그 기념비는 사망자와 실종자를 위한 제단이 되었다.

shrink /ʃrɪŋk/ (shrinks, shrinking, shrank, shrunk) **1** V-I If cloth or clothing shrinks, it becomes smaller in size, usually as a result of being washed. ☐ *People were short in those days – or else those military uniforms all shrank in the wash!* **2** V-T/V-I If something shrinks or something else shrinks it, it becomes smaller. ☐ *The vast forests of West Africa have shrunk.* **3** V-I If you shrink away from someone or something, you move away from them because you are frightened, shocked, or disgusted by them. ☐ *One child shrinks away from me when I try to talk to him.* **4** V-I If you do not shrink from a task or duty, you do it even though it is unpleasant or dangerous. [usu with neg] ☐ *We must not shrink from the legitimate use of force if we are to remain credible.* **5** N-COUNT A shrink is a psychiatrist. [INFORMAL] ☐ *I've seen a shrink already.* **6** no shrinking violet →see violet

1 자동사 줄어들다 ☐ 그 시절엔 사람들 키가 작았잖아. 그게 아니면 그 군복이 전부 세탁 과정에서 줄어들었거나. **2** 타동사/자동사 줄어들다; 줄이다 ☐ 서아프리카의 방대한 숲이 줄어들었다. **3** 자동사 피하다, 움츠리다 ☐ 한 아이가 내가 말을 걸려 할 때마다 나를 피한다. **4** 자동사 피하다 ☐ 우리가 신뢰를 받으려면 정당한 무력 사용을 피하지 말아야 한다. **5** 가산명사 정신과 의사 [비격식체] ☐ 나는 벌써 정신과 진료를 받았다.

shriv|el /ˈʃrɪvᵊl/ (shrivels, shriveling, shriveled) [BRIT, sometimes AM **shrivelling, shrivelled**] V-T/V-I When something shrivels or when something shrivels it, it becomes dryer and smaller, often with lines in its surface, as a result of losing the water it contains. ☐ *The plant shrivels and dies.* ● PHRASAL VERB Shrivel up means the same as shrivel. ☐ *The leaves started to shrivel up.* ● shriv|eled ADJ ☐ *...a shriveled chestnut.*

[영국영어, 미국영어 가끔 shrivelling, shrivelled] 타동사/자동사 쪼글쪼글해지다, 오그라들다 ☐ 초목이 쪼글쪼글해져서 죽는다. ● 구동사 쪼글쪼글해지다, 오그라들다 ☐ 나뭇잎이 오그라들기 시작했다. ● 쪼글쪼글해진, 오그라든 형용사 ☐ 쪼글쪼글해진 밤

shroud /ʃraʊd/ (shrouds, shrouding, shrouded) **1** N-COUNT A shroud is a cloth which is used for wrapping a dead body. ☐ *...the burial shroud.* **2** V-T If something has been shrouded in mystery or secrecy, very little information about it has been made available. ☐ *For years the teaching of acting has been shrouded in mystery.* **3** V-T If darkness, fog, or smoke shrouds an area, it covers it so that it is difficult to see. ☐ *Mist shrouded the outline of Buckingham Palace.*

1 가산명사 수의 ☐ 수의 **2** 타동사 싸여 있다, 가려져 있다 ☐ 연기술 가르치는 일은 오랜 동안 미스터리에 싸여 있었다. **3** 타동사 뒤덮다 ☐ 버킹검 궁전의 윤곽이 안개로 뒤덮여 있었다.

shrub /ʃrʌb/ (shrubs) N-COUNT Shrubs are plants that have several woody stems. ☐ *...flowering shrubs.*

가산명사 관목 ☐ 꽃이 피는 관목

shrug /ʃrʌg/ (shrugs, shrugging, shrugged) V-T/V-I If you shrug, you raise your shoulders to show that you are not interested in something or that you do not know or care about something. ☐ *I shrugged, as if to say, "Why not?"* ● N-COUNT Shrug is also a noun. ☐ *"I suppose so," said Anna with a shrug.*

타동사/자동사 어깨를 으쓱하다 ☐ 나는 "안 될 거 없지."하고 말하는 양, 어깨를 으쓱했다. ● 가산명사 어깨를 으쓱하기 ☐ "그런 것 같아."라고 안나가 어깨를 으쓱 하며 말했다.

▶ **shrug off** PHRASAL VERB If you shrug something off, you ignore it or treat it as if it is not really important or serious. ☐ *He shrugged off the criticism.*

구동사 떨쳐 버리다, 무시하다 ☐ 그는 그런 비판 따위는 무시했다.

shrunk /ʃrʌŋk/ Shrunk is the past participle of shrink.

shrink의 과거 분사

shud|der /ˈʃʌdər/ (shudders, shuddering, shuddered) **1** V-I If you shudder, you shake with fear, horror, or disgust, or because you are cold. ☐ *Lloyd had urged her to eat caviar. She had shuddered at the thought.* ● N-COUNT Shudder is also a noun. [usu sing] ☐ *She gave a violent shudder.* **2** V-I If something such as a machine or vehicle shudders, it shakes suddenly and violently. ☐ *The train began to pull out of the station – then suddenly shuddered to a halt.* **3** N-COUNT If something sends shudders or a shudder through a group of people, it makes them worried or afraid. ☐ *The next crisis sent a shudder of fear through the UN community.*

1 자동사 몸서리치다, 전율하다 ☐ 로이드가 그녀에게 캐비아를 먹으라고 강력히 권했다. 그녀는 생각만 해도 몸서리가 쳐졌었다. ● 가산명사 몸서리, 전율 ☐ 그녀가 부들부들 떨었다. **2** 자동사 마구 흔들리다 ☐ 기차가 역을 빠져나가기 시작하더니 갑자기 마구 흔들리면서 멈춰 섰다. **3** 가산명사 전율 ☐ 그 다음 위기가 유엔 공동체를 공포의 전율에 빠뜨렸다.

shuf|fle /ˈʃʌfᵊl/ (shuffles, shuffling, shuffled) **1** V-I If you shuffle somewhere, you walk there without lifting your feet properly off the ground. ☐ *Moira shuffled across the kitchen.* ● N-SING Shuffle is also a noun. ☐ *She noticed her own proud walk had become a shuffle.* **2** V-I If you shuffle around, you move your feet about while standing or you move your bottom about while sitting, often because you feel uncomfortable or embarrassed. ☐ *He shuffles around in his chair.* **3** V-T If you shuffle playing cards, you mix them up before you begin a game. ☐ *There are various ways of shuffling and dealing the cards.*

1 자동사 발을 질질 끌며 걷다 ☐ 모이라가 발을 질질 끌며 부엌을 가로질러 갔다. ● 단수명사 발을 질질 끌며 걷기 ☐ 그녀는 더 이상 당당한 걸음이 아니라 축 쳐져서 걷는 자신을 발견했다. **2** 자동사 안절부절 못하다, 시설시리다 ☐ 그는 의자에 앉아 안절부절 못했다. **3** 타동사 카드를 섞다 ☐ 카드를 섞어 패를 돌리는 방법은 여러 가지가 있다.

a b c d e f g h i j k l m n o p q r s t u v w x y z

A

shun /ʃʌn/ (shuns, shunning, shunned) V-T If you **shun** someone or something, you deliberately avoid them or keep away from them. □ *From that time forward everybody shunned him.*

타동사 피하다, 멀리하다 □ 그때부터 쭉 모든 사람들이 그를 멀리했다.

B

shunt /ʃʌnt/ (shunts, shunting, shunted) V-T If a person or thing **is shunted** somewhere, they are moved or sent there, usually because someone finds them inconvenient. [DISAPPROVAL] [usu passive] □ *He has spent most of his life being shunted between his mother, father and various foster families.*

타동사 보내지다 [탐탁찮음] □ 그는 인생 대부분을 엄마와 아빠 그리고 여러 수양부모 사이를 전전하며 살았다.

C

shut ◆◇◇ /ʃʌt/ (shuts, shutting)

> The form **shut** is used in the present tense and is the past tense and past participle.

shut은 동사의 현재, 과거, 과거 분사로 쓰인다.

D

1 V-T/V-I If you **shut** something such as a door or if it **shuts**, it moves so that it fills a hole or a space. □ *Just make sure you shut the gate after you.* ● ADJ **Shut** is also an adjective. [v-link ADJ] □ *They have warned residents to stay inside and keep their doors and windows shut.* **2** V-T If you **shut** your eyes, you lower your eyelids so that you cannot see anything. □ *Lucy shut her eyes so she wouldn't see it happen.*

E

● ADJ **Shut** is also an adjective. [v-link ADJ] □ *His eyes were shut and he seemed to have fallen asleep.* **3** V-T/V-I If your mouth **shuts** or if you **shut** your mouth, you place your lips firmly together. □ *Daniel's mouth opened, and then shut again.* ● ADJ **Shut** is also an adjective. [v-link ADJ] □ *She was silent for a moment, lips tight shut, eyes distant.* **4** V-T/V-I When a store, bar, or other public building **shuts** or when someone **shuts** it, it is closed and you cannot use it until it is open again.

F

□ *There is a tendency to shut museums or shops at a moment's notice.* □ *Shops usually shut from noon to 3 p.m., and stay open late.* ● ADJ **Shut** is also an adjective. [v-link ADJ] □ *Make sure you have food to tide you over when the local shop may be shut.* **5** PHRASE If someone tells you to **keep** your **mouth shut** about something, they are telling you not to let anyone else know about it. □ *I don't have to tell you how important it is for you to keep your mouth shut about all this.* **6** PHRASE If you **keep** your **mouth shut**, you do not express your opinions about something, even though you would like to. □ *If she had kept her mouth shut she would still have her job now.*

G

1 타동사/자동사 닫다 □ 나가신 다음에 대문을 꼭 닫아 주세요. ● 형용사 닫힌 □ 그들은 주민들에게 밖에 나가지 말고 문과 창문을 닫아 두라고 경고했다. **2** 타동사 (눈을) 감다 □ 루시는 그 일이 일어나는 광경을 보지 않으려고 눈을 감았다. ● 형용사 감긴 □ 그의 두 눈은 감겨 있고 그는 잠든 것 같아 보였다. **3** 타동사/자동사 (입을) 다물다 □ 대니얼의 입을 벌렸다가 다시 다물었다. ● 형용사 다문 □ 그녀는 잠시 말이 없었다. 입술을 굳게 다물고 먼 곳을 바라보며. **4** 타동사/자동사 닫히다; 닫다 □ 충분한 사전 예고 없이 박물관과 가게 문을 닫는 경향이 있다. □ 가게는 보통 정오 12시부터 오후 3시까지 문을 닫고 그 이후에까지 문을 연다. ● 형용사 닫힌 □ 현지 가게가 문을 닫을 경우를 대비해서 식품을 꼭 가져가세요. **5** 구 입 다물다, 비밀을 지키다 □ 이 모든 사실에 대해 당신이 입 다물고 있는 것이 얼마나 중요한지 내가 말 안 해도 되겠지. **6** 구 입 다물다, 하고 싶은 말을 참다 □ 그녀가 하고 싶은 말만 참았어도 직장을 잃지는 않았을 것이다.

H

I

J

Thesaurus shut의 참조어

V. close, fasten, secure; (ant.) open **1**

K

Word Partnership shut의 연어

V.	force *something* shut, pull *something* shut, push *something* shut, slam *something* shut **1**
ADV.	shut tight **1**-**3**
N.	shut a door, shut a gate, shut a window **1** shut your eyes **2**

L

M

▶**shut down** PHRASAL VERB If a factory or business **shuts down** or if someone **shuts** it **down**, work there stops or it no longer trades as a business. □ *Smaller contractors have been forced to shut down.* □ *It is required by law to shut down banks which it regards as chronically short of capital.* →see also **shutdown**

N

구동사 폐쇄되다, 폐점되다; 폐쇄하다, 문을 닫다 □ 소규모 하청업자들이 문을 닫을 수밖에 없었다. □ 법률상 고질적인 자금난에 시달리는 은행은 문을 닫아야 한다.

▶**shut in** PHRASAL VERB If you **shut** someone or something **in** a room, you close the door so that they cannot leave it. □ *The door enables us to shut the birds in the shelter in bad weather.*

O

구동사 가두다 □ 날씨가 나쁠 때는 그 문을 사용해서 새들을 우리 안에 가둬 둘 수 있다.

P

▶**shut off** **1** PHRASAL VERB If you **shut off** something such as an engine or an electrical item, you turn it off to stop it working. □ *They pulled over and shut off the engine.* **2** PHRASAL VERB If you **shut yourself off**, you avoid seeing other people, usually because you are feeling depressed. □ *Billy tends to keep things to himself more and shut himself off.* **3** PHRASAL VERB If an official organization **shuts off** the supply of something, they no longer send it to the people they supplied in the past. □ *The State Water Project has shut off all supplies to farmers.*

Q

1 구동사 끄다, 잠그다 □ 그들이 차를 세우고 엔진을 껐다. **2** 구동사 혼자 틀어박히다 □ 빌리는 남들에게 이야기를 하지 않고 혼자 틀어박혀 지내는 편이다. **3** 구동사 중단하다, 차단하다 □ 주 수자원공사가 농장에 수도 공급을 전면 차단했다.

R

▶**shut out** **1** PHRASAL VERB If you **shut** something or someone **out**, you prevent them from getting into a place, for example by closing the doors. □ *"I shut him out of the bedroom," says Maureen.* **2** PHRASAL VERB If you **shut out** a thought or a feeling, you prevent yourself from thinking or feeling it. □ *I shut out the memory which was too painful to dwell on.* **3** PHRASAL VERB If you **shut** someone **out** of something, you prevent them from having anything to do with it. □ *She is very reclusive, to the point of shutting me out of her life.*

S

1 구동사 막다, 들어가지 못하게 하다 □ "나는 그가 침실에 들어오지 못하게 한다."라고 모린이 말한다. **2** 구동사 (생각 등을) 막다 □ 나는 생각만 해도 너무나 아픈 그 기억을 떠올리지 않으려 했다. **3** 구동사 배제하다, 제외하다 □ 그녀는 내가 자기 삶에 끼어들지 못하게 할 정도로 세상을 등지고 산다.

T

▶**shut up** PHRASAL VERB If someone **shuts up** or if someone **shuts** them **up**, they stop talking. You can say **"shut up"** as an impolite way to tell a person to stop talking. □ *Just shut up, will you?*

U

구동사 입 다물다; 입 다물게 하다; 입 닥쳐 □ 입 좀 다물어, 알았어?

shut|down /ʃʌtdaʊn/ (shutdowns) N-COUNT A **shutdown** is the closing of a factory, store, or other business, either for a short time or forever. □ *The shutdown is the latest in a series of painful budget measures.*

V

가산명사 폐쇄, 폐업, 휴업 □ 공장 폐쇄는 뼈를 깎는 일련의 예산정책 중 가장 최근에 나온 조치이다.

shut|ter /ʃʌtər/ (shutters) **1** N-COUNT The **shutter** in a camera is the part which opens to allow light through the lens when a photograph is taken. □ *There are a few things you should check before pressing the shutter release.* **2** N-COUNT **Shutters** are wooden or metal covers fitted on the outside of a window. They can be opened to let in the light, or closed to keep out the sun or the cold. □ *She opened the shutters and gazed out over village roofs.* →see **photography**

W

1 가산명사 (카메라) 셔터 □ 셔터를 누르기 전에 확인해 봐야 할 사항이 몇 가지 있다. **2** 가산명사 덧창, 겉창 □ 그녀는 겉창을 열고 마을 지붕들을 내다보았다.

X

shut|tle /ʃʌtl/ (shuttles, shuttling, shuttled) **1** N-COUNT A **shuttle** is the same as a **space shuttle**. **2** N-COUNT A **shuttle** is a plane, bus, or train which makes frequent journeys between two places. □ *...shuttle flights between London and Manchester.* **3** V-T/V-I If someone or something **shuttles** or **is shuttled** from one place to another place, they frequently go from one place to the other. □ *He and colleagues have shuttled back and forth between the three capitals.*

Y

1 가산명사 우주 왕복선 **2** 가산명사 두 지역을 정기적으로 왕복하는 비행기나 버스, 기차 □ 런던과 맨체스터 구간 왕복 비행기 **3** 타동사/자동사 왕복하다; 왕복 운행되다 □ 그와 동료들은 지금까지 그 수도들 세 곳을 오가며 다녔다.

Z

shy /ʃaɪ/ (**shyer, shyest, shies, shying, shied**) **1** ADJ A **shy** person is nervous and uncomfortable in the company of other people. ❑ *She was a shy, quiet-spoken girl.* ❑ *She was a shy and retiring person off-stage.* ● **shy**|**ly** ADV ❑ *The children smiled shyly.* ● **shy**|**ness** N-UNCOUNT ❑ *Eventually he overcame his shyness.* **2** ADJ If you are **shy about** or **shy of** doing something, you are unwilling to do it because you are afraid of what might happen. ❑ *They feel shy about showing their feelings.*

Thesaurus	*shy*의 참조어
ADJ.	nervous, quiet, uncomfortable; (*ant.*) confident **1**

▶**shy away from** PHRASAL VERB If you **shy away from** doing something, you avoid doing it, often because you are afraid or not confident enough. ❑ *We frequently shy away from making decisions.*

sib|**ling** /sɪblɪŋ/ (**siblings**) N-COUNT Your **siblings** are your brothers and sisters. [FORMAL] ❑ *His siblings are mostly in their early twenties.*

> Note that there is no common English word that can refer to both a brother and a sister. You simply have to use both words. The word **sibling** exists, but it is very formal. Some Americans use **sib** as an informal substitute for **sibling**. ❑ *All my sibs were home for Thanksgiving.*

sic You write **sic** in brackets after a word or expression when you want to indicate to the reader that although the word looks odd or wrong, you intended to write it like that or the original writer wrote it like that. ❑ *How many more day (sic) till the end of term?*

sick ◆◇◇ /sɪk/ (**sicker, sickest**) **1** ADJ If you are **sick**, you are ill. **Sick** usually means physically ill, but it can sometimes be used to mean mentally ill. ❑ *He's very sick. He needs medication.* ❑ *She found herself with two small children, a sick husband, and no money.* ● N-PLURAL **The sick** are people who are sick. ❑ *There were no doctors to treat the sick.* **2** ADJ If you are **sick**, the food that you have eaten comes up from your stomach and out of your mouth. If you **feel sick**, you feel as if you are going to be sick. [v-link ADJ] ❑ *She got up and was sick in the handbasin.* ❑ *The very thought of food made him feel sick.* **3** N-UNCOUNT **Sick** is vomit. [BRIT, INFORMAL] ❑ *The floor was covered in sick and that made it slippery.* **4** ADJ If you say that you are **sick of** something or **sick and tired of** it, you are emphasizing that you are very annoyed by it and want it to stop. [INFORMAL, EMPHASIS] [v-link ADJ of n/-ing] ❑ *I am sick and tired of hearing all these people moaning.* **5** ADJ If you describe something such as a joke or story as **sick**, you mean that it deals with death or suffering in an unpleasantly humorous way. [DISAPPROVAL] ❑ *...a sick joke about a cat.*

6 PHRASE If you say that something or someone **makes** you **sick**, you mean that they make you feel angry or disgusted. [INFORMAL] ❑ *It makes me sick that this wasn't disclosed.* **7** PHRASE If you are **off sick**, you are not at work because you are ill. ❑ *When we are off sick, we only receive half pay.* **8** PHRASE If you say that you are **worried sick**, you are emphasizing that you are extremely worried. [INFORMAL, EMPHASIS] ❑ *He was worried sick about what our mothers would say.*

> The words **ill** and **sick** are very similar in meaning, but are used in slightly different ways. **Ill** is generally not used before a noun, and can be used in verbal expressions such as **fall ill** and **be taken ill**. ❑ *He fell ill shortly before Christmas... One of the jury members was taken ill.* **Sick** is often used before a noun. ❑ *...sick children.* In British English, **ill** is a slightly more polite, less direct word than **sick**. **Sick** often suggests the actual physical feeling of being ill, for example nausea or vomiting. ❑ *I spent the next 24 hours in bed, groaning and being sick.* In American English, **sick** is often used where British people would say **ill**. ❑ *Some people get hurt in accidents or get sick.*

Word Partnership	*sick*의 연어
N.	sick **children**, sick **mother**, sick **patients**, sick **people**, sick **person** **1**
ADV.	really sick, very sick **1**
V.	care for the sick **1**
	become sick, feel sick, get sick **1** **2**
ADJ.	worried sick **8**

sick|**en** /sɪkən/ (**sickens, sickening, sickened**) V-T If something **sickens** you, it makes you feel disgusted. ❑ *The notion that art should be controlled by intellectuals sickened him.*

sick|**en**|**ing** /sɪkənɪŋ/ ADJ You describe something as **sickening** when it gives you feelings of horror or disgust, or makes you feel sick in your stomach. ❑ *...the sickening rise in the number of suicide bombings.*

sick leave N-UNCOUNT **Sick leave** is the time that a person spends away from work because of illness or injury. [BUSINESS] ❑ *I have been on sick leave for seven months with depression.*

sick|**ly** /sɪkli/ (**sicklier, sickliest**) **1** ADJ A **sickly** person or animal is weak, unhealthy, and often ill. ❑ *He had been a sickly child.* **2** ADJ A **sickly** smell or taste is unpleasant and makes you feel slightly sick, often because it is extremely sweet. ❑ *...the sickly smell of rum.*

1 형용사 수줍은, 부끄럼 타는 ❑ 그녀는 숫기 없이 말을 조용히 하는 소녀였다. ❑ 그녀는 무대 밖에선 수줍고 비사교적이었다. ● 수줍게, 부끄러워하며 부사 ❑ 아이들이 수줍게 미소 지었다. ● 수줍음, 부끄러움 불가산명사 ❑ 결국 그는 수줍은 성격을 극복했다. **2** 형용사 꺼리는 ❑ 그들은 자신의 감정 표현을 꺼린다.

구동사 _을 피하다, _을 꺼리다 ❑ 우리는 종종 결정 내리기를 피한다.

가산명사 동기(同氣), 형제자매 [격식체] ❑ 그의 동기(同氣)들은 대부분 20대 초반이다.

> 영어에는 남자형제와 여자형제를 함께 지칭하는 말이 없음을 유념하시오. 두 단어를 모두 써야 한다. ❑ 그녀는 남녀 형제가 13명이 있다. sibling이라는 말이 있지만 아주 격식체이다. 일부 미국인들은 sibling을 대신하는 구어체로 sib을 쓴다. ❑ 내 형제들이 모두 추수감사절에 집에 와 있었다.

원문 그대로임 (부정확한 표현이 원문 대로임) ❑ 학기가 끝나려면 며칠이나(원문 그대로임) 남았지?

1 형용사 아픈, 병든 ❑ 그가 너무 아파요. 약물 치료를 해야겠어요. ❑ 그녀는 어린아이들에 병든 남편에 땡전 한 푼 없는 처지가 되었다. ● 복수명사 아픈 사람들, 병든 사람들 ❑ 아픈 사람들을 치료해 줄 의사가 한 명도 없었다. **2** 형용사 구토하는 ❑ 그녀는 일어나 세면기에 대고 토했다. ❑ 그는 음식 생각만 해도 토할 것 같았다. **3** 불가산명사 토사물 [영국영어, 비격식체] ❑ 바닥이 토사물로 덮여 미끄러웠다. **4** 형용사 지긋지긋한, 질리는 [비격식체, 강조] ❑ 나는 이 사람들의 신음 소리를 듣는 것도 이제 지긋지긋하다. **5** 형용사 역겨운, 기분 나쁜 [탐탁찮음] ❑ 고양이에 관한 역겨운 농담

6 구 불쾌하게 하다 [비격식체] ❑ 나는 이것이 공개되지 않아서 불쾌하다. **7** 구 아파서 결근한 ❑ 우리는 아파서 결근하면 급여의 반밖에 받지 못한다. **8** 구 노심초사하는 [비격식체, 강조] ❑ 그는 우리 어머니들이 뭐라고 말할지 노심초사했다.

> ill과 sick은 그 의미에 있어 아주 비슷하지만 조금 다르게 쓰인다. ill은 보통 명사 앞에는 쓰이지 않고 fall ill과 be taken ill과 같은 숙어로 쓸 수 있다. ❑ 그는 성탄절 직전에 병이 났다...배심원 한명이 병이 났다. sick은 흔히 명사 앞에 쓰인다. ❑ ...아픈 아이들. 영국영어에서, ill은 sick보다 약간 더 공손하고, 완곡한 말이다. sick은 흔히 병의 실제 신체적 느낌, 예를 들면, 메스꺼림이나 구토 같은 것을 의미한다. ❑ 나는 이후 24시간을 신음하고 토하며 앓아 누워있었다. 영국사람들이 ill을 쓰는 곳에 미국영어에서는 흔히 sick을 사용한다. ❑ 어떤 사람들은 사고로 다치거나 병이 든다.

타동사 억겁게 하다 ❑ 그는 예술이 지식인의 통제를 받아야 한다는 생각에 역겨움을 느꼈다.

형용사 구역질 나는, 소름끼치는 ❑ 자살 폭파범 수의 소름끼칠 정도의 증가

불가산명사 병가 [경제] ❑ 나는 우울증으로 7개월 동안 병가 중이다.

1 형용사 병약한 ❑ 그는 병약한 아이였다. **2** 형용사 메스꺼운 ❑ 럼주에서 나는 메스꺼운 냄새

a
b
c
d
e
f
g
h
i
j
k
l
m
n
o
p
q
r
s
t
u
v
w
x
y
z

A

sick|ness /sɪknɪs/ (**sicknesses**) **1** N-UNCOUNT **Sickness** is the state of being ill or unhealthy. ❑ *In fifty-two years of working he had one week of sickness.* **2** N-UNCOUNT **Sickness** is the uncomfortable feeling that you are going to vomit. ❑ *After a while, the sickness gradually passed and she struggled to the mirror.* **3** N-VAR A **sickness** is a particular illness. ❑ *More than 930 local people are registered as suffering from radiation sickness.*

B

sick pay N-UNCOUNT When you are ill and unable to work, **sick pay** is the money that you get from your employer instead of your normal wages. [BUSINESS] ❑ *...if they are not eligible for sick pay.*

C

side ♦♦♦ /saɪd/ (**sides, siding, sided**) **1** N-COUNT The **side of** something is a position to the left or right of it, rather than in front of it, behind it, or on it. ❑ *On one side of the main entrance there's a red plaque.* ❑ *...a photograph with Joe and Ken on each side of me.* ❑ *...the nations on either side of the Pacific.* **2** N-COUNT The **side** of an object, building, or vehicle is any of its flat surfaces which is not considered to be its front, its back, its top, or its bottom. ❑ *We put a notice on the side of the box.* ❑ *A carton of milk lay on its side.* **3** N-COUNT The **sides** of a hollow or a container are its inside vertical surfaces. ❑ *The rough rock walls were like the sides of a deep canal.* ❑ *Line the base of the dish with greaseproof paper and lightly grease the sides.* **4** N-COUNT The **sides** of an area or surface are its edges. ❑ *Park on the side of the road.* ❑ *...a small beach on the north side of the peninsula.* **5** N-COUNT The two **sides of** an area, surface, or object are its two halves. ❑ *She turned over on her stomach on the other side of the bed.* ❑ *The major centre for language is in the left side of the brain.* **6** N-COUNT The two **sides** of a road are its two halves on which traffic travels in opposite directions. ❑ *It had gone on to the wrong side of the road and hit a car coming in the other direction.* **7** N-COUNT If you talk about the other **side** of a town or of the world, you mean a part of the town or of the world that is very far from where you are. ❑ *He lives the other side of London.* ❑ *He saw the ship that was to transport them to the other side of the world.* **8** N-COUNT Your **sides** are the parts of your body between your front and your back, from under your arms to your hips. ❑ *His arms were limp at his sides.* **9** N-COUNT If someone is **by** your **side** or **at** your **side**, they stay near you and give you comfort or support. ❑ *He was constantly at his wife's side.* ❑ *He calls me 20 times a day and needs me by his side in the evening.* **10** N-COUNT The two **sides** of something flat, for example a piece of paper, are its two flat surfaces. You can also refer to one **side** of a piece of paper filled with writing as one **side** of writing. ❑ *The new copiers only copy onto one side of the paper.* ❑ *Fry the chops until brown on both sides.* **11** N-COUNT One **side** of a tape or record is what you can hear or record if you play the tape or record from beginning to end without turning it over. ❑ *We want to hear side A.* **12** ADJ **Side** is used to describe things that are not the main or most important ones of their kind. [ADJ n] ❑ *She slipped in and out of the theater by a side door.* **13** N-COUNT The different **sides** in a war, argument, or negotiation are the groups of people who are opposing each other. ❑ *Both sides appealed for a new ceasefire.* ❑ *Any solution must be acceptable to all sides.* **14** N-COUNT The different **sides** of an argument or deal are the different points of view or positions involved in it. ❑ *His words drew sharp reactions from people on both sides of the issue.* **15** V-I If one person or country **sides with** another, they support them in an argument or a war. If people or countries **side against** another person or country, they support each other against them. ❑ *There has been much speculation that America might be siding with the rebels.* **16** N-COUNT In sports, a **side** is a team. [mainly BRIT; AM usually **team**] ❑ *Italy were definitely a better side than Germany.* **17** N-COUNT A particular **side** of something such as a situation or someone's character is one aspect of it. ❑ *He is in charge of the civilian side of the UN mission.* **18** N-COUNT The **mother's side** and the **father's side** of your family are your mother's relatives and your father's relatives. ❑ *So was your father's side more well off?* **19** PHRASE If two people or things are **side by side**, they are next to each other. ❑ *We sat side by side on two wicker seats.* **20** PHRASE If people work or live **side by side**, they work or live closely together in a friendly way. ❑ *...areas where different nationalities have lived side by side for centuries.* **21** PHRASE If something moves **from side to side**, it moves repeatedly to the left and to the right. ❑ *She was shaking her head from side to side.* **22** PHRASE If you are **on** someone's **side**, you are supporting them in an argument or a war. ❑ *He has the Democrats on his side.* **23** PHRASE If something is **on your side** or if you have it **on your side**, it helps you when you are trying to achieve something. ❑ *The weather is rather on our side.* **24** PHRASE If you say that something is **on the** small **side**, you are saying politely that you think it is slightly too small. If you say that someone is **on the young side**, you are saying politely that you think they are slightly too young. [POLITENESS] ❑ *He's quiet and on the shy side.* **25** PHRASE If someone does something **on the side**, they do it in addition to their main work. ❑ *...ways of making a little bit of money on the side.* **26** PHRASE If you **put** something **to one side** or **put** it **on one side**, you temporarily ignore it in order to concentrate on something else. ❑ *In order to maintain profit margins health and safety regulations are often put to one side.* **27** PHRASE If you **take** someone **to one side** or **draw** them **to one side**, you speak to them privately, usually in order to give them advice or a warning. ❑ *He took Sabrina to one side and told her about the safe.* **28** PHRASE If you **take sides** or **take** someone's **side** in an argument or war, you support one of the sides against the other. ❑ *We cannot take sides in a civil war.* **29** **the other side of the coin** →see **coin**. **to err on the side of** something →see **err**. **to be on the safe side** →see **safe**. someone's **side of the story** →see **story**

side-effect (**side-effects**) also **side effect 1** N-COUNT The **side-effects** of a drug are the effects, usually bad ones, that the drug has on you in addition to its function of curing illness or pain. ❑ *The treatment has a whole host of extremely unpleasant side-effects including weight gain, acne, skin rashes, and headaches.* **2** N-COUNT A **side-effect of** a situation is something unplanned and usually unpleasant that happens in addition to the main effects of that situation. ❑ *One side-effect of modern life is stress.*

1 불가산명사 아픈 상태 ❑ 52년간 일하면서 그가 아팠던 날은 총 일주일이었다. **2** 불가산명사 메스꺼움 ❑ 시간이 지나면서 메스꺼움이 조금씩 사라지자 그녀는 힘겹게 거울로 다가갔다. **3** 가산명사 또는 불가산명사 질병 ❑ 주민 930명 이상이 방사능 관련 질병에 걸린 것으로 등록되어 있다.

불가산명사 질병 수당 [경제] ❑ 질병 수당을 받을 자격이 없는 사람들의 경우

1 가산명사 옆 ❑ 현관 한쪽 옆에 빨간색 명판이 있다. ❑ 내 양쪽 옆에 각각 조와 켄을 두고 찍은 사진 ❑ 태평양 양안에 있는 국가들 **2** 가산명사 옆면, 측면 ❑ 우리는 박스 옆면에 메모를 써 붙였다. ❑ 우유 한 팩이 옆으로 넘어져 있었다. **3** 가산명사 안쪽 면 ❑ 거친 바위벽이 마치 깊은 운하의 안쪽 면과 같았다. ❑ 접시 바닥에 기름이 배지 않는 종이를 깔고 안쪽 측면에는 기름을 살짝 바르세요. **4** 가산명사 가장자리 ❑ 길가에 차를 세우세요. ❑ 반도 북쪽 가장자리에 있는 작은 해변 **5** 가산명사 - 쪽 ❑ 그녀는 침대 다른 한쪽으로 몸을 굴려 엎드렸다. ❑ 언어 기능을 주로 담당하는 부분은 뇌의 왼쪽에 있다. **6** 가산명사 (길의 한) 방향 ❑ 그 차가 길에서 방향을 잘못 들어서서 맞은편에서 오는 차를 받았다. **7** 가산명사 반대편, 반대쪽 ❑ 그는 런던 반대쪽에 산다. ❑ 그는 그들을 지구 반대편으로 실어나를 줄 배를 보았다. **8** 가산명사 옆구리, 옆 ❑ 그는 팔을 옆으로 축 늘어뜨리고 있었다. **9** 가산명사 - 곁에, - 가까이에 ❑ 그는 항상 아내 곁에 있었다. 그는 하루에도 20번 나에게 전화를 하고 저녁이면 내가 곁에 있기를 바란다. **10** 가산명사 면 ❑ 새 복사기는 종이 한쪽 면에만 복사가 된다. ❑ 고깃덩이 양쪽 면이 모두 노릇노릇해질 때까지 기름에 튀기세요. **11** 가산명사 (카세트테이프 등의) 면 ❑ 우리는 A면을 듣고 싶어요. **12** 형용사 부차적인 ❑ 그는 쪽문을 통해 극장을 몰래 드나들었다. **13** 가산명사 편, 측 ❑ 양측 모두 휴전 재개를 촉구했다. ❑ 어떤 해결책이든 모든 당사자가 수용할 수 있는 것이어야 한다. **14** 가산명사 관점 ❑ 그의 발언이 문제의 찬반 양측으로부터 날카로운 반응을 불러일으켰다. **15** 자동사 편들다 ❑ 그간 미국이 반군을 편을 들고 있을 듯이도 모른다는 추측이 난무했다. **16** 가산명사 팀 [주로 영국영어; 미국영어 대개 team] ❑ 이탈리아가 분명 독일보다 나은 팀이었다. **17** 가산명사 측면 ❑ 그는 유엔 임무의 민간 부문을 맡고 있다. **18** 가산명사 외가; 친가 ❑ 그래서 친가가 더 잘 살았니? **19** 구 나란히 ❑ 우리는 고리버들 의자 두 개를 놓고 나란히 앉았다. **20** 구 사이좋게 ❑ 서로 다른 민족의 사람들이 수세기 동안 사이좋게 살아온 지역 **21** 구 좌우로 ❑ 그녀가 머리를 좌우로 흔들고 있었다. **22** 구 -편을 지지하여, -의 편인 ❑ 그는 민주당원들의 지지를 얻고 있다. **23** 구 -에게 유리한 ❑ 날씨가 우리에게 다소 유리하다. **24** 구 -한 편인 [공손체] ❑ 그는 조용하고 조금 수줍어하는 편이다. **25** 구 부업으로 ❑ 부업으로 돈을 조금 버는 방법 **26** 구 잠시 제쳐 두다 ❑ 수익 마진을 유지하기 위해서 건강 및 안전 규정을 잠시 제쳐 두는 경우가 흔히 있다. **27** 구 따로 불러서 이야기하다 ❑ 그는 사브리나를 따로 불러서 금고에 관한 이야기를 했다. **28** 구 한 쪽 편을 들다 ❑ 우리는 내전이 일어날 경우 한쪽 편만 들 수 없다.

1 가산명사 부작용 ❑ 치료에는 체중증가, 여드름, 발진, 두통 등 각종 극심한 부작용이 따른다. **2** 가산명사 부작용 ❑ 현대 생활의 부작용 중 하나가 스트레스이다.

D
E
F
G
H
I
J
K
L
M
N
O
P
Q
R
S
T
U
V
W
X
Y
Z

side|line /saɪdlaɪn/ (**sidelines, sidelining, sidelined**) **1** N-COUNT A **sideline** is something that you do in addition to your main job in order to earn extra money. ❑ *It was quite a lucrative sideline.* **2** N-PLURAL The **sidelines** are the lines marking the long sides of the playing area, for example on a football field or tennis court. **3** N-PLURAL If you are **on the sidelines** in a situation, you do not influence events at all, either because you have chosen not to be involved, or because other people have not involved you. ❑ *France no longer wants to be left on the sidelines when critical decisions are taken.* **4** V-T If someone or something **is sidelined,** they are made to seem unimportant and not included in what people are doing. [usu passive] ❑ *For months he had been under pressure to resign and was about to be sidelined anyway.* →see **basketball, football, soccer, tennis**

side road (**side roads**) N-COUNT A **side road** is a road which leads off a busier, more important road.

side|step /saɪdstɛp/ (**sidesteps, sidestepping, sidestepped**) also **side-step** V-T If you **sidestep** a problem, you avoid discussing it or dealing with it. ❑ *Rarely, if ever, does he sidestep a question.*

side street (**side streets**) N-COUNT A **side street** is a quiet, often narrow street which leads off a busier street.

side|walk /saɪdwɔk/ (**sidewalks**) N-COUNT A **sidewalk** is a path with a hard surface by the side of a road. [AM; BRIT **pavement**] ❑ *Two men and a woman were walking briskly down the sidewalk toward him.*

side|ways /saɪdweɪz/ **1** ADV **Sideways** means from or toward the side of something or someone. [ADV after v] ❑ *Piercey glanced sideways at her.* ❑ *The ladder blew sideways.* ● ADJ **Sideways** is also an adjective. [ADJ n] ❑ *Alfred shot him a sideways glance.* **2** ADV If you are moved **sideways** at work, you move to another job at the same level as your old job. [ADV after v] ❑ *He would be moved sideways, rather than demoted.* ● ADJ **Sideways** is also an adjective. [ADJ n] ❑ *...her recent sideways move.*

siege /sidʒ/ (**sieges**) **1** N-COUNT A **siege** is a military or police operation in which soldiers or police surround a place in order to force the people there to come out or give up control of the place. [also under n] ❑ *We must do everything possible to lift the siege.* **2** PHRASE If police, soldiers, or journalists **lay siege to** a place, they surround it in order to force the people there to come out or give up control of the place. ❑ *The rebels laid siege to the governor's residence.*

<table>
<tr><td colspan="2">**Word Partnership**   *siege*의 연어</td></tr>
<tr><td>PREP.</td><td>**after a** siege, **during a** siege, **under** siege **1**</td></tr>
<tr><td>V.</td><td>**end a** siege, **lift a** siege **1**</td></tr>
</table>

sieve /sɪv/ (**sieves, sieving, sieved**) **1** N-COUNT A **sieve** is a tool used for separating solids from liquids or larger pieces of something from smaller pieces. It consists of a metal or plastic ring with a wire or plastic net underneath, which the liquid or smaller pieces pass through. ❑ *Press the raspberries through a fine sieve to form a puree.* **2** V-T When you **sieve** a substance, you put it through a sieve. ❑ *Cream the margarine in a small bowl, then sieve the icing sugar into it.*

sift /sɪft/ (**sifts, sifting, sifted**) **1** V-T If you **sift** a powder such as flour or sand, you put it through a sieve in order to remove large pieces or lumps. ❑ *Sift the flour and baking powder into a medium-sized mixing bowl.* **2** V-I If you **sift through** something such as evidence, you examine it thoroughly. ❑ *Police officers have continued to sift through the wreckage following yesterday's bomb attack.*

sigh /saɪ/ (**sighs, sighing, sighed**) **1** V-I When you **sigh,** you let out a deep breath, as a way of expressing feelings such as disappointment, tiredness, or pleasure. ❑ *Michael sighed wearily.* ❑ *Roberta sighed with relief.* ● N-COUNT **Sigh** is also a noun. ❑ *She kicked off her shoes with a sigh.* **2** PHRASE If people breathe or heave a **sigh of relief,** they feel happy that something unpleasant has not happened or is no longer happening. ❑ *With monetary mayhem now retreating into memory, European countries can breathe a collective sigh of relief.*

<table>
<tr><td colspan="2">**Word Partnership**   *sigh*의 연어</td></tr>
<tr><td>ADJ.</td><td>**collective** sigh, **deep** sigh, **long** sigh **1**</td></tr>
<tr><td>V.</td><td>**breathe a** sigh, **give a** sigh, **hear a** sigh, **heave a** sigh, **let out a** sigh **1 2**</td></tr>
</table>

sight ♦♦◊ /saɪt/ (**sights, sighting, sighted**) **1** N-UNCOUNT Someone's **sight** is their ability to see. ❑ *My sight is failing, and I can't see to read any more.* **2** N-SING The **sight** of something is the act of seeing it or an occasion on which you see it. ❑ *I faint at the sight of blood.* **3** N-COUNT A **sight** is something that you see. ❑ *The practice of hanging clothes across the street is a common sight in many parts of the city.* **4** V-T If you **sight** someone or something, you suddenly see them, often briefly. ❑ *The security forces sighted a group of young men that had crossed the border.* **5** N-PLURAL The **sights** are the places that are interesting to see and that are often visited by tourists. ❑ *We'd toured the sights of Paris.* **6** →see also **sighting** **7** PHRASE If you **catch sight of** someone, you suddenly see them, often briefly. ❑ *Then he caught sight of her small black velvet hat in the crowd.* **8** PHRASE If you say that something seems to have certain characteristics **at first sight,** you mean that it appears to have the features you describe when you first see it but later it is found to be different. ❑ *It promised to be a more difficult undertaking than might appear at first sight.* **9** PHRASE If something is **in sight** or **within sight,** you can see it. If it is **out of sight,** you cannot see it. ❑ *The sandy beach was in sight.* ❑ *The Atlantic coast is within sight of the hotel.* **10** PHRASE If a result or a decision is **in sight** or **within sight,** it is likely to happen within a short time. ❑ *An agreement*

1 가산명사 부업 ❑ 이는 꽤나 짭짤한 부업이었다. **2** 복수명사 사이드라인 **3** 복수명사 방관자 ❑ 프랑스는 중요한 결정이 내려질 때 더 이상 방관자로 남지 않기를 바란다. **4** 타동사 제외되다 ❑ 몇 달 동안 그는 사임 압력을 받았으며 어쨌든 곧 회사에서 잘릴 운명이었다.

가산명사 샛길, 지선도로

타동사 회피하다 ❑ 그는 좀처럼 질문을 회피하지 않는다.

가산명사 골목, 옆길

가산명사 인도, 보도 [미국영어; 영국영어 pavement] ❑ 남자 둘과 여자 한 명이 인도를 따라 그를 향해 빠르게 걸어오고 있었다.

1 부사 옆으로, 비스듬히 ❑ 피어시가 그녀를 힐끔 곁눈질했다. ❑ 바람에 날려 사다리가 비스듬해졌다. ● 형용사 옆의, 비스듬한 ❑ 알프레드가 그에게 힐끔 곁눈질을 보냈다. **2** 부사 (인사 이동에서) 비슷한 위치로 ❑ 그는 좌천되기보다 비슷한 위치의 다른 자리로 이동될 것이다. ● 형용사 비슷한 위치의 ❑ 그녀가 최근 비슷한 위치로 이동함

1 가산명사 포위 ❑ 우리는 포위를 풀 수 있도록 가능한 모든 수단을 동원해야 한다. **2** 구 포위하다 ❑ 반군이 사령관 관저를 포위했다.

1 가산명사 체 ❑ 산딸기를 고운체에 내려서 퓨레를 만드세요. **2** 타동사 체로 거르다 ❑ 작은 그릇에 마가린을 부드럽게 으깬 다음 가루설탕을 체에 밭쳐 넣으세요.

1 타동사 체로 거르다 ❑ 중간 크기의 혼합용 그릇에 밀가루와 베이킹파우더를 체에 걸러 넣어라. **2** 자동사 철저히 조사하다 ❑ 어제 폭격 공격 후 경찰이 계속해서 잔해를 샅샅이 조사해 왔다.

1 자동사 한숨 쉬다, 탄식하다 ❑ 마이클이 맥없이 한숨을 내쉬었다. ❑ 로베르타가 안도의 한숨을 쉬었다. ● 가산명사 한숨, 탄식 ❑ 그녀는 한숨을 쉬며 신발을 벗어 던졌다. **2** 구 안도의 한숨 ❑ 이제 통화 대란이 기억의 한편으로 사라지면서 유럽 국가들 모두 안도의 한숨을 쉴 수 있게 되었다.

1 불가산명사 시력 ❑ 나는 시력이 나빠지고 있어 아무것도 읽을 수 없다. **2** 단수명사 봄, 보기 ❑ 나는 피를 보기만 해도 기절한다. **3** 가산명사 광경, 풍경 ❑ 도로를 가로질러 옷을 걸어 두는 행위는 그 도시 곳곳에서 흔하게 볼 수 있는 광경이다. **4** 타동사 목격하다, 발견하다 ❑ 보안대가 국경을 건넌 젊은 남자들 무리를 목격했다. **5** 복수명사 관광지, 명소 ❑ 우리는 파리 명소를 돌아본 상태였다. **7** 구 목격하다, 발견하다 ❑ 그러다가 그가 사람들 속에서 그녀의 작고 까만 벨벳 모자를 발견했다. **8** 구 첫눈에, 언뜻 보면 ❑ 처음 봤을 때보다 일이 더 어려울 것 같았다. **9** 구 보이는; 안 보이는 ❑ 모래사장이 눈에 보였다. ❑ 호텔에서 대서양 연안이 보인다. **10** 구 눈앞에 다가온, 임박한 ❑ 통상 정책의 다양한 측면에 대한 합의를 눈앞에 두고 있었다. **11** 구 지나자마자, 간파하다 ❑ 일부 경우들에 있어서 미국 산업이 제품 디자인에서 고객의 요구를 간파해 온 측면이 있다. **12** 구 보자마자 ❑ 군이 수상해 보이는 사람은 모두

on many aspects of trade policy was in sight. ⓫ PHRASE If you **lose sight of** an important aspect of something, you no longer pay attention to it because you are worrying about less important things. ❑ *In some cases, U.S. industry has lost sight of customer needs in designing products.* ⓬ PHRASE If someone is ordered to do something **on sight**, they have to do it without delay, as soon as a person or thing is seen. ❑ *Troops shot anyone suspicious on sight.* ⓭ PHRASE If you **set** your **sights on** something, you decide that you want it and try hard to get it. ❑ *They have set their sights on the world record.*

보는 즉시 쏴 버렸다. ⓭ 구 노리다, 목표로 하다 ❑ 그들은 세계 기록을 노려 왔다.

Word Partnership sight의 연어

ADJ.	**common** sight, **familiar** sight, **welcome** sight ❸
	the end is in sight ❿
V.	**disappear from** sight, **vanish from** sight ❶
	catch sight of *someone/something* ❼
	come into sight, **keep** *someone/something* **in** sight ❾
PREP.	**in plain** sight ❾
	drop out of sight, **lose** sight of *something* ⓫

---

sight|ing /ˈsaɪtɪŋ/ (**sightings**) N-COUNT A **sighting of** something, especially something unusual or unexpected is an occasion on which it is seen. ❑ *...the sighting of a rare sea bird at Lundy island.*

〉 가산명사 목격 ❑ 룬디 섬에서의 바닷새 희귀종 목격

sight|see|ing /ˈsaɪtsiːɪŋ/ also **sight-seeing** N-UNCOUNT If you go **sightseeing** or do some **sightseeing**, you travel around visiting the interesting places that tourists usually visit. ❑ *...a day's sightseeing in Venice.* →see **city**

불가산명사 관광 ❑ 베니스 1일 관광

sign ◆◆◆ /saɪn/ (**signs, signing, signed**) ❶ N-COUNT A **sign** is a mark or shape that always has a particular meaning, for example in mathematics or music. ❑ *Equations are generally written with a two-bar equals sign.* ❷ N-COUNT A **sign** is a movement of your arms, hands, or head which is intended to have a particular meaning. ❑ *They gave Lavalle the thumbs-up sign.* ❸ V-T If you **sign**, you communicate with someone using sign language. If a program or performance **is signed**, someone uses sign language so that deaf people can understand it. ❑ *All programmes will be either "signed" or subtitled.* ❹ N-COUNT A **sign** is a piece of wood, metal, or plastic with words or pictures on it. Signs give you information about something, or give you a warning or an instruction. ❑ *...a sign saying that the highway was closed because of snow.* ❺ N-VAR If there is a **sign of** something, there is something which shows that it exists or is happening. ❑ *They are prepared to hand back a hundred prisoners of war a day as a sign of good will.* ❑ *His face and movements rarely betrayed a sign of nerves.* ❻ V-T When you **sign** a document, you write your name on it, usually at the end or in a special space. You do this to indicate that you have written the document, that you agree with what is written, or that you were present as a witness. ❑ *World leaders are expected to sign a treaty pledging to increase environmental protection.* ❼ V-T/V-I If an organization **signs** someone or if someone **signs** for an organization, they sign a contract agreeing to work for that organization for a specified period of time. ❑ *It cost the Minnesota Vikings 12 players to sign Herschel Walker from the Dallas Cowboys.* ❽ N-COUNT In astrology, a **sign** or a **sign of the zodiac** is one of the twelve areas into which the heavens are divided. ❑ *The New Moon takes place in your opposite sign of Libra on the 15th.* ❾ →see also **signing** ❿ PHRASE If you say that there is **no sign of** someone, you mean that they have not yet arrived, although you are expecting them to come. ❑ *The London train was on time, but there was no sign of my Finnish friend.*

❶ 가산명사 기호, 부호 ❑ 등식은 보통 막대기 두 개로 된 등호를 사용해 쓴다. ❷ 가산명사 손짓, 몸짓 ❑ 그들이 라발에게 엄지손가락을 치켜 올려 보였다. ❸ 타동사 수화하다; 수화가 제공되다 ❑ 모든 프로그램에 수화나 자막이 제공될 것이다. ❹ 가산명사 표지판 ❑ 눈 때문에 고속도로가 봉쇄되었다는 내용의 표지판 ❺ 가산명사 또는 불가산명사 조짐, 기미 ❑ 그들이 전쟁포로를 하루에 백 명씩 양도할 준비를 하면서 화해 조짐을 보이고 있다. ❑ 그의 얼굴이나 행동에 긴장하는 기색이라고는 거의 없었다. ❻ 타동사 서명하다 ❑ 세계 지도자들이 환경 보호 강화를 약속하는 조약에 서명할 것으로 예상된다. ❼ 타동사/자동사 계약하다 ❑ 미네소타 바이킹스가 달라스 카우보이스에서 허설 워커를 계약하여 데려오면서 다른 선수 12명을 포기해야 했다. ❽ 가산명사 별자리 (황도 12궁 중 하나) ❑ 15일 초승달이 당신 별자리 정 반대편에 있는 천칭자리에 들어선다. ❿ 구 아직 나타나지 않음 ❑ 런던행 기차가 제시간에 도착했지만 내 핀란드 친구는 아직 보이지 않았다.

Word Partnership sign의 연어

V.	**give** a sign ❷
	hang a sign, **read** a sign ❹
	see a sign ❹ ❺
	show no sign of *something* ❺
	refuse to sign ❻
	see no sign of *someone/something* ❿
N.	sign **on a door**, sign **over an entrance**, **neon** sign, **stop** sign, sign **in a window** ❹
	sign **an agreement**, sign **an autograph**, sign **a contract**, sign **legislation**, sign *your* **name**, sign **a petition**, sign **a treaty** ❻
ADJ.	**bad/good** sign, **encouraging** sign, **positive** sign, **a sure** sign, **warning** sign ❺
PREP.	sign **of progress**, sign **of the times**, sign **of trouble**, sign **of weakness** ❺

Thesaurus sign의 참조어

N.	nod, signal, wave ❷
V.	authorize, autograph, endorse ❻

▶**sign for** PHRASAL VERB If you **sign for** something, you officially state that you have received it, by signing a form or book. ❑ *When the postal clerk delivers your order, check the carton before signing for it.*

구동사 수취인 서명을 하다 ❑ 우체국 직원이 주문한 물건을 배달해 주면 수취인 서명을 하기 전에 상자를 확인하세요.

▶**sign in** PHRASAL VERB If you **sign in**, you officially indicate that you have arrived at a hotel or club by signing a book or form. ❑ *I signed in and crunched across the gravel to my room.*

구동사 서명하고 들어가다 ❑ 나는 서명하고 들어가서 자갈밭을 지나 내 방으로 갔다.

▶**sign over** PHRASAL VERB If you **sign** something **over**, you sign documents that give someone else property, possessions, or rights that were previously yours. ❑ *Two years ago, he signed over his art collection to the New York Metropolitan Museum of Art.*

구동사 양도 서명을 하다 ❑ 2년 전 그는 자신의 미술 수집품을 뉴욕 미술박물관에 정식으로 양도하는 서명을 했다.

▶**sign up** PHRASAL VERB If you **sign up** for an organization or if an organization **signs** you **up**, you sign a contract officially agreeing to do a job or course of study. ❑ *He signed up as a steward with Korean Air.*

구동사 계약하다, 등록하다; 영입하다 ❑ 그는 승무원으로 대한항공과 계약을 맺었다.

sig|nal ♦♦♢ /sɪɡnəl/ (**signals, signaling, signaled**) [BRIT, sometimes AM **signalling, signalled**] **1** N-COUNT A **signal** is a gesture, sound, or action which is intended to give a particular message to the person who sees or hears it. ❑ *They fired three distress signals.* ❑ *As soon as it was dark, Mrs. Evans gave the signal.* **2** V-T/V-I If you **signal to** someone, you make a gesture or sound in order to send them a particular message. ❑ *Mandy started after him, signaling to Jesse to follow.* ❑ *She signaled to Tank that she was moving forward.* **3** N-COUNT If an event or action is a **signal** of something, it suggests that this thing exists or is going to happen. ❑ *Kurdish leaders saw the visit as an important signal of support.* **4** V-T If someone or something **signals** an event, they suggest that the event is happening or likely to happen. ❑ *He seemed to be signaling important shifts in U.S. government policy.* **5** N-COUNT A **signal** is a piece of equipment beside a railroad, which indicates to train drivers whether they should stop the train or not. ❑ *A signal failure contributed to the crash.* **6** N-COUNT A **signal** is a series of radio waves, light waves, or changes in electrical current which may carry information. ❑ *...high-frequency radio signals.* →see **cellphone, television**

[영국영어, 미국영어 가끔 signalling, signalled] **1** 가산명사 신호 ❑ 그들은 세 차례 조난 조난 신호를 보냈다. ❑ 어두워지자마자 에반스 여사가 신호를 보냈다. **2** 타동사/자동사 신호를 보내다 ❑ 맨디가 그의 뒤를 따라 출발하면서 제시에게 따라오라는 신호를 보냈다. ❑ 그녀가 탱크에게 자신이 앞으로 나아가고 있다고 신호를 보냈다. **3** 가산명사 표시, 징조 ❑ 쿠르드 지도자들은 이번 방문을 지원의 뜻으로 중요하게 받아들였다. **4** 타동사 암시하다, 시사하다 ❑ 그가 미국 정부 정책의 중요한 전환을 암시하고 있는 것으로 보였다. **5** 가산명사 철도 신호기 ❑ 철도 신호기 고장으로 그 충돌 사고가 났다. **6** 가산명사 신호 ❑ 고주파 무선 신호

Word Partnership	signal의 연어
V.	**give a** signal **1** **3**
	send a signal **1** **3** **6**
ADJ.	**wrong** signal **1** **3**
	clear signal, **strong** signal **1** **3** **6**
	important signal **3**

sig|na|tory /sɪɡnətɔri, BRIT sɪɡnətri/ (**signatories**) N-COUNT The **signatories** of an official document are the people, organizations, or countries that have signed it. [FORMAL] ❑ *Both countries are signatories to the Nuclear Non-Proliferation Treaty.*

가산명사 서명인; 조인(국) [격식체] ❑ 양국 모두 핵비확산조약 조인국이다.

sig|na|ture /sɪɡnətʃər, -tʃʊər/ (**signatures**) N-COUNT Your **signature** is your name, written in your own characteristic way, often at the end of a document to indicate that you wrote the document or that you agree with what it says. ❑ *I was writing my signature at the bottom of the page.*

가산명사 서명 ❑ 나는 페이지 하단에 서명을 하고 있었다.

sig|nifi|cance /sɪɡnɪfɪkəns/ N-UNCOUNT The **significance** of something is the importance that it has, usually because it will have an effect on a situation or shows something about a situation. ❑ *Ideas about the social significance of religion have changed over time.*

불가산명사 의의, 중요성 ❑ 시간이 흐르면서 종교의 사회적 의의에 대한 인식이 바뀌어 왔다.

Word Partnership	significance의 연어
ADJ.	**cultural** significance, **great** significance, **historic/historical** significance, **political** significance, **religious** significance
V.	**explain the** significance of *something*, **understand the** significance of *something*

sig|nifi|cant ♦♦♢ /sɪɡnɪfɪkənt/ **1** ADJ A **significant** amount or effect is large enough to be important or affect a situation to a noticeable degree. ❑ *Most 11-year-olds are not encouraged to develop reading skills; a small but significant number are illiterate.* ● **sig|nifi|cant|ly** ADV ❑ *The number of MPs now supporting him had increased significantly.* **2** ADJ A **significant** fact, event, or thing is one that is important or shows something. ❑ *I think it was significant that he never knew his own father.* ● **sig|nifi|cant|ly** ADV ❑ *Significantly, the company recently opened a huge store in Atlanta.*

1 형용사 상당한 ❑ 열한 살 어린이 대부분이 읽기 능력 개발 기회조차 없는 상태이다. 많진 않지만 상당수의 아이들이 글을 읽을 줄 모른다. ● 상당히 부사 ❑ 이제 그를 지지하는 의원 수가 상당히 증가한 상태였다. **2** 형용사 중요한, 의미심장한 ❑ 나는 그가 자기 아버지를 전혀 몰랐다는 사실이 중요하다고 생각한다. ● 중요하게, 의미심장하게 부사 ❑ 최근 회사가 애틀랜타에 대형 매장을 연 것은 중요한 일이다.

Thesaurus	significant의 참조어
ADJ.	big, important, large; (*ant.*) insignificant, minor, small **1**

sig|ni|fy /sɪɡnɪfaɪ/ (**signifies, signifying, signified**) **1** V-T If an event, a sign, or a symbol **signifies** something, it is a sign of that thing or represents that thing. ❑ *The contrasting approaches to Europe signified a sharp difference between the major parties.* **2** V-T If you **signify** something, you make a sign or gesture in order to communicate a particular meaning. ❑ *Two jurors signified their dissent.*

1 타동사 나타내다, 의미하다 ❑ 유럽에 대한 대조적인 접근방식은 주요 정당들 간에 현격한 차이가 있음을 의미했다. **2** 타동사 표시하다, 알리다 ❑ 배심원 두 명이 반대 의사를 표시했다.

sign|ing /saɪnɪŋ/ (**signings**) **1** N-UNCOUNT The **signing of** a document is the act of writing your name to indicate that you agree with what it says or to say that you have been present to witness other people writing their signature. ❑ *Spain's top priority is the signing of an EMU treaty.* **2** N-COUNT A **signing** is someone who has recently signed a contract agreeing to play for a sports team or work for a record company. [usu with supp] ❑ *...the salary paid to the club's latest signing.* **3** N-UNCOUNT The **signing of** a player by a sports team or a group by a record company is the act of drawing up a legal document setting out the length and terms of the association between them. ❑ *...Manchester United's signing of the Australian goalkeeper Mark Bosnich.* **4** N-UNCOUNT **Signing** is the use of sign language to communicate with someone who is deaf. ❑ *The two deaf actors converse solely in signing.*

1 불가산명사 조인, 서명 ❑ 스페인의 최우선 과제는 유럽경제통화동맹에의 조인이다. **2** 가산명사 계약 선수; 계약 가수 ❑ 가장 최근에 구단에 들어온 계약 선수에게 지급되는 연봉 **3** 불가산명사 계약 ❑ 맨체스터 유나이티드와 호주 골키퍼 마크 보스니치 사이의 계약 **4** 불가산명사 수화 ❑ 청각 장애인 배우 두 명은 수화로만 대화한다.

a b c d e f g h i j k l m n o p q r s t u v w x y z

Picture Dictionary — sign language

The American Manual Alphabet

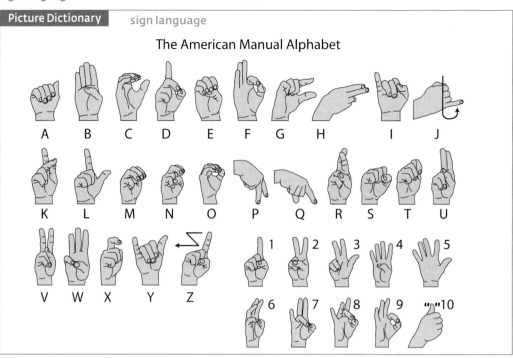

A B C D E F G H I J

K L M N O P Q R S T U

V W X Y Z   1 2 3 4 5

6 7 8 9 "10"

sign lan|guage (**sign languages**) N-VAR **Sign language** is movements of your hands and arms used to communicate. There are several official systems of sign language, used for example by deaf people. Movements are also sometimes invented by people when they want to communicate with someone who does not speak the same language. ❑ *Her son used sign language to tell her what happened.* →see Picture Dictionary: **sign language**

가산명사 또는 불가산명사 수화 ❑ 아들이 그녀에게 수화로 무슨 일이 일어났는지 설명했다.

Sikh /siːk/ (**Sikhs**) N-COUNT A **Sikh** is a person who follows the Indian religion of Sikhism. ❑ *The rise of racism concerns Sikhs because they are such a visible minority.* ❑ *...a Sikh temple.*

가산명사 시크교도 ❑ 시크교도들은 눈에 잘 띄는 소수민족인 까닭에 인종주의 확산이 걱정이다. ❑ 시크교 사원

Sikh|ism /siːkɪzəm/ N-UNCOUNT **Sikhism** is an Indian religion which separated from Hinduism in the sixteenth century and which teaches that there is only one God.

불가산명사 시크교

si|lence ♦♢♢ /saɪləns/ (**silences, silencing, silenced**) **1** N-VAR If there is **silence**, nobody is speaking. ❑ *They stood in silence.* ❑ *He never lets those long silences develop during dinner.* **2** N-UNCOUNT Someone's **silence** about something is their failure or refusal to speak to other people about it. ❑ *The district court ruled that Popper's silence in court today should be entered as a plea of not guilty.* ● PHRASE If someone **breaks** their **silence** about something, they talk about something that they have not talked about before or for a long time. **3** V-T If someone **silences** you, they stop you from expressing opinions that they do not agree with. ❑ *Like other tyrants, he tried to silence anyone who spoke out against him.*

1 가산명사 또는 불가산명사 침묵 ❑ 그들은 아무 말 없이 서 있었다. ❑ 그는 저녁식사 동안 그처럼 긴 침묵이 흐르도록 절대 그냥 두지 않는다. **2** 불가산명사 침묵 ❑ 지방 법원은 오늘 법정에 출두한 포퍼의 침묵을 무죄 주장으로 받아들여야 한다는 판결을 내렸다. ● 구 침묵을 깨다 **3** 타동사 입을 못 열게 만들다, 침묵하게 만들다 ❑ 다른 폭군들과 마찬가지로 그도 자신을 반대하는 사람은 모두 침묵하게 만들려고 했다.

Word Partnership   silence의 연어

ADJ.	**awkward** silence, **complete** silence, **long** silence, **sudden** silence, **total** silence **1**
V.	**listen in** silence, **observe a** silence, **sit in** silence, **watch** *something* in silence **1** **break a/***your* silence **2**

si|lent ♦♢♢ /saɪlənt/ **1** ADJ Someone who is **silent** is not speaking. [v-link ADJ] ❑ *Trish was silent because she was reluctant to put her thoughts into words.* ❑ *He spoke no English and was completely silent during the visit.* ● **si|lent|ly** ADV [ADV with v] ❑ *She and Ned sat silently for a moment, absorbing the peace of the lake.* **2** ADJ A place that is **silent** is completely quiet, with no sound at all. Something that is **silent** makes no sound at all. ❑ *The room was silent except for the slight crunching coming from John's mouth as he ground his teeth together.* ● **si|lent|ly** ADV [ADV with v] ❑ *Strange shadows moved silently in the almost permanent darkness.* **3** ADJ A **silent** movie has pictures usually accompanied by music but does not have the actors' voices or any other sounds. [ADJ n] ❑ *...one of the famous silent films of Charlie Chaplin.*

1 형용사 조용한, 말없는 ❑ 트리시는 자신의 생각을 말로 옮기는 것이 내키지 않아 침묵을 지켰다. ❑ 그는 영어를 하나도 못했고 방문 기간 동안 한마디도 하지 않았다. ● 조용히, 묵묵히 부사 ❑ 그녀와 네드는 호수의 평화로움을 만끽하며 잠시 동안 묵묵히 앉아 있었다. **2** 형용사 조용한, 적막한 ❑ 존이 이를 갈 때 그의 입에서 작게 나는 뽀드득거리는 소리를 빼고는 방안이 조용했다. ● 조용히, 고요하게 부사 ❑ 이상한 그림자들이 끝이 없을 것 같은 어둠 속에서 조용히 움직였다. **3** 형용사 무성의 ❑ 찰리 채플린의 유명한 무성 영화 중 하나

Thesaurus   silent의 참조어

ADJ.	hushed, mute, speechless **1** quiet **2**

Word Partnership   silent의 연어

V.   **go** silent, **keep** silent, **remain** silent, **sit** silent ■

N.   silent **prayer**, silent **reading** ■

si|lent part|ner (**silent partners**) N-COUNT A **silent partner** is a person who provides some of the capital for a business but who does not take an active part in managing the business. [AM, BUSINESS; BRIT **sleeping partner**] ❑ ...*firms run by his friends in which he was a silent partner.*

가산명사 익명의 동업자 [미국영어, 경제; 영국영어 sleeping partner] ❑ 자신은 자금만 대고 친구들이 운영을 맡은 회사들

sil|hou|ette /sɪluˈet/ (**silhouettes**) ■ N-COUNT A **silhouette** is the solid dark shape that you see when someone or something has a bright light or pale background behind them. ❑ *The dark silhouette of the castle ruins stood out boldly against the fading light.* ◻ N-COUNT The **silhouette** of something is the outline that it has, which often helps you to recognize it. ❑ *He put on a hat that came down over his squarish skull and changed the distinctive silhouette of his ears.*

■ 가산명사 실루엣 ❑ 성과 잔해의 검은 실루엣이 희미해져 가는 빛을 배경으로 선명하게 드러났다. ◻ 가산명사 윤곽 ❑ 그가 모자를 쓰자 각진 두상이 덮이고 특이했던 귀의 윤곽이 바뀌었다.

sili|con /sɪˈlɪkən/ N-UNCOUNT **Silicon** is an element that is found in sand and in minerals such as quartz and granite. Silicon is used to make parts of computers and other electronic equipment. ❑ *Each new chip will contain over three million transistors on a piece of silicon about the size of a standard postage stamp.*

불가산명사 규소, 실리콘 ❑ 새로운 각각의 칩은 기본 우표 크기의 실리콘 조각 위에 3백만 개가 넘는 트랜지스터를 담는다.

Silicon Valley is an area in the US, near San Francisco, where the computer industry dominates the local economy. These days the name may also be given to other locations where computer companies are gathered.

Silicon Valley(실리콘 밸리)는 미국 샌프란시스코 인근 지역인데 이 곳에서는 컴퓨터 산업이 지역 경제를 지배하고 있다. 요즘에는 실리콘 밸리란 이름을 컴퓨터 회사가 모여 있는 다른 지역에도 붙일 수 있다.

sili|con chip (**silicon chips**) N-COUNT A **silicon chip** is a very small piece of silicon inside a computer. It has electronic circuits on it and can hold large quantities of information or perform mathematical or logical operations.

가산명사 실리콘 칩

sili|cone /sɪˈlɪkoʊn/ N-UNCOUNT **Silicone** is a tough artificial substance made from silicon, which is used to make polishes, and also used in cosmetic surgery and plastic surgery. ❑ ...*women who suffered health problems from silicone breast implants that leak.*

불가산명사 실리콘 ❑ 가슴에 이식한 실리콘이 새는 바람에 건강상의 문제를 겪은 여성들

silk /sɪlk/ (**silks**) N-MASS **Silk** is a substance which is made into smooth fine cloth and sewing thread. ❑ *They continued to get their silks from China.* ❑ *Pauline wore a silk dress with a strand of pearls.*

물질명사 실크, 비단 ❑ 그들은 계속 중국에서 실크를 수입했다. ❑ 폴린은 한 줄로 진주가 장식된 실크 드레스를 입고 있었다.

silky /sɪˈlki/ (**silkier, silkiest**) ADJ If something has a **silky** texture, it is smooth, soft, and shiny, like silk. ❑ ...*dresses in seductively silky fabrics.*

형용사 부드러운, 비단결 같은 ❑ 매혹적일 만큼 부드러운 천으로 만든 드레스

sill /sɪl/ (**sills**) N-COUNT A **sill** is a shelf along the bottom edge of a window, either inside or outside a building. ❑ *Whitlock was perched on the sill of the room's only window.*

가산명사 창문턱 ❑ 위트록은 방에 딱 하나 있는 창문턱에 걸터앉아 있었다.

sil|ly /sɪˈli/ (**sillier, silliest**) ADJ If you say that someone or something is **silly**, you mean that they are foolish, childish, or ridiculous. ❑ *My best friend tells me that I am silly to be upset about this.* ❑ *I thought it would be silly to be too rude at that stage.*

형용사 어리석은, 철없는, 바보 같은 ❑ 제일 친한 친구가 내가 이런 일에 화를 내면 바보라고 말한다. ❑ 나는 그 단계에서 너무 무례하게 구는 것은 어리석은 것이라고 생각했다.

silt /sɪlt/ N-UNCOUNT **Silt** is fine sand, soil, or mud which is carried along by a river. ❑ *The lake was almost solid with silt and vegetation.* →see **erosion**

불가산명사 침적토 ❑ 호수는 침적토와 초목으로 거의 땅처럼 되어 있는 상태였다.

sil|ver ♦◇◇ /sɪˈlvər/ (**silvers**) ■ N-UNCOUNT **Silver** is a valuable pale gray metal that is used for making jewelry and ornaments. ❑ ...*a hand-crafted brooch made from silver.* ❑ ...*amber earrings set in silver.* ◻ N-UNCOUNT **Silver** consists of coins that are made from silver or that look like silver. ❑ ...*the basement where £150,000 in silver was buried.* ◼ N-UNCOUNT You can use **silver** to refer to all the things in a house that are made of silver, especially the flatware and dishes. [also the N] ❑ *He beat the rugs and polished the silver.* ◻ COLOR **Silver** is used to describe things that are shiny and pale gray in color. ❑ *He had thick silver hair which needed cutting.* →see **mineral, money, silverware**

■ 불가산명사 은 ❑ 수공예 은 브로치 ❑ 은에 호박을 박아 만든 귀걸이 ◻ 불가산명사 은화 ❑ 은화 15만 파운드가 묻혀 있었던 지하실 ◼ 불가산명사 은제품; 은식기류 ❑ 그는 바닥 깔개를 털고 은식기를 닦았다. ◻ 색채어 은색, 회백색 ❑ 그는 덥수룩해서 잘라야 할 것 같은 백발을 하고 있었다.

sil|ver med|al (**silver medals**) N-COUNT If you win a **silver medal**, you come second in a competition, especially a sports contest, and are given a medal made of silver as a prize. ❑ *Gillingham won the silver medal in the 200 meters at Seoul.*

가산명사 은메달 ❑ 길링엄은 서울에서 2백 미터 은메달을 획득했다.

silver|ware /sɪˈlvərweər/ ■ N-UNCOUNT You can use **silverware** to refer to all the things in a house that are made of silver, especially the flatware and dishes. ❑ *There was a serving spoon missing when Nina put the silverware back in its box.* ◻ N-UNCOUNT Journalists sometimes use **silverware** to refer to silver cups and other prizes won by sports teams or players. ❑ *Everton paraded their recently acquired silverware.* →see Word Web: **silverware**

■ 불가산명사 은식기류 ❑ 니나는 은식기를 박스에 도로 넣으면서 서빙스푼 하나가 없어진 것을 발견했다. ◻ 불가산명사 은제 우승컵, 은제 상패 ❑ 에버턴이 그들이 최근에 획득한 은제 우승컵을 자랑스럽게 보였다.

Word Web   silverware

Anthropologists tell us that the first knives were simple cutting instruments made from flint that were first used about two million years ago. The first modern knife with a metal **blade** and wooden **handle** appeared about 1000 years BC. During the Middle Ages, people carried their own eating knives with them because no one provided knives for guests. The earliest **spoons** were made from scooped-out bones or shells tied to the end of sticks. Later the Romans introduced bronze and **silver** spoons. The earliest **forks** had only two tines and were used only for carving and serving meat.

dessert spoon
dessert fork
butter knife
teaspoon
salad fork
dinner fork
dinner knife

a b c d e f g h i j k l m n o p q r s t u v w x y z

sil|very /sɪlvəri/ ADJ **Silvery** things look like silver or are the color of silver. ❑ ...a small, intense man with silvery hair.

형용사 은색의, 회백색의 ❑ 회백색 머리에 키가 작고 열정적인 남자

sim /sɪm/ (**sims**) N-COUNT A **sim** is a computer game that simulates an activity such as playing a sport or flying an aircraft. [COMPUTING] ❑ World Cricket is more than a simple sports sim, with loads of management potential, too.

가산명사 시뮬레이션 게임 [컴퓨터] ❑ 월드크리켓은 다양한 관리 기능이 있어 단순한 스포츠 시뮬레이션 게임을 넘어선 제품이다.

SIM card /sɪm kɑrd/ (**SIM cards**) N-COUNT A **SIM card** is a microchip in a cell phone that connects it to a particular phone network. **SIM** is an abbreviation for "Subscriber Identity Module."

가산명사 (휴대 전화) 심카드

sim|i|lar ♦♦◇ /sɪmɪlər/ ADJ If one thing is **similar to** another, or if two things are **similar**, they have features that are the same. ❑ ...a savoury cake with a texture similar to that of carrot cake. ❑ The accident was similar to one that happened in 1973.

형용사 비슷한 ❑ 당근 케이크와 질감이 비슷한 맛 좋은 케이크 ❑ 그 사고는 1973년에 일어난 사고와 비슷한 사고였다.

sim|i|lar|ity /sɪmɪlærɪti/ (**similarities**) ◼ N-UNCOUNT If there is a **similarity between** two or more things, they are similar to each other. ❑ The astonishing similarity between my brother and my first-born son. ❑ There was a very basic similarity in our philosophy. ◻ N-COUNT **Similarities** are features that things have which make them similar to each other. ❑ There were significant similarities between mother and son.

◼ 불가산명사 비슷함, 유사성 ❑ 내 남동생과 내 첫째 아들 사이의 놀라울 정도의 유사성 ❑ 우리의 철학은 아주 기본적으로 비슷했다. ◻ 가산명사 닮은 점, 비슷한 점 ❑ 엄마와 아들이 여러 면에서 많이 닮아 있었다.

sim|i|lar|ly /sɪmɪlərli/ ◼ ADV You use **similarly** to say that something is similar to something else. ❑ Most of the men who now gathered round him again were similarly dressed. ◻ ADV You use **similarly** when mentioning a fact or situation that is similar to the one you have just mentioned. [ADV with cl] ❑ A mother somehow memorises the feel of her child's skin from the very first touches and can recognise it even when blindfolded. Similarly a baby's cry is instantly identified by the mother.

◼ 부사 비슷하게 ❑ 그의 주변에 다시 모여든 남자들 대부분이 비슷한 옷을 입고 있었다. ◻ 부사 이와 비슷하게 ❑ 어머니는 아이를 처음 만진 순간부터 용케 그 감촉을 기억하며 눈을 가렸을 때조차도 이를 알아볼 수 있다. 이와 비슷하게 어머니는 아이의 울음소리도 즉각 구분할 수 있다.

sim|mer /sɪmər/ (**simmers, simmering, simmered**) ◼ V-T/V-I When you **simmer** food or when it **simmers**, you cook it by keeping it at boiling point or just below boiling point. ❑ Make an infusion by boiling and simmering the rhubarb and camomile together. ● N-SING **Simmer** is also a noun. ❑ Combine the stock, whole onion and peppercorns in a pan and bring to a simmer. ◻ V-I If a conflict or a quarrel **simmers**, it does not actually happen for a period of time, but eventually builds up to the point where it does. ❑ ...bitter divisions that have simmered for more than half a century.

◼ 타동사/자동사 고다, 뭉근히 끓이다; 부글부글 끓다, 뭉근히 끓다 ❑ 대황과 카모밀을 함께 넣고 처음에는 팔팔 끓이다가 나중에는 뭉근히 끓여서 차를 만드세요. ● 단수명사 부글부글 끓는 상태, 뭉근히 끓는 상태 ❑ 냄비에 육수와 후추 열매를 넣고 양파도 통째로 넣어서 부글부글 끓이세요. ◻ 자동사 고조되다 ❑ 반세기 이상 고조되어 온 극심한 반목

sim|ple ♦♦◇ /sɪmpəl/ (**simpler, simplest**) ◼ ADJ If you describe something as **simple**, you mean that it is not complicated, and is therefore easy to understand. ❑ ...simple pictures and diagrams. ❑ ...pages of simple advice on filling in your tax form. ● **simply** ADV [ADV with v] ❑ When applying for a visa extension state simply and clearly the reasons why you need an extension. ◻ ADJ If you describe people or things as **simple**, you mean that they have all the basic or necessary things they require, but nothing extra. ❑ He ate a simple dinner of rice and beans. ❑ ...the simple pleasures of childhood. ● **simply** ADV [ADV after v] ❑ The living room is furnished simply with white wicker furniture and blue-and-white fabrics. ◼ ADJ If a problem is **simple** or if its solution is **simple**, the problem can be solved easily. ❑ Some puzzles look difficult but once the solution is known are actually quite simple. ◻ ADJ A **simple** task is easy to do. ❑ The job itself had been simple enough. ● **simply** ADV [ADV after v] ❑ We can do things that were not possible before, and they can be done simply. ◼ ADJ You use **simple** to emphasize that the thing you are referring to is the only important or relevant reason for something. [EMPHASIS] [ADJ n] ❑ His refusal to talk was simple stubbornness. ◼ ADJ In grammar, **simple** tenses are ones which are formed without an auxiliary verb "be," for example "I dressed and went for a walk" and "This tastes nice." **Simple** verb groups are used especially to refer to completed actions, regular actions, and situations. Compare **continuous**. ◼ →see also **simply**

◼ 형용사 간단한, 단순한 ❑ 단순한 그림과 도형 ❑ 세금 신고서를 작성하는 것에 관한 간단한 도움말 여러 페이지 ● 간단하게 부사 ❑ 비자 연장을 신청할 때는 간단명료하게 왜 연장이 필요한지를 설명하세요. ◻ 형용사 소박한, 간소한 ❑ 그는 쌀과 콩으로 만든 조촐한 저녁 식사를 했다. ❑ 유년기의 소박한 즐거움들 ● 소박하게, 간소하게 부사 ❑ 거실은 고리버들 세공으로 만들어진 가구와 파랗고 하얀 천으로 꾸며졌다. ◼ 형용사 간단한, 단순한 ❑ 어떤 수수께끼들은 어려워 보이지만 일단 답을 알면 사실은 아주 단순하다. ◼ 형용사 쉬운 ❑ 일 자체는 아주 쉬웠다. ● 쉽게 부사 ❑ 이전에 할 수 없었던 것들을 이제는 할 수 있고 그것도 쉽게 할 수 있다. ◼ 형용사 순전한 [강조] ❑ 그는 순전히 고집 때문에 이야기를 안 하려고 했다. ◼ 형용사 (문법) 단순시제의

sim|ple in|ter|est N-UNCOUNT **Simple interest** is interest that is calculated on an original sum of money and not also on interest which has previously been added to the sum. Compare **compound interest**. [BUSINESS] ❑ ...an investment that pays only simple interest.

불가산명사 단리 (원금에 지불되는 이자) [경제] ❑ 단리만을 지불하는 투자

sim|plic|ity /sɪmplɪsɪti/ N-UNCOUNT The **simplicity** of something is the fact that it is not complicated and can be understood or done easily. ❑ The apparent simplicity of his plot is deceptive.

불가산명사 간단함, 단순함 ❑ 그의 계획은 겉으로 보기에만 간단하다.

sim|pli|fi|ca|tion /sɪmplɪfɪkeɪʃən/ (**simplifications**) ◼ N-COUNT You can use **simplification** to refer to the thing that is produced when you make something simpler or when you reduce it to its basic elements. ❑ Like any such

◼ 가산명사 단순화한 것 ❑ 여느 도표처럼 그것은 단순한 것이다. ◻ 불가산명사 단순화 ❑ 모든 사람들이 사법 절차의 간소화를 원한다.

diagram, it is a simplification. **2** N-UNCOUNT **Simplification** is the act or process of making something simpler. ❑ *Everyone favors the simplification of court procedures.*

타동사 단순화하다 ❑ 이 계획의 목적은 복잡한 사회 보장 제도를 단순하게 만드는 것이다.

sim|pli|fy /sɪmplɪfaɪ/ (**simplifies, simplifying, simplified**) V-T If you **simplify** something, you make it easier to understand or you remove the things which make it complex. ❑ *The aim of the scheme is to simplify the complex social security system.*

형용사 단순화된 ❑ 그는 습진의 치료에 대해 지극히 단순한 견해를 갖고 있다.

sim|plis|tic /sɪmplɪstɪk/ ADJ A **simplistic** view or interpretation of something makes it seem much simpler than it really is. ❑ *He has a simplistic view of the treatment of eczema.*

1 부사 단지 [강조] ❑ 그 탁자는 단지 받침대 위에 둥근 합판을 얹어 놓은 것에 불과하였다. ❑ 발생한 피해 대부분은 단지 나무가 쓰러진 때문이었다. **2** 부사 그저 [강조] ❑ 이런 종류의 증가는 그저 정당화될 수가 없다.

sim|ply ♦♦◇ /sɪmpli/ **1** ADV You use **simply** to emphasize that something consists of only one thing, happens for only one reason, or is done in only one way. [EMPHASIS] ❑ *The table is simply a chipboard circle on a base.* ❑ *Most of the damage that's occurred was simply because of fallen trees.* **2** ADV You use **simply** to emphasize what you are saying. [EMPHASIS] ❑ *This sort of increase simply cannot be justified.* **3** →see also **simple**

1 타동사 흉내 내다, 모의 훈련을 하다 ❑ 그들은 유혈 전쟁을 하듯 모의 훈련을 하며 길리간 로드 위에서 이리저리 뒹굴었다. **2** 타동사 모의실험을 하다 ❑ 그 과학자는 지구 기후 일년 치를 모의실험을 하기 위한 모델을 하나 개발했다.

simu|late /sɪmyəleɪt/ (**simulates, simulating, simulated**) **1** V-T If you **simulate** an action or a feeling, you pretend that you are doing it or feeling it. ❑ *They rolled about on the Gilligan Road, simulating a bloodthirsty fight.* **2** V-T If you **simulate** a set of conditions, you create them artificially, for example in order to conduct an experiment. ❑ *The scientist developed one model to simulate a full year of the globe's climate.*

가산명사 또는 불가산명사 모의훈련, 모의실험, 시뮬레이션 ❑ 부상자 처리 절차를 실제처럼 모의훈련하는 것이 훈련에 포함된다.

simu|la|tion /sɪmyəleɪⁱn/ (**simulations**) N-VAR **Simulation** is the process of simulating something or the result of simulating it. ❑ *Training includes realistic simulation of casualty procedures.*

형용사 동시의 ❑ 책과 앨범의 동시 발표 ● 동시에 부사 ❑ 그 두 총이 거의 동시에 발사했다.

simul|ta|neous /saɪməlt`eɪniəs, BRIT sɪməlt`eɪniəs/ ADJ Things which are **simultaneous** happen or exist at the same time. ❑ *...the simultaneous release of the book and the album.* ● **simul|ta|neous|ly** ADV ❑ *The two guns fired almost simultaneously.*

1 가산명사 또는 불가산명사 (종교적) 죄, 죄악 ❑ 낙태에 관한 바티칸의 가르침은 명확하게 그것을 죄로 본다. **2** 자동사 죄를 짓다 ❑ 스페인 종교재판소는 그를 하느님과 인간에 대해 죄를 지은 혐의로 기소했다. ● 죄인 가산명사 ❑ 내가 죄인이라는 것과 죄를 참회할 필요가 있다는 것을 나에게 보여주었다. **3** 가산명사 잘못 ❑ 거만한 비정함이라는 잘못

sin /sɪn/ (**sins, sinning, sinned**) **1** N-VAR **Sin** or a **sin** is an action or type of behavior which is believed to break the laws of God. ❑ *The Vatican's teaching on abortion is clear: it is a sin.* **2** V-I If you **sin**, you do something that is believed to break the laws of God. ❑ *The Spanish Inquisition charged him with sinning against God and man.* ● **sin|ner** /sɪnər/ (**sinners**) N-COUNT ❑ *I was shown that I am a sinner, that I needed to repent of my sins.* **3** N-COUNT A **sin** is any action or behavior that people disapprove of or consider morally wrong. ❑ *...the sin of arrogant hard-heartedness.*

1 전치사 -부터 ❑ 그는 1959년부터 인도에서 망명 생활을 하고 있다. ❑ 그녀는 몇 년 전에 일종의 신경 쇠약을 겪었는데, 그때부터 매우 소심해졌다. ● 부사 그때 이래로 ❑ 그들은 1960년대에 같이 일을 했고 그때 이래로 계속 연락을 유지하고 지낸다. ● 접속사 -한 때부터, -한 이후로 ❑ 나는 일곱 살이었을 때부터 온갖 일을 하며 내 밥벌이를 해 왔다. **2** 전치사 - 이후, - 이래 ❑ 올해 보고 된 영국과 웨일스의 범죄 증가율은 전쟁 이후 최고이다. ● 접속사 - 이후로 ❑ 내가 십대였을 때 이후로 그 종목이 너무 많이 변했다. ❑ 내가 엄마가 된 이후로 아이들의 목소리가 더 이상 매력적이지 않다. **3** 부사 이후에 ❑ 약 6천 명이 체포되었으며 그 중 몇 백 명은 이후에 석방되었다. **4** 접속사 - 때문에 ❑ 나는 체중이 쉽게 붙기 때문에 항상 다이어트를 한다.

since ♦♦♦ /sɪns/ **1** PREP You use **since** when you are mentioning a time or event in the past and indicating that a situation has continued from then until now. ❑ *He's been in exile in India since 1959.* ❑ *She had a sort of breakdown some years ago, and since then she has been very shy.* ● ADV **Since** is also an adverb. [ADV with v] ❑ *They worked together in the 1960s, and have kept in contact ever since.* ● CONJ **Since** is also a conjunction. ❑ *I've earned my own living since I was seven, doing all kinds of jobs.* **2** PREP You use **since** to mention a time or event in the past when you are describing an event or situation that has happened after that time. ❑ *The percentage increase in reported crime in England and Wales this year is the highest since the war.* ● CONJ **Since** is also a conjunction. ❑ *So much has changed in the sport since I was a teenager.* ❑ *Since I have become a mother, the sound of children's voices has lost its charm.* **3** ADV When you are talking about an event or situation in the past, you use **since** to indicate that another event happened at some point later in time. [ADV with v] ❑ *About six thousand people were arrested, several hundred of whom have since been released.* **4** CONJ You use **since** to introduce reasons or explanations. ❑ *I'm forever on a diet, since I put on weight easily.*

형용사 진실한 [마음에 듦] ❑ 그의 견해는 진실하다. ● 진실성 불가산명사 ❑ 나는 그의 깊은 진실성에 감명받았다.

sin|cere /sɪnsɪər/ ADJ If you say that someone is **sincere**, you approve of them because they really mean the things they say. You can also describe someone's behavior and beliefs as **sincere**. [APPROVAL] ❑ *He's sincere in his views.* ● **sin|cer|ity** /sɪnsɛrɪti/ N-UNCOUNT ❑ *I was impressed with his deep sincerity.*

1 부사 진심으로 ❑ "축하해."라고 그가 진심으로 말했다. ❑ 진심으로 믿는 종교적 신념 **2** 관용 표현 올림 (편지 끝에 쓰는 말) ❑ 로비 와인즈 올림

sin|cere|ly /sɪnsɪərli/ **1** ADV If you say or feel something **sincerely**, you really mean or feel it, and are not pretending. ❑ *"Congratulations," he said sincerely.* ❑ *...sincerely held religious beliefs.* **2** CONVENTION In the United States, people write **"Sincerely yours"** or **"Sincerely"** before their signature at the end of a formal letter when they have addressed it to someone by name. In Britain and sometimes in the United States, people usually write **"Yours sincerely"** instead. ❑ *Sincerely yours, Robbie Weinz.*

형용사 죄 많은, 나쁜 ❑ "나는 죄 많은 남자야, 마그다."라고 그가 조용히 말했다. ❑ 죄 많은 세상이다. ● 죄악 불가산명사 ❑ 남아공 인종 차별 정책의 죄악

sin|ful /sɪnfəl/ ADJ If you describe someone or something as **sinful**, you mean that they are wicked or immoral. ❑ *"I am a sinful man, Magda," he said quietly.* ❑ *...this is a sinful world.* ● **sin|ful|ness** N-UNCOUNT ❑ *...the sinfulness of apartheid.*

1 타동사/자동사 노래하다 ❑ 나는 노래 못해. ❑ 나는 대체로 사랑에 대해서 노래한다. ❑ 그들은 모두 같은 노래를 부르고 있었다.

sing ♦♦◇ /sɪŋ/ (**sings, singing, sang, sung**) **1** V-T/V-I When you **sing**, you make musical sounds with your voice, usually producing words that fit a tune. ❑ *I can't sing.* ❑ *I sing about love most of the time.* ❑ *They were all singing the same song.* **2** →see also **singing**

Thesaurus	sing의 참조어
V.	chant, hum

Word Partnership	sing의 연어
V.	begin to sing, can/can't sing, dance and sing, hear *someone* sing, like to sing
N.	birds sing, sing **a song**

a b c d e f g h i j k l m n o p q r s t u v w x y z

▶**sing along** PHRASAL VERB If you **sing along with** a piece of music, you sing it while you are listening to someone else perform it. ❑ *We listen to children's shows on the radio, and Janey can sing along with all the tunes.* ❑ *Would-be Elvis Presleys can sing along to "Jailhouse Rock," "Love me Tender" and "Blue Suede Shoes."*

구동사 따라 부르다 ❑ 우리는 라디오의 어린이 프로를 듣는데 제이니는 모든 노래를 따라 부를 줄 안다. ❑ 엘비스 프레슬리처럼 되고 싶어 하는 사람들은 "제일하우스 락", "러브 미 텐더", "블루 스웨이드 슈즈" 등을 따라 부를 줄 안다.

sing|er ♦♢♢ /sɪŋər/ (**singers**) N-COUNT A **singer** is a person who sings, especially as a job. ❑ *My mother was a singer in a dance band.* →see **concert**

가산명사 가수 ❑ 우리 어머니는 댄스 그룹의 가수였다.

sing|ing /sɪŋɪŋ/ N-UNCOUNT **Singing** is the activity of making musical sounds with your voice. ❑ *...a people's carnival, with singing and dancing in the streets.* ❑ *...the singing of a traditional hymn.*

불가산명사 노래 부르기 ❑ 길거리에서 노래하고 춤추는 시민들의 카니발 ❑ 전통 찬송가를 부름

sin|gle ♦♦♦ /sɪŋɡ²l/ (**singles, singling, singled**) ◳ ADJ You use **single** to emphasize that you are referring to one thing, and no more than one thing. [EMPHASIS] [ADJ n] ❑ *A single shot rang out.* ❑ *Over six hundred people were wounded in a single day.* ◳ ADJ You use **single** to indicate that you are considering something on its own and separately from other things like it. [EMPHASIS] [det ADJ] ❑ *Every single house in town had been damaged.* ◳ ADJ Someone who is **single** is not married. You can also use **single** to describe someone who does not have a girlfriend or boyfriend. ❑ *Is it difficult being a single mother?* ◳ ADJ A **single** room is a room intended for one person to stay or live in. ❑ *Each guest has her own single room, or shares, on request, a double room.* ● N-COUNT **Single** is also a noun. ❑ *It's £65 for a single, £98 for a double and £120 for an entire suite.* ◳ ADJ A **single** bed is wide enough for one person to sleep in. ❑ *...his bedroom with its single bed.* ◳ ADJ A **single** ticket is a ticket for a trip from one place to another but not back again. [BRIT; AM **one-way**] ❑ *The price of a single ticket is thirty-nine pounds.* ● N-COUNT **Single** is also a noun. ❑ *...a Club Class single to Los Angeles.* ◳ N-COUNT A **single** is a small record which has one song on each side. A **single** is also a CD which has a few short songs on it. You can also refer to the main song on a record or CD as a **single**. ❑ *The winners will pocket a cash sum and get a chance to release their debut CD single.* ◳ N-UNCOUNT **Singles** is a game of tennis or badminton in which one player plays another. The plural **singles** can be used to refer to one or more of these matches. ❑ *Boris Becker of Germany won the men's singles.* ◳ →see also **single-. in single file** →see **file**
→see **hotel, tennis**

◳ 형용사 한 개의, 단 하나의 [강조] ❑ 한 발의 총성이 울려 퍼졌다. ❑ 단 하루 만에 6백 명이 넘는 사람들이 부상을 입었다. ◳ 형용사 개개의 [강조] ❑ 마을의 모든 주택 하나하나가 피해를 입었다. ◳ 형용사 독신의, 혼자인 ❑ 남편 없이 혼자 아이를 키우는 것이 힘든가요? ◳ 형용사 1인용의 ❑ 각 손님에게는 1인실이 주어지며 요청할 경우 2인실을 공유할 수 있다. ● 가산명사 1인실 ❑ 1인실은 65파운드, 2인실은 98파운드, 그리고 스위트룸은 120파운드이다. ◳ 형용사 1인용의 ❑ 1인용 침대가 있는 그의 침실 ◳ 형용사 편도의 [영국영어; 미국영어 one-way] ❑ 편도 차표 값은 39파운드이다. ● 가산명사 편도 차표 ❑ 로스앤젤레스행 클럽클래스 편도표 ◳ 가산명사 싱글 레코드; 싱글 시디; 싱글 곡 ❑ 우승자들은 상금과 데뷔 싱글 시디를 발표할 수 있는 기회를 갖게 될 것이다. ◳ 불가산명사 단식 ❑ 독일의 보리스 베커가 남자 단식에서 우승했다.

▶**single out** PHRASAL VERB If you **single** someone **out** from a group, you choose them and give them special attention or treatment. ❑ *The gunman had singled Debilly out and waited for him.* ❑ *His immediate superior has singled him out for a special mention.*

구동사 선발하다, 지목하다 ❑ 그 총잡이는 데빌리를 지목하고 그를 기다렸다. ❑ 그의 직속상관이 그를 특별 표창감으로 지목했다.

single- /sɪŋɡ²l-/ COMB IN ADJ **single-** is used to form words which describe something that has one part or feature, rather than having two or more of them. ❑ *The single-engine plane landed in western Arizona.*

복합형-형용사 한 개의 ❑ 그 단발 엔진 비행기는 애리조나 서부에 착륙했다.

single-handed ADV If you do something **single-handed**, you do it on your own, without help from anyone else. [ADV after v] ❑ *I brought up my seven children single-handed.*

부사 혼자서, 홀로 ❑ 나는 내 아이 일곱을 혼자서 키웠다.

single-minded ADJ Someone who is **single-minded** has only one aim or purpose and is determined to achieve it. ❑ *They were effective politicians, ruthless and single-minded in their pursuit of political power.*

형용사 외골수인 ❑ 그들은 유능한 정치인들이었고 무자비하고 외골수로 정치권력을 추구했다.

sin|gle par|ent (**single parents**) N-COUNT A **single parent** is someone who is bringing up a child on their own, because the other parent is not living with them. ❑ *I was bringing up my three children as a single parent.* ❑ *...single parent families.*

가산명사 한 부모 ❑ 나는 한 부모로서 아이 셋을 기르고 있었다. ❑ 한 부모 가정

sin|gle sup|ple|ment (**single supplements**) also **single person supplement** N-COUNT A **single supplement** is an additional sum of money that a hotel charges for one person to stay in a room meant for two people. ❑ *You can avoid the single supplement by agreeing to share a twin room.*

가산명사 객실 추가 사용료 ❑ 트윈 룸을 공동으로 사용하기로 하면 객실 추가 사용료를 면할 수 있다.

sin|gu|lar /sɪŋɡyələr/ ◳ ADJ The **singular** form of a word is the form that is used when referring to one person or thing. ❑ *...the fifteen case endings of the singular form of the Finnish noun.* ◳ N-SING The **singular** of a noun is the form of it that is used to refer to one person or thing. ❑ *The inhabitants of the Arctic are known as the Inuit. The singular is Inuk.*

◳ 형용사 단수의 ❑ 핀란드 어 단수 명사의 15개 격 어미 ◳ 단수명사 단수형 ❑ 북극의 주민들은 이누잇이라는 명칭으로 알려져 있다. 그 단수형은 이눅이다.

sin|is|ter /sɪnɪstər/ ADJ Something that is **sinister** seems evil or harmful. ❑ *There was something sinister about him that she found disturbing.*

형용사 사악한 ❑ 그에게는 그녀가 불안하게 여기는 뭔가 사악한 면이 있었다.

sink ♦♢♢ /sɪŋk/ (**sinks, sinking, sank, sunk**) ◳ N-COUNT A **sink** is a large fixed container in a kitchen or bathroom, with faucets to supply water. In the kitchen, it is used for washing dishes, and in the bathroom, it is used to wash your hands and face. ❑ *The sink was full of dirty dishes.* ❑ *The bathroom is furnished with 2 toilets, 2 showers, and 2 sinks.* ◳ V-T/V-I If a boat **sinks** or if someone or something **sinks** it, it disappears below the surface of a mass of water. ❑ *In a naval battle your aim is to sink the enemy's ship.* ❑ *The boat was beginning to sink fast.* ◳ V-I If something **sinks**, it disappears below the surface of a mass of water. ❑ *A fresh egg will sink and an old egg will float.* ◳ V-I If something **sinks**, it moves slowly downward. ❑ *Far off to the west the sun was sinking.* ◳ V-I If something **sinks to** a lower level or standard, it falls to that level or standard. ❑ *Share prices would have sunk – hurting small and big investors.* ❑ *Pay increases have sunk to around seven per cent.* ◳ ADJ People use **sink** school or **sink** estate to refer to a school or housing estate that is in a very poor area with few resources. [BRIT, JOURNALISM] [ADJ n] ❑ *...unemployed teenagers from sink estates.* ◳ V-I If your heart or your spirits **sink**, you become depressed or lose hope. ❑ *My heart sank because I thought he was going to dump me for another girl.* ◳ V-T/V-I If something sharp **sinks** or **is sunk into** something solid, it goes deeply into it. ❑ *I sank my teeth into a peppermint cream.* ◳ V-T If someone **sinks** a well, mine, or other large hole, they make a deep hole in the ground, usually by digging or drilling. ❑ *...the site*

◳ 가산명사 싱크대 ❑ 싱크대에 더러운 접시가 가득했다. ❑ 화장실은 두 개의 변기, 두 개의 샤워기, 두 개의 싱크대를 갖추고 있다. ◳ 타동사/자동사 가라앉다; 가라앉히다 ❑ 해전에서는 적선을 침몰시키는 것이 목표이다. ❑ 배는 빠르게 가라앉고 있었다. ◳ 자동사 가라앉다 ❑ 신선한 계란은 가라앉고 오래된 계란은 뜬다. ◳ 자동사 천천히 내려가다 ❑ 멀리 서쪽에서 해가 지고 있었다. ◳ 자동사 떨어지다 ❑ 주가가 소액 및 거액 투자자 모두에게 피해를 주며 떨어졌을 것이다. ❑ 임금 상승률이 약 7퍼센트로 낮아졌다. ◳ 형용사 저소득 지역의 [영국영어, 언론] ❑ 저소득 주거 지구 출신의 실업 청소년들 ◳ 자동사 철렁하다, 낙심하다 ❑ 그가 다른 여자 때문에 나를 버릴 것 같아서 나는 가슴이 철렁했다. ◳ 타동사/자동사 깊이 들어가다; 깊이 박아 넣다 ❑ 나는 박하 아이스크림을 깊숙이 베어 물었다. ◳ 타동사 파다 ❑ 스텝슨슨이 최초의 수갱을 판 곳 ◳ 타동사 투자하다 ❑ 그는 그 프로젝트에 이미 2천5백만 달러를 투자한 상태이다. ◳ 구 흥하든 망하든 알아서 하다 ❑ 정부는 너무 빨리 비공식적인

where Stephenson sank his first mineshaft. **10** V-T If you **sink** money **into** a business or project, you spend money on it in the hope of making more money. ❑ *He has already sunk $25million into the project.* **11** PHRASE If you say that someone will have to **sink or swim**, you mean that they will have to succeed through their own efforts, or fail. ❑ *The government doesn't want to force inefficient firms to sink or swim too quickly.* to **sink without trace** →see **trace**

기업들에게 흥하든 망하든 알아서 하라고 강요하기를 원하지는 않는다.

Word Partnership	*sink*의 연어
N.	bathroom sink, **dishes in a** sink, **kitchen** sink **1** sink **a ship** **2**

▶**sink in** PHRASAL VERB When a statement or fact **sinks in**, you finally understand or realize it fully. ❑ *The implication took a while to sink in.*

구동사 완전히 이해되다 ❑ 함축된 의미를 완전히 이해하는 데 약간 시간이 걸렸다.

sip /sɪp/ (**sips, sipping, sipped**) **1** V-T/V-I If you **sip** a drink or **sip at** it, you drink by taking just a small amount at a time. ❑ *Jessica sipped her drink thoughtfully.* ❑ *He sipped at the glass and then put it down.* **2** N-COUNT A **sip** is a small amount of drink that you take into your mouth. ❑ *Harry took a sip of bourbon.*

1 타동사/자동사 홀짝이다, 조금 마시다 ❑ 제시카는 생각에 잠겨 음료수를 홀짝였다. ❑ 그는 잔을 조금 마시고는 내려놓았다. **2** 가산명사 한 모금 ❑ 해리는 버번 한 모금을 마셨다.

si|phon /ˈsaɪfⁿn/ (**siphons, siphoning, siphoned**) also **syphon** **1** V-T If you **siphon** liquid from a container, you make it come out through a tube and down into a lower container by enabling the pressure of the air on it to push it out. ❑ *She puts a piece of plastic tubing in her mouth and starts siphoning gas from a huge metal drum.* ● PHRASAL VERB **Siphon off** means the same as **siphon**. ❑ *Surgeons siphoned off fluid from his left lung.* **2** N-COUNT A **siphon** is a tube that you use for siphoning liquid. ❑ *The little containers are filled by siphon from the big ones.* **3** V-T If you **siphon** money or resources from something, you cause them to be used for a purpose for which they were not intended. ❑ *He siphoned $1.2 billion from his companies to prop up his crumbling media empire.* ● PHRASAL VERB **Siphon off** means the same as **siphon**. ❑ *He had siphoned off a small fortune in aid money from the United Nations.*

1 타동사 흡입관으로 빼내다 ❑ 그녀가 입 안에 플라스틱 관을 넣고 그걸 흡입관 삼아 쇠 드럼통에서 기름을 빼낸다. ● 구동사 흡입관으로 빼내다 ❑ 외과 의사들이 흡입관으로 그의 왼쪽 허파에서 액체를 뽑아냈다. **2** 가산명사 사이펀, 흡입관 ❑ 흡입관을 이용해 큰 통에서 작은 통으로 액체를 옮긴다. **3** 타동사 유용하다, 빼내다 ❑ 그는 자신의 무너져가는 미디어 제국을 지탱하기 위해 그의 회사들에서 12억 달러를 유용했다. ● 구동사 유용하다, 빼내다 ❑ 그는 국제 연합의 원조금에서 적지 않은 돈을 빼냈다.

sir ♦♦◇ /sɜr/ (**sirs**) **1** N-VOC People sometimes say **sir** as a very formal and polite way of addressing a man whose name they do not know or a man of superior rank. For example, a store clerk might address a male customer as **sir**. [POLITENESS] ❑ *Excuse me sir, but would you mind telling me what sort of car that is?* **2** N-TITLE **Sir** is the title used in front of the name of a knight or baronet. ❑ *She introduced me to Sir Tobias and Lady Clarke.* **3** CONVENTION You use the expression **Dear Sir** at the beginning of a formal letter or a business letter when you are writing to a man. You use **Dear Sirs** when you are writing to an organization. ❑ *Dear Sir, Enclosed is a copy of my rÿsumÝ for your consideration.*

1 호격명사 선생님 (남자에 대한 경칭) [공손체] ❑ 저, 선생님, 죄송하지만 저것이 어떤 종류의 차인지 말씀해 주실 수 있나요? **2** 경칭명사 경(卿) ❑ 그녀가 나를 토비아스 경과 클라크 귀부인에게 소개했다. **3** 관용 표현 담당자께 (공식 편지의 시두) ; 관계 기관 귀하 ❑ 담당자께, 참고하실 수 있도록 저의 이력서를 동봉합니다.

si|ren /ˈsaɪrən/ (**sirens**) N-COUNT A **siren** is a warning device which makes a long, loud noise. Most fire engines, ambulances, and police cars have sirens. ❑ *It sounds like an air raid siren.*

가산명사 사이렌 ❑ 마치 공습경보 사이렌 같다.

sis|ter ♦♦◇ /ˈsɪstər/ (**sisters**) **1** N-COUNT Your **sister** is a girl or woman who has the same parents as you. ❑ *His sister Sarah helped him.* ❑ *...Vanessa Bell, the sister of Virginia Woolf.* →see also **half-sister, stepsister**

1 가산명사 누이, 자매 ❑ 그의 누이인 새러가 그를 도와줬다. ❑ 버지니아 울프의 자매인 바네사 벨

Note that there is no common English word that can refer to both a brother and a sister. You simply have to use both words. ❑ *She has 13 brothers and sisters.* The word **sibling** exists, but it is very formal. Some Americans use **sib** as an informal substitute for **sibling**. ❑ *All my sibs were home for Thanksgiving.*

영어에는 남자형제와 여자형제를 함께 지칭하는 말이 없음을 유념하시오. 두 단어를 모두 써야 한다. ❑ 그녀는 남녀 형제가 13명이다. sibling이라는 말이 있지만 아주 격식체이다. 일부 미국인들은 sibling을 대신하는 구어체로 sib을 쓴다. ❑ 내 형제들이 모두 추수감사절에 집에 와 있었다.

2 N-COUNT; N-TITLE; N-VOC **Sister** is a title given to a woman who belongs to a religious community. ❑ *Sister Francesca entered the chapel.* **3** N-COUNT; N-TITLE; N-VOC A **sister** is a senior female nurse who supervises part of a hospital. [BRIT] ❑ *Ask to speak to the sister on the ward.* **4** N-COUNT You can describe a woman as your **sister** if you feel a connection with her, for example because she belongs to the same race, religion, country, or profession. ❑ *Modern woman has been freed from many of the duties that befell her sisters in times past.* **5** ADJ You can use **sister** to describe something that is of the same type or is connected in some way to another thing you have mentioned. For example, if a company has a **sister** company, they are connected. [ADJ n] ❑ *...the International Monetary Fund and its sister organisation, the World Bank.* →see **family**

2 가산명사; 경칭명사; 호격명사 수녀 ❑ 프란체스카 수녀가 성당에 들어갔다. **3** 가산명사; 경칭명사; 호격명사 수간호사 [영국영어] ❑ 병동의 수간호사와 면담을 요청하세요. **4** 가산명사 여성 동포, 여성 동지 ❑ 현대 여성은 자신의 전시대 동지들에게 떨어졌던 많은 책임들로부터 해방되었다. **5** 형용사 자매 관계의 ❑ 국제 통화 기금과 그 자매기관인 세계은행

sister-in-law (**sisters-in-law**) N-COUNT Someone's **sister-in-law** is the sister of their husband or wife, or the woman who is married to their brother. →see **family**

가산명사 형수; 제수; 처형; 처제; 시누이; 올케

sit ♦♦♦ /sɪt/ (**sits, sitting, sat**) **1** V-I If you **are sitting** somewhere, for example in a chair, your bottom is resting on the chair and the upper part of your body is upright. ❑ *Mother was sitting in her chair in the kitchen.* ❑ *They had been sitting watching television.* **2** V-I When you **sit** somewhere, you lower your body until you are sitting on something. ❑ *He set the cases against a wall and sat on them.* ❑ *Eva pulled over a chair and sat beside her husband.* ● PHRASAL VERB **Sit down** means the same as **sit**. ❑ *I sat down, stunned.* **3** V-T If you **sit** someone somewhere, you tell them to sit there or put them in a sitting position. ❑ *He used to sit me on his lap.* ● PHRASAL VERB To **sit** someone **down** somewhere means to **sit** them there. ❑ *She helped him out of the water and sat him down on the rock.* **4** V-T If you **sit** an examination, you take it. [BRIT] ❑ *June and July are the traditional months for sitting exams.* **5** V-I If you **sit on** a committee or other official group, you are a member of it. [no cont] ❑ *He was asked to sit on numerous committees.* **6** V-I When a legislature, court, or other official body **sits**, it officially carries out its work. [FORMAL] ❑ *Parliament sits for only 28 weeks out of 52.* **7** PHRASE If you **sit tight**, you remain in the same place or situation and do not take any action, usually because you are waiting for

1 자동사 앉아 있다 ❑ 어머니께서는 부엌의 의자에 앉아 계셨다. ❑ 그들은 앉아서 텔레비전을 보고 있었다. **2** 자동사 앉다 ❑ 그는 상자들을 벽에 대고 놓은 다음 그 위에 앉았다. ❑ 에바는 의자를 끌어와 남편 옆에 앉았다. ● 구동사 앉다 ❑ 나는 충격을 받은 채 앉았다. **3** 타동사 앉히다 ❑ 그는 나를 무릎에 앉히곤 했다. ● 구동사 앉히다 ❑ 그녀는 그가 물에서 나오는 것을 도와준 후 그를 바위에 앉혔다. **4** 타동사 (시험을) 보다 [영국영어] ❑ 6월과 7월이 전통적으로 시험을 보는 기간이다. **5** 자동사 (위원 등의) 일원이 되다 ❑ 그는 무수한 위원회의 위원이 되어 달라는 요청을 받았다. **6** 자동사 (공공 기관의) 업무를 보다 [격식체] ❑ 의회는 52주 중 단 28주 동안만 개원한다. **7** 구 가만히 있다 ❑ 가만히 있어. 금방 올게.

something to happen. ❑ *Sit tight. I'll be right back.* **to sit on the fence** →see **fence**

▶**sit back** PHRASAL VERB If you **sit back** while something is happening, you relax and do not become involved in it. [INFORMAL] ❑ *They didn't have to do anything except sit back and enjoy life.*

▶**sit in on** PHRASAL VERB If you **sit in on** a lesson, meeting, or discussion, you are present while it is taking place but do not take part in it. ❑ *Will they permit you to sit in on a few classes?*

▶**sit on** PHRASAL VERB If you say that someone **is sitting on** something, you mean that they are delaying dealing with it. [INFORMAL] ❑ *He had been sitting on the document for at least two months.*

▶**sit out** PHRASAL VERB If you **sit** something **out**, you wait for it to finish, without taking any action. ❑ *The only thing I can do is keep quiet and sit this one out.*

▶**sit through** PHRASAL VERB If you **sit through** something such as a movie, lecture, or meeting, you stay until it is finished although you are not enjoying it. ❑ *...movies so bad you can hardly bear to sit through them.*

▶**sit up** ▮ PHRASAL VERB If you **sit up**, you move into a sitting position when you have been leaning back or lying down. ❑ *Her head spins dizzily as soon as she sits up.* ▮ PHRASAL VERB If you **sit** someone **up**, you move them into a sitting position when they have been leaning back or lying down. ❑ *She sat him up and made him comfortable.* ▮ PHRASAL VERB If you **sit up**, you do not go to bed although it is very late. ❑ *We sat up drinking and talking.* ▮ →see also **sit-up**

site ♦♦◊ /saɪt/ (**sites, siting, sited**) ▮ N-COUNT A **site** is a piece of ground that is used for a particular purpose or where a particular thing happens. ❑ *I was working as a foreman on a building site.* ▮ N-COUNT **The site of** an important event is the place where it happened. ❑ *Scientists have described the Aral sea as the site of the worst ecological disaster on earth.* ▮ N-COUNT A **site** is a piece of ground where something such as a statue or building stands or used to stand. ❑ *...the site of Moses' tomb.* ▮ N-COUNT A **site** is the same as a **website**. ▮ V-T If something **is sited** in a particular place or position, it is put there or built there. [usu passive] ❑ *He said chemical weapons had never been sited in Germany.* ● **siting** N-SING ❑ *...controls on the siting of gas storage vessels.* ▮ PHRASE If someone or something is **on site**, they are in a particular area or group of buildings where people work, study, or stay. ❑ *It is cheaper to have extra building work done when the builder is on site, rather than bringing him back for a small job.* ▮ PHRASE If someone or something is **off site**, they are away from a particular area or group of buildings where people work, study, or stay. ❑ *There is ample car parking off site.*

sit-in (**sit-ins**) N-COUNT A **sit-in** is a protest in which people go to a public place and stay there for a long time. [BUSINESS] ❑ *The campaigners held a sit-in outside the Supreme Court.*

sit|ting room (**sitting rooms**) also **sitting-room** N-COUNT A **sitting room** is a room in a house where people sit and relax. [BRIT; AM usually **living room**]

sit|uat|ed /sɪtʃueɪtɪd/ ADJ If something is **situated** in a particular place or position, it is in that place or position. [v-link ADJ prep, adv ADJ] ❑ *His hotel is situated in one of the loveliest places on the Loire.*

situa|tion ♦♦◊ /sɪtʃueɪʃⁿn/ (**situations**) ▮ N-COUNT You use **situation** to refer generally to what is happening in a particular place at a particular time, or to refer to what is happening to you. ❑ *Army officers said the situation was under control.* ❑ *And now for a look at the travel situation in the rest of the country.* ▮ PHRASE **Situations Vacant** is the title of a column or page in a newspaper where jobs are advertised. [mainly BRIT; AM **Employment**] ❑ *...the Situations Vacant column in the local newspaper.*

구동사 가만히 있다 [비격식체] ❑ 그들은 가만히 앉아서 인생을 즐기는 것 말고는 할 일이 없었다.

구동사 참관하다 ❑ 강의 몇 개를 청강하는 것도 허락할까요?

구동사 미적거리다, 뭉개다, 쥐고 아무 짓도 안 하다 [비격식체] ❑ 그는 그 문건을 갖고 최소 두 달 동안 뭉개기만 하고 있었다.

구동사 -이 끝나기만 가만히 기다리다 ❑ 지금 내가 할 수 있는 것이라고는 조용히 이것이 끝나기만 기다리는 것뿐이다.

구동사 억지로 끝까지 앉아 있다 ❑ 끝까지 보고 앉아 있기가 힘든 형편없는 영화들

▮ 구동사 똑바로 앉다 ❑ 그녀는 똑바로 앉자마자 머리가 어지럽게 돌기 시작한다. ▮ 구동사 똑바로 앉히다 ❑ 그녀는 그를 똑바로 앉혀 편안하게 해 줬다. ▮ 구동사 늦게까지 안 자다 ❑ 우리는 밤샘하며 술 마시며 이야기했다.

▮ 가산명사 현장, 부지 ❑ 나는 건설 현장에서 십장으로 일하고 있었다. ▮ 가산명사 현장 ❑ 과학자들은 아랄 해를 지구상 최악의 환경 재앙을 겪은 현장이라고 설명한다. ▮ 가산명사 터, 장소 ❑ 모세의 무덤이 있는 장소 ▮ 가산명사 웹사이트 ▮ 타동사 배치되다 ❑ 그는 독일에 화학 무기를 둔 적이 없다고 말했다. ● 배치 단수명사 ❑ 기름 저장 선박의 배치에 관한 규제 ▮ 구 현장에 있을 때, 작업 중인 ❑ 건축업자가 현장에 있을 때 추가 건설 작업을 맡기는 것이 작은 일 때문에 나중에 다시 부르는 것보다 싸다. ▮ 구 부지 밖에, 작업장 밖에 있는 ❑ 부지 밖에 주차 공간이 넉넉하게 있다.

가산명사 연좌 농성 [경제] ❑ 운동가들은 대법원 밖에서 연좌 농성을 벌였다.

가산명사 거실 [영국영어; 미국영어 대개 living room]

형용사 위치한 ❑ 그의 호텔은 루아르 강변에서 가장 아름다운 곳 중 한 곳에 위치해 있다.

▮ 가산명사 상황 ❑ 육군 장교들은 상황이 통제하에 있다고 했다. ❑ 이제 전국 다른 지역의 교통 상황을 살펴보겠습니다. ▮ 구 구인 광고 [주로 영국영어; 미국영어 employment] ❑ 지역 신문의 구인 광고란

sit-up (**sit-ups**) [AM also **situp**] N-COUNT **Sit-ups** are exercises that you do to strengthen your stomach muscles. They involve sitting up from a lying position while keeping your legs straight on the floor. ❏ *He does 100 sit-ups each day.*

six ◆◆◆ /sɪks/ (**sixes**) NUM **Six** is the number 6. ❏ *...a glorious career spanning more than six decades.*

six|teen ◆◆◆ /sɪkstin/ (**sixteens**) NUM **Sixteen** is the number 16. ❏ *...exams taken at the age of sixteen.* ❏ *He worked sixteen hours a day.*

six|teenth ◆◇◇ /sɪkstinθ/ (**sixteenths**) ◼ ORD The **sixteenth** item in a series is the one that you count as number sixteen. ❏ *...the sixteenth century AD.* ◻ FRACTION A **sixteenth** is one of sixteen equal parts of something. ❏ *...a sixteenth of a second.*

sixth ◆◆◇ /sɪksθ/ (**sixths**) ◼ ORD The **sixth** item in a series is the one that you count as number six. ❏ *...the sixth round of the World Cup.* ◻ FRACTION A **sixth** is one of six equal parts of something. ❏ *The company yesterday shed a sixth of its workforce.*

sixth form (**sixth forms**) also **sixth-form** N-COUNT The **sixth form** in a British school consists of the classes that students go into at the age of about sixteen, usually in order to study for A levels. ❏ *She was offered her first modelling job while she was still in the sixth form.*

six|ti|eth ◆◆◇ /sɪkstiəθ/ (**sixtieths**) ◼ ORD The **sixtieth** item in a series is the one that you count as number sixty. ❏ *He is to retire on his sixtieth birthday.* ◻ FRACTION A **sixtieth** is one of sixty equal parts of something.

six|ty ◆◆◇ /sɪksti/ (**sixties**) ◼ NUM **Sixty** is the number 60. ❏ *...the sunniest April in Britain for more than sixty years.* ◻ N-PLURAL When you talk about the **sixties**, you are referring to numbers between 60 and 69. For example, if you are **in your sixties**, you are aged between 60 and 69. If the temperature is **in the sixties**, it is between 60 and 69 degrees. ❏ *...a lively widow in her sixties.* ◼ N-PLURAL The **sixties** is the decade between 1960 and 1969. ❏ *In the sixties there were the deaths of the two Kennedy brothers and Martin Luther King.*

siz|able /saɪzəbəl/ →see **sizeable**

size ◆◆◇ /saɪz/ (**sizes**) ◼ N-VAR The **size of** something is how big or small it is. Something's size is determined by comparing it to other things, counting it, or measuring it. ❏ *In 1970 the average size of a French farm was 19 hectares.* ❏ *...shelves containing books of various sizes.* ◻ N-UNCOUNT The **size** of something is the fact that it is very large. ❏ *He knows the size of the task.* ◼ N-COUNT A **size** is one of a series of graded measurements, especially for things such as clothes or shoes. ❏ *My sister is the same height but only a size 12.*

Word Partnership		*size의 연어*
ADJ.	**average** size, **full** size ◼	
	sheer size ◻	
	right size, size **large/medium/small** ◼	
N.	**bite** size, **class** size, **family** size, **life** size, **pocket** size ◼	
	size **chart** ◼	
V.	**double in** size, **increase in** size, **vary in** size ◼	
	a size **fits** ◼	

▶**size up** PHRASAL VERB If you **size up** a person or situation, you carefully look at the person or think about the situation, so that you can decide how to act. [INFORMAL] ❏ *Some U.S. manufacturers have been sizing up the UK as a possible market for their clothes.*

size|able /saɪzəbəl/ also **sizable** ADJ **Sizeable** means fairly large. ❏ *Harry has inherited the house and a sizeable chunk of land that surrounds it.*

siz|zle /sɪzəl/ (**sizzles, sizzling, sizzled**) V-I If something such as hot oil or fat **sizzles**, it makes hissing sounds. ❏ *The sausages and burgers sizzled on the barbecue.*

skate /skeɪt/ (**skates, skating, skated**) ◼ N-COUNT **Skates** are ice-skates. ◻ N-COUNT **Skates** are roller-skates. ◼ V-I If you **skate**, you move about wearing ice-skates or roller-skates. ❏ *I actually skated, and despite some teetering I did not fall on the ice.* ● **skat|ing** N-UNCOUNT ❏ *They all went skating together in the winter.* ● **skat|er** (**skaters**) N-COUNT ❏ *West Lake, an outdoor ice-skating rink, attracts skaters during the day and night.*

skate|board /skeɪtbɔrd/ (**skateboards**) N-COUNT A **skateboard** is a narrow board with wheels at each end, which people stand on and ride for pleasure. →see **skateboarding**

skate|board|ing /skeɪtbɔrdɪŋ/ N-UNCOUNT **Skateboarding** is the activity of riding on a skateboard. ❏ *...a skateboarding competition.* →see Picture Dictionary: **skateboarding**

skel|etal /skɛlɪtəl/ ◼ ADJ **Skeletal** means relating to the bones in your body. [ADJ n] ❏ *...the skeletal remains of seven adults.* ◻ ADJ A **skeletal** person is so thin that you can see their bones through their skin. ❏ *...a hospital filled with skeletal children.*

skel|eton /skɛlɪtən/ (**skeletons**) ◼ N-COUNT Your **skeleton** is the framework of bones in your body. ❏ *...a human skeleton.* ◻ N-COUNT A **skeleton** staff is the smallest number of staff necessary in order to run an organization or service. [ADJ n] ❏ *Only a skeleton staff remains to show anyone interested around the site.* ◼ N-COUNT The **skeleton** of something such as a building or a plan is its basic framework.

[미국영어 situp] 가산명사 윗몸 일으키기 ❏ 그는 윗몸 일으키기를 매일 100회씩 한다.

수사 6, 여섯 ❏ 60년이 넘는 기간 동안의 화려한 경력

수사 16, 열여섯 ❏ 열여섯 살에 치른 시험 ❏ 그는 매일 열여섯 시간을 일했다.

◼ 서수 열여섯 번째, 열여섯 번째 ❏ 서기 16세기 ◻ 분수 16분의 1 ❏ 16분의 1초

◼ 서수 여섯 번째, 열여섯 번째 ❏ 월드컵 6차전 ◻ 분수 6분의 1 ❏ 그 회사는 어제 전체 인력의 6분의 1을 감원했다.

가산명사 영국에서 16~18세 학생들이 다니는 대학 준비 과정 (한국의 고등학교에 해당) ❏ 그녀는 아직 고등학생일 때 처음으로 모델 일을 제안받았다.

◼ 서수 예순 번째, 예순 번째 ❏ 그는 예순 번째 생일 때 은퇴할 것이다. ◻ 분수 60분의 1

◼ 수사 60, 예순 ❏ 60여 년 동안 영국에서 가장 화창했던 4월 ◻ 복수명사 60대; 60대의; (온도가) 60도 내의 ❏ 60대의 팔팔한 과부 ◼ 복수명사 60년대 ❏ 60년대에는 두 케네디 형제와 마틴 루터 킹이 죽었다.

◼ 가산명사 또는 불가산명사 크기 ❏ 1970년에 프랑스 농장의 평균 크기는 19헥타르였다. ◻ 다양한 크기의 책이 꽂힌 책꽂이 ◻ 불가산명사 (엄청난) 규모 ❏ 그는 그 일의 규모가 어느 정도인지를 안다. ◼ 가산명사 크기, 치수 ❏ 내 누이는 키가 같지만 옷 치수는 12를 입는다.

구동사 가늠하다 [비격식체] ❏ 일부 미국 제조사들은 자신들이 생산하는 옷의 잠재적 시장으로 영국을 가늠해 보고 있다.

형용사 꽤 큰, 상당한 ❏ 해리는 집과 그 주변의 상당한 땅을 물려받았다.

자동사 지글거리다 ❏ 소시지와 버거용 고기가 바비큐 판 위에서 지글거리고 있었다.

◼ 가산명사 아이스스케이트 ◻ 가산명사 롤러스케이트 ◼ 자동사 스케이트를 타다 ❏ 나는 실제로 스케이트를 탔는데, 약간 비틀거리긴 했지만 얼음판에 넘어지지는 않았다. ● 스케이트 타기 불가산명사 ❏ 그들은 겨울에는 모두 같이 스케이트를 타러 갔다. ● 스케이트를 타는 사람 가산명사 ❏ 실외 아이스스케이트 링크인 웨스트 레이크는 밤낮으로 사람들이 스케이트를 타러 몰려든다.

가산명사 스케이트보드

불가산명사 스케이트보드 타기 ❏ 스케이트보드 대회

◼ 형용사 뼈의 ❏ 성인 7명의 유골 ◻ 형용사 뼈가 앙상한 ❏ 뼈가 앙상한 아이들이 가득한 병원

◼ 가산명사 골격, 뼈대 ❏ 인간의 골격 ◻ 형용사 최소 인원의 ❏ 최소한의 직원만이 남아 관심을 가진 사람들에게 현장을 보여 준다. ◼ 가산명사 뼈대, 골조 ❏ 루드바에는 건물의 뼈대만이 남아 있고 마을로서의 존재는 끝난 상태였다.

a
b
c
d
e
f
g
h
i
j
k
l
m
n
o
p
q
r
s
t
u
v
w
x
y
z

Picture Dictionary

skateboarding

elbow pad

helmet

knee pad

skateboard

platform

wheel

ramp

❏ *The town of Rudbar had ceased to exist, with only skeletons of buildings remaining.*
→see **shark**
→see Word Web: **skeleton**

skep|tic skɛptɪk (**skeptics**) [BRIT **sceptic**] N-COUNT A **skeptic** is a person who has doubts about things that other people believe. ❏ *He is a skeptic who tries to keep an open mind.*

skep|ti|cal /skɛptɪkᵊl/ [BRIT **sceptical**] ADJ If you are **skeptical about** something, you have doubts about it. ❏ *Others here are more skeptical about the chances for justice being done.*

skep|ti|cism /skɛptɪsɪzəm/ [BRIT **scepticism**] N-UNCOUNT **Skepticism** is great doubt about whether something is true or useful. ❏ *A survey reflects business skepticism about the strength of the economic recovery.*

sketch /skɛtʃ/ (**sketches, sketching, sketched**) ◼ N-COUNT A **sketch** is a drawing that is done quickly without a lot of details. Artists often use sketches as a preparation for a more detailed painting or drawing. ❏ *...a sketch of a soldier by Orpen.* ◻ V-T/V-I If you **sketch**, or **sketch** something, you make a quick, rough drawing of it. ❏ *Clare and David Astor are sketching a view of far Spanish hills.* ◼ N-COUNT A **sketch of** a situation, person, or incident is a brief description of it without many details. ❏ *...thumbnail sketches of heads of state and political figures.* ◼ V-T If you **sketch** a situation or incident, you give a short description of it, including only the most important facts. ❏ *Cross sketched the story briefly, telling the facts just as they had happened.* ● PHRASAL VERB **Sketch out** means the same as **sketch**. ❏ *Luxembourg sketched out an acceptable compromise between Britain, France, and Germany.* ◼ N-COUNT A **sketch** is a short humorous piece of acting, usually forming part of a comedy show. ❏ *...a five-minute sketch about a folk singer.* →see **animation, drawing**

sketchy /skɛtʃi/ (**sketchier, sketchiest**) ADJ **Sketchy** information about something does not include many details and is therefore incomplete or inadequate. ❏ *Details of what actually happened are still sketchy.*

skew /skyu/ (**skews, skewing, skewed**) V-T If something **is skewed**, it is changed or affected to some extent by a new or unusual factor, and so is not correct or normal. ❏ *The arithmetic of nuclear running costs has been skewed by the fall in the cost of other fuels.*

[영국영어 sceptic] 가산명사 회의론자 ❏ 그는 항상 열린 마음을 가지려는 회의론자이다.

[영국영어 sceptical] 형용사 회의적인 ❏ 이곳의 다른 사람들은 정의가 구현될 가능성에 대해 좀 더 회의적이다.

[영국영어 scepticism] 불가산명사 회의론 ❏ 한 조사는 경기 회복력에 대한 업계의 회의를 반영하고 있다.

◼ 가산명사 스케치 ❏ 오르펜이 한 군인을 그린 스케치 ◻ 타동사/자동사 스케치하다 ❏ 클레어와 데이비드 애스터는 멀리 스페인의 구릉이 펼쳐진 광경을 스케치하고 있다. ◼ 가산명사 개요, 요약문 ❏ 국가 정상과 정치인들에 대한 간단한 묘사 ◼ 타동사 개요를 말하다 ❏ 크로스는 사건의 개요를 간략하게 추려 발생한 사실들을 그대로 말했다. ● 구동사 개요를 말하다 ❏ 룩셈부르크는 영국과 프랑스와 독일 사이에 합의 가능한 타협안의 개요를 제시했다. ◼ 가산명사 촌극 ❏ 포크 송 가수에 대한 5분짜리 촌극

형용사 대강의, 불분명한 ❏ 사건의 상세한 실제 경위는 아직도 미흡하다.

타동사 왜곡되다, 빗나가다 ❏ 핵발전소의 운영비 산출이 다른 연료들의 가격 하락으로 인하여 빗나가게 되었다.

Word Web   skeleton

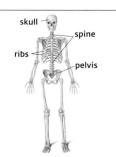

skull

spine

ribs

pelvis

Australian scientists recently discovered some unusual **skeletons** on the Indonesian island of Flores. The **bones** are about 18,000 years old and indicate that a race of human-like creatures, only about the size of three-year-old children, once lived there. The overall skeleton and the **skull** are much smaller than those of modern human beings. The femur and tibia bones are also differently shaped. However, in most other ways they seem very closely related to humans.

skew|er /skyu̲ər/ (**skewers**) N-COUNT A **skewer** is a long metal pin which is used to hold pieces of food together during cooking.

ski ♦♢♢ /ski̲/ (**skis, skiing, skied**) **1** N-COUNT **Skis** are long, flat, narrow pieces of wood, metal, or plastic that are fastened to boots so that you can move easily on snow or water. □ ...*a pair of skis.* **2** V-I When people **ski**, they move over snow or water on skis. □ *They surf, ski, and ride.* ● **ski|er** /ski̲ər/ (**skiers**) N-COUNT □ *He is an enthusiastic skier.* ● **ski|ing** N-UNCOUNT □ *My hobbies were skiing and scuba diving.* **3** ADJ You use **ski** to refer to things that are concerned with skiing. [ADJ n] □ ...*the Swiss ski resort of Klosters.* □ ...*a private ski instructor.*

skid /ski̲d/ (**skids, skidding, skidded**) V-I If a vehicle **skids**, it slides sideways or forward while moving, for example when you are trying to stop it suddenly on a wet road. □ *The car pulled up too fast and skidded on the dusty shoulder of the road.* ● N-COUNT **Skid** is also a noun. □ *I slammed the brakes on and went into a skid.*

skil|ful /ski̲lfəl/ →see **skillful**

skill ♦♢♢ /ski̲l/ (**skills**) **1** N-COUNT A **skill** is a type of work or activity which requires special training and knowledge. □ *Most of us will know someone who is always learning new skills, or studying new fields.* **2** N-UNCOUNT **Skill** is the knowledge and ability that enables you to do something well. □ *The cut of a diamond depends on the skill of its craftsman.*

Thesaurus	skill의 참조어
N.	ability, proficiency, talent **1** **2**

skilled /ski̲ld/ **1** ADJ Someone who is **skilled** has the knowledge and ability to do something well. □ *Few doctors are actually trained, and not all are skilled, in helping their patients make choices.* **2** ADJ **Skilled** work can only be done by people who have had some training. □ *New industries demanded skilled labour not available locally.*

skill|ful /ski̲lfəl/ [BRIT **skilful**] ADJ Someone who is **skillful** at something does it very well. □ *He actually is quite a skillful campaigner.* ● **skill|ful|ly** ADV [ADV with v] □ *The city's rulers skillfully played both powers off against each other.*

skim /ski̲m/ (**skims, skimming, skimmed**) **1** V-T If you **skim** something **from** the surface of a liquid, you remove it. □ *Rough seas today prevented specially equipped ships from skimming oil off the water's surface.* **2** V-T If something **skims** a surface, it moves quickly along just above it. □ ...*seagulls skimming the waves.* **3** V-T If you **skim** a piece of writing, you read through it quickly. □ *He skimmed the pages quickly, then read them again more carefully.*

skim milk [BRIT, sometimes AM **skimmed milk**] N-UNCOUNT **Skim milk** is milk from which the cream has been removed.

skimpy /ski̲mpi/ (**skimpier, skimpiest**) ADJ Something that is **skimpy** is too small in size or quantity. □ ...*skimpy underwear.*

skin ♦♦♢ /ski̲n/ (**skins, skinning, skinned**) **1** N-VAR Your **skin** is the natural covering of your body. □ *His skin is clear and smooth.* □ *There are three major types of skin cancer.* **2** N-VAR An animal **skin** is skin which has been removed from a dead animal. Skins are used to make things such as coats and rugs. □ *That was real crocodile skin.* **3** N-VAR The **skin** of a fruit or vegetable is its outer layer or covering. □ *The outer skin of the orange is called the "zest."* **4** N-SING If a **skin** forms on the surface of a liquid, a thin, fairly solid layer forms on it. □ *Stir the custard occasionally to prevent a skin forming.* **5** V-T If you **skin** a dead animal, you remove its skin. □ ...*with the expertise of a chef skinning a rabbit.*
→see Word Web: **skin**

Word Partnership	skin의 연어
N.	**skin and bones**, **skin cancer**, **skin cells**, **skin color** (or color of *someone's* skin), **skin cream**, **skin problems**, **skin type** **1** **leopard skin** **2**
ADJ.	**dark skin**, **dry skin**, **fair skin**, **oily skin**, **pale skin**, **sensitive skin**, **smooth skin**, **soft skin** **1**

skin|ny /ski̲ni/ (**skinnier, skinniest**) ADJ A **skinny** person is extremely thin, often in a way that you find unattractive. [INFORMAL] □ *He was quite a skinny little boy.*

skip /ski̲p/ (**skips, skipping, skipped**) **1** V-I If you **skip** along, you move almost as if you are dancing, with a series of little jumps from one foot to the other.

가산명사 꼬치

1 가산명사 스키 □ 스키 한 벌 **2** 자동사 스키를 타다 □ 그들은 서핑도 하고 스키도 타고 말도 탄다. ● 스키어 가산명사 □ 그는 열렬한 스키어이다. ● 스키 타기 불가산명사 □ 나의 취미는 스키와 스쿠버 다이빙이었다. **3** 형용사 스키의 □ 스위스의 스키 휴양지인 클로스터즈 □ 개인 스키 강사

자동사 미끄러지다 □ 차가 너무 빨리 정지하다가 모래가 덮인 갓길에서 미끄러졌다. ● 가산명사 미끄러짐 □ 나는 브레이크를 있는 대로 밟았고 차는 미끄러졌다.

1 가산명사 기술 □ 우리들 대부분은 항상 새로운 기술을 배우거나 새로운 영역을 공부하는 사람을 적어도 한 사람은 안다. **2** 불가산명사 기량 □ 가공된 다이아몬드의 모양은 기술자의 기량에 달려 있다.

1 형용사 능숙한, 숙련된 □ 소수의 의사들만이 환자들이 선택을 할 수 있도록 도움을 주는 훈련을 받으며 그것에 능숙한 사람은 더 드물다. **2** 형용사 숙련을 요하는 □ 새로운 산업들은 지역 내에서 구하기 어려운 숙련 노동력을 필요로 하였다.

[영국영어 skilful] 형용사 유능한, 능숙한 □ 그는 사실 상당히 유능한 운동원이다. ● 유능하게, 능숙하게 부사 □ 그 도시의 지도자들은 능숙하게 두 강대 세력을 서로 대치시켜 어부지리를 취했다.

1 타동사 (수면에 뜬 것을) 걷어 내다 □ 오늘 거친 파도 때문에 특수 장비를 갖춘 선박들이 수면에서 기름을 걷어 내지 못했다. **2** 타동사 스쳐 지나가다, 미끄러져 가다 □ 파도 위를 미끄러지듯 날아가는 갈매기들 **3** 타동사 훑어보다 □ 그는 책장들을 훑어보고 난 뒤 다시 더 자세히 읽었다.

[영국영어, 미국영어 가끔 skimmed milk] 불가산명사 탈지 우유

형용사 빈약한; 너무 작은 □ 너무 작은 속옷

1 가산명사 또는 불가산명사 피부 □ 그의 피부는 깨끗하고 매끄럽다. □ 피부암에는 크게 세 가지 유형이 있다. **2** 가산명사 또는 불가산명사 가죽 □ 그것은 진짜 악어가죽이었다. **3** 가산명사 또는 불가산명사 (과일 등의) 껍질 □ 오렌지의 바깥 껍질을 '제스트'라고 부른다. **4** 단수명사 막 □ 커스터드에 막이 생기지 않도록 간간이 저으세요. **5** 타동사 가죽을 벗기다 □ 토끼의 가죽을 벗기는 주방장의 능숙한 솜씨

형용사 깡마른, 비쩍 마른 [비격식체] □ 그는 상당히 깡마른 아이였다.

1 자동사 깡충깡충 뛰다, 팔짝팔짝 뛰다 □ 그들은 그 남자와 그 뒤를 깡충깡충 따라가는 작은 소녀를 봤다.

Word Web	skin

What is the best thing you can do for your **skin**? Stay out of the sun. When skin **cells** grow normally, the skin remains smooth and firm. However, the sun's **ultraviolet** rays sometimes cause damage. This can lead to **sunburn**, **wrinkles**, and skin cancer. The damage may not be apparent for several years. However, doctors have discovered that even a light **suntan** can be dangerous. **Sunlight** makes the melanin in skin turn dark. This is the body's attempt to protect itself from the ultraviolet radiation. Dermatologists recommend limiting exposure to the sun and always using a **sunscreen**.

They saw the man with a little girl skipping along behind him. *We went skipping down the street arm in arm.* ● N-COUNT **Skip** is also a noun. *The boxer gave a little skip as he came out of his corner.* **2** V-T/V-I When someone **skips rope**, they jump up and down over a rope which they or two other people are holding at each end and turning around and around. In British English, you say that someone **skips**. *Outside a dozen children were skipping and singing a complicated rhyme.* ● **skipping** N-UNCOUNT *Skipping is one of the most enjoyable aerobic activities.* **3** V-T If you **skip** something that you usually do or something that most people do, you decide not to do it. *It is important not to skip meals.* **4** V-T/V-I If you **skip** or **skip over** a part of something you are reading or a story you are telling, you miss it out or pass over it quickly and move on to something else. *You might want to skip the exercises in this chapter.* **5** V-I If you **skip from** one subject or activity **to** another, you move quickly from one to the other, although there is no obvious connection between them. *She kept up a continuous chatter, skipping from one subject to the next.* **6** N-COUNT A **skip** is a large, open, metal container which is used to hold and take away large unwanted items and trash. [BRIT; AM **Dumpster**]

skip|per /skɪpər/ (**skippers**) **1** N-COUNT; N-VOC You can use **skipper** to refer to the captain of a ship or boat. *...the skipper of an English fishing boat.* **2** N-COUNT You can use **skipper** to refer to the captain of a sports team. [mainly BRIT] *The England skipper is confident.*

skir|mish /skɜrmɪʃ/ (**skirmishes, skirmishing, skirmished**) **1** N-COUNT A **skirmish** is a minor battle. *Border skirmishes between India and Pakistan were common.* **2** V-RECIP If people **skirmish**, they fight. *They were skirmishing close to the minefield now.*

skirt /skɜrt/ (**skirts, skirting, skirted**) **1** N-COUNT A **skirt** is a piece of clothing worn by women and girls. It fastens at the waist and hangs down around the legs. **2** V-T Something that **skirts** an area is situated around the edge of it. *We raced across a large field that skirted the slope of a hill.* **3** V-T If you **skirt** a problem or question, you avoid dealing with it. *He skirted the hardest issues, concentrating on areas of possible agreement.* →see **clothing**

skull /skʌl/ (**skulls**) N-COUNT Your **skull** is the bony part of your head which encloses your brain. *Her husband was later treated for a fractured skull.* →see **skeleton**

sky ♦◇◇ /skaɪ/ (**skies**) N-VAR The **sky** is the space around the earth which you can see when you stand outside and look upward. *The sun is already high in the sky.* *...warm sunshine and clear blue skies.*

Word Partnership	*sky*의 연어
ADV.	sky **above, the** sky **overhead, up in the** sky
ADJ.	**black** sky, **blue** sky, **bright** sky, **clear** sky, **dark** sky, **empty** sky, **high in the** sky

sky|line /skaɪlaɪn/ (**skylines**) N-COUNT The **skyline** is the line or shape that is formed where the sky meets buildings or the land. *The village church dominates the skyline.*

sky|scraper /skaɪskreɪpər/ (**skyscrapers**) N-COUNT A **skyscraper** is a very tall building in a city. →see **city** →see Word Web: **skyscraper**

slab /slæb/ (**slabs**) N-COUNT A **slab of** something is a thick, flat piece of it. [with supp] *...slabs of stone.*

slack /slæk/ (**slacker, slackest, slacks, slacking, slacked**) **1** ADJ Something that is **slack** is loose and not firmly stretched or tightly in position. *The boy's jaw went slack.* **2** ADJ A **slack** period is one in which there is not much work or activity. *The workload can be evened out, instead of the shop having busy times and slack periods.* **3** ADJ Someone who is **slack** in their work does not do it properly. [DISAPPROVAL] *Many publishers have simply become far too slack.* **4** V-I If someone **is slacking**, they are not working as hard as they should. [DISAPPROVAL] [only cont] *He had never let a foreman see him slacking.* ● PHRASAL VERB **Slack off** means the same as **slack**. *If someone slacks off, Bill comes down hard.*

slack|en /slækən/ (**slackens, slackening, slackened**) **1** V-T/V-I If something **slackens** or if you **slacken** it, it becomes slower, less active, or less intense. *Inflationary pressures continued to slacken last month.* **2** V-T/V-I If your grip or a part of your body **slackens** or if you **slacken** your grip, it becomes looser or more relaxed. *Her grip slackened on Arnold's arm.*

slam /slæm/ (**slams, slamming, slammed**) **1** V-T/V-I If you **slam** a door or window or if it **slams**, it shuts noisily and with great force. *She slammed the door and locked it behind her.* *I was relieved to hear the front door slam.* **2** V-T If you

---

1 가산명사; 호격명사 선장 *영국 어선의 선장* **2** 가산명사 주장 [주로 영국영어] *영국의 주장은 자신감에 차 있다.*

1 가산명사 작은 전투, 소규모 접전 *인도와 파키스탄 간의 국경에서 작은 전투가 자주 벌어졌다.* **2** 상호동사 싸우다, 접전을 벌이다 *그들은 이제 지뢰밭 근처에서 싸우고 있었다.*

1 가산명사 치마, 스커트 **2** 타동사 두르다 *언덕 경사 주변을 두르는 커다란 들판이 가로질러 달렸다.* **3** 타동사 회피하다 *그는 가장 어려운 문제들은 회피하고 합의가 가능한 영역에만 집중했다.*

가산명사 두개골 *그녀의 남편은 나중에 두개골 골절로 치료를 받았다.*

가산명사 또는 불가산명사 하늘 *태양은 이미 하늘 높이 떠 있다.* *따뜻한 햇볕과 맑고 푸른 하늘*

가산명사 스카이라인 *마을 교회가 하늘 위로 윤곽이 가장 두드러진다.*

가산명사 마천루

가산명사 두껍고 평평한 조각, 판 *석판*

1 형용사 느슨한 *소년의 입이 벌어졌다.* **2** 형용사 한산한 *작업장의 일이 바쁘다가 한산하다가 하지 않게 작업량을 균등하게 분산시킬 수 있다.* **3** 형용사 태만한 [탐탁잖음] *많은 출판업자들이 그저 너무 태만해졌다.* **4** 자동사 게으름 피우다 [탐탁잖음] *그는 게으름 피우다 감독한테 걸린 적이 한 번도 없었다.* ● 구동사 게으름 피우다 *누군가가 게으름을 피우면 빌이 호되게 나무란다.*

1 타동사/자동사 완화되다; 완화하다 *물가 인상 압력이 지난달 계속 완화되었다.* **2** 타동사/자동사 느슨해지다 *아놀드의 팔을 잡았던 그녀의 손아귀가 느슨해졌다.*

1 타동사/자동사 쾅 닫다, 세게 닫다 *그녀는 문을 쾅 닫고 잠갔다.* *나는 앞문이 쾅 닫히는 소리를 듣고 마음이 편해졌다.* **2** 타동사 쾅 하고 내려놓다

Word Web	skyscraper

Large American **cities** were expanding rapidly in the early 1900s. As this happened, **land** became scarce and expensive. **Real estate developers** soon felt the need for taller **buildings** and the **skyscraper** was born. Two things made these buildings possible—mass-produced steel and the invention of the **elevator**. The **construction** of the Empire State Building set two important records. At 102 **stories**, it was the tallest building in the world for 41 years. And 3,000 workers completed it in only 14 months. To accomplish this, they worked day and night, seven days a week, including holidays.

slam something **down**, you put it there quickly and with great force. ❑ *She listened in a mixture of shock and anger before slamming the phone down.* ❸ v-T To **slam** someone or something means to criticize them very severely. [JOURNALISM] ❑ *The famed film-maker slammed the claims as "an outrageous lie."* ❹ v-I If one thing **slams** into or against another, it crashes into it with great force. ❑ *The plane slammed into the building after losing an engine shortly after take-off.*

> **Word Partnership**   slam의 연어
>
> | | |
> |---|---|
> | N. | slam **a door** ❶ |
> | V. | hear *something* slam ❶ |
> | ADV. | slam *(something)* **shut** ❶ |

slan|der /slǽndər/ (**slanders, slandering, slandered**) ❶ N-VAR **Slander** is an untrue spoken statement about someone which is intended to damage their reputation. Compare **libel**. ❑ *Dr. Bach is now suing the company for slander.* ❷ v-T To **slander** someone means to say untrue things about them in order to damage their reputation. ❑ *He has been questioned on suspicion of slandering the Prime Minister.*

slang /slǽŋ/ N-UNCOUNT **Slang** consists of words, expressions, and meanings that are informal and are used by people who know each other very well or who have the same interests. ❑ *Archie liked to think he kept up with current slang.*

slant /slǽnt/ (**slants, slanting, slanted**) ❶ v-I Something that **slants** is sloping, rather than horizontal or vertical. ❑ *The morning sun slanted through the glass roof.* ❷ N-SING If something is **on a slant**, it is in a slanting position. ❑ *...long pockets cut on the slant.* ❸ v-T If information or a system **is slanted**, it is made to show favor toward a particular group or opinion. [usu passive] ❑ *The program was deliberately slanted to make the home team look good.* ❹ N-SING A particular **slant** on a subject is a particular way of thinking about it, especially one that is unfair. ❑ *The political slant at Focus can be described as centre-right.*

slap /slǽp/ (**slaps, slapping, slapped**) ❶ v-T If you **slap** someone, you hit them with the palm of your hand. ❑ *He would push or slap her once in a while.* ❑ *I slapped him hard across the face.* ● N-COUNT **Slap** is also a noun. ❑ *He reached forward and gave her a slap.* ❷ v-T If you **slap** something **onto** a surface, you put it there quickly, roughly, or carelessly. ❑ *"Coffee!" bellowed the barman, slapping the cup on to the waiting saucer.* ❸ v-T If journalists say that the authorities **slap** something such as a tax or a ban **on** something, they think it is unreasonable or put on without careful thought. [INFORMAL, DISAPPROVAL] ❑ *The government slapped a ban on the export of unprocessed logs.*

> **Word Partnership**   slap의 연어
>
> | | |
> |---|---|
> | N. | a slap **on the back**, a slap **in the face**, a slap **on the wrist** ❶ |

slash /slǽʃ/ (**slashes, slashing, slashed**) ❶ v-T If you **slash** something, you make a long, deep cut in it. ❑ *He came within two minutes of bleeding to death after slashing his wrists.* ● N-COUNT **Slash** is also a noun. ❑ *Make deep slashes in the meat and push in the spice paste.* ❷ v-I If you **slash at** a person or thing, you quickly hit at them with something such as a knife. ❑ *She slashed at her, aiming carefully.* ❸ v-T To **slash** something such as costs or jobs means to reduce them by a large amount. [JOURNALISM] ❑ *Car makers could be forced to slash prices after being accused of overcharging yesterday.* ❹ You say **slash** to refer to a sloping line that separates letters, words, or numbers. For example, if you are giving the number 340/21/K you say "Three four zero, slash two one, slash K." [SPOKEN]

slate /sleɪt/ (**slates, slating, slated**) ❶ N-UNCOUNT **Slate** is a dark grey rock that can be easily split into thin layers. Slate is often used for covering roofs. ❑ *... a stone-built cottage, with a traditional slate roof.* ❷ N-COUNT A **slate** is one of the small flat pieces of slate that are used for covering roofs. ❑ *Thieves had stolen the slates from the roof.* ❸ v-T PASSIVE If something **is slated** to happen, it is planned to happen at a particular time or on a particular occasion. [mainly AM] ❑ *Bromfield was slated to become U.S. Secretary of Agriculture.* ❹ v-T If something **is slated**, it is criticized very severely. [BRIT, JOURNALISM] [usu passive] ❑ *Arnold Schwarzenegger's new restaurant has been slated by a top food critic.* ❺ PHRASE If you start **with a clean slate**, you do not take account of previous mistakes or failures and make a fresh start. ❑ *The proposal is to pay everything you owe, so that you can start with a clean slate.*

slaugh|ter /slɔ́ːtər/ (**slaughters, slaughtering, slaughtered**) ❶ v-T If large numbers of people or animals **are slaughtered**, they are killed in a way that is cruel or unnecessary. [usu passive] ❑ *Thirty four people were slaughtered while queuing up to cast their votes.* ● N-UNCOUNT **Slaughter** is also a noun. ❑ *This was only a small part of a war where the slaughter of civilians was commonplace.* ❷ v-T To **slaughter** animals such as cows and sheep means to kill them for their meat. ❑ *Lack of chicken feed means that chicken farms are having to slaughter their stock.* ● N-UNCOUNT **Slaughter** is also a noun. ❑ *More than 491,000 sheep were exported to the Continent for slaughter last year.* →see **kill**

slave /sleɪv/ (**slaves, slaving, slaved**) ❶ N-COUNT A **slave** is someone who is the property of another person and has to work for that person. ❑ *The state of Liberia was formed a century and a half ago by freed slaves from the United States.* ❷ N-COUNT You can describe someone as a **slave** when they are completely under the control of another person or of a powerful influence. ❑ *She may no longer be a slave to the studio system, but she still has a duty to her fans.* ❸ v-I If you say that a person **is slaving over** something or **is slaving for** someone, you mean that they are working very hard. ❑ *When you're busy all day the last thing you want to do is spend hours slaving over a hot stove.* ● PHRASAL VERB **Slave away** means the same as **slave**. ❑ *He stares at the hundreds of workers slaving away in the intense sun.*

---

❸ 그녀는 충격과 분노가 섞인 감정으로 듣고 있다가 전화를 쾅 하고 내려놓다. ❸ 타동사 혹평하다 [언론] ❑ 그 유명한 영화 제작자는 그 주장들을 '터무니없는 거짓말'이라고 강하게 비난했다. ❹ 자동사 들이받다 ❑ 그 비행기는 이륙 직후 엔진 한 개를 잃고서는 건물을 들이받았다.

❶ 가산명사 또는 불가산명사 중상, 비방 ❑ 바크 박사는 이제 그 회사를 명예 훼손으로 고소 중이다. ❷ 타동사 중상하다, 비방하다 ❑ 그는 수상을 중상한 혐의로 심문을 받았다.

불가산명사 속어, 은어 ❑ 아치는 자신이 최신 속어에 밝다고 기분 좋게 생각했다.

❶ 자동사 기울어지다, 비스듬해지다 ❑ 아침 해가 유리 지붕을 통해 비스듬히 들어왔다. ❷ 단수명사 경사 ❑ 비스듬하게 나 있는 긴 주머니 ❸ 타동사 왜곡되다 ❑ 그 프로그램은 홈팀을 잘 보이게 하려고 의도적으로 편향이었다. ❹ 단수명사 관점 ❑ 포커스 지의 정치적 편향성은 중도 우익으로 묘사될 수 있다.

❶ 타동사 찰싹 때리다 ❑ 그는 그녀를 간혹 밀거나 따귀를 때리곤 했다. ❑ 나는 그의 따귀를 갈겼다. ● 가산명사 찰싹 때리기 ❑ 그는 앞으로 손을 내밀어 그녀를 찰싹 때렸다. ❷ 타동사 털썩 놓다 ❑ 바텐더는 "커피요!"라고 소리 지르며 컵을 놓아 있던 받침 위에 털썩 놓았다. ❸ 타동사 부과하다, 강제하다 [비격식체, 탐탁찮음] ❑ 정부는 가공되지 않은 목재에 대한 수출 금지령을 갑자기 발표했다.

❶ 타동사 (깊숙이) 베다 ❑ 그는 자신의 손목을 자른 후 2분만 더 있으면 출혈로 죽을 지경까지 이르렀다. ● 가산명사 베기 ❑ 고기에 깊은 칼자국들을 낸 다음 양념 반죽을 밀어 넣으세요. ❷ 자동사 (칼 같은 것을) 휘두르다 ❑ 그녀는 조심스럽게 조준하며 그녀에게 칼을 휘둘렀다. ❸ 타동사 대폭 줄이다, 대폭 낮추다 [언론] ❑ 자동차 회사들이 어제 부당 가격 부과 혐의를 받은 후, 가격을 대폭 내려야 하는 요구를 받을 수도 있다. ❹ 사선(斜線) (/) [구어체]

❶ 불가산명사 슬레이트 ❑ 전통적인 슬레이트 지붕을 인 석조 오두막 ❷ 가산명사 슬레이트 ❑ 도둑들이 지붕에서 슬레이트를 훔쳐 가 버린 상태였다. ❸ 수동 타동사 예정이다, 계획되다 [주로 미국영어] ❑ 브롬필드가 농림부 장관이 될 예정이었다. ❹ 타동사 혹평을 받다 [영국영어, 언론] ❑ 아놀드 슈왈제네거의 새 식당은 유력 음식 평론가로부터 혹평을 받았다. ❺ 구 새 출발 ❑ 당신이 빚진 모든 것을 갚고 새 출발을 하라는 게 제안이다.

❶ 타동사 도살당하다, 학살당하다 ❑ 34명이 투표하기 위해 줄을 서 있다가 학살당했다. ● 불가산명사 도살, 학살 ❑ 민간인의 학살이 흔하게 벌어지는 전쟁에서 이것은 일부분에 불과했다. ❷ 타동사 도축하다 ❑ 닭 모이가 부족하면 양계 농장들이 닭들을 도축해야 한다. ● 불가산명사 도축 ❑ 작년에 491,000마리가 넘는 양이 도축용으로 유럽에 수출되었다.

❶ 가산명사 노예 ❑ '라이베리아'라는 나라는 150년 전에 미국에서 해방된 노예들에 의해 세워졌다. ❷ 가산명사 노예, 꼼짝 못하는 사람 ❑ 그녀는 더 이상 스튜디오 시스템에 얽매이지 않을 수도 있지만, 여전히 자신의 팬들에 대한 의무는 있다. ❸ 자동사 노예처럼 고되게 일하다 ❑ 온종일 바쁜데 뜨거운 난로 위에서 음식 한다고 몇 시간 동안 씨름하고 싶을 리는 만무합니다. ● 구동사 노예처럼 고되게 일하다 ❑ 그는 강렬한 태양 아래 고되게 일하고 있는 수백 명의 일꾼들을 응시한다.

slav|ery /sleɪvəri, sleɪvri/ N-UNCOUNT **Slavery** is the system by which people are owned by other people as slaves. ❑ *My people have survived 400 years of slavery.*

불가산명사 노예 제도 ❑ 우리 민족은 4백년간의 노예 제도를 견디고 살아남았다.

sleaze /sliz/ N-UNCOUNT You use **sleaze** to describe activities that you consider immoral, dishonest, or not respectable, especially in politics, business, journalism, or entertainment. [INFORMAL, DISAPPROVAL] ❑ *She claimed that an atmosphere of sleaze and corruption now surrounded the Government.*

불가산명사 저속함, 추잡함 [비격식체, 탐탁잖음] ❑ 그녀는 현재 정부가 저속하고 타락한 분위기에 휩싸여 있다고 주장했다.

slea|zy /slizi/ (sleazier, sleaziest) **1** ADJ If you describe a place as **sleazy**, you dislike it because it looks dirty and badly cared for, and not respectable. [INFORMAL, DISAPPROVAL] ❑ *...sleazy bars.* **2** ADJ If you describe something or someone as **sleazy**, you disapprove of them because you think they are not respectable and are rather disgusting. [INFORMAL, DISAPPROVAL] ❑ *The accusations are making the government's conduct appear increasingly sleazy.*

1 형용사 누추한, 초라한 [비격식체, 탐탁잖음] ❑ 누추한 술집 **2** 형용사 추잡한, 저속한 [비격식체, 탐탁잖음] ❑ 그와 같은 비난이 정부의 행동을 더욱 더 추잡하게 보이도록 만들고 있다.

sled /slɛd/ (sleds, sledding, sledded) **1** N-COUNT A **sled** is an object used for traveling over snow. It consists of a framework which slides on two strips of wood or metal. [AM] ❑ *I saw her pulling three children through the snow on a sled.* **2** V-I If you **sled** or go **sledding**, you ride on a sled. [AM] ❑ *We got home and went sledding on the small hill in our back yard.*

1 가산명사 썰매 [미국영어] ❑ 그녀가 눈 속을 헤치며 세 아이를 썰매에 태워 끌고 가는 것을 보았다. **2** 자동사 썰매를 타다 [미국영어] ❑ 우리는 집에 가서 뒤뜰에 있는 작은 둔덕에 썰매를 타러 갔다.

sledge /slɛdʒ/ (sledges, sledging, sledged) **1** N-COUNT A **sledge** is the same as a **sled** [BRIT] [also by N] ❑ *She travelled 14,000 miles by sledge across Siberia to Kamchatka.* **2** V-I If you **sledge** or go **sledging**, you ride on a sledge. [BRIT] ❑ *Our hill is marvellous for sledging and we always have snow in January.*

1 가산명사 썰매 [영국영어] ❑ 그녀는 시베리아를 가로질러 캄차카 반도까지 썰매로 14,000마일을 이동했다. **2** 자동사 썰매를 타다 [영국영어] ❑ 우리 고장의 구릉은 썰매를 타기에 아주 훌륭하며 1월에는 항상 눈이 내린다.

sleek /slik/ (sleeker, sleekest) **1** ADJ **Sleek** hair or fur is smooth and shiny and looks healthy. ❑ *...sleek black hair.* **2** ADJ If you describe someone as **sleek**, you mean that they look rich and stylish. ❑ *Lord White is as sleek and elegant as any other millionaire businessman.* **3** ADJ **Sleek** vehicles, furniture, or other objects look smooth, shiny, and expensive. ❑ *... a sleek white BMW.*

1 형용사 윤기 있는, 매끄러운 ❑ 윤기가 흐르는 검은 머리 **2** 형용사 부티 나는, 멋있는 ❑ 화이트 경은 다른 어떤 백만장자 사업가 못지않게 부티가 나고 멋지다. **3** 형용사 번쩍번쩍한, 부티 나는 ❑ 번쩍번쩍한 흰색 비엠더블유 자동차

sleep ♦♦♢ /slip/ (sleeps, sleeping, slept) **1** N-UNCOUNT **Sleep** is the natural state of rest in which your eyes are closed, your body is inactive, and your mind does not think. ❑ *They were exhausted from lack of sleep.* ❑ *Be quiet and go to sleep.* **2** V-I When you **sleep**, you rest with your eyes closed and your mind and body inactive. ❑ *During the car journey, the baby slept.* ❑ *I've not been able to sleep for the last few nights.* **3** N-COUNT A **sleep** is a period of sleeping. ❑ *I think he may be ready for a sleep soon.* **4** V-T If a building or room **sleeps** a particular number of people, it has beds for that number of people. [no cont, no passive] ❑ *The villa sleeps 10 and costs £530 per person for two weeks.* **5** PHRASE If you cannot **get to sleep**, you are unable to sleep. ❑ *I can't get to sleep with all that singing.* **6** PHRASE If you say that you didn't **lose** any **sleep over** something, you mean that you did not worry about it at all. ❑ *I didn't lose too much sleep over that investigation.* **7** PHRASE If you are trying to make a decision and you say that you will **sleep on it**, you mean that you will delay making a decision on it until the following day, so you have time to think about it. ❑ *I need more time to sleep on it. It's a big decision and I want to make the right one.* **8** PHRASE If a sick or injured animal **is put to sleep**, it is killed by a vet in a way that does not cause it pain. ❑ *I'm going take the dog down to the vet's and have her put to sleep.* **9** to **sleep rough** →see **rough**
→see **dream**
→see Word Web: **sleep**

1 불가산명사 잠, 수면 ❑ 그들은 수면 부족으로 녹초가 되어 있었다. ❑ 조용히 하고 주무세요. **2** 자동사 잠자다 ❑ 자동차 여행을 하는 동안, 아기는 잠을 잤다. ❑ 지난 며칠간 잠을 잘 수가 없었다. **3** 가산명사 잠자는 시간 ❑ 내 생각에 그는 곧 잠잘 준비가 될 것 같다. **4** 타동사 ~ 만큼의 침상이 있다 ❑ 그 별장은 10개의 침상이 있고 숙박비는 1인당 2주일에 530파운드이다. **5** 구 잠들다 ❑ 그 모든 노랫소리들 때문에 잠들 수가 없다. **6** 구 ~에 신경 쓰다 ❑ 나는 그 조사에 그다지 신경을 많이 쓰지 않았다. **7** 구 자면서 생각해 보다, 하룻밤 생각해 보다 ❑ 하룻밤쯤 생각할 시간이 더 필요해요. 그건 중대한 결정이니 옳은 결정을 내리고 싶어요. **8** 구 안락사하다 ❑ 그 개를 수의사에게 데려가 안락사 시킬 것이다.

There are several verbal expressions in English using the noun **sleep** which refer to the moment when you start to sleep. When you go to bed at night, you normally **go to sleep** or **fall asleep**. When you **go to sleep**, it is usually a deliberate action. ❑ *He didn't want to go to sleep.* You can **fall asleep** by accident, or at a time when you should be awake. ❑ *I've seen doctors fall asleep in the operating room.* If you have difficulty sleeping, you can say that you cannot **get to sleep**. ❑ *Sometimes the fever prevents the child from getting to sleep.*

영어에는 잠을 자기 시작하는 순간을 일컫는 명사 sleep을 쓰는 동사 표현이 여러 가지가 있다. 밤에 잠자리에 들면, 보통은 go to sleep 또는 fall asleep한다. go to sleep하면, 대개 의도적인 행동이다. ❑ 그는 잠자리에 들고 싶지 않았다. 우연히/실수로 또는 깨어있어야 할 시간에 fall asleep할 수 있다. ❑ 나는 의사들이 수술실에서 잠이 드는 것을 본 적이 있다. 잠들기가 힘들면, get to sleep할 수 없다고 말할 수 있다. ❑ 때때로 열이 나서 그 아이가 잠들 수 없다.

Thesaurus   sleep의 참조어

N.   nap, rest, slumber **1** **3**

V.   doze, rest, snooze; *(ant.)* wake **2**

Word Partnership   sleep의 연어

N.   sleep **deprivation**, sleep **disorder**, sleep **on the floor**, **hours of** sleep, **lack of** sleep, sleep **nights** **1**

ADJ.   **deep** sleep **1**
      good sleep **3**

V.   **can't/couldn't** sleep, **drift off to** sleep, **get enough** sleep, **get some** sleep, **go to** sleep, **need** sleep **2**

Word Web   sleep

Do you ever go to **bed** and then discover you can't **fall asleep**? You start **yawning** and you feel **tired**. But somehow your body isn't ready for a good night's **rest**. You **toss and turn** and pound the **pillow** for hours. After a while you may start to **doze**, but then five minutes later you're **wide awake**. The scientific name for this condition is **insomnia**. There are many causes for sleeplessness like this. If you **nap** too late in the day it may interrupt your normal sleep cycle. Health and job-related worries can also affect sleep patterns.

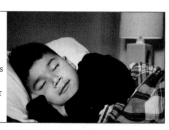

▶**sleep around** PHRASAL VERB If you say that someone **sleeps around**, you disapprove of them because they have sex with a lot of different people. [INFORMAL, DISAPPROVAL] ❏ *I don't sleep around.*

▶**sleep off** PHRASAL VERB If you **sleep off** the effects of too much traveling, drink, or food, you recover from it by sleeping. ❏ *It's a good idea to spend the first night of your holiday sleeping off the jet lag.*

▶**sleep together** PHRASAL VERB If two people **are sleeping together**, they are having a sexual relationship, but are not usually married to each other. ❏ *I'm pretty sure they slept together before they were married.*

▶**sleep with** PHRASAL VERB If you **sleep with** someone, you have sex with them. ❏ *He was old enough to sleep with a girl and make her pregnant.*

sleep|er /slipər/ (**sleepers**) **1** N-COUNT You can use **sleeper** to indicate how well someone sleeps. For example, if someone is a light **sleeper**, they are easily woken up. ❏ *I'm a very light sleeper and I can hardly get any sleep at all.* **2** N-COUNT A **sleeper** is a train with beds for its passengers to sleep in at night. [BRIT] ❏ *...the sleeper to London.*

sleep|ing bag (**sleeping bags**) N-COUNT A **sleeping bag** is a large deep bag with a warm lining, used for sleeping in, especially when you are camping.

sleep|ing part|ner (**sleeping partners**) N-COUNT A **sleeping partner** is a person who provides some of the capital for a business but who does not take an active part in managing the business. [BRIT, BUSINESS; AM **silent partner**] ❏ *I'm the sleeping partner in the restaurant while David runs it.*

sleep|less /sliplɪs/ **1** ADJ A **sleepless** night is one during which you do not sleep. ❏ *I have sleepless nights worrying about her.* **2** ADJ Someone who is **sleepless** is unable to sleep. ❏ *A sleepless baby can seem to bring little reward.*

sleep|over /slipoʊvər/ (**sleepovers**) also **sleep-over** N-COUNT A **sleepover** is an occasion when someone, especially a child, sleeps for one night in a place such as a friend's home. ❏ *Emily couldn't ask a friend for a sleepover until she cleaned her room.*

sleep|walk /slipwɔk/ (**sleepwalks, sleepwalking, sleepwalked**) V-I If someone **is sleepwalking**, they are walking around while they are asleep. ❏ *He once sleepwalked to the middle of the road outside his home at 1 a.m.*

sleepy /slipi/ (**sleepier, sleepiest**) **1** ADJ If you are **sleepy**, you are very tired and are almost asleep. ❏ *I was beginning to feel amazingly sleepy.* ● **sleep|ily** ADV [ADV with v] ❏ *Joanna sat up, blinking sleepily.* **2** ADJ A **sleepy** place is quiet and does not have much activity or excitement. ❏ *Valence is a sleepy little town just south of Lyon.*

sleet /slit/ N-UNCOUNT **Sleet** is rain that is partly frozen. ❏ *...blinding snow, driving sleet and wind.* →see **water**

sleeve /sliv/ (**sleeves**) **1** N-COUNT The **sleeves** of a coat, shirt, or other item of clothing are the parts that cover your arms. ❏ *His sleeves were rolled up to his elbows.* **2** N-COUNT A record **sleeve** is the stiff envelope in which a record is kept. [mainly BRIT; AM usually **jacket**] ❏ *There are to be no pictures of him on the sleeve of the new record.* **3** PHRASE If you have something **up** your **sleeve**, you have an idea or plan which you have not told anyone about. You can also say that someone has **an ace, card,** or **trick up** their **sleeve**. ❏ *He wondered what Shearson had up his sleeve.*

sleigh /sleɪ/ (**sleighs**) N-COUNT A **sleigh** is a vehicle which can slide over snow. Sleighs are usually pulled by horses.

slen|der /slɛndər/ **1** ADJ A **slender** person is attractively thin and graceful. [WRITTEN, APPROVAL] ❏ *She was slender, with delicate wrists and ankles.* ❏ *...a tall, slender figure in a straw hat.* **2** ADJ You can use **slender** to describe a situation which exists but only to a very small degree. [WRITTEN] ❏ *The United States held a slender lead.*

slept /slɛpt/ **Slept** is the past tense and past participle of **sleep**.

slice ◆◇◇ /slaɪs/ (**slices, slicing, sliced**) **1** N-COUNT A **slice of** bread, meat, fruit, or other food is a thin piece that has been cut from a larger piece. ❏ *Try to eat at least four slices of bread a day.* **2** V-T If you **slice** bread, meat, fruit, or other food, you cut it into thin pieces. ❏ *Helen sliced the cake.* ● PHRASAL VERB **Slice up** means the same as **slice**. ❏ *I sliced up an onion.* **3** N-COUNT You can use **slice** to refer to a part of a situation or activity. ❏ *Fiction takes up a large slice of the publishing market.* **4** **slice of the action** →see **action**

Word Partnership	*slice*의 연어	
ADJ.	**thin** slice, **small** slice **1**	
N.	slice **of bread**, slice **of pie**, slice **of pizza** **1**	
	slice **a cake** **2**	
	slice **of life** **3**	
PREP.	slice **into**, slice **off**, slice **through** **2**	

slick /slɪk/ (**slicker, slickest**) **1** ADJ A **slick** performance, production, or advertisement is skillful and impressive. ❏ *There's a big difference between an amateur video and a slick Hollywood production.* **2** ADJ A **slick** action is done quickly and smoothly, and without any obvious effort. ❏ *They were outplayed by the Colombians' slick passing and decisive finishing.* **3** ADJ A **slick** person speaks easily in a way that is likely to convince people, but is not sincere. [DISAPPROVAL] ❏ *Don't be fooled by slick politicians.* **4** N-COUNT A **slick** is the same as an **oil slick**. ❏ *Experts are trying to devise ways to clean up the huge slick.*

구동사 아무하고나 자다, 여러 사람과 성관계를 갖다 [비격식체, 탐탁찮음] ❏ 난 아무하고나 자지 않아요.

구동사 잠을 자서 낫게 하다, 잠으로 떨쳐 내다 ❏ 휴가의 첫날 밤에 잠을 자서 시차증에서 벗어나는 것은 좋은 생각이다.

구동사 성관계를 갖다, 같이 자다 ❏ 그들이 결혼 전에 같이 잤다고 나는 거의 확신한다.

구동사 성관계를 갖다 ❏ 그는 여자와 성관계를 갖고 임신시킬 수 있을 만큼 충분히 나이가 들어 있었다.

1 가산명사 (어떠어떠하게) 잠자는 사람 ❏ 나는 잠을 아주 얕게 자는 사람이라 거의 잠을 자지 못한다. **2** 가산명사 침대차 [영국영어] ❏ 런던행 침대차

가산명사 침낭

가산명사 익명의 동업자 [영국영어, 경제; 미국영어 silent partner] ❏ 데이비드가 그 식당을 경영하고 나는 익명의 동업자이다.

1 형용사 잠 못 이루는 ❏ 나는 그녀에 대한 걱정으로 며칠 밤잠을 못 이룬다. **2** 형용사 잠을 못 자는, 불면증의 ❏ 잠을 못 자는 아기는 별로 보람을 가져다주지 못하는 것처럼 보일 수 있다.

가산명사 (친구 집에서) 자고 가기 ❏ 에밀리는 방 청소를 하기 전까지는 친구를 불러 놀다가 자고 가라고 할 수 없었다.

자동사 잠결에 걸어 다니다, 몽유병이 있다 ❏ 그는 예전에 몽유병 증세로 새벽 1시에 집 밖 도로 한가운데까지 걸어 나간 적이 있다.

1 형용사 졸린 ❏ 나는 굉장히 졸리기 시작했다. ● 졸리게, 졸린 듯이 부사 ❏ 조안나는 졸린 듯이 눈을 깜박이며 일어나 앉았다. **2** 형용사 나른한 분위기의, 활기 없는 ❏ 발랑스는 리옹 바로 남쪽에 있는 나른한 분위기의 작은 읍이다.

불가산명사 진눈깨비 ❏ 눈앞을 가리며 내리는 눈, 휘몰아치는 진눈깨비와 바람

1 가산명사 소매 ❏ 그의 소매가 팔꿈치까지 걷어 올려져 있었다. **2** 가산명사 레코드 재킷 [주로 영국영어; 미국영어 대개 jacket] ❏ 신보 레코드 재킷에는 그의 사진이 실리지 않을 예정이다. **3** 구 (생각 등을) 숨기고 있다; (카드를) 숨겨 가지고 있다 ❏ 그는 쉬어슨이 무슨 속셈인지 궁금했다.

가산명사 (말이 끄는) 썰매

1 형용사 날씬한, 호리호리한 [문어체, 마음에 듦] ❏ 그녀는 날씬했고, 손목과 발목이 가늘었다. ❏ 밀짚모자를 쓴 키가 크고 호리호리한 사람 **2** 형용사 얼마 안 되는, 빈약한 [문어체] ❏ 미국이 아주 약간의 우위를 점했다.

sleep의 과거, 과거 분사

1 가산명사 얇게 썬 조각 ❏ 하루에 최소한 빵 네 조각을 먹도록 하세요. **2** 타동사 얇게 썰다, 저미다 ❏ 헬렌이 케이크를 얇게 썰었다. ● 구동사 얇게 썰다, 저미다 ❏ 나는 양파 한 개를 얇게 썰었다. **3** 가산명사 부분 ❏ 소설이 출판 시장의 큰 부분을 차지한다.

---

1 형용사 깔끔한, 매끄러운 ❏ 아마추어 비디오와 깔끔한 할리우드 제작품 사이에는 큰 차이가 있다. **2** 형용사 능란한 ❏ 그들은 콜롬비아 선수들의 능란한 패스와 결정력 있는 마무리에 압도당했다. **3** 형용사 언변이 좋은, 말만 번지르르한 [탐탁찮음] ❏ 말만 번지르르한 정치가들에게 우롱당하지 마세요. **4** 가산명사 (수면에 형성된) 기름막 ❏ 전문가들이 거대한 기름막을 걷어 내기 위한 방법을 고안하기 위해 노력하고 있다.

a b c d e f g h i j k l m n o p q r s t u v w x y z

slide ♦♦♦ /slaɪd/ (**slides, sliding, slid**) **1** V-T/V-I When something **slides** somewhere or when you **slide** it there, it moves there smoothly over or against something. ❑ *She slid the door open.* ❑ *I slid the wallet into his pocket.* **2** V-I If you **slide** somewhere, you move there smoothly and quietly. ❑ *He slid into the driver's seat.* **3** V-I To **slide into** a particular mood, attitude, or situation means to gradually start to have that mood, attitude, or situation, often without intending to. ❑ *She had slid into a depression.* **4** V-I If currencies or prices **slide**, they gradually become worse or lower in value. [JOURNALISM] ❑ *The U.S. dollar continued to slide.* • N-COUNT **Slide** is also a noun. ❑ *...the dangerous slide in oil prices.* **5** N-COUNT A **slide** is a small piece of photographic film which you project onto a screen so that you can see the picture. ❑ *...a slide show.* **6** N-COUNT A **slide** is a piece of glass on which you put something that you want to examine through a microscope. ❑ *...a drop of blood on a slide.* **7** N-COUNT A **slide** is a piece of playground equipment that has a steep slope for children to go down for fun. ❑ *... two young children playing on a slide.*

Word Partnership	slide의 연어
V.	**begin to** slide, **continue to** slide **1**-**4** **7**
ADJ.	**downward** slide, **recent** slide, **steep** slide **4**

slight ♦♦◇ /slaɪt/ (**slighter, slightest, slights, slighting, slighted**) **1** ADJ Something that is **slight** is very small in degree or quantity. ❑ *Doctors say he has made a slight improvement.* ❑ *He's not the slightest bit worried.* **2** ADJ A **slight** person has a fairly thin and delicate looking body. ❑ *She is smaller and slighter than Christie.* • **slight|ly** ADV [ADV -ed] ❑ *...a slightly built man.* **3** V-T If you **are slighted**, someone does or says something that insults you by treating you as if your views or feelings are not important. [usu passive] ❑ *They felt slighted by not being adequately consulted.* • N-COUNT **Slight** is also a noun. ❑ *It's difficult to persuade my husband that it isn't a slight on him that I enjoy my evening class.* **4** PHRASE You use **in the slightest** to emphasize a negative statement. [EMPHASIS] ❑ *That doesn't interest me in the slightest.*

slight|ly ♦♦◇ /slaɪtli/ ADV **Slightly** means to some degree but not to a very large degree. ❑ *His family then moved to a slightly larger house.* ❑ *Each person learns in a slightly different way.*

slim ♦◇◇ /slɪm/ (**slimmer, slimmest, slims, slimming, slimmed**) **1** ADJ A **slim** person has an attractively thin and well-shaped body. ❑ *The young woman was tall and slim.* **2** V-I If you **are slimming**, you are trying to make yourself thinner and lighter by eating less food. [BRIT] ❑ *Some people will gain weight, no matter how hard they try to slim.* **3** ADJ A **slim** book, wallet, or other object is thinner than usual. ❑ *The slim booklets describe a range of services and facilities.* **4** ADJ A **slim** chance or possibility is a very small one. ❑ *There's still a slim chance that he may become Prime Minister.* **5** V-T If an organization **slims** its products or workers, it reduces the number of them that it has. [BUSINESS] ❑ *The company recently slimmed its product line.*

Word Partnership	slim의 연어
ADJ.	**tall and** slim **1**
ADV.	**pretty** slim, **very** slim **1** **4**
N.	slim **chance**, slim **lead**, slim **margin** **4**

▶**slim down 1** PHRASAL VERB If you **slim down**, you lose weight and become thinner. [AM] ❑ *People will lose weight when they slim down with a friend.* **2** PHRASAL VERB If a company or other organization **slims down** or **is slimmed down**, it employs fewer people, in order to save money or become more efficient. [BUSINESS] ❑ *Many firms have had little choice but to slim down.*

slime /slaɪm/ N-UNCOUNT **Slime** is a thick, wet substance which covers a surface or comes from the bodies of animals such as snails. ❑ *He swam down and retrieved his glasses from the muck and slime at the bottom of the pond.*

slimy /slaɪmi/ (**slimier, slimiest**) ADJ **Slimy** substances are thick, wet, and unpleasant. **Slimy** objects are covered in a slimy substance. ❑ *His feet slipped in the slimy mud.*

sling /slɪŋ/ (**slings, slinging, slung**) **1** V-T If you **sling** something somewhere, you throw it there carelessly. ❑ *Marla was recently seen slinging her shoes at Trump.* **2** V-T If you **sling** something over your shoulder or over something such as a chair, you hang it there loosely. ❑ *She slung her coat over her desk chair.* ❑ *He had a small green rucksack slung over one shoulder.* **3** V-T If a rope, blanket, or other object **is slung** between two points, someone has hung it loosely between them. [usu passive] ❑ *...two long poles with a blanket slung between them.* **4** N-COUNT A **sling** is an object made of ropes, straps, or cloth that is used for carrying things. ❑ *They used slings of rope to lower us from one set of arms to another.* **5** N-COUNT A **sling** is a piece of cloth which supports someone's broken or injured arm and is tied around their neck. ❑ *She was back at work with her arm in a sling.*

sling|shot /slɪŋʃɒt/ (**slingshots**) N-COUNT A **slingshot** is a device for shooting small stones. It is made of a Y-shaped stick with a piece of elastic tied between the two top posts. [AM; BRIT **catapult**]

slip ♦♦◇ /slɪp/ (**slips, slipping, slipped**) **1** V-I If you **slip**, you accidentally slide and lose your balance. ❑ *He had slipped on an icy pavement.* **2** V-I If something **slips**, it slides out of place or out of your hand. ❑ *His glasses had slipped.* **3** V-I If you **slip** somewhere, you go there quickly and quietly. ❑ *Amy slipped downstairs and out of the house.* **4** V-T If you **slip** something somewhere, you put it there quickly in a way that does not attract attention. ❑ *I slipped a note under Louise's door.* ❑ *He found a coin in his pocket and slipped it into her collecting tin.* **5** V-T If you

1 타동사/자동사 미끄러져 가다; 미끄러뜨리듯 움직이다 ❑ 그녀는 문을 스르르 열었다. ❑ 나는 그의 주머니에 지갑을 슬그머니 밀어 넣었다. **2** 자동사 미끄러지듯이 움직이다 ❑ 그가 미끄러지듯이 운전석으로 들어갔다. **3** 자동사 어느새 -이 되다 ❑ 그녀는 어느새 우울해져 있었다. **4** 자동사 (가치가) 하락하다 [언론] ❑ 미국 달러화 가치가 계속해서 떨어졌다. ● 가산명사 하락 ❑ 위험한 유가 하락 **5** 가산명사 (환등기의) 슬라이드 ❑ 슬라이드 쇼 **6** 가산명사 (현미경의) 슬라이드 ❑ 슬라이드 위의 피 한 방울 **7** 가산명사 미끄럼틀 ❑ 미끄럼틀 위에서 놀고 있는 어린 아이 두 명

1 형용사 약간의, 조금의 ❑ 의사들은 그의 병세가 약간 호전되었다고 말한다. ❑ 그는 조금도 걱정하지 않는다. **2** 형용사 홀쭉한, 가냘픈 ❑ 그녀는 크리스티보다 더 작고 가냘프다. ● 홀쭉하게 부사 ❑ 홀쭉한 체격의 남자 **3** 타동사 무시당하다 ❑ 그들은 자신들의 의견이 충분히 참고 되지 않아 무시당한 기분이었다. ● 가산명사 무시, 얕봄 ❑ 내가 원하는 저녁 수업을 듣는 것이 자기를 무시하는 것이 아니라는 것을 남편에게 납득시키기가 어렵다. **4** 구 전혀, 조금도 [강조] ❑ 나는 그것에 전혀 흥미가 없다.

부사 약간, 조금 ❑ 그러고 나서 그의 가족은 약간 더 큰 집으로 이사했다. ❑ 사람은 각자가 약간씩 다른 방식으로 배운다.

1 형용사 호리호리한, 날씬한 [마음에 듦] ❑ 그 젊은 여자는 키가 크고 호리호리했다. **2** 자동사 살을 빼다, 체중을 줄이다 [영국영어] ❑ 어떤 사람들은 아무리 살을 빼려고 노력을 해도 체중이 는다. **3** 형용사 얇은 ❑ 그 얇은 소책자에 서비스와 편의 시설 종류가 나와 있습니다. **4** 형용사 (가능성 등이) 희박한 ❑ 아직도 그가 수상이 될 수 있는 아주 적은 가능성이 있다. **5** 타동사 줄이다, 감축하다 [경제] ❑ 그 회사는 최근에 제품 라인을 줄였다.

1 구동사 살을 빼다 [미국영어] ❑ 사람들은 친구와 함께 살을 뺄 때 체중이 주는 법이다. **2** 구동사 규모를 줄이다, 군살을 빼다 [경제] ❑ 많은 회사들이 군살을 빼는 것 외에는 선택의 여지가 거의 없었다.

불가산명사 끈적끈적한 물질; 점액 ❑ 그는 헤엄쳐 내려가 연못 바닥의 오물과 끈적거리는 진흙 구덩이에서 안경을 찾아 가지고 왔다.

형용사 끈적끈적한, 미끈미끈한 ❑ 미끈미끈한 진창에서 그의 발이 미끄러졌다.

1 타동사 내던지다 ❑ 최근 말라가 트럼프에게 신발을 내던지는 모습이 목격되었다. **2** 타동사 걸치다 ❑ 그녀는 책상 의자에 외투를 걸쳤다. ❑ 그는 한쪽 어깨에 작은 녹색 배낭을 걸치고 있었다. **3** 타동사 걸쳐지다 ❑ 그 사이에 담요가 걸쳐져 늘어져 있는 두 개의 긴 장대 **4** 가산명사 (끈 등으로 된) 운반 도구 ❑ 그들은 밧줄로 된 운반 도구를 이용하여 이 팔에서 저 팔로 우리를 내려 주었다. **5** 가산명사 삼각건 ❑ 그녀는 팔에 삼각건을 한 채로 다시 일하고 있었다.

가산명사 고무줄 새총 [미국영어; 영국영어 catapult]

1 자동사 미끄러지다 ❑ 그는 얼음이 덮인 보도 위에서 미끄러졌다. **2** 자동사 미끄러져 떨어지다 ❑ 그의 안경이 미끄러져 떨어져 버렸다. **3** 자동사 슬그머니 가다 ❑ 에이미는 슬그머니 아래층으로 내려가서 집 밖으로 나갔다. **4** 타동사 슬그머니 놓다 ❑ 나는 루이스의 문 밑에 쪽지를 슬쩍 넣어 놓았다. ❑ 그는 주머니에서 동전 하나를 찾아서 그녀의 모금통에

slip something **to** someone, you give it to them secretly. ❏ *Robert had slipped her a note in school.* ⑥ V-I To **slip into** a particular state or situation means to pass gradually into it, in a way that is hardly noticed. ❏ *It amazed him how easily one could slip into a routine.* ⑦ V-T/V-I If something **slips to** a lower level or standard, it falls to that level or standard. ❏ *Shares slipped to 117p.* ❏ *In June, producer prices slipped 0.1% from May.* ● N-SING **Slip** is also a noun. ❏ *...a slip in consumer confidence.* ⑧ V-I If you **slip into** or **out of** clothes or shoes, you put them on or take them off quickly and easily. ❏ *She slipped out of the jacket and tossed it on the couch.* ⑨ N-COUNT A **slip** is a small or unimportant mistake. ❏ *We must be well prepared, there must be no slips.* ⑩ N-COUNT A **slip of** paper is a small piece of paper. ❏ *...little slips of paper he had torn from a notebook.* ❏ *I put her name on the slip.* ⑪ PHRASE If you **let slip** information, you accidentally tell it to someone, when you wanted to keep it secret. ❏ *I bet he let slip that I'd gone to America.* ⑫ PHRASE If something **slips** your **mind**, you forget about it. ❏ *The reason for my visit had obviously slipped his mind.*

슬그머니 넣었다. ⑤ 타동사 슬쩍 건네다 ❏ 학교에서 로버트가 그녀에게 쪽지를 슬쩍 건넸다. ⑥ 자동사 (부지불식간에) 빠져들다 ❏ 그는 사람이 판에 박힌 일상에 얼마나 쉽게 빠져들 수 있는가 하는 것에 깜짝 놀랐다. ⑦ 타동사/자동사 떨어지다 ❏ 주식이 117포인트로 떨어졌다. ❏ 6월에, 생산자 가격이 5월 대비 0.1퍼센트 떨어졌다. ● 단수명사 하락, 저하 ❏ 소비자 신뢰 저하 ⑧ 자동사 (옷 등을) 후딱 입다; 후딱 벗다 ❏ 그녀는 옷을 후딱 벗어서 소파 위로 던졌다. ⑨ 가산명사 사소한 실수, 잘못 ❏ 준비를 잘 해야 해, 실수가 없어야 돼. ⑩ 가산명사 종잇조각 ❏ 그가 공책에서 찢어 낸 작은 종이조각 ❏ 종잇조각에 그녀의 이름을 썼다. ⑪ 구 무심코 입 밖에 내다, 발실수하다 ❏ 장담컨대 내가 미국에 갔다는 걸 그가 무심코 입 밖에 냈을 거야. ⑫ 구 잊히지다 ❏ 그는 분명히 내가 방문한 이유를 잊어버렸었다.

Thesaurus
slip의 참조어

V.	fall, slide, trip ①
N.	blunder, failure, mistake ⑨
	leaf, page, paper, sheet ⑩

Word Partnership
slip의 연어

ADJ.	slip **resistant** ①
N.	slip **of paper**, **sales** slip ⑩
V.	**let** (*something*) slip ⑪

▶**slip up** PHRASAL VERB If you **slip up**, you make a small or unimportant mistake. ❏ *There were occasions when we slipped up.*

구동사 (작은) 실수를 하다 ❏ 우리가 실수할 때가 있었다.

slip|page /slɪpɪdʒ/ (**slippages**) N-VAR **Slippage** is a failure to maintain a steady position or rate of progress, so that a particular target or standard is not achieved. ❏ *...a substantial slippage in the value of sterling.*

가산명사 또는 불가산명사 지하 ❏ 영국 파운드화 가치의 대폭 저하

slip|per /slɪpər/ (**slippers**) N-COUNT **Slippers** are loose, soft shoes that you wear at home. ❏ *...a pair of old slippers.*

가산명사 실내화, 슬리퍼 ❏ 낡은 실내화 한 켤레

slip|pery /slɪpəri/ ① ADJ Something that is **slippery** is smooth, wet, or oily and is therefore difficult to walk on or to hold. ❏ *The tiled floor was wet and slippery.* ② ADJ You can describe someone as **slippery** if you think that they are dishonest in a clever way and cannot be trusted. [DISAPPROVAL] ❏ *He is a slippery customer, and should be carefully watched.* ③ PHRASE If someone is on a **slippery slope**, they are involved in a course of action that is difficult to stop and that will eventually lead to failure or trouble. ❏ *The company started down the slippery slope of believing that they knew better than the customer.*

① 형용사 미끄러운 ❏ 타일이 깔린 바닥은 젖어서 미끄러웠다. ② 형용사 (사람이) 반들반들한, 약삭빠른 [탐탁찮음] ❏ 그는 약삭빠른 손님이라 주의 깊게 지켜봐야 한다. ③ 구 (비유적) 위험한 비탈길 ❏ 그 회사는 자신들이 고객보다 더 잘 안다고 믿는 위험한 비탈길을 내려가기 시작했다.

slit /slɪt/ (**slits, slitting**)

The form **slit** is used in the present tense and is the past tense and past participle.

slit은 동사의 현재, 과거, 과거 분사로 쓰인다.

① V-T If you **slit** something, you make a long narrow cut in it. ❏ *They say somebody slit her throat.* ❏ *He began to slit open each envelope.* ② N-COUNT A **slit** is a long narrow cut. ❏ *Make a slit in the stem about half an inch long.* ③ N-COUNT A **slit** is a long narrow opening in something. ❏ *She watched them through a slit in the curtains.* →see **shark**

① 타동사 길게 베다, 죽 찢다 ❏ 누군가가 그녀의 목을 길게 벴다고 한다. ❏ 그는 봉투 하나하나를 죽죽 찢어 열기 시작했다. ② 가산명사 길게 벤 자국, 죽 찢긴 자국 ❏ 줄기에 0.5인치 정도 칼자국을 내세요. ③ 가산명사 갈라진 틈 ❏ 그녀는 커튼 사이 틈을 통해 그들을 주시했다.

slith|er /slɪðər/ (**slithers, slithering, slithered**) ① V-I If you **slither** somewhere, you slide along in an uneven way. ❏ *Robert lost his footing and slithered down the bank.* ② V-I If an animal such as a snake **slithers**, it moves along in a curving way. ❏ *The snake slithered into the water.*

① 자동사 미끄러져 가다 ❏ 로버트는 발을 헛디뎌 둑 아래로 미끄러졌다. ② 자동사 (뱀 등이) 스르르 기어가다 ❏ 그 뱀은 물속으로 스르르 기어 들어갔다.

sliv|er /slɪvər/ (**slivers**) N-COUNT A **sliver of** something is a small thin piece or amount of it. ❏ *Not a sliver of glass remains where the windows were.*

가산명사 얇은 조각 ❏ 창이 있던 곳에 유리한 조각도 남아 있지 않다.

slog /slɒg/ (**slogs, slogging, slogged**) ① V-I If you **slog through** something, you work hard and steadily through it. [INFORMAL] ❏ *They secure their degrees by slogging through an intensive 11-month course.* ● PHRASAL VERB **Slog away** means the same as **slog**. ❏ *Edward slogged away, always learning.* ② N-SING If you describe a task as a **slog**, you mean that it is tiring and requires a lot of effort. [INFORMAL] [also no det] ❏ *There is little to show for the two years of hard slog.*

① 자동사 힘겹게 해 나가다, 꾸준히 노력하다 [비격식체] ❏ 그들은 강도 높은 11개월간의 과정을 힘들게 공부해서 학위를 획득한다. ● 구동사 힘겹게 해 나가다, 꾸준히 노력하다 ❏ 에드워드는 언제나 애써서 꾸준히 공부했다. ② 단수명사 힘겨운 일; 고투 [비격식체] ❏ 2년간의 고된 노력의 성과가 별로 없다.

slo|gan /sloʊgən/ (**slogans**) N-COUNT A **slogan** is a short phrase that is easy to remember. Slogans are used in advertisements and by political parties and other organizations who want people to remember what they are saying or selling. ❏ *They could campaign on the slogan "We'll take less of your money."*

가산명사 슬로건, 구호 ❏ 그들은 '여러분의 돈을 덜 가져가겠습니다.'라는 구호를 내걸고 선거 운동을 할 수 있었다.

slop /slɒp/ (**slops, slopping, slopped**) V-T/V-I If liquid **slops** from a container or if you **slop** liquid somewhere, it comes out over the edge of the container, usually accidentally. ❏ *A little cognac slopped over the edge of the glass.*

타동사/자동사 넘치다 ❏ 약간의 코냑이 잔 가장자리를 넘쳤다.

slope /sloʊp/ (**slopes, sloping, sloped**) ① N-COUNT A **slope** is the side of a mountain, hill, or valley. ❏ *Saint-Christo is perched on a mountain slope.* ② N-COUNT A **slope** is a surface that is at an angle, so that one end is higher than the other. ❏ *The street must have been on a slope.* ③ V-I If a surface **slopes**, it is at an angle, so that one end is higher than the other. ❏ *The bank sloped down sharply to the river.* ● **slop|ing** ADJ ❏ *...a brick building, with a sloping roof.* ④ V-I If something **slopes**, it leans to the right or to the left rather than being upright. ❏ *The writing sloped backwards.* ⑤ N-COUNT The **slope** of something is the angle at which it slopes. ❏ *The slope increases as you go up the curve.* ⑥ **slippery slope** →see **slippery**

① 가산명사 비탈 ❏ 세인트 크리스토는 산비탈에 자리 잡고 있다. ② 가산명사 경사면 ❏ 그 거리는 틀림없이 경사면에 있었을 것이다. ③ 자동사 경사지다, 비탈지다 ❏ 강둑이 강 쪽으로 급경사져 있었다. ● 경사진 형용사 ❏ 지붕이 경사진 벽돌 건물 ④ 자동사 기울어지다 ❏ 그 필체는 뒤쪽으로 기울어져 있었다. ⑤ 가산명사 경사도 ❏ 곡선 도로를 올라갈수록 경사가 가팔라진다.

slop|py /slɒpi/ (**sloppier, sloppiest**) ADJ If you describe someone's work or activities as **sloppy**, you mean they have been done in a careless and lazy way. [DISAPPROVAL] ❑ *He has little patience for sloppy work from colleagues.*

형용사 엉성한 [탐탁잖음] ❑ 그는 동료들의 엉성한 솜씨를 쉽게 보아 넘기지 못한다.

slot /slɒt/ (**slots, slotting, slotted**) **1** N-COUNT A **slot** is a narrow opening in a machine or container, for example a hole that you put coins in to make a machine work. ❑ *He dropped a coin into the slot and dialed.* **2** V-T/V-I If you **slot** something into something else, or if it **slots** into it, you put it into a space where it fits. ❑ *He was slotting a CD into a CD player.* ❑ *The car seat belt slotted into place easily.* **3** N-COUNT A **slot** in a schedule or program is a place in it where an activity can take place. ❑ *Visitors can book a time slot a week or more in advance.*

1 가산명사 동전 넣는 구멍 ❑ 그는 주화 투입구에 동전을 넣고 다이얼을 돌렸다. **2** 타동사/자동사 끼워 넣다; 끼워져 들어가다 ❑ 그가 시디플레이어에 시디를 끼워 넣고 있었다. ❑ 그 자동차 안전벨트는 쉽게 제자리에 채워졌다. **3** 가산명사 시간대 ❑ 방문객들은 일주일 또는 그 이상 미리 시간대를 예약할 수 있다.

slouch /slaʊtʃ/ (**slouches, slouching, slouched**) V-I If someone **slouches**, they sit or stand with their shoulders and head bent so they look lazy and unattractive. ❑ *Try not to slouch when you are sitting down.*

자동사 구부정한 자세를 취하다 ❑ 앉을 때 몸을 구부정하게 하지 않도록 하여라.

slow ♦♦◇ /sloʊ/ (**slower, slowest, slows, slowing, slowed**) **1** ADJ Something that is **slow** moves, happens, or is done without much speed. ❑ *The traffic is heavy and slow.* ❑ *Electric whisks should be used on a slow speed.* ● **slow|ly** ADV [ADV with v] ❑ *He spoke slowly and deliberately.* ● **slow|ness** N-UNCOUNT ❑ *She lowered the glass with calculated slowness.* **2** ADV In informal English, **slower** is used to mean "at a slower speed" and **slowest** is used to mean "at the slowest speed." In nonstandard English, **slow** is used to mean "with little speed." [ADV after v] ❑ *I began to walk slower and slower.* **3** ADJ Something that is **slow** takes a long time. ❑ *The distribution of passports has been a slow process.* ● **slow|ly** ADV [ADV with v] ❑ *My resentment of her slowly began to fade.* ● **slow|ness** N-UNCOUNT ❑ *...the slowness of political and economic progress.* **4** ADJ If someone is **slow** to do something, they do it after a delay. [v-link ADJ, usu ADJ to-inf, ADJ in -ing] ❑ *The world community has been slow to respond to the crisis.* **5** V-T/V-I If something **slows** or if you **slow** it, it starts to move or happen more slowly. ❑ *The rate of bombing has slowed considerably.* ❑ *She slowed the car and began driving up a narrow road.* **6** ADJ Someone who is **slow** is not very clever and takes a long time to understand things. ❑ *He got hit on the head and he's been a bit slow since.* **7** ADJ If you describe a situation, place, or activity as **slow**, you mean that it is not very exciting. ❑ *Don't be faint-hearted when things seem a bit slow or boring.* **8** ADJ If a clock or watch is **slow**, it shows a time that is earlier than the correct time. ❑ *The clock is about two and a half minutes slow.* **9 slowly but surely** →see **surely**

1 형용사 느린 ❑ 교통량이 많고 차량 소통이 더디다. ❑ 전기 거품기는 느린 속도로 사용해야 한다. ● 느리게, 천천히 부사 ❑ 그는 느리고 신중하게 말했다. ● 느림 불가산명사 ❑ 그녀는 일부러 천천히 잔을 내렸다. **2** 부사 느리게, 천천히 ❑ 나는 더욱 더 느리게 걷기 시작했다. **3** 형용사 시간이 오래 걸리는 ❑ 여권 배포는 시간이 오래 걸리는 과정이었다. ● 더디게 부사 ❑ 그녀에 대한 나의 분노는 더디게 사라지기 시작했다. ● 더딤 불가산명사 ❑ 더딘 정치적.경제적 발전 **4** 형용사 굼뜬, 둔한 ❑ 세계 공동체는 위기에 굼뜨게 반응해 왔다. **5** 타동사/자동사 속도가 줄어들다; 속도를 늦추다, 느리게 하다 ❑ 폭격 빈도가 상당히 둔화되어 왔다. ❑ 그녀는 차의 속도를 늦추고 좁은 도로로 차를 몰고 올라가기 시작했다. **6** 형용사 이해가 더딘, (머리가) 둔한 ❑ 그는 머리에 타격을 입었고 그때 이후로 약간 둔해졌다. **7** 형용사 지루한 ❑ 만사가 약간 지루하고 따분해 보일 때 무기력해지지 마세요. **8** 형용사 (시계가) 느리게 가는 ❑ 그 시계는 2분 30초 가량 늦다.

Word Partnership   slow의 연어

ADJ.	slow **but steady** **1** **3**
N.	slow **movements**, slow **speed**, slow **traffic** **1**
	slow **death**, slow **growth**, slow **pace**, slow **process**, slow **progress**, slow **recovery**, slow **response**, slow **sales**, slow **start**, slow **stop** **3**

▶**slow down** **1** PHRASAL VERB If something **slows down** or if something **slows** it **down**, it starts to move or happen more slowly. ❑ *The car slowed down as they passed Customs.* ❑ *There is no cure for the disease, although drugs can slow down its rate of development.* **2** PHRASAL VERB If someone **slows down** or if something **slows** them **down**, they become less active. ❑ *You will need to slow down for a while.* **3** →see also **slowdown**

1 구동사 속도가 줄다; 속도를 늦추다, 느리게 하다 ❑ 그들이 세관을 지나갈 때 자동차가 속도를 늦추었다. ❑ 약으로 진행 속도를 늦출 수는 있지만, 그 병을 치료할 수 있는 방법은 없다. **2** 구동사 느긋해지다; 느긋하게 만들다 ❑ 너는 잠시 느긋해질 필요가 있을 거야.

▶**slow up** PHRASAL VERB **Slow up** means the same as **slow down 1**. ❑ *Sales are slowing up.*

구동사 속도가 줄다; 속도를 늦추다, 느리게 하다 ❑ 판매 속도가 줄어들고 있다.

slow|down /sloʊdaʊn/ (**slowdowns**) **1** N-COUNT A **slowdown** is a reduction in speed or activity. ❑ *There has been a sharp slowdown in economic growth.* **2** N-COUNT A **slowdown** is a protest in which workers deliberately work slowly and cause problems for their employers. [AM, BUSINESS; BRIT **go-slow**] ❑ *It's impossible to assess how many officers are participating in the slowdown.*

1 가산명사 감속; 둔화 ❑ 경제 성장이 급속히 둔화되어 왔다. **2** 가산명사 태업 [미국영어, 경제; 영국영어 go-slow] ❑ 얼마나 많은 수의 경찰관들이 태업에 참가하고 있는지 산정하는 것은 불가능하다.

slow mo|tion also **slow-motion** N-UNCOUNT When film or television pictures are shown **in slow motion**, they are shown much more slowly than normal. ❑ *It seemed almost as if he were falling in slow motion.*

불가산명사 느린 동작, 슬로 모션 ❑ 마치 그가 거의 슬로 모션으로 떨어지고 있는 것처럼 보였다.

sludge /slʌdʒ/ (**sludges**) N-VAR **Sludge** is thick mud, sewage, or industrial waste. ❑ *All dumping of sludge will be banned by 1998.*

가산명사 또는 불가산명사 진창, 오물; 산업 폐기물 ❑ 1998년까지 모든 산업 폐기물 투기 행위가 금지될 것이다.

slug /slʌg/ (**slugs**) **1** N-COUNT A **slug** is a small slow-moving creature with a long soft body and no legs, like a snail without a shell. **2** N-COUNT If you take a **slug of** an alcoholic drink, you take a large mouthful of it. [INFORMAL] ❑ *Edgar took a slug of his drink.*

1 가산명사 민달팽이, 괄태충 **2** 가산명사 (술 등의) 큰 한 모금 [비격식체] ❑ 에드거는 술을 한 모금 크게 들이켰다.

slug|gish /slʌgɪʃ/ ADJ You can describe something as **sluggish** if it moves, works, or reacts much slower than you would like or is normal. ❑ *The economy remains sluggish.* ❑ *Circulation is much more sluggish in the feet than in the hands.*

형용사 굼뜬; 불경기의 ❑ 경제가 여전히 불경기이다. ❑ 손보다 발에서 혈액 순환이 훨씬 더 부진하다.

slum /slʌm/ (**slums**) N-COUNT A **slum** is an area of a city where living conditions are very bad and where the houses are in bad condition. ❑ *...a slum area of St Louis.*

가산명사 빈민굴, 슬럼가 ❑ 세인트루이스의 빈민가

slum|ber /slʌmbər/ (**slumbers, slumbering, slumbered**) N-VAR **Slumber** is sleep. [LITERARY] ❑ *He had fallen into exhausted slumber.* ● V-I **Slumber** is also a verb. ❑ *The older three girls are still slumbering peacefully.*

가산명사 또는 불가산명사 잠 [문예체] ❑ 그는 녹초가 되어 잠에 빠져들었다. ● 자동사 잠자다 ❑ 나이가 더 많은 세 여자아이들은 여전히 평온하게 잠을 자고 있었다.

slum|ber par|ty (**slumber parties**) N-COUNT A **slumber party** is an occasion when a group of young friends spend the night together at the home of one of the group. [mainly AM] ❑ *I'm having a slumber party for my birthday.*

가산명사 (10대 소녀들의) 밤샘 파티 [주로 미국영어] ❑ 내 생일날 밤샘 파티를 할 예정이다.

slump /slʌmp/ (**slumps, slumping, slumped**) **1** V-I If something such as the value of something **slumps**, it falls suddenly and by a large amount. ❑ *Net profits slumped by 41%.* ● N-COUNT **Slump** is also a noun. ❑ *The council's land is now worth much less than originally hoped because of a slump in property prices.* **2** N-COUNT A **slump** is a time when many people in a country are unemployed and poor. ❑ *...the slump of the early 1980s.* **3** V-I If you **slump** somewhere, you fall or sit

1 자동사 폭락하다 ❑ 순이익이 41퍼센트 폭락했다. ● 가산명사 폭락 ❑ 부동산 가격의 폭락 탓에 지방 의회 보유지의 현재 가치는 애초에 기대했던 것보다 훨씬 낮다. **2** 가산명사 불황 ❑ 1980년대 초기의 불황 **3** 자동사 푹 쓰러지다; 털썩 주저앉다 ❑ 그녀는 의자에 털썩 주저앉았다.

down there heavily, for example because you are very tired or you feel ill. ❑ *She slumped into a chair.*

slung /slʌŋ/ **Slung** is the past tense and past participle of **sling**.

slur /slɜːr/ (**slurs, slurring, slurred**) **1** N-COUNT A **slur** is an insulting remark which could damage someone's reputation. ❑ *This is yet another slur on the integrity of the Metropolitan Police.* **2** V-T/V-I If someone **slurs** their speech or if their speech **slurs**, they do not pronounce each word clearly, because they are drunk, ill, or sleepy. ❑ *He repeated himself and slurred his words more than usual.*

slurp /slɜːrp/ (**slurps, slurping, slurped**) **1** V-T If you **slurp** a liquid, you drink it noisily. ❑ *He blew on his soup before slurping it off the spoon.* **2** N-COUNT A **slurp** is a noise that you make with your mouth when you drink noisily, or a mouthful of liquid that you drink noisily. ❑ *He takes a slurp from a cup of black coffee.*

slush /slʌʃ/ N-UNCOUNT **Slush** is snow that has begun to melt and is therefore very wet and dirty. ❑ *Front-drive cars work better in the snow and slush.*

slush fund (**slush funds**) N-COUNT A **slush fund** is a sum of money collected to pay for an illegal activity, especially in politics or business. ❑ *He's accused of misusing $17.5 million from a secret government slush fund.*

sly /slaɪ/ **1** ADJ A **sly** look, expression, or remark shows that you know something that other people do not know or that was meant to be a secret. ❑ *His lips were spread in a sly smile.* ● **sly|ly** ADV ❑ *Anna grinned slyly.* **2** ADJ If you describe someone as **sly**, you disapprove of them because they keep their feelings or intentions hidden and are clever at deceiving people. [DISAPPROVAL] ❑ *She is devious and sly and manipulative.*

smack /smæk/ (**smacks, smacking, smacked**) **1** V-T If you **smack** someone, you hit them with your hand. ❑ *She smacked me on the side of the head.* ● N-COUNT **Smack** is also a noun. ❑ *Sometimes he just doesn't listen and I end up shouting at him or giving him a smack.* **2** V-T If you **smack** something somewhere, you put it or throw it there so that it makes a loud, sharp noise. ❑ *He smacked his hands down on his knees.* **3** V-I If one thing **smacks of** another thing that you consider bad, it reminds you of it or is like it. ❑ *The engineers' union was unhappy with the motion, saying it smacked of racism.* **4** ADV Something that is **smack** in a particular place is exactly in that place. [INFORMAL] [ADV prep] ❑ *In part that's because industry is smack in the middle of the city.* **5** N-UNCOUNT **Smack** is heroin. [INFORMAL] ❑ *...a smack addict.* **6** PHRASE If you **smack** your **lips**, you open and close your mouth noisily, especially before or after eating, to show that you are eager to eat or enjoyed eating. ❑ *"I really want some dessert," Keaton says, smacking his lips.*

small ♦♦♦ /smɔːl/ (**smaller, smallest**) **1** ADJ A **small** person, thing, or amount of something is not large in physical size. ❑ *She is small for her age.* ❑ *Stick them on using a small amount of glue.* **2** ADJ A **small** group or quantity consists of only a few people or things. ❑ *A small group of students meets regularly to learn Japanese.* **3** ADJ A **small** child is a very young child. ❑ *I have a wife and two small children.* **4** ADJ You use **small** to describe something that is not significant or great in degree. ❑ *It's quite easy to make quite small changes to the way that you work.* ❑ *No detail was too small to escape her attention.* **5** ADJ **Small** businesses or companies employ a small number of people and do business with a small number of clients. ❑ *...shops, restaurants and other small businesses.* **6** ADJ If someone makes you look or feel **small**, they make you look or feel stupid or ashamed. [v-link ADJ] ❑ *This may just be another of her schemes to make me look small.* **7** N-SING The **small of** your back is the bottom part of your back that curves in slightly. ❑ *Place your hands on the small of your back and breathe out.* **8** the **small hours** →see hour. **small wonder** →see wonder

You can use the adjective **small** rather than **little** to draw attention to the fact that something is small. For instance, you cannot say "The town is little" or "I have a very little car," but you can say "**The town is small**" or "**I have a very small car**." **Little** is a less precise word than **small**, and may be used to suggest the speaker's feelings or attitude toward the person or thing being described. For that reason, **little** is often used after another adjective. ❑ *What a nice little house you've got here!...* ❑ *Shut up, you horrible little boy!*

Thesaurus   *small*의 참조어

ADJ.	little, minute, petite, slight; (*ant.*) big, large **1**
	young **3**
	insignificant, minor; (*ant.*) important, major, significant **4**

small print N-UNCOUNT The **small print** of a contract or agreement is the part of it that is written in very small print. You refer to it as **the small print** especially when you think that it might include unfavorable conditions which someone might not notice or understand. ❑ *Read the small print in your contract to find out exactly what you are insured for.*

small-scale ADJ A **small-scale** activity or organization is small in size and limited in extent. ❑ *...the small-scale production of farmhouse cheeses in Devon.*

smart ♦♦♦ /smɑːrt/ (**smarter, smartest, smarts, smarting, smarted**) **1** ADJ You can describe someone who is clever or intelligent as **smart**. ❑ *He thinks he's smarter than Sarah is.* **2** ADJ **Smart** people and things are pleasantly neat and clean in appearance. [mainly BRIT] ❑ *He was smart and well groomed but not good looking.* ❑ *I was dressed in a smart navy blue suit.* ● **smart|ly** ADV [ADV with v] ❑ *He dressed very smartly, which was important in those days.* **3** ADJ A **smart** place or event is connected with wealthy and fashionable people. [mainly BRIT] ❑ *...smart London dinner parties.* **4** V-I If a part of your body or a wound **smarts**, you feel a sharp stinging pain in it. ❑ *My eyes smarted from the smoke.* **5** V-I If you **are smarting from** something such as criticism or failure, you feel upset about it. [JOURNALISM] [usu cont] ❑ *The Americans were still smarting from their defeat in the Vietnam War.*

sling의 과거, 과거 분사

1 가산명사 중상, 비방 ❑이것은 런던 경찰의 청렴성에 대한 또 다른 중상이다. **2** 타동사/자동사 불분명하게 발음하다; 불분명하게 발음되어 나오다 ❑그는 한 말을 또 하고 발음도 평소보다 더 불분명하게 했다.

1 타동사 후루룩 마시다 ❑그는 수프를 숟가락으로 떠서 후후 불어서 후루룩거리며 먹었다. **2** 가산명사 후루룩 하는 소리; 후루룩 하고 들이키기 ❑그는 블랙커피를 한 입 후루룩 들이켰다.

불가산명사 (반쯤 녹은) 진창 ❑눈길이나 진창에서는 전륜 구동 자동차가 더 잘 나간다.

가산명사 부정 자금 ❑그는 정부의 비밀 부정 자금에서 천 7백 5십만 달러를 유용한 혐의로 고발되었다.

1 형용사 뭔가를 숨기고 있는, 비밀스러운 ❑그의 입술이 비밀스러운 미소를 띠며 씩 벌어졌다. ● 뭔가를 숨기고 있는 듯이, 비밀스럽게 부사 ❑애너가 비밀스럽게 씩 웃었다. **2** 형용사 교활한, 음흉한 [탐탁잖음] ❑그녀는 사악하고 음흉하며 교활하다.

1 타동사 (손바닥으로) 철썩 때리다 ❑그녀가 내 머리 옆쪽을 철썩 갈겼다. ● 가산명사 철썩 때리기 ❑때때로 그가 말을 듣지 않아서 나는 결국 소리를 지르거나 손바닥으로 때리고 만다. **2** 타동사 털썩 놓다, 털썩 던지다 ❑그가 양손을 무릎 위에다 털썩 내려놓았다. **3** 자동사 -한 대가 있다, -을 연상케 하다 ❑기관사 노조는 그 제안에서 인종 차별주의 경향이 느껴진다며 불쾌했다. **4** 부사 정통으로 [비격식체] ❑부분적으로 그것은 산업체가 도시의 한가운데 있기 때문이다. **5** 불가산명사 헤로인 [비격식체] ❑헤로인 중독자 **6** 구 입맛을 쩝쩝 다시다 ❑"정말로 디저트를 좀 먹고 싶어."라고 키턴이 입맛을 쩝쩝 다시며 말한다.

1 형용사 작은 ❑그녀는 나이에 비해 작다. **2** 소량의, 접착제를 사용해서 그것들을 붙이세요. **2** 형용사 (규모가) 작은 ❑학생들이 작은 그룹을 이루어 정기적으로 모여서 일본어를 배운다. **3** 형용사 어린 ❑나는 아내와 어린 자녀 두 명이 있다. **4** 형용사 사소한, 시시한 ❑작업 방식에 사소한 변화를 주기는 아주 쉽다. ❑그녀의 주의를 벗어날 만큼 사소한 세부 사항은 아무것도 없었다. **5** 형용사 소규모의 ❑상점과 식당, 그리고 여타의 소규모 사업체들 **6** 형용사 하찮은, 부끄러운 ❑이는 그저 나를 하찮게 보이도록 만들려는 그녀의 또 다른 계략일지도 모른다. **7** 단수명사 허리의 잘록한 부분 ❑양 손을 허리의 잘록한 부분에 대고 숨을 들이쉬세요.

어떤 것이 작다는 사실에 주의를 끌기 위해 little 보다는 형용사 small을 쓸 수 있다. 예를 들어, 일반적으로 'The town is little'이나 'I have a very little car'라고 할 수 없고, 'The town is small'이나 'I have a very small car'라고 할 수 있다. little은 small보다 정확하지 못한 말로, 묘사하고 있는 사람이나 사물에 대한 화자의 느낌이나 태도를 나타내는데 쓴다. 그러한 이유로, little은 흔히 다른 형용사 뒤에 쓴다. ❑당신은 이곳에 얼마나 멋진 작은 집을 가지고 있는지!... ❑입닥쳐, 끔찍한 꼬마 녀석 같으니라고!

불가산명사 (계약서 등의) 세목; (계약서의 숨겨진) 불리한 조건 ❑계약서의 세목을 읽고 정확히 무엇을 보증 받는지 알아내세요.

형용사 소규모의 ❑대본 주에서 소규모로 생산되는 농장 치즈

1 형용사 똑똑한, 영리한 ❑그는 자신이 새러보다 똑똑하다고 생각한다. **2** 형용사 말쑥한, 맵시 있는 [주로 영국영어] ❑그는 말쑥하고 단정했지만 잘 생긴 건 아니었다. ❑나는 맵시 있는 짙은 감색 정장을 입고 있었다. ● 말쑥하게, 맵시 있게 부사 ❑그는 아주 말쑥하게 옷을 차려 입었는데, 그 시절에는 옷차림이 중요했다. **3** 형용사 부유층의 [주로 영국영어] ❑부유층의 런던 만찬회 **4** 자동사 (몸이) 쑤시다, 쓰리다 ❑연기 때문에 눈이 쓰렸다. **5** 자동사 괴로워하다, 상심하다 [언론] ❑미국인들은 아직도 베트남 전쟁에서의 패배 때문에 괴로워하고 있었다.

a b c d e f g h i j k l m n o p q r s t u v w x y z

smart card (**smart cards**) N-COUNT A **smart card** is a plastic card which looks like a credit card and can store and process computer data. ❑ *...the use of smart cards for online payments.*

smart|en /smɑrtʰn/ (**smartens, smartening, smartened**)

▶ **smarten up** PHRASAL VERB If you **smarten yourself** or a place **up**, you make yourself or the place look neater and tidier. ❑ *...a 10-year programme to smarten up the London Underground.* ❑ *She had wisely smartened herself up.*

smash ◆◇◇ /smæʃ/ (**smashes, smashing, smashed**) **1** V-T/V-I If you **smash** something or if it **smashes**, it breaks into many pieces, for example when it is hit or dropped. ❑ *Someone smashed a bottle.* ❑ *A crowd of youths started smashing windows.* **2** V-I If you **smash** through a wall, gate, or door, you get through it by hitting and breaking it. ❑ *The demonstrators used trucks to smash through embassy gates.* **3** V-T/V-I If something **smashes** or is **smashed** against something solid, it moves very fast and with great force against it. ❑ *The bottle smashed against a wall.* **4** V-T To **smash** a political group or system means to deliberately destroy it. [INFORMAL] ❑ *Their attempts to clean up politics and smash the power of party machines failed.* **5** →see also **smashing**

▶ **smash up** **1** PHRASAL VERB If you **smash** something **up**, you completely destroy it by hitting it and breaking it into many pieces. ❑ *She took revenge on her ex-boyfriend by smashing up his home.* **2** PHRASAL VERB If you **smash up** your car, you damage it by crashing it into something. ❑ *All you told me was that he'd smashed up yet another car.*

smash|ing /smæʃɪŋ/ ADJ If you describe something or someone as **smashing**, you mean that you like them very much. [BRIT, OLD-FASHIONED] ❑ *It was smashing. I really enjoyed it.*

smear /smɪɑr/ (**smears, smearing, smeared**) **1** V-T If you **smear** a surface **with** an oily or sticky substance or **smear** the substance onto the surface, you spread a layer of the substance over the surface. ❑ *My sister smeared herself with suntan oil and slept by the swimming pool.* **2** N-COUNT A **smear** is a dirty or oily mark. ❑ *There was a smear of gravy on his chin.* **3** V-T To **smear** someone means to spread unpleasant and untrue rumors or accusations about them in order to damage their reputation. [JOURNALISM] ❑ *The BBC last night launched an inquiry into an apparently crude attempt to smear its director-general.* **4** N-COUNT A **smear** is an unpleasant and untrue rumor or accusation that is intended to damage someone's reputation. [JOURNALISM] ❑ *He puts all the accusations down to a smear campaign by his political opponents.* **5** N-COUNT A **smear** or a **smear test** is a medical test in which a few cells are taken from a woman's cervix and examined to see if any cancer cells are present. [BRIT; AM **Pap smear, Pap test**] ❑ *Ideally women over 35 should have a smear every two years.*

smell ◆◇◇ /smɛl/ (**smells, smelling, smelled, smelt**)

> American English usually uses the form **smelled** as the past tense and past participle. British English uses either **smelled** or **smelt**.

1 N-COUNT The **smell** of something is a quality it has which you become aware of when you breathe in through your nose. ❑ *...the smell of freshly baked bread.* ❑ *...horrible smells.* **2** N-UNCOUNT Your sense of **smell** is the ability that your nose has to detect things. ❑ *...people who lose their sense of smell.* **3** V-LINK If something **smells** in a particular way, it has a quality which you become aware of through your nose. ❑ *The room smelled of lemons.* ❑ *It smells delicious.* **4** V-I If you say that something **smells**, you mean that it smells unpleasant. ❑ *Ma threw that out. She said it smelled.* **5** V-T If you **smell** something, you become aware of it when you breathe in through your nose. ❑ *As soon as we opened the front door we could smell the gas.* **6** V-T If you **smell** something, you put your nose near to it and breathe in, so that you can discover its smell. ❑ *I took a fresh rose out of the vase on our table, and smelled it.* **7** to **smell a rat** →see **rat**
→see **taste**
→see Word Web: **smell**

Thesaurus   smell의 참조어

N.   aroma, fragrance, odor, scent **1**
V.   reek, stink **4**
      breathe, inhale, sniff **5**

---

smell|y /smɛli/ (**smellier, smelliest**) ADJ Something that is **smelly** has an unpleasant smell. ❑ *He had extremely smelly feet.*

smelt /smɛlt/ **Smelt** is a past tense and past participle of **smell**. [mainly BRIT]

smile ◆◆◇ /smaɪl/ (**smiles, smiling, smiled**) **1** V-I When you **smile**, the corners of your mouth curve up and you sometimes show your teeth. People smile when they are pleased or amused, or when they are being friendly. ❑ *When he saw me, he smiled and waved.* ❑ *He rubbed the back of his neck and smiled ruefully at me.* **2** N-COUNT A **smile** is the expression that you have on your face when you smile. ❑ *She gave a wry smile.* ❑ *"There are some sandwiches if you're hungry," she said with a smile.*

Word Partnership   smile의 연어

V.   smile **and** laugh, make *someone* smile, smile **and** nod,
     see *someone* smile, try to smile **1**
     smile fades, flash a smile, give *someone* a smile **2**
ADJ.   big/little/small smile, broad smile, friendly smile, half smile,
     sad smile, shy smile, warm smile, wide smile, wry smile **2**

---

smi|ley /smaɪli/ (**smileys**) **1** ADJ A **smiley** person smiles a lot or is smiling. [INFORMAL] [usu ADJ n] ❑ *Two smiley babies are waiting for their lunch.* **2** N-COUNT A

가산명사 스마트 카드 ❑ 온라인 결제용으로 스마트 카드 사용

구동사 말쑥하게 하다, 산뜻하게 하다 ❑ 런던 지하철의 미관 개선을 위한 10개년 계획 ❑ 그녀는 빈틈없이 말쑥하게 몸단장을 했었다.

1 타동사/자동사 박살내다; 박살이 나다 ❑ 누군가 병을 박살냈다. ❑ 다수의 젊은이들이 창문을 박살내기 시작했다. **2** 자동사 돌파하다 ❑ 시위 참가자들이 트럭을 이용하여 대사관 정문을 돌파했다. **3** 타동사/자동사 세게 충돌하다; 세게 부딪다 ❑ 병이 벽에 세게 부딪혔다. **4** 타동사 분쇄하다 [비격식체] ❑ 정계를 일소하고 정당 조직의 권력을 분쇄하려는 그들의 시도는 실패했다.

1 구동사 박살내다, 때려 부수다 ❑ 그녀는 이전 남자 친구의 집을 때려 부수는 것으로 그에게 복수를 했다. **2** 구동사 (차를) 들이받다 ❑ 네가 내게 말한 것이라고는 그가 또 다른 차를 들이받았다는 것뿐이었다.

형용사 아주 멋진, 굉장한 [영국영어, 구식어] ❑ 그것은 아주 멋졌어. 정말 마음에 들었어.

1 타동사 바르다 ❑ 누이는 몸에 선탠오일을 바르고 풀장 옆에서 잠을 잤다. **2** 가산명사 얼룩 ❑ 그의 턱에 고깃국물 얼룩이 묻어 있었다. **3** 타동사 중상하다, 비방하다 [언론] ❑ 비비시는 지난밤 자사 사장을 중상하려는 명백히 노골적인 시도에 대한 조사에 착수했다. **4** 가산명사 중상, 비방 [언론] ❑ 그는 모든 혐의를 정적들에 의한 흑색선전 탓으로 돌린다. **5** 가산명사 자궁 경부암 검사 [영국영어; 미국영어 Pap smear, Pap test] ❑ 이상적으로는 서른다섯 살을 넘긴 여성들은 2년마다 한 번씩 자궁 경부암 검사를 받아야 한다.

미국영어에서 대개 과거 및 과거 분사로 smelled를 쓴다. 영국영어에서는 smelled 또는 smelt를 쓴다.

1 가산명사 냄새 ❑ 갓 구운 빵 냄새 ❑ 지독한 냄새 **2** 불가산명사 후각 ❑ 후각을 잃은 사람들 **3** 연결동사 냄새가 나다 ❑ 그 방에는 레몬 냄새가 났다. ❑ 맛있는 냄새가 나는데. **4** 자동사 악취가 나다, 냄새가 나다 ❑ 엄마가 그걸 내버렸다. 엄마는 그게 악취가 난다고 했다. **5** 타동사 -의 냄새를 느끼다 ❑ 현관을 열자마자 가스 냄새가 났다. **6** 타동사 -의 냄새를 맡다 ❑ 나는 탁자 위 꽃병에서 싱싱한 장미 한 송이를 꺼내 냄새를 맡았다.

형용사 냄새가 고약한, 악취가 나는 ❑ 그는 발 냄새가 아주 고약했다.

smell의 과거, 과거 분사 [주로 영국영어]

1 자동사 미소 짓다 ❑ 그는 나를 보자 미소 지으며 손을 흔들었다. ❑ 그는 목 뒤쪽을 문지르며 나를 향해 서글프게 미소 지었다. **2** 가산명사 미소 ❑ 그녀가 짓궂은 미소를 지었다. ❑ "배고프면 샌드위치가 약간 있어."라고 그녀가 미소 지으며 말했다.

1 형용사 생글거리는, 미소 띤 [비격식체] ❑ 생글거리는 아기 둘이 점심 식사를 기다리고

Word Web   smell

Scientists believe that the average person can recognize about 10,000 separate **odors**. Until recently, however, the **sense** of smell was a mystery. We now know that most substances release odor molecules into the air. They enter the body through the **nose**. When they reach the **nasal cavity**, they attach to **sensory** cells. The olfactory nerve carries the information to the brain and we identify the smell. The eyes, mouth, and throat also contain receptors that add to the olfactory experience. Interestingly, our sense of smell is more accurate later in the day than it is in the morning.

smiley is a symbol used in e-mail to show how someone is feeling. :-) is a smiley showing happiness. [COMPUTING]

smirk /smɜrk/ (**smirks, smirking, smirked**) V-I If you **smirk**, you smile in an unpleasant way, often because you believe that you have gained an advantage over someone else or know something that they do not know. ❏ *Two men standing nearby looked at me, nudged each other and smirked.*

smog /smɒg/ (**smogs**) N-VAR **Smog** is a mixture of fog and smoke which occurs in some busy industrial cities. ❏ *Cars cause pollution, both smog and acid rain.* →see **pollution**

smoke ♦♦◇ /smoʊk/ (**smokes, smoking, smoked**) ■ N-UNCOUNT **Smoke** consists of gas and small bits of solid material that are sent into the air when something burns. ❏ *A cloud of black smoke blew over the city.* ② V-I If something **is smoking**, smoke is coming from it. ❏ *The chimney was smoking fiercely.* ③ V-T/V-I When someone **smokes** a cigarette, cigar, or pipe, they suck the smoke from it into their mouth and blow it out again. If you **smoke**, you regularly smoke cigarettes, cigars, or a pipe. ❏ *He was sitting alone, smoking a big cigar.* ❏ *It's not easy to quit smoking cigarettes.* ● N-SING **Smoke** is also a noun. ❏ *Someone came out for a smoke.* ● **smok|er** (**smokers**) N-COUNT ❏ *He was not a heavy smoker.* ④ V-T If fish or meat **is smoked**, it is hung over burning wood so that the smoke preserves it and gives it a special flavor. [usu passive] ❏ *...the grid where the fish were being smoked.* ⑤ →see also **smoking** ⑥ PHRASE If someone says **there's no smoke without fire** or **where there's smoke there's fire**, they mean that there are rumors or signs that something is true so it must be at least partly true. ❏ *The story was the main item on the news and people were bound to think there was no smoke without fire.* ⑦ PHRASE If something **goes up in smoke**, it is destroyed by fire. ❏ *More than 900 years of British history went up in smoke in the Great Fire of Windsor.* ⑧ PHRASE If something that is very important to you **goes up in smoke**, it fails or ends without anything being achieved. ❏ *The dreams of hundreds of holidaymakers went up in smoke after the collapse of their travel agency.* →see **fire**

Word Partnership   smoke의 연어

ADJ.	**black** smoke, **dense** smoke, **heavy** smoke, **secondhand** smoke, **thick** smoke ■
N.	**cigarette** smoke, **cloud of** smoke, smoke **damage**, smoke **from a fire**, **smell of** smoke, **tobacco** smoke ■ smoke **a cigar/cigarette**, smoke **tobacco** ③
V.	**see** smoke, **smell** smoke ■ smoke **and drink** ③

smok|ing ♦◇◇ /smoʊkɪŋ/ ■ N-UNCOUNT **Smoking** is the act or habit of smoking cigarettes, cigars, or a pipe. ❏ *Smoking is now banned in many places of work.* ② ADJ A **smoking** area is intended for people who want to smoke. [ADJ n] ❏ *...the decision to scrap smoking compartments on Kent trains.* ③ →see also **smoke**

Word Partnership   smoking의 연어

V.	**ban** smoking, **quit** smoking, **stop** smoking ■
N.	**ban on** smoking, **dangers of** smoking, **effects of** smoking, smoking **habits**, **risk of** smoking ■ **(no)** smoking **section** ②

smoky /smoʊki/ (**smokier, smokiest**) also **smokey** ■ ADJ A place that is **smoky** has a lot of smoke in the air. ❏ *His main problem was the extremely smoky atmosphere at work.* ② ADJ You can use **smoky** to describe something that looks like smoke, for example because it is slightly blue or grey or because it is not clear. [ADJ n, ADJ color] ❏ *At the center of the dial is a piece of smoky glass.* ③ ADJ Something that has a **smoky** flavor tastes as if it has been smoked. ❏ *The fish had just the right amount of smoky flavor.*

smol|der /smoʊldər/ (**smolders, smoldering, smoldered**) [BRIT **smoulder**] ■ V-I If something **smolders**, it burns slowly, producing smoke but not flames. ❏ *The wreckage was still smoldering several hours after the crash.* ② V-I If a feeling such as anger or hatred **smolders** inside you, you continue to feel it but do not show it. ❏ *...the guilt that had so long smoldered in her heart.* ③ V-I If you say that someone **smolders**, you mean that they are sexually attractive, usually in a mysterious or very intense way. ❏ *He was good-looking, with dark eyes which could smolder with just the right intimation of passion.* →see **fire**

smooth ♦◇◇ /smuð/ (**smoother, smoothest, smooths, smoothing, smoothed**) ■ ADJ A **smooth** surface has no roughness, lumps, or holes. ❏ *...a rich cream that keeps skin soft and smooth.* ❏ *...a smooth surface such as glass.* ② ADJ A **smooth** liquid

있다. ② 가산명사 (이메일의) 스마일리, 미소 표시 [컴퓨터]

자동사 능글맞게 웃다, 히죽히죽 웃다 ❏ 가까이에 서 있던 두 남자가 나를 보더니, 서로 옆구리를 슬쩍 지르며 능글맞게 웃었다.

가산명사 또는 불가산명사 스모그 ❏ 자동차들은 스모그와 산성비라는 공해를 둘 다 유발한다.

■ 불가산명사 연기 ❏ 검은 연기구름이 도시 위로 날렸다. ② 자동사 연기를 뿜다 ❏ 굴뚝이 무섭게 연기를 내뿜고 있었다. ③ 타동사/자동사 (담배를) 피우다 ❏ 그는 커다란 시가를 피우면서 혼자 앉아 있었다. ❏ 담배를 끊는 일은 쉽지 않다. ● 단수명사 담배 피우기 ❏ 누군가가 담배를 피우러 나왔다. ● 흡연자 가산명사 ❏ 그는 골초가 아니었다. ④ 타동사 훈제 처리되다 ❏ 생선을 훈제 처리하는 데 쓰이고 있던 석쇠 ⑤ 구 아니 땐 굴뚝에 연기 나랴 ❏ 그 이야기가 뉴스의 주된 항목이었고 사람들은 아니 땐 굴뚝에 연기나겠느냐고 생각하기 마련이었다. ⑥ 구 불에 타서 사라지다 ❏ 윈저 대화재 때 900년 이상의 영국 역사가 불에 타서 사라졌다. ⑧ 구 인기처럼 사라지다, 수포로 돌아가다 ❏ 여행사가 파산한 후 수백 명에 달하는 휴가객들의 꿈이 연기처럼 사라졌다.

■ 불가산명사 흡연 ❏ 요즘 많은 직장에서 흡연이 금지되어 있다. ② 형용사 흡연용의 ❏ 켄트 철도의 흡연 객차를 없애는 결정

■ 형용사 연기가 자욱한 ❏ 그의 주된 문제는 몹시 연기가 자욱한 직장의 공기였다. ② 형용사 흐릿한, 침침한 ❏ 다이얼의 한가운데에 흐릿한 유리 조각이 있다. ③ 형용사 훈제한 듯한 ❏ 그 생선 요리는 아주 적당한 만큼의 훈제 맛이 났다.

[영국영어 smoulder] ■ 자동사 (불꽃은 없고) 연기만 피워 올리다 ❏ 추락 후 몇 시간이 지난 후에도 잔해에서는 여전히 연기가 나고 있었다. ② 자동사 (분노 능이) 들끓다 ❏ 그녀의 마음속에서 아주 오랫동안 들끓던 죄책감 ③ 자동사 묘한 성적 매력을 풍기다 ❏ 그는 잘 생겼고, 눈이 적당히 은밀한 욕정을 품은 듯 묘한 성적 매력을 풍기는 짙은 색이었다.

■ 형용사 매끄러운 ❏ 피부를 부드럽고 매끄럽게 유지해 주는 영양 크림 ❏ 유리 같은 매끄러운 표면 ② 형용사 고루 잘 섞인, 잘 이겨진 ❏ 반죽이 잘 섞여서

or mixture has been mixed well so that it has no lumps. ❑ *Continue whisking until the mixture looks smooth and creamy.* ❸ ADJ If you describe a drink such as wine, whiskey, or coffee as **smooth**, you mean that it is not bitter and is pleasant to drink. ❑ *This makes the whiskeys much smoother.* ❹ ADJ A **smooth** line or movement has no sudden breaks or changes in direction or speed. ❑ *This exercise is done in one smooth motion.* ● **smooth|ly** ADV [ADV with v] ❑ *Make sure that you execute all movements smoothly and without jerking.* ❺ ADJ A **smooth** ride, flight, or sea crossing is very comfortable because there are no unpleasant movements. ❑ *The active suspension system gives the car a very smooth ride.* ❻ ADJ You use **smooth** to describe something that is going well and is free of problems or trouble. ❑ *Political hopes for a swift and smooth transition to democracy have been dashed.* ● **smooth|ly** ADV [ADV with v] ❑ *So far, talks at GM have gone smoothly.* ❼ ADJ If you describe a man as **smooth**, you mean that he is extremely smart, confident, and polite, often in a way that you find rather unpleasant. ❑ *Twelve extremely good-looking, smooth young men have been picked as finalists.* ❽ V-T If you **smooth** something, you move your hands over its surface to make it smooth and flat. ❑ *She stood up and smoothed down her frock.*

▶**smooth out** PHRASAL VERB If you **smooth out** a problem or difficulty, you solve it, especially by talking to the people concerned. ❑ *Baker was smoothing out differences with European allies.*

smoth|er /smΛðər/ (**smothers, smothering, smothered**) ❶ V-T If you **smother** a fire, you cover it with something in order to put it out. ❑ *The girl's parents were also burned as they tried to smother the flames.* ❷ V-T To **smother** someone means to kill them by covering their face with something so that they cannot breathe. ❑ *He tried to smother me with a pillow.* ❸ V-T Things that **smother** something cover it completely. ❑ *Once the shrubs begin to smother the little plants, we have to move them.* ❹ V-T If you **smother** someone, you show your love for them too much and protect them too much. ❑ *She loved her own children, almost smothering them with love.* ❺ V-T If you **smother** an emotion or a reaction, you control it so that people do not notice it. ❑ *She summoned up all her pity for him, to smother her self-pity.*

smoul|der /smoʊldər/ →see **smolder**

SMS /ɛs ɛm ɛs/ N-UNCOUNT **SMS** is a way of sending short written messages from one cellphone to another. **SMS** is an abbreviation for "short message system" or "short message service."

smudge /smΛdʒ/ (**smudges, smudging, smudged**) ❶ N-COUNT A **smudge** is a dirty mark. ❑ *There was a dark smudge on his forehead.* ❷ V-T If you **smudge** a substance such as ink, paint, or make-up that has been put on a surface, you make it less neat by touching or rubbing it. ❑ *She rubbed her eyes, smudging her make-up.* ❸ V-T If you **smudge** a surface, you make it dirty by touching it and leaving a substance on it. ❑ *She kissed me, careful not to smudge me with her fresh lipstick.* →see **drawing**

smug /smΛg/ ADJ If you say that someone is **smug**, you are criticizing the fact they seem very pleased with how good, clever, or lucky they are. [DISAPPROVAL] ❑ *Thomas and his wife looked at each other in smug satisfaction.*

smug|gle /smΛgᵊl/ (**smuggles, smuggling, smuggled**) V-T If someone **smuggles** things or people into a place or out of it, they take them there illegally or secretly. ❑ *My message is "If you try to smuggle drugs you are stupid."* ❑ *Police have foiled an attempt to smuggle a bomb into Belfast airport.* ● **smug|gling** N-UNCOUNT ❑ *An air hostess was arrested and charged with drug smuggling.*

smug|gler /smΛglər/ (**smugglers**) N-COUNT **Smugglers** are people who take goods into or out of a country illegally. ❑ *...drug smugglers.*

snack /snæk/ (**snacks, snacking, snacked**) ❶ N-COUNT A **snack** is a simple meal that is quick to cook and to eat. ❑ *Lunch was a snack in the fields.* ❷ N-COUNT A **snack** is something such as a chocolate bar that you eat between meals. ❑ *Do you eat sweets, cakes, or sugary snacks?* ❸ V-I If you **snack**, you eat snacks between meals. ❑ *Instead of snacking on crisps and chocolate, nibble on celery or carrot.* →see **peanut**

snack bar (**snack bars**) N-COUNT A **snack bar** is a place where you can buy drinks and simple meals such as sandwiches.

snag /snæg/ (**snags, snagging, snagged**) ❶ N-COUNT A **snag** is a small problem or disadvantage. ❑ *A police clampdown on car thieves hit a snag when villains stole one of their cars.* ❷ V-T/V-I If you **snag** part of your clothing **on** a sharp or rough object or if it **snags**, it gets caught on the object and tears. ❑ *She snagged a heel on a root and tumbled to the ground.* ❑ *Brambles snagged his suit.*

snail /sneɪl/ (**snails**) ❶ N-COUNT A **snail** is a small animal with a long, soft body, no legs, and a spiral-shaped shell. Snails move very slowly. ❷ PHRASE If you say that someone does something **at a snail's pace**, you are emphasizing that they are doing it very slowly, usually when you think it would be better if they did it much more quickly. [EMPHASIS] ❑ *The train was moving now at a snail's pace.*

snail mail N-UNCOUNT Some computer users refer to the postal system as **snail mail**, because it is very slow in comparison with e-mail. ❑ *The price of stamps has risen 725 percent, causing many disgruntled consumers to abandon snail mail for e-mail.*

snake /sneɪk/ (**snakes, snaking, snaked**) ❶ N-COUNT A **snake** is a long, thin reptile without legs. ❷ V-I Something that **snakes** in a particular direction goes in that direction in a line with a lot of bends. [LITERARY] ❑ *The road snaked through forested mountains.* →see **desert**

snap ♦◇◇ /snæp/ (**snaps, snapping, snapped**) ❶ V-T/V-I If something **snaps** or if you **snap** it, it breaks suddenly, usually with a sharp cracking noise. ❑ *He*

크림같이 보일 때까지 계속 휘저으세요. ❸ 형용사 (술 등의 맛이) 부드러운 ❑ 이것이 위스키 맛을 훨씬 더 부드럽게 만들어 준다. ❹ 형용사 (움직임 등이) 부드러운 ❑ 이 운동은 하나의 부드러운 동작으로 이루어진다. ● 부드럽게 부사 ❑ 반드시 모든 동작을 급격한 움직임 없이 부드럽게 실시하세요. ❺ 형용사 편안한 ❑ 액티브 서스펜션 시스템이 차량에 매우 편안한 승차감을 줍니다. ❻ 형용사 순조로운 ❑ 신속하고 순조롭게 민주주의로 이행하기를 바라는 정치적 희망이 좌절을 겪어 왔다. ● 순조롭게 부사 ❑ 지금까지, 지엠사에서의 협의는 순조롭게 진행되어 왔다. ❼ 형용사 능글능글한 ❑ 아주 잘 생기고 능글능글한 열두 명의 젊은 남자들이 결선 진출자로 선발되었다. ❽ 타동사 (손으로 쓸어) 매끈하게 하다, 주름을 펴다 ❑ 그녀는 일어서서 드레스를 쓸어내려 주름을 폈다.

구동사 (문제를) 해결하다, 바로잡다 ❑ 베이커가 유럽 동맹국들과의 의견 차이를 해결하고 있었다.

❶ 타동사 (불을) 덮어 끄다 ❑ 소녀의 부모 역시 불길을 덮어 끄려고 하다가 불에 탔다. ❷ 타동사 질식시켜 죽이다 ❑ 그가 나를 베개로 덮어 질식사시키려 했다. ❸ 타동사 덮어 가리다 ❑ 일단 관목이 작은 묘목을 덮어 가리기 시작하면 그것들을 옮겨야 한다. ❹ 타동사 숨 막힐 정도로 애정을 퍼붓다 ❑ 그녀는 자기 자식들에게 거의 숨 막힐 정도로 사랑을 퍼부었다. ❺ 타동사 (감정 등을) 억제하다, 억누르다 ❑ 그녀는 자기 연민을 억누르기 위해 그에 대한 동정심을 최대한 끌어냈다.

불가산명사 문자 메시지 전송

❶ 가산명사 얼룩 ❑ 그의 이마에 까만 얼룩이 묻어 있었다. ❷ 타동사 얼룩지게 하다 ❑ 그녀가 눈을 비비自 화장이 번져 얼룩이 졌다. ❸ 타동사 묻히다, 더럽히다 ❑ 그녀는 금방 바른 립스틱이 묻지 않도록 신경 쓰면서 나에게 키스했다.

형용사 자기만족의, 자아도취의 [탐탁잖음] ❑ 토머스와 그의 아내는 자아도취에 빠져 서로를 바라보았다.

타동사 밀수하다; 몰래 데리고 들어오다 ❑ 저는 "마약 밀수를 하려는 자는 어리석은 자이다."라고 말씀 드리고 싶습니다. ❑ 벨파스트 공항으로 폭탄을 밀반입하려는 시도가 경찰에 의해 좌절됐다. ● 밀수, 밀항 불가산명사 ❑ 항공기 여 승무원 한 사람이 마약 밀매 혐의로 체포되어 기소되었다.

가산명사 밀수자, 밀수범 ❑ 마약 밀수범

❶ 가산명사 간단한 식사 ❑ 점심은 야외에서 간단히 먹었다. ❷ 가산명사 간식 ❑ 단것이나 케이크 또는 단맛 위주의 간식을 드십니까? ❸ 자동사 간식을 먹다 ❑ 감자 칩이나 초콜릿을 간식으로 먹는 대신 셀러리나 당근을 썰어 드세요.

가산명사 간이식당, 스낵 바

❶ 가산명사 걸림돌, 차질 ❑ 악당들이 경찰차 한 대를 훔치면서 경찰의 자동차 강도 강력 단속이 걸림돌을 만났다. ❷ 타동사/자동사 걸려서 찢어지다, 걸리다 ❑ 그녀는 신발굽이 나무뿌리에 걸리는 바람에 땅바닥으로 넘어졌다. ❑ 브램블즈의 옷이 걸려서 찢어졌다.

❶ 가산명사 달팽이 ❷ 구 달팽이같이 느리게 [강조] ❑ 이제는 기차가 달팽이처럼 느리게 움직이고 있었다.

불가산명사 (이메일과 대조되는) 재래식 우편 제도 ❑ 우표 값이 725퍼센트 인상되면서 이에 불만을 품은 소비자 상당수가 재래식 우편제도 대신 이메일을 사용하게 되었다.

❶ 가산명사 뱀 ❷ 자동사 꾸불꾸불 나아가다 [문예체] ❑ 숲이 울창한 산 속으로 길이 꾸불꾸불 나 있었다.

❶ 타동사/자동사 툭 부러지다; 툭 부러뜨리다 ❑ 그가 무게 중심을 바꾸자 나뭇가지가 툭 부러졌다.

shifted his weight and a twig snapped. ❑ *The brake pedal had just snapped off.* ● N-SING **Snap** is also a noun. ❑ *Every minute or so I could hear a snap, a crack and a crash as another tree went down.* ❷ V-T/V-I If you **snap** something into a particular position, or if it **snaps** into that position, it moves quickly into that position, with a sharp sound. ❑ *He snapped the notebook shut.* ❑ *He snapped the cap on his ballpoint.* ● N-SING **Snap** is also a noun. ❑ *He shut the book with a snap and stood up.* ❸ V-T If you **snap** your **fingers**, you make a sharp sound by moving your middle finger quickly across your thumb, for example in order to accompany music or to order someone to do something. ❑ *She had millions of listeners snapping their fingers to her first single.* ❑ *He snapped his fingers, and Wilson produced a sheet of paper.* ● N-SING **Snap** is also a noun. [N of n] ❑ *I could obtain with the snap of my fingers anything I chose.* ❹ V-T/V-I If someone **snaps at** you, they speak to you in a sharp, unfriendly way. ❑ *"Of course I don't know her," Roger snapped.* ❺ V-I If someone **snaps**, or if something **snaps** inside them, they suddenly stop being calm and become very angry because the situation has become too tense or too difficult for them. ❑ *He finally snapped when she prevented their children from visiting him one weekend.* ❻ V-I If an animal such as a dog **snaps at** you, it opens and shuts its jaws quickly near you, as if it were going to bite you. ❑ *His teeth clicked as he snapped at my ankle.* ❼ ADJ A **snap** decision or action is one that is taken suddenly, often without careful thought. [ADJ n] ❑ *I think this is too important for a snap decision.* ❽ N-COUNT A **snap** is a photograph. [INFORMAL] ❑ *...a snap my mother took last year.*

▶**snap up** PHRASAL VERB If you **snap** something **up**, you buy it quickly because it is cheap or is just what you want. ❑ *...a millionaire ready to snap them up at the premium price of $200 a gallon.*

snap|shot /snǽpʃɒt/ (**snapshots**) ❶ N-COUNT A **snapshot** is a photograph that is taken quickly and casually. ❑ *Let me take a snapshot of you guys, so friends back home can see you.* ❷ N-COUNT If something provides you with a **snapshot of** a place or situation, it gives you a brief idea of what that place or situation is like. [usu sing, usu N of n] ❑ *The interviews present a remarkable snapshot of Britain in these dark days of recession.*

snare /snéər/ (**snares, snaring, snared**) ❶ N-COUNT A **snare** is a trap for catching birds or small animals. It consists of a loop of wire or rope which pulls tight around the animal. ❑ *I felt like an animal caught in a snare.* ❷ N-COUNT If you describe a situation as a **snare**, you mean that it is a trap from which it is difficult to escape. [FORMAL] ❑ *Given data which are free from bias there are further snares to avoid in statistical work.* ❸ V-T If someone **snares** an animal, they catch it using a snare. ❑ *He'd snared a rabbit earlier in the day.*

snarl /snɑ́rl/ (**snarls, snarling, snarled**) V-I When an animal **snarls**, it makes a fierce, rough sound in its throat while showing its teeth. ❑ *He raced ahead up into the bush, barking and snarling.* ● N-COUNT **Snarl** is also a noun. ❑ *With a snarl, the second dog made a dive for his heel.*

snatch /snætʃ/ (**snatches, snatching, snatched**) ❶ V-T/V-I If you **snatch** something or **snatch at** something, you take it or pull it away quickly. ❑ *Mick snatched the cards from Archie's hand.* ❑ *He snatched up the telephone.* ❷ V-T If something **is snatched** from you, it is stolen, usually using force. If a person **is snatched**, they are taken away by force. [usu passive] ❑ *If your bag is snatched, let it go.* ❸ V-T If you **snatch** an opportunity, you take it quickly. If you **snatch** something to eat or a rest, you have it quickly in between doing other things. ❑ *I snatched a glance at the mirror.* ❹ V-T If you **snatch** victory in a competition, you defeat your opponent by a small amount or just before the end of the contest. ❑ *The American came from behind to snatch victory by a mere eight seconds.* ❺ N-COUNT A **snatch of** a conversation or a song is a very small piece of it. ❑ *I heard snatches of the conversation.*

sneak /sniːk/ (**sneaks, sneaking, sneaked**)

The form **snuck** is also used in American English for the past tense and past participle.

❶ V-I If you **sneak** somewhere, you go there very quietly on foot, trying to avoid being seen or heard. ❑ *Sometimes he would sneak out of his house late at night to be with me.* ❷ V-T If you **sneak** something somewhere, you take it there secretly. ❑ *He smuggled papers out each day, photocopied them, and snuck them back.* ❸ V-T If you **sneak** a look at someone or something, you secretly have a quick look at them. ❑ *You sneak a look at your watch to see how long you've got to wait.*

sneak|er /sniːkər/ (**sneakers**) N-COUNT **Sneakers** are casual shoes with rubber soles that people wear often for running or other sports. [mainly AM; BRIT usually **trainers**] [usu pl] ❑ *...a new pair of sneakers.*
→see **clothing**

Athletic shoes have many names. The simplest name is **sneakers**. Other names may specify where the shoe was designed to be worn: **tennis shoe, gym shoe, basketball shoe, running shoe** and so on. In the UK, the term **trainers** is usually used.

sneer /snɪ́ər/ (**sneers, sneering, sneered**) V-T/V-I If you **sneer**, or **sneer at** someone or something, you express your contempt for them by the expression on your face or by what you say. ❑ *There is too great a readiness to sneer at anything the Opposition does.* ❑ *If you go to a club and you don't look right, you're sneered at.* ● N-COUNT **Sneer** is also a noun. ❑ *Canete's mouth twisted in a contemptuous sneer.*

sneeze /sniːz/ (**sneezes, sneezing, sneezed**) ❶ V-I When you **sneeze**, you suddenly take in your breath and then blow it down your nose noisily without being able to stop yourself, for example because you have a cold.

❑ 브레이크 페달이 방금 톡 부러진 상태였다. ● 단수명사 톡 (부러지는 소리) ❑ 거의 1분마다 나무가 새로 넘어지면서 톡 부러지고, 쩍 갈라지고, 쿵 쓰러지는 소리가 들렸다. ❷ 타동사/자동사 탁 하는 소리 나게 놓다; 톡 하고 움직이다 ❑ 그가 공책을 탁 덮었다. ❑ 그가 볼펜 뚜껑을 탁 닫았다. ● 단수명사 탁, 딱, 찰칵 ❑ 그는 책을 탁 덮고 일어섰다. ❸ 타동사 (엄지와 중지로) 딱 소리를 내다 ❑ 수백만 명의 사람들이 그녀의 첫 싱글 곡을 들으며 손가락을 딱딱거리며 장단을 맞췄다. ❑ 그가 손가락으로 딱 소리를 내자 윌슨이 종이 한 장을 꺼냈다. ● 단수명사 손가락을 딱 튕기기 ❑ 나는 손가락을 딱 튕겨서 신호만 보내면 원하는 뭐든지 얻을 수 있었다. ❹ 타동사/자동사 쏘아붙이다, 딱딱거리다 ❑ "물론 나는 그 여자 몰라." 라고 로저가 쏘아붙였다. ❺ 자동사 (감정이) 폭발하다, 한 순간 무너지다 ❑ 어느 주말엔가 아내가 아이들한테 아빠를 못 만나게 하자 그가 마침내 폭발했다. ❻ 자동사 물려고 하다, 달려들다 ❑ 내 발목으로 달려들면서 놈이 이빨을 딱딱 맞부딪혔다. ❼ 형용사 성급한 ❑ 내 생각에 이것은 성급한 결정을 내리기엔 너무나 중대한 사안 같아. ❽ 가산명사 사진 [비격식체] ❑ 작년에 어머니가 찍어 주신 사진

구동사 잽싸 사다 ❑ 갤런당 2백 달러라는 고가에 당장이라도 그걸 살 준비가 된 백만장자

❶ 가산명사 스냅 사진 ❑ 집에 돌아온 친구들이 볼 수 있게 내가 너희 스냅 사진 찍어 줄게. ❷ 가산명사 간략한 묘사 ❑ 그 인터뷰들은 불황 속에서 암울한 나날을 보내고 있는 영국을 엿볼 수 있는 훌륭한 기회를 제공한다.

❶ 가산명사 덫, 올가미 ❑ 나는 덫에 걸린 동물 같은 심정이었다. ❷ 가산명사 함정 [격식체] ❑ 데이터가 편견에서 자유롭다 할지라도 통계에서 피해야 할 함정이 몇 군데 더 있다. ❸ 타동사 덫으로 잡다 ❑ 그는 그날 일찍 덫을 놓아 토끼를 잡았었다.

자동사 (이빨을 드러내고) 으르렁거리다 ❑ 그 놈은 큰소리로 짖고 으르렁거리며 수풀 속으로 뛰어 들어갔다. ● 가산명사 으르렁거림 ❑ 두 번째 개가 으르렁거리며 그의 발뒤꿈치를 향해 달려들었다.

❶ 타동사/자동사 와락 잡다, 잡아채다 ❑ 믹이 아치의 손에서 카드를 와락 집어 들었다. ❷ 타동사 강탈하다; 강제로 끌려가다 ❑ 가방을 강탈당하더라도 그냥 놔두세요. ❸ 타동사 재빨리 붙잡다, 재빨리 하다 ❑ 나는 재빨리 거울을 쳐다봤다. ❹ 타동사 (승리를) 낚아채다 ❑ 미국 선수가 추월하면서 단 8초 차이로 승리를 낚아챘다. ❺ 가산명사 조각, 단편 ❑ 나는 그 대화의 몇 마디만 간간이 들었다.

snuck도 미국영어에서 과거 및 과거 분사로 쓰인다.

❶ 자동사 살금살금 가다 ❑ 가끔씩 그가 밤늦게 조용히 집을 빠져나와서 나와 함께 있기도 했다. ❷ 타동사 몰래 가지고 가다 ❑ 그는 매일 문서를 빼돌려서 복사를 한 다음에 몰래 되돌려 놨다. ❸ 타동사 훔쳐보다 ❑ 당신은 얼마나 오래 기다려야 하는지 보려고 시계를 훔쳐본다.

가산명사 운동화 [주로 미국영어; 영국영어 대개 trainers] ❑ 새 운동화 한 켤레

운동화는 이름이 많다. 가장 간단한 이름이 sneakers이다. 다른 명칭들은 tennis shoe(테니스화), gym shoe(체조화), basketball shoe(농구화), running shoe(육상화) 등처럼 그 신발이 어디에서 신도록 만들어졌는지를 명시한다. 영국에서는 대개 trainers라는 말을 쓴다.

타동사/자동사 비웃다, 경멸하다 ❑ 야당이 하는 일이라면 무엇이든 비웃기부터 하려는 경향이 지나치게 많다. ❑ 클럽에 갈 때 제대로 차려 입지 않으면 비웃음을 사게 된다. ● 가산명사 비웃음, 경멸 ❑ 카네테가 입술을 실룩거리며 경멸 섞인 비웃음을 지었다.

❶ 자동사 재채기하다 ❑ 우리가 재채기를 할 때 정확히 어떤 일이 일어날까? ● 가산명사 재채기 ❑ 기침과 재채기는 전염병을 퍼뜨린다. ❷ 구 얕잡아 볼 수 없다,

❑ *What exactly happens when we sneeze?* ● N-COUNT **Sneeze** is also a noun. ❑ *Coughs and sneezes spread infections.* ② PHRASE If you say that something is **not to be sneezed at**, you mean that it is worth having. [INFORMAL] ❑ *The money's not to be sneezed at.*

무시 못할 정도이다 [비격식체] ❑ 무시할 수 없는 액수의 돈이다.

sniff /snɪf/ (**sniffs, sniffing, sniffed**) ① V-I When you **sniff**, you breathe in air through your nose hard enough to make a sound, for example when you are trying not to cry, or in order to show disapproval. ❑ *She wiped her face and sniffed loudly.* ❑ *Then he sniffed. There was a smell of burning.* ● N-COUNT **Sniff** is also a noun. ❑ *At last the sobs ceased, to be replaced by sniffs.* ② V-T/V-I If you **sniff** something or **sniff at** it, you smell it by sniffing. ❑ *Suddenly, he stopped and sniffed the air.* ③ V-T You can use **sniff** to indicate that someone says something in a way that shows their disapproval or contempt. ❑ *"Tourists!" she sniffed.* ④ V-I If you say that something is **not to be sniffed at**, you think it is very good or worth having. If someone **sniffs at** something, they do not think it is good enough, or they express their contempt for it. [usu passive, usu with brd-neg] ❑ *The salary was not to be sniffed at either.* ⑤ V-T If someone **sniffs** a substance such as glue, they deliberately breathe in the substance or the gases from it as a drug. ❑ *He felt light-headed, as if he'd sniffed glue.*

① 자동사 코를 훌쩍거리다, 코를 킁킁거리다, 콧방귀 뀌다 ❑ 그녀가 얼굴을 훔치더니 큰소리로 코를 훌쩍거렸다. ❑ 그리고 그가 코를 킁킁거렸다. 타는 냄새가 났다. ● 가산명사 훌쩍임, 킁킁거림, 콧방귀 ❑ 마침내 흐느낌이 멈추고 이제는 훌쩍이는 소리가 났다. ② 타동사/자동사 킁킁대어 냄새 맡다 ❑ 갑자기 그가 멈춰 서서 킁킁대며 냄새를 맡았다. ③ 타동사 콧방귀 뀌다 ❑ "여행자들이라고!"라고 그녀가 콧방귀를 뀌었다. ④ 자동사 비웃을 수 있다, 무시할 수 없다; 비웃다, 무시하다 ❑ 연봉도 무시할 수 없는 액수였다. ⑤ 타동사 흡입하다 ❑ 그는 본드를 마신 것처럼 정신이 혼미해졌다.

snig|ger /snɪgər/ (**sniggers, sniggering, sniggered**) V-I If someone **sniggers**, they laugh quietly in a disrespectful way, for example at something rude or unkind. ❑ *Suddenly, three schoolkids sitting near me started sniggering.* ● N-COUNT **Snigger** is also a noun. ❑ *...trying to suppress a snigger.*

자동사 킬킬대다, 키득거리다 ❑ 갑자기 내 옆에 앉은 어린 학생 세 명이 키득거리기 시작했다. ● 가산명사 킬킬댐, 키득거림 ❑ 키득거리지 않으려고 애쓰면서

snip /snɪp/ (**snips, snipping, snipped**) ① V-T/V-I If you **snip** something, or if you **snip at** or **through** something, you cut it quickly using sharp scissors. ❑ *He has now begun to snip away at the piece of paper.* ② N-SING If you say that something is **a snip**, you mean that it is very good value. [BRIT, INFORMAL] [a N] ❑ *The beautifully made briefcase is a snip at £74.25.*

① 타동사/자동사 싹둑 자르다 ❑ 그가 이제 종이를 싹둑 잘라 내기 시작했다. ② 단수명사 저렴하고 좋은 물건 [영국영어, 비격식체] ❑ 이처럼 훌륭한 서류 가방이 74.25파운드면 거저나 다름없다.

snipe /snaɪp/ (**snipes, sniping, sniped**) ① V-I If someone **snipes at** you, they criticize you. ❑ *The Spanish media were still sniping at the British press yesterday.* ② V-I To **snipe at** someone means to shoot at them from a hidden position. ❑ *Gunmen have repeatedly sniped at U.S. Army positions.*

① 자동사 비난하다 ❑ 어제까지도 스페인 언론이 영국 언론을 공격하고 있었다. ② 자동사 저격하다 ❑ 저격수들이 미국 육군 위치에 여러 차례 총을 쏘았다.

snip|er /snaɪpər/ (**snipers**) N-COUNT A **sniper** is someone who shoots at people from a hidden position. ❑ *...a sniper attack.*

가산명사 저격수 ❑ 저격 공격

snip|pet /snɪpɪt/ (**snippets**) N-COUNT A **snippet of** something is a small piece of it. ❑ *...snippets of popular classical music.*

가산명사 일부분, 조금 ❑ 인기 있는 클래식 음악을 조금씩 딴 것

snob /snɒb/ (**snobs**) N-COUNT If you call someone a **snob**, you disapprove of them because they behave as if they are superior to other people because of their intelligence or taste. [DISAPPROVAL] ❑ *She was an intellectual snob.*

가산명사 속물, 잘난 척 하는 사람 [탐탁잖음] ❑ 그녀는 똑똑한 척하는 속물이었다.

snob|bery /snɒbəri/ N-UNCOUNT **Snobbery** is the attitude of a snob. ❑ *There has often been an element of snobbery in British golf.*

불가산명사 속물근성, 우월의식 ❑ 지금까지 영국 골프계에서는 우월의식이 종종 드러났었다.

snook|er /snʊkər, BRIT snuːkər/ N-UNCOUNT **Snooker** is a game involving balls on a large table. The players use a long stick to hit a white ball, and score points by knocking colored balls into the pockets at the sides of the table. ❑ *...a game of snooker.*

불가산명사 스누커 (당구의 일종) ❑ 스누커 한 판

snoop /snuːp/ (**snoops, snooping, snooped**) ① V-I If someone **snoops** around a place, they secretly look around it in order to find out things. ❑ *Ricardo was the one she'd seen snooping around Kim's hotel room.* ● N-COUNT **Snoop** is also a noun. ❑ *The second house that Grossman had a snoop around contained "strong simple furniture."* ● **snoop|er** (**snoopers**) N-COUNT ❑ *Even if the information is intercepted by a snooper, it is impossible for them to decipher it.* ② V-I If someone **snoops on** a person, they watch them secretly in order to find out things about their life. ❑ *Governments have been known to snoop on and harass innocent citizens in the past.*

① 자동사 기웃거리다, 염탐하다 ❑ 킴의 호텔 방을 기웃거리다 그녀에게 목격된 사람이 바로 리카르도였다. ● 가산명사 기웃거림, 염탐 ❑ 그로스맨이 두 번째로 염탐한 집에는 '튼튼하고 소박한 가구'가 있었다. ● 기웃거리는 사람, 염탐꾼 가산명사 ❑ 염탐꾼이 정보를 가로챘다 하더라도 해독은 불가능하게 되어 있다. ② 자동사 몰래 감시하다 ❑ 과거에 정부들이 무고한 시민을 몰래 감시하고 괴롭힌 것은 이미 알려진 사실이다.

snooze /snuːz/ (**snoozes, snoozing, snoozed**) ① N-COUNT A **snooze** is a short, light sleep, especially during the day. [INFORMAL] ❑ *I lay down on the bed with my shoes off to have a snooze.* ② V-I If you **snooze**, you sleep lightly for a short period of time. [INFORMAL] ❑ *Mark snoozed in front of the television.*

① 가산명사 선잠, 낮잠 [비격식체] ❑ 나는 낮잠을 자려고 신발을 벗고 침대에 누웠다. ② 자동사 졸다 [비격식체] ❑ 마크는 텔레비전 앞에서 졸았다.

snore /snɔːr/ (**snores, snoring, snored**) V-I When someone who is asleep **snores**, they make a loud noise each time they breathe. ❑ *His mouth was open, and he was snoring.* ● N-COUNT **Snore** is also a noun. ❑ *Uncle Arthur, after a loud snore, woke suddenly.*

자동사 코를 골다 ❑ 그는 입을 벌리고 코를 골고 있었다. ● 가산명사 코골기 ❑ 아서 삼촌이 한 번 크게 코를 골더니 갑자기 깨어났다.

snor|kel /snɔːrkᵊl/ (**snorkels, snorkeling, snorkeled**) [BRIT **snorkelling, snorkelled**] ① N-COUNT A **snorkel** is a tube through which a person swimming just under the surface of the sea can breathe. ② V-I When someone **snorkels**, they swim under water using a snorkel. ❑ *Swim off the side of the ship and snorkel in some of the clearest waters imaginable.*

[영국영어 snorkelling, snorkelled] ① 가산명사 스노클 (잠수용 호흡 기구) ② 자동사 스노클을 물고 수영하다 ❑ 배의 측면에서 헤엄쳐나가 가장 깨끗한 물이 있는 곳에서 스노클을 끼고 수영하세요.

snort /snɔːrt/ (**snorts, snorting, snorted**) ① V-I When people or animals **snort**, they breathe air noisily out through their noses. People sometimes snort in order to express disapproval or amusement. ❑ *Harrell snorted with laughter.* ● N-COUNT **Snort** is also a noun. ❑ *...snorts of laughter.* ② V-T To **snort** a drug such as cocaine means to breathe in it quickly through your nose. ❑ *He died of cardiac arrest after snorting cocaine at a party.*

① 자동사 콧김을 내뿜다, 코웃음 치다, 콧방귀 뀌다 ❑ 하렐이 크게 코웃음을 쳤다. ● 가산명사 콧김, 코웃음, 콧방귀 ❑ 코웃음 소리 ② 타동사 코로 흡입하다 ❑ 그는 파티에서 코카인을 코로 흡입한 후 심장 마비로 죽었다.

snow ♦◇◇ /snoʊ/ (**snows, snowing, snowed**) ① N-UNCOUNT **Snow** consists of a lot of soft white bits of frozen water that fall from the sky in cold weather. ❑ *In Mid-Wales six inches of snow blocked roads.* ② V-I When **it snows**, snow falls from the sky. ❑ *It had been snowing all night.* →see **storm, water**

① 불가산명사 눈 ❑ 웨일스 중부지방에 눈이 6인치 쌓여 길이 막혔다. ② 자동사 눈이 오다 ❑ 밤새 눈이 온 터였다.

snow|ball /snoʊbɔːl/ (**snowballs, snowballing, snowballed**) ① N-COUNT A **snowball** is a ball of snow. Children often throw snowballs at each other. ② V-I If something such as a project or campaign **snowballs**, it rapidly increases and grows. ❑ *From those early days the business has snowballed.*

① 가산명사 눈 뭉치, 눈덩이 ② 자동사 눈덩이처럼 불어나다 ❑ 그 초창기 시절부터 사업이 눈덩이처럼 불어났다.

snow|board /snoʊbɔːrd/ (**snowboards**) N-COUNT A **snowboard** is a narrow board that you stand on in order to slide quickly down snowy slopes as a sport or for fun.

가산명사 스노보드

snow|board|ing /snoʊbɔrdɪŋ/ N-UNCOUNT **Snowboarding** is the sport or activity of traveling down snowy slopes using a snowboard. ❑ *New snowboarding facilities should attract more people.*

불가산명사 스노보드 타기 ❑ 새로 생긴 스노보드 시설에 사람들이 더 몰려와 한다.

snow|plow /snoʊplaʊ/ (**snowplows**) [BRIT **snowplough**] N-COUNT A **snowplow** is a vehicle which is used to push snow off roads or railroad tracks.

[영국영어 snowplough] 가산명사 제설차

snowy /snoʊi/ (**snowier**, **snowiest**) ADJ A **snowy** place is covered in snow. A **snowy** day is a day when a lot of snow has fallen. ❑ *...the snowy peaks of the Bighorn Mountains.*

형용사 눈 덮인, 눈이 내리는 ❑ 빅혼산맥의 눈 덮인 정상

snub /snʌb/ (**snubs, snubbing, snubbed**) ◼ V-T If you **snub** someone, you deliberately insult them by ignoring them or by behaving or speaking rudely toward them. ❑ *He snubbed her in public and made her feel an idiot.* ◻ N-COUNT If you **snub** someone, your behavior or your remarks can be referred to as a **snub**. ❑ *Ryan took it as a snub.*

◼ 타동사 무시하다, 망신을 주다 ❑ 그는 사람들이 보는 앞에서 그녀에게 망신을 주어 그녀가 바보 같은 기분이 들게 했다. ◻ 가산명사 무시, 모욕 ❑ 라이언은 그 일을 모욕적으로 받아들였다.

snuck /snʌk/ **Snuck** is a past tense and past participle of **sneak** in American English.

sneak의 과거, 과거 분사

snuff /snʌf/ (**snuffs, snuffing, snuffed**) ◼ N-UNCOUNT **Snuff** is powdered tobacco which people take by breathing it in quickly through their nose. ❑ *...the old man's habit of taking snuff.* ◻ V-T If someone **snuffs it**, they die. [BRIT, INFORMAL] ❑ *Perhaps he thought he was about to snuff it.*

◼ 불가산명사 코담배 ❑ 그 노인의 코담배를 피는 버릇 ◻ 타동사 죽다 [영국영어, 비격식체] ❑ 어쩌면 그가 이제 갈 때가 됐다고 생각했을지도 모른다.

▶**snuff out** PHRASAL VERB To **snuff out** something such as a disagreement means to stop it, usually in a forceful or sudden way. ❑ *Every time a new flicker of resistance appeared, the government snuffed it out.*

구동사 막다, 저지하다 ❑ 저항의 기미가 새로 보일 때마다 정부가 탄압했다.

snug /snʌg/ (**snugger, snuggest**) ◼ ADJ If you feel **snug** or are in a **snug** place, you are very warm and comfortable, especially because you are protected from cold weather. ❑ *They lay snug and warm amid the blankets and watched their sister hard at work.* ◻ ADJ Something such as a piece of clothing that is **snug** fits very closely or tightly. ❑ *...a snug black T-shirt and skin-tight black jeans.*

◼ 형용사 아늑한, 안락한 ❑ 그들은 담요 속에 편안하고 따뜻하게 누워 누나가 열심히 일하는 모습을 지켜봤다. ◻ 형용사 꼭 맞는 ❑ 꼭 맞는 까만 티셔츠와 몸에 딱 붙는 까만 면바지

snug|gle /snʌgəl/ (**snuggles, snuggling, snuggled**) V-I If you **snuggle** somewhere, you settle yourself into a warm, comfortable position, especially by moving closer to another person. ❑ *Jane snuggled up against his shoulder.*

자동사 바싹 파고들다, 바싹 달라붙다 ❑ 제인이 그의 어깨에 몸을 바싹 붙이며 파고들었다.

so ♦♦♦ /soʊ/ ◼ ADV You use **so** to refer back to something that has just been mentioned. [ADV after v] ❑ *"Do you think that made much of a difference to the family?" — "I think so."* ❑ *If you can't play straight, then say so.* ◻ ADV You use **so** when you are saying that something which has just been said about one person or thing is also true of another one. [ADV cl] ❑ *I enjoy Ann's company and so does Martin.* ❑ *They had a wonderful time and so did I.* ◼ CONJ You use the structures **as...so** and **just as...so** when you want to indicate that two events or situations are similar in some way. ❑ *As computer systems become even more sophisticated, so too do the methods of those who exploit the technology.* ❑ *Just as John has changed, so has his wife.* ◼ ADV If you say that a state of affairs **is so**, you mean that it is the way it has been described. [v-link ADV] ❑ *In those days English dances as well as songs were taught at school, but that seems no longer to be so.* ❑ *It is strange to think that she held strong views on many things, but it must have been so.* ◼ ADV You can use **so** with actions and gestures to show a person how to do something, or to indicate the size, height, or length of something. [ADV after v] ❑ *Clasp the chain like so.* ◼ CONJ You use **so** and **so that** to introduce the result of the situation you have just mentioned. ❑ *I am not an emotional type and so cannot bring myself to tell him I love him.* ❑ *People are living longer than ever before, so even people who are 65 or 70 have a surprising amount of time left.* ◼ CONJ You use **so**, **so that**, and **so as** to introduce the reason for doing the thing that you have just mentioned. ❑ *Come to my suite so I can tell you all about this wonderful play I saw in Boston.* ❑ *He took her arm and hurried her upstairs so that they wouldn't be overheard.* ◼ ADV You can use **so** in conversations to introduce a new topic, or to introduce a question or comment about something that has been said. [ADV cl] ❑ *So how was your day?* ❑ *So you're a runner, huh?* ❑ *So as for your question, Miles, the answer still has to be no.* ◼ ADV You can use **so** in conversations to show that you are accepting what someone has just said. [ADV cl] ❑ *"It makes me feel, well, important..." — "And so you are."* ❑ *"You can't possibly use this word." — "So I won't."* ◼ CONVENTION You say **"So?"** and **"So what?"** to indicate that you think that something that someone has said is unimportant. [INFORMAL] ❑ *"My name's Bruno." — "So?"* ◼ ADV You can use **so** in front of adjectives and adverbs to emphasize the quality that they are describing. [EMPHASIS] [ADV adj/adv] ❑ *He was surprised they had married – they had seemed so different.* ◼ ADV You can use **so...that** and **so...as** to emphasize the degree of something by mentioning the result or consequence of it. [EMPHASIS] ❑ *The tears were streaming so fast she could not see.* ❑ *He's not so daft as to listen to rumors.* ◼ →see also **insofar as**. ◼ PHRASE You use **and so on** or **and so forth** at the end of a list to indicate that there are other items that you could also mention. ❑ *...the Government's policies on such important issues as health, education, tax, and so on.* ◼ PHRASE You use **so much** and **so many** when you are saying that there is a definite limit to something but you are not saying what this limit is. ❑ *There is only so much time in the day for answering letters.* ❑ *There is only so much fuel in the tank and if you burn it up too quickly you are in trouble.* ◼ PHRASE You use the structures **not...so much** and **not so much...as** to say that something is one kind of thing rather than another kind. ❑ *I did not really object to Will's behavior so much as his personality.* ◼ PHRASE You use **so** or **so** when you are giving an approximate amount. [VAGUENESS] ❑ *Though rates are heading down, they still offer real returns of 8% or so.* ◼ **so much the better** →see **better**. **so far so good** →see **far**. **so long** →see **long**. **so much so** →see **much**. **every so often** →see **often**. **so there** →see **there**

◼ 부사 그렇게 ❑ "네 생각에 그 일이 가족에게 큰 영향을 미친 것 같아?" "그런 것 같아." ❑ 바로 이어서 경기를 못할 것 같으면 그렇게 이야기하세요. ◻ 부사 역시, 또한 ❑ 나도 그렇고 마틴도 그렇고 앤이랑 함께 있으면 즐겁다. ❑ 그들은 아주 즐거운 시간을 보냈다. 나도 마찬가지였다. ◼ 접속사 꼭 ~와 마찬가지로 또 ...인, 꼭 ~인 것처럼 ...인 ❑ 컴퓨터 시스템이 훨씬 더 정교해지면서 또 사람들이 컴퓨터 기술을 사용하는 방법 역시 복잡해졌다. ❑ 존이 변한 것처럼 그의 아내도 변했다. ◼ 부사 그러하다 ❑ 그 시절에는 학교에서 잉글랜드 노래나 춤을 가르쳤지만 이제 더 이상 그렇지 않은 것 같다. ❑ 그가 많은 문제에 확고한 견해를 가졌다고 생각하니 이상하지만, 그래도 그랬음에 틀림없다. ◼ 부사 이렇게, 이 정도 ❑ 체인을 그렇게 고정시키세요. ◼ 접속사 따라서, 그러므로 ❑ 나는 감정에 솔직한 사람이 아니기 때문에 그에게 사랑 고백을 용기가 나질 않는다. ❑ 평균 수명이 전에 없이 길어지면서 예순다섯 살이나 일흔 살 노인들까지도 남은 여생이 놀라울 정도로 길다. ◼ 접속사 ~하도록 ❑ 보스턴에서 본 훌륭한 연극 이야기를 해 줄 테니 내 스위트룸으로 오세요. ❑ 다른 사람들이 듣지 못하게 그가 그녀의 팔을 잡고 위층으로 급히 데려갔다. ◼ 부사 새로운 화제로 넘어가거나 질문이나 의견을 말할 때 쓰는 말 ❑ 그래, 오늘 하루는 어땠어? ❑ 그럼 당신은 달리기 선수군요? ❑ 자, 마일스, 네 질문에 대해선 여전히 아니라는 답밖에 없다. ◼ 부사 상냥도, 실제로 ❑ "그냥 뼈만 내 때린 끼 내가 중요한 사람처럼 느껴져." "실제로 그래." ❑ "이 단어는 절대 사용할 수 없어." "정말 사용 안 할 거야." ◼ 관용 표현 그래서 어떻다는 거야? [비격식체] ❑ "저는 브루노라고 합니다." "그래서?" ◼ 부사 매우, 너무나 [강조] ❑ 그는 그들이 결혼했다는 사실에 놀랐다. 그들이 너무나 다른 것 같았었기 때문이다. ◼ 부사 너무나 ~해서 ...하다, ~할 정도로 ...하다 [강조] ❑ 그녀는 눈물이 너무나 빨리 흘러내려 앞이 보이지 않았다. ❑ 그가 소문에 귀 기울일 만큼 바보는 아니다. ◼ 구동등 ❑ 보건, 교육, 세금 등등 중요한 문제에 대한 정부 정책 ◼ 구 그 정도의, 그만큼의 ❑ 하루 동안 답장하는 데 쓸 수 있는 시간도 그만큼 밖에 없다. ❑ 탱크에 연료가 그만큼 밖에 없어서 너무 빨리 다 써버리면 곤란하다. ◼ 구 ~라기보다 ...이나 ❑ 나는 윌의 행동보다는 성격이 마음에 안 들었다. ◼ 구 ~ 정도, ~쯤 [짐작틀] ❑ 금리 하락세에도 불구하고 그들은 여전히 8퍼센트 정도의 실질적인 수익률을 제시하고 있다.

So, very, and too can all be used to intensify the meaning of an adjective, an adverb, or a word like **much** or **many**. However, they are not used in the same way. **Very** is the simplest intensifier. It has no other meaning beyond that. **So** can suggest an emotional reaction on the part of the speaker, such as

so, very, too는 모두 형용사, 부사, 그리고 much나 many와 같은 단어의 의미를 강화하는 데 쓸 수 있다. 그러나, 이들이 모두 똑같이 쓰이지는 않는다. very는 가장 간단한 강화사이며 그 이상의

pleasure, surprise, or disappointment. ❑ *John makes me so angry!... ❑ Oh thank you so much!* **So** can also refer forward to a result clause introduced by *that*. ❑ *The procession was forced to move so slowly that he arrived three hours late.* **Too** suggests an excessive or undesirable amount, often so much that a particular result does not or cannot happen. ❑ *She does wear too much make-up at times... He was too late to save her.*

의미가 없다. so는 화자의 입장에서 기쁨, 놀람, 실망과 같은 감정적 반응을 암시할 수 있다. ❑ 존이 나를 너무도 화나게 만든다!... ❑ 아, 너무나 감사합니다! so는 that이 이끄는 결과절을 선행하여 지칭할 수도 있다. ❑ 그 행렬은 아주 천천히 움직일 수 밖에 없어서 그는 세시간이나 늦게 도착했다. too는 과도하거나 바람직하지 않은 양을 암시하는데, 종종 너무 지나쳐서 특정한 결과가 일어나지 않거나 일어나지 못할 수도 있다. ❑ 그녀는 가끔 너무 지나치게 화장을 한다... 그는 그녀를 구하기에는 너무 늦었다.

soak /soʊk/ (**soaks, soaking, soaked**) **1** V-T/V-I If you **soak** something or leave it **to soak**, you put it into a liquid and leave it there. ❑ *Soak the beans for 2 hours.* **2** V-T If a liquid **soaks** something or if you **soak** something **with** a liquid, the liquid makes the thing very wet. ❑ *The water had soaked his jacket and shirt.* **3** V-I If a liquid **soaks through** something, it passes through it. ❑ *There was so much blood it had soaked through my boxer shorts.* **4** V-I If someone **soaks**, they spend a long time in a hot bath, because they enjoy it. ❑ *What I need is to soak in a hot tub.* ● N-COUNT **Soak** is also a noun. ❑ *I was having a long soak in the bath.* **5** →see also **soaked, soaking**

1 타동사/자동사 담그다 ❑ 콩을 2시간 동안 담가 놓으세요. **2** 타동사 흠뻑 적시다 ❑ 물에 그의 재킷과 셔츠가 다 젖어 있었다. **3** 자동사 스며들다 ❑ 피가 너무 많이 나서 내 사각팬티까지 스며들었다. **4** 자동사 몸을 푹 담그다, 목욕을 즐기다 ❑ 내가 필요한 것은 뜨거운 욕조에 몸을 푹 담그는 것이다. ● 가산명사 몸을 푹 담그기, 목욕 ❑ 나는 욕조에서 한참 동안 목욕을 즐기고 있었다.

▶**soak up** **1** PHRASAL VERB If a soft or dry material **soaks up** a liquid, the liquid goes into the substance. ❑ *The cells will promptly start to soak up moisture.* **2** PHRASAL VERB If you **soak up** the atmosphere in a place that you are visiting, you observe or get involved in the way of life there, because you enjoy it or are interested in it. [INFORMAL] ❑ *Keaton comes here once or twice a year to soak up the atmosphere.* **3** PHRASAL VERB If something **soaks up** something such as money or other resources, it uses a great deal of money or other resources. ❑ *Defense soaks up forty per cent of the budget.*

1 구동사 흡수하다, 빨아들이다 ❑ 세포가 즉각 수분을 흡수하기 시작할 것이다. **2** 구동사 분위기에 흠뻑 젖다, 만끽하다 [비격식체] ❑ 키턴은 일년에 한두 번 찾아와 이곳 분위기에 흠뻑 젖는다. **3** 구동사 상당 부분을 차지하다 ❑ 국방비가 예산의 40퍼센트나 차지한다.

soaked /soʊkt/ ADJ If someone or something gets **soaked** or **soaked through**, water or some other liquid makes them extremely wet. ❑ *I have to check my tent – it got soaked last night in the storm.* ❑ *We got soaked to the skin.*

형용사 흠뻑 젖은 ❑ 텐트 좀 보고 와야겠어. 어젯밤 폭풍우에 흠뻑 젖었거든. ❑ 우리는 온몸이 흠뻑 젖었다.

soak|ing /soʊkɪŋ/ ADJ If something is **soaking** or **soaking wet**, it is very wet. ❑ *My face and raincoat were soaking wet.*

형용사 흠뻑 젖은 ❑ 내 얼굴과 우의가 흠뻑 젖어 있었다.

so-and-so PRON-SING You use **so-and-so** instead of a word, expression, or name when you are talking generally rather than giving a specific example of a particular thing. [INFORMAL] ❑ *It would be a case of "just do so-and-so and here's your cash."*

단수대명사 이러이러한 것; 이러이러한 사람 [비격식체] ❑ "그냥 이러이러한 일을 하면 돈을 주겠다."라는 경우일 것이다.

soap /soʊp/ (**soaps**) **1** N-MASS **Soap** is a substance that you use with water for washing yourself or sometimes for washing clothes. ❑ *...a bar of lavender soap.* ❑ *...a large packet of soap powder.* **2** N-COUNT A **soap** is the same as a **soap opera**. [INFORMAL]
→see Word Web: soap

1 물질명사 비누 ❑ 라벤더 비누 한 개 ❑ 가루비누 큰 통으로 하나 **2** 가산명사 드라마, 연속극 [비격식체]

soap op|era (**soap operas**) N-COUNT A **soap opera** is a popular television drama series about the daily lives and problems of a group of people who live in a particular place.

가산명사 드라마, 연속극

soar /sɔr/ (**soars, soaring, soared**) **1** V-I If the amount, value, level, or volume of something **soars**, it quickly increases by a great deal. [JOURNALISM] ❑ *Insurance claims are expected to soar.* ❑ *Shares soared on the stock exchange.* **2** V-I If something such as a bird **soars** into the air, it goes quickly up into the air. [LITERARY] ❑ *If you're lucky, a splendid golden eagle may soar into view.*

1 자동사 치솟다, 급증하다 [언론] ❑ 보험금 청구 건수가 급증할 것으로 예상된다. ❑ 주식 거래소에서 주가가 폭등했다. **2** 자동사 날아오르다, 솟구치다 [문예체] ❑ 운이 좋으면 눈부신 황금 독수리가 날아오르는 모습이 보일지도 모른다.

sob /sɒb/ (**sobs, sobbing, sobbed**) **1** V-I When someone **sobs**, they cry in a noisy way, breathing in short breaths. ❑ *She began to sob again, burying her face in the pillow.* ● **sob|bing** N-UNCOUNT ❑ *The room was silent except for her sobbing.* **2** N-COUNT A **sob** is one of the noises that you make when you are crying. ❑ *Her sobs grew louder.*

1 자동사 흐느끼다 ❑ 그녀가 베개에 얼굴을 묻고 다시 흐느끼기 시작했다. ● 흐느낌 불가산명사 ❑ 그녀의 흐느낌 빼고는 방이 조용했다. **2** 가산명사 흐느낌 ❑ 그녀가 흐느끼는 소리가 점점 더 커졌다.

so|ber /soʊbər/ **1** ADJ When you are **sober**, you are not drunk. ❑ *He'd been drunk when I arrived. Now he was sober.* **2** ADJ A **sober** person is serious and thoughtful. ❑ *We are now far more sober and realistic.* ❑ *It was a room filled with sad, sober faces.* ● **so|ber|ly** ADV ❑ *"There's a new development," he said soberly.* **3** ADJ **Sober** colors and clothes are plain and rather dull. ❑ *He dresses in sober grey suits.* ● **so|ber|ly** ADV [ADV with v] ❑ *She saw Ellis, soberly dressed in a well-cut dark suit.* **4** →see also **sobering**

1 형용사 술 취하지 않은, 정신이 말짱한 ❑ 그는 내가 도착할 때까지만 해도 술에 취해 있었지만 이제 말짱했다. **2** 형용사 엄숙한, 냉정한, 진지한 ❑ 이제 우리는 훨씬 더 냉정하고 현실적이다. ❑ 슬프고 엄숙한 표정의 얼굴로 가득 찬 방이었다. ● 엄숙하게, 진지하게 부사 ❑ "상황 변화가 있습니다."라고 그가 엄숙하게 말했다. **3** 형용사 수수한, 밋밋한 ❑ 그는 수수한 회색 정장을 입고 있다. ● 수수하게, 밋밋하게 부사 ❑ 그녀는 깔끔한 검은 정장을 수수하게 차려 입은 엘리스를 보았다.

▶**sober up** PHRASAL VERB If someone **sobers up**, or if something **sobers** them **up**, they become sober after being drunk. ❑ *He was left to sober up in a police cell.*

구동사 술이 깨다; 술이 깨게 하다 ❑ 술이 깰 때까지 그들 경찰서 유치장에 내버려 뒀다.

so|ber|ing /soʊbərɪŋ/ ADJ You say that something is a **sobering** thought or has a **sobering** effect when a situation seems serious and makes you become serious and thoughtful. ❑ *It is a sobering thought that in the 17th century she could have been burnt as a witch.*

형용사 정신이 번쩍 드는 ❑ 17세기였다면 그녀가 마녀로 몰려 화형 당했을 수도 있다고 생각하니 정신이 번쩍 든다.

Word Web   soap

Soap is an important part of everyday life. We **wash** our hands before we eat. We lather up with a **bar** of soap in the **shower** or **tub**. We use liquid **detergent** to **clean** our dishes. We use **laundry** detergent to get our clothes clean. But why do we use soap? How does it work? It works almost like a magnet. Only instead of attracting and repelling metal, soap attracts dirt and grease. It makes a **bubble** around the dirt, and water washes it all away.

Picture Dictionary soccer

player
uniform
shin guard
soccer ball
center spot
center circle
halfway line
goal line
goal
side line

---

so-called ◆◇◇ also **so called** **1** ADJ You use **so-called** to indicate that you think a word or expression used to describe someone or something is in fact wrong. [ADJ n] ❏ *These are the facts that explode their so-called economic miracle.* **2** ADJ You use **so-called** to indicate that something is generally referred to by the name that you are about to use. [ADJ n] ❏ *...a summit of the world's seven leading market economies, the so-called G-7.*

soc|cer ◆◇◇ /sɒkər/ N-UNCOUNT **Soccer** is a game played by two teams of eleven players using a round ball. Players kick the ball to each other and try to score goals by kicking the ball into a large net. Outside the United States, this game is also referred to as **football.** ❏ *...a soccer match.*
→see Picture Dictionary: **soccer**

soc|cer play|er /sɒkər pleɪər/ (**soccer players**) N-COUNT A **soccer player** is a person who plays football, especially as a profession. [AM; BRIT **footballer**]

so|cia|ble /soʊʃəbəl/ ADJ **Sociable** people are friendly and enjoy talking to other people. ❏ *She was, and remained, extremely sociable, enjoying dancing, golf, tennis, skating and bicycling.*

Word Link soci ≈ companion : as*soci*ate, *soci*al, *soci*ology

so|cial ◆◆◆ /soʊʃəl/ **1** ADJ **Social** means relating to society or to the way society is organized. [ADJ n] ❏ *...the worst effects of unemployment, low pay and other social problems.* ❏ *...long-term social change.* ❏ *...changing social attitudes.* ● **so|cial|ly** ADV [ADV adj/-ed] ❏ *Let's face it – drinking is a socially acceptable habit.* **2** ADJ **Social** means relating to the status or rank that someone has in society. [ADJ n] ❏ *Higher education is unequally distributed across social classes.* ● **so|cial|ly** ADV ❏ *For socially ambitious couples this is a problem.* **3** ADJ **Social** means relating to leisure activities that involve meeting other people. [ADJ n] ❏ *We ought to organize more social events.* ● **so|cial|ly** ADV ❏ *We have known each other socially for a long time.* →see **myth**

so|cial|ism /soʊʃəlɪzəm/ N-UNCOUNT **Socialism** is a set of left-wing political principles whose general aim is to create a system in which everyone has an equal opportunity to benefit from a country's wealth. Under socialism, the country's main industries are usually owned by the state.

so|cial|ist ◆◇◇ /soʊʃəlɪst/ (**socialists**) **1** ADJ **Socialist** means based on socialism or relating to socialism. ❏ *...members of the ruling Socialist Party.* **2** N-COUNT A **socialist** is a person who believes in socialism or who is a member of a socialist party. ❏ *Esperanto has always been popular among socialists.*

so|cial|ize /soʊʃəlaɪz/ (**socializes, socializing, socialized**) [BRIT also **socialise**] V-I If you **socialize**, you meet other people socially, for example at parties. ❏ *...an open meeting, where members socialized and welcomed any new members.*

so|cial sci|ence (**social sciences**) **1** N-UNCOUNT **Social science** is the scientific study of society. ❏ *The research methods of social science generate two kinds of data.* **2** N-COUNT The **social sciences** are the various types of social science, for example sociology and politics. ❏ *...a degree in a social science.*

so|cial se|cu|rity N-UNCOUNT **Social security** is a system under which a government pays money regularly to certain groups of people, for example the sick, the unemployed, or older people. ❏ *...women who did not have jobs and were on social security.*

so|cial ser|vices N-PLURAL **Social services** in a district are the services provided by the local authority or government to help people who have serious family problems or financial problems. ❏ *Schools and social services are also struggling to absorb the influx.*

so|cial work N-UNCOUNT **Social work** is work which involves giving help and advice to people with serious family problems or financial problems.

so|cial work|er (**social workers**) N-COUNT A **social worker** is a person whose job is to do social work.

so|ci|ety ◆◆◆ /səsaɪɪti/ (**societies**) **1** N-UNCOUNT **Society** is people in general, thought of as a large organized group. ❏ *This reflects attitudes and values prevailing in society.* **2** N-VAR A **society** is the people who live in a country or region, their organizations, and their way of life. ❏ *We live in a capitalist society.* **3** N-COUNT A **society** is an organization for people who have the same interest or aim. ❏ *...the North of England Horticultural Society.* **4** N-UNCOUNT **Society** is the rich, fashionable people in a particular place who meet on social occasions. ❏ *The couple quickly became a fixture of society pages.* →see **culture**

1 형용사 이른바, 소위 ●이와 같은 사실들은 소위 그들이 말하는 경제 기적이라는 것의 허위성을 증명해 준다. **2** 형용사 이른바, 소위 ❏세계 7대 시장 경제대국의 정상 회담을 일컫는 이른바 지세븐

불가산명사 축구 ❏축구 경기

가산명사 축구 선수 [미국영어; 영국영어 footballer]

형용사 사교적인, 붙임성 있는 ❏그녀는 춤, 골프, 테니스, 스케이트, 자전거 등을 즐기는 사교적인 사람이었고, 또 항상 그래 왔다.

1 형용사 사회의, 사회적인 ❏실업과 저임금 및 다른 사회 문제의 가장 큰 악영향 ❏장기적인 사회 변화 ❏사회인식의 변화 ●사회적으로 부사 ❏인정할 것은 인정합시다. 음주는 사회적으로 용납되는 습관입니다. **2** 형용사 사회의 ❏고등 교육이 사회 계층에 따라 불평등하게 제공된다. ●사회적으로 부사 ❏이는 사회적으로 성공하고자 하는 부부에게 문제가 된다. **3** 형용사 사회생활의, 친목의 ❏우리는 함께 모일 수 있는 자리를 더 만들어야 한다. ●사교적으로, 친하게 부사 ❏우리는 오랫동안 개인적으로 서로 알고 지냈다.

불가산명사 사회주의

1 형용사 사회주의 성향의 ❏집권당인 사회당 당원들 **2** 가산명사 사회주의자 ❏에스페란토 어는 사회주의자들 사이에서 항상 인기가 많았다.

[영국영어 socialise] 자동사 사람들과 사귀다, 사교생활을 하다 ❏회원들 간에 친목을 도모하고 새로운 회원을 환영하던 공개 모임

1 불가산명사 사회과학 ❏사회과학 연구 방법에 따라 두 가지 종류의 데이터가 나온다. **2** 가산명사 사회과학의 여러 분야 ❏사회과학 학위

불가산명사 사회 보장 제도 ❏직업 없이 사회 보장 제도 수혜자였던 여성들

복수명사 사회 복지 ❏학교와 사회복지 부문도 유입된 인구를 감당하는 데 애를 먹고 있다.

불가산명사 사회사업

가산명사 사회 복지사, 사회사업가

1 불가산명사 사회 ❏이는 사회 보편적인 태도와 가치관을 반영한다. **2** 가산명사 또는 불가산명사 사회 ❏우리는 자본주의 사회에 산다. **3** 가산명사 단체, 모임, 학회 ❏잉글랜드 북부 원예학회 **4** 불가산명사 상류 사회, 사교계 ❏그 커플은 곧 상류 사회 잡지에 고정적으로 등장하게 되었다.

a b c d e f g h i j k l m n o p q r s t u v w x y z

so|ci|o|e|co|nom|ic /sousiouɛkənɒmɪk, -ikə-/ also **socio-economic** ADJ **Socioeconomic** circumstances or developments involve a combination of social and economic factors. [ADJ n] ❑ *The age, education, and socioeconomic status of these young mothers led to less satisfactory child care.*

형용사 사회경제적인 ❑ 이와 같이 나이 어린 엄마들은 나이, 교육 수준, 사회경제적 지위상의 자녀 양육을 제대로 할 수 없었다.

Word Link	*soci ≈ companion : associate, social, sociology*

so|ci|ol|o|gy /sousiɒlədʒi/ N-UNCOUNT **Sociology** is the study of society or of the way society is organized. ● **so|ci|o|logi|cal** /sousiəlɒdʒɪkəl/ ADJ ❑ *Psychological and sociological studies were emphasizing the importance of the family.* ● **so|ci|olo|gist** (**sociologists**) N-COUNT ❑ *By the 1950s some sociologists were confident that they had identified the key characteristics of capitalist society.*

불가산명사 사회학 ● 사회학의, 사회학적인 형용사 ❑ 심리학 및 사회학 연구들이 가족의 중요성을 강조하고 있었다. ● 사회학자 가산명사 ❑ 1950년대에 이르러 몇몇 사회학자들은 자본주의 사회의 주요 특징을 밝혀냈다고 자신했다.

so|ci|o|po|liti|cal /sousioupəlɪtɪkəl/ also **socio-political** ADJ **Sociopolitical** systems and problems involve a combination of social and political factors. [ADJ n] ❑ *...contemporary sociopolitical issues such as ecology, human rights, and nuclear arms.*

형용사 사회정치적인 ❑ 생태, 인권, 핵무기와 같은 현대의 사회정치적 사안들

sock /sɒk/ (**socks**) N-COUNT **Socks** are pieces of clothing which cover your foot and ankle and are worn inside shoes. ❑ *...a pair of knee-length socks.* →see **clothing**

가산명사 양말 ❑ 무릎까지 오는 양말 한 켤레

sock|et /sɒkɪt/ (**sockets**) ◼ N-COUNT A **socket** is a device on a piece of electrical equipment into which you can put a bulb or plug. ❑ *On the stairway to the basement, he took the light bulb out of the socket.* ◼ N-COUNT A **socket** is a device or point in a wall where you can connect electrical equipment to the power supply. [mainly BRIT; AM usually **outlet**] ❑ *Behind her the television stood mute, its plug lying disconnected from the socket.* ◼ N-COUNT You can refer to any hollow part or opening in a structure which another part fits into as a **socket**. ❑ *Rotate the shoulders in their sockets five times.*

◼ 가산명사 소켓 ❑ 지하실로 내려가는 계단에서 그가 소켓에서 전구를 뺐다. ◼ 가산명사 콘센트 [주로 영국영어; 미국영어 대개 outlet] ❑ 그녀 뒤에는 플러그가 콘센트에서 빠져 작동되지 않 나는 텔레비전이 있었다. ◼ 가산명사 푹 들어간 곳, 구멍 ❑ 겨드랑이를 중심으로 어깨를 다섯 번 돌리세요.

sod /sɒd/ (**sods**) ◼ N-COUNT If someone calls another person or something such as a job a **sod**, they are expressing anger or annoyance toward that person or thing. [BRIT, INFORMAL, VULGAR, DISAPPROVAL] ❑ *When I saw him sunbathing, I thought, "You lucky sod."* ◼ PHRASE **Sod all** means "nothing at all." [BRIT, INFORMAL, VULGAR, EMPHASIS] ❑ *But you know sod all about theater.* ◼ PHRASE **Sod's Law** or **sod's law** is the idea that if something can go wrong, it will go wrong. [BRIT, INFORMAL] ❑ *It was sod's law, she supposed, that the day after Anne moved into her new flat in Royal Circus she and Jon had their first serious row.*

◼ 가산명사 망할 놈, 망할 것 [영국영어, 비격식체, 비속어, 탐탁찮음] ❑ 그가 일광욕하는 모습을 보면서 나는 "망할 놈! 복은 많이 가졌군."라고 생각했다. ◼ 구 쥐뿔도 [영국영어, 비격식체, 비속어, 강조] ❑ 하지만 너 연극에 대해서 쥐뿔도 모르잖아. ◼ 구 머피의 법칙 ❑ 앤은 로열 서커스의 새 아파트에 이사 온 다음날부터 존과 처음으로 심하게 다툰 것이 머피의 법칙 같다고 생각했다.

▶**sod off** PHRASAL VERB If someone tells someone else to **sod off**, they are telling them in a very rude way to go away or leave them alone. [BRIT, INFORMAL, VULGAR] [only imper] ❑ *She'd told a woman at the golf club to sod off and had been rude to the chief constable's wife.*

구동사 꺼져 [영국영어, 비격식체, 비속어] ❑ 그녀는 골프장에서 어떤 여자에게 꺼지라고 말한 적도 있고 경찰서장 부인에게 무례하게 군 적도 있었다.

soda /soudə/ (**sodas**) ◼ N-MASS **Soda** is a sweet carbonated drink. [AM] ❑ *...a glass of diet soda.* ● N-COUNT A **soda** is a bottle of soda. ❑ *They had liquor for the adults and sodas for the children.*

◼ 물질명사 탄산음료 [미국영어] ❑ 다이어트 탄산음료 한 잔 ● 가산명사 탄산음료 한 병 ❑ 그들은 어른들을 위한 술과 아이들을 위한 탄산음료를 준비했다.

Carbonated drinks containing no alcohol are called **soda** or **soda pop**. They are usually very sweet. Another name is **soft drinks**, and this is the term usually used in the UK.

알코올이 들어있지 않은 탄산 음료를 soda(소다) 또는 soda pop(소다 팝)이라고 하는데 이 음료는 대개 아주 달다. 다른 이름으로는 soft drinks라고도 하는데 이는 주로 영국에서 쓰는 말이다.

◼ N-UNCOUNT **Soda** is the same as **soda water**.

◼ 불가산명사 탄산수, 소다수

soda pop (**soda pops**) N-UNCOUNT **Soda pop** is a sweet carbonated drink. [AM] ❑ *Beer and soda pop are served before the bus departs.* ● N-COUNT A **soda pop** is a bottle or a glass of soda pop. ❑ *He bought me a soda pop.*

◼ 불가산명사 탄산음료 [미국영어] ❑ 버스가 출발하기 전 맥주와 탄산음료가 제공된다. ● 가산명사 탄산음료 한 병; 탄산음료 한 잔 ❑ 그가 나에게 탄산음료를 한 잔 가져다 주었다.

soda wa|ter also **soda-water** N-UNCOUNT **Soda water** is carbonated water used for mixing with alcoholic drinks and fruit juice.

불가산명사 탄산수, 소다수

sod|den /sɒdən/ ADJ Something that is **sodden** is extremely wet. ❑ *We stripped off our sodden clothes.*

형용사 흠뻑 젖은 ❑ 우리는 흠뻑 젖은 옷을 벗었다.

so|dium /soudiəm/ N-UNCOUNT **Sodium** is a silvery-white chemical element which combines with other chemicals. Salt is a sodium compound. ❑ *The fish or seafood is heavily salted with pure sodium chloride.*

불가산명사 나트륨 ❑ 생선이나 해산물은 정제염을 잔뜩 뿌려 절여 놨다.

sofa /soufə/ (**sofas**) N-COUNT A **sofa** is a long, comfortable seat with a back and usually with arms, which two or three people can sit on.

가산명사 소파

soft ♦♦◊ /sɒft, BRIT sɒft/ (**softer, softest**) ◼ ADJ Something that is **soft** is pleasant to touch, and not rough or hard. ❑ *Regular use of a body lotion will keep the skin soft and supple.* ❑ *When it's dry, brush the hair using a soft, nylon baby brush.* ● **soft|ness** N-UNCOUNT ❑ *The sea air robbed her hair of its softness.* ◼ ADJ Something that is **soft** changes shape or bends easily when you press it. ❑ *She lay down on the soft, comfortable bed.* ❑ *Add enough milk to form a soft dough.* ◼ ADJ Something that has a **soft** appearance has smooth curves rather than sharp or distinct edges. ❑ *This is a smart, yet soft and feminine look.* ● **soft|ly** ADV [ADV with v] ❑ *She wore a softly tailored suit.* ◼ ADJ Something that is **soft** is very gentle and has no force. For example, a **soft** sound or voice is quiet and not harsh. A **soft** light or color is pleasant to look at because it is not bright. ❑ *There was a soft tapping on my door.* ● **soft|ly** ADV [ADV with v] ❑ *She crossed the softly lit room.* ◼ ADJ If you are **soft** on someone, you do not treat them as strictly or severely as you should do. [DISAPPROVAL] ❑ *The president says the measure is soft and weak on criminals.* ◼ ADJ If you say that someone has a **soft heart**, you mean that they are sensitive and sympathetic toward other people. [APPROVAL] ❑ *Her rather tough and worldly exterior hides a very soft and sensitive heart.* ◼ ADJ You use **soft** to describe a way of life that is easy and involves very little work. ❑ *The regime at Latchmere could be seen as a soft option.* ◼ ADJ **Soft** drugs are drugs, such as cannabis, which are illegal but which many people do not consider to be strong or harmful. [ADJ n] ❑ *Her drinking was moderate, there was no dependency on drugs, hard or soft.* ◼ ADJ **Soft** water does not contain much of the mineral

◼ 형용사 부드러운, 매끄러운 ❑ 바디 로션을 규칙적으로 사용하면 부드럽고 유연한 피부를 유지할 수 있을 것이다. ❑ 머리가 건조할 때에는 부드러운 나일론 소재의 유아용 빗을 사용하세요. ● 부드러움, 매끄러움 불가산명사 ❑ 바다 공기 때문에 그녀의 비단실 같던 머리도 예전 같지 않았다. ◼ 형용사 유연한, 말랑말랑한 ❑ 그녀는 푹신푹신하고 편안한 침대 위에 누웠다. ❑ 우유를 충분히 넣어서 말랑말랑하게 반죽하세요. ◼ 형용사 선이 부드러운 ❑ 단정하면서도 선이 부드럽고 여성스러운 스타일이다. ● 부드럽게 부사 ❑ 그녀는 선이 부드러운 정장을 입고 있었다. ◼ 형용사 부드러운, 조용한, 은은한 ❑ 누군가 내 방문을 조용히 두드렸다. ● 부드럽게, 조용히 부사 은은하게 ❑ 그녀가 조명이 은은한 방을 가로질러 갔다. ◼ 형용사 관대한 [탐탁찮음] ❑ 대통령은 그 조치가 범죄자에게 너무 너그럽고 불충분하다고 말한다. ◼ 형용사 여린 [마음이 듦] ❑ 그녀는 다소 거칠고 세파에 찌든 겉모습과 달리 마음이 아주 여리고 예민하다. ◼ 형용사 편한, 편리한 ❑ 래치미어에서 채택한 제도가 편리한 선택으로 비춰질 수도 있다. ◼ 형용사 중독성이 약한 ❑ 그녀는 술도 많이 안 마셨고 중독성이 강하든 약하든 약물에도 의존하지

calcium and so makes bubbles easily when you use soap. ❑ ...*an area where the water is very soft.*

알았다. ⑨ 형용사 칼슘 함량이 낮은, 인수의 ❑ 물의 칼슘 함량이 매우 낮은 지역

soft drink (soft drinks) N-COUNT A **soft drink** is a cold, nonalcoholic drink such as lemonade or fruit juice, or a carbonated drink.

가산명사 무알코올음료, 청량음료

sof|ten /sɒfᵊn, BRIT sɒfᵊn/ (**softens, softening, softened**) ■ V-T/V-I If you **soften** something or if it **softens**, it becomes less hard, stiff, or firm. ❑ *Soften the butter mixture in a small saucepan.* ■ V-T If one thing **softens** the damaging effect of another thing, it makes the effect less severe. ❑ *There were also pledges to soften the impact of the subsidy cuts on the poorer regions.* ■ V-T/V-I If you **soften** your position, if your position **softens**, or if you **soften**, you become more sympathetic and less hostile or critical. ❑ *The letter shows no sign that the Americans have softened their position.* ❑ *His party's policy has softened a lot in recent years.* ■ V-T/V-I If your voice or expression **softens** or if you **soften** it, it becomes much more gentle and friendly. ❑ *All at once, Mick's serious expression softened into a grin.* ■ V-T If you **soften** something such as light, a color, or a sound, you make it less bright or harsh. ❑ *We wanted to soften the light without destroying the overall effect of space.* ■ V-T Something that **softens** your skin makes it very smooth and pleasant to touch. ❑ *...products designed to moisturize and soften the skin.*

■ 타동사/자동사 부드럽게 하다; 부드러워지다 ❑ 작은 소스팬에 버터 혼합물을 부드럽게 녹이세요. ■ 타동사 완화하다, 덜다 ❑ 빈곤 지역에 대한 보조금 삭감의 충격을 완화하겠다는 약속도 나왔다. ■ 타동사/자동사 누그러뜨리다; 누그러지다 ❑ 공식 서한에서 미국이 입장을 누그러뜨린 기미를 전혀 찾아볼 수 없다. ❑ 그가 속한 당의 정책이 최근 상당히 누그러졌다. ■ 타동사/자동사 부드러워지다; 부드럽게 하다 ❑ 갑자기 믹의 심각한 표정이 부드러워지면서 환한 미소로 바뀌었다. ■ 타동사 약하게 하다 ❑ 우리는 공간의 전체적인 효과를 해치지 않고 조명을 약하게 하고 싶었다. ■ 타동사 매끄럽게 하다 ❑ 촉촉하고 매끄러운 피부를 위해 개발된 제품들

soft land|ing (soft landings) N-COUNT In economics, a **soft landing** is a situation in which the economy stops growing but this does not produce a recession. ❑ *...the belief that the economy is on course for a so-called soft landing.*

가산명사 연착륙 ❑ 경제가 이른바 연착륙의 수순을 밟고 있다는 믿음

soft loan (soft loans) N-COUNT A **soft loan** is a loan with a very low interest rate. Soft loans are usually made to developing countries or to businesses in developing countries. [BUSINESS]

가산명사 연화 차관 (대출 조건이 좋은 차관) [경제]

soft sell also **soft-sell** N-SING A **soft sell** is a method of selling or advertising that involves persuading people in a gentle way rather than putting a lot of pressure on people to buy things. [BUSINESS] ❑ *I think more customers probably prefer a soft sell.*

단수명사 (부드러운 설득 위주의) 온건한 판매 방식 (물건 판매나 광고 시 설득에 의존하는 방법) [경제] ❑ 나는 온건한 판매 방식을 선호하는 소비자들이 더 많다고 생각한다.

soft|ware ♦♢♢ /sɒftweər, BRIT sɒftweəʳ/ N-UNCOUNT Computer programs are referred to as **software**. Compare **hardware**. [COMPUTING] ❑ *...the people who write the software for big computer projects.* →see **computer**

불가산명사 소프트웨어 [컴퓨터] ❑ 대형 컴퓨터 프로젝트에 쓰일 소프트웨어를 제작하는 사람들

sog|gy /sɒgi/ (**soggier, soggiest**) ADJ Something that is **soggy** is unpleasantly wet. ❑ *...soggy cheese sandwiches.*

형용사 축축한, 눅눅한 ❑ 눅눅한 치즈 샌드위치

soil ♦♢♢ /sɔɪl/ (**soils**) N-MASS **Soil** is the substance on the surface of the earth in which plants grow. ❑ *We have the most fertile soil in Europe.* →see **erosion, farm**

물질명사 흙, 땅 ❑ 우리 땅이 유럽에서 가장 기름진 땅이다.

sol|ace /sɒlɪs/ N-UNCOUNT **Solace** is a feeling of comfort that makes you feel less sad. [FORMAL] ❑ *I found solace in writing when my father died three years ago.*

불가산명사 위안 [격식체] ❑ 3년 전 아버지가 돌아가셨을 때 나는 글쓰기를 위안으로 삼았다.

so|lar /soʊlər/ ■ ADJ **Solar** is used to describe things relating to the sun. ❑ *A total solar eclipse is due to take place some time tomorrow.* ■ ADJ **Solar** power is obtained from the sun's light and heat. ❑ *...the financial savings from solar energy.* →see **energy, greenhouse effect**

■ 형용사 태양의 ❑ 개기 일식이 내일 중으로 일어날 예정이다. ■ 형용사 태양의 ❑ 태양 에너지 사용을 통한 비용 절감

so|lar sys|tem (solar systems) N-COUNT The **solar system** is the sun and all the planets that go round it. ❑ *Saturn is the second biggest planet in the solar system.* →see **galaxy**
→see Word Web: **solar system**

가산명사 태양계 ❑ 토성은 태양계에서 두 번째로 큰 행성이다.

sold /soʊld/ **Sold** is the past tense and past participle of **sell**.

sell의 과거, 과거 분사

sol|dier ♦♦♢ /soʊldʒər/ (**soldiers**) N-COUNT A **soldier** is a member of an army, especially a person who is not an officer. →see **war**

가산명사 군인, 병사

sold out ■ ADJ If a performance, sports event, or other entertainment is **sold out**, all the tickets for it have been sold. [v-link ADJ] ❑ *The premiere on Monday is sold out.* ■ ADJ If a store is **sold out of** something, it has sold all of it that it had. [v-link ADJ, oft ADJ of n] ❑ *The stores are sometimes sold out of certain groceries.* →see also **sell out**

■ 형용사 매진된 ❑ 월요일 초연 표가 매진되었다. ■ 형용사 매진된 ❑ 식료품점에서 특정 상품이 매진될 때도 있다.

sole /soʊl/ (**soles**) ■ ADJ The **sole** thing or person of a particular type is the only one of that type. [ADJ n] ❑ *Their sole aim is to destabilize the Indian government.* ■ ADJ If you have **sole** charge or ownership of something, you are the only person in charge of it or who owns it. [ADJ n] ❑ *Many women are left as the sole providers in families after their husband has died.* ■ N-COUNT The **sole** of your foot or of a shoe or sock is the underneath surface of it. ❑ *...shoes with rubber soles.* →see **foot**

■ 형용사 유일한 ❑ 그들의 유일한 목적은 인도 정부를 와해시키는 것이다. ■ 형용사 혼자의, 단독의 ❑ 많은 여성들이 남편 사망 후에 혼자서 가족을 부양해야 할 처지에 놓인다. ■ 가산명사 발바닥; 밑창이 고무로 된 ❑ 고무 밑창 신발

The **sun** formed when a nebula turned into a star almost 5 billion years ago. All the **planets**, **comets**, and asteroids in our **solar system** started out in this nebula. Today they all **orbit** around the sun. The four planets closest to the sun are small and rocky. The next four consist mostly of **gases**. Scientists aren't sure about outermost planet, Pluto. They think it may be composed of rock and ice. Many of the planets have **moons** orbiting them. Most asteroids are irregularly shaped and covered with **craters**. Only about 200 asteroids have diameters of over 100 kilometers.

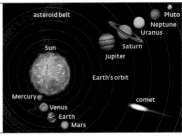

A

sole|ly /soʊlli/ ADV If something involves **solely** one thing, it involves only this thing and no others. ❑ *Too often we make decisions based solely upon what we see in the magazines.*

부사 오로지, 유일하게 ❑ 우리는 너무나 자주 잡지에서 본 내용에만 의존해 결정을 내린다.

B

sol|emn /sɒləm/ ■ ADJ Someone or something that is **solemn** is very serious rather than cheerful or humorous. ❑ *His solemn little face broke into smiles.* ● **sol|em|nity** /səlɛmnɪti/ N-UNCOUNT ❑ *The setting for this morning's signing ceremony matched the solemnity of the occasion.* ② ADJ A **solemn** promise or agreement is one that you make in a very formal, sincere way. ❑ *She made a solemn promise to him when they became engaged that she would give up cigarettes for good.*

■ 형용사 엄숙한, 심각한, 장엄한 ❑ 그의 작은 얼굴 위의 심각한 표정이 미소로 바뀌었다. ● 엄숙, 장엄 불가산명사 ❑ 오늘 아침 조인식 장소가 행사의 무게와 잘 어울렸다. ② 형용사 정식의, 엄숙한 ❑ 그녀는 약혼하면서 평생 담배를 끊겠다고 그에게 엄숙히 약속했다.

C

D

so|lic|it /səlɪsɪt/ (**solicits, soliciting, solicited**) ■ V-T If you **solicit** money, help, support, or an opinion **from** someone, you ask them for it. [FORMAL] ❑ *He's already solicited their support on health care reform.* ② V-I When prostitutes **solicit**, they offer to have sex with people in return for money. ❑ *Prostitutes were forbidden to solicit on public roads and in public places.* ● **so|lic|it|ing** N-UNCOUNT ❑ *Girls could get very heavy sentences for soliciting – nine months or more.*

■ 타동사 간청하다 [격식체] ❑ 그는 이미 의료 서비스 개혁에 대한 그들의 지지를 간청했다. ② 자동사 (매춘부가) 호객 행위를 하다 ❑ 공공도로나 공공장소에서 매춘부의 호객 행위는 금지였다. ● 성매매 제의 행위 불가산명사 ❑ 여학생들은 성매매 제의 행위가 징역 9개월 이상의 심한 처벌을 받을 수 있다.

E

F

so|lic|i|ta|tion /səlɪsɪteɪʃ°n/ (**solicitations**) N-VAR **Solicitation** is the act of asking someone for money, help, support, or an opinion. [mainly AM] ❑ *Republican leaders are making open solicitation of the Italian-American vote.*

가산명사 또는 불가산명사 간청 [주로 미국영어] ❑ 공화당 지도부가 이탈리아계 미국인을 상대로 공개적으로 표를 간청하고 있다.

G

so|lic|i|tor ♦◇◇ /səlɪsɪtər/ (**solicitors**) ■ N-COUNT In the United States, a **solicitor** is the chief lawyer in a government or city department. ② N-COUNT In Britain, a **solicitor** is a lawyer who gives legal advice, prepares legal documents and cases, and represents clients in the lower courts of law. Compare **barrister**. →see **lawyer**

■ 가산명사 법무관 ② 가산명사 사무 변호사

H

sol|id ♦♦◇ /sɒlɪd/ (**solids**) ■ ADJ A **solid** substance or object stays the same shape whether it is in a container or not. ❑ *...the potential of greatly reducing our solid waste problem.* ② N-COUNT A **solid** is a substance that stays the same shape whether it is in a container or not. ❑ *Solids turn to liquids at certain temperatures.* ③ ADJ A substance that is **solid** is very hard or firm. ❑ *The snow had melted, but the lake was still frozen solid.* ④ ADJ A **solid** object or mass does not have a space inside it, or holes or gaps in it. ❑ *...a tunnel carved through 50ft of solid rock.* ❑ *The car park was absolutely packed solid with people.* ⑤ ADJ If an object is made of **solid** gold or **solid** wood, for example, it is made of gold or wood all the way through, rather than just on the outside. [ADJ n] ❑ *The taps appeared to be made of solid gold.* ❑ *...solid wood doors.* ⑥ ADJ A structure that is **solid** is strong and is not likely to collapse or fall over. ❑ *Banks are built to look solid to reassure their customers.* ● **sol|id|ly** ADV [ADV with v] ❑ *Their house, which was solidly built, resisted the main shock.* ● **so|lid|ity** N-UNCOUNT ❑ *...the solidity of walls and floors.* ⑦ ADJ If you describe someone as **solid**, you mean that they are very reliable and respectable. [APPROVAL] ❑ *You want a husband who is solid and stable, someone who will devote himself to you.* ● **sol|id|ly** ADV ❑ *Graham is so solidly consistent.* ● **so|lid|ity** N-UNCOUNT ❑ *He had the proverbial solidity of the English.* ⑧ ADJ **Solid** evidence or information is reliable because it is based on facts. ❑ *We don't have good solid information on where the people are.* ⑨ ADJ You use **solid** to describe something such as advice or a piece of work which is useful and reliable. ❑ *The CIU provides churches with solid advice on a wide range of subjects.* ● **sol|id|ly** ADV [ADV with v] ❑ *She's played solidly throughout the spring.* ⑩ ADJ You use **solid** to describe something such as the basis for a policy or support for an organization when it is strong, because it has been developed carefully and slowly. ❑ *...a Democratic nominee with solid support within the party and broad appeal beyond.* ● **sol|id|ly** ADV ❑ *The Los Alamos district is solidly Republican.* ● **so|lid|ity** N-UNCOUNT ❑ *...doubts over the solidity of European backing for the American approach.* ⑪ ADJ If you do something for a **solid** period of time, you do it without any pause or interruption throughout that time. [ADJ n, -ed ADJ] ❑ *We had worked together for two solid years.* ● **sol|id|ly** ADV [ADV with v] ❑ *People who had worked solidly since Christmas enjoyed the chance of a Friday off.* →see **matter**

■ 형용사 고체의, 고형의 ❑ 고형 폐기물 문제를 크게 경감시킬 수 있는 가능성 ② 가산명사 고체, 고형 ❑ 고체는 특정 온도에서 액체로 변한다. ③ 형용사 단단한 ❑ 눈은 녹았지만 호수는 아직도 꽁꽁 얼어붙어 있었다. ④ 형용사 빈틈없는, 견고한, 속이 꽉 찬 ❑ 견고한 암석 50피트를 뚫고 만든 터널 ❑ 주차장에 사람들이 빈틈없이 꽉 들어차 있었다. ⑤ 형용사 순수한, 안과 밖이 같은 재료인 ❑ 수도꼭지가 순금으로 만든 것처럼 보였다. ❑ 순수 목재 문들 ⑥ 형용사 튼튼한, 견고한 ❑ 은행은 고객에게 안심을 줄 수 있도록 견고하게 보이게끔 건설된다. ● 튼튼하게, 견고하게 부사 ❑ 그들의 집은 튼튼하게 지어져 강한 충격도 버텨냈다. ● 튼튼함, 견고함 불가산명사 ❑ 벽과 바닥의 견고함 ⑦ 형용사 믿음직한 [마음에 듦] ❑ 당신은 믿음직스럽고 한결같으며 당신에게 헌신할 누군가가 남편이 되었으면 한다. ● 믿음직스럽게 부사 ❑ 그레이엄은 한결같이 믿음직하다. ● 믿음직스러움 불가산명사 ❑ 그는 잉글랜드 사람 특유의 믿음직한 구석이 있었다. ⑧ 형용사 믿을 만한, 확실한 ❑ 우리는 그 사람들의 행방에 대한 믿을 만한 좋은 정보가 없다. ⑨ 형용사 실속 있는, 알찬 ❑ 시아이유(CIU)는 교회를 상대로 다양한 주제에 대해 실속 있는 조언을 제공합니다. ● 알차게 부사 ❑ 그녀는 봄 내내 알찬 경기를 펼쳤다. ⑩ 형용사 탄탄한 ❑ 당 안으로 탄탄한 지지 기반과 당 밖으로 폭넓은 호소력을 가진 민주당 지명자 ● 탄탄하게 부사 ❑ 로스알라모스 선거구는 공화당 기반이 탄탄하다. ● 탄탄함 불가산명사 ❑ 미국식 접근법에 대한 유럽의 지지가 탄탄한지를 둘러싼 의혹 ⑪ 형용사 쉼 없이 이어지는 ❑ 우리는 2년 내내 함께 일했었다. ● 줄곧, 내내 부사 ❑ 크리스마스 이후 쉬지 않고 줄곧 일한 사람들은 금요일 하루를 쉴 수 있는 기회를 누렸다.

I

J

K

L

M

N

O

P

Q

R

Word Partnership   solid의 연어

N.	solid **food**, solid **waste** ■
	solid **ground**, **rock** solid ③
	solid **rock** ⑤
	solid **base**, solid **foundation** ⑥ ⑩
	solid **evidence** ⑧
	solid **performance** ⑨
	solid **growth**, solid **majority**, solid **support** ⑩
ADJ.	**frozen** solid ③
	good and solid ⑥ ⑩

S

T

U

soli|dar|ity /sɒlɪdæriti/ N-UNCOUNT If a group of people show **solidarity**, they show support for each other or for another group, especially in political or international affairs. ❑ *Supporters want to march tomorrow to show solidarity with their leaders.*

불가산명사 단결, 결속력 ❑ 지지자들은 지도자들에 대한 결속력을 보여 주기 위해 내일 행진을 하길 원한다.

V

so|lid|ify /səlɪdɪfaɪ/ (**solidifies, solidifying, solidified**) ■ V-T/V-I When a liquid **solidifies** or **is solidified**, it changes into a solid. ❑ *The thicker lava would have taken two weeks to solidify.* ❑ *The Energy Department plans to solidify the deadly waste in a high-tech billion-dollar factory.* ② V-T/V-I If something such as a position or opinion **solidifies**, or if something **solidifies** it, it becomes firmer and more definite and unlikely to change. ❑ *Her attitudes solidified through privilege and habit.* ❑ *...his attempt to solidify his position as chairman.*

■ 타동사/자동사 굳어지다, 고체로 변하다; 굳히다, 고체로 만들다 ❑ 농밀한 용암이 굳어지는 데는 2주가 걸렸을 것이다. ❑ 산업 자원부는 인간에게 치명적인 쓰레기를 막대한 돈을 들여 세운 최첨단 공장에서 고형화시킬 계획을 하고 있다. ② 타동사/자동사 고착되다; 고착시키다 ❑ 그녀의 태도는 특권과 자신의 습성 때문에 고착되었다. ❑ 의장직을 고착시키기 위한 그의 노력

W

X

Y

soli|tary /sɒlɪtɛri, BRIT sɒlɪtri/ ■ ADJ A person or animal that is **solitary** spends a lot of time alone. ❑ *Paul was a shy, pleasant, solitary man.* ② ADJ A **solitary**

■ 형용사 혼자 잘 지내는 ❑ 폴은 수줍음이 많고, 상냥하며, 혼자 있기를 좋아하는 사람이었다.

Z

activity is one that you do alone. [ADJ n] □ *His evenings were spent in solitary drinking.* **3** ADJ A **solitary** person or object is alone, with no others near them. [ADJ n] □ *...the occasional solitary figure making a study of wildflowers or grasses.*

soli|tude /sɒlɪtud, BRIT sɒlɪtyuːd/ N-UNCOUNT **Solitude** is the state of being alone, especially when this is peaceful and pleasant. □ *He enjoyed his moments of solitude before the pressures of the day began.*

solo /soʊloʊ/ (**solos**) **1** ADJ You use **solo** to indicate that someone does something alone rather than with other people. □ *He had just completed his final solo album.* □ *...Daniel Amokachi's spectacular solo goal.* ● ADV **Solo** is also an adverb. [ADV after v] □ *Charles Lindbergh became the very first person to fly solo across the Atlantic.* **2** N-COUNT A **solo** is a piece of music or a dance performed by one person. □ *The original version featured a guitar solo.*

so|lo|ist /soʊloʊɪst/ (**soloists**) N-COUNT A **soloist** is a musician or dancer who performs a solo. □ *...the relationship between soloist and orchestra.*

sol|uble /sɒlyəbəl/ **1** ADJ A substance that is **soluble** will dissolve in a liquid. □ *Uranium is soluble in sea water.* **2** COMB in ADJ If something is **water-soluble** or **fat-soluble**, it will dissolve in water or in fat. □ *The red dye on the leather is water-soluble.*

so|lu|tion ♦♦◇ /səluʃən/ (**solutions**) **1** N-COUNT A **solution to** a problem or difficult situation is a way of dealing with it so that the difficulty is removed. □ *Although he has sought to find a peaceful solution, he is facing pressure to use greater military force.* **2** N-COUNT The **solution to** a puzzle is the answer to it. □ *...the solution to crossword No. 19721.* **3** N-COUNT A **solution** is a liquid in which a solid substance has been dissolved. [also in N] □ *...a warm solution of liquid detergent.*

Word Partnership	solution의 연어
ADJ.	**best** solution, **peaceful** solution, **perfect** solution, **possible** solution, **practical** solution, **temporary** solution **1** **easy** solution, **obvious** solution, **simple** solution **1 2**
N.	solution **to a conflict**, solution **to a crisis** **1** solution **to a problem** **1 2**
V.	**propose** a solution, **reach** a solution, **seek** a solution **1** **find** a solution **1 2**

solve ♦◇◇ /sɒlv/ (**solves, solving, solved**) V-T If you **solve** a problem or a question, you find a solution or an answer to it. □ *Their domestic reforms did nothing to solve the problem of unemployment.*

Word Partnership	solve의 연어
N.	**ability to** solve *something*, solve **a crisis**, solve **a mystery**, solve **a problem**, solve **a puzzle**, **way to** solve *something*
V.	**attempt/try to** solve *something*, **help** solve *something*

sol|ven|cy /sɒlvənsi/ N-UNCOUNT A person or organization's **solvency** is their ability to pay their debts. [BUSINESS] □ *... unsound investments that could threaten the company's solvency.*

sol|vent /sɒlvənt/ (**solvents**) **1** ADJ If a person or a company is **solvent**, they have enough money to pay all their debts. [BUSINESS] □ *They're going to have to show that the company is now solvent.* **2** N-MASS A **solvent** is a liquid that can dissolve other substances. □ *...a small amount of cleaning solvent.* →see **dry cleaning**

som|ber /sɒmbər/ [BRIT **sombre**] **1** ADJ If someone is **somber**, they are serious or sad. □ *Spencer cried as she described the somber mood of her co-workers.* **2** ADJ **Somber** colors and places are dark and dull. □ *His room is somber and dark.*

some ♦♦♦ /səm, STRONG sʌm/ **1** DET You use **some** to refer to a quantity of something or to a number of people or things, when you are not stating the quantity or number precisely. □ *Robin opened some champagne.* □ *He went to fetch some books.* ● PRON **Some** is also a pronoun. □ *This year all the apples are all red. My niece and nephew are going out this morning with step-ladders to pick some.* **2** DET You use **some** to emphasize that a quantity or number is fairly large. For example, if an activity takes **some** time, it takes quite a lot of time. [EMPHASIS] □ *I have discussed this topic in some detail.* □ *He remained silent for some time.* **3** DET You use **some** to emphasize that a quantity or number is fairly small. For example, if something happens to **some** extent, it happens a little. [EMPHASIS] □ *"Isn't there some chance that William might lead a normal life?" asked Jill.* □ *All mothers share to some extent in the tension of a wedding.* **4** QUANT If you refer to **some of** the people or things in a group, you mean a few of them but not all of them. If you refer to **some of** a particular thing, you mean a part of it but not all of it. [QUANT of n-uncount/pl-n] □ *Some of the people already in work will lose their jobs.* □ *Remove the cover and spoon some of the sauce into a bowl.* ● PRON **Some** is also a pronoun. □ *When the chicken is cooked I'll freeze some.*

You use **not any** instead of **some** in negative sentences. □ *There isn't any money.*

5 DET If you refer to **some** person or thing, you are referring to that person or thing but in a vague way, without stating precisely which person or thing you mean. [VAGUENESS] □ *If you are worried about some aspect of your child's health, call us.* **6** ADV You can use **some** in front of a number to indicate that it is approximate. [VAGUENESS] [ADV num] □ *I have kept birds for some 30 years.* **7** ADV **Some** is used to mean to a small extent or degree. [AM] [ADV after v] □ *If Susanne*

2 형용사 혼자의 □ 그는 저녁마다 혼자 술을 마시며 시간을 보냈다. **3** 형용사 단독의 □ 간혹 단독으로 야생화나 야생초를 연구하는 사람

불가산명사 호젓함, 고독 □ 그는 하루의 분주함이 시작되기 전에 호젓한 자신의 시간을 즐겼다.

1 형용사 혼자서 하는 □ 그는 자신의 마지막 독집 앨범을 막 완성한 참이었다. □ 대니얼 아모카치의 혼자서 따낸 멋진 골 ● 부사 혼자서 □ 찰스 린드버그는 혼자서 대서양 비행 횡단을 한 최초의 인물이 되었다. **2** 가산명사 독주곡; 독창곡; 독무 □ 그 원곡은 기타 독주곡이었다.

가산명사 독주자; 독창자; 독무 추는 무용수 □ 독주자와 오케스트라 간의 관계

1 형용사 녹는, 용해성의 □ 우라늄은 바닷물에 녹는다. **2** 복합형-형용사 수용성의; 지용성의 □ 그 가죽에 물들인 붉은 염료는 수용성이다.

1 가산명사 해결책 □ 그가 비록 평화로운 해결책을 찾고 있었지만, 더 막강한 군사력을 사용하라는 압력에 봉착하고 있다. **2** 가산명사 해답 □ 십자말풀이 19721번의 해답 **3** 가산명사 용액 □ 따뜻한 세제 용액

타동사 해결하다, 풀다 □ 그들의 국내 개혁은 실업 문제를 해결하기 위해 아무것도 하지 않았다.

불가산명사 지불 능력 [경제] □ 그 회사의 지불 능력을 위협할지도 모르는 불안정한 투자

1 형용사 지불 능력이 있는 [경제] □ 그들은 그 회사가 이제는 지불 능력이 있다는 것을 보여 줘야만 할 것이다. **2** 물질명사 용매, 용액 □ 소량의 세탁 용액

[영국영어 sombre] **1** 형용사 침울한 □ 그녀가 동료들의 침울한 기분을 전해 주자 스펜서는 울어 버렸다. **2** 형용사 (색이) 칙칙한; 어두컴컴한 □ 그의 방은 칙칙하고 어둡다.

1 한정사 몇몇의 □ 로빈은 샴페인 몇 병을 땄다. □ 그는 책 몇 권을 가지러 갔다. ● 대명사 몇몇 □ 올해 사과가 모두 빨갛게 익었다. 오늘 아침에 내 조카들이 사과를 몇 개 따러 사다리를 가지고 나갈 것이다. **2** 한정사 상당한 [강조] □ 나는 이 주제에 대해서 상당히 자세하게 토론해 왔다. □ 그는 꽤 오랫동안 침묵했다. **3** 한정사 조금의, 약간의 [강조] □ "윌리엄이 정상적인 생활을 할 가능성이 좀 없습니까?"라고 질이 물었다. □ 모든 어머니들이 어느 정도는 결혼식에 대한 긴장감을 갖고 있다. **4** 수량사 - 중 몇몇, - 중 얼마 □ 이미 일자리를 갖고 있는 사람들 중 몇몇이 직장을 잃을 것이다. □ 뚜껑을 열고 숟가락으로 소스를 조금 떠서 그릇에 넣으세요. ● 대명사 조금, 일부 □ 그 닭고기가 익으면, 나는 그 중 일부는 얼릴 것이다.

부정문에서는 some 대신 not any를 쓴다. □ 돈이 전혀 없다.

5 한정사 어떤 [짐작투] □ 당신 아이의 건강의 어떤 면이 걱정되면 우리에게 전화하세요. **6** 부사 약 [짐작투] □ 나는 약 30년째 새들을 키우고 있다. **7** 부사 조금, 약간 [미국영어] □ 만약 수잰이 어디 가 있으면, 나는 여기저기를 좀 둘러보며 시간을 보낼 것이다. **8** 한정사 대단한; 형편없는 [비격식체, 감정

is off somewhere, I'll kill time by looking around some. **8** DET You can use **some** in front of a noun in order to express your approval or disapproval of the person or thing you are mentioning. [INFORMAL, FEELINGS] ❏ *"Some party!" — "Yep. One hell of a party."*

some|body ♦♦◇ /sʌmbədi, -bʌdi, BRIT sʌmbədi/ PRON-INDEF **Somebody** means the same as **someone**.

> You use **not anybody** instead of **somebody** in negative sentences. ❏ *There isn't anybody here.*

some|how ♦♦◇ /sʌmhaʊ/ **1** ADV You use **somehow** to say that you do not know or cannot say how something was done or will be done. ❏ *We'll manage somehow, you and me. I know we will.* ❏ *Somehow Karin managed to cope with the demands of her career.* **2** **somehow or other** →see **other**

some|one ♦♦◇ /sʌmwʌn/

> The form **somebody** is also used.

1 PRON-INDEF You use **someone** or **somebody** to refer to a person without saying exactly who you mean. ❏ *Her father was shot by someone trying to rob his small retail store.* ❏ *I need someone to help me.* **2** PRON-INDEF If you say that a person is **someone** or **somebody** in a particular kind of work or **in** a particular place, you mean that they are considered to be important in that kind of work or in that place. ❏ *"Before she came around," she says, "I was somebody in this town."*

> You use **not anyone** instead of **someone** in negative sentences. ❏ *There isn't anyone here.*

some|place /sʌmpleɪs/ ADV **Someplace** means the same as **somewhere**. [AM] [ADV after v] ❏ *Maybe if we could go someplace together, just you and I.*

som|er|sault /sʌmərsɔlt/ (**somersaults, somersaulting, somersaulted**) **1** N-COUNT If someone or something does a **somersault**, they turn over completely in the air. ❏ *Trained dogs did somersaults on a man's shoulders.* **2** V-I If someone or something **somersaults**, they perform one or more somersaults. ❏ *His boat hit a wave and somersaulted at speed.*

some|thing ♦♦♦ /sʌmθɪŋ/ **1** PRON-INDEF You use **something** to refer to a thing, situation, event, or idea, without saying exactly what it is. ❏ *He realized right away that there was something wrong.* ❏ *There was something vaguely familiar about him.* ❏ *"You said there was something you wanted to ask me," he said politely.* **2** PRON-INDEF You can use **something** to say that the description or amount that you are giving is not exact. ❏ *Clive made a noise, something like a grunt.* ❏ *Their membership seems to have risen to something over 10,000.* **3** PRON-INDEF If you say that a person or thing is **something** or is really **something**, you mean that you are very impressed by them. [INFORMAL] ❏ *You're really something.* **4** PRON-INDEF You can use **something** in expressions like **"that's something"** when you think that a situation is not very good but is better than it might have been. ❏ *Well, at least he was in town. That was something.* **5** PRON-INDEF If you say that a thing is **something of** a disappointment, you mean that it is quite disappointing. If you say that a person is **something of** an artist, you mean that they are quite good at art. [PRON of n] ❏ *The city proved to be something of a disappointment.* **6** PRON-INDEF If you say that there is **something in** an idea or suggestion, you mean that it is quite good and should be considered seriously. [PRON in n] ❏ *Could there be something in what he said?* **7** PRON-INDEF You use **something** in expressions such as **"or something"** and **"or something like that"** to indicate that you are referring to something similar to what you have just mentioned but you are not being exact. [VAGUENESS] ❏ *This guy, his name was Briarly or Beardly or something.* **8** **something like** →see **like**

> You use **not anything** instead of **something** in negative sentences. ❏ *There isn't anything here.*

some|time /sʌmtaɪm/ ADV You use **sometime** to refer to a time in the future or the past that is unknown or that has not yet been decided. ❏ *The sales figures won't be released until sometime next month.* ❏ *Why don't you come and see me sometime?*

some|times ♦♦◇ /sʌmtaɪmz/ ADV You use **sometimes** to say that something happens on some occasions rather than all the time. ❏ *During the summer, my skin sometimes gets greasy.* ❏ *Sometimes I think he dislikes me.*

some|what ♦♦◇ /sʌmwʌt, -wɒt/ ADV You use **somewhat** to indicate that something is the case to a limited extent or degree. [FORMAL] [ADV with cl/group] ❏ *He concluded that Oswald was somewhat abnormal.* ❏ *He explained somewhat unconvincingly that the company was paying for everything.*

some|where ♦♦◇ /sʌmweər/ **1** ADV You use **somewhere** to refer to a place without saying exactly where you mean. ❏ *I've got a feeling I've seen him before somewhere.* ❏ *I'm not going home yet. I have to go somewhere else first.* ❏ *I needed somewhere to live in London.* **2** ADV You use **somewhere** when giving an approximate amount, number, or time. [ADV prep] ❏ *The Queen is believed to earn somewhere between seven million and one hundred million pounds.* ❏ *Caray is somewhere between 73 and 80 years of age.* **3** PHRASE If you say that you **are getting somewhere**, you mean that you are making progress toward achieving something. ❏ *At last they were agreeing, at last they were getting somewhere.*

> You use **not anywhere** instead of **somewhere** in negative sentences. ❏ *He isn't going anywhere.* Informally, Americans also use the forms **someplace** and **anyplace.**

son ♦♦♦ /sʌn/ (**sons**) **1** N-COUNT Someone's **son** is their male child. ❏ *He shared a pizza with his son Laurence.* ❏ *Sam is the seven-year-old son of Eric Davies.* **2** N-COUNT A man, especially a famous man, can be described as a **son** of the place he comes from. [JOURNALISM] ❏ *...New Orleans's most famous son, Louis Armstrong.* **3** N-VOC Some people use **son** as a form of address when they are showing kindness or affection to a boy or a man who is younger than them. [INFORMAL, FEELINGS] ❏ *Don't be frightened by failure, son.* →see **child**

개입]❏ *"형편없는 파티야!" "그래, 진절머리 나는 파티군."*

부정(不定)대명사 어떤 사람, 누구

> 부정문에서는 somebody 대신 not anybody를 쓴다. ❏ *여기에 아무도 없다.*

1 부사 어떻게든지, 아무튼 ❏ *너와 나 우리 둘이 어떻게든지 해낼 거야. 우리가 해낼 거라는 걸 난 알아.* ❏ *카린은 그녀 직업상 해야 했던 일을 아무튼 성공적으로 해냈다.*

somebody도 쓰인다.

1 부정(不定)대명사 어떤 사람, 누구 ❏ *그녀의 아버지는 그의 작은 소매점을 털러 했던 누군가가 쏜 총에 맞았다.* ❏ *나는 누군가의 도움이 필요하다.* **2** 부정(不定)대명사 중요한 사람, 대단한 인물 ❏ *"그녀가 돌아오기 전에는 내가 이 마을에서 중요한 사람이었다."라고 그녀가 말한다.*

> 부정문에서는 someone 대신 not anyone을 쓴다. ❏ *여기에 아무도 없다.*

부사 어딘가에 [미국영어] ❏ *아마도 우리가 함께 어딘가로 갈 수 있다면, 너와 나 단 둘이.*

1 가산명사 공중제비, 재주넘기 ❏ *훈련받은 개들이 한 남자 어깨 위에서 공중제비를 했다.* **2** 자동사 공중제비를 하다, 재주를 넘다 ❏ *그의 배가 파도에 부딪히고 고속으로 한 바퀴 완전히 돌았다.*

1 부정(不定)대명사 어떤 것, 무엇 ❏ *그는 무엇인가 잘못되었다는 것을 곧 깨달았다.* ❏ *그에게는 희미하게 뭔가 친근한 면이 있었다.* ❏ *"제게 무엇인가 물어보고 싶은 게 있다고 말씀하셨지요."라며 그가 정중하게 말했다.* **2** 부정(不定)대명사 무슨 - 같은 것, -인가 뭔가 ❏ *클라이브는 무슨 투덜거림 같은 소리를 냈다.* ❏ *그들의 회원 수가 10,000명 이상 인가 얼마로 증가한 것 같다.* **3** 부정(不定)대명사 대단한 사람; 대단한 것 [비격식체] ❏ *너는 정말로 대단해.* **4** 부정(不定)대명사 그나마 괜찮은 것; 그 정도면 괜찮은 ❏ *글쎄, 적어도 그가 시내에 있었잖아. 그나마 다행이었어.* **5** 부정(不定)대명사 상당히 ❏ *그 도시는 상당히 실망스러운 것으로 밝혀졌다.* **6** 부정(不定)대명사 뭔가 대단한 것 ❏ *그가 한 말 속에 뭔가 대단한 것이 있었을까?* **7** 부정(不定)대명사 뭐 그런 것 [짐작투] ❏ *이 남자 그의 이름이 브리알리인가 비어들리인가 뭐 그랬어.*

> 부정문에서는 something 대신 not anything을 쓴다. ❏ *여기에 아무것도 없다.*

부사 언젠가, 언제쯤 ❏ *판매 가격이 다음 달 언제쯤 되어서야 나올 것이다.* ❏ *언제 저를 한 번 만나러 오시는 것이 어때요?*

부사 때때로, 가끔 ❏ *여름 동안에는 내 피부가 가끔 번들거린다.* ❏ *가끔 나는 그가 나를 싫어하는 것 같은 생각이 든다.*

부사 약간, 다소 [격식체] ❏ *그는 오스왈드가 약간 비정상적이었다고 결론지었다.* ❏ *그는 회사가 모든 걸 지불한다고 다소 납득이 가지 않게 설명했다.*

1 부사 어디에선가, 어딘가 ❏ *나는 그를 전에 어디에선가 만난 적이 있다는 느낌이 든다.* ❏ *나는 아직 집에 안 갈 거야. 먼저 어디 다른 곳에 좀 봐야 하거든.* ❏ *나는 런던 내에 어딘가 살 곳이 필요했다.* **2** 부사 대략 ❏ *여왕은 대략 7백만 파운드에서 1억 파운드 정도 버는다고 생각된다.* ❏ *캐라이는 대략 일흔세 살에서 여든 살 정도이다.* **3** 구 진척되어 가다 ❏ *마침내 그들은 의견의 일치를 보았다. 마침내 진척이 있은 것이다.*

> 부정문에서는 somewhere 대신 not anywhere를 쓴다. ❏ *그는 아무데도 가지 않는다.* 구어체로 미국인들은 someplace와 anyplace 형태도 쓴다.

1 가산명사 아들 ❏ *그는 자신의 아들 로렌스와 피자를 나누어 먹었다.* ❏ *샘은 에릭 데이비스의 일곱 살 난 아들이다.* **2** 가산명사 - 출신인 사람 [언론] ❏ *뉴올리언스 출신의 가장 유명한 인물, 루이 암스트롱* **3** 호격사 (호칭으로) 젊은이, 여보게 [비격식체, 감정 개입] ❏ *여보게, 실패를 두려워하지 말거나.*

so|na|ta /sənɑːtə/ (**sonatas**) N-COUNT A **sonata** is a piece of classical music written either for a single instrument, or for one instrument and a piano.

가산명사 (음악) 소나타

song ♦♦◊ /sɒŋ, BRIT sɒn/ (**songs**) **1** N-COUNT A **song** is words and music sung together. ❑ ...*a voice singing a Spanish song.* **2** N-UNCOUNT **Song** is the art of singing. ❑ ...*dance, music, mime, and song.* **3** N-COUNT A bird's **song** is the pleasant, musical sounds that it makes. ❑ *It's been a long time since I heard a blackbird's song in the evening.* **4** PHRASE If someone **bursts into song** or **breaks into song**, they start singing. ❑ *I feel as if I should break into song.* →see **concert**, **music**

1 가산명사 노래 ❑ 스페인 노래를 부르는 목소리 **2** 불가산명사 성악 ❑ 춤, 음악, 무언극, 성악 **3** 가산명사 새소리 ❑ 저녁에 검정새 지저귀는 소리를 들은 지도 꽤 오래되었다. **4** 구 노래를 시작하다 ❑ 내가 노래를 시작해야 할 것 같은 느낌이 든다.

Word Partnership   song의 연어

ADJ.	**beautiful** song, **favorite** song, **old** song, **popular** song **1**
N.	**hit** song, **love** song, song **lyrics**, song **music**, **pop** song, **rap** song, song **title**, **theme** song, **words** of a song **1**
V.	**hear** a song, **play** a song, **record** a song, **sing** a song, **write** a song **1**

---

son|ic /sɒnɪk/ ADJ **Sonic** is used to describe things related to sound. [TECHNICAL] [ADJ n] ❑ ...*the sonic boom of enemy fighter-bombers.*

형용사 소리의 [과학 기술] ❑ 적의 전폭기가 내는 엄청난 폭발음

son-in-law (**sons-in-law**) N-COUNT Someone's **son-in-law** is the husband of their daughter.

가산명사 사위

son|net /sɒnɪt/ (**sonnets**) N-COUNT A **sonnet** is a poem that has 14 lines. Each line has 10 syllables, and the poem has a fixed pattern of rhymes.

가산명사 소네트, 14행시

son of a bitch (**sons of bitches**) also **son-of-a-bitch** N-COUNT If someone is very angry with another person, or if they want to insult them, they sometimes call them a **son of a bitch**. [INFORMAL, VULGAR, DISAPPROVAL]

가산명사 개자식 (욕설) [비격식체, 비속어, 탐탁찮음]

soon ♦♦♦ /suːn/ (**sooner, soonest**) **1** ADV If something is going to happen **soon**, it will happen after a short time. If something happened **soon** after a particular time or event, it happened a short time after it. ❑ *You'll be hearing from us very soon.* ❑ *This chance has come sooner than I expected.* **2** PHRASE If you say that something happens **as soon as** something else happens, you mean that it happens immediately after the other thing. ❑ *As soon as relations improve they will be allowed to go.* **3** PHRASE If you say that you **would just as soon** do something or you**'d just as soon** do it, you mean that you would prefer to do it. ❑ *These people could afford to retire to Florida but they'd just as soon stay put.* ❑ *I'd just as soon not have to make this public.*

1 부사 곧, 빨리 ❑ 우리가 너에게 곧 연락할게. ❑ 이번 기회가 생각보다 더 빨리 왔다. **2** 구 –하자마자 ❑ 관계가 개선되자마자 그들은 갈 수 있도록 허락받을 것이다. **3** 구 차라리 – 하려 하다, –하기를 더 원하다 ❑ 이 사람들은 은퇴 후 플로리다로 갈 형편이 되지만 차라리 그냥 머물러 있으려 할 것이다. ❑ 이것을 공개하지 않았으면 좋겠다.

soot /sʊt, suːt/ N-UNCOUNT **Soot** is black powder which rises in the smoke from a fire and collects on the inside of chimneys. ❑ ... *a wall blackened by soot.*

불가산명사 검댕 ❑ 검댕에 그을린 담벼락

soothe /suːð/ (**soothes, soothing, soothed**) **1** V-T If you **soothe** someone who is angry or upset, you make them feel calmer. ❑ *He would take her in his arms and soothe her.* ● **sooth|ing** ADJ ❑ *Put on some nice soothing music.* **2** V-T Something that **soothes** a part of your body where there is pain or discomfort makes the pain or discomfort less severe. ❑ ...*body lotion to soothe dry skin.* ● **sooth|ing** ADJ ❑ *Cold tea is very soothing for burns.*

1 타동사 달래다, 진정시키다 ❑ 그가 그녀를 끌어안고 달래 주곤 했다. ● 진정시키는 형용사 ❑ 마음을 진정시키는 좋은 음악을 트세요. **2** 타동사 (통증을) 완화시키다, 누그러뜨리다 ❑ 건성 피부를 완화시켜 주는 바디 로션 ● 완화시키는 형용사 ❑ 차가운 차는 화상의 열기를 아주 잘 완화시킨다.

so|phis|ti|cat|ed ♦◊◊ /səfɪstɪkeɪtɪd/ **1** ADJ A **sophisticated** machine, device, or method is more advanced or complex than others. ❑ *Honeybees use one of the most sophisticated communication systems of any insect.* **2** ADJ Someone who is **sophisticated** is comfortable in social situations and knows about culture, fashion, and other matters that are considered socially important. ❑ *Claude was a charming, sophisticated companion.* **3** ADJ A **sophisticated** person is intelligent and knows a lot, so that they are able to understand complicated situations. ❑ *These people are very sophisticated observers of the foreign policy scene.*

1 형용사 정교한, 복잡한 ❑ 꿀벌의 의사소통 체계는 곤충의 세계에서 가장 복잡한 체계에 속한다. **2** 형용사 세련된 ❑ 클로드는 매력적이고 세련된 친구였다. **3** 형용사 박식한 ❑ 이 사람들은 외교 정책 현장의 매우 박식한 관찰자들이다.

Thesaurus   sophisticated의 참조어

ADJ.	advanced, complex, elaborate, intricate **1**
	cultured, experienced, refined, worldly; (*ant.*) backward, crude **2**

---

so|phis|ti|ca|tion /səfɪstɪkeɪʃ°n/ N-UNCOUNT The **sophistication** of people, places, machines, or methods is their quality of being sophisticated. ❑ *It would take many decades to build up the level of education and sophistication required.*

불가산명사 교양, 세련 ❑ 필요한 교육 정도와 교양 수준을 형성하는 데는 수십 년이 걸릴 것이다.

so|pra|no /səprɑːnoʊ, -præn-/ (**sopranos**) N-COUNT A **soprano** is a woman, girl, or boy with a high singing voice. ❑ *She was the main soprano at the Bolshoi theater.*

가산명사 소프라노 ❑ 그녀는 볼쇼이 극장의 주연 소프라노였다.

sor|did /sɔːrdɪd/ **1** ADJ If you describe someone's behavior as **sordid**, you mean that it is immoral or dishonest. [DISAPPROVAL] ❑ *He sat with his head buried in his hands as his sordid double life was revealed.* **2** ADJ If you describe a place as **sordid**, you mean that it is dirty, unpleasant, or depressing. [DISAPPROVAL] ❑ ...*the attic windows of their sordid little rooms.*

1 형용사 비도덕적인 [탐탁찮음] ❑ 그는 자신의 비도덕적인 이중생활이 밝혀지자, 머리를 두 손으로 감싸 쥐고 앉아 있었다. **2** 형용사 지저분한 [탐탁찮음] ❑ 그들의 지저분한 작은 방 다락 창문들

sore /sɔːr/ (**sorer, sorest, sores**) **1** ADJ If part of your body is **sore**, it causes you pain and discomfort. ❑ *It's years since I've had a sore throat like I did last night.* **2** ADJ If you are **sore** about something, you are angry and upset about it. [mainly AM, INFORMAL] [v-link ADJ, oft ADJ at/about n/-ing] ❑ *The result is that they are now all feeling very sore at you.* **3** N-COUNT A **sore** is a painful place on the body where the skin is infected. ❑ *Our backs and hands were covered with sores and burns from the ropes.* **4** PHRASE If something is a **sore point** with someone, it is likely to make them angry or embarrassed if you try to discuss it. ❑ *His lack of stature was a very sore point with him.*

1 형용사 아픈, 따가운 ❑ 어젯밤처럼 목이 아픈 것이 오래됐다. **2** 형용사 화난 [주로 미국영어, 비격식체] ❑ 결과적으로 그들이 지금 모두 네게 아주 많이 화가 나 있다. **3** 가산명사 상처 ❑ 우리는 밧줄 때문에 등과 손이 화끈거리면서 온통 상처투성이였다. **4** 구 민감한 사안, 약점 ❑ 그에게는 왜소한 신장이 민감한 사안이었다.

sore|ly /sɔːrli/ ADV **Sorely** is used to emphasize that a feeling such as disappointment or need is very strong. [EMPHASIS] ❑ *I for one was sorely disappointed.* ❑ *He will be sorely missed.*

부사 몹시 [강조] ❑ 나야말로 정말 실망했다. ❑ 그는 몹시 보고 싶을 것이다.

sor|row /sɒroʊ/ N-UNCOUNT Sorrow is a feeling of deep sadness or regret. □ *Words cannot express my sorrow.*

불가산명사 슬픔 □ 말로는 내 슬픔을 다 표현할 수 없다.

sor|rows /sɒroʊz/ N-PLURAL Sorrows are events or situations that cause deep sadness. □ *...the joys and sorrows of everyday living.* to **drown** one's **sorrows** →see **drown**

복수명사 슬픈 일 □ 일상생활에서 일어나는 기쁜 일과 슬픈 일

sor|ry ♦♦◇ /sɒri/ (**sorrier, sorriest**) **1** CONVENTION You say "Sorry" or "I'm sorry" as a way of apologizing to someone for something that you have done which has upset them or caused them difficulties, or when you bump into them accidentally. [FORMULAE] □ *"We're all talking at the same time." — "Yeah. Sorry."* □ *Sorry I took so long.* □ *I'm really sorry if I said anything wrong.* **2** ADJ If you are **sorry** about a situation, you feel regret, sadness, or disappointment about it. [v-link ADJ, usu ADJ about n, ADJ that/to-inf] □ *She was very sorry about all the trouble she'd caused.* □ *I'm sorry he's gone.* **3** CONVENTION You use **I'm sorry** or **sorry** as an introduction when you are telling a person something that you do not think they will want to hear, for example when you are disagreeing with them or giving them bad news. □ *No, I'm sorry, I can't agree with you.* □ *"I'm sorry," he told the real estate agent, "but we really must go now."* **4** PHRASE You use the expression **I'm sorry to say** to express regret together with disappointment or disapproval. [FEELINGS] □ *I've only done half of it, I'm sorry to say.* **5** CONVENTION You say "I'm sorry" to express your regret and sadness when you hear sad or unpleasant news. [FEELINGS] □ *"I'm afraid he's ill." — "I'm sorry to hear that."* **6** ADJ If you feel **sorry for** someone who is unhappy or in an unpleasant situation, you feel sympathy and sadness for them. [v-link ADJ for n] □ *I felt sorry for him and his colleagues – it must have been so frustrating for them.* **7** ADJ You say that someone is feeling **sorry for themselves** when you disapprove of the fact that they keep thinking unhappily about their problems, rather than trying to be cheerful and positive. [DISAPPROVAL] [v-link ADJ for pron-refl] □ *What he must not do is to sit around at home feeling sorry for himself.* **8** CONVENTION You say "Sorry?" when you have not heard something that someone has said and you want them to repeat it. [FORMULAE] □ *Once or twice I heard her muttering, but when I said, "Sorry? What did you say?" she didn't respond.* **9** CONVENTION You use **sorry** when you correct yourself and use different words to say what you have just said, especially when what you say the second time does not use the words you would normally choose to use. □ *Barcelona will be hoping to bring the trophy back to Spain (sorry, Catalonia) for the first time.* **10** ADJ If someone or something is in a **sorry** state, they are in a bad state, mentally or physically. [ADJ n] □ *The fire left Kuwait's oil industry in a sorry state.* **11 better safe than sorry** →see **safe**

1 관용 표현 미안해요 [의례적인 표현] □ "우리 모두가 지금 동시에 말하고 있어." "응, 미안해." □ 미안합니다. 제가 너무 오래 끌었네요. □ 제 말에 실수한 부분이 있다면 정말 미안합니다. **2** 형용사 후회하는, 애석해하는 □ 그녀는 자기가 초래한 모든 논란에 대해 매우 크게 후회했다. □ 그가 가 버려서 애석하다. **3** 관용 표현 죄송합니다만 □ 죄송합니다만, 당신 의견에 동의할 수 없습니다. □ "죄송합니다만, 우리는 이제 정말 가야겠습니다."라고 그가 부동산 중개인에게 말했다. **4** 구 말씀드리기 죄송하지만 [감정 개입] □ 말씀드리기 죄송하지만, 절반밖에 하지 못했어요. **5** 관용 표현 안됐군요 [감정 개입] □ "그 사람이 아파요." "그것 참 안됐군요." **6** 형용사 안쓰럽게 느끼는 □ 나는 그 남자와 그의 동료들이 안됐다는 생각이 들었다. 얼마나 실망스러웠을까 싶었다. **7** 형용사 관용 한탄하는 [탐탁잖음] □ 그가 하지 말아야 할 일은 집에 앉아 자신을 신세 한탄이나 하는 것이다. **8** 관용 표현 뭐라고요?, 뭐라고 그러셨나요? [의례적인 표현] □ 그녀가 중얼거리는 소리를 한두 번 들었지만, 내가, "뭐라고? 뭐라고 그랬냐?"라고 물었을 때, 그녀는 아무런 대답이 없었다. **9** 관용 표현 아, 죄송합니다 □ 바르셀로나는 처음으로 그 트로피를 스페인으로 (아, 죄송합니다, 카탈로니아로) 되가져오기를 희망하고 있을 겁니다. **10** 형용사 비참한, 딱한 □ 그 화재로 인해서 쿠웨이트 정유 산업은 비참한 상태가 되었다.

sort ♦♦♦ /sɔrt/ (**sorts, sorting, sorted**) **1** N-COUNT If you talk about a particular **sort** of something, you are talking about a class of things that have particular features in common and that belong to a larger group of related things. □ *What sort of school did you go to?* □ *There are so many different sorts of mushrooms available these days.* □ *A dozen trees of various sorts were planted.* **2** N-SING You describe someone as a particular **sort** when you are describing their character. [with supp] □ *He seemed to be just the right sort for the job.* □ *She was a very vigorous sort of person.* **3** V-T/V-I If you **sort** things, you separate them into different classes, groups, or places, for example so that you can do different things with them. □ *He sorted the materials into their folders.* □ *He unlatched the box and sorted through the papers.* **4** V-T If you get a problem or the details of something **sorted**, you do what is necessary to solve the problem or organize the details. [INFORMAL] [usu passive] □ *I'm trying to get my script sorted.* **5** PHRASE **All sorts of** things or people means a large number of different things or people. □ *There are all sorts of animals, including bears, pigs, kangaroos, and penguins.* □ *It was used by all sorts of people.* **6** PHRASE If you describe something as a thing **of sorts** or as a thing **of a sort**, you are suggesting that the thing is of a rather poor quality or standard. □ *He made a living of sorts selling pancakes from a van.* **7** PHRASE You use **sort of** when you want to say that your description of something is not very accurate. [INFORMAL, VAGUENESS] □ *You could even order windows from a catalogue – a sort of mail order stained glass service.* **8 nothing of the sort** →see **nothing**

1 가산명사 종류, 부류 □ 어떤 학교에 다녔니? □ 오늘날에는 너무나 많은 여러 종류의 버섯을 먹을 수 있다. □ 다양한 종류의 나무 십여 그루를 심었다. **2** 단수명사 성격, 부류 □ 그는 성격상 그 직업이 딱 맞는 것 같았다. □ 그녀는 아주 에너지가 넘치는 부류의 사람이었다. **3** 타동사/자동사 분류하다 □ 그는 자료들을 폴더에 분류해 넣었다. □ 그는 상자를 열어서 그 속에 있는 논문들을 분류했다. **4** 타동사 해결하다 [비격식체] □ 나는 내 대본을 해결하려고 애쓰는 중이다. **5** 구 모든 종류, 모든 부류 □ 곰, 돼지, 캥거루, 펭귄을 포함한 모든 종류의 동물들이 있다. □ 모든 부류의 사람들이 그것을 사용했다. **6** 구 이류의 □ 그는 소형 트럭에서 팬케이크를 팔면서 이류 생활을 했다. **7** 구 일종의 [비격식체, 짐작투] □ 당신은 카탈로그로 창문까지도 주문할 수 있어요. 일종의, 스테인드글라스 창 우편 주문 서비스 같은 거죠.

▶ **sort out** **1** PHRASAL VERB If you **sort out** a group of things, you separate them into different classes, groups, or places, for example so that you can do different things with them. □ *Sort out all your bills, receipts, invoices and expenses as quickly as possible and keep detailed accounts.* □ *Davina was sorting out scraps of material.* **2** PHRASAL VERB If you **sort out** a problem or the details of something, you do what is necessary to solve the problem or organize the details. □ *India and Nepal have sorted out their trade and security dispute.* **3** PHRASAL VERB If you **sort** someone **out**, you make them realize that they have behaved wrongly, for example by talking to them or by punishing them. [mainly BRIT] □ *It was the older women and young mothers who sorted all the troublemakers out.* **4** PHRASAL VERB If you **sort yourself out**, you organize yourself or calm yourself so that you can act effectively and reasonably. □ *We're in a state of complete chaos here and I need a little time to sort myself out.*

1 구동사 분류하다 □ 모든 고지서, 영수증, 청구서, 비용 내역서를 가능한 한 빨리 분류하고 자세한 장부를 작성하세요. □ 다비나는 자료 스크랩을 분류하고 있었다. **2** 구동사 해결하다, 정리하다 □ 인도와 네팔은 그들 사이의 무역과 안보에 관한 분쟁을 해결했다. **3** 구동사 (나무라거나 벌해서) 잘못을 깨닫게 하다 [주로 영국영어] □ 모든 문제아들이 잘못을 깨닫도록 만드는 사람은 바로 나이 많은 여자들과 젊은 엄마들이었다. **4** 구동사 진정시키다 □ 우리는 지금 완전히 혼돈 상태라서 제 마음을 진정시킬 시간이 좀 필요합니다.

sor|tie /sɔrti/ (**sorties**) N-COUNT If a military force makes a **sortie**, it leaves its own position and goes briefly into enemy territory to make an attack. [FORMAL] □ *His men made a sortie to Guazatan and took a prisoner.*

가산명사 출격 [격식체] □ 그의 부하들이 과자탄으로 출격해서 포로 한 명을 붙잡았다.

SOS /ɛs oʊ ɛs/ N-SING An SOS is a signal which indicates to other people that you are in danger and need help quickly. □ *The ferry did not even have time to send out an SOS.*

단수명사 조난 신호, 구조 신호 □ 그 배는 조난 신호 보낼 시간조차도 없었다.

souf|flé /sufleɪ, BRIT suːfleɪ/ (**soufflés**) also **souffle** N-VAR A **soufflé** is a light food made from a mixture of beaten egg whites and other ingredients that is baked in the oven. It can be either sweet or savory. □ *...a superb cheese soufflé.*

가산명사 또는 불가산명사 수플레 (요리) □ 훌륭한 치즈 수플레

sought /sɔt/ **Sought** is the past tense and past participle of **seek**.

seek의 과거, 과거 분사

sought-after ADJ Something that is **sought-after** is in great demand, usually because it is rare or of very good quality. □ *An Olympic gold medal is the most sought-after prize in world sport.*

형용사 많은 사람들이 갖고 싶어 하는, 염원하는 □ 올림픽 금메달은 전 세계 스포츠 대회에서 가장 받고 싶어 하는 상이다.

soul ◆◇◇ /soʊl/ (souls) **1** N-COUNT Your **soul** is the part of you that consists of your mind, character, thoughts, and feelings. Many people believe that your soul continues existing after your body is dead. □ *She went to pray for the soul of her late husband.* **2** N-COUNT You can refer to someone as a particular kind of **soul** when you are describing their character or condition. □ *He's a jolly soul.* **3** N-SING You use **soul** in negative statements like **not a soul** to mean nobody at all. □ *I've never harmed a soul in my life.* **4** N-UNCOUNT **Soul** or **soul music** is a type of pop music performed mainly by black American musicians. It developed from gospel and blues music and often expresses deep emotions. □ *...American soul singer Anita Baker.* **5** to **bare** one's **soul** →see **bare**. **body and soul** →see **body**

가산명사 영혼 □ 그녀는 사망한 남편의 영혼을 위한 기도를 하러 갔다. **2** 가산명사 (- 한 성격의) 사람 □ 그는 쾌활한 사람이다. **3** 단수명사 (특정 부정문에서) 사람 □ 나는 내 평생 단 한 사람에게도 해를 끼치지 않았다. **4** 불가산명사 흑인 음악, 소울 뮤직 □ 미국 흑인 음악 가수 애니타 베이커

---

sound

① NOUN AND VERB USES
② ADJECTIVE USES

---

① **sound** ◆◆◆ /saʊnd/ (sounds, sounding, sounded) →**Please look at category 10 to see if the expression you are looking for is shown under another headword.** **1** N-COUNT A **sound** is something that you hear. □ *Peter heard the sound of gunfire.* □ *Liza was so frightened she couldn't make a sound.* **2** N-UNCOUNT **Sound** is energy that travels in waves through air, water, or other substances, and can be heard. □ *The aeroplane will travel at twice the speed of sound.* **3** N-SING **The sound** on a television, radio, or CD player is what you hear coming from the machine. Its loudness can be controlled. □ *She went and turned the sound down.* **4** N-COUNT A singer's or band's **sound** is the distinctive quality of their music. □ *They have started showing a strong soul element in their sound.* **5** V-T/V-I If something such as a horn or a bell **sounds** or if you **sound** it, it makes a noise. □ *The buzzer sounded in Daniel's office.* **6** V-T If you **sound** a warning, you publicly give it. If you **sound** a note of caution or optimism, you say publicly that you are cautious or optimistic. □ *The Archbishop of Canterbury has sounded a warning to Europe's leaders on third world debt.* **7** V-LINK When you are describing a noise, you can talk about the way it **sounds**. □ *They heard what sounded like a huge explosion.* □ *The creaking of the hinges sounded very loud in that silence.* **8** V-LINK When you talk about the way someone **sounds**, you are describing the impression you have of them when they speak. □ *She sounded a bit worried.* □ *Murphy sounds like a child.* **9** V-LINK When you are describing your impression or opinion of something you have heard about or read about, you can talk about the way it **sounds**. □ *It sounds like a wonderful idea to me, does it really work?* □ *It sounds as if they might have made a dreadful mistake.* **10** N-SING You can describe your impression of something you have heard about or read about by talking about **the sound of** it. □ *Here's a new idea we liked the sound of.* □ *I don't like the sound of Toby Osborne.* **11** to **sound the alarm** →see **alarm**. **safe and sound** →see **safe**
→see **ear, echo**
→see Word Web: **sound**

1 가산명사 소리 □ 피터가 총 소리를 들었다. □ 리자는 너무나 놀라서 아무 소리도 못 냈다. **2** 불가산명사 음, 소리 □ 그 비행기는 음속의 두 배 속도로 날 것이다. **3** 단수명사 소리 □ 그녀는 가서 소리를 낮췄다. **4** 가산명사 (특유한) 음악 스타일 □ 그들은 자신들의 음악에서 강한 흑인 음악적 요소를 보이기 시작했다. **5** 타동사/자동사 소리가 나다; 소리를 내다 □ 다니엘의 사무실에서 버저 소리가 났다. **6** 타동사 공식적으로 말하다 □ 캔터베리 대주교는 유럽의 지도자들에게 제 3세계 국가의 부채에 대해 공식적으로 경고했다. **7** 연결동사 -한 소리가 나다 □ 그들은 엄청난 폭발음 같은 소리를 들었다. □ 그렇게 조용한 가운데 문 경첩이 삐걱거리는 소리는 매우 크게 들렸다. **8** 연결동사 (말하는 것이) -인 것 같다 □ 그녀는 약간 걱정스러운 것 같았다. □ 머피는 말하는 것이 어린아이 같다. **9** 연결동사 -처럼 들린다, -인 것 같다 □ 내가 듣기엔 정말 좋은 생각인 것 같은데, 정말로 효과가 있는 거야? □ 그들이 마치 엄청난 실수를 했을 수도 있을 것 같다. **10** 단수명사 인상, 느낌 □ 우리가 괜찮게 생각했던 새로운 아이디어가 있다. □ 나는 토비 오스본의 인상이 별로 좋지 않다.

Thesaurus   sound의 참조어

ADJ.   safe, sturdy, whole ② **1**
            logical, valid, wise; (ant.) illogical, unreliable ② **2**

▶**sound out** PHRASAL VERB If you **sound** someone **out**, you question them in order to find out what their opinion is about something. □ *He is sounding out Middle Eastern governments on ways to resolve the conflict.*

구동사 (의견을) 타진하다 □ 그는 그 갈등을 해결할 방법에 대해 중동 지역 국가들의 의견을 타진하고 있다.

② **sound** /saʊnd/ (sounder, soundest) **1** ADJ If a structure, part of someone's body, or someone's mind is **sound**, it is in good condition or healthy. □ *When we bought the house, it was structurally sound.* □ *Although the car is basically sound, I was worried about certain areas.* **2** ADJ **Sound** advice, reasoning, or evidence is reliable and sensible. □ *They are trained nutritionists who can give sound advice on diets.* □ *Buy a policy only from an insurance company that is financially sound.* **3** ADJ If you describe someone's ideas as **sound**, you mean that you approve of them and think they are correct. [APPROVAL] □ *I am not sure that this is sound democratic practice.* **4** ADJ If someone is in a **sound sleep**, they are sleeping very deeply. □ *She had woken me out of a sound sleep.* • ADV **Sound** is also an adverb. [ADV adj] □ *He was lying in bed, sound asleep.* **5** →see also **soundly**

1 형용사 튼튼한, 건강한 □ 우리가 그 집을 샀을 때, 그 집은 구조가 튼튼했다. □ 그 차는 기본적으로 튼튼하지만, 몇몇 부분이 걱정스러웠다. **2** 형용사 믿을 만한, 타당한 □ 그들은 다이어트에 대한 믿을 만한 조언을 해 줄 수 있는 교육받은 영양사들이다. □ 재정적으로 믿을 만한 보험 회사에서만 보험에 가입하세요. **3** 형용사 올바른 [마음에 듦] □ 나는 과연 이것이 올바른 민주주의의 실천인지 잘 모르겠다. **4** 형용사 (잠이) 깊은 □ 그녀는 깊이 잠든 나를 깨웠다. • 부사 깊이 □ 그는 침대에 누워 깊이 잠들어 있었다.

sound|card /saʊndkɑrd/ (soundcards) also sound card N-COUNT A **soundcard** is a piece of equipment which can be put into a computer so that the computer can produce music or other sounds. [COMPUTING]

가산명사 (컴퓨터) 사운드 카드 [컴퓨터]

Word Web   sound

Sound is the only form of energy we can hear. It consists of vibrating molecules of air. Rapid vibrations called high **frequencies** produce high-pitched sounds. Slower vibrations produce lower frequencies. Sound vibrations travel in waves, just like **waves** in water. Each wave has a **crest** and a **trough**. Amplitude is a measure of how high above the medium line a sound wave moves. When a **sound wave** bounces off an object, it produces an **echo**. When an airplane reaches **supersonic** speed, it generates **shock waves**. As these waves move toward the ground, a sonic boom occurs.

sound|ly /sa͡ʊndli/ **1** ADV If someone is **soundly** defeated or beaten, they are defeated or beaten thoroughly. [ADV -ed] ❑ *Needing just a point from their match at St. Helens, they were soundly beaten, going down by 35 points to 10.* **2** ADV If a decision, opinion, or statement is **soundly** based, there are sensible or reliable reasons behind it. [APPROVAL] [ADV -ed] ❑ *Changes must be soundly based in economic reality.* **3** ADV If you sleep **soundly**, you sleep deeply and do not wake during your sleep. ❑ *How can he sleep soundly at night? He's the one responsible for all those crimes.*

1 부사 완전히 ❑ 그들은 세인트 헬렌스 팀과의 경기에서 단 1점만 득점하면 됐는데, 결국 35대 10으로 완패했다. **2** 부사 (근거가) 타당하게 [마음에 듦] ❑ 변화는 경제적 현실에 타당한 기반을 두고 있어야 한다. **3** 부사 깊이 (잠들) ❑ 어떻게 그가 밤에 깊이 잠들 수가 있을까? 그는 그 모든 범죄에 대해 책임이 있는 사람이다.

sound sys|tem (**sound systems**) N-COUNT A **sound system** is a set of equipment for playing recorded music, or for making a band's music able to be heard by everyone at a concert.

가산명사 사운드 시스템

sound|track /sa͡ʊndtræk/ (**soundtracks**) also **sound track** N-COUNT The **soundtrack** of a movie is its sound, speech, and music. It is used especially to refer to the music. ❑ *...the forthcoming release of the soundtrack to a movie called "Judgment Night."*

가산명사 영화 음악, 사운드 트랙 ❑ 곧 발매될 '심판의 밤'이라는 영화의 영화 음악

soup /su͡p/ (**soups**) N-MASS **Soup** is liquid food made by boiling meat, fish, or vegetables in water. ❑ *...home-made chicken soup.*

물질명사 수프 ❑ 집에서 만든 닭고기 수프

sour /sa͡ʊər/ (**sours, souring, soured**) **1** ADJ Something that is **sour** has a sharp, unpleasant taste like the taste of a lemon. ❑ *The stewed apple was sour even with honey.* **2** ADJ **Sour** milk is milk that has an unpleasant taste because it is no longer fresh. ❑ *The milk had gone sour.* **3** ADJ Someone who is **sour** is bad-tempered and unfriendly. ❑ *She made a sour face in his direction.* ● **sour|ly** ADV [ADV with v] ❑ *"Leave my mother out of it," he said sourly.* **4** ADJ If a situation or relationship **turns sour** or **goes sour**, it stops being enjoyable or satisfactory. ❑ *Everything turned sour for me there.* ❑ *Even the European dream is beginning to turn sour.* **5** V-T/V-I If a friendship, situation, or attitude **sours** or if something **sours** it, it becomes less friendly, enjoyable, or hopeful. ❑ *If anything sours the relationship, it is likely to be real differences in their world-views.* →see **fruit, taste**

1 형용사 신맛이 나는, 신 ❑ 사과 스튜가 꿀을 넣었는데도 신맛이 났다. **2** 형용사 (우유가) 상한 ❑ 그 우유는 상해 있었다. **3** 형용사 통한, 심술궂은 ❑ 그녀가 그의 지시에 통한 표정을 지었다. ● 통하게, 심술궂게 부사 "우리 어머니는 끌어들이지 마."라고 그가 심술궂게 말했다. **4** 형용사 (상황 등이) 틀어진, 언짢은 ❑ 그곳에서 모든 것이 내게 언짢게 돌아갔다. ❑ 유럽에서 성공하려는 꿈조차 틀어지기 시작하고 있다. **5** 타동사/자동사 잘못되다, 틀어지다; 잘못되게 만들다, 틀어지게 만들다 ❑ 어떤 것이든 관계를 틀어지게 만드는 것이 있다면, 그것은 그들의 세계관에 진정한 차이가 있기 때문일 가능성이 크다.

source ♦♦◇ /sɔ͡ːrs/ (**sources, sourcing, sourced**) **1** N-COUNT The **source of** something is the person, place, or thing which you get it from. ❑ *...over 40 per cent of British adults use television as their major source of information about the arts.* ❑ *Renewable sources of energy must be used.* **2** V-T In business, if a person or firm **sources** a product or a raw material, they find someone who will supply it. [BUSINESS] ❑ *Together they travel the world, sourcing clothes for the small, privately owned company.* **3** N-COUNT A **source** is a person or book that provides information for a news story or for a piece of research. ❑ *Military sources say the boat was heading south at high speed.* **4** N-COUNT The **source of** a difficulty is its cause. ❑ *This gave me a clue as to the source of the problem.* **5** N-COUNT The **source of** a river or stream is the place where it begins. ❑ *...the source of the Tiber.* →see **diary**

1 가산명사 출처 ❑ 영국 성인의 40퍼센트 이상이 예술에 대한 정보를 얻는 주된 출처로서 텔레비전을 이용한다. ❑ 재생 가능 에너지원을 이용해야만 한다. **2** 타동사 공급자를 찾다 [경제] ❑ 그들은 소규모 민간 회사에 옷감을 공급할 사람을 찾아, 함께 전 세계를 다닌다. **3** 가산명사 정보원, 소식통 ❑ 군 소식통이 그 배가 남쪽을 향해서 고속으로 항해하고 있었다고 말한다. **4** 가산명사 원인 ❑ 이것이 나에게 그 문제의 원인에 대한 단서를 제공했다. **5** 가산명사 (강의) 수원, 원천 ❑ 테베레 강의 수원

Thesaurus　　　source의 참조어

N.　beginning, origin, root, start **1** **4** **5**

---

south ♦♦♦ /sa͡ʊθ/ also **South** **1** N-UNCOUNT The **south** is the direction which is on your right when you are looking toward the direction where the sun rises. [also the N] ❑ *The town lies ten miles to the south of here.* **2** N-SING The **south of** a place, country, or region is the part which is in the south. [usu the N, oft N of n] ❑ *...holidays in the south of France.* **3** ADV If you go **south**, you travel toward the south. [ADV after v] ❑ *We did an extremely fast U-turn and shot south up the Boulevard St. Michel.* **4** ADV Something that is **south of** a place is positioned to the south of it. [ADV of n] ❑ *They now own and operate a farm 50 miles south of Rochester.* **5** ADJ The **south** edge, corner, or part of a place or country is the part which is toward the south. [ADJ n] ❑ *...the south coast of Alderney.* **6** ADJ "**South**" is used in the names of some countries, states, and regions in the south of a larger area. ❑ *Next week the President will visit five South American countries in six days.* **7** ADJ A **south** wind is a wind that blows from the south. ❑ *...a mild south wind.* **8** N-SING **The South** is used to refer to the poorer, less developed countries of the world. [the N] ❑ *The debate will pit the industrial North against developing countries in the South.*

1 불가산명사 남쪽 ❑ 그 마을은 여기에서 남쪽으로 10마일 떨어진 곳에 있다. **2** 단수명사 남부 지방 ❑ 프랑스 남부 지방에서의 휴가 **3** 부사 남쪽으로 ❑ 우리는 엄청나게 빠르게 유턴을 해서 생미셸 대로를 타고 남쪽으로 총알같이 달렸다. **4** 부사 남쪽에 ❑ 그들은 로체스터에서 남쪽으로 50마일 떨어진 곳에 있는 농장을 사서 경영하고 있다. **5** 형용사 남쪽의 ❑ 알더니 섬의 남해안 **6** 형용사 남부의 ❑ 다음 주에 대통령은 6일 동안 남미 5개국을 방문할 것이다. **7** 형용사 남쪽에서 불어오는 ❑ 따뜻한 남풍 **8** 단수명사 남반구 개발도상국들 ❑ 그 논쟁은 북반구 선진국과 남반구 개발도상국 간의 싸움을 유발시킬 것이다.

south|east ♦♦◇ /sa͡ʊθi͡ːst/ also **south-east** **1** N-UNCOUNT The **southeast** is the direction which is halfway between south and east. [also the N] ❑ *It shook buildings as far away as Galveston, 90 miles to the southeast.* **2** N-SING The **southeast** of a place, country, or region is the part which is in the southeast. ❑ *Record levels of rainfall fell over the southeast of the country.* **3** ADV If you go **southeast**, you travel toward the southeast. [ADV after v] ❑ *I know we have to go southeast, more or less.* **4** ADV Something that is **southeast of** a place is positioned to the southeast of it. [ADV of n] ❑ *...a vessel that is believed to have sunk 500 miles southeast of Nova Scotia.* **5** ADJ The **southeast** part of a place, country, or region is the part which is toward the southeast. [ADJ n] ❑ *...rural southeast Kansas.* ❑ *...Southeast Asia.* **6** ADJ A **southeast** wind is a wind that blows from the southeast. [ADJ n] ❑ *Thick clothes keeping the chill southeast wind from freezing his bones.*

1 불가산명사 남동쪽 ❑ 그것은 남동쪽으로 90마일이나 떨어진 갤버스턴에 있는 건물까지 뒤흔들었다. **2** 단수명사 동남부 ❑ 나라 동남부 전역에 기록적인 양의 비가 내렸다. **3** 부사 남동쪽으로 ❑ 우리가 약간 남동쪽으로 가야 한다는 것을 나는 알고 있다. **4** 부사 남동쪽에 ❑ 노바 스코샤 남동쪽 5백 마일 지점에서 침몰된 것으로 여겨지는 배 **5** 형용사 남동부의 ❑ 캔자스 동남부의 전원 지역 ❑ 동남아시아 **6** 형용사 남동쪽에서 불어오는 ❑ 차가운 남동풍이 그의 뼛속까지 스며 들어오는 것을 막아 주는 두꺼운 옷

south|eastern /sa͡ʊθi͡ːstərn/ also **south-eastern** ADJ **Southeastern** means in or from the southeast of a region or country. ❑ *...this city on the southeastern edge of the United States.*

형용사 남동부 지역의 ❑ 미국 남동부 끝자락에 있는 이 도시

south|er|ly /sʌ͡ðərli/ **1** ADJ A **southerly** point, area, or direction is to the south or toward the south. ❑ *We set off in a southerly direction.* **2** ADJ A **southerly** wind is a wind that blows from the south. ❑ *...a strong southerly wind.*

1 형용사 남쪽의 ❑ 우리는 남쪽 방향으로 출발했다. **2** 형용사 남쪽에서 불어오는 ❑ 강한 남풍

south|ern ♦♦◇ /sʌ͡ðərn/ also **Southern** ADJ **Southern** means in or from the south of a region, state, or country. [ADJ n] ❑ *The Everglades National Park stretches across the southern tip of Florida.*

형용사 남부의 ❑ 에버글레이즈 국립공원은 플로리다 남부 지역 끝을 가로질러 뻗어 있다.

south|ern|er /sʌðərnər/ (**southerners**) N-COUNT A **southerner** is a person who was born in or lives in the south of a country. ❏ *Bob Wilson is a Southerner, from Texas.*

가산명사 남부 사람 ❏ 밥 윌슨은 텍사스 출신의 남부 사람이다.

south|ward /saʊθwərd/

The form **southwards** is also used.

southwards도 쓰인다.

ADV **Southward** or **southwards** means toward the south. [ADV after v] ❏ *They drove southward.* ● ADJ **Southward** is also an adjective. ❏ *Instead of her normal southward course towards Alexandria and home, she headed west.*

부사 남쪽으로 ❏ 그들은 남쪽으로 차를 몰았다. ● 형용사 남쪽의 ❏ 그녀는 평소에 자신이 알렉산드리아의 집으로 가는 남쪽 코스 대신, 서쪽으로 향했다.

south|west ♦♦◇ /saʊθwɛst/ also **south-west** ■ N-UNCOUNT The **southwest** is the direction which is halfway between south and west. [also the n] ❏ *...some 500 kilometers to the southwest of Johannesburg.* ② N-SING The **southwest** of a place, country, or region is the part which is in the southwest. ❏ *...the southwest of France.* ③ ADV If you go **southwest**, you travel toward the southwest. [ADV after v] ❏ *We took a plane southwest across the Anatolian plateau to Cappadocia.* ④ ADV Something that is **southwest** of a place is positioned to the southwest of it. [ADV of n] ❏ *It's some 65 miles southwest of Houston.* ⑤ ADJ The **southwest** part of a place, country, or region is the part which is toward the southwest. [ADJ n] ❏ *...a Labor Day festival in southwest Louisiana.* ⑥ ADJ A **southwest** wind is a wind that blows from the southwest. [ADJ n] ❏ *Then the southwest wind began to blow.*

■ 불가산명사 남서쪽 ❏ 요하네스버그의 남서쪽까지 5백 킬로미터 정도 ② 단수명사 남서부 ❏ 프랑스 남서부 ③ 부사 남서쪽으로 ❏ 우리는 아나토리안 고원을 가로질러 카파도키아까지 남서쪽으로 가는 비행기를 탔다. ④ 부사 남서쪽에 ❏ 그곳은 휴스턴의 남서쪽 65마일 정도 지점이다. ⑤ 형용사 남서부의 ❏ 루이지애나 남서부의 노동절 축제 ⑥ 형용사 남서쪽에서 불어오는 ❏ 그러더니 남서풍이 불어오기 시작했다.

south|western /saʊθwɛstərn/ also **south-western** ADJ **Southwestern** means in or from the southwest of a region or country. ❏ *...remote areas in the southwestern part of the country.*

형용사 남서부의 ❏ 국가 남서부에 있는 벽지들

sou|venir /suːvənɪər, BRIT suːvənɪəʳ/ (**souvenirs**) N-COUNT A **souvenir** is something which you buy or keep to remind you of a vacation, place, or event. ❏ *...a souvenir of the summer of 1992.*

가산명사 기념품 ❏ 1992년 여름 행사 기념품

sov|er|eign /sɒvrɪn/ (**sovereigns**) ■ ADJ A **sovereign** state or country is independent and not under the authority of any other country. ❏ *Lithuania and Armenia signed a treaty in Vilnius recognising each other as independent sovereign states.* ② ADJ **Sovereign** is used to describe the person or institution that has the highest power in a country. ❏ *Sovereign power will continue to lie with the Supreme People's Assembly.* ③ N-COUNT A **sovereign** is a king, queen, or other royal ruler of a country. ❏ *In March 1889, she became the first British sovereign to set foot on Spanish soil.*

■ 형용사 자주적인, 독립된 ❏ 리투아니아와 아르메니아는 빌니우스에서 서로를 독립적인 자주 국가로 인정하는 조약에 서명했다. ② 형용사 최고 권력을 가진, 최고의 ❏ 최고 권력은 계속 최고인민회의에 있을 것이다. ③ 가산명사 군주, 국왕 ❏ 1889년 3월, 그녀는 스페인 땅에 발을 디딘 최초의 영국 국왕이 되었다.

sov|er|eign|ty /sɒvrɪnti/ N-UNCOUNT **Sovereignty** is the power that a country has to govern itself or another state or state. ❏ *Britain's concern to protect national sovereignty is far from new.*

불가산명사 통치권 ❏ 국가 통치권을 지키려는 영국의 관심은 전혀 새로운 것이 아니다.

---
                                    sow
---

① VERB USES
② NOUN USE

---

① **sow**/soʊ/ (**sows, sowing, sowed, sown**) ■ V-T If you **sow** seeds or **sow** an area of land **with** seeds, you plant the seeds in the ground. ❏ *Sow the seed in a warm place in February/March.* ② V-T If someone **sows** an undesirable feeling or situation, they cause it to begin and develop. ❏ *He cleverly sowed doubts into the minds of his rivals.* ③ PHRASE If one thing **sows the seeds of** another, it starts the process which leads eventually to the other thing. ❏ *Rich industrialised countries have sown the seeds of global warming.*

■ 타동사 씨를 뿌리다 ❏ 2-3월이 되면 따뜻한 곳에 그 씨를 뿌리세요. ② 타동사 (종지 않은 감정 등을) 싹트게 하다 ❏ 그는 교묘하게 자신의 경쟁자들을 마음속에 의구심을 싹트게 했다. ③ 구 ∼의 씨를 뿌리다 ❏ 부유한 선진 산업 국가들이 지구 온난화의 빌미를 만들었다.

② **sow**/saʊ/ (**sows**) N-COUNT A **sow** is an adult female pig.

가산명사 암퇘지

spa /spɑː/ (**spas**) ■ N-COUNT A **spa** is a place where water with minerals in it comes out of the ground. People drink the water or go in it in order to improve their health. ❏ *...Fiuggi, a spa town famous for its water.* ② N-COUNT A health **spa** is a kind of hotel where people go to exercise and have special treatments in order to improve their health. ❏ *There's also an excellent spa with a large pool, steam room, and sauna.* →see **hotel**

■ 가산명사 온천, 광천 ❏ 약수로 유명한 온천 마을, 퓨기 ② 가산명사 (건강 관련 시설이 있는) 휴양 시설 ❏ 넓은 수영장, 한증탕, 사우나를 구비한 아주 좋은 휴양 시설도 있다.

space ♦♦◇ /speɪs/ (**spaces, spacing, spaced**) ■ N-VAR You use **space** to refer to an area that is empty or available. The area can be any size. For example, you can refer to a large area outside as a large open **space** or to a small area between two objects as a small **space**. ❏ *...cutting down yet more trees to make space for houses.* ❏ *I had plenty of space to write and sew.* ❏ *The space underneath could be used as a storage area.*

■ 가산명사 또는 불가산명사 공간, 여백 ❏ 택지 조성을 위해 아직도 더 많은 나무를 베어 쓰러뜨리는 ❏ 나는 글씨를 쓰고 제본도 할 수 있는 여백이 충분했다. ❏ 아래쪽 공간을 창고로 이용할 수도 있다. C

You should use **space** or **room** to refer to an open or empty area. You do not use **place** as an uncount noun in this sense. **Room** is more likely to be used when you are talking about space inside an enclosed area. ❏ *There's not enough room in the bathroom for both of us... Leave plenty of space between you and the car in front.*

열린 공간이나 빈 공간을 지칭할 때에는 space나 room을 써야 한다. 이런 의미로는 place를 불가산 명사로 쓰지 않는다. room은 둘러싸인 영역 내에 있는 공간을 말할 때 쓰는 경향이 있다. ❏ 욕실에는 우리 둘이 들어갈 공간이 없다... 당신과 앞 차 사이에 충분한 공간을 두세요.

② N-VAR A particular kind of **space** is the area that is available for a particular activity or for putting a particular kind of thing in. ❏ *...the high cost of office space.* ❏ *You don't want your living space to look like a bedroom.* ③ N-UNCOUNT If a place gives a feeling of **space**, it gives an impression of being large and open. ❏ *Large paintings can enhance the feeling of space in small rooms.* ④ N-UNCOUNT If you give someone **space** to think about something or to develop as a person, you allow them the time and freedom to do this. ❏ *You need space to think everything over.* ⑤ N-UNCOUNT The amount of **space** for a topic to be discussed in a document is the number of pages available to discuss the topic. ❏ *We can't promise to publish a reply as space is limited.* ⑥ N-SING A **space of** time is a period of time. ❏ *They've come a long way in a short space of time.* ⑦ N-UNCOUNT **Space** is the area beyond the Earth's atmosphere, where the stars and planets are. ❏ *The six astronauts on board will spend ten days in space.* ❏ *...launching satellites into space.* ⑧ N-UNCOUNT **Space** is the whole area within which everything exists. ❏ *She*

② 가산명사 또는 불가산명사 공간, 장소 ❏ 사무실 공간에 들어가는 많은 경비 ❏ 당신은 당신의 생활공간이 침실처럼 보이는 것은 원하지 않는다. ③ 불가산명사 (장소가) 시원스러움, 널찍함 ❏ 큰 그림을 걸면 작은 방도 시원스러운 느낌을 줄 수 있다. ④ 불가산명사 여지, 이유 ❏ 너는 모든 것을 잘 생각해 볼 수 있는 여유가 필요하다. ⑤ 불가산명사 (내용은 다룰) 공간 ❏ 공간이 제한되어 있기 때문에 답변을 실을 수 있으리라 장담할 수는 없다. ⑥ 단수명사 시간, 기간 ❏ 그들은 짧은 시간에 먼 길을 왔다. ⑦ 불가산명사 우주 ❏ 탑승한 여섯 명의 우주 비행사들은 우주에서 열흘간 지낼 것이다. ❏ 우주로 인공위성을 쏘아 올리기 ⑧ 불가산명사 (사물이 존재하는) 공간 ❏ 그녀는 자신이 시공을 넘나들고

felt herself transcending time and space. **9** V-T If you **space** a series of things, you arrange them so that they are not all together but have gaps or intervals of time between them. □ *Women once again are having fewer children and spacing them further apart.* ● PHRASAL VERB **Space out** means the same as **space**. □ *He talks quite slowly and spaces his words out.* ● **spac|ing** N-UNCOUNT □ *Generous spacing gives healthier trees and better crops.* **10** →see also **spacing, airspace, breathing space, outer space** **11** PHRASE If you are staring **into space**, you are looking straight in front of you, without actually looking at anything in particular, for example because you are thinking or because you are feeling shocked. □ *He just sat in the dressing-room staring into space.* →see **meteor, moon, satellite**

있다는 느낌을 받았다. **9** 타동사 간격을 두다 □ 또다시 여성들이 자녀를 적게 낳고, 자녀들의 나이 터울도 더 크게 벌어지고 있다. ● 구동사 간격을 두다 □ 그는 말을 아주 천천히 하고 단어도 띄엄띄엄 뱉는다. ● 간격 두기 불가산명사 □ 충분한 간격을 두고 나무를 심으면 나무도 더 실해지고 착황도 더 좋다. **11** 구 허공을 □ 그는 분장실에서 허공을 응시하며 그냥 앉아 있었다.

space|craft /spe͟ɪskræft/

Spacecraft is both the singular and the plural form.

spacecraft는 단수형 및 복수형이다.

N-COUNT A **spacecraft** is a rocket or other vehicle that can travel in space. □ *...the world's largest and most expensive unmanned spacecraft.*

가산명사 우주선 □ 세계에서 가장 크고 비싼 무인 우주선

space|ship /spe͟ɪʃɪp/ (**spaceships**) N-COUNT A **spaceship** is a spacecraft that carries people through space. □ *...an alien spaceship.*

가산명사 우주선 □ 외계의 우주선

space shut|tle (**space shuttles**) N-COUNT A **space shuttle** or a **shuttle** is a spacecraft that is designed to travel into space and back to earth several times.

가산명사 우주 왕복선

space sta|tion (**space stations**) N-COUNT A **space station** is a place built for astronauts to live and work in, which is sent into space and then keeps going around the earth. →see **satellite**

가산명사 우주 정거장

spac|ing /spe͟ɪsɪŋ/ N-UNCOUNT **Spacing** refers to the way that typing or printing is arranged on a page, especially in relation to the amount of space that is left between words or lines. □ *Single spacing is used within paragraphs, double spacing between paragraphs.* →see also **space**

불가산명사 자간, 행간 □ 단락 내 행간은 한 줄이고, 단락 간 행간은 두 줄이다.

spa|cious /spe͟ɪʃəs/ ADJ A **spacious** room or other place is large in size or area, so that you can move around freely in it. □ *The house has a spacious kitchen and dining area.*

형용사 넓은, 널찍한 □ 그 집은 주방과 식당이 넓다.

spade /spe͟ɪd/ (**spades**) **1** N-COUNT A **spade** is a tool used for digging, with a flat metal blade and a long handle. □ *... a garden spade.* **2** N-UNCOUNT-COLL **Spades** is one of the four suits in a pack of playing cards. Each card in the suit is marked with one or more black symbols: ♠. □ *...the ace of spades.* ● N-COUNT A **spade** is a playing card of this suit. □ *He would have done better to play a spade now.*

1 가산명사 삽 □ 원예용 삽 **2** 불가산명사-집합 (카드놀이) 스페이드 □ 스페이드의 에이스 카드 ● 가산명사 스페이드 카드 □ 그가 이때 스페이드를 냈으면 더 잘 됐을 텐데.

spa|ghet|ti /spəge͟ti/ N-UNCOUNT **Spaghetti** is a type of pasta. It looks like long pieces of string and is usually served with a sauce.

불가산명사 스파게티

spam /spæ͟m/ (**spams, spamming, spammed**) V-T In computing, to **spam** people or organizations means to send unwanted e-mails to a large number of them, usually as advertising. [COMPUTING] □ *...programs that let you spam the newspapers.* ● N-VAR **Spam** is also a noun. □ *...a small group of people fighting the spam plague.* →see **advertising**

타동사 (컴퓨터) 스팸 메일을 보내다 [컴퓨터] □ 그 신문들을 스팸 메일로 보낼 수 있는 프로그램 ● 가산명사 또는 불가산명사 스팸 메일 □ 골칫거리 스팸 메일과 싸우고 있는 소수의 집단

span /spæ͟n/ (**spans, spanning, spanned**) **1** N-COUNT A **span** is the period of time between two dates or events during which something exists, functions, or happens. □ *The batteries had a life span of six hours.* **2** N-COUNT Your concentration **span** or your attention **span** is the length of time you are able to concentrate on something or be interested in it. □ *His ability to absorb information was astonishing, but his concentration span was short.* **3** V-T If something **spans** a long period of time, it lasts throughout that period of time or relates to that whole period of time. [no passive] □ *His professional career spanned 16 years.* **4** V-T If something **spans** a range of things, all those things are included in it. [no passive] □ *Bernstein's compositions spanned all aspects of music, from symphonies to musicals.* **5** N-COUNT The **span** of something that extends or is spread out sideways is the total width of it from one end to the other. [usu with supp] □ *It is a very pretty butterfly, with a 2 inch wing span.* **6** V-T A bridge or other structure that **spans** something such as a river or a valley stretches right across it. □ *Travellers get from one side to the other by walking across a footbridge that spans a little stream.*

1 가산명사 (활동 등의) 기간 □ 그 건전지는 수명이 6시간이었다. **2** 가산명사 (주의를 집중하는) 시간, 기간 □ 그가 정보를 받아들이는 능력은 놀라울 정도였지만, 집중력이 지속되는 시간이 짧았다. **3** 타동사 (일정한 기간 동안) 지속되다 □ 그의 프로 경력이 16년이었다. **4** 타동사 미치다, 포괄하다 □ 번스타인의 작곡은 심포니에서 뮤지컬에 이르는 모든 종류의 음악을 포괄했다. **5** 가산명사 폭 □ 그것은 날개폭이 2인치인 아주 예쁜 나비이다. **6** 타동사 (다리가 강을) 가로지르다 □ 여행객들은 작은 시내를 가로지르는 인도교를 걸어서 이쪽저쪽으로 오간다.

Word Partnership		span의 연어
N.	life span, time span **1**	
	attention span **2**	
	span years **3**	
ADJ.	short span **1** **5**	
	brief span **1**	

spank /spæ͟ŋk/ (**spanks, spanking, spanked**) V-T If someone **spanks** a child, they punish them by hitting them on the bottom several times with their hand. □ *When I used to do that when I was a kid, my mom would spank me.*

타동사 (손바닥으로) 엉덩이를 때리다 □ 내가 어릴 때 그런 짓을 하면, 엄마가 내 엉덩이를 때리곤 하셨다.

span|ner /spæ͟nər/ (**spanners**) **1** N-COUNT A **spanner** is a metal tool whose end fits around a nut so that you can turn it to loosen or tighten it. [mainly BRIT; AM usually **wrench, monkey wrench**] **2** PHRASE If someone **throws a spanner in the works**, they prevent something happening smoothly in the way that it was planned, by causing a problem or difficulty. [BRIT; AM **throw a wrench, throw a monkey wrench**] □ *A bad result is sure to throw a spanner in the works.*

1 가산명사 스패너 (공구) [주로 영국영어; 미국영어 대개 wrench, monkey wrench] **2** 구 제동을 걸다 [영국영어; 미국영어 throw a wrench, throw a monkey wrench] □ 나쁜 결과가 분명히 일에 제동을 걸 것이다.

spar /spɑ͟ːr/ (**spars, sparring, sparred**) V-RECIP If you **spar with** someone, you box using fairly gentle blows instead of hitting your opponent hard, either when you are training or when you want to test how quickly your opponent reacts. □ *He entered the ring to spar a few one-minute rounds with an old friend.*

상호동사 권투 연습을 하다, 스파링 하다 □ 그는 옛 친구와 1분짜리 스파링을 몇 회전 하기 위해 링으로 올라갔다.

spare ♦◇◇ /spe͟ər/ (**spares, sparing, spared**) **1** ADJ You use **spare** to describe something that is the same as something that you are already using, but that you do not need yet and are keeping ready in case another one is needed. □ *If*

1 형용사 예비의 □ 가능하면 지금 쓰고 있는 안경이 깨지거나 분실될 경우를 대비해서 예비 안경을 하나 마련해 두세요. □ 그가 예비 열쇠를 가지고 있을

possible keep a spare pair of glasses accessible in case your main pair is broken or lost. ❑ He could have taken a spare key. ● N-COUNT **Spare** is also a noun. ❑ Give me the trunk key and I'll get the spare. **2** ADJ You use **spare** to describe something that is not being used by anyone, and is therefore available for someone to use. ❑ They don't have a lot of spare cash. ❑ The spare bedroom is on the second floor. **3** V-I If you have something such as time, money, or space **to spare**, you have some extra time, money, or space that you have not used or which you do not need. [only to-inf] ❑ You got here with ninety seconds to spare. **4** V-T If you **spare** time or another resource **for** a particular purpose, you make it available for that purpose. ❑ She said that she could only spare 35 minutes for our meeting. **5** V-T If a person or a place **is spared**, they are not harmed, even though other people or places have been. [LITERARY] [usu passive] ❑ We have lost everything, but thank God, our lives have been spared. **6** V-T If you **spare** someone an unpleasant experience, you prevent them from suffering it. ❑ I wanted to spare Frances the embarrassment of discussing this subject. ❑ Prisoners are spared the indignity of wearing uniforms. **7** →see also **sparing** **8** PHRASE If you **spare a thought for** an unfortunate person, you make an effort to think sympathetically about them and their bad luck. ❑ Spare a thought for the nation's shopkeepers – consumer sales slid again in May.

수도 있다. ● 가산명사 예비용 ❑ 트렁크 열쇠를 주면 내가 예비 타이어를 가져올게. **2** 형용사 여분의, 예비의 ❑ 그들은 여분의 현금이 많지 않다. ❑ 여분의 방이 2층에 있다. **3** 자동사 여유를 두다, 남다 ❑ 당신은 90초를 남겨 두고 이곳에 도착했다. **4** 타동사 할애하다 ❑ 그녀는 우리 모임에 단 35분밖에 할애할 수 없다고 말했다. **5** 타동사 해를 입지 않다 [문예체] ❑ 우리는 모든 것을 잃었지만, 감사하게도 목숨만은 건졌다. **6** 타동사 (나쁜 일을) 모면하게 하다 ❑ 나는 프란체스가 이 주제에 대해 논의하는 당혹감을 모면하게 해 주고 싶었다. ❑ 죄수들이 죄수복을 입어야 하는 모멸은 면하고 있다. **8** 구 (남의 불행에 대해) 생각하다, 가여워 하는 마음을 갖다 ❑ 이 나라 상인들의 고통을 생각해 보세요. 5월 달에 소비자 매출이 또다시 떨어졌어요.

Thesaurus　　spare의 참조어

ADJ.　additional, backup, emergency, extra, reserve **1** **2**

Word Partnership　　spare의 연어

N.　spare **change**, spare **equipment** **1**
　　spare **bedroom** **2**
　　a **moment** to spare, **time** to spare **3**
　　spare **someone's life** **5**

spare part (**spare parts**) N-COUNT **Spare parts** are parts that you can buy separately to replace old or broken parts in a piece of equipment. They are usually parts that are designed to be easily removed or fitted. ❑ In the future the machines will need spare parts and maintenance.

가산명사 예비 부품 ❑ 앞으로 그 기계는 예비 부품과 정비가 필요할 것이다.

spare time N-UNCOUNT Your **spare time** is the time during which you do not have to work and you can do whatever you like. ❑ In her spare time she read books on cooking.

불가산명사 여가 시간 ❑ 그녀는 여가 시간에 요리에 관한 책을 읽는다.

spar|ing /spɛərɪŋ/ ADJ Someone who is **sparing with** something uses it or gives it only in very small quantities. ❑ I've not been sparing with the garlic. ● **spar|ing|ly** ADV [ADV after v] ❑ Medication is used sparingly.

형용사 -을 아끼는 ❑ 나는 마늘을 아끼지 않고 넣어 왔다. ● 아껴서, 조금씩 부사 ❑ 약물은 조금씩 사용해야 한다.

spark ◆◇◇ /spɑrk/ (**sparks, sparking, sparked**) **1** N-COUNT A **spark** is a tiny bright piece of burning material that flies up from something that is burning. ❑ The fire gradually got bigger and bigger. Sparks flew off in all directions. **2** N-COUNT A **spark** is a flash of light caused by electricity. It often makes a loud sound. ❑ He passed an electric spark through a mixture of gases. **3** V-I If something **sparks**, sparks of fire or light come from it. ❑ The wires were sparking above me. **4** V-T If a burning object or electricity **sparks** a fire, it causes a fire. ❑ A dropped cigarette may have sparked the fire. **5** N-COUNT A **spark of** a quality or feeling, especially a desirable one, is a small but noticeable amount of it. ❑ His music lacked that vital spark of imagination. **6** V-T If one thing **sparks** another, the first thing causes the second thing to start happening. ❑ My teacher organized a unit on space exploration that really sparked my interest. ● PHRASAL VERB **Spark off** means the same as **spark**. ❑ That incident sparked it off. **7** PHRASE If **sparks fly** between people, they discuss something in an excited or angry way. ❑ They are not afraid to tackle the issues or let the sparks fly when necessary. →see **fire**

1 가산명사 불똥 ❑ 갈수록 불이 점점 더 커져 갔다. 불똥이 사방으로 날렸다. **2** 가산명사 불꽃, 스파크 ❑ 그는 혼합 기체 속으로 전기 스파크를 통하게 했다. **3** 자동사 불꽃이 튀다 ❑ 내 머리 위 전선에서 불꽃이 튀고 있었다. **4** 타동사 불을 내다, 화재를 촉발시키다 ❑ 버려진 담배꽁초 하나 때문에 그 불이 난 것이었는지도 모른다. **5** 가산명사 (재능 등의) 번득임 ❑ 그의 음악에는 결정적으로 번득이는 상상력이 없었다. **6** 타동사 촉발시키다, 유발하다 ● 선생님이 정말 내 관심을 유발하는 우주 탐험대를 편성했다. ● 구동사 촉발시키다, 유발하다 ❑ 그 일이 그것을 유발했다. **7** 구 (비유적) 불꽃이 튀다 ❑ 그들은 그런 문제들에 달려들거나 필요하다면 불꽃 튀는 설전을 벌이는 것을 두려워하지 않는다.

Word Partnership　　spark의 연어

N.　spark **from a fire** **1**
　　spark **conflict**, spark **debate**, spark **interest**, spark **a reaction** **6**
V.　**ignite** a spark, **provide** a spark **5**

spar|kle /spɑrk³l/ (**sparkles, sparkling, sparkled**) **1** V-I If something **sparkles**, it is clear and bright and shines with a lot of very small points of light. ❑ The jewels on her fingers sparkled. ❑ His bright eyes sparkled. ● N-UNCOUNT **Sparkle** is also a noun. ❑ ...the sparkle of colored glass. **2** N-COUNT **Sparkles** are small points of light caused by light reflecting off a clear bright surface. ❑ ...sparkles of light. **3** V-I Someone who **sparkles** is lively, intelligent, and witty. [APPROVAL] ❑ She sparkles, and has as much zest as a person half her age. ● N-UNCOUNT **Sparkle** is also a noun. ❑ There was little sparkle in their performance. ● **spar|kling** ADJ ❑ He is sparkling and versatile in front of the camera.

1 자동사 반짝이다 ❑ 그녀 손가락의 보석들이 반짝였다. ❑ 그의 빛나는 눈이 반짝였다. ● 반짝임 불가산명사 반짝임 ❑ 채색 유리의 반짝임 **2** 가산명사 광채 ❑ 빛의 광채 **3** 자동사 생기가 있다; 재기 발랄하다 [마음에 듦] ❑ 그녀는 재기발랄하고, 자기 나이의 절반밖에 안 되는 사람만큼 활력이 넘친다. ● 불가산명사 생기, 재기 ❑ 그들의 공연에는 생기가 별로 없었다. ● 생기에 찬, 재기 넘치는 형용사 ❑ 카메라 앞에서 그는 생기 넘치고 다재다능하다.

spar|kling /spɑrklɪŋ/ ADJ **Sparkling** drinks are slightly carbonated. ❑ ...a glass of sparkling wine. →see also **sparkle**

형용사 거품이 이는; 탄산을 첨가한 ❑ 탄산이 든 와인 한 잔

spar|row /spærou/ (**sparrows**) N-COUNT A **sparrow** is a small brown bird that is very common in the United States and Britain.

가산명사 참새

sparse /spɑrs/ (**sparser, sparsest**) ADJ Something that is **sparse** is small in number or amount and spread out over an area. ❑ Many slopes are rock fields with sparse vegetation. ❑ He was a tubby little man in his fifties, with sparse hair. ● **sparse|ly** ADV ❑ ...the sparsely populated interior region, where there are few roads.

형용사 성긴, 드문드문한, 희박한 ❑ 많은 경사지들이 초목이 드문드문한 암반 지대이다. ❑ 그는 머리숱이 적은 오십 대의 땅딸막한 남자였다. ● 드문드문, 희박하게 부사 ❑ 도로가 별로 없는, 인구가 희박한 내륙 지방

spar|tan /spɑrt³n/ ADJ A **spartan** lifestyle or existence is very simple or strict, with no luxuries. ❑ Their spartan lifestyle prohibits a fridge or a phone.

형용사 스파르타식의; 검소하고 엄격한 ❑ 그들의 검소하고 엄격한 생활양식은 냉장고나 전화도 금지한다.

A

spasm /spǽzəm/ (spasms) N-VAR A spasm is a sudden tightening of your muscles, which you cannot control. ❑ A muscular spasm in the coronary artery can cause a heart attack.

가산명사 또는 불가산명사 경련, 쥐 ❑ 관상 동맥 부위의 근육 경련은 심장 발작을 유발할 수 있다.

B

spat /spǽt/ (spats) Spat is a past tense and past participle of **spit**.

spit의 과거, 과거 분사

spate /spéɪt/ (spates) N-COUNT A spate of things, especially unpleasant things, is a large number of them that happen or appear within a short period of time. ❑ ...the recent spate of attacks on horses.

가산명사 (안 좋은 일의) 빈발 ❑ 최근 빈발하는 말 습격 사건

C

spa|tial /spéɪʃ°l/ ■ ADJ Spatial is used to describe things relating to areas. [ADJ n] ❑ ...the spatial distribution of black employment and population in South Africa. ■ ADJ Your spatial ability is your ability to see and understand the relationships between shapes, spaces, and areas. [ADJ n] ❑ His manual dexterity and fine spatial skills were wasted on routine tasks.

■ 형용사 지역적인 ❑ 남아프리카 공화국 내 흑인 고용과 흑인 인구의 지역적 분포 ■ 형용사 공간적인 ❑ 그의 뛰어난 손재주와 훌륭한 공간 지각 능력이 틀에 박힌 업무에 낭비되었다.

D

E

spat|ter /spǽtər/ (spatters, spattering, spattered) V-T/V-I If a liquid spatters a surface or you spatter a liquid over a surface, drops of the liquid fall on an area of the surface. ❑ He stared at the rain spattering on the glass. ❑ Gently turn the fish, being careful not to spatter any hot butter on yourself.

타동사/자동사 튀다; 튀기다 ❑ 그는 유리창에 부딪쳐 튀는 빗물을 지켜보았다. ❑ 몸에 뜨거운 버터가 튀지 않도록 주의하면서, 천천히 생선을 뒤집으세요.

F

speak ♦♦♦ /spíːk/ (speaks, speaking, spoke, spoken) ■ V-I When you speak, you use your voice in order to say something. ❑ He tried to speak, but for once, his voice had left him. ❑ I rang the hotel and spoke to Louie. ❑ She cried when she spoke of Oliver. ● spo|ken ADJ [ADJ n] ❑ ...a marked decline in the standards of written and spoken English in Britain. ■ V-I When someone speaks to a group of people, they make a speech. ❑ When speaking to the seminar Mr. Franklin spoke of his experience, gained on a recent visit to Trinidad. ❑ He's determined to speak at the Democratic Convention. ■ V-I If you speak for a group of people, you make their views and demands known, or represent them. ❑ He said it was the job of the Church to speak for the underprivileged. ❑ I speak for all 7,000 members of our organization. ■ V-T If you speak a foreign language, you know the language and are able to have a conversation in it. ❑ He doesn't speak English. ■ V-I People sometimes mention something that has been written by saying what the author speaks of. ❑ Throughout the book Liu speaks of the abuse of Party power. ■ V-RECIP If two people are not speaking, they no longer talk to each other because they have quarreled. [with neg] ❑ He is not speaking to his mother because of her friendship with his ex-wife. ■ V-I If you say that something speaks for itself, you mean that its meaning or quality is so obvious that it does not need explaining or pointing out. [no cont] ❑ ...the figures speak for themselves – low order books, bleak prospects at home and a worsening outlook for exports. ■ PHRASE If a person or thing is spoken for or has been spoken for, someone has claimed them or asked for them, so no-one else can have them. ❑ She'd probably drop some comment about her "fiancé" into the conversation so that he'd think she was already spoken for. ■ PHRASE If you speak well of someone or speak highly of someone, you say good things about them. If you speak ill of someone, you criticize them. ❑ Both spoke highly of the Russian president. ■ PHRASE You use so to speak to draw attention to the fact that you are describing or referring to something in a way that may be amusing or unusual rather than completely accurate. ❑ I ought not to tell you but I will, since you're in the family, so to speak. ■ to speak your mind →see mind. to speak volumes →see volume

■ 자동사 말하다, 이야기하다 ❑ 그는 말하려고 했지만, 이번에는 목소리가 나오지 않았다. ❑ 나는 호텔에 전화를 해서 루이와 통화했다. ❑ 그녀는 올리버에 관한 이야기를 하면서 울었다. ● 구두의, 구어의 형용사 ❑ 영국 내에서 문어와 구어 수준의 두드러진 퇴보 ■ 자동사 연설하다 ❑ 세미나에서 연설할 때 프랭클린 씨는 최근의 트리니다드 방문 때 얻은 자신의 경험에 대해 이야기했다. ❑ 그는 민주당 전당 대회에서 연설하기로 결심했다. ■ 자동사 대변하다 ❑ 그는 사회적으로 혜택 받지 못하는 이들을 대변하는 것이 교회의 의무라고 말했다. ❑ 내가 우리 단체 7천 명 회원 모두를 대변한다. ■ 타동사 (외국어를) 구사하다 ❑ 그는 영어를 못한다. ■ 자동사 (책에서) ~에 관해 이야기하다 ❑ 리우는 그 책 전반에서 권력의 남용에 관해 이야기한다. ■ 상호동사 말을 하지 않다 ❑ 그는 전처와 어머니의 친분 때문에 어머니와 말을 하지 않고 있다. ■ 자동사 자명하다 ❑ 그 수치들이 보여 주는 건 자명하다. 수주량이 낮고 내수 전망도 없고 수출 전망도 악화되고 있다. ■ 구 예약되다 ❑ 그녀는 자신이 이미 임자 있는 사람이라고 대화 중에 자신의 '약혼자'에 대한 이야기를 넌지시 흘렸을 것이다. ■ 구 칭찬하다; ~을 헐뜯다 ❑ 둘 다 러시아 대통령을 칭찬했다. ■ 구 말하자면 ❑ 내가 너에게 말해 줄 의무는 없지만 말해 주겠어, 말하자면 너도 한 가족이니까.

G

H

I

J

K

L

M

N

There are some differences in the way the verbs speak and talk are used. When you speak, you could, for example, be addressing someone or making a speech. Talk is more likely to be used when you are referring to a conversation or discussion. ❑ I talked about it with my family at dinner... Sometimes we'd talk all night. Talk can also be used to emphasize the activity of saying things, rather than the words that are spoken. ❑ She thought I talked too much.

동사 speak와 talk를 쓰는 방식에는 차이가 있다. speak는, 누구에게 말을 하거나 연설을 하는 것이다. talk는 대화나 토론을 지칭할 때 쓰는 경향이 있다. ❑ 나는 그것에 관해 내 가족과 저녁식사 때 얘기했다... 가끔 우리는 밤새도록 얘기하곤 했다. talk는 하는 말보다는 말하는 행위를 강조하기 위해서 쓸 수도 있다. ❑ 그녀는 내가 말을 너무 많이 한다고 생각했다.

O

P

Q

Thesaurus
speak의 참조어

V.   articulate, communicate, declare, talk ■

R

S

Word Partnership
speak의 연어

ADV.   speak **directly** ■

N.   chance to speak, opportunity to speak, speak the truth ■ ■

speak **English**, speak **a (foreign) language** ■

T

▶**speak out** PHRASAL VERB If you speak out against something or in favor of something, you say publicly that you think it is bad or good. ❑ As tempers rose, he spoke out strongly against some of the radical ideas for selling off state-owned property.

구동사 (의견 등을) 거리낌 없이 말하다 ❑ 화가 치밀어 오르자, 그는 국가 소유의 자산을 매각하려는 급진적인 생각에 대해 거리낌 없이 강하게 비난했다.

U

▶**speak up** ■ PHRASAL VERB If you speak up, you say something, especially to defend a person or protest about something, rather than just saying nothing. ❑ Uncle Herbert never argued, never spoke up for himself. ■ PHRASAL VERB If you ask someone to speak up, you are asking them to speak more loudly. [no cont] ❑ I'm quite deaf – you'll have to speak up.

■ 구동사 (침묵하지 않고) 자기 의견을 말하다 ❑ 허버트 삼촌은 언쟁하는 법이 없었고, 자기 주장을 내세우는 법이 없었다. ■ 구동사 더 크게 말하다 ❑ 나는 귀가 잘 안 들려. 네가 좀 더 크게 말해야 할 거야.

V

W

-speak /-spíːk/ COMB IN N-UNCOUNT -speak is used to form nouns which refer to the kind of language used by a particular person or by people involved in a particular activity. You use -speak when you disapprove of this kind of language because it is difficult for other people to understand. [DISAPPROVAL] ❑ Team building, motivation and performance feature widely in modern business-speak.

복합형-불가산명사 - 분야의 전문 용어 [탐탁잖음] ❑ 팀 구성, 동기 부여, 직무 수행 등은 현대 사업체들에서 널리 쓰이는 용어들이다.

X

Y

speak|er ♦◇◇ /spíːkər/ (speakers) ■ N-COUNT A speaker at a meeting, conference, or other gathering is a person who is making a speech or giving a talk. ❑ Among the speakers at the gathering was Treasury Secretary Nicholas Brady. ❑ Bruce Wyatt will be the guest speaker at next month's meeting. ■ N-COUNT A speaker

■ 가산명사 연사 ❑ 그 회합의 연사들 중에는 재무 장관 니콜라스 브래디가 있었다. ❑ 브루스 와이어트가 다음 달 모임의 초청 연사가 될 것이다. ■ 가산명사 특정 언어 구사자 ❑ 인구의 5분의 1이 러시아 어를

Z

of a particular language is a person who speaks it, especially one who speaks it as their first language. ❑ *...in the Ukraine, where a fifth of the population are Russian speakers.* ◼ N-PROPER; N-VOC In the legislature or parliament of many countries, the **Speaker** is the person who is in charge of meetings. [*Mr/Madam N*] ❑ *...the Speaker of the Polish Parliament.* ◼ N-COUNT A **speaker** is a person who is speaking. ❑ *From a simple gesture or the speaker's tone of voice, the Japanese listener gleans the whole meaning.* ◼ N-COUNT A **speaker** is a piece of electrical equipment, for example part of a radio or set of equipment for playing CDs or tapes, through which sound comes out. ❑ *For a good stereo effect, the speakers should not be too wide apart.*

구사하는 우크라이나에서 ◼ 고유명사; 호격명사 의장 ❑ 폴란드 의회 의장 ◼ 가산명사 말하는 사람 ❑ 그 일본인 청자는 간단한 제스처나 화자의 목소리 톤에서 전체적인 의미를 알아낸다. ◼ 가산명사 확성기, 스피커 ❑ 양질의 입체 음향 효과를 위해서는, 확성기가 서로 너무 멀리 떨어져 있어서는 안 됩니다.

speak|ing /spíːkɪŋ/ ◼ N-UNCOUNT **Speaking** is the activity of giving speeches and talks. ❑ *It would also train women union members in public speaking and decision-making.* ◼ PHRASE You can say "**speaking as** a parent" or "**speaking as** a teacher," for example, to indicate that the opinion you are giving is based on your experience as a parent or as a teacher. ❑ *Well, speaking as a journalist I'm dismayed by the amount of pressure there is for pictures of combat.* ◼ PHRASE You use **speaking** in expressions such as **generally speaking** and **technically speaking** to indicate which things or which particular aspect of something you are talking about. [PHR with cl] ❑ *Generally speaking there was no resistance to the idea.*

◼ 불가산명사 말하기; 연설 ❑ 그곳에서는 여성 조합원들에게 대중 연설과 의사 결정도 교육을 것이다. ◼ 구 - 입장에서 말하면 ❑ 글쎄, 기자 입장에서 말하면, 나는 전투 장면을 찍은 사진을 구해 오라는 엄청난 압력에 곤혹스럽다. ◼ 구 -하게 말하면 ❑ 전반적으로 말하면 그 안에 대해 아무런 반대도 없었다.

spear /spíər/ (spears, spearing, speared) ◼ N-COUNT A **spear** is a weapon consisting of a long pole with a sharp metal point attached to the end. ◼ V-T If you **spear** something, you push or throw a pointed object into it. ❑ *Spear a piece of fish with a carving fork and dip it in the batter.* →see **army**

◼ 가산명사 창 ◼ 타동사 찌르다 ❑ 큰 포크로 생선 한 조각을 찔러서 반죽에 담그세요.

spear|head /spíərhed/ (spearheads, spearheading, spearheaded) V-T If someone **spearheads** a campaign or an attack, they lead it. [JOURNALISM] ❑ *...Esther Rantzen, who is spearheading a national campaign against bullying.*

타동사 선봉에 서다, 진두지휘하다 [언론] ❑ 전국적인 왕따 반대 운동을 진두지휘하고 있는 에스더 란첸

spec /spɛk/ (specs) ◼ N-PLURAL Someone's **specs** are their glasses. [INFORMAL] [also a pair of N] ❑ *...a young businessman in his specs and suit.* ◼ N-COUNT The **spec** for something, especially a machine or vehicle, is its design and the features included in it. [INFORMAL] ❑ *The standard spec includes stainless steel holding tanks.* ◼ PHRASE If you do something **on spec**, you do it hoping to get something that you want, but without being asked or without being certain to get it. [INFORMAL] ❑ *When searching for a job Adrian favors networking and writing letters on spec.*

◼ 복수명사 안경 [비격식체] ❑ 안경을 끼고 정장을 갖춰 입은 한 젊은 사업가 ◼ 가산명사 사양(仕樣) [비격식체] ❑ 표준 사양에는 스테인리스강 저장 탱크가 포함되어 있다. ◼ 구 무기적으로, 요행수를 바라고 [비격식체] ❑ 일자리를 구할 때 에이드리언은 요행수를 바라고 사람들과 연락을 취하며 편지를 쓰는 방법을 선호한다.

spe|cial ♦♦♦ /spɛ́ʃəl/ (specials) ◼ ADJ Someone or something that is **special** is better or more important than other people or things. ❑ *You're very special to me, darling.* ❑ *My special guest will be comedian Ben Elton.* ◼ ADJ **Special** means different from normal. [ADJ n] ❑ *In special cases, a husband can deduct the travel expenses of his wife who accompanies him on a business trip.* ❑ *So you didn't notice anything special about him?* ◼ ADJ You use **special** to describe someone who is officially appointed or who has a particular position specially created for them. [ADJ n] ❑ *Due to his wife's illness, he returned to the State Department as special adviser to the President.* ◼ ADJ **Special** institutions are for people who have serious physical or mental problems. [ADJ n] ❑ *Police are still searching for a convicted rapist, who escaped from Broadmoor special hospital yesterday.* ◼ ADJ You use **special** to describe something that relates to one particular person, group, or place. [ADJ n] ❑ *Every anxious person will have his or her own special problems or fears.* ◼ N-COUNT A **special** is a product, program, or meal which is not normally available, or which is made for a particular purpose. ❑ *...complaints about the Hallowe'en special, "Ghostwatch."* ❑ *Grocery stores have to offer enough specials to bring people into the store.*

◼ 형용사 특별한 ❑ 당신은 내게 매우 특별해, 여보. ❑ 특별 손님으로 코미디언 벤 엘턴을 모실 겁니다. ◼ 형용사 특수한, 특별한 ❑ 특별한 경우에는, 남편이 출장 여행에 동반한 아내의 여행 경비를 공제할 수도 있다. ❑ 그럼 너는 그에 대해서 특이한 걸 아무 것도 알아채지 못했니? ◼ 형용사 특별 직책의 ❑ 아내의 병 때문에, 그는 대통령 특별 고문으로서 국무부에 복귀했다. ◼ 형용사 특수한 (수용 시설) ❑ 경찰이 아직, 어제 브로드무어 특수 병원을 탈출한, 유죄 선고를 받은 강간범을 찾아 수색 중이다. ◼ 형용사 특유의, 특별한 ❑ 모든 불안해하는 사람들은 자신만의 특별한 문제나 두려움을 갖고 있기 마련이다. ◼ 가산명사 특별 프로그램; 특별 상품 ❑ 핼러윈 데이 특별 프로그램 '고스트위치'에 대한 불평 ❑ 식료품점에서는 손님을 불러들일 수 있을 만큼 충분히 특별 상품을 제공해야 한다.

Thesaurus	*special*의 참조어
ADJ.	distinctive, exceptional, unique; (ant.) ordinary ◼ ◼

spe|cial ef|fect (special effects) N-COUNT In a movie, **special effects** are unusual pictures or sounds that are created by using special techniques. ❑ *...a Hollywood horror film with special effects that are not for the nervous.*

가산명사 특수 효과 ❑ 집 많은 사람들은 관람을 삼가야 할, 특수 효과가 가미된 할리우드 공포 영화

spe|cial|ise /spɛ́ʃəlaɪz/ →see **specialize**

spe|cial|ist ♦♢♢ /spɛ́ʃəlɪst/ (specialists) N-COUNT A **specialist** is a person who has a particular skill or knows a lot about a particular subject. [usu N n, n N, N in/on n] ❑ *Peckham, himself a cancer specialist, is well aware of the wide variations in medical practice.*

가산명사 전문가, 전공자 ❑ 그 자신이 암 전문가인 페컴은 다양한 형태의 의료 시술에 대해 잘 알고 있다.

spe|cial|ity /spɛ̀ʃiǽlɪti/ (specialities) ◼ N-COUNT Someone's **speciality** is a particular type of work that they do most or do best, or a subject that they know a lot about. [mainly BRIT; AM usually **specialty**] ❑ *My father was a historian of repute. His speciality was the history of Germany.* ◼ N-COUNT A **speciality** of a particular place is a special food or product that is always very good there. [mainly BRIT; AM usually **specialty**] [with supp] ❑ *Rhineland dishes are a speciality of the restaurant.*

◼ 가산명사 전공, 전문 [주로 영국영어; 미국영어 대개 specialty] ❑ 내 아버지는 저명한 역사학자였다. 아버지의 전공은 독일 역사였다. ◼ 가산명사 특산품, 명물 [주로 영국영어; 미국영어 대개 specialty] ❑ 라인란트 요리가 그 식당의 명물이다.

spe|cial|ize ♦♢♢ /spɛ́ʃəlaɪz/ (specializes, specializing, specialized) [BRIT also **specialise**] V-I If you **specialize in** a thing, you know a lot about it and concentrate a great deal of your time and energy on it, especially in your work or when you are studying or training. You also use **specialize** to talk about a restaurant which concentrates on a particular type of food. ❑ *...a University professor who specializes in the history of the Russian empire.* ● **spe|cial|i|za|tion** /spɛ̀ʃəlaɪzéɪʃən/ (specializations) N-VAR ❑ *This degree offers a major specialization in Social Policy alongside a course in Sociology.*

[영국영어 specialise] 자동사 -을 전공하다, -을 전문으로 다루다 ❑ 러시아 제국사를 전공하는 대학 교수 ● 전문화; 전문 분야 가산명사 또는 불가산명사 ❑ 이 학위 과정은 사회학 강좌와 함께 사회 정책에 대한 주 전공 과정을 제공한다.

spe|cial|ized /spɛ́ʃəlaɪzd/ [BRIT also **specialised**] ADJ Someone or something that is **specialized** is trained or developed for a particular purpose or area of knowledge. ❑ *Cocaine addicts get specialized support from knowledgeable staff.*

[영국영어 specialised] 형용사 전문의, 전문화된 ❑ 코카인 중독자들은 지식을 갖춘 직원들로부터 전문적인 지원을 받는다.

spe|cial|ly /spɛ́ʃəli/ ◼ ADV If something has been done **specially for** a particular person or purpose, it has been done only for that person or purpose.

◼ 부사 특별히 ❑ 피부가 민감한 사람들을 위해 특별히 고안된 비누 ❑ 패트릭은 특별히 개조된 컴퓨터 장비를

A

...*a soap specially designed for those with sensitive skins.* □ *Patrick needs to use specially adapted computer equipment.* ◻ ADV **Specially** is used to mean more than usually or more than other things. [INFORMAL] □ *Stay in bed extra late or get up specially early.*

사용할 필요가 있다. ◻ 부사 특별히, 유달리 [비격식체] □ 아주 늦게까지 침대에 누워 있거나 특별히 일찍 일어나세요.

B

spe|cial of|fer (special offers) N-COUNT A **special offer** is a product, service, or program that is offered at reduced prices or rates. □ *Ask about special offers on our new 2-week holidays.*

가산명사 특별 제품 □ 저희 회사에서 새로 내놓은 2주간의 휴가 여행 특별 상품에 대해 문의하세요.

C

spe|cial|ty /spɛʃəlti/ (specialties) ◻ N-COUNT Someone's **specialty** is a particular type of work that they do most or do best, or a subject that they know a lot about. [AM; BRIT **speciality**] □ *His specialty is international law.* ◻ N-COUNT A **specialty** of a particular place is a special food or product that is always very good there. [AM; BRIT **speciality**] □ *...seafood, paella, empanadas, and other specialties.*

D

◻ 가산명사 전문, 전공 [미국영어; 영국영어 speciality] □ 그의 전공은 국제법이다. ◻ 가산명사 명물, 특제품 [미국영어; 영국영어 speciality] □ 해산물 요리, 파엘랴, 엠파나다, 그리고 기타 명물 요리

E

spe|cies ♦◇◇ /spiʃiz/

Species is both the singular and the plural form.

species는 단수형 및 복수형이다.

F

N-COUNT A **species** is a class of plants or animals whose members have the same main characteristics and are able to breed with each other. □ *Pandas are an endangered species.* →see **plant**, **zoo**

가산명사 종(種) □ 팬더는 멸종 위기에 처한 종이다.

G

spe|cif|ic ♦♦◇ /spɪsɪfɪk/ ◻ ADJ You use **specific** to refer to a particular fixed area, problem, or subject. [ADJ n] □ *Massage may help to increase blood flow to specific areas of the body.* □ *There are several specific problems to be dealt with.* ◻ ADJ If someone is **specific**, they give a description that is precise and exact. You can also use **specific** to describe their description. □ *She declined to be more specific about the reasons for the separation.* ◻ ADJ Something that is **specific to** a particular thing is connected with that thing only. □ *Send your résumé with a cover letter that is specific to that particular job.* ◻ COMB IN ADJ **Specific** is also used after nouns. □ *Most studies of trade have been country-specific.*

H

◻ 형용사 특정한 □ 마사지는 신체의 특정 부위의 혈액 순환 증진을 도울 수 있다. □ 처리해야 할 특정한 문제가 몇 가지 있다. ◻ 형용사 명확한, 구체적인 □ 그녀는 별거 이유에 대해 더 구체적으로 밝히기를 거부했다. ◻ 형용사 ~에 특별히 관련된 □ 해당 특정 업무와 관련된 자기소개서와 함께 이력서를 보내십시오. ● 복합형-형용사 -별의 □ 교역에 관한 대부분의 연구는 국가별로 이루어져 왔다.

I

spe|cif|cal|ly ♦◇◇ /spɪsɪfɪkli/ ◻ ADV You use **specifically** to emphasize that something is given special attention and considered separately from other things of the same kind. [EMPHASIS] [ADV with v] □ *...the first nursing home designed specifically for people with AIDS.* □ *We haven't specifically targeted school children.* ◻ ADV You use **specifically** to add something more precise or exact to what you have already said. [ADV with group] □ *Death frightens me, specifically my own death.* □ *...the Christian, and specifically Protestant, religion.* ◻ ADV You use **specifically** to indicate that something has a restricted nature, as opposed to being more general in nature. [ADV adj] □ *...a specifically female audience.* ◻ ADV If you state or describe something **specifically**, you state or describe it precisely and clearly. [ADV with v] □ *I specifically asked for this steak rare.*

J

K

◻ 부사 특별히 [강조] □ 에이즈 환자들을 위해 특별히 고안된 최초의 요양소 □ 우리는 특별히 학생들을 표적으로 삼은 적은 없다. ◻ 부사 특히 □ 죽음은, 특히 내 자신의 죽음은 나를 두렵게 한다. ◻ 기독교, 특히 신교 ◻ 부사 특히 □ 특히 여성 관객층 ◻ 부사 똑똑히, 분명히 □ 제가 이 스테이크를 설익혀 달라고 분명히 부탁했어요.

L

spe|cif|ca|tion /spɛsɪfɪkeɪʃən/ (specifications) N-COUNT A **specification** is a requirement which is clearly stated, for example about the necessary features in the design of something. □ *I'd like to buy some land and have a house built to my specification.*

M

가산명사 명세 사항; 설계 명세서 □ 땅을 좀 사서 내 설계 명세서대로 집을 짓고 싶다.

N

spe|cif|ics /spɪsɪfɪks/ N-PLURAL The **specifics** of a subject are the details of it that need to be considered. □ *Things improved when we got down to the specifics.*

복수명사 세부 사항 □ 우리가 세부 사항에 신경을 쓰자 사정이 나아졌다.

O

spe|ci|fy /spɛsɪfaɪ/ (specifies, specifying, specified) ◻ V-T If you **specify** something, you give information about what is required or should happen in a certain situation. □ *They specified a spacious entrance hall.* ◻ V-T If you **specify** what should happen or be done, you explain it in an exact and detailed way. □ *Each recipe specifies the size of egg to be used.* □ *A new law specified that houses must be a certain distance back from the water.*

P

◻ 타동사 조건으로서 지정하다, 명시하다 □ 그들은 넓은 현관홀을 조건으로 들었다. ◻ 타동사 상술하다, 자세히 밝히다 □ 각각의 조리법에는 사용되는 계란의 크기가 구체적으로 밝혀져 있다. □ 새 법안에는 주택들이 물에서 일정한 거리를 두고 있어야 한다고 상술되어 있다.

Q

spe|ci|men /spɛsɪmɪn/ (specimens) ◻ N-COUNT A **specimen** is a single plant or animal which is an example of a particular species or type and is examined by scientists. [usu with supp] □ *200,000 specimens of fungus are kept at the Komarov Botanical Institute.* ◻ N-COUNT A **specimen of** something is an example of it which gives an idea of what the whole of it is like. [usu with supp] □ *Job applicants have to submit a specimen of handwriting.* ◻ N-COUNT A **specimen** is a small quantity of someone's urine, blood, or other body fluid which is examined in a medical laboratory, in order to find out if they are ill or if they have been drinking alcohol or taking drugs. □ *He refused to provide a specimen.*

R

S

◻ 가산명사 표본 □ 코마로프 식물 연구소에는 20만 가지의 버섯 표본이 보존되어 있다. ◻ 가산명사 견본 □ 구직 지원자들은 육필 견본을 제출해야 한다. ◻ 가산명사 (의학 검사용) 시료 □ 그는 시료 제출을 거부했다.

T

speck /spɛk/ (specks) ◻ N-COUNT A **speck** is a very small stain, mark, or shape. [oft N of n] □ *He has even cut himself shaving. There is a speck of blood by his ear.* ◻ N-COUNT A **speck** is a very small piece of a powdery substance. [oft N of n] □ *Billy leaned forward and brushed a speck of dust off his shoes.*

◻ 가산명사 (작은) 얼룩, 자국, 반점 □ 그는 면도를 하다 베기까지 했다. 귀 옆에 핏자국이 있다. ◻ 가산명사 작은 알갱이, 입자 □ 빌리는 몸을 앞으로 숙여 구두에 묻은 먼지를 털어 냈다.

U

specs /spɛks/ →see **spec**

V

Word Link	spect ≈ looking : spect**acle**, spect**acular**, spect**ator**

W

spec|ta|cle /spɛktək⁰l/ (spectacles) ◻ N-PLURAL Glasses are sometimes referred to as **spectacles**. [FORMAL] [also a pair of N] □ *He looked at me over the tops of his spectacles.* ◻ N-COUNT A **spectacle** is a strange or interesting sight. □ *It was a spectacle not to be missed.* ◻ N-VAR A **spectacle** is a grand and impressive event or performance. □ *94,000 people turned up for the spectacle.*

◻ 복수명사 안경 [격식체] □ 그가 안경테 너머로 나를 보았다. ◻ 가산명사 장관, 기이한 광경 □ 그것은 놓칠 수 없는 장관이었다. ◻ 가산명사 또는 불가산명사 구경거리, 쇼 □ 그 구경거리를 보기 위해 9만 4천 명의 사람들이 모여들었다.

X

spec|tacu|lar ♦◇◇ /spɛktækyələr/ (spectaculars) ◻ ADJ Something that is **spectacular** is very impressive or dramatic. □ *...spectacular views of the Sugar Loaf Mountain.* ● **spec|tacu|lar|ly** ADV □ *My turnover increased spectacularly.* ◻ N-COUNT A **spectacular** is a show or performance which is very grand and impressive. [usu n N] □ *...a television spectacular.*

Y

◻ 형용사 장관을 이루는; 극적인 □ 슈가로프 산의 장관을 이루는 풍경 ● 극적으로 부사 □ 내 거래액이 극적으로 증가했다. ◻ 가산명사 (호화로운) 구경거리, 쇼 □ 호화판 텔레비전 쇼

Z

spec|ta|tor /spɛkteɪtər, BRIT spɛkteɪtər/ (spectators) N-COUNT A **spectator** is someone who watches something, especially a sports event. □ *Thirty thousand spectators watched the final game.*

가산명사 관중, 관객 □ 삼만 명의 관중이 그 결승전을 지켜보았다.

spec|ter /spɛktər/ (**specters**) [BRIT **spectre**] N-COUNT If you refer to the **specter of** something unpleasant, you are referring to something that you are frightened might occur. [usu the N of n] ❑ *The arrests raised the specter of revenge attacks.*

[영국영어 spectre] 가산명사 두려운 것; 위험 ❑ 그 체포로 인해 보복 공격의 위험이 제기되었다.

spec|trum /spɛktrəm/ (**spectra** or **spectrums**) **1** N-SING **The spectrum** is the range of different colors which is produced when light passes through a glass prism or through a drop of water. A rainbow shows the colors in the spectrum. **2** N-COUNT A **spectrum** is a range of a particular type of thing. ❑ *She'd seen his moods range across the emotional spectrum.* ❑ *Politicians across the political spectrum have denounced the act.*

1 단수명사 스펙트럼, 분광 **2** 가산명사 범위, 영역 ❑ 그녀는 그의 기분을 형성하는 감정의 영역이 아주 다양함을 보았었다. ❑ 정치권 전반의 정치가들이 그 행위를 비난해 왔다.

spec|u|late ♦◇◇ /spɛkyəleɪt/ (**speculates, speculating, speculated**) **1** V-T/V-I If you **speculate** about something, you make guesses about its nature or identity, or about what might happen. ❑ *Critics of the project speculate about how many hospitals could be built instead.* ❑ *The doctors speculate that he died of a cerebral haemorrhage caused by a blow on the head.* ● **spec|u|la|tion** /spɛkyəleɪʃⁿn/ (**speculations**) N-VAR ❑ *The President has given out of his way to dismiss speculation over the future of the economy minister.* **2** V-I If someone **speculates** financially, they buy property, stocks, or shares, in the hope of being able to sell them again at a higher price and make a profit. ❑ *The banks made too many risky loans which now can't be repaid, and they speculated in property whose value has now dropped.*

1 타동사/자동사 추측하다 ❑ 그 사업에 대한 비판자들은 그 사업 대신에 얼마나 많은 병원을 지을 수 있는지를 추정한다. ❑ 의사들은 그가 두부 타격으로 인한 뇌출혈로 사망한 것으로 추측한다. ● 추측 가산명사 또는 불가산명사 ❑ 대통령은 경제 장관의 미래에 대한 추측을 잠재우기 위해 각별히 노력해 왔다. **2** 자동사 투기하다 ❑ 은행들은 현재 상황이 불가능한 위험한 대출을 너무 많이 해 주었고, 이제 가치가 떨어져 버린 부동산에 투기를 했다.

Word Partnership speculate의 연어

N. **analysts** speculate, speculate **about a game,** speculate **about an outcome 1**

---

spec|u|la|tive /spɛkyəleɪtɪv, -lətɪv, BRIT spɛkyʊlətɪv/ **1** ADJ A piece of information that is **speculative** is based on guesses rather than knowledge. ❑ *The papers ran speculative stories about the mysterious disappearance of Eddie Donagan.* **2** ADJ **Speculative** is used to describe activities which involve buying goods or shares, or buildings and properties, in the hope of being able to sell them again at a higher price and make a profit. ❑ *Thousands of pensioners were persuaded to mortgage their homes to invest in speculative bonds.*

1 형용사 추측에 근거한 ❑ 신문들은 에디 도너건의 수수께끼 같은 실종에 대한 추측성 기사들을 실었다. **2** 형용사 투기적인 ❑ 수천 명의 연금 생활자들이 설득에 넘어가 집을 저당 잡히고 투기성 채권에 투자했다.

spec|u|la|tor /spɛkyəleɪtər/ (**speculators**) N-COUNT A **speculator** is a person who speculates financially. ❑ *A speculator buys cheap and sells dear.*

가산명사 투기자 ❑ 투기자는 싸게 사서 비싸게 판다.

sped /spɛd/ **Sped** is a past tense and past participle of **speed.**

speed의 과거, 과거 분사

speech ♦♦◇ /spitʃ/ (**speeches**) **1** N-UNCOUNT **Speech** is the ability to speak or the act of speaking. ❑ *...the development of speech in children.* ❑ *Intoxication interferes with speech and coordination.* **2** N-SING Your **speech** is the way in which you speak. ❑ *His speech became increasingly thick and nasal.* **3** N-UNCOUNT **Speech** is spoken language. ❑ *He could imitate in speech or writing most of those he admired.* **4** N-COUNT A **speech** is a formal talk which someone gives to an audience. ❑ *She is due to make a speech on the economy next week.* ❑ *He delivered his speech in French.* **5** →see also **direct speech, indirect speech** →see **election**

1 불가산명사 언어 능력; 언어 행위 ❑ 아이들의 언어 능력 발달 ❑ 취하면 언어 능력과 신체 통제력에 지장이 생긴다. **2** 단수명사 말투, 화법 ❑ 그의 말투는 더욱더 비음이 섞이고 불분명해졌다. **3** 불가산명사 말, 구두 언어 ❑ 그는 말이나 글로 자신이 존경하는 사람들 대부분을 흉내 낼 수 있었다. **4** 가산명사 연설, 담화 ❑ 그녀는 다음 주에 경제에 대해 담화를 발표할 예정이다. ❑ 그는 프랑스 어로 연설을 했다.

Word Partnership speech의 연어

ADJ. **free** speech **3**
famous speech, **major** speech, **political** speech, **recent** speech **4**
N. **acceptance** speech, **campaign** speech, **keynote** speech, speech **writing 4**
V. **deliver a** speech, **give a** speech, **make a** speech, **prepare a** speech **4**

---

speech|less /spitʃlɪs/ ADJ If you are **speechless**, you are temporarily unable to speak, usually because something has shocked you. ❑ *Alex was almost speechless with rage and despair.*

형용사 말을 못 하는 ❑ 앨릭스는 분노와 절망으로 거의 말을 할 수가 없었다.

speed ♦♦◇ /spid/ (**speeds, speeding, sped, speeded**)

The form of the past tense and past participle is **sped** in meaning **5** but **speeded** for the phrasal verb.

과거 및 과거 분사는 **5**의미로 sped이지만, 구동사는 speeded이다.

---

1 N-VAR The **speed** of something is the rate at which it moves or travels. ❑ *He drove off at high speed.* ❑ *Wind speeds reached force five.* **2** N-COUNT The **speed** of something is the rate at which it happens or is done. ❑ *In the late 1850s the speed of technological change quickened.* **3** N-UNCOUNT **Speed** is very fast movement or travel. ❑ *Speed is the essential ingredient of all athletics.* ❑ *He put on a burst of speed.* **4** N-UNCOUNT **Speed** is a very fast rate at which something happens or is done. ❑ *I was amazed at his speed of working.* **5** V-I If you **speed** somewhere, you move or travel there quickly, usually in a vehicle. ❑ *Trains will speed through the Channel Tunnel at 186mph.* **6** V-I Someone who **is speeding** is driving a vehicle faster than the legal speed limit. [usu cont] ❑ *This man was not qualified to drive and was speeding.* ● **speed|ing** N-UNCOUNT ❑ *He was fined for speeding last year.* **7** N-UNCOUNT **Speed** is an illegal drug such as amphetamine which some people take to increase their energy and excitement. [INFORMAL] ❑ *I take speed most days and cocaine every weekend.* **8** to **pick up speed** →see **pick up**

1 가산명사 또는 불가산명사 속도 ❑ 그는 빠른 속도로 차를 몰고 떠났다. ❑ 풍속이 강도 5에 도달했다. **2** 가산명사 속도 ❑ 1850년대 후반에 기술 변화 속도가 빨라졌다. **3** 불가산명사 빠름 ❑ 빠르기는 모든 육상 경기의 필수 요소이다. ❑ 그는 폭발적으로 속도를 늘렸다. **4** 불가산명사 빠름 ❑ 나는 그가 일하는 신속성에 놀랐다. **5** 자동사 빠르게 가다 ❑ 기차는 시속 186마일로 해서 터널을 주파할 것이다. **6** 자동사 속도위반을 하다 ❑ 이 사람은 무면허에 속도위반을 하고 있었다. ● 속도위반 불가산명사 ❑ 그는 작년에 속도위반으로 벌금을 냈다. **7** 불가산명사 각성제 [비격식체] ❑ 나는 거의 매일 각성제를 먹고 주말마다 코카인을 마신다.

▶**speed up 1** PHRASAL VERB When something **speeds up** or when you **speed it up**, it moves or travels faster. ❑ *You notice that your breathing has speeded up a bit.* **2** PHRASAL VERB When a process or activity **speeds up** or when something **speeds it up**, it happens at a faster rate. ❑ *Job losses are speeding up.* ❑ *I had already taken steps to speed up a solution to the problem.*

1 구동사 속도가 늘다; 속도를 높이다 ❑ 여러분은 자신의 호흡 속도가 약간 빨라졌음을 인식합니다. **2** 구동사 속도가 늘다; 속도를 높이다 ❑ 실업 속도가 증가하고 있다. ❑ 나는 이미 그 문제의 해결을 서두르기 위한 조처를 취한 참이다.

speed dial (**speed dials**) N-VAR **Speed dial** is a facility on a telephone that allows you to call a number by pressing a single button rather than by dialing the full number. ❑ *Who's at the top of your speed dial list?*

가산명사 또는 불가산명사 단축 다이얼 ❑ 당신의 단축 다이얼 목록 맨 처음에 있는 사람은 누구입니까?

speed lim|it (speed limits) N-COUNT The **speed limit** on a road is the maximum speed at which you are legally allowed to drive. ❑ *I was fined $158 for exceeding the speed limit by 15km/h.*

가산명사 제한 속도 ❑ 제한 속도보다 시속 15킬로미터 빨리 달려서 벌금 158달러를 징수당했다.

speed|om|eter /spidɒmɪtər/ (speedometers) N-COUNT A **speedometer** is the instrument in a vehicle which shows how fast the vehicle is moving.

가산명사 속도계

speedy /spidi/ (speedier, speediest) ADJ A **speedy** process, event, or action happens or is done very quickly. ❑ *We wish Bill a speedy recovery.*

형용사 빠른, 신속한 ❑ 빌이 속히 회복하기를 바랍니다.

spell ♦◇◇ /spɛl/ (spells, spelling, spelled, spelt)

> The forms **spelled** and **spelt** can both be used for the past tense and past participle, but **spelt** is more common in British English than in American English.

> spelled와 spelt 모두 과거 및 과거 분사로 쓸 수 있지만, spelt가 미국영어보다 영국영어에서 더 일반적이다.

◻ V-T When you **spell** a word, you write or speak each letter in the word in the correct order. ❑ *He gave his name and then helpfully spelt it.* ❑ *How do you spell "potato"?* ● PHRASAL VERB **Spell out** means the same as **spell**. ❑ *If I don't know a word, I ask them to spell it out for me.* ◻ V-I Someone who can **spell** knows the correct order of letters in words. [no cont] ❑ *It's shocking how students can't spell these days.* ◻ V-T If something **spells** a particular result, often an unpleasant one, it suggests that this will be the result. [no cont] ❑ *If the irrigation plan goes ahead, it could spell disaster for the birds.* ◻ N-COUNT A **spell of** a particular type of weather or a particular activity is a short period of time during which this type of weather or activity occurs. ❑ *There has been a long spell of dry weather.* ◻ N-COUNT A **spell** is a situation in which events are controlled by a magical power. ❑ *They say she died after a witch cast a spell on her.* ◻ →see also **spelling**

◻ 타동사 철자를 쓰다; 철자를 말해 주다 ❑ 그는 자기 이름을 말하고 친절하게 철자를 불러 주었다. ❑ 'potato'를 어떻게 쓰지? ● 구동사 철자를 쓰다; 철자를 말해 주다 ❑ 나는 어떤 단어를 모르면 그들에게 철자를 불러 달라고 부탁한다. ◻ 자동사 철자를 알다, 맞춤법을 알다 ❑ 요즈음 학생들은 충격적일 정도로 맞춤법을 모른다. ◻ 타동사 의미하다, 가져오다 ❑ 그 관개 사업 계획이 계속 추진된다면, 새들에게는 재앙을 가져다줄지도 모른다. ◻ 가산명사 (특정한 날씨 등이 지속되는) 한동안 ❑ 오랫동안 건조한 기후가 계속되고 있다. ◻ 가산명사 주문; 마법 ❑ 사람들은 마녀가 그녀에게 주문을 건 후 그녀가 죽었다고 말한다.

Thesaurus   spell의 참조어

N.   period, phase ◻

Word Partnership   spell의 연어

N.   spell **a name/word** ◻
     spell **the end of** *something*, spell **trouble** ◻
V.   **can/can't** spell *something* ◻
     break a spell, **cast a** spell ◻

▶**spell out** ◻ PHRASAL VERB If you **spell** something **out**, you explain it in detail or in a very clear way. ❑ *Be assertive and spell out exactly how you feel.* ◻ →see **spell** 1

◻ 구동사 상세히 설명하다 ❑ 단호한 태도로 당신이 느끼는 바를 상세히 설명하세요.

spell|check /spɛltʃɛk/ (spellchecks, spellchecking, spellchecked) also spell check ◻ V-T If you **spellcheck** something you have written on a computer, you use a special program to check whether you have made any spelling mistakes. [COMPUTING] ❑ *This model allows you to spellcheck over 100,000 different words.* ◻ N-COUNT If you run a **spellcheck** over something you have written on a computer, you use a special program to check whether you have made any spelling mistakes. [COMPUTING]

◻ 타동사 맞춤법 검사를 하다 [컴퓨터] ❑ 이 모델로는 10만 개 이상의 단어에 대해 맞춤법 검사를 할 수 있습니다. ◻ 가산명사 맞춤법 검사 [컴퓨터]

spell|check|er /spɛltʃɛkər/ (spellcheckers) also spell checker N-COUNT A **spellchecker** is a special program on a computer which you can use to check whether something you have written contains any spelling mistakes. [COMPUTING]

가산명사 맞춤법 검사 프로그램 [컴퓨터]

spell|ing /spɛlɪŋ/ (spellings) ◻ N-COUNT A **spelling** is the correct order of the letters in a word. ❑ *In most languages adjectives have slightly different spellings for masculine and feminine.* ◻ N-UNCOUNT **Spelling** is the ability to spell words in the correct way. It is also an attempt to spell a word in the correct way. ❑ *His spelling is very bad.* ◻ →see also **spell**

◻ 가산명사 철자, 맞춤법 ❑ 대부분의 언어에서 형용사는 남성형과 여성형의 철자가 약간 다르다. ◻ 불가산명사 맞춤법[철자법]에 맞게 쓰는 능력 ❑ 그는 맞춤법 실력이 아주 형편없다.

spelt /spɛlt/ **Spelt** is a past tense and past participle form of **spell**. [mainly BRIT]

spell의 과거, 과거 분사 [주로 영국영어]

spend ♦♦♦ /spɛnd/ (spends, spending, spent) ◻ V-T When you **spend** money, you pay money for things that you want or need. ❑ *By the end of the holiday I had spent all my money.* ❑ *Businessmen spend enormous amounts advertising their products.* ◻ V-T If you **spend** time or energy doing something, you use your time or effort doing it. ❑ *Engineers spend much time and energy developing brilliant solutions.* ◻ V-T If you **spend** a period of time in a place, you stay there for a period of time. ❑ *We spent the night in a hotel.* ◻ N-COUNT The **spend** on a particular thing is the amount of money that is spent on it, or will be spent. [BUSINESS] ❑ *...the marketing and advertising spend.*

◻ 타동사 (돈을) 쓰다, 소비하다 ❑ 휴가가 끝날 무렵 나는 돈을 이미 다 써 버렸다. ❑ 사업가들은 자신들의 상품을 광고하는 데 막대한 금액을 쓴다. ◻ 타동사 (노력 등을) 들이다, 기울이다 ❑ 기술자들은 훌륭한 해결책을 개발하는 데 많은 시간과 정력을 들인다. ◻ 타동사 (시간을) 보내다, 지내다 ❑ 우리는 한 호텔에서 그날 밤을 보냈다. ◻ 가산명사 비용 [경제] ❑ 마케팅 및 광고 비용

> Do not confuse **spend** and **pass**. If you **spend** a period of time doing something or **spend** time in a place, you do that thing or stay in that place for all of the time you are talking about. ❑ *I spent three days cleaning our apartment....a hotel where we could spend the night.* If you do something while you are waiting for something else, you can say you do it to "**pass the time.**" ❑ *He had brought along a book to pass the time.* You can say that time **has passed** in order to show that a period of time has finished. ❑ *The first few days passed... The time seems to have passed so quickly.*

> spend와 pass를 혼동하지 마시오. 무엇을 하면서 일정 기간의 시간을 spend하거나 어떤 장소에서 시간을 광고하는 데 막대한 금액을 쓴다. ❑ 타동사 그것을 하거나 그 장소에 머무는 것이다. ❑ 나는 내 아파트를 청소하면서 3일을 보냈다....우리가 그날 밤을 보낼 수 있었던 호텔. 무엇을 기다리면서 다른 무엇을 하면, 'pass the time'하기 위해 그것을 한다고 말할 수 있다. ❑ 그는 시간을 보내려고 책을 한 권 가져왔었다. 일정 기간의 시간이 끝났음을 알려주기 위해 시간이 has passed라고 말할 수 있다. ❑ 처음 며칠이 지나갔다... 시간이 너무도 빨리 지나간 것 같다.

Word Partnership   spend의 연어

N.   spend **billions/millions**, **companies** spend, **consumers** spend, spend **money** ◻
     spend **an amount** ◻ ◻
     spend **energy**, spend **time** ◻
     spend **a day**, spend **hours/minutes**, spend **months/ weeks/years**, spend **a night**, spend **a weekend** ◻
V.   **afford to** spend, **expect to** spend, **going to** spend, **plan to** spend ◻-◻

A B C D E F G H I J K L M N O P Q R S T U V W X Y Z

spend|er /spɛndər/ (**spenders**) N-COUNT If a person or organization is a big spender or a compulsive spender, for example, they spend a lot of money or are unable to stop themselves from spending money. ❑ *The Swiss are Europe's biggest spenders on food.*

spent /spɛnt/ Spent is the past tense and past participle of **spend**.

sperm /spɜrm/ (**sperms**)

> Sperm can also be used as the plural form.

1 N-COUNT A **sperm** is a cell which is produced in the sex organs of a male animal and can enter a female animal's egg and fertilize it. ❑ *Conception occurs when a single sperm fuses with an egg.* **2** N-UNCOUNT **Sperm** is used to refer to the liquid that contains sperm when it is produced. ❑ *...a sperm donor.*

spew /spyu/ (**spews, spewing, spewed**) V-T/V-I When something **spews** out a substance or when a substance **spews** from something, the substance flows out quickly in large quantities. ❑ *The volcano spewed out more scorching volcanic ashes, gases and rocks.*

sphere /sfɪər/ (**spheres**) **1** N-COUNT A **sphere** is an object that is completely round in shape like a ball. ❑ *Because the earth spins, it is not a perfect sphere.* **2** N-COUNT A **sphere of** activity or interest is a particular area of activity or interest. ❑ *...the sphere of international politics.* →see **volume**

spice /spaɪs/ (**spices, spicing, spiced**) **1** N-MASS A **spice** is a part of a plant, or a powder made from that part, which you put in food to give it flavor. Cinnamon, ginger, and paprika are spices. ❑ *...herbs and spices.* **2** V-T If you **spice** something that you say or do, you add excitement or interest to it. ❑ *They spiced their conversations and discussions with intrigue.* • PHRASAL VERB **Spice up** means the same as **spice**. ❑ *Her publisher wants her to spice up her stories with sex.* →see Word Web: **spice**

spiced /spaɪst/ ADJ Food that is **spiced** has had spices or other strong-tasting foods added to it. ❑ *Every dish was served heavily spiced.*

spicy /spaɪsi/ (**spicier, spiciest**) ADJ **Spicy** food is strongly flavored with spices. ❑ *Thai food is hot and spicy.* →see **spice**

spi|der /spaɪdər/ (**spiders**) N-COUNT A **spider** is a small creature with eight legs. Most types of spider make structures called webs in which they catch insects for food.

spike /spaɪk/ (**spikes**) N-COUNT A **spike** is a long piece of metal with a sharp point. ❑ *...a 15-foot wall topped with iron spikes.*

spike heels N-PLURAL **Spike heels** are women's shoes with very high narrow heels. [AM; BRIT **stilettos**] [also *a pair of n*] ❑ *..women wearing spike heels.*

spiky /spaɪki/ ADJ Something that is **spiky** has one or more sharp points. ❑ *Her short spiky hair is damp with sweat.*

spill /spɪl/ (**spills, spilling, spilled, spilt**)

> The forms **spilled** and **spilt** can both be used for the past tense and past participle, but **spilt** is more common in British English than in American English.

1 V-T/V-I If a liquid **spills** or if you **spill** it, it accidentally flows over the edge of a container. ❑ *70,000 tonnes of oil spilled from the tanker.* ❑ *He always spilled the drinks.* **2** N-COUNT A **spill** is an amount of liquid that has spilled from a container. ❑ *She wiped a spill of milkshake off the counter.* **3** V-T/V-I If the contents of a bag, box, or other container **spill** or **are spilled**, they come out of the container onto a surface. ❑ *A number of bags had split and were spilling their contents.* **4** V-I If people or things **spill** out of a place, they come out of it in large numbers. ❑ *Tears began to spill out of the boy's eyes.*

spill|age /spɪlɪdʒ/ (**spillages**) N-VAR If there is a **spillage**, a substance such as oil escapes from its container. **Spillage** is also used to refer to the substance that escapes. ❑ *...an oil spillage off the coast of Texas.*

spin ♦◇◇ /spɪn/ (**spins, spinning, spun**) **1** V-T/V-I If something **spins** or if you **spin** it, it turns quickly around a central point. ❑ *The latest discs, used for small portable computers, spin 3600 times a minute.* ❑ *He spun the wheel sharply and made a U turn in the middle of the road.* • N-VAR **Spin** is also a noun. ❑ *This driving mode allows you to move off in third gear to reduce wheel-spin in icy conditions.* **2** V-I If your head **is**

가산명사 소비자 ❑ 스위스 인들은 유럽 최대 식품 소비자이다.

spend의 과거, 과거 분사

> sperm은 복수형으로도 쓰일 수 있다.

1 가산명사 정자 ❑ 하나의 정자가 난자와 결합할 때 수정이 이루어진다. **2** 불가산명사 정액 ❑ 정액 기증자

타동사/자동사 뿜어내다, 분출하다; 뿜어져 나오다, 분출되다 ❑ 그 화산이 더 많은 뜨거운 화산재와 가스, 암석 등을 뿜어냈다.

1 가산명사 구체, 구 ❑ 지구는 자전하기 때문에 완벽한 구체가 아니다. **2** 가산명사 (활동 등의) 영역, 분야 ❑ 국제 정치 분야

1 물질명사 양념, 향신료 ❑ 약초와 향신료류 **2** 타동사 흥취를 돋우다, 묘미를 더하다 ❑ 그들은 일부러 궁금증을 자아냄으로써 대화와 토론에 묘미를 더했다. • 구동사 흥취를 돋우다, 묘미를 더하다 ❑ 출판사는 그녀가 이야기에 성적인 요소를 가미하기를 원한다.

형용사 양념을 넣은 ❑ 모든 요리는 양념을 듬뿍 넣어 차려져 나왔다.

형용사 양념 맛이 강한 ❑ 태국 음식은 양념 맛이 강하다.

가산명사 거미

가산명사 긴 못, 대못 ❑ 꼭대기에 쇠못을 박은 15피트 높이의 담

복수명사 뾰족구두 [미국영어; 영국영어 stilettos] ❑ 뾰족구두를 신은 여자들

형용사 뾰족뾰족한 ❑ 그녀의 짧고 삐죽삐죽한 머리는 땀으로 축축하게 젖었다.

> spilled와 spilt 모두 과거 및 과거 분사로 쓸 수 있지만, spilt는 미국영어보다 영국영어에서 더 일반적이다.

1 타동사/자동사 쏟아지다, 엎질러지다; 쏟다, 엎지르다 ❑ 유조선으로부터 7만 톤의 기름이 유출되었다. ❑ 그는 늘 음료수를 엎질렀다. **2** 가산명사 쏟은 액체 ❑ 그녀는 카운터에 엎지른 밀크셰이크를 닦아 냈다. **3** 타동사/자동사 새다, 흐르다 ❑ 여러 개의 가방이 찢어져서 내용물이 새고 있었다. **4** 자동사 쏟아져 나오다 ❑ 소년의 두 눈에서 눈물이 쏟아지기 시작했다.

가산명사 또는 불가산명사 유출; 유출물 ❑ 텍사스 연안에서의 기름 유출

1 타동사/자동사 돌다, 회전하다; 돌리다, 회전시키다 ❑ 소형 휴대용 컴퓨터에 쓰이는 최신형 디스크는 분당 3,600회 회전한다. ❑ 그는 도로 한가운데서 핸들을 급격히 돌려 유턴을 했다. • 가산명사 또는 불가산명사 회전 ❑ 이 주행 모드는 빙판길에서 3단 기어로 출발할

Word Web   spice

While researching the use of **spices** in cooking, scientists discovered that many of them have strong disease-prevention properties. Bacteria can grow quickly on food and cause a variety of serious illnesses in humans. The researchers found that many spices are extremely antibacterial. For example, **garlic**, **onion**, allspice, and oregano kill almost all common germs. **Cinnamon**, tarragon, cumin and **chili peppers** also eliminate about 75% of bacteria. And even common, everyday **black pepper** destroys about 25% of all microbes. The research also found a connection between hot climates and **spicy** food and cold climates and **bland** food.

garlic

onion

chili pepper

ginger

black pepper

cinnamon

cloves

spinning, you feel unsteady or confused, for example because you are drunk, ill, or excited. ❑ *My head was spinning from the wine.* ◳ N-SING If someone puts a certain **spin** on an event or situation, they interpret it and try to present it in a particular way. [INFORMAL] ❑ *He interpreted the vote as support for the constitution and that is the spin his supporters are putting on the results today.* ◳ N-UNCOUNT In politics, **spin** is the way in which political parties try to present everything they do in a positive way to the public and the media. ❑ *The public is sick of spin and tired of promises. It's time for performance politics.* ◳ N-SING If you go for **a spin** or take a car for **a spin**, you make a short trip in a car just to enjoy yourself. ❑ *Tom Wright celebrated his 99th birthday by going for a spin in his sporty Mazda.* ◳ V-T When people **spin**, they make thread by twisting together pieces of a fiber such as wool or cotton using a device or machine. ❑ *Michelle will also spin a customer's wool fleece to specification at a cost of $2.25 an ounce.* ◳ N-UNCOUNT In a game such as tennis or baseball, if you put **spin** on a ball, you deliberately make it spin rapidly when you hit it or throw it. ❑ *He threw it back again, putting a slight spin on the ball.*

수 있게 해서 차바퀴의 공회전을 줄어 줍니다. ◳ 자동사 어지럽다, (눈앞이) 빙빙 돈다 ❑ 와인을 마셨더니 머리가 어지러웠다. ◳ 단수명사 (특정한) 해석 [비격식체] ❑ 그는 그 투표를 헌법에 대한 지지로 이해했고 그것이 그의 지지자들이 오늘 결과에 부여하고 있는 해석이다. ◳ 불가산명사 (정당 등의) 자화자찬 ❑ 대중은 자화자찬과 공약에 넌더리가 난다. 이제는 실행하는 정치를 해야 할 때이다. ◳ 단수명사 드라이브, 한바탕 달리기 ❑ 톰 라이트는 자기 마즈다 스포츠카를 타고 한바탕 드라이브하는 것으로 99번째 생일을 자축했다. ◳ 타동사 (실을) 잣다 ❑ 미셸은 온스당 2.25달러의 비용에 손님의 양털을 주문 내역대로 잣는 일도 할 것이다. ◳ 불가산명사 (테니스 등의) 스핀, 회전 ❑ 그는 공에 살짝 회전을 걸어서 되던졌다.

Word Partnership		spin의 연어
N.	spin **a wheel** ◳	
ADJ.	**positive** spin ◳ ◳	

▶**spin off** PHRASAL VERB To **spin off** something such as a company means to create a new company that is separate from the original organization. [BUSINESS] ❑ *He rescued the company and later spun off its textile division into a separate quoted entity.*

구동사 (회사 등을) 분리 신설하다 [경제] ❑ 그는 그 회사를 구제하여 나중에 섬유 분야를 분리해서 독립 상장 법인을 신설했다.

▶**spin out** PHRASAL VERB If you **spin** something **out**, you make it last longer than it normally would. ❑ *My wife's solicitor was anxious to spin things out for as long as possible.*

구동사 오래가게 하다 ❑ 내 아내의 변호사는 사태를 가능한 한 오래 끌고 싶어 했다.

spin|ach /spɪnɪtʃ/ N-UNCOUNT **Spinach** is a vegetable with large dark green leaves that you chop up and boil in water before eating.

불가산명사 시금치

spi|nal /spaɪnªl/ ADJ **Spinal** means relating to your spine. [ADJ n] ❑ ...*spinal fluid.* →see **nervous system**

형용사 척추의 ❑ 척수액

spin doc|tor (**spin doctors**) N-COUNT In politics, a **spin doctor** is someone who is skilled in public relations and who advises political parties on how to present their policies and actions. [INFORMAL] ❑ ...*two spin doctors in the transport department.*

가산명사 공보 비서관, 언론 담당자 [비격식체] ❑ 교통성 내 두 명의 공보 비서관

spine /spaɪn/ (**spines**) ◳ N-COUNT Your **spine** is the row of bones down your back. ❑ ...*injuries to his spine.* ◳ N-COUNT The **spine** of a book is the narrow stiff part which the pages and covers are attached to. ❑ ...*a book with "Lifestyle" on the spine.* ◳ N-COUNT **Spines** are also long, sharp points on an animal's body or on a plant. ❑ *An adult hedgehog can boast 7,500 spines.*

◳ 가산명사 등뼈, 척추 ❑ 그의 척추 손상 ◳ 가산명사 책등 ❑ 책등에 '생활양식'이라고 쓰인 책 ◳ 가산명사 가시 ❑ 성장한 고슴도치는 7,500개의 가시를 낸다.

spin-off (**spin-offs**) ◳ N-COUNT A **spin-off** is an unexpected but useful or valuable result of an activity that was designed to achieve something else. ❑ *The company put out a report on commercial spin-offs from its research.* ◳ N-COUNT A **spin-off** is a book, film, or television series that comes after and is related to a successful book, film, or television series. ❑ *The film is a spin-off from the American TV series "Sabrina The Teenage Witch."*

◳ 가산명사 부산물, 파생 효과 ❑ 그 회사는 자사의 연구로부터 발생한 상업적 파생 효과에 관한 보고서를 발표했다. ◳ 가산명사 파생 상품 ❑ 그 영화는 미국 텔레비전 시리즈 '십 대 마녀 사브리나'의 파생 상품이다.

spi|ral /spaɪrəl/ (**spirals**, **spiraling**, **spiraled**) [BRIT, sometimes AM **spiralling**, **spiralled**] ◳ N-COUNT A **spiral** is a shape which winds round and round, with each curve above or outside the previous one. ❑ *The maze is actually two interlocking spirals.* ● ADJ **Spiral** is also an adjective. [ADJ n] ❑ ...*a spiral staircase.* ◳ V-T/V-I If something **spirals** or **is spiraled** somewhere, it grows or moves in a spiral curve. ❑ *Vines spiraled upward toward the roof.* ❑ *The aircraft began spiraling out of control.* ● N-COUNT **Spiral** is also a noun. ❑ *Larks were rising in spirals from the ridge.* ◳ V-I If an amount or level **spirals**, it rises quickly and at an increasing rate. ❑ *Production costs began to spiral.* ❑ ...*spiraling health care costs.* ● N-SING **Spiral** is also a noun. ❑ ...*an inflationary spiral.* ◳ V-I If an amount or level **spirals** downward, it falls quickly and at an increasing rate. ❑ *House prices will continue to spiral downwards.* ● N-SING **Spiral** is also a noun. ❑ ...*a spiral of debt.* →see **circle**

[영국영어, 미국영어 가끔 spiralling, spiralled] ◳ 가산명사 나선 ❑ 그 미로는 사실상 맞물려 있는 두 개의 나선이다. ● 형용사 나선형의 ❑ 나선형 계단 ◳ 타동사/자동사 나선형을 그리다, 나선형으로 움직이다 ❑ 덩굴이 지붕 쪽으로 나선을 그리며 뻗어 올라갔다. ❑ 그 비행기는 제어가 안 되고 나선형으로 돌기 시작했다. ● 가산명사 나선형 움직임 ❑ 종달새들이 산등성이에서 나선형으로 날아오르고 있었다. ◳ 자동사 급상승하다 ❑ 생산 비용이 급상승하기 시작했다. ❑ 급상승하는 의료비 ● 단수명사 급상승 ❑ 인플레이션 급상승 ◳ 자동사 소용돌이치다 ❑ 집값이 계속 급격히 하락할 것이다. ● 단수명사 소용돌이 ❑ 빚의 소용돌이

spire /spaɪər/ (**spires**) N-COUNT The **spire** of a building such as a church is the tall pointed structure on the top. ❑ ...*a church spire poking above the trees.*

가산명사 첨탑 ❑ 나무들 위로 뾰족 솟은 교회 첨탑

spir|it ♦♦◇ /spɪrɪt/ (**spirits**, **spiriting**, **spirited**) ◳ N-SING Your **spirit** is the part of you that is not physical and that consists of your character and feelings. ❑ *The human spirit is virtually indestructible.* ◳ N-COUNT A person's **spirit** is the nonphysical part of them that is believed to remain alive after their death. ❑ *His spirit has left him and all that remains is the shell of his body.* ◳ N-COUNT A **spirit** is a ghost or supernatural being. ❑ *In the Middle Ages branches were hung outside country houses as a protection against evil spirits.* ◳ N-UNCOUNT **Spirit** is the courage and determination that helps people to survive in difficult times and to keep their way of life and their beliefs. ❑ *She was a very brave girl and everyone who knew her admired her spirit.* ◳ N-UNCOUNT **Spirit** is the liveliness and energy that someone shows in what they do. ❑ *They played with spirit.* ◳ N-SING The **spirit** in which you do something is the attitude you have when you are doing it. ❑ *Their problem can only be solved in a spirit of compromise.* ◳ N-UNCOUNT A particular kind of **spirit** is the feeling of loyalty to a group that is shared by the people who belong to the group. ❑ *There is a great sense of team spirit among the British Olympic squad.* ◳ N-SING A particular kind of **spirit** is the set of ideas, beliefs, and aims that are held by a group of people. ❑ ...*the real spirit of the Labour movement.* ◳ N-SING The **spirit** of something such as a law or an agreement is the way that it was intended to be interpreted or applied. ❑ *The requirement for work permits violates the spirit of the 1950 treaty.* ◳ N-COUNT You can refer to a person as a particular kind of **spirit** if they show a certain

◳ 단수명사 정신 ❑ 인간의 정신은 사실상 파괴할 수 없다. ◳ 가산명사 영혼 ❑ 그의 영혼은 그를 떠나 버렸고 남은 것은 그의 껍데기인 육신이다. ◳ 가산명사 유령 ❑ 중세 시대에는 악령을 막기 위해 시골집들이 집 밖에 나뭇가지를 내걸었다. ◳ 불가산명사 기백, 용기 ❑ 그녀는 매우 용감한 여자였고 그녀를 아는 사람들은 모두 그녀의 기백을 칭찬했다. ◳ 불가산명사 활기 ❑ 그들은 활기차게 경기를 했다. ◳ 단수명사 태도, 자세 ❑ 그들의 문제는 양보하는 자세로만 해결될 수 있다. ◳ 불가산명사 충성심 ❑ 영국 올림픽 참가단은 공동체 정신이 대단히 높다. ◳ 단수명사 정신, 이념 ❑ 노동 운동의 진정한 정신 ◳ 단수명사 (조약 등의) 정신, 참뜻 ❑ 노동 허가증을 요구하는 것은 1950년 조약의 정신을 어기는 것이다. ◳ 가산명사 정신적 특징을 지닌 사람 ❑ ...한 영혼의 소유자 ❑ 나는 나 스스로를 자유로운 영혼의 소유자로 여기기를 좋아한다. ◳ 복수명사 기분 ❑ 저녁 식사 때, 모두들 기분이 아주 좋았다. ◳ 복수명사 (위스키나 진 같은) 증류주 ❑ 이곳의 유일한 문제점은 와인과 증류주만 있고 맥주를 팔지 않는다는 것이다.

characteristic or if they show a lot of enthusiasm in what they are doing. ❑ *I like to think of myself as a free spirit.* **11** N-PLURAL Your **spirits** are your feelings at a particular time, especially feelings of happiness or unhappiness. ❑ *At supper, everyone was in high spirits.* **12** N-PLURAL **Spirits** are strong alcoholic drinks such as whiskey and gin. ❑ *The only problem here is that they don't serve beer - only wine and spirits.*

Word Partnership	spirit의 연어
N.	**human** spirit **1** **2**
	evil spirit **3**
	team spirit **7**
ADJ.	**free** spirit, **independent** spirit **5** **10**
	competitive spirit, **generous** spirit **6**

spir|it|ed /spɪrɪtɪd/ **1** ADJ A **spirited** action shows great energy and courage. ❑ *This television program provoked a spirited debate in the United Kingdom.* **2** ADJ A **spirited** person is very active, lively, and confident. ❑ *He was by nature a spirited little boy.*

spir|itu|al ♦◇◇ /spɪrɪtʃuəl/ **1** ADJ **Spiritual** means relating to people's thoughts and beliefs, rather than to their bodies and physical surroundings. ❑ *She lived entirely by spiritual values, in a world of poetry and imagination.* ● **spir|itu|al|ly** ADV ❑ *Our whole programme is spiritually oriented but not religious.* ● **spir|itu|al|ity** /spɪrɪtʃuælɪti/ N-UNCOUNT ❑ *...the peaceful spirituality of Japanese culture.* **2** ADJ **Spiritual** means relating to people's religious beliefs. ❑ *The spiritual leader of Ireland's 3.7 million Catholics.* →see **myth**

spit /spɪt/ (**spits, spitting, spit, spat**)

The forms **spit** and **spat** can both be used for the past tense and past participle.

1 N-UNCOUNT **Spit** is the watery liquid produced in your mouth. You usually use **spit** to refer to an amount of it that has been forced out of someone's mouth. ❑ *A trickle of spit collected at the corner of her mouth.* **2** V-I If someone **spits,** they force an amount of liquid out of their mouth, often to show hatred or contempt. ❑ *The gang thought of hitting him too, but decided just to spit.* ❑ *They spat at me and taunted me.* **3** V-T If you **spit** liquid or food somewhere, you force a small amount of it out of your mouth. ❑ *Spit out that gum and pay attention.* **4** N-COUNT A **spit** is a long rod which is pushed through a piece of meat and hung over an open fire to cook the meat. ❑ *She roasted the meat on a spit.* **5** PHRASE If you say that one person is **the spitting image** of another, you mean that they look very similar. [INFORMAL] ❑ *Nina looks the spitting image of Sissy Spacek.*

spite ♦◇◇ /spaɪt/ **1** PHRASE You use **in spite of** to introduce a fact which makes the rest of the statement you are making seem surprising. ❑ *Josef Krips at the State Opera hired her in spite of the fact that she had never sung on stage.* **2** PHRASE If you do something **in spite of yourself,** you do it although you did not really intend to or expect to. ❑ *The blunt comment made Richard laugh in spite of himself.* **3** N-UNCOUNT If you do something cruel **out of spite,** you do it because you want to hurt or upset someone. ❑ *I refused her a divorce, out of spite I suppose.* **4** V-T If you do something cruel **to spite** someone, you do it in order to hurt or upset them. [only to-inf] ❑ *Pantelaras was giving his art collection away for nothing, to spite Marie and her husband.*

splash /splæʃ/ (**splashes, splashing, splashed**) **1** V-I If you **splash** around in water, you hit or disturb the water in a noisy way, causing some of it to fly up into the air. ❑ *A lot of people were in the water, swimming or simply splashing about.* ❑ *She could hear the voices of her friends as they splashed in a nearby rock pool.* **2** V-T/V-I If you **splash** a liquid somewhere or if it **splashes,** it hits someone or something and scatters in a lot of small drops. ❑ *He closed his eyes tight, and splashed the water on his face.* ❑ *A little wave, the first of many, splashed in my face.* **3** N-SING A **splash** is the sound made when something hits water or falls into it. ❑ *There was a splash and something fell clumsily into the water.* **4** N-COUNT A **splash** of a liquid is a small quantity of it that falls on something or is added to something. ❑ *Wallcoverings and floors should be able to withstand steam and splashes.* **5** N-COUNT A **splash** of color is an area of a bright color which contrasts strongly with the colors around it. ❑ *...shady walks punctuated by splashes of color.* **6** V-T If a magazine or newspaper **splashes** a story, it prints it in such a way that it is very noticeable. ❑ *The newspapers splashed the story all over their front pages.* **7** PHRASE If you **make a splash,** you become noticed or become popular because of something that you have done. ❑ *Now she's made a splash in the American television show "Civil Wars."*

▸**splash out** PHRASAL VERB If you **splash out on** something, especially on a luxury, you buy it even though it costs a lot of money. [BRIT] [no passive] ❑ *If he wanted to splash out on a new car it would take him a couple of days to get his hands on the cash.*

splat|ter /splætər/ (**splatters, splattering, splattered**) V-T/V-I If a thick wet substance **splatters** on something or **is splattered** on it, it drops or is thrown over it. ❑ *The rain splattered against the windows.* ❑ *"Sorry Edward," I said, splattering the cloth with jam.*

splen|did /splɛndɪd/ ADJ If you say that something is **splendid,** you mean that it is very good. ❑ *The book includes a wealth of splendid photographs.* ● **splen|did|ly** ADV [ADV with v] ❑ *I have heard him tell people that we get along splendidly.*

splen|dor /splɛndər/ (**splendors**) [BRIT **splendour**] **1** N-UNCOUNT The **splendor** of something is its beautiful and impressive appearance. ❑ *She gazed down upon*

1 형용사 활발한; 용기 있는 ❑ 이 텔레비전 프로그램은 영국 내에 활발한 토론을 불러일으켰다. **2** 형용사 활기찬 ❑ 그는 천성적으로 활기찬 소년이었다.

1 형용사 정신의, 정신적인 ❑ 그녀는 시와 상상의 세계 속에서 전적으로 정신적 가치에 따라 살았다. ● 정신적으로 부사 ❑ 우리의 모든 프로그램은 정신 지향적이지만 종교적이지는 않다. ● 정신성 불가산명사 ❑ 일본 문화의 평온한 정신성 **2** 형용사 종교적인 ❑ 3백 7십만 아일랜드 가톨릭교도들의 종교적 지도자

spit와 spat 모두 과거 및 과거 분사로 쓰일 수 있다.

1 불가산명사 침 ❑ 그녀의 입 귀퉁이에 침이 좀 고였다. **2** 자동사 침을 뱉다 ❑ 그 깡패들은 그를 때릴 생각도 했지만, 그냥 침만 뱉기로 결심했다. ❑ 그들은 내게 침을 뱉으며 조롱했다. **3** 타동사 뱉다 ❑ 그 껌 뱉고 주의를 기울여. **4** 가산명사 꼬치, 꼬챙이 ❑ 그녀는 고기를 꼬치에 끼워서 구웠다. **5** 구 ~을 쏙 빼닮다 [비격식체] ❑ 니나는 시시 스페이식을 쏙 빼닮았다.

1 구 ~에도 불구하고 ❑ 주립 오페라 극장의 요제프 크립스는 그녀가 무대에서 노래를 해 본 경험이 없다는 사실에도 불구하고 그녀를 채용했다. **2** 구 자신도 모르게, 무심코 ❑ 그런 생각 없이 내뱉는 말을 듣고 리처드는 자신도 모르게 웃었다. **3** 불가산명사 악의, 앙심 ❑ 나는 그녀의 이혼 제의를 받아들이지 않았는데, 아마 분풀이로 그랬을 게다. **4** 타동사 괴롭히다 ❑ 판텔라라스는 마리와 그녀의 남편을 괴롭히기 위해 자신의 소장 미술품을 다른 사람들에게 거저 주어 버리고 있었다.

1 자동사 첨벙거리다 ❑ 많은 사람들이 물속에서 수영을 하거나 그저 첨벙거리고 있었다. ❑ 그녀는 근처 바위 수영장에서 첨벙거리는 친구들의 목소리를 들을 수 있었다. **2** 타동사/자동사 튀기다, 끼얹다; 튀다 ❑ 그는 눈을 꼭 감고서 얼굴에 물을 끼얹었다. ❑ 여러 가지 중에서 첫 번째로, 작은 파도가 내 얼굴을 찰싹 때렸다. **3** 단수명사 첨벙 하는 소리 ❑ 첨벙 하고 뭔가가 물속으로 꼴사납게 떨어지는 소리가 났다. **4** 가산명사 (어디에 떨어지는) 소량의 액체 ❑ 벽지와 바닥재는 증기와 낙숫물을 견딜 수 있어야 한다. **5** 가산명사 (주변 색과 대조되는) 밝은 색 부분 ❑ 군데군데 밝은 빛이 비치는 그늘진 보도 **6** 타동사 대서특필하다 ❑ 신문들은 그 이야기를 일 면에 대서특필했다. **7** 구 유명해지다 ❑ 이제 그녀는 미국 텔레비전 쇼 '남북 전쟁'을 통해 유명해졌다.

구동사 ~에 돈을 뿌리다 [영국영어] ❑ 만일 그가 새 자동차에 돈을 쓰고 싶다 해도 그만한 현찰을 손에 쥐려면 이틀은 걸릴 것이다.

타동사/자동사 튀다; 튀기다 ❑ 빗물이 창문에 후드득 떨어졌다. ❑ "미안해, 에드워드."라고 내가 그 천에 잼을 튀겨서 이렇게 말했다.

형용사 훌륭한, 멋진 ❑ 그 책에는 훌륭한 사진들이 많이 들어 있다. ● 훌륭하게 부사 ❑ 나는 그가 사람들에게 우리가 아주 사이좋게 잘 지낸다고 말하는 것을 들은 적이 있다.

[영국영어 **splendour**] **1** 불가산명사 장관 ❑ 그녀는 장관을 이루고 있는 도시의 야경을 내려다보았다.

the nighttime splendor of the city. **2** N-PLURAL The **splendors of** a place or way of life are its beautiful and impressive features. □ *...such splendors as the Acropolis and the Parthenon.*

2 복수명사 장려한 것들, 장관을 이루는 것들 □ 아크로폴리스와 파르테논 같은 장려한 건축물들

splin|ter /splɪntər/ (**splinters, splintering, splintered**) **1** N-COUNT A **splinter** is a very thin, sharp piece of wood, glass, or other hard substance, which has broken off from a larger piece. □ *...splinters of glass.* **2** V-T/V-I If something **splinters** or is **splintered**, it breaks into thin, sharp pieces. □ *The ruler cracked and splintered into pieces.*

1 가산명사 쪼개진 조각 □ 유리 조각들
2 타동사/자동사 쪼개지다, 조각나다; 쪼개다, 조각내다 □ 자가 깨져서 산산조각이 났다.

split ♦♦◇ /splɪt/ (**splits, splitting**)

> The form **split** is used in the present tense and is the past tense and past participle of the verb.

> split은 동사의 현재, 과거, 과거 분사로 쓰인다.

1 V-T/V-I If something **splits** or if you **split** it, it is divided into two or more parts. □ *In a severe gale the ship split in two.* □ *If the chicken is fairly small, you may simply split it in half.* **2** V-T/V-I If an organization **splits** or is **split**, one group of members disagree strongly with the other members, and may form a group of their own. □ *They accused both radicals and conservatives of trying to provoke a split in the party.* ● ADJ **Split** is also an adjective. □ *The Kremlin is deeply split in its approach to foreign policy.* **3** N-COUNT A **split in** an organization is a disagreement between its members. □ *They accused both radicals and conservatives of trying to provoke a split in the party.* **4** N-SING A **split between** two things is a division or difference between them. □ *...a split between what is thought and what is felt.* **5** V-T/V-I If something such as wood or a piece of clothing **splits**, or is **split**, a long crack or tear appears in it. □ *The seat of his short grey trousers split.* **6** N-COUNT A **split** is a long crack or tear. □ *The plastic-covered seat has a few small splits around the corners.* **7** V-T If two or more people **split** something, they share it between them. □ *I would rather pay for a meal than watch nine friends pick over and split a bill.*

1 타동사/자동사 쪼개지다, 나뉘다; 쪼개다, 나누다 □ 모진 폭풍 속에서 그 배가 두 동강이 났다. □ 닭고기가 꽤 작긴 하지만, 그냥 절반으로 나눌 수도 있다. **2** 타동사/자동사 분열되다; 분열시키다 □ 그렇지만 공화당 지도부가 그 협약을 놓고 분열될까 염려된다. ● 형용사 분열된 □ 소련 정부는 대외 정책에 대한 접근법에 있어서 심각하게 분열되어 있다. **3** 가산명사 분열, 분화 □ 그들은 당내 분열을 야기하려 한다고 급진파와 보수파 모두를 비난했다. **4** 단수명사 괴리, 차이 □ 사고와 느낌의 괴리 **5** 타동사/자동사 찢다; 찢어지다 □ 그의 짧은 회색 바지 엉덩이 부분이 찢어졌다. **6** 가산명사 쪼개진 틈, 갈라진 금 □ 덮개가 플라스틱으로 된 그 좌석은 모서리 부분에 작은 갈라진 금이 몇 개 나 있다. **7** 타동사 분배하다, 나눠 갖다 □ 친구 아홉이서 계산서를 따져 가며 나눠서 내는 것을 보느니 차라리 내가 한 끼 사겠다.

Thesaurus　　　split의 참조어

V.	break, divide, part, separate; (ant.) combine **1 2 5**
N.	crack, separation, tear **6**

Word Partnership　　　split의 연어

PREP.	split into **1**
	split over *something* **2**
	split between **4**
	split among **7**
N.	split shares, split wood **1**
	split in a party **3**
ADV.	split apart **1 2**

▶**split up** **1** PHRASAL VERB-RECIP If two people **split up**, or if someone or something **splits** them **up**, they end their relationship or marriage. □ *Research suggests that children whose parents split up are more likely to drop out of high school.* □ *I was beginning to think that nothing could ever split us up.* **2** PHRASAL VERB If a group of people **split up** or are **split up**, they go away in different directions. □ *Did the two of you split up in the woods?* □ *This situation has split up the family.* **3** PHRASAL VERB If you **split** something **up**, or if it **splits up**, you divide it so that it is in a number of smaller separate sections. □ *Any thought of splitting up the company was unthinkable, they said.* □ *Even though museums have begged to borrow her collection, she could never split it up.*

1 상호 구동사 갈라서다; 헤어지게 만들다 □ 연구에 따르면 이혼한 부모를 둔 아이들이 고등학교를 중퇴할 확률이 더 높다고 한다. □ 나는 그 무엇도 우리를 갈라놓을 수 없다고 생각하기 시작했다. **2** 구동사 갈라지다; 갈라놓다 □ 너희 둘은 숲 속에서 갈라졌니? □ 이런 사정 때문에 그 가족은 뿔뿔이 헤어졌다. **3** 구동사 분할하다; 분할되다 □ 회사를 분할하는 것은 상상할 수도 없는 일이라고 그들은 말했다. □ 소장품을 빌려 달라고 박물관에서 간청해 왔지만, 그녀는 절대로 그것을 쪼개 놓을 수 없었다.

split se|cond also **split-second** N-SING A **split second** is an extremely short period of time. □ *Her gaze met Michael's for a split second.*

단수명사 눈 깜짝할 사이, 아주 잠시 □ 아주 잠시 그녀는 마이클과 눈이 마주쳤다.

splut|ter /splʌtər/ (**splutters, spluttering, spluttered**) **1** V-T/V-I If someone **splutters**, they make short sounds and have difficulty speaking clearly, for example because they are embarrassed or angry. □ *"But it cannot be," he spluttered.* **2** V-I If something **splutters**, it makes a series of short, sharp sounds. □ *Suddenly the engine coughed, spluttered, and died.*

1 타동사/자동사 말을 더듬다 □ "하지만 그럴 리 없어."라고 그가 더듬거리며 말했다. **2** 자동사 털털거리다 □ 갑자기 엔진이 캑캑거리더니 털털거리다가 꺼져 버렸다.

spoil /spɔɪl/ (**spoils, spoiling, spoiled, spoilt**)

> The forms **spoiled** and **spoilt** can both be used for the past tense and past participle, but **spoilt** is more common in British English than in American English.

> spoiled와 spoilt 모두 과거 및 과거 분사로 쓸 수 있지만, spoilt는 미국영어보다 영국영어에서 더 일반적이다.

1 V-T If you **spoil** something, you prevent it from being successful or satisfactory. □ *It's important not to let mistakes spoil your life.* **2** V-T If you **spoil** children, you give them everything they want or ask for. This is considered to have a bad effect on a child's character. □ *Grandparents are often tempted to spoil their grandchildren whenever they come to visit.* **3** V-T If you **spoil yourself** or **spoil** another person, you give yourself or them something nice as a treat or do something special for them. □ *Spoil yourself with a new perfume this summer.* **4** V-T/V-I If food **spoils** or if it **is spoiled**, it is no longer fit to be eaten. □ *We all know that fats spoil by becoming rancid.* **5** PHRASE If you say that someone is **spoiled for choice** or **spoilt for choice**, you mean that they have a great many things of the same type to choose from. □ *The business traveller has never been so spoiled for choice, in travel and accommodation.*

1 타동사 망치다 □ 실수 때문에 인생을 망치는 일이 없도록 해야 한다. **2** 타동사 응석을 다 받아 주다 □ 할머니 할아버지는 손주가 찾아올 때마다 응석을 다 받아 주고 싶은 마음이 생기곤 한다. **3** 타동사 마음껏 -하다; 마음껏 -하게 하다 □ 이번 여름에는 새 향수를 마음껏 뿌려 보세요. **4** 타동사/자동사 상하다; 상하게 하다 □ 지방이 상하면서 악취가 나는 것은 다 아는 사실이다. **5** 구 선택의 폭이 무진장한 □ 출장객의 여행과 숙박에서 이처럼 무진장한 선택권을 누려 본 적이 없다.

spoilt /spɔɪlt/ **Spoilt** is a past participle and past tense of **spoil**. [mainly BRIT]

spoil의 과거, 과거 분사 [주로 영국영어]

spoke /spoʊk/ (**spokes**) **Spoke** is the past tense of **speak**.

speak의 과거

spo|ken /spoʊkən/ **Spoken** is the past participle of **speak**.

speak의 과거 분사

spokes|man ♦♦◇ /spoʊksmən/ (**spokesmen**) N-COUNT A **spokesman** is a male spokesperson. □ *A UN spokesman said that the mission will carry 20 tons of relief supplies.*

가산명사 (남성) 대변인 □ 사절단을 통해 구호물자 20톤이 전달될 것이라고 유엔 대변인이 밝혔다.

spokes|person /spoʊkspɜːrsᵊn/ (**spokespersons** or **spokespeople**) N-COUNT A **spokesperson** is a person who speaks as the representative of a group or organization. ❑ *A spokesperson for Amnesty, Norma Johnston, describes some cases.*

가산명사 대변인 ❑ 국제 사면 위원회 대변인인 노마 존슨이 몇몇 사례를 자세히 설명한다.

spokes|woman /spoʊkswʊmən/ (**spokeswomen**) N-COUNT A **spokeswoman** is a female spokesperson. ❑ *A United Nations spokeswoman in New York said the request would be considered.*

가산명사 (여성) 대변인 ❑ 뉴욕 주재 유엔 대변인이 이 요청을 고려해 볼 것이라고 밝혔다.

sponge /spʌndʒ/ (**sponges, sponging, sponged**) ◻ N-COUNT **Sponge** is a very light soft substance with lots of little holes in it, which can be either artificial or natural. It is used to clean things or as a soft layer. ❑ *...a sponge mattress.* ◻ N-COUNT A **sponge** is a piece of sponge that you use for washing yourself or for cleaning things. ❑ *He wiped off the table with a sponge.* ◻ V-T If you **sponge** something, you clean it by wiping it with a wet sponge. ❑ *Fill a bowl with water and gently sponge your face and body.* ● PHRASAL VERB **Sponge down** means the same as **sponge**. ❑ *If your child's temperature rises, sponge her down gently with tepid water.* ◻ N-VAR A **sponge** is a light cake or pudding made from flour, eggs, sugar, and sometimes fat. ❑ *It makes a superb filling for cakes and sponges.* ◻ V-I If you say that someone **sponges off** other people or **sponges on** them, you mean that they regularly get money from other people when they should be trying to support themselves. [INFORMAL, DISAPPROVAL] ❑ *He should just get an honest job and stop sponging off the rest of us!*

◻ 가산명사 스펀지 ❑ 스펀지 매트리스 ◻ 가산명사 스펀지 ❑ 그가 스펀지로 테이블을 닦았다. ◻ 타동사 스펀지로 닦다 ❑ 대야에 물을 채우고 스펀지로 얼굴과 몸을 부드럽게 닦으세요. ● 구동사 스펀지로 닦다 ❑ 아이의 체온이 올라가면 미지근한 물을 스펀지에 적셔 부드럽게 닦아 주세요. ◻ 가산명사 또는 불가산명사 스펀지케이크 ❑ 이는 일반 케이크나 스펀지 케이크 속재료로 아주 훌륭하다. ◻ 자동사 빌붙다 [비격식체, 탐탁찮음] ❑ 그는 떳떳한 직장을 구해서 우리한테 그만 빌붙어 살아야 한다.

spon|sor ♦♢♢ /spɒnsər/ (**sponsors, sponsoring, sponsored**) ◻ V-T If an organization or an individual **sponsors** something such as an event or someone's training, they pay some or all of the expenses connected with it, often in order to get publicity for themselves. ❑ *Mercury, in association with "The Independent," is sponsoring Britain's first major Pop Art exhibition for over 20 years.* ◻ V-T If you **sponsor** someone who is doing something to raise money for charity, for example trying to walk a certain distance, you agree to give them a sum of money for the charity if they succeed in doing it. ❑ *Please could you sponsor me for my school's campaign for Help the Aged?* ◻ V-T If you **sponsor** a proposal or suggestion, you officially put it forward and support it. ❑ *Eight senators sponsored legislation to stop the military funding.* ◻ V-T When a country or an organization such as the United Nations **sponsors** negotiations between countries, it suggests holding the negotiations and organizes them. ❑ *Given the strength of pressure on both sides, the superpowers may well have difficulties sponsoring negotiations.* ◻ V-T If one country accuses another of **sponsoring** attacks on it, they mean that the other country does not do anything to prevent the attacks, and may even encourage them. ❑ *We have to make the states that sponsor terrorism pay a price.* ◻ V-T If a company or organization **sponsors** a television program, they pay to have a special advertisement shown at the beginning and end of the program, and at each commercial break. ❑ *The company plans to sponsor television programs as part of its marketing strategy.* ◻ N-COUNT A **sponsor** is a person or organization that sponsors something or someone. ❑ *I understand Coca-Cola are to be named as the new sponsors of the League Cup later this week.*

◻ 타동사 후원하다, 스폰서가 되다 ❑ 머큐리는 인디펜던트 지와 함께 영국에서 20여 년 만에 처음으로 열리는 대규모 팝아트 전시회를 후원하고 있다. ◻ 타동사 후원하다 ❑ 학내 노인 봉사 캠페인에서 제 후원사가 되어 주시겠습니까? ◻ 타동사 지지하다 ❑ 상원의원 여덟 명이 군사 자금 지원 중단을 위한 법안을 지지했다. ◻ 타동사 주선하다 ❑ 양측이 모두 커다란 압박을 받고 있기 때문에 강대국이 협상을 주선하는 데 분명히 어려움이 있을 것이다. ◻ 타동사 지원하다 ❑ 우리는 테러 지원 국가가 반드시 대가를 치르게 해야 한다. ◻ 타동사 (특정 프로그램을) 광고하다 ❑ 회사가 마케팅 전략의 일환으로 텔레비전 프로그램에 광고를 낼 계획이다. ◻ 가산명사 후원자, 스폰서 ❑ 나는 코카콜라가 이번 주 말에 리그컵 새 후원사로 지명된다고 알고 있다.

spon|sor|ship /spɒnsərʃɪp/ N-UNCOUNT **Sponsorship** is financial support given by a sponsor. [also N in pl] ❑ *Campbell is one of an ever-growing number of skiers in need of sponsorship.*

불가산명사 후원, 협찬 ❑ 캠벨을 비롯해서 스폰서가 필요한 스키어들이 계속 증가하고 있다.

spon|ta|neity /spɒntəniːɪti, -neɪ-/ N-UNCOUNT **Spontaneity** is spontaneous, natural behavior. ❑ *He had the spontaneity of a child.*

불가산명사 자연스러운 행동거지 ❑ 그는 어린 아이처럼 행동이 자연스러웠다.

spon|ta|neous /spɒnteɪniəs/ ◻ ADJ **Spontaneous** acts are not planned or arranged, but are done because someone suddenly wants to do them. ❑ *Diana's house was crowded with happy people whose spontaneous outbursts of song were accompanied by lively music.* ● **spon|ta|neous|ly** ADV ❑ *As soon as the tremor passed, many people spontaneously arose and cheered.* ◻ ADJ A **spontaneous** event happens because of processes within something rather than being caused by things outside it. ❑ *I had another spontaneous miscarriage at around the 16th to 18th week.* ● **spon|ta|neous|ly** ADV [ADV after v] ❑ *Usually a woman's breasts produce milk spontaneously after the birth.*

◻ 형용사 자발적인, 즉흥적인 ❑ 다이애나의 집에는 사람들이 가득 모여 즉흥적인 반주에 맞춰 즉흥적으로 노래를 부르며 행복해했다. ● 자발적으로, 즉흥적으로 부사 ❑ 떨리던 음성이 잦아들자마자 많은 사람들이 자발적으로 일어나 박수를 쳤다. ◻ 형용사 자연발생적인 ❑ 임신 16주에서 18주 즈음에 나는 또 한 번 자연 유산을 했다. ● 자연히 부사 ❑ 보통 여성의 가슴에서는 출산 후에 자연히 모유가 나온다.

spooky /spuːki/ (**spookier, spookiest**) ADJ A place that is **spooky** has a frightening atmosphere, and makes you feel that there are ghosts around. [INFORMAL] ❑ *The whole place has a slightly spooky atmosphere.*

형용사 으스스한, 귀신이 나올 듯한 [비격식체] ❑ 사방에서 귀신이 나올 것만 같은 분위기이다.

spool /spuːl/ (**spools**) N-COUNT A **spool** is a round object onto which thread, tape, or film can be wound, especially before it is put into a machine. ❑ *...the hissing of a tape rewinding on its spool.*

가산명사 (실 등을 감는) 얼레, 릴 ❑ 테이프가 릴에 되감기며 나는 소리

spoon /spuːn/ (**spoons, spooning, spooned**) ◻ N-COUNT A **spoon** is an object used for eating, stirring, and serving food. One end of it is shaped like a shallow bowl and it has a long handle. ❑ *He stirred his coffee with a spoon.* ◻ V-T If you **spoon** food into something, you put it there with a spoon. ❑ *He spooned instant coffee into two of the mugs.* →see **silverware**

◻ 가산명사 숟가락, 스푼 ❑ 그가 스푼으로 커피를 저었다. ◻ 타동사 스푼으로 떠 넣다 ❑ 그가 머그잔 두 개에 인스턴트커피를 떠 넣었다.

spo|rad|ic /spərædɪk/ ADJ **Sporadic** occurrences of something happen at irregular intervals. ❑ *...a year of sporadic fighting over northern France.* ● **spo|radi|cal|ly** ADV [ADV with v] ❑ *The distant thunder from the coast continued sporadically.*

형용사 산발적인, 이따금 일어나는 ❑ 프랑스 북부를 두고 이따금 싸움이 일어난 해 ● 산발적으로, 이따금 부사 ❑ 멀리 해변에서 천둥 치는 소리가 이따금 들려왔다.

sport ♦♦♢ /spɔːrt/ (**sports**) N-VAR **Sports** are games such as football and basketball and other competitive leisure activities which need physical effort and skill. ❑ *I chose boxing because it is my favorite sport.* ❑ *She excels at sport.*

가산명사 또는 불가산명사 스포츠, 운동, 경기 ❑ 내가 복싱을 선택한 이유는 가장 좋아하는 운동이기 때문이다. ❑ 그녀는 스포츠에 뛰어나다.

sport|ing /spɔːrtɪŋ/ ADJ **Sporting** means relating to sports or used for sports. [ADJ n] ❑ *...major sporting events, such as Wimbledon and the World Cup finals.*

형용사 스포츠의, 스포츠 용품의 ❑ 윔블던이나 월드컵 결승전과 같은 주요 스포츠 행사

sports car (**sports cars**) N-COUNT A **sports car** is a low, fast car, usually with room for only two people. →see **car**

가산명사 스포츠카

sports|man /spɔːrtsmən/ (**sportsmen**) N-COUNT A **sportsman** is a man who takes part in sports.

가산명사 스포츠맨

sports|woman /spɔ:rtswʊmən/ (**sportswomen**) N-COUNT A **sportswoman** is a woman who takes part in sports.

가산명사 스포츠우먼

sporty /spɔ:rti/ (**sportier, sportiest**) **1** ADJ You can describe a car as **sporty** when it performs like a racing car but can be driven on normal roads. ❑ *The steering and braking are exactly what you want from a sporty car.* **2** ADJ Someone who is **sporty** likes playing sports. ❑ *I'm an outdoor, sporty type and don't want to sit behind a desk all day.*

1 형용사 스포츠카의, 경주용 차와 성능이 비슷한 ❑ 핸들이나 브레이크가 경주용 차와 같은 성능의 차에 제격이다. **2** 형용사 활동적인, 운동을 좋아하는 ❑ 나는 활동적이고 운동을 좋아하는 타입이라 하루 종일 책상에 앉아 있기 싫다.

spot ♦♦◇ /spɒt/ (**spots, spotting, spotted**) **1** N-COUNT **Spots** are small, round, colored areas on a surface. ❑ *The leaves have yellow areas on the top and underneath are powdery orange spots.* **2** N-COUNT **Spots** on a person's skin are small lumps or marks. ❑ *Never squeeze blackheads, spots, or pimples.* **3** N-COUNT A **spot of** a liquid is a small amount of it. [mainly BRIT] ❑ *Spots of rain had begun to fall.* **4** N-COUNT You can refer to a particular place as a **spot**. ❑ *They stayed at several of the island's top tourist spots.* **5** N-COUNT A **spot** in a television or radio show is a part of it that is regularly reserved for a particular performer or type of entertainment. ❑ *Unsuccessful at screen writing, he got a spot on a CNN film show.* **6** V-T If you **spot** something or someone, you notice them. ❑ *Vicenzo failed to spot the error.* **7** PHRASE If you do something **on the spot**, you do it immediately. ❑ *James was called to see the producer and got the job on the spot.* **8** **rooted to the spot** →see **rooted**

1 가산명사 점, 반점 ❑ 그 나뭇잎은 위쪽에는 노란색 부분이 아래쪽에는 가루 같은 주황색 점들이 있다. **2** 가산명사 발진, 여드름 ❑ 블랙헤드나 여드름, 뾰루지는 절대 짜면 안 된다. **3** 가산명사 조금 [주로 영국영어] ❑ 비가 조금씩 떨어지기 시작했다. **4** 가산명사 장소 ❑ 그들은 섬에서 가장 유명한 관광지 몇 군데에 머물렀다. **5** 가산명사 (텔레비전 프로그램 등의) 고정 코너 ❑ 시나리오 작가로 실패한 그는 시엔엔 영화 프로그램의 한 고정 코너를 맡게 됐다. **6** 타동사 발견하다, 알아채다 ❑ 빈센조가 오류를 잡아내지 못했다. **7** 구 당장에서, 즉각 ❑ 제임스는 프로듀서를 만나보라는 연락을 받았고 즉석에서 일자리를 얻었다.

Word Partnership	spot의 연어

| ADJ. | **good** spot, **perfect** spot, **popular** spot, **quiet** spot, **the right** spot **4** |
| N. | **parking** spot, **vacation** spot **4** |

spot|less /spɒtlɪs/ ADJ Something that is **spotless** is completely clean. ❑ *Each morning cleaners make sure everything is spotless.* ● **spot|less|ly** ADV [ADV adj] ❑ *The house had huge, spotlessly clean rooms.*

형용사 티 없이 깨끗한 ❑ 매일 아침 청소부들은 온 세상을 티 없이 깨끗하게 만든다. ● 부사 티 없이 깨끗하게 ❑ 그 집에는 아주 크고 티끌 하나 없이 깨끗한 방들이 있었다.

spot|light /spɒtlaɪt/ (**spotlights, spotlighting, spotlighted**) **1** N-COUNT A **spotlight** is a powerful light, for example in a theater, which can be directed so that it lights up a small area. **2** V-T If something **spotlights** a particular problem or situation, it makes people notice it and think about it. ❑ *The budget crisis also spotlighted a weakening American economy.* **3** PHRASE Someone or something that is **in the spotlight** is getting a great deal of public attention. ❑ *Webb is back in the spotlight.*

1 가산명사 스포트라이트 **2** 타동사 주의를 환기시키다, 스포트라이트를 비추다 ❑ 예산 위기는 점점 약해지는 미국 경제를 돌아볼 기회가 되기도 했다. **3** 구 각광을 받는, 세인의 주목을 받는 ❑ 웹이 다시금 각광받고 있다.

spouse /spaʊs/ (**spouses**) N-COUNT Someone's **spouse** is the person they are married to. ❑ *You, or your spouse, must be at least 60 to participate.*

가산명사 배우자 ❑ 본인이나 배우자가 최소한 예순 살은 되어야 참여할 수 있다.

spout /spaʊt/ (**spouts, spouting, spouted**) **1** V-T/V-I If something **spouts** liquid or fire or if liquid or fire **spouts** out of something, it comes out very quickly with a lot of force. ❑ *He replaced the boiler when the last one began to spout flames.* ❑ *The main square has a fountain that spouts water 40 feet into the air.* **2** V-T If you say that a person **spouts** something, you disapprove of them because they say something which you do not agree with or which you think they do not honestly feel. [DISAPPROVAL] ❑ *My mother would go red in the face and spout bitter recriminations.* **3** N-COUNT A **spout** is a long, hollow part of a container through which liquids can be poured out easily. ❑ *She lifted the kettle a little and tilted its spout over the teapot.*

1 타동사/자동사 내뿜다; 솟구치다 ❑ 그는 이전 보일러에서 불꽃이 튀기 시작하자 그것을 교체했다. ❑ 중앙 광장에는 공중 40피트까지 물을 내뿜는 분수가 있다. **2** 타동사 지껄이다, 내뱉다 [탐탁찮음] ❑ 어머니는 얼굴이 빨개지면서 신랄하게 말을 맞받아치곤 했다. **3** 가산명사 (주전자 등의) 주둥이 ❑ 그녀는 물주전자를 약간 들어 올려 찻주전자 위로 주둥이를 기울였다.

sprain /spreɪn/ (**sprains, spraining, sprained**) **1** V-T If you **sprain** a joint such as your ankle or wrist, you accidentally damage it by twisting it or bending it violently. ❑ *He fell and sprained his ankle.* **2** N-COUNT A **sprain** is the injury caused by spraining a joint. ❑ *Rubin suffered a right ankle sprain when she rolled over on her ankle.*

1 타동사 삐다 ❑ 그는 넘어져서 발목을 삐었다. **2** 가산명사 삠, 인좌 ❑ 루빈은 굴러 넘어지면서 오른쪽 발목을 잘못 디뎌 삐고 말았다.

sprang /spræŋ/ **Sprang** is the past tense of **spring**.

spring의 과거

sprawl /sprɔ:l/ (**sprawls, sprawling, sprawled**) **1** V-I If you **sprawl** somewhere, you sit or lie down with your legs and arms spread out in a careless way. ❑ *She sprawled on the bed as he had left her, not even moving to cover herself up.* ● PHRASAL VERB **Sprawl out** means the same as **sprawl**. ❑ *He would take two aspirin and sprawl out on his bed.* **2** V-I If you say that a place **sprawls**, you mean that it covers a large area of land. ❑ *The State Recreation Area sprawls over 900 acres on the southern tip of Key Biscayne.* **3** N-UNCOUNT You can use **sprawl** to refer to an area where a city has grown outward in an uncontrolled way. ❑ *The whole urban sprawl of Ankara contains over 2.6m people.*

1 자동사 팔다리를 아무렇게나 벌리고 앉다; 큰 대자로 눕다 ❑ 그가 떠나자 그녀는 침대에 큰 대자로 누워 몸을 가릴 생각도 않고 그대로 있었다. ● 구동사 팔다리를 아무렇게나 벌리고 있다; 큰 대자로 눕다 ❑ 그는 아스피린 두 알을 먹고 침대 위에 큰 대자로 뻗곤 했다. **2** 자동사 죽 뻗어 있다, 죽 펼쳐져 있다 ❑ 주립 휴양지는 키비스케인 남단 900에이커에 걸쳐 펼쳐져 있다. **3** 불가산명사 무질서하게 뻗어 나간 도시 외곽 지역 ❑ 무질서하게 뻗어 나간 앙카라 외곽 지역에 2백 6십만 명이 살고 있다.

spray ♦◇◇ /spreɪ/ (**sprays, spraying, sprayed**) **1** N-VAR **Spray** is a lot of small drops of water which are being thrown into the air. ❑ *The moon was casting a rainbow through the spray from the waterfall.* **2** N-MASS A **spray** is a liquid kept under pressure in a can or other container, which you can force out in very small drops. ❑ *...hair spray.* **3** V-T/V-I If you **spray** a liquid somewhere or if it **sprays** somewhere, drops of the liquid cover a place or shower someone. ❑ *A sprayer hooked to a tractor can spray five gallons onto ten acres.* ❑ *Two inmates hurled slates at prison officers spraying them with a hose.* **4** V-T/V-I If a lot of small things **spray** somewhere or if something **sprays** them, they are scattered somewhere with a lot of force. ❑ *A shower of mustard seeds sprayed into the air and fell into the grass.* ❑ *The intensity of the blaze shattered windows, spraying glass on the streets below.* **5** V-T If someone **sprays** bullets somewhere, they fire a lot of bullets at a group of people or things. ❑ *He ran to the top of the building spraying bullets into shoppers below.* **6** V-T If something **is sprayed**, it is painted using paint kept under pressure in a container. [usu passive] ❑ *The bare metal was sprayed with several coats of primer.* **7** V-T/V-I When someone **sprays** against insects, they cover plants or crops with a chemical which prevents insects feeding on them. ❑ *He doesn't spray against pests or diseases.* ❑ *Confine the use of insecticides to the evening and do not spray plants that are in flower.* **8** N-COUNT A **spray** is a piece of

1 가산명사 또는 불가산명사 물보라, 물안개 ❑ 폭포 주변 물안개에 달빛이 쏟아지면서 무지개를 이루고 있었다. **2** 물질명사 스프레이 ❑ 헤어 스프레이 **3** 타동사/자동사 뿌리다; 뿌려지다 ❑ 트랙터에 장착된 분무기 하나가 10에이커의 땅에 5갤런을 뿌릴 수 있다. ❑ 수감자 두 명이 호스를 들고 물을 뿌리는 교도관들에게 슬레이트를 던졌다. **4** 타동사/자동사 흩날리다; 흩뿌리다 ❑ 수많은 겨자씨가 공중에 흩날렸다가 잔디 속으로 떨어졌다. ❑ 세찬 불길에 창문이 산산조각 나면서 길 위로 유리 파편을 흩뿌렸다. **5** 타동사 총알을 퍼붓다, 마구 쏘아 대다 ❑ 그는 건물 옥상으로 달려가 밑에서 쇼핑하는 사람들을 향해 총알 세례를 퍼부었다. **6** 타동사 스프레이로 칠해지다 ❑ 맨 금속에 스프레이가 애벌칠을 몇 차례 했다. **7** 타동사/자동사 살충제를 뿌리다, 방충제를 뿌리다 ❑ 그는 해충 때문이든 질병 때문이든 살충제를 뿌리지 않는다. ❑ 살충제는 저녁에만 사용하도록 하고 꽃이 핀 식물에는 쓰지 마세요. **8** 가산명사 분무기 ❑ 농부들은 분무기를

equipment for spraying water or another liquid, especially over growing plants. ❑ *Farmers can use the spray to kill weeds without harming the soya crop.*

사용해 콩작물에 피해를 주지 않고 잡초를 죽일 수 있다.

Word Partnership   *spray*의 연어

N.	spray **can**, **pepper** spray **2**
N.	spray **with water** **3**

---

spread ♦♦◊ /sprɛd/ (**spreads**, **spreading**, **spread**) **1** V-T If you **spread** something somewhere, you open it out or arrange it over a place or surface, so that all of it can be seen or used easily. ❑ *She spread a towel on the sand and lay on it.* ● PHRASAL VERB **Spread out** means the same as **spread**. ❑ *He extracted several glossy prints and spread them out on a low coffee table.* **2** V-T If you **spread** your arms, hands, fingers, or legs, you stretch them out until they are far apart. ❑ *Sitting on the floor, spread your legs as far as they will go without overstretching.* ● PHRASAL VERB **Spread out** means the same as **spread**. ❑ *David made a gesture, spreading out his hands as if he were showing that he had no explanation to make.* **3** V-T If you **spread** a substance on a surface or **spread** the surface **with** the substance, you put a thin layer of the substance over the surface. ❑ *Spread the mixture in the cake tin and bake for 30 minutes.* **4** V-T/V-I If something **spreads** or **is spread** by people, it gradually reaches or affects a larger and larger area or more and more people. ❑ *The industrial revolution which started a couple of hundred years ago in Europe is now spreading across the world.* ❑ *...the sense of fear spreading in residential neighborhoods.* ● N-SING **Spread** is also a noun. ❑ *The greatest hope for reform is the gradual spread of information.* **5** V-T/V-I If something such as a liquid, gas, or smoke **spreads** or **is spread**, it moves outward in all directions to cover a larger area. ❑ *Fire spread rapidly after a chemical truck exploded.* ❑ *A dark red stain was spreading across his shirt.* ● N-SING **Spread** is also a noun. ❑ *The situation was complicated by the spread of a serious forest fire.* **6** V-T If you **spread** something **over** a period of time, it takes place regularly or continuously over that period, rather than happening at one time. ❑ *There seems to be little difference whether you eat all your calorie allowance in one go, or spread it over the day.* **7** V-T If you **spread** something such as wealth or work, you distribute it evenly or equally. ❑ *...policies that spread the state's wealth more evenly.* ● N-SING **Spread** is also a noun. ❑ *There are easier ways to encourage the even spread of wealth.* **8** N-SING A **spread** of ideas, interests, or other things is a wide variety of them. ❑ *A topic-based approach can be hard to assess in primary schools with a typical spread of ability.* **9** N-COUNT A **spread** is two pages of a book, magazine, or newspaper that are opposite each other when you open it at a particular place. ❑ *There was a double-page spread of a dinner for 46 people.* **10** N-SING **Spread** is used to refer to the difference between the price that a seller wants someone to pay for a particular stock or share and the price that the buyer is willing to pay. [BUSINESS] ❑ *Market makers earn their livings from the spread between buying and selling prices.* **11** to **spread** your **wings** →see **wing**

Thesaurus   *spread*의 참조어

V.	arrange, disperse, prepare **1**
N.	range, variety **8**

Word Partnership   *spread*의 연어

N.	spread **of an epidemic**, spread **of technology**, spread **of a virus**, spread **fear**, **fires** spread, spread **an infection**, spread **a message**, spread **news**, spread **rumors** **4**
V.	**continue to** spread, **prevent/stop the** spread **of** *something* **4** **5**

▶**spread out** **1** PHRASAL VERB If people, animals, or vehicles **spread out**, they move apart from each other. ❑ *Felix watched his men move like soldiers, spreading out into two teams.* **2** PHRASAL VERB If something such as a city or forest **spreads out**, it gets larger and gradually begins to covers a larger area. ❑ *Cities such as Tokyo are spreading out.* **3** →see **spread 1** **4** →see **spread 2**

spread out ADJ If people or things are **spread out**, they are a long way apart. ❑ *The Kurds are spread out across five nations.*

spread|sheet /sprɛdʃit/ (**spreadsheets**) N-COUNT A **spreadsheet** is a computer program that is used for displaying and dealing with numbers. Spreadsheets are used mainly for financial planning. [COMPUTING]

spree /spri/ (**sprees**) N-COUNT If you spend a period of time doing something in an excessive way, you can say that you are going on a particular kind of **spree**. ❑ *Some Americans went on a spending spree in December to beat the new tax.*

spring ♦♦◊ /sprɪŋ/ (**springs**, **springing**, **sprang**, **sprung**) **1** N-VAR **Spring** is the season between winter and summer when the weather becomes warmer and plants start to grow again. ❑ *The Labor government of Western Australia has an election due next spring.* **2** N-COUNT A **spring** is a spiral of wire which returns to its original shape after it is pressed or pulled. ❑ *Unfortunately, as a standard mattress wears, the springs soften and do not support your spine.* **3** N-COUNT A **spring** is a place where water comes up through the ground. It is also the water that comes from that place. ❑ *To the north are the hot springs.* **4** V-I When a person or animal **springs**, they jump upward or forward suddenly or quickly. ❑ *He sprang to his feet, grabbing his keys off the coffee table.* ❑ *The lion roared once and sprang.* **5** V-I If something **springs** in a particular direction, it moves suddenly and quickly. ❑ *Sadly when the lid of the boot sprang open, it was empty.* **6** V-I If one thing **springs from** another thing, it is the result of it. ❑ *Ethiopia's art springs from her early Christian as well as her Muslim heritage.* **7** V-T If you **spring** some news or a surprise **on** someone, you tell them something that they did not expect to

---

1 타동사 펼치다 ❑ 그녀는 모래 위에 수건을 펼쳐 그 위에 누웠다. ● 구동사 펼치다 ❑ 그는 윤이 나는 사진 몇 장을 뽑아서 낮은 커피 테이블 위에 펼쳐 놓았다. **2** 타동사 뻗다, 펴다 ❑ 바닥에 앉아 지나치게 당기지 않는 선에서 다리를 가능한 한 죽 뻗으세요. ● 구동사 뻗다, 펴다 ❑ 데이비드가 해명할 게 없다는 듯 양 손을 펴 보이는 몸짓을 취했다. **3** 타동사 펴 바르다 ❑ 반죽을 케이크 통에 펴 바른 후 30분간 구우세요. **4** 타동사/자동사 확산되다; 확산시키다 ❑ 2백 년 전 유럽에서 시작된 산업 혁명이 이제 전 세계로 확산되고 있다. ❑ 인근 주택지에 퍼지고 있는 공포감 ● 단수명사 확산, 보급, 유포 ❑ 점차적인 정보의 보급이야 말로 개혁의 가장 큰 희망이다. **5** 타동사/자동사 번지다, 퍼지다; 번지게 하다, 퍼뜨리다 ❑ 화학 약품을 실은 트럭이 폭발한 후 불이 급속도로 번졌다. ❑ 그의 셔츠 위에 검붉은색 얼룩이 번지고 있었다. ● 단수명사 번짐, 퍼짐 ❑ 큰 산불이 번지면서 상황이 복잡해졌다. **6** 타동사 여러 번 나눠 하다 ❑ 칼로리 권장량을 한번에 섭취하든 하루 동안 여러 번 나누어 먹든 별 차이가 없는 것으로 보인다. **7** 타동사 분배하다 ❑ 국가의 부를 더 골고루 분배하기 위한 정책 ● 단수명사 분배 ❑ 더 쉬운 방법으로 부의 평등 분배를 장려할 수 있다. **8** 단수명사 폭넓음, 다양함 ❑ 전형적으로 학생들의 능력 간에 폭이 큰 초등학교에서는 주제 중심의 접근 방식은 평가하기가 어려울 수 있다. **9** 가산명사 양면에 걸친 실린 내용, 양면 기사 ❑ 두 페이지에 걸쳐 46명의 만찬을 담은 사진이 나와 있었다. **10** 단수명사 차액, 마진 [경제] ❑ 증권 중개인은 매매 차액을 통해 벌어먹고 산다.

---

1 구동사 퍼지다, 흩어지다 ❑ 펠릭스는 부하들이 군인처럼 움직여 두 팀으로 흩어지는 모습을 지켜봤다. **2** 구동사 확장되다, 뻗어 나가다 ❑ 도쿄와 같은 도시들이 점점 확장되고 있다.

형용사 멀리 떨어져 있는 ❑ 쿠르드족은 다섯 개 국가에 걸쳐 널리 퍼져 있다.

가산명사 스프레드시트 [컴퓨터]

가산명사 흥청망청하기 ❑ 일부 미국인들은 새로운 세금을 안 내려고 12월에 흥청망청 돈을 썼다.

1 가산명사 또는 불가산명사 봄 ❑ 웨스턴 오스트레일리아 노동당 주정부가 다음 봄에 선거를 한다. **2** 가산명사 용수철 ❑ 안타깝게도 표준 규격의 매트리스는 낡으면서 용수철의 탄력이 떨어지고 결국 척추를 받쳐 주지 못한다. **3** 가산명사 샘; 샘물 ❑ 북쪽으로는 온천들이 있다. **4** 자동사 벌떡 일어서다, 뛰어오르다 ❑ 그가 벌떡 일어서며 커피 테이블에서 열쇠를 움켜쥐었다. ❑ 사자가 한 번 으르렁거리더니 뛰어올랐다. **5** 자동사 휙 움직이다 ❑ 안타깝게도 차 트렁크 뚜껑이 휙 열렸을 때 트렁크는 비어 있었다. **6** 자동사 ...로부터 발생하다 ❑ 에티오피아 미술은 이슬람 유산뿐만이 아니라 초기 기독교의 소산이기도 하다. **7** 타동사 불쑥 알려주다 ❑ 맥클라렌이 그에게 불쑥 새로운 아이디어를 말해 주었다.

hear, without warning them. ❑ *Mclaren sprang a new idea on him.* ❽ to **spring to mind** →see **mind**
→see **river**

구동사 (갑자기) 생겨나다 ❑ 새 극장과 예술회관이 전국적으로 생겨났다.

▶**spring up** PHRASAL VERB If something **springs up**, it suddenly appears or begins to exist. ❑ *New theaters and arts centres sprang up all over the country.*

spring|board /sprɪŋbɔrd/ (**springboards**) ❶ N-COUNT If something is a **springboard for** something else, it makes it possible for that thing to happen or start. ❑ *The 1981 budget was the springboard for an economic miracle.* ❷ N-COUNT A **springboard** is a flexible board from which you jump into a swimming pool or onto a piece of gymnastic equipment.

❶ 가산명사 발판, 출발점 ❑ 1981년 예산은 경제 기적을 향한 발판이었다. ❷ 가산명사 도약판; 다이빙대

sprin|kle /sprɪŋkªl/ (**sprinkles, sprinkling, sprinkled**) ❶ V-T If you **sprinkle** a thing **with** something such as a liquid or powder, you scatter the liquid or powder over it. ❑ *Sprinkle the meat with salt and place in the pan.* ❑ *At the festival, candles are blessed and sprinkled with holy water.* ❷ V-T If something **is sprinkled with** particular things, it has a few of them throughout it and they are far apart from each other. ❑ *Unfortunately, the text is sprinkled with errors.*

❶ 타동사 뿌리다 ❑ 고기에 소금을 뿌려서 팬에 넣으세요. ❑ 축제에서는 촛불에 축성을 내리고 성수를 뿌린다. ❷ 타동사 산재하다 ❑ 안타깝게도 글 곳곳에 틀린 부분이 있다.

sprint /sprɪnt/ (**sprints, sprinting, sprinted**) ❶ N-SING The **sprint** is a short, fast running race. ❑ *Rob Harmeling won the sprint in Bordeaux.* ❷ N-COUNT A **sprint** is a short race in which the competitors run, drive, ride, or swim very fast. ❑ *Lewis will compete in both sprints in Stuttgart.* ❸ N-SING A **sprint** is a fast run that someone does, either at the end of a race or because they are in a hurry. ❑ *Gilles Delion, of France, won the Tour of Lombardy in a sprint finish at Monza yesterday.* ❹ V-I If you **sprint**, you run or ride as fast as you can over a short distance. ❑ *Sergeant Horne sprinted to the car.*

❶ 단수명사 스프린트, 단거리 경주 ❑ 롭 하멜링이 보르도에서 열린 단거리 경주에서 우승했다. ❷ 가산명사 스프린트 ❑ 루이스는 슈투트가르트에서 펼쳐질 스프린트 두 종목에 출전할 것이다. ❸ 단수명사 전력 질주 ❑ 프랑스의 질레스 델리온이 어제 몬자에서 열린 '투어 오브 롬바르디'에서 마지막 전력 질주로 우승했다. ❹ 자동사 전력 질주하다 ❑ 혼 경사는 차를 향해 전력 질주했다.

sprint|er /sprɪntər/ (**sprinters**) N-COUNT A **sprinter** is a person who takes part in short, fast races.

가산명사 스프린터, 단거리 주자

sprout /spraʊt/ (**sprouts, sprouting, sprouted**) ❶ V-I When plants, vegetables, or seeds **sprout**, they produce new shoots or leaves. ❑ *It only takes a few days for beans to sprout.* ❷ V-I When leaves, shoots, or plants **sprout** somewhere, they grow there. ❑ *Leaf-shoots were beginning to sprout on the hawthorn.* ❸ V-T/V-I If something such as hair **sprouts** from a person or animal, or if they **sprout** it, it grows on them. [no passive] ❑ *She is very old now, with little, round, wire-rimmed glasses and whiskers sprouting from her chin.* ❹ N-COUNT **Sprouts** are vegetables that look like tiny cabbages. They are also called **brussels sprouts**. [usu pl]
→see **tree**

❶ 자동사 싹트다, 나다 ❑ 콩은 며칠만 있으면 싹이 튼다. ❷ 자동사 자라나다 ❑ 산사나무에 새잎이 자라나기 시작하고 있었다. ❸ 타동사/자동사 나다, 생기다 ❑ 그녀는 이제 많이 늙었다. 작고 동그란 금속테 안경을 쓰고 턱에는 구레나룻이 생기기 시작했다. ❹ 가산명사 싹양배추

spruce /sprus/ (**spruces**)

Spruce is both the singular and the plural form.

❶ N-VAR A **spruce** is a kind of evergreen tree. ❑ *Trees such as spruce, pine, and oak have been planted.* ❑ *...a young blue spruce.* ❷ ADJ Someone who is **spruce** is very neat and clean in appearance. ❑ *Chris was looking spruce in his stiff-collared black shirt and new short hair cut.*

spruce은 단수형 및 복수형이다.

❶ 가산명사 또는 불가산명사 가문비나무 ❑ 가문비나무나 소나무, 떡갈나무 같은 나무들을 심었다. ❷ 싱그럽고 푸른 가문비나무 ❷ 형용사 말쑥한 ❑ 크리스는 깃이 빳빳한 검은 셔츠를 입고 새로 짧게 머리를 깎아 말쑥해 보였다.

▶**spruce up** PHRASAL VERB If something **is spruced up**, its appearance is improved. If someone **is spruced up**, they have made themselves look very smart. ❑ *Many buildings have been spruced up.*

구동사 치장하다, 모양내다 ❑ 상당수의 건물이 새로 단장했다.

sprung /sprʌŋ/ **Sprung** is the past participle of **spring**.

spring의 과거 분사

spun /spʌn/ **Spun** is the past tense and past participle of **spin**.

spin의 과거, 과거 분사

spur ♦◇◇ /spɜr/ (**spurs, spurring, spurred**) ❶ V-T If one thing **spurs** you to do another, it encourages you to do it. ❑ *It's the money that spurs these fishermen to risk a long ocean journey in their flimsy boats.* ● PHRASAL VERB **Spur on** means the same as **spur**. ❑ *Their attitude, rather than reining him back, only seemed to spur Philip on.* ❷ V-T If something **spurs** a change or event, it makes it happen faster or sooner. [JOURNALISM] ❑ *The administration may put more emphasis on spurring economic growth.* ❸ N-COUNT Something that acts as a **spur** to something else encourages a person or organization to do that thing or makes it happen more quickly. ❑ *...a belief in competition as a spur to efficiency.* ❹ PHRASE If you do something **on the spur of the moment**, you do it suddenly, without planning it beforehand. ❑ *They admitted they had taken a vehicle on the spur of the moment.*

❶ 타동사 자극하다, 동기가 되다 ❑ 어민들이 금방이라도 부서질 것 같은 배를 타고 바다를 향해 긴 여정에 나서는 이유는 돈 때문이다. ● 구동사 자극하다, 동기가 되다 ❑ 그들의 태도가 필립을 제지하기보다 오히려 자극시키는 것만 같았다. ❷ 타동사 박차를 가하다 [언론] ❑ 정부가 경제 성장 활성화를 더욱 강조할지도 모른다. ❸ 가산명사 박차, 자극, 원동력 ❑ 경쟁이 효율성 향상의 원동력이라는 믿음 ❹ 구 순간적인 충동에서, 충동적으로 ❑ 그들은 순간적인 충동에서 차 한 대를 훔쳤다고 시인했다.

spu|ri|ous /spyʊəriəs/ ❶ ADJ Something that is **spurious** seems to be genuine, but is false. [DISAPPROVAL] ❑ *He was arrested in 1979 on spurious corruption charges.* ❷ ADJ A **spurious** argument or way of reasoning is incorrect, and so the conclusion is probably incorrect. [DISAPPROVAL] ❑ *...a spurious framework for analysis.*

❶ 형용사 그럴싸한, 신빙성 없는 [탐탁찮음] ❑ 그는 1979년 신빙성 없는 부패 혐의로 체포되었다. ❷ 형용사 비논리적인 [탐탁찮음] ❑ 비논리적인 분석틀

spurn /spɜrn/ (**spurns, spurning, spurned**) V-T If you **spurn** someone or something, you reject them. ❑ *He spurned the advice of management consultants.*

타동사 일축하다, 퇴짜 놓다 ❑ 그는 경영 컨설턴트들의 조언을 일축했다.

spurt /spɜrt/ (**spurts, spurting, spurted**) ❶ V-T/V-I When liquid or fire **spurts** from somewhere or when something **spurts** liquid or fire, it comes out quickly in a thin, powerful stream. ❑ *They spurted blood all over me. I nearly passed*

❶ 타동사/자동사 분출하다, 뿜어 나오다, 솟구치다 ❑ 그들의 피가 내 온몸에 튀었다. 나는 거의 기절할 뻔했다. ❑ 그가 그녀의 머리를 쳐서 그녀에게서도 피가

out. ❑ *He hit her on the head, causing her too to spurt blood.* ❑ *I saw flames spurt from the roof.* ● PHRASAL VERB **Spurt out** means the same as **spurt**. ❑ *When the washing machine spurts out water at least we can mop it up.* ② N-COUNT A **spurt of** liquid is a stream of it which comes out of something very forcefully. ❑ *A spurt of diesel came from one valve and none from the other.* ③ N-COUNT A **spurt of** activity, effort, or emotion is a sudden, brief period of intense activity, effort, or emotion. ❑ *The average boy of 14 years old is only beginning his adolescent growth spurt.* ④ V-I If someone or something **spurts** somewhere, they suddenly increase their speed for a short while in order to get there. ❑ *The back wheels spun and the van spurted up the last few feet.* ⑤ PHRASE If something happens **in spurts**, there are periods of activity followed by periods in which it does not happen. ❑ *The deals came in spurts: three in 1977, none in 1978, three more in 1979.*

spy /spaɪ/ (**spies, spying, spied**) ① N-COUNT A **spy** is a person whose job is to find out secret information about another country or organization. ❑ *He was jailed for five years as an alleged British spy.* ② ADJ A **spy** satellite or **spy** plane obtains secret information about another country by taking photographs from the sky. [ADJ n] ❑ *...pictures from unmanned spy planes operated by the U.S. military.* ③ V-I Someone who **spies for** a country or organization tries to find out secret information about another country or organization. ❑ *The agent spied for East Germany for more than twenty years.* ❑ *East and West are still spying on one another.* ● **spying** N-UNCOUNT ❑ *...a ten-year sentence for spying.* ④ V-I If you **spy on** someone, you watch them secretly. ❑ *That day he spied on her while pretending to work on the shrubs.*

sq

The spelling **sq.** is also used.

sq is used as a written abbreviation for **square** when you are giving the measurement of an area. ❑ *The building provides about 25,500 sq ft of air-conditioned offices.*

squab|ble /skwɒbəl/ (**squabbles, squabbling, squabbled**) V-RECIP When people **squabble**, they quarrel about something that is not really important. ❑ *Mother is devoted to Dad although they squabble all the time.* ❑ *The children were squabbling over the remote-control gadget for the television.* ● **squabbling** N-UNCOUNT ❑ *In recent months its government has been paralysed by political squabbling.* ● N-COUNT **Squabble** is also a noun. ❑ *There have been minor squabbles about phone bills.*

squad ◆◇◇ /skwɒd/ (**squads**) ① N-COUNT A **squad** is a section of a police force that is responsible for dealing with a particular type of crime. ❑ *The building was evacuated and the bomb squad called.* ② N-COUNT A **squad** is a group of players from which a sports team will be chosen. ❑ *Sean O'Leary has been named in the England squad to tour Argentina.*

squad|ron /skwɒdrən/ (**squadrons**) N-COUNT-COLL A **squadron** is a section of one of the armed forces, especially the air force. ❑ *The government said it was preparing a squadron of eighteen Mirage fighter planes.*

squal|id /skwɒlɪd/ ADJ A **squalid** place is dirty, untidy, and in bad condition. ❑ *The early industrial cities were squalid and unhealthy places.*

squal|or /skwɒlər/ N-UNCOUNT You can refer to very dirty, unpleasant conditions as **squalor**. ❑ *He was out of work and living in squalor.*

squan|der /skwɒndər/ (**squanders, squandering, squandered**) V-T If you **squander** money, resources, or opportunities, you waste them. ❑ *Hooker didn't squander his money on flashy cars or other vices.*

square ◆◆◇ /skweər/ (**squares, squaring, squared**) ① N-COUNT A **square** is a shape with four sides that are all the same length and four corners that are all right angles. ❑ *Serve the cake warm or at room temperature, cut in squares.* ❑ *There was a calendar on the wall, with large squares around the dates.* ② N-COUNT; N-IN-NAMES In a town or city, a **square** is a flat open place, often in the shape of a square. ❑ *The house is located in one of Pimlico's prettiest garden squares.* ③ ADJ Something that is **square** has a shape the same as a square or similar to a square. ❑ *Round tables seat more people in the same space as a square table.* ④ ADJ **Square** is used before units of length when referring to the area of something. For example, if something is three feet long and two feet wide, its area is six square feet. [ADJ n] ❑ *Canary Wharf was set to provide 10 million square feet of office space.* ⑤ ADJ **Square** is used after units of length when you are giving the length of each side of something that is square in shape. [amount ADJ] ❑ *...a linen cushion cover, 45 cm square.* ⑥ V-T To **square** a number means to multiply it by itself. For example, **3 squared** is 3 x 3, or 9. **3 squared** is usually written as 3². ❑ *Take the time in seconds, square it, and multiply by 5.12.* ⑦ N-COUNT The **square** of a number is the number produced when you multiply that number by itself. For example, the **square of 3** is 9. ❑ *...the square of the speed of light, an exceedingly large number.* ⑧ V-T/V-I If you **square** two different ideas or actions **with** each other or if they **square with** each other, they fit or match each other. ❑ *That explanation squares with the facts, doesn't it?* ⑨ V-T If you **square** something **with** someone, you ask their permission or check with them that what you are doing is acceptable to them. ❑ *I squared it with Dan, who said it was all right so long as I was back next Monday morning.* ⑩ →see also **squarely** ⑪ PHRASE If you are **back to square one**, you have to start dealing with something from the beginning again because the way you were dealing with it has failed. ❑ *If your complaint is not upheld, you may feel you are back to square one.* ⑫ **fair and square** →see **fair**

square|ly /skweərli/ ① ADV **Squarely** means directly or in the middle, rather than indirectly or at an angle. [ADV with v] ❑ *I kept the gun aimed squarely at his eyes.* ② ADV If something such as blame or responsibility lies **squarely** with someone, they are definitely the person responsible. [ADV with v] ❑ *The president put the blame squarely on his opponent.*

뿜어져 나왔다. ❑ 나는 지붕에서 불꽃이 솟구치는 것을 보았다. ● 구동사 분출하다, 뿜어 나오다, 솟구치다 ❑ 세탁기에서 물이 뿜어져 나오면 최소한 닦을 수는 있다. ② 가산명사 분출 ❑ 디젤 연료가 밸브 하나에서만 분출되고 다른 밸브에서는 아무것도 나오지 않았다. ③ 가산명사 한창, (감정의) 용솟음침 ❑ 열네 살밑 보통 소년은 한창을 때 시기에 접어든 청소년에 불과하다. ④ 자동사 갑자기 속도를 내다, 신속하게 달리다 ❑ 트럭 뒷바퀴가 돌더니 밴이 마지막 몇 피트를 전속력으로 달렸다. ⑤ 구 단속적으로, 띄엄띄엄 ❑ 계약이 띄엄띄엄 성사되었다. 1977년에는 세 건이 있었으나, 1978년에는 단 한 건도 없었고, 1979년에 세 건이 더 성사되었다.

① 가산명사 스파이, 첩보원, 간첩 ❑ 그는 영국 스파이라는 혐의로 5년 동안 수감되었다. ② 형용사 정찰의, 첩보의 ❑ 미군 소속 무인 정찰기에 찍힌 사진 ③ 자동사 첩보 활동을 하다, 스파이 노릇을 하다 ❑ 이 요원은 20년 넘게 동독 스파이 노릇을 했다. ● 첩보 활동 불가산명사 ❑ 첩보 활동에 대한 혐의로 징역 10년 ④ 자동사 염탐하다, 몰래 감시하다 ❑ 그날 그는 관목을 다듬는 척하면서 그녀를 몰래 지켜봤다.

철자 sq.도 쓴다.

square의 약자, 재곱, 평방 ❑ 건물 내에는 에어컨 시설이 갖춰진 사무실이 대략 25,500평방피트가 있다.

상호동사 티격태격하다, 다투다 ❑ 비록 늘 다투기는 해도 엄마는 아빠에게 헌신적이다. ❑ 아이들이 텔레비전 리모컨을 두고 티격태격하고 있었다. ● 티격태격, 다툼 불가산명사 ❑ 최근 몇 달간 정치판이 다투느라 정부 기능이 마비됐다. ● 가산명사 티격태격, 다툼 ❑ 전화 요금 청구서를 두고 사소한 다툼이 있어 왔다.

① 가산명사 (경찰서의) 반, 계 ❑ 건물에 소개명령이 떨어졌고 폭탄 제거반이 호출되었다. ② 가산명사 선수단 ❑ 숀 오리어리가 아르헨티나 원정 경기 잉글랜드 선수단에 뽑혔다.

가산명사-집합 비행 중대 ❑ 정부가 미라주 전투기 18대로 구성된 비행 중대를 준비 중이라고 밝혔다.

형용사 누추한, 꾀죄한 ❑ 초기의 산업 도시들은 불결하고 비위생적인 곳이었다.

불가산명사 누추한 상태, 너저분함 ❑ 그는 직장을 잃고 누추한 곳에서 살고 있었다.

타동사 허비하다, 낭비하다 ❑ 후커는 화려한 차나 다른 죄악을 부르는 것에 돈을 낭비하지 않았다.

① 가산명사 정사각형 ❑ 케이크를 정사각형으로 잘라서 따뜻하게 데우거나 상온으로 내놓으세요. ❑ 커다란 정사각형 안에 날짜가 적힌 달력이 벽에 걸려 있었다. ② 가산명사; 이름명사 광장 ❑ 그 집은 핌리코에서 가장 예쁜 정원형 광장 중 한 곳에 위치해 있다. ③ 형용사 정사각형 모양의, 사각형 모양의 ❑ 같은 공간이라면 사각형 탁자보다 둥근 탁자에 더 많은 사람이 앉을 수 있다. ④ 형용사 평방의, 제곱의 ❑ 카나리 워프는 총 1천만 평방피트의 사무실 공간을 제공하기 위해 건축되었다. ⑤ 형용사 사각형의 -의 ❑ 가로세로 45센티미터의 리넨 쿠션 커버 ⑥ 타동사 제곱하다 ❑ 초 단위로 시간을 재서 제곱한 뒤 5.12를 곱하세요. ⑦ 가산명사 제곱, 자승 ❑ 빛의 속도를 제곱하면 어마어마하게 큰 숫자가 나온다. ⑧ 타동사/자동사 일치시키다, 맞추다; 일치하다, 맞다 ❑ 설명이 사실과 맞아떨어지는군. 그렇지? ⑨ 타동사 허락을 구하다 ❑ 내가 댄한테 물어봤더니 다음주 월요일 아침에 돌아오기만 하면 괜찮다고 했어. ⑪ 구 원점으로 돌아가다 ❑ 고소가 받아들여지지 않을 경우 원점으로 돌아간 기분이 들지도 모른다.

① 부사 정면으로, 똑바로 ❑ 나는 똑바로 그의 눈을 향해 총을 겨누었다. ② 부사 전적으로 ❑ 대통령은 야당 당수에게 전적인 책임을 물었다.

A

Square Mile N-PROPER **The Square Mile** is the part of London where many important financial institutions have their main offices. □ ...*one of the Square Mile's most prestigious banks.* →see also **City**

고유명사 스퀘어 마일 (런던 금융 중심지) □ 스퀘어마일에서 가장 명성 높은 은행 가운데 하나

B

square root (**square roots**) N-COUNT The **square root of** a number is another number which produces the first number when it is multiplied by itself. For example, the **square root of 16 is 4**.

가산명사 제곱근

C

squash /skwɒʃ/ (**squashes, squashing, squashed**) ■ V-T If someone or something **is squashed**, they are pressed or crushed with such force that they become injured or lose their shape. □ *Robert was lucky to escape with just a broken foot after being squashed against a fence by a car.* □ *Whole neighborhoods have been squashed flat by shelling.* ■ ADJ If people or things are **squashed into** a place, they are put or pushed into a place where there is not enough room for them to be. [v-link ADJ into n] □ *There were 2000 people squashed into her recent show.* ■ N-SING If you say that getting a number of people into a small space is **a squash**, you mean that it is only just possible for them all to get into it. [INFORMAL] □ *It all looked a bit of a squash as they squeezed inside the small hatchback.* ■ V-T If you **squash** something that is causing you trouble, you put a stop to it, often by force. □ *The troops would stay in position to squash the first murmur of trouble.* ■ N-UNCOUNT **Squash** is a game in which two players hit a small rubber ball against the walls of a court using rackets. □ *I also play squash.*

■ 타동사 깃눌리다 □ 로버트는 교통사고로 차와 담장 사이에 끼이고서야 다행히 한쪽 발만 부러진 채 빠져 나왔다. □ 폭격으로 온 동네가 초토화되었다. ■ 형용사 밀어 넣다, 쑤셔 넣다 □ 최근 그녀의 공연을 보기 위해 2천 명의 사람들이 객석을 가득 메웠다. ■ 단수명사 꽉 들어찬 상태, 비좁은 상태 □ 그들이 조그만 해치백형 자동차 안으로 비집고 들어가는데 상당히 비좁아 보였다. ■ 타동사 진압하다 □ 소란이 일어날 기미만 보이면 진압을 하려고 군대가 대기할 것이다. ■ 불가산명사 스쿼시 □ 나는 스쿼시도 친다.

D

E

F

G

squat /skwɒt/ (**squats, squatting, squatted**) ■ V-I If you **squat**, you lower yourself toward the ground, balancing on your feet with your legs bent. □ *We squatted beside the pool and watched the diver sink slowly down.* ● PHRASAL VERB **Squat down** means the same as **squat**. □ *Albert squatted down and examined it.* ● N-SING **Squat** is also a noun. □ *He bent to a squat and gathered the puppies on his lap.* ■ ADJ If you describe someone or something as **squat**, you mean they are short and thick, usually in an unattractive way. □ *Eddie was a short squat fellow in his forties with thinning hair.* ■ V-I People who **squat** occupy an unused building or unused land without having a legal right to do so. □ *You can't simply wander around squatting on other people's property.* ■ N-COUNT A **squat** is an empty building that people are living in illegally, without paying any rent or any property tax. □ *After returning from Paris, David moved to a squat in Brixton.*

■ 자동사 쪼그리고 앉다 □ 우리는 수영장 옆에 쪼그리고 앉아 다이버가 천천히 가라앉는 모습을 지켜봤다. ● 구동사 쪼그리고 앉다 □ 앨버트가 쪼그리고 앉아 그것을 자세히 살펴봤다. ● 단수명사 쪼그리고 앉은 자세 □ 그가 쪼그리고 앉아 강아지들을 무릎 위에 올려놓았다. ■ 형용사 땅딸막한 □ 에디는 땅딸막하고 머리가 듬성듬성 빠지는 40대 아저씨였다. ■ 자동사 불법 거주하다 □ 다른 사람들 땅에 불법 거주하면서 떠돌며 생활할 수는 없다. ■ 가산명사 불법 거주지 □ 데이비드는 파리로 돌아온 후 브릭스턴의 한 건물에서 불법 거주하기 시작했다.

H

I

J

K

squat|ter /skwɒtər/ (**squatters**) N-COUNT A **squatter** is someone who lives in an unused building without having a legal right to do so and without paying any rent or any property tax. □ *...another violent clash as police evicted squatters from empty buildings.*

가산명사 불법 점거자, 무단 입주자 □ 경찰이 빈 건물들에서 무단 입주자들을 쫓아내면서 또 한 차례 충돌이 벌어졌다.

L

squeak /skwiːk/ (**squeaks, squeaking, squeaked**) V-I If something or someone **squeaks**, they make a short, high-pitched sound. □ *My boots squeaked a little as I walked.* □ *The door squeaked open.* ● N-COUNT **Squeak** is also a noun. □ *He gave an outraged squeak.*

자동사 소리를 꽥 지르다, 끽끽거리다, 삐걱거리다 □ 걸을 때 내 부츠에서 끽끽 소리가 났다. □ 문이 삐걱거리며 열렸다. ● 가산명사 꽥 하는 소리, 끽끽거리는 소리 □ 그는 화를 내며 소리를 꽥 질렀다.

M

squeal /skwiːl/ (**squeals, squealing, squealed**) V-I If someone or something **squeals**, they make a long, high-pitched sound. □ *Jennifer squealed with delight and hugged me.* ● N-COUNT **Squeal** is also a noun. □ *At that moment there was a squeal of brakes and the angry blowing of a car horn.*

자동사 비명을 지르다, 끽 소리 나다 □ 제니퍼가 행복해하며 끽 소리를 지르며 나를 껴안았다. ● 가산명사 비명 소리, 끽 하는 소리 □ 바로 그 순간 끽 하고 브레이크 밟는 소리와 시끄럽게 울려 대는 경적 소리가 들렸다.

N

squeam|ish /skwiːmɪʃ/ ADJ If you are **squeamish**, you are easily upset by unpleasant sights or situations. □ *I'm terribly squeamish. I can't bear gory films.*

형용사 비위가 약한 □ 나는 비위가 심하게 약하다. 잔학한 영화는 도무지 볼 수가 없다.

O

squeeze ◆◇◇ /skwiːz/ (**squeezes, squeezing, squeezed**) ■ V-T If you **squeeze** something, you press it firmly, usually with your hands. □ *He squeezed her arm reassuringly.* ● N-COUNT **Squeeze** is also a noun. □ *I liked her way of reassuring you with a squeeze of the hand.* ■ V-T If you **squeeze** a liquid or a soft substance out of an object, you get the liquid or substance out by pressing the object. □ *Joe put the plug in the sink and squeezed some detergent over the dishes.* ■ V-T/V-I If you **squeeze** a person or thing somewhere or if they **squeeze** there, they manage to get through or into a small space. □ *They lowered him gradually into the cockpit. Somehow they squeezed him in the tight space, and strapped him in.* ■ N-SING If you say that getting a number of people into a small space is **a squeeze**, you mean that it is only just possible for them all to get into it. [INFORMAL] □ *It was a squeeze in the car with five of them.* ■ V-T If a government **squeezes** the economy, they put strict controls on people's ability to borrow money or on their own departments' freedom to spend money, in order to control the country's rate of inflation. □ *If a voluntary agreement is not reached the government will squeeze the economy into a severe recession to force inflation down.* ● N-SING **Squeeze** is also a noun. □ *The CBI also says the squeeze is slowing down inflation.*

■ 타동사 꼭 쥐다, 꼭 짜다 □ 그는 안심시키려는 듯 그녀의 팔을 꼭 잡아 줬다. ● 가산명사 꼭 쥠, 꼭 잡음 □ 나는 그녀가 손을 꼭 잡아 주면서 너를 안심시키는 모습이 좋았다. ■ 타동사 짜내다 □ 조는 싱크대 구멍을 막고 그릇들 위에 대고 주방세제를 좀 짰다. ■ 타동사/자동사 밀어 넣다, 쑤셔 넣다 □ 그들은 그의 몸을 낮춰 천천히 조정석으로 들여보냈다. ● 가산명사 밀침, 쑤셔 넣은 상태 [비격식체] □ 차 안이 그들 5명으로 꽉 차 있었다. ■ 타동사 긴축 정책을 펴다 □ 자발적인 합의가 도출되지 않으면 정부가 인위적으로 물가를 끌어내리기 위한 긴축 정책을 펴 심각한 경기 침체로 맞이할 것이다. ● 단수명사 긴축 정책 □ 영국경제인연합회(CBI)는 긴축 정책이 인플레이션을 완화시키고 있다고 말한다.

P

Q

R

S

T

squid /skwɪd/ (**squids**)

| Squid can also be used as the plural form. |

squid도 복수형으로 쓰일 수 있다.

U

N-COUNT A **squid** is a sea creature with a long soft body and many soft arms called tentacles. ● N-UNCOUNT **Squid** is pieces of this creature eaten as food. □ *Add the prawns and squid and cook for 2 minutes.*

가산명사 오징어 ● 불가산명사 오징어 □ 새우와 오징어를 넣고 2분간 조리하세요.

V

squint /skwɪnt/ (**squints, squinting, squinted**) ■ V-I If you **squint at** something, you look at it with your eyes partly closed. □ *The girl squinted at the photograph.* □ *The bright sunlight made me squint.* ■ N-COUNT If someone has a **squint**, their eyes look in different directions from each other. □ *...a pimple-faced man with a squint.*

■ 자동사 눈을 찡그리고 보다, 눈을 가늘게 뜨고 보다 □ 소녀가 눈을 가늘게 뜨고 사진을 보았다. □ 나는 밝은 햇살에 눈살을 찌푸렸다. ■ 가산명사 사팔뜨기, 사시 □ 사팔뜨기에다 얼굴에 여드름이 난 남자

W

squirm /skwɜːrm/ (**squirms, squirming, squirmed**) ■ V-I If you **squirm**, you move your body from side to side, usually because you are nervous or uncomfortable. □ *He had squirmed and wriggled and screeched when his father had washed his face.* □ *He gave a feeble shrug and tried to squirm free.* ■ V-I If you **squirm**, you are very embarrassed or ashamed. □ *Mentioning religion is a sure way to make him squirm.*

■ 자동사 꿈틀거리다, 몸부림치다 □ 아빠가 세수를 시켜 주는 동안 아이는 꿈틀거리고 바둥거리며 소리를 빽 질렀다. □ 그는 가볍게 어깨를 으쓱 하더니 발버둥쳐서 빠져나가려 했다. ■ 자동사 어색해하다, 안절부절못하다 □ 그는 종교 이야기만 하면 꼭 안절부절못한다.

X

Y

squir|rel /skwɜːrəl, BRIT skwɪrəl/ (**squirrels**) N-COUNT A **squirrel** is a small animal with a long furry tail. Squirrels live mainly in trees.

가산명사 다람쥐

Z

squirt /skwɜrt/ (**squirts, squirting, squirted**) ◼ V-T/V-I If you **squirt** a liquid somewhere or if it **squirts** somewhere, the liquid comes out of a narrow opening in a thin fast stream. ◻ *Norman cut open his pie and squirted tomato sauce into it.* ● N-COUNT **Squirt** is also a noun. ◻ *It just needs a little squirt of oil.* ◼ V-T If you **squirt** something **with** a liquid, you squirt the liquid at it. ◻ *They squirted the politicians with manure.*

◼ 타동사/자동사 쩍 짜다; 쩍 나오다 ◻ 노먼은 파이를 잘라 그 안에 토마토소스를 쩍 짜 넣었다. ● 가산명사 쩍 짜기, 쩍 나오는 줄기 ◻ 기름을 조금만 쩍 짜 넣으면 된다. ◼ 타동사 -을 짝 뿌리다 ◻ 그들은 정치인들에게 거름을 뿌렸다.

St.

> The spelling **st.** is also used. The form **SS.** or **SS** is used as the plural for meaning ◼.

> 철자 st.도 쓰인다. SS. 또는 SS는 ◼의미의 복수로 쓰인다.

[BRIT also **St**] ◼ **St.** is a written abbreviation for **Street**. ◻ *...116 Princess St.* ◼ **St.** is a written abbreviation for **Saint**. ◻ *...St. Thomas.*

[영국영어 st] ◼ Street의 약자, - 가(街) ◻ 프린세스 가 116번지 ◼ Saint의 약자, 성(聖) - ◻ 성토머스

stab /stæb/ (**stabs, stabbing, stabbed**) ◼ V-T If someone **stabs** you, they push a knife or sharp object into your body. ◻ *Somebody stabbed him in the stomach.* ◻ *Dean tried to stab him with a screwdriver.* ◼ V-T/V-I If you **stab** something or **stab at** it, you push at it with your finger or with something pointed that you are holding. ◻ *Bess stabbed a slice of cucumber.* ◻ *Goldstone flipped through the pages and stabbed his thumb at the paragraph he was looking for.* ◼ N-SING If you have a **stab at** something, you try to do it. [INFORMAL] ◻ *Several tennis stars have had a stab at acting.* ◼ N-SING You can refer to a sudden, usually unpleasant feeling as a **stab** of that feeling. [LITERARY] ◻ *...a stab of pain just above his eye.* ◼ PHRASE If you say that someone **has stabbed** you **in the back**, you mean that they have done something very harmful to you when you thought that you could trust them. You can refer to an action of this kind as a **stab in the back**. ◻ *She felt betrayed, as though her daughter had stabbed her in the back.* ◼ **a stab in the dark** →see **dark**

◼ 타동사 -을 드라이버로 그를 찌르려 했다. ◼ 타동사/자동사 찌르다, 찔러 넣다 ◻ 베스가 오이 한 조각을 찔러 넣었다. ◻ 골드스톤은 책장을 넘기다가 찾고 있던 단락에 엄지손가락을 댔다. ◼ 단수명사 시도 [비격식체] ◻ 테니스 선수 몇 명이 연기를 시도해 봤었다. ◼ 단수명사 찌르는 듯한 아픔, 쑤시는 느낌 [문예체] ◻ 그의 눈 바로 위쪽이 욱신거림 ◼ 구 뒤통수를 치다, 배신하다; 뒤통수치기 ◻ 그녀는 딸에게 뒤통수를 얻어맞은 듯한 배신감을 느꼈다.

stab|bing /stæbɪŋ/ (**stabbings**) ◼ N-COUNT A **stabbing** is an incident in which someone stabs someone else with a knife. ◻ *...the victim of a stabbing.* ◼ ADJ A **stabbing** pain is a sudden sharp pain. [ADJ n] ◻ *He was struck by a stabbing pain in his midriff.*

◼ 가산명사 사람을 칼로 찌른 사건 ◻ 칼에 찔린 사람 ◼ 형용사 찌르는 듯한, 통렬한 ◻ 그는 몸통 중앙이 찌르는 듯이 아팠다.

sta|bil|ity /stəbɪlɪti/ →see **stable**

sta|bi|lize /steɪbɪlaɪz/ (**stabilizes, stabilizing, stabilized**) [BRIT also **stabilise**] V-T/V-I If something **stabilizes**, or is **stabilized**, it becomes stable. ◻ *Although her illness is serious, her condition is beginning to stabilize.* ● **sta|bi|li|za|tion** /steɪbɪlɪzeɪʃ³n/ N-UNCOUNT ◻ *...the stabilization of property prices.*

[영국영어 stabilise] 타동사/자동사 안정되다; 안정시키다 ◻ 그녀의 병이 심각하기는 해도 상태가 안정되기 시작하고 있다. ● 안정화 불가산명사 ◻ 부동산 가격 안정화

sta|ble ◆◇◇ /steɪb³l/ (**stabler, stablest, stables**) ◼ ADJ If something is **stable**, it is not likely to change or come to an end suddenly. ◻ *The price of oil should remain stable for the rest of 1992.* ● **sta|bil|ity** /stəbɪlɪti/ N-UNCOUNT ◻ *It was a time of political stability and progress.* ◼ ADJ If someone has a **stable** personality, they are calm and reasonable and their mood does not change suddenly. ◻ *Their characters are fully formed and they are both very stable children.* ◼ ADJ You can describe someone who is seriously ill as **stable** when their condition has stopped getting worse. ◻ *The injured man was in a stable condition.* ◼ ADJ Chemical substances are described as **stable** when they tend to remain in the same chemical or atomic state. [TECHNICAL] ◻ *The less stable compounds were converted into a compound called Delta-A THC.* ◼ ADJ If an object is **stable**, it is firmly fixed in position and is not likely to move or fall. ◻ *This structure must be stable.* ◼ N-COUNT A **stable** or **stables** is a building in which horses are kept. ◼ N-COUNT A **stable** or **stables** is an organization that breeds and trains horses for racing. ◻ *Miss Curling won on two horses from Mick Trickey's stable.*

◼ 형용사 안정된 ◻ 1992년 남은 기간 동안 유가가 안정세를 유지해야 한다. ● 안정, 안정성 불가산명사 ◻ 그 때는 정치적으로 안정되고 발전한 시기였다. ◼ 형용사 (성격이) 안정된 ◻ 두 아이 모두 성숙한 인격을 지녔고 매우 안정되어 있다. ◼ 형용사 (병의 상태가) 안정된 ◻ 그 부상자는 상태가 안정되어 있었다. ◼ 형용사 [과학 기술] 안정성이 떨어지는 화합물은 '델타-에이 티에이취시'로 명명된 화합물로 전환되었다. ◼ 형용사 튼튼한, 흔들림 없는 ◻ 이 구조물은 튼튼한 것이 분명해. ◼ 가산명사 마구간 ◼ 가산명사 경주마 훈련소 ◻ 컬링 양은 믹트리키에서 훈련받은 말 두 마리에 걸어 이겼다.

stack /stæk/ (**stacks, stacking, stacked**) ◼ N-COUNT A **stack of** things is a pile of them. ◻ *There were stacks of books on the bedside table and floor.* ◼ V-T If you **stack** a number of things, you arrange them in neat piles. ◻ *Mme Cathiard was stacking the clean bottles in crates.* ● PHRASAL VERB **Stack up** means the same as **stack**. ◻ *He ordered them to stack up pillows behind his back.* ◼ N-PLURAL If you say that someone has **stacks of** something, you mean that they have a lot of it. [INFORMAL] ◻ *If the job's that good, you'll have stacks of money.*

◼ PHRASE If you say that **the odds are stacked against** someone, or that particular factors **are stacked against** them, you mean that they are unlikely to succeed in what they want to do because the conditions are not favorable. ◻ *The odds are stacked against civilians getting a fair trial.*

◼ 가산명사 무더기, 더미 ◻ 침대 옆 탁자와 바닥에 책이 쌓여 있었다. ◼ 타동사 쌓다, 쌓아올리다 ◻ 카티아드 부인이 깨끗한 병을 나무 상자에 넣어 쌓아올리고 있었다. ● 구동사 쌓다, 쌓아올리다 ◻ 그는 그들을 시켜 자기 등 뒤에 베개를 쌓아 올리도록 했다. ◼ 복수명사 많음, 다량 [비격식체] ◻ 그 직장이 그렇게 좋으면 돈을 엄청 벌겠군.

◼ 구 사정이 -에게 불리하다, 가능성이 희박하다 ◻ 민간인들이 공정한 재판을 받을 가능성이 희박하다.

> A **stack** of things is usually tidy, and often consists of flat objects placed directly on top of each other. ◻ *...a neat stack of dishes.* A **heap** of things is usually untidy, and often has the shape of a hill or mound. ◻ *Now, the house is a heap of rubble.* A **pile** can be tidy or untidy. ◻ *...a neat pile of clothes.*

> 물건의 stack은 대개 정돈되어 있으며, 종종 납작한 사물을 겹겹이 쌓아둔 것을 말한다. ◻ ...깔끔하게 쌓아 놓은 접시들. 물건의 heap은 대개 정돈되어 있지 않고, 종종 언덕이나 마운드의 모양을 하고 있다. ◻ 자, 집이 파편 더미다. pile은 정돈되어 있을 수도 있고 그렇지 않을 수도 있다. ◻ ...차곡차곡 깔끔하게 쌓아 놓은 옷.

sta|dium ◆◇◇ /steɪdiəm/ (**stadiums** or **stadia**) /steɪdiə/ N-COUNT; N-IN-NAMES A **stadium** is a large sports ground with rows of seats all around it. ◻ *...a baseball stadium.*

가산명사; 이름명사 경기장, 스타디움 ◻ 야구장

staff ◆◆◆ /stæf/ (**staffs, staffing, staffed**) ◼ N-COUNT-COLL The **staff** of an organization are the people who work for it. ◻ *The staff were very good.* ◻ *The outpatient program has a staff of six people.* →see also **Chief of Staff** ◼ N-PLURAL People who are part of a particular staff are often referred to as **staff**. ◻ *10 staff were allocated to the task.* ◼ V-T If an organization **is staffed by** particular people, they are the people who work for it. [usu passive] ◻ *They are staffed by volunteers.* ● **staffed** ADJ [adv ADJ] ◻ *The house allocated to them was pleasant and spacious, and well-staffed.*

◼ 가산명사-집합 (집합적) 직원 ◻ 직원들이 매우 훌륭했다. ◻ 외래 환자 프로그램 담당 직원이 총 6명이다. ◼ 복수명사 (개개인의) 직원 ◻ 그 일에 직원 열 명이 할당되었다. ◼ 타동사 -로 구성되다, -을 직원으로 두다 ◻ 이들 기관은 자원 봉사자로 구성되어 있다. ● 직원이 -한 형용사 ◻ 그들이 할당받은 집은 쾌적하고 널찍했으며 일하는 사람들도 잘 갖춰져 있었다.

staff|ing /stæfɪŋ/ N-UNCOUNT **Staffing** refers to the number of workers employed to work in a particular organization or building. [BUSINESS] ◻ *Staffing levels in prisons are too low.*

불가산명사 직원 수, 인적 구성 [경제] ◻ 교도소 내의 교도관 수가 매우 저조하다.

stag /stæg/ (**stags**) N-COUNT A **stag** is an adult male deer belonging to one of the larger species of deer. Stags usually have large branch-like horns called antlers.

가산명사 수사슴

stage ♦♦♦ /steɪdʒ/ (stages, staging, staged) **1** N-COUNT A **stage of** an activity, process, or period is one part of it. □ *The way children talk about or express their feelings depends on their age and stage of development.* **2** N-COUNT In a theater, the **stage** is an area where actors or other entertainers perform. [also on N] □ *The road crew needed more than 24 hours to move and rebuild the stage after a concert.* **3** V-T If someone **stages** a play or other show, they organize and present a performance of it. □ *Maya Angelou first staged the play "And I Still Rise" in the late 1970s.* **4** V-T If you **stage** an event or ceremony, you organize it and usually take part in it. □ *Russian workers have staged a number of strikes in protest at the republic's declaration of independence.* **5** N-SING You can refer to a particular area of activity as a particular **stage**, especially when you are talking about politics. □ *He was finally forced off the political stage last year by the deterioration of his physical condition.* **6** to **set the stage** →see **set**
→see **concert**

1 가산명사 단계, 시기 □ 아이들이 자신의 감정에 대해 이야기하고 표현하는 방식은 나이와 발달 단계에 따라 다르다. **2** 가산명사 무대 □ 콘서트가 끝난 후 현장 요원이 무대를 옮겨 다시 짓는 데 24시간 이상이 필요했다. **3** 타동사 선보이다, 무대에 올리다 □ 마야 앤젤루우가 1970년대 후반에 연극 '나는 그래도 일어선다'를 처음 무대에 올렸다. **4** 타동사 조직하다, 벌이다 □ 러시아 노동자들이 공화국 독립 선언에 항의하면서 수차례 파업을 벌여 왔다. **5** 단수명사 활동 무대 □ 그는 결국 건강 악화로 작년에 정계에서 물러나야 했다.

| | **Word Partnership** | *stage*의 연어 |

ADJ.	**advanced** stage, **critical** stage, **crucial** stage, **early** stage, **final** stage, **late/later** stage **1**
V.	**reach** a stage **1**
	leave the stage, **take** the stage **2**
N.	stage **of development**, stage **of a disease**, stage **of a process 1**
	actors on stage, **center** stage, **concert** stage, stage **fright**, stage **manager 2**

stag|fla|tion /stægfleɪʃⁿn/ N-UNCOUNT If an economy is suffering from **stagflation**, inflation is high but there is no increase in the demand for goods or in the number of people who have jobs. [BUSINESS] □ *Many of the industrialized economies would be pushed into a cycle of stagflation.*

불가산명사 스태그플레이션 [경제] □ 많은 경제 선진국들이 스태그플레이션 주기에 빠질지도 모른다.

stag|ger /stægər/ (staggers, staggering, staggered) **1** V-I If you **stagger**, you walk very unsteadily, for example because you are ill or drunk. □ *He lost his balance, staggered back against the rail and toppled over.* **2** V-T If something **staggers** you, it surprises you very much. □ *The whole thing staggers me.* ● **stag|gered** ADJ [v-link ADJ] □ *I was simply staggered by the heat of the Argentinian high summer.* **3** V-T To **stagger** things such as people's vacations or hours of work means to arrange them so that they do not all happen at the same time. □ *During the past few years the government has staggered the summer vacation periods for students.*

1 자동사 비틀거리다 □ 그가 몸의 균형을 잃고 비틀거리며 난간 쪽으로 뒷걸음질하다 넘어지고 말았다. **2** 타동사 깜짝 놀라게 하다, 충격을 주다 □ 그 모든 일이 나에게는 충격이다. ● 깜짝 놀란, 충격받은 형용사 □ 나는 아르헨티나의 한여름 무더위에 정말이지 깜짝 놀랐다. **3** 타동사 서로 엇갈리게 배열하다, 서로 시간 차를 두다 □ 정부가 지난 몇 해 동안 학생들의 여름 방학 기간을 서로 시간 차가 나게 잡아왔다.

stag|ger|ing /stægərɪŋ/ ADJ Something that is **staggering** is very surprising. □ *...a staggering $900 million in short and long-term debt.*

형용사 경악스러운, 어마어마한 □ 자그마치 9백만 달러에 달하는 단기 및 장기 부채

stag|nant /stægnənt/ **1** ADJ If something such as a business or society is **stagnant**, there is little activity or change. [DISAPPROVAL] □ *He is seeking advice on how to revive the stagnant economy.* **2** ADJ **Stagnant** water is not flowing, and therefore often smells unpleasant and is dirty. □ *...a stagnant pond.*

1 형용사 부진한, 침체된 [탐탁찮음] □ 그는 침체된 경기를 회생시킬 방안에 대한 조언을 구하고 있다. **2** 형용사 고여 있는 □ 고여 있는 연못

stag|nate /stægneɪt, BRIT stægneɪt/ (stagnates, stagnating, stagnated) V-I If something such as a business or society **stagnates**, it stops changing or progressing. [DISAPPROVAL] □ *Industrial production is stagnating.* ● **stag|na|tion** /stægneɪʃⁿn/ N-UNCOUNT □ *...the stagnation of the steel industry.*

자동사 침체되다, 부진해지다 [탐탁찮음] □ 산업생산이 부진해지고 있다. ● 침체, 부진 불가산명사 □ 철강 산업 침체

staid /steɪd/ ADJ If you say that someone or something is **staid**, you mean that they are serious, dull, and rather old-fashioned. □ *...a staid seaside resort.*

형용사 고루한, 너무 차분한 □ 재미없는 해변 휴양지

stain /steɪn/ (stains, staining, stained) **1** N-COUNT A **stain** is a mark on something that is difficult to remove. □ *Remove stains by soaking in a mild solution of bleach.* **2** V-T If a liquid **stains** something, the thing becomes colored or marked by the liquid. □ *Some foods can stain the teeth, as of course can smoking.* ● **stained** ADJ □ *His clothing was stained with mud.* ● **-stained** COMB in ADJ □ *...ink-stained fingers.* →see **dry cleaning**

1 가산명사 얼룩 □ 표백제를 희석한 물에 담가 얼룩을 제거하세요. **2** 타동사 얼룩지게 하다, 변색되게 하다 □ 담배와 마찬가지로 일부 음식 때문에 치아가 변색될 수도 있다. ● 얼룩진, 변색된 형용사 □ 그의 옷은 진흙으로 얼룩져 있었다. ● -로 얼룩진 복합형-형용사 □ 잉크가 묻은 손가락

stained glass also **stained-glass** N-UNCOUNT **Stained glass** consists of pieces of glass of different colors which are fixed together to make decorative windows or other objects. □ *...the stained glass window in St. John's Cathedral.*

불가산명사 스테인드글라스 □ 세인트 존 성당에 있는 스테인드글라스 창문

stain|less steel /steɪnlɪs stil/ N-UNCOUNT **Stainless steel** is a metal made from steel and chromium which does not rust. □ *...a stainless steel sink.* →see **pan**

불가산명사 스테인리스 스틸 (녹슬지 않는 금속) □ 스테인리스 스틸로 만든 싱크대

stair /steər/ (stairs) N-PLURAL **Stairs** are a set of steps inside a building which go from one floor to another. □ *Nancy began to climb the stairs.* □ *We walked up a flight of stairs.*

복수명사 (한 단 한 단의) 계단 □ 낸시는 그 계단을 오르기 시작했다. □ 우리는 계단참 하나를 걸어 올라갔다.

stair|case /steərkeɪs/ (staircases) N-COUNT A **staircase** is a set of stairs inside a building. □ *They walked down the staircase together.* →see **house**

가산명사 (죽 이어진) 계단 □ 그들은 함께 계단을 걸어 내려왔다.

stair|way /steərweɪ/ (stairways) N-COUNT A **stairway** is a staircase or a flight of steps, inside or outside a building. □ *...the stairway leading to the top floor.*

가산명사 (죽 이어진) 계단 □ 꼭대기 층으로 연결된 계단

stake /steɪk/ (stakes, staking, staked) **1** PHRASE If something is **at stake**, it is being risked and might be lost or damaged if you are not successful. □ *The tension was naturally high for a game with so much at stake.* **2** N-PLURAL The **stakes** involved in a contest or a risky action are the things that can be gained or lost. □ *The game was usually played for high stakes between two large groups.* **3** V-T If you **stake** something such as your money or your reputation **on** the result of something, you risk your money or reputation on it. □ *He has staked his political future on an election victory.* **4** N-COUNT If you have a **stake in** something such as a business, it matters to you, for example because you own part of it or because its success or failure will affect you. □ *He was eager to return to a more entrepreneurial role in which he had a big financial stake in his own efforts.* **5** N-PLURAL You can use **stakes** to refer to something that is like a contest. For example, you can refer to the choosing of a leader as the **leadership stakes**. □ *Britain lags behind in the European childcare stakes.* **6** N-COUNT A **stake** is a pointed wooden

1 구 위험에 처한, 위태로운 □ 아주 위태로운 경기라서 자연히 긴장감이 고조되어 있었다. **2** 복수명사 내기에 건 돈, 내기에 걸린 물건 □ 평소에는 대규모의 두 단체 간에 큰 돈을 걸고 경기를 했다. **3** 타동사 (돈, 명예 등을) 걸다 □ 그는 자신의 정치 생명을 선거에서의 승리에 걸었다. **4** 가산명사 -에 관여, -의 이해관계 □ 그는 자신의 노력으로 크게 관여하게 된 기업가의 역할로 되돌아가기를 간절히 바랐다. **5** 복수명사 경쟁 □ 영국은 유럽의 육아 정책 경쟁에서 뒤져 있다. **6** 가산명사 지주, 말뚝 □ 그가 똑바로 누워 있게 하기 위해서 그의 두 팔을 나무 말뚝에 묶어 두고 있었다. **7** 구 권리를 주장하다 □ 제인은 배우로서의 권리를 주장하기로 마음먹었다.

post which is pushed into the ground, for example in order to support a young tree. ❏ *His arms were tied to wooden stakes to hold him flat.* **7** PHRASE If you **stake a claim**, you say that something is yours or that you have a right to it. ❏ *Jane is determined to stake her claim as an actress.*

Word Partnership   *stake*의 연어

N.	interests at **stake**, issues at stake **1**
	stake lives on *something* **3**
	stake in a company/firm, majority/minority stake **4**
ADJ.	personal **stake** **4**

---

stake|hold|er /steɪkhoʊldər/ (**stakeholders**) N-COUNT **Stakeholders** are people who have an interest in a company's or organization's affairs. [BUSINESS] ❏ *...the Delaware River Port Authority, a major stakeholder in Penn's Landing.*

stake|hold|er pen|sion (**stakeholder pensions**) N-COUNT In Britain, a **stakeholder pension** is a flexible pension plan with low charges. Both employees and the state contribute to the plan, which is optional, and is in addition to the basic state pension. [BUSINESS] ❏ *New stakeholder pensions will aim to give all workers a retirement pension they can live on.*

가산명사 근로자 연금 [경제] ❏ 새로운 근로자 연금 제도는 모든 근로자들이 퇴직 후 생활이 가능하도록 퇴직 연금을 주는 것을 추구할 것이다.

stale /steɪl/ (**staler, stalest**) **1** ADJ **Stale** food is no longer fresh or good to eat. ❏ *Their daily diet consisted of a lump of stale bread, a bowl of rice and stale water.* **2** ADJ **Stale** air or smells are unpleasant because they are no longer fresh. ❏ *...the smell of stale sweat.* **3** ADJ If you say that a place, an activity, or an idea is **stale**, you mean that it has become boring because it is always the same. [DISAPPROVAL] ❏ *Her relationship with Mark has become stale.*

1 형용사 (식품이) 신선하지 않은 ❏ 그들이 매일 먹는 음식은 오래된 빵 한 덩이와 밥 한 그릇, 신선하지 않은 물이었다. **2** 형용사 (냄새가) 퀴퀴한 ❏ 퀴퀴한 땀 냄새 **3** 형용사 신선미가 없는, 진부한 [탐탁찮음] ❏ 그녀와 마크와의 관계는 더 이상 신선미가 없어졌다.

stale|mate /steɪlmeɪt/ (**stalemates**) N-VAR **Stalemate** is a situation in which neither side in an argument or contest can win or in which no progress is possible. ❏ *The proportional representation system was widely blamed for two inconclusive election results and a year of political stalemate.*

가산명사 또는 불가산명사 교착 상태 ❏ 비례 대표제는 결론이 나지 않는 두 가지 선거 결과와 1년간의 정치적 교착 상태 때문에 비난을 많이 받았다.

stalk /stɔk/ (**stalks, stalking, stalked**) **1** N-COUNT The **stalk** of a flower, leaf, or fruit is the thin part that joins it to the plant or tree. ❏ *A single pale blue flower grows up from each joint on a long stalk.* **2** V-T If you **stalk** a person or a wild animal, you follow them quietly in order to kill them, catch them, or observe them carefully. ❏ *He stalks his victims like a hunter after a deer.* **3** V-T If someone **stalks** someone else, especially a famous person or a person they used to have a relationship with, they keep following them or contacting them in an annoying and frightening way. ❏ *Even after their divorce he continued to stalk and threaten her.*

1 가산명사 (식물의) 줄기 ❏ 대가 긴 줄기 마디마다 연한 파란색 꽃이 하나씩 핀다. **2** 타동사 몰래 접근하다 ❏ 그는 마치 사슴을 쫓는 사냥꾼처럼 자신의 피해자들에게 살금살금 따라 간다. **3** 타동사 쫓아다니며 괴롭히다, 스토킹하다 ❏ 그는 이혼을 한 후에도 그녀를 계속 쫓아다니며 괴롭혔다.

stalk|er /stɔkər/ (**stalkers**) N-COUNT A **stalker** is someone who keeps following or contacting someone else, especially a famous person or a person they used to have a relationship with, in an annoying and frightening way. ❏ *She had been followed and then trapped by a stalker.*

가산명사 남을 따라다니며 괴롭히는 사람, 스토커 ❏ 한 스토커가 그녀를 집요하게 따라다니다가 결국 그녀를 가두어 버렸다.

stall /stɔl/ (**stalls, stalling, stalled**) **1** V-T/V-I If a process **stalls**, or if someone or something **stalls** it, the process stops but may continue at a later time. ❏ *The Social Democratic Party has vowed to try to stall the bill until the current session ends.* ❏ *...but the peace process stalled.* **2** V-I If you **stall**, you try to avoid doing something until later. ❏ *Thomas had spent all week stalling over his decision.* **3** V-T If you **stall** someone, you prevent them from doing something until a later time. ❏ *Shop manager Brian Steel stalled the man until the police arrived.* **4** V-T/V-I If a vehicle **stalls** or if you accidentally **stall** it, the engine stops suddenly. ❏ *The engine stalled.* **5** N-COUNT A **stall** is a large table on which you put goods that you want to sell, or information that you want to give people. ❏ *...market stalls selling local fruits.* **6** N-PLURAL The **stalls** in a theater or concert hall are the seats on the ground floor directly in front of the stage. [mainly BRIT; AM **orchestra**] ❏ *...a lady in the third row of the stalls.* **7** N-COUNT A **stall** is a small enclosed area in a room which is used for a particular purpose, for example a shower. [AM; BRIT usually **cubicle**] ❏ *She went into the shower stall, turned on the water, and grabbed the soap.* →see **traffic**

1 타동사/자동사 지연되다, 중단되다; 지연시키다, 중단시키다 ❏ 사회 민주당이 현 회기가 끝날 때까지 그 법안을 중단시키겠다고 다짐했다. ❏ 그러나 그 평화 정착 절차가 지연되었다. **2** 자동사 지연시키다, 회피하려 하다 ❏ 토머스는 일 주일 내내 그가 내려야 할 결정을 미루면 보냈었다. **3** 타동사 (시간을 끌며) ─를 잡고 있다 ❏ 경찰이 도착할 때까지 가게 관리인 브라이언 스틸이 그 남자를 붙잡고 있었다. **4** 타동사/자동사 (엔진이) 갑자기 멈추다; (엔진을) 갑자기 세우다 ❏ 엔진이 갑자기 멈췄다. **5** 가산명사 진열대, 가판대 ❏ 지방 특산 과일을 파는 가판절들 **6** 복수명사 1층 무대 앞좌석 [주로 영국영어; 미국영어 orchestra] ❏ 1층 무대 앞좌석 세 번째 줄에 앉은 한 숙녀 **7** 가산명사 칸, 칸막이를 한 곳 [미국영어; 영국영어 대개 cubicle] ❏ 그녀는 샤워 박스로 들어가서 물을 틀고 비누를 집었다.

stal|lion /stælɪən/ (**stallions**) N-COUNT A **stallion** is a male horse, especially one kept for breeding.

가산명사 종마

stal|wart /stɔlwərt/ (**stalwarts**) N-COUNT A **stalwart** is a loyal worker or supporter of an organization, especially a political party. ❏ *His free-trade policies aroused suspicion among Tory stalwarts.*

가산명사 충복, 충실한 신봉자 ❏ 그의 자유 무역 정책이 토리당의 충복들 간에 의혹을 불러일으켰다.

stami|na /stæmɪnə/ N-UNCOUNT **Stamina** is the physical or mental energy needed to do a tiring activity for a long time. ❏ *You have to have a lot of stamina to be a top-class dancer.*

불가산명사 체력, 스테미나 ❏ 최고 무용수가 되려면 강인한 체력을 가져야만 한다.

stam|mer /stæmər/ (**stammers, stammering, stammered**) **1** V-T/V-I If you **stammer**, you speak with difficulty and repeating words or sounds. ❏ *Five per cent of children stammer at some point.* ❏ *"Forgive me," I stammered.* ● **stam|mer|ing** N-UNCOUNT ❏ *Of all speech impediments stammering is probably the most embarrassing.* **2** N-SING Someone who has a **stammer** tends to stammer when they speak. ❏ *A speech-therapist cured his stammer.*

1 타동사/자동사 말을 더듬다 ❏ 아이들 중 5퍼센트가 어떤 단계에서는 말을 더듬는다. ❏ "용서해 주세요."라고 나는 더듬거리며 말했다. ● 말 더듬기 불가산명사 ❏ 모든 언어 장애 중에서 말을 더듬는 것이 아마도 가장 당혹스러울 것이다. **2** 단수명사 말 더듬기 ❏ 언어 장애 치료사가 그의 말 더듬기를 치료했다.

stamp ♦♢♢ /stæmp/ (**stamps, stamping, stamped**) **1** N-COUNT A **stamp** or a **postage stamp** is a small piece of paper which you lick and stick on an envelope or package before you mail it to pay for the cost of the postage. ❏ *...a book of stamps.* ❏ *As of February 3rd, the price of a first class stamp will go up to 29 cents.* **2** N-COUNT A **stamp** is a small block of wood or metal which has a pattern or a group of letters on one side. You press it onto a pad of ink and then onto a piece of paper in order to produce a mark on the paper. The mark that you produce is also called a **stamp**. ❏ *...a date stamp and an ink pad.* **3** V-T If you **stamp** a mark or word on an object, you press the mark or word onto the object using

1 가산명사 우표 ❏ 우표책 ❏ 2월 3일자로 1등급 우표 값이 29센트로 오를 것이다. **2** 가산명사 도장, 스탬프 ❏ 날짜 스탬프와 잉크 패드 **3** 타동사 스탬프를 찍다, 압인을 찍다 ❏ 자동차 제조사들은 도난 차량을 추적할 수 있도록 새 차의 이곳저곳에 자동차 인식 번호를 찍는다. **4** 타동사/자동사 발을 구르다 ❏ 그가 종종 내가 성질이 돌을 때까지 나를 놀리면, 나는 화가 나서 어쩔 줄 몰라 하며 발을 구르고 소리를 질렀다. ❏ 그의 발이 액셀을 꾹 밟았다. ● 가산명사 발 구르기 ❏ 문이

a stamp or other device. ❑ *Car manufacturers stamp a vehicle identification number at several places on new cars to help track down stolen vehicles.* ◪ V-T/V-I If you **stamp** or **stamp** your **foot**, you lift your foot and put it down very hard on the ground, for example because you are angry or because your feet are cold. ❑ *Often he teased me till my temper went and I stamped and screamed, feeling furiously helpless.* ❑ *His foot stamped down on the accelerator.* ● N-COUNT **Stamp** is also a noun. ❑ *...hearing the creak of a door and the stamp of cold feet.* ◪ V-I If you **stamp** somewhere, you walk there putting your feet down very hard on the ground because you are angry. ❑ *"I'm going before things get any worse!" he shouted as he stamped out of the bedroom.* ◪ V-I If you **stamp on** something, you put your foot down on it very hard. ❑ *He received the original ban last week after stamping on the referee's foot during the supercup final.* ◪ N-SING If something bears **the stamp of** a particular quality or person, it clearly has that quality or was done by that person. ❑ *Most of us want to make our home a familiar place and put the stamp of our personality on its walls.* ◪ →see also **rubber stamp**

Word Partnership   stamp의 연어

| N. | stamp **collection**, **postage** stamp ◪ |
| | stamp **of approval** ◪ |

▶**stamp out** PHRASAL VERB If you **stamp** something **out**, you put an end to it. ❑ *Dr. Muffett stressed that he was opposed to bullying in schools and that action would be taken to stamp it out.*

stamped ad|dressed en|velope (**stamped addressed envelopes**) N-COUNT A **stamped addressed envelope** is an envelope with a stamp on it and your own name and address, which you send to someone so that something can be sent back to you. The abbreviation **s.a.e.** is also used. [BRIT; AM **SASE**] ❑ *All enquiries should include a stamped addressed envelope.*

stam|pede /stæmˈpiːd/ (**stampedes, stampeding, stampeded**) ◪ N-COUNT If there is a **stampede**, a group of people or animals run in a wild, uncontrolled way. ❑ *There was a stampede for the exit.* ◪ V-T/V-I If a group of animals or people **stampede** or if something **stampedes** them, they run in a wild, uncontrolled way. ❑ *The crowd stampeded and many were crushed or trampled underfoot.* ❑ *...a herd of stampeding cattle.* ◪ N-COUNT If a lot of people all do the same thing at the same time, you can describe it as a **stampede**. ❑ *...a stampede of consumers rushing to buy merchandise at bargain prices.*

stance /stæns/ (**stances**) ◪ N-COUNT Your **stance** on a particular matter is your attitude to it. ❑ *The Congress had agreed to reconsider its stance on the armed struggle.* ◪ N-COUNT Your **stance** is the way that you are standing. [FORMAL] ❑ *Take a comfortably wide stance and flex your knees a little.*

Word Partnership   stance의 연어

PREP.	stance **against/on/toward** *something* ◪
ADJ.	**aggressive** stance, **critical** stance, **tough** stance ◪
V.	**adopt** a stance, **take** a stance ◪ ◪

stand ♦♦♦ /stænd/ (**stands, standing, stood**) ◪ V-I When you **are standing**, your body is upright, your legs are straight, and your weight is supported by your feet. ❑ *She was standing beside my bed staring down at me.* ❑ *They told me to stand still and not to turn round.* ● PHRASAL VERB **Stand up** means the same as **stand**. ❑ *We waited, standing up, for an hour.* ◪ V-I When someone who is sitting **stands**, they change their position so that they are upright and on their feet. ❑ *Becker stood and shook hands with Ben.* ● PHRASAL VERB **Stand up** means the same as **stand**. ❑ *When I walked in, they all stood up and started clapping.* ◪ V-I If you **stand aside** or **stand back**, you move a short distance sideways or backward, so that you are standing in a different place. ❑ *I stood aside to let her pass me.* ◪ V-I If something such as a building or a piece of furniture **stands** somewhere, it is in that position, and is upright. [WRITTEN] ❑ *The house stands alone on top of a small hill.* ◪ V-I You can say that a building **is standing** when it remains after other buildings around it have fallen down or been destroyed. ❑ *The palace, which was damaged by bombs in World War II, still stood.* ◪ V-T If you **stand** something somewhere, you put it there in an upright position. ❑ *Stand the plant in the open in a sunny, sheltered place.* ◪ V-I If you leave food or a mixture of something **to stand**, you leave it without disturbing it for some time. ❑ *The salad improves if made in advance and left to stand.* ◪ N-COUNT If you take or make a **stand**, you do something or say something in order to make it clear what your attitude to a particular thing is. ❑ *He felt the need to make a stand against racism in South Africa.* ◪ V-I If you ask someone **where** or **how** you **stand on** a particular issue, you are asking them what their attitude or view is. ❑ *The amendment will force senators to show where they stand on the issue of sexual harassment.* ◪ V-I If you do not know **where** you **stand with** someone, you do not know exactly what their attitude to you is. ❑ *No-one knows where they stand with him; he is utterly unpredictable.* ◪ V-LINK You can use **stand** instead of "be" when you are describing the present state or condition of something or someone. ❑ *The alliance stands ready to do what is necessary.* ◪ V-I If a decision, law, or offer **stands**, it still exists and has not been changed or canceled. ❑ *Although exceptions could be made, the rule still stands.* ◪ V-I If something that can be measured **stands at** a particular level, it is at that level. ❑ *The inflation rate now stands at 3.6 per cent.* ◪ V-T If something can **stand** a situation or a test, it is good enough or strong enough to experience it without being damaged, harmed, or shown to be inadequate. ❑ *These are the first machines that can stand the wear and tear of continuously crushing glass.* ◪ V-T If you cannot **stand** something, you cannot bear it or tolerate it. ❑ *I can't stand any more. I'm going to run away.* ❑ *Stoddart can stand any amount of personal criticism.* ◪ V-T If you cannot **stand** someone or

삐걱거리는 소리와 언 발을 구르는 소리를 들으며 ◪ 자동사 발을 쿵쾅거리다 ❑ "일이 더 악화되기 전에 갈 거야." 그는 침대에서 쿵쾅거리고 내려서며 소리쳤다. ◪ 자동사 발로 짓밟다 ❑ 그는 지난주에 수퍼컵 결승전에서 심판의 발을 짓밟은 후 최초로 출전 금지를 당했다. ◪ 단수명사 (뚜렷이) 흔적 ❑ 우리들 대부분은 자기 집을 친근한 장소로 만들고 벽에서 자신의 개성이 뚜렷이 드러나기를 원한다.

구동사 근절하다, 종지부를 찍다 ❑ 머페트 박사가 자신은 학교에서의 왕따에 반대하며 그것을 근절하기 위한 조치를 취해야 한다고 강조했다.

가산명사 우표 첨부 회신용 봉투 (줄여서 s.a.e라고도 함) [영국영어; 미국영어 SASE] ❑ 모든 문의 편지는 우표 첨부 회신용 봉투를 동봉해야 한다.

◪ 가산명사 우르르 몰리는 사태 ❑ 비상구 쪽으로 사람들이 우르르 몰리는 일이 벌어졌다. ◪ 타동사/자동사 우르르 몰려가다 ❑ 군중들이 우르르 몰려가면서 많은 사람들이 발 밑에 깔리거나 짓밟혔다. ❑ 우르르 몰려가는 한 무리의 소 떼 ◪ 가산명사 우르르 몰려감 ❑ 세일 가격으로 물건을 사기 위해 소비자들이 우르르 몰려 뛰어감

◪ 가산명사 (특정한 일에 대한) 태도 ❑ 의회가 무장 투쟁에 대한 의회 측의 태도를 재고하는 것에 동의했다. ◪ 가산명사 서 있는 자세 [격식체] ❑ 섰을 때 발의 위치를 편안할 정도로 넓게 하고 무릎을 약간 구부리세요.

◪ 자동사 서다 ❑ 그녀가 나를 내려다보면서 내 침대 옆에 서 있었다. ❑ 그들은 나에게 꼼짝 말고 서서 뒤돌아보지 말라고 말했다. ● 구동사 서다 ❑ 우리는 선 채로 한 시간을 기다렸다. ◪ 자동사 일어서다 ❑ 베커는 일어서서 벤과 악수했다. ● 구동사 일어서다 ❑ 내가 들어가자, 그들이 모두 일어서서 박수를 치기 시작했다. ◪ 자동사 비켜서다; 물러서다 ❑ 나는 그녀가 지나가도록 비켜서 주었다. ◪ 자동사 (건물이) 서 있다 [문어체] ❑ 그 집은 작은 언덕 꼭대기 위에 홀로 서 있다. ◪ 자동사 (건물이) 남아 있다 ❑ 2차 세계 대전 때 폭격으로 훼손된 궁전이 아직도 남아 있었다. ◪ 타동사 두다, 세워 두다 ❑ 그 식물을 훤히 트이고 햇볕이 잘 드는 안전한 곳에 두세요. ◪ 자동사 (건드리지 않고) 놓아두다 ❑ 샐러드는 미리 만들어서 놔두면 맛이 더 좋아진다. ◪ 가산명사 태도, 입장 ❑ 그는 남아프리카의 인종 차별주의에 반대하는 태도를 분명히 밝힐 필요를 느꼈다. ◪ 자동사 (특정 사안에 대해) 입장을 취하다 ❑ 그 수정안 때문에 상원의원들은 성 희롱 문제에 대한 자신의 입장을 분명히 밝혀야만 할 것이다. ◪ 자동사 (누구에 대해 어떤) 처지에 있다 ❑ 아무도 그들에 대한 그의 마음을 모른다. 그는 전혀 예측할 수 없는 사람이니까. ◪ 연결동사 ❑ 그 동맹국들은 필요한 일을 할 준비가 되어 있다. ◪ 자동사 유효하다, 존속하다 ❑ 예외가 있을 수도 있지만, 그 규칙은 여전히 유효하다. ◪ 자동사 (수치가) -이다 [영국영어; 미국영어 run] ❑ 물가 상승률이 현재 3.6퍼센트이다. ◪ 타동사 견디다 ❑ 이것은 유리를 계속 부숨으로써 생기는 마모도 견딜 수 있는 최초의 기계이다. ◪ 타동사 참다, 견디다 ❑ 더 이상은 못 참겠어. 도망갈 거야. ❑ 스토다트는 개인적인 비난을 얼마든지 견딜 수 있다. ◪ 타동사 참고 봐주다 [비격식체] ❑ 나는 그의 오만함을 못 봐주겠다. ◪ 타동사 인을 것 같다; 잃을 것 같다 ❑ 회사가 매각되면 경영진이 수백만 달러를 벌 수도 있을 것이다. ◪ 자동사 입후보하다 [영국영어; 미국영어 run] ❑ 그는 선거에 입후보할지 여부를 아직 발표하지 않았다. ◪ 가산명사 가판점 ❑ 그는 아메리칸 익스프레스 사무실 밖에서 신문 가판점을 했다.

something, you dislike them very strongly. [INFORMAL] ❑ *I can't stand that man and his arrogance.* ⏀ V-T If you **stand to gain** something, you are likely to gain it. If you **stand to lose** something, you are likely to lose it. ❑ *The management group would stand to gain millions of dollars if the company were sold.* ⏀ V-I If you **stand in** an election, you are a candidate in it. [BRIT; AM **run**] ❑ *He has not yet announced whether he will stand in the election.* ⏀ N-COUNT A **stand** is a small store or stall, outdoors or in a large public building. ❑ *He ran a newspaper stand outside the American Express office.* ⏀ N-PLURAL The **stands** at a sports stadium or arena are a large structure where people sit or stand to watch what is happening. ❑ *The people in the stands at Candlestick Park are standing and cheering with all their might.* ● N-COUNT In British English, **stand** is used with the same meaning. ❑ *I was sitting in the stand for the first game.* ⏀ N-COUNT A **stand** is an object or piece of furniture that is designed for supporting or holding a particular kind of thing. ❑ *The teapot came with a stand to catch the drips.* ⏀ N-COUNT A **stand** is an area where taxis or buses can wait to pick up passengers. ❑ *Luckily there was a taxi stand nearby.* ⏀ N-SING In a law court, **the stand** is the place where a witness stands to answer questions. ❑ *When the father took the stand today, he contradicted his son's testimony.* ⏀ →see also **standing** ⏀ PHRASE If you say **it stands to reason that** something is true or likely to happen, you mean that it is obvious. ❑ *It stands to reason that if you are considerate and friendly to people you will get a lot more back.* ⏀ PHRASE If you **stand in the way of** something or **stand in** a person's **way**, you prevent that thing from happening or prevent that person from doing something. ❑ *The British government would not stand in the way of such a proposal.* ⏀ to **stand a chance** →see **chance**. to **stand firm** →see **firm**. to **stand on your own two feet** →see **foot**. to **stand your ground** →see **ground**. to **stand someone in good stead** →see **stead**. to **stand trial** →see **trial**

▶**stand aside** PHRASAL VERB If someone **stands aside**, they resign from an important job or position, often in order to let someone else take their place. [BRIT; AM **stand down**] ❑ *The President said he was willing to stand aside if that would stop the killing.*

▶**stand back** PHRASAL VERB If you **stand back** and think about a situation, you think about it as if you were not involved in it. ❑ *Stand back and look objectively at the problem.*

▶**stand by** ⏀ PHRASAL VERB If you **are standing by**, you are ready and waiting to provide help or to take action. ❑ *British and American warships are standing by to evacuate their citizens if necessary.* →see also **standby** ⏀ PHRASAL VERB If you **stand by** and let something bad happen, you do not do anything to stop it. [DISAPPROVAL] ❑ *The Secretary of Defense has said that he would not stand by and let democracy be undermined.* ⏀ PHRASAL VERB If you **stand by** someone, you continue to give them support, especially when they are in trouble. [APPROVAL] ❑ *I wouldn't break the law for a friend, but I would stand by her if she did.* ⏀ PHRASAL VERB If you **stand by** an earlier decision, promise, or statement, you continue to support it or keep it. ❑ *The decision has been made and I have got to stand by it.*

▶**stand down** PHRASAL VERB If someone **stands down**, they resign from an important job or position, often in order to let someone else take their place. ❑ *Four days later, the despised leader finally stood down, just 17 days after taking office.*

▶**stand for** ⏀ PHRASAL VERB If you say that a letter **stands for** a particular word, you mean that it is an abbreviation for that word. ❑ *AIDS stands for Acquired Immune Deficiency Syndrome.* ⏀ PHRASAL VERB The ideas or attitudes that someone or something **stands for** are the ones that they support or represent. ❑ *The party is trying to give the impression that it alone stands for democracy.* ⏀ PHRASAL VERB If you will **not stand for** something, you will not allow it to happen or continue. [with neg] ❑ *It's outrageous, and we won't stand for it any more.*

▶**stand in** PHRASAL VERB If you **stand in for** someone, you take their place or do their job, because they are ill or away. ❑ *I had to stand in for her on Tuesday when she didn't show up.* →see also **stand-in**

▶**stand out** ⏀ PHRASAL VERB If something **stands out**, it is very noticeable. ❑ *Every tree, wall and fence stood out against dazzling white fields.* ⏀ PHRASAL VERB If something **stands out** from a surface, it rises up from it. ❑ *His tendons stood out like rope beneath his skin.*

▶**stand up** ⏀ →see **stand 1, 2** ⏀ PHRASAL VERB If something such as a claim or a piece of evidence **stands up**, it is accepted as true or satisfactory after being carefully examined. ❑ *He made wild accusations that did not stand up.* ⏀ PHRASAL VERB If a boyfriend or girlfriend **stands** you **up**, they fail to keep an arrangement to meet you. [INFORMAL] ❑ *We were to have had dinner together yesterday evening, but he stood me up.*

▶**stand up for** PHRASAL VERB If you **stand up for** someone or something, you defend them and make your feelings or opinions very clear. [APPROVAL] ❑ *They stood up for what they believed to be right.*

▶**stand up to** ⏀ PHRASAL VERB If something **stands up to** bad conditions, it is not damaged or harmed by them. ❑ *Is this building going to stand up to the strongest gales?* ⏀ PHRASAL VERB If you **stand up to** someone, especially someone more powerful than you are, you defend yourself against their attacks or demands. ❑ *He hit me, so I hit him back – the first time in my life I'd stood up to him.*

stand-alone ⏀ ADJ A **stand-alone** business or organization is independent and does not receive financial support from another organization. [BUSINESS] [ADJ n] ❑ *They plan to relaunch it as a stand-alone company.* ⏀ ADJ A **stand-alone** computer is one that can operate on its own and does not have to be part of a network. [COMPUTING] [ADJ n] ❑ *...an operating system that can work on networks and stand-alone machines.*

stand|ard ◆◇◇ /stǽndərd/ (**standards**) ⏀ N-COUNT A **standard** is a level of quality or achievement, especially a level that is thought to be acceptable. ❑ *The standard of professional cricket has never been lower.* ⏀ N-COUNT A **standard** is

---

⏀ 복수명사 관중석 ❑ 캔들스 구장의 관람석에 앉아 있는 사람들이 일어서서 온 힘을 다해 응원하고 있다. ● 가산명사 관중석 ❑ 나는 첫 경기를 보기 위해서 관중석에 앉아 있었다. ⏀ 가산명사 받침대 ❑ 그 찻주전자에는 물방울 받침대가 딸려 있었다. ⏀ 가산명사 정류장 ❑ 다행스럽게도 근처에 택시 정류장이 있었다. ⏀ 단수명사 증인석 ❑ 오늘 그 아버지가 증인석에 섰을 때, 그는 아들의 증언과 상반된 진술을 했다. ⏀ 구 – 이 분명하다 ❑ 당신이 사람들에게 사상하고 친절하게 대한다면 당신에게 그보다 훨씬 많은 것이 돌아올 것이 분명하다. ⏀ 구 –을 방해하다, –을 막다 ❑ 영국 정부가 그런 제안을 막지는 않을 것이다.

구동사 사임하다 [영국영어; 미국영어 stand down] ❑ 그것이 살해를 막을 수 있다면 자신이 기꺼이 사임할 것이라고 대통령은 말했다.

구동사 한 발 물러서다 ❑ 한 발 물러서서 그 문제를 객관적으로 보세요.

⏀ 구동사 대기하다 ❑ 필요하다면 자국민을 피난시키기 위해서 영국 군함과 미국 군함이 대기하고 있다. ⏀ 구동사 좌시하다 [탐탁찮음] ❑ 국방 장관이 민주주의가 훼손되는 것을 좌시하지 않을 것이라고 말했다. ⏀ 구동사 – 을 지키다, 변함없이 지지하다 [마음에 듦] ❑ 내가 친구를 위해서 법을 어기지는 않겠지만, 그녀가 법을 어긴다 한다 해도 나는 그녀를 외면하지 않을 것이다. ⏀ 구동사 고수하다, 계속 지키다 ❑ 결정은 이미 내려졌고 나는 그것을 고수해야만 한다.

구동사 사임하다, 물러나다 ❑ 나흘 후, 취임한 지 단 17일 만에, 존경을 못 받던 그 지도자가 마침내 물러났다.

⏀ 구동사 의미하다 ❑ 에이즈는 후천성 면역 결핍증을 의미한다. ⏀ 구동사 대표하다 ❑ 그 정당은 자신들만이 민주주의를 대표한다는 인상을 주려고 하고 있다. ⏀ 구동사 허용하지 않다 ❑ 그것은 말도 안 되는 일이고, 우리는 더 이상 그것을 허용하지 않을 것이다.

구동사 대신하다 ❑ 그녀가 화요일에 나오지 않아서 나는 그녀 대신 일해야 했다.

⏀ 구동사 쉽게 눈에 띄다, 두드러지다 ❑ 눈부시게 하얀 들판을 배경으로 모든 나무와 담과 울타리가 두드러져 보였다. ⏀ 구동사 튀어나오다, 도드라지다 ❑ 그의 피부 아래로 밧줄처럼 힘줄이 튀어나와 있었다.

⏀ 구동사 사실로 인정되다 ❑ 그는 사실로 인정되지 않은 마구잡이 비난을 해댔다. ⏀ 구동사 바람맞히다 [비격식체] ❑ 어제 저녁에 우리는 함께 식사하기로 했으나, 그가 나를 바람맞혔다.

구동사 옹호하다 [마음에 듦] ❑ 그들은 자신들이 옳다고 믿는 것을 옹호했다.

⏀ 구동사 견뎌 내다 ❑ 이 건물이 아주 강한 돌풍도 견뎌 낼까요? ⏀ 구동사 맞서다 ❑ 그가 나를 치길래 나도 맞받아 쳤다. 내 평생 그에게 맞서 보기는 처음이었다.

⏀ 형용사 (재정적으로) 독립적인 [경제] ❑ 그들은 그 회사를 독립적인 회사로 다시 출범시킬 계획이다. ⏀ 형용사 독립형의 [컴퓨터] ❑ 네트워크와 스탠드 얼론 컴퓨터에 작동할 수 있는 운영 시스템

⏀ 가산명사 수준 ❑ 프로 크리켓의 수준이 이보다 더 낮은 적이 없었다. ⏀ 가산명사 기준 ❑ 이후 기준으로 봤을 때 틀림없이 원시적이었던 체제 ⏀ 복수명사 규범

something that you use in order to judge the quality of something else. ❑ *...systems that were by later standards absurdly primitive.* ➌ N-PLURAL **Standards** are moral principles which affect people's attitudes and behavior. ❑ *My father has always had high moral standards.* ➍ ADJ You use **standard** to describe things which are usual and normal. ❑ *It was standard practice for untrained clerks to advise in serious cases such as murder.* ➎ ADJ A **standard** work or text on a particular subject is one that is widely read and often recommended. [ADJ n] ❑ *At twenty he translated Euler's standard work on algebra into English.*

❑ 아버지께서는 항상 도덕규범이 높으셨다. ➍ 형용사 보통의, 일반적인 ❑ 훈련받지 않은 사무직원들이 살인과 같은 심각한 사건에서 조언을 하는 것이 일반적인 관행이었다. ➎ 형용사 기본적인, 표준적인 ❑ 그는 스무 살에 율러의 대수학 기본서를 영어로 번역했다.

Word Partnership	*standard*의 연어
V.	**become a** standard, **maintain a** standard, **meet a** standard, **raise a** standard, **set a** standard, **use a** standard ➊ ➋
N.	standard **of excellence**, **industry** standard ➊ ➋ standard **English**, standard **equipment**, standard **practice**, standard **procedure** ➍

stand|ard|ize /stǽndərdaɪz/ (**standardizes, standardizing, standardized**) [BRIT also **standardise**] V-T To standardize things means to change them so that they all have the same features. ❑ *There is a drive both to standardize components and to reduce the number of models on offer.* ● **stand|ard|i|za|tion** /stændərdɪzeɪʃ⁰n, BRIT stændaˈdaɪzeɪʃ⁰n/ N-UNCOUNT ❑ *...the standardization of working hours in Community countries.*

[영국영어 standardise] 타동사 표준화하다 ❑ 제공하는 부품을 표준화하면서 그 모델 수도 감소시키려는 움직임이 있다. ● 표준화 불가산명사 ❑ 유럽 공동체 국가의 근로 시간 표준화

stand|ard of liv|ing (**standards of living**) N-COUNT Your **standard of living** is the level of comfort and wealth which you have. ❑ *We'll continue to fight for a decent standard of living for our members.*

가산명사 생활수준 ❑ 우리는 회원들의 품위 있는 생활수준을 위해 계속 싸울 것이다.

stand|ard time N-UNCOUNT **Standard time** is the official local time of a region or country. ❑ *French standard time is GMT plus 1 hr.*

불가산명사 표준시 ❑ 프랑스의 표준시는 그리니치 표준시에 한 시간을 더한다.

stand|by /stǽndbaɪ/ (**standbys**) also **stand-by** ➊ N-COUNT A **standby** is something or someone that is always ready to be used if they are needed. ❑ *Canned varieties of beans and pulses are a good standby.* ➋ PHRASE If someone or something is **on standby**, they are ready to be used if they are needed. ❑ *Five ambulances are on standby at the port.* ➌ ADJ A **standby** ticket for something such as the theater or a plane trip is a cheap ticket that you buy just before the performance starts or the plane takes off, if there are still some seats left. [ADJ n] ❑ *He bought a standby ticket to New York at 5:30 a.m. the following morning and flew to JFK airport six hours later.* ● ADV **Standby** is also an adverb. [ADV after v] ❑ *Magda was going to fly standby.*

➊ 가산명사 예비용; 대기자 ❑ 다양한 콩 통조림은 훌륭한 예비 식량이다. ➋ 구 대기 중인 ❑ 다섯 대의 구급차가 항구에서 대기 중이다. ➌ 형용사 대기자의 빈 좌석이 있는 경우 살 수 있는 할인 가격의 ❑ 그는 다음날 새벽 5시 30분에 뉴욕 행 대기자 티켓을 사서 6시간 후에 제이에프케이 공항으로 날아갔다. ● 부사 대기자로 ❑ 마그다는 비행기를 대기자 티켓으로 탈 예정이었다.

stand-in (**stand-ins**) N-COUNT A **stand-in** is a person who takes someone else's place or does someone else's job for a while, for example because the other person is ill or away. ❑ *He was a stand-in for my regular doctor.*

가산명사 대리인 ❑ 그는 내 주치의의 대리인이었다.

stand|ing /stǽndɪŋ/ (**standings**) ➊ N-UNCOUNT Someone's **standing** is their reputation or status. ❑ *...an artist of international standing.* ❑ *He has improved his country's standing abroad.* ➋ N-COUNT A party's or person's **standing** is their popularity. ❑ *But, as the opinion poll shows, the party's standing with the people at large has never been so low.* ➌ ADJ You use **standing** to describe something which is permanently in existence. [ADJ n] ❑ *Israel has a relatively small standing army and its strength is based on its reserves.* ➍ →see also **long-standing**

➊ 불가산명사 명성, 지위 ❑ 국제적인 명성이 있는 예술가 ❑ 그는 고국의 대외적인 지위를 드높였다. ➋ 가산명사 인기도 ❑ 그러나 여론 조사가 보여 주듯이 일반 국민들 사이에서 그 정당의 인기도가 이렇게 낮았던 적은 없었다. ➌ 형용사 영속적인 ❑ 이스라엘은 상대적으로 상비군의 수가 적고 병력을 예비군에 토대를 두고 있다.

stand|ing or|der (**standing orders**) N-COUNT A **standing order** is an instruction to your bank to pay a fixed amount of money to someone at regular times. [BRIT] [also by n] ❑ *Payments made by standing order generally take at least four working days to reach us.*

가산명사 자동 이체 [영국영어] ❑ 자동 이체로 우리가 돈을 지급받는 데는 평일 기준으로 보통 나흘이 걸린다.

stand-off (**stand-offs**) also **standoff** N-COUNT A **stand-off** is a situation in which neither of two opposing groups or forces will make a move until the other one does something, so nothing can happen until one of them gives way. ❑ *There is no sign of an end to the stand-off between Mohawk Indians and the Quebec provincial police.*

가산명사 대치 상황 ❑ 모호크 인디언들과 퀘백 주 경찰과의 대치 상황이 끝날 조짐이 보이지 않는다.

stand|point /stǽndpɔɪnt/ (**standpoints**) N-COUNT From a particular **standpoint** means looking at an event, situation, or idea in a particular way. ❑ *He believes that from a military standpoint the situation is under control.*

가산명사 견지, 관점 ❑ 군의 견지에서 볼 때, 그 사태는 진압되고 있다고 그는 믿고 있다.

stand|still /stǽndstɪl/ N-SING If movement or activity comes **to** or is brought **to a standstill**, it stops completely. ❑ *Abruptly the group ahead of us came to a standstill.*

단수명사 정지, 멈춤 ❑ 우리 앞에 가던 그룹이 갑자기 정지를 했다.

stand-up also **standup** ADJ A **stand-up** comic or comedian stands alone in front of an audience and tells jokes. [ADJ n] ❑ *He does all kinds of accents, he can do jokes – he could be a stand-up comic.*

형용사 (관객 앞에 서서) 단독으로 재담하는 ❑ 그는 모든 사투리를 구사하고 재담도 잘 한다. 그래서 혼자 재담하는 코미디언이 될 수 있을 거다.

stank /stǽŋk/ **Stank** is the past tense of **stink**.

stink의 과거

sta|ple /steɪp⁰l/ (**staples, stapling, stapled**) ➊ ADJ A **staple** food, product, or activity is one that is basic and important in people's everyday lives. [ADJ n] ❑ *Rice is the staple food of more than half the world's population.* ❑ *The Chinese also eat a type of pasta as part of their staple diet.* ● N-COUNT **Staple** is also a noun. ❑ *Fish is a staple in the diet of many Africans.* ➋ N-COUNT A **staple** is something that forms an important part of something else. ❑ *Political reporting has become a staple of American journalism.* ➌ N-COUNT **Staples** are small pieces of bent wire that are used mainly for holding sheets of paper together firmly. You put the staples into the paper using a device called a stapler. ➍ V-T If you **staple** something, you fasten it to something else or fix it in place using staples. ❑ *Staple some sheets of paper together into a book.*

➊ 형용사 주요한 ❑ 쌀은 전 세계 인구의 절반 이상 사람들에게 주식이다. ❑ 중국 사람도 주식의 일부로서 파스타 종류를 먹는다. ● 가산명사 주식 ❑ 생선은 많은 아프리카인들에게 주식이다. ➋ 가산명사 주요소 ❑ 정치 관련 보도는 미국 언론에 있어서 주요소가 되고 있다. ➌ 가산명사 스테이플러의 철침 ➍ 타동사 스테이플러로 철하다 ❑ 여러 장의 종이를 스테이플러로 함께 묶어 책으로 만드세요.

sta|pler /steɪplər/ (**staplers**) N-COUNT A **stapler** is a device used for putting staples into sheets of paper. →see **office**

가산명사 재봉못, 스테이플러

star ♦♦♦ /stɑr/ (**stars, starring, starred**) ➊ N-COUNT A **star** is a large ball of burning gas in space. Stars appear to us as small points of light in the sky on clear nights. ❑ *The nights were pure with cold air and lit with stars.* ➋ N-COUNT You can refer to a shape or an object as a **star** when it has four, five, or more points sticking out of it in a regular pattern. ❑ *Children at school receive colored stars for*

➊ 가산명사 별 ❑ 밤에는 차가운 공기가 맑았고 별들이 빛났다. ➋ 가산명사 별 모양 ❑ 아이들은 학교에서 잘하면 색색의 별 모양을 받는다. ➌ 가산명사 (호텔 등급의) 별 ❑ 별 다섯 개짜리 호텔 ➍ 가산명사 (연예계 등의) 스타 ❑ 텔레비전 연속극 '페니스 프럼 헤번'의

Word Web   star

Astronomy is the oldest science. It is the study of **stars** and other objects in the **night sky**. People sometimes confuse astronomy and **astrology**. Astrology is the belief that the stars influence people's lives. Long ago people named groups of stars after gods, heroes, and imaginary animals. One of the most famous of these **constellations** is the Big Dipper. Its original name meant "the big bear." It is easy to find and it points toward the North Star*. For centuries sailors have used the North Star to **navigate**. The best-known star in our **galaxy** is the **sun**.

North Star: the star that the earth's northern axis points toward.

North Star

Big Dipper

---

work well done. ⑤ N-COUNT You can say how many **stars** something such as a hotel or restaurant has as a way of talking about its quality, which is often indicated by a number of star-shaped symbols. The more stars something has, the better it is. ❏ *...five star hotels.* ④ N-COUNT Famous actors, musicians, and sports players are often referred to as **stars**. ❏ *...Gemma, 41, star of the TV series "Pennies From Heaven."* ❏ *By now Murphy is Hollywood's top male comedy star.* ⑤ V-I If an actor or actress **stars in** a play or movie, he or she has one of the most important parts in it. ❏ *The previous star Adolphson had starred in a play in which Ingrid had been an extra.* ⑥ V-T If a play or movie **stars** a famous actor or actress, he or she has one of the most important parts in it. ❏ *...a Hollywood film, "The Secret of Santa Vittoria," directed by Stanley Kramer and starring Anthony Quinn.* ⑦ N-PLURAL Predictions about people's lives which are based on astrology and appear regularly in a newspaper or magazine are sometimes referred to as **the stars**. ❏ *There was nothing in my stars to say I'd have travel problems!*
→see galaxy, navigation
→see Word Web: star

Word Partnership   star의 연어

ADJ.	**bright** star ①
	big star, **former** star ④
N.	**bronze** star, **gold** star ②
	basketball/football/tennis star, **guest** star, **film/movie** star, **pop/rap** star, **porn** star, **TV** star ④
	star **in a film/movie/show** ⑤

star|board /stɑrbərd/ ADJ In sailing, the **starboard** side of a ship is the right side when you are on it and facing toward the front. [TECHNICAL] ❏ *He detected a ship moving down the starboard side of the submarine.* ● N-UNCOUNT **Starboard** is also a noun. ❏ *I could see the fishing boat to starboard.*

starch /stɑrtʃ/ (**starches**) ① N-MASS **Starch** is a substance that is found in foods such as bread, potatoes, pasta, and rice and gives you energy. ❏ *She reorganised her eating so that she was taking more fruit and vegetables and less starch, salt, and fat.* ② N-UNCOUNT **Starch** is a substance that is used for making cloth stiffer, especially cotton and linen. ❏ *He never puts enough starch in my shirts.*
→see rice

star|dom /stɑrdəm/ N-UNCOUNT **Stardom** is the state of being very famous, usually as an actor, musician, or athlete. ❏ *In 1929 she shot to stardom on Broadway in a Noel Coward play.*

stare ♦◇◇ /steər/ (**stares, staring, stared**) ① V-I If you **stare at** someone or something, you look at them for a long time. ❏ *Tamara stared at him in disbelief, shaking her head.* ❏ *Ben continued to stare out the window.* ● N-COUNT **Stare** is also a noun. ❏ *Hlasek gave him a long, cold stare.* ② PHRASE If a situation or the answer to a problem **is staring** you **in the face**, it is very obvious, although you may not be immediately aware of it. [INFORMAL] ❏ *Then the answer hit me. It had been staring me in the face ever since Lullington.*

The verbs **stare** and **gaze** are both used to talk about looking at something for a long time. If you **stare** at something or someone, it is often because you think they are strange or shocking. ❏ *Various families came out and stared at us.* If you **gaze at** something, it is often because you think it is marvelous or impressive. ❏ *A fresh-faced little girl gazes in wonder at the bright fairground lights.*

Word Partnership   stare의 연어

ADJ.	**blank** stare ①
V.	**continue to** stare, **turn to** stare ①

stark /stɑrk/ (**starker, starkest**) ① ADJ **Stark** choices or statements are harsh and unpleasant. ❏ *UK companies face a stark choice if they want to stay competitive.* ● **stark|ly** ADV ❏ *That issue is presented starkly and brutally by Bob Graham and David Cairns.* ② ADJ If two things are in **stark** contrast to one another, they are very different from each other in a way that is very obvious. ❏ *...secret cooperation between London and Washington that was in stark contrast to official policy.* ● **stark|ly** ADV ❏ *Angus's child-like paintings contrast starkly with his adult subject matter in these portraits.* ③ ADJ Something that is **stark** is very plain in appearance. ❏ *...the*

스타인 41세의 젬마 ❏ 이제 머피는 할리우드 최고의 남성 코미디 스타이다. ⑤ 자동사 -에서 주역을 맡다 ❏ 그 전년도에 아돌프슨은 잉그리드가 단역으로 나왔던 연극에서 주역을 맡았었다. ⑥ 타동사 주연으로 등장시키다 ❏ 스탠리 크레이머가 감독하고 앤소니 퀸이 주역으로 나오는 할리우드 영화, '산타 비토리아의 비밀' ⑦ 복수명사 운세 ❏ 내 운세에 역마살이 끼어 있다고 하지는 않았다.

형용사 (선박) 우현 쪽의 [과학 기술] ❏ 그는 잠수함의 우현 쪽이 가라앉는 것을 탐지했다. ● 불가산명사 (선박) 우현 ❏ 나는 그 고깃배를 우현 방향에서 볼 수 있었다.

① 물질명사 녹말, 탄수화물 ❏ 그녀는 자신의 식습관을 과일과 야채를 더 많이 먹고 탄수화물, 염분, 지방은 덜 섭취하는 쪽으로 바꾸었다. ② 불가산명사 풀, 녹말 성분 ❏ 그는 내 셔츠에 한 번도 충분히 풀을 먹이지 않는다.

불가산명사 스타의 지위, 스타덤 ❏ 1929년에 그녀는 노엘 카워드의 연극으로 브로드웨이에서 스타 자리에 올랐다.

① 자동사 응시하다 ❏ 타마라는 머리를 내저으면서 못 미더운 듯, 그를 응시했다. ❏ 벤은 계속 창밖을 응시했다. ● 가산명사 응시 ❏ 라섹이 그를 오랫동안 차가운 눈초리로 응시했다. ② 구 (의식하지는 못해도) 바로 눈앞에 있다, 아주 분명하다 [비격식체] ❏ 그러자 답이 번쩍 떠올랐다. 그것은 내가 룰링턴에 온 이후로 늘 눈앞에 있던 것이었다.

동사 stare와 gaze는 둘 다 어떤 것을 오랫동안 쳐다보는 것을 말할 때 쓴다. 사람이나 사물을 stare at 하는 것은 그것이 이상하거나 충격적이라고 여기기 때문인 경우가 많다. ❏ 여러 가족들이 나와서 우리를 빤히 쳐다 보았다. 무엇을 gaze at 하는 것은 흔히 그것이 멋지거나 인상적이라고 생각하기 때문이다. ❏ 새로운 얼굴의 어린 소녀가 환한 박람회장의 불빛을 신기한 듯 바라본다.

① 형용사 (진술 등이) 냉정한 ❏ 영국 기업들이 계속 경쟁력이 있으려면 냉정한 선택을 해야 한다. ● 냉정하게 부사 ❏ 그 사안은 밥 그레엄과 데이비드 카이른스가 잔인하리만큼 냉정하게 제기했다. ② 형용사 (대조가) 뚜렷한 ❏ 공식적인 정책과는 뚜렷한 대조를 이루는 런던과 워싱턴 간의 비밀 공조 ● 뚜렷하게 부사 ❏ 앵거스의 아이 같은 그림들은 이 초상화들에 나타난 성인 관련 주제와는 뚜렷하게

stark white, characterless fireplace in the drawing room. ● **stark|ly** ADV ❑ *The room was starkly furnished.*

대조를 보인다. ❸ 형용사 순수한, 별 장식 없는 ❑ 거실에 있는 그냥 흰색의 특징 없는 벽난로로 ● 별 장식 없이 부사 ❑ 그 방은 별 장식 없이 가구를 비치해 놓았다.

star prize (**star prizes**) N-COUNT The **star prize** in a competition is the most valuable prize. ❑ *The star prize in the raffle is a holiday for two in Gran Canaria.*

가산명사 최상상 ❑ 그 복권의 최고상은 두 사람이 그랜 카나리아로 휴가 가는 것이다.

star sign (**star signs**) N-COUNT Your **star sign** is the sign of the zodiac under which you were born. ❑ *What star sign are you?*

가산명사 별자리 ❑ 네 별자리는 뭐니?

start ♦♦♦ /stɑrt/ (**starts, starting, started**) ❶ V-T If you **start to** do something, you do something that you were not doing before and you continue doing it. ❑ *John then unlocked the front door and I started to follow him up the stairs.* ❑ *It was 1956 when Susanna started the work on the garden.* ● N-COUNT **Start** is also a noun. ❑ *After several starts, she read the report properly.* ❷ V-T/V-I When something **starts**, or if someone **starts** it, it takes place from a particular time. ❑ *The fire is thought to have started in an upstairs room.* ❑ *All of the passengers started the day with a swim.* ● N-SING **Start** is also a noun. ❑ *...1918, four years after the start of the Great War.* ❸ V-I If you **start by** doing something, or if you **start with** something, you do that thing first in a series of actions. ❑ *I started by asking how many day-care centers were located in the United States.* ❹ V-I You use **start** to say what someone's first job was. For example, if their first job was that of a factory worker, you can say that they **started as** a factory worker. ❑ *Betty started as a shipping clerk at the clothes factory.* ● PHRASAL VERB **Start off** means the same as **start**. ❑ *Mr. Dambar had started off as an assistant to Mrs. Spear's husband.* ❺ V-T When someone **starts** something such as a new business, they create it or cause it to happen. ❑ *George Granger has started a health centre and I know he's looking for qualified staff.* ● PHRASAL VERB **Start up** means the same as **start**. ❑ *The cost of starting up a day-care center for children ranges from $150,000 to $300,000.* →see also **start-up** ❻ V-T/V-I If you **start** an engine, car, or machine, or if it **starts**, it begins to work. ❑ *He started the car, which hummed smoothly.* ● PHRASAL VERB **Start up** means the same as **start**. ❑ *He waited until they went inside the building before starting up the car and driving off.* ❑ *Put the key in the ignition and turn it to start the car up.*

❶ 타동사 시작하다 ❑ 그때 존이 열쇠로 현관문을 열었고 나는 그를 따라 계단을 올라가기 시작했다. ❑ 수재너가 그 정원에서 일을 시작했던 때는 바로 1956년이었다. ● 가산명사 시작 ❑ 가산명사 시작 ❑ 여러 번 시작을 한 후에야, 그것을 제대로 읽어 보았다. ❷ 타동사/자동사 시작되다; 시작하다 ❑ 그 화재는 위층 방에서부터 시작되었다고 생각된다. ❑ 모든 승객들은 수영으로 하루를 시작했다. ● 단수명사 시작 ❑ 제 1차 세계 대전이 시작된 지 4년 뒤인 1918년 ❸ 자동사 ~으로 시작하다; ~와 함께 시작하다 ❑ 나는 미국 내에 몇 개의 주간 보육 시설이 있는지에 대한 질문으로 시작을 했다. ❹ 자동사 직장 생활을 시작하다 ❑ 베티는 의류 공장에서 선적 담당자로서 직장 생활을 시작했다. ● 구동사 직장 생활을 시작하다 ❑ 댐버 씨는 스피어 부인 남편의 조수로서 직장 생활을 시작했었다. ❺ 타동사 (사업을) 시작하다, 개업하다 ❑ 조지 그랜저는 헬스 센터를 개업해서 내가 알기로는 자격 있는 직원을 찾고 있다. ● 구동사 (사업을) 시작하다, 개업하다 ❑ 주간 유아 개업 비용이 150,000달러에서 300,000달러가 든다. ❻ 타동사/자동사 시동을 걸다 ❑ 그가 차의 시동을 걸자, 부드럽게 웡 하는 소리가 났다. ● 구동사 시동을 걸다 ❑ 그는 그들이 건물 안으로 들어갈 때까지 기다렸다가 차의 시동을 걸고 떠났다. ❑ 차에 시동을 걸려면 차 열쇠를 점화에 꽂은 뒤 돌리세요.

❼ V-I If you **start**, your body suddenly moves slightly as a result of surprise or fear. ❑ *She put the bottle on the coffee table beside him, banging it down hard. He started at the sound, his concentration broken.* ● N-COUNT **Start** is also a noun. ❑ *Sylvia woke with a start.* ❽ →see also **head start, false start** ❾ PHRASE You use **for a start** or **to start with** to introduce the first of a number of things or reasons that you want to mention or could mention. ❑ *You must get her name and address, and that can be a problem for a start.* ❿ PHRASE **To start with** means at the very first stage of an event or process. ❑ *To start with, the pressure on her was very heavy, but it's eased off a bit now.* ⓫ to **get off to a flying start** →see **flying**

❼ 자동사 움찔하다 ❑ 그녀가 그 남자 옆에 있는 커피 테이블 위에 병을 쾅 하고 내려놓았다. 그는 골똘히 생각에 잠겨 있다가 그 소리에 놀라 움찔했다. ● 가산명사 움찔함 ❑ 실비아가 움찔하더니 잠에서 깼다. ❾ 구 우선 ❑ 너는 그녀의 이름과 주소를 알아야 하는데, 우선 그것이 문제가 될 수 있다. ❿ 구 처음에는 ❑ 처음에는, 그녀가 느끼는 중압감이 매우 컸지만, 이제는 조금 나아졌다.

Start, begin, and commence all have a similar meaning, although commence is more formal and is not normally used in conversation. ❑ *The meeting is ready to begin... He tore the list up and started a fresh one... The space probe commenced taking a series of photographs.* Note that **begin**, **start**, and **commence** can all be followed by an -ing form or a noun, but only **begin** and **start** can be followed by a "to" infinitive.

start, begin, commence는 모두 비슷한 뜻이다. 그 중 commence는 더 문어체적이며 대화에서는 잘 쓰지 않는다. ❑ 회의를 시작할 준비가 되어있다... 그는 리스트를 찢어버리고 새 것을 쓰기 시작했다....유럽 통합 과정 착수에 대한 대안. begin, start, commence 다음에는 모두 -ing 또는 명사가 올 수 있으나, begin과 start 다음에만 'to' 부정사가 올 수 있다.

Thesaurus   start의 참조어

V.	begin, commence, originate; (ant.) end ❶ ❷
	establish, found, launch ❺
N.	beginning, onset; (ant.) ending, finish ❶ ❷
	jump, scare, shock ❼

▶**start off** ❶ PHRASAL VERB If you **start off by** doing something, you do it as the first part of an activity. ❑ *She started off by accusing him of blackmail but he more or less ignored her.* ❷ PHRASAL VERB To **start** someone **off** means to cause them to begin doing something. ❑ *Her mother started her off acting in children's theater.* ❸ PHRASAL VERB To **start** something **off** means to cause it to begin. ❑ *He became more aware of the things that started that tension off.* ❹ →see **start 4**

❶ 구동사 시작하다, 착수하다 ❑ 그녀는 그가 공갈 협박을 했다고 비난하기 시작했지만 그는 그녀를 거의 무시했다. ❷ 구동사 ~가 ...을 시작하게 하다 ❑ 그녀의 어머니는 그녀가 아동 극단에서 연극을 시작하게 했다. ❸ 구동사 시작하게 하다 ❑ 그는 그 긴장 상태를 야기했던 것들에 대해 더 잘 알게 되었다.

▶**start on** PHRASAL VERB If you **start on** something that needs to be done, you start dealing with it. ❑ *Before you start on these chapters, clear your head.*

구동사 시작하다 ❑ 이 장들을 시작하기 전에, 머리부터 맑게 하세요.

▶**start out** ❶ PHRASAL VERB If someone or something **starts out as** a particular thing, they are that thing at the beginning although they change later. ❑ *Daly was a fast-talking Irish-American who had started out as a salesman.* ❷ PHRASAL VERB If you **start out by** doing something, you do it at the beginning of an activity. ❑ *We start out by advising people to sit down and identify seven experiences from any time of their life.*

❶ 구동사 ~로서 출발하다 ❑ 달리는 영업 사원으로 출발했던 언변 좋은 아일랜드 계 미국인이었다. ❷ 구동사 ~부터 하기 시작하다 ❑ 우리는 먼저 사람들을 앉게 하고 그들이 어느 때든 살아오면서 겪었던 경험 중 일곱 가지를 말하게 한다.

▶**start over** PHRASAL VERB If you **start over** or **start** something **over**, you begin something again from the beginning. [mainly AM; BRIT **start again**] ❑ *...moving the kids to some other schools, closing them down and starting over with a new staff.*

구동사 처음부터 다시 시작하다 [주로 미국영어; 영국영어 start again] ❑ 아이들을 다른 학교로 전학시키고, 그 학교들을 폐교하고, 또 새로운 교직원들과 처음부터 시작하고.

▶**start up** →see **start 5, 6**

start|er /stɑrtər/ (**starters**) N-COUNT A **starter** is a small quantity of food that is served as the first course of a meal. [mainly BRIT; AM **appetizer**] ❑ *Mushrooms are also very popular as a starter - often served on toast.*

가산명사 (식사의) 첫 코스 [주로 영국영어; 미국영어 appetizer] ❑ 버섯 요리도 매우 인기 있는 첫 코스 요리입니다. 흔히 토스트 위에 얹어서 나오지요.

start|ing point (**starting points**) also **starting-point** ❶ N-COUNT Something that is a **starting point for** a discussion or process can be used to begin it or act as a basis for it. ❑ *These proposals represent a realistic starting point for negotiation.*

❶ 가산명사 출발점 ❑ 이러한 제안들은 협상을 위한 현실적인 출발점이 된다. ❷ 가산명사 출발지 ❑ 그들은 이미 출발지로부터 2-3 마일 이상 걸어간 상태였다.

2 N-COUNT When you make a journey, your **starting point** is the place from which you start. ❏ *They had already walked a couple of miles or more from their starting point.*

타동사 깜짝 놀라게 하다 ❏ 전화벨 소리에 그가 깜짝 놀랐다. ● 깜짝 놀란 형용사 ❏ 마서는 그녀를 보고 깜짝 놀란 표정을 했다.

star|tle /stɑːrtʲl/ (startles, startling, startled) V-T If something sudden and unexpected **startles** you, it surprises and frightens you slightly. ❏ *The telephone startled him.* ● **startled** ADJ ❏ *Martha gave her a startled look.*

형용사 아주 놀라운 ❏ 때로는 그 결과가 좀 놀라울 수도 있다.

star|tling /stɑːrtʲlɪŋ/ ADJ Something that is **startling** is so different, unexpected, or remarkable that people react to it with surprise. ❏ *Sometimes the results may be rather startling.*

1 형용사 착수하는, 개시의 [경제] ❏ 그것은 14건의 연구 사업에 대한 착수 비용으로 충분하다. **2** 형용사 신규의 [경제] ❏ 수천 개의 신규 회사들이 컴퓨터 시장으로 쏟아져 들어왔다. ● 가산명사 신규 업체 ❏ 지금은 노동 시장에서 유일하게 전망이 밝은 곳은 소규모 업체들과 하이테크 신규 업체들이다.

start-up (start-ups) **1** ADJ The **start-up** costs of something such as a new business or new product are the costs of starting to run or produce it. [BUSINESS] [ADJ n] ❏ *That is enough to pay the start-up costs for fourteen research projects.* **2** ADJ A **start-up** company is a small business that has recently been started by someone. [BUSINESS] [ADJ n] ❏ *Thousands and thousands of start-up firms have poured into the computer market.* ● N-COUNT **Start-up** is also a noun. ❏ *For now the only bright spots in the labor market are small businesses and high-tech start-ups.*

불가산명사 기아, 굶주림 ❏ 올해 초부터 3백 명 이상의 사람들이 아사했다.

star|va|tion /stɑːrveɪʃⁿn/ N-UNCOUNT **Starvation** is extreme suffering or death, caused by lack of food. ❏ *Over three hundred people have died of starvation since the beginning of the year.*

1 자동사 굶주리다; 굶어 죽다 ❏ 우리가 본 많은 죄수들이 굶어 죽어 가고 있다. ❏ 1930년대에 수백만의 우크라이나 사람들이 굶어 죽거나 외국으로 추방되었다. **2** 타동사 굶기다 ❏ 유일한 대안은 그 사람들을 굶기는 것이지만, 이런 일이 발생하게 해서는 안 된다고 그가 말했다. **3** 타동사 갈망하다, 굶주리다 ❏ 투자에 굶주려 온 분야가 전기 산업만이 아니다.

starve /stɑːrv/ (starves, starving, starved) **1** V-I If people **starve**, they suffer greatly from lack of food which sometimes leads to their death. ❏ *A number of the prisoners we saw are starving.* ❏ *In the 1930s, millions of Ukrainians starved to death or were deported.* **2** V-T To **starve** someone means not to give them any food. ❏ *He said the only alternative was to starve the people, and he said this could not be allowed to happen.* **3** V-T If a person or thing **is starved of** something that they need, they are suffering because they are not getting enough of it. ❏ *The electricity industry is not the only one to have been starved of investment.*

형용사 몹시 배고픈 [비격식체] ❏ 다른 무엇보다도 나는 너무나 배가 고팠다.

starv|ing /stɑːrvɪŋ/ ADJ If you say that you are **starving**, you mean that you are very hungry. [INFORMAL] [v-link ADJ] ❏ *Apart from anything else I was starving.*

1 타동사 숨겨 두다 [비격식체] ❏ 우리는 책장 뒤에 몰래 숨겨 두었던 위스키 한 병을 가지러 갔다. **2** 가산명사 은닉처 [비격식체] ❏ 그 요트에서 엄청난 마약 은닉처가 발견되었다.

stash /stæʃ/ (stashes, stashing, stashed) **1** V-T If you **stash** something valuable in a secret place, you store it there to keep it safe. [INFORMAL] ❏ *We went for the bottle of whiskey that we had stashed behind the bookcase.* **2** N-COUNT A **stash of** something valuable is a secret store of it. [INFORMAL] ❏ *A large stash of drugs had been found aboard the yacht.*

1 가산명사 국가 ❏ 멕시코는 비종교 국가이고 바티칸과 외교적 관계를 맺고 있지 않다.

state ♦♦♦ /steɪt/ (states, stating, stated) **1** N-COUNT You can refer to countries as **states**, particularly when you are discussing politics. ❏ *Mexico is a secular state and does not have diplomatic relations with the Vatican.*

country는 세계가 나누어져 있는 주요 정치 단위에 대해 얘기할 때 가장 평범한 말이다. state는 정치나 정부 기관에 대해 얘기할 때 쓴다. **3** 통일 과정에 의해 만들어진 새 독일 정부.... 정부가 통제하는 이태리 통신 회사. state는 특정 국가의 정치 단위를 지칭할 수도 있다. ❏ ...캘리포니아 주. nation은 나라의 거주자, 거주자의 문화적이나 인종적 배경을 얘기할 때 종종 쓴다. ❏ 웨일스는 고유의 전통을 지닌 자부심이 있는 나라이다... 정부 고위 대변인이 나라 전체에 연설할 것이다. land는 덜 정확하고 더 문학적인 말이며, 예를 들면 특정 국가에 대한 감정을 얘기할 때 쓸 수 있다. ❏ 그녀는 유럽의 가장자리에 있는 그 낯선 땅에 대해 배우는 데 매료되었다.

> **Country** is the most usual word to use when you are talking about the major political units that the world is divided into. **State** is used when you are talking about politics or government institutions. ❏ *...the new German state created by the unification process. ...Italy's state-controlled telecommunications company.* **State** can also refer to a political unit within a particular country. ❏ *...the state of California.* **Nation** is often used when you are talking about a country's inhabitants, and their cultural or ethnic background. ❏ *Wales is a proud nation with its own traditions... A senior government spokesman will address the nation.* **Land** is a less precise and more literary word, which you can use, for example, to talk about the feelings you have for a particular country. ❏ *She was fascinated to learn about this strange land at the edge of Europe.*

2 N-COUNT Some large countries such as the U.S. are divided into smaller areas called **states**. ❏ *Leaders of the Southern states are meeting in Louisville.* **3** N-PROPER The U.S. is sometimes referred to as **the States**. [INFORMAL] ❏ *She bought it last year in the States.* **4** N-SING You can refer to the government of a country as **the state**. ❏ *The state does not collect enough revenue to cover its expenditure.* **5** ADJ **State** industries or organizations are financed and organized by the government rather than private companies. [ADJ n] ❏ *...reform of the state social-security system.* →see **state school** **6** ADJ A **state** occasion is a formal one involving the head of a country. [ADJ n] ❏ *The president of Czechoslovakia is in Washington on a state visit.* **7** N-COUNT When you talk about the **state** of someone or something, you are referring to the condition they are in or what they are like at a particular time. ❏ *For the first few months after Daniel died, I was in a state of clinical depression.* **8** V-T If you **state** something, you say or write it in a formal or definite way. ❏ *Clearly state your address and telephone number.* ❏ *The police report stated that he was arrested for allegedly assaulting his wife.* **9** →see also **head of state**, **welfare state** **10** PHRASE If you say that someone is **not in a fit state to** do something, you mean that they are too upset or ill to do it. ❏ *When you left our place, you weren't in a fit state to drive.* **11** PHRASE If you are **in a state** or if you get **into a state**, you are very upset or nervous about something. ❏ *I was in a terrible state because nobody could understand why I had this illness.* **12** PHRASE If the dead body of an important person **lies in state**, it is publicly displayed for a few days before it is buried. ❏ *...the 30,000 people who filed past the cardinal's body while it lay in state last week.* →see **matter**

2 가산명사 주(州) ❏ 미국 남부 지역의 주 대표들이 루이빌에서 만날 예정이다. **3** 고유명사 미국 [비격식체] ❏ 그녀는 그것을 작년에 미국에서 샀다. **4** 단수명사 정부 ❏ 정부는 지출을 감당할 만큼 충분한 세금을 거두지 못하고 있다. **5** 형용사 국가의, 국영의 ❏ 국가 사회 보장 제도의 개혁 **6** 형용사 국가적인, 공식적인 ❏ 체코슬로바키아 대통령이 워싱턴을 국빈 방문 중이다. **7** 가산명사 상태 ❏ 대니얼이 사망한 후 처음 몇 달 동안, 나는 병적으로 우울한 상태였다. **8** 타동사 진술하다 ❏ 당신 주소와 전화번호를 분명하게 진술하세요. ❏ 경찰 보고서에는 그가 부인을 폭행한 혐의로 체포되었다고 진술되어 있었다. **10** 구 -을 할 수 있는 상태가 아니다 ❏ 당신이 우리 집을 떠날 때, 운전할 수 있는 상태가 아니었다. **11** 구 흥분한, 초조한 ❏ 내가 왜 이 병에 걸리게 되었는지 아무도 몰랐기 때문에 나는 몹시 초조한 상태였다. **12** 구 (유해가) 안치되다 ❏ 지난 한 주 동안 안치되어 있던 추기경의 시신에 조문한 3만 명의 추모객들

State De|part|ment ♦♢♢ N-PROPER In the United States, **the State Department** is the government department that is concerned with foreign affairs. ❏ *Officials at the State Department say the issue is urgent.*

고유명사 미 국무성 ❏ 미 국무성 관리들이 이번 사안은 긴급히 처리해야 한다고 말한다.

a b c d e f g h i j k l m n o p q r **s** t u v w x y z

A B C D E F G H I J K L M N O P Q R S T U V W X Y Z

state|ment ♦♦◊ /stéɪtmənt/ (**statements**) **1** N-COUNT A **statement** is something that you say or write which gives information in a formal or definite way. ❑ *Andrew now disowns that statement, saying he was depressed when he made it.* **2** N-COUNT A **statement** is an official or formal announcement that is issued on a particular occasion. ❑ *The statement by the military denied any involvement in last night's attack.* **3** N-COUNT You can refer to the official account of events which a suspect or a witness gives to the police as a **statement**. ❑ *The 350-page report was based on statements from witnesses to the events.* **4** N-COUNT If you describe an action or thing as a **statement**, you mean that it clearly expresses a particular opinion or idea that you have. ❑ *The following recipe is a statement of another kind – food is fun!* **5** N-COUNT A printed document showing how much money has been paid into and taken out of a bank or building society account is called a **statement**. ❑ *...the address at the top of your monthly statement.*

1 가산명사 진술 ❑ 앤드류는 자신이 그 진술을 했을 당시, 우울증에 걸려 있었다고 말하면서, 이제는 그 진술을 무시해 달라고 말하고 있다. **2** 가산명사 성명서 ❑ 군부는 성명서를 통해 어제 밤 공격에 대한 개입을 부인했다. **3** 가산명사 진술서 ❑ 350페이지 분량의 그 보고서는 그 사건에 대한 목격자들의 진술서에 근거했다. **4** 가산명사 표현, 표명 ❑ 다음의 요리법은 또 다른 표명입니다. 즉, 요리는 즐겁다, 이거죠! **5** 가산명사 예출금 내역서 ❑ 당신의 월별 입출금 내역서 맨 위에 있는 주소

Word Partnership	statement의 연어
ADJ.	**brief** statement, **formal** statement, **written** statement **1**-**3**
	political statement, **public** statement, **strong** statement **1** **2** **4**
	false/true statement **1** **3**
	official statement **2**
	financial statement, **monthly** statement **5**
N.	**mission** statement **1**
	response to a statement **1**-**4**
	statement **of support 1** **2** **4**
	policy statement **2**

state of af|fairs N-SING If you refer to a particular **state of affairs**, you mean the general situation and circumstances connected with someone or something. ❑ *This state of affairs cannot continue for too long, if parliament is to recover.*

단수명사 상황 ❑ 의회가 제 기능을 다시 찾으려면, 이런 상황이 오랫동안 계속될 수 없다.

state of mind (**states of mind**) N-COUNT Your **state of mind** is your mood or mental state at a particular time. ❑ *I want you to get into a whole new state of mind.*

가산명사 심리 상태 ❑ 나는 네가 완전히 새로운 심리 상태를 갖게 되길 바란다.

state-of-the-art ADJ If you describe something as **state-of-the-art**, you mean that it is the best available because it has been made using the most modern techniques and technology. ❑ *...the production of state-of-the-art military equipment.* →see **technology**

형용사 최첨단의 기술, 최신식의 ❑ 최첨단 군 장비 생산

state school (**state schools**) **1** N-COUNT A **state school** is the same as a **state university**. [AM] **2** N-COUNT A **state school** is a school that is controlled and funded by the government or a local authority, and which children can attend without having to pay. [BRIT; AM **public school**]

1 가산명사 주립 대학 [미국영어] **2** 가산명사 공립학교 [영국영어; 미국영어 public school]

states|man /stéɪtsmən/ (**statesmen**) N-COUNT A **statesman** is an important and experienced politician, especially one who is widely known and respected. ❑ *Hamilton is a great statesman and political thinker.*

가산명사 (존경받는) 정치인 ❑ 해밀턴은 위대한 정치인이자 지략가이다.

state university (**state universities**) N-COUNT A **state university** is a university that is partly funded by an American state. [AM] ❑ *He was a professor at the local state university.*

가산명사 주립 대학 [미국영어] ❑ 그는 지방 주립 대학의 교수였다.

Word Link	stat ≈ standing : static, station, stationary

stat|ic /stǽtɪk/ **1** ADJ Something that is **static** does not move or change. ❑ *The number of young people obtaining qualifications has remained static or decreased.* **2** N-UNCOUNT **Static** or **static electricity** is electricity which can be caused by things rubbing against each other and which collects on things such as your body or metal objects. ❑ *When the weather turns cold and dry, my clothes develop a static problem.* **3** N-UNCOUNT If there is **static** on the radio or television, you hear a series of loud noises which spoils the sound. ❑ *After only a minute an authoritative voice came through the static on the radio.*

1 형용사 변화가 없는, 움직임이 없는 ❑ 자격증을 따는 젊은이들의 수가 변화가 없거나 감소했다. **2** 불가산명사 정전기 ❑ 날씨가 춥고 건조해지면, 옷에 정전기가 생긴다. **3** 불가산명사 잡음 ❑ 겨우 1분 후에 라디오에서 권위적인 목소리가 잡음에 섞여 나왔다.

sta|tion ♦♦◊ /stéɪʃn/ (**stations, stationing, stationed**) **1** N-COUNT A **station** is a building by a railroad track where trains stop so that people can get on or off. ❑ *Ingrid went with him to the railway station to see him off.* **2** N-COUNT A bus **station** is a building, usually in a town or city, where buses stop, usually for a while, so that people can get on or off. ❑ *I walked the two miles back to the bus station and bought a ticket home.* **3** N-COUNT If you talk about a particular radio or television **station**, you are referring to the company that broadcasts programs. ❑ *...an independent local radio station.* **4** V-T PASSIVE If soldiers or officials **are stationed** in a place, they are sent there to do a job or to work for a period of time. ❑ *Reports from the capital, Lome, say troops are stationed on the streets.* **5** →see also **gas station, petrol station, police station, power station, service station, space station**
→see **cellphone, radio, television**

1 가산명사 역(驛) ❑ 잉그리드는 그를 배웅하기 위해서 그와 함께 역으로 갔다. **2** 가산명사 정류장 ❑ 나는 2마일을 되돌아 걸어가 버스 정류장에서 집으로 가는 표를 샀다. **3** 가산명사 방송국 ❑ 독자적인 지방 라디오 방송국 **4** 수동 타동사 배치되다, 주둔되다 ❑ 수도인 롬 발 보도에 따르면 군대가 거리에 주둔하고 있다고 한다.

Word Partnership	station의 연어
N.	**railroad** station, **subway** station **1**
	radio station, **television/TV** station **3**
ADJ.	**local** station **3**

sta|tion|ary /stéɪʃənɛri, BRIT stéɪʃənri/ ADJ Something that is **stationary** is not moving. ❑ *Stationary cars in traffic jams cause a great deal of pollution.*

형용사 정지한 ❑ 교통 체증으로 인해 정지해 있는 차량들이 엄청난 오염을 유발한다.

sta|tion|ery /stéɪʃənɛri, BRIT stéɪʃənri/ N-UNCOUNT **Stationery** is paper, envelopes, and other materials or equipment used for writing. ❑ *...envelopes and other office stationery.* →see **office**

불가산명사 문구류 ❑ 봉투와 다른 사무용품

sta|tion wag|on (station wagons) N-COUNT A **station wagon** is a car with a long body, a door at the rear, and space behind the back seats. [AM; BRIT **estate car**] →see car

가산명사 스테이션 웨건 [미국영어; 영국영어 estate car]

sta|tis|tic ♦♦♦ /stətɪstɪk/ (statistics) **1** N-COUNT **Statistics** are facts which are obtained from analyzing information expressed in numbers, for example information about the number of times that something happens. ◻ *Official statistics show real wages declining by 24%.* **2** N-UNCOUNT **Statistics** is a branch of mathematics concerned with the study of information that is expressed in numbers. ◻ *...a professor of Mathematical Statistics.*

1 가산명사 통계 ◻ 공식 통계에 의하면 실질 임금이 24퍼센트 하락하고 있다. **2** 불가산명사 통계학 ◻ 수리 통계학 교수

sta|tis|ti|cal /stətɪstɪkˤl/ ADJ **Statistical** means relating to the use of statistics. ◻ *The report contains a great deal of statistical information.* ● **sta|tis|ti|cal|ly** /stətɪstɪkli/ ADV ◻ *The results are not statistically significant.*

형용사 통계적인 ◻ 그 보고서에는 통계적인 정보가 상당히 많이 들어 있다. ● 통계적으로 부사 ◻ 그 결과는 통계적으로 의미가 없다.

stat|ue /stætʃu/ (statues) N-COUNT A **statue** is a large sculpture of a person or an animal, made of stone or metal. ◻ *...a bronze statue of an Arabian horse.*

가산명사 상(像), 조상(彫像) ◻ 아랍종 말의 청동상

stat|ure /stætʃər/ **1** N-UNCOUNT Someone's **stature** is their height. ◻ *It's more than his physical stature that makes him remarkable.* ◻ *Mother was of very small stature, barely five feet tall.* **2** N-UNCOUNT The **stature** of a person is the importance and reputation that they have. ◻ *Who can deny his stature as the world's greatest cellist?*

1 불가산명사 신장 ◻ 그를 돋보이게 하는 것이 그의 큰 신장뿐은 아니다. ◻ 어머니는 채 5피트도 안 되는 작은 키였다. **2** 불가산명사 명성, 지명도 ◻ 세계 최고의 첼리스트로서의 그의 명성을 누가 부인할 수 있겠는가?

sta|tus ♦♦♦ /steɪtəs, stæt-/ **1** N-UNCOUNT Your **status** is your social or professional position. ◻ *People of higher status tend to use certain drugs.* ◻ *...women and men of wealth and status.* **2** N-UNCOUNT **Status** is the importance and respect that someone has among the public or a particular group. ◻ *Nurses are undervalued, and they never enjoy the same status as doctors.* **3** N-UNCOUNT The **status** of something is the importance that people give it. ◻ *Those things that can be assessed by external tests are being given unduly high status.* **4** N-UNCOUNT A particular **status** is an official description that says what category a person, organization, or place belongs to, and gives them particular rights or advantages. ◻ *Bristol regained its status as a city in the local government reorganisation.* **5** N-UNCOUNT The **status** of something is its state of affairs at a particular time. ◻ *The Council unanimously directed city staff to prepare a status report on the project.*

1 불가산명사 지위 ◻ 고위층 사람들이 마약을 복용할 가능성이 더 높다. ◻ 부와 지위가 있는 남녀들 **2** 불가산명사 지위, 신망 ◻ 간호사들은 과소평가당하고, 결코 의사들과 동등한 지위를 누리지 못 한다. **3** 불가산명사 중요도, 의미 ◻ 외부 시험으로나 평가될 수 있는 그런 부분들에 부당하게 높은 의미를 부여하고 있다. **4** 불가산명사 신분, 자격 ◻ 브리스톨이 지방 정부 개편 때 시의 자격을 다시 얻었다. **5** 불가산명사 현황 ◻ 시 의회가 입수 모아 공무원들에게 그 프로젝트에 대한 현황 보고서를 준비하라고 지시했다.

Word Partnership	status의 연어
V.	**achieve** status, **maintain/preserve** *one's* status **1** **2**
N.	**celebrity** status, **wealth and** status **1** **2**
	change of status **1**-**5**
	marital status, **tax** status **4**
ADJ.	**current** status **1**-**5**
	economic status, **financial** status **5**

sta|tus quo /steɪtəs kwoʊ, stæt-/ N-SING The **status quo** is the state of affairs that exists at a particular time, especially in contrast to a different possible state of affairs. ◻ *By 492 votes to 391, the federation voted to maintain the status quo.*

단수명사 현재의 상황, 현황 ◻ 투표 결과, 492 대 391로 그 연합체는 현 상태를 유지하기로 결정했다.

stat|ute /stætʃut/ (statutes) N-VAR A **statute** is a rule or law which has been made by a government or other organization and formally written down. ◻ *The new statute covers the care for, bringing up and protection of children.*

가산명사 또는 불가산명사 법규, 법령 ◻ 그 새 법규는 아동 부양, 양육, 보호에 관한 것을 포괄하고 있다.

statu|tory /stætʃʊtəri, BRIT stætʃʊtəri/ ADJ **Statutory** means relating to rules or laws which have been formally written down. [FORMAL] ◻ *We had a statutory duty to report to Parliament.*

형용사 법령의, 법에 명시된 [격식체] ◻ 우리는 법에 명시된 대로 의회에 보고해야 할 의무가 있었다.

staunch /stɔntʃ/ (stauncher, staunchest) ADJ A **staunch** supporter or believer is very loyal to a person, organization, or set of beliefs, and supports them strongly. ◻ *He's a staunch supporter of controls on government spending.* ● **staunch|ly** ADV ◻ *He was staunchly opposed to a public confession.*

형용사 충실한, 확고한 ◻ 그는 정부 지출 제한 안에 대한 확고한 지지자이다. ● 충실하게, 확고하게 부사 ◻ 그는 공개적인 자백에 대해 확고하게 반대했다.

stay ♦♦♦ /steɪ/ (stays, staying, stayed) **1** V-I If you **stay** where you are, you continue to be there and do not leave. ◻ *"Stay here," Trish said. "I'll bring the car down the drive to take you back."* **2** V-I If you **stay** in a town or hotel, or at someone's house, you live there for a short time. ◻ *Gordon stayed at The Park Hotel, Milan.* ● N-COUNT **Stay** is also a noun. ◻ *An experienced Indian guide is provided during your stay.* **3** V-LINK If someone or something **stays** in a particular state or situation, they continue to be in it. ◻ *The Republican candidate said he would "work like crazy to stay ahead."* ◻ *...community care networks that offer classes on how to stay healthy.* **4** V-I If you **stay away from** a place, you do not go there. ◻ *Employers and officers also stayed away from work during the strike.* **5** V-I If you **stay out of** something, you do not get involved in it. ◻ *In the past, the UN has stayed out of the internal affairs of countries unless invited in.* **6** PHRASE If you **stay put**, you remain somewhere. ◻ *He was forced by his condition to stay put and remain out of politics.* **7** PHRASE If you **stay the night** in a place, you sleep there for one night. ◻ *They had invited me to come to supper and stay the night.*

1 자동사 (다른 곳에 가지 않고) 그대로 있다, 머무르다 ◻ "여기 있어," 트리시가 말했다. "진입로 아래로 차 가지고 와서 데려다 줄게." **2** 자동사 묵다 ◻ 고든은 밀란에 있는 파크 호텔에 묵었다. ● 가산명사 체류 ◻ 당신이 체류하는 동안 경험 많은 인디언 가이드를 보내겠다. **3** 연결동사 계속 ~이다, ~한 상태를 유지하다 ◻ 그 공화당 입후보자는 "계속 앞서기 위해 미친 듯이 일할 것"이라고 말했다. ◻ 건강 유지 관련 강좌를 제공하는 지역 보건 네트워크 **4** 자동사 ~에 가지 않다 ◻ 고용주들과 간부들도 파업 중에는 일을 하러 가지 않았다. **5** 자동사 ~에 관여하지 않다 ◻ 과거에는, 유엔이 개입 요청을 받지 않는 한 각 국의 국내 문제에는 관여하지 않았다. **6** 구 가만히 있다 ◻ 그는 건강 상태 때문에 어쩔 수 없이 정치에 관여하지 못하고 가만히 있어야 했다. **7** 구 하룻밤 묵다 ◻ 저녁 식사를 함께 하고 하룻밤 묵어가라고 그들이 나를 초대했었다.

▶**stay in** PHRASAL VERB If you **stay in** during the evening, you remain at home and do not go out. ◻ *If I stay in, my boyfriend cooks a wonderful lasagne or chicken or steak.*

구동사 (나가지 않고) 집에 있다 ◻ 내가 집에 있을 때는, 남자 친구가 맛있는 라자냐나 닭요리, 스테이크 같은 음식을 해 준다.

▶**stay on** PHRASAL VERB If you **stay on** somewhere, you remain there after other people have left or after the time when you were going to leave. ◻ *He had managed to arrange to stay on in Adelaide.*

구동사 계속 남아 있다 ◻ 그는 아델레이드에 계속 남아 있을 수 있도록 겨우 일정을 조정했었다.

▶**stay out** PHRASAL VERB If you **stay out** at night, you remain away from home, especially when you are expected to be there. ◻ *That was the first time Elliot stayed out all night.*

구동사 집에 안 들어오다, 외박하다 ◻ 엘리어트가 밤새 집에 안 들어오기는 그때가 처음이었다.

a
b
c
d
e
f
g
h
i
j
k
l
m
n
o
p
q
r
s
t
u
v
w
x
y
z

►stay up PHRASAL VERB If you **stay up**, you remain out of bed at a time when most people have gone to bed or at a time when you are normally in bed yourself. ❑ *I used to stay up late with my mom and watch movies.*

구동사 자지 않고 깨어 있다 ❑ 나는 엄마와 밤늦게까지 자지 않고 영화를 보곤 했다.

stead /stɛd/ PHRASE If you say that something will **stand** someone **in good stead**, you mean that it will be very useful to them in the future. ❑ *These two games here will stand them in good stead for the future.*

구 크게 도움이 되다 ❑ 이곳에서 두 경기가 장차 그들에게 큰 도움이 될 것이다.

stead·fast /stɛdfæst/ ADJ If someone is **steadfast in** something that they are doing, they are convinced that what they are doing is right and they refuse to change it or to give it up. ❑ *He remained steadfast in his belief that he had done the right thing.*

형용사 확고한, 변함없는 ❑ 자신이 올바른 일을 했다는 그의 믿음은 변함이 없었다.

steady ♦◇◇ /stɛdi/ (**steadier, steadiest, steadies, steadying, steadied**) **1** ADJ A **steady** situation continues or develops gradually without any interruptions and is not likely to change quickly. ❑ *Despite the steady progress of building work, the campaign against it is still going strong.* ❑ *The improvement in standards has been steady and persistent, but has attracted little comment from educationalists.* ● **steadi·ly** /stɛdili/ ADV [ADV with v] ❑ *Relax as much as possible and keep breathing steadily.* **2** ADJ If an object is **steady**, it is firm and does not shake or move about. ❑ *Get as close to the subject as you can and hold the camera steady.* **3** ADJ If you look at someone or speak to them in a **steady** way, you look or speak in a calm, controlled way. ❑ *"Well, go on," said Camilla, her voice fairly steady.* ● **steadi·ly** /stɛdili/ ADV [ADV after v] ❑ *He moved back a little and stared steadily at Elaine.* **4** ADJ If you describe a person as **steady**, you mean that they are sensible and reliable. ❑ *He was firm and steady unlike other men she knew.* **5** V-T/V-I If you **steady** something or if it **steadies**, it stops shaking or moving around. ❑ *Two men were on the bridge-deck, steadying a ladder.* **6** V-T If you **steady yourself**, you control your voice or expression, so that people will think that you are calm and not nervous. ❑ *Somehow she steadied herself and murmured, "Have you got a cigarette?"*

1 형용사 꾸준한 ❑ 건설 작업이 꾸준히 진행되고 있음에도 불구하고 이를 반대하는 운동이 여전히 강력하게 계속되고 있다. **2** 수준 향상은 꾸준히 지속적으로 이뤄지고 있지만 교육자들은 이에 대한 언급이 거의 없었다. ● 꾸준히 부사 ❑ 최대한 휴식을 많이 취하고 숨을 고르게 쉬세요. **2** 형용사 견고한, 안정된 ❑ 피사체에 최대한 다가가 카메라를 흔들리지 않게 잡으세요. **3** 형용사 침착한 ❑ "그래, 계속해." 라고 카밀라는 꽤 침착한 목소리로 말했다. ● 침착하게 부사 ❑ 그는 뒤로 약간 물러나 일레인을 침착하게 바라봤다. **4** 형용사 한결같은, 충실한 ❑ 그는 그녀가 아는 다른 남자들과는 달리 안정되고 한결같았다. **5** 타동사/자동사 고정시키다 ❑ 남자 둘이 선교 갑판에서 사다리를 고정시키고 있었다. **6** 타동사 진정시키다 ❑ 그녀는 가까스로 마음을 진정시키고는 중얼거렸다. "담배 있어?"

Thesaurus   steady의 참조어

ADJ.	consistent, continuous, uninterrupted **1**
	constant, fixed, stable **2**
	calm, cool, reserved, sedate **3** **4**

Word Partnership   steady의 연어

N.	steady **decline/increase**, steady **diet**, steady **growth**, steady **improvement**, steady **income**, steady **progress**, steady **rain**, steady **rate**, steady **supply** **1**
V.	**remain** steady **1** **4**
	hold/keep *something* steady, **hold** steady **2**

---

steak /steɪk/ (**steaks**) **1** N-VAR A **steak** is a large flat piece of beef without much fat on it. You cook it by grilling or frying it. ❑ *...a steak sizzling on the grill.* **2** N-UNCOUNT **Steak** is beef that is used for making stews. It is often cut into cubes to be sold. [BRIT] ❑ *...steak and kidney pie.* A fish **steak** is a large piece of fish that contains few bones. ❑ *...fresh salmon steaks.*

1 가산명사 또는 불가산명사 스테이크 ❑ 석쇠에서 지글거리고 있는 스테이크 **2** 불가산명사 쇠고기 국거리 [영국영어] ❑ 쇠고기 국거리와 콩팥이 들어간 파이 **3** 가산명사 (생선 살로 된) 스테이크 ❑ 신선한 연어 스테이크

steal ♦◇◇ /stil/ (**steals, stealing, stole, stolen**) **1** V-T/V-I If you **steal** something **from** someone, you take it away from them without their permission and without intending to return it. ❑ *He was accused of stealing a small boy's bicycle.* ❑ *People who are drug addicts come in and steal.* ● **stolen** ADJ ❑ *We have now found the stolen car.* **2** V-T If you **steal** someone else's ideas, you pretend that they are your own. ❑ *A writer is suing director Steven Spielberg for allegedly stealing his film idea.*

1 타동사/자동사 훔치다 ❑ 그는 어린 소년의 자전거를 훔친 혐의로 고발되었다. ❑ 마약 중독자들이 들어와 물건을 훔친다. ● 도난당한 형용사 ❑ 도난 차량을 이제 찾았다. **2** 타동사 도용하다 ❑ 한 작가가 자신의 영화 아이디어를 훔쳤다고 주장하며 스티븐 스필버그 감독을 고소했다.

Do not confuse **steal** and **rob**. If someone **steals** something, for example, money or a car, they take it without asking and without intending to give it back. ❑ *My car was stolen on Friday evening.* Note that you cannot say that someone **steals** someone. If someone **robs** someone or somewhere, they take something, often violently, from that person or place without asking and without intending to give it back. ❑ *They planned to rob an old widow... They joined forces to rob a factory.* You can also say that someone **robs** you of something when referring to what has been taken. ❑ *The two men were robbed of more than $700.*

steal과 rob을 혼동하지 마시오. 어떤 사람이 무엇을, 예를 들어 돈이나 자동차를 steal하면, 그것을 요청하지 않거나 되돌려 줄 의사가 없이 가져가는 것이다. ❑ 내 자동차를 금요일 저녁에 도둑맞았다. 어떤 사람이 누구를 steal할 수는 없음을 유념하시오. 어떤 사람이 누구를 또는 어디를 rob하면, 그 사람이 누구 또는 어디로부터 무엇을 요청하지 않거나 되돌려 줄 의사가 없이 종종 폭력을 써서 취하는 것이다. ❑ 그들은 나이든 미망인을 강탈하려고 계획했다... 그들은 공장을 털려고 힘을 합쳤다. 빼앗긴 것을 지정할 때 누가 당신에게서 무엇을 rob했다고 말할 수도 있다. ❑ 그 두 남자는 700 달러 이상을 강탈당했다.

Thesaurus   steal의 참조어

V.	burglarize, embezzle, swipe, take **1**

---

stealth /stɛlθ/ N-UNCOUNT If you use **stealth** when you do something, you do it quietly and carefully so that no one will notice what you are doing. ❑ *Wild animals demand secrecy and a certain amount of stealth from the photographer.*

불가산명사 몰래 함, 잠행 ❑ 야생 동물을 촬영하려면 사진작가가 은밀함과 어느 정도의 잠행 능력을 발휘해야 한다.

steam ♦◇◇ /stim/ (**steams, steaming, steamed**) **1** N-UNCOUNT **Steam** is the hot mist that forms when water boils. **Steam** vehicles and machines are operated using steam as a means of power. ❑ *In an electric power plant the heat converts water into high-pressure steam.* **2** V-I If something **steams**, it gives off steam. ❑ *...restaurants where coffee pots steamed on their burners.* **3** V-T/V-I If you **steam** food or if it **steams**, you cook it in steam rather than in water. ❑ *Steam the carrots until they are just beginning to be tender.* ❑ *Leave the vegetables to steam over the rice for the 20 minutes cooking time.* →see **cook** **4** PHRASE If something such as a plan or a project goes **full steam ahead**, it progresses quickly. ❑ *The Government was determined to go full steam ahead with its privatization programme.* **5** PHRASE If you **run out of steam**, you stop doing something because you have no more

1 불가산명사 증기 ❑ 발전소에서는 열이 물을 고압력 증기로 전환시킨다. **2** 자동사 김을 내다 ❑ 불 위에서 커피 주전자가 김을 내뿜고 있던 식당들 **3** 타동사/자동사 찌다 ❑ 당근을 살짝 부드러워지려고 할 때까지만 찌세요. ❑ 야채를 20분 동안 쌀 위에 얹어 두고 찌세요. **4** 구 전속력으로 ❑ 정부는 민영화 계획을 전속력으로 밀고 나갈 생각이었다. **5** 구 기력이 다하다 [비격식체] ❑ 욕실 천장을 도색하려고 했으나 도중에 기력이 다했다.

energy or enthusiasm left. [INFORMAL] ❑ *I decided to paint the bathroom ceiling but ran out of steam halfway through.* →see **cook**

Word Partnership　　*steam의 연어*

N.　　steam **bath**, **clouds of** steam, steam **engine**, steam **pipes**, steam **turbine** 　❶

▶**steam up** PHRASAL VERB When a window, mirror, or pair of glasses **steams up**, it becomes covered with steam or mist. ❑ *...the irritation of living with lenses that steam up when you come in from the cold.*

구동사 김이 서리다 ❑ 추운 곳에서 들어오면 김이 서리는 안경을 쓰고 살아야 하는 불편함

steamy /stimi/ ❶ ADJ **Steamy** means involving exciting sex. [INFORMAL] ❑ *He'd had a steamy affair with an office colleague.* ❷ ADJ A **steamy** place has hot, wet air. ❑ *...a steamy café.*

❶ 형용사 성적인, 에로틱한 [비격식체] ❑ 그는 사무실 동료와 육체관계를 맺었다. ❷ 형용사 찜통 같은 ❑ 통 같은 카페

steel ◆◇◇ /stil/ (**steels, steeling, steeled**) ❶ N-MASS **Steel** is a very strong metal which is made mainly from iron. Steel is used for making many things, for example bridges, buildings, vehicles, and flatware. ❑ *...steel pipes.* ❑ *...the iron and steel industry.* →see also **stainless steel** ❷ V-T If you **steel yourself**, you prepare to deal with something unpleasant. ❑ *Those involved are steeling themselves for the coming battle.* →see **train**

❶ 물질명사 강철 ❑ 강철 파이프 ❑ 철강 산업 ❷ 타동사 마음을 굳게 먹다 ❑ 관련된 사람들은 다가올 전투에 대비해 마음을 굳게 먹고 있다.

steely /stili/ ADJ **Steely** is used to emphasize that a person is hard, strong, and determined. [EMPHASIS] ❑ *Their indecision has been replaced by confidence and steely determination.*

형용사 강철 같은 [강조] ❑ 그들의 우유부단함이 자신감과 강철 같은 의지로 바뀌었다.

steep /stip/ (**steeper, steepest**) ❶ ADJ A **steep** slope rises at a very sharp angle and is difficult to go up. ❑ *San Francisco is built on 40 hills and some are very steep.* ● **steep**|**ly** ADV [ADV with v] ❑ *The road climbs steeply, with good views of Orvieto through the trees.* ❑ *...steeply terraced valleys.* ❷ ADJ A **steep** increase or decrease in something is a very big increase or decrease. ❑ *Consumers are rebelling at steep price increases.* ● **steep**|**ly** ADV [ADV with v] ❑ *Unemployment is rising steeply.* ❸ ADJ If you say that the price of something is **steep**, you mean that it is expensive. [INFORMAL] ❑ *The annual premium can be a little steep, but will be well worth it if your dog is injured.*

❶ 형용사 가파른 ❑ 샌프란시스코는 40개의 언덕 위에 자리하고 있는데 그 중 일부는 매우 가파르다. ● 가파르게 부사 ❑ 길은 가파르게 올라가며 나무 사이로 오르비에토를 시원하게 볼 수 있다. ❑ 가파른 계단식 골짜기들 ❷ 형용사 급격한 ❑ 소비자들은 급격한 가격 인상에 반발하고 있다. ● 급격하게 부사 ❑ 실업이 급격하게 증가하고 있다. ❸ 형용사 비싼 [비격식체] ❑ 연간 납입 금액이 약간 비싸다 싶을 수도 있지만 개가 다친다면 그만한 가치는 충분히 있다.

steeped /stipt/ ADJ If a place or person is **steeped in** a quality or characteristic, they are surrounded by it or deeply influenced by it. [v-link ADJ in n] ❑ *The castle is steeped in history and legend.*

형용사 ~한 특성에 넘치는 ❑ 그 성을 둘러싼 역사와 전설은 무궁무진하다.

steer /stɪər/ (**steers, steering, steered**) ❶ V-T When you **steer** a car, boat, or plane, you control it so that it goes in the direction that you want. ❑ *What is it like to steer a ship this size?* ❷ V-T If you **steer** people toward a particular course of action or attitude, you try to lead them gently in that direction. ❑ *The new government is seen as one that will steer the country in the right direction.* ❸ V-T If you **steer** someone in a particular direction, you guide them there. ❑ *Nick steered them into the nearest seats.* ❹ PHRASE If you **steer clear of** someone or something, you deliberately avoid them. ❑ *I think a lot of people, women in particular, steer clear of these sensitive issues.*

❶ 타동사 조종하다 ❑ 이 정도 크기의 배를 조종하는 기분은 어떻습니까? ❷ 타동사 인도하다 ❑ 새 정부는 국가를 올바른 방향으로 인도할 것으로 여겨진다. ❸ 타동사 이끌다 ❑ 닉은 그들을 가장 가까운 좌석으로 이끌었다. ❹ 구 피하다 ❑ 많은 사람들, 특히 여성들이 이들 민감한 사안을 피하는 것 같다.

steer|**ing wheel** (**steering wheels**) N-COUNT In a car or other vehicle, the **steering wheel** is the wheel which the driver holds when he or she is driving.

가산명사 핸들

stem ◆◇◇ /stɛm/ (**stems, stemming, stemmed**) ❶ V-I If a condition or problem **stems from** something, it was caused originally by that thing. ❑ *All my problems stem from drink.* ❷ V-T If you **stem** something, you stop it spreading, increasing, or continuing. [FORMAL] ❑ *Austria has sent three army battalions to its border with Hungary to stem the flow of illegal immigrants.* ❸ N-COUNT The **stem** of a plant is the thin, upright part on which the flowers and leaves grow. ❑ *He stooped down, cut the stem for her with his knife and handed her the flower.*

❶ 자동사 ~에서 기인하다 ❑ 나의 모든 문제는 음주에서 기인한다. ❷ 타동사 막다 [격식체] ❑ 오스트리아는 불법 이민자의 유입을 막기 위해 헝가리와의 국경에 세 개 육군 대대를 보냈다. ❸ 가산명사 줄기 ❑ 그는 그녀를 위해 몸을 구부리고 칼로 줄기를 자른 다음 그녀에게 꽃을 건넸다.

Word Partnership　　*stem의 연어*

N.　　**charges** stem from *something*, **problems** stem from *something* 　❶
V.　　stem **the flow of** *something*, stem **losses**, stem **the tide of** *something* 　❷

stem cell (**stem cells**) N-COUNT A **stem cell** is a type of cell that can produce other cells which are able to develop into any kind of cell in the body. ❑ *Stem-cell research is supported by many doctors.*

가산명사 줄기세포 ❑ 많은 의사들이 줄기세포 연구를 지지한다.

stench /stɛntʃ/ (**stenches**) N-COUNT A **stench** is a strong and very unpleasant smell. ❑ *The stench of burning rubber was overpowering.*

가산명사 악취 ❑ 고무 타는 악취가 지독하게 났다.

sten|**cil** /stɛnsᵊl/ (**stencils, stenciling, stenciled**) [BRIT, sometimes AM **stencilling, stencilled**] ❶ N-COUNT A **stencil** is a piece of paper, plastic, or metal which has a design cut out of it. You place the stencil on a surface and paint it so that paint goes through the holes and leaves a design on the surface. ❷ V-T If you **stencil** a design or if you **stencil** a surface **with** a design, you put a design on a surface using a stencil. ❑ *He then stenciled the ceiling with a moon and stars motif.*

[영국영어, 미국영어 가끔 stencilling, stencilled] ❶ 가산명사 스텐실 ❷ 타동사 스텐실로 찍다 ❑ 그런 뒤 그는 천장에 달과 별을 모티브로 한 모양들을 스텐실로 찍었다.

step ◆◆◆ /stɛp/ (**steps, stepping, stepped**) ❶ N-COUNT If you take a **step**, you lift your foot and put it down in a different place, for example when you are walking. ❑ *I took a step towards him.* ❑ *She walked on a few steps.* ❷ V-I If you **step on** something or **step in** a particular direction, you put your foot on the thing or move your foot in that direction. ❑ *This was the moment when Neil Armstrong became the first man to step on the Moon.* ❑ *She accidentally stepped on his foot on a crowded commuter train.* ❸ N-COUNT **Steps** are a series of surfaces at increasing or decreasing heights, on which you put your feet in order to walk up or down to a different level. ❑ *This little room was along a passage and down some steps.* ❹ N-COUNT A **step** is a raised flat surface in front of a door. ❑ *A little girl was sitting on the step of the end house.* →see also **doorstep** ❺ N-COUNT A **step** is one of a

❶ 가산명사 걸음 ❑ 나는 그에게 한 걸음 다가갔다. ❑ 그녀는 몇 걸음 더 걸어갔다. ❷ 자동사 밟다, 디디다 ❑ 이 때가 닐 암스트롱이 달에 발을 디딘 최초의 인간이 되는 순간이었다. ❑ 그녀는 붐비는 통근 열차에서 실수로 그의 발을 밟았다. ❸ 가산명사 계단 ❑ 이 작은 방은 복도를 따라간 다음 계단을 몇 개 내려가면 있었다. ❹ 가산명사 문 앞의 발판 ❑ 어린 여자아이가 끝에 있는 집의 문에 앉아 있었다. ❺ 가산명사 조치 ❑ 그는 그 합의를 평화를 향한 첫 조치로 환영했다. ❻ 가산명사 단계 ❑ 다음 단계는 이론을 실천으로 옮기는 것이다. ❼ 가산명사 (춤의)

series of actions that you take in order to achieve something. ☐ *He greeted the agreement as the first step towards peace.* **6** N-COUNT A **step** in a process is one of a series of stages. ☐ *The next step is to put the theory into practice.* **7** N-COUNT The **steps** of a dance are the sequences of foot movements which make it up. ☐ *She was a better dancer than Gordon. At least she knew the steps.* **8** N-SING Someone's **step** is the way they walk. ☐ *He quickened his step.* **9** PHRASE If you stay **one step ahead** of someone or something, you manage to achieve more than they do or avoid competition or danger from them. ☐ *Successful travel is partly a matter of keeping one step ahead of the crowd.* **10** PHRASE If people who are walking or dancing are **in step**, they are moving their feet forward at exactly the same time as each other. If they are **out of step**, their feet are moving forward at different times. ☐ *They were almost the same height and they moved perfectly in step.* **11** PHRASE If people are **in step with** each other, their ideas or opinions are the same. If they are **out of step with** each other, their ideas or opinions are different. ☐ *Moscow is anxious to stay in step with Washington.* **12** PHRASE If you do something **step by step**, you do it by progressing gradually from one stage to the next. ☐ *I am not rushing things and I'm taking it step by step.* **13** PHRASE If someone tells you to **watch** your **step**, they are warning you to be careful about how you behave or what you say so that you do not get into trouble. ☐ *David Beckham will have to watch his step because he was booked in the first half.*

Word Partnership	step의 연어
ADV.	step **outside** 2
	step **ahead**, step **backward**, step **forward** 2 5 6
N.	step **in a process** 6
ADJ.	**big** step, **bold** step, **giant** step, **the right** step 5
	critical step, **important** step, **positive** step 5 6

▶**step aside** →see **step down**

▶**step back** PHRASAL VERB If you **step back** and think about a situation, you think about it as if you were not involved in it. ☐ *I stepped back and analyzed the situation.*

▶**step down** or **step aside** PHRASAL VERB If someone **steps down** or **steps aside**, they resign from an important job or position, often in order to let someone else take their place. ☐ *Judge Ito said that if his wife was called as a witness, he would step down as trial judge.*

▶**step in** PHRASAL VERB If you **step in**, you get involved in a difficult situation because you think you can or should help with it. ☐ *If no agreement was reached, the army would step in.*

▶**step up** PHRASAL VERB If you **step up** something, you increase it or increase its intensity. ☐ *He urged donors to step up their efforts to send aid to Somalia.*

step|brother /stɛpbrʌðər/ (stepbrothers) also step-brother N-COUNT Someone's **stepbrother** is the son of their stepfather or stepmother.

step|daughter /stɛpdɔtər/ (stepdaughters) also step-daughter N-COUNT Someone's **stepdaughter** is a daughter that was born to their husband or wife during a previous relationship.

Word Link	step ≈ related by remarriage : *step*father, *step*mother, *step*sister

step|father /stɛpfɑðər/ (stepfathers) also step-father N-COUNT Someone's **stepfather** is the man who has married their mother after the death or divorce of their father.

step|mother /stɛpmʌðər/ (stepmothers) also step-mother N-COUNT Someone's **stepmother** is the woman who has married their father after the death or divorce of their mother.

step|ping|stone /stɛpɪŋstoʊn/ (steppingstones) also stepping-stone, stepping stone **1** N-COUNT You can describe a job or event as a **steppingstone** when it helps you to make progress, especially in your career. ☐ *It is just another steppingstone to bigger and better things.* **2** N-COUNT **Steppingstones** are a line of large stones which you can walk on in order to cross a shallow stream or river.

step|sister /stɛpsɪstər/ (stepsisters) also step-sister N-COUNT Someone's **stepsister** is the daughter of their stepfather or stepmother.

step|son /stɛpsʌn/ (stepsons) also step-son N-COUNT Someone's **stepson** is a son that was born to their husband or wife during a previous relationship.

ste|reo /stɛrioʊ/ (stereos) **1** ADJ. **Stereo** is used to describe a sound system in which the sound is played through two speakers. Compare **mono**. ☐ *...loudspeakers that give all-around stereo sound.* **2** N-COUNT A **stereo** is a CD player with two speakers.

ste|reo|type /stɛriətaɪp, stɪər-/ (stereotypes, stereotyping, stereotyped) **1** N-COUNT A **stereotype** is a fixed general image or set of characteristics that a lot of people believe represent a particular type of person or thing. ☐ *There's always been a stereotype about successful businessmen.* **2** V-T If someone **is stereotyped** as something, people form a fixed general idea or image of them, so that it is assumed that they will behave in a particular way. [usu passive] ☐ *He was stereotyped by some as a renegade.*

ste|reo|typi|cal /stɛriətɪpɪkᵊl, stɪər-/ ADJ A **stereotypical** idea of a type of person or thing is a fixed general idea that a lot of people have about it, that may be false in many cases. ☐ *These are men whose masculinity does not conform to stereotypical images of the unfeeling male.*

ster|ile /stɛrəl, BRIT stɛraɪl/ **1** ADJ Something that is **sterile** is completely clean and free from germs. ☐ *He always made sure that any cuts were protected by*

스텝 ☐ 그녀는 고든보다 나은 무용수였다. 최소한 스텝은 알고 있었다. **8** 단수명사 걸음걸이, 걸음 ☐ 그는 걸음을 빨리 했다. **7** 구 한 걸음 앞선 ☐ 성공적인 여행은 부분적으로 다른 사람들보다 한 걸음 앞서서 다니는 것이라고 할 수 있다. **10** 구 발을 맞춰; 발을 안 맞춰 ☐ 그들은 키가 거의 같았고 완벽히 발을 맞춰서 움직였다. **11** 구 생각이 같은; 생각이 다른 ☐ 러시아 정부는 무척이나 미국 정부와 생각을 같이 하고 싶어 한다. **12** 구 차근차근 ☐ 나는 일을 서두르지 않고 차근차근 밟아 나가고 있다. **13** 구 조심하다 ☐ 데이비드 베컴은 전반전에 경고를 받았기 때문에 조심해야 할 것이다.

구동사 물러서다 ☐ 나는 잠깐 물러서서 상황을 분석했다.

구동사 물러나다 ☐ 이토 판사는 자기 부인이 증인으로 소환되면 자기는 담당 판사 자리를 물러나겠다고 했다.

구동사 개입하다 ☐ 합의가 이루어지지 않으면 군대가 개입할 것이다.

구동사 증가시키다, 강화하다 ☐ 그는 소말리아에 원조를 보내는 노력을 강화하라고 기부자들에게 촉구했다.

가산명사 의붓형; 의붓동생

가산명사 의붓딸

가산명사 계부, 의붓아버지

가산명사 계모, 의붓어머니

1 가산명사 발판 ☐ 그것은 보다 크고 좋은 것들을 향한 하나의 발판에 불과하다. **2** 가산명사 징검돌

가산명사 의붓언니; 의붓동생

가산명사 의붓아들

1 형용사 스테레오의 ☐ 전면적인 스테레오 사운드를 들려주는 스피커 **2** 가산명사 스테레오

1 가산명사 전형(典型), 정형(定型) ☐ 성공한 사업가에 관한 어떤 정형이 항상 존재해 왔었다. **2** 타동사 정형화되다, 인식이 박히다 ☐ 일부 사람들에게 그는 변절자라는 인식이 박혀 있었다.

형용사 정형화된, 판에 박힌 ☐ 이 남자들의 남성은 무뚝뚝한 남성이라는 고정관념에 들어맞지 않는다.

1 형용사 살균한, 무균의 ☐ 그는 항상 모든 자상에는 반드시 살균한 붕대를 감도록 했다. ● 무균 불가산명사

sterile dressings. ● **ste|ril|ity** /stərɪlɪti/ N-UNCOUNT ☐ *...the antiseptic sterility of the hospital.* **2** ADJ A person or animal that is **sterile** is unable to have or produce babies. ☐ *George was sterile.* ● **ste|ril|ity** N-UNCOUNT ☐ *This disease causes sterility in both males and females.*

ster|il|ize /stɛrɪlaɪz/ (**sterilizes, sterilizing, sterilized**) [BRIT also **sterilise**] **1** V-T If you **sterilize** a thing or a place, you make it completely clean and free from germs. ☐ *Sulphur is also used to sterilize equipment.* ● **ster|ili|za|tion** /stɛrɪlɪzeɪʃn, BRIT stɛrɪlaɪzeɪʃn/ N-UNCOUNT ☐ *...the pasteurization and sterilization of milk.* **2** V-T If a person or an animal **is sterilized**, they have a medical operation that makes it impossible for them to have or produce babies. [usu passive] ☐ *My wife was sterilized after the birth of her fourth child.* ● **ster|ili|za|tion** (**sterilizations**) N-VAR ☐ *In some cases, a sterilization is performed through the vaginal wall.*

ster|ling ♦◇◇ /stɜrlɪŋ/ **1** N-UNCOUNT **Sterling** is the money system of Great Britain. ☐ *The stamps had to be paid for in sterling.* **2** ADJ **Sterling** means very good in quality; used to describe someone's work or character. [FORMAL, APPROVAL] ☐ *Those are sterling qualities to be admired in anyone.*

stern /stɜrn/ (**sterner, sternest, sterns**) **1** ADJ **Stern** words or actions are very severe. ☐ *Mr. Straw issued a stern warning to those who persist in violence.* ● **stern|ly** ADV ☐ *"We will take the necessary steps," she said sternly.* **2** ADJ Someone who is **stern** is very serious and strict. ☐ *Her father was stern and hard to please.*

ster|oid /stɪrɔɪd, stɛr-, BRIT stɪərɔɪd/ (**steroids**) N-COUNT A **steroid** is a type of chemical substance found in your body. Steroids can be artificially introduced into the bodies of athletes to improve their strength.

stew /stu, BRIT styuː/ (**stews, stewing, stewed**) **1** N-VAR A **stew** is a meal which you make by cooking meat and vegetables in liquid at a low temperature. ☐ *She served him a bowl of beef stew.* **2** V-T When you **stew** meat, vegetables, or fruit, you cook them slowly in liquid in a covered pot. ☐ *Stew the apple and blackberries to make a thick pulp.*

stew|ard /stuərd, BRIT styuːərd/ (**stewards**) **1** N-COUNT A **steward** is a man who works on a ship, plane, or train, taking care of passengers and serving meals to them. **2** N-COUNT A **steward** is a man or woman who helps to organize a race, march, or other public event. ☐ *The steward at the march stood his ground while the rest of the marchers decided to run.*

stew|ard|ess /stuərdɛs, BRIT styuːərdɛs/ (**stewardesses**) N-COUNT A **stewardess** is a woman who works on a ship, plane, or train, taking care of passengers and serving meals to them.

---
stick
① NOUN USES
② VERB USES
---

① **stick** ♦◇◇ /stɪk/ (**sticks**) **1** N-COUNT A **stick** is a thin branch which has fallen off a tree. ☐ *...people carrying bundles of dried sticks to sell for firewood.* **2** N-COUNT A **stick** is a long thin piece of wood which is used for supporting someone's weight or for hitting people or animals. ☐ *He looks old, has diabetes, and walks with a stick.* **3** N-COUNT A **stick** is a long thin piece of wood which is used for a particular purpose. ☐ *...kebab sticks.* **4** N-COUNT Some long thin objects that are used in sports are called **sticks**. ☐ *...lacrosse sticks.* ☐ *...hockey sticks.* **5** N-COUNT A **stick** of something is a long thin piece of it. ☐ *...a stick of celery.* **6** PHRASE If someone **gets the wrong end of the stick** or **gets hold of the wrong end of the stick**, they do not understand something correctly and get the wrong idea about it. [INFORMAL] ☐ *I think someone has got the wrong end of the stick. They should have established the facts before speaking out.*

② **stick** ♦◇◇ /stɪk/ (**sticks, sticking, stuck**) **1** V-T If you **stick** something somewhere, you put it there in a rather casual way. [INFORMAL] ☐ *He folded the papers and stuck them in his desk drawer.* **2** V-T/V-I If you **stick** a pointed object **in** something, or if it **sticks in** something, it goes into it or through it by making a cut or hole. ☐ *They sent in loads of male nurses and stuck a needle in my back.* **3** V-I If something **is sticking out** from a surface or object, it extends up or away from it. If something **is sticking into** a surface or object, it is partly in it. ☐ *They lay where they had fallen from the crane, sticking out of the water.* **4** V-T If you **stick** one thing to another, you attach it using glue, Scotch tape, or another sticky substance. ☐ *Don't forget to clip the token and stick it on your card.* **5** V-I If one thing **sticks to** another, it becomes attached to it and is difficult to remove. ☐ *The soil sticks to the blade and blocks the plough.* ☐ *Peel away the waxed paper if it has stuck to the bottom of the cake.* **6** V-I If something **sticks in** your mind, you remember it for a long time. ☐ *The incident stuck in my mind because it was the first example I had seen of racism in that country.* **7** V-I If something which can usually be moved **sticks**, it becomes fixed in one position. ☐ *The needle on the dial went right round to fifty feet, which was as far as it could go, and there it stuck.* **8** →see also **stuck**

Word Partnership	*stick의 연어*		
PREP.	stick **out** ②③		
	stick **to** *something* ②⑤		
ADV.	stick **together** ②⑤		

▶**stick around** PHRASAL VERB If you **stick around**, you stay where you are, often because you are waiting for something. [INFORMAL] ☐ *Stick around a while and see what develops.*

▶**stick by** **1** PHRASAL VERB If you **stick by** someone, you continue to give them help or support. ☐ *...friends who stuck by me during the difficult times as Council*

☐ 병원의 소독한 무균 환경 **2** 형용사 불임의 ☐ 조지는 불임이었다. ● 불임 불가산명사 ☐ 이 병은 남녀 모두에게 불임을 유발한다.

[영국영어 sterilise] **1** 타동사 살균하다, 소독하다 ☐ 유황도 장비를 소독하기 위해 사용된다. ● 살균, 소독 불가산명사 ☐ 우유의 저온 살균법 및 일반 살균법 **2** 타동사 불임 시술을 받다 ☐ 내 아내는 넷째 아이를 낳은 이후 불임 시술을 받았다. ● 불임 시술 가산명사 또는 불가산명사 ☐ 일부 경우 질 벽을 통해 불임 시술을 행한다.

1 불가산명사 영국 화폐 제도 ☐ 우표를 영국 돈으로 사야 했다. **2** 형용사 훌륭한 [격식체, 마음에 듦] ☐ 그러한 자질은 누구에게서나 존경할 만한 훌륭한 자질이다.

1 형용사 엄중한 ☐ 스트로 씨는 폭력을 고집하는 이들에게 엄중한 경고를 보냈다. ● 엄중하게 부사 ☐ "필요한 조치를 취하겠다."라고 그녀가 엄중하게 말했다. **2** 형용사 엄격한, 준엄한 ☐ 그녀의 아버지는 엄격하고 마음에 들기가 어려웠다.

가산명사 스테로이드

1 가산명사 또는 불가산명사 스튜 ☐ 그녀는 그에게 쇠고기 스튜 한 그릇을 차려 주었다. **2** 타동사 뭉근한 불로 끓이다 ☐ 사과와 검은 딸기를 뭉근한 불에 끓여 걸쭉한 죽처럼 만드세요.

1 가산명사 (남자) 승무원 **2** 가산명사 (행사) 진행원 ☐ 행진을 하던 다른 사람들은 달리기로 결정을 했으나 행진의 진행원들은 뜻을 굽히지 않았다.

가산명사 (여자) 승무원

1 가산명사 (잔가지) 나뭇가지 ☐ 땔감으로 팔 마른 나뭇가지 묶음들을 들고 가는 사람들 **2** 가산명사 지팡이, 막대기 ☐ 그는 늙어 보이고 당뇨병이 있으며 지팡이를 짚고 다닌다. **3** 가산명사 막대기 ☐ 케밥 꼬챙이 **4** 가산명사 (스포츠에서 사용하는) 채 ☐ 라크로스 채 ☐ 하키 채 **5** 가산명사 막대기 모양의 것, 대 ☐ 셀러리 한 대 **6** 구 오해하다 [비격식체] ☐ 누군가 뭔가를 오해하는 것 같다. 이야기를 하기 전에 사실을 확인했어야 했다.

1 타동사 대충 놓다 [비격식체] ☐ 그는 서류를 접어서 이를 자기 책상 서랍에 대충 집어넣었다. **2** 타동사/자동사 찔러 넣다, 박다 ☐ 남자 간호사를 무더기로 들여보낸 다음 내 등에 바늘을 찔러 넣었다. **3** 자동사 쑥 나와 되어나와 있다; 쑥 들어가 있다 ☐ 그것들은 기중기에서 떨어진 위치에 그대로 수면 위로 쑥 나온 상태로 있었다. **4** 타동사 붙이다 ☐ 잊지 말고 선물권을 잘라서 카드에 붙이세요. **5** 자동사 달라붙다 ☐ 흙이 날에 달라붙어 쟁기질을 방해한다. ☐ 기름종이가 케이크의 바닥에 달라붙었다면 벗겨 내세요. **6** 자동사 (마음속에) 박히다, 잊히지 않다 ☐ 그 사건은 그 나라에서 최초로 목격한 인종 차별 사례였기 때문에 내 머릿속에 박혀 지워지지 않았다. **7** 자동사 (움직이려 해도) 꼼짝 않다 ☐ 다이얼의 바늘이 최고치인 50피트까지 돌아간 다음에 그곳에서 꼼짝을 하지 않았다.

구동사 머무르다 [비격식체] ☐ 잠깐 머물러서 일이 어떻게 되어 가는지 보세요.

1 구동사 -의 곁을 지키다, -를 떠나지 않다 ☐ 위원회 지도자로서의 어려웠던 시기에 내 곁을 지켰던 친구들

Leader. **2** PHRASAL VERB If you **stick by** a promise, agreement, decision, or principle, you do what you said you would do, or do not change your mind. ❑ *But I made my decision then and stuck by it.*

▶**stick out** **1** PHRASAL VERB If you **stick out** part of your body, you extend it away from your body. ❑ *She made a face and stuck out her tongue at him.* to **stick your neck out** →see **neck** **2** PHRASAL VERB If something **sticks out**, it is very noticeable because it is unusual. ❑ *What had Cutter done to make him stick out from the crowd?* **3** PHRASE If someone in an unpleasant or difficult situation **sticks it out**, they do not leave or give up. ❑ *I really didn't like New York, but I wanted to stick it out a little bit longer.*

▶**stick to** **1** PHRASAL VERB If you **stick to** something or someone when you are traveling, you stay close to them. ❑ *There are interesting hikes inland, but most ramblers stick to the clifftops.* **2** PHRASAL VERB If you **stick to** something, you continue doing, using, saying, or talking about it, rather than changing to something else. ❑ *Perhaps he should have stuck to writing.* **3** PHRASAL VERB If you **stick to** a promise, agreement, decision, or principle, you do what you said you would do, or do not change your mind. ❑ *Immigrant support groups are waiting to see if he sticks to his word.* to **stick to your guns** →see **gun**

▶**stick together** PHRASAL VERB If people **stick together**, they stay with each other and support each other. ❑ *If we all stick together, we ought to be okay.*

▶**stick up for** PHRASAL VERB If you **stick up for** a person or a principle, you support or defend them forcefully. ❑ *Dad spoils me. He loves me. He sticks up for me.*

▶**stick with** **1** PHRASAL VERB If you **stick with** something, you do not change to something else. ❑ *If you're in a job that keeps you busy, stick with it.* **2** PHRASAL VERB If you **stick with** someone, you stay close to them. ❑ *Tugging the woman's arm, she pulled her to her side saying: "You just stick with me, dear."*

stick|er /stɪkər/ (**stickers**) N-COUNT A **sticker** is a small piece of paper or plastic, with writing or a picture on one side, which you can stick onto a surface. ❑ *...a bumper sticker that said, "Flowers Make Life Lovelier."*

stick|ing point (**sticking points**) also **sticking-point** N-COUNT A **sticking point** in a discussion or series of negotiations is a point on which the people involved cannot agree and which may delay or stop the talks. A **sticking point** is also one aspect of a problem which you have trouble dealing with. ❑ *The main sticking point was the question of taxes.*

stick shift (**stick shifts**) N-COUNT A **stick shift** is the lever that you use to change gear in a car or other vehicle. [mainly AM; BRIT usually **gear lever**] ❑ *I'm having trouble with this stick shift because I'm left-handed.*

sticky /stɪki/ (**stickier, stickiest**) **1** ADJ A **sticky** substance is soft, or thick and liquid, and can stick to other things. **Sticky** things are covered with a sticky substance. ❑ *...sticky toffee.* ❑ *If the dough is sticky, add more flour.* **2** ADJ A **sticky** situation involves problems or is embarrassing. [mainly BRIT, INFORMAL] ❑ *Inevitably the transition will yield some sticky moments.* **3** ADJ **Sticky** weather is unpleasantly hot and damp. ❑ *...four desperately hot, sticky days in the middle of August.*

stiff /stɪf/ (**stiffer, stiffest**) **1** ADJ Something that is **stiff** is firm or does not bend easily. ❑ *The furniture was stiff, uncomfortable, too delicate, and too neat.* ❑ *His gaberdine trousers were brand new and stiff.* ● **stiff|ly** ADV ❑ *Moira sat stiffly upright in her straight-backed chair.* **2** ADJ Something such as a door or drawer that is **stiff** does not move as easily as it should. ❑ *Train doors have handles on the inside. They are stiff so that they cannot be opened accidentally.* **3** ADJ If you are **stiff**, your muscles or joints hurt when you move, because of illness or because of too much exercise. ❑ *The Mud Bath is particularly recommended for relieving tension and stiff muscles.* ● **stiff|ly** ADV ❑ *He climbed stiffly from the Volkswagen.* **4** ADJ **Stiff** behavior is rather formal and not very friendly or relaxed. ❑ *They always seemed a little awkward with each other, a bit stiff and formal.* ● **stiff|ly** ADV ❑ *"Why don't you borrow your sister's car?" said Cassandra stiffly.* **5** ADJ **Stiff** can be used to mean difficult or severe. ❑ *The film faces stiff competition for the Best Film nomination.* **6** ADV If you are bored **stiff**, worried **stiff**, or scared **stiff**, you are extremely bored, worried, or scared. [INFORMAL, EMPHASIS] [adj ADV] ❑ *Anna tried to look interested. Actually, she was bored stiff.* ● ADJ **Stiff** is also an adjective. [v n ADJ] ❑ *Even if he bores you stiff, it is good manners not to let him know it.*

stiff|en /stɪfⁿn/ (**stiffens, stiffening, stiffened**) **1** V-I If you **stiffen**, you stop moving and stand or sit with muscles that are suddenly tense, for example because you feel afraid or angry. ❑ *Ada stiffened at the sound of his voice.* **2** V-T/V-I If your muscles or joints **stiffen**, or if something **stiffens** them, they become difficult to bend or move. ❑ *The blood supply to the skin is reduced when muscles stiffen.* ● PHRASAL VERB **Stiffen up** means the same as **stiffen**. ❑ *These clothes restrict your freedom of movement and stiffen up the whole body.* **3** V-T If something such as cloth **is stiffened**, it is made firm so that it does not bend easily. [usu passive] ❑ *This special paper was actually thin, soft Sugiwara paper that had been stiffened with a kind of paste.*

sti|fle /staɪfᵊl/ (**stifles, stifling, stifled**) **1** V-T If someone **stifles** something you consider to be a good thing, they prevent it from continuing. [DISAPPROVAL] ❑ *Regulations on children stifled creativity.* **2** V-T If you **stifle** a yawn or laugh, you prevent yourself from yawning or laughing. ❑ *She makes no attempt to stifle a yawn.* **3** V-T If you **stifle** your natural feelings or behavior, you prevent yourself from having those feelings or behaving in that way. ❑ *It is best to stifle curiosity and leave birds' nests alone.*

---

2 구동사 지키다 ❑ 그러나 나는 그때 결정을 내렸고 그것을 지켰다.

1 구동사 내밀다 ❑ 그녀는 놀리는 표정을 지으며 그를 보고 혀를 내밀었다. **2** 구동사 눈에 띄다, 특이하다 ❑ 커터가 어떤 짓을 했기에 사람들 가운데서 눈에 띄게 되었을까? **3** 구 버티다 ❑ 나는 뉴욕이 정말 싫었으나 좀 더 그곳에서 버티고 싶었다.

1 구동사 ~의 근처에만 머무르다 ❑ 내륙으로 들어가면 하이킹을 할 수 있는 흥미로운 길들이 있는데도 대부분의 하이킹족들이 절벽 꼭대기 근처만 다닌다. **2** 구동사 ~을 계속하다 ❑ 글쓰기를 계속 하는 것이 그에게 나았을 수도 있다. **3** 구동사 ~을 지키다, ~을 고수하다 ❑ 이민자 지원 단체들은 그가 자신의 약속을 지킬지 지켜보고 있다.

구동사 함께 뭉치다, 단결하다 ❑ 우리가 함께 뭉친다면 괜찮을 것이다.

구동사 지지하다, 옹호하다 ❑ 아빠께서는 내가 하고 싶은 것을 다 하게 해 주셔. 나를 사랑하고, 항상 열렬히 지지하셔.

1 구동사 ~을 계속하다 ❑ 바쁘게 할 수 있는 일을 하고 계시면 그것을 계속 하세요. **2** 구동사 ~의 곁에 머물다 ❑ 그녀는 여자의 팔을 잡아 자기 곁으로 끌어당기면서 말했다. "내 곁에 있기만 하면 돼요, 아가씨."

가산명사 스티커 ❑ "꽃은 인생을 보다 아름답게 한다."라는 내용의 자동차 스티커

가산명사 골치 아픈 사항, 난제 ❑ 주요 난제는 세금 문제였다.

가산명사 수동 변속기 [주로 미국영어; 영국영어 대개 gear lever] ❑ 나는 왼손잡이라서 이 수동 변속기를 다루는 데 애로가 있다.

1 형용사 끈적거리는, 달라붙는 ❑ 끈적거리는 연사탕 ❑ 반죽이 끈적거리면 밀가루를 추가하세요. **2** 형용사 난감한 [주로 영국영어, 비격식체] ❑ 불가피하게 과도기에는 난감한 순간들이 좀 생긴다. **3** 형용사 끈적거리는, 무더운 ❑ 8월 중순의 절망적일 정도로 덥고 끈적거리는 나흘

1 형용사 뻣뻣한 ❑ 가구는 뻣뻣하고 불편하고 너무 섬세하고 너무 깔끔했다. ❑ 그의 개버딘 바지는 산 새 것이었고 뻣뻣했다. ● 뻣뻣하게 부사 ❑ 모이라는 등받이가 곧은 의자에 뻣뻣하게 똑바로 앉아 있었다. **2** 형용사 경직된 ❑ 기차 문은 손잡이가 안쪽에 달려 있다. 그 손잡이들은 잘못 열리는 일이 없도록 빡빡하게 만들어져 있다. **3** 형용사 경직된 ❑ 긴장과 경직된 근육을 푸는 데 진흙 목욕을 특별히 추천한다. ● 경직되게 부사 ❑ 그는 경직된 동작으로 폭스바겐에서 내렸다. **4** 형용사 경직된, 딱딱한 ❑ 그들은 서로를 대할 때 항상 조금 경직되고 정중하면서 약간 어색해 보인다. ● 경직되게, 딱딱하게 부사 ❑ "왜 네 누이의 차를 빌리지 그러니"라고 카산드라가 딱딱한 어조로 말했다. **5** 형용사 어려운, 심한 ❑ 이 영화는 최우수작품상 후보로 오르는 데 심한 경쟁을 물리쳐야 한다. **6** 부사 몹시, 극심하게 [비격식체, 강조] ❑ 애너는 흥미가 있는 것처럼 보이려고 애를 썼다. 사실 그녀는 지루해 죽을 것 같았다. ● 형용사 극심한 ❑ 그가 죽을 정도로 지루하게 해도 티를 내지 않는 것이 예의다.

1 자동사 몸이 굳다, 경직되다 ❑ 에이다는 그의 목소리에 온몸이 굳었다. **2** 타동사/자동사 경직되다, 뻣뻣해지다; 경직시키다, 뻣뻣하게 만들다 ❑ 근육이 경직되면 피부로 가는 혈액의 양이 줄어든다. **2** 구동사 경직되다, 뻣뻣해지다; 뻣뻣하게 만들다 ❑ 이 옷들은 움직임의 자유를 제한하며 온몸을 경직시킨다. **3** 타동사 뻣뻣해지다 ❑ 이 특수종이는 원래는 얇고 부드러운 스기와라 종이였는데 일종의 풀로 뻣뻣하게 만든 것이었다.

1 타동사 억압하다 [탐탁찮음] ❑ 아이들에 대한 규정들이 창의력을 억압했다. **2** 타동사 (하품이나 웃음을) 참다 ❑ 그녀는 하품을 참으려는 노력도 하지 않는다. **3** 타동사 억제하다, 억누르다 ❑ 호기심을 억제하고 새 둥지를 가만 놔두는 것이 제일 잘 하는 것이다.

sti|fling /ˈstaɪflɪŋ/ ■ ADJ **Stifling** heat is so intense that it makes you feel uncomfortable. You can also use **stifling** to describe a place that is extremely hot. ❑ *The stifling heat of the little room was beginning to make me nauseous.* ■ ADJ If a situation is **stifling**, it makes you feel uncomfortable because you cannot do what you want. ❑ *Life at home with her parents and two sisters was stifling.* ■ →see also **stifle**

stig|ma /ˈstɪgmə/ (**stigmas**) N-VAR If something has a **stigma** attached to it, people think it is something to be ashamed of. ❑ *There is still a stigma attached to cancer.*

stig|ma|tize /ˈstɪgmətaɪz/ (**stigmatizes, stigmatizing, stigmatized**) [BRIT also **stigmatise**] V-T If someone or something **is stigmatized**, they are unfairly regarded by many people as being bad or having something to be ashamed of. ❑ *Children in single-parent families must not be stigmatized.*

sti|let|to /stɪˈlɛtoʊ/ (**stilettos**) N-COUNT **Stilettos** are women's shoes that have high, very narrow heels. [mainly BRIT; AM usually **spike heels**] ❑ *Off came her sneakers and on went a pair of stilettos.*

---

still

① ADVERB USES
② NOT MOVING OR MAKING A NOISE
③ EQUIPMENT

---

① **still** ♦♦♦ /stɪl/ ■ ADV If a situation that used to exist **still** exists, it has continued and exists now. ❑ *I still dream of home.* ❑ *Brian's toe is still badly swollen and he cannot put on his shoe.* ■ ADV If something that has not yet happened could **still** happen, it is possible that it will happen. If something that has not yet happened is **still to** happen, it will happen at a later time. [ADV before v] ❑ *Big money could still be made if the crisis keeps oil prices high.* ❑ *We could still make it, but we won't get there till three.* ■ ADV If you say that there **is still** an amount of something left, you are emphasizing that there is that amount left. [be ADV n] ❑ *There are still some outstanding problems.* ■ ADV You use **still** to emphasize that something remains the case or is true in spite of what you have just said. [ADV before v] ❑ *I'm average for my height. But I still feel I'm fatter than I should be.* ■ ADV You use **still** to indicate that a problem or difficulty is not really worth worrying about. [ADV with cl] ❑ *Their luck had simply run out. Still, never fear.* ■ ADV You use **still** in expressions such as **still further, still another,** and **still more** to show that you find the number or quantity of things you are referring to surprising or excessive. [EMPHASIS] [ADV n/adv] ❑ *We look forward to strengthening still further our already close co-operation with the police service.* ■ ADV You use **still** with comparatives to indicate that something has even more of a quality than something else. [EMPHASIS] [ADV with compar] ❑ *Formula One motor car racing is supposed to be dangerous. "Indycar" racing is supposed to be more dangerous still.*

> If you say that something is **still** happening or is **still** the case, you are usually emphasizing your surprise that it has been happening or has been the case for so long. ❑ *She was still looking at me... There are still plenty of horses around here.* **Already** is often used to add emphasis or to suggest that it is surprising that something has happened so soon. ❑ *They were already eating their lunch.* You use **yet** in negative sentences and in questions. It is often used to add emphasis, to suggest surprise that something has not happened, or to say that it will happen later. ❑ *Have you seen it yet?... The troops could not yet see the shore... It isn't dark yet.*

② **still** ♦♦♦ /stɪl/ (**stiller, stillest, stills**) ■ ADJ If you stay **still**, you stay in the same position and do not move. [ADJ after v, v-link ADJ, ADJ n] ❑ *David had been dancing about like a child, but suddenly he stood still and looked at Brad.* ■ ADJ If air or water is **still**, it is not moving. ❑ *The night air was very still.* ■ ADJ Drinks that are **still** do not contain any bubbles of carbon dioxide. [mainly BRIT] ❑ *...a glass of still orange.* ■ ADJ If a place is **still**, it is quiet and shows no sign of activity. ❑ *In the room it was very still.* ● **still|ness** N-UNCOUNT ❑ *Four deafening explosions shattered the stillness of the night air.* ■ N-COUNT A **still** is a photograph taken from a movie which is used for publicity purposes. ❑ *...stills from the James Bond movie series.*

③ **still** /stɪl/ (**stills**) N-COUNT A **still** is a piece of equipment used to make strong alcoholic drinks by a process called distilling.

still|born /ˈstɪlbɔrn/ ADJ A **stillborn** baby is dead when it is born. ❑ *It was a miracle that she survived the birth of her stillborn baby.*

still life (**still lifes**) N-VAR A **still life** is a painting or drawing of an arrangement of objects such as flowers or fruit. It also refers to this type of painting or drawing. ❑ *...a still life by one of France's finest artists.* →see **painting**

stimu|lant /ˈstɪmyələnt/ (**stimulants**) N-COUNT A **stimulant** is a drug that makes your body work faster, often increasing your heart rate and making you less likely to sleep. ❑ *It is not a good idea to fight fatigue by taking stimulants.*

stimu|late ♦♦♦ /ˈstɪmyəleɪt/ (**stimulates, stimulating, stimulated**) ■ V-T To **stimulate** something means to encourage it to begin or develop further. ❑ *America's priority is simply to stimulate its economy.* ● **stimu|la|tion** /ˌstɪmyəˈleɪʃⁿn/ N-UNCOUNT ❑ *...an economy in need of stimulation.* ■ V-T If you **are stimulated by** something, it makes you feel full of ideas and enthusiasm. [usu passive] ❑ *Bill was stimulated by the challenge.* ● **stimu|lat|ing** ADJ ❑ *It is a complex yet stimulating book.* ● **stimu|la|tion** N-UNCOUNT ❑ *Many enjoy the mental stimulation of a*

■ 형용사 질식할 듯한, 숨막힐 정도의 ❑ 그 작은 방의 질식할 듯한 열기 때문에 나는 속이 메슥거리기 시작했다. ■ 형용사 답답한 ❑ 그녀가 집에서 부모하고 두 명의 자매와 같이 지내는 삶은 답답했다. ■ →see also **stifle**

가산명사 또는 불가산명사 오명 ❑ 암에 대해서는 아직도 오명이 붙어 있다.

[영국영어 stigmatise] 타동사 오명을 쓰다, 낙인이 찍히다 ❑ 한 부모 가정의 아이들에게 낙인을 찍어서는 안 된다.

가산명사 뾰족구두 [주로 영국영어; 미국영어 대개 spike heels] ❑ 그녀는 운동화를 벗고 뾰족구두를 신었다.

■ 부사 아직 ❑ 나는 아직도 집에 대한 꿈을 꾼다. ❑ 브라이언은 발가락이 아직 심하게 부어 있어서 신발을 신지 못한다. ■ 부사 아직 ❑ 위기로 석유 가격이 높게 유지된다면 아직 큰 돈을 벌 수 있을 것이다. ❑ 아직도 갈 수는 있겠지만 3시 이전에 도착하는 것은 불가능하다. ■ 부사 ～이 아직도 있다 ❑ 아직도 몇 가지 해결 안 된 문제가 있다. ■ 부사 그런데도 ❑ 내 신장은 평균 정도이다. 그런데도 내 정상 체중보다 더 뚱뚱하다는 느낌이 든다. ■ 부사 그래도 ❑ 그들은 그저 운이 다 한 상태였어요. 그래도 너무 걱정하지 마세요. ■ 부사 보다, 한층 더 [강조] ❑ 우리는 이미 경찰과 기존에 맺어 온 긴밀한 협조를 강화할 수 있기를 기대한다. ■ 부사 훨씬 [강조] ❑ 포뮬러원 자동차 경주는 위험하다고 알려져 있다. '인디카' 경주는 그보다 훨씬 더 위험하다고 알려져 있다.

어떤 일이 아직도(still) 일어나거나 사실이라고 말하면, 대개 그 일이 오랫동안 계속 일어나고 있었거나 사실이었음에 대한 놀라움을 강조하는 것이다. ❑ 그녀가 여전히 나를 보고 있었다... 여기에는 아직도 말이 충분히 많이 있다. already는 종종 강조를 하거나 어떤 일이 그렇게 빨리 일어난 것에 대해 놀라움을 표시할 때 쓴다. ❑ 그들은 벌써 점심을 먹고 있었다. yet은 부정문과 의문문에서 쓴다. yet은 종종 강조를 하거나, 어떤 일이 일어나지 않은 것에 대해 놀라움을 표시하거나, 어떤 일이 나중에 일어날 것이라고 말할 때 쓴다. ❑ 그것을 아직 안 보았나요?... 군대는 아직도 해변을 볼 수 없었다... 아직 어둡지 않다.

■ 형용사 가만히 있는, 정지한 ❑ 데이비드는 아이처럼 이리저리 움직고 있다가 갑자기 가만히 서서는 브래드를 쳐다봤다. ■ 형용사 움직이지 않는, 고요한 ❑ 밤공기는 매우 고요했다. ■ 형용사 탄산이 안 든 [주로 영국영어] ❑ 탄산이 안 든 오렌지 주스 한 잔 ■ 형용사 고요한 ❑ 방안은 매우 고요했다. ● 고요 불가산명사 ❑ 네 번의 엄청난 폭발이 밤공기의 고요를 깨뜨렸다. ■ 가산명사 스틸 사진 ❑ 제임스 본드 영화 시리즈의 스틸 사진

가산명사 증류기

형용사 사산된 ❑ 그녀가 아이를 사산하고도 살아남은 것은 기적이었다.

가산명사 또는 불가산명사 정물화 ❑ 프랑스 최고의 화가 중 한 명이 그린 정물화

가산명사 흥분제 ❑ 피로를 이기려고 흥분제를 먹는 것은 좋은 생각이 아니다.

■ 타동사 격려하다, 부양하다 ❑ 미국의 최우선 과제는 당연히 경제를 부양하는 것이다. ● 격려, 부양 불가산명사 ❑ 부양이 필요한 경제 ■ 타동사 자극을 받은 ❑ 빌은 그 도전에 자극을 받았다. ● 자극을 주는 형용사 ❑ 그것은 복잡하면서도 자극을 주는 책이다. ● 자극 불가산명사 ❑ 많은 사람들이 도전적인 직업이 주는 정신적 자극을 즐긴다. ■ 타동사 자극하다

challenging job. ❸ V-T If something **stimulates** a part of a person's body, it causes it to move or start working. ❑ *Exercise stimulates the digestive and excretory systems.* ● **stimu|lat|ing** ADJ ❑ *...the stimulating effect of adrenaline.* ● **stimu|la|tion** N-UNCOUNT [usu with supp] ❑ *...physical stimulation.*

□ 운동은 소화 및 배설 기관을 자극한다. ● 자극적인 형용사 □ 아드레날린의 자극적인 효과 ● 자극 불가산명사 □ 신체적 자극

stimu|la|tive /stɪmyələtɪv/ ADJ If a government policy has a **stimulative** effect on the economy, it encourages the economy to grow. ❑ *It is possible that a tax cut might have some stimulative effect.*

형용사 부양하는 □ 세금 감면이 약간의 부양 효과를 가질지도 모른다.

stimu|lus /stɪmyələs/ (**stimuli** /stɪmyəlaɪ/) N-VAR A **stimulus** is something that encourages activity in people or things. ❑ *Interest rates could fall soon and be a stimulus to the U.S. economy.*

가산명사 또는 불가산명사 자극, 고무 □ 금리가 곧 떨어지면 미국 경제에 자극이 될 수도 있다.

sting /stɪŋ/ (**stings, stinging, stung**) ❶ V-T If a plant, animal, or insect **stings** you, a sharp part of it, usually covered with poison, is pushed into your skin so that you feel a sharp pain. ❑ *The nettles stung their legs.* ❷ N-COUNT The **sting** of an insect or animal is the part that stings you. ❑ *Remove the bee sting with tweezers.* ❸ N-COUNT If you feel a **sting**, you feel a sharp pain in your skin or other part of your body. ❑ *This won't hurt – you will just feel a little sting.* ❹ V-T/V-I If a part of your body **stings**, or if a substance **stings** it, you feel a sharp pain there. ❑ *His cheeks were stinging from the icy wind.* ❺ V-T If someone's remarks **sting** you, they make you feel hurt and annoyed. [no cont] ❑ *He's a sensitive lad and some of the criticism has stung him.*

❶ 타동사 (곤충 등이) 찌르다, 쏘다 □ 쐐기풀이 그들의 다리를 찔렀다. ❷ 가산명사 (곤충 등의) 침 □ 벌의 침을 집게로 제거하세요. ❸ 가산명사 따끔함 □ 아프지 않을 거예요. 그냥 좀 따끔할 겁니다. ❹ 타동사/자동사 따끔거리다; 따끔하게 하다, 얼얼하게 하다 □ 얼음같이 찬 바람에 그는 볼이 얼얼했다. ❺ 타동사 마음을 상하게 하다 □ 그는 예민한 청년인데 그 비판 중 일부가 그의 마음을 상하게 했다.

stin|gy /stɪndʒi/ (**stingier, stingiest**) ADJ If you describe someone as **stingy**, you are criticizing them for being unwilling to spend money. [INFORMAL, DISAPPROVAL] ❑ *The West is stingy with aid.*

형용사 인색한 [비격식체, 탐탁잖음] □ 서방 세계가 원조에 대해 인색하다.

stink /stɪŋk/ (**stinks, stinking, stank, stunk**) ❶ V-I To **stink** means to smell extremely unpleasant. ❑ *We all stank and nobody minded.* ❑ *The place stinks of fried onions.* ● N-SING **Stink** is also a noun. ❑ *He was aware of the stink of stale beer on his breath.* ❷ V-I If you say that something **stinks**, you mean that you disapprove of it because it involves ideas, feelings, or practices that you do not like. [INFORMAL, DISAPPROVAL] ❑ *I think their methods stink.* ❸ N-SING If someone makes **a stink** about something they are angry about, they show their anger in order to make people take notice. [INFORMAL] ❑ *The family's making a hell of a stink.*

❶ 자동사 악취가 나다, 고약한 냄새가 나다 □ 우리 모두에게서 악취가 났으며 어느 누구도 신경 쓰지 않았다. □ 그곳은 튀긴 양파 냄새가 진동을 한다. ● 단수명사 악취, 고약한 냄새 □ 그는 자기 입에서 김빠진 맥주 냄새가 고약하게 난다는 것을 알고 있었다. ❷ 자동사 형편없다 [비격식체, 탐탁잖음] □ 내 생각에 그들의 방식은 형편없다. ❸ 단수명사 소동 [비격식체] □ 그 가족은 엄청난 소동을 벌이고 있다.

stint /stɪnt/ (**stints**) N-COUNT A **stint** is a period of time which you spend doing a particular job or activity or working in a particular place. ❑ *He is returning to this country after a five-year stint in Hong Kong.*

가산명사 (활동 등을 한) 기간 □ 그는 5년을 홍콩에서 보낸 다음 이 나라로 돌아오고 있다.

stipu|late /stɪpyəleɪt/ (**stipulates, stipulating, stipulated**) V-T If you **stipulate** a condition or **stipulate that** something must be done, you say clearly that it must be done. ❑ *She could have stipulated that she would pay when she collected the computer.* ● **stipu|la|tion** /stɪpyəleɪʃən/ (**stipulations**) N-COUNT ❑ *Clifford's only stipulation is that his clients obey his advice.*

타동사 조건을 달다, 명기하다 □ 그녀가 컴퓨터를 수령하면 돈을 주겠다고 조건을 달 수도 있었다. ● 조건 가산명사 □ 클리퍼드의 유일한 조건은 고객이 자신의 충고를 따라야 한다는 것이다.

stir ◆◇◇ /stɜr/ (**stirs, stirring, stirred**) ❶ V-T If you **stir** a liquid or other substance, you move it around or mix it in a container using something such as a spoon. ❑ *Stir the soup for a few seconds.* ❑ *There was Mrs. Bellingham, stirring sugar into her tea.* ❷ V-I If you **stir**, you move slightly, for example because you are uncomfortable or beginning to wake up. [WRITTEN] ❑ *Eileen shook him, and he started to stir.* ❸ V-I If you do not **stir from** a place, you do not move from there. [WRITTEN] [usu with brd-neg] ❑ *She had not stirred from the house that evening.* ❹ V-T/V-I If something **stirs** or if the wind **stirs** it, it moves gently in the wind. [WRITTEN] ❑ *Palm trees stir in the soft Pacific breeze.* ❺ V-T/V-I If a particular memory, feeling, or mood **stirs** or **is stirred in** you, you begin to think about it or feel it. [WRITTEN] ❑ *Then a memory stirs in you and you start feeling anxious.* ❑ *Amy remembered the anger he had stirred in her.* ❻ N-SING If an event causes a **stir**, it causes great excitement, shock, or anger among people. ❑ *His film has caused a stir in America.* ❼ →see also **stirring**

❶ 타동사 젓다 □ 수프를 몇 초간 저으세요. □ 벨링엄 부인이 차에 설탕을 넣어 젓고 있었다. ❷ 자동사 약간 움직이다, 뒤척이다 [문어체] □ 아일린이 그를 흔들었더니 그가 뒤척이기 시작했다. ❸ 자동사 나서다 [문어체] □ 그녀는 그 날 저녁 집 밖으로 나서지 않았다. ❹ 타동사/자동사 살랑이다, 하늘거리다; 살랑거리게 하다 [문어체] □ 야자수가 부드러운 태평양 바람에 하늘거린다. ❺ 타동사/자동사 (분위기 등이) 일어나다, 꿈틀거리다 [문어체] □ 그리고 당신 안에서 어떤 기억이 꿈틀거리고 당신은 불안을 느끼기 시작한다. □ 에이미는 그가 자기 안에 불러일으켰던 분노를 기억했다. ❻ 단수명사 소동, 술렁거림 □ 그의 영화는 미국을 술렁이게 했다.

Word Partnership	stir의 연어
N.	stir **a mixture**, stir **in sugar** ❶
V.	**cause a** stir, **create a** stir ❻

▶**stir up** ❶ PHRASAL VERB If something **stirs up** dust or **stirs up** mud in water, it causes it to rise up and move around. ❑ *They saw first a cloud of dust and then the car that was stirring it up.* ❷ PHRASAL VERB If you **stir up** a particular mood or situation, usually a bad one, you cause it. [DISAPPROVAL] ❑ *As usual, Harriet is trying to stir up trouble.*

❶ 구동사 (먼지 등을) 일으키다 □ 그들은 먼저 먼지 구름을 봤고 그 다음 그것을 일으키는 차를 봤다. ❷ 구동사 (말썽 등을) 일으키다 [탐탁잖음] □ 여느 때처럼 해리엇이 말썽을 일으키려고 한다.

stir|ring /stɜrɪŋ/ (**stirrings**) ❶ ADJ A **stirring** event, performance, or account of something makes people very excited or enthusiastic. ❑ *The Prime Minister made a stirring speech.* ❷ N-COUNT A **stirring of** a feeling or thought is the beginning of one. [usu N of n] ❑ *I feel a stirring of curiosity.*

❶ 형용사 감동적인, 흥미진진한 □ 수상은 감동적인 연설을 했다. ❷ 가산명사 (감정 등이) 동함 □ 호기심이 동하는 것이 느껴진다.

stitch /stɪtʃ/ (**stitches, stitching, stitched**) ❶ V-T/V-I If you **stitch** cloth, you use a needle and thread to join two pieces together or to make a decoration. ❑ *Fold the fabric and stitch the two layers together.* ❑ *We stitched incessantly.* ❷ N-COUNT **Stitches** are the short pieces of thread that have been sewn in a piece of cloth. ❑ *...a row of straight stitches.* ❸ N-COUNT In knitting and crochet, a **stitch** is a loop made by one turn of wool around a knitting needle or crochet hook. ❑ *Her mother counted the stitches on her knitting needles.* ❹ N-UNCOUNT If you sew or knit something in a particular **stitch**, you sew or knit in a way that produces a particular pattern. ❑ *The design can be worked in cross stitch.* ❺ V-T When doctors **stitch** a wound, they use a special needle and thread to sew the skin together. ❑ *Jill washed and stitched the wound.* ❻ N-COUNT A **stitch** is a piece of thread that has been used to sew the skin of a wound together. ❑ *He had six stitches in a head wound.* ❼ N-SING A **stitch** is a sharp pain in your side, usually caused by running or laughing a lot. ❑ *One of them was laughing so much he got a stitch.*

❶ 타동사/자동사 바느질하다, 꿰매다 □ 천을 접고 두 겹을 함께 꿰매세요. □ 우리는 쉬지 않고 바느질을 했다. ❷ 가산명사 바늘땀 □ 일직선으로 나 있는 바늘땀 한 줄 ❸ 가산명사 (뜨개질의) 코 □ 그녀의 어머니는 뜨개질바늘에 감은 코를 셌다. ❹ 불가산명사 (특정 형태의) 수 □ 이 도안은 십자수로도 놓을 수 있다. ❺ 타동사 봉합하다 □ 질은 상처를 씻고 봉합했다. ❻ 가산명사 바늘 (상처를 꿰맨 횟수) □ 그는 머리 상처에 여섯 바늘을 꿰맸다. ❼ 단수명사 옆구리가 땅김 □ 그 중 한 명은 너무 많이 웃어서 옆구리에 쥐가 났다.

stock ♦♦♢ /stɒk/ (**stocks, stocking, stocked**) **1** N-COUNT **Stocks** are shares in the ownership of a company, or investments on which a fixed amount of interest will be paid. [BUSINESS] ❏ ...the buying and selling of stocks and shares. **2** N-UNCOUNT A company's **stock** is the amount of money which the company has through selling shares. [BUSINESS] ❏ Two years later, when Compaq went public, their stock was valued at $38 million. **3** V-T If a store **stocks** particular goods, it keeps a supply of them to sell. [no cont] ❏ The shop stocks everything from cigarettes to recycled loo paper. **4** N-UNCOUNT A store's **stock** is the total amount of goods which it has available to sell. ❏ We took the decision to withdraw a quantity of stock from sale. **5** V-T If you **stock** something such as a cupboard, shelf, or room, you fill it with food or other things. ❏ I worked stocking shelves in a grocery store. ❏ Some families stocked their cellars with food and water. ● PHRASAL VERB **Stock up** means the same as **stock**. ❏ I had to stock the boat up with food. **6** N-COUNT If you have a **stock of** things, you have a supply of them stored in a place ready to be used. ❏ I keep a stock of cassette tapes describing various relaxation techniques. **7** ADJ A **stock** answer, expression, or way of doing something is one that is very commonly used, especially because people cannot be bothered to think of something new. [ADJ n] ❏ My boss had a stock response – "If it ain't broke, don't fix it!" **8** N-MASS **Stock** is a liquid, usually made by boiling meat, bones, or vegetables in water, that is used to give flavor to soups and sauces. ❏ Finally, add the beef stock. **9** PHRASE If goods are **in stock**, a shop has them available to sell. If they are **out of stock**, it does not. ❏ Check that your size is in stock. **10** PHRASE If you **take stock**, you pause to think about all the aspects of a situation or event before deciding what to do next. ❏ It was time to take stock of the situation. **11** lock, stock, and barrel →see barrel

▶**stock up** **1** →see stock 5 **2** PHRASAL VERB If you **stock up on** something, you buy a lot of it, in case you cannot get it later. ❏ The authorities have urged people to stock up on fuel. →see **company**

stock|broker /stɒkbroʊkər/ (**stockbrokers**) N-COUNT A **stockbroker** is a person whose job is to buy and sell stocks and shares for people who want to invest money. [BUSINESS]

stock|broking /stɒkbroʊkɪŋ/ N-UNCOUNT **Stockbroking** is the professional activity of buying and selling stocks and shares for clients. [BUSINESS] ❏ His stockbroking firm was hit by the 1987 crash.

stock con|trol N-UNCOUNT **Stock control** is the activity of making sure that a company always has exactly the right amount of goods available to sell. [BUSINESS] ❏ Better stock control helped Wal-Mart to reduce its expenses by $2 billion in 1997.

stock ex|change ♦♢♢ (**stock exchanges**) N-COUNT A **stock exchange** is a place where people buy and sell stocks and shares. **The stock exchange** is also the trading activity that goes on there and the trading organization itself. [BUSINESS] ❏ The shortage of good stock has kept some investors away from the stock exchange. →see **stock market**

stock|holder /stɒkhoʊldər/ (**stockholders**) N-COUNT A **stockholder** is a person who owns shares in a company. [AM, BUSINESS; BRIT **shareholder**] ❏ He was a stockholder in a hotel corporation.

stock|ing /stɒkɪŋ/ (**stockings**) N-COUNT **Stockings** are items of women's clothing which fit closely over their feet and legs. Stockings are usually made of nylon and are held in place by garters. ❏ ...a pair of nylon stockings.

stock|ist /stɒkɪst/ (**stockists**) N-COUNT A **stockist** of a particular product is someone who sells this product in their store. [BRIT] ❏ The name of your nearest stockist is available from the company.

stock mar|ket ♦♢♢ (**stock markets**) N-COUNT The **stock market** consists of the general activity of buying and selling stocks and shares, and the people and institutions that organize it. [BUSINESS] ❏ He's been studying and playing the stock market since he was 14. →see **company**
→see Word Web: **stock market**

stock op|tion (**stock options**) N-COUNT A **stock option** is an opportunity for the employees of a company to buy shares at a special price. [AM, BUSINESS; BRIT **share option**] ❏ He made a huge profit from the sale of shares purchased in January under the company's stock option program.

stock|pile /stɒkpaɪl/ (**stockpiles, stockpiling, stockpiled**) **1** V-T If people **stockpile** things such as food or weapons, they store large quantities of them for future use. ❏ People are stockpiling food for the coming winter. **2** N-COUNT A **stockpile of** things is a large quantity of them that have been stored for future use. ❏ The two leaders also approved treaties to cut stockpiles of chemical weapons.

stock|taking /stɒkteɪkɪŋ/ N-UNCOUNT **Stocktaking** is the activity of counting and checking all the goods that a store or business has. [BUSINESS]

stocky /stɒki/ (**stockier, stockiest**) ADJ A **stocky** person has a body that is broad, solid, and often short. ❏ ...a short stocky man in his forties.

---

1 가산명사 주식 [경제] ❏ 주식과 지분의 매매
2 불가산명사 주식 처분액 [경제] ❏ 2년 후, 컴팩이 상장되었을 때 그들의 주식 평가 가치는 3천8백만 달러였다. **3** 타동사 (물건을) 갖추다 ❏ 그 가게는 담배부터 재생 화장지까지 모든 것을 갖추고 있다. **4** 불가산명사 재고 ❏ 우리는 재고의 일부분을 세일에서 제외하기로 결정했다. **5** 타동사 물품을 채우다, 비축물을 채워 넣다 ❏ 나는 식료품점에서 선반에 물품을 채우는 일을 했다. ❏ 어떤 가족들은 지하실에 물과 식품을 가득 비축했다. ● 구동사 물품을 채우다, 비축물을 채워 넣다 ❏ 나는 배에 식품을 가득 실어야 했다. **6** 가산명사 비축물, 재고품 ❏ 나는 긴장을 푸는 다양한 기법을 설명하는 카세트테이프를 여러 개 구비하고 있다. **7** 형용사 상투적인 ❏ 내 상사는 늘 반응이 상투적이었다. "고장 나지 않았으면 고치지 마!" ❏ 물질명사 육수 ❏ 마지막으로 쇠고기 육수를 넣으세요. **9** 구 재고가 있는, 재고가 없는 ❏ 당신의 사이즈가 재고가 있는지를 확인하세요. **10** 구 검토하다, 꼼꼼히 살피다 ❏ 상황을 검토할 시점이었다.

2 구동사 비축하다 ❏ 당국은 사람들에게 연료를 비축할 것을 촉구했다.

가산명사 증권 중개인 [경제]

불가산명사 증권 중개업 [경제] ❏ 그의 증권 회사는 1987년의 폭락 때 된서리를 맞았다.

불가산명사 재고 관리 [경제] ❏ 우수한 재고 관리 덕분에 월마트는 1997년에 비용을 20억 달러 줄일 수 있었다.

가산명사 증권 거래소 [경제] ❏ 우량 주식 부족 때문에 일부 투자자들은 증권 거래소를 멀리했다.

가산명사 주주 [미국영어, 경제; 영국영어 shareholder] ❏ 그는 한 호텔 회사의 주주였다.

가산명사 스타킹 ❏ 나일론 스타킹 한 켤레

가산명사 (특정 상품의) 판매자 [영국영어] ❏ 가장 가까운 영업자의 이름은 회사에서 얻을 수 있다.

가산명사 주식 시장 [경제] ❏ 그는 열네 살 때부터 주식 시장을 공부하고 관여해 왔다.

가산명사 스톡옵션 [미국영어, 경제; 영국영어 share option] ❏ 그는 회사 스톡옵션 제도를 통해 1월에 매수한 주식을 매도하여 엄청난 이윤을 남겼다.

1 타동사 대량으로 비축하다 ❏ 사람들이 다가올 겨울을 대비해 식품을 대량으로 비축하고 있다. **2** 가산명사 대량 비축 ❏ 두 지도자는 또한 화학 무기의 대량 보유고를 감축하는 조약을 승인했다.

불가산명사 재고 조사 [경제]

형용사 (체격이) 다부진 ❏ 키가 작고 체격이 다부진 40대

Word Web — stock market

The Dutch established the first **stock exchange** in Amsterdam in 1611. Its purpose was to raise **capital** to **invest** in the spice trade with the Far East. It also **traded** in metals and grains such as wheat and rye. The Dutch also experienced the world's first **stock market crash**. Tulips were an important **commodity** in seventeenth century Holland. By 1636 a single tulip bulb sold for the equivalent of $76,000. However, **confidence** in the tulip market suddenly dropped. Soon a tulip bulb was worth only $1. **Commerce** in Holland did not recover for many years.

stoke /stoʊk/ (stokes, stoking, stoked) **1** V-T If you **stoke** a fire, you add coal or wood to it to keep it burning. ❑ *She was stoking the stove with sticks of maple.* ● PHRASAL VERB **Stoke up** means the same as **stoke**. ❑ *He stoked up the fire in the hearth.* **2** V-T If you **stoke** something such as a feeling, you cause it to be felt more strongly. ❑ *These demands are helping to stoke fears of civil war.* ● PHRASAL VERB **Stoke up** means the same as **stoke**. ❑ *He has sent his proposals in the hope of stoking up interest for the idea.*

stole /stoʊl/ (stoles) Stole is the past tense of **steal**.

stol|en /stoʊlᵊn/ Stolen is the past participle of **steal**.

stom|ach ◆◇◇ /stʌmək/ (stomachs, stomaching, stomached) **1** N-COUNT Your **stomach** is the organ inside your body where food is digested before it moves into the intestines. ❑ *He had an upset stomach.* **2** N-COUNT You can refer to the front part of your body below your waist as your **stomach**. ❑ *The children lay down on their stomachs.* **3** N-COUNT If the front part of your body below your waist feels uncomfortable because you are feeling worried or frightened, you can refer to it as your **stomach**. ❑ *His stomach was in knots.* **4** N-COUNT If you say that someone has a strong **stomach**, you mean that they are not disgusted by things that disgust most other people. ❑ *Surgery often demands actual physical strength, as well as the possession of a strong stomach.* **5** V-T If you cannot **stomach** something, you cannot accept it because you dislike it or disapprove of it. [with brd-neg] ❑ *I could never stomach the cruelty involved in the wounding of animals.* **6** PHRASE If you do something **on an empty stomach**, you do it without having eaten. ❑ *Avoid drinking on an empty stomach.*

stomp /stɒmp/ (stomps, stomping, stomped) V-I If you **stomp** somewhere, you walk there with very heavy steps, often because you are angry. ❑ *He turned his back on them and stomped off up the hill.*

stone ◆◆◇ /stoʊn/ (stones, stoning, stoned)

The plural is usually **stone** in meaning **9**.

1 N-MASS **Stone** is a hard solid substance found in the ground and often used for building houses. ❑ *He could not tell whether the floor was wood or stone.* ❑ *People often don't appreciate that marble is a natural stone.* **2** N-COUNT A **stone** is a small piece of rock that is found on the ground. ❑ *He removed a stone from his shoe.* **3** N-COUNT A **stone** is a large piece of stone put somewhere in memory of a person or event, or as a religious symbol. ❑ *The monument consists of a circle of gigantic stones.* **4** N-UNCOUNT **Stone** is used in expressions such as **set in stone** and **tablets of stone** to suggest that an idea or rule is firm and fixed, and cannot be changed. ❑ *He is merely throwing the idea forward for discussion, it is not cast in stone.* **5** N-COUNT You can refer to a jewel as a **stone**. ❑ *...a diamond ring with three stones.* **6** N-COUNT A **stone** is a small hard ball of minerals and other substances which sometimes forms in a person's kidneys or gallbladder. ❑ *He had kidney stones.* **7** N-COUNT The **stone** in a plum, cherry, or other fruit is the large hard seed in the middle of it. [mainly BRIT; AM usually **pit**] ❑ *Halve each peach and remove the stone.* **8** V-T If people **stone** someone or something, they throw stones at them. ❑ *Youths burned cars and stoned police.* **9** N-COUNT A **stone** is a measurement of weight, especially the weight of a person, equal to 14 pounds or 6.35 kilograms. [BRIT] ❑ *I weighed around 16 stone.* →see **weight** **10** →see also **stoned**, **steppingstone** →see **fruit**

stoned /stoʊnd/ ADJ If someone is **stoned**, their mind is greatly affected by a drug such as cannabis. [INFORMAL] ❑ *Half of them were so stoned they couldn't even see.*

stony /stoʊni/ (stonier, stoniest) **1** ADJ **Stony** ground is rough and contains a lot of stones. ❑ *The steep, stony ground is well drained.* **2** ADJ A **stony** expression or attitude does not show any sympathy or friendliness. ❑ *She gave me the stoniest look I ever got.*

stood /stʊd/ Stood is the past tense and past participle of **stand**.

stool /stuːl/ (stools) N-COUNT A **stool** is a seat with legs but no support for your arms or back. ❑ *O'Brien sat on a bar stool and leaned his elbows on the counter.*

stoop /stuːp/ (stoops, stooping, stooped) **1** V-I If you **stoop**, you stand or walk with your shoulders bent forward. ❑ *She was taller than he was and stooped slightly.* ● N-SING **Stoop** is also a noun. ❑ *He was a tall, thin fellow with a slight stoop.* **2** V-I If you **stoop**, you bend your body forward and downward. ❑ *He stooped to pick up the carrier bag of groceries.* ❑ *Two men in shirt sleeves stooped over the car.* **3** V-I If you say that a person **stoops to** doing something, you are criticizing them because they do something wrong or immoral that they would not normally do. [DISAPPROVAL] ❑ *He had not, until recently, stooped to personal abuse.*

stop ◆◆◆ /stɒp/ (stops, stopping, stopped) **1** V-T If you stop doing something and then you stop doing it, you no longer do it. ❑ *Stop throwing those stones!* ❑ *Does either of the parties want to stop the fighting?* ❑ *She stopped in mid-sentence.* **2** V-T If you **stop** something from happening, or you **stop** something happening, you prevent it from happening or prevent it from continuing. ❑ *He proposed a new diplomatic initiative to try to stop the war.* ❑ *He would do what he must to stop her from destroying him.* **3** V-I If an activity or process **stops**, it is no longer happening. ❑ *The rain had stopped and a star or two was visible over the mountains.* ❑ *The system overheated and filming had to stop.* **4** V-T/V-I If something such as machine **stops** or **is stopped**, it is no longer moving or working. ❑ *The clock stopped at 11:59 Saturday night.* ❑ *Arnold stopped the engine and got out of the car.* **5** V-T/V-I When a moving person or vehicle **stops** or **is stopped**, they no longer move and they remain in the same place. ❑ *The car failed to stop at an army checkpoint.* ❑ *He stopped and let her catch up with him.* **6** N-SING If something that is moving comes **to a stop** or is brought **to a stop**, it slows down and no longer moves. ❑ *People often wrongly open doors before the train has come to a stop.* **7** V-I If someone does not **stop to** think or **to** explain, they continue with what they

---

❶ 타동사 불을 때다 ❑ 그녀는 단풍나무 가지로 난로에 불을 때고 있었다. ● 구동사 불을 때다 ❑ 그는 화로에 불을 땠다. ❷ 타동사 (감정을) 더 돋우다, 강화하다 ❑ 이러한 요구들이 내전의 공포를 강화시키고 있다. ● 구동사 (감정을) 더 돋우다, 강화하다 ❑ 그는 그 아이디어에 대해 흥미를 돋울 수 있으리라는 희망으로 제안서를 보냈다.

steal의 과거

steal의 과거 분사

❶ 가산명사 위, 배 ❑ 그는 배탈이 나 있었다. ❷ 가산명사 복부, 배 ❑ 아이들은 배를 깔고 엎드려 있었다. ❸ 가산명사 비위 ❑ 외과 수술을 하려면 대개 실질적인 근력이 필요하고 또한 비위도 강해야 한다. ❺ 타동사 견디다 ❑ 동물을 잔인하게 하는 것과 관련된 잔혹함을 나는 항상 견디지 못했다. ❻ 구 빈속에 ❑ 빈속에 음주하지 마세요.

자동사 (화가 나서) 쿵쿵거리며 걷다 ❑ 그는 그들에게 등을 돌리고 화난 걸음으로 언덕 위로 올라갔다.

❾ 의미의 복수는 stone이다.

❶ 물질명사 돌 ❑ 그는 바닥이 나무인지 돌인지 분간할 수가 없었다. ❑ 사람들은 흔히 대리석이 자연석이라는 것을 제대로 이해하지 못한다. ❷ 가산명사 돌멩이 ❑ 그는 신발에서 돌멩이 하나를 꺼냈다. ❸ 가산명사 기념석 ❑ 그 기념물은 원형으로 배치된 거대한 기념석들로 이루어져 있다. ❹ 불가산명사 (변치 않는 것의 상징으로) 돌 ❑ 그는 단지 논의를 위해 그 제안을 내놓는 것이지 그것이 고정불변의 것은 아니다. ❺ 가산명사 보석 ❑ 다이아몬드 세 개가 박힌 반지 ❻ 가산명사 결석 ❑ 그는 신장 결석이 있었다. ❼ 가산명사 (자두 등의) 씨 [주로 영국영어]; 미국영어 대개 pit] ❑ 복숭아를 반으로 가른 다음 씨를 제거하세요. ❽ 타동사 돌을 던지다 ❑ 청년들이 차에 불을 지르고 경찰에게 돌을 던졌다. ❾ 가산명사 스톤 (약 6.35킬로그램의 무게) [영국영어] ❑ 나는 무게가 약100킬로그램이었다.

형용사 마약에 취한 [비격식체] ❑ 그들 절반은 너무도 마약에 취해서 제대로 보지도 못했다.

❶ 형용사 돌이 많은 ❑ 가파르고 돌이 많은 터는 물이 잘 빠진다. ❷ 형용사 무정한 ❑ 그녀는 내가 본 것 중 최고로 무정한 표정을 내게 지었다.

stand의 과거, 과거 분사

가산명사 (등받이 없는) 의자 ❑ 오브라이언은 바 의자에 앉아 팔꿈치를 카운터에 기댔다.

❶ 자동사 구부정하다 ❑ 그녀는 그보다 키가 컸으며 등이 약간 구부정했다. ● 단수명사 구부정함 ❑ 그는 약간 구부정하고 키가 크며 살이 마른 친구였다. ❷ 자동사 몸을 구부리다 ❑ 그는 식료품이 담긴 봉지를 들기 위해 몸을 구부렸다. ❑ 와이셔츠 차림의 두 남자가 자동차 위로 몸을 구부렸다. ❸ 자동사 비굴한 짓을 하다 [탐탁찮음] ❑ 그는 최근까지는 인신공격 같은 비굴한 짓을 한 적이 없었다.

❶ 타동사/자동사 그만두다, 중단하다 ❑ 그 돌 그만 던져! ❑ 양측 중 어느 쪽이라도 싸움을 그만두고 싶어 하는가? ❑ 그녀는 말을 하다가 중간에 멈췄다. ❷ 타동사 막다 ❑ 그는 전쟁을 막기 위해 새로운 외교적 방안을 제시했다. ❑ 그는 그녀가 그를 파멸시키는 것을 막기 위해서 해야 할 일은 뭐든 다 할 것이다. ❸ 자동사 그치다 ❑ 비가 그치고 산 위로 별 한두 개가 보였다. ❑ 시스템이 과열되어서 촬영을 멈춰야 했다. ❹ 타동사/자동사 멈다; 멈게 하다 ❑ 시계가 토요일 밤 11시 59분에 멈췄다. ❑ 아놀드는 엔진을 끄고 차에서 내렸다. ❺ 타동사/자동사 멈추다, 서다; 멈추게 하다, 세우다 ❑ 그 자동차는 군대 검문소에서 서지 않았다. ❑ 그는 멈춰 서서 그녀가 따라 올 때까지 기다렸다. ❻ 단수명사 멈춤, 정지 ❑ 기차가 완전히 정지하기 전에 사람들이 흔히 가끔 문을 여는데 이는 잘못이다. ❼ 자동사 멈추다 ❑ 그녀는 생각도 안 하고 말한다. ❑ 잠깐

are doing without taking any time to think about or explain it. ❑ *She doesn't stop to think about what she's saying.* ❑ *There is something rather strange about all this if one stops to consider it.*

❽ V-I If you say that a quality or state **stops** somewhere, you mean that it exists or is true up to that point, but no further. ❑ *The cafe owner has put up the required "no smoking" signs, but thinks his responsibility stops there.* ❾ N-COUNT A **stop** is a place where buses or trains regularly stop so that people can get on and off. ❑ *There was an Underground map above one of the windows and I counted the stops to West Hampstead.* ❿ V-I If you **stop** somewhere on a journey, you stay there for a short while. ❑ *He insisted we stop at a small restaurant just outside of Atlanta.* ⓫ N-COUNT A **stop** is a time or place at which you stop during a journey. ❑ *The last stop in Mr. Cook's lengthy tour was Paris.* ⓬ PHRASE If you say that someone will **stop at nothing** to get something, you are emphasizing that they are willing to do things that are extreme, wrong, or dangerous in order to get it. [EMPHASIS] ❑ *Their motive is money, and they will stop at nothing to get it.* ⓭ PHRASE If you **put a stop to** something that you do not like or approve of, you prevent it from happening or continuing. ❑ *His daughter should have stood up and put a stop to all these rumors.* ⓮ PHRASE If you say that someone does not **know when to stop**, you mean that they do not control their own behavior very well and so they often annoy or upset other people. ❑ *Like many politicians before him, Mr. Bentley did not know when to stop.* ⓯ to **stop dead** →see **dead**. to **stop short of** →see **short**. to **stop** someone **in their tracks** →see **track**

> When an action comes to an end or **stops**, you can say that someone **stops doing** it. ❑ *She stopped reading and closed the book.* However, if you say that someone **stops to do** something, you mean that they interrupt their movement or another activity in order to do that thing. The "to" infinitive indicates purpose. ❑ *I stopped to read the notices on the bulletin board.*

▶**stop by** PHRASAL VERB If you **stop by** somewhere, you make a short visit to a person or place. [INFORMAL] ❑ *Perhaps I'll stop by the hospital.*

▶**stop off** PHRASAL VERB If you **stop off** somewhere, you stop for a short time in the middle of a journey. ❑ *The president stopped off in Poland on his way to Munich for the economic summit.*

stop|light /stɒplaɪt/ (**stoplights**) also **stop light** N-COUNT A **stoplight** is a set of colored lights which controls the flow of traffic on a road. [AM; BRIT **traffic light**] ❑ *Holly waited at a stoplight, impatient for the signal to change.*

stop|over /stɒpoʊvər/ (**stopovers**) N-COUNT A **stopover** is a short stay in a place in between parts of a journey. ❑ *The Sunday flights will make a stopover in Paris.*

stop|page /stɒpɪdʒ/ (**stoppages**) ❶ N-COUNT When there is a **stoppage**, people stop working because of a disagreement with their employers. [BUSINESS] ❑ *Mineworkers in the Ukraine have voted for a one-day stoppage next month.* ❷ N-COUNT In soccer and some other sports, when there is a **stoppage**, the game stops for a short time, for example because a player is injured. The referee may add some extra time at the end of the game because of this. [BRIT; AM **time out**] ❑ *Poyet could even have equalized in time added on for stoppages.*

stop|watch /stɒpwɒtʃ/ (**stopwatches**) also **stop-watch** N-COUNT A **stopwatch** is a watch with buttons which you press at the beginning and end of an event, so that you can measure exactly how long it takes.

stor|age /stɔːrɪdʒ/ N-UNCOUNT If you refer to the **storage** of something, you mean that it is kept in a special place until it is needed. ❑ *...the storage of toxic waste.* ❑ *Some of the space will at first be used for storage.*

store ♦♦♢ /stɔːr/ (**stores, storing, stored**) ❶ N-COUNT A **store** is a building or part of a building where things are sold. In American English, a **store** can be any size, but in British English, it is usually a large building selling a variety of goods. ❑ *Bombs were planted in stores in Manchester and Blackpool.* ❑ *...grocery stores.* ❷ V-T When you **store** things, you put them in a container or other place and leave them there until they are needed. ❑ *Store the cookies in an airtight tin.* ● PHRASAL VERB **Store away** means the same as **store**. ❑ *He simply stored the tapes away.* ❸ V-T When you **store** information, you keep it in your memory, in a file, or in a computer. ❑ *Where in the brain do we store information about colors?* ❹ N-COUNT A **store of** things is a supply of them that you keep somewhere until you need them. ❑ *I handed over my secret store of chocolate biscuits.* ❺ N-COUNT A **store** is a place where things are kept while they are not being used. ❑ *...a store for spent fuel from submarines.* ❻ →see also **department store** ❼ PHRASE If something is **in store for** you, it is going to happen at some time in the future. ❑ *Surprises were also in store for me.* →see **city**

Thesaurus	*store*의 참조어
N.	business, market, shop ❶
	collection, reserve, stock ❹
V.	accumulate, keep, save ❷ ❸

▶**store away** →see **store 2**

▶**store up** PHRASAL VERB If you **store** something **up**, you keep it until you think that the time is right to use it. ❑ *Investors were storing up a lot of cash in anticipation of disaster.*

store|card /stɔːrkɑːrd/ (**storecards**) also **store card** N-COUNT A **storecard** is a plastic card that you use to buy goods on credit from a particular store or group of stores. [mainly BRIT; AM usually **charge card**]

store|keeper /stɔːrkiːpər/ (**storekeepers**) N-COUNT A **storekeeper** is a shopkeeper. [mainly AM]

멈추고 생각해 본다면 이 모든 것이 약간 수상하기는 하다.

❽ 자동사 끝나다 ❑ 카페 주인은 규정대로 "금연" 표지판을 붙이긴 했으나 자신의 책임이 거기서 끝난다고 생각한다. ❾ 가산명사 정류장, 정거장 ❑ 창문 위에 지하철 지도가 있어서 나는 웨스트 햄스테드까지 몇 정거장이 남았는지 세어 보았다. ❿ 자동사 (여행 도중) 잠시 머무르다, 들르다 ❑ 그는 애틀랜타 바로 외곽에 있는 작은 식당에 잠깐 들렀다 가자고 주장했다. ⓫ 가산명사 잠시 머묾, 들름 ❑ 쿡 씨가 긴 장정에서 마지막으로 들른 곳은 파리였다. ⓬ 구 어떤 일도 서슴지 않다 [강조] ❑ 그들의 동기는 돈이며 그것을 구하기 위해선 어떤 일도 서슴지 않을 것이다. ⓭ 구 저지하다, 중지시키다 ❑ 그의 딸이 나서서 이 모든 소문을 중지시켰어야 했다. ⓮ 구 적당한 선에서 그만두다 ❑ 이전의 많은 정치인들처럼 벤틀리 씨도 적당한 선에서 그만둘 줄을 몰랐다.

> 어떤 행위가 끝나거나 멈추었다(stop)고 하면, 'someone stops doing it'이라고 말할 수 있다. ❑ 그녀가 책 읽기를 그치고 덮었다. 그러나, 'someone stops to do something'이라고 말하면, 그 사람이 그것을 하기 위해 자신의 움직임이나 다른 활동을 중지함을 의미한다. 'to' 부정사는 목적을 나타낸다. ❑ 나는 게시판의 공고를 읽기 위해 멈추어 섰다.

구동사 들르다, 잠시 머물다 [비격식체] ❑ 병원에 들를지도 모르겠다.

구동사 들르다 ❑ 대통령은 경제 정상 회담 때문에 뮌헨으로 가는 길에 폴란드에 들렀다.

가산명사 신호등 [미국영어; 영국영어 traffic light] ❑ 할리는 신호가 바뀌기를 겨우 참으며 신호등에서 기다렸다.

가산명사 잠깐 들름, 단기 체류 ❑ 일요일발 비행기는 파리에 들렀다 간다.

❶ 가산명사 휴업 [경제] ❑ 우크라이나 광부들은 다음 달에 하루 휴업하기로 투표했다. ❷ 가산명사 경기 중단 [영국영어; 미국영어 time out] ❑ 심지어는 뽀옛이 경기 중단 때문에 생긴 연장 시간에 동점골을 넣을 수도 있었다.

가산명사 스톱워치, 초시계

불가산명사 저장, 보관 ❑ 유독성 폐기물의 저장 ❑ 일부 공간은 처음에는 저장용으로 활용될 것이다.

❶ 가산명사 가게, 상점 ❑ 맨체스터와 블랙풀의 상점들에 폭탄이 몰래 설치되어 있었다. ❑ 식료품점 ❷ 타동사 보관하다, 저장하다 ❑ 쿠키를 공기 밀폐 주석 통에 보관하세요. ● 구동사 보관하다, 저장하다 ❑ 그는 테이프를 단지 보관할 뿐이었다. ❸ 타동사 (정보를) 저장하다 ❑ 색깔에 대한 정보는 우리 뇌 어디에 저장하는가? ❹ 가산명사 비축된 것 ❑ 나는 몰래 감춰 뒀던 초콜릿 비스킷을 건네주었다. ❺ 가산명사 창고, 저장소 ❑ 잠수에서 사용할 연료를 두는 창고 ❼ 구 예비 된, 앞으로 겪게 될 ❑ 내가 놀랄 일들이 아직도 더 있었다.

구동사 비축하다 ❑ 투자자들이 재난을 예상하며 많은 현금을 비축하고 있었다.

가산명사 백화점 신용 카드 [주로 영국영어; 미국영어 대개 charge card]

가산명사 가게 운영자 [주로 미국영어]

sto|rey /stɔ́ri/ (storeys) →see story 6

storm ♦♢♢ /stɔ́rm/ (storms, storming, stormed) **1** N-COUNT A **storm** is very bad weather, with heavy rain, strong winds, and often thunder and lightning. ❑ *...the violent storms which whipped America's East Coast.* **2** N-COUNT If something causes a **storm**, it causes an angry or excited reaction from a large number of people. ❑ *The photos caused a storm when they were first published.* **3** N-COUNT A **storm of** applause or other noise is a sudden loud amount of it made by an audience or other group of people in reaction to something. ❑ *His speech was greeted with a storm of applause.* **4** V-I If you **storm into** or **out of** a place, you enter or leave it quickly and noisily, because you are angry. ❑ *After a bit of an argument, he stormed out.* **5** V-T If a place that is being defended **is stormed**, a group of people attack it, usually in order to get inside it. ❑ *Government buildings have been stormed and looted.* ● **storm|ing** N-UNCOUNT ❑ *...the storming of the Bastille.* **6** PHRASE If someone or something **takes** a place **by storm**, they are extremely successful. ❑ *Kenya's long distance runners have taken the athletics world by storm.* →see **disaster, forecast, weather, hurricane**

1 가산명사 폭풍, 폭풍우 ❑ 미국의 동해안을 강타한 거센 폭풍 **2** 가산명사 (비유적) 폭풍, 평지풍파 ❑ 처음 출판되었을 때 그 사진들은 평지풍파를 일으켰다. **3** 가산명사 우레 (같은 박동) ❑ 그의 연설에 우레와 같은 박수가 터졌다. **4** 자동사 뛰어 들어오다; 뛰쳐나가다 ❑ 약간의 말다툼 뒤에 그는 뛰쳐나갔다. **5** 타동사 급습당하다, 난입당하다 ❑ 정부 건물은 사람들이 난입해 약탈을 자행했다. ● 급습, 난입 불가산명사 ❑ 바스티유 감옥 급습 **6** 구 휩쓸다 ❑ 케냐의 장거리 달리기 선수들이 육상계를 휩쓸어 왔다.

Word Partnership   storm의 연어

ADJ.	**heavy** storm, **severe** storm, **tropical** storm **1**
V.	**hit by a** storm, **weather the** storm **1**
	cause a storm **2**
N.	**center of a** storm, storm **clouds**, storm **damage**, **eye of a** storm, **ice/rain/snow** storm, storm **warning**, storm **winds** **1**
	storm **a building** **5**

stormy /stɔ́rmi/ (stormier, stormiest) **1** ADJ If there is **stormy** weather, there are strong winds and heavy rain. ❑ *It had been a night of stormy weather, with torrential rain and high winds.* **2** ADJ **Stormy** seas have very large strong waves because there are strong winds. ❑ *They make the treacherous journey across stormy seas.* **3** ADJ If you describe a situation as **stormy**, you mean it involves a lot of angry argument or criticism. ❑ *The letter was read at a stormy meeting.*

1 형용사 폭풍우가 몰아치는, (날씨가) 험악한 ❑ 호우와 강풍이 몰아치는 날씨가 험악한 밤이었다. **2** 형용사 풍랑이 거센, 거친 ❑ 그들은 거친 바다를 헤치며 위험천만한 여행을 한다. **3** 형용사 고성이 오가는, 소란스러운 ❑ 그 편지는 고성이 오가는 회의에서 낭독되었다.

story ♦♦♦ /stɔ́ri/ (stories) **1** N-COUNT A **story** is a description of imaginary people and events, which is written or told in order to entertain. ❑ *The second story in the book is titled "The Scholar."* ❑ *I shall tell you a story about four little rabbits.* **2** N-COUNT A **story** is a description of an event or something that happened to someone, especially a spoken description of it. ❑ *The parents all shared interesting stories about their children.* **3** N-COUNT The **story of** something is a description of all the important things that have happened to it since it began. ❑ *...the story of the women's movement in Ireland.* **4** N-COUNT If someone invents a **story**, they give a false explanation or account of something. ❑ *He invented some story about a cousin.* **5** N-COUNT A news **story** is a piece of news in a newspaper or in a news broadcast. ❑ *Those are some of the top stories in the news.* ❑ *They'll do anything for a story.* **6** N-COUNT A **story** of a building is one of its different levels, which is situated above or below other levels. [BRIT **storey**] ❑ *...long brick buildings, two stories high.* **7** PHRASE You use a **different story** to refer to a situation, usually a bad one, which exists in one set of circumstances when you have mentioned that it does not exist in another set of circumstances. ❑ *Where Marcella lives, the rents are fairly cheap, but a little further north it's a different story.* **8** PHRASE If you say **it's the same old story** or **it's the old story**, you mean that something unpleasant or undesirable seems to happen again and again. ❑ *It's the same old story. They want one person to do three people's jobs.* **9** PHRASE If you say that something is **only part of the story** or is **not the whole story**, you mean that the explanation or information given is not enough for a situation to be fully understood. ❑ *This may be true but it is only part of the story.* **10** PHRASE If someone tells you their **side of the story**, they tell you why they behaved in a particular way and why they think they were right, when other people think that person behaved wrongly. ❑ *He had already made up his mind before even hearing her side of the story.* →see **myth**

1 가산명사 (허구적인) 이야기 ❑ 그 책 속 두 번째 이야기의 제목은 '학자'이다. ❑ 네 마리 작은 토끼에 대한 이야기를 해 드릴게요. **2** 가산명사 (실제 일에 대한) 이야기 ❑ 부모들은 모두 자녀들에 대해 재미있는 이야기를 나누었다. **3** 가산명사 역사, 기술 ❑ 아일랜드 여성 운동의 역사 **4** 가산명사 거짓말 ❑ 그는 사촌에 대한 무슨 거짓말을 지어냈다. **5** 가산명사 기사 ❑ 오늘의 뉴스 톱기사들이었습니다. ❑ 그들은 기사를 위해서라면 무슨 짓이든 한다. **6** 가산명사 층 [영국영어 storey] ❑ 2층 높이의 긴 벽돌 건물 **7** 구 다른 내막, 다른 사정 ❑ 마르셀라가 사는 곳은 임대료가 꽤 싸지만 조금만 북쪽으로 가면 사정은 다르다. **8** 구 뻔한 이야기이다 ❑ 뻔한 이야기야. 그들은 한 사람이 세 사람 일을 하기를 원해. **9** 구 전체 내용의 일부분에 불과한 ❑ 이것이 사실일지도 모르지만 전체 내용의 일부분에 불과하다. **10** 구 자신의 입장에서 하는 이야기, -의 말 ❑ 그는 그녀의 말을 들어보기도 전에 이미 결정을 내린 상태였다.

Thesaurus   story의 참조어

N.	epic, fable, fairy tale, romance, saga, tale **1**
	account, description, report **2**
	lie **4**
	article, feature **5**

Word Partnership   story의 연어

N.	**character in a** story, **horror** story, story **hour**, story **line**, **title of a** story, story **writer** **1**
	beginning of a story, **end of a** story, **version of a** story **1**-**5**
	life story **2**
	front-page story, **news** story **5**
ADJ.	**classic** story, **compelling** story, **funny** story, **good** story, **interesting** story **1**-**5**
	familiar story **2**-**5**
	the full story, **untold** story **2** **3** **5**
	the whole story **2** **3** **5** **9**
	big story, **related** story, **top** story **5**
V.	**publish a** story, **read a** story, **write a** story **1** **5**
	hear a story, **tell a** story **1**-**4**

stout /staʊt/ (**stouter, stoutest**) **1** ADJ A **stout** person is rather fat. ❑ *He was a tall, stout man with gray hair.* **2** ADJ **Stout** shoes, branches, or other objects are thick and strong. ❑ *I hope you've both got stout shoes.*

stove /stoʊv/ (**stoves**) N-COUNT A **stove** is a piece of equipment which provides heat, either for cooking or for heating a room. ❑ *She put the kettle on the gas stove.*

stow /stoʊ/ (**stows, stowing, stowed**) V-T If you **stow** something somewhere, you carefully put it there until it is needed. ❑ *Luke stowed his camera bags into the trunk.*

stow|away /stoʊəweɪ/ (**stowaways**) N-COUNT A **stowaway** is a person who hides in a ship, airplane, or other vehicle in order to make a journey secretly or without paying. ❑ *The crew discovered the stowaway about two days into their voyage.*

strad|dle /stræd³l/ (**straddles, straddling, straddled**) **1** V-T If you **straddle** something, you put or have one leg on either side of it. ❑ *He looked at her with a grin and sat down, straddling the chair.* **2** V-T If something **straddles** a river, road, border, or other place, it stretches across it or exists on both sides of it. ❑ *A small wooden bridge straddled the dike.* **3** V-T Someone or something that **straddles** different periods, groups, or fields of activity exists in, belongs to, or takes elements from them all. ❑ *He straddles two cultures, having been brought up in Britain and later converted to Islam.*

straight ♦♦◇ /streɪt/ (**straighter, straightest, straights**) **1** ADJ A **straight** line or edge continues in the same direction and does not bend or curve. ❑ *Keep the boat in a straight line.* ❑ *His teeth were perfectly straight.* ● ADV **Straight** is also an adverb. [ADV after v] ❑ *Stand straight and stretch the left hand to the right foot.* **2** ADJ **Straight** hair has no curls or waves in it. ❑ *Grace had long straight dark hair which she wore in a bun.* **3** ADV You use **straight** to indicate that the way from one place to another is very direct, with no changes of direction. [ADV prep/adv] ❑ *...squirting the medicine straight to the back of the child's throat.* ❑ *He finished his conversation and stood up, looking straight at me.* **4** ADV If you go **straight** to a place, you go there immediately. [ADV prep/adv] ❑ *As always, we went straight to the experts for advice.* **5** ADJ If you give someone a **straight** answer, you answer them clearly and honestly. [ADJ n] ❑ *What a shifty arguer he is, refusing ever to give a straight answer to a straight question.* ● ADV **Straight** is also an adverb. [ADV after v] ❑ *I lost my temper and told him straight that I hadn't been looking for any job.* **6** ADJ **Straight** means following one after the other, with no gaps or intervals. [ADJ n] ❑ *They'd won 12 straight games before they lost.* ● ADV **Straight** is also an adverb. [n ADV] ❑ *He called from Weddington, having been there for 31 hours straight.* **7** ADJ A **straight** choice or a **straight** fight involves only two people or things. [ADJ n] ❑ *It's a straight choice between low-paid jobs and no jobs.* **8** ADJ If you describe someone as **straight**, you mean that they are normal and conventional, for example in their opinions and in the way they live. ❑ *Dorothy was described as a very straight woman who was married to her job.* **9** ADJ If you describe someone as **straight**, you mean they are heterosexual rather than homosexual. [INFORMAL] ❑ *His sexual orientation was a lot more gay than straight.* ● N-COUNT **Straight** is also a noun. ❑ *...a standard of sexual conduct that applies equally to gays and straights.* **10** PHRASE If you **get** something **straight**, you make sure that you understand it properly or that someone else does. [SPOKEN] ❑ *You need to get your facts straight.* **11** **a straight face** →see **face**

<table>
<tr><td colspan="3">**Word Partnership**　　　*straight의 연어*</td></tr>
<tr><td>N.</td><td colspan="2">straight **line**, straight **nose** **1**
second/third straight **loss/victory/win**, second/third
straight **season/year** **6**</td></tr>
<tr><td>v.</td><td colspan="2">**drive** straight, **keep going** straight, **look** straight, **point** straight **3**</td></tr>
</table>

straight ar|row (**straight arrows**) N-COUNT A **straight arrow** is someone who is very traditional, honest, and moral. [mainly AM] [oft N n] ❑ *...a well-scrubbed, straight-arrow group of young people.*

straight away also **straightaway** ADV If you do something **straight away**, you do it immediately and without delay. [ADV with v] ❑ *I should go and see a doctor straight away.*

straight|en /streɪt³n/ (**straightens, straightening, straightened**) **1** V-T If you **straighten** something, you make it neat or put it in its proper position. ❑ *She sipped her coffee and straightened a picture on the wall.* ● PHRASAL VERB **Straighten up** means the same as **straighten**. ❑ *This is my job, to straighten up, to file things.* **2** V-I If you are standing in a relaxed or slightly bent position and then you **straighten**, you make your back or body straight and upright. ❑ *The three men straightened and stood waiting.* ● PHRASAL VERB **Straighten up** means the same as **straighten**. ❑ *He straightened up and slipped his hands in his pockets.* **3** V-T/V-I If you **straighten** something, or it **straightens**, it becomes straight. ❑ *Straighten both legs until they are fully extended.* ● PHRASAL VERB **Straighten out** means the same as **straighten**. ❑ *No one would dream of straightening out the knobbly spire at Empingham Church.*

▶**straighten out** **1** PHRASAL VERB If you **straighten out** a confused situation, you succeed in getting it organized and tidied up. ❑ *He would make an appointment with him to straighten out a couple of things.* **2** →see **straighten 1**

straight|for|ward /streɪtfɔrwərd/ **1** ADJ If you describe something as **straightforward**, you approve of it because it is easy to do or understand. [APPROVAL] ❑ *Disposable nappies are fairly straightforward to put on.* ❑ *The question seemed straightforward enough.* **2** ADJ If you describe a person or their behavior as **straightforward**, you approve of them because they are honest and direct, and do not try to hide their feelings. [APPROVAL] ❑ *She is very blunt, very straightforward, and very honest.*

1 형용사 뚱뚱한 ❑ 그는 머리가 허연 키가 크고 뚱뚱한 남자였다. **2** 형용사 튼튼한, 견실한 ❑ 둘 다 튼튼한 신발이 있는 것이 좋다.

가산명사 난로, 스토브 ❑ 그녀는 가스스토브 위에 주전자를 올려놓았다.

타동사 (조심스럽게) 집어넣다 ❑ 루크는 카메라 가방을 트렁크에 집어넣었다.

가산명사 밀항자, 밀입국자 ❑ 선원들은 출발한 지 약 이틀이 지난 다음에 그 밀항자를 발견했다.

1 타동사 - 위로 다리를 벌려 걸치다 ❑ 그는 그녀를 보고 씩 웃으며 의자 위로 다리를 벌리고 걸터앉았다. **2** 타동사 가로지르다, 양쪽에 걸치다 ❑ 작은 나무다리가 제방 위에 걸쳐져 있었다. **3** 타동사 아우르다 ❑ 그는 영국에서 자랐고 후에 이슬람교로 개종하여 두 가지의 문화를 아우른다.

1 형용사 곧은, 똑바른 ❑ 보트를 똑바로 몰아라. ❑ 그의 치아는 완벽하게 가지런했다. ● 부사 곧게, 똑바로 ❑ 똑바로 서서 왼손을 오른발 쪽으로 뻗으세요. **2** 형용사 (머리가) 직모의 ❑ 그레이스는 길고 검은 직모를 쪽을 찌고 있었다. **3** 부사 바로, 똑바로 ❑ 아이 목구멍의 바로 뒤쪽에 약을 뿜으며 ❑ 그는 대화를 마치고는 나를 똑바로 보며 일어났다. **4** 부사 바로 ❑ 여느 때처럼 우리는 조언을 들으러 바로 전문가들에게 갔다. **5** 형용사 솔직한, 직설적인 ❑ 꾸밈없는 질문에 솔직한 대답을 절대로 하지 않고, 그는 참 교활한 논쟁가이다. ● 부사 솔직하게 ❑ 나는 성질이 나서 그에게 직장을 알아보고 있는 것이 아니었다고 직설적으로 말했다. **6** 형용사 연속의 ❑ 그들은 지기 전까지 열두 경기를 연속으로 이겼었다. ● 부사 연속으로, 줄곧 ❑ 31시간 동안 줄곧 웨딩턴에 머물다가 그곳에서 전화를 했다. **7** 형용사 양자 간의, 양자 간의 ❑ 저임금 일자리와 무직 사이의 양자택일이다. **8** 형용사 올곧은 ❑ 도로시는 일과 결혼한 아주 올곧은 여성으로 묘사되었다. **9** 형용사 동성애자가 아닌, 이성애의 [비격식체] ❑ 그의 성적 취향은 이성애적이기보다는 동성애적인 데가 훨씬 더 많았다. ● 가산명사 이성애자 ❑ 동성애자 및 이성애자 모두에게 균등하게 적용되는 성행위 규범 **10** 구 제대로 알다; 제대로 알리다 [구어체] ❑ 사실을 제대로 알아야 한다.

가산명사 올곧은 사람 [주로 미국영어] ❑ 말쑥하고 올곧은 젊은이들의 집단

부사 곧바로, 곧장 ❑ 곧바로 의사에게 진찰을 받아야겠다.

1 타동사 똑바르게 하다, 정돈하다 ❑ 그녀는 커피를 홀짝이고서 벽에 있는 그림을 바로 세웠다. ● 구동사 똑바르게 하다, 정돈하다 ❑ 이것저것을 정돈하고 철하는 것, 이것이 내 일이다. **2** 자동사 허리를 펴다, 곧추세우다 ❑ 세 남자는 허리를 곧추세우고 기다리며 서 있었다. ● 구동사 허리를 곧추세우다 ❑ 그는 허리를 곧추세우고 두 손을 주머니에 찔러 넣었다. **3** 타동사/자동사 똑바르게 펴다; 똑바르게 펴지다 ❑ 두 다리를 최대한 똑바로 펴세요. ● 구동사 똑바르게 펴다; 똑바르게 펴지다 ❑ 엠핑엄 교회의 울퉁불퉁한 뾰족탑을 똑바르게 펴는다는 것은 감히 꿈도 못 꿀 일이다.

1 구동사 정리하다 ❑ 그는 그와 두어 가지 일을 정리하기 위해 약속을 할 것이다.

1 형용사 간단한 [마음에 듦] ❑ 일회용 기저귀는 입히기가 꽤 간단하다. ❑ 질문은 아주 간단해 보였다. **2** 형용사 솔직한 [마음에 듦] ❑ 그녀는 굉장히 무뚝뚝하고, 굉장히 솔직하며, 굉장히 정직하다.

strain ◆◇◇ /streɪn/ (strains, straining, strained) **1** N-VAR If **strain** is put **on** an organization or system, it has to do more than it is able to do. ❑ *The prison service is already under considerable strain.* **2** V-T To **strain** something means to make it do more than it is able to do. ❑ *The volume of scheduled flights is straining the air traffic control system.* **3** N-UNCOUNT **Strain** is a state of worry and tension caused by a difficult situation. [also N in pl] ❑ *She was tired and under great strain.* **4** N-SING If you say that a situation is a **strain**, you mean that it makes you worried and tense. ❑ *I sometimes find it a strain to be responsible for the mortgage.* **5** N-UNCOUNT **Strain** is a force that pushes, pulls, or stretches something in a way that may damage it. ❑ *Place your hands under your buttocks to take some of the strain off your back.* **6** N-VAR **Strain** is an injury to a muscle in your body, caused by using the muscle too much or twisting it. ❑ *Avoid muscle strain by warming up with slow jogging.* **7** V-T If you **strain** a muscle, you injure it by using it too much or twisting it. ❑ *He strained his back during a practice session.* **8** V-T If you **strain** to do something, you make a great effort to do it when it is difficult to do. ❑ *I had to strain to hear.* **9** V-T When you **strain** food, you separate the liquid part of it from the solid parts. ❑ *Strain the stock and put it back into the pan.* **10** N-COUNT A **strain of** a germ, plant, or other organism is a particular type of it. ❑ *Every year new strains of influenza develop.*

Word Partnership   strain의 연어

ADJ.	**great** strain **1 3 4**
	virulent strain **10**
N.	**stress and** strain **3**
	muscle strain, strain **a muscle 6 7**
	strain **of bacteria/virus 10**

---

strained /streɪnd/ **1** ADJ If someone's appearance, voice, or behavior is **strained**, they seem worried and nervous. ❑ *She looked a little pale and strained.* **2** ADJ If relations between people are **strained**, those people do not like or trust each other. ❑ *...a period of strained relations between the prime minister and his deputy.*

strait /streɪt/ (straits) **1** N-COUNT; N-IN-NAMES You can refer to a narrow strip of sea which joins two large areas of sea as a **strait** or **the straits**. ❑ *An estimated 1600 vessels pass through the strait annually.* **2** N-PLURAL If someone is **in** dire or desperate **straits**, they are in a very difficult situation, usually because they do not have much money. [adj N] ❑ *The company's closure has left many small businessmen in desperate financial straits.*

straitjacket /streɪtdʒækɪt/ (straitjackets) **1** N-COUNT A **straitjacket** is a special jacket used to tie the arms of a violent person tightly around their body. ❑ *Occasionally his behavior became so uncontrollable that he had to be placed in a straitjacket.* **2** N-COUNT If you describe an idea or a situation as a **straitjacket**, you mean that it is very limited and restricting. ❑ *The national curriculum must be a guide, not a straitjacket.*

strand /strænd/ (strands, stranding, stranded) **1** N-COUNT A **strand of** something such as hair, wire, or thread is a single thin piece of it. ❑ *She tried to blow a gray strand of hair from her eyes.* **2** V-T If you **are stranded**, you are prevented from leaving a place, for example because of bad weather. ❑ *The climbers had been stranded by a storm.* →see **rope**

strange ◆◇◇ /streɪndʒ/ (stranger, strangest) **1** ADJ Something that is **strange** is unusual or unexpected, and makes you feel slightly nervous or afraid. ❑ *Then a strange thing happened.* ❑ *There was something strange about the flickering blue light.* ● **strange|ly** ADV ❑ *She noticed he was acting strangely.* ● **strange|ness** N-UNCOUNT ❑ *...the breathy strangeness of the music.* **2** ADJ A **strange** place is one that you have never been to before. A **strange** person is someone that you have never met before. [ADJ n] ❑ *I ended up alone in a strange city.* **3** →see also **stranger**

Thesaurus   strange의 참조어

ADJ.	bizarre, different, eccentric, odd, peculiar, unusual, weird; (ant.) ordinary, usual **1**
	exotic, foreign, unfamiliar **2**

---

strange|ly /streɪndʒli/ ADV You use **strangely** to emphasize that what you are saying is surprising. [EMPHASIS] [ADV with cl] ❑ *Strangely, they hadn't invited her to join them.* →see also **strange**

stran|ger /streɪndʒər/ (strangers) **1** N-COUNT A **stranger** is someone you have never met before. ❑ *Telling a complete stranger about your life is difficult.* **2** N-PLURAL If two people are **strangers**, they do not know each other. ❑ *The women knew nothing of the dead girl. They were strangers.* **3** N-COUNT If you are a **stranger to** something, you have had no experience of it or do not understand it. ❑ *He is no stranger to controversy.* →see also **strange**

> You do not use **stranger** to talk about someone who comes from a country which is not your own. You can refer to him or her as a **foreigner**, but this word can sound rather rude. It is better to say specifically where someone comes from. ❑ *He's Egyptian... She's from Finland.*

stran|gle /stræŋgᵊl/ (strangles, strangling, strangled) **1** V-T To **strangle** someone means to kill them by squeezing their throat tightly so that they cannot breathe. ❑ *He tried to strangle a border policeman and steal his gun.* **2** V-T To **strangle** something means to prevent it from succeeding or developing. ❑ *The country's economic plight is strangling its scientific institutions.*

1 가산명사 또는 불가산명사 부담, 중압 ❑ 교도소들은 이미 상당한 중압감을 느끼고 있다. **2** 타동사 중압하다, 무리를 주다 ❑ 편성 항공편의 수가 항공관제 시스템에 무리를 주고 있다. **3** 불가산명사 긴장 ❑ 그녀는 피곤했고 엄청난 긴장에 시달리고 있었다. **4** 단수명사 부담 ❑ 융자에 대해 책임을 지는 것이 때로는 부담스럽다. **5** 불가산명사 압력 ❑ 손으로 엉덩이 밑을 받쳐서 등이 받는 압력을 조금 줄이세요. **6** 가산명사 또는 불가산명사 삠, 접질림 ❑ 느린 조깅으로 워밍업해서 근육 부상을 피하세요. **7** 타동사 삐다, 접질리다 ❑ 그는 연습 도중에 허리를 접질렸다. **8** 타동사 무진 애를 쓰다, 분투하다 ❑ 나는 듣기 위해 귀를 열심히 기울여야 했다. **9** 타동사 거르다 ❑ 육수를 거른 다음 냄비에 다시 담으세요. **10** 가산명사 유형, 종류 ❑ 매년 새로운 독감 종류가 생긴다.

1 형용사 긴장한 ❑ 그녀는 약간 창백하고 긴장한 듯 보였다. **2** 형용사 (관계가) 껄끄러운 ❑ 수상과 부수상 사이의 관계가 껄끄러웠던 시기

1 가산명사; 이름명사 해협 ❑ 매년 약 1600척의 배가 그 해협을 통과하는 것으로 추정된다. **2** 복수명사 궁핍, 곤경 ❑ 그 회사의 폐업으로 인하여 많은 소기업들이 엄청난 재정적 어려움을 겪고 있다.

1 가산명사 (죄수 등의) 구속복 ❑ 때로는 그의 행동이 통제가 불가능할 정도로 심해져서 구속복을 입혀야 했다. **2** 가산명사 심한 구속 ❑ 국가 교육 과정은 지침이어야지 구속이 되어서는 안 된다.

1 가산명사 가닥 ❑ 그녀는 눈 앞에 흘러내린 흰머리 한 가닥을 날려 버리려고 했다. **2** 타동사 오도 가도 못하게 되다, 발이 묶이다 ❑ 등반가들은 폭풍 때문에 발이 묶인 상태였다.

1 형용사 이상한 ❑ 그리고 이상한 일이 벌어졌다. ❑ 깜빡이는 푸른 불이 심상치 않았다. ● 이상하게 부사 ❑ 그가 행동이 이상하다는 걸 그녀가 알아챘다. ● 이상함 불가산명사 ❑ 사람의 숨소리 같은 그 음악의 기묘함 **2** 형용사 낯선 ❑ 나는 낯선 도시에 홀로 남겨지게 되었다.

부사 이상하게도 [강조] ❑ 이상하게도 그들이 그녀를 동참하자고 초대하지 않았다.

1 가산명사 낯선 사람 ❑ 전혀 낯선 사람에게 자신의 삶에 대해 이야기하는 것은 어렵다. **2** 복수명사 서로 모르는 사이 ❑ 그 여자들은 죽은 여자애에 대해 아는 것이 없었다. 그들은 서로 모르는 사이였다. **3** 가산명사 문외한, 무경험자 ❑ 그가 논쟁을 안 겪어본 것이 아니다.

> 자신과 다른 나라에서 온 사람을 얘기할 때 stranger를 쓰지 않는다. 그런 사람을 foreigner라고 지칭하지만, 이 말은 다소 무례하게 들릴 수 있다. 그 사람이 어느 나라 출신인지 구체적으로 말하는 것이 더 좋다. ❑ 그는 이집트인이다... 그녀는 핀란드 출신이다.

1 타동사 교살하다, 목 졸라 죽이다 ❑ 그는 국경 순찰 경찰을 교살하고 총을 훔치려고 시도했다. **2** 타동사 목을 조이다 ❑ 국가의 경제적 곤경이 과학 연구 기관들의 목을 죄고 있다.

stran|gle|hold /stræŋgᵊlhoʊld/ N-SING To have a **stranglehold on** something means to have control over it and prevent it from being free or from developing. ❑ *These companies are determined to keep a stranglehold on the banana industry.*

단수명사 목 조르기 ❑이 회사들이 작정하고 계속 바나나 산업의 목을 움켜쥐고 있다.

strap /stræp/ (**straps, strapping, strapped**) ◘ N-COUNT A **strap** is a narrow piece of leather, cloth, or other material. Straps are used to carry things, fasten things together, or to hold a piece of clothing in place. ❑ *Nancy gripped the strap of her beach bag.* ❑ *She pulled the strap of her nightgown onto her shoulder.* ◙ V-T If you **strap** something somewhere, you fasten it there with a strap. ❑ *Strapping the skis on the roof, we boarded the hovercraft in Dover.*

◘ 가산명사 띠, 끈 ❑낸시는 비치백의 끈을 잡았다. ❑그녀는 잠옷 끈을 어깨 위로 끌어 올렸다. ◙ 타동사 (끈으로) 매다, 묶다 ❑우리는 도버에서 차 지붕에 스키를 묶고 호버크라프트에 올라탔다.

stra|te|gic ♦◇◇ /strətiːdʒɪk/ ◘ ADJ **Strategic** means relating to the most important, general aspects of something such as a military operation or political policy, especially when these are decided in advance. ❑ *...the new strategic thinking which NATO leaders produced at the recent London summit.* ● **stra|te|gi|cal|ly** /strətiːdʒɪkli/ ADV ❑ *...strategically important roads, bridges and buildings.* ◙ ADJ **Strategic** weapons are very powerful missiles that can be fired only after a decision to use them has been made by a political leader. ❑ *...strategic nuclear weapons.* ◚ ADJ If you put something in a **strategic** position, you place it cleverly in a position where it will be most useful or have the most effect. ❑ *...the marble benches Eve had placed at strategic points throughout the gardens, where the views were spectacular.* ● **stra|te|gi|cal|ly** ADV ❑ *We had kept its presence hidden with a strategically placed chair.*

◘ 형용사 전략적인 ❑나토의 지도자들이 최근의 런던 정상 회담에서 내놓은 새로운 전략적 발상 ● 전략적으로 부사 ❑전략적으로 중요한 도로, 교각, 건물들 ◙ 형용사 전략적인 ❑전략적 핵무기 ◚ 형용사 전략적인 ❑이브가 정원 내에 경치가 환상적인 곳만을 골라 효과적으로 배치한 대리석 벤치들 ● 전략적으로, 효과가 극대화되도록 부사 ❑우리는 기막힌 위치에 놓은 의자 덕택에 그것의 존재를 계속 숨겼었다.

strat|e|gist /strætədʒɪst/ (**strategists**) N-COUNT A **strategist** is someone who is skilled in planning the best way to gain an advantage or to achieve success, especially in war. ❑ *Military strategists had devised a plan that guaranteed a series of stunning victories.*

가산명사 전략가 ❑군사 전략가들이 일련의 놀라운 승리를 보장하는 계획을 마련했었다.

strat|e|gy ♦♦◇ /strætədʒi/ (**strategies**) ◘ N-VAR A **strategy** is a general plan or set of plans intended to achieve something, especially over a long period. ❑ *The Energy Secretary will present the strategy tomorrow afternoon.* ◙ N-UNCOUNT **Strategy** is the art of planning the best way to gain an advantage or achieve success, especially in war. ❑ *I've just been explaining the basic principles of strategy to my generals.*

◘ 가산명사 또는 불가산명사 전략, 계획 ❑에너지 장관이 내일 오후에 전략을 발표할 것이다. ◙ 불가산명사 전략 ❑나는 전략의 기본 원칙들을 장군들에게 막 설명하고 있었다.

straw /strɔː/ (**straws**) ◘ N-UNCOUNT **Straw** consists of the dried, yellowish stalks from crops such as wheat or barley. ❑ *The barn was full of bales of straw.* ❑ *I stumbled through mud to a yard strewn with straw.* ◙ N-COUNT A **straw** is a thin tube of paper or plastic, which you use to suck a drink into your mouth. ❑ *...a bottle of lemonade with a straw in it.* ◚ PHRASE If you **are clutching at straws** or **grasping at straws**, you are trying unusual or extreme ideas or methods because other ideas or methods have failed. ❑ *...a badly thought-out scheme from a Government clutching at straws.* ◛ PHRASE If an event is **the last straw** or **the straw that broke the camel's back**, it is the latest in a series of unpleasant or undesirable events, and makes you feel that you cannot tolerate a situation any longer. ❑ *For him the Church's decision to allow the ordination of women had been the last straw.* ◜ PHRASE If you **draw the short straw**, you are chosen from a number of people to perform a job or duty that you will not enjoy. ❑ *...if a few of your guests have drawn the short straw and agreed to drive others home after your summer barbecue.* →see **rice**

◘ 불가산명사 짚 ❑헛간은 짚 뭉치로 가득 차 있었다. ❑나는 비틀거리다 진창을 지나 짚이 널린 마당으로 갔다. ◙ 가산명사 빨대 ❑빨대가 꽂힌 레모네이드 한 병 ◚ 구 지푸라기라도 잡으려 하다 ❑정부가 지푸라기라도 잡는 심정으로 내놓은 허점투성이의 계획 ◛ 구 최후의 결정타 ❑그에겐 여성에게 서품을 허용하는 교단의 결정이 최후의 결정타였다. ◜ 구 (제비 뽑기에 걸려) 싫은 일을 떠맡게 됨 ❑만약 여름 바비큐 파티가 끝난 다음에 당신 손님 중 몇 명이 다른 사람들을 집까지 태워다 주는 귀찮은 일을 맡게 되었다면

straw|ber|ry /strɔːbəri, BRIT strɔːbri/ (**strawberries**) N-COUNT A **strawberry** is a small red fruit which is soft and juicy and has tiny yellow seeds on its skin. ❑ *...strawberries and cream.*

가산명사 딸기 ❑크림을 끼얹은 딸기

stray /streɪ/ (**strays, straying, strayed**) ◘ V-I If someone **strays** somewhere, they wander away from where they are supposed to be. ❑ *Tourists often get lost and stray into dangerous areas.* ◙ ADJ A **stray** dog or cat has wandered away from its owner's home. [ADJ n] ❑ *A stray dog came up to him.* ● N-COUNT **Stray** is also a noun. ❑ *The dog was a stray which had been adopted.* ◚ V-I If your mind or your eyes **stray**, you do not concentrate on or look at one particular subject, but start thinking about or looking at other things. ❑ *Even with the simplest cases I find my mind straying.* ◛ ADJ You use **stray** to describe something that exists separated from other similar things. [ADJ n] ❑ *An 8-year-old boy was killed by a stray bullet.*

◘ 자동사 길을 벗어나다, 옆길로 새다 ❑관광객들이 종종 길을 잃고 위험한 지역으로 샌다. ◙ 형용사 (개 등이) 주인 없는 ❑주인 없는 개 한 마리가 그에게 다가왔다. ● 가산명사 주인 없는 짐승 ❑그 개는 예전에 주인이 없어 입양된 개였다. ◚ 자동사 다른 곳으로 새다 ❑가장 단순한 경우에도 나는 생각이 다른 곳으로 새게 된다. ◛ 형용사 한쪽으로 샌, 빗나간 ❑여덟 살 소년이 빗나간 총탄에 맞아 숨졌다.

streak /striːk/ (**streaks, streaking, streaked**) ◘ N-COUNT A **streak** is a long stripe or mark on a surface which contrasts with the surface because it is a

◘ 가산명사 (바탕과 대조되는) 줄, 줄무늬 ❑달의 표면에 이런 어두운 줄무늬들이 있다. ◙ 타동사 ~에

different color. ❑ *There are these dark streaks on the surface of the moon.* **2** V-T If something **streaks** a surface, it makes long stripes or marks on the surface. ❑ *Rain had begun to streak the windowpanes.* **3** N-COUNT If someone has a **streak** of a particular type of behavior, they sometimes behave in that way. [usu sing, with supp] ❑ *We're both alike – there is a streak of madness in us both.* **4** V-I If something or someone **streaks** somewhere, they move there very quickly. ❑ *A meteorite streaked across the sky.* **5** N-COUNT A winning **streak** or a lucky **streak** is a continuous series of successes, for example in gambling or sports. A losing **streak** or an unlucky **streak** is a series of failures or losses. ❑ *The casinos had better watch out since I'm obviously on a lucky streak!*

줄을 긋다, -에 줄무늬를 그리다 ❑ 비가 창문에 줄무늬를 그리기 시작한 참이었다. **3** 가산명사 (어떤 상황을 보여 주는) 요소 ❑ 우리 둘은 비슷하다. 즉 우린 둘 다 광기 같은 게 있다. **4** 자동사 쏜살같이 가다 ❑ 운석이 하늘을 쏜살같이 가로질렀다. **5** 가산명사 -의 연속 ❑ 내 운에 불이 붙은 것 같으니 카지노들이 조심하는 게 좋을 것 같은데!

stream ◆◇◇ /striːm/ (**streams**, **streaming**, **streamed**) **1** N-COUNT A **stream** is a small narrow river. ❑ *There was a small stream at the end of the garden.* **2** N-COUNT A **stream** of smoke, air, or liquid is a narrow moving mass of it. ❑ *He breathed out a stream of cigarette smoke.* **3** N-COUNT A **stream** of vehicles or people is a long moving line of them. ❑ *There was a stream of traffic behind him.* **4** N-COUNT A **stream of** things is a large number of them occurring one after another. ❑ *The discovery triggered a stream of readers' letters.* ❑ *...a never-ending stream of jokes.* **5** V-I If a liquid **streams** somewhere, it flows or comes out in large amounts. ❑ *Tears streamed down their faces.* **6** V-I If your eyes **are streaming**, liquid is coming from them, for example because you have a cold. You can also say that your nose **is streaming**. [usu cont] ❑ *Her eyes were streaming now from the wind.* **7** V-I If people or vehicles **stream** somewhere, they move there quickly and in large numbers. ❑ *Refugees have been streaming into Travnik for months.* **8** V-I When light **streams** into or out of a place, it shines strongly into or out of it. ❑ *Sunlight was streaming into the courtyard.* **9** PHRASE If something such as a new factory or a new system comes **on stream** or is brought **on stream**, it begins to operate or becomes available. ❑ *As new mines come on stream, Chile's share of world copper output will increase sharply.* →see **river**

1 가산명사 개울 ❑ 정원의 끝에 작은 개울이 있었다. **2** 가산명사 (연기 등의) 줄기 ❑ 그가 담배 연기를 줄기 내뿜었다. **3** 가산명사 (차량 등이) 줄 ❑ 그의 뒤에 많은 차들이 줄지어 늘어서 있었다. **4** 가산명사 연속 ❑ 그 발견이 독자 편지가 쇄도했다. **5** 끝없이 이어지는 농담 **5** 자동사 계속 흐르다, 줄줄 이어지다 ❑ 그들의 얼굴 위로 눈물이 줄줄 흘렀다. **6** 자동사 (액체가) 흘러나오다 ❑ 이제 바람 때문에 그녀의 눈에서 눈물이 줄줄 흘렀다. **7** 자동사 (물줄기처럼) 끊임없이 이어지다 ❑ 여러 달 동안 난민들이 트래브닉으로 끊임없이 밀려들고 있다. **8** 자동사 (빛줄기가) 쏟아지다 ❑ 햇빛이 뜰 안에 쏟아져 내리고 있었다. **9** 구 가동 중인, 시작된 ❑ 새로운 광산들이 가동되면서 세계 구리 생산에서 칠레가 차지하는 비중이 급격히 증가할 것이다.

stream|line /striːmlaɪn/ (**streamlines**, **streamlining**, **streamlined**) V-T To **streamline** an organization or process means to make it more efficient by removing unnecessary parts of it. ❑ *They're making efforts to streamline their normally cumbersome bureaucracy.* →see **mass production**

타동사 간소화하다, 능률화하다 ❑ 그들은 보통 때 거추장스러운 관료 제도를 간소화하기 위해 노력을 기울이고 있다.

stream|lined /striːmlaɪnd/ ADJ A **streamlined** vehicle, animal, or object has a shape that allows it to move quickly or efficiently through air or water. ❑ *...these beautifully streamlined and efficient cars.*

형용사 유선형의 ❑ 아름다운 유선형의 효율적인 이 차들

street ◆◆◆ /striːt/ (**streets**) **1** N-COUNT; N-IN-NAMES A **street** is a road in a city, town, or village, usually with houses along it. ❑ *He lived at 66 Bingfield Street.* **2** N-COUNT You can use **street** or **streets** when talking about activities that happen out of doors in a city or town rather than inside a building. ❑ *Changing money on the street is illegal – always use a bank.* ❑ *Their aim is to raise a million pounds to get the homeless off the streets.* **3** →see also **Downing Street, high street, Wall Street**

1 가산명사; 이름명사 거리, -가(街) ❑ 그는 빙필드가 66번지에 살았다. **2** 가산명사 길거리, 길 ❑ 길거리에서 환전을 하는 것은 불법입니다. 항상 은행을 이용하세요. ❑ 그들의 목표는 노숙자들이 길거리에서 벗어날 수 있게 하기 위해 백만 파운드를 모으는 것이다.

Thesaurus	street의 참조어
N.	avenue, drive, road **1**

street|car /striːtkɑr/ (**streetcars**) N-COUNT A **streetcar** is an electric vehicle for carrying people which travels on rails in the streets of a city or town. [AM; BRIT **tram**] →see **transportation**

가산명사 전차 [미국영어; 영국영어 tram]

strength ◆◆◇ /streŋkθ, streŋθ/ (**strengths**) **1** N-UNCOUNT Your **strength** is the physical energy that you have, which gives you the ability to perform various actions, such as lifting or moving things. ❑ *She has always been encouraged to swim to build up the strength of her muscles.* ❑ *He threw it forward with all his strength.* **2** N-UNCOUNT Someone's **strength** in a difficult situation is their confidence or courage. [also a N] ❑ *Something gave me the strength to overcome the difficulty.* ❑ *He copes incredibly well. His strength is an inspiration to me in my life.* **3** N-UNCOUNT The **strength** of an object or material is its ability to be treated roughly, or to carry heavy weights, without being damaged or destroyed. [also N in pl] ❑ *He checked the strength of the cables.* **4** N-UNCOUNT The **strength** of a person, organization, or country is the power or influence that they have. [also N in pl] ❑ *America values its economic leadership, and the political and military strength that goes with it.* ❑ *The Alliance in its first show of strength drew a hundred thousand-strong crowd to a rally.* **5** N-UNCOUNT If you refer to the **strength of** a feeling, opinion, or belief, you are talking about how deeply it is felt or believed by people, or how much they are influenced by it. ❑ *He was surprised at the strength of his own feeling.* **6** N-VAR Someone's **strengths** are the qualities and abilities that they have which are an advantage to them, or which make them successful. ❑ *Take into account your own strengths and weaknesses.* ❑ *Tact was never Mr. Moore's strength.* **7** N-UNCOUNT If you refer to the **strength** of a currency, economy, or industry, you mean that its value or success is steady or increasing. ❑ *...the long-term competitive strength of the American economy.* **8** N-UNCOUNT The **strength** of a group of people is the total number of people in it. [also N in pl] ❑ *...elite forces, comprising about one-tenth of the strength of the army.* **9** N-UNCOUNT The **strength** of a wind, current, or other force is its power or speed. [also N in pl] ❑ *Its oscillation depends on the strength of the gravitational field.* **10** N-UNCOUNT The **strength** of a drink, chemical, or drug is the amount of the particular substance in it that gives it its particular effect. [also N in pl] ❑ *It is very alcoholic, sometimes near the strength of port.* **11** PHRASE If a person or organization **goes from strength to strength**, they become more and more successful or confident. ❑ *A decade later, the company has gone from strength to strength.* **12** PHRASE If a team or army is at **full strength**, all the members that it needs or usually has are present. ❑ *He needed more time to bring U.S. forces there up to full strength.* **13** PHRASE If one thing is done **on the strength of** another, it is done because of the influence of that other thing. ❑ *He was elected to power on the strength of his charisma.* →see **muscle**

1 불가산명사 힘 ❑ 근력을 기르려면 수영을 하라고 그녀는 항상 권고를 받아 왔다. ❑ 그가 그것을 힘껏 앞으로 던졌다. **2** 불가산명사 힘, 정신력, 용기 ❑ 뭔가가 내게 어려움을 극복할 수 있는 힘을 주었다. ❑ 그는 정말 잘 버티고 있다. 그의 정신력이 내 인생의 영감이다. **3** 불가산명사 내구력 ❑ 그는 케이블의 내구력을 시험했다. **4** 불가산명사 힘, 영향력 ❑ 미국은 자국의 경제적 지도력과 그에 동반되는 정치적, 군사적 힘을 중요하게 생각한다. ❑ 그 연합체가 그것의 영향력을 처음으로 드러내며 집회에 10만 명의 군중을 끌어들였다. **5** 불가산명사 강도 ❑ 그는 자기 감정의 강도에 놀랐다. **6** 가산명사 또는 불가산명사 강점, 장점 ❑ 자신의 장점과 약점을 고려하세요. ❑ 무어 씨는 도대체 눈치가 없었다. **7** 불가산명사 힘, -력 ❑ 미국 경제의 장기적인 경쟁력 **8** 불가산명사 인원 ❑ 육군 전체 병력의 10분의 1 가량을 구성하는 정예군 **9** 불가산명사 힘 ❑ 진동은 중력장의 힘에 달려있다. **10** 불가산명사 농도, 도수 ❑ 그것은 알코올 도수가 굉장히 높으며 때로는 포트와인의 도수에 가깝다. **11** 구 점점 강해지다 ❑ 10년 뒤 회사는 점점 강해졌다. **12** 구 전원 집결 ❑ 그가 그곳에 미군을 전원 집결시키기 위해서는 시간이 더 필요했다. **13** 구 -에 힘입어 ❑ 그는 자신의 카리스마에 힘입어 권좌에 선출되었다.

strength|en ◆◇◇ /strɛŋθ°n/ (**strengthens, strengthening, strengthened**) **1** v-т
If something **strengthens** a person or group or if they **strengthen** their
position, they become more powerful and secure, or more likely to succeed.
❑ *Giving the president the authority to go to war would strengthen his hand for peace.*
2 v-т If something **strengthens** a case or argument, it supports it by
providing more reasons or evidence for it. ❑ *He does not seem to be familiar with
research which might have strengthened his own arguments.* **3** v-т/v-ı If a currency,
economy, or industry **strengthens**, or if something **strengthens** it, it increases
in value or becomes more successful. ❑ *The dollar strengthened against most other
currencies.* **4** v-т If something **strengthens** you or **strengthens** your resolve or
character, it makes you more confident and determined. ❑ *Any experience can
teach and strengthen you, but particularly the more difficult ones.* ❑ *This merely
strengthens our resolve to win the league.* **5** v-т/v-ı If something **strengthens** a
relationship or link, or if a relationship or link **strengthens**, it makes it closer
and more likely to last for a long time. ❑ *It will draw you closer together, and it will
strengthen the bond of your relationship.* **6** v-т/v-ı If something **strengthens** an
impression, feeling, or belief, or if it **strengthens**, it becomes greater or affects
more people. ❑ *His speech strengthens the impression he is the main power in the
organization.* ❑ *Every day of sunshine strengthens the feelings of optimism.* **7** v-т If
something **strengthens** your body or a part of your body, it makes it healthier,
often in such a way that you can move or carry heavier things. ❑ *Cycling is good
exercise. It strengthens all the muscles of the body.* **8** v-т If something **strengthens**
an object or structure, it makes it able to be treated roughly or able to support
heavy weights, without being damaged or destroyed. ❑ *The builders will have to
strengthen the existing joists with additional timber.*

strenu|ous /strɛnyuəs/ ADJ A **strenuous** activity or action involves a lot of
energy or effort. ❑ *Avoid strenuous exercise in the evening.* ❑ *Strenuous efforts had been
made to improve conditions in the jail.*

stress ◆◆◇ /strɛs/ (**stresses, stressing, stressed**) **1** v-т If you **stress** a point in a
discussion, you put extra emphasis on it because you think it is important.
❑ *The spokesman stressed that the measures did not amount to an overall ban.* ❑ *China's
leaders have stressed the need for increased co-operation between Third World countries.*
● N-VAR **Stress** is also a noun. ❑ *Japanese car makers are laying ever more stress on
European sales.* **2** N-VAR If you feel under **stress**, you feel worried and tense
because of difficulties in your life. ❑ *Katy could think clearly when not under stress.*
3 v-т If you **stress** a word or part of a word when you say it, you put emphasis
on it so that it sounds slightly louder. ❑ *She stresses the syllables as though teaching
a child.* ● N-VAR **Stress** is also a noun. ❑ *...the misplaced stress on the first syllable of
this last word.* →see **emotion**

Word Partnership	*stress*의 연어
N.	stress **the importance of** *something* **1**
	anxiety and stress, **effects of** stress, stress **management**, stress
	reduction, response to stress, **symptoms of** stress, stress **test** **2**
ADJ.	**emotional** stress, **excessive** stress, **high** stress, **physical** stress,
	stress **related, severe** stress **2**
V.	**cause** stress, **cope with** stress, **deal with** stress, **experience** stress,
	induce stress, **reduce** stress, **relieve** stress **2**

stressed /strɛst/ ADJ If you are **stressed**, you feel tense and anxious because of
difficulties in your life. ❑ *Work out what situations or people make you feel stressed
and avoid them.*

stressed out ADJ If someone is **stressed out**, they are very tense and anxious
because of difficulties in their lives. [INFORMAL] ❑ *I can't imagine sitting in traffic,
getting stressed out.*

stress|ful /strɛsfəl/ ADJ If a situation or experience is **stressful**, it causes the
person involved to feel stress. ❑ *I think I've got one of the most stressful jobs there is.*

stretch ◆◇◇ /strɛtʃ/ (**stretches, stretching, stretched**) **1** v-т/v-ı Something
that **stretches** over an area or distance covers or exists in the whole of that
area or distance. [no cont] ❑ *The procession stretched for several miles.* **2** N-COUNT A
stretch of road, water, or land is a length or area of it. ❑ *It's a very dangerous
stretch of road.* **3** v-т/v-ı When you **stretch**, you put your arms or legs out
straight and tighten your muscles. ❑ *He yawned and stretched.* ❑ *Try stretching
your legs and pulling your toes upwards.* ● N-COUNT **Stretch** is also a noun. ❑ *At the
end of a workout spend time cooling down with some slow stretches.* **4** N-COUNT A
stretch of time is a period of time. ❑ *...after an 18-month stretch in the army.* **5** v-ı If
something **stretches from** one time **to** another, it begins at the first time and
ends at the second, which is longer than expected. ❑ *...a working day that
stretches from seven in the morning to eight at night.* **6** v-ı If a group of things **stretch
from** one type of thing **to** another, the group includes a wide range of things.
❑ *...a trading empire, with interests that stretched from chemicals to sugar.* **7** v-т/v-ı
When something soft or elastic **stretches** or **is stretched**, it becomes longer as well as
bigger as well as thinner, usually because it is pulled. ❑ *The cables are designed
not to stretch.* **8** v-т If you **stretch** an amount of something or if it **stretches**,
you make it last longer than it usually would by being careful and not
wasting any of it. ❑ *They're used to stretching their budgets.* **9** v-т If something
stretches your money or resources, it uses them up so you have hardly
enough for your needs. ❑ *The drought there is stretching American resources.* **10** v-т If
you say that a job or task **stretches** you, you mean that you like it because it
makes you work hard and use all your energy and skills so that you do not
become bored or achieve less than you should. [APPROVAL] ❑ *I'm trying to move on
and stretch myself with something different.* **11** PHRASE If you say that something is
not true or possible **by any stretch of the imagination**, you are emphasizing

형용사 힘이 많이 드는, 격렬한 ❑ 저녁에는 격렬한
운동을 피하세요. ❑ 교도소의 환경을 개선하기 위해
많은 노력을 기울여 왔었다.

1 타동사 강조하다, 역설하다 ❑ 대변인은 그 조치가
전면적인 금지를 뜻하는 것은 아니라는 점을 강조했다.
❑ 중국의 지도자들은 제 3 세계 국가들 간에 공조
강화의 필요성을 역설해 왔다. ● 가산명사 또는
불가산명사 강조, 중점 ❑ 일본의 자동차 제조 회사들은
유럽 시장 판매에 그 어느 때보다 더 많은 중점을 두고
있다. **2** 가산명사 또는 불가산명사 스트레스
❑ 케이티가 스트레스를 받지 않으면 생각을 똑바로 할
수 있을 것이다. **3** 타동사 강세를 두다 ❑ 그녀는 마치
아이를 가르치듯이 각 음절에 강세를 두었다.
● 가산명사 또는 불가산명사 강세 ❑ 이 마지막 단어의
첫 음절에 잘못 둔 강세

형용사 스트레스를 받은 ❑ 스트레스를 주는 상황과
사람이 누구인지 파악해서 그들을 피하세요.

형용사 스트레스로 지친 [비격식체] ❑ 스트레스를
잔뜩 받으며 교통 체증 속에 앉아 있는 것은 상상도
못하겠다.

형용사 스트레스를 주는 ❑ 내 생각엔 내 직업이 가장
스트레스가 많은 직업 중의 하나인 것 같다.

1 타동사/자동사 뻗어 있다, 이어지다 ❑ 행렬이 몇
마일에 걸쳐 뻗어 있었다. **2** 가산명사 뻗은 지역, 구간
❑ 그곳은 굉장히 위험한 도로 구간이다.
3 타동사/자동사 기지개를 켜다, (팔, 다리를) 뻗다
❑ 그가 하품을 하며 기지개를 켰다. ❑ 두 다리를
뻗으며 발가락을 위로 당기세요. ● 가산명사 팔다리
운동 ❑ 운동 후에는 천천히 팔다리 운동을 하면서 몸을
식히세요. **4** 가산명사 기간 ❑ 군대에서 18개월의
기간을 보낸 후 **5** 자동사 (시간이) 이어지다 ❑ 아침
7시에 시작해서 저녁 8시까지 이어지는 일과 **6** 자동사
포괄하다, 아우르다 ❑ 관심 품목이 화학 약품부터
설탕까지를 아우르는 무역 왕국 **7** 타동사/자동사
(길이가) 늘어나다; (길이를) 늘리다 ❑ 이 케이블들은
늘어나게 만들어졌다. **8** 타동사/자동사 오래 가게
하게 하다, 아껴 쓰다; 오래 가다 ❑ 그들은 예산을 오래
가게 아껴 쓰는 데 익숙하다. **9** 타동사 부담을 주다
❑ 가뭄 때문에 미국의 자원에 부담이 가고 있다.
10 타동사 능력을 최대한 발휘하게 하다 [마음에 듦]
❑ 나는 다른 곳으로 옮겨서 뭔가 다른 일을 하면서 내
능력을 최대한 발휘해 보려고 한다. **11** 구 아무리
생각해도 (-일 수 없는), 도저히 상상할 수 없는 [강조]
❑ 그녀는 남편이 여색에 빠져 있다는 것은 도저히
상상할 수 없었다.

1 타동사 강화하다 ❑ 전쟁을 개시할 권한을
대통령에게 주면 평화를 수립하려는 그의 계획에 힘을 실어
줄 것이다. **2** 타동사 뒷받침하다 ❑ 그는 자신의
주장을 뒷받침해줄 주었을지도 모르는 연구를 알고 있는
것 같지 않다. **3** 타동사/자동사 (가치가) 강화되다;
(가치를) 강화하다 ❑ 달러가 대부분의 다른 화폐에
대비해서 가치가 상승했다. **4** 타동사 강화하다,
굳건히 하다 ❑ 어떤 경험이든 교훈을 주고 사람을
강하게 만들지만 어려운 경험은 특히 그렇다. ❑ 이는
리그전에서 이기겠다는 우리의 결심을 더 굳게 만들
뿐이다. **5** 타동사/자동사 강화하다, 공고히 하다
❑ 이것은 서로를 더욱 가깝게 만들 것이며 관계의 끈을
더욱 공고히 해 줄 것이다. **6** 타동사/자동사
강화되다 ❑ 그의 연설을 들으니 그가 조직 내 권력의
핵심이라는 인상이 강해진다. **7** 화장한 나날은
낙관적인 기분을 강화해 준다. **7** 타동사 강화하다
❑ 자전거는 좋은 운동이다. 온 몸의 근육을 강화해
준다. **8** 타동사 보강하다 ❑ 건축업자들은 기존의
들보에 추가로 목재를 덧붙여 보강을 해야 할 것이다.

that it is completely untrue or absolutely impossible. [EMPHASIS] □ Her husband was not a womaniser by any stretch of the imagination.

Word Partnership	stretch의 연어
PREP.	stretch **across** 1
	during a stretch 3
N.	stretch **of** highway/road, stretch **of** a river, **along** a stretch **of** road, **down** the road a stretch 2

▶**stretch out** 1 PHRASAL VERB If you **stretch out** or **stretch yourself out**, you lie with your legs and body in a straight line. □ The jacuzzi was too small to stretch out in. 2 PHRASAL VERB If you **stretch out** a part of your body, you hold it out straight. □ He was about to stretch out his hand to grab me.

stretch|er /strɛtʃər/ (**stretchers, stretchered**) 1 N-COUNT A **stretcher** is a long piece of canvas with a pole along each side, which is used to carry an injured or sick person. □ The two ambulance attendants quickly put Plover on a stretcher and got him into the ambulance. 2 V-T PASSIVE If someone **is stretchered** somewhere, they are carried there on a stretcher. □ I was close by as Lester was stretchered into the ambulance.

strewn /struːn/ ADJ If a place is **strewn with** things, they are lying scattered there. [v-link ADJ with n] □ The front room was strewn with books and clothes. ● COMB in ADJ **Strewn** is also a combining form. □ ...a litter-strewn street.

strick|en /strɪkən/ 1 **Stricken** is the past participle of some meanings of **strike**. 2 ADJ If a person or place is **stricken by** something such as an unpleasant feeling, an illness, or a natural disaster, they are severely affected by it. □ ...a family stricken by genetically inherited cancer. ● COMB in ADJ **Stricken** is also a combining form. □ ...a leukaemia-stricken child. □ ...drought-stricken areas.

strict ♦◇◇ /strɪkt/ (**stricter, strictest**) 1 ADJ A **strict** rule or order is very clear and precise or severe and must always be obeyed completely. □ The officials had issued strict instructions that we were not to get out of the jeep. □ French privacy laws are very strict. ● **strict|ly** ADV [ADV with v] □ The acceptance of new members is strictly controlled. 2 ADJ If a parent or other person in authority is **strict**, they regard many actions as unacceptable and do not allow them. □ My parents were very strict. ● **strict|ly** ADV □ My own mother was brought up very strictly and correctly. 3 ADJ If you talk about the **strict** meaning of something, you mean the precise meaning of it. [ADJ n] □ It's not quite peace in the strictest sense of the word, rather the absence of war. ● **strict|ly** ADV [ADV adj] □ Actually, that is not strictly true. 4 ADJ You use **strict** to describe someone who never does things that are against their beliefs. [ADJ n] □ Four million Britons are now strict vegetarians.

strict|ly /strɪktli/ ADV You use **strictly** to emphasize that something is of one particular type, or intended for one particular thing or person, rather than any other. [EMPHASIS] [ADV group] □ He seemed fond of her in a strictly professional way.

stride /straɪd/ (**strides, striding, strode**) 1 V-I If you **stride** somewhere, you walk there with quick, long steps. □ They were joined by a newcomer who came striding across a field. 2 N-COUNT A **stride** is a long step which you take when you are walking or running. □ With every stride, runners hit the ground with up to five times their body-weight. 3 N-COUNT If you **make strides** in something that you are doing, you make rapid progress in it. □ The country has made enormous strides politically but not economically. 4 PHRASE If you **get into** your **stride** or **hit** your **stride**, you start to do something easily and confidently, after being slow and uncertain. □ The campaign is just getting into its stride. 5 PHRASE In American English, if you **take** a problem or difficulty **in stride**, you deal with it calmly and easily. The British expression is **take** something **in your stride**. □ He took the ridiculous accusation in stride.

Word Partnership	stride의 연어
V.	**break** *(your)* stride, **lengthen** *your* stride 2
ADJ.	**long** stride 2
	in stride 5

stri|dent /straɪdᵊnt/ ADJ If you use **strident** to describe someone or the way they express themselves, you mean that they make their feelings or opinions known in a very strong way that perhaps makes people uncomfortable. [DISAPPROVAL] □ She was increasingly seen as a strident feminist.

strife /straɪf/ N-UNCOUNT **Strife** is strong disagreement or fighting. [FORMAL] □ Money is a major cause of strife in many marriages.

strike ♦♦◇ /straɪk/ (**strikes, striking, struck, stricken**)

The form **struck** is the past tense and past participle. The form **stricken** can also be used as the past participle for meanings 6 and 17.

1 N-COUNT When there is a **strike**, workers stop doing their work for a period of time, usually in order to try to get better pay or conditions for themselves. [BUSINESS] [also on n] □ French air traffic controllers have begun a three-day strike in a dispute over pay. □ Staff at the hospital went on strike in protest at the incidents. 2 V-I When workers **strike**, they go on strike. [BUSINESS] □ ...their recognition of the workers' right to strike. □ They shouldn't be striking for more money. ● **strik|er** (**strikers**) N-COUNT □ The strikers want higher wages, which state governments say they can't afford. 3 V-T If you **strike** someone or something, you deliberately hit them. [FORMAL] □ She took two quick steps forward and struck him across the mouth. □ It is impossible to say who struck the fatal blow. 4 V-T If something that is falling or moving **strikes** something, it hits it. [FORMAL] □ His head struck the bottom when he dived into the 6ft end of the pool. □ One 16-inch shell struck the control tower.

1 구동사 몸을 쭉 빼다 □ 거품 욕조가 몸을 쭉 뻗기에는 너무 작았다. 2 구동사 내뻗다 □ 그는 나를 잡기 위해 손을 내뻗는 찰나였다.

1 가산명사 들것 □ 구급차 요원 두 명이 플로버를 재빨리 들것에 옮긴 다음 구급차에 태웠다. 2 수동 타동사 들것으로 옮겨지다 □ 레스터가 들것으로 구급차에 실리고 있을 때 내가 근처에 있었다.

형용사 -이 널브러진, -으로 어질러진 □ 거실에는 책과 옷이 마구 널브러져 있었다. ● 복합형-형용사 -이 널브러진 □ 쓰레기가 널브러진 거리

1 strike의 과거 분사 2 형용사 시달리는, 고통을 받는 □ 유전적으로 대물림되는 암으로 고통 받는 가족 ● 복합형-형용사 -에 시달리는, -으로 고통 받는 □ 백혈병을 앓고 있는 아이 □ 가뭄에 시달리는 지역

1 형용사 엄격한 □ 관리들은 우리가 지프에서 내리면 안 된다는 엄격한 지시를 내렸었다. □ 프랑스의 사생활 보호법은 매우 엄격하다. ● 엄격하게 부사 □ 새 회원 가입은 엄격히 통제된다. 2 형용사 엄한 □ 우리 부모님은 매우 엄하셨다. ● 엄하게 부사 □ 우리 어머니께서는 매우 엄하게 그리고 올바르게 교육을 받으셨다. 3 형용사 엄밀한 □ 엄밀히 말하자면 평화는 아니고 전쟁이 없는 상태라고 할 수 ● 엄밀히 부사 □ 사실 그것은 엄밀히 말하면 사실이 아니다. 4 형용사 엄격한 □ 지금 영국인 4백만 명이 엄격한 채식주의자이다.

부사 엄격히 [강조] □ 그는 엄격히 직업적인 측면에서 그녀를 좋아하는 것 같았다.

1 자동사 성큼성큼 걷다 □ 새로 한 사람이 들판을 가로질러 성큼성큼 걸어와 그들과 합류했다. 2 가산명사 큰 걸음 □ 달리기 선수들이 한 번 성큼 발을 내디딜 때마다 지면에 가해지는 힘이 체중의 최대 다섯 배까지 된다. 3 가산명사 발전 □ 그 나라는 정치적으로는 엄청난 발전을 이뤘으나 경제적으로는 그렇지 못했다. 4 구 본격적으로 진행하다 □ 선거 운동이 이제 막 본격적으로 진행되기 시작했다. 5 구 침착하게 대처하다, 수월하게 받아들이다 □ 그는 터무니없는 비난에 침착하게 대처했다.

형용사 귀에 거슬리는, 공격적인 [탐탁찮음] □ 그녀는 점점 더 공격적인 페미니스트로 인식되었다.

불가산명사 불화, 다툼 [격식체] □ 많은 결혼에서 돈이 불화의 주된 요인이 된다.

struck은 과거 및 과거 분사이다. stricken은 6과 17의 의미로 과거분사로 쓰일 수 있다.

1 가산명사 파업 [경제] □ 프랑스 항공 관제요원들이 임금 분쟁으로 사흘간의 파업을 시작했다. □ 병원 직원들이 그 사건들에 대한 항의 표시로 파업에 들어갔다. 2 자동사 파업하다 [경제] □ 노동자의 쟁의권에 대한 그들의 인정 □ 그들이 더 많은 돈을 위해서 파업해서는 안 된다. ● 파업 참가자 가산명사 □ 파업 참가자들은 임금 인상을 원하지만 주 정부들은 그럴 형편이 안 된다고 한다. 3 타동사 때리다, 치다 [격식체] □ 그녀는 재빨리 두 걸음 앞으로 가더니 그의 입 부분을 후려쳤다. □ 누가 치명타를 가했는지를 알기가 불가능하다. 4 타동사 부딪치다, 찧다 [격식체] □ 그가 깊이 6피트인 풀장 속으로 다이빙을 할 때

⑤ V-T/V-I If you **strike** one thing against another, or if one thing **strikes** against another, the first hits the second thing. [FORMAL] ❑ *Wilde fell and struck his head on the stone floor.* ⑥ V-I If something such as an illness or disaster **strikes**, it suddenly happens. ❑ *Bank of England officials continued to insist that the pound would soon return to stability but disaster struck.* ⑦ V-I To **strike** means to attack someone or something quickly and violently. ❑ *He was the only cabinet member out of the country when the terrorists struck.* ⑧ N-COUNT A military **strike** is a military attack, especially an air attack. ❑ *...a punitive air strike.* ⑨ V-T If an idea or thought **strikes** you, it suddenly comes into your mind. [no cont] ❑ *A thought struck her. Was she jealous of her mother, then?* ⑩ V-T If something **strikes** you **as** being a particular thing, it gives you the impression of being that thing. ❑ *He struck me as a very serious but friendly person.* ⑪ V-T If you **are struck** by something, you think it is very impressive, noticeable, or interesting. ❑ *She was struck by his simple, spellbinding eloquence.* ⑫ V-RECIP If you **strike** a deal or a bargain with someone, you come to an agreement with them. ❑ *They struck a deal with their paper supplier, getting two years of newsprint on credit.* ❑ *The two struck a deal in which Rendell took half of what a manager would.* ⑬ V-T If you **strike** a balance, you do something that is halfway between two extremes. ❑ *At times like that you have to strike a balance between sleep and homework.* ⑭ V-T If you **strike** a pose or attitude, you put yourself in a particular position, for example when someone is taking your photograph. ❑ *She struck a pose, one hand on her hip and the other waving an imaginary cigarette.* ⑮ V-T If something **strikes** fear **into** people, it makes them very frightened or anxious. [LITERARY] ❑ *If there is a single subject guaranteed to strike fear in the hearts of parents, it is drugs.* ⑯ V-T/V-I When a clock **strikes**, its bells make a sound to indicate what the time is. ❑ *The clock struck nine.* ⑰ V-T If you **strike** words **from** a document or an official record, you remove them. [FORMAL] ❑ *Strike that from the minutes.* ● PHRASAL VERB **Strike out** means the same as **strike**. ❑ *The censor struck out the next two lines.* ⑱ V-T When you **strike** a match, you make it produce a flame by moving it quickly against something rough. ❑ *Robina struck a match and held it to the crumpled newspaper in the grate.* ⑲ V-T If someone **strikes** oil or gold, they discover it in the ground as a result of mining or drilling. ❑ *Hamilton Oil announced that it had struck oil in the Liverpool Bay area of the Irish Sea.* ⑳ →see also **stricken, striking, hunger strike** ㉑ to **strike** a **chord** →see **chord.** to **strike home** →see **home**

▶**strike down** PHRASAL VERB If someone **is struck down**, especially by an illness, they are killed or severely harmed. [WRITTEN] ❑ *Frank had been struck down by a massive heart attack.*

▶**strike off** PHRASAL VERB If someone such as a doctor or lawyer **is struck off**, their name is removed from the official register and they are not allowed to do medical or legal work anymore. [BRIT] ❑ *...a company lawyer who had been struck off for dishonest practices.*

▶**strike out** ① PHRASAL VERB If you **strike out**, you begin to do something different, often because you want to become more independent. ❑ *She wanted me to strike out on my own, buy a business.* ② PHRASAL VERB If you **strike out at** someone, you hit, attack, or speak angrily to them. ❑ *He seemed always ready to strike out at anyone and for any cause.* ③ →see also **strike 17**

▶**strike up** PHRASAL VERB When you **strike up** a conversation or friendship with someone, you begin one. [WRITTEN] ❑ *I trailed her into Penney's and struck up a conversation.*

strik|er /straɪkər/ (**strikers**) ① N-COUNT In soccer and some other team sports, a **striker** is a player who mainly attacks and scores goals, rather than defends. ❑ *...and the England striker scored his sixth goal of the season.* ② →see also **strike**

strik|ing ◆◇◇ /straɪkɪŋ/ ① ADJ Something that is **striking** is very noticeable or unusual. ❑ *The most striking feature of those statistics is the high proportion of suicides.* ❑ *He bears a striking resemblance to Lenin.* ● **strik|ing|ly** ADV ❑ *In one respect, however, the men were strikingly similar.* ❑ *...a strikingly handsome man.* ② ADJ Someone who is **striking** is very attractive, in a noticeable way. ❑ *She was a striking woman with long blonde hair.* ③ →see also **strike**

string ◆◇◇ /strɪŋ/ (**strings, stringing, strung**) ① N-VAR **String** is thin rope made of twisted threads, used for tying things together or tying up packages. ❑ *He held out a small bag tied with string.* ② N-COUNT A **string** of things is a number of them on a piece of string, thread, or wire. ❑ *She wore a string of pearls around her neck.* ③ N-COUNT A **string of** places or objects is a number of them that form a line. ❑ *The landscape is broken only by a string of villages.* ④ N-COUNT A **string of** similar events is a series of them that happen one after the other. ❑ *The incident was the latest in a string of attacks.* ⑤ N-COUNT The **strings** on a musical instrument such as a violin or guitar are the thin pieces of wire or nylon stretched across it that make sounds when the instrument is played. ❑ *He went off to change a guitar string.* ⑥ N-PLURAL The **strings** are the section of an orchestra which consists of stringed instruments played with a bow. ❑ *The strings provided a melodic background to the passages played by the soloist.* ⑦ PHRASE If something is offered to you with **no strings attached** or with **no strings**, it is offered without any special conditions. ❑ *Aid should be given to developing countries with no strings attached.* ⑧ PHRASE If you **pull strings**, you use your influence with other people in order to get something done, often unfairly. ❑ *Tony is sure he can pull a few strings and get you in.* →see **orchestra**

Thesaurus   *string*의 참조어

N.   cord, fiber, rope ①
      chain, line, row, sequence, series ③ ④

머리를 바닥에 찧었다. ❑ 16인치짜리 포탄이 관제탑을 가격했다. ⑤ 타동사/자동사 부딪다, 충돌시키다; 부딪치다, 충돌하다 [격식체] ❑ 와일드는 넘어지면서 머리를 돌바닥에 부딪혔다. ⑥ 자동사 (안 좋은 일이) 닥치다 ❑ 영국은행 관계자들은 파운드가 곧 안정될 것이라고 계속 주장했지만 재앙이 닥쳤다. ⑦ 자동사 습격하다 ❑ 그는 테러리스트들이 습격해 왔을 때 외국에 나가 있었던 유일한 각료였다. ⑧ 가산명사 공격, 공습 ❑ 응징의 성격을 띤 공습 ⑨ 타동사 문득 떠오르다 ❑ 그녀에게 갑자기 생각이 떠올랐다. 그렇다면 그녀가 어머니를 시기했다는 것인가? ⑩ 타동사 인상을 주다 ❑ 그는 매우 진지하지만 다정한 사람이라는 인상을 주었다. ⑪ 타동사 감명을 받다, 인상 깊게 생각하다 ❑ 그녀는 그의 간단하면서도 매혹적인 웅변에 깊은 인상을 받았다. ⑫ 상호동사 타협을 보다 ❑ 그들은 종이 공급자와 타협을 봐서 신문 용지 2년치를 외상으로 받았다. ❑ 둘은 타협을 봐서 렌델이 매니저들이 보통 받는 것의 절반을 받기로 했다. ⑬ 타동사 절충을 하다 ❑ 그럴 때에는 잠과 숙제 사이에서 절충을 해야 한다. ⑭ 타동사 (자세 등을) 취하다 ❑ 그녀는 한 손은 엉덩이에 얹고 다른 한 손은 담배를 쥔 듯한 포즈를 취했다. ⑮ 타동사 (공포 속으로) 몰아넣다 [문예체] ❑ 부모들의 가슴을 틀림없이 공포감에 떨게 할 수 있는 단 하나의 소재가 있다면 그것은 마약이다. ⑯ 타동사/자동사 (시계가 시간을) 알리다 ❑ 시계가 아홉 시를 알렸다. ⑰ 타동사 삭제하다 [격식체] ❑ 회의록에서 그것을 삭제하세요. ● 구동사 삭제하다 ❑ 검열관이 그 다음 두 줄을 삭제했다. ⑱ 타동사 (성냥을) 켜다 ❑ 로비나는 성냥을 켜서 벽난로 안의 구겨진 신문에 갖다 댔다. ⑲ 타동사 발견하다 ❑ 해밀턴 정유사는 아일랜드 해의 리버풀 만 지역에서 석유를 발견했다고 발표했다.

구동사 쓰러지다 [문어체] ❑ 프랭크는 심한 심장 마비로 쓰러졌다.

구동사 자격이 정지되다 [영국영어] ❑ 부정 영업으로 자격 정지된 한 회사 변호사

① 구동사 스스로의 길을 개척하다, 독립해서 시작하다 ❑ 그녀는 내가 사업체를 하나 인수하든지 해서 독립하기를 원했다. ② 구동사 공격하다, 폭언을 하다 ❑ 그는 누구에게 어떤 이유로든 항상 공격을 퍼부을 준비를 하고 있는 사람처럼 보였다.

구동사 (대화 등을) 시작하다 [문어체] ❑ 나는 그녀를 페네이스까지 따라간 다음 말을 붙였다.

① 가산명사 공격수 ❑ 그리고 영국 팀 공격수가 시즌 여섯 번째 골을 기록했다.

① 형용사 현저한, 두드러진 ❑ 그 통계의 가장 현저한 특징은 높은 자살 비율이다. ❑ 그는 레닌을 아주 많이 닮았다. ● 현저하게, 두드러지게 부사 ❑ 그러나, 한 가지 측면에서 그 남자들은 정말 두드러지게 비슷했다. ❑ 두드러지게 잘 생긴 남자 ② 형용사 멋있는, 인상적인 ❑ 그녀는 긴 금발 머리를 가진 멋진 여자였다.

① 가산명사 또는 불가산명사 끈, 줄 ❑ 그는 끈으로 묶은 작은 가방을 내밀었다. ② 가산명사 한 줄로 꿴 것 ❑ 그녀는 목에 진주 목걸이를 걸었다. ③ 가산명사 열을 지어 늘어선 것 ❑ 그 경치를 어지럽히는 것은 오직 일렬로 늘어선 촌락뿐이다. ④ 가산명사 일련 ❑ 그 사건은 일련의 습격 사건 중 최근의 것이었다. ⑤ 가산명사 (악기의) 현, 줄 ❑ 그는 기타 줄을 갈기 위해 자리를 떴다. ⑥ 복수명사 (오케스트라의) 현악기부 ❑ 독주자가 연주하는 악절에 현악기부가 배경 선율을 연주해 주었다. ⑦ 구 아무런 조건 없이 ❑ 개발도상국에 아무런 조건 없이 원조가 제공되어야 한다. ⑧ 구 영향력을 행사하다 ❑ 토니는 자신이 영향력을 행사해서 너를 끼워 줄 수 있을 것으로 확신한다.

a b c d e f g h i j k l m n o p q r s t u v w x y z

Word Partnership   string의 연어

N.	**piece of** string **1**
	string **of pearls 2**
	string **of attacks**, string **of losses**, string **of scandals 4**
	guitar string **5**
ADJ.	**long** string **1**-**4**
	latest string **of** *something*, **recent** string **of** *something* **4**

▶**string together** PHRASAL VERB If you **string** things **together**, you form something from them by adding them to each other, one at a time. ❏ *As speech develops, the child starts to string more words together.*

strin|gent /strɪndʒ³nt/ ADJ **Stringent** laws, rules, or conditions are very severe or are strictly controlled. [FORMAL] ❏ *He announced that there would be more stringent controls on the possession of weapons.*

strip ◆◇◇ /strɪp/ (**strips, stripping, stripped**) **1** N-COUNT A **strip of** something such as paper, cloth, or food is a long, narrow piece of it. ❏ *...a new kind of manufactured wood made by pressing strips of wood together and baking them.* ❏ *The simplest rag-rugs are made with strips of fabric plaited together.* **2** N-COUNT A **strip of** land or water is a long narrow area of it. ❏ *The coastal cities of Liguria sit on narrow strips of land lying under steep mountains.* **3** N-COUNT A **strip** is a long street in a city or town, where there are a lot of stores, restaurants, and hotels. [AM] ❏ *...Goff's Charcoal Hamburgers on Lover's Lane, a busy commercial strip in North Dallas.* **4** V-I If you **strip**, you take off your clothes. ❏ *They stripped completely, and lay and turned in the damp grass.* ● PHRASAL VERB **Strip off** means the same as **strip.** ❏ *The children were brazenly stripping off and leaping into the sea.* **5** V-T If someone **is stripped,** their clothes are taken off by another person, for example in order to search for hidden or illegal things. [usu passive] ❏ *One prisoner claimed he'd been dragged to a cell, stripped and beaten.* **6** V-T To **strip** something means to remove everything that covers it. ❏ *After Mike left for work I stripped the beds and vacuumed the carpets.* **7** V-T If you **strip** an engine or a piece of equipment, you take it to pieces so that it can be cleaned or repaired. ❏ *Volvo's three-man team stripped the car and treated it to a restoration.* ● PHRASAL VERB **Strip down** means the same as **strip.** ❏ *In five years I had to strip the water pump down four times.* **8** V-T To **strip** someone **of** their property, rights, or titles means to take those things away from them. ❏ *The soldiers have stripped the civilians of their passports, and every other type of document.* **9** N-COUNT In a newspaper or magazine, a **strip** is a series of drawings which tell a story. The words spoken by the characters are often written on the drawings. [AM] ❏ *...the Doonesbury strip.*

Word Partnership   strip의 연어

ADJ.	**long** strip, **narrow** strip **1 2**
	commercial strip **3**
	strip (*someone*) **naked 4 5**

▶**strip away** PHRASAL VERB To **strip away** something, especially something that hides the true nature of a thing, means to remove it completely. ❏ *Altman strips away the pretense and mythology to expose the film industry as a business like any other.*

▶**strip off** PHRASAL VERB If you **strip off** your clothes, you take them off. ❏ *He stripped off his wet clothes and stepped into the shower.* →see also **strip 4**

stripe /straɪp/ (**stripes**) N-COUNT A **stripe** is a long line which is a different color from the areas next to it. ❏ *She wore a bright green jogging suit with a white stripe down the sides.*

striped /straɪpt/ ADJ Something that is **striped** has stripes on it. ❏ *...a bottle green and maroon striped tie.*

strip|per /strɪpər/ (**strippers**) N-COUNT A **stripper** is a person who earns money by stripping their clothes off. ❏ *She worked as a stripper and did some acting.*

strive /straɪv/ (**strives, striving**)

The past tense is either **strove** or **strived,** and the past participle is either **striven** or **strived.**

V-T/V-I If you **strive to** do something or **strive for** something, you make a great effort to do it or get it. ❏ *He strives hard to keep himself very fit.*

strode /stroʊd/ **Strode** is the past tense and past participle of **stride.**

stroke ◆◇◇ /stroʊk/ (**strokes, stroking, stroked**) **1** V-T If you **stroke** someone or something, you move your hand slowly and gently over them. ❏ *Carla, curled up on the sofa, was smoking a cigarette and stroking her cat.* **2** N-COUNT If someone has a **stroke,** a blood vessel in their brain bursts or becomes blocked, which may kill them or make them unable to move one side of their body. ❏ *He had a minor stroke in 1987, which left him partly paralyzed.* **3** N-COUNT The **strokes** of a pen or brush are the movements or marks that you make with it when you are writing or painting. ❏ *Fill in gaps by using short, upward strokes of the pencil.* **4** N-COUNT When you are swimming or rowing, your **strokes** are the repeated movements that you make with your arms or the oars. ❏ *I turned and swam a few strokes further out to sea.* **5** N-COUNT A swimming **stroke** is a particular style or method of swimming. ❏ *She spent hours practicing the breast stroke.* **6** N-COUNT The **strokes** of a clock are the sounds that indicate each hour. ❏ *On the stroke of 12, fireworks suddenly exploded into the night.* **7** N-COUNT In sports such as tennis, baseball, golf, and cricket, a **stroke** is the action of hitting the ball. ❏ *Compton was sending the ball here, there, and everywhere with each stroke.* **8** N-SING A **stroke of** luck or good fortune is something lucky that happens. ❏ *It didn't rain, which*

구동사 결합시키다 ❏ 언어 능력이 발달할수록, 아이는 더 많은 단어들을 결합시키기 시작한다.

형용사 엄격한, 엄중한 [격식체] ❏ 그는 무기 소지에 대해 보다 엄격한 통제가 있을 것이라고 발표했다.

1 가산명사 (헝겊 등의) 길고 가는 조각 ❏ 여러 개의 길고 가는 나뭇조각을 압착하여 굽는 새로운 방식으로 제조된 목재 ❏ 헌 천을 모아 만드는 바닥 깔개의 가장 간단한 형태는 기다란 천불 조각을 한데 엮어서 만든다. **2** 가산명사 (땅 등의) 좁고 긴 지역 ❏ 리구리아의 해안 도시들은 가파른 산맥 밑에 놓여 있는 좁고 긴 지대에 위치하고 있다. **3** 가산명사 각종 가게가 즐비한 거리 [미국영어] ❏ 노스 댈러스의 번화한 상가 거리인 러버스 레인에 위치한 '고프스 차콜 햄버거스' **4** 자동사 옷을 벗다 ❏ 그들은 옷을 완전히 벗고, 축축한 잔디에 누워 몸을 뒤척였다. ● 구동사 옷을 벗다 ❏ 그 아이들은 뻔뻔하게 옷을 벗어젖히고 바다 속으로 뛰어들고 있었다. **5** 타동사 벌거벗기다 ❏ 한 죄수가 감방으로 끌려가서 벌거벗겨지고 구타당했었다고 주장했다. **6** 타동사 (껍질 등을) 벗기다, 벗어내다 ❏ 마이크가 출근한 후 나는 침대 커버를 벗기고 진공청소기로 양탄자를 청소했다. **7** 타동사 분해하다, 해체하다 ❏ 볼보의 삼인조 팀이 그 차를 분해했다가 복구시켰다. ● 구동사 분해하다, 해체하다 ❏ 5년 동안 그 양수기를 네 번 분해해야 했다. **8** 타동사 ~에게서 ...을 빼앗다 ❏ 병사들이 민간인들에게서 여권과 기타 모든 종류의 서류를 빼앗았다. **9** 가산명사 (잡지 등의) 만화 [미국영어] ❏ 만화 '둔스베리'

구동사 (껍데기 등을) 벗겨 버리다 ❏ 앨트먼은 영화 산업은 다른 어느 사업과 같은 사업이라는 것을 드러내기 위해 그 겉치레와 신화를 벗겨 버린다.

구동사 (옷을) 벗다 ❏ 그는 젖은 옷을 벗고 샤워실로 걸어 들어갔다.

가산명사 줄무늬, 줄 ❏ 그녀는 옆에 흰 줄무늬가 있는 밝은 초록색 조깅복을 입고 있었다.

형용사 줄무늬가 있는 ❏ 암녹색과 밤색 줄무늬가 있는 넥타이

가산명사 스트리퍼 (스트립쇼를 하는 사람) ❏ 그녀는 스트리퍼로 일했고 연기도 조금 했다.

과거는 strove 또는 strived, 과거 분사는 striven 또는 strived이다.

타동사/자동사 노력하다, 분투하다 ❏ 그는 건강을 아주 좋게 유지하려고 열심히 노력한다.

stride의 과거, 과거 분사

1 타동사 쓰다듬다, 어루만지다 ❏ 칼라는 소파에 웅크리고 누워서 담배를 피우며 고양이를 쓰다듬고 있었다. **2** 가산명사 뇌졸중 ❏ 그는 1987년에 경미한 뇌졸중을 앓아 몸의 일부가 마비되었다. **3** 가산명사 획 ❏ 연필로 위쪽을 향해 짧게 획을 그어 가며 빈 곳을 채우세요. **4** 가산명사 (수영에서) 팔을 젓기; 노 젓기 ❏ 나는 방향을 돌려 몇 번 더 팔을 저어 바다 쪽으로 더 멀리 헤엄쳐 나갔다. **5** 가산명사 (특정한) 수영법 ❏ 그녀는 평영을 연습하며 몇 시간을 보냈다. **6** 가산명사 (시계가) 치는 소리 ❏ 시계가 12시를 알리자, 갑자기 불꽃들이 피우며 고양이 속에 작렬했다. **7** 가산명사 (구기 종목에서) 한 번 치기 ❏ 콤튼은 매번 타구를 여기저기 구석구석으로 보내고 있었다. **8** 가산명사 (행운 등의) 뜻밖에 찾아듦 ❏ 비가 오지 않았는데, 그것은 뜻밖의 행운으로 드러났다. **9** 단수명사 (영감 등의) 반짝 떠오름 ❏ 그 당시 그의 임명은 기가 막힌 생각인 것처럼 보였다. **10** 구

turned out to be a stroke of luck. ◙ N-SING A **stroke of** genius or inspiration is a very good idea that someone suddenly has. ❑ *At the time, his appointment seemed a stroke of genius.* ◙ PHRASE If someone does not **do a stroke of** work, they are very lazy and do no work at all. [INFORMAL, EMPHASIS] ❑ *I never did a stroke of work at college.*

틀끝만큼 하다 [비격식체, 강조] ❑ 나는 대학에서 공부라고는 틸끝만큼도 하지 않았다.

Word Partnership   stroke의 연어

V.	**die from a** stroke, **have a** stroke, **suffer a** stroke ◙
N.	**risk of a** stroke ◙
	stroke **of a pen** ◙

stroll /stroʊl/ (**strolls, strolling, strolled**) V-I If you **stroll** somewhere, you walk there in a slow, relaxed way. ❑ *He collected some orange juice from the refrigerator and, glass in hand, strolled to the kitchen window.* ● N-COUNT **Stroll** is also a noun. ❑ *After dinner, I took a stroll round the city.* →see park

자동사 거닐다, 산책하다 ❑ 그는 냉장고에서 오렌지 주스를 좀 모아 부어, 잔을 손에 들고 부엌 창문 쪽으로 느릿느릿 걸어갔다. ● 가산명사 어슬렁어슬렁 거닐기, 산책 ❑ 저녁 식사 후, 나는 도시를 한 바퀴 거닐었다.

stroll|er /stroʊlər/ (**strollers**) N-COUNT A **stroller** is a small chair on wheels, in which a baby or small child can sit and be wheeled around. [AM; BRIT **pushchair**]

가산명사 유모차 [미국영어; 영국영어 pushchair]

strong ◆◆◆ /strɒŋ, BRIT strɔŋ/ (**stronger** /strɒŋɡər, BRIT strɔŋɡər/, **strongest** /strɒŋɡɪst, BRIT strɔŋɡɪst/) ◙ ADJ Someone who is **strong** is healthy with good muscles and can move or carry heavy things, or do hard physical work. ❑ *I'm not strong enough to carry him.* ◙ ADJ Someone who is **strong** is confident and determined, and is not easily influenced or worried by other people. ❑ *He is sharp and manipulative with a strong personality.* ❑ *It's up to managers to be strong and do what they believe is right.* ◙ ADJ **Strong** objects or materials are not easily broken and can support a lot of weight or resist a lot of strain. ❑ *The vacuum flask has a strong casing, which won't crack or chip.* ❑ *Glue the mirror in with a strong adhesive.* ● **strongly** ADV [ADV -ed] ❑ *The fence was very strongly built, with very large posts.* ◙ ADJ A **strong** wind, current, or other force has a lot of power or speed, and can cause heavy things to move. ❑ *Strong winds and torrential rain combined to make conditions terrible for golfers in the Scottish Open.* ❑ *A fairly strong current seemed to be moving the whole boat.* ● **strongly** ADV [ADV with v] ❑ *The metal is strongly attracted to the surface.* ◙ ADJ A **strong** impression or influence has a great effect on someone. ❑ *We're glad if our music makes a strong impression, even if it's a negative one.* ❑ *There will be a strong incentive to enter into a process of negotiation.* ● **strongly** ADV [ADV with v] ❑ *He is strongly influenced by Spanish painters such as Goya and El Greco.* ◙ ADJ If you have **strong** opinions on something or express them using **strong** words, you have extreme or very definite opinions which you are willing to express or defend. ❑ *She is known to hold strong views on Cuba.* ❑ *I am a strong supporter of the NHS.* ● **strongly** ADV ❑ *Obviously you feel very strongly about this.* ❑ *We are strongly opposed to the presence of America in this region.* ◙ ADJ If someone in authority takes **strong** action, they act firmly and severely. ❑ *The government has said it will take strong action against any further strikes.* ◙ ADJ If there is a **strong** case or argument for something, it is supported by a lot of evidence. ❑ *The testimony presented offered a strong case for acquitting her on grounds of self-defense.* ● **strongly** ADV ❑ *He argues strongly for retention of NATO as a guarantee of peace.* ◙ ADJ If there is a **strong** possibility or chance that something is true or will happen, it is very likely to be true or to happen. ❑ *There is a strong possibility that the cat contracted the condition by eating contaminated pet food.* ◙ ADJ Your **strong** points are your best qualities or talents, or the things you are good at. [ADJ n, v-link ADJ on n] ❑ *Discretion is not Jeremy's strong point.* ❑ *Exports may be the only strong point in the economy over the next six to 12 months.* ◙ ADJ A **strong** competitor, candidate, or team is good or likely to succeed. ❑ *She was a strong contender for Britain's Olympic team.* ◙ ADJ If a relationship or link is **strong**, it is close and likely to last for a long time. ❑ *He felt he had a relationship strong enough to talk frankly to Sarah.* ❑ *This has tested our marriage, and we have come through it stronger than ever.* ◙ ADJ A **strong** currency, economy, or industry has a high value or is very successful. ❑ *The U.S. dollar continued its strong performance in Tokyo today.* ◙ ADJ If something is a **strong** element or part of something else, it is an important or large part of it. ❑ *We are especially encouraged by the strong representation, this year, of women in information technology disciplines.* ◙ ADJ You can use **strong** when you are saying how many people there are in a group. For example, if a group is twenty strong, there are twenty people in it. [num ADJ] ❑ *Ukraine indicated that it would establish its own army, 400,000 strong.* ◙ ADJ A **strong** drink, chemical, or drug contains a lot of the particular substance which makes it effective. ❑ *Strong coffee or tea late at night may cause sleeplessness.* ◙ ADJ A **strong** color, flavor, smell, sound, or light is intense and easily noticed. ❑ *As she went past there was a gust of strong perfume.* ● **strongly** ADV [ADV with v] ❑ *He leaned over her, smelling strongly of sweat.* ◙ ADJ If someone has a **strong** accent, they speak in a distinctive way that shows very clearly what country or region they come from. ❑ *"Good, Mr. Ryle," he said in English with a strong French accent.* ◙ PHRASE If someone or something is still **going strong**, they are still alive, in good condition, or popular after a long time. [INFORMAL] ❑ *The old machinery was still going strong.*

◙ 형용사 힘이 센, 강한 ❑ 나는 그를 들어 옮길 수 있을 만큼 힘이 세지 못하다. ◙ 형용사 단호한, 심지가 굳은 ❑ 그는 단호한 성격에 예리하고 수완도 좋다. ❑ 확고한 태도로 자기가 옳다고 믿는 일을 하는 것이 관리자의 의무이다. ◙ 형용사 튼튼한, 강한 ❑ 그 진공 플라스크는 튼튼한 포장재로 포장되어 금이 가거나 깨지지 않습니다. ❑ 강력 접착제로 거울을 붙여 넣으세요. ● 튼튼하게, 강하게 부사 ❑ 그 담장은 아주 큰 말뚝을 써서 매우 튼튼하게 세워졌다. ◙ 형용사 강한 ❑ 강한 바람과 호우가 어우러져 스코티시 오픈에 출전한 골퍼들에게 악조건을 만들었다. ❑ 상당히 강한 해류가 그 보트 전체를 움직이는 것처럼 보였다. ● 강하게 부사 ❑ 금속은 그 표면에 강하게 끌린다. ◙ 형용사 (정도가) 강한, 큰 ❑ 우리의 음악이, 부정적인 것일지언정 강한 인상을 남긴다면 기쁘다. ❑ 협상 과정에 착수하게 할 강한 유인 수단이 있을 것이다. ● 강하게, 크게 부사 ❑ 그는 고야나 엘 그레코 같은 스페인 화가들로부터 강한 영향을 받았다. ◙ 형용사 강경한, 확고한; 열렬한 ❑ 그녀는 쿠바에 대해 강경한 견해를 갖고 있는 것으로 알려져 있다. ❑ 나는 국민 건강 보험의 열렬 지지자이다. ● 강경히, 확고히; 열렬히 부사 ❑ 명백히 너는 이 일에 대해 아주 확고한 생각을 갖게 될 것이다. ❑ 우리는 이 지역에서의 미국의 존재에 대해 강력히 반대한다. ◙ 형용사 엄중한 ❑ 정부는 더 이상의 어떠한 파업에 대해서도 엄중한 조처를 취할 것이라고 얘기해 왔다. ◙ 형용사 강력한, 확실한 ❑ 제시된 증언은 정당방위로 석방하는 데 강력한 논거를 제공했다. ● 강력하게 부사 ❑ 그는 평화를 보증하는 존재로서 나토 유지 찬성론을 강력하게 주장한다. ◙ 형용사 (가능성이) 큰 ❑ 고양이가 오염된 애완동물 사료를 먹음으로써 그런 병에 걸렸을 가능성이 크다. ◙ 형용사 잘하는, 장하는 ❑ 신중함은 제러미의 강점이 아니다. ❑ 추후 6개월 내지 12개월 동안은 수출이 경제의 유일한 강점이 될지도 모른다. ◙ 형용사 유력한 ❑ 그녀는 영국 올림픽 팀의 유력한 후보자였다. ◙ 형용사 돈독한; (유대 관계가) 강한 ❑ 그는 솔직하게 이야기할 만큼 자신과 새라가 돈독한 사이라고 생각했다. ❑ 이 일이 우리의 결혼 생활을 시험했고, 우리는 어느 때보다도 더 돈독하게 헤쳐 나갔다. ◙ 형용사 (경제적으로) 강세인; 번창하는 ❑ 오늘 도쿄에서는 미 달러화가 강세를 이어 나갔다. ◙ 형용사 중요한, 큰 부분을 차지하는 ❑ 우리는 특히 올해 정보 기술분야에서 여성들이 두각을 나타낸 것에 고무되었다. ◙ 형용사 총 –명의, (–명에) 달하는 ❑ 우크라이나는 총 40만 명 규모의 자체 군대를 창설할 뜻을 나타냈다. ◙ 형용사 (약 등이) 독한, 진한 ❑ 밤늦게 진한 커피나 차를 마시면 잠이 오지 않을 수도 있다. ◙ 형용사 강렬한, 선명한 ❑ 그녀가 지나가자 강렬한 향수 냄새가 확 풍겼다. ● 강렬하게, 선명하게 부사 ❑ 그는 강한 땀 냄새를 풍기며 그녀에게 기댔다. ◙ 형용사 (억양이) 강한 ❑ "좋아요, 라일 씨." 라고 강한 프랑스 억양의 영어로 그가 말했다. ◙ 구 건재하다 [비격식체] ❑ 낡은 기계들이 아직도 건재했다.

Thesaurus   strong의 참조어

ADJ.	mighty, powerful, tough; (ant.) weak ◙
	confident, determined; (ant.) cowardly ◙
	solid, sturdy ◙

strong|hold /strɒŋhoʊld, BRIT strɔŋhoʊld/ (**strongholds**) N-COUNT If you say that a place or region is a **stronghold of** a particular attitude or belief, you mean that most people there share this attitude or belief. ❑ *The westernmost part of north Wales is a stronghold of Welsh-speakers.*

가산명사 (사상 등의) 중심지, 본거지 ❑ 북웨일스 서단 지역이 웨일스 어 사용자들의 본거지이다.

strove /stroʊv/ **Strove** is a past tense of **strive**.

strive의 과거

struck /strʌk/ Struck is the past tense and past participle of **strike**.

strike의 과거, 과거 분사

struc|tur|al /strʌktʃərəl/ ADJ **Structural** means relating to or affecting the structure of something. ❏ *The explosion caused little structural damage to the office towers themselves.* ● **struc|tur|al|ly** ADV ❏ *When we bought the house, it was structurally sound, but I decided to redecorate throughout.*

형용사 구조적, 구조상의 ❏ 그 폭발은 사무실이 밀집된 빌딩들 자체에는 구조적 손상을 별로 입히지 않았다. ● 구조적으로 부사 ❏ 우리가 샀을 때 그 집은 구조적으로 튼튼했지만, 장식은 완전히 다시 하기로 나는 결정했다.

struc|tur|al en|gi|neer (structural engineers) N-COUNT A **structural engineer** is an engineer who works on large structures such as roads, bridges, and large buildings.

가산명사 구조 기술자

struc|ture ♦♦◊ /strʌktʃər/ (structures, structuring, structured) **1** N-VAR The **structure** of something is the way in which it is made, built, or organized. ❏ *The typical family structure of Freud's patients involved two parents and two children.* **2** N-COUNT A **structure** is something that consists of parts connected together in an ordered way. ❏ *The feet are highly specialised structures made up of 26 small delicate bones.* **3** N-COUNT A **structure** is something that has been built. ❏ *About half of those funds has gone to repair public roads, structures and bridges.* **4** V-T If you **structure** something, you arrange it in a careful, organized pattern or system. ❏ *By structuring the course this way, we're forced to produce something the companies think is valuable.*

1 가산명사 또는 불가산명사 구조, 체계 ❏ 프로이트 환자들의 전형적인 가족 구조에는 양친과 두 명의 자녀가 있었다. **2** 가산명사 조직체 ❏ 발은 26개의 작고 섬세한 뼈들로 만들어진 분화된 조직체이다. **3** 가산명사 구조물, 건축물 ❏ 그 기금들의 절반가량은 공공 도로와 건축물, 교량을 수리하는 데 쓰였다. **4** 타동사 조직하다, 구조화하다 ❏ 공정을 이런 식으로 조직함에 따라, 우리는 기업들이 가치 있다고 여기는 것들을 생산해야만 하게 된다.

strug|gle ♦♦◊ /strʌgəl/ (struggles, struggling, struggled) **1** V-I If you **struggle to** do something, you try hard to do it, even though other people or things may be making it difficult for you to succeed. ❏ *They had to struggle against all kinds of adversity.* **2** N-VAR A **struggle** is a long and difficult attempt to achieve something such as freedom or political rights. ❏ *Life became a struggle for survival.* ❏ *...a young lad's struggle to support his poverty-stricken family.* **3** V-I If you **struggle** when you are being held, you twist, kick, and move violently in order to get free. ❏ *I struggled, but he was a tall man, well-built.* **4** V-RECIP If two people **struggle with** each other, they fight. ❏ *She screamed at him to "stop it" as they struggled on the ground.* ● N-COUNT **Struggle** is also a noun. ❏ *He died in a struggle with prison officers less than two months after coming to Britain.* **5** V-I If you **struggle to** move yourself or to move a heavy object, you try to do it, but it is difficult. ❏ *I could see the young boy struggling to free himself.* **6** V-I If a person or organization **is struggling**, they are likely to fail in what they are doing, even though they might be trying very hard. [only cont] ❏ *The company is struggling to find buyers for its new product.* ❏ *One in five young adults was struggling with everyday mathematics.* **7** N-SING An action or activity that is **a struggle** is very difficult to do. ❏ *Losing weight was a terrible struggle.*

1 자동사 분투하다, 고투하다 ❏ 그들은 온갖 종류의 역경에 맞서 고투해야 했다. **2** 가산명사 또는 불가산명사 분투, 고투 ❏ 삶은 생존을 위한 고투가 되었다. ❏ 가난에 찌든 가족을 부양하기 위한 한 청년의 고투 **3** 자동사 버둥거리다 ❏ 나는 버둥거렸지만, 그는 키가 크고 체격이 건장한 남자였다. **4** 상호동사 싸우다 ❏ 그들이 땅바닥에서 싸울 때 그녀가 그를 향해 "그만 둬."라고 소리쳤다. ● 가산명사 싸움, 전투 ❏ 그는 영국에 온 지 두 달이 안 되어 교도관들과 싸우다 죽었다. **5** 자동사 애쓰다 ❏ 나는 그 어린 소년이 자유로워지기 위해 애쓰고 있는 것을 볼 수 있었다. **6** 자동사 (가망 없이) 기를 쓰다, 고생하다 ❏ 그 회사는 신상품의 구매자를 찾으며 기를 쓰고 있다. ❏ 젊은 성인 다섯 명 중 한 명은 일상적인 계산 때문에 고생하고 있다. **7** 단수명사 매우 어려운 일 ❏ 살을 빼는 것은 끔찍이 어려운 일이다.

Word Partnership *struggle의 연어*

ADJ.	**bitter** struggle, **internal** struggle, **long** struggle, **ongoing** struggle, **uphill** struggle **2** **7** **political** struggle **2**
N.	struggle **for democracy**, struggle **for equality**, struggle **for freedom/independence**, **power** struggle, struggle **for survival** **2**

strum /strʌm/ (strums, strumming, strummed) V-T If you **strum** a stringed instrument such as a guitar, you play it by moving your fingers backward and forward across the strings. ❏ *In the corner, one youth sat alone, softly strumming a guitar.*

타동사 (현악기를) 치다 ❏ 모퉁이에 한 젊은이가 홀로 앉아서 작은 소리로 기타를 치고 있었다.

strung /strʌŋ/ Strung is the past tense and past participle of **string**.

string의 과거, 과거 분사

strut /strʌt/ (struts, strutting, strutted) **1** V-I Someone who **struts** walks in a proud way, with their head held high and their chest out, as if they are very important. [DISAPPROVAL] ❏ *He struts around town like he owns the place.* **2** N-COUNT A **strut** is a piece of wood or metal which holds the weight of other pieces in a building or other structure. ❏ *...the struts of a suspension bridge.*

1 자동사 뽐내며 걷다 [탐탁찮음] ❏ 그는 자기가 주인이라도 되는 것처럼 읍내 여기저기를 뽐내며 걸어 다닌다. **2** 가산명사 지주, 버팀대 ❏ 현수교의 지주

stub /stʌb/ (stubs, stubbing, stubbed) **1** N-COUNT The **stub** of a cigarette or a pencil is the last short piece of it which remains when the rest has been used. ❏ *He pulled the stub of a pencil from behind his ear.* **2** N-COUNT A ticket **stub** is the part that you keep when you go in to watch a performance. ❏ *Fans who still have their original ticket stubs should contact Sheffield Arena by July 3.* **3** N-COUNT A check **stub** is the small part that you keep as a record of what you have paid. ❏ *I have every check stub we've written since 1959.* **4** V-T If you **stub** your **toe**, you hurt it by accidentally kicking something hard. ❏ *I stubbed my toes against a table leg.*

1 가산명사 동강이, 꽁초 ❏ 그는 귀 뒤에서 연필 동강이를 꺼냈다. **2** 가산명사 (입장권의) 보관용 부분 ❏ 입장권 원본 관객 보관분을 아직까지 갖고 계신 팬들께서는 7월 3일까지 셰필드 경기장으로 연락을 주셔야 합니다. **3** 가산명사 (수표책의) 떼어 주고 남은 쪽 ❏ 나는 1959년 이래로 우리가 쓴 수표표의 보관본을 모두 가지고 있다. **4** 타동사 (발부리를) 채이다 ❏ 탁자 다리에 발부리를 채었다.

▶stub out PHRASAL VERB When someone **stubs out** a cigarette, they put it out by pressing it against something hard. ❏ *Signs across the entrances warn all visitors to stub out their cigarettes.*

구동사 비벼 끄다 ❏ 입구에 걸려 있는 표지판에 모든 방문객들은 담배를 비벼 끄라는 경고문이 적혀 있다.

stub|ble /stʌbəl/ **1** N-UNCOUNT **Stubble** is the short stalks which are left standing in fields after corn or wheat has been cut. ❏ *The stubble was burning in the fields.* **2** N-UNCOUNT The very short hairs on a man's face when he has not shaved recently are referred to as **stubble**. ❏ *His face was covered with the stubble of several nights.*

1 불가산명사 그루터기 ❏ 들판에서 그루터기가 불타고 있었다. **2** 불가산명사 짧은 수염, 다박나룻 ❏ 그의 얼굴은 며칠 밤 새 자란 다박나룻으로 덮여 있었다.

stub|born /stʌbərn/ **1** ADJ Someone who **is stubborn** or who behaves in a **stubborn** way is determined to do what they want and is very unwilling to change their mind. ❏ *He is a stubborn character used to getting his own way.* ● **stub|born|ly** ADV ❏ *He stubbornly refused to tell her how he had come to be in such a state.* ● **stub|born|ness** N-UNCOUNT ❏ *I couldn't tell if his refusal to talk was simple stubbornness.* **2** ADJ A **stubborn** stain or problem is difficult to remove or to deal with. ❏ *This treatment removes the most stubborn stains.* ● **stub|born|ly** ADV ❏ *Some interest rates have remained stubbornly high.*

1 형용사 완고한, 완강한 ❏ 그는 자기만의 방법을 고수하는 데 익숙한 완고한 인물이다. ● 완고하게, 완강하게 부사 ❏ 그는 자신이 어떻게 그와 같은 상태에 처하게 되었는지 그녀에게 말하기를 완강히 거부했다. ● 완고함, 완강함 불가산명사 ❏ 나는 그의 대화 거부가 단순히 완고함 때문인지 알 수 없었다. **2** 형용사 잘 지지 않는; 다루기 어려운 ❏ 이 처리법은 가장 지우기 힘든 얼룩도 지운다. ● 다루기 어렵게 부사 ❏ 일부 이율이 여전히 다루기 어려울 정도로 높은 상태로 유지되어 왔다.

A B C D E F G H I J K L M N O P Q R S T U V W X Y Z

stuck /stʌk/ **1** **Stuck** is the past tense and past participle of **stick**. **2** ADJ If something is **stuck** in a particular position, it is fixed tightly in this position and is unable to move. [v-link ADJ, oft ADJ prep/adv] □ *He said his car had got stuck in the snow.* **3** ADJ If you are **stuck** in a place, you want to get away from it, but are unable to. [v-link ADJ prep/adv] □ *I was stuck at home with flu.* **4** ADJ If you are **stuck** in a boring or unpleasant situation, you are unable to change it or get away from it. [v-link ADJ prep/adv] □ *I don't want to get stuck in another job like that.* **5** ADJ If something is **stuck** at a particular level or stage, it is not progressing or changing. [v-link ADJ prep/adv] □ *I think the economy is stuck on a plateau of slow growth.* □ *U.S. unemployment figures for March showed the jobless rate stuck at 7 percent.* **6** ADJ If you are **stuck with** something that you do not want, you cannot get rid of it. [v-link ADJ with n] □ *Many people are now stuck with expensive fixed-rate mortgages.* **7** ADJ If you get **stuck** when you are trying to do something, you are unable to continue doing it because it is too difficult. [v-link ADJ, oft ADJ on n] □ *They will be there to help if you get stuck.*

stud /stʌd/ (**studs**) **1** N-COUNT **Studs** are small pieces of metal which are attached to a surface for decoration. □ *You see studs on lots of London front doors.* **2** N-COUNT **Studs** are small round objects attached to the bottom of boots, especially sports boots, so that the person wearing them does not slip. [BRIT; AM **cleats**] □ *...the sound of the studs of our boots on the concrete.* **3** N-UNCOUNT Horses or other animals that are kept for **stud** are kept to be used for breeding. □ *He was retired near the end of the year and then was retired to stud.*

stud|ded /stʌdɪd/ ADJ Something that is **studded** is decorated with studs or things that look like studs. □ *...studded leather jackets.*

stu|dent ♦♦♦ /stjuːdᵊnt/ (**students**) **1** N-COUNT In the United States, a **student** is a person who is studying at an elementary school, secondary school, college, or university. In Britain, a **student** is a person who is studying at college or university. □ *Warren's eldest son is an art student, at St Martin's.* →see also **graduate student** **2** N-COUNT Someone who is a **student of** a particular subject is interested in the subject and spends time learning about it. □ *...a passionate student of history and an expert on nineteenth century prime ministers.* →see **graduation**

stu|dio ♦♦◇ /stjuːdioʊ/ (**studios**) **1** N-COUNT A **studio** is a room where a painter, photographer, or designer works. □ *She was in her studio again, painting onto a large canvas.* **2** N-COUNT A **studio** is a room where radio or television programs are recorded, CDs are produced, or movies are made. □ *She's much happier performing live than in a recording studio.* **3** N-COUNT You can also refer to film-making or recording companies as **studios**. □ *She wrote to Paramount Studios and asked if they would audition her.* **4** N-COUNT A **studio** is a small apartment with one room for living and sleeping in, a kitchen, and a bathroom. You can also talk about a **studio apartment** in American English or a **studio flat** in British English. □ *Home for a couple of years was a studio apartment.*

Word Partnership	*studio*의 연어
N.	studio **album**, studio **audience**, **music** studio, **recording** studio, **television/TV** studio **2**
	studio **executives**, **film/movie** studio **3**

study ♦♦♦ /stʌdi/ (**studies**, **studying**, **studied**) **1** V-T/V-I If you **study**, you spend time learning about a particular subject or subjects. □ *...a relaxed and happy atmosphere that will allow you to study to your full potential.* □ *He went to Hull University, where he studied History and Economics.* **2** N-UNCOUNT **Study** is the activity of studying. [also N in pl] □ *...the use of maps and visual evidence in the study of local history.* **3** N-COUNT A **study** is a piece of research on it. □ *Recent studies suggest that as many as 5 in 1000 new mothers are likely to have this problem.* **4** N-PLURAL You can refer to educational subjects or courses that contain several elements as **studies** of a particular kind. □ *Oxford established a centre for Islamic studies following a grant from a Saudi prince.* **5** V-T If you **study** something, you look at it or watch it very carefully, in order to find something out. □ *Debbie studied her friend's face for a moment.* **6** V-T If you **study** something, you consider it or observe it carefully in order to be able to understand it fully. □ *I know that you've been studying chimpanzees for thirty years now.* **7** N-COUNT A **study** is a room in a house which is used for reading, writing, and studying. □ *That evening we sat together in his study.* **8** →see also **case study** →see **laboratory**

stuff ♦♦◇ /stʌf/ (**stuffs**, **stuffing**, **stuffed**) **1** N-UNCOUNT You can use **stuff** to refer to things such as a substance, a collection of things, events, or ideas, or the contents of something in a general way without mentioning the thing itself by name. [INFORMAL] [usu with supp] □ *I'd like some coffee, and if it's the powdered stuff it's all you've got.* □ *He pointed to a duffle bag. "That's my stuff."* **2** V-T If you **stuff** something somewhere, you push it there quickly and roughly. □ *I stuffed my hands in my pockets.* **3** V-T If you **stuff** a container or space **with** something, you fill it with something or with a quantity of things until it is full. □ *He grabbed my purse, opened it and stuffed it full, then gave it back to me.* **4** V-T If you **stuff yourself**, you eat a lot of food. [INFORMAL] □ *I could stuff myself with ten chocolate bars and half an hour later eat a big meal.* **5** V-T If you **stuff** a bird such as a chicken or a vegetable such as a pepper, you put a mixture of food inside it before cooking it. □ *Will you stuff the turkey and shove it in the oven for me?* **6** V-T If a dead animal **is stuffed**, it is filled with a substance so that it can be preserved and displayed. [usu passive] □ *...his collections of stamps and books and stuffed birds.* **7** PHRASE If you say that someone

1 stick의 과거, 과거 분사 **2** 형용사 (-에 빠져서) 꼼짝 못하는 □ 그는 차가 눈 속에 빠져서 꼼짝 못했다고 말했다. **3** 형용사 붙잡혀 있는, 빠져나갈 수 없는 □ 나는 독감에 걸려 집에 갇혀 있었다. **4** 형용사 (지루한 상황에) 빠진 □ 나는 그와 같은 일에 또다시 빠져들고 싶지 않다. **5** 형용사 고착된 □ 내 생각에는 경제가 저성장이라는 안정기에 고착되어 있는 것 같다. □ 3월의 미국 실업 수치에 따르면 실업률이 7퍼센트에 고착되어 있다. **6** 형용사 -을 떨치지 못하는, -을 떠안은 있는 □ 현재 많은 사람들이 비싼 고정 이율 담보 대출을 떠안고 있다. **7** 형용사 (어떤 일을 하다가) 막힌 □ 네가 막히면 그들이 나서서 도와줄 것이다.

1 가산명사 장식 못, 장식용 금속 단추 □ 런던의 많은 건물 정문에서 장식 못을 볼 수 있습니다. **2** 가산명사 징 [영국영어; 미국영어 cleats] □ 콘크리트 위에 우리가 신은 구두의 징이 부딪쳐 나는 소리 **3** 불가산명사 종마; 번식용 수컷 □ 그 말은 투표를 통해 그해의 말로 선정되었고 그 후 퇴역하여 종마가 되었다.

형용사 장식용 금속 단추가 박힌 □ 장식용 금속 단추가 박힌 가죽 재킷

1 가산명사 학생 □ 워렌의 맏아들은 세인트 마틴스 대학에서 미술을 전공하는 학생이다. **2** 가산명사 연구가, 학자 □ 열성적인 역사 연구가이자 19세기 수상들에 대한 전문가

1 가산명사 (예술가의) 작업장 □ 그녀는 다시 작업장에 돌아와, 커다란 화폭 위에 그림을 그리고 있었다. **2** 가산명사 방송실; 녹음실 □ 그녀는 녹음실에 있을 때보다 라이브 공연을 할 때가 훨씬 더 행복하다. **3** 가산명사 영화사; 음반사 □ 그녀는 파라마운트 영화사에 편지를 써서 오디션을 받을 수 있는지 문의했다. **4** 가산명사 원룸 아파트, 원룸 □ 2년 동안 원룸에서 살았다.

1 타동사/자동사 공부하다, 배우다 □ 최대한의 잠재력을 활용하여 공부할 수 있도록 해 줄 편안하고 즐거운 분위기 □ 그는 헐 대학에 가서 역사와 경제학을 공부했다. **2** 불가산명사 공부, 학습 □ 지역사 학습에 있어서 지도와 시각적 증거의 활용 **3** 가산명사 연구 □ 최근의 연구들에 따르면 새로 어머니가 된 여성 천 명 중 무려 다섯 명이 이런 문제를 가질 수 있는 것으로 나타난다. **4** 복수명사 학과; 과정 □ 옥스퍼드에서 사우디 왕자의 보조금을 받아 이슬람학 센터를 개설했다. **5** 타동사 유심히 보다 □ 데비는 잠시 동안 친구의 얼굴을 유심히 바라보았다. **6** 타동사 관찰하다, 살펴보다 □ 당신이 지금껏 삼십 년간 침팬지들을 관찰해 왔다는 걸 알고 있다. **7** 가산명사 서재 □ 그날 저녁 우리는 그의 서재에 모여 앉았다.

1 불가산명사 물건, 것 [비격식체] □ 커피를 좀 마시고 싶은데, 그리고 가루로 된 것밖에 없다면 그것도 괜찮아. □ 그는 더플백을 하나 가리켰다. "저거 내 물건이야." **2** 타동사 쑤셔 넣다 □ 나는 주머니에 양손을 쑤셔 넣었다. **3** 타동사 채워 넣다 □ 그가 내 지갑을 잡아채서는, 그걸 열어서 가득 채운 다음, 내게 돌려주었다. **4** 타동사 배불리 먹다, 포식하다 [비격식체] □ 나는 초코바 열 개를 포식하고 나서 30분 후에 푸짐하게 식사를 할 수 있다. **5** 타동사 (요리에) 소를 넣다 □ 저 대신 칠면조 속을 채워서 오븐에 넣어 주시겠어요? **6** 타동사 (동물이) 박제되다 □ 그의 우표와 서적, 그리고 박제된 조류 수집품 □ 구 만사들을 말하고 있다, 숙녀이면서 [비격식체, 마음속 들] □ 이 친구들은 7년간 전쟁을 겪은 후라 만사에 훤하다.

knows their **stuff**, you mean that they are good at doing something because they know a lot about it. [INFORMAL, APPROVAL] ❏ *These chaps know their stuff after seven years of war.*

Thesaurus   *stuff*의 참조어

N.	belongings, goods, material, substance **1**
V.	crowd, fill, jam, squeeze **2 3**

---

stuff|ing /stʌfɪŋ/ (**stuffings**) **1** N-MASS **Stuffing** is a mixture of food that is put inside a bird such as a chicken, or a vegetable such as a pepper, before it is cooked. ❏ *Chestnuts can be used at Christmas time, as a stuffing for turkey, guinea fowl, or chicken.* **2** N-UNCOUNT **Stuffing** is material that is used to fill things such as cushions or toys in order to make them firm or solid. ❏ *...a rag doll with all the stuffing coming out.*

1 물질명사 소 (요리 속에 채워 넣는 재료) ❏ 밤은 크리스마스 때 칠면조나 뿔닭, 또는 닭의 배에 채워 넣는 소로 쓸 수 있다. **2** 불가산명사 (방석 등에 채워 넣는) 충전제 ❏ 속의 솜이 온통 비어져 나온 봉제 인형

stuffy /stʌfi/ (**stuffier**, **stuffiest**) ADJ If it is **stuffy** in a place, it is unpleasantly warm and there is not enough fresh air. ❏ *It was hot and stuffy in the classroom even though two of the windows at the back had been opened.*

형용사 (환기가 안 되어) 답답한 ❏ 뒤쪽 창문 두 개를 열어 놓았음에도 불구하고 교실 안은 덥고 답답했다.

stum|ble /stʌmbᵊl/ (**stumbles**, **stumbling**, **stumbled**) **V-I** If you **stumble**, you put your foot down awkwardly while you are walking or running and nearly fall over. ❏ *He stumbled and almost fell.* ● N-COUNT **Stumble** is also a noun. ❏ *I make it into the darkness with only one stumble.*

자동사 비틀거리다; 발을 헛디디다 ❏ 그는 발을 헛디뎌 하마터면 넘어질 뻔했다. ● 가산명사 비틀거림; 발을 헛디딤 ❏ 나는 단 한 번만 발을 헛디디고서 어둠 속을 헤쳐 간다.

▶**stumble across** or **stumble on** PHRASAL VERB If you **stumble across** something or **stumble on** it, you find it or discover it unexpectedly. ❏ *I stumbled across an extremely simple but very exact method for understanding where my money went.*

구동사 우연히 찾아내다 ❏ 내 돈이 어디로 갔는지 알 수 있는 대단히 간단하고도 아주 정확한 방법을 우연히 찾아냈다.

stum|bling block (**stumbling blocks**) N-COUNT A **stumbling block** is a problem which stops you from achieving something. ❏ *The major stumbling block in the talks has been money.*

가산명사 장애물 ❏ 회담에서 주요 장애물은 돈 문제이었다.

stump /stʌmp/ (**stumps**, **stumping**, **stumped**) **1** N-COUNT A **stump** is a small part of something that remains when the rest of it has been removed or broken off. ❏ *If you have a tree stump, check it for fungus.* **2** V-T If you **are stumped** by a question or problem, you cannot think of any solution or answer to it. ❏ *John Diamond is stumped by an unexpected question.*

1 가산명사 그루터기 ❏ 혹시 나무 그루터기가 있으면, 버섯이 있는지 확인해 보세요. **2** 타동사 (질문 등으로) 쩔쩔매다 ❏ 존 다이아몬드는 예상치 못했던 질문에 쩔쩔맨다.

stun /stʌn/ (**stuns**, **stunning**, **stunned**) **1** V-T If you **are stunned** by something, you are extremely shocked or surprised by it and are therefore unable to speak or do anything. [usu passive] ❏ *He's stunned by today's resignation of his longtime ally.* ● **stunned** ADJ ❏ *When they told me she had gone missing I was totally stunned.* **2** V-T If something such as a blow on the head **stuns** you, it makes you unconscious or confused and unsteady. ❏ *Sam stood his ground and got a blow that stunned him.* **3** →see also **stunning**

1 타동사 망연자실하다 ❏ 그는 자신의 오랜 협력자가 오늘 사임한 것에 망연자실했다. ● 망연자실한 형용사 ❏ 그녀가 실종되었다고 그들이 말했을 때, 나는 완전히 망연자실했다. **2** 타동사 실신시키다 ❏ 샘은 자기 자리를 지키고 서 있다가 일격을 받고 실신했다.

stung /stʌŋ/ **Stung** is the past tense and past participle of **sting**.

sting의 과거, 과거 분사

stunk /stʌŋk/ **Stunk** is the past participle of **stink**.

stink의 과거 분사

stun|ning /stʌnɪŋ/ **1** ADJ A **stunning** person or thing is extremely beautiful or impressive. ❏ *She was 55 and still a stunning woman.* **2** ADJ A **stunning** event is extremely unusual or unexpected. ❏ *The minister resigned last night after a stunning defeat in Sunday's vote.*

1 형용사 굉장히 멋진 ❏ 그녀는 55세였고 아직도 굉장히 멋진 여자였다. **2** 형용사 충격적인; 전혀 뜻밖의 ❏ 일요일 투표에서 충격적인 패배를 겪고 나서 장관은 지난밤 사임했다.

Word Partnership   *stunning*의 연어

N.	stunning **images**, stunning **views 1**
	stunning **blow**, stunning **defeat/loss**, stunning **success**, stunning **upset**, stunning **victory 2**

---

stunt /stʌnt/ (**stunts**, **stunting**, **stunted**) **1** N-COUNT A **stunt** is something interesting that is done in order to attract attention and get publicity for the person or company responsible for it. ❏ *In a bold promotional stunt for the movie, he smashed his car into a passing truck.* **2** N-COUNT A **stunt** is a dangerous and exciting piece of action in a movie. ❏ *Sean Connery insisted on living dangerously for his new film by performing his own stunts.* **3** V-T If something **stunts** the growth or development of a person or thing, it prevents it from growing or developing as much as it should. ❏ *The heart condition had stunted his growth a bit.* ● **stunt|ed** ADJ ❏ *Damage may result in stunted growth and sometimes death of the plant.*

1 가산명사 이목을 끌기 위한 행위 ❏ 이목을 끌어 그 영화를 선전하기 위해 용감하게도, 그는 자신의 자동차로 지나가는 트럭을 들이받았다. **2** 가산명사 스턴트 ❏ 숀 코네리는 자신의 새 영화를 위해 위험을 무릅쓰고 직접 스턴트 연기를 하겠다고 고집했다. **3** 타동사 (성장을) 방해하다 ❏ 심장 질환이 그의 성장을 약간 방해해 왔었다. ● 성장을 방해당한 형용사 ❏ 손상을 입으면 식물은 발육 부전을 겪을 수도 있고 가끔은 죽을 수도 있다.

stu|pid ◆◇◇ /stjuːpɪd, BRIT styuːpɪd/ (**stupider**, **stupidest**) **1** ADJ If you say that someone or something is **stupid**, you mean that they show a lack of good judgment or intelligence and they are not at all sensible. ❏ *I'll never do anything so stupid again.* ❏ *I made a stupid mistake.* ● **stu|pid|ly** ADV ❏ *We had stupidly been looking at the wrong column of figures.* ● **stu|pid|ity** /stjuːpɪdɪti, BRIT styuːpɪdɪti/ (**stupidities**) N-VAR ❏ *I stared at him, astonished by his stupidity.* **2** ADJ You say that something is **stupid** to indicate that you do not like it or that it annoys you. [DISAPPROVAL] ❏ *I wouldn't call it art. It's just stupid and tasteless.*

1 형용사 어리석은 ❏ 그렇게 어리석은 일은 다시는 하지 않겠다. ❏ 내가 어리석은 실수를 했어. ● 어리석게도 부사 ❏ 우리는 어리석게도 틀린 줄의 숫자들을 보고 있었던 것이었다. ● 어리석음 가산명사 또는 불가산명사 ❏ 나는 그의 어리석음에 깜짝 놀라 그를 응시했다. **2** 형용사 바보 같은; 싱거운 [탐탁찮음] ❏ 나는 그걸 예술이라고 부르지 않겠다. 그것은 그저 바보 같고 몰취미하다.

Word Partnership   *stupid*의 연어

N.	stupid **idea**, stupid **man**, stupid **mistake**, stupid **people**, stupid **question 1**
	stupid **things 1 2**
V.	(**don't**) **do** anything/*something* stupid, **feel** stupid, **look** stupid **1**
	think *something* is stupid **1 2**

---

stur|dy /stɜːrdi/ (**sturdier**, **sturdiest**) ADJ Someone or something that is **sturdy** looks strong and is unlikely to be easily injured or damaged. ❏ *She was a short, sturdy woman in her early sixties.* ● **stur|di|ly** ADV ❏ *It was a good table too, sturdily constructed of elm.*

형용사 튼튼한, 억센 ❏ 그녀는 60대 초반의 키가 작고 튼튼한 여자였다. ● 튼튼하게 부사 ❏ 그것은 또 느릅나무로 튼튼하게 조립한 훌륭한 탁자였다.

stut|ter /stʌtər/ (**stutters, stuttering, stuttered**) **1** N-COUNT If someone has a **stutter**, they find it difficult to say the first sound of a word, and so they often hesitate or repeat it two or three times. [usu sing] ❏ *He spoke with a pronounced stutter.* **2** V-I If someone **stutters**, they have difficulty speaking because they find it hard to say the first sound of a word. ❏ *I was trembling so hard, I thought I would stutter when I spoke.* ● **stut|ter|ing** N-UNCOUNT ❏ *He had to stop talking because if he'd kept on, the stuttering would have started.*

style ♦♦◇ /staɪl/ (**styles, styling, styled**) **1** N-COUNT The **style** of something is the general way in which it is done or presented, which often shows the attitudes of the people involved. [with supp, also in adj N] ❏ *Our children's different needs and learning styles created many problems.* ❏ *Belmont Park is a broad sweeping track which will suit the European style of running.* **2** N-UNCOUNT If people or places have **style**, they are fashionable and elegant. ❏ *Bournemouth, you have to admit, has style.* ❏ *Both love doing things in style.* **3** N-VAR The **style** of a product is its design. ❏ *His 50 years of experience have given him strong convictions about style.* **4** N-COUNT In the arts, a particular **style** is characteristic of a particular period or group of people. ❏ *...six scenes in the style of a classical Greek tragedy.* ❏ *...a mixture of musical styles.* **5** V-T If something such as a piece of clothing, a vehicle, or someone's hair **is styled** in a particular way, it is designed or shaped in that way. [usu passive] ❏ *His thick blond hair had just been styled before his trip.* **6** →see also **self-styled**

Word Partnership	*style*의 연어

ADJ.   **personal** style **1**
      distinctive style, **particular** style **1**-**4**
N.   **leadership** style, **learning** style, style **of life**, **management** style **1**
      differences in style **1**-**4**
      music style, **prose** style, **writing** style **4**

styl|ish /staɪlɪʃ/ ADJ Someone or something that is **stylish** is elegant and fashionable. ❏ *...a very attractive and very stylish woman of 27.* ● **styl|ish|ly** ADV ❏ *...stylishly dressed middle-aged women.*

styl|is|tic /staɪlɪstɪk/ ADJ **Stylistic** describes things relating to the methods and techniques used in creating a piece of writing, music, or art. ❏ *There are some stylistic elements in the statue that just don't make sense.*

styl|ized /staɪlaɪzd/ [BRIT also **stylised**] ADJ Something that is **stylized** is shown or done in a way that is not natural in order to create an artistic effect. ❏ *Some of it has to do with recent stage musicals, which have been very, very stylised.*

suave /swɑːv/ (**suaver, suavest**) ADJ Someone who is **suave** is charming, polite, and elegant, but may be insincere. ❏ *He is a suave, cool, and cultured man.*

sub /sʌb/ (**subs**) **1** N-COUNT A **sub** is the same as a **substitute**. **2** N-COUNT A **sub** is the same as a **substitute teacher**. [AM] **3** N-COUNT In team games such as football, a **sub** is a player who is brought into a game to replace another player. [INFORMAL] ❏ *We had a few injuries and had to use youth team kids as subs.* **4** N-COUNT A **sub** is the same as a **submarine**. [INFORMAL]

sub|com|mit|tee /sʌbkəmɪti/ (**subcommittees**) also **sub-committee** N-COUNT-COLL A **subcommittee** is a small committee made up of members of a larger committee.

sub|con|scious /sʌbkɒnʃəs/ **1** N-SING Your **subconscious** is the part of your mind that can influence you or affect your behavior even though you are not aware of it. ❏ *...the hidden power of the subconscious.* **2** ADJ A **subconscious** feeling or action exists in or is influenced by your subconscious. ❏ *He caught her arm in a subconscious attempt to detain her.* ● **sub|con|scious|ly** ADV ❏ *Subconsciously I had known that I would not be in personal danger.* →see **hypnosis**

sub|con|tract /sʌbkəntrækt/ (**subcontracts, subcontracting, subcontracted**) V-T If one firm **subcontracts** part of its work to another firm, it pays the other firm to do part of the work that it has been employed to do. [BUSINESS] ❏ *The company is subcontracting production of most of the parts.*

sub|con|trac|tor /sʌbkəntræktər, BRIT sʌbkəntræktə/ (**subcontractors**) also **sub-contractor** N-COUNT A **subcontractor** is a person or firm that has a contract to do part of a job which another firm is responsible for. [BUSINESS] ❏ *The company was considered as a possible subcontractor to build the aeroplane.*

sub|cul|ture /sʌbkʌltʃər/ (**subcultures**) also **sub-culture** N-COUNT A **subculture** is the ideas, art, and way of life of a group of people within a society, which are different from the ideas, art, and way of life of the rest of the society. ❏ *...the latest American subculture.* →see **culture**

Word Link	*sub ≈ below* : *sub*division, *sub*marine, *sub*missive

sub|di|vi|sion /sʌbdɪvɪʒən/ (**subdivisions**) also **sub-division** **1** N-COUNT A **subdivision** is an area, part, or section of something which is itself a part of something larger. ❏ *Months are a conventional subdivision of the year.* **2** N-COUNT A **subdivision** is an area of land for building houses on. [AM] ❏ *Rammick lives high on a ridge in a 400-home subdivision.*

sub|due /səbduː, BRIT səbdjuː/ (**subdues, subduing, subdued**) **1** V-T If soldiers or the police **subdue** a group of people, they defeat them or bring them under control by using force. ❏ *Senior government officials admit they have not been able to subdue the rebels.* **2** V-T To **subdue** feelings means to make them less strong. ❏ *He forced himself to subdue and overcome his fears.*

sub|dued /səbduːd, BRIT səbdjuːd/ **1** ADJ Someone who is **subdued** is very quiet, often because they are sad or worried about something. ❏ *He faced the*

---

1 가산명사 말 더듬기 ❏ 그는 심하게 말을 더듬었다. **2** 자동사 말을 더듬다 ❏ 나는 심하게 몸이 떨렸고, 말할 때 말을 더듬을 것 같았다. ● 말 더듬기 불가산명사 ❏ 계속했다가는 말을 더듬기 시작할지도 몰랐기 때문에 그는 말을 멈춰야 했다.

1 가산명사 방식 ❏ 우리 아이들의 서로 다른 필요와 학습 방식 때문에 많은 문제가 생겼다. ❏ 벨몬트 파크는 유럽식의 경주에 적합할 넓고 길게 뻗은 트랙이다. **2** 불가산명사 멋, 품격 ❏ 본머스가 멋이 있다는 것은 인정해야 해. ❏ 두 사람 모두 일을 품격 있게 하기를 좋아한다. **3** 가산명사 또는 불가산명사 디자인, 스타일 ❏ 그는 50년 경력을 통해 디자인에 대한 강한 확신을 얻었다. **4** 가산명사 양식 ❏ 고대 그리스 비극 양식의 여섯 개 장 ❏ 여러 음악 양식의 혼합 **5** 타동사 (특정 양식으로) 디자인하다; (머리 스타일을) 손질하다 ❏ 그의 숱이 많은 금발 머리는 여행 직전에 손질한 것이었다.

형용사 멋진; 유행을 따른 ❏ 아주 매력적이고 대단히 멋진 27세 여성 ● 멋지게; 유행을 따라 부사 ❏ 유행 따라 멋지게 차려입은 중년 여인들

형용사 양식적인 ❏ 그 조각상에는 전혀 말이 되지 않는 양식적 요소가 있다.

[영국영어 stylised] 형용사 양식화된 ❏ 그 중 일부는 매우 많이 양식화되어 온 최근의 스테이지 뮤지컬과 관계가 있다.

형용사 상냥하고 매력적인 ❏ 그는 상냥하고 침착하며 세련된 사람이다.

1 가산명사 대리인 **2** 가산명사 대리 교사 [미국영어] **3** 가산명사 교체 선수 [비격식체] ❏ 약간의 부상이 있어서 청소년 팀 아이들을 교체 선수로 활용해야 했다. **4** 가산명사 잠수함 [비격식체]

가산명사-집합 소위원회, 분과 위원회

1 단수명사 잠재의식 ❏ 잠재의식의 숨겨진 힘 **2** 형용사 잠재의식적인 ❏ 그는 잠재의식적으로 그녀를 붙들려 하며 그녀의 팔을 잡았다. ● 잠재의식적으로 부사 ❏ 나는 신변상의 위험에 처하지 않으리라는 것을 잠재의식적으로 알고 있었다.

타동사 하도급을 주다 [경제] ❏ 그 회사는 대부분의 부속품 생산을 하도급으로 주고 있다.

가산명사 하도급 입자 [경제] ❏ 그 회사는 비행기를 제작할 하도급 업체 후보로 여겨졌다.

가산명사 하위문화; 이(異)문화 ❏ 최신 미국 하위문화

1 가산명사 일부분; 분할 ❏ 달은 한 해를 관습적으로 분할한 것이다. **2** 가산명사 구획된 택지 [미국영어] ❏ 래믹은 높은 산등성이의 400가구가 있는 택지 지구에 산다.

1 타동사 진압하다 ❏ 정부 원로 관리들은 반란을 진압할 수 없었음을 시인한다. **2** 타동사 (감정을) 억제하다, 가라앉히다 ❏ 그는 억지로 두려움을 억제하고 극복하려고 했다.

1 형용사 조용한, 가라앉은 ❏ 그는 처음에는 약간 가라앉은 기분으로 기자들을 대했다. **2** 형용사 (빛

A

press, initially, in a somewhat subdued mood. ☐ ADJ **Subdued** lights or colors are not very bright. ☐ *The lighting was subdued.*

둥이) 부드러운 ☐ 조명은 부드러웠다.

sub|ject ♦♦◇ (**subjects, subjecting, subjected**)

B

The noun and adjective are pronounced /sʌbdʒɪkt/. The verb is pronounced /səbdʒɛkt/.

명사와 형용사는 /sʌbdʒɪkt /로 발음된다. 동사는 /səbdʒɛkt /로 발음된다.

C

1 N-COUNT The **subject** of something such as a conversation, letter, or book is the thing that is being discussed or written about. ☐ *It was I who first raised the subject of plastic surgery.* ☐ *...the president's own views on the subject.* **2** N-COUNT Someone or something that is the **subject** of criticism, study, or an investigation is being criticized, studied, or investigated. ☐ *Over the past few years, some of the positions Mr. Meredith has adopted have made him the subject of criticism.* **3** N-COUNT A **subject** is an area of knowledge or study, especially one that you study at school or college. ☐ *Surprisingly, mathematics was voted their favorite subject.* **4** N-COUNT In an experiment or piece of research, the **subject** is the person or animal that is being tested or studied. ☐ *"White noise" was played into the subject's ears through headphones.* **5** N-COUNT An artist's **subjects** are the people, animals, or objects that he or she paints, models, or photographs. ☐ *Her favorite subjects are shells spotted on beach walks.* **6** N-COUNT In grammar, the **subject** of a clause is the noun group that refers to the person or thing that is doing the action expressed by the verb. For example, in "My cat keeps catching birds," "my cat" is the subject. **7** ADJ To be **subject to** something means to be affected by it or to be likely to be affected by it. [v-link ADJ to n] ☐ *Prices may be subject to alteration.* **8** ADJ If someone is **subject to** a particular set of rules or laws, they have to obey those rules or laws. [v-link ADJ to n] ☐ *The tribunal is unique because Mr. Jones is not subject to the normal police discipline code.* **9** V-T If you **subject** someone **to** something unpleasant, you make them experience it. ☐ *...the man who had subjected her to four years of beatings and abuse.* **10** N-COUNT The people who live in or belong to a particular country, usually one ruled by a monarch, are the **subjects** of that monarch or country. ☐ *...his subjects regarded him as a great and wise monarch.* **11** PHRASE When someone involved in a conversation **changes the subject**, they start talking about something else, often because the previous subject was embarrassing. ☐ *He tried to change the subject, but she wasn't to be put off.* **12** PHRASE If an event will take place **subject to** a condition, it will take place only if that thing happens. ☐ *They denied a report that Egypt had agreed to a summit, subject to certain conditions.* →see **hypnosis**

D

E

F

G

H

I

J

1 가산명사 주제 ☐ 성형 수술이라는 주제를 처음으로 꺼낸 사람이 바로 나였다. ☐ 그 주제에 대한 대통령 자신의 견해 **2** 가산명사 -의 대상 ☐ 지난 몇 년간에 걸쳐, 메러디스 씨가 취해 온 몇몇 입장들이 그를 비판의 대상으로 만들어 왔다. **3** 가산명사 학과, 과목 ☐ 놀랍게도, 수학이 투표를 통해 그들이 가장 좋아하는 과목으로 선정되었다. **4** 가산명사 피실험자, 실험 대상 [격식체] ☐ '백색 소음'을 헤드폰을 통해 피실험자들의 귀에 들려주었다. **5** 가산명사 (그림 둥의) 대상, 피사체 ☐ 그녀가 좋아하는 대상은 해변 산책로에 점점이 깔려 있는 조가비들이다. **6** 가산명사 주어 **7** 형용사 -의 영향을 받는, -에 종속된 ☐ 개정에 의해 물가가 영향을 받을지도 모른다. **8** 형용사 -의 지배를 받는 ☐ 존스 씨는 일반적인 경찰 징계 규칙의 지배를 받지 않으므로 그 징계 위원회가 유일하다. **9** 타동사 (좋지 않은 일을) 당하게 하다 ☐ 4년 동안 그녀에게 구타와 학대를 저질러 왔던 그 남자 **10** 가산명사 국민, 신하 ☐ 그의 신하들은 그를 위대하고 현명한 군주로 여겼다. **11** 구 화제를 바꾸다 ☐ 그는 화제를 바꾸려 했지만, 그녀를 말릴 수가 없었다. **12** 구 -을 조건으로 하여 ☐ 그들은 이집트가 특정한 조건하에, 정상 회담에 동의했다는 보도를 부인했다.

K

L

M

N

O

P

sub|jec|tive /səbdʒɛktɪv/ ADJ Something that is **subjective** is based on personal opinions and feelings rather than on facts. [LITERARY, APPROVAL] ☐ *We know that taste in art is a subjective matter.* ● **sub|jec|tive|ly** ADV ☐ *Our preliminary results suggest that people do subjectively find the speech clearer.* ● **sub|jec|tiv|ity** /sʌbdʒɛktɪvɪti/ N-UNCOUNT ☐ *They accused her of flippancy and subjectivity in her reporting of events in their country.*

형용사 주관적인 ☐ 우리는 예술에서의 취향이 주관적인 문제임을 알고 있다. ● 주관적으로 부사 ☐ 우리의 1차 예비 결과에 따르면 사람들은 실제 주관적으로 그 담화를 더 명료하다고 생각한다. ● 주관성 불가산명사 ☐ 그들은 자국 사건들을 보도하는 데 있어 그녀가 경솔하고 주관적이라고 비난했다.

Q

R

sub|ject mat|ter also **subject-matter** N-UNCOUNT The **subject matter** of something such as a book, lecture, movie, or painting is the thing that is being written about, discussed, or shown. ☐ *Then, attitudes changed and artists were given greater freedom in their choice of subject matter.*

불가산명사 주제, 제재 ☐ 그 후, 태도가 변화하여 예술가들은 주제를 선택하는 데 있어 더 큰 자유를 누리게 되었다.

S

sub|lime /səblaɪm/ ADJ If you describe something as **sublime**, you mean that it has a wonderful quality that affects you deeply. [LITERARY, APPROVAL] ☐ *Sublime music floats on a scented summer breeze to the spot where you lie.* ● N-SING You can refer to sublime things as **the sublime**. ☐ *She elevated every rare small success to the sublime.* ● PHRASE If you describe something as going **from the sublime to the ridiculous**, you mean that it involves a change from something very good or serious to something silly or unimportant.

형용사 숭고한, 장엄한 [문예체, 마음에 듦] ☐ 장엄한 음악이 향기로운 여름 미풍을 타고 당신이 누워 있는 곳으로 흘러간다. ● 단수명사 숭고한 것; 극치 ☐ 그녀는 얼마 안 되는 드문 성취를 모두 최고로 끌어올렸다. ● 구 최고에서 최악으로

T

U

sub|limi|nal /sʌblɪmɪnəl/ ADJ **Subliminal** influences or messages affect your mind without you being aware of it. ☐ *Color has a profound, though often subliminal influence on our senses and moods.* →see **advertising**

형용사 잠재의식적인 ☐ 색채는 우리의 감각과 기분에 종종 잠재의식적이긴 하지만 심대한 영향을 미친다.

V

W

sub|ma|rine /sʌbmərin, BRIT sʌbməriːn/ (**submarines**) N-COUNT A **submarine** is a type of ship that can travel both above and below the surface of the sea. The abbreviation **sub** is also used. ☐ *...a nuclear submarine.*

가산명사 잠수함 ☐ 핵 잠수함

X

Y

Z

sub|merge /səbmɜrdʒ/ (**submerges, submerging, submerged**) V-T/V-I If something **submerges** or if you **submerge** it, it goes below the surface of some water or another liquid. ☐ *Hippos are unable to submerge in the few remaining water holes.*

타동사/자동사 물속에 잠기다; 물속에 잠그다 ☐ 하마들은 몇 개 안 남은 물구덩이에서 물속에 몸을 잠글 수가 없다.

sub|mis|sion /səbmɪʃ³n/ (**submissions**) N-UNCOUNT **Submission** is a state in which people can no longer do what they want to do because they have been brought under the control of someone else. ❑ *The army intends to take the city or simply starve it into submission.*

불가산명사 복종; 항복 ❑ 군대는 그 도시를 점령하거나 아니면 간단히 굶겨서 항복을 받아 내거나 할 작정이다.

| **Word Link** | *sub* ≈ *below* : *subdivision, submarine, submissive* |

sub|mis|sive /səbmɪsɪv/ ADJ If you are **submissive**, you obey someone without arguing. ❑ *Most doctors want their patients to be submissive.* ● **sub|mis|sive|ly** ADV ❑ *The troops submissively laid down their weapons.*

형용사 순종적인, 고분고분한 ❑ 대부분의 의사들은 고분고분한 환자를 원한다. ● 고분고분 부사 ❑ 그 군인들은 고분고분 무기를 내려놓았다.

sub|mit /səbmɪt/ (**submits, submitting, submitted**) **1** V-I If you **submit to** something, you unwillingly allow something to be done to you, or you do what someone wants, for example because you are not powerful enough to resist. ❑ *In desperation, Mrs. Jones submitted to an operation on her right knee to relieve the pain.* **2** V-T If you **submit** a proposal, report, or request **to** someone, you formally send it to them so that they can consider it or decide about it. ❑ *They submitted their reports to the Chancellor yesterday.*

1 자동사 굴복하다; 감수하다 ❑ 필사적인 심정으로, 존스 여사는 고통을 덜기 위해 오른쪽 무릎 수술을 받았다. **2** 타동사 제출하다 ❑ 그들은 어제 재무 장관에게 보고서를 제출했다.

sub|or|di|nate (**subordinates, subordinating, subordinated**)

The noun and adjective are pronounced /səbɔːrdªnɪt/. The verb is pronounced /səbɔːrdªneɪt/.

명사와 형용사는 /səbɔːrdªnɪt/로 발음된다. 동사는 /səbɔːrdªneɪt/로 발음된다.

1 N-COUNT If someone is your **subordinate**, they have a less important position than you in the organization that you both work for. ❑ *Haig tended not to seek guidance from subordinates.* **2** ADJ Someone who is **subordinate to** you has a less important position than you and has to obey you. ❑ *Sixty of his subordinate officers followed his example.* **3** ADJ Something that is **subordinate to** something else is less important than the other thing. ❑ *It was an art in which words were subordinate to images.* **4** V-T If you **subordinate** something **to** another thing, you regard it or treat it as less important than the other thing. ❑ *He was both willing and able to subordinate all else to this aim.* ● **sub|or|di|na|tion** /səbɔːrdªneɪʃ³n/ N-UNCOUNT ❑ *...the social subordination of women.*

1 가산명사 부하, 하급자 ❑ 헤이그는 하급자로부터 조언을 구하길 꺼리는 경향이 있었다. **2** 형용사 부하의 ❑ 그의 부하 장교 육십 명이 그의 본보기를 따랐다. **3** 형용사 부차적인, 부수적인 ❑ 그것은 말이 이미지보다 부차적인 예술이었다. **4** 타동사 –보다 경시하다; –에 종속시키다 ❑ 그는 기꺼이 다른 모든 것들보다 이 목표를 중시하려 했고 또 그렇게 할 수 있었다. ● 경시; 종속 불가산명사 ❑ 여성에 대한 사회적 경시

sub|poe|na /səpiːnə/ (**subpoenas, subpoenaing, subpoenaed**) **1** N-COUNT A **subpoena** is a legal document telling someone that they must attend a court of law and give evidence as a witness. ❑ *He has been served with a subpoena to answer the charges in court.* **2** V-T If someone **subpoenas** a person, they give them a legal document telling them to attend a court of law and give evidence. If someone **subpoenas** a piece of evidence, the evidence must be produced in a court of law. ❑ *Select committees have the power to subpoena witnesses.*

1 가산명사 소환장, 호출장 ❑ 그는 법정에 출두해 혐의에 대한 답변을 하라는 소환장을 받은 상태이다. **2** 타동사 소환하다, 소환장을 발부하다 ❑ 특별 위원회는 증인을 소환할 수 있는 권한을 가지고 있다.

sub|scribe /səbskraɪb/ (**subscribes, subscribing, subscribed**) **1** V-I If you **subscribe to** an opinion or belief, you are one of a number of people who have this opinion or belief. ❑ *I've personally never subscribed to the view that either sex is superior to the other.* **2** V-I If you **subscribe to** a magazine or a newspaper, you pay to receive copies of it regularly. ❑ *My main reason for subscribing to New Scientist is to keep abreast of advances in science.* **3** V-I If you **subscribe to** an online newsgroup or service, you send a message saying that you wish to receive it or belong to it. [COMPUTING] ❑ *Usenet is a collection of discussion groups, known as newsgroups, to which anybody can subscribe.* **4** V-I If you **subscribe for** shares in a company, you apply to buy shares in that company. [BUSINESS] ❑ *Employees subscribed for far more shares than were available.*

1 자동사 –에 동의하다, –에 찬성하다 ❑ 나는 개인적으로 어느 한쪽 성별이 다른 쪽보다 더 우수하다는 견해에 동의한 적이 없다. **2** 자동사 –을 구독하다 ❑ 내가 '뉴 사이언티스트' 지를 구독하는 주된 이유는 과학 분야의 진보에 뒤지지 않고 따라가기 위함이다. **3** 자동사 (인터넷 서비스에) 가입하다 [컴퓨터] ❑ 유스네트는 뉴스그룹으로 알려진 토론 그룹을 모아 놓은 것으로, 누구나 가입할 수 있다. **4** 자동사 (주식을) 청약하다 [경제] ❑ 피고용인들이 할당 가능한 주식보다 훨씬 더 많이 청약했다.

sub|scrib|er /səbskraɪbər/ (**subscribers**) **1** N-COUNT A magazine's or a newspaper's **subscribers** are the people who pay to receive copies of it regularly. ❑ *I have been a subscriber to "Railway Magazine" for many years.* **2** N-COUNT **Subscribers to** a service are the people who pay to receive the service. ❑ *China has almost 15 million subscribers to satellite and cable television.*

1 가산명사 구독자 ❑ 나는 다년간 '레일웨이 매거진'을 구독해 왔다. **2** 가산명사 (특정 서비스의) 가입자 ❑ 중국은 거의 1천 5백만 명의 위성 및 케이블 텔레비전 가입자를 보유하고 있다.

sub|scrip|tion /səbskrɪpʃ³n/ (**subscriptions**) **1** N-COUNT A **subscription** is an amount of money that you pay regularly in order to belong to an organization, to help a charity or campaign, or to receive copies of a magazine or newspaper. ❑ *You can become a member by paying the yearly subscription.* **2** ADJ **Subscription** television is television that you can watch only if you pay a subscription. A **subscription** channel is a channel that you can watch only if you pay a subscription. [ADJ n] ❑ *Premiere, a subscription channel which began in 1991, shows live football covering the top two divisions.*

1 가산명사 회비; 구독료 ❑ 연회비를 내시면 회원이 되실 수 있습니다. **2** 형용사 유료 (방송) ❑ 1991년에 개설된 유료 채널인 프리미어 채널에서는 최상위 두 개 디비전을 망라한 축구 경기를 생중계한다.

sub|se|quent ◆◇◇ /sʌbsɪkwənt/ ADJ You use **subsequent** to describe something that happened or existed after the time or event that has just been referred to. [FORMAL] [ADJ n] ❑ *...the increase of population in subsequent years.* ● **sub|se|quent|ly** ADV ❑ *She subsequently became the Faculty's President.*

형용사 그 다음의, 차후의 [격식체] ❑ 차후 몇 년간의 인구 증가 ● 그 후, 그 뒤에 부사 ❑ 그녀는 그 후 학장이 되었다.

sub|ser|vi|ent /səbsɜːrviənt/ **1** ADJ If you are **subservient**, you do whatever someone wants you to do. ❑ *Her willingness to be subservient to her children isolated her.* ● **sub|ser|vi|ence** /səbsɜːrviəns/ N-UNCOUNT ❑ *...an austere regime stressing obedience and subservience to authority.* **2** ADJ If you treat one thing as **subservient to** another, you treat it as less important than the other thing. [v-link ADJ to n] ❑ *The woman's needs are seen as subservient to the group interest.*

1 형용사 굴종하는, 뭐든지 다 해 주는 ❑ 자식들에게 기꺼이 뭐든지 다 해 주고자 하는 그녀의 태도가 그녀를 고립시켰다. ● 굴종 불가산명사 ❑ 당국에 복종하고 굴종할 것을 강조하는 엄혹한 정권 **2** 형용사 –보다 부수적인 ❑ 그 여자의 요구는 집단의 이익에 비해 부수적인 것으로 여겨진다.

sub|side /səbsaɪd/ (**subsides, subsiding, subsided**) **1** V-I If a feeling or noise **subsides**, it becomes less strong or loud. ❑ *The pain had subsided during the night.* **2** V-I If fighting **subsides**, it becomes less intense or general. ❑ *Violence has subsided following two days of riots.* **3** V-I If the ground or a building **is subsiding**, it is very slowly sinking to a lower level. ❑ *Does that mean the whole house is subsiding?* **4** V-I If a level of water, especially flood water, **subsides**, it goes down. ❑ *Local officials say the flood waters have subsided.*

1 자동사 가라앉다 ❑ 통증이 밤사이에 가라앉아 있었다. **2** 자동사 진정되다 ❑ 이틀간의 폭동 뒤에 폭력 사태는 진정되었다. **3** 자동사 내려앉다, 침하되다 ❑ 그 말은 집 전체가 내려앉고 있다는 뜻인가? **4** 자동사 (물이) 빠지다 ❑ 지역 관계자들은 홍수 물이 빠졌다고 말한다.

sub|sidi|ary /səbsɪdieri, BRIT səbsɪdiəri/ (**subsidiaries**) **1** N-COUNT A **subsidiary** or a **subsidiary** company is a company which is part of a larger and more important company. [BUSINESS] ❑ *...British Asia Airways, a subsidiary of British Airways.* **2** ADJ If something is **subsidiary**, it is less important than something else with which it is connected. ❑ *The economics ministry has increasingly played a subsidiary role to the finance ministry.*

1 가산명사 자회사 [경제] ❑ 브리티시 항공의 자회사인 브리티시 아시아 항공 **2** 형용사 보조의, 종속적인 ❑ 경제부는 점점 더 재무부에 종속적인 역할을 해 왔다.

a
b
c
d
e
f
g
h
i
j
k
l
m
n
o
p
q
r
s
t
u
v
w
x
y
z

sub|si|dize /sʌbsɪdaɪz/ (**subsidizes, subsidizing, subsidized**) [BRIT also **subsidise**] V-T If a government or other authority **subsidizes** something, they pay part of the cost of it. ❑ *Around the world, governments have subsidized the housing of middle and upper-income groups.* ● **sub|si|dized** ADJ ❑ *...heavily subsidized prices for housing, bread, and meat.*

[영국영어 subsidise] 타동사 보조금을 주다 ❑ 세계 각국에서, 정부가 중산층 및 고소득층의 주택 공급에 보조금을 지원해 왔다. ● 보조금을 지원받는 형용사 ❑ 많은 보조금을 지원받는 주택 가격과 빵, 고기 가격

sub|si|dy ♦◇◇ /sʌbsɪdi/ (**subsidies**) N-COUNT A **subsidy** is money that is paid by a government or other authority in order to help an industry or business, or to pay for a public service. ❑ *European farmers are planning a massive demonstration against farm subsidy cuts.*

가산명사 보조금 ❑ 유럽 농부들은 농업 보조금 삭감에 반대하는 대규모 시위를 계획하고 있다.

sub|sist|ence /səbsɪstəns/ **1** N-UNCOUNT **Subsistence** is the condition of just having enough food or money to stay alive. ❑ *...below the subsistence level.* **2** ADJ In **subsistence** farming or **subsistence** agriculture, farmers produce food to eat themselves rather than to sell. [ADJ n] ❑ *Many black Namibians are subsistence farmers who live in the arid borderlands.*

1 불가산명사 최저 생활, 호구지책 ❑ 최저 생활수준 이하 **2** 형용사 자급적 ❑ 다수의 나미비아 흑인들은 국경 지대의 불모지에서 사는 자급 농업인들이다.

sub|stance ♦◇◇ /sʌbstəns/ (**substances**) **1** N-COUNT A **substance** is a solid, powder, liquid, or gas with particular properties. ❑ *There's absolutely no regulation of cigarettes to make sure that they don't include poisonous substances.* **2** N-UNCOUNT **Substance** is the quality of being important or significant. [FORMAL] ❑ *It's questionable whether anything of substance has been achieved.* **3** N-SING The **substance of** what someone says or writes is the main thing that they are trying to say. ❑ *The substance of his discussions doesn't really matter.* **4** N-UNCOUNT If you say that something has no **substance**, you mean that it is not true. [FORMAL] ❑ *There is no substance in any of these allegations.*

1 가산명사 물질 ❑ 담배에 독성 물질이 없어야 한다는 것을 분명히 명시한 규제가 전혀 없다. **2** 불가산명사 본질 [격식체] ❑ 뭔든 본질적인 것을 이루어 냈는지가 의심스럽다. **3** 단수명사 취지 ❑ 그의 토론의 취지는 정말이지 문제가 되지 않는다. **4** 불가산명사 실체 ❑ 이런 근거 없는 주장들은 전혀 실체가 없다.

Word Partnership　　substance의 연어

ADJ.	**natural** substance **1**
N.	**lack of** substance **2** **4**

---

sub|stan|tial ♦◇◇ /səbstænʃəl/ ADJ **Substantial** means large in amount or degree. [FORMAL] ❑ *A substantial number of mothers with young children are deterred from undertaking paid work because they lack access to childcare.* →see **important**

형용사 상당한 [격식체] ❑ 어린 아이들이 있는 상당수의 어머니들은 탁아 시설을 구하기 어렵기 때문에 보수를 받는 직장을 갖지 못한다.

Word Partnership　　substantial의 연어

ADV.	**fairly** substantial, **very** substantial
N.	substantial **amount**, substantial **changes**, substantial **difference**, substantial **evidence**, substantial **improvement**, substantial **increase**, substantial **loss**, substantial **number**, substantial **part**, substantial **progress**, substantial **savings**, substantial **support**

---

sub|stan|tial|ly /səbstænʃəli/ ADV If something changes **substantially** or is **substantially** different, it changes a lot or is very different. [FORMAL] ❑ *The percentage of girls in engineering has increased substantially.*

부사 상당히 [격식체] ❑ 공학 계열에서 여학생들이 차지하는 비율이 상당히 증가했다.

sub|stan|ti|ate /səbstænʃieɪt/ (**substantiates, substantiating, substantiated**) V-T To **substantiate** a statement or a story means to supply evidence which proves that it is true. [FORMAL] ❑ *There is little scientific evidence to substantiate the claims.*

타동사 입증하다 [격식체] ❑ 그 주장을 입증할 만한 과학적인 증거가 거의 없다.

sub|stan|tive /sʌbstəntɪv/ ADJ **Substantive** negotiations or issues deal with the most important and central aspects of a subject. [FORMAL] ❑ *They plan to meet again in Rome very soon to begin substantive negotiations.*

형용사 실질적인 [격식체] ❑ 그들은 실질적인 협상을 시작하기 위해서 로마에서 곧 다시 만날 계획이다.

sub|sti|tute ♦◇◇ /sʌbstɪtut, BRIT sʌbstɪtyu:t/ (**substitutes, substituting, substituted**) **1** V-T/V-I If you **substitute** one thing **for** another, or if one thing **substitutes for** another, it takes the place or performs the function of the other thing. ❑ *They were substituting violence for dialogue.* ❑ *He was substituting for the injured William Wales.* ● **sub|sti|tu|tion** /sʌbstɪtuʃn, BRIT sʌbstɪtyu:ʃn/ (**substitutions**) N-VAR ❑ *In my experience a straight substitution of carob for chocolate doesn't work* **2** N-COUNT A **substitute** is something that you have or use instead of something else. ❑ *She is seeking a substitute for the very man whose departure made her cry.* **3** N-COUNT If you say that one thing is no **substitute for** another, you mean that it does not have certain desirable features that the other thing has, and is therefore unsatisfactory. If you say that there is no **substitute for** something, you mean that it is the only thing which is really satisfactory. ❑ *The printed word is no substitute for personal discussion with a great thinker.* **4** N-COUNT In team games such as football, a **substitute** is a player who is brought into a game to replace another player. ❑ *Jeremies entered as a substitute in the 60th minute.*

1 타동사/자동사 대치하다; 대치되다, 대신하다 ❑ 그들은 대화 대신에 폭력을 쓰고 있었다. ❑ 그는 부상당한 윌리엄 웨일스를 대신하고 있었다. ● 대응: 대치 가산명사 또는 불가산명사 ❑ 내 경험으로 볼 때, 초콜릿 대신 구주콩나무를 바로 대신 쓰는 것은 효과가 없다. **2** 가산명사 대신하는 것 ❑ 그녀는 자신을 울게 하고 떠나 버린 바로 그 남자를 대신할 사람을 찾고 있다. **3** 가산명사 -을 대신할 수 있는 것 ❑ 인쇄되어 나온 활자는 위대한 사상가와 직접 토론하는 것을 대신할 만한 게 못 된다. **4** 가산명사 교체 선수 ❑ 제레미스는 경기 시작 60분 후에 교체 선수로 투입됐다.

Word Partnership　　substitute의 연어

ADJ.	**good** substitute **2**
	temporary substitute **2** **4**
V.	**use** *someone/something* **as a** substitute **2** **4**

---

sub|sti|tute teach|er (**substitute teachers**) N-COUNT A **substitute teacher** is a teacher whose job is to take the place of other teachers at different schools when they are unable to be there. [AM; BRIT **supply teacher**]

가산명사 대리 교사 [미국영어; 영국영어 supply teacher]

sub|ter|ra|nean /sʌbtəreɪniən/ ADJ A **subterranean** river or tunnel is under the ground. [FORMAL] ❑ *London has 9 miles of such subterranean passages.*

형용사 지하의 [격식체] ❑ 런던에는 그런 지하 통로 길이가 9마일에 이른다.

sub|ti|tle /sʌbtaɪtl/ (**subtitles**) **1** N-COUNT The **subtitle** of a piece of writing is a second title which is often longer and explains more than the main title.

1 가산명사 부제 ❑ '캐틀린'은 1892년 부제가 말해 주듯이, '아일랜드 드라마'이다. **2** 복수명사 (영화)

❶ "Kathleen" was, as its 1892 subtitle asserted, "An Irish Drama." ❷ N-PLURAL **Subtitles** are a printed translation of the words of a foreign film that are shown at the bottom of the picture. ❑ *The dialogue is in Spanish, with English subtitles.*

자막 ❑ 그 대사는 스페인 어로 되어 있고 영어 자막이 붙는다.

sub|ti|tled /sʌbtaɪt³ld/ ❶ V-T PASSIVE If you say how a book or play **is subtitled**, you say what its subtitle is. ❑ *"Lorna Doone" is subtitled "a Romance of Exmoor."* ❷ ADJ If a foreign film is **subtitled**, a printed translation of the words is shown at the bottom of the picture. ❑ *Much of the film is subtitled.*

❶ 수동 타동사 부제가 붙다 ❑ '로나 둔'은 '엑스무어의 연애담'이라는 부제가 붙어 있다. ❷ 형용사 자막이 있는 ❑ 그 영화의 많은 부분에 자막이 나온다.

sub|tle /sʌt³l/ (**subtler**, **subtlest**) ❶ ADJ Something that is **subtle** is not immediately obvious or noticeable. ❑ *...the slow and subtle changes that take place in all living things.* ● **sub|tly** ADV ❑ *The truth is subtly different.* ❷ ADJ A **subtle** person cleverly uses indirect methods to achieve something. ❑ *I even began to exploit him in subtle ways.* ● **sub|tly** ADV [ADV with v] ❑ *Nathan is subtly trying to turn her against Barry.* ❸ ADJ **Subtle** smells, tastes, sounds, or colors are pleasantly complex and delicate. ❑ *...subtle shades of brown.* ● **sub|tly** ADV ❑ *...a white sofa teamed with subtly colored rugs.*

❶ 형용사 미묘한 ❑ 모든 생명체에게 일어나는 더디고도 미묘한 변화들 ● 미묘하게, 아주 약간 부사 ❑ 진실은 아주 약간 다르다. ❷ 형용사 교묘한 ❑ 나는 심지어 그를 교묘한 방법으로 이용하기 시작했다. ● 교묘하게 부사 ❑ 네이던은 그녀가 배리에게서 마음을 돌리게 만들기 위해서 교묘하게 수를 쓰고 있다. ❸ 형용사 미묘한(微妙한), 오묘한 ❑ 오묘한 갈색의 색조 ● 미묘하게, 오묘하게 부사 ❑ 오묘한 색깔의 양탄자와 짝을 이루는 흰색 소파

sub|tle|ty /sʌt³lti/ (**subtleties**) ❶ N-COUNT **Subtleties** are very small details or differences which are not obvious. ❑ *His fascination with the subtleties of human behavior makes him a good storyteller.* ❷ N-UNCOUNT **Subtlety** is the quality of being not immediately obvious or noticeable, and therefore difficult to describe. ❑ *African dance is vigorous, but full of subtlety, requiring great strength and control.* ❸ N-UNCOUNT **Subtlety** is the ability to notice and recognize things which are not obvious, especially small differences between things. ❑ *She analyzes herself with great subtlety.* ❹ N-UNCOUNT **Subtlety** is the ability to use indirect methods to achieve something, rather than doing something that is obvious. ❑ *They had obviously been hoping to approach the topic with more subtlety.*

❶ 가산명사 미묘한 차이 ❑ 인간 행동의 미묘한 차이에 대한 큰 관심이 그를 훌륭한 작가로 만든다. ❷ 불가산명사 미묘함 ❑ 아프리카 민속춤은 힘과 제어력이 필요한 열정적인 춤이지만, 또한 아주 미묘하다. ❸ 불가산명사 (관찰력이) 예민함, 예리함 ❑ 그녀는 자신을 대단히 예리하게 분석한다. ❹ 불가산명사 교묘함 ❑ 그들은 분명히 그 주제에 좀 더 교묘하게 접근하기를 바라고 있었다.

sub|to|tal /sʌbtoʊt³l/ (**subtotals**) also **sub-total** N-COUNT A **subtotal** is a figure that is the result of adding some numbers together but is not the final total. ❑ *...the subtotals for each category of investments.*

가산명사 소계 ❑ 각 분야 투자액의 소계

Word Link   tract ≈ dragging, drawing : con**tract**, sub**tract**, **tract**or

sub|tract /səbtrækt/ (**subtracts**, **subtracting**, **subtracted**) V-T If you **subtract** one number **from** another, you do a calculation in which you take it away from the other number. For example, if you subtract 3 from 5, you get 2. ❑ *Mandy subtracted the date of birth from the date of death.* ● **sub|trac|tion** /səbtrækʃ³n/ (**subtractions**) N-VAR ❑ *She's ready to learn simple addition and subtraction.*

타동사 빼다 ❑ 맨디는 사망일에서 출생일을 뺐다. ● 빼기 가산명사 또는 불가산명사 ❑ 그녀는 간단한 더하기와 빼기를 배울 때가 되었다.

sub|urb /sʌbɜrb/ (**suburbs**) ❶ N-COUNT A **suburb** of a city or large town is a smaller area which is part of the city or large town but is outside its center. ❑ *Anna was born in 1923 in Ardwick, a suburb of Manchester.* ❷ N-PLURAL If you live **in the suburbs**, you live in an area of houses outside the center of a city or large town. ❑ *His family lived in the suburbs.* →see **city**, **transportation**

❶ 가산명사 근교 ❑ 애너는 1923년 맨체스터 근교 아드윅에서 태어났다. ❷ 복수명사 교외 ❑ 그의 가족은 교외에서 살았다.

sub|ur|ban /səbɜrbən/ ADJ **Suburban** means relating to a suburb. [ADJ n] ❑ *...a comfortable suburban home.*

형용사 교외의 ❑ 교외에 있는 안락한 집

sub|ur|bia /səbɜrbiə/ N-UNCOUNT Journalists often use **suburbia** to refer to the suburbs of cities and large towns considered as a whole. ❑ *...images of bright summer mornings in leafy suburbia.*

불가산명사 (전체적인) 교외 ❑ 나무가 우거진 교외의 눈부신 여름 아침 이미지

Word Link   vers ≈ turning : sub**vers**ion, **vers**atile, **vers**ion

sub|ver|sion /səbvɜrʒ³n, BRIT səbvɜːʃ³n/ N-UNCOUNT **Subversion** is the attempt to weaken or destroy a political system or a government. ❑ *He was arrested in parliament on charges of subversion for organizing the demonstration.*

불가산명사 전복 ❑ 그는 시위를 조직하여 체제를 전복하려 한다는 혐의로 의회에서 체포되었다.

sub|ver|sive /səbvɜrsɪv/ (**subversives**) ❶ ADJ Something that is **subversive** is intended to weaken or destroy a political system or government. ❑ *The play was promptly banned as subversive and possibly treasonous.* ❷ N-COUNT **Subversives** are people who attempt to weaken or destroy a political system or government. ❑ *Agents regularly rounded up suspected subversives.*

❶ 형용사 전복시키는, 체제 전복적인 ❑ 그 연극은 체제 전복적이고 반역적인 데가 있다는 이유로 즉각 상영 금지되었다. ❷ 가산명사 불순분자 ❑ 정보부 요원들이 정기적으로 불순분자 혐의자들을 색출했다.

Word Link   verg, vert ≈ turning : con**verg**e, di**verg**e, sub**vert**

sub|vert /səbvɜrt/ (**subverts**, **subverting**, **subverted**) V-T To **subvert** something means to destroy its power and influence. [FORMAL] ❑ *...an alleged plot to subvert the state.*

타동사 전복시키다 [격식체] ❑ 국가 전복을 의도하는 것으로 추정되는 음모

sub|way /sʌbweɪ/ (**subways**) ❶ N-COUNT A **subway** is an underground railroad. [mainly AM; BRIT **underground, tube**] [oft N n, also by N] ❑ *I don't ride the subway late at night.* ❷ N-COUNT A **subway** is a passage underneath a busy road or a railroad track for people to walk through. [BRIT; AM **underpass**] ❑ *The majority of us feel worried if we walk through a subway.* →see **transportation**

❶ 가산명사 지하철 [주로 미국영어; 영국영어 underground, tube] ❑ 나는 밤늦게 지하철을 타지 않는다. ❷ 가산명사 지하보도 [영국영어; 미국영어 underpass] ❑ 우리들 대다수는 지하보도를 걸어갈 경우 두려움을 느낀다.

suc|ceed ♦♦◇ /səksid/ (**succeeds**, **succeeding**, **succeeded**) ❶ V-I If you **succeed** in doing something, you manage to do it. ❑ *We have already succeeded in working out ground rules with the Department of Defense.* ❷ V-I If something **succeeds**, it works in a satisfactory way or has the result that is intended. ❑ *The talks can succeed if both sides are flexible and serious.* ❸ V-I Someone who **succeeds** gains a high position in what they do, for example in business or politics. ❑ *...the skills and qualities needed to succeed in small and medium-sized businesses.* ❹ V-T/V-I If you **succeed** another person, you are the next person to have their job or position. ❑ *David Rowland is almost certain to succeed him as chairman on January 1.* ❺ V-T If one thing **is succeeded by** another thing, the other thing happens or

❶ 자동사 ~을 해내다 ❑ 우리는 이미 국방부와 기본 원칙을 도출해 냈다. ❷ 자동사 성과를 거두다 ❑ 그 회담은 양국이 모두 융통성 있고 진지하게 임한다면 성과를 거둘 수 있다. ❸ 자동사 성공하다 ❑ 중소 기업체에서 성공하기 위해 필요한 기술과 자질 ❹ 타동사/자동사 승계하다 ❑ 데이비드 로우랜드가 1월 1일 자로 그를 이어 의장직을 승계할 것이 거의 확실하다. ❺ 타동사 이어지다 ❑ 그 발표 뒤에 원탁회의가 이어졌다.

comes after it. [usu passive] ❑ *The presentation was succeeded by a roundtable discussion.*

Thesaurus   *succeed*의 참조어

> v.   accomplish, conquer, master; (ant.) fail **1**
>   displace, replace; (ant.) precede **4**

---

suc|cess ♦♦◊ /səksɛs/ (**successes**) **1** N-UNCOUNT **Success** is the achievement of something that you have been trying to do. ❑ *It's important for the long-term success of any diet that you vary your meals.* **2** N-UNCOUNT **Success** is the achievement of a high position in a particular field, for example in business or politics. ❑ *Nearly all of the young people interviewed believed that work was the key to success.* **3** N-UNCOUNT The **success** of something is the fact that it works in a satisfactory way or has the result that is intended. ❑ *Most of the cast was amazed by the play's success.* **4** N-COUNT Someone or something that is a **success** achieves a high position, makes a lot of money, or is admired a great deal. ❑ *We hope it will be a commercial success.*

Word Partnership   *success*의 연어

> N.   **success** of a business **1**
>   key to **success**, **success** or failure **1** **2**
>   chance for/of **success**, lack of **success**, measure of **success** **1**-**4**
> ADJ.   great **success**, huge **success**, recent **success**,
>   tremendous **success** **1**-**4**
>   academic **success**, commercial **success** **4**
> V.   achieve **success**, **success** depends on *something*,
>   enjoy **success** **1**-**4**

---

suc|cess|ful ♦♦◊ /səksɛsfəl/ ADJ Something that is **successful** achieves what it was intended to achieve. Someone who is **successful** achieves what they intended to achieve. ❑ *How successful will this new treatment be?* ❑ *I am looking forward to a long and successful partnership with him.* ● **suc|cess|ful|ly** ADV [ADV with v] ❑ *The doctors have successfully concluded preliminary tests.* **2** ADJ Something that is **successful** is popular or makes a lot of money. ❑ *...the hugely successful movie that brought Robert Redford an Oscar for his directing.* **3** ADJ Someone who is **successful** achieves a high position in what they do, for example in business or politics. ❑ *Women do not necessarily have to imitate men to be successful in business.*

suc|ces|sion /səksɛʃᵊn/ (**successions**) **1** N-SING A **succession** of things of the same kind is a number of them that exist or happen one after the other. [oft N of n, also in n] ❑ *Adams took a succession of jobs which have stood him in good stead.* **2** N-UNCOUNT **Succession** is the act or right of being the next person to have an important job or position. ❑ *She is now seventh in line of succession to the throne.*

suc|ces|sive /səksɛsɪv/ ADJ **Successive** means happening or existing one after another without a break. ❑ *Jackson was the winner for a second successive year.*

suc|ces|sor /səksɛsər/ (**successors**) N-COUNT Someone's **successor** is the person who takes their job after they have left. ❑ *He set out several principles that he hopes will guide his successors.*

suc|cinct /səksɪŋkt/ ADJ Something that is **succinct** expresses facts or ideas clearly and in few words. [APPROVAL] ❑ *The book gives an admirably succinct account of the technology and its history.* ● **suc|cinct|ly** ADV ❑ *He succinctly summed up his manifesto as "Work hard, train hard and play hard."*

suc|cu|lent /sʌkyələnt/ ADJ **Succulent** food, especially meat or vegetables, is juicy and good to eat. [APPROVAL] ❑ *Cook pieces of succulent chicken with ample garlic and a little sherry.*

suc|cumb /səkʌm/ (**succumbs**, **succumbing**, **succumbed**) V-I If you **succumb to** temptation or pressure, you do something that you want to do, or that other people want you to do, although you feel it might be wrong. [FORMAL] ❑ *Don't succumb to the temptation to have just one cigarette.*

such ♦♦♦ /sʌtʃ/

> When **such** is used as a predeterminer, it is followed by "a" and a count noun in the singular. When it is used as a determiner, it is followed by a count noun in the plural or by an uncount noun.

1 DET You use **such** to refer back to the thing or person that you have just mentioned, or a thing or person like the one that you have just mentioned. You use **such as** and **such...as** to introduce a reference to the person or thing that has just been mentioned. ❑ *There have been previous attempts at coups. We regard such methods as entirely unacceptable.* ● PREDET **Such** is also a predeterminer. [PREDET a n] ❑ *If your request is for information about a child, please contact the Registrar to find out how to make such a request.* ❑ *She has told us that when she goes back to stay with her family, they make her pay rent. We could not believe such a thing.* ● PRON **Such** is also used before be. ❑ *We are scared because we are being watched – such is the atmosphere in Pristina and other cities in Kosovo.* **2** DET You use **such...as** or **such as** to link something or someone with a clause in which you give a description of the kind of thing or person that you mean. ❑ *Britain is not enjoying such prosperity as it was in the mid-1980s.* ❑ *Children do not use inflections such as are used in mature adult speech.* **3** DET You use **such...as** or **such as** to introduce one or more examples of the kind of thing or person that you have just mentioned. ❑ *...such careers as teaching, nursing, hairdressing, and catering.* ❑ *...serious offenses, such as assault on a police officer.* **4** DET You use **such** before

---

1 불가산명사 성공, 성과 ❑ 다이어트의 장기적인 성공을 위해서는 음식 종류를 다양하게 하는 것이 중요하다. **2** 불가산명사 성공 ❑ 인터뷰에 응했던 거의 모든 젊은이들은 일이 성공의 열쇠라고 믿고 있었다. **3** 불가산명사 성공 ❑ 출연자들 대부분이 그 연극의 성공에 놀라워했다. **4** 가산명사 성공한 사람, 성공한 것 ❑ 우리는 그것이 상업적으로 성공하기를 희망한다.

1 형용사 성공적인, 성공한 ❑ 이 새로운 처치법이 얼마나 성공할까요? ❑ 나는 그와 장기적이고도 성공적인 동업 관계를 맺기를 기대하고 있다. ● 성공적으로 부사 ❑ 그 의사들은 예비 테스트를 성공적으로 끝냈다. **2** 형용사 성공한 ❑ 감독을 한 로버트 레드퍼드에게 오스카상을 안겨 준 엄청 성공한 영화 **3** 형용사 성공한 ❑ 사업에 성공하기 위해서 여성들이 남성들을 반드시 흉내낼 필요는 없다.

1 단수명사 연속, 잇따름 ❑ 애덤스는 자신에게 도움이 되었던 자리들을 잇따라 거쳤다. **2** 불가산명사 승계, 계승 ❑ 그녀는 이제 왕위 계승권 순위 7위이다.

형용사 연속적인 ❑ 잭슨은 2년 연속 우승자였다.

가산명사 후임자 ❑ 그는 자신의 후임자들에게 지침이 됐으면 싶은 원칙을 몇 가지 작성했다.

형용사 간단명료한 [마음에 듦] ❑ 그 책은 과학 기술과 그것의 역사에 대해 칭찬할 정도로 간단명료한 설명을 하고 있다. ● 간단명료하게 부사 ❑ 그는 자신의 선언문을 '열심히 일하고, 배우고, 놀아라'로 간단명료하게 요약했다.

형용사 즙이 많은 [마음에 듦] ❑ 육즙이 많은 닭고기 토막에 마늘을 듬뿍 넣고 셰리주를 약간 넣어서 조리하세요.

자동사 굴복하다 [격식체] ❑ 담배를 딱 한대만 하는 유혹에 넘어가지 마세요.

such는 전치 한정사로 쓸 때, 뒤에 'a'와 가산명사 단수가 온다. 한정사로 쓸 때에는, 뒤에 가산명사 복수 또는 불가산명사가 온다.

1 한정사 그런; -와 같은 ❑ 이전에도 여러 번 쿠데타 시도가 있었다. 우리는 그런 방식을 절대 용납할 수 없다고 생각한다. ● 전치 한정사 그런 ❑ 당신이 어떤 아이에 대한 정보를 요청하는 것이라면, 어떻게 그런 청구를 하는지 등기계에 가서 알아보세요. ❑ 그녀는 자신이 가족들에게 돌아가 같이 지내게 되면 임대료를 내야 한다고 우리에게 말했다. 우리는 그런 일을 믿을 수가 없었다. ● 대명사 그런 것 ❑ 우리는 늘 주시받고 있어서 무섭다. 그런 것이 프리스티나와 코소보에 있는 여러 도시들의 분위기이다. **2** 한정사 -와 같은; 그런 ❑ 영국은 1980년대 중반에 누렸던 그런 번영을 누리고 못하고 있다. ❑ 아이들은 어른들 사이에서 잘 쓰이는 그런 굴절형을 사용하지 않는다. **3** 한정사 -와 같은; 그런 ❑ 가르치고, 간호하고, 미용하고, 음식 조달하는 그런 직업들 ❑ 예를 들어 경찰관을 폭행하는 것과 같은 중대 범죄 **4** 한정사 그 정도의, 그런 [강조] ❑ 우리 대부분은 신문에 난 기사를 그 정도로 자세한 것까지는

noun groups to emphasize the extent of something or to emphasize that something is remarkable. [EMPHASIS] ❑ *I think most of us don't want to read what's in the newspaper anyway in such detail.* ❑ *One will never be able to understand why these political issues can acquire such force.* ● PREDET **Such** is also a predeterminer. [PREDET *a* n] ❑ *You know the health service is in such a state and it's getting desperate now.* ● PREDET You use **such...that** or **such that** in order to emphasize the degree of something by mentioning the result or consequence of it. [EMPHASIS] [PREDET *a* n that] ❑ *The weather has brought such a demand for beer that one brewery will operate over the weekend.* ❑ *This is something where you can earn such a lot of money that there is not any risk that you will lose it.* ❑ *Though Vivaldi had earned a great deal in his lifetime, his extravagance was such that he died in poverty.* 4 DET **Such** is also a determiner. ❑ *She looked at him in such distress that he had to look away.* 5 DET You use **such...that** or **such...as** in order to say what the result or consequence of something that you have just mentioned is. ❑ *The operation has uncovered such backstreet dealing in stolen property that police might now press for changes in the law.* ● PREDET **Such** is also a predeterminer. [PREDET *a* n that/*as* to] ❑ *He could put an idea in such a way that Alan would believe it was his own.* 6 PHRASE You use **such and such** to refer to a thing or person when you do not want to be exact or precise. [SPOKEN, VAGUENESS] ❑ *I said, "Well what time'll I get to Leeds?" and he said such and such a time but I missed my connection.* 7 PHRASE You use **as such** with a negative to indicate that a word or expression is not a very accurate description of the actual situation. ❑ *I am not a learner as such – I used to ride a bike years ago.* 8 PHRASE You use **as such** after a noun to indicate that you are considering that thing on its own, separately from other things or factors. ❑ *Mr. Simon said he was not against taxes as such, "but I do object when taxation is justified on spurious or dishonest grounds," he says.* 9 **no such thing** →see **thing**

Such is followed by **a** when the noun is something that can be counted. ❑ *...such a pleasant surprise.* It is not followed by **a** when the noun is plural or something that cannot be counted. ❑ *...such beautiful girls. ...such power.* You do not use **such** when you are talking about something that is present, or about the place where you are. You need to use the phrases **like that** or **like this**. For example, if you are admiring someone's watch, you do not say "I'd like such a watch." You say "**I'd like a watch like that.**" Similarly, you do not say about the place where you are living "There's not much to do in such a town." You say "**There's not much to do in a town like this.**" **Such** in other contexts is quite formal.

---

suck /sʌk/ (**sucks, sucking, sucked**) 1 V-T/V-I If you **suck** something, you hold it in your mouth and pull at it with the muscles in your cheeks and tongue, for example in order to get liquid out of it. ❑ *They waited in silence and sucked their sweets.* ❑ *He sucked on his cigarette.* 2 V-T If something **sucks** a liquid, gas, or object in a particular direction, it draws it there with a powerful force. ❑ *The pollution-control team is at the scene and is due to start sucking up oil any time now.* 3 V-T PASSIVE If you **are sucked into** a bad situation, you are unable to prevent yourself from becoming involved in it. ❑ *...the extent to which they have been sucked into the cycle of violence.*

sud|den ♦♢♢ /sʌdⁿn/ 1 ADJ **Sudden** means happening quickly and unexpectedly. ❑ *He had been deeply affected by the sudden death of his father-in-law.* ❑ *It was all very sudden.* ● **sud|den|ness** N-UNCOUNT ❑ *The enemy seemed stunned by the suddenness of the attack.* 2 PHRASE If something happens **all of a sudden**, it happens quickly and unexpectedly. ❑ *All of a sudden she didn't look sleepy any more.*

sud|den|ly ♦♦♢ /sʌdⁿnli/ ADV If something happens **suddenly**, it happens quickly and unexpectedly. ❑ *Suddenly, she looked ten years older.* ❑ *Her expression suddenly altered.*

sue /su/ (**sues, suing, sued**) V-T/V-I If you **sue**, or **sue** someone, you start a legal case against them, usually in order to claim money from them because they have harmed you in some way. ❑ *Mr. Warren sued him for libel over the remarks.* ❑ *The company could be sued for damages.*

suede /sweɪd/ N-UNCOUNT **Suede** is leather with a soft, slightly rough surface. ❑ *Albert wore a brown suede jacket and jeans.*

suf|fer ♦♦♢ /sʌfər/ (**suffers, suffering, suffered**) 1 V-T If you **suffer** pain, you feel it in your body or in your mind. ❑ *Within a few days she had become seriously ill, suffering great pain and discomfort.* 2 V-I If you **suffer from** an illness or from some other bad condition, you are badly affected by it. ❑ *He was eventually diagnosed as suffering from terminal cancer.* 3 V-T If you **suffer** something bad, you are in a situation in which something painful, harmful, or very unpleasant happens to you. ❑ *The peace process has suffered a serious blow now.* 4 V-I If you **suffer**, you are badly affected by an event or situation. ❑ *There are few who have not suffered.* 5 V-I If something **suffers**, it becomes worse because it has not been given enough attention or is in a bad situation. ❑ *I'm not surprised that your studies are suffering.*

suf|fer|ing /sʌfərɪŋ/ (**sufferings**) N-UNCOUNT **Suffering** is serious pain which someone feels in their body or their mind. [also N in pl] ❑ *They began to recover slowly from their nightmare of pain and suffering.* ❑ *It has caused terrible suffering to animals.* →see also **long-suffering**

suf|fice /səfaɪs/ (**suffices, sufficing, sufficed**) 1 V-I If you say that something will **suffice**, you mean it will be enough to achieve a purpose or to fulfill a need. [FORMAL] [no cont] ❑ *A cover letter should never exceed one page; often a far*

읽고 싶어 하지 않는다고 나는 생각한다. ❑ 왜 이런 정치적인 화제가 그 정도로 큰 힘을 얻을 수 있는지 누구도 결코 이해할 수 없을 것이다. ● 전치 한정사 그 정도의, 그런 ❑ 당신은 공공 의료가 그런 백주 회사는 점점 더 절망적으로 되어 가고 있다는 것을 당신은 알고 있다. ● 전치 한정사 너무나...해서 －하다 [강조] ❑ 날씨 때문에 맥주 수요가 너무 많아서 한 백주 회사는 주말에도 일을 할 것이다. ❑ 이 일은 당신이 돈을 너무나 많이 벌 수 있어서 손해날 위험이 전혀 없는 그런 일입니다. ❑ 비발디는 생전에 엄청난 돈을 벌었었지만, 낭비가 너무 심해서 가난 속에서 죽었다. ● 한정사 너무 심한 ❑ 그녀가 너무 괴로워하며 그를 쳐다봐서 그는 눈길을 피해야 했다. 5 한정사 ...해서 －하게 되다 ❑ 그 작전으로 그런 장물 암거래를 적발했으므로 경찰이 이제 법 개정을 재촉할지도 모른다. ● 전치 한정사 그런 ❑ 그는 앨런이 그 아이디어가 그의 것인 양 믿게 될 그런 정도로 아이디어를 작성했다. 6 구 이러저러한, 여차여차한 [구어체, 짐작투] ❑ "언제 리즈에 도착할까요?"라고 내가 물었을 때, 그가 이러저러한 시간이라고 말했지만 나는 바뀐 타야 할 기차를 놓쳤다. 7 구 싶은, 실제로는 ❑ 나는 실은 새로 배우는 사람이 아니에요. 수년 전에 자전거를 타곤 했거든요. 8 구 그 자체로 ❑ 사이먼 씨는 세금 그 자체에 대해서는 반대하지 않는다고 말했다. "하지만 세제가 신빙성이 없거나 부정직한 것을 근거로 정당화된다면 나는 분명히 반대한다."라고 그는 말한다.

---

such는 뒤에 셀 수 있는 명사가 오면 such 다음에 a를 쓴다. ❑ ...그렇게 즐거운 놀라움. 명사가 복수이거나 셀 수 없으면 such 다음에 a를 쓰지 않는다. ❑ 그렇게 아름다운 소녀들....그런 힘. 현재 있는 것이나 현재 있는 장소를 말할 때에는 such를 쓰지 않고 like that이나 like this와 같은 구를 써야 한다. 예를 들면, 어떤 사람의 시계에 감탄을 하면, 'I'd like such a watch.'라고 하지 않고 'I'd like a watch like that.'이라고 말한다. 이와 비슷하게, 지금 살고 있는 마을에 대해 'There's not much to do in such a town.'라고 하지 않고 'There's not much to do in a town like this.'라고 말한다. 다른 문맥에서 such는 상당히 격식체이다.

---

1 타동사/자동사 빨다 ❑ 그들은 말없이 기다리며 사탕을 빨아 먹고 있었다. ❑ 그는 담배를 빨아들였다. 2 타동사 빨아들이다 ❑ 오염 처리반이 현장에 도착해서 지금부터 당장 기름을 빨아들이는 작업을 시작할 예정이다. 3 수동 타동사 (나쁜 상황으로) 휩쓸려 들어가다 ❑ 그들이 반복되는 폭력 사태로 휩쓸려 들어갔던 정도

1 형용사 갑작스러운 ❑ 그는 장인의 갑작스러운 죽음으로 깊이 상심했었다. ❑ 그것은 너무 갑작스러운 일이었다. ● 갑작스러움 불가산명사 ❑ 적군은 갑작스러운 공격에 아연실색하는 것 같았다. 2 구 갑자기 ❑ 갑자기 그녀는 더 이상 졸린 것 같지 않았다.

부사 갑자기 ❑ 갑자기 그녀는 10년은 더 늙어 보였다. ❑ 그녀의 표정이 갑자기 변했다.

타동사/자동사 고소하다, 소송을 제기하다 ❑ 워렌 씨는 그 논평에 대해 명예 훼손죄로 그를 고소했다. ❑ 그 회사는 손해 배상 청구 소송을 당할 수도 있다.

불가산명사 스웨이드 천 ❑ 앨버트는 갈색 스웨이드 재킷과 면바지를 입고 있었다.

1 타동사 (통증을) 느끼다, (고통을) 겪다 ❑ 며칠 지나지 않아 그녀는 크게 병이 나서 몹시 아파하고 힘들어했다. 2 자동사 (병을) 앓다 ❑ 그는 마침내 말기 암을 앓고 있다는 진단을 받았다. 3 타동사 (좋지 않은 일을) 겪다 ❑ 평화 추진 절차가 현재 심각한 타격을 받고 있다. 4 자동사 고통 받다 ❑ 고통 받지 않은 사람은 거의 없다. 5 자동사 나빠지다 ❑ 나는 네 학업 성적이 나빠지고 있다는 것이 전혀 놀랍지 않다.

불가산명사 고통 ❑ 그들은 통증과 고통의 악몽에서 서서히 회복되기 시작했다. ❑ 그것은 동물들에게 심각한 통증을 야기했다.

1 자동사 충분하다 [격식체] ❑ 자기소개서는 절대로 한 페이지를 넘으면 안 된다. 흔히 훨씬 더 짧은 소개서도 충분할 것이다. 2 구 －정도로만 말하겠다

shorter letter will suffice. ② PHRASE **Suffice it to say** or **suffice to say** is used at the beginning of a statement to indicate that what you are saying is obvious, or that you will only give a short explanation. ☐ *Suffice it to say that afterwards we never met again.*

☐ 우리 앞으로는 절대 다시 만나는 일이 없을 것이라는 정도로만 말하겠다.

suf|fi|cient ◆◇◇ /səfɪʃ⁰nt/ ADJ If something is **sufficient for** a particular purpose, there is enough of it for the purpose. ☐ *One meter of fabric is sufficient to cover the exterior of an 18-in.-diameter hatbox.* ☐ *Lighting levels should be sufficient for photography without flash.* ● **suf|fi|cient|ly** ADV ☐ *She recovered sufficiently to accompany Chou on his tour of Africa in 1964.*

형용사 충분한 ☐ 직경이 18인치인 모자 상자를 씌우는 데는 1미터짜리 천이면 충분하다. ☐ 플래시 없이 사진을 찍을 수 있을 정도로 조명도가 충분해야 한다. ● 충분하게 부사 ☐ 그녀는 1964년 아프리카 여행에 초우와 동행할 수 있을 정도로 충분히 회복되었다.

Word Link   *fix ≈ fastening : fixture, prefix, suffix*

suf|fix /sʌfɪks/ (suffixes) N-COUNT A **suffix** is a letter or group of letters, for example "-ly" or "-ness", which is added to the end of a word in order to form a different word, often of a different word class. For example, the suffix "-ly" is added to "quick" to form "quickly." Compare **affix** and **prefix**.

가산명사 접미사

suf|fo|cate /sʌfəkeɪt/ (suffocates, suffocating, suffocated) ① V-T/V-I If someone **suffocates** or **is suffocated**, they die because there is no air for them to breathe. ☐ *He either suffocated, or froze to death.* ● **suf|fo|ca|tion** /sʌfəkeɪʃ⁰n/ N-UNCOUNT ☐ *Many of the victims died of suffocation.* ② V-T/V-I If you say that you **are suffocating** or that something **is suffocating** you, you mean that you feel very uncomfortable because there is not enough fresh air and it is difficult to breathe. ☐ *That's better. I was suffocating in that cell of a room.*

① 타동사/자동사 질식사하다; 질식사하게 하다 ☐ 그는 질식사했거나 동사했다. ● 질식 불가산명사 ☐ 많은 희생자들이 질식사했다. ② 타동사/자동사 질식하다, 숨막히다; 질식시키다, 숨막히게 하다 ☐ 좀 낫다. 그 감방 같은 방에 있으니 질식할 것 같았다.

sug|ar ◆◇◇ /ʃʊgər/ (sugars) ① N-UNCOUNT **Sugar** is a sweet substance that is used to make food and drinks sweet. It is usually in the form of small white or brown crystals. ☐ *...bags of sugar.* ② N-COUNT If someone has one **sugar** in their tea or coffee, they have one small spoon of sugar or one sugar lump in it. ☐ *How many sugars do you take?* ③ N-COUNT **Sugars** are substances that occur naturally in food. When you eat them, the body converts them into energy. ☐ *Plants produce sugars and starch to provide themselves with energy.* ④ to **sugar the pill** →see **pill**
→see **fruit**
→see Word Web: **sugar**

① 불가산명사 설탕 ☐ 설탕 부대 ② 가산명사 설탕 ☐ 설탕 몇 숟가락 넣을까요? ③ 가산명사 당분 ☐ 식물은 스스로 에너지를 공급하기 위해서 당분과 전분을 생산한다.

sug|gest ◆◆◆ /səgdʒest, BRIT sədʒest/ (suggests, suggesting, suggested) ① V-T If you **suggest** something, you put forward a plan or idea for someone to think about. ☐ *He suggested a link between class size and test results of seven-year-olds.* ☐ *I suggest you ask him some specific questions about his past.* ☐ *No one has suggested how this might occur.* ② V-T If you **suggest** the name of a person or place, you recommend it to someone. ☐ *Could you suggest someone to advise me how to do this?* ③ V-T If you **suggest that** something is the case, you say something which you believe is the case. ☐ *I'm not suggesting that this is what is happening.* ☐ *It is wrong to suggest that there are easy alternatives.* ④ V-T If one thing **suggests** another, it implies it or makes you think that it might be the case. ☐ *Earlier reports suggested that a meeting would take place on Sunday.*

① 타동사 제안하다, 제기하다 ☐ 그는 일곱 살짜리 학생들의 학급 규모와 시험 성적 사이의 연관성을 제기했다. ☐ 나는 네가 그의 과거에 대해 세부적인 질문 몇 가지를 했으면 하고 생각한다. ☐ 아무도 어떻게 이런 일이 발생할 수 있었는지에 대해 말을 꺼내지 않았다. ② 타동사 추천하다 ☐ 내게 이것을 하는 방법에 대해 조언해 줄 사람을 추천해 주시겠습니까? ③ 타동사 ...라고 말하다 ☐ 내가 현재의 사태가 그렇다고 말하는 것은 아니다. ④ 타동사 시사하다, 암시하다 ☐ 지난번 보도들은 회담이 일요일에 이루어질 것임을 암시했다.

Note that **suggest** cannot usually be followed directly by a noun or pronoun referring to a person; you generally have to put the preposition **to** in front of it. You do not "suggest someone something," you "**suggest** something **to** someone." ☐ *John Caskey first suggested this idea to me.* Nor do you "suggest someone to do something." You "**suggest that** someone **do** something." ☐ *Beatrice suggested that he spend the summer at their place.* Do not confuse **suggest** and **advise**. If you **suggest** something, you mention it as an idea or plan for someone to think about. If you **advise** someone to do something, you tell them what you think they should do. ☐ *I advised him to leave as soon as possible.*

suggest는 대개 명사나 사람을 지칭하는 대명사가 바로 뒤에 올 수 없고, 대개 그 앞에 전치사 to를 써야 함을 유념하시오. 즉, 'suggest someone something'이라고 하지 않고 'suggest something to someone.'이라고 한다. ☐ 존 캐스키가 먼저 이런 생각을 내게 제안했다. 그리고 'suggest someone to do something'이라고도 하지 않고 'suggest that someone do something'이라고 한다. ☐ 비에트리스는 그들의 집에서 여름을 보내겠다고 제안했다. suggest와 advise를 혼동하지 마시오. 당신이 무엇을 suggest하면, 당신은 그것을 다른 사람이 하나의 아이디어나 계획으로 생각해 보도록 언급하는 것이다. 당신이 누구에게 무엇을 하도록 advise하면, 당신은 생각하기에 그 사람이 무엇을 해야 한다고 말하는 것이다. ☐ 나는 그에게 가능하면 빨리 떠나라고 조언했다.

Word Partnership   *suggest의 연어*

N.   **analysts** suggest, **experts** suggest, **researchers** suggest ①-③
       data suggest, **findings** suggest, **results** suggest, **studies** suggest, **surveys** suggest ④

sug|ges|tion ◆◇◇ /səgdʒestʃ⁰n, BRIT sədʒestʃⁿ/ (suggestions) ① N-COUNT If you make a **suggestion**, you put forward an idea or plan for someone to think about. ☐ *The dietitian was helpful, making suggestions as to how I could improve my diet.* ☐ *Perhaps he'd followed her suggestion of a stroll to the river.* ② N-COUNT A **suggestion** is something that a person says which implies that something is the case.

① 가산명사 제안, 제의 ☐ 내 식생활 개선법에 대해 여러 가지 제안을 해 준 그 영양사가 도움이 되었다. ☐ 아마도 그는 강가지 거닐어 보라는 그녀의 제의를 따랐던 것 같았다. ② 가산명사 제안, 제의 ☐ 우리는 그 법을 수정해야 한다는 어떤 제의도 기각한다.

Word Web   sugar

Sugar cane was discovered in prehistoric New Guinea*. As people migrated across the Pacific Islands and into India and China, they brought sugar cane with them. At first, people just chewed on the cane. They liked the **sweet taste**. When sugar cane reached the Middle East, people discovered how to **refine** it into **crystals**. **Brown sugar** is created by stopping the refining process earlier. This leaves some of the molasses syrup in the sugar. Today two-fifths of sugar comes from **beets**. Refined sugar is used in many **foods** and **beverages**. The overuse of sugar can cause many problems, such as obesity and **diabetes**.

New Guinea: a large island in the southern Pacific Ocean.

❑ *We reject any suggestion that the law needs amending.* ❸ N-SING If there is no **suggestion that** something is the case, there is no reason to think that it is the case. ❑ *There is no suggestion whatsoever that the two sides are any closer to agreeing.*

❸ 단수명사 암시, 기미 ❑ 양측이 합의에 좀 더 가까워지고 있다는 기미가 조금도 없다.

Word Partnership   suggestion의 연어

| v. | **follow** a suggestion, **make** a suggestion ❶ |
| | **reject** a suggestion ❶ ❷ |

---

sug|ges|tive /səgdʒɛstɪv, BRIT sədʒɛstɪv/ ❶ ADJ Something that is **suggestive of** something else is quite like it or may be a sign of it. [v-link ADJ of n] ❑ *The fingers were gnarled, lumpy, with long, curving nails suggestive of animal claws.* ❷ ADJ **Suggestive** remarks or looks cause people to think about sex, often in a way that makes them feel uncomfortable. ❑ *…another former employee who claims Thomas made suggestive remarks to her.*

❶ 형용사 _을 시사하는, 꼭 – 같은 ❑ 그 손가락들은 우툴두툴 굳은살이 박이고 손톱은 길고 짐승의 발톱같이 굽어 있었다. ❷ 형용사 도발적인 ❑ 토머스가 자기에게 도발적인 말을 건넸다고 주장하는 또 한 명의 이전 여직원

sui|cid|al /suɪsaɪdəl/ ADJ People who are **suicidal** want to kill themselves. ❑ *I was suicidal and just couldn't stop crying.*

형용사 자살의, 자살 충동을 느끼는 ❑ 나는 죽고 싶기만 했고 그저 울음을 멈출 수가 없었다.

sui|cide ♦♢♢ /suɪsaɪd/ (**suicides**) N-VAR People who commit **suicide** deliberately kill themselves because they do not want to continue living. ❑ *She tried to commit suicide on several occasions.* ❑ *…a case of attempted suicide.*

가산명사 또는 불가산명사 자살 ❑ 그녀는 여러 번 자살을 시도했다. ❑ 자살 미수 사건

Word Partnership   suicide의 연어

| v. | **attempt** suicide, **commit** suicide |
| N. | suicide **bomber**, suicide **rate**, **risk of** suicide |

---

suit ♦♦♢ /sut/ (**suits, suiting, suited**) ❶ N-COUNT A man's **suit** consists of a jacket, pants, and sometimes a vest, all made from the same fabric. ❑ *…a dark pin-striped business suit.* ❷ N-COUNT A woman's **suit** consists of a jacket and skirt, or sometimes pants, made from the same fabric. ❑ *I was wearing my tweed suit.* ❸ N-COUNT A particular type of **suit** is a piece of clothing that you wear for a particular activity. ❑ *The six survivors only lived through their North Sea ordeal because of the special rubber suits they were wearing.* ❹ V-T If something **suits** you, it is convenient for you or is the best thing for you in the circumstances. [no cont] ❑ *They will only release information if it suits them.* ❺ V-T If something **suits** you, you like it. [no cont] ❑ *I don't think a sedentary life would altogether suit me.* ❻ V-T If a piece of clothing or a particular style or color **suits** you, it makes you look attractive. [no cont] ❑ *Green suits you.*

❶ 가산명사 (남성용) 정장 ❑ 가는 세로줄무늬의 검정 신사복 ❷ 가산명사 (여성용) 정장 ❑ 나는 트위드 정장을 입고 있었다. ❸ 가산명사 (특정 목적을 위한) 옷 한 벌 ❑ 여섯 명의 생존자들은 특수 고무복을 입고 있었기 때문에 북해에서의 시련을 이겨 내고 살아남았다. ❹ 타동사 편리하다, 맞다 ❑ 그들은 자신들에게 편리할 때만 정보를 유출시킬 것이다. ❺ 타동사 만족시키다 ❑ 나는 정적인 생활이 내게 전적으로 만족스러울 것이라고 생각하지 않는다. ❻ 타동사 _에게 어울리다 ❑ 녹색이 네게 어울린다.

❼ V-T If you **suit yourself**, you do something just because you want to do it, without bothering to consider other people. ❑ *The British have tended to suit themselves, not paying much heed to the reformers.* ❽ N-COUNT In a court of law, a **suit** is a case in which someone tries to get a legal decision against a person or company, often so that the person or company will have to pay them money for having done something wrong to them. ❑ *Up to 2,000 former employees have filed personal injury suits against the company.* ● N-UNCOUNT In American English, you can say that someone **files** or **brings suit against** another person. ❑ *One insurance company has already filed suit against the city of Chicago.* ❾ →see also **pant suit** ❿ PHRASE If people **follow suit**, they do the same thing that someone else has just done. ❑ *Efforts to persuade the remainder to follow suit have continued.* →see **clothing**

❼ 타동사 좋을 대로 하다 ❑ 영국인들은 개혁가들을 별로 의식하지 않고 자신들이 좋을 대로 해 온 경향이 있다. ❽ 가산명사 소송 ❑ 2천 명에 가까운 전 종업원들이 그 회사를 상대로 개인 상해 소송을 제기했다. ● 불가산명사 소송 ❑ 한 보험 회사가 시카고 시를 상대로 이미 소송을 제기했다. ❿ 구 남이 하는 대로 따라 하다 ❑ 그 나머지 사람들에게 다른 사람이 하는 대로 따라 하도록 설득하려는 노력이 계속되고 있다.

You do not use the verb **suit** if clothes are simply not the right size for you. The verb you need is **fit**. ❑ *The size 12 gown was gorgeous and fit perfectly… The gloves didn't fit.* You can say that something **suits** a person or place if it looks attractive on that person or in that place. ❑ *It is really feminine and pretty and it certainly suits you.* However, you cannot usually say that one color, pattern, or object **suits** another. The verb you need is **match**. ❑ *She wears a straw hat with a yellow ribbon to match her yellow cheesecloth dress… His clothes don't quite match.*

옷이 딱 맞지 않을 경우에는 동사 suit를 쓰지 않는다. 필요한 동사는 fit이다. ❑ 사이즈 12인 가운이 멋졌고 아주 잘 맞았다… 장갑이 맞지 않았다. 무엇이 어떤 사람이나 어떤 장소에 suit한다고 말할 수 있다. ❑ 그게 정말 여성스럽고 예쁘며 네게 확실히 잘 어울린다. 그러나, 대개 한가지 색, 문양, 사물이 다른 색, 문양, 사물에 suit한다고는 말할 수 없다. 여기에 필요한 동사는 match이다. ❑ 그녀는 노란색 무명 드레스에 어울리게 노란 리본이 달린 밀짚 모자를 쓰고 있다… 그 옷이 서로 잘 어울리지 않는다.

---

suit|able ♦♢♢ /sutəbəl/ ADJ Someone or something that is **suitable for** a particular purpose or occasion is right or acceptable for it. ❑ *Employers usually decide within five minutes whether someone is suitable for the job.* ● **suit|abil|ity** /sutəbɪlɪti/ N-UNCOUNT ❑ *…information on the suitability of a product for use in the home.*

형용사 적합한 ❑ 고용주들은 어떤 사람이 그 일에 적합한지를 보통 5분 내에 결정한다. ● 적합성 불가산명사 ❑ 어떤 상품이 가정용으로 적합한지에 관한 정보

Word Partnership   suitable의 연어

| v. | **find (a)** suitable *something*, **use (a)** suitable *something* |

---

suit|ably /sutəbli/ ADV You use **suitably** to indicate that someone or something has the right qualities or things for a particular activity, purpose, or situation. [ADV adj/-ed] ❑ *There are problems in recruiting suitably qualified scientific officers for NHS laboratories.*

부사 적합하게, 어울리게 ❑ 국민 건강 보험 실험실에서 일하기에 적절한 자격을 갖춘 관리자급 과학자들을 구하는 데 문제가 있다.

Word Link   cas = box, hold : case, encase, suitcase

---

suit|case /sutkeɪs/ (**suitcases**) N-COUNT A **suitcase** is a box or bag with a handle and a hard frame in which you carry your clothes when you are traveling. ❑ *It did not take Andrew long to pack a suitcase.*

가산명사 여행용 가방 ❑ 앤드류가 여행 가방을 싸는 데 오래 걸리지 않았다.

suite /swit/ (**suites**) ❶ N-COUNT A **suite** is a set of rooms in a hotel or other building. ❑ *They had a fabulous time during their week in a suite at the Paris Hilton.*

❶ 가산명사 스위트룸 ❑ 그들은 파리 힐튼 호텔 스위트룸에서 일주일을 멋지게 보냈다. ❷ 가산명사

→see also **en suite** ❷ N-COUNT A **suite** is a set of matching armchairs and a sofa. ❑ *...a three-piece suite.* ❸ N-COUNT A bathroom **suite** is a matching bathtub, sink, and toilet. ❑ *...the horrible pink suite in the bathroom.* →see **hotel**

소파 세트 ❑ 세 점 한 벌짜리 소파 세트 ❸ 가산명사 (욕조 등) 욕실 세트 ❑ 욕실에 있는 보기 싫은 분홍색 욕실 세트

suit|ed /súːtɪd/ ADJ If something is well **suited** to a particular purpose, it is right or appropriate for that purpose. If someone is well **suited** to a particular job, they are right or appropriate for that job. [v-link ADJ, usu adv ADJ to n/-ing, ADJ to-inf] ❑ *The area is well suited to road cycling as well as off-road riding.*

형용사 적합한 ❑ 그 지역은 오프로드 운전뿐 아니라 로드 사이클링에도 아주 적합하다.

Word Partnership	suited의 연어
ADV.	**ill** suited, **perfectly** suited, **well** suited
PREP.	suited **to something**

suit|or /súːtər/ (**suitors**) ❶ N-COUNT A woman's **suitor** is a man who wants to marry her. [OLD-FASHIONED] ❑ *My mother had a suitor who adored her.* ❷ N-COUNT A **suitor** is a company or organization that wants to buy another company. [BUSINESS] ❑ *The company was making little progress in trying to find a suitor.*

❶ 가산명사 구혼자 [구식어] ❑ 어머니께는 어머니를 너무나 사랑하던 구혼자가 있었다. ❷ 가산명사 기업 인수 희망자 [경제] ❑ 그 회사는 인수 희망자를 찾는 데 별 진전이 없었다.

sul|fur /sʌ́lfər/ [BRIT **sulphur**] N-UNCOUNT **sulfur** is a yellow chemical which has a strong smell. ❑ *Burning sulfur creates poisonous fumes.*

[영국영어 sulphur] 불가산명사 황, 유황 ❑ 황을 태우면 독가스가 생긴다.

sulk /sʌ́lk/ (**sulks, sulking, sulked**) V-I If you **sulk**, you are silent and bad-tempered for a while because you are annoyed about something. ❑ *He turned his back and sulked.* ● N-COUNT **Sulk** is also a noun. ❑ *He went off in a sulk.*

자동사 부루퉁하다 ❑ 그는 돌아서서 부루퉁해 있었다. ● 가산명사 부루퉁함 ❑ 그는 부루퉁해졌다.

sul|len /sʌ́lən/ ADJ Someone who is **sullen** is bad-tempered and does not speak much. ❑ *The offenders lapsed into a sullen silence.*

형용사 뚱한 ❑ 그 범법자들은 점점 뚱해져서 말을 하지 않았다.

sul|phur /sʌ́lfər/ →see **sulfur**

sul|tan /sʌ́ltən/ (**sultans**) N-TITLE; N-COUNT A **sultan** is a ruler in some Muslim countries. ❑ *...during the reign of Sultan Abdul Hamid.*

경칭명사; 가산명사 회교국 군주 ❑ 압둘 하미드 군주의 치세 기간 동안

sul|try /sʌ́ltri/ ❶ ADJ **Sultry** weather is hot and damp. [WRITTEN] ❑ *The climax came one sultry August evening.* ❷ ADJ Someone who is **sultry** is attractive in a way that suggests hidden passion. [WRITTEN] ❑ *...a dark-haired sultry woman.*

❶ 형용사 후텁지근한 [문어체] ❑ 더위의 절정은 8월의 후텁지근한 어느 저녁이었다. ❷ 형용사 관능적인 [문어체] ❑ 검은 머리의 관능적인 한 여성

sum ♦◇◇ /sʌ́m/ (**sums, summing, summed**) ❶ N-COUNT A **sum** of money is an amount of money. ❑ *Large sums of money were lost.* ❷ N-COUNT A **sum** is a simple calculation in arithmetic. ❑ *I can't do my sums.* ❸ N-SING In mathematics, **the sum of** two numbers is the number that is obtained when they are added together. ❑ *The sum of all the angles of a triangle is 180 degrees.* ❹ N-SING **The sum of** something is all of it. You often use **sum** in this way to indicate that you are disappointed because the extent of something is rather small, or because it is not very good. ❑ *To date, the sum of my gardening experience had been futile efforts to rid the flower beds of grass.* ❺ →see also **lump sum**

❶ 가산명사 액수, 금액 ❑ 많은 액수의 돈이 분실되었다. ❷ 가산명사 산수 ❑ 나는 산수를 못한다. ❸ 단수명사 총합 ❑ 삼각형 세 각의 총합은 180도이다. ❹ 단수명사 전부 ❑ 그때까지, 내 조경술 경력의 전부는 화단에서 풀을 없애기 위해 부질없이 노력했던 것뿐이었다.

Word Partnership	sum의 연어
ADJ.	**equal** sum, **large** sum, **substantial** sum, **undisclosed** sum ❶
N.	sum **of money** ❶

▶**sum up** ❶ PHRASAL VERB If you **sum** something **up**, you describe it as briefly as possible. ❑ *One voter in Brasilia summed up the mood – "Politicians have lost credibility," he complained.* ❷ PHRASAL VERB If something **sums** a person or situation **up**, it represents their most typical characteristics. ❑ *"I love my wife, my horse, and my dog," he said, and that summed him up.* ❸ PHRASAL VERB If you **sum up** after a speech or at the end of a piece of writing, you briefly state the main points again. When a judge **sums up** after a trial, he reminds the jury of the evidence and the main arguments of the case they have heard. ❑ *When the judge summed up, it was clear he wanted a guilty verdict.*

❶ 구동사 요약하다 ❑ 브라질리아의 한 유표권자가 그 분위기를 다음과 같이 요약하며 불평했다. "정치인들은 이미 신임을 잃어버렸어요." ❷ 구동사 − 을 압축해서 보여 주다 ❑ "나는 내 아내와 내 말과 내 개를 사랑한다."라고 그가 말했는데, 그것이 그를 압축적으로 보여 준다. ❸ 구동사 요점을 정리하다 ❑ 그 판사가 요점을 정리했을 때, 그가 유죄 평결을 원한다는 것이 분명했다.

sum|ma|rize /sʌ́məraɪz/ (**summarizes, summarizing, summarized**) [BRIT also **summarise**] V-T/V-I If you **summarize** something, you give a summary of it. ❑ *Table 3.1 summarizes the information given above.* ❑ *Basically, the article can be summarized in three sentences.*

[영국영어 summarise] 타동사/자동사 요약하다 ❑ 표 3.1은 위에서 설명한 내용을 요약한 것이다. ❑ 기본적으로 이 글은 세 문장으로 요약될 수 있다.

sum|mary /sʌ́məri/ (**summaries**) ❶ N-COUNT A **summary of** something is a short account of it, which gives the main points but not the details. ❑ *What follows is a brief summary of the process.* ● PHRASE You use **in summary** to indicate that what you are about to say is a summary of what has just been said. ❑ *In summary, it is my opinion that this complete treatment process was very successful.* ❷ ADJ **Summary** actions are done without delay, often when something else should have been done first or done instead. [FORMAL] [ADJ n] ❑ *It says torture and summary execution are common.*

❶ 가산명사 요약 ❑ 다음은 그 과정의 간략한 요약이다. ● 구 요약하면 ❑ 요약하면, 이런 철저한 치료 과정이 아주 성공적이었다는 것이 나의 생각이다. ❷ 형용사 즉결의 [격식체] ❑ 고문과 즉결 처형이 일반적이라고 한다.

sum|mer ♦♦◇ /sʌ́mər/ (**summers**) N-VAR **Summer** is the season between spring and fall. In the summer the weather is usually warm or hot. ❑ *I escaped the heatwave in London earlier this summer and flew to Cork.* ❑ *It was a perfect summer's day.*

가산명사 또는 불가산명사 여름 ❑ 나는 올 여름 일찌감치 런던의 열기를 피해서 코크로 떠났다. ❑ 완벽한 여름날이었다.

sum|mer camp (**summer camps**) N-COUNT In the United States, a **summer camp** is a place in the country where parents can pay to send their children during the school summer vacation. The children staying there can take part in many outdoor and social activities.

가산명사 여름 캠프

sum|mit ♦♦◇ /sʌ́mɪt/ (**summits**) ❶ N-COUNT A **summit** is a meeting at which the leaders of two or more countries discuss important matters. ❑ *...next week's Washington summit.* ❷ N-COUNT The **summit** of a mountain is the top of it. ❑ *...the first man to reach the summit of Mount Everest.*

❶ 가산명사 정상 회담 ❑ 다음 주에 열리는 워싱턴 정상 회담 ❷ 가산명사 (산의) 정상 ❑ 에베레스트 산 정상에 최초로 오른 사람

sum|mon /sʌ́mən/ (**summons, summoning, summoned**) ❶ V-T If you **summon** someone, you order them to come to you. [FORMAL] ❑ *Howe summoned a doctor and hurried over.* ❑ *Suddenly we were summoned to the interview room.* ❷ V-T If you **summon** a quality, you make a great effort to have it. For example, if you **summon** the courage or strength to do something, you make a great effort to

❶ 타동사 호출하다 [격식체] ❑ 하우는 의사를 호출하고 서둘러 왔다. ❑ 갑자기 우리는 면회실로 호출되었다. ❷ 타동사 (용기 등을) 내다 ❑ 그녀가 어머니께 말씀드릴 용기를 내는 데 꼬박 한 달이 걸렸다. ● 구동사 (용기 등을) 내다 ❑ 꽹장히

be brave or strong, so that you will be able to do it. ❑ *It took her a full month to summon the courage to tell her mother.* ● PHRASAL VERB **Summon up** means the same as **summon**. ❑ *Painfully shy, he finally summoned up courage to ask her to a game.*

sum|mons /sʌmənz/ (summonses, summonsing, summonsed) ◼ N-COUNT A **summons** is an order to come and see someone. ❑ *I received a summons to the Palace from Sir Robert Fellowes, the Queen's private secretary.* ◻ N-COUNT A **summons** is an official order to appear in court. ❑ *She had received a summons to appear in court.* ◼ V-T If someone **is summonsed**, they are officially ordered to appear in court. [usu passive] ❑ *The men were summonsed and last week 30 appeared before Hove magistrates.*

sump|tu|ous /sʌmptʃuəs/ ADJ Something that is **sumptuous** is grand and obviously very expensive. ❑ *...a sumptuous feast.*

sun ♦♦◇ /sʌn/ ◼ N-SING **The sun** is the ball of fire in the sky that the Earth goes around, and that gives us heat and light. ❑ *The sun was now high in the southern sky.* ❑ *The sun came out, briefly.* ◻ N-UNCOUNT You refer to the light and heat that reach us from the sun as **the sun**. ❑ *Dena took them into the courtyard to sit in the sun.* →see **earth, eclipse, navigation, solar system, star**

Sun. **Sun.** is a written abbreviation for **Sunday.** ❑ *The Palace is open Mon.-Sun.*

sun|bathe /sʌnbeɪð/ (sunbathes, sunbathing, sunbathed) V-I When people **sunbathe**, they sit or lie in a place where the sun shines on them, so that their skin becomes browner. ❑ *Franklin swam and sunbathed at the pool every morning.* ● sun|bath|ing N-UNCOUNT ❑ *Nearby there is a stretch of white sand beach perfect for sunbathing.*

sun|burn /sʌnbɜrn/ (sunburns) N-VAR If someone has **sunburn**, their skin is bright pink and sore because they have spent too much time in hot sunshine. ❑ *The risk and severity of sunburn depend on the body's natural skin color.* →see **skin**

sun|burned /sʌnbɜrnd/ also **sunburnt** ADJ Someone who is **sunburned** has sore bright pink skin because they have spent too much time in hot sunshine. ❑ *A badly sunburned face or back is extremely painful.*

Sun|day ♦♦♦ /sʌndeɪ, -di/ (Sundays) N-VAR **Sunday** is the day after Saturday and before Monday. ❑ *I thought we might go for a drive on Sunday.*

sun|dries /sʌndriz/ N-PLURAL When someone is making a list of things, items that are not important enough to be listed separately are sometimes referred to together as **sundries**. [FORMAL] ❑ *The inn gift shop stocks quality Indian crafts and sundries.*

sun|dry /sʌndri/ ◼ ADJ If someone refers to **sundry** people or things, they are referring to several people or things that are all different from each other. [FORMAL] [ADJ n] ❑ *Scientists, business people, and sundry others gathered on Monday for the official opening.* ◻ PHRASE **All and sundry** means everyone. ❑ *I made tea for all and sundry at the office.*

sun|flower /sʌnflaʊər/ (sunflowers) N-COUNT A **sunflower** is a very tall plant with large yellow flowers. Oil from sunflower seeds is used in cooking and to make margarine.

sung /sʌŋ/ **Sung** is the past participle of **sing**.

sun|glasses /sʌnglæsɪz/ N-PLURAL **Sunglasses** are glasses with dark lenses which you wear to protect your eyes from bright sunlight. [also a pair of N] ❑ *She slipped on a pair of sunglasses.*

sunk /sʌŋk/ **Sunk** is the past participle of **sink**.

sunk|en /sʌŋkən/ ◼ ADJ **Sunken** ships have sunk to the bottom of a sea, ocean, or lake. [ADJ n] ❑ *The sunken sailing-boat was a glimmer of white on the bottom.* ◻ ADJ **Sunken** gardens, roads, or other features are below the level of their surrounding area. [ADJ n] ❑ *Steps lead down to the sunken garden.* ◼ ADJ **Sunken** eyes, cheeks, or other parts of the body curve inward and make you look thin and unwell. ❑ *Her eyes were sunken and black-ringed.*

sun|light /sʌnlaɪt/ N-UNCOUNT **Sunlight** is the light that comes from the sun during the day. ❑ *I saw her sitting at a window table, bathed in sunlight.* →see **rainbow, skin**

sun|ny /sʌni/ (sunnier, sunniest) ◼ ADJ When it is **sunny**, the sun is shining brightly. ❑ *The weather was surprisingly warm and sunny.* ◻ ADJ **Sunny** places are brightly lit by the sun. ❑ *Most roses like a sunny position in a fairly fertile soil.*

sun|rise /sʌnraɪz/ (sunrises) ◼ N-UNCOUNT **Sunrise** is the time in the morning when the sun first appears in the sky. ❑ *The rain began before sunrise.* ◻ N-COUNT A **sunrise** is the colors and light that you see in the eastern part of the sky when the sun first appears. ❑ *There was a spectacular sunrise yesterday.*

sun|roof /sʌnruf/ (sunroofs) N-COUNT A **sunroof** is a panel in the roof of a car that opens to let sunshine and air enter the car. ❑ *...extras like a sunroof, a CD player, or chrome wheels.*

sun|screen /sʌnskrin/ (sunscreens) N-MASS A **sunscreen** is a cream that protects your skin from the sun's rays, especially in hot weather. ❑ *Use a sunscreen suitable for your skin type.* →see **skin**

sun|set /sʌnset/ (sunsets) ◼ N-UNCOUNT **Sunset** is the time in the evening when the sun disappears out of sight from the sky. ❑ *The dance ends at sunset.* ◻ N-COUNT A **sunset** is the colors and light that you see in the western part of the sky when the sun disappears in the evening. ❑ *There was a red sunset over Paris.*

sun|shine /sʌnʃaɪn/ N-UNCOUNT **Sunshine** is the light and heat that comes from the sun. ❑ *In the marina yachts sparkle in the sunshine.* ❑ *She was sitting outside a cafe in bright sunshine.*

수줍어하면서, 마침내 그가 그녀를 경기에 나오도록 부탁할 용기를 냈다.

◼ 가산명사 호출, 호출장 ❑ 나는 여왕의 개인 비서인 로버트 펠로우스 경으로부터 궁으로 오라는 호출을 받았다. ◻ 가산명사 출두 명령, 소환장 ❑ 그녀는 법정 출두 명령을 받았었다. ◼ 타동사 소환되다 ❑ 그 남자들은 소환되었고 지난주에 30명이 호브 치안 판사 앞에 출두했다.

형용사 호화스러운 ❑ 호화스러운 축제

◼ 단수명사 태양, 해 ❑ 이제는 태양이 남쪽 하늘 높이 떠 있었다. ❑ 해가 잠깐 나왔다. ◻ 불가산명사 햇빛, 햇볕 ❑ 데나는 앉아서 햇볕을 쬐려고 그들을 뜰로 데리고 나왔다.

일 ❑ 버킹엄 궁전은 월요일에서 일요일까지 개방한다.

자동사 일광욕하다 ❑ 프랭클린은 아침마다 수영장에서 수영을 하고 일광욕을 했다. ● 일광욕 불가산명사 ❑ 근처에 일광욕하기에 최상인 흰 모래사장이 펼쳐져 있다.

가산명사 또는 불가산명사 햇볕에 탐 ❑ 햇볕에 탈 위험성과 심각성은 사람의 피부색에 달려 있다.

형용사 햇볕에 탄 ❑ 얼굴과 등이 햇볕에 심하게 타면 몹시 따갑다.

가산명사 또는 불가산명사 일요일 ❑ 나는 우리가 일요일에 드라이브하러 갈지도 모른다고 생각했다.

복수명사 잡다한 것, 여러 가지 [격식체] ❑ 그 숙소 선물 가게에는 고급 인도 공예품 외 여러 가지가 구비되어 있다.

◼ 형용사 가양각색의, 여러 가지의 [격식체] ❑ 과학자들, 사업가들, 그리고 각양각색의 사람들이 월요일에 그 개통식을 위해서 모였다. ◻ 구 모든 사람들 ❑ 나는 사무실에 있는 모든 사람들을 위해 차를 끓였다.

가산명사 해바라기

sing의 과거 분사

복수명사 선글라스 ❑ 그녀가 선글라스를 썼다.

sink의 과거 분사

◼ 형용사 침몰한 ❑ 침몰한 범선은 바닥이 흐릿한 흰색이었다. ◻ 형용사 움푹 들어간 ❑ 발길을 옮기다 보니 정원의 움푹 들어간 쪽으로 가게 되었다. ◼ 형용사 (눈 등이) 꽹한 ❑ 그녀는 두 눈이 꽹하고 눈 주위가 거무스름했다.

불가산명사 햇빛 ❑ 나는 그녀가 햇빛을 쬐며 창가 식탁에 앉아 있는 것을 보았다.

◼ 형용사 화창한 ❑ 날씨가 놀랄 정도로 따뜻하고 화창했다. ◻ 형용사 햇빛이 잘 드는 ❑ 대부분의 장미는 토양이 상당히 비옥하고 햇빛이 잘 드는 곳에서 잘 자란다.

◼ 불가산명사 동틀 녘 ❑ 동틀 녘이 되기 전에 비가 오기 시작했다. ◻ 가산명사 일출 ❑ 어제는 일출이 장관이었다.

가산명사 (자동차의) 선루프 ❑ 선루프, 시디플레이어, 크롬 휠과 같은 추가 사양들

물질명사 자외선 차단제 ❑ 당신의 피부 타입에 맞는 자외선 차단제를 쓰세요.

◼ 불가산명사 해질 녘 ❑ 댄스파티는 해질 녘에 끝난다. ◻ 가산명사 일몰 ❑ 파리 하늘 위로 붉은 노을이 지고 있었다.

불가산명사 햇빛, 햇살 ❑ 요트 정박장에서는 요트들이 햇빛에 반짝이고 있다. ❑ 그녀가 눈부신 햇살 아래 야외 카페에 앉아 있었다.

sun|stroke /sʌnstroʊk/ N-UNCOUNT **Sunstroke** is an illness caused by spending too much time in hot sunshine. ❑ *I was suffering from acute sunstroke, starvation, and exhaustion.*

불가산명사 일사병 ❑ 나는 심한 일사병과 굶주림과 극심한 피로에 시달리고 있었다.

sun|tan /sʌntæn/ (suntans) also sun-tan **1** N-COUNT If you have a **suntan**, the sun has turned your skin an attractive brown color. ❑ *They want to go to the Bahamas and get a suntan.* **2** ADJ **Suntan** lotion, oil, or cream protects your skin from the sun. [ADJ n] ❑ *She playfully rubs suntan lotion on his neck.* →see **skin**

1 가산명사 햇볕에 피부를 태우기, 선탠 ❑ 그들은 바하마로 가서 선탠을 하고 싶어 한다. **2** 형용사 선탠용의 ❑ 그녀는 선탠로션을 그의 목에 장난스럽게 발라 준다.

Word Link   super ≈ above : super, superficial, superpower

su|per ♦◇◇ /supər/ **1** ADV **Super** is used before adjectives to indicate that something has a lot of a quality. [ADV adj] ❑ *I'm going to Greece in the summer so I've got to be super slim.* **2** ADJ **Super** is used before nouns to indicate that something is larger, better, or more advanced than similar things. [ADJ n] ❑ *We wouldn't build a super highway through Yellowstone National Park.* **3** ADJ Some people use **super** to mean very nice or very good. [INFORMAL, OLD-FASHIONED] ❑ *We had a super time.* ❑ *That's a super idea.*

1 부사 극도로, 굉장히 ❑ 나는 여름에 그리스로 가려고 한다. 그러니 아주 날씬해져야 한다. **2** 형용사 엄청난, 굉장한 ❑ 우리라면 옐로스톤 국립공원을 관통하는 엄청난 고속도로를 건설하지는 않을 것이다. **3** 형용사 멋진, 기막힌 [비격식체, 구식어] ❑ 우리는 멋진 시간을 보냈다. ❑ 그것은 기막힌 아이디어이다.

super|an|nua|tion /supərænyueɪʃ°n/ N-UNCOUNT **Superannuation** is money which people pay regularly into a special fund so that when they retire from their job they will receive money regularly as a pension. [mainly BRIT, BUSINESS] ❑ *The union pressed for a superannuation scheme.*

불가산명사 연금 불입금 [주로 영국영어, 경제] ❑ 그 조합은 연금 불입 계획 수립을 촉구했다.

su|perb ♦◇◇ /supɜrb/ **1** ADJ If something is **superb**, its quality is very good indeed. ❑ *There is a superb 18-hole golf course 6 miles away.* ● **su|perb|ly** ADV ❑ *The orchestra played superbly.* **2** ADJ If you say that someone has **superb** confidence, control, or skill, you mean that they have very great confidence, control, or skill. ❑ *With superb skill he managed to make a perfect landing.* ● **su|perb|ly** ADV ❑ *...his superbly disciplined opponent.*

1 형용사 최고급의 ❑ 6마일 떨어진 곳에 최고급 18홀 골프장이 있다. ● 최고로 부사 ❑ 그 오케스트라는 최고의 연주를 했다. **2** 형용사 최상의 ❑ 그는 최상의 기술로 완벽한 착륙을 해냈다. ● 최상으로 부사 ❑ 최상으로 훈련된 그의 상대자

super|fi|cial /supərfɪʃ°l/ **1** ADJ If you describe someone as **superficial**, you disapprove of them because they do not think deeply, and have little understanding of anything serious or important. [DISAPPROVAL] ❑ *This guy is a superficial yuppie with no intellect whatsoever.* **2** ADJ If you describe something such as an action, feeling, or relationship as **superficial**, you mean that it includes only the simplest and most obvious aspects of that thing, and not those aspects which require more effort to deal with or understand. ❑ *Their arguments do not withstand the most superficial scrutiny.* **3** ADJ **Superficial** is used to describe the appearance of something or the impression that it gives, especially if its real nature is very different. ❑ *Despite these superficial resemblances, this is a darker work than her earlier novels.* **4** ADJ **Superficial** injuries are not very serious, and affect only the surface of the body. You can also describe damage to an object as **superficial**. ❑ *The 69-year-old clergyman escaped with superficial wounds.*

1 형용사 깊이가 없는, 얕은 [탐탁찮음] ❑ 이 사람은 지성이라고는 전혀 없는 깊이 없는 여피족이다. **2** 형용사 피상적인 ❑ 그들의 주장은 아주 피상적으로 살펴보아도 그 허점이 드러난다. **3** 형용사 표면상의 ❑ 표면상의 이런 유사점들에도 불구하고, 이것은 그녀가 쓴 초기 소설들보다 더 어두운 작품이다. **4** 형용사 (상처가) 깊지 않은, 표피상의 ❑ 69세 된 성직자가 가벼운 외상만 입고 무사했다.

super|flu|ous /supɜrfluəs/ ADJ Something that is **superfluous** is unnecessary or is no longer needed. ❑ *My presence at the afternoon's proceedings was superfluous.*

형용사 불필요한, (더 이상) 필요치 않은 ❑ 오후 행사에까지 내가 참석하는 것은 불필요했다.

super|high|way /supərhaɪweɪ/ (superhighways) **1** N-COUNT A **superhighway** is a large, fast highway or freeway with several lanes. [AM] ❑ *He took off for the city on the eight-lane superhighway.* **2** N-COUNT The information **superhighway** is the network of computer links that enables computer users all over the world to communicate with each other. [COMPUTING] ❑ *...a superhighway using digital and fibre-optic technology to provide new telecommunications links.*

1 가산명사 고속도로 [미국영어] ❑ 그는 8차선 고속도로를 타고 그 도시를 향해 출발했다. **2** 가산명사 초고속 정보 통신망 [컴퓨터] ❑ 새로운 통신 회선을 제공하기 위한 디지털과 광섬유 기술을 사용한 초고속 정보 통신망

super|im|pose /supərɪmpoʊz/ (superimposes, superimposing, superimposed) **1** V-T If one image **is superimposed on** another, it is put on top of it so that you can see the second image through it. [usu passive] ❑ *The image of a seemingly tiny dancer was superimposed on the image of the table.* **2** V-T If features or characteristics from one situation **are superimposed onto** or **on** another, they are transferred onto or used in the second situation, though they may not fit. [usu passive] ❑ *Patterns of public administration and government are superimposed on traditional societies.*

1 타동사 겹쳐지다, 포개지다 ❑ 자그마한 무희 같아 보이는 것의 영상이 탁자의 영상 위로 겹쳐졌다. **2** 타동사 겹쳐지다, 덧씌워지다 ❑ 행정부라는 통치 방식들이 전통 사회들에 덧씌워졌다.

Word Link   ent ≈ one who does, has : dependent, resident, superintendent

super|in|ten|dent /supərɪntɛndənt, suprɪn-/ (superintendents) **1** N-COUNT; N-TITLE In the United States, a **superintendent** is the head of a police department. In Britain, a **superintendent** is a senior police officer of the rank above an inspector. ❑ *He was stopped at the airport by an assistant superintendent of police.* **2** N-COUNT A **superintendent** is a person who is responsible for a particular thing or the work done in a particular department. ❑ *He became superintendent of the bank's East African branches.* **3** N-COUNT A **superintendent** is a person whose job is to take care of a large building such as a school or an apartment building and deal with small repairs to it. [AM; BRIT caretaker] ❑ *The superintendent, a bundle of keys hanging from his belt, was standing at the door.*

1 가산명사; 경칭명사 경찰서장, 경정 ❑ 공항에서 그는 부경찰서장에게 제지당했다. **2** 가산명사 책임자 ❑ 그는 그 은행의 동아프리카 지점 책임자가 되었다. **3** 가산명사 (건물 등의) 관리인 [미국영어; 영국영어 caretaker] ❑ 허리춤에 한 움큼의 열쇠를 매단 관리인이 문 앞에 서 있었다.

su|peri|or ♦◇◇ /supɪəriər/ (superiors) **1** ADJ If one thing or person is **superior to** another, the first is better than the second. ❑ *We have a relationship infinitely superior to those of many of our friends.* ● **su|peri|or|ity** N-UNCOUNT ❑ *The technical superiority of laser discs over tape is well established.* **2** ADJ If you describe something as **superior**, you mean that it is good, and better than other things of the same kind. ❑ *A few years ago it was virtually impossible to find superior quality coffee in local shops.* **3** ADJ A **superior** person or thing is more important than another person or thing in the same organization or system. ❑ *...negotiations between the mutineers and their superior officers.* **4** N-COUNT Your **superior** in an organization that you work for is a person who has a higher rank than you. ❑ *Other army units are completely surrounded and cut off from communication with their superiors.* **5** ADJ If you describe someone as **superior**, you disapprove of them because they behave as if they are better, more important, or more intelligent than other people. [DISAPPROVAL] ❑ *Finch gave a superior smile.* ● **su|peri|or|ity**

1 형용사 -보다 좋은, -보다 나은 ❑ 우리는 다른 많은 친구들보다 훨씬 더 좋은 관계를 맺고 있다. ● 우위 불가산명사 ❑ 테이프에 비해 레이저 디스크가 갖는 기술적 우위가 잘 확립되었다. **2** 형용사 고급의, 우수한 ❑ 몇 년 전에만 해도 현지 지역 상점에서 고급 품질의 커피를 찾는다는 것은 사실상 불가능했다. **3** 형용사 상급의 ❑ 반란자들과 그들의 상급 장교들 간의 협상 **4** 가산명사 상관 ❑ 다른 군부대들은 완전히 포위되어 그들의 상관과 연락이 두절되어 있다. **5** 형용사 거만한 [탐탁찮음] ❑ 핀치는 거만한 미소를 지었다. ● 우월감 불가산명사 ❑ 단순한 언론인보다는 자신이 더 낫다는 그의 잘못된 우월감 **6** 형용사 (수적으로) 우세한 [격식체] ❑ 시위자들은 수적으로 우세한 경찰을 보고 도망쳤다.

N-UNCOUNT ❑ ...*a false sense of his superiority over mere journalists.* ☑ ADJ If one group of people has **superior** numbers to another group, the first has more people than the second, and therefore has an advantage over it. [FORMAL] ❑ *The demonstrators fled when they saw the authorities' superior numbers.*

Word Partnership	superior의 연어
ADV.	**far** superior, **vastly** superior ☑
N.	superior **performance**, superior **quality**, superior **service** ☑

su|peri|or|ity /supɪəriɒrɪti, BRIT su:pɪəriɒrɪti/ N-UNCOUNT If one side in a war or conflict has **superiority**, it has an advantage over its enemy, for example because it has more soldiers or better equipment. [FORMAL] ❑ *We have air superiority.* →see also **superior**

불가산명사 우세 [격식체] ❑ 우리는 공군력이 우세하다.

su|per|la|tive /supɜrlətɪv/ (superlatives) ☑ ADJ If you describe something as **superlative**, you mean that it is extremely good. ❑ *Some superlative wines are made in this region.* ☑ N-COUNT If someone uses **superlatives** to describe something, they use adjectives and expressions which indicate that it is extremely good. ❑ *...a spectacle which has critics world-wide reaching for superlatives.* ☒ ADJ In grammar, the **superlative** form of an adjective or adverb is the form that indicates that something has more of a quality than anything else in a group. For example, "biggest" is the superlative form of "big." Compare **comparative**. [ADJ n] ● N-COUNT **Superlative** is also a noun. ❑ *...his tendency towards superlatives and exaggeration.*

☑ 형용사 최상의 ❑ 최상급 와인 몇 종류가 이 지역에서 만들어진다. ☑ 가산명사 최고의 찬사 ❑ 전 세계적으로 비평가들로부터 최고의 찬사를 받은 공연 ☒ 형용사 (문법) 최상급의 ● 가산명사 최상급 ❑ 최상급과 과장법을 주로 쓰는 그의 경향

su|per|mar|ket /supɜrmɑrkɪt/ (supermarkets) N-COUNT A **supermarket** is a large store which sells all kinds of food and some household goods. ❑ *Most of us do our food shopping in the supermarket.*

가산명사 슈퍼마켓 ❑ 우리들 대다수는 슈퍼마켓에서 식료품을 산다.

su|per|mod|el /supɜrmɒdəl/ (supermodels) N-COUNT A **supermodel** is a very famous fashion model.

가산명사 슈퍼 모델

su|per|natu|ral /supɜrnætʃərəl, -nætʃrəl/ ADJ **Supernatural** creatures, forces, and events are believed by some people to exist or happen, although they are impossible according to scientific laws. ❑ *The Nakani were evil spirits who looked like humans and possessed supernatural powers.* ● N-SING **The supernatural** is things that are supernatural. ❑ *He writes short stories with a touch of the supernatural.*

형용사 초자연적인 ❑ 나카니는 인간의 모습을 하고서 초자연적인 힘을 지녔던 악령이었다. ● 단수명사 초자연적인 것 ❑ 그는 초자연적인 것을 가미한 단편 소설을 쓴다.

Word Link	super ≈ above : super, superficial, superpower

su|per|pow|er /supɜrpaʊər/ (superpowers) N-COUNT A **superpower** is a very powerful and influential country, usually one that is rich and has nuclear weapons. ❑ *The United States could claim to be both a military and an economic superpower.*

가산명사 강대국 ❑ 미국은 군사적, 경제적 강대국임을 주장할 수 있을 것이다.

su|per|sede /supɜrsid/ (supersedes, superseding, superseded) V-T If something **is superseded by** something newer, it is replaced because it has become old-fashioned or unacceptable. [usu passive] ❑ *Hand tools are relics of the past that have now been superseded by the machine.*

타동사 대체되다 ❑ 수공구들은 이제 기계로 대체되어 버린 과거의 유물이다.

su|per|son|ic /supɜrsɒnɪk/ ADJ **Supersonic** aircraft travel faster than the speed of sound. [ADJ n] ❑ *There was a huge bang; it sounded like a supersonic jet.* →see **sound**

형용사 초음속의 ❑ 엄청나게 크게 쾅 하는 소리가 났다. 그것은 마치 초음속 제트기 소리 같았다.

su|per|star /supɜrstɑr/ (superstars) N-COUNT A **superstar** is a very famous entertainer or athlete. [INFORMAL] ❑ *He was more than a footballing superstar, he was a celebrity.*

가산명사 유명 스타 [비격식체] ❑ 그는 유명한 축구 스타 이상이었다. 그는 유명 인사였다.

su|per|sti|tion /supɜrstɪʃən/ (superstitions) N-VAR **Superstition** is belief in things that are not real or possible, for example magic. ❑ *Fortune-telling is a very much debased art surrounded by superstition.*

가산명사 또는 불가산명사 미신 ❑ 점치는 것은 미신에 둘러싸인, 거의 존중을 못 받는 기술이다.

su|per|sti|tious /supɜrstɪʃəs/ ☑ ADJ People who are **superstitious** believe in things that are not real or possible, for example magic. ❑ *Jean was extremely superstitious and believed the color green brought bad luck.* ☑ ADJ **Superstitious** fears or beliefs are irrational and not based on fact. [ADJ n] ❑ *A wave of superstitious fear spread among the townspeople.*

☑ 형용사 미신을 믿는 ❑ 장은 미신을 너무 많이 믿어서 녹색이 불행을 가져온다고 생각했다. ☑ 형용사 미신적인 ❑ 미신적인 공포의 물결이 마을 사람들 사이로 퍼져 갔다.

su|per|store /supɜrstɔr/ (superstores) N-COUNT **Superstores** are very large supermarkets or stores selling household goods and equipment. Superstores are usually built outside cities and away from other stores. ❑ *...a Do-It-Yourself superstore.*

가산명사 대형 슈퍼마켓 ❑ 손수 제작 용품 대형 슈퍼마켓

su|per|vise /supɜrvaɪz/ (supervises, supervising, supervised) V-T If you **supervise** an activity or a person, you make sure that the activity is done correctly or that the person is doing a task or behaving correctly. ❑ *University teachers have refused to supervise students' examinations.*

타동사 감독하다, 지도하다 ❑ 대학 교수들이 학생들의 시험 감독을 거부해 오고 있다.

su|per|vi|sion /supɜrvɪʒən/ N-UNCOUNT **Supervision** is the supervising of people, activities, or places. ❑ *A toddler requires close supervision and firm control at all times.*

불가산명사 감독, 지도 ❑ 아장아장 걷는 아이는 늘 세심한 지도와 철저한 관리가 필요하다.

su|per|vi|sor /supɜrvaɪzər/ (supervisors) N-COUNT A **supervisor** is a person who supervises activities or people, especially workers or students. ❑ *...a full-time job as a supervisor at a factory.*

가산명사 감독자 ❑ 공장 감독관으로서의 상근직

sup|per /sʌpər/ (suppers) ☑ N-VAR Some people refer to the main meal eaten in the early part of the evening as **supper**. ❑ *Some guests like to dress for supper.* →see **meal** ☑ N-VAR **Supper** is a simple meal eaten just before you go to bed at night. ❑ *She gives the children their supper, then puts them to bed.*

☑ 가산명사 또는 불가산명사 만찬 ❑ 일부 손님들은 만찬을 위해 옷을 갖춰 입는 것을 좋아한다. ☑ 가산명사 또는 불가산명사 저녁 식사 ❑ 그녀는 아이들에게 저녁을 주고, 그 후에 재운다.

sup|ple /sʌpəl/ (suppler, supplest) ☑ ADJ A **supple** object or material bends or changes shape easily without cracking or breaking. ❑ *The leather is supple and sturdy enough to last for years.* ☑ ADJ A **supple** person can move and bend their body very easily. ❑ *Paul was incredibly supple and strong.*

☑ 형용사 유연한 ❑ 그 가죽은 유연하고 수년 동안 충분히 사용할 정도로 튼튼하다. ☑ 형용사 유연성 있는 ❑ 폴은 믿기 힘들 정도로 유연성이 있으며 강했다.

sup|ple|ment /sʌplɪmənt/ (supplements, supplementing, supplemented)
1 V-T If you **supplement** something, you add something to it in order to improve it. ❑ ...people doing extra jobs outside their regular jobs to supplement their incomes. ● N-COUNT **Supplement** is also a noun. ❑ Business sponsorship must be a supplement to, not a substitute for, public funding. **2** N-COUNT A **supplement** is a pill that you take or a special kind of food that you eat in order to improve your health. ❑ ...a multiple vitamin and mineral supplement. **3** N-COUNT A **supplement** is a separate part of a magazine or newspaper, often dealing with a particular topic. ❑ ...a special supplement to a monthly financial magazine. **4** N-COUNT A **supplement** to a book is an additional section, written some time after the main text and published either at the end of the book or separately. ❑ ...the supplement to the Encyclopedia Britannica. **5** N-COUNT A **supplement** is an extra amount of money that you pay in order to obtain special facilities or services, for example when you are traveling or staying at a hotel. ❑ If you are traveling alone, the single room supplement is £11 a night.

1 타동사 보충하다 ❑ 소득을 보충하기 위해 정규 직업 외에 추가로 다른 일을 하는 사람들 ● 가산명사 보충 ❑ 재계의 후원은 공공 재정 지원을 보충하기 위해 사용되어야지 그 자체를 대신해서는 안 된다. **2** 가산명사 보충재 ❑ 복합 비타민과 무기질 보충제 **3** 가산명사 부록 ❑ 경제 월간지의 특별 부록 한 권 **4** 가산명사 증보판 ❑ 브리태니커 백과사전 증보판 **5** 가산명사 추가 비용 ❑ 혼자 여행하면 독방 추가 비용은 하룻밤에 11파운드이다.

sup|ple|men|ta|ry /sʌplɪmentri, BRIT sʌplɪmentri/ ADJ **Supplementary** things are added to something in order to improve it. ❑ ...the question of whether or not we need to take supplementary vitamins.

형용사 보충의 ❑ 우리가 비타민 보충제를 섭취할 필요가 있는가의 문제

sup|pli|er /səplaɪər/ (suppliers) N-COUNT A **supplier** is a person, company, or organization that sells or supplies something such as goods or equipment to customers. [BUSINESS] ❑ ...Hillsdown Holdings, one of the UK's biggest food suppliers.

가산명사 공급업자 [경제] ❑ 영국 최대 식품 공급 업체 중 하나인 힐스다운 홀딩스

sup|ply ♦♦◇ /səplaɪ/ (supplies, supplying, supplied) **1** V-T If you **supply** someone with something that they want or need, you give them a quantity of it. ❑ ...an agreement not to produce or supply chemical weapons. ❑ ...a pipeline which will supply the major Greek cities with Russian natural gas. **2** N-PLURAL You can use **supplies** to refer to food, equipment, and other essential things that people need, especially when these are provided in large quantities. ❑ What happens when food and gasoline supplies run low? **3** N-VAR A **supply of** something is an amount of it which someone has or which is available for them to use. ❑ The brain requires a constant supply of oxygen. **4** N-UNCOUNT **Supply** is the quantity of goods and services that can be made available for people to buy. [BUSINESS] ❑ Prices change according to supply and demand. **5** PHRASE If something is in short **supply**, there is very little of it available and it is difficult to find or obtain. ❑ Food is in short supply all over the country.

1 타동사 공급하다 ❑ 화학 무기를 생산하거나 공급하지 않는다는 협정 ❑ 그리스 대도시들에 러시아산 천연가스를 공급할 수송관 **2** 복수명사 공급품 ❑ 식품과 가솔린 공급품이 떨어진다면 어떻게 될까? **3** 가산명사 또는 불가산명사 공급 ❑ 두뇌에는 끊임없이 산소가 공급되어야 한다. **4** 불가산명사 공급 [경제] ❑ 공급과 수요에 따라 가격이 변동한다. **5** 구 공급이 부족한 ❑ 식량 공급이 그 나라 전국적으로 부족하다.

Word Partnership	supply의 연어
N.	supply **electricity**, supply **equipment**, supply **information** **1**
ADJ.	**abundant** supply, **large** supply, **limited** supply **3**

sup|port ♦♦♦ /səpɔrt/ (supports, supporting, supported) **1** V-T If you **support** someone or their ideas or aims, you agree with them, and perhaps help them because you want them to succeed. ❑ The vice president insisted that he supported the hard-working people of New York. ● N-UNCOUNT **Support** is also a noun. ❑ The prime minister gave his full support to the government's reforms. **2** N-UNCOUNT If you give **support** to someone during a difficult or unhappy time, you are kind to them and help them. ❑ It was hard to come to terms with her death after all the support she gave to me and the family. **3** N-UNCOUNT Financial **support** is money provided to enable an organization to continue. This money is usually provided by the government. ❑ ...the government's proposal to cut agricultural support by only about 15%. **4** V-T If you **support** someone, you provide them with money or the things that they need. ❑ I have children to support, money to be earned, and a home to be maintained. **5** V-T If a fact **supports** a statement or a theory, it helps to show that it is true or correct. ❑ The Freudian theory about daughters falling in love with their father has little evidence to support it. ● N-UNCOUNT **Support** is also a noun. ❑ The two largest powers in any system must always be major rivals. History offers some support for this view. **6** V-T If something **supports** an object, it is underneath the object and holding it up. ❑ ...the thick wooden posts that supported the ceiling. **7** N-COUNT A **support** is a bar or other object that supports something. ❑ Each slab was backed up to two straight wooden supports. **8** V-T If you **support yourself**, you prevent yourself from falling by holding onto something or by leaning on something. ❑ He supported himself by means of a nearby post. ● N-UNCOUNT **Support** is also a noun. ❑ Alice, very pale, was leaning against him as if for support. **9** V-T If you **support** a sports team, you always want them to win and perhaps go regularly to their games. ❑ Tim, 17, supports Manchester United.

1 타동사 지지하다 ❑ 부통령은 뉴욕의 근면하게 일하는 사람들을 지지한다고 주장했다. ● 불가산명사 지지 ❑ 수상은 정부 개혁을 전적으로 지지했다. **2** 불가산명사 지원하다 ❑ 나와 가족들을 지원했던 그녀의 죽음을 감수해 내기 어려웠다. **3** 불가산명사 지원 ❑ 약 15퍼센트만큼만 영농 지원을 삭감하자는 정부 측 제안 **4** 타동사 부양하다 ❑ 나는 부양할 아이들이 있고, 돈을 벌어야 하고, 유지해야 할 집도 있다. **5** 타동사 뒷받침하다 ❑ 딸들이 자기 아버지에게 연정을 느낀다는 프로이트 이론은 이를 뒷받침할 증거가 부족하다. ● 불가산명사 뒷받침 ❑ 어느 체제에서든 가장 큰 두 세력은 항상 틀림없이 주경쟁자가 된다. 역사가 어느 정도 이런 견해를 뒷받침한다. **6** 타동사 떠받치다 ❑ 천장을 떠받치던 두꺼운 나무 기둥 **7** 가산명사 버팀대 ❑ 각각의 널빤지는 못으로 두 개의 곧은 나무 버팀대에 고정되어 있었다. **8** 타동사 지탱하다 ❑ 그는 근처 기둥에 몸을 지탱했다. ● 불가산명사 지탱 ❑ 매우 창백한 앨리스는 몸을 지탱하듯 그에게 기대고 있었다. **9** 타동사 응원하다 ❑ 열일곱 살인 팀은 맨체스터 유나이티드를 응원한다.
C

If you dislike something very much or get annoyed by it, you do not say "I can't support it." You say "**I can't bear it.**" or "**I can't stand it.**" ❑ She can't bear the new Republican governor... I cannot stand going shopping.

무엇을 아주 싫어하거나 그것에 화가 나면, 'I can't support it.'이라고 하지 않고 'I can't bear it.' 또는 'I can't stand it.'이라고 말한다. ❑ 그녀는 새 공화당 지사를 참을 수 없다... 나는 쇼핑하러 가는 것을 참을 수 없다.

sup|port|er ♦♦◇ /səpɔrtər/ (supporters) N-COUNT **Supporters** are people who support someone or something, for example a political leader or a sports team. ❑ The fourth night of violence in the German city of Rostock was triggered by football supporters.

가산명사 지지자, 후원자 ❑ 독일의 도시 로스토크에서 일어난 나흘째 밤의 폭력 사태는 축구 지지자들에 의해 촉발되었다.

Word Partnership	supporter의 연어
ADJ.	**active** supporter, **big** supporter, **enthusiastic** supporter, **former** supporter, **staunch** supporter, **strong** supporter

sup|port|ive /səpɔrtɪv/ ADJ If you are **supportive**, you are kind and helpful to someone at a difficult or unhappy time in their life. ❑ They were always supportive of each other.

형용사 협력적인 ❑ 그들은 항상 서로에게 협력적이었다.

sup|pose ♦♦◇ /səpoʊz/ (supposes, supposing, supposed) **1** V-T You can use **suppose** or **supposing** before mentioning a possible situation or action. You usually then go on to consider the effects that this situation or action might have. ❑ *Suppose someone gave you an egg and asked you to describe exactly what was inside.* **2** V-T If you **suppose that** something is true, you believe that it is probably true, because of other things that you know. ❑ *The policy is perfectly clear and I see no reason to suppose that it isn't working.* ❑ *I knew very well that the problem was more complex than he supposed.* **3** PHRASE You can say "**I suppose**" when you want to express slight uncertainty. [SPOKEN, VAGUENESS] ❑ *I suppose I'd better do some homework.* ❑ "*Is that the right way up?*" — "*Yeah. I suppose so.*" **4** PHRASE You can say "**I suppose**" or "**I don't suppose**" before describing someone's probable thoughts or attitude, when you are impatient or slightly angry with them. [SPOKEN, FEELINGS] ❑ *I suppose you think you're funny.* **5** PHRASE You can say "**I don't suppose**" as a way of introducing a polite request. [SPOKEN, POLITENESS] ❑ *I don't suppose you could tell me where James Street is, could you?* **6** PHRASE You can use "**do you suppose**" to introduce a question when you want someone to give their opinion about something, although you know that they are unlikely to have any more knowledge or information about it than you. [SPOKEN] ❑ *Do you suppose he was telling the truth?*

Note that when you are using the verb **suppose** with a "that"-clause in order to state a negative opinion or belief, you normally make **suppose** negative, rather than the verb in the "that"-clause. For instance, it is more usual to say ❑ "*I don't suppose he ever saw it.*" than "I suppose he didn't ever see it." The same pattern applies to other verbs with a similar meaning, such as **believe**, **consider**, and **think**.

Word Partnership	suppose의 연어
ADV.	**now** suppose **1**
V.	**let's** suppose **1**

sup|posed ♦♦◇

Pronounced /səpoʊzd/ or /səpoʊst/ for meanings **1** to **4**, and /səpoʊzɪd/ for meaning **5**.

1 PHRASE If you say that something **is supposed to** happen, you mean that it is planned or expected. Sometimes this use suggests that the thing does not really happen in this way. ❑ *He produced a hand-written list of nine men he was supposed to kill.* **2** PHRASE If something **was supposed to** happen, it was planned or intended to happen, but did not in fact happen. ❑ *He was supposed to go back to Bergen on the last bus, but of course the accident prevented him.* **3** PHRASE If you say that something **is supposed to** be true, you mean that people say it is true but you do not know for certain that it is true. ❑ "*The Whipping Block*" *has never been published, but it's supposed to be a really good poem.* **4** PHRASE You can use "**be supposed to**" to express annoyance at someone's ideas, or because something is not happening in the proper way. [FEELINGS] ❑ *You're supposed to be my friend!* **5** ADJ You can use **supposed** to suggest that something that people talk about or believe in may not in fact exist, happen, or be as it is described. [ADJ n] ❑ *Not all indigenous regimes were willing to accept the supposed benefits of British trade.* ● **sup|pos|ed|ly** /səpoʊzɪdli/ ADV ❑ *He was more of a victim than any of the women he supposedly offended.*

sup|press /səpres/ (suppresses, suppressing, suppressed) **1** V-T If someone in authority **suppresses** an activity, they prevent it from continuing, by using force or making it illegal. ❑ *...drug traffickers, who continue to flourish despite international attempts to suppress them.* ● **sup|pres|sion** /səpreʃⁿn/ N-UNCOUNT ❑ *...people who were imprisoned after the violent suppression of the pro-democracy movement protests.* **2** V-T If a natural function or reaction of your body **is suppressed**, it is stopped, for example by drugs or illness. ❑ *The reproduction and growth of the cancerous cells can be suppressed by bombarding them with radiation.* ● **sup|pres|sion** N-UNCOUNT ❑ *Eye problems can indicate an unhealthy lifestyle with subsequent suppression of the immune system.* **3** V-T If you **suppress** your feelings or reactions, you do not express them, even though you might want to. ❑ *Liz thought of Barry and suppressed a smile.* ● **sup|pres|sion** N-UNCOUNT ❑ *A mother's suppression of her own feelings can cause problems.* **4** V-T If someone **suppresses** a piece of information, they prevent other people from learning it. ❑ *At no time did they try to persuade me to suppress the information.* ● **sup|pres|sion** N-UNCOUNT ❑ *The inspectors found no evidence which supported any allegation of suppression of official documents.* **5** V-T If someone or something **suppresses** a process or activity, they stop it continuing or developing. ❑ "*The Government is suppressing inflation by devastating the economy,*" *he said.*

su|prema|cy /suprɛməsi/ **1** N-UNCOUNT If one group of people has **supremacy** over another group, they have more political or military power than the other group. ❑ *The conservative old guard had re-established its political supremacy.* **2** N-UNCOUNT If someone or something has **supremacy** over another person or thing, they are better. ❑ *In the United States Open final, Graf retained overall supremacy.*

su|preme ♦♦◇ /suprim/ **1** ADJ **Supreme** is used in the title of a person or an official group to indicate that they are at the highest level in a particular organization or system. [ADJ n] ❑ *MacArthur was Supreme Commander for the allied powers in the Pacific.* ❑ *...the Supreme Court.* **2** ADJ You use **supreme** to emphasize that a quality or thing is very great. [EMPHASIS] ❑ *Her approval was of supreme importance.* ● **su|preme|ly** ADV [ADV adj/adv] ❑ *She gets on with her job and does it supremely well.*

1 타동사 가정하다 ❑ 누군가가 당신에게 계란 한 개를 준 후 안에 무엇이 들어 있는지 묘사해 보라고 한다고 가정해 보세요. **2** 타동사 생각하다, 추측하다 ❑ 그 정책은 더할 나위 없이 명백하고 실패할 거라고 생각할 이유가 없다고 본다. ❑ 나는 그 문제가 그가 생각했던 것보다 더 복잡했음을 매우 잘 알고 있었다. **3** 구 아마 -일 거다 [구어체, 짐작] ❑ 숙제 좀 하는 게 나을 것 같아. ❑ "그 길이 맞아요?" "그래, 아마 그럴 거야." **4** 구 (약간 화나 부아); 인 것 같다; -가 아닌 것 같다 [구어체, 감정 개입] ❑ 너는 네가 재미있다고 생각하는 것 같군. **5** 구 -하지 않겠지요 (정중한 요청을 나타냄) [구어체, 공손체] ❑ 제임스 스트리트가 어디 있는지 알려 주실 수 없으시겠죠? **6** 구 -라고 생각합니까 [구어체] ❑ 그가 진실을 말하고 있었다고 생각하니?

부정의 의견이나 믿음을 진술하기 위해 동사 suppose를 that-절과 함께 쓸 때, 보통 that-절의 동사보다는 suppose를 부정으로 만든다는 점을 유념하시오. 예를 들면, "I suppose he didn't ever see it." 보다는 "I don't suppose he ever saw it."이라고 말하는 것이 보통이다. believe, consider, think와 같이 유사한 의미의 다른 동사에도 같은 유형이 적용된다.

1부터 **4**까지의 의미일 때 /səpoʊzd/ 또는 /səpoʊst/ 로, **5** 의미일 때 /səpoʊzɪd/ 로 발음된다.

1 구 -하기로 되어 있다 ❑ 그는 자기가 살해하기로 되어 있는 남자 9명의 이름을 손으로 쓴 명단을 내보였다. **2** 구 -하기로 되어 있었다 ❑ 그는 그 마지막 버스를 타고 베르겐으로 돌아가기로 되어 있었으나, 당연히 그 사고로 인해 그렇지 못했다. **3** 구 -라고 여겨지다 ❑ '위핑 블록'은 결코 출판된 적이 없으나, 정말 훌륭한 시라고 여겨진다. **4** 구 -라는 게 뭐 그런가 [감정 개입] ❑ 넌 내 친구라는 게 뭐 그래! **5** 형용사 추정상의 ❑ 모든 토착 정권이 영국과의 무역을 통해 추정되는 혜택들을 기꺼이 수락한 것은 아니었다. ● 아마도 부사 ❑ 그가 아마도 상처를 줬던 그 어떤 여성들보다도 그가 오히려 더 피해자였다.

1 타동사 억제하다, 진압하다 ❑ 국제 사회의 억제 노력에도 불구하고 계속 번성하는 마약 밀매상 ● 억제, 진압 불가산명사 ❑ 민주화 운동 시위의 폭력 진압 후 수감된 사람들 **2** 타동사 억제되다 ❑ 암세포의 번식과 성장은 방사선을 집중적으로 쏘아 억제될 수 있다. ● 억제 불가산명사 ❑ 안과 질환은 건강하지 못한 생활 방식과 그에 따른 면역 체계 억제를 시사하는 것일 수 있다. **3** 타동사 자제하다 ❑ 리즈는 배리를 떠올리며 웃음을 자제했다. ● 자제 불가산명사 ❑ 엄마가 자신의 감정을 자제하는 것이 문제를 유발할 수도 있다. **4** 타동사 (정보를) 숨기다 ❑ 그 정보를 누설하지 말라고 나를 설득하려 한 적은 절대 없었다. ● 숨김 불가산명사 ❑ 조사관들은 공식 문서를 숨겼다는 어떤 의혹도 뒷받침하는 증거를 발견하지 못했다. **5** 타동사 억제하다 ❑ "정부가 경제를 황폐화시키면서 인플레이션을 억제하고 있다."라고 그는 말했다.

1 불가산명사 패권 ❑ 보수 성향의 구세력이 정치적 패권을 회복했다. **2** 불가산명사 우위, 우월 ❑ 유에스 오픈 결승전에서 그라프가 계속 전반적인 우위를 점했다.

1 형용사 최고의 ❑ 맥아더는 태평양 연합군의 최고 사령관이었다. ❑ 대법원 **2** 형용사 지대한, 극도의 [강조] ❑ 그녀의 승낙이 대단히 중요했다. ● 대단히, 극도로 부사 ❑ 그녀는 자기 일을 계속하고 있고 대단히 잘 해 내고 있다.

a b c d e f g h i j k l m n o p q r s t u v w x y z

Word Link   sur ≈ above : surcharge, surface, surplus

sur|charge /sɜːrtʃɑːrdʒ/ (surcharges) N-COUNT A **surcharge** is an extra payment of money in addition to the usual payment for something. It is added for a specific reason, for example by a company because costs have risen or by a government as a tax. ❏ *The government introduced a 15% surcharge on imports.*

가산명사 추가 요금 ❏ 정부는 수입품에 대한 15퍼센트의 추가 요금을 도입했다.

sure ♦♦♦ /ʃʊər/ (surer, surest) **1** ADJ If you are **sure** that something is true, you are certain that it is true. If you are not **sure** about something, you do not know for certain what the true situation is. [v-link ADJ, ADJ that, ADJ wh, ADJ about/of n] ❏ *He'd never been in a class before and he was not even sure that he should have been teaching.* ❏ *The president has never been sure which direction he wanted to go in on this issue.* **2** ADJ If someone is **sure** of getting something, they will definitely get it or they think they will definitely get it. [v-link ADJ of -ing/n] ❏ *A lot of people think that it's better to pay for their education so that they can be sure of getting quality.* **3** PHRASE If you say that something is **sure to** happen, you are emphasizing your belief that it will happen. [EMPHASIS] ❏ *With over 80 beaches to choose from, you are sure to find a place to lay your towel.* **4** ADJ **Sure** is used to emphasize that something such as a sign or ability is reliable or accurate. [EMPHASIS] [ADJ n] ❏ *Sharpe's leg and shoulder began to ache, a sure sign of rain.* **5** ADJ If you tell someone to **be sure to** do something, you mean that they must not forget to do it. [EMPHASIS] [v-link ADJ, ADJ to-inf, ADJ that] ❏ *Be sure to read about how mozzarella is made, on page 65.* **6** CONVENTION **Sure** is an informal way of saying "yes" or "all right." [FORMULAE] ❏ *"Do you know where she lives?" — "Sure."* **7** ADV You can use **sure** in order to emphasize what you are saying. [INFORMAL, EMPHASIS] [ADV before v] ❏ *"Has the whole world just gone crazy?" — "Sure looks that way, doesn't it?"* **8** PHRASE You say **sure enough**, especially when telling a story, to confirm that something was really true or was actually happening. ❏ *We found the English treacle pudding too good to resist. Sure enough, it was delicious.* **9** PHRASE If you say that something is **for sure** or that you know it **for sure**, you mean that it is definitely true. ❏ *One thing's for sure, Astbury's vocal style hasn't changed much over the years.* **10** PHRASE If you **make sure that** something is done, you take action so that it is done. ❏ *Make sure that you follow the instructions carefully.* **11** PHRASE If you **make sure that** something is the way that you want or expect it to be, you check that it is that way. ❏ *He looked in the bathroom to make sure that he was alone.* **12** PHRASE If you are **sure of yourself**, you are very confident about your own abilities or opinions. ❏ *I'd never seen him like this, so sure of himself, so in command.*

1 형용사 확신하는 ❏ 그는 전에 한 번도 수업을 한 적이 없었고 심지어 자기가 가르치는 일을 해야 했는지 확신하지도 못했다. ❏ 대통령은 이 사안에 대해 자신이 어떤 입장을 취하고 싶은지 확신이 든 적이 없었다. **2** 형용사 확신한; 확신하는 ❏ 많은 사람들이 그렇게 해야 확실히 질 높은 교육을 받을 수 있다고 생각해서 자기가 받는 교육에 대해 돈을 지불하는 게 더 낫다고 생각한다. **3** 구 반드시 ~할 [강조] ❏ 선택할 수 있는 해변이 80곳이 넘기 때문에 여러분은 타월을 깔고 쉴 수 있는 곳을 반드시 찾으실 수 있을 겁니다. **4** 형용사 확실한 [강조] ❏ 샤프의 다리와 어깨가 쑤시기 시작했는데 그것은 비가 올 확실한 조짐이다. **5** 형용사 꼭 ~하시오 [강조] ❏ 65쪽에 있는 모차렐라 제조 방법을 꼭 읽어 보세요. **6** 관용 표현 물론이지, 그럼 [의례적인 표현] ❏ "그녀가 사는 곳을 아세요?" "물론이죠." **7** 부사 확실히 [비격식체, 강조] ❏ "그냥 세상 전체가 미쳐 버린 건가?" "확실히 그래 보여, 그렇지 않아?" **8** 구 정말로 ❏ 우리는 영국 당밀 푸딩이 너무 훌륭해 먹지 않을 수 없다는 것을 알게 되었다. 정말이지 맛있었다. **9** 구 확실히 ❏ 한 가지는 확실해. 애스트베리의 창법이 세월이 지났어도 별로 변하지 않았어. **10** 구 확실히 하다 ❏ 반드시 지시를 주의 깊게 따르세요. **11** 구 확인하다 ❏ 그는 자기 혼자뿐인지 확인하기 위해 목욕탕 안을 들여다보았다. **12** 구 확신에 찬 ❏ 나는 이와 같이 그렇게 확신에 차고, 그렇게 통솔력이 있는 그를 본 적이 없었다.

sure-fire also **surefire** ADJ A **sure-fire** thing is something that is certain to succeed or win. [INFORMAL] [ADJ n] ❏ *If something's a sure-fire hit then Radio One will play it.*

형용사 틀림없이 성공할 [비격식체] ❏ 만약 틀림없이 성공할 만한 히트곡이 있다면 라디오 원은 그것을 틀 것이다.

sure|ly ♦♦♦ /ʃʊərli/ **1** ADV You use **surely** to emphasize that you think something should be true, and you would be surprised if it was not true. [EMPHASIS] [ADV with cl/group] ❏ *You're an intelligent woman, surely you realize by now that I'm helping you.* ❏ *You surely haven't forgotten Dr. Walters?* **2** ADV If something will **surely** happen or is **surely** the case, it will definitely happen or is definitely the case. [FORMAL] ❏ *He knew that under the surgeon's knife he would surely die.* **3** PHRASE If you say that something is happening **slowly but surely**, you mean that it is happening gradually but it is definitely happening. ❏ *Slowly but surely she started to fall in love with him.*

1 부사 확실히, 틀림없이 [강조] ❏ 너는 머리가 좋은 여자야. 너는 지금쯤이면 틀림없이 내가 너를 도와주고 있다는 걸 알아차리겠지. ❏ 너 틀림없이 월터스 박사를 잊지 않았겠지? **2** 부사 분명히 [격식체] ❏ 그는 그 외과 의사가 수술을 한다면 자신이 분명히 죽으리라는 것을 알았다. **3** 구 서서히 그러나 분명히 ❏ 서서히 그러나 분명히 그녀는 그를 사랑하기 시작하고 있었다.

You use **surely** to express disagreement or surprise. ❏ *Surely you care about what happens to her.* You use **certainly** to emphasize that what you say is definitely true. ❏ *His death was certainly not an accident.* Both British and American speakers use **certainly** to agree with requests and statements. ❏ *"It is still a difficult world for women." — "Oh, certainly."* Note that American speakers also use **surely** in this way.

surely는 동의하지 않음 또는 놀람을 표현할 때 쓴다. ❏ 확실히 당신은 그녀에게 일어난 일을 걱정하지요. certainly는 말하는 내용이 분명히 사실임을 강조할 때 쓴다. ❏ 그의 죽음은 분명히 사고가 아니에요. certainly는 영국인과 미국인 모두 요청이나 진술에 동의할 때 쓴다. ❏ '세상은 아직도 여성들에게는 힘들지요.' — '네, 물론입니다.' 미국인들은 이런 식으로 surely도 쓴다는 점을 유념하시오.

Word Partnership   surely의 연어

v.   surely know *something*, surely think *something* **1**
     surely die **2**

sure|ty /ʃʊərɪti/ (sureties) N-VAR A **surety** is money or something valuable which you give to someone to show that you will do what you have promised. ❏ *The insurance company will take warehouse stocks or treasury bonds as surety.*

가산명사 또는 불가산명사 담보 ❏ 보험 회사는 창고 물건과 장기 재정 증권을 담보로 잡을 것이다.

surf /sɜːrf/ (surfs, surfing, surfed) **1** N-UNCOUNT **Surf** is the mass of white bubbles that is formed by waves as they fall upon the shore. ❏ *...surf rolling onto white sand beaches.* **2** V-I If you **surf**, you ride on big waves in the sea on a special board. ❏ *I'm going to buy a surfboard and learn to surf.* ● **surf|er** (surfers) N-COUNT ❏ *...this small fishing village, which continues to attract painters and surfers.* **3** V-T If you **surf** the Internet, you spend time finding and looking at things on the Internet. [COMPUTING] ❏ *No one knows how many people currently surf the Net.* ● **surf|er** (surfers) N-COUNT ❏ *Net surfers can use their credit cards to pay for anything from toys to train tickets.* →see **beach**

1 불가산명사 (하얗게 부서지는) 파도 ❏ 백사장 위로 밀려오는 파도 **2** 자동사 파도타기를 하다 ❏ 나는 서핑보드를 사서 파도타기를 배울 거야. ● 파도타기를 하는 사람 가산명사 ❏ 화가들과 파도타기를 하는 사람들이 계속 찾아드는 이 작은 어촌 **3** 타동사 (인터넷에서) 정보를 검색하다 [컴퓨터] ❏ 요즘에 얼마나 많은 사람들이 인터넷에서 정보를 검색하는지 아무도 모른다. ● 검색자 가산명사 ❏ 인터넷 검색자들은 신용 카드를 이용해 장난감에서 기차표까지 뭐든지 살 수 있다.

sur|face ♦♦♦ /sɜːrfɪs/ (surfaces, surfacing, surfaced) **1** N-COUNT The **surface** of something is the flat top part of it or the outside of it. ❏ *Ozone forms a protective layer between 12 and 30 miles above the Earth's surface.* ❏ *...tiny little waves on the surface of the water.* **2** N-COUNT A work **surface** is a flat area, for example the top of a table, desk, or kitchen counter, on which you can work. ❏ *It can simply be left on the work surface.* **3** N-SING When you refer to **the surface** of a situation, you are talking about what can be seen easily rather than what is hidden or not immediately obvious. ❏ *Back in Britain, things appear, on the surface, simpler.* **4** V-I If someone or something under water **surfaces**, they come up to the surface of the water. ❏ *He surfaced, gasping for air.* **5** V-I When something such as a piece of

1 가산명사 표면 ❏ 오존은 지구 표면으로부터 12마일에서 30마일 떨어진 곳에서 보호층을 형성한다. ❏ 수면 위의 아주 작은 물결 **2** 가산명사 표면 ❏ 그것은 간단히 작업대 표면 위에 둘 수 있다. **3** 단수명사 외관, 표면 ❏ 영국으로 돌아오니 외관상으로는 사정이 더 간단해 보인다. **4** 자동사 수면 위로 올라오다 ❏ 그는 수면 위로 나와 헐떡거리며 숨을 쉬었다. **5** 자동사 표면으로 떠오르다 ❏ 신문은 그 증거가 표면으로 떠오르면 분명히 대소동이 일어날 것이라고 말한다.

news, a feeling, or a problem **surfaces**, it becomes known or becomes obvious. ❑ *The paper says the evidence, when it surfaces, is certain to cause uproar.*

	Word Partnership surface의 연어
ADJ.	**flat** surface, **rough** surface, **smooth** surface ■
N.	surface **area**, **Earth's** surface, surface **of the water** ■
	surface **level** ■ ⑤
V.	**break the** surface ■
	scratch the surface ■ ⑤

sur|face mail N-UNCOUNT **Surface mail** is the system of sending letters and packages by road, rail, or sea, not by air. ❑ *Goods may be sent by surface mail or airmail.*

불가산명사 (항공 우편이 아닌) 보통 우편 ❑ 물품들은 보통 우편이나 항공 우편으로 보낼 것이다.

surf|ing /sɜrfɪŋ/ ■ N-UNCOUNT **Surfing** is the sport of riding on the top of a wave while standing or lying on a special board. ❑ *...every type of watersport from jetskiing and surfing to sailing and fishing.* ② N-UNCOUNT **Surfing** is the activity of looking at different sites on the Internet, especially when you are not looking for anything in particular. [COMPUTING] ❑ *The simple fact is that, for most people, surfing is too expensive.*

■ 불가산명사 파도타기, 서핑 ❑ 제트 스키 타기와 파도타기부터 요트 타기와 낚시에 이르는 온갖 형태의 수상 스포츠 ② 불가산명사 인터넷 검색 [컴퓨터] ❑ 분명한 사실은 대부분의 사람들에게는 인터넷 검색이 너무 비용이 많이 든다는 것이다.

surge /sɜrdʒ/ (**surges, surging, surged**) ■ N-COUNT A **surge** is a sudden large increase in something that has previously been steady, or has only increased or developed slowly. ❑ *Specialists see various reasons for the recent surge in inflation.* ② V-I If something **surges**, it increases suddenly and greatly, after being steady or developing only slowly. ❑ *The Freedom Party's electoral support surged from just under 10 per cent to nearly 17 per cent.* ③ V-I If a crowd of people **surge** forward, they suddenly move forward together. ❑ *The photographers and cameramen surged forward.* ④ N-COUNT A **surge** is a sudden powerful movement of a physical force such as wind or water. ❑ *The whole car shuddered with an almost frightening surge of power.* ⑤ V-I If a physical force such as water or electricity **surges** through something, it moves through it suddenly and powerfully. ❑ *Thousands of volts surged through his car after he careered into a lamp post, ripping out live wires.*

■ 가산명사 급등 ❑ 전문가들은 최근 인플레이션 급등에는 여러 가지 이유가 있다고 본다. ② 자동사 급등하다 ❑ 선거에서 자유당에 대한 지지가 겨우 10퍼센트를 밑돌다가 약17퍼센트로 급등했다. ③ 자동사 (갑자기) 밀려들다 ❑ 사진사들과 촬영 기사들이 앞으로 밀려들었다. ④ 가산명사 요동, 격동 ❑ 차 전체가 거의 겁이 날 정도로 세차게 요동치며 흔들렸다. ⑤ 자동사 뒤흔들다 ❑ 그가 차를 몰고 가로등을 들이받으면서 전류가 흐르는 전선이 뜯겨 나와 수천 볼트의 전류가 순식간에 그의 차를 뒤흔들고 지나갔다.

sur|geon /sɜrdʒən/ (**surgeons**) N-COUNT A **surgeon** is a doctor who is specially trained to perform surgery. ❑ *...a heart surgeon.*

가산명사 외과 의사 ❑ 심장 전문 외과 의사

sur|gery ◆◇◇ /sɜrdʒəri/ (**surgeries**) ■ N-UNCOUNT **Surgery** is medical treatment in which someone's body is cut open so that a doctor can repair, remove, or replace a diseased or damaged part. ❑ *His father has just recovered from heart surgery.* →see also **cosmetic surgery, plastic surgery** ② N-COUNT A **surgery** is the room in a hospital where surgeons operate on their patients. [AM; BRIT **theatre, operating theatre**] ③ N-COUNT A **surgery** is the room or house where a doctor or dentist works. [BRIT; AM **doctor's office, dentist's office**] ❑ *Bill was in the doctor's surgery demanding to know what was wrong with him.* ④ N-COUNT A doctor's **surgery** is the period of time each day when a doctor sees patients at his or her surgery. [BRIT; AM **office hours**] ❑ *His surgery always ends at eleven.* →see **cancer, laser**

■ 불가산명사 수술 ❑ 그의 아버지는 심장 수술을 받고 막 회복된 참이다. ② 가산명사 수술실 [미국영어; 영국영어 theatre, operating theatre] ③ 가산명사 진료소, 진료소 [미국영어; 미국영어 doctor's office, dentist's office] ❑ 빌은 그 의사의 진료실에서 자기에게 무슨 문제가 있는 건지 알려 달라고 요구하고 있었다. ④ 가산명사 진료 시간 [영국영어; 미국영어 office hours] ❑ 그의 진료 시간은 항상 11시에 끝난다.

sur|gi|cal /sɜrdʒɪkəl/ ■ ADJ **Surgical** equipment and clothing are used in surgery. [ADJ n] ❑ *...an array of surgical instruments.* ② ADJ **Surgical** treatment involves surgery. [ADJ n] ❑ *A biopsy is usually a minor surgical procedure.* ● **sur|gi|cal|ly** ADV [ADV with v] ❑ *In very severe cases, bunions may be surgically removed.*

■ 형용사 외과의 ❑ 배치해 놓은 수술 도구들 ② 형용사 수술의 ❑ 조직 검사는 대체로 수술 절차가 간단하다. ● 외과적으로, 수술로 부사 ❑ 아주 심각한 경우에는 건막류를 수술로 제거할 수도 있다.

sur|mise /sərmaɪz/ (**surmises, surmising, surmised**) ■ V-T If you **surmise** that something is true, you guess it from the available evidence, although you do not know for certain. [FORMAL] ❑ *There's so little to go on, we can only surmise what happened.* ② N-VAR If you say that a particular conclusion is **surmise**, you mean that it is a guess based on the available evidence and you do not know for certain that it is true. [FORMAL] ❑ *It is mere surmise that Bosch had Brant's poem in mind when doing this painting.*

■ 타동사 추측하다 [격식체] ❑ 계속 진행되고 있는 일이 거의 없다. 전에 무슨 일이 있었는지는 추측만 할 뿐이다. ② 가산명사 또는 불가산명사 추측 [격식체] ❑ 보쉬가 이 그림을 그릴 때 브란트의 시를 마음에 두고 있었다는 것은 어디까지나 추측일 뿐이다.

sur|name /sɜrneɪm/ (**surnames**) N-COUNT Your **surname** is the name that you share with other members of your family. In English speaking countries and many other countries it is your last name. ❑ *She'd never known his surname.*

가산명사 성(姓) ❑ 그녀는 결코 그의 성을 알지 못했다.

sur|pass /sərpæs/ (**surpasses, surpassing, surpassed**) ■ V-T If one person or thing **surpasses** another, the first is better than, or has more of a particular quality than, the second. ❑ *He was determined to surpass the achievements of his older brothers.* ② V-T If something **surpasses** expectations, it is much better than it was expected to be. ❑ *Conrad Black gave an excellent party that surpassed expectations.*

■ 타동사 능가하다 ❑ 그는 형들의 성적을 능가하기로 결심했다. ② 타동사 뛰어넘다, 초과하다 ❑ 콘래드 블랙은 기대를 뛰어넘는 훌륭한 파티를 열었다.

	Word Link sur ≈ above : surcharge, surface, surplus

sur|plus ◆◇◇ /sɜrplʌs, -pləs/ (**surpluses**) ■ N-VAR If there is a **surplus of** something, there is more than is needed. ❑ *Germany suffers from a surplus of teachers.* ② ADJ **Surplus** is used to describe something that is extra or that is more than is needed. ❑ *Few people have large sums of surplus cash.* ❑ *I sell my surplus birds to a local pet shop.* ③ N-COUNT If a country has a trade **surplus**, it exports more than it imports. ❑ *Japan's annual trade surplus is in the region of 100 billion dollars.* ④ N-COUNT If a government has a budget **surplus**, it has spent less than it received in taxes. ❑ *Norway's budget surplus has fallen from 5.9% in 1986 to an expected 0.1% this year.*

■ 가산명사 또는 불가산명사 과잉 ❑ 독일은 교사 과잉 문제를 안고 있다. ② 형용사 여분의, 과잉의 ❑ 여분으로 많은 현금을 보유하고 있는 사람은 거의 없다. ❑ 나는 여분의 새들을 동네 애완동물 가게에 팔았다. ③ 가산명사 (무역) 흑자 ❑ 일본의 연간 무역 흑자는 1,000억 달러 정도 된다. ④ 가산명사 흑자 ❑ 노르웨이의 예산 흑자는 1986년 5.9 퍼센트에서 올해는 예상대로 0.1퍼센트로 하락했다.

sur|prise ◆◆◇ /sərpraɪz/ (**surprises, surprising, surprised**) ■ N-COUNT A **surprise** is an unexpected event, fact, or piece of news. ❑ *I have a surprise for you: we are moving to Switzerland!* ❑ *It may come as a surprise to some that a normal, healthy child is born with many skills.* ● ADJ **Surprise** is also an adjective. [ADJ n] ❑ *Baxter*

■ 가산명사 뜻밖의 일, 놀라운 소식 ❑ 너에게 알려 줄 뜻밖의 소식이 있어. 우리 스위스로 이사 가! ❑ 정상이고 건강한 아이가 많은 재주를 갖고 태어나는 것이 일부 사람들에게는 뜻밖의 일로 다가올 수도

arrived here this afternoon, on a surprise visit. ◨ N-UNCOUNT **Surprise** is the feeling that you have when something unexpected happens. ❑ The Foreign Office in London has expressed surprise at these allegations. ❑ "You mean he's going to vote against her?" Scobie asked in surprise. ◱ V-T If something **surprises** you, it gives you a feeling of surprise. ❑ We'll solve the case ourselves and surprise everyone. ❑ It surprised me that a driver of Alain's experience should make those mistakes. ◳ V-T If you **surprise** someone, you give them, tell them, or do something pleasant that they are not expecting. ❑ Surprise a new neighbor with one of your favorite home-made dishes. ◵ N-COUNT If you describe someone or something as a **surprise**, you mean that they are very good or pleasant although you were not expecting this. ❑ ...Senga MacFie, one of the surprises of the World Championships three months ago. ◷ V-T If you **surprise** someone, you attack, capture, or find them when they are not expecting it. ❑ Marlborough led his armies across the Rhine and surprised the French and Bavarian armies near the village of Blenheim. ◸ →see also **surprised, surprising** ◺ PHRASE If something **takes** you **by surprise**, it happens when you are not expecting it or when you are not prepared for it. ❑ His question took his two companions by surprise.

Word Partnership   surprise의 연어

N.	surprise **announcement**, surprise **attack**, surprise **move**, surprise **visit** ◨
	a bit of a surprise ◨ ◵
	element of surprise ◨
ADJ.	**big** surprise, **complete** surprise, **great** surprise, **pleasant** surprise ◨ ◵

sur|prised ♦♦♦ /sərpraɪzd/ ◨ ADJ If you are **surprised** at something, you have a feeling of surprise, because it is unexpected or unusual. ❑ This lady was genuinely surprised at what happened to her pet. ◩ →see also **surprise**

sur|pris|ing ♦♦♦ /sərpraɪzɪŋ/ ◨ ADJ Something that is **surprising** is unexpected or unusual and makes you feel surprised. ❑ It is not surprising that children learn to read at different rates. ● **sur|pris|ing|ly** ADV ❑ ...the Flemish Bloc, which did surprisingly well in the general election last year. ◩ →see also **surprise**

sur|re|al /sərɪəl/ ADJ If you describe something as **surreal**, you mean that the elements in it are combined in a strange way that you would not normally expect, like in a dream. ❑ "Performance" is undoubtedly one of the most surreal movies ever made.

sur|ren|der ♦♦♦ /sərendər/ (surrenders, surrendering, surrendered) ◨ V-I If you **surrender**, you stop fighting or resisting someone and agree that you have been beaten. ❑ General Martin Bonnet called on the rebels to surrender. ● N-VAR **Surrender** is also a noun. ❑ ...the government's apparent surrender to demands made by the religious militants. ◩ V-T If you **surrender** something you would rather keep, you give it up or let someone else have it, for example after a struggle. ❑ Nadja had to fill out forms surrendering all rights to her property. ● N-UNCOUNT **Surrender** is also a noun. ❑ ...the sixteen-day deadline for the surrender of weapons and ammunition. ◪ V-T If you **surrender** something such as a ticket or your passport, you give it to someone in authority when they ask you to. [FORMAL] ❑ They have been ordered to surrender their passports. →see **flag, war**

Thesaurus   surrender의 참조어

v.	abandon, give in, give up ◨ ◩

sur|ren|der value (surrender values) N-COUNT The **surrender value** of a life insurance policy is the amount of money you receive if you decide that you no longer wish to continue with the policy. [BUSINESS] ❑ An ordinary life policy may have a cash surrender value of $50,000.

sur|ro|gate /sɜrəgeɪt, -gɪt, BRIT sʌrəgɪt/ (surrogates) ADJ You use **surrogate** to describe a person or thing that is given a particular role because the person or thing that should have the role is not available. [ADJ n] ❑ Martin had become Howard Cosell's surrogate son. ● N-COUNT **Surrogate** is also a noun. ❑ Arms control should not be made into a surrogate for peace.

sur|ro|gate moth|er (surrogate mothers) N-COUNT A **surrogate mother** is a woman who has agreed to give birth to a baby on behalf of another woman.

sur|round ♦♦◊ /səraʊnd/ (surrounds, surrounding, surrounded) ◨ V-T If a person or thing **is surrounded** by something, that thing is situated all around them. ❑ The small churchyard was surrounded by a rusted wrought-iron fence. ❑ The shell surrounding the egg has many important functions. ◩ V-T If you **are surrounded** by soldiers or police, they spread out so that they are in positions all the way around you. ❑ When the car stopped in the town square it was surrounded by soldiers and militiamen. ◪ V-T The circumstances, feelings, or ideas which **surround** something are those that are closely associated with it. ❑ The decision had been agreed in principle before today's meeting, but some controversy surrounded it. ◫ V-T If you **surround yourself with** certain people or things, you make sure that you have a lot of them near you all the time. ❑ He had made it his business to surround himself with a hand-picked group of bright young officers.

sur|round|ings /səraʊndɪŋz/ N-PLURAL When you are describing the place where you are at the moment, or the place where you live, you can refer to it as your **surroundings**. ❑ Schumacher adapted effortlessly to his new surroundings.

sur|tax /sɜrtæks/ N-UNCOUNT **Surtax** is an additional tax on incomes higher than the level at which ordinary tax is paid. [BUSINESS] ❑ ...a 10% surtax for Americans earning more than $250,000 a year.

있다. ● 형용사 뜻밖의 ❑ 백스터는 오늘 오후에 여기 도착했는데 뜻밖의 방문이다. ◨ 불가산명사 놀라움 ❑ 런던에 위치한 외무성이 이러한 의혹에 대해서 놀라움을 표시했다. ❑ "그가 그녀에게 반대표를 던질 거라는 말씀인가요?"라고 스코비가 놀라서 물었다. ◱ 타동사 놀라게 하다 ❑ 우리는 이 사건을 우리 스스로 해결해서 모든 사람들을 놀라게 할 것이다. ❑ 앨레인같이 경험 많은 운전자가 그러한 실수를 하다니 나는 놀라웠다. ◳ 타동사 (반가운 일로) 깜짝 놀라게 하다 ❑ 당신이 가장 좋아하는, 집에서 만든 요리들 중 하나로 새 이웃을 깜짝 놀라게 해 보세요. ◵ 가산명사 놀라운 사람, 놀라운 것 ❑ 석 달 전 세계 선수권 대회에 등장한 놀라운 인물들 중 한 사람인 센가 맥피 ◷ 타동사 기습하다 ❑ 말보로는 군대를 이끌고 라인 강을 건너 블렌하임 마을 근처에서 프랑스와 바바리아 군대를 기습 공격했다. ◺ 구 깜짝 놀라게 하다 ❑ 그의 질문에 그의 동료 두 명은 깜짝 놀랐다.

◨ 형용사 깜짝 놀란 ❑ 이 부인은 자기 애완동물에게 일어난 일에 대해 정말 놀랐다.

◨ 형용사 놀라운 ❑ 아이들이 글 읽기를 익히는 속도가 개인별로 다르다는 것은 놀라운 일이 아니다. ● 놀랍게도 부사 ❑ 지난해 총선 때 놀랄 정도로 선전한 플랑드르 블록

형용사 초현실적인 ❑ '공연'은 의심할 바 없이 역대 가장 초현실적인 영화 중의 하나이다.

◨ 자동사 항복하다 ❑ 마틴 보넷 장군은 반군들에게 항복할 것을 요구했다. ● 가산명사 또는 불가산명사 항복, 굴복 ❑ 종교 과격 단체의 요구에 대한 정부의 명백한 굴복 ◩ 타동사 포기하다, 내주다 ❑ 나디아는 자기의 재산에 대한 모든 권리를 포기하는 서류를 작성해야 했다. ● 불가산명사 포기, 인도 ❑ 무기 및 탄약 인도를 위한 16일간의 기한 ◪ 타동사 건네주다, 양도하다 [격식체] ❑ 그들은 여권을 제시하라는 명령을 받았다.

가산명사 중도 해약 반환금 [경제] ❑ 일반 생명 보험은 중도 해약 반환금 5만 달러를 현금으로 받는다.

형용사 대리의 ❑ 마틴은 하워드 코젤의 아들을 대신하게 되었다. ● 가산명사 대리, 대용물 ❑ 군비 제한이 평화를 대신하는 것이 되어서는 안 된다.

가산명사 대리모

◨ 타동사 둘러싸이다 ❑ 조그마한 그 교회 마당은 녹이 슨 연철 울타리로 둘러싸였다. ❑ 알을 둘러싸고 있는 껍데기는 많은 중요한 기능을 한다. ◩ 타동사 포위하다 ❑ 그 자동차가 마을 광장에 멈춰 서자 군인과 민병대들이 그 차를 포위했다. ◪ 타동사 둘러싸다 ❑ 원칙적으로 그 결정은 오늘 모임 전에 이미 합의가 되었지만 그것을 둘러싼 논란이 어느 정도 여전히 남아 있었다. ◫ 타동사 (자기 주위에) ~을 포진시키다 ❑ 그는 일을 삼고 똑똑하고 젊은 장교들 일단을 세심히 선발하여 자기 주위에 포진시켰다.

복수명사 환경 ❑ 슈마허는 수월하게 새로운 환경에 적응했다.

불가산명사 부가세 [경제] ❑ 미국 내 연간 25만 달러 이상의 소득자에게 적용되는 10퍼센트의 부가세

sur|veil|lance /sərveɪləns/ N-UNCOUNT **Surveillance** is the careful watching of someone, especially by an organization such as the police or the army. ❑ *He was arrested after being kept under constant surveillance.* ❑ *Police swooped on the home after a two-week surveillance operation.*

불가산명사 감시 ❑ 그는 지속적인 감시를 받다가 체포되었다. ❑ 경찰은 2주간의 감시 작전 후에 그 집을 급습했다.

sur|vey ◆◇ (**surveys, surveying, surveyed**)

> The noun is pronounced /sɜrveɪ/. The verb is pronounced /sərveɪ/, and can also be pronounced /sɜrveɪ/ in meanings ② and ⑤.

> 명사는 /sɜrveɪ /로 발음된다. 동사는 /sərveɪ /로 발음되고, ②와 ⑤ 의미는 /sɜrveɪ /로도 발음될 수 있다.

❶ N-COUNT If you carry out a **survey**, you try to find out detailed information about a lot of different people or things, usually by asking people a series of questions. ❑ *The council conducted a survey of the uses to which farm buildings are put.* ❷ V-T If you **survey** a number of people, companies, or organizations, you try to find out information about their opinions or behavior, usually by asking them a series of questions. ❑ *Business Development Advisers surveyed 211 companies for the report.* ❸ V-T If you **survey** something, you look at or consider the whole of it carefully. ❑ *He pushed himself to his feet and surveyed the room.* ❹ N-COUNT If someone carries out a **survey** of an area of land, they examine it and measure it, usually in order to make a map of it. ❑ *...the organizer of the geological survey of India.* ❺ V-T If someone **surveys** an area of land, they examine it and measure it, usually in order to make a map of it. ❑ *Scarborough Council commissioned geological experts earlier this year to survey the cliffs.* ❻ N-COUNT A **survey** is a careful examination of the condition and structure of a house, usually carried out in order to give information to a person who wants to buy it. [mainly BRIT; AM **inspection**] ❑ *...a structural survey undertaken by a qualified surveyor.* ❼ V-T If someone **surveys** a house, they examine it carefully and report on its structure, usually in order to give advice to a person who is thinking of buying it. [mainly BRIT; AM **inspect**] ❑ *...the people who surveyed the house for the mortgage.* →see **census**

❶ 가산명사 (설문) 조사 ❑ 위원회는 농장 건물 용도에 대한 조사를 실시했다. ❷ 타동사 (설문) 조사하다 ❑ 사업 발전 고문들은 그 보고서를 위해 211개 회사를 대상으로 설문 조사를 했다. ❸ 타동사 유심히 살피다 ❑ 그는 발을 내딛으며 그 방을 유심히 살폈다. ❹ 가산명사 측량 ❑ 인도 지질 측량 작업 주최자 ❺ 타동사 측량하다 ❑ 스카버러 시의회가 올해 초 지질 전문가들에게 의뢰하여 그 절벽을 측량했다. ❻ 가산명사 (건물의) 검사 [주로 영국영어; 미국영어 inspection] ❼ 타동사 (건물을) 검사하다 [주로 영국영어; 미국영어 inspect] ❑ 담보 대출을 위해 그 집을 검사한 사람들

sur|vey|or /sərveɪr/ (**surveyors**) ❶ N-COUNT A **surveyor** is a person whose job is to survey land. ❑ *...the surveyor's maps of the Queen Alexandra Range.* ❷ N-COUNT A **surveyor** is a person whose job is to survey buildings. [BRIT; AM **structural engineer, inspector**] ❑ *Our surveyor warned us that the house needed totally rebuilding.* ❸ →see also **quantity surveyor**

❶ 가산명사 측량관 ❑ 그 측량관의 퀸 알렉산드라 레인지 지도 ❷ 가산명사 (건물) 조사관 [영국영어; 미국영어 structural engineer, inspector] ❑ 조사관은 우리에게 그 집은 전면적인 재건축을 해야 한다고 경고했다.

sur|viv|al ◆◆◇ /sərvaɪvəl/ ❶ N-UNCOUNT If you refer to the **survival** of something or someone, you mean that they manage to continue or exist in spite of difficult circumstances. ❑ *...companies which have been struggling for survival in the advancing recession.* ❷ N-UNCOUNT If you refer to the **survival** of a person or living thing, you mean that they live through a dangerous situation in which it was possible that they might die. ❑ *If cancers are spotted early there's a high chance of survival.*

❶ 불가산명사 생존 ❑ 계속되는 불경기 속에서 생존 투쟁을 해 오고 있는 기업들 ❷ 불가산명사 생존, 살아남음 ❑ 암은 조기 발견 시 생존 가능성이 높다.

Word Link	viv ≈ living : revival, survive, vivacious

sur|vive ◆◆◇ /sərvaɪv/ (**survives, surviving, survived**) ❶ V-I If a person or living thing **survives** in a dangerous situation such as an accident or an illness, they do not die. ❑ *...the sequence of events that left the eight pupils battling to survive in icy seas for over four hours.* ❑ *Those organisms that are most suited to the environment will be those that will survive.* ❷ V-I If you **survive** in difficult circumstances, you manage to live or continue in spite of them and do not let them affect you very much. ❑ *On my first day here I thought, "Ooh, how will I survive?"* ❑ *...people who are struggling to survive without jobs.* ❸ V-I If something **survives**, it continues to exist even after being in a dangerous situation or existing for a long time. ❑ *When the market economy is introduced, many factories will not survive.* ❹ V-T If you **survive** someone, you continue to live after they have died. ❑ *Most women will survive their spouses.*

❶ 자동사 살아남다 ❑ 8명의 어린 학생들이 얼어 붙일 듯한 바닷물 속에서 생존을 위해 4시간 넘게 몸부림을 치게 만든 일련의 사건들 ❑ 환경에 가장 적합한 그런 유기체가 살아남는 것들이다. ❷ 자동사 견디다 ❑ 여기 온 첫날 난 '아, 어떻게 견딜 것인가?'하고 생각했다. ❑ 일자리도 없이 견뎌 내려고 노력하는 사람들 ❸ 자동사 살아남다 ❑ 시장 경제가 도입된다면, 많은 공장들이 살아남지 못할 것이다. ❹ 타동사 -보다 오래 살다 ❑ 대부분의 여성들은 배우자보다 오래 산다.

sur|vi|vor /sərvaɪvər/ (**survivors**) ❶ N-COUNT A **survivor of** a disaster, accident, or illness is someone who continues to live afterward in spite of coming close to death. ❑ *Officials said there were no survivors of the plane crash.* ❷ N-COUNT A **survivor of** a very unpleasant experience is a person who has had such an experience, and who is still affected by it. ❑ *This book is written with survivors of child sexual abuse in mind.* ❸ N-COUNT A person's **survivors** are the members of their family who continue to live after they have died. [AM] ❑ *The compensation bill offers the miners or their survivors as much as $100,000 apiece.*

❶ 가산명사 생존자 ❑ 관계자들은 그 비행기 추락 사건의 생존자가 없다고 했다. ❷ 가산명사 (힘든 일을) 겪은 사람, 피해자 ❑ 이 책은 아동 성학대 피해자들을 염두에 두고 쓰여졌다. ❸ 가산명사 유족 [미국영어] ❑ 보상 법안으로 광부들이나 유족들은 무려 10만 달러를 각자 받게 된다.

sus|cep|ti|ble /səsɛptɪbəl/ ❶ ADJ If you are **susceptible to** something or someone, you are very likely to be influenced by them. [v-link ADJ to n] ❑ *Young people are the most susceptible to advertisements.* ❑ *James was extremely susceptible to flattery.* ❷ ADJ If you are **susceptible to** a disease or injury, you are very likely to be affected by it. ❑ *Walking with weights makes the shoulders very susceptible to injury.*

❶ 형용사 민감한, 쉽게 영향을 받는 ❑ 젊은 사람들이 광고에 가장 민감하다. ❑ 제임스는 지나치게 칭찬에 민감했다. ❷ 형용사 (부상을) 당하기 쉬운, (병에) 걸리기 쉬운 ❑ 무거운 물건을 메고 걸으면 어깨에 부상을 입기 매우 쉽다.

sus|pect ◆◆◇ (**suspects, suspecting, suspected**)

> The verb is pronounced /səspɛkt/. The noun and adjective are pronounced /sʌspɛkt/.

> 동사는 /səspɛkt /로 발음된다. 명사와 형용사는 /sʌspɛkt /로 발음된다.

❶ V-T You use **suspect** when you are stating something that you believe is probably true, in order to make it sound less direct. [VAGUENESS] ❑ *I suspect they were right.* ❑ *The above complaints are, I suspect, just the tip of the iceberg.* ❷ V-T If you **suspect** that something dishonest or unpleasant has been done, you believe that it has probably been done. If you **suspect** someone **of** doing an action of this kind, you believe that they probably did it. ❑ *I Ie suspected that the woman staying in the flat above was using heroin.* ❑ *It was perfectly all right, he said, because the police had not suspected him of anything.* ❸ N-COUNT A **suspect** is a person who the police or authorities think may be guilty of a crime. ❑ *Police have arrested a suspect in a series of killings and sexual assaults in the city.* ❹ ADJ **Suspect** things or people are ones that you think may be dangerous or may be less good or genuine than they appear. ❑ *Delegates evacuated the building when a suspect package was found.*

❶ 타동사 -이 아닌가 싶다 [짐작투] ❑ 그들이 옳았던 게 아닌가 싶다. ❑ 상기의 불만 사항은 아마 빙산의 일각이라 생각해. ❷ 타동사 의심하다 ❑ 그는 아파트 위층에 머물렀던 그 여자가 헤로인을 할 거라고 의심했다. ❑ 경찰이 무엇에 대해서도 그를 의심하지 않았기 때문에 이무런 문제가 없었다고 그는 말했다. ❸ 가산명사 용의자 ❑ 경찰이 도시에서 발생한 일련의 살인 및 성폭행 용의자를 체포했다. ❹ 형용사 의심스러운, 수상한 ❑ 대표단들은 수상한 꾸러미가 발견되자 그 건물에서 철수했다.

A

sus|pend ♦◇◇ /səspɛnd/ (**suspends, suspending, suspended**) **1** V-T If you **suspend** something, you delay it or stop it from happening for a while or until a decision is made about it. ❑ *The union suspended strike action this week.* **2** V-T If someone **is suspended**, they are prevented from holding a particular job or position for a fixed length of time or until a decision is made about them. ❑ *Julie was suspended from her job shortly after the incident.* **3** V-T If something **is suspended** from a high place, it is hanging from that place. [usu passive] ❑ *...instruments that are suspended on cables.*

1 타동사 연기하다, 잠시 중단하다 ❑ 노조는 이번 주 파업 행위를 연기했다. **2** 타동사 정직을 당하다 ❑ 줄리는 그 사건 후에 곧 정직을 당했다. **3** 타동사 매달려 있다 ❑ 케이블에 매달려 있는 기구들

B

C

sus|pend|er /səspɛndər/ (**suspenders**) **1** N-PLURAL **Suspenders** are a pair of straps that go over someone's shoulders and are fastened to their pants at the front and back to prevent the pants from falling down. [AM; BRIT **braces**] [also a pair of N] ❑ *He also wore a pair of suspenders.* **2** N-COUNT **Suspenders** are the fastenings which hold up a woman's stockings. [BRIT; AM **garters**] ❑ *...women who wear stockings and suspenders.*

1 복수명사 바지 멜빵 [미국영어; 영국영어 braces] ❑ 그는 또한 바지 멜빵도 하고 있었다. **2** 가산명사 가터벨트 [영국영어; 미국영어 garters] ❑ 스타킹에 가터벨트를 맨 여자들

D

E

sus|pense /səspɛns/ **1** N-UNCOUNT **Suspense** is a state of excitement or anxiety about something that is going to happen very soon, for example about some news that you are waiting to hear. ❑ *The suspense over the two remaining hostages ended last night when the police discovered the bullet-ridden bodies.* **2** PHRASE If you **keep** or **leave** someone **in suspense**, you deliberately delay telling them something that they are very eager to know about. ❑ *Keppler kept all his men in suspense until that morning before announcing which two would be going.*

1 불가산명사 긴장감, 불안 ❑ 남아 있는 두 명의 인질들을 둘러싼 긴장감은 지난밤 경찰이 총알투성이의 사체들을 발견함으로써 끝났다. **2** 구 마음을 졸이게 하다 ❑ 케플러는 그날 아침까지 어느 두 사람이 가게 될지의 발표를 미루어 모든 부하들의 마음을 졸이게 했다.

F

G

sus|pen|sion /səspɛnʃn/ (**suspensions**) **1** N-UNCOUNT The **suspension** of something is the act of delaying or stopping it for a while or until a decision is made about it. ❑ *A strike by British Airways ground staff has led to the suspension of flights between London and Manchester.* **2** N-VAR Someone's **suspension** is their removal from a job or position for a period of time or until a decision is made about them. ❑ *The minister warned that any civil servant not at his desk faced immediate suspension.* **3** N-VAR A vehicle's **suspension** consists of the springs and other devices attached to the wheels, which give a smooth ride over uneven ground. ❑ *...the only small car with independent front suspension.*

1 불가산명사 연기, 중단 ❑ 영국 항공 지상 근무자들의 파업으로 런던과 맨체스터 간의 항공기 운행이 중단되었다. **2** 가산명사 또는 불가산명사 정직 ❑ 장관은 어떠한 공무원도 자리를 지키지 않으면 즉각 정직시킬 것이라고 경고했다. **3** 가산명사 또는 불가산명사 현가장치 ❑ 별도의 전면 현가장치가 있는 유일한 소형차

H

I

J

sus|pi|cion ♦◇◇ /səspɪʃn/ (**suspicions**) **1** N-VAR **Suspicion** or a **suspicion** is a belief or feeling that someone has committed a crime or done something wrong. ❑ *There was a suspicion that this runner attempted to avoid the procedures for dope testing.* ❑ *The police said their suspicions were aroused because Mr. Owens had other marks on his body.* **2** N-VAR If there is **suspicion of** someone or something, people do not trust them or consider them to be reliable. ❑ *This tendency in his thought is deepened by his suspicion of all Utopian political programmes.* **3** N-COUNT A **suspicion** is a feeling that something is probably true or is likely to happen. ❑ *I have a sneaking suspicion that they are going to succeed.*

1 가산명사 또는 불가산명사 혐의, 의혹 ❑ 이 주자가 약물 검사 절차를 기피하려 했다는 의혹이 있었다. ❑ 경찰은 오웬스 씨의 몸에서 다른 흔적들이 발견되었기 때문에 그에 대해 혐의를 품게 되었다고 말했다. **2** 가산명사 또는 불가산명사 의심 ❑ 그의 사고에서 이러한 경향은 유토피아적인 정치 프로그램에 대한 의심 때문에 심화된다. **3** 가산명사 (막연한) 느낌 ❑ 나는 그들이 성공할 것이라는 막연한 느낌이 든다.

K

L

M

Word Partnership	suspicion의 연어
V.	**arouse** suspicion **1**
	view *someone/something* **with** suspicion **1** **2**

N

sus|pi|cious /səspɪʃəs/ **1** ADJ If you are **suspicious of** someone or something, you do not trust them, and are careful when dealing with them. ❑ *He was rightly suspicious of meeting me until I reassured him I was not writing about him.* ● **sus|pi|cious|ly** ADV [ADV after v] ❑ *"What is it you want me to do?" Adams asked suspiciously.* **2** ADJ If you are **suspicious of** someone or something, you believe that they are probably involved in a crime or some dishonest activity. ❑ *Two officers on patrol became suspicious of two men in a car.* **3** ADJ If you describe someone or something as **suspicious**, you mean that there is some aspect of them which makes you think that they are involved in a crime or a dishonest activity. ❑ *He reported that two suspicious-looking characters had approached Callendar.* ● **sus|pi|cious|ly** ADV [ADV with v, ADV adj/adv] ❑ *They'll question them as to whether anyone was seen acting suspiciously in the area over the last few days.*

1 형용사 의심하는, 불신하는 ❑ 그는 내가 자기에 대한 기사를 쓰고 있지 않다는 것을 확신시켜 주기 전까지는 당연히 있는 나를 만나는 것을 의심했다. ● 의심하듯 형용사 ❑ "도대체 내가 했으면 하는 일이 뭐냐?"라고 애덤스가 의심하듯 물었다. **2** 형용사 수상쩍어 하는, 의혹을 가지는 ❑ 순찰 중인 경관 두 명이 자동차 안에 있던 두 남자를 수상쩍게 여기게 되었다. **3** 형용사 수상한 ❑ 그는 수상스러워 보이는 인물 두 명이 캘린더에게 접근했다고 보고했다. ● 수상하게 부사 ❑ 그들은 지난 며칠 동안 그 지역에서 수상한 행동을 하는 사람을 보았는지를 물어볼 것이다.

O

P

Q

R

S

Do not confuse **suspicious**, **doubtful**, and **dubious**. If you are **suspicious** of a person, you do not trust them and think they might be involved in something dishonest or illegal. ❑ *I am suspicious of his intentions. ...Miss Lenaut had grown suspicious.* If you describe something as **suspicious**, it suggests behavior that is dishonest, illegal, or dangerous. ❑ *He listened for any suspicious sounds. ...in suspicious circumstances.* If you feel **doubtful** about something, you are unsure about it or about whether it will happen or be successful. ❑ *Do you feel insecure and doubtful about your ability?... It was doubtful he would ever see her again.* If you are **dubious** about something, you are not sure whether it is the right thing to do. ❑ *Alison sounded very dubious. ...The men in charge were a bit dubious about taking women on.* If you describe something as **dubious**, you think it is not completely honest, safe, or reliable. ❑ *...his dubious abilities as a teacher.*

suspicious, doubtful, dubious를 혼동하지 마시오. 어떤 사람에 대해 suspicious하면, 그 사람을 믿지 않고 또 정직하지 못하거나 불법적인 일에 연루되어 있을 것이라고 생각하는 것이다. ❑ 나는 그의 의도가 의심스럽다... 르노 양은 의심을 품게 되었다. 무엇을 suspicious하다고 기술하면, 정직하지 못하거나, 불법이거나, 위험한 행동을 의미한다. ❑ 그는 의심스러운 소리에는 다 주의를 기울이려고 했다....미심쩍은 환경에서. 무엇에 대해 doubtful한 생각이 들면, 그것에 대해 확신이 없거나 그것이 일어날지 또는 성공할지에 대해 확신이 없는 것이다. ❑ 너는 네 능력에 대해 불안하고 확신이 없니?... 그가 그녀를 다시 보게 될지는 분명치 않았다. 무엇에 대해 dubious하면, 그것을 하는 것이 올바른 일인지 아닌지 확신이 없는 것이다. ❑ 앨리슨은 반신반의하는 것 같아 보였다... 책임을 맡고 있는 남자들은 여자들을 고용하는 것에 조금 반신반의했다. 무엇을 dubious하다고 기술하면, 그것이 아주 정직하거나, 안전하거나, 믿을 만하지 않다고 생각하는 것이다. ❑ ...선생님으로서 그의 의심스러운 능력.

T

U

V

W

X

Y

sus|pi|cious|ly /səspɪʃəsli/ **1** ADV If you say that one thing looks or sounds **suspiciously** like another thing, you mean that it probably is that thing, or something very similar to it, although it may be intended to seem different. [ADV prep] ❑ *The tan-colored dog looks suspiciously like an American pit bull terrier.* **2** ADV You can use **suspiciously** when you are describing something that you think is slightly strange or not as it should be. [ADV adj/adv] ❑ *He lives alone in a suspiciously tidy flat in Notting Hill Gate.* **3** →see also **suspicious**

1 부사 이상하게도 ❑ 그 황갈색 개는 이상하게도 미국 투견 테리어처럼 보인다. **2** 부사 어딘가 이상하게 ❑ 그는 노팅 힐 게이트에 있는, 어딘가 이상할 만큼 깔끔한 작은 아파트에서 혼자 산다.

Z

a

sustain ◆◇◇ /səsteɪn/ (sustains, sustaining, sustained) **1** V-T If you **sustain** something, you continue it or maintain it for a period of time. □ *But he has sustained his fierce social conscience from young adulthood through old age.* □ *The parameters within which life can be sustained on Earth are extraordinarily narrow.* **2** V-T If you **sustain** something such as a defeat, loss, or injury, it happens to you. [FORMAL] □ *Every aircraft in there has sustained some damage.* **3** V-T If something **sustains** you, it supports you by giving you help, strength, or encouragement. [FORMAL] □ *The cash dividends they get from the cash crop would sustain them during the lean season.*

sustainable /səsteɪnəbʰl/ **1** ADJ You use **sustainable** to describe the use of natural resources when this use is kept at a steady level that is not likely to damage the environment. □ *...the management, conservation, and sustainable development of forests.* **2** ADJ A **sustainable** plan, method, or system is designed to continue at the same rate or level of activity without any problems. □ *The creation of an efficient and sustainable transport system is critical to the long-term future of London.*

SUV /ɛs yu vi/ (SUVs) N-COUNT An **SUV** is a powerful vehicle with four-wheel drive that can be driven over rough ground. **SUV** is an abbreviation for "sport utility vehicle." →see **car**

swab /swɒb/ (swabs) N-COUNT A **swab** is a small piece of cotton used by a doctor or nurse for cleaning a wound or putting a substance on it. □ *"Okay," he replied and winced as she dabbed the cotton swab over the gash.*

swagger /swæɡər/ (swaggers, swaggering, swaggered) V-I If you **swagger**, you walk in a very proud, confident way, holding your body upright and swinging your hips. □ *A broad shouldered man wearing a dinner jacket swaggered confidently up to the bar.* ● N-SING **Swagger** is also a noun. □ *He walked with something of a swagger.*

swallow /swɒloʊ/ (swallows, swallowing, swallowed) **1** V-T If you **swallow** something, you cause it to go from your mouth down into your stomach. □ *You are asked to swallow a capsule containing vitamin B.* ● N-COUNT **Swallow** is also a noun. □ *Jan lifted her glass and took a quick swallow.* **2** V-I If you **swallow**, you make a movement in your throat as if you are swallowing something, often because you are nervous or frightened. □ *Nancy swallowed hard and shook her head.* **3** V-T If someone **swallows** a story or a statement, they believe it completely. □ *They cast doubt on his words when it suited their case, but swallowed them whole when it did not.* **4** N-COUNT A **swallow** is a kind of small bird with pointed wings and a forked tail. **5 a bitter pill to swallow** →see **pill**

▶**swallow up** **1** PHRASAL VERB If one thing **is swallowed up** by another, it becomes part of the first thing and no longer has a separate identity of its own. □ *During the 1980s monster publishing houses started to swallow up smaller companies.* **2** PHRASAL VERB If something **swallows up** money or resources, it uses them entirely while giving very little in return. □ *A seven-day TV ad campaign could swallow up the best part of £50,000.*

swam /swæm/ **Swam** is the past tense of **swim**.

swamp /swɒmp/ (swamps, swamping, swamped) **1** N-VAR A **swamp** is an area of very wet land with wild plants growing in it. □ *I spent one whole night by a swamp behind the road listening to frogs.* **2** V-T If something **swamps** a place or object, it fills it with water. □ *Their electronic navigation failed and a rogue wave swamped the boat.* **3** V-T If you **are swamped** by things or people, you have more of them than you can deal with. [usu passive] □ *He is swamped with work.*

swan /swɒn/ (swans, swanning, swanned) **1** N-COUNT A **swan** is a large bird with a very long neck. Swans live on rivers and lakes and are usually white. **2** V-I If you describe someone as **swanning around** or **swanning off**, you mean that they go and have fun, rather than working or taking care of their responsibilities. [BRIT, INFORMAL] □ *She spends her time swanning around the world.*

swap /swɒp/ (swaps, swapping, swapped) [BRIT also swop] **1** V-RECIP If you **swap** something with someone, you give it to them and receive a different thing in exchange. □ *Next week they will swap places and will repeat the switch weekly.* □ *I know a sculptor who swaps her pieces for drawings by a well-known artist.* ● N-COUNT **Swap** is also a noun. □ *If she ever fancies a job swap, I could be interested.* **2** V-T If you **swap** one thing **for** another, you remove the first thing and replace it with the second, or you stop doing the first thing and start doing the second. □ *Despite the heat, he'd swapped his overalls for a suit and tie.* □ *He has swapped his hectic rock star's lifestyle for that of a country gentleman.*

Word Partnership	*swap*의 연어
N.	debt swap, interest rate swap, stock swap **2**

swarm /swɔrm/ (swarms, swarming, swarmed) **1** N-COUNT-COLL A **swarm of** bees or other insects is a large group of them flying together. □ *...a swarm of locusts.* **2** V-I When bees or other insects **swarm**, they move or fly in a large group. □ *A dark cloud of bees comes swarming out of the hive.* **3** V-I When people **swarm** somewhere, they move there quickly in a large group. □ *People swarmed to the shops, buying up everything in sight.* **4** N-COUNT-COLL A **swarm of** people is a large group of them moving about quickly. □ *A swarm of people encircled the hotel.* **5** V-I If a place **is swarming with** people, it is full of people moving about in a busy way. [usu cont] □ *Within minutes the area was swarming with officers who began searching a nearby wood.*

swat /swɒt/ (swats, swatting, swatted) V-T If you **swat** something such as an insect, you hit it with a quick, swinging movement, using your hand or a flat object. □ *Hundreds of flies buzz around us, and the workman keeps swatting them.*

1 타동사 계속하다, 지속하다 □ 그러나 그는 청소년 때부터 노년에 이르기까지 줄곧 자신의 확고한 사회적 양심을 계속 지켜 왔다. □ 지구상에서 삶이 유지될 수 있는 한계 범위는 놀랄 정도로 제한적이다. **2** 타동사 (피해 등을) 입다 [격식체] □ 그곳에 있던 모든 항공기가 어느 정도 피해를 입었다. **3** 타동사 살아가게 하다, 지탱하다 [격식체] □ 환금 작물에서 얻은 현금 배당금으로 그들은 흉작기 동안 살아갈 수 있을 것이다.

1 형용사 환경 파괴 없이 지속 가능한 □ 산림의 관리와 보존, 그리고 환경 파괴 없이 지속 가능한 발전 **2** 형용사 유지 가능한 □ 효과적이고 유지 가능한 운송 체계를 세우는 것이 런던의 장기적인 미래를 위해 매우 중요하다.

가산명사 스포츠 실용차, 4륜 구동 승용차

가산명사 소독면, 약솜 □ "좋아."라고 그는 대답하며 그녀가 깊게 베인 상처 부위에 약솜을 문지르자 얼굴을 찌푸렸다.

자동사 으스대며 걷다, 활보하다 □ 턱시도를 입은 어깨가 넓은 남자가 자신감에 찬 모습으로 카운터로 으스대며 걸어갔다. ● 단수명사 으스대며 걷기 □ 그는 으스대듯 걸었다.

1 타동사 삼키다 □ 비타민 비가 든 정제 하나를 삼켜야 한다. ● 가산명사 삼킴 □ 잰은 유리잔을 들더니 재빨리 한 모금 삼켰다. **2** 자동사 침을 꿀꺽 삼키다 □ 낸시는 힘들게 침을 꿀꺽 삼키더니 머리를 내저었다. **3** 타동사 곧이듣다 □ 그들은 그가 하는 말이 자신들의 경우에 적용될 때는 의심을 했지만, 그렇지 않을 때는 모두 곧이들었다. **4** 가산명사 제비

1 구동사 흡수되다, 잡아삼켜지다 □ 1980년대에 거대 출판사들이 소규모 출판사들을 흡수하기 시작했다. **2** 구동사 다 써 버리다 □ 7일 동안 텔레비전 광고 캠페인으로 5만 파운드의 대부분을 다 써 버릴 수도 있다.

swim의 과거

1 가산명사 또는 불가산명사 늪, 습지 □ 나는 도로 뒤편 늪가에서 개구리 소리를 들으며 하룻밤을 꼬박 보냈다. **2** 타동사 물에 잠기게 하다, 침수시키다 □ 그들의 전자 항법 장치가 말을 듣지 않았고 사나운 파도가 보트를 뒤덮어 버렸다. **3** 타동사 -에 압도당하다 □ 그는 일에 압도당해 있다.

1 가산명사 백조 **2** 자동사 (속 편하게) 유람하다 [영국영어, 비격식체] □ 그녀는 세계를 유람하며 시간을 보낸다.

[영국영어 swop] **1** 상호동사 교환하다 □ 다음 주에 그들은 장소를 교환하고 매주 이것을 반복할 것이다. □ 나는 자기 작품들을 유명 화가의 그림과 교환하는 조각가를 알고 있다. ● 가산명사 교환 □ 그녀가 업무 교환을 생각해 본다면, 내가 관심을 가질 텐데. **2** 타동사 바꾸다 □ 더운 날씨에도 불구하고, 그는 작업 바지를 정장으로 바꿔 입고 넥타이를 맸다. □ 그는 분주한 록스타로서의 생활 방식에서 시골 신사의 생활 방식으로 바꾸었다.

1 가산명사-집합 떼 □ 메뚜기 떼 **2** 자동사 떼 지어 다니다 □ 벌집에서 벌들이 검은 구름처럼 떼 지어 나오고 있다. **3** 자동사 떼로 쉬어 이동하나 □ 사람들은 떼를 지어 상점들로 가서 눈에 보이는 대로 사재기를 했다. **4** 가산명사-집합 무리, 군중 군중이 호텔을 에워쌌다. **5** 자동사 붐비다 ● 수분 내로 그 지역은 근처 숲 수색을 시작한 경찰관들로 붐볐다.

타동사 찰싹 때리다 □ 수백 마리의 파리가 우리 주위를 윙윙거리고 그 일꾼은 그 파리들을 계속 찰싹 때려잡는다.

b
c
d
e
f
g
h
i
j
k
l
m
n
o
p
q
r
s
t
u
v
w
x
y
z

sway /sweɪ/ (**sways, swaying, swayed**) **1** v-I When people or things **sway**, they lean or swing slowly from one side to the other. □ *The people swayed back and forth with arms linked.* □ *The whole boat swayed and tipped.* **2** v-T If you **are swayed by** someone or something, you are influenced by them. □ *Don't ever be swayed by fashion.* **3** PHRASE If someone or something **holds sway**, they have great power or influence over a particular place or activity. □ *Powerful traditional chiefs hold sway over more than 15 million people in rural areas.*

1 자동사 (전후좌우로 천천히) 움직이다, 흔들리다 □ 사람들은 팔을 엮은 채로 앞뒤로 움직였다. □ 보트 전체가 흔들리더니 기울어졌다. **2** 타동사 동요되다, 흔들리다 □ 유행에 맞서 싸울 것을 맹세했다. **3** 구 쥐고 흔들다, 지배하다 □ 농촌 지역에서는 전통적인 막강한 추장들이 1,500만 명 이상을 지배하고 있다.

swear /swɛər/ (**swears, swearing, swore, sworn**) **1** v-I If someone **swears**, they use language that is considered to be vulgar or offensive, usually because they are angry. □ *It's wrong to swear and shout.* **2** v-T If you **swear to** do something, you promise in a serious way that you will do it. □ *Alan swore that he would do everything in his power to help us.* □ *We have sworn to fight cruelty wherever we find it.* **3** v-T/v-I If you say that you **swear** that something is true or that you can **swear** to it, you are saying very firmly that it is true. [EMPHASIS] □ *I swear I've told you all I know.* □ *I swear on all I hold dear that I had nothing to do with this.* **4** v-T If someone **is sworn to** secrecy or **is sworn to** silence, they promise another person that they will not reveal a secret. [usu passive] □ *She was bursting to announce the news but was sworn to secrecy.* **5** →see also **sworn**

1 자동사 욕을 하다 □ 욕을 하고 소리치는 것은 나쁜 것이다. **2** 타동사 맹세하다 □ 앨런은 있는 힘껏 우리를 돕겠다고 맹세했다. □ 우리는 어느 곳에서든지 잔인함에 맞서 싸울 것을 맹세했다. **3** 타동사/자동사 맹세하다 [강조] □ 맹세코 내가 아는 모든 것을 너에게 말했어. □ 나는 이것과 아무 관계가 없음을 내가 소중하게 여기는 모든 것을 걸고 맹세한다. **4** 타동사 (비밀 등을) 지킬 것을 맹세하다 □ 그녀는 그 소식을 말하고 싶어 좀이 쑤셨지만 비밀을 지킬 것을 맹세했다.

▶**swear by** PHRASAL VERB If you **swear by** something, you believe that it can be relied on to have a particular effect. [INFORMAL] □ *Many people swear by vitamin C's ability to ward off colds.*

구동사 –을 확실히 믿다 [비격식체] □ 많은 사람들이 비타민 시가 감기를 물리치는 효능이 있다고 확실히 믿는다.

▶**swear in** PHRASAL VERB When someone **is sworn in**, they formally promise to fulfill the duties of a new job or appointment. □ *Mary Robinson has been formally sworn in as Ireland's first woman president.*

구동사 취임 선서를 하다 □ 매리 로빈슨은 아일랜드의 첫 여성 대통령으로 공식 취임 선서를 했다.

sweat /swɛt/ (**sweats, sweating, sweated**) **1** N-UNCOUNT **Sweat** is the salty colorless liquid which comes through your skin when you are hot, ill, or afraid. □ *Both horse and rider were dripping with sweat within five minutes.* **2** v-I When you **sweat**, sweat comes through your skin. □ *Already they were sweating as the sun beat down upon them.* ● **sweat**ing N-UNCOUNT *…symptoms such as sweating, irritability, anxiety, and depression.* **3** N-COUNT If someone is **in a sweat**, they are sweating a lot. □ *Every morning I would break out in a sweat.* □ *Cool down very gradually after working up a sweat.* **4** PHRASE If someone is **in a cold sweat** or **in a sweat**, they feel frightened or embarrassed. □ *The very thought brought me out in a cold sweat.*
→see Word Web: **sweat**

1 불가산명사 땀 □ 말과 기수 둘 다 5분도 되기 전에 땀방울을 뚝뚝 흘리고 있었다. **2** 자동사 땀을 흘리다 □ 태양이 그들에게 쨍쨍 내리쬐어서 이미 그들은 땀을 흘리고 있었다. ● 발한 불가산명사 □ 발한, 성마름, 불안, 우울함 같은 증상 **3** 가산명사 흠뻑 땀이 나는 상태 □ 매일 아침 나는 갑자기 흠뻑 땀에 젖곤 했다. □ 땀을 흠뻑 흘린 후에는 아주 천천히 몸을 식히세요. **4** 구 식은땀을 흘리는, 땀을 흘리는 □ 그걸 생각만 해도 나는 식은땀이 났다.

sweat|er /swɛtər/ (**sweaters**) N-COUNT A **sweater** is a warm knitted piece of clothing which covers the upper part of your body and your arms. →see **clothing**

가산명사 스웨터

sweat|shirt /swɛtʃɜrt/ (**sweatshirts**) also **sweat shirt** N-COUNT A **sweatshirt** is a loose warm piece of casual clothing, usually made of thick stretchy cotton, which covers the upper part of your body and your arms. →see **clothing**

가산명사 스웨트 셔츠

sweat|suit /swɛtsut/ (**sweatsuits**) also **sweat suit** N-COUNT A **sweatsuit** is a loose, warm, stretchy suit consisting of long pants and a top which people wear to relax and do exercise.

가산명사 운동복

sweaty /swɛti/ (**sweatier, sweatiest**) **1** ADJ If parts of your body or your clothes are **sweaty**, they are soaked or covered with sweat. □ *…sweaty hands.* **2** ADJ A **sweaty** place or activity makes you sweat because it is hot or tiring. □ *…a sweaty nightclub.*

1 형용사 땀에 젖은 □ 땀에 젖은 손 **2** 형용사 땀을 흘리게 하는 □ 땀을 흘리게 하는 나이트클럽

sweep ♦◇◇ /swip/ (**sweeps, sweeping, swept**) **1** v-T If you **sweep** an area of floor or ground, you push dirt or garbage off it using a brush with a long handle. □ *The owner of the store was sweeping his floor when I walked in.* □ *She was in the kitchen sweeping crumbs into a dust pan.* **2** v-T If you **sweep** things off something, you push them off with a quick smooth movement of your arm. □ *I swept rainwater off the flat top of a gravestone.* □ *With a gesture of frustration, she swept the cards from the table.* **3** v-T If someone with long hair **sweeps** their hair into a particular style, they put it into that style. □ *…stylish ways of sweeping your hair off your face.* **4** v-T/v-I If your arm or hand **sweeps** in a particular direction, or if you **sweep** it there, it moves quickly and smoothly in that direction. □ *His arm swept around the room.* □ *Daniels swept his arm over his friend's shoulder.* ● N-COUNT **Sweep** is also a noun. □ *With one sweep of her hand she threw back the sheets.* **5** v-T If wind, a stormy sea, or another strong force **sweeps** someone or something along, it moves them quickly along. □ *…landslides that buried homes and swept cars into the sea.* **6** v-T If you **are swept** somewhere, you are taken there very quickly. □ *The visitors were swept past various monuments.* **7** v-I If something **sweeps** from one place to another, it moves there extremely

1 타동사 쓸다 □ 내가 들어갔을 때 상점 주인은 바닥을 쓸고 있었다. □ 그녀는 부엌에서 쓰레받기로 빵 부스러기를 쓸어 담고 있었다. **2** 타동사 훔치다, 쓸어 내다 □ 나는 비석의 평평한 위쪽에 고인 빗물을 훔쳐 냈다. □ 좌절스러운 몸짓을 하며 그녀가 탁자에서 카드를 쓸어 냈다. **3** 타동사 (머리카락을) 빗어 넘기다 □ 얼굴에서 머리카락을 우아하게 빗어 넘기는 방법 **4** 타동사/자동사 확 움직이다, 스쳐 지나가다; 확 움직이게 하다, 스치게 하다 □ 그는 방 이리저리로 팔을 휘획 움직여 보았다. □ 대니얼즈가 친구의 어깨 위로 휘획 팔을 둘렀다. ● 가산명사 휘획 움직임 □ 그녀가 손을 한 번 휘획 움직여 그 종이들을 도로 내던졌다. **5** 타동사 휩쓸다 □ 주택을 매몰시키고 차량을 바다로 휩쓸어 보낸 산사태 **6** 타동사 급히 끌려 다니다 □ 방문객들은 급히 끌려 다니며 여러 기념비들을 훑어보았다. **7** 자동사 확 지나가다 [문어체] □ 얼음처럼 차가운 바람이 길거리를 휘획 지나갔다.

quickly. [WRITTEN] ❑ *An icy wind swept through the streets.* ⑧ V-I If events, ideas, or beliefs **sweep** through a place, they spread quickly through it. ❑ *A flu epidemic is sweeping through Moscow.* ⑨ V-T/V-I If a person or group **sweeps** an election or **sweeps** to victory, they win the election easily. ❑ *...a man who's promised to make radical changes to benefit the poor has swept the election.* ⑩ N-COUNT If someone makes a **sweep of** a place, they search it, usually because they are looking for people who are hiding or for an illegal activity. ❑ *Two of the soldiers swiftly began making a sweep of the premises.* ⑪ →see also **sweeping** ⑫ PHRASE If someone **sweeps** something bad or wrong **under the carpet**, or if they **sweep** it **under the rug**, they try to prevent people from hearing about it. ❑ *For a long time this problem has been swept under the carpet.* ⑬ PHRASE If you **make a clean sweep of** something such as a series of games or tournaments, you win them all. ❑ *...the first club to make a clean sweep of all three trophies.* ⑭ to **sweep the board** →see **board**

Word Partnership	*sweep의 연어*
ADV.	sweep *someone/something* away ⑤ ⑥
PREP.	sweep through *someplace* ⑦ ⑧
	sweep into *someplace* ⑦

▶**sweep up** PHRASAL VERB If you **sweep up** rubbish or dirt, you push it together with a brush and then remove it. ❑ *Get a broom and sweep up that glass will you?*

sweep|ing /swiːpɪŋ/ ① ADJ A **sweeping** curve is a long wide curve. [ADJ n] ❑ *...the long sweeping curve of Rio's Guanabara Bay.* ② ADJ If someone makes a **sweeping** statement or generalization, they make a statement which applies to all things of a particular kind, although they have not considered all the relevant facts carefully. [DISAPPROVAL] ❑ *It is far too early to make sweeping statements about gene therapy.* ③ ADJ **Sweeping** changes are large and very important or significant. ❑ *The new government has started to make sweeping changes in the economy.* ④ →see also **sweep**

sweet ◆◇◇ /swiːt/ (**sweeter**, **sweetest**, **sweets**) ① ADJ **Sweet** food and drink contain a lot of sugar. ❑ *If the sauce seems too sweet, add a dash of red wine vinegar.* ● **sweet|ness** N-UNCOUNT ❑ *Florida oranges have a natural sweetness.* ② ADJ A **sweet** smell is a pleasant one, for example the smell of a flower. ❑ *...the sweet smell of her shampoo.* ③ ADJ A **sweet** sound is pleasant, smooth, and gentle. ❑ *Her voice was as soft and sweet as a young girl's.* ● **sweet|ly** ADV ❑ *He sang much more sweetly than he has before.* ④ ADJ If you describe something as **sweet**, you mean that it gives you great pleasure and satisfaction. [WRITTEN] ❑ *There are few things quite as sweet as revenge.* ⑤ ADJ If you describe someone as **sweet**, you mean that they are pleasant, kind, and gentle toward other people. ❑ *He was a sweet man but when he drank he tended to quarrel.* ● **sweet|ly** ADV ❑ *I just smiled sweetly and said no.* ⑥ ADJ If you describe a small person or thing as **sweet**, you mean that they are attractive in a simple or unsophisticated way. [INFORMAL] ❑ *...a sweet little baby girl.* ⑦ N-PLURAL **Sweets** are foods that have a lot of sugar. [AM] ❑ *To maintain her weight, she simply chooses fruits and vegetables over fats and sweets.* ⑧ N-COUNT **Sweets** are small sweet things such as chocolates and mints. [BRIT; AM **candy**] ❑ *...packets of brightly colored sweets.* ⑨ N-VAR A **sweet** is something sweet, such as fruit or a pudding, that you eat at the end of a meal, especially in a restaurant. [BRIT; AM **dessert**] ❑ *The sweet was a mousse flavored with whiskey.* ⑩ →see also **sweetness** ⑪ a **sweet tooth** →see **tooth**
→see **fruit, sugar, taste**

sweet|corn /swiːtkɔːrn/ also **sweet corn** N-UNCOUNT **Sweetcorn** is a long rounded vegetable covered in small yellow seeds. It is part of the maize plant. The seeds themselves can also be referred to as **sweetcorn**.

sweet|en /swiːtən/ (**sweetens**, **sweetening**, **sweetened**) ① V-T If you **sweeten** food or drink, you add sugar, honey, or another sweet substance to it. ❑ *He liberally sweetened his coffee.* ② V-T If you **sweeten** something such as an offer or a business deal, you try to make someone want it more by improving it or by increasing the amount you are willing to pay. ❑ *Kalon Group has sweetened its takeover offer for Manders.*

sweet|en|er /swiːtənər/ (**sweeteners**) ① N-MASS **Sweetener** is an artificial substance that can be used in drinks instead of sugar. ② N-COUNT A **sweetener** is something that you give or offer someone in order to persuade them to accept an offer or business deal. ❑ *A corporation can buy back its bonds by paying investors the face value (plus a sweetener).*

sweet|heart /swiːthɑːrt/ (**sweethearts**) ① N-VOC You call someone **sweetheart** if you are very fond of them. ❑ *Happy birthday, sweetheart.* ② N-COUNT Your **sweetheart** is your boyfriend or your girlfriend. [OLD-FASHIONED] ❑ *I married Shurla, my childhood sweetheart, in Liverpool.*

sweet|ness /swiːtnɪs/ ① PHRASE If you say that a relationship or situation is not **all sweetness and light**, you mean that it is not as pleasant as it appears to be. ❑ *It has not all been sweetness and light between him and the Prime Minister.* ② →see also **sweet**

swell /swel/ (**swells**, **swelling**, **swelled**, **swollen**)

The forms **swelled** and **swollen** are both used as the past participle.

① V-T/V-I If the amount or size of something **swells** or if something **swells** it, it becomes larger than it was before. ❑ *The human population swelled, at least temporarily, as migrants moved south.* ❑ *His bank balance has swelled by £222,000 in the last three weeks.* ② V-I If something such as a part of your body **swells**, it becomes larger and rounder than normal. ❑ *Do your ankles swell at night?* ● PHRASAL VERB **Swell up** means the same as **swell**. ❑ *When you develop a throat infection or catch a cold the glands in the neck swell up.* ③ →see also **swollen**

⑧ 자동사 휩쓸다 ❑ 유행성 감기가 모스크바를 휩쓸고 있다. ⑨ 타동사/자동사 낙승하다 ❑ 빈곤층에게 혜택을 주기 위한 급진적인 변화를 약속한 사람이 이번 선거에서 낙승했다. ⑩ 가산명사 수색하다 ❑ 군인 두 명이 재빨리 그 구내를 수색하기 시작했다. ⑫ 구 ~을 비밀에 부치다 ❑ 오랫동안 이 문제는 비밀에 부쳐져 있었다. ⑬ 구 압승을 거두다 ❑ 세 트로피를 모두 거머쥐는 압승을 거둔 최초의 클럽

구동사 청소하다, 쓸어 모으다 ❑ 빗자루를 들고 그 유리를 치워 주겠니?

① 형용사 넓고 긴 ❑ 넓고 길게 휘어진 리오의 구아나바라 만 ② 형용사 포괄적인 [탐탁잖음] ❑ 유전자 치료에 대해 포괄적으로 이야기하는 것은 아직 시기상조이다. ③ 형용사 전면적인 ❑ 새 정부는 전면적인 경제 개혁에 착수했다.

① 형용사 달콤한, 단 ❑ 달콤한 차 한 잔 ❑ 소스가 너무 단 것 같으면, 적포도주 식초를 약간 첨가하세요. ● 달콤함, 단맛 불가산명사 ❑ 플로리다 산 오렌지는 원래 달콤한 맛이 난다. ② 형용사 향기로운 ❑ 그녀에게서 나는 향기로운 샴푸 냄새 ③ 형용사 감미로운 ❑ 그녀의 목소리는 어린 소녀의 목소리처럼 부드럽고 감미로웠다. ● 감미롭게 부사 ❑ 그는 예전보다 훨씬 더 감미롭게 노래를 불렀다. ④ 형용사 통쾌한 [문어체] ❑ 복수만큼 통쾌한 일도 없을 것이다. ⑤ 형용사 상냥한 ❑ 그는 상냥한 남자였으나 술만 취하면 싸우려고 했다. ● 상냥하게 부사 ❑ 나는 그냥 상냥하게 미소를 지으면서 안 된다고 말했다. ⑥ 형용사 예쁜 [비격식체] ❑ 예쁘고 작은 아기 ⑦ 복수명사 단 음식 [미국영어] ❑ 몸무게를 유지하기 위해 그녀는 지방과 단 음식 대신 간단히 과일과 채소를 먹는다. ⑧ 가산명사 단 것, 사탕 [영국영어; 미국영어 candy] ❑ 선명한 색깔의 사탕들을 넣어 놓은 봉지들 ⑨ 가산명사 또는 불가산명사 디저트용 단 음식 [영국영어; 미국영어 dessert] ❑ 그 디저트용 단 음식은 위스키 향이 나는 무스였다.

불가산명사 사탕옥수수

① 타동사 설탕을 넣다, 달게 하다 ❑ 그는 커피에 설탕을 듬뿍 넣었다. ② 타동사 매혹적으로 만들다 ❑ 칼론 그룹은 맨더스 인수 제안에 매혹적인 조건들을 제시해 왔다.

① 물질명사 감미료 ② 가산명사 우대 조건 ❑ 회사는 투자가들에게 액면가(더하기 우대 조건)를 지불하고 채권을 다시 매입할 수 있다.

① 호격명사 사랑하는 사람을 부르는 호칭 ❑ 생일 축하해요, 여보. ② 가산명사 이성 친구 [구식어] ❑ 나는 리버풀에서 어린 시절 여자 친구인 쉴라와 결혼했다.

① 구 좋기만 한 ❑ 그와 수상 사이에 항상 기분 좋은 일만 있는 건 아니다.

swelled와 swollen 모두 과거 분사로 쓰인다

① 타동사/자동사 팽창하다, 증가하다; 팽창시키다, 증가시키다 ❑ 이주자들이 남쪽으로 이동했기 때문에 적어도 일시적으로는 인구가 팽창했다. ❑ 그의 은행 잔고가 지난 3주 동안 222,000파운드나 증가했다. ② 자동사 부어오르다, 붓다 ❑ 밤에 발목이 부어오르나? ● 구동사 부어오르다 ❑ 목 감염이나 감기에 걸리면 갑상선이 붓는다.

swell|ing /swelɪŋ/ (swellings) N-VAR A **swelling** is a raised, curved shape on the surface of your body which appears as a result of an injury or an illness. ❑ *His eye was partly closed, and there was a swelling over his lid.*

가산명사 또는 불가산명사 부어오른 것 ❑ 그는 한쪽 눈이 반쯤 감겨 있었고 눈꺼풀이 부어 있었다.

swel|ter|ing /sweltərɪŋ/ ADJ If you describe the weather as **sweltering**, you mean that it is extremely hot and makes you feel uncomfortable. ❑ *...the sweltering heat of the St Petersburg summer.*

형용사 찌는 듯이 더운 ❑ 상트페테르부르크 여름의 찌는 듯한 더위

swept /swept/ **Swept** is the past tense and past participle of **sweep**.

sweep의 과거, 과거 분사

swerve /swɜrv/ (swerves, swerving, swerved) V-T/V-I If a vehicle or other moving thing **swerves** or if you **swerve** it, it suddenly changes direction, often in order to avoid hitting something. ❑ *Drivers coming in the opposite direction swerved to avoid the bodies.* ❑ *Her car swerved off the road into a 6ft high brick wall.* ● N-COUNT **Swerve** is also a noun. ❑ *He swung the car to the left and that swerve saved Malone's life.*

타동사/자동사 획 방향을 틀다 ❑ 반대 차선의 운전자들이 사체들을 피하기 위해 획 방향을 틀었다. ❑ 그녀의 차가 획 방향을 틀며 도로를 벗어나 6피트 높이 벽돌 벽을 들이받았다. ● 가산명사 급선회 ❑ 그가 획 차의 방향을 왼쪽으로 튼 덕분에 말론이 목숨을 건졌다.

swift /swɪft/ (swifter, swiftest, swifts) **1** ADJ A **swift** event or process happens very quickly or without delay. ❑ *Our task is to challenge the UN to make a swift decision.* ● **swift|ly** ADV ❑ *The French have acted swiftly and decisively to protect their industries.* **2** ADJ Something that is **swift** moves very quickly. ❑ *With a swift movement, Matthew Jerrold sat upright.* ● **swift|ly** ADV [ADV with v] ❑ *Lenny moved swiftly and silently across the front lawn.* **3** N-COUNT A **swift** is a small bird with long curved wings.

1 형용사 신속한 ❑ 우리의 과제는 유엔을 촉구해 결정을 신속히 내리게 하는 것이다. ● 신속하게 부사 ❑ 프랑스인들은 신속하고 단호하게 행동함으로써 자국 산업을 보호하고 오고 있다. **2** 형용사 재빠른 ❑ 재빠른 행동으로 매튜 제롤드가 곧바로 앉았다. ● 재빠르게 부사 ❑ 레니는 재빠르게 조용히 앞 잔디밭을 가로질러 갔다. **3** 가산명사 칼새

swim ♦♢♢ /swɪm/ (swims, swimming, swam, swum) **1** V-I When you **swim**, you move through water by making movements with your arms and legs. ❑ *She learned to swim when she was really tiny.* ❑ *He was rescued only when an exhausted friend swam ashore.* ● N-SING **Swim** is also a noun. ❑ *When can we go for a swim, Mom?* **2** V-T If you **swim** a race, you take part in a swimming race. ❑ *She swam the 400 meters medley ten seconds slower than she did in 1980.* **3** V-T If you **swim** a stretch of water, you keep swimming until you have crossed it. ❑ *In 1875, Captain Matthew Webb became the first man to swim the English Channel.* **4** V-I When a fish **swims**, it moves through water by moving its body. ❑ *The barriers are lethal to fish trying to swim upstream.* **5** V-I If your head **is swimming**, you feel unsteady and slightly ill. ❑ *The musty aroma of incense made her head swim.* **6** sink or swim →see sink

1 자동사 수영하다, 헤엄치다 ❑ 그녀는 아주 어렸을 때 수영을 배웠다. ❑ 그는 기진맥진한 친구가 물가로 헤엄쳐 닿았을 때에서야 구출되었다. ● 단수명사 수영, 헤엄 ❑ 엄마, 우리 언제 수영하러 갈 수 있어요? **2** 타동사 수영 대회에 참가하다 ❑ 그녀는 4백 미터 메들리 경영(競泳)에 참가했는데 1980년 때보다 10초가 느렸다. **3** 타동사 헤엄쳐 건너다 ❑ 1875년, 캡틴 매튜 웹이 최초로 영국 해협을 헤엄쳐 건너간 사람이 되었다. **4** 자동사 헤엄치다 ❑ 그 울타리는 강물을 거슬러 헤엄쳐 나아가려고 하는 물고기에게는 치명적이다. **5** 자동사 현기증이 나다 ❑ 케케묵은 향냄새에 그녀는 현기증이 났다.

swim|mer /swɪmər/ (swimmers) N-COUNT A **swimmer** is a person who swims, especially for sport or pleasure, or a person who is swimming. ❑ *You don't have to worry about me. I'm a good swimmer.*

가산명사 수영 선수, 헤엄을 치는 사람 ❑ 나 때문에 걱정할 필요 없어. 난 수영 잘해.

swim|ming /swɪmɪŋ/ N-UNCOUNT **Swimming** is the activity of swimming, especially as a sport or for pleasure. ❑ *Swimming is probably the best form of exercise you can get.*

불가산명사 수영 ❑ 수영이 아마 너에게 가장 적합한 운동일 거야.

swim|ming pool (swimming pools) N-COUNT A **swimming pool** is a large hole in the ground that has been made and filled with water so that people can swim in it.

가산명사 수영장

swim|ming trunks N-PLURAL **Swimming trunks** are the shorts that a man wears when he goes swimming. [BRIT; AM **trunks**] [also a pair of N]

복수명사 (남자) 수영복 [영국영어; 미국영어 trunks]

swim|suit /swɪmsut/ (swimsuits) N-COUNT A **swimsuit** is a piece of clothing that is worn for swimming, especially by women and girls. ❑ *... pictures of models in swimsuits.*

가산명사 (여자) 수영복 ❑ 수영복 차림의 모델 사진

swin|dle /swɪndᵊl/ (swindles, swindling, swindled) V-T If someone **swindles** a person or an organization, they deceive them in order to get something valuable from them, especially money. ❑ *A City businessman swindled investors out of millions of pounds.* ● N-COUNT **Swindle** is also a noun. ❑ *He fled to Switzerland rather than face trial for a tax swindle.*

타동사 속여 빼앗다, 사취하다 ❑ 런던 금융가의 한 사업가가 투자자들에게서 수백만 파운드를 사취했다. ● 가산명사 사취, 사기 ❑ 그는 세금 사기로 인한 재판을 받는 대신 스위스로 도망을 쳤다.

swing ♦♢♢ /swɪŋ/ (swings, swinging, swung) **1** V-T/V-I If something **swings** or if you **swing** it, it moves repeatedly backward and forward or from side to side from a fixed point. ❑ *The sail of the little boat swung crazily from one side to the other.* ❑ *She was swinging a bottle of wine by its neck.* ● N-COUNT **Swing** is also a noun. ❑ *...a woman in a tight red dress, walking with a slight swing to her hips.* **2** V-T/V-I If something **swings** in a particular direction or if you **swing** it in that direction, it moves in that direction with a smooth, curving movement. ❑ *The torchlight swung across the little beach and out over the water, searching.* ❑ *The canoe found the current and swung around.* ● N-COUNT **Swing** is also a noun. ❑ *When he's not on the tennis court, you'll find him practicing his golf swing.* **3** V-T/V-I If a vehicle **swings** in a particular direction, or if the driver **swings** it in a particular direction, they turn suddenly and quickly. ❑ *Joanna swung back onto the main approach and headed for the airport.* **4** V-I If someone **swings around**, they turn around quickly, usually because they are surprised. ❑ *She swung around to him, spilling her tea without noticing it.* **5** V-I If you **swing at** a person or thing, you try to hit them with your arm or with something that you are holding. ❑ *Blanche swung at her but she moved her head back and Blanche missed.* ● N-COUNT **Swing** is also a noun. ❑ *I often want to take a swing at someone to relieve my feelings.* **6** N-COUNT A **swing** is a seat hanging by two ropes or chains from a metal frame or from the branch of a tree. You can sit on the seat and move forward and backward through the air. ❑ *Go to the neighborhood park. Run around, push the kids on the swings.* **7** N-COUNT A **swing** in people's opinions, attitudes, or feelings is a change in them, especially a sudden or big change. ❑ *There was a massive twenty per cent swing away from the Conservatives to the Liberal Democrats.* ❑ *Educational practice is liable to sudden swings and changes.* **8** V-I If people's opinions, attitudes, or feelings **swing**, they change, especially in a sudden or extreme way. ❑ *In two years' time there is a presidential election, and the voters could swing again.* **9** PHRASE If something is **in full swing**, it is operating fully and is no longer in its early stages. ❑ *When we returned, the party was in full swing and the dance floor was crowded.* **10** PHRASE If you **get into the swing of** something, you become very involved in

1 타동사/자동사 흔들리다; 흔들다 ❑ 작은 보트의 돛이 이리저리 심하게 흔들렸다. ❑ 그녀는 와인 병의 목을 잡고 흔들고 있었다. ● 가산명사 흔듦 ❑ 몸에 꼭 끼는 빨간 드레스를 입고 가볍게 엉덩이를 흔들며 걷는 여자 **2** 타동사/자동사 빙 돌다; 빙 돌리다 ❑ 횃불이 빙 돌아 작은 해안을 훑고 그 너머 바다 위를 비추며 무언가를 찾고 있었다. ❑ 카누가 물살을 만나 돌았다. ● 가산명사 빙 돎, 스윙 ❑ 그가 테니스장에 없다면, 골프 스윙을 연습하는 거야. **3** 타동사/자동사 획 돌다; 획 돌리다 ❑ 조애너는 다시 주 진입로로 쪽으로 획 차를 돌려 공항으로 향했다. **4** 자동사 획 몸을 돌리다 ❑ 그녀가 그에게로 휙 돌아서면서 자신도 모르게 차를 엎질렀다. **5** 자동사 (때리려고 팔 등을) 휘두르다, 후려치다 ❑ 블랑쉬가 그녀에게 팔을 휘둘렀으나 그녀가 머리를 뒤로 움직이는 바람에 치지 못했다. ● 가산명사 휘두름, 후려침 ❑ 난 자주 기분을 풀 수 있도록 누군가를 후려패고 싶어. **6** 가산명사 그네 ❑ 근처 공원에 가 보세요. 공원에서 뛰어다니며, 그네에 탄 아이들을 밀어 주기도 하세요. **7** 가산명사 큰 변동 ❑ 보수당에서 자유 민주당으로 무려 20퍼센트의 엄청난 변동이 있었다. ❑ 교육 현장에서 갑작스런 변경과 변화는 흔한 것이다. **8** 자동사 (생각 등을) 바꾸다 ❑ 2년 있으면 대통령 선거가 있는데 유권자들이 또다시 생각을 바꿀 수도 있다. **9** 구 한창 진행 중인 ❑ 우리가 돌아왔을 때는 파티가 한창이었고 무도장은 춤추는 사람들로 북적댔다. **10** 구 ~에 익숙해지다 ❑ 그렇게 오래 자리를 비웠다가 다시 일에 익숙해지는 것이 얼마나 힘든 것인지를 모두가 이해해 주었다.

it and enjoy what you are doing. ❏ *Everyone understood how hard it was to get back into the swing of things after such a long absence.*

Word Partnership	*swing*의 연어

N.	swing **a bat**, **golf** swing **2**
	swing **at a ball** **5**
	porch swing **6**
	voters swing **8**
ADJ.	**good** swing, **perfect** swing **2**
	big swing **2 5 8**
	in full swing **9**

swipe /swaɪp/ (**swipes, swiping, swiped**) **1** V-T/V-I If you **swipe at** a person or thing, you try to hit them with a stick or other object, making a swinging movement with your arm. ❏ *She swiped at Rusty as though he was a fly.* ● N-COUNT **Swipe** is also a noun. ❏ *He took a swipe at Andrew that deposited him on the floor.* **2** V-T If you **swipe** something, you steal it quickly. [INFORMAL] ❏ *Five soldiers were each fined £140 for swiping a wheelchair from a disabled tourist.* **3** N-COUNT If you take a **swipe at** a person or an organization, you criticize them, usually in an indirect way. ❏ *Genesis recorded a song which took a swipe at greedy property developers who bought up and demolished people's homes.* **4** V-T If you **swipe** a credit card or swipe card through a machine, you pass it through a narrow space in the machine so that the machine can read information on the card's magnetic strip. ❏ *Swipe your card through the phone, then dial.*

swipe card (**swipe cards**) also **swipecard** N-COUNT A **swipe card** is a plastic card with a magnetic strip on it which contains information that can be read or transferred by passing the card through a special machine. ❏ *They use a swipe card to go in and out of their offices.*

swirl /swɜrl/ (**swirls, swirling, swirled**) V-T/V-I If you **swirl** something liquid or flowing, or if it **swirls**, it moves around and around quickly. ❏ *She smiled, swirling the wine in her glass.* ❏ *The black water swirled around his legs, reaching almost to his knees.* ● N-COUNT **Swirl** is also a noun. ❏ *...small swirls of chocolate cream.*

swish /swɪʃ/ (**swishes, swishing, swished**) V-T/V-I If something **swishes** or if you **swish** it, it moves quickly through the air, making a soft sound. ❏ *A car swished by steady and fast heading for the coast.* ❏ *He swished his cape around his shoulders.* ● N-COUNT **Swish** is also a noun. ❏ *She turned with a swish of her skirt.*

switch ◆◇◇ /swɪtʃ/ (**switches, switching, switched**) **1** N-COUNT A **switch** is a small control for an electrical device which you use to turn the device on or off. ❏ *Leona put some detergent into the dishwasher, shut the door and pressed the switch.* **2** N-PLURAL On a railroad track, the **switches** are the levers and rails at a place where two tracks join or separate. The **switches** enable a train to move from one track to another. [AM; BRIT **points**] ❏ *...a set of railroad tracks – including switches – and a model train.* **3** V-I If you **switch to** something different, for example to a different system, task, or subject of conversation, you change to it from what you were doing or saying before. ❏ *Estonia is switching to a market economy.* ❏ *The law would encourage companies to switch from coal to cleaner fuels.* ● N-COUNT **Switch** is also a noun. [usu with supp] ❏ *The spokesman implicitly condemned the United States policy switch.* ● PHRASAL VERB **Switch over** means the same as **switch**. ❏ *Everywhere communists are tending to switch over to social democracy.* **4** V-T/V-I If you **switch** your attention from one thing **to** another or if your attention **switches**, you stop paying attention to the first thing and start paying attention to the second. ❏ *My mother's interest had switched to my health.* **5** V-T If you **switch** two things, you replace one with the other. ❏ *In half an hour, they'd switched the tags on every cable.*

Word Partnership	*switch*의 연어

N.	**ignition** switch, **light** switch, **power** switch **1**
	switch **sides** **3**
V.	**flick** a switch, **flip** a switch, **turn** a switch **1**
	make a switch **3**

▶**switch off** **1** PHRASAL VERB If you **switch off** a light or other electrical device, you stop it working by operating a switch. ❏ *She switched off the coffee machine.* **2** PHRASAL VERB If you **switch off**, you stop paying attention or stop thinking or worrying about something. [INFORMAL] ❏ *Thankfully, I've learned to switch off and let it go over my head.*

▶**switch on** PHRASAL VERB If you **switch on** a light or other electrical device, you make it start working by operating a switch. ❏ *She emptied both their mugs and switched on the electric kettle.*

switch|board /swɪtʃbɔrd/ (**switchboards**) N-COUNT A **switchboard** is a place in a large office or business where all the telephone calls are connected. ❏ *He asked to be connected to the central switchboard at London University.*

swiv|el /swɪvᵊl/ (**swivels, swiveling, swiveled**) [BRIT **swivelling, swivelled**] V-T/V-I If something **swivels** or if you **swivel** it, it turns around a central point so that it is facing in a different direction. ❏ *She swiveled her chair and stared out the window.*

1 타동사/자동사 후려치다 ❏ 그녀는 러스티가 파리라도 되는 양 그를 후려쳤다. ● 가산명사 후려침 ❏ 그가 앤드류를 후려쳐서 앤드류가 바닥에 쓰러졌다. **2** 타동사 훔치다 [비격식체] ❏ 군인 다섯 명이 장애인 관광객에게서 휠체어를 훔쳐서 각각 140파운드의 벌금형을 받았다. **3** 가산명사 -에 대한 비난 ❏ 창세기에는 사람들의 집을 다 사들인 후 헐어 버린 탐욕스런 부동산 개발업자를 비난한 노래가 기록되어 있다. **4** 타동사 (신용 카드 등을) 판독기에 넣다 ❏ 전화기에 카드를 넣고 다이얼을 돌리세요.

가산명사 전자 카드 ❏ 그들은 사무실 출입 시 전자 카드를 사용한다.

타동사/자동사 (물 등을) 소용돌이치게 하다; 소용돌이치다, (물 등이) 빙빙 돌다 ❏ 그녀는 미소를 지으며 잔에 든 와인을 빙빙 돌렸다. ❏ 검은 물이 그의 다리 주위에서 소용돌이를 일으키더니 거의 그의 무릎까지 올라왔다. ● 가산명사 소용돌이, 소용돌이 모양 ❏ 작은 소용돌이 모양의 초콜릿 크림

타동사/자동사 휙 소리 내며 지나가다, 쌩하고 가다; 휙 소리 내며 지나가게 하다, 휙 휘두르다 ❏ 자동차 한 대가 일정하게 빠른 속도로 해안을 향해 쌩 소리 내며 지나갔다. ❏ 그는 망토를 어깨 위로 휙 걸쳤다. ● 가산명사 휙 하는 소리, 쌩 하는 소리 ❏ 그녀는 치마에서 쌩 바람 소리가 나게 돌아섰다.

1 가산명사 스위치 ❏ 레오나는 식기 세척기에 세제를 넣고 문을 닫은 후 스위치를 눌렀다. **2** 복수명사 선로 변환기 [미국영어; 영국영어 points] ❏ 선로 변환기와 모형 기차를 포함한 철로 세트 **3** 자동사 전환하다 ❏ 에스토니아는 시장 경제로 전환하고 있다. ❏ 그 법규는 기업들이 석탄에서 청정연료로 전환할 것을 권장하게 될 것이다. ● 가산명사 전환 ❏ 그 대변인은 미국의 정책 전환을 암시적으로 비난했다. ● 구동사 전환하다 ❏ 모든 곳에서 공산주의자들이 사회주의적 민주주의로 전환하려는 경향을 보이고 있다. **4** 타동사/자동사 바꾸다; 바뀌다 ❏ 어머니의 관심사가 내 건강으로 바뀌어 있었다. **5** 타동사 교체하다 ❏ 30분이 지나자 그들은 모든 케이블에 붙은 꼬리표들을 교체했다.

1 구동사 스위치를 끄다 ❏ 그녀는 커피 기계의 스위치를 껐다. **2** 구동사 신경을 끄다 [비격식체] ❏ 다행히도 나는 신경을 끄고 내 머릿속에서 그 일을 잊어버릴 줄 알게 되었다.

구동사 스위치를 켜다 ❏ 그녀는 그들의 머그잔을 비우고 전기 주전자의 스위치를 켰다.

가산명사 교환대 ❏ 그는 런던 대학교 중앙 교환대로 연결해 달라고 부탁했다.

[영국영어 swivelling, swivelled] 타동사/자동사 (축을 중심으로) 회전하다; 회전시키다 ❏ 그녀는 앉은 의자를 빙 돌려 창밖을 응시했다.

a b c d e f g h i j k l m n o p q r s t u v w x y z

swollen /swooʊlᵊn/ ■ ADJ If a part of your body is **swollen**, it is larger and rounder than normal, usually as a result of injury or illness. ❑ *My eyes were so swollen I could hardly see.* ■ ADJ A **swollen** river has more water in it and flows faster than normal, usually because of heavy rain. ❑ *The river, brown and swollen with rain, was running fast.* ■ **Swollen** is the past participle of **swell**.

■ 형용사 부은 ❑ 나는 내 두 눈이 너무 부어서 거의 앞을 볼 수 없었다. ■ 형용사 물이 불어난 ❑ 비가 내려 탁해지고 불어난 강은 빠르게 흐르고 있었다. ■ swell의 과거 분사

swoop /swup/ (**swoops, swooping, swooped**) ■ V-I If police or soldiers **swoop on** a place, they go there suddenly and quickly, usually in order to arrest someone or to attack the place. [JOURNALISM] ❑ *The terror ended when armed police swooped on the car.* ● N-COUNT **Swoop** is also a noun. ❑ *Police held 10 suspected illegal immigrants after a swoop on a German lorry.* ■ V-I When a bird or airplane **swoops**, it suddenly moves downwards through the air in a smooth curving movement. ❑ *More than 20 helicopters began swooping in low over the ocean.* ■ PHRASE If something is done **in one fell swoop** or **at one fell swoop**, it is done on a single occasion or by a single action. ❑ *In one fell swoop the bank wiped away the tentative benefits of this policy.*

■ 자동사 급습하다 [언론] ❑ 무장 경찰들이 그 차를 급습함으로써 테러는 종식되었다. ● 가산명사 급습 ❑ 경찰이 독일에서 온 트럭을 급습해서 불법 이민자로 의심되는 사람을 열 명을 잡았다. ■ 자동사 하강하다 ❑ 20여기가 넘는 헬리콥터들이 바다 수면 위로 낮게 하강하기 시작했다. ■ 구 단번에 ❑ 그 은행이 이 정책의 일시적인 혜택을 단번에 일소시켜 버렸다.

swop /swɒp/ →see **swap**

sword /sɔrd/ (**swords**) ■ N-COUNT A **sword** is a weapon with a handle and a long sharp blade. ■ PHRASE If you **cross swords with** someone, you disagree with them and argue with them about something. ❑ *...a candidate who's crossed swords with Labor by supporting the free-trade pact.* ■ PHRASE If you say that something is a **double-edged sword** or a **two-edged sword**, you mean that it has negative effects as well as positive effects. ❑ *A person's looks are a double-edged sword. Sometimes it works in your favor, sometimes it works against you.* →see **army**

■ 가산명사 칼 ■ 구 불화하다 ❑ 자유 무역 협약을 지지함으로써 노동당과 불화를 빚은 후보 ■ 구 양날의 검 ❑ 사람의 인상은 양날의 칼과 같다. 때로는 본인에게 유리하지만 때로는 불리하다.

swore /swɔr/ **Swore** is the past tense of **swear**.

swear의 과거

sworn /swɔrn/ ■ **Sworn** is the past participle of **swear**. ■ ADJ If you make a **sworn** statement or declaration, you swear that everything that you have said in it is true. [ADJ n] ❑ *The allegations against them were made in sworn evidence to the inquiry.* ■ ADJ If two people or two groups of people are **sworn** enemies, they dislike each other very much. [ADJ n] ❑ *It somehow seems hardly surprising that Ms. Player is now his sworn enemy.*

■ swear의 과거 분사 ■ 형용사 맹세한 ❑ 그들에 대한 혐의는 그 조사 과정에서 맹세를 하고 제시된 증거에 의해 이뤄졌다. ■ 형용사 불구대천의 ❑ 아무튼 이제 플레이어 씨가 그의 불구대천의 원수라는 것은 거의 놀랄 일이 아니다.

swot /swɒt/ (**swots, swotting, swotted**) V-I If you **swot**, you study very hard, especially when you are preparing for an examination. [BRIT, INFORMAL] ❑ *They swotted for their A levels.*

자동사 기를 쓰고 공부하다 [영국영어, 비격식체] ❑ 그들은 에이 레벨 시험을 위해 기를 쓰고 공부했다.

swum /swʌm/ **Swum** is the past participle of **swim**.

swim의 과거 분사

swung /swʌŋ/ **Swung** is the past tense and past participle of **swing**.

swing의 과거, 과거 분사

syl|la|ble /sɪləbᵊl/ (**syllables**) N-COUNT A **syllable** is a part of a word that contains a single vowel sound and that is pronounced as a unit. So, for example, "book" has one syllable, and "reading" has two syllables. ❑ *We children called her Oma, accenting both syllables.*

가산명사 음절 ❑ 우리 어린이들은 그녀를 양 음절 모두에 강세를 붙여 오마라고 불렀다.

syl|la|bus /sɪləbəs/ (**syllabuses**) ■ N-COUNT A **syllabus** is an outline or summary of the subjects to be covered in a course. [mainly AM] ❑ *The course syllabus consisted mainly of novels by African-American authors, male and female.* ■ N-COUNT You can refer to the subjects that are studied in a particular course as the **syllabus**. [mainly BRIT] ❑ *...the GCSE history syllabus.*

■ 가산명사 교수요목 [주로 미국영어] ❑ 그 과정의 교수요목은 주로 미국 흑인 남녀 작가들의 소설로 이뤄져 있었다. ■ 가산명사 과목 [주로 영국영어] ❑ 지시에스이의 역사 과목

sym|bol ◇◇◇ /sɪmbᵊl/ (**symbols**) ■ N-COUNT Something that is a **symbol of** a society or an aspect of life seems to represent it because it is very typical of it. ❑ *To them, the monarchy is the special symbol of nationhood.* ■ N-COUNT A **symbol of** something such as an idea is a shape or design that is used to represent it. ❑ *Later in this same passage Yeats resumes his argument for the Rose as an Irish symbol.* ■ N-COUNT A **symbol for** an item in a calculation or scientific formula is a number, letter, or shape that represents that item. ❑ *What's the chemical symbol for mercury?* ■ →see also **sex symbol** →see **flag, myth**

■ 가산명사 상징 ❑ 그들에게, 군주제는 독립 국가임을 나타내는 특별한 상징이다. ■ 가산명사 상징 ❑ 여기 같은 구절 후반부에서 예이츠는 다시 그 장미가 아일랜드의 상징이라는 주장을 펼친다. ■ 가산명사 기호 ❑ 수은을 나타내는 화학 기호는 무엇입니까?

sym|bol|ic /sɪmbɒlɪk/ ■ ADJ If you describe an event, action, or procedure as **symbolic**, you mean that it represents an important change, although it has little practical effect. ❑ *A lot of Latin-American officials are stressing the symbolic importance of the trip.* ● **sym|boli|cal|ly** /sɪmbɒlɪkli/ ADV ❑ *It was a simple enough gesture, but symbolically important.* ■ ADJ Something that is **symbolic** of a person or thing is regarded or used as a symbol of them. ❑ *Yellow clothes are worn as symbolic of spring.* ● **sym|boli|cal|ly** ADV [ADV with v] ❑ *Each circle symbolically represents the whole of humanity.* ■ ADJ **Symbolic** is used to describe things involving or relating to symbols. [ADJ n] ❑ *...symbolic representations of landscape.*

■ 형용사 상징적인 ❑ 많은 라틴 아메리카 관계자들이 그 여행의 상징적인 중요성을 강조하고 있다. ● 상징적으로 부사 ❑ 그것은 극히 간단한 제스처였지만 상징적으로 중요했다. ■ 형용사 ~을 상징하는 ❑ 노란색 옷은 봄을 상징하기 위해 입는다. ● 상징적으로 부사 ❑ 각 원은 상징적으로 인류 전체를 나타냅니다. ■ 형용사 기호를 사용한 ❑ 풍경을 기호를 사용한 표현

sym|bol|ism /sɪmbəlɪzəm/ ■ N-UNCOUNT **Symbolism** is the use of symbols in order to represent something. ❑ *The scene is so rich in symbolism that any explanation risks spoiling the effect.* ■ N-UNCOUNT You can refer to the **symbolism** of an event or action when it seems to show something important about a situation. ❑ *The symbolism of every gesture will be of vital importance during the short state visit.*

■ 불가산명사 상징주의 ❑ 그 장면은 상징주의 색채가 아주 풍부해서 어떤 설명도 그 효과를 망칠 위험이 있다. ■ 불가산명사 상징성 ❑ 국가 원수의 단기간 공식 방문 시에는 제스처 하나하나가 지닌 상징성이 매우 중요하다.

sym|bol|ize /sɪmbəlaɪz/ (**symbolizes, symbolizing, symbolized**) [BRIT also **symbolise**] V-T If one thing **symbolizes** another, it is used or regarded as a symbol of it. ❑ *The fall of the Berlin Wall symbolized the end of the Cold War between East and West.* →see **flag**

[영국영어 symbolise] 타동사 상징하다 ❑ 베를린 장벽의 붕괴는 동서 양대 진영의 냉전 종식을 상징했다.

sym|met|ri|cal /sɪmetrɪkᵊl/ ADJ If something is **symmetrical**, it has two halves which are exactly the same, except that one half is the mirror image of the other. ❑ *...the neat rows of perfectly symmetrical windows.* ● **sym|met|ri|cal|ly** /sɪmetrɪkli/ ADV [ADV with v] ❑ *The south garden at Sissinghurst was composed symmetrically.*

형용사 대칭적인 ❑ 완벽하게 대칭을 이루며 깔끔하게 늘어선 창문들 ● 대칭적으로 부사 ❑ 시싱허스트의 남쪽 정원은 대칭적으로 구성되어 있었다.

sym|me|try /sɪmɪtri/ (**symmetries**) ■ N-VAR Something that has **symmetry** is symmetrical in shape, design, or structure. ❑ *...the incredible beauty and symmetry of a snowflake.* ■ N-UNCOUNT **Symmetry** in a relationship or agreement is the fact of both sides giving and receiving an equal amount. ❑ *The superpowers pledged to maintain symmetry in their arms shipments.*

■ 가산명사 또는 불가산명사 대칭 ❑ 눈송이의 믿기 어려운 아름다움과 대칭 ■ 불가산명사 균형 ❑ 강대국들은 무기 수송의 균형을 유지하기로 약속했다.

sym|pa|thet|ic /sɪmpəθɛtɪk/ **1** ADJ If you are **sympathetic** to someone who is in a bad situation, you are kind to them and show that you understand their feelings. ❑ *She was very sympathetic to the problems of adult students.* ● **sym|pa|theti|cal|ly** /sɪmpəθɛtɪkli/ ADV [ADV with v] ❑ *She nodded sympathetically.* **2** ADJ If you are **sympathetic to** a proposal or action, you approve of it and are willing to support it. ❑ *Many of these early visitors were sympathetic to the Chinese socialist experiment.* ● **sym|pa|theti|cal|ly** ADV [ADV with v] ❑ *After a year we will sympathetically consider an application for reinstatement.*

> Do not confuse **sympathetic** and **friendly**. If you have a problem and someone is **sympathetic** or shows a **sympathetic** attitude, they show that they care and would like to help you. ❑ *My boyfriend was very sympathetic.* A person who is **friendly** or has a **friendly** attitude is kind and pleasant and behaves the way a friend would. ❑ *...a friendly woman who offered me cakes and tea. ...a pleasant, friendly smile.* Note that people sometimes refer to characters in a play or novel who are easy to like as **sympathetic**. ❑ *There were no sympathetic characters in my book.* You usually say that real people are "nice" or "likable."

sym|pa|thize /sɪmpəθaɪz/ (sympathizes, sympathizing, sympathized) [BRIT also **sympathise**] **1** V-I If you **sympathize** with someone who is in a bad situation, you show that you are sorry for them. ❑ *I must tell you how much I sympathize with you for your loss, Professor.* **2** V-I If you **sympathize with** someone's feelings, you understand them and are not critical of them. ❑ *Some Europeans sympathize with the Americans over the issue.* **3** V-I If you **sympathize with** a proposal or action, you approve of it and are willing to support it. ❑ *Most of the people living there sympathized with the guerrillas.*

sym|pa|thiz|er /sɪmpəθaɪzər/ (sympathizers) [BRIT also **sympathiser**] N-COUNT The **sympathizers** of an organization or cause are the people who approve of it and support it. ❑ *Safta Hashmi was a well-known playwright and Communist sympathizer.*

| **Word Link** | path ≈ feeling : apathy, empathy, sympathy |

| **Word Link** | sym ≈ together : sympathy, symphony, symposium |

sym|pa|thy ♦◊◊ /sɪmpəθi/ (sympathies) **1** N-UNCOUNT If you have **sympathy** for someone who is in a bad situation, you are sorry for them, and show this in the way you behave toward them. [also N in pl] ❑ *We expressed our sympathy for her loss.* ❑ *I have had very little help from doctors and no sympathy whatsoever.* **2** N-UNCOUNT If you have **sympathy** with someone's ideas or opinions, you agree with them. [also N in pl, oft N with/for n] ❑ *I have some sympathy with this point of view.* ❑ *Lithuania still commands considerable international sympathy for its cause.* **3** N-UNCOUNT If you take some action **in sympathy with** someone else, you do it in order to show that you support them. ❑ *Several hundred workers struck in sympathy with their colleagues.*

Word Partnership	sympathy의 연어
ADJ.	deep sympathy, great sympathy, public sympathy **1**
V.	express sympathy, feel sympathy, gain sympathy, have sympathy **1 2**

sym|pho|ny /sɪmfəni/ (symphonies) N-COUNT; N-IN-NAMES A **symphony** is a piece of music written to be played by an orchestra. Symphonies are usually made up of four separate sections called movements. ❑ *...Beethoven's Ninth Symphony.* →see **music, orchestra**

sym|pho|ny or|ches|tra (symphony orchestras) N-COUNT; N-IN-NAMES A **symphony orchestra** is a large orchestra that plays classical music.

sym|po|sium /sɪmpoʊziəm/ (symposia /sɪmpoʊziə/ or symposiums) N-COUNT A **symposium** is a conference in which experts or academics discuss a particular subject. ❑ *He had been taking part in an international symposium on population.*

symp|tom ♦◊◊ /sɪmptəm/ (symptoms) **1** N-COUNT A **symptom** of an illness is something wrong with your body or mind that is a sign of the illness. ❑ *One of the most common symptoms of schizophrenia is hearing imaginary voices.* ❑ *...patients with flu symptoms.* **2** N-COUNT A **symptom of** a bad situation is something that happens which is considered to be a sign of this situation. ❑ *Your problem with keeping boyfriends is just a symptom of a larger problem: making and keeping friends.* →see **diagnosis, illness**

symp|to|mat|ic /sɪmptəmætɪk/ ADJ If something is **symptomatic of** something else, especially something bad, it is a sign of it. [FORMAL] [v-link ADJ, usu ADJ of n] ❑ *The city's problems are symptomatic of the crisis that is spreading throughout the country.*

syna|gogue /sɪnəgɒg/ (synagogues) N-COUNT; N-IN-NAMES A **synagogue** is a building where Jewish people meet to worship or to study their religion.

| **Word Link** | syn ≈ together : synchronize, synergy, synopsis |

syn|chro|nize /sɪŋkrənaɪz/ (synchronizes, synchronizing, synchronized) [BRIT also **synchronise**] V-RECIP If you **synchronize** two activities, processes, or movements, or if you **synchronize** one activity, process, or movement **with**

1 형용사 동정적인 ❑ 그녀는 성인 학생들의 문제에 매우 동정적이었다. ● 동정적으로 부사 ❑ 그는 동정적으로 고개를 끄덕였다. **2** 형용사 호의적인 ❑ 이들 초기 방문객들중 많은 사람들이 중국의 사회주의 실험에 호의적이었다. ● 호의적으로 부사 ❑ 1년 후 우리는 복직 신청을 호의적으로 고려할 것이다.

> sympathetic과 friendly를 혼동하지 마시오. 당신에게 고민이 있고 누군가가 sympathetic한 태도를 보이면, 그들이 당신에 대해 염려하고 도와주고 싶어 하는 것이다. ❑ 내 남자친구는 무척 인정이 많았다. friendly하거나 friendly한 태도를 가진 사람은 친절하고 상냥하고 친구처럼 행동한다. ❑ ...내게 케이크와 차를 권했던 친절한 여자....상냥하고 친근한 미소. 때때로 연극이나 소설의 공감하기 쉬운 등장인물들을 sympathetic하다고 표현하는 것을 유념하시오. ❑ 내 책에는 공감이 가는 인물이 하나도 없다. 실제 사람들에 대해서는 대개 'nice'나 'likable'을 쓴다.

[영국영어 sympathise] **1** 자동사 동정하다, 측은히 여기다 ❑ 교수님께서 나쁜 일을 당하신 데 대해 정말 마음이 아프다는 말씀을 드리고 싶습니다. **2** 자동사 이해하다 ❑ 일부 유럽인들은 그 사안에 대해 미국인들을 이해한다. **3** 자동사 공감하다, 호의적이다 ❑ 그곳에 사는 대부분의 사람들은 게릴라들에게 호의적이었다.

[영국영어 sympathiser] 가산명사 동조자 ❑ 사프타 하시미는 유명한 극작가였으며 공산주의 동조자였다.

1 불가산명사 동정 ❑ 우리는 그녀가 상을 당한 것에 대해 동정을 표했다. ❑ 나는 의사들에게 거의 도움을 받지도 못했고 동정은 전혀 받지 못했다. **2** 불가산명사 동의, 공감 ❑ 나는 이 견해에 어느 정도 동의한다. ❑ 리투아니아는 여전히 그 명분에 대해 국제 사회의 상당한 동의를 얻고 있다. **3** 불가산명사 동조 ❑ 수백 명의 근로자들이 동료들에게 동조하여 파업을 벌였다.

가산명사; 이름명사 교향곡 ❑ 베토벤 교향곡 9번

가산명사; 이름명사 교향악단

가산명사 심포지엄 ❑ 그는 인구 문제에 대한 국제 심포지엄에 참가하고 있었다.

1 가산명사 증상 ❑ 정신 분열증의 가장 일반적인 증상 중 하나는 환청을 듣는 것이다. ❑ 독감 증상을 보이는 환자들 **2** 가산명사 조짐 ❑ 남자 친구들과 관계를 유지하면서 갖게 되는 문제가 더 큰 문제인, 친구를 사귀고 관계를 유지하는 것과 관련된 문제의 조짐에 불과할 수도 있다.

형용사 징후를 보이는 [격식체] ❑ 그 도시의 문제들은 국가 전체에 퍼지고 있는 위기의 징후를 보여 준다.

가산명사; 이름명사 유대교 회당

[영국영어 synchronise] 상호동사 동시에 일어나게 하다, (시간적으로) 일치시키다 ❑ 휴일과 주말을 함께 할 수 있도록 우리 생활을 맞추는 것이 사실상

a b c d e f g h i j k l m n o p q r **s** t u v w x y z

another, you cause them to happen at the same time and speed as each other. ❑ *It was virtually impossible to synchronize our lives so as to take holidays and weekends together.* ❑ *Synchronize the score with the film action.*

불가능했다. ❑ 영화 액션과 음악을 일치시키세요.

syn|di|cate /ˈsɪndɪkɪt/ (**syndicates, syndicating, syndicated**) **1** N-COUNT A **syndicate** is an association of people or organizations that is formed for business purposes or in order to carry out a project. ❑ *They formed a syndicate to buy the car in which they competed in the race.* ❑ *...a syndicate of 152 banks.* **2** V-T When newspaper articles or television programs **are syndicated**, they are sold to several different newspapers or television stations, who then publish the articles or broadcast the programs. [usu passive] ❑ *Today his program is syndicated to 500 stations.* **3** N-COUNT A press **syndicate** is a group of newspapers or magazines that are all owned by the same person or company.

1 가산명사 신디케이트, 연합체 ❑ 그들은 신디케이트를 결성해서 그들이 경주에서 겨룬 차를 구입했다. ❑ 152개 은행의 신디케이트 **2** 타동사 (기사 등이 언론사에) 판매되어 발표되다 ❑ 그가 만든 프로그램은 5백 개 방송국에 판매되어 방송된다. **3** 가산명사 기업 연합, 언론 그룹

syn|drome /ˈsɪndroʊm/ (**syndromes**) N-COUNT; N-IN-NAMES A **syndrome** is a medical condition that is characterized by a particular group of signs and symptoms. ❑ *Irritable bowel syndrome seems to affect more women than men.*

가산명사; 이름명사 증후군 ❑ 과민대장증후군은 남자보다는 여자들에게서 더 많이 나타나는 것 같다.

| Word Link | syn ≈ together : synchronize, synergy, synopsis |

---

syn|er|gy /ˈsɪnərdʒi/ (**synergies**) N-VAR If there is **synergy** between two or more organizations or groups, they are more successful when they work together than when they work separately. [BUSINESS] ❑ *Of course, there's quite obviously a lot of synergy between the two companies.*

가산명사 또는 불가산명사 동반 상승효과 [경제] ❑ 물론, 그 두 회사 간의 동반 상승효과가 크다는 것이 꽤 명백하다.

| Word Link | onym ≈ name : acronym, anonymous, synonym |

---

syno|nym /ˈsɪnənɪm/ (**synonyms**) N-COUNT A **synonym** is a word or expression which means the same as another word or expression. ❑ *The term "industrial democracy" is often used as a synonym for worker participation.*

가산명사 동의어 ❑ '산업 민주주의'라는 용어는 흔히 '노동자 참여'의 동의어로 쓰인다.

syn|ony|mous /sɪˈnɒnɪməs/ ADJ If you say that one thing is **synonymous with** another, you mean that the two things are very closely associated with each other so that one suggests the other or one cannot exist without the other. ❑ *Paris has always been synonymous with elegance, luxury and style.*

형용사 동의어의 ❑ 파리는 언제나 우아, 호화, 품위의 동의어를 이루어 왔다.

syn|op|sis /sɪˈnɒpsɪs/ (**synopses** /sɪˈnɒpsiːz/) N-COUNT A **synopsis** is a summary of a longer piece of writing or work. ❑ *For each title there is a brief synopsis of the book.*

가산명사 개요 ❑ 각 제목마다 책의 개요가 간략히 나와 있다.

syn|the|sis /ˈsɪnθɪsɪs/ (**syntheses** /ˈsɪnθɪsiːz/) **1** N-COUNT A **synthesis of** different ideas or styles is a mixture or combination of these ideas or styles. [FORMAL] ❑ *His novels are a rich synthesis of Balkan history and mythology.* **2** N-VAR The **synthesis** of a substance is the production of it by means of chemical or biological reactions. [TECHNICAL] ❑ *...the genes that regulate the synthesis of these compounds.*

1 가산명사 종합 [격식체] ❑ 그의 소설들은 발칸 반도의 역사와 신화를 풍부히 종합한 것이다. **2** 가산명사 또는 불가산명사 합성 [과학 기술] ❑ 이러한 복합물들의 합성을 통제하는 유전자들

syn|the|size /ˈsɪnθɪsaɪz/ (**synthesizes, synthesizing, synthesized**) [BRIT also **synthesise**] **1** V-T To **synthesize** a substance means to produce it by means of chemical or biological reactions. [TECHNICAL] ❑ *After extensive research, Albert Hoffman first succeeded in synthesizing the acid in 1938.* **2** V-T If you **synthesize** different ideas, facts, or experiences, you combine them to form a single idea or impression. [FORMAL] ❑ *The movement synthesized elements of modern art that hadn't been brought together before, such as Cubism and Surrealism.*

[영국영어 synthesise] **1** 타동사 합성하다 [과학 기술] ❑ 광범위한 연구 후에 앨버트 호프만은 1938년 처음으로 산 합성에 성공했다. **2** 타동사 종합하다 [격식체] ❑ 그 운동은 입체파와 초현실주의와 같이 이전에는 함께 다루어지지 않았던 현대 미술의 요소들을 종합했다.

syn|the|siz|er /ˈsɪnθɪsaɪzər/ (**synthesizers**) [BRIT also **synthesiser**] N-COUNT A **synthesizer** is an electronic machine that produces speech, music, or other sounds, usually by combining individual syllables or sounds that have been previously recorded. ❑ *Now he can only communicate through a voice synthesizer.* →see **keyboard**

[영국영어 synthesiser] 가산명사 신시사이저, 전자 음향 합성 장치 ❑ 그는 이제 전자 음향 합성 장치를 통해서만 의사소통을 할 수 있다.

syn|thet|ic /sɪnˈθetɪk/ ADJ **Synthetic** products are made from chemicals or artificial substances rather than from natural ones. ❑ *Boots made from synthetic materials can usually be washed in a machine.*

형용사 합성의, 인조의 ❑ 인조 재료로 만든 장화는 보통 기계에 넣어 세탁할 수 있다.

sy|phon /ˈsaɪfᵊn/ →see **siphon**

sy|ringe /sɪˈrɪndʒ/ (**syringes**) N-COUNT A **syringe** is a small tube with a thin hollow needle at the end. Syringes are used for putting liquids into things and for taking liquids out, for example for injecting drugs or for taking blood from someone's body. ❑ *As he reached over, Azrak slid a hypodermic syringe into his left arm.*

가산명사 주사기 ❑ 그가 팔을 뻗자, 아즈락이 그의 왼쪽 팔에 피하 주사기를 찔러 넣었다.

syr|up /ˈsɪrəp, ˈsɜːr-/ (**syrups**) **1** N-MASS **Syrup** is a sweet liquid made by cooking sugar with water, and sometimes with fruit juice as well. ❑ *...canned fruit with sugary syrup.* **2** N-MASS **Syrup** is a medicine in the form of a thick, sweet liquid. ❑ *...cough syrup.*

1 물질명사 시럽 ❑ 달콤한 시럽으로 절인 과일 통조림 **2** 물질명사 (약물) 시럽 ❑ 기침 시럽

sys|tem ♦♦♦ /ˈsɪstəm/ (**systems**) **1** N-COUNT A **system** is a way of working, organizing, or doing something which follows a fixed plan or set of rules. You can use **system** to refer to an organization or institution that is organized in this way. ❑ *The present system of funding for higher education is unsatisfactory.* ❑ *...a flexible and relatively efficient filing system.* **2** N-COUNT A **system** is a set of devices powered by electricity, for example a computer or an alarm. ❑ *Viruses tend to be good at surviving when a computer system crashes.* **3** N-COUNT A **system** is a set of equipment or parts such as water pipes or electrical wiring, which is used to supply water, heat, or electricity. ❑ *...a central heating system.* **4** N-COUNT A **system** is a network of things that are linked together so that people or things can travel from one place to another or communicate. ❑ *Australia's road and rail system.* **5** N-COUNT Your **system** is your body's organs and other parts that together perform particular functions. ❑ *He had slept for over fourteen hours, and his system seemed to have recuperated admirably.* **6** N-COUNT A **system** is a particular set of rules, especially in mathematics or science, which is used to count or measure things. ❑ *...the decimal system of metric weights and measures.* **7** N-SING People sometimes refer to the government or administration of a

1 가산명사 체계 ❑ 현 고등 교육 기금 체계는 만족스럽지 못하다. ❑ 유연하고 상대적으로 효율적인 서류 체계 **2** 가산명사 (기기의) 시스템 ❑ 바이러스는 컴퓨터 시스템이 고장 나도 없어지지 않는 경향이 있다. **3** 가산명사 (수도 등의) 시스템, 장치 ❑ 중앙난방 시스템 **4** 가산명사 (통신 등의) 조직망 ❑ 오스트레일리아의 도로 및 철로망 **5** 가산명사 신체, 몸 ❑ 14시간을 자고 나니 그는 몸이 감탄할 정도로 회복되는 것 같았다. **6** 가산명사 (체계적) 방식 ❑ 무게와 길이 측정의 십진법 방식 **7** 단수명사 체제 ❑ 이러한 감정으로 인해 사람들은 체제 전복을 기도하기 쉽다.

country as **the system**. ❏ *These feelings are likely to make people attempt to overthrow the system.* 🛲 →see also **ecosystem, immune system, nervous system, solar system, sound system**

sys|tem|at|ic /sɪstəmǽtɪk/ ADJ Something that is done in a **systematic** way is done according to a fixed plan, in a thorough and efficient way. ❏ *They went about their business in a systematic way.* ● sys|tem|ati|cal|ly /sɪstəmǽtɪkli/ ADV ❏ *The army has systematically violated human rights.*

형용사 체계적인 ❏ 그들은 체계적으로 사업을 해 나갔다. ● 체계적으로 부사 ❏ 군대는 체계적으로 인권을 유린해 왔다.

sys|tem|ic /sɪstɛmɪk/ ADJ **Systemic** means affecting the whole of something. [FORMAL] ❏ *The economy is locked in a systemic crisis.*

형용사 조직의 [격식체] ❏ 경제가 조직의 위기 속에 갇혀 있다.

sys|tems ana|lyst (**systems analysts**) N-COUNT A **systems analyst** is someone whose job is to decide what computer equipment and software a company needs, and to provide it.

가산명사 (컴퓨터) 시스템 분석가

a b c d e f g h i j k l m n o p q r s t u v w x y z

Tt

T, t /tiː/ (**T's, t's**) N-VAR T is the twentieth letter of the English alphabet.

tab /tæb/ (**tabs**) **1** N-COUNT A **tab** is a small piece of cloth or paper that is attached to something, usually with information about that thing written on it. ❑ *A stupid medical clerk had slipped the wrong tab on his X-ray while reaching for a mug of tea.* **2** N-COUNT A **tab** is the total cost of goods or services that you have to pay, or the bill or check for those goods or services. [mainly AM] ❑ *At least one estimate puts the total tab at $7 million.* **3** PHRASE If someone **keeps tabs on** you, they make sure that they always know where you are and what you are doing, often in order to control you. [INFORMAL] ❑ *It was obvious Hill had come over to keep tabs on Johnson and make sure he didn't do anything drastic.* **4** PHRASE If you **pick up the tab**, you pay a bill on behalf of a group of people or provide the money that is needed for something. [INFORMAL] ❑ *Pollard picked up the tab for dinner that night.*

ta|ble ♦♦◇ /ˈteɪbəl/ (**tables, tabling, tabled**) **1** N-COUNT A **table** is a piece of furniture with a flat top that you put things on or sit at. ❑ *She was sitting at the kitchen table eating a currant bun.* **2** V-T If someone **tables** a proposal or plan which has been put forward, they decide to discuss it or deal with it at a later date, rather than straight away. [AM] ❑ *We will table that for later.* **3** V-T If someone **tables** a proposal, they say formally that they want it to be discussed at a meeting. [mainly BRIT] ❑ *They've tabled a motion criticizing the Government for doing nothing about the problem.* **4** N-COUNT A **table** is a written set of facts and figures arranged in columns and rows. [also N num] ❑ *Consult the table on page 104.* **5** →see also **negotiating table**

table|cloth /ˈteɪbəlklɒθ, BRIT teɪbəlklɒθ/ (**tablecloths**) N-COUNT A **tablecloth** is a cloth used to cover a table.

table|spoon /ˈteɪbəlspuːn/ (**tablespoons**) N-COUNT A **tablespoon** is a fairly large spoon used for serving food and in cooking.

tab|let /ˈtæblɪt/ (**tablets**) **1** N-COUNT A **tablet** is a small solid round mass of medicine which you swallow. ❑ *It is never a good idea to take sleeping tablets regularly for this kind of wakefulness.* **2** N-COUNT Clay **tablets** or stone **tablets** are the flat pieces of clay or stone which people used to write on before paper was invented. **tablets of stone** →see **stone**

tab|loid /ˈtæblɔɪd/ (**tabloids**) N-COUNT A **tabloid** is a newspaper that has small pages, short articles, and a lot of photographs. Tabloids are often considered to be less serious than other newspapers. Compare **broadsheet**. ❑ *The broadsheet papers set the political agenda and the tabloids were regarded as a bit of fun.*

ta|boo /təˈbuː/ (**taboos**) N-COUNT If there is a **taboo** on a subject or activity, it is a social custom to avoid doing that activity or talking about that subject, because people find them embarrassing or offensive. ❑ *The topic of addiction remains something of a taboo.* ● ADJ **Taboo** is also an adjective. ❑ *Cancer is a taboo subject and people are frightened or embarrassed to talk openly about it.*

tac|it /ˈtæsɪt/ ADJ If you refer to someone's **tacit** agreement or approval, you mean they are agreeing to something or approving it without actually saying so, often because they are unwilling to admit to doing so. ❑ *The question was a tacit admission that a mistake had indeed been made.* ● **tac|it|ly** ADV [ADV with v] ❑ *He tacitly admitted that the government had breached regulations.*

tack /tæk/ (**tacks, tacking, tacked**) **1** N-COUNT A **tack** is a short nail with a broad, flat head, especially one that is used for fastening carpets to the floor. ❑ *...a box of carpet tacks.* →see also **thumbtack** **2** V-T If you **tack** something to a surface, you pin it there with tacks or thumbtacks. ❑ *He had tacked this note to her door.* **3** N-SING If you change **tack** or try a different **tack**, you try a different method for dealing with a situation. [also no det] ❑ *In desperation I changed tack.* **4** V-T If you **tack** pieces of material together, you sew them together with big, loose stitches in order to hold them firmly or check that they fit, before sewing them properly. ❑ *Tack them together with a 1.5 cm seam.*

▶**tack on** PHRASAL VERB If you say that something **is tacked on** to something else, you think that it is added in a hurry and in an unsatisfactory way. ❑ *The child-care bill is to be tacked on to the budget plan now being worked out in the Senate.*

tack|le ♦◇◇ /ˈtækəl/ (**tackles, tackling, tackled**) **1** V-T If you **tackle** a difficult problem or task, you deal with it in a very determined or efficient way. ❑ *The first reason to tackle these problems is to save children's lives.* **2** V-T If you **tackle** someone in a game such as football or rugby, you knock them to the ground. If you **tackle** someone in soccer or hockey, you try to take the ball away from them. ❑ *Foley tackled the quarterback.* ● N-COUNT **Tackle** is also a noun. ❑ *...a tackle by full-back Brian Burrows.* **3** V-T If you **tackle** someone about a particular matter, you speak to them honestly about it, usually in order to get it changed or

---

가산명사 또는 불가산명사 영어 알파벳의 스무 번째 글자

1 가산명사 색인표 ❑ 멍청한 병원 직원이 찻잔을 집느라 그의 엑스선 사진에 엉뚱한 색인표를 밀어 넣어 버렸다. **2** 가산명사 계산서 [주로 미국영어] ❑ 최소한 한 추정치에 따르면 전체 비용이 7백만 달러이다. **3** 구 감시하다 [비격식체] ❑ 존슨을 감시하고 그가 과격한 짓을 하지 않도록 막기 위해 힐이 왔다는 것은 명백했다. **4** 구 지불하다, 쏘다 [비격식체] ❑ 폴라드가 그 날 저녁을 쏐다.

1 가산명사 식탁 ❑ 그녀는 건포도 빵을 먹으며 부엌 식탁에 앉아 있었다. **2** 타동사 심의를 보류하다 [미국영어] ❑ 그것은 심의를 추후로 보류하겠다. **3** 타동사 (의안) 상정하다 [주로 영국영어] ❑ 그들은 그 문제에 대해 아무것도 안 하는 정부를 비판하며 의안을 상정했다. **4** 가산명사 표 ❑ 104페이지의 표를 참조하시오.

가산명사 식탁보

가산명사 테이블스푼, 큰 스푼

1 가산명사 알약 ❑ 이런 종류의 불면증 때문에 정기적으로 수면제를 먹는 것은 절대로 좋은 생각이 아니다. **2** 가산명사 석판, 평판

가산명사 타블로이드판 신문 ❑ 주요 일간지들은 정치적 사안들에 영향력을 행사했고 타블로이드판 신문들은 단순히 재미를 주는 것으로 여겨졌다.

가산명사 금기, 터부 ❑ 중독이라는 소재는 여전히 금기시되고 있다. ● 형용사 금기의 ❑ 암은 금기시되는 주제이고 사람들은 그것을 공개하거나 이야기하는 것을 두려워하거나 곤란해 한다.

형용사 무언의 ❑ 그 질문은 잘못이 범해졌다는 무언의 시인이었다. ● 무언으로 부사 ❑ 그는 정부가 규정을 어겼다는 것을 암묵적으로 인정했다.

1 가산명사 압정 ❑ 카펫용 압정 한 통 **2** 타동사 압정으로 붙이다 ❑ 그는 이 메모를 그녀의 문에 압정으로 붙여 놓았었다. **3** 단수명사 방침 ❑ 필사적인 심정으로 나는 방침을 바꿨다. **4** 타동사 시치다, 시침질하다 ❑ 1.5센티미터 길이의 솔기로 그것들을 함께 시쳐라.

구동사 (대충) 부가하다 ❑ 현재 상원에서 다루고 있는 예산안에 육아 법안을 부가할 것이다.

1 타동사 (문제에) 씨름하다 ❑ 이 문제들과 씨름을 해야 하는 첫째 이유는 아이들의 목숨을 살리기 위해서이다. **2** 타동사 태클하다 ❑ 폴리는 쿼터백을 태클했다. ● 가산명사 태클 ❑ 풀백 브라이언 버로우스의 태클 **3** 타동사 솔직하게 따지다 ❑ 나는 그렇게 심한 빈곤 속에서 도대체 누가 살 수 있는지를 그에게 솔직하게 따졌다. **4** 타동사 덤벼들다 ❑ 그는 파솔리니가 자신을 뒤따라와 덤벼들더니 땅바닥에

done. ❏ *I tackled him about how anyone could live amidst so much poverty.* **4** V-T If you **tackle** someone, you attack them and fight them. ❏ *He claims Pasolini overtook and tackled him, pushing him into the dirt.* **5** N-UNCOUNT **Tackle** is the equipment that you need for a sport or activity, especially fishing. ❏ *...fishing tackle.*

내팽개쳤다고 주장하다. **5** 불가산명사 (스포츠용) 도구 ❏ 낚시 도구

tacky /tǽki/ (**tackier, tackiest**) **1** ADJ If you describe something as **tacky**, you dislike it because it is cheap and badly made or vulgar. [INFORMAL, DISAPPROVAL] ❏ *...a woman in a fake leopard-skin coat and tacky red sunglasses.* **2** ADJ If something such as paint or glue is **tacky**, it is slightly sticky and not yet dry. ❏ *Test to see if the finish is tacky, and if it is, leave it to harden.*

1 형용사 싸구려의, 천박한 [비격식체, 탐탁찮음] ❏ 모조 표범 가죽 외투를 입고 싸구려 붉은색 선글라스를 쓴 여자 **2** 형용사 끈적끈적한, 마르지 않은 ❏ 마무리 칠이 아직 안 말랐는지 살펴보고 안 말랐으면 굳게 놔둬라.

tact /tækt/ N-UNCOUNT **Tact** is the ability to avoid upsetting or offending people by being careful not to say or do things that would hurt their feelings. ❏ *Her tact and intuition never failed. She was a discreet and sympathetic confidante.*

불가산명사 눈치 ❏ 그녀의 눈치와 직관은 틀리는 법이 없었다. 그녀는 비밀을 잘 지키고 이해심도 많아서 마음을 편하게 털어놓을 수 있었다.

tactful /tæktfʊl/ ADJ If you describe a person or what they say as **tactful** you approve of them because they are careful not to offend or upset another person. [APPROVAL] ❏ *He had been extremely tactful in dealing with the financial question.* ● **tactfully** ADV ❏ *Alex tactfully refrained from further comment.*

형용사 눈치 빠른, 요령 있는 [마음에 듦] ❏ 그는 재정적 문제를 다루는 데 있어서 매우 요령 있게 행동했었다. ● 눈치 빠르게, 요령 있게 부사 ❏ 알렉스는 눈치 빠르게 더 이상 토를 달지 않았다.

tactic ◆◇◇ /tæktɪk/ (**tactics**) N-COUNT **Tactics** are the methods that you choose to use in order to achieve what you want in a particular situation. ❏ *The rebels would still be able to use guerrilla tactics to make the country ungovernable.*

가산명사 전법, 작전 ❏ 반군들은 그래도 게릴라 전법을 사용하여 국가의 통치를 굉장히 어렵게 만들 수도 있을 것이다.

Word Partnership   tactic의 연어

ADJ.	**effective** tactic, **similar** tactic
N.	**scare** tactic

tactical /tæktɪkᵊl/ **1** ADJ You use **tactical** to describe an action or plan which is intended to help someone achieve what they want in a particular situation. ❏ *It's not yet clear whether the Prime Minister's resignation offer is a serious one, or whether it's simply a tactical move.* ● **tactically** /tæktɪkli/ ADV ❏ *The electorate is astute enough to vote tactically against the Government.* **2** ADJ **Tactical** weapons or forces are those which a military leader can decide for themselves to use in a battle, rather than waiting for a decision by a political leader. [ADJ n] ❏ *They have removed all tactical nuclear missiles that could strike Europe.*

1 형용사 작전상의 ❏ 수상의 사임 의사가 진심인지 아니면 단순한 책략에 불과한지는 아직 불분명하다. ● 작전적으로 부사 ❏ 유권자들이 전략적으로 정부를 반대하는 표를 던질 수 있을 만큼 냉철하다. **2** 형용사 전략의 ❏ 그들은 유럽을 공격할 수 있는 모든 전략적 핵무기를 제거했다.

taffy /tæfi/ N-UNCOUNT **Taffy** is a sticky candy that you chew. It is made by boiling sugar and butter together with water. [AM; BRIT **toffee**]

불가산명사 토피 [미국영어; 영국영어 toffee]

tag /tæg/ (**tags, tagging, tagged**) **1** N-COUNT A **tag** is a small piece of card or cloth which is attached to an object or person and has information about that object or person on it. ❏ *Staff wore name tags and called inmates by their first names.* →see also **price tag** **2** N-COUNT An electronic **tag** is a device that is firmly attached to someone or something and sets off an alarm if that person or thing moves away or is removed. ❏ *A hospital is to fit new-born babies with electronic tags to foil kidnappers.* **3** V-T If you **tag** something, you attach something to it or mark it so that it can be identified later. ❏ *Professor Orr has developed interesting ways of tagging chemical molecules using existing laboratory lasers.*

1 가산명사 꼬리표, 정가표 ❏ 직원들은 명찰을 달고 수감자들을 대했다. **2** 가산명사 꼬리표 ❏ 한 병원이 신생아들에게 전자 꼬리표를 달아 유괴를 방지할 계획이다. **3** 타동사 꼬리표를 달다, 표시를 달다 ❏ 오르 교수는 기존의 실험실 레이저를 이용하여 화학 분자에 표시를 달 수 있는 흥미로운 방법들을 개발했다.

▶**tag along** PHRASAL VERB If someone goes somewhere and you **tag along**, you go with them, especially when they have not asked you to. ❏ *I let him tag along because he had not been too well recently.*

구동사 (귀찮게) 따라가다 ❏ 나는 그가 최근에 몸이 좋지 않았으므로 따라오도록 놔뒀다.

tail ◆◇◇ /teɪl/ (**tails, tailing, tailed**) **1** N-COUNT The **tail** of an animal, bird, or fish is the part extending beyond the end of its body. ❏ *...a black dog with a long tail.* **2** N-COUNT You can use **tail** to refer to the end or back of something, especially something long and thin. ❏ *...the horizontal stabilizer bar on the plane's tail.* **3** N-PLURAL If a man is wearing **tails**, he is wearing a formal jacket which has two long pieces hanging down at the back. ❏ *...men in tails and women in party dresses.* **4** V-T To **tail** someone means to follow close behind them and watch where they go and what they do. [INFORMAL] ❏ *Officers had tailed the gang from London during a major undercover inquiry.* **5** ADV If you toss a coin and it comes down **tails**, you can see the side of it that does not have a picture of a head on it. [ADV after v] ❏ *The England skipper called heads as usual — and the coin came down tails.* **6** cannot **make head or tail of** something →see **head**

1 가산명사 꼬리 ❏ 꼬리가 긴 검은 개 **2** 가산명사 꼬리 ❏ 비행기 꼬리의 수평 미익 **3** 복수명사 연미복 ❏ 연미복을 입은 남자들과 파티 드레스를 입은 여자들 **4** 타동사 미행하다 [비격식체] ❏ 대규모 잠복 수사에서 경관들이 그 갱 단원들을 런던에서부터 미행해 왔었다. **5** 부사 (동전의) 뒷면 ❏ 영국 팀 주장은 여느 때처럼 앞면을 불렀는데 동전의 뒷면이 나왔다.

▶**tail off** PHRASAL VERB When something **tails off**, it gradually becomes less in amount or value, often before coming to an end completely. ❏ *Last year, economic growth tailed off to below four percent.*

구동사 점차 감소하다 ❏ 작년 경제 성장률은 계속 감소해서 4퍼센트 미만에서 한 해를 마쳤다.

tailor /teɪlər/ (**tailors, tailoring, tailored**) **1** N-COUNT A **tailor** is a person whose job is to make men's clothes. **2** V-T If you **tailor** something such as a plan or system **to** someone's needs, you make it suitable for a particular person or purpose by changing the details of it. ❏ *We can tailor the program to the patient's needs.*

1 가산명사 남성복 재단사 **2** 타동사 맞추어 만들다, 요구에 맞추다 ❏ 환자의 필요에 맞춰 프로그램을 짤 수 있다.

tailor-made **1** ADJ If something is **tailor-made**, it has been specially designed for a particular person or purpose. ❏ *Each client's portfolio is tailor-made.* **2** ADJ If you say that someone or something is **tailor-made** for a particular task, purpose, or need, you are emphasizing that they are perfectly suitable for it. [EMPHASIS] ❏ *He was tailor-made, it was said, for the task ahead.* **3** ADJ **Tailor-made** clothes have been specially made to fit a particular person. ❏ *He was wearing a tweed suit that looked tailor-made.*

1 형용사 맞춤형으로 만든 ❏ 모든 고객의 포트폴리오는 맞춤형으로 만들어진다. **2** 형용사 적격인, 안성맞춤인 [강조] ❏ 사람들이 말하기를 앞으로의 일을 맡기에 그가 적격이라고 했다. **3** 형용사 맞춘 ❏ 그는 맞춘 것 같은 트위드 양복을 입고 있었다.

tailpipe /teɪlpaɪp/ (**tailpipes**) N-COUNT A **tailpipe** is the end pipe of a car's exhaust system. [AM; BRIT also **exhaust pipe**] ❏ *...a dramatic reduction in tailpipe emissions.*

가산명사 (자동차) 배기관 [미국영어; 영국영어 exhaust pipe] ❏ 배기가스 배출량의 급격한 감소

taint /teɪnt/ (**taints, tainting, tainted**) **1** V-T If a person or thing **is tainted by** something bad or undesirable, their status or reputation is harmed because they are associated with it. ❏ *Opposition leaders said that the elections had been tainted by corruption.* ● **tainted** ADJ ❏ *He came out only slightly tainted by telling millions of viewers he and his wife had had marital problems.* **2** N-COUNT A **taint** is an undesirable quality which spoils the status or reputation of someone or

1 타동사 오명을 얻다, 더러워지다 ❏ 야당 지도자들은 선거가 부패로 얼룩졌다고 말했다. ● 더럽혀진, 오명을 입은 형용사 ❏ 그가 수백만의 시청자에게 자신과 아내가 결혼 생활에 문제가 있었다고 밝힌 것이 그에게는 작은 흠집만을 남겼을 뿐이다. **2** 가산명사 오점 ❏ 그녀의 정부는 부패의 오명을 결코 완전히 씻어

A

something. □ *Her government never really shook off the taint of corruption.* **3** V-T If an unpleasant substance **taints** food or medicine, the food or medicine is spoiled or damaged by it. □ *Rancid oil will taint the flavor.*

내지 못했다. **3** 타동사 오염시키다 □ 묵은 냄새가 나는 기름은 맛을 버려 놓는다.

B

---
take
① USED WITH NOUNS DESCRIBING ACTIONS
② OTHER USES

C

① **take** ♦♦♦ /teɪk/ (takes, taking, took, taken)

D

Take is used in combination with a wide range of nouns, where the meaning of the combination is mostly given by the noun. Many of these combinations are common idiomatic expressions whose meanings can be found at the appropriate nouns. For example, the expression **take care** is explained at **care**.

take는 다양한 종류의 명사와 결합하여 쓰이는데 그 결합체의 의미는 주로 명사에 의해 결정된다. 이런 결합체는 많은 경우 일반적 관용 표현인데 그 의미는 해당 명사에서 찾아볼 수 있다. 예를 들어, take care라는 표현은 care에서 설명된다.

E

1 V-T You can use **take** followed by a noun to talk about an action or event, when it would also be possible to use the verb that is related to that noun. For example, you can say "she took a shower" instead of "she showered." □ *She was too tired to take a shower.* □ *Betty took a photograph of us.* **2** V-T In ordinary spoken or written English, people use **take** with a range of nouns instead of using a more specific verb. For example people often say "he took control" or "she took a positive attitude" instead of "he assumed control" or "she adopted a positive attitude." □ *The Patriotic Front took power after a three-month civil war.* □ *I felt it was important for women to join and take a leading role.*

1 타동사 (-을) 하다 □ 그녀는 샤워를 하기엔 너무 지쳐 있었다. □ 베티는 우리의 사진을 찍었다. **2** 타동사 잡다, 취하다 □ 애국 전선이 3개월 동안의 내전 끝에 권력을 잡았다. □ 나는 여성들이 참여해서 주도적 역할을 하는 것이 중요하다고 생각했다.

F

G

H

② **take** ♦♦♦ /teɪk/ (takes, taking, took, taken) →Please look at category ① to see if the expression you are looking for is shown under another headword.
1 V-T If you **take** something, you reach out for it and hold it. □ *Here, let me take your coat.* □ *Colette took her by the shoulders and shook her.* **2** V-T If you **take** something with you when you go somewhere, you carry it or have it with you. □ *Mark often took his books to Bess's house to study.* □ *You should take your passport with you when changing money.*

1 타동사 잡다, 쥐다 □ 자, 외투를 제게 주세요. □ 콜레트가 그녀의 어깨를 잡고 흔들었다. **2** 타동사 가져가다 □ 마크는 자주 책을 가지고 베스의 집에 공부하러 갔다. □ 환전할 때는 여권을 가지고 가야 한다.

I

J

3 V-T If a person, vehicle, or path **takes** someone somewhere, they transport or lead them there. □ *She took me to a Mexican restaurant.* **4** V-T If something such as a job or interest **takes** you to a place, it is the reason for you going there. □ *He was a poor student from Madras whose genius took him to Cambridge.* **5** V-T If you **take** something such as your problems or your business to someone, you go to that person when you have problems you want to discuss or things you want to buy. □ *You need to take your problems to a trained counsellor.* **6** V-T If one thing **takes** another to a particular level, condition, or state, it causes it to reach that level or condition. □ *A combination of talent, hard work and good looks have taken her to the top.* **7** V-T If you **take** something from a place, you remove it from there. □ *He took a handkerchief from his pocket and lightly wiped his mouth.* **8** V-T If you **take** something from someone who owns it, you steal it or go away with it without their permission. □ *He has taken my money, and I have no chance of getting it back.* **9** V-T If an army or political party **takes** something or someone, they win them from their enemy or opponent. □ *A Serb army unit took the town.* **10** V-T If you **take** one number or amount from another, you subtract it or deduct it. □ *Take off the price of the house, that's another five thousand.* **11** V-T If you cannot **take** something difficult, painful, or annoying, you cannot tolerate it without becoming upset, ill, or angry. [no passive, usu with brd-neg] □ *Don't ever ask me to look after those kids again. I just can't take it!* **12** V-T If you **take** something such as damage or loss, you suffer it, especially in war or in a battle. □ *They have taken heavy casualties.* **13** V-T If something **takes** a certain amount of time, that amount of time is needed in order to do it. [no passive] □ *Since the roads are very bad, the journey took us a long time.* □ *I had heard an appeal could take years.* □ *The sauce takes 25 minutes to prepare and cook.* □ *It takes 15 minutes to convert the car into a car by removing the wings and the tail.* **14** V-T If something **takes** a particular quality or thing, that quality or thing is needed in order to do it. [no passive] □ *At one time, walking across the room took all her strength.* □ *It takes courage to say what you think.* **15** V-T If you **take** something that is given or offered to you, you agree to accept it. □ *When I took the job I thought I could change the system, but it's hard.* **16** V-T If you **take** a feeling such as pleasure, pride, or delight in a particular thing or activity, the thing or activity gives you that feeling. □ *They take great pride in their heritage.* **17** V-T If a store, restaurant, theater, or other business **takes** a certain amount of money, they get that amount from people buying goods or services. [mainly BRIT, BUSINESS; AM usually **take in**] □ *The firm took £100,000 in bookings.* **18** N-SING You can use **take** to refer to the amount of money that a business such as a store or theater gets from selling its goods or tickets during a particular period. [mainly AM, BUSINESS; BRIT usually **takings**] □ *It added another $11.8 million in take, for a grand total of $43 million.* **19** V-T If you **take** a prize or medal, you win it. □ *"Poison" took first prize at the 1991 Sundance Film Festival.* **20** V-T If you **take** the blame, responsibility, or credit for something, you agree to accept it. □ *His brother Raoul did it, but Leonel took the blame and kept his mouth shut.* **21** V-T If you **take** patients or clients, you accept them as your patients or clients. □ *Some universities would be forced to take more students than they wanted.* **22** V-T If you **take** a telephone call, you speak to someone who is telephoning you. □ *Douglas telephoned Catherine at her office. She refused to take his calls.* **23** V-T If you **take** something in a particular way, you react in the way mentioned to a situation or to someone's beliefs or behavior. □ *Unfortunately, no one took my messages seriously.* **24** V-T You use **take** when you are discussing or explaining a particular question, in order to introduce an example or to say how the question is being considered. [usu imper] □ *There's confusion and resentment, and it's almost never expressed out in the open. Take this office, for example.* **25** V-T If you **take** someone's meaning or point, you understand and accept what they are saying. □ *They've*

K

L

M

N

O

P

Q

R

S

1 타동사 데리고 가다; (길이 -로) 이어지다 □ 그녀는 나를 멕시코 음식점에 데리고 갔다. **4** 타동사 -로 가게 하다 □ 그는 천재성 덕분에 케임브리지까지 간 마드라스 출신의 가난한 학생이었다. **5** 타동사 가져가다 □ 넌 전문 상담원에게 너의 문제를 갖고 가 봐야 한다. **6** 타동사 -에 이르게 하다 □ 재능, 노력, 외모를 모두 갖춘 덕분에 그녀는 최고의 자리에까지 오를 수 있었다. **7** 타동사 꺼내다 □ 그는 주머니에서 손수건을 꺼내 입을 가볍게 닦았다. **8** 타동사 훔치다, (허락 없이) 가져가다 □ 그가 내 돈을 훔쳐 갔는데 그것을 되찾을 가망성은 없다. **9** 타동사 쟁취하다 □ 세르비아 군부대가 그 마을을 확보했다. **10** 타동사 (수나 양을) 빼다 □ 집값을 빼면 5천이 추가로 빠진다. **11** 타동사 받아들이다 □ 다시는 그 애들을 돌봐 달라고 부탁하지 마. 도저히 받아들일 수 없어! **12** 타동사 (피해 등을) 입다 □ 그들에게 많은 사상자가 발생했다. **13** 타동사 (시간이) 걸리다 □ 도로가 너무 안 좋아서 여정이 오래 걸렸다. □ 상소하는 데 몇 년이 걸릴 수도 있다고 들었다. □ 그 소스를 준비하고 요리하는 데에 25분이 걸린다. □ 비행기를 날개와 꼬리를 제거하고 자동차로 전환시키는 데 15분이 걸린다. **14** 타동사 요구하다, 필요로 하다 □ 한 때는 그녀가 방을 가로질러 가는 것도 모든 힘을 들여야 했다. □ 자신의 생각을 말하기 위해서는 용기가 필요하다. **15** 타동사 받아들이다 □ 내가 그 자리를 받아들였을 때는 체제를 바꿀 수 있을 줄 알았으나 어렵다. **16** 타동사 (느낌을) 가지다 □ 그들은 자신들의 문화유산에 굉장한 자부심을 가진다. **17** 타동사 거두다, 벌어들이다 [주로 영국영어, 경제; 미국영어 대개 take in] □ 회사는 예약으로 10만 파운드를 거둬들였다. **18** 단수명사 수익 [주로 미국영어, 경제; 영국영어 대개 takings] □ 수익에 1,180만 달러가 추가되어 총 4,300만 달러가 되었다. **19** 타동사 (상 등을) 받다 □ '포이즌'이 1991년 선댄스 영화제에서 1등 상을 받았다. **20** 타동사 (비난 등을) 받아들이다 □ 그것은 동생 라울이 저질렀지만 레오넬이 대신 비난을 받으면서도 아무 말을 하지 않았다. **21** 타동사 (환자 등을) 받다 □ 일부 대학은 원하는 것보다 많은 학생을 받도록 강요받을 것이다. **22** 타동사 (전화를) 받다 □ 더글라스는 캐서린에게 사무실로 전화했다. 그녀는 그의 전화를 받기를 거부했다. **23** 타동사 받아들이다, 반응을 보이다 □ 불행히 어느 누구도 나의 말을 심각하게 받아들이지 않았다. **24** 타동사 (예를) 들다 □ 혼란스러움과 분해하는 마음은 공개적으로는 거의 표현되지 않는다. 가령, 이 사무실의 경우를 봐라. **25** 타동사 이해하다, 수긍하다 □ 그들이 현명해졌어. 무슨 말인지 알지? **26** 타동사 착각하다 □ 그녀는 그가 기자라고 착각했다. **27** 타동사 (길을) 택하다 □ 렉싱 센터에서 체스터 로드를 타고 시 외곽까지 가시오. **28** 타동사 (차 등을) 타다 □ 그것은 중심가 철길에 있어. 차를 탈래? **29** 타동사 수강하다 □ 학생들은 유럽사와 미국사를 수강할 수 있다. **30** 타동사 (시험을) 보다 □ 그녀는 그린포드에서 운전면허 시험을 봤다. **31** 타동사 가르치다 [주로 영국영어] □ 우리에게

T

U

V

W

X

Y

Z

turned sensible, if you take my meaning. ᴤ V-T If you **take** someone **for** something, you believe wrongly that they are that thing. ❑ *She had taken him for a journalist.* ᴤ V-T If you **take** a road or route, you choose to travel along it. ❑ *From Wrexham centre take the Chester Road to the outskirts of town.* ᴤ V-T If you **take** a car, train, bus, or plane, you use it to go from one place to another. ❑ *It's the other end of the High Street. We'll take the car, shall we?* ᴤ V-T If you **take** a subject or course at school or college, you choose to study it. ❑ *Students are allowed to take European history and American history.* ᴤ V-T If you **take** a test or examination, you do it in order to show your knowledge or ability. ❑ *She took her driving test in Greenford.* ᴤ V-T If you **take** a subject, you give them lessons in that subject. [mainly BRIT] ❑ *The teacher that took us for economics was Miss Humphrey.* ᴤ V-T If someone **takes** drugs, pills, or other medicines, they take them into their body, for example by swallowing them. ❑ *She's been taking sleeping pills.* ᴤ V-T If you **take** a note or a letter, you write down something you want to remember or the words that someone says. ❑ *She sat expressionless, carefully taking notes.* ᴤ V-T If you **take** a measurement, you find out what it is by measuring. ❑ *By drilling, geologists can take measurements at various depths.* ᴤ V-T If a place or container **takes** a particular amount or number, there is enough space for that amount or number. [no passive] ❑ *The place could just about take 2,000 people.* ᴤ V-T If you **take** a particular size in shoes or clothes, that size fits you. ❑ *47 per cent of women in the UK take a size 16 or above.* ᴤ N-COUNT A **take** is a short piece of action which is filmed in one continuous process for a movie. ❑ *She couldn't get it right – she never knew the lines and we had to do several takes.* ᴤ N-SING Someone's **take on** a particular situation or fact is their attitude to it or their interpretation of it. ❑ *What's your take on the new government? Do you think it can work?* ᴤ CONVENTION If you say to someone "**take it or leave it,**" you are telling them that they can accept something or not accept it, but that you are not prepared to discuss any other alternatives. ❑ *A 72-hour week, 12 hours a day, six days a week, take it or leave it.* ᴤ PHRASE If someone **takes** an insult or attack **lying down,** they accept it without protesting. ❑ *The government is not taking such criticism lying down.* ᴤ PHRASE If something **takes a lot out of you** or **takes it out of you,** it requires a lot of energy or effort and makes you feel very tired and weak afterward. ❑ *He looked tired, as if the argument had taken a lot out of him.* ᴤ PHRASE If someone tells you to **take five** or **take ten,** they are telling you to have a five or ten minute break from what you are doing. [mainly AM, INFORMAL] ᴤ to **be taken aback** →see aback. to **take up arms** →see arm. to **take the biscuit** →see biscuit. to **take the cake** →see cake. to **take your hat off** to someone →see hat. to **take the piss out of** someone →see piss. to **be taken for a ride** →see ride. to **take** someone **by surprise** →see surprise. **take my word for it** →see word

Take and bring are both used to talk about carrying something or accompanying someone somewhere, but take is used to suggest movement away from the speaker, and bring is used to suggest movement toward the speaker. ❑ *Anna took the book to school with her... Bring your calculator to every lesson.* In the first sentence, **took** suggests that Anna left the speaker when she went to school. In the second sentence, **bring** suggests that the person and the calculator should come to the place where the speaker is. You could also say "Anna brought the book to school with her" to suggest that Anna and the speaker were both at school, and "Take your calculator to every lesson" to suggest that the speaker will not be not present at the lesson. The difference between **take** and **bring** is equivalent to that between **go** and **come.** **Fetch** suggests that someone goes away to get something and comes back with it. ❑ *O'Leary went to fetch tickets and was soon back.*

Thesaurus
take의 참조어

v. grab, grasp, hold ② ᴤ
    drive, escort, transport ② ᴤ
    steal ② ᴤ
    capture, seize ② ᴤ

▶**take after** PHRASAL VERB If you **take after** a member of your family, you resemble them in your appearance, your behavior, or your character. [no passive] ❑ *Ted's always been difficult, Mr. Kemp – he takes after his dad.*

▶**take apart** PHRASAL VERB If you **take** something **apart,** you separate it into the different parts that it is made of. ❑ *When the clock stopped, he took it apart, found what was wrong, and put the whole thing together again.*

▶**take away** ᴤ PHRASAL VERB If you **take** something **away from** someone, you remove it from them, so that they no longer possess it or have it with them. ❑ *They're going to take my citizenship away.* "Give me the knife," he said softly, "or I'll take it away from you." ᴤ PHRASAL VERB If you **take** one number or amount **away from** another, you subtract one number from the other. ❑ *We take the time when he goes and we take the time when he comes back, take one away from the other and we know how long the horse has been out.* ᴤ PHRASAL VERB To **take** someone **away** means to bring them from their home to an institution such as a prison or hospital. ❑ *Two men claiming to be police officers called at the pastor's house and took him away.* ᴤ →see also **takeaway**

▶**take back** ᴤ PHRASAL VERB If you **take** something **back,** you return it to the place where you bought it or where you borrowed it from, because it is unsuitable or broken, or because you have finished with it. ❑ *If I buy something and he doesn't like it I'll take it back.* ᴤ PHRASAL VERB If you **take** something **back,** you admit that something that you said or thought is wrong. ❑ *Take back what*

경제학을 가르쳐 준 사람은 험프리 선생님이었다. ᴤ 타동사 (약을) 먹다, 복용하다 ❑ 그녀는 요즘 수면제를 먹고 있다. ᴤ 타동사 쓰다 ❑ 그녀는 표정 없이 메모 내용을 주의 깊게 받아 적으며 앉아 있었다. ᴤ 타동사 재다, 측정하다 ❑ 지질학자들은 시추를 통해 다양한 깊이에서 측정을 할 수 있다. ᴤ 타동사 수용하다 ❑ 그 장소는 겨우 2,000명 정도를 수용할 수 있을 것이다. ᴤ 타동사 입다 ❑ 영국 여성의 47퍼센트가 16사이즈 이상을 입는다. ᴤ 가산명사 (1회분의) 촬영 장면 ❑ 그녀가 계속 틀렸다. 그녀는 대사를 전혀 못 외워서 우리는 그 장면을 여러 번 찍어야 했다. ᴤ 단수명사 입장 ❑ 새 정부에 대한 당신의 입장은 무엇입니까? 제대로 할 수 있을 것 같습니까? ᴤ 관용 표현 하려면 하고 싫으면 관둬라, 다른 선택의 여지는 없다 ❑ 일주일에 6일, 하루 12시간, 일주일에 72시간 근무다. 하려면 하고 말려면 말아라. ᴤ 구 가만히 당하고만 있다 ❑ 정부가 그러한 비판을 가만히 당하고만 있지는 않다. ᴤ 구 지치게 하다 ❑ 그 논쟁이 많이 힘들었는지 그는 지쳐 보였다. ᴤ 구 5분 휴식; 10분 휴식 [주로 미국영어, 비격식체]

take와 bring은 둘 다 무엇을 옮기거나 누구를 동행하는 것을 말할 때 쓰지만, take는 화자로부터 멀어져 가는 이동을 나타낼 때, bring은 화자 쪽으로 가는 이동을 나타낼 때 쓴다. ❑ 안나가 그 책을 학교에 가지고 갔다... 수업 때마다 계산기를 가지고 오시오. 첫 번째 문장에서 took은 안나가 학교에 가면서 화자로부터 떠났음을 나타낸다. 두 번째 문장에서 bring은 화자가 있는 곳으로 사람과 계산기가 와야 함을 말한다. 안나와 화자가 모두 학교에 있음을 시사할 때에는 "안나가 그 책을 학교에 가지고 왔다."고 하고, 화자가 수업 현장에 가지 않음을 시사할 때에는 "수업마다 계산기를 가지고 가시오."라고 말할 수 있다. take와 bring 사이의 차이는 go와 come 사이의 차이에 해당한다. fetch는 누가 무엇을 가지러 갔다가 그것을 갖고 돌아 오는 것을 나타낸다. ❑ 오리어리는 입장권을 가지러 갔다가 곧 돌아왔다.

구동사 닮다 ❑ 테드는 항상 성깔이 있었어요, 켐프 씨. 그런 면에선 그의 아버질 닮았죠.

구동사 분해하다 ❑ 시계가 멈추자 그는 그것을 분해해서 문제를 찾아내고 그것을 다시 원상태로 조립했다.

ᴤ 구동사 빼앗다 ❑ 그들이 나의 시민권을 빼앗으려 한다. "내게 칼을 줘, 안 그러면 내가 뺏겠어." 그는 조용히 말했다. ᴤ 구동사 빼다 ❑ 말이 나간 시간을 기록하고 돌아온 시간을 기록한 다음 들어온 시간에서 나간 시간을 빼면 그것이 얼마 동안 나가 있었는지를 알 수 있다. ᴤ 구동사 (감금 시설로) 데려가다 ❑ 경찰이라고 주장하는 두 명의 남자가 목사의 집을 방문하여 그를 데려갔다.

ᴤ 구동사 반납하다; 반품하다 ❑ 내가 무엇을 샀는데 그가 그것을 좋아하지 않으면 나는 그것을 반품한다. ᴤ 구동사 철회하다, 취소하다 ❑ 제레미에 대해서 한 말 취소해! ᴤ 구동사 다시 받아들이다 ❑ 그녀는 왜 그를 다시 받아들였을까? ᴤ 구동사 상기시키다 ❑ 나는

you said about Jeremy! **3** PHRASAL VERB If you **take** someone **back**, you allow them to come home again, after they have gone away because of a quarrel or other problem. ❑ *Why did she take him back?* **4** PHRASAL VERB If you say that something **takes** you **back**, you mean that it reminds you of a period of your past life and makes you think about it again. ❑ *I enjoyed experimenting with colors – it took me back to being five years old.*

색깔을 가지고 실험하는 것이 즐거웠다. 다시 내가 다섯 살이었던 때로 돌아간 것 같았다.

▶**take down** **1** PHRASAL VERB If you **take** something **down**, you reach up and get it from a high place such as a shelf. ❑ *Alberg took the portrait down from the wall.* **2** PHRASAL VERB If you **take down** a structure, you remove each piece of it. ❑ *The Canadian army took down the barricades erected by the Indians.* **3** PHRASAL VERB If you **take down** a piece of information or a statement, you write it down. ❑ *We've been trying to get back to you, Tom, but we think we took your number down incorrectly.*

1 구동사 끌어내리다 ❑ 앨버그는 벽에 걸렸던 초상화를 내렸다. **2** 구동사 뜯어내다, 허물다 ❑ 캐나다 군대가 인디언들이 설치한 바리케이드를 제거했다. **3** 구동사 받아 적다 ❑ 톰, 네게 다시 연락을 하려고 계속 시도했지만 아무래도 우리가 네 번호를 잘못 받아 적은 것 같다.

▶**take in** **1** PHRASAL VERB If you **take** someone **in**, you allow them to stay in your house or your country, especially when they do not have anywhere to stay or are in trouble. ❑ *He persuaded Jo to take him in.* **2** PHRASAL VERB If the police **take** someone **in**, they remove them from their home in order to question them. ❑ *The police have taken him in for questioning in connection with the murder of a girl.* **3** PHRASAL VERB If you **are taken in by** someone or something, you are deceived by them, so that you get a false impression of them. ❑ *I married in my late teens and was taken in by his charm – which soon vanished.* **4** PHRASAL VERB If you **take** something **in**, you pay attention to it and understand it when you hear it or read it. ❑ *Lesley explains complicated treatments but you can tell she's not taking it in.* **5** PHRASAL VERB If you **take** something **in**, you see all of it at the same time or with just one look. ❑ *The eyes behind the lenses were dark and quick-moving, taking in everything at a glance.* **6** PHRASAL VERB If people, animals, or plants **take in** air, drink, or food, they allow it to enter their body, usually by breathing or swallowing. ❑ *They will certainly need to take in plenty of liquid.* **7** PHRASAL VERB If a store, restaurant, theater, or other business **takes in** a certain amount of money, they get that amount from people buying goods or services. [mainly AM, BUSINESS; BRIT usually **take**] ❑ *They plan to take in $1.6 billion.*

1 구동사 (집에 등으로) 받아들이다 ❑ 그는 자기를 받아들이도록 조를 설득했다. **2** 구동사 (경찰이) 데려가다, 연행해 가다 ❑ 경찰이 한 소녀의 살해 사건과 관련하여 취조를 하기 위해 그를 연행해 갔다. **3** 구동사 속다, 현혹되다 ❑ 나는 십 대 후반에 결혼했고 그의 매력에 현혹되었다. 하지만 매력은 곧 사라졌다. **4** 구동사 받아들이다, 이해하다 ❑ 레슬리가 가능한 치료들을 설명하지만 그녀가 그것을 받아들이지 못한다는 것을 알 수 있다. **5** 구동사 파악하다 ❑ 렌즈 뒤의 짙은 눈이 재빨리 움직이며 모든 것을 한꺼번에 파악했다. **6** 구동사 섭취하다; 들이쉬다 ❑ 그들은 분명히 액체를 많이 섭취해야 할 것이다. **7** 구동사 벌어들이다 [주로 미국영어, 경제; 영국영어 대개 take] ❑ 그들은 16억 달러를 벌어들일 계획이다.

▶**take off** **1** PHRASAL VERB When an airplane **takes off**, it leaves the ground and starts flying. ❑ *We eventually took off at 11 o'clock and arrived in Venice at 1.30.* **2** PHRASAL VERB If something such as a product, an activity, or someone's career **takes off**, it suddenly becomes very successful. ❑ *In 1944, he met Edith Piaf, and his career took off.* **3** PHRASAL VERB If you **take off** or **take yourself off**, you go away, often suddenly and unexpectedly. ❑ *He took off at once and headed back to the motel.* **4** PHRASAL VERB If you **take** a garment **off**, you remove it. ❑ *He wouldn't take his hat off.* **5** PHRASAL VERB If you **take** time **off**, you obtain permission not to go to work for a short period of time. ❑ *Mitchel's schedule had not permitted him to take time off.*

1 구동사 이륙하다 ❑ 우리는 결국 11시에 이륙해서 1시 반에 베니스에 도착했다. **2** 구동사 성공가도를 달리기 시작하다 ❑ 1944년에 그는 에디뜨 피아프를 만나고 그 때부터 그는 성공가도를 달렸다. **3** 구동사 갑자기 떠나다 ❑ 그는 갑자기 자리를 떠서 모텔로 돌아갔다. **4** 구동사 벗다 ❑ 그는 모자를 벗지 않으려 했다. **5** 구동사 (업무에서) 쉬다 ❑ 미첼은 일정 때문에 쉬지를 못했다.

▶**take on** **1** PHRASAL VERB If you **take on** a job or responsibility, especially a difficult one, you accept it. ❑ *No other organisation was able or willing to take on the job.* **2** PHRASAL VERB If something **takes on** a new appearance or quality, it develops that appearance or quality. [no passive] ❑ *Believing he had only a year to live, his writing took on a feverish intensity.* **3** PHRASAL VERB If a vehicle such as a bus or ship **takes on** passengers, goods, or fuel, it stops in order to allow them to get on or to be loaded on. ❑ *This is a brief stop to take on passengers and water.* **4** PHRASAL VERB If you **take** someone **on**, you employ them to do a job. ❑ *He's spoken to a publishing firm. They're going to take him on.* **5** PHRASAL VERB If you **take** someone **on**, you fight them or compete against them, especially when they are bigger or more powerful than you are. [no passive] ❑ *Democrats were reluctant to take on a president whose popularity ratings were historically high.* **6** PHRASAL VERB If you **take** something **on** or **upon yourself**, you decide to do it without asking anyone for permission or approval. [no passive] ❑ *Knox had taken it on himself to choose the wine.* ❑ *He took upon himself the responsibility for protecting her.*

1 구동사 떠맡다 ❑ 다른 어떤 조직도 그 일을 떠맡을 수 없었고 떠맡으려 하지도 않았다. **2** 구동사 (양상 등을) 띠다 ❑ 자신이 1년밖에 더 못 산다고 믿은 그의 글은 열병에 걸린 듯한 치열함을 띠기 시작했다. **3** 구동사 싣다, 채우다 ❑ 승객과 물을 싣기 위해 잠깐 섭니다. **4** 구동사 고용하다 ❑ 그는 한 출판사와 이야기를 했다. 그들이 그를 고용할 것이다. **5** 구동사 넘비다, 도전하다 ❑ 민주당은 역사적으로 유례없이 높은 대중 지지율을 얻고 있는 대통령에게 도전하기를 꺼렸다. **6** 구동사 (임의로) 행동하다 ❑ 녹스는 임의로 와인을 골랐다. ❑ 그는 임의로 그녀의 보호에 관한 책임을 떠맡았다.

▶**take out** **1** PHRASAL VERB If you **take** something **out**, you remove it permanently from its place. ❑ *I got an abscess so he took the tooth out.* **2** PHRASAL VERB If you **take out** something such as a loan, a license, or an insurance policy, you obtain it by fulfilling the conditions and paying the money that is necessary. ❑ *I'll have to stop by the bank and take out a loan.* **3** PHRASAL VERB If you **take** someone **out**, they go to something such as a restaurant or theater with you after you have invited them, and usually you pay for them. ❑ *Jessica's grandparents took her out for the day.* ❑ *Reichel took me out to lunch.*

1 구동사 제거하다 ❑ 내게 농양이 생겨서 그가 이빨을 뽑아 주었다. **2** 구동사 (대출 등을) 얻다, (보험 등을) 들다 ❑ 은행에 들러서 대출을 얻어야 한다. **3** 구동사 외출을 시켜 주다, 데리고 나가 대접하다 ❑ 제시카의 조부모가 그녀를 하루 동안 구경을 시켜 주었다. ❑ 레이첼은 나에게 점심 대접을 해 줬다.

▶**take over** **1** PHRASAL VERB If you **take over** a company, you get control of it, for example by buying its shares. [BUSINESS] ❑ *A British newspaper says British Airways plan to take over Trans World Airways.* **2** PHRASAL VERB If someone **takes over** a country or building, they get control of it by force, for example with the help of the army. ❑ *The Belgians took over Rwanda under a League of Nations mandate.* **3** PHRASAL VERB If you **take over** a job or role or if you **take over**, you become responsible for the job after someone else has stopped doing it. ❑ *His widow has taken over the running of his empire, including six London theaters.* ❑ *In 1966, Pastor Albertz took over from him as governing mayor.* **4** PHRASAL VERB If one thing **takes over** from something else, it becomes more important, successful, or powerful than the other thing, and eventually replaces it. ❑ *Cars gradually took over from horses.* **5** →see also takeover

1 구동사 인수하다 [경제] ❑ 한 영국 신문은 영국 항공이 트랜스월드 항공을 인수할 계획이라고 한다. **2** 구동사 접수하다 ❑ 벨기에가 국제 연맹의 위임하에 르완다를 접수했다. **3** 구동사 넘겨받다 ❑ 그의 미망인이 런던 극장 여섯 개를 포함하여 그의 제국의 운영권을 넘겨받았다. ❑ 1966년에 앨버츠 목사가 그로부터 시장의 자리를 넘겨받았다. **4** 구동사 대체하다 ❑ 자동차가 차츰 말을 대체했다.

▶**take to** **1** PHRASAL VERB If you **take to** someone or something, you like them, especially after knowing them or thinking about them for only a short time. ❑ *Did the children take to him?* **2** PHRASAL VERB If you **take to** doing something, you begin to do it as a regular habit. ❑ *They had taken to wandering through the streets arm-in-arm.*

1 구동사 좋아하다 ❑ 아이들이 그를 좋아했니? **2** 구동사 ~하는 버릇이 생기다 ❑ 그들은 팔짱을 끼고 거리를 돌아다니는 버릇이 생겼었다.

▶**take up** **1** PHRASAL VERB If you **take up** an activity or a subject, you become interested in it and spend time doing it, either as a hobby or as a career. ❑ *He did not particularly want to take up a competitive sport.* **2** PHRASAL VERB If you **take**

1 구동사 (취미 등을) 시작하다 ❑ 그는 특히 남과 겨뤄야 하는 스포츠를 시작하고 싶어 하지는 않았다. **2** 구동사 다루다 ❑ 환경적인 위험에 대한 증거를

up a question, problem, or cause, you act on it or discuss how you are going to act on it. ❑ *Most scientists who can present evidence of an environmental threat can reasonably assume that a pressure group will take up the issue.* ❑ *Dr. Mahathir intends to take up the proposal with the prime minister.* ◼ PHRASAL VERB If you **take up** a job, you begin to work at it. ❑ *He will take up his post as the head of the civil courts at the end of next month.* ◼ PHRASAL VERB If you **take up** an offer or a challenge, you accept it. ❑ *Increasingly, more wine-makers are taking up the challenge of growing Pinot Noir.* ◼ PHRASAL VERB If something **takes up** a particular amount of time, space, or effort, it uses that amount. ❑ *I know how busy you must be and naturally I wouldn't want to take up too much of your time.* ❑ *A good deal of my time is taken up with reading critical essays and reviews.*

▶**take upon** →see **take on 6**

take|away /ˈteɪkəweɪ/ (**takeaways**) ◼ N-COUNT A **takeaway** is a store or restaurant which sells hot cooked food that you eat somewhere else. [BRIT; AM **takeout**] ❑ *...delicious Thai food from the takeaway.* ◼ N-COUNT A **takeaway** is hot cooked food that you buy from a store or restaurant and eat somewhere else. [BRIT; AM **takeout**] ❑ *...a Chinese takeaway.*

take-home pay N-UNCOUNT Your **take-home pay** is the amount of your wages or salary that is left after income tax and other payments have been subtracted. [BUSINESS] ❑ *He was earning £215 a week before tax: take-home pay, £170.*

tak|en /ˈteɪkən/ ◼ **Taken** is the past participle of **take**. ◼ ADJ If you are **taken with** something or someone, you are very interested in them or attracted to them. [INFORMAL] [v-link ADJ, usu ADJ with n] ❑ *She seems very taken with the idea.*

take|off /ˈteɪkɔf, BRIT ˈteɪkɒf/ (**takeoffs**) also **take-off** N-VAR **Takeoff** is the beginning of a flight, when an aircraft leaves the ground. ❑ *The plane crashed seconds after takeoff.*

take|out /ˈteɪkaʊt/ (**takeouts**) ◼ N-COUNT A **takeout** is a store or restaurant which sells hot cooked food that you eat somewhere else. [AM; BRIT **takeaway**] ❑ *...a Chinese takeout restaurant.* ◼ N-COUNT A **takeout** or **takeout** food is hot cooked food which you buy from a store or restaurant and eat somewhere else. [AM; BRIT **takeaway**] ❑ *...a takeout pizza.* →see **restaurant**

take|over ♦◇◇ /ˈteɪkoʊvər/ (**takeovers**) ◼ N-COUNT A **takeover** is the act of gaining control of a company by buying more of its shares than anyone else. [BUSINESS] ❑ *...the proposed £3.4 billion takeover of Midland Bank by the Hong Kong and Shanghai.* ◼ N-COUNT A **takeover** is the act of taking control of a country, political party, or movement by force. ❑ *There's been a military takeover of some kind.*

tak|ings /ˈteɪkɪŋz/ N-PLURAL You can use **takings** to refer to the amount of money that a business such as a store or a movie theater gets from selling its goods or tickets during a particular period. [BUSINESS] ❑ *The pub said that their takings were fifteen to twenty thousand pounds a week.*

tale ♦◇◇ /teɪl/ (**tales**) ◼ N-COUNT; N-IN-NAMES A **tale** is a story, often involving magic or exciting events. ❑ *...a collection of stories, poems and folk tales.* ◼ N-COUNT You can refer to an interesting, exciting, or dramatic account of a real event as a **tale**. ❑ *The media have been filled with tales of horror and loss resulting from Monday's earthquake.* ◼ →see also **fairy tale**

tal|ent ♦◇◇ /ˈtælənt/ (**talents**) N-VAR **Talent** is the natural ability to do something well. ❑ *She is proud that both her children have a talent for music.* ❑ *He's got lots of talent.*

Thesaurus	*talent*의 참조어
N.	ability, aptitude, gift

Word Partnership	*talent*의 연어
ADJ.	**great** talent, **musical** talent, **natural** talent
V.	**have (a)** talent, **have got** talent

tal|ent|ed /ˈtæləntɪd/ ADJ Someone who is **talented** has a natural ability to do something well. ❑ *Howard is a talented pianist.*

talk ♦♦♦ /tɔk/ (**talks, talking, talked**) ◼ V-I When you **talk**, you use spoken language to express your thoughts, ideas, or feelings. ❑ *He was too distressed to talk.* ❑ *The boys all began to talk at once.* ● N-UNCOUNT **Talk** is also a noun. ❑ *That's not the kind of talk one usually hears from accountants.* ◼ V-RECIP If you **talk** to someone, you have a conversation with them. You can also say that two people **talk**. ❑ *We talked and laughed a great deal.* ❑ *I talked to him yesterday.* ❑ *When she came back, they were talking about American food.* ● N-COUNT **Talk** is also a noun. ❑ *We had a long talk about her father, Tony, who was a friend of mine.* ◼ V-RECIP If you **talk to** someone, you tell them about the things that are worrying you. You can also say that two people **talk**. ❑ *Your first step should be to talk to a teacher or school counselor.* ❑ *Do ring if you want to talk about it.* ● N-COUNT **Talk** is also a noun. ❑ *I think it's time we had a talk.* ◼ V-I If you **talk on** or **about** something, you make an informal speech telling people what you know or think about it. ❑ *She will talk on the issues she cares passionately about including education and nursery care.* ● N-COUNT **Talk** is also a noun. ❑ *A guide gives a brief talk on the history of the site.* ◼ N-PLURAL **Talks** are formal discussions intended to produce an agreement, usually between different countries or between employers and employees. ❑ *...the next round of Middle East peace talks.* ◼ V-RECIP If one group of people **talks to** another, or if two groups **talk**, they have formal discussions in order to do a deal or produce an agreement. ❑ *We're talking to some people about opening an*

제시할 수 있는 대부분의 과학자들이 당연히 압력 집단이 그 사안을 다르게 될 것이라고 여긴다. ❑ 마하티르 박사는 수상과 그 안건을 논의할 계획이다. ◼ 구동사 (일을) 맡다 ❑ 그는 다음 달 말에 민사법원장의 직책을 맡을 것이다. ◼ 구동사 받아들이다 ❑ 점점 많은 와인 양조자들이 피노 누와를 재배하는 도전을 받아들이고 있다. ◼ 구동사 (공간 등을) 차지하다 ❑ 네가 얼마나 바쁜지 아니까 당연히 네 시간을 너무 많이 뺏고 싶지는 않다. ❑ 나는 많은 시간을 여러 평론을 읽는 데 들인다.

◼ 가산명사 테이크아웃 전문점 [영국영어; 미국영어 takeout] ❑ 테이크아웃 전문점에서 산 맛있는 태국 음식 ◼ 가산명사 테이크아웃 음식 [영국영어; 미국영어 takeout] ❑ 테이크아웃 중국 음식

불가산명사 세후 임금, 실제 소득 [경제] ❑ 그의 주급은 세전 215파운드, 세후 170파운드였다.

◼ take의 과거 분사 ◼ 형용사 끌리는, 매혹된 [비격식체] ❑ 그녀가 그 생각에 굉장히 끌리는 것 같다.

가산명사 또는 불가산명사 이륙 ❑ 비행기가 이륙하자마자 추락했다.

◼ 가산명사 테이크아웃 전문점 [미국영어; 영국영어 takeaway] ❑ 중국 음식 테이크아웃 전문점 ◼ 가산명사 테이크아웃 음식 [미국영어; 영국영어 takeaway] ❑ 테이크아웃 피자

◼ 가산명사 경영권 인수 [경제] ❑ 홍콩상하이은행이 미드랜드 은행의 경영권을 34억 파운드에 인수하겠다는 제안 ◼ 가산명사 탈취 ❑ 모종의 군사적 정권 탈취가 있었다.

복수명사 매출액 [경제] ❑ 그 술집은 주당 매출액이 만 5천에서 2만 파운드가 된다고 했다.

◼ 가산명사; 이름명사 이야기 ❑ 이야기, 시, 민간 설화 모음집 ◼ 가산명사 이야기 ❑ 언론에 월요일에 발생한 지진 때문에 생긴 공포와 상실의 이야기가 넘쳐 난다.

가산명사 또는 불가산명사 재능 ❑ 그녀는 자신의 아이 둘 다 음악적 재능이 있다는 것을 자랑스럽게 생각한다. ❑ 그에겐 많은 재능이 있다.

형용사 재능 있는 ❑ 하워드는 재능 있는 피아니스트이다.

◼ 자동사 말하다 ❑ 그는 너무 당혹해서 말을 못했다. ❑ 소년들이 모두 한꺼번에 말하기 시작했다. ● 불가산명사 말 ❑ 그것은 회계사들의 입에서 보통 나오는 말이 아니다. ◼ 상호동사 이야기하다, 수다 떨다 ❑ 우리는 많이 웃고 떠들었다. ❑ 나는 어제 그와 이야기했다. ❑ 그녀가 돌아왔을 때 그들은 미국 음식에 대해서 이야기하고 있었다. ● 가산명사 이야기 ❑ 우리는 그녀의 아버지이자 나의 친구였던 토니에 대해 오래 이야기했다. ◼ 상호동사 대화하다, (심각하게) 이야기하다 ❑ 가장 먼저 교사나 학교 상담 전문가와 대화를 해야 한다. ❑ 그것에 대해 이야기하고 싶으면 꼭 전화를 해. ● 가산명사 대화 ❑ 우리가 대화를 해야 할 때가 온 것 같아. ◼ 자동사 설명하다, 논하다 ❑ 그녀는 교육이나 육아 등 본인이 열성적인 관심을 가지고 있는 사안에 대해 논할 것이다. ● 가산명사 해설 ❑ 안내원이 그곳의 역사에 관해 간략하게 설명을 한다. ◼ 복수명사 회담 ❑ 차기 중동 평화 회담 ◼ 상호동사 협의하다 ❑ 런던에서 사무실을 열기 위해 몇몇 사람과 협의하고 있다. ❑ 회사는 여러 잠재적 투자가와 협의를 했다. ◼ 상호동사 협상하다 ❑ 외부무 장관은 적대적

office in London. □ The company talked with many potential investors. **7** V-RECIP When different countries or different sides in a dispute **talk**, or **talk to** each other, they discuss their differences in order to try and settle the dispute. □ The Foreign Minister said he was ready to talk to any country that had no hostile intentions. □ They are collecting information in preparation for the day when the two sides sit down and talk. **8** V-I If people **are talking about** another person or **are talking**, they are discussing that person. □ Everyone is talking about him. ● N-UNCOUNT **Talk** is also a noun. □ There has been a lot of talk about me getting married. **9** V-I If someone **talks** when they are being held by police or soldiers, they reveal important or secret information, usually unwillingly. □ They'll talk, they'll implicate me. **10** V-T/V-I If you **talk** a particular language or **talk** with a particular accent, you use that language or have that accent when you speak. [no passive] □ You don't sound like a foreigner talking English. **11** V-T If you **talk** something such as politics or sports, you discuss it. [no passive] □ The guests were mostly middle-aged men talking business. **12** V-T You can use **talk** to say what you think of the ideas that someone is expressing. For example, if you say that someone **is talking sense**, you mean that you think the opinions they are expressing are sensible. □ You must admit George, you're talking absolute rubbish. **13** V-T You can say that you **are talking** a particular thing to draw attention to your topic or to point out a characteristic of what you are discussing. [SPOKEN] [no passive] □ We're talking megabucks this time. **14** N-UNCOUNT If you say that something such as an idea or threat is just **talk**, or **all talk**, you mean that it does not mean or matter much, because people are exaggerating about it or do not really intend to do anything about it. □ Has much of this actually been tried here? Or is it just talk? **15** PHRASE You can say **talk about** before mentioning a particular expression or situation, when you mean that something is a very striking or clear example of that expression or situation. [INFORMAL, EMPHASIS] □ Took us quite a while to get here, didn't it? Talk about Fate moving in a mysterious way! **16** PHRASE You can use the expression **talking of** to introduce a new topic that you want to discuss, and to link it to something that has already been mentioned. □ I'll give a prize to the best idea. Talking of good ideas, here's one to break the ice at a wedding party. **17** to **talk shop** →see **shop**

There are some differences in the way the verbs **speak** and **talk** are used. When you **speak**, you could, for example, be addressing someone or making a speech. **Talk** is more likely to be used when you are referring to a conversation or discussion. □ I talked about it with my family at dinner... Sometimes we'd talk all night. **Talk** can also be used to emphasize the activity of saying things, rather than the words that are spoken. □ She thought I talked too much.

Thesaurus
talk의 참조어

v. chat, converse, discuss, gossip, say, share, speak, tell; (ant.) listen **1**-**4**
N. argument, conversation, dialog, discussion, interview, negotiation; (ant.) silence **2**
chatter, conversation, gossip, rumor **8**

▶**talk into 1** PHRASAL VERB If you **talk** a person **into** doing something they do not want to do, especially something wrong or stupid, you persuade them to do it. □ He talked me into marrying him. He also talked me into having a baby.

▶**talk out of 1** PHRASAL VERB If you **talk** someone **out of** doing something they want or intend to do, you persuade them not to do it. □ My mother tried to talk me out of getting a divorce.

▶**talk over** PHRASAL VERB If you **talk** something **over**, you discuss it thoroughly and honestly. □ He always talked things over with his friends. □ We should go somewhere quiet, and talk it over.

▶**talk through 1** PHRASAL VERB-RECIP If you **talk** something **through** with someone, you discuss it with them thoroughly. □ I and I have talked through this whole tricky problem. □ Now her children are grown-up and she has talked through with them what happened. **2** PHRASAL VERB If someone **talks** you **through** something that you do not know, they explain it to you carefully. □ Now she must talk her sister through the process a step at a time.

▶**talk up** PHRASAL VERB If someone **talks up** a particular thing, they make it sound more interesting, valuable, or likely than it originally seemed. □ Politicians accuse the media of talking up the possibility of a riot.

talka|tive /tɔ́kətɪv/ ADJ Someone who is **talkative** talks a lot. □ He suddenly became very talkative, his face slightly flushed, his eyes much brighter.

talk show (**talk shows**) also **talk-show** N-COUNT A **talk show** is a television or radio show in which famous people talk to a host in an informal way and are asked questions about different topics.

tall ♦♢♢ /tɔl/ (**taller, tallest**) **1** ADJ Someone or something that is **tall** has a greater height than is normal or average. □ Being tall can make you feel incredibly self-confident. **2** ADJ You use **tall** to ask or talk about the height of someone or something. [how ADJ, amount ADJ, as ADJ as, ADJ-compar than] □ How tall are you? →see **high 3** PHRASE If something is a **tall order**, it is very difficult. □ Financing your studies may seem like a tall order, but there is plenty of help available. **4** PHRASE If you say that someone **walks tall**, you mean that they behave in a way that shows that they have pride in themselves and in what they are doing. □ They shouldn't be disappointed or let their heads fall, but walk tall.

tal|ly /tǽli/ (**tallies, tallying, tallied**) **1** N-COUNT A **tally** is a record of amounts or numbers which you keep changing and adding to as the activity which

의도가 없는 모든 국가들과 협상할 준비가 되어 있다고 말했다. □ 양측이 마주 앉아 대화하는 그 날을 위하여 그들은 정보를 수집하고 있다. **8** 자동사 이야기하다 ● 모두가 그에 대해 이야기하고 있다. ● 불가산명사 이야기 □ 내가 결혼하는 것에 대해 많은 이야기가 있었다. **9** 자동사 (마지못해) 누설하다 □ 그들은 누설을 해서 나를 연루시킬 것이다. **10** 타동사/자동사 (특정 언어를) 말하다 □ 당신은 영어를 외국인처럼 말하지 않는다. **11** 타동사 논하다 □ 손님들은 대부분 사업을 논하는 중년 남성들이었다. **12** 타동사 말하다 ; 사리에 맞게 말하다 □ 조지, 넌 인정해야 해. 넌 지금 완전 헛소리를 하고 있어. **13** 타동사 내 말은 ~라는 것이다 [구어체] □ 우리 말은 이번에는 틀림없이 대박이라는 거야. **14** 불가산명사 말뿐인 말 □ 이 중 많은 걸 실제로 해 보긴 한 거야? 아니면 말뿐인 거야? **15** 구 ~라더니 딱 그 짝이다 [비격식체, 강조] □ 여기까지 오는 데 꽤 걸렸지? 운명의 장난이라더니, 참 이런 때를 두고 하는 말이군! **16** 구 화제 전환을 위해 쓰임 □ 가장 좋은 아이디어에 상을 주겠어요. 좋은 아이디어라니 말인데, 여기 결혼식 잔치에서 어색한 분위기를 깨기 위한 아이디어 하나를 알려드릴게요.

동사 speak와 talk를 쓰는 방식에는 차이가 있다. 예를 들어 speak는, 누구에게 말을 하거나 연설을 하는 것이다. talk는 대화나 토론을 가리킬 때 쓸 가능성이 더 크다. □ 나는 그것에 관해서 내 가족과 저녁 식사 때 얘기했다... 가끔 우리는 밤새도록 얘기하곤 했다. talk는 하는 말보다는 말하는 행위를 강조하기 위해서 쓸 수도 있다. □ 그녀는 내가 말을 너무 많이 한다고 생각했다.

1 구동사 (~ 하도록) 설득하다 □ 그가 나를 자기와 결혼하도록 설득했어요. 애도 그의 말에 넘어가서 갖게 된 거요.

1 구동사 ~하지 않도록 설득하다 □ 어머님께서는 내가 이혼을 안 하도록 설득해 보려고 하셨다.

구동사 충분히 상의하다 □ 그는 항상 친구들과 모든 것을 충분히 상의했다. □ 어딘가 조용한 데로 가서 제대로 이야기를 좀 하자.

1 상호 구동사 철저히 논의하다 □ 이 까다로운 문제에 대해 그와 나는 모든 논의를 끝마쳤다. □ 이제 아이들이 장성했으므로 그녀는 무슨 일이 있었는지를 처음부터 끝까지 이야기해 줬다. **2** 구동사 차근차근 설명하다 □ 이제 그녀는 언니에게 절차를 단계별로 차근차근 설명해야 한다.

구동사 부풀려 말하다 □ 정치인들은 언론이 폭동의 가능성을 부풀린다고 비난한다.

형용사 수다스러운 □ 그는 갑자기 얼굴이 살짝 상기되고 눈에서 빛이 나면서 말이 아주 많아지기 시작했다.

가산명사 토크 쇼

1 형용사 키가 큰 □ 키가 크면 엄청난 자신감을 느낄 수 있다. **2** 형용사 키가 ~인 □ 키가 어떻게 돼? **3** 구 매우 힘든 요구 □ 스스로 학비를 조달하는 것은 매우 힘든 요구처럼 들릴지도 모르나 도움을 얻을 수 있는 방법이 많다. **4** 구 가슴을 펴고 다니다 □ 그들은 실망하거나 고개를 숙이지 말고 가슴을 펴고 다녀야 한다.

1 가산명사 총계 □ 왕궁 방문객의 총수를 세지는 않지만 그곳은 인기가 매우 좋다. **2** 상호동사

affects it progresses. ❑ *They do not keep a tally of visitors to the palace, but it is very popular.* ② V-RECIP If one number or statement **tallies with** another, they agree with each other or are exactly the same. You can also say that two numbers or statements **tally**. ❑ *Its own estimate of three hundred tallies with that of another survey.*

일치하다 ❑ 300이라는 그 자체의 추정치는 다른 조사의 추정치와 일치한다.

tame /teɪm/ (tames, taming, tamed, tamer, tamest) ① ADJ A **tame** animal or bird is one that is not afraid of humans. ❑ *They never became tame; they would run away if you approached them.* ② ADJ If you say that something or someone is **tame**, you are criticizing them for being weak and uninteresting, rather than forceful or shocking. [DISAPPROVAL] ❑ *Some of today's political demonstrations look rather tame.* ③ V-T If someone **tames** a wild animal or bird, they train it not to be afraid of humans and to do what they say. ❑ *The Amazons were believed to have been the first to tame horses.*

① 형용사 길들여진 ❑ 그들은 결코 길들지 않았다. 그들에게 다가가면 항상 도망을 가 버리곤 했다. ② 형용사 활기 없는, 재미없는 [탐탁찮음] ❑ 오늘날의 일부 정치적 시위는 좀 활기가 없어 보인다. ③ 타동사 길들이다 ❑ 아마존 사람들이 말을 처음 길들인 것으로 추정되었다.

tam|per /tæmpər/ (tampers, tampering, tampered) V-I If someone **tampers with** something, they interfere with it or try to change it when they have no right to do so. ❑ *I don't want to be accused of tampering with the evidence.*

자동사 조작하다 ❑ 나는 증거를 조작했다는 혐의를 받고 싶지 않다.

tam|pon /tæmpɒn/ (tampons) N-COUNT A **tampon** is a tube made of cotton that a woman puts inside her vagina in order to absorb blood during menstruation.

가산명사 탐폰 (생리대)

tan /tæn/ (tans, tanning, tanned) ① N-SING If you have a **tan**, your skin has become darker than usual because you have been in the sun. ❑ *She is tall and blonde, with a permanent tan.* ② V-T/V-I If a part of your body **tans** or if you **tan** it, your skin becomes darker than usual because you spend a lot of time in the sun. ❑ *I have very pale skin that never tans.* ● **tanned** ADJ ❑ *Their skin was tanned and glowing from their weeks at the sea.*

① 단수명사 그을린 피부 ❑ 그녀는 큰 키에 금발이며 원래 가무잡잡한 피부이다. ② 타동사/자동사 햇볕에 타다; 햇볕에 태우다 ❑ 나는 절대로 햇볕에 타지 않는 매우 창백한 피부를 가지고 있다. ● 햇볕에 탄 형용사 ❑ 해변에서 몇 주 보낸 그들은 피부가 그을리고 건강한 광채가 났다.

tan|dem /tændəm/ (tandems) ① N-COUNT A **tandem** is a bicycle designed for two riders, on which one rider sits behind the other. ② PHRASE If one thing happens or is done **in tandem with** another thing, the two things happen at the same time. ❑ *Malcolm's contract will run in tandem with his existing one.* →see **bicycle**

① 가산명사 앞뒤로 앉는 2인승 자전거 ② 구 동시에, 나란히 ❑ 말콤의 계약은 기존의 것과 동시에 운용될 것이다.

tan|gible /tændʒɪbəl/ ADJ If something is **tangible**, it is clear enough or definite enough to be easily seen, felt, or noticed. ❑ *There should be some tangible evidence that the economy is starting to recover.*

형용사 만질 수 있는, 실체가 있는 ❑ 경제가 회복되기 시작했다는 뚜렷한 증거가 있어야 한다.

tan|gle /tæŋgəl/ (tangles, tangling, tangled) ① N-COUNT A **tangle of** something is a mass of it twisted together in a messy way. ❑ *A tangle of wires is all that remains of the computer and phone systems.* ② V-T/V-I If something **is tangled** or **tangles**, it becomes twisted together in a messy way. ❑ *Animals get tangled in fishing nets and drown.* ❑ *Her hair tends to tangle.*

① 가산명사 엉킴, 얽힘 ❑ 컴퓨터와 전화 장치의 흔적이라고는 뒤엉킨 전선들밖에 없다. ② 타동사/자동사 엉키다; 얽히다, 엉키다 ❑ 동물들이 어망에 엉켜 익사한다. ❑ 그녀의 머리는 엉키는 경향이 있다.

tank ♦♢♢ /tæŋk/ (tanks) ① N-COUNT A **tank** is a large container for holding liquid or gas. ❑ *...an empty fuel tank.* ❑ *Two water tanks provide a total capacity of 400 litres.* ② N-COUNT A **tank** is a large military vehicle that is equipped with weapons and moves along on metal tracks that are fitted over the wheels. →see **scuba diving**

① 가산명사 (액체나 가스) 탱크 ❑ 빈 연료 탱크 ❑ 물탱크 두 개가 총 용량 400리터의 설비이다. ② 가산명사 전차, 탱크

tank|er /tæŋkər/ (tankers) ① N-COUNT A **tanker** is a very large ship used for transporting large quantities of gas or liquid, especially oil. [oft supp N, also by N] ❑ *A Greek oil tanker has run aground.* ② N-COUNT A **tanker** is a large truck, railroad vehicle, or aircraft used for transporting large quantities of a substance. [usu supp N, also by N] ❑ *...an accident involving a petrol tanker on the M27, east of Southampton.* →see **oil, ship**

① 가산명사 유조선 ❑ 그리스 유조선이 좌초했다. ② 가산명사 대형 유조 트럭; 공중 급유기 ❑ 사우샘프턴 동쪽 27번 고속도로에서 대형 유조 트럭이 관련된 사고

tan|ta|lize /tænt°laɪz/ (tantalizes, tantalizing, tantalized) [BRIT also **tantalise**] V-T If someone or something **tantalizes** you, they make you feel hopeful and excited about getting what you want, usually before disappointing you by not letting you have what they appeared to offer. ❑ *...the dreams of democracy that have so tantalized them.* ● **tan|ta|liz|ing** ADJ ❑ *A tantalizing aroma of roast beef fills the air.*

[영국영어 tantalise] 타동사 감질나게 하다 ❑ 그들을 그렇게 감질나게 해 온 민주주의의 꿈 ● 감질나는 형용사 ❑ 감질나는 구운 쇠고기 냄새가 진동을 한다.

tan|ta|mount /tæntəmaʊnt/ ADJ If you say that one thing is **tantamount to** a second, more serious thing, you are emphasizing how bad, unacceptable, or unfortunate the first thing is by comparing it to the second. [FORMAL, EMPHASIS] [v-link ADJ to n/-ing] ❑ *What Bracey is saying is tantamount to heresy.*

형용사 -와 동등한, -와 유사한 [격식체, 강조] ❑ 브레이시가 하는 말은 이단에 가깝다.

tan|trum /tæntrəm/ (tantrums) N-COUNT If a child has a **tantrum**, they lose their temper in a noisy and uncontrolled way. If you say that an adult is throwing a **tantrum**, you are criticizing them for losing their temper and acting in a childish way. [DISAPPROVAL] ❑ *He immediately threw a tantrum, screaming and stomping up and down like a child.*

가산명사 발끈함, 떼씀 [탐탁찮음] ❑ 그는 금방 발끈하여 아이처럼 악을 쓰며 발을 쿵쿵거렸다.

tap ♦♢♢ /tæp/ (taps, tapping, tapped) ① N-COUNT A **tap** is a device that controls the flow of a liquid or gas from a pipe or container, for example on a sink or on a cask or barrel. [mainly BRIT; AM usually **faucet**] ❑ *She turned on the taps.* ❑ *...a cold-water tap.* ② V-T/V-I If you **tap** something, you hit it with a quick light blow or a series of quick light blows. ❑ *He tapped the table to still the shouts of protest.* ● N-COUNT Tap is also a noun. ❑ *A tap on the door interrupted him and Sally Pierce came in.* ③ V-T If you **tap** your fingers or feet, you make a regular pattern of sound by hitting a surface lightly and repeatedly, especially while you are listening to music. ❑ *The song's so catchy it makes you bounce round the living room or tap your feet.* ④ V-T If someone **taps** your telephone, they attach a special device to the line so that they can secretly listen to your conversations. ❑ *The government passed laws allowing the police to tap telephones.* ● N-COUNT Tap is also a noun. ❑ *He assured MPs that ministers and MPs were not subjected to phone taps.*

① 가산명사 수도꼭지 [주로 영국영어; 미국영어 대개 faucet] ❑ 그녀는 꼭지를 돌렸다. ❑ 찬물 수도꼭지 ② 타동사/자동사 톡톡 치다 ❑ 항의의 고함 소리들을 조용히 시키기 위해 그가 탁자를 똑똑 두드렸다. ● 가산명사 톡톡 침 ❑ 문을 두드리는 소리에 그는 하던 일을 멈추었고, 샐리 피어스가 들어왔다. ③ 타동사 (박자를 맞추며) 톡톡 치다 ❑ 그 곡은 아주 매력적이어서 듣게 되면 거실을 뛰어다니며 춤을 추거나 발로 박자를 맞추게 된다. ④ 타동사 도청하다 ❑ 정부가 경찰에게 전화 도청을 허용하는 법을 통과시켰다. ● 가산명사 도청 ❑ 그는 장관과 국회의원들은 전화 도청을 당하지 않는다고 국회의원들을 안심시켰다.

Word Partnership	tap의 연어
N.	cold/hot water **tap** ①
	tap on a door, **tap** *someone* on the shoulder ②
	tap your feet ③
	tap a (tele)phone ④
V.	turn on a **tap** ①

tape ♦♦◇ /teɪp/ (**tapes, taping, taped**) **1** N-UNCOUNT **Tape** is a narrow plastic strip covered with a magnetic substance. It is used to record sounds, pictures, and computer information. ❑ *Tape is expensive and loses sound quality every time it is copied.* **2** N-COUNT A **tape** is a cassette or spool with magnetic tape wound around it. ❑ *...a new cassette tape.* **3** V-T/V-I If you **tape** music, sounds, or television pictures, you record them using a tape recorder or a video recorder. ❑ *She has just taped an interview.* ❑ *He shouldn't be taping without the singer's permission.* **4** N-VAR A **tape** is a strip of cloth used to tie things together or to identify who a piece of clothing belongs to. ❑ *The books were all tied up with tape.* **5** N-COUNT A **tape** is a ribbon that is stretched across the finishing line of a race. ❑ *...the finishing tape.* **6** N-UNCOUNT **Tape** is a sticky strip of plastic used for sticking things together. ❑ *...strong adhesive tape.* **7** V-T If you **tape** one thing to another, you attach it using adhesive tape. ❑ *I taped the base of the feather onto the velvet.* **8** →see also **red tape, videotape** →see **office**

Word Partnership	*tape*의 연어
N.	**reel of** tape **1**
	cassette tape, **music** tape, tape **player 2**
	tape **a conversation,** tape **an interview,** tape **a show 3**
	piece of tape, **roll of** tape **6**
V.	**listen to a** tape, **make a** tape, **play a** tape, **watch a** tape **2**

tape meas|ure (**tape measures**) N-COUNT A **tape measure** is a strip of metal, plastic, or cloth which has numbers marked on it and is used for measuring.

ta|per /teɪpər/ (**tapers, tapering, tapered**) V-T/V-I If something **tapers**, or if you **taper** it, it becomes gradually thinner at one end. ❑ *Unlike other trees, it doesn't taper very much. It stays fat all the way up.* ● **ta|pered** ADJ ❑ *...the elegantly tapered legs of the dressing-table.*

tape re|cord|er (**tape recorders**) also **tape-recorder** N-COUNT A **tape recorder** is a machine used for recording and playing music, speech, or other sounds.

tape stream|er (**tape streamers**) N-COUNT A **tape streamer** is a piece of computer equipment that you use for copying data from a hard disk onto magnetic tape for security or storage. [COMPUTING] ❑ *Do not use a bit-image method of backup (like a tape streamer), because this will copy the virus.*

tap|es|try /tæpɪstri/ (**tapestries**) N-VAR A **tapestry** is a large piece of heavy cloth with a picture sewn on it using colored threads. ❑ *He stared in wonder at the tapestries on the walls.*

tar /tɑr/ **1** N-UNCOUNT **Tar** is a thick black sticky substance that is used especially for making roads. ❑ *The oil has hardened to tar.* **2** N-UNCOUNT **Tar** is one of the poisonous substances contained in tobacco. ❑ *...strict guidelines as to the amount of tar contained in cigarettes.*

tar|get ♦♦◇ /tɑrgɪt/ (**targets, targeting, targeted**) [BRIT, sometimes AM **targetting, targetted**] **1** N-COUNT A **target** is something at which someone is aiming a weapon or other object. ❑ *The village lies beside a main road, making it an easy target for bandits.* **2** N-COUNT A **target** is a result that you are trying to achieve. ❑ *He's won back his place too late to achieve his target of 20 goals this season.* **3** V-T To **target** a particular person or thing means to decide to attack or criticize them. ❑ *Republicans targeted Unsoeld as vulnerable in her bid for reelection this year.* ● N-COUNT **Target** is also a noun. [oft N *of/for* n] ❑ *In the past they have been the target of racist abuse.* **4** V-T If you **target** a particular group of people, you try to appeal to those people or affect them. ❑ *The campaign will target American insurance companies.* ● N-COUNT **Target** is also a noun. ❑ *Yuppies are a prime target group for marketing strategies.* **5** PHRASE If someone or something is **on target**, they are making good progress and are likely to achieve the result that is wanted. ❑ *We were still right on target for our deadline.*

Word Partnership	*target*의 연어
V.	**attack a** target **1**
	hit a target, **miss a** target **1 2**
ADJ.	**easy** target, **moving** target **1**
	likely target, **possible** target, **prime** target **1**-**4**
N.	target **practice 1**
	target **date 2**
	target **of criticism 3**
	target **audience,** target **group,** target **population 4**

tar|iff /tærɪf/ (**tariffs**) **1** N-COUNT A **tariff** is a tax that a government collects on goods coming into a country. [BUSINESS] ❑ *America wants to eliminate tariffs on items such as electronics.* **2** N-COUNT A **tariff** is the rate at which you are charged for public services such as gas and electricity, or for accommodations and services in a hotel. [BRIT, FORMAL] ❑ *The daily tariff includes unlimited use of the pool and gymnasium.*

tar|mac /tɑrmæk/ **1** N-UNCOUNT **Tarmac** is a material used for making road surfaces, consisting of crushed stones mixed with tar. [BRIT, TRADEMARK; AM usually **blacktop**] ❑ *...a strip of tarmac.* **2** N-SING **The tarmac** is an area with a surface made of tarmac, especially the area from which planes take off and land at an airport. ❑ *Standing on the tarmac were two American planes.*

1 불가산명사 (녹음용) 테이프 ❑ 테이프는 비싸며 복사될 때마다 음질이 저하된다. **2** 가산명사 카세트테이프 ❑ 새 카세트테이프 **3** 타동사/자동사 녹음하다, 녹화하다 ❑ 그녀는 방금 인터뷰를 녹음했다. ❑ 그는 가수의 허락 없이 녹음해서는 안 된다. **4** 가산명사 또는 불가산명사 끈 ❑ 책은 모두 끈으로 묶여 있었다. **5** 가산명사 (결승 지점의) 테이프 ❑ 결승 테이프 **6** 불가산명사 (접착용) 테이프 ❑ 접착력이 강한 테이프 **7** 타동사 테이프로 붙이다 ❑ 깃털의 기부를 벨벳에 테이프로 붙였다.

가산명사 줄자

타동사/자동사 점점 가늘어지다; 점점 가늘게 만들다 ❑ 다른 나무와는 달리 그 나무는 별로 가늘어지지 않는다. 꼭대기까지 두께를 유지한다. ● 점점 가늘어지는 형용사 ❑ 우아하게 가늘어지는 화장대의 다리

가산명사 녹음기

가산명사 테이프 스트리머 (백업용 테이프에 하드의 내용을 저장하기 위한 기록 장치) [컴퓨터] ❑ 모든 비트를 원본 그대로 복사해 버리는 (테이프 스트리머와 같은) 백업 방식을 사용하지 말아라. 이러면 바이러스까지 복사하게 된다.

가산명사 또는 불가산명사 태피스트리 ❑ 그는 벽에 걸린 태피스트리를 신기한 눈으로 봤다.

1 불가산명사 타르 ❑ 석유가 굳어서 타르가 됐다. **2** 불가산명사 타르 ❑ 담배에 함유된 타르의 양에 관한 엄격한 지침

[영국영어, 미국영어 가끔 targetting, targetted] **1** 가산명사 표적 ❑ 그 마을은 주요 도로 옆에 있어서 산적들에게 쉬운 표적이 된다. **2** 가산명사 목표 ❑ 그가 올 시즌 20득점이라는 목표를 이루기에는 자신의 자리를 너무 늦게 되찾았다. **3** 타동사 표적으로 삼다 ❑ 공화당은 올해 운소엘드의 재선 운동이 취약하다고 보고 이를 표적으로 삼았다. ● 가산명사 표적 ❑ 과거에는 그들이 인종 차별적 학대의 표적이었다. **4** 타동사 겨냥하다 ❑ 이 캠페인은 미국 보험 회사들을 겨냥할 것이다. ● 가산명사 표적 ❑ 여피족은 마케팅 전략의 주요 표적이다. **5** 구 예정대로 가는 ❑ 우리는 여전히 기한에 맞춰 예정대로 잘 가고 있었다.

1 가산명사 관세 [경제] ❑ 미국은 전자 제품 같은 물품에 대한 관세를 철폐하고 싶어 한다. **2** 가산명사 요금; 요율 [영국영어, 격식체] ❑ 일일 요금에는 수영장과 실내 체육관의 무제한 사용이 포함되어 있다.

1 불가산명사 타맥 (아스팔트 포장재) [영국영어, 상표; 미국영어 대개 blacktop] ❑ 타맥으로 포장된 가설 활주로 **2** 단수명사 (활주로 등) 타맥 포장 도로 ❑ 두 대의 미국 비행기가 활주로에 서 있었다.

tar|nish /ˈtɑrnɪʃ/ (**tarnishes**, **tarnishing**, **tarnished**) **1** V-T If you say that something **tarnishes** someone's reputation or image, you mean that it causes people to have a worse opinion of them than they would otherwise have had. ❏ *The affair could tarnish the reputation of the prime minister.* ● **tar|nished** ADJ ❏ *He says he wants to improve the tarnished image of his country.* **2** V-T/V-I If a metal **tarnishes** or if something **tarnishes** it, it becomes stained and loses its brightness. ❏ *It never rusts or tarnishes.*

tart /tɑrt/ (**tarts**) **1** N-VAR A **tart** is a shallow pastry case with a filling of food, especially sweet food. ❏ *...jam tarts.* **2** ADJ If something such as fruit is **tart**, it has a sharp taste. ❏ *The blackberries were a bit too tart on their own, so we stewed them gently with some apples.* **3** ADJ A **tart** remark or way of speaking is sharp and unpleasant, often in a way that is rather cruel. ❏ *The words were more tart than she had intended.* **4** N-COUNT If someone refers to a woman or girl as a **tart**, they are criticizing her because they think she is sexually immoral or dresses in a way that makes her look sexually immoral. [INFORMAL, OFFENSIVE, DISAPPROVAL] ❏ *I've often heard him call women "tarts" when they just dress a bit sexily.*

tar|tan /ˈtɑrtən/ (**tartans**) N-VAR **Tartan** is a design for cloth traditionally associated with Scotland, and which has a number of distinctive types. The design is made up of lines of different widths and colors crossing each other at right angles. **Tartan** is also used to refer to cloth which has this pattern. ❏ *...traditional tartan kilts.*

task ♦♦◇ /tæsk/ (**tasks**) N-COUNT A **task** is an activity or piece of work which you have to do, usually as part of a larger project. ❏ *Walker had the unenviable task of breaking the bad news to Hill.*

Thesaurus   task의 참조어

N.	assignment, job, responsibility

Word Partnership   task의 연어

V.	accomplish a task, assign *someone* a task, complete a task, face a task, give *someone* a task, perform a task
ADJ.	complex task, difficult task, easy task, enormous task, important task, impossible task, main task, simple task

---

taste ♦♦◇ /teɪst/ (**tastes**, **tasting**, **tasted**) **1** N-UNCOUNT **Taste** is one of the five senses that people have. When you have food or drink in your mouth, your sense of taste makes it possible for you to recognize what it is. ❏ *...a keen sense of taste.* **2** N-COUNT The **taste** of something is the individual quality which it has when you put it in your mouth and which distinguishes it from other things. For example, something may have a sweet, bitter, sour, or salty taste. ❏ *I like the taste of wine and enjoy trying different kinds.* **3** N-SING If you have a **taste** of some food or drink, you try a small amount of it in order to see what the flavor is like. ❏ *Yves sometimes gives customers a taste of a wine before they order.* **4** V-I If food or drink **tastes of** something, it has that particular flavor, which you notice when you eat or drink it. [no cont] ❏ *I drank a cup of tea that tasted of diesel.* ❏ *It tastes like chocolate.* **5** V-T If you **taste** some food or drink, you eat or drink a small amount of it in order to try its flavor, for example to see if you like it or not. ❏ *He finished his aperitif and tasted the wine the waiter had produced.* **6** V-T If you can **taste** something that you are eating or drinking, you are aware of its flavor. [no passive] ❏ *You can taste the chilli in the dish but it is a little sweet.* **7** N-SING If you have a **taste of** a particular way of life or activity, you have a brief experience of it. ❏ *This voyage was his first taste of freedom.* **8** V-T If you **taste** something such as a way of life or a pleasure, you experience it for a short period of time. [no passive] ❏ *Once you have tasted the outdoor life in southern California, it takes a peculiar kind of masochism to return to a Nottingham winter.* **9** N-SING If you have a **taste for** something, you have a liking or preference for it. ❏ *That gave me a taste for reading.* **10** N-UNCOUNT A person's **taste** is their choice in the things that they like or buy, for example their clothes, possessions, or music. If you say that someone has good **taste**, you mean that you approve of their choices. If you say that they have poor **taste**, you disapprove of their choices. [also N in pl] ❏ *His taste in clothes is extremely good.* **11** PHRASE If you say that something that is said or done is **in bad taste** or **in poor taste**, you mean that it is offensive, often because it concerns death or sex and is inappropriate for the situation. If you say that something is **in good taste**, you mean that it is not offensive and that it is appropriate for the situation. ❏ *He rejects the idea that his film is in bad taste.* →see **sugar**
→see Word Web: **taste**

Word Partnership   taste의 연어

N.	sense of taste **1**
ADJ.	bitter/salty/sour/sweet taste **2**
	taste bitter/salty/sour/sweet, taste good **4**
	bad/good/poor taste **10**
	in bad/good/poor taste **11**
V.	like the taste of *something* **2**
	get a taste of *something* **7**

---

taste|ful /ˈteɪstfəl/ ADJ If you say that something is **tasteful**, you consider it to be attractive, elegant, and in good taste. ❏ *The decor is tasteful and restrained.* ● **taste|ful|ly** ADV ❏ *...a large and tastefully decorated home.*

---

1 타동사 더럽히다, (평판 등을) 손상시키다 ❏ 그 사건이 총리의 평판을 손상시킬 수도 있다. ● 더럽혀진, 손상된 형용사 ❏ 그는 자기 나라의 손상된 이미지를 개선하긴 원한다고 말한다. **2** 타동사/자동사 흐려지다, 변색되다; 흐리게 하다, 변색시키다 ❏ 그것은 절대로 녹슬거나 변색되지 않는다.

1 가산명사 또는 불가산명사 타트 (속에 단 것을 넣은 파이) ❏ 잼 타트 **2** 형용사 시큼한 ❏ 검은 딸기는 그냥 먹기에 좀 너무 시큼해서, 약간의 사과와 함께 살짝 익혔다. **3** ADJ 형용사 신랄한, 호된 ❏ 그 말은 그녀가 의도했던 것보다 더 신랄했다. **4** 가산명사 행실이 단정치 못한 여자, 창녀 [비격식체, 모욕어, 탐탁찮음] ❏ 나는 그가 옷만 약간 섹시하게 입어도 여자들을 '창녀 같은 계집들'이라고 부르는 것을 종종 들었다.

가산명사 또는 불가산명사 격자무늬, 체크무늬; 격자무늬의 모직물 ❏ 전통적인 격자무늬 킬트

가산명사 일, 과업 ❏ 워커는 힐에게 나쁜 소식을 털어 놓는 내키지 않는 과업을 맡았다.

1 불가산명사 미각 ❏ 민감한 미각 **2** 가산명사 맛 ❏ 나는 와인의 맛을 좋아하며 다양한 종류의 와인을 시음하는 것을 즐긴다. **3** 단수명사 시식, 맛보기 ❏ 이브는 종종 손님들이 주문을 하기 전에 와인을 시음할 수 있도록 한다. **4** 자동사 ~한 맛이 나다 ❏ 디젤 기름 같은 맛이 나는 차를 한 잔 마셨다. ❏ 그것은 초콜릿 맛이 난다. **5** 타동사 맛을 보다 ❏ 그는 아페리티프를 다 마시고 나서 웨이터가 내놓은 와인을 맛보았다. **6** 타동사 ~의 맛을 느끼다 ❏ 그 요리는 고추 맛이 나지만 약간 달콤합니다. **7** 단수명사 (약간의) 경험 ❏ 이 항해가 그가 처음으로 맛본 자유의 경험이었다. **8** 타동사 경험하다, 맛보다 ❏ 한번 캘리포니아 남부에서 야외 생활을 맛보고 나면, 노팅엄의 겨울로 돌아가는 데는 일종의 자기 학대 심리가 필요하다. **9** 단수명사 좋아함, 기호 ❏ 그것 때문에 나는 독서를 좋아하게 되었다. **10** 불가산명사 감식력; 감각 ❏ 그는 옷 입는 감각이 매우 뛰어나다. **11** 구 천박한; 고상한 ❏ 그는 자신의 영화가 천박하다는 생각을 거부한다.

형용사 우아한, 고상한 ❏ 그 실내 장식은 우아하고 절제미가 있다. ● 우아하게 부사 ❏ 크고 우아하게 장식된 집

Word Web taste

What we think of as **taste** is mostly **odor**. The sense of **smell** accounts for about 80% of the experience. We actually taste only four **sensations**: **sweet**, **salty**, **sour**, and **bitter**. We experience sweetness and saltiness through taste buds near the tip of the **tongue**. We sense sourness at the sides and bitterness at the back of the tongue. Saltiness is felt all over the tongue. Some people have more taste buds than others. Scientists have discovered some "supertasters" with 425 taste buds per square centimeter. Most of us have about 184 and some "nontasters" have only about 96.

taste|less /teɪstlɪs/ ■ ADJ If you describe something such as furniture, clothing, or the way that a house is decorated as **tasteless**, you consider it to be vulgar and unattractive. □ ...a flat crammed with spectacularly tasteless objets d'art. ■ ADJ If you describe something such as a remark or joke as **tasteless**, you mean that it is offensive. □ I think that is the most vulgar and tasteless remark I ever heard in my life. ■ ADJ If you describe food or drink as **tasteless**, you mean that it has very little or no flavor. □ The fish was mushy and tasteless.

■ 형용사 몰취미한 □ 엄청나게 몰취미한 미술품들이 가득가득 들어찬 아파트 ■ 형용사 천박한 □ 내 생각에 그것은 내 평생에 들어 본 것 중 가장 저속하고 천박한 말이다. ■ 형용사 맛없는 □ 그 생선 요리는 흐물흐물하고 맛이 없었다.

tasty /teɪsti/ (**tastier**, **tastiest**) ADJ If you say that food, especially savory food, is **tasty**, you mean that it has a fairly strong and pleasant flavor which makes it good to eat. □ Try this tasty dish for supper with a crispy salad.

형용사 맛있는 □ 저녁 식사로 아삭아삭한 샐러드를 곁들여서 이 맛있는 요리를 드셔 보세요.

tat|tered /tætərd/ ADJ If something such as clothing or a book is **tattered**, it is damaged or torn, especially because it has been used a lot over a long period of time. □ He fled wearing only a sarong and a tattered shirt.

형용사 누더기가 된 □ 그는 사롱과 누더기가 된 셔츠만 걸친 채로 도망쳤다.

tat|ters /tætərz/ ■ N-PLURAL Clothes that are **in tatters** are badly torn in several places, so that pieces can easily come off. □ His jersey was left in tatters. ■ N-PLURAL If you say that something such as a plan or a person's state of mind is **in tatters**, you are emphasizing that it is weak, has suffered a lot of damage, and is likely to fail completely. [EMPHASIS] □ The economy is in tatters.

■ 복수명사 누더기 □ 그의 운동복 상의가 누더기가 되어 있었다. ■ 복수명사 만신창이 [강조] □ 경제는 만신창이가 된 상태이다.

tat|too /tætu/ (**tattoos**, **tattooing**, **tattooed**) ■ N-COUNT A **tattoo** is a design that is drawn on someone's skin using needles to make little holes and filling them with colored dye. □ On the back of his neck he has a tattoo of a cross. ■ V-T If someone **tattoos** you, they give you a tattoo. □ In the old days, they would paint and tattoo their bodies for ceremonies.

■ 가산명사 문신 □ 그는 목 뒤에 십자가 문신이 있다. ■ 타동사 문신을 새기다 □ 옛날에는, 의식을 위해 몸에 그림을 그리고 문신을 새기곤 했다.

taught /tɔt/ **Taught** is the past tense and past participle of **teach**.

teach의 과거, 과거 분사

taunt /tɔnt/ (**taunts**, **taunting**, **taunted**) V-T If someone **taunts** you, they say unkind or insulting things to you, especially about your weaknesses or failures. □ A gang taunted a disabled man. ● N-COUNT **Taunt** is also a noun. □ For years they suffered racist taunts.

타동사 조롱하다, 놀리다 □ 어떤 패거리가 한 장애인을 조롱했다. ● 가산명사 조롱, 놀림 □ 그들은 수년간 인종 차별주의적 조롱을 받았다.

taut /tɔt/ (**tauter**, **tautest**) ■ ADJ Something that is **taut** is stretched very tight. □ The clothes line is pulled taut and secured. ■ ADJ If someone has a **taut** expression, they look very worried and tense. □ Ben sat up quickly, his face taut and terrified.

■ 형용사 팽팽한 □ 빨랫줄은 팽팽하게 당겨져서 고정되었다. ■ 형용사 긴장된 □ 벤은 긴장되고 겁먹은 얼굴을 하고 재빨리 일어나 앉았다.

tax ♦♦♦ /tæks/ (**taxes**, **taxing**, **taxed**) ■ N-VAR **Tax** is an amount of money that you have to pay to the government so that it can pay for public services. [BUSINESS] □ No-one enjoys paying tax. □ ...a pledge not to raise taxes on people below a certain income. ■ V-T When a person or company **is taxed**, they have to pay a part of their income or profits to the government. When goods **are taxed**, a percentage of their price has to be paid to the government. [BUSINESS] □ Husband and wife are now taxed separately on their incomes. ■ →see also **taxing, income tax, value added tax**

■ 가산명사 또는 불가산명사 세금 [경제] □ 세금 내는 것을 즐기는 사람은 아무도 없다. □ 일정 수준이하의 소득자를 대상으로 세금을 올리지 않겠다는 약속 ■ 타동사 과세되다 [경제] □ 이제는 남편과 아내가 각자의 소득에 대해 따로 세금을 부과받는다.

tax|able /tæksəbəl/ ADJ **Taxable** income is income on which you have to pay tax. [BUSINESS] □ It is worth consulting the guide to see whether your income is taxable.

형용사 세금이 붙는, 과세 대상인 [경제] □ 소득에 세금이 붙는지 알아보기 위해 가이드의 충고를 구할 만한 가치가 있다.

taxa|tion /tækseɪʃən/ ■ N-UNCOUNT **Taxation** is the system by which a government takes money from people and spends it on things such as education, health, and defense. [BUSINESS] □ ...the proposed reforms to taxation. ■ N-UNCOUNT **Taxation** is the amount of money that people have to pay in taxes. □ The result will be higher taxation.

■ 불가산명사 과세; 세제 [경제] □ 제안된 세제 개혁안 ■ 불가산명사 조세액, 세수 [경제] □ 그 결과 세수가 더 늘어날 것이다.

tax break (**tax breaks**) N-COUNT If the government gives a **tax break** to a particular group of people or type of organization, it reduces the amount of tax they have to pay or changes the tax system in a way that benefits them. [mainly AM, BUSINESS] □ Today they'll consider tax breaks for businesses that create jobs in inner cities.

가산명사 세금 우대 조치, 세제상 특전 [주로 미국영어, 경제] □ 오늘 그들은 도심에 일자리를 창출하는 기업들에 대해 세금 우대 조치를 고려할 것이다.

tax cred|it (**tax credits**) N-COUNT A **tax credit** is an amount of money on which you do not have to pay tax. □ The president proposed to provide tax credits to businesses that allow workers time off.

가산명사 세액 공제 [경제] □ 대통령은 노동자들에게 일을 쉬는 시간을 주는 기업들에 세액 공제 혜택을 줄 것을 제안했다.

tax-deductible /tæks dɪdʌktɪbəl/ ADJ If an expense is **tax-deductible**, it can be paid out of the part of your income on which you do not pay tax, so that the amount of tax you pay is reduced. [BUSINESS] □ The cost of private childcare should be made tax-deductible.

형용사 소득 공제의 [경제] □ 개인 육아 비용은 소득 공제가 가능하게 해야 한다.

tax eva|sion N-UNCOUNT **Tax evasion** is the crime of not paying the full amount of tax that you should pay. [BUSINESS] □ Mr. Kozlowski was charged with tax evasion.

불가산명사 탈세 [경제] □ 코즐로우스키 씨는 탈세 혐의로 고발되었다.

Word Link   free ≈ without : care*free*, duty-*free*, tax-*free*

tax-free ADJ **Tax-free** is used to describe income on which you do not have to pay tax. [BUSINESS] [ADJ n, amount ADJ, v-link ADJ] ❑ ...*a tax-free investment plan.*

형용사 면세의, 비과세의 [경제] ❑ 비과세 투자 계획

tax ha|ven (**tax havens**) N-COUNT A **tax haven** is a country or place which has a low rate of tax so that people choose to live there or register companies there in order to avoid paying higher tax in their own countries. [BUSINESS] ❑ *The Caribbean has become an important location for international banking because it is a tax haven.*

가산명사 조세 피난처 (세제상 특전이 많은 지역) [경제] ❑ 카리브 해는 조세 피난지이기 때문에 국제 은행업의 요지가 되었다.

taxi /tǽksi/ (**taxis, taxiing, taxied**) 1 N-COUNT A **taxi** is a car driven by a person whose job is to take people where they want to go in return for money. [also by N] ❑ *The taxi drew up in front of the Riviera Club.* 2 V-T/V-I When an aircraft **taxis** along the ground or when a pilot **taxis** a plane somewhere, it moves slowly along the ground. ❑ *She gave permission to the plane to taxi into position and hold for takeoff.*

1 가산명사 택시 ❑ 그 택시는 리비에라 클럽 앞에 멈춰 섰다. 2 타동사/자동사 (비행기가) 이동하다; (비행기를 유상에서) 이동시키다 ❑ 그녀는 비행기에 제 위치로 이동하여 이륙 준비를 취하라는 허가를 내렸다.

tax|ing /tǽksɪŋ/ ADJ A **taxing** task or problem is one that requires a lot of mental or physical effort. ❑ *They were comparing notes on each other's progress towards solving that most taxing of all puzzles: the riddle of the human genome.*

형용사 부담이 큰, 어려운 ❑ 그들은 모든 난제 중에서 가장 어려운 문제인 인간 게놈이라는 수수께끼의 해결을 향한 각자의 경과를 적은 기록을 서로 비교하고 있었다.

taxi rank (**taxi ranks**) N-COUNT A **taxi rank** is the same as a **taxi stand**. [BRIT]

가산명사 택시 승차장 [영국영어]

taxi stand (**taxi stands**) N-COUNT A **taxi stand** is a place where taxis wait for passengers, for example at an airport or outside a station. [mainly AM; BRIT usually **taxi rank**]

가산명사 택시 승차장 [주로 미국영어; 영국영어 대개 taxi rank]

tax|payer /tǽkspeɪər/ (**taxpayers**) N-COUNT **Taxpayers** are people who pay a percentage of their income to the government as tax. [BUSINESS] ❑ *This is not going to cost the taxpayer anything. The company will bear the costs for the delay.*

가산명사 납세자 [경제] ❑ 이 일은 납세자에게 아무런 부담을 끼치지 않을 것이다. 기업이 지연에 대한 손실을 감수할 것이다.

tax re|lief N-UNCOUNT **Tax relief** is a reduction in the amount of tax that a person or company has to pay, for example because of expenses associated with their business or property. [BUSINESS] ❑ ...*mortgage interest tax relief.*

불가산명사 세금 감감 [경제] ❑ 주택 융자 이자 세금 경감

tax re|turn (**tax returns**) N-COUNT A **tax return** is an official form that you fill in with details about your income and personal situation, so that the tax you owe can be calculated. [BUSINESS]

가산명사 소득 신고서 [경제]

tax shel|ter (**tax shelters**) N-COUNT A **tax shelter** is a way of arranging the finances of a business or a person so that they have to pay less tax. [BUSINESS] ❑ *The consultancy offers advice on ethical tax-shelters.*

가산명사 감세 수단 [경제] ❑ 그 컨설팅 회사는 윤리적인 감세 수단에 대한 조언을 제공한다.

tax year (**tax years**) N-COUNT A **tax year** is a particular period of twelve months which is used by the government as a basis for calculating taxes and for organizing its finances and accounts. In the United States, the tax year begins on January 1st and ends on December 31st. In Britain, the tax year begins on April 6th and ends on April 5th. [BUSINESS]

가산명사 과세 연도 [경제]

TB /tí bí/ N-UNCOUNT **TB** is an extremely serious infectious disease that affects someone's lungs and other parts of their body. **TB** is an abbreviation for **tuberculosis**.

불가산명사 결핵

tba also **TBA** **tba** is sometimes written in announcements to indicate that something such as the place where something will happen or the people who will take part is not yet known and will be announced at a later date. **tba** is an abbreviation for "to be announced." ❑ *July 24: Australia v New Zealand (venue TBA).*

추후 공고; 미정 ❑ 7월 24일: 호주 대 뉴질랜드 (장소는 추후 공고)

tbc also **TBC** **tbc** is sometimes written in announcements about future events to indicate that details of the event are not yet certain and will be confirmed later. **tbc** is an abbreviation for "to be confirmed." ❑ *11 Feb: European Skating Championships, time tbc, BBC1.*

추후 확정; 미정 ❑ 2월 11일: 유럽 스케이트 선수권 대회, 시간 미정, 비비시 1 채널.

tea ♦♦◇ /tí/ (**teas**) 1 N-MASS **Tea** is a drink made by adding boiling water to tea leaves or tea bags. ❑ ...*a cup of tea.* ❑ *Would you like some tea?* ● N-COUNT A cup of tea can be referred to as a **tea**. ❑ *Would anybody like a tea or coffee?* 2 N-MASS The chopped dried leaves of the plant that tea is made from is referred to as **tea**. ❑ ...*a packet of tea.* 3 N-VAR **Tea** is a meal some people eat in the late afternoon. It consists of food such as sandwiches and cakes, with tea to drink. [BRIT] ❑ *I'm doing the sandwiches for tea.* →see **meal** 4 N-VAR Some people refer to the main meal that they eat in the early part of the evening as **tea**. [BRIT] ❑ *At five o'clock he comes back for his tea.*
→see Word Web: **tea**

1 물질명사 차 ❑ 차 한 잔 ❑ 차 좀 드실래요? ● 가산명사 차 한 잔 ❑ 차나 커피 한 잔 할 사람 있어? 2 물질명사 찻잎, 차 ❑ 차 한 통 3 가산명사 또는 불가산명사 오후 간식 [영국영어] ❑ 오후 간식으로 먹으려고 샌드위치를 만들고 있다. 4 가산명사 또는 불가산명사 이른 저녁 식사 [영국영어] ❑ 5시에 그는 이른 저녁 식사를 위해 돌아온다.

teach ♦♦◇ /tíʧ/ (**teaches, teaching, taught**) 1 V-T If you **teach** someone something, you give them instructions so that they know about it or how to do it. ❑ *The trainers have a programme to teach them vocational skills.* ❑ *George had taught him how to ride a horse.* 2 V-T To **teach** someone something means to make them think, feel, or act in a new or different way. ❑ *Their daughter's death had taught him humility.* ❑ *He taught his followers that they could all be members of the kingdom of God.* 3 V-T/V-I If you **teach** or **teach** a subject, you help students to learn about it by explaining or showing them how to do it, usually as a job

1 타동사 가르치다, 교육하다 ❑ 교관들은 그들에게 직업 기술을 가르치는 프로그램을 가지고 있다. ❑ 조지가 그에게 말 타는 법을 가르쳤었다. 2 타동사 가르치다, 알게 하다 ❑ 그들의 딸의 죽음은 그에게 겸손을 알게 해 주었다. ❑ 그는 신도들에게 그들 모두 하느님의 왕국 백성이 될 수 있다고 가르쳤다. 3 타동사/자동사 (학교에서) 가르치다, 교수하다 ❑ 잉그리드는 현재 쉼라 공립학교에서 수학을

Word Web   tea

If you want to **brew** a good cup of **tea**, don't use a tea bag. For the best taste, try using fresh **tea leaves**. Begin by bringing a **teakettle** of water to a full boil. Use some of the water to warm the inside of a china **teapot**. Then empty the pot and add the tea leaves. Pour in more boiling water and let the tea steep for at least five minutes. Cover the pot with a tea cozy to keep it hot. Serve the tea in thin china teacups. Add milk and sugar if you wish.

A

at a school or college. ❑ *Ingrid is currently teaching Mathematics at Shimla Public School.* ❑ *She taught English to Japanese business people.* ◳ →see also **teaching**. to **teach** someone **a lesson** →see **lesson**

가르치고 있다. ❑ 그녀는 일본 회사원들에게 영어를 가르쳤다.

B

Thesaurus	*teach*의 참조어
v.	educate, school, train ◳ ◲ ◱

C

Word Partnership	*teach*의 연어
ADV.	teach *someone* how ◳
N.	teach *someone* a skill, teach students ◳
	teach children ◳–◱
	teach *someone* a lesson ◲
	teach classes, teach courses, teach English/history/reading/science, teach school ◱
v.	try to teach ◳–◱

F

teach|er ♦♦◇ /títʃər/ (**teachers**) N-COUNT A **teacher** is a person who teaches, usually as a job at a school or similar institution. ❑ *I'm a teacher with 21 years' experience.*

가산명사 선생, 교사 ❑ 나는 21년 경력의 교사이다.

G

Thesaurus	*teacher*의 참조어
N.	instructor, professor, trainer

H

I

teach|ing ♦♦◇ /títʃɪŋ/ (**teachings**) ◳ N-UNCOUNT **Teaching** is the work that a teacher does in helping students to learn. ❑ *The Government funds university teaching.* ◲ N-COUNT The **teachings** of a particular person, school of thought, or religion are all the ideas and principles that they teach. ❑ *...the teachings of Jesus.*

◳ 불가산명사 교육, 수업 ❑ 정부는 대학 교육에 자금을 지원한다. ◲ 가산명사 가르침, 교리 ❑ 예수의 가르침

J

teak /tik/ N-UNCOUNT **Teak** is the wood of a tall tree with very hard, light-colored wood which grows in Southeast Asia. ❑ *The door is beautifully made in solid teak.*

불가산명사 티크 (나무 목재) ❑ 그 문은 견고한 티크로 아름답게 만들어졌다.

K

tea|kettle /tíkɛtəl/ (**teakettles**) also **tea kettle** N-COUNT A **teakettle** is a kettle that is used for boiling water to make tea. [mainly AM] →see **tea**

가산명사 찻주전자 [주로 미국영어]

L

team ♦♦♦ /tim/ (**teams, teaming, teamed**) ◳ N-COUNT-COLL A **team** is a group of people who play a particular sport or game together against other similar groups of people. ❑ *The team failed to qualify for the African Nations Cup finals.* ◲ N-COUNT-COLL You can refer to any group of people who work together as a **team**. ❑ *Each specialist consultant has a team of doctors under him.*

◳ 가산명사·집합 팀 ❑ 그 팀은 아프리카 네이션스컵 대회 결선에 진출하지 못했다. ◲ 가산명사·집합 조, 작업조 ❑ 각 전문의는 자기 밑에 한 조의 의사들을 거느리고 있다.

M

▶**team up** PHRASAL VERB-RECIP If you **team up with** someone, you join them in order to work together for a particular purpose. You can also say that two people or groups **team up**. ❑ *Elton teamed up with Eric Clapton to wow thousands at a Wembley rock concert.*

상호 구동사 팀을 이루다 ❑ 엘튼은 에릭 클랩턴과 팀을 이뤄 웸블리 록 콘서트에서 수천 명의 관중을 열광시켰다.

N

team|mate /tímmeɪt/ (**teammates**) also **team-mate** N-COUNT In a game or sport, your **teammates** are the other members of your team. ❑ *He was always a solid player, a hard worker, a great example to his teammates.*

가산명사 팀 동료 ❑ 그는 언제나 견실한 선수이자 성실한 일꾼이었으며, 팀 동료들에게는 뛰어난 본보기였다.

O

P

team|work /tímwɜrk/ N-UNCOUNT **Teamwork** is the ability a group of people have to work well together. ❑ *Today's complex buildings require close teamwork between the architect and the builders.*

불가산명사 팀워크 ❑ 오늘날의 복합 건물에는 건축가와 시공자 사이에 긴밀한 팀워크가 요구된다.

Q

tea|pot /típɒt/ (**teapots**) also **tea pot** N-COUNT A **teapot** is a container with a lid, a handle, and a spout, used for making and serving tea. →see **tea**

가산명사 찻주전자

tear
① CRYING
② DAMAGING OR MOVING

R

S

T

① **tear** ♦◇◇ /tɪər/ (**tears**) ◳ N-COUNT **Tears** are the drops of salty liquid that come out of your eyes when you are crying. ❑ *Her eyes filled with tears.* ❑ *I just broke down and wept with tears of joy.* ◲ N-PLURAL You can use **tears** in expressions such as **in tears**, **burst into tears**, and **close to tears** to indicate that someone is crying or is almost crying. ❑ *He was in floods of tears on the phone.* ❑ *She burst into tears and ran from the kitchen.* →see **cry**

◳ 가산명사 눈물 ❑ 그녀의 두 눈에 눈물이 그렁그렁했다. ❑ 나는 그냥 울음을 터뜨리며 기쁨의 눈물을 흘렸다. ◲ 복수명사 울음, 눈물 ❑ 그는 전화를 받으며 눈물을 펑펑 쏟았다. ❑ 그녀는 왈칵 울음을 터뜨리며 부엌에서 뛰쳐나갔다.

U

V

② **tear** ♦♦◇ /tɛər/ (**tears, tearing, tore, torn**) →Please look at category ◳ to see if the expression you are looking for is shown under another headword. ◳ V-T/V-I If you **tear** paper, cloth, or another material, or if it **tears**, you pull it into two pieces or you pull it so that a hole appears in it. ❑ *She very nearly tore my overcoat.* ● PHRASAL VERB **Tear up** means the same as **tear**. ❑ *She tore the letter up.* ❑ *Don't you dare tear up her ticket.* ◲ N-COUNT A **tear** in paper, cloth, or another material is a hole that has been made in it. ❑ *I peered through a tear in the van's curtains.* ◳ V-T/V-I If you **tear** one of your muscles or ligaments, or if it **tears**, you injure it by accidentally moving it in the wrong way. ❑ *He tore a muscle in his right thigh.* ❑ *If the muscle is stretched again it could even tear.* ◱ V-T To **tear** something from somewhere means to remove it roughly and violently. ❑ *She tore the windscreen wipers from his car.* ◵ V-I If a person or animal **tears at** something, they pull it violently and try to break it into pieces. ❑ *Female fans fought their way past bodyguards and tore at his clothes.* ◶ V-I If you **tear** somewhere, you move there very quickly, often in an uncontrolled or dangerous way. ❑ *The door flew open and Miranda tore into the room.* ◷ V-T PASSIVE If you say that a place **is**

◳ 타동사/자동사 찢다; 찢어지다 ❑ 그녀는 내 외투를 거의 찢을 뻔했다. ● 구동사 찢다; 찢어지다 ❑ 그녀는 편지를 찢었다. ❑ 감히 그녀의 표를 찢을 생각일랑 하지 마라. ◲ 가산명사 째진 틈, 찢어진 곳 ❑ 나는 그 밴에 달린 커튼의 찢어진 틈으로 유심히 보았다. ◳ 타동사/자동사 (근육 등을) 찢다; 찢어지다 ❑ 그는 오른쪽 넓적다리 근육이 찢어졌다. ❑ 그 근육을 다시 늘이면 찢어질 수도 있다. ◱ 타동사 거칠게 뜯어내다 ❑ 그녀는 그의 차 앞 유리 와이퍼를 거칠게 뜯어냈다. ◵ 자동사 잡아채다, 쥐어뜯다 ❑ 여성 팬들이 경호원들을 헤치고 나가서 그의 옷을 잡아챘다. ◶ 자동사 질주하다; 날뛰다 ❑ 문이 확 열리더니 미란다가 방 안으로 뛰어 들어왔다. ◷ 수동 타동사 분열되다 ❑ 독립된 이래 내전과 외세의 침략으로 분열된 나라

W

X

Y

Z

torn by particular events, you mean that unpleasant events which cause suffering and division among people are happening there. ❑ *...a country that has been torn by civil war and foreign invasion since its independence.* ◍ →see also **torn, wear and tear**

▸**tear apart** ❶ PHRASAL VERB If something **tears** people **apart**, it causes them to quarrel or to leave each other. ❑ *The quarrel tore the party apart.* ❷ PHRASAL VERB If something **tears** you **apart**, it makes you feel very upset, worried, and unhappy. ❑ *Don't think it hasn't torn me apart to be away from you.*

▸**tear away** PHRASAL VERB If you **tear** someone **away from** a place or activity, you force them to leave the place or stop doing the activity, even though they want to remain there or carry on. ❑ *Fame hasn't torn her away from her beloved Liverpool.* ❑ *Japan's education ministry ordered the change to encourage students to tear themselves away from textbooks.*

▸**tear down** PHRASAL VERB If you **tear** something **down**, you destroy it or remove it completely. ❑ *Angry Russians may have torn down the statue of Felix Dzerzhinsky.*

▸**tear off** PHRASAL VERB If you **tear off** your clothes, you take them off in a rough and violent way. ❑ *Totally exhausted, he tore his clothes off and fell into bed.*

▸**tear up** ❶ PHRASAL VERB If something such as a road, railroad, or area of land **is torn up**, it is completely removed or destroyed. ❑ *Dozens of miles of railway track have been torn up.* ❷ →see **tear 1**

tear|ful /tɪərfəl/ ADJ If someone is **tearful**, their face or voice shows signs that they have been crying or that they want to cry. ❑ *She became very tearful when pressed to talk about it.*

tear gas /tɪər gæs/ N-UNCOUNT **Tear gas** is a gas that causes your eyes to sting and fill with tears so that you cannot see. It is sometimes used by the police or army to control crowds. ❑ *Police used tear gas to disperse the demonstrators.*

tease /tiz/ (**teases, teasing, teased**) ❶ V-T To **tease** someone means to laugh at them or make jokes about them in order to embarrass, annoy, or upset them. ❑ *He told her how the boys in East Poldown had set on him, teasing him.* ❑ *He teased me mercilessly about going Hollywood.* ● N-COUNT **Tease** is also a noun. ❑ *Calling her by her real name had always been one of his teases.* ❷ N-COUNT If you refer to someone as a **tease**, you mean that they like laughing at people or making jokes about them. ❑ *My brother's such a tease.*

Thesaurus   *tease*의 참조어

V.   aggravate, bother, provoke ❶

tea|spoon /tispun/ (**teaspoons**) N-COUNT A **teaspoon** is a small spoon used for putting sugar into tea or coffee, and in cooking. ❑ *Drop the dough onto a baking sheet with a teaspoon.*

Word Link   techn ≈ art, skill : techn**ical**, techn**ician**, techn**ology**

tech|ni|cal ♦◇◇ /tɛknɪkəl/ ❶ ADJ **Technical** means involving the sorts of machines, processes, and materials that are used in industry, transportation, and communications. ❑ *In order to reach this limit a number of technical problems will have to be solved.* ● **tech|ni|cal|ly** /tɛknɪkli/ ADV [ADV adj] ❑ *...the largest and most technically advanced furnace company in the world.* ❷ ADJ You use **technical** to describe the practical skills and methods used to do an activity such as an art, a craft, or a sport. ❑ *Their technical ability is exceptional.* ● **tech|ni|cal|ly** ADV [ADV adj] ❑ *While Sade's voice isn't technically brilliant it has a quality which is unmistakable.* ❸ ADJ **Technical** language involves using special words to describe the details of a specialized activity. ❑ *The technical term for sunburn is erythema.* ❹ →see also **technically**

Word Partnership   *technical*의 연어

N.   technical **knowledge** ❶
        technical **assistance**, technical **difficulties**, technical **expertise**,
        technical **experts**, technical **information**, technical **issues**,
        technical **problems**, technical **services**, technical **skills**,
        technical **support**, technical **training** ❷
ADV.   **highly** technical ❶ ❷

tech|ni|cal|ity /tɛknɪkæliti/ (**technicalities**) ❶ N-PLURAL The **technicalities** of a process or activity are the detailed methods used to do it or to carry it out. ❑ *...the technicalities of classroom teaching.* ❷ N-COUNT A **technicality** is a point, especially a legal one, that is based on a strict interpretation of the law or of a set of rules. ❑ *The earlier verdict was overturned on a legal technicality.*

tech|ni|cal|ly /tɛknɪkli/ ADV If something is **technically** the case, it is the case according to a strict interpretation of facts, laws, or rules, but may not be important or relevant in a particular situation. ❑ *Nude bathing is technically illegal but there are plenty of unspoilt beaches where no one would ever know.* →see also **technical**

tech|ni|cal sup|port N-UNCOUNT **Technical support** is a repair and advice service that some companies such as computer companies provide for their customers, usually by telephone, fax, or e-mail. ❑ *The branch, which provides technical support for America Online users, had planned to close.*

tech|ni|cian /tɛknɪʃ°n/ (**technicians**) ❶ N-COUNT A **technician** is someone whose job involves skilled practical work with scientific equipment, for

❶ 구동사 분열시키다 ❑ 그 싸움으로 인해 그 당은 분열되었다. ❷ 구동사 마음을 찢어 놓다 ❑ 당신과 떨어져 있는 것이 내 마음을 찢어 놓지 않았다고는 생각지 말아 주오.

구동사 ~로부터 억지로 떼어 놓다 ● 명성이 그녀를 그녀가 사랑하는 리버풀로부터 떼어 놓지는 못했다. ❑ 일본 교육부는 학생들로 하여금 교과서에서 벗어나도록 장려하는 변화를 지시했다.

구동사 부수다, 무너뜨리다 ❑ 성난 러시아 군중들이 펠릭스 제르진스키의 동상을 무너뜨렸는지도 모른다.

구동사 황급히 벗다 ❑ 그는 완전히 탈진해서 급하게 옷을 벗어 던지고 침대 속으로 빠져 들어갔다.

❶ 구동사 완전히 제거되다, 붕괴되다 ❑ 수십 마일에 달하는 철로가 붕괴되었다.

형용사 눈물 어린 ❑ 그녀는 그것에 대해 말하라고 강요받자 금방이라도 울 것처럼 눈물이 그렁그렁해졌다.

불가산명사 최루 가스 ❑ 경찰이 시위대를 해산시키기 위해 최루 가스를 사용했다.

❶ 타동사 집적거리다, 못살게 굴다, 놀려 대다 ❑ 그는 이스트 폴다운의 사내애들이 어떻게 자기를 덮쳐서 못살게 굴곤 했는지 그녀에게 얘기해 주었다. ❑ 그는 할리우드에 가는 걸 가지고 나를 무자비하게 못살게 굴었다. ● 가산명사 집적거림, 군더더기 끼움질 ❑ 그녀의 본명을 부르는 것은 항상 그가 집적거리는 수법 중 하나였다. ❷ 가산명사 집적거리는 사람, 남을 못살게 구는 사람 ❑ 내 남동생은 정말 지독하게 남을 못살게 군다.

가산명사 찻숟가락 ❑ 찻숟가락으로 떠서 반죽을 구움판 위에 떨어뜨리세요.

❶ 형용사 기술적, 과학 기술의 ❑ 이러한 한계에 도달하기 위해서는 수많은 기술적 문제들이 해결되어야 할 것이다. ● 기술적으로 부사 ❑ 세계에서 규모가 가장 크고 기술적으로 가장 발달한 용광로 회사 ❷ 형용사 기법상의, 기술적인 ❑ 그들의 기술적 기량은 비범하다. ● 기법상으로, 기술적으로 부사 ❑ 사드의 목소리는 기술적으로 화려하진 않지만 두드러진 음색을 지니고 있다. ❸ 형용사 전문의, 특수한 ❑ 햇볕에 탄 것을 가리키는 전문 용어는 홍반이다.

❶ 복수명사 전문적 활동, 전문적 절차 ❑ 교실 수업의 전문적 활동 ❷ 가산명사 전문적 사항 ❑ 앞선 평결은 법의 전문적 사항에 의거하여 뒤집혔다.

부사 엄격히 따지면 ❑ 나체 해수욕은 엄격히 따지면 불법이지만, 아무도 알 수 없는 사람들 발길이 닿지 않는 해변이 많이 있다.

불가산명사 기술 지원 ❑ 아메리카 온라인 사용자들에게 기술 지원을 제공하는 그 분과는 폐쇄할 계획을 했었다.

❶ 가산명사 기술자 ❑ 연구소 기술자 ❷ 가산명사 기교가 ❑ 다재다능한 베테랑 선수이자, 뛰어난 기교과

example in a laboratory. ❑ ...a laboratory technician. ◆2 N-COUNT A **technician** is someone who is very good at the detailed technical aspects of an activity. ❑ ...a versatile, veteran player, a superb technician.

tech|nique ♦♦◇ /tɛknik/ (techniques) ◆1 N-COUNT A **technique** is a particular method of doing an activity, usually a method that involves practical skills. ❑ ...tests performed using a new technique. ◆2 N-UNCOUNT **Technique** is skill and ability in an artistic, sporting, or other practical activity that you develop through training and practice. ❑ He went off to the Amsterdam Academy to improve his technique.

■ 가산명사 기술 ❑ 신기술을 사용하여 수행된 검사
■ 불가산명사 기법 ❑ 그는 자신의 기법을 향상시키기 위해 암스테르담 아카데미로 떠났다.

tech|no|logi|cal /tɛknəlɒdʒɪkᵊl/ ADJ **Technological** means relating to or associated with technology. [ADJ n] ❑ ...an era of very rapid technological change. ● tech|no|logi|cal|ly /tɛknəlɒdʒɪkli/ ADV ❑ ...technologically advanced aircraft.

형용사 기술의 ❑ 대단히 급속한 기술 변화의 시대
● 기술적으로 부사 ❑ 기술적으로 발달한 항공기

Word Link techn ≈ art, skill : technical, technician, technology

tech|nol|ogy ♦♦◇ /tɛknɒlədʒi/ (technologies) N-VAR **Technology** refers to methods, systems, and devices which are the result of scientific knowledge being used for practical purposes. ❑ Technology is changing fast. ❑ They should be allowed to wait for cheaper technologies to be developed.
→see Word Web: **technology**

가산명사 또는 불가산명사 과학 기술 ❑ 과학 기술은 급속히 변화하고 있다. ❑ 그들에게 더 저렴한 기술이 개발되는 것을 기다리도록 허락해야 한다.

Word Partnership   technology의 연어

ADJ.	**advanced** technology, **available** technology, **educational** technology, **high** technology, **latest** technology, **medical** technology, **modern** technology, **new** technology, **sophisticated** technology, **wireless** technology
N.	**computer** technology, **information** technology, **science and** technology

te|di|ous /tidiəs/ ADJ If you describe something such as a job, task, or situation as **tedious**, you mean it is boring and rather frustrating. ❑ Such lists are long and tedious to read. ● te|di|ous|ly ADV ❑ ...the most tediously boring aspects of international relations.

형용사 지루한, 싫증나는 ❑ 그런 명단은 길고 읽기 지루하다. ● 지루하게 부사 ❑ 국제 관계에서 가장 지루하고 따분한 측면

teem /tim/ (teems, teeming, teemed) V-I If you say that a place **is teeming with** people or animals, you mean that it is crowded and the people and animals are moving around a lot. [usu cont] ❑ For most of the year, the area is teeming with tourists.

자동사 들끓다, 많이 있다 ❑ 거의 연중 내내, 그 지역에는 관광객들이 들끓는다.

teen /tin/ (teens) ◆1 N-PLURAL If you are in your **teens**, you are between thirteen and nineteen years old. ❑ Most people who smoke began smoking in their teens. ◆2 ADJ **Teen** is used to describe things such as movies, magazines, bands, or activities that are aimed at or are done by people who are in their teens. [ADJ n] ❑ ...a teen movie starring George Carlin.

■ 복수명사 십 대 (13세에서 19세) ❑ 대부분의 흡연자들은 십 대 때 담배를 피우기 시작했다.
■ 형용사 십 대를 대상으로 한; 십 대가 만든 ❑ 조지 칼린이 출연한 십 대 영화

teen|age /tineɪdʒ/ ◆1 ADJ **Teenage** children are aged between thirteen and nineteen years old. [ADJ n] ❑ Almost one in four teenage girls now smoke. ◆2 ADJ **Teenage** is used to describe things such as movies, magazines, bands, or activities that are aimed at or are done by teenage children. [ADJ n] ❑ ..."Smash Hits," a teenage magazine.

■ 형용사 십 대의 (13세에서 19세의) ❑ 오늘날 십 대 소녀들은 거의 네 명 중 한 명꼴로 담배를 피운다.
■ 형용사 십 대를 대상으로 한; 십 대가 만든 ❑ 십 대 잡지인 '스매시 히츠'

Word Link teen ≈ plus ten, from 13-19 : eighteen, seventeen, teenager

teen|ager ♦◇◇ /tineɪdʒər/ (teenagers) N-COUNT A **teenager** is someone who is between thirteen and nineteen years old. ❑ As a teenager he attended Tulse Hill Senior High School. →see **age, child**

가산명사 십 대 (소년·소녀) ❑ 그는 십 대일 때 털스 힐 고등학교에 다녔다.

tee|ter /titər/ (teeters, teetering, teetered) ◆1 V-I **Teeter** is used in expressions such as **teeter on the brink** and **teeter on the edge** to emphasize that something seems to be in a very unstable situation or position. [EMPHASIS] ❑ Three of the hotels are in receivership, and others are teetering on the brink of bankruptcy. ◆2 V-I If someone or something **teeters**, they shake in an unsteady way, and seem to be about to lose their balance and fall over. ❑ Hyde shifted his weight and felt himself teeter forward, beginning to overbalance.

■ 자동사 -의 위기에 처하다 [강조] ❑ 그 호텔들 중 세 곳은 법정 관리에 들어가 있고, 다른 곳들은 파산 위기에 처해 있다. ■ 자동사 기우뚱거리다, 흔들리다 ❑ 하이드는 무게 중심을 이동시키자 몸이 앞쪽으로 기우뚱거리는 것을 느끼며 균형을 잃기 시작했다.

teeth /tiθ/ **Teeth** is the plural of **tooth**. →see **face**
→see Word Web: **teeth**

tooth의 복수형

teeth|ing prob|lems /tiðɪŋ prɒbləmz/ N-PLURAL If a project or new product has **teething problems**, it has problems in its early stages or when it first becomes available. [BRIT] ❑ There are bound to be teething problems with something so new.

복수명사 초창기 문제 [영국영어] ❑ 그렇게 새로운 것에는 초창기 문제가 있기 마련이다.

Word Web   technology

Innovative **technologies** affect every aspect of our lives. **State-of-the-art** computer systems coordinate heating, lighting, communication, and entertainment systems in new homes. **Gadgets** such as **digital** music players the size of a pack of gum are common. The high-tech trend also has a more serious side. **Biotechnology** may help us find cures for diseases, but it also raises many ethical questions. **Cutting-edge** biometric technology is replacing old-fashioned security systems. Soon your ATM will check your identity by scanning the iris of your eye and your laptop will scan your fingerprint.

Word Web   teeth

Dentists suggest **brushing** and flossing every day to help prevent **cavities**. Brushing removes food from the surface of the **teeth**. Flossing helps remove the **plaque** that forms between teeth and **gums**. In many places, the water supply contains **fluoride** which also helps keep teeth healthy. If **tooth decay** does develop, a dentist can use a metal or plastic **filling** to repair the tooth. A badly damaged or broken tooth may require a **crown**. Orthodontists use **braces** to straighten uneven rows of teeth. Occasionally, a dentist must remove all of a patient's teeth. Then **dentures** take the place of natural teeth.

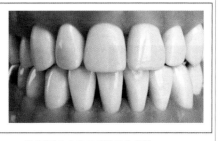

tele|com|mu|ni|ca|tions /tɛlɪkəmyunɪkeɪʃ⁰nz/ N-UNCOUNT
Telecommunications is the technology of sending signals and messages over long distances using electronic equipment, for example by radio and telephone. ❏ *...the UK telecommunications industry.*

불가산명사 통신 ❏ 영국 통신 산업

tele|com|mut|ing /tɛlɪkəmyutɪŋ/ N-UNCOUNT **Telecommuting** is the same as **teleworking**. [BUSINESS]

불가산명사 재택 근무 [경제]

tele|con|fer|ence /tɛlɪkɒnfərəns, -frəns/ (**teleconferences**) N-COUNT A **teleconference** is a meeting involving people in various places around the world who use telephones or video links to communicate with each other. [BUSINESS] ❏ *Managers at their factory in Birmingham hold a two-hour teleconference with head office in Stuttgart every day.* ● **tele|con|fer|enc|ing** N-UNCOUNT ❏ *...teleconferencing facilities.*

가산명사 원격 회의 [경제] ❏ 버밍엄 공장에 있는 관리자들은 슈투트가르트의 본사와 매일 두 시간씩 원격 회의를 한다. ● 원격 회의 불가산명사 ❏ 원격 회의 설비

Word Link   gram ≈ writing : dia*gram*, pro*gram*, tele*gram*

tele|gram /tɛlɪgræm/ (**telegrams**) N-COUNT A **telegram** is a message that is sent by telegraph and then printed and delivered to someone's home or office. [also *by* N] ❏ *The President received a briefing by telegram.*

가산명사 전보, 전신 ❏ 대통령은 전보로 요약 보고를 받았다.

tele|mar|ket|ing /tɛlɪmɑrkɪtɪŋ/ N-UNCOUNT **Telemarketing** is a method of selling in which someone employed by a company telephones people to try and persuade them to buy the company's products or services. [BUSINESS] ❏ *As postal rates go up, many businesses have been turning to telemarketing as a way of contacting new customers.*

불가산명사 전화 판촉, 텔레마케팅 [경제] ❏ 우편 요금이 상승함에 따라, 많은 사업체들이 새로운 고객들을 접촉하는 방법으로 전화 판촉에 의존해 오고 있다.

tele|path|ic /tɛlɪpæθɪk/ ADJ If you believe that someone is **telepathic**, you believe that they have mental powers which cannot be explained by science, such as being able to communicate with other people's minds, and know what other people are thinking. ❏ *About half the subjects considered themselves to be telepathic.*

형용사 정신 감응 능력이 있는 ❏ 피실험자들의 절반 가량이 자신이 정신 감응 능력이 있다고 생각했다.

Word Link   tele ≈ distance : *tele*vision, *tele*pathy, *tele*phone

te|lepa|thy /tɪlɛpəθi/ N-UNCOUNT If you refer to **telepathy**, you mean the direct communication of thoughts and feelings between people's minds, without the need to use speech, writing, or any other normal signals. ❏ *Many of us find it very difficult to state our needs. We expect people to know by telepathy what we are feeling.*

불가산명사 텔레파시, 정신 감응 ❏ 우리들 중 많은 사람들이 자기 요구를 진술하는 데 몹시 어려움을 겪는다. 우리는 사람들이 우리가 느끼는 바를 텔레파시로 알기를 기대한다.

tele|phone ♦♦◇ /tɛlɪfoʊn/ (**telephones, telephoning, telephoned**)
■ N-UNCOUNT The **telephone** is the electrical system of communication that you use to talk directly to someone else in a different place. You use the telephone by dialing a number on a piece of equipment and speaking into it. ❏ *They usually exchanged messages by telephone.* ❏ *I dread to think what our telephone bill is going to be.* ■ N-COUNT A **telephone** is the piece of equipment that you use when you talk to someone by telephone. ❏ *He got up and answered the telephone.* ■ V-T/V-I If you **telephone** someone, you dial their telephone number and speak to them by telephone. ❏ *I felt so badly I had to telephone Owen to say I was sorry.* ■ PHRASE If you are **on the telephone**, you are speaking to someone by telephone. ❏ *Linda remained on the telephone to the police for three hours.*

■ 불가산명사 전화 ❏ 그들은 보통 전화로 연락을 주고받았다. ❏ 우리 전화 요금이 얼마나 나올지 생각하면 두렵다. ■ 가산명사 전화기 ❏ 그는 일어나서 전화를 받았다. ■ 타동사/자동사 전화를 걸다, 전화로 이야기하다 ❏ 나는 기분이 아주 좋지 않아서 오웬에게 전화를 걸어 미안하다고 말해야 했다. ■ 구 통화 중인 ❏ 린다는 세 시간 동안 계속 경찰과 통화 중이었다.

tele|sales /tɛlɪseɪlz/ N-UNCOUNT **Telesales** is the selling of a company's products or services by telephone, either by phoning possible customers or by answering calls from customers. [BUSINESS] ❏ *Many people start their careers in telesales.*

불가산명사 전화 판매 [경제] ❏ 많은 사람들이 직장 생활을 전화 판매로 시작한다.

tele|scope /tɛlɪskoʊp/ (**telescopes**) N-COUNT A **telescope** is a long instrument shaped like a tube. It has lenses inside it that make distant things seem larger and nearer when you look through it. ❏ *It's hoped that the telescope will enable scientists to see deeper into the universe than ever before.*

가산명사 망원경 ❏ 과학자들이 망원경으로 지금껏 어느 때보다도 더 깊이 우주를 들여다볼 수 있을 것이 기대된다.

tele|vise /tɛlɪvaɪz/ (**televises, televising, televised**) V-T If an event or program is **televised**, it is broadcast so that it can be seen on television. [usu passive] ❏ *The Grand Prix will be televised by the BBC.*

타동사 텔레비전으로 방송되다 ❏ 비비시가 그랑프리 경주를 방송할 것이다.

tele|vi|sion ♦♦◇ /tɛlɪvɪʒ⁰n, -vɪʒ-/ (**televisions**) ■ N-COUNT A **television** or **television set** is a piece of electrical equipment consisting of a box with a glass screen on it on which you can watch programs with pictures and sounds. ❏ *She turned the television on and flicked around between news programmes.* ■ N-UNCOUNT **Television** is the system of sending pictures and sounds by electrical signals over a distance so that people can receive them on a television in their home. ❏ *Toy manufacturers began promoting some of their products on television.* ■ N-UNCOUNT **Television** refers to all the programs that you can watch. ❏ *I don't have much time to watch very much television.* ■ N-UNCOUNT **Television** is the business or industry concerned with making programs and broadcasting them on television. ❏ *British commercial television has been steadily losing its lead as the most advanced sector of the industry in Europe.* →see **advertising** →see Word Web: **television**

■ 가산명사 텔레비전 ❏ 그녀는 텔레비전을 켜서 뉴스 프로그램을 이리저리 돌려 댔다. ■ 불가산명사 텔레비전 (방송 체계) ❏ 장난감 제조사들이 일부 상품의 텔레비전 광고를 시작했다. ■ 불가산명사 텔레비전 (프로그램) ❏ 나는 텔레비전을 많이 볼 시간이 많지 않다. ■ 불가산명사 텔레비전 관련 산업 ❏ 영국 상업 텔레비전 산업은 유럽에서 가장 앞선 산업 분야로서의 우위를 계속 상실해 오고 있다.

a
b
c
d
e
f
g
h
i
j
k
l
m
n
o
p
q
r
s
t
u
v
w
x
y
z

Word Web   television

For many years, all **televisions** used cathode-ray tubes to produce a picture. In the tube, a stream of **electrons** from one end strikes a **screen** at the other end. This creates tiny lighted areas called **pixels**. The average cathode-ray TV screen has about 200,000 pixels. Recently, however, high definition TV has become very popular. Ground **stations**, **satellites**, and **cables** still supply the TV **signal**. However, high definition television creates its picture using **digital** information on a flat screen. Digital **receivers** can display two million pixels per square inch. This produces an extraordinarily clear **image**.

tele|work|ing /tɛliwɜrkɪŋ/ N-UNCOUNT **Teleworking** is working from home using equipment such as telephones, fax machines, and modems to contact people. [BUSINESS] ❑ *There is also the potential to develop teleworking and other more flexible working practices.*

불가산명사 재택근무 [경제] ❑ 재택근무와 보다 융통성 있는 여타의 근무 방식을 발전시킬 가능성 역시 존재한다.

tell ♦♦♦ /tɛl/ (**tells, telling, told**) **1** V-T If you **tell** someone something, you give them information. ❑ *In the evening I returned to tell Phyllis our relationship was over.* ❑ *I called Andie to tell her how spectacular the stuff looked.* ❑ *Claire had made me promise to tell her the truth.* **2** V-T If you **tell** something such as a joke, a story, or your personal experiences, you communicate it to other people using speech. ❑ *His friends say he was always quick to tell a joke.* ❑ *He told his story to The Sunday Times and produced photographs.* **3** V-T If you **tell** someone **to** do something, you order or advise them to do it. ❑ *A passer-by told the driver to move his car so that it was not causing an obstruction.* **4** V-T If you **tell yourself** something, you put it into words in your own mind because you need to encourage or persuade yourself about something. ❑ *"Come on," she told herself.*

1 타동사 알리다, 말하다 ❑ 나는 저녁 때 돌아와서 필리스에게 우리의 관계가 끝났음을 알렸다. ❑ 나는 앤디에게 전화해서 그것이 얼마나 봐 만했는지 알려 주었다. ❑ 클레어는 내가 자기한테 사실을 말하겠다고 약속하도록 만들어 났었다. **2** 타동사 말하다, 이야기하다 ❑ 그는 언제나 농담을 잘 했다고 그의 친구들이 말한다. ❑ 그는 '선데이 타임스'에 자신의 이야기를 하고 사진을 제출했다. **3** 타동사 지시하다, 충고하다 ❑ 지나가는 사람 하나가 운전사에게 길을 막지 않도록 차를 옮기라고 말했다. **4** 타동사 (마음속으로) 말하다 ❑ "힘내." 그녀는 스스로에게 말했다.

5 V-T If you can **tell** what is happening or what is true, you are able to judge correctly what is happening or what is true. [no cont, oft with brd-neg] ❑ *It was already impossible to tell where the bullet had entered.* **6** V-T If you can **tell** one thing **from** another, you are able to recognize the difference between it and other similar things. [no cont, oft with brd-neg] ❑ *I can't really tell the difference between their policies and ours.* ❑ *How do you tell one from another?* **7** V-I If you **tell**, you reveal or give away a secret. [INFORMAL] ❑ *Many of the children know who they are but are not telling.* **8** V-T If facts or events **tell** you something, they reveal certain information to you through ways other than speech. ❑ *The facts tell us that this is not true.* ❑ *I don't think the unemployment rate ever tells us much about the future.* **9** V-I If an unpleasant or tiring experience begins to **tell**, it begins to have a serious effect. ❑ *It wasn't long before the strain began to tell on our relationship.* **10** →see also **telling** **11** PHRASE You use **as far as I can tell** or **so far as I could tell** to indicate that what you are saying is based on the information you have, but that there may be things you do not know. [VAGUENESS] ❑ *As far as I can tell, Jason is basically a nice guy.* **12** CONVENTION You can say "**I tell you**," "**I can tell you**," or "**I can't tell you**" to add emphasis to what you are saying. [INFORMAL, EMPHASIS] ❑ *I tell you this, I will not rest until that day has come.* **13** CONVENTION If someone disagrees with you or refuses to do what you suggest and you are eventually proved to be right, you can say "**I told you so.**" [INFORMAL] ❑ *Her parents did not approve of her decision and, if she failed, her mother would say, "I told you so."* **14** CONVENTION You use **I'll tell you what** or **I tell you what** to introduce a suggestion or a new topic of conversation. [SPOKEN] ❑ *I tell you what, I'll bring the water in a separate glass.* **15** to **tell the time** →see **time. time will tell** →see **time**

5 타동사 분간하다, 알다 ❑ 총알이 어디로 들어갔는지 아는 것은 이미 불가능하다. **6** 타동사 구별하다 ❑ 정말이지 그들의 정책과 우리의 정책 사이의 차이점을 구별할 수가 없다. ❑ 어떻게 하나를 다른 것과 구별하지? **7** 자동사 말하다, 털어 놓다 [비격식체] ❑ 많은 아이들이 그들이 누군지 알지만 털어놓지 않고 있다. **8** 타동사 알려 주다, 보여 주다 ❑ 그 사실은 우리에게 이것이 사실이 아님을 알려 준다. ❑ 실업률이 미래에 대해 많은 것을 우리에게 알려 준다고 생각하지 않는다. **9** 자동사 문제가 생기다, 좋지 않은 영향을 미치다 ❑ 오래지 않아 그런 긴장으로 말미암아 우리의 관계에 문제가 생기기 시작했다. **11** 구 -가 말할 수 있는 한에서 [짐작투] ❑ 내가 말할 수 있는 한에서, 제이슨은 원래 멋진 녀석이다. **12** 관용 표현 정말이지, 참으로 [비격식체, 강조] ❑ 정말이지 난 그 날이 올 때까지 쉬지 않을 것이다. **13** 관용 표현 그러게 내가 뭤어 [비격식체] ❑ 그녀의 부모는 그녀의 결정에 찬성하지 않았고, 그녀가 실패한다면 어머니는 이렇게 말할 것이었다. "그러게 내가 뭤랬니." **14** 관용 표현 내 말 좀 들어 봐 [구어체] ❑ 내 말 좀 들어 봐, 내가 다른 잔에다가 물을 받아 올게.

Note that the verb **tell** is usually followed by a direct object indicating the person who is being addressed. ❑ *He told Alison he was suffering from leukemia... What did she tell you?* "What did she tell to you?" is wrong. With the verb **say**, however, if you want to mention the person who is being addressed, you should use the preposition **to**. "What did she say you?" is wrong. "**What did she say to you?**" is correct. **Tell** is used to report information that is given to someone. ❑ *The manufacturer told me that the product did not contain corn.* **Tell** can also be used with a "to" infinitive to report an order or instruction. ❑ *My mother told me to shut up and eat my dinner.* **Say** is the most general verb for reporting the words that someone speaks.

동사 tell은 대개 말을 듣는 사람을 나타내는 직접 목적어가 뒤에 온다. ❑ 그는 자기가 백혈병을 앓고 있다고 앨리슨에게 말했다... 그녀가 당신에게 뭐라고 했나요? "What did she tell to you?"는 틀렸다. 동사 say로 쓸 때 말을 듣는 사람을 언급하고 싶으면, 전치사 to를 써야 한다는 점을 유의하라. "What did she say you?"는 틀렸고, "What did she say to you?"가 맞다. tell은 누군가에게 주어진 정보를 전달할 때 쓴다. ❑ 제조업자가 내게 그 상품에는 옥수수가 들어 있지 않다고 말했다. tell은 to부정사와 함께 써서 명령문이나 지시문을 전달할 수 있다. ❑ 우리 어머니가 내게 그만 떠들고 저녁을 먹으라고 하셨다. say는 누가 하는 말을 전달하는 데 쓰는 가장 일반적인 동사다.

Thesaurus   tell의 참조어

v.   communicate, disclose, inform, state **1** **2**
     advise, declare, order **3**

▶**tell apart** PHRASAL VERB If you can **tell** people or things **apart**, you are able to recognize the differences between them and can therefore identify each of them. ❑ *Perhaps it is the almost universal use of flavorings that makes it so hard to tell the products apart.*

구동사 식별하다, 구별하다 ❑ 아마도 각기 다른 제품들을 그처럼 구별하기 어렵게 만드는 것은 바로, 거의 보편적인 조미료 사용일 것이다.

▶**tell off** PHRASAL VERB If you **tell** someone **off**, you speak to them angrily or seriously because they have done something wrong. ❑ *He never listened to us when we told him off.* ❑ *I'm always being told off for being so awkward.*

구동사 야단치다, 책망하다 ❑ 그는 우리가 야단칠 때 우리 얘기를 듣는 법이 없었다. ❑ 나는 항상 서투르다고 야단을 맞는다.

tell|er /tɛlər/ (**tellers**) N-COUNT A **teller** is someone who works in a bank and who customers pay money to or get money from. [mainly AM or SCOTTISH] ❑ *Every bank pays close attention to the speed and accuracy of its tellers.*

가산명사 금전 출납원 [주로 미국영어 또는 스코틀랜드영어] ❑ 모든 은행은 금전 출납원의 속도와 정확성에 세심한 주의를 기울인다.

tell|ing /tɛlɪŋ/ (**tellings**) **1** N-VAR The **telling** of a story or of something that has happened is the reporting of it to other people. ❑ *Herbert sat quietly through the telling of this saga.* **2** ADJ If something is **telling**, it shows the true nature of a

1 가산명사 또는 불가산명사 이야기하기 ❑ 허버트는 이 무용담이 이야기되는 내내 조용히 앉아 있었다. **2** 형용사 (성격 등을) 드러내 주는 ❑ 남자가 면도하는

person or situation. ❑ *How a man shaves may be a telling clue to his age.* ● **tell|ing|ly** ADV ❑ *Most tellingly, perhaps, chimpanzees do not draw as much information from the world around them as we do.*

tel|ly /tɛli/ (**tellies**) N-VAR A **telly** is a television. [BRIT, INFORMAL; AM **TV**] ❑ *After a hard day's work most people want to relax in front of the telly.*

temp /tɛmp/ (**temps, temping, temped**) ◼ N-COUNT A **temp** is a person who is employed by an agency that sends them to work in different offices for short periods of time, for example to replace someone who is ill or on vacation. [BUSINESS] ❑ *She began working for the company as a temp.* ◼ V-I If someone is **temping**, they are working as a temp. [BUSINESS] [only cont] ❑ *Like so many aspiring actresses, she ended up waiting tables and temping in office jobs.*

tem|per /tɛmpər/ (**tempers**) ◼ N-VAR If you refer to someone's **temper** or say that they have a **temper**, you mean that they become angry very easily. ❑ *He had a temper and could be nasty.* ❑ *His short temper had become notorious.* ◼ N-VAR Your **temper** is the way you are feeling at a particular time. If you are in a good **temper**, you feel cheerful. If you are in a bad **temper**, you feel angry and impatient. ❑ *I was in a bad temper last night.* ◼ PHRASE If someone is **in a temper** or gets **into a temper**, the way that they are behaving shows that they are feeling angry and impatient. ❑ *She was still in a temper when Colin arrived.* ◼ PHRASE If you **lose** your **temper**, you become so angry that you shout at someone or show in some other way that you are no longer in control of yourself. ❑ *I've never seen him get cross or lose his temper.*

Word Partnership	*temper*의 연어
ADJ.	**bad** temper, **explosive** temper, **quick** temper, **short** temper, **violent** temper ◼
N.	temper **tantrum** ◼
V.	**control** your temper, **have a** temper ◼
	lose your temper ◼

tem|pera|ment /tɛmprəmənt/ (**temperaments**) ◼ N-VAR Your **temperament** is your basic nature, especially as it is shown in the way that you react to situations or to other people. ❑ *His impulsive temperament regularly got him into difficulties.* ◼ N-UNCOUNT **Temperament** is the tendency to behave in an uncontrolled, bad-tempered, or unreasonable way. ❑ *Some of the models were given to fits of temperament.*

tem|pera|men|tal /tɛmprəment°l/ ◼ ADJ If you say that someone is **temperamental**, you are criticizing them for not being calm or quiet by nature, but having moods that change often and suddenly. [DISAPPROVAL] ❑ *He is very temperamental and critical.* ◼ ADJ If you describe something such as a machine or car as **temperamental**, you mean that it often does not work properly. ❑ *I first started cruising in yachts with temperamental petrol engines.*

tem|per|ate /tɛmpərit, -prit/ ADJ **Temperate** is used to describe a climate or a place which is never extremely hot or extremely cold. ❑ *The Nile Valley keeps a temperate climate throughout the year.*

tem|pera|ture ♦◇◇ /tɛmprətʃər/ (**temperatures**) ◼ N-VAR The **temperature** of something is a measure of how hot or cold it is. ❑ *Winter closes in and the temperature drops below freezing.* ◼ N-UNCOUNT Your **temperature** is the temperature of your body. A normal temperature is about 98.6° Fahrenheit. ❑ *His temperature continued to rise and the cough worsened until Tania finally persuaded a doctor to come.* ◼ N-COUNT You can use **temperature** to talk about the feelings and emotions that people have in particular situations. ❑ *There's also been a noticeable rise in the political temperature.* ◼ PHRASE If you **are running a temperature** or if you **have a temperature**, your temperature is higher than it usually is. ❑ *He began to run an extremely high temperature. I begged him to let me call a doctor.* ◼ PHRASE If you **take** someone's **temperature** you use an instrument called a thermometer to measure the temperature of their body in order to see if they are ill. ❑ *He will probably take your child's temperature too.*
→see calories, climate, forecast, greenhouse effect, refrigerator, wind

Word Partnership	*temperature*의 연어
ADJ.	**average** temperature, **high/low** temperature, **normal** temperature ◼
V.	**reach a** temperature ◼
N.	**changes in/of** temperature, temperature **increase**, **ocean** temperature, **rise in** temperature, **room** temperature, **surface** temperature, **water** temperature ◼
	body temperature ◼

In the United States, two different scales are commonly used for measuring temperature. On the **Celsius** (formerly **Centigrade**) scale, used for scientific purposes, water freezes at zero degrees and boils at 100 degrees. On the **Fahrenheit** scale, used for everyday subjects such as the weather and cooking, water freezes at 32 degrees and boils at 212 degrees. In Britain, the Celsius scale is used for most things, including the weather, but some people use the Fahrenheit scale informally.

방법은 그 나이를 드러내 주는 단서가 될 수도 있다. ● **뚜렷이 부사** ❑ 아마도 가장 뚜렷하게는, 침팬지들은 우리만큼 많은 정보를 주변 세계에서 얻지 않는다.

가산명사 또는 불가산명사 텔레비전 [영국영어, 비격식체; 미국영어 TV] ❑ 힘든 하루를 마치고 나면 대부분의 사람들은 텔레비전 앞에서 편히 쉬고 싶어 한다.

◼ 가산명사 임시 직원 [경제] ❑ 그녀는 임시 직원으로 그 회사에서 일하기 시작했다. ◼ 자동사 임시 직원으로서 일하다 [경제] ❑ 많은 야심만만한 여배우들과 마찬가지로, 그녀도 결국 식탁 시중을 들고 임시 사무직 일을 하게 되었다.

◼ 가산명사 또는 불가산명사 성미, 성질 ❑ 그는 성깔이 있었고 심술궂게 굴 수도 있었다. ❑ 그의 성마른 성미는 이미 평판이 나 있었다. ◼ 가산명사 또는 불가산명사 기분 ❑ 그는 지난밤에 기분이 나빴다. ◼ 구 화가 나 ❑ 콜린이 도착했을 때 그녀는 여전히 화가 나 있었다. ◼ 구 성질을 부리다 ❑ 나는 그가 화를 내거나 성질을 부리는 것을 본 적이 없다.

◼ 가산명사 또는 불가산명사 기질, 성질 ❑ 그의 충동적인 기질이 자주 그를 곤란에 처하게 했다. ◼ 불가산명사 신경질, 괴팍함 ❑ 몇몇 모델들은 발작적으로 신경질을 부렸다.

◼ 형용사 괴팍한, 변덕스러운 [탐탁찮음] ❑ 그는 매우 괴팍하고 흠잡기를 좋아한다. ◼ 형용사 말을 잘 안 듣는, 고장이 잦은 ❑ 나는 처음에 말을 잘 듣지 않는 가솔린 엔진이 달린 요트를 타고 항해를 시작했다.

형용사 온화한 ❑ 나일 계곡은 연중 내내 온화한 기후를 유지한다.

◼ 가산명사 또는 불가산명사 온도; 기온 ❑ 겨울이 다가오니 기온이 영하로 떨어진다. ◼ 불가산명사 체온 ❑ 마침내 타냐가 의사를 설득해서 오게 할 때까지 그의 체온은 계속 상승했고 기침도 심해졌다. ◼ 가산명사 감정, 정서 ❑ 정치적 감정 역시 현저히 고조되어 왔다. ◼ 구 열이 있다, 열이 나다 ❑ 그는 아주 심하게 열이 나기 시작했다. 나는 의사를 부르게 해 달라고 그에게 간청했다. ◼ 구 체온을 재다 ❑ 그는 아마 당신 아이의 체온도 잴 것입니다.

미국에서는, 온도 측정에 두 가지 다른 단위가 일반적으로 쓰인다. 과학적인 용도로 쓰이는 Celsius (이전에는 Centigrade) 온도계에서는, 물이 0도일 때 얼고 100도일 때 끓는다. 날씨나 요리같이 일상적인 일에 쓰이는 Fahrenheit 온도계에서는, 물이 32도에서 얼고, 212도일 때 끓는다. 영국에서는, 날씨를 포함해서 대부분의 경우에 Celsius 온도계를 쓰지만, 사람에 따라 비격식적으로 Fahrenheit 온도계를 쓰기도 한다.

a b c d e f g h i j k l m n o p q r s t u v w x y z

tem|plate /ˈtemplɪt, BRIT ˈtempleɪt/ (**templates**) **1** N-COUNT A **template** is a thin piece of metal or plastic which is cut into a particular shape. It is used to help you cut wood, paper, metal, or other materials accurately, or to reproduce the same shape many times. □ *Trace around your template and transfer the design onto a sheet of card.* **2** N-COUNT If one thing is a **template for** something else, the second thing is based on the first thing. □ *The template for Adair's novel is not somebody else's fiction, but fact.*

1 가산명사 형판, 본 □ 형판을 따라서 선을 그은 다음 도안을 마분지에 옮기세요. 2 가산명사 토대, 본 □ 아데어가 쓴 소설의 토대는 다른 사람의 소설이 아니라, 사실이다.

tem|ple ♦◇◇ /ˈtempᵊl/ (**temples**) **1** N-COUNT; N-IN-NAMES A **temple** is a building used for the worship of a god or gods, especially in the Buddhist and Hindu religions, and in ancient Greek and Roman times. □ *...a small Hindu temple.* **2** N-COUNT Your **temples** are the flat parts on each side of the front part of your head, near your forehead. □ *Threads of silver ran through his beard and the hair at his temples.*

1 가산명사; 이름명사 신전, 절, 사원 □ 작은 힌두교 사원 2 가산명사 관자놀이 □ 그의 수염과 관자놀이 부분의 머리카락 사이에는 은빛 백발이 나 있었다.

tem|po /ˈtempoʊ/ (**tempos**)

Tempi can also be used as the plural form.

tempi도 복수형으로 쓸 수 있다.

1 N-SING The **tempo** of an event is the speed at which it happens. □ *...owing to the slow tempo of change in an overwhelmingly rural country.* **2** N-VAR The **tempo** of a piece of music is the speed at which it is played. □ *In a new recording, the Boston Philharmonic tried the original tempo.*

1 단수명사 속도 □ 굉장히 외딴 시골의 느린 변화 속도 때문에 2 가산명사 또는 불가산명사 빠르기, 박자 □ 새 녹음에서, 보스턴 교향악단은 원래 박자를 시도했다.

Word Link	tempo ≈ time : contemporary, temporal, temporary

tem|po|ral /ˈtempərəl/ **1** ADJ **Temporal** powers or matters relate to ordinary institutions and activities rather than to religious or spiritual ones. [FORMAL] [ADJ n] □ *...the spiritual and temporal leader of the Tibetan people.* **2** ADJ **Temporal** means relating to time. [FORMAL] [ADJ n] □ *One is also able to see how specific acts are related to a temporal and spatial context.*

1 형용사 현세의, 속세의 [격식체] □ 티베트 인들의 영적, 현세적 지도자 2 형용사 시간의 [격식체] □ 특정한 행동이 어떻게 시간적·공간적 맥락과 관련을 맺는지도 알 수 있습니다.

tem|po|rary ♦◇◇ /ˈtempəri, BRIT ˈtempərəri/ ADJ Something that is **temporary** lasts for only a limited time. □ *His job here is only temporary.* □ *Most adolescent problems are temporary.* ● **tem|po|rar|ily** /ˌtempəˈreərɪli/ ADV □ *The peace agreement has at least temporarily halted the civil war.*

형용사 임시의, 일시적인 □ 그의 이곳에서의 일자리는 단지 임시직일 뿐이다. □ 청소년기의 문제 대부분은 일시적인 것이다. ● 임시로, 일시적으로 부사 □ 평화 협정이 최소한 일시적으로나마 내전을 중지시켰다.

tempt /tempt/ (**tempts, tempting, tempted**) **1** V-T Something that **tempts** you attracts you and makes you want it, even though it may be wrong or harmful. □ *Reducing the income will further impoverish these families and could tempt an offender into further crime.* □ *It is the fresh fruit that tempts me at this time of year.* **2** V-T If you **tempt** someone, you offer them something they want in order to encourage them to do what you want them to do. □ *...a million dollar marketing campaign to tempt American tourists back to Britain.* □ *Don't let credit tempt you to buy something you can't afford.* **3** →see also **tempted**

1 타동사 유혹하다, 부추기다 □ 소득을 떨어뜨리게 되면 이 가구들은 한층 더 가난해지고 범죄자들로 하여금 더 많은 범죄를 저지르도록 부추길 수도 있다. □ 한 해 중 이맘때 나를 유혹하는 것은 바로 신선한 과일이다. 2 타동사 (뭔가를 주어) 유혹하다, 유도하다 □ 미국 관광객들을 영국으로 돌아오게 하기 위한 백만 달러 예산의 마케팅 캠페인 □ 신용 거래에 혹해서 감당할 여유가 없는 물건을 사지 않도록 하세요.

Word Link	tempt ≈ trying : attempt, temptation, tempted

temp|ta|tion /tempˈteɪʃᵊn/ (**temptations**) N-VAR If you feel you want to do something or have something, even though you know you really should avoid it, you can refer to this feeling as **temptation**. You can also refer to the thing you want to have or do as a **temptation**. □ *Will they be able to resist the temptation to buy?*

가산명사 또는 불가산명사 유혹; 유혹물 □ 그들이 사려는 유혹을 견딜 수 있을 것인가?

tempt|ed /ˈtemptɪd/ ADJ If you say that you are **tempted to** do something, you mean that you would like to do it. [v-link ADJ, usu ADJ to-inf] □ *I'm very tempted to sell my house.*

형용사 -하고 싶은 □ 나는 몹시 집을 팔고 싶다.

tempt|ing /ˈtemptɪŋ/ ADJ If something is **tempting**, it makes you want to do it or have it. □ *In the end, I turned down Raoul's tempting offer of the Palm Beach trip.* ● **tempt|ing|ly** ADV □ *The good news is that prices are still temptingly low.*

형용사 마음을 끄는, 솔깃한 □ 결국, 나는 팜비치 여행을 가자는 라울의 솔깃한 제안을 거절했다. ● 마음을 끌 만큼, 구미가 당기게 부사 □ 좋은 소식은 물가가 여전히 구미가 당기게 낮다는 것이다.

ten ♦♦♦ /ten/ (**tens**) NUM **Ten** is the number 10. □ *Over the past ten years things have changed.*

수사 10, 십, 열 □ 지난 십 년간에 걸쳐 사정이 변해 왔다.

te|na|cious /tɪˈneɪʃəs/ ADJ If you are **tenacious**, you are very determined and do not give up easily. □ *He is regarded at the BBC as a tenacious and persistent interviewer.* ● **te|na|cious|ly** ADV □ *In spite of his illness, he clung tenaciously to his job.*

형용사 고집이 센, 집요한 □ 그는 비비시에서 집요하고 끈질긴 탐방 기자로 여겨진다. ● 집요하게 부사 □ 그는 병에도 불구하고 집요하게 자기 일에 매달렸다.

te|nac|ity /tɪˈnæsɪti/ N-UNCOUNT If you have **tenacity**, you are very determined and do not give up easily. □ *Talent, hard work and sheer tenacity are all crucial to career success.*

불가산명사 고집, 끈기 □ 재능과 노력, 그리고 순전한 끈기 모두가 일에서 성공하는 데 필수적이다.

ten|an|cy /ˈtenənsi/ (**tenancies**) N-VAR **Tenancy** is the use that you have of land or property belonging to someone else, for which you pay rent. □ *His father took over the tenancy of the farm 40 years ago.*

가산명사 또는 불가산명사 (땅 등의) 차용, 임차 □ 그의 아버지는 40년 전에 그 농장을 임차로 넘겨받았다.

ten|ant /ˈtenənt/ (**tenants**) N-COUNT A **tenant** is someone who pays rent for the place they live in, or for buildings or land that they use. □ *Regulations placed clear obligations on the landlord for the benefit of the tenant.*

가산명사 임차인, 세입자 □ 법규에 의하면 집주인에게는 세입자의 권익을 위한 뚜렷한 의무가 주어져 있었다.

tend ♦♦◇ /tend/ (**tends, tending, tended**) **1** V-T If something **tends to** happen, it usually happens or it often happens. □ *A problem for manufacturers is that lighter cars tend to be noisy.* **2** V-I If you **tend toward** a particular characteristic, you often display that characteristic. □ *Artistic and intellectual people tend towards left-wing views.* **3** V-T You can say that you **tend to** think something when you want to give your opinion, but do not want it to seem too forceful or definite. [VAGUENESS] □ *I tend to think that members of parliament by and large do a good job.*

1 타동사 (-하는) 경향이 있다 □ 제조사들에게 한 가지 문제는 경차가 소음이 큰 경향이 있다는 것이다. 2 자동사 성향을 띠다 □ 예술가나 지식인들은 좌파적 성향을 띤다. 3 타동사 -이지 않나 싶다 (의견을 완곡하게 표현할 때) [짐작투] □ 국회의원들이 대체로 일을 잘 하고 있지 않나 싶다.

Word Partnership	tend의 연어
V.	tend **to avoid**, tend **to become**, tend **to develop**, tend **to forget**, tend **to happen**, tend **to lose**, tend **to stay 1**
	tend **to agree**, tend **to blame**, tend **to feel**, tend **to think 1 3**
N.	**Americans** tend, **children/men/women** tend, **people** tend **1 2**

ten|den|cy ◆◇◇ /tɛndənsi/ (**tendencies**) ■ N-COUNT A **tendency** is a worrying or unpleasant habit or action that keeps occurring. ❑ *The army has become increasingly restless over the mounting separatist tendencies of the northern republics.* ❷ N-COUNT A **tendency** is a part of your character that makes you behave in an unpleasant or worrying way. ❑ *He is spoiled, arrogant and has a tendency towards snobbery.*

■ 가산명사 경향 ❑ 군대는 북부 공화국의 커져 가는 분리주의자 성향 때문에 점점 더 가만히 못 있게 되었다. ❷ 가산명사 (좋지 않은) 성향, 기질 ❑ 그는 버릇없고 거만하며 속물 기질이 있다.

Thesaurus	tendency의 참조어
N.	habit, inclination, predisposition, weakness ■ ❷

--- **tender** ---

① ADJECTIVE USES
② NOUN AND VERB USES

① **ten|der** /tɛndər/ (**tenderer, tenderest**) ■ ADJ Someone or something that is **tender** expresses gentle and caring feelings. ❑ *Her voice was tender, full of pity.* ● **ten|der|ly** ADV [ADV with v] ❑ *Mr. White tenderly embraced his wife.* ● **ten|der|ness** N-UNCOUNT ❑ *She smiled, politely rather than with tenderness or gratitude.* ❷ ADJ If you say that someone does something at a **tender** age, you mean that they do it when they are still young and have not had much experience. [ADJ n] ❑ *He had become attracted to the game at the tender age of seven.* ❸ ADJ Meat or other food that is **tender** is easy to cut or chew. ❑ *Cook for a minimum of 2 hours, or until the meat is tender.* ❹ ADJ If part of your body is **tender**, it is sensitive and painful when it is touched. ❑ *My tummy felt very tender.* ● **ten|der|ness** N-UNCOUNT ❑ *There is still some tenderness in her tummy.*

■ 형용사 상냥한, 친절한 ❑ 그녀의 목소리는 상냥하고 동정심이 가득 담겨 있었다. ● 상냥하게, 친절하게 부사 ❑ 화이트 씨는 상냥하게 아내를 껴안았다. ● 상냥함, 친절함 불가산명사 ❑ 그녀는 상냥하다거나 감사하는 마음으로라기보다는, 공손하게 미소를 지었다. ❷ 형용사 어린, 미숙한 ❑ 그는 일곱 살이라는 어린 나이에 그 경기에 끌렸다. ❸ 형용사 부드러운 ❑ 최소 2시간 동안, 아니면 고기가 부드러워질 때까지 익히세요. ❹ 형용사 예민한, 만지면 아픈 ❑ 배를 만지면 무척 아팠다. ● 만지면 느껴지는 통증 불가산명사 ❑ 그녀는 여전히 배에 만지면 느껴지는 통증이 약간 있다.

② **ten|der** /tɛndər/ (**tenders, tendering, tendered**) ■ N-VAR A **tender** is a formal offer to supply goods or to do a particular job, and a statement of the price that you or your company will charge. If a contract is **put out to tender**, formal offers are invited. If a company **wins a tender**, their offer is accepted. [BUSINESS] ❑ *Builders will then be sent the specifications and asked to submit a tender for the work.* ❷ V-I If a company **tenders for** something, it makes a formal offer to supply goods or do a job for a particular price. [BUSINESS] ❑ *The staff are forbidden to tender for private-sector work.* ❸ →see also **legal tender**

■ 가산명사 또는 불가산명사 입찰 [경제] ❑ 그런 다음 건축업자들은 설계 명세서를 받고 그 공사에 대해 입찰하라는 요구를 받을 것이다. ❷ 자동사 입찰하다 [경제] ❑ 그 직원들이 민간 부문 공사에 입찰하는 것은 금지되어 있다.

ten|don /tɛndən/ (**tendons**) N-COUNT A **tendon** is a strong cord in a person's or animal's body which joins a muscle to a bone. ❑ *...a torn tendon in his right shoulder.*

가산명사 힘줄, 건(腱) ❑ 그의 오른쪽 어깨에 찢어진 힘줄

ten|ement /tɛnəmənt/ (**tenements**) ■ N-COUNT A **tenement** is a large, old building which is divided into a number of individual apartments. ❑ *...elegant 19th century tenement buildings.* ❷ N-COUNT A **tenement** is one of the apartments in a tenement. ❑ *...the cramped Edinburgh tenement in which Connery grew up.*

■ 가산명사 공동 주택, 아파트 ❑ 격조 있는 19세기 아파트 건물 ❷ 가산명사 공동 주택 (내의 한 집) ❑ 코너리가 자란 비좁은 에든버러의 공동 주택

ten|et /tɛnɪt/ (**tenets**) N-COUNT The **tenets** of a theory or belief are the main principles on which it is based. [FORMAL] ❑ *Non-violence and patience are the central tenets of their faith.*

가산명사 주의, 교의 [격식체] ❑ 비폭력과 인내가 그들 신앙의 중심 교의이다.

ten|nis ◆◇◇ /tɛnɪs/ N-UNCOUNT **Tennis** is a game played by two or four players on a rectangular court. The players use an oval bat with strings across it to hit a ball over a net across the middle of the court. →see **park** →see Picture Dictionary: **tennis**

불가산명사 테니스

ten|or /tɛnər/ (**tenors**) ■ N-COUNT A **tenor** is a male singer whose voice is fairly high. ❑ *...a free, open-air concert given by the Italian tenor, Luciano Pavarotti.* ❷ ADJ A **tenor** saxophone or other musical instrument has a range of notes that are of a fairly low pitch. ❑ *...one of the best tenor sax players ever.*

■ 가산명사 테너 ❑ 이탈리아 테너 루치아노 파바로티가 연 무료 야외 콘서트 ❷ 형용사 (악기) 테너의 ❑ 역대 최고의 테너 색소폰 연주자 중 한 명

tense /tɛns/ (**tenser, tensest, tenses, tensing, tensed**) ■ ADJ A **tense** situation or period of time is one that makes people anxious, because they do not know what is going to happen next. ❑ *This gesture of goodwill did little to improve the tense atmosphere at the talks.* ❷ ADJ If you are **tense**, you are anxious and nervous and

■ 형용사 긴박한, 긴장시키는 ❑ 이런 친선 제스처는 회담에서의 긴박한 분위기를 개선하는 데 별 도움이 되지 않았다. ❷ 형용사 긴장한 ❑ 처음에 매우 긴장했었던 다트가 마침내 긴장을 풀었다. ❸ 형용사

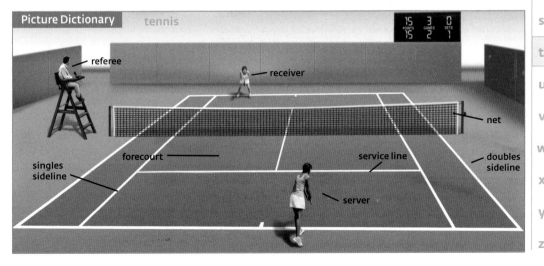

Picture Dictionary   tennis

15 3 0
POINTS GAMES SETS
15 2 1

referee
receiver
net
forecourt
service line
doubles sideline
singles sideline
server

A | cannot relax. ❑ *Dart, who had at first been very tense, at last relaxed.* ◳ ADJ If your body is **tense**, your muscles are tight and not relaxed. ❑ *A bath can relax tense muscles.* ◳ V-T/V-I If your muscles **tense**, if you **tense**, or if you **tense** your muscles, your muscles become tight and stiff, often because you are anxious or frightened. ❑ *Newman's stomach muscles tensed.* ● PHRASAL VERB **Tense up** means the same as **tense**. ❑ *When we are under stress our bodies tend to tense up.* ◳ N-COUNT The **tense** of a verb group is its form, which usually shows whether you are referring to past, present, or future time. ❑ *It was as though Corinne was already dead: they were speaking of her in the past tense.*

긴장된 ❑ 목욕을 하면 긴장된 근육을 풀 수 있다. ◳ 타동사/자동사 긴장하다; 긴장시키다 ❑ 뉴먼의 복근이 긴장되었다. ● 구동사 긴장하다; 긴장시키다 ❑ 스트레스를 받을 때 우리 몸은 긴장되는 경향이 있다. ◳ 가산명사 시제 ❑ 마치 코린이 이미 죽은 것 같았다. 그들은 그녀에 대해 과거 시제로 이야기하고 있었다.

Word Partnership | tense의 연어

N.	tense **atmosphere**, tense **moment**, tense **situation** ◳
	tense **mood** ◳
	muscles tense ◳ ◳
	future/past/present tense ◳
ADV.	**very** tense ◳-◳
V.	**feel** tense ◳ ◳

ten|sion ◆◇◇ /tɛnʃ°n/ (tensions) ◳ N-UNCOUNT **Tension** is the feeling that is produced in a situation when people are anxious and do not trust each other, and when there is a possibility of sudden violence or conflict. [also N in pl] ❑ *The tension between the two countries is likely to remain.* ◳ N-UNCOUNT **Tension** is a feeling of worry and anxiety which makes it difficult for you to relax. [also N in pl] ❑ *Smiling and laughing has actually been shown to relieve tension and stress.* ◳ N-VAR If there is a **tension** between forces, arguments, or influences, there are differences between them that cause difficulties. ❑ *The film explored the tension between public duty and personal affections.* ◳ N-UNCOUNT The **tension** in something such as a rope or wire is the extent to which it is stretched tight. ❑ *As the cable wraps itself around the wheel, there is provision for adjusting the tension of the cable.*

◳ 불가산명사 긴장 ❑ 그 두 나라 간의 긴장은 지속될 것 같다. ◳ 불가산명사 긴장감, 불안 ❑ 미소와 웃음이 실제로 불안과 스트레스를 경감하는 것으로 증명되었다. ◳ 가산명사 또는 불가산명사 긴장, 갈등 ❑ 그 영화는 공적인 의무감과 사적인 애정 사이의 갈등을 탐구했다. ◳ 불가산명사 장력 ❑ 케이블이 바퀴에 감길 때, 케이블의 장력을 조절해 주는 설비가 있다.

Word Partnership | tension의 연어

V.	**ease** tension, tension **grows**, tension **mounts**, **relieve** tension ◳ ◳ ◳
N.	**source of** tension ◳ ◳ ◳ ◳
ADJ.	**racial** tension ◳ ◳

tent /tɛnt/ (tents) N-COUNT A **tent** is a shelter made of canvas or nylon which is held up by poles and ropes, and is used mainly by people who are camping.

가산명사 텐트, 천막

ten|ta|cle /tɛntək°l/ (tentacles) ◳ N-COUNT The **tentacles** of an animal such as an octopus are the long thin parts that are used for feeling and holding things, for getting food, and for moving. ◳ N-COUNT If you talk about the **tentacles** of a political, commercial, or social organization, you are referring to the power and influence that it has in the outside community. [DISAPPROVAL] ❑ *Free speech is being gradually eroded year after year by new tentacles of government control.*

◳ 가산명사 촉수 ◳ 가산명사 (비유적) 촉수 [탐탁찮음] ❑ 정부 통제라는 새로운 촉수가 언론의 자유를 해를 거듭할수록 점차 좁먹고 있다.

ten|ta|tive /tɛntətɪv/ ◳ ADJ **Tentative** agreements, plans, or arrangements are not definite or certain, but have been made as a first step. ❑ *Political leaders have reached a tentative agreement to hold a preparatory conference next month.* ● **ten|ta|tive|ly** ADV [ADV with v] ❑ *The next round of talks is tentatively scheduled to begin October 21st in Washington.* ◳ ADJ If someone is **tentative**, they are cautious and not very confident because they are uncertain or afraid. ❑ *My first attempts at complaining were rather tentative.* ● **ten|ta|tive|ly** ADV [ADV with v] ❑ *Perhaps, he suggested tentatively, they should send for Dr. Band.*

◳ 형용사 잠정적인 ❑ 정치 지도자들이 다음 달 사전 회의를 열기로 잠정 합의를 봤다. ● 잠정적으로 부사 ❑ 차기 회담은 10월 21일 워싱턴에서 시작하는 것으로 잠정적으로 일정이 잡혀 있다. ◳ 형용사 망설이는, 자신 없는 ❑ 나는 처음 불만을 제기하려 할 때 다소 망설였다. ● 망설이며, 자신 없어 하며 부사 ❑ 아마 그가 망설이면서 그들에 밴드 박사를 불러와야 할 것이라고 말했을 것이다.

tenth ◆◇◇ /tɛnθ/ (tenths) ◳ ORD The **tenth** item in a series is the one that you count as number ten. ❑ *...her tenth birthday.* ◳ FRACTION A **tenth** is one of ten equal parts of something. ❑ *He finished three-tenths of a second behind Prost.*

◳ 서수 열 번째의 ❑ 그녀의 열 번째 생일 ◳ 분수 10분의 1, 1/10 ❑ 그는 프로스트보다 0.3초 늦게 결승선을 통과했다.

tenu|ous /tɛnyuəs/ ADJ If you describe something such as a connection, a reason, or someone's position as **tenuous**, you mean that it is very uncertain or weak. ❑ *The cultural and historical links between the many provinces were seen to be very tenuous.*

형용사 빈약한, 보장성없는 ❑ 여러 지방 간의 문화적·역사적인 관계가 매우 빈약해 보였다.

ten|ure /tɛnyər/ ◳ N-UNCOUNT **Tenure** is the legal right to live in a particular building or to use a particular piece of land during a fixed period of time. ❑ *Lack of security of tenure was a reason for many families becoming homeless.* ◳ N-UNCOUNT **Tenure** is the period of time during which someone holds an important job. ❑ *...the three-year tenure of President Bush.*

◳ 불가산명사 (건물이나 토지의) 거주권, 사용권 ❑ 건물 사용권이 보장되지 않아 집 없는 가족들이 많이 생겨나기도 했다. ◳ 불가산명사 재임 기간, 임기 ❑ 부시 대통령 임기 3년

tep|id /tɛpɪd/ ADJ Water or another liquid that is **tepid** is slightly warm. ❑ *She bent her mouth to the tap and drank the tepid water.*

형용사 미지근한 ❑ 그녀는 몸을 숙여 수도꼭지에 입을 대고 미지근한 물을 마셨다.

term ◆◆◆ /tɜrm/ (terms, terming, termed) ◳ PHRASE If you talk about something **in terms of** something or in particular **terms**, you are specifying which aspect of it you are discussing or from what point of view you are considering it. ❑ *Our goods compete in terms of product quality, reliability and above all variety.* ◳ PHRASE If you say something **in particular terms**, you say it using a particular type or level of language or using language which clearly shows your attitude. ❑ *The video explains in simple terms how the new tax works.* ◳ N-COUNT A **term** is a word or expression with a specific meaning, especially one which is used in relation to a particular subject. ❑ *Myocardial infarction is the medical term for a heart attack.* ◳ V-T If you say that something **is termed** a particular thing, you mean that that is what people call it or that is their opinion of it. ❑ *He had been termed a temporary employee.* ◳ N-VAR A **term** is one of the periods of time that a school, college, or university divides the year into. ❑ *...the summer*

◳ 구 - 측면에서 ❑ 우리 상품은 품질과 신뢰성 그리고 무엇보다도 다양성 측면에서 경쟁력이 있다. ◳ 구 - 한 말로 ❑ 그 비디오에서 새로운 세금이 운영되는 방식을 쉬운 말로 설명해 준다. ◳ 가산명사 용어, 전문 용어 ❑ 심근 경색이란 심장 마비를 뜻하는 의학 용어이다. ◳ 타동사 불리다 ❑ 그는 임시 노동자라고 불렸다. ◳ 가산명사 또는 불가산명사 ◳ 가산명사 임기 ❑ 스페인의 펠리페 곤잘레스가 재선에 성공해 세 번째 임기를 맡게 됐다. ◳ 가산명사 기간 ❑ 12개월의 근무 기간 ◳ 가산명사 계약 기간 ❑ 보험료는 보험 계약 기간 내내 보장된다. ◳ 불가산명사 임신 기간; 출산 예정 시기 ❑ 이로써 그녀는 텔레비전 뉴스 진행자 중에 최초로 임신 기간

term. ⑥ N-COUNT A **term** is a period of time between two elections during which a particular party or government is in power. ❑ *Felipe Gonzalez won a fourth term of office in Spain's election.* ⑦ N-COUNT A **term** is a period of time that someone spends doing a particular job or in a particular place. ❑ *...a 12 month term of service.* ⑧ N-COUNT A **term** is the period for which a legal contract or insurance policy is valid. ❑ *Premiums are guaranteed throughout the term of the policy.* ⑨ N-UNCOUNT The **term** of a woman's pregnancy is the nine month period that it lasts. **Term** is also used to refer to the end of the nine month period. ❑ *That makes her the first TV presenter to work the full term of her pregnancy.* ⑩ N-PLURAL The **terms** of an agreement, treaty, or other arrangement are the conditions that must be accepted by the people involved in it. ❑ *...the terms of the Helsinki agreement.* ⑪ PHRASE If you **come to terms with** something difficult or unpleasant, you learn to accept and deal with it. ❑ *She had come to terms with the fact that her husband would always be crippled.* ⑫ PHRASE If two people or groups compete **on equal terms** or **on the same terms**, neither of them has an advantage over the other. ❑ *I had at last found a sport where I could compete on equal terms with able-bodied people.* ⑬ PHRASE If two people are **on good terms** or **on friendly terms**, they are friendly with each other. ❑ *Madeleine is on good terms with Sarah.* ⑭ PHRASE You use the expressions **in the long term**, **in the short term**, and **in the medium term** to talk about what will happen over a long period of time, over a short period of time, and over a medium period of time. ❑ *The agreement should have very positive results in the long term.* →see also **long-term**, **medium-term**, **short-term** ⑮ PHRASE If you do something **on** your **terms**, you do it under conditions that you decide because you are in a position of power. ❑ *They will sign the union treaty only on their terms.* ⑯ PHRASE If you say that you **are thinking in terms of** doing a particular thing, you mean that you are considering it. ❑ *United should be thinking in terms of winning the European Cup.* ⑰ **in no uncertain terms** →see **uncertain**. **in real terms** →see **real**

내내 일한 여성이 된다. ⑩ 복수명사 조건 ❑ 헬싱키 협약 조건 ⑪ 구 받아들이다, 타협하다 ❑ 그녀는 남편이 영원히 불구로 살아야 한다는 사실을 받아들이게 됐다. ⑫ 구 동등한 조건에서 ❑ 나는 드디어 신체 건강한 사람과 동등한 조건에서 경쟁할 수 있는 스포츠를 발견했다. ⑬ 구 사이좋은 ❑ 마들렌은 사라와 사이가 좋다. ⑭ 구 장기적으로; 단기적으로; 중기적으로 ❑ 협약은 장기적으로 매우 긍정적인 결과를 낳아야 한다. ⑮ 구 ~가 원하는 조건으로 ❑ 그들은 자신이 원하는 조건으로만 동맹 협약을 맺을 것이다. ⑯ 구 고려하고 있다 ❑ 유나이티드는 유러피언 컵 우승을 고려하고 있을 것이다.

ter|mi|nal /tˈɜrmɪnᵊl/ (**terminals**) ① ADJ A **terminal** illness or disease causes death, often slowly, and cannot be cured. ❑ *...terminal cancer.* ● **ter|mi|nal|ly** ADV [ADV adj] ❑ *The patient is terminally ill.* ② N-COUNT A **terminal** is a place where vehicles, passengers, or goods begin or end a journey. [usu supp N] ❑ *Plans are underway for a fifth terminal at Heathrow airport.* ③ N-COUNT A computer **terminal** is a piece of equipment consisting of a keyboard and a screen that is used for putting information into a computer or getting information from it. [COMPUTING] ❑ *Carl sits at a computer terminal 40 hours a week.* ④ N-COUNT On a piece of electrical equipment, a **terminal** is one of the points where electricity enters or leaves it. ❑ *...the positive terminal of the battery.*

① 형용사 말기의, 불치의 ❑ 말기 암 ● 말기에, 불치병에 걸려 부사 ❑ 그 사람은 불치병 환자이다. ② 가산명사 터미널 ❑ 히드로 공항 다섯 번째 터미널 건설 계획이 진행 중이다. ③ 가산명사 (컴퓨터) 단말기 [컴퓨터] ❑ 칼은 일주일에 40시간을 컴퓨터 단말기 앞에서 보낸다. ④ 가산명사 전극, 단자 ❑ 건전지 양극

ter|mi|nate /tˈɜrmɪneɪt/ (**terminates, terminating, terminated**) ① V-T/V-I When you **terminate** something or when it **terminates**, it ends completely. [FORMAL] ❑ *Her next remark abruptly terminated the conversation.* ● **ter|mi|na|tion** /tˌɜrmɪnˈeɪʃᵊn/ N-UNCOUNT ❑ *...a dispute which led to the abrupt termination of trade.* ② V-T To **terminate** a pregnancy means to end it. [MEDICAL] ❑ *After a lot of agonizing she decided to terminate the pregnancy.* ● **ter|mi|na|tion** (**terminations**) N-VAR ❑ *You should also have a medical check-up after the termination of a pregnancy.* ③ V-I When a train or bus **terminates** somewhere, it ends its journey there. [FORMAL] ❑ *This train will terminate at Taunton.*

① 타동사/자동사 끝내다, 종결시키다 [격식체] ❑ 그녀의 다음 발언으로 대화가 갑자기 중단됐다. ● 중단, 종결 불가산명사 ❑ 갑작스런 무역 중단으로 이어진 분쟁 ② 타동사 낙태하다 [의학] ❑ 그녀는 수많은 번민 끝에 낙태하기로 결심했다. ● 유산, 낙태 가산명사 또는 불가산명사 ❑ 낙태 후에는 건강 검진도 받아야 한다. ③ 자동사 종착하다, 끝나다 [격식체] ❑ 이 열차의 종착역은 톤턴이다.

ter|mi|nol|ogy /tˌɜrmɪnˈɒlədʒi/ (**terminologies**) N-VAR The **terminology** of a subject is the set of special words and expressions used in connection with it. ❑ *...gastritis, which in medical terminology means an inflammation of the stomach.*

가산명사 또는 불가산명사 용어, 전문 용어 ❑ 의학 용어로 위에 생긴 염증을 뜻하는 위염

ter|race /tˈɛrɪs/ (**terraces**) ① N-COUNT A **terrace** is a flat area of stone or grass next to a building where people can sit. ❑ *Some guests recline in lounge chairs on the sea-facing terrace.* ② N-COUNT **Terraces** are a series of flat areas built like steps on the side of a hill so that crops can be grown there. ❑ *...massive terraces of maize and millet carved into the mountainside like giant steps.* ③ N-COUNT; N-IN-NAMES A **terrace** is a row of similar houses joined together by their side walls. [BRIT] ❑ *...a terrace of stylish Victorian houses.*

① 가산명사 테라스 ❑ 손님 몇 명이 바다가 보이는 테라스 안락의자에 편하게 앉아 있다. ② 가산명사 계단식 논밭 ❑ 마치 산 경사면을 따라 새긴 거대한 층계 같은, 옥수수와 기장을 심은 계단식 밭 ③ 가산명사; 이름명사 연립 주택 [영국영어] ❑ 빅토리아조 양식으로 지은 우아한 연립 주택

ter|raced house /tˈɛrɪst haʊs/ (**terraced houses**) N-COUNT A **terraced house** or a **terrace house** is one of a row of similar houses joined together by their side walls. [BRIT; AM **row house**]

가산명사 연립 주택 한 채 [영국영어; 미국영어 row house]

terra|cotta /tˌɛrəkˈɒtə/ also **terra-cotta** N-UNCOUNT **Terracotta** is a brownish-red clay that has been baked and is used for making things such as flower pots, small statues, and tiles. ❑ *...plants in terracotta pots.*

불가산명사 테라코타 ❑ 테라코타 화분에 담긴 화초

ter|rain /tˈɛreɪn/ (**terrains**) N-VAR **Terrain** is used to refer to an area of land or a type of land when you are considering its physical features. ❑ *The terrain changed quickly from arable land to desert.*

가산명사 또는 불가산명사 지형, 지역 ❑ 그 지역은 경작지에서 사막으로 급격히 바뀌었다.

ter|res|trial /tɪrˈɛstriəl/ ① ADJ **Terrestrial** means relating to the planet Earth rather than to some other part of the universe. [ADJ n] ❑ *...terrestrial life forms.* ② ADJ **Terrestrial** television channels are transmitted using equipment situated at ground level, and not by satellite. [BRIT] ❑ *...the BBC's terrestrial channels.*

① 형용사 지구의 ❑ 지구 생명체 ② 형용사 지상의 [영국영어] ❑ 비비시 지상파 방송

ter|ri|ble ♦♦◇ /tˈɛrɪbᵊl/ ① ADJ A **terrible** experience or situation is very serious or very unpleasant. ❑ *Tens of thousands more suffered terrible injuries in the world's worst industrial disaster.* ❑ *I often have the most terrible nightmares.* ● **ter|ri|bly** ADV [ADV after v] ❑ *My son has suffered terribly. He has lost his best friend.* ② ADJ If something is **terrible**, it is very bad or of very poor quality. ❑ *She admits her French is terrible.* ③ ADJ You use **terrible** to emphasize the great extent or degree of something. [EMPHASIS] [ADJ n] ❑ *I was a terrible fool, you know. I remember that now.* ● **ter|ri|bly** ADV ❑ *I'm terribly sorry to bother you at this hour.*

① 형용사 끔찍한, 심한 ❑ 지상 최악의 산업 재해로 수만 명의 사람들이 추가로 끔찍한 부상을 당했다. ❑ 나는 종종 아주 무시무시한 악몽을 꾼다. ● 끔찍하게, 심하게 부사 ❑ 내 아들은 심하게 앓았다. 가장 친한 친구를 잃은 것이다. ② 형용사 형편없는 ❑ 그녀도 자기 불어 실력이 형편없다고 인정한다. ③ 형용사 지독한 [강조] ❑ 자네도 알다시피 나는 지독한 바보였네. 이제야 기억이 나는군. ● 굉장히 부사 ❑ 이 시간에 귀찮게 해서 너무 죄송해요.

A

ter|rif|ic /tərɪfɪk/ **1** ADJ If you describe something or someone as **terrific**, you are pleased with them or very impressed by them. [INFORMAL] ❑ *What a terrific idea!* **2** ADJ **Terrific** means very great in amount, degree, or intensity. [EMPHASIS] [ADJ n] ❑ *All of a sudden there was a terrific bang and a flash of smoke.*

　　■ 형용사 멋진, 훌륭한 [비격식체] ❑ 아주 멋진 생각이야! ■ 형용사 굉장한, 엄청난 [강조] ❑ 갑자기 엄청난 소리와 함께 연기가 폭발했다.

B

ter|ri|fy /tɛrɪfaɪ/ **(terrifies, terrifying, terrified)** V-T If something **terrifies** you, it makes you feel extremely frightened. ❑ *Flying terrifies him.* ● **ter|ri|fied** ADJ ❑ *He was terrified of heights.*

　　타동사 무섭게 하다, 겁먹게 하다 ❑ 그는 비행기 타는 것을 무서워한다. ● 무서워 하는, 겁먹은 형용사 ❑ 그는 고소 공포증이 있었다.

C

ter|ri|fy|ing /tɛrɪfaɪɪŋ/ ADJ If something is **terrifying**, it makes you very frightened. ❑ *I still find it terrifying to find myself surrounded by large numbers of horses.*

　　형용사 무서운, 겁나는 ❑ 나는 아직도 말 여러 마리에 둘러싸이면 겁이 난다.

D

ter|ri|to|rial /tɛrɪtɔriəl/ **1** ADJ **Territorial** means concerned with the ownership of a particular area of land or water. ❑ *It is the only republic which has no territorial disputes with the others.* **2** ADJ If you describe an animal or its behavior as **territorial**, you mean that it has an area which it regards as its own, and which it defends when other animals try to enter it. ❑ *Two cats or more in one house will also exhibit territorial behavior.*

E

　　■ 형용사 영토의 ❑ 이 나라는 다른 나라와 영토 분쟁이 없는 유일한 공화국이다. ■ 형용사 (동물의) 영역 다툼과 관련된 ❑ 한 집에 고양이가 두 마리 이상 있을 때도 영역 다툼과 관련된 행동이 나타날 것이다.

F

ter|ri|to|ry ◆◇◇ /tɛrətɔri, BRIT tɛrətri/ **(territories)** **1** N-VAR **Territory** is land which is controlled by a particular country or ruler. ❑ *The government denies that any of its territory is under rebel control.* **2** N-COUNT A **territory** is a country or region that is controlled by another country. ❑ *He toured some of the disputed territories now under UN control.* **3** N-UNCOUNT You can use **territory** to refer to an area of knowledge or experience. [with supp] ❑ *Following the futuristic The Handmaid's Tale, Margaret Atwood's seventh novel, Cat's Eye, returns to more familiar territory.* **virgin territory** →see **virgin** **4** N-VAR An animal's **territory** is an area which it regards as its own and which it defends when other animals try to enter it. ❑ *The territory of a cat only remains fixed for as long as the cat dominates the area.* **5** N-UNCOUNT **Territory** is land with a particular character. ❑ *...mountainous territory.*

G

H

I

　　■ 가산명사 또는 불가산명사 영토 ❑ 정부는 반군의 통제하에 있는 영토가 전혀 없다고 주장한다. ■ 가산명사 관할지, 보호령 ❑ 그는 현재 유엔 관할하에 있는 분쟁 지역 일부를 돌아봤다. ■ 불가산명사 영역 ❑ 마가렛 애트우드는 미래주의적인 '하녀 이야기' 다음에 출판된 일곱 번째 소설 '고양이의 눈'에서 좀 더 친숙한 영역으로 돌아왔다. ■ 가산명사 또는 불가산명사 세력권, 영역 ❑ 한 고양이의 세력권은 그 고양이가 해당 지역을 지배하는 동안에만 그대로 남아 있다. ■ 불가산명사 지역 ❑ 산간 지역

Word Partnership
*territory*의 연어

N.	**enemy** territory, **part of a** territory **1 2**
ADJ.	**vast** territory **1**-**3**
	familiar territory **3**

J

K

L

ter|ror /tɛrər/ **(terrors)** **1** N-UNCOUNT **Terror** is very great fear. ❑ *I shook with terror whenever I was about to fly in an aeroplane.* **2** N-UNCOUNT **Terror** is violence or the threat of violence, especially when it is used for political reasons. ❑ *The bomb attack on the capital could signal the start of a pre-election terror campaign.* **3** N-COUNT A **terror** is something that makes you very frightened. ❑ *As a boy, he had a real terror of facing people.*

M

　　■ 불가산명사 공포 ❑ 나는 비행기를 타고 날아오르는 순간이 올 때마다 공포에 떨었다. ■ 불가산명사 테러 ❑ 수도 폭탄 공격은 선거 전 테러 공격의 시작을 알리는 신호일 수 있다. ■ 가산명사 공포의 대상 ❑ 그는 어린 시절 사람을 대하는 것을 정말 두려워했다.

Word Partnership
*terror*의 연어

N.	**acts of** terror, terror **alert**, terror **attack**, terror **campaign**, **fight against** terror, **reign of** terror, terror **suspects 2**

N

O

ter|ror|ism /tɛrərɪzəm/ N-UNCOUNT **Terrorism** is the use of violence, especially murder and bombing, in order to achieve political aims or to force a government to do something. [DISAPPROVAL] ❑ *...the threat of global terrorism.*

　　불가산명사 테러리즘, 테러 행위 [탐탁잖음] ❑ 국제 테러리즘 위협

P

ter|ror|ist ◆◇◇ /tɛrərɪst/ **(terrorists)** N-COUNT A **terrorist** is a person who uses violence, especially murder and bombing, in order to achieve political aims. [DISAPPROVAL] ❑ *One American was killed and three were wounded in terrorist attacks.*

　　가산명사 테러리스트 [탐탁잖음] ❑ 테러 공격으로 미국인 한 명이 죽고 세 명이 부상당했다.

Q

ter|ror|ize /tɛrəraɪz/ **(terrorizes, terrorizing, terrorized)** [BRIT also **terrorise**] V-T If someone **terrorizes** you, they keep you in a state of fear by making it seem likely that they will attack you. ❑ *Bands of gunmen have hijacked food shipments and terrorized relief workers.*

　　[영국영어 terrorise] 타동사 공포의 도가니로 몰아넣다, 위협하다 ❑ 저격수 일당이 수송 중인 음식을 강탈하고 구조 요원들을 위협했다.

R

terse /tɜrs/ **(terser, tersest)** ADJ A **terse** statement or comment is brief and unfriendly. ❑ *He issued a terse statement, saying he is discussing his future with colleagues before announcing his decision on Monday.* ● **terse|ly** ADV [ADV with v] ❑ *"It's too late," he said tersely.*

　　형용사 간단한, 퉁명스러운 ❑ 그는 월요일에 결정을 발표하기 전에 동료들과 자신의 장래에 대해 의논하고 있다고 짧게 말할 것이다. ● 짧게, 퉁명스럽게 부사 ❑ "너무 늦었어."라고 그가 짧게 쏘아붙였다.

S

T

ter|ti|ary /tɜrʃiɛri, BRIT tɜːʃəri/ **1** ADJ **Tertiary** means third in order, third in importance, or at a third stage of development. [FORMAL] ❑ *He must have come to know those philosophers through secondary or tertiary sources.* **2** ADJ **Tertiary education** is education at university or college level. [BRIT; AM **higher education**] [ADJ n] ❑ *...institutions of tertiary education.*

　　■ 형용사 제 3의, 제 3차의 [격식체] ❑ 그는 분명히 아는 사람이나 제 3자를 통해 그와 같은 철학자들을 알게 되었을 것이다. ■ 형용사 고등 교육 [영국영어; 미국영어 higher education] ❑ 고등 교육 기관

U

test ◆◆◆ /tɛst/ **(tests, testing, tested)** **1** V-T When you **test** something, you try it, for example by touching it or using it for a short time, in order to find out what it is, what condition it is in, or how well it works. ❑ *Either measure the temperature with a bath thermometer or test the water with your wrist.* **2** N-COUNT A **test** is a deliberate action or experiment to find out how well something works. ❑ *...the banning of nuclear tests.* **3** V-T If you **test** someone, you ask them questions or tell them to perform certain actions in order to find out how much they know about a subject or how well they are able to do something. ❑ *There was a time when each teacher spent an hour, one day a week, testing pupils in every subject.* **4** N-COUNT A **test** is a series of questions that you must answer or actions that you must perform in order to show how much you know about a subject or how well you are able to do something. ❑ *Out of a total of 2,602 pupils only 922 passed the test.* **5** V-T If you **test** someone, you deliberately make things difficult for them in order to see how they react. ❑ *From the first day, Rudolf was testing me, seeing if I would make him tea, bring him a Coke.* **6** N-COUNT If an event or situation is a **test of** a person or thing, it reveals their qualities or effectiveness. ❑ *It is a commonplace fact that holidays are a major test of any*

V

W

X

Y

Z

　　■ 타동사 시험해 보다, 실험하다 ❑ 욕조용 온도계로 온도를 재거나 물에 손목을 대어 보아라. ■ 가산명사 시험, 실험 ❑ 핵 실험 금지 ■ 타동사 시험하다, 테스트하다 ❑ 선생님이라면 모두 일주일에 한 번 한 시간씩 각 과목에 대해 학생들에게 시험을 치게 하던 시절이 있었다. ■ 가산명사 시험 ❑ 총 학생 2,602명 가운데 922명만이 그 시험에 통과했다. ■ 타동사 시험하다 ❑ 루돌프는 내가 차를 끓여 주거나 콜라를 갖다 주는지 보면서 첫날부터 나를 시험하고 있었다. ■ 가산명사 시금석, 시험대 ❑ 명절은 모든 인간관계의 깊이를 가늠할 수 있는 좋은 기회라는 것은 다들 아는 사실이다. ■ 타동사 검사받다 ❑ 내 주치의가 당뇨병 검사를 받아 보라고 했다. ■ 가산명사 검사, 검진 ❑ 필요할 경우 진단을 돕기 위해 엑스레이나 피 검사도 할 것이다. ■ 구 시험하다 ❑ 연구팀이 개발한 이론이 이제 시험 단계에 들어갔다. ■ 구 시험하다 ❑ 조만간 삶이 관계를 시험할 것이다. 가장 탄탄한 기반을 가진

relationship. **7** V-T If you **are tested for** a particular disease or medical condition, you are examined or go through various procedures in order to find out whether you have that disease or condition. [usu passive] ❑ *My doctor wants me to be tested for diabetes.* **8** N-COUNT A medical **test** is an examination of a part of your body in order to check that you are healthy or to find out what is wrong with you. ❑ *If necessary X-rays and blood tests will also be used to aid diagnosis.* **9** PHRASE If you **put** something **to the test**, you find out how useful or effective it is by using it. ❑ *The team are now putting their theory to the test.* **10** PHRASE If new circumstances or events **put** something **to the test**, they put a strain on it and indicate how strong or stable it really is. ❑ *Sooner or later, life will put the relationship to the test – and it's those relationships with the strongest foundations that weather the course.* **11** PHRASE If you say that something **will stand the test of time**, you mean that it is strong or effective enough to last for a very long time. ❑ *It says a lot for her culinary skills that so many of her recipes have stood the test of time.* **12** **test the waters →**see **water**

Student knowledge or skill can be measured by a **test**. If the test is not long or a significant share of the total grade, it may be called a **quiz**. An **examination** is a comprehensive test that contributes either all or a major portion of the final grade.

학생의 지식이나 기능은 test(평가)를 통해 측정할 수 있다. 평가가 길지 않거나 전체 성적의 중요한 몫을 차지하지 않을 때는 이를 quiz라고 부르기도 한다. examination(시험)은 최종 성적에서 전체 또는 주된 부분을 차지하는 종합적인 평가이다.

Word Partnership   test의 연어

N.	test **a** drug, test **a** hypothesis **1**
	flight test, strength test, stress test **2**
	achievement test, aptitude test, test data/results, intelligence test, test items, math/reading test, test preparation, test scores **4**
	blood test, drug test, HIV test, pregnancy test **8**
ADJ.	nuclear test **2**
	diagnostic test **2 4 8**
	test negative/positive **7**
V.	administer a test, fail a test, give *someone* a test, pass a test, study for a test, take a test **4**

tes|ta|ment /tɛstəmənt/ (**testaments**) **1** N-VAR If one thing is a **testament to** another, it shows that the other thing exists or is true. [FORMAL] ❑ *Braka's house, just off Sloane Square, is a testament to his Gothic tastes.* **2** PHRASE Someone's **last will and testament** is the most recent will that they have made, especially the last will that they make before they die. [LEGAL]

test case (**test cases**) N-COUNT A **test case** is a legal case which becomes an example for deciding other similar cases. ❑ *If this test case is successful, it could open the door for anyone knowingly transmitting a sexual disease to be charged.*

tes|ti|cle /tɛstɪkᵊl/ (**testicles**) N-COUNT A man's **testicles** are the two sex glands between his legs that produce sperm.

tes|ti|fy /tɛstɪfaɪ/ (**testifies, testifying, testified**) V-T/V-I When someone **testifies** in a court of law, they give a statement of what they saw someone do or what they know of a situation, after having promised to tell the truth. ❑ *Several eyewitnesses testified that they saw the officers hit Miller in the face.* ❑ *Eva testified to having seen Herndon with his gun on the stairs.*

tes|ti|mo|nial /tɛstɪmoʊniəl/ (**testimonials**) **1** N-COUNT A **testimonial** is a written statement about a person's character and abilities, often written by their employer. ❑ *She could hardly expect her employer to provide her with testimonials to her character and ability.* **2** N-COUNT A **testimonial** is an event which is held to honor someone for their services or achievements. ❑ *...a testimonial dinner held in New York.*

tes|ti|mo|ny /tɛstɪmoʊni, BRIT tɛstɪməni/ (**testimonies**) **1** N-VAR In a court of law, someone's **testimony** is a formal statement that they make about what they saw someone do or what they know of a situation, after having promised to tell the truth. ❑ *His testimony was an important element of the Prosecution case.* **2** N-UNCOUNT If you say that one thing is **testimony to** another, you mean that it shows clearly that the second thing has a particular quality. [also *a* N, usu N to n] ❑ *The environmental movement is testimony to the widespread feelings of support for nature's inherent worth.*
→see **trial**

test|ing ◆◇◇ /tɛstɪŋ/ **1** ADJ A **testing** problem or situation is very difficult to deal with and shows a lot about the character of the person who is dealing with it. ❑ *The most testing time is undoubtedly in the early months of your return to work.* **2** N-UNCOUNT **Testing** is the activity of testing something or someone in order to find out information. ❑ *...product testing and labelling.*

tes|tos|ter|one /tɛstɒstəroʊn/ N-UNCOUNT **Testosterone** is a hormone found in men and male animals, which can also be produced artificially. It is thought to be responsible for the male sexual instinct and other male characteristics.

teth|er /tɛðər/ (**tethers, tethering, tethered**) **1** PHRASE If you say that you are **at the end of** your **tether**, you mean that you are so worried, tired, and unhappy because of your problems that you feel you cannot cope. ❑ *She was jealous, humiliated, and emotionally at the end of her tether.* **2** N-COUNT A **tether** is a rope or chain which is used to tie an animal to a post or fence so that it can only move around within a small area. ❑ *...a dog that choked to death on its tether.* **3** V-T If you **tether** an animal or object to something, you attach it there with a rope or chain so that it cannot move very far. ❑ *The officer dismounted, tethering his horse to a tree.*

text ◆◇◇ /tɛkst/ (**texts, texting, texted**) **1** N-SING The **text** of a book is the main part of it, rather than the pictures, notes, or notes. ❑ *The text is precise*

관계만이 이 과정을 견뎌 낸다. **11** 구 오랜 세월에도 불구하고 견뎌하다 ❑ 그녀가 개발한 많은 조리법이 이 오랜 세월을 견뎌 냈다는 사실이 그녀의 음식 솜씨를 잘 말해 준다.

1 가산명사 또는 불가산명사 증거 [격식체] ❑ 슬로안 스퀘어 바로 옆에 있는 자택은 브라카의 고딕 취향을 잘 보여 준다. **2** 구 가장 최근에 작성한 유언장, 유서 [법률]

가산명사 판례가 되는 소송 사건 ❑ 이번 소송이 성공하여 판례가 되면 알면서도 성병을 전염시키는 사람들을 처벌할 수 있는 길이 열릴 수 있게 된다.

가산명사 고환

타동사/자동사 증언하다 ❑ 경찰관들이 밀러의 얼굴을 때리는 장면을 봤다고 목격 증인 몇 명이 증언했다. ❑ 헌던이 총을 들고 계단에 서 있는 모습을 목격했다고 에바가 증언했다.

1 가산명사 추천서, 증명서 ❑ 그녀는 사장이 그녀의 인품과 능력을 증명하는 추천서를 써 주리라고 거의 기대할 수 없었다. **2** 가산명사 (한 사람의 업적을 기리는) 기념식 ❑ 뉴욕에서 열린 기념식 만찬

1 가산명사 또는 불가산명사 증언 ❑ 그의 증언은 검사 측 주장의 중요한 요소였다. **2** 불가산명사 증명, 증거 ❑ 환경 운동은 많은 사람들이 자연의 내재적 가치를 옹호한다는 증거이다.

1 형용사 힘겨운, 힘난한 ❑ 가장 힘든 시기는 두말 할 필요 없이 직장에 복귀한 후 처음 몇 달 동안이다. **2** 불가산명사 시험 ❑ 제품 시험 및 분류

불가산명사 테스토스테론

1 구 막다른 지경에 이른 ❑ 그녀는 질투심과 모욕감을 느꼈으며 막다른 지경에 이른 기분이었다. **2** 가산명사 줄, 사슬 ❑ 개줄에 묶여 질식해 죽은 개 **3** 타동사 사슬로 묶다, 밧줄로 묶다 ❑ 경관이 말에서 내려와 말을 나무에 묶었다.

1 단수명사 본문 ❑ 본문 자체가 정확하고 유익하며 사진과 삽화가 많아 내용이 더욱 명확하게 전달된다.

a b c d e f g h i j k l m n o p q r s t u v w x y z

and informative, while the many photographs and illustrations enhance its clarity. **2** N-UNCOUNT **Text** is any written material. ❑ *The machine can recognize handwritten characters and turn them into printed text.* **3** N-COUNT The **text** of a speech, broadcast, or recording is the written version of it. ❑ *A spokesman said a text of Dr. Runcie's speech had been circulated to all of the bishops.* **4** N-COUNT A **text** is a book or other piece of writing, especially one connected with science or learning. ❑ *Her text is believed to be the oldest surviving manuscript by a female physician.* **5** N-COUNT A **text** is a written or spoken passage, especially one that is used in a school or university for discussion or in an examination. ❑ *His early plays are set texts in universities.* **6** N-COUNT A **text** is the same as a **text message**. ❑ *The new system can send a text to a cellphone, or to another landline phone.* **7** V-T If you **text** someone, you send them a text message on a cellphone. ❑ *Mary texted me when she got home.* →see **diary**

text|book /tɛkstbʊk/ (**textbooks**) also **text book** **1** N-COUNT A **textbook** is a book containing facts about a particular subject that is used by people studying that subject. ❑ *She wrote a textbook on international law.* **2** ADJ If you say that something is a **textbook** case or example, you are emphasizing that it provides a clear example of a type of situation or event. [EMPHASIS] [ADJ n] ❑ *The house is a textbook example of medieval domestic architecture.*

tex|tile /tɛkstaɪl/ (**textiles**) **1** N-COUNT **Textiles** are types of cloth or fabric, especially ones that have been woven. ❑ *...decorative textiles for the home.* **2** N-PLURAL **Textiles** are the industries concerned with the manufacture of cloth. [no det] ❑ *Another 75,000 jobs will be lost in textiles and clothing.* →see **industry**, **quilt**

text|ing /tɛkstɪŋ/ N-UNCOUNT **Texting** is the same as **text messaging**.

text mes|sage (**text messages**) N-COUNT A **text message** is a message that you send using a cellphone. ❑ *She has sent text messages to her family telling them not to worry.*

text mes|sag|ing N-UNCOUNT **Text messaging** is the sending of written messages using a cellphone. ❑ *...the popularity of text messaging.*

tex|ture /tɛkstʃər/ (**textures**) **1** N-VAR The **texture** of something is the way that it feels when you touch it, for example how smooth or rough it is. ❑ *It is used in moisturizers to give them a wonderfully silky texture.* **2** N-VAR The **texture** of something, especially food or soil, is its structure, for example whether it is light with lots of holes, or very heavy and solid. ❑ *Matured over 18 months, this cheese has an open, crumbly texture with a strong flavor.*

than ♦♦♦ /ðən, STRONG ðæn/ **1** PREP You use **than** after a comparative adjective or adverb in order to link two parts of a comparison. [compar PREP group] ❑ *The radio only weighs a few ounces and is smaller than a cigarette packet.* ● CONJ **Than** is also a conjunction. ❑ *He wished he could have helped her more than he did.* **2** PREP You use **than** when you are stating a number, quantity, or value approximately by saying that it is above or below another number, quantity, or value. [more/less PREP n] ❑ *They talked on the phone for more than an hour.* **3** CONJ You use **than** in order to link two parts of a contrast, for example in order to state a preference. ❑ *The arrangement was more a formality than a genuine partnership of two nations.* **4** less than →see **less**. more. more often than not →see **often**. other than →see **other**. rather than →see **rather**

thank ♦♦♦ /θæŋk/ (**thanks, thanking, thanked**) **1** CONVENTION You use **thank you** or, in more informal English, **thanks** to express your gratitude when someone does something for you or gives you what you want. [FORMULAE] ❑ *Thank you very much for your call.* ❑ *Thanks for the information.* **2** CONVENTION You use **thank you** or, in more informal English, **thanks** to politely accept or refuse something that has just been offered to you. [FORMULAE] ❑ *"You'd like a cup as well, would you, Mr. Secombe?" — "Thank you, Jane, I'd love one."* **3** CONVENTION You use **thank you** or, in more informal English, **thanks** to politely acknowledge what someone has said to you, especially when they have answered your question or said something nice to you. [FORMULAE] ❑ *The policeman smiled at her. "Pretty dog." — "Oh well, thank you."* **4** CONVENTION You use **thank you** or **thank you very much** in order to say firmly that you do not want someone's help or to tell them that you do not like the way that they are behaving towards you. [EMPHASIS] ❑ *I can stir my own tea, thank you.* **5** V-T When you **thank** someone **for** something, you express your gratitude to them for it. ❑ *I thanked them for their long and loyal service.* **6** N-PLURAL When you express your **thanks** to someone, you express your gratitude to them for something. ❑ *They accepted their certificates with words of thanks.* **7** PHRASE You say "**Thank God**," "**Thank Goodness**," or "**Thank heavens**" when you are very relieved about something. [FEELINGS] ❑ *I was wrong, thank God.* **8** PHRASE If you say that you **have** someone **to thank for** something, you mean that you are grateful to them because they caused it to happen. ❑ *I have her to thank for my life.* **9** PHRASE If you say that something happens **thanks to** a particular person or thing, you mean that they are responsible for it happening or caused it to happen. ❑ *It is thanks to this committee that many new sponsors have come forward.*

thank|ful /θæŋkfəl/ ADJ When you are **thankful**, you are very happy and relieved that something has happened. ❑ *Most of the time I'm just thankful that I've got a job.*

thank|ful|ly /θæŋkfəli/ ADV You use **thankfully** in order to express approval or happiness about a statement that you are making. [ADV with cl/group] ❑ *Thankfully, she was not injured.*

Thanks|giving (**Thanksgivings**) N-VAR In the United States, **Thanksgiving** or **Thanksgiving Day** is a public holiday on the fourth Thursday in November. In Canada, it is on the second Monday in October. It was originally a day when people celebrated the end of the harvest and thanked God for it. ❑ *No matter where his business took him, he always managed to be home for Thanksgiving.*

2 불가산명사 글, 문서 ❑ 이 기계는 손으로 쓴 글자를 인식해 환자 문서로 변환시킬 수 있다. **3** 가산명사 원문, 기록 ❑ 룬시 박사 연설 원문이 모든 주교에게 배포되었다고 대변인이 밝혔다. **4** 가산명사 글, 문서 ❑ 그녀의 글은 여의사가 쓴 것으로 지금까지 남아 있는 원고 가운데 가장 오래된 것으로 생각된다. **5** 가산명사 교재 ❑ 그의 초기 희곡들은 대학들의 고정 교재이다. **6** 가산명사 문자 메시지 ❑ 새 시스템을 사용해서 휴대 전화나 다른 유선 전화에 문자 메시지를 보낼 수 있다. **7** 타동사 문자 메시지를 보내다 ❑ 메리가 집에 도착했을 때 나에게 문자 메시지를 보냈다.

1 가산명사 교과서, 교재 ❑ 그녀는 국제법 교재를 썼다. **2** 형용사 교과서적인, 전형적인 [강조] ❑ 이 집은 중세 시대 국내 건축의 전형적인 예이다.

1 가산명사 직물, 옷감 ❑ 집안 장식용 직물 **2** 복수명사 섬유 산업 ❑ 섬유 및 의류 산업에서 일자리 75,000개가 더 줄어들 것이다.

불가산명사 문자 메시지 전송

가산명사 문자 메시지 ❑ 그녀는 가족에게 걱정하지 말라고 문자 메시지를 보냈다.

불가산명사 문자 메시지 전송 ❑ 문자 메시지 전송의 인기

1 가산명사 또는 불가산명사 감촉, 질감 ❑ 이는 놀라울 정도로 부드러운 감촉을 더하기 위해 보습제에 사용된다. **2** 가산명사 또는 불가산명사 조직 ❑ 이 치즈는 18개월 동안 숙성되어 향이 강하고 조직은 구멍이 많아 부서지기 쉽다.

1 전치사 -보다 ❑ 그 라디오는 무게가 몇 온스밖에 안 되며 크기는 담뱃갑보다 작다. ● 접속사 (접속사로) -보다 ❑ 그는 그녀를 실제로 도왔던 것보다 더 도울 수 있었으면 하고 바랬다. **2** 전치사 (more와 함께 쓰여) 이상; (less와 함께 쓰여) 이하 ❑ 그들은 한 시간 이상 전화 통화를 했다. **3** 접속사 -보다는 ❑ 그 협정은 두 국가 간의 진정한 동반자 관계를 뜻한다기보다는 형식적인 것이었다.

1 관용 표현 고맙습니다, 고마워 [의례적인 표현] ❑ 전화 주셔서 매우 감사합니다. ❑ 정보 고맙습니다. **2** 관용 표현 고맙습니다, 고마워 [의례적인 표현] ❑ "세콤 씨 컵도 하나 드릴까요?" "제인, 그래 주시면 고맙겠어요." **3** 관용 표현 고맙습니다, 고마워 [의례적인 표현] ❑ 경찰관이 그녀를 향해 미소지었다. "강아지가 예쁜걸요" "아 네, 고마워요." **4** 관용 표현 됐어요, 됐어 [강조] ❑ 됐어요. 내 차는 내가 저어 마실 수 있어요. **5** 타동사 감사하다, 감사의 뜻을 표하다 ❑ 나는 그들이 오랫동안 성실하게 일해 준 것에 감사의 뜻을 표했다. **6** 복수명사 감사의 뜻, 고마움 ❑ 그들은 감사의 말과 함께 수료증을 받았다. **7** 구 다행이다 [감정 개입] ❑ 내가 잘못 알았던 거구나. 다행이다. **8** 구 -에게 감사하다 ❑ 내게 생명을 준 그분에게 감사한다. **9** 구 -덕분에 ❑ 이 위원회 덕분에 새 스폰서가 많이 생기게 되었다.

형용사 고맙게 생각하는, 감사하는 ❑ 평소에는 내가 직장이 있다는 사실에 감사할 뿐이다.

부사 고맙게도, 다행히도 ❑ 고맙게도 그녀가 다치지 않았다.

가산명사 또는 불가산명사 추수 감사절 ❑ 그는 사업상 어디를 가더라도 항상 추수 감사절만큼은 용케 집에서 보냈다.

A national holiday in the US and a big family occasion, **Thanksgiving** falls on the fourth Thursday in November. It commemorates the first harvest reaped by the **Pilgrims**, the first English settlers, in 1621, for which they gave thanks to God – hence the name of the festival. The traditional meal centers around a roast turkey, followed by "pumpkin pie" for dessert.

미국의 국경일이자 큰 명절인 Thanksgiving(추수감사절)은 11월 네 번째 목요일이다. 추수감사절은 1621년에 미국에 처음 정착한 영국인들인 Pilgrims(청교도들)가 거둔 첫 수확을 기념하는 날인데, 그들은 그런 수확을 거둘 수 있게 해준 하느님께 감사를 드렸고, 거기에서 이 명절의 이름이 나왔다. 이 날의 전통적인 식사에서는 구운 칠면조 요리가 중심이 되고 후식으로는 '호박 파이'가 나온다.

---

that

① DEMONSTRATIVE USES
② CONJUNCTION AND RELATIVE PRONOUN USES

① **that** ♦♦♦ /ðæt/ →Please look at category 20 to see if the expression you are looking for is shown under another headword. **1** PRON You use **that** to refer back to an idea or situation expressed in a previous sentence or sentences. ❑ They said you particularly wanted to talk to me. Why was that? ❑ "Hey, is there anything the matter with my sisters?" — "Is that why you're phoning?" ● DET **That** is also a determiner. ❑ The most important purpose of our Health Care is to support you when making a claim for medical treatment. For that reason the claims procedure is as simple and helpful as possible. **2** DET You use **that** to refer to someone or something already mentioned. ❑ The Commissioners get between £50,000 and £60,000 a year in various allowances. But that amount can soar to £90,000 a year. **3** DET When you have been talking about a particular period of time, you use **that** to indicate that you are still referring to the same period. You use expressions such as **that morning** or **that afternoon** to indicate that you are referring to an earlier period of the same day. ❑ The story was published in a Sunday newspaper later that week. **4** PRON You use **that** in expressions such as **that of** and **that which** to introduce more information about something already mentioned, instead of repeating the noun which refers to it. [FORMAL] [PRON of n, PRON pron-rel] ❑ A recession like that of 1973-74 could put one in ten American companies into bankruptcy. **5** PRON You use **that** in front of words or expressions which express agreement, responses, or reactions to what has just been said. ❑ "She said she'd met you in England." — "That's true." **6** DET You use **that** to introduce a person or thing that you are going to give details or information about. [FORMAL] ❑ In my case I chose that course which I considered right. **7** DET You use **that** when you are referring to someone or something which is a distance away from you in position or time, especially when you indicate or point to them. When there are two or more things near you, **that** refers to the more distant one. ❑ Look at that guy. He's got red socks. ● PRON **That** is also a pronoun. ❑ Leo, what's that you're writing? **8** PRON You use **that** when you are identifying someone or asking about their identity. ❑ "Who's that with you?" — "A friend of mine." **9** DET You can use **that** when you expect the person you are talking to to know what or who you are referring to, without needing to identify the particular person or thing fully. [SPOKEN] ❑ I really thought I was something when I wore that hat and my patent leather shoes. ● PRON **That** is also a pronoun. ❑ That was a terrible case of blackmail in the paper today. **10** ADV If something is **not that** bad, funny, or expensive for example, it is not as bad, funny, or expensive as it might be or as has been suggested. [with brd-neg, ADV adj/adv] ❑ Not even Gary, he said, was that stupid. **11** ADV You can use **that** to emphasize the degree of a feeling or quality. [INFORMAL, EMPHASIS] [ADV adj/adv] ❑ I would have walked out, I was that angry. **12** →see also **those 13** PHRASE You use **and all that** or **and that** to refer generally to everything else which is associated with what you have just mentioned. [INFORMAL, VAGUENESS] ❑ I'm not a cook myself but I am interested in nutrition and that. **14** PHRASE You use **at that** after a statement which modifies or emphasizes what you have just said. [EMPHASIS] ❑ Success never seems to come but through hard work, often physically demanding work at that. **15** PHRASE You use **that is** or **that is to say** to indicate that you are about to express the same idea more clearly or precisely. ❑ I am a disappointing, though generally dutiful, student. That is, I do as I'm told. **16** PHRASE You use **that's it** to indicate that nothing more needs to be done or that the end has been reached. ❑ When he left the office, that was it, the workday was over. **17** CONVENTION You use **that's it** to express agreement with or approval of what has just been said or done. [FORMULAE] ❑ "You got married, right?" — "Yeah, that's it." **18** PHRASE You use **just like that** to emphasize that something happens or is done immediately or in a very simple way, often without much thought or discussion. [INFORMAL, EMPHASIS] ❑ Just like that, I was in love. **19** PHRASE You use **that's that** to say there is nothing more you can do or say about a particular matter. [SPOKEN] ❑ "Well, if that's the way you want it," he replied, tears in his eyes, "I guess that's that." **20** **like that** →see **like**. **this and that** →see **this**. **this, that and the other** →see **this**

② **that** ♦♦♦ /ðət, STRONG ðæt/ **1** CONJ You can use **that** after many verbs, adjectives, nouns, and expressions to introduce a clause in which you report what someone has said, or what they think or feel. ❑ He called her up one day and said that he and his wife were coming to New York. **2** CONJ You use **that** after "it" and a linking verb and an adjective to comment on a situation or fact. ❑ It's interesting that you like him. **3** PRON-REL You use **that** to introduce a clause which gives more information to help identify the person or thing you are talking about. ❑ ...pills that will make the problem disappear. **4** CONJ You use **that** after expressions with "so" and "such" in order to introduce the result or effect of something. ❑ She became so nervous that she shook violently.

thatched /θætʃt/ ADJ A **thatched** house or a house with a **thatched** roof has a roof made of straw or reeds. ❑ ...a 400-year-old thatched cottage.

that's /ðæts/ **That's** is a spoken form of "that is."

1 대명사 그것 ❑ 그들이 말하길 특히 당신이 나와 얘기하고 싶어 했다던데 왜 그런 겁니까? ❑ "이봐, 내 여동생들한테 무슨 문제라도 생긴 거야?" "그래서 당신이 지금 전화하는 거 아니에요?" ● 한정사 그, 그러한 ❑ 건강 보험의 가장 중요한 목표는 치료에 대한 비용을 청구할 때 여러분을 돕는 것입니다. 그러한 이유로 청구 과정이 가능한 한 유용하고 간단하게 되어 있습니다. **2** 한정사 그 ❑ 이사들은 각종 수당으로 일년에 5만–6만 파운드를 받는다. 하지만 그 금액이 일년에 9만 파운드까지 치솟을 수 있다. **3** 한정사 그 ❑ 이 이야기는 그 주 주말 일요판 신문에 실렸다. **4** 대명사 그것, 것 [격식체] ❑ 1973-74년에 일어난 것과 같은 경기 침체가 오면 미국 기업 10개 중 1개가 파산할 수도 있다. **5** 대명사 앞에 언급한 내용을 받아 ❑ "그녀가 영국에서 널 만났다고 하던데." "맞아." **6** 한정사 그런 [격식체] ❑ 나의 경우 내가 옳다고 생각되는 그런 길을 택했다. **7** 한정사 저 ❑ 저 사람 좀 봐. 빨간 양말을 신었어. ● 대명사 저것, 그것 ❑ 레오, 네가 쓰고 있는 게 뭐야? **8** 대명사 그 사람, 저 사람 ❑ "너랑 같이 있는 그 사람 누구니?" "내 친구." **9** 한정사 그 [구어체] ❑ 나는 내가 그 모자랑 에나멜가죽 신발을 신었을 때 뭔 정말 대단한 사람이라도 된 것 같았다. ● 대명사 그것, 그일 ❑ 오늘 신문에 나온 그것은 끔찍한 협박 사건이었다. **10** 부사 그렇게, 그다지 ❑ 심지어 게리도 그렇게 멍청하지는 않았다고 그가 말했다. **11** 부사 그만큼 [비격식체, 강조] ❑ 나는 그냥 나가 버리려고 했었다. 그만큼 화가 났던 것이다. **12** 구 뭐 그런 것 [비격식체, 점작투] ❑ 나 자신이 요리를 잘하는 건 아니지만 영양이나 뭐 그런 것에 관심은 있다. **13** 구 그것도, 게다가 [강조] ❑ 성공은 항상 노력을 통해서만 거둘 수 있을 것 같다. 그것도 종종 육체적으로 힘든 일을 열심히 할 때 그렇다. **14** 구 즉, 말하자면 ❑ 나는 전반적으로 성실하기는 해도 기대에 미치지 못하는 학생이다. 즉 나는 시키는 대로만 한다. **15** 구 다 하는, 그것으로 끝이다 ❑ 그가 사무실을 나서면 그것으로 끝이었다. 하루 일과는 끝나는 것이었다. **16** 관용 표현 그렇다 [의례적인 표현] ❑ "결혼했죠?" "네, 그래요." **17** 구 끝내, 아주 간단히 [비격식체, 강조] ❑ 나는 금세 사랑에 빠졌다. **18** 구 그렇다, 그것으로 끝이다 [구어체] ❑ "뭐, 당신이 그러길 바란다면 할 수 없지." 그가 눈물을 머금고 답했다. "그럼 그것으로 끝인 것 같군."

1 접속사 –라고, –라서 ❑ 하루는 그가 그녀에게 전화를 걸어서 그와 아내가 뉴욕에 올 예정이라고 말했다. **2** 접속사 ('it'과 함께 쓰여) –라니 ❑ 네가 그를 좋아한다니 재밌구나. **3** 관계대명사 (명사를 수식하며) – 하는 ❑ 그 문제를 사라지게 하는 약 **4** 접속사 'so' 또는 'such'와 함께 쓰여서 결과를 나타냄 ❑ 그녀는 너무 긴장해서 몸을 심하게 떨었다.

형용사 초가의 ❑ 4백 년 된 초가집

that is의 축약형

thaw /θɔː/ (thaws, thawing, thawed) **1** V-I When ice, snow, or something else that is frozen **thaws**, it melts. □ *It's so cold the snow doesn't get a chance to thaw.* **2** N-COUNT A **thaw** is a period of warmer weather when snow and ice melt, usually at the end of winter. □ *We slogged through the mud of an early spring thaw.* **3** V-T/V-I When you **thaw** frozen food or when it **thaws**, you leave it in a place where it can reach room temperature so that it is ready for use. □ *Always thaw pastry thoroughly.* ● PHRASAL VERB **Thaw out** means the same as **thaw**. □ *Thaw it out completely before reheating in a saucepan.*

the ♦♦♦

The is the definite article. It is used at the beginning of noun groups. **The** is usually pronounced /ðə/ before a consonant and /ði/ before a vowel, but pronounced /ðiː/ when you are emphasizing it.

1 DET You use **the** at the beginning of noun groups to refer to someone or something that you have already mentioned or identified. □ *A waiter came and hovered. John caught my look and we both got up and, ignoring the waiter, made our way to the buffet.* **2** DET You use **the** at the beginning of a noun group when the first noun is followed by an "of" phrase or a clause which identifies the person or thing. □ *There has been a slight increase in the consumption of meat.* **3** DET You use **the** in front of some nouns that refer to something in our general experience of the world. □ *It's always hard to speculate about the future.* **4** DET You use **the** in front of nouns that refer to people, things, services, or institutions that are associated with everyday life. □ *The doctor's on his way.* **5** DET You use **the** instead of a possessive determiner, especially when you are talking about a part of someone's body or a member of their family. □ *"How's the family?" — "Just fine, thank you."* **6** DET You use **the** in front of a singular noun when you want to make a general statement about things or people of that type. □ *An area in which the computer has made considerable strides in recent years is in playing chess.* **7** DET You use **the** with the name of a musical instrument when you are talking about someone's ability to play the instrument. □ *Did you play the piano as a child?* **8** DET You use **the** with nationality adjectives and nouns to talk about the people who live in a country. □ *The Japanese, Americans, and even the French and Germans, judge economic policies by results.* **9** DET You use **the** with words such as "rich," "poor," "old," or "unemployed" to refer to all people of a particular type. □ *Conditions for the poor in Los Angeles have not improved.* **10** DET If you want to refer to a whole family or to a married couple, you can make their surname into a plural and use **the** in front of it. □ *The Taylors decided that they would employ an architect to do the work.* **11** DET You use **the** in front of an adjective when you are referring to a particular thing that is described by that adjective. □ *He knows he's wishing for the impossible.* **12** DET You use **the** to indicate that you have enough of the thing mentioned for a particular purpose. □ *She may not have the money to maintain or restore her property.* **13** DET You use **the** with some titles, place names, and other names. □ *...the SUN, the DAILY STAR and the DAILY EXPRESS.* **14** DET You use **the** in front of numbers such as first, second, and third. □ *The meeting should take place on the fifth of May.* **15** DET You use **the** in front of numbers when they refer to decades. □ *It's sometimes hard to imagine how bad things were in the thirties.* **16** DET You use **the** in front of superlative adjectives and adverbs. □ *Brisk daily walks are still the best exercise for young and old alike.* **17** DET You use **the** in front of each of two comparative adjectives or adverbs when you are describing how one amount or quality changes in relation to another. □ *The longer the therapy goes on, the more successful it will be.* **18** DET When you express rates, prices, and measurements, you can use **the** to say how many units apply to each of the items being measured. □ *New Japanese cars averaged 13 km to the litre in 1981.* **19** DET You use **the** to indicate that something or someone is the most famous, important, or best thing of its kind. In spoken English, you put more stress on it, and in written English, you often underline it or write it in capitals or italics. □ *Camden Market is the place to be on a Saturday or Sunday.*

thea|ter ♦♦♦ /ˈθiːətər/ (theaters) [BRIT **theatre**] **1** N-COUNT; N-IN-NAMES A **theater** is a building with a stage in it, on which plays, shows, and other performances take place. □ *They brought her to the theater where their new musical was in production.* **2** N-SING You can refer to work in the theater such as acting or writing plays as **the theater**. □ *The story of her career in the theater is told in a new biography.* **3** N-UNCOUNT **Theater** is entertainment that involves the performance of plays. □ *...American musical theater.* **4** N-COUNT A **theater** or a **movie theater** is a place where people go to watch movies for entertainment. [AM; BRIT **cinema**] □ *A movie theater and roller rink attracted customers and profit.* **5** N-COUNT In a hospital, a **theatre** is a special room where surgeons carry out medical operations. [BRIT] [also prep N] □ *She is back from theatre and her condition is comfortable.* →see **city**
→see Word Web: **theater**

---

1 자동사 녹다 □ 날씨가 너무 추워서 눈이 녹을 틈조차 없다. **2** 가산명사 해빙기 □ 우리는 이른 봄 눈이 녹을 때 진흙을 헤치며 강행군을 했다. **3** 타동사/자동사 해동시키다; 녹다 □ 항상 패스추리를 완전히 해동시켜라. ● 구동사 해동시키다; 녹다 □ 프라이팬에 다시 데우기 전에 완전히 해동시켜라.

the은 정관사로서 명사군 앞에 쓴다. the는 자음 앞에서는 /ðə/로, 모음 앞에서는 /ði/로 발음하는 것이 일반적이지만 강조하고자 할 때는 /ðiː/로 발음한다.

1 한정사 이미 언급한 명사 앞에 사용하는 정관사 □ 웨이터가 와서 서성거렸다. 존과 나는 눈이 마주친 후 함께 일어나서, 웨이터를 무시하고 뷔페 쪽으로 걸어갔다. **2** 한정사 뒤에서 'of – 구'의 수식을 받는 명사 앞에 사용 □ 육류 소비량이 소폭 증가했다. **3** 한정사 일반적으로 통용되는 의미로 명사를 쓸 때 그 앞에 사용 □ 미래에 대한 측은 항상 어렵다. **4** 한정사 일상생활과 관련된 모든 명사 앞에 사용 □ 의사가 오는 중이다. **5** 한정사 신체 일부분이나 가족 구성원에 대한 말을 할 때 소유격처럼 사용 □ "식구들은 어때요?" "잘 지내요. 고마워요." **6** 한정사 단수 명사 앞에 붙여서 대표 명사로 사용 □ 최근 몇 년간 컴퓨터가 장족의 발전을 이룬 분야 중 하나가 체스 게임이다. **7** 한정사 악기 앞에 사용 □ 어릴 때 피아노 쳤어요? **8** 한정사 국가와 관련된 명사나 형용사 앞에 쓰여 그 나라 사람들을 지칭 □ 일본인, 미국인, 심지어 프랑스인과 독일인까지 경제 정책을 평가할 때 결과를 기준으로 삼는다. **9** 한정사 형용사 앞에 붙어서 특정한 부류의 사람들을 일컬음 □ 로스앤젤레스 빈민층의 생활환경이 아직 개선되지 않았다. **10** 한정사 성 앞에 붙여서 가족 전체나 부부를 지칭 □ 테일러 씨 가족은 그 일을 하기 위해 건축가를 쓰기로 결정했다. **11** 한정사 형용사 앞에 붙어서 형용사의 특징을 갖는 명사처럼 사용 □ 그도 자신이 불가능한 것을 바라고 있음을 안다. **12** 한정사 충분히 □ 그녀는 재산을 유지하거나 복구할 돈이 충분치 않을지도 모른다. **13** 한정사 제목이나 장소를 비롯해 여러 이름 앞에 사용 □ 선지(紙), 데일리 스타 지, 그리고 데일리 익스프레스 지 **14** 한정사 서수 앞에 붙임 □ 회의가 5월 5일 열릴 예정이다. **15** 한정사 10 단위로 쓰인 숫자 앞에 붙임 □ 가끔씩 30년대의 상황이 얼마나 열악했는지 상상하기 힘들 때가 있다. **16** 한정사 형용사나 부사 최상급 앞에 붙임 □ 매일 빠르게 걷는 것이 여전히 나이를 막론하고 가장 좋은 운동이다. **17** 한정사 비례적인 관계를 나타낼 때 형용사나 부사 비교급 앞에 붙임 □ 치료를 오래하면 할수록 성공률이 더 높다. **18** 한정사 단위 앞에 붙임 □ 1981년 새로 출시된 일제 차의 평균 연료 효율은 리터당 13킬로미터였다. **19** 한정사 가장 유명한, 가장 중요한, 가장 좋은 □ 캄덴마켓은 토요일이나 일요일을 보내기에 가장 좋은 곳이다.

[영국영어 theatre] **1** 가산명사; 이름명사 극장 □ 그들은 그들의 새 뮤지컬이 제작되고 있는 극장으로 그녀를 데려왔다. **2** 단수명사 연극 관련 일 □ 그녀의 연극 분야 경력이 관련된 전기에 나와 있다. **3** 불가산명사 연극 □ 미국 뮤지컬 **4** 가산명사 영화관, 극장 [미국영어; 영국영어 cinema] □ 영화관 겸 롤러스케이트장이 고객과 수익을 끌어 모았다. **5** 가산명사 수술실 [영국영어] □ 그녀는 수술실에서 나왔고 안정된 상태이다.

Word Web   theater

Plays in ancient Greece were very different from those of today. **Performances** happened outdoors in open air **theaters**. Two or three male **actors** played all of the **roles** in the **production**. Women could not appear onstage. The actors would go **backstage**, change their **masks** and **costumes**, and re-emerge as new **characters**. A group of people, called the chorus, explained what was happening to the **audience**. Traditional Greek **tragedies** came from stories of the distant past. **Comedies** often made fun of contemporary public figures. Several **plays** appeared together as a contest. The **audience** voted for their favorite **show**.

the|at|ri|cal /θiˈætrɪkᵊl/ (**theatricals**) **1** ADJ **Theatrical** means relating to the theater. [ADJ n] ❑ *These are the prizes given for the most outstanding British theatrical performances of the year.* ● **the|at|ri|cal|ly** /θiˈætrɪkli/ ADV ❑ *Shaffer's great gift lies in his ability to animate ideas theatrically.* **2** ADJ **Theatrical** behavior is exaggerated and unnatural, and intended to create an effect. ❑ *In a theatrical gesture Glass clamped his hand over his eyes.* ● **the|at|ri|cal|ly** ADV ❑ *He looked theatrically at his watch.*

theft /θɛft/ (**thefts**) N-VAR **Theft** is the crime of stealing. ❑ *Over the last decade, auto theft has increased by over 56 percent.*

their ♦♦♦ /ðɛər/

> **Their** is the third person plural possessive determiner.

1 DET You use **their** to indicate that something belongs or relates to the group of people, animals, or things that you are talking about. ❑ *Janis and Kurt have announced their engagement.* **2** DET You use **their** instead of "his or her" to indicate that something belongs or relates to a person without saying whether that person is a man or a woman. Some people think this use is incorrect. ❑ *It is up to the student to improve their own lot by regular and proper practice of yoga techniques.*

theirs /ðɛərz/

> **Theirs** is the third person plural possessive pronoun.

1 PRON-POSS You use **theirs** to indicate that something belongs or relates to the group of people, animals, or things that you are talking about. ❑ *There was a big group of a dozen people at the table next to theirs.* ❑ *It would cost about £3000 to install a new heating system in a flat such as theirs.* **2** PRON-POSS You use **theirs** instead of "his or hers" to indicate that something belongs or relates to a person without saying whether that person is a man or a woman. Some people think this use is incorrect. ❑ *He would leave the trailer unlocked. If there was something inside someone wanted, it would be theirs for the taking.*

them ♦♦♦ /ðəm, STRONG ðɛm/

> **Them** is a third person plural pronoun. **Them** is used as the object of a verb or preposition.

1 PRON-PLURAL You use **them** to refer to a group of people, animals, or things. [v PRON, prep PRON] ❑ *The Beatles – I never get tired of listening to them.* **2** PRON-PLURAL You use **them** instead of "him or her" to refer to a person without saying whether that person is a man or a woman. Some people think this use is incorrect. [v PRON, prep PRON] ❑ *It takes great courage to face your child and tell them the truth.*

theme ♦♦◊ /θiːm/ (**themes**) **1** N-COUNT A **theme** in a piece of writing, a talk, or a discussion is an important idea or subject that runs through it. ❑ *The theme of the conference is renaissance Europe.* **2** N-COUNT A **theme** in an artist's work or in a work of literature is an idea in it that the artist or writer develops or repeats. ❑ *The novel's central theme is the perennial conflict between men and women.* **3** N-COUNT A **theme** is a short simple tune on which a piece of music is based. ❑ *...variations on themes from Mozart's The Magic Flute.* **4** N-COUNT **Theme** music or a **theme** song is a piece of music that is played at the beginning and end of a movie or of a television or radio program. ❑ *...the theme from Dr. Zhivago.* →see **myth**

	Word Partnership	*theme*의 연어
ADJ.	**central** theme, **common** theme, **dominant** theme, **main** theme, **major** theme, **new** theme **1** **2**	
N.	**campaign** theme **1**	
	theme **of a book/movie/story** **2**	
	theme **and variations** **3**	
	theme **music**, theme **song** **4**	

them|selves ♦♦♦ /ðəmˈsɛlvz/

> **Themselves** is the third person plural reflexive pronoun.

1 PRON-REFL You use **themselves** to refer to people, animals, or things when the object of a verb or preposition refers to the same people or things as the subject of the verb. [v PRON, prep PRON] ❑ *They all seemed to be enjoying themselves.* **2** PRON-REFL-EMPH You use **themselves** to emphasize the people or things that you are referring to. **Themselves** is also sometimes used instead of "them" as the object of a verb or preposition. [EMPHASIS] ❑ *Many mentally ill people are themselves unhappy about the idea of community care.* **3** PRON-REFL You use **themselves** instead of "himself or herself" to refer back to the person who is the subject of sentence without saying whether it is a man or a woman. Some people think this use is incorrect. [v PRON, prep PRON] ❑ *What can a patient with emphysema do to help themselves?* **4** PRON-REFL-EMPH You use **themselves** instead of "himself or herself" to emphasize the person you are referring to without saying whether it is a man or a woman. **Themselves** is also sometimes used as the object of a verb or preposition. Some people think this use is incorrect. [EMPHASIS] ❑ *Each student makes only one item themselves.*

then ♦♦♦ /ðɛn/ **1** ADV **Then** means at a particular time in the past or in the future. ❑ *He wanted to have a source of income after his retirement; until then, he wouldn't require additional money.* ❑ *She eventually decided to go professional. Since then she's had considerable success across the Atlantic as well as one hit single.* **2** ADJ **Then** is used when you refer to something which was true at a particular time in the past but is not true now. [ADJ n] ❑ *...the Race Relations Act of 1976 (enacted by the then Labour Government).* ● ADV **Then** is also an adverb. [ADV group] ❑ *Richard*

---

1 형용사 연극의, 극장의 ❑ 이는 한 해 동안 가장 두드러진 영국 공연 작품에 주어지는 상이다. ● 극으로 부사 ❑ 섀퍼의 뛰어난 재능은 아이디어를 무대 위에 올리는 능력에 있다. **2** 형용사 과장된, 연극조의 ❑ 글래스가 과장된 몸짓으로 손을 눈 위에 딱 갖다 댔다. ● 과장되게, 연극조로 부사 ❑ 그는 과장된 제스처를 취하며 시계를 보았다.

가산명사 또는 불가산명사 절도 ❑ 지난 10년간 차량 절도가 56퍼센트 이상 증가했다.

their은 3인칭 복수 소유 한정사이다.

1 한정사 그들의; 그것들의 ❑ 재니스와 커트가 약혼을 발표했다. **2** 한정사 성별 구분 없이 제 3자의 것이라는 뜻으로 사용 ❑ 규칙적이고 정확한 요가 기술 연습을 통한 실력 향상은 학생들 몫이다.

theirs는 3인칭 복수 소유 대명사이다.

1 소유대명사 그들의 것; 그것들의 것 ❑ 그들 옆 테이블에 12명으로 구성된 일행이 앉아 있었다. ❑ 그들의 아파트 같은 곳에 난방 시설을 새로 설치하려면 3천 파운드 정도 들 것이다. **2** 소유대명사 성별 구분 없이 제 3자의 것을 지칭할 때 ❑ 그는 트레일러 문을 잠그지 않고 놔두곤 했다. 누군가 원하는 물건이 그 안에 있으면 그냥 가져가기만 하면 자기 것이 되었다.

them은 3인칭 복수 대명사이다. them은 동사 또는 전치사의 목적어로 쓰인다.

1 복수대명사 그들; 그것들 ❑ 비틀스, 나는 그들의 음악을 들으며 싫증난 적이 한 번도 없었다. **2** 요즘 아이들은 옳고 그름을 가르쳐 줄 사람이 없다. **2** 복수대명사 제 3자를 지칭하며 성별의 구분을 두지 않을 때 ❑ 자식과 마주하면서 진실을 말해 줄 수 있으려면 커다란 용기가 필요하다.

1 가산명사 주제 ❑ 학회의 주제는 르네상스 시대의 유럽이다. **2** 가산명사 주제, 테마 ❑ 소설의 주된 테마는 남녀 간의 영원한 갈등이다. **3** 가산명사 주제 ❑ 모차르트의 마술 피리의 주제를 바탕으로 한 변주곡 **4** 가산명사 테마 음악 ❑ 영화 '닥터 지바고'의 테마 음악

themselves는 3인칭 복수 재귀 대명사이다.

1 재귀대명사 동사의 주어나 목적어로 다시 올 때 쓰임 ❑ 그들 모두 즐거운 시간을 보내고 있는 것 같았다. **2** 강조 재귀대명사 그들 자신; 그것들 자체 [강조] ❑ 상당수의 정신질환자 자신들이 지역 중심의 복지 제도라는 개념에 불만이 있다. **3** 재귀대명사 3인칭 단수 주어를 성별 구분 없이 다시 언급할 때 ❑ 폐기종 환자들이 자구책으로 사용할 수 있는 방법에 무엇이 있을까요? **4** 강조 재귀대명사 3인칭 단수 주어를 성별 구분 없이 강조할 때 [강조] ❑ 학생들은 각각 항목을 하나씩만 만든다.

1 부사 그때 ❑ 그는 퇴직 후에 소득원을 갖고 싶었다. 그때까지는 그가 돈이 추가로 필요하지 않을 것이었다. ❑ 그녀는 결국 프로로 나서기로 결심했다. 그때 이후로 그녀는 싱글 앨범 하나를 히트시킬 뿐만 아니라 대서양 건너편에서도 크게 성공했다. **2** 형용사 당시의 ❑ 1976년(당시 노동당 정부가 제정한 인종관계 특별법) ● 부사 당시 ❑ 당시 일흔여섯 살이었던 리처드

A

Strauss, then 76 years old, suffered through the war years in silence. ᴇ ADV You use **then** to say that one thing happens after another, or is after another on a list. □ *Add the oil and then the scallops to the pan, leaving a little space for the garlic.* ᴈ ADV You use **then** in conversation to indicate that what you are about to say follows logically in some way from what has just been said or implied. [cl/group ADV] □ *"I wasn't a very good scholar at school." — "What did you like doing best then?"* ᴉ ADV You use **then** at the end of a topic or at the end of a conversation. [cl/group ADV] □ *"I'll talk to you on Friday anyway." — "Yep. Okay then."* ᴊ ADV You use **then** with words like "now," "well," and "okay," to introduce a new topic or a new point of view. [adv ADV] □ *Now then, I'm going to explain everything to you before we do it.* ᴋ ADV You use **then** to introduce the second part of a sentence which begins with "if." The first part of the sentence describes a possible situation, and **then** introduces the result of the situation. [ADV cl] □ *If the answer is "yes," then we must decide on an appropriate course of action.* ᴌ ADV You use **then** at the beginning of a sentence or after "and" or "but" to introduce a comment or an extra piece of information to what you have already said. [ADV cl] □ *He sounded sincere, but then, he always did.* ᴍ **now and then** →see **now. there and then** →see **there**

스트라우스는 전쟁 몇 년 내내 침묵하며 고통의 나날을 보냈다. ᴇ 부사 그리고 나서, 그 다음에 □ 팬에 기름을 두른 다음 가리비를 넣어라. 이때 마늘이 들어갈 자리를 조금 남겨 둔다. ᴉ 부사 그러면, 그럴 다면 □ "나는 학교에서 그렇게 훌륭한 학생이 아니었어요." "그러면 제일 좋아했던 것이 뭐였어요?" ᴊ 부사 대화나 화제 끝에 쓰는 말 □ "어쨌든 금요일에 이야기해 줄게." "그래, 그러지 뭐." ᴋ 부사 (새 주제를 소개하며) 그러면, 이제 □ 그러면 이제 우리가 직접 해 보기 전에 제가 여러분께 모든 것을 설명 드리겠습니다. ᴌ 부사 그렇다면 □ 만약 이에 대한 대답이 긍정이라면, 그렇다면 우리는 적절한 행동 방침을 결정해야 한다. ᴍ 부사 게다가, 하기는 □ 그는 진지하게 말했다. 하긴 그는 항상 그랬다.

the|ol|ogy /θiˈɒlədʒi/ N-UNCOUNT **Theology** is the study of the nature of God and of religion and religious beliefs. □ *...questions of theology.* ● **theo|logi|cal** /ˌθiəˈlɒdʒɪkʰl/ ADJ □ *...theological books.*

불가산명사 신학 □ 신학에서 다루는 문제 ● 신학의 형용사 □ 신학 관련 서적

theo|reti|cal /ˌθiəˈrɛtɪkʰl/ ᴉ ADJ A **theoretical** study or explanation is based on or uses the ideas and abstract principles that relate to a particular subject, rather than the practical aspects or uses of it. □ *...theoretical physics.* ᴉ ADJ If you describe a situation as a **theoretical** one, you mean that although it is supposed to be true or to exist in the way stated, it may not in fact be true or exist in that way. □ *This is certainly a theoretical risk but in practice there is seldom a problem.*

ᴉ 형용사 이론의 □ 이론 물리학 ᴉ 형용사 이론적인 □ 이는 이론적으로는 분명 위험 요소가 되지만 실제로는 거의 문제가 되지 않는다.

theo|reti|cal|ly /ˌθiəˈrɛtɪkli/ ADV You use **theoretically** to say that although something is supposed to be true or to happen in the way stated, it may not in fact be true or happen in that way. [ADV with cl/group] □ *Theoretically, the price is supposed to be marked on the shelf.*

부사 이론상, 원칙상 □ 원칙상으로는 가격이 선반에 표시되어야 한다.

theo|rist /ˈθiərɪst/ (**theorists**) N-COUNT A **theorist** is someone who develops an abstract idea or set of ideas about a particular subject in order to explain it. □ *...theorists unaligned with any particular doctrine.*

가산명사 이론가 □ 특정 학파에 속하지 않는 이론가

theo|ry ♦♦◇ /ˈθiəri/ (**theories**) ᴉ N-VAR A **theory** is a formal idea or set of ideas that is intended to explain something. □ *Marx produced a new theory about historical change based upon conflict between competing groups.* ᴉ N-COUNT If you have a **theory** about something, you have your own opinion about it which you cannot prove but which you think is true. □ *There was a theory that he wanted to marry her.* ᴉ N-UNCOUNT The **theory** of a practical subject or skill is the set of rules and principles that form the basis of it. □ *He taught us music theory.* ᴉ PHRASE You use **in theory** to say that although something is supposed to be true or to happen in the way stated, it may not in fact be true or happen in that way. □ *A school dental service exists in theory, but in practice, there are few dentists to work in them.* →see **science**

ᴉ 가산명사 또는 불가산명사 이론, 학설 □ 마르크스는 경쟁 관계에 있는 계층 간의 갈등에 기초해 역사의 변화를 설명하는 새 이론을 내놓았다. ᴉ 가산명사 의견, 사견 □ 그가 그녀와 결혼하고 싶어 한다는 의견이 있었다. ᴉ 불가산명사 이론 □ 그는 우리에게 음악 이론을 가르쳤다. ᴉ 구 이론상, 원칙상 □ 원칙상 학교에서 치과 치료를 해줘야 하지만 실제로 학교에서 일하는 치과 의사들이 거의 없다.

Word Partnership	*theory의 연어*		
N.	**evidence for** a theory, **support for** a theory ᴉ ᴉ		
	conspiracy theory ᴉ		
	learning theory ᴉ		
	theory **and practice** ᴉ		
ADJ.	**scientific** theory ᴉ		
	economic theory, **literary** theory ᴉ		
V.	**advance** a theory, **propose** a theory ᴉ-ᴉ		
	develop a theory, **test** a theory ᴉ ᴉ		

thera|peu|tic /ˌθɛrəˈpjutɪk/ ADJ If something is **therapeutic**, it helps you to relax or to feel better about things, especially about a situation that made you unhappy. □ *It's so therapeutic, a bit like meditation.*

형용사 치료의, 치료를 돕는 □ 이는 치유 효과가 커 명상과 약간 비슷하다.

thera|pist /ˈθɛrəpɪst/ (**therapists**) N-COUNT A **therapist** is a person who is skilled in a particular type of therapy. □ *My therapist helped me feel my anger.*

가산명사 치료사 □ 치료사는 내가 분노를 느낄 수 있게 도와줬다.

thera|py ♦♦◇ /ˈθɛrəpi/ (**therapies**) ᴉ N-UNCOUNT **Therapy** is the treatment of someone with mental illness without the use of drugs or operations. □ *In therapy, she began to let go of her obsession with Mike.* ᴉ N-VAR A **therapy** is a particular treatment of someone with a particular illness or medical condition. [MEDICAL] □ *...hormonal therapies.* →see **cancer**

ᴉ 불가산명사 치료 □ 그녀는 치료를 받으면서 마이크에 대한 집착을 버리기 시작했다. ᴉ 가산명사 또는 불가산명사 요법 [의학] □ 호르몬 요법

there ♦♦♦

Pronounced /ðər, STRONG ðɛər/ for meanings ᴉ and ᴉ, and /ðɛər/ for meanings ᴉ to ᴉ.

ᴉ과 ᴉ의 의미일 때는 /ðər, 강형은 ðɛər /로 발음되고, ᴉ부터 ᴉ까지의 의미일 때 /ðɛər /로 발음된다.

ᴉ PRON **There** is used as the subject of the verb "be" to say that something exists or does not exist, or to draw attention to it. [PRON be n] □ *There's roadworks and temporary traffic lights between Camblesforth and Carlton.* □ *Are there some countries that have been able to tackle these problems successfully?*

ᴉ 대명사 무엇이 존재함을 말하거나 주의를 환기시킬 때 □ 캠블스포스와 칼튼 사이에 도로 공사가 진행 중이어서 임시 신호등이 설치되어 있다. □ 이와 같은 문제를 성공적으로 해결할 수 있었던 국가가 있습니까?

There is normally followed by a plural form of the verb **be** when it is used to introduce a count noun in the plural. □ *There were policemen everywhere.* However, when it introduces a series of nouns in the singular, linked by **and**, a singular form of the verb **be** is normally used. □ *There is a time and a place for everything... There was a street fair and an old-fashioned brass band.* Take care not to confuse **there** and **their**.

there가 복수형으로 된 가산명사를 유도하기 위해 사용될 때는, 그 뒤에 일반적으로 be동사의 복수형이 따라온다. □ 어딜 가나 경찰이 있었다. 그러나, 단수형 명사가 and로 연결되어 연속적으로 언급될 때는, 대개 be동사의 단수형이 쓰인다. □ 모든 것에는 알맞은 때와 장소가 있다. 거리 축제와 구식 취주악단이 있었다. there와 their를 혼동하지 않도록 주의하라.

2 PRON You use **there** in front of certain verbs when you are saying that something exists, develops, or can be seen. Whether the verb is singular or plural depends on the noun which follows the verb. [PRON v n] ❑ *There remains considerable doubt over when the intended high-speed rail link will be complete.* **3** CONVENTION **There** is used after "hello" or "hi" when you are greeting someone. ❑ *"Hello there," said the woman, smiling at them. — "Hi!" they chorused.* **4** ADV If something is **there**, it exists or is available. ❑ *The group of old buildings on the corner by the main road is still there today.* **5** ADV You use **there** to refer to a place which has already been mentioned. ❑ *The next day we drove the 33 miles to Siena (the Villa Arceno is a great place to stay while you are there) for the Palio.* ❑ *"Come on over, if you want." — "How do I get there?"* **6** ADV You use **there** to indicate a place that you are pointing to or looking at, in order to draw someone's attention to it. ❑ *There it is, on the corner over there.* ❑ *There she is on the left up there.* **7** ADV You use **there** in expressions such as "there he was" or "there we were" to sum up part of a story or to slow a story down for dramatic effect. [SPOKEN] [ADV cl] ❑ *So there we were with Amy and she was driving us crazy.* **8** ADV You use **there** when speaking on the telephone to ask if someone is available to speak to you. [ADV with be] ❑ *Hello, is Gordon there please?* **9** ADV You use **there** to refer to a point that someone has made in a conversation. [ADV after v] ❑ *I think you're right there John.* **10** ADV You use **there** to refer to a stage that has been reached in an activity or process. ❑ *We are making further investigations and will take the matter from there.* **11** ADV You use **there** to indicate that something has reached a point or level which is completely successful. ❑ *We had hoped to fill the back page with extra news; we're not quite there yet.* **12** ADV You can use **there** in expressions such as **there you go** or **there we are** when accepting that an unsatisfactory situation cannot be changed. [SPOKEN] [ADV cl] ❑ *I'm the oldest and, according to all the books, should be the achiever, but there you go.* **13** ADV You can use **there** in expressions such as **there you go** and **there we are** when emphasizing that something proves that you were right. [SPOKEN, EMPHASIS] [ADV cl] ❑ *You see? There you go. That's why I didn't mention it earlier. I knew you'd take it the wrong way.* **14** PHRASE Phrases such as **there you go again** are used to show annoyance at someone who is repeating something that has annoyed you in the past. [SPOKEN] ❑ *"There you go again, upsetting the child!" said Shirley.* **15** PHRASE You can add "**so there**" to what you are saying to show that you will not change your mind about a decision you have made, even though the person you are talking to disagrees with you. [INFORMAL] ❑ *I think that's sweet, so there.* **16** PHRASE If something happens **there and then** or **then and there**, it happens immediately. ❑ *Many felt that he should have resigned there and then.* **17** CONVENTION You say "**there there**" to someone who is very upset, especially a small child, in order to comfort them. [SPOKEN] ❑ *"There, there," said Mom. "You've been having a really bad dream."* **18** CONVENTION You say "**there you are**" or "**there you go**" when you are offering something to someone. [SPOKEN, FORMULAE] ❑ *"There you go, Mr. Walters," she said, giving him his documents.* **19** PHRASE If someone **is there for** you, they help and support you, especially when you have problems. [INFORMAL] ❑ *Despite what happened in the past I want her to know I am there for her.*

there|af|ter /ðɛərˈæftər/ ADV **Thereafter** means after the event or date mentioned. [FORMAL] [ADV with cl] ❑ *It was the only time she had ever discouraged him from dangerous activities and she regretted it thereafter.*

there|by /ðɛərˈbaɪ/ ADV You use **thereby** to introduce an important result or consequence of the event or action you have just mentioned. [FORMAL] [ADV with cl] ❑ *Our bodies can sweat, thereby losing heat by evaporation.*

there|fore ♦♦◇ /ðɛərfɔr/ ADV You use **therefore** to introduce a logical result or conclusion. [ADV with cl/group] ❑ *Muscle cells need lots of fuel and therefore burn lots of calories.*

there|in /ðɛərˈɪn/ **1** ADV **Therein** means contained in the place that has been mentioned. [LITERARY] [n ADV] ❑ *By burning tree branches, pine needles, and pine cones, many not only warm their houses but improve the smell therein.* **2** ADV **Therein** means relating to something that has just been mentioned. [FORMAL] [n ADV] ❑ *Afternoon groups relate to the specific addictions and problems therein.*

ther|mal /θɜrmᵊl/ (**thermals**) **1** ADJ **Thermal** means relating to or caused by heat or by changes in temperature. [ADJ n] ❑ *...thermal power stations.* **2** ADJ **Thermal** streams or baths contain water which is naturally hot or warm. [ADJ n] ❑ *Volcanic activity has created thermal springs and boiling mud pools.* **3** ADJ **Thermal** clothes are specially designed to keep you warm in cold weather. [ADJ n] ❑ *My feet were like blocks of ice despite the thermal socks.* ● N-PLURAL **Thermals** are thermal clothes. ❑ *Have you got your thermals on?* **4** N-COUNT A **thermal** is a movement of rising warm air. ❑ *Birds use thermals to lift them through the air.*

ther|mom|eter /θɜrmɒmɪtər/ (**thermometers**) N-COUNT A **thermometer** is an instrument for measuring temperature. It usually consists of a narrow glass tube containing a thin column of a liquid which rises and falls as the temperature rises and falls.

the|sau|rus /θɪsɔrəs/ (**thesauruses**) N-COUNT A **thesaurus** is a reference book in which words with similar meanings are grouped together.

these ♦♦♦

The determiner is pronounced /ðiz/. The pronoun is pronounced /ðiz/.

1 DET You use **these** at the beginning of noun groups to refer to someone or something that you have already mentioned or identified. ❑ *A steering committee has been formed. These people can make decisions in ten minutes which would usually take us months.* ● PRON **These** is also a pronoun. ❑ *AIDS kills mostly the young population of a nation. These are the people who contribute most to a country's economic development.* **2** DET You use **these** to introduce people or things that you are going to talk about. ❑ *Your camcorder should have these basic features: autofocus, playback facility, zoom lens.* ● PRON **These** is also a pronoun. ❑ *Look after yourself*

---

2 대명사 있다, 발전하다, 보이다 등의 뜻을 가진 동사 앞에 사용 ❑ 계획된 고속 철도의 완공 시점을 둘러싸고 회의적인 시각이 여전히 지배적이다. **3** 관용 표현 인사할 때 상대방을 가리키며 쓰는 말 ❑ "안녕하세요!" 여자가 웃으면서 그들에게 인사했다. "안녕하세요!" 그들도 이구동성으로 인사했다. **4** 부사 존재하여, 사용할 수 있는 ❑ 큰 주요 도로 옆 모퉁이에 위치한 오래된 건물들이 지금도 여전히 남아 있다. **5** 부사 거기에, 그곳에 ❑ 다음날 우리는 팔리오 축제를 보러 시에나까지 33마일을 달렸다. (거기 머무는 동안 숙소로는 빌라아르세노가 추천할 만하다.) ❑ "오고 싶으면 이리 와 봐." "거길 어떻게 가?" **6** 부사 거기에 ❑ 저기 모퉁이에, 저쪽 모퉁이에. ❑ 저기 왼쪽에 그녀가 있다. **7** 부사 (이야기의 극적 효과를 더할 때) 결국 [구어체] ❑ 그래서 결국 우리는 에이미랑 있게 되었는데 그녀가 우릴 미치게 만들었다. **8** 부사 전화 통화에서 누구를 바꿔달라고 할 때 ❑ 여보세요. 고든 있으면 바꿔 주시겠어요? **9** 부사 그 점에서 ❑ 존, 그 점에 대해서 네가 옳는 것 같아. **10** 부사 그 단계에서 ❑ 우리는 추가 조사를 하고 있으며 앞으로 그 단계에서 한 걸음 더 나아갈 것이다. **11** 부사 (목표 지점인) 거기까지 ❑ 우리는 뒷면을 기타 뉴스로 채우고 싶었지만 아직 거기까지는 못했다. **12** 부사 어쩔 수 없다 [구어체] ❑ 모든 책에 나와 있듯이 나는 맏이이기 때문에 뭔든지 잘해야 하는데. 어쩔 수 없다. **13** 부사 그것 봐 [구어체, 강조] ❑ 이제 알겠지? 그것 봐. 그래서 내가 더 일찍 이야기 안 한 거야. 네가 이상하게 받아들일 줄 알았다고. **14** 구 또 시작이군 [구어체] ❑ "애나 울리고 또 시작이군!"이라고 셜리가 말했다. **15** 구 상대방이 동의하지 않더라도 자신의 견정을 바꾸지 않겠다는 확고한 의사 표시 [비격식체] ❑ 난 좋은데. 이제 이게 이야긴 하지 말자. **16** 구 바로, 즉시 ❑ 그가 바로 사임했어야 한다고 많은 사람들이 생각했다. **17** 관용 표현 사람을 달래면서 하는 말 [구어체] ❑ "괜찮아, 괜찮아. 정말 나쁜 꿈을 꾼 것뿐이야."라고 엄마가 말했다. **18** 관용 표현 여기 있어요 [구어체, 의례적인 표현] ❑ "월터스 씨, 여기 있어요." 그녀에게 서류를 건네며 그녀가 말했다. **19** 구 돕다 [비격식체] ❑ 과거는 접어 두고 내가 그녀를 도울 준비가 되어 있다는 사실을 그녀가 알았으면 한다.

부사 그 후에 [격식체] ❑ 그녀는 그때 유일하게 그가 위험한 활동을 하지 못하게 했으며 나중에 이를 후회했다.

부사 그렇게 함으로써, 그 때문에 [격식체] ❑ 우리 몸은 땀을 흘려서 증발을 통해 열을 방출시킬 수 있다.

부사 그러므로, 그 결과 ❑ 근육 세포는 연료가 많이 필요하다. 그 결과 칼로리 소모량이 높다.

1 부사 그 안에 [문예체] ❑ 나뭇가지, 솔잎, 솔방울을 태우면 집을 따뜻하게 할 뿐 아니라 그 집안의 냄새도 좋아지게 한다. **2** 부사 그것과 관련해서 [격식체] ❑ 오후 그룹은 특정 중독과 그것과 관련된 문제점에 관해서 이야기한다.

1 형용사 열의 ❑ 화력 발전소 **2** 형용사 온천의 ❑ 화산 활동으로 인해서 온천과 끓는 진흙탕이 만들어졌다. **3** 형용사 보온성이 좋은 ❑ 나는 보온성 좋은 양말을 신었는데도 발이 얼음덩어리처럼 찼다. ● 복수명사 보온 내의 ❑ 보온 내의 입었니? **4** 가산명사 상승 온난 기류 ❑ 새들은 하늘로 날아오르기 위해 상승 온난 기류를 이용한다.

가산명사 온도계

가산명사 유의어 사전

한정사는 /ðiz/ 로 발음되고, 대명사는 /ðiz/ 로 발음된다.

1 한정사 (this의 복수형) 이 ❑ 운영 위원회가 소집되었다. 이 사람들은 우리라면 몇 달이 걸릴 결정을 단 10분만에 내릴 수 있다. ● 대명사 이 사람들 ❑ 한 나라에서 보통 젊은 사람들이 에이즈에 걸려서 사망한다. 이 사람들은 국가 경제 발전의 주역이다. **2** 한정사 (곧 말하려는 사람, 사물 앞에 쓰이) 이런 ❑ 캠코더는 자동 초점 맞추기, 다시 보기, 줌 렌즈와 같은 이런 기본 기능들이 있어야 한다. ● 대명사 이런

---

a
b
c
d
e
f
g
h
i
j
k
l
m
n
o
p
q
r
s
t
u
v
w
x
y
z

properly while you are pregnant. These are some of the things you can do for yourself. ❸ DET In spoken English, people use **these** to introduce people or things into a story. ❑ *I was on my own and these fellows came along towards me.* ❹ PRON You use **these** when you are identifying someone or asking about their identity. ❑ *These are my children.* ❺ DET You use **these** to refer to people or things that are near you, especially when you touch them or point to them. ❑ *These scissors are awfully heavy.* ● PRON **These** is also a pronoun. ❑ *These are the people who are doing our loft conversion for us.* ❻ DET You use **these** when you refer to something which you expect the person you are talking to to know about, or when you are checking that you are both thinking of the same person or thing. ❑ *You know these last few months when we've been expecting it to warm up a little bit?* ❼ DET You use **these** in the expression **these days** to mean "at the present time." ❑ *Living in Bootham these days can be depressing.*

사람들; 이런 것들 ❑ 임신 중에는 몸조심을 잘 해라. 스스로를 위해 할 수 있는 일로는 이런 것들이 있다. ❸ 한정사 이 ❑ 나는 혼자였는데 이 녀석들이 나에게로 왔다. ❹ 대명사 이 사람들 ❑ 얘들은 제 아이들이다. ❺ 한정사 이 ❑ 이 가위는 엄청나게 무겁다. ● 대명사 이 사람들; 이것들 ❑ 이 사람들은 우리 다락을 개조하고 있는 사람들이다. ❻ 한정사 이 ❑ 이 지난 몇 달 동안 날씨가 좀 따뜻해지기를 우리가 기대하고 있다는 것을 알고 있지요? ❼ 한정사 요즘에 ❑ 요즘 부쌈에서의 생활은 우울할 수도 있다.

the|sis /θˈiːsɪs/ (**theses**) /θˈiːsiːz/ ❶ N-COUNT A **thesis** is an idea or theory that is expressed as a statement and is discussed in a logical way. ❑ *This thesis does not stand up to close inspection.* ❷ N-COUNT A **thesis** is a long piece of writing based on your own ideas and research that you do as part of a university degree, especially a higher degree such as a Ph.D. ❑ *I wrote my masters thesis on Herman Melville.* →see **graduation**

❶ 가산명사 논지 ❑ 이 논지는 엄밀하게 검토해 보면 그 논리성이 입증되지 못한다. ❷ 가산명사 학위 논문 ❑ 나는 헤르만 멜빌에 대해 석사 논문을 썼다.

they ♦♦♦ /ðˈeɪ/

> **They** is a third person plural pronoun. **They** is used as the subject of a verb.

❶ PRON-PLURAL You use **they** to refer to a group of people, animals, or things. ❑ *The two men were far more alike than they would ever admit.* ❑ *People matter because of what they are, not what they have.* ❷ PRON-PLURAL You use **they** instead of "he or she" to refer to a person without saying whether that person is a man or a woman. Some people think this use is incorrect. ❑ *The teacher is not responsible for the student's success or failure. They are only there to help the student learn.* ❸ PRON-PLURAL You use **they** in expressions such as "they say" or "they call it" to refer to people in general when you are making general statements about what people say, think, or do. [VAGUENESS] ❑ *They say there's plenty of opportunities out there, you just have to look carefully and you'll find them.*

> they는 3인칭 복수 대명사이다. they는 동사의 주어로 쓰인다.

❶ 복수대명사 그들; 그것들 ❑ 그 두 남자는 그들이 인정하는 것보다 훨씬 더 닮았었다. ❑ 사람들은 그들이 가진 재산 때문이 아니라 그들의 됨됨이 때문에 중요하다. ❷ 복수대명사 (성별 구별 없이 한 사람을 가리켜) 그 ❑ 교사는 학생의 성공이나 실패에 책임이 있는 것이 아니다. 그는 단지 학생들이 배울 수 있도록 돕기 위해 그곳에 있을 뿐이다. ❸ 복수대명사 (일반 사람들 [잘못투]) ❑ 기회는 충분히 있으니까, 그저 잘 살펴보기만 하면 그 기회를 찾을 것이라고 사람들은 말한다.

they'd /ðˈeɪd/ ❶ **They'd** is a spoken form of "they had," especially when "had" is an auxiliary verb. ❑ *They'd both lived in this road all their lives.* ❷ **They'd** is a spoken form of "they would." ❑ *He agreed that they'd visit her after they stopped at Jan's for coffee.*

❶ they had의 축약형 ❑ 그들은 둘 다 평생 동안 이 거리에서 살았었다. ❷ they would의 축약형 ❑ 커피 한 잔 하러 잔의 집에 잠깐 들렀다가 그녀에게 가자는 말에 그는 동의했다.

they'll /ðˈeɪl/ **They'll** is the usual spoken form of "they will." ❑ *They'll probably be here Monday and Tuesday.*

they will의 축약형 ❑ 그들은 아마도 월요일과 화요일에 여기에 올 것이다.

they're /ðˈɛər/ **They're** is the usual spoken form of "they are." ❑ *People eat when they're depressed.*

they are의 축약형 ❑ 사람들은 우울할 때 음식을 먹는다.

they've /ðˈeɪv/ **They've** is the usual spoken form of "they have," especially when "have" is an auxiliary verb. ❑ *The worst thing is when you call friends and they've gone out.*

they have의 축약형 ❑ 최악의 경우는 당신이 친구들에게 전화를 했는데 그들이 이미 나가고 없을 때이다.

thick ♦♦♢ /θˈɪk/ (**thicker, thickest**) ❶ ADJ Something that is **thick** has a large distance between its two opposite sides. ❑ *He wore glasses with thick rims.* ● **thick|ly** ADV [ADV with v] ❑ *Slice the meat thickly.* ❷ ADJ You can use **thick** to talk or ask about how wide or deep something is. [n ADJ, *how* ADJ, *amount* ADJ, *as* ADJ *as*] ❑ *The folder was two inches thick.* ● COMB in ADJ **Thick** is also a combining form. [ADJ n] ❑ *His life was saved by a quarter-inch-thick bullet-proof steel screen.* ● **thick|ness** (**thicknesses**) N-VAR ❑ *The size of the fish will determine the thickness of the steaks.* ❸ ADJ If something that consists of several things is **thick**, it has a large number of them very close together. ❑ *She inherited our father's thick, wavy hair.* ● **thick|ly** ADV ❑ *I rounded a bend where the trees and brush grew thickly.* ❹ ADJ If something is **thick with** another thing, the first thing is full of or covered with the second. [v-link ADJ with n] ❑ *The air is thick with acrid smoke from the fires.* ❺ ADJ **Thick** clothes are made from heavy cloth, so that they will keep you warm in cold weather. ❑ *In the winter she wears thick socks, Wellington boots and gloves.* ❻ ADJ **Thick** smoke, fog, or cloud is difficult to see through. ❑ *The smoke was bluish-black and thick.* ❼ ADJ **Thick** liquids are fairly stiff and solid and do not flow easily. ❑ *They had to battle through thick mud to reach construction workers.* ❽ ADJ If you describe someone as **thick**, you think they are stupid. [BRIT, INFORMAL, DISAPPROVAL] ❑ *How could she have been so thick?*

❶ 형용사 두꺼운 ❑ 나는 아침 식사로 두꺼운 빵 한 조각을 시럽에 찍어 먹었다. ❑ 그는 테가 두꺼운 안경을 쓰고 있었다. ● 두껍게 부사 ❑ 고기를 두껍게 저며라. ❷ 형용사 두께가 -인 ❑ 그 폴더는 2인치 두께였다. ● 복합형-형용사 -두께의 ❑ 4분의 1인치 두께인 강철 방탄 막이 그의 목숨을 살렸다. ● 명사 가산명사 또는 불가산명사 ❑ 생선의 크기가 스테이크의 두께를 결정할 것이다. ❸ 형용사 빽빽한, 무성한 ❑ 그녀는 우리 아버지의 숱 많은 곱슬머리를 물려받았다. ● 빽빽하게, 무성하게 부사 ❑ 나는 나무와 덤불이 무성하게 자라고 있는 모퉁이를 돌아갔다. ❹ 형용사 -로 가득 찬 ❑ 공기가 불에서 나오는 매운 연기로 가득 차 있다. ❺ 형용사 두꺼운 ❑ 그녀는 겨울에 두꺼운 양말과 웰링턴 부츠를 신고, 장갑을 낀다. ❻ 형용사 자욱한, 짙은 ❑ 푸르스름한 검은 연기가 자욱했다. ❼ 형용사 걸쭉한 ❑ 그들은 공사장 인부들에게 가기 위해 걸쭉한 진흙탕 길을 힘들게 걸어가야 했다. ❽ 형용사 둔한 [영국영어, 비격식체, 탐탁잖음] ❑ 그녀가 어떻게 그렇게 둔할 수가 있었을까?

Word Partnership	*thick*의 연어
N.	thick **glass**, thick **ice**, thick **layer**, thick **lips**, thick **neck**, thick **slice**, thick **wall** ❶
	thick **carpet**, **feet/inches** thick ❷
	thick **beard**, thick **fur**, thick **grass**, thick **hair** ❸
	thick **with smoke** ❹
	thick **air, clouds**, thick **fog**, thick **smoke** ❻
ADV.	so thick, too thick, very thick ❶–❼

thick|en /θˈɪkən/ (**thickens, thickening, thickened**) ❶ V-T/V-I When you **thicken** a liquid or when it **thickens**, it becomes stiffer and more solid. ❑ *Thicken the broth with the cornflour.* ❷ V-I If something **thickens**, it becomes more closely grouped together or more solid than it was before. ❑ *The crowds around him began to thicken.*

❶ 타동사/자동사 걸쭉하게 하다 ❑ 옥수수녹말을 넣어서 국물을 걸쭉하게 만들어라. ❷ 자동사 더 많아지다, 더 빽빽해지다 ❑ 그의 주위로 군중들이 많이 모여들기 시작했다.

thief /θˈiːf/ (**thieves**) /θˈiːvz/ N-COUNT A **thief** is a person who steals something from another person. ❑ *The thieves snatched the camera.*

가산명사 도둑 ❑ 그 도둑들이 사진기를 낚아챘다.

Anyone who steals can be called a **thief**. A **robber** often uses violence or the threat of violence to steal things from places such as banks or businesses. A **burglar** breaks into houses or other buildings and steals things.

물건을 훔치는 사람은 누구든 thief이라고 부를 수 있다. robber는 흔히 은행이나 사무실 같은 장소에서 물건을 훔치기 위해 폭력을 사용하거나, 폭력을 사용하겠다고 위협한다. burglar는 집이나 여타 건물에 침입하여 물건을 훔친다.

thigh /θaɪ/ (thighs) N-COUNT Your **thighs** are the top parts of your legs, between your knees and your hips. ❑ *The shorts are so small I can't fit my thighs into any of them.* →see **body**

가산명사 허벅지 ❑ 그 반바지가 나한테 너무 작아서 허벅지도 들어가지 않는다.

thin ◆◇◇ /θɪn/ (thinner, thinnest, thins, thinning, thinned) **1** ADJ Something that is **thin** is much narrower than it is long. ❑ *A thin cable carries the signal to a computer.* **2** ADJ A person or animal that is **thin** has no extra fat on their body. ❑ *He was a tall, thin man with grey hair that fell in a wild tangle to his shoulders.* **3** ADJ Something such as paper or cloth that is **thin** is flat and has only a very small distance between its two opposite surfaces. ❑ *...a small, blue-bound book printed in fine type on thin paper.* ● **thinly** ADV [ADV with v] ❑ *Peel and thinly slice the onion.* **4** ADJ Liquids that are **thin** are weak and watery. ❑ *The soup was thin and clear, yet mysteriously rich.* **5** ADJ A crowd or audience that is **thin** does not have many people in it. ❑ *The crowd, which had been thin for the first half of the race, had now grown considerably.* ● **thinly** ADV [ADV -ed] ❑ *The island is thinly populated.* **6** ADJ **Thin** clothes are made from light cloth and are not warm to wear. ❑ *Her gown was thin, and she shivered, partly from cold.* ● **thinly** ADV [ADV adj/-ed] ❑ *Mrs. Brown wrapped the thinly clad man in her own fur coat and very likely saved his life.* **7** ADJ If you describe an argument or explanation as **thin**, you mean that it is weak and difficult to believe. ❑ *However, the evidence is thin and, to some extent, ambiguous.* ● **thinly** ADV ❑ *Much of the speech was a thinly disguised attack on British Airways.* **8** ADJ If someone's hair is described as **thin**, they do not have a lot of hair. ❑ *She had pale thin yellow hair she pulled back into a bun.* **9** V-T/V-I When you thin something or when it **thins**, it becomes less crowded because people or things have been removed from it. ❑ *It would have been better to have thinned the trees over several winters rather than all at one time.* ● PHRASAL VERB **Thin out** means the same as **thin**. ❑ *NATO will continue to thin out its forces.* **10** PHRASE If someone's patience, for example, **is wearing thin**, they are beginning to become impatient or angry with someone. ❑ *Parliament has not yet begun to combat the deepening economic crisis, and public patience is wearing thin.* **11 on thin ice** →see **ice**. **thin air** →see **air**

1 형용사 가는 ❑ 가는 전선이 그 신호를 컴퓨터로 전달한다. **2** 형용사 마른, 여윈 ❑ 그는 키가 크고 백발이 헝클어져 어깨까지 늘어져 있는 마른 사람이었다. **3** 형용사 얇은 ❑ 얇은 종이에 가는 활자로 인쇄한 파란색 표지의 작은 책 ● 얇게 부사 ❑ 양파의 껍질을 벗기고 얇게 썰어라. **4** 형용사 묽은 ❑ 그 수프는 묽고 멀겠지만, 이상하게도 기름졌다. **5** 형용사 (사람이) 많지 않은 ❑ 관객이 경기 초반부에는 많지 않았었는데, 지금은 상당히 많아져 있었다. ● 드문드문하게 부사 ❑ 그 섬은 인구 밀도가 낮다. **6** 형용사 얇은 ❑ 그녀의 가운이 얇기도 했지만 추위 때문에도 그녀가 몸을 떨었다. ● 얇게 부사 ❑ 브라운 여사는 옷을 얇게 입은 그 남자를 자신의 털 코트로 감싸주어 그의 목숨을 거의 구해 주었다. **7** 형용사 (신빙성이) 약한 ❑ 그러나, 그 증거는 신빙성이 약하고 어느 정도는 모호하기까지 하다. ● 살짝, 얄팍하게 부사 ❑ 연설 중 많은 부분이 영국 항공에 대해 살짝 위장한 공격이었다. **8** 형용사 숱이 적은 ❑ 그녀는 옅은 노란색의 숱이 적은 머리를 뒤로 빗어 쪽진 머리를 하고 있었다. **9** 타동사/자동사 솎다, (수를) 줄이다; 솎아지다 ❑ 나무를 한번에 다 솎아 내는 것보다 겨울마다 몇 차례에 걸쳐 솎아 내는 것이 더 좋았을 것 같다. ● 구동사 솎다, (수를) 줄이다; 솎아지다 ❑ 나토는 병력을 계속 줄일 것이다. **10** 구 (인내심 등이) 약해지다 ❑ 의회는 침체되고 있는 경제 위기 해결을 위한 싸움을 아직 시작도 하지 않았는데, 국민들의 인내심은 약해지고 있다.

Thesaurus

thin의 참조어

ADJ.	lean, skinny, slender, slim; (ant.) fat, heavy **2**
	flimsy, transparent; (ant.) dense, solid, thick **3**
	watery, weak; (ant.) thick **4**

Word Partnership

thin의 연어

N.	thin **face**, thin **fingers**, thin **legs**, thin **line**, thin **lips**, thin **mouth**, thin **smile**, thin **strips 1**
	thin **body**, thin **man/woman 2**
	thin **film**, thin **ice**, thin **layer**, thin **slice 3**
ADJ.	**long and** thin **1**
	tall and thin **2**
ADV.	**extremely** thin, **too** thin, **very** thin **1**-**8**

---

thing ◆◆◆ /θɪŋ/ (things) **1** N-COUNT You can use **thing** to refer to any object, feature, or event when you cannot, need not, or do not want to refer to it more precisely. ❑ *"What's that thing in the middle of the fountain?" — "Some kind of statue, I guess."* ❑ *She was in the middle of clearing the breakfast things.* **2** N-COUNT **Thing** is used in lists and descriptions to give examples or to increase the range of what you are referring to. ❑ *These are genetic disorders that only affect males normally. They are things like muscular dystrophy and haemophilia.* **3** N-COUNT **Thing** is often used after an adjective, where it would also be possible just to use the adjective. For example, you can say **it's a different thing** instead of **it's different**. ❑ *Of course, literacy isn't the same thing as intelligence.* **4** N-SING **Thing** is often used instead of the pronouns "anything," or "everything" in order to emphasize what you are saying. [EMPHASIS] ❑ *One thing is to solve a single thing.* **5** N-COUNT **Thing** is used in expressions such as **such a thing** or **things like that**, especially in negative statements, in order to emphasize the bad or difficult situation you are referring back to. [EMPHASIS] ❑ *I don't believe he would tell Leo such a thing.* **6** N-COUNT You can use **thing** to refer in a vague way to a situation, activity, or idea, especially when you want to suggest that it is not very important. [INFORMAL, VAGUENESS] ❑ *I'm a bit unsettled tonight. This war thing's upsetting me.* **7** N-COUNT You often use **thing** to indicate to the person you are addressing that you are about to mention something important, or something that you particularly want them to know. ❑ *One thing I am sure of was that she was scared.* **8** N-COUNT **Thing** is often used to refer back to something that has just been mentioned, either to emphasize it or to give more information about it. ❑ *Getting drunk is a thing all young men do.* **9** N-COUNT A **thing** is a physical object that is considered as having no life of its own. ❑ *It's not a thing, Beauchamp. It's a human being!* **10** N-COUNT **Thing** is used to refer to something, especially a physical object, when you want to express your feelings of anger toward it. [SPOKEN, DISAPPROVAL] ❑ *Turn that thing off!* **11** N-COUNT You can call a person or an animal a particular **thing** when you want to mention a particular quality that they have and express your feelings toward them, usually affectionate feelings. [INFORMAL] ❑ *You really are quite a clever little thing.* **12** N-PLURAL Your **things** are your clothes or possessions. ❑ *Sara told him to take all his things and not to return.* **13** N-PLURAL **Things** can refer to the situation or life

1 가산명사 것 ❑ "분수 한가운데 있는 저것이 뭐니?" "내 생각에 조각상 종류인 것 같은데." ❑ 그녀는 아침 먹은 것들을 치우고 있는 중이었다. **2** 가산명사 (– 같은) 것 ❑ 이것들은 보통 남자들만 걸리는 유전적 질환이다. 근육축소나 혈우병 같은 것들이다. **3** 가산명사 것 ❑ 물론, 읽고 쓰는 능력은 지능과는 다른 것이다. **4** 난수명사 (anything이나 everything 대신에 쓰여) 것 [강조] ❑ 것은 단 한 가지 일도 해결하지 못할 것이다. **5** 가산명사 것 [강조] ❑ 나는 그가 레오에게 그런 말을 했을 것이라고 생각하지 않는다. **6** 가산명사 (모호하게 뭘 가리킬 때의) 것 [비격식체, 점작도] ❑ 오늘 밤은 좀 불안하다. 이 전쟁이니 뭐니 하는 것이 나를 불안하게 하고 있다. **7** 가산명사 것 ❑ 내가 확신하고 있는 것 하나는 그녀가 무서워했다는 것이었다. **8** 가산명사 것 ❑ 술 취하는 것은 모든 젊은 남자들이 하는 것이다. **9** 가산명사 물건 ❑ 그것은 물건이 아니야, 보샹. 그것은 인간이야. **10** 가산명사 그 놈의 것 [구어체, 탐탁찮음] ❑ 그 놈의 것 꺼 버려! **11** 가산명사 녀석 [비격식체] ❑ 너는 정말로 똑똑한 녀석이구나. **12** 복수명사 소지품들, (개인 소유의) 물건 ❑ 사라는 그에게 물건을 모두 챙겨 가지고 가서 돌아오지 말라고 말했다. **13** 복수명사 상황, 사정 ❑ 상황에 모든 사람이 동의하는

in general and the way it is changing or affecting you. ❑ *Everyone agrees things are getting better.* ⚹ PHRASE If, for example, you **do the** right **thing** or **do the** decent **thing** in a situation, you do something which is considered correct or socially acceptable in that situation. ❑ *People want to do the right thing and buy "green."* ⚹ PHRASE If you do something **first thing**, you do it at the beginning of the day, before you do anything else. If you do it **last thing**, you do it at the end of the day, before you go to bed or go to sleep. ❑ *I'll go see her, first thing.* ⚹ PHRASE You say **it is a** good **thing to** do something to introduce a piece of advice or a comment on a situation or activity. ❑ *Can you tell me whether it is a good thing to prune an apple tree and does it apply to other fruit trees apart from apples?* ⚹ PHRASE You can say that the first of two ideas, actions, or situations **is one thing** when you want to contrast it with a second idea, action, or situation and emphasize that the second one is much more difficult, important, or extreme. [EMPHASIS] ❑ *It was one thing to talk about leaving; it was another to physically walk out the door.* ⚹ PHRASE You can say **for one thing** when you are explaining a statement or answering a question, to suggest that you are not giving the whole explanation or answer, and that there are other points that you could add to it. ❑ *She was a monster. For one thing, she really enjoyed cruelty.* ⚹ PHRASE You can use the expression **"one thing and another"** to suggest that there are several reasons for something or several items on a list, but you are not going to explain or mention them all. [SPOKEN] ❑ *What with one thing and another, it was fairly late in the day when we returned to Shrewsbury.* ⚹ PHRASE If you say **it is just one of those things** you mean that you cannot explain something because it seems to happen by chance. ❑ *"I wonder why." Mr. Dambar shrugged. "It must be just one of those things, I guess."* ⚹ PHRASE If you say that someone **is seeing** or **hearing things**, you mean that they believe they are seeing or hearing something that is not really there. ❑ *Dr. Payne led Lana back into the examination room and told her she was seeing things.* ⚹ PHRASE You can say there is **no such thing as** something to emphasize that it does not exist or is not possible. [EMPHASIS] ❑ *There really is no such thing as a totally risk-free industry.* ⚹ PHRASE You say **the thing is** to introduce an explanation, comment, or opinion, that relates to something that has just been said. **The thing is** is often used to identify a problem relating to what has just been said. [SPOKEN] ❑ *"What does your market research consist of?" — "Well, the thing is, it depends on our target age group."* ⚹ **other things being equal** →see **equal**

Thesaurus *thing*의 참조어

N. device, figure, gadget, item, object, tool ⚹ ⚹

think ♦♦♦ /θɪŋk/ (**thinks, thinking, thought**) ⚹ V-T/V-I If you **think** that something is the case, you have the opinion that it is the case. [no cont] ❑ *I certainly think there should be a ban on tobacco advertising.* ❑ *A generation ago, it was thought that babies born this small could not survive.* ❑ *Tell me, what do you think of my theory?* ⚹ V-T If you say that you **think** that something is true or will happen, you mean that you have the impression that it is true or will happen, although you are not certain of the facts. [no cont] ❑ *Nora thought he was seventeen years old.* ❑ *The storm is thought to be responsible for as many as four deaths.* ⚹ V-T/V-I If you **think** in a particular way, you have those general opinions or attitudes. [no cont, no passive] ❑ *You were probably brought up to think like that.* ❑ *If you think as I do, vote as I do.* ⚹ V-I When you **think** about ideas or problems, you make a mental effort to consider them. ❑ *She closed her eyes for a moment, trying to think.* ❑ *I have often thought about this problem.* ● N-SING **Think** is also a noun. [mainly BRIT] [a N] ❑ *I'll have a think about that.* ⚹ V-T/V-I If you **think** in a particular way, you consider things, solve problems, or make decisions in this way, for example because of your job or your background. [no passive] ❑ *To make the computer work at full capacity, the programmer has to think like the machine.* ⚹ V-T/V-I If you **think of** something, it comes into your mind or you remember it. [no cont] ❑ *Nobody could think of anything to say.* ⚹ V-I If you **think of** an idea, you make a mental effort and use your imagination and intelligence to create it or develop it. ❑ *He thought of another way of getting out of the marriage.* ⚹ V-T If you **are thinking** something at a particular moment, you have words or ideas in your mind without saying them out loud. [no passive] ❑ *She must be ill, Tatiana thought.* ❑ *I remember thinking how lovely she looked.* ⚹ V-T/V-I If you **think of** someone or something as having a particular quality or purpose, you regard them as having this quality or purpose. [no cont] ❑ *We all thought of him as a father.* ❑ *He thinks of it as his home.* ⚹ V-T/V-I If you **think** a lot of someone or something, you admire them very much or think they are very good. [no cont] ❑ *To tell the truth, I don't think much of psychiatrists.* ⚹ V-I If you **think of** someone, you show consideration for them and pay attention to their needs. ❑ *I'm only thinking of you.* ⚹ V-I If you **are thinking of** taking a particular course of action, you are considering it as a possible course of action. ❑ *Martin was thinking of taking legal action against Zuckerman.* ⚹ V-I You can say that you **are thinking of** a particular aspect or subject, in order to introduce an example or explain more exactly what you are talking about. [usu cont] ❑ *The parts of the enterprise which are scientifically the most exciting are unlikely to be militarily useful. I am thinking here of the development of new kinds of lasers.* ⚹ V-I You use **think** in questions where you are expressing your anger or shock at someone's behavior. [DISAPPROVAL] [only interrog] ❑ *What were you thinking of? You shouldn't steal.* ⚹ V-T/V-I You use **think** when you are commenting on something which you did or experienced in the past and which now seems surprising, foolish, or shocking to you. [no cont, no passive] ❑ *To think I left you alone in a place with a madman at large!* ⚹ →see also **thinking, thought** ⚹ PHRASE You use expressions such as **come to think of it, when you think about it**, or **thinking about it**, when you mention something that you have suddenly remembered or realized. ❑ *He was her distant relative, as was everyone else on the island, come to think of it.* ⚹ PHRASE You use **"I think"** as a way of being polite when you are explaining or suggesting to

괴물이었다. 우선 첫째로, 그녀는 잔인함을 정말로 즐겼다. ⚹ 구 이런저런 일 [구어체] ❑ 이런저런 일 때문에, 우리가 슈르즈베리로 돌아갔을 때는 많이 늦어 있었다. ⚹ 구 어쩌다 우연히 생긴 일이다 ❑ "나도 이유는 모르겠어." 댐버 씨가 어깨를 으쓱거렸다. "내 생각에 그냥 어쩌다 그런 일이 생긴 게 분명해." ⚹ 구 허깨비를 보다; 헛것을 듣다 ❑ 페인 박사는 라나를 진찰실로 다시 데리고 가서 그녀에게 허깨비를 본 것이라고 말했다. ⚹ 구 (∼와 같은) 그런 것이 없는 [강조] ❑ 전혀 손해 볼 가능성이 없는 사업 같은 것은 정말로 없다. ⚹ 구 문제는, 실은 [구어체] ❑ "당신이 했던 시장 연구에는 어떤 내용이 들어 있었습니까?" "실은, 우리가 어떤 나이대의 사람들을 대상으로 하느냐에 따라 다릅니다."

⚹ 타동사/자동사 생각하다 ❑ 나는 담배 광고를 분명히 금지해야 한다고 생각한다. ❑ 한 세대 전에는, 이 정도로 작게 태어난 아기는 살지 못할 거라고 생각했었다. ❑ 내 이론에 대해서 어떻게 생각하는지 말해 봐. ⚹ 타동사 생각하다 ❑ 노라는 그가 열일곱 살이라고 생각했다. ❑ 그 폭풍 때문에 네 사람까지 죽었다고 사람들은 생각한다. ⚹ 타동사/자동사 생각하다 ❑ 너는 아마도 그런 식으로 생각하도록 키워졌을 거다. ❑ 너도 나처럼 생각한다면, 내가 하는 쪽으로 투표해라. ⚹ 자동사 (깊이) 생각을 하다 ❑ 그녀는 생각을 하려고 잠시 두 눈을 감았다. ❑ 나는 이 문제에 대해서 자주 생각을 해 보았다. ● 단수명사 생각 [주로 영국영어] ❑ 그것에 대해 한 번 생각해 보겠다. ⚹ 타동사/자동사 생각하다, 사고하다 ❑ 컴퓨터를 최대한 활용하려면, 프로그래머가 그 컴퓨터처럼 생각해야 한다. ⚹ 타동사/자동사 (생각이) 떠오르다, 생각해 내다 ❑ 아무도 할 말이 떠오르지 않았다. ⚹ 자동사 ∼에 대해 생각하다 ❑ 그는 결혼에서 벗어날 다른 방법에 대해 생각해 보았다. ⚹ 타동사 (마음속으로) 생각하다 ❑ 그녀는 분명히 아플 거라고 타티아나는 생각했다. ❑ 나는 그가 굉장히 멋져 보인다고 생각했던 것을 기억한다. ⚹ 타동사/자동사 (∼로) 여기다, 생각하다 ❑ 우리 모두는 그를 아버지로 생각했다. ❑ 그는 그곳을 자신의 집으로 생각한다. ⚹ 타동사/자동사 존경하다, 대단하다고 생각하다 ❑ 사실대로 말하자면, 나는 정신과 의사를 대단하다고 생각하지는 않는다. ⚹ 자동사 생각하다 ❑ 나는 오로지 네 생각뿐이야. ⚹ 자동사 ∼를 하려고 생각 중이다 ❑ 마틴은 주커만에 대해서 법적 행동에 나설 생각을 하고 있었다. ⚹ 자동사 ∼을 고려 중이다 ❑ 과학적으로 아주 흥미로운 기획이라도 군사적으로는 유용할 것 같지 않다. 그래서 나는 새로운 종류의 레이저 개발을 고려하고 있다. ⚹ 자동사 생각하다 [탐탁잖음] ❑ 도대체 넌 뭘 생각하고 있었니? 도둑질을 해서는 안 돼. ⚹ 타동사/자동사 (놀람 등의 감정을 담아) 생각하다 ❑ 내가 너를 미친 사람이 나돌아 다니는 곳에 혼자 내버려 두었다니 생각만 해도! ⚹ 구 생각해 보니 ❑ 그 섬에 사는 다른 모든 사람들처럼 그도 그녀의 먼 친척뻘 되는 사람이었다. ⚹ 구 ∼하는 게 좋겠다 [공손체] ❑ 나는 집에 가서 샤워를 하는 게 좋겠어. ⚹ 구 (완곡하게 의사를 말할 때) 내 생각으로는 [짐작투] ❑ 고맙습니다, 제가 할 수 있을 것 같은데요. ⚹ 구 한 번 생각해 봐 ❑ 한 번 생각하면, 내일 그 일이 이곳을 떠나 이 모든 것과 영원히 작별한다는 것을. ⚹ 구 재고하다 ❑ 그 사건 때문에 정치인들이 피난민들을 대피시키려고 했던 것이 과연 현명한 것인가에 대해서 재고해야만 했다.

someone what you want to do, or when you are accepting or refusing an offer. [POLITENESS] ❑ *I think I'll go home and have a shower.* 19 PHRASE You use "**I think**" in conversations or speeches to make your statements and opinions sound less forceful, rude, or direct. [VAGUENESS] ❑ *Thanks, but I think I can handle it.* 20 PHRASE You say **just think** when you feel excited, fascinated, or shocked by something, and you want the person to whom you are talking to feel the same. ❑ *Just think; tomorrow we shall walk out of this place and leave it all behind us forever.* 21 PHRASE If you **think again about** an action or decision, you consider it very carefully, often with the result that you change your mind and decide to do things differently. ❑ *It has forced politicians to think again about the wisdom of trying to evacuate refugees.* 22 PHRASE If you **think nothing of** doing something that other people might consider difficult, strange, or wrong, you consider it to be easy or normal, and you do it often or would be quite willing to do it. ❑ *I thought nothing of betting £1,000 on a horse.* 23 PHRASE If something happens and you **think nothing of it**, you do not pay much attention to it or think of it as strange or important, although later you realize that it is. ❑ *When she went off to see her parents for the weekend I thought nothing of it.* 24 you **can't hear** yourself **think** →see **hear**. **to think better of it** →see **better**. **to think big** →see **big**. **to think twice** →see **twice**

> Note that when you are using the verb **think** with a "that"-clause in order to state a negative opinion or belief, you normally make **think** negative, rather than the verb in the "that"-clause. For instance, it is more usual to say "I don't think he saw me" than "I think he didn't see me." The same pattern applies to other verbs with a similar meaning, such as **believe**, **consider**, and **suppose**.

Thesaurus   think의 참조어

v.   believe, feel, judge 1
     analyze, evaluate, meditate, reflect, study 4
     recall, remember; (ant.) forget 6

▶**think back** PHRASAL VERB If you **think back**, you make an effort to remember things that happened to you in the past. ❑ *I thought back to the time in 1975 when my son was desperately ill.*

▶**think over** PHRASAL VERB If you **think** something **over**, you consider it carefully before making a decision. ❑ *She said she needs time to think it over.*

▶**think through** PHRASAL VERB If you **think** a situation **through**, you consider it thoroughly, together with all its possible effects or consequences. ❑ *I didn't think through the consequences of promotion.* ❑ *The administration has not really thought through what it plans to do once the fighting stops.*

▶**think up** PHRASAL VERB If you **think** something **up**, for example an idea or plan, you invent it using mental effort. ❑ *Julian has been thinking up new ways of raising money.*

think|er ◆◇◇ /θɪŋkər/ (thinkers) N-COUNT A **thinker** is a person who spends a lot of time thinking deeply about important things, especially someone who is famous for thinking of new or interesting ideas. ❑ *...some of the world's greatest thinkers.*

think|ing ◆◆◇ /θɪŋkɪŋ/ 1 N-UNCOUNT The general ideas or opinions of a person or group can be referred to as their **thinking**. ❑ *There was undeniably a strong theoretical dimension to his thinking.* 2 N-UNCOUNT **Thinking** is the activity of using your brain by considering a problem or possibility or creating an idea. ❑ *This is a time of decisive action and quick thinking.* 3 →see also **wishful thinking**. **to** my **way of thinking** →see **way**

third ◆◆◇ /θɜrd/ (thirds) 1 ORD The **third** item in a series is the one that you count as number three. ❑ *I sleep on the third floor.* 2 FRACTION A **third** is one of three equal parts of something. ❑ *A third of the cost went into technology and services.* 3 ADV You say **third** when you want to make a third point or give a third reason for something. [ADV with cl (not last in cl)] ❑ *First, interest rates may take longer to fall than is hoped. Second, lending may fall. Third, bad loans could wipe out much of any improvement.* 4 N-COUNT A **third** is the lowest honors degree that can be obtained from a British university. ❑ *...Mrs. Hodge, who graduated in 1966 with a third in economics.*

third|ly /θɜrdli/ ADV You use **thirdly** when you want to make a third point or give a third reason for something. [ADV with cl (not last in cl)] ❑ *First of all, there are not many of them, and secondly, they have little money and, thirdly, they have few big businesses.*

thirst /θɜrst/ (thirsts) 1 N-VAR **Thirst** is the feeling that you need to drink something. ❑ *Instead of tea or coffee, drink water to quench your thirst.* 2 N-UNCOUNT **Thirst** is the condition of not having enough to drink. ❑ *They died of thirst on the voyage.*

thirsty /θɜrsti/ (thirstier, thirstiest) ADJ If you are **thirsty**, you feel a need to drink something. ❑ *If a baby is thirsty, it feeds more often.*

thir|teen ◆◆◇ /θɜrtin/ (thirteens) NUM **Thirteen** is the number 13.

thir|teenth ◆◆◇ /θɜrtinθ/ ORD The **thirteenth** item in a series is the one that you count as number thirteen. ❑ *...his thirteenth birthday.*

thir|ti|eth ◆◆◇ /θɜrtiəθ/ ORD The **thirtieth** item in a series is the one that you count as number thirty. ❑ *...the thirtieth anniversary of my parents' wedding.*

thir|ty ◆◆◆ /θɜrti/ (thirties) 1 NUM **Thirty** is the number 30. 2 N-PLURAL When you talk about the **thirties**, you are referring to numbers between 30

Korean column:

22 구 아무렇지도 않게 생각하다 ❑ 나는 경마에 1,000파운드를 거는 것에 대해 아무렇지 않게 생각했다. 23 구 예사로 생각하다 ❑ 그녀가 주말 동안 부모님을 뵙기 위해 갔을 때도 나는 예사로 생각했다.

> 부정적인 의견이나 확신을 말하기 위해 think를 that 절과 함께 쓸 때에는, 보통 that 절 안의 동사가 아니라 think를 부정형으로 만든다. 예를 들어, "I think he didn't see me."라고 하기보다 "I don't think he saw me."라고 하는 것이 더 일반적이다. believe, consider, suppose와 같이 비슷한 뜻을 갖는 다른 동사들에도 같은 패턴이 적용된다.

구동사 회고하다 ❑ 나는 내 아들이 몹시 아팠던 1975년의 그 때를 회고했다.

구동사 심사숙고하다 ❑ 그녀는 그것에 대해 심사숙고할 시간이 필요하다고 말했다.

구동사 충분히 생각하다 ❑ 나는 승진의 결과에 대해서 충분히 생각하지 않았다. ❑ 군 당국은 전투가 일단 끝나면 하려고 계획했던 안에 대해서 충분히 생각하지 않았다.

구동사 고안하다 ❑ 줄리안은 새로운 기금 마련 방법을 고안하고 있는 중이다.

가산명사 사상가 ❑ 세계적으로 가장 위대한 사상가들 몇 명

1 불가산명사 의견 ❑ 그의 의견에는 부인할 수 없을 정도로 강력한 이론적 측면이 있었다. 2 불가산명사 사고 ❑ 지금은 결정적인 행동과 빠른 사고를 해야 할 시기이다.

1 서수 세 번째의 ❑ 나는 3층에서 잔다. 2 분수 3분의 1 ❑ 비용의 3분의 1은 기술과 서비스에 들어간다. 3 부사 셋째로 ❑ 첫째, 금리 하락이 원하는 것보다 시간이 더 걸릴 수도 있다. 둘째, 대출 건수가 하락할 것이다. 셋째, 부실 대출 때문에 개선이 되어도 별 효과가 없을 수도 있다. 4 가산명사 3등급 (영국 대학 성적의 최하위 등급) ❑ 1966년 경제학과를 3등급으로 졸업했던 호지 부인

부사 셋째로 ❑ 우선, 그런 업체들이 많지 않고, 둘째로, 그들이 돈도 별로 없고, 셋째로, 큰 일거리도 거의 없다.

1 가산명사 또는 불가산명사 갈증 ❑ 갈증을 해소하려면, 차나 커피대신 물을 마셔라. 2 불가산명사 갈증 ❑ 그들은 여행 중에 갈증으로 인해 죽었다.

형용사 목마른 ❑ 아기가 목이 마르면 젖을 더 자주 먹는다.

수사 13, 열셋

서수 열세 번째 ❑ 그의 열세 번째 생일

서수 서른 번째 ❑ 부모님의 서른 번째 결혼기념일

1 수사 30, 서른 2 복수명사 30대 ❑ 모차르트는 20대에서 30대 초반까지는 분명히 건강이 좋았다.

and 39. For example, if you are **in** your **thirties**, you are aged between 30 and 39. If the temperature is **in the thirties**, the temperature is between 30 and 39 degrees. ☐ *Mozart clearly enjoyed good health throughout his twenties and early thirties.* ◾ N-PLURAL **The thirties** is the decade between 1930 and 1939. ☐ *She became quite a notable director in the thirties and forties.*

◼ 복수명사 1930년대 ☐ 그녀는 1930년대와 1940년대에 상당히 유명한 감독이 되었다.

this ♦♦♦

> The determiner is pronounced /ðɪs/. In other cases, **this** is pronounced /ðɪs/.

> 한정사는 /ðɪs /로 발음되고, 그 밖의 경우에는 this가 /ðɪs /로 발음된다.

1 DET You use **this** to refer back to a particular person or thing that has been mentioned or implied. ☐ *When food comes out of any oven, it should stand a while. During this delay the center carries on cooking.* ● PRON **This** is also a pronoun. ☐ *I don't know how bad the injury is, because I have never had one like this before.* **2** PRON You use **this** to introduce someone or something that you are going to talk about. ☐ *This is what I will do. I will telephone Anna and explain.* ● DET **This** is also a determiner. ☐ *This report is from David Cook of our Science Unit: "One of the biggest questions surrounding animal evolution is why did the dinosaurs become extinct about 70 million years ago?"* **3** PRON You use **this** to refer back to an idea or situation expressed in a previous sentence or sentences. ☐ *You feel that it's uneconomic to insist that people work together in groups. Why is this?* ● DET **This** is also a determiner. ☐ *There have been continual demands for action by the political authorities to put an end to this situation.* **4** DET In spoken English, people use **this** to introduce a person or thing into a story. ☐ *I came here by chance and was just watching what was going on, when this girl attacked me.* **5** PRON You use **this** to refer to a person or thing that is near you, especially when you touch them or point to them. When there are two or more people or things near you, **this** refers to the nearest one. ☐ *"If you'd prefer something else I'll gladly have it changed for you." — "No, this is great."* ● DET **This** is also a determiner. ☐ *David beckons me to an archway behind the lectern. "This church was built by the Emperor Constantine Monomarchus in the eleventh century."* **6** PRON You use **this** when you refer to a general situation, activity, or event which is happening or has just happened and which you feel involved in. [PRON with be] ☐ *I thought, this is why I've travelled thousands of miles.* **7** DET You use **this** when you refer to the place you are in now or to the present time. ☐ *We've stopped shipping weapons to this country by train.* ☐ *This place is run like a hotel ought to be run.* ● PRON **This** is also a pronoun. ☐ *This is the worst place I've come across.* **8** DET You use **this** to refer to the next occurrence in the future of a particular day, month, season, or festival. ☐ *...this Sunday's 7.45 performance.* **9** ADV You use **this** when you are indicating the size or shape of something with your hands. [ADV adj] ☐ *"They'd said the wound was only about this big," and he showed me with his fingers.* **10** ADV You use **this** when you are going to specify how much you know or how much you can tell someone. [ADV adv] ☐ *I am not going to reveal what my seven-year plan is, but I will tell you this much, if it works out, the next seven years will be very interesting.* **11** CONVENTION If you say **this is it**, you are agreeing with what someone else has just said. [FORMULAE] ☐ *"You know, people conveniently forget the things they say." — "Well this is it."* **12** PRON You use **this** in order to say who you are or what organization you are representing, when you are speaking on the telephone, radio, or television. ☐ *Hello, this is John Thompson.* **13** DET You use **this** to refer to the medium of communication that you are using at the time of speaking or writing. ☐ *What I'm going to do in this lecture is focus on something very specific.* **14** →see also **these 15** PHRASE If you say that you are doing or talking about **this and that**, or **this, that, and the other** you mean that you are doing or talking about a variety of things that you do not want to specify. ☐ *"And what are you doing now?" — "Oh this and that."*

1 한정사 이 ☐ 오븐에서 음식을 꺼내면 잠시 동안 그대로 두어야 한다. 이 시간 동안 가운데 부분이 익는다. ● 대명사 이것; 이 사람 ☐ 나는 전에 이런 상처를 입어 본 적이 한 번도 없어서 이 상처가 어느 정도로 심각한 것인지 모르겠다. **2** 대명사 이것; 이 사람 ☐ 내가 할 일은 이것이다. 나는 안나에게 전화를 해서 설명을 할 것이다. ● 한정사 이 ☐ 이 보고서는 우리 과학부의 데이비드 쿡이 쓴 것이다. 그 내용은 "동물 진화를 둘러싼 가장 큰 의문점 중 하나는 공룡이 왜 약 칠천만 년 전에 멸종했는가 하는 것이다." **3** 대명사 이것 ☐ 사람들이 집단으로 함께 일해야 한다고 주장하는 것이 비경제적이라고 당신은 생각하는 것 같은데, 이것은 왜 그럴까요? ● 한정사 이 ☐ 정치권이 이 상황을 종결짓기 위한 조치를 취해야 한다는 지속적인 요구가 있어 왔다. **4** 한정사 이 ☐ 나는 이곳에 우연히 왔고 무슨 일이 일어나고 있는지 그냥 지켜보고 있던 중이었는데, 그 때 이 소녀가 나를 공격했다. **5** 대명사 이 사람; 이것 ☐ "당신이 다른 것을 더 좋아한다면, 기꺼이 바꿔 드리겠습니다." "아니에요. 이것도 훌륭한데요." ● 한정사 이 ☐ 데이비드가 독서대 뒤쪽 통로로 나를 손짓해서 불렀다. "이 교회는 11세기에 콘스탄틴 모노마르쿠스 황제가 건립했어." **6** 대명사 이것 ☐ 이것이 내가 수천 마일을 여행했던 이유라고 나는 생각했다. **7** 한정사 이 ☐ 우리는 기차로 이 나라에 무기를 실어 보내는 것을 중단했다. ☐ 호텔을 운영하는 식으로 이 곳을 운영한다. ● 대명사 이곳 ☐ 이곳은 내가 들렀던 곳 중에 최악의 장소이다. **8** 한정사 이번의, 이 ☐ 이번 주 일요일 7시 45분 공연 **9** 부사 이만큼 ☐ "그들이 말하기를 그 상처는 겨우 이 정도였다."라며 그가 손가락으로 내게 가리켜 보이며 말했다. **10** 부사 이 정도로 ☐ 내 7년 계획은 밝히지는 않겠지만, 그것이 만약 성공하게 되면, 다음 7년이 굉장히 흥미로울 거라고, 이 정도는 네게 말해 주겠다. **11** 관용 표현 내 말이 그 말이야 [의례적인 표현] ☐ "있잖아, 사람들은 참 편리하게도 자신들이 말한 것들을 잊어버리지." "글쎄, 내 말이 그 말이야." **12** 대명사 나 (전화에서 자신을 밝힐 때) ☐ 여보세요, 저는 존 톰슨입니다. **13** 한정사 이번의 이 ☐ 이번 강연에서 제가 하려고 하는 것은 매우 세부적인 것에 초점을 맞추는 것입니다. **15** 구 이것저것 ☐ "당신은 지금 뭘 하고 있나요?" "아, 뭐 이것저것요."

thorn /θɔrn/ (**thorns**) **1** N-COUNT **Thorns** are the sharp points on some plants and trees, for example on a rose bush. ☐ *Roses will always have thorns but with care they can be avoided.* **2** N-VAR A **thorn** bush or a **thorn tree** is a bush or tree which has a lot of thorns on it. ☐ *...the shade of a thorn bush.*

1 가산명사 가시 ☐ 장미에는 가시가 있긴 하지만 조심하면 안 찔릴 수도 있다. **2** 가산명사 또는 불가산명사 가시; 가시덤불; 가시나무 ☐ 가시덤불 그늘

thorny /θɔrni/ (**thornier, thorniest**) **1** ADJ A **thorny** plant or tree is covered with thorns. ☐ *...thorny hawthorn trees.* **2** ADJ If you describe a problem as **thorny**, you mean that it is very complicated and difficult to solve, and that people are often unwilling to discuss it. ☐ *...the thorny issue of immigration policy.*

1 형용사 가시가 많은 ☐ 가시가 많은 산사나무 **2** 형용사 (문제가) 골치 아픈, 곤란한 ☐ 이민 정책에 있어서 골치 아픈 문제

thorough ♦♢♢ /θɜroʊ, BRIT θʌrə/ **1** ADJ A **thorough** action or activity is one that is done very carefully and in a detailed way so that nothing is forgotten. ☐ *We are making a thorough investigation.* ☐ *This very thorough survey goes back to 1784.* ● **thor|ough|ly** ADV [ADV with v] ☐ *Food that is being offered must be reheated thoroughly.* ● **thor|ough|ness** N-UNCOUNT ☐ *The thoroughness of the evaluation process we went through was impressive.* **2** ADJ Someone who is **thorough** is always very careful in their work, so that nothing is forgotten. ☐ *Martin would be a good judge, I thought. He was calm and thorough.* ● **thor|ough|ness** N-UNCOUNT ☐ *His thoroughness and attention to detail is legendary.* **3** ADJ **Thorough** is used to emphasize the great degree or extent of something. [EMPHASIS] [det ADJ] ☐ *We regard the band as a thorough shambles.* ● **thor|ough|ly** ADV ☐ *I thoroughly enjoy your programme.*

1 형용사 철저한 ☐ 우리는 철저한 수사를 하고 있다. ☐ 아주 철저한 이 조사는 1784년까지 거슬러 올라간다. ● 철저히, 완전히 부사 ☐ 뜨겁게 내야 할 음식은 완전히 다시 데워야 한다. ● 철저함 불가산명사 ☐ 우리가 치렀던 평가 과정의 그 철저함이 인상적이었다. **2** 형용사 철두철미한 ☐ 내 생각에 마틴은 훌륭한 판사가 될 것 같았다. 그는 침착하면서도 철두철미했다. ● 철두철미함 불가산명사 ☐ 그의 철두철미함과 세부적인 일에도 신경을 쓰는 면모는 전설적이다. **3** 형용사 완전한 [강조] ☐ 그 악단은 완전 엉망이라고 우리는 생각한다. ● 정말로 부사 ☐ 당신 프로그램 정말 잘 봤어요.

those ♦♦♦

> The determiner is pronounced /ðoʊz/. The pronoun is pronounced /ðoʊz/.

> 한정사는 /ðoʊz /로 발음되고, 대명사는 /ðoʊz /로 발음된다.

1 DET You use **those** to refer to people or things which have already been mentioned. ☐ *They have the aircraft capable of doing significant damage, because most of those aircraft are capable of launching anti-ship missiles.* ● PRON **Those** is also a pronoun. ☐ *I understand that there are a number of projects going on. Could you tell us a little bit about those?* **2** DET You use **those** when you are referring to people or things that are a distance away from you in position or time, especially when you indicate or point to them. ☐ *What are those buildings?* ● PRON **Those** is also a pronoun. ☐ *Those are nice shoes. Where'd you get them?* **3** DET You use **those** to refer to someone or something when you are going to give details or information

1 한정사 (that의 복수형) 그 ☐ 그들은 그 항공기들이 상당한 파괴력을 갖도록 만든다. 왜냐하면 그 항공기 대부분이 대함 미사일을 쏠 수 있기 때문이다. ● 대명사 그것들 ☐ 지금 많은 프로젝트가 진행되고 있는 것으로 알고 있는데 그것들에 대해서 좀 말씀해 주시겠습니까? ● 대명사 저들; 저것들 ☐ 저 신발 괜찮군요. 어디에서 사셨습니까? **3** 한정사 그 [격식체] ☐ 자신들을 방어하기 위해서 무기를 들었던 그 사람들은 정치범들이다.

about them. [FORMAL] ❑ *Those people who took up weapons to defend themselves are political prisoners.* ◆ PRON You use **those** to introduce more information about something already mentioned, instead of repeating the noun which refers to it. [FORMAL] [PRON pron-rel, PRON of n] ❑ *The interests he is most likely to enjoy will be those which enable him to show off himself or his talents.* ◆ PRON You use **those** to mean "people." [PRON prep/adj/-ed, PRON pron-rel] ❑ *A little selfish behavior is unlikely to cause real damage to those around us.* ◆ DET You use **those** when you refer to things that you expect the person you are talking to to know about or when you are checking that you are both thinking of the same people or things. ❑ *He did buy me those daffodils a week or so ago.*

though ♦♦♦ /ðoʊ/ ◆ CONJ You use **though** to introduce a statement in a subordinate clause which contrasts with the statement in the main clause. You often use **though** to introduce a fact which you regard as less important than the fact in the main clause. ❑ *Gaelic has been a dying language for many years, though children are nowadays taught it in school.* ◆ CONJ You use **though** to introduce a subordinate clause which gives some information that is relevant to the main clause and weakens the force of what it is saying. ❑ *I look back on it as the bloodiest (though not literally) winter of the war.* ◆ ADV You use **though** to indicate that the information in a clause contrasts with or modifies information given in a previous sentence or sentences. [ADV with cl] ❑ *I like him. Though he makes me angry sometimes.* ◆ **as though** →see **as**. **even though** →see **even**

thought ♦♦♦ /θɔt/ (thoughts) ◆ **Thought** is the past tense and past participle of **think**. ◆ N-COUNT A **thought** is an idea that you have in your mind. ❑ *The thought of Nick made her throat tighten.* ❑ *I've just had a thought.* ◆ N-PLURAL A person's **thoughts** are their mind, or all the ideas in their mind when they are concentrating on one particular thing. ❑ *I jumped to my feet so my thoughts wouldn't start to wander.* ❑ *Usually at this time our thoughts are on Christmas.* ◆ N-PLURAL A person's **thoughts** are their opinions on a particular subject. ❑ *Many of you have written to us to express your thoughts on the conflict.* ◆ N-UNCOUNT **Thought** is the activity of thinking, especially deeply, carefully, or logically. ❑ *Alice had been so deep in thought that she had walked past her car without even seeing it.* ❑ *He had given some thought to what she had told him.* ◆ N-COUNT A **thought** is an intention, hope, or reason for doing something. ❑ *Sarah's first thought was to run back and get Max.* ◆ N-UNCOUNT **Thought** is the group of ideas and beliefs which belongs, for example, to a particular religion, philosophy, science, or political party. ❑ *Aristotle's scientific theories dominated Western thought for fifteen hundred years.* ◆ →see also **second thought**

thought|ful /θɔtfəl/ ◆ ADJ If you are **thoughtful**, you are quiet and serious because you are thinking about something. ❑ *Nancy, who had been thoughtful for some time, suddenly spoke.* ● **thought|ful|ly** ADV [ADV with v] ❑ *Daniel nodded thoughtfully.* ◆ ADJ If you describe someone as **thoughtful**, you approve of them because they remember what other people want, need, or feel, and try not to upset them. [APPROVAL] ❑ *...a thoughtful and caring man.* ● **thought|ful|ly** ADV [ADV with v] ❑ *...the bottle of wine he had thoughtfully purchased for the celebrations.* ◆ ADJ If you describe something such as a book, film, or speech as **thoughtful**, you mean that it is serious and well thought out. ❑ *...a thoughtful and scholarly book.* ● **thought|ful|ly** ADV [ADV with v] ❑ *...these thoughtfully designed machines.*

thought|less /θɔtlɪs/ ◆ ADJ If you describe someone as **thoughtless**, you are critical of them because they forget or ignore other people's wants, needs, or feelings. [DISAPPROVAL] ❑ *...a small minority of thoughtless and inconsiderate people.* ● **thought|less|ly** ADV [ADV with v] ❑ *They thoughtlessly planned a picnic without him.*

thou|sand ♦♦♦ /θaʊzᵊnd/ (thousands)

The plural form is **thousand** after a number, or after a word or expression referring to a number, such as "several" or "a few."

◆ NUM A **thousand** or one **thousand** is the number 1,000. ❑ *...five thousand acres.* ◆ QUANT If you refer to **thousands** of things or people, you are emphasizing that there are very many of them. [EMPHASIS] [QUANT of pl-n] ❑ *Thousands of refugees are packed into over-crowded towns and villages.* ● PRON You can also use **thousands** as a pronoun. ❑ *Hundreds have been killed in the fighting and thousands made homeless.* ◆ **a thousand and one** →see **one**

thou|sandth /θaʊzᵊnθ/ (thousandths) ◆ ORD The **thousandth** item in a series is the one that you count as number one thousand. ❑ *The magazine has just published its six thousandth edition.* ● ORD If you say that something has happened for the **thousandth** time, you are emphasizing that it has happened again and that it has already happened a great many times. [EMPHASIS] ❑ *The phone rings for the thousandth time.* ◆ FRACTION A **thousandth** is one of a thousand equal parts of something. ❑ *...a dust particle weighing only a thousandth of a gram.*

thrash /θræʃ/ (thrashes, thrashing, thrashed) ◆ V-T If one player or team **thrashes** another in a game or contest, they defeat them easily or by a large score. [INFORMAL] ❑ *Second-placed Rangers thrashed St Johnstone 5-nil.* ◆ V-T If you **thrash** someone, you hit them several times as a punishment. ❑ *"Liar!" Sarah screamed, as she thrashed the child. "You stole it."* ◆ V-T/V-I If someone **thrashes around** or **about**, or **thrashes** their arms or legs **around** or **about**, they move in a wild or violent way, often hitting against something. You can also say that someone's arms or legs **thrash around** or **about**. ❑ *She would thrash around in her hospital bed and remove her intravenous line.* ❑ *Many of the crew died a terrible death as they thrashed about in shark-infested waters.* ◆ V-T/V-I If a person or thing **thrashes** something, or **thrashes at** something, they hit it continually in a violent and noisy way. ❑ *...a magnificent paddle-steamer with the mighty Mississippi, her huge wheel thrashing the muddy water.* ◆ →see also **thrashing**

▶**thrash out** ◆ PHRASAL VERB If people **thrash out** something such as a plan or an agreement, they decide on it after a great deal of discussion. ❑ *The foreign*

◆ 대명사 그런 이들; 그런 것들 [격식체] ❑ 그가 가장 좋아하는 취미 활동은 자신을 과시하거나 자신의 재능을 자랑할 수 있는 그런 것들일 것이다. ◆ 대명사 사람들 ❑ 약간 이기적인 행동이 우리 주변 사람들에게 진짜 피해를 끼치지는 않을 것 같다. ◆ 한정사 그 ❑ 그가 내게 일주일 전쯤에 그 수선화를 정말 사줬다.

◆ 접속사 비록 ~이지만, ~일지라도 ❑ 비록 아이들이 요즘 학교에서 배우기는 하지만, 게일 어는 여러 해 전에 이미 사어가 되었다. ◆ 접속사 ~이지만 ❑ 나는 그 때를 전쟁 중 가장 피비린내 나는 (글자 그대로는 아니었지만) 겨울로 기억한다. ◆ 부사 그렇지만 ❑ 나는 그를 좋아한다. 그렇지만 때로는 그가 나를 화나게도 한다.

◆ think의 과거, 과거 분사 ◆ 가산명사 생각 ❑ 닉 생각을 하면 그녀는 목이 메었다. ❑ 내가 생각이 막 떠올랐다. ◆ 복수명사 생각 ❑ 나는 생각이 흐트러지지 않도록 벌떡 일어났다. ❑ 보통 이맘때쯤이면 우리는 크리스마스를 생각한다. ◆ 복수명사 의견 ❑ 여러분들 중 많은 분들이 이번 갈등에 대한 의견을 저희에게 글로써 표현해 주셨습니다. ◆ 불가산명사 사색 ❑ 앨리스는 너무나 깊이 사색에 잠긴 나머지 자기 차를 보지도 못한 채 그냥 지나쳤다. ❑ 그는 그녀가 자신에게 했던 말을 곰곰이 생각했었다. ◆ 가산명사 생각, 의도 ❑ 사라의 첫 번째 생각은 다시 뛰어가서 맥스를 잡는 것이었다. ◆ 불가산명사 사상, 사조 ❑ 아리스토텔레스의 과학 이론이 1,500년간 서양 사상을 지배했다.

◆ 형용사 생각에 잠긴 ❑ 한참 동안 생각에 잠겼던 낸시가 갑자기 입을 열었다. ● 생각에 잠겨서 부사 ❑ 다니엘이 생각에 잠긴 채 고개를 끄덕였다. ◆ 형용사 사려 깊은 [마음이 듦] ❑ 사려 깊고 다정한 남자 ● 사려 깊게 부사 ❑ 그가 사려 깊게도 축하용으로 산 와인 한 병 ◆ 형용사 심사숙고한 ❑ 깊은 생각이 담긴 학술적인 책 ● 심사숙고해서 부사 ❑ 심사숙고해서 디자인된 이 기계들

형용사 무심한 [탐탁찮음] ❑ 무심하고 배려심 없는 소수의 사람들 ● 무심하게 부사 ❑ 그들은 무심하게도 그를 빼고 야유회를 계획했다.

숫자 또는 'several', 'a few'와 같이 수를 지칭하는 단어나 표현 뒤에서 복수형은 thousand이다.

◆ 수사 1,000, 천 ❑ 5천 에이커 ◆ 수량사 수천의 [강조] ❑ 수천 명의 피난민들이 이미 사람이 넘치는 도시와 마을로 꽉득 들어간다. ● 대명사 수천 ❑ 수백 명이 그 전투에서 사망했고, 수천 명이 집을 잃었다.

◆ 서수 천 번째 ❑ 그 잡지는 6천 호가 막 발간되었다. ● 서수 수천 번의 [강조] ❑ 전화가 수천 번도 더 울린다. ◆ 분수 1,000분의 1 ❑ 단 1,000분의 1그램 무게의 먼지 입자

◆ 타동사 완파하다 [비격식체] ❑ 2위인 레인저스 팀이 세인트 존스턴 팀을 5대 0으로 완파했다. ◆ 타동사 (벌로) 마구 때리다 ❑ "거짓말쟁이! 네가 훔쳤지." 사라가 그 아이를 마구 때리면서 소리 질렀다. ◆ 자동사/타동사 몸부림치다 ❑ 그녀는 병실 침대에서 몸부림치다가 정맥 주사 줄이 빠져 버리곤 했다. ❑ 많은 선원들이 상어가 우글거리는 바다 속에서 몸부림치다가 처참하게 죽었다. ◆ 타동사/자동사 철썩철썩 치다 ❑ 거대한 미시시피 강에서 커다란 바퀴로 흙탕물을 철썩철썩 치고 있는 멋진 외륜선

◆ 구동사 (고심해서) 결정하다 ❑ 외무 장관들이 적절한 타협안을 고심 끝에 내놓았다. ◆ 구동사

ministers have thrashed out a suitable compromise formula. ② PHRASAL VERB If people **thrash out** a problem or a dispute, they discuss it thoroughly until they reach an agreement. ❑ ...a sincere effort by two people to thrash out differences about which they have strong feelings.

thrash|ing /θræʃɪŋ/ (thrashings) ❶ N-COUNT If one player or team gives another one a **thrashing**, they defeat them easily or by a large score. [INFORMAL] ❑ She dropped only eight points in the 43-minute thrashing of the former Wimbledon champion. ② N-COUNT If someone gives someone else a **thrashing**, they hit them several times as a punishment. ❑ If Sarah caught her, she would get a thrashing. ③ →see also **thrash**

❶ 가산명사 완파 [비격식체] ❑ 전 윔블던 챔피언의 완파한 43분간의 그 경기에서 그녀는 단 8 포인트만 잃었을 뿐이다. ② 가산명사 심하게 때림 ❑ 만약 그녀가 사라에게 잡힌다면, 심하게 맞을 것이다.

thread /θrɛd/ (threads, threading, threaded) ❶ N-VAR **Thread** or a **thread** is a long very thin piece of a material such as cotton, nylon, or silk, especially one that is used in sewing. ❑ This time I'll do it properly with a needle and thread. ② N-COUNT The **thread** of an argument, a story, or a situation is an aspect of it that connects all the different parts together. ❑ The thread running through many of these proposals was the theme of individual power and opportunity. ③ N-COUNT A **thread** of something such as liquid, light, or color is a long thin line or piece of it. ❑ A thin, glistening thread of moisture ran along the rough concrete sill. ④ N-COUNT The **thread** on a screw, or on something such as a lid or a pipe, is the raised spiral line of metal or plastic around it which allows it to be fixed in place by twisting. ❑ The screw threads will be able to get a good grip. ⑤ V-T/V-I If you **thread** your **way** through a group of people or things, or **thread through** it, you move through it carefully or slowly, changing direction frequently as you move. ❑ Slowly she threaded her way back through the moving mass of bodies. ⑥ V-T If you **thread** a long thin object **through** something, you pass it through one or more holes or narrow spaces. ❑ ...threading the laces through the eyelets of his shoes. ⑦ V-T If you **thread** small objects such as beads onto a string or thread, you join them together by pushing the string through them. ❑ Wipe the mushrooms clean and thread them on a string. ⑧ V-T When you **thread** a needle, you put a piece of thread through the hole in the top of the needle in order to sew with it. ❑ I sit down, thread a needle, snip off an old button. →see **rope**

❶ 가산명사 또는 불가산명사 실 ❑ 이번에는 실과 바늘로 잘 꿰맬게요. ② 가산명사 (이야기 등의) 맥락, 기조 ❑ 이들 중 많은 제안서들의 공통된 기조는 개인의 힘과 기회라는 주제였다. ③ 가산명사 가는 줄기, 가닥 ❑ 반짝이는 가는 물줄기가 거칠거칠한 콘크리트 창틀을 따라 흘러내렸다. ④ 가산명사 나삿니, 나사 홈 ❑ 나삿니가 단단히 죌 수 있을 것이다. ⑤ 타동사/자동사 요리조리 빠져나가다 ❑ 그녀는 밀리는 군중들 사이를 천천히 요리조리 빠져 가며 되돌아갔다. ⑥ 타동사 꿰다 ❑ 그가 신발 구멍에 신발 끈을 꿰면서 ⑦ 타동사 꿰다 ❑ 버섯을 깨끗이 닦아서 줄에 꿰어라. ⑧ 타동사 (바늘에) 실을 꿰다 ❑ 나는 앉아서 바늘에 실을 꿰고 헌 단추를 싹둑 잘라 낸다.

threat ♦♦◊ /θrɛt/ (threats) ❶ N-VAR A **threat to** a person or thing is a danger that something unpleasant might happen to them. A **threat** is also the cause of this danger. ❑ Some couples see single women as a threat to their relationships. ② N-COUNT A **threat** is a statement by someone that they will do something unpleasant, especially if you do not do what they want. ❑ He may be forced to carry out his threat to resign. ③ PHRASE If a person or thing is **under threat**, there is a danger that something unpleasant might be done to them, or that they might cease to exist. ❑ His position as leader will be under threat at a party congress due next month.

❶ 가산명사 또는 불가산명사 위협적인 존재 ❑ 어떤 커플들은 애인이 없는 여자들을 그들의 관계에 위협적인 존재로 여긴다. ② 가산명사 협박 ❑ 그는 사임하겠던 협박을 실행하게 될지도 모른다. ③ 구 위협받는 ❑ 다음 달로 예정된 당대회에서 당대표로서의 그의 자리가 위협받을 것이다.

Word Partnership	threat의 연어
N.	threat to *someone's* health ❶
	threat of attack, death threat, threat to peace, threat to stability, threat of a strike, terrorist threat, threat of violence, threat of war ❶ ②
ADJ.	major threat ❶
	credible threat, potential threat, real threat, serious threat, significant threat ❶-②

threat|en ♦♦◊ /θrɛtᵊn/ (threatens, threatening, threatened) ❶ V-T If a person **threatens to** do something unpleasant to you, or if they **threaten** you, they say or imply that they will do something unpleasant to you, especially if you do not do what they want. ❑ He said army officers had threatened to destroy the town. ❑ He tied her up and threatened her with a six-inch knife. ② V-T If something or someone **threatens** a person or thing, they are likely to harm that person or thing. ❑ The newcomers directly threaten the livelihood of the established workers. ③ V-T If something unpleasant **threatens to** happen, it seems likely to happen. ❑ The fighting is threatening to turn into full-scale war. ④ →see also **threatening**

❶ 타동사 협박하다, 위협하다 ❑ 군 장교들이 그 마을을 파괴할 거라고 협박했었다고 그는 말했다. ❑ 그는 그녀를 묶어 놓고 6인치짜리 칼로 위협했다. ② 타동사 위협하다 ❑ 신참자들이 기존 노동자들의 생계를 직접적으로 위협한다. ③ 타동사 조짐을 보이다 ❑ 그 싸움이 전면전으로 비화할 조짐을 보이고 있다.

Word Partnership	threaten의 연어
N.	threaten safety, threaten security, threaten stability, threaten survival ②

threat|en|ing ♦◊◊ /θrɛtᵊnɪŋ/ ADJ You can describe someone's behavior as **threatening** when you think that they are trying to harm you. ❑ Firing women because of a husband's or boyfriend's threatening behavior might amount to sex discrimination. →see also **threaten**

형용사 위협적인 ❑ 남편이나 애인의 위협적인 행동 때문에 여성을 해고하는 것은 성차별에 해당할 수 있다.

three ♦♦♦ /θri/ (threes) NUM **Three** is the number 3. ❑ We waited three months before going back to see the specialist.

수사 3, 셋, 세 ❑ 우리는 3달 동안 기다린 후 전문의에게 다시 갔다.

three-dimensional /θri dɪmɛnʃənᵊl, BRIT θri: daɪmɛnʃənəl/ ❶ ADJ A **three-dimensional** object is solid rather than flat, because it can be measured in three different directions, usually the height, length, and width. The abbreviation **3-D** can also be used. ❑ ...a three-dimensional model. ② ADJ A **three-dimensional** picture, image, or movie looks real, is deep or solid rather than flat. The abbreviation **3-D** can also be used. ❑ ...new software, which generates both two-dimensional drawings and three-dimensional images.

❶ 형용사 3차원의 ❑ 3차원 모델 ② 형용사 3차원의 ❑ 2차원 그림과 3차원 이미지를 둘 다 만들어 내는 새로운 소프트웨어

three-quarters QUANT **Three-quarters** is an amount that is three out of four equal parts of something. [QUANT of n] ❑ Three-quarters of the country's workers took part in the strike. ● PRON **Three-quarters** is also a pronoun. ❑ Road deaths have increased by three-quarters. ● ADV **Three-quarters** is also an adverb. [ADV adj/-ed] ❑ We were left with an open bottle of champagne three-quarters full.

수량사 4분의 3 ❑ 전국 노동자의 4분의 3이 파업에 동참했다. ● 대명사 4분의 3, 75퍼센트 ❑ 객사하는 사람들의 수가 75퍼센트 증가했다. ● 부사 4분의 3으로 ❑ 4분의 3 정도 남아 있는 샴페인이 뚜껑이 열린 채 우리에게 맡겨졌다.

thresh|old /ˈθrɛʃhoʊld/ (**thresholds**) **1** N-COUNT The **threshold** of a building or room is the floor in the doorway, or the doorway itself. ❑ *He stopped at the threshold of the bedroom.* **2** N-COUNT A **threshold** is an amount, level, or limit on a scale. When the **threshold** is reached, something else happens or changes. ❑ *She has a low threshold of boredom and needs the constant stimulation of physical activity.* **3** PHRASE If you are **on the threshold of** something exciting or new, you are about to experience it. ❑ *We are on the threshold of a new era in astronomy.*

threw /θruː/ **Threw** is the past tense of **throw**.

thrift /θrɪft/ N-UNCOUNT **Thrift** is the quality and practice of being careful with money and not wasting things. [APPROVAL] ❑ *They were rightly praised for their thrift and enterprise.*

> **Thrift stores** (or **charity shops** in the UK) are a great source of pleasure for the bargain-hunter. When people no longer need clothes, books, toys and other items, they may take them along to these shops, which rely on this type of donation. The proceeds all go to a particular charity.

thrill /θrɪl/ (**thrills, thrilling, thrilled**) **1** N-COUNT If something gives you a **thrill**, it gives you a sudden feeling of great excitement, pleasure, or fear. ❑ *I can remember the thrill of not knowing what I would get on Christmas morning.* **2** V-T/V-I If something **thrills** you, or if you **thrill at** it, it gives you a feeling of great pleasure and excitement. ❑ *The electric atmosphere both terrified and thrilled him.* **3** →see also **thrilled, thrilling**

thrilled /θrɪld/ **1** ADJ If someone is **thrilled**, they are extremely pleased about something. [v-link ADJ, oft ADJ to-inf, ADJ prep, ADJ that] ❑ *I was so thrilled to get a good report from him.* **2** →see also **thrill**

thrill|er /ˈθrɪlər/ (**thrillers**) N-COUNT A **thriller** is a book, movie, or play that tells an exciting fictional story about something such as criminal activities or spying. ❑ *...a tense psychological thriller.*

thrill|ing /ˈθrɪlɪŋ/ **1** ADJ Something that is **thrilling** is very exciting and enjoyable. ❑ *Our wildlife trips offer a thrilling encounter with wildlife in its natural state.* **2** →see also **thrill**

thrive /θraɪv/ (**thrives, thriving, thrived**) **1** V-I If someone or something **thrives**, they do well and are successful, healthy, or strong. ❑ *Today his company continues to thrive.* **2** V-I If you say that someone **thrives on** a particular situation, you mean that they enjoy it or that they can deal with it very well, especially when other people find it unpleasant or difficult. ❑ *Many people thrive on a stressful lifestyle.*

throat ♦♢♢ /θroʊt/ (**throats**) **1** N-COUNT Your **throat** is the back of your mouth and the top part of the tubes that go down into your stomach and your lungs. ❑ *She had a sore throat.* **2** N-COUNT Your **throat** is the front part of your neck. ❑ *His striped tie was loosened at his throat.* **3** PHRASE If you **clear** your **throat**, you cough once in order to make it easier to speak or to attract people's attention. ❑ *Cross cleared his throat and spoke in low, polite tones.* **4** PHRASE If you **ram** something **down** someone's **throat** or **force** it **down** their **throat**, you keep mentioning a situation or idea in order to make them accept it or believe it. ❑ *I've always been close to my dad but he's never rammed his career down my throat.* **5** PHRASE If two people or groups are **at each other's throats**, they are quarreling or fighting violently with each other. ❑ *The idea that Billy and I are at each other's throats couldn't be further from the truth.* **6** a **lump in** your **throat** →see **lump**

throb /θrɒb/ (**throbs, throbbing, throbbed**) **1** V-I If part of your body **throbs**, you feel a series of strong and usually painful beats there. ❑ *His head throbbed.* **2** V-I If something **throbs**, it vibrates and makes a steady noise. [LITERARY] ❑ *The engines throbbed.*

throne /θroʊn/ (**thrones**) **1** N-COUNT A **throne** is a decorative chair used by a king, queen, or emperor on important official occasions. **2** N-SING You can talk about the **throne** as a way of referring to the position of being king, queen, or emperor. ❑ *...the Queen's 40th anniversary on the throne.*

throng /θrɒŋ/, BRIT θrɒŋ/ (**throngs, thronging, thronged**) **1** N-COUNT A **throng** is a large crowd of people. [LITERARY] ❑ *An official pushed through the throng.* **2** V-I When people **throng** somewhere, they go there in great numbers. [LITERARY] ❑ *The crowds thronged into the mall.*

throt|tle /ˈθrɒtᵊl/ (**throttles, throttling, throttled**) **1** V-T To **throttle** someone means to kill or injure them by squeezing their throat or tightening something around it and preventing them from breathing. ❑ *The attacker then tried to throttle her with wire.* **2** N-COUNT The **throttle** of a motor vehicle or aircraft is the device, lever, or pedal that controls the quantity of fuel entering the engine and is used to control the vehicle's speed. ❑ *He gently opened the throttle, and the ship began to ease forward.*

through ♦♦♦

> The preposition is pronounced /θruː/. In other cases, **through** is pronounced /θruː/

> In addition to the uses shown below, **through** is used in phrasal verbs such as "see through," "think through," and "win through."

1 PREP To move **through** something such as a hole, opening, or pipe means to move directly from one side or end of it to the other. ❑ *The theatre was evacuated when rain poured through the roof at the Liverpool Playhouse.* ❑ *Go straight through that door under the EXIT sign.* ● ADV **Through** is also an adverb. [ADV after v] ❑ *He went straight through to the kitchen and took a can of beer from the fridge.* **2** PREP To cut **through** something means to cut it in two pieces or to make a hole in it. ❑ *Use*

1 가산명사 문지방 ❑ 그는 침실 문지방에서 발을 멈췄다. **2** 가산명사 한계, 수준 ❑ 그녀는 지루함을 빨리 느끼기 때문에 육체적인 활동을 하도록 지속적인 자극이 필요하다. **3** 구 ─의 문턱에 서 있는 ❑ 우리는 천문학의 새로운 지평으로 가는 문턱에 서 있다.

throw의 과거

불가산명사 검소함 [마음에 듦] ❑ 그들은 검소함과 진취성으로 당연한 찬사를 받았다.

> thrift store(알뜰 상점: 영국에서는 charity shop이라고 함)은 싼 물건을 찾는 사람들에게는 아주 즐거운 곳이다. 사람들은 옷, 책, 장난감, 기타 물품이 더 이상 필요 없어지면 이 물건들을 이런 형태의 기부에 의존하는 알뜰 상점들에 가져간다. 이익금은 모두 특정 자선 단체로 간다.

1 가산명사 설렘, 전율 ❑ 크리스마스 날 아침에 무슨 선물을 받을지 몰라 설레던 그 마음을 기억할 수 있다. **2** 타동사/자동사 설레게 하다, 열광시키다 ❑ 격앙된 그 분위기 때문에 그는 겁도 났지만 설레기도 했다.

1 형용사 (기뻐서) 몹시 흥분한 ❑ 나는 그로부터 좋은 성적표를 받고 몹시 흥분했다.

가산명사 (영화 등의) 스릴러물 ❑ 긴장감 넘치는 심리 스릴러물

1 형용사 흥미진진한 ❑ 저희 야생 동물 여행은 자연 상태에 있는 야생 동물과의 흥미진진한 만남을 제공합니다.

1 자동사 번창하다 ❑ 요즘 그의 회사는 계속 번창하고 있다. **2** 자동사 잘 헤쳐 나가다 ❑ 많은 사람들이 스트레스 많은 생활을 잘 헤쳐 나간다.

1 가산명사 목구멍, 목 ❑ 그녀는 목이 아팠다. **2** 가산명사 목 ❑ 줄무늬 타이가 그의 목에 느슨하게 매어져 있었다. **3** 구 헛기침하다 ❑ 크로스는 헛기침을 하고 나서 점잖고 나지막한 톤으로 말했다. **4** 구 강요하다 ❑ 나는 항상 아빠와 친했지만 아빠께서는 내게 그의 직업을 강요하지 않으셨다. **5** 구 서로 으르렁대는 ❑ 빌리와 내가 서로 으르렁댄다는 말은 전혀 사실이 아니다.

1 자동사 욱신거리다, 지끈거리다 ❑ 그는 머리가 지끈거렸다. **2** 자동사 진동 소리를 내다 [문예체] ❑ 엔진이 진동 소리를 냈다.

1 가산명사 왕좌 **2** 단수명사 왕위 ❑ 여왕의 즉위 40주년 기념일

1 가산명사 인파, 군중 [문예체] ❑ 한 관리가 그 인파 속을 밀치고 나갔다. **2** 자동사 모여들다 [문예체] ❑ 군중들이 쇼핑몰로 모여들었다.

1 타동사 목을 조르다 ❑ 그리고 나서 그 폭행범은 철사로 그녀의 목을 조르려고 했다. **2** 가산명사 조절판 ❑ 그가 살짝 조절판을 여니, 배가 앞으로 부드럽게 나가기 시작했다.

> 전치사는 /θruː/로 발음되고, 그 밖의 경우에는 through가 /θruː/로 발음된다.

> through는 아래 용법 외에도 'see through', 'think through', 'win through'와 같은 구동사에 쓰인다.

1 전치사 ─를 통하여, ─으로 ❑ 리버풀 플레이하우스 지붕으로 폭우가 들이치자, 그 극장에서는 사람들을 대피시켰다. ● 부사 줄곧, 곧장 ❑ 그는 부엌으로 곧장 가서 냉장고에서 캔 맥주 하나를 꺼냈다. **2** 전치사 ─을 관통하여 ❑ 생선용 칼과 포크는 가시가 아닌 살만

A

a proper fish knife and fork if possible as they are designed to cut through the flesh but not the bones. ● ADV **Through** is also an adverb. [ADV after v] □ *Score lightly at first and then repeat, scoring deeper each time until the board is cut through.* ▪ PREP To go **through** a town, area, or country means to travel across it or in it. □ *Go up to Ramsgate, cross into France, go through Andorra and into Spain.* ● ADV **Through** is also an adverb. [ADV after v] □ *Few know that the tribe was just passing through.* ▪ PREP If you move **through** a group of things or a mass of something, it is on either side of you or all around you. □ *We made our way through the crowd to the river.* ● ADV **Through** is also an adverb. [ADV after v] □ *He pushed his way through to the edge of the crowd where he waited.* ▪ PREP To get **through** a barrier or obstacle means to get from one side of it to the other. □ *Allow twenty-five minutes to get through Passport Control and Customs.* ● ADV **Through** is also an adverb. [ADV after v] □ *...a maze of concrete and steel barriers, designed to prevent vehicles driving straight through.* ▪ PREP If a driver goes **through** a red light, they keep driving even though they should stop. □ *He was killed at a road junction by a van driver who went through a red light.* ▪ PREP If something goes into an object and comes out of the other side, you can say that it passes **through** the object. □ *The ends of the net pass through a wooden bar at each end.* ● ADV **Through** is also an adverb. [ADV after v] □ *I bored a hole so that the fixing bolt would pass through.* ▪ PREP To go **through** a system means to move around it or to pass from one end of it to the other. □ *...electric currents traveling through copper wires.* ● ADV **Through** is also an adverb. [ADV after v] □ *It is also expected to consider a resolution which would allow food to go through immediately with fewer restrictions.* ▪ PREP If you see, hear, or feel something **through** a particular thing, that thing is between you and the thing you can see, hear, or feel. □ *Alice gazed pensively through the wet glass.* ▪ PREP If something such as a feeling, attitude, or quality happens **through** an area, organization, or a person's body, it happens everywhere in it or affects all of it. □ *An atmosphere of anticipation vibrated through the crowd.* ▪ PREP If something happens or exists **through** a period of time, it happens or exists from the beginning until the end. □ *She kept quiet all through breakfast.* ● ADV **Through** is also an adverb. [ADV after v] □ *We've got a tough programme, hard work right through to the summer.* ▪ PREP If something happens from a particular period of time **through** another, it starts at the first period and continues until the end of the second period. [AM; BRIT **to**] □ *...open Monday through Sunday from 7:00 am to 10:00 pm.* ▪ PREP If you go **through** a particular experience or event, you experience it, and if you behave in a particular way **through** it, you behave in that way while it is happening. □ *Men go through a change of life emotionally just like women.* ▪ ADJ If you are **through with** something or if it is **through**, you have finished doing it and will never do it again. If you are **through with** someone, you do not want to have anything to do with them again. [v-link ADJ, oft ADJ with n] □ *I'm through with the explaining.* ▪ PREP You use **through** in expressions such as **half-way through** and **all the way through** to indicate to what extent an action or task is completed. [n PREP n] □ *A thirty-nine-year-old competitor collapsed half-way through the marathon and died shortly afterwards.* ● ADV **Through** is also an adverb. [n ADV] □ *Stir the pork about until it turns white all the way through.* ▪ PREP If something happens because of something else, you can say that it happens **through** it. □ *They are understood to have retired through age or ill health.* ▪ PREP You use **through** when stating the means by which a particular thing is achieved. □ *Those who seek to grab power through violence deserve punishment.* ▪ PREP If you do something **through** someone else, they take the necessary action for you. □ *Do I need to go through my doctor or can I make an appointment direct?* ▪ ADV If something such as a proposal or idea goes **through**, it is accepted by people in authority and is made legal or official. [ADV after v] □ *It is possible that the present Governor General will be made interim President, if the proposals go through.* ● PREP **Through** is also a preposition. □ *They want to get the plan through Congress as quickly as possible.* ▪ PREP If someone gets **through** an examination or a round of a competition, they succeed or win. □ *She was bright, learned languages quickly, and sailed through her exams.* ● ADV **Through** is also an adverb. [ADV after v] □ *Nigeria also go through from that group.* ▪ ADV When you get **through** while making a telephone call, the call is connected and you can speak to the person you are phoning. [ADV after v] □ *He may find the line cut on the telephone so that he can't get through.* ▪ PREP If you look or go **through** a lot of things, you look at them or deal with them one after the other. □ *Let's go through the numbers together and see if a workable deal is possible.* ▪ PREP If you read **through** something, you read it from beginning to end. □ *She read through pages and pages of the music I had brought her.* ● ADV **Through** is also an adverb. [ADV after v] □ *The article had been authored by Raymond Kennedy. He read it straight through, looking for any scrap of information that might have passed him by.* ▪ ADV If you say that someone or something is wet **through**, you are emphasizing how wet they are. [EMPHASIS] [adj ADV] □ *I returned to the inn cold and wet, soaked through by the drizzling rain.*

through|out ♦♦◇ /θruaʊt/ ▪ PREP If you say that something happens **throughout** a particular period of time, you mean that it happens during the whole of that period. □ *The national tragedy of rival groups killing each other continued throughout 1990.* □ *Movie music can be made memorable because its themes are repeated throughout the film.* ● ADV **Throughout** is also an adverb. [ADV with cl] □ *The first song, "Blue Moon," didn't go too badly except that everyone talked throughout.* ▪ PREP If you say that something happens or exists **throughout** a place, you mean that it happens or exists in all parts of that place. □ *"Sight Savers," founded in 1950, now runs projects throughout Africa, the Caribbean and South East Asia.* ● ADV **Throughout** is also an adverb. [ADV with cl] □ *The route is well sign-posted throughout.*

throw ♦♦◇ /θroʊ/ (**throws, throwing, threw, thrown**) ▪ V-T When you **throw** an object that you are holding, you move your hand or arm quickly and let go of the object, so that it moves through the air. □ *He spent hours throwing a tennis ball against a wall.* □ *The crowd began throwing stones.* ● N-COUNT **Throw** is also a noun. □ *A throw of the dice allows a player to move himself forward.* ▪ V-T If you **throw** your body or part of your body into a particular position or place, you move it

골라내도록 고안된 것이니까 가능하다면 그런 알맞은 도구를 사용해라. ● 부사 완전히 □ 그 판자가 완전히 잘라질 때까지 매번 조금씩 더 깊게 파면서, 처음에는 얇게 칼로 금을 긋고 또 다시 반복해라. ▪ 전치사 -를 통과하여 □ 램스게이트까지 가서 프랑스 본토를 가로질러, 안도라를 통과하여 스페인으로 가라. ● 부사 통과하여 □ 그 부족은 그저 지나가고 있는 중이었다는 것을 아는 사람은 거의 없다. ▪ 전치사 -을 통과하여 □ 우리는 군중 속을 뚫고 그 강까지 갔다. ● 부사 뚫고서 □ 그는 그 남자가 기다리고 있는 군중들 맨 끝까지 사람들 사이를 뚫고 갔다. ▪ 전치사 -을 통과하여 □ 여권 심사와 세관을 통과하는 데 25분이 걸릴 것으로 감안하라. ● 부사 통과하여 □ 차량이 바로 통과하지 못하도록 디자인된, 콘크리트와 강철 방벽으로 만든 미로 ▪ 전치사 -을 (정지하지 않고) 통과하여 □ 그는 교차로에서 정지 신호를 무시하고 통과하던 트럭 운전자에게 치어서 사망했다. ▪ 전치사 -에 끼워져, -을 통과하여 □ 그물 그녀의 양 끝은 양쪽에 있는 나무 기둥에 끼워져 있다. ● 부사 통과하여, 끼워져 □ 나는 그 볼트 나사가 잘 끼워지도록 구멍을 하나 뚫었다. ▪ 전치사 -를 통과하여 □ 구리선을 통해 흐르는 전류 ● 부사 통과하여 □ 식품이 규제를 덜 받고 바로 통과되게 하는 결의안이 고려될 것으로 예상된다. ▪ 전치사 -을 통해서 □ 앨리스는 수심에 잠긴 모습으로 젖어 있는 유리창 밖을 응시했다. ▪ 전치사 -에 온통 □ 기대에 찬 분위기가 군중들 사이로 온통 퍼져 나갔다. ▪ 전치사 -동안 내내 □ 그녀는 아침 식사 동안 내내 아무 말이 없었다. ● 부사 내내, 줄곧 □ 우리는 여름까지 내내 힘든 일을 해야 하는 어려운 프로그램이 있다. ▪ 전치사 (중간에 끊김이 없이) ~까지 계속 [미국영어; 영국영어 to] □ 일요일부터 일요일까지 계속 오전 7시부터 오후 10시까지 개방 ▪ 전치사 -을 겪는 □ 남자들도 여자들만큼 정서적으로 삶의 변화를 겪는다. ▪ 형용사 (일을) 완전히 끝낸; (일이) 완전히 끝난, (사람 간의 관계가) 완전히 끝난 □ 나는 설명을 완전히 끝냈다. ▪ 전치사 -을 반쯤 끝내고, -을 모두 끝내고 □ 서른아홉 살 된 선수가 마라톤을 반쯤 끝내고 쓰러져서 이후 곧 숨졌다. ● 부사 완전히 □ 돼지고기를 모든 면이 완전히 하얗게 될 때까지 이리저리 뒤적여라. ▪ 전치사 -을 이유로 □ 그들은 나이, 혹은 건강상 이유로 퇴직했었다고 알려져 있다. ▪ 전치사 -을 이용해서, -을 통해서 □ 폭력을 이용해서 권력을 잡으려는 사람들은 벌 받아 마땅하다. ▪ 전치사 -를 거쳐서 □ 내 주치의를 거쳐야 하나요, 아니면 직접 예약을 할까요? ▪ 부사 통과하여 □ 그 제의가 통과된다면, 현 총독이 임시 대통령이 될 수도 있다. ● 전치사 -을 통과하여 □ 그들은 그 안이 가능하면 빨리 국회를 통과하기를 바란다. ▪ 전치사 (시험, 경기에서) -을 통과하여 □ 그녀는 똑똑해서 언어도 빨리 배웠으며 시험도 순조롭게 통과했다. ● 부사 통과하여 □ 나이지리아도 그 그룹에서 통과한다. ▪ 부사 (전화가) 연결되어 □ 그는 전화선이 끊어져서 전화가 연결이 안 된다는 것을 알게 될지도 모른다. ▪ 전치사 -을 하나하나 □ 우리 함께 숫자들을 하나하나 살펴 가며 계약을 성사시킬 수 있겠는지 봅시다. ▪ 전치사 -을 처음부터 끝까지 □ 그녀는 내가 사 준 악보 책을 한 페이지씩 처음부터 끝까지 다 읽었다. ● 부사 처음부터 끝까지 □ 그 글은 저자가 레이몬드 케네디였었다. 그는 자신이 간과했을 수도 있는 정보 한 자락이라도 찾을 수 있을까 살펴보며 그 글을 처음부터 끝까지 읽었다. ▪ 부사 완전히 [강조] □ 나는 이슬비에 흠뻑 젖어서, 추위에 떨며 젖은 채 여관으로 돌아왔다.

▪ 전치사 -동안 죽 □ 1990년 내내 경쟁 집단들이 서로를 죽이는 국가적 비극이 계속 벌어졌다. □ 영화 음악은 그 주제가 영화 내내 반복되기 때문에 인상에 남겨질 수 있다. ● 부사 처음부터 끝까지 □ 첫 번째 곡인 '블루문'은 사람들이 연주 내내 떠들었다는 것 말고는 그렇게 나쁘지 않았다. ▪ 전치사 -의 도처에 □ 1950년에 설립된 "사이트 세이버스"는 이제 아프리카, 카리브 해, 동남아 도처에서 사업을 운영한다. ● 부사 도처에 □ 그 길에는 거리 표지판이 곳곳에 잘 설치되어 있다.

▪ 타동사 던지다 □ 그는 테니스공을 벽에 던지며 여러 시간을 보냈다. □ 군중들은 돌을 던지기 시작했다. ● 가산명사 던짐 □ 주사위를 한 번 던지고 나면 선수가 전진할 수 있다. ▪ 타동사 (신체 일부를 던지듯) 움직이다 □ 그녀가 갑자기 두 팔로 그의 어깨를 얼싸안았다. □ 그녀는 기차 앞으로 뛰어들겠다고

there suddenly and with a lot of force. ❑ *She threw her arms around his shoulders.* ❑ *She threatened to throw herself in front of a train.* ■ V-T If you **throw** something into a particular place or position, you put it there in a quick and careless way. ❑ *He struggled out of his bulky jacket and threw it on to the back seat.* ■ V-T To **throw** someone into a particular place or position means to force them roughly into that place or position. ❑ *He threw me to the ground and started to kick.* ■ V-T If you say that someone **is thrown into** prison, you mean that they are put there by the authorities, especially if this seems unfair or cruel. ❑ *Those two should have been thrown in jail.* ■ V-T If a horse **throws** its rider, it makes him or her fall off, by suddenly jumping or moving violently. ❑ *The horse reared, throwing its rider and knocking down a youth standing beside it.* ■ V-T If a person or thing **is thrown into** an unpleasant situation or state, something causes them to be in that situation or state. ❑ *Abidjan was thrown into turmoil because of a protest by taxi drivers.* ■ V-T If something **throws** light or a shadow **on** a surface, it causes that surface to have a light or a shadow on it. ❑ *The sunlight is white and blinding, throwing hard-edged shadows on the ground.* ■ V-T If something **throws** doubt **on** a person or thing, it causes people to doubt or suspect them. ❑ *This new information does throw doubt on their choice.* ⑩ V-T If you **throw** a look or smile at someone or something, you look or smile at them quickly and suddenly. [no cont] ❑ *Emily turned and threw her a suggestive grin.* ⑪ V-T If you **throw** yourself, your energy, or your money **into** a particular job or activity, you become involved in it very actively or enthusiastically. ❑ *She threw herself into a modelling career.* ⑫ V-T If you **throw** a fit or a tantrum, you suddenly start to behave in an uncontrolled way. ❑ *I used to get very upset and scream and swear, throwing tantrums all over the place.* ⑬ V-T If something such as a remark or an experience **throws** you, it surprises you or confuses you because it is unexpected. ❑ *The professor rather threw me by asking if I went in for martial arts.* ⑭ V-T If you **throw** a punch, you punch someone. ❑ *Everything was fine until someone threw a punch.* ⑮ V-T When someone **throws** a party, they organize one, usually in their own home. [INFORMAL] ❑ *Why not throw a party for your friends?* ⑯ **to throw** someone **in at the deep end** →see **end**. **to throw down the gauntlet** →see **gauntlet**. **to throw light on** something →see **light**. **to throw money at** something →see **money**. **to throw a spanner in the works** →see **spanner**. **to throw in the towel** →see **towel**. **to throw your weight about** →see **weight**. **to throw a wrench** →see **wrench**

Word Partnership   throw의 연어

N.   throw **a ball**, throw **a pass**, throw **a pitch**, throw **a rock/stone** ■

▶**throw away** or **throw out** ■ PHRASAL VERB When you **throw away** or **throw out** something that you do not want, you get rid of it, for example by putting it in a trash container. ❑ *I never throw anything away.* ■ PHRASAL VERB If you **throw away** an opportunity, advantage, or benefit, you waste it, rather than using it sensibly. ❑ *Failing to tackle the deficit would be throwing away an opportunity we haven't had for a generation.*

▶**throw out** ■ →see **throw away 1** ■ PHRASAL VERB If a judge **throws out** a case, he or she rejects it and the accused person does not have to stand trial. ❑ *The defense wants the district Judge to throw out the case.* ■ PHRASAL VERB If you **throw** someone **out**, you force them to leave a place or group. ❑ *He was thrown out of the Olympic team after testing positive for drugs.* ❑ *I wanted to kill him, but instead I just threw him out of the house.*

▶**throw up** ■ PHRASAL VERB When someone **throws up**, they vomit. [INFORMAL] ❑ *She said she had thrown up after reading reports of the trial.* ■ PHRASAL VERB If something **throws up** dust, stones, or water, when it moves or hits the ground, it causes them to rise up into the air. ❑ *If it had hit the Earth, it would have made a crater 100 miles across and thrown up an immense cloud of dust.*

thrown /θroʊn/ **Thrown** is the past participle of **throw**.

thrush /θrʌʃ/ (**thrushes**) ■ N-COUNT A **thrush** is a fairly small bird with a brown back and a spotted breast. ■ N-UNCOUNT **Thrush** is a medical condition cause by a fungus. It most often occurs in a baby's mouth or in a woman's vagina. ❑ *...a medicine that's used to prevent and treat thrush and other fungal infections.*

thrust /θrʌst/ (**thrusts, thrusting, thrust**) ■ V-T If you **thrust** something or someone somewhere, you push or move them there quickly with a lot of force. ❑ *They thrust him into the back of a jeep.* ● N-COUNT **Thrust** is also a noun. ❑ *Two of the knife thrusts were fatal.* ■ V-T If you **thrust** your **way** somewhere, you move there, pushing between people or things which are in your way. ❑ *She thrust her way into the crowd.* ■ V-I If something **thrusts** up or out of something else, it sticks up or sticks out in a noticeable way. [LITERARY] ❑ *...a seedling ready to thrust up into any available light.* ■ N-UNCOUNT **Thrust** is the power or force that is required to make a vehicle move in a particular direction. ❑ *It provides the thrust that makes the craft move forward.* →see **flight**

Word Partnership   thrust의 연어

ADV.   thrust **someone/something** aside ■
thrust **something/yourself** forward ■ ■
N.   thrust **your** hands, thrust **your** head ■

thud /θʌd/ (**thuds, thudding, thudded**) ■ N-COUNT A **thud** is a dull sound, such as that which a heavy object makes when it hits something soft. ❑ *She tripped and fell with a sickening thud.* ■ V-I If something **thuds** somewhere, it makes a dull sound, usually when it falls onto or hits something else. ❑ *She ran up the stairs, her bare feet thudding on the wood.* ■ V-I When your heart **thuds**, it beats

협박했다. ■ 타동사 던지다 ❑ 그는 거추장스러운 잠바를 힘겹게 벗어 뒷좌석에 던졌다. ■ 타동사 내던지다 ❑ 그가 나를 바닥으로 내던지고 발길질을 하기 시작했다. ■ 타동사 치넣어지다, 내동댕이쳐지다 ❑ 그 둘을 감옥에 처넣었어야 했다. ■ 타동사 내팽개치다, 내동댕이치다 ❑ 말이 앞다리를 들어 올리며 기수를 내동댕이치고 옆에 서 있던 청년을 넘어뜨렸다. ■ 타동사 (어떤 상태에) 내몰다 ❑ 아비장은 택시 기사들의 시위 때문에 아수라장이 되었다. ■ 타동사 (빛, 그림자를) 던지다 ❑ 순백의 눈부신 햇살에 바닥에 선명한 그림자들이 드리워진다. ■ 타동사 (의심이) 들게 하다 ❑ 이 새로운 정보 때문에 그들의 선택에 정말 의심이 든다. ⑩ 타동사 (눈길 등을) 던지다 ❑ 에밀리는 돌아서서 그녀에게 의미심장한 미소를 던졌다. ⑪ 타동사 내던지다, 쏟아 붓다 ❑ 그녀는 모델 일에 자신을 완전히 내던졌다. ⑫ 타동사 (성질 등을) 부리다 ❑ 나는 심하게 골이 나서 비명을 지르고 욕하며 아무데나 성질을 부리곤 했다. ⑬ 타동사 혼란시키다 ❑ 교수가 지구에 무술을 즐기냐고 물어서 약간 얼떨떨했다. ⑭ 타동사 (주먹을) 날리다 ❑ 누군가가 주먹을 날리기 전까지는 모든 것이 괜찮았다. ⑮ 타동사 (파티를) 열다 [비격식체] ❑ 친구들을 위해 파티를 여는 것은 어때?

■ 구동사 버리다 ❑ 나는 어떤 것도 절대로 버리지 않는다. ■ 구동사 (기회 등을) 낭비하다 ❑ 적자를 바로 잡지 않는다면 한 세대 동안 갖지 못한 기회를 헛되게 하는 것이 될 것이다.

■ 구동사 기각하다 ❑ 피고 측은 지역 판사가 소송을 기각하기를 원한다. ■ 구동사 내쫓다 ❑ 그는 약물 양성 반응을 보여서 올림픽 팀에서 쫓겨났다. ❑ 나는 그를 죽이고 싶었지만 그냥 집에서 내쫓았다.

■ 구동사 토하다 [비격식체] ❑ 그녀는 그 재판 보도를 읽은 다음 토했다고 했다. ■ 구동사 피워 올리다, 솟구쳐 올리다 ❑ 만약 그것이 지구에 충돌했다면 지름 100마일의 운석 구멍을 형성하고 엄청난 먼지 구름을 피워 올렸을 것이다.

throw의 과거 분사

■ 가산명사 개똥지빠귀 ■ 불가산명사 아구창 ❑ 아구창과 기타 세균성 감염을 예방하고 치료하기 위한 약

■ 타동사 밀다; 찌르다 ❑ 그들은 그를 지프의 뒷좌석에 밀어 넣었다. ● 가산명사 밀침, 찌름 ❑ 칼에 찔린 상처 중 두 개는 치명적이었다. ■ 타동사 밀치고 가다 ❑ 그녀는 군중 사이로 밀치고 들어갔다. ■ 자동사 뚫고 나오다 [문예체] ❑ 빛이 있기만 하다면 뚫고 나올 준비가 되어 있는 씨앗 ■ 불가산명사 추진력 ❑ 그것이 기체를 앞으로 가게 하는 추진력을 제공한다.

■ 가산명사 퍽, 툭 (무거운 물건이 떨어지는 둔탁한 소리) ❑ 그녀는 일이 걸려 퍽 하는 끔찍한 소리와 함께 넘어졌다. ■ 자동사 탁탁 소리를 내다, 퍽 하는 소리를 내다 ❑ 그녀는 맨발로 탁탁 소리를 내며 나무 계단을 뛰어 올라갔다. ■ 자동사 두근거리다

strongly and rather quickly, for example because you are very frightened or very happy. ❑ *My heart had started to thud, and my mouth was dry.*

thug /θʌg/ (**thugs**) N-COUNT You can refer to a violent person or criminal as a **thug**. [DISAPPROVAL] ❑ *...the cowardly thugs who mug old people.*

thumb /θʌm/ (**thumbs, thumbing, thumbed**) **1** N-COUNT Your **thumb** is the short thick piece on the side of your hand next to your four fingers. ❑ *She bit the tip of her left thumb, not looking at me.* **2** V-T If you **thumb** a lift or **thumb** a ride, you stand by the side of the road holding out your thumb until a driver stops and gives you a lift. ❑ *It may interest you to know that a boy answering Rory's description thumbed a ride to Howth.* **3** PHRASE If you are **under** someone's **thumb**, you are under their control, or very heavily influenced by them. ❑ *I cannot tell you what pain I feel when I see how much my mother is under my father's thumb.* **4** **green thumb** →see **green**. **rule of thumb** →see **rule** →see **hand**

thumb|tack /θʌmtæk/ (**thumbtacks**) N-COUNT A **thumbtack** is a short pin with a broad flat top which is used for fastening papers or pictures to a board, wall, or other surface. [AM; BRIT **drawing pin**] →see **office**

thump /θʌmp/ (**thumps, thumping, thumped**) **1** V-T/V-I If you **thump** something, you hit it hard, usually with your fist. ❑ *He thumped my shoulder affectionately, nearly knocking me over.* ● N-COUNT **Thump** is also a noun. ❑ *He felt a thump on his shoulder.* **2** V-T If you **thump** someone, you attack them and hit them with your fist. [mainly BRIT, INFORMAL] ❑ *Don't say it serves me right or I'll thump you.* **3** V-T If you **thump** something somewhere or if it **thumps** there, it makes a loud, dull sound by hitting something else. ❑ *She thumped her hand on the witness box.* ❑ *...paving stones and bricks which have been thumping down on police shields and helmets.* ● N-COUNT **Thump** is also a noun. ❑ *There was a loud thump as the horse crashed into the van.* **4** V-I When your heart **thumps**, it beats strongly and quickly, usually because you are afraid or excited. ❑ *My heart was thumping wildly but I didn't let my face show any emotion.*

thun|der /θʌndər/ (**thunders, thundering, thundered**) **1** N-UNCOUNT **Thunder** is the loud noise that you hear from the sky after a flash of lightning, especially during a storm. ❑ *There was frequent thunder and lightning, and torrential rain.* **2** V-I When **it thunders**, a loud noise comes from the sky after a flash of lightning. ❑ *The day was heavy and still. It would probably thunder later.* **3** N-UNCOUNT The **thunder of** something that is moving or making a sound is the loud deep noise it makes. ❑ *The thunder of the sea on the rocks seemed to blank out their thoughts.* **4** V-I If something or someone **thunders** somewhere, they move there quickly and with a lot of noise. ❑ *The horses thundered across the valley floor.*

thun|der|ous /θʌndərəs/ ADJ If you describe a noise as **thunderous**, you mean that it is very loud and deep. ❑ *The audience responded with thunderous applause.*

thun|der|storm /θʌndərstɔrm/ (**thunderstorms**) N-COUNT A **thunderstorm** is a storm in which there is thunder and lightning and a lot of heavy rain. →see **erosion**

Thurs.

The spellings **Thur.** and **Thu.** are also used.

Thurs. is a written abbreviation for **Thursday**.

Thurs|day ♦♦♦ /θɜrzdeɪ, -di/ (**Thursdays**) N-VAR **Thursday** is the day after Wednesday and before Friday. ❑ *On Thursday Barrett invited me for a drink.* ❑ *We go and do the weekly shopping every Thursday morning.*

thus ♦♦◇ /ðʌs/ **1** ADV You use **thus** to show that what you are about to mention is the result or consequence of something else that you have just mentioned. [FORMAL] [ADV with cl/group] ❑ *Neither of them thought of turning on the lunch-time news. Thus Caroline didn't hear of John's death until Peter telephoned.* **2** ADV If you say that something is **thus** or happens **thus** you mean that it is, or happens, as you have just described or as you are just about to describe. [FORMAL] ❑ *Joanna was pouring the drink. While she was thus engaged, Charles sat on one of the bar-stools.*

thwart /θwɔrt/ (**thwarts, thwarting, thwarted**) V-T If you **thwart** someone or **thwart** their plans, you prevent them from doing or getting what they want. ❑ *The security forces were doing all they could to thwart terrorists.*

thyme /taɪm/ N-UNCOUNT **Thyme** is a type of herb used in cooking.

tick /tɪk/ (**ticks, ticking, ticked**) **1** V-I When a clock or watch **ticks**, it makes a regular series of short sounds as it works. ❑ *A wind-up clock ticked busily from the kitchen counter.* ● PHRASAL VERB **Tick away** means the same as **tick**. ❑ *A grandfather clock ticked away in a corner.* ● **tick|ing** N-UNCOUNT ❑ *...the endless ticking of clocks.* **2** N-COUNT The **tick** of a clock or watch is the series of short sounds it makes when it is working, or one of those sounds. ❑ *He sat listening to the tick of the grandfather clock.* **3** N-COUNT A **tick** is a written mark like a V: ✓. It is used to show that something is correct or has been selected or dealt with. [mainly BRIT; AM usually **check**] ❑ *Place a tick in the appropriate box.* **4** V-T If you **tick** something that is written on a piece of paper, you put a tick next to it. [mainly BRIT; AM usually **check**] ❑ *Please tick this box if you do not wish to receive such mailings.*

▶**tick off** PHRASAL VERB If you **tick off** items on a list, you write a tick or other mark next to them, in order to show that they have been dealt with. [mainly BRIT; AM usually **check off**] ❑ *He ticked off my name on a piece of paper.*

▶**tick over** PHRASAL VERB If an engine **is ticking over**, it is running at a low speed or rate, for example when it is switched on but you are not actually using it. [BRIT] ❑ *Very slowly he moved forward, the engine ticking over.*

❑ 심장은 두근거리기 시작했고 입은 바짝 마른 상태였다.

가산명사 흉악범 [탐탁잖음] ❑ 노인들을 대상으로 노상 강도짓을 하는 비열한 흉악범들

1 가산명사 엄지손가락 ❑ 그녀는 왼쪽 엄지손가락 끝을 물며 내 시선을 피했다. **2** 타동사 (엄지손가락을 들어) 히치하이크하다 ❑ 로리의 설명과 맞아 떨어지는 소년이 하우스까지 히치하이크해서 갔다는 사실에 흥미를 가지실지도 모르겠네요. **3** 구 -에게 쥐여사는 ❑ 어머니가 아버지의 손아귀에 얼마나 심하게 쥐여사는지를 볼 때마다 내가 어떤 고통을 받는지를 이루 말할 수 없다.

가산명사 압정 [미국영어; 영국영어 drawing pin]

1 타동사/자동사 탁 소리 나게 치다 ❑ 그가 내 어깨를 다정하게 탁 쳤는데 내가 거의 넘어갈 뻔했다. ● 가산명사 탁 치기 ❑ 그는 무엇이 자기 어깨를 탁 치는 것을 느꼈다. **2** 타동사 두들겨 패다 [주로 영국영어, 비격식체] ❑ 당해도 싸다는 말을 하기만 해 봐라. 아주 두들겨 패줄 테니까. **3** 타동사 탁 소리 나게 놓다; 탁 소리 내며 놓이다 ❑ 그녀는 손으로 증인석을 탁하고 소리 나게 쳤다. ❑ 경찰의 방패와 헬멧에 퍽퍽 하며 줄기차게 떨어지는 보도의 돌과 벽돌들 ● 가산명사 퍽하는 소리를 냄 ❑ 말이 봉고에 부딪치며 퍽 하고 큰 소리가 났다. **4** 자동사 두근거리다, (심장이) 쿵쾅거리다 ❑ 나는 심장이 미친 듯이 쿵쾅거렸으나 얼굴에 어떤 감정도 드러내지 않았다.

1 불가산명사 천둥 ❑ 천둥과 번개가 자주 쳤으며 폭우가 쏟아졌다. **2** 자동사 천둥 치다 ❑ 그날은 날씨가 후텁지근하고 바람은 미동도 안 했다. 아마도 나중에 천둥이 칠 것 같았다. **3** 불가산명사 -의 우레와 같은 소리 ❑ 파도가 바위에 부딪치며 내는 우레와 같은 소리는 다른 모든 생각을 몰아내는 것 같았다. **4** 자동사 큰 소리를 내며 질주하다 ❑ 말들이 우레 같은 소리를 내며 계곡 아래를 가로질러 달렸다.

형용사 우레 같은 ❑ 청중은 우레 같은 박수 소리로 화답했다.

가산명사 뇌우

철자 Thur.와 Thu.도 쓴다.

목

가산명사 또는 불가산명사 목요일 ❑ 목요일에 바레트가 한 잔 하자며 나를 불렀다. ❑ 우리는 매주 목요일 오전에 일주일치의 쇼핑을 한다.

1 부사 그래서 [격식체] ❑ 그들은 둘 다 점심시간 뉴스를 들을 생각을 하지 않았다. 그래서 캐롤라인은 피터가 전화할 때까지 존의 죽음에 대해 듣지 못했다. **2** 부사 이렇게 [격식체] ❑ 조안나는 음료수를 따르고 있었다. 그녀가 그러는 동안 찰스는 바의 의자에 앉아 있었다.

타동사 방해하다, 좌절시키다 ❑ 보안 유지군은 테러리스트들을 좌절시키기 위해 최선을 다하고 있었다.

불가산명사 백리향

1 자동사 똑딱거리다 ❑ 태엽시계가 부엌 카운트에서 부지런히 똑딱거렸다. ● 구동사 똑딱거리다 ❑ 대형 괘종시계가 한쪽 구석에서 똑딱거렸다. ● 똑딱거리는 소리 불가산명사 ❑ 시계들이 끊임없이 똑딱거리는 소리 **2** 가산명사 똑딱똑딱 소리 ❑ 그는 대형 괘종시계의 똑딱똑딱 소리를 들으며 앉아 있었다. **3** 가산명사 체크 표시 [주로 영국영어; 미국영어 대개 check] ❑ 해당 네모에 체크를 하세요. **4** 타동사 체크 표시를 하다 [주로 영국영어; 미국영어 대개 check] ❑ 그러한 우편물을 받기를 원치 않으시면 이 네모에 체크 표시를 하십시오.

구동사 (확인했다는 의미에서) 체크 표시를 하다 [주로 영국영어; 미국영어 대개 check off] ❑ 그가 종이에 적힌 내 이름에 체크 표시를 했다.

구동사 (엔진이 시동만 걸린 채) 서서히 작동하다 [영국영어] ❑ 엔진은 시동만 걸어 놓은 채로 그는 아주 천천히 앞으로 나아갔다.

tick|et ♦♦◇ /tɪkɪt/ (**tickets**) **1** N-COUNT A **ticket** is a small, official piece of paper or card which shows that you have paid to enter a place such as a theater or a sports stadium, or shows that you have paid for a trip. [also by N] ❏ *He had a ticket for a flight on Friday.* ❏ *Entrance is free, but by ticket only.* **2** N-COUNT A **ticket** is an official piece of paper which orders you to pay a fine or to appear in court because you have committed a driving or parking offense. ❏ *I want to know at what point I break the speed limit and get a ticket.* **3** N-COUNT A **ticket** for a game of chance such as a raffle or a lottery is a piece of paper with a number on it. If the number on your ticket matches the number chosen, you win a prize. ❏ *She bought a lottery ticket and won more than $33 million.* **4** →see also **season ticket**

1 가산명사 표 ❏ 그는 금요일 비행기 표를 가지고 있었다. ❏ 입장은 무료지만 표가 있어야 한다. **2** 가산명사 교통 위반 딱지 ❏ 어떤 속도를 지나야 딱지를 떼이게 되는지 알고 싶다. **3** 가산명사 – 권 ❏ 그녀는 복권을 사서 3천 3백만 달러 이상을 땄다.

Word Partnership　ticket의 연어

N.	ticket **agent**, ticket **booth**, ticket **counter**, ticket **holder**, **plane** ticket, ticket **price** **1**
	parking ticket **2**
	lottery ticket **3**
ADJ.	**free** ticket **1**
	winning ticket **3**
V.	**get** a ticket **1** **2**
	buy/pay for a ticket **1** **3**

---

tick|le /tɪkəl/ (**tickles, tickling, tickled**) **1** V-T When you **tickle** someone, you move your fingers lightly over a sensitive part of their body, often in order to make them laugh. ❏ *I was tickling him, and he was laughing and giggling.* **2** V-T/V-I If something **tickles** you or **tickles**, it causes an irritating feeling by lightly touching a part of your body. ❏ *...a yellow hat with a great feather that tickled her ear.*

1 타동사 간질이다 ❏ 나는 그를 간질이고 있었고 그는 킬킬거리며 웃고 있었다. **2** 타동사/자동사 간질이다 ❏ 그녀의 귀를 간질이는 거대한 깃털이 달린 노란 모자

tid|al /taɪdəl/ ADJ **Tidal** means relating to or produced by tides. ❏ *The tidal stream or current gradually decreases in the shallows.*

형용사 조수의 ❏ 조류는 여울에서 점점 약해진다.

tid|al wave (**tidal waves**) N-COUNT A **tidal wave** is a very large wave, often caused by an earthquake, that flows onto the land and destroys things. ❏ *...a massive tidal wave swept the ship up and away.*

가산명사 해일 ❏ 거대한 해일이 그 선박을 들어올려서는 삼켜 버렸다.

tide ♦◇◇ /taɪd/ (**tides**) **1** N-COUNT The **tide** is the regular change in the level of the sea on the shore. ❏ *The tide was at its highest.* ❏ *The tide was going out, and the sand was smooth and glittering.* **2** N-COUNT A **tide** is a current in the sea that is caused by the regular and continuous movement of large areas of water toward and away from the shore. ❏ *Roman vessels used to sail with the tide from Boulogne to Richborough.* **3** N-SING The **tide of** opinion, for example, is what the majority of people think at a particular time. ❏ *The tide of opinion seems overwhelmingly in his favor.* →see **ocean**
→see Word Web: **tide**

1 가산명사 조수 ❏ 조수가 최고조였다. ❏ 물이 빠지고 있었으며 모래는 매끄럽고 반짝였다. **2** 가산명사 조류 ❏ 로마의 선박은 조류에 맞춰 불로뉴에서 리치버로우까지 항해하곤 했다. **3** 단수명사 – 의 흐름 ❏ 여론의 흐름은 압도적으로 그에게 유리한 것 같다.

tidy /taɪdi/ (**tidier, tidiest, tidies, tidying, tidied**) **1** ADJ Someone who is **tidy** likes everything to be neat and arranged in an organized way. ❏ *John was very neat, tidy and domestic.* **2** ADJ Something that is **tidy** is neat and is arranged in an organized way. ❏ *Having a tidy desk can seem impossible if you have a busy, demanding job.* ● **tidi|ly** /taɪdɪli/ ADV ❏ *...books and magazines stacked tidily on shelves.* ● **tidi|ness** N-UNCOUNT ❏ *Employees are expected to maintain a high standard of tidiness in their dress and appearance.* **3** V-T When you **tidy** a place such as a room or closet, you make it neat by putting things in their proper places. ❏ *She made her bed, and tidied her room.*

1 형용사 깔끔한 ❏ 존은 매우 단정하고 깔끔하며 가정적이었다. **2** 형용사 깔끔한 ❏ 바쁘고 힘든 일을 하고 있으면 책상을 깔끔하게 유지하는 것은 불가능해 보일 수도 있다. ● 깔끔하게 부사 ❏ 책꽂이에 깔끔하게 꽂혀 있는 책과 잡지들 ● 깔끔함 불가산명사 ❏ 직원들은 복장과 외모를 매우 깔끔하게 유지해야 한다. **3** 타동사 정돈하다 ❏ 그녀는 침대 이불을 정리한 다음 방을 정돈했다.

▶**tidy away** PHRASAL VERB When you **tidy** something **away**, you put it in something else so that it is not in the way. [mainly BRIT] ❏ *The large log basket can be used to tidy toys away.*

구동사 넣어 두다, 치워 두다 [주로 영국영어] ❏ 큰 장작 바구니는 장난감을 넣어 두는 데 쓸 수도 있다.

▶**tidy up** PHRASAL VERB When you **tidy up** or **tidy** a place **up**, you put things back in their proper places so that everything is neat. ❏ *I really must start tidying the place up.* ❏ *He tried to tidy up, not wanting the maid to see the disarray.*

구동사 정돈하다 ❏ 정말로 이곳을 정돈하기 시작해야겠다. ❏ 그는 하녀에게 너저분한 것을 보여 주고 싶지 않아서 정돈을 하려고 했다.

tie ♦♦◇ /taɪ/ (**ties, tying, tied**) **1** V-T If you **tie** two things **together** or **tie** them, you fasten them together with a knot. ❏ *He tied the ends of the plastic bag together.* **2** V-T If you **tie** something or someone in a particular place or position, you put them there and fasten them using rope or string. ❏ *He had tied the dog to one of the trees near the canal.* **3** V-T If you **tie** a piece of string or cloth around something or **tie** something with a piece of string or cloth, you put the piece of string or cloth around it and fasten the ends together. ❏ *She tied her scarf over her head.* ❏ *Roll the meat and tie it with string.* **4** V-T If you **tie** a knot or bow **in** something or **tie** something **in** a knot or bow, you fasten the ends together. ❏ *He took a short length of rope and swiftly tied a slip knot.* ❏ *She tied a knot in a cherry stem.* **5** V-T/V-I When you **tie** something or when something **ties**, you close or fasten it using a bow or knot. ❏ *He pulled on his heavy suede shoes and tied the laces.* **6** N-COUNT A **tie** is a long narrow piece of cloth that is worn around the neck under a shirt collar and tied in a knot at the front. Ties are worn mainly by

1 타동사 묶다 ❏ 그는 플라스틱 봉지의 양끝을 묶었다. **2** 타동사 묶어 두다 ❏ 그는 운하 옆의 나무 중 하나에 개를 묶어 뒀었다. **3** 타동사 묶다 ❏ 그녀는 스카프를 머리에 쓰고 묶었다. ❏ 고기를 만 다음 실로 묶어라. **4** 타동사 묶다 ❏ 그는 짧은 밧줄을 잡더니 재빨리 풀매듭을 묶었다. ❏ 그녀는 체리 꼭지에 매듭을 묶었다. **5** 타동사/자동사 묶다 ❏ 그는 무거운 스웨이드 신발을 당겨 신고 끈을 묶었다. **6** 가산명사 넥타이 ❏ 제이슨은 재킷을 벗고 넥타이를 느슨하게 푼 상태였다. **7** 타동사 연관되다 ❏ 그들의 암은 방사능 노출과 그다지 명확한 관련이 있지는 않다. **8** 타동사 얽매이다 ❏ 그들에겐 애들이 있었고 그래서 학교 방학에 얽매여 있었다. **9** 가산명사 연관 ❏ 퀘벡은 항상 프랑스와 매우 가까운 관계를 유지해

Word Web　tide

The **gravitational** pull of the **moon** on the earth's **oceans** causes **tides**. **High tides** occur twice a day at any given point on the earth's surface. During the next six hours, the water gradually **ebbs** away, producing a **low tide**. In some places tidal energy powers hydroelectric plants. Rip tides are responsible for the deaths of hundreds of swimmers each year. However, a riptide is not really a tide. It is a strong ocean **current**.

men. ❏ *Jason had taken off his jacket and loosened his tie.* **7** V-T If one thing **is tied to** another or two things **are tied**, the two things have a close connection or link. [usu passive] ❏ *Their cancers are not so clearly tied to radiation exposure.* **8** V-T If you **are tied to** a particular place or situation, you are forced to accept it and cannot change it. [usu passive] ❏ *They had children and were consequently tied to the school holidays.* **9** N-COUNT **Ties** are the connections you have with people or a place. [usu pl, oft N prep] ❏ *Quebec has always had particularly close ties to France.* **10** V-RECIP If two people **tie** in a competition or game or if they **tie with** each other, they have the same number of points or the same degree of success. ❏ *Ronan Rafferty had tied with Frank Nobilo.* ● N-COUNT **Tie** is also a noun. ❏ *The first game ended in a tie.* **11** N-COUNT In sports, a **tie** is a match that is part of a competition. The losers leave the competition and the winners go on to the next round. [mainly BRIT] ❏ *They'll meet the winners of the first round tie.* **12** your **hands are tied** →see hand
→see clothing

▶**tie up** **1** PHRASAL VERB When you **tie** something **up**, you fasten string or rope around it so that it is firm or secure. ❏ *He tied up the bag and took it outside.* **2** PHRASAL VERB If someone **ties** another person **up**, they fasten ropes or chains around them so that they cannot move or escape. ❏ *Masked robbers broke in, tied him up, and made off with $8,000.* **3** PHRASAL VERB If you **tie** an animal **up**, you fasten it to a fixed object with a piece of rope so that it cannot run away. ❏ *Would you go and tie your horse up please.*

tier /tɪər/ (**tiers**) **1** N-COUNT A **tier** is a row or layer of something that has other layers above or below it. ❏ *...the auditorium with the tiers of seats around and above it.* ● COMB in ADJ **Tier** is also a combining form. ❏ *...a three-tier wedding cake.* **2** N-COUNT A **tier** is a level in an organization or system. ❏ *Islanders have campaigned for the abolition of one of the three tiers of municipal power on the island.* ● COMB in ADJ **Tier** is also a combining form. ❏ *...the possibility of a two-tier system of universities.*

ti|ger /taɪgər/ (**tigers**) N-COUNT A **tiger** is a large fierce animal belonging to the cat family. Tigers are orange with black stripes.

tight ◆◇◇ /taɪt/ (**tighter**, **tightest**) **1** ADJ **Tight** clothes or shoes are rather small and fit closely to your body. ❏ *She walked off the plane in a miniskirt and tight top.* ● **tight|ly** ADV [ADV with v] ❏ *He buttoned his collar tightly round his thick neck.* **2** ADV If you hold someone or something **tight**, you hold them firmly and securely. [ADV after v] ❏ *She just fell into my arms, clutching me tight for a moment.* ❏ *Just hold tight to my hand and follow along.* ● ADJ **Tight** is also an adjective. ❏ *As he and Henrietta passed through the gate he kept a tight hold of her arm.* ● **tight|ly** ADV [ADV after v] ❏ *She climbed back into bed and wrapped her body tightly round her body.* **3** ADJ **Tight** controls or rules are very strict. ❏ *The measures include tight control of media coverage.* ❏ *The Government were prepared to keep a tight hold on public sector pay rises.* ● **tight|ly** ADV ❏ *The internal media was tightly controlled by the government during the war.* **4** ADV Something that is shut **tight** is shut very firmly. ❏ *The baby lay on his back with his eyes closed tight.* ❏ *I keep the flour and sugar in individual jars, sealed tight with their glass lids.* ● **tight|ly** ADV ❏ *Pemberton frowned and closed his eyes tightly.* **5** ADJ Skin, cloth, or string that is **tight** is stretched or pulled so that it is smooth or straight. ❏ *My skin feels tight and lacking in moisture.* ● **tight|ly** ADV [ADV with v] ❏ *Her sallow skin was drawn tightly across the bones of her face.* **6** ADJ **Tight** is used to describe a group of things or an amount of something that is closely packed together. ❏ *She curled up in a tight ball, with her knees tucked up at her chin.* ● ADV **Tight** is also an adverb. ❏ *The people sleep on sun lounges packed tight, end to end.* ● **tight|ly** ❏ *Many animals travel in tightly packed lorries and are deprived of food, water and rest.* **7** ADJ If a part of your body is **tight**, it feels rather uncomfortable and painful, for example because you are ill, anxious, or angry. ❏ *It is better to stretch the tight muscles first.* **8** ADJ A **tight** group of people is one whose members are closely linked by beliefs, feelings, or interests. ❏ *We're a tight group, so we do keep in touch.* **9** ADJ A **tight** bend or corner is one that changes direction very quickly so that you cannot see very far round it. ❏ *They collided on a tight bend and both cars were extensively damaged.* **10** ADJ A **tight** schedule or budget allows very little time or money for unexpected events or expenses. ❏ *It's difficult to cram everything into a tight schedule.* ❏ *Emma is on a tight budget for clothes.* **11** →see also **airtight** **12** to **keep a tight rein on** →see rein. to **sit tight** →see sit

Word Partnership	*tight*의 연어
N.	tight **dress/jeans/pants** **1**
	tight **fit** **1** **5**
	tight **grip**, tight **hold** **2**
	tight **control**, tight **security** **3**
	tight **squeeze** **6**
	tight **lips**, tight **muscles** **7**
ADV.	**extremely** tight, **a little** tight, **so** tight, **too** tight, **very** tight **1**-**10**
ADJ.	**shut** tight **4**
	tight **knit** **8**

tight|en /taɪtᵊn/ (**tightens**, **tightening**, **tightened**) **1** V-T/V-I If you **tighten** your grip on something, or if your grip **tightens**, you hold the thing more firmly or securely. ❏ *Luke answered by tightening his grip on her shoulder.* ❏ *Her arms tightened about his neck in gratitude.* **2** V-T/V-I If you **tighten** a rope or chain, or if it **tightens**, it is stretched or pulled hard until it is straight. ❏ *The anchorman flung his whole weight back, tightening the rope.* **3** V-T/V-I If a government or organization **tightens** its grip on a group of people or an activity, or if its grip **tightens**, it begins to have more control over it. ❏ *He knows he has considerable support for his plans to tighten his grip on the machinery of central government.* **4** V-T

왔다. **10** 상호동사 비기다 ❏ 로난 래퍼티는 프랭크 노빌로와 비긴 상태였다. ● 가산명사 동점 ❏ 첫 번째 경기는 무승부로 끝났다. **11** 가산명사 승자 진출 시합 [주로 영국영어] ❏ 그들은 첫 번째 라운드의 승자들과 만날 것이다.

1 구동사 묶다, 동여매다 ❏ 그는 봉지를 동여매어 밖으로 가지고 나갔다. **2** 구동사 묶다 ❏ 복면강도들이 쳐들어와서 그를 묶고는 8천 달러를 훔쳐 달아냈다. **3** 구동사 묶다, 매다 ❏ 가서 당신의 말을 매주세요.

1 가산명사 층, 단 ❏ 둘레에 그리고 위에 좌석이 층층이 놓인 강당 ● 복합형-형용사 층, 단 ❏ 3단으로 된 결혼 케이크 **2** 가산명사 등급 ❏ 섬 주민들은 섬에서의 3등급으로 된 자치 권력 체계에서 한 등급을 철폐하라고 운동을 벌이고 있다. ● 복합형-형용사 등급 ❏ 대학들이 두 등급으로 나뉠 가능성

가산명사 호랑이

1 형용사 꽉 끼는 ❏ 그녀는 미니스커트와 꽉 끼는 상의를 입고 비행기에서 내렸다. ● 꽉 끼게 부사 ❏ 그는 두꺼운 목에 깃이 꽉 끼게 단추를 채웠다. **2** 부사 꽉 ❏ 그녀는 그냥 내 팔 안으로 쓰러져 잠시 나를 꽉 움켜잡고 있었다. ❏ 내 손을 꽉 잡고 따라 오기만 해. ● 형용사 단단한 ❏ 그와 헨리에타가 정문을 통과하는 동안 그는 그녀의 팔을 단단히 잡고 있었다. ● 단단히, 꽉 부사 ❏ 그녀는 침대 안으로 다시 들어가서 두 팔로 자기 몸을 꽉 껴안았다. **3** 형용사 엄격한 ❏ 조치 중에는 언론 보도에 관한 엄격한 규제도 포함되어 있다. ❏ 정부는 공공 부문의 임금 인상을 엄격히 통제할 준비가 되어 있었다. ● 엄격하게 부사 ❏ 내부 언론이 전쟁 기간 동안 정부의 엄격한 통제를 받았다. **4** 부사 꼭, 단단히 ❏ 아기는 눈을 꼭 감고 반듯이 누워 있었다. ❏ 개별 병에 밀가루와 설탕을 각각 따로 담아 나는 유리 뚜껑으로 꼭 닫아 보관한다. ● 꼭, 단단히 부사 ❏ 펨버튼은 눈을 꼭 감고 인상을 찌푸렸다. **5** 형용사 팽팽한 ❏ 피부가 바짝 쬐고 수분이 없는 것 같다. ● 바짝 부사 ❏ 그녀의 누런 피부는 얼굴뼈에 바짝 달라붙어 있었다. **6** 형용사 꽉 들어찬 ❏ 그녀는 무릎을 턱까지 갖다 대며 단단한 공처럼 몸을 꽉 움츠렸다. ● 부사 꽉 ❏ 사람들은 일광욕실에서 방 끝에서 끝까지 꽉 들어차서 잔다. ● 꽉꽉 부사 ❏ 많은 동물들은 트럭에 꽉꽉 실려 다니며 먹이, 물, 휴식을 얻지 못한다. **7** 형용사 뭉친 ❏ 뭉친 근육을 먼저 푸는 것이 낫다. **8** 형용사 유대가 강한 ❏ 유대가 강한 집단이므로 서로 꼭 연락을 유지한다. **9** 형용사 (커브가) 급격한 ❏ 그들은 급커브에서 충돌했으며 두 차 모두 심하게 파손되었다. **10** 형용사 빡빡한, 빠듯한 ❏ 빡빡한 일정에 모든 것을 집어넣기란 어렵다. ❏ 엠마는 옷을 사기에는 돈이 빠듯하다.

1 타동사/자동사 더 단단히 잡다; 더 단단해지다 ❏ 루크는 그녀의 어깨에 얹은 손에 더 힘을 주는 것으로 답변을 대신했다. ❏ 그녀는 고마워하며 그의 목을 더 단단히 껴안았다. **2** 타동사/자동사 바짝 당기다; 팽팽해지다 ❏ 줄다리기에서 맨 중심이 되는 남자가 자신의 몸무게를 모두 실어 뒤로 바짝 당기자 밧줄이 팽팽해졌다. **3** 타동사/자동사 강화하다; 강화되다 ❏ 그는 중앙 정부 조직에 대한 자신의 지배력을 더욱 강화하려는 계획에 대해 상당한

When you **tighten** a screw, nut, or other device, you turn it or move it so that it is more firmly in place or holds something more firmly. □ *I used my thumbnail to tighten the screw on my lamp.* ● PHRASAL VERB **Tighten up** means the same as **tighten.** □ *It's important to tighten up the wheels properly, otherwise they vibrate loose and fall off.* ⑤ V-I If a part of your body **tightens,** the muscles in it become tense and stiff, for example because you are angry or afraid. □ *Sofia's throat had tightened and she couldn't speak.* ⑥ V-T If someone in authority **tightens** a rule, a policy, or a system, they make it stricter or more efficient. □ *The United States plans to tighten the economic sanctions currently in place.* ● PHRASAL VERB **Tighten up** means the same as **tighten.** □ *Until this week, every attempt to tighten up the law had failed.* ⑦ to **tighten** your **belt** →see **belt**

tights /taɪts/ N-PLURAL **Tights** are a piece of clothing, worn by women and girls. They are usually made of nylon and cover the hips, legs, and feet. [BRIT; AM **pantyhose**] [also *a pair of* N] □ *...a new pair of tights.*

tile /taɪl/ (tiles) ① N-VAR **Tiles** are flat, square pieces of baked clay, carpet, cork, or other substance, which are fixed as a covering onto a floor or wall. □ *Amy's shoes squeaked on the tiles as she walked down the corridor.* ② N-VAR **Tiles** are flat pieces of baked clay which are used for covering roofs. □ *...a fine building, with a neat little porch and ornamental tiles on the roof.*

till ♦◇◇ /tɪl/ (tills) ① PREP In spoken English and informal written English, **till** is often used instead of **until.** □ *They had to wait till Monday to ring the bank manager.* ● CONJ **Till** is also a conjunction. □ *I hadn't left home till I was nineteen.* ② N-COUNT A **till** is the drawer of a cash register, in which the money is kept. [AM] □ *He checked the register. There was money in the till.* ③ N-COUNT In a store or other place of business, a **till** is a counter or cash register where money is kept, and where customers pay for what they have bought. [BRIT; AM **cash register**] □ *...long queues at tills that make customers angry.*

> Note that you only use **until** or **till** when you are talking about time. You do not use these words to talk about place or position. Instead, you should use **as far as** or **up to.** □ *Then you'll be riding with us as far as the village?... We walked up to where his bicycle was.*

tilt /tɪlt/ (tilts, tilting, tilted) ① V-T/V-I If you **tilt** an object or if it **tilts,** it moves into a sloping position with one end or side higher than the other. □ *She tilted the mirror and began to comb her hair.* □ *Leonard tilted his chair back on two legs and stretched his long body.* ② V-T If you **tilt** part of your body, usually your head, you move it slightly upward or to one side. □ *Mari tilted her head back so that she could look at him.* □ *His wife tilted his head to the side and inspected the wound.* ● N-COUNT **Tilt** is also a noun. □ *He opened the rear door for me with an apologetic tilt of his head.* ③ N-COUNT The **tilt** of something is the fact that it tilts or slopes, or the angle at which it tilts or slopes. □ *...calculations based on our understanding of the tilt of the earth's axis.* ④ V-I If a person or thing **tilts toward** a particular opinion or if something **tilts** them **toward** it, they change slightly so that they become more in agreement with that opinion or position. □ *Political will might finally tilt toward some sort of national health plan.*

tim|ber /tɪmbər/ N-UNCOUNT **Timber** is wood that is used for building houses and making furniture. You can also refer to trees that are grown for this purpose as **timber.** □ *These Severn Valley woods have been exploited for timber since Saxon times.* →see **forest**

time ♦♦♦ /taɪm/ (times, timing, timed) ① N-UNCOUNT **Time** is what we measure in minutes, hours, days, and years. □ *...a two-week period of time.* □ *Time passed, and still Ma did not appear.* ② N-SING You use **time** to ask or talk about a specific point in the day, which is stated in hours and minutes and is shown on clocks. □ *"What time is it?" — "Eight o'clock."* □ *He asked me the time.* ③ N-COUNT The **time** when something happens is the point in the day when it happens or is supposed to happen. □ *Departure times are 08.15 from St Quay, and 18.15 from St Helier.* ④ N-UNCOUNT You use **time** to refer to the system of expressing time and counting hours that is used in a particular part of the world. □ *The incident happened just after ten o'clock local time.* ⑤ N-UNCOUNT You use **time** to refer to the period that you spend doing something or when something has been happening. [also *a* N] □ *Adam spent a lot of time in his grandfather's office.* □ *He wouldn't have the time or money to take care of me.* □ *Listen to me, I haven't got much time.* □ *It's obvious that you need more time to think.* ⑥ N-SING If you say that something has been happening for **a time,** you mean that it has been happening for a fairly long period of time. □ *He was also for a time the art critic of "The Scotsman".* □ *He stayed for quite a time.* ⑦ N-COUNT You use **time** to refer to a period of time or a point in time, when you are describing what is happening then. For example, if something happens **at a particular time,** that is when it happened. If it happens **at all times,** it always happens. □ *We were in the same college, which was male-only at that time.* □ *By this time he was thirty.* □ *It was a time of terrible uncertainty.* ⑧ N-COUNT You use **time** or **times** to talk about a particular period in history or in your life. □ *They were hard times and his parents had been struggling to raise their family.* □ *We'll be alone together, quite like old times.* ⑨ N-PLURAL You can use **the times** to refer to the present time and to modern fashions, tastes, and developments. For example, if you say that someone **keeps up with the times,** you mean they are fashionable or aware of modern developments. If you say they are **behind the times,** you mean they are unfashionable or not aware of them. □ *This approach is now seriously out of step with the times.* ⑩ N-COUNT When you describe the **time** that you had on a particular occasion or during a particular part of your life, you are describing the sort of experience that you had then. □ *Sarah and I had a great time while the kids were away.* ⑪ N-SING Your **time** is the amount of time that you have to live, or to do a particular thing. □ *Now Martin has begun to suffer the effects of AIDS, and*

지지를 받고 있다는 것을 안다. ④ 타동사 죄다 □ 나는 엄지손톱으로 램프의 나사를 조였다. ● 구동사 죄다 □ 바퀴를 제대로 죄는 게 중요하다. 그렇지 않으면 진동하면서 풀려 떨어져 나간다. ⑤ 자동사 (근육이) 뻣뻣해지다 □ 소피아의 목이 뻣뻣해져 말을 할 수 없었다. ⑥ 타동사 강화하다 □ 미국은 기존의 경제 제재를 더욱 강화할 방침이다. ● 구동사 강화하다 □ 이번 주까지는 법을 강화하려는 모든 시도가 실패했었다.

복수명사 팬티스타킹, 타이츠 [영국영어; 미국영어 pantyhose] □ 새 팬티스타킹 하나

① 가산명사 또는 불가산명사 타일 □ 에이미가 복도를 따라 걸어갈 때 신발이 타일 위에서 삐걱거렸다. ② 가산명사 또는 불가산명사 기와 □ 작고 단아한 현관에, 장식용 기와로 지붕을 인 멋진 건물

① 전치사 ～까지 □ 그들이 은행 지점장에게 전화를 걸기 위해선 월요일까지 기다려야 했다. ● 접속사 ～한 때까지 □ 나는 열아홉 살이 될 때까지 집을 떠난 적이 없었다. ② 가산명사 현금 서랍 [미국영어] □ 그는 금전 등록기를 확인했다. 현금 서랍에 돈이 있었다. ③ 가산명사 계산대, 금전 등록기 [영국영어; 미국영어 cash register] □ 고객들을 화나게 하는 계산대 앞의 긴 줄

> until이나 till은 시간에 대해 말할 때만 쓴다는 점을 유의하라. 장소나 위치에 대해 말할 때는 이런 말은 사용하지 않고, 대신, as far as나 up to를 써야 한다. □ 그러면 당신은 마을까지 우리와 함께 타고 가시나요?... 우리는 그의 자전거가 있는 곳까지 걸어갔다.

① 타동사/자동사 기울이다; 기울어지다 □ 그녀는 거울을 기울이고 머리를 빗기 시작했다. □ 레너드는 의자가 두 다리로만 받쳐지게 뒤로 기울이며 긴 몸을 쭉 폈다. ② 타동사 젖히다 □ 마리는 그를 보기 위해 고개를 젖히고 □ 아내가 남자의 고개를 옆으로 젖히고 상처를 살펴봤다. ● 가산명사 기울임, 젖힘 □ 그가 사과의 뜻으로 고개를 약간 기울이며 나를 위해 뒷문을 열어 주었다. ③ 가산명사 기울기 □ 지구 축의 기울기에 대한 우리의 이해를 근거로 한 계산 ④ 자동사 기울어지다; 기울어지게 하다 □ 정치적인 중론이 드디어 어떤 형태로든 국가적 보건 계획 쪽으로 기울어질지도 모른다.

불가산명사 재목 □ 이 세번 계곡의 숲은 색슨족 시대 이래로 재목을 위해 벌채되어 왔다.

① 불가산명사 시간 □ 2주의 시간 □ 시간은 흘러도 엄마는 나타나지 않았다. ② 단수명사 시간 □ "몇 시야?" "여덟 시." □ 그는 나에게 시간을 물었다. ③ 가산명사 시각 □ 출발 시각은 세인트키에서는 8시 15분, 세인트 헬리어에서는 18시 15분입니다. ④ 불가산명사 시간 □ 그 사건은 현지 시간으로 10시 갓 지나서 발생했다. ⑤ 불가산명사 시간 □ 아담은 많은 시간을 할아버지의 사무실에서 보냈다. □ 그는 나를 돌볼 시간도 돈도 없을 것이다. □ 내 말 들어봐, 시간이 얼마 없단 말이야. □ 너는 분명히 더 생각할 시간이 필요해. ⑥ 단수명사 한 동안 □ 그는 꽤 한 동안 '스코츠맨' 지의 미술 평론가였다. □ 그는 한 동안 머물렀다. ⑦ 가산명사 시기, 때 □ 당시에는 남자로만 다닐 수 있었던 대학에 우리는 같이 다녔다. □ 이때쯤 나이가 이미 서른이었다. □ 엄청난 불확실성의 시기였다. ⑧ 가산명사 시기 □ 그들이 어려운 시기였고 그의 부모는 가족을 부양하기 위해 애쓰고 있었다. □ 꼭 옛날처럼 우리만 함께 있을 거야. ⑨ 복수명사 시대 □ 변화가 있어야 할 시기가 온 것 같다는 인식이 대중 사이에 존재한다는 것이 여론 조사로 드러났다. □ 그가 일하려 할 시기가 왔다. ⑩ 가산명사 시기 □ 그녀가 버스를 탈 때마다 최소한 3시간은 연착된다. ⑪ 단수명사 시기 □ 마틴에게 이제 에이즈의 영향이 나타나기 시작했고 그는 살 시간이 많지 않다는 것을 안다. ⑫ 불가산명사 시간, 때, 시기 □ 그들이 집을 떠난 동안 사람과 나는 아주 즐거운 시간을 보냈다. ⑬ 가산명사 때 □ 하루에 세 번 차를 타는 것이 그녀의 일이었다. ⑭ 복수명사 배 □ 그 회사의 수익은 네 회사보다 네 배 빨리 증가하고 있다. ⑮ 접속사 ～에 곱하기 □ 4 곱하기 6은 24이다. ⑯ 가산명사 (경주에서) 시간 기록 □ 그는 종전의 최고 기록보다 1초 이상 빠른 기록을 남겼다. ⑰ 타동사

A

he says his time is running out. **12** N-UNCOUNT If you say it is **time for** something, **time to** do something, or **time** you did something, you mean that this thing ought to happen or be done now. ❑ _Opinion polls indicated a feeling among the public that it was time for a change._ ❑ _It was time for him to go to work._ **13** N-COUNT

B

When you talk about a **time** when something happens, you are referring to a specific occasion when it happens. ❑ _Every time she travels on the bus it's delayed by at least three hours._ **14** N-COUNT You use **time** after numbers to say how often something happens. ❑ _It was her job to make tea three times a day._ **15** N-PLURAL You

C

use **times** after numbers when comparing one thing to another and saying, for example, how much bigger, smaller, better, or worse it is. ❑ _Its profits are rising four times faster than the average company._ **16** CONJ You use **times** in arithmetic to link numbers or amounts that are multiplied together to reach

D

a total. ❑ _Four times six is 24._ **17** N-COUNT Someone's **time** in a race is the amount of time it takes them to finish the race. ❑ _He was over a second faster than his previous best time._ **18** V-T If you **time** something **for** a particular time, you plan or decide to do it or cause it to happen at this time. ❑ _He timed the election to coincide_

E

with new measures to boost the economy. ❑ _We had timed our visit for March 7._ **19** V-T If you **time** an action or activity, you measure how long someone takes to do it or

F

how long it lasts. ❑ _A radar gun timed the speed of the baseball._ **20** →see also **timing** **21** PHRASE If you say it is **about time** that something was done, you are saying in an emphatic way that it should happen or be done now, and really should have happened or been done sooner. [EMPHASIS] ❑ _It's about time a few movie_

G

makers with original ideas were given a chance. **22** PHRASE If you do something **ahead of time**, you do it before a particular event or before you need to, in order to be well prepared. ❑ _Find out ahead of time what regulations apply to your situation._

H

23 PHRASE If someone is **ahead** of their **time** or **before** their **time**, they have new ideas a long time before other people start to think in the same way. ❑ _Bond was also ahead of his time in appreciating the power of marketing._ **24** PHRASE If

I

something happens or is done **all the time**, it happens or is done continually. ❑ _We can't be together all the time._ **25** PHRASE You say **at a time** after an amount to say how many things or how much of something is involved in one action, place, or group. ❑ _Beat in the eggs, one at a time._ **26** PHRASE If something could

J

happen **at any time**, it is possible that it will happen very soon, though nobody can predict exactly when. ❑ _Conditions are still very tense and the fighting could escalate at any time._ **27** PHRASE If you say that something was the case **at**

K

one time, you mean that it was the case during a particular period in the past. ❑ _At one time 400 men, women and children lived in the village._ **28** PHRASE If two or more things exist, happen, or are true **at the same time**, they exist, happen, or

L

are true together although they seem to contradict each other. ❑ _I was afraid of her, but at the same time I really liked her._ **29** PHRASE **At the same time** is used to introduce a statement that slightly changes or contradicts the previous statement. ❑ _I don't think I set out to come up with a different sound for each album. At_

M

the same time, I do have a sense of what is right for the moment. **30** PHRASE You use **at times** to say that something happens or is true on some occasions or at some moments. ❑ _The debate was highly emotional at times._ **31** PHRASE If you say that something will be the case **for all time**, you mean that it will always be the

N

case. ❑ _The desperate condition of the world is that madness has always been here, and that it will remain so for all time._ **32** PHRASE If something is the case or will happen **for the time being**, it is the case and will happen now, but only until something else becomes possible or happens. ❑ _For the time being, however, immunotherapy is_

O

still in its experimental stages. **33** PHRASE If you do something **from time to time**, you do it occasionally but not regularly. ❑ _Her daughters visited him from time to_

P

time when he was ill. **34** PHRASE If you say that something is the case **half the time** you mean that it often is the case. [INFORMAL] ❑ _Half the time, I don't have the slightest idea what he's talking about._ **35** PHRASE If you are **in time for** a particular event, you are not too late for it. ❑ _I arrived just in time for my flight to London._

Q

36 PHRASE If you say that something will happen **in time** or **given time**, you mean that it will happen eventually, when a lot of time has passed. ❑ _He would sort out his own problems, in time._ **37** PHRASE If you are playing, singing, or

R

dancing **in time** with a piece of music, you are following the rhythm and speed of the music correctly. If you are **out of time** with it, you are not following the rhythm and speed of the music correctly. ❑ _Her body swayed in time with the music._ **38** PHRASE If you say that something will happen, for

S

example, **in a week's time** or **in two years' time**, you mean that it will happen a week from now or two years from now. ❑ _Presidential elections are due to be held in ten days' time._ **39** PHRASE If you arrive somewhere **in good time**, you arrive early

T

so that there is time to spare before a particular event. ❑ _If we're out, we always make sure we're home in good time for the programme._ **40** PHRASE If something happens **in no time** or **in next to no time**, it happens almost immediately or very quickly. ❑ _He's going to be just fine. At his age he'll heal in no time._ **41** PHRASE If

U

you **keep time** when playing or singing music, you follow or play the beat, without going too fast or too slowly. ❑ _As he sang he kept time on a small drum._

V

42 PHRASE When you talk about how well a watch or clock **keeps time**, you are talking about how accurately it measures time. ❑ _Some pulsars keep time better than the earth's most accurate clocks._ **43** PHRASE If you **make time for** a particular activity or person, you arrange to have some free time so that you can do the

W

activity or spend time with the person. ❑ _Before leaving the city, be sure to make time for a shopping trip._ **44** PHRASE If you say that you **made good time** on a trip, you mean it did not take you very long compared to the length of time you expected it to take. ❑ _They had left early in the morning, on quiet roads, and made good_

X

time. **45** PHRASE If someone is **making up for lost time**, they are doing something actively and with enthusiasm because they have not had the opportunity to do it before or when they were younger. ❑ _Five years older than the majority of officers of his same rank, he was determined to make up for lost time._

Y

46 PHRASE If you say that something happens or is the case **nine times out of ten** or **ninety-nine times out of a hundred**, you mean that it happens on nearly every occasion or is almost always the case. ❑ _When they want something, nine times out of ten they get it._ **47** PHRASE If you say that someone or something is,

Z

시기를 맞추다 ❑ 그는 경제를 진작시키기 위한 새로운 조치와 맞어떨어지도록 선거 시기를 맞추었다. ❑ 우리는 방문 시기를 3월 7일로 잡아 놓은 상태다. **19** 타동사 시간을 재다 ❑ 속도 측정기가 야구공의 속도를 쟀다. **21** 구 –해야 할 때 [강조] ❑ 독창적인 생각을 가진 영화 제작자들에게 기회를 주어야 할 때이다. **22** 구 미리 ❑ 당신의 상황에 어떤 규제가 적용되는지 미리 알아두시오. **23** 구 시대를 앞선 ❑ 본드 또한 마케팅의 힘을 인식하는 데는 시대를 앞서 있었다. **24** 구 항상 ❑ 항상 같이 있을 수는 없다. **25** 구 한번에 ❑ 계란을 한번에 하나씩 넣으면서 저어라. **26** 구 언제라도 ❑ 여전히 일촉즉발의 상황이며 언제라도 싸움이 더 치열해질 수 있다. **27** 구 한때에는 ❑ 한때에는 그 마을에 남녀노소 4백 명이 살았다. **28** 구 동시에 ❑ 나는 그녀가 무서웠지만 또 동시에 그녀가 정말로 좋았다. **29** 구 그렇지만, 한편으로는 ❑ 내가 각 앨범을 위해 각각 다른 소리를 내려고 작정을 하지는 않는 것 같다. 하지만 한편으로는 그 순간에 뭐가 맞는지에 대한 감이 가지고 있다. **30** 구 때로는 ❑ 토론이 때로 굉장히 격앙된 가운데 진행되었다. **31** 구 영원히 ❑ 세상의 절망적인 사정은 이곳에 항상 광기가 존재해왔었다는 것 그리고 앞으로도 영원히 존재할 것이라는 것이다. **32** 구 지금으로서는, 당분간은 ❑ 하지만 지금으로서는 면역 치료가 아직도 실험 단계에 있다. **33** 구 종종 ❑ 그녀의 딸들이 그가 아플 때 종종 그를 찾아갔다. **34** 구 거의 언제나 [비격식체] ❑ 거의 언제나 나는 그가 무슨 얘기를 하는지 도통 모르겠다. **35** 구 –하는 시간에 맞춰 ❑ 나는 런던 행 비행기 출발 시간에 가까스로 맞춰 도착했다. **36** 구 언젠가는 ❑ 언젠가는 그가 자기 문제를 해결할 것이다. **37** 구 박자에 맞춰, 박자에 어긋나게 ❑ 그녀는 음악에 맞춰 몸을 흔들었다. **38** 구 – 뒤에, –의 시간이 흐르면 ❑ 대통령 선거가 10일 뒤에 처러질 예정이다. **39** 구 시간이 넉넉하게 미리 ❑ 우리가 만약 외출을 하면 그 프로그램에 맞춰 시간이 넉넉하게 집에 도착할 수 있도록 신경을 쓴다. **40** 구 곧, 금방 ❑ 그는 괜찮을 것이다. 그 나이면 금방 나을 것이다. **41** 구 장단을 맞추다 ❑ 그는 노래를 부르면서 작은 북으로 장단을 맞추었다. **42** 구 (시계가) 시간이 정확하다 ❑ 일부 맥동성은 지구의 가장 정확한 시계보다 시간이 더 정확하다. **43** 구 시간을 내다 ❑ 그 도시를 떠나기 전에 꼭 시간을 내어 쇼핑을 해라. **44** 구 시간이 예상보다 적게 걸리다 ❑ 그들은 길이 한산한 이른 아침에 떠나서 예상보다 빨리 도착했다. **45** 구 잃어버린 시간을 보완하다 ❑ 동일한 계급의 대부분의 다른 장교들보다 다섯 살이나 많은 그는 잃어버린 시간을 보완할 작정을 하고 있었다. **46** 구 십중팔구 ❑ 그들은 무엇을 원할 경우 십중팔구는 그것을 갖게 된다. **47** 구 역대, 지금껏 ❑ 모노폴리는 역대 최고로 잘 팔리는 게임 중 하나이다. **48** 구 제시간에 맞춰 ❑ 걱정하지 마, 그녀는 시간 맞춰 올 거야. **49** 구 단지 시간문제 ❑ 그들이 퇴임하기까지는 이제 단지 시간문제인 것 같다. **50** 구 시간을 때우다 ❑ 별다른 관심 없이 단지 시간을 때우기 위해 나는 이야기를 하나 읽었다. **51** 구 시간이 걸리다 ❑ 변화는 오겠지만 시간이 걸릴 것이다. **52** 구 천천히 하다 ❑ "천천히 해." 크로스가 그에게 말했다. "나 안 급해." **53** 구 시계를 볼 줄 안다 ❑ 내 4살배기 딸은 아직 시계를 제대로 못 본다. **54** 구 여러 번, 거듭거듭 ❑ 버스는 여러 번 탈출했었다. **55** 구 시간이 금방 가다 ❑ 재미가 있으면 시간이 금방 간다. **56** 구 낭비할 시간이 없다 ❑ 낭비할 시간이 없다는 것을 알고 그는 집으로 서둘러 갔다. **57** 구 시간이 지나 봐야 안다 ❑ 브라운턴의 낙관론이 정당한지는 시간이 지나 봐야 안다. **58** 구 바로 –하다 ❑ 톰은 자신이 왜 왔는지를 내게 바로 말했다.

for example, the best writer **of all time**, or the most successful movie **of all time**, you mean that they are the best or most successful that there has ever been. ❑ *"Monopoly" is one of the best-selling games of all time.* ⓮ PHRASE If you are **on time**, you are not late. ❑ *Don't worry, she'll be on time.* ⓯ PHRASE If you say that it is **only a matter of time** or **only a question of time** before something happens, you mean that it cannot be avoided and will definitely happen at some future date. ❑ *It now seems only a matter of time before they resign.* ⓰ PHRASE If you do something to **pass the time** you do it because you have some time available and not because you really want to do it. ❑ *Without particular interest and just to pass the time, I read a story.* ⓱ PHRASE If you say that something will **take time**, you mean that it will take a long time. ❑ *Change will come, but it will take time.* ⓲ PHRASE If you **take** your **time** doing something, you do it quite slowly and do not hurry. ❑ *"Take your time," Cross told him. "I'm in no hurry."* ⓳ PHRASE If a child can **tell the time**, they are able to find out what the time is by looking at a clock or watch. ❑ *My four-year-old daughter cannot quite tell the time.* ⓴ PHRASE If something happens **time after time**, it happens in a similar way on many occasions. ❑ *Burns had escaped from jail time after time.* ㉕ PHRASE If you say that **time flies**, you mean that it seems to pass very quickly. ❑ *Time flies when you're having fun.* ㉖ PHRASE If you say there is **no time to lose** or **no time to be lost**, you mean you must hurry as fast as you can to do something. ❑ *He rushed home, realising there was no time to lose.* ㉗ PHRASE If you say that **time will tell** whether something is true or correct, you mean that it will not be known until some time in the future whether it is true or correct. ❑ *Only time will tell whether Broughton's optimism is justified.* ㉘ PHRASE If you **waste no time in** doing something, you take the opportunity to do it immediately or quickly. ❑ *Tom wasted no time in telling me why he had come.* ㉙ **time and again** →see **again**

You do not say "one time a year" or "two times a year"; you say **once a year** or **twice a year**. You also do not say "two times as much"; you say **twice as much**.

time-consuming also time consuming ADJ If something is **time-consuming**, it takes a lot of time. [oft it v-link ADJ to-inf] ❑ *It's just very time consuming to get such a large quantity of data.*

time|less /ˈtaɪmlɪs/ ADJ If you describe something as **timeless**, you mean that it is so good or beautiful that it cannot be affected by changes in society or fashion. ❑ *There is a timeless quality to his best work.*

time|line /ˈtaɪmlaɪn/ (**timelines**) also time line ■ N-COUNT A **timeline** is a visual representation of a sequence of events, especially historical events. ❑ *A unique 13,000-word timeline runs through the full-color volume, detailing events from the Earth's creation to the present day.* ❷ N-COUNT A **timeline** is the length of time that a project is expected to take. [BUSINESS] ❑ *Use your deadlines to establish the timeline for your research plan.* →see **history**

time|ly /ˈtaɪmli/ ADJ If you describe an event as **timely**, you approve of it because it happens exactly at the moment when it is most useful, effective, or relevant. [APPROVAL] ❑ *The recent outbreaks of cholera are a timely reminder that this disease is still a serious health hazard.*

time out (**time outs**) also time-out ■ N-VAR In basketball, football, ice hockey, and some other sports, when a team calls a **time out**, they call a stop to the game for a few minutes in order to rest and discuss how they are going to play. The referee may also call **time out** when a player is injured. ❑ *With 22.2 seconds to go before halftime, Brown wanted to call a time-out.* ❷ N-UNCOUNT If you take **time out from** a job or activity, you have a break from it and do something different instead. [oft N from n, N to-inf] ❑ *He took time out from campaigning to accompany his mother to dinner.*

time|scale /ˈtaɪmskeɪl/ (**timescales**) also time scale N-COUNT The **timescale** of an event is the length of time during which it happens or develops. ❑ *The likelihood is that these companies now will show excellent profits on a two-year timescale.*

time-share (**time-shares**) also time share N-VAR If you have a **time-share**, you have the right to use a particular property as vacation accommodations for a specific amount of time each year. ❑ *Other prizes include hotel discounts and a time-share at a Scottish castle.*

time|table /ˈtaɪmteɪbəl/ (**timetables**) ■ N-COUNT A **timetable** is a plan of the times when particular events are to take place. ❑ *The timetable was hopelessly optimistic.* ❑ *Don't you realize we're working to a timetable? We have to have results.* ❷ N-COUNT A **timetable** is a list of the times when trains, boats, buses, or airplanes are supposed to arrive at or leave from a particular place. [mainly BRIT; AM usually **schedule**] ❑ *...the 24-hour system as used in bus and train timetables.* ❸ N-COUNT In a school or college, a **timetable** is a list that shows the times in the week at which particular subjects are taught. You can also refer to the range of subjects that a student learns or the classes that a teacher teaches as their **timetable**. [BRIT; AM usually **class schedule**] ❑ *Options are offered subject to staff availability and the constraints of the timetable.*

tim|id /ˈtɪmɪd/ ADJ **Timid** people are shy, nervous, and have no courage or confidence in themselves. ❑ *A timid child, Isabella had learned obedience at an early age.* ● **ti|mid|ity** /tɪˈmɪdɪti/ N-UNCOUNT ❑ *She doesn't ridicule my timidity.* ● **tim|id|ly** ADV ❑ *The little boy stepped forward timidly and shook Leo's hand.*

tim|ing /ˈtaɪmɪŋ/ ■ N-UNCOUNT **Timing** is the skill or action of judging the right moment in a situation or activity at which to do something. ❑ *His photo is a wonderful happy moment caught with perfect timing.* ❷ N-UNCOUNT **Timing** is used to refer to the time at which something happens or is planned to happen, or to the length of time that something takes. ❑ *The timing of the minister's visit, however, could somewhat detract from the goodwill it's supposed to generate.* ❸ →see also **time**

one time a year나 two times a year라고는 하지 않고, once a year나 twice a year라고 한다. 마찬가지로 two times as much가 아니라 twice as much이다.

형용사 시간이 많이 걸리는 ❑ 그렇게 많은 양의 데이터를 얻는 데는 정말 시간이 많이 걸린다.

형용사 시대를 초월한 ❑ 그의 가장 뛰어난 작품에는 시대를 뛰어넘는 요소가 있다.

■ 가산명사 연대기 ❑ 그 완전 컬러로 된 책에는 지구의 생성부터 오늘에 이르기까지의 사건들을 상세히 설명하는, 13,000단어 길이로 된 연대기가 실려 있다. ❷ 가산명사 일정, 시간표 [경제] ❑ 연구 계획을 위한 시간표를 만들 때는 스스로 기한을 정해 놓는 방법을 써라.

형용사 시기적절한 [마음에 듦] ❑ 최근의 콜레라 발병이, 이 병이 아직도 보건에 심각한 위협이 되고 있다는 것을 시기적절하게 다시 상기시켜 주었다.

■ 가산명사 또는 불가산명사 타임아웃 ❑ 전반 종료 22.2초 전에 브라운은 타임아웃을 부르고 싶어 했다. ❷ 불가산명사 잠깐 중단, 휴식 ❑ 그는 선거 운동을 잠깐 중단하고 어머니와 동행하여 저녁 식사를 하러 갔다.

가산명사 기간 ❑ 이제 2년이라는 기간 내에 이 회사들이 훌륭한 수익을 거둘 가능성이 높다.

가산명사 또는 불가산명사 휴양 시설의 공동 사용권 ❑ 다른 상품 중에는 호텔 할인권과 스코틀랜드의 성에서 일정 기간 휴가를 보낼 수 있는 사용권이 있다.

■ 가산명사 계획표 ❑ 계획표가 지나치게 낙관적이었다. ❑ 우리가 계획표에 맞춰서 일하고 있다는 것을 모르나요? 결과를 내야죠. ❷ 가산명사 (운행) 시간표 [주로 영국영어; 미국영어 대개 schedule] ❑ 버스와 열차 시간표에 사용하는 것과 같은 24시간제 ❸ 가산명사 (수업) 시간표 [영국영어; 미국영어 대개 class schedule] ❑ 개강되는 선택 과목은 교원 수급 상황과 시간표상의 제약에 따라 달라진다.

형용사 소심한, 수줍은 ❑ 소심한 아이였던 이사벨라는 어린 나이에 순종하는 것을 배워 버렸다. ● 소심함, 수줍음 불가산명사 ❑ 그녀는 나의 소심함을 비웃지 않는다. ● 소심하게, 수줍게 부사 ❑ 어린 소년은 수줍게 앞으로 다가가 레오와 악수를 했다.

■ 불가산명사 타이밍 ❑ 그의 사진은 절묘한 타이밍으로 황홀하게 행복한 순간을 포착하고 있다. ❷ 불가산명사 시기 ❑ 그러나 장관의 방문이 시기 때문에 의도하던 만큼 친선 효과를 못 가져올 수도 있다.

tin /tɪn/ (**tins**) **1** N-UNCOUNT **Tin** is a soft silvery-white metal. ❑ ...*a factory that turns scrap metal into tin cans.* **2** N-COUNT A **tin** is a metal container with a lid in which things such as cookies, cakes, or tobacco can be kept. ❑ *Store the cookies in an airtight tin.* ● N-COUNT A **tin** of something is the amount contained in a tin. ❑ *They emptied out the remains of the tin of paint and smeared it on the inside of the van.* **3** N-COUNT A **tin** is a metal container which is filled with food and sealed in order to preserve the food for long periods of time. [mainly BRIT] ❑ *She popped out to buy a tin of soup.* ● N-COUNT A **tin of** food is the amount of food contained in a tin. [mainly BRIT; AM usually **can**] ❑ *He had survived by eating a small tin of fruit every day.* **4** N-COUNT A baking **tin** is a metal container used for baking things such as cakes and bread in an oven. [BRIT; AM **pan, baking pan**] ❑ *Pour the mixture into the cake tin and bake for 45 minutes.* →see **can, pan**

1 불가산명사 주석 **2** 가산명사 (뚜껑이 있는) 깡통 ❑ 쿠키는 공기가 들어가는 깡통에 넣어 두어라. ● 가산명사 깡통에 든 것 ❑ 그들은 통에 남아 있는 페인트를 다 부어 내어 밴 안에다 마구 발랐다. **3** 가산명사 통조림 [주로 영국영어] ❑ 그녀는 통조림 수프를 사기 위해 잠깐 나갔다. ● 가산명사 한 통조림 분량의 것 [주로 영국영어; 미국영어 대개 can] ❑ 그는 매일 작은 과일 통조림 한 통씩을 먹고 연명했었다. **4** 가산명사 (빵 굽는) 틀 [영국영어; 미국영어 pan, baking pan] ❑ 케이크 틀에 반죽을 부은 다음 45분간 오븐에서 구워라.

tinge /tɪndʒ/ (**tinges**) N-COUNT A **tinge** of a color, feeling, or quality is a small amount of it. ❑ *His skin had an unhealthy greyish tinge.*

가산명사 엷은 색조, 기색 ❑ 그의 피부에는 건강하지 못한 잿빛 색이 돌았다.

tinged /tɪndʒd/ **1** ADJ If something is **tinged with** a particular color, it has a small amount of that color in it. ❑ *His dark hair was just tinged with grey.* **2** ADJ If something is **tinged with** a particular feeling or quality, it has or shows a small amount of that feeling or quality. ❑ *Her homecoming was tinged with sadness.*

1 형용사 (색조를 띤, - 기가 나는 ❑ 그의 검은 머리는 아주 조금 희끗희끗했다. **2** 형용사 - 기색이 어린 ❑ 그녀의 귀향에는 슬픔이 어려 있었다.

tingle /tɪŋgᵊl/ (**tingles, tingling, tingled**) **1** V-I When a part of your body **tingles**, you have a slight stinging feeling there. ❑ *The backs of his thighs tingled.* ● **tingling** N-UNCOUNT ❑ *Its effects on the nervous system include weakness, paralysis, and tingling in the hands and feet.* **2** V-I If you **tingle with** a feeling such as excitement, you feel it very strongly. ❑ *She tingled with excitement.* ● N-COUNT **Tingle** is also a noun. ❑ *I felt a sudden tingle of excitement.*

1 자동사 따끔거리다, 욱신거리다 ❑ 그의 허벅지 뒤쪽이 욱신거렸다. ● 따끔거림, 욱신거림 불가산명사 ❑ 그것이 신경에 미치는 영향으로는 체력 저하, 마비, 손발 욱신거림 등이 있다. **2** 자동사 좀이 쑤시다, 마구 설레다 ❑ 그녀는 흥분해서 가만 있을 수가 없었다. ● 가산명사 마구 설렘, 좀이 쑤심 ❑ 나는 갑자기 마음이 마구 설레었다.

tinker /tɪŋkər/ (**tinkers, tinkering, tinkered**) V-I If you **tinker with** something, you make some small changes to it, in an attempt to improve it or repair it. ❑ *Instead of the Government admitting its error, it just tinkered with the problem.*

자동사 어설프게 손보다 ❑ 정부는 실수를 인정하는 대신 어설프게 문제를 해결하려 할 뿐이었다.

tinned /tɪnd/ ADJ **Tinned** food is food that has been preserved by being sealed in a tin. [mainly BRIT; AM usually **canned**] ❑ ...*tinned tomatoes.*

형용사 통조림으로 만든 [주로 영국영어; 미국영어 대개 canned] ❑ 토마토 통조림

tint /tɪnt/ (**tints, tinting, tinted**) **1** N-COUNT A **tint** is a small amount of color. ❑ *Its olive leaves often show a delicate purple tint.* **2** V-T If something **is tinted**, it has a small amount of a particular color or dye in it. [usu passive] ❑ *Eyebrows can be tinted with the same dye.*

1 가산명사 엷은 색, 색조 ❑ 그것의 큰 이파리에는 흔히 약간 자주색 기운이 돈다. **2** 타동사 엷게 염색하다, 엷은 색조를 띠게 만들다 ❑ 같은 염료로 눈썹을 엷게 염색할 수 있다.

tiny ♦♢♢ /taɪni/ (**tinier, tiniest**) ADJ Something or someone that is **tiny** is extremely small. ❑ *The living room is tiny.* ❑ *Though she was tiny, she had a very loud voice.*

형용사 아주 작은 ❑ 거실은 아주 작다. ❑ 그녀는 아주 작았지만 목소리는 아주 컸다.

tip ♦♢♢ /tɪp/ (**tips, tipping, tipped**) **1** N-COUNT The **tip** of something long and narrow is the end of it. ❑ *The sleeves covered his hands to the tips of his fingers.* **2** V-T/V-I If you **tip** an object or part of your body or if it **tips**, it moves into a sloping position with one end or side higher than the other. ❑ *He leaned away from her, and she had to tip her head back to see him.* **3** V-T If you **tip** something somewhere, you pour it there. ❑ *Tip the vegetables into a bowl.* **4** V-T If you **tip** someone such as a waiter in a restaurant, you give them some money in order to thank them for their services. ❑ *Do you really think it's customary to tip the waiters?* **5** N-COUNT If you give a **tip** to someone such as a waiter in a restaurant, you give them some money to thank them for their services. ❑ *I gave the barber a tip.* **6** N-COUNT A **tip** is a useful piece of advice. ❑ *It shows how to prepare a CV, and gives tips on applying for jobs.* **7** N-COUNT A **tip** is a place where garbage is left. [BRIT; AM **garbage dump**] ❑ *Officers had found a large bread knife on the rubbish tip.* **8** N-COUNT If you describe a place as a **tip**, you mean it is very messy. [BRIT, INFORMAL] ❑ *The flat is an absolute tip.* **9** V-T If a person **is tipped to** do something or **is tipped for** success at something, experts or journalists believe that they will do that thing or achieve that success. [BRIT] [usu passive] ❑ *He is tipped to be the country's next foreign minister.* **10** PHRASE If you say that a problem is **the tip of the iceberg**, you mean that it is one small part of a much larger problem. ❑ *Unless we're all a lot more careful, the people who have died so far will be just the tip of the iceberg.* **11** PHRASE If something **tips the scales** or **tips the balance**, it gives someone a slight advantage. ❑ *Today's slightly shorter race could well help to tip the scales in his favor.* →see **restaurant**

1 가산명사 뾰족한 끝, 첨단 ❑ 소매가 그의 손가락 끝까지 덮고 있었다. **2** 타동사/자동사 기울이다; 기울다 ❑ 그가 그녀에게서 멀어지게 몸을 기울이자 그녀가 그를 보기 위해 고개를 뒤로 젖혀야 했다. **3** 타동사 붓다 ❑ 야채를 사발에 부어라. **4** 타동사 팁을 주다 ❑ 웨이터에게 팁을 주는 것이 진짜로 관례인 것 같아? **5** 가산명사 팁 ❑ 나는 이발사에게 팁을 주었다. **6** 가산명사 조언, (도움이 되는) 정보 ❑ 그것은 이력서를 어떻게 준비하는지를 알려주고 구직 지원을 하는 것에 대한 정보들을 준다. **7** 가산명사 쓰레기 하치장 [영국영어; 미국영어 garbage dump] ❑ 경찰들이 쓰레기 하치장에서 큰 빵칼을 발견했었다. **8** 가산명사 쓰레기장 같은 곳 [영국영어, 비격식체] ❑ 그 아파트는 완전히 쓰레기장이다. **9** 타동사 -으 하리라 예상되다 [영국영어] ❑ 그가 그 나라의 차기 외무부 장관이 되리라 예상된다. **10** 구 빙산의 일각 ❑ 우리가 훨씬 더 조심하지 않는 한 지금까지 죽은 사람들은 그저 빙산의 일각에 불과하게 될 것이다. **11** 구 국면을 바꾸다 ❑ 오늘 치러질 약간 더 짧은 경주가 국면을 그에게 유리하게 바꿔 줄 수도 있다.

> ## Word Partnership ｜ tip의 연어
>
> | | |
> |---|---|
> | N. | **tip of your finger/nose** **1** |
> | | **tip your hat** **2** |
> | ADJ. | **northern/southern tip of an island** **1** |
> | | **anonymous tip** **6** |

▶**tip off** PHRASAL VERB If someone **tips** you **off**, they give you information about something that has happened or is going to happen. ❑ *Greg tipped police off on his car phone about a suspect drunk driver.*

구동사 -에게 귀띔하다 ❑ 그레그가 카폰으로 경찰에게 음주 운전자로 의심되는 사람을 귀띔해 주었다.

▶**tip over** PHRASAL VERB If you **tip** something **over** or if it **tips over**, it falls over or turns over. ❑ *He tipped the table over in front of him.* ❑ *She tipped over the chair and collapsed into the corner with a splintering crash.*

구동사 -을 넘어뜨리다, -을 뒤집어엎다 ❑ 그가 자기 앞에 있는 탁자를 넘어뜨렸다. ❑ 그녀는 의자를 넘어뜨리고 뭔가가 깨지는 소리와 함께 구석으로 쓰러졌다.

tip-off (**tip-offs**) N-COUNT A **tip-off** is a piece of information or a warning that you give to someone, often privately or secretly. ❑ *The man was arrested at his home after a tip-off to police from a member of the public.*

가산명사 비밀 정보, 귀띔 ❑ 그 남자는 한 일반 시민이 경찰에 제공한 비밀 정보에 의해 자택에서 체포되었다.

tiptoe /tɪptoʊ/ (**tiptoes, tiptoeing, tiptoed**) **1** V-I If you **tiptoe** somewhere, you walk there very quietly without putting your heels on the floor when you walk. ❑ *She slipped out of bed and tiptoed to the window.* **2** PHRASE If you do something **on tiptoe** or **on tiptoes**, you do it standing or walking on the front

1 자동사 발끝으로 걷다 ❑ 그녀는 슬그머니 침대를 빠져 나와 창 쪽으로 발끝으로 걸어갔다. **2** 구 발끝으로 ❑ 그녀는 돌담에 자전거를 기대어 놓고 건너편을 넘겨다보려고 까치발을 세웠다.

part of your foot, without putting your heels on the ground. ❑ *She leaned her bike against the stone wall and stood on tiptoe to peer over it.*

ti|rade /taɪreɪd/ (tirades) N-COUNT A **tirade** is a long angry speech in which someone criticizes a person or thing. ❑ *She launched into a tirade against the policies that ruined her business.*

가산명사 장광설 ❑ 그녀는 자기 사업을 망쳐 놓은 그 정책을 비난하는 장광설을 늘어놓기 시작했다.

tire /taɪər/ (tires, tiring, tired) **1** V-T/V-I If something **tires** you or you **tire**, you feel that you have used a lot of energy and you want to rest or sleep. ❑ *If driving tires you, take the train.* **2** V-I If you **tire of** something, you no longer wish to do it, because you have become bored of it or unhappy with it. [no passive] ❑ *He felt he would never tire of international cricket.* **3** N-COUNT A **tire** is a thick piece of rubber which is fitted onto the wheels of vehicles such as cars, buses, and bicycles. [BRIT **tyre**] →see **bicycle**

1 타동사/자동사 피로하게 하다; 피로하다 ❑ 차를 모는 게 피곤하면, 기차를 타세요. **2** 자동사 -에 싫증나다 ❑ 그는 국제 크리켓 경기에 절대로 싫증나지 않을 거라고 생각했다. **3** 가산명사 타이어 [영국영어 tyre]

tired ◆◇◇ /taɪərd/ **1** ADJ If you are **tired**, you feel that you want to rest or sleep. ❑ *Michael is tired and he has to rest after his long trip.* ● **tired|ness** N-UNCOUNT ❑ *He had to cancel some engagements because of tiredness.* **2** ADJ You can describe a part of your body as **tired** if it looks or feels as if you need to rest it or sleep. ❑ *Cucumber is good for soothing tired eyes.* **3** ADJ If you are **tired of** something, you do not want it to continue because you are bored of it or unhappy with it. [v-link ADJ of n/-ing] ❑ *I am tired of all the speculation.* →see **sleep**

1 형용사 피로한, 지친 ❑ 마이클은 긴 여행을 마친 후 지쳐서 휴식을 취해야 한다. ● 피로 불가산명사 ❑ 그는 피로 때문에 몇 가지 일정을 취소해야 했다. **2** 형용사 피로한, 지친 ❑ 오이는 피로한 눈을 진정시키는 데 좋다. **3** 형용사 -에 싫증난 ❑ 나는 그 모든 억측에 넌더리가 난다.

Word Partnership   *tired*의 연어

V.	feel tired, look tired **1** **2**
	be tired, get tired, grow tired **1**-**3**
ADV.	a little tired, (just) too tired, very tired **1**-**3**
ADJ.	tired and hungry **1**
	sick and tired of *something* **3**

---

tire|less /taɪərlɪs/ ADJ If you describe someone or their efforts as **tireless**, you approve of the fact that they put a lot of hard work into something, and refuse to give up or take a rest. [APPROVAL] ❑ *...Mother Teresa's tireless efforts to help the poor.* ● **tire|less|ly** ADV [ADV with v] ❑ *He worked tirelessly for the cause of health and safety.*

형용사 지칠 줄 모르는 [마음에 듦] ❑ 가난한 이들을 돕기 위한 테레사 수녀의 지칠 줄 모르는 노력 ● 지칠 줄 모르고 부사 ❑ 그는 건강과 안전이라는 대의를 위해 지칠 줄 모르고 일했다.

tire|some /taɪərsəm/ ADJ If you describe someone or something as **tiresome**, you mean that you find it irritating or boring. ❑ *...the tiresome old lady next door.*

형용사 지루한; 성가신 ❑ 옆집의 성가신 늙은 여자

tir|ing /taɪərɪŋ/ ADJ If you describe something as **tiring**, you mean that it makes you tired so that you want to rest or sleep. ❑ *It had been a long and tiring day.*

형용사 지치게 하는 ❑ 그 날은 길고 지치는 하루였다.

tis|sue ◆◇◇ /tɪʃu, tɪsyu/ (tissues) **1** N-UNCOUNT In animals and plants, **tissue** consists of cells that are similar to each other in appearance and that have the same function. [also N in pl] ❑ *As we age we lose muscle tissue.* **2** N-UNCOUNT **Tissue** or **tissue paper** is thin paper that is used for wrapping things that are easily damaged, such as objects made of glass or china. ❑ *...a small package wrapped in tissue paper.* **3** N-COUNT A **tissue** is a piece of thin soft paper that you use to blow your nose. ❑ *...a box of tissues.* →see **cancer**

1 불가산명사 (세포) 조직 ❑ 나이를 먹을수록 우리의 근육 조직은 감소한다. **2** 불가산명사 박엽지 ❑ 박엽지로 싼 작은 꾸러미 **3** 가산명사 화장지 ❑ 화장지 한 통

tit|il|late /tɪt³leɪt/ (titillates, titillating, titillated) V-T If something **titillates** someone, it pleases and excites them, especially in a sexual way. ❑ *The pictures were not meant to titillate audiences.* ● **tit|il|lat|ing** ADJ ❑ *...deliberately titillating lyrics.*

타동사 (성적으로) 자극하다, 흥분시키다 ❑ 그 사진들은 관객들을 자극하려는 의도는 없었다. ● 자극적인 형용사 ❑ 일부러 자극적으로 쓴 가사

title ◆◇◇ /taɪt³l/ (titles, titling, titled) **1** N-COUNT The **title** of a book, play, movie, or piece of music is its name. ❑ *"Patience and Sarah" was first published in 1969 under the title "A Place for Us".* **2** V-T When a writer, composer, or artist **titles** a work, they give it a title. ❑ *Pirandello titled his play "Six Characters in Search of an Author".* ❑ *The single is titled "White Love".* **3** N-COUNT Publishers and booksellers often refer to books or magazines as **titles**. ❑ *It has become the biggest publisher of new poetry in Britain, with 50 new titles a year.* **4** N-COUNT A person's **title** is a word such as "Sir", "Lord", or "Lady" that is used in front of their name, or a phrase that is used instead of their name, and indicates that they have a high rank in society. ❑ *Her husband was also honored with his title "Sir Denis."* **5** N-COUNT Someone's **title** is a word such as "Mr," "Mrs," or "Doctor," that is used before their own name in order to show their status or profession. ❑ *She has been awarded the title Professor.* **6** N-COUNT Someone's **title** is a name that describes their job or status in an organization. ❑ *He was given the title of deputy prime minister.* **7** N-COUNT If a person or team wins a particular **title**, they win a sports competition that is held regularly. Usually a person keeps a title until someone else defeats them. ❑ *He became Jamaica's first Olympic gold medallist when he won the 400m title in 1948.* →see **graph**

1 가산명사 표제, 제목 ❑ '페이션스와 사라'는 1969년 '우리를 위한 곳'이라는 제목으로 처음 출판되었다. **2** 타동사 제목을 붙이다 ❑ 피란델로는 자신의 희곡에 '작가를 찾는 6인의 등장인물'이라는 제목을 붙였다. ❑ 그 싱글 앨범에는 '화이트 러브'라는 제목이 붙었다. **3** 가산명사 서적, 출판물 ❑ 그 회사는 연간 50권의 신간 서적을 내는 영국 최대의 신작 시 출판사가 되었다. **4** 가산명사 칭호; 경칭 ❑ 그녀의 남편은 '데니스 경'이라는 경칭도 수여받았다. **5** 가산명사 직함 ❑ 그녀는 교수 직함을 수여받았다. **6** 가산명사 관직, 직위 ❑ 그는 부총리 직위를 받았다. **7** 가산명사 선수권, 타이틀 ❑ 그는 1948년 400미터 달리기에서 우승하여 자메이카 선수로는 처음으로 올림픽 금메달리스트가 되었다.

---

to

① PREPOSITION AND ADVERB USES
② USED BEFORE THE BASE FORM OF A VERB

① **to** ◆◆◆

Usually pronounced /tə/ before a consonant and /tu/ before a vowel, but pronounced /tu/ when you are emphasizing it.

대개 자음 앞에서는 /tə/로, 모음 앞에서는 /tu/로 발음하지만 강조할 때는 /tu/로 발음한다.

In addition to the uses shown below, **to** is used in phrasal verbs such as "see to" and "come to." It is also used with some verbs that have two objects in order to introduce the second object.

to는 아래 용법 외에도 'see to', 'come to'와 같은 구동사에도 쓰인다. 또한 to는 두 개의 목적어를 취하는 동사에서 두번째 목적어를 소개할 때도 사용한다.

1 PREP You use **to** when indicating the place that someone or something visits, moves toward, or points at. ❑ *Two friends and I drove to Florida during college spring break.* ❑ *She went to the window and looked out.* **2** PREP If you go **to** an event,

1 전치사 -로, -쪽으로 ❑ 대학 봄방학 동안 두 명의 친구와 나는 차를 몰고 플로리다로 갔다. ❑ 그녀는 창문 쪽으로 가서 내다보았다. **2** 전치사 (행사) 에

you go where it is taking place. ❑ *We went to a party at the leisure centre.* ❑ *He came to dinner.* ❸ PREP If something is attached **to** something larger or fixed **to** it, the two things are joined together. ❑ *There was a piece of cloth tied to the dog's collar.* ❹ PREP You use **to** when indicating the position of something. For example, if something is **to** your left, it is nearer your left side than your right side. ❑ *Hemingway's studio is to the right.* ❺ PREP When you give something to someone, they receive it. [v n PREP n] ❑ *He picked up the knife and gave it to me.* ❻ PREP You use **to** to indicate who or what an action or a feeling is directed toward. [adj/n PREP n] ❑ *Marcus has been most unkind to me today.* ❑ *...troops loyal to the government.* ❼ PREP You use **to** with certain nouns and adjectives to show that a following noun is related to them. [adj/n PREP n] ❑ *He is a witty man, and an inspiration to all of us.* ❽ PREP If you say something **to** someone, you want that person to listen and understand what you are saying. ❑ *I'm going to have to explain to them that I can't pay them.* ❾ PREP You use **to** when indicating someone's reaction to something or their feelings about a situation or event. For example, if you say that something happens **to** someone's surprise you mean that they are surprised when it happens. ❑ *To his surprise, the bedroom door was locked.* ❿ PREP You use **to** when indicating the person whose opinion you are stating. ❑ *It was clear to me that he respected his boss.* ⓫ PREP You use **to** when indicating what something or someone is becoming, or the state or situation that they are progressing toward. ❑ *The shouts changed to screams of terror.* ❑ *...an old ranch house that has been converted to a nature center.* ⓬ PREP **To** can be used as a way of introducing the person or organization you are employed by, when you perform some service for them. [n PREP n] ❑ *Rickman worked as a dresser to Nigel Hawthorne.* ⓭ PREP You use **to** to indicate that something happens until the time or amount mentioned is reached. ❑ *From 1977 to 1985 the United States gross national product grew 21 percent.* ⓮ PREP You use **to** when indicating the last thing in a range of things, usually when you are giving two extreme examples of something. [from n PREP n] ❑ *I read everything from fiction to history.* ⓯ PREP If someone goes from place to place or from job to job, they go to several places, or work in several jobs, and spend only a short time in each one. [from n PREP n] ❑ *Larry and Andy had drifted from place to place, worked at this and that.* ⓰ PHRASE If someone moves **to and fro**, they move repeatedly from one place to another and back again, or from side to side. ❑ *She stood up and began to pace to and fro.* ⓱ PREP You use **to** when you are stating a time which is less than thirty minutes before an hour. For example, if it is "five to eight," it is five minutes before eight o'clock. [num/n PREP num] ❑ *At twenty to six I was waiting by the entrance to the station.* ⓲ PREP You use **to** when giving ratios and rates. [amount PREP amount] ❑ *...engines that can run at 60 miles to the gallon.* ⓳ PREP You use **to** when indicating that two things happen at the same time. For example, if something is done **to** music, it is done at the same time as music is being played. ❑ *Romeo left the stage, to enthusiastic applause.* ⓴ CONVENTION If you say "**There's nothing to it**," "**There's not much to it**," or "**That's all there is to it**," you are emphasizing how simple you think something is. [EMPHASIS] ❑ *"There is nothing to it,"* those I asked about it told me. ㉑ →see also **according to**

② to ♦♦♦

Pronounced /tə/ before a consonant and /tu/ before a vowel.

❶ to inf You use **to** before the base form of a verb to form the to-infinitive. You use the to-infinitive after certain verbs, nouns, and adjectives, and after words such as "how," "which," and "where." ❑ *The management wanted to know what I was doing there.* ❑ *She told ministers of her decision to resign.* ❷ to inf You use **to** before the base form of a verb to indicate the purpose or intention of an action. ❑ *...using the experience of big companies to help small businesses.* ❸ to inf You use **to** before the base form of a verb when you are commenting on a statement that you are making, for example when saying that you are being honest or brief, or that you are summing up or giving an example. ❑ *I'm disappointed, to be honest.* ❹ to inf You use **to** before the base form of a verb when indicating what situation follows a particular action. ❑ *From the garden you walk down to discover a large and beautiful lake.* ❺ You use **to** with "too" and "enough" in expressions like **too much to** and **old enough to**; see **too** and **enough**.

toad /toʊd/ (**toads**) N-COUNT A **toad** is a creature which is similar to a frog but which has a drier skin and spends less time in water.

toast /toʊst/ (**toasts, toasting, toasted**) ❶ N-UNCOUNT **Toast** is bread which has been cut into slices and made brown and crisp by cooking at a high temperature. ❑ *...a piece of toast.* ❷ V-T When you **toast** something such as bread, you cook it at a high temperature so that it becomes brown and crisp. ❑ *Toast the bread lightly on both sides.* →see **cook** ❸ N-COUNT When you drink a **toast** to someone or something, you drink some wine or another alcoholic drink as a symbolic gesture, in order to show your appreciation of them or to wish them success. ❑ *Eleanor and I drank a toast to Miss Jacobs.* ❹ V-T When you **toast** someone or something, you drink to them. ❑ *Party officials and generals toasted his health.* →see **cook**

toast|er /toʊstər/ (**toasters**) N-COUNT A **toaster** is a piece of electric equipment used to toast bread.

to|bac|co /təbækoʊ/ (**tobaccos**) ❶ N-MASS **Tobacco** is dried leaves which people smoke in pipes, cigars, and cigarettes. You can also refer to pipes, cigars, and cigarettes as a whole as **tobacco**. ❑ *Try to do without tobacco and alcohol.* ❷ N-UNCOUNT **Tobacco** is the plant from which tobacco is obtained. ❑ *...Cuba's tobacco crop.*

to|day ♦♦♦ /tədeɪ/ ❶ ADV You use **today** to refer to the day on which you are speaking or writing. [ADV with cl] ❑ *How are you feeling today?* ● N-UNCOUNT **Today** is also a noun. ❑ *Today is Friday, September 14th.* ❷ ADV You can refer to the present period of history as **today**. ❑ *The United States is in a serious recession today.* ● N-UNCOUNT **Today** is also a noun. ❑ *In today's America, health care is one of the very biggest businesses.*

우리는 레저 센터에서 열린 파티에 갔다. ❑ 그가 저녁 식사를 하러 왔다. ❸ 전치사 -에 (붙어) ❑ 그 개의 목덜미에는 천 조각이 매어져 있었다. ❹ 전치사 (위치) 에 ❑ 헤밍웨이의 작업장은 오른쪽에 있다. ❺ 전치사 -에게 ❑ 그는 칼을 집어서 나에게 주었다. ❻ 전치사 -에게, -에 대해 ❑ 마커스는 오늘 나에게 매우 불친절했다. ❑ 정부에 충성하는 군대 ❼ 전치사 -에게, -에 대해 ❑ 그는 재치 있는 사람이고, 우리 모두에게 자극이 된다. ❽ 전치사 -에게 (말하다) ❑ 나는 그들에게 돈을 줄 수 없음을 설명해야 할 것이다. ❾ 전치사 (주로 감정을 나타내는 명사를 수반하여) -하게도 ❑ 그가 놀랍게도, 침실 문이 잠겨 있었다. ❿ 전치사 -가 볼 때, -에게 ❑ 그가 자기 상관을 존경한다는 것이 내게는 명백했다. ⓫ 전치사 -로 ❑ 그 외침은 공포의 절규로 바뀌었다. ❑ 자연 센터로 개조된 오래 된 대농장 저택 ⓬ 전치사 -에 소속된, -에 딸린 ❑ 릭맨은 나이젤 호손의 의상 담당으로 일했다. ⓭ 전치사 -까지 ❑ 1977년에서 1985년까지 미국의 국민 총생산은 21퍼센트 성장했다. ⓮ 전치사 -에 이르기까지 ❑ 나는 소설에서 역사서에 이르기까지 모든 것을 읽는다. ⓯ 전치사 (-에서)...로 ❑ 래리와 앤디는 이곳저곳 떠돌면서 이런저런 일을 해 왔었다. ⓰ 구 이리저리, 앞뒤로 ❑ 그녀는 일어나서 이리저리 서성거리기 시작했다. ⓱ 전치사 (- 분) 전 ❑ 6시 20분 전에 나는 역 출입구 옆에서 기다리고 있었다. ⓲ 전치사 -당, -에 대비 ❑ 갤런당 60마일을 달릴 수 있는 엔진 ⓳ 전치사 -에 맞추어; -와 함께 ❑ 로미오는 열광적인 박수갈채와 함께 무대를 떠났다. ⓴ 관용 표현 그건 별 거 아니다 [강조] ❑ "그건 별 거 아니다."라고 그 일에 대해 질문을 받은 사람들이 내게 말했다.

자음 앞에서는 /tə/로, 모음 앞에서는 /tu/로 발음된다.

❶ to 부정사 뒤에 따라오는 동사 원형과 함께 to부정사를 만드는 다양한 용법으로 쓰임 ❑ 경영자 측은 내가 그곳에서 무슨 일을 하고 있는지 알기를 원했다. ❑ 그녀는 사임하기로 한 자신의 결심을 각료들에게 말했다. ❷ to 부정사 - 하기 위해 ❑ 소기업들을 돕기 위해 대기업들의 경험을 이용하는 것 ❸ to 부정사 -하자면 (독립부사구 유도) ❑ 솔직히 말하면, 나는 실망했다. ❹ to 부정사 (결과를 나타내어) - 하게 되어 ❑ 정원에서 걸어 내려가면 커다랗고 아름다운 호수를 발견하게 됩니다. ❺ -하기에는 너무...한; -하기에 충분한

가산명사 두꺼비

❶ 불가산명사 토스트, 구운 식빵 ❑ 토스트 한 조각 ❷ 타동사 노릇하게 굽다 ❑ 빵을 양쪽 다 조금만 구우세요. ❸ 가산명사 -를 위한 축배, 건배 ❑ 엘리너와 나는 제이콥스 양을 위해 건배를 했다. ❹ 타동사 -을 위해 건배하다 ❑ 당 임원과 장성들이 그의 건강을 위해 건배했다.

가산명사 토스터, 빵 굽는 기구

❶ 물질명사 담배 ❑ 담배와 술 없이 지내려고 노력해 봐라. ❷ 불가산명사 (식물) 담배 ❑ 쿠바의 담배 수확

❶ 부사 오늘 ❑ 오늘 기분이 어때? ● 불가산명사 오늘 ❑ 오늘은 9월 14일 금요일이다. ❷ 부사 현재, 오늘날 ❑ 미국은 현재 심각한 경기 침체에 빠져 있다. ● 불가산명사 현재, 오늘날 ❑ 오늘날 미국에서, 건강관리는 가장 거대한 사업 중 하나이다.

tod|dler /ˈtɒdlər/ (**toddlers**) N-COUNT A **toddler** is a young child who has only just learned to walk or who still walks unsteadily with small, quick steps. ❑ *I had a toddler at home and two other children at school.* →see **age, child**

toe /toʊ/ (**toes**) **1** N-COUNT Your **toes** are the five movable parts at the end of each foot. ❑ *She wiggled her toes against the packed sand.* **2** PHRASE If you say that someone or something **keeps** you **on** your **toes**, you mean that they cause you to remain alert and ready for anything that might happen. ❑ *His fiery campaign rhetoric has kept opposition parties on their toes for months.*

toe|nail /ˈtoʊneɪl/ (**toenails**) also **toe nail** N-COUNT Your **toenails** are the thin hard areas at the end of each of your toes. →see **foot**

tof|fee /ˈtɒfi, BRIT ˈtɒfi/ (**toffees**) **1** N-UNCOUNT **Toffee** is a sticky candy that you chew. It is made by boiling sugar and butter together with water. [BRIT; AM **taffy**] **2** N-COUNT A **toffee** is an individual piece of toffee. [BRIT] ❑ *...a bag of toffees.*

to|geth|er ♦♦♦ /təˈgɛðər/

> In addition to the uses shown below, **together** is used in phrasal verbs such as "piece together," "pull together," and "sleep together."

1 ADV If people do something **together**, they do it with each other. ❑ *We went on long bicycle rides together.* ❑ *He and I worked together on a book.* **2** ADV If things are joined **together**, they are joined with each other so that they touch or form one whole. [ADV after v] ❑ *Mix the ingredients together thoroughly.* **3** ADV If things or people are situated **together**, they are in the same place and very near to each other. [ADV after v] ❑ *The trees grew close together.* ❑ *Ginette and I gathered our things together.* **4** ADV If a group of people are held or kept **together**, they are united with each other in some way. [ADV after v] ❑ *He has done enough to pull the party together.* ● ADJ **Together** is also an adjective. ❑ *We are together in the way we're looking at this situation.* **5** ADJ If two people are **together**, they are married or having a sexual relationship with each other. [v-link ADJ, n ADJ, v n ADJ] ❑ *We were together for five years.* **6** ADV If two things happen or are done **together**, they happen or are done at the same time. [ADV after v] ❑ *Three horses crossed the finish line together.* **7** ADV You use **together** when you are adding two or more amounts or things to each other in order to consider a total amount or effect. ❑ *The two main right-wing opposition parties together won 29.8 per cent.* **8** PHRASE If you say that two things **go together**, or that one thing **goes together with** another, you mean that they go well with each other or cannot be separated from each other. ❑ *I can see that some colors go together and some don't.* **9** PHRASE You use **together with** to mention someone or something else that is also involved in an action or situation. ❑ *Every month we'll deliver the very best articles, together with the latest fashion and beauty news.* **10** to **get** your **act together** →see **act**. to **put** your **heads together** →see **head**. **put together** →see **put**

| **Word Partnership** | *together의 연어* |

V.	**live** together, **play** together, **spend time** together, **work** together **1**
	come together **1 4**
	get together **1 5**
	go together **1 8**
	bound together, **fit** together, **glue** together, **join** together, **lump** together, **mix** together, **string** together, **stuck** together, **tied** together **2**
	bring together, **keep** together, **stay** together **2 4 5**
	gather together, **sit** together, **stand** together **3**
	hold together **4**
	stick together **4 5**
	close together **3**

toil /tɔɪl/ (**toils, toiling, toiled**) V-T/V-I When people **toil**, they work very hard doing unpleasant or tiring tasks. [LITERARY] ❑ *People who toiled in dim, dank factories were too exhausted to enjoy their family life.* ● PHRASAL VERB **Toil away** means the same as **toil**. ❑ *She has toiled away at the violin for years.*

toi|let /ˈtɔɪlɪt/ (**toilets**) **1** N-COUNT A **toilet** is a large bowl with a seat, or a platform with a hole, which is connected to a water system and which you use when you want to get rid of urine or feces from your body. ❑ *She made Tina flush the pills down the toilet.* **2** N-COUNT A **toilet** is a room in a house or public building that contains a toilet. [mainly BRIT; AM usually **bathroom, rest room**] ❑ *Annette ran and locked herself in the toilet.* **3** PHRASE You can say that someone **goes to the toilet** to mean that they get rid of waste substances from their body, especially when you want to avoid using words that you think may offend people. [mainly BRIT; AM usually **go to the bathroom**] ❑ *He needed to go to the toilet because of a stomach upset.* →see **plumbing**

toi|let|ries /ˈtɔɪlətriz/ N-PLURAL **Toiletries** are things that you use when washing or taking care of your body, for example soap and toothpaste.

to|ken /ˈtoʊkən/ (**tokens**) **1** ADJ You use **token** to describe things or actions which are small or unimportant but are meant to show particular intentions or feelings which may not be sincere. [ADJ n] ❑ *The announcement was welcomed as a step in the right direction, but was widely seen as a token gesture.* **2** N-COUNT A **token** is a round flat piece of metal or plastic that is sometimes used instead of money. ❑ *Some of the older telephones still only accept tokens.* **3** N-COUNT A **token** is a piece of paper or card that can be exchanged for goods, either in a particular store or as part of a special offer. [BRIT; AM **coupon**] ❑ *...£10 book tokens.* **4** PHRASE You use **by the same token** to introduce a statement that you think is true for the same reasons that were given for a previous statement. ❑ *If you give up*

가산명사 걸음마를 배우는 아기 ❑ 나는 집에 걸음마를 배우는 아이가 있고 학교에 다니는 아이가 둘 더 있었다.

1 가산명사 발가락 ❑ 그녀는 단단히 다져 놓은 모래에 대고 발가락을 꼼틀거렸다. **2** 구 -에게 방심하지 못하게 하다 ❑ 그의 열띤 유세 공·변론이 야당으로 하여금 몇 달 동안 방심할 수 없도록 해 왔다.

가산명사 발톱

1 불가산명사 토피 (설탕·버터 등으로 만든 사탕) [영국영어; 미국영어 taffy] **2** 가산명사 토피 한 개 [영국영어] ❑ 토피 한 봉지

> together는 아래 용법 외에도 'piece together', 'pull together', 'sleep together'와 같은 구동사에 쓰인다.

1 부사 함께, 같이 ❑ 우리는 같이 장거리 자전거 여행을 갔다. ❑ 그와 나는 함께 책을 한 권 쓰고 있다. **2** 부사 합쳐서 ❑ 여러 재료를 완전히 혼합하세요. **3** 부사 모여 ❑ 나무들이 서로 가까이 모여 자랐다. ❑ 지네뜨와 나는 우리 물건들을 그러모았다. **4** 부사 결집하여, 함께하여 ❑ 그는 당을 결속시켜 끌고 나가기 위해 할 만큼 했다. ● 형용사 결집된, 함께하는 ❑ 우리는 이 사태를 바라보는 방식에 있어서 의견이 일치한다. **5** 형용사 (남녀가) 함께 지내는 ❑ 우리는 5년 동안 함께 지내고 있었다. **6** 부사 동시에 ❑ 세 마리의 말이 동시에 결승선을 통과했다. **7** 부사 통틀어, 전부 ❑ 양대 우익 야당이 합쳐서 29.8퍼센트를 획득했다. **8** 구 어울리다; 떼어 놓을 수 없다 ❑ 어떤 색은 어울리고 어떤 색은 어울리지 않음을 알 수 있다. **9** 구 -와 더불어, -도 또한 ❑ 매달 최신 패션·미용 뉴스와 더불어 최고의 기사들을 전해 드리겠습니다.

타동사/자동사 고생하다, 애써 일하다 [문예체] ❑ 침침하고 습기 찬 공장에서 고생하는 사람들은 너무 지쳐 빠져서 각자의 가정생활을 즐길 수가 없었다. ● 구동사 고생하다, 애써 일하다 ❑ 그녀는 몇 년 동안 바이올린 연습을 힘들게 해 왔다.

1 가산명사 변기 ❑ 그녀는 티나에게 알약을 변기에 넣고 물을 내리게 했다. **2** 가산명사 화장실 [주로 영국영어; 미국영어 대개 bathroom, rest room] ❑ 아네트는 화장실로 달려 들어가 문을 잠갔다. **3** 구 (용변을 보러) 화장실에 가다 [주로 영국영어; 미국영어 대개 go to the bathroom] ❑ 그는 복통 때문에 화장실에 가야 했다.

복수명사 세면 용품

1 형용사 형식적인, 명목상의 ❑ 그 성명은 올바른 방향으로 가는 조치로 받아들여지긴 했지만, 대부분의 사람들로부터 형식적인 제스처로 여겨졌다. **2** 가산명사 (화폐 대용인) 토큰 ❑ 아직도 어떤 구형 전화기들은 토큰으로만 쓸 수 있다. **3** 가산명사 상품권, 교환권 [영국영어; 미국영어 coupon] ❑ 10파운드짜리 도서 상품권 **4** 구 마찬가지로, 같은 식으로 ❑ 운동을 그만두면, 근육이 줄고 지방이 증가한다. 같은 식으로, 에너지를 더 많이 소비하면 지방이 줄게 되어 있다.

exercise, your muscles shrink and fat increases. By the same token, if you expend more energy you will lose fat.

told /toʊld/ **1** Told is the past tense and past participle of **tell**. **2** PHRASE You can use **all told** to introduce or follow a summary, general statement, or total. ❑ *All told there were 104 people on the payroll.*

1 tell의 과거, 과거 분사 **2** 구 모두 통틀어 ❑ 모두 통틀어 종업원 명부에는 104명이 올라 있었다.

tol|er|able /tɒlərəbᵊl/ ADJ If you describe something as **tolerable**, you mean that you can bear it, even though it is unpleasant or painful. ❑ *The levels of tolerable pain vary greatly from individual to individual.* ● **tol|er|ably** /tɒlərəbli/ ADV ❑ *Their captors treated them tolerably well.*

형용사 참을 수 있는, 견딜 만한 ❑ 참을 수 있는 통증의 정도는 사람마다 크게 다르다. ● 견딜 만하게 부사 ❑ 인질범들은 그들을 견딜 만하게 잘 대해 주었다.

tol|er|ance /tɒlərəns/ (**tolerances**) **1** N-UNCOUNT Tolerance is the quality of allowing other people to say and do as they like, even if you do not agree or approve of it. [APPROVAL] ❑ *...his tolerance and understanding of diverse human nature.* **2** N-UNCOUNT Tolerance is the ability to bear something painful or unpleasant. ❑ *There is lowered pain tolerance, lowered resistance to infection.*

1 불가산명사 관용, 아량 [마음에 듦] ❑ 다양한 인간성에 대한 그의 관용과 이해 **2** 불가산명사 인내력, 내성 ❑ 통증 내성과 감염 저항력이 떨어졌다.

tol|er|ant /tɒlərənt/ **1** ADJ If you describe someone as **tolerant**, you approve of the fact that they allow other people to say and do as they like, even if they do not agree with or like it. [APPROVAL] ❑ *They need to be tolerant of different points of view.* **2** ADJ If a plant, animal, or machine is **tolerant of** particular conditions or types of treatment, it is able to bear them without being damaged or hurt. [v-link ADJ of n] ❑ *...plants which are more tolerant of dry conditions.*

1 형용사 관대한, 아량 있는 [마음에 듦] ❑ 그들은 다른 관점들에 대해 관대해질 필요가 있다. **2** 형용사 -에 대한 내성이 있는, -을 잘 견디는 ❑ 건조한 환경에 더 강한 식물들

tol|er|ate /tɒləreɪt/ (**tolerates, tolerating, tolerated**) **1** V-T If you **tolerate** a situation or person, you accept them although you do not particularly like them. ❑ *She can no longer tolerate the position that she's in.* **2** V-T If you can **tolerate** something unpleasant or painful, you are able to bear it. ❑ *The ability to tolerate pain varies from person to person.*

1 타동사 참다, 받아들이다 ❑ 그녀는 더 이상 자신의 처지를 받아들일 수가 없다. **2** 타동사 참다, 견디다 ❑ 통증을 견딜 수 있는 능력은 사람마다 다르다.

toll /toʊl/ (**tolls, tolling, tolled**) **1** V-T/V-I When a bell **tolls** or when someone **tolls** it, it rings slowly and repeatedly, often as a sign that someone has died. ❑ *Church bells tolled and black flags fluttered.* **2** N-COUNT A **toll** is a small sum of money that you have to pay in order to use a particular bridge or road. ❑ *You can pay a toll to drive on Pike's Peak Highway or relax and take the Pike's Peak Cog Railway.* **3** N-COUNT A **toll** road or **toll** bridge is a road or bridge where you have to pay in order to use it. [N n] ❑ *Most people who drive the toll roads don't use them every day.* **4** N-COUNT A **toll** is a total number of deaths, accidents, or disasters that occur in a particular period of time. [JOURNALISM] ❑ *There are fears that the casualty toll may be higher.* →see also **death toll** **5** PHRASE If you say that something **takes its toll** or **takes a heavy toll**, you mean that it has a bad effect or causes a lot of suffering. ❑ *Winter takes its toll on your health.*

1 타동사/자동사 (종이) 울리다 ❑ 교회종이 울리고 검은색 깃발이 펄럭였다. **2** 가산명사 통행료 ❑ 통행료를 내고 파이크스 피크 대로를 드라이브하든가 휴식을 취하며 파이크스 피크 톱니 궤도 열차를 탈 수 있습니다. **3** 가산명사 통행료 (을 내야 하는) ❑ 유료 도로를 지나다니는 사람들은 대부분이 그 도로를 매일 사용하지는 않는다. **4** 가산명사 희생자 수 [언론] ❑ 사상자 수가 더 많을지도 모른다는 우려가 있다. **5** 구 피해를 주다, 타격을 입히다 ❑ 겨울은 우리 건강에 타격을 준다.

to|ma|to /təmeɪtoʊ, BRIT təmɑːtoʊ// (**tomatoes**) N-VAR Tomatoes are small, soft, red fruit that you can eat raw in salads or cooked as a vegetable.

가산명사 또는 불가산명사 토마토

tomb /tum/ (**tombs**) N-COUNT A **tomb** is a large grave that is above ground and that usually has a sculpture or other decoration on it. ❑ *...the continuing excavation of the emperor's tomb.*

가산명사 무덤, 묘 ❑ 계속되는 황제 묘 발굴

to|mor|row ◆◇ /təmɒroʊ, BRIT təmɒroʊ/ (**tomorrows**) **1** ADV You use **tomorrow** to refer to the day after today. [ADV with cl] ❑ *Bye, see you tomorrow.* ● N-UNCOUNT Tomorrow is also a noun. ❑ *What's on your agenda for tomorrow?* **2** ADV You can refer to the future, especially the near future, as **tomorrow**. [ADV with cl] ❑ *What is education going to look like tomorrow?* ● N-UNCOUNT Tomorrow is also a noun. [also N in pl] ❑ *...tomorrow's computer industry.*

1 부사 내일 ❑ 안녕, 내일 봐. ● 불가산명사 내일 ❑ 내일 일정이 어떻게 돼? **2** 부사 장래 ❑ 장래의 교육은 어떤 모습일까? ● 불가산명사 장래 ❑ 장래의 컴퓨터 산업

ton ◆◇◇ /tʌn/ (**tons**) **1** N-COUNT A **ton** is a unit of weight that is equal to 2000 pounds in the United States and to 2240 pounds in Britain. ❑ *Hundreds of tons of oil spilled into the sea.* **2** N-COUNT A **ton** is the same as a **tonne**.

1 가산명사 톤 ❑ 수백 톤의 기름이 바다에 누출되었다. **2** 가산명사 톤 (1000킬로그램)

tone ◆◇◇ /toʊn/ (**tones, toning, toned**) **1** N-COUNT The **tone** of a sound is its particular quality. ❑ *Cross could hear him speaking in low tones to Sarah.* **2** N-COUNT Someone's **tone** is a quality in their voice which shows what they are feeling or thinking. ❑ *I still didn't like his tone of voice.* **3** N-SING The **tone** of a speech or piece of writing is its style and the opinions or ideas expressed in it. [also in N] ❑ *The spokesman said the tone of the letter was very friendly.* **4** N-SING The **tone** of a place or an event is its general atmosphere. ❑ *The high tone of the occasion was assured by the presence of a dozen wealthy patrons.* **5** N-UNCOUNT The **tone** of someone's body, especially their muscles, is its degree of firmness and strength. ❑ *...stretch exercises that aim to improve muscle tone.* **6** V-T/V-I Something that **tones** your body makes it firm and strong. ❑ *This movement lengthens your spine and tones the spinal nerves.* ❑ *Try these toning exercises before you start the day.* ● PHRASAL VERB **Tone up** means the same as **tone**. ❑ *Exercise tones up your body.* **7** N-VAR A **tone** is one of the lighter, darker, or brighter shades of the same color. ❑ *Each brick also varies slightly in tone, texture, and size.* **8** N-SING A **tone** is one of the sounds that you hear when you are using a telephone, for example the sound that tells you that a number is busy, or no longer exists. ❑ *A high-pitched tone erupted in the phone.* **9** →see also **dial tone, ring tone** →see **drum**

1 가산명사 음성, 음색 ❑ 크로스는 그가 낮은 소리로 사라에게 말하는 것을 들을 수 있었다. **2** 가산명사 어조, 말씨 ❑ 나는 그의 어투가 여전히 맘에 들지 않았다. **3** 단수명사 논조 ❑ 그 서한의 논조는 매우 우호적이라고 대변인이 말했다. **4** 단수명사 분위기 ❑ 그 행사의 고급스런 분위기는 십여 명의 부유한 후원자들의 참석으로 확실해졌다. **5** 불가산명사 (몸이나 근육의) 탄력, 탄탄함 ❑ 근육의 탄력 향상을 목표로 하는 맨손 체조 **6** 타동사/자동사 (몸이나 근육을) 탄탄하게 하다 ❑ 이 운동은 척추를 길게 해 주며 척수 신경을 탄탄하게 합니다. ❑ 하루 일과를 시작하기 전에 이 근육 강화 운동을 해 보세요. ● 구동사 (몸이나 근육을) 탄탄하게 하다 ❑ 운동은 신체를 탄탄하게 한다. **7** 가산명사 또는 불가산명사 색조, 농담 ❑ 각각의 벽돌은 색조와 결, 크기에서도 서로 약간씩 다릅니다. **8** 단수명사 (전화) 신호음 ❑ 높은 음의 신호음이 수화기에서 흘러 나왔다.

Word Partnership	tone의 연어
ADJ.	**clear** tone, **low** tone **1**
	different tone **2**
	serious tone **2** **3**
V.	**change your** tone **2**
	set a tone **4**
N.	tone **of voice** **2**
	muscle tone **5**
	skin tone **7**

►**tone down** ▪ PHRASAL VERB If you **tone down** something that you have written or said, you make it less forceful, severe, or offensive. ❑ *The fiery right-wing leader toned down his militant statements after the meeting.* ▪ PHRASAL VERB If you **tone down** a color or a flavor, you make it less bright or strong. ❑ *When Ken Hom wrote his first book for the BBC he was asked to tone down the spices and garlic in his recipes.*

tongue /tʌŋ/ (**tongues**) ▪ N-COUNT Your **tongue** is the soft movable part inside your mouth which you use for tasting, eating, and speaking. ❑ *I walked over to the mirror and stuck my tongue out.* ▪ N-COUNT You can use **tongue** to refer to the kind of things that a person says. ❑ *She had a nasty tongue, but I liked her.* ▪ N-COUNT A **tongue** is a language. [LITERARY] ❑ *The French feel passionately about their native tongue.* ▪ PHRASE A **tongue-in-cheek** remark or attitude is not serious, although it may seem to be. ❑ *...a lighthearted, tongue-in-cheek approach.* ▪ to **bite** your **tongue** →see **bite** →see **diagnosis, face, taste**

Word Partnership		*tongue*의 연어
V.	bite your tongue, stick out your tongue ▪	
ADJ.	pink tongue ▪	
	sharp tongue ▪	
N.	native tongue ▪	

tonic /tɒnɪk/ (**tonics**) ▪ N-MASS **Tonic** or **tonic water** is a colorless carbonated drink that has a slightly bitter flavor and is often mixed with alcoholic drinks, especially gin. ❑ *Keeler sipped at his gin and tonic.* ▪ N-MASS A **tonic** is a medicine that makes you feel stronger, healthier, and less tired. ❑ *Britons are spending twice as much on health tonics as they were five years ago.*

tonight ♦♦◊ /tənaɪt/ ADV **Tonight** is used to refer to the evening of today or the night that follows today. ❑ *I'm at home tonight.* ❑ *Tonight, I think he proved to everybody what a great player he was.* ● N-UNCOUNT **Tonight** is also a noun. ❑ *Tonight is the opening night of the opera.*

tonne /tʌn/ (**tonnes**) N-COUNT A **tonne** is a metric unit of weight that is equal to 1000 kilograms. ❑ *...65.5 million tonnes of coal.*

---
too
---

① ADDING SOMETHING OR RESPONDING
② INDICATING EXCESS

---

① **too** ♦♦♦ /tuː/ ▪ ADV You use **too** after mentioning another person, thing, or aspect that a previous statement applies to or includes. [cl/group ADV] ❑ *"Nice to talk to you." — "Nice to talk to you too."* ❑ *"I've got a great feeling about it." — "Me too."* ▪ ADV You use **too** after adding a piece of information or a comment to a statement, in order to emphasize that it is surprising or important. [EMPHASIS] [cl/group ADV] ❑ *We did learn to read, and quickly too.* ▪ ADV You use **too** at the end of a sentence to emphasize an opinion that you have added after a statement made by you or by another person. [EMPHASIS] [cl ADV] ❑ *"That money's mine." — "Of course it is, and quite right too."*

② **too** ♦♦♦ /tuː/ →Please look at category ▪ to see if the expression you are looking for is shown under another headword. ▪ ADV You use **too** in order to indicate that there is a greater amount or degree of something than is desirable, necessary, or acceptable. ❑ *Leather jeans that are too big will make you look larger.* ❑ *Eggs shouldn't be kept in the fridge, it's too cold.* ▪ ADV You use **too** with a negative to make what you are saying sound less forceful or more polite or cautious. [VAGUENESS] [with brd-neg, ADV adj] ❑ *I wasn't too happy with what I'd written so far.* ▪ PHRASE You use **all too** or **only too** to emphasize that something happens to a greater extent or degree than is pleasant or desirable. [EMPHASIS] ❑ *She remembered it all too well.* ▪ **none too** →see **none**

Too can be used to intensify the meaning of an adjective, an adverb, or a word like **much** or **many**. **Too**, however, also suggests an excessive or undesirable amount, often so much that a particular result does not or cannot happen. ❑ *She does wear too much makeup at times... He was too late to save her.* **Too** is not generally used to modify an adjective inside a noun group. For instance, you cannot say "the too heavy boxes" or "too expensive jewelry." There is one exception to this rule, which is when the noun group begins with **a** or **an**. Notice the word order in the following examples. ❑ *...if the products have been stored at too high a temperature... He found it too good an opportunity to miss... It was too long a drive for one day.*

took /tʊk/ **Took** is the past tense of **take**.

tool ♦◊◊ /tuːl/ (**tools**) ▪ N-COUNT A **tool** is any instrument or simple piece of equipment that you hold in your hands and use to do a particular kind of work. For example, spades, hammers, and knives are all tools. ❑ *I find the best tool for the purpose is a pair of shears.* ▪ N-COUNT You can refer to anything that

▪ 구동사 (어조나 강도를) 누그러뜨리다, 순화하다 ❑ 그 성미 사나운 우익 지도자가 회합 후에 호전적인 성명의 강도를 누그러뜨렸다. ▪ 구동사 (색조나 맛을) 부드럽게 하다, 약화시키다 ❑ 켄 홈이 비비시를 위해 첫 책을 쓸 때, 그는 조리법에서 향신료와 마늘 맛을 약하게 해 달라는 부탁을 받았다.

▪ 가산명사 혀 ❑ 나는 거울 쪽으로 걸어가서 혀를 내밀어 보았다. ▪ 가산명사 말; 말씨 ❑ 그녀는 말씨가 고약했지만, 나는 그녀를 좋아했다. ▪ 가산명사 언어 [문예체] ❑ 프랑스인들은 자기 모국어에 대해 열정적인 감정을 가진다. ▪ 구 우스개조의, 농담조의 ❑ 가볍게 농담조로 접근

▪ 물질명사 토닉 (진 등에 섞어 마시는 탄산음료) ❑ 킬러는 진토닉을 홀짝였다. ▪ 물질명사 강장제 ❑ 영국인들은 자양강장제에 5년 전에 비해 두 배나 많은 돈을 쓰고 있다.

부사 오늘밤 ❑ 나는 오늘밤 집에 있다. ❑ 오늘밤, 그가 자신이 얼마나 대단한 선수인지를 모두에게 증명했다고 나는 생각한다. ● 불가산명사 오늘밤 ❑ 오늘밤이 그 오페라의 첫 공연 날이다.

가산명사 톤 (1000킬로그램) ❑ 석탄 6,550만 톤

▪ 부사 ~도 역시 ❑ "함께 이야기하게 되어서 기쁩니다." "저 역시 마찬가지입니다." ❑ "그것에 대해 커다란 인상을 받았어." "나 역시 그래." ▪ 부사 그것도 [강조] ❑ 우리는 정말 읽기를 배웠다. 그것도 빠르게. ▪ 부사 앞의 진술에 대한 의견을 강조하는 표현에서 쓴다. [강조] ❑ "그 돈은 내 거야." "물론이지, 아주 정당한 거고."

▪ 부사 너무 ~하다 ❑ 너무 큰 가죽바지를 입으면 더 커 보일 것이다. ❑ 계란을 냉장고에 보관해서는 안 된다. 너무 차가우니까. ▪ 부사 부정어와 함께 쓰여 어조를 누그러뜨리거나 공손함을 나타낼 수 있다. [짐작투] ❑ 내가 그때까지 써 왔던 글들이 아주 만족스럽지는 않았다. ▪ 구 너무나 [강조] ❑ 그녀는 그 모든 것을 너무나도 잘 기억하고 있었다.

too는 형용사나 부사 또는 much나 many와 같은 단어의 뜻을 강조할 때 쓴다. 그러나, too는 또한 지나치거나 바람직하지 않은 정도임을 시사하는데, 흔히 그 정도가 너무 지나쳐서 어떤 특정한 결과가 나오지 않거나 나올 수 없음을 뜻한다. ❑ 그녀는 때로는 정말 너무 지나치게 짙은 화장을 한다... 그는 너무 늦게 와서 그녀를 구할 수 없었다. too는 일반적으로 명사구 안에 있는 형용사를 수식하는데는 않는다. 예를 들어, the too heavy boxes라거나 too expensive jewelry라고 하지는 않는다. 이 규칙에 한 가지 예외가 있는데, 명사구가 a나 an으로 시작하는 경우이다. 다음 예문들에서 어순에 주의하라. ❑ ...만일 이 제품이 지나치게 높은 온도에서 보관되어 왔다면... 그는 그것이 놓치기에는 너무도 아까운 기회라는 것을 알았다... 그것은 하루에 운전해 가기에는 너무 먼 거리였다.

take의 과거

▪ 가산명사 연장, 도구 ❑ 나는 그 용도에는 최적의 도구가 큰 가지치기 가위라는 것을 안다. ▪ 가산명사 수단, 방편 ❑ 글쓰기는 주체할 수 없는 감정을 방출하기에 좋은 수단이다.

you use for a particular purpose as a particular type of **tool**. ❑ *Writing is a good tool for discharging overwhelming feelings.*

Thesaurus
*tool*의 참조어

N. appliance, device, instrument 🔢 🔢

Word Partnership
*tool*의 연어

N. tool **belt** 🔢
communication tool, **learning** tool, **management** tool,
marketing tool, **teaching** tool 🔢
V. **use a** tool 🔢 🔢
ADJ. **effective** tool, **important** tool, **valuable** tool 🔢 🔢
powerful tool 🔢

tool|bar /túlbɑr/ (**toolbars**) N-COUNT A **toolbar** is a narrow gray strip across a computer screen containing pictures, called icons, which represent different computer functions. When you want to use a particular function, you move the cursor onto its icon using a mouse. [COMPUTING]

가산명사 (컴퓨터) 도구 모음 [컴퓨터]

tooth ♦♢♢ /túθ/ (**teeth**) 🔢 N-COUNT Your **teeth** are the hard white objects in your mouth, which you use for biting and chewing. ❑ *She had very pretty straight teeth.* 🔢 N-PLURAL The **teeth** of something such as a comb, saw, cog, or zipper are the parts that stick out in a row on its edge. ❑ *The front cog has 44 teeth.* 🔢 PHRASE If you have **a sweet tooth**, you like sweet food very much. ❑ *Add more honey if you have a sweet tooth.* 🔢 to **grit** your **teeth** →see **grit**. a **kick in the teeth** →see **kick** →see **teeth**

🔢 가산명사 이, 치아 ❑ 그녀는 치아가 아주 예쁘고 가지런했다. 🔢 복수명사 (톱 등의) 이 모양 ❑ 전면 톱니바퀴에는 이가 44개 있다. 🔢 구 단 것을 좋아함 ❑ 단 것을 좋아하신다면 꿀을 더 넣으세요.

Word Partnership
*tooth*의 연어

N. tooth **decay**, tooth **enamel** 🔢
lose a tooth, **pull a** tooth 🔢

tooth|brush /túθbrʌʃ/ (**toothbrushes**) N-COUNT A **toothbrush** is a small brush that you use for cleaning your teeth.

가산명사 칫솔

tooth|paste /túθpeɪst/ (**toothpastes**) N-MASS **Toothpaste** is a thick substance which you put on your toothbrush and use to clean your teeth.

물질명사 치약

top ♦♦♦ /tɒp/ (**tops, topping, topped**) 🔢 N-COUNT The **top** of something is its highest point or part. ❑ *I waited at the top of the stairs.* ❑ *...the picture at the top of the page.* ● ADJ **Top** is also an adjective. [ADJ n] ❑ *...the top corner of his newspaper.* 🔢 ADJ The **top** thing or layer in a series of things or layers is the highest one. [ADJ n] ❑ *I can't reach the top shelf.* 🔢 N-COUNT The **top** of something such as a bottle, jar, or tube is a cap, lid, or other device that fits or screws onto one end of it. ❑ *...the plastic tops from aerosol containers.* 🔢 N-SING The **top** of a street, garden, bed, or table is the end of it that is farthest away from where you usually enter it or from where you are. [mainly BRIT] ❑ *...a little shop at the top of the street.* ● ADJ **Top** is also an adjective. [ADJ n] ❑ *...the hill near the top end of the garden.* 🔢 N-COUNT A **top** is a piece of clothing that you wear on the upper half of your body, for example a blouse or shirt. [INFORMAL] ❑ *Look at my new top.* 🔢 ADJ You can use **top** to indicate that something or someone is at the highest level of a scale or measurement. [ADJ n] ❑ *The vehicles have a top speed of 80 kilometers per hour.* 🔢 N-SING The **top** of an organization or career structure is the highest level in it. ❑ *We started from the bottom and we had to work our way up to the top.* ❑ *...his dramatic rise to the top of the military hierarchy.* ● ADJ **Top** is also an adjective. [ADJ n] ❑ *I need to have the top people in this company pull together.* 🔢 ADJ You can use **top** to describe the most important or famous people or things in a particular area of work or activity. [ADJ n] ❑ *So you want to be a top model.* 🔢 N-SING If someone is **at the top of**, for example, a table or league or is the **top of** the table or league, their performance is better than that of all the other people involved. ❑ *The United States will be at the top of the medal table.* ● ADJ **Top** is also an adjective. ❑ *He was the top student in physics.* 🔢 ADJ You can use **top** to indicate that something is the first thing you are going to do, because you consider it to be the most important. ❑ *Cleaning up the water supply is their top priority.* 🔢 ADJ You can use **top** to indicate that someone does a particular thing more times than anyone else or that something is chosen more times than anything else. [ADJ n] ❑ *Schillaci was Italy's top scorer during the World Cup matches.* 🔢 V-T To **top** a list means to be mentioned or chosen more times than anyone or anything else. [JOURNALISM] ❑ *It was the first time a Japanese manufacturer had topped the list for imported vehicles.* 🔢 PHRASE If you say that you clean or examine something **from top to bottom**, you are emphasizing that you do it completely and thoroughly. [EMPHASIS] ❑ *She would clean the house from top to bottom.* 🔢 PHRASE You can use **from top to toe** to emphasize that the whole of someone's body is covered or dressed in a particular thing or type of clothing. [EMPHASIS] ❑ *They were sensibly dressed from top to toe in rain gear.* 🔢 PHRASE When something **gets on top of** you, it makes you feel unhappy or depressed because it is very difficult or worrying, or because it involves more work than you can manage. ❑ *Things have been getting on top of me lately.* 🔢 PHRASE If you say something **off the top of** your **head**, you say it without thinking about it much before you speak, especially because you do not have enough time. ❑ *It was the best I could think of off the top of my head.* 🔢 PHRASE If one thing is **on top of** another, it is placed over it or on its highest part. ❑ *He was sound asleep on top of the bedclothes.* 🔢 PHRASE You can use **on top** or **on top of** to indicate that a particular problem exists in addition to a number of other problems. ❑ *A*

🔢 가산명사 꼭대기, 맨 위 ❑ 나는 계단 맨 위에서 기다렸다. ❑ 그 페이지 맨 위에 있는 사진 ● 형용사 맨 위의 ❑ 그의 신문 맨 위쪽 귀퉁이 🔢 형용사 맨 위의 ❑ 맨 위쪽 선반에 내 손이 안 닿는다. 🔢 가산명사 뚜껑, 마개 ❑ 스프레이 통의 플라스틱 뚜껑 🔢 단수명사 (맞은편) 끝 [주로 영국영어] ❑ 그 거리 끝의 작은 상점 ● 형용사 (맞은편) 끝의 ❑ 정원 맞은편 끝 가까이에 있는 언덕 🔢 가산명사 윗도리, 윗옷 [비격식체] ❑ 내 새 윗옷을 봐. 🔢 형용사 최고의 ❑ 그 운송 수단은 최고 속도가 시속 80킬로미터이다. 🔢 단수명사 최고위, 최상위 ❑ 우리는 밑바닥에서부터 시작했고 가장 높은 자리에 이를 때까지 노력해 나가야 했다. ❑ 군대 서열 최고위에 오른 그의 극적인 출세 ● 형용사 최고위의 ❑ 이 회사의 최고위 인사들로 하여금 서로 협력하여 일하게 해야 한다. 🔢 형용사 일류의 ❑ 그러니까 너는 일류 모델이 되기를 원하는구나. 🔢 단수명사 최상위, 선두 ❑ 미국이 메달 획득 순위 선두에 오를 것이다. ● 형용사 최상위의 ❑ 그는 물리학 과목 성적이 가장 좋은 학생이었다. 🔢 형용사 최우선의, 가장 중요한 ❑ 상수도 청소가 그들의 최고 급선무이다. 🔢 형용사 최고의, 뛰어난 ❑ 스킬라치는 월드컵 대회 동안 이탈리아의 최고 선수였다. 🔢 타동사 최고에 오르다 [언론] ❑ 일본 제조사가 수입 차 부문 1위에 오른 것은 그때가 처음이었다. 🔢 구 완전히, 샅샅이 [강조] ❑ 그녀는 집을 구석구석 청소하곤 했다. 🔢 구 머리끝에서 발끝까지 [강조] ❑ 그들은 현명하게 머리끝에서 발끝까지 우비를 착용했다. 🔢 구 ~을 벅차게 하다, ~을 압박하다 ❑ 요즈음 들어 사태가 나를 벅차게 해 왔다. 🔢 구 준비 없이, 즉석에서 ❑ 그것이 내가 즉석에서 생각해 낼 수 있는 최선이었다. 🔢 구 ~ 위에 ❑ 그는 이불 위에서 곤히 잠들어 있었다. 🔢 구 ~에 더하여; ~ 외에 ❑ 재혼 가족은 일반 가족이 겪는 모든 문제에 대해 일련의 추가적인 문제를 겪는다. 🔢 구 최고 지위에 올라 ❑ 외무 장관이 된 지 17년 후에도, 그가 어떻게 계속 최고 지위에 머물러 있는가? 🔢 구 ~을 잘 처리하여 ❑ 정부가 그 사태를 잘 처리할 능력이 없음 🔢 구 기분이 최고인, 전하늘 다 얻은 것 같은 [강조] ❑ 그녀는 제이슨을 낳기 두 달 전에 천하를 다 얻은 것 같은 기분으로 일을 그만두었다. 🔢 구 ~ 위에, ~을 덮어 ❑ 나는 용기 위에 얇은 폴리에틸렌 종이 한 장 덮어서 이 문제를 극복해 냈다. 🔢 구 과장되어 [주로 영국영어, 비격식체] ❑ 특수 효과가 약간 과장이 심하지만 나는 재미있었다. 🔢 구 목청껏 ❑ "스티븐!" 하고 마시아가 목청껏 외쳤다.

stepfamily faces all the problems that a normal family has, with a set of additional problems on top. 🔟 PHRASE You say that someone is **on top** when they have reached the most important position in an organization or business. ❑ *How does he stay on top, 17 years after becoming foreign minister?* 🔞 PHRASE If you **are on top of** or **get on top of** something that you are doing, you are dealing with it successfully. ❑ *...the government's inability to get on top of the situation.* 🔞 PHRASE If you say that you feel **on top of the world**, you are emphasizing that you feel extremely happy and healthy. [EMPHASIS] ❑ *Two months before she gave birth to Jason she left work feeling on top of the world.* 🔞 PHRASE If one thing is **over the top** of another, it is placed over it so that it is completely covering it. ❑ *I have overcome this problem by placing a sheet of polythene over the top of the container.* 🔞 PHRASE You describe something as **over the top** when you think that it is exaggerated, and therefore unacceptable. [mainly BRIT, INFORMAL] ❑ *The special effects are a bit over the top but I enjoyed it.* 🔞 PHRASE If you say something **at the top of** your **voice**, you say it very loudly. ❑ *"Stephen!" shouted Marcia at the top of her voice.*

Thesaurus   *top*의 참조어

N.	peak, summit, zenith; (ant.) base, bottom ❶
ADJ.	best, first-rate ❽

▶**top up** PHRASAL VERB If you **top** something **up**, you make it full again when part of it has been used. [mainly BRIT] ❑ *We topped up the water tanks.* →see also **top-up**

구동사 다시 가득 채우다 [주로 영국영어] ❑ 우리는 물탱크를 다시 가득 채웠다.

top-end ADJ **Top-end** products are expensive and of extremely high quality. [BUSINESS] ❑ *...top-end camcorders.*

형용사 최고급의 [경제] ❑ 최고급 캠코더

top|ic /tɒpɪk/ (**topics**) N-COUNT A **topic** is a particular subject that you discuss or write about. ❑ *The weather is a constant topic of conversation in Britain.*

가산명사 화제, 주제 ❑ 영국에서 날씨는 변치 않는 대화 주제이다.

top|ical /tɒpɪkəl/ ADJ **Topical** is used to describe something that concerns or relates to events that are happening at the present time. ❑ *The magazine's aim is to discuss topical issues within a Christian framework.*

형용사 시사 문제의 ❑ 그 잡지의 목표는 기독교 틀 안에서 시사 문제를 논하는 것이다.

top|less /tɒplɪs/ ADJ If a woman goes **topless**, she does not wear anything to cover her breasts. [ADJ after v, ADJ n, v-link ADJ] ❑ *I wouldn't sunbathe topless if I thought I might offend anyone.*

형용사 윗옷을 입지 않은, 가슴을 드러낸 ❑ 만약 내가 누군가를 불쾌하게 만들 수도 있다는 생각이 들면 가슴을 드러낸 채로 일광욕을 하지는 않을 것이다.

top|ple /tɒpəl/ (**topples, toppling, toppled**) ❶ V-T/V-I If someone or something **topples** somewhere or if you **topple** them, they become unsteady or unstable and fall over. ❑ *He just released his hold and toppled slowly backwards.* ● PHRASAL VERB **Topple over** means the same as **topple**. ❑ *The tree is so badly damaged they are worried it might topple over.* ❷ V-T To **topple** a government or leader, especially one that is not elected by the people, means to cause them to lose power. [JOURNALISM] ❑ *...the revolution which toppled the regime.*

❶ 타동사/자동사 쓰러지다; 쓰러뜨리다 ❑ 그가 그냥 잡았던 손을 놓더니 천천히 뒤로 쓰러졌다. ● 구동사 쓰러지다; 쓰러뜨리다 ❑ 그 나무는 아주 심하게 손상을 입어서 쓰러지지 않을까 사람들이 걱정한다. ❷ 타동사 전복시키다 [언론] ❑ 그 정권을 전복시킨 혁명

top se|cret ADJ **Top secret** information or activity is intended to be kept completely secret, for example in order to prevent a country's enemies from finding out about it. ❑ *The top secret documents had to do with the most advanced military equipment.*

형용사 극비의 ❑ 그 극비 문서는 가장 발달한 군사 장비와 관련이 있었다.

top-up (**top-ups**) ❶ N-COUNT A **top-up** is another serving of a drink in the same glass that you have just used. [BRIT] ❑ *I couldn't have a top-up of vodka, could I?* ❷ ADJ A **top-up** loan or payment is added to an amount of money in order to bring it up to a required level. [BRIT, BUSINESS] [ADJ n] ❑ *Student grants will be frozen at existing levels and top-up loans made available.*

❶ 가산명사 (술을 마셨던 잔에) 다시 채움 [영국영어] ❑ 보드카를 한 잔 더 채워 주시면 안 될까요? ❷ 형용사 추가의, 보충 [영국영어, 경제] ❑ 학비 보조금은 현행 수준으로 동결되며 추가 융자를 이용할 수 있게 될 것이다.

torch /tɔːtʃ/ (**torches**) ❶ N-COUNT A **torch** is a long stick with burning material at one end, used to provide light or to set things on fire. ❑ *They lit a torch and set fire to the chapel's thatch.* ❷ N-COUNT A **torch** is a device that produces a hot flame and is used for tasks such as cutting or joining pieces of metal. ❑ *The gang worked for up to ten hours with acetylene torches to open the vault.* ❸ N-COUNT A **torch** is a small electric light which is powered by batteries and which you can carry in your hand. [BRIT; AM **flashlight**] ❑ *He shone a torch in my face.*

❶ 가산명사 횃불 ❑ 그들은 횃불을 붙여서 예배당 초가지붕에 불을 질렀다. ❷ 가산명사 토치램프 ❑ 그 갱단들은 귀중품 보관실을 열기 위해 아세틸렌 토치램프로 최고 열 시간 동안 작업을 했다. ❸ 가산명사 손전등 [영국영어; 미국영어 flashlight] ❑ 그가 내 얼굴에 손전등을 비췄다.

tore /tɔː/ **Tore** is the past tense of **tear**.

tear의 과거

tor|ment (**torments, tormenting, tormented**)

The noun is pronounced /tɔːmɛnt/. The verb is pronounced /tɔːmɛnt/.

명사는 /tɔːmɛnt/로 발음되고, 동사는 /tɔːmɛnt/로 발음된다.

❶ N-UNCOUNT **Torment** is extreme suffering, usually mental suffering. ❑ *She is my first ever girlfriend, a source both of wonder and torment.* ❷ N-COUNT A **torment** is something that causes extreme suffering, usually mental suffering. ❑ *Sooner or later most writers end up making books about the torments of being a writer.* ❸ V-T If something **torments** you, it causes you extreme mental suffering. ❑ *At times the memories returned to torment her.*

❶ 불가산명사 고통, 고뇌 ❑ 그녀는 내 생애 최초의 여자친구로, 내게 경이로움과 고뇌 둘 다 안겨 준다. ❷ 가산명사 고민거리 ❑ 조만간 대부분의 작가들이 작가로서 갖는 고민거리에 대한 책을 써 내게 된다. ❸ 타동사 괴롭히다 ❑ 이따금씩 그 기억이 되살아나 그녀를 괴롭혔다.

torn /tɔːn/ ❶ **Torn** is the past participle of **tear**. ❷ ADJ If you are **torn between** two or more things, you cannot decide which to choose, and so you feel anxious or troubled. ❑ *Robb is torn between becoming a doctor and a career in athletics.*

❶ tear의 과거 분사 ❷ 형용사 고민하는, 이러지도 저러지도 못 하는 ❑ 로브는 의사가 되는 것과 운동선수가 되는 것 사이에서 고민하고 있다.

tor|na|do /tɔːneɪdoʊ/ (**tornadoes** or **tornados**) N-COUNT A **tornado** is a violent wind storm consisting of a tall column of air which spins around very fast and causes a lot of damage.

가산명사 회오리바람

tor|pe|do /tɔːpiːdoʊ/ (**torpedoes, torpedoing, torpedoed**) ❶ N-COUNT A **torpedo** is bomb that is shaped like a tube and that travels under water. ❷ V-T If a ship **is torpedoed**, it is hit, and usually sunk, by a torpedo or torpedoes. [usu passive] ❑ *More than a thousand people died when the Lusitania was torpedoed.*

❶ 가산명사 어뢰 ❷ 타동사 어뢰에 맞아 격침되다 ❑ 루시타니아호가 어뢰에 맞아 격침되었을 때 천 명 이상이 죽었다.

tor|rent /tɒrənt, BRIT tɒrənt/ (**torrents**) ❶ N-COUNT A **torrent** is a lot of water falling or flowing rapidly or violently. ❑ *Torrents of water gushed into the reservoir.*

❶ 가산명사 급류 ❑ 급류가 저수지로 세차게 흘러들었다. ❷ 가산명사 (질문 등의) 마구 퍼부음,

A

2 N-COUNT A **torrent of** abuse or questions is a lot of abuse or questions directed continuously at someone. ❏ *He turned round and directed a torrent of abuse at me.*

B

tor|ren|tial /tɔrenʃ°l, BRIT tərenʃ°l/ ADJ **Torrential** rain pours down very rapidly and in great quantities. ❏ *The storms and torrential rain caused traffic chaos across the country.*

C

tor|so /tɔrsoʊ/ (torsos) N-COUNT Your **torso** is the main part of your body, and does not include your head, arms, and legs. [FORMAL] ❏ *The man had the bulky upper torso of a weightlifter.*

D

tor|toise /tɔrtəs/ (tortoises) N-COUNT A **tortoise** is a slow-moving animal with a shell into which it can pull its head and legs for protection.

tor|tu|ous /tɔrtʃuəs/ **1** ADJ A **tortuous** road is full of bends and twists. ❏ *The only road access is a tortuous mountain route.* **2** ADJ A **tortuous** process or piece of writing is very long and complicated. ❏ *...these long and tortuous negotiations aimed at ending the conflict.*

E

F

tor|ture ♦◇◇ /tɔrtʃər/ (tortures, torturing, tortured) **1** V-T If someone **is tortured**, another person deliberately causes them great pain over a period of time, in order to punish them or to make them reveal information. ❏ *French police are convinced that she was tortured and killed.* ● N-VAR **Torture** is also a noun. ❏ *...alleged cases of torture and murder by the security forces.* **2** V-T To **torture** someone means to cause them to suffer mental pain or anxiety. ❏ *He would not torture her further by trying to argue with her.*

G

H

Tory ♦◇◇ /tɔri/ (Tories) ADJ In Britain, a **Tory** politician or voter is a member of or votes for the Conservative Party. ❏ *...the former Tory Party chairman, Chris Patten.* ● N-COUNT **Tory** is also a noun. ❏ *...the first budget since the Tories won the 1992 general election.*

I

J

toss /tɔs, BRIT tɒs/ (tosses, tossing, tossed) **1** V-T If you **toss** something somewhere, you throw it there lightly, often in a rather careless way. ❏ *He screwed the paper into a ball and tossed it into the fire.* **2** V-T If you **toss** your head or **toss** your hair, you move your head backward, quickly and suddenly, often as a way of expressing an emotion such as anger or contempt. ❏ *"I'm sure I don't know." Cook tossed her head.* ● N-COUNT **Toss** is also a noun. ❏ *With a toss of his head and a few hard gulps, Bob finished the last of his beer.* **3** V-T In sports and informal situations, if you decide something by **tossing** a coin, you spin a coin into the air and guess which side of the coin will face upward when it lands. ❏ *We tossed a coin to decide who would go out and buy the buns.* ● N-COUNT **Toss** is also a noun. ❏ *It would be better to decide it on the toss of a coin.* **4** PHRASE If you **toss and turn**, you keep moving around in bed and cannot sleep properly, for example because you are ill or worried. ❏ *I try to go back to sleep and toss and turn for a while.*

K

L

M

to|tal ♦♦♦ /toʊt°l/ (totals, totalling, totalled) **1** N-COUNT A **total** is the number that you get when you add several numbers together or when you count how many things there are in a group. ❏ *The companies have a total of 1,776 employees.* **2** ADJ The **total** number or cost of something is the number or cost that you get when you add together or count all the parts in it. [ADJ n] ❏ *They said that the total number of cows dying from BSE would be twenty thousand.* **3** PHRASE If there are a number of things **in total**, there are that number when you count or add them all together. ❏ *I was with my husband for eight years in total.* **4** V-T If several numbers or things **total** a certain figure, that figure is the total of all the numbers or all the things. ❏ *The unit's exports will total $85 million this year.* **5** ADJ You can use **total** to emphasize that something is as great in extent, degree, or amount as it possibly can be. [EMPHASIS] ❏ *You were a total failure if you hadn't married by the time you were about twenty-three.* ● **to|tal|ly** ADV ❏ *Young people want something totally different from the old ways.*

N

O

P

Q

Word Partnership	total의 연어		
N.	total **area**, total **population**, **sum** total **1**		
	total **amount**, total **cost**, total **expenses**, total **sales**, total **savings**, total **value 2 5**		
ADJ.	**grand** total **1 2**		

R

S

to|tali|tar|ian /toʊtælɪteəriən/ ADJ A **totalitarian** political system is one in which there is only one political party which controls everything and does not allow any opposition parties. [DISAPPROVAL] ❏ *...a brutal totalitarian regime.*

T

tot|ter /tɒtər/ (totters, tottering, tottered) V-I If someone **totters** somewhere, they walk there in an unsteady way, for example because they are ill or drunk. ❏ *He tottered to the fridge, got a beer and slumped at the table.*

U

touch ♦♦◇ /tʌtʃ/ (touches, touching, touched) **1** V-T/V-I If you **touch** something, you put your hand onto it in order to feel it or to make contact with it. ❏ *Her tiny hands gently touched my face.* ❏ *Don't touch that dial.* ● N-COUNT **Touch** is also a noun. ❏ *Sometimes even a light touch on the face is enough to trigger off this pain.* **2** V-RECIP If two things **are touching**, or if one thing **touches** another, or if you **touch** two things, their surfaces come into contact with each other. ❏ *Their knees were touching.* ❏ *A cyclist crashed when he touched wheels with another rider.* **3** N-UNCOUNT Your sense of **touch** is your ability to tell what something is like when you feel it with your hands. ❏ *The evidence suggests that our sense of touch is programmed to diminish with age.* **4** V-T To **touch** something means to strike it, usually quite gently. ❏ *He scored the first time he touched the ball.* **5** V-T If something **has not been touched**, nobody has dealt with it or taken care of it. [usu passive, with brd-neg] ❏ *When John began to restore the house in the 1960s, nothing had been touched for 40 years.* **6** V-T If you say that you did not **touch** someone or something, you are emphasizing that you did not attack, harm or destroy them, especially when you have been accused of doing so. [EMPHASIS]

V

W

X

Y

Z

쇄도 ❏ 그는 돌아서서 나에게 욕지거리를 마구 퍼부었다.

형용사 억수 같은 ❏ 폭풍우와 억수 같은 비로 전국적으로 교통난이 일어났다.

가산명사 몸통 [격식체] ❏ 그 남자는 역도 선수 같이 윗몸통이 컸다.

가산명사 거북

1 형용사 구불구불한 ❏ 유일한 접근 도로는 구불구불한 산길뿐이다. **2** 형용사 길고 복잡한, 지난한 ❏ 분쟁 종식을 목표로 한 이런 길고 지난한 협상들

1 타동사 고문을 당하다 ❏ 프랑스 경찰은 그녀가 고문을 받고 살해되었다고 확신하고 있다. ● 가산명사 또는 불가산명사 고문 ❏ 보안군에 의해 저질러졌다고 주장되는 고문과 살인 사건들 **2** 타동사 (정신적으로) 괴롭히다 ❏ 그는 그녀와 논쟁을 해서 더 이상 그녀를 괴롭히고 싶지 않았다.

형용사 (영국) 토리당의 ❏ 전 토리당 의장, 크리스 패튼 ● 가산명사 토리당원 ❏ 토리당이 1992년 총선거에서 승리한 이후 첫 예산안

1 타동사 (가볍게) 던지다 ❏ 그는 종이를 공처럼 뭉쳐서 불 속에 던져 넣었다. **2** 타동사 (머리를 뒤로) 홱 젖히다 ❏ "난 확실히 몰라."하고 쿡은 머리를 홱 젖혔다. ● 가산명사 홱 젖히기 ❏ 밥은 머리를 홱 젖히고 몇 번 세차게 꿀꺽꿀꺽 들이켜서 자기 몫의 마지막 맥주를 다 마셔 버렸다. **3** 타동사 (결정하기 위해 동전을) 던지다 ❏ 우리는 누가 나가서 롤빵을 사올지 결정하기 위해 동전을 던졌다. ● 가산명사 (동전) 던지기 ❏ 동전 던지기로 결정하는 편이 더 낫겠다. **4** 구 뒤척거리다, 뒤척이다 ❏ 나는 다시 잠들려고 애쓰며 잠시 동안 뒤척거린다.

1 가산명사 합계, 총수 ❏ 그 회사들은 총 1,776명의 종업원을 거느리고 있다. **2** 형용사 합계의, 총계의 ❏ 광우병으로 죽는 소의 총수가 2만 마리는 될 거라고 그들은 말했다. **3** 구 합계하여, 전부 ❏ 나는 모두 8년 동안 남편과 함께 했다. **4** 타동사 합계 ~이 되다 ❏ 그 부서의 올해 수출액은 총 8,500만 달러에 달할 것이다. **5** 형용사 완전한, 전적인 [강조] ❏ 만약 스물세 살 무렵까지 결혼을 하지 않았다면 완전 실패작이다. ● 완전히, 전적으로 부사 ❏ 젊은이들은 옛 방식과는 완전히 다른 뭔가를 원한다.

형용사 전체주의의 [탐탁잖음] ❏ 엄혹한 전체주의 정권

자동사 비틀거리다 ❏ 그는 비틀거리며 냉장고로 가서, 맥주 한 병을 꺼내 들고 식탁에 무너지듯이 앉았다.

1 타동사/자동사 만지다 ❏ 그녀의 작은 손이 부드럽게 내 얼굴을 만졌다. ❏ 그 눈금판 만지지 마. ● 가산명사 접촉, 만지기 ❏ 때로는 얼굴을 가볍게 만지는 것만으로도 이 통증을 일으키기에 충분하다. **2** 상호동사 닿다; 닿게 하다 ❏ 그들의 무릎이 맞닿았다. ❏ 사이클 선수 한 명이 다른 선수와 바퀴가 부딪쳐 쓰러졌다. **3** 불가산명사 촉각 ❏ 그 증거는 우리의 촉각이 나이를 먹으면 감퇴하도록 되어 있다는 것을 시사한다. **4** 타동사 건드리다 ❏ 그는 처음 공을 건드렸을 때 득점을 올렸다. **5** 타동사 손길이 닿다 ❏ 존이 1960년대에 그 집을 복원하기 시작했을 때, 40년 동안 어느 곳의 손길도 닿지 않은 상태였다. **6** 타동사 (해칠 목적으로) 손을 대다 [강조] ❏ 피어스는 여전히 완강하게, "난 그 사람한테 손도 안 댔어."라고 말했다. **7** 타동사 손을 대다, 사용하다 [강조] ❏ 그는 술을 많이 안 마시고 약물에는 손도 대지

[with brd-neg] ❑ *Pearce remained adamant, saying "I didn't touch him."* **7** V-T You say that you never **touch** something or that you have not **touched** something for a long time to emphasize that you never use it, or you have not used it for a long time. [EMPHASIS] [no passive, with brd-neg] ❑ *He doesn't drink much and doesn't touch drugs.* **8** V-I If you **touch on** a particular subject or problem, you mention it or write briefly about it. ❑ *The film touches on these issues, but only superficially.* **9** V-T If something **touches** you, it affects you in some way for a short time. ❑ *...a guilt that in some sense touches everyone.* **10** V-T If something that someone says or does **touches** you, it affects you emotionally, often because you see that they are suffering a lot or that they are being very kind. ❑ *It has touched me deeply to see how these people live.* ● **touched** ADJ [v-link ADJ] ❑ *I was touched to find that he regards me as engaging.* **11** N-COUNT A **touch** is a detail which is added to something to improve it. [supp N] ❑ *They called the event "a tribute to heroes," which was a nice touch.* **12** N-SING If someone has a particular kind of **touch**, they have a particular way of doing something. ❑ *The dishes he produces all have a personal touch.* **13** QUANT A **touch of** something is a very small amount of it. [QUANT of n-uncount] ❑ *She thought she just had a touch of flu.* **14** →see also **touching** **15** PHRASE You use **at the touch of** in expressions such as **at the touch of a button** and **at the touch of a key** to indicate that something is possible by simply touching a switch or one of the keys of a keyboard. ❑ *Staff will be able to trace calls at the touch of a button.* **16** PHRASE If you get **in touch with** someone, you contact them by writing to them or telephoning them. If you are, keep, or stay **in touch with** them, you write, phone, or visit each other regularly. ❑ *I will get in touch with solicitors about this.* **17** PHRASE If you are **in touch with** a subject or situation, or if someone keeps you **in touch with** it, you know the latest news or information about it. If you are **out of touch with** it, you do not know the latest news or information about it. ❑ *...keeping the unemployed in touch with the labour market.* **18** PHRASE If you **lose touch with** someone, you gradually stop writing, telephoning, or visiting them. ❑ *In my job one tends to lose touch with friends.* **19** PHRASE If you **lose touch with** something, you no longer have the latest news or information about it. ❑ *Their leaders have lost touch with what is happening in the country.* **20** the finishing touch →see finish. touch wood →see wood

▶**touch down** PHRASAL VERB When an aircraft **touches down**, it lands. ❑ *Spacecraft Columbia touched down yesterday.*

touch|ing /tʌtʃɪŋ/ ADJ If something is **touching**, it causes feelings of sadness or sympathy. ❑ *Her story is the touching tale of a wife who stood by the husband she loved.* →see also **touch**

touch|screen /tʌtʃskriːn/ (touchscreens) also touch-screen N-COUNT A **touchscreen** is a computer screen that allows the user to give commands to the computer by touching parts of the screen rather than by using the keyboard or mouse. [COMPUTING] ❑ *...touchscreen voting machines.*

touch-tone ADJ A **touch-tone** telephone has numbered buttons that make different sounds when you press them. Some automatic telephone services can only be used with this kind of telephone. [ADJ n]

touchy /tʌtʃi/ (touchier, touchiest) ADJ If you describe someone as **touchy**, you mean that they are easily upset, offended, or irritated. [DISAPPROVAL] ❑ *She is very touchy about her past.*

tough ♦♦◇ /tʌf/ (tougher, toughest) **1** ADJ A **tough** person is strong and determined, and can tolerate difficulty or suffering. ❑ *He built up a reputation as a tough businessman.* ● **tough|ness** N-UNCOUNT ❑ *Mrs. Potter has won a reputation for toughness and determination on her way to the top.* **2** ADJ If you describe someone as **tough**, you mean that they are hard and violent. ❑ *He had shot three people dead earning himself a reputation as a tough guy.* **3** ADJ A **tough** place or area is considered to have a lot of crime and violence. ❑ *She doesn't seem cut out for this tough neighborhood.* **4** ADJ A **tough** way of life or period of time is difficult or full of suffering. ❑ *She had a pretty tough childhood.* **5** ADJ A **tough** task or problem is difficult to do or solve. ❑ *It was a very tough decision but we feel we made the right one.* **6** ADJ **Tough** policies or actions are strict and firm. ❑ *He is known for taking a tough line on security.* **7** ADJ A **tough** substance is strong, and difficult to break, cut, or tear. ❑ *In industry, diamond can form a tough, non-corrosive coating for tools.* **8** ADJ **Tough** meat is difficult to cut and chew. ❑ *The steak was tough and the peas were like bullets.*

tough|en /tʌfⁿn/ (toughens, toughening, toughened) **1** V-T If you **toughen** something or if it **toughens**, you make it stronger so that it will not break

---

않는다. **8** 자동사 언급하다, 다루다 ❑ 그 영화는 이런 문제들을 다루지만, 단지 피상적으로일 뿐이다. **9** 타동사 영향을 주다 ❑ 어떤 의미에서 모든 사람들에게 영향을 미치는 범죄 행위 **10** 타동사 감동시키다 ❑ 나는 이 사람들이 사는 모습을 보고 깊이 감동받았다. ● 감동받은 형용사 ❑ 나는 그가 나를 매력적이라고 생각한다는 것을 알고 감동받았다. **11** 가산명사 손질, 솜씨 ❑ 그들은 그 행사를 '영웅들을 기림'이라고 불렀는데, 그것은 멋진 솜씨였다. **12** 단수명사 특색 ❑ 그가 만든 요리들은 모두 그만의 특색이 있다. **13** 수량사 조금, 기미 ❑ 그녀는 독감 기운이 약간 있는 것뿐이라고 생각했다. **15** 구 -를 누르기만 하면 ❑ 직원들이 버튼을 누르기만 하면 전화를 추적할 수 있게 될 것이다. **16** 구 -와 연락을 취하여 ❑ 이 일에 관해 변호사들과 연락을 취할 것이다. **17** 구 -와 연락이 끊고; 뒤떨어져 ❑ 실업자들을 노동 시장의 추세에 뒤떨어지지 않게 하는 것 **18** 구 -와 연락이 끊기다 ❑ 내 직업은 친구들과 연락이 끊기게 만드는 경향이 있다. **19** 구 -에 뒤떨어지다 ❑ 그들의 지도자들은 지방에서 무슨 일이 벌어지는지 실정에 뒤떨어져 있다.

구동사 착륙하다 ❑ 우주선 컬럼비아호가 어제 착륙했다.

형용사 감동적인 ❑ 그녀의 이야기는 자기가 사랑하는 남편 곁을 지켰던 한 아내에 대한 감동적인 이야기다.

가산명사 터치스크린 (화면을 누르면 입력이 되는 컴퓨터 장치) [컴퓨터] ❑ 터치스크린 투표기

형용사 터치톤식의 (버튼을 누르면 각기 다른 소리가 남)

형용사 성마른, 과민한 [탐탁찮음] ❑ 그녀는 자기 과거에 대해 매우 과민하다.

1 형용사 강인한, 굳센 ❑ 그는 강인한 사업가로서의 평판을 쌓았다. ● 강인함, 굳셈 불가산명사 ❑ 포터 여사는 최고의 자리까지 나아가는 과정에서 강인하고 결단력이 있다는 평판을 얻었다. **2** 형용사 음악한, 난폭한 ❑ 그는 세 사람을 쏘아 죽여서 흉악한 자라는 평판을 얻었었다. **3** 형용사 무법의, 폭력이 난무하는 ❑ 그녀는 이 무법 지대에 어울릴 것 같지 않다. **4** 형용사 고달픈, 힘든 ❑ 그녀는 상당히 힘든 어린 시절을 보냈다. **5** 형용사 힘든, 까다로운 ❑ 대단히 힘든 결정이었지만 우리가 옳은 결정을 했다고 생각한다. **6** 형용사 강경한 ❑ 그는 안보에 대해 강경 노선을 취하는 것으로 알려져 있다. **7** 형용사 단단한 ❑ 산업계에서는, 다이아몬드로 공구에 단단하고 부식되지 않는 코팅을 입힐 수 있다. **8** 형용사 (고기가) 질긴 ❑ 스테이크는 질겼고 완두콩은 총알 같았다.

1 타동사 질기게 하다, 단단하게 하다 ❑ 소금은 보통 콩의 껍질을 질기게 하므로 조리할 때 넣지 마라.

easily. ❑ *Do not add salt to beans when cooking as this tends to toughen the skins.* ❑ V-T If a person, institution, or law **toughens** its policies, regulations, or punishments, it makes them firmer or stricter. ❑ *Talks are under way to toughen trade restrictions.* ● PHRASAL VERB **Toughen up** means the same as **toughen.** ❑ *The new law toughens up penalties for those that misuse guns.* ❑ V-T If an experience **toughens** you, it makes you stronger and more independent in character. ❑ *They believe that participating in fights toughens boys and shows them how to be men.* ● PHRASAL VERB **Toughen up** means the same as **toughen.** ❑ *He thinks boxing is good for kids, that it toughens them up.*

tour ♦♦◇ /tʊər/ (**tours, touring, toured**) ❶ N-COUNT A **tour** is an organized trip that people such as musicians, politicians, or theater companies go on to several different places, stopping to meet people or perform. ❑ *The band are currently on a two-month tour of Europe.* ● PHRASE When people are traveling on a tour, you can say that they are **on tour.** ❑ *The band will be going on tour.* ❷ V-T/V-I When people such as musicians, politicians, or theater companies **tour,** they go on a tour, for example in order to perform or to meet people. ❑ *A few years ago they toured the country in a roadshow.* ❸ N-COUNT A **tour** is a trip during which you visit several places that interest you. ❑ *It was week five of my tour of the major cities of Europe.* ❹ N-COUNT A **tour** is a short trip that you make around a place, for example around a historical building, so that you can look at it. ❑ *...a guided tour of a ruined Scottish castle.* ❺ V-T If you **tour** a place, you go on a trip or journey around it. ❑ *You can also tour the site on modern coaches equipped with videos.*

Word Partnership	tour의 연어
N.	concert tour, farewell tour ❶
	world tour ❸
	tour bus, tour guide, walking tour ❸ ❹
	museum tour ❹
V.	begin a tour, finish a tour ❶ ❸ ❹
	take a tour ❸ ❹

tour|ism /tʊərɪzəm/ N-UNCOUNT **Tourism** is the business of providing services for people on vacation, for example hotels, restaurants, and trips. ❑ *Tourism is vital for the Spanish economy.* →see **industry**

tour|ist ♦◇◇ /tʊərɪst/ (**tourists**) N-COUNT A **tourist** is a person who is visiting a place for pleasure and interest, especially when they are on vacation. ❑ *...foreign tourists.* ❑ *Blackpool is the top tourist attraction in England.* →see **city**

tour|na|ment ♦◇◇ /tʊərnəmənt, tɜr-/ (**tournaments**) N-COUNT A **tournament** is a sports competition in which players who win a match continue to play further matches in the competition until just one person or team is left. ❑ *...the biggest golf tournament to be held in Australia.*

tout /taʊt/ (**touts, touting, touted**) ❶ V-T If someone **touts** something, they try to sell it or convince people that it is good. [DISAPPROVAL] ❑ *It has the trappings of an election campaign in the United States, with slick television ads touting the candidates.* ❷ V-I If someone **touts for** business or custom, they try to obtain it. [mainly BRIT] ❑ *He visited Thailand and Singapore to tout for investment.* ❸ V-T If someone **touts** tickets, they sell them outside a sports stadium or theater, usually for more than their original value. [BRIT; AM **scalp**] ❑ *...a man who made his money touting tickets.* ❹ N-COUNT A **tout** is someone who sells things such as tickets unofficially, usually at prices which are higher than the official ones. [BRIT; AM **scalper**] ❑ *Genuine tickets were being bought from touts at up to £1,600 a pair.*

tow /toʊ/ (**tows, towing, towed**) V-T If one vehicle **tows** another, it pulls it along behind it. ❑ *He had been using the vehicle to tow his work trailer.* ❑ *They threatened to tow away my car.*

to|ward ♦♦♦ /tɔrd, BRIT təwɔːˈdz/ also **towards**

In addition to the uses shown below, **toward** is used in phrasal verbs such as "count toward" and "lean toward."

❶ PREP If you move, look, or point **toward** something or someone, you move, look, or point in their direction. ❑ *They were all moving toward him down the stairs.* ❑ *When he looked towards me, I smiled and waved.* ❷ PREP If things develop **toward** a particular situation, that situation becomes nearer in time or more likely to happen. [PREP n/-ing] ❑ *The agreement is a major step toward peace.* ❸ PREP If you have a particular attitude **toward** something or someone, you have that attitude when you think about them or deal with them. ❑ *My attitude toward religion has been shaped by this man.* ❹ PREP If something happens **toward** a particular time, it happens just before that time. ❑ *There was a forecast of cooler weather toward the end of the week.* ❺ PREP If something is **toward** part of a place or thing, it is near that part. ❑ *Gulls are nesting on a small island toward the eastern shore.* ❻ PREP If you give money **toward** something, you give it to help pay for that thing. ❑ *Taxes only get part of the way toward a $50 billion deficit.*

tow|el /taʊəl/ (**towels, toweling, toweled**) [BRIT, sometimes AM **towelling, towelled**] ❶ N-COUNT A **towel** is a piece of thick soft cloth that you use to dry yourself. ❑ *...a bath towel.* ❷ V-T If you **towel** something or **towel** it dry, you dry it with a towel. ❑ *James came out of his bedroom, toweling his wet hair.* ❑ *I toweled myself dry.* ❸ PHRASE If you **throw in the towel,** you stop trying to do something because you realize that you cannot succeed. [INFORMAL] ❑ *It seemed as if the police had thrown in the towel and were abandoning the investigation.*

tow|er /taʊər/ (**towers, towering, towered**) ❶ N-COUNT; N-IN-NAMES A **tower** is a tall, narrow building, that either stands alone or forms part of another building such as a church or castle. ❑ *...an eleventh century castle with 120-foot high towers.* ❷ V-I Someone or something that **towers over** surrounding people or things is a lot taller than they are. ❑ *He stood up and towered over her.*

---

② 타동사 강화하다 ❑ 무역 규제 강화를 위한 회담이 진행 중이다. ● 구동사 강화하다 ❑ 새 법률에 따라 총을 오용하는 사람에 대한 처벌이 강화됐다. ③ 타동사 강인하게 만들다 ❑ 그들은 남자아이들이 싸우면서 강인해지고 남자다워지는 법을 배운다고 믿는다. ● 구동사 강인하게 만들다 ❑ 그는 복싱이 강인함을 키워 주기 때문에 아이들에게 좋다고 생각한다.

❶ 가산명사 순회 ❑ 밴드는 현재 두 달 일정의 유럽 순회공연을 하고 있다. ● 구 순회 중인 ❑ 밴드가 순회공연에 들어갈 것이다. ❷ 타동사/자동사 순회하다 ❑ 그들은 몇 년 전 순회공연을 하며 전국을 돌았다. ❸ 가산명사 여행, 관광 ❑ 내가 유럽 주요 도시 관광을 시작한 지 5주가 되던 때였다. ❹ 가산명사 관광, 견학 ❑ 스코틀랜드 고성 가이드 투어 ❺ 타동사 여행하다, 관광하다, 견학하다 ❑ 또한 여러분은 비디오가 장착된 현대식 버스를 타고 유적 관광을 하실 수 있습니다.

불가산명사 관광업 ❑ 관광업은 스페인 경제에 없어서는 안 될 산업이다.

가산명사 관광객 ❑ 외국인 관광객 ❑ 블랙풀은 잉글랜드 최고의 관광지이다.

가산명사 토너먼트 ❑ 호주에서 개최되는 사상 최대 규모의 골프 토너먼트

❶ 타동사 -의 장점을 늘어놓다, 선전하다 [탐탁찮음] ❑ 이는 후보를 선전하는 그럴듯한 텔레비전 광고를 포함해 미국 선거전에서 볼 수 있는 다양한 면모를 갖추고 있다. ❷ 자동사 (손님을) 끌다 [주로 영국영어] ❑ 그는 투자 유치 차원에서 태국과 싱가포르를 방문했다. ❸ 타동사 암표를 팔다 [영국영어; 미국영어 scalp] ❑ 암표를 팔아 돈을 번 남자 ❹ 가산명사 암표상 [영국영어; 미국영어 scalper] ❑ 암표상에게서는 진짜 표가 두 장 당 1,600파운드에 팔리고 있었다.

타동사 끌어가다, 끌다 ❑ 그는 작업 트레일러를 끄는 데 항상 그 차량을 사용했었다. ❑ 그들이 내 차를 끌어가겠다고 위협했다.

toward는 아래 용법 외에도 'count toward', 'lean toward'와 같은 구동사에 쓰인다.

❶ 전치사 ~쪽으로, ~을 향하여 ❑ 그들 모두 그를 향해 계단을 내려가고 있었다. ❑ 그가 내 쪽을 바라봤을 때 나는 미소 지으며 손을 흔들었다. ❷ 전치사 ~을 향하여 ❑ 이번 합의로 평화를 향해 한걸음 성큼 나아갔다. ❸ 전치사 ~에 대하여 ❑ 나의 종교관은 이 사람의 영향을 받아 형성되었다. ❹ 전치사 ~ 무렵에 ❑ 이번 주말 무렵 날씨가 차가워진다는 예보가 있었다. ❺ 전치사 ~쪽에 ❑ 갈매기들이 동부 해안 쪽 작은 섬에 둥지를 틀고 있다. ❻ 전치사 ~을 위하여 ❑ 세금으로는 적자 5백 억 달러의 일부만 메울 수 있다.

[영국영어, 미국영어 가끔 towelling, towelled] ❶ 가산명사 수건 ❑ 목욕 수건 ❷ 타동사 수건으로 닦다 ❑ 제임스가 수건으로 머리를 말리며 침실 밖으로 나왔다. ❑ 나는 수건으로 몸을 닦았다. ❸ 구 항복하다, 포기하다 [비격식체] ❑ 경찰이 포기하고 수사를 중단한 것처럼 보였다.

❶ 가산명사; 이름명사 고층 빌딩, 탑, 타워 ❑ 120피트 높이의 탑 여러 개를 갖춘 11세기의 성 ❷ 자동사 키가 훨씬 크다, 훨씬 높다 ❑ 그가 일어섰다. 그녀에 비해 훨씬 큰 키였다. ❸ 가산명사 송신탑 ❑ 군이 아직도 텔레비전과 라디오 송신탑을 통제하고 있다.

3 N-COUNT A **tower** is a tall structure that is used for sending radio or television signals. ❑ *Troops are still in control of the television and radio tower.*
4 N-COUNT A **tower** is a tall box that contains the main parts of a computer, such as the hard disk and the drives. [COMPUTING]

tow|er|ing /ˈtaʊərɪŋ/ **1** ADJ If you describe something such as a mountain or cliff as **towering**, you mean that it is very tall and therefore impressive. [LITERARY] [ADJ n] ❑ *...towering cliffs of black granite which rise straight out of the sea.*
2 ADJ If you describe someone or something as **towering**, you are emphasizing that they are impressive because of their importance, skill, or intensity. [LITERARY, EMPHASIS] [ADJ n] ❑ *He remains a towering figure in modern British politics.*

town ♦♦♦ /taʊn/ (**towns**) **1** N-COUNT A **town** is a place with many streets and buildings, where people live and work. Towns are larger than villages and smaller than cities. In informal American English and in British English, cities are sometimes called towns. ❑ *...the northern California town of Albany.*
● N-COUNT You can use **the town** to refer to the people of a town. ❑ *The town takes immense pride in recent achievements.* **2** N-UNCOUNT You use **town** in order to refer to the town where you live. ❑ *He admits he doesn't even know when his brother is in town.* **3** N-UNCOUNT You use **town** in order to refer to the central area of a town where most of the stores and offices are. ❑ *I walked around town.*

town hall (**town halls**) also **Town Hall** N-COUNT A **town hall** is a building or hall used for local government business, usually a building which is the main office of a town council.

tox|ic /ˈtɒksɪk/ ADJ A **toxic** substance is poisonous. ❑ *...the cost of cleaning up toxic waste.* →see **cancer**

toy ♦♦◇ /tɔɪ/ (**toys, toying, toyed**) N-COUNT A **toy** is an object that children play with, for example a doll or a model car. ❑ *He was really too old for children's toys.*
▶**toy with 1** PHRASAL VERB If you **toy with** an idea, you consider it casually without making any decisions about it. ❑ *He toyed with the idea of going to China.* **2** PHRASAL VERB If you **toy with** food or drink, you do not eat or drink it with any enthusiasm, but only take a bite or a little drink from time to time. ❑ *She had no appetite, and merely toyed with the bread and cheese.*

trace ♦♦◇ /treɪs/ (**traces, tracing, traced**) **1** V-T If you **trace** the origin or development of something, you find out or describe how it started or developed. ❑ *The exhibition traces the history of graphic design in America from the 19th century to the present.* ● PHRASAL VERB **Trace back** means the same as **trace**. ❑ *...Bronx residents who trace their families back to Dutch settlers.* **2** V-T If you **trace** someone or something, you find them after looking for them. ❑ *Police are anxious to trace two men seen leaving the house just before 8am.* **3** V-T If you **trace** something such as a pattern or a shape, for example with your finger or toe, you mark its outline on a surface. ❑ *I traced the course of the river on the map spread out on my briefcase.* **4** V-T If you **trace** a picture, you copy it by covering it with a piece of transparent paper and drawing over the lines underneath. ❑ *She learned to draw by tracing pictures out of old storybooks.* **5** N-COUNT A **trace of** something is a very small amount of it. ❑ *Wash them in cold water to remove all traces of sand.* **6** PHRASE If you say that someone or something **sinks without trace** or **sinks without a trace**, you mean that they stop existing or stop being successful very suddenly and completely. ❑ *The Social Democratic Party has sunk without trace at these elections.* →see **fossil**

Word Partnership | *trace*의 연어
N. | trace *your* ancestry/origins/roots, trace **the** history **of** *something*, trace **the** origins/roots **of** *something* **1**
 | trace **of an** accent, trace amount, trace minerals **5**

---

track ♦♦◇ /træk/ (**tracks, tracking, tracked**) **1** N-COUNT A **track** is a narrow road or path. ❑ *We set off once more, over a rough mountain track.* **2** N-COUNT A **track** is a piece of ground, often oval-shaped, that is used for races involving running, cars, bicycles, horses, or dogs called greyhounds. ❑ *The two men turned to watch the horses going round the track.* **3** N-COUNT Railroad **tracks** are the rails that a train travels along. ❑ *A woman fell on to the tracks.* **4** N-COUNT A **track** is one of the songs or pieces of music on a CD, record, or tape. ❑ *Graeme Naysmith has produced two of the ten tracks on this album.* **5** N-PLURAL **Tracks** are marks left in the ground by the feet of animals or people. ❑ *The only evidence of pandas was their tracks in the snow.* **6** V-T If you **track** animals or people, you try to follow them by looking for the signs that they have left behind, for example the marks left by their feet. ❑ *He thought he had better track this wolf and kill it.* **7** V-T To **track** someone or something means to follow their movements by means of a special device, such as a satellite or radar. ❑ *Our radar began tracking the jets.* **8** →see also **fast track, racetrack, soundtrack 9** PHRASE If you **keep track of** a situation or a person, you make sure that you have the newest and most accurate information about them all the time. ❑ *With eleven thousand employees, it's very difficult to keep track of them all.* **10** PHRASE If you **lose track of** someone or something, you no longer know where they are or what is happening. ❑ *You become so deeply absorbed in an activity that you lose track of time.* **11** PHRASE If someone or something is **on track**, they are acting or progressing in a way that is likely to result in success. ❑ *It may take some time to get the British economy back on track.* **12** PHRASE If you are **on the right track**, you are acting or progressing in a way that is likely to result in success. If you are **on the wrong track**, you are acting or progressing in a way that is likely to result in failure. ❑ *Guests are returning in increasing numbers – a sign that we are on the right track.* **13** PHRASE If someone or something **stops** you **in** your **tracks**, or if you **stop dead in** your **tracks**, you suddenly stop moving because you are very surprised, impressed, or frightened. ❑ *This magnificent church cannot fail to stop you in your*

4 가산명사 타워 (컴퓨터 본체 케이스의 일종) [컴퓨터]

1 형용사 우뚝 솟은, 높이 치솟은 [문예체] ❑ 바다에서 바로 불쑥 솟아 나온 듯 우뚝 치솟은 검은색 화강암 절벽 **2** 형용사 대단히; 걸출한 [문예체, 강조] ❑ 그는 여전히 영국 현대 정치의 거물로 남아 있다.

1 가산명사 소도시, 읍 ❑ 캘리포니아 북부에 위치한 작은 도시 올버니 ● 가산명사 읍민, 소도시 주민 ❑ 최근 성과에 대한 주민들의 자부심이 대단하다. **2** 불가산명사 마을, 고장 ❑ 그는 형이 언제 마을에 있는지조차 모른다고 털어놓는다. **3** 불가산명사 시내 ❑ 나는 시내를 돌아다녔다.

가산명사 읍사무소, 시청

형용사 유독성의 ❑ 유독성 폐기물 처리 비용

가산명사 장난감 ❑ 그는 어린이용 장난감을 가지고 놀기에는 정말 나이가 너무 많았다.
1 구동사 ~할까 한 번 생각해 보다 ❑ 그는 중국에 갈까 한 번 생각해 봤다. **2** 구동사 깨지락거리다 ❑ 그녀는 입맛이 전혀 없었다. 그래서 빵이랑 치즈를 깨지락거리기만 했다.

1 타동사 자취를 더듬다 ❑ 그 전시회는 19세기부터 현재에 이르기까지 미국 그래픽 디자인의 역사를 더듬는다. ● 구동사 자취를 더듬다 ❑ 자신들의 가족사를 더듬다 보면 네덜란드 정착민까지 거슬러 올라가는 브롱크스 주민들 **2** 타동사 추적하다 ❑ 경찰이 오전 8시 직전에 그 집을 떠나는 것이 목격된 두 남자의 추적에 열을 올리고 있다. **3** 타동사 윤곽을 따라가다 ❑ 나는 서류 가방 위에 지도를 펼쳐 놓고 지도에 표시된 강줄기를 손가락으로 따라가 봤다. **4** 타동사 원본을 대고 따라 그리다 ❑ 그녀는 오래된 이야기책 그림에 종이를 대고 따라 그리면서 그림 그리기를 배웠다. **5** 가산명사 흔적, 자취, 소량 ❑ 그것들을 차가운 물에 씻어서 모래 흔적을 모두 없애라. **6** 구 흔적도 없이 사라지다, 갑자기 자취를 감추다 ❑ 사회 민주당이 이번 선거에서 갑자기 자취를 감추었다.

1 가산명사 좁은 길, 한적한 통로 ❑ 우리는 험한 산길을 따라 한 번 더 출발했다. **2** 가산명사 경주로, 트랙 ❑ 두 남자가 말이 트랙을 도는 모습을 보려고 몸을 돌렸다. **3** 가산명사 선로 ❑ 한 여성이 선로 위로 떨어졌다. **4** 가산명사 (음반의 음악이나 노래) 한 곡 ❑ 그래미 네이스미스가 이 앨범의 10곡 중 2곡을 만들었다. **5** 복수명사 발자국, 발자국 ❑ 판다의 존재를 증명하는 유일한 증거는 눈 위에 찍힌 판다 발자국뿐이다. **6** 타동사 추적하다, 뒤를 밟다 ❑ 그는 늑대를 추적해서 죽이는 편이 나을 거라고 생각했다. **7** 타동사 추적하다, 탐지하다 ❑ 우리 레이더에 제트기가 잡히기 시작했다. **9** 구 ~에 대해 최신 정보를 파악하다 ❑ 직원이 만천 명이나 되니 그들에 대한 최신 정보를 일일이 파악하기란 매우 어렵다. **10** 구 ~을 놓치다 ❑ 사람이 한 가지 활동에 깊이 몰입하면 시간가는 줄도 모르게 된다. **11** 구 착착 진행 중인, 정상 궤도에 오른 ❑ 영국 경제가 다시 정상을 회복하는 데 시간이 좀 걸릴지도 모른다. **12** 구 올바른 방향으로; 잘못된 방향으로 ❑ 다시 오는 손님들이 점점 더 많아지고 있다. 우리가 제대로 하고 있다는 명백한 증거이다. **13** 구 가던 길을 딱 멈추게 하다; 가던 길을 딱 멈추다 ❑ 이 웅장한 교회를 보면 가던 길을 딱 멈출 수밖에 없을 것이다. **14** 구 중단하다, 중단되다 ❑ 프란시스는 이 대화를 중단하고 싶어졌다.

a b c d e f g h i j k l m n o p q r s t u v w x y z

tracks. ⏰ PHRASE If someone or something **stops** a process or activity **in its tracks**, or if it **stops dead in its tracks**, they prevent the process or activity from continuing. ❑ *Francis felt he would like to stop this conversation in its tracks.* ⏰ **off the beaten track** →see **beaten**
→see **fossil, transportation**

▶**track down** PHRASAL VERB If you **track down** someone or something, you find them, or find information about them, after a difficult or long search. ❑ *She had spent years trying to track down her parents.*

구동사 찾아내다 ❑ 그녀가 부모님을 찾아내는 데 수년이 걸렸다.

track and field N-UNCOUNT **Track and field** refers to sports that are played or performed on a racetrack and a nearby field, such as running, the high jump, and the javelin. ❑ *...events that range from track and field to soccer, rugby, and hockey.*

불가산명사 육상 경기 ❑ 육상에서부터 축구, 럭비, 하키에 이르는 경기들

track|er fund /trǽkərfʌnd/ (**tracker funds**) N-COUNT A **tracker fund** is an investment in which shares in different companies are bought and sold so that the value of the shares held always matches the average value of shares in all or part of a stock market. [mainly BRIT, BUSINESS]

가산명사 트래커 펀드 [주로 영국영어, 경제]

track rec|ord (**track records**) N-COUNT If you talk about the **track record** of a person, company, or product, you are referring to their past performance, achievements, or failures in it. ❑ *The job needs someone with a good track record in investment.*

가산명사 실적, 업적 ❑ 그 일은 투자 실적이 좋은 사람이 맡아야 한다.

track|suit /trǽksut/ (**tracksuits**) also **track suit** N-COUNT A **tracksuit** is a loose, warm suit consisting of pants and a top which people wear to relax and to do exercise. [mainly BRIT; AM usually **sweatsuit**]

가산명사 운동복 [주로 영국영어; 미국영어 대개 sweatsuit]

trac|tor /trǽktər/ (**tractors**) N-COUNT A **tractor** is a farm vehicle that is used to pull farm machinery and to provide the energy needed for the machinery to work.

가산명사 트랙터, 견인차

tractor-trailer (**tractor-trailers**) N-COUNT A **tractor-trailer** is a truck that is made in two or more sections which are joined together by metal bars, so that the vehicle can turn more easily. [AM; BRIT **articulated lorry**] ❑ *Driving a tractor-trailer is not an easy job.*

가산명사 트랙터트레일러 [미국영어; 영국영어 articulated lorry] ❑ 트랙터트레일러 운전은 쉽지가 않다.

trade ♦♦♦ /treɪd/ (**trades, trading, traded**) ⏰ N-UNCOUNT **Trade** is the activity of buying, selling, or exchanging goods or services between people, firms, or countries. [BUSINESS] ❑ *MOFTEC offers assistance in various areas of foreign trade* ❑ *...negotiations on a new international trade agreement.* ⏰ V-I When people, firms, or countries **trade**, they buy, sell, or exchange goods or services between themselves. [BUSINESS] ❑ *They may refuse to trade, even when offered attractive prices.* ❑ *They had years of experience of trading with the West.* ● **trad|ing** N-UNCOUNT ❑ *Trading on the stock exchange may be suspended.* ⏰ N-COUNT A **trade** is a particular area of business or industry. [BUSINESS] ❑ *They've completely ruined the tourist trade for the next few years.* ⏰ N-COUNT Someone's **trade** is the kind of work that they do, especially when they have been trained to do it over a period of time. [BUSINESS] [oft poss N, also by N] ❑ *He learnt his trade as a diver in the North Sea.* ❑ *Allyn was a jeweler by trade.* ⏰ V-RECIP If someone **trades** one thing **for** another or if two people **trade** things, they agree to exchange one thing for the other thing. [mainly AM] ❑ *They traded land for goods and money.* ❑ *Kids used to trade baseball cards.* ● N-COUNT **Trade** is also a noun. [BRIT usually **exchange**] ❑ *I am willing to make a trade with you.* ⏰ V-RECIP If you **trade** places **with** someone or if the two of you **trade** places, you move into the other person's position or situation, and they move into yours. [mainly AM] ❑ *Mike asked George to trade places with him so he could ride with Tod.* ⏰ V-RECIP If two people or groups **trade** something such as blows, insults, or jokes, they hit each other, insult each other, or tell each other jokes. [mainly AM] ❑ *Children would settle disputes by trading punches or insults in the schoolyard.* →see **company, stock market**

⏰ 불가산명사 거래, 교역, 무역 [경제] ❑ 모프테크는 해외 무역과 관련된 제반 사항에 대한 도움을 제공하고 있다. ❑ 새로운 국제 무역 협정에 관한 협상 ⏰ 자동사 거래하다, 교역하다, 무역하다 [경제] ❑ 매력적인 가격을 제시한다 하더라도 그들이 거래를 거절할지 모른다. ❑ 그들은 수년 동안 서방 세계와 교역해 왔었다. ● 거래, 교역, 무역 불가산명사 ❑ 주식시장 거래가 잠정 중단될지도 모른다. ⏰ 가산명사 -업, -업계 [경제] ❑ 그들이 향후 몇 년간의 관광업을 완전히 망쳐 놓았다. ⏰ 가산명사 직업, 일 [경제] ❑ 그는 북해에서 잠수부 일을 배웠다. ❑ 알린의 생업은 보석상이었다. ⏰ 상호동사 교환하다, 거래하다 [주로 미국영어] ❑ 그들은 땅을 주고 물건과 돈을 받았다. ❑ 아이들이 서로 야구 카드를 교환하곤 했다. ● 교환, 거래 가산명사 [영국영어 대개 exchange] ❑ 나는 당신과 거래할 의향이 있다. ⏰ 상호동사 (자리 등을) 바꾸다 [주로 미국영어] ❑ 마이크는 토드와 함께 탈 수 있도록 조지한테 자리를 바꾸자고 했다. ⏰ 상호동사 (욕설 등을) 주고받다 [주로 미국영어] ❑ 아이들이라면 학교 운동장에서 주먹다짐이나 욕설을 주고받으며 싸움을 끝낼 것이다.

▶**trade down** PHRASAL VERB If someone **trades down**, they sell something such as their car or house and buy a less expensive one. ❑ *They are selling their five-bedroom house and trading down to a two-bedroom cottage.*

구동사 (원래 물건을 팔고) 더 싼 물건으로 바꾸다 ❑ 그들은 방 다섯 개짜리 집을 팔고 방 두 개짜리 오두막으로 옮길 계획이다.

▶**trade up** PHRASAL VERB If someone **trades up**, they sell something such as their car or their house and buy a more expensive one. ❑ *Mini-car owners are trading up to "real" cars.*

구동사 (원래 물건을 팔고) 더 비싼 물건으로 바꾸다 ❑ 소형차 주인들이 '차다운' 차로 바꾸고 있다.

trade fair (**trade fairs**) N-COUNT A **trade fair** is an exhibition where manufacturers show their products to other people in industry and try to get business. [BUSINESS] ❑ *...the world's largest IT trade fair.*

가산명사 무역 박람회, 산업 박람회 [경제] ❑ 세계 최대 규모의 아이티(IT) 산업 박람회

trade gap (**trade gaps**) N-COUNT If a country imports goods worth more than the value of the goods that it exports, this is referred to as a **trade gap**. [BUSINESS] [usu sing] ❑ *The trade gap surprised most analysts by shrinking, rather than growing.*

가산명사 무역적자 [경제] ❑ 무역 적자가 증가하지 않고 오히려 줄어들어서 분석가 대부분이 놀라움을 금치 못했다.

trade-in (**trade-ins**) N-COUNT A **trade-in** is an arrangement in which someone buys something such as a new car or washing machine at a reduced price by giving their old one, as well as money, in payment. [BUSINESS] ❑ *...the trade-in value of the car.*

가산명사 보상 판매 [경제] ❑ 자동차 보상 판매 가격

trade|mark /treɪdmɑrk/ (**trademarks**) also **trade mark** ⏰ N-COUNT A **trademark** is a name or symbol that a company uses on its products and that

⏰ 가산명사 상표 [경제] ❑ 크리스틴 드비에르 종쿠르가 새로 출시된 향수 제품 군의 상표를

cannot legally be used by another company. [BUSINESS] ❑ *Christine Deviers-Joncour has registered a trademark for a new range of perfumes.* ◻ N-COUNT If you say that something is the **trademark** of a particular person or place, you mean that it is characteristic of them or typically associated with them. ❑ *...the spiky punk hairdo that became his trademark.*

trade name (**trade names**) N-COUNT A **trade name** is the name which manufacturers give to a product or to a range of products. [BUSINESS] ❑ *It's marketed under the trade name "Tattle."*

trad|er ♦◇◇ /trɛɪdər/ (**traders**) N-COUNT A **trader** is a person whose job is to trade in goods or stocks. [BUSINESS] ❑ *Market traders display an exotic selection of the island's produce.*

trade se|cret (**trade secrets**) N-COUNT A **trade secret** is information that is known, used, and kept secret by a particular firm, for example about a method of production or a chemical process. [BUSINESS] ❑ *The nature of the polymer is currently a trade secret.*

trades|man /trɛɪdzmən/ (**tradesmen**) N-COUNT A **tradesman** is a person, usually a man, who sells goods or services, especially one who owns and runs a store. [BUSINESS] ❑ *...tradesmen such as electricians or plumbers.*

trade sur|plus (**trade surpluses**) N-COUNT If a country has a **trade surplus**, it exports more than it imports. [BUSINESS] ❑ *The country's trade surplus widened to 16.5 billion dollars.*

trade un|ion (**trade unions**) also **trades union** N-COUNT A **trade union** is an organization that has been formed by workers in order to represent their rights and interests to their employers, for example in order to improve working conditions or wages. [mainly BRIT; AM usually **labor union**]

trade un|ion|ist /trɛɪd yunyənɪst/ (**trade unionists**) also **trades unionist** N-COUNT A **trade unionist** is an active member of a trade union. [BRIT] ❑ *...a senior trade unionist in Australia.*

tra|di|tion ♦◇◇ /trədɪʃⁿn/ (**traditions**) N-VAR A **tradition** is a custom or belief that has existed for a long time. ❑ *...the rich traditions of Afro-Cuban music, and dance.*

Thesaurus   *tradition*의 참조어

N.   culture, custom, practice, ritual

tra|di|tion|al ♦♦◇ /trədɪʃⁿⁿl/ ◻ ADJ **Traditional** customs, beliefs, or methods are ones that have existed for a long time without changing. ❑ *Traditional teaching methods sometimes only succeeded in putting students off learning.* ● **tra|di|tion|al|ly** ADV [ADV with cl/group] ❑ *Married women have traditionally been treated as dependent on their husbands.* ◻ ADJ A **traditional** organization or person prefers older methods and ideas to modern ones. ❑ *We're still a traditional school in a lot of ways.* ● **tra|di|tion|al|ly** ADV ❑ *He is loathed by some of the more traditionally minded officers.*

traf|fic ♦◇◇ /træfɪk/ (**traffics, trafficking, trafficked**) ◻ N-UNCOUNT **Traffic** refers to all the vehicles that are moving along the roads in a particular area. [also the N] ❑ *There was heavy traffic on the roads.* ❑ *Traffic was unusually light for that time of day.* ◻ N-UNCOUNT **Traffic** refers to the movement of ships, trains, or aircraft between one place and another. **Traffic** also refers to the people and goods that are being transported. ❑ *Air traffic had returned to normal.* ◻ N-UNCOUNT **Traffic in** something such as drugs or stolen goods is an illegal trade in them. ❑ *...the widespread traffic in stolen cultural artifacts.* ◻ V-I Someone who **traffics in** something such as drugs or stolen goods buys and sells them even though it is illegal to do so. ❑ *The president said illegal drugs are hurting the entire world and anyone who traffics in them should be brought to justice.* ● **traf|fick|ing** N-UNCOUNT ❑ *He was sentenced to ten years in prison on charges of drug trafficking.*
→see Word Web: **traffic**

Word Partnership   *traffic*의 연어

ADJ.   **heavy** traffic, **light** traffic, **stuck in** traffic ◻
N.   traffic **accident**, **city** traffic, traffic **congestion**, traffic **flow**, traffic **pollution**, traffic **problems**, **rush hour** traffic, traffic **safety**, traffic **signals**, traffic **violation** ◻
          air traffic ◻
          drug traffic ◻

Word Web   traffic

Boston's Southeast Expressway was built to handle 75,000 **vehicles** a day. But from the day it opened in 1959, **commuter traffic** crawled. Sometimes it **stalled** completely. The 27 entrance **ramps** and lack of **breakdown lanes** caused frequent **gridlock**. By the 1990s, **traffic congestion** was even worse. Nearly 200,000 cars a day were using the **highway** and there were constant **traffic jams**. In 1994, a ten-year **road** construction project called the Big Dig began. The project built underground roadways, six-**lane** bridges, and improved **tunnels**. As a result of the project traffic **flows** more smoothly through the city.

등록했다. ◻ 가산명사 트레이드마크 ❑ 그의 트레이드마크가 되어 버린 삐쭉삐쭉한 펑크 머리

가산명사 상품명, 상표명 [경제] ❑ 이는 "태틀"이라는 상품명으로 판매되고 있다.

가산명사 상인, 거래자 [경제] ❑ 시장 상인들이 섬 특산물 가운데 이국적인 것을 골라 내놓았다.

가산명사 영업 비밀, 기업 비밀 [경제] ❑ 중합체의 성질은 현재 기업 비밀이다.

가산명사 자영업자 [경제] ❑ 전기공이나 배관공 같은 자영업자들

가산명사 무역 흑자 [경제] ❑ 국내 무역 흑자가 165억 달러로 늘어났다.

가산명사 노조 [주로 영국영어; 미국영어 대개 labor union]

가산명사 노조원 [영국영어] ❑ 호주 노조 간부

가산명사 또는 불가산명사 전통 ❑ 아프리카계 쿠바 음악의 풍부한 전통과 춤

◻ 형용사 전통적인, 기존의 ❑ 기존 교수법은 때때로 학생들이 학습에 흥미를 잃게 하는 결과만 낳기도 했다. ● 전통적으로 부사 ❑ 기혼 여성들은 전통적으로 남편에게 종속된 사람으로 취급받았다. ◻ 형용사 보수적인 ❑ 우리는 많은 면에서 아직까지 보수적인 학교이다. ● 보수적으로 부사 ❑ 보수적인 성향이 더 강한 당국자들 중에 그를 몹시 싫어하는 사람들이 있다.

◻ 불가산명사 차량 ❑ 도로에 차량이 많았다. ❑ 시간대에 비해 도로가 유별나게 한산했다. ◻ 불가산명사 운행, 교통; 수송객, 수송 물자 ❑ 항공 운행이 정상을 되찾은 상태였다. ◻ 불가산명사 불법거래, 밀매 ❑ 만연하고 있는 도난 문화재 불법 거래 ◻ 자동사 밀매하다 ❑ 대통령은 불법 마약이 전 세계에 해가 되고 있으며 이를 밀매하는 사람은 모두 법의 심판을 받아야 한다고 밝혔다. ● 밀매 불가산명사 ❑ 그는 마약밀매 혐의로 징역 10년을 선고받았다.

a
b
c
d
e
f
g
h
i
j
k
l
m
n
o
p
q
r
s
t
u
v
w
x
y
z

traf|fic cir|cle (traffic circles) N-COUNT A **traffic circle** is a circular structure in the road at a place where several roads meet. You drive around it until you come to the road that you want. [AM; BRIT **roundabout**]

가산명사 로터리 [미국영어; 영국영어 roundabout]

traf|fick|er /trǽfɪkər/ (traffickers) N-COUNT A **trafficker** in particular goods, especially drugs, is a person who illegally buys or sells these goods. ❑ *They have been arrested as suspected drug traffickers.*

가산명사 밀매자 ❑ 그들은 마약 밀매 용의자로 체포되었다.

traf|fic light (traffic lights) N-COUNT **Traffic lights** are sets of red, amber, and green lights at the places where roads meet. They control the traffic by signaling when vehicles have to stop and when they can go. ❑ *The car hit a traffic light before it stopped.*

가산명사 신호등 ❑ 차가 신호등을 들이받고 멈췄다.

trag|edy ♦♢♢ /trǽdʒɪdi/ (tragedies) **1** N-VAR A **tragedy** is an extremely sad event or situation. ❑ *They have suffered an enormous personal tragedy.* **2** N-VAR **Tragedy** is a type of literature, especially drama, that is serious and sad, and often ends with the death of the main character. ❑ *The story has elements of tragedy and farce.* →see **theater**

1 가산명사 또는 불가산명사 비극, 참사 ❑ 그들은 개인적으로 엄청난 비극을 겪었다. **2** 가산명사 또는 불가산명사 비극 ❑ 그 이야기는 비극과 소극의 요소를 고루 갖추고 있다.

trag|ic /trǽdʒɪk/ **1** ADJ A **tragic** event or situation is extremely sad, usually because it involves death or suffering. ❑ *It was just a tragic accident.* ❑ *...the tragic loss of so many lives.* ● **tragi|cal|ly** /trǽdʒɪkli/ ADV ❑ *Tragically, she never saw the completed building because she died before it was finished.* **2** ADJ **Tragic** is used to refer to tragedy as a type of literature. [ADJ n] ❑ *...Michael Henchard, the tragic hero of "The Mayor of Casterbridge."*

1 형용사 비극적인, 안타까운 ❑ 그것은 참으로 안타까운 사건이었다. ❑ 수많은 사람들이 목숨을 잃은 비극 ● 비극적으로 부사 ❑ 안타깝게도 그녀는 건물이 완공되기 전에 세상을 떠나 완성된 건물을 보지 못했다. **2** 형용사 비극의, 비극적인 ❑ '캐스터브리지의 시장'의 비극적인 주인공 마이클 헨차드

trail ♦♢♢ /treɪl/ (trails, trailing, trailed) **1** N-COUNT A **trail** is a rough path across open country or through forests. ❑ *He was following a broad trail through the trees.* **2** N-COUNT A **trail** is a route along a series of paths or roads, often one that has been planned and marked out for a particular purpose. ❑ *...a large area of woodland with hiking and walking trails.* **3** N-COUNT A **trail** is a series of marks or other signs of movement or other activities left by someone or something. ❑ *Everywhere in the house was a sticky trail of orange juice.* **4** V-T If you **trail** someone or something, you follow them secretly, often by finding the marks or signs that they have left. ❑ *Two detectives were trailing him.* **5** N-COUNT You can refer to all the places that a politician visits in the period before an election as their campaign **trail**. ❑ *During a recent speech on the campaign trail, he was interrupted by hecklers.* **6** V-T/V-I If you **trail** something or it **trails**, it hangs down loosely behind you as you move along. ❑ *She came down the stairs slowly, trailing the coat behind her.* **7** PHRASE If you are **on the trail of** a person or thing, you are trying hard to find them or find out about them. ❑ *The police were hot on his trail.*

1 가산명사 산길, 시골길 ❑ 그는 숲 속의 넓은 길을 따라가고 있었다. **2** 가산명사 특정 용도에 맞춰 계획되거나 표시된 길 ❑ 하이킹 도로와 산책로가 있는 넓은 삼림 지대 **3** 가산명사 자국, 흔적 ❑ 집안 곳곳에 끈득끈득한 오렌지 주스 자국이 남아 있었다. **4** 타동사 추적하다 ❑ 형사 두 명이 그를 추적하고 있었다. **5** 가산명사 유세지 ❑ 그는 최근 유세지 연설 도중 야유 공세를 받았다. **6** 타동사/자동사 질질 끌다; 질질 끌리다 ❑ 그녀가 코트를 질질 끌면서 계단을 천천히 내려왔다. **7** 구 추적 중인 ❑ 경찰이 그를 맹렬히 추적하고 있었다.

Word Partnership	trail의 연어
V.	**follow a trail** **1**-**3**
	leave a trail, pick up a trail **3**
N.	**campaign trail** **5**

trail|er /treɪlər/ (trailers) **1** N-COUNT A **trailer** is a container on wheels which is pulled by a car or other vehicle and which is used for transporting large or heavy items. **2** N-COUNT A **trailer** is the long rear section of a lorry or truck, in which the goods are carried. **3** N-COUNT A **trailer** is a long vehicle without an engine which people use as a home or as an office and which can be pulled behind a car. [mainly AM; BRIT **caravan**] **4** N-COUNT A **trailer** for a film or television programme is a set of short extracts which are shown to advertise it. ❑ *...a misleadingly violent trailer for the film.*

1 가산명사 트레일러 **2** 가산명사 트럭 화물칸 **3** 가산명사 이동식 주택 [주로 미국영어; 영국영어 caravan] **4** 가산명사 예고편 ❑ 오해를 살 정도로 폭력적인 영화 예고편

trail|er park (trailer parks) also **trailer court** N-COUNT A **trailer park** is an area where people can pay to park their trailers and live in them. [AM; BRIT **caravan site**]

가산명사 야영용 자동차 야영지 [미국영어; 영국영어 caravan site]

train

① NOUN USES
② VERB USES

① **train** ♦♦♢ /treɪn/ (trains) **1** N-COUNT A **train** is a number of cars which are all connected together and which are pulled by an engine along a railroad. Trains carry people and goods from one place to another. [also by N] ❑ *The train pulled into a station.* ❑ *We can catch the early morning train.* **2** N-COUNT A **train of** vehicles, people, or animals is a long line of them traveling slowly in the same direction. ❑ *In the old days this used to be done with a baggage train of camels.* **3** N-COUNT A **train** of thought or a **train** of events is a connected sequence, in which each thought or event seems to occur naturally or logically as a result of the previous one. ❑ *He lost his train of thought for a moment, then recovered it.* →see **transportation** →see Word Web: **train**

1 가산명사 열차, 기차 ❑ 열차가 역에 정차했다. ❑ 우리는 새벽 기차를 탈 수 있다. **2** 가산명사 행렬 ❑ 예전에는 짐을 실은 낙타 행렬을 가지고 이 일을 했다. **3** 가산명사 이어짐, 일련 ❑ 그는 잠시 생각의 꼬리를 놓쳤다가 다시 생각에 잠겼다.

Thesaurus	train의 참조어
N.	caravan, procession, series ① **2**
V.	coach, educate, guide, prepare ② **1**

② **train** ♦♦♢ /treɪn/ (trains, training, trained) **1** V-T/V-I If someone **trains** you to do something, they teach you the skills that you need in order to do it. If you **train to** do something, you learn the skills that you need in order to do it. ❑ *The U.S. was ready to train its troops to participate.* ● **-trained** COMB in ADJ ❑ *Mr. Koutab is an American-trained lawyer.* ● **train|er** (trainers) N-COUNT ❑ *...a book for both teachers and teacher trainers.* **2** V-T To **train** a natural quality or talent that someone has, for example their voice or musical ability, means to help them to develop it. ❑ *I see my degree as something which will train my mind and improve my*

1 타동사/자동사 훈련시키다, 교육하다; 훈련하다, 배우다 ❑ 미국은 참전군을 훈련시킬 준비가 되어 있었다. ● 훈련받은, 교육받은 복합형·형용사 ❑ 쿠탑 씨는 미국에서 수학한 변호사이다. ● 지도자, 트레이너 가산명사 ❑ 교사와 교사 연수자 모두를 위한 책 **2** 타동사 연마하다 ❑ 나는 학위란 마음을 연마하고 직장을 구할 확률을 높여 줄 무엇이라고 생각한다. **3** 타동사/자동사 훈련하다; 훈련시키다 ❑ 스트라찬이

In sixteenth-century Germany, a **railway** was a horse-drawn **wagon** traveling along wooden **rails**. By the 19th century, steam locomotives and **steel rails** had replaced the older system. At first, railroads operated only **freight lines**. Later, they began to run **passenger** trains. And soon Pullman cars were added to make overnight trips more comfortable. Today, Japan's bullet trains carry people at speeds up to 300 miles per hour. This type of train doesn't have an engine or use tracks. Instead, an electromagnetic field allows the **cars** to float just above the ground. This electromagnetic field also propels them ahead.

A Japanese Bullet Train

chances of getting a job. **3** V-T/V-I If you **train for** a physical activity such as a race or if someone **trains** you **for** it, you prepare for it by doing particular physical exercises. ❑ *Strachan is training for the new season.* ● **trainer** N-COUNT ❑ *She went to the gym with her trainer.* **4** V-T If an animal or bird **is trained to** do particular things, it is taught to do them, for example in order to be able to work for someone or to be a good pet. ❑ *Sniffer dogs could be trained to track them down.* ● **trainer** N-COUNT ❑ *The horse made a winning start for his new trainer.* **5** →see also **training**

▶**train up** PHRASAL VERB If someone **trains** you **up**, they teach you new skills or give you the necessary preparation so that you will reach the standard required for a particular job or activity. [BRIT, INFORMAL, BUSINESS] ❑ *The first companies to go in took a policy of employing East Germans and training them up.*

trainee /treɪniː/ (**trainees**) N-COUNT A **trainee** is someone who is employed at a low level in a particular job in order to learn the skills needed for that job. [BUSINESS] [oft N n] ❑ *He is a 24-year-old trainee reporter.*

trainer /treɪnər/ (**trainers**) N-COUNT **Trainers** are shoes that people wear, especially for running and other sports. [BRIT; AM **sneakers**] ❑ *...a new pair of trainers.* →see also **train**

training /treɪnɪŋ/ **1** N-UNCOUNT **Training** is the process of learning the skills that you need for a particular job or activity. [BUSINESS] ❑ *He called for much higher spending on education and training.* ❑ *Kennedy had no formal training as a decorator.* **2** N-UNCOUNT **Training** is physical exercise that you do regularly in order to keep fit or to prepare for an activity such as a race. ❑ *The emphasis is on developing fitness through exercises and training.*

trait /treɪt/ (**traits**) N-COUNT A **trait** is a particular characteristic, quality, or tendency that someone or something has. ❑ *The study found that some alcoholics had clear personality traits showing up early in childhood.* →see **culture**

traitor /treɪtər/ (**traitors**) **1** N-COUNT If you call someone a **traitor**, you mean that they have betrayed beliefs that they used to hold, or that their friends hold, by their words or actions. [DISAPPROVAL] ❑ *Some say he's a traitor to the working class.* **2** N-COUNT If someone is a **traitor**, they betray their country or a group of which they are a member by helping its enemies, especially during time of war. ❑ *...rumors that there were traitors among us who were sending messages to the enemy.*

tram /træm/ (**trams**) **1** N-COUNT A **tram** is the same as a **cable car**. [AM] **2** N-COUNT A **tram** is a public transport vehicle, usually powered by electricity from wires above it, which travels along rails laid in the surface of a street. [mainly BRIT; AM usually **streetcar**] [also by n] ❑ *You can get to the beach easily from the center of town by tram.* →see **transportation**

tramp /træmp/ (**tramps, tramping, tramped**) **1** N-COUNT A **tramp** is a person who has no home or job, and very little money. Tramps go from place to place, and get food or money by asking people or by doing casual work. ❑ *Undiagnosed hypothermia is common among tramps sleeping rough.* **2** V-T/V-I If you **tramp** somewhere, you walk there slowly and with regular, heavy steps, for a long time. ❑ *They put on their coats and tramped through the falling snow.* **3** N-UNCOUNT The **tramp** of people is the sound of their heavy, regular walking. ❑ *He heard the slow, heavy tramp of feet on the stairs.* **4** N-COUNT If someone refers to a woman as a **tramp**, they are insulting her, because they think that she is immoral in her sexual behavior. [mainly AM, OFFENSIVE, DISAPPROVAL] ❑ *He'd think I was a tramp, a cheap slut, and he'd lose all respect for me.*

trample /træmpᵊl/ (**tramples, trampling, trampled**) **1** V-T/V-I To **trample on** someone's rights or values or to **trample** them means to deliberately ignore them. ❑ *They say loggers are destroying rain forests and trampling on the rights of natives.* **2** V-T If someone **is trampled**, they are injured or killed by being stepped on by animals or by other people. [usu passive] ❑ *Many people were trampled in the panic that followed.* **3** V-T/V-I If someone **tramples** something or **tramples on** it, they step heavily and carelessly on it and damage it. ❑ *They don't want people trampling the grass, pitching tents or building fires.*

trance /trɑːns/ (**trances**) N-COUNT A **trance** is a state of mind in which someone seems to be asleep and to have no conscious control over their thoughts or actions, but in which they can see and hear things and respond to commands given by other people. ❑ *Like a man in a trance, Blake found his way back to his rooms.* →see **hypnosis**

tranche /trɑːnʃ/ (**tranches**) **1** N-COUNT In economics, a **tranche** of shares in a company, or a **tranche** of a company, is a number of shares in that company. [mainly BRIT, BUSINESS] [usu N of n] ❑ *On February 12th he put up for sale a second tranche of 32 state-owned companies.* **2** N-COUNT A **tranche** of something is a piece, section, or part of it. A **tranche** of things is a group of them. [FORMAL] [usu N of n] ❑ *They risk losing the next tranche of funding.*

새 시즌을 대비해 훈련하고 있다. ● 코치, 트레이너 ⑤ 가산명사 ❑ 그녀가 트레이너와 함께 체육관에 갔다. **4** 타동사 훈련받다 ❑ 탐지견을 훈련시켜서 그들을 추적하게 할 수도 있을 것이다. ● 훈련사, 조련사 ⑤ 가산명사 ❑ 그 말은 새 조련사에게 처음부터 승리를 안겨 주었다.

구동사 연수하다, 교육하다 [영국영어, 비격식체, 경제] ❑ 처음 참가한 기업들은 동독인들을 고용하고 교육시키는 정책을 취했다.

가산명사 훈련받는 사람, 수습 직원 [경제] ❑ 그는 스물네 살의 수습기자이다.

가산명사 운동화 [영국영어; 미국영어 sneakers] ❑ 새 운동화 한 켤레

1 불가산명사 교육, 연수 [경제] ❑ 그는 교육 및 연수 부문 지출을 훨씬 늘려야 한다고 요구했다. ❑ 케네디는 실내 장식가로 정식 교육을 받지 못했다. **2** 불가산명사 훈련 ❑ 여기서 중요한 것은 운동과 훈련을 통한 건강한 신체 단련이다.

가산명사 특성, 특징 ❑ 연구 결과 일부 알코올 중독자들은 어린 시절에 뚜렷한 성격상의 특성을 보인 것으로 나타났다.

1 가산명사 배신자 [탐탁잖음] ❑ 몇몇 사람들은 그가 노동자 계층에 대한 배신자라고 한다. **2** 가산명사 반역자, 매국노 ❑ 우리 중에 적에게 메시지를 보낸 반역자가 있다는 소문

1 가산명사 케이블카 [미국영어] **2** 가산명사 시내 전차 [주로 영국영어; 미국영어 대개 streetcar] ❑ 시내에서 해변까지 시내 전차를 타고 쉽게 갈 수 있다.

1 가산명사 떠돌이, 부랑자 ❑ 원인 불명의 저체온증이 한데서 자는 부랑자 사이에 흔하게 나타난다. **2** 타동사/자동사 터벅터벅 걷다, 쿵쿵거리며 걷다 ❑ 그들은 코트를 입고 내리는 눈 사이로 터벅터벅 걸어갔다. **3** 불가산명사 터벅터벅 걷는 소리, 쿵쿵거리는 소리 ❑ 그는 느리고 육중하게 계단 위를 걸어가는 발소리를 들었다. **4** 가산명사 잡년 [주로 미국영어, 모욕어, 탐탁잖음] ❑ 그는 내가 추잡하고 싸구려 창녀 같다고 생각해서 나를 무시할지도 몰라.

1 타동사/자동사 (남의 권리 등을) 짓밟다 ❑ 그들은 벌목꾼이 열대 우림을 파괴하고 토착민의 권리를 짓밟고 있다고 말한다. **2** 타동사 짓밟히다 ❑ 뒤따른 공황 상태에서 많은 사람들이 짓밟혔다. **3** 타동사/자동사 짓밟다, 밟아 뭉개다 ❑ 그들은 사람들이 잔디를 짓밟거나 텐트를 치고 모닥불을 피우는 것을 원치 않는다.

가산명사 최면 ❑ 블레이크는 최면에 걸린 사람처럼 자기 방까지 길을 찾아 되돌아왔다.

1 가산명사 지분 [주로 영국영어, 경제] ❑ 그는 2월 12일 국유 기업 32개의 2차 지분을 시장에 내놓았다. **2** 가산명사 부분 [격식체] ❑ 그들은 다음 번 자금 지원을 받지 못할 위험을 무릅쓰고 있다.

a b c d e f g h i j k l m n o p q r s t u v w x y z

tran|quil /trǽŋkwɪl/ ADJ Something that is **tranquil** is calm and peaceful. ❑ *The tranquil atmosphere of The Connaught allows guests to feel totally at home.* ● **tran|quil|lity** /træŋkwɪlɪti/ N-UNCOUNT ❑ *The hotel is a haven of peace and tranquillity.*

형용사 고요한, 평온한 ❑ 코노트의 평온한 분위기는 방문객들에게 집처럼 편안한 느낌을 준다. ● 고요, 평온 불가산명사 ❑ 그 호텔은 평화롭고 고요한 안식처이다.

tran|quil|ize /trǽŋkwɪlaɪz/ (**tranquilizes, tranquilizing, tranquilized**)

> In BRIT and sometimes in AM use **tranquillize**. The spelling **tranquillise** is also used in British English

영국영어와 가끔 미국영어에서 tranquillize을 쓴다. 철자 tranquillise도 영국영어에서 쓴다.

V-T To **tranquilize** a person or an animal means to make them become calm, sleepy, or unconscious by means of a drug. ❑ *This powerful drug is used to tranquilize patients undergoing surgery.*

타동사 안정시키다, 진정시키다 ❑ 이 강력한 약은 수술 환자 진정제로 사용된다.

tran|quil|iz|er /trǽŋkwɪlaɪzər/ (**tranquilizers**)

> In BRIT and sometimes in AM, use **tranquillizer**. The spelling **tranquilliser** is also used in British English.

영국영어와 가끔 미국영어에서 tranquillizer을 쓴다. 철자 tranquilliser도 영국영어에서 쓴다.

N-COUNT A **tranquilizer** is a drug that makes people feel calmer or less anxious. Tranquilizers are sometimes used to make people or animals become sleepy or unconscious. ❑ *If a tranquilizer is prescribed, be sure your physician informs you of its possible side effects.*

가산명사 진정제, 신경 안정제 ❑ 진정제를 처방받으면 반드시 담당 의사로부터 부작용으로 나타날 수 있는 증상이 무엇인지 설명을 들어야 한다.

trans|ac|tion ♦♦◇ /trænzǽkʃən/ (**transactions**) N-COUNT A **transaction** is a piece of business, for example an act of buying or selling something. [FORMAL, BUSINESS] ❑ *The transaction is completed by payment of the fee.* →see **bank**

가산명사 거래, 매매 [격식체, 경제] ❑ 수수료 지급으로 거래가 완료되었다.

> ### Word Partnership   transaction의 연어
> N.   **cash** transaction, transaction **costs**, transaction **fee**
> V.   **complete a** transaction

trans|at|lan|tic /trænzətlǽntɪk/ ❶ ADJ **Transatlantic** flights or signals go across the Atlantic Ocean, usually between the United States and Britain. [ADJ n] ❑ *Many transatlantic flights land there.* ❷ ADJ **Transatlantic** is used to refer to something that happens, exists, or begins on the other side of the Atlantic Ocean. [BRIT] [ADJ n] ❑ *...transatlantic fashions.*

❶ 형용사 대서양을 횡단하는 ❑ 대서양을 횡단하는 비행기가 그곳에 많이 착륙한다. ❷ 형용사 대서양 건너편의 [영국영어] ❑ 대서양 건너편 패션

tran|scend /trænsénd/ (**transcends, transcending, transcended**) V-T Something that **transcends** normal limits or boundaries goes beyond them, because it is more significant than them. ❑ *...issues like European union that transcend party loyalty.*

타동사 초월하다 ❑ 유럽국가 간 연합과 같은 초당적 성격의 문제들

tran|scribe /trænskráɪb/ (**transcribes, transcribing, transcribed**) V-T If you **transcribe** a speech or text, you write it out in a different form from the one in which it exists, for example by writing it out in full from notes or from a tape recording. ❑ *She is transcribing, from his dictation, the diaries of Simon Forman.*

타동사 필사하다, (구술 등을) 받아쓰다 ❑ 그녀는 그가 읽어 주는 사이먼 포만의 일기를 받아쓰고 있다.

> ### Word Link   script ≈ writing : manuscript, scripture, transcript

tran|script /trǽnskrɪpt/ (**transcripts**) N-COUNT A **transcript of** a conversation or speech is a written text of it, based on a recording or notes. ❑ *They wouldn't let me have a transcript of the interview.*

가산명사 필기록, (인설 등의) 원고 ❑ 그들은 인터뷰 원고를 나에게 주지 않으려 했다.

> ### Word Link   trans ≈ across : transfer, transition, translate

trans|fer ♦♦◇ (**transfers, transferring, transferred**)

> The verb is pronounced /trænsfɜ́r/. The noun is pronounced /trǽnsfɜr/.

동사는 /trænsfɜ́r/로 발음되고, 명사는 /trǽnsfɜr/로 발음된다.

❶ V-T/V-I If you **transfer** something or someone **from** one place **to** another, or they **transfer from** one place **to** another, they go from the first place to the second. ❑ *Remove the wafers with a spoon and transfer them to a plate.* ● N-VAR **Transfer** is also a noun. [oft N of n] ❑ *Arrange for the transfer of medical records to your new doctor.* ❷ V-T/V-I If something **is transferred**, or **transfers, from** one person or group of people to another, the second person or group gets it instead of the first. ❑ *I realized she'd transferred all her love from me to you.* ● N-VAR **Transfer** is also a noun. ❑ *...the transfer of power from the old to the new regimes.* ❸ V-T/V-I If you **are transferred**, or you **transfer, to** a different job or place, you move to a different job or start working in a different place. ❑ *I was transferred to the book department.* ❑ *I suspect that she is going to be transferred.* ● N-VAR **Transfer** is also a noun. [oft N to n] ❑ *They will be offered transfers to other locations.* ❹ V-T When information **is transferred onto** a different medium, it is copied from one medium to another. ❑ *Such information is easily transferred onto microfilm.* ● N-UNCOUNT **Transfer** is also a noun. ❑ *It can be connected to a PC for the transfer of information.*

❶ 타동사/자동사 옮기다; 이동하다 ❑ 스푼으로 와퍼를 들어내서 접시에 옮겨 놓아라. ● 가산명사 또는 불가산명사 이동 ❑ 새 주치의한테 진료 기록을 넘기도록 조치를 해라. ❷ 타동사/자동사 전이되다, 이양되다 ❑ 나는 그녀가 사랑하는 대상이 내가 아닌 너로 바뀌었음을 깨달았다. ● 가산명사 또는 불가산명사 전이, 이양 ❑ 구정권에서 신정권으로의 정권 교체 ❸ 타동사/자동사 전임되다, 전근하다 ❑ 나는 서적부로 전임됐다. ❑ 내 생각에 그녀가 다른 곳으로 발령 날 것 같다. ● 가산명사 또는 불가산명사 전임, 전근 ❑ 그들은 다른 곳으로 전임 제안을 받을 것이다. ❹ 타동사 전사되다, 전송되다 ❑ 그와 같은 정보는 마이크로필름에 쉽게 전사된다. ● 불가산명사 전사, 전송 ❑ 이것을 피시에 연결하여 정보를 전송할 수 있다.

> ### Word Partnership   transfer의 연어
> N.   **balance** transfer, transfer **funds**, transfer **money** ❶
>   transfer **ownership**, transfer **of power** ❷
>   transfer **schools, students** transfer ❸
>   transfer **data**, transfer **information** ❹

trans|fer|able /trænsfɜ́rəbəl/ ADJ If something is **transferable**, it can be passed or moved from one person or organization to another and used by them. ❑ *Use the transferable skills acquired from your previous working background.*

형용사 양도할 수 있는, 이전할 수 있는 ❑ 전에 일하던 곳에서 습득한 기술 중 이전 가능한 기술을 사용하라.

trans|form ♦◇◇ /trænsfɔ́rm/ (**transforms, transforming, transformed**) ❶ V-T To **transform** something **into** something else means to change or convert it into that thing. ❑ *Your metabolic rate is the speed at which your body transforms food into*

❶ 타동사 바꾸다, 전환시키다 ❑ 신진대사율이란 신체가 음식물을 에너지로 바꾸는 속도를 말한다. ● 변화, 전환 가산명사 또는 불가산명사 ❑ 노라가

energy. ● **trans|for|ma|tion** /trænsfərmeɪʃᵊn/ (**transformations**) N-VAR ❑ *Norah made plans for the transformation of an attic room into a study.* **2** V-T To **transform** something or someone means to change them completely and suddenly so that they are much better or more attractive. ❑ *The Minister said the Urban Development Corporation was now transforming the area.* ● **trans|for|ma|tion** N-VAR ❑ *In the last five years he's undergone a personal transformation.*

다락방을 서재로 개조시키기 위한 계획을 세웠다. **2** 타동사 변신시키다, 탈바꿈시키다 ❑ 장관은 도시 개발 공사가 이제 그 지역을 탈바꿈시키고 있다고 밝혔다. ● 변모, 변신 가산명사 또는 불가산명사 ❑ 지난 5년간 그는 사람이 많이 바뀌었다.

<table>
<tr><td>Thesaurus</td><td>transform의 참조어</td></tr>
<tr><td>v.</td><td>alter, change, convert 1 2</td></tr>
</table>

trans|fu|sion /trænsfjuːʒᵊn/ (**transfusions**) N-VAR A **transfusion** is the same as a **blood transfusion**.

가산명사 또는 불가산명사 수혈

tran|sient /trænʃənt, BRIT trænzɪənt/ ADJ **Transient** is used to describe a situation that lasts only a short time or is constantly changing. [FORMAL] ❑ *...the transient nature of high fashion.*

형용사 일시적인, 끊임없이 변하는 [격식체] ❑ 최신 유행의 일시적인 성격

trans|it /trænzɪt/ **1** N-UNCOUNT **Transit** is the carrying of goods or people by vehicle from one place to another. ❑ *During their talks, the two presidents discussed the transit of goods between the two countries.* ❑ *...a transit time of about 42 minutes.* ● PHRASE If people or things are **in transit**, they are travelling or being carried from one place to another. **2** ADJ A **transit** area is an area where people wait or where goods are kept between different stages of a journey. [ADJ n] ❑ *...refugees arriving at the two transit camps.* **3** N-UNCOUNT A **transit system** is a system for moving people or goods from one place to another, for example using buses or trains. [AM; BRIT **transport system**] ❑ *The president wants to improve the nation's highways and mass transit systems.* →see **transportation**

1 불가산명사 수송, 이동 ❑ 두 대통령은 회담 중에 양국 간 물자 수송에 대해 논의했다. ❑ 42분 가량의 이동 시간 ● 구 이동 중인, 수송 중인 **2** 형용사 중간 기착지의 ❑ 중간 임시 수용소 두 곳에 도착한 난민들 **3** 불가산명사 수송 체계 [미국영어; 영국영어 transport system] ❑ 대통령이 국내 고속도로 및 대량 수송 체계를 개선하고자 한다.

<table>
<tr><td>Word Link</td><td>trans ≈ across : transfer, transition, translate</td></tr>
</table>

tran|si|tion ♦◇◇ /trænzɪʃᵊn/ (**transitions, transitioning, transitioned**) **1** N-VAR **Transition** is the process in which something changes from one state to another. ❑ *The transition to a multi-party democracy is proving to be difficult.* **2** V-T/V-I If someone **transitions from** one state or activity to another, they move gradually from one to the other. [BUSINESS] ❑ *Most of the discussion was on what needed to be done now as we transitioned from the security issues to the challenging economic issues.*

1 가산명사 또는 불가산명사 변화, 변천, 이행 ❑ 다당제 민주주의로의 이행이 힘겨운 과정임이 드러나고 있다. **2** 타동사/자동사 서서히 바뀌다 [경제] ❑ 안보 현안에서 경제 문제로 주제가 바뀌면서 우리는 토론 시간 대부분을 지금 해야 할 일이 무엇인지 논의하는 데 썼다.

tran|si|tion|al /trænzɪʃᵊnᵊl/ **1** ADJ A **transitional** period is one in which things are changing from one state to another. [ADJ n] ❑ *...a transitional period following more than a decade of civil war.* **2** ADJ **Transitional** is used to describe something that happens or exists during a transitional period. [ADJ n] ❑ *The main rebel groups have agreed to join in a meeting to set up a transitional government.*

1 형용사 과도적인 ❑ 10년 넘게 진행된 내전 후의 과도기 **2** 형용사 과도기의 ❑ 주요 반군 단체들이 과도 정부 수립을 위한 회의에 참석하기로 동의했다.

tran|si|tive /trænzɪtɪv/ ADJ A **transitive** verb has a direct object.

형용사 타동사의

trans|late /trænzleɪt/ (**translates, translating, translated**) **1** V-T/V-I If something that someone has said or written **is translated from** one language **into** another, it is said or written again in the second language. ❑ *Only a small number of Kadare's books have been translated into English.* ❑ *The Celtic word "geis" is usually translated as "taboo."* ❑ *The girls waited for Mr. Esch to translate.* ● **trans|la|tion** N-UNCOUNT ❑ *The papers have been sent to Saudi Arabia for translation.* **2** V-I If a name, a word, or an expression **translates as** something in a different language, that is what it means in that language. ❑ *His family's Cantonese nickname for him translates as Never Sits Still.* **3** V-T/V-I If one thing **translates** or is **translated into** another, the second happens or is done as a result of the first. ❑ *Reforming Warsaw's stagnant economy requires harsh measures that would translate into job losses.*

1 타동사/자동사 통역되다, 번역되다 ❑ 지금까지 카다르 작품의 극히 일부만이 영어로 번역되었다. ❑ 켈트어 단어 'geis'는 보통 '금기'로 번역된다. ❑ 여학생들은 에쉬 씨의 통역을 기다렸다. ● 번역, 통역 불가산명사 ❑ 그 서류들을 번역 때문에 사우디아라비아로 보냈다. **2** 자동사 해석되다, 뜻하다 ❑ 가족이 그를 부를 때 사용하는 광동어 별명의 뜻은 '절대로 가만히 있지 않는다'이다. **3** 타동사/자동사 ...는 결과로 이어지다 ❑ 바르샤바의 침체된 경제를 개혁하기 위해서는 고용 축소로 이어질 수도 있는 엄격한 대책이 필요하다.

trans|la|tion /trænzleɪʃᵊn/ (**translations**) N-COUNT A **translation** is a piece of writing or speech that has been translated from a different language. [also in N] ❑ *...MacNiece's excellent English translation of "Faust".*

가산명사 번역, 통역 ❑ 맥니스가 훌륭히 번역한 '파우스트' 영문판

trans|la|tor /trænzleɪtər/ (**translators**) N-COUNT A **translator** is a person whose job is translating writing or speech from one language to another.

가산명사 번역가, 통역사

trans|lu|cent /trænzluːsᵊnt/ ADJ If a material is **translucent**, some light can pass through it. ❑ *The building is roofed entirely with translucent corrugated plastic.* →see **pottery**

형용사 반투명한 ❑ 건물 지붕 전체가 반투명 플라스틱 골판 패널로 되어 있다.

trans|mis|sion /trænzmɪʃᵊn/ (**transmissions**) **1** N-UNCOUNT The **transmission** of something is the passing or sending of it to a different person or place. ❑ *Heterosexual contact is responsible for the bulk of HIV transmission.* **2** N-UNCOUNT The **transmission** of television or radio programs is the broadcasting of them. ❑ *The transmission of the programme was brought forward due to its unexpected topicality.* **3** N-COUNT A **transmission** is a broadcast. ❑ *...foreign television transmissions.*

1 불가산명사 전송, 전파; 전염 ❑ 면역 결핍 바이러스의 전염 원인은 대부분 이성 간의 성 접촉이다. **2** 불가산명사 방송 ❑ 예상치 않게 프로그램이 시사성을 띠면서 방송이 앞당겨졌다. **3** 가산명사 방송 ❑ 외국 텔레비전 방송

trans|mit /trænzmɪt/ (**transmits, transmitting, transmitted**) **1** V-T/V-I When radio and television programs, computer data, or other electronic messages **are transmitted**, they are sent from one place to another, using wires, radio waves, or satellites. ❑ *The game was transmitted live in Spain and Italy.* ❑ *This is currently the most efficient way to transmit certain types of data like electronic mail.* **2** V-T If one person or animal **transmits** a disease to another, they have the disease and cause the other person or animal to have it. [FORMAL] ❑ *...mosquitoes that transmit disease to humans.* **3** V-T If an object or substance **transmits** something such as sound or electrical signals, the sound or signals are able to pass through it. ❑ *These thin crystals transmit much of the power.*

1 타동사/자동사 전송되다, 방송되다 ❑ 그 경기는 스페인과 이탈리아에서 생방송되었다. ❑ 이는 현재 이메일과 같은 특정 데이터 전송 방법으로는 가장 효율적이다. **2** 타동사 전염시키다 [격식체] ❑ 사람에게 질병을 전염시키는 모기 **3** 타동사 전달하다 ❑ 이와 같이 얇은 크리스털이 전력 대부분을 전달한다.

trans|mit|ter /trænzmɪtər/ (**transmitters**) N-COUNT A **transmitter** is a piece of equipment that is used for broadcasting television or radio programs. ❑ *...a homemade radio transmitter.* →see **cellphone, radio**

가산명사 송신기 ❑ 손수 만든 무선 송신기

trans|par|en|cy /trænspɛərənsi, -pær-, BRIT trænspærənsi/ (**transparencies**)
1 N-COUNT A **transparency** is a small piece of photographic film with a frame around it which can be projected onto a screen so that you can see the picture. ❑ ...transparencies of masterpieces from Lizzie's art collection. **2** N-UNCOUNT **Transparency** is the quality that an object or substance has when you can see through it. ❑ Cataracts is a condition that affects the transparency of the lenses.

① 가산명사 슬라이드 ❑ 리지의 예술 작품 중에 걸작을 선별해서 만든 슬라이드 ② 불가산명사 투명도, 투명성 ❑ 백내장은 수정체의 투명도를 떨어뜨리는 병이다.

trans|par|ent /trænspɛərənt, -pær-, BRIT trænspærənt/ **1** ADJ If an object or substance is **transparent**, you can see through it. ❑ ...a sheet of transparent colored plastic. **2** ADJ If a situation, system, or activity is **transparent**, it is easily understood or recognized. ❑ The company has to make its accounts and operations as transparent as possible. **3** ADJ You use **transparent** to describe a statement or action that is obviously dishonest or wrong, and that you think will not deceive people. ❑ He thought he could fool people with transparent deceptions.

① 형용사 투명한 ❑ 색깔이 있는 투명 플라스틱 한 장 ② 형용사 투명한, 알기 쉬운 ❑ 회사는 회계와 경영을 최대한 투명하게 해야 한다. ③ 형용사 명백한, 뻔한 ❑ 그는 뻔한 속임수를 가지고 사람들을 속일 수 있으리라고 생각했다.

tran|spire /trænspaɪər/ (**transpires, transpiring, transpired**) **1** V-T When it **transpires that** something is the case, people discover that it is the case. [FORMAL] ❑ It transpired that Paolo had left his driving license at home. **2** V-I When something **transpires**, it happens. Some speakers of English consider this use to be incorrect. ❑ Nothing is known as yet about what transpired at the meeting.

① 타동사 알고 보니 ─이다 [격식체] ❑ 알고 보니 파올로가 집에 운전면허증을 놔두고 왔던 것이다. ② 자동사 일어나다, 발생하다 ❑ 아직까지 그 회의에서 무슨 일이 있었는지 아무것도 알려지지 않았다.

trans|plant (**transplants, transplanting, transplanted**)

> The noun is pronounced /trænsplænt/. The verb is pronounced /trænsplænt/.

명사는 /trænsplænt/로 발음되고, 동사는 /trænsplænt/로 발음된다.

1 N-VAR A **transplant** is a medical operation in which a part of a person's body is replaced because it is diseased. ❑ He was recovering from a heart transplant operation. **2** V-T If doctors **transplant** an organ such as a heart or a kidney, they use it to replace a patient's diseased organ. ❑ The operation to transplant a kidney is now fairly routine. **3** V-T To **transplant** someone or something means to move them to a different place. ❑ Marriage had transplanted Rebecca from London to Manchester. →see **donor, hospital**

① 가산명사 또는 불가산명사 이식 ❑ 그는 심장이식 수술을 받고 회복 중이었다. ② 타동사 이식하다 ❑ 신장 이식 수술은 이제 상당히 일반화됐다. ③ 타동사 이주시키다 ❑ 레베카는 결혼하면서 런던에서 맨체스터로 거처를 옮겼었다.

trans|port ♦♦◇ (**transports, transporting, transported**)

> The verb is pronounced /trænspɔrt/. The noun is pronounced /trænspɔrt/.

동사는 /trænspɔrt/로 발음되고, 명사는 /trænspɔrt/로 발음된다.

1 V-T To **transport** people or goods somewhere is to take them from one place to another in a vehicle. ❑ They are banned from launching any flights except to transport people. **2** N-UNCOUNT **Transport** refers to any vehicle that you can travel in or carry goods in. [mainly BRIT; AM usually **transportation**] ❑ Have you got your own transport? **3** N-UNCOUNT **Transport** is a system for taking people or goods from one place to another, for example using buses or trains. [mainly BRIT; AM usually **transportation**] ❑ The extra money could be spent on improving public transport. **4** N-UNCOUNT **Transport** is the activity of taking goods or people from one place to another in a vehicle. [mainly BRIT; AM usually **transportation**] ❑ Local production virtually eliminates transport costs.

① 타동사 운송하다, 수송하다 ❑ 그들은 사람을 실어 나르는 용도 외에는 비행기를 전혀 띄워서는 안 된다. ② 불가산명사 교통수단, 운송 수단 [주로 영국영어; 미국영어 대개 transportation] ❑ 타고 가실 차편은 있습니까? ③ 불가산명사 교통 [주로 영국영어; 미국영어 대개 transportation] ❑ 추가 금액을 대중교통을 향상시키는 데 사용할 수도 있을 것이다. ④ 불가산명사 운송, 수송 [주로 영국영어; 미국영어 대개 transportation] ❑ 지역 내에서 생산하면 운송비가 사실상 없어진다.

trans|por|ta|tion /trænspərteɪʃn/ **1** N-UNCOUNT **Transportation** refers to any type of vehicle that you can travel in or carry goods in. [mainly AM; BRIT usually **transport**] ❑ The company will provide transportation. **2** N-UNCOUNT **Transportation** is a system for taking people or goods from one place to another, for example using buses or trains. [mainly AM; BRIT usually **transport**] ❑ Campuses are usually accessible by public transportation. **3** N-UNCOUNT **Transportation** is the activity of taking goods or people from one place to another in a vehicle. [mainly AM; BRIT usually **transport**] ❑ The baggage was being rapidly stowed away for transportation. →see Word Web: **transportation**

① 불가산명사 교통수단, 운송 수단 [주로 미국영어; 영국영어 대개 transport] ❑ 회사가 교통편을 제공할 것이다. ② 불가산명사 교통 [주로 미국영어; 영국영어 대개 transport] ❑ 캠퍼스는 보통 대중교통편으로 연결되어 있다. ③ 불가산명사 운송, 수송 [주로 미국영어; 영국영어 대개 transport] ❑ 운송물들이 빠르게 실리고 있었다.

trap ♦♦◇ /træp/ (**traps, trapping, trapped**) **1** N-COUNT A **trap** is a device which is placed somewhere or a hole which is dug somewhere in order to catch animals or birds. ❑ Nathan's dog ends up caught in a trap. **2** V-T If a person **traps** animals or birds, he or she catches them using traps. ❑ The locals were encouraged to trap and kill the birds. **3** N-COUNT A **trap** is a trick that is intended to catch or deceive someone. ❑ He failed to keep a rendezvous after sensing a police trap. **4** V-T If you **trap** someone **into** doing or saying something, you trick them so that they do or say it, although they did not want to. ❑ Were you just trying to trap her into making some admission? **5** V-T To **trap** someone, especially a criminal, means to capture them. [JOURNALISM] ❑ The police knew that to trap the killer they had to play him at his own game. **6** N-COUNT A **trap** is an unpleasant situation that you cannot easily escape from. ❑ The Government has found it's caught in a trap of its own making. **7** V-T If you **are trapped** somewhere, something falls onto you or blocks your way and prevents you from moving or escaping. ❑ The train was trapped underground by a fire. ❑ The light aircraft then cartwheeled, trapping both men. **8** V-T When something **traps** gas, water, or energy, it prevents it from

① 가산명사 덫, 함정 ❑ 나단의 개가 덫에 걸리고 만다. ② 타동사 덫으로 잡아 죽이다 ❑ 그 지역에서는 덫으로 그 새들을 잡아 죽이는 행위가 장려됐다. ③ 가산명사 속임수, 함정 ❑ 그는 경찰이 파 놓은 함정을 감지한 후에 약속 장소에 나가지 못했다. ④ 타동사 속이다 ❑ 당신 그 여자를 속여서 시인이라도 하게끔 만들려고 했던 거야? ⑤ 타동사 잡다 [언론] ❑ 경찰은 그 살인범을 잡으려면 살인범이 사용한 것과 똑같은 수법을 사용해야 함을 알았다. ⑥ 가산명사 곤경, 덫 ❑ 정부가 스스로 판 덫에 빠지게 되었다. ⑦ 타동사 간히다 ❑ 화재로 인해 기차가 지하에 갇혔다. ❑ 그 후 경비행기가 옆으로 넘어지면서 두 남자가 밑에 깔렸다. ⑧ 타동사 가두다, 흐름을 막다 ❑ 모직물은 체온을 새어나가지 못하게 하고 찬바람은 막아 준다.

Word Web   transportation

Urban **mass transportation** began more than 200 years ago. By 1830, there were horse-drawn **streetcars** in New York City and New Orleans. They ran on **rails** built into the right of way of city streets. The first electric **tram** opened in Berlin in 1881. Later on, **buses** became more popular because they didn't require **tracks**. Today, **commuter trains** link **suburbs** to cities everywhere. Many large cities also have an underground train system. It's called the **subway, metro,** or **tube** depending on where you live. In cities with steep hills, cable cars are a popular form of mass **transit**.

escaping. ❑ *Wool traps your body heat, keeping the chill at bay.* 🔟 →see also **trapped, death trap, poverty trap**

Word Partnership *trap*의 연어

V. **avoid a trap, caught in a trap, fall into a trap, set a trap** 🔟 🔟 🔟

trapped /træpt/ ADJ If you feel **trapped**, you are in an unpleasant situation in which you lack freedom, and you feel you cannot escape from it. ❑ *...people who think of themselves as trapped in mundane jobs.* →see also **trap**

형용사 위매인, 갇힌 ❑ 스스로를 시시한 일의 노예라고 생각하는 사람들

trap|pings /træpɪŋz/ N-PLURAL The **trappings** of power, wealth, or a particular job are the extra things, such as decorations and luxury items, that go with it. [DISAPPROVAL] ❑ *The family were in government for several generations and evidently loved the trappings of power.*

복수명사 장식물, 부속물 [탐탁잖음] ❑ 그 집안은 몇 세대에 걸쳐 정부 요직을 차지했으며 권력의 장식물을 좋아했음은 물론이다.

trash /træʃ/ 🔟 N-UNCOUNT **Trash** consists of unwanted things or waste material such as used paper, empty containers and bottles, and waste food. [AM; BRIT **rubbish**] [also the N] ❑ *The yards are overgrown and cluttered with trash.* 🔟 N-UNCOUNT If you say that something such as a book, painting, or movie is **trash**, you mean that it is of very poor quality. [INFORMAL] ❑ *Pop music doesn't have to be trash, it can be art.*

🔟 불가산명사 쓰레기 [미국영어; 영국영어 rubbish] ❑ 뜰에는 잡초가 무성하고 쓰레기가 어지럽게 널려 있다. 🔟 불가산명사 쓰레기 같은 것, 졸작 [비격식체] ❑ 대중음악이 꼭 쓰레기 같을 필요는 없다. 예술이 될 수도 있다.

In American English, the words **trash** and **garbage** are most commonly used to refer to waste material that is thrown away. ❑ *...the smell of rotting garbage... She threw the bottle into the trash.* In British English, **rubbish** is the usual word. **Trash** and **garbage** are are sometimes used in British English, but only informally and metaphorically. ❑ *I don't have to listen to this garbage... The book was trash.*

미국 영어에서는 버리는 물건을 가리킬 때 trash와 garbage가 가장 흔히 사용된다. ❑ ...쓰레기 썩는 냄새... 그녀는 그 병을 쓰레기 속에 던져 넣었다. 영국 영어에서는 rubbish가 흔히 쓰인다. trash와 garbage가 때때로 영국 영어에서 쓰이기도 하지만, 비격식체나 은유적으로만 쓴다. ❑ 난 이런 쓰레기 같은 이야기를 들을 필요가 없다... 그 책은 허섭스레기였다.

Thesaurus *trash*의 참조어

N. debris, garbage, junk, litter 🔟

trash can (**trash cans**) N-COUNT A **trash can** is a large round container which people put their trash in and which is usually kept outside their house. [AM; BRIT **dustbin**]

가산명사 쓰레기통 [미국영어; 영국영어 dustbin]

trau|ma /trɑːmə, trɔ-, BRIT trɔːmə/ (**traumas**) N-VAR **Trauma** is a very severe shock or very upsetting experience, which may cause psychological damage. ❑ *I'd been through the trauma of losing a house.*

가산명사 또는 불가산명사 큰 충격, 정신적 외상, 가슴 아픈 경험 ❑ 나는 집을 잃는 가슴 아픈 경험을 했었다.

trau|mat|ic /trəmætɪk, BRIT trɔːmætɪk/ ADJ A **traumatic** experience is very shocking and upsetting, and may cause psychological damage. ❑ *I suffered a nervous breakdown. It was a traumatic experience.*

형용사 깊은 상처를 주는 ❑ 나는 신경 쇠약을 앓았다. 잊지 못할 정도로 힘든 경험이었다.

trau|ma|tize /trɑːmətaɪz, trɔ-, BRIT trɔːmətaɪz/ (**traumatizes, traumatizing, traumatized**) [BRIT also **traumatise**] V-T If someone **is traumatized** by an event or situation, it shocks or upsets them very much, and may cause them psychological damage. ❑ *My wife was traumatized by the experience.* ● **trau|ma|tized** ADJ ❑ *He left her in the middle of the road, shaking and deeply traumatized.*

[영국영어 traumatise] 타동사 정신적인 충격을 받다 ❑ 아내는 그 일로 정신적인 충격을 받았다. ● 충격을 받은 형용사 ❑ 그는 그녀가 부들부들 떨며 심한 충격을 받은 채 길 한가운데 서 있도록 내버려 두었다.

trav|el ♦♦◇ /trævˀl/ (**travels, traveling, traveled**) [BRIT, sometimes AM **travelling, travelled**] 🔟 V-T/V-I If you **travel**, you go from one place to another, often to a place that is far away. ❑ *You had better travel to Helsinki tomorrow.* ❑ *I've been traveling all day.* ❑ *Students often travel hundreds of miles to get here.* 🔟 N-UNCOUNT **Travel** is the activity of traveling. ❑ *Information on travel in New Zealand is available at the hotel.* ❑ *He detested air travel.* 🔟 V-T If you **travel** the world, the country, or the area, you go to many different places in the world or in a particular country or area. ❑ *He was a very wealthy man who had traveled the world.* 🔟 V-I When light or sound from one place reaches another, you say that it **travels** to the other place. ❑ *When sound travels through water, strange things can happen.* 🔟 V-I When news becomes known by people in different places, you can say that it **travels** to them. ❑ *News of his work traveled all the way to Asia.* 🔟 N-PLURAL Someone's **travels** are the journeys that they make to places a long way from their home. ❑ *He also collects things for the house on his travels abroad.* 🔟 PHRASE If you **travel light**, you travel without taking much luggage. ❑ *It would be good to be able to travel light, but I end up taking 28 T-shirts, wearing four and buying lots more.*

[영국영어, 미국영어 가끔 travelling, travelled] 🔟 타동사/자동사 가다, 다니다, 여행하다 ❑ 내일 헬싱키까지 가 보는 편이 좋을 것 같아요. 그는 하루 종일 돌아다녔다. ❑ 학생들은 이곳에 오기 위해 수백 마일이라는 먼 길을 여행하기도 한다. 🔟 불가산명사 여행 ❑ 뉴질랜드 여행 정보는 호텔에서 얻을 수 있다. ❑ 그는 비행기 여행을 몹시 싫어했다. 🔟 타동사 여행하다, 돌아다니다 ❑ 그는 전 세계를 돌아다녀 본 매우 부유한 남자였다. 🔟 자동사 (빛, 소리 등이) 이동하다 ❑ 빛이 물 속에서 이동할 때 신기한 현상이 일어나기도 한다. 🔟 자동사 (소식이) 전해지다, 알려지다 ❑ 그의 작품 소식이 아시아에까지 전해졌다. 🔟 복수명사 여행 ❑ 그는 해외여행 중에 집을 장식할 만한 것들을 수집하기도 한다. 🔟 구 가볍게 여행하다 ❑ 짐을 가볍게 싸서 여행하면 좋겠지만, 나는 결국 가져가는 티셔츠만 28장에 4장은 직접 입고 새로 사는 옷도 많다.

The noun **travel** is used to talk about the general activity of traveling. It is either uncount or plural. You cannot say "a travel," you would use the word **trip** or **journey** instead. ❑ *First-class rail travel to Paris or Brussels is included... We were going to go on a trip to Florida together.*

명사 travel은 일반적인 여행 행위에 대해 말할 때 쓰는데, 불가산 명사나 복수로 쓴다. a travel 이라고는 하지 않고, 대신 trip이나 journey를 쓸 수 있다. ❑ 파리나 브뤼셀로 가는 일등칸 기차 여행이 포함되어 있다... 우리는 플로리다로 함께 여행을 가려고 했다.

Thesaurus *travel*의 참조어

V. explore, trek, visit 🔟 🔟
N. expedition, journey, trip 🔟

Word Partnership *travel*의 연어

ADV. travel **abroad** 🔟-🔟
N. **air** travel, travel **arrangements**, travel **books, car** travel, travel **delays**, travel **expenses**, travel **guide**, travel **industry**, travel **insurance**, travel **plans**, travel **reports**, travel **reservations** 🔟 travel **the world** 🔟

trav|el agent (**travel agents**) **1** N-COUNT A **travel agent** or **travel agent's** is a store or office where you can go to arrange a vacation or trip. □ *He worked in a travel agent's.* **2** N-COUNT A **travel agent** is a person or business that arranges people's vacations and trips.

1 가산명사 여행사 □ 그는 여행사에서 일했다.
2 가산명사 여행사 직원; 여행사 일

trav|el|er ◆◇◇ /trǽvələr/ (**travelers**) [BRIT, sometimes AM **traveller**] N-COUNT A **traveler** is a person who is making a journey or a person who travels a lot. □ *Airline travelers need to be confident that their bookings will be honored.*

[영국영어, 미국영어 가끔 traveller] 가산명사 여행자 □ 비행기 여행객들은 예약이 분명히 되어 있는지 확실히 해 둘 필요가 있다.

trav|el|er's check (**traveler's checks**) [BRIT **traveller's cheque**] N-COUNT **Traveler's checks** are checks that you buy at a bank and take with you when you travel, for example so that you can exchange them for the currency of the country that you are in. □ *She refused to accept cash, credit cards, or traveler's checks.*

[영국영어 traveller's cheque] 가산명사 여행자 수표 □ 그녀는 현금도 신용 카드도 여행자 수표도 받지 않았다.

trav|es|ty /trǽvəsti/ (**travesties**) N-COUNT If you describe something as a **travesty of** another thing, you mean that it is a very bad representation of that other thing. □ *Her research suggests that Smith's reputation today is a travesty of what he really stood for.*

가산명사 억지 해석 □ 그녀는 연구를 통해 오늘날 스미스의 명성은 그가 실제로 상징했던 것을 억지 해석한 결과라는 점을 시사한다.

trawl /trɔl/ (**trawls, trawling, trawled**) **1** V-T/V-I If you **trawl through** a large number of similar things, you search through them looking for something that you want or something that is suitable for a particular purpose. □ *A team of officers is trawling through the records of thousands of petty thieves.* **2** V-T/V-I When fishermen **trawl for** fish, they pull a wide net behind their ship in order to catch fish. □ *They had seen him trawling and therefore knew that there were fish.*

1 타동사/자동사 대대적인 조사를 하다, 샅샅이 조사하다 □ 경찰관 한 팀이 좀도둑 수천 명의 기록을 대대적으로 조사하고 있다. **2** 타동사/자동사 트롤 어업을 하다, 저인망으로 고기를 잡다 □ 그들은 그가 저인망으로 고기를 잡는 것을 보았고, 그래서 물고기가 있다는 사실을 알았다.

trawl|er /trɔ́lər/ (**trawlers**) N-COUNT A **trawler** is a fishing boat that is used for trawling.

가산명사 트롤선, 저인망 어선

tray /treɪ/ (**trays**) N-COUNT A **tray** is a flat piece of wood, plastic, or metal, which usually has raised edges and which is used for carrying things, especially food and drinks.

가산명사 쟁반

treach|er|ous /trɛ́tʃərəs/ **1** ADJ If you describe someone as **treacherous**, you mean that they are likely to betray you and cannot be trusted. [DISAPPROVAL] □ *He publicly left the party and denounced its treacherous leaders.* **2** ADJ If you say that something is **treacherous**, you mean that it is very dangerous and unpredictable. □ *The current of the river is fast flowing and treacherous.*

1 형용사 기만적인, 신뢰할 수 없는 [탐탁찮음] □ 그는 당을 공식적으로 떠나면서 기만적인 당 지도자들을 비난했다. **2** 형용사 위험한 □ 그 강물은 급류라서 위험하다.

treach|ery /trɛ́tʃəri/ (**treacheries**) N-UNCOUNT **Treachery** is behavior or an action in which someone betrays their country or betrays a person who trusts them. □ *He was deeply wounded by the treachery of close aides and old friends.*

불가산명사 배반 □ 그는 측근 참모들과 옛 친구들이 자신을 배반한 것에 대해 크게 상처 입었다.

tread /trɛd/ (**treads, treading, trod, trodden**) **1** V-I If you **tread on** something, you put your foot on it when you are walking or standing. □ *Oh, sorry, I didn't mean to tread on your foot.* **2** V-I If you **tread** in a particular way, you walk that way. □ *She trod casually, enjoying the touch of the damp grass on her feet.* **3** V-I If you **tread** carefully, you behave in a careful or cautious way. □ *If you are hoping to form a new relationship tread carefully and slowly to begin with.* **4** N-VAR The **tread** of a tire or shoe is the pattern of thin lines cut into its surface that stops it from slipping. □ *The fat, broad tires had a good depth of tread.* **5** PHRASE If someone is **treading a fine line** or **path**, they are acting carefully because they have to avoid making a serious mistake, especially in a situation where they have to deal with two opposing demands. □ *They have to tread the delicate path between informing children and boring them.* **6** PHRASE If you **tread** a particular **path**, you take a particular course of action or do something in a particular way. □ *He continues to tread an unconventional path.*

1 자동사 밟다 □ 아, 미안합니다. 일부러 발을 밟으려 했던 것은 아니었어요. **2** 자동사 걷다 [문예체] □ 그녀는 발끝에 닿는 촉촉한 잔디의 감촉을 느끼면서 가볍게 걸었다. **3** 자동사 행동하다, 접근하다 □ 만약 당신이 새로운 관계 형성을 원하고 있다면, 우선 조심성 있게 그리고 천천히 접근하세요. **4** 가산명사 또는 불가산명사 (타이어 등의) 접지 면 □ 두껍고 넓은 그 타이어는 접지 면이 매우 깊게 패어 있었다. **5** 구 아주 조심해서 행동하다 □ 그들은 아이들에게 정보를 주는 것과 그들을 지루하게 하는 것 사이의 미묘한 길에서 아주 조심스럽게 행동을 해야 한다. **6** 구 (특정한) 길을 걷다 □ 그는 계속 비통념적인 길을 걷고 있다.

tread|mill /trɛ́dmɪl/ (**treadmills**) **1** N-COUNT You can refer to a task or a job as a **treadmill** when you have to keep doing it although it is unpleasant and exhausting. □ *Mr. Stocks can expect a gruelling week on the publicity treadmill.* **2** N-COUNT A **treadmill** is a piece of equipment, for example an exercise machine, consisting of a wheel with steps around its edge or a continuous moving belt. The weight of a person or animal walking on it causes the wheel or belt to turn.

1 가산명사 재미없고 피곤한 일 □ 스톡스 씨는 재미없고 피곤한 홍보 일로 녹초가 될 한 주를 예상할 수 있다. **2** 가산명사 발로 밟아 돌리는 기구

trea|son /tríz⁽ⁿ⁾n/ N-UNCOUNT **Treason** is the crime of betraying your country, for example by helping its enemies or by trying to remove its government using violence. □ *They were tried and found guilty of treason.*

불가산명사 반역죄 □ 그들을 심리한 후 반역죄로 평결했다.

treas|ure /trɛ́ʒər/ (**treasures, treasuring, treasured**) **1** N-UNCOUNT **Treasure** is a collection of valuable old objects such as gold coins and jewels that has been hidden or lost. [LITERARY] □ *It was here, the buried treasure, she knew it was.* **2** N-COUNT **Treasures** are valuable objects, especially works of art and items of historical value. □ *The house was large and full of art treasures.* **3** V-T If you **treasure** something that you have, you keep it or care for it carefully because it gives you great pleasure and you think it is very special. □ *She treasures her memories of those joyous days.* ● N-COUNT **Treasure** is also a noun. □ *His greatest treasure is his collection of rock records.* ● **treas|ured** ADJ [ADJ n] □ *These books are still among my most treasured possessions.*

1 불가산명사 보물 [문예체] □ 숨겨진 보물이 여기 있다는 것을 그녀는 알고 있었다. **2** 가산명사 보물 □ 그 집은 컸고 보물 같은 예술품들이 가득했다. **3** 타동사 보물처럼 소중히 여기다 □ 그녀는 즐거웠던 그 시절에 대한 기억들을 보물처럼 소중히 여긴다. ● 가산명사 보물처럼 여기는 것 □ 그가 가장 보물처럼 여기는 것은 자신이 모아 둔 록 음반이다. ● 귀중한 형용사 □ 이 책들은 여전히 나의 가장 귀중한 재산 목록에 들어간다.

treas|ur|er /trɛ́ʒərər/ (**treasurers**) N-COUNT The **treasurer** of a society or organization is the person who is in charge of its finances and keeps its accounts.

가산명사 회계 담당자

treas|ury ◆◇◇ /trɛ́ʒəri/ (**treasuries**) N-COUNT-COLL In the United States and Britain, and some other countries, **the Treasury** is the government department that deals with the country's finances. □ *...a senior official at the Treasury.*

가산명사-집합 재무부 □ 재무부 고위 관리

treat ◆◆◇ /trit/ (**treats, treating, treated**) **1** V-T If you **treat** someone or something in a particular way, you behave toward them or deal with them in that way. □ *Artie treated most women with indifference.* □ *Police say they're treating it as a case of attempted murder.* **2** V-T When a doctor or nurse **treats** a patient or an illness, he or she tries to make the patient well again. □ *Doctors treated her with aspirin.* □ *The boy was treated for a minor head wound.* **3** V-T If something **is treated with** a particular substance, the substance is put onto or into it in order to

1 타동사 대하다, 처리하다 □ 아티는 대부분의 여성들을 무관심하게 대했다. □ 경찰은 그것을 살인 미수 사건으로 처리할 것이라고 말한다. **2** 타동사 치료하다, 치료하다 □ 의사들은 그녀에게 아스피린을 처방했다. □ 그 소년은 머리에 난 작은 상처 때문에 치료를 받았다. **3** 타동사 (화학 약품 등으로) 처리하다 □ 코코아 경작지의 약 70퍼센트가 살충제 처리된다.

clean it, to protect it, or to give it special properties. ❑ *About 70% of the cocoa acreage is treated with insecticide.* ◢ V-T If you **treat** someone **to** something special which they will enjoy, you buy it or arrange it for them. ❑ *She was always treating him to ice cream.* ❑ *Tomorrow I'll treat myself to a day's gardening.* ◣ N-COUNT If you give someone a **treat**, you buy or arrange something special for them which they will enjoy. ❑ *Lettie had never yet failed to return from town without some special treat for him.*

◢ 타동사 대접하다 ❑ 그녀는 항상 그에게 아이스크림을 사주었다. ❑ 내일은 하루 종일 정원 가꾸기를 하며 즐겁게 보낼 것이다. ◣ 가산명사 특별 선물, 한턱 ❑ 레티는 그때까지 한 번도 시내에서 돌아올 때 그에게 특별 선물을 잊은 적이 없었다.

Word Partnership   *treat*의 연어

ADV.	treat **equally**, treat **fairly**, treat **well** ◢
N.	treat **with contempt/dignity/respect** ◢
	treat **people**, treat **women** ◢ ◣
	treat **AIDS**, treat **cancer**, treat **a disease**, **doctors** treat ◣

---

treat|ment ♦♦◇ /trítmənt/ (**treatments**) ◢ N-VAR **Treatment** is medical attention given to a sick or injured person or animal. ❑ *Many patients are not getting the medical treatment they need.* ❑ *...a veterinary surgeon who specializes in the treatment of cage birds.* ◣ N-UNCOUNT Your **treatment** of someone is the way you behave toward them or deal with them. ❑ *We don't want any special treatment.* ◤ N-VAR **Treatment** of something involves putting a particular substance onto or into it, in order to clean it, to protect it, or to give it special properties. ❑ *There should be greater treatment of sewage before it is discharged.* →see **cancer**, **illness**

◢ 가산명사 또는 불가산명사 치료 ❑ 많은 환자들이 필요한 의학적 치료를 받지 못하고 있다. ❑ 새장에 넣어 기르는 새들 치료에 전문인 수의사 ◣ 불가산명사 대우 ❑ 우리는 어떠한 특별 대우를 원하지 않는다. ◤ 가산명사 또는 불가산명사 처리 ❑ 하수를 내보내기 전에 더 광범위한 처리 과정이 있어야만 한다.

Word Partnership   *treatment*의 연어

V.	**get/receive** treatment, **give** treatment, **undergo** treatment ◢
N.	treatment **of addiction**, **AIDS** treatment, **cancer** treatment,
	treatment **center**, treatment **of an illness** ◢
	treatment **of prisoners** ◣
	treatment **plant**, **water** treatment ◤
ADJ.	**effective** treatment, **medical** treatment ◢
	better treatment, **equal** treatment, **fair** treatment, **humane** treatment ◣
	special treatment ◣ ◤

---

trea|ty ♦♦◇ /tríti/ (**treaties**) N-COUNT A **treaty** is a written agreement between countries in which they agree to do a particular thing or to help each other. ❑ *...negotiations over a 1992 treaty on global warming.*

가산명사 조약 ❑ 지구 온난화에 관한 1992년 조약에 대한 협상

tre|ble /trébəl/ (**trebles, trebling, trebled**) ◢ V-T/V-I If something **trebles** or if you **treble** it, it becomes three times greater in number or amount than it was. ❑ *They will have to pay much more when rents treble in January.* ◣ PREDET If one thing is **treble** the size or amount of another thing, it is three times greater in size or amount. [PREDET det n] ❑ *More than 7 million shares changed hands, treble the normal daily average.*

◢ 타동사/자동사 3배로 되다; 3배로 하다 ❑ 그들은 1월에 임대료가 세 배가 되면 훨씬 돈을 더 많이 내야 할 것이다. ◣ 전치 한정사 3배의 ❑ 평일 평균의 3배인 7백만 이상의 주식이 다른 사람들 손에 넘어갔다.

tree ♦♦◇ /trí/ (**trees**) N-COUNT A **tree** is a tall plant that has a hard trunk, branches, and leaves. ❑ *I planted those apple trees.* →see **forest**, **plant** →see Word Web: **tree**

가산명사 나무 ❑ 내가 저 사과나무들을 심었다.

trek /trék/ (**treks, trekking, trekked**) ◢ V-I If you **trek** somewhere, you go on a journey across difficult country, usually on foot. ❑ *...trekking through the jungles.* ● N-COUNT **Trek** is also a noun. ❑ *He is on a trek through the South Gobi desert.* ◣ V-I If you **trek** somewhere, you go there rather slowly and unwillingly, usually because you are tired. ❑ *They trekked from shop to shop in search of white knee-length socks.*

◢ 자동사 (주로 걸어서) 힘들게 여행하다 ❑ 정글 트레킹 ● 가산명사 오지 여행 ❑ 그는 지금 남고비 사막을 오지 여행 중이다. ◣ 자동사 천천히 가다 ❑ 그들은 무릎까지 오는 흰 양말을 찾으려고 가게마다 돌아다녔다.

Word Link   *trem* ≈ shaking : *tremble, tremendous, tremor*

---

trem|ble /trémbəl/ (**trembles, trembling, trembled**) ◢ V-I If you **tremble**, you shake slightly because you are frightened or cold. ❑ *His mouth became dry, his eyes widened, and he began to tremble all over.* ❑ *Gil was white and trembling with anger.* ● N-SING **Tremble** is also a noun. ❑ *I will never forget the look on the patient's face, the tremble in his hand.* ◣ V-I If something **trembles**, it shakes slightly. [LITERARY] ❑ *He felt the earth tremble under him.* ◤ V-I If your voice **trembles**, it sounds unsteady and uncertain, usually because you are upset or nervous. [LITERARY] ❑ *His voice trembled, on the verge of tears.* ● N-SING **Tremble** is also a noun. ❑ *"Please understand this," she began, a tremble in her voice.*

◢ 자동사 떨다 ❑ 그는 입이 말랐고, 눈은 휘둥그레졌으며, 온몸을 떨기 시작했다. ❑ 질은 화가 나서 하얗게 질려서 떨고 있었다. ● 단수명사 떨림 ❑ 나는 그 환자의 표정과 떨고 있던 손을 결코 잊을 수 없을 것이다. ◣ 자동사 진동하다 [문예체] ❑ 그는 발밑에서 땅이 진동하는 것을 느꼈다. ◤ 자동사 떨리다 [문예체] ❑ 그는 목소리가 떨리며 금방이라도 울 것 같았다. ● 단수명사 떨림 ❑ "제발 이걸 좀 이해해 주세요." 그녀는 떨리는 목소리로 말을 시작했다.

Word Web   tree

Trees are one of the oldest living things. They are also the largest **plant**. Some scientists believe that the largest living thing on Earth is a **coniferous** giant **redwood** tree named General Grant. Other scientists point to a huge **grove** of **deciduous** aspen trees known as Pando. This grove is a single plant because all of the trees grow from the root system of just one tree. Pando covers more than 106 acres. Some aspen trees **germinate** from seeds, but most result from natural cloning. In this process the parent tree sends up new **sprouts** from its root system. Fossil records show tree clones may live up to a million years.

A

Word Link

trem ≈ shaking : tremble, tremendous, tremor

tre|men|dous ♦◇◇ /trɪmɛndəs/ ■ ADJ You use **tremendous** to emphasize how strong a feeling or quality is, or how large an amount is. [INFORMAL, EMPHASIS] ❑ I felt a tremendous pressure on my chest. ● **tre|men|dous|ly** ADV ❑ I thought they played tremendously well, didn't you? ■ ADJ You can describe someone or something as **tremendous** when you think they are very good or very impressive. [INFORMAL] ❑ I thought it was absolutely tremendous.

■ 형용사 엄청난 [비격식체, 강조] ❑ 나는 가슴에 엄청난 압박감을 느꼈다. ● 굉장히 부사 ❑ 나는 그들이 굉장히 잘한다고 생각했는데, 넌? ■ 형용사 근사한, 대단한 [비격식체] ❑ 내 생각에 그것은 아주 근사했다.

trem|or /trɛmər/ (**tremors**) ■ N-COUNT A **tremor** is a small earthquake. ❑ The earthquake sent tremors through the region. ■ N-COUNT If an event causes a **tremor** in a group or organization, it threatens to make the group or organization less strong or stable. ❑ News of 160 redundancies had sent tremors through the community. ■ N-COUNT A **tremor** is a shaking of your body or voice that you cannot control. ❑ He felt a tremor in his arms.

■ 가산명사 미진(微震) ❑ 그 지진이 일어날 때 그 지방 전체에 미진이 있었다. ■ 가산명사 불안감 ❑ 160명이 감원된다는 소식은 그 사람들 모두에게 불안감을 퍼뜨렸다. ■ 가산명사 전율 ❑ 그는 두 팔에 전율을 느꼈다.

trench /trɛntʃ/ (**trenches**) ■ N-COUNT A **trench** is a long narrow channel that is cut into the ground, for example in order to lay pipes or get rid of water. ■ N-COUNT A **trench** is a long narrow channel in the ground used by soldiers in order to protect themselves from the enemy. People often refer to the battle grounds of the First World War in Northern France and Belgium as **the trenches**. ❑ We fought with them in the trenches.

■ 가산명사 도랑 ■ 가산명사 참호; 제1차 세계 대전 때의 전장 ❑ 우리는 전장에서 그들과 함께 싸웠다.

trend ♦◇◇ /trɛnd/ (**trends**) ■ N-COUNT A **trend** is a change or development towards something new or different. ❑ This is a growing trend. ❑ ...a trend towards part-time employment. ■ N-COUNT To set a **trend** means to do something that becomes accepted or fashionable, and that a lot of other people copy. ❑ The record has already proved a success and may well start a trend.
→see **population**

■ 가산명사 추세 ❑ 이것은 점점 성장해 가는 추세이다. ❑ 임시직 채용으로 가는 추세 ■ 가산명사 유행 ❑ 그 음반은 이미 성공을 했고 당연히 유행이 될 것이다.

Thesaurus

trend의 참조어

N.   craze, fad, style ■

Word Partnership

trend의 연어

ADJ.   **overall** trend, **upward** trend ■
current trend, **disturbing** trend, **latest** trend, **new** trend, **recent** trend ■ ■
V.   **continue a** trend, **reverse a** trend, **start a** trend ■ ■

trendy /trɛndi/ (**trendier, trendiest**) ADJ If you say that something or someone is **trendy**, you mean that they are very fashionable and modern. [INFORMAL] ❑ ...a trendy London night club.

형용사 최신 유행의 [비격식체] ❑ 런던의 최신 유행 나이트클럽

trepi|da|tion /trɛpɪdeɪʃⁿn/ N-UNCOUNT **Trepidation** is fear or anxiety about something that you are going to do or experience. [FORMAL] ❑ It was with some trepidation that I viewed the prospect of cycling across Uganda.

불가산명사 불안함 [격식체] ❑ 나는 약간 불안해 하면서 자전거로 우간다를 횡단하는 계획을 살펴보았다.

tres|pass /trɛspəs, -pæs/ (**trespasses, trespassing, trespassed**) V-I If someone **trespasses**, they go onto someone else's land without their permission. ❑ They were trespassing on private property. ● N-VAR **Trespass** is the act of trespassing. ❑ You could be prosecuted for trespass.

자동사 무단 침입하다 ❑ 그들은 사유지를 무단 침입하고 있었다. ● 가산명사 또는 불가산명사 무단 침입 ❑ 너는 무단 침입으로 고소당할 수도 있다.

tri|al ♦◇◇ /traɪəl/ (**trials**) ■ N-VAR A **trial** is a formal meeting in a law court, at which a judge and jury listen to evidence and decide whether a person is guilty of a crime. ❑ New evidence showed the police lied at the trial. ❑ He's awaiting trial in a military court on charges of plotting against the state. ■ N-COUNT A **trial** is an experiment in which you test something by using it or doing it for a period of time to see how well it works. If something is **on trial**, it is being tested in this way. ❑ They have been treated with this drug in clinical trials. ❑ I took the car out for a trial on the roads. ■ N-COUNT If someone gives you a **trial** for a job, or if you are **on trial**, you do the job for a short period of time to see if you are suitable for it. [usu sing, also on N] ❑ He had just given a trial to a young woman who said she had previous experience. ■ N-COUNT If you refer to the **trials of** a situation, you mean the unpleasant things that you experience in it. ❑ ...the trials of adolescence. ■ PHRASE If you do something **by trial and error**, you try several different methods of doing it until you find the method that works properly. ❑ Many drugs were found by trial and error. ■ PHRASE If someone is **on trial**, they are being tried in a court of law. ❑ He is currently on trial accused of serious drugs charges. ■ PHRASE If you say that someone or something is **on trial**, you mean that they are in a situation where people are observing them to see whether they succeed or fail. ❑ The President will be drawn into a damaging battle in which his credentials will be on trial. ■ PHRASE If someone **stands trial**, they are tried in court for a crime they are accused of. ❑ He was found to be mentally unfit to stand trial.
→see Word Web: **trial**

■ 가산명사 또는 불가산명사 재판 ❑ 새로운 증거로 경찰 측이 재판에서 거짓말을 했다는 사실이 드러났다. ❑ 그는 국가에 대한 반역 음모를 꾸민 죄로 군사 법정에서의 재판을 기다리고 있다. ■ 가산명사 또는 불가산명사 시험, 실험; 시험 중에 있는 ❑ 임상 실험에서 그들에게 이 약을 투여해 보았다. ❑ 나는 도로 시운전을 해 보려고 차를 가지고 나왔다. ■ 가산명사 시보; 시보로 일하는 ❑ 그는 이전 경험이 있다고 말했던 한 젊은 여자에게 막 시보 자리를 준 참이었다. ■ 가산명사 시련 ❑ 사춘기 때의 시련 ■ 구 시행착오를 통해 ❑ 많은 약품들이 시행착오를 거치면서 개발되었다. ■ 구 재판을 받는 중인 ❑ 그는 현재 심각한 마약 혐의들로 고발되어 재판을 받고 있다. ■ 구 시험받는 ❑ 대통령은 그의 능력을 시험하게 될 그 불리한 전투에 개입되게 될 것이다. ■ 구 재판받다 ❑ 그는 재판을 받을 만큼 정신이 온전하지 않은 것으로 밝혀졌다.

Word Partnership

trial의 연어

ADJ.   **civil** trial, **fair** trial, **federal** trial, **speedy** trial, **upcoming** trial ■
clinical trial ■
N.   trial **date**, **jury** trial, **murder** trial, **outcome of a** trial ■
trial **and error** ■
V.   **await** trial, **bring** someone **to** trial, **face** trial, **go on** trial, **put on** trial ■ ■

Word Web   trial

Many countries guarantee the right to a **trial** by jury. The **judge** begins by explaining the **charges** against the **defendant**. Next the defendant **pleads guilty** or not guilty. Then the **lawyers** for the **plaintiff** and the defendant present **evidence**. Both **attorneys** interview **witnesses**. They can also question each other's **clients**. Sometimes the lawyers go back and **cross-examine** witnesses about **testimony** they gave earlier. When they finish, the **jury** meets to **deliberate**. They deliver their **verdict** and the judge **pronounces** the **sentence**. At this point, the plaintiff may be able to **appeal** the verdict and request a new trial.

Word Link   tri ≈ three : triangle, trilogy, trio

tri|an|gle /traɪæŋgᵊl/ (**triangles**) **1** N-COUNT A **triangle** is an object, arrangement, or flat shape with three straight sides and three angles. ❑ *This design is in pastel colors with three rectangles and three triangles.* ❑ *Its outline roughly forms an equilateral triangle.* **2** N-COUNT The **triangle** is a musical instrument that consists of a piece of metal shaped like a triangle. You play it by hitting it with a short metal bar. ❑ *My musical career consisted of playing the triangle in kindergarten.* →see **circle**

1 가산명사 삼각형 ❑ 이 디자인에는 직사각형 세 개와 삼각형 세 개가 들어 있고 파스텔 색조이다. ❑ 그것의 외형은 대략 등변 삼각형을 이룬다. **2** 가산명사 트라이앵글 (악기) ❑ 내 연주 경력은 유치원 시절에 트라이앵글을 연주했던 것뿐이다.

tri|an|gu|lar /traɪæŋgyələr/ ADJ Something that is **triangular** is in the shape of a triangle. ❑ *...cottages around a triangular green.*

형용사 삼각의 ❑ 삼각형의 풀밭에 둘러싸인 오두막들

trib|al /traɪbᵊl/ ADJ **Tribal** is used to describe things relating to or belonging to tribes and the way that they are organized. ❑ *They would go back to their tribal lands.*

형용사 부족의 ❑ 그들은 자신들의 부족의 땅으로 되돌아갈 것이었다.

tribe /traɪb/ (**tribes**) N-COUNT-COLL **Tribe** is sometimes used to refer to a group of people of the same race, language, and customs, especially in a developing country. Some people disapprove of this use. ❑ *...three-hundred members of the Xhosa tribe.*

가산명사-집합 부족, 종족 ❑ 300명의 코사 족 사람들

tribu|la|tion /trɪbyəleɪᵊn/ (**tribulations**) N-VAR You can refer to the suffering or difficulty that you experience in a particular situation as **tribulations**. [FORMAL] ❑ *...the trials and tribulations of everyday life.*

가산명사 또는 불가산명사 고난 [격식체] ❑ 일상 생활의 시련과 고난

tri|bu|nal /traɪbyun ᵊl/ (**tribunals**) N-COUNT-COLL A **tribunal** is a special court or committee that is appointed to deal with particular problems. ❑ *His case comes before an industrial tribunal in March.*

가산명사-집합 특별 위원회, 심사 위원회 ❑ 그의 사건은 3월에 산업 특별 위원회에 제기된다.

tribute /trɪbyut/ (**tributes**) **1** N-VAR A **tribute** is something that you say, do, or make to show your admiration and respect for someone. ❑ *The song is a tribute to Roy Orbison.* **2** N-SING If one thing is **a tribute to** another, the first thing is the result of the second and shows how good it is. ❑ *His success has been a tribute to hard work, to professionalism.*

1 가산명사 또는 불가산명사 (감사나 존경의 표시로) 바치는 것 ❑ 이 곡은 로이 오비슨에게 바치는 노래이다. **2** 단수명사 ~의 가치를 입증하는 것 ❑ 그의 성공은 근면과 전문가 정신의 가치를 입증해 주는 것이었다.

trick ◇◇◇ /trɪk/ (**tricks, tricking, tricked**) **1** N-COUNT A **trick** is an action that is intended to deceive someone. ❑ *We are playing a trick on a man who keeps bothering me.* **2** V-T If someone **tricks** you, they deceive you, often in order to make you do something. ❑ *Stephen is going to be pretty upset when he finds out how you tricked him.* ❑ *His family tricked him into going to Pakistan, and once he was there, they took away his passport.* **3** N-COUNT A **trick** is a clever or skillful action that someone does in order to entertain people. ❑ *He shows me card tricks.* **4** N-COUNT A **trick** is a clever way of doing something. ❑ *Everything I cooked was a trick of my mother's.* **5** →see also **hat-trick 6** PHRASE If something **does the trick**, it achieves what you wanted. [INFORMAL] ❑ *Sometimes a few choice words will do the trick.* **7** PHRASE If someone tries **every trick in the book**, they try every possible thing that they can think of in order to achieve something. [INFORMAL] ❑ *Companies are using every trick in the book to stay one step in front of their competitors.* **8** PHRASE The **tricks of the trade** are the quick and clever ways of doing something that are known by people who regularly do a particular activity. ❑ *To get you started, we have asked five successful writers to reveal some of the tricks of the trade.*

1 가산명사 골탕 먹임, 속임수 ❑ 우리는 나를 계속 괴롭히는 사람을 골탕 먹이려고 한다. **2** 타동사 속이다 ❑ 스티븐이 네가 그를 어떻게 속였는지 알면 굉장히 화낼 거야. ❑ 그의 가족들이 그를 속여서 파키스탄으로 가도록 했고, 일단 그곳에 가자 그의 여권을 빼앗아 버렸다. **3** 가산명사 묘기 ❑ 그는 내게 카드 묘기를 보여 준다. **4** 가산명사 비법, 비결 ❑ 내가 하는 요리는 모두 엄마에게서 배운 비법이었다. **6** 구 목적을 달성하다, 효과가 있다 [비격식체] ❑ 때로는 몇 마디 가려 뽑은 말로도 목적을 달성할 수 있을 것이다. **7** 구 모든 가능한 방법 [비격식체] ❑ 회사들은 경쟁 업체들보다 한 발이라도 앞서기 위해 가능한 모든 방법을 사용하고 있다. **8** 구 요령, 비법 ❑ 당신을 준비시키기 위해서, 우리는 다섯 명의 성공한 작가들에게 그들의 성공 요령을 알려 달라고 요청했습니다.

Word Partnership   trick의 연어

ADJ.	cheap trick	**1**
	old trick	**1 3**
	clever trick	**1 3 4**
V.	play a trick	**1**
	try to trick *someone*	**2**
	do the trick	**6**
N.	card trick	**3**
	every trick in the book	**7**

trick|le /trɪkᵊl/ (**trickles, trickling, trickled**) **1** V-T/V-I When a liquid **trickles**, or when you **trickle** it, it flows slowly in very small amounts. ❑ *A tear trickled down the old man's cheek.* ● N-COUNT **Trickle** is also a noun. ❑ *There was not so much as a trickle of water.* **2** V-I When people or things **trickle** in a particular direction, they move there slowly in small groups or amounts, rather than all together. ❑ *Some donations are already trickling in.* ● N-COUNT **Trickle** is also a noun. ❑ *The flood of cars has now slowed to a trickle.*

1 타동사/자동사 (액체가) 조금 흐르다 ❑ 그 노인의 볼을 타고 눈물이 한 줄기 흘러내렸다. ● 가산명사 물방울; 약간 흐름 ❑ 물이 한 방울도 없었다. **2** 자동사 조금씩 움직이다 ❑ 기부금이 이미 조금씩 들어오고 있다. ● 가산명사 조금씩 움직임 ❑ 밀려드는 차량이 이제 점점 줄어들고 있다.

tricky /trɪki/ (**trickier, trickiest**) ADJ If you describe a task or problem as **tricky**, you mean that it is difficult to do or deal with. ❑ *Parking can be tricky in the town center.*

형용사 곤란한 ❑ 시내 중심가에서는 주차하기가 곤란할 것 같다.

tried /traɪd/ ADJ **Tried** is used in the expressions **tried and tested**, **tried and trusted**, and **tried and true**, which describe a product or method that has already been used and has been found to be successful. [ADJ and adj] ❑ ...over 1000 tried-and-tested recipes.
→see also **try**

형용사 테스트를 통해 효능이 입증된; 효능이 입증되어 믿을 수 있는 ❑ 테스트를 통해 맛이 입증된 천 가지도 넘는 요리법

tri|fle /traɪfᵊl/ (trifles) ■ PHRASE You can use **a trifle** to mean slightly or to a small extent, especially in order to make something you say seem less extreme. [VAGUENESS] ❑ As a photographer, he'd found both locations just a trifle disappointing. ② N-COUNT A **trifle** is something that is considered to have little importance, value, or significance. ❑ He had no money to spare on trifles. ③ N-VAR **Trifle** is a cold British dessert made of layers of sponge cake, jelly, fruit, and custard, and usually covered with cream. ❑ ...a bowl of trifle.

■ 구 조금 [짐작투] ❑ 사진작가로서, 그는 그 두 장소 모두 조금 실망스럽다고 느꼈다. ② 가산명사 사소한 일 ❑ 그는 사소한 일에 쓸 돈은 전혀 없었다. ③ 가산명사 또는 불가산명사 트라이플 (스펀지 케이크 등에 크림을 바른 영국식 디저트) ❑ 트라이플 한 접시

trig|ger ♦◇◇ /trɪgər/ (triggers, triggering, triggered) ■ N-COUNT The **trigger** of a gun is a small lever which you pull to fire it. ❑ A man pointed a gun at them and pulled the trigger. ② N-COUNT The **trigger** of a bomb is the device which causes it to explode. ❑ ...trigger devices for nuclear weapons. ③ V-T To **trigger** a bomb or system means to cause it to work. ❑ The thieves must have deliberately triggered the alarm and hidden inside the house. ④ V-T If something **triggers** an event or situation, it causes it to begin to happen or exist. ❑ ...the incident which triggered the outbreak of the First World War. ● PHRASAL VERB **Trigger off** means the same as. ❑ It is still not clear what events triggered off the demonstrations. ⑤ N-COUNT If something acts as a **trigger for** another thing such as an illness, event, or situation, the first thing causes the second thing to begin to happen or exist. ❑ Stress may act as a trigger for these illnesses.

■ 가산명사 방아쇠 ❑ 어떤 남자가 그들에게 총을 겨누고 방아쇠를 당겼다. ② 가산명사 (폭탄의) 폭발 장치 ❑ 핵무기의 폭발 장치 ③ 타동사 작동시키다 ❑ 그 도둑들은 일부러 경보 장치를 울리게 하고 집안에 숨어 있었음이 분명하다. ④ 타동사 야기하다 ❑ 1차 세계 대전의 발발을 야기했던 사건 ● 구동사 야기하다 ❑ 무슨 사건들이 그 시위를 야기했는지 아직도 분명하지 않다. ⑤ 가산명사 (유발시키는) 원인 ❑ 스트레스가 이런 질병을 유발시키는 원인으로 작용할지도 모른다.

tril|lion /trɪlyən/ (trillions)

> The plural form is **trillion** after a number, or after a word or expression referring to a number, such as "several" or "a few."

숫자 또는 'several', 'a few'와 같이 수를 지칭하는 단어나 표현 뒤에서 복수형은 trillion이다.

NUM A **trillion** is a million million. ❑ Between July 1st and October 1st, the central bank printed over 2 trillion roubles.

수사 1조 ❑ 7월 1일부터 10월 1일까지, 중앙은행은 2조 루브르 이상의 화폐를 발행했다.

┃ **Word Link**   tri ≈ three : triangle, trilogy, trio

tril|ogy /trɪlədʒi/ (trilogies) N-COUNT A **trilogy** is a series of three books, plays, or movies that have the same subject or the same characters. ❑ ...Laurie Lee's trilogy of autobiographical novels.

가산명사 (연극 등의) 3부작 ❑ 로리 리의 자서전적 소설 3부작

trim /trɪm/ (trimmer, trimmest, trims, trimming, trimmed) ■ ADJ Something that is **trim** is neat, and attractive. ❑ The neighbors' gardens were trim and neat. ② ADJ If you describe someone's figure as **trim**, you mean that it is attractive because there is no extra fat on their body. [APPROVAL] ❑ The driver was a trim young woman of perhaps thirty. ③ V-T If you **trim** something, for example someone's hair, you cut off small amounts of it in order to make it look neater. ❑ My friend trims my hair every eight weeks. ● N-SING **Trim** is also a noun. ❑ His hair needed a trim. ④ V-T If a government or other organization **trims** something such as a plan, policy, or amount, they reduce it slightly in extent or size. ❑ American companies looked at ways they could trim these costs. ⑤ V-T If something such as a piece of clothing **is trimmed with** a type of material or design, it is decorated with it, usually along its edges. [usu passive] ❑ ...jackets, which are then trimmed with crocheted flowers. ⑥ N-VAR The **trim** on something such as a piece of clothing is, for example along its edges, that is in a different color or material. ❑ ...a white satin scarf with black trim.

■ 형용사 손질이 잘 된 ❑ 이웃집 정원은 손질이 잘 되어 있고 말쑥했다. ② 형용사 (군살이 없이) 균형 잡힌 [마음에 듦] ❑ 그 운전자는 서른 살쯤으로 보이는 균형 잡힌 몸매의 젊은 여자였다. ③ 타동사 (머리를) 다듬다, 조금 깎다 ❑ 내 친구가 8주마다 내 머리를 깎아 준다. ● 단수명사 다듬기 ❑ 그의 머리를 다듬을 때가 되어 있었다. ④ 타동사 축소하다 ❑ 미국ական 회사들은 이런 비용을 축소할 방법을 모색했다. ⑤ 타동사 (가장자리가) 장식되다 ❑ 꽃 모양 코바늘뜨기로 가장자리를 장식한 재킷 ⑥ 가산명사 또는 불가산명사 (가장자리) 장식 ❑ 검은색 가장자리 장식이 되어 있는 흰색 공단 스카프

trim|ming /trɪmɪŋ/ (trimmings) ■ N-VAR The **trimming** on something such as a piece of clothing is the decoration, for example along its edges, that is in a different color or material. ❑ ...the lace trimming on her satin nightgown. ② N-PLURAL **Trimmings** are pieces of something, usually food, which are left over after you have cut away what you need. ❑ Use any pastry trimmings to decorate the apples.

■ 가산명사 또는 불가산명사 (가장자리의) 장식 ❑ 그녀의 공단 잠옷에 되어 있는 레이스 장식 ② 복수명사 (원하는 부분을 잘라 내고) 남은 부분 ❑ 사과를 장식할 때는 페스트리를 만들고 남은 부분을 사용해라.

trio /triou/ (trios) N-COUNT-COLL A **trio** is a group of three people together, especially musicians or singers, or a group of three things that have something in common. ❑ ...classy American songs from a Texas trio.

가산명사-집합 3인조 그룹 ❑ 텍사스 3인조 그룹이 부른 수준 높은 미국 노래들

trip ♦♦◇ /trɪp/ (trips, tripping, tripped) ■ N-COUNT A **trip** is a journey that you make to a particular place. ❑ On the Thursday we went out on a day trip. →see also **round trip**

■ 가산명사 여행 ❑ 목요일에 우리는 당일 여행을 떠났다.

② V-I If you **trip** when you are walking, you knock your foot against something and fall or nearly fall. ❑ She tripped and fell last night and broke her hip. ● PHRASAL VERB **Trip up** means the same as. ❑ I tripped up and hurt my foot. ③ V-T If you **trip** someone who is walking or running, you put your foot or something else in front of them, so that they knock their own foot against it and fall or nearly fall. ❑ One guy stuck his foot out and tried to trip me. ● PHRASAL VERB **Trip up** means the same as. ❑ He made a sudden dive for Uncle Jim's legs to try to trip him up.

② 자동사 헛디뎌 넘어지다, -에 걸려 비틀거리다 ❑ 그녀는 어젯밤에 발을 헛디뎌 넘어져서 고관절이 부러졌다. ● 구동사 헛디뎌 넘어지다, -에 걸려 비틀거리다 ❑ 나는 헛디뎌 넘어져서 발을 다쳤다. ③ 타동사 발을 걸어 넘어뜨리다 ❑ 어떤 남자가 발을 뻗어서 내 발을 걸어 넘어뜨리려고 했다. ● 구동사 발을 걸어 넘어뜨리다 ❑ 그는 짐 아저씨의 발을 걸어 넘어뜨리려고 갑자기 아저씨의 다리를 잡으러 뛰어들었다.

> The noun **travel** is used to talk about the general activity of traveling. It is either uncount or plural. You cannot say "a travel," you would use the word **trip** or **journey** instead. ❑ First-class rail travel to Paris or Brussels is included... We were going to go on a trip to Florida together.

명사 travel은 일반적인 여행 행위에 대해 말할 때 쓰는데, 불가산 명사나 복수로 쓴다. a travel 이라고는 하지 않고, 대신 trip이나 journey를 쓸 수 있다. ❑ 파리나 브뤼셀로 가는 일등칸 기차 여행이 포함되어 있다... 우리는 플로리다로 함께 여행을 가려고 했다.

┃ **Thesaurus**   trip의 참조어

N.   excursion, expedition, journey, voyage ■
V.   fall, slip, stumble ②

	Word Partnership	*trip*의 연어
N.	boat trip, bus trip, business trip, field trip, trip home, return trip, shopping trip, train trip, vacation trip 🔟	
V.	cancel a trip, make a trip, plan a trip, return from a trip, take a trip 🔟	
ADJ.	free trip, last trip, long trip, next trip, recent trip, safe trip, short trip 🔟	

tri|ple /trɪpᵊl/ (triples, tripling, tripled) 🔟 ADJ **Triple** means consisting of three things or parts. [ADJ n] ❑ *...a triple somersault.* 🔟 V-T/V-I If something **triples** or if you **triple** it, it becomes three times as large in size or number. ❑ *I got a fantastic new job and my salary tripled.* ❑ *The Exhibition has tripled in size from last year.* 🔟 PREDET If something is **triple the** amount or size of another thing, it is three times as large. [PREDET the n] ❑ *The mine reportedly had an accident rate triple the national average.*

tri|plet /trɪplɪt/ (triplets) N-COUNT **Triplets** are three children born at the same time to the same mother. ❑ *"Guess what? Katinka had triplets - all healthy."*

tri|pod /traɪpɒd/ (tripods) N-COUNT A **tripod** is a stand with three legs that is used to support something such as a camera or a telescope.

tri|umph ♦◇◇ /traɪʌmf/ (triumphs, triumphing, triumphed) 🔟 N-VAR A **triumph** is a great success or achievement, often one that has been gained with a lot of skill or effort. ❑ *The championships proved to be a personal triumph for the coach, Dave Donovan.* 🔟 N-UNCOUNT **Triumph** is a feeling of great satisfaction and pride resulting from a success or victory. ❑ *Her sense of triumph was short-lived.* 🔟 V-I If someone or something **triumphs**, they gain complete success, control, or victory, often after a long or difficult struggle. ❑ *All her life, Kelly has stuck with difficult tasks and challenges, and triumphed.*

tri|um|phant /traɪʌmfənt/ ADJ Someone who is **triumphant** has gained a victory or succeeded in something and feels very happy about it. ❑ *The captain's voice was triumphant.* ● **tri|um|phant|ly** ADV ❑ *They marched triumphantly into the capital.*

triv|ia /trɪviə/ N-UNCOUNT **Trivia** is unimportant facts or details that are considered to be interesting rather than serious or useful. ❑ *The two men chatted about such trivia as their favorite kinds of fast food.*

triv|ial /trɪviəl/ ADJ If you describe something as **trivial**, you think that it is unimportant and not serious. ❑ *The director tried to wave aside these issues as trivial details that could be settled later.*

triv|ial|ize /trɪviəlaɪz/ (trivializes, trivializing, trivialized) [BRIT also **trivialise**] V-T If you say that someone **trivializes** something important, you disapprove of them because they make it seem less important, serious, and complex than it is. [DISAPPROVAL] ❑ *It never ceases to amaze me how the business world continues to trivialize the world's environmental problems.*

trod /trɒd/ **Trod** is the past tense of **tread**.

trod|den /trɒdᵊn/ **Trodden** is the past participle of **tread**.

trol|ley /trɒli/ (trolleys) 🔟 N-COUNT A **trolley** or **trolley car** is an electric vehicle for carrying people which travels on rails in the streets of a city or town. [AM; BRIT **tram**] ❑ *He took a northbound trolley on State Street.* 🔟 N-COUNT A **trolley** is an object with wheels that you use to transport heavy things such as shopping or luggage. [BRIT; AM **cart**] ❑ *A porter relieved her of the three large cases she had been pushing on a trolley.* 🔟 N-COUNT A **trolley** is a small table on wheels which is used for serving drinks or food. [BRIT; AM **cart**] ❑ *The waiter had brought the sweet trolley.* 🔟 N-COUNT A **trolley** is a bed on wheels for moving patients in a hospital. [BRIT; AM **gurney**] ❑ *She was left on a hospital trolley for 14 hours without even a glass of water.*

trom|bone /trɒmboʊn/ (trombones) N-VAR A **trombone** is a large musical instrument of the brass family. It consists of two long oval tubes, one of which can be pushed backward and forward to play different notes. [oft the n] ❑ *Her husband had played the trombone in the band for a decade.* →see **orchestra**

troop ♦♦◇ /trup/ (troops, trooping, trooped) 🔟 N-PLURAL **Troops** are soldiers, especially when they are in a large organized group doing a particular task. ❑ *The next phase of the operation will involve the deployment of more than 35,000 troops from a dozen countries.* 🔟 N-COUNT-COLL A **troop** is a group of soldiers. ❑ *...a troop of American Marines.* 🔟 N-COUNT A **troop** of people or animals is a group of them. ❑ *The whole troop of men and women wore their hair fairly short.* 🔟 V-I If people **troop** somewhere, they walk there in a group, often in a sad or tired way. [INFORMAL] ❑ *They all trooped back to the house for a rest.* →see **army**

troop|er /trupər/ (troopers) 🔟 N-COUNT; N-TITLE A **trooper** is a soldier of low rank in the cavalry or in an armored regiment in the army. ❑ *...a trooper from the 7th Cavalry.* 🔟 N-COUNT In the United States, a **trooper** is a police officer in a state police force. ❑ *Once long ago he had considered becoming a state trooper.*

tro|phy /troʊfi/ (trophies) 🔟 N-COUNT A **trophy** is a prize, for example a silver cup, that is given to the winner of a competition or race. ❑ *The special trophy for the best foreign rider went to the U.S.A.'s Chris Read.* 🔟 N-COUNT A **trophy** is something that you keep in order to show that you have done something very difficult. ❑ *His office was lined with animal heads, trophies of his hunting hobby.*

tropi|cal /trɒpɪkᵊl/ 🔟 ADJ **Tropical** means belonging to or typical of the tropics. [ADJ n] ❑ *...tropical diseases.* 🔟 ADJ **Tropical** weather is hot and damp weather that people believe to be typical of the tropics. ❑ *The cool, sweet milk is just what you need in the tropical heat.* →see **hurricane**

🔟 형용사 3회의, 3종의, 3종의 ❑ 3회 공중제비 넘기 🔟 타동사/자동사 3배가 되다; ~을 3배로 만들다 ❑ 나는 너무나 괜찮은 새 직장을 얻었는데, 월급이 3배나 돼. ❑ 그 전시회는 작년의 3배 규모이다. 🔟 전치 한정사 ~의 3배의 ❑ 보도에 의하면, 그 광산에서는 전국 평균 사고율의 3배나 되는 사고가 일어난다고 했다.

가산명사 세 쌍둥이 ❑ "너 이거 아니? 카틴카가 세 쌍둥이를 나았대. 모두 다 건강하게."

가산명사 삼각대

🔟 가산명사 또는 불가산명사 승리 ❑ 그 우승은 코치인 데이브 도노반 개인의 승리임이 입증되었다. 🔟 불가산명사 승리의 기쁨 ❑ 그녀의 승리의 기쁨은 오래가지 않았다. 🔟 자동사 승리를 거두다 ❑ 켈리는 평생 동안 어려운 임무와 도전들을 치뤄냈고 승리도 거두었다.

형용사 의기양양한 ❑ 그 선장의 목소리는 의기양양했다. ● 의기양양하게 부사 ❑ 그들은 의기양양하게 수도로 행진해 들어왔다.

불가산명사 하찮은 것 ❑ 그 두 남자는 자신들이 제일 좋아하는 패스트푸드 같은 하찮은 것에 관해 잡담했다.

형용사 하찮은 ❑ 그 감독은 이런 문제들을 나중에 해결해도 될 하찮은 것으로 무시하려 했다.

[영국영어 trivialise] 타동사 하찮게 여기다 [탐탁찮음] ❑ 기업계가 지구의 환경 문제를 얼마나 하찮게 여기는가에 대해 나는 늘 놀라고 있다.

tread의 과거

tread의 과거 분사

🔟 가산명사 시내 전차 [미국영어; 영국영어 tram] ❑ 그는 스테이트 스트리트에서 북쪽행 시내 전차를 탔다. 🔟 가산명사 손수레 [영국영어; 미국영어 cart] ❑ 어떤 짐꾼이 그녀가 손수레에 싣고 밀고 가던 큰 가방 세 개를 대신 밀어 주었다. 🔟 가산명사 (음식 등을 나르는) 손수레식 탁자 [영국영어; 미국영어 cart] ❑ 웨이터가 디저트를 손수레식 탁자에 내왔다. 🔟 가산명사 환자 운반용 침대 [영국영어; 미국영어 gurney] ❑ 그녀는 물 한 잔 마시지 못하고 14시간 동안 환자 운반용 침대에 남겨져 있었다.

가산명사 또는 불가산명사 트롬본 (악기) ❑ 그녀의 남편은 그 밴드에서 십 년간 트롬본을 연주했다.

🔟 복수명사 병력, 군대 ❑ 그 작전의 다음 단계에는 십여 개의 국가에서 3만 5천 명 이상의 병력이 배치될 것이다. 🔟 가산명사-집합 부대 ❑ 미 해병대 부대 🔟 가산명사 ~의 무리 ❑ 그 무리의 모든 남녀는 머리가 아주 짧았다. 🔟 자동사 무리지어 걸어가다 [비격식체] ❑ 그들은 쉬기 위해서 모두 무리지어 집으로 돌아갔다.

🔟 가산명사; 경칭명사 기병대 ❑ 제7 기병대의 기병 🔟 가산명사 (미국) 주 경찰관 ❑ 그는 옛날에 주 경찰이 되는 것을 한번 고려해 봤었다.

🔟 가산명사 우승컵 ❑ 가장 우수한 외국인 기수에게 수여하는 특별 우승컵은 미국의 크리스 리드에게 돌아갔다. 🔟 가산명사 전리품 ❑ 그의 사무실에는 자신이 취미로 하는 사냥의 전리품으로 동물들의 머리가 줄지어 나열되어 있었다.

🔟 형용사 열대 지방의 ❑ 열대병 🔟 형용사 열대성의 ❑ 열대성 더위에서는 시원하고 달콤한 우유가 바로 네게 필요한 것이다.

trop|ics /trɒpɪks/ N-PLURAL The **tropics** are the parts of the world that lie between two lines of latitude, the tropic of Cancer, 23½° north of the equator, and the tropic of Capricorn, 23½° south of the equator. ❑ *Being in the tropics meant that insects formed a large part of our life.*

복수명사 열대 지방 ❑ 열대 지방에서 산다는 것은 곤충들이 우리 생활의 아주 많은 부분을 차지하고 있다는 뜻이었다.

trot /trɒt/ (**trots, trotting, trotted**) ⓵ V-I If you **trot** somewhere, you move fairly fast at a speed between walking and running, taking small quick steps. ❑ *I trotted down the steps and out to the shed.* ● N-SING **Trot** is also a noun. ❑ *He walked briskly, but without breaking into a trot.* ② V-I When an animal such as a horse **trots**, it moves fairly fast, taking quick small steps. You can also say that the rider of the animal **is trotting**. ❑ *Alan took the reins and the small horse started trotting.* ● N-SING **Trot** is also a noun. ❑ *As they started up again, the horse broke into a brisk trot.*

⓵ 자동사 빠른 걸음으로 걷다, 종종걸음으로 걷다 ❑ 나는 계단을 빠르게 걸어 내려가서 헛간 쪽으로 갔다. ● 단수명사 빠른 걸음 ❑ 그는 빠르게 걷기는 않았지만 기운차게 걸어갔다. ② 자동사 (말이) 빨리 걷다; (기수가 말을) 빨리 걷게 하다 ❑ 알란은 고삐를 잡았고 그 작은 말은 빨리 걷기 시작했다. ● 단수명사 속보 ❑ 그들이 다시 고삐를 당기자, 그 말이 기운차게 빨리 걸었다.

trou|ble ♦♦◇ /trʌbʰl/ (**troubles, troubling, troubled**) ⓵ N-UNCOUNT You can refer to problems or difficulties as **trouble**. [oft in N, also N in pl] ❑ *I had trouble parking.* ❑ *You've caused us a lot of trouble.* ② N-SING If you say that one aspect of a situation is **the trouble**, you mean that it is the aspect which is causing problems or making the situation unsatisfactory. ❑ *The trouble is that these restrictions have remained while other things have changed.* ③ N-PLURAL Your **troubles** are the things that you are worried about. ❑ *She tells me her troubles. I tell her mine.* ④ N-UNCOUNT If you have kidney **trouble** or back **trouble**, for example, there is something wrong with your kidneys or your back. ❑ *An unsuitable bed is the most likely cause of back trouble.* ❑ *Her husband had never before had any heart trouble.* ⑤ N-UNCOUNT If there is **trouble** somewhere, especially in a public place, there is fighting or rioting there. [also N in pl] ❑ *Riot police are being deployed throughout the city to prevent any trouble.* ❑ *Fans who make trouble during the World Cup will be severely dealt with.* ⑥ N-UNCOUNT If you tell someone that it is **no trouble** to do something for them, you are saying politely that you can or will do it, because it is easy or convenient for you. [POLITENESS] ❑ *It's no trouble at all; on the contrary, it will be a great pleasure to help you.* ⑦ N-UNCOUNT If you say that a person or animal is **no trouble**, you mean that they are very easy to look after. ❑ *My little grandson is no trouble at all, but his 6-year-old elder sister is rude and selfish.* ⑧ V-T If something **troubles** you, it makes you feel rather worried. ❑ *Is anything troubling you?* ● **trou|bling** ADJ ❑ *But most troubling of all was the simple fact that nobody knew what was going on.* ⑨ V-T If a part of your body **troubles** you, it causes you physical pain or discomfort. ❑ *The ulcer had been troubling her for several years.* ⑩ V-T If you say that someone does **not trouble to** do something, you are critical of them because they do not do something that they should do and do not behave in the way that they should, and you think that this would require very little effort. [DISAPPROVAL] ❑ *He yawns, not troubling to cover his mouth.* ⑪ V-T You use **trouble** in expressions such as **I'm sorry to trouble you** when you are apologizing to someone for disturbing them in order to ask them something. [FORMULAE] ❑ *I'm sorry to trouble you, but I wondered if by any chance you know where he is.* ⑫ PHRASE If someone is **in trouble**, they are in a situation in which a person in authority is angry with them or is likely to punish them because they have done something wrong. ❑ *He was in trouble with his teachers.* ⑬ PHRASE If you **take the trouble to** do something, you do something which requires a small amount of additional effort. ❑ *He did not take the trouble to see the film before he attacked it.*

⓵ 불가산명사 고생 ❑ 나는 주차하느라 고생했다. ❑ 나 때문에 우리가 고생을 아주 많이 하고 있다. ② 단수명사 문제 ❑ 문제는, 다른 것들이 변했는데 이러한 규제들은 남아 있다는 것이다. ③ 복수명사 걱정거리 ❑ 그녀는 내게 자신의 걱정거리를 말하고 나는 내 걱정거리를 그녀에게 말한다. ④ 불가산명사 문제, 병 ❑ 부적합한 침대가 허리에 문제를 일으킬 가능성이 가장 높다. ❑ 그녀의 남편은 전에는 심장에 문제가 있었던 적이 한 번도 없었다. ⑤ 불가산명사 소요 사태, 발병 ❑ 폭동 진압 경찰이 한 건의 소요 사태라도 막기 위해 시 전역에 배치되고 있다. ❑ 월드컵 경기 동안 말썽을 피운 팬들을 엄하게 다룰 것이다. ⑥ 불가산명사 수고 [공손체] ❑ 전혀 수고로울 게 없어요. 오히려 당신을 돕게 된다면 너무나 기쁠 겁니다. ⑦ 불가산명사 성가시게 하다 [의례적인 표현] ❑ 내 어린 손자는 전혀 말썽을 피우지 않지만, 여섯 살 된 그 누나는 예의가 없고 이기적이다. ⑧ 타동사 걱정시키다 ❑ 무슨 걱정되는 게 있나요? ● 걱정스러운 형용사 ❑ 그러나 가장 걱정스러운 것은 누구도 무슨 일이 벌어지고 있는지를 모른다는 그 간단한 사실이었다. ⑨ 타동사 (병 등이) 괴롭히다 ❑ 궤양이 수년 동안 그녀를 괴롭히고 있었다. ⑩ 타동사 (해야 할 일을) 하다 [탐탁잖음] ❑ 그는 입을 가리지도 않고 하품을 한다. ⑪ 타동사 성가시게 하다 [의례적인 표현] ❑ 성가시게 해서 죄송합니다만, 혹시 그가 어디 있는지 아세요? ⑫ 구 문제가 생긴 ❑ 그는 선생님들과 문제가 좀 있었다. ⑬ 구 수고라서 ❑ 그는 그 영화를 혹평하기 전에 그것을 보는 것조차도 하지 않았다.

trou|bled /trʌbʰld/ ⓵ ADJ Someone who is **troubled** is worried because they have problems. ❑ *Rose sounded deeply troubled.* ② ADJ A **troubled** place, situation, organization, or time has many problems or conflicts. ❑ *There is much we can do to help this troubled country.*

⓵ 형용사 걱정스러워 하는 ❑ 로즈의 목소리는 꽹장히 걱정스러워 하는 것처럼 들렸다. ② 형용사 문제가 많은 ❑ 문제가 많은 이 나라를 위해서 우리가 할 수 있는 일은 많다.

trouble|maker /trʌbʰlmeɪkər/ (**troublemakers**) N-COUNT If you refer to someone as a **troublemaker**, you mean that they cause unpleasantness, quarrels, or fights, especially by encouraging people to oppose authority. [DISAPPROVAL] ❑ *The regional governor has been given powers to outlaw strikes and expel suspected troublemakers.*

가산명사 문제를 일으키는 사람, 말썽꾼 [탐탁잖음] ❑ 주 지사에게 파업을 불법화하고 문제를 일으키는 것으로 의심되는 사람들을 제명할 수 있는 권한이 부여되어 있다.

trouble|shooter /trʌbʰlʃutər/ (**troubleshooters**) also **trouble-shooter** N-COUNT A **troubleshooter** is a person whose job is to solve major problems or difficulties that occur in a company or government. ❑ *The United Nations dispatched a team of troubleshooters to Somalia today.*

가산명사 (회사나 국가 간의) 분쟁 중재자 ❑ 유엔은 오늘 소말리아로 분쟁 중재 팀을 파견했다.

Word Link   some ≈ causing: awesome, fearsome, troublesome

trou|ble|some /trʌbʰlsəm/ ADJ You use **troublesome** to describe something or someone that causes annoying problems or difficulties. ❑ *He needed surgery to cure a troublesome back injury.*

형용사 골칫거리인 ❑ 그는 골칫거리인 허리 부상을 치료하기 위해서 수술이 필요했다.

trough /trɒf, BRIT trɒf/ (troughs) ◼ N-COUNT A **trough** is a long narrow container from which farm animals drink or eat. ❑ *The old stone cattle trough still sits by the main entrance.* ◻ N-COUNT A **trough** is a low area between two big waves on the sea. ❑ *The boat rolled heavily in the troughs between the waves.* ◼ N-COUNT A **trough** is a low point in a process that has regular high and low points, for example a period in business when people do not produce as much as usual. ❑ *Looking back afterwards you will see that this was not a terminal trough in your career.* ◻ N-COUNT A **trough** of low pressure is a long narrow area of low air pressure between two areas of higher pressure. [TECHNICAL] ❑ *The trough of low pressure extended over about 1000 kilometers.* →see **sound**

troupe /truːp/ (troupes) N-COUNT-COLL A **troupe** is a group of actors, singers, or dancers who work together and often travel around together, performing in different places. ❑ *...troupes of traveling actors.*

trousers /ˈtraʊzərz/

> The form **trouser** is used as a modifier.

N-PLURAL **Trousers** are a piece of clothing that you wear over your body from the waist downward, and that cover each leg separately. [mainly BRIT; AM usually **pants**] [also *a pair of* N] ❑ *He was smartly dressed in a shirt, dark trousers, and boots.*

trouser suit (trouser suits) N-COUNT A **trouser suit** is women's clothing consisting of a pair of trousers and a jacket which are made from the same material. [BRIT; AM **pantsuit, pants suit**]

trout /traʊt/

> The plural can be either **trout** or **trouts**.

N-VAR A **trout** is a fairly large fish that lives in rivers and streams. ● N-UNCOUNT **Trout** is this fish eaten as food. ❑ *Grilled trout needs only a squeeze of lemon.*

truant /ˈtruːənt/ (truants, truanting, truanted) ◼ N-COUNT A **truant** is a student who stays away from school without permission. ❑ *...the parents of persistent truants.* ◻ PHRASE If a student **plays truant**, he or she stays away from school without permission. ❑ *She was getting into trouble over playing truant from school.*

truce /truːs/ (truces) N-COUNT A **truce** is an agreement between two people or groups of people to stop fighting or quarreling for a short time. ❑ *The fighting of recent days has given way to an uneasy truce between the two sides.*

truck ◆◇◇ /trʌk/ (trucks, trucking, trucked) ◼ N-COUNT A **truck** is a large vehicle that is used to transport goods by road. [mainly AM; BRIT usually **lorry**] ❑ *Now and then they heard the roar of a heavy truck.* ◻ N-COUNT A **truck** is an open vehicle used for carrying goods on a railroad. [BRIT; AM **freight car**] ❑ *They were loaded on the railway trucks to go to Liverpool.* ◼ V-T When something or someone is **trucked** somewhere, they are driven there in a truck. [mainly AM] [usu passive] ❑ *The liquor was sold legally and trucked out of the state.*

trucker /ˈtrʌkər/ (truckers) N-COUNT A **trucker** is someone who drives a truck as their job. [mainly AM; BRIT **lorry driver**] ❑ *...the type of place where truckers and farmers stopped for coffee and pie.*

trudge /trʌdʒ/ (trudges, trudging, trudged) V-I If you **trudge** somewhere, you walk there slowly and with heavy steps, especially because you are tired or unhappy. ❑ *We had to trudge up the track back to the station.* ● N-SING **Trudge** is also a noun. ❑ *We were reluctant to start the long trudge home.*

true ◆◆◇ /truː/ (truer, truest) ◼ ADJ If something is **true**, it is based on facts rather than being invented or imagined, and is accurate and reliable. ❑ *Everything I had heard about him was true.* ❑ *He said it was true that a collision had happened.* ◻ ADJ You use **true** to emphasize that a person or thing is sincere or genuine, often in contrast to something that is pretended or hidden. [EMPHASIS] [ADJ n] ❑ *I allowed myself to acknowledge my true feelings.* ◼ ADJ If you use **true** to describe something or someone, you approve of them because they have all the characteristics or qualities that such a person or thing typically has. [APPROVAL] ❑ *This country professes to be a true democracy.* ❑ *Maybe one day you'll find true love.* ◻ ADJ If you say that a fact is **true of** a particular person or situation, you mean that it is valid or relevant for them. [v-link ADJ of/for n] ❑ *I accept that the romance may have gone out of the marriage, but surely this is true of many couples.* ◼ ADJ If you are **true to** someone, you remain committed and loyal to them. If you are **true to** an idea or promise, you remain committed to it and continue to act according to it. [v-link ADJ to n] ❑ *David was true to his wife.* ❑ *India has remained true to democracy.* ◼ PHRASE If a dream, wish, or prediction **comes true**, it actually happens. ❑ *Many of his predictions are coming true.* ◼ PHRASE If a general statement **holds true** in particular circumstances, or if your previous statement **holds true** in different circumstances, it is true or valid in those circumstances. [FORMAL] ❑ *This law is known to hold true for galaxies at a distance of at least several billion light years.* ◼ PHRASE If you say that something seems **too good to be true**, you are suspicious of it because it seems better than you had expected, and you think there may something wrong with it that you have not noticed. ❑ *On the whole the celebrations were remarkably good-humored and peaceful. Indeed, it seemed almost too good to be true.* ◼ to ring **true** →see **ring**. **tried and true** →see **tried**

truly ◆◇◇ /ˈtruːli/ ◼ ADV You use **truly** to emphasize that something has all the features or qualities of a particular thing, or is the case to the fullest possible extent. [EMPHASIS] ❑ *...a truly democratic system.* ❑ *Not all doctors truly understand the reproductive cycle.* ◻ ADV You can use **truly** in order to emphasize your description of something. [EMPHASIS] [ADV adj] ❑ *...a truly splendid man.* ◼ ADV You use **truly** to emphasize that feelings are genuine and sincere. [EMPHASIS] ❑ *Believe me, Susan, I am truly sorry.* ◼ **well and truly** →see **well**

◼ 가산명사 여물통 ❑ 돌로 된 옛날 소 여물통이 아직도 출입구 옆에 놓여 있다. ◻ 가산명사 (높은 물결 사이의) 골 ❑ 배가 파도와 파도 사이에서 심하게 요동쳤다. ◼ 가산명사 (경기의) 저점 ❑ 나중에 되돌아보면 이것이 너의 경력에서 최종 저점이 아니었다는 것을 알게 될 것이다. ◼ 가산명사 기압골 [과학 기술] ❑ 기압골의 저기압이 약 1,000킬로미터 정도 걸쳐 있었다.

가산명사·집합 공연단, 극단 ❑ 순회 극단

trouser은 수식어구로 쓴다.

복수명사 바지 [주로 영국영어; 미국영어 대개 pants] ❑ 그는 셔츠와 검정 바지를 말쑥하게 차려 입고 부츠를 신고 있었다.

가산명사 (여성용) 바지 정장 [영국영어; 미국영어 pantsuit, pants suit]

복수는 trout 또는 trouts이다.

가산명사 또는 불가산명사 송어 ● 불가산명사 송어요리 ❑ 송어 구이에는 레몬만 짜 넣으면 된다.

◼ 가산명사 무단결석생 ❑ 지속적으로 무단결석하는 학생들의 부모들 ◻ 구 무단결석하다 ❑ 그녀는 학교를 무단결석하는 바람에 곤란해지고 있었다.

가산명사 휴전 ❑ 최근 며칠간 있었던 그 싸움 대신 양측 간에 불안한 휴전이 실시되었다.

◼ 가산명사 트럭 [주로 미국영어; 영국영어 대개 lorry] ❑ 그들은 가끔 큰 트럭이 지나갈 때 나는 굉음을 들었다. ◻ 가산명사 (철도) 무개화차 [영국영어; 미국영어 freight car] ❑ 그것들을 리버풀로 가는 무개화차에 실었다. ◼ 타동사 트럭으로 운반되다 [주로 미국영어] ❑ 그 술은 합법적으로 팔렸고 트럭에 실려 주 외부로 운반되었다.

가산명사 트럭 운전사 [주로 미국영어; 영국영어 lorry driver] ❑ 트럭 운전사들과 농부들이 커피와 파이를 먹기 위해 잠깐 들르는 그런 장소

자동사 터벅터벅 걷다 ❑ 우리는 역으로 다시 터벅터벅 걸어서 되돌아가야만 했다. ● 단수명사 터벅터벅 걷기 ❑ 우리는 할 수 없이 멀리 집까지 터벅터벅 걷기 시작했다.

◼ 형용사 사실인 ❑ 내가 그에 관해서 들었던 모든 것은 사실이었다. ❑ 충돌 사건이 발생한 것은 사실이라고 그가 말했다. ◻ 형용사 진심인 [강조] ❑ 나는 내 진심을 인정하기로 했다. ◼ 형용사 진정한 [마음에 듦] ❑ 이 나라는 진정한 민주주의 국가임을 공언하는 바이다. ❑ 아마 너도 언젠가는 진정한 사랑을 만날 것이다. ◼ 형용사 적용되는 ❑ 결혼과 함께 연애 감정이 사라진 모양이라는 걸 인정한다. 하지만 분명히 이것은 다른 부부들에게도 마찬가지일 것이다. ◼ 형용사 충실한 ❑ 데이비드는 부인에게 충실했다. ❑ 인도는 민주주의를 충실하게 이행하고 있다. ◼ 구 실현되다, 현실화되다 ❑ 그가 했던 많은 예언들이 현실로 나타나고 있다. ◼ 구 적용되다 [격식체] ❑ 이 법칙은 수십억 광년 떨어져 있는 은하계에도 적용되는 것으로 알려져 있다. ◼ 구 너무 좋아 의심스러운 ❑ 대체로 그 기념식은 상당히 화기애애하고 평화로웠다. 사실, 너무 좋아 의심스러울 정도였다.

◼ 부사 진실로, 진짜로 [강조] ❑ 진실로 민주적인 체제 ❑ 모든 의사들이 진정으로 생식 주기를 이해하는 것은 아니다. ◻ 부사 정말로 [강조] ❑ 정말로 대단한 사람 ◼ 부사 정말 [강조] ❑ 수잔, 믿어 줘. 정말 미안해. ◼ 관용 표현 그럼 안녕히 계십시오 (편지 맺음말) ❑ 그럼 안녕히 계십시오. 필 터너 올림.

A

5 CONVENTION You write **Yours truly** at the end of a formal letter to someone you do not know very well. You write your signature after the words "Yours truly." ❏ *Yours truly, Phil Turner.*

B

trump /trʌmp/ (**trumps, trumping, trumped**) **1** N-UNCOUNT-COLL In a game of cards, **trumps** is the suit which is chosen to have the highest value in one particular game. ❏ *Hearts are trumps.* **2** N-COUNT In a game of cards, a **trump** is a playing card which belongs to the suit which has been chosen as trumps. ❏ *He played a trump.* **3** V-T If you **trump** what someone has said or done, you beat it by saying or doing something else that seems better. ❏ *The Socialists tried to trump this with their slogan.* **4** PHRASE Your **trump card** is something powerful that you can use or do, which gives you an advantage over someone. ❏ *In the end, the ten took their appeal to the Supreme Court; this, they had believed from the outset, would be their trump card.*

C

D

1 불가산명사-집합 으뜸 패 (짝패 한 조) ❏ 하트가 으뜸 패이다. **2** 가산명사 으뜸 패 (한 장) ❏ 그가 으뜸 패를 내놓았다. **3** 타동사 물리치다 ❏ 사회주의자들은 그들이 내거는 구호로 이것을 억누르려 노력했다. **4** 구 비장의 수 ❏ 마지막에는 그 열 명의 고소인들이 대법원에 항소했다. 왜냐하면 처음부터 그들이 비장의 수라고 믿고 있던 것이었다.

E

trum|pet /trʌmpɪt/ (**trumpets**) N-VAR A **trumpet** is a musical instrument of the brass family which plays quite high notes. [oft the N] ❏ *He played the trumpet in the school orchestra.*
→see **orchestra**

가산명사 또는 불가산명사 트럼펫 (악기) ❏ 그는 학교 오케스트라에서 트럼펫을 불었다.

F

trun|dle /trʌndᵊl/ (**trundles, trundling, trundled**) **1** V-I If a vehicle **trundles** somewhere, it moves there slowly, often with difficulty or an irregular movement. ❏ *The truck was trundling along the escarpment of the Zambesi valley.* **2** V-T If you **trundle** something somewhere, especially a small, heavy object with wheels, you move or roll it along slowly. ❏ *The old man lifted the barrow and trundled it away.*

G

1 자동사 (자동차가 천천히) 굴러가다 ❏ 트럭이 잠베시 계곡의 급경사를 따라 천천히 가고 있었다. **2** 타동사 (바퀴 달린 것을 천천히) 밀다 ❏ 그 노인은 손수레를 들어올리더니 그것을 천천히 밀고 갔다.

H

trunk /trʌŋk/ (**trunks**) **1** N-COUNT The **trunk** of a tree is the large main stem from which the branches grow. ❏ *...the gnarled trunk of a birch tree.* **2** N-COUNT A **trunk** is a large, strong case or box used for storing things or for taking on a trip. ❏ *Maloney unlocked his trunk and took out some coveralls.* **3** N-COUNT An elephant's **trunk** is its very long nose that it uses to lift food and water to its mouth. ❏ *Manfred reached out with his trunk and gently scooped up the baby.* **4** N-COUNT The **trunk** of a car is a covered space at the back or front in which you put luggage or other things. [AM; BRIT **boot**] ❏ *She opened the trunk of the car and started to take out a bag of groceries.* **5** N-PLURAL **Trunks** are shorts that a man wears when he goes swimming. ❏ *I wear these trunks because they have a streamline effect in the water.* **6** N-COUNT Your **trunk** is the central part of your body, from your neck to your waist. [FORMAL] [usu sing] ❏ *The leg to be stretched should be positioned behind your trunk with your knee bent.*

I

J

K

L

1 가산명사 나무의 몸통 ❏ 자작나무의 뒤틀린 몸통 **2** 가산명사 트렁크 (여행길 큰 가방) ❏ 말로니는 트렁크를 열고 작업복 몇 벌을 꺼냈다. **3** 가산명사 코끼리의 코 ❏ 맨프레드는 자신의 긴 코를 뻗어서 그 아기를 부드럽게 들어올렸다. **4** 가산명사 (자동차의) 트렁크 [미국영어; 영국영어 boot] ❏ 그녀는 차 트렁크를 열고 식료품 봉지를 꺼내기 시작했다. **5** 복수명사 남성용 수영복 ❏ 나는 이 수영복이 물속에서 유선형 효과를 볼 수 있기 때문에 이것을 입는다. **6** 가산명사 몸통, 상반신 [격식체] ❏ 뻗은 다리는 무릎을 굽혀 몸통 뒤로 가게 한다.

trust ♦♦◇ /trʌst/ (**trusts, trusting, trusted**) **1** V-T If you **trust** someone, you believe that they are honest and sincere and will not deliberately do anything to harm you. ❏ *"I trust you completely," he said.* **2** N-UNCOUNT Your **trust in** someone is your belief that they are honest and sincere and will not deliberately do anything to harm you. ❏ *He destroyed me and my trust in men.* ❏ *You've betrayed their trust.* **3** V-T If you **trust** someone **to** do something, you believe that they will do it. ❏ *That's why I must trust you to keep this secret.* **4** V-T If you **trust** someone **with** something important or valuable, you allow them to look after it or deal with it. ❏ *This could make your superiors hesitate to trust you with major responsibilities.* ● N-UNCOUNT **Trust** is also a noun. [also a N] ❏ *She was organizing and running a large household, a position of trust which was generously paid.* **5** V-T If you do not **trust** something, you feel that it is not safe or reliable. ❏ *She nodded, not trusting her own voice.* ❏ *For one thing, he didn't trust his legs to hold him up.* **6** V-T If you **trust** someone's judgment or advice, you believe that it is good or right. ❏ *Jake has raised two smashing kids and I trust his judgement.* **7** V-T If you say you **trust that** something is true, you mean you hope and expect that it is true. [FORMAL] ❏ *I trust you will take the earliest opportunity to make a full apology.* **8** V-I If you **trust in** someone or something, you believe strongly in them, and do not doubt their powers or their good intentions. [FORMAL] ❏ *For a believer, replies to all the questions about life and work are far different because he trusts in God.* **9** N-COUNT A **trust** is a financial arrangement in which a group of people or an organization keeps and invests money for someone. [BUSINESS] ❏ *You could also set up a trust so the children can't spend any inheritance until they are a certain age.* **10** N-COUNT A **trust** is a group of people or an organization that has control of an amount of money or property and invests it on behalf of other people or as a charity. [BUSINESS] ❏ *He had set up two charitable trusts.* **11** →see also **unit trust** **12** **tried and trusted** →see **tried**

M

N

O

P

Q

R

S

T

1 타동사 믿다, 신뢰하다 ❏ "당신을 전적으로 믿습니다."라고 그가 말했다. **2** 불가산명사 믿음, 신뢰 ❏ 그는 나를 파멸시켰고 남자에 대한 나의 신뢰를 버렸다. ❏ 너는 그들의 믿음을 저버렸다. **3** 타동사 -하리라고 믿다 ❏ 그것 때문에 나는 분명히 네가 이 비밀을 지킬 거라고 믿는 거야. **4** 타동사 -을 믿고 맡기다 ❏ 이것 때문에 자네 상사들이 자네에게 주요 임무를 믿고 맡기기를 주저할지 모른다. ● 불가산명사 믿고 맡김 ❏ 그녀는 대가족의 집안일을 유지하며 관리하고 있는데, 보수가 후한 책임자의 자리였다. **5** 타동사 믿다 ❏ 그녀는 자신의 목소리를 믿을 수 없어 고개를 끄덕였다. ❏ 우선, 그는 자기 두 다리가 자기를 지탱할 수 있을지가 믿기지 않았다. **6** 타동사 믿다 ❏ 제이크는 정말 괜찮은 아이 둘을 키워 냈으니 나는 그의 판단을 믿는다. **7** 타동사 -하기를 바라다 [격식체] ❏ 나는 당신이 충분한 사과를 할 기회를 최대한 빨리 갖기를 바랍니다. **8** 자동사 -을 강력히 믿다 [격식체] ❏ 그는 신을 믿으니까, 신앙인에게는 삶과 노동에 관련된 그 모든 질문에 대한 대답이 아주 다르다. **9** 가산명사 신탁 [경제] ❏ 아이들이 일정한 나이가 될 때까지 상속 재산을 쓰지 못하도록 신탁을 설정할 수도 있다. **10** 가산명사 신탁 기관 [경제] ❏ 그는 두 개의 자선 투자 신탁 기관을 세웠다.

	Word Partnership	trust의 연어
V.	build trust, **create** trust, **learn** to trust, **place** trust **in** *someone* **2**	
ADJ.	mutual trust **2**	
	charitable trust **10**	
N.	trust *your* instincts, trust *someone's* judgment **6**	
	investment trust **9**	

U

V

W

X

trus|tee /trʌstiː/ (**trustees**) N-COUNT A **trustee** is someone with legal control of money or property that is kept or invested for another person, company, or organization. [BUSINESS] ❏ *The trustees of your pension fund decide which fund manager will invest some or all of your future income.*

가산명사 신탁 관리자 [경제] ❏ 당신의 연금 관리인이 당신의 장래 수입의 전부 혹은 일부를 투자할 펀드 매니저를 결정한다.

Y

trust fund (**trust funds**) N-COUNT A **trust fund** is an amount of money or property that someone owns, usually after inheriting it, but which is kept and invested for them. [BUSINESS] ❏ *The money will be placed in a trust fund for her daughter.*

가산명사 신탁 자금 [경제] ❏ 그 돈은 그녀의 딸 앞으로 신탁 자금에 넣을 것이다.

Z

trust|worthy /trʌstwɜrði/ ADJ A **trustworthy** person is reliable, responsible, and can be trusted completely. ❑ *He is a trustworthy and level-headed leader.*

형용사 믿을 만한 ❑ 그는 믿을 만하고 신중한 지도자이다.

truth ♦♦◇ /truθ/ (**truths**) **1** N-UNCOUNT The **truth** about something is all the facts about it, rather than things that are imagined or invented. ❑ *Is it possible to separate truth from fiction?* ❑ *I must tell you the truth about this business.* **2** N-UNCOUNT If you say that there is some **truth in** a statement or story, you mean that it is true, or at least partly true. ❑ *There is no truth in this story.* ❑ *Is there any truth to the rumors?* **3** N-COUNT A **truth** is something that is believed to be true. ❑ *It is an almost universal truth that the more we are promoted in a job, the less we actually exercise the skills we initially used to perform it.* **4** PHRASE You say **to tell you the truth** or **truth to tell** in order to indicate that you are telling someone something in an open and honest way, without trying to hide anything. ❑ *To tell you the truth, I was afraid to see him.*

1 불가산명사 사실, 진상 ❑ 사실과 거짓을 구별할 수 있습니까? ❑ 당신께 이 일의 진상에 대해서 말씀드려야겠습니다. **2** 불가산명사 진실 ❑ 이 이야기는 전혀 진실이 아니다. ❑ 그 소문에 진실성이 있습니까? **3** 가산명사 진리 ❑ 우리가 직장에서 승진을 하면 할수록, 그 직장을 위해 처음에 썼던 그 기술을 활용할 기회가 더 적어진다는 것은 거의 보편적인 진리이다. **4** 구 사실을 말하자면 ❑ 사실을 말하자면, 나는 그를 만나기가 두려웠다.

truth|ful /truθfʊl/ ADJ If a person or their comments are **truthful**, they are honest and do not tell any lies. ❑ *Most religions teach you to be truthful.* ❑ *We've all learnt to be fairly truthful about our personal lives.* ● **truth|ful|ly** ADV [ADV with v] ❑ *I answered all their questions truthfully.* ● **truth|ful|ness** N-UNCOUNT ❑ *I can say, with absolute truthfulness, that I did not injure her.*

형용사 정직한 ❑ 대부분의 종교는 정직하라고 가르친다. ❑ 우리는 모두 각자의 사생활에 대해 매우 정직하도록 배웠다. ● 정직하게 부사 ❑ 나는 그들의 질문에 모두 정직하게 답했다. ● 정직함 불가산명사 ❑ 정말로 정직하게, 나는 그녀를 다치게 하지 않았다고 말할 수 있다.

try ♦♦♦ /traɪ/ (**tries**, **trying**, **tried**) **1** V-T/V-I If you **try** to do something, you want to do it, and you take action which you hope will help you to do it. ❑ *He secretly tried to block her advancement in the Party.* ❑ *Does it annoy you if others do things less well than you do, or don't seem to try hard enough?* ● N-COUNT **Try** is also a noun. ❑ *It wasn't that she'd really expected to get any money out of him; it had just seemed worth a try.* **2** V-T To **try and** do something means to try to do it. [INFORMAL] ❑ *I must try and see him.* **3** V-I If you **try for** something, you make an effort to get it or achieve it. ❑ *My partner and I have been trying for a baby for two years.* **4** V-T If you **try** something new or different, you use it, do it, or experience it in order to discover its qualities or effects. ❑ *It's best not to try a new recipe for the first time on such an important occasion.* ● N-COUNT **Try** is also a noun. ❑ *If you're still sceptical about exercising, we can only ask you to trust us and give it a try.* **5** V-T If you **try** a particular place or person, you go to that place or person because you think that they may be able to provide you with what you want. ❑ *Have you tried the local music shops?* **6** V-T If you **try** a door or window, you try to open it. ❑ *Bob tried the door. To his surprise it opened.* **7** V-T When a person **is tried**, he or she has to appear in a law court and is found innocent or guilty after the judge and jury have heard the evidence. When a legal case **is tried**, it is considered in a court of law. ❑ *He suggested that those responsible should be tried for crimes against humanity.* ❑ *Whether he is innocent or guilty is a decision that will be made when the case is tried in court.* **8** N-COUNT In the game of rugby, a **try** is the action of scoring by putting the ball down behind the goal line of the opposing team. ❑ *The French, who led 21-3 at half time, scored eight tries.* **9** →see also **tried**, **trying**. **10** to **try** your **best** →see **best**. to **try** your **hand** →see **hand**. to **try** someone's **patience** →see **patience**

1 타동사/자동사 노력하다 ❑ 그는 당 내에서 그녀의 승진을 막기 위해 비밀스럽게 노력했다. ❑ 당신은 다른 사람들이 당신보다 일을 잘 못하거나, 아주 열심히 하지 않는 것 같으면 화가 나나요? ● 가산명사 노력 ❑ 그녀가 그에게서 꼭 돈을 받으리라고 기대했던 것은 아니다. 단지 한번 노력해 볼 만해 보였을 뿐이다. **2** 타동사 노력하다, 애쓰다 [비격식체] ❑ 나는 그를 만나기 위해 노력해야 한다. **3** 자동사 ~을 위해 노력하다 ❑ 내 파트너와 나는 2년째 아기를 갖기 위해 노력하고 있는 중이다. **4** 타동사 시험해 보다, 시도하다 ❑ 그렇게 중요한 기회에 처음으로 새로운 요리법을 시도하는 일은 안 하는 것이 상책이다. ● 가산명사 시도 ❑ 아직도 운동하는 것에 대해 미심쩍다면, 그냥 우리를 믿고 한번 시도해 보시지요. **5** 타동사 (찾는 게 있나 하고) 들러 보다 ❑ 지역 음반 가게들에 들러 보셨나요? **6** 타동사 (문이나 창문을) 열어 보다 ❑ 봅이 그 문을 열어 봤더니, 놀랍게도 문이 열렸다. **7** 타동사 재판받다, 심리받다 ❑ 그는 비인도적인 범죄에 대해서 그 책임자들을 재판하도록 제안했다. ❑ 그가 무죄인지 유죄인지에 대한 결정은 그 사건을 법정에서 심리하면 내려질 것이다. **8** 가산명사 트라이 (럭비에서 득점) ❑ 전반전에 21대 3으로 이기고 있던 프랑스 팀이 8점을 얻었다.

Try and is often used instead of **try to** in spoken English, but you should avoid it in writing. ❑ *Just try and stop me!* Notice also the difference between **try to** and **try** with the "-ing" form of the verb, which often suggests doing something. ❑ *I'm going to try to open a jammed door... Try opening the windows to freshen the air.*

구어체 영어에서는 try to대신 흔히 try and를 쓰지만, 글을 쓸 때는 피해야 한다. ❑ 날 한번 막아 보시지! 또한 try to와, 흔히 무엇을 하고 있음을 시사하는 try -ing와의 차이에도 유의하라. ❑ 나는 꽉 낀 문을 열어 보려고 하고 있다... 창문을 열어서 환기를 하도록 해 봐.

▶**try on** **1** PHRASAL VERB If you **try on** a piece of clothing, you put it on to see if it fits you or if it looks nice. ❑ *Try on clothing and shoes to make sure they fit.* **2** PHRASAL VERB If you say that a person **is trying it on**, you mean that they are trying to obtain something or to impress someone, often in a slightly dishonest way and without much hope of success. [BRIT, INFORMAL] ❑ *They're just trying it on – I don't believe they'll go this far.*

1 구동사 (옷을) 입어 보다, (신을) 신어 보다 ❑ 잘 맞는지 확인하게 옷을 입어 보고 신도 신어 봐. **2** 구동사 그냥 한번 해보다 [영국영어, 비격식체] ❑ 그들은 그저 그냥 한번 해 보려고 한 것뿐일 거야. 그들이 이렇게까지 하리라고는 생각하지 않아.

▶**try out** PHRASAL VERB If you **try** something **out**, you test it in order to find out how useful or effective it is or what it is like. ❑ *She knew I wanted to try the boat out at the weekend.*

구동사 시험해 보다 ❑ 그녀는 내가 주말에 그 배를 시험해 보기를 원한다는 것을 알고 있었다.

try|ing /traɪɪŋ/ ADJ If you describe something or someone as **trying**, you mean that they are difficult to deal with and make you feel impatient or annoyed. ❑ *Support from those closest to you is vital in these trying times.* →see also **try**

형용사 견디기 힘든 ❑ 이렇게 힘든 시기에는 가장 가까운 사람들의 도움이 꼭 필요하다.

T-shirt (**T-shirts**) also **tee-shirt** N-COUNT A **T-shirt** is a cotton shirt with no collar or buttons. T-shirts usually have short sleeves. →see **clothing**

가산명사 티셔츠

tub /tʌb/ (**tubs**) **1** N-COUNT A **tub** is a deep container of any size. ❑ *He peeled the paper top off a little white tub and poured the cream into his coffee.* ● N-COUNT A **tub of** something is the amount of it contained in a tub. ❑ *She would eat four tubs of ice cream in one sitting.* **2** N-COUNT A **tub** is the same as a **bathtub**. [AM] ❑ *She lay back in the tub.* →see **soap**

1 가산명사 통 ❑ 그는 작은 흰색 통 윗부분의 종이를 벗겨 내고 커피에 그 크림을 부었다. ● 가산명사 통 ❑ 그녀는 앉은자리에서 아이스크림 네 통을 먹곤 했다. 2 가산명사 욕조 [미국영어] ❑ 그녀는 욕조 속에서 뒤로 누웠다.

tube ♦◇◇ /tjuːb, BRIT tjuːb/ (**tubes**) **1** N-COUNT A **tube** is a long hollow object that is usually round, like a pipe. ❑ *He is fed by a tube that enters his nose.* **2** N-COUNT A **tube of** something such as paste is a long, thin container which you squeeze in order to force the paste out. ❑ *I went out today and bought a tube of toothpaste.* **3** N-COUNT Some long, thin, hollow parts in your body are referred to as **tubes**. ❑ *The lungs are in fact constructed of thousands of tiny tubes.* **4** N-SING **The tube** is the underground railroad system in London. [BRIT] [*the N, also by N*] ❑ *I took the tube then the train and came straight here.* **5** N-COUNT You can refer to the television as the **tube**. [AM, INFORMAL; BRIT **the box**] ❑ *The only baseball he saw was on the tube.* →see **transportation**

1 가산명사 관, 튜브 ❑ 그는 코에 끼워진 관을 통해 음식물을 주입받는다. 2 가산명사 통, 튜브 ❑ 난 오늘 나가서 치약 한 통을 샀다. ● 가산명사 관, 관상 기관 ❑ 폐는 사실 수천 개의 작은 관으로 구성되어 있다. 4 단수명사 (영국) 지하철 [영국영어] ❑ 나는 지하철을 탄 다음에 기차를 타고 이리로 곧장 왔다. 5 가산명사 텔레비전 [미국영어, 비격식체; 영국영어 the box] ❑ 그가 유일하게 야구를 본 것은 텔레비전에서였다.

tu|ber|cu|lo|sis /tjuːbɜːrkjəloʊsɪs, BRIT tjuːbɜːʳkjʊloʊsɪs/ N-UNCOUNT **Tuberculosis** is a serious infectious disease that affects someone's lungs and other parts of their body. The abbreviation **TB** is also used.

불가산명사 결핵

tub|ing /tjuːbɪŋ, BRIT tjuːbɪŋ/ N-UNCOUNT **Tubing** is plastic, rubber, or another material in the shape of a tube. ❑ *...meters of plastic tubing.*

불가산명사 배관재 ❑ 플라스틱 배관재 몇 미터

tuck /tʌk/ (**tucks**, **tucking**, **tucked**) **1** V-T If you **tuck** something somewhere, you put it there so that it is safe, comfortable, or neat. ❑ *He tried to tuck his flapping shirt inside his trousers.* **2** N-COUNT You can use **tuck** to refer to a form of plastic surgery which involves reducing the size of a part of someone's body. ❑ *She'd undergone 13 operations, including a tummy tuck.*

1 타동사 쑤셔 넣다, 밀어 넣다 ❑ 그는 너풀거리는 셔츠 자락을 바지 속에 쑤셔 넣으려 했다. ● 가산명사 축소술, 지방 제거 수술 ❑ 그녀는 복부 지방 제거 수술을 포함해서 13번 수술을 받았다.

▶**tuck away 1** PHRASAL VERB If you **tuck away** something such as money, you store it in a safe place. ❑ *The extra income has meant Phillippa can tuck away the rent.* **2** PHRASAL VERB If someone or something **is tucked away**, they are well hidden in a quiet place where very few people go. ❑ *We were tucked away in a secluded corner of the room.*

1 구동사 (안전한 곳으로) 치우다, 감추다 ❑ 추가 소득 덕분에 필리파는 임대료를 따로 모을 수 있다. 2 구동사 숨다; 숨겨 두다 ❑ 우리는 방의 으슥한 구석에 숨어 있었다.

▶**tuck in 1** PHRASAL VERB If you **tuck in** a piece of material, you keep it in position by placing one edge or end of it behind or under something else. For example, if you **tuck in** your shirt, you place the bottom part of it inside your pants or skirt. ❑ *"Probably," I said, tucking in my shirt.* **2** PHRASAL VERB If you **tuck** a child in or **tuck** them in, you make them comfortable in bed by straightening the sheets and blankets and pushing the loose ends under the mattress. ❑ *I read Lili a story and tucked her in her own bed.*

1 구동사 집어 넣다, 밀어 넣다 ❑ "아마도"라고 나는 셔츠를 허리춤에 집어넣으며 말했다. 2 구동사 이불을 잘 덮어 주다 ❑ 나는 릴리에게 이야기를 읽어 주고 침대 이불을 잘 덮어 주었다.

▶**tuck into** or **tuck in** PHRASAL VERB If someone **tucks into** a meal or **tucks in**, they start eating enthusiastically or hungrily. [BRIT, INFORMAL] ❑ *She tucked into a breakfast of bacon and eggs.*

구동사 게걸스레 먹다, 왕성하게 먹다 [영국영어, 비격식체] ❑ 그녀는 베이컨과 계란으로 된 조반을 게걸스레 먹었다.

Tues.

The spelling **Tue.** is also used.

Tues. is a written abbreviation for **Tuesday**.

철자 Tue.도 쓴다.

Tues|day ♦♦◇ /tjuːzdeɪ, -di, BRIT tjuːzdeɪ, -di/ (**Tuesdays**) N-VAR **Tuesday** is the day after Monday and before Wednesday. ❑ *He phoned on Tuesday, just before you came.* ❑ *Talks are likely to start next Tuesday.*

화 가산명사 또는 불가산명사 화요일 ❑ 그는 화요일에, 당신이 오기 직전에 전화를 했다. ❑ 회담은 다음 화요일에 시작될 것 같다.

tug /tʌg/ (**tugs**, **tugging**, **tugged**) **1** V-T/V-I If you **tug** something or **tug at** it, you give it a quick and usually strong pull. ❑ *A little boy came running up and tugged at his sleeve excitedly.* ● N-COUNT **Tug** is also a noun. ❑ *I felt a tug at my sleeve.* **2** N-COUNT A **tug** or a **tug boat** is a small powerful boat which pulls large ships, usually when they come into a port. ❑ *...a 76,000-ton barge pulled by five tug boats.*

1 타동사/자동사 세게 당기다 ❑ 어린 소년이 뛰어와서는 그의 소매를 마구 잡아당겼다. ● 가산명사 세게 당김 ❑ 나는 누가 내 소매를 잡아당기는 것을 느꼈다. 2 가산명사 예인선 ❑ 다섯 척의 예인선이 끄는 76,000톤 급 바지선

tui|tion /tjuːɪʃ°n, BRIT tjuːɪʃ°n/ N-UNCOUNT **1** If you are given **tuition** in a particular subject, you are taught about that subject. ❑ *The courses will give the beginner personal tuition in all types of outdoor photography.* **2** N-UNCOUNT You can use **tuition** to refer to the amount of money that you have to pay for being taught particular subjects, especially in a university, college, or private school. ❑ *Angela's $7,000 tuition at University this year will be paid for with scholarships.*

1 불가산명사 수업, 지도 ❑ 강좌 중 모든 종류의 야외 촬영에서는 초보자에게 개인 지도를 해 준다. 2 불가산명사 수업료 ❑ 안젤라의 올해 대학 등록금 7천 달러는 장학금으로 납부될 것이다.

tu|lip /tjuːlɪp, BRIT tjuːlɪp/ (**tulips**) N-COUNT **Tulips** are flowers that grow in the spring, and have oval or pointed petals packed closely together.

가산명사 튤립

tum|ble /tʌmb°l/ (**tumbles**, **tumbling**, **tumbled**) **1** V-I If someone or something **tumbles** somewhere, they fall there with a rolling or bouncing movement. ❑ *A small boy tumbled off a third floor fire escape.* ● N-COUNT **Tumble** is also a noun. [usu sing] ❑ *He injured his ribs in a tumble from his horse.* **2** V-I If prices or levels of something **are tumbling**, they are decreasing rapidly. [JOURNALISM] ❑ *Profit after taxes tumbled by half to $15.8 million.* ❑ *Share prices continued to tumble today on the Tokyo stock market.* ● N-COUNT **Tumble** is also a noun. ❑ *Oil prices took a tumble yesterday.* **3** V-I If water **tumbles**, it flows quickly over an uneven surface. ❑ *Waterfalls crash and tumble over rocks.*

1 자동사 굴러 떨어지다 ❑ 어린 소년이 3층 화재 비상구에서 굴러 떨어졌다. ● 가산명사 추락, 떨어짐 ❑ 그는 말에서 떨어져 갈비뼈를 다쳤다. 2 자동사 폭락하다 [언론] ❑ 세후 이익이 반 토막이 나서 1,580만 달러가 되었다. ❑ 오늘 도쿄증시에서는 주가가 계속해서 폭락했다. ● 가산명사 폭락 ❑ 유가가 어제 폭락했다. 3 자동사 (물이) 거세게 요동치다 ❑ 폭포가 바위 위로 요동을 치며 떨어져 내린다.

tum|ble dry|er (**tumble dryers**) also **tumble drier** N-COUNT A **tumble dryer** is an electric machine which dries washing by turning it over and over and blowing warm air onto it. [mainly BRIT; AM **dryer**]

가산명사 (회전식) 세탁물 건조기 [주로 영국영어; 미국영어 dryer]

tum|my /tʌmi/ (**tummies**) **1** N-COUNT Your **tummy** is the part of the front of your body below your waist. **Tummy** is often used by children or by adults talking to children. ❑ *Your baby's tummy should feel warm, but not hot.* **2** N-COUNT You can use **tummy** to refer to the parts inside your body where food is digested. **Tummy** is often used by children or by adults talking to children. ❑ *I've got a sore tummy.*

1 가산명사 배 ❑ 아기의 배는 따뜻해야 되지만 뜨거워선 안 된다. 2 가산명사 배, 속 ❑ 나는 속이 쓰리다.

tu|mor /tjuːmər, BRIT tjuːməʳ/ (**tumors**) [BRIT **tumour**] N-COUNT A **tumor** is a mass of diseased or abnormal cells that has grown in a person's or animal's body. ❑ *...a malignant brain tumor.*

[영국영어 tumour] 가산명사 종양 ❑ 악성 뇌종양

tu|mul|tu|ous /tumʌltʃuəs, BRIT tyuːmʌltʃuəs/ **1** ADJ A **tumultuous** event or period of time involves many exciting and confusing events or feelings. ❑ ...the tumultuous changes in Eastern Europe. **2** ADJ A **tumultuous** reaction to something is very noisy, because the people involved are very happy or excited. ❑ A tumultuous welcome from a 2,000 strong crowd greeted the champion.

tuna /tunə, BRIT tyuːnə/

The plural can be either **tuna** or **tunas**.

N-VAR **Tuna** or **tuna fish** are large fish that live in warm seas and are caught for food. ❑ ...a shoal of tuna. ● N-UNCOUNT **Tuna** or **tuna fish** is this fish eaten as food. ❑ She began opening a tin of tuna.

tune ◆◇◇ /tun, BRIT tyuːn/ (**tunes, tuning, tuned**) **1** N-COUNT A **tune** is a series of musical notes that is pleasant and easy to remember. ❑ She was humming a merry little tune. **2** N-COUNT You can refer to a song or a short piece of music as a **tune**. ❑ She'll also be playing your favorite pop tunes. **3** V-T When someone **tunes** a musical instrument, they adjust it so that it produces the right notes. ❑ "We do tune our guitars before we go on," he insisted. ● PHRASAL VERB **Tune up** means the same as **tune**. ❑ Others were quietly tuning up their instruments. **4** V-T When an engine or machine **is tuned**, it is adjusted so that it works well. [usu passive] ❑ Drivers are urged to make sure that car engines are properly tuned. ● PHRASAL VERB **Tune up** means the same as **tune**. ❑ The shop charges up to $500 to tune up a Porsche. **5** V-T If your radio or television **is tuned to** a particular broadcasting station, you are listening to or watching the programs being broadcast by that station. [usu passive] ❑ A small color television was tuned to an afternoon soap opera. **6** →see also **fine-tune** **7** PHRASE If you say that a person or organization **is calling the tune**, you mean that they are in a position of power or control in a particular situation. ❑ It is Coulthard who is calling the tune so far this season. **8** PHRASE If you say that someone **has changed** their **tune**, you are criticizing them because they have changed their opinion or way of doing things. [DISAPPROVAL] ❑ You've changed your tune since this morning, haven't you? **9** PHRASE A person or musical instrument that is **in tune** produces exactly the right notes. A person or musical instrument that is **out of tune** does not produce exactly the right notes. ❑ It was just an ordinary voice, but he sang in tune.

▶**tune in** **1** PHRASAL VERB If you **tune in** to a particular television or radio station or program, you watch or listen to it. ❑ More than six million youngsters tune in to Blockbusters every day. **2** PHRASAL VERB If you **tune in to** something such as your own or other people's feelings, you become aware of them. ❑ You can start now to tune in to your own physical, social, and spiritual needs.

tu|nic /tunɪk, BRIT tyuːnɪk/ (**tunics**) N-COUNT A **tunic** is a long sleeveless garment that is worn on the top part of your body. ❑ ...a cotton tunic.

tun|nel ◆◇◇ /tʌnᵊl/ (**tunnels, tunneling, tunneled**) [BRIT, sometimes AM **tunnelling, tunnelled**] **1** N-COUNT A **tunnel** is a long passage which has been made under the ground, usually through a hill or under the sea. ❑ ...two new railway tunnels through the Alps. **2** V-I To **tunnel** somewhere means to make a tunnel there. ❑ The thieves tunneled under all the security devices. →see **traffic** →see Word Web: **tunnel**

tur|bine /tɜrbɪn, -baɪn, BRIT tɜːʳbaɪn/ (**turbines**) N-COUNT A **turbine** is a machine or engine which uses a stream of air, gas, water, or steam to turn a wheel and produce power. ❑ The new ship will be powered by two gas turbines and four diesel engines. →see **electricity**

tur|bu|lence /tɜrbyələns/ **1** N-UNCOUNT **Turbulence** is a state of confusion and disorganized change. ❑ The 1960s and early 1970s were a time of change and turbulence. **2** N-UNCOUNT **Turbulence** is violent and uneven movement within a particular area of air, liquid, or gas. ❑ His plane encountered severe turbulence and winds of nearly two-hundred miles an hour.

tur|bu|lent /tɜrbyələnt/ **1** ADJ A **turbulent** time, place, or relationship is one in which there is a lot of change, confusion, and disorder. ❑ They had been together for five or six turbulent years of rows and reconciliations. **2** ADJ **Turbulent** water or air contains strong currents which change direction suddenly. ❑ I had to have a boat that could handle turbulent seas.

turf /tɜrf/ **1** N-UNCOUNT **Turf** is short, thick, even grass. [also the N] ❑ They shuffled slowly down the turf towards the cliff's edge. **2** N-UNCOUNT Someone's **turf** is

1 형용사 격동의 ❑ 동유럽의 격변 **2** 형용사 떠들썩한 ❑ 그 우승자는 2천 명 인원의 군중들로부터 떠들썩한 환영을 받았다.

복수는 tuna 또는 tunas이다.

가산명사 또는 불가산명사 참치 ❑ 참치 떼 ● 불가산명사 참치 ❑ 그녀가 참치 통조림 하나를 따기 시작했다.

1 가산명사 가락, 선율 ❑ 그녀는 흥겹고 단순한 가락을 흥얼거리고 있었다. **2** 가산명사 곡조, 노래 ❑ 그녀는 네가 좋아하는 팝도 몇 곡 연주할 것이다. **3** 타동사 (악기를) 조율하다 ❑ "우리는 계속하기 전에 반드시 기타를 조율한다."라고 그가 고집했다. ● 구동사 (악기를) 조율하다 ❑ 다른 사람들은 조용히 자기 악기를 조율하고 있었다. **4** 타동사 (엔진이) 정비되다 ❑ 운전자들에게 자동차 엔진이 제대로 정비되었는지 확인할 것을 권한다. ● 구동사 (엔진을) 정비하다 ❑ 그 정비소에서는 포르쉐 엔진을 정비하는 데 5백 달러까지 받는다. **5** 타동사 -에 주파수가 맞추어지다 ❑ 작은 컬러텔레비전에서는 오후 연속극이 방송되고 있었다. **7** 구 장악하다, 지배하다 ❑ 이번 시즌에 지금까지 선두를 장악하고 있는 사람은 쿨타드이다. **8** 구 의견을 싹 바꾸다, 태도를 싹 바꾸다 [탐탁찮음] ❑ 오늘 아침 이후로 태도를 싹 바꾸셨네요, 그렇지 않아요? **9** 구 음이 잘 맞는; 음이 맞지 않는 ❑ 그저 평범한 목소리였지만, 그는 음정을 잘 맞게 노래를 불렀다.

1 구동사 -을 시청하다, -을 청취하다 ❑ 육백만 명 이상의 젊은이들이 매일 블럭버스터스를 시청한다. **2** 구동사 -에 맞추다 ❑ 당신은 이제 자신의 신체적, 사회적, 정신적 요구에 맞추기 시작할 수 있다.

가산명사 튜닉 (소매 없는 긴 웃옷) ❑ 면 튜닉

[영국영어, 미국영어 가끔 tunnelling, tunnelled] **1** 가산명사 터널, 굴 ❑ 알프스 산맥을 관통하는 두 개의 새 철도 터널 **2** 자동사 터널을 파다 ❑ 도둑들이 모든 보안 장치 아래로 터널을 뚫었다.

가산명사 터빈 ❑ 새 선박은 두 개의 가스 터빈과 네 개의 디젤 엔진으로 추진될 것이다.

1 불가산명사 격동 ❑ 1960년대와 1970년대 초반은 변화와 격동의 시기였다. **2** 불가산명사 난기류 ❑ 그가 탄 비행기는 심한 난기류와 시속 2백 마일가량의 바람을 만났다.

1 형용사 격동의 ❑ 그들은 분란과 화해가 반복되었던 격동의 오륙 년을 함께 보낸 사이였다. **2** 형용사 거친, 난기류의 ❑ 나는 거친 바다를 견딜 수 있는 배가 있어야 했다.

1 불가산명사 잔디, 뗏장 ❑ 그들은 절벽 끝을 향해 발을 끌며 잔디 위를 천천히 걸어 내려갔다.

Word Web tunnel

The Egyptians built the first **tunnels** as entrances to tombs. Later the Babylonians* built a tunnel under the Euphrates River*. It linked the royal palace with the Temple of Jupiter*. The Romans **dug** tunnels when **mining** for gold. By the late 1600s, **explosives** had replaced digging. Gunpowder was used to build the **underground** section of a canal in France in 1679. Nitroglycerin explosions helped create a railroad tunnel in Massachusetts in 1867. The longest continuous tunnel in the world is the Delaware Aqueduct. It carries water from the Catskill Mountains* to New York City and is 105 miles long.

Babylonians: people who lived in the ancient city of Babylon.
Euphrates River: a large river in the Middle East.
Temple of Jupiter: a religious building.
Catskill Mountains: a mountain range in the northeastern U.S.

a b c d e f g h i j k l m n o p q r s t u v w x y z

A

the area which is most familiar to them or where they feel most confident. ❑ *Their turf was Paris: its streets, theaters, homes, and parks.*

B

tur|key /tˈɜːrki/ (**turkeys**) N-COUNT A **turkey** is a large bird that is kept on a farm for its meat. ● N-UNCOUNT **Turkey** is the flesh of this bird eaten as food. ❑ *They will sit down to a traditional turkey dinner early this afternoon.*

tur|moil /tˈɜːrmɔɪl/ (**turmoils**) N-VAR **Turmoil** is a state of confusion, disorder, uncertainty, or great anxiety. ❑ ...*the political turmoil of 1989.*

C

turn ♦♦♦ /tˈɜːrn/ (**turns, turning, turned**)

D

> **Turn** is used in a large number of other expressions which are explained under other words in the dictionary. For example, the expression "turn over a new leaf" is explained at **leaf**.

E

1 V-T/V-I When you **turn** or when you **turn** part of your body, you move your body or part of your body so that it is facing in a different or opposite direction. ❑ *He turned abruptly and walked away.* ❑ *He sighed, turning away and surveying the sea.* ● PHRASAL VERB **Turn around** or **turn round** means the same as **turn**. ❑ *I felt a tapping on my shoulder and I turned around.* **2** V-T When you **turn** something, you move it so that it is facing in a different or opposite direction, or is in a very different position. ❑ *They turned their telescopes towards other nearby galaxies.* ❑ *She had turned the bedside chair to face the door.* **3** V-T/V-I When something such as a wheel **turns**, or when you **turn** it, it continually moves around in a particular direction. ❑ *As the wheel turned, the potter shaped the clay.* **4** V-T/V-I When you **turn** something such as a key, knob, or switch, or when it **turns**, you hold it and twist your hand, in order to open something or make it start working. ❑ *Turn a special key, press the brake pedal, and your car's brakes lock.* ❑ *Turn the heat to very low and cook for 20 minutes.* **5** V-T/V-I When you **turn** in a particular direction or **turn** a corner, you change the direction in which you are moving or traveling. ❑ *He turned into the narrow street where he lived.* ❑ *Now turn right to follow West Ferry Road.* ● N-COUNT **Turn** is also a noun. ❑ *You can't do a right-hand turn here.* **6** V-I The point where a road, path, or river **turns** is the point where it has a bend or curve in it. ❑ ...*the corner where Tenterfield Road turned into the main road.* ● N-COUNT **Turn** is also a noun. ❑ ...*a sharp turn in the road.* **7** V-I When the tide **turns**, it starts coming in or going out. ❑ *There was not much time before the tide turned.* **8** V-T When you **turn** a page of a book or magazine, you move it so that it is flat against the previous page, and you can read the next page. ❑ *He turned the pages of a file in front of him.* **9** V-T If you **turn** a weapon or an aggressive feeling **on** someone, you point it at them or direct it at them. ❑ *He tried to turn the gun on me.* **10** V-I If you **turn to** a particular page in a book or magazine, you open it at that page. ❑ *To order, turn to page 236.* **11** V-T/V-I If you **turn** your attention or thoughts **to** a particular subject or if you **turn to** it, you start thinking about it or discussing it. ❑ *We turned our attention to the practical matters relating to forming a company.* **12** V-I If you **turn to** someone, you ask for their help or advice. ❑ *For assistance, they turned to one of the city's most innovative museums.* **13** V-I If you **turn to** a particular activity, job, or way of doing something, you start doing or using it. ❑ *These communities are now turning to recycling in large numbers.* **14** V-T/V-I To **turn** or be **turned into** something means to become that thing. ❑ *A prince turns into a frog in this cartoon fairytale.* **15** V-LINK You can use **turn** before an adjective to indicate that something or someone changes by acquiring the quality described by the adjective. ❑ *If the bailiff thinks that things could turn nasty he will enlist the help of the police.* **16** V-LINK If something **turns** a particular color or if something **turns** it a particular color, it becomes that color. ❑ *The sea would turn pale pink and the sky blood red.* **17** V-LINK You can use **turn** to indicate that there is a change to a particular kind of weather. For example, if it **turns** cold, the weather starts being cold. ❑ *If it turns cold, cover plants.* **18** N-COUNT If a situation or trend takes a particular kind of **turn**, it changes so that it starts developing in a different or opposite way. ❑ *The scandal took a new turn over the weekend.* **19** V-T If a business **turns** a profit, it earns more money than it spends. [BUSINESS] [no passive] ❑ *The firm will be able to service debt and still turn a modest profit.* **20** V-T When someone **turns** a particular age, they pass that age. When it **turns** a particular time, it passes that time. ❑ *It was his ambition to accumulate a million dollars before he turned thirty.* **21** N-SING **Turn** is used in expressions such as **the turn of the century** and **the turn of the year** to refer to a period of time when one century or year is ending and the next one is beginning. ❑ *They fled to South America around the turn of the century.* **22** N-COUNT If it is your **turn** to do something, you now have the duty, chance, or right to do it, when other people have done it before you or will do it after you. ❑ *Tonight it's my turn to cook.* **23** →see also **turning 24** PHRASE If there is a particular **turn of events**, a particular series of things happen. ❑ *They were horrified at this unexpected turn of events.* **25** PHRASE If you say that something happens **at every turn**, you are emphasizing that it happens frequently or all the time, usually so that it prevents you from achieving what you want. [EMPHASIS] ❑ *Its operations were hampered at every turn by inadequate numbers of trained staff.* **26** PHRASE If you do someone **a good turn**, you do something that helps or benefits them. ❑ *He did you a good turn by resigning.* **27** PHRASE You use **in turn** to refer to actions or events that are in a sequence one after the other, for example because one causes the other. ❑ *One of the members of the surgical team leaked the story to a fellow physician who, in turn, confided in a reporter.* **28** PHRASE If each person in a group does something **in turn**, they do it one after the other in a fixed or agreed order. ❑ *There were cheers for each of the women as they spoke in turn.* **29** PHRASE If two or more people **take turns to** do something, or in British English **take it in turns to** do something, they do it one after the other several times, rather than doing it together. ❑ *We took turns to drive the car.* **30** PHRASE If a situation **takes a turn for the worse**, it suddenly becomes worse. If a situation **takes a turn for the better**, it suddenly becomes better. ❑ *Her condition took a sharp turn for the worse.*

2 불가산명사 주 활동 무대, 본고장 **3** 그들의 주 활동 무대는 파리였다. 파리의 거리와 극장과 집과 공원들이었다.

가산명사 칠면조 ● 불가산명사 칠면조 고기 ❑ 그들은 오늘 오후에 일찍 전통 칠면조 고기 만찬을 시작할 것이다.

가산명사 또는 불가산명사 혼란, 소요 ❑ 1989년의 정치적 혼란

이 사전에서 turn이 포함된 많은 표현들이 다른 표제어에서 설명된다. 예를 들어, 'turn over a new leaf'는 leaf에서 설명된다.

1 타동사/자동사 돌다; 돌리다 ❑ 그는 갑자기 몸을 돌려 걸어가 버렸다. ❑ 그는 한숨을 쉬며 몸을 돌려 바다를 바라보았다. ● 구동사 돌다; 돌리다 ❑ 누가 내 어깨를 툭툭 쳐서 내가 뒤돌아보았다. **2** 타동사 돌리다, 방향을 돌리다 ❑ 그들은 망원경을 근처의 다른 성운 쪽으로 돌렸다. ❑ 그녀는 침대 머리맡의 의자를 문을 향하도록 돌려놓았다. **3** 타동사/자동사 회전하다, 돌아가다; 회전시키다, 돌리다 ❑ 물레가 회전하면 도공은 진흙으로 모양을 빚었다. **4** 타동사/자동사 돌리다, 켜다; 켜지다 ❑ 별도 열쇠를 돌리고 브레이크 페달을 밟으면, 자동차의 브레이크가 잠긴다. ❑ 불을 아주 약하게 낮추고 20분간 익히시오. **5** 타동사/자동사 방향을 바꾸다; (모퉁이를) 돌다 ❑ 그는 길을 꺾어 자기가 살고 있는 좁은 거리로 들어섰다. ❑ 이제 오른쪽으로 돌아 웨스트 페리 로드를 따라 가시오. ● 가산명사 (방향) 전환 ❑ 여기서는 우회전을 할 수 없다. **6** 자동사 구부러지다, 방향이 바뀌다 ❑ 텐터필드 로드가 큰길로 이어지는 모퉁이 ● 가산명사 굽이 ❑ 도로가 급히 꺾이는 곳 **7** 자동사 (조수가) 바뀌다 ❑ 조수가 바뀌기 전까지 시간이 얼마 남지 않았다. **8** 타동사 (책장을) 넘기다 ❑ 그는 자기 앞에 놓인 파일의 페이지를 넘겼다. **9** 타동사 -에 향하게 하다 ❑ 그는 나에게 총을 겨누려고 했다. **10** 자동사 (책 등의 어느 부분을) 펴다 ❑ 주문하려면 236쪽을 펴시오. **11** 타동사/자동사 (생각 등을) -로 돌리다 ❑ 우리는 회사의 설립과 관련된 실제적인 문제로 주의를 돌렸다. **12** 자동사 -에 의지하다 ❑ 도움을 받으려고 그들은 그 도시의 가장 혁신적인 박물관 중 하나에 문의했다. **13** 자동사 -에 착수하다 ❑ 이 지역 사회들은 이제 대규모로 재활용을 시작하고 있다. **14** 타동사/자동사 -으로 변하다 ❑ 이 만화의 본 동화에서는 왕자가 개구리로 변한다. **15** 연결동사 -이 되다 ❑ 집행관이 일이 어렵게 될지 모르겠다고 생각하면 경찰의 도움을 청할 것이다. **16** 연결동사 (-색으로) 변하다; (-색으로) 변하게 하다 ❑ 바다는 엷은 분홍빛으로, 하늘은 붉은 핏빛으로 바뀌곤 했다. **17** 연결동사 (날씨가) -로 변하다 ❑ 날씨가 추워지면 화초를 덮으시오. **18** 가산명사 (정세의) 전환 ❑ 그 스캔들은 주말에 새로운 전환점을 맞았다. **19** 타동사 (이익을) 내다 [경제] ❑ 그 회사는 부채의 이자를 지급하고도 조금은 이익을 낼 수 있을 것이다. **20** 타동사 (나이가) 넘다; (시간이) 지나다 ❑ 서른이 넘기 전에 백만 달러를 모으는 것이 그의 야망이었다. **21** 단수명사 전환기; 세기가 바뀌는 시기; 해가 바뀌는 시기 ❑ 그들은 세기가 바뀌는 그 무렵에 남아메리카로 달아났다. **22** 가산명사 차례, 순번 ❑ 오늘밤은 내가 요리할 차례다. **23** →구 한바탕 사건들, 일련의 사건들 ❑ 그들은 이 예기치 않은 일련의 사건들로 겁에 질려 있었다. **24** 구 매번, 항상 [강조] ❑ 그 작업은 매번 훈련된 직원이 모자라서 지장을 받았다. **26** 구 친절, 도움 ❑ 그는 사임하는 것으로써 당신에게 도움을 주었다. **27** 구 이번에는 ❑ 그 수술 팀 중 한 사람이 그 이야기를 동료 의사에게 누설했고, 그 의사가 이번에는 기자에게 털어놓았다. **28** 구 차례로 ❑ 그 여자들이 한 사람씩 차례로 말을 할 때마다 환성이 터졌다. **29** 구 교대로 하다 ❑ 우리는 교대로 운전을 했다. **30** 구 (갑자기) 악화되다; (갑자기) 호전되다 ❑ 그녀의 상태가 갑자기 악화되었다.

Thesaurus	turn의 참조어
v.	pivot, revolve, rotate, spin, twist **1**-**4**
	become **14**-**17**
n.	chance, opportunity **22**

▶**turn against** PHRASAL VERB If you **turn against** someone or something, or if you **are turned against** them, you stop supporting them, trusting them, or liking them. ❏ *A kid I used to be friends with turned against me after being told that I'd been insulting him.*

구동사 -에게 등을 돌리다 ❏ 나하고 친했던 아이 하나가, 내가 그를 욕하고 다녔다는 소리를 듣고 나서는 나에게 등을 돌렸다.

▶**turn around** or **turn round** **1** →see turn **1** **2** PHRASAL VERB If you **turn** something **around**, or if it **turns around**, it is moved so that it faces the opposite direction. ❏ *Bud turned the truck around, and started back for Dalton Pond.* ❏ *He had reached over to turn round a bottle of champagne so that the label didn't show.* **3** PHRASAL VERB If something such as a business or economy **turns around**, or if someone **turns** it **around**, it becomes successful, after being unsuccessful for a period of time. [BUSINESS] ❏ *Turning the company around won't be easy.* ❏ *In his long career at BP, Horton turned around two entire divisions.*

2 구동사 (반대 방향으로) 돌리다; (반대 방향으로) 돌다 ❏ 버드는 트럭의 방향을 돌려서 달튼 폰드로 되돌아가기 시작했다. ❏ 그는 상표가 안 보이게 샴페인 병을 돌려놓으려고 팔을 뻗었었다. **3** 구동사 (사업 등이) 나아지다; (사업 등을) 나아지게 하다 [경제] ❏ 회사가 나아지게 만드는 게 쉽지 않을 것이다. ❏ 영국 석유에서 오래 근무하면서, 홀튼은 2개 부서 전체를 개선시켰다.

▶**turn away** **1** PHRASAL VERB If you **turn** someone **away**, you do not allow them to enter your country, home, or other place. ❏ *Turning boat people away would be an inhumane action.* **2** PHRASAL VERB To **turn away from** something such as a method or an idea means to stop using it or to become different from it. ❏ *Japanese corporations have been turning away from production and have diverted into finance and real estate.*

1 구동사 (못 들어오게) 쫓아 버리다 ❏ 표류 난민의 입국을 거부하는 것은 잔혹한 처사일 것이다. **2** 구동사 (-로부터) 멀어지다, 지양하다 ❏ 일본 기업들은 생산업을 외면하고 금융과 부동산 쪽으로 방향을 바꾸었다.

▶**turn back** **1** PHRASAL VERB If you **turn back** or if someone **turns** you **back** when you are going somewhere, you change direction and go toward where you started from. ❏ *She turned back towards the crossroads.* ❏ *Police attempted to turn back protesters marching towards the offices of President Ershad.* **2** PHRASAL VERB If you **cannot turn back**, you cannot change your plans and decide not to do something, because the action you have already taken makes it impossible. [with brd-neg] ❏ *The administration has now endorsed the bill and can't turn back.*

1 구동사 되돌아가다; 되돌아가게 하다 ❏ 그녀는 교차로 방향으로 되돌아갔다. ❏ 경찰은 에르샤드 대통령 집무실을 향해 행진하는 시위대를 되돌아가게 하려고 했다. **2** 구동사 돌이킬 수 없다 ❏ 정부가 이제 그 법안을 승인했기 때문에 돌이킬 수가 없다.

▶**turn down** **1** PHRASAL VERB If you **turn down** a person or their request or offer, you refuse their request or offer. ❏ *I thanked him for the offer but turned it down.* **2** PHRASAL VERB When you **turn down** a radio, heater, or other piece of equipment, you reduce the amount of sound or heat being produced, by adjusting the controls. ❏ *He kept turning the central heating down.*

1 구동사 거절하다 ❏ 나는 그 제안을 해 준 데 대해 그에게 감사는 표시했지만 그 제안은 거절했다. **2** 구동사 (소리 등을) 낮추다 ❏ 그는 중앙난방의 온도를 계속 낮추었다.

▶**turn off** **1** PHRASAL VERB If you **turn off** the road or path you are going along, you start going along a different road or path which leads away from it. ❏ *The truck turned off the main road along the gravelly track which led to the farm.* **2** PHRASAL VERB When you **turn off** a piece of equipment or a supply of something, you stop heat, sound, or water from being produced by adjusting the controls. ❏ *The light's a bit too harsh. You can turn it off.*

1 구동사 (다른 길로) 빠지다 ❏ 트럭은 중심 도로로 빠져 나와 농장으로 가는 자갈길을 따라 갔다. **2** 구동사 (장치를) 끄다 ❏ 불빛이 너무 강한 편이야. 꺼도 좋아.

▶**turn on** **1** PHRASAL VERB When you **turn on** a piece of equipment or a supply of something, you cause heat, sound, or water to be produced by adjusting the controls. ❏ *I want to turn on the television.* **2** PHRASAL VERB If someone or something **turns** you **on**, they attract you and make you feel sexually excited. [INFORMAL] ❏ *The body that turns men on doesn't have to be perfect.* **3** PHRASAL VERB If someone **turns on** you, they attack you or speak angrily to you. ❏ *Demonstrators turned on police, overturning vehicles and setting fire to them.*

1 구동사 (장치를) 켜다 ❏ 나는 텔레비전을 켜고 싶다. **2** 구동사 흥분시키다 [비격식체] ❏ 몸매가 꼭 완벽해야만 남자들이 흥분하는 것은 아니다. **3** 구동사 공격하다 ❏ 시위대는 경찰을 공격하여 차량을 전복시키고 불태웠다.

▶**turn out** **1** PHRASAL VERB-LINK If something **turns out** a particular way, it happens in that way or has the result or degree of success indicated. ❏ *If I had known my life was going to turn out like this, I would have let them kill me.* ❏ *I was positive things were going to turn out fine.* **2** PHRASAL VERB If something **turns out to** be a particular thing, it is discovered to be that thing. ❏ *Cosgrave's forecast turned out to be quite wrong.* **3** PHRASAL VERB When you **turn out** something such as a light, you move the switch or knob that controls it so that it stops giving out light or heat. ❏ *The janitor comes round to turn the lights out.* **4** →see also **turnout**

1 연결 구동사 (결과가) -로 되다 ❏ 내 인생이 결국 이렇게 될 줄 알았더라면, 그들이 나를 죽이도록 내버려두었을 텐데. ❏ 나는 일이 잘 되어 가리라고 확신했다. **2** 구동사 (결국) -로 드러나다 ❏ 코스그레이브의 예측이 크게 빗나간 것으로 드러났다. **3** 구동사 (불 등을) 끄다 ❏ 관리인이 한 바퀴 돌며 불을 끈다.

▶**turn over** **1** PHRASAL VERB If you **turn** something **over**, or if it **turns over**, it is moved so that the top part is now facing downward. ❏ *Liz picked up the blue envelope and turned it over curiously.* ❏ *The buggy turned over and Nancy was thrown out.* **2** PHRASAL VERB If you **turn over**, for example when you are lying in bed, you move your body so that you are lying in a different position. ❏ *Ann turned over in her bed once more.* **3** PHRASAL VERB If you **turn** something **over** in your mind, you think carefully about it. ❏ *Even when she didn't say anything you could see her turning things over in her mind.* **4** PHRASAL VERB If you **turn** something **over to** someone, you give it to them when they ask for it, because they have a right to it. ❏ *I would, indeed, turn the evidence over to the police.* **5** PHRASAL VERB If you **turn over** when you are watching television, you change to another channel. ❏ *Whenever he's on TV, I turn over.* **6** →see also **turnover**

1 구동사 뒤집다; 뒤집히다 ❏ 리즈는 파란 봉투를 집어 들고 호기심에 뒤집어 보았다. ❏ 마차가 뒤집혀 낸시가 내동댕이쳐졌다. **2** 구동사 몸을 뒤굴다, 뒤척이다 ❏ 앤이 침대에서 다시 한 번 뒤척였다. **3** 구동사 숙고하다 ❏ 그녀가 아무 말도 하지 않을 때에도 마음속으로 이것저것 숙고하고 있는 것을 알 수 있었다. **4** 구동사 -에게 인도하다, -에게 넘겨주다 ❏ 나는 정말 경찰에 증거를 넘겨줄 수도 있다. **5** 구동사 채널을 돌리다 ❏ 그가 텔레비전에 나오기만 하면 나는 채널을 돌려버린다.

▶**turn round** →see **turn around**

▶**turn up** **1** PHRASAL VERB If you say that someone or something **turns up**, you mean that they arrive, often unexpectedly or after you have been waiting a long time. ❏ *Richard had turned up on Christmas Eve with Tony.* **2** PHRASAL VERB If you **turn** something **up** or if it **turns up**, you find, discover, or notice it. ❏ *Investigations have never turned up any evidence.* **3** PHRASAL VERB When you **turn up** a radio, heater, or other piece of equipment, you increase the amount of sound, heat, or power being produced, by adjusting the controls. ❏ *Bill would turn up the TV in the other room.* ❏ *I turned the volume up.*

1 구동사 모습을 나타내다, 나타나다 ❏ 리처드는 토니와 함께 성탄절 전야에 모습을 나타냈다. **2** 구동사 발견하다, 찾아내다; 나타나다 ❏ 몇 차례 조사를 통해 어떤 증거도 찾아내지 못했다. **3** 구동사 (소리를) 크게 하다; (난방을) 올리다 ❏ 빌이 다른 방에서 텔레비전을 크게 틀곤 했다. ❏ 나는 음량을 올렸다.

turn|ing /tɜːrnɪŋ/ (**turnings**) N-COUNT If you take a particular **turning**, you go along a road which leads away from the side of another road. [mainly BRIT] ❏ *Take the next turning on the right.* →see also **turn**

가산명사 (방향) 전환 [주로 영국영어] ❏ 다음 모퉁이에서 오른쪽으로 도시오.

turn|ing point (**turning points**) N-COUNT A **turning point** is a time at which an important change takes place which affects the future of a person or thing. ❑ *The vote yesterday appears to mark something of a turning point in the war.*

가산명사 전환기, 전기 ❑ 어제의 투표가 그 전쟁에 있어 일종의 전환기를 나타내는 것처럼 보인다.

tur|nip /tɜrnɪp/ (**turnips**) N-VAR A **turnip** is a round vegetable with a cream-colored skin that is the root of a crop.

가산명사 또는 불가산명사 순무

turn|out /tɜrnaʊt/ (**turnouts**) also **turn-out** N-COUNT The **turnout** at an event is the number of people who go to it or take part in it. ❑ *On the big night there was a massive turnout.*

가산명사 (집회 등의) 참가자 수 ❑ 그 큰 야간 행사에 엄청난 수가 참가했다.

turn|over /tɜrnoʊvər/ (**turnovers**) **1** N-VAR The **turnover** of a company is the value of the goods or services sold during a particular period of time. [BUSINESS] ❑ *The company had a turnover of £3.8 million.* **2** N-VAR The **turnover** of people in an organization or place is the rate at which people leave and are replaced. [BUSINESS] ❑ *Short-term contracts increase staff turnover.*

1 가산명사 또는 불가산명사 총매상고 [경제] ❑ 그 회사는 380만 파운드의 총매상고를 올렸다. **2** 가산명사 또는 불가산명사 이직률, 노동 이동률 [경제] ❑ 단기 계약은 직원들의 이직률을 증가시킨다.

turn sig|nal (**turn signals**) N-COUNT A car's **turn signals** are the flashing lights that tell you it is going to turn left or right. [AM; BRIT **indicators**] ❑ *He flipped his turn signal, and took a left.*

가산명사 방향 지시등, 깜박이 [미국영어; 영국영어 indicators] ❑ 그는 깜박이를 켜고 좌회전을 했다.

tur|quoise /tɜrkwɔɪz/ (**turquoises**) COLOR **Turquoise** or **turquoise blue** is used to describe things that are of a light greenish-blue color. ❑ *...a clear turquoise sea.*

색채어 밝은 청록색, 터키옥색 ❑ 맑고 밝은 청록색 바다

tur|tle /tɜrtəl/ (**turtles**) **1** N-COUNT A **turtle** is any reptile that has a thick shell around its body, for example a tortoise or terrapin. [AM] **2** N-COUNT A **turtle** is a large reptile which has a thick shell covering its body and which lives in the sea most of the time. [BRIT; AM **sea turtle**]

1 가산명사 거북 [미국영어] **2** 가산명사 바다거북 [영국영어; 미국영어 sea turtle]

tusk /tʌsk/ (**tusks**) N-COUNT The **tusks** of an elephant, wild boar, or walrus are its two very long, curved, pointed teeth.

가산명사 (코끼리 등의) 엄니

tus|sle /tʌsəl/ (**tussles, tussling, tussled**) V-RECIP If one person **tussles with** another, or if they **tussle**, they get hold of each other and struggle or fight. ❑ *They ended up ripping down perimeter fencing and tussling with the security staff.* ❑ *He grabbed my microphone and we tussled over that.* ● N-COUNT **Tussle** is also a noun. ❑ *The referee booked him for a tussle with the goalie.*

상호동사 드잡이하다, 몸싸움을 벌이다 ❑ 그들은 결국 방호 울타리를 무너뜨리고 보안 요원과 몸싸움을 벌이게 되었다. ❑ 그가 내 마이크를 잡아채서 우리는 그걸 서로 뺏으려고 몸싸움을 벌였다. ● 가산명사 드잡이 ❑ 심판이 골키퍼와 드잡이를 했다는 이유로 그의 이름을 적었다.

tu|tor /tutər, BRIT tyuːtəʳ/ (**tutors**) **1** N-COUNT A **tutor** is someone who gives private lessons to one student or a very small group of students. ❑ *Whitney had accepted a position as private tutor with a nearby family.* **2** N-COUNT A **tutor** is a teacher at a British university or college. In some American universities or colleges, a **tutor** is a teacher of the lowest rank. ❑ *He is course tutor in archaeology at the University of Southampton.*

1 가산명사 개인 교사 ❑ 휘트니는 이웃집의 개인 교사 일을 수락했었다. **2** 가산명사 (대학의) 강사 ❑ 그는 사우샘프턴대학교의 고고학 강사이다.

tu|to|rial /tutɔriəl, BRIT tyuːtɔːriəl/ (**tutorials**) **1** N-COUNT In a university or college, a **tutorial** is a regular meeting between a tutor or professor and one or several students, for discussion of a subject that is being studied. ❑ *The methods of study include lectures, tutorials, case studies and practical sessions.* **2** N-COUNT A **tutorial** is part of a book or a computer program which helps you learn something step-by-step without a teacher. ❑ *There is an excellent tutorial section, which carefully walks you through how to play.* **3** ADJ **Tutorial** means relating to a tutor or tutors, especially one at a university or college. [ADJ n] ❑ *Students may decide to seek tutorial guidance.*

1 가산명사 개별 지도, 그룹 지도 ❑ 학습 방법에는 강의, 개별 지도, 사례 연구, 실습 활동이 포함된다. **2** 가산명사 지침서, 설명 프로그램 ❑ 아주 훌륭한 설명 부분이 있는데, 여기서 게임 방법을 꼼꼼하게 안내해 준다. **3** 형용사 개별 지도의 ❑ 학생이 개별 지도가 필요한지 결정할 수도 있다.

tux|edo /tʌksidoʊ/ (**tuxedos**) N-COUNT A **tuxedo** is a black or white jacket worn by men for formal social events. [mainly AM; BRIT usually **dinner jacket**]

가산명사 턱시도 [주로 미국영어; 영국영어 대개 dinner jacket]

TV ◆◇◇ /tiː viː/ (**TVs**) N-VAR **TV** means the same as **television**. ❑ *The TV was on.* ❑ *I prefer going to the cinema to watching TV.*

가산명사 또는 불가산명사 텔레비전 ❑ 텔레비전이 켜져 있었다. ❑ 나는 텔레비전을 보는 것보다 영화관에 가는 게 더 좋다.

tweed /twid/ (**tweeds**) N-MASS **Tweed** is a thick woolen cloth, often woven from different colored threads. ❑ *...shooting coats in tweed or rubberized cotton.*

물질명사 트위드 천 ❑ 트위드나 고무를 입힌 면으로 만든 사냥용 외투

twelfth ◆◇◇ /twelfθ/ (**twelfths**) **1** ORD The **twelfth** item in a series is the one that you count as number twelve. ❑ *...the twelfth anniversary of the April revolution.* **2** FRACTION A **twelfth** is one of twelve equal parts of something. ❑ *She is entitled to a twelfth of the cash.*

1 서수 열두 번째 ❑ 사월 혁명의 12주년 기념일 **2** 분수 12분의 1 ❑ 그녀는 그 현금의 12분의 1을 받을 권리가 있다.

twelve ◆◆◇ /twelv/ (**twelves**) NUM **Twelve** is the number 12.

수사 12, 열둘

twen|ti|eth ◆◇◇ /twentiəθ/ (**twentieths**) **1** ORD The **twentieth** item in a series is the one that you count as number twenty. ❑ *...the twentieth century.* **2** FRACTION A **twentieth** is one of twenty equal parts of something. ❑ *A few twentieths of a gram can be critical.*

1 서수 스무 번째의 ❑ 20세기 **2** 분수 20분의 1 ❑ 1그램의 20분의 몇만 되어도 치명적일 수 있다.

twen|ty ◆◆◇ /twenti/ (**twenties**) **1** NUM **Twenty** is the number 20. **2** N-PLURAL When you talk about the **twenties**, you are referring to numbers between 20 and 29. For example, if you are in your **twenties**, you are aged between 20 and 29. If the temperature is **in the twenties**, the temperature is between 20 and 29 degrees. ❑ *They're both in their twenties and both married with children of their own.* **3** N-PLURAL The **twenties** is the decade between 1920 and 1929. ❑ *It was written in the Twenties, but it still really stands out.*

1 수사 20, 스물 **2** 복수명사 (나이가) 20대의; (수가) 20대의 ❑ 그들은 둘 다 20대이며, 모두 자기 아이들을 데리고 결혼했다. **3** 복수명사 1920년대 ❑ 그것은 20년대에 쓰였지만, 아직도 정말 뛰어나다.

24-7 /twentiforsevⁿn/ also **twenty-four seven** ADV If something happens **24-7**, it happens all the time without ever stopping. **24-7** means twenty-four hours a day, seven days a week. [mainly AM, INFORMAL] [ADV after v] ❑ *I feel like sleeping 24-7.* ● ADJ **24-7** is also an adjective. [ADJ n] ❑ *Now it is a 24-7 radio station that generates $30 million a year in advertising revenue.*

부사 언제나 끊임없이; 1주일 내내 매일 24 시간 동안 [주로 미국영어, 비격식체] ❑ 나는 1주일 내내 매일 24 시간 동안 잤으면 좋겠다. ● 형용사 끊임없는 ❑ 이제 그것은 광고 수익으로 일년에 3천만 달러를 창출하는 연중무휴 전일 라디오 방송국이다.

Word Link	twi ≈ two : twice, twilight, twin

twice ◆◆◆ /twaɪs/ **1** ADV If something happens **twice**, there are two actions or events of the same kind. ❑ *He visited me twice that fall and called me on the telephone often.* ❑ *The government has twice declined to back the scheme.* **2** ADV You use **twice** in expressions such as **twice a day** and **twice a week** to indicate that two events or actions of the same kind happen in each day or week. [ADV a n] ❑ *I phoned twice a day, leaving messages with his wife.* **3** ADV If one thing is, for example, **twice**

1 부사 두 번 ❑ 그는 그 해 가을 내게 두 번 찾아와서 전화도 자주 했다. ❑ 정부가 그 계획에 대한 지원을 두 번 거부했다. **2** 부사 두 번 ❑ 나는 하루에 두 번씩 전화를 해서 그의 부인에게 메시지를 남겨 놓았다. **3** 부사 -보다 두 배, -보다 갑절로 ❑ 7천만 파운드는 예상보다 두 배나 큰 액수였다. ● 전치 한정사 두 배의

as big or old **as** another, the first thing is two times as big or old as the second. People sometimes say that one thing is **twice as** good or hard **as** another when they want to emphasize that the first thing is much better or harder than the second. [ADV as adj/adv] ❑ *The figure of seventy-million pounds was twice as big as expected.* ● PREDET Twice is also a predeterminer. [PREDET the n] ❑ *Unemployment in Northern Ireland is twice the national average.* ◪ PHRASE If you **think twice** about doing something, you consider it again and decide not to do it, or decide to do it differently. ❑ *She'd better shut her mouth and from now on think twice before saying stupid things.* ◪ **once or twice** →see **once**. **twice over** →see **over**

□ 북아일랜드의 실업은 국가 평균의 두 배이다. ◪ 구 재고하다, 다시 생각하다 ❑ 그녀는 입 닥치고 이제부터는 멍청한 얘기하기 전에 다시 한 번 생각해 보는 게 좋을 거다.

twig /twɪɡ/ (**twigs**) N-COUNT A **twig** is a very small thin branch that grows out from a main branch of a tree or bush. ❑ *There is the bird, sitting on a twig halfway up a tree.*

가산명사 작은 가지, 잔가지 ❑ 새 한 마리가 나무의 중간에 있는 가지에 앉아 있다.

Word Link   twi ≈ two : *twice*, *twilight*, *twin*

twi|light /ˈtwaɪlaɪt/ N-UNCOUNT **Twilight** is the time just before night when the daylight has almost gone but when it is not completely dark. ❑ *They returned at twilight, and set off for one of the promenade bars.*

불가산명사 황혼, 땅거미 ❑ 그들은 어스름할 무렵에 돌아와서 해변가 술집 한 곳으로 갔다.

twin ◆◇◇ /twɪn/ (**twins**) ◯ N-COUNT If two people are **twins**, they have the same mother and were born on the same day. ❑ *Sarah was looking after the twins.* ❑ *I think there are many positive aspects to being a twin.* ◪ ADJ **Twin** is used to describe a pair of things that look the same and are close together. [ADJ n] ❑ *...the twin spires of the cathedral.* ◪ ADJ **Twin** is used to describe two things or ideas that are similar or connected in some way. [ADJ n] ❑ *...the twin concepts of liberty and equality.* →see **clone**

◯ 가산명사 쌍둥이 ❑ 사라가 쌍둥이를 돌보고 있었다. ❑ 나는 쌍둥이들에게는 긍정적인 측면이 많다고 생각한다. ◪ 형용사 같은 모양의, 쌍둥이의 ❑ 대성당의 쌍둥이 첨탑 ◪ 형용사 닮은, 결부된 ❑ 자유와 평등이라는 서로 결부되어 있는 두 개념

twin|kle /ˈtwɪŋkᵊl/ (**twinkles**, **twinkling**, **twinkled**) ◯ V-I If a star or a light **twinkles**, it shines with an unsteady light which rapidly and constantly changes from bright to faint. ❑ *At night, lights twinkle in distant villages across the valleys.* ◪ V-I If you say that someone's eyes **twinkle**, you mean that their face expresses good humor or amusement. ❑ *She saw her mother's eyes twinkle with amusement.* ● N-SING **Twinkle** is also a noun. ❑ *A kindly twinkle came into her eyes.*

◯ 자동사 반짝이다, 반짝반짝 빛나다 ❑ 밤에는 계곡 건너 먼 마을에서 불빛이 반짝거린다. ◪ 자동사 (눈이) 반짝거리다 ❑ 그녀는 어머니의 눈이 재미있어 하며 반짝이는 것을 보았다. ● 단수명사 반짝거림 ❑ 그녀의 눈에 다정한 빛이 반짝였다.

twirl /twɜrl/ (**twirls**, **twirling**, **twirled**) ◯ V-T/V-I If you **twirl** something or if it **twirls**, it turns around and around with a smooth, fairly fast movement. ❑ *Bonnie twirled her empty glass in her fingers.* ◪ V-I If you **twirl**, you turn around and around quickly, for example when you are dancing. ❑ *Several hundred people twirl around the ballroom dance floor.*

◯ 타동사/자동사 빙빙 돌리다; 빙빙 돌다 ❑ 보니는 손가락으로 빈 잔을 빙빙 돌렸다. ◪ 자동사 빙빙 돌다 ❑ 수백 명의 사람들이 무도장의 댄스 플로어를 빙빙 돈다.

twist ◆◇◇ /twɪst/ (**twists**, **twisting**, **twisted**) ◯ V-T If you **twist** something, you turn it to make a spiral shape, for example by turning the two ends of it in opposite directions. ❑ *Her hands began to twist the handles of the bag she carried.* ◪ V-T/V-I If you **twist** something, especially a part of your body, or if it **twists**, it moves into an unusual, uncomfortable, or bent position, for example because of being hit or pushed, or because you are upset. ❑ *He twisted her arms behind her back and clipped a pair of handcuffs on her wrists.* ❑ *Sophia's face twisted in perplexity.* ◪ V-T/V-I If you **twist** part of your body such as your head or your shoulders, you turn that part while keeping the rest of your body still. ❑ *She twisted her head sideways and looked towards the door.* ◪ V-T If you **twist** a part of your body such as your ankle or wrist, you injure it by turning it too sharply, or in an unusual direction. ❑ *He fell and twisted his ankle.* ◪ V-T If you **twist** something, you turn it so that it moves around in a circular direction. ❑ *She was staring down at her hands, twisting the ring on her finger.* ● N-COUNT **Twist** is also a noun. ❑ *Just a twist of the handle is all it takes to wring out the mop.* ◪ V-I If a road or river **twists**, it has a lot of sudden changes of direction in it. ❑ *The roads twist round hairpin bends.* ● N-COUNT **Twist** is also a noun. [usu pl] ❑ *It allows the train to maintain a constant speed through the twists and turns of existing track.* ◪ V-T If you say that someone **has twisted** something that you have said, you disapprove of them because they have repeated it in a way that changes its meaning, in order to harm you or benefit themselves. [DISAPPROVAL] ❑ *It's a shame the way that the media can twist your words and misrepresent you.* ◪ N-COUNT A **twist** in something is an unexpected and significant development. ❑ *The battle of the sexes also took a new twist.* **to twist** someone's **arm** →see **arm**. **to get** your **knickers in a twist** →see **knickers**. **to twist the knife** →see **knife**

◯ 타동사 꼬다 ❑ 그녀는 갖고 있던 가방 손잡이를 배배 꼬기 시작했다. ◪ 타동사/자동사 비틀어 돌리다; 뒤틀리다 ❑ 그는 그녀의 등 뒤로 팔을 비틀어 손목에 수갑을 채웠다. ❑ 소피아는 당황하여 얼굴을 찡그렸다. ◪ 타동사/자동사 (머리나 어깨를) 돌리다 ❑ 그녀는 머리를 옆으로 돌려 문 쪽을 바라보았다. ◪ 타동사 (발목 또는 손목을) 삐다 ❑ 그는 넘어져서 발목을 삐었다. ◪ 타동사 돌리다 ❑ 그녀는 자기 손을 내려다보면서 손가락의 반지를 빙빙 돌리고 있었다. ● 가산명사 돌리기 ❑ 손잡이를 한 번 돌리기만 하면 대걸레를 짤 수 있다. ◪ 자동사 굽이치다, 굽다 ❑ 길들이 머리핀처럼 굽어져 있다. ● 가산명사 굽이, 만곡 ❑ 그것 덕분에 기차가 기존 선로의 구불구불한 곳을 지나면서도 일정한 속도를 유지할 수 있다. ◪ 타동사 곡해하다, 왜전시키다 [탐탁잖음] ❑ 언론이 당신의 말을 왜전시키고 당신을 부정확하게 전달할 수 있다는 점이 유감스럽다. ◪ 가산명사 예상 밖의 진전 ❑ 남녀의 성 대결 또한 예상 밖으로 새로운 진전을 보였다.

Word Partnership   twist의 연어

ADV.	twist **around** ◯ ◪
V.	twist **and turn** ◪
	plot twist, **story** twist ◪
ADJ.	**added** twist, **bizarre** twist, **interesting** twist, **latest** twist, **new** twist, **unexpected** twist ◪

twist|er /ˈtwɪstər/ (**twisters**) N-COUNT A **twister** is the same as a **tornado**. [AM]

가산명사 돌개바람, 회오리바람 [미국영어]

twitch /twɪtʃ/ (**twitches**, **twitching**, **twitched**) V-T/V-I If something, especially a part of your body, **twitches** or if you **twitch** it, it makes a little jumping movement. ❑ *When I stood up to her, her right cheek would begin to twitch.* ● N-COUNT **Twitch** is also a noun. ❑ *He developed a nervous twitch and began to blink constantly.*

타동사/자동사 실룩거리다; ~을 실룩대다 ❑ 내가 그녀에게 맞서면, 그녀의 오른쪽 뺨이 실룩거리곤 했다. ● 가산명사 실룩거림, 경련 ❑ 그는 신경성 경련이 생겨서 계속 눈을 깜박거리기 시작했다.

two ◆◆◆ /tu/ (**twos**) ◯ NUM **Two** is the number 2. ◪ PHRASE If you say **it takes two** or **it takes two to tango**, you mean that a situation or argument involves two people and they are both therefore responsible for it. ❑ *Divorce is never the fault of one partner; it takes two.* ◪ PHRASE If you **put two and two together**, you work out the truth about something for yourself, by using the information that is available to you. ❑ *Putting two and two together, I assume that this was the car he used.* ◪ **to kill two birds with one stone** →see **bird**

◯ 수사 2, 둘 ◪ 구 손뼉도 마주쳐야 소리가 난다 ❑ 이혼은 결코 한 쪽만의 잘못이 아니다. 손뼉도 마주쳐야 소리가 난다. ◪ 구 정보를 종합하여 결론을 내리다 ❑ 정보를 종합해 보면, 나는 이것이 그가 사용한 차량이라고 생각한다.

two-faced ADJ If you describe someone as **two-faced**, you are critical of them because they say they do or believe one thing when their behavior or words show that they do not do it or do not believe it. [DISAPPROVAL] ❑ *The scientists saw the*

형용사 두 얼굴의, 위선적인 [탐탁잖음] ❑ 과학자들은 가축이 어떻게 취급받는지를 볼 때 사람들이 동물 복지에 대해 특히 이중적이라고 생각했다.

a b c d e f g h i j k l m n o p q r s t u v w x y z

public as being particularly two-faced about animal welfare in view of the way domestic animals are treated.

two|fold /ˈtuːfoʊld/ also **two-fold** ADJ You can use **twofold** to introduce a topic that has two equally important parts. [FORMAL] ❑ *The purpose of the ambassador's visit is twofold – to step up pressure on the invaders to withdraw peacefully, and to intensify preparations for war if that pressure fails.*

형용사 두 요소의, 두 가지의 [격식체] ❑ 대사의 방문 목적은 두 가지이다. 그것은 평화롭게 철수하도록 침략자들에게 더욱 압력을 가하는 것과 그러한 압박이 효과가 없으면 전쟁 준비를 강화하는 것이다.

two-way ❶ ADJ **Two-way** means moving or working in two opposite directions or allowing something to move or work in two opposite directions. ❑ *The bridge is now open to two-way traffic.* ❷ ADJ A **two-way** radio can send and receive signals. [ADJ n] ❑ *Each squad has a two-way radio to stay in touch.*

❶ 형용사 양 방향의 ❑ 그 다리는 이제 양방향 통행이 자유롭다. ❷ 형용사 송수신용의 ❑ 각 분대에는 서로 연락하기 위한 송수신용 무전기가 있다.

ty|coon /taɪkuːn/ (**tycoons**) N-COUNT A **tycoon** is a person who is successful in business and so has become rich and powerful. ❑ *...a self-made Irish property tycoon.*

가산명사 재계의 거물 ❑ 자수성가한 아일랜드 출신의 부동산 거물

---

type

① SORT OR KIND
② WRITING AND PRINTING

---

① type ♦♦◇ /taɪp/ (**types**) ❶ N-COUNT A **type of** something is a group of those things that have particular features in common. ❑ *...several types of lettuce.* ❑ *There are various types of the disease.*

❶ 가산명사 종류 ❑ 여러 종류의 상추 ❑ 그 병에는 여러 종류가 있다.

❷ N-COUNT If you refer to a particular thing or person as a **type of** something more general, you are considering that thing or person as an example of that more general group. ❑ *Have you done this type of work before?* ❑ *Rates of interest for this type of borrowing can be high.* ❸ N-COUNT If you refer to a person as a particular type, you mean that they have that particular appearance, character, or type of behavior. ❑ *It's the first time I, a fair-skinned, freckly type, have sailed in the sun without burning.*

❷ 가산명사 유형, 종류 ❑ 전에 이런 종류의 일을 해 본 적이 있나요? ❑ 이런 유형의 융자는 금리가 높을 수도 있다. ❸ 가산명사 -형, -타입 ❑ 피부가 희고 주근깨 타입인 내가 햇빛 속에서 항해했는데 타지 않은 것은 처음이다.

The **brand** of a product such as jeans, tea, or soap is its name, which can also be the name of the company that makes or sells it. The **make** of a car or electrical appliance such as a radio or washing machine is the name of the company that produces it. If you talk about what **type** of product or service you want, you are talking about its quality and what features it should have. You can also talk about **types** of people or of abstract things. ❑ *...which type of coffeemaker to choose....a new type of bank account....looking for a certain type of actor.* A **model** of car or of some other devices is a name that is given to a particular **type**, for example, Ford Escort or Nissan Micra. Note that **type** can also be used informally to mean either **make** or **model**. For example, if someone asks what **type** of car you have got, you could reply "an SUV," "a Ford," or perhaps "an Escort."

청바지, 차, 비누와 같은 상품의 brand는 그 상품의 이름인데, 상품명이 그것을 만들거나 파는 회사명일 수도 있다. 자동차 또는 라디오나 세탁기 같은 전기제품의 make는 그것을 생산하는 회사명이다. 원하는 상품이나 서비스의 type을 얘기하는 것은 그 상품이나 서비스가 지녀야 할 품질이나 특성을 말하는 것이다. 사람이나 추상적 사물에 대해서도 type을 말할 수 있다. ❑ ...어떤 종류의 커피 메이커를 선택할지....새로운 종류의 은행 계좌....어떤 특정한 유형의 배우를 찾는. 자동차나 다른 일부 장치의 model은 특정 type에 붙여진 이름으로, 예를 들면 포드 에스코트나 니산 마이크라와 같은 것이다. type은 또한 비격식체로 make나 model을 뜻할 수도 있다. 예를 들어 어떤 type의 자동차를 가지고 있느냐고 누가 물으면, '스포츠 유틸리티 차량,' 또는 '포드,' 또는 '에스코트'라고 대답할 수 있다.

② type ♦♦◇ /taɪp/ (**types, typing, typed**) ❶ V-T/V-I If you **type** something, you use a typewriter or computer keyboard to write it. ❑ *I can type your essays for you.* ❑ *I had never really learnt to type properly.* ❷ N-UNCOUNT **Type** is printed text as it appears in a book or newspaper, or the small pieces of metal that are used to create this. ❑ *The correction had already been set in type.* ❸ →see also **typing**
→see **printing**

❶ 타동사/자동사 타이프 치다 ❑ 내가 네 대신 에세이를 타이프 쳐줄 수 있다. ❑ 나는 정말 타이프 치는 법을 제대로 배운 적이 없었다. ❷ 불가산명사 인쇄본; 활자 ❑ 수정 부분이 이미 조판되어 있었다.

Thesaurus	*type*의 참조어
N.	class, kind, sort ① ❶ ❷ ❸
print ② ❷
V.	transcribe, write ② ❶

▶**type in** or **type into** PHRASAL VERB If you **type** information **into** a computer or **type** it **in**, you press keys on the keyboard so that the computer stores or processes the information. ❑ *Officials type each passport number into a computer.* ❑ *You have to type in commands, such as "help" and "print."*

구동사 –을 입력하다 ❑ 관리들이 각 여권 번호를 컴퓨터에 입력한다. ❑ '도움말'이나 '인쇄'와 같은 명령어를 입력해야 한다.

▶**type up** PHRASAL VERB If you **type up** a text that has been written by hand, you produce a typed copy of it. ❑ *When the first draft was completed, Nichols typed it up.*

구동사 (손으로 쓴 것을) 타자기로 치다 ❑ 초고가 완성되자 니콜스가 그것을 타자기로 쳤다.

type|face /taɪpfeɪs/ (**typefaces**) N-COUNT In printing, a **typeface** is a set of alphabetical characters, numbers, and other characters that all have the same design. There are many different typefaces. ❑ *...the ubiquitous Times New Roman typeface.*

가산명사 서체, 활자체 ❑ 어디서나 볼 수 있는 타임스 뉴로만 서체

type|writ|er /taɪpraɪtər/ (**typewriters**) N-COUNT A **typewriter** is a machine with keys which are pressed in order to print letters, numbers, or other characters onto paper.

가산명사 타자기

ty|phoon /taɪfuːn/ (**typhoons**) N-COUNT A **typhoon** is a very violent tropical storm. →see **disaster, hurricane**

가산명사 태풍

typi|cal ♦◇◇ /tɪpɪkəl/ ❶ ADJ You use **typical** to describe someone or something that shows the most usual characteristics of a particular type of person or thing, and is therefore a good example of that type. ❑ *Cheney is everyone's image of a typical cop: a big white guy, six foot, 220 pounds.* ❷ ADJ If a particular action or feature is **typical of** someone or something, it shows their usual qualities or characteristics. ❑ *This reluctance to move towards a democratic state is typical of totalitarian regimes.* ❸ ADJ If you say that something is **typical of** a person, situation, or thing, you are criticizing them or complaining about them and saying that they are just as bad or disappointing as you expected them to be. [FEELINGS] ❑ *She threw her hands into the air. "That is just typical of you, isn't it?"*

❶ 형용사 전형적인, 대표적인 ❑ 채니는 모든 사람들이 생각하는 전형적인 경관의 모습으로, 몸집 큰 백인 남자에 키는 6피트이고 몸무게는 220파운드이다. ❷ 형용사 전형적인 ❑ 민주국가로 향해 나아가기를 이렇게 꺼려하는 것이 전체주의 체제의 전형적인 특징이다. ❸ 형용사 늘 그런 식의, 매사 똑같은 방식의 [감정 개입] ❑ 그녀는 두 손을 번쩍 들었다. "넌 맨날 그런 식이지, 안 그러니?"

typi|cal|ly /tɪpɪkli/ **1** ADV You use **typically** to say that something usually happens in the way that you are describing. [ADV with cl/group] ❑ *It typically takes a day or two, depending on size.* **2** ADV You use **typically** to say that something shows all the most usual characteristics of a particular type of person or thing. [ADV adj] ❑ *Philip paced the floor, a typically nervous expectant father.* **3** ADV You use **typically** to indicate that someone has behaved in the way that they normally do. ❑ *Typically, the Norwegians were on the mountain two hours before anyone else.*

1 부사 일반적으로, 대체로 ❑ 그것은 크기에 따라서 대체로 하루나 이틀이 걸린다. **2** 부사 전형적으로 ❑ 필립은 복도를 서성거렸는데, 전형적으로 안절부절 못하며 출산을 기다리는 아버지의 모습이었다. **3** 부사 으레 그렇듯이 ❑ 으레 그렇듯이 노르웨이 사람들이 다른 사람들보다 두 시간 먼저 산에 올라가 있었다.

typi|fy /tɪpɪfaɪ/ (**typifies, typifying, typified**) V-T If something or someone **typifies** a situation or type of thing or person, they have all the usual characteristics of it and are a typical example of it. ❑ *These two buildings typify the rich extremes of Irish architecture.*

타동사 전형이 되다, 특징을 나타내다 ❑ 이 두 건물은 아일랜드 건축의 극치를 보여 주는 전형이다.

typ|ing /taɪpɪŋ/ **1** N-UNCOUNT **Typing** is the work or activity of typing something by means of a typewriter or computer keyboard. ❑ *She didn't do any typing till the evening.* **2** N-UNCOUNT **Typing** is the skill of using a typewriter or keyboard quickly and accurately. ❑ *My typing is quite dreadful.*

1 불가산명사 타자, 타이프 치기 ❑ 그녀는 저녁까지 전혀 타이프를 치지 않았다. **2** 불가산명사 타자 기술 ❑ 내 타자 기술은 엉망이다.

typ|ist /taɪpɪst/ (**typists**) N-COUNT A **typist** is someone who works in an office typing letters and other documents.

가산명사 타자수

tyr|an|ny /tɪrəni/ (**tyrannies**) **1** N-VAR A **tyranny** is a cruel, harsh, and unfair government in which a person or small group of people have power over everyone else. ❑ *Self-expression and individuality are the greatest weapons against tyranny.* **2** N-UNCOUNT If you describe someone's behavior and treatment of others that they have authority over as **tyranny**, you mean that they are severe with them or unfair to them. ❑ *I'm the sole victim of Mother's tyranny.*

1 가산명사 또는 불가산명사 전제 정치 ❑ 자기표현과 개성이 전제 정치에 대항하는 가장 큰 무기이다. **2** 불가산명사 포학, 횡포 ❑ 나는 어머니의 횡포의 유일한 희생자이다.

tyr|ant /taɪrənt/ (**tyrants**) N-COUNT You can use **tyrant** to refer to someone who treats the people they have authority over in a cruel and unfair way. ❑ *...households where the father was a tyrant.*

가산명사 폭군 ❑ 아버지가 폭군인 가정들

tyre /taɪər/ →see **tire**

a b c d e f g h i j k l m n o p q r s t u v w x y z

Uu

U, u (U's, u's) /yu/ N-VAR **U** is the twenty-first letter of the English alphabet.

ubiquitous /yubɪkwɪtəs/ ADJ If you describe something or someone as **ubiquitous**, you mean that they seem to be everywhere. [FORMAL] ❑ *Sugar is ubiquitous in the diet.* ❑ *In the U.S., the camcorder has become ubiquitous.*

ugly /ʌgli/ (**uglier, ugliest**) **1** ADJ If you say that someone or something is **ugly**, you mean that they are very unattractive and unpleasant to look at. ❑ *...an ugly little hat.* ● **ug|li|ness** N-UNCOUNT ❑ *The Arndale Centre, despite its ugliness, is popular with shoppers.* **2** ADJ If you refer to an event or situation as **ugly**, you mean that it is very unpleasant, usually because it involves violent or aggressive behavior. ❑ *There have been some ugly scenes.* ❑ *The confrontation turned ugly.* ● **ug|li|ness** N-UNCOUNT ❑ *...the subtlety and ugliness of sexual harassment.* **3** to **rear** its **ugly head** →see **head**

<table>
<tr><td colspan="2">Thesaurus   ugly의 참조어</td></tr>
<tr><td>ADJ.</td><td>hideous, unattractive; (ant.) beautiful 1
offensive, unpleasant 2</td></tr>
</table>

UK ◆◇◇ /yu keɪ/ N-PROPER **The UK** is Great Britain and Northern Ireland. **UK** is an abbreviation for "United Kingdom." [the N]

ul|cer /ʌlsər/ (**ulcers**) N-COUNT An **ulcer** is a sore area on the outside or inside of your body which is very painful and may bleed or produce an unpleasant poisonous substance. ❑ *In addition to headaches, you may develop stomach ulcers as well.*

ul|te|ri|or /ʌltɪəriər/ ADJ If you say that someone has an **ulterior** motive for doing something, you believe that they have a hidden reason for doing it. [ADJ n] ❑ *Sheila had an ulterior motive for trying to help Stan.*

ul|ti|mate ◆◇◇ /ʌltɪmɪt/ **1** ADJ You use **ultimate** to describe the final result or aim of a long series of events. [ADJ n] ❑ *He said it is still not possible to predict the ultimate outcome.* **2** ADJ You use **ultimate** to describe the original source or cause of something. [ADJ n] ❑ *Plants are the ultimate source of all foodstuffs.* **3** ADJ You use **ultimate** to describe the most important or powerful thing of a particular kind. [ADJ n] ❑ *...the ultimate power of the central government.* ❑ *My experience as player, coach and manager has prepared me for this ultimate challenge.* **4** ADJ You use **ultimate** to describe the most extreme and unpleasant example of a particular thing. [ADJ n] ❑ *Bringing back the death penalty would be the ultimate abuse of human rights.* ❑ *Treachery was the ultimate sin.* **5** ADJ You use **ultimate** to describe the best possible example of a particular thing. [ADJ n] ❑ *He is the ultimate English gentleman.* **6** PHRASE **The ultimate in** something is the best or most advanced example of it. ❑ *Ballet is the ultimate in human movement.* ❑ *This hotel is the ultimate in luxury.*

<table>
<tr><td colspan="2">Word Partnership   ultimate의 연어</td></tr>
<tr><td>N.</td><td>ultimate aim/goal/objective, ultimate outcome 1
ultimate authority, ultimate decision, ultimate power,
ultimate weapon 3
ultimate experience 3 5</td></tr>
</table>

ul|ti|mate|ly ◆◇◇ /ʌltɪmɪtli/ **1** ADV **Ultimately** means finally, after a long and often complicated series of events. ❑ *Whatever the scientists ultimately conclude, all of their data will immediately be disputed.* **2** ADV You use **ultimately** to indicate that what you are saying is the most important point in a discussion. [ADV with cl] ❑ *Ultimately, Bismarck's revisionism scarcely affected or damaged British interests at all.*

<table>
<tr><td colspan="2">Thesaurus   ultimately의 참조어</td></tr>
<tr><td>ADV.</td><td>eventually, finally 1</td></tr>
</table>

ul|ti|ma|tum /ʌltɪmeɪtəm/ (**ultimatums**) N-COUNT An **ultimatum** is a warning to someone that unless they act in a particular way, action will be taken against them. ❑ *They issued an ultimatum to the police to rid an area of racist attackers, or they will take the law into their own hands.*

ultra|sound /ʌltrəsaʊnd/ N-UNCOUNT **Ultrasound** is sound waves which travel at such a high frequency that they cannot be heard by humans. Ultrasound is used in medicine to get pictures of the inside of people's bodies. ❑ *I had an ultrasound scan to see how the pregnancy was progressing.*

가산명사 또는 불가산명사 영이 알파벳의 스물한 번째 글자

형용사 어디에나 있는, 편재하는 [격식체] ❑ 설탕은 어느 식단에나 다 들어 있다. ❑ 미국에서 캠코더는 어디서나 볼 수 있는 흔한 것이 되었다.

1 형용사 추한, 보기 싫은 ❑ 보기 싫은 작은 모자 ● 추함, 꼴사나움 불가산명사 ❑ 안데일 센터는 흉물스럽지만 쇼핑객들에게 인기가 있다. **2** 형용사 추잡한, 험악한 ❑ 몇몇 꼴사나운 장면이 있었다. ❑ 대립 사태가 험악해졌다. ● 추잡함 불가산명사 ❑ 성추행의 미묘함과 추잡함

고유명사 영국

가산명사 궤양 ❑ 당신은 두통에 위궤양까지도 생길 수 있다.

형용사 이면의, 숨은 ❑ 실라가 스탄을 도와주려고 한 데는 숨은 동기가 있었다.

1 형용사 궁극적인, 최후의 ❑ 그는 최종 결과는 여전히 예측 불가능하다고 말했다. **2** 형용사 근원적인 ❑ 식물은 모든 식품의 근원이다. **3** 형용사 최고의 ❑ 중앙 정부의 최고 권력 ❑ 선수, 코치, 감독 경험이 있기 때문에 내가 이 최대 도전에 대비할 수 있다. **4** 형용사 최악의 ❑ 사형 제도를 다시 도입하는 것은 최악의 인권 유린이 될 것이다. ❑ 반역은 최악의 죄였다. **5** 형용사 최상의, 최고의 ❑ 그는 최고의 영국 신사이다. **6** 구 ∼의 정수 ❑ 발레는 인체 동작의 정수를 보여 준다. ❑ 이 호텔은 사치의 정수를 보여준다.

1 부사 궁극적으로 ❑ 과학자들이 궁극적으로 어떤 결론을 내리든, 그들의 모든 자료는 즉각 논박을 받을 것이다. **2** 부사 결론적으로 ❑ 결론적으로, 비스마르크의 수정주의는 영국의 이해관계에 거의 어떤 영향을 주거나 손상을 입히지 않았다.

가산명사 최후통첩 ❑ 그들은 경찰에 어떤 지역에서 인종 차별주의자인 범죄자들을 제거하지 않으면 자기들이 직접 법을 행사하겠다는 최후통첩을 보냈다.

불가산명사 초음파 ❑ 나는 임신 진행 상황을 알아보기 위해 초음파 검사를 했다.

ultra|vio|let /ˌʌltrəvaɪəlɪt/ ADJ **Ultraviolet** light or radiation is what causes your skin to become darker in color after you have been in sunlight. In large amounts ultraviolet light is harmful. ❑ *The sun's ultraviolet rays are responsible for both tanning and burning.* →see **skin**, **wave**

형용사 자외선의 ❑ 태양의 자외선은 피부를 그을리게 하고 화상을 초래한다.

um|brel|la /ʌmbrelə/ (**umbrellas**) **1** N-COUNT An **umbrella** is an object which you use to protect yourself from the rain or hot sun. It consists of a long stick with a folding frame covered in cloth. ❑ *Harry held an umbrella over Dawn.* **2** N-SING **Umbrella** is used to refer to a single group or description that includes a lot of different organizations or ideas. ❑ *Does coincidence come under the umbrella of the paranormal?* ❑ *...Socialist International, an umbrella group comprising almost a hundred Social Democrat parties.*

1 가산명사 우산, 양산 ❑ 해리는 도운에게 우산을 씌워 주었다. **2** 단수명사 (포괄적) 개념, 총체 ❑ 우연이 초자연적 현상이라는 포괄적인 개념 안에 포함됩니까? ❑ 거의 백 개에 달하는 사회 민주당들을 포괄하는 총체인 사회주의 국제 연맹

um|pire /ʌmpaɪr/ (**umpires**, **umpiring**, **umpired**) **1** N-COUNT An **umpire** is a person whose job is to make sure that a sports contest or game is played fairly and that the rules are not broken. ❑ *The umpire's decision is final.* **2** V-T/V-I To **umpire** means to be the umpire in a sports contest or game. ❑ *He umpired baseball games.*

1 가산명사 심판 ❑ 심판의 결정은 최종적이다. **2** 타동사/자동사 심판을 보다 ❑ 그는 야구 경기 심판을 보았다.

UN ◆◇◇ /yu ɛn/ N-PROPER The **UN** is the same as the **United Nations**. ❑ *...a UN peacekeeping force.*

고유명사 국제 연합 ❑ 국제 연합의 평화 유지 사절단

un|able ◆◇◇ /ʌneɪbᵊl/ ADJ If you are **unable to** do something, it is impossible for you to do it, for example because you do not have the necessary skill or knowledge, or because you do not have enough time or money. [v-link ADJ to-inf] ❑ *The military may feel unable to hand over power to a civilian President next year.*

형용사 -할 수 없는, -할 능력이 없는 ❑ 군부는 내년에 민간인 대통령에게 권력을 이양할 수 없다고 느낄지도 모른다.

Word Partnership	*unable*의 연어
V.	unable **to afford**, unable **to agree**, unable **to attend**, unable **to control**, unable **to cope**, unable **to decide**, unable **to explain**, unable **to find**, unable **to hold**, unable **to identify**, unable **to make**, unable **to move**, unable **to pay**, unable **to perform**, unable **to reach**, unable **to speak**, unable **to walk**, unable **to work**

un|ac|cep|table /ʌnəksɛptəbᵊl/ ADJ If you describe something as **unacceptable**, you strongly disapprove of it or object to it and feel that it should not be allowed to continue. ❑ *It is totally unacceptable for children to swear.*

형용사 용인할 수 없는 ❑ 아이들이 욕하는 것은 절대 용인할 수 없다.

Word Partnership	*unacceptable*의 연어
ADV.	**absolutely** unacceptable, **simply** unacceptable,
N.	unacceptable **behavior**, unacceptable **conditions**

un|af|fect|ed /ʌnəfɛktɪd/ **1** ADJ If someone or something is **unaffected by** an event or occurrence, they are not changed by it in any way. [v-link ADJ, oft ADJ by n] ❑ *She seemed totally unaffected by what she'd drunk.* **2** ADJ If you describe someone as **unaffected**, you mean that they are natural and genuine in their behavior, and do not act as though they are more important than other people. [APPROVAL] ❑ *...this unaffected, charming couple.*

1 형용사 영향을 받지 않는 ❑ 그녀는 자기가 마신 것에 전혀 영향을 받지 않는 것처럼 보였다. **2** 형용사 있는 그대로의, 꾸밈없는 [마음에 듦] ❑ 이 꾸밈없는 멋진 한 쌍

Thesaurus	*unaffected*의 참조어
ADJ.	unchanged **1**
	genuine, honest, natural **2**

una|nim|ity /yunənɪmɪti/ N-UNCOUNT When there is **unanimity** among a group of people, they all agree about something or all vote for the same thing. ❑ *All decisions would require unanimity.*

불가산명사 만장일치 ❑ 모든 결정은 만장일치를 요할 것이다.

unan|i|mous /yunænɪməs/ **1** ADJ When a group of people are **unanimous**, they all agree about something or all vote for the same thing. ❑ *Editors were unanimous in their condemnation of the proposals.* ● **unani|mous|ly** ADV [ADV with v] ❑ *The board of ministers unanimously approved the project last week.* **2** ADJ A **unanimous** vote, decision, or agreement is one in which all the people involved agree. ❑ *...the unanimous vote for Hungarian membership.*

1 형용사 만장일치의 ❑ 편집자들은 입을 모아 그 제안들을 비난했다. ● 만장일치로 부사 ❑ 각료 회의는 지난주에 그 계획을 만장일치로 승인했다. **2** 형용사 만장일치의 ❑ 헝가리의 회원 가입에 대한 만장일치 가결

un|an|nounced /ʌnənaʊnst/ ADJ If someone arrives or does something **unannounced**, they do it unexpectedly and without anyone having being told about it beforehand. ❑ *He had just arrived unannounced from South America.*

형용사 예고 없는 ❑ 그는 남미에서 예고 없이 막 도착한 참이었다.

un|an|swered /ʌnænsərd/ ADJ Something such as a question or letter that is **unanswered** has not been answered. [v-link ADJ, ADJ n, ADJ after v] ❑ *Some of the most important questions remain unanswered.* ❑ *Readers should send a copy of unanswered letters to their MP.*

형용사 답변 없는, 응답 없는 ❑ 몇몇 가장 중요한 물음은 답변이 안 된 상태이다. ❑ 독자들은 응답 없는 편지들은 그 사본을 그들의 국회의원에게 보내야 한다.

un|ap|pe|tiz|ing /ʌnæpɪtaɪzɪŋ/ [BRIT also **unappetising**] ADJ If you describe food as **unappetizing**, you think it will be unpleasant to eat because of its appearance. ❑ *...cold and unappetizing chicken.*

[영국영어 unappetising] 형용사 맛없어 보이는 ❑ 차갑고 맛없어 보이는 닭고기

un|armed /ʌnɑrmd/ ADJ If a person or vehicle is **unarmed**, they are not carrying any weapons. ❑ *The soldiers concerned were unarmed at the time.* ● ADV **Unarmed** is also an adverb. [ADV after v] ❑ *He says he walks inside the prison without guards, unarmed.*

형용사 무장하지 않은 ❑ 문제의 군인들은 당시 비무장 상태였다. ● 부사 비무장인 상태로 ❑ 그는 자기가 호위병 없이 비무장 상태로 감옥 안을 걸어 다닌다고 말한다.

un|ashamed /ʌnəʃeɪmd/ ADJ If you describe someone's behavior or attitude as **unashamed**, you mean that they are open and honest about things that other people might find embarrassing or shocking. ❑ *I grinned at him in unashamed delight.* ● **un|asham|ed|ly** /ʌnəʃeɪmɪdli/ ADV ❑ *Drugs are sold unashamedly in broad daylight.*

형용사 부끄러워하지 않는, 수치심 모르는 ❑ 나는 부끄럼도 없이 기뻐하면서 그를 보고 씩 웃었다. ● 부끄러운 줄 모르고 부사 ❑ 마약이 대낮에 버젓이 팔린다.

un|at|tend|ed /ʌnətɛndɪd/ ADJ When people or things are left **unattended**, they are not being watched or taken care of. [ADJ after v, ADJ n, v-link ADJ] ❑ *Never leave young children unattended near any pool or water tank.* ❑ *An unattended bag was spotted near the platform at Gatwick.*

형용사 내버려 둔, 방치된 ❑ 절대로 어린 아이들을 수영장이나 물탱크 가까이에 혼자 내버려 두지 마시오. ❑ 방치된 가방이 개트윅 승강장 근처에서 발견되었다.

a
b
c
d
e
f
g
h
i
j
k
l
m
n
o
p
q
r
s
t
u
v
w
x
y
z

A

un|at|trac|tive /ˌʌnətræktɪv/ **1** ADJ **Unattractive** people and things are unpleasant in appearance. ❑ *I'm 27, have a good job and I'm not unattractive.* ❑ *...an unattractive shade of orange.* **2** ADJ If you describe something as **unattractive**, you mean that people do not like it and do not want to be involved with it. ❑ *The market is still unattractive to many insurers.*

❶ 형용사 못생긴, 볼품없는 ❑ 난 스물일곱 살이고, 좋은 직장이 있으며, 못생기지 않았다. ❑ 보기에 별로 좋지 않은 오렌지 빛깔 ❷ 형용사 매력 없는, 흥미 없는 ❑ 그 시장은 많은 보험업자들에게 여전히 매력이 없다.

B

un|author|ized /ʌnˈɔːθəraɪzd/ [BRIT also **unauthorised**] ADJ If something is **unauthorized**, it has been produced or is happening without official permission. ❑ *...a new unauthorized biography of the Russian President.* ❑ *It has also been made quite clear that the trip was unauthorized.*

[영국영어 unauthorised] 형용사 인가받지 않은 ❑ 러시아 대통령에 관한 인가받지 않은 새 전기 ❑ 그 여행이 인가받지 않은 것도 또한 아주 명백해졌다.

C

un|avail|able /ʌnəˈveɪləbəl/ ADJ When things or people are **unavailable**, you cannot obtain them, meet them, or talk to them. ❑ *Mr. Hicks is out of the country and so unavailable for comment.*

형용사 입수할 수 없는, 부재의 ❑ 힉스 씨는 해외에 나가 있어서 논평을 해 줄 수 없다.

D

un|avoid|able /ˌʌnəˈvɔɪdəbəl/ ADJ If something is **unavoidable**, it cannot be avoided or prevented. ❑ *Managers said the job losses were unavoidable.*

형용사 피할 수 없는 ❑ 관리자들은 실직은 피할 수 없는 것이라고 말했다.

E

un|aware /ˌʌnəˈwɛər/ ADJ If you are **unaware of** something, you do not know about it. [v-link ADJ, usu ADJ of n, ADJ that] ❑ *Many people are unaware of just how much food and drink they consume.*

형용사 알지 못하는 ❑ 많은 사람들은 자신들이 정확히 얼마나 많이 먹고 마시는지 모른다.

F

un|bal|anced /ʌnˈbælənst/ **1** ADJ If you describe someone as **unbalanced**, you mean that they appear disturbed and upset or they seem to be slightly mad. ❑ *I knew how unbalanced Paula had been since my uncle Peter died.* **2** ADJ If you describe something such as a report or argument as **unbalanced**, you think that it is unfair or inaccurate because it emphasizes some things and ignores others. ❑ *UN officials argued that the report was unbalanced.*

❶ 형용사 불안정한, 약간 제 정신이 아닌 ❑ 나는 피터 아저씨가 돌아가신 이후로 폴라가 얼마나 불안정했는지 알고 있었다. ❷ 형용사 일방적인, 형평을 잃은 ❑ 유엔 당국자들은 그 보고서가 형평성이 결여되었다고 주장했다.

G

un|bear|able /ʌnˈbɛərəbəl/ ADJ If you describe something as **unbearable**, you mean that it is so unpleasant, painful, or upsetting that you feel unable to accept it or deal with it. ❑ *War has made life almost unbearable for the civilians remaining in the capital.* ● **un|bear|ably** /ʌnˈbɛərəbli/ ADV ❑ *By the evening it had become unbearably hot.*

형용사 견딜 수 없는, 참을 수 없는 ❑ 전쟁은 수도에 남아 있는 민간인들의 삶을 거의 견딜 수 없는 상태로 만들었다. ● 견딜 수 없을 만큼 부사 ❑ 저녁 무렵이 되자 참을 수 없을 만큼 더워져 있었다.

H

I

un|beat|able /ʌnˈbiːtəbəl/ **1** ADJ If you describe something as **unbeatable**, you mean that it is the best thing of its kind. [EMPHASIS] ❑ *These resorts, like Magaluf and Arenal, remain unbeatable in terms of price.* **2** ADJ In a game or competition, if you describe a person or team as **unbeatable**, you mean that they win so often, or perform so well that they are unlikely to be beaten by anyone. ❑ *With two more days of competition to go China in an unbeatable position.*

❶ 형용사 타의 추종을 불허하는 [강조] ❑ 이 휴양지들은 마가루프나 아래날처럼 가격에 있어서 여전히 타의 추종을 불허한다. ❷ 형용사 무적의 ❑ 경기가 이틀 더 남아 있고 중국은 무적의 위치에 있다.

J

K

un|beat|en /ʌnˈbiːtən/ ADJ In sports, if a person or their performance is **unbeaten**, nobody else has performed well enough to beat them. ❑ *He's unbeaten in 20 fights.*

형용사 패배를 모르는, 무패의 ❑ 그는 20경기 무패이다.

L

un|be|liev|able /ˌʌnbɪˈliːvəbəl/ **1** ADJ If you say that something is **unbelievable**, you are emphasizing that it is very good, impressive, intense, or extreme. [EMPHASIS] ❑ *His guitar solos are just unbelievable.* ❑ *The pressure they put us under was unbelievable.* ● **un|be|liev|ably** /ˌʌnbɪˈliːvəbli/ ADV [ADV with cl/group] ❑ *It was unbelievably dramatic as lightning crackled all round the van.* ❑ *Our car was still going unbelievably well.* **2** ADJ You can use **unbelievable** to emphasize that you think something is very bad or shocking. [EMPHASIS] ❑ *I find it unbelievable that people can accept this sort of behavior.* ● **un|be|liev|ably** ADV [ADV with cl/group] ❑ *What you did was unbelievably stupid.* **3** ADJ If an idea or statement is **unbelievable**, it seems so unlikely to be true that you cannot believe it. ❑ *I still find this story both fascinating and unbelievable.* ● **un|be|liev|ably** ADV [ADV with cl/group] ❑ *Lainey was, unbelievably, pregnant again.*

❶ 형용사 (믿을 수 없을 만큼) 좋은, 감동적인; 심한 [강조] ❑ 그의 기타 독주는 정말 믿을 수 없을 정도로 좋다. ❑ 그들이 우리에게 주는 압박이 믿을 수 없을 만큼 심했다. ● 믿을 수 없을 정도로 부사 ❑ 번개가 온통 밴 주위에 번쩍이는데 믿을 수 없을 정도로 극적이었다. ❑ 우리 차는 여전히 기막히게 잘 굴러갔다. ❷ 형용사 (믿을 수 없을 만큼) 심한 [강조] ❑ 나는 이런 식의 행동이 용납된다는 것은 너무 심하다고 본다. ● 믿을 수 없을 정도로 부사 ❑ 네가 한 것은 믿어지지 않을 만큼 어리석었다. ❸ 형용사 믿기 어려운 ❑ 내게는 이 이야기가 매혹적이기도 하고 믿기지도 않는다. ● 믿어지지 않게 부사 ❑ 레이니가 다시 임신을 했다니 믿어지지 않았다.

M

N

O

P

Thesaurus
unbelievable의 참조어

ADJ. astounding, incredible, remarkable **1**
inconceivable, preposterous, unimaginable **3**

Q

R

un|born /ʌnˈbɔːrn/ ADJ An **unborn** child has not yet been born and is still inside its mother's womb. ❑ *...her unborn baby.* ● N-PLURAL **The unborn** are children who are not born yet. ❑ *...a law that protects the lives of pregnant women and the unborn.*

형용사 아직 태어나지 않은, 태중의 ❑ 그녀의 태중 아기 ● 복수명사 태아 ❑ 임신한 여성과 태아의 생명을 보호하는 법

S

un|bro|ken /ʌnˈbroʊkən/ ADJ If something is **unbroken**, it is continuous or complete and has not been interrupted or broken. ❑ *...an unbroken string of victories.* ❑ *We've had ten days of almost unbroken sunshine.*

형용사 중단 없는, 연속의 ❑ 연승 행진 ❑ 열흘간 거의 연이어 해가 났다.

T

un|can|ny /ʌnˈkæni/ ADJ If you describe something as **uncanny**, you mean that it is strange and difficult to explain. ❑ *The hero, Danny, bears an uncanny resemblance to Kirk Douglas.* ● **un|can|ni|ly** /ʌnˈkænɪli/ ADV ❑ *They have uncannily similar voices.*

형용사 이상한, 묘한 ❑ 주인공 데니는 묘하게 커크 더글러스를 닮았다. ● 이상하게 부사 ❑ 그들은 목소리가 묘하게 비슷하다.

U

un|cer|tain /ʌnˈsɜːrtən/ **1** ADJ If you are **uncertain about** something, you do not know what you should do, what is going to happen, or what the truth is about something. ❑ *He was uncertain about his brother's intentions.* ❑ *They were uncertain of the total value of the transaction.* ● **un|cer|tain|ly** ADV ❑ *He entered the hallway and stood uncertainly.* **2** ADJ If something is **uncertain**, it is not known or definite. ❑ *How far the republics can give practical help, however, is uncertain.* ❑ *It's uncertain whether they will accept the plan.* **3** PHRASE If you say that someone tells a person something **in no uncertain terms**, you are emphasizing that they say it strongly and clearly so that there is no doubt about what they mean. [EMPHASIS] ❑ *She told him in no uncertain terms to go away.*

❶ 형용사 확신이 없는, 잘 알지 못하는 ❑ 그는 자기 형의 의도를 잘 몰랐다. ❑ 그들은 그 거래의 총 가치에 대해 잘 몰랐다. ● 확신이 없이 부사 ❑ 그는 현관으로 들어가서 망설이며 서 있었다. ❷ 형용사 불확실한, 미정의 ❑ 그렇지만 공화국이 얼마나 실질적인 도움을 줄 수 있을런지는 미지수이다. ❑ 그들이 그 계획을 받아들일지는 불확실하다. ❸ 구 아주 분명하게, 의심의 여지없이 [강조] ❑ 그녀는 그에게 가라고 아주 분명하게 말했다.

V

W

X

Word Partnership
uncertain의 연어

PREP. uncertain **about** *something* **1**
V. **be** uncertain, **remain** uncertain **1 2**
ADV. **highly** uncertain, **still** uncertain **1 2**

Y

Z

un|cer|tain|ty /ʌnsɜ̃rtⁿti/ (**uncertainties**) N-VAR **Uncertainty** is a state of doubt about the future or about what is the right thing to do. ❏ ...a period of political uncertainty.

가산명사 또는 불가산명사 불확실성 ❏ 정치적 불확실성의 시대

Word Partnership   uncertainty의 연어

ADJ.   **economic** uncertainty, **great** uncertainty, **political** uncertainty

---

un|chal|lenged /ʌntʃælɪndʒd/ **1** ADJ When something goes **unchallenged** or is **unchallenged**, people accept it without asking questions about whether it is right or wrong. [ADJ after v, ADJ n, v-link ADJ] ❏ These views have not gone unchallenged. ❏ His integrity was unchallenged. **2** ADJ If you say that someone's position of authority is **unchallenged**, you mean that it is strong and no one tries to replace them. [ADJ n, ADJ after v, v-link ADJ] ❏ He is the unchallenged leader of the strongest republic.

1 형용사 문제 삼지 않은, 이의가 제기되지 않은 ❏ 이 견해들은 문제없이 그냥 넘어가지지 않았다. ❏ 그의 성실성에는 이의가 제기되지 않았다. **2** 형용사 도전받지 않은 ❏ 그는 가장 강력한 공화국의 넘볼 수 없는 지도자이다.

un|changed /ʌntʃeɪndʒd/ ADJ If something is **unchanged**, it has stayed the same for a particular period of time. ❏ For many years prices have remained virtually unchanged.

형용사 변함없는 ❏ 수년 동안 가격은 거의 변함이 없었다.

un|char|ac|ter|is|tic /ʌnkærɪktərɪstɪk/ ADJ If you describe something as **uncharacteristic of** someone, you mean that it is not typical of them. ❏ It was uncharacteristic of her father to disappear like this. ● **un|char|ac|ter|is|ti|cal|ly** /ʌnkærɪktərɪstɪkli/ ADV ❏ Owen has been uncharacteristically silent.

형용사 전형적이지 않은, 특성에 맞지 않은 ❏ 이렇게 사라지는 것은 그녀의 아버지답지 않았다. ● 특성에 맞지 않게 부사 ❏ 오언은 평소 그답지 않게 계속 조용했다.

un|checked /ʌntʃekt/ ADJ If something harmful or undesirable is left **unchecked**, nobody controls it or prevents it from growing or developing. [ADJ after v, ADJ n, v-link ADJ] ❏ If left unchecked, weeds will flourish. ❏ ...a world in which brutality and lawlessness are allowed to go unchecked.

형용사 억제되지 않는, 방해받지 않는 ❏ 만일 그대로 두면, 잡초가 무성할 것이다. ❏ 잔인과 무법이 날뛰도록 허용된 세계

un|civi|lized /ʌnsɪvɪlaɪzd/ [BRIT also **uncivilised**] ADJ If you describe someone's behavior as **uncivilized**, you find it unacceptable, for example because it is very cruel or very rude. [DISAPPROVAL] ❏ The campaign has abounded in mutual accusations of uncivilized behavior.

[영국영어 uncivilised] 형용사 야만적인 [탐탁찮음] ❏ 지금까지 그 선거전은 야만적인 행위에 대한 상호 비방으로 가득 찼다.

un|cle ♦♦◇ /ʌŋkᵊl/ (**uncles**) N-FAMILY; N-TITLE Someone's **uncle** is the brother of their mother or father, or the husband of their aunt. ❏ My uncle was the mayor of Memphis. ❏ A telegram from Uncle Fred arrived. →see **family**

친족명사; 경칭명사 삼촌, 외삼촌, 고모부, 이모부 ❏ 우리 삼촌은 멤피스 시장이었다. ❏ 프레드 삼촌으로부터 전보가 왔다.

un|clear /ʌnklɪər/ **1** ADJ If something is **unclear**, it is not known or not certain. ❏ It is unclear how much popular support they have among the island's population. ❏ Just what the soldier was doing there is unclear. **2** ADJ If you are **unclear** about something, you do not understand it properly or are not sure about it. [v-link ADJ, oft ADJ about n/wh, ADJ as to wh/n, ADJ wh] ❏ He is still unclear about his own future.

1 형용사 분명하지 않은 ❏ 그들이 섬 인구 중 얼마나 많은 주민의 지지를 받고 있는지는 분명하지 않다. ❏ 그 군인이 거기서 도대체 무엇을 하고 있었는지는 분명하지 않다. **2** 형용사 분명하지 않은 ❏ 그는 아직 자기 자신의 미래에 대해 불분명하다.

un|com|fort|able /ʌnkʌmftəbᵊl, -kʌmfərtə-/ **1** ADJ If you are **uncomfortable**, you are slightly worried or embarrassed, and not relaxed and confident. ❏ The request for money made them feel uncomfortable. ❏ If you are uncomfortable with your counsellor or therapist, you must discuss it. ● **un|com|fort|ably** /ʌnkʌmftəbli, -kʌmfərtə-/ ADV ❏ Sandy leaned across the table, his face uncomfortably close to Brad's. ❏ I became uncomfortably aware that the people at the next table were watching me. **2** ADJ Something that is **uncomfortable** makes you feel slight pain or physical discomfort when you experience it or use it. ❏ Wigs are hot and uncomfortable to wear constantly. ❏ The journey back to the center of the town was hot and uncomfortable. ● **un|com|fort|ably** [ADV adj] ❏ The water was uncomfortably cold. **3** ADJ If you are **uncomfortable**, you are not physically content and relaxed, and feel slight pain or discomfort. ❏ I sometimes feel uncomfortable after eating in the evening. ● **un|com|fort|ably** ADV ❏ He felt uncomfortably hot.

1 형용사 마음이 편치 못한, 불편한 ❏ 돈 요청에 그들은 마음이 편치 못했다. ❏ 당신의 상담사나 치료사에 대해 불편하다면, 그것을 상의해야 한다. ● 불편하게 부사 ❏ 샌디가 테이블 너머로 몸을 기대서 그의 얼굴이 브래드의 얼굴에 불편할 정도로 가까웠다. ❏ 나는 옆 테이블 사람들이 나를 지켜보고 있다는 것을 알아채고는 불편해졌다. **2** 형용사 불편한 ❏ 가발은 계속 쓰고 있기에 덥고 불편하다. ❏ 시내로 되돌아오는 길이 덥고 불편했다. ● 불편하게 부사 ❏ 물이 불편할 정도로 차가웠다. **3** 형용사 (몸이) 불편한, 거북한 ❏ 나는 저녁을 먹고 나면 가끔 거북하다. ● (몸이) 불편하게 부사 ❏ 그는 더워서 힘들었다.

Thesaurus   uncomfortable의 참조어

ADJ.   awkward, embarrassed, troubled; (ant.) comfortable **1**
irritating, painful **2**

---

un|com|mon /ʌnkɒmən/ ADJ If you describe something as **uncommon**, you mean that it does not happen often or is not often seen. ❏ Cancer of the breast in young women is uncommon.

형용사 보기 드문 ❏ 젊은 여성의 유방암은 드물다.

un|com|pli|cat|ed /ʌnkɒmplɪkeɪtɪd/ ADJ If you describe someone or something as **uncomplicated**, you approve of them because they are easy to deal with or understand. [APPROVAL] ❏ She is a beautiful, uncomplicated girl.

형용사 복잡하지 않은 [마음에 듦] ❏ 그녀는 아름답고 복잡하지 않은 여자이다.

un|com|pro|mis|ing /ʌnkɒmprəmaɪzɪŋ/ **1** ADJ If you describe someone as **uncompromising**, you mean that they are determined not to change their opinions or aims in any way. ❏ Mrs. Thatcher was a tough and uncompromising politician. **2** ADJ If you describe something as **uncompromising**, you mean that it does not attempt to make something that is shocking or unpleasant any more acceptable to people. ❏ ...a film of uncompromising brutality.

1 형용사 단호한, 타협하지 않는 ❏ 대처 여사는 강하고 단호한 정치가였다. **2** 형용사 적나라한 ❏ 적나라하게 잔인한 영화

un|con|cerned /ʌnkənsɜ̃rnd/ ADJ If a person is **unconcerned about** something, usually something that most people would care about, they are not interested in it or worried about it. ❏ Paul was unconcerned about what he had done.

형용사 개의치 않는, 태연한 ❏ 폴은 그가 한 일에 대해 태연했다.

un|con|di|tion|al /ʌnkəndɪʃᵊnᵊl/ ADJ If you describe something as **unconditional**, you mean that the person doing or giving it does not require anything to be done by other people in exchange. ❏ Children need unconditional love. ● **un|con|di|tion|al|ly** ADV [ADV with v] ❏ The hostages were released unconditionally.

형용사 무조건의 ❏ 아이들은 조건 없는 사랑을 필요로 한다. ● 무조건으로 부사 ❏ 인질들은 조건 없이 풀려났다.

un|con|firmed /ʌnkənfɜ̃rmd/ ADJ If a report or a rumor is **unconfirmed**, there is no definite proof as to whether it is true or not. ❏ There are unconfirmed reports of several small villages buried by mudslides.

형용사 미확인의 ❏ 몇몇 작은 마을이 흙 속에 파묻혔다는 미확인된 보도들이 있다.

un|con|nect|ed /ʌnkənektɪd/ ADJ If one thing is **unconnected with** another or the two things are **unconnected**, the things are not related to each other

형용사 관련이 없는 ❏ 그녀에게는 자기 결혼 생활과는 관련이 없는 개인적인 문제들이 있었다고 알려졌다.

a
b
c
d
e
f
g
h
i
j
k
l
m
n
o
p
q
r
s
t
u
v
w
x
y
z

A

in any way. ❏ *She was known to have had personal problems unconnected with her marriage.*

B

un|con|scious /ʌnkɒnʃəs/ **1** ADJ Someone who is **unconscious** is in a state similar to sleep, usually as the result of a serious injury or a lack of oxygen. [v-link ADJ, ADJ n, ADJ after v] ❏ *By the time ambulancemen arrived he was unconscious.* ● **un|con|scious|ness** N-UNCOUNT ❏ *He knew that he might soon lapse into unconsciousness.* **2** ADJ If you are **unconscious** of something, you are unaware of it. [v-link ADJ of n] ❏ *He himself seemed totally unconscious of his failure.* ● **un|con|scious|ly** ADV *"I was very unsure of myself after the divorce," she says, unconsciously sweeping back the curls from her forehead.* **3** ADJ If feelings or attitudes are **unconscious**, you are not aware that you have them, but they show in the way that you behave. ❏ *Unconscious envy manifests itself very often as this kind of arrogance.* ● **un|con|scious|ly** ADV ❏ *Many women whose fathers left home unconsciously expect to be betrayed by their own mates.* →see **dream**

C

D

E

Thesaurus	unconscious의 참조어
ADJ.	subconscious, subliminal; (ant.) conscious **3**

F

un|con|sti|tu|tion|al /ʌnkɒnstɪtuːʃən³l, BRIT ʌnkɒnstɪtjuːʃən³l/ ADJ If something is **unconstitutional**, it breaks the rules of a political system. ❏ *Banning cigarette advertising would be unconstitutional, since selling cigarettes is legal.*

G

un|con|trol|lable /ʌnkəntroʊləb³l/ **1** ADJ If you describe a feeling or physical action as **uncontrollable**, you mean that you cannot control it or prevent yourself from feeling or doing it. ❏ *It had been a time of almost uncontrollable excitement.* ❏ *William was seized with uncontrollable rage.* ● **un|con|trol|lably** /ʌnkəntroʊləbli/ ADV ❏ *I started shaking uncontrollably and began to cry.* **2** ADJ If you describe a person as **uncontrollable**, you mean that their behavior is bad and that nobody can make them behave more sensibly. ❏ *Mark was withdrawn and uncontrollable.* **3** ADJ If you describe a situation or series of events as **uncontrollable**, you believe that nothing can be done to control them or to prevent things from getting worse. ❏ *If political and ethnic problems are not resolved the situation could become uncontrollable.*

H

I

J

un|con|trolled /ʌnkəntroʊld/ **1** ADJ If you describe someone's behavior as **uncontrolled**, you mean they appear unable to stop it or to make it less extreme. [ADJ n, ADJ after v, v-link ADJ] ❏ *His uncontrolled behavior disturbed the entire class.* **2** ADJ If a situation or activity is **uncontrolled**, no one is controlling it or preventing it from continuing or growing. ❏ *The capital, Nairobi, is choking on uncontrolled immigration.*

K

L

un|con|ven|tion|al /ʌnkənvenʃən³l/ **1** ADJ If you describe a person or their attitude or behavior as **unconventional**, you mean that they do not behave in the same way as most other people in their society. ❏ *Linus Pauling is an unconventional genius.* ❏ *He was known for his unconventional behavior.* **2** ADJ An **unconventional** way of doing something is not the usual way of doing it, and may be rather surprising. ❏ *The vaccine had been produced by an unconventional technique.* ❏ *Despite his unconventional methods, he has inspired pupils more than anyone else.*

M

N

un|con|vinc|ing /ʌnkənvɪnsɪŋ/ **1** ADJ If you describe something such as an argument or explanation as **unconvincing**, you find it difficult to believe because it does not seem real. ❏ *Mr. Patel phoned the University for an explanation, and he was given the usual unconvincing excuses.* ● **un|con|vinc|ing|ly** ADV [ADV with v] ❏ *"It's not that I don't believe you, Meg," Jack said, unconvincingly.* **2** ADJ If you describe a story or a character in a story as **unconvincing**, you think they do not seem likely or real. ❏ *...an unconvincing love story.*

O

P

un|count|able noun /ʌnkaʊntəb³l naʊn/ (**uncountable nouns**) N-COUNT An **uncountable noun** is the same as an **uncount noun**.

Q

un|count noun /ʌnkaʊnt naʊn/ (**uncount nouns**) N-COUNT An **uncount noun** is a noun such as "gold," "information," or "furniture" which has only one form and can be used without a determiner.

R

un|cov|er /ʌnkʌvər/ (**uncovers, uncovering, uncovered**) **1** V-T If you **uncover** something, especially something that has been kept secret, you discover or find out about it. ❏ *Auditors said they had uncovered evidence of fraud.* **2** V-T To **uncover** something means to remove something that is covering it. ❏ *When the seedlings sprout, uncover the tray.*

S

T

Word Partnership	uncover의 연어
N.	uncover **evidence**, uncover **a plot**, uncover **the truth** **1**
V.	**help** uncover *something* **1 2**

U

un|daunt|ed /ʌndɔːntɪd/ ADJ If you are **undaunted**, you are not at all afraid or worried about dealing with something, especially something that would frighten or worry most people. ❏ *Undaunted by the scale of the job, Lesley set about planning how each room should look.*

V

W

un|de|cid|ed /ʌndɪsaɪdɪd/ ADJ If someone is **undecided**, they cannot decide about something or have not yet decided about it. ❏ *After university she was still undecided as to what career she wanted to pursue.*

X

un|demo|crat|ic /ʌndeməkrætɪk/ ADJ A system, process, or decision that is **undemocratic** is one that is controlled or made by one person or a small number of people, rather than by all the people involved. ❏ *...the undemocratic rule of the former political establishment.* ❏ *Opponents denounced the decree as undemocratic and unconstitutional.*

Y

un|de|ni|able /ʌndɪnaɪəb³l/ ADJ If you say that something is **undeniable**, you

Z

(Korean translations column)

1 형용사 의식이 없는 ❏ 구급대원들이 도착했을 때 그는 의식 불명이었다. ● 의식 불명 불가산명사 ❏ 그는 자기가 곧 의식 불명 상태에 빠질 수도 있다는 것을 알았다. **2** 형용사 ~을 모르는 ❏ 그 자신은 자기의 실패를 전혀 모르는 것 같아 보였다. ● 부지불식간에 부사 ❏ "나는 이혼 후 내 자신에 대한 확신이 없었어."라고 그녀는 부지불식간에 이마의 곱슬머리를 뒤로 쓸어 올리며 말한다. **3** 형용사 자각하지 않은, 무의식적인 ❏ 무의식적인 시기심이 아주 흔히 이런 종류의 오만으로 나타난다. ● 무의식적으로 부사 ❏ 집 나간 아버지를 둔 많은 여자들이 무의식적으로 자신의 배우자에게 배신당할지도 모른다고 생각한다.

형용사 위헌의, 헌법에 위배되는 ❏ 담배 판매가 합법적이기 때문에 담배 광고를 금지하는 것은 위헌일 것이다.

1 형용사 억제할 수 없는 ❏ 거의 억제가 불가능한 흥분의 시간이었다. ❏ 윌리엄은 억제할 수 없는 분노에 사로잡혔다. ● 억제할 수 없이 부사 ❏ 나는 걷잡을 수 없이 떨기 시작하며 울음을 터뜨렸다. **2** 형용사 말을 안 듣는, 다스릴 수 없는 ❏ 마크는 내성적이고 말을 듣지 않았다. **3** 형용사 통제할 수 없는 ❏ 정치 문제와 소수 민족 문제가 해결되지 않으면 상황이 통제 불가능하게 될 수도 있다.

1 형용사 (행동이) 절제되지 않은 ❏ 그의 절제되지 않은 행동이 수업 전체를 방해했다. **2** 형용사 통제되지 않은 ❏ 수도 나이로비는 통제되지 않은 이민으로 숨통이 막힐 지경이다.

1 형용사 인습에 얽매이지 않는 ❏ 리너스 폴링은 인습에 얽매이지 않는 천재이다. ❏ 그는 관습에 얽매이지 않는 행동으로 유명했다. **2** 형용사 통례를 벗어난 ❏ 그 백신은 통례를 벗어난 기술로 만들어졌다. ❏ 그는 통례를 벗어난 방법들을 썼음에도 불구하고 누구보다도 제자들을 더 고무시켰다.

1 형용사 설득력이 없는 ❏ 페이틀 씨는 설명을 들으려고 대학에 전화를 걸었으나 의례적인 설득력 없는 변명만을 들었다. ● 설득력 없이 부사 ❏ "내가 너를 못 믿기 때문이 아니야, 맥."이라고 잭이 설득력 없이 말했다. **2** 형용사 비현실적인, 설득력 없는 ❏ 비현실적인 사랑 이야기

가산명사 불가산 명사

가산명사 불가산 명사

1 타동사 알아내다, 적발하다 ❏ 회계 감사원들은 사기 증거를 찾아냈다고 말했다. **2** 타동사 덮개를 벗기다 ❏ 묘목들이 싹이 나면 모판의 덮개를 벗기시오.

형용사 두려워하지 않는, 겁먹지 않는 ❏ 일의 규모에 겁먹지 않고, 레스리는 각각의 방을 어떤 모습으로 할지 계획을 세우기 시작했다.

형용사 결심이 서지 않은 ❏ 대학 졸업 후에도 그녀는 아직 어떤 진로를 추구하고 싶은지에 대해 결심이 서 있지 않았다.

형용사 비민주적인 ❏ 이전 정부의 비민주적인 통치 ❏ 반대파들은 그 법령이 비민주적이고 위헌적이라고 비난했다.

형용사 부인할 수 없는, 명백한 ❏ 그녀의 매력은

mean that it is definitely true. ❏ *Her charm is undeniable.* ● **un|de|ni|ably** /ʌndɪnaɪəbli/ ADV ❏ *Bringing up a baby is undeniably hard work.*

부인할 수 없다. ● 부인할 수 없이 부사 ❏ 아기를 키우는 일은 부인할 수 없이 힘든 일이다.

un|der ◆◆◆ /ʌndər/

> In addition to the uses shown below, **under** is also used in phrasal verbs such as "go under" and "knuckle under."

under는 아래 용법 외에도 'go under', 'knuckle under'와 같은 구동사에 쓰인다.

1 PREP If a person or thing is **under** something, they are at a lower level than that thing, and may be covered or hidden by it. ❏ *They found a labyrinth of tunnels under the ground.* ❏ *...swimming in the pool or lying under an umbrella.* ❏ *A path runs under the trees.* **2** PREP In a place such as a sea, river, or swimming pool, if someone or something is **under** the water, they are fully in the water and covered by it. ❏ *They said he'd been held under the water and drowned.* ● ADV **Under** is also an adverb. [ADV after v] ❏ *When the water was up to his neck, a hand came from behind and pushed his head under.* **3** PREP If you go **under** something, you move from one side to the other of something that is at a higher level than you. ❏ *He went under a brick arch.* **4** PREP Something that is **under** a layer of something, especially clothing, is covered by that layer. ❏ *I was wearing two sweaters under the green army jacket.* ❏ *...a faded striped shirt under a knit sweater.* **5** PREP You can use **under** before a noun to indicate that a person or thing is being affected by something or is going through a particular process. ❏ *...fishermen whose livelihoods are under threat.* ❏ *Firemen said they had the blaze under control.* **6** PREP If something happens **under** particular circumstances or conditions, it happens when those circumstances or conditions exist. ❏ *His best friend was killed by police under extremely questionable circumstances.* ❏ *Under normal conditions, only about 20 to 40 per cent of vitamin E is absorbed.* **7** PREP If something happens **under** a law, agreement, or system, it happens because that law, agreement, or system says that it should happen. ❏ *Under law, your employer has the right to hire a temporary worker to replace you.* ❏ *We believe an offence was committed under EU regulations.* **8** PREP If something happens **under** a particular person or government, it happens when that person or government is in power. ❏ *There would be no new taxes under his leadership.* ❏ *...the realities of life under a brutal dictatorship.* **9** PREP If you study or work **under** a particular person, that person teaches you or tells you what to do. ❏ *Kiefer was just one of the artists who had studied under Beuys in the early Sixties.* ❏ *General Lewis Hyde had served under General Mitchell.* **10** PREP If you do something **under** a particular name, you use that name instead of your real name. ❏ *Were any of your books published under the name Amanda Fairchild?* **11** PREP You use **under** to say which section of a list, book, or system something is in. ❏ *This study is described under "General Diseases of the Eye."* ❏ *"Where would it be?" — "Filed under C, second drawer down."* **12** PREP If something or someone is **under** a particular age or amount, they are less than that age or amount. [PREP amount] ❏ *...jobs for those under 65.* ❏ *Nearly half of mothers with children under five have a job.* ● ADV **Under** is also an adverb. [amount and ADV] ❏ *...free or subsidized health insurance for children 13 and under.* **13 under wraps** →see **wrap**

1 전치사 - 아래에 ❏ 그들은 땅속에서 복잡하게 얽힌 굴들을 찾아냈다. ❏ 수영장에서 수영하거나 파라솔 아래에 누워 있기 ❏ 나무들 아래에 작은 길이 나 있다. **2** 전치사 - 속에 ❏ 그들은 그가 물에서 나오지 못하고 익사했다고 했다. ● 부사 - 속에 ❏ 물이 그의 목까지 찼을 때, 뒤에서 손이 다가와 그의 머리를 물속에 밀어 넣었다. **3** 전치사 - 아래로 ❏ 그는 벽돌 아치 아래로 갔다. **4** 전치사 - 밑에, - 속에 ❏ 나는 녹색 군복 상의 속에 스웨터 두 벌을 입고 있었다. ❏ 스웨터 속에 입은 빛바랜 줄무늬 셔츠 **5** 전치사 - 을 ❏ 생계를 위협받고 있는 어민들 ❏ 소방대원들이 화재를 진압했다고 말했다. **6** 전치사 (상황 또는 조건) 하에 ❏ 그의 가장 절친한 친구가 아주 미심쩍은 상황에서 경찰에게 살해당했다. ❏ 정상적인 조건하에서는 비타민 이(E)의 약 20내지 40퍼센트만 흡수된다. **7** 전치사 (법 또는 체계) 하에 ❏ 법적으로 당신의 고용주는 당신을 대체할 임시 근로자를 고용할 권리가 있다. ❏ 우리는 유럽 연합의 법규하에 위법이 행해졌다고 믿는다. **8** 전치사 (특정한 사람 또는 정부) 아래에 ❏ 그의 통치하에서는 새로운 세금은 없을 것이다. ❏ 잔인한 독재 치하의 삶의 현실 **9** 전치사 (특정한 사람) 밑에서 ❏ 키퍼는 60년대 초기에 베이스 밑에서 공부한 예술가 중 한 사람일 뿐이다. ❏ 루이스 하이드 장군은 미첼 장군 밑에서 복무했다. **10** 전치사 (-라는 이름)으로 ❏ 당신의 책 중 '아만다 페어차일드'라는 이름으로 출판된 것이 있나요? **11** 전치사 - 항목 하에 ❏ 이 연구는 '눈의 일반 질병'이라는 항목 하에 기술되어 있다. ❏ "그게 어디에 있을까요?" "아래쪽 두 번째 서랍 씨 항목에 정리되어 있어요." **12** 전치사 - 미만의 ❏ 65세 미만을 위한 직장 ❏ 5세 미만의 자녀를 둔 어머니들의 거의 절반이 직장이 있다. ● 부사 - 미만 ❏ 13세 이하 어린이를 위한 무료 또는 국가 보조 건강 보험

under|brush /ʌndərbrʌʃ/ N-UNCOUNT **Underbrush** consists of bushes and plants growing close together under trees in a forest. [AM; BRIT **undergrowth**] ❏ *...the cool underbrush of the rain forest.*

불가산명사 (숲속 나무 밑) 덤불 [미국영어; 영국영어 undergrowth] ❏ 열대 우림의 시원한 덤불숲

under|cov|er /ʌndərkʌvər/ ADJ **Undercover** work involves secretly obtaining information for the government or the police. ❏ *...an undercover operation designed to catch drug smugglers.* ❏ *...undercover FBI agents.* ● ADV **Undercover** is also an adverb. [ADV after v] ❏ *Swanson persuaded Hubley to work undercover to capture the killer.*

형용사 비밀로 행해지는, 첩보의 ❏ 마약 밀수업자들을 잡기 위해 고안된 비밀 작전 ❏ 에프비아이(FBI) 첩보 요원들 ● 부사 비밀로 ❏ 스완슨은 후블리에게 살인자를 체포하기 위해 비밀로 활동하도록 설득했다.

under|cur|rent /ʌndərkɜrənt/ (**undercurrents**) **1** N-COUNT If there is an **undercurrent** of a feeling, you are hardly aware of the feeling, but it influences the way you think or behave. ❏ *...a deep undercurrent of racism in British society.* **2** N-COUNT An **undercurrent** is a strong current of water that is moving below the surface current and in a different direction to it. ❏ *Colin tried to swim after him but the strong undercurrent swept them apart.*

1 가산명사 저의(底意) ❏ 영국 사회 저변 깊숙이 흐르는 인종 차별 **2** 가산명사 (역방향의) 저류(低流) ❏ 콜린은 그를 뒤쫓아 헤엄쳐나가려고 애썼으나 강한 저류가 그들을 휩쓸어 갈라놓았다.

under|cut /ʌndərkʌt/ (**undercuts, undercutting**)

> The form **undercut** is used in the present tense and is also the past tense and past participle.

undercut은 현재, 과거 및 과거 분사로 쓴다.

V-T If you **undercut** someone or **undercut** their prices, you sell a product more cheaply than they do. [BUSINESS] ❏ *Subsidies allow growers to undercut competitors and depress world prices.* ❏ *...promises to undercut air fares on some routes by 40 percent.*

타동사 -보다 가격을 내리다 [경제] ❏ 보조금 때문에 재배자들이 경쟁자들보다 값을 내려 국제 가격을 하락시킬 수 있다. ❏ 일부 노선의 항공료를 40퍼센트 내리겠다는 약속

under|de|vel|oped /ʌndərdɪveləpt/ ADJ An **underdeveloped** country or region does not have modern industries and usually has a low standard of living. Some people dislike this term and prefer to use **developing**. ❏ *Underdeveloped countries should be assisted by allowing them access to modern technology.*

형용사 저개발의 ❏ 저개발 국가들이 최신 기술을 접할 수 있도록 도와주어야 한다.

under|dog /ʌndərdɔg, BRIT ʌndəˈdɒg/ (**underdogs**) N-COUNT The **underdog** in a competition or situation is the person who seems least likely to succeed or win. ❏ *Most of the crowd were cheering for the underdog to win just this one time.*

가산명사 이길 승산이 제일 없는 사람 ❏ 대부분의 관중들은 만년 꼴찌가 이번 한번만이라도 이기라고 응원하고 있었다.

under|es|ti|mate /ʌndərestɪmeɪt/ (**underestimates, underestimating, underestimated**) **1** V-T If you **underestimate** something, you do not realize how large or great it is or will be. ❏ *None of us should ever underestimate the degree of difficulty women face in career advancement.* **2** V-T If you **underestimate** someone, you do not realize what they are capable of doing. ❏ *I think a lot of people still underestimate him.*

1 타동사 과소평가하다 ❏ 우리는 누구도 여성이 직장 승진에서 직면하는 어려움의 정도를 결코 과소평가해서는 안 된다. **2** 타동사 과소평가하다 ❏ 나는 많은 사람들이 여전히 그를 과소평가한다고 생각한다.

under|fund|ed /ʌndərfʌndɪd/ also **under-funded** ADJ An organization or institution that is **underfunded** does not have enough money to spend, and so it cannot function properly. ❏ *For years we have argued that the health service is underfunded.*

형용사 재원이 부족한 ❏ 수년 동안 우리는 보건 서비스의 재원이 부족하다고 주장해 왔다.

under|go /ʌndərgoʊ/ (**undergoes, undergoing, underwent, undergone**) V-T If

타동사 겪다, 받다 ❏ 신입 사원들은 최근 몇 주 동안

A

you **undergo** something necessary or unpleasant, it happens to you. ❑ *New recruits have been undergoing training in recent weeks.*

교육을 받고 있다.

under|gradu|ate /ʌndərgrædʒuɪt/ (**undergraduates**) N-COUNT An **undergraduate** is a student at a university or college who is studying for his or her first degree. ❑ *Economics undergraduates are probably the brightest in the university.*

가산명사 대학생, 학부생 ❑ 경제학 학부생들이 아마 그 대학에서 가장 똑똑할 것이다.

B

under|ground ♦◇◇

> The adverb is pronounced /ʌndərgraʊnd/. The noun and adjective are pronounced /ʌndərgraʊnd/.

> 부사는 /ʌndərgraʊnd/로 발음되고, 명사와 형용사는 /ʌndərgraʊnd/로 발음된다.

C

1 ADV Something that is **underground** is below the surface of the ground. [ADV after v] ❑ *Solid low-level waste will be disposed of deep underground.* ● ADJ **Underground** is also an adjective. [ADJ n] ❑ *...a run-down shopping area with an underground car park.* **2** N-SING **The underground** in a city is the railroad system in which electric trains travel below the ground in tunnels. [BRIT; AM **subway**] [the N, also by N] ❑ *...a woman alone in the underground waiting for a train.* ❑ *He crossed London by underground.* **3** ADJ **Underground** groups and activities are secret because their purpose is to oppose the government and they are illegal. [ADJ n] ❑ *...the underground Kashmir Liberation Front.* **4** ADV If you go **underground**, you hide from the authorities or the police because your political ideas or activities are illegal. [ADV after v] ❑ *After the violent clashes of 1981 they either went underground or left the country.* →see **tunnel**

1 부사 지하에, 땅속에 ❑ 유해성이 적은 경질 폐기물은 땅속 깊이 폐기될 것이다. ● 형용사 지하의, 땅속의 ❑ 지하 주차장이 있는 퇴락한 쇼핑 지역 **2** 단수명사 (영국) 지하철 [영국영어; 미국영어 subway] ❑ 지하철에서 홀로 열차를 기다리고 있는 한 여인 ❑ 그는 지하철로 런던을 지나갔다. **3** 형용사 지하 조직의 ❑ 지하 카슈미르 해방 전선 **4** 부사 지하에 ❑ 1981년 폭력 충돌 후에 그들은 지하에 숨거나 나라를 떠났다.

D

E

F

G

under|growth /ʌndərgroʊθ/ N-UNCOUNT **Undergrowth** consists of bushes and plants growing together under the trees in a forest. [mainly BRIT; AM usually **underbrush**] ❑ *...plunging through the undergrowth.*

불가산명사 (나무 밑의) 덤불 [주로 영국영어; 미국영어 대개 underbrush] ❑ 덤불 속을 휙 헤치며

H

under|hand /ʌndərhænd/ or **underhanded** **1** ADJ If an action is **underhand** or if it is done in an **underhand** way, it is done secretly and dishonestly. [DISAPPROVAL] [usu ADJ n] ❑ *...underhand financial deals.* ❑ *...a list of the underhanded ways in which their influence operates in the United States.* **2** ADJ You use **underhand** or **underhanded** to describe actions, such as throwing a ball, in which you do not raise your arm above your shoulder. [AM] [ADJ n] ❑ *...an underhanded pitch.* ● ADV **Underhand** is also an adverb. [BRIT **underarm**] [ADV after v] ❑ *In softball, pitches are tossed underhand.*

1 형용사 비밀의, 속임수를 쓰는 [탐탁찮음] ❑ 비밀 금융 거래들 ❑ 그들이 미국 내에서 비밀리에 영향력을 행사하는 방법 목록 **2** 형용사 밑으로 던지는, 언더핸드의 [미국영어] ❑ 언더핸드 투구 ● 부사 아래로 던져 [영국영어 underarm] ❑ 소프트볼에서 투구는 아래로 한다.

I

J

under|lie /ʌndərlaɪ/ (**underlies, underlying, underlay, underlain**) V-T If something **underlies** a feeling or situation, it is the cause or basis of it. ❑ *Try to figure out what feeling underlies your anger.* →see also **underlying**

타동사 (감정 등의) 근거가 되다 ❑ 어떤 감정 때문에 화가 났는지 생각해 보아라.

K

under|line /ʌndərlaɪn/ (**underlines, underlining, underlined**) **1** V-T If one thing, for example an action or an event, **underlines** another, it draws attention to it and emphasizes its importance. ❑ *The report underlined his concern that standards were at risk.* ❑ *This incident underlines the danger of traveling in the border area.* **2** V-T If you **underline** something such as a word or a sentence, you draw a line underneath it in order to make people notice it or to give it extra importance. ❑ *Underline the following that apply to you.*

1 타동사 분명히 나타내다, 강조하다 ❑ 보고서는 도덕이 위태롭다는 그의 우려를 강조했다. ❑ 이 사건은 국경 지역 여행의 위험을 분명히 보여 준다. **2** 타동사 밑줄을 치다 ❑ 다음 중 당신에게 해당되는 것에 밑줄을 치시오.

L

M

N

Word Partnership	underline의 연어
N.	underline **the need for** *something* **1** underline **passages**, underline **text**, underline **titles**, underline **words** **2**

O

P

un|der|ly|ing /ʌndərlaɪɪŋ/ **1** ADJ The **underlying** features of an object, event, or situation are not obvious, and it may be difficult to discover or reveal them. [ADJ n] ❑ *To stop a problem you have to understand its underlying causes.* **2** ADJ You describe something as **underlying** when it is below the surface of something else. [ADJ n] ❑ *...hills with the hard underlying rock poking through the turf.* **3** →see also **underlie**

1 형용사 밑에 숨은, 잠재적인 ❑ 문제를 막기 위해서는 숨은 원인들을 이해해야 한다. **2** 형용사 밑에 있는 ❑ 풀 위로 삐죽 솟아난 단단한 바위가 밑에 깔려 있는 언덕들

Q

under|mine ♦◇◇ /ʌndərmaɪn/ (**undermines, undermining, undermined**) **1** V-T If you **undermine** something such as a feeling or a system, you make it less strong or less secure than it was before, often by a gradual process or by repeated efforts. ❑ *Offering advice on each and every problem will undermine her feeling of being adult.* **2** V-T If you **undermine** someone or **undermine** their position or authority, you make their authority or position less secure, often by indirect methods. ❑ *She undermined him and destroyed his confidence in his own talent.* **3** V-T If you **undermine** someone's efforts or **undermine** their chances of achieving something, you behave in a way that makes them less likely to succeed. ❑ *The continued fighting threatens to undermine efforts to negotiate an agreement.*

1 타동사 조금씩 해치다, 잠식하다 ❑ 사사건건 조언을 하면 그녀가 다 큰 성인이라는 느낌을 갖지 못하게 할 것이다. **2** 타동사 (권위 등을) 손상시키다 ❑ 그녀는 그의 자신감을 훼손시켜 자신의 재능에 대한 확신을 말살시켰다. **3** 타동사 (기회 등을) 손상시키다 ❑ 지속된 싸움은 협정을 교섭하기 위한 노력을 손상시킬 우려가 있다.

R

S

T

Word Partnership	undermine의 연어
N.	undermine **confidence**, undermine **government**, undermine **peace**, undermine **security** **1** undermine **authority** **1** **2**
V.	**threaten to** undermine, **try to** undermine **1**-**3**

U

V

W

under|neath /ʌndərniθ/ **1** PREP If one thing is **underneath** another, it is directly under it, and may be covered or hidden by it. ❑ *The device exploded underneath a van.* ❑ *...using dogs to locate people trapped underneath collapsed buildings.* ● ADV **Underneath** is also an adverb. ❑ *He has on his jeans and a long-sleeved blue denim shirt with a white T-shirt underneath.* ❑ *The shooting-range is lit from underneath by rows of ruby-red light fittings.* **2** N-T The part of something which is **underneath** is the part which normally touches the ground or faces toward the ground. ❑ *Check the actual construction of the chair by looking underneath.* ❑ *The sand martin is a brown bird with white underneath.* ● ADJ **Underneath** is also an adjective. [ADJ n] ❑ *Some objects had got entangled with the underneath mechanism of*

1 전치사 -의 바로 밑에 ❑ 폭발 장치는 밴 바로 밑에서 터졌다. ❑ 붕괴된 건물 밑에 갇힌 사람들을 찾아내기 위해 개를 이용하는 것 ● 부사 바로 밑에 ❑ 그는 진바지와 흰 티셔츠 위에 긴 팔 하늘색 데님 셔츠를 입고 있다. ❑ 사격장은 줄지어 늘어선 진홍색 조명 기구가 밑에서 불을 밝히고 있다. **2** 부사 밑면에 ❑ 밑면을 보고 의자의 실제 구조를 확인하시오. ❑ 갈색제비는 배 부분이 하얀 갈색 새이다. ● 형용사 밑면의 ❑ 어떤 물체들이 엔진의 하부 기계 장치에 얽혀 있었다. ● 단수명사 밑면, 하부 ❑ 나는 이제 자동차의

X

Y

Z

the engine. ● N-SING **Underneath** is also a noun. ❏ *Now I know what the underneath of a car looks like.* ❸ ADV You use **underneath** when talking about feelings and emotions that people do not show in their behavior. [ADV with cl] ❏ *He was as violent as Nick underneath.* ● PREP **Underneath** is also a preposition. ❏ *Underneath his outgoing behavior Luke was shy.*

하부가 어떤지 안다. ❸ 부사 속에 ❏ 그는 속으로는 닉과 마찬가지로 폭력적이었다. ● 전치사 _의 속에 ❏ 루크는 외향적인 행동 속에 수줍음이 있었다.

under|paid /ˌʌndərˈpeɪd/ ADJ People who are **underpaid** are not paid enough money for the job that they do. ❏ *Women are frequently underpaid for the work that they do.*

형용사 (일에 비해) 보수가 적은 ❏ 여성들은 종종 하는 일에 비해 보수가 적다.

under|pants /ˈʌndərˌpænts/ N-PLURAL **Underpants** are a piece of underwear which have two holes to put your legs through and elastic around the top to hold them up around your waist or hips. In American English **underpants** refers to both men's and women's underwear but in British English it refers to only men's. [also *a pair of* N] ❏ *Half of men admit that their underpants are their oldest item of clothing.*

복수명사 팬티 ❏ 남자들의 절반이 팬티가 자기들 옷 중에서 가장 오래된 것이라고 인정한다.

under|pass /ˈʌndərˌpæs/ (underpasses) N-COUNT An **underpass** is a road or path that goes underneath a railroad or another road. ❏ *The Hanger Lane underpass was closed through flooding.*

가산명사 (교차로의) 지하도 ❏ 행거 레인 지하도가 침수로 폐쇄되었다.

under|rate /ˌʌndərˈreɪt/ (underrates, underrating, underrated) V-T If you **underrate** someone or something, you do not recognize how clever, important, or significant they are. ❏ *We women have a lot of good business skills, although we tend to underrate ourselves.* ● under|rat|ed ADJ ❏ *He is a very underrated poet.*

타동사 과소평가하다 ❏ 우리 여성들은 비록 스스로 과소평가하는 경향이 있긴 하지만 훌륭한 사업 수완을 많이 갖고 있다. ● 과소평가된 형용사 ❏ 그는 매우 과소평가된 시인이다.

under|score /ˌʌndərˈskɔːr/ (underscores, underscoring, underscored) ❶ V-T If something such as an action or an event **underscores** another, it draws attention to the other thing and emphasizes its importance. [mainly AM; BRIT usually **underline**] ❏ *The Labor Department figures underscore the shaky state of the economic recovery.* ❷ V-T If you **underscore** something such as a word or a sentence, you draw a line underneath it in order to make people notice it or give it extra importance. [mainly AM; BRIT usually **underline**] ❏ *He heavily underscored his note to Shelley.*

❶ 타동사 분명히 보여 주다, 강조하다 [주로 미국영어; 영국영어 대개 underline] ❏ 노동부의 수치들은 경제 회복의 불안정한 상태를 분명히 보여 준다. ❷ 타동사 밑줄을 치다 [주로 미국영어; 영국영어 대개 underline] ❏ 그는 셜리에게 보내는 쪽지에 밑줄을 잔뜩 쳤다.

under|shirt /ˈʌndərˌʃɜːrt/ (undershirts) N-COUNT An **undershirt** is a piece of clothing that you wear on the top half of your body next to your skin in order to keep warm. [AM; BRIT **vest**] ❏ *He put on a pair of short pants and an undershirt.*

가산명사 속옷 윗도리 [미국영어; 영국영어 vest] ❏ 그는 반바지와 속옷 윗도리를 입었다.

under|side /ˈʌndərˌsaɪd/ (undersides) N-COUNT The **underside** of something is the part of it which normally faces towards the ground. ❏ *...the underside of the car.*

가산명사 밑면, 아래쪽 ❏ 차의 아래쪽

under|spend /ˌʌndərˈspɛnd/ (underspends, underspending, underspent) V-T/V-I If an organization or country **underspends**, it spends less money than it plans to or less money than it can afford. [BUSINESS] ❏ *...a country that underspends on health and overspends on statisticians.* ● N-COUNT **Underspend** is also a noun. ❏ *There has been an underspend in the department's budget.*

타동사/자동사 적게 지출하다 [경제] ❏ 보건에는 과소 지출하고 통계학자에게는 과대 지출하는 나라 ● 가산명사 과소 지출 ❏ 이 부처의 예산이 계획보다 적게 지출되었다.

under|stand ♦♦♦ /ˌʌndərˈstænd/ (understands, understanding, understood) ❶ V-T If you **understand** someone or **understand** what they are saying, you know what they mean. [no cont] ❏ *I think you heard and also understand me.* ❏ *I don't understand what you are talking about.* ❷ V-T If you **understand** a language, you know what someone is saying when they are speaking that language. [no cont] ❏ *I couldn't read or understand a word of Yiddish, so I asked him to translate.* ❸ V-T To **understand** someone means to know how they feel and why they behave in the way that they do. [no cont] ❏ *It would be nice to have someone who really understood me, a friend.* ❏ *Trish had not exactly understood his feelings.* ❹ V-T You say that you **understand** something when you know why or how it happens. [no cont] ❏ *They are too young to understand what is going on.* ❏ *She didn't understand why the TV was kept out of reach of the patients.* ❺ V-T If you **understand** that something is the case, you think it is true because you have heard or read that it is. You can say that something **is understood** to be the case to mean that people generally think it is true. [no cont] ❏ *We understand that she's in the studio recording her second album.* ❏ *As I understand it, you came round the corner by the cricket field and there was the man in the road.* ❏ *The management is understood to be very unwilling to agree to this request.* →see **philosophy**

❶ 타동사 (-의 말을) 이해하다 ❏ 너는 내가 하는 말을 들었고 또한 이해한다고 생각한다. ❏ 당신이 무슨 말을 하고 있는지 모르겠다. ❷ 타동사 (언어를) 알아듣다 ❏ 나는 이디시 말을 한마디도 읽거나 알아듣지 못해서 그에게 번역을 부탁했다. ❸ 타동사 (사람을) 이해하다 ❏ 나를 진정으로 이해해 주는 어떤 사람, 즉 친구가 있었으면 좋겠다. ❏ 트리쉬가 그의 감정을 제대로 이해한 것은 아니다. ❹ 타동사 (상황을) 이해하다 ❏ 그들은 지금 일어나고 있는 일을 이해하기에는 너무 어리다. ❏ 그녀는 왜 텔레비전을 환자들의 손이 닿지 않는 곳에 두는지 이해하지 못했다. ❺ 타동사 (-라고) 알고 있다; (-라고) 알려져 있다 ❏ 우리는 그녀가 스튜디오에서 자신의 두 번째 앨범을 녹음하고 있는 것으로 알고 있다. ❏ 내가 알기로는, 당신이 크리켓 구장 옆의 모퉁이를 돌아 나오자 길에 그 남자가 있었지요. ❏ 경영진이 이 요구를 수용하기를 매우 꺼린다고 한다.

<table>
<tr><td>**Thesaurus**</td><td>*understand*의 참조어</td></tr>
<tr><td>v.</td><td>catch on, comprehend, get, grasp; *(ant.)* misunderstand ❶</td></tr>
</table>

under|stand|able /ˌʌndərˈstændəbəl/ ❶ ADJ If you describe someone's behavior or feelings as **understandable**, you think that they have reacted to a situation in a natural way or in the way you would expect. ❏ *His unhappiness was understandable.* ● under|stand|ably /ˌʌndərˈstændəbli/ ADV ❏ *The duke is understandably proud of Lady Helen and her achievements.* ❷ ADJ If you say that something such as a statement or theory is **understandable**, you mean that people can easily understand it. ❏ *Roger Neuberg writes in a simple and understandable way.*

❶ 형용사 이해할 수 있는, 당연한 ❏ 그가 불만족스러워 하는 것은 이해할 만했다. ● 이해할 수 있게, 당연하게도 부사 ❏ 공작이 레이디 헬렌과 그녀의 업적을 자랑스러워하는 것은 이해할 만하다. ❷ 형용사 이해하기 쉬운 ❏ 로저 뉴버그는 간결하고 이해하기 쉽게 글을 쓴다.

under|stand|ing ♦◇◇ /ˌʌndərˈstændɪŋ/ (understandings) ❶ N-VAR If you have an **understanding** of something, you know how it works or know what it means. ❏ *They have to have a basic understanding of computers in order to use the advanced technology.* ❷ ADJ If you are **understanding** toward someone, you are kind and forgiving. ❏ *My boss, who was very understanding, gave her time off.* ❸ N-UNCOUNT If you show **understanding**, you show that you realize how someone feels or why they did something, and are not hostile toward them. ❏ *We would like to thank them for their patience and understanding.* ❹ N-UNCOUNT If there is **understanding between** people, they are friendly toward each other and trust each other. ❏ *There was complete understanding between Wilson and myself.* ❺ N-COUNT An **understanding** is an informal agreement about something. ❏ *We had not set a date for marriage but there was an understanding between us.* ❻ N-SING If you say that it is your **understanding that** something is the case,

❶ 가산명사 또는 불가산명사 이해, 지식 ❏ 고도의 기술을 이용하려면 컴퓨터에 대해 기본적인 이해를 갖고 있어야 한다. ❷ 형용사 이해심 있는 ❏ 그녀의 상사는 무척 이해심이 많아서 그녀에게 휴가를 주었다. ❸ 불가산명사 사려 ❏ 우리는 그들의 인내심과 사려에 감사드리고 싶습니다. ❹ 불가산명사 이해심, 공감 ❏ 윌슨과 나는 서로를 완전히 이해했다. ❺ 가산명사 합의, 약혼 ❏ 결혼 날짜는 정하지 않았지만 우리 사이엔 합의가 되어 있었다. ❻ 단수명사 (듣거나 읽어서) 알고 있음 ❏ 저는 이런 고문이 수년 동안 계속되어 온 것으로 알고 있습니다. ❼ 구 _이라는 조건하에 ❏ 가난 때문에 그녀는 그를 수양 가정에 보낼 수밖에 없었지만, 그것은 단지

a b c d e f g h i j k l m n o p q r s t u v w x y z

you mean that you believe it to be the case because you have heard or read that it is. ❑ *It is my understanding that this torture has been going on for many years.* **7 PHRASE** If you agree to do something **on the understanding that** something else will be done, you do it because you have been told that the other thing will definitely be done. ❑ *Poverty forced her to surrender him to foster families, but only on the understanding that she could eventually regain custody.*

그녀가 나중에 양육권을 되찾을 수 있다는 조건하에서였다.

Word Partnership   *understanding*의 연어

V.	**develop** understanding, **difficulty** understanding, **have trouble** understanding, **lack** understanding **1**
ADJ.	**basic** understanding, **clear** understanding, **complete** understanding **1**
	deep understanding **1 4**
	better understanding **1 4**
	mutual understanding **3 4**

under|state /ʌndərsteɪt/ (**understates, understating, understated**) **V-T** If you **understate** something, you describe it in a way that suggests that it is less important or serious than it really is. ❑ *The government chooses deliberately to understate the increase in prices.*

타동사 (실제보다) 축소해 말하다 ❑ 정부는 물가 인상에 대해 일부러 축소하여 발표하는 방향을 택한다.

under|stat|ed /ʌndərsteɪtɪd/ **ADJ** If you describe a style, color, or effect as **understated**, you mean that it is not obvious. [ADJ n] ❑ *I have always liked understated clothes – simple shapes which take a lot of hard work to get right.*

형용사 절제된, 삼가는 ❑ 나는 항상 절제된 의상, 즉 제대로 만들어 내기 무척 어려운 단순한 모양을 좋아했다.

under|state|ment /ʌndərsteɪtmənt/ (**understatements**) **1 N-COUNT** If you say that a statement is an **understatement**, you mean that it does not fully express the extent to which something is true. ❑ *To say I'm disappointed is an understatement.* **2 N-UNCOUNT Understatement** is the practice of suggesting that things have much less of a particular quality than they really have. ❑ *He informed us with massive understatement that he was feeling disappointed.*

1 가산명사 절제된 표현 ❑ 내가 실망했다고 말하는 것은 절제된 표현이다. **2** 불가산명사 삼가서 하는 말 ❑ 그는 아주 삼가는 표현을 써서, 유감스럽다고 우리에게 알려 왔다.

un|der|stood /ʌndərstʊd/ **Understood** is the past tense and past participle of **understand**.

understand의 과거, 과거 분사

under|take /ʌndərteɪk/ (**undertakes, undertaking, undertook, undertaken**) **1 V-T** When you **undertake** a task or job, you start doing it and accept responsibility for it. ❑ *She undertook the arduous task of monitoring the elections.* **2 V-T** If you **undertake to** do something, you promise that you will do it. ❑ *He undertook to edit the text himself.*

1 타동사 (책무 등을) 맡다 ❑ 그녀는 선거를 감시하는 힘든 책무를 맡았다. **2** 타동사 –을 약속하다 ❑ 그는 원문을 직접 편집하겠다고 약속했다.

Word Partnership   *undertake*의 연어

| N. | undertake **an action**, undertake **a project**, undertake **reforms**, undertake **a task**, undertake **work** **1** |

under|tak|er /ʌndərteɪkər/ (**undertakers**) **N-COUNT** An **undertaker** is a person whose job is to deal with the bodies of people who have died and to arrange funerals. ❑ *An undertaker had already collected the body.*

가산명사 장의사 ❑ 장의사가 이미 시신을 수습해 온 참이었다.

under|tak|ing /ʌndərteɪkɪŋ/ (**undertakings**) **1 N-COUNT** An **undertaking** is a task or job, especially a large or difficult one. ❑ *Organizing the show has been a massive undertaking.* **2 N-COUNT** If you give an **undertaking** to do something, you formally promise to do it. ❑ *He gave an undertaking to increase spending on health by 7.4 per cent.*

1 가산명사 사업, 과업 ❑ 그 공연을 기획하는 것은 엄청난 사업이었다. **2** 가산명사 약속 ❑ 그가 보건에 대한 지출을 7.4퍼센트 늘리겠다고 공약했다.

un|der|took /ʌndərtʊk/ **Undertook** is the past tense of **undertake**.

undertake의 과거

under|value /ʌndərvælyu/ (**undervalues, undervaluing, undervalued**) **V-T** If you **undervalue** something or someone, you fail to recognize how valuable or important they are. ❑ *We must never undervalue freedom.*

타동사 과소평가하다, 경시하다 ❑ 우리는 자유를 절대 경시해서는 안 된다.

under|wa|ter /ʌndərwɔtər/ **1 ADV** Something that exists or happens **underwater** exists or happens below the surface of the sea, a river, or a lake. ❑ *...giant submarines able to travel at high speeds underwater.* ❑ *Some stretches of beach are completely underwater at high tide.* ● **ADJ Underwater** is also an adjective. [ADJ n] ❑ *...underwater exploration.* ❑ *...underwater fishing with harpoons.* **2 ADJ Underwater** devices are specially made so that they can work in water. [ADJ n] ❑ *...underwater camera equipment.*

1 부사 물속에서, 수중에서 ❑ 수중에서 빠른 속도로 운행할 수 있는 거대한 잠수함들 ❑ 해변의 일부는 만조 때 완전히 물에 잠긴다. ● 형용사 수중의, 물속의 ❑ 수중 탐험 ❑ 작살을 이용한 수중 낚시 **2** 형용사 수중용의 ❑ 수중용 카메라 장비

under|way /ʌndərweɪ/ **ADJ** If an activity is **underway**, it has already started. If an activity gets **underway**, it starts. [v-link ADJ] ❑ *An investigation is underway to find out how the disaster happened.* ❑ *It was a cold evening, winter well underway.*

형용사 진행 중인 ❑ 참사가 어떻게 일어났는지 알아내려고 조사가 진행 중이다. ❑ 겨울이 한창인 추운 저녁이었다.

under|wear /ʌndərwɛər/ **N-UNCOUNT Underwear** is clothing such as undershirts and underpants which you wear next to your skin under your other clothes. ❑ *...a couple who went for a late-night swim in their underwear.*

불가산명사 속옷 ❑ 속옷 바람에 심야 수영을 간 한 쌍의 남녀

un|der|went /ʌndərwɛnt/ **Underwent** is the past tense of **undergo**.

undergo의 과거

under|world /ʌndərwɜrld/ **N-SING** The **underworld** in a city is the organized crime there and the people who are involved in it. ❑ *...a Spanish Harlem underworld of gangs, drugs and violence.* ❑ *Some claim that she still has connections to the criminal underworld.*

단수명사 암흑가 ❑ 갱, 마약, 폭력이 난무하는 스페인계 할렘의 암흑가 ❑ 몇몇 사람들은 그녀가 아직도 범죄 세계와 관련되어 있다고 주장한다.

under|write /ʌndərraɪt/ (**underwrites, underwriting, underwrote, underwritten**) **V-T** If an institution or company **underwrites** an activity or **underwrites** the cost of it, they agree to provide any money that is needed to cover losses or buy special equipment, often for an agreed upon fee. [BUSINESS] ❑ *The government will have to create a special agency to underwrite small business loans.*

타동사 승인하다 [경제] ❑ 정부는 소기업 융자를 승인해 줄 특별 부처를 만들어야 할 것이다.

under|writ|er /ʌndərraɪtər/ (**underwriters**) **1 N-COUNT** An **underwriter** is someone whose job involves agreeing to provide money for a particular

1 가산명사 증권 인수인; 보증인 [경제] ❑ 시장이 주식을 사려고 하지 않으면, 증권 인수 회사가 산다.

activity or to pay for any losses. [BUSINESS] ❑ *If the market will not buy the shares, the underwriter buys them.* **2** N-COUNT An **underwriter** is someone whose job is to judge the risks involved in certain activities and decide how much to charge for insurance. [BUSINESS] ❑ *AIG is an organization of insurance underwriters.*

un|de|sir|able /ˌʌndɪzaɪərəb^əl/ ADJ If you describe something or someone as **undesirable**, you think they will have harmful effects. ❑ *Inflation is considered to be undesirable because of its adverse effects on income distribution.*

🟦 가산명사 보험업자 [경제] ❑ 에이아이지는 보험업자들의 조합이다.

형용사 바람직하지 않은, 달갑지 않은 ❑ 인플레는 그것이 소득 분배에 미치는 역효과 때문에 바람직하지 않다고 여겨진다.

un|did /ʌndɪd/ **Undid** is the past tense of **undo**.

undo의 과거

un|dis|closed /ˌʌndɪskloʊzd/ ADJ **Undisclosed** information is not revealed to the public. ❑ *The company has been sold for an undisclosed amount.*

형용사 비밀에 붙여진 ❑ 그 회사는 발표되지 않은 액수에 팔렸다.

un|dis|put|ed /ˌʌndɪspyutɪd/ ADJ **1** If you describe a fact or opinion as **undisputed**, you are trying to persuade someone that it is generally accepted as true or correct. ❑ *...the undisputed fact that he had broken the law.* ❑ *...his undisputed genius.* **2** ADJ If you describe someone as the **undisputed** leader or champion, you mean that everyone accepts their position as leader or champion. ❑ *Seles won 10 tournaments, and was the undisputed world champion.* ❑ *At 78 years of age, he's still undisputed leader of his country.*

🟦 형용사 이의 없는, 명백한 ❑ 그가 법을 어겼다는 명백한 사실 ❑ 논의의 여지가 없는 그의 천재성 🟦 형용사 의심할 바 없는, 모두가 인정하는 ❑ 셀레스는 10개 대회에서 우승했고, 모두가 인정하는 세계 챔피언이었다. ❑ 78세의 나이에 그는 여전히 자기 나라에서 모두가 인정하는 지도자이다.

un|dis|turbed /ˌʌndɪstɜrbd/ **1** ADJ Something that remains **undisturbed** is not touched, moved, or used by anyone. [v-link ADJ, ADJ after v, ADJ n] ❑ *The desk looked undisturbed.* **2** ADJ A place that is **undisturbed** is peaceful and has not been affected by changes that have happened in other places. [v-link ADJ, ADJ after v, ADJ n] ❑ *In the Balearics pockets of rural life and inland villages are undisturbed.* **3** ADJ If you are **undisturbed** in something that you are doing, you are able to continue doing it and are not affected by something that is happening. [ADJ after v, ADJ n, v-link ADJ] ❑ *I can spend the whole day undisturbed at the warehouse.* ❑ *There was a small restaurant on Sullivan Street where we could talk undisturbed.* **4** ADJ If someone is **undisturbed by** something, it does not affect, bother, or upset them. ❑ *Victoria was strangely undisturbed by this symptom, even though her husband and family were frightened.*

🟦 형용사 손대지 않은, 건드리지 않은 ❑ 그 책상은 아무도 손대지 않은 것 같았다. 🟦 형용사 평온한 ❑ 발레아릭스 제도의 전원생활 지역과 내륙 마을들은 평온하다. 🟦 형용사 (외부의) 방해를 받지 않는 ❑ 나는 창고에서 하루 종일 방해를 받지 않고 지낼 수 있다. ❑ 설리번 스트리트에서 우리가 방해받지 않고 이야기할 수 있는 작은 식당이 있었다. 🟦 형용사 괴롭힘을 받지 않는 ❑ 자기 남편과 가족들은 겁을 먹었지만 빅토리아는 이상하게도 이 증상에 태연했다.

undo /ʌndu/ (**undoes, undoing, undid, undone**) **1** V-T If you **undo** something that is closed, tied, or held together, or if you **undo** the thing holding it, you loosen or remove the thing holding it. ❑ *I managed secretly to undo a corner of the parcel.* ❑ *I undid the bottom two buttons of my yellow and grey shirt.* **2** V-T To **undo** something that has been done means to reverse its effect. ❑ *A heavy-handed approach from the police could undo that good impression.* ❑ *She knew it would be difficult to undo the damage that had been done.* **3** →see also **undoing**

🟦 타동사 (묶인 것을) 풀다 ❑ 나는 소포의 한 귀퉁이를 몰래 풀어냈다. ❑ 나는 노란색과 회색이 섞인 내 셔츠의 아래쪽 단추 두 개를 풀었다. 🟦 타동사 원상태로 돌리다 ❑ 경찰의 강압적인 처리법은 그 좋은 인상을 망칠 수 있다. ❑ 그녀는 일단 생겨난 피해를 원상 복구하는 것은 어려울 것임을 알고 있었다.

un|do|ing /ʌndu.ɪŋ/ N-SING If something is someone's **undoing**, it is the cause of their failure. ❑ *His lack of experience may prove to be his undoing.*

단수명사 실패의 원인 ❑ 그의 경험 부족이 그가 실패한 원인일지도 모른다.

un|doubt|ed /ʌndaʊtɪd/ ADJ You can use **undoubted** to emphasize that something exists or is true. [EMPHASIS] ❑ *The event was an undoubted success.* ❑ *...a man of your undoubted ability.* ● **un|doubt|ed|ly** ADV ❑ *Undoubtedly, political and economic factors have played their part.*

형용사 의심할 여지없는, 확실한 [강조] ❑ 그 행사는 의심할 여지없는 성공이었다. ❑ 당신같이 확실한 능력의 소유자 ● 의심할 여지없이 부사 의심할 여지없이, 정치적 및 경제적 요인들이 개입되었다.

un|dress /ʌndrɛs/ (**undresses, undressing, undressed**) V-T/V-I When you **undress** or **undress** someone, you take off your clothes or someone else's clothes. ❑ *She went out, leaving Rachel to undress and have her shower.* →see **wear**

타동사/자동사 (옷을) 벗다; (옷을) 벗기다 ❑ 그녀는 레이첼이 옷을 벗고 샤워를 하도록 놔두고 밖으로 나갔다.

un|dressed /ʌndrɛst/ ADJ If you are **undressed**, you are wearing no clothes or your nightclothes. If you get **undressed**, you take off your clothes. ❑ *Fifteen minutes later he was undressed and in bed.*

형용사 옷을 벗은, 잠옷 바람의 ❑ 15분 후 그는 옷을 벗고 잠자리에 들었다.

un|due /ʌndu, BRIT ʌndyu:/ ADJ If you describe something bad as **undue**, you mean that it is greater or more extreme than you think is reasonable or appropriate. [ADJ n] ❑ *This would help the families to survive the drought without undue suffering.* ❑ *It is unrealistic to put undue pressure on ourselves by saying we are the best.*

형용사 과도한, 필요 이상의 ❑ 이것이 그 가족들이 필요 이상으로 고통받지 않고 가뭄을 이겨 내도록 도와줄 겁니다. ❑ 우리가 최고라고 말하면서 우리 자신에게 지나친 압박감을 주는 것은 비현실적이다.

Word Partnership	undue의 연어
N.	undue **attention**, undue **burden**, undue **delay**, undue **emphasis**, undue **hardship**, undue **influence**, undue **interference**, undue **pressure**, undue **risk**

un|du|ly /ʌnduli, BRIT ʌndyu:li/ ADV If you say that something does not happen or is not done **unduly**, you mean that it does not happen or is not done to an excessive or unnecessary extent. ❑ *"But you're not unduly worried about doing this report?" — "No."* ❑ *This will achieve greater security without unduly burdening the consumers or the economy.*

부사 과도하게, 필요 이상으로 ❑ "하지만 당신이 이 보고서를 쓰는 것에 대해 필요 이상으로 걱정하는 것은 아니잖아요?" "그렇죠." ❑ 이것으로 소비자나 경제에 지나치게 부담을 주지 않고 더 큰 안정을 얻을 수 있다.

un|earned in|come /ʌnɜrnd ɪnkʌm/ N-UNCOUNT **Unearned income** is money that people gain from interest or profit from property or investment, rather than money that they earn from a job. [BUSINESS] ❑ *... reduction in the tax on unearned income could be a boost for small businesses.*

불가산명사 불로 소득 [경제] ❑ 불로 소득에 대한 세금 삭감이 영세업을 부양시킬 수 있을 것이다.

un|earth /ʌnɜrθ/ (**unearths, unearthing, unearthed**) **1** V-T If someone **unearths** facts or evidence about something bad, they discover them with difficulty, usually because they were being kept secret or were being lied about. ❑ *Researchers have unearthed documents indicating her responsibility for the forced adoption of children.* ❑ *The frauds have been unearthed by investigators working for the Camden and Islington Health Authority* **2** V-T If someone **unearths** something that is buried, they find it by digging in the ground. ❑ *Fossil hunters have unearthed the bones of an elephant believed to be 500,000 years old.* ❑ *More human remains have been unearthed in the north.* **3** V-T If you say that someone **has unearthed** something, you mean that they have found it after it had been hidden or lost for some time. ❑ *From somewhere, he had unearthed a black silk suit.* ❑ *Today I unearthed a copy of "90 Minutes" and had a chuckle at your article.*

🟦 타동사 찾아내다, 밝혀내다 ❑ 조사원들은 아이들의 강제 입양에 그녀가 책임이 있음을 나타내는 서류들을 찾아냈다. ❑ 그 사기 사건들이 캠덴과 이스링턴 보건국 수사관들에 의해 밝혀졌다. 🟦 타동사 발굴하다, 파내다 ❑ 화석을 찾는 사람들이 50만 년 된 것으로 보이는 코끼리 뼈를 발굴했다. ❑ 더 많은 유해가 북쪽에서 발굴되었다. 🟦 타동사 찾아내다 ❑ 어딘가에서 그가 검은 비단 양복을 찾아냈다. ❑ 오늘 나는 '90분' 한 권을 찾아내 당신의 글을 읽고 쿡쿡 웃었다.

un|ease /ʌniz/ **1** N-UNCOUNT If you have a feeling of **unease**, you feel rather anxious or afraid, because you think that something is wrong. ❑ *Sensing my*

🟦 불가산명사 불안, 걱정 ❑ 다가오는 오후에 대한 나의 불안을 알아채고, 그는 "이 사람들은 말

A

unease about the afternoon ahead, he told me, "These men are pretty easy to talk to." ❑ *We left with a deep sense of unease, because we knew something was being hidden from us.* **2** N-UNCOUNT If you say that there is **unease** in a situation, you mean that people are dissatisfied or angry, but have not yet started to take any action. ❑ *He faces growing unease among the Democrats about the likelihood of war.* ❑ *...the depth of public unease about the economy.*

B

상대하기가 아주 쉬워요."라고 내게 말했다.
❑ 우리한테 뭔가 숨기는 것이 있다는 걸 알았기 때문에 우리는 몹시 불안한 마음으로 떠났다. **2** 불가산명사 불안, 걱정 ❑ 그는 내게 음흉한 미소만 지었는데 그게 나를 너무도 불안하게 만들었다. ❑ 경제에 대한 국민적 불안의 깊이

C

un|eas|y /ʌníːzi/ **1** ADJ If you are **uneasy**, you feel anxious, afraid, or embarrassed, because you think that something is wrong or that there is danger. ❑ *He said nothing but gave me a sly grin that made me feel terribly uneasy.* ❑ *He looked uneasy and refused to answer questions.* ● **un|eas|i|ly** /ʌníːzɪli/ ADV ❑ *Meg shifted uneasily on her chair.* ● **un|easi|ness** N-UNCOUNT ❑ *With a small degree of uneasiness, he pushed it open and stuck his head inside.* **2** ADJ If you are **uneasy about** doing something, you are not sure that it is correct or wise. ❑ *Richard was uneasy about how best to approach his elderly mother.* ● **un|easi|ness** N-UNCOUNT ❑ *I felt a great uneasiness about meeting her again.* **3** ADJ If you describe a situation or relationship as **uneasy**, you mean that the situation is not settled and may not last. [JOURNALISM] ❑ *An uneasy calm has settled over Los Angeles.* ❑ *There is an uneasy relationship between us and the politicians.* ● **un|eas|i|ly** ADV ❑ *...a country whose component parts fit uneasily together.*

D

1 형용사 불안한, 염려스러운 ❑ 그는 아무 말도 하지 않고 내게 음흉한 미소만 지었는데 그게 나를 너무도 불안하게 만들었다. ❑ 그는 불안해 보였고 질문에 대답하기를 거부했다. ● 불안하게 부사 ❑ 메그는 자리에서 초조하게 자세를 고쳐 앉았다. ● 불안, 걱정 불가산명사 ❑ 약간 불안해하면서 그는 그것을 밀어젖히고 머리를 안으로 들이밀었다. **2** 형용사 불안한 ❑ 리처드는 연로하신 어머니에게 어떻게 접근하는 것이 최선일지 확신이 서지 않았다. ● 불안감, 걱정 불가산명사 ❑ 나는 그녀를 다시 만나는 것이 무척 걱정스러웠다. **3** 형용사 불안정한, 불안한 [언론] ❑ 불안한 고요가 로스앤젤레스를 뒤덮고 있다. ❑ 우리와 정치인들은 불안정한 관계에 있다. ● 불안정하게 부사 ❑ 각 구성 요소들이 불안정하게 엮여 있는 나라

E

F

G

un|em|ployed /ʌnɪmplɔ́ɪd/ ADJ Someone who is **unemployed** does not have a job. ❑ *The problem is millions of people are unemployed.* ❑ *This workshop helps young unemployed people in Grimsby.* ● N-PLURAL **The unemployed** are people who are unemployed. ❑ *We want to create jobs for the unemployed.*

형용사 실직한, 실업자인 ❑ 문제는 수백만 명의 사람들이 실업자라는 것이다. ❑ 이 연수회는 그림스비의 청년 실업자들에게 도움이 된다. ● 복수명사 실업 ❑ 우리는 실업자들을 위한 일자리를 창출하고 싶다.

H

un|em|ploy|ment ♦♢♢ /ʌnɪmplɔ́ɪmənt/ N-UNCOUNT **Unemployment** is the fact that people who want jobs cannot get them. ❑ *...an area that had the highest unemployment rate in western Europe.*

I

불가산명사 실업 ❑ 서유럽에서 실업률이 가장 높은 지역

un|em|ploy|ment ben|efit (**unemployment benefits**) N-UNCOUNT **Unemployment benefit** is the same as **unemployment compensation.** [BRIT] [also N in pl] ❑ *More than three million were receiving unemployment benefit.*

J

불가산명사 실업 수당 [영국영어] ❑ 3백만 명 이상이 실업 수당을 받고 있었다.

un|em|ploy|ment com|pen|sa|tion N-UNCOUNT **Unemployment compensation** is money that some people receive from the state when they do not have a job and are unable to find one. [AM] ❑ *He has to get by on unemployment compensation.*

K

불가산명사 실업 수당 [미국영어] ❑ 그는 실업 수당으로 꾸려 나가야 한다.

un|equivo|cal /ʌnɪkwɪ́vəkəl/ ADJ If you describe someone's attitude as **unequivocal**, you mean that it is completely clear and very firm. [FORMAL] ❑ *...Richardson's unequivocal commitment to fair play.* ● **un|equivo|cal|ly** /ʌnɪkwɪ́vəkli/ ADV ❑ *He stated unequivocally that the French forces were ready to go to war.*

L

형용사 명백한, 뚜렷한 [격식체] ❑ 리처드슨의 정정당당한 경기를 하겠다는 뚜렷한 의지 ● 분명하게, 뚜렷하게 부사 ❑ 그는 프랑스군이 전쟁에 나설 준비가 되어 있다고 분명하게 말했다.

M

un|ethi|cal /ʌnéθɪkəl/ ADJ If you describe someone's behavior as **unethical**, you think it is wrong and unacceptable according to a society's rules or people's beliefs. ❑ *It's simply unethical to promote and advertise such a dangerous product.* ❑ *I thought it was unethical for doctors to operate upon their wives.*

N

형용사 비윤리적인 ❑ 그렇게 위험한 상품을 선전하고 광고하는 것은 정말 비윤리적이다. ❑ 나는 의사들이 자기 아내를 수술하는 것이 비윤리적이라고 생각했다.

un|even /ʌníːvən/ **1** ADJ An **uneven** surface or edge is not smooth, flat, or straight. ❑ *He staggered on the uneven surface.* ❑ *The pathways were uneven, broken and dangerous.* **2** ADJ Something that is **uneven** is not regular or consistent. ❑ *He could hear that her breathing was uneven.* **3** ADJ An **uneven** system or situation is unfairly arranged or organized. ❑ *Some of the victims are complaining loudly about the uneven distribution of emergency aid.*

O

1 형용사 평평하지 않은, 울퉁불퉁한 ❑ 그는 평평하지 않은 바닥에서 비틀거렸다. ❑ 좁은 길들은 울퉁불퉁하고, 파손되어 있고, 위험했다. **2** 형용사 고르지 않은 ❑ 그는 그녀의 숨소리가 고르지 않은 것을 들을 수 있었다. **3** 형용사 불공평한 ❑ 몇몇 피해자들은 비상 구급 물자의 불공평한 분배에 대해 큰소리로 불평하고 있다.

P

R

un|event|ful /ʌnɪvéntfəl/ ADJ If you describe a period of time as **uneventful**, you mean that nothing interesting, exciting, or important happened during it. ❑ *The return journey was uneventful, the car running without a hitch.*

S

형용사 사건이 없는, 무사 평온한 ❑ 돌아오는 여행길은 무사 평온해서 차가 아무 일 없이 굴러갔다.

un|ex|pec|ted ♦♢♢ /ʌnɪkspéktɪd/ ADJ If an event or someone's behavior is **unexpected**, it surprises you because you did not think that it was likely to happen. ❑ *His death was totally unexpected.* ❑ *He made a brief, unexpected appearance at the office.* ● **un|ex|pect|ed|ly** ADV ❑ *Moss had clamped an unexpectedly strong grip on his arm.*

T

형용사 예기치 않은, 뜻밖의 ❑ 그의 죽음은 전혀 예기치 않은 일이었다. ❑ 그는 예기치 않게 사무실에 잠시 모습을 보였다. ● 뜻밖에, 예상외로 부사 ❑ 모스가 예상외로 강하게 그의 팔을 꽉 잡았었다.

U

V

un|ex|plained /ʌnɪkspléɪnd/ ADJ If you describe something as **unexplained**, you mean that the reason for it or cause of it is unclear or is not known. ❑ *The demonstrations were provoked by the unexplained death of an opposition leader.* ❑ *Soon after leaving Margate, for some unexplained reason, the train was brought to a standstill.*

W

형용사 이유가 밝혀지지 않은 ❑ 그 시위들은 한 야당 지도자의 의문사에 자극을 받아 일어났다. ❑ 마게이트를 떠난 직후, 알 수 없는 이유로, 기차가 멈췄다.

X

un|fair ♦♢♢ /ʌnféər/ ADJ An **unfair** action or situation is not right or fair. ❑ *She was awarded £5,000 in compensation for unfair dismissal.* ❑ *It was unfair that he should suffer so much.* ● **un|fair|ly** ADV ❑ *An industrial tribunal has no jurisdiction to decide whether an employee was fairly or unfairly dismissed.*

Y

형용사 부당한, 불공평한 ❑ 그녀는 부당 해고에 대한 보상으로 5,000파운드를 받았다. ❑ 그가 그렇게 많이 고생하는 것은 부당했다. ● 부당하게 부사 ❑ 산업 재판소는 피고용인이 정당하게 해고되었는지 부당하게 해고되었는지의 여부를 결정할 사법권이 없다.

Z

un|faith|ful /ʌnfeɪθfəl/ ADJ If someone is **unfaithful to** their lover or to the person they are married to, they have a sexual relationship with someone else. ❑ *James had been unfaithful to Christine for the entire four years they'd been together.*

형용사 외도를 한 ❑ 제임스는 크리스틴과 함께 살았던 4년 내내 바람을 피웠다.

un|fa|mil|iar /ʌnfəmɪlyər/ **1** ADJ If something is **unfamiliar to** you, you know nothing or very little about it, because you have not seen or experienced it before. ❑ *She grew many wonderful plants that were unfamiliar to me.* **2** ADJ If you are **unfamiliar with** something, it is unfamiliar to you. [v-link ADJ with n] ❑ *She speaks no Japanese and is unfamiliar with Japanese culture.*

1 형용사 익숙지 않은, 낯선 ❑ 그녀는 내게는 낯선 멋진 식물을 많이 키웠다. **2** 형용사 -을 잘 모르는 ❑ 그녀는 일본말을 하지 못하며 일본 문화도 잘 모른다.

un|fash|ion|able /ʌnfæʃənəbəl/ ADJ If something is **unfashionable**, it is not approved of or done by most people. ❑ *Wearing fur has become deeply unfashionable.*

형용사 유행하지 않는 ❑ 모피를 입는 것은 크게 한물갔다.

un|fa|vor|able /ʌnfeɪvərəbəl/ [BRIT **unfavourable**] **1** ADJ **Unfavorable** conditions or circumstances cause problems for you and reduce your chances of success. ❑ *The decision to delay the launch stems from unfavorable weather conditions.* ❑ *The whole international economic situation is very unfavorable for the countries in the south.* **2** ADJ If you have an **unfavorable** reaction to something, you do not like it. ❑ *The President is drawing unfavorable comments on his new forest policy.* ❑ *...views unfavorable to the capitalist system.* ● **un|fa|vor|ably** /ʌnfeɪvərəbli/ ADV [ADV after v] ❑ *Other medications or foods may react unfavorably with it.* **3** ADJ If you make an **unfavorable** comparison between two things, you say that one thing seems worse than the other. [ADJ n] ❑ *I didn't expect unfavorable comparisons between my sons and their friends.* ● **un|fa|vor|ably** ADV [ADV with v] ❑ *Tax rates compare unfavorably with the less heavy-handed North American agreement.*

[영국영어 unfavourable] **1** 형용사 불리한, 순조롭지 않은 ❑ 발사 연기 결정은 기상 조건이 순조롭지 않아서이다. ❑ 국제 경제의 전반적인 상황이 남쪽 나라들에게 아주 불리하다. **2** 형용사 좋지 않은, 부정적인 ❑ 대통령은 그의 새로운 산림 정책에 대해 좋지 않은 평을 내리고 있다. ❑ 자본주의 체제에 부정적인 견해들 ● 좋지 않게 부사 ❑ 다른 약이나 음식이 그것에 부정적인 반응을 보일 수도 있다. **3** 형용사 (한쪽이) 불리한 ❑ 나는 내 아들들과 그들의 친구들을 불리하게 비교할 것을 예상치 않았다. ● 불리하게 부사 ❑ 세율이 그보다 덜 엄격한 북미 협약보다도 불리하다.

un|fin|ished /ʌnfɪnɪʃt/ ADJ If you describe something such as a work of art or a piece of work as **unfinished**, you mean that it is not complete, for example because it was abandoned or there was no time to complete it. [ADJ n, v-link ADJ, ADJ after v] ❑ *...Jane Austen's unfinished novel.* ❑ *The cathedral was eventually completed in 1490, though the Gothic facade remains unfinished.*

형용사 미완성의 ❑ 제인 오스틴의 미완성 소설 ❑ 그 대성당은 마침내 1490년에 완성되었지만 고딕 양식의 정면은 미완성으로 남아 있다.

un|fit /ʌnfɪt/ **1** ADJ If you are **unfit**, your body is not in good condition because you have not been getting regular exercise. ❑ *Many children are so unfit they are unable to do even basic exercises.* **2** ADJ If someone is **unfit** for something, he or she is unable to do it because of injury or illness. ❑ *He had a third examination and was declared unfit for duty.* **3** ADJ If you say that someone or something is **unfit** for a particular purpose or job, you are criticizing them because they are not good enough for that purpose or job. [DISAPPROVAL] ❑ *Existing houses are becoming totally unfit for human habitation.* ❑ *They were utterly unfit to govern America.*

1 형용사 건강하지 않은 ❑ 많은 어린이들이 건강하지 못해서 기본적인 운동조차도 하지 못할 정도이다. **2** 형용사 부적합한 ❑ 그는 세 번째 검사를 했는데 직무에 부적합한 것으로 선고받았다. **3** 형용사 부적합한 [탐탁찮음] ❑ 기존 주택들이 사람이 거주하기에 완전히 부적합해지고 있다. ❑ 그들은 미국을 통치하기에는 완전히 부적합했다.

un|fold /ʌnfoʊld/ (**unfolds, unfolding, unfolded**) **1** V-I If a situation **unfolds**, it develops and becomes known or understood. ❑ *The outcome depends on conditions as well as how events unfold.* **2** V-T/V-I If a story **unfolds** or if someone **unfolds** it, it is told to someone else. ❑ *Don's story unfolded as the cruise got under way.* **3** V-T/V-I If someone **unfolds** something which has been folded or if it **unfolds**, it is opened out and becomes flat. ❑ *He quickly unfolded the blankets and spread them on the mattress.*

1 자동사 전개되다 ❑ 결과는 사건이 어떻게 전개되는가 뿐만 아니라 상황에 따라서도 좌우된다. **2** 타동사/자동사 펼쳐지다; 펼치다 ❑ 유람선 항해가 시작되자 돈의 이야기가 펼쳐졌다. **3** 타동사/자동사 펴다; 펴지다 ❑ 그는 재빨리 담요들을 펴서 매트 위에 깔았다.

un|fore|seen /ʌnfɔrsin/ ADJ If something that has happened was **unforeseen**, it was not expected to happen or known about beforehand. ❑ *Radiation may damage cells in a way that was previously unforeseen.* ❑ *Unfortunately, due to unforeseen circumstances, this year's show has been cancelled.*

형용사 예기치 못한 ❑ 방사선이 사전에 예기치 못한 방식으로 세포에 해를 끼칠 수 있다. ❑ 불행하게도 예기치 못한 상황으로 올해 공연이 취소되었다.

un|for|get|table /ʌnfərɡetəbəl/ ADJ If you describe something as **unforgettable**, you mean that it is, for example, extremely beautiful, enjoyable, or unusual, so that you remember it for a long time. You can also refer to extremely unpleasant things as **unforgettable**. ❑ *A visit to the Museum is an unforgettable experience.* ❑ *...the leisure activities that will make your holiday unforgettable.*

형용사 잊을 수 없는 ❑ 그 박물관 방문은 잊을 수 없는 경험이다. ❑ 당신의 휴가를 잊을 수 없게 만들어 줄 여가 활동들

un|for|tu|nate /ʌnfɔrtʃənɪt/ (**unfortunates**) **1** ADJ If you describe someone as **unfortunate**, you mean that something unpleasant or unlucky has happened to them. You can also describe the unpleasant things that happen to them as **unfortunate**. ❑ *Some unfortunate person passing below could all too easily be seriously injured.* ❑ *Apparently he had been unfortunate enough to fall victim to a gang of thugs.* **2** ADJ If you describe something that has happened as **unfortunate**, you think that it is inappropriate, embarrassing, awkward, or undesirable. ❑ *It really is desperately unfortunate that this should have happened just now.* ❑ *...the unfortunate incident of the upside-down Canadian flag.* **3** ADJ You can describe someone as **unfortunate** when they are poor or have a difficult life. ❑ *Every year we have charity days to raise money for unfortunate people.* ● N-COUNT An **unfortunate** is someone who is unfortunate. ❑ *Dorothy was another of life's unfortunates.*

1 형용사 모욕한, 불행한 ❑ 운수 나쁜 사람이 지나가다가 너무도 쉽게 심한 부상을 당할 수 있다. ❑ 그는 분명 범죄 조직의 희생자가 될 정도로 불운했던 것 같다. **2** 형용사 적절치 않은, 난처한 ❑ 이게 하필이면 지금 발생하다니 정말로 심히 난처하다. ❑ 캐나다 국기가 거꾸로 걸린 난처한 사건 **3** 형용사 불행한 ❑ 해마다 우리는 불행한 사람들을 위해 며칠 동안 돈을 모으는 자선 행사를 한다. ● 가산명사 불행한 사람 ❑ 도로시는 불행한 삶을 사는 또 한 명의 사람이었다.

un|for|tu|nate|ly ◆◇◇ /ʌnfɔrtʃənɪtli/ ADV You can use **unfortunately** to introduce or refer to a statement when you consider that it is sad or disappointing, or when you want to express regret. [FEELINGS] ❑ *Unfortunately, my time is limited.* ❑ *Unfortunately for the Prince, his title brought obligations as well as privileges.*

부사 불행하게도 [감정 개입] ❑ 불행하게도 내 시간은 제한되어 있다. ❑ 왕자에게는 불행하게도, 그의 지위에는 특권뿐 아니라 의무도 수반되었다.

un|found|ed /ʌnfaʊndɪd/ ADJ If you describe a rumor, belief, or feeling as **unfounded**, you mean that it is wrong and is not based on facts or evidence. ❑ *Unfounded rumors of accounting problems hit stocks of other companies.* ❑ *The allegations were totally unfounded.*

형용사 사실 무근의 ❑ 사실 무근의 회계 관련 소문이 다른 회사들의 주식을 강타했다. ❑ 그 혐의들은 완전히 사실무근이었다.

un|friend|ly /ʌnfrendli/ ADJ If you describe a person, organization, or their behavior as **unfriendly**, you mean that they behave toward you in an unkind or rather hostile way. ❑ *It is not fair for him to be permanently unfriendly to someone who has hurt him.* ❑ *People always complain that the big banks and big companies are unfriendly and unhelpful.*

형용사 불친절한, 적의 있는 ❑ 그가 자기를 다치게 한 사람에게 영원히 적의를 품는 것은 정당하지 않다. ❑ 사람들은 대형 은행과 대형 회사들이 불친절하고 잘 도와주지 않는다고 항상 불평한다.

Thesaurus   unfriendly의 참조어

ADJ.   cold, unkind; (ant.) friendly

A

un|ful|filled /ˌʌnfʊlˈfɪld/ ADJ If you use **unfulfilled** to describe something such as a promise, ambition, or need, you mean that what was promised, hoped for, or needed has not happened. ❑ *Do you have any unfulfilled ambitions?* ❑ *...angry at unfulfilled promises of jobs and decent housing.* ❷ ADJ If you describe someone as **unfulfilled**, you mean that they feel dissatisfied with life or with what they have done. ❑ *You must let go of the idea that to be single is to be unhappy and unfulfilled.*

B

un|furl /ˌʌnˈfɜrl/ (unfurls, unfurling, unfurled) ❶ V-T/V-I If you **unfurl** something rolled or folded such as an umbrella, sail, or flag, you open it, so that it is spread out. You can also say that it **unfurls**. ❑ *Once outside the inner breakwater, we began to unfurl all the sails.* ❷ V-I If you say that events, stories, or scenes **unfurl** before you, you mean that you are aware of them or can see them as they happen or develop. ❑ *The dramatic changes in Europe continue to unfurl.*

C

un|grate|ful /ʌnˈgreɪtfəl/ ADJ If you describe someone as **ungrateful**, you are criticizing them for not showing thanks or for being unkind to someone who has helped them or done them a favor. [DISAPPROVAL] ❑ *I thought it was rather ungrateful.*

D

E

un|hap|pi|ly /ʌnˈhæpɪli/ ADV You use **unhappily** to introduce or refer to a statement when you consider it is sad and wish that it was different. [ADV with cl] ❑ *On May 23rd, unhappily, the little boy died.* ❑ *Unhappily the facts do not wholly bear out the theory.*

F

un|hap|py ◆◇◇ /ʌnˈhæpi/ (unhappier, unhappiest) ❶ ADJ If you are **unhappy**, you are sad and depressed. ❑ *Her marriage is in trouble and she is desperately unhappy.* ❑ *He was a shy, sometimes unhappy man.* ● **un|hap|pi|ly** ADV ❑ *"I don't have your imagination," King said unhappily.* ● **un|hap|pi|ness** N-UNCOUNT ❑ *There was a lot of unhappiness in my adolescence.* ❷ ADJ If you are **unhappy about** something, you are not pleased about it or not satisfied with it. [v-link ADJ, oft ADJ about/at n/-ing, ADJ that] ❑ *He has been unhappy with his son's political leanings.* ❑ *I suspect he isn't altogether unhappy about my absence.* ● **un|hap|pi|ness** N-UNCOUNT ❑ *He has, by submitting his resignation, signalled his unhappiness with the government's decision.* ❸ ADJ An **unhappy** situation or choice is not satisfactory or desirable. [ADJ n] ❑ *It is our hope that this unhappy chapter in the history of relations between our two countries will soon be closed.* ❑ *The legislation represents in itself an unhappy compromise.*

G

H

I

J

Thesaurus
unhappy의 참조어

ADJ. depressed, miserable, sad; (ant.) happy ❶

K

L

un|harmed /ʌnˈhɑrmd/ ADJ If someone or something is **unharmed** after an accident or violent incident, they are not hurt or damaged in any way. [ADJ after v, v-link ADJ] ❑ *They both escaped unharmed.*

M

un|healthy /ʌnˈhɛlθi/ (unhealthier, unhealthiest) ❶ ADJ Something that is **unhealthy** is likely to cause illness or poor health. ❑ *Avoid unhealthy foods such as hamburger and chips.* ❷ ADJ If you are **unhealthy**, you are not very fit or well. ❑ *I'm quite unhealthy really.* ❸ ADJ An **unhealthy** economy or company is financially weak and unsuccessful. ❑ *If you have an unhealthy economy, the poor will get hurt worst because they are the weakest.* ❹ ADJ If you describe someone's behavior or interests as **unhealthy**, you do not consider them to be normal and think they may involve mental problems. ❑ *Frank has developed what I would term an unhealthy relationship with these people.*

N

O

un|heard of /ʌnˈhɜrd ʌv/ ADJ You can say that an event or situation is **unheard of** when it never happens. [v-link ADJ] ❑ *It's almost unheard of in France for a top politician not to come from the social elite.*

P

un|help|ful /ʌnˈhɛlpfəl/ ADJ If you say that someone or something is **unhelpful**, you mean that they do not help you or improve a situation, and may even make things worse. ❑ *The criticism is both unfair and unhelpful.*

Q

R

un|hurt /ʌnˈhɜrt/ ADJ If someone who has been attacked, or involved in an accident, is **unhurt**, they are not injured. [ADJ after v, v-link ADJ] ❑ *The lorry driver escaped unhurt, but a pedestrian was injured.*

S

Word Link
ident ≈ same : identical, identification, unidentified

T

un|iden|ti|fied ◆◇◇ /ˌʌnaɪˈdɛntɪfaɪd/ ❶ ADJ If you describe someone or something as **unidentified**, you mean that nobody knows who or what they are. ❑ *He was shot this morning by unidentified intruders at his house.* ❷ ADJ If you use **unidentified** to describe people, groups, and organizations, you do not want to give their names. [JOURNALISM] ❑ *...his claims, which were based on the comments of anonymous and unidentified sources.*

U

uni|fi|ca|tion /ˌjunɪfɪˈkeɪʃən/ N-UNCOUNT **Unification** is the process by which two or more countries join together and become one country. ❑ *...the process of European unification.*

V

Word Link
uni ≈ one : uniform, unilateral, union

W

uni|form ◆◇◇ /ˈjunɪfɔrm/ (uniforms) ❶ N-VAR A **uniform** is a special set of clothes which some people, for example soldiers or the police, wear to work in and which some children wear at school. ❑ *The town police wear dark blue uniforms.* ❑ *Philippe was in uniform, wearing a pistol holster on his belt.* ❷ ADJ If something is **uniform**, it does not vary, but is even and regular throughout. ❑ *Cut down between the bones so that all the chops are of uniform size.* ❑ *All flowing water, though it appears to be uniform, is actually divided into extensive inner surfaces, or layers, moving against one another.* ● **uni|form|ity** /ˌjunɪˈfɔrmɪti/ N-UNCOUNT ❑ *...the caramel that was used to maintain uniformity of color in the brandy.*

X

Y

Z

[Korean translation column]

❶ 형용사 실현되지 않은, 충족되지 않은 ❑ 당신이 이루지 못한 야망의 ❑ 일자리와 적당한 집을 제공하겠다는 약속이 지켜지지 않아서 화가 난 ❷ 형용사 만족을 못 느끼는 ❑ 당신은 혼자 사는 것이 불행하고 만족스럽지 못하다는 생각을 버려야 한다.

❶ 타동사/자동사 (우산 등을) 펼치다 ❑ 내부 방파제를 벗어나자 우리는 돛을 모두 펼치기 시작했다. ❷ 자동사 (눈앞에) 펼쳐지다 ❑ 유럽에서 극적인 변화가 계속 펼쳐지고 있다.

형용사 은혜를 모르는, 배은망덕한 [탐탁찮음] ❑ 나는 그게 좀 배은망덕하다고 생각했다.

부사 불행히도 ❑ 5월 23일에 불행하게도 그 어린 소년은 죽었다. ❑ 불행히도 그 사실들이 그 이론을 완전히 밑받침해 주지는 않는다.

❶ 형용사 불행한, 비참한 ❑ 그녀는 결혼 생활에 문제가 있어서 극도로 불행한 상태이다. ❑ 그는 수줍을 때로는 침울해 보이는 남자였다. ● 침울하게 부사 ❑ "나는 너와 같은 상상력이 없어."라고 왕은 침울하게 말했다. ● 불행, 침울함 불가산명사 ❑ 나는 청소년기에 마음 아픈 일이 많았다. ❷ 형용사 불만스러운 ❑ 그는 자기 아들의 정치적 성향이 계속해 불만스러웠다. ❑ 나는 내가 없는 것에 대해 그가 아주 불만스러워 하지는 않을 거라고 생각한다. ● 불만족 불가산명사 ❑ 그는 사표를 제출함으로써 정부의 결정에 대한 불만을 나타냈다. ❸ 형용사 불만족스러운, 바람직하지 못한 ❑ 우리의 희망은 우리 두 나라 관계가 역사적으로 이렇게 바람직하지 못한 시기가 하루 빨리 끝나는 것이다. ❑ 입법은 그 자체로 불만족스러운 타협이다.

형용사 해를 입지 않은 ❑ 그들은 둘 다 무사했다.

❶ 형용사 몸에 나쁜, 건강에 좋지 않은 ❑ 햄버거나 감자튀김 같이 건강에 나쁜 음식은 피하시오. ❷ 형용사 건강이 좋지 않은 ❑ 나는 정말로 건강이 아주 좋지 않다. ❸ 형용사 건실하지 못한 ❑ 경제가 건실하지 못하면 가난한 사람들이 가장 취약하기 때문에 가장 심하게 피해를 입는다. ❹ 형용사 건강하지 못한, 비정상적인 ❑ 프랭크는 이런 사람들과 소위 건강하지 못한 관계를 맺어 왔다.

형용사 들어 본 일이 없는, 전례가 없는 ❑ 프랑스에서 고위 정치인이 사회의 엘리트 출신이 아닌 경우는 거의 전례가 없다.

형용사 도움이 되지 않는 ❑ 그 비판은 공정하지도 않고 도움이 되지도 않는다.

형용사 다치지 않은, 해를 입지 않은 ❑ 트럭 기사는 무사했지만 보행자 한 사람이 다쳤다.

❶ 형용사 미확인의, 정체불명의 ❑ 그는 오늘 아침 자기 집에서 정체불명의 침입자의 총에 맞았다. ❷ 형용사 미확인의 [언론] 익명에 미확인된 출처의 논평에 근거를 둔 그의 주장

불가산명사 통일 ❑ 유럽 통일의 과정

❶ 가산명사 또는 불가산명사 제복, 교복, 유니폼 ❑ 시 경찰은 암청색 제복을 입는다. ❑ 필립은 제복을 입고 벨트에는 권총집을 차고 있었다. ❷ 형용사 일정한, 균일한 ❑ 갈비살의 크기가 모두 균일하도록 뼈를 자르시오. ❑ 모든 흐르는 물은 보기에는 일사불란한 것 같지만 실제로는 서로 어긋나게 흐르는 광범위한 내부 수면, 즉 여러 층으로 나누어진다. ● 균일성 불가산명사 ❑ 브랜디 색의 균일성을 유지하기 위해 사용된 물엿 ● 균일하게 부사 ❑ 창 너머로 보이는

● **uni|form|ly** ADV ❑ *Beyond the windows, a November midday was uniformly gray.*
3 ADJ If you describe a number of things as **uniform**, you mean that they are all the same. ❑ *Along each wall stretched uniform green metal filing cabinets.*
● **uni|form|ity** N-UNCOUNT ❑ *...the dull uniformity of the houses.* ● **uni|form|ly** ADV ❑ *They are all about twenty years old, serious, smart, a bit conventional perhaps, but uniformly pleasant.* →see **basketball, football, soccer**

11월의 한낮은 회색 일색이었다. **3** 형용사 똑같은, 동일한 ❑ 각 벽을 따라 똑같은 서류 정리용 녹색 철제 캐비닛이 늘어서 있었다. ● 동일성, 획일성 불가산명사 ❑ 집들의 단조로운 획일성 ● 똑같이, 동일하게 부사 ❑ 그들은 모두 스무 살 정도인데 진지하고, 똑똑하며, 조금 틀에 박힌 듯하긴 하지만 한결같이 명랑하다.

uni|formed /y_ni_fɔrmd/ ADJ If you use **uniformed** to describe someone who does a particular job, you mean that they are wearing a uniform. ❑ *...uniformed policemen.*

형용사 제복을 입은 ❑ 제복 차림의 경찰들

uni|form|ity /y_ni_fɔrmiti/ N-UNCOUNT If there is **uniformity** in something such as a system, organization, or group of countries, the same rules, ideas, or methods are applied in all parts of it. ❑ *Spanish liberals sought to create linguistic as well as administrative uniformity.* →see also **uniform**

불가산명사 일률성, 통일성 ❑ 스페인의 진보주의자들은 행정상의 통일성뿐만 아니라 언어의 통일성도 이루어 내고자 했다.

uni|fy /y_ni_faɪ/ (**unifies, unifying, unified**) V-RECIP If someone **unifies** different things or parts, or if the things or parts **unify**, they are brought together to form one thing. ❑ *He pledged to unify the city's political factions.* ❑ *...constitutional reforms designed to unify the country.* ● **uni|fied** ADJ ❑ *...a unified system of taxation.*

상호동사 통합하다, 동일하다; 통합되다 ❑ 그는 시의 정치 파벌들을 통합하겠다고 맹세했다. ❑ 나라를 통일하기 위해 입안된 헌법 개혁 ● 통합된, 동일된 형용사 ❑ 통합된 세금 제도

Word Link	uni ≈ one : **uni**form, **uni**lateral, **uni**on

uni|lat|er|al /y_ni_læt_ər_ol/ ADJ A **unilateral** decision or action is taken by only one of the groups, organizations, or countries that are involved in a particular situation, without the agreement of the others. ❑ *...unilateral nuclear disarmament.*

형용사 일방적인, 단독의 ❑ 일방적인 핵 군축

un|im|ag|in|able /ʌnɪmædʒɪnəbəl/ ADJ If you describe something as **unimaginable**, you are emphasizing that it is difficult to imagine or understand properly, because it is not part of people's normal experience. [EMPHASIS] ❑ *The scale of the fighting is almost unimaginable.* ● **un|im|ag|in|ably** /ʌnɪmædʒɪnəbli/ ADV [ADV adj] ❑ *Conditions in prisons out there are unimaginably bad.*

형용사 상상할 수 없는 [강조] ❑ 그 전투의 규모는 거의 상상할 수 없다. ● 상상할 수 없이 부사 ❑ 그곳의 교도소 형편은 상상할 수 없을 정도로 나쁘다.

un|im|por|tant /ʌnɪmpɔrtənt/ ADJ If you describe something or someone as **unimportant**, you mean that they do not have much influence, effect, or value, and are therefore not worth serious consideration. ❑ *When they had married, six years before, the difference in their ages had seemed unimportant.*

형용사 중요하지 않은, 하찮은 ❑ 6년 전 그들이 결혼했을 때는 나이 차이가 중요하지 않아 보였었다.

Thesaurus	unimportant의 참조어
ADJ.	frivolous, insignificant, trivial; (ant.) important

un|im|pressed /ʌnɪmpr_est/ ADJ If you are **unimpressed by** something or someone, you do not think they are very good, clever, or useful. [v-link ADJ, oft ADJ by/with n] ❑ *He was also very unimpressed by his teachers.*

형용사 감동을 받지 않은 ❑ 그는 자기 선생님들 또한 별로 대단치 않게 생각했다.

un|in|hib|it|ed /ʌnɪnhɪbɪtɪd/ ADJ If you describe a person or their behavior as **uninhibited**, you mean that they express their opinions and feelings openly, and behave as they want to, without worrying what other people think. ❑ *...a commanding and uninhibited entertainer.* ❑ *The dancing is uninhibited and as frenzied as an aerobics class.*

형용사 남을 의식하지 않는, 아무 제약을 받지 않는 ❑ 당당하고 남을 의식하지 않는 연예인 ❑ 그 춤은 아무 제약을 받지 않으며 에어로빅 하듯 미친 듯이 춘다.

un|in|stall /ʌnɪnstɔl/ (**uninstalls, uninstalling, uninstalled**) V-T If you **uninstall** a computer program, you remove it permanently from your computer. [COMPUTING] ❑ *If you don't like the program, just uninstall it and forget it.*

타동사 (컴퓨터 프로그램을) 삭제하다 [컴퓨터] ❑ 그 프로그램이 마음에 들지 않으면 삭제하고 잊어버리시오.

un|in|tel|li|gible /ʌnɪntelɪdʒɪbəl/ ADJ **Unintelligible** language is impossible to understand, for example because it is not written or pronounced clearly, or because its meaning is confused or complicated. ❑ *He muttered something unintelligible.*

형용사 이해할 수 없는, 난해한 ❑ 그가 뭐라고 알아들을 수 없는 말을 중얼거렸다.

un|in|ten|tion|al /ʌnɪntenʃənəl/ ADJ Something that is **unintentional** is not done deliberately, but happens by accident. ❑ *Perhaps he had slightly misled them, but it was quite unintentional.* ● **un|in|ten|tion|al|ly** ADV ❑ *...an overblown and unintentionally funny adaptation of "Dracula."*

형용사 고의가 아닌 ❑ 아마 그가 그들을 약간 오도한 것 같은데 그건 전혀 고의가 아니었다. ● 의도치 않게, 어쩌다 부사 ❑ 과장되고 어쩌다 보니 우습게 각색된 '드라큘라'

un|in|ter|rupt|ed /ʌnɪntərʌptɪd/ **1** ADJ If something is **uninterrupted**, it is continuous and has no breaks or interruptions in it. [ADJ after v, v-link ADJ, ADJ n] ❑ *This enables the healing process to continue uninterrupted.* ❑ *His hearing remained good, so that his contact with the world was uninterrupted.* **2** ADJ An **uninterrupted** view of something is a clear view of it, without any obstacles in the way. ❑ *Diners can enjoy an uninterrupted view of the garden.*

1 형용사 중단되지 않은, 연속된 ❑ 이것은 치유 과정이 중단되지 않고 계속될 수 있게 해 준다. ❑ 그는 청력이 여전히 좋았고 그래서 세계와의 접촉은 중단되지 않았다. **2** 형용사 막히지 않은 ❑ 식사 손님들은 탁 트인 정원을 조망할 수 있다.

un|ion ◆◆◇ /y_ny_ən/ (**unions**) **1** N-COUNT A **union** is a workers' organization which represents its members and which aims to improve things such as their working conditions and pay. ❑ *I feel that women in all types of employment can benefit from joining a union.* **2** N-UNCOUNT When the **union** of two or more things occurs, they are joined together and become one thing. ❑ *In 1918 the Romanian majority in this former tsarist province voted for union with Romania.* **3** N-SING When two or more things, for example countries or organizations, have been joined together to form one thing, you can refer to them as a **union**. ❑ *Tanzania is a union of the states of Tanganyika and Zanzibar.* →see **empire, factory** →see Word Web: **union**

1 가산명사 노동조합 ❑ 나는 여성이 모든 종류의 직장에서 노동조합에 가입하면 혜택을 볼 수 있다고 생각한다. **2** 불가산명사 연합, 합병 ❑ 1918년에 이곳 과거 제정 러시아 지역의 루마니아 사람 대다수가 루마니아와의 합병에 찬성투표를 했다. **3** 단수명사 연합체 ❑ 탄자니아는 탕가니카와 잔지바르 두 나라가 합병한 것이다.

unique ◆◇◇ /y_nik/ **1** ADJ Something that is **unique** is the only one of its kind. ❑ *Each person's signature is unique.* ● **unique|ly** ADV ❑ *Because of the extreme cold, the Antarctic is a uniquely fragile environment.* ● **unique|ness** N-UNCOUNT ❑ *...the uniqueness of China's own experience.* **2** ADJ You can use **unique** to describe things that you admire because they are very unusual and special. [APPROVAL] ❑ *Brett's vocals are just unique.* ● **unique|ly** ADV ❑ *There'll never be a shortage of people who consider themselves uniquely qualified to be president of the United States.* **3** ADJ If something is **unique to** one thing, person, group, or place, it concerns or belongs only to that thing, person, group, or place. [v-link ADJ to n] ❑ *No one*

1 형용사 유일한 ❑ 개개인의 서명은 유일무이하다. ● 유일하게 부사 ❑ 극심한 추위 때문에 남극은 유독 환경이 취약하다. ● 유일함 불가산명사 ❑ 중국 자체의 유일한 경험 **2** 형용사 독특한 [마음에 듦] ❑ 브렛의 창법은 아주 독특하다. ● 특별하게 부사 ❑ 자신이 미합중국 대통령에 특별히 적임이라고 여기는 사람들이 부족한 일은 결코 없을 것이다. **3** 형용사 -에 특유한, -에 고유한 ❑ 왜 사춘기가 인간에게만 특별히 있는 건지 아무도 확실히 알지 못한다. ● 특유하게,

A B C D E F G H I J K L M N O P Q R S T U V W X Y Z

Word Web union

In some places, **laborers** work long hours with little chance for a **raise** in **wages**. **Workdays** of 10 to 12 hours are not uncommon. Some people even work seven days a week. Conditions like this lead to unrest among **workers**. At that point, **organizers** can sometimes get them to join a **union**. Union leaders engage in **collective bargaining** with business owners. They try to win a shorter workday or better working conditions for workers. If the **employees** are not satisfied with the results, they may **strike**. In Sweden, 85% of laborers and 75% of **white-collar** employees belong to unions.

knows for sure why adolescence is unique to humans. ● **unique|ly** ADV [ADV adj] ❏ *The problem isn't uniquely American.*

고유하게 부사 ❏ 그 문제가 미국 고유의 것은 아니다.

Thesaurus unique의 참조어

ADJ. different, special, uncommon; (ant.) common, standard, usual **2**

uni|sex /yuniseks/ ADJ **Unisex** is used to describe things, usually clothes or places, which are designed for use by both men and women rather than by only one sex. ❏ *...the classic unisex hair salon.*

형용사 남녀 공용의 ❏ 고전적인 남녀 공용 미장원

uni|son /yunisən, -zən/ **1** PHRASE If two or more people do something **in unison**, they do it together at the same time. ❏ *The students gave him a rapturous welcome, chanting in unison: "We want the king!"* **2** PHRASE If people or organizations act **in unison**, they act the same way because they agree with each other or because they want to achieve the same aims. ❏ *The international community is ready to work in unison against him.*

1 구 일제히 ❏ 학생들은 "우리는 왕을 원한다!"라고 일제히 외치면서 그를 열광적으로 환영했다. **2** 구 합심하여 ❏ 국제 사회가 그에 대항해 합심하여 움직일 준비가 되어 있다.

unit ♦♦◇ /yunɪt/ (**units**) **1** N-COUNT If you consider something as a **unit**, you consider it as a single, complete thing. ❏ *Agriculture was based in the past on the family as a unit.* **2** N-COUNT A **unit** is a group of people who work together at a specific job, often in a particular place. ❏ *the health services research unit.* **3** N-COUNT A **unit** is a group within an armed force or police force, whose members fight or work together or carry out a particular task. ❏ *One secret military unit tried to contaminate the drinking water of the refugees.* **4** N-COUNT A **unit** is a small machine which has a particular function, often part of a larger machine. ❏ *The unit plugs into any TV set.* **5** N-COUNT A **unit** of measurement is a fixed standard quantity, length, or weight that is used for measuring things. The quart, the inch, and the ounce are all units. ❏ *...the Malay kati, a unit of weight for tea, approximately 1.3 lbs.* **6** N-COUNT A **unit** is one of the parts that a textbook is divided into. ❏ *Unit V of this book explains those errors in detail and shows you ways to correct them.* →see graph

1 가산명사 구성 단위, 부분 ❏ 과거에는 농사를 가족 단위로 지었다. **2** 가산명사 (구성 단위로서의) 부서 ❏ 보건 서비스 연구과 **3** 가산명사 (특정 임무를 위한) 부대, 단 ❏ 한 비밀 군사 부대가 난민들의 식수를 오염시키려고 했다. **4** 가산명사 (작은) 장치 ❏ 그 장치는 어떤 텔레비전에나 꽂으면 다 맞는다. **5** 가산명사 (계량의) 단위 ❏ 차의 무게를 재는 단위이며 대략 1.3파운드에 해당하는 말레이시아 카티 **6** 가산명사 (책의) 단원 ❏ 이 책의 단원 5에는 그런 오류들이 자세하게 설명되어 있고 그것을 바로잡는 방법이 나와 있다.

unit cost (**unit costs**) N-COUNT **Unit cost** is the amount of money that it costs a company to produce one article. [BUSINESS] ❏ *They aim to reduce unit costs through extra sales.*

가산명사 단위 원가, 단가 [경제] ❏ 추가 판매를 통해 단가를 줄이는 것이 그들의 목표이다.

unite /yunaɪt/ (**unites, uniting, united**) V-T/V-I If a group of people or things **unite** or if something **unites** them, they join together and act as a group. ❏ *The two parties have been trying to unite since the New Year.*

타동사/자동사 연합하다, 결합하다; 결합시키다 ❏ 두 정당은 새해 첫날부터 연합하려고 노력해 왔다.

Thesaurus unite의 참조어

V. blend, combine, incorporate; (ant.) separate

unit|ed ♦◇◇ /yunaɪtɪd/ **1** ADJ When people are **united** about something, they agree about it and act together. ❏ *Every party is united on the need for parliamentary democracy.* **2** ADJ **United** is used to describe a country which has been formed from two or more states or countries. ❏ *...the first elections to be held in a united Germany for fifty eight years.*

1 형용사 연합된, 합심한 ❏ 각 정당은 의회 민주주의의 필요성에 대해 의기투합해 있다. **2** 형용사 연합한, 통일된 ❏ 58년 만에 통일 독일에서 최초로 실시된 선거

Unit|ed Na|tions ♦♦◇ N-PROPER **The United Nations** is an organization which most countries belong to. Its role is to encourage international peace, cooperation, and friendship.

고유명사 국제 연합, 유엔

unit sales N-PLURAL **Unit sales** refers to the number of individual items that a company sells. [BUSINESS] ❏ *Unit sales of T-shirts increased 6%.*

복수명사 판매 수량 [경제] ❏ 티셔츠 항목의 판매 수량은 6퍼센트 증가했다.

unit trust (**unit trusts**) N-COUNT A **unit trust** is an organization which invests money in many different types of business and which offers units for sale to the public as an investment. You can also refer to an investment of this type as a **unit trust**. [BRIT, BUSINESS; AM **mutual fund**] ❏ *Many unit trusts charge an initial fee of up to 5.5%.*

가산명사 개방형 투자 신탁 회사; 개방형 신탁 투자 [영국영어, 경제; 미국영어 mutual fund] ❏ 많은 개방형 투자 신탁 회사들은 초기 수수료를 5.5퍼센트까지 부과한다.

unity ♦◇◇ /yuniti/ **1** N-UNCOUNT **Unity** is the state of different areas or groups being joined together to form a single country or organization. ❏ *Senior politicians met today to discuss the future of European economic unity.* **2** N-UNCOUNT When there is **unity**, people are in agreement and act together for a particular purpose. ❏ *...a renewed unity of purpose.* ❏ *Speakers at the rally mouthed sentiments of unity.*

1 불가산명사 통합 ❏ 원로 정치인들이 오늘 회동하여 유럽 경제 통합의 미래에 대해 논의하였다. **2** 불가산명사 통일, 화합 ❏ 목표의 새로운 통일 ❏ 그 집회에서 연사들이 입으로는 화합을 강조했다.

Word Partnership unity의 연어

ADJ.	**economic** unity, **national** unity, **political** unity **1** **2**
V.	**maintain** unity, **promote** unity **1** **2**
N.	**party** unity, unity **of purpose**, **sense of** unity, **show of** unity, **spirit of** unity **2**

uni|ver|sal /yunɪvɜrsᵊl/ ■ ADJ Something that is **universal** relates to everyone in the world or everyone in a particular group or society. ❑ *The insurance industry has produced its own proposals for universal health care.* ② ADJ Something that is **universal** affects or relates to every part of the world or the universe. ❑ *...universal diseases.*

uni|ver|sal bank (**universal banks**) N-COUNT A **universal bank** is a bank that offers both banking and stockbroking services to its clients. [BUSINESS] ❑ *...universal banks offering a wide range of services.*

uni|ver|sal|ly /yunɪvɜrsəli/ ■ ADV If something is **universally** believed or accepted, it is believed or accepted by everyone with no disagreement. ❑ *...a universally accepted point of view.* ② ADV If something is **universally** true, it is true everywhere in the world or in all situations. ❑ *The disadvantage is that it is not universally available.*

uni|verse ◆◇◇ /yunɪvɜrs/ (**universes**) ■ N-COUNT The **universe** is the whole of space and all the stars, planets, and other forms of matter and energy in it. ❑ *Einstein's equations showed the Universe to be expanding.* ② N-COUNT If you talk about someone's **universe**, you are referring to the whole of their experience or an important part of it. ❑ *Good writers suck in what they see of the world, re-creating their own universe on the page.* ❑ *They marked out the boundaries of our visual universe.* →see **galaxy**

uni|ver|sity ◆◆◆ /yunɪvɜrsiti/ (**universities**) N-VAR; N-IN-NAMES A **university** is an institution where students study for degrees and where academic research is done. ❑ *Patrick is now at London University.* ❑ *Maybe next year I'll go to university, as I planned.*

un|just /ʌndʒʌst/ ADJ If you describe an action, system, or law as **unjust**, you think that it treats a person or group badly in a way that they do not deserve. ❑ *The attack on Charles was deeply unjust.* ● **un|just|ly** ADV ❑ *She was unjustly accused of stealing money and then given the sack.*

un|jus|ti|fied /ʌndʒʌstɪfaɪd/ ADJ If you describe a belief or action as **unjustified**, you think that there is no good reason for having it or doing it. ❑ *Your report last week was unfair. It was based upon wholly unfounded and totally unjustified allegations.*

un|kind /ʌnkaɪnd/ (**unkinder**, **unkindest**) ■ ADJ If someone is **unkind**, they behave in an unpleasant, unfriendly, or slightly cruel way. You can also describe someone's words or actions as **unkind**. ❑ *All last summer he'd been unkind to her.* ❑ *No one has an unkind word to say about him.* ● **un|kind|ly** ADV ❑ *Several viewers commented unkindly on her costumes.* ● **un|kind|ness** N-UNCOUNT ❑ *He realized the unkindness of the remark and immediately regretted having hurt her with it.* ② ADJ If you describe something bad that happens to someone as **unkind**, you mean that they do not deserve it. [WRITTEN] ❑ *The weather was unkind to those pipers who played in the morning.*

Thesaurus *unkind*의 참조어

ADJ. harsh, mean, unfriendly; (ant.) kind ■

---

un|known ◆◇◇ /ʌnnoʊn/ (**unknowns**) ■ ADJ If something is **unknown** to you, you have no knowledge of it. ❑ *An unknown number of demonstrators were arrested.* ❑ *The motive for the killing is unknown.* ● N-COUNT An **unknown** is something that is unknown. ❑ *The length of the war is one of the biggest unknowns.* ② ADJ An **unknown** person is someone whose name you do not know or whose character you do not know anything about. ❑ *Unknown thieves had forced their way into the apartment.* ③ ADJ An **unknown** person is not famous or publicly recognized. ❑ *He was an unknown writer.* ● N-COUNT An **unknown** is a person who is unknown. ❑ *Within a short space of time a group of complete unknowns had established a wholly original form of humor.* ④ ADJ If you say that a particular problem or situation is **unknown**, you mean that it never occurs. ❑ *A hundred years ago coronary heart disease was virtually unknown in Europe and America.* ⑤ N-SING **The unknown** refers generally to things or places that people do not know about or understand. ❑ *Ignorance of people brings fear, fear of the unknown.*

un|law|ful /ʌnlɔfəl/ ADJ If something is **unlawful**, the law does not allow you to do it. [FORMAL] ❑ *...employees who believe their dismissal was unlawful.* ● **un|law|ful|ly** ADV [ADV with v] ❑ *...the councils' assertion that the government acted unlawfully in imposing the restrictions.*

un|lead|ed /ʌnlɛdɪd/ ADJ **Unleaded** fuel contains a smaller amount of lead than most fuels so that it produces less harmful substances when it is burned. ❑ *The new Metro is designed to run on unleaded fuel.* ● N-UNCOUNT **Unleaded** is also a noun. ❑ *All its V8 engines will run happily on unleaded.*

un|leash /ʌnliʃ/ (**unleashes**, **unleashing**, **unleashed**) V-T If you say that someone or something **unleashes** a powerful force, feeling, activity, or group, you mean that they suddenly start it or send it somewhere. ❑ *Then he unleashed his own, unstoppable, attack.* ❑ *The officers were still reluctant to unleash their troops in pursuit of a defeated enemy.*

un|less ◆◆◇ /ʌnlɛs/ CONJ You use **unless** to introduce the only circumstances in which an event you are mentioning will not take place or in which a statement you are making is not true. ❑ *Unless you are trying to lose weight to please yourself, it's going to be tough to keep your motivation level high.* ❑ *We cannot understand disease unless we understand the person who has the disease.*

> Do not confuse **unless**, **except**, **except for**, and **besides**. **Unless** is used to introduce the only situation in which something will take place or be true. ❑ *In the 1940s, unless she wore gloves a woman was not properly dressed... You must not give compliments unless you mean them.* You use **except** to introduce the only

---

■ 형용사 일반적인, 보편적인 ❑ 보험업계는 일반 의료보험을 위한 자체 안을 제시했다. ② 형용사 전 세계적인 ❑ 전 세계적인 질병

가산명사 유니버설 뱅크 [경제] ❑ 다양한 서비스를 제공하는 유니버설 뱅크

■ 부사 일반적으로 ❑ 일반적으로 인정되는 관점 ② 부사 어디서나 ❑ 불편한 점은 그것을 어디서나 사용할 수 없다는 것이다.

■ 가산명사 우주 ❑ 아인슈타인의 방정식은 우주가 팽창하고 있다는 것을 보여주었다. ② 가산명사 (개인의) 경험 세계 ❑ 훌륭한 작가는 자기가 세상에서 보는 것을 흡수하여 페이지 위에 자신의 경험을 재창조한다. ❑ 그들은 우리의 가시적 세계의 경계선을 표시했다.

가산명사 또는 불가산명사; 이름명사 대학 ❑ 패트릭은 지금 런던 대학에 다닌다. ❑ 나는 아마도 내년에 계획한 대로 대학에 갈 것이다.

형용사 부당한 ❑ 찰스에 대한 공격은 매우 부당한 것이었다. ● 부당하게 부사 ❑ 그녀는 돈을 훔쳤다고 부당하게 고발당한 뒤 해고되었다.

형용사 정당하지 않은 ❑ 지난주 당신의 보도는 편파적이었다. 그것은 전적으로 사실 무근이고 완전히 터무니없는 주장에 근거하고 있었다.

■ 형용사 불친절한, 인정 없는 ❑ 지난여름 내내 그는 그녀에게 불친절했다. ❑ 아무도 그에 대해 나쁜 말을 하지 않는다. ● 불친절하게, 몰인정하게 부사 ❑ 몇몇 시청자들이 그녀의 복장에 대해서 심하게 말했다. ● 불친절, 몰인정 불가산명사 ❑ 그는 그 논평이 심했다는 것을 깨닫고 곧 그것으로 인해 그녀를 상처 입게 한 것을 후회했다. ② 형용사 가혹한 [문어체] ❑ 날씨는 아침에 연주하는 파이프 연주자들에게 가혹했다.

■ 형용사 알려지지 않은 ❑ 몇 명인가 밝혀지지 않은 시위 참가자들이 체포되었다. ❑ 살인의 동기는 알려지지 않고 있다. ● 가산명사 알려지지 않은 것 ❑ 그 전쟁의 기간이 가장 불명확한 것들 중 하나이다. ② 형용사 신원 미상의 ❑ 신원 미상의 도둑들이 그 아파트 안으로 침입했다. ③ 형용사 무명의 ❑ 그는 무명 작가였다. ● 가산명사 무명인, 알려지지 않은 사람 ❑ 짧은 기간 안에 완전히 무명인 그룹이 매우 독창적인 유머의 형태를 확립시켰다. ④ 형용사 발생하지 않는, 들어 보지도 못한 ❑ 백 년 전에는 심장 동맥 질환이 유럽과 미국에서 실질적으로 발생하지 않았다. ⑤ 단수명사 미지 ❑ 사람들에 대한 무지는 공포, 즉 미지에 대한 공포를 낳는다.

형용사 불법의 [격식체] ❑ 자신들의 해고가 불법이라고 믿는 직원들 ● 불법으로 부사 ❑ 정부가 제한 규정을 불법적으로 부과했다는 위원회의 주장

형용사 (연료가) 무연의 ❑ 새 지하철은 무연 연료로 움직이도록 설계되어 있다. ● 불가산명사 무연 휘발유 ❑ 그것의 브이8 엔진은 모두 무연 휘발유로 잘 작동될 것이다.

타동사 폭발시키다; 퍼뜨리다 ❑ 그리고 나서 그는 제지할 수 없는 공격을 퍼부었다. ❑ 장교들은 패배한 적을 추격하기 위하여 자신들의 군대를 보내는 것이 여전히 내키지 않았다.

접속사 - 하지 않으면, -이 아닌 한 ❑ 자기 자신의 만족을 위해 살을 빼려고 하는 것이 아니라면, 계속 살을 빼려는 열의를 가지기는 어려울 것이다. ❑ 그 병에 걸린 사람을 이해하지 않는 한 병을 이해할 수는 없다.

> unless, except, except for, besides를 혼동하지 않도록 하라. unless는 어떤 일이 발생하거나 사실이 될 수 있는 유일한 상황을 언급할 때 쓴다. ❑ 1940년대에는 여자가 장갑을 끼지 않으면

things, situations, people, or ideas that a statement does not apply to. ❑ *All of his body relaxed except his right hand... Traveling was impossible, except in the cool of the morning.* You use **except for** before something that prevents a statement from being completely true. ❑ *The classrooms were silent, except for the scratching of pens on paper... I had absolutely no friends except for Tom.* You use **besides** to introduce extra things in addition to the ones you are mentioning already. ❑ *Fruit will give you, besides enjoyment, a source of vitamins.* However, note that if you talk about "the only thing" or "the only person **besides**" a particular person or thing, **besides** means the same as "apart from." ❑ *He was the only person besides Gertrude who talked to Guy.*

복장을 갖추어 입지 않은 것이었다... 진심이 아니면 칭찬을 하면 안 된다. except는 진술이 적용되지 않는 유일한 사물, 상황, 사람, 생각을 말할 때 쓴다. ❑ 그는 오른손을 제외한 몸 전체가 긴장이 풀렸다... 아침에 서늘한 때를 제외하면 여행은 불가능했다. except for는 진술이 완벽한 진실이 되지 못하게 하는 것 앞에 쓴다. ❑ 교실은 고요했고 종이 위에 펜 긁히는 소리만 들렸다... 나는 톰을 빼면 친구가 한 명도 없었다. besides는 이미 언급한 것에 더하여 추가로 다른 것을 소개할 때 쓴다. ❑ 과일은 즐거움뿐만 아니라 비타민도 제공한다. 그러나 특정한 사람이나 물건 이외(besides)의 the only thing 또는 the only person이라고 하면, 이 때 besides는 apart from과 같은 뜻이다. ❑ 그는 거트루드를 제외하고는 가이에게 말을 건 유일한 사람이었다.

un|like ♦♦◇ /ʌnlaɪk/ **1** PREP If one thing is **unlike** another thing, the two things have different qualities or characteristics from each other. ❑ *This was a foreign country, so unlike San Jose.* **2** PREP You can use **unlike** to contrast two people, things, or situations, and show how they are different. ❑ *Unlike aerobics, walking entails no expensive fees for classes or clubs.* **3** PREP If you describe something that a particular person has done as being **unlike** them, you mean that you are surprised by it because it is not typical of their character or normal behavior. ❑ *It was so unlike him to say something like that, with such intensity, that I was astonished.*

1 전치사 다른 ❑ 이곳은 외국이었고, 산호세와 너무 달랐다. **2** 전치사 -와 다르게 ❑ 에어로빅과는 다르게, 걷는 비싼 강습료나 클럽 사용료가 들지 않는다. **3** 전치사 -답지 않은 ❑ 그렇게 격렬하게 그런 말을 하는 건 너무 그답지 않은 일이어서 나는 놀랐다.

un|like|ly ♦♦◇ /ʌnlaɪkli/ (**unlikeliest**) ADJ If you say that something is **unlikely to** happen or **unlikely to** be true, you believe that it will not happen or that it is not true, although you are not completely sure. ❑ *A military coup seems unlikely.* ❑ *It's now unlikely that future parliaments will bring back the death penalty.*

형용사 -할 것 같지 않은 ❑ 군사 쿠데타는 일어날 것 같지 않다. ❑ 지금 보면 나중에라도 의회에서 사형 제도를 부활시킬 것 같지는 않다.

Word Partnership	unlikely의 연어
ADV.	**extremely** unlikely, **highly** unlikely, **most** unlikely, **very** unlikely
N.	unlikely **event**
V.	unlikely **to change**, unlikely **to happen**, **seem** unlikely

un|lim|it|ed /ʌnlɪmɪtɪd/ ADJ If there is an **unlimited** quantity of something, you can have as much or as many of that thing as you want. ❑ *An unlimited number of copies can still be made from the original.* ❑ *You'll also have unlimited access to the swimming pool.*

형용사 무제한의, 무한정한 ❑ 여전히 원본에서 무한정한 복사본이 만들어질 수 있다. ❑ 또한 수영장을 무제한으로 사용해도 될 것이다.

un|list|ed /ʌnlɪstɪd/ **1** ADJ If a person or their telephone number is **unlisted**, the number is not listed in the telephone book, and the telephone company will refuse to give it to people who ask for it. [mainly AM; BRIT usually **ex-directory**] ❑ *Mr. Marra, whose New York telephone number is unlisted, could not be contacted yesterday.* **2** ADJ An **unlisted** company or **unlisted** stock is not listed officially on a stock exchange. [BUSINESS] ❑ *Its shares are traded on the Unlisted Securities Market.*

1 형용사 전화번호부에 실리지 않은 [주로 미국영어; 영국영어 대개 ex-directory] ❑ 마라 씨의 연락처가 뉴욕 전화번호부에 나와 있지 않아서 어제 연락할 수 없었다. **2** 형용사 (주식 시장에) 상장되지 않은 [경제] ❑ 그것의 주식은 장외 주식 시장에서 거래되고 있다.

un|load /ʌnloʊd/ (**unloads, unloading, unloaded**) V-T If you **unload** goods from a vehicle, or you **unload** a vehicle, you remove the goods from the vehicle, usually after they have been transported from one place to another. ❑ *Unload everything from the boat and clean it thoroughly.*

타동사 짐을 내리다 ❑ 보트에서 모든 짐을 내리고 철저히 청소해라.

un|lock /ʌnlɒk/ (**unlocks, unlocking, unlocked**) **1** V-T If you **unlock** something such as a door, a room, or a container that has a lock, you open it using a key. ❑ *He unlocked the car and threw the coat on to the back seat.* **2** V-T If you **unlock** the potential or the secrets of something or someone, you release them. ❑ *Education and training is the key that will unlock our nation's potential.*

1 타동사 (열쇠로) 열다 ❑ 그는 차 문을 열고 뒷좌석에 코트를 던졌다. **2** 타동사 드러내다, 튀어놓다 ❑ 교육과 훈련은 우리나라의 잠재력을 드러낼 열쇠이다.

un|lucky /ʌnlʌki/ (**unluckier, unluckiest**) **1** ADJ If someone is **unlucky**, they have bad luck. ❑ *Cantona was unlucky not to score on two occasions.* **2** ADJ You can use **unlucky** to describe unpleasant things which happen to someone, especially when you feel that the person does not deserve them. ❑ *...Argentina's unlucky defeat by Ireland.* **3** ADJ **Unlucky** is used to describe something that is thought to cause bad luck. ❑ *Some people think it is unlucky to look at a new moon through glass.*

1 형용사 운이 나쁜 ❑ 칸토나는 득점 기회를 두 번 놓치는 불운을 겪었다. **2** 형용사 불행한 ❑ 아일랜드에 의한 아르헨티나의 불행한 패배 **3** 형용사 불길한 ❑ 유리창 너머로 초승달을 보는 것은 불길하다고 어떤 사람들은 생각한다.

un|marked /ʌnmɑrkt/ **1** ADJ Something that is **unmarked** has no marks on it. ❑ *Her shoes are still white and unmarked.* **2** ADJ Something that is **unmarked** has no marking on it which identifies what it is or whose it is. ❑ *He had seen them come out and get into the unmarked police car.*

1 형용사 아무 표가 없는, 아무 흔적이 없는 ❑ 그녀의 신발은 여전히 하얗고 아무 흔적도 없다. **2** 형용사 표시를 안 한 ❑ 그는 그들이 밖으로 나가서 표시가 안 된 경찰차에 올라타는 것을 보았다.

un|me|tered /ʌnmitərd/ ADJ An **unmetered** service for something such as water supply or telephone access is one that allows you to use as much as you want for a basic cost, rather than paying for the amount you use. ❑ *Clients are not charged by the minute but given unmetered access to the Internet for a fixed fee.*

형용사 정액제의 ❑ 이용자는 분당 요금을 내지 않고 일정 사용료를 내면 무제한으로 인터넷에 접속할 수 있다.

un|mis|tak|able /ʌnmɪsteɪkəb°l/ also **unmistakeable** ADJ If you describe something as **unmistakable**, you mean that it is so obvious that it cannot be mistaken for anything else. ❑ *He didn't give his name, but the voice was unmistakable.* ● **un|mis|tak|ably** ♦◇ /ʌnmɪsteɪkəbli/ ADV ❑ *It's still unmistakably a Minnelli movie.* ❑ *She's unmistakably Scandinavian.*

형용사 명백한, 틀림없는 ❑ 그는 이름을 대지 않았지만, 그 목소리는 틀림없었다. ● 명백히 부사 ❑ 그래도 명백히 그것은 미넬리 영화이다. ❑ 그녀는 틀림없이 스칸디나비아 사람이다.

un|miti|gat|ed /ʌnmɪtɪgeɪtɪd/ ADJ You use **unmitigated** to emphasize that a bad situation or quality is totally bad. [EMPHASIS] [ADJ n] ❑ *Last year's cotton crop was an unmitigated disaster.*

형용사 (더할 나위 없이) 악화된 [강조] ❑ 지난해의 목화 수확은 완전 흉작이었다.

un|moved /ʌnmuvd/ ADJ If you are **unmoved by** something, you are not emotionally affected by it. [v-link ADJ] ❑ *Mr. Bird remained unmoved by the corruption allegations.*

형용사 확고한, 흔들리지 않는 ❑ 버드 씨는 부정부패 의혹에도 흔들리지 않았다.

un|named /ʌnneɪmd/ **1** ADJ **Unnamed** people or things are talked about but

1 형용사 이름이 밝혀지지 않은 ❑ 이름이 밝혀지지

their names are not mentioned. ❑ *An unnamed man collapsed and died while he was walking near Dundonald.* ❷ ADJ **Unnamed** things have not been given a name. ❑ *...unnamed comets and asteroids.*

un|nat|ural /ʌnnætʃərᵊl/ ❶ ADJ If you describe something as **unnatural**, you mean that it is strange and often frightening, because it is different from what you normally expect. ❑ *The aircraft rose with unnatural speed on take-off.* ● **un|nat|ural|ly** ADV [ADV adj] ❑ *The house was unnaturally silent.* ❷ ADJ Behavior that is **unnatural** seems artificial and not normal or genuine. ❑ *She gave him a bright, determined smile which seemed unnatural.* ● **un|nat|ural|ly** ADV [ADV with v] ❑ *Try to avoid shouting or speaking unnaturally.*

un|nat|ural|ly /ʌnnætʃərəli/ PHRASE You can use **not unnaturally** to indicate that the situation you are describing is exactly as you would expect in the circumstances. ❑ *It was a question that Roy not unnaturally found impossible to answer.* →see also **unnatural**

un|nec|es|sary /ʌnnɛsəsɛri, BRIT ʌnnɛsəsri/ ADJ If you describe something as **unnecessary**, you mean that it is not needed or does not have to be done, and is undesirable. ❑ *The slaughter of whales is unnecessary and inhuman.* ● **un|nec|es|sari|ly** /ʌnnɛsəsɛərili/ ADV ❑ *I didn't want to upset my husband or my daughter unnecessarily.*

Thesaurus		*unnecessary*의 참조어
ADJ.	dispensable, superfluous, useless; *(ant.)* necessary	

un|nerve /ʌnnɜrv/ (**unnerves, unnerving, unnerved**) V-T If you say that something **unnerves** you, you mean that it worries or troubles you. ❑ *The news about Dermot had unnerved me.*

un|nerv|ing /ʌnnɜrvɪŋ/ ADJ If you describe something as **unnerving**, you mean that it makes you feel worried or uncomfortable. ❑ *It is very unnerving to find out that someone you see every day is carrying a potentially deadly virus.*

un|no|ticed /ʌnnoʊtɪst/ ADJ If something happens or passes **unnoticed**, it is not seen or noticed by anyone. ❑ *I tried to slip up the stairs unnoticed.*

un|ob|tru|sive /ʌnəbtrusɪv/ ADJ If you describe something or someone as **unobtrusive**, you mean that they are not easily noticed or do not draw attention to themselves. [FORMAL] ❑ *The coffee-table is glass, to be as unobtrusive as possible.* ● **un|ob|tru|sive|ly** ADV ❑ *They slipped away unobtrusively.*

un|of|fi|cial /ʌnəfɪʃᵊl/ ADJ An **unofficial** action or statement is not organized or approved by a person or group in authority. ❑ *Staff voted to continue an unofficial strike in support of seven colleagues who were dismissed last week.* ● **un|of|fi|cial|ly** ADV ❑ *Some workers are legally employed, but the majority work unofficially with neither health nor wage security.*

un|or|tho|dox /ʌnɔrθədɒks/ ADJ If you describe someone's behavior, beliefs, or customs as **unorthodox**, you mean that they are different from what is generally accepted. ❑ *She spent an unorthodox girlhood traveling with her father throughout Europe.*

un|pack /ʌnpæk/ (**unpacks, unpacking, unpacked**) ❶ V-T/V-I When you **unpack** a suitcase, box, or similar container, you take the things inside it, you take the things out of the container. ❑ *He unpacked his bag.* ❷ V-T If you **unpack** an idea or problem, you analyze it and consider it in detail. ❑ *A lot of ground has been covered in unpacking the issues central to achieving this market-led strategic change.*

un|paid /ʌnpeɪd/ ❶ ADJ If you do **unpaid** work or are an **unpaid** worker, you do a job without receiving any money for it. [ADJ n] ❑ *Even unpaid work for charity is better than nothing.* ❷ ADJ **Unpaid** taxes or bills, for example, are bills or taxes which have not been paid yet. ❑ *The taxman caught up with him and demanded £17,000 in unpaid taxes.*

un|pal|at|able /ʌnpælɪtəbᵊl/ ❶ ADJ If you describe an idea as **unpalatable**, you mean that you find it unpleasant and difficult to accept. ❑ *It was only then that I began to learn the unpalatable truth about John.* ❷ ADJ If you describe food as **unpalatable**, you mean that it is so unpleasant that you can hardly eat it. ❑ *...a lump of dry, unpalatable cheese.*

un|par|al|leled /ʌnpærəleld/ ADJ If you describe something as **unparalleled**, you are emphasizing that it is, for example, bigger, better, or worse than anything else of its kind, or anything that has happened before. [EMPHASIS] ❑ *Germany's unparalleled prosperity is based on wise investments.*

un|pleas|ant /ʌnplɛzᵊnt/ ❶ ADJ If something is **unpleasant**, it gives you bad feelings, for example by making you feel upset or uncomfortable. ❑ *The symptoms can be uncomfortable, unpleasant and serious.* ❑ *The vacuum has an unpleasant smell.* ● **un|pleas|ant|ly** ADV ❑ *The water moved darkly around the body, unpleasantly thick and brown.* ❑ *The smell was unpleasantly strong.* ❷ ADJ An **unpleasant** person is very unfriendly and rude. ❑ *She thought him an unpleasant man.* ❑ *Don't start giving me problems otherwise I'll have to be very unpleasant indeed.* ● **un|pleas|ant|ly** ADV ❑ *Melissa laughed unpleasantly.*

Thesaurus		*unpleasant*의 참조어
ADJ.	irksome, troublesome; *(ant.)* pleasant ❶	
	mean, rude, unkind ❷	

un|plug /ʌnplʌg/ (**unplugs, unplugging, unplugged**) V-T If you **unplug** an electrical device or telephone, you pull a wire out of an outlet so that it stops working. ❑ *I had to unplug the phone.*

않은 한 남자가 던도날드 근처를 걸어가는 도중에 쓰러져 죽었다. ❷ 형용사 이름이 없는 ❑ 이름 없는 혜성과 소행성들

❶ 형용사 비정상적인, 이상한 ❑ 그 비행기는 이륙할 때 비정상적인 속도로 올라갔다. ● 이상하게 부사 ❑ 그 집은 이상하게도 조용했다. ❷ 형용사 인위적인, 인위적으로 ❑ 그녀는 인위적으로 보이는 밝고 결연한 미소를 그에게 지어 보였다. ● 인위적으로 부사 ❑ 소리 지르거나 부자연스럽게 말하지 않도록 해라.

구 예상했던 대로 ❑ 그것은 예상됐던 대로 로이가 대답하기 불가능한 질문이었다.

형용사 불필요한 ❑ 고래 도살은 불필요하고 잔인한 일이다. ● 불필요하게 부사 ❑ 나는 불필요하게 남편과 딸을 화나게 하고 싶지 않았다.

타동사 걱정시키다, 당황하게 만들다 ❑ 더모트에 관한 뉴스를 듣고 나는 걱정이 되었다.

형용사 걱정하게 하는, 불안하게 하는 ❑ 매일 만나는 사람이 치명적일 수 있는 바이러스를 가지고 있음을 알게 되는 것은 매우 당황스런 일이다.

형용사 주의를 끌지 않은 ❑ 나는 눈치 채지 못하게 계단을 살짝 올라가려고 했다.

형용사 쉽게 눈에 띄지 않은 [격식체] ❑ 커피 테이블은 가능한 한 눈에 띄지 않게 유리로 되어 있다. ● 눈에 띄지 않게 부사 ❑ 그들은 눈에 띄지 않게 살짝 떠났다.

형용사 비공식적인 ❑ 지난주 해고되었던 일곱 명의 동료를 지지하여 비공식적인 파업을 계속하기 위해 직원들은 투표를 하였다. ● 비공식적으로 부사 ❑ 어떤 직원들은 정규직으로 고용되어 있으나 대부분은 건강 보험 혜택도 없고 임금도 안정적이지 않은 비정규직으로 일한다.

형용사 정통이 아닌, 남다른 ❑ 그녀는 아버지와 유럽 전역을 여행하면서 남다른 소녀 시절을 보냈다.

❶ 타동사/자동사 (가방 등을) 풀다 ❑ 그는 가방을 풀었다. ❷ 타동사 분석하다 ❑ 이 시장 주도적인 전략 변화를 달성하는 데 중점이 되는 쟁점들을 분석하는 논의가 많이 이루어져 왔다.

❶ 형용사 무급의 ❑ 자선 단체를 위해 무급으로라도 일을 하는 것이 아무것도 안 하는 것보다는 낫다. ❷ 형용사 미납의 ❑ 세무서 직원이 그를 추적해서 찾아내어 미납된 세금 17,000파운드를 요구했다.

❶ 형용사 불쾌한 ❑ 겨우 그때가 되어서야 나는 존에 대한 불쾌한 진실을 알기 시작했다. ❷ 형용사 입에 맞지 않는, 맛없는 ❑ 건조하고 맛없는 치즈 한 덩어리

형용사 유례없는, 비길 데 없는 [강조] ❑ 독일의 유례없는 번영은 현명한 투자에 기반을 두고 있다.

❶ 형용사 불쾌한 ❑ 그 증상들은 불편하고, 불쾌하고, 그리고 심각하다. ❑ 그 진공청소기는 불쾌한 냄새가 난다. ● 불쾌하게 부사 ❑ 불쾌할 정도로 탁하고 갈색인 물이 시체 주위를 음산하게 움직였다. ❑ 냄새가 불쾌하게 강했다. ❷ 형용사 기분 나쁜, 무례한 ❑ 그녀는 그가 기분 나쁜 사람이라고 생각했다. ❑ 나를 성가시게 하지 마라. 안 그러면 나도 정말로 무례해질 수밖에 없다. ● 무례하게, 기분 나쁘게 부사 ❑ 멜리사는 기분 나쁘게 웃었다.

타동사 플러그를 뽑다 ❑ 나는 전화선을 뽑아야 했다.

un|pop|u|lar /ʌnpɒpyʊlər/ ADJ If something or someone is **unpopular**, most people do not like them. ❑ *It was a painful and unpopular decision.* ❑ *In high school, I was very unpopular, and I did encounter a little prejudice.* ● un|pop|u|lar|ity /ʌnpɒpyəlærɪti/ N-UNCOUNT ❑ *...his unpopularity among his colleagues.*

형용사 인기가 없는 ❑ 그것은 힘들면서 호응이 좋지 않은 결정이었다. ❑ 고등학교 때 나는 매우 인기가 없었고 약간은 나에 대한 편견과 맞부딪쳤다. ● 인기 없음 불가산명사 ❑ 동료 사이에서 그의 인기 없음

un|prec|edent|ed /ʌnpresɪdentɪd/ **1** ADJ If something is **unprecedented**, it has never happened before. ❑ *Such a move is rare, but not unprecedented.* **2** ADJ If you describe something as **unprecedented**, you are emphasizing that it is very great in quality, amount, or scale. [EMPHASIS] ❑ *The scheme has been hailed as an unprecedented success.*

1 형용사 전례 없는 ❑ 그러한 조치는 드물지만, 전례가 없는 것은 아니다. **2** 형용사 비길 데 없는, 미증유의 [강조] ❑ 그 계획은 유례를 찾아보기 힘든 성공으로 환영받았다.

un|pre|dict|able /ʌnprɪdɪktəbəl/ ADJ If you describe someone or something as **unpredictable**, you mean that you cannot tell what they are going to do or how they are going to behave. ❑ *He is utterly unpredictable.* ● un|pre|dict|abil|ity /ʌnprɪdɪktəbɪlɪti/ N-UNCOUNT [oft with poss] ❑ *...the unpredictability of the weather.*

형용사 예측할 수 없는 ❑ 그는 정말로 예측할 수 없는 사람이다. ● 예측할 수 있음 불가산명사 ❑ 날씨의 예측할 수 없음

un|pre|pared /ʌnprɪpeərd/ **1** ADJ If you are **unprepared for** something, you are not ready for it, and you are therefore surprised or at a disadvantage when it happens. ❑ *I was totally unprepared for the announcement on the next day.* ❑ *Faculty members complain that their students are unprepared to do college-level work.* **2** ADJ If you are **unprepared to** do something, you are not willing to do it. [v-link ADJ to-inf] ❑ *They are unprepared to accept the real reasons for their domestic and foreign situation.*

1 형용사 준비가 되지 않은 ❑ 그 다음 날 나온 발표에 대해 나는 전혀 준비가 안 되어 있었다. ❑ 교수들은 학생들이 대학 수준의 학업을 할 준비가 되어 있지 않다고 불평한다. **2** 형용사 마음이 내키지 않는 ❑ 그들은 국내외 상황의 진정한 이유를 선뜻 받아들이려 하지 않는다.

un|pro|duc|tive /ʌnprədʌktɪv/ ADJ Something that is **unproductive** does not produce any good results. ❑ *Research workers are well aware that much of their time and effort is unproductive.*

형용사 비생산적인 ❑ 연구자들은 자신들의 시간과 노력의 많은 부분이 비생산적이라는 것을 잘 알고 있다.

un|pro|fes|sion|al /ʌnprəfeʃənəl/ ADJ If you use **unprofessional** to describe someone's behavior at work, you are criticizing them for not behaving according to the standards that are expected of a person in their profession. [DISAPPROVAL] ❑ *He was also fined $150 for unprofessional conduct.*

형용사 전문가답지 않은 [탐탁찮음] ❑ 그는 전문가답지 못한 행동으로 150달러의 벌금도 부과받았다.

un|prof|it|able /ʌnprɒfɪtəbəl/ **1** ADJ An industry, company, or product that is **unprofitable** does not make any profit or does not make enough profit. [BUSINESS] ❑ *...unprofitable state-owned industries.* **2** ADJ **Unprofitable** activities or efforts do not produce any useful or helpful results. ❑ *...an endless, unprofitable argument.*

1 형용사 이익이 없는 [경제] ❑ 이익이 없는 국가 소유의 산업들 **2** 형용사 무익한 ❑ 끝이 없는, 무익한 논쟁

un|pro|tect|ed /ʌnprətektɪd/ **1** ADJ An **unprotected** person or place is not watched over or defended, and so they may be harmed or attacked. [ADJ n, v-link ADJ, ADJ after v] ❑ *The landing beaches would be unprotected.* **2** ADJ If something is **unprotected**, it is not covered or treated with anything, and so it may easily be damaged. [ADJ n, v-link ADJ, ADJ after v] ❑ *Exposure of unprotected skin to the sun carries the risk of developing skin cancer.* **3** ADJ If two people have **unprotected** sex, they do not use a condom when they have sex. [ADJ n] ❑ *...the dangers of unprotected sex.*

1 형용사 무방비의 ❑ 상륙할 해변은 무방비 상태일 것이다. **2** 형용사 보호 수단을 쓰지 않은 ❑ 자외선 차단제를 바르거나 옷을 가리고 있지 않은 피부를 태양에 노출하는 것은 피부암 유발 위험을 수반한다. **3** 형용사 콘돔을 사용하지 않은 ❑ 콘돔을 사용하지 않은 성관계의 위험

un|pub|lished /ʌnpʌblɪʃt/ ADJ An **unpublished** book, letter, or report has never been published. An **unpublished** writer has never had his or her work published. ❑ *Much of his writing remains unpublished.*

형용사 출판되지 않은 ❑ 그의 많은 글들이 출판되지 않은 채로 남아 있다.

un|quali|fied /ʌnkwɒlɪfaɪd/ **1** ADJ If you are **unqualified**, you do not have any qualifications, or you do not have the right qualifications for a particular job. ❑ *She was unqualified for the job.* **2** ADJ **Unqualified** means total or unlimited. [EMPHASIS] ❑ *The event was an unqualified success.*

1 형용사 자격이 없는 ❑ 그녀는 그 일을 할 수 있는 자격이 없었다. **2** 형용사 무조건적인, 절대적인 [강조] ❑ 그 행사는 절대적인 성공이었다.

un|ques|tion|able /ʌnkwestʃənəbəl/ ADJ If you describe something as **unquestionable**, you are emphasizing that it is so obviously true or real that nobody can doubt it. [EMPHASIS] ❑ *He inspires affection and respect as a man of unquestionable integrity.* ● un|ques|tion|ably /ʌnkwestʃənəbli/ ADV [ADV with cl/group] ❑ *They have seen the change as unquestionably beneficial to the country.*

형용사 의문의 여지가 없는 [강조] ❑ 그는 의문의 여지가 없을 정도로 성실한 사람으로 애정과 존경을 불러일으킨다. ● 의문의 여지없이, 확실하게 부사 ❑ 그들은 그 변화가 나라에 확실히 이익이 되는 것으로 보아 왔다.

un|rav|el /ʌnrævəl/ (unravels, unraveling, unraveled) [BRIT, sometimes AM **unravelling, unravelled**] **1** V-T/V-I If you **unravel** something that is knotted, woven, or knitted, or if it **unravels**, it becomes one straight piece again or separates into its different threads. ❑ *He could unravel a knot that others wouldn't even attempt.* **2** V-T/V-I If you **unravel** a mystery or puzzle, or it **unravels**, it gradually becomes clearer and you can work out the answer to it. ❑ *A young mother has flown to Iceland to unravel the mystery of her husband's disappearance.* →see **rope**

[영국영어, 미국영어 가끔 unravelling, unravelled] **1** 타동사/자동사 (매듭 등을) 풀다; (매듭 등이) 풀리다 ❑ 그는 다른 사람들이 시도조차 하지 않으려 할 매듭을 풀 수 있을 것이다. **2** 타동사/자동사 풀다, 해명하다 ❑ 한 젊은 아기 엄마가 실종된 남편의 미스터리를 풀기 위해서 아이슬란드로 비행기를 타고 갔다.

un|real /ʌnrɪl/ **1** ADJ If you say that a situation is **unreal**, you mean that it is so strange that you find it difficult to believe it is happening. [v-link ADJ] ❑ *It was unreal. Like some crazy childhood nightmare.* ● un|real|ity /ʌnriælɪti/ N-UNCOUNT ❑ *To his surprise he didn't feel too weak. Light-headed certainly, and with a sense of unreality, but able to walk.* **2** ADJ If you use **unreal** to describe something, you are critical of it because you think that it is not like, or not related to, things you expect to find in the real world. [DISAPPROVAL] ❑ *Almost all fictional detectives are unreal.*

1 형용사 믿을 수 없을 정도인 ❑ 그것은 도저히 믿을 수가 없었다. 마치 유년기의 어떤 기이한 악몽 같았다. ● 비현실성 불가산명사 ❑ 그는 놀랍게도 몸이 그렇게 약하게 느껴지지 않았다. 확실히 어질어질하고 몽롱한 느낌이었지만 걸을 수는 있었다. **2** 형용사 비현실적인 [탐탁찮음] ❑ 거의 모든 소설 속 탐정들은 비현실적이다.

un|re|al|is|tic /ʌnrɪəlɪstɪk/ ADJ If you say that someone is being **unrealistic**, you mean that they do not recognize the truth about a situation, especially about the difficulties involved in something they want to achieve. ❑ *There are many who feel that the players are being completely unrealistic in their demands.* ❑ *It would be unrealistic to expect such a process ever to be completed.*

형용사 비현실적인 ❑ 선수들의 요구가 완전히 비현실적이라고 생각하는 사람이 많이 있다. ❑ 그러한 과정이 완성되기를 기대하는 것 자체가 비현실적일 것이다.

un|rea|son|able /ʌnrizənəbəl/ **1** ADJ If you say that someone is being **unreasonable**, you mean that they are behaving in a way that is not fair or sensible. ❑ *The strikers were being unreasonable in their demands, having rejected the deal two weeks ago.* ❑ *It was her unreasonable behavior with a Texas playboy which broke up her marriage.* ● un|rea|son|ably /ʌnrizənəbli/ ADV ❑ *We unreasonably expect near perfect behavior from our children.* **2** ADJ An **unreasonable** decision, action, price, or amount seems unfair and difficult to justify. ❑ *...unreasonable increases in the price of petrol.* ● un|rea|son|ably ADV ❑ *The banks' charges are unreasonably high.*

1 형용사 분별이 없는 ❑ 2주 전의 제안을 거절하면서 파업 중인 노동자들은 비현실적인 요구를 하고 있었다. ❑ 그녀의 결혼 생활이 파탄 난 것은 그녀가 한 텍사스 바람둥이와 분별없는 행동을 한 때문이다. ● 분별없이 부사 ❑ 우리는 분별없이 자녀가 거의 완벽한 행동을 할 것이라고 기대한다. **2** 형용사 터무니없는, 불합리한 ❑ 터무니없는 기름값 인상 ● 터무니없게 부사 ❑ 은행의 수수료는 터무니없이 높다.

un|rec|og|niz|able /ʌnrɛkəgnaɪzəbl, -naɪz-/ [BRIT also **unrecognisable**] ADJ If someone or something is **unrecognizable**, they have become impossible to recognize or identify, for example because they have been greatly changed or damaged. [oft ADJ to n] ❑ *The corpses of the prisoners were nearly unrecognizable from the number of bullet wounds they'd received.*

[영국영어 unrecognisable] 형용사 인지할 수 없는, 알아볼 수 없는 ❑ 죄수들의 시신은 수많은 총탄 자국으로 거의 알아볼 수가 없었다.

un|re|lat|ed /ʌnrɪleɪtɪd/ ❶ ADJ If one thing is **unrelated to** another, there is no connection between them. You can also say that two things are **unrelated**. ❑ *My line of work is entirely unrelated to politics.* ❷ ADJ If one person is **unrelated to** another, they are not members of the same family. You can also say that two people are **unrelated**. [WRITTEN] ❑ *Jimmy is adopted and thus unrelated to Beth by blood.*

❶ 형용사 관계가 없는 ❑ 내가 하는 일은 전적으로 정치와는 무관하다. ❷ 형용사 혈연이 아닌 [문어체] ❑ 지미는 입양되어 베스와 혈연관계는 아니다.

un|re|lent|ing /ʌnrɪlɛntɪŋ/ ❶ ADJ If you describe someone's behavior as **unrelenting**, you mean that they are continuing to do something in a very determined way, often without caring whether they hurt or embarrass other people. ❑ *She established her authority with unrelenting thoroughness.* ❷ ADJ If you describe something unpleasant as **unrelenting**, you mean that it continues without stopping. ❑ *...an unrelenting downpour of rain.*

❶ 형용사 가차 없는, 무자비한 ❑ 그녀는 무자비하고 철두철미하게 자기 권위를 세웠다. ❷ 형용사 끊임없는, 꾸준한 ❑ 끊임없이 쏟아지는 비

un|re|li|able /ʌnrɪlaɪəbᵊl/ ADJ If you describe a person, machine, or method as **unreliable**, you mean that you cannot trust them. ❑ *Diplomats can be a notoriously unreliable and misleading source of information.* ❑ *His judgement was unreliable.*

형용사 믿을 수 없는 ❑ 외교관들은 신뢰할 수 없고 오해의 소지가 있는 정보의 근원으로 악명 높을 수 있다. ❑ 그의 판단은 믿을 수가 없었다.

un|re|mark|able /ʌnrɪmɑrkəbᵊl/ ADJ If you describe someone or something as **unremarkable**, you mean that they are very ordinary, without many exciting, original, or attractive qualities. ❑ *...a tall, lean man, with an unremarkable face.*

형용사 평범한, 보통의 ❑ 평범한 얼굴에 키 크고 마른 남자

un|re|pent|ant /ʌnrɪpɛntənt/ ADJ If you are **unrepentant**, you are not ashamed of your beliefs or actions. ❑ *Pamela was unrepentant about her strong language and abrasive remarks.*

형용사 뉘우치지 않는 ❑ 파멜라는 욕설을 하고 남의 비위를 거스르는 발언을 한 것에 대해서 뉘우치지 않았다.

un|re|solved /ʌnrɪzɒlvd/ ADJ If a problem or difficulty is **unresolved**, no satisfactory solution has been found to it. [FORMAL] [v-link ADJ, ADJ n, ADJ after v] ❑ *The murder remains unresolved.*

형용사 미해결의 [격식체] ❑ 그 살인 사건은 미해결된 채로 남아 있다.

un|rest /ʌnrɛst/ N-UNCOUNT If there is **unrest** in a particular place or society, people are expressing anger and dissatisfaction about something, often by demonstrating or rioting. [JOURNALISM] ❑ *The real danger is civil unrest in the east of the country.*

불가산명사 (정치적) 불만 [언론] ❑ 정말 위험한 것은 그 나라 동부 주민들의 불만이다.

un|re|strict|ed /ʌnrɪstrɪktɪd/ ❶ ADJ If an activity is **unrestricted**, you are free to do it in the way that you want, without being limited by any rules. ❑ *Freedom to pursue extra-curricular activities is totally unrestricted.* ❷ ADJ If you have an **unrestricted** view of something, you can see it fully and clearly, because there is nothing in the way. ❑ *Nearly all seats have an unrestricted view.*

❶ 형용사 제한을 받지 않는, 구속을 받지 않는 ❑ 과외 활동을 하고자 하는 자유는 전혀 제한을 받지 않는다. ❷ 형용사 툭 트인 ❑ 거의 모든 자리에서 툭 트인 전망이 보인다.

un|ri|valed /ʌnraɪvᵊld/ [BRIT, sometimes AM **unrivalled**] ADJ If you describe something as **unrivaled**, you are emphasizing that it is better than anything else of the same kind. [EMPHASIS] ❑ *He acquired unrivaled knowledge of party affairs.*

[영국영어, 미국영어 가끔 unrivalled] 형용사 견줄 상대가 없는, 무적의 [강조] ❑ 그는 당의 일에 대해서 누구보다도 많은 지식을 습득했다.

un|ru|ly /ʌnruli/ ADJ If you describe people, especially children, as **unruly**, you mean that they behave badly and are difficult to control. ❑ *...unruly behavior.*

형용사 고분고분하지 않은, 제멋대로인 ❑ 제멋대로인 행동

un|safe /ʌnseɪf/ ❶ ADJ If a building, machine, activity, or area is **unsafe**, it is dangerous. ❑ *Critics claim the trucks are unsafe.* ❷ ADJ If you are **unsafe**, you are in danger of being harmed. [v-link ADJ] ❑ *In the larger neighborhood, I felt very unsafe.* ❸ ADJ If a criminal conviction is **unsafe**, it is not based on enough evidence or is based on false evidence. [BRIT, LEGAL] ❑ *An appeal court decided their convictions were unsafe.*

❶ 형용사 안전하지 않은 ❑ 비판하는 사람들이 그 트럭들이 안전하지 못하다고 주장한다. ❷ 형용사 불안한 ❑ 더 큰 동네에 살 때는 나는 매우 불안했다. ❸ 형용사 충분한 증거가 없는, 거짓 증거에 의한 [영국영어, 법률] ❑ 항소 법원은 그들의 판결이 증거가 불충분하다고 결정을 내렸다.

un|sat|is|fac|to|ry /ʌnsætɪsfæktəri/ ADJ If you describe something as **unsatisfactory**, you mean that it is not as good as it should be, and cannot be considered acceptable. ❑ *The inspectors said just under a third of lessons were unsatisfactory.*

형용사 만족스럽지 못한 ❑ 감독관들은 수업의 3분의 1 이하가 만족스럽지 못하다고 말했다.

Thesaurus	unsatisfactory의 참조어
ADJ.	inadequate, insufficient, unacceptable; (ant.) satisfactory

un|sa|vory /ʌnseɪvəri/ [BRIT **unsavoury**] ADJ If you describe a person, place, or thing as **unsavory**, you mean that you find them unpleasant or morally unacceptable. [DISAPPROVAL] ❑ *Police officers meet more unsavory characters in a week than most of us encounter in a lifetime.*

[영국영어 unsavoury] 형용사 불미스러운 [탐탁찮음] ❑ 경찰관들은 일주일 동안에 우리들 대부분이 평생 동안 만나게 되는 것보다 더 많은 떳떳치 못한 사람들을 만난다.

un|scathed /ʌnskeɪðd/ ADJ If you are **unscathed** after a dangerous experience, you have not been injured or harmed by it. [ADJ after v, v-link ADJ] ❑ *Tony emerged unscathed apart from a severely bruised finger.* ❑ *East Los Angeles was left relatively unscathed by the riots.*

형용사 다치지 않은 ❑ 토니는 손가락 하나가 심하게 멍이 든 것을 빼고는 하나도 다치지 않았다. ❑ 로스앤젤레스 동부는 비교적 폭동의 피해를 입지 않았다.

un|scru|pu|lous /ʌnskrupyələs/ ADJ If you describe a person as **unscrupulous**, you are critical of the fact that they are prepared to act in a dishonest or immoral way in order to get what they want. [DISAPPROVAL] ❑ *These kids are being exploited by very unscrupulous people.*

형용사 파렴치한, 부도덕한 [탐탁찮음] ❑ 이 아이들은 매우 부도덕한 사람들에 의해 착취당하고 있다.

un|se|cured /ʌnsɪkyʊərd/ ADJ **Unsecured** is used to describe loans or debts that are not guaranteed by a particular asset such as a person's home. [BUSINESS] ❑ *We can arrange unsecured loans for any amount from £500 to £7,500.*

형용사 무담보의 [경제] ❑ 우리는 500파운드부터 7,500파운드까지는 얼마든 무담보 대출을 해 줄 수 있다.

un|seen /ʌnsin/ ❶ ADJ If you describe something as **unseen**, you mean that it has not been seen for a long time. ❑ *...a spectacular ballroom, unseen by the public for over 30 years.* ❷ ADJ You can use **unseen** to describe things which people cannot see. [ADJ n, ADJ after v] ❑ *For me, a performance is in front of a microphone, over the radio, to an unseen audience.*

❶ 형용사 본 적이 없는 ❑ 30년이 넘도록 대중들이 본 적이 없는 굉장한 무도회장 ❷ 형용사 보이지 않는 ❑ 나에게 있어서 연주는 마이크 앞에서 라디오를 통해 보이지 않는 청중에게 하는 것이다.

un|set|tled /ʌnsetəld/ ❶ ADJ In an **unsettled** situation, there is a lot of uncertainty about what will happen. ❑ Britain's unsettled political scene also worries some investors. ❷ ADJ If you are **unsettled**, you cannot concentrate on anything because you are worried. [v-link ADJ] ❑ To tell the truth, I'm a bit unsettled tonight. ❸ ADJ An **unsettled** argument or dispute has not yet been resolved. ❑ They were in the process of resolving all the unsettled issues. ❹ ADJ **Unsettled** weather is unpredictable and changes a lot. ❑ Despite the unsettled weather, we had a marvellous weekend.

un|set|tling /ʌnsetəlɪŋ/ ADJ If you describe something as **unsettling**, you mean that it makes you feel rather worried or uncertain. ❑ The prospect of change of this kind has an unsettling effect on any organisation.

un|sight|ly /ʌnsaɪtli/ ADJ If you describe something as **unsightly**, you mean that it is unattractive to look at. ❑ The Polish market in Berlin was considered unsightly and shut down.

un|skilled /ʌnskɪld/ ❶ ADJ People who are **unskilled** do not have any special training for a job. ❑ He went to Paris in search of work as an unskilled labourer. ❷ ADJ **Unskilled** work does not require any special training. ❑ In the U.S., minorities and immigrants have generally gone into low-paid, unskilled jobs.

un|so|lic|it|ed /ʌnsəlɪsɪtɪd/ ADJ Something that is **unsolicited** has been given without being asked for and may not have been wanted. ❑ "If I were you," she adds by way of some unsolicited advice, "I'd watch out for that girl of yours."

un|solved /ʌnsɒlvd/ ADJ An **unsolved** mystery or problem has never been solved. ❑ ...America's unsolved problems of poverty and racism.

un|speak|able /ʌnspiːkəbəl/ ADJ If you describe something as **unspeakable**, you are emphasizing that it is extremely unpleasant. [EMPHASIS] ❑ ...the unspeakable horrors of chemical weapons. ❑ The pain is unspeakable. ● **un|speak|ably** /ʌnspiːkəbli/ ADV ❑ The novel was unspeakably boring.

un|speci|fied /ʌnspesɪfaɪd/ ADJ You say that something is **unspecified** when you are not told exactly what it is. ❑ The government said an unspecified number of bandits were killed.

un|spoiled /ʌnspɔɪld/ [BRIT also **unspoilt** /ʌnspɔɪlt/] ADJ If you describe a place as **unspoiled**, you think it is beautiful because it has not been changed or built on for a long time. ❑ The port is quiet and unspoiled.

un|spo|ken /ʌnspoʊkən/ ❶ ADJ If your thoughts, wishes, or feelings are **unspoken**, you do not speak about them. ❑ His face was expressionless, but Alex felt the unspoken criticism. ❷ ADJ When there is an **unspoken** agreement or understanding between people, their behavior shows that they agree about something or understand it, even though they have never spoken about it. [ADJ n] ❑ There had been an unspoken agreement between them that he would not call for her at Seymour House.

un|sta|ble /ʌnsteɪbəl/ ❶ ADJ You can describe something as **unstable** if it is likely to change suddenly, especially if this creates difficulty or danger. ❑ The situation is unstable and potentially dangerous. ❷ ADJ **Unstable** objects are likely to move or fall. ❑ Both clay and sandstone are unstable rock formations. ❸ ADJ If people are **unstable**, their emotions and behavior keep changing because their minds are disturbed or upset. ❑ He was emotionally unstable.

un|steady /ʌnstedi/ ❶ ADJ If you are **unsteady**, you have difficulty doing something, for example walking, because you cannot completely control your legs or your body. ❑ The boy was very unsteady and had staggered around when he got up. ● **un|stead|ily** /ʌnstedɪli/ ADV [ADV with v] ❑ She pulled herself unsteadily from the bed to the dresser. ❷ ADJ If you describe something as **unsteady**, you mean that it is not regular or stable, but unreliable or unpredictable. ❑ His voice was unsteady and only just audible. ❸ ADJ **Unsteady** objects are not held, fixed, or balanced securely. ❑ ...a slightly unsteady item of furniture.

un|sub|scribe /ʌnsəbskraɪb/ (**unsubscribes**, **unsubscribing**, **unsubscribed**) V-I If you **unsubscribe** from an online service, you send a message saying that you no longer wish to receive that service. [COMPUTING] ❑ Go to the website today and you can unsubscribe online.

un|sub|stan|ti|at|ed /ʌnsəbstænʃieɪtɪd/ ADJ A claim, accusation, or story that is **unsubstantiated** has not been proved to be valid or true. ❑ I do object to their claim, which I find totally unsubstantiated.

un|suc|cess|ful /ʌnsəksesfəl/ ❶ ADJ Something that is **unsuccessful** does not achieve what it was intended to achieve. ❑ His efforts were unsuccessful. ❑ ...a second unsuccessful operation on his knee. ● **un|suc|cess|ful|ly** ADV [ADV with v] ❑ He has been trying unsuccessfully to sell the business in one piece since early last year. ❷ ADJ Someone who is **unsuccessful** does not achieve what they intended to achieve, especially in their career. ❑ The difference between successful and unsuccessful people is that successful people put into practice the things they learn.

un|suit|able /ʌnsuːtəbəl/ ADJ Someone or something that is **unsuitable for** a particular purpose or situation does not have the right qualities for it. ❑ Amy's shoes were unsuitable for walking any distance.

un|sure /ʌnʃʊər/ ❶ ADJ If you are **unsure of yourself**, you lack confidence. ❑ The evening show was terrible, with hesitant unsure performances from all. ❷ ADJ If you are **unsure about** something, you feel uncertain about it. [v-link ADJ, oft ADJ about/of n] ❑ Fifty-two per cent were unsure about the idea.

un|sus|pect|ing /ʌnsəspektɪŋ/ ADJ You can use **unsuspecting** to describe someone who is not at all aware of something that is happening or going to happen. ❑ ...his unsuspecting victim.

un|sym|pa|thet|ic /ˌʌnsɪmpəˈθɛtɪk/ ☐ ADJ If someone is **unsympathetic**, they are not kind or helpful to a person in difficulties. ☐ *Her husband was unsympathetic and she felt she had no one to turn to.* ☐ ADJ An **unsympathetic** person is unpleasant and difficult to like. ☐ *...a very unsympathetic main character.* ☐ ADJ If you are **unsympathetic to** a particular idea or aim, you are not willing to support it. [v-link ADJ to n] ☐ *I'm highly unsympathetic to what you are trying to achieve.*

un|ten|able /ʌnˈtɛnəbəl/ ADJ An argument, theory, or position that is **untenable** cannot be defended successfully against criticism or attack. ☐ *This argument is untenable from an intellectual, moral and practical standpoint.*

un|think|able /ʌnˈθɪŋkəbəl/ ☐ ADJ If you say that something is **unthinkable**, you are emphasizing that it cannot possibly be accepted or imagined as a possibility. [EMPHASIS] ☐ *Her strong Catholic beliefs made abortion unthinkable.* ● N-SING **The unthinkable** is something that is unthinkable. [the N] ☐ *Edward VIII had done the unthinkable and abdicated the throne.*

un|ti|dy /ʌnˈtaɪdi/ ☐ ADJ If you describe something as **untidy**, you mean that it is not neat or well arranged. ☐ *The place quickly became untidy.* ☐ *...a thin man with untidy hair.* ● **un|ti|di|ly** /ʌnˈtaɪdɪli/ ADV ☐ *...the desk piled untidily with books and half-finished homework.* ☐ ADJ If you describe a person as **untidy**, you mean that they do not care about whether things are neat and well arranged, for example in their house. ☐ *I'm untidy in most ways.*

Word Link	**un ≈ reversal : untie, unusual, unwrap**

un|tie /ʌnˈtaɪ/ (**unties, untying, untied**) ☐ V-T If you **untie** something that is tied to another thing or if you **untie** two things that are tied together, you remove the string or rope that holds them or that has been tied round them. ☐ *Nicholas untied the boat from her mooring.* ☐ *Just untie my hands.* ☐ V-T If you **untie** something such as string or rope, you undo it so that there is no knot or so that it is no longer tying something. ☐ *She hurriedly untied the ropes binding her ankles.* ☐ V-T When you **untie** your shoelaces or your shoes, you loosen or undo the laces of your shoes. ☐ *She untied the laces on one of her sneakers.*

un|til ♦♦♦ /ʌnˈtɪl/ ☐ PREP If something happens **until** a particular time, it happens during the period before that time and stops at that time. [PREP n/prep] ☐ *Until 1971, he was a high-ranking official in the Central Communist Committee.* ● CONJ **Until** is also a conjunction. ☐ *I waited until it got dark.* ☐ PREP You use **until** with a negative to emphasize the moment in time after which the rest of your statement becomes true, or the condition which would make it true. [PREP after neg] ☐ *The traffic laws don't take effect until the end of the year.* ● CONJ **Until** is also a conjunction. ☐ *The EU will not lift its sanctions until that country makes political changes.* ☐ **up until** →see **up**

> Note that you only use **until** or **till** when you are talking about time. You do not use these words to talk about place or position. Instead, you should use **as far as** or **up to**. ☐ *Then you'll be riding with us as far as the village?... We walked up to where his bicycle was.*

un|told /ʌnˈtoʊld/ ☐ ADJ You can use **untold** to emphasize how bad or unpleasant something is. [EMPHASIS] [ADJ n] ☐ *The demise of the industry has caused untold misery to thousands of hard-working tradesmen.* ☐ ADJ You can use **untold** to emphasize that an amount or quantity is very large, especially when you are not sure how large it is. [EMPHASIS] [ADJ n] ☐ *...the nation's untold millions of anglers.*

un|touched /ʌnˈtʌtʃt/ ☐ ADJ Something that is **untouched by** something else is not affected by it. [v-link ADJ, ADJ after v] ☐ *Asian airlines remain untouched by the deregulation that has swept America.* ☐ ADJ If something is **untouched**, it is not damaged in any way, although it has been in a situation where it could easily have been damaged. [v-link ADJ, ADJ after v] ☐ *Michael pointed out to me that amongst the rubble, there was one building that remained untouched.* ☐ ADJ An **untouched** area or place is thought to be beautiful because it is still in its original state and has not been changed or damaged in any way. [ADJ n, v-link ADJ, ADJ after v] ☐ *Ducie is one of the world's last untouched islands.* ☐ ADJ If food or drink is **untouched**, none of it has been eaten or drunk. [v-link ADJ, ADJ after v, ADJ n] ☐ *The coffee was untouched, the toast had cooled.*

un|trained /ʌnˈtreɪnd/ ADJ Someone who is **untrained** has not been taught the skills that they need for a particular job, activity, or situation. ☐ *It is a nonsense to say we have untrained staff dealing with emergencies.*

un|treat|ed /ʌnˈtriːtɪd/ ☐ ADJ If an injury or illness is left **untreated**, it is not given medical treatment. [ADJ after v, ADJ n, v-link ADJ] ☐ *If left untreated the condition may become chronic.* ☐ ADJ **Untreated** materials, water, or chemicals are harmful and have not been made safe. ☐ *...the dumping of nuclear waste and untreated sewage.* ☐ ADJ **Untreated** materials are in their natural or original state, often before being prepared for use in a particular process. ☐ *All the bedding is made of simple, untreated cotton.*

un|true /ʌnˈtruː/ ADJ If a statement or idea is **untrue**, it is false and not based on facts. ☐ *The allegations were completely untrue.* ☐ *It was untrue to say that all political prisoners have been released.*

un|used

> Pronounced /ʌnˈyuːzd/ for meaning ☐, and /ʌnˈyuːst/ for meaning ☐.

☐ ADJ Something that is **unused** has not been used or is not being used at the moment. [ADJ n, ADJ after v, v-link ADJ] ☐ *...unused containers of food and drink.* ☐ ADJ If you are **unused to** something, you have not often done it or experienced it

---

☐ 형용사 인정 없는, 냉담한 ☐ 그녀의 남편은 인정이 없었고, 그녀가 의지할 사람이 아무도 없다고 생각했다. ☐ 형용사 마음에 안 드는 ☐ 아주 마음에 안 드는 주인공 ☐ 형용사 지지하지 않는 ☐ 나는 네가 하고자 하는 것을 전혀 지지하지 않아.

형용사 변호할 수 없는, 방어할 수 없는 ☐ 이러한 주장은 지적이고 도덕적이며 실용적인 견지에서 보면 변론할 수 없다.

형용사 생각할 수 없는, 상상할 수 없는 [강조] ☐ 그녀의 독실한 가톨릭 믿음이 낙태는 생각할 수도 없게 했다. ● 단수명사 생각할 수 없는 것, 상상할 수 없는 것 ☐ 에드워드 8세는 상상할 수도 없는 일을 했고 왕위를 포기했다.

☐ 형용사 어수선한, 난잡한 ☐ 그 장소는 빠르게 어수선해졌다. ☐ 머리가 부스스한 마른 남자 ● 난잡하게 부사 ☐ 책과 반쯤 끝난 숙제 등이 어수선하게 쌓여 있는 책상 ☐ 형용사 깔끔하지 못한 ☐ 나는 여러 면에서 깔끔하지 못하다.

☐ 타동사 풀다 ☐ 니콜라스는 정박해 있던 곳에서 배를 풀어놓았다. ☐ 내 손 좀 풀어 줘. ☐ 타동사 풀다 ☐ 그녀는 서둘러 발목을 묶고 있는 밧줄을 풀었다. ☐ 타동사 풀다 ☐ 그녀는 운동화 한쪽 끈을 풀었다.

☐ 전치사 – 때까지 ☐ 1971년까지 그는 중앙 공산당 위원회의 고위 당원이었다. ● 접속사 –할 때까지 ☐ 나는 어두워질 때까지 기다렸다. ☐ 전치사 – 때까지 ☐ 그 교통 법규들은 올해 말까지 시행되지 않는다. ● 접속사 –할 때까지 ☐ 그 나라에 정치적 변화가 있을 때까지 유럽 연합은 제재를 풀지 않을 것이다.

until이나 till은 시간에 대해 말할 때만 쓴다는 점을 유의하라. 장소나 위치에 대해 말할 때는 이런 말은 사용하지 않고, 대신 as far as나 up to를 써야 ☐ 그러면 당신은 마을까지 우리와 함께 타고 가시나요?... 우리는 그의 자전거가 있는 곳까지 걸어갔다.

☐ 형용사 말로 표현할 수 없는, 정말 끔찍한 [강조] ☐ 그 산업 분야의 종말은 성실한 수천 명의 상인들에게 말할 수 없는 불행을 가져다주었다. ☐ 형용사 막대한 [강조] ☐ 전국 수백만 명의 엄청난 낚시꾼들

☐ 형용사 영향을 받지 않은 ☐ 아시아 항공사들은 미국을 휩쓴 규제 완화의 영향을 받지 않고 있다. ☐ 형용사 손상되지 않은 ☐ 마이클은 내게 파편 더미 사이에 손상되지 않은 건물이 하나 남아 있다는 사실을 지적했다. ☐ 형용사 본래 그대로의, 인간의 손이 미치지 않은 ☐ 듀시는 세계에서 마지막으로 남은 자연 그대로의 섬 중 하나이다. ☐ 형용사 손도 대지 않은 ☐ 커피는 손도 대지 않았고, 토스트는 이미 식어 있었다.

형용사 훈련받지 않은, 미숙한 ☐ 우리가 훈련도 되지 않은 직원들에게 위급 상황을 처리하게 한다는 것은 말도 안 된다.

☐ 형용사 치료하지 않은 ☐ 만일 치료하지 않고 내버려 두면 이 병은 만성이 될 수 있다. ☐ 형용사 처리하지 않은 ☐ 핵폐기물과 미처리 하수의 방기 ☐ 형용사 가공하지 않은 ☐ 모든 침구는 수수하고 가공하지 않은 면으로 만들어졌다.

형용사 거짓의, 허위의 ☐ 그 주장은 완전히 거짓이었다. ☐ 모든 정치범들이 석방되었다고 말하는 것은 허위였다.

☐의 의미일 때는 /ʌnˈyuːzd/로, ☐의 의미일 때는 /ʌnˈyuːst/로 발음된다.

☐ 형용사 사용하지 않은 ☐ 사용하지 않은 식품과 음료 용기 ☐ 형용사 –에 익숙하지 않은 ☐ 어머니는 그렇게 힘든 일에는 전혀 익숙하지 않았다.

before, so it feels unusual and unfamiliar to you. [v-link ADJ to n] ❑ *Mother was entirely unused to such hard work.*

Word Link

un ≈ reversal : untie, unusual, unwrap

un|usual ♦◇◇ /ʌnjuːʒuəl/ **1** ADJ If something is **unusual**, it does not happen very often or you do not see it or hear it very often. ❑ *They have replanted many areas with rare and unusual plants.* **2** ADJ If you describe someone as **unusual**, you think that they are interesting and different from other people. ❑ *He was an unusual man with great business talents.*

1 형용사 드문, 희귀한 ❑ 그들은 여러 지역에 드물고 희귀한 식물들을 이식했다. **2** 형용사 비범한 ❑ 그는 대단한 사업 수완을 지닌 비범한 사람이었다.

Thesaurus   unusual의 참조어

ADJ.   abnormal, rare, strange, uncommon; (ant.) usual **1**
different, interesting, unconventional **2**

un|usu|al|ly /ʌnjuːʒuəli/ **1** ADV You use **unusually** to emphasize that someone or something has more of a particular quality than is usual. [EMPHASIS] [ADV adj] ❑ *He was an unusually complex man.* **2** ADV You can use **unusually** to suggest that something is not what normally happens. ❑ *Unusually among British prime ministers, he was not a man of natural authority.*

1 부사 유별나게, 대단히 [강조] ❑ 그는 유별나게 복잡한 사람이었다. **2** 부사 특이하게, 남달리 ❑ 영국 수상들 중에서는 특이하게도, 그는 타고난 권위가 있는 인물이 아니었다.

un|veil /ʌnveɪl/ (**unveils, unveiling, unveiled**) **1** V-T If someone formally **unveils** something such as a new statue or painting, they draw back the curtain which is covering it. ❑ *...a ceremony to unveil a monument to the victims.* **2** V-T If you **unveil** a plan, new product, or some other thing that has been kept secret, you introduce it to the public. ❑ *Mr. Werner unveiled his new strategy this week.*

1 타동사 덮개를 벗기다, 제막식을 하다 ❑ 희생자들을 기리는 기념비 제막식 **2** 타동사 발표하다, 밝히다 ❑ 워너 씨는 이번 주에 자기의 새 전략을 발표했다.

un|waged /ʌnweɪdʒd/ N-PLURAL You can refer to people who do not have a paid job as **the unwaged**. [BRIT, BUSINESS] ❑ *There are special rates for the under 18s, full-time students, over 60s, and the unwaged.* ● ADJ **Unwaged** is also an adjective. ❑ *...the effect on male wage-earners, unwaged females, and children.*

복수명사 급여 소득이 없는 사람, 실업자 [영국영어, 경제] ❑ 18세 미만, 전업 학생, 60세 이상 및 급여 소득이 없는 사람들을 위한 특별 요금이 있습니다. ● 형용사 급여 소득이 없는 ❑ 남성 급여 소득자, 급여 소득이 없는 여성 및 아이들에 미치는 영향

un|want|ed /ʌnwɒntɪd/ ADJ If you say that something or someone is **unwanted**, you mean that you do not want them, or that nobody wants them. ❑ *...the misery of unwanted pregnancies.* ❑ *She felt unwanted.*

형용사 원치 않는, 쓸모없는 ❑ 원치 않는 임신의 고통 ❑ 그녀는 자신이 쓸모없다고 느꼈다.

un|war|rant|ed /ʌnwɒrəntɪd, BRIT ʌnwɒrəntɪd/ ADJ If you describe something as **unwarranted**, you are critical of it because there is no need or reason for it. [FORMAL, DISAPPROVAL] ❑ *Any attempt to discuss the issue of human rights was rejected as an unwarranted interference in the country's internal affairs.*

형용사 부당한, 불필요한 [격식체, 탐탁잖음] ❑ 인권 문제에 대해 논의하려는 어떠한 시도도 그 나라의 내정에 대한 부당한 간섭으로 여겨져 거부되었다.

un|wel|come /ʌnwelkəm/ **1** ADJ An **unwelcome** experience is one that you do not like and did not want. ❑ *The media has brought more unwelcome attention to the Royal Family.* **2** ADJ If you say that a visitor is **unwelcome**, you mean that you did not want them to come. ❑ *...an unwelcome guest.*

1 형용사 달갑지 않은, 환영받지 못하는 ❑ 언론 때문에 왕실 가족에게로 달갑지 않은 세인들의 관심이 더 쏠리게 되었다. **2** 형용사 달갑지 않은, 귀찮은 ❑ 달갑지 않은 손님

un|well /ʌnwel/ ADJ If you are **unwell**, you are ill. [v-link ADJ] ❑ *He had been riding in Hyde Park, but felt unwell as he was being driven back to his office late this afternoon.*

형용사 몸이 편치 않은, 아픈 ❑ 그는 하이드 파크에서 승마를 했었는데, 오늘 오후 늦게 자기 사무실로 돌아가던 중 몸이 불편한 것을 느꼈다.

un|wieldy /ʌnwiːldi/ **1** ADJ If you describe an object as **unwieldy**, you mean that it is difficult to move or carry because it is so big or heavy. ❑ *They came panting up to his door with their unwieldy baggage.* **2** ADJ If you describe a system as **unwieldy**, you mean that it does not work very well as a result of it being too large or badly organized. ❑ *His firm must contend with the unwieldy Russian bureaucracy.*

1 형용사 부피가 큰, (무거워서) 다루기 힘든 ❑ 그들은 거대한 짐을 가지고 헐떡거리며 그의 집 문까지 올라왔다. **2** 형용사 비대한 ❑ 그의 회사는 비대한 러시아 관료 체제를 상대해야 한다.

un|will|ing /ʌnwɪlɪŋ/ **1** ADJ If you are **unwilling** to do something, you do not want to do it and will not agree to do it. ❑ *Initially the government was unwilling to accept the defeat.* ● **un|will|ing|ness** N-UNCOUNT ❑ *...their unwillingness to accept responsibility for mistakes.* **2** ADJ You can use **unwilling** to describe someone who does not really want to do the thing they are doing. ❑ *A youthful teacher, he finds himself an unwilling participant in school politics.* ● **un|will|ing|ly** ADV ❑ *My beard had started to grow, and I had unwillingly complied with the order to shave it off.*

1 형용사 꺼리는, 싫어하는 ❑ 정부가 처음에는 패배를 인정하려 하지 않았다. ● 꺼림, 싫어함 불가산명사 ❑ 그들이 실수에 대한 책임 인정을 꺼림 **2** 형용사 마지못해 하는, 본의 아닌 ❑ 젊은 교사인 그는 교내 세력 다툼에 어쩔 수 없이 말려들었다. ● 마지못해, 본의 아니게 부사 ❑ 내 턱수염이 자라기 시작했고, 나는 면도하라는 명령에 마지못해 따랐다.

un|wind /ʌnwaɪnd/ (**unwinds, unwinding, unwound**) **1** V-I When you **unwind**, you relax after you have done something that makes you tense or tired. ❑ *It helps them to unwind after a busy day at work.* **2** V-T/V-I If you **unwind** a length of something that is wrapped around something else or around itself, you loosen it and make it straight. You can also say that it **unwinds**. ❑ *One of them unwound a length of rope from around his waist.*

1 자동사 (긴장을) 풀다 ❑ 그것은 그들이 직장에서 바쁜 하루를 보낸 뒤 긴장을 풀게 해 준다. **2** 타동사/자동사 (묶인 것을) 풀다 ❑ 그들 중 한 사람이 그의 허리에 묶인 밧줄을 풀었다.

un|wise /ʌnwaɪz/ ADJ If you describe something as **unwise**, you think that it is foolish and likely to lead to a bad result. ❑ *It would be unwise to expect too much.* ❑ *I think this is extremely unwise.* ● **un|wise|ly** ADV ❑ *She accepted that she had acted unwisely and mistakenly.*

형용사 어리석은, 현명하지 못한 ❑ 지나치게 많이 기대하는 것은 어리석은 일일 것이다. ❑ 나는 이것이 극도로 분별없는 것이라고 생각한다. ● 어리석게 부사 ❑ 그녀는 자기가 분별없이 잘못 행동했다는 것을 인정했다.

un|wit|ting /ʌnwɪtɪŋ/ ADJ If you describe a person or their actions as **unwitting**, you mean that the person does something or is involved in something without realizing it. ❑ *We're unwitting victims of the system.* ● **un|wit|ting|ly** ADV ❑ *He was unwittingly caught up in the confrontation.*

형용사 의식하지 못한, 고의가 아닌 ❑ 우리는 모르고 당하는 제도의 희생자들이다. ● 부지불식간에 부사 ❑ 그는 저도 모르게 충돌 상황에 말려들었다.

un|work|able /ʌnwɜːrkəbəl/ ADJ If you describe something such as a plan, law, or system as **unworkable**, you believe that it cannot be successful. ❑ *There is the strong possibility that such cooperation will prove unworkable.*

형용사 실행 불가능한 ❑ 그러한 협력은 실행 불가능한 것으로 판명될 가능성이 아주 높다.

un|wor|thy /ʌnwɜːrði/ ADJ If a person or thing is **unworthy of** something good, they do not deserve it. ❑ *You may feel unworthy of the attention and help people offer you.*

형용사 자격이 없는, 가치가 없는 ❑ 당신은 사람들이 당신에게 보여 주는 관심과 도움을 받을 자격이 없다고 느낄지도 모른다.

un|wound /ʌnwaʊnd/ **Unwound** is the past tense and past participle of **unwind**.

unwind의 과거, 과거 분사

un|wrap /ʌnræp/ (**unwraps, unwrapping, unwrapped**) V-T When you **unwrap**

타동사 (포장 등을) 풀다 ❑ 나는 리본을 풀고 작은

something, you take off the paper, plastic, or other covering that is around it. ❑ *I untied the bow and unwrapped the small box.*

un|writ|ten /ʌnrɪtᵊn/ **1** ADJ Something such as a book that is **unwritten** has not been printed or written down. ❑ *Universal have agreed to pay £2.5 million for Grisham's next, as yet unwritten, novel.* **2** ADJ An **unwritten** rule, law, or agreement is one that is understood and accepted by everyone, although it may not have been formally or officially established. ❑ *They obey the one unwritten rule that binds them all – no talking.*

un|zip /ʌnzɪp/ (unzips, unzipping, unzipped) **1** V-T/V-I When you **unzip** something which is fastened by a zipper or when it **unzips**, you open it by pulling open the zipper. ❑ *James unzipped his bag.* **2** V-T To **unzip** a computer file means to open a file that has been compressed. [COMPUTING] ❑ *Unzip the icons into a sub-directory.*

---

up

① PREPOSITION, ADVERB, AND ADJECTIVE USES
② USED IN COMBINATION AS A PREPOSITION
③ VERB USES

---

① **up** ♦♦♦

The preposition is pronounced /ʌp/. The adverb and adjective are pronounced /ʌp/.

Up is often used with verbs of movement such as "jump" and "pull," and also in phrasal verbs such as "give up" and "wash up."

→Please look at category **16** to see if the expression you are looking for is shown under another headword. **1** PREP If a person or thing goes **up** something such as a slope, ladder, or chimney, they move away from the ground or to a higher position. ❑ *They were climbing up a narrow mountain road.* ❑ *I ran up the stairs and saw Alison lying at the top.* ● ADV **Up** is also an adverb. ❑ *Finally, after an hour, I went up to Jeremy's room.* ❑ *Intense balls of flame rose up into the sky.* **2** PREP If a person or thing is **up** something such as a ladder or a mountain, they are near the top of it. ❑ *He was up a ladder sawing off the tops of his apple trees.* ● ADV **Up** is also an adverb. [ADV after v] ❑ *...a research station perched 4000 meters up on the lip of the crater.* **3** ADV You use **up** to indicate that you are looking or facing in a direction that is away from the ground or toward a higher level. [ADV after v] ❑ *Keep your head up, and look around you from time to time.* **4** ADV If someone stands **up**, they move so that they are standing. [ADV after v] ❑ *He stood up and went to the window.* **5** PREP If you go or look **up** something such as a road or river, you go or look along it. If you are **up** a road or river, you are somewhere along it. [V PREP n] ❑ *A line of tanks came up the road from the city.* ❑ *We leaned on the wooden rail of the bridge and looked up the river.* **6** ADV If you are traveling to a particular place, you can say that you are going **up** to that place, especially if you are going toward the north or to a higher level of land. If you are already in such a place, you can say that you are **up** there. [mainly SPOKEN] ❑ *I'll be up to see you tomorrow.* ❑ *He was living up North.* **7** ADV To go **up** to something or someone, you move to the place where they are and stop there. ❑ *The girl ran the rest of the way across the street and up to the car.* ❑ *On the way out a boy of about ten came up on roller skates.* **8** ADV If an amount of something goes **up**, it increases. If an amount of something is **up**, it has increased and is at a higher level than it was. ❑ *They recently put my rent up.* ❑ *Tourism is up, jobs are up, individual income is up.* **9** ADJ If you are **up**, you are not in bed. [v-link ADJ] ❑ *Are you sure you should be up?* ❑ *These days all sorts of people were up at the crack of dawn.* **10** ADJ If a period of time is **up**, it has come to an end. [v-link ADJ] ❑ *The moment the half-hour was up, Brooks rose.* **11** ADJ If a computer or computer system is **up**, it is working. Compare **down**. [v-link ADJ] ❑ *The new system is up and ready to run.* **12** PHRASE If someone who has been in bed for some time, for example because they have been ill, is **up and about**, they are now out of bed and living their normal life. ❑ *How are you Lennox? Good to see you up and about.* **13** PHRASE If you say that **something is up**, you mean that something is wrong or that something worrying is happening. [INFORMAL] ❑ *What is it then? Something's up, isn't it?* **14** PHRASE If you say to someone "**What's up?**" or if you tell them **what's up**, you are asking them or telling them what is wrong or what is worrying them. [INFORMAL] ❑ *"What's up?" I said to him. – "Nothing much," he answered.* **15** PHRASE If you move **up and down** somewhere, you move there repeatedly in one direction and then in the opposite direction. ❑ *I used to jump up and down to keep warm.* ❑ *I strolled up and down thoughtfully before calling a taxi.* **16** up in arms →see arm

② **up** ♦♦♦ /ʌp/ →Please look at category **3** to see if the expression you are looking for is shown under another headword. **1** PHRASE If you feel **up to** doing something, you are well enough to do it. ❑ *Those patients who were up to it could move to the adjacent pool.* ❑ *His fellow-directors were not up to running the business without him.* **2** PHRASE To be **up to** something means to be secretly doing something that you should not be doing. [INFORMAL] ❑ *Why did you need a room unless you were up to something?* ❑ *They must have known what their father was up to.* **3** PHRASE If you say that it is **up to** someone to do something, you mean that it is their responsibility to do it. ❑ *It was up to him to make it right, no matter how long it took.* ❑ *I'm sure I'd have spotted him if it had been up to me.* **4** PHRASE **Up until** or **up to** are used to indicate the latest time at which something can happen, or the end of the period of time that you are referring to. ❑ *Please feel free to call me any time up until half past nine at night.* **5** PHRASE You use **up to** to say how large something can be or what level it has reached. ❑ *Up to twenty thousand students paid between five and six thousand dollars.* **6** PHRASE If someone or something is **up**

---

1 형용사 인쇄되지 않은, 집필되지 않은 ❑ 유니버설 사는 그리샴의 아직 집필되지도 않은 다음 소설에 2백 5십만 파운드를 지불하기로 했다. **2** 형용사 불문의, 성문화되지 않은 ❑ 그들은 그들 모두를 결속하는 유일한 불문율인 묵언을 지킨다.

1 타동사/자동사 지퍼를 열다; 지퍼가 열리다 ❑ 제임스는 자기 가방의 지퍼를 열었다. **2** 타동사 압축 파일을 풀다 [컴퓨터] ❑ 그 아이콘들을 하부 디렉터리에 압축을 푸시오.

전치사는 /ʌp/으로 발음되고, 부사와 형용사는 /ʌp/으로 발음된다.

up은 종종 'jump', 'pull'과 같은 이동 동사와 함께 쓰여 'give up', 'wash up'과 같은 구동사에도 쓰인다.

1 전치사 -의 위에, -의 위로 ❑ 그들은 좁은 산길 위로 올라가고 있었다. ❑ 나는 계단 위로 달려 올라가서 앨리슨이 맨 위에 누워 있는 것을 보았다. ● 부사 위에, 위로 ❑ 마침내 한 시간 후, 나는 제레미의 방으로 올라갔다. ❑ 작열하는 불덩이가 하늘로 솟아올랐다. **2** 전치사 -의 위쪽에, -의 위쪽으로 ❑ 그는 사다리 위에서 톱으로 사과나무 윗부분을 잘라내고 있었다. ● 부사 위쪽에 ❑ 지상 4천 미터 위의 분화구 가장자리에 자리 잡은 연구소 **3** 부사 위로, 위쪽으로 ❑ 머리를 위로 들고 가끔 당신의 주변을 살펴보시오. **4** 부사 (몸을) 일으켜 ❑ 그는 일어서서 창가로 갔다. **5** 전치사 -을 따라 ❑ 탱크가 줄지어 도시로부터 도로를 따라 나왔다. ❑ 우리는 다리의 나무 난간에 기대어 강줄기를 바라보았다. **6** 부사 북쪽으로, 북쪽에, 위쪽으로, 위쪽에 [주로 구어체] ❑ 내일 널 보러 올라갈게. ❑ 그는 저 위 북쪽에 살고 있었다. **7** 부사 -까지 ❑ 그 소녀는 거리를 가로질러 차까지 남은 길을 달려갔다. ❑ 나가는 길에 열 살 정도 된 소년이 롤러스케이트를 타고 다가왔다. **8** 부사 상승하여, 증가하여 ❑ 그들은 최근 내 집세를 올렸다. ❑ 관광 사업이 번창하고, 일자리가 많아졌으며, 개인 소득이 증가했다. **9** 형용사 일어나 있는, 자고 있지 않은 ❑ 꼭 자지 않고 있어야 하니? ❑ 그 당시는 온갖 사람들이 동이 틀 때나 일어나 있었다. **10** 형용사 (시간이) 끝난, 종료된 ❑ 30분이 다 되자, 브룩스가 일어났다. **11** 형용사 (컴퓨터가) 켜진 ❑ 새 시스템이 켜져서 작동할 준비가 되어 있다. **12** 구 (병상에서) 회복한, 일어나 다니는 ❑ 좀 어떠니, 레녹스? 일어나 다니는 것을 보니 기쁘구나. **13** 구 무슨 일이 일어나다, 어떤 문제가 발생하다 [비격식체] ❑ 그게 뭔데 그래? 뭔가 문제가 있지, 그렇지? **14** 구 무슨 일이지, 뭐가 문제인지 [비격식체] ❑ "무슨 일이지?" 하고 나는 그에게 물었다. "별일 아니에."라고 그가 대답했다. **15** 구 아래위로 ❑ 나는 체온을 유지하기 위해 아래위로 뛰곤 했다. ❑ 나는 택시를 부르기 전에 생각에 잠겨 천천히 거리를 오르내렸다.

1 구 -을 감당할 수 있는 ❑ 그것을 해낼 수 있는 환자들은 바로 옆 수영장으로 갈 수 있었다. ❑ 그의 동료 중역들이 그가 없으면 사업을 해 나갈 수가 없었다. **2** 구 (비밀로 일을) 꾸미는 [비격식체] ❑ 당신이 뭔가를 꾸미고 있지 않다면 왜 방이 필요했나요? ❑ 그들은 자기 아버지가 무슨 일을 꾸미고 있는지 알고 있었음에 틀림없다. **3** 구 -의 책임인 ❑ 시간이 얼마나 걸리는 간에 그것을 세대로 해 놓는 것은 그의 책임이었다. ❑ 내 책임이었다면 난 분명히 그를 찾아냈을 거야. **4** 구 (시간 또는 시기가) -까지 ❑ 밤 9시 반까지는 언제고 부담없이 제게 전화하세요. **5** 구 (양이나 크기가) -까지 ❑ 2만 명까지나 되는 학생들이 5천에서 6천 달러 사이를 지불했다. **6** 구 (선거에) 입후보한; (논의에) 올라 있는 ❑ 상원의 3분의 1과 하원 전체가 재선에 출마하고 있다. **7** 구 (곤경 등에)

for election, review, or discussion, they are about to be considered. ❑ *A third of the Senate and the entire House are up for re-election.* ◼ PHRASE If you are **up against** something, you have a very difficult situation or problem to deal with. ❑ *The chairwoman is up against the greatest challenge to her position.* ◼ **up to par** →see **par**

③ **up** /ʌp/ (**ups, upping, upped**) ◼ V-T If you **up** something such as the amount of money you are offering for something, you increase it. ❑ *He upped his offer for the company.* ❑ *Chemist stores upped sales by 63 percent.* ◼ V-I If you **up** and leave a place, you go away from it, often suddenly or unexpectedly. ❑ *One day he just upped and left.*

타동사 (금액 등을) 올리다 ❑ 그는 그 회사에 액수를 올려 제안했다. ❑ 약국들의 매출이 63퍼센트 올랐다. ◼ 자동사 갑자기 -하다 ❑ 어느 날 그는 그냥 갑자기 떠났다.

up-and-coming ADJ **Up-and-coming** people are likely to be successful in the future. [ADJ n] ❑ *...his readiness to share the limelight with young, up-and-coming stars.*

형용사 전도가 유망한, 떠오르는 ❑ 떠오르는 젊은 스타들과 기꺼이 함께 인기를 나누려는 그의 태도

up|beat /ʌpbiːt/ ADJ If people or their opinions are **upbeat**, they are cheerful and hopeful about a situation. [INFORMAL] ❑ *The Defense Secretary gave an upbeat assessment of the war so far.* ❑ *Neil's colleagues say he was actually in a joking, upbeat mood.*

형용사 낙관적인, 즐거운 [비격식체] ❑ 국방부 장관은 지금까지의 전쟁에 대해 낙관적인 평가를 내렸다. ❑ 닐의 동료들은 그가 실은 장난스럽고 흥겨운 기분이었다고 말한다.

up|bring|ing /ʌpbrɪŋɪŋ/ N-UNCOUNT Your **upbringing** is the way that your parents treat you and the things that they teach you when you are growing up. ❑ *Martin's upbringing shaped his whole life.*

불가산명사 양육, 훈육 ❑ 마틴의 양육 과정이 그의 일생을 결정지었다.

up|com|ing /ʌpkʌmɪŋ/ ADJ **Upcoming** events will happen in the near future. [ADJ n] ❑ *We'll face a tough fight in the upcoming election.*

형용사 다가오는 ❑ 우리는 다가오는 선거에서 치열한 싸움에 직면할 것이다.

up|date /ʌpdeɪt/ (**updates, updating, updated**)

The verb is pronounced /ʌpdeɪt/. The noun is pronounced /ʌpdeɪt/.

동사는 /ʌpdeɪt /으로 발음되고, 명사는 /ʌpdeɪt/ 으로 발음된다.

◼ V-T/V-I If you **update** something, you make it more modern, usually by adding new parts to it or giving new information. ❑ *He was back in the office, updating the work schedule on the computer.* ❑ *Airlines would prefer to update rather than retrain crews.* ◼ N-COUNT An **update** is a news item containing the latest information about a particular situation. ❑ *She had heard the news-flash on a TV channel's news update.* ❑ *...a weather update.* ◼ V-T If you **update** someone **on** a situation, you tell them the latest developments in that situation. ❑ *We'll update you on the day's top news stories.*

◼ 타동사/자동사 갱신하다, 새롭게 하다 ❑ 그는 사무실로 돌아와서 컴퓨터에 작업 일정을 갱신하고 있었다. ❑ 항공사들은 승무원들을 계속 근속시키기보다 새로 뽑기를 원할 것이다. ◼ 가산명사 최신 정보, 최신판 ❑ 그녀는 텔레비전 방송의 최신 뉴스에서 그 속보를 들었다. ❑ 최신 날씨 정보 ◼ 타동사 -에 관한 최근 소식을 전하다 ❑ 오늘의 가장 중요한 최신 뉴스를 알려 드리겠습니다.

up front also **up-front** ◼ ADJ If you are **up front about** something, you act openly or publicly so that people know what you are doing or what you believe. [INFORMAL] ❑ *You can't help being biased so you may as well be up front about it.* ◼ ADV If a payment is made **up front**, it is made in advance and openly, so that the person being paid can see that the money is there. [ADV after v] ❑ *For the first time the government's actually put some money up front.* ● ADJ **Up front** is also an adjective. [ADJ n] ❑ *The eleven percent loan has no up-front costs.*

◼ 형용사 솔직한, 정직한 [비격식체] ❑ 당신이 편견을 갖지 않을 수 없으니까 그것에 대해 솔직히 하는 것이 좋겠다. ◼ 부사 선불로 ❑ 처음으로 정부가 정말 약간의 선불을 내놓았다. ● 형용사 선불의 ❑ 11퍼센트 이자 대출에는 선불 비용이 없다.

up|grade /ʌpgreɪd, -greɪd/ (**upgrades, upgrading, upgraded**) ◼ V-T If equipment or services **are upgraded**, they are improved or made more efficient. [usu passive] ❑ *Helicopters have been upgraded and modernized.* ❑ *Medical facilities are being reorganized and upgraded.* ● N-COUNT **Upgrade** is also a noun. ❑ *...equipment which needs expensive upgrades.* ◼ V-T If someone **is upgraded**, their job or status is changed so that they become more important or receive more money. [usu passive] ❑ *He was upgraded to security guard.* ◼ V-T/V-I If you **upgrade** or **are upgraded**, you change something such as your plane ticket or your hotel room to one that is more expensive. ❑ *His family were upgraded from economy to business class.* →see **hotel**

◼ 타동사 개선되다, 개량되다 ❑ 헬리콥터는 개량되었고 첨단화되었다. ❑ 의료 시설이 개편 및 개선되고 있다. ● 가산명사 개선, 개량 ❑ 값비싼 성능 개선이 요구되는 장비 ◼ 타동사 승진되다 ❑ 그는 경비원으로 승진되었다. ◼ 타동사/자동사 격상되다, 격상하다 ❑ 그의 가족은 보통석에서 비지니스 석으로 격상되었다.

up|heav|al /ʌphiːvˀl/ (**upheavals**) N-COUNT An **upheaval** is a big change which causes a lot of trouble, confusion, and worry. ❑ *Algeria has been going through political upheaval for the past two months.*

가산명사 격변, 대변동 ❑ 알제리는 지난 2개월간 정치적 격변을 겪어 왔다.

up|held /ʌpheld/ **Upheld** is the past tense and past participle of **uphold**.

uphold의 과거, 과거 분사

up|hill /ʌphɪl/ ◼ ADV If something or someone is **uphill** or is moving **uphill**, they are near the top of a hill or are going up a slope. ❑ *He had been running uphill a long way.* ❑ *The man was no more than ten yards away and slightly uphill.* ● ADJ **Uphill** is also an adjective. ❑ *...a long, uphill journey.* ◼ ADJ If you refer to something as an **uphill** struggle or an **uphill** battle, you mean that it requires a great deal of effort and determination, but it should be possible to achieve it. [ADJ n] ❑ *It had been an uphill struggle to achieve what she had wanted.*

◼ 부사 비탈 위에, 비탈 위로 ❑ 그는 비탈길을 쭉 달려 올라오고 있었다. ❑ 그 남자는 10야드밖에 떨어지어 있지 않았고 약간 비탈진 곳에 있었다. ● 형용사 오르막의 ❑ 긴 오르막길 여정 ◼ 형용사 힘겨운, 애쓰는 ❑ 그녀가 바라는 바를 성취하는 것은 힘겨운 투쟁이었다.

up|hold /ʌphoʊld/ (**upholds, upholding, upheld**) ◼ V-T If you **uphold** something such as a law, a principle, or a decision, you support and maintain it. ❑ *Our policy has been to uphold the law.* ❑ *It is the responsibility of every government to uphold certain basic principles.* ◼ V-T If a court of law **upholds** a legal decision that has already been made, it decides that it was the correct decision. ❑ *The crown court, however, upheld the magistrate's decision.*

◼ 타동사 (법, 원칙 등을) 유지하다 ❑ 우리 정책은 지금까지 그 법을 유지하는 것이었다. ❑ 어느 정도의 기본 원칙을 유지하는 것은 모든 정부의 책임이다. ◼ 타동사 지지하다 ❑ 그러나 대법원은 치안 판사의 평결을 지지했다.

up|hol|stery /ʌphoʊlstəri, əpoʊl-/ N-UNCOUNT **Upholstery** is the soft covering on chairs and seats that makes them more comfortable to sit on. ❑ *...white leather upholstery.*

불가산명사 (소파 등의) 커버 ❑ 흰 가죽 커버

up|keep /ʌpkiːp/ ◼ N-UNCOUNT The **upkeep** of a building or place is the work of keeping it in good condition. ❑ *The money will be used for the estate's upkeep.* ◼ N-UNCOUNT The **upkeep** of a group of people or services is the process of providing them with the things that they need. ❑ *He offered to pay £100 a month towards his son's upkeep.*

◼ 불가산명사 유지, 보존 ❑ 그 돈은 그 사유지를 유지하는 데 사용될 것이다. ◼ 불가산명사 부양 ❑ 그는 아들의 부양비로 매달 100파운드를 내겠다고 제안했다.

up|lift|ing /ʌplɪftɪŋ/ ADJ You describe something as **uplifting** when it makes you feel very cheerful and happy. ❑ *...a charming and uplifting love story.*

형용사 기분을 좋게 하는 ❑ 매혹적이고 기분 좋게 하는 사랑 이야기

up|load /ʌploʊd/ (**uploads, uploading, uploaded**) V-T If you **upload** data, you transfer it to your computer or from your computer to another computer. [COMPUTING] ❑ *All you need to do is upload the files on to your web space.*

타동사 (자료를) 올리다, 전송하다 [컴퓨터] ❑ 당신의 웹 공간에 파일들을 올려놓기만 하면 됩니다.

up|market /ʌpmɑrkɪt/ also **up-market** ADJ **Upmarket** products or services are expensive, of good quality, and intended to appeal to people in a high social class. [mainly BRIT] ❑ *Anne chose an upmarket agency aimed at professional people.* ● ADV **Upmarket** is also an adverb. [AM usually **upscale**] [ADV after v] ❑ *Japanese firms have moved steadily upmarket.*

upon ♦♦◇ /əpɒn/

In addition to the uses shown below, **upon** is used in phrasal verbs such as "come upon" and "look upon," and after some other verbs such as "decide" and "depend."

1 PREP If one thing is **upon** another, it is on it. [FORMAL] ❑ *He set the tray upon the table.* ❑ *He bent forward and laid a kiss softly upon her forehead.* **2** PREP You use **upon** when mentioning an event that is followed immediately by another event. [FORMAL] [PREP -ing/n] ❑ *The door on the left, upon entering the church, leads to the Crypt of St Issac.* **3** PREP You use **upon** between two occurrences of the same noun in order to say that there are large numbers of the thing mentioned. [n PREP n] ❑ *Row upon row of women surged forwards.* **4** PREP If an event is **upon** you, it is just about to happen. [PREP pron] ❑ *The long-threatened storm was upon us.* ❑ *The wedding season is upon us.*

up|per ♦♦◇ /ʌpər/ **1** ADJ You use **upper** to describe something that is above something else. [ADJ n, *the* ADJ] ❑ *There is a smart restaurant on the upper floor.* **2** ADJ You use **upper** to describe the higher part of something. [ADJ n] ❑ *...the upper part of the foot.* ❑ *...the muscles of the upper back and chest.* **3** PHRASE If you have **the upper hand** in a situation, you have more power than the other people involved and can make decisions about what happens. ❑ *The government was beginning to gain the upper hand.*

upper|case /ʌpərkeɪs/ also **upper case** ADJ **Uppercase** letters are capital letters. ❑ *Most schools teach children lowercase letters first, and uppercase letters later.* ● N-UNCOUNT **Uppercase** is also a noun. ❑ *They should use uppercase.*

up|per class (**upper classes**) also **upper-class** N-COUNT-COLL The **upper class** or the **upper classes** are the group of people in a society who own the most property and have the highest social status, and who may not need to work for money. ❑ *...goods specifically designed to appeal to the tastes of the upper class.* ● ADJ **Upper class** is also an adjective. ❑ *All of them came from wealthy, upper class families.*

up|right /ʌpraɪt/ (**uprights**) **1** ADJ If you are sitting or standing **upright**, you are sitting or standing with your back straight, rather than bending or lying down. ❑ *Helen sat upright in her chair.* ❑ *He moved into an upright position.* **2** ADJ An **upright** vacuum cleaner or freezer is tall rather than wide. [ADJ n] ❑ *...the latest state-of-the-art upright vacuum cleaners.* **3** ADJ An **upright** chair has a straight back and no arms. ❑ *He was sitting on an upright chair beside his bed, reading.* **4** N-COUNT You can refer to vertical posts or the vertical parts of an object as **uprights**. ❑ *...the uprights of a four-poster bed.* **5** ADJ You can describe people as **upright** when they are careful to follow acceptable rules of behavior and behave in a moral way. ❑ *...a very upright, trustworthy man.*

up|ris|ing /ʌpraɪzɪŋ/ (**uprisings**) N-COUNT When there is an **uprising**, a group of people start fighting against the people who are in power in their country, because they want to bring about a political change. ❑ *...a popular uprising against the authoritarian government.*

up|roar /ʌprɔr/ **1** N-UNCOUNT If there is **uproar**, there is a lot of shouting and noise because people are very angry or upset about something. [also a N, oft in N] ❑ *The announcement caused uproar in the crowd.* **2** N-UNCOUNT You can also use **uproar** to refer to a lot of public criticism and debate about something that has made people angry. [also a N] ❑ *The town is in uproar over the dispute.*

up|root /ʌprut/ (**uproots, uprooting, uprooted**) **1** V-T If you **uproot yourself** or if you **are uprooted**, you leave, or are made to leave, a place where you have lived for a long time. ❑ *...the trauma of uprooting themselves from their homes.* ❑ *He had no wish to uproot Dena from her present home.* **2** V-T If someone **uproots** a tree or plant, or if the wind **uproots** it, it is pulled out of the ground. ❑ *They had been forced to uproot their vines and plant wheat.* ❑ *...fallen trees which have been uprooted by the storm.*

up|scale /ʌpskeɪl/ ADJ **Upscale** is used to describe products or services that are expensive, of good quality, and intended to appeal to people in a high social class. [AM] [usu adj n] ❑ *...upscale department-store chains such as Bloomingdale's and Saks Fifth Avenue.* ● ADV **Upscale** is also an adverb. [BRIT **upmarket**] [ADV after v] ❑ *T-shirts, the epitome of American casualness, have moved upscale.*

up|set ♦♦◇ (**upsets, upsetting, upset**)

The verb and adjective are pronounced /ʌpsɛt/. The noun is pronounced /ʌpset/.

1 ADJ If you are **upset**, you are unhappy or disappointed because something unpleasant has happened to you. ❑ *After she died I felt very, very upset.* ❑ *Marta looked upset.* ● N-COUNT **Upset** is also a noun. ❑ *...stress and other emotional upsets.* **2** V-T If something **upsets** you, it makes you feel worried or unhappy. ❑ *The whole incident had upset me and my fiancee terribly.* ❑ *She warned me not to say anything to upset him.* ● **up|set|ting** ADJ *Childhood illness can be upsetting for children and parents alike.* **3** V-T If events **upset** something such as a procedure or a state of affairs, they cause it to go wrong. ❑ *Political problems could upset agreements between Moscow and Kabul.* ● N-COUNT **Upset** is also a noun. ❑ *Markets are very sensitive to any upsets in the Japanese economic machine.* **4** V-T If you **upset** an object, you accidentally knock or push it over so that it scatters over a large area. ❑ *Don't upset the piles of sheets under the box.* **5** N-COUNT A stomach **upset** is a slight illness in your stomach caused by an infection or by something that you have eaten. ❑ *Paul was unwell last night with a stomach*

❑ 앤은 전문직 종사자들을 대상으로 삼는 고급 대행사를 선택했다. ● 부사 고급으로 [미국영어 대개 upscale] ❑ 일본 회사들은 꾸준히 고가품 시장 쪽으로 이동해 왔다.

upon은 아래 용법 외에도 'come upon', 'look upon'과 같은 구동사에 쓰며 'decide', 'depend'와 같은 동사 뒤에도 쓰인다.

1 전치사 ~ 위에 [격식체] ❑ 그는 쟁반을 식탁 위에 놓았다. ❑ 그는 앞으로 몸을 숙이고 그녀의 이마에 부드럽게 키스를 했다. **2** 전치사 ~하자 곧 [격식체] ❑ 교회에 들어가자마자 보이는 왼쪽 문은 성 아이삭 묘지로 통한다. **3** 전치사 ~에 더하여 ❑ 여자들의 행렬이 끊임없이 앞으로 쏟아져 나왔다. **4** 전치사 ~에게 막 닥치다 ❑ 오래전부터 염려해 온 폭풍우가 우리에게 이제 막 닥쳐왔다. ❑ 결혼 시즌이 다가왔다.

1 형용사 더 위의 ❑ 위층에 깨끗한 식당이 있다. **2** 형용사 상부의 ❑ 발 윗부분 ❑ 등 위쪽과 가슴 부분의 근육 **3** 구 우세, 우위 ❑ 정부가 우위를 점하기 시작하고 있었다.

형용사 대문자의 ❑ 대부분의 학교에서는 아이들에게 소문자를 먼저 가르치고 대문자를 나중에 가르친다. ● 불가산명사 대문자 ❑ 그들은 대문자를 써야 한다.

가산명사-집합 상류 사회, 상류층 ❑ 상류층의 구미에 맞도록 특별히 고안된 상품 ● 형용사 상류층의 ❑ 그들 모두는 부유하고 상류층인 집안 출신이었다.

1 형용사 꼿꼿한, 똑바른 ❑ 헬렌은 자기 의자에 꼿꼿이 앉았다. ❑ 그는 똑바른 자세를 취하였다. **2** 형용사 (가전제품이) 봉통보다) 키가 큰 ❑ 키가 큰 최신식 첨단 진공청소기들 **3** 형용사 (팔걸이가 없고) 수직 등받이 있는 ❑ 그는 자기 침대 옆에서 수직 등받이가 있는 의자에 앉아 책을 읽고 있었다. **4** 가산명사 수직 기둥 ❑ 사주식 침대의 수직 기둥들 **5** 형용사 정직한 ❑ 아주 정직하고 신뢰할 수 있는 남자

가산명사 반란, 봉기 ❑ 독재 정부에 항거하는 민중 봉기

1 불가산명사 대소동, 소란 ❑ 그 발표로 군중들 사이에 소동이 일어났다. **2** 불가산명사 야단법석 ❑ 시대가 온통 그 논쟁으로 야단법석이다.

1 타동사 (오래 살던 곳을) 떠나다; (오래 살던 곳에서) 떠나게 되다 ❑ 그들이 정든 집을 떠나는 데 대한 정신적 충격 ❑ 그는 디나를 지금 살고 있는 집에서 내보낼 뜻이 없었다. **2** 타동사 뿌리뽑다 ❑ 그들은 자기들의 포도나무를 뽑고 밀을 심도록 강요받았다. ❑ 폭풍우에 뿌리째 뽑혀 넘어진 나무들

형용사 고급의, 상류층을 겨냥한 [미국영어] ❑ 브루밍데일스와 삭스 피프스 애버뉴와 같은 고급 백화점 체인들 ● 부사 고급으로 [영국영어 upmarket] ❑ 미국식 평상복의 대명사인 티셔츠가 고급품으로 바뀌었다.

동사와 형용사는 /ʌpsɛt/으로 발음되고, 명사는 /ʌpset/으로 발음된다.

1 형용사 속상한, 좌절한 ❑ 그녀가 죽은 뒤 나는 아주 깊이 속상해졌다. ❑ 마르타는 속상해하는 것 같았다. ● 가산명사 좌절, 혼란 ❑ 스트레스 및 다른 감정적인 혼란 **2** 타동사 낭패를 보게 하다, 혼란스럽게 하다 ❑ 그 모든 사건 때문에 나와 내 약혼자는 몹시 화나고 걱정되었다. ❑ 그녀는 그를 흥분시킬 수 있는 어떤 말도 하지 말라고 내게 주의를 주었다. ● 괴로움을 주는 형용사 ❑ 유년기의 질병은 아이들과 부모에게 똑같이 괴로울 수 있다. **3** 타동사 망쳐 놓다 ❑ 정치적 문제가 러시아와 아프가니스탄 사이의 협정을 망쳐 놓을 수도 있다. ● 가산명사 혼란 ❑ 시장의 일본 경제 장치의 어떤 혼란에도 매우 민감하다. **4** 타동사 뒤엎다 ❑ 그 상자 아래의 종이 더미들을 뒤엎지 마시오. **5** 가산명사 (위 등의) 탈 ❑ 폴은 지난밤 위장에 탈이 나서 상태가 좋지

upset. ● ADJ **Upset** is also an adjective. [ADJ n] ❑ *Larry is suffering from an upset stomach.*

않았다. ● 형용사 탈이 난 ❑ 래리는 위장에 탈이 나서 고생하고 있다.

Thesaurus   upset의 참조어

ADJ.	disappointed, hurt, unhappy; (ant.) happy **1**
	ill, sick, unsettled **5**
V.	overturn, spill, topple **4**

Word Partnership   upset의 연어

PREP.	upset **about/by/over** *something* **1 2**
ADV.	**really** upset, **so** upset, **very** upset **1 2**
V.	**become** upset, **feel** upset, **get** upset **1 2 5**
N.	**stomach** upset (or upset **stomach**) **5**

---

up|shot /ʌpʃɒt/ N-SING The **upshot** of a series of events or discussions is the final result of them, usually a surprising result. ❑ *The upshot is that we have lots of good but not very happy employees.*

단수명사 최종 결과 ❑ 최종적인 결론은 우리 직원들이 우수한 사람은 많지만 그다지 만족해하지는 못한다는 것이다.

up|side down /ʌpsaɪd daʊn/ also **upside-down** ADV If something has been moved **upside down**, it has been turned around so that the part that is usually lowest is above the part that is usually highest. ❑ *The painting was hung upside down.* ● ADJ **Upside down** is also an adjective. ❑ *Tony had an upside-down map of Britain on his wall.*

부사 (아래위가) 거꾸로, 뒤집혀 ❑ 그 그림은 거꾸로 걸려 있었다. ● 형용사 거꾸로인 ❑ 토니의 방 벽에는 거꾸로 붙은 영국 지도가 있었다.

up|stage /ʌpsteɪdʒ/ (upstages, upstaging, upstaged) V-T If someone **upstages** you, they draw attention away from you by being more attractive or interesting. ❑ *He had a younger brother who always publicly upstaged him.*

타동사 -에게서 인기를 가로채다, -보다 돋보이다 ❑ 그에게는 항상 자기보다 남들의 주목을 더 끄는 남동생이 있었다.

up|stairs /ʌpsteərz/ **1** ADV If you go **upstairs** in a building, you go up a staircase toward a higher floor. [ADV after v] ❑ *He went upstairs and changed into fresh clothes.* **2** ADV If something or someone is **upstairs** in a building, they are on a floor that is higher than the ground floor. ❑ *The restaurant is upstairs and consists of a large, open room.* **3** ADJ An **upstairs** room or object is situated on a floor of a building that is higher than the ground floor. [ADJ n] ❑ *Marsani moved into the upstairs apartment.* **4** N-SING The **upstairs** of a building is the floor or floors that are higher than the ground floor. ❑ *Together we went through the upstairs.*

1 부사 위층으로 ❑ 그는 위층으로 올라가서 깨끗한 옷으로 갈아입었다. **2** 부사 2층에, 위층에 ❑ 식당은 위층에 있는데 넓고, 탁 트인 방이다. **3** 형용사 2층의, 위층의 ❑ 마사니는 위층 아파트로 입주했다. **4** 단수명사 2층, 위층 ❑ 우리는 함께 위층을 모두 샅샅이 조사했다.

up|start /ʌpstɑrt/ (upstarts) N-COUNT You can refer to someone as an **upstart** when they behave as if they are important, but you think that they are too new in a place or job to be treated as important. [DISAPPROVAL] ❑ *Many prefer a familiar authority figure to a young upstart.*

가산명사 벼락출세한 사람, 벼락부자 [탐탁찮음] ❑ 많은 사람들이 벼락출세한 젊은 사람보다는 잘 아는 권위 있는 인물을 선호한다.

up|stream /ʌpstrim/ ADV Something that is moving **upstream** is moving toward the source of a river, from a point further down the river. Something that is **upstream** is toward the source of a river. ❑ *The water rose high enough for them to continue upstream.* ❑ *...the river police, whose headquarters are just upstream of the Isle St Louis.* ● ADJ **Upstream** is also an adjective. [ADJ n] ❑ *We'll go to the upstream side of that big rock.*

부사 상류로, 상류 방향으로 ❑ 물은 그들이 상류로 계속 나아갈 수 있을 만큼 충분히 불어 있었다. ❑ 세인트루이스 섬 바로 상류 지점에 본부를 둔 수상 경찰 ● 형용사 상류의 ❑ 우리는 저 큰 바위의 상류 쪽으로 갈 것이다.

up|surge /ʌpsɜrdʒ/ N-SING If there is an **upsurge in** something, there is a sudden, large increase in it. [FORMAL] ❑ *...the upsurge in oil prices.*

단수명사 급증 [격식체] ❑ 석유 가격의 급증

up|tight /ʌptaɪt/ ADJ Someone who is **uptight** is tense, nervous, or annoyed about something and so is difficult to be with. [INFORMAL] ❑ *Penny never got uptight about exams.*

형용사 긴장한, 초조해 하는 [비격식체] ❑ 페니는 시험에 절대 긴장하지 않았다.

up-to-date also up to date **1** ADJ If something is **up-to-date**, it is the newest thing of its kind. ❑ *...Germany's most up to date electric power station.* ❑ *Web services are always up-to-date and available.* **2** ADJ If you are **up-to-date** about something, you have the latest information about it. ❑ *We'll keep you up to date with any news.*

1 형용사 최신의 ❑ 독일의 가장 최신식 발전소 ❑ 웹 서비스는 항상 최신이며 언제든 이용 가능하다. **2** 형용사 최신 소식을 아는 ❑ 네게 새로운 소식들을 다 전해 줄게.

up|town /ʌptaʊn/ ADV If you go **uptown**, or go to a place **uptown**, you go away from the center of a city or town toward the edge. **Uptown** sometimes refers to a part of the city other than the main business district. [mainly AM] [ADV after v] ❑ *He rode uptown and made his way to Bob's apartment.* ❑ *Susan continued to live uptown.* ● ADJ **Uptown** is also an adjective. [ADJ n] ❑ *...uptown clubs.* ❑ *...a small uptown radio station.*

부사 도심을 벗어나, 외곽으로 [주로 미국영어] ❑ 그는 도심 밖으로 차를 몰아 밥의 아파트로 향했다. ❑ 수잔은 내내 도심 밖에서 살았다. ● 형용사 도심을 벗어난 ❑ 도심 밖의 클럽들 ❑ 도심 밖의 작은 라디오 방송국

up|trend /ʌptrend/ N-SING An **uptrend** is a general improvement in something such as a market or the economy. ❑ *Racal Electronics shares have been in a strong uptrend.*

단수명사 오름세, 상승세 ❑ 라칼 전자 주식이 강한 상승세를 이어 왔다.

up|turn /ʌptɜrn/ (upturns) N-COUNT If there is an **upturn** in the economy or in a company or industry, it improves or becomes more successful. [BUSINESS] ❑ *They do not expect an upturn in the economy until the end of the year.*

가산명사 호전, 상승 [경제] ❑ 그들은 올해 말까지는 경제가 호전될 것을 기대하지 않는다.

up|ward /ʌpwərd/ **1** ADJ An **upward** movement or look is directed towards a higher place or a higher level. [ADJ n] ❑ *She started once again on the steep upward climb.* ❑ *She gave him a quick, upward look, then lowered her eyes.* **2** ADJ If you refer to an **upward** trend or an **upward** spiral, you mean that something is increasing in quantity or price. [ADJ n] ❑ *...the Army's concern that the upward trend in the numbers avoiding military service may continue.* **3** ADV If someone moves or looks **upward**, they move or look up toward a higher place. [BRIT, sometimes AM **upwards**] ❑ *They climbed upward along the steep cliffs surrounding the village.* ❑ *"There," said Jack, pointing upwards.* **4** ADV If an amount or rate moves **upward**, it increases. [BRIT, sometimes AM **upwards**] [ADV after v] ❑ *...with prices soon heading upward in high street stores.* ❑ *Unemployment will continue upward for much of this year.* **5** PHRASE A quantity that is **upwards of** a particular number is more than that number. ❑ *It costs upward of $40,000 a year to keep some prisoners in prison.*

1 형용사 올라가는, 위로 향한 ❑ 그녀는 다시 한 번 가파른 비탈을 오르기 시작했다. ❑ 그녀는 그를 재빨리 한번 올려다보고는 시선을 내렸다. **2** 형용사 오르는, 증가하는 ❑ 군 복무를 피하는 사람 수의 증가 추세가 계속될지 모른다는 군의 염려 **3** 부사 위쪽으로 [영국영어, 미국영어 가끔 upwards] ❑ 그들은 마을을 둘러싸고 있는 가파른 절벽을 따라 위로 올라갔다. ❑ "저기."라고 잭이 위를 가리키면서 말했다. **4** 부사 상승하여, 증가하여 [영국영어, 미국영어 가끔 upwards] ❑ 번화가 상점들에서 물가가 곧 오르면서 ❑ 실업이 올해 상당한 기간 동안 계속 증가할 것이다. **5** 구 (특정한 수) 이상 ❑ 일부 죄수들은 감옥에 수감하는 비용이 일 년에 4만 달러 이상 든다.

ura|nium /yʊreɪniəm/ N-UNCOUNT **Uranium** is a naturally occurring radioactive metal that is used to produce nuclear energy and weapons.

불가산명사 우라늄

ur|ban ♦♢♢ /ˈɜrbən/ ADJ **Urban** means belonging to, or relating to, a city or town. ❑ *Most of the population is an urban population.* ❑ *Most urban areas are close to a park.* →see **city**

형용사 도시의 ❑ 인구의 대부분은 도시 인구이다. ❑ 도시 지역 대부분은 공원에 인접해 있다.

urge ♦♦♢ /ˈɜrdʒ/ (**urges, urging, urged**) ■ V-T If you **urge** someone **to** do something, you try hard to persuade them to do it. ❑ *They urged parliament to approve plans for their reform programme.* ■ V-T If you **urge** someone somewhere, you make them go there by touching them or talking to them. ❑ *He slipped his arm around her waist and urged her away from the window.* ■ V-T If you **urge** a course of action, you strongly advise that it should be taken. ❑ *He urged restraint on the security forces.* ■ N-COUNT If you have an **urge to** do or have something, you have a strong wish to do or have it. ❑ *He had an urge to open a shop of his own.*

■ 타동사 (하도록) 재촉하다 ❑ 그들은 자기들의 개혁 프로그램 계획을 승인하도록 의회에 촉구했다. ■ 타동사 (움직이게 하도록) 재촉하다 ❑ 그는 그녀의 허리를 팔로 감싸 안고 창가에서 데리고 들어오려고 했다. ■ 타동사 촉구하다 ❑ 그는 보안군을 제지할 것을 촉구했다. ■ 가산명사 충동, 욕망 ❑ 그는 자기 가게를 열고 싶은 욕심이 있었다.

Word Partnership   urge의 연어

N.	urge **people**, urge **voters** ■
	leaders/officials urge ■ ■
	urge **action**, urge **caution**, urge **restraint**, urge **support** ■
V.	**feel** an urge, **fight** an urge, **get** an urge, **resist** an urge ■

---

ur|gent ♦♢♢ /ˈɜrdʒənt/ ■ ADJ If something is **urgent**, it needs to be dealt with as soon as possible. ❑ *There is an urgent need for food and water.* ● **ur|gen|cy** N-UNCOUNT ❑ *The urgency of finding a cure attracted some of the best minds in medical science.* ● **ur|gent|ly** ADV [ADV with v] ❑ *Red Cross officials said they urgently needed bread and water.* ■ ADJ If you speak in an **urgent** way, you show that you are anxious for people to notice something or to do something. ❑ *His voice was low and urgent.* ● **ur|gen|cy** N-UNCOUNT ❑ *She was surprised at the urgency in his voice.* ● **ur|gent|ly** ADV [ADV with v] ❑ *They hastened to greet him and asked urgently, "Did you find it?"*

■ 형용사 긴급한, 촉박한 ❑ 음식과 물이 긴급히 필요하다. ● 긴급, 절박 불가산명사 ❑ 치료법을 찾아야 하는 절박감 때문에 의학계 최고 지성의 일부가 모이게 되었다. ● 긴급하게 부사 ❑ 적십자사 당국자들은 빵과 물이 긴급히 필요하다고 말했다. ■ 형용사 다급한 ❑ 그의 목소리는 낮고 다급했다. ● 다급함 불가산명사 ❑ 그녀는 그의 목소리가 다급한 데 놀랐다. ● 다급하게 부사 ❑ 그들은 서둘러서 그를 맞이하고, 다급하게 "그것을 찾았나요?"라고 물었다.

Word Partnership   urgent의 연어

N.	urgent **action**, urgent **business**, urgent **care**, urgent **matter**,
	urgent **meeting**, urgent **mission**, urgent **need**, urgent **problem** ■
	urgent **appeal**, urgent **message** ■

---

uri|nate /ˈyʊərɪneɪt/ (**urinates, urinating, urinated**) V-I When someone **urinates**, they get rid of urine from their body. [v] ❑ *I experience pain with sex and it hurts to urinate.*

자동사 소변을 보다 ❑ 나는 성관계 시 통증이 있고 소변을 볼 때 아프다.

urine /ˈyʊərɪn/ N-UNCOUNT **Urine** is the liquid that you get rid of from your body when you go to the toilet. ❑ *The doctor took a urine sample and a blood sample.*

불가산명사 소변 ❑ 의사는 소변과 혈액 샘플을 채취했다.

URL /ˌyu ɑr ˈɛl/ (**URLs**) N-COUNT A **URL** is an address that shows where a particular page can be found on the World Wide Web. **URL** is an abbreviation for "Uniform Resource Locator." [COMPUTING] ❑ *The URL for the Lonely Planet travel center is http://www.lonelyplanet.com.*

가산명사 인터넷 주소 [컴퓨터] ❑ 론리 플래닛 여행사의 인터넷 주소는 http://www.lonelyplanet.com이다.

urn /ˈɜrn/ (**urns**) ■ N-COUNT An **urn** is a container in which a dead person's ashes are kept. ❑ *...a funeral urn.* ■ N-COUNT An **urn** is a metal container used for making a large quantity of tea or coffee and keeping it hot. ❑ *...the ten gallon coffee urn.*

■ 가산명사 유골 단지 ❑ 납골 단지 ■ 가산명사 (차, 커피 등의) 대형 보온통 ❑ 10갤런짜리 커피 보온통

us ♦♦♦ /əs, STRONG ʌs/

us는 1인칭 복수 대명사이다. us는 동사 또는 전치사의 목적어로 쓰인다.

Us is the first person plural pronoun. **Us** is used as the object of a verb or a preposition.

■ PRON-PLURAL A speaker or writer uses **us** to refer both to himself or herself and to one or more other people. You can use **us** before a noun to make it clear which group of people you are referring to. [v PRON, prep PRON] ❑ *Neither of us forgot about it.* ❑ *Heather went to the kitchen to get drinks for us.* ❑ *They don't like us much.* ■ PRON-PLURAL **Us** is sometimes used to refer to people in general. [v PRON, prep PRON] ❑ *All of us will struggle fairly hard to survive if we are in danger.* ■ PRON-PLURAL A speaker or writer may use **us** instead of "me" in order to include the audience or reader in what they are saying. [mainly FORMAL] [v PRON, prep PRON] ❑ *This brings us to the second question I asked.* ■ PRON-SING In non-standard English, **us** is sometimes used instead of "me." [BRIT, SPOKEN] [v PRON, prep PRON] ❑ *"Hang on a bit," said Eileen. "I'm not finished yet. Give us a chance."*

■ 복수대명사 우리, 우리를, 우리에게 ❑ 우리들 다 그것을 잊지 않았다. ❑ 헤더는 우리에게 마실 것을 갖다 주려고 부엌으로 갔다. ❑ 그들은 우리를 별로 좋아하지 않는다. ■ 복수대명사 우리, 일반 사람들 ❑ 우리는 모두 위험에 처하면 살기 위해 아주 열심히 발버둥을 친다. ■ 복수대명사 (독자, 청중을 포함한) 우리 [주로 격식체] ❑ 이것과 함께 제가 던진 두 번째 질문으로 이어지게 됩니다. ■ 단 수대명사 내게, 나를 [영국영어, 구어체] ❑ "잠깐만" 하고 아일린이 말했다. "난 아직 안 끝났어. 내게도 기회를 줘."

US ♦♦♦ /ˌyu ˈɛs/ also **U.S.** N-PROPER The **US** is an abbreviation for **the United States**. [the N, N n] ❑ *The first time I saw TV was when I arrived in the U.S. in 1956.*

고유명사 미국, 미합중국, United States의 약자 ❑ 내가 텔레비전을 처음 본 것은 1956년 미국에 와서였다.

USA ♦♢♢ /ˌyu ɛs ˈeɪ/ also **U.S.A.** N-PROPER The **USA** is an abbreviation for **the United States of America**. [the N]

고유명사 미합중국, United States of America의 약자

us|able /ˈyuːzəbəl/ ADJ If something is **usable**, it is in a good enough state or condition to be used. ❑ *It's been reported that no usable fingerprints were found at the scene.*

형용사 쓸 수 있는, 쓸모 있는 ❑ 현장에서 전혀 쓸 만한 지문이 발견되지 않았다고 보도되었다.

us|age /ˈyuːsɪdʒ/ (**usages**) ■ N-UNCOUNT **Usage** is the way in which words are actually used in particular contexts, especially with regard to their meanings. ❑ *He was a stickler for the correct usage of English.* ■ N-COUNT A **usage** is a meaning that a word has or a way in which it can be used. ❑ *It's very definitely a usage which has come over to Britain from America.* ■ N-UNCOUNT **Usage** is the degree to which something is used or the way in which it is used. ❑ *Parts of the motor wore out because of constant usage.*

■ 불가산명사 (단어의) 용법 ❑ 그는 올바른 영어 용법을 철저하게 고수하는 사람이었다. ■ 가산명사 의미, 어법 ❑ 그것은 틀림없이 미국에서 영국으로 건너온 어법이다. ■ 불가산명사 사용, 사용법 ❑ 계속된 사용으로 모터 부품들이 마모되어 있었다.

USB /ˌyu ɛs ˈbi/ (**USBs**) N-COUNT A **USB** on a computer is a place where you can attach another piece of equipment, for example a printer. **USB** is an abbreviation for "Universal Serial Bus." [COMPUTING] ❑ *The device plugs into one of the laptop's USB ports.*

■ 가산명사 (컴퓨터) 유에스비, Universal Serial Bus의 약자 [컴퓨터] ❑ 그 장치는 노트북의 유에스비 포트 중 하나에 연결된다.

a b c d e f g h i j k l m n o p q r s t u v w x y z

A

use
① VERB USES
② NOUN USES

① **use** ♦♦♦ /yuz/ (uses, using, used) **1** V-T If you **use** something, you do something with it in order to do a job or to achieve a particular result or effect. ❑ *Trim off the excess pastry using a sharp knife.* ❑ *The U.S. has used ships to bring most of its heavy material, like tanks, to the region.* **2** V-T If you **use** a supply of something, you finish it so that none of it is left. ❑ *You used all the ice cubes and didn't put the ice trays back.* ● PHRASAL VERB **Use up** means the same as **use.** ❑ *It isn't them who use up the world's resources.* **3** V-T If someone **uses** drugs, they take drugs regularly, especially illegal ones. ❑ *He denied he had used drugs.* **4** V-T You can say that someone **uses** the toilet or bathroom as a polite way of saying that they go to the toilet. [POLITENESS] ❑ *Wash your hands after using the toilet.* **5** V-T If you **use** a particular word or expression, you say or write it, because it has the meaning that you want to express. ❑ *The judge liked using the word "wicked" of people he had sent to jail.* **6** V-T If you **use** a particular name, you call yourself by that name, especially when it is not the name that you usually call yourself. ❑ *Now I use a false name if I'm meeting people for the first time.* **7** V-T If you say that someone **uses** people, you disapprove of them because they make others do things for them in order to benefit or gain some advantage from it, and not because they care about the other people. [DISAPPROVAL] ❑ *Why do I have the feeling I'm being used again?* **8** →see also **used**

② **use** ♦♦◇ /yus/ (uses) **1** N-UNCOUNT Your **use** of something is the action or fact of your using it. [also a N, usu N of n] ❑ *The treatment does not involve the use of any artificial drugs.* ❑ *...research related to microcomputers and their use in classrooms.* **2** N-SING If you have **a use for** something, you need it or can find something useful to do with it. ❑ *You will no longer have a use for the magazines.* **3** N-VAR If something has a particular **use,** it is intended for a particular purpose. ❑ *Infrared detectors have many uses.* ❑ *It's an interesting scientific phenomenon, but of no practical use whatever.* ❑ *The report outlined possible uses for the new weapon.* **4** N-UNCOUNT If you have the **use of** something, you have the permission or ability to use it. [also the N, usu N of n] ❑ *She will have the use of the car one night a week.* ❑ *...young people who at some point in the past have lost the use of their limbs.* **5** N-COUNT A **use** of a word is a particular meaning that it has or a particular way in which it can be used. ❑ *There are new uses of words coming in and old ones dying out.* **6** N-UNCOUNT Your **use of** a particular name is the fact of your calling yourself by it. ❑ *Police have been hampered by Mr. Urquhart's use of bogus names.* **7** PHRASE If something is **for the use of** a particular person or group of people, it is for that person or group to use. ❑ *The leisure facilities are there for the use of guests.* **8** PHRASE If you say that being something or knowing someone **has** its **uses,** you mean that it makes it possible for you to do what you otherwise would not be able to do. [INFORMAL] ❑ *Being a hospital Sister had its uses.* **9** PHRASE If something such as a technique, building, or machine is **in use,** it is used regularly by people. If it has gone **out of use,** it is no longer used regularly by people. ❑ *...the methods of making Champagne which are still in use today.* **10** PHRASE If you **make use of** something, you do something with it in order to do a job or achieve a particular result or effect. [WRITTEN] ❑ *Not all nursery schools make use of the opportunities open to them.* **11** PHRASE If you say **it's no use,** you mean that you have failed to do something and realize that it is useless to continue trying because it is impossible. ❑ *It's no use. Let's hang up and try for a better time.* **12** PHRASE If something or someone is **of use,** they are useful. If they are **no use,** they are not at all useful. ❑ *The contents of this booklet should be of use to all students.*

Thesaurus   use의 참조어
v.   utilize ① **1**
N.   application, function, purpose ② **1** **3**

used
① MODAL USES AND PHRASES
② ADJECTIVE USES

① **used** ♦♦◇ /yust/ **1** PHRASE If something **used to** be done or **used to** be the case, it was done regularly in the past or was the case in the past. ❑ *People used to come and visit him every day.* ❑ *He used to be one of the professors at the School of Education.* **2** PHRASE If something **used not to** be done or **used not to** be the case, it was not done in the past or was not the case in the past. The forms **did not use to** and **did not used to** are also found, especially in spoken English. ❑ *Borrowing used not to be recommended.* ❑ *At some point kids start doing things they didn't use to do. They get more independent.* **3** PHRASE If you **are used to** something, you are familiar with it because you have done it or experienced it many times before. ❑ *I'm used to having my sleep interrupted.* **4** PHRASE If you **get used to** something or someone, you become familiar with it or get to know them, so that you no longer feel that the thing or person is unusual or surprising. ❑ *This is how we do things here. You'll soon get used to it.* ❑ *You quickly get used to using the brakes.*

② **used** /yuzd/ **1** ADJ A **used** object is dirty or spoiled because it has been used, and usually needs to be thrown away or washed. ❑ *...a used cotton ball stained with makeup.* **2** ADJ A **used** car has already had one or more owners. ❑ *Would you buy a used car from this man?*

use|ful ♦♦◇ /yusfəl/ **1** ADJ If something is **useful,** you can use it to do something or to help you in some way. ❑ *The slow cooker is very useful for people who go out all day.* ❑ *Hypnotherapy can be useful in helping you give up smoking.* ● **use|ful|ly** ADV [ADV with v] ❑ *...the problems to which computers could be usefully*

1 타동사 사용하다, 이용하다 ❑ 남는 반죽은 잘 드는 칼을 사용하여 잘라 내시오. ❑ 미국은 탱크와 같은 중장비 대부분을 그 지역에 가져오기 위해 배를 사용했다. **2** 타동사 다 써 버리다 ❑ 네가 각얼음을 다 쓰고 나서 제빙 용기를 다시 넣어 놓지 않았어. ● 구동사 다 써 버리다 ❑ 세계의 자원을 고갈시키는 건 그들이 아니다. **3** 타동사 (약물을) 사용하다 ❑ 그는 약물 사용을 부인했다. **4** 타동사 (화장실을) 사용하다 [공손체] ❑ 화장실을 사용한 다음에는 손을 씻으시오. **5** 타동사 (단어, 표현 등을) 사용하다 ❑ 그 판사는 자기가 감옥으로 보낸 사람들에 대해 '사악한'이란 단어를 즐겨 사용했다. **6** 타동사 (특정한 이름을) 사용하다 ❑ 이제 나는 처음 만나는 사람에겐 가명을 쓴다. **7** 타동사 (사람을) 이용하다 [탐탁찮음] ❑ 왜 내가 다시 이용당하고 있다는 느낌이 들지?

1 불가산명사 사용 ❑ 그 치료에는 어떠한 인공 약물도 사용되지 않는다. ❑ 마이크로컴퓨터 및 그것의 교실 내 사용에 관한 연구 **2** 단수명사 -에 대한 필요 ❑ 너는 더 이상 그 잡지가 필요하지 않을 거야. **3** 가산불가산 명사 용도 ❑ 적외선 감지기는 여러 용도로 쓰인다. ❑ 그것은 흥미로운 과학 현상이지만 실제로는 어떠한 용도로도 쓸 수가 없다. ❑ 그 보고서는 신무기의 가능한 용도에 대한 개요를 제시했다. **4** 불가산명사 사용권, 사용 능력 ❑ 그녀는 일주일에 하룻밤은 그 차를 사용할 수 있는 권리를 갖게 될 것이다. ❑ 과거 어느 시점에 사지를 쓸 수 있는 능력을 잃어버린 젊은이들 **5** 가산명사 용법 ❑ 단어에는 새로운 용법이 생기기도 하고 시대에 뒤진 용법은 사라지기도 한다. **6** 불가산명사 -을 사용함 ❑ 경찰은 우르크하트 씨의 가명 사용으로 인해 방해를 받았다. **7** 구 -용으로, -가 사용하도록 ❑ 그 여가 시설은 손님용으로 마련된 것이다. **8** 구 나름의 쓸모가 있다 [비격식체] ❑ 병원 수간호사가 되는 것은 나름의 의미가 있는 일이었다. **9** 구 사용되고 있는; 사용되지 않는 ❑ 오늘날에도 여전히 사용되고 있는 샴페인 제조법들 **10** 구 이용하다 [문어체] ❑ 모든 유치원이 그들에게 주어진 기회들을 이용하는 것은 아니다. **11** 구 소용없다 ❑ 소용없어. 그만 끊고 좀 더 좋은 회선을 찾아보자. **12** 구 쓸모 있는, 도움이 되는; 쓸모없는 ❑ 이 소책자에 담긴 내용은 모든 학생들에게 쓸모가 있어야 한다.

1 구 -하곤 했다; 예전에는 -이었다 ❑ 사람들이 매일 그를 찾아오곤 했다. ❑ 그는 예전에 사범 대학 교수들 중의 한 사람이었다. **2** 구 전에는 -하지 않았었다, 예전에는 -가 아니었었다 ❑ 전에는 차용이 권장되지 않았었다. ❑ 어느 시점에서 어린아이들이 예전에 하지 않았던 일들을 시작하면서 더 독립적이게 된다. **3** 구 -에 익숙하다 ❑ 난 자다가 방해받는 것에 익숙해. **4** 구 -에 익숙해지다 ❑ 이것이 우리가 여기서 일을 하는 방식이야. 너도 곧 이 방식에 익숙해질 거야. ❑ 너는 금세 브레이크 사용에 익숙해지는구나.

1 형용사 써서 낡은 ❑ 화장을 닦아 얼룩이 진 화장솜 **2** 형용사 중고의 ❑ 이 사람에게서 중고차를 사시겠습니까?

1 형용사 유용한 ❑ 그 저온 조리 기구는 하루 종일 밖에서 일하는 사람들에게 매우 유용하다. ❑ 최면 요법은 담배를 끊는 데 유용할 수 있다. ● 유용하게 부사 ❑ 컴퓨터를 유용하게 적용할 수 있는 문제들

applied. ● **use|ful|ness** N-UNCOUNT ❏ *His interest lay in the usefulness of his work, rather than in any personal credit.* **2** PHRASE If an object or skill **comes in useful**, it can help you achieve something in a particular situation. [mainly BRIT] ❏ *Rae brought a brush hook to the island, thinking the machete-like tool might come in useful.*

● 유용성 불가산명사 ❏ 그의 관심은 자신의 업무 유용성에 있었지 어떤 개인적인 명성에 있지 않았다. **2** 구 쓸모 있게 되다 [주로 영국영어] ❏ 라에가 그 섬에 덤불 베는 낫을 가지고 왔는데, 날이 넓은 칼처럼 생긴 이 도구가 쓸모 있게 될 수도 있다고 생각해서였다.

Word Partnership　　useful의 연어

ADV.	**also** useful, **especially** useful, **extremely** useful, **less/more** useful, **particularly** useful, **very** useful **1**
N.	useful **information**, useful **knowledge**, useful **life**, useful **purpose**, useful **strategy**, useful **tool** **1**

---

use|less /yuslɪs/ **1** ADJ If something is **useless**, you cannot use it. ❏ *He realized that his money was useless in this country.* **2** ADJ If something is **useless**, it does not achieve anything helpful or good. ❏ *She knew it was useless to protest.* **3** ADJ If you say that someone or something is **useless**, you mean that they are no good at all. [INFORMAL] ❏ *Their education system is useless.* **4** ADJ If someone feels **useless**, they feel bad because they are unable to help someone or achieve anything. ❏ *She sits at home all day, watching TV and feeling useless.*

1 형용사 쓸모없는 ❏ 그는 그 사람들의 돈이 이 나라에서는 쓸모없다는 것을 깨달았다. **2** 형용사 소용없는 ❏ 그녀는 저항해도 소용없다는 것을 알고 있었다. **3** 형용사 아무짝에도 쓸모없는 [비격식체] ❏ 그들의 교육 제도는 아무짝에도 쓸모없다. **4** 형용사 무능한 ❏ 그녀는 온종일 집에서 텔레비전을 보며 무능함을 느끼며 앉아 있다.

user ♦◇◇ /yuzər/ (**users**) N-COUNT A **user** is a person or thing that uses something such as a place, facility, product, or machine. ❏ *Beach users have complained that the bikes are noisy.* ❏ *...a regular user of Holland's health-care system.* →see **Internet**

가산명사 이용자 ❏ 해변 이용자들은 자전거 소리가 시끄럽다고 불평을 해 왔다. ❏ 네덜란드의 보건 제도를 정기적으로 이용하는 사람

user-friendly ADJ If you describe something such as a machine or system as **user-friendly**, you mean that it is well designed and easy to use. ❏ *This is an entirely computer operated system which is very user friendly.*

형용사 사용하기 쉬운 ❏ 이것은 전적으로 컴퓨터로 작동되는 방식으로서 매우 사용하기 쉽다.

ush|er /ʌʃər/ (**ushers, ushering, ushered**) **1** V-T If you **usher** someone somewhere, you show them where they should go, often by going with them. [FORMAL] ❏ *I ushered him into the office.* **2** N-COUNT An **usher** is a person who shows people where to sit, for example at a wedding or at a concert. ❏ *He did part-time work as an usher in a theater.*

1 타동사 안내하다 [격식체] ❏ 나는 그 사무실로 그를 안내했다. **2** 가산명사 좌석 안내원 ❏ 그는 극장에서 좌석 안내원으로 시간제 근무를 했다.

USP /yu ɛs pi/ (**USPs**) N-COUNT The **USP** of a product or service is a particular feature of it which can be used in advertising to show how it is different from, and better than, other similar products or services. **USP** is an abbreviation for "Unique Selling Point." [BUSINESS] ❏ *With Volvo, safety was always the USP.*

가산명사 (상품의) 차별화 특성 [경제] ❏ 볼보로 대해서는 항상 안전성이 차별화 특성이었다.

usu|al ♦♦◇ /yuʒuəl/ **1** ADJ **Usual** is used to describe what happens or what is done most often in a particular situation. [det ADJ, v-link ADJ, oft it v-link ADJ to-inf] ❏ *It is a neighborhood beset by all the usual inner-city problems.* ❏ *After lunch there was a little more clearing up to do than usual.* ● N-SING **Usual** is also a noun. ❏ *The stout barman in a bow tie presented himself to take their order. "Good morning, sir. The usual?"* **2** PHRASE You use **as usual** to indicate that you are describing something that normally happens or that is normally the case. ❏ *As usual there will be the local and regional elections on June the twelfth.* **3** PHRASE If something happens **as usual**, it happens in the way that it normally does, especially when other things have changed. ❏ *When somebody died everything went on as usual, as if it had never happened.* **4 business as usual** →see **business**

1 형용사 흔히 있는, 보통의 ❏ 그곳은 도시 저소득층 지역에서 흔히 볼 수 있는 갖가지 문제들에 시달리는 지역이다. ❏ 점심을 먹고 나서 치울 거리가 평소보다 조금 더 많았다. ● 단수명사 늘 하는 일, 늘 먹는 것 ❏ 나비넥타이를 한 뚱뚱한 바텐더가 나타나 주문을 받았다. "안녕하십니까, 손님? 늘 드시는 걸로 하시겠어요?" **2** 구 평소 그러하듯이 ❏ 항상 그러하듯이 6월 12일에 지방 및 지역 선거가 있을 것이다. **3** 구 여느 때처럼 ❏ 누군가가 죽었어도 마치 아무 일도 없었다는 듯이 모든 일이 여느 때처럼 이루어졌다.

Word Partnership　　usual의 연어

ADV.	**less/more than** usual **1**
N.	usual **place**, usual **routine**, usual **self**, usual **stuff**, usual **suspects**, usual **way** **1**

---

usu|al|ly ♦♦◇ /yuʒuəli/ **1** ADV If something **usually** happens, it is the thing that most often happens in a particular situation. ❏ *The best information about hotels usually comes from friends and acquaintances who have been there.* ❏ *Usually, the work is boring.* **2** PHRASE You use **more than usually** to show that something shows even more of a particular quality than it normally does. ❏ *She felt more than usually hungry after her excursion.*

1 부사 대개, 일반적으로 ❏ 호텔에 관한 가장 좋은 정보는 대개 그곳에 묵었던 친구나 아는 사람들에게서 나온다. ❏ 일반적으로 그 업무는 따분하다. **2** 구 어느 때보다도 더 ❏ 그녀는 소풍을 갔다 온 후에 여느 때보다도 더 배고픔을 느꼈다.

usurp /yusɜrp, -zɜrp/ (**usurps, usurping, usurped**) V-T If you say that someone **usurps** a job, role, title, or position, they take it from someone when they have no right to do this. [FORMAL] ❏ *Did she usurp his place in his mother's heart?*

타동사 (직장 등을) 빼앗다, 강탈하다 [격식체] ❏ 그녀가 그의 어머니 마음속에 자리 잡고 있는 그의 자리를 빼앗았는가?

uten|sil /yutɛnsəl/ (**utensils**) N-COUNT **Utensils** are tools or objects that you use in order to help you to cook, serve food, or eat. ❏ *...utensils such as bowls, steamers, and frying pans.*

가산명사 요리 기구, 식기 및 수저류 ❏ 사발, 찜통, 프라이팬과 같은 요리 기구들

uter|us /yutərəs/ (**uteruses**) N-COUNT The **uterus** of a woman or female mammal is her womb. [MEDICAL] ❏ *...an ultrasound scan of the uterus.*

가산명사 자궁 [의학] ❏ 자궁 초음파 검사

uti|lise /yutɪlaɪz/ →see **utilize**

util|i|tar|ian /yutɪlɪtɛəriən/ (**utilitarians**) **1** ADJ **Utilitarian** means based on the idea that the morally correct course of action is the one that produces benefit for the greatest number of people. [TECHNICAL] ❏ *It was James Mill who was the best publicist for utilitarian ideas on government.* ● N-COUNT A **utilitarian** is someone with utilitarian views. ❏ *One of the greatest utilitarians was Claude Helvetius.* **2** ADJ **Utilitarian** objects and buildings are designed to be useful rather than attractive. ❏ *Bruce's office is a corner one, utilitarian and unglamorous.*

1 형용사 공리주의의 [과학 기술] ❏ 정부에 대해 공리주의적 사상을 주창했던 최고의 정치 평론가가 바로 제임스 밀이었다. ● 가산명사 공리주의자 ❏ 가장 위대한 공리주의자들 중의 한 사람이 클로드 엘베시우스였다. **2** 형용사 실용적인 ❏ 브루스의 사무실은 길모퉁이에 있는데, 실용적이지만 멋지지는 않다.

util|ity /yutɪlɪti/ (**utilities**) N-COUNT A **utility** is an important service such as water, electricity, or gas that is provided for everyone, and that everyone pays for. ❏ *...public utilities such as gas, electricity and phones.*

가산명사 공익 시설 ❏ 가스와 전기, 그리고 전화와 같은 공익 시설

uti|lize /yutɪlaɪz/ (**utilizes, utilizing, utilized**) [BRIT also **utilise**] V-T If you **utilize** something, you use it. [FORMAL] ❏ *Sound engineers utilize a range of techniques to enhance the quality of the recordings.* ● **uti|li|za|tion** /yutɪlɪzeɪʃən/ N-UNCOUNT ❏ *...the utilization of human resources.*

[영국영어 utilise] 타동사 이용하다, 활용하다 [격식체] ❏ 유능한 기술자들이 다양한 기술을 활용해서 녹음의 질을 향상시킨다. ● 활용 불가산명사 ❏ 인적 자원 활용

a
b
c
d
e
f
g
h
i
j
k
l
m
n
o
p
q
r
s
t
u
v
w
x
y
z

ut|most /ˈʌtmoʊst/ **1** ADJ You can use **utmost** to emphasize the importance or seriousness of something or to emphasize the way that it is done. [EMPHASIS] [ADJ n] ❑ *It is a matter of the utmost urgency to find out what has happened to these people.* ❑ *Security matters are treated with the utmost seriousness.* **2** N-SING If you say that you are doing your **utmost to** do something, you are emphasizing that you are trying as hard as you can to do it. [FORMAL, EMPHASIS] ❑ *He would have done his utmost to help her.*

■ 형용사 최고의, 극단의 [강조] ❑ 이 사람들에게 무슨 일이 일어났는지를 알아내는 것이 최고로 긴급한 사안이다. ❑ 안보 문제는 극히 중대하게 다루어진다. ② 단수명사 최선 [격식체, 강조] ❑ 그가 그녀를 돕기 위해 최선을 다할 수도 있었을 것이다.

uto|pia /yuˈtoʊpiə/ (**utopias**) N-VAR If you refer to an imaginary situation as a **utopia**, you mean that it is one in which society is perfect and everyone is happy, but which you feel is not possible. ❑ *We weren't out to design a contemporary utopia.*

가산명사 또는 불가산명사 이상향, 유토피아 ❑ 우리가 이 시대의 이상향을 세우려고 애를 쓴 것은 아니었다.

uto|pian /yuˈtoʊpiən/ **1** ADJ If you describe a plan or idea as **utopian**, you are criticizing it because it is unrealistic and shows a belief that things can be improved much more than is possible. [DISAPPROVAL] ❑ *He was pursuing a utopian dream of world prosperity.* **2** ADJ **Utopian** is used to describe political or religious philosophies which claim that it is possible to build a new and perfect society in which everyone is happy. [FORMAL] ❑ *His was a utopian vision of nature in its purest form.*

■ 형용사 비현실적인 [탐탁찮음] ❑ 그는 세계 변영이라는 비현실적인 이상을 추구하고 있었다. ② 형용사 이상적인, 유토피아적인 [격식체] ❑ 그의 이상적인 미래상은 가장 순수한 형태의 자연 속에 있었다.

ut|ter /ˈʌtər/ (**utters, uttering, uttered**) **1** V-T If someone **utters** sounds or words, they say them. [LITERARY] ❑ *He uttered a snorting laugh.* **2** ADJ You use **utter** to emphasize that something is great in extent, degree, or amount. [EMPHASIS] [ADJ n] ❑ *This, of course, is utter nonsense.* ❑ *...this utter lack of responsibility.*

■ 타동사 입 밖에 내다, 말하다 [문예체] ❑ 그는 코웃음을 쳤다. ② 형용사 전적인, 완전한 [강조] ❑ 이것은 물론 전적으로 말이 안 된다. ❑ 이러한 전적인 책임감의 결여

ut|ter|ance /ˈʌtərəns/ (**utterances**) N-COUNT Someone's **utterances** are the things that they say. [FORMAL] ❑ *...the Queen's public utterances.*

가산명사 발언 [격식체] ❑ 여왕의 공적인 발언

ut|ter|ly /ˈʌtərli/ ADV You use **utterly** to emphasize that something is very great in extent, degree, or amount. [EMPHASIS] ❑ *China is utterly different.* ❑ *The new laws coming in are utterly ridiculous.*

부사 전적으로 [강조] ❑ 중국은 전적으로 다르다. ❑ 시행되는 신규 법안은 전적으로 터무니없는 것이다.

U-turn (**U-turns**) **1** N-COUNT If you make a **U-turn** when you are driving or riding a bicycle, you turn in a half circle in one movement, so that you are then going in the opposite direction. ❑ *Wade made a U-turn on North Main and drove back to Depot Street.* **2** N-COUNT If you describe a change in a politician's policy, plans, or actions as a **U-turn**, you mean that it is a complete change and that they made the change because they were weak or were wrong. [DISAPPROVAL] ❑ *...a humiliating U-turn by the Prime Minister.*

■ 가산명사 유턴 ❑ 웨이드는 노스 메인에서 유턴을 한 후 다시 디포트 가로 차를 몰았다. ② 가산명사 180도 전환 [탐탁찮음] ❑ 수상의 굴욕적인 180도 정책 전환

V, v /viː/ (**V's, v's**) N-VAR **V** is the twenty-second letter of the English alphabet.

va|can|cy /ˈveɪkənsi/ (**vacancies**) ◼ N-COUNT A **vacancy** is a job or position which has not been filled. ❑ *Most vacancies are at senior level, requiring appropriate qualifications.* ◼ N-COUNT If there are **vacancies** at a building such as a hotel, some of the rooms are available to rent. ❑ *This year hotels that usually are jammed had vacancies all summer.*

va|cant /ˈveɪkənt/ ◼ ADJ If something is **vacant**, it is not being used by anyone. ❑ *Half way down the coach was a vacant seat.* ◼ ADJ If a job or position is **vacant**, no one is doing it or in it at present, and people can apply for it. ❑ *The post of chairman has been vacant for some time.* ◼ ADJ A **vacant** look or expression is one that suggests that someone does not understand something or that they are not thinking about anything in particular. ❑ *She had a kind of vacant look on her face.* ● **va|cant|ly** ADV [ADV after v] ❑ *He looked vacantly out of the window.*

va|cate /ˈveɪkeɪt, BRIT vəˈkeɪt/ (**vacates, vacating, vacated**) V-T If you **vacate** a place or a job, you leave it or give it up, making it available for other people. [FORMAL] ❑ *He quickly vacated the gym after the workout.*

va|ca|tion /veɪˈkeɪʃ°n, BRIT vəˈkeɪʃ°n/ (**vacations, vacationing, vacationed**) ◼ N-COUNT A **vacation** is a period of time during which you relax and enjoy yourself away from home. [AM; BRIT **holiday**] [also on/from N] ❑ *They planned a late summer vacation in Europe.*

> American workers generally get 2 weeks a year of paid **vacation**. Most people take their vacation time in the summer when their children are not in school. In the UK, workers usually get 4-5 weeks of paid vacation per year.

◼ N-COUNT A **vacation** is a period of the year when universities and colleges, and in the United States also schools, are officially closed. ❑ *During his summer vacation he visited Russia.* ◼ N-UNCOUNT If you have a particular number of days' or weeks' **vacation**, you do not have to go to work for that number of days or weeks. [AM; BRIT **holiday**] ❑ *The French get five to six weeks' vacation a year.* ◼ V-I If you **are vacationing** in a place away from home, you are on vacation there. [AM; BRIT **holiday**] ❑ *Myles vacationed in Jamaica.*

va|ca|tion|er /veɪˈkeɪʃ°nər/ (**vacationers**) N-COUNT **Vacationers** are people who are on vacation in a particular place. [mainly AM; BRIT usually **holidaymakers**] [usu pl] ❑ *Camping, biking, hiking, and swimming are all available for the vacationer.*

vac|ci|nate /ˈvæksɪneɪt/ (**vaccinates, vaccinating, vaccinated**) V-T If a person or animal **is vaccinated**, they are given a vaccine, usually by injection, to prevent them from getting a disease. [usu passive] ❑ *Dogs must be vaccinated against distemper.* ❑ *Have you had your child vaccinated against whooping cough?* ● **vac|ci|na|tion** /ˌvæksɪˈneɪʃ°n/ (**vaccinations**) N-VAR ❑ *Anyone who wants to avoid the flu should consider getting a vaccination.*

vac|cine /ˈvæksiːn, BRIT ˈvæksiːn/ (**vaccines**) N-MASS A **vaccine** is a substance containing a harmless form of the germs that cause a particular disease. It is given to people, usually by injection, to prevent them from getting that disease. ❑ *Anti-malarial vaccines are now undergoing trials.* →see **hospital**

vacuum /ˈvækyuːm, -yuəm/ (**vacuums, vacuuming, vacuumed**) ◼ N-COUNT If someone or something creates a **vacuum**, they leave a place or position which then needs to be filled by another person or thing. ❑ *His presence should fill the power vacuum which has been developing over the past few days.* ◼ PHRASE If something is done **in a vacuum**, it is not affected by any outside influences or information. ❑ *Moral values cannot be taught in a vacuum.* ◼ V-T/V-I If you **vacuum** something, you clean it using a vacuum cleaner. ❑ *I vacuumed the carpets today.* ◼ N-COUNT A **vacuum** is a space that contains no air or other gas. ❑ *Wind is a current of air caused by a vacuum caused by hot air rising.*

vacuum clean|er (**vacuum cleaners**) also **vacuum-cleaner** N-COUNT A **vacuum cleaner** or a **vacuum** is an electric machine which sucks up dust and dirt from carpets.

va|gi|na /vəˈdʒaɪnə/ (**vaginas**) N-COUNT A woman's **vagina** is the passage connecting her outer sex organs to her womb.

vag|i|nal /ˈvædʒɪn°l/ ADJ **Vaginal** means relating to or involving the vagina. [ADJ n] ❑ *The creams have been used to reduce vaginal infections.*

vague /veɪg/ (**vaguer, vaguest**) ◼ ADJ If something written or spoken is

---

가산명사 또는 불가산명사 영어 알파벳의 스물두 번째 글자

◼ 가산명사 결원 ❑ 대부분의 결원은 적절한 자격 요건을 요하는 고위급이었다. ◼ 가산명사 빈 방 ❑ 보통 꽉꽉 채워지는 호텔들에 올해는 여름 내내 빈 방이 있었다.

◼ 형용사 비어 있는 ❑ 버스의 중간쯤에 빈 자리가 있었다. ◼ 형용사 공석인, 결원의 ❑ 의장 자리가 한동안 공석이었다. ◼ 형용사 멍한, 얼빠진 ❑ 그녀는 얼굴에 얼빠진 듯한 표정을 하고 있었다. ● 멍하니 부사 ❑ 그는 멍하니 창밖을 바라보았다.

타동사 떠나가다, 사퇴하다 [격식체] ❑ 그는 운동 후에 재빨리 체육관을 떠났다.

◼ 가산명사 휴가 [미국영어; 영국영어 holiday] ❑ 그들을 유럽에서 늦여름 휴가를 보낼 계획을 세웠다.

> 미국 근로자는 일반적으로 1년에 2주간의 유급 vacation(휴가)를 갖는다. 대부분의 사람들이 자녀가 학교에 가지 않는 여름에 휴가를 갖는다. 영국의 근로자는 대개 1년에 4-5주의 유급 휴가를 갖는다.

◼ 가산명사 방학 ❑ 이번 여름 방학 동안 그는 러시아를 방문했다. ◼ 불가산명사 정기 휴가 [미국영어; 영국영어 holiday] ❑ 프랑스 사람들은 일년에 5-6주의 정기 휴가를 갖는다. ◼ 자동사 휴가를 보내다 [미국영어; 영국영어 holiday] ❑ 마일스는 자메이카에서 휴가를 보냈다.

가산명사 휴가객, 행락객 [주로 미국영어; 영국영어 대개 holidaymakers] ❑ 캠핑과 자전거 타기, 하이킹, 수영 모두를 휴가객들이 즐길 수 있다.

타동사 예방 접종하다 ❑ 개들은 반드시 견온병 예방 접종을 해야 한다. ❑ 당신 아이는 백일해 예방 접종을 시켰습니까? ● 예방 접종 가산명사 또는 불가산명사 ❑ 독감에 걸리고 싶지 않은 사람은 누구나 예방 접종을 고려해야 한다.

물질명사 백신 ❑ 말라리아 백신이 지금 사용 단계를 거치고 있다.

◼ 가산명사 공백, 구멍 ❑ 그의 존재가 지난 며칠 동안 생겨난 권력의 공백을 메워 줄 것이다. ◼ 구 고립된 채, 외부와 절연된 상태에서 ❑ 도덕적 가치는 외부와 절연된 상태에서 가르칠 수 없다. ◼ 타동사/자동사 진공청소기로 청소하다 ❑ 나는 오늘 진공청소기로 양탄자를 청소했다. ◼ 가산명사 진공 상태 ❑ 바람은 뜨거운 공기의 상승에 따라 생겨난 진공 상태에 의해 만들어지는 공기의 흐름이다.

가산명사 진공청소기

가산명사 (여성의) 질

형용사 질의 ❑ 그 크림들은 질 감염을 줄이기 위해 사용되어 왔다.

◼ 형용사 모호한, 애매한 ❑ 그 연설의 많은 부분이

vague, it does not explain or express things clearly. ❑ *A lot of the talk was apparently vague and general.* ❑ *The description was pretty vague.* ● **vague|ly** ADV ❑ *"I'm not sure," Liz said vaguely.* **2** ADJ If you have a **vague** memory or idea of something, the memory or idea is not clear. ❑ *They have only a vague idea of the amount of water available.* ● **vague|ly** ADV [ADV with v] ❑ *Judith could vaguely remember her mother lying on the sofa.* **3** ADJ If you are **vague** about something, you deliberately do not tell people much about it. ❑ *He was vague, however, about just what U.S. forces might actually do.* **4** ADJ If something such as a feeling is **vague**, you experience it only slightly. ❑ *He was conscious of that vague feeling of irritation again.* **5** ADJ A **vague** shape or outline is not clear and is therefore not easy to see. ❑ *The bus was a vague shape in the distance.*

분명 모호하고 막연했다. ❑ 그 묘사는 상당히 모호했다. ● 모호하게, 애매하게 부사 ❑ "난 잘 모르겠어."라고 리즈가 애매하게 말했다. **2** 형용사 희미한, 어렴풋한 ❑ 그들은 사용 가능한 물의 양에 대해 막연하게만 알고 있을 뿐이다. ● 희미하게, 어렴풋이 부사 ❑ 주디스는 어머니가 소파에 누워 계셨던 것을 어렴풋이 기억할 수 있었다. **3** 형용사 (대답이) 애매모호한 ❑ 그는 그러나 미군이 실제로 어떤 일을 할 수 있는지에 대해서는 분명한 대답을 피했다. **4** 형용사 약간의 ❑ 그는 약간 짜증나는 그런 기분을 다시 느꼈다. **5** 형용사 희미한, 흐릿한 ❑ 그 버스는 멀리서 형체가 분명치 않았다.

Word Partnership   vague의 연어

ADV.	**a little** vague, **rather** vague, **too** vague, **very** vague **1-5**
N.	vague **references**, vague **terms 1 3**
	vague **idea/notion/sense 2**
V.	**have (only) a** vague **idea/notion/sense of** *something* **2**

---

vague|ly /veɪgli/ **1** ADV **Vaguely** means to some degree but not to a very large degree. [ADV adj] ❑ *The voice on the line was vaguely familiar, but Crook couldn't place it at first.* **2** →see also **vague**

1 부사 조금, 약간 ❑ 전화 목소리는 좀 귀에 익었지만 크룩은 처음에는 누군지 알 수 없었다.

vain /veɪn/ (**vainer, vainest**) **1** ADJ A **vain** attempt or action is one that fails to achieve what was intended. [ADJ n] ❑ *The drafting committee worked through the night in a vain attempt to finish on schedule.* ● **vain|ly** ADV [ADV with v] ❑ *He hunted vainly through his pockets for a piece of paper.* **2** ADJ If you describe a hope that something will happen as a **vain** hope, you mean that there is no chance of it happening. [ADJ n] ❑ *He married his fourth wife, Susan, in the vain hope that she would improve his health.* ● **vain|ly** ADV [ADV with v] ❑ *He then set out for Virginia for what he vainly hoped would be a peaceful retirement.* **3** ADJ If you describe someone as **vain**, you are critical of their extreme pride in their own beauty, intelligence, or other good qualities. [DISAPPROVAL] ❑ *He wasn't so vain as to think he was smarter than his boss.* **4** PHRASE If you do something **in vain**, you do not succeed in achieving what you intend. ❑ *He stopped at the door, waiting in vain for her to acknowledge his presence.* **5** PHRASE If you say that something such as someone's death, suffering, or effort was **in vain**, you mean that it was useless because it did not achieve anything. ❑ *He wants the world to know his son did not die in vain.*

1 형용사 헛된, 소용없는 ❑ 기초 위원회는 일정에 맞추어 끝내려고 밤새 일했지만 소용없었다. ● 공연히, 헛되이 부사 ❑ 그는 종이 한 장을 찾으려고 공연히 주머니를 모두 뒤졌다. **2** 형용사 헛된 ❑ 그는 네 번째 아내인 수잔과 결혼했는데 그녀가 자기 건강을 좋아지게 할 거라는 헛된 희망에서였다. ● 헛되이 부사 ❑ 그는 그리고는 평온한 노후를 보내게 될 곳으로 기대했던 버지니아를 향해 떠났지만 헛된 일이었다. **3** 형용사 자만심이 강한, 허영심 많은 [탐탁잖음] ❑ 그는 자기 사장보다 더 똑똑하다고 생각할 만큼 그렇게 자만심이 강하지는 않았다. **4** 구 소득 없이, 소용없이 ❑ 그는 문간에 멈춰 서서 그녀가 자기가 와 있는 것을 알아주기를 기다렸으나 소용없었다. **5** 구 헛되이, 쓸데없이 ❑ 그는 세상 사람들이 자기 아들이 헛되이 죽지 않았다는 것을 알아주길 원한다.

val|iant /vælyənt/ ADJ A **valiant** action is very brave and determined, though it may lead to failure or defeat. ❑ *Despite valiant efforts by the finance minister, inflation rose to 36%.* ● **val|iant|ly** ADV [ADV with v] ❑ *He suffered further heart attacks and strokes, all of which he fought valiantly.*

형용사 용감한, 대담한 ❑ 재무 장관의 대담한 노력에도 불구하고 인플레가 36퍼센트로 증가했다. ● 용감하게, 대담하게 부사 ❑ 그는 또 다시 몇 차례 심장 마비와 뇌졸중 발작을 일으켰지만, 이 모든 것과 용감하게 싸웠다.

val|id /vælɪd/ **1** ADJ A **valid** argument, comment, or idea is based on sensible reasoning. ❑ *They put forward many valid reasons for not exporting.* ● **va|lid|ity** /vəlɪdɪti/ N-UNCOUNT ❑ *The editorial says this argument has lost much of its validity.* **2** ADJ Something that is **valid** is important or serious enough to make it worth saying or doing. ❑ *Most designers share the unspoken belief that fashion is a valid form of visual art.* ● **va|lid|ity** N-UNCOUNT ❑ *...the validity of making children wear bicycle helmets.* **3** ADJ If a ticket or other document is **valid**, it can be used and will be accepted by people in authority. ❑ *All tickets are valid for two months.* **4** →see also **validity**

1 형용사 타당한, 근거가 확실한 ❑ 그들은 수출하지 않는 데 대해 타당한 이유를 많이 들었다. ● 타당성 불가산명사 ❑ 그 사설은 이러한 주장이 타당성을 많이 잃었다고 한다. **2** 형용사 중요한, 유효한 ❑ 대부분의 디자이너들은 패션이 하나의 중요한 시각 예술 형태라는 암묵적인 믿음을 공유하고 있다. ● 중요성 불가산명사 ❑ 아이들에게 자전거 헬멧을 착용시키는 것의 중요성 **3** 형용사 유효한, 합법적인 ❑ 모든 표는 두 달 동안 유효하다.

val|i|date /vælɪdeɪt/ (**validates, validating, validated**) **1** V-T To **validate** something such as a claim or statement means to prove or confirm that it is true or correct. [FORMAL] ❑ *This discovery seems to validate the claims of popular astrology.* ● **val|i|da|tion** /vælɪdeɪʃᵊn/ (**validations**) N-VAR ❑ *This validation process ensures that the data conforms to acceptable formats.* **2** V-T To **validate** a person, state, or system means to prove or confirm that they are valuable or worthwhile. ❑ *The Academy Awards appear to validate his career.* ● **val|i|da|tion** N-VAR ❑ *I think the film is a validation of our lifestyle.*

1 타동사 (주장 등의) 타당성을 입증하다 [격식체] ❑ 이 발견은 통속적인 점성술의 주장을 입증해 주는 것 같다. ● 확인, 입증 가산명사 또는 불가산명사 ❑ 이러한 확인 과정은 그 자료가 확실히 적합한 형식을 따르도록 해 준다. **2** 타동사 확인하다, 비준하다, 승인하다 ❑ 아카데미상이 그의 출세를 보장해 주는 것 같다. ● 비준, 확인 가산명사 또는 불가산명사 ❑ 나는 그 영화가 우리의 생활 방식을 인준해 준다고 생각한다.

va|lid|ity /vəlɪdɪti/ N-UNCOUNT The **validity of** something such as a result or a piece of information is whether it can be trusted or believed. ❑ *Shocked by the results of the elections, they now want to challenge the validity of the vote.* ❑ *Some people, of course, denied the validity of any such claim.* →see also **valid**

불가산명사 타당성, 유효성 ❑ 그들은 선거 결과에 충격을 받아서 이제 투표의 타당성에 대한 이의를 제기하고 싶어 한다. ❑ 물론 일부 사람들은 그러한 어떤 주장에 대해서도 그 타당성을 부인했다.

Va|lium /væliəm/

Valium is both the singular and the plural form.

N-VAR **Valium** is a drug given to people to calm their nerves when they are very depressed or upset. [TRADEMARK] ❑ *Do you have any Valium?*

Valium은 단수형 및 복수형이다.

가산명사 또는 불가산명사 바륨 (신경 안정제) [상표] ❑ 바륨이 있나요?

val|ley ♦♢♢ /væli/ (**valleys**) N-COUNT; N-IN-NAMES A **valley** is a low stretch of land between hills, especially one that has a river flowing through it. ❑ *...a wooded valley set against the backdrop of Monte Rosa.* →see **river**

가산명사; 이름명사 계곡, 골짜기 ❑ 몬테로사 산을 배경으로 자리 잡은 숲이 우거진 계곡

valu|able ♦♢♢ /vælyuəbᵊl/ **1** ADJ If you describe something or someone as **valuable**, you mean that they are very useful and helpful. ❑ *Many of our teachers also have valuable academic links with Heidelberg University.* **2** ADJ **Valuable** objects are objects which are worth a lot of money. ❑ *Just because a camera is old does not mean it is valuable.*

1 형용사 소중한, 귀중한 ❑ 많은 우리 선생님들이 하이델베르크 대학과 소중한 학문적 유대를 또한 맺고 있다. **2** 형용사 값비싼, 고가의 ❑ 카메라가 오래됐다는 것만으로 값이 나가는 것은 아니다.

Thesaurus   valuable의 참조어

ADJ.	helpful, important, useful; (*ant.*) useless **1**
	costly, expensive, priceless; (*ant.*) worthless **2**

Word Partnership   *valuable*의 연어

V.	**learn** a valuable **lesson** ■
N.	valuable **experience**, valuable **information**, valuable **lesson**, **time is** valuable ■
	valuable **asset**, valuable **resource** ■ ■
	valuable **property** ■
ADV.	**extremely** valuable, **less** valuable, **very** valuable ■ ■

valu|ables /vǽlyuəbᵊlz/ N-PLURAL **Valuables** are things that you own that are worth a lot of money, especially small objects such as jewelry. ❑ *Leave your valuables in the hotel safe.*
복수명사 귀중품 ❑귀중품은 호텔 금고에 맡기시오.

valua|tion /vælyuéɪʃn/ (valuations) N-VAR A **valuation** is a judgment that someone makes about how much money something is worth. ❑ *Valuation lies at the heart of all takeovers.*
가산명사 또는 불가산명사 가치 평가 ❑가치 평가가 모든 경영권 인수에서 가장 중요하다.

value ◆◆◆ /vǽlyu/ (values, valuing, valued) ■ N-UNCOUNT The **value** of something such as a quality, attitude, or method is its importance or usefulness. If you place a particular **value** on something, that is the importance or usefulness you think it has. [also a N, usu with supp] ❑ *The value of this work experience should not be underestimated.* ● PHRASE If something is **of value**, it is useful or important. If it is **of no value**, it has no usefulness or importance. ❑ *This weekend course will be of value to everyone interested in the Pilgrim Route.* ■ V-T If you **value** something or someone, you think that they are important and you appreciate them. ❑ *I value the opinion of my husband and we agree on most things.* ■ N-VAR The **value** of something is how much money it is worth. ❑ *The value of his investment has risen by more than $50,000.* ● PHRASE If something is **of value**, it is worth a lot of money. If it is **of no value**, it is worth very little money. ❑ *...a brooch which is really of no value.* ■ V-T When experts **value** something, they decide how much money it is worth. ❑ *Your lender will then send their own surveyor to value the property.* ❑ *I asked him if he would have my jewelry valued for insurance purposes.* ■ N-UNCOUNT You use **value** in certain expressions to say whether something is worth the money that it costs. For example, if something is or gives **good value**, it is worth the money that it costs. ❑ *The restaurant is informal, stylish, and extremely good value.* ■ N-PLURAL The **values** of a person or group are the moral principles and beliefs that they think are important. ❑ *The countries of South Asia also share many common values.* ■ N-UNCOUNT **Value** is used after another noun when mentioning an important or noticeable feature about something. ❑ *The script has lost all of its shock value over the intervening 24 years.*
■ 불가산명사 가치, 유용성 ❑이 업무 경력의 가치가 과소평가되어서는 안 된다. ●구 가치 있는; 가치 없는 ❑이 주말 과정은 청교도의 이주 경로에 관심이 있는 모든 사람들에게 중요할 것이다. ■ 타동사 소중히 여기다, 높이 평가하다 ❑나는 남편의 의견을 존중하며 우리는 대부분의 일에 의견이 일치한다. ■ 가산명사 또는 불가산명사 가치, 가격 ❑그가 투자한 것의 가치가 5만 달러 이상 올랐다. ●구 값비싼; 값싼 ❑전혀 가치 없는 브로치 ■ 타동사 (가치 등을) 평가하다 ❑당신의 대출 기관은 그 다음에 부동산의 가치를 평가할 자기 측 조사관을 보낼 것이다. ❑나는 그에게 보험에 들기 위해 내 보석에 대한 감정을 의뢰할 것인지 물어보았다. ■ 불가산명사 (돈을 치른 만큼의) 가치; 상당한 값어치 ❑그 식당은 격식을 따지지 않고, 멋지고, 정말 상당히 값어치를 한다. ■ 복수명사 가치관, 가치 기준 ❑남아시아 국가들은 또한 많은 공통된 가치관을 공유하고 있다. ■ 불가산명사 -상의 가치 ❑그 원고는 그 24년 사이에 충격을 줄 수 있는 가치를 모두 잃어버렸다.

Thesaurus   *value*의 참조어

N.	importance, merit ■
	cost, price, worth ■
V.	admire, honor, respect ■
	appraise, estimate, price ■

Word Partnership   *value*의 연어

ADJ.	**artistic** value ■
	actual value, **equal** value, **great** value ■ ■
V.	**decline in** value, **increase in** value, **lose** value ■ ■
N.	**cash** value, **dollar** value, value **of an investment**, **market** value ■

value add|ed tax N-UNCOUNT **Value added tax** is a tax that is added to the price of goods or services. The abbreviation **VAT** is also used. [BRIT]
불가산명사 부가 가치세 [영국영어]

valve /vǽlv/ (valves) N-COUNT A **valve** is a device attached to a pipe or a tube which controls the flow of air or liquid through the pipe or tube. →see **engine**
가산명사 밸브

vam|pire /vǽmpaɪər/ (vampires) N-COUNT A **vampire** is a creature in legends and horror stories. Vampires are said to come out of graves at night and suck the blood of living people.
가산명사 흡혈귀

van ◆◇◇ /vǽn/ (vans) N-COUNT A **van** is a small or medium-sized road vehicle with one row of seats at the front and a space for carrying goods behind. →see **car**
가산명사 밴, 유개 운반차

van|dal /vǽndᵊl/ (vandals) N-COUNT A **vandal** is someone who deliberately damages things, especially public property. ❑ *All information systems that have been fitted at Ashford station have now been destroyed by vandals.*
가산명사 공공 기물 파괴자, 반달 ❑애쉬포드 역에 설치된 모든 정보 시스템이 현재 공공 기물 파괴자들에 의해 부서져 있다.

van|dal|ism /vǽndᵊlɪzəm/ N-UNCOUNT **Vandalism** is the deliberate damaging of things, especially public property. ❑ *...a 13-year-old boy whose crime file includes violence, theft, vandalism, and bullying.*
불가산명사 공공 기물 파괴, 문화 예술의 파괴 ❑폭력, 절도, 공공 기물 파괴, 행패의 범죄 기록이 있는 13세 소년

van|dal|ize /vǽndᵊlaɪz/ (vandalizes, vandalizing, vandalized) [BRIT also **vandalise**] V-T If something such as a building or part of a building **is vandalized** by someone, it is damaged on purpose. ❑ *The walls had been horribly vandalized with spray paint.*
[영국영어 vandalise] 타동사 (공공 기물이) 파괴되다, 훼손되다 ❑그 벽들은 스프레이 페인트로 끔찍하게 훼손되어 있었다.

van|guard /vǽngɑrd/ N-SING If someone is **in the vanguard of** something such as a revolution or an area of research, they are involved in the most advanced part of it. You can also refer to the people themselves as **the vanguard**. ❑ *Students and intellectuals have been in the vanguard of revolutionary change in China.*
단수명사 -의 선봉에, -의 전위에; 선봉 ❑학생과 지식인들이 중국 혁명적 변화의 선봉에 있었다.

va|nil|la /vənɪ́lə/ N-UNCOUNT **Vanilla** is a flavoring used in ice cream and other sweet food. ❑ *I added a dollop of vanilla ice-cream to the pie.*
불가산명사 바닐라 ❑나는 파이에 바닐라 아이스크림 한 덩이를 얹었다.

van|ish /vǽnɪʃ/ (vanishes, vanishing, vanished) ■ V-I If someone or something **vanishes**, they disappear suddenly or in a way that cannot be explained. ❑ *He*
■ 자동사 (갑자기) 사라지다 ❑그는 그냥 사라져 버렸고 다시는 눈에 띄지 않았다. ❑앤이 지난 수요일

just vanished and was never seen again. ❑ *Anne vanished from outside her home last Wednesday.* **2** V-I If something such as a species of animal or a tradition **vanishes**, it stops existing. ❑ *Near the end of Devonian times, thirty percent of all animal life vanished.*

자기 집 밖에서 사라졌다. **2** 자동사 멸종되다 ❑ 데본기 말 무렵에 모든 동물의 30퍼센트가 멸종되었다.

van|ity /vǽnɪti/ N-UNCOUNT If you refer to someone's **vanity**, you are critical of them because they take great pride in their appearance or abilities. [DISAPPROVAL] ❑ *Men who use steroids are motivated by sheer vanity.*

불가산명사 허영심 [탐탁잖음] ❑ 스테로이드를 사용하는 남자는 순전히 허영심에 그런다.

van|tage point /vǽntɪdʒ pɔɪnt/ (**vantage points**) **1** N-COUNT A **vantage point** is a place from which you can see a lot of things. ❑ *From a concealed vantage point, he saw a car arrive.* **2** N-COUNT If you view a situation **from** a particular **vantage point**, you have a clear understanding of it because of the particular period of time you are in. ❑ *From today's vantage point, the 1987 crash seems just a blip in the upward progress of the market.*

1 가산명사 유리한 위치 ❑ 밖이 잘 보이게 은닉된 지점에서, 그는 차가 도착하는 것을 보았다. **2** 가산명사 (시간적으로) 유리한 입장 ❑ 오늘날의 유리한 입장에서 보면, 1987년의 폭락은 시장이 상승되는 가운데 일어난 일시적 하락 정도로 보인다.

va|por /véɪpər/ (**vapours**) [AM **vapour**] N-VAR **Vapor** consists of tiny drops of water or other liquids in the air, which appear as mist. ❑ *...water vapor.* →see **greenhouse effect**, **lake**, **water**

[미국영어 vapour] 가산명사 또는 불가산명사 증기, 김 ❑ 수증기

vari|able /véɪriəbᵊl/ (**variables**) **1** ADJ Something that is **variable** changes quite often, and there usually seems to be no fixed pattern to these changes. ❑ *The potassium content of foodstuffs is very variable.* ● **vari|abil|ity** /vèɪriəbɪ́lɪti/ N-UNCOUNT ❑ *There's a great deal of variability between individuals.* **2** N-COUNT A **variable** is a factor that can change in quality, quantity, or size, which you have to take into account in a situation. ❑ *Decisions could be made on the basis of price, delivery dates, after-sales service or any other variable.*

1 형용사 변하기 쉬운, 가변성의 ❑ 식품에 들어 있는 칼륨은 아주 쉽게 변성된다. ● 변화성, 변이성 불가산명사 ❑ 사람들 사이에는 개인차가 아주 크다. **2** 가산명사 변수 ❑ 결정은 가격, 배달, 사후 관리, 또는 다른 변수에 근거하여 내려질 수 있다.

vari|ance /véɪriəns/ PHRASE If one thing is **at variance with** another, the two things seem to contradict each other. [FORMAL] ❑ *Many of his statements were at variance with the facts.*

구 상충하는, 모순되는 [격식체] ❑ 그의 진술 중 많은 부분이 사실과 상충되었다.

vari|ant /véɪriənt/ (**variants**) N-COUNT A **variant** of a particular thing is something that has a different form from that thing, although it is related to it. ❑ *The quagga was a strikingly beautiful variant of the zebra.*

가산명사 변종, 변이 ❑ 콰가는 얼룩말의 굉장히 아름다운 변종이었다.

vari|ation /vèɪriéɪʃᵊn/ (**variations**) **1** N-COUNT A **variation on** something is the same thing presented in a slightly different form. ❑ *This delicious variation on an omelette is quick and easy to prepare.* **2** N-VAR A **variation** is a change or slight difference in a level, amount, or quantity. ❑ *The survey found a wide variation in the prices charged for canteen food.*

1 가산명사 –의 변형, –의 변주 ❑ 오믈렛의 이 맛있는 변형은 빠르고 손쉽게 만들 수 있다. **2** 가산명사 또는 불가산명사 변화; (정도의) 차이 ❑ 조사 결과 구내식당 음식 가격에 많은 차이가 있음이 드러났다.

vari|ied /véɪrid/ ADJ Something that is **varied** consists of things of different types, sizes, or qualities. ❑ *It is essential that your diet is varied and balanced.* →see also **vary**

형용사 다양한 ❑ 다양하고 균형 잡힌 식사를 하는 것이 매우 중요하다.

vari|ety ♦♦◇ /vəráɪɪti/ (**varieties**) **1** N-UNCOUNT If something has **variety**, it consists of things which are different from each other. ❑ *Susan's idea of freedom was to have variety in her life style.* **2** N-SING A **variety of** things is a number of different kinds or examples of the same thing. ❑ *West Hampstead has a variety of good shops and supermarkets.* ❑ *The island offers such a wide variety of scenery and wildlife.* **3** N-COUNT A **variety of** something is a type of it. ❑ *I'm always pleased to try out a new variety.*

1 불가산명사 다양성, 변화 ❑ 수잔의 자유에 대한 생각은 자신의 생활 양식에 다양성을 갖는 것이었다. **2** 단수명사 갖가지, 각양각색 ❑ 웨스트 햄프스테드에는 각종 좋은 가게와 슈퍼마켓이 있다. ❑ 그 섬에는 너무도 다양한 갖가지 경치와 야생 생물들이 있다. **3** 가산명사 종류 ❑ 나는 항상 새로운 종류를 시험해 사용해 보는 것을 즐긴다.

Thesaurus
*variety*의 참조어

N.	assortment, diversity, variation; (ant.) uniformity **2**
	breed, sort, type **3**

Word Partnership
*variety*의 연어

N.	variety **of activities**, variety **of colors**, variety **of foods**,
	variety **of issues**, variety **of problems**, variety **of products**,
	variety **of reasons**, variety **of sizes**, variety **of styles**,
	variety **of ways** **2**
V.	**choose** a variety, **offer** a variety, **provide** a variety **2**

---

vari|ous ♦♦◇ /véɪriəs/ **1** ADJ If you say that there are **various** things, you mean there are several different things of the type mentioned. ❑ *His plan is to spread the capital between various building society accounts.* **2** ADJ If a number of things are described as **various**, they are very different from one another. ❑ *The methods are many and various.*

1 형용사 여러 개의 ❑ 그의 계획은 여러 개의 주택 금융 기관 계좌에 자본을 분산하는 것이다. **2** 형용사 다양한, 가지각색의 ❑ 방법은 많고 다양하다.

vari|ous|ly /véɪriəsli/ ADV You can use **variously** to introduce a number of different ways in which something can be described. ❑ *...the crowds, which were variously estimated at two to several thousand.*

부사 여러 가지로 ❑ 2천에서 수천까지 여러 가지로 달리 추산되는 군중

var|nish /vɑ́rnɪʃ/ (**varnishes, varnishing, varnished**) **1** N-MASS **Varnish** is an oily liquid which is painted onto wood or other material to give it a hard, clear, shiny surface. ❑ *The varnish comes in six natural wood shades.* **2** V-T If you **varnish** something, you paint it with varnish. ❑ *Varnish the table with two or three coats of water-based varnish.*

1 물질명사 광택제, 니스 ❑ 그 광택제는 여섯 가지 천연 원목색으로 나온다. **2** 타동사 광택제를 칠하다 ❑ 탁자에 수성 광택제를 두세 겹 칠하시오.

vary ♦♦◇ /véɪri/ (**varies, varying, varied**) **1** V-I If things **vary**, they are different from each other in size, amount, or degree. ❑ *As they're handmade, each one varies slightly.* ❑ *The text varies from the earlier versions.* **2** V-T/V-I If something **varies** or if you **vary** it, it becomes different or changed. ❑ *The cost of the alcohol duty varies according to the amount of wine in the bottle.* **3** →see also **varied**

1 자동사 다르다 ❑ 그것들은 손으로 만들기 때문에 제각각 조금씩 다르다. ❑ 그 판본은 이전 판들과는 다르다. **2** 타동사/자동사 변화하다, 달라지다; 달리하다, 변화를 주다 ❑ 주세는 병에 든 와인의 양에 따라 달라진다.

Word Partnership
*vary*의 연어

N.	**prices** vary, **rates** vary, **styles** vary **1**
	vary **by location**, vary **by size**, vary **by state**, vary **by store** **1 2**
ADV.	vary **greatly**, vary **slightly** **1 2**

vase /veɪs, vaz, BRIT vɑːz/ (**vases**) N-COUNT A **vase** is a jar, usually made of glass or pottery, used for holding cut flowers or as an ornament. ❑ *...a vase of red roses.*

가산명사 꽃병 ❑ 붉은 장미가 담긴 꽃병

vast ♦◇◇ /væst/ (**vaster, vastest**) ADJ Something that is **vast** is extremely large. ❑ *...Afrikaner farmers who own vast stretches of land.*

형용사 거대한, 광대한 ❑ 거대한 땅을 소유한 남아공의 백인 농장주들

Thesaurus   *vast*의 참조어

ADJ.   broad, endless, large, massive; (ant.) limited

Word Partnership   *vast*의 연어

N.   vast **amounts**, vast **distance**, vast **expanse**, vast **knowledge**, vast **majority**, vast **quantities**

---

vast|ly /væstli/ ADV **Vastly** means to an extremely great degree or extent. ❑ *The jury has heard two vastly different accounts of what happened.*

부사 대단히, 엄청나게 ❑ 배심원단은 일어난 일에 대해 두 가지의 아주 서로 다른 이야기를 들었다.

VAT /vi ti, væt/ N-UNCOUNT **VAT** is a tax that is added to the price of goods or services. **VAT** is an abbreviation for **value added tax**. ❑ *All prices include VAT.* [BRIT]

불가산명사 부가 가치세, value added tax의 약자 ❑ 모든 가격은 부가 가치세를 포함한다. [영국영어]

Vati|can /vætɪkən/ N-PROPER **The Vatican** is the city state in Rome ruled by the Pope which is the center of the Roman Catholic Church. You can also use **the Vatican** to refer to the Pope or his officials. ❑ *The president had an audience with the Pope in the Vatican.*

고유명사 바티칸 시국; 로마 교황청 ❑ 대통령은 바티칸에서 교황과 공식 회견을 가졌다.

vault /vɔlt/ (**vaults, vaulting, vaulted**) ◼ N-COUNT A **vault** is a secure room where money and other valuable things can be kept safely. ❑ *Most of the money was in storage in bank vaults.* ◻ N-COUNT A **vault** is a room underneath a church or in a cemetery where people are buried, usually the members of a single family. ❑ *He ordered that Matilda's body should be buried in the family vault.* ◾ V-T/V-I If you **vault** something or **vault over** it, you jump quickly onto or over it, especially by putting a hand on top of it to help you balance while you jump. ❑ *He could easily vault the wall.*

◼ 가산명사 금고실 ❑ 대부분의 돈은 은행 금고에 보관되어 있었다. ◻ 가산명사 납골당 ❑ 그는 마틸다의 유해를 가족 납골당에 묻도록 지시했다. ◾ 타동사/자동사 뛰어넘다 ❑ 그는 그 벽을 쉽게 뛰어넘을 수 있을 것이다.

VCR /vi si ar/ (**VCRs**) N-COUNT A **VCR** is a machine that can be used to record television programmes or films onto videotapes, so that people can play them back and watch them later on a television set. **VCR** is an abbreviation for "video cassette recorder." ❑ *Panasonic's Program Director lets you program your VCR so easily!*

가산명사 비디오 녹화기, video cassette recorder의 약자 ❑ 파나소닉의 프로그램 디렉터를 쓰면 비디오 녹화기를 아주 쉽게 조작할 수 있습니다!

VDT /vi di ti/ (**VDTs**) N-COUNT A **VDT** is a machine with a screen which is used to display information from a computer. **VDT** is an abbreviation for "video display terminal." [mainly AM; BRIT usually **VDU**]

가산명사 화상 표시기, video display terminal의 약자 [주로 미국영어; 영국영어 대개 VDU]

VDU /vi di yu/ (**VDUs**) N-COUNT A **VDU** is the same as a **VDT**. **VDU** is an abbreviation for "visual display unit." [BRIT] ❑ *I work at a VDU screen for hours each day.*

가산명사 화상 표시기, visual display unit의 약자 [영국영어] ❑ 나는 매일 몇 시간씩 화상 표시기 화면 앞에서 일한다.

veal /vil/ N-UNCOUNT **Veal** is meat from a calf. ❑ *...a veal cutlet.*

불가산명사 송아지고기 ❑ 송아지고기 커틀릿

veer /vɪər/ (**veers, veering, veered**) ◼ V-I If something **veers** in a certain direction, it suddenly moves in that direction. ❑ *The plane veered off the runway and careered through the perimeter fence.* ◻ V-I If someone or something **veers** in a certain direction, they change their position or direction in a particular situation. ❑ *He is unlikely to veer from his boss's strongly held views.*

◼ 자동사 (~ 쪽으로 갑자기) 움직이다 ❑ 그 비행기가 갑자기 활주로를 벗어나서 경계 벽을 뚫고 나갔다. ◻ 자동사 방향을 바꾸다 ❑ 그가 자기 사장의 고집스런 생각에서 벗어날 수 있을 것 같지 않다.

Word Link   an, ian ≈ one of, relating to : Christian, pedestrian, vegan

---

ve|gan /vigən/ (**vegans**) ADJ Someone who is **vegan** never eats meat or any animal products such as milk, butter, or cheese. ❑ *The menu changes weekly and usually includes a vegan option.* ● N-COUNT A **vegan** is someone who is vegan. ❑ *...vegetarians and vegans.* →see **vegetarian**

형용사 (유제품도 먹지 않는) 극단적 채식주의자의 ❑ 식단은 매주 바뀌며 대개 극단적 채식주의자가 선택할 수 있는 것도 포함한다. ● 가산명사 극단적 채식주의자 ❑ 채식주의자와 극단적 채식주의자

vege|ta|ble ♦◇◇ /vedʒtəbªl, vedʒə-/ (**vegetables**) ◼ N-COUNT **Vegetables** are plants such as cabbages, potatoes, and onions which you can cook and eat. ❑ *A good general diet should include plenty of fresh vegetables.* ◻ ADJ **Vegetable** matter comes from plants. [FORMAL] ❑ *...compounds of animal, vegetable or mineral origin.* →see **vegetarian** →see Word Web: **vegetables**

◼ 가산명사 야채 ❑ 좋은 일반적 식단은 신선한 야채를 많이 포함해야 한다. ◻ 형용사 식물성 [격식체] ❑ 동물, 식물, 또는 광물성 혼합물

vege|tar|ian /vedʒɪtɛəriən/ (**vegetarians**) ◼ ADJ Someone who is **vegetarian** never eats meat or fish. ❑ *Yasmin sticks to a strict vegetarian diet.* ● N-COUNT A **vegetarian** is someone who is vegetarian. ❑ *...a special menu for vegetarians.* ◻ ADJ **Vegetarian** food does not contain any meat or fish. ❑ *...vegetarian lasagnes.* →see Word Web: **vegetarian**

◼ 형용사 채식주의자의 ❑ 야스민은 엄격한 채식주의 식단만을 고수한다. ● 가산명사 채식주의자 ❑ 채식주의자를 위한 특별 식단 ◻ 형용사 야채만의 ❑ 야채로 만든 라자냐

Word Web   vegetables

Fresh vegetables are good for you! They're low in fat and calories so they may help you lose weight. **Broccoli** contains vitamin C. It can help you avoid colds and other infections. **Carrots** are a good source of vitamin A, which is good for the eyes. Because they grow in soil, vegetables also contain minerals such as calcium and iron. These substances help keep bones, teeth, and hair healthy. **Leafy** green vegetables like **cabbage** contain antioxidants. These natural chemicals may help prevent cancer. Vegetables also contain **fiber**. This aids digestion and helps carry toxins out of the body quickly.

a
b
c
d
e
f
g
h
i
j
k
l
m
n
o
p
q
r
s
t
u
v
w
x
y
z

Word Web   vegetarian

The Greek philosopher Pythagoras was a **vegetarian**. He believed that as long as humans kept killing animals, they would keep killing each other. He decided not to eat **meat**. Vegetarians eat more than just **vegetables**. They also eat fruits, grains, oils, fats, and sugar. **Vegans** are vegetarians who don't eat eggs or dairy products. Some people choose this **diet** for health reasons. A well-balanced veggie diet can be healthy. Some people choose this diet for religious reasons. Others want to make the world's **food** supply go further. It takes fifteen pounds of grain to produce one pound of meat.

veg|eta|tion /vɛdʒɪteɪʃⁿn/ N-UNCOUNT Plants, trees, and flowers can be referred to as **vegetation**. [FORMAL] ❑ *The inn has a garden of semi-tropical vegetation.* →see **erosion**

불가산명사 초목, 식물 [격식체] ❑ 그 여관에는 반열대성 식물 정원이 있다.

ve|he|ment /viəmənt/ ADJ If a person or their actions or comments are **vehement**, the person has very strong feelings or opinions and expresses them forcefully. ❑ *She suddenly became very vehement and agitated, jumping around and shouting.* ● **ve|he|mence** N-UNCOUNT ❑ *He spoke more loudly and with more vehemence than he had intended.* ● **ve|he|ment|ly** ADV ❑ *Krabbe has always vehemently denied using drugs.*

형용사 격렬한, 맹렬한 ❑ 그녀는 갑자기 이리저리 뛰고 고함지르면서 매우 격렬해지며 흥분했다. ● 격렬함 불가산명사 ❑ 그는 의도한 것보다 더 크고 격렬하게 말했다. ● 격렬하게 부사 ❑ 크랩은 항상 약물 사용을 강하게 부인해 왔다.

ve|hi|cle ♦♦◇ /viːkⁿl/ (**vehicles**) ■ N-COUNT A **vehicle** is a machine with an engine, for example a bus, car, or truck, that carries people or things from place to place. ❑ *...a vehicle which was somewhere between a tractor and a truck.* ☑ N-COUNT You can use **vehicle** to refer to something that you use in order to achieve a particular purpose. ❑ *Her art became a vehicle for her political beliefs.* →see **car, traffic**

■ 가산명사 차량, 운송 수단 ❑ 트랙터와 트럭의 중간쯤 되는 차량 ☑ 가산명사 매개, 수단 ❑ 그녀의 미술은 자신의 정치적 신념을 표현하는 수단이 되었다.

veil /veɪl/ (**veils**) ■ N-COUNT A **veil** is a piece of thin soft cloth that women sometimes wear over their heads and which can also cover their face. ❑ *She's got long fair hair but she's got a veil over it.* ☑ N-COUNT You can refer to something that hides or partly hides a situation or activity as a **veil**. ❑ *The country is ridding itself of its disgraced prime minister in a veil of secrecy.* ☑ N-COUNT You can refer to something that you can partly see through, for example a mist, as a **veil**. [LITERARY] ❑ *The eruption has left a thin veil of dust in the upper atmosphere.*

■ 가산명사 베일, 면사포 ❑ 그녀는 긴 금발인데 그 위에 베일을 쓰고 있다. ☑ 가산명사 장막 ❑ 그 나라는 명예가 실추된 자기 나라 수상을 비밀리에 제거하고 있다. ☑ 가산명사 엷은 막 [문예체] ❑ 그 화산 폭발로 상층 대기권에 엷은 먼지 막이 생겼다.

veiled /veɪld/ ■ ADJ A **veiled** comment is expressed in a disguised form rather than directly and openly. [ADJ n] ❑ *He made only a veiled reference to international concerns over human rights issues.* ☑ ADJ A woman or girl who is **veiled** is wearing a veil. ❑ *A veiled woman gave me a kindly smile.*

■ 형용사 숨겨진, 가려진 ❑ 그는 인권 문제에 대한 국제적 우려에 관해 간접적인 언급만을 했다. ☑ 형용사 베일을 쓴 ❑ 어떤 베일을 쓴 여인이 내게 친절한 미소를 보냈다.

vein /veɪn/ (**veins**) ■ N-COUNT Your **veins** are the thin tubes in your body through which your blood flows toward your heart. Compare **artery**. ❑ *Many veins are found just under the skin.* ☑ N-COUNT Something that is written or spoken in a particular **vein** is written or spoken in that style or mood. ❑ *It is one of his finest works in a lighter vein.* ☑ N-COUNT A **vein of** a particular quality is evidence of that quality which someone often shows in their behavior or work. ❑ *A rich vein of humor runs through the book.* ☑ N-COUNT The **veins** on a leaf are the thin lines on it. ❑ *...the serrated edges and veins of the feathery leaves.*

■ 가산명사 정맥 ❑ 정맥은 피부 바로 아래에 많이 있다. ☑ 가산명사 분위기, 스타일 ❑ 그것은 좀 더 가벼운 분위기를 지닌 그의 걸작 중 하나이다. ☑ 가산명사 맥, 흔적 ❑ 풍부한 해학의 맥이 시종일관 그 책 속에 흐른다. ☑ 가산명사 잎맥 ❑ 깃털 같은 잎들의 톱니 모양 가장자리와 잎맥

ve|loc|ity /vəlɒsɪti/ (**velocities**) N-VAR **Velocity** is the speed at which something moves in a particular direction. [TECHNICAL] ❑ *...the velocities at which the stars orbit.*

가산명사 또는 불가산명사 속도 [과학 기술] ❑ 별들이 공전하는 속도

vel|vet /vɛlvɪt/ (**velvets**) N-MASS **Velvet** is soft material made from cotton, silk, or nylon, which has a thick layer of short cut threads on one side. ❑ *...a charcoal-gray overcoat with a velvet collar.*

물질명사 벨벳, 우단 ❑ 벨벳 깃이 달린 짙은 회색 외투

ven|det|ta /vɛndetə/ (**vendettas**) N-VAR If one person has a **vendetta against** another, the first person wants revenge for something the second person did to them in the past. ❑ *The vice president said the cartoonist has a personal vendetta against him.*

가산명사 또는 불가산명사 앙갚음, 복수 ❑ 부통령은 만화가가 자기에게 개인적인 앙갚음을 하고 싶어 한다고 말했다.

vend|ing ma|chine /vɛndɪŋ məʃiːn/ (**vending machines**) N-COUNT A **vending machine** is a machine from which you can get things such as cigarettes, chocolate, or coffee by putting in money and pressing a button.

가산명사 자동판매기

ven|dor /vɛndər/ (**vendors**) ■ N-COUNT A **vendor** is someone who sells things such as newspapers, cigarettes, or food from a small stall or cart. ❑ *...ice-cream vendors.* ☑ N-COUNT The **vendor** of a house or piece of land is the person who owns it and is selling it. [LEGAL] ❑ *The estate agent is working for the vendor, from whom he will be receiving his commission.*

■ 가산명사 노점상인 ❑ 아이스크림 노점상들 ☑ 가산명사 (집 또는 토지의) 매도인 [법률] ❑ 그 부동산 중개업자는 매도인을 위해 일하는데 그에게서 자기 몫의 수수료를 받을 것이다.

ve|neer /vɪnɪər/ (**veneers**) ■ N-SING If you refer to the pleasant way that someone or something appears as a **veneer**, you are critical of them because you believe that their true, hidden nature is not good. [DISAPPROVAL] ❑ *He was able to fool the world with his veneer of education.* ☑ N-VAR **Veneer** is a thin layer of wood or plastic which is used to improve the appearance of something. ❑ *The wood was cut into large sheets of veneer.*

■ 단수명사 겉치장, 허식 [탐탁찮음] ❑ 그는 교육받은 사람인 체하면서 세상을 속일 수 있었다. ☑ 가산명사 또는 불가산명사 베니어판, 화장판 ❑ 그 목재는 큰 베니어판들로 잘려졌다.

ven|er|able /vɛnərəbⁿl/ ■ ADJ A **venerable** person deserves respect because they are old and wise. ❑ *Her Chinese friends referred to the Empress as their venerable ancestor.* ☑ ADJ Something that is **venerable** is impressive because it is old or important historically. ❑ *May Day has become a venerable institution.*

■ 형용사 공경할 만한, 덕망 있는 ❑ 그녀의 중국 친구들은 그 황후를 자기들의 존경스런 조상이라 불렀다. ☑ 형용사 유서 깊은, 숭고한 ❑ 노동절은 숭고한 제도가 되었다.

venge|ance /vɛndʒⁿns/ ■ N-UNCOUNT **Vengeance** is the act of killing, injuring, or harming someone because they have harmed you. ❑ *He swore vengeance on everyone involved in the murder.* ☑ PHRASE If you say that something happens **with a vengeance**, you are emphasizing that it happens to a much greater extent than was expected. [EMPHASIS] ❑ *It began to rain again with a vengeance.*

■ 불가산명사 복수, 앙갚음 ❑ 그는 그 살인에 연루된 모든 사람들에 대해 복수를 맹세했다. ☑ 구 맹렬히 [강조] ❑ 비가 다시 맹렬히 내리기 시작했다.

ven|i|son /ˈvɛnɪsᵊn, -zᵊn/ N-UNCOUNT Venison is the meat of a deer. ❑ ...*a wonderful lunch of salmon salad and roast venison.*

불가산명사 사슴고기 ❑ 연어 샐러드와 오븐 구이 사슴고기로 된 멋진 점심

ven|om /ˈvɛnəm/ (venoms) ◢ N-UNCOUNT You can use **venom** to refer to someone's feelings of great bitterness and anger toward someone. ❑ *He reserved particular venom for critics of his foreign policy.* ◢ N-MASS The **venom** of a creature such as a snake or spider is the poison that it puts into your body when it bites or stings you. ❑ *...snake handlers who grow immune to snake venom.*

◢ 불가산명사 앙심, 원한 ❑ 그는 자기 외교 정책을 비판하는 사람들에게 유독 앙심을 품었다. ◢ 물질명사 (뱀 등의) 독, 독액 ❑ 뱀의 독에 면역이 생기는 땅꾼들

ven|om|ous /ˈvɛnəməs/ ◢ ADJ If you describe a person or their behavior as **venomous**, you mean that they show great bitterness and anger towards someone. ❑ *...his terrifying and venomous Aunt Bridget.* ◢ ADJ A **venomous** snake, spider, or other creature uses poison to attack other creatures. ❑ *The adder is Britain's only venomous snake.*

◢ 형용사 악의에 찬 ❑ 그의 무섭고 악의에 찬 브리지트 숙모 ◢ 형용사 독이 있는 ❑ 살무사는 영국에 있는 유일한 독사이다.

vent /vɛnt/ (vents, venting, vented) ◢ N-COUNT A **vent** is a hole in something through which air can come in and smoke, gas, or smells can go out. ❑ *Quite a lot of steam escaped from the vent at the front of the machine.* ◢ V-T If you **vent** your feelings, you express them forcefully. ❑ *She telephoned her best friend to vent her frustration.* ◢ PHRASE If you **give vent to** your feelings, you express them forcefully. [FORMAL] ❑ *She gave vent to her anger and jealousy.*

◢ 가산명사 환풍구, 통풍구 ❑ 상당히 많은 증기가 그 기계 앞의 통풍구에서 빠져 나갔다. ◢ 타동사 (감정을) 터뜨리다 ❑ 그녀는 가장 친한 친구에게 전화를 걸어 자기의 좌절감을 토로했다. ◢ 구 (감정을) 터뜨리다, 발산하다 [격식체] ❑ 그녀는 노여움과 질투심을 발산했다.

ven|ti|late /ˈvɛntᵊleɪt/ (ventilates, ventilating, ventilated) V-T If you **ventilate** a room or building, you allow fresh air to get into it. ❑ *Ventilate the room properly when paint stripping.* ● **ven|ti|la|tion** /ˌvɛntᵊleɪʃᵊn/ N-UNCOUNT ❑ *The only ventilation comes from tiny sliding windows.*

타동사 환기하다 ❑ 페인트를 벗겨 낼 때에는 방을 환기를 잘 하시오. ● 환기 불가산명사 ❑ 작은 미닫이창들을 통해서만 환기가 된다.

ven|ture ◆◇◇ /ˈvɛntʃər/ (ventures, venturing, ventured) ◢ N-COUNT A **venture** is a project or activity which is new, exciting, and difficult because it involves the risk of failure. ❑ *...a Russian-American joint venture.* ◢ V-I If you **venture** somewhere, you go somewhere that might be dangerous. [LITERARY] ❑ *People are afraid to venture out for fear of sniper attacks.* ◢ V-T If you **venture** a question or statement, you say it in an uncertain way because you are afraid it might be stupid or wrong. [WRITTEN] ❑ *"So you're Leo's girlfriend?" he ventured.* ❑ *He ventured that plants draw part of their nourishment from the air.* ◢ V-T If you **venture** to do something that requires courage or is risky, you do it. ❑ *"Don't ask," he said, whenever Ginny ventured to raise the subject.* ◢ V-I If you **venture into** an activity, you do something that involves the risk of failure because it is new and different. ❑ *He enjoyed little success when he ventured into business.*

◢ 가산명사 벤처, 모험적 사업 ❑ 러시아와 미국의 합작 벤처 ◢ 자동사 위험을 무릅쓰고 가다 [문어체] ❑ 사람들은 저격병의 공격이 두려워서 감히 밖으로 나갈 용기를 내지 못한다. ◢ 타동사 주저하며 말하다 [문어체] ❑ "그래 당신이 리오의 여자 친구라고요?"라고 그가 머뭇거리며 말했다. ❑ 그는 식물이 공기로부터 일부 양분을 흡수한다고 주저하며 말했다. ◢ 타동사 감히 –하다 ❑ 지니가 감히 그 문제를 꺼내 보면 그때마다 그는 "묻지 마."라고 말했다. ◢ 자동사 위험을 무릅쓰고 –을 하다 ❑ 그는 위험을 무릅쓰고 사업을 해서 별로 재미를 못 보았다.

ven|ture capi|tal N-UNCOUNT **Venture capital** is capital that is invested in projects that have a high risk of failure, but that will bring large profits if they are successful. [BUSINESS] ❑ *Successful venture capital investment is a lot harder than it sometimes looks.*

불가산명사 벤처 투기 자본 [경제] ❑ 벤처 자본 투자가 성공하기는 가끔 생각보다 훨씬 더 어렵다.

ven|ture capi|tal|ist (venture capitalists) N-COUNT A **venture capitalist** is someone who makes money by investing in high risk projects. [BUSINESS]

가산명사 위험 투자가 [경제]

ven|ue ◆◇◇ /ˈvɛnjuː/ (venues) N-COUNT The **venue** for an event or activity is the place where it will happen. ❑ *Birmingham's International Convention Centre is the venue for a three-day arts festival.* →see **concert**

가산명사 (행사 등의) 장소 ❑ 버밍엄의 국제 컨벤션 센터가 3일간 예술 축제가 열릴 장소이다.

ve|ran|da /vəˈrændə/ (verandas) also **verandah** N-COUNT A **veranda** is a roofed platform along the outside of a house. ❑ *They had their coffee and tea on the veranda.*

가산명사 베란다 ❑ 그들은 베란다에서 커피와 차를 마셨다.

verb /vɜːrb/ (verbs) N-COUNT A **verb** is a word such as "sing," "feel," or "die" which is used with a subject to say what someone or something does or what happens to them, or to give information about them. →see also **phrasal verb**

가산명사 동사

Word Link	verb ≈ word : *proverb*, *verbal*, *verbatim*

ver|bal /ˈvɜːrbᵊl/ ◢ ADJ You use **verbal** to indicate that something is expressed in speech rather than in writing or action. ❑ *They were jostled and subjected to a torrent of verbal abuse.* ● **ver|bal|ly** ADV ❑ *Teachers were threatened with kitchen knives, physically assaulted, and verbally abused.* ◢ ADJ You use **verbal** to indicate that something is connected with words and the use of words. ❑ *The test has scores for verbal skills, mathematical skills, and abstract reasoning skills.* ◢ ADJ In grammar, **verbal** means relating to a verb. ❑ *...a verbal noun.*

◢ 형용사 말의 ❑ 그들은 떠밀리고 마구 퍼붓는 욕설을 들었다. ● 말로 부사 ❑ 교사들은 식칼로 위협을 받고, 폭행을 당하고, 욕설을 들었다. ◢ 형용사 언어의 ❑ 그 시험에서는 언어 능력, 수학 능력, 추상적 추론 능력에 대해 점수를 매긴다. ◢ 형용사 동사의 ❑ 동사적 명사

ver|ba|tim /vɜːrˈbeɪtɪm/ ADV If you repeat something **verbatim**, you use exactly the same words as were used originally. [ADV after v] ❑ *The President's speeches are regularly reproduced verbatim in the state-run newspapers.* ● ADJ **Verbatim** is also an adjective. [ADJ n] ❑ *I was treated to a verbatim report of every conversation she's taken part in over the past week.*

부사 글자 그대로, 말 그대로 ❑ 대통령의 연설은 정기적으로 국영 신문에 그대로 전재된다. ● 형용사 글자 그대로의 ❑ 나는 지난 한 주 동안 그녀가 참석한 모든 대화를 한 자도 빼놓지 않고 보고받았다.

ver|dict ◆◇◇ /ˈvɜːrdɪkt/ (verdicts) ◢ N-COUNT In a court of law, the **verdict** is the decision that is given by the jury or judge at the end of a trial. ❑ *The jury returned a unanimous guilty verdict.* ◢ N-COUNT Someone's **verdict** on something is their opinion of it, after thinking about it or investigating it. ❑ *The doctor's verdict was that he was entirely healthy.* →see **trial**

◢ 가산명사 평결, 판결 ❑ 배심원단은 만장일치로 유죄 평결을 제출했다. ◢ 가산명사 의견 ❑ 의사의 소견은 그가 완전히 건강하다는 것이었다.

verge /vɜːrdʒ/ (verges, verging, verged) ◢ PHRASE If you are **on the verge of** something, you are going to do it very soon or it is likely to begin or happen very soon. ❑ *The country was on the verge of becoming prosperous and successful.* ◢ N-COUNT The **verge** of a road is a narrow piece of ground by the side of a road, which is usually covered with grass or flowers. [mainly BRIT; AM usually **shoulder**] ❑ *The ambulance veered off the road and onto a grass verge.*

◢ 구 –하기 직전에 ❑ 그 나라는 번영과 성공의 문턱에 있었다. ◢ 가산명사 길가 풀밭, 길가 화단 [주로 영국영어; 미국영어 대개 shoulder] ❑ 그 구급차가 도로를 벗어나 길가 풀밭으로 올라갔다.

▶ **verge on** PHRASAL VERB If someone or something **verges on** a particular state or quality, they are almost the same as that state or quality. ❑ *...a fury that verged on madness.*

구동사 (상태 등이) –에 가깝다 ❑ 광기에 가까운 분노

veri|fy /ˈvɛrɪfaɪ/ (verifies, verifying, verified) ◢ V-T If you **verify** something, you check that it is true by careful examination or investigation. ❑ *I verified the source from which I had that information.* ● **veri|fi|ca|tion** /ˌvɛrɪfɪkeɪʃᵊn/ N-UNCOUNT

◢ 타동사 입증하다, 확인하다 ❑ 나는 내가 그 정보를 얻은 출처를 확인했다. ● 입증, 확인 불가산명사 ❑ 그녀의 이야기가 확인될 때까지 그녀에 대한 모든

A □ *All charges against her are dropped pending the verification of her story.* ◻ V-T If you **verify** something, you state or confirm that it is true. [no cont] □ *The government has not verified any of those reports.*

고소가 취하되었다. ◻ 타동사 확인하다, 확인해 주다 □ 정부는 그 보도들에 대해 아무것도 확인해 주지 않았다.

B **veri|table** /vɛrɪtəbəl/ ADJ You can use **veritable** to emphasize the size, amount, or nature of something. [EMPHASIS] □ *...a veritable feast of pre-match entertainment.*

형용사 진정한 [강조] □ 시합 전 여흥의 진정한 향연

C **ver|nacu|lar** /vərnækyələr/ (**vernaculars**) N-COUNT The **vernacular** is the language or dialect that is most widely spoken by ordinary people in a region or country. □ *...books or plays written in the vernacular.*

가산명사 자국어, 토착어 □ 토착어로 쓰인 책이나 희곡들

D

Word Link	*vers* ≈ turning : sub*version*, *versatile*, *version*

E **ver|sa|tile** /vɜrsətªl, BRIT vɜːˈsətaɪl/ ADJ If you say that a person is **versatile**, you approve of them because they have many different skills. [APPROVAL] □ *He had been one of the game's most versatile athletes.* ● **ver|sa|til|ity** /vɜrsətɪlɪti/ N-UNCOUNT □ *Aileen stands out for her incredible versatility as an actress.* ◻ ADJ A tool, machine, or material that is **versatile** can be used for many different purposes. □ *Never before has computing been so versatile.* ● **ver|sa|til|ity** N-UNCOUNT □ *Velvet is not known for its versatility.*

F ◼ 형용사 다재다능한 [마음에 듦] □ 그는 그 경기에서 가장 다재다능한 선수 중 한 명이었다. ● 다재다능함 불가산명사 □ 아일린은 배우로서 놀라운 다재다능함이 돋보인다. ◻ 형용사 다목적의, 다용도의 □ 컴퓨터가 지금처럼 이렇게 다양하게 쓰인 적이 없었다. ● 다목적성 불가산명사 □ 벨벳은 용도가 다양하지 않다.

G **verse** /vɜrs/ (**verses**) ◼ N-UNCOUNT **Verse** is writing arranged in lines which have rhythm and which often rhyme at the end. □ *I have been moved to write a few lines of verse.* ◻ N-COUNT A **verse** is one of the parts into which a poem, a song, or a chapter of the Bible or the Koran is divided. □ *This verse describes three signs of spring.*

◼ 불가산명사 운문, 시 □ 나는 시를 몇 줄 쓰고 싶은 감흥이 들었다. ◻ 가산명사 (시의) 연, (노래 등의) 절 □ 이 연은 봄의 세 가지 전조를 묘사한다.

H

I **ver|sion** ♦♦◇ /vɜrʒªn/ (**versions**) ◼ N-COUNT A **version** of something is a particular form of it in which some details are different from earlier or later forms. □ *...an updated version of his book.* □ *Ludo is a version of an ancient Indian racing game.* ◻ N-COUNT Someone's **version** of an event is their own description of it, especially when it is different from other people's. □ *Some former hostages contradicted the official version of events.*

◼ 가산명사 ~판; 변형 □ 그의 책의 최신 개정판 □ 루도는 고대 인디언들 경주 놀이의 변형이다. ◻ 가산명사 설명, 견해 □ 몇 명의 과거 인질들이 사건에 대한 공식적인 설명을 반박했다.

J

K **ver|sus** /vɜrsəs/ ◼ PREP You use **versus** to indicate that two figures, ideas, or choices are opposed. □ *Only 18.8% of the class of 1982 had some kind of diploma four years after high school, versus 45% of the class of 1972.* ◻ PREP **Versus** is used to indicate that two teams or people are competing against each other in a sports event. □ *Italy versus Japan is turning out to be a surprisingly well matched competition.*

◼ 전치사 ~에 대비하여 □ 1972년도 입학생의 학급당 45퍼센트에 대비하여, 1982년도 학급은 18.8퍼센트만이 고등학교 졸업 후 4년 만에 일종의 수료증을 받았다. ◻ 전치사 ~ 대(對) □ 이태리 대 일본전은 의외로 호적수의 경기인 것으로 드러나고 있다.

L **ver|te|bra** /vɜrtɪbreɪ, -bri/ (**vertebrae**) /vɜrtɪbreɪ/ N-COUNT **Vertebrae** are the small circular bones that form the spine of a human being or animal.

가산명사 등뼈, 척추

M

N **ver|ti|cal** /vɜrtɪkªl/ ADJ Something that is **vertical** stands or points straight up. □ *The climber inched up a vertical wall of rock.* ● **ver|ti|cal|ly** ADV [ADV after v] □ *Cut each bulb in half vertically.* →see **graph**

형용사 수직의 □ 그 등반가는 수직 암벽을 조금씩 올라갔다. ● 수직으로 부사 □ 각 알뿌리를 수직으로 반씩 자르시오.

O **very** ♦♦♦ /vɛri/ ◼ ADV **Very** is used to give emphasis to an adjective or adverb. [EMPHASIS] [ADV adj/adv] □ *The problem and the answer are very simple.* □ *I'm very sorry.* □ *They are getting the hang of it very quickly.* ◻ PHRASE **Not very** is used with an adjective or adverb to say that something is not at all true, or that it is true only to a small degree. □ *She's not very impressed with them.* □ *"How well do you know her?" — "Not very."* ◾ ADV You use **very** to give emphasis to a superlative adjective or adverb. For example, if you say that something is **the very best**, you are emphasizing that it is the best. [EMPHASIS] [ADV superl] □ *They will be helped by the very latest in navigation aids.* □ *I am feeling in the very best of spirits.* ◼ ADJ You use **very** with certain nouns in order to specify an extreme position or extreme point in time. [EMPHASIS] [ADJ n] □ *At the very back of the yard was a wooden shack.* □ *I turned to the very end of the book, to read the final words.* ◼ ADJ You use **very** with nouns to emphasize that something is exactly the right one or exactly the same one. [EMPHASIS] [ADJ n] □ *Everybody says he is the very man for the case.* ◼ ADJ You use **very** with nouns to emphasize the importance or seriousness of what you are saying. [EMPHASIS] [ADJ n] □ *At one stage his very life was in danger.* □ *History is taking place before your very eyes.* ◼ PHRASE The expression **very much so** is an emphatic way of answering "yes" to something or saying that it is true or correct. [EMPHASIS] □ *"Are you enjoying your holiday?" — "Very much so."* ◼ CONVENTION **Very well** is used to say that you agree to do something or you accept someone's answer, even though you might not be completely satisfied with it. [FORMULAE] □ *"We need proof, sir." Another pause. Then, "Very well."* ◼ PHRASE If you say that you **cannot very well** do something, you mean that it would not be right or possible to do it. □ *I said yes. I can't very well say no.*

P ◼ 부사 매우, 아주 [강조] □ 문제와 해답은 아주 간단하다. □ 정말 미안합니다. □ 그들은 아주 빨리 그것의 요령을 파악하고 있다. ◻ 구 전혀; 별로 □ 그녀는 그들에게서 전혀 감동받지 않았다. □ "그녀를 얼마나 잘 아니?" "별로." ◾ 부사 가장; 가장 좋은 것 [강조] □ 그들은 가장 최신식 항법 보조 기구의 도움을 받을 것이다. □ 나는 지금 기분이 최고로 좋다. ◼ 형용사 맨 ~ [강조] □ 뜰 맨 뒤에 나무 오두막이 하나 있었다. □ 나는 마지막 말을 읽으려고 책을 맨 뒤로 넘겼다. ◼ 형용사 바로 그 [강조] □ 모든 사람들이 그가 그 사건에 적임이라고 말한다. ◼ 형용사 바로 그, 다름 아닌 그 [강조] □ 어떤 단계에서는 다름 아닌 그의 목숨이 위험했다. □ 역사가 바로 당신의 눈앞에서 펼쳐지고 있다. ◼ 구 정말 그렇다 [강조] □ "휴가 잘 보내고 있나요?" "정말 잘 보내고 있어요." ◼ 관용 표현 그러지, 하는 수 없지 [의례적인 표현] □ "증거가 필요합니다, 선생님." 또 잠시 말이 없다. 그리고는, "그러죠." ◼ 구 쉽게 ~할 수 없다 □ 나는 승낙했지. 나는 쉽게 거절하지 못해.

Q

R

S

T

U

V Very, so, and too can all be used to intensify the meaning of an adjective, an adverb, or a word like **much** or **many**. However, they are not used in the same way. **Very** is the simplest intensifier. It has no other meaning beyond that. **So** can suggest an emotional reaction on the part of the speaker, such as pleasure, surprise, or disappointment. □ *John makes me so angry!... Oh thank you so much!* **So** can also refer forward to a result clause introduced by **that**. □ *The procession was forced to move so slowly that he arrived three hours late.* **Too** suggests an excessive or undesirable amount, often so much that a particular result does not or cannot happen. □ *She does wear too much makeup at times... He was too late to save her.*

W very, so, too는 모두 형용사나, 부사, 또 much나 many와 같은 단어의 의미를 강화하는 데 쓸 수 있다. 그러나, 이들이 모두 똑같이 쓰이지는 않는다. very는 가장 단순한 강화사이며 그 이상의 의미가 없다. so는 화자의 입장에서 기쁨, 놀람, 실망과 같은 감정적인 반응을 시사할 수 있다. □ 존 때문에 너무 화가 나!... 아, 너무나 감사합니다! so는 또 that이 이끄는 결과 절을 선행하여 지칭할 수도 있다. □ 그 행렬은 아주 천천히 움직일 수밖에 없어서 그는 세 시간이나 늦게 도착했다. too는 과도하거나 바람직하지 않을 정도임을 시사하는데, 흔히 그 정도가 너무 지나쳐서 특정한 결과가 일어나지 않거나 일어나지 못하게 된다. □ 그녀는 가끔 너무 지나치게 화장을 한다... 그는 너무 늦게 와서 그녀를 구할 수 없었다.

X

Y

Thesaurus	very의 참조어
ADV.	absolutely, extremely, greatly, highly ◼

Z

ves|sel ◆◇◇ /vɛsᵊl/ (vessels) **1** N-COUNT A **vessel** is a ship or large boat. [FORMAL] ❏ ...a New Zealand navy vessel. **2** →see also **blood vessel** →see **ship**

1 가산명사 배, 선박 [격식체] ❏ 뉴질랜드 군함

vest /vɛst/ (vests) **1** N-COUNT A **vest** is a sleeveless piece of clothing with buttons which people usually wear over a shirt. [AM; BRIT **waistcoat**] **2** N-COUNT A **vest** is a piece of underwear which you can wear on the top half of your body in order to keep warm. [BRIT; AM **undershirt**]

1 가산명사 조끼 [미국영어; 영국영어 waistcoat] **2** 가산명사 속옷 윗도리 [영국영어; 미국영어 undershirt]

vest|ed in|ter|est (vested interests) N-VAR If you have a **vested interest in** something, you have a very strong reason for acting in a particular way, for example to protect your money, power, or reputation. ❏ The administration has no vested interest in proving public schools good or bad.

가산명사 또는 불가산명사 기득 권익 ❏ 행정부는 공립학교를 좋거나 나쁘다고 입증하는 데 있어서 기득 권익이 없다.

ves|tige /vɛstɪdʒ/ (vestiges) N-COUNT A **vestige of** something is a very small part that still remains of something that was once much larger or more important. [FORMAL] ❏ We represent the last vestige of what made this nation great – hard work.

가산명사 자취, 흔적 [격식체] ❏ 우리는 이 나라를 위대하게 만들었던 것, 즉 근면의 마지막 자취를 대표한다.

vet /vɛt/ (vets, vetting, vetted) **1** N-COUNT A **vet** is someone who is qualified to treat sick or injured animals. [INFORMAL] ❏ She's at the vet, with her dog, right now. **2** N-COUNT A **vet** is someone who has served in the armed forces of their country, especially during a war. [AM, INFORMAL] ❏ The New England Shelter in Boston will serve Christmas dinner for 200 vets. **3** V-T If someone **is vetted**, they are investigated fully before being given a particular job, role, or position, especially one which involves military or political secrets. [usu passive] ❏ She was secretly vetted before she ever undertook any work for me. ● **vet|ting** N-UNCOUNT ❏ The government is to make major changes to the procedure for carrying out security vetting.

1 가산명사 수의사 [비격식체] ❏ 그녀는 지금 자기 개와 동물 병원에 가 있다. **2** 가산명사 참전 용사, 재향 군인 [미국영어, 비격식체] ❏ 보스턴의 뉴잉글랜드 쉘터는 200명의 참전 용사에게 성탄절 만찬을 열 것이다. **3** 타동사 신원 조회를 받다 ❏ 그녀는 나를 위해 무슨 일을 시작하기 전에 비밀리에 신원 조회를 했다. ● 신원 조회 불가산명사 ❏ 정부는 보안을 위한 신원 조회 과정을 대대적으로 바꾸려고 한다.

vet|er|an ◆◇◇ /vɛtᵊrən/ (veterans) **1** N-COUNT A **veteran** is someone who has served in the armed forces of their country, especially during a war. ❏ They approved a $1.1 billion package of pay increases for the veterans of the Persian Gulf War. **2** N-COUNT You use **veteran** to refer to someone who has been involved in a particular activity for a long time. ❏ ...Tony Benn, the veteran Labour MP and former Cabinet minister.

1 가산명사 참전 용사, 재향 군인 ❏ 그들은 걸프전 참전 용사들을 위한 11억 달러의 봉급 증액을 승인했다. **2** 가산명사 경험이 풍부한 사람, 베테랑 ❏ 노동당의 베테랑 의원이며 전직 각료인 토니 벤

vet|eri|nar|ian /vɛtᵊrɪnɛəriən/ (veterinarians) N-COUNT A **veterinarian** is a person who is qualified to treat sick or injured animals. [mainly AM; BRIT usually **vet**]

가산명사 수의사 [주로 미국영어; 영국영어 대개 vet]

vet|eri|nary /vɛtᵊrənɛri, BRIT vɛtᵊrənəri/ ADJ **Veterinary** is used to describe the work of a person whose job is to treat sick or injured animals, or to describe the medical treatment of animals. [ADJ n] ❏ It was decided that our veterinary screening of horses at events should be continued.

형용사 수의사의, 수의학의 ❏ 대회에 참가하는 말은 우리 수의사의 검사를 계속 받도록 결정되었다.

veto /vitoʊ/ (vetoes, vetoing, vetoed) **1** V-T If someone in authority **vetoes** something, they forbid it, or stop it from being put into action. ❏ The President vetoed the economic package passed by Congress. ● N-COUNT **Veto** is also a noun. ❏ The veto was a calculated political risk taken by a President beset by rising domestic troubles. **2** N-UNCOUNT **Veto** is the right that someone in authority has to forbid something. ❏ ...the President's power of veto.

1 타동사 거부권을 행사하다, (행위 등을) 금지하다 ❏ 대통령이 하원에서 통과된 경제 종합 정책을 거부했다. ● 가산명사 거부권 행사 ❏ 거부권 행사는 점점 고개를 드는 국내 문제로 고심하던 대통령의 계산된 정치적 모험이었다. **2** 불가산명사 거부권 ❏ 대통령의 거부권

vex /vɛks/ (vexes, vexing, vexed) V-T If someone or something **vexes** you, they make you feel annoyed, puzzled, and frustrated. ❏ It vexed me to think of others gossiping behind my back. ● **vexed** ADJ ❏ Exporters, farmers and industrialists alike are vexed and blame the government. ● **vex|ing** ADJ ❏ There remains, however, another and more vexing problem. →see also **vexed**

타동사 성가시게 하다, 화나게 하다 ❏ 남들이 등 뒤에서 내 험담을 하고 있다는 생각을 하면 화가 났다. ● 성난, 화난 형용사 ❏ 수출업자, 농부, 제조업자가 다 같이 화가 나서 정부를 비난했다. ● 화나게 하는, 성가신 형용사 ❏ 그러나 또 하나 더 성가신 문제가 남아 있다.

vexed /vɛkst/ ADJ A **vexed** problem or question is very difficult and causes people a lot of trouble. ❏ Ministers have begun work on the vexed issue of economic union. →see also **vex**

형용사 골치 아픈, 말썽 많은 ❏ 장관들은 경제적 통합이라는 골치 아픈 문제를 다루기 시작했다.

via ◆◇◇ /vaɪə, viə/ **1** PREP If you go somewhere **via** a particular place, you go through that place on the way to your destination. ❏ We drove via Lovech to the old Danube town of Ruse. **2** PREP If you do something **via** a particular means or person, you do it by making use of that means or person. ❏ The technology to allow relief workers to contact the outside world via satellite already exists.

1 전치사 –을 거쳐, –을 경유하여 ❏ 우리는 로베치를 거쳐 다뉴브 강변의 고도인 루세까지 차를 몰았다. **2** 전치사 –을 매체로 하여, –을 통해서 ❏ 구조 요원들로 하여금 위성을 이용하여 바깥 세계와 접촉하게 해 주는 기술이 이미 존재한다.

vi|able /vaɪəbᵊl/ ADJ Something that is **viable** is capable of doing what it is intended to do. ❏ Cash alone will not make Eastern Europe's banks viable. ● **vi|abil|ity** /vaɪəbɪliti/ N-UNCOUNT ❏ ...the shaky financial viability of the nuclear industry.

형용사 생존 가능한, 실행 가능한 ❏ 현찰만으로는 동부 유럽 은행들을 생존하게 만들 수 없을 것이다. ● 생존 능력 불가산명사 ❏ 원자력 산업의 위태로운 재정적 생존 가능성

vibe /vaɪb/ (vibes) N-COUNT **Vibes** are the good or bad atmosphere that you sense with a person or in a place. [INFORMAL] ❏ Sorry, Chris, but I have bad vibes about this guy.

가산명사 인상, 느낌 [비격식체] ❏ 미안하지만, 크리스, 난 이 사람 느낌이 안 좋아.

vi|brant /vaɪbrənt/ **1** ADJ Someone or something that is **vibrant** is full of life, energy, and enthusiasm. ❏ Tom felt himself being drawn towards her vibrant personality. ❏ ...Shakespeare's vibrant language. ● **vi|bran|cy** /vaɪbrənsi/ N-UNCOUNT ❏ She was a woman with extraordinary vibrancy and extraordinary knowledge. **2** ADJ **Vibrant** colors are very bright and clear. ❏ Horizon Blue, Corn Yellow, and Pistachio Green are just three of the vibrant colors in this range. ● **vi|brant|ly** ADV [ADV adj] ❏ ...a selection of vibrantly colored French cast-iron saucepans.

1 형용사 원기 왕성한, 활기가 넘치는 ❏ 톰은 자신이 그녀의 활기 넘치는 성격에 끌리는 것을 느꼈다. ❏ 셰익스피어의 생기가 넘치는 언어 ● 활기참 불가산명사 ❏ 그녀는 유난히 활기차고 비범한 지식을 갖춘 여자였다. **2** 형용사 (색이) 강렬한, 선명한 ❏ 수평선의 푸른색, 옥수수의 노란색, 피스타치오의 초록색은 이 계열에 속하는 바로 세 가지의 선명한 색채들이다. ● 강렬하게, 선명하게 부사 ❏ 선명하게 채색된 프랑스제 주물 냄비 특선

vi|brate /vaɪbreɪt, BRIT vaɪbreɪt/ (vibrates, vibrating, vibrated) V-T/V-I If something **vibrates** or if you **vibrate** it, it shakes with repeated small, quick movements. ❏ The ground shook and the cliffs seemed to vibrate. ● **vi|bra|tion** /vaɪbreɪʃᵊn/ (vibrations) N-VAR ❏ The vibrations of the vehicles rattled the shop windows. →see **ear**

타동사/자동사 떨다, 진동하다; 진동시키다 ❏ 땅이 흔들리고 절벽이 떨리는 것 같았다. ● 떨림, 진동 가산명사 또는 불가산명사 ❏ 차량의 진동에 가게 창문이 덜컹거렸다.

A
B
C
D
E
F
G
H
I
J
K
L
M
N
O
P
Q
R
S
T
U
V
W
X
Y
Z

vi|car /vɪkər/ (vicars) ■ N-COUNT; N-VOC A **vicar** is a priest who is in charge of a chapel that is associated with a parish church in the Episcopal Church in the United States. [AM] ■ N-COUNT; N-VOC A **vicar** is an Anglican priest who is in charge of a church and the area it is in, which is called a parish. [mainly BRIT]

vice ♦♢♢ /vaɪs/ (vices) ■ N-COUNT A **vice** is a habit which is regarded as a weakness in someone's character, but not usually as a serious fault. ❏ *His only vice is to get drunk on champagne after concluding a successful piece of business.* ■ N-UNCOUNT **Vice** refers to criminal activities, especially those connected with pornography or prostitution. ❏ *He said those responsible for offenses connected with vice, gaming, and drugs should be deported on conviction.* ■ →see **vise**

vice ver|sa /vaɪsə vɜrsə, vaɪs/ PHRASE **Vice versa** is used to indicate that the reverse of what you have said is true. For example "women may bring their husbands with them, and vice versa" means that men may also bring their wives with them. ❏ *Teachers qualified to teach in England are not accepted in Scotland and vice versa.*

vi|cin|ity /vɪsɪnɪti/ N-SING If something is **in the vicinity of** a particular place, it is near it. [FORMAL] ❏ *There were a hundred or so hotels in the vicinity of the railway station.*

vi|cious /vɪʃəs/ ■ ADJ A **vicious** person or a **vicious** blow is violent and cruel. ❏ *He was a cruel and vicious man.* ❏ *He suffered a vicious attack by a gang of white youths.* ● **vi|cious|ly** ADV ❏ *She had been viciously attacked with a hammer.* ● **vi|cious|ness** N-UNCOUNT ❏ *...the intensity and viciousness of these attacks.* ■ ADJ A **vicious** remark is cruel and intended to upset someone. ❏ *It is a deliberate, nasty and vicious attack on a young man's character.* ● **vi|cious|ly** ADV [ADV with v] ❏ *"He deserved to die," said Penelope viciously.*

Thesaurus   vicious의 참조어

ADJ.   brutal, cruel, violent; (ant.) nice ■ ■

vi|cious cir|cle (vicious circles) also **vicious cycle** N-COUNT A **vicious circle** is a problem or difficult situation that has the effect of creating new problems which then cause the original problem or situation to occur again. ❏ *The more pesticides are used, the more resistant the insects become so the more pesticides have to be used. It's a vicious circle.*

vic|tim ♦♦♢ /vɪktəm/ (victims) ■ N-COUNT A **victim** is someone who has been hurt or killed. ❏ *Statistically our chances of being the victims of violent crime are remote.* ■ N-COUNT A **victim** is someone who has suffered as a result of someone else's actions or beliefs, or as a result of unpleasant circumstances. ❏ *He was a victim of racial prejudice.* ❏ *He described himself and Altman as victims rather than participants in the scandal.*

vic|tim|ize ♦♢♢ /vɪktəmaɪz/ (victimizes, victimizing, victimized) [BRIT also **victimise**] V-T If someone **is victimized**, they are deliberately treated unfairly. ❏ *He felt the students had been victimized because they'd voiced opposition to the government.* ● **vic|tim|za|tion** /vɪktəmaɪzeɪʃⁿn/ N-UNCOUNT ❏ *...society's cruel victimization of women.*

vic|tor /vɪktər/ (victors) N-COUNT The **victor** in a battle or contest is the person who wins. [LITERARY] ❏ *Oliver Townsend and co-driver Kirk Lee eventually emerged as victors after five different cars had led the event.*

Vic|to|rian /vɪktɔriən/ (Victorians) ■ ADJ **Victorian** means belonging to, connected with, or typical of Britain in the middle and last parts of the 19th century, when Victoria was Queen. ❏ *We have a lovely old Victorian house.* ❏ *...a Victorian-style family portrait.* ■ ADJ You can use **Victorian** to describe people who have old-fashioned attitudes, especially about good behavior and morals. ❏ *Victorian values are much misunderstood.* ■ N-COUNT The **Victorians** were the British people who lived in the time of Queen Victoria. ❏ *The Victorians were the last people to invest properly in the railways.*

vic|to|ri|ous /vɪktɔriəs/ ADJ You use **victorious** to describe someone who has won a victory in a struggle, war, or competition. ❏ *In 1978 he played for the victorious Argentinian side in the World Cup.*

vic|to|ry ♦♦♢ /vɪktəri, vɪktri/ (victories) ■ N-VAR A **victory** is a success in a struggle, war, or competition. ❏ *Union leaders are heading for victory in their battle over workplace rights.* ■ PHRASE If you say that someone has won a **moral victory**, you mean that although they have officially lost a contest or dispute, they have succeeded in showing they are right about something. ❏ *She said her party had won a moral victory.*

Thesaurus   victory의 참조어

N.   conquest, success, win; (ant.) defeat ■

video ♦♦♢ /vɪdioʊ/ (videos, videoing, videoed) ■ N-COUNT A **video** is a movie or television program recorded on tape for people to watch on a television set. ❏ *...sports and exercise videos.* ■ N-UNCOUNT **Video** is the system of recording movies and events on tape so that people can watch them on a television set. ❏ *She has watched the race on video.* ❏ *...manufacturers of audio and video equipment.* ■ N-COUNT A **video** is a machine that you can use to record television programs and play videotapes on a television set. [mainly BRIT; AM usually **VCR**] ❏ *He'd set the video for 8:00.* ■ V-T If you **video** a television program or event, you record it on tape using a video recorder or video camera, so that you can watch it later. [mainly BRIT; AM usually **tape**, **videotape**] ❏ *She had been videoing the highlights of the tournament.*

■ 가산명사; 호격명사 부목사, (미국 성공회의) 회당 목사 [미국영어] ■ 가산명사; 호격명사 (영국 국교회의) 교구 목사 [주로 영국영어]

■ 가산명사 나쁜 버릇 ❏ 그의 유일한 나쁜 버릇은 성공적으로 업무를 한 건 마치면 샴페인에 취하는 것이다. ■ 불가산명사 (매춘 같은) 죄, 비행 ❏ 그는 매춘, 도박, 마약과 연관된 죄를 저지른 사람들은 유죄 판결이 나면 추방되어야 한다고 말했다.

구 그 반대도 마찬가지임 ❏ 영국의 교사 자격을 지닌 교사가 스코틀랜드에서 가르칠 수 없고, 그 반대도 또한 마찬가지다.

단수명사 (~의) 부근 [격식체] ❏ 기차역 부근에는 백여 개의 호텔이 있었다.

■ 형용사 잔인한, 포악한 ❏ 그는 잔인하고 포악한 사람이었다. ❏ 그는 백인 청년 패거리에게 잔인한 공격을 당했다. ● 잔인하게 부사 ❏ 그녀는 망치로 잔인하게 공격을 당했다. ● 잔인함 불가산명사 ❏ 이 공격들의 격렬함과 잔인함 ■ 형용사 악의 있는, 비열한 ❏ 그것은 한 젊은이의 인격에 대한 의도적이고 비열하며 악의에 찬 공격이다. ● 악독하게 부사 ❏ "그는 죽어 마땅해."라고 페넬로프는 악독하게 말했다.

가산명사 악순환 ❏ 살충제를 많이 사용할수록 해충은 더 내성이 생겨서 더 많은 살충제를 사용해야 한다. 그것은 악순환이다.

■ 가산명사 희생자, 피해자 ❏ 통계적으로 우리가 폭력 범죄의 피해자가 될 가능성은 매우 낮다. ■ 가산명사 희생자, 피해자 ❏ 그는 인종적 편견의 희생자였다. ❏ 그는 자신과 알트만이 그 스캔들에 가담한 사람이라기보다 희생자라고 말했다.

[영국영어 victimise] 타동사 부당한 취급을 받다, 희생되다 ❏ 그는 그 학생들이 정부에 대해 반대 의사를 표명했기 때문에 피해를 당했다고 느꼈다. ● 부당한 대우 불가산명사 ❏ 여성에 대한 사회의 부당한 처우

가산명사 승리자 [문예체] ❏ 올리버 타운젠드와 동승 운전자인 커크 리가 경기의 선두를 달리던 다른 다섯 대의 차를 제치고 결국 승자로 부상했다.

■ 형용사 빅토리아 여왕 시대의, 빅토리아조 풍의 ❏ 우리는 멋진 빅토리아풍의 고택이 있다. ❏ 빅토리아조 양식의 가족 초상화 ■ 형용사 (도덕적으로) 엄격한, 근엄한 ❏ 빅토리아조의 근엄한 가치관은 상당히 잘못 인식되어 있다. ■ 가산명사 빅토리아 시대 영국 사람들 ❏ 빅토리아 시대 영국 사람들은 철도에 제대로 투자한 마지막 사람이었다.

형용사 승리한 ❏ 1978년에 그는 월드컵에서 우승한 아르헨티나 팀에서 뛰었다.

■ 가산명사 또는 불가산명사 승리 ❏ 노조 지도자들은 직장에서의 권리를 획득하기 위한 투쟁에서 승리를 향해 나아가고 있다. ■ 구 도덕적 승리, 정신적 승리 ❏ 그녀는 자기 당이 도덕적 승리를 거두었다고 말했다.

■ 가산명사 비디오, 비디오 영상물 ❏ 스포츠와 운동 비디오 ■ 불가산명사 비디오 ❏ 그녀는 그 경주를 비디오로 보았다. ❏ 오디오 및 비디오 기기 제조사들 ■ 가산명사 비디오, 비디오 기기 [주로 영국영어; 미국영어 대개 VCR] ❏ 그는 비디오를 8시로 맞춰 놓았다. ■ 타동사 비디오로 녹화하다 [주로 영국영어; 미국영어 대개 tape, videotape] ❏ 그녀는 그 선수권 경기 전체의 주요 부분을 비디오로 녹화해 왔다.

video cas|sette (**video cassettes**) also **videocassette** N-COUNT A **video cassette** is a cassette containing videotape, on which you can record or watch moving pictures and sounds.

가산명사 비디오테이프

video-conference (**video-conferences**) also **videoconference** N-COUNT A **video-conference** is a meeting that takes place using video conferencing. [BUSINESS] ❑ *It is now possible to hold a video conference in real time on a mobile phone.*

가산명사 (텔레비전) 화상 회의 [경제] ❑ 이제는 이동 전화로 실시간 화상 회의를 여는 것이 가능하다.

video con|fer|enc|ing /vɪdioʊ kɒnfrənsɪŋ/ also **video-conferencing**, **videoconferencing** N-UNCOUNT **Video conferencing** is a system that enables people in various places around the world to have a meeting by seeing and hearing each other on a screen. [BUSINESS] ❑ *Couple Counselling also hopes to use video conferencing to train and supervise counsellors.*

불가산명사 화상 회의 시스템 [경제] ❑ 커플 카운슬링 사는 또한 상담사를 훈련시키고 감독하는 데 화상 회의 시스템 사용을 희망한다.

video game (**video games**) N-COUNT A **video game** is an electronic or computerized game that you play on your television or on a computer screen.

가산명사 비디오 게임

video|phone /vɪdioʊfoʊn/ (**videophones**) also **video phone** N-COUNT A **videophone** is a telephone which has a camera and screen so that people who are using the phone can see and hear each other.

가산명사 비디오 폰, 화상 전화

video re|cord|er (**video recorders**) N-COUNT A **video recorder** or a **video cassette recorder** is the same as a VCR.

가산명사 비디오, 비디오 녹화기

| Word Link | *vid, vis* ≈ *seeing* : *audiovisual*, *videotape*, *visible* |

---

video|tape /vɪdioʊteɪp/ (**videotapes, videotaping, videotaped**) also **video tape** ◼ N-UNCOUNT **Videotape** is magnetic tape that is used to record moving pictures and sounds to be shown on television. ❑ *...the use of videotape in criminal court rooms.* ◼ N-COUNT A **videotape** is the same as a **video cassette**. ◼ V-T If you **videotape** a television program or event, you record it on tape using a video recorder or video camera, so that you can watch it later. [mainly AM] ❑ *She videotaped the entire trip.*

◼ 불가산명사 비디오테이프 ❑ 형사 재판정에서의 비디오테이프 사용 ◻ 가산명사 비디오테이프 ◼ 타동사 비디오로 녹화하다 [주로 미국영어] ❑ 그녀는 여행 전체를 비디오로 녹화했다.

vie /vaɪ/ (**vies, vying, vied**) V-RECIP If one person or thing **is vying with** another for something, the people or things are competing for it. [FORMAL] ❑ *California is vying with other states to capture a piece of the growing communications market.* ❑ *The two are vying for the support of New York voters.*

상호동사 각축을 벌이다, 경쟁하다 [격식체] ❑ 캘리포니아는 성장하는 통신 시장의 일부를 장악하려고 다른 주들과 각축을 벌이고 있다. ❑ 그 둘은 뉴욕 유권자들의 지지를 얻으려고 경쟁하고 있다.

view ◆◆◆ /vyu/ (**views, viewing, viewed**) ◼ N-COUNT Your **views** on something are the beliefs or opinions that you have about it, for example whether you think it is good, bad, right, or wrong. ❑ *Washington and Moscow are believed to have similar views on Kashmir.* ❑ *You should also make your views known to your local MP.* ◻ N-SING Your **view of** a particular subject is the way that you understand and think about it. ❑ *The whole point was to get away from a Christian-centered view of religion.* ◼ V-T If you **view** something in a particular way, you think of it in that way. ❑ *First-generation Americans view the United States as a land of golden opportunity.* ❑ *Abigail's mother Linda views her daughter's behavior with a mixture of pride and worry.* ◼ N-COUNT The **view** from a window or high place is everything which can be seen from that place, especially when it is considered to be beautiful. ❑ *The view from our window was one of beautiful green countryside.* ◼ N-SING If you have a **view of** something, you can see it. ❑ *He stood up to get a better view of the blackboard.* ◼ N-UNCOUNT You use **view** in expressions to do with being able to see something. For example, if something is **in view**, you can see it. If something is **in full view of everyone**, everyone can see it. ❑ *She was lying there in full view of anyone who walked by.* ◼ V-T If you **view** something, you look at it for a particular purpose. [FORMAL] ❑ *They came back to view the house again.* ◼ V-T If you **view** a television program, video, or movie, you watch it. [FORMAL] ❑ *We have viewed the video recording of the incident.* ◼ N-SING **View** refers to the way in which a piece of text or graphics is displayed on a computer screen. [COMPUTING] ❑ *To see the current document in full-page view, click the Page Zoom Full button.* ◼ PHRASE You use **in my view** when you want to indicate that you are stating a personal opinion, which other people might not agree with. ❑ *In my view things won't change.* ◼ PHRASE You use **in view of** when you are taking into consideration facts that have just been mentioned or are just about to be mentioned. ❑ *In view of the fact that Hobson was not a trained economist his achievements were remarkable.* ◼ PHRASE If something such as a work of art is **on view**, it is shown in public for people to look at. ❑ *A significant exhibition of contemporary sculpture will be on view at the Portland Gallery.* ◼ PHRASE If you do something **with a view to** doing something else, you do it because you hope it will result in that other thing being done. ❑ *He has called a meeting of all parties tomorrow, with a view to forming a national reconciliation government.*

상호동사 각축을 벌이다, 경쟁하다 [격식체] ❑ 캘리포니아는 성장하는 통신 시장의 일부를 장악하려고 다른 주들과 각축을 벌이고 있다. ❑ 그 둘은 뉴욕 유권자들의 지지를 얻으려고 경쟁하고 있다.

◼ 가산명사 견해 ❑ 워싱턴과 모스크바는 캐슈미르에 관해 비슷한 견해를 갖고 있다고 생각된다. ❑ 또한 당신의 견해를 지역구 국회의원에게 알려야 한다. ◻ 단수명사 관점 ❑ 핵심은 기독교 중심적인 종교관에서 벗어나는 것이었다. ◼ 타동사 (-라고) 여기다, (-으로) 보다 ❑ 1세대 미국인들은 미국을 황금 같은 기회의 땅으로 여긴다. ❑ 아비게일의 어머니 린다는 자기 딸의 재능을 자랑 반 걱정 반으로 바라본다. ◼ 가산명사 전망, 경관 ❑ 우리 집 창에서는 아름다운 녹색의 전원이 내려다보였다. ◼ 단수명사 시야, 시계 ❑ 그는 칠판을 더 잘 보려고 일어섰다. ◼ 불가산명사 바라봄; 보이는; 누구나 볼 수 있는 ❑ 그녀는 지나다니는 사람 누구나 볼 수 있게 저기에 누워있었다. ◼ 타동사 살펴보다 [격식체] ❑ 그들은 그 집을 다시 살펴보기 위해 되돌아왔다. ◼ 타동사 시청하다 [격식체] ❑ 우리는 그 사건의 비디오 녹화물을 보았다. ◼ 단수명사 화면 모양 [컴퓨터] ❑ 현재 사용 중인 문서를 페이지 단위로 보려면, 전체 화면 최대 버튼을 클릭하시오. ◼ 구 내 견해로는, 내 생각에는 ❑ 내 생각에는 상황이 변하지 않을 것이다. ◼ 구 -을 고려하여, -을 감안하면 ❑ 홉슨이 정식으로 교육받은 경제학자가 아니라는 것을 감안하면, 그의 업적은 놀랄 만하다. ◼ 구 전시되어, 진열 중에 ❑ 중요한 현대 조각 전시회가 포트랜드 화랑에서 열릴 것이다. ◼ 구 -할 목적으로 ❑ 그는 국민 화합 정부를 구성할 목적으로 내일 모든 정당이 참여하는 회의를 소집했다.

view|er /vyuər/ (**viewers**) ◼ N-COUNT **Viewers** are people who watch television, or who are watching a particular program on television. ❑ *These programmes are each watched by around 19 million viewers every week.* ◻ N-COUNT A **viewer** is someone who is looking carefully at a picture or other interesting object. ❑ *...the relationship between the art object and the viewer.*

◼ 가산명사 시청자 ❑ 이 프로그램들은 각각 매주 약 1천 9백만 명의 시청자가 본다. ◻ 가산명사 보는 사람, 관찰자 ❑ 미술품과 감상자 간의 관계

view|point /vyupɔɪnt/ (**viewpoints**) ◼ N-COUNT Someone's **viewpoint** is the way that they think about things in general, or the way they think about a particular thing. ❑ *The novel is shown from the girl's viewpoint.* ◻ N-COUNT A **viewpoint** is a place from which you can get a good view of something. ❑ *You have to know where to stand for a good viewpoint.*

◼ 가산명사 관점, 시각 ❑ 그 소설은 그 소녀의 관점에서 서술된다. ◻ 가산명사 조망점 ❑ 잘 보려면 설 자리를 잘 잡아야 한다.

vig|il /vɪdʒɪl/ (**vigils**) N-COUNT A **vigil** is a period of time when people remain quietly in a place, especially at night, for example because they are praying or are making a political protest. ❑ *Protesters are holding a twenty-four hour vigil outside the socialist party headquarters.* ● PHRASE If someone **keeps a vigil** or **keeps vigil** somewhere, they remain there quietly for a period of time, especially at night, for example because they are praying or are making a political protest.

가산명사 철야 기도; 철야 농성 ❑ 항의자들이 사회당 본부 밖에서 24시간 철야 농성을 하고 있다. ● 구 밤새 지키다, 철야 기도하다; 철야 농성하다
가산명사 철야 기도; 철야 농성 ❑ 항의자들이 사회당 본부 밖에서 24시간 철야 농성을 하고 있다. ● 구 밤새 지키다, 철야 기도하다; 철야 농성하다

A

vig|i|lant /vɪdʒɪlənt/ ADJ Someone who is **vigilant** gives careful attention to a particular problem or situation and concentrates on noticing any danger or trouble that there might be. ❑ *He warned the public to be vigilant and report anything suspicious.* ● **vigi|lance** N-UNCOUNT ❑ *Drugs are a problem that requires constant vigilance.*

형용사 경계하고 있는, 방심하지 않는 ❑ 그는 국민들에게 방심하지 말고 조금이라도 수상한 것은 보고하라고 주의시켰다. ● 경계 불가산명사 ❑ 마약이 끊임없는 경계를 요하는 문제이다.

B

vigi|lan|te /vɪdʒɪlænti/ (vigilantes) N-COUNT **Vigilantes** are people who organize themselves into an unofficial group to protect their community and to catch and punish criminals. ❑ *The vigilantes dragged the men out.*

가산명사 자경단원 ❑ 자경단원들이 그 남자들을 끌어냈다.

C

vig|or /vɪgər/ [BRIT **vigour**] N-UNCOUNT **Vigor** is physical or mental energy and enthusiasm. ❑ *He has approached his job with renewed vigor.*

[영국영어 vigour] 불가산명사 활력, 활기 ❑ 그는 새로운 활력을 가지고 자기 일에 접근했다.

D

vig|or|ous /vɪgərəs/ ❶ ADJ **Vigorous** physical activities involve using a lot of energy, usually to do short and repeated actions. ❑ *Very vigorous exercise can increase the risk of heart attacks.* ● **vig|or|ous|ly** ADV [ADV after v] ❑ *He shook his head vigorously.* ❷ ADJ A **vigorous** person does things with great energy and enthusiasm. A **vigorous** campaign or activity is done with great energy and enthusiasm. ❑ *Sir Robert was a strong and vigorous politician.* ● **vig|or|ous|ly** ADV [ADV with v] ❑ *The police vigorously denied that excessive force had been used.*

❶ 형용사 활기찬; 격렬한 ❑ 너무 격렬한 운동은 심장 마비의 위험을 증가시킬 수 있다. ● 활기차게; 격렬히 부사 ❑ 그는 머리를 격렬히 흔들었다. ❷ 형용사 활력이 넘치는, 정력적인; 강력한 ❑ 로버트 경은 강하고 활력이 넘치는 정치인이었다. ● 정력적으로; 강력히 부사 ❑ 경찰은 과도한 무력 사용을 강력히 부인했다.

E

F

vig|our /vɪgər/ →see **vigor**

G

vile /vaɪl/ (**viler**, **vilest**) ADJ If you say that someone or something is **vile**, you mean that they are very unpleasant. ❑ *The weather is consistently vile.*

형용사 몹시 불쾌한, 몹시 나쁜 ❑ 날씨가 시종일관 몹시 나쁘다.

vil|la /vɪlə/ (**villas**) N-COUNT A **villa** is a fairly large house, especially one that is used for vacations in Mediterranean countries. ❑ *He lives in a secluded five-bedroom luxury villa.*

가산명사 저택, 별장 ❑ 그는 호젓한 곳에서 침실이 다섯 개인 고급 저택에 산다.

H

vil|lage ♦♦◇ /vɪlɪdʒ/ (**villages**) N-COUNT A **village** consists of a group of houses, together with other buildings such as a church and a school, in a country area. ❑ *He lives quietly in the country in a village near Lahti.*

가산명사 마을 ❑ 그는 라티 근처 시골의 한 마을에서 조용히 살고 있다.

I

vil|lain /vɪlən/ (**villains**) ❶ N-COUNT A **villain** is someone who deliberately harms other people or breaks the law in order to get what he or she wants. ❑ *The victims of this epidemic, the farmers, were smeared as the villains.* ❷ N-COUNT The **villain** in a novel, movie, or play is the main bad character. ❑ *He also played a villain opposite Sylvester Stallone in Demolition Man (1992).*

❶ 가산명사 나쁜 사람, 범죄자 ❑ 이 전염병의 피해자인 농부들이 전염병의 원흉이라는 오명을 뒤집어썼다. ❷ 가산명사 악당 ❑ 그는 또한 1992년 영화 '디몰리션 맨'에서 실베스터 스탤론의 상대 악당 역을 했다.

J

K

vin|di|cate /vɪndɪkeɪt/ (**vindicates**, **vindicating**, **vindicated**) V-T If a person or their decisions, actions, or ideas **are vindicated**, they are proved to be correct, after people have said that they were wrong. [FORMAL] ❑ *The director said he had been vindicated by the experts' report.* ● **vin|di|ca|tion** /vɪndɪkeɪʃən/ N-UNCOUNT [also a N, usu N of n] ❑ *He called the success a vindication of his party's free-market economic policy.*

타동사 정당함이 입증되다 [격식체] ❑ 소장은 전문가들의 보고서에 의해 자신의 정당함이 입증되었다고 말했다. ● 정당성 입증 불가산명사 ❑ 그는 그 성공을 자기 당의 자유 시장 경제 정책의 정당성을 입증하는 것이라고 칭했다.

L

M

vin|dic|tive /vɪndɪktɪv/ ADJ If you say that someone is **vindictive**, you are critical of them because they deliberately try to upset or cause trouble for someone who they think has done them harm. [DISAPPROVAL] ❑ *...a vindictive woman desperate for revenge against the man who loved and left her.* ● **vin|dic|tive|ness** N-UNCOUNT ❑ *...a dishonest person who is operating completely out of vindictiveness.*

형용사 앙심을 품은 [탐탁찮음] ❑ 자기를 사랑하다가 떠나 버린 남자에 대한 복수심에 불타는 한 맺힌 여자 ● 앙심 불가산명사 ❑ 순전히 앙심에 차서 행동하고 있는 정직하지 못한 사람

N

vine /vaɪn/ (**vines**) N-VAR A **vine** is a plant that grows up or over things, especially one which produces grapes. ❑ *Every square meter of soil was used, mainly for olives, vines, and almonds.*

가산명사 또는 불가산명사 덩굴 식물, 포도나무 ❑ 한 치도 빈 땅이 없이 주로 올리브, 포도, 아몬드 나무가 심어져 있었다.

O

P

vin|egar /vɪnɪgər/ (**vinegars**) N-MASS **Vinegar** is a sharp-tasting liquid, usually made from sour wine or malt, which is used to make things such as salad dressing.

물질명사 식초

Q

vine|yard /vɪnyərd/ (**vineyards**) N-COUNT A **vineyard** is an area of land where grape vines are grown in order to produce wine. You can also use **vineyard** to refer to the set of buildings in which the wine is produced.

가산명사 포도원; 포도주 공장

R

vin|tage /vɪntɪdʒ/ (**vintages**) ❶ N-COUNT The **vintage** of a good quality wine is the year and place that it was made before being stored to improve it. You can also use **vintage** to refer to the wine that was made in a certain year. ❑ *This wine is from one of the two best vintages of the decade in this region.* ❷ ADJ **Vintage** wine is good quality wine that has been stored for several years in order to improve its quality. [ADJ n] ❑ *If you can buy only one case at auction, it should be vintage port.* ❸ ADJ **Vintage** cars or airplanes are old but are admired because they are considered to be the best of their kind. [ADJ n] ❑ *The museum will have a permanent exhibition of 60 vintage and racing cars.*

❶ 가산명사 (고급 포도주의) 수확 연도와 장소; 특정 양조 연도의 포도주 ❑ 이 포도주는 이 지역에서 10년간 생산된 두 가지 최고급 포도주 중 하나이다. ❷ 형용사 (몇 년간 숙성시킨) 고급의 ❑ 경매에서 딱 한 상자만 살 수 있다면 고급 포트와인이어야 한다. ❸ 형용사 (자동차 등의) 고전적 구형의 ❑ 그 박물관은 60대의 고전적 구형 자동차와 경주용 자동차를 영구적으로 전시할 것이다.

S

T

vi|nyl /vaɪnɪl/ (**vinyls**) ❶ N-MASS **Vinyl** is a strong plastic used for making things such as floor coverings and furniture. ❑ *...a modern vinyl floor covering.* ❷ N-UNCOUNT You can use **vinyl** to refer to records, especially in contrast to cassettes or compact discs. ❑ *This compilation was first issued on vinyl in 1984.*

❶ 물질명사 비닐, 플라스틱 ❑ 현대식 비닐 장판 ❷ 불가산명사 레코드판 ❑ 이 모음집은 1984년에 레코드판으로 처음 나왔다.

U

V

vi|o|la /vioʊlə/ (**violas**) N-VAR A **viola** is a musical instrument with four strings that is played with a bow. It is like a violin, but is slightly larger and can play lower notes. ❑ *She also played the viola in some of the amateur orchestras conducted by Grandpa Green.* →see **orchestra**

가산명사 또는 불가산명사 비올라 ❑ 그녀는 또한 그랜드파 그린이 지휘하는 몇몇 아마추어 오케스트라에서 비올라를 연주했다.

W

X

vio|late ♦◇◇ /vaɪəleɪt/ (**violates**, **violating**, **violated**) ❶ V-T If someone **violates** an agreement, law, or promise, they break it. [FORMAL] ❑ *They went to prison because they violated the law.* ● **vio|la|tion** /vaɪəleɪʃən/ (**violations**) N-VAR ❑ *To deprive the boy of his education is a violation of state law.* ❷ V-T If you **violate** someone's privacy or peace, you disturb it. [FORMAL] ❑ *These men were violating her family's privacy.* ❸ V-T If someone **violates** a special place, for example a grave, they damage it or treat it with disrespect. ❑ *Detectives are still searching for those who violated the graveyard.* ● **vio|la|tion** N-UNCOUNT ❑ *The violation of the graves is not the first such incident.*

❶ 타동사 위반하다, 어기다 [격식체] ❑ 그들은 법을 어겨서 감옥에 갔다. ● 위반 가산명사 또는 불가산명사 ❑ 그 소년이 교육을 받지 못하게 하는 것은 주법 위반이다. ❷ 타동사 침해하다 [격식체] ❑ 이 남자들이 그녀 가족의 사생활을 침해하고 있었다. ❸ 타동사 훼손하다, 유린하다 ❑ 형사들이 아직도 그 묘지를 훼손한 사람들을 찾고 있다. ● 훼손 불가산명사 ❑ 묘지를 훼손한 것은 그것이 처음이 아니다.

Y

Z

Word Partnership   violate의 연어

N.   violate **an agreement**, violate **the constitution**, violate **the law**,
violate **rights**, violate **rules** ■
violate *someone's* **privacy** ■

vio|lence ♦♦◇ /vaɪələns/ ■ N-UNCOUNT **Violence** is behavior which is
intended to hurt, injure, or kill people. ❑ *Twenty people were killed in the violence.*
❑ *...domestic violence between husband and wife.* ■ N-UNCOUNT If you do or say
something with **violence**, you use a lot of force and energy in doing or saying
it, often because you are angry. [LITERARY] ❑ *The violence in her tone gave Alistair a
shock.*

■ 불가산명사 폭력 ❑ 그 폭력 사태에서 스무 명이
죽었다. ❑ 남편과 아내 사이의 가정 폭력
■ 불가산명사 격렬함, 맹렬함 [문예체] ❑ 그녀의
격렬한 말투가 알리스테어에게 충격을 주었다.

Word Partnership   violence의 연어

N.   **acts of** violence, **outbreak of** violence, **victims of** violence,
violence **against women** ■
V.   **condemn** violence, violence **erupts**, **prevent** violence, **resort to**
violence, **stop** violence ■
ADJ.   **ethnic** violence, **physical** violence, **racial** violence, **widespread**
violence ■

vio|lent ♦◇◇ /vaɪələnt/ ■ ADJ If someone is **violent**, or if they do
something which is **violent**, they use physical force or weapons to hurt,
injure, or kill other people. ❑ *A quarter of current inmates have committed
violent crimes.* ❑ *...violent anti-government demonstrations.* ● **vio|lent|ly** ADV
[ADV with v] ❑ *Some opposition activists have been violently attacked.* ■ ADJ
A **violent** event happens suddenly and with great force. ❑ *A violent impact
hurtled her forward.* ● **vio|lent|ly** ADV [ADV with v] ❑ *A nearby volcano erupted
violently, sending out a hail of molten rock and boiling mud.* ■ ADJ If you describe
something as **violent**, you mean that it is said, done, or felt very strongly.
❑ *Violent opposition to the plan continues.* ❑ *He had violent stomach pains.*
● **vio|lent|ly** ADV ❑ *He was violently scolded.* ■ ADJ A **violent** death is painful
and unexpected, usually because the person who dies has been murdered.
❑ *...an innocent man who had met a violent death.* ● **vio|lent|ly** ADV [ADV with v] ❑ *...a
girl who had died violently nine years earlier.* ■ ADJ A **violent** movie or television
program contains a lot of scenes which show violence. ❑ *It was the most violent
film that I have ever seen.*

■ 형용사 폭력적인, 난폭한 ❑ 현재 수감자의 4분의
1은 폭력 범죄를 저지른 사람들이다. ❑ 폭력적인
반정부 시위들 ● 난폭하게 부사 ❑ 몇몇 야당
활동가들이 난폭하게 공격을 당했다. ■ 형용사
격렬한, 강력한 ❑ 강력한 충격에 그녀가 앞으로 확
튕겨 나갔다. ● 격렬하게, 강력하게 부사 ❑ 인근
화산이 세차게 폭발하면서 용암과 부글부글 끓는
진흙을 우박처럼 쏟아 냈다. ■ 형용사 극심한 ❑ 그
계획에 대한 극심한 반대가 계속되고 있다. ❑ 그는
극심한 복통을 일으켰다. ● 극심하게 부사 ❑ 그는
호되게 야단을 맞았다. ■ 형용사 무참한 ❑ 무참하게
살해당한 무고한 남자 ❑ 무참히 부사 ❑ 9년 전에
무참히 죽은 소녀 ■ 형용사 폭력 장면이 많은,
폭력적인 ❑ 그것은 내가 본 가장 폭력적인 영화였다.

Word Partnership   violent의 연어

N.   violent **acts**, violent **attacks**, violent **behavior**, violent **clash**,
violent **conflict**, violent **confrontations**, violent **crime**,
violent **criminals**, violent **demonstrations**, violent **incidents**,
violent **offenders** ■
violent **protests**, violent **reaction** ■ ■
violent **death** ■
violent **films/movies** ■
ADV.   **extremely** violent, **increasingly** violent ■ ■

vio|let /vaɪələt/ (**violets**) ■ N-COUNT A **violet** is a small plant that has purple
or white flowers in the spring. ■ COLOR Something that is **violet** is a
bluish-purple color. ❑ *The light was beginning to drain from a violet sky.* ■ PHRASE If
you say that someone is no **shrinking violet**, you mean that they are not
at all shy. ❑ *When it comes to expressing himself he is no shrinking violet.* →see
rainbow

■ 가산명사 제비꽃 ■ 색채어 보라색, 청자색
❑ 햇빛이 보랏빛 하늘에서 서서히 스러지기 시작하고
있었다. ■ 구 내성적인 사람 ❑ 자신을 표현하는 일에
있어서라면 그는 전혀 내성적인 사람이 아니다.

vio|lin /vaɪəlɪn/ (**violins**) N-VAR A **violin** is a musical instrument. Violins are
made of wood and have four strings. You play the violin by holding it under your
chin and moving a bow across the strings. ❑ *Lizzie used to play the violin.* →see
orchestra

가산명사 또는 불가산명사 바이올린 ❑ 리지는 한때
바이올린을 연주했다.

vio|lin|ist /vaɪəlɪnɪst/ (**violinists**) N-COUNT A **violinist** is someone who plays the
violin. ❑ *Rose's father was a talented violinist.*

가산명사 바이올린 연주자 ❑ 로즈의 아버지는 재능
있는 바이올린 연주자였다.

VIP /vi aɪ pi/ (**VIPs**) N-COUNT A **VIP** is someone who is given better treatment
than ordinary people because they are famous, influential, or important. **VIP** is
an abbreviation for "very important person." ❑ *...such VIPs as Prince Charles and
Richard Nixon.*

가산명사 요인, 귀빈, very important person의 약자
❑ 찰스 왕자와 리처드 닉슨 같은 요인들

Word Link   vir ≈ poison : viral, virulent, virus

vi|ral /vaɪrəl/ ADJ A **viral** disease or infection is caused by a virus. ❑ *...a 65-year-old
patient suffering from severe viral pneumonia.*

형용사 바이러스성의 ❑ 심한 바이러스성 폐렴에 걸린
65세의 환자

vir|gin /vɜrdʒɪn/ (**virgins**) ■ N-COUNT A **virgin** is someone, especially a woman
or girl, who has never had sex. ❑ *I was a virgin until I was thirty years old.*
● **vir|gin|ity** /vərdʒɪnɪti/ N-UNCOUNT ❑ *She lost her virginity when she was 20.* ■ ADJ
You use **virgin** to describe something such as land that has never been used or
spoiled. ❑ *Within 40 years there will be no virgin forest left.* ■ PHRASE If you say that a
situation is **virgin territory**, you mean that you have no experience of it and it
is completely new for you. ❑ *The World Cup is virgin territory for Ecuador.*
■ N-COUNT You can use **virgin** to describe someone who has never done or
used a particular thing before. ❑ *Until he appeared in "In the Line of Fire" Malkovich
had been an action-movie virgin.*

■ 가산명사 처녀 ❑ 나는 30세가 될 때까지 처녀였다.
● 순결, 처녀성 불가산명사 ❑ 그녀는 스무 살에 순결을
잃었다. ■ 형용사 미답의, 미개발의 ❑ 40년도 못
지나서 개간되지 않는 숲은 남아 있지 않게 될 것이다.
■ 구 미답의 영역 ❑ 월드컵은 에콰도르에게 미답의
영역이다. ■ 가산명사 초보자, 미경험자
❑ '탄도에서'에 출연할 때까지 말코비치는 액션
영화에는 출연해 본 적이 없었다.

vir|ile /ˈvɪrᵊl, BRIT ˈvɪraɪl/ ADJ If you describe a man as **virile**, you mean that he has the qualities that a man is traditionally expected to have, such as strength and sexual power. ❑ *He wanted his sons to become strong, virile, and athletic like himself.* ● **vi|ril|ity** /vɪˈrɪlɪti/ N-UNCOUNT ❑ *Children are also considered proof of a man's virility.*

형용사 남성적인, 강건한 ❑ 그는 자기의 아들들이 자기처럼 힘세고, 남성적이며, 강건하기를 원했다. ● 남성성, 생식력 불가산명사 ❑ 자녀들 또한 남자의 남성성의 증거로 여겨진다.

vir|tual /ˈvɜːrtʃuəl/ ■ ADJ You can use **virtual** to indicate that something is so nearly true that for most purposes it can be regarded as true. [ADJ n] ❑ *Argentina came to a virtual standstill while the game was being played.* ❷ ADJ **Virtual** objects and activities are generated by a computer to simulate real objects and activities. [COMPUTING] [ADJ n] ❑ *Up to four players can compete in a virtual world of role playing.* ● **vir|tu|al|ity** N-UNCOUNT ❑ *People speculate about virtuality systems, but we're already working on it.*

■ 형용사 사실상의, 실질상의 ❑ 그 경기가 진행되는 동안에 아르헨티나가 사실상 정지 상태가 되었다. ❷ 형용사 가상의 [컴퓨터] ❑ 네 명까지 가상 세계의 역할 체험에 참가해서 겨룰 수 있다. ● 가상 세계 불가산명사 ❑ 사람들은 가상세계 시스템에 관해 생각만 하고 있지만, 우리는 이미 그것에 대해 작업을 하고 있다.

vir|tu|al|ly ◆◇◇ /ˈvɜːrtʃuəli/ ADV You can use **virtually** to indicate that something is so nearly true that for most purposes it can be regarded as true. [ADV with group] ❑ *Virtually all cooking was done over coal-fired ranges.*

부사 사실상, 거의 ❑ 사실상 모든 요리가 갈탄 화덕에서 만들어졌다.

vir|tual memo|ry N-UNCOUNT **Virtual memory** is a computing technique in which you increase the size of a computer's memory by arranging or storing the data in it in a different way. [COMPUTING] ❑ *...with 4mb RAM and 8mb virtual memory.*

불가산명사 가상 메모리 [컴퓨터] ❑ 4메가 램과 8메가 가상 메모리를 가진

vir|tual re|al|ity N-UNCOUNT **Virtual reality** is an environment which is produced by a computer and seems very like reality to the person experiencing it. [COMPUTING] ❑ *One day virtual reality will revolutionize the entertainment industry.*

불가산명사 가상현실 [컴퓨터] ❑ 언젠가는 가상현실이 오락 산업에 혁명을 일으킬 것이다.

vir|tual stor|age N-UNCOUNT **Virtual storage** is the same as **virtual memory**. [COMPUTING]

불가산명사 가상 메모리 [컴퓨터]

vir|tue /ˈvɜːrtʃuː/ (**virtues**) ■ N-UNCOUNT **Virtue** is thinking and doing what is right and avoiding what is wrong. ❑ *Virtue is not confined to the Christian world.* ❷ N-COUNT A **virtue** is a good quality or way of behaving. ❑ *His virtue is patience.* ❸ N-COUNT The **virtue** of something is an advantage or benefit that it has, especially in comparison with something else. ❑ *There was no virtue in returning to Calvi the way I had come.* ❹ PHRASE You use **by virtue of** to explain why something happens or is true. [FORMAL] ❑ *The article stuck in my mind by virtue of one detail.*

■ 불가산명사 선, 선행 ❑ 선은 기독교 세계에만 국한된 것이 아니다. ❷ 가산명사 미덕, 덕목 ❑ 그의 미덕은 인내이다. ❸ 가산명사 장점, 이점 ❑ 내가 캘비까지 왔던 길로 되돌아가는 것에는 이점이 없었다. ❹ 구 ~ 덕분에, ~ 때문에 [격식체] ❑ 그 기사는 한 가지 세부 사항 덕분에 내 기억에 계속 남았다.

vir|tuo|so /ˌvɜːrtʃuˈoʊsoʊ/ (**virtuosos** or **virtuosi**) /ˌvɜːrtʃuˈoʊsi/ ■ N-COUNT A **virtuoso** is someone who is extremely good at something, especially at playing a musical instrument. ❑ *He was gaining a reputation as a remarkable virtuoso.* ❷ ADJ A **virtuoso** performance or display shows great skill. [ADJ n] ❑ *England's football fans were hoping for a virtuoso performance against Cameroon.*

■ 가산명사 (특히 음악의) 거장, 명인 ❑ 그는 비범한 거장으로서 명성을 얻고 있었다. ❷ 형용사 대가의, 명인의 ❑ 잉글랜드의 축구 팬들은 카메룬전에서 대가다운 기량을 보여 주길 기대하고 있었다.

vir|tu|ous /ˈvɜːrtʃuəs/ ■ ADJ A **virtuous** person behaves in a moral and correct way. ❑ *Louis was shown as an intelligent, courageous and virtuous family man.* ❷ ADJ If you describe someone as **virtuous**, you mean that they have done what they ought to have and feel very pleased with themselves, perhaps too pleased. ❑ *I cleaned the flat, which left me feeling virtuous.* ● **vir|tu|ous|ly** ADV ❑ *"I've already done that," said Ronnie virtuously.*

■ 형용사 도덕적인, 고결한 ❑ 루이스는 지적이고, 용기 있고, 도덕적이며 가정적인 남자로 나왔다. ❷ 형용사 버젓한 ❑ 나는 아파트를 청소하고 나서 버젓해진 기분이 들었다. ● 버젓하게 부사 ❑ "그건 이미 다 했어."라고 로니가 버젓하게 말했다.

Word Link vir ≈ poison : viral, virulent, virus

viru|lent /ˈvɪrjələnt/ ■ ADJ **Virulent** feelings or actions are extremely bitter and hostile. [FORMAL] ❑ *Now he faces virulent attacks from the Italian media.* ● **viru|lent|ly** ADV ❑ *The talk was virulently hostile to the leadership.* ❷ ADJ A **virulent** disease or poison is extremely powerful and dangerous. ❑ *A very virulent form of the disease appeared in Belgium.*

■ 형용사 매서운, 신랄한 [격식체] ❑ 이제 그는 이태리 언론의 매서운 공격에 직면하고 있다. ● 매섭게, 신랄하게 부사 ❑ 그 연설은 지도부에 대해 신랄하게 적대적이었다. ❷ 형용사 악성의, 치명적인 ❑ 그 병의 매우 치명적인 형태가 벨기에에 나타났다.

vi|rus ◆◇◇ /ˈvaɪrəs/ (**viruses**) ■ N-COUNT A **virus** is a kind of germ that can cause disease. ❑ *There are many different strains of flu virus.* ❷ N-COUNT In computer technology, a **virus** is a program that introduces itself into a system, altering or destroying the information stored in the system. [COMPUTING] ❑ *Hackers are said to have started a computer virus.* →see **illness**

■ 가산명사 바이러스 ❑ 독감 바이러스는 다른 변종이 많다. ❷ 가산명사 (컴퓨터) 바이러스 [컴퓨터] ❑ 해커들이 컴퓨터 바이러스를 창시했다고 한다.

visa /ˈviːzə/ (**visas**) N-COUNT A **visa** is an official document, or a stamp put in your passport, which allows you to enter or leave a particular country. ❑ *His visitor's visa expired.* ❑ *...an exit visa.*

가산명사 비자, 사증 ❑ 그의 방문 비자는 만기가 지났다. ❑ 출국 사증

vise /vaɪs/ (**vices**) N-COUNT A **vise** is a tool with a pair of parts that hold an object tightly while you do work on it. [AM; BRIT **vice**]

가산명사 바이스 [미국영어; 영국영어 vice]

vis|ibil|ity /ˌvɪzɪˈbɪlɪti/ ■ N-UNCOUNT **Visibility** means how far or how clearly you can see in particular weather conditions. ❑ *Visibility was poor.* ❷ N-UNCOUNT If you refer to the **visibility** of something such as a situation or problem, you mean how much it is seen or noticed by other people. ❑ *The plight of the Kurds gained global visibility.*

■ 불가산명사 시계(視界) ❑ 시계가 나빴다. ❷ 불가산명사 가시성, 눈에 보임 ❑ 쿠르드 족의 곤경이 세계적인 이목을 끌었다.

vis|ible ◆◇◇ /ˈvɪzɪbᵊl/ ■ ADJ If something is **visible**, it can be seen. ❑ *The warning lights were clearly visible.* ❷ ADJ You use **visible** to describe something or someone that people notice or recognize. ❑ *The most visible sign of the intensity of the crisis is unemployment.* ● **vis|ibly** /ˈvɪzɪbli/ ADV ❑ *The Russians were visibly wavering.* →see **wave**

■ 형용사 알아볼 수 있는, 보이는 ❑ 경고등이 분명하게 잘 보였다. ❷ 형용사 인지할 수 있는, 명백한 ❑ 위기의 강도를 가장 잘 보여 주는 징후는 실업이다. ● 눈에 띄게, 분명히 부사 ❑ 러시아 사람들은 분명히 동요하고 있었다.

Word Partnership	visible의 연어
ADV.	**barely** visible, **highly** visible, **less** visible, **more** visible, **still** visible, **very** visible ■ ❷
V.	**become** visible ■ ❷

vi|sion ◆◇◇ /ˈvɪʒᵊn/ (**visions**) ■ N-COUNT Your **vision of** a future situation or society is what you imagine or hope it would be like, if things were very different from the way they are now. ❑ *I have a vision of a society that is free of exploitation and injustice.* ❑ *That's my vision of how the world could be.* ❷ N-COUNT If you have a **vision of** someone in a particular situation, you imagine them in

■ 가산명사 시각, 전망, 미래상 ❑ 나는 착취와 부정이 없는 사회를 꿈꾼다. ❑ 그게 세계의 가능성에 대한 나의 시각이다. ❷ 가산명사 환상, 상상 ❑ 그는 체릴이 대기실 플라스틱 의자에 축 처져 있는 모습을 상상했다. ❸ 가산명사 환영, 환각 ❑ 마을 젊은이들이

that situation, for example because you are worried that it might happen, or hope that it will happen. ❑ *He had a vision of Cheryl, slumped on a plastic chair in the waiting-room.* **3** N-COUNT A **vision** is the experience of seeing something that other people cannot see, for example in a religious experience or as a result of madness or taking drugs. ❑ *It was on 24th June 1981 that young villagers first reported seeing the Virgin Mary in a vision.* **4** N-UNCOUNT Your **vision** is your ability to see clearly with your eyes. ❑ *It causes blindness or serious loss of vision.* **5** N-UNCOUNT Your **vision** is everything that you can see from a particular place or position. ❑ *Jane blocked Cross's vision and he could see nothing.*

성모 마리아의 환영을 보았다고 처음 알려 온 것은 1981년 6월 24일이었다. **4** 불가산명사 시력 ❑ 그것은 실명 또는 심각한 시력 저하를 일으킨다. **5** 불가산명사 시야 ❑ 제인이 크로스의 시야를 가려서 그는 아무것도 볼 수 없었다.

Word Partnership		*vision*의 연어
V.	share a vision **1**	
	have a vision **1**-**3**	
	see a vision **3**	
ADJ.	clear vision **1** **2** **4**	
N.	vision **of the future**, vision **of peace**, vision **of reality** **1**	
	color vision **4**	
	field of vision **5**	

vi·sion·ary /vɪ́ʒənɛri, BRIT vɪ́ʒənri/ (**visionaries**) **1** N-COUNT If you refer to someone as a **visionary**, you mean that they have strong, original ideas about how things might be different in the future, especially about how things might be improved. ❑ *An entrepreneur is more than just a risk taker. He is a visionary.* **2** ADJ You use **visionary** to describe the strong, original ideas of a visionary. ❑ *...the visionary architecture of Etienne Boullé.*

1 가산명사 예견가, 이상가 ❑ 기업가는 단순한 모험가 이상이다. 그는 예견가이다. **2** 형용사 예견력 있는, 이상적인 ❑ 에띠엔느 불레의 예견력 있는 건축 양식

vis·it ♦♦♦ /vɪ́zɪt/ (**visits, visiting, visited**) **1** V-T/V-I If you **visit** someone, you go to see them and spend time with them. ❑ *He wanted to visit his brother in Worcester.* ● N-COUNT **Visit** is also a noun. ❑ *Helen had recently paid him a visit.* **2** V-T/V-I If you **visit** a place, you go there for a short time. ❑ *He'll be visiting four cities including Cagliari in Sardinia.* ❑ *Caroline visited all the big stores.* ● N-COUNT **Visit** is also a noun. ❑ *...the Pope's visit to Canada.* **3** V-T If you **visit** a website, you look at it. [COMPUTING] ❑ *For details visit our website at www.collins.co.uk.* **4** V-T If you **visit** a professional person such as a doctor or lawyer, you go and see them in order to get professional advice. If they **visit** you, they come to see you in order to give you professional advice. [mainly BRIT] ❑ *If necessary the patient can then visit his doctor for further advice.* ● N-COUNT **Visit** is also a noun. ❑ *You may have regular home visits from a neonatal nurse.*

1 타동사/자동사 방문하다 ❑ 그는 우스터에 있는 형을 방문하고 싶어 했다. ● 가산명사 방문 ❑ 헬렌은 최근 그를 방문했었다. **2** 타동사/자동사 들르다 ❑ 그는 사르디니아의 카글리아리를 포함하여 네 도시를 들를 것이다. ❑ 캐롤라인은 모든 큰 상점에 들렀다. ● 가산명사 방문 ❑ 교황의 캐나다 방문 **3** 타동사 (웹사이트를) 보다 [컴퓨터] ❑ 자세한 사항은 저희 웹사이트 www.collins.co.uk 을 보세요. **4** 타동사 (의사 등에게) 가다; (의뢰인을) 방문하다 [주로 영국영어] ❑ 필요하면 환자가 그 다음에 조언을 더 들으러 자기 의사에게 찾아갈 수 있다. ● 가산명사 출장 ❑ 당신은 신생아 간호사의 정기적 가정 출장 방문을 받을 수 있다.

Thesaurus		*visit*의 참조어
V.	call on, go, see, stop by **1**	

Word Partnership		*visit*의 연어
N.	visit **family/relatives**, visit **friends**, visit *your* **mother** **1**	
	weekend visit **1** **2**	
	visit **a museum**, visit **a restaurant** **2**	
	visit **a website** **3**	
	visit **a doctor** **4**	
V.	**come to** visit, **go to** visit, **invite** *someone* **to** visit, **plan to** visit **1** **2**	
ADJ.	**brief** visit, **last** visit, **next** visit, **recent** visit, **short** visit, **surprise** visit **1** **2**	
	foreign visit, **official** visit **2**	

▶**visit with** PHRASAL VERB If you **visit with** someone, you go to see them and spend time with them. [AM] ❑ *I visited with him in San Francisco.*

구동사 ~에게 가서 지내다 [미국영어] ❑ 나는 샌프란시스코에 가서 그와 지냈다.

vis·i·tor ♦♦♦ /vɪ́zɪtər/ (**visitors**) N-COUNT A **visitor** is someone who is visiting a person or place. ❑ *The other day we had some visitors from Switzerland.*

가산명사 손님 ❑ 저번에 스위스에서 손님이 몇 분 오셨다.

vis·ta /vɪ́stə/ (**vistas**) N-COUNT A **vista** is a view from a particular place, especially a beautiful view from a high place. [WRITTEN] ❑ *From my bedroom window I looked out on a crowded vista of hills and rooftops.*

가산명사 조망, 전망 [문어체] ❑ 내 침실 창에서 나는 언덕과 지붕이 가득한 전망을 내다보았다.

vis·ual /vɪ́ʒuəl/ (**visuals**) **1** ADJ **Visual** means relating to sight, or to things that you can see. ❑ *...the graphic visual depiction of violence.* ● **visu·al·ly** ADV ❑ *...visually handicapped boys and girls.* **2** N-COUNT A **visual** is something such as a picture, diagram, or piece of film that is used to show or explain something. ❑ *Remember you want your visuals to reinforce your message, not detract from what you are saying.*

1 형용사 시각의 ❑ 폭력의 생생한 시각적 묘사 ● 시각적으로 부사 ❑ 시각 장애가 있는 소년 소녀들 **2** 가산명사 시각 자료 ❑ 시각 자료는 당신이 말하는 내용에서 주의를 벗어나게 하는 것이 아니라 메시지 전달을 보완하도록 해야 한다는 것을 명심하시오.

Word Partnership		*visual*의 연어
N.	visual **arts**, visual **effects**, visual **information**, visual **memory**, visual **perception** **1**	

vis·ual aid (**visual aids**) N-COUNT **Visual aids** are things that you can look at, such as a film, model, map, or slides, to help you understand something or to remember information.

가산명사 시청각 교재

vis·ual·ize /vɪ́ʒuəlaɪz/ (**visualizes, visualizing, visualized**) [BRIT also **visualise**] V-T If you **visualize** something, you imagine what it is like by forming a mental picture of it. ❑ *Susan visualized her wedding day and saw herself walking down the aisle on her father's arm.* ❑ *He could not visualize her as old.*

[영국영어 visualise] 타동사 마음속에 그리다, 상상하다 ❑ 수잔은 자기의 결혼식 날을 마음속에 그리며 아버지의 팔을 잡고 통로를 걸어가는 자신의 모습을 보았다. ❑ 그는 나이가 든 그녀의 모습을 상상할 수가 없었다.

a b c d e f g h i j k l m n o p q r s t u **v** w x y z

Word Link vita ≈ life : revitalize, vital, vitality

vi|tal ◆◇◇ /vaɪtəl/ ADJ If you say that something is **vital**, you mean that it is necessary or very important. ❑ The port is vital to supply relief to millions of drought victims. ❑ Nick Wileman is a school caretaker so it is vital that he gets on well with young people. ● **vi|tal|ly** ADV ❑ Lesley's career in the church is vitally important to her.

형용사 필수적인, 중대한 ❑ 그 항구는 수백만의 가뭄 피해자들에게 구호품을 보내는 데 매우 중요하다. ❑ 닉 와일만은 학교 관리인이어서 그가 젊은이들과 잘 지내는 것이 필수적이다. ● 중대하게 부사 ❑ 레스리의 교회 이력은 그녀에게 참으로 중요하다.

Thesaurus vital의 참조어

ADJ. crucial, essential, necessary; (ant.) unimportant

Word Partnership vital의 연어

ADV. **absolutely** vital
N. vital **importance**, vital **information**, vital **interests**, vital **link**, vital **part**, vital **role**

vi|tal|ity /vaɪtæliti/ N-UNCOUNT If you say that someone or something has **vitality**, you mean that they have great energy and liveliness. ❑ Without continued learning, graduates will lose their intellectual vitality.

불가산명사 활력, 원기, 생명력 ❑ 계속 배우지 않으면 졸업생들은 지적 활력을 잃을 것이다.

vita|min ◆◇◇ /vaɪtəmɪn, BRIT vɪtəmɪn/ (**vitamins**) N-COUNT **Vitamins** are substances that you need in order to remain healthy, which are found in food or can be eaten in the form of pills. ❑ Lack of vitamin D is another factor to consider.

가산명사 비타민 ❑ 비타민 디(D)의 결핍도 고려해야 할 또 다른 요인이다.

viva /vaɪvə/ (**vivas**) N-COUNT A **viva** is a university examination in which a student answers questions in speech rather than writing. [BRIT]

가산명사 구술시험 [영국영어]

Word Link viv ≈ living : revival, survive, vivacious

vi|va|cious /vɪveɪʃəs/ ADJ If you describe someone as **vivacious**, you mean that they are lively, exciting, and attractive. [WRITTEN, APPROVAL] ❑ She's beautiful, vivacious, and charming.

형용사 활기 있는, 쾌활한 [문어체, 마음에 듦] ❑ 그녀는 아름답고 쾌활하고 매력적이다.

viv|id /vɪvɪd/ ◼ ADJ If you describe memories and descriptions as **vivid**, you mean that they are very clear and detailed. ❑ People of my generation who lived through World War II have vivid memories of confusion and incompetence. ● **viv|id|ly** ADV ❑ I can vividly remember the feeling of panic. ◼ ADJ Something that is **vivid** is very bright in color. ❑ ...a vivid blue sky. ● **viv|id|ly** ADV [ADV -ed/adj] ❑ ...vividly colored birds.

◼ 형용사 생생한 ❑ 2차 세계 대전을 겪은 우리 세대의 사람들은 혼란과 무능을 생생히 기억하고 있다. ● 생생하게 부사 ❑ 나는 그 공포감을 생생하게 기억할 수 있다. ◼ 형용사 밝은, 선명한 ❑ 선명하게 푸른 하늘 ● 선명하게 부사 ❑ 선명한 빛깔의 새들

vivi|sec|tion /vɪvɪsekʃⁿn/ N-UNCOUNT **Vivisection** is the practice of using live animals for scientific experiments. ❑ ...a fierce opponent of vivisection.

불가산명사 생체 실험, 생체 해부 ❑ 생체 실험을 맹렬히 반대하는 사람

viz. viz. is used in written English to introduce a list of specific items or examples. ❑ The school offers two modules in Teaching English as a Foreign Language, viz. Principles and Methods of Language Teaching and Applied Linguistics.

즉 ❑ 학교에서는 외국어로서의 영어 교육을 2개 모듈, 즉 언어 교수 원리와 방법 및 응용 언어학으로 개설하고 있다.

Word Link voc ≈ speaking : advocate, vocabulary, vocal

vo|cabu|lary /voʊkæbyələri, BRIT voʊkæbyʊləri/ (**vocabularies**) ◼ N-VAR Your **vocabulary** is the total number of words you know in a particular language. ❑ His speech is immature, his vocabulary limited. ◼ N-SING The **vocabulary** of a language is all the words in it. ❑ ...a new word in the German vocabulary. ◼ N-VAR The **vocabulary** of a subject is the group of words that are typically used when discussing it. ❑ ...the vocabulary of natural science. →see English

◼ 가산명사 또는 불가산명사 (개인이 구사하는) 어휘 ❑ 그의 연설은 생경하고 그의 어휘는 한정되어 있다. ◼ 단수명사 (한 언어에 속한) 어휘 ❑ 독일어 어휘에서 새로운 단어 ◼ 가산명사 또는 불가산명사 (전문 분야의) 용어 ❑ 자연 과학 용어

Word Partnership vocabulary의 연어

N. **part of** someone's vocabulary ◼
vocabulary **development** ◼ ◼
V. **learn** vocabulary ◼ ◼
ADJ. **specialized** vocabulary, **technical** vocabulary ◼

vo|cal /voʊkⁿl/ ◼ ADJ You say that people are **vocal** when they speak forcefully about something that they feel strongly about. ❑ He has been very vocal in his displeasure over the results. ◼ ADJ **Vocal** means involving the use of the human voice, especially in singing. [ADJ n] ❑ ...a wider range of vocal styles.

◼ 형용사 강경하게 말하는 ❑ 그는 그 결과에 대한 불만을 아주 강경하게 표현해 왔다. ◼ 형용사 목소리의, 발성의 ❑ 더 다양한 음색의 목소리들

vo|cal|ist /voʊkəlɪst/ (**vocalists**) N-COUNT A **vocalist** is a singer who sings with a pop group. ❑ He and Carla Torgerson take turns as the band's lead vocalist.

가산명사 (팝 그룹의) 가수, 보컬 ❑ 그와 칼라 토거슨이 번갈아 가며 그 밴드의 리드 보컬을 한다.

vo|cals /voʊkⁿlz/ N-PLURAL In a pop song, the **vocals** are the singing, in contrast to the playing of instruments. ❑ Johnson now sings backing vocals for Mica Paris.

복수명사 (노래의) 보컬 부분 ❑ 존슨이 이제 미카 파리의 보컬 부분을 보조한다.

vo|ca|tion /voʊkeɪʃⁿn/ (**vocations**) ◼ N-VAR If you have a **vocation**, you have a strong feeling that you are especially suited to do a particular job or to fulfill a particular role in life, especially one which involves helping other people. ❑ It could well be that he has a real vocation. ◼ N-VAR If you refer to your job or profession as your **vocation**, you feel that you are particularly suited to it. ❑ Her vocation is her work as an actress.

◼ 가산명사 또는 불가산명사 사명감, 소명 의식 ❑ 그는 분명 진정한 사명감이 있을 것이다. ◼ 가산명사 또는 불가산명사 천직 ❑ 그녀의 천직은 배우라는 직업이다.

vo|ca|tion|al /voʊkeɪʃənⁿl/ ADJ **Vocational** training and skills are the training and skills needed for a particular job or profession. ❑ ...a course designed to provide vocational training in engineering.

형용사 직업상의 ❑ 기술직 직업 훈련을 제공하기 위해 만들어진 과정

vo|cif|er|ous /voʊsɪfərəs, BRIT vəsɪfərəs/ ADJ If you describe someone as **vociferous**, you mean that they speak with great energy and determination, because they want their views to be heard. ❑ He was a vociferous opponent of Conservatism. ● **vo|cif|er|ous|ly** ADV ❑ He vociferously opposed the state of emergency imposed by the government.

형용사 소리 높여 외치는 ❑ 그는 보수주의를 소리 높여 반대했다. ● 소리 높여 부사 ❑ 그는 정부가 선포한 비상사태에 소리 높여 반대했다.

vod|ka /vɒdkə/ (**vodkas**) N-MASS **Vodka** is a strong, clear, alcoholic drink.

물질명사 보드카

vogue /voʊg/ ◼ N-SING If there is a **vogue for** something, it is very popular and fashionable. ❑ Despite the vogue for so-called health teas, there is no evidence that they are any healthier. ◼ PHRASE If something is **in vogue**, is very popular and fashionable. If it comes **into vogue**, it becomes very popular and fashionable. ❑ Pale colors are much more in vogue than autumnal bronzes and coppers.

◼ 단수명사 유행 ❑ 소위 건강차(茶)라는 것들이 유행하지만 그것들이 건강에 더 좋다는 증거는 전혀 없다. ◼ 구 유행하는; 유행하게 된 ❑ 가을 느낌 나는 청동색과 구릿빛보다 무채색 계열 색깔들이 훨씬 더 유행하고 있다.

voice ♦♦◇ /vɔɪs/ (**voices, voicing, voiced**) ◼ N-COUNT When someone speaks or sings, you hear their **voice**. ❑ Miriam's voice was strangely calm. ❑ "The police are here," she said in a low voice. ◼ N-COUNT Someone's **voice** is their opinion on a particular topic and what they say about it. ❑ What does one do when a government simply refuses to listen to the voice of the opposition? ◼ V-T If you **voice** something such as an opinion or an emotion, you say what you think or feel. ❑ Some scientists have voiced concern that the disease could be passed on to humans. ◼ PHRASE If you **give voice to** an opinion, a need, or a desire, you express it aloud. ❑ ...a community radio run by the Catholic Church which gave voice to the protests of the slum-dwellers. ◼ PHRASE If someone tells you to **keep** your **voice down**, they are asking you to speak more quietly. ❑ Keep your voice down, for goodness sake. ◼ PHRASE If you **lose** your **voice**, you cannot speak for a while because of an illness. ❑ I had to be careful not to get a sore throat and lose my voice. ◼ PHRASE If you **raise** your **voice**, you speak more loudly. If you **lower** your **voice**, you speak more quietly. ❑ He raised his voice for the benefit of the other two women. ◼ PHRASE If you say something **at the top of** your **voice**, you say it as loudly as possible. [EMPHASIS] ❑ "Damn!" he yelled at the top of his voice.

◼ 가산명사 목소리, 음성 ❑ 미리암의 목소리는 묘하게 차분했다. ❑ "경찰이 왔어."라고 그녀가 낮은 음성으로 말했다. ◼ 가산명사 목소리, 의견 ❑ 정부가 그저 반대 의견에 전혀 귀를 기울이려 하지 않을 때 사람은 어떤 행동을 하는가? ◼ 타동사 목소리를 내다, 표명하다 ❑ 일부 과학자들은 그 질병이 인간에게도 전염될 수 있다고 우려를 표명해 왔다. ◼ 구 공개하다, 표명하다 ❑ 빈민가 주민들의 시위를 공개한 천주교회가 운영하는 지역 라디오 방송국 ◼ 구 목소리를 낮춰 말하다, 작게 말하다 ❑ 목소리를 낮춰, 제발! ◼ 구 목소리가 나오지 않는다 ❑ 나는 목이 아파서 목소리가 안 나오는 일이 없도록 조심해야 했다. ◼ 구 더 큰 소리로 말하다, 목소리를 높이는; 더 작은 소리로 말하다, 목소리를 낮추다 ❑ 그는 다른 두 여자들이 들을 수 있도록 더 큰 소리로 말했다. ◼ 구 목청껏 [강조] ❑ "제기랄!" 하고 그가 목청껏 소리 질렀다.

voice mail N-UNCOUNT **Voice mail** is a system of sending messages over the telephone. Calls are answered by a machine which connects you to the person you want to leave a message for, and they can listen to their messages later. ❑ He was on a call, so I left a message on his voice mail.

불가산명사 음성 사서함 ❑ 그가 통화 중이어서 나는 그의 음성 사서함에 메시지를 남겼다.

voice-over (**voice-overs**) also **voiceover** N-COUNT The **voice-over** of a film, television program, or advertisement consists of words which are spoken by someone who is not seen. ❑ 89% of advertisements had a male voice-over.

가산명사 (화면에 나타나지 않는) 해설자의 목소리 ❑ 광고의 89퍼센트에 남성의 목소리가 해설자로 등장했다.

void /vɔɪd/ (**voids, voiding, voided**) ◼ N-COUNT If you describe a situation or a feeling as a **void**, you mean that it seems empty because there is nothing interesting or worthwhile about it. ❑ His death has left a void in the cricketing world which can never be filled. ◼ N-COUNT You can describe a large or frightening space as a **void**. ❑ He stared into the dark void where the battle had been fought. ◼ ADJ Something that is **void** or **null and void** is officially considered to have no value or authority. [v-link ADJ] ❑ The original elections were declared void by the former military ruler. ◼ ADJ If you are **void of** something, you do not have any of it. [FORMAL] [v-link ADJ of n] ❑ He rose, his face void of emotion as he walked towards the door. ◼ V-T To **void** something means to officially say that it is not valid. [FORMAL] ❑ The Supreme Court threw out the confession and voided his conviction for murder.

◼ 가산명사 공허감 ❑ 그의 죽음은 크리켓 세계에 다시 채워질 수 없는 공허감을 남겼다. ◼ 가산명사 텅 빈 큰 공간 ❑ 그는 전투가 벌어졌던 어두운 공간을 응시했다. ◼ 형용사 무효의 ❑ 원래 선거는 이전 군부 통치자에 의해 무효라고 선언되었다. ◼ 형용사 ~의 없는 [격식체] ❑ 그는 아무 표정 없는 얼굴로 문을 향해 걸어갔다. ◼ 타동사 무효로 하다 [격식체] ❑ 연방 대법원이 그 자백을 기각하고 그의 살인죄 유죄 판결에 대해 무효 판결을 내렸다.

vol. ♦◇◇ (**vols.**) **Vol.** is used as a written abbreviation for **volume** when you are referring to one or more books in a series of books.

(전집 등의) 권, volume의 축약형

volatile /vɒlətl, BRIT vɒlətaɪl/ ◼ ADJ A situation that is **volatile** is likely to change suddenly and unexpectedly. ❑ There have been riots before and the situation is volatile. ◼ ADJ If someone is **volatile**, their mood often changes quickly. ❑ He accompanied the volatile actress to Hollywood the following year. ◼ ADJ A **volatile** liquid or substance is one that will quickly change into a gas. [TECHNICAL] ❑ It's thought that the blast occurred when volatile chemicals exploded.

◼ 형용사 폭발 직전의, 일촉즉발의 ❑ 전에도 여러 차례 폭동이 있어 왔으며 현 상황은 폭발 직전이다. ◼ 형용사 변덕스러운 ❑ 그는 이듬해에 그 변덕스러운 여배우와 함께 할리우드로 갔다. ◼ 형용사 휘발성의 [과학 기술] ❑ 그 폭발은 휘발성 화학 물질이 터지면서 일어난 것으로 여겨진다.

volcanic /vɒlkænɪk/ ADJ **Volcanic** means coming from or created by volcanoes. ❑ Over 200 people have been killed by volcanic eruptions. →see **volcano**

형용사 화산의, 화산 작용에 의한 ❑ 화산 폭발로 200명 이상이 사망했다.

volcano /vɒlkeɪnoʊ/ (**volcanoes**) N-COUNT A **volcano** is a mountain from which hot melted rock, gas, steam, and ash from inside the earth sometimes burst. ❑ The volcano erupted last year killing about 600 people. →see Word Web: **volcano**

가산명사 화산 ❑ 작년에 그 화산이 분출하면서 600명 가량이 사망했다.

volley /vɒli/ (**volleys, volleying, volleyed**) ◼ V-T/V-I In sports, if someone **volleys** the ball, they hit it before it touches the ground. ❑ He volleyed the ball spectacularly into the far corner of the net. ● N-COUNT **Volley** is also a noun. ❑ She hit most of the winning volleys. ◼ N-COUNT A **volley** of gunfire is a lot of bullets that travel through the air at the same time. ❑ It's still not known how many died in the volleys of gunfire.

◼ 타동사/자동사 (공이 땅에 닿기 전에) 되받아치다, 발리를 하다 ❑ 그는 멋지게 발리를 해서 네트에서 멀리 떨어진 구석으로 공을 보냈다. ● 가산명사 발리 ❑ 그녀는 결정적인 발리 대부분을 해냈다. ◼ 가산명사 일제 사격 ❑ 화포의 일제 사격으로 몇 명이나 죽었는지는 아직 알려져 있지 않다.

a
b
c
d
e
f
g
h
i
j
k
l
m
n
o
p
q
r
s
t
u
v
w
x
y
z

Word Web   volcano

The most famous **volcano** in the world is Mount Vesuvius, near Naples, Italy. This mountain sits in the middle of the much older **volcanic cone** of Mount Somma. In 79 AD the sleeping volcano **erupted** and magma surged to the surface. The people of the nearby city of Pompeii were terrified. Soon huge black clouds of **ash** and pumice came rushing toward them. The clouds blocked out the sun and smothered thousands of people. Pompeii was buried under hot ash and **molten lava**. Centuries later the remains of the people and town were exposed. The discovery made this active volcano world famous.

volley|ball /vɒlibɔl/ N-UNCOUNT **Volleyball** is a game in which two teams hit a large ball with their hands backward and forwards over a high net. If you allow the ball to touch the ground, the other team wins a point.

불가산명사 배구

volt /voʊlt/ (**volts**) N-COUNT A **volt** is a unit used to measure the force of an electric current.

가산명사 볼트

volt|age /voʊltɪdʒ/ (**voltages**) N-VAR The **voltage** of an electrical current is its force measured in volts. ❑ *The systems are getting smaller and using lower voltages.*

가산명사 또는 불가산명사 전압 ❑ 기계 장치들이 크기는 점점 더 작아지고 사용 전압은 점점 더 낮아지고 있다.

vol|ume ♦♦◇ /vɒlyum/ (**volumes**) **1** N-COUNT The **volume** of something is the amount of it that there is. ❑ *Senior officials will be discussing how the volume of sales might be reduced.* **2** N-COUNT The **volume** of an object is the amount of space that it contains or occupies. ❑ *When egg whites are beaten they can rise to seven or eight times their original volume.* **3** N-COUNT A **volume** is one book in a series of books. ❑ *...the first volume of his autobiography.* **4** N-COUNT A **volume** is a collection of several issues of a magazine, for example all the issues for one year. ❑ *...bound volumes of the magazine.* **5** N-UNCOUNT **The volume** of a radio, television, or sound system is the loudness of the sound it produces. ❑ *He turned down the volume.* **6** PHRASE If something such as an action **speaks volumes about** a person or thing, it gives you a lot of information about them. ❑ *What you wear speaks volumes about you.*
→see Picture Dictionary: volume

1 가산명사 양, 분량 ❑ 고위 관계자들이 판매량 감소의 가능한 원인에 대해 논의할 것이다. **2** 가산명사 부피 ❑ 달걀 흰자위는 휘저으면 원래 부피의 일곱 내지 여덟 배까지 부풀어 오른다. **3** 가산명사/자동사 (전집 등의) 권 ❑ 그의 자서전 1권 **4** 가산명사 합본 ❑ 그 잡지의 합본 **5** 불가산명사 음량, 소리의 크기 ❑ 그는 소리를 줄였다. **6** 구 많은 것을 말해 주다 ❑ 당신의 옷차림은 당신에 대해 많은 것을 말해 줍니다.

vol|un|tary ♦◇◇ /vɒlənteri, BRIT vɒləntri/ **1** ADJ **Voluntary** actions or activities are done because someone chooses to do them and not because they have been forced to do them. ❑ *Attention is drawn to a special voluntary course in Commercial French.* ● **vol|un|tar|ily** /vɒlənteərɪli, BRIT vɒləntrəli/ ADV [ADV with v] ❑ *I would only leave here voluntarily if there was a big chance to play abroad.* **2** ADJ **Voluntary** work is done by people who are not paid for it, but who do it because they want to do it. ❑ *In her spare time she does voluntary work.* **3** ADJ A **voluntary** organization is controlled and organized by the people who have chosen to work for it, often without being paid, rather than receiving help or money from the government. [ADJ n] ❑ *Some local authorities and voluntary organizations also run workshops for disabled people.*

1 형용사 자발적인, 자원의 ❑ 실무 상업불어 특별 자원 강좌가 관심을 끌고 있다. ● 자발적으로, 자진하여 부사 ❑ 해외에서 운동할 큰 기회가 있기만 하면 그냥 여기는 자진해서 떠나 버릴 텐데. **2** 형용사 자원 봉사의 ❑ 여가 시간에 그녀는 자원 봉사를 한다. **3** 형용사 자원 봉사의 ❑ 일부 지역 기관들과 자원 봉사 단체들도 장애인을 위한 작업장을 운영한다.

Word Partnership   *voluntary*의 연어

N.   voluntary **action**, voluntary **basis**, voluntary **compliance**, voluntary **contributions**, voluntary **program**, voluntary **retirement**, voluntary **test 1**
voluntary **organizations 3**

Word Link   eer ≈ one who does : auction*eer*, mountain*eer*, volunt*eer*

vol|un|teer ♦◇◇ /vɒləntɪər/ (**volunteers, volunteering, volunteered**) **1** N-COUNT A **volunteer** is someone who does work without being paid for it, because they want to do it. ❑ *She now helps in a local school as a volunteer three days a week.* **2** N-COUNT A **volunteer** is someone who offers to do a particular task or job without being forced to do it. ❑ *Right. What I want now is two volunteers to come down to the front.* **3** V-T/V-I If you **volunteer** to do something, you offer to do it without being forced to do it. ❑ *Aunt Mary volunteered to clean up the kitchen.* ❑ *He volunteered for the army in 1939.* **4** V-T If you **volunteer** information, you tell someone something without being asked. [FORMAL] ❑ *The room was quiet; no one volunteered any further information.* ❑ *"They were both great supporters of Franco," Ryle volunteered.* **5** N-COUNT A **volunteer** is someone who chooses to join the armed forces, especially during a war, as opposed to

1 가산명사 자원 봉사자 ❑ 그녀는 지금 지역 학교에서 일주일에 삼 일간 자원 봉사자로 일을 거들고 있다. **2** 가산명사 지원자 ❑ 맞아. 지금 내가 원하는 건 지원자 두 사람이 앞으로 나와 주는 것이야. **3** 타동사/자동사 자진하여 하다, 지원하다 ❑ 메리 이모가 자진하여 부엌을 치웠다. ❑ 그는 1939년에 군에 지원했다. **4** 타동사 자진해서 말하다 [격식체] ❑ 방 안은 조용했고 아무도 자진해서 더 이상의 정보를 말하려 들지 않았다. ❑ "그들 둘 다 프랑코를 대단히 지지했었지."라고 라일이 자진해서 말했다. **5** 가산명사 지원병 ❑ 그들은 지원병으로 참전해서 아프가니스탄 게릴라들과 싸웠다.

Picture Dictionary   volume

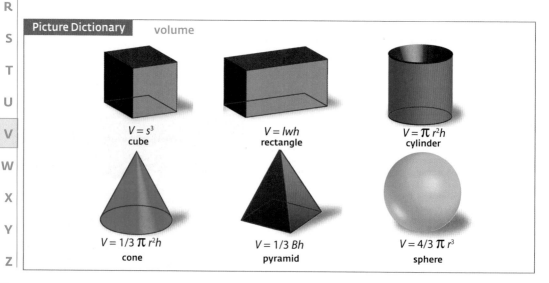

$V = s^3$
cube

$V = lwh$
rectangle

$V = \pi\, r^2 h$
cylinder

$V = 1/3\, \pi\, r^2 h$
cone

$V = 1/3\, Bh$
pyramid

$V = 4/3\, \pi\, r^3$
sphere

someone who is forced to join by law. ❏ *They fought as volunteers with the Afghan guerrillas.*

Word Partnership   *volunteer의 연어*

N.   **community** volunteer **1**
     volunteer **organization**, volunteer **program**, volunteer **work** **1 2**
     volunteer **for service**, volunteer **for the army** **3**
     volunteer **information** **4**
V.   **need a** volunteer **1 2 5**
     volunteer **to help**, volunteer **to work** **3**

---

vom|it /vɒmɪt/ (**vomits, vomiting, vomited**) **1** V-T/V-I If you **vomit**, food and drink comes back up from your stomach and out through your mouth. ❏ *Any product made from cow's milk made him vomit.* ❏ *She began to vomit blood a few days before she died.* **2** N-UNCOUNT **Vomit** is partly digested food and drink that has come back up from someone's stomach and out through their mouth. ❏ *Zimmer slipped and nearly fell on a pool of vomit.*

vo|ra|cious /vɔreɪʃəs, BRIT vəreɪʃəs/ ADJ If you describe a person, or their appetite for something, as **voracious**, you mean that they want a lot of something. [LITERARY] ❏ *Joseph Smith was a voracious book collector.*

vote ♦♦♦ /voʊt/ (**votes, voting, voted**) **1** N-COUNT A **vote** is a choice made by a particular person or group in a meeting or an election. ❏ *He walked to the local polling center to cast his vote.* ❏ *The government got a massive majority – well over 400 votes.* **2** N-COUNT A **vote** is an occasion when a group of people make a decision by each person indicating his or her choice. The choice that most people support is accepted by the group. ❏ *Why do you think we should have a vote on that?* **3** N-SING The **vote** is the total number of votes or voters in an election, or the number of votes received or cast by a particular group. ❏ *Opposition parties won about fifty-five per cent of the vote.* **4** N-SING If you have **the vote** in an election, or have **a vote** in a meeting, you have the legal right to indicate your choice. ❏ *Before that, women did not have a vote at all.* **5** V-T/V-I When you **vote**, you indicate your choice officially at a meeting or in an election, for example by raising your hand or writing on a piece of paper. ❏ *Two-thirds of the national electorate had the chance to vote in these elections.* ❏ *It seems many people would vote for the government, at a general election, if there was a new leader.* ❏ *The residents of Leningrad voted to restore the city's original name of St Petersburg.* ● **vot|ing** N-UNCOUNT ❏ *Voting began about two hours ago.* **6** V-T If you **vote** a particular political party or leader, or **vote yes** or **no**, you make that choice with the vote that you have. ❏ *52.5% of those questioned said they'd vote Labour.* **7** V-T If people **vote** someone a particular title, they choose that person to have that title. ❏ *His class voted him the man "who had done the most for Yale."* **8** PHRASE If you **vote with** your **feet**, you show that you do not support something by leaving the place where it is happening or leaving the organization that is supporting it. ❏ *Thousands of citizens are already voting with their feet, and leaving the country.* **9** PHRASE If you say "**I vote that**" a particular thing should happen, you are suggesting that this is what should happen. [INFORMAL] ❏ *I vote that we all go to Holland immediately.* **10** PHRASE **One man one vote** or **one person one vote** is a system of voting in which every person in a group or country has the right to cast their vote, and in which each individual's vote is counted and has equal value. ❏ *Mr. Gould called for a move towards "one man one vote."* →see **election**
→see Word Web: **vote**

vote of thanks (**votes of thanks**) N-COUNT A **vote of thanks** is an official speech in which the speaker formally thanks a person for doing something. ❏ *I would like to propose a vote of thanks to our host.*

vot|er ♦♦◇ /voʊtər/ (**voters**) N-COUNT **Voters** are people who have the legal right to vote in elections, or people who are voting in a particular election. ❏ *The turnout was at least 62 percent of registered voters.* →see **election**

vouch /vaʊtʃ/ (**vouches, vouching, vouched**)

▶**vouch for** **1** PHRASAL VERB If you say that you can or will **vouch for** someone, you mean that you can guarantee their good behavior. ❏ *Kim's mother agreed to vouch for Maria and get her a job.* **2** PHRASAL VERB If you say that you can **vouch for** something, you mean that you have evidence from your own personal experience that it is true or correct. ❏ *He cannot vouch for the accuracy of the story.*

vouch|er /vaʊtʃər/ (**vouchers**) N-COUNT A **voucher** is a ticket or piece of paper that can be used instead of money to pay for something. ❏ *The winners will each receive a voucher for a pair of cinema tickets.*

---

1 타동사/자동사 토하다, 게우다 ❏ 우유로 만든 제품을 먹기만 하면 그는 토했다. ❏ 그녀는 죽기 며칠 전에 피를 토하기 시작했다. **2** 불가산명사 토사물 ❏ 짐머가 미끄러져서 하마터면 흥건히 고인 토사물 위로 넘어질 뻔했다.

형용사 게걸스러운 [문예체] ❏ 조셉 스미스는 게걸스러운 도서 수집가였다.

1 가산명사 투표 ❏ 그는 지역 투표소로 걸어가서 투표를 했다. ❏ 정부가 과반수 득표했는데 400표가 족히 넘었다. **2** 가산명사 투표, 표결 ❏ 왜 우리가 그것을 놓고 투표해야 한다고 생각하십니까? **3** 단수명사 투표수 ❏ 야당들이 투표수의 약 55퍼센트를 획득했다. **4** 단수명사 선거권, 투표권 ❏ 그 이전에는 여성에게는 선거권이 전혀 없었다. **5** 타동사/자동사 투표하다, 찬반 의사 표시를 하다 ❏ 전국 유권자의 3분의 2가 이러한 선거들에서 투표할 기회가 있었다. ❏ 새로운 지도자가 있다면 총선거에서 많은 사람들이 정부 측에 찬성표를 던질 것 같다. ❏ 레닌그라드 주민들은 그 도시의 본래 이름인 상트페테르부르크를 되찾자고 투표했다. ● 투표 불가산명사 ❏ 투표가 두 시간 전쯤 시작되었다. **6** 타동사 투표로 -에 투표하다 ❏ 질문을 받은 사람들 중 52.5퍼센트가 노동당에 투표하겠다고 말했다. **7** 타동사/자동사 뽑다 ❏ 그의 동기생들이 투표를 해서 '예일 대학에 가장 많이 기여한' 사람으로 그를 뽑았다. **8** 구 떠나는 것으로 반대 의사를 표시하다, 체제가 싫어 망명하다 ❏ 이미 시민 수천 명이 체제에 반대하여 그 나라를 뜨고 있다. **9** 구 나는 제안한다 [비격식체] ❏ 나는 모두 함께 당장 네덜란드로 갈 것을 제안한다. **10** 구 일인 일표주의 ❏ 골드 씨는 '일인 일표주의'를 향한 조치를 요구했다.

가산명사 감사 결의 ❏ 주최자께 드리는 감사 결의를 제의하고 싶습니다.

가산명사 유권자들 ❏ 투표자 수는 최소한 선거인 명부에 등록된 유권자 수의 62퍼센트는 되었다.

1 구동사 -을 보장하다, -의 보증인이 되다 ❏ 김의 모친은 마리아의 보증인이 되어 그녀의 직장을 구해 주겠다고 동의했다. **2** 구동사 -을 보증하다 ❏ 그는 그 이야기의 정확성을 보증할 수 없다.

가산명사 상품권, 쿠폰 ❏ 우승자들은 각각 영화 표 두 장에 해당하는 상품권을 받게 됩니다.

Word Web   vote

Today in almost all **democracies** any adult can **vote** for the **candidate** of his or her choice. However, this hasn't always been true. Until the suffrage movement revolutionized voting rights, women had been **disenfranchised**. In 1893, New Zealand became the first country to give women full voting rights. Women could finally enter a **polling place** and **cast** a **ballot**. Countries such as Canada, Finland, Germany, Sweden, and the U.S. soon followed. However, China, France, India, Italy, and Japan didn't grant suffrage until the mid-1900s.

vow /va͟ʊ/ (**vows, vowing, vowed**) **1** V-T If you **vow** to do something, you make a serious promise or decision that you will do it. □ *While many models vow to go back to college, few do.* □ *I solemnly vowed that someday I would return to live in Europe.* **2** N-COUNT A **vow** is a serious promise or decision to do a particular thing. □ *I made a silent vow to be more careful in the future.* **3** N-COUNT **Vows** are a particular set of serious promises, such as the promises two people make when they are getting married. □ *I took my marriage vows and kept them.*

vow|el /va͟ʊəl/ (**vowels**) N-COUNT A **vowel** is a sound such as the ones represented in writing by the letters "a," "e," "i," "o," and "u," which you pronounce with your mouth open, allowing the air to flow through it. Compare **consonant.** ● The vowel in words like "my" and "thigh" is not very difficult.

voy|age /vɔ͟ɪɪdʒ/ (**voyages**) N-COUNT A **voyage** is a long journey on a ship or in a spacecraft. □ *He aims to follow Columbus's voyage to the West Indies.*

vs. vs. is a written abbreviation for **versus.** □ *...England vs. Brazil in the U.S. Cup.*

vul|gar /vʌ͟lgər/ **1** ADJ If you describe something as **vulgar**, you think it is in bad taste or of poor artistic quality. [DISAPPROVAL] □ *I think it's a very vulgar house.* ● **vul|gar|ity** /vʌlgæ͟rɪti/ N-UNCOUNT □ *I hate the vulgarity of this room.* **2** ADJ If you describe pictures, gestures, or remarks as **vulgar**, you dislike them because they refer to sex or parts of the body in an offensive way that you find unpleasant. [DISAPPROVAL] □ *The women laughed coarsely at some vulgar jokes.* ● **vul|gar|ity** N-UNCOUNT □ *There's a good deal of vulgarity.* **3** ADJ If you describe a person or their behavior as **vulgar**, you mean that they lack taste or behave offensively. [DISAPPROVAL] □ *He was a vulgar old man, but he never swore in front of a woman.* ● **vul|gar|ity** N-UNCOUNT □ *It's his vulgarity that I can't take.*

vul|ner|able ♦◇◇ /vʌ͟lnərəbəl/ **1** ADJ Someone who is **vulnerable** is weak and without protection, with the result that they are easily hurt physically or emotionally. □ *Old people are particularly vulnerable members of our society.* ● **vul|ner|abil|ity** /vʌlnərəbɪ͟lɪti/ (**vulnerabilities**) N-VAR □ *David accepts his own vulnerability.* **2** ADJ If a person, animal, or plant is **vulnerable to** a disease, they are more likely to get it than other people, animals, or plants. □ *People with high blood pressure are especially vulnerable to diabetes.* ● **vul|ner|abil|ity** N-UNCOUNT □ *Taking long-term courses of certain medicines may increase vulnerability to infection.* **3** ADJ Something that is **vulnerable** can be easily harmed or affected by something bad. □ *Their tanks would be vulnerable to attack from the air.* ● **vul|ner|abil|ity** N-UNCOUNT □ *...anxieties about the country's vulnerability to invasion.*

Word Partnership　　vulnerable의 연어

N.	vulnerable **children/people/women** **1** **2**
	vulnerable **to attack** **3**
V.	**become** vulnerable, **remain** vulnerable **1**-**3**
	feel vulnerable **1** **3**
ADV.	**especially** vulnerable, **extremely** vulnerable, **highly** vulnerable, **particularly** vulnerable, **so** vulnerable, **too** vulnerable, **very** vulnerable **1**-**3**

---

vul|ture /vʌ͟ltʃər/ (**vultures**) **1** N-COUNT A **vulture** is a large bird which lives in hot countries and eats the flesh of dead animals. **2** N-COUNT If you describe a person as a **vulture**, you disapprove of them because you think they are trying to gain from another person's troubles. [JOURNALISM, DISAPPROVAL] □ *With no buyer in sight for the company as a whole, the vultures started to circle.*

vy|ing /va͟ɪɪŋ/ **Vying** is the present participle of **vie.**

---

1 타동사 맹세하다, 서약하다 □ 많은 모델이 대학으로 돌아가겠다고 맹세하지만, 거의 지키지 않는다. □ 나는 언젠가 유럽에 돌아와 살겠다고 엄숙하게 맹세했다. **2** 가산명사 맹세 □ 나는 앞으로 더욱 신중하겠다고 조용히 맹세했다. **3** 가산명사 서약 □ 나는 혼인 서약을 했고 서약한 바를 지켰다.

가산명사 모음 □ 'my'와 'thigh' 같은 단어들에 들어 있는 모음은 별로 어렵지 않다.

가산명사 긴 여행, 긴 항해 □ 그는 콜럼버스가 항해한 대로 서인도 제도로 갈 작정이다.

versus의 축약형, - 대(對) □ 유에스 컵 대회에서 잉글랜드 대 브라질 경기

1 형용사 멋없는, 안목 없는 [탐탁잖음] □ 나는 그 집이 아주 멋없다고 생각한다. ● 멋없음, 안목 없음 불가산명사 □ 난 이 방의 안목 없음을 혐오한다. **2** 형용사 저속한, 천박한 [탐탁잖음] □ 그 여자들은 저속한 농담에 천박하게 웃었다. ● 저속함, 천박함 불가산명사 □ 상당히 천박한 데가 있다. **3** 형용사 상스러운, 노골적인 [탐탁잖음] □ 그는 상스러운 노인이었지만 여자 앞에서 욕을 하지는 않았다. ● 상스러움, 무례함 불가산명사 □ 내가 참을 수 없는 것은 그의 상스러움이다.

1 형용사 상처받기 쉬운, 연약한 □ 노인들은 우리 사회의 특히나 상처받기 쉬운 구성원이다. ● 상처받기 쉬움, 연약함 가산명사 또는 불가산명사 □ 데이비드는 자신의 연약함을 인정한다. **2** 형용사 (질병에) 걸리기 쉬운, 저항력이 없는 □ 고혈압이 있는 사람들은 특히 당뇨병에 걸리기 쉽다. ● 저항력이 약함 불가산명사 □ 특정 약품으로 장기간 치료하면 감염에 대한 저항력을 더 약화시킬 수 있다. **3** 형용사 피해를 입기 쉬운, 공격받기 쉬운 □ 그들이 탄 전차는 공습을 받기 쉬울 것이다. ● 취약성 불가산명사 □ 그 나라가 침략에 취약한 데 대한 염려

1 가산명사 독수리, 콘도르 **2** 가산명사 남의 불행을 이용해 먹는 사람, 사기꾼 [언론, 탐탁잖음] □ 회사 전체를 구매하려는 사람이 전혀 나서지 않는 상황에서 남의 불행을 이용해 먹는 그 사기꾼들이 주위에 모여들기 시작했다.

vie의 현재 분사

Ww

W, w /dʌbᵊlyu/ (**W's, w's**) N-VAR W is the twenty-third letter of the English alphabet.

wacky /wæki/ (**wackier, wackiest**) also **whacky** ADJ If you describe something or someone as **wacky**, you mean that they are eccentric, unusual, and often funny. [INFORMAL] ❑ ...a wacky new television comedy series.

wad /wɒd/ (**wads**) N-COUNT A **wad of** something such as paper or cloth is a tight bundle or ball of it. ❑ ...a wad of banknotes.

wade /weɪd/ (**wades, wading, waded**) ◼ V-I If you **wade** through something that makes it difficult to walk, usually water or mud, you walk through it. ❑ Her mother came to find them, wading across a river to reach them. ◼ V-I To **wade through** a lot of documents or pieces of information means to spend a lot of time and effort reading them or dealing with them. ❑ It has taken a long time to wade through the "incredible volume" of evidence.

▶**wade in** or **wade into** PHRASAL VERB If someone **wades in** or **wades into** something, they get involved in a very determined and forceful way, often without thinking enough about the consequences of their actions. ❑ They don't just listen sympathetically, they wade in with remarks like, "If I were you..."

wa|fer /weɪfər/ (**wafers**) N-COUNT A **wafer** is a thin crisp cookie which is usually eaten with ice cream.

waf|fle /wɒfᵊl/ (**waffles, waffling, waffled**) ◼ V-I If someone **waffles** on an issue or question, they cannot decide what to do or what their opinion is about it. [AM] ❑ He's waffled on abortion and gay rights. ◼ V-I If you say that someone **waffles**, you are critical of them because they talk or write a lot without actually making any clear or important points. [BRIT, INFORMAL, DISAPPROVAL] ❑ My wife often tells me I waffle. ● PHRASAL VERB **Waffle on** means the same as **waffle**. ❑ Whenever I open my mouth I don't half waffle on. ● N-UNCOUNT **Waffle** is also a noun. ❑ He writes smug, sanctimonious waffle.

waft /wɒft, wæft/ (**wafts, wafting, wafted**) V-T/V-I If sounds or smells **waft** through the air, or if something such as a light wind **wafts** them, they move gently through the air. ❑ The scent of climbing roses wafts through the window.

wag /wæg/ (**wags, wagging, wagged**) ◼ V-T When a dog **wags** its tail, it repeatedly waves its tail from side to side. ❑ The dog was biting, growling, and wagging its tail. ◼ V-T If you **wag** your finger, you shake it repeatedly and quickly from side to side, usually because you are annoyed with someone. ❑ He wagged a disapproving finger.

wage ♦◇◇ /weɪdʒ/ (**wages, waging, waged**) ◼ N-COUNT Someone's **wages** are the amount of money that is regularly paid to them for the work that they do. ❑ His wages have gone up. ◼ V-T If a person, group, or country **wages** a campaign or a war, they start it and continue it over a period of time. ❑ The government, along with the three factions that had been waging a civil war, signed a peace agreement.
→see **factory**

When used as a noun, **pay** is a general word which you can use to refer to the money you get from your employer for doing your job. Manual workers are paid **wages**, or **a wage**. The plural is more common than the singular, especially when you are talking about the actual cash that someone receives. ❑ Every week he handed all his wages in cash to his wife. Wages are usually paid, and quoted, as a weekly sum. ❑ ...a starting wage of five dollars an hour. Professional people and office workers receive a **salary**, which is paid monthly. However, when talking about someone's salary, you usually give the annual figure. ❑ I'm paid a salary of $29,000 a year. Your **income** consists of all the money you receive from all sources, including your pay.

Thesaurus   *wage*의 참조어

N.   earnings, pay, salary ◼

가산명사 또는 불가산명사 영어 알파벳의 스물세 번째 글자

형용사 별난 [비격식체] ❑ 별난 새 텔레비전 코미디 시리즈

가산명사 뭉치 ❑ 지폐 뭉치

◼ 자동사 (힘겹게) 헤치며 걷다 ❑ 그녀의 어머니가 그들을 찾으러 나와, 강을 힘겹게 헤쳐 그들에게로 왔다. ◼ 자동사 힘들어 해내다, 헤쳐 나가다 ❑ '엄청난 양'의 증거를 힘들여 읽어 내느라 시간이 오래 걸렸다.

구동사 (정신없이) 덤벼들다 ❑ 그들은 단지 공감하며 듣기만 하는 게 아냐. "내가 너라면..."과 같은 말을 하면서 그냥 덤벼든다니까.

가산명사 웨이퍼 (과자)

◼ 자동사 생각이 이랬다저랬다 하다 [미국영어] ❑ 그는 낙태와 동성애자들의 권리에 대해 생각이 이랬다저랬다 한다. ◼ 자동사 두서없이 지껄이다 [영국영어, 비격식체, 탐탁찮음] ❑ 내 아내는 내가 말을 두서없이 지껄인다고 자주 이야기한다. ● 구동사 두서없이 지껄이다 ❑ 내가 입을 열 때는 두서없이 지껄이는 경우가 전혀 없다. ● 불가산명사 두서없는 말 ❑ 그는 점잔 빼며 독실한 체 글을 쓰지만 두서가 없다.

타동사/자동사 (내가에) 퍼지다; 퍼뜨리다 ❑ 피어오르는 장미 향기가 창문으로 날아 들어왔다.

◼ 타동사 (개가 꼬리를) 흔들다 ❑ 그 개는 물어뜯고, 으르렁거리며 꼬리를 흔들고 있었다. ◼ 타동사 까딱거리다 ❑ 그는 안 된다는 뜻으로 손가락을 까딱거렸다.

◼ 가산명사 임금 ❑ 그의 임금이 올랐다. ◼ 타동사 벌이다, 수행하다 ❑ 정부는 내전을 벌여 왔던 세 파벌들과 함께 평화 협정에 조인했다.

pay는 명사로 쓰면, 자기가 일을 한 것에 대해 고용주로부터 받는 돈을 가리킬 때 쓸 수 있는 일반적인 말이다. 육체노동자는 wages 또는 a wage를 받는다. 특히 실제로 받는 현금을 말할 때는 단수보다 복수가 더 일반적이다. ❑ 매주 그는 현금으로 된 자기 임금 전부를 자기 아내에게 주었다. 임금은 대개 시급 또는 주급으로 지불하고 매긴다. ❑ ...시간당 5달러의 초임. 전문직과 사무직 종사자들은 매달 시급되는 salary를 받는다. 그러나, 누구의 salary를 말할 때에는 대개 연봉을 말한다. ❑ 나는 일년에 29,000달러의 연봉을 받는다. income은 급료를 포함해서 모든 소득원으로부터 받는 총액으로 구성된다.

A
B
C

Word Partnership	*wage의 연어*

ADJ.	**average** wage, **high/higher** wage, **hourly** wage, **low/lower** wage **1**
V.	**offer** a wage, **pay** a wage, **raise** a wage **1**
N.	wage **cuts**, wage **earners**, wage **increases**, wage **rates** **1** wage a **campaign**, wage **war** **2**

가산명사 임금, 봉급 [주로 영국영어; 미국영어 대개 paycheck] ❑ 그들은 두둑한 봉급을 집에 가져가려고 장시간 근무한다.

wage pack|et (**wage packets**) N-COUNT People's wages can be referred to as their **wage packet**. [mainly BRIT; AM usually **paycheck**] ❑ *They work long hours in order to take home a fat wage packet.*

wa|ger /weɪdʒər/ (**wagers, wagering, wagered**) V-I If you **wager on** the result of a horse race, baseball game, or other event, you give someone a sum of money which they give you back with extra money if the result is what you predicted, or which they keep if it is not. [JOURNALISM] ❑ *Just because people wagered on the Yankees did not mean that they liked them.* ● N-COUNT **Wager** is also a noun. ❑ *There have been various wagers on certain candidates since the Bishop announced his retirement.*

자동사 (돈을) 걸다 [언론] ❑ 사람들이 양키스 팀에 돈을 걸었다고 해서 그들이 그 팀을 좋아했다는 뜻은 아니었다. ● 가산명사 내기 ❑ 주교가 은퇴를 발표한 후에 특정 후보들을 두고 갖가지 내기가 있어 왔다.

wag|on /wægən/ (**wagons**) [BRIT also **waggon**] **1** N-COUNT A **wagon** is a strong vehicle with four wheels, usually pulled by horses or oxen and used for carrying heavy loads. **2** N-COUNT A **wagon** is a large container on wheels which is pulled by a train. [BRIT; AM **freight car**] ❑ *Only one of the 15 wagons on the train came off the rails.* →see **train**

[영국영어 waggon] **1** 가산명사 사륜 짐마차 **2** 가산명사 화차 [영국영어; 미국영어 freight car] ❑ 열차에 달린 열다섯 량의 화차 중 한 량만이 철로에서 탈선했다.

wail /weɪl/ (**wails, wailing, wailed**) **1** V-I If someone **wails**, they make long, loud, high-pitched cries which express sorrow or pain. ❑ *The women began to wail in mourning.* ● N-COUNT **Wail** is also a noun. ❑ *Wails of grief were heard as visitors filed past the site of the disaster.* **2** V-T If you **wail** something, you say it in a loud, high-pitched voice that shows that you are unhappy or in pain. ❑ *"Now look what you've done!" Shirley wailed.* **3** V-I If something such as a siren or an alarm **wails**, it makes a long, loud, high-pitched sound. ❑ *Police cars, their sirens wailing, accompanied the lorries.* ● N-UNCOUNT **Wail** is also a noun. ❑ *The wail of the bagpipe could be heard in the distance.*

1 자동사 통곡하다 ❑ 여자들이 죽음을 애도하며 통곡하기 시작했다. ● 가산명사 통곡 ❑ 방문객들이 줄지어 재해 현장을 지나갈 때 비탄에 찬 통곡 소리가 들렸다. **2** 타동사 울부짖다 ❑ "자 이제 네가 한 짓을 봐!"라며 셜리가 울부짖었다. **3** 자동사 (길고 높은) 소리를 내다 ❑ 경찰차들이 긴 사이렌 소리를 내며 트럭들을 따라갔다. ● 불가산명사 긴 소리, 구슬픈 소리 ❑ 멀리서 백파이프의 구슬픈 소리를 들을 수 있었다.

waist /weɪst/ (**waists**) **1** N-COUNT Your **waist** is the middle part of your body where it narrows slightly above your hips. ❑ *Ricky kept his arm round her waist.* **2** N-COUNT The **waist** of a garment such as a dress, coat, or pair of pants is the part of it which covers the middle part of your body. ❑ *She tucked her thumbs into the waist of her trousers.* →see **body**

1 가산명사 허리 ❑ 리키는 계속 팔로 그녀의 허리를 감싸고 있었다. **2** 가산명사 (의복의) 허리 부분 ❑ 그녀는 바지허리 안으로 양 엄지손가락을 찌르고 있었다.

waist|coat /weɪstkoʊt, wɛskət/ (**waistcoats**) N-COUNT A **waistcoat** is a sleeveless piece of clothing with buttons which people usually wear over a shirt. [BRIT; AM **vest**]

가산명사 조끼 [영국영어; 미국영어 vest]

wait ♦♦♦ /weɪt/ (**waits, waiting, waited**) **1** V-I When you **wait** for something or someone, you spend some time doing very little, because you cannot act until that thing happens or that person arrives. [no passive] ❑ *I walk to a street corner and wait for the school bus.* ❑ *Stop waiting for things to happen. Make them happen.* ❑ *I waited to see how she responded.* ● N-UNCOUNT **waiting** ❑ *The waiting became almost unbearable.* **2** N-COUNT A **wait** is a period of time in which you do very little, before something happens or before you can do something. ❑ *...the four-hour wait for the organizers to declare the result.* **3** V-I If something **is waiting for** you, it is ready for you to use, have, or do. [usu cont] ❑ *There'll be a car waiting for you.* ❑ *When we came home we had a meal waiting for us.* **4** V-I If you say that something can **wait**, you mean that it is not important or urgent and so you will deal with it or do it later. [no cont] ❑ *I want to talk to you, but it can wait.* **5** V-I You can use **wait** when you are trying to make someone feel excited, or to encourage or threaten them. ❑ *If you think this all sounds very exciting, just wait until you read the book.* **6** V-T **Wait** is used in expressions such as **wait a minute**, **wait a second**, and **wait a moment** to interrupt someone when they are speaking, for example because you object to what they are saying or because you want them to repeat something. [SPOKEN] [only imper] ❑ *"Wait a minute!" he broke in. "This is not giving her a fair hearing!"* **7** V-I If an employee **waits on** you, for example in a restaurant or hotel, they take orders from you and bring you what you want. ❑ *There were plenty of servants to wait on her.* **8** PHRASE If you say that you **can't wait** to do something or **can hardly wait** to do it, you are emphasizing that you are very excited about it and eager to do it. [SPOKEN, EMPHASIS] ❑ *We can't wait to get started.* **9** PHRASE If you tell someone to **wait and see**, you tell them that they must be patient or that they must not worry about what is going to happen in the future because they have no control over it. [BRIT also **wait about**] ❑ *We'll have to wait and see what happens.*

1 자동사 기다리다 ❑ 나는 거리 모퉁이로 걸어가서 학교 버스를 기다린다. ❑ 상황이 만들어지기를 기다리지 말고 네가 그런 상황을 만들어 봐. ❑ 나는 그녀가 어떻게 반응할까를 보려고 기다렸다. ● 기다림 불가산명사 ❑ 기다림은 거의 참을 수 없는 지경이 되었다. **2** 가산명사 기다리는 시간 ❑ 주최측이 결과를 발표하기까지 4시간 동안의 기다림 **3** 자동사 준비되어 있다 ❑ 당신을 위한 승용차가 준비되어 있을 겁니다. ❑ 우리가 집에 오니 우리를 위해 식사가 준비되어 있었다. **4** 자동사 잠시 미루다 ❑ 너랑 얘기하고 싶지만, 나중으로 미루어도 돼. **5** 자동사 기다리다 ❑ 이것이 아주 흥미로울 것 같다는 생각이 들면, 그 책을 읽을 때까지 좀 기다리세요. **6** 타동사 기다리다 [구어체] ❑ "잠깐만!"이라며 그가 말참견을 했다. "이건 그녀의 말을 호의적으로 들어주는 게 아니잖아!" **7** 자동사 시중들다 ❑ 많은 하인들이 그녀의 시중을 들었다. **8** 구 어서 -하기를 무척 바라다, 빨리 -하고 싶어 기다릴 수가 없다 [구어체, 강조] ❑ 우리는 어서 시작되기를 무척 바란다. **9** 구 두고 보다 [영국영어 wait about] ❑ 무슨 일이 일어날지 두고 봐야지.

구동사 (서정이며) 기다리다 ❑ 공격자가 일격을 가할 기회를 노리며 기다리고 있는지도 모른다. ❑ 나는 그 의사와 말하기 위해 기다렸다.

Do not confuse **wait for**, **expect**, and **look forward to**. When you **wait for** someone or something, you stay in the same place until the person arrives or the thing happens. ❑ *Soft drinks were served while we waited for him... We got off the plane and waited for our luggage.* When you are **expecting** someone or something, you think that the person or thing is going to arrive or that the thing is going to happen. ❑ *I sent a postcard, so they were expecting me... We are expecting rain.* When you **look forward to** something that is going to happen, you feel happy because you think you will enjoy it. ❑ *I'll bet you're looking forward to your holidays... I always looked forward to seeing her.*

wait for, expect, look forward to를 혼동하지 않도록 하라. 누구를 또는 무엇을 wait for하면 그 사람이 도착하거나 그것이 일어날 때까지 같은 장소에 머무르는 것이다. ❑ 우리가 그를 기다리는 동안 음료수가 제공되었다. ❑ 우리는 비행기에서 내려 짐을 기다렸다. 누구를 또는 무엇을 expect하면, 그 사람 또는 그것이 도착하거나 그것이 일어날 것이라고 생각하는 것이다. ❑ 내가 엽서를 보내서 그들이 나를 기다리고 있었다... 우리는 비가 오리라고 생각하고 있다. 일어날 무엇을 look forward to하면, 그것이 즐거울 것이라고 생각해서 기분이 좋음을 나타낸다. ❑ 너는 틀림없이 휴가를 고대하고 있을 거야... 나는 항상 그녀 보게 되기를 고대했다.

Thesaurus   *wait*의 참조어

| V. | anticipate, expect, hold on, stand by; *(ant.)* carry out, go ahead **1** |
| N. | delay, halt, hold-up, pause **2** |

Word Partnership   *wait*의 연어

V.	**(can't) afford to** wait **1**
	can/can't/couldn't wait, **have to** wait, **will/won't/wouldn't** wait **1 4**
	wait **to hear**, wait **to say** **1 4**
	can't wait, **can hardly** wait **8**
	wait **and see** **9**
N.	wait **for an answer**, wait **days/hours**, wait **a long time**, wait *your* turn **1**
	wait **a minute**, wait **until tomorrow** **1 4 6**
ADV.	wait **forever**, wait **here**, wait **outside** **1**
	just wait **1 5**
ADJ.	**worth the** wait **2**

▶**wait around** PHRASAL VERB If you **wait around** or **wait about**, you stay in the same place, usually doing very little, because you cannot act before something happens or before someone arrives. ❑ *The attacker may have been waiting around for an opportunity to strike.* ❑ *I waited around to speak to the doctor.*

▶**wait in** PHRASAL VERB If you **wait in**, you deliberately stay at home and do not go out, for example because someone is coming to see you. [mainly BRIT] ❑ *If I'd waited in for you I could have waited all day.*

▶**wait up** PHRASAL VERB If you **wait up**, you deliberately do not go to bed, especially because you are expecting someone to return home late at night. ❑ *I hope he doesn't expect you to wait up for him.*

wait|er /ˈweɪtər/ (**waiters**) N-COUNT A **waiter** is a man who works in a restaurant, serving people with food and drink. →see **restaurant**

Waiter and **waitress** are used less often in the US these days, although they are still the usual terms in the UK. Restaurant staff, especially in the US, can be called **servers** or **waitpersons**, and these terms are used to refer to both men and women.

wait|ing list (**waiting lists**) N-COUNT A **waiting list** is a list of people who have asked for something which cannot be given to them immediately, for example medical treatment, housing, or training, and who must therefore wait until it is available. ❑ *There were 20,000 people on the waiting list for a home.*

wait|ress /ˈweɪtrɪs/ (**waitresses**) N-COUNT A **waitress** is a woman who works in a restaurant, serving people with food and drink. →see **restaurant**

waive /weɪv/ (**waives, waiving, waived**) **1** V-T If you **waive** your right to something, for example legal representation, you choose not to have it or do it. ❑ *He pled guilty to the murders of three boys and waived his right to appeal.* **2** V-T If someone **waives** a rule, they say that people do not have to obey it in a particular situation. ❑ *The art gallery waives admission charges on Sundays.*

waiv|er /ˈweɪvər/ (**waivers**) N-COUNT A **waiver** is when a person, government, or organization agrees to give up a right or says that people do not have to obey a particular rule or law. ❑ *...a waiver of constitutional rights.*

wake ♦◇◇ /weɪk/ (**wakes, waking, woke, woken**)

The form **waked** is used in American English for the past tense.

1 V-T/V-I When you **wake** or when someone or something **wakes** you, you become conscious again after being asleep. ❑ *It was cold and dark when I woke at 6.30.* ❑ *She went upstairs to wake Milton.* ● PHRASAL VERB **Wake up** means the same as **wake**. ❑ *One morning I woke up and felt something was wrong.* **2** N-COUNT A **wake** is a gathering or social event that is held before or after someone's funeral. ❑ *A funeral wake was in progress.* **3** PHRASE If one thing follows **in the wake of** another, it happens after the other thing is over, often as a result of it. ❑ *The governor has enjoyed a huge surge in the polls in the wake of last week's convention.* →see **funeral**

Word Partnership   *wake*의 연어

| PREP-P. | wake **up during the night**, wake **up in the middle of the night**, wake **up in the morning** **1** |
| ADV. | wake *(someone)* **up** **1** |

▶**wake up** PHRASAL VERB If something such as an activity **wakes** you **up**, it makes you more alert and ready to do things after you have been lazy or inactive. ❑ *A cool shower wakes up the body and boosts circulation.* →see also **wake 1**

wake-up call (**wake-up calls**) N-COUNT A **wake-up call** is a telephone call that you can book through an operator or at a hotel to make sure that you wake up at a particular time. ❑ *I book a wake-up call for 4.45 am.*

walk ♦♦♦ /wɔk/ (**walks, walking, walked**) **1** V-T/V-I When you **walk**, you move forward by putting one foot in front of the other in a regular way. ❑ *Rosanna*

구동사 집에서 기다리다 [주로 영국영어] ❑ 내가 너를 집에서 기다렸더라면 하루 종일 기다릴 수 있었을 텐데.

구동사 자지 않고 기다리다 ❑ 그가 자신이 집에 돌아갈 때까지 네가 자지 않고 기다릴 거라 기대하지 말았으면 해.

가산명사 웨이터, (식당) 종업원

waiter와 waitress는 영국에서는 아직도 흔히 사용되는 말이지만 미국에서는 요즘 잘 사용되지 않는다. 특히 미국에서는 식당 직원을 servers 또는 waitpersons라고 하는데 이 말은 남녀 모두에 대해 쓴다.

가산명사 대기자 명단 ❑ 2만 명이 주택 마련을 위한 대기자 명단에 올라 있었다.

가산명사 웨이트리스, (식당의) 여 종업원

1 타동사 포기하다, 철회하다 ❑ 그는 세 명의 남자아이들에 대한 살인죄를 인정했고 항소권도 포기했다. **2** 타동사 면제하다 ❑ 그 미술관은 일요일이면 입장료를 받지 않는다.

가산명사 권리 포기 ❑ 헌법상의 권리에 대한 권리 포기

waked는 미국영어에서 과거 시제로 쓰인다.

1 타동사/자동사 (잠이) 깨다; (잠을) 깨우다 ❑ 내가 6시 30분에 잠이 깼을 때는 춥고 어두웠다. ❑ 그녀는 밀턴을 깨우러 위층으로 올라갔다. ● 구동사 (잠이) 깨다; (잠을) 깨우다 ❑ 어느 날 아침 내가 잠이 깼을 때 뭔가가 잘못되었다는 것을 느꼈다. **2** 가산명사 (초상집에서) 경야(警夜) ❑ 장례식 경야가 진행 중이었다. **3** 구 ~의 결과로서 ❑ 주지사는 지난주 집회의 결과로 여론 조사에서 엄청난 지지율 상승을 누렸다.

구동사 정신을 차리게 하다, 각성시키다 ❑ 찬물로 샤워를 하면 몸이 깨어나고 혈액 순환이 잘 된다.

가산명사 모닝콜 ❑ 나는 새벽 4시 45분에 모닝콜을 해달라고 예약한다.

1 타동사/자동사 걷다 ❑ 로재너와 포브스는 얼마 동안 말없이 걸었다. ❑ 우리는 휴게실로 걸어 들어갔다.

and Forbes walked in silence for some while. ❑ *We walked into the foyer.* ❷ N-COUNT A **walk** is a trip that you make by walking, usually for pleasure. ❑ *I went for a walk.* ❸ N-SING A **walk** of a particular distance is the distance which a person has to walk to get somewhere. ❑ *It was only a three-mile walk to Kabul from there.* ❹ N-COUNT A **walk** is a route suitable for walking along for pleasure. ❑ *There is a 2 mile coastal walk from Craster to Newton.* ❺ N-SING A **walk** is the action of walking rather than running. ❑ *She slowed to a steady walk.* ❻ N-SING Someone's **walk** is the way that they walk. ❑ *George, despite his great height and gangling walk, was a keen dancer.* ❼ V-T If you **walk** someone somewhere, you walk there with them in order to show politeness or to make sure that they get there safely. ❑ *She walked me to my car.* ❽ to **walk tall** →see **tall**

Thesaurus   *walk*의 참조어

V.	hike, stroll ❶
N.	hike, march, parade, stroll ❷ ❸

Word Partnership   *walk*의 연어

ADV.	walk **alone**, walk **away**, walk **back**, walk **home** ❶
V.	**begin** to walk, **start** to walk ❶
	go for a walk, **take** a walk ❷ ❸
ADJ.	**(un)able** to walk ❶
	brisk walk, **long** walk, **short** walk ❷-❹
N.	walk a **dog** ❷

▶**walk away** PHRASAL VERB If you **walk away** from a problem or a difficult situation, you do nothing about it or do not face any bad consequences from it. ❑ *The most appropriate strategy may simply be to walk away from the problem.*

▶**walk away with** PHRASAL VERB If you **walk away with** something such as a prize, you win it or get it very easily. [JOURNALISM] ❑ *Enter our competition and you could walk away with £10,000.*

▶**walk into** PHRASAL VERB If you **walk into** an unpleasant situation, you become involved in it without expecting to, especially because you have been careless. ❑ *He's walking into a situation that he absolutely can't control.*

▶**walk off with** PHRASAL VERB If you **walk off with** something such as a prize, you win it or get it very easily. [JOURNALISM] ❑ *We'd like nothing better than to see him walk off with the big prize.*

▶**walk out** ❶ PHRASAL VERB If you **walk out of** a meeting, a performance, or an unpleasant situation, you leave it suddenly, usually in order to show that you are angry or bored. ❑ *Several dozen councillors walked out of the meeting in protest.* ❷ PHRASAL VERB If someone **walks out on** their family or their partner, they leave them suddenly and go to live somewhere else. ❑ *Her husband walked out on her.* ❸ PHRASAL VERB If workers **walk out**, they stop doing their work for a period of time, usually in order to try to get better pay or conditions for themselves. ❑ *Nationwide industrial action began earlier this week, when staff at most banks walked out.*

walk|ing /wɔ:kɪŋ/ N-UNCOUNT **Walking** is the activity of taking walks for exercise or pleasure, especially in the country. ❑ *Recently I've started to do a lot of walking and cycling.*

Walk|man /wɔ:kmən/ (**Walkmans**) N-COUNT A **Walkman** is a small cassette player with light headphones which people carry around so that they can listen to music, for example while they are traveling. [TRADEMARK]

walk of life (**walks of life**) N-COUNT The **walk of life** that you come from is the position that you have in society and the kind of job you have. ❑ *One of the greatest pleasures of this job is meeting people from all walks of life.*

walk|out /wɔ:kaʊt/ (**walkouts**) ❶ N-COUNT A **walkout** is a strike. ❑ *But union leaders are holding off on calling the walkout while talks are showing progress.* ❷ N-COUNT If there is a **walkout** during a meeting, some or all of the people attending it leave in order to show their disapproval of something that has happened at the meeting. ❑ *The commission's proceedings have been wrecked by tantrums and walkouts.*

walk|way /wɔ:kweɪ/ (**walkways**) N-COUNT A **walkway** is a passage or path for people to walk along. Walkways are often raised above the ground. ❑ *...a new concrete walkway between two rows of apartment blocks.*

wall ♦♦♢ /wɔ:l/ (**walls**) ❶ N-COUNT A **wall** is one of the vertical sides of a building or room. ❑ *Kathryn leaned against the wall of the church.* ❑ *The bedroom walls would be papered with chintz.* ❷ N-COUNT A **wall** is a long narrow vertical structure made of stone or brick that surrounds or divides an area of land. ❑ *He sat on the wall in the sun.* ❸ N-COUNT The **wall** of something that is hollow is its side. ❑ *He ran his fingers along the inside walls of the box.* ❹ →see also **fly-on-the-wall** ❺ PHRASE If you say that something or someone **is driving** you **up the wall**, you are emphasizing that they annoy and irritate you. [INFORMAL, EMPHASIS] ❑ *The heat is driving me up the wall.*

Word Partnership   *wall*의 연어

N.	**back to the** wall, **brick** wall, **concrete** wall, **glass** wall, **stone** wall ❶ ❷
PREP.	**against** a wall, **along** a wall, **behind** a wall, **near** a wall, **on** a wall ❶ ❷
V.	**lean against/on** a wall, **build** a wall, **climb** a wall ❶ ❷

---

❷ 가산명사 산책 ❑ 나는 산책을 갔다. ❸ 단수명사 보행거리 ❑ 거기서 카불까지는 걸어서 겨우 3마일이었다. ❹ 가산명사 산책길 ❑ 2마일에 이르는 해변 산책로가 크라스터에서 뉴턴까지 이어져 있다. ❺ 단수명사 걷기, 보행 ❑ 그녀는 속도를 늦춰 꾸준히 걸었다. ❻ 단수명사 걸음걸이 ❑ 조지는 키가 엄청 크고 걸음걸이가 좀 흐느적거렸지만 춤추는 걸 아주 좋아했다. ❼ 타동사 ~와 함께 걷다, 걸어서 바래다주다 ❑ 그녀는 내 차까지 나와 함께 걸었다.

구동사 그만두다, 외면하다 ❑ 가장 적절한 전략은 그저 그 문제를 외면해 버리는 것일지도 모른다.

구동사 쉽게 차지하다 [언론] ❑ 저희 경연대회에 참가하셔서 손쉽게 10,000파운드를 벌어 가세요.

구동사 (나쁜 상황에) 빠지다 ❑ 그는 결코 통제할 수 없는 상황으로 빠져들고 있다.

구동사 수월하게 따내다 [언론] ❑ 그가 그 큰 상을 수월하게 따내는 걸 보는 것보다 우리가 더 바라는 건 없다.

❶ 구동사 박차고 나가다 ❑ 의원들 수십 명이 항의의 표시로 회의장을 박차고 나갔다. ❷ 구동사 버리고 떠나다 ❑ 그녀의 남편은 그녀를 버리고 떠났다. ❸ 구동사 작업을 중단하다, 파업하다 ❑ 이번 주 초 대부분의 은행 직원들이 파업했을 때, 전국적으로 쟁의 행위가 시작됐다.

불가산명사 걷기 ❑ 최근 들어 나는 많이 걷고 자전거를 타기 시작했다.

가산명사 워크맨, 휴대용 카세트 플레이어 [상표]

가산명사 (사회의) 위치 ❑ 이 직업을 통해 느낄 수 있는 가장 큰 즐거움 중 하나는 사회 각계각층의 사람들과 만날 수 있다는 것이다.

❶ 가산명사 파업 ❑ 그러나 회담이 진전을 보이고 있는 동안 노조 지도자들이 파업 지령을 연기하고 있다. ❷ 가산명사 항의 퇴장 ❑ 사람들이 분통을 터뜨리고 불만과 항의 퇴장을 하는 바람에 위원회 진행이 엉망이 되었다.

가산명사 보도 ❑ 두 아파트 단지 사이에 새로 만들어진 콘크리트 보도

❶ 가산명사 벽 ❑ 캐서린이 교회 벽에 몸을 기대었다. ❑ 침실 벽은 사라사 무늬로 도배되었을 것이다. ❷ 가산명사 담 ❑ 그는 햇빛을 받으며 담 위에 앉아 있었다. ❸ 가산명사 내벽 ❑ 그는 그 상자의 내벽을 손가락으로 만져 보았다. ❺ 구 짜증나게 하다, 몹시 화나게 하다 [비격식체, 강조] ❑ 더워서 짜증나 죽겠다.

walled /wɔld/ ADJ If an area of land or a city is **walled**, it is surrounded or enclosed by a wall. ❑ *The city was walled and built upon a rock.*

형용사 담으로 둘러싸인 ❑ 그 도시는 담으로 둘러싸였으며 암석 위에 건설되어 있었다.

wal|let /wɒlɪt/ (wallets) N-COUNT A **wallet** is a small flat folded case, usually made of leather or plastic, in which you can keep money and credit cards.

가산명사 지갑

wal|low /wɒloʊ/ (wallows, wallowing, wallowed) **1** V-I If you say that someone is **wallowing** in an unpleasant situation, you are criticizing them for being deliberately unhappy. [DISAPPROVAL] ❑ *His tired mind continued to wallow in self-pity.* **2** V-I If a person or animal **wallows in** water or mud, they lie or roll about in it slowly for pleasure. ❑ *Never have I had such a good excuse for wallowing in deep warm baths.*

1 자동사 젖어 있다, 빠져 있다 [탐탁찮음] ❑ 심적으로 지친 그는 계속 자기 연민에 젖어 있었다. **2** 자동사 뒹굴다 ❑ 지금까지 내가 따뜻한 물을 가득 채운 욕조에서 뒹굴어도 되는 그렇게 좋은 구실이 한 번도 없었다.

wall|paper /wɔlpeɪpər/ (wallpapers, wallpapering, wallpapered) **1** N-MASS **Wallpaper** is thick colored or patterned paper that is used for covering and decorating the walls of rooms. ❑ *...the wallpaper in the bedroom.* **2** V-T If someone **wallpapers** a room, they cover the walls with wallpaper. ❑ *We were going to wallpaper that room anyway.* **3** N-UNCOUNT **Wallpaper** is the background on a computer screen. [COMPUTING] ❑ *... pre-installed wallpaper images.*

1 물질명사 벽지 ❑ 침실 벽지 **2** 타동사 도배하다 ❑ 어쨌든 우리는 그 방에 도배를 하려고 했었다. **3** 불가산명사 (컴퓨터) 배경 화면 [컴퓨터] ❑ 사전 설치된 배경 화면 이미지들

Wall Street ♦◇◇ N-PROPER **Wall Street** is a street in New York where the Stock Exchange and important banks are. **Wall Street** is often used to refer to the financial business carried out there and to the people who work there. [BUSINESS] ❑ *On Wall Street, stocks closed at their second highest level today.*

고유명사 월 가 (뉴욕의 금융가) [경제] ❑ 오늘 월 가에서는 주가가 사상 두 번째 높은 가격으로 마감했다.

wal|nut /wɔlnʌt, -nət/ (walnuts) N-VAR **Walnuts** are edible nuts which have a wrinkled shape and a hard round shell that is light brown in color. ❑ *...chopped walnuts.*

가산명사 또는 불가산명사 호두 ❑ 잘게 다진 호두

waltz /wɔlts, wɒls/ (waltzes, waltzing, waltzed) **1** N-COUNT; N-IN-NAMES A **waltz** is a piece of music with a rhythm of three beats in each bar, which people can dance to. ❑ *...Tchaikovsky's "Waltz of the Flowers".* **2** N-COUNT A **waltz** is a dance in which two people hold each other and move around the floor using special steps in time to waltz music. ❑ *Arthur Murray taught the foxtrot, the tango and the waltz.* **3** V-RECIP If you **waltz** with someone, you dance a waltz with them. ❑ *"Waltz with me," he said, taking her hand.*

1 가산명사; 이름명사 왈츠 (곡) ❑ 차이코프스키의 '꽃의 왈츠' **2** 가산명사 왈츠 (춤) ❑ 아서 머리가 폭스트롯, 탱고, 왈츠를 가르쳤다. **3** 상호동사 왈츠를 추다 ❑ "나와 함께 왈츠를 춰요."라고 그가 그녀의 손을 잡으며 말했다.

wan|der /wɒndər/ (wanders, wandering, wandered) **1** V-I If you **wander** in a place, you walk around there in a casual way, often without intending to go in any particular direction. ❑ *When he got bored he wandered around the fair.* ❑ *They wandered off in the direction of the nearest store.* ● N-SING **Wander** is also a noun. ❑ *A wander around any market will reveal stalls piled high with vegetables.* **2** V-I If a person or animal **wanders** from a place where they are supposed to stay, they move away from the place without going in a particular direction. ❑ *Because Mother is afraid we'll get lost, we aren't allowed to wander far.* **3** V-I If your mind **wanders** or your thoughts **wander**, you stop concentrating on something and start thinking about other things. ❑ *His mind would wander, and he would lose track of what he was doing.* **4** V-I If your eyes **wander**, you stop looking at one thing and start looking around at other things. ❑ *His eyes wandered restlessly around the room.*

1 자동사 돌아다니다, 헤매다 ❑ 그는 지루해지자 박람회장을 이리저리 돌아다녔다. ❑ 그들은 가장 가까운 상점으로 가는 방향을 잃고 헤맸다. ● 단수명사 돌아다님 ❑ 어느 시장에서든 이리저리 돌아다니면 채소를 가득 쌓아 놓은 노점들을 보게 된다. **2** 자동사 (있을 곳에) 있지 않다 ❑ 다른 데로 가는 우리가 길을 잃을까 봐 걱정해서, 우리가 멀리 가지 못하게 하신다. **3** 자동사 산만해지다 ❑ 그는 마음이 산만해지고 자신이 무엇을 하고 있는지 갈피를 잡지 못할 것이다. **4** 자동사 두리번거리다 ❑ 그의 두 눈동자는 방 안을 이리저리 쉴새없이 두리번거렸다.

wane /weɪn/ (wanes, waning, waned) V-I If something **wanes**, it becomes gradually weaker or less, often so that it eventually disappears. ❑ *While his interest in these sports began to wane, a passion for rugby developed.*

자동사 줄어들다 ❑ 이 스포츠에 대한 그의 관심이 줄어드는 한편, 럭비에 대한 열정은 계속 커져 갔다.

want ♦♦♦ /wɒnt/ (wants, wanting, wanted) **1** V-T If you **want** something, you feel a desire or a need for it. [no cont, no passive] ❑ *I want a drink.* ❑ *People wanted to know who this talented designer was.* ❑ *They began to want their father to be the same as other daddies.* ❑ *They didn't want people staring at them as they sat on the lawn, so they put up high walls.*

1 타동사 원하다, -하고 싶어 하다 ❑ 마실 것 좀 주세요. ❑ 사람들은 이 재능 있는 디자이너가 누군지 알고 싶어 했다. ❑ 그들은 자신들의 아버지가 다른 아버지들과 같기를 원하기 시작했다. ❑ 그들은 잔디밭에 앉아 있을 때 사람들이 쳐다보기를 원하지 않았기 때문에 높은 담을 쳤다.

> Note that **want** and **wish** have similar meanings, but are used differently. If you **want** something, you feel a need for it or a desire to have it. You can say that you **want** to do something, that you **want** someone to do something, or that you **want** something to happen. If you use **wish** with a "to" infinitive, this has the same meaning as **want** but is more formal. ❑ *I want to get out of here... She wished to consult him about her future.*

> want와 wish가 비슷한 뜻을 가졌지만 다르게 쓰인다는 점을 유의하라. 만일 무엇을 want하면, 그것을 필요로 하거나, 갖고 싶어 하는 것이다. want to do something, want someone to do something이나 want something to happen이라고 쓴다. 만일 wish를 to 부정사와 같이 사용하면, 이것은 want와 같은 뜻이지만 좀 더 격식적이다. ❑ 나는 여기서 벗어나고 싶다... 그녀는 자신의 미래에 관해서 그와 상의하기를 희망했다.

2 V-T You can say that you **want to** say something to indicate that you are about to say it. [no cont, no passive] ❑ *I want to say how really delighted I am that you're having a baby.* **3** V-T If you say to someone that you **want** something, or ask them if they **want to** do it, you are firmly telling them what you want or what you want them to do. [no cont, no passive] ❑ *I want an explanation from you, Jeremy.* ❑ *Do you want to tell me what all this is about?* **4** V-T If you say that something **wants** doing, you think that it needs to be done. [mainly BRIT, INFORMAL] [no cont, no passive] ❑ *The windows wanted cleaning.* **5** V-T If you tell someone that they **want to** do a particular thing, you are advising them to do it. [INFORMAL] [no cont, no passive] ❑ *You want to be very careful not to have a man like Crevecoeur for an enemy.* **6** V-T If someone **is wanted** by the police, they are searching for them because they are thought to have committed a crime. [usu passive] ❑ *He was wanted for the murder of a magistrate.* ● **want|ed** ADJ [ADJ n] ❑ *He is one of the most wanted criminals in Europe.* **7** N-PLURAL Your **wants** are the things that you want. ❑ *She couldn't lift a spoon without a servant anticipating her wants and getting it for her.* **8** PHRASE If you do something **for want of** something else, you do it because the other thing is not available or not possible. ❑ *Many of them had gone into teaching for want of anything better to do.*

2 타동사 하고 싶다 ❑ 당신이 아이를 가져서 내가 정말로 기쁘게 생각한다는 말을 해 주고 싶어요. **3** 타동사 바라다 ❑ 제레미, 나는 당신이 설명해 주기를 바래요. ❑ 이게 모두 어떻게 된 일인지 내게 말하고 싶어요? **4** 타동사 필요하다 [주로 영국영어, 비격식체] ❑ 유리창은 청소가 필요했다. **5** 타동사 -할 필요가 있다 [비격식체] ❑ 너는 크레브쾨르와 같은 사람과 적이 되지 않도록 매우 조심할 필요가 있다. **6** 타동사 지명수배를 받다 ❑ 그는 한 행정 장관을 살해해서 지명수배를 받고 있었다. ● 수배 중인 형용사 ❑ 그는 유럽에서 최고 지명 수배범 중 한 명이다. **7** 복수명사 원하는 것 ❑ 그녀는 그녀가 원하는 것을 미리 알아차리고 그것을 해 주는 하인 없이는 숟가락을 들 수도 없었다. **8** 구 -이 없기 때문에 ❑ 그들 대부분은 할 수 있는 더 나은 일이 없었기 때문에 가르치는 일을 선택했었다.

Thesaurus		want의 참조어
v.		covet, desire, long, need, require, wish **1**

want|ing /wɒntɪŋ/ ADJ If you find something or someone **wanting**, they are not of as high a standard as you think they should be. [v-link ADJ, oft ADJ in n] ❏ *He analysed his game and found it wanting.*

형용사 부족한 ❏ 그는 자신의 경기를 분석했고 부족하다는 걸 알게 되었다.

WAP /wæp/ N-UNCOUNT **WAP** is a system which allows devices such as mobile phones to connect to the Internet. **WAP** is an abbreviation for "Wireless Application Protocol." ❏ *...a WAP phone.*

불가산명사 무선 응용 통신 규약 ❏ 무선 응용 통신 규약을 이용하는 전화기

war ♦♦♦ /wɔr/ (**wars**) **1** N-VAR A **war** is a period of fighting or conflict between countries or states. ❏ *He spent part of the war in the National Guard.* ❏ *...matters of war and peace.* **2** N-VAR **War** is intense economic competition between countries or organizations. ❏ *The most important thing is to reach an agreement and to avoid a trade war.* **3** N-VAR If you make **war on** someone or something that you are opposed to, you do things to stop them from succeeding. ❏ *She has been involved in the war against organized crime.* **4** →see also **warring, civil war** **5** PHRASE If a country **goes to war**, it starts fighting a war. ❏ *Do you think this crisis can be settled without going to war?* →see **army, history** →see Word Web: **war**

1 가산명사 또는 불가산명사 전쟁 ❏ 그는 전쟁 중에 얼마간 주 방위군으로 참가했다. ❏ 전쟁이나 평화냐가 걸린 문제들 **2** 가산명사 또는 불가산명사 무역 전쟁 ❏ 가장 중요한 사항은 합의를 하고 무역 전쟁을 피하는 것이다. **3** 가산명사 또는 불가산명사 전쟁, 투쟁 ❏ 그녀는 조직범죄 퇴치를 위한 전쟁에 관여해 왔다. **5** 구 전쟁을 시작하다 ❏ 당신은 이번 위기가 전쟁을 시작하지 않고 진정되리라고 생각하십니까?

war|ble /wɔrbʰl/ (**warbles, warbling, warbled**) **1** V-I When a bird **warbles**, it sings pleasantly. ❏ *The bird continued to warble.* **2** V-I If someone **warbles**, they sing in a high-pitched, rather unsteady voice. ❏ *She warbled as she worked.*

1 자동사 지저귀다 ❏ 그 새가 계속 지저귀었다. **2** 자동사 (높고 가는 목소리로) 노래하다 ❏ 그녀는 일할 때 노래를 불렀다.

ward /wɔrd/ (**wards, warding, warded**) N-COUNT A **ward** is a room in a hospital which has beds for many people, often people who need similar treatment. ❏ *A toddler was admitted to the emergency ward with a wound in his chest.* →see **hospital**

가산명사 병동 ❏ 걸음마를 겨우 할 수 있는 아기가 가슴에 상처를 입고 응급 병동에 입원하였다.

▶**ward off** PHRASAL VERB To **ward off** a danger or illness means to prevent it from affecting you or harming you. ❏ *She may have put up a fight to try to ward off her assailant.*

구동사 피하다, 막다 ❏ 그녀가 공격범을 피하려고 애쓰느라 싸움이 벌어졌을 수도 있다.

war|den /wɔrdʰn/ (**wardens**) **1** N-COUNT A **warden** is a person who is responsible for a particular place or thing, and for making sure that the laws or regulations that relate to it are obeyed. ❏ *He was a warden at the local parish church.* **2** N-COUNT The **warden** of a prison is the person in charge of it. [AM; BRIT **governor**] ❏ *A new warden took over the prison.*

1 가산명사 관리인 ❏ 그는 지역 교구 교회의 관리인이었다. **2** 가산명사 교도소장 [미국영어; 영국영어 governor] ❏ 신임 교도소장이 그 교도소를 인계받았다.

war|der /wɔrdər/ (**warders**) N-COUNT A **warder** is someone who works in a prison supervising the prisoners. [BRIT; AM **guard**]

가산명사 간수 [영국영어; 미국영어 guard]

ward|robe /wɔrdroʊb/ (**wardrobes**) **1** N-COUNT A **wardrobe** is a tall closet or cabinet in which you can hang your clothes. **2** N-COUNT Someone's **wardrobe** is the total collection of clothes that they have. ❏ *Her wardrobe consists primarily of huge cashmere sweaters and tiny Italian sandals.*

1 가산명사 옷장 **2** 가산명사 개인 소유 의상 ❏ 그녀가 소유한 의상은 주로 커다란 캐시미어 스웨터와 작은 샌들들로 이뤄져 있다.

ware|house /wɛərhaʊs/ (**warehouses**) N-COUNT A **warehouse** is a large building where raw materials or manufactured goods are stored until they are exported to other countries or distributed to stores to be sold.

가산명사 창고

war|fare /wɔrfɛər/ **1** N-UNCOUNT **Warfare** is the activity of fighting a war. ❏ *...the threat of chemical warfare.* **2** N-UNCOUNT **Warfare** is sometimes used to refer to any violent struggle or conflict. ❏ *Much of the violence is related to drugs and gang warfare.*

1 불가산명사 전쟁, 교전 행위 ❏ 화학전의 위협 **2** 불가산명사 무력 충돌 ❏ 그 폭력 사태의 대부분이 마약과 갱들 간의 무력 충돌과 관계가 있다.

war|head /wɔrhɛd/ (**warheads**) N-COUNT A **warhead** is the front part of a bomb or missile where the explosives are carried. ❏ *...nuclear warheads.*

가산명사 탄두 ❏ 핵탄두

warm ♦♦◇ /wɔrm/ (**warmer, warmest, warms, warming, warmed**) **1** ADJ Something that is **warm** has some heat but not enough to be hot. ❏ *Wheat is grown in places which have cold winters and warm, dry summers.* ❏ *Because it was warm, David wore only a white cotton shirt.*

1 형용사 따뜻한 ❏ 밀은 겨울엔 춥고 여름엔 따뜻하고 건조한 지역에서 자란다. ❏ 날씨가 따뜻해서 데이비드는 흰색 면셔츠만 걸치고 있었다.

> In informal English, if you want to emphasize how hot the weather is, you can say that it is **boiling** or **scorching**. In winter, if the temperature is above average, you can say that it is **mild**. In general, **hot** suggests a higher temperature than **warm**, and **warm** things are usually pleasant. ❏ *...a warm evening.*

> 비격식체 영어에서는, 날씨가 얼마나 더운지를 강조하고 싶으면, boiling이나 scorching을 쓸 수 있다. 겨울에 기온이 평균보다 높으면, 날씨가 mild하다고 할 수 있다. 대체로, hot은 warm보다 더 기온이 높은 것을 나타내고, warm한 것은 대개 쾌적하다. ❏ ...따스한 저녁

2 ADJ **Warm** clothes and blankets are made of a material such as wool which protects you from the cold. ❏ *They have been forced to sleep in the open without food or warm clothing.* ● **warm|ly** ADV ❏ *Remember to wrap up warmly on cold days.* **3** ADJ **Warm** colors have red or yellow in them rather than blue or green, and make you feel comfortable and relaxed. ❏ *The basement hallway is painted a warm yellow.* **4** ADJ A **warm** person is friendly and shows a lot of affection or enthusiasm in their behavior. ❏ *She was a warm and loving mother.* ● **warm|ly** ADV [ADV with v]

2 형용사 따뜻한, 보온성의 ❏ 그들은 먹을 것과 따뜻한 옷도 없는 상태에서 지금까지 계속 한뎃잠을 자야만 했다. ● 따뜻하게 부사 ❏ 날씨가 추울 때 따뜻하게 몸을 감싸는 것을 잊지 마세요. **3** 형용사 따뜻한 느낌을 주는 ❏ 그 지하실 복도는 따뜻한 느낌을 주는 노란색으로 칠해져 있다. **4** 형용사 마음씨가 따뜻한 ❏ 그녀는 마음씨가 따뜻하고 애정이 넘치는

❏ *New members are warmly welcomed.* ⑤ V-T If you **warm** a part of your body or if something hot **warms** it, it stops feeling cold and starts to feel hotter. ❏ *The sun had come out to warm his back.* ⑥ V-I If you **warm to** a person or an idea, you become fonder of the person or more interested in the idea. ❏ *Those who got to know him better warmed to his openness and honesty.*

어머니였다. ● 열렬히 부사 ❏ 신입 회원들은 열렬히 환영받는다. ⑤ 타동사 따뜻하게 하다 ❏ 해가 나와 그의 등이 따뜻해졌다. ⑥ 자동사 ~에 마음이 끌리다 ❏ 그를 잘 알게 된 사람들은 그의 솔직함과 정직함에 마음이 끌렸다.

① 구동사 따뜻하게 하다, 데우다; 따뜻해지다, 데워지다 ❏ 그는 손에 입김을 불어 손을 따뜻하게 했다. ❏ 그녀가 해야 했던 일이라고는 푸딩을 데우는 일뿐이었다. ② 구동사 준비 운동을 하다 ❏ 한 시간 있으면 운전자들이 주 경기를 위해 준비 운동을 하게 될 것이다. ③ 구동사 예열하다; 예열시키다 ❏ 그는 자동차가 예열되기를 기다렸다.

Word Partnership   warm의 연어

ADJ.	warm and sunny ①
	warm and cozy, warm and dry ① ②
	soft and warm ②
	warm and friendly ④
N.	warm air, warm bath, warm breeze, warm hands, warm water, warm weather ①
	warm clothes ②
	warm smile, warm welcome ④

▶**warm up** ① PHRASAL VERB If you **warm** something **up** or if it **warms up**, it gets hotter. ❏ *He blew on his hands to warm them up.* ❏ *All that she would have to do was warm up the pudding.* ② PHRASAL VERB If you **warm up** for an event such as a race, you prepare yourself for it by doing exercises or by practicing just before it starts. ❏ *In an hour the drivers will be warming up for the main event.* ③ PHRASAL VERB When a machine or engine **warms up** or someone **warms** it **up**, it becomes ready for use a little while after being switched on or started. ❏ *He waited for his car to warm up.*

warmth /wɔrmθ/ ① N-UNCOUNT The **warmth** of something is the heat that it has or produces. ❏ *She went further into the room, drawn by the warmth of the fire.* ② N-UNCOUNT The **warmth** of something such as a garment or blanket is the protection that it gives you against the cold. ❏ *The blanket will provide additional warmth and comfort in bed.*

① 불가산명사 온기 ❏ 그녀는 화롯불의 온기에 이끌려 그 방안으로 더 깊숙이 들어갔다. ② 불가산명사 보온력 ❏ 잘 때 그 담요를 덮으면 더 보온이 잘 되고 더 안락할 것이다.

warm-up (warm-ups) N-COUNT A **warm-up** is something that prepares you for an activity or event, usually because it is a short practice or example of what the activity or event will involve. ❏ *The exercises can be fun and a good warm-up for the latter part of the programme.*

가산명사 준비 운동 ❏ 그 운동은 프로그램의 후반부를 위한 재미있고 좋은 준비 운동이 될 수 있다.

warn ♦♦◇ /wɔrn/ (warns, warning, warned) ① V-T If you **warn** someone about something such as a possible danger or problem, you tell them about it so that they are aware of it. ❏ *When I had my first baby friends warned me that children were expensive.* ❏ *They warned him of the dangers of sailing alone.* ② V-T If you **warn** someone not to do something, you advise them not to do it so that they can avoid possible danger or punishment. ❏ *Mrs. Blount warned me not to interfere.* ❏ *"Don't do anything yet," he warned. "Too risky."*

① 타동사 주의를 주다, 경고하다 ❏ 내가 첫 아이를 가졌을 때 친구들은 아이를 기르는 데 돈이 많이 든다고 주의를 주었다. ❏ 그들은 그에게 혼자 항해하는 것은 위험하다고 경고했다. ② 타동사 충고하다 ❏ 블라운트 부인은 간섭하지 말라고 나에게 충고했다. ❏ "아직 아무것도 하지 마."라고 그가 충고했다. "너무 위험해."

Thesaurus   warn의 참조어

V.	alert, caution, notify ① ②

warn|ing ♦◇◇ /wɔrnɪŋ/ (warnings) ① N-COUNT A **warning** is something which is said or written to tell people of a possible danger, problem, or other unpleasant thing that might happen. ❏ *The minister gave a warning that if war broke out, it would be catastrophic.* ❏ *He was killed because he ignored a warning to put stronger cords on his parachute.* ② N-VAR A **warning** is an advance notice of something that will happen, often something unpleasant or dangerous. ❏ *The soldiers opened fire without warning.* ③ ADJ **Warning** actions or signs give a warning. [ADJ n] ❏ *She ignored the warning signals and did not check the patient's medical notes.*

① 가산명사 경고 ❏ 장관은 전쟁이 발발하면 파국이 올 것이라고 경고를 했다. ❏ 그는 낙하산에 좀더 튼튼한 끈을 사용하라는 경고를 무시했기 때문에 목숨을 잃었다. ② 가산명사 또는 불가산명사 경고, 주의 ❏ 군인들은 경고없이 발포를 했다. ③ 형용사 경고의 ❏ 그녀는 경고 신호를 무시하고 그 환자의 진료 기록을 확인하지 않았다.

Word Partnership   warning의 연어

ADJ.	stern warning ①
	advance warning, early warning ① ②
N.	warning of danger, hurricane warning, storm warning ①
	warning labels, warning signs ③
V.	give (a) warning, ignore a warning, receive (a) warning, send a warning ① ②

warp /wɔrp/ (warps, warping, warped) V-T/V-I If something **warps** or **is warped**, it becomes damaged by bending or curving, often because of the effect of heat or water. ❏ *Left out in the heat of the sun, tapes easily warp or get stuck in their cases.*

타동사/자동사 휘다 ❏ 태양열에 방치된 테이프는 쉽게 휘거나 케이스 안에 달라붙게 된다.

war|rant /wɔrənt, BRIT wɒrənt/ (warrants, warranting, warranted) ① V-T If something **warrants** a particular action, it makes the action seem necessary or appropriate for the circumstances. ❏ *The allegations are serious enough to warrant an investigation.* ② N-COUNT A **warrant** is a legal document that allows someone to do something, especially one that is signed by a judge or magistrate and gives the police permission to arrest someone or search their house. [oft N for n, also by N] ❏ *Police confirmed that they had issued a warrant for his arrest.*

① 타동사 정당화하다 ❏ 그 혐의는 조사를 정당화할 정도로 중대하다. ② 가산명사 영장 ❏ 경찰이 그들이 그 남자의 체포영장을 발부했다고 확인했다.

war|ran|ty /wɔrənti, BRIT wɒrənti/ (warranties) N-COUNT A **warranty** is a written promise by a company that, if you find a fault in something they have sold you within a certain time, they will repair it or replace it free of charge. [also under N] ❏ *...a twelve month warranty.*

가산명사 품질 보증서 ❏ 12개월간의 품질 보증서

war|ring /wɔrɪŋ/ ADJ **Warring** is used to describe groups of people who are involved in a conflict or quarrel with each other. [ADJ n] ❏ *An official said the warring factions have not yet turned in all their heavy weapons.*

형용사 전쟁 중인 ❏ 한 관계자가 전쟁 중인 파벌들이 아직 자신들의 중화기를 모두 내놓지 않았다고 말했다.

A

war|ri|or /wɒriər, BRIT wɒriəʳ/ (warriors) N-COUNT A **warrior** is a fighter or soldier, especially one in former times who was very brave and experienced in fighting. ❑ ...the tale of Bima, the great warrior of Indonesian folklore.

가산명사 전사 ❑인도네시아 민담에 나오는 위대한 전사인 비마 이야기

B

war|ship /wɔrʃɪp/ (warships) N-COUNT A **warship** is a ship with guns that is used for fighting in wars. →see ship

가산명사 전함

wart /wɔrt/ (warts) N-COUNT A **wart** is a small lump which grows on your skin.

가산명사 사마귀; 혹

C

war|time /wɔrtaɪm/ also war-time N-UNCOUNT **Wartime** is a period of time when a war is being fought. ❑ The government will commandeer ships only in wartime.

불가산명사 전시 ❑정부는 전시에만 선박들을 징발할 것이다.

D

wary /weəri/ (warier, wariest) ADJ If you are **wary** of something or someone, you are cautious because you do not know much about them and you believe they may be dangerous or cause problems. ❑ People did not teach their children to be wary of strangers. ● **wari|ly** /weərɪli/ ADV ❑ She studied me warily, as if I might turn violent.

형용사 경계하는, 조심하는 ❑사람들은 낯선 사람을 경계하라고 아이들에게 가르치지 않았다. ● 경계하여, 조심하여 부사 ❑그녀는 마치 내가 난폭하게 굴지도 모른다는 듯이 나를 경계하며 살폈다.

E

was /wəz, STRONG wɒz, wʌz, BRIT wɒz/ **Was** is the first and third person singular of the past tense of **be**.

be동사의 1인칭 및 3인칭 단수 과거

F

wash ◆◇◇ /wɒʃ/ (washes, washing, washed) **1** V-T If you **wash** something, you clean it using water and usually a substance such as soap or detergent. ❑ We did odd jobs like farm work and washing dishes. ❑ It took a long time to wash the mud out of his hair. ● N-COUNT **Wash** is also a noun. ❑ That coat could do with a wash. **2** V-T/V-I If you **wash** or if you **wash** part of your body, especially your hands and face, you clean part of your body using soap and water. ❑ They looked as if they hadn't washed in days. ❑ She washed her face with cold water. ● N-COUNT **Wash** is also a noun. ❑ They are clean birds. Once every day they pop down to the river for a wash. **3** V-T/V-I If a sea or river **washes** somewhere, it flows there gently. You can also say that something carried by a sea or river **washes** or **is washed** somewhere. ❑ The sea washed against the shore. **4** V-I If a feeling **washes over** you, you suddenly feel it very strongly and cannot control it. [WRITTEN] ❑ A wave of self-consciousness can wash over her when someone new enters the room. **5** →see also **washing** **6** PHRASE If you say that something such as an item of clothing **is in the wash**, you mean that it is being washed, is waiting to be washed, or has just been washed and should therefore not be worn or used. [INFORMAL] ❑ Your jeans are in the wash. **7** to **wash** your **hands of** something →see hand →see **dry cleaning, soap**

1 타동사 씻다 ❑우리는 농장일과 접시닦이 같은 생각지 못한 일을 했다. ❑그가 머리에 묻은 진흙을 씻어 내는 데 오랜 시간이 걸렸다. ● 가산명사 씻기, 세탁 ❑그 코트는 세탁이 가능할 것이다. **2** 타동사/자동사 씻다 ❑그들은 며칠 동안 씻지 않은 것처럼 보였다. ❑그녀는 찬물로 얼굴을 씻었다. ● 가산명사 씻기 ❑그들은 청결한 새들이다. 매일 한 번씩은 몸을 씻기 위해 강물 속으로 풍덩 들어간다. **3** 타동사/자동사 (물이) 밀려오다; (물에) 떠내려 오다; 떠내려 보내다 ❑바닷물이 해변으로 밀려왔다. **4** 자동사 엄습하다 [문어체] ❑새로 온 누군가가 그 방에 들어간다면 한 차례 자의식이 그녀를 엄습할 수 있다. **6** 구 세탁 중이다 [비격식체] ❑네 청바지는 세탁 중이야.

G

H

I

J

K

L

> **Thesaurus** wash의 참조어
>
> V. clean, rinse, scrub **1**
> bathe, clean, soap **2**

M

> **Word Partnership** wash의 연어
>
> N. wash **a car**, wash **clothes**, wash **dishes** **1**
> wash *your* **face/hair/hands** **2**

N

O

▶**wash away** PHRASAL VERB If rain or floods **wash away** something, they destroy it and carry it away. ❑ Flood waters washed away one of the main bridges in Pusan.

구동사 떠내려 가게 하다, 쓸어 가다 ❑홍수로 인해 부산의 주요 교량 중 하나가 떠내려 갔다.

▶**wash down** **1** PHRASAL VERB If you **wash** something, especially food, **down** with a drink, you drink the drink after eating the food, especially to make the food easier to swallow or digest. ❑ He took two aspirin immediately and washed them down with three cups of water. **2** PHRASAL VERB If you **wash down** an object, you wash it all, from top to bottom. ❑ The prisoner started to wash down the walls of his cell.

1 구동사 (물과 함께 먹어) 넘기다 ❑그는 즉시 아스피린 두 알을 복용하고 물 세 잔을 마시면서 넘겼다. **2** 구동사 씻어 내리다 ❑그 죄수는 감방의 벽들을 씻어 내리기 시작했다.

P

▶**wash up** **1** PHRASAL VERB If you **wash up**, you clean part of your body with soap and water, especially your hands and face. [AM; BRIT **wash**] ❑ He headed to the bathroom to wash up. **2** PHRASAL VERB If something **is washed up on** a piece of land, it is carried by a river or sea and left there. ❑ Thousands of herring and crab are washed up on the beaches during every storm. **3** PHRASAL VERB If you **wash up**, you wash the plates, cups, flatware, and pans which have been used for cooking and eating a meal. [BRIT; AM **wash the dishes**] ❑ I ran some hot water and washed up.

1 구동사 씻다 [미국영어; 영국영어 wash] ❑그는 씻기 위해 화장실로 향했다. **2** 구동사 떠내려 가다 ❑태풍이 올 때마다 수천 마리의 청어와 게들이 해안가로 떠내려 온다. **3** 구동사 설거지하다 [영국영어; 미국영어 wash the dishes] ❑나는 뜨거운 물을 좀 틀어 놓고 설거지를 했다.

Q

R

S

T

wash|able /wɒʃəbəl/ ADJ **Washable** clothes or materials can be washed in water without being damaged. ❑ Choose washable curtains.

형용사 물세탁이 가능한 ❑물세탁이 가능한 커튼을 고르세요.

wash|basin /wɒʃbeɪsən/ (washbasins) also wash basin N-COUNT A **washbasin** is a large bowl, usually with faucets for hot and cold water, for washing your hands and face. [mainly BRIT; AM usually **sink**]

가산명사 대야, 세면기 [주로 영국영어; 미국영어 대개 sink]

U

wash|cloth /wɒʃklɔθ, BRIT wɒʃklɒθ/ (washcloths) N-COUNT A **washcloth** is a small cloth that you use for washing yourself. [AM; BRIT **flannel, facecloth**]

가산명사 목욕 수건 [미국영어; 영국영어 flannel, facecloth]

V

wash|er /wɒʃər/ (washers) **1** N-COUNT A **washer** is a thin flat ring of metal or rubber which is placed over a bolt before the nut is screwed on. **2** N-COUNT A **washer** is the same as a **washing machine**. [INFORMAL]

1 가산명사 (나사의) 와서 **2** 가산명사 세탁기 [비격식체]

W

wash|ing /wɒʃɪŋ/ N-UNCOUNT **Washing** is a collection of clothes, sheets, and other things which are waiting to be washed, are being washed, or have just been washed. ❑ ...plastic bags full of dirty washing.

불가산명사 세탁물 ❑더러운 세탁물로 가득한 비닐봉지들

X

wash|ing ma|chine (washing machines) N-COUNT A **washing machine** is a machine that you use to wash clothes in.

가산명사 세탁기

Y

washing-up **1** N-UNCOUNT To **do** the **washing-up** means to wash the plates, cups, flatware, and pans which have been used for cooking and eating a meal. [BRIT; AM **wash the dishes**] ❑ Martha volunteered to do the washing-up. **2** N-UNCOUNT **Washing-up** is the plates, cups, flatware, and pans which you have to wash after a meal. [BRIT; AM **dirty dishes, the dishes**] ❑ You are faced with a brimming bowl of washing-up.

1 불가산명사 설거지 [영국영어; 미국영어 wash the dishes] ❑마샤는 자진해서 설거지를 했다. **2** 불가산명사 설거지 거리 [영국영어; 미국영어 dirty dishes, the dishes] ❑설거지 거리가 한 통 가득하게 된다.

Z

wasn't /wʌzᵊnt, wɒz-, BRIT wɒzᵊnt/ **Wasn't** is the usual spoken form of "was not."

wasp /wɒsp/ (**wasps**) N-COUNT A **wasp** is an insect with wings and yellow and black stripes across its body. Wasps have a painful sting like a bee but do not produce honey.

wast|age /weɪstɪdʒ/ **1** N-UNCOUNT **Wastage** of something is the act of wasting it or the amount of it that is wasted. ❑ *There was a lot of wastage and many wrong decisions were hastily taken.* **2** N-UNCOUNT **Wastage** refers to the number of people who leave a company, college, or other organization, especially before they have completed their education or training. [BRIT] ❑ *British universities have very little wastage and their graduates are good.* →see also **natural wastage**

waste ♦♦♢ /weɪst/ (**wastes, wasting, wasted**) **1** V-T If you **waste** something such as time, money, or energy, you use too much of it doing something that is not important or necessary, or is unlikely to succeed. ❑ *There could be many reasons and he was not going to waste time speculating on them.* ❑ *I resolved not to waste money on a hotel.* ● N-SING **Waste** is also a noun. ❑ *It is a waste of time going to the doctor with most mild complaints.* **2** N-UNCOUNT **Waste** is the use of money or other resources on things that do not need it. ❑ *The packets are measured to reduce waste.* **3** N-UNCOUNT **Waste** is material which has been used and is no longer wanted, for example because the valuable or useful part of it has been taken out. [also N in pl] ❑ *Congress passed a law that regulates the disposal of waste.* ❑ *Up to 10 million tonnes of toxic wastes are produced every year in the UK.* **4** V-T If you **waste** an opportunity for something, you do not take advantage of it when it is available. ❑ *Let's not waste an opportunity to see the children.* **5** ADJ **Waste** land is land, especially in or near a city, which is not used or looked after by anyone, and so is covered by wild plants and garbage. ❑ *There was a patch of waste land behind the church.* **6** PHRASE If something **goes to waste,** it remains unused or has to be thrown away. ❑ *So much of his enormous effort and talent will go to waste if we are forced to drop one hour of the film.* **7** to **waste no time** →see **time**

Thesaurus		waste의 참조어
V.	misuse, squander; (ant.) conserve **1**	
N.	garbage, junk, trash **3**	

Word Partnership		waste의 연어
N.	waste **energy**, waste **money**, waste **time**, waste **water** **1**	
V.	reduce waste **2** **3**	
	recycle waste **3**	
ADJ.	**hazardous** waste, **human** waste, **industrial** waste, **nuclear** waste, **toxic** waste **3**	

▶**waste away** PHRASAL VERB If someone **wastes away,** they become extremely thin or weak because they are ill or worried and they are not eating properly. ❑ *Persons dying from cancer grow thin and visibly waste away.*

waste|ful /weɪstfəl/ ADJ Action that is **wasteful** uses too much of something valuable such as time, money, or energy. ❑ *This kind of training is ineffective, and wasteful of scarce resources.*

waste|land /weɪstlænd/ (**wastelands**) **1** N-VAR A **wasteland** is an area of land on which not much can grow or which has been spoiled in some way. ❑ *The pollution has already turned vast areas into a wasteland.* **2** N-COUNT If you refer to a place, situation, or period in time as a **wasteland,** you are criticizing it because you think there is nothing interesting or exciting in it. [DISAPPROVAL] ❑ *...the cultural wasteland of Franco's repressive rule.*

watch
① LOOKING AND PAYING ATTENTION
② INSTRUMENT THAT TELLS THE TIME

① **watch** ♦♦♦ /wɒtʃ/ (**watches, watching, watched**) →Please look at category **1** to see if the expression you are looking for is shown under another headword. **1** V-T/V-I If you **watch** someone or something, you look at them, usually for a period of time, and pay attention to what is happening. ❑ *The man was standing in his doorway watching him.* ❑ *He watched the barman prepare the beer he had ordered.* **2** V-T If you **watch** something on television or an event such as a sports match, you spend time looking at it, especially when you see it from the beginning to the end. ❑ *I'd stayed up late to watch the film.* **3** V-T/V-I If you **watch** a situation or event, you pay attention to it or you are aware of it, but you do not influence it. ❑ *Human rights groups have been closely watching the case.* **4** V-T If you **watch** people, especially children or animals, you are responsible for them, and make sure that they are not in danger. ❑ *Parents can't be expected to watch their children 24 hours a day.* **5** V-T If you tell someone to **watch** a particular person or thing, you are warning them to be careful that the person or thing does not get out of control or do something unpleasant. ❑ *You really ought to watch these quiet types.* **6** PHRASE If someone **keeps watch,** they look and listen all the time, while other people are asleep or doing something else, so that they can warn them of danger or an attack. ❑ *Jose, as usual, had climbed a tree to keep watch.* **7** PHRASE If you **keep watch** on events or a situation, you pay attention to what is happening, so that you can take action at the right moment. ❑ *U.S. officials have been keeping close watch on the situation.* **8** PHRASE

---

was not의 축약형

가산명사 말벌

1 불가산명사 낭비 ❑ 많은 낭비가 있었고 수많은 잘못된 결정이 성급하게 내려졌다. **2** 불가산명사 중도 탈락자 [영국영어] ❑ 영국의 대학교들은 중도 탈락자가 거의 없고 졸업생들은 우수하다.

1 타동사 낭비하다 ❑ 거기엔 많은 이유가 있을 수 있었고 그는 그것들을 추측하느라 시간을 낭비하지는 않을 참이었다. ❑ 나는 호텔에 돈을 낭비하지 않기로 결심했다. ● 단수명사 낭비 ❑ 대부분 가벼운 병으로 병원에 가는 것은 시간 낭비이다. **2** 불가산명사 낭비 ❑ 낭비를 줄이기 위해 포장 용기들을 잰다. **3** 불가산명사 폐기물, 쓰레기 ❑ 의회는 폐기물 처리를 규제하는 법안을 통과시켰다. ❑ 매년 영국에서는 천만 톤에 이르는 유독성 폐기물이 나온다. **4** 타동사 (기회를) 놓치다 ❑ 그 아이들을 만날 수 있는 기회를 놓치지 맙시다. **5** 형용사 버려진 ❑ 그 교회 뒤에는 버려진 땅이 조금 있었다. **6** 구 낭비되다 ❑ 우리가 그 영화에서 억지로 한 시간 분량을 줄여야 한다면 그가 기울인 엄청난 노력과 재능의 너무 많은 부분이 낭비될 것이다.

구동사 쇠약해지다 ❑ 암으로 사망하는 사람들은 몸이 마르고 눈에 띄게 쇠약해진다.

형용사 낭비적인 ❑ 이러한 훈련은 비효과적이며, 부족한 자원을 낭비하는 것이다.

1 가산명사 또는 불가산명사 불모지 ❑ 오염으로 인해 이미 광대한 지역이 불모지가 되었다. **2** 가산명사 (정신적 또는 문화적) 황무지 [탐탁찮음] ❑ 프랑코의 억압 통치라는 문화적 황무지.

1 타동사/자동사 지켜보다 ❑ 그 남자는 출입구 안쪽에 서서 그를 지켜보고 있었다. ❑ 그는 자신이 주문한 맥주를 준비하는 바텐더를 지켜보았다. **2** 타동사 (영화 등을) 보다 ❑ 나는 늦게까지 안 자고 그 영화를 봤어. **3** 타동사/자동사 주시하다 ❑ 인권 단체들은 주의 깊게 그 사건을 주시하고 있다. **4** 타동사 지키다, 지켜보다 ❑ 부모들이 하루 24시간 동안 자녀들을 지키리라고 기대할 수는 없다. **5** 타동사 조심하다 ❑ 너는 정말로 이 조용한 타입의 사람들을 조심해야 해. **6** 구 망을 보다 ❑ 호세는 여느 때처럼 망을 보기 위해 나무 위로 올라갔다. **7** 구 주시하다 ❑ 미국 관리들이 그 상황을 면밀히 주시해 오고 있다. **8** 구 조심해 ❑ "자 조심해요, 펫."라고 경사가 그녀에게 말했다. **9** 구 주시받고 있는 ❑ 의사들이 조세핀의 상태가 얼마나 심각한지를 확인했고, 그녀를 아직도 지켜보고 있는 중이다. **10** 구 두고 봐 ❑ 두고 봐. 그들이 낫기 전에 사정이 더 악화될 거야.

A You say "**watch it**" in order to warn someone to be careful, especially when you want to threaten them about what will happen if they are not careful. ❏ *"Now watch it, Patsy," the Sergeant told her.* **9** PHRASE If someone is being kept **under watch**, they are being guarded or observed all the time. ❏ *Doctors confirmed how serious Josephine's condition was, and she is still being kept under watch.*
B
10 PHRASE You say to someone "**you watch**" or "**just watch**" when you are predicting that something will happen, and you are very confident that it will happen as you say. ❏ *You watch. Things will get worse before they get better.*
C **11** to **watch** your **step** →see **step**

▶**watch for** or **watch out for** PHRASAL VERB If you **watch for** something or **watch out for** it, you pay attention so that you notice it, either because you do not want to miss it or because you want to avoid it. ❏ *We'll be watching for any developments.*
D

구동사 예의 주시하다 ❏ 우리는 어떠한 사태 변화에 대해서도 예의 주시할 것이다.

▶**watch out** PHRASAL VERB If you tell someone to **watch out**, you are warning them to be careful, because something unpleasant might happen to them or they might get into difficulties. ❏ *You have to watch out because there are land mines all over the place.*
E

구동사 조심하다 ❏ 그 장소에는 도처에 지뢰가 매설되어 있으므로 조심해야 합니다.

▶**watch out for** →see **watch for**
F

If you want to say that someone is paying attention to something they can see, you say they **are watching** or **looking at** it. In general, you **watch** something that is moving or changing, and you **look at** something that is not moving. ❏ *I asked him to look at the picture above his bed... He watched Blake run down the stairs.* You use **see** to talk about things that you are aware of because a visual impression reaches your eyes. You often use **can** in this case. ❏ *I can see the fax here on the desk.*
G

H

누군가가 자신이 볼 수 있는 어떤 것에 주의를 기울이고 있다고 말하려면, watch나 look을 써서 they are watching it 또는 they are looking at it이라고 한다. 대개, 움직이거나 변하는 것은 watch하는 반면에, 움직이지 않는 것은 look at한다. ❏ 나는 그에게 그의 침대 위에 걸려 있는 그림을 보라고 했다... 그는 블레이크가 계단을 달려 내려가는 것을 지켜보았다. 시각적 인상이 눈에 들어와서 의식하게 되는 것에 대해 말할 때는 see를 쓴다. 이런 경우에는 흔히 can을 쓴다. ❏ 난 여기 책상 위에 팩스가 보인다.

J ② **watch** ♦◇◇ /wɒtʃ/ (**watches**) N-COUNT A **watch** is a small clock which you wear on a strap on your wrist, or on a chain. →see **jewelry**, **time zone**

가산명사 손목시계, 회중시계

K | **Word Partnership** | watch의 연어 |

L N. watch **people** ① **1**
watch **a DVD**, watch **a film/movie**, watch **fireworks**, watch **a game**, watch **the news**, watch **a video**, watch **television/TV** ① **2**
watch **children** ① **4**
M V. **check** *your* watch, **glance at** *your* watch, **look at** *your* watch ② **1**

N **watch|dog** /wɒtʃdɒg, BRIT wɒtʃdɒg/ (**watchdogs**) N-COUNT A **watchdog** is a person or committee whose job is to make sure that companies do not act illegally or irresponsibly. ❏ *...an anti-crime watchdog group funded by New York businesses.*

가산명사 감시인 ❏ 뉴욕 실업계가 지원하는 방범 감시단

O **watch|ful** /wɒtʃfəl/ ADJ Someone who is **watchful** notices everything that is happening. ❏ *The best thing is to be watchful and see the family doctor for any change in your normal health.*

형용사 경계하는, 방심하지 않는 ❏ 주의하며 평소 건강에 조금이라도 변화가 있으면 가정의에게 진찰을 받는 것이 최선이다.

P **watch|word** /wɒtʃwɜrd/ (**watchwords**) N-COUNT Someone's **watchword** is a word or phrase that sums up their attitude or approach to a particular subject or to things in general. ❏ *Caution has been one of Mr. Allan's watchwords.*

가산명사 좌우명 ❏ 조심은 앨런 씨가 가지고 있는 좌우명의 하나이다.

Q **wa|ter** ♦♦♦ /wɔtər/ (**waters, watering, watered**) **1** N-UNCOUNT **Water** is a clear thin liquid that has no color or taste when it is pure. It falls from clouds as rain and enters rivers and seas. All animals and people need water in order to live. ❏ *Get me a glass of water.* ❏ *...the sound of water hammering on the metal roof.* **2** N-PLURAL You use **waters** to refer to a large area of sea, especially the area of sea which is near to a country and which is regarded as belonging to it. ❏ *The ship will remain outside Chinese territorial waters.* **3** V-T If you **water** plants, you pour water over them in order to help them to grow. ❏ *He went out to water the plants.* **4** V-I If your eyes **water**, tears build up in them because they are hurting or because you are upset. ❏ *His eyes watered from cigarette smoke.* **5** V-I If you say that your mouth **is watering**, you mean that you can smell or see some nice food and you might mean that your mouth is producing a liquid. ❏ *...cookies to make your mouth water.* **6** PHRASE If you say that an event or incident is **water under the bridge**, you mean that it has happened and cannot now be changed, so there is no point in worrying about it anymore. ❏ *He was relieved his time in jail was over and regarded it as water under the bridge.* **7** PHRASE If you are **in deep water**, you are in a difficult or awkward situation. ❏ *You certainly seem to be in deep water.* **8** PHRASE If an argument or theory does not **hold water**, it does not seem to be reasonable or be in accordance with the facts. ❏ *This argument simply cannot hold water in Europe.* **9** PHRASE If you are **in hot water**, you are in trouble. [INFORMAL] ❏ *The company has already been in hot water over high prices this year.* **10** PHRASE If you **pour cold water on** an idea or suggestion, you show that you have a low opinion of it. ❏ *City economists pour cold water on the idea that the economic recovery has begun.* **11** PHRASE If you **test the water** or **test the waters**, you try to find out what reaction an action or idea will get before you do it or tell it to people. ❏ *You should be cautious when getting involved and test the water before committing yourself.* **12** **like water off a duck's back** →see **duck**. **to take to something like a duck to water** →see **duck**. **to keep your head above water** →see **head**
→see **erosion**, **greenhouse effect**, **lake**, **plumbing**
→see Word Web: **water**

R
S
T
U
V
W
X
Y
Z

1 불가산명사 물 ❏ 물 한 잔 갖다 주세요. ❏ 금속 지붕 위를 두드려 대는 물소리 **2** 복수명사 바다, 영해, 근해 ❏ 그 배는 중국 영해 바깥에 머무를 것이다. **3** 타동사 (식물에) 물을 주다 ❏ 그는 화초들에 물을 주러 나갔다. **4** 자동사 눈물이 나다 ❏ 그는 담배 연기 때문에 눈물이 났다. **5** 자동사 군침을 흘리다 ❏ 군침이 돌게 하는 쿠키 **6** 구 이미 지나간 일, 과거지사 ❏ 그는 복역 기간이 끝나서 안도했고 복역을 과거지사로 치부했다. **7** 구 곤란한 처지의, 난국에 처한 ❏ 당신은 분명 난국에 처한 것 같다. **8** 구 (논리가) 옳다, 이치에 맞다 ❏ 이 주장은 유럽에서는 전혀 말이 되지 않는다. **9** 구 곤경에 처하여 [비격식체] ❏ 회사가 올해 높은 물가로 인해 이미 어려움에 빠져 있다. **10** 구 찬물을 끼얹다 ❏ 시 경제학자들은 경제가 회복되기 시작했다는 의견에 찬물을 끼얹었다. **11** 구 미리 상황을 살피다, 미리 탐색해 보다 ❏ 관련된 경우에는 조심해야 하고, 동의를 하기 전에 미리 탐색을 해 보아야 한다.

Word Web — water

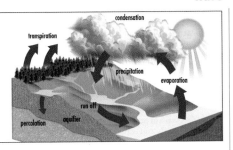

Water changes its form in the hydrologic **cycle**. The sun warms oceans, lakes, and rivers. This causes some water to **evaporate**. Evaporation creates a gas called **water vapor**. Plants also give off water vapor through transpiration. Water vapor rises into the **atmosphere**. When it hits cooler air, it **condenses** into drops of water and forms **clouds**. When these drops get heavy enough, they begin to fall. They form different types of precipitation. Rain forms in warm air. Cold air creates **freezing rain**, **sleet**, and **snow**.

▶**water down** ■ PHRASAL VERB If you **water down** a substance, for example food or drink, you add water to it to make it weaker. ❑ *You can water down a glass of wine and make it last twice as long.* ❷ V-T If something such as a proposal, speech, or statement **is watered down**, it is made much weaker and less forceful, or less likely to make people angry. ❑ *Proposed legislation affecting bird-keepers has been watered down.*

water|color /wɔtərkʌlər/ (**watercolors**) [BRIT **watercolour**] ■ N-VAR **Watercolors** are colored paints, used for painting pictures, which you apply with a wet brush or dissolve in water first. ❑ *Oil paints can be replaced with watercolors.* ❷ N-COUNT A **watercolor** is a picture which has been painted with watercolors. ❑ *...a lovely watercolor by J. M. W. Turner.*

water|fall /wɔtərfɔl/ (**waterfalls**) N-COUNT A **waterfall** is a place where water flows over the edge of a steep, high cliff in hills or mountains, and falls into a pool below. ❑ *...Angel Falls, the world's highest waterfall.*

water|front /wɔtərfrʌnt/ (**waterfronts**) N-COUNT A **waterfront** is a street or piece of land which is next to an area of water, for example a harbor or the sea. ❑ *They went for a stroll along the waterfront.*

water|proof /wɔtərpruf/ ADJ Something which is **waterproof** does not let water pass through it. ❑ *Take waterproof clothing – Orkney weather is unpredictable.*

water|shed /wɔtərʃed/ (**watersheds**) N-COUNT If something such as an event is a **watershed** in the history or development of something, it is very important because it represents the beginning of a new stage in it. ❑ *The election of Mary Robinson in 1990 was a watershed in Irish politics.*

water|tight /wɔtərtaɪt/ also **water-tight** ■ ADJ Something that is **watertight** does not allow water to pass through it, for example because it is tightly sealed. ❑ *The flask is completely watertight, even when laid on its side.* ❷ ADJ A **watertight** case, argument, or agreement is one that has been so carefully put together that nobody will be able to find a fault in it. ❑ *The police had a watertight case. They even got his fingerprints from that glass cabinet.*

water|way /wɔtərweɪ/ (**waterways**) N-COUNT A **waterway** is a canal, river, or narrow channel of sea which ships or boats can sail along. ❑ *There are more than 400 miles of waterways to explore in the area.*

wa|tery /wɔtəri/ ■ ADJ Something that is **watery** is weak or pale. ❑ *A watery light began to show through the branches.* ❷ ADJ If you described food or drink as **watery**, you dislike it because it contains too much water, or has no flavor. [DISAPPROVAL] ❑ *...a plateful of watery soup.* ❸ ADJ Something that is **watery** contains, resembles, or consists of water. ❑ *There was a watery discharge from her ear.*

watt /wɒt/ (**watts**) N-COUNT A **watt** is a unit of measurement of electrical power. ❑ *Use a 3 amp fuse for equipment up to 720 watts.*

wave ◆◇◇ /weɪv/ (**waves, waving, waved**) ■ V-T/V-I If you **wave** or **wave** your hand, you move your hand from side to side in the air, usually in order to say hello or goodbye to someone. ❑ *Jessica caught sight of Lois and waved to her.* ❑ *He grinned, waved, and said, "Hi!"* ● N-COUNT **Wave** is also a noun. ❑ *Steve stopped him with a wave of the hand.* ❷ V-T If you **wave** someone away or **wave** them on, you make a movement with your hand to indicate that they should move in a particular direction. ❑ *Leshka waved him away with a show of irritation.* ❑ *He waited for a policeman to stop the traffic and wave the people on.* ❸ V-T If you **wave** something, you hold it up and move it rapidly from side to side. ❑ *Hospital staff were outside to welcome him, waving flags and applauding.* ❹ V-I If something **waves**, it moves gently from side to side or up and down. ❑ *...grass and flowers waving in the wind.* ❺ N-COUNT A **wave** is a raised mass of water on the surface of water, especially the sea, which is caused by the wind or by tides making the surface of the water rise and fall. ❑ *...the sound of the waves breaking on the shore.* ❻ N-COUNT If someone's hair has **waves**, it curves slightly instead of being straight. ❑ *Her blue eyes shone and caught the light, and so did the platinum waves in her hair.* ❼ N-COUNT A **wave** is a sudden increase in heat or energy that spreads out from an earthquake or explosion. ❑ *The shock waves of the earthquake were felt in Teheran.* ❽ N-COUNT **Waves** are the form in which things such as sound, light, and radio signals travel. ❑ *Regular repeating actions such as sound waves, light waves, or radio waves have a certain frequency, or number of waves per second.* ❾ N-COUNT If you refer to a **wave** of a particular feeling, you mean that it increases quickly and becomes very intense, and then often decreases again. ❑ *She felt a wave of panic, but forced herself to leave the room calmly.* ❿ N-COUNT A **wave** is a sudden increase in a particular activity or type of behavior, especially an undesirable or

■ 구동사 물을 타다 ❑ 와인 한 잔에 물을 타서 두 배로 오래 마실 수 있다. ❷ 타동사 (방언 등의) 수위가 조절되다, 강도가 낮춰지다 ❑ 조류 사육자에게 영향을 미치는 입법안이 강도가 낮아졌다.

[영국영어 watercolour] ■ 가산명사 또는 불가산명사 수채화 물감 ❑ 유화 재료는 수채 물감으로 대치할 수 있다. ❷ 가산명사 수채화 ❑ 제이 엠 더블유 터너가 그린 멋진 수채화

가산명사 폭포 ❑ 세계에서 가장 높은 폭포인 엔젤 폭포

가산명사 물가, 부두, 선창가 ❑ 그들은 부둣가를 따라 산책을 나갔다.

형용사 방수의 ❑ 방수가 되는 옷을 입으세요. 오크니의 날씨는 예측할 수가 없거든요.

가산명사 분수령, 분기점 ❑ 1990년 메리 로빈슨의 당선이 아일랜드 정치의 분수령이었다.

■ 형용사 물이 새지 않는, 물이 들어오지 못하는 ❑ 그 보온병은 심지어 옆으로 눕혀 놓아도 완벽하게 물이 새지 않는다. ❷ 형용사 완벽한, 빈틈없는 ❑ 경찰은 빈틈없는 수사를 했다. 그들은 심지어 저 유리 캐비닛에서 그의 지문까지 채취했다.

가산명사 수로 ❑ 그 지역에는 탐사할 수로가 400마일이 넘게 있다.

■ 형용사 옅은, 희미한 ❑ 나뭇가지 사이로 옅은 빛이 들기 시작했다. ❷ 형용사 묽은, 싱거운 [탐탁찮음] ❑ 묽은 수프 한 그릇 ❸ 형용사 물의 ❑ 그녀의 귀에서 물 같은 분비물이 나왔다.

가산명사 와트 ❑ 720와트까지의 장비에는 3암페어짜리 퓨즈를 사용하세요.

■ 타동사/자동사 손을 흔들다; (손을) 흔들다 ❑ 제시카가 로이스의 모습을 보고 그녀에게 손을 흔들었다. ❑ 그는 싱긋 웃고, 손을 흔들며 "안녕!" 하고 말했다. ● 가산명사 흔들기 ❑ 스티브가 손을 흔들어 그를 멈춰 세웠다. ❷ 타동사 손을 흔들어 지시하다 ❑ 레쉬카는 짜증난 표를 내며 그에게 가라고 손짓했다. ❑ 그는 경찰관이 차량 통행을 막고 수신호로 사람들을 지나가게 할 때까지 기다렸다. ❸ 타동사 흔들다, 휘두르다 ❑ 병원 직원들은 밖에서 깃발을 흔들고 환호하며 그를 맞이했다. ❹ 자동사 물결치다, 나부끼다, 너울거리다 ❑ 바람에 너울거리는 풀과 꽃들 ❺ 가산명사 파도, 물결 ❑ 해변에 부서지는 파도 소리 ❻ 가산명사 (머리의) 웨이브 ❑ 그녀의 푸른 눈이 빛나며 빛을 받아 반짝였고, 그녀 머리칼의 백금빛 웨이브도 그랬다. ❼ 가산명사 파장, 물결 ❑ 지진의 충격파가 테헤란에서 감지되었다. ❽ 가산명사 파동 ❑ 음파, 광파, 전파와 같은 규칙적으로 반복되는 작용에는 일정한 빈도수, 즉 초당 파동수가 있다. ❾ 가산명사 고조 ❑ 그녀는 공포가 고조되는 것을 느꼈지만, 애써 침착하게 방을 나왔다. ❿ 가산명사 급증 ❑ 최근 폭력의 급증

A

unpleasant one. ❏ ...*the current wave of violence.* ⓫ →see also **new wave, tidal wave**
→see **beach, ear, earthquake, echo, ocean, radio, sound**
→see Word Web: **wave**

B

C

D

E

F

wave|length /wéɪvlɛŋθ/ (**wavelengths**) ⓵ N-COUNT A **wavelength** is the distance between a part of a wave of energy such as light or sound and the next similar part. ❏ *Sunlight consists of different wavelengths of radiation.*
⓶ N-COUNT A **wavelength** is the size of radio wave which a particular radio station uses to broadcast its programs. ❏ *She found the wavelength of their broadcasts, and left the radio tuned to their station.* ⓷ PHRASE If two people are **on the same wavelength,** they find it easy to understand each other and they tend to agree, because they share similar interests or opinions. ❏ *We could complete each other's sentences because we were on the same wavelength.*

⓵ 가산명사 파장 ❏ 햇빛은 다른 파장의 복사 에너지로 구성되어 있다. ⓶ 가산명사 주파수 ❏ 그녀는 그들 방송의 주파수를 찾아 라디오를 그 방송국에 맞추어 두었다. ⓷ 구 마음이 잘 맞는, 의기투합하여 ❏ 우리는 마음이 잘 맞기 때문에 서로 상대방의 말을 대신 마무리 지어 줄 수도 있었다.

G

H

wa|ver /wéɪvər/ (**wavers, wavering, wavered**) ⓵ V-I If you **waver,** you cannot decide about something or you consider changing your mind about something. ❏ *Some military commanders wavered over whether to support the coup.*
⓶ V-I If something **wavers,** it shakes with very slight movements or changes. ❏ *The shadows of the dancers wavered continually.*

⓵ 자동사 주저하다, 결정을 못 내리다 ❏ 일부 군 사령관들은 쿠데타를 지지할 것인지를 두고 주저하고 있었다. ⓶ 자동사 너울거리다, 흔들리다 ❏ 춤추는 사람들의 그림자가 계속해서 너울거렸다.

I

wavy /wéɪvi/ (**wavier, waviest**) ⓵ ADJ **Wavy** hair is not straight or curly, but curves slightly. ❏ *She had short, wavy brown hair.* ⓶ ADJ A **wavy** line has a series of regular curves along it. ❏ *The boxes were decorated with a wavy gold line.*

⓵ 형용사 웨이브가 있는, 약간 곱슬거리는 ❏ 그녀는 약간 곱슬거리는 갈색 머리를 짧게 하고 있었다. ⓶ 형용사 물결 모양의 ❏ 상자들은 물결 모양의 금색 선으로 장식되어 있었다.

J

K

wax /wǽks/ (**waxes, waxing, waxed**) ⓵ N-MASS **Wax** is a solid, slightly shiny substance made of fat or oil which is used to make candles and polish. It melts when it is heated. ❏ *There were colored candles which had spread pools of wax on the furniture.* ⓶ V-T If you **wax** a surface, you put a thin layer of wax onto it, especially in order to polish it. ❏ *We'd have long talks while she helped me wax the floor.* ⓷ N-UNCOUNT **Wax** is the sticky yellow substance found in your ears. ❏ *I seem to be going a little bit deaf and I think this is due to wax in my ears.*

⓵ 물질명사 밀랍, 왁스 ❏ 가구 위에는 흘러내린 여러 색의 촛농이 흘러내린 여러 색의 양초가 있었다. ⓶ 타동사 왁스를 내다 ❏ 그녀가 내가 마루에 왁스칠하는 것을 도와주는 동안 우리는 긴 이야기를 나누었다. ⓷ 불가산명사 귀지 ❏ 나는 귀가 잘 안 들리는 것 같은데 귓속의 귀지 때문인 것 같다.

L

M

way ♦♦♦ /wéɪ/ (**ways**) ⓵ N-COUNT If you refer to a **way** of doing something, you are referring to how you can do it, for example the action you can take or the method you can use to achieve it. ❏ *Freezing isn't a bad way of preserving food.* ❏ *I worked myself into a frenzy plotting ways to make him jealous.* ❏ *There just might be a way.* ⓶ N-COUNT If you talk about the **way** someone does something, you are talking about the qualities their action has. ❏ *She smiled in a friendly way.* ❏ *He had a strange way of talking.* ⓷ N-COUNT If a general statement or description is true **in** a particular **way,** this is the form of it that is true in a particular case. ❏ *Computerized reservation systems help airline profits in several ways.* ❏ *She was afraid in a way that was quite new to her.* ⓸ N-COUNT You use **way** in expressions such as **in some ways, in many ways,** and **in every way** to indicate the degree or extent to which a statement is true. ❏ *In some ways, the official opening is a formality.* ⓹ N-PLURAL The **ways** of a particular person or group of people are their customs or their usual behavior. ❏ *He denounces people who urge him to alter his ways.* ❏ *I think you've been too long in Cornwall. You've forgotten the ways of the city.* ⓺ N-SING If you refer to someone's **way,** you are referring to their usual or preferred type of behavior. ❏ *She is now divorced and, in her usual resourceful way, has started her own business.* ⓻ N-COUNT You use **way** to refer to one particular opinion or interpretation of something, when others are possible. ❏ *I suppose that's one way of looking at it.* ❏ *With most of Dylan's lyrics, however, there are other ways of interpreting the words.* ⓼ N-COUNT You use **way** when mentioning one of a number of possible, alternative results or decisions. ❏ *There is no indication which way the vote could go.* ⓽ N-SING The **way** you feel about something is your attitude to it or your opinion about it. ❏ *I'm terribly sorry – I had no idea you felt that way.* ⓾ N-SING If you mention the **way** that something happens, you are mentioning the fact that it happens. ❏ *I hate the way he manipulates people.*
⓫ N-SING You use **way** in expressions such as **push your way, work your way,**

⓵ 가산명사 방법, 수단 ❏ 냉동은 음식을 보관하는 괜찮은 방법이다. ❏ 나는 그가 질투하게 만들려고 미친 듯이 계략을 꾸미게 되었다. ❏ 아마도 무슨 방법이 꼭 있을 것이다. ⓶ 가산명사 방식, 버릇 ❏ 그녀가 친근하게 미소 지었다. ❏ 그는 이상한 말버릇이 있었다. ⓷ 가산명사 (–한) 면, 사항 ❏ 전산 예약 시스템은 여러모로 항공사 수익에 도움이 된다. ❏ 그녀는 스스로도 아주 생소하게 겁이 났다. ⓸ 가산명사 (–한) 점, (–한) 정도 ❏ 어떤 점에서 공식 개장은 격식 갖추기이다. ⓹ 복수명사 습관, 방식 ❏ 그는 자기 생활 방식을 바꾸도록 강요하는 사람을 비난한다. ❏ 내 생각엔 당신이 콘월에 너무 오래 있은 것 같아. 당신은 도시의 생활 방식을 잊어버렸군. ⓺ 단수명사 (자기만의 평상시 행동) 방식 ❏ 그녀는 이제 이혼을 했고, 평상시처럼 수완 좋게 자신의 사업을 시작했다. ⓻ 가산명사 (해석, 이해하는) 방식 ❏ 난 그걸 그렇게 볼 수도 있다고 생각한다. ❏ 그러나 딜런의 노랫말 대부분은 단어들을 다른 식으로도 해석할 수 있다. ⓼ 가산명사 방향, 쪽 ❏ 표결이 어느 방향으로 진행될지 아무런 조짐이 없다. ⓽ 단수명사 방식, 의견 ❏ 정말 미안해, 네가 그렇게 생각하는 줄 몰랐어. ⓾ 단수명사 –하는 것 ❏ 나는 그가 사람들을 교묘하게 조종하는 것이 싫다. ⓫ 단수명사 진행, 나아감 ❏ 그녀는 군중 속으로 밀치고 나아갔다. ⓬ 가산명사 길 ❏ 누가 화장실 가는 길 아세요? ❏ 유감스럽게도 가는 길이 생각나지 않는다. ⓭ 단수명사 방향, 쪽 ❏ 그는 부엌으로 성큼성큼

V

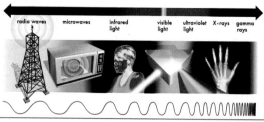

Word Web   wave

As **wind** blows across water, it creates **waves**. It does this by transferring energy to the water. If the waves encounter an object, they bounce off it. Light also travels in waves and behaves the same way. We are able to see an object only if light waves bounce off it. Light waves can be categorized by their **frequency**. Wave frequency is usually the measure of the number of waves per second. **Radio waves** and microwaves are examples of low-frequency light waves. **Visible light** consists of medium-frequency light waves. **Ultraviolet radiation** and **X-rays** are high-frequency light waves.

THE ELECTROMAGNETIC SPECTRUM

radio waves   microwaves   infrared light   visible light   ultraviolet light   X-rays   gamma rays

or **eat your way**, followed by a prepositional phrase or adverb, in order to indicate movement, progress, or force as well as the action described by the verb. ❑ *She thrust her way into the crowd.* ⏱ N-COUNT **The way** somewhere consists of the different places that you go through or the route that you take in order to get there. ❑ *Does anybody know the way to the bathroom?* ❑ *I'm afraid I can't remember the way.* ⏱ N-SING If you go or look a particular **way**, you go or look in that direction. ❑ *As he strode into the kitchen, he passed Pop coming the other way.* ❑ *They paused at the top of the stairs, doubtful as to which way to go next.* ⏱ N-SING You can refer to the direction you are traveling in as your **way**. [SPOKEN] ❑ *She would say she was going my way and offer me a lift.* ⏱ N-SING If you **lose your way**, you take a wrong or unfamiliar route, so that you do not know how to get to the place that you want to go to. If you find your **way**, you manage to get to the place that you want to go to. ❑ *The men lost their way in a sandstorm and crossed the border by mistake.* ⏱ N-COUNT You talk about people going their different **ways** in order to say that their lives develop differently and they have less contact with each other. ❑ *It wasn't until we each went our separate ways that I began to learn how to do things for myself.* ⏱ N-SING If something comes your **way**, you get it or receive it. ❑ *Take advantage of the opportunities coming your way in a couple of months.* ⏱ N-SING If someone or something is in the **way**, they prevent you from moving forward or seeing clearly. ❑ *"You're standing in the way," she said. "Would you mind moving aside."* ⏱ N-SING You use **way** in expressions such as **the right way up** and **the other way around** to refer to one of two or more possible positions or arrangements that something can have. ❑ *The flag was held the wrong way up by some spectators.* ⏱ ADV You can use **way** to emphasize, for example, that something is a great distance away or is very much below or above a particular level or amount. [EMPHASIS] [ADV adv/prep] ❑ *Way down in the valley to the west is the town of Freiburg.* ⏱ N-PLURAL If you split something a number of **ways**, you divide it into a number of different parts or quantities, usually fairly equal in size. ❑ *The region was split three ways, between Greece, Serbia, and Bulgaria.* ● COMB in ADJ **Way** is also a combining form. [ADJ n] ❑ *...a simple three-way division.* ⏱ N-SING **Way** is used in expressions such as **a long way**, **a little way**, and **quite a way**, to say how far away something is or how far you have traveled. ❑ *Some of them live in places quite a long way from here.* ❑ *A little way further down the lane we passed the driveway to a house.* ⏱ N-SING **Way** is used in expressions such as **a long way**, **a little way**, and **quite a way**, to say how far away in time something is. ❑ *Success is still a long way off.* ⏱ N-SING You use **way** in expressions such as **all the way**, **most of the way** and **half the way** to refer to the extent to which an action has been completed. ❑ *He had unscrewed the caps most of the way.* ⏱ PHRASE You use **all the way** to emphasize how long a distance is. [EMPHASIS] ❑ *He had to walk all the way home.* ⏱ PHRASE You can use **all the way** to emphasize that your remark applies to every part of a situation, activity, or period of time. [EMPHASIS] ❑ *Having started a revolution we must go all the way.* ⏱ PHRASE If someone says that you **can't have it both ways**, they are telling you that you have to choose between two things and cannot do or have them both. ❑ *Countries cannot have it both ways: the cost of a cleaner environment may sometimes be fewer jobs in dirty industries.* ⏱ PHRASE You say **by the way** when you add something to what you are saying, especially something that you have just thought of. [SPOKEN] ❑ *The name Latifah, by the way, means "delicate."* ⏱ PHRASE If you **clear the way**, **open the way**, or **prepare the way** for something, you create an opportunity for it to happen. ❑ *The talks are meant to clear the way for formal negotiations on a new constitution.* ⏱ PHRASE If you say that someone takes **the easy way out**, you disapprove of them because they do what is easiest for them in a difficult situation, rather than dealing with it properly. [DISAPPROVAL] ❑ *As soon as things got difficult he took the easy way out.* ⏱ PHRASE You use **either way** in order to introduce a statement which is true in each of the two possible or alternative cases that you have just mentioned. ❑ *The sea may rise or the land may fall; either way the sand dunes will be gone in a short time.* ⏱ PHRASE If you say that a particular type of action or development is **the way forward**, you approve of it because it is likely to lead to success. [APPROVAL] ❑ *...people who genuinely believe that anarchy is the way forward.* ⏱ PHRASE If someone **gets their way** or **has their way**, nobody stops them from doing what they want to do. You can also say that someone **gets their own way** or **has their own way**. ❑ *She is very good at using her charm to get her way.* ⏱ PHRASE If one thing **gives way to** another, the first thing is replaced by the second. ❑ *First he had been numb. Then the numbness gave way to anger.* ⏱ PHRASE If an object that is supporting something **gives way**, it breaks or collapses, so that it can no longer support that thing. ❑ *The hook in the ceiling had given way and the lamp had fallen blazing on to the table.* ⏱ PHRASE You use **in no way** or **not in any way** to emphasize that a statement is not at all true. [EMPHASIS] ❑ *In no way am I going to adopt any of his methods.* ⏱ PHRASE If you say that something is true **in a way**, you mean that although it is not completely true, it is true to a limited extent or in certain respects. You use **in a way** to reduce the force of a statement. [VAGUENESS] ❑ *In a way, I suppose I'm frightened of failing.* ⏱ PHRASE If you say that someone **gets in the way** or **is in the way**, you are annoyed because their presence or their actions stop you from doing something properly. ❑ *"We wouldn't get in the way," Suzanne promised. "We'd just stand quietly in a corner."* ⏱ PHRASE To **get in the way of** something means to make it difficult for it to happen, continue, or be appreciated properly. ❑ *She had a job which never got in the way of her leisure interests.* ⏱ PHRASE If you **know** your **way around** a particular subject, system, or job, or if you **know** your **way about** it, you know all the procedures and facts about it. ❑ *He knows his way around the intricate maze of European law.* ⏱ PHRASE If you **lead the way** along a particular route, you go along it in front of someone in order to show them where to go. ❑ *She grabbed his suitcase and led the way.* ⏱ PHRASE If a person or group **leads the way** in a particular activity, they are the first person or group to do it or they make the most new developments in it. ❑ *Sony has also led the way in shrinking the size of compact-disc players.* ⏱ PHRASE If you say that someone or something **has come a long way**, you mean that they have developed, progressed, or become very

들어오다가 맞은편에서 오던 팝과 스쳐 지나쳤다. ❑ 그들은 다음에 어느 쪽으로 가야 할지 몰라서 계단 꼭대기에서 멈추어 서 있다. ⏱ 단수명사 방향 [구어체] ❑ 그녀는 내게 같은 방향으로 가니 태워 주겠다고 말하곤 했다. ⏱ 단수명사 길 ❑ 그 남자들은 모래 폭풍 속에 길을 잃고 실수로 국경을 넘었다. ⏱ 가산명사 길 ❑ 우리가 서로 각자의 길을 가게 된 후에야 비로소 나는 혼자 힘으로 일을 처리하는 법을 배우기 시작했다. ⏱ 단수명사 수증 ❑ 두어 달 후에 당신에게 다가올 기회를 잘 이용하세요. ⏱ 단수명사 길 ❑ "길을 막고 있네요."라고 그녀가 말했다. "옆으로 좀 비켜 주시겠어요." ⏱ 단수명사 방식, 바르게, 반대로 ❑ 일부 관중들은 기를 거꾸로 들고 있었다. ⏱ 부사 훨씬, 한참 [강조] ❑ 계곡 한참 아래 서쪽으로 프라이버그 시가 있다. ⏱ 복수명사 부분 ❑ 그 지역은 그리스, 세르비아, 불가리아의 세 부분으로 분리되었다. ● 복합형-형용사 부분의 ❑ 단순히 세 부분으로 분할 ⏱ 단수명사 (떨어진) 거리, 곳, 먼 곳에, 조금 떨어진 곳 ❑ 그들 일부는 여기서 아주 멀리 떨어진 곳에 산다. ❑ 좁은 길을 따라 조금 더 아래로 내려가서 우리는 어느 집 진입로를 지나갔다. ⏱ 단수명사 (시간적인) 거리; (시간적으로) 멀리; (시간적으로) 가까이; (시간적으로) 상당히 멀리 ❑ 성공은 아직 멀었다. ⏱ 단수명사 진행 정도; 전부 다; 거의 다; 절반 ❑ 그가 마개들을 거의 다 돌려 따 놓았었다. ⏱ 구 내내 [강조] ❑ 그는 내내 걸어서 집으로 와야 했다. ⏱ 구 완전히, 끝까지 [강조] ❑ 혁명을 시작했으니 우리는 끝까지 가야 한다. ⏱ 구 두 마리의 토끼를 다 잡을 수 없다 ❑ 국가가 두 마리의 토끼를 다 잡을 수는 없다. 깨끗한 환경을 위한 대가로 때로는 오염을 초래하는 산업에서 일자리가 줄어들 수도 있다. ⏱ 구 많이 난 김에, 그런데 [구어체] ❑ 그런데, 라티파라는 이름은 '섬세하다'는 뜻이다. ⏱ 구 길을 트다, 기회를 만들다 ❑ 그 회담들은 새 헌법을 위한 공식 협상으로 가는 길을 트기 위한 것이다. ⏱ 구 아이한 해결책 [탐탁잖음] ❑ 일이 어렵게 되자마자 그는 안이한 해결책을 취했다. ⏱ 구 어느 쪽이든 ❑ 바다가 솟아올 수도 있고 땅이 꺼질 수도 있다. 어느 쪽이든 그 사구들은 곧 사라질 것이다. ⏱ 구 나아갈 길 [마음에 듦] ❑ 무정부 상태가 나아갈 길이라고 진심으로 믿는 사람들 ⏱ 구 자기 마음대로 하다, 자기 뜻대로 하다 ❑ 그녀는 자기 뜻대로 하기 위해 자신의 매력을 아주 잘 이용한다. ⏱ 구 ~로 바뀌다 ❑ 처음에 그는 멍했었다. 그 다음에는 멍하던 기분이 화로 바뀌었다. ⏱ 구 부러지다, 무너지다 ❑ 천장의 고리가 부러져서 등불이 타오르면서 탁자 위로 떨어졌다. ⏱ 구 결코 ~않다 [강조] ❑ 결단코 나는 그의 어떤 방식도 받아들이지 않을 것이다. ⏱ 구 어떤 면에서는, 어느 정도, 다소 [점작투] ❑ 어떤 면에서 나는 실패가 두려운 것 같다. ⏱ 구 방해가 되다 ❑ "우리가 방해하지 않을게요."라고 수잔이 약속했다. "그냥 구석에 조용히 서 있을게요." ⏱ 구 ~에 방해가 되다 ❑ 그녀는 자기 여가 취미에 전혀 방해가 되지 않는 직업을 가졌다. ⏱ 구 ~에 정통하다, 익숙하다 ❑ 그는 미로같이 복잡한 유럽 법률에 정통하고 있다. ⏱ 구 길을 안내하다, 앞장서 가다 ❑ 그녀가 그의 여행 가방을 집어 들고 앞장서 갔다. ⏱ 구 선도하다 ❑ 소니는 또한 콤팩트디스크 플레이어의 크기를 줄이는 것도 선도했다. ⏱ 구 크게 성공했다, 장족의 발전을 했다 ❑ 그는 하루에 단지 한 끼밖에 못 먹던 시절에서 지금은 크게 성공했다. ⏱ 구 단연코, 가장 [강조] ❑ 그것은 내가 지금까지 참석한 회의 중 단연코 최악이었다. ⏱ 구 절대로 ~이 아니다, 아주 거리가 멀다 [강조] ❑ 그녀는 영국 최고의 부자와는 아주 거리가 멀다. ⏱ 구 효과가 있다, 중요한 요소이다 ❑ 공손하고 예의 바른 것이 친분을 쌓는 데 중요한 요소이다. ⏱ 구 방향을 잃다 [탐탁잖음] ❑ 왜 백악관이 세금과 예산 정책에서 방향을 잃었습니까? ⏱ 구 가다, 나아가다 ❑ 그는 시장으로 갔다. ⏱ 구 길을 내주다 ❑ 그는 당의 더 젊은 사람들을 위해서 자리를 내줄 준비가 되어 있다고 말했다. ⏱ 구 절대로 ~ 아니다 [강조] ❑ 우리는 절대로 그것을 되풀이 하지 못할 것이다. ⏱ 구 절대로 아니다 [비격식체, 강조] ❑ 마이크야, 나는 너와 돈내기 카드놀이는 절대로 하지 않아. ⏱ 구 오는 중이다; 가는 중이다 ❑ 그 나라를 떠나도록 허가를 받아서 영국으로 오는 중이다. ⏱ 구 도중에, 그 사이에 ❑ 당신은 도중에 몇 가지 새로운 기술을 배워야 될지도 모른다. ⏱ 구 한창 ~하는 중, 거의 ~하는 중 ❑ 나는 이제 퇴원하여 거의 회복되어 가고 있는 중이다. ⏱ 구 다가오는 ❑ 기상정보관에 의하면 눈이 더 올 것이라고 한다, 어찌 됐든 [점작투] ❑ 당신은 여기 있는 모든 사람들을 상당히 잘 알고 있다. ⏱ 구 어느 쪽으로든 ❑ 우리는 어느 쪽이든 결정을 내려야만 한다. ⏱ 구 반대 ❑ 당신은 당신이 내게 호의를 베풀었고, 그 반대는 아니라고 생각하겠지요. ⏱ 구 소멸하고 있는, 사라지고 있는 ❑ 냉전 사고방식이 사라지고 있다는 고무적인 징후가 있다. ⏱ 구 애써 ~하다, 각별히 ~하다 ❑ 그는 내게 아주

a b c d e f g h i j k l m n o p q r s t u v **w** x y z

successful. ❏ *He has come a long way since the days he could only afford one meal a day.* 🆎 PHRASE You can use **by a long way** to emphasize that something is, for example, much better, worse, or bigger than any other thing of that kind. [EMPHASIS] ❏ *It was, by a long way, the worst meeting I have ever attended.* 🆎 PHRASE If you say that something is **a long way from** being true, you are emphasizing that it is definitely not true. [EMPHASIS] ❏ *She is a long way from being the richest person in Britain.* 🆎 PHRASE If you say that something **goes a long way toward** doing a particular thing, you mean that it is an important factor in achieving that thing. ❏ *Being respectful and courteous goes a long way toward building a relationship.* 🆎 PHRASE If you say that someone has **lost** their **way**, you are criticizing them because they do not have any good ideas anymore, or seem to have become unsure about what to do. [DISAPPROVAL] ❏ *Why has the White House lost its way on tax and budget policy?* 🆎 PHRASE When you **make** your **way** somewhere, you walk or travel there. ❏ *He made his way to the marketplace.* 🆎 PHRASE If one person or thing **makes way for** another, the first is replaced by the second. ❏ *He said he was prepared to make way for younger people in the party.* 🆎 PHRASE If you say **there's no way** that something will happen, you are emphasizing that you think it will definitely not happen. [EMPHASIS] ❏ *There was absolutely no way that we were going to be able to retrieve it.* 🆎 PHRASE You can say **no way** as an emphatic way of saying no. [INFORMAL, EMPHASIS] ❏ *Mike, no way am I playing cards with you for money.* 🆎 PHRASE If you **are on** your **way**, you have started your trip somewhere. ❏ *He has been allowed to leave the country and is on his way to Britain.* 🆎 PHRASE If something happens **on the way** or **along the way**, it happens during the course of a particular event or process. ❏ *You may have to learn a few new skills along the way.* 🆎 PHRASE If you are **on** your **way** or **well on** your **way** to something, you have made so much progress that you are almost certain to achieve that thing. ❏ *I am now out of hospital and well on the way to recovery.* 🆎 PHRASE If something is **on the way**, it will arrive soon. ❏ *The forecasters say more snow is on the way.* 🆎 PHRASE You can use **one way or another** or **one way or the other** when you want to say that something definitely happens, but without giving any details about how it happens. [VAGUENESS] ❏ *You know pretty well everyone here, one way or the other.* 🆎 PHRASE You use **one way or the other** or **one way or another** to refer to two possible decisions or conclusions that have previously been mentioned, without stating which one is reached or preferred. ❏ *We've got to make our decision one way or the other.* 🆎 PHRASE You use **the other way around** or **the other way round** to refer to the opposite of what you have just said. ❏ *You'd think you were the one who did me the favor, and not the other way around.* 🆎 PHRASE If something or someone is **on the way out** or **on their way out**, they are likely to disappear or to be replaced very soon. ❏ *There are encouraging signs that cold war attitudes are on the way out.* 🆎 PHRASE If you **go out of** your **way** to do something, for example to help someone, you make a special effort to do it. ❏ *He was very kind to me and seemed to go out of his way to help me.* 🆎 PHRASE If you **keep out of** someone's **way** or **stay out of** their **way**, you avoid them or do not get involved with them. ❏ *I'd kept out of his way as much as I could.* 🆎 PHRASE When something is **out of the way**, it has finished or you have dealt with it, so that it is no longer a problem or needs no more time spent on it. ❏ *The plan has to remain confidential at least until the local elections are out of the way.* 🆎 PHRASE If you **go** your **own way**, you do what you want rather than what everyone else does or expects. ❏ *In school I was a loner. I went my own way.* 🆎 PHRASE You use **in the same way** to introduce a situation that you are comparing with one that you have just mentioned, because there is a strong similarity between them. ❏ *There is no reason why a gifted aircraft designer should also be a capable pilot. In the same way, a brilliant pilot can be a menace behind the wheel of a car.* 🆎 PHRASE You can use **that way** or **this way** to refer to a statement or comment that you have just made. ❏ *We have a beautiful city and we pray it stays that way.* 🆎 PHRASE You can use **that way** or **this way** to refer to an action or situation that you have just mentioned, when you go on to mention the likely consequence or effect of it. ❏ *Keep the soil moist. That way, the seedling will flourish.* 🆎 PHRASE If an activity or plan is **under way**, it has begun and is now taking place. ❏ *A full-scale security operation is now under way.* 🆎 to see **the error of** your **ways** →see **error**

Thesaurus
way의 참조어

N. method, practice, style, technique 🆎
    behavior, characteristic, habit, personality 🆎 🆎 🆎

---

way of life (ways of life) 🆎 N-COUNT A **way of life** is the behavior and habits that are typical of a particular person or group, or that are chosen by them. ❏ *Mining activities have totally disrupted the traditional way of life of the Yanomami Indians.* 🆎 N-COUNT If you describe a particular activity as a **way of life** for someone, you mean that it has become a very important and regular thing in their life, rather than something they do or experience occasionally. ❏ *She likes it so much it's become a way of life for her.*

way|ward /ˈweɪwərd/ ADJ If you describe a person or their behavior as **wayward**, you mean that they behave in a selfish, bad, or unpredictable way, and are difficult to control. ❏ *...wayward children with a history of severe emotional problems.*

WC /ˌdʌbᵊlˌjuː ˈsiː/ (WCs) N-COUNT A toilet is sometimes referred to as a **WC**, especially on signs or in advertisements for houses, apartments, or hotels. **WC** is an abbreviation for "water closet." [BRIT] ❏ *Other features include a separate utility room, cloakroom, and WC.*

we ♦♦♦ /wi, STRONG wiː/

We is the first person plural pronoun. We is used as the subject of a verb.

🆎 PRON-PLURAL A speaker or writer uses **we** to refer both to himself or herself and to one or more other people as a group. You can use **we** before a noun to

친절했고 각별히 나를 돕는 것 같았다. 🆎구 -을 피하다 ❏ 나는 가능한 그를 피했었다. 🆎구 끝이 난, 이미 해결된 ❏ 그 계획은 적어도 지방 선거가 끝이 날 때까지는 기밀로 해야 한다. 🆎구 자기 생각대로 하다 ❏ 학교에서 나는 외톨이였다. 나는 독자적으로 행동했다. 🆎구 같은 방식으로, 마찬가지로 ❏ 천부적인 비행기 설계사가 유능한 조종사이기도 해야 할 이유는 없다. 마찬가지로 훌륭한 조종사가 자동차 운전대를 잡으면 위험인물이 될 수도 있다. 🆎구 그렇게; 이렇게 ❏ 우리에게는 아름다운 도시가 있고 그 도시가 그대로 남아 있기를 빈다. 🆎구 그렇게 하면; 이렇게 하면 ❏ 흙을 계속 촉촉하게 하세요. 그렇게 하면, 묘목이 잘 자랄 거예요. 🆎구 진행 중인 ❏ 전면적인 안보 작전이 현재 진행 중이다.

🆎 가산명사 생활 방식 ❏ 광산 활동이 야노마미 인디언의 전통적인 생활 방식을 완전히 붕괴시켰다. 🆎 가산명사 삶의 일부, 삶의 양식 ❏ 그녀는 그것을 너무 좋아해서 그게 그녀에게는 삶의 일부가 되었다.

형용사 제멋대로인, 외고집의 ❏ 과거에 심한 정서적 문제가 있었던, 제멋대로 행동하는 아이들

가산명사 화장실, water closet의 약자 [영국영어] ❏ 다른 특징으로는 별도 다용도실, 옷장, 화장실이 있다.

we는 1인칭 복수 대명사이다. we는 동사의 주어로 쓰인다.

🆎 복수대명사 우리 ❏ 우리 둘은 이후로 쭉 친구가 되기로 맹세했다. ❏ 우리는 샴페인을 한 병 더

make it clear which group of people you are referring to. ❑ *We both swore we'd be friends ever after.* ❑ *We ordered another bottle of champagne.* ◻ PRON-PLURAL **We** is sometimes used to refer to people in general. ❑ *We need to take care of our bodies.* ◻ PRON-PLURAL A speaker or writer may use **we** instead of "I" in order to include the audience or reader in what they are saying, especially when discussing how a talk or book is organized. [FORMAL] ❑ *We will now consider the raw materials from which the body derives energy.*

weak ♦♦◇◇ /wik/ (**weaker**, **weakest**) ◻ ADJ If someone is **weak**, they are not healthy or do not have good muscles, so that they cannot move quickly or carry heavy things. ❑ *I was too weak to move or think or speak.* ● **weak|ly** ADV [ADV with v] ❑ *"I'm all right," Max said weakly, but his breathing came in jagged gasps.* ● **weak|ness** N-UNCOUNT ❑ *Symptoms of anemia include weakness, fatigue, and iron deficiency.* ◻ ADJ If someone has an organ or sense that is **weak**, it is not very effective or powerful, or is likely to fail. ❑ *She tired easily and had a weak heart.* ◻ ADJ If you describe someone as **weak**, you mean that they are not very confident or determined, so that they are often frightened or worried, or easily influenced by other people. ❑ *He was a nice doctor, but a weak man who wasn't going to stick his neck out.* ● **weak|ness** N-UNCOUNT ❑ *Many people felt that admitting to stress was a sign of weakness.* ◻ ADJ If you describe someone's voice or smile as **weak**, you mean that it not very loud or big, suggesting that the person lacks confidence, enthusiasm, or physical strength. ❑ *His weak voice was almost inaudible.* ● **weak|ly** ADV [ADV after v] ❑ *He smiled weakly at reporters.* ◻ ADJ If an object or surface is **weak**, it breaks easily and cannot support a lot of weight or resist a lot of strain. ❑ *The owner said the bird may have escaped through a weak spot in the aviary.* ◻ ADJ A **weak** physical force does not have much power or intensity. ❑ *The molecules in regular liquids are held together by relatively weak bonds.* ❑ *Strong winds can turn boats when the tide is weak.* ● **weak|ly** ADV ❑ *The mineral is weakly magnetic.* ◻ ADJ If individuals or groups are **weak**, they do not have any power or influence. ❑ *The council was too weak to do anything about it.* ● N-PLURAL **The weak** are people who are weak. ❑ *He voiced his solidarity with the weak and defenseless.* ● **weak|ness** N-UNCOUNT ❑ *It made me feel patronised, in a position of weakness.* ◻ ADJ A **weak** government or leader does not have much control, and is not prepared or able to act firmly or severely. ❑ *The changes come after mounting criticism that the government is weak and indecisive.* ● **weak|ly** ADV ❑ *...the weakly-led movement for reform.* ● **weak|ness** N-UNCOUNT ❑ *Officials fear that he might interpret the emphasis on diplomacy as a sign of weakness.* ◻ ADJ If you describe something such as a country's currency, economy, industry, or government as **weak**, you mean that it is not successful, and may be likely to fail or collapse. ❑ *The weak dollar means American goods are relative bargains for foreigners.* ● **weak|ness** N-UNCOUNT ❑ *The weakness of his regime is showing more and more.* ◻ ADJ If something such as an argument or case is **weak**, it is not convincing or there is little evidence to support it. ❑ *Do you think the prosecution made any particular errors, or did they just have a weak case?* ● **weak|ly** ADV [ADV before v] ❑ *Bush listened to that statement and responded rather weakly.* ● **weak|ness** (**weaknesses**) N-VAR ❑ *Critical thinking requires that you examine the weaknesses of any argument.* ◻ ADJ A **weak** drink, chemical, or drug contains very little of a particular substance, for example because a lot of water has been added to it. ❑ *Grace poured a cup of weak tea.* ◻ ADJ Your **weak** points are the qualities or talents you do not possess, or the things you are not very good at. ❑ *Geography was my weak subject.* ● **weak|ness** N-VAR ❑ *His only weakness is his temperament.* ◻ →see also **weakness**
→see **muscle**

Thesaurus   weak의 참조어

ADJ.	feeble, frail; (ant.) strong ◻
	cowardly, insecure; (ant.) strong ◻

Word Partnership   weak의 연어

ADV.	**relatively** weak, **still** weak, **too** weak, **very** weak ◻-◻
N.	weak **dollar**, weak **economy**, weak **sales** ◻

---

weak|en ♦◇◇ /wikən/ (**weakens**, **weakening**, **weakened**) ◻ V-T/V-I If you **weaken** something or if it **weakens**, it becomes less strong or less powerful. ❑ *The recession has weakened so many firms that many can no longer survive.* ❑ *Family structures are weakening and breaking up.* ◻ V-T/V-I If your resolve **weakens** or if something **weakens** it, you become less determined or less certain about taking a particular course of action that you had previously decided to take. ❑ *I looked at the list and felt my resolve weakening.* ❑ *Jennie weakened, and finally relented.* ◻ V-T If something **weakens** you, it causes you to lose some of your physical strength. ❑ *Malnutrition obviously weakens the patient.* ◻ V-T If something **weakens** an object, it does something to it which causes it to become less firm and more likely to break. ❑ *A bomb blast had weakened an area of brick on the back wall.*

Word Partnership   weaken의 연어

N.	weaken **the economy** ◻
	weaken *someone's* **ability**, weaken *someone's* **resolve** ◻

---

weak|ling /wiklɪŋ/ (**weaklings**) N-COUNT If you describe a person or an animal as a **weakling**, you mean that they are physically weak. [DISAPPROVAL] ❑ *One classmate told me that he'd grown from the six-stone weakling into a 15-stone body builder.*

weak|ness /wiknɪs/ (**weaknesses**) N-COUNT If you have a **weakness for** something, you like it very much, although this is perhaps surprising or

---

주문했다. ◻ 복수대명사 우리 (인간), 사람 ❑ 우리는 우리 몸을 잘 돌볼 필요가 있다. ◻ 복수대명사 우리 (필자가 독자를 포함하기 위해 'I' 대신 사용) [격식체] ❑ 이제 몸이 에너지를 생성해 내는 원료를 살펴보기로 하자.

◻ 형용사 (몸이) 약한, 허약한 ❑ 나는 너무 허약해서 움직이거나, 생각하거나, 말할 수가 없었다. ● 약하게, 힘없이 부사 ❑ "난 괜찮아."라고 맥스가 힘없이 말했지만 그의 호흡은 거칠게 헐떡거렸다. ● 허약 불가산명사 ❑ 빈혈의 증상은 허약, 피로, 철분 결핍을 포함한다. ◻ 형용사 약한 ❑ 그녀는 쉽게 지치고 심장이 약했다. ◻ 형용사 심약한 ❑ 그는 좋은 의사였으나 위험한 일은 하지 못할 심약한 사람이었다. ● 심약함 불가산명사 ❑ 많은 사람들이 스트레스를 받는다고 인정하는 것이 심약한 표시라고 생각한다. ◻ 형용사 약한, 희미한 ❑ 그의 작은 목소리는 거의 들리지 않았다. ● 약하게, 희미하게 부사 ❑ 그는 기자들에게 희미하게 미소를 지어 보였다. ◻ 형용사 약한 ❑ 새 주인은 그 새가 새장의 약한 부분을 통해 탈출했을지도 모른다고 말했다. ◻ 형용사 약한 ❑ 보통 액체의 분자는 비교적 약하게 결합되어 있다. ◻ 조수가 약할 때에는 강한 바람에 배가 뒤집힐 수 있다. ● 약하게 부사 ❑ 그 광물은 약하게 자성을 띤다. ◻ 형용사 힘이 없는, 약소한 ❑ 지방 의회는 너무 힘이 없어서 그것에 관해 어떤 것도 할 수 없었다. ● 복수명사 약자 ❑ 그는 약하고 방어 능력이 없는 사람들과의 연대를 표명했다. ● 무력(無力) 불가산명사 ❑ 그것은 내가 무력한 처지에서 하수 취급을 받는다는 느낌이 들게 했다. ◻ 형용사 무기력한 ❑ 정부가 무기력하고 결단력이 없다는 비판이 고조된 후에 그런 변화들이 온다. ● 무기력하게 부사 ❑ 주도 세력이 무기력한 개혁 운동 ● 무기력감 불가산명사 ❑ 관료들은 그가 외교에 대한 강조를 무기력의 표시로 해석하지 않을까 걱정한다. ◻ 형용사 약한, 약세의 ❑ 달러화가 약세이면 미국 상품이 외국인에게 상대적으로 싼 값이 된다. ● 약세 불가산명사 ❑ 그의 정권의 약세가 점점 더 많이 드러나고 있다. ◻ 형용사 약한, 설득력 없는 ❑ 검찰이 특별한 잘못을 저질렀다고 생각합니까, 아니면 단지 검찰의 증거가 불충분했다고 생각합니까? ● 설득력 없게 부사 ❑ 부시는 그 진술을 듣고 다소 설득력 없게 대답했다. ● 취약점 가산명사 또는 불가산명사 ❑ 비판적 사고를 하려면 어느 주장에서나 그 취약점을 점검해 볼 필요가 있다. ◻ 형용사 묽은, 약한 ❑ 그레이스가 연한 차 한 잔을 따랐다. ◻ 형용사 못하는, 뒤떨어진 ❑ 지리는 내가 못하는 과목이었다. ● 약점, 견점 가산명사 또는 불가산명사 ❑ 그의 유일한 약점은 자기 성질이다.

◻ 타동사/자동사 약화시키다; 약화되다 ❑ 불경기 때문에 너무도 많은 회사들이 약화되어 많은 회사가 더 이상 살아남을 수가 없다. ❑ 가정의 틀이 약화되고 무너지고 있다. ◻ 타동사/자동사 (결심이) 흔들리다; (결심을) 흔들다 ❑ 나는 명단을 보고 내 결심이 흔들리는 것을 느꼈다. ❑ 제니는 결심이 흔들렸고 마침내 누그러졌다. ◻ 타동사 (건강을) 약화시키다 ❑ 영양실조는 분명히 환자를 약하게 만든다. ◻ 타동사 약화시키다 ❑ 폭탄 폭발로 인해 뒷벽의 벽돌 부분 일부가 약화되어 있었다.

가산명사 허약자, 약골 [탐탁잖음] ❑ 한 급우는 자기가 6스톤의 약골에서 15스톤의 보디빌더로 자랐다고 내게 말했다.

가산명사 지나치게 좋아함 ❑ 스티븐 자신이 고양이라면 사족을 못 썼다.

A

undesirable. ❑ *Stephen himself had a weakness for cats.* →see also **weak**

wealth ♦♢♢ /wɛlθ/ N-UNCOUNT **Wealth** is the possession of a large amount of money, property, or other valuable things. You can also refer to a particular person's money or property as their **wealth**. ❑ *Economic reform has brought relative wealth to peasant farmers.* →see **economics**

불가산명사 부, 재물 ❑ 경제 개혁이 소작농들에게 상대적 부를 가져왔다.

B

Thesaurus   *wealth*의 참조어

| N. | affluence, funds, money; *(ant.)* poverty |

C

wealthy /wɛlθi/ (**wealthier**, **wealthiest**) ADJ Someone who is **wealthy** has a large amount of money, property, or valuable possessions. ❑ *...a wealthy international businessman.* ● N-PLURAL **The wealthy** are people who are wealthy. ❑ *The best education should not be available only to the wealthy.*

형용사 재산이 많은, 부유한 ❑ 재산이 많은 국제적인 사업가 ● 복수명사 부유한 사람들 ❑ 최상의 교육을 부유한 사람들만 누릴 수 있어서는 안 된다.

D

wean /win/ (**weans**, **weaning**, **weaned**) 🔳 V-T When a baby or baby animal **is weaned**, its mother stops feeding it milk and starts giving it other food, especially solid food. ❑ *When would be the best time to start weaning my baby?* 🔳 V-T If you **wean** someone **off** a habit or something they like, you gradually make them stop doing it or liking it, especially when you think is bad for them. ❑ *You are given capsules or pills with small quantities of nicotine to wean you from the habit.*

🔳 타동사 젖을 떼다 ❑ 우리 아기의 이유는 언제 시작하는 것이 가장 좋을까요? 🔳 타동사 (나쁜 습관 등을) 버리게 하나 ❑ 당신이 흡연 습관을 버리도록 적은 양의 니코틴이 든 정제나 알약을 준다.

E

F

weap|on ♦♦♢ /wɛpən/ (**weapons**) N-COUNT A **weapon** is an object such as a gun, a knife, or a missile, which is used to kill or hurt people in a fight or a war. ❑ *...nuclear weapons.* →see **army**, **war**

가산명사 무기 ❑ 핵무기

G

weap|on|ry /wɛpənri/ N-UNCOUNT **Weaponry** is all the weapons that a group or country has or that are available to it. ❑ *...rich nations, armed with superior weaponry.*

불가산명사 무기류 ❑ 우수한 무기류로 무장한 부유한 국가들

H

wear ♦♦♢ /wɛər/ (**wears**, **wearing**, **wore**, **worn**) 🔳 V-T When you **wear** something such as clothes, shoes, or jewelry, you have them on your body or on part of your body. ❑ *He was wearing a brown uniform.* ❑ *I sometimes wear contact lenses.*

🔳 타동사 입다, 신다, 쓰다, 끼다 ❑ 그는 갈색 유니폼을 입고 있었다. ❑ 나는 가끔 콘택트렌즈를 낀다.

I

After you get up in the morning, you **get dressed**, or you **dress**, by **putting on** your clothes. ❑ *He put on his shoes and socks.* Small children and sick people may be unable to **dress themselves**, so someone else has to **dress** them. When you **are dressed**, you **are wearing** your clothes, or you **have** them **on**. ❑ *Edith had her hat on... They ought to stop walking around the house with nothing on.* During the day you might want to **get changed**, or to **change** your clothes. ❑ *She returned having changed from pants into a skirt... Adams changed his shirt a couple of times a day.* Before you go to bed, you **get undressed**, or you **undress**, by **taking off** your clothes. ❑ *He won't take his clothes off in front of me.* See also note at **clothes**.

아침에 일어나면 옷을 put on함으로써 get dressed 또는 dress한다. 그는 양말과 신발을 신었다. 어린 아이나 환자는 스스로 옷을 입을(dress themselves) 수 없을 수도 있고, 그러면 다른 사람이 그들에게 옷을 입혀 주어야(dress) 한다. you are dressed(옷을 입고 있다)는 you are wearing your clothes 또는 you have your clothes on과 같은 뜻이다. ❑ 에디스는 모자를 쓰고 있었다... 그들은 알몸으로 집안을 돌아다니는 것을 그만 둬야 한다. 낮 동안 당신은 get changed(옷을 갈아입다)하거나, 옷을 change하고 싶을 수도 있다. ❑ 그녀는 바지를 치마로 갈아입고 돌아왔다... 아담스는 하루에 두어 번 씩 셔츠를 갈아입었다. 잠자리에 들기 전에는 옷을 take off함으로써, get undressed하거나 undress한다. ❑ 그는 내 앞에서 옷을 벗으려 하지 않는다. clothes에 있는 주석도 보라.

J

K

L

M

N

🔳 V-T If you **wear** your hair or beard in a particular way, you have it cut or styled in that way. ❑ *She wore her hair in a long braid.* 🔳 N-UNCOUNT You use **wear** to refer to clothes that are suitable for a certain time or place. For example, **evening wear** is clothes suitable for the evening. ❑ *The shop stocks an extensive range of beach wear.* 🔳 N-UNCOUNT **Wear** is the amount or type of use that something has over a period of time. ❑ *You'll get more wear out of a hat if you choose one in a neutral color.* 🔳 N-UNCOUNT **Wear** is the damage or change that is caused by something being used a lot or for a long time. ❑ *...a large, well-upholstered armchair which showed signs of wear.* 🔳 V-I If something **wears**, it becomes thinner or weaker because it is constantly being used over a long period of time. ❑ *The stone steps, dating back to 1855, are beginning to wear.* 🔳 V-I You can use **wear** to talk about how well something lasts over a period of time. For example, if something **wears well**, it still seems quite new or useful after a long time or a lot of use. ❑ *Ten years on, the original concept was wearing well.* →see **makeup**

🔳 타동사 (수염 등을 어떻게) 하고 있다 ❑ 그녀는 길게 땋은 머리를 하고 있었다. 🔳 불가산명사 (특정 상황에 어울리는) 의류; 야회복 ❑ 그 상점은 다양한 종류의 해변용 의류를 구비하고 있다. 🔳 불가산명사 착용, 사용 ❑ 튀지 않는 색의 모자를 고르면 더 다양하게 착용할 수 있을 것이다. 🔳 불가산명사 닳아 해짐, 마모 ❑ 낡은 흔적이 뚜렷한, 좋은 가죽을 씌운 커다란 안락의자 🔳 자동사 닳다 ❑ 그 돌계단은 1855년에 만들어진 것인데 닳기 시작하고 있다. 🔳 자동사 오래가다; 오래도록 유용하다 ❑ 10년 동안 계속 원래의 개념이 유용하게 사용되고 있었다.

O

P

Q

R

S

T

Word Partnership   *wear*의 연어

| N. | wear **black/red/white**, wear **clothes**, wear **contact lenses**, wear **glasses**, wear **gloves**, wear **a hat/helmet**, wear **a jacket**, wear **jeans**, wear **makeup**, wear **a mask**, wear **a suit**, wear **a uniform** 🔳 |
| ADJ. | **casual** wear, **day** wear, **evening** wear 🔳 |

U

V

▶**wear away** PHRASAL VERB If you **wear** something **away** or if it **wears away**, it becomes thin and eventually disappears because it is used a lot or rubbed a lot. ❑ *It had a saddle with springs sticking out, which wore away the seat of my pants.*

구동사 닳아 없애다; 닳아 없어지다 ❑ 그것은 안장의 스프링이 튀어나와 있어서, 그것 때문에 내 바지의 엉덩이 부분이 다 닳아 버렸다.

W

▶**wear down** 🔳 PHRASAL VERB If you **wear** something **down** or if it **wears down**, it becomes flatter or smoother as a result of constantly rubbing against something else. ❑ *Pipe smokers sometimes wear down the tips of their teeth where they grip their pipes.* ❑ *The machines start to wear down, they don't make as many nuts and bolts as they used to.* 🔳 PHRASAL VERB If you **wear** someone **down**, you make them gradually weaker or less determined until they eventually do what you want. ❑ *None can match your sheer will-power and persistence in wearing down the opposition.* ❑ *They hoped the waiting and the uncertainty would wear down my resistance.*

🔳 구동사 마모시키다; 마모되다 ❑ 파이프 담배를 피우는 사람들은 간혹 파이프를 무는 이빨 끝부분이 마모된다. ❑ 기계가 마모되기 시작해서 너트와 볼트를 이전만큼 많이 만들지 못한다. 🔳 구동사 조금씩 지치게 하다 ❑ 상대를 서서히 지치게 만드는 데는 당신의 더없는 의지력과 끈기 이상 가는 게 없다. ❑ 그들은 기다림과 불확실함으로 내 저항이 서서히 지쳐서 약화될 것을 기대했다.

X

Y

▶**wear off** PHRASAL VERB If a sensation or feeling **wears off**, it disappears slowly

구동사 점점 사라져 없어지다 ❑ 많은 사람에게 그

Z

until it no longer exists or has any effect. ❑ *For many the philosophy was merely a fashion, and the novelty soon wore off.*

▶**wear out** 🄸 PHRASAL VERB When something **wears out** or when you **wear** it **out**, it is used so much that it becomes thin or weak and unable to be used anymore. ❑ *Every time she consulted her watch, she wondered if the batteries were wearing out.* ❑ *Horses used for long-distance riding tend to wear their shoes out more quickly.* 🄰 PHRASAL VERB If something **wears** you **out**, it makes you feel extremely tired. [INFORMAL] ❑ *The past few days had really worn him out.* ❑ *The young people run around kicking a ball, wearing themselves out.* 🄱 →see also **worn out**

wear and tear /wɛər ən tɛər/ N-UNCOUNT **Wear and tear** is the damage or change that is caused to something when it is being used normally. ❑ *...the problem of wear and tear on the equipment in the harsh desert conditions.*

wea|ry /wɪəri/ (**wearier**, **weariest**) 🄸 ADJ If you are **weary**, you are very tired. ❑ *Rachel looked pale and weary.* 🄰 ADJ If you are **weary of** something, you have become tired of it and have lost your enthusiasm for it. [v-link ADJ of n/-ing] ❑ *They're getting awfully weary of this silly war.*

weath|er ♦♦◇ /wɛðər/ (**weathers**, **weathering**, **weathered**) 🄸 N-UNCOUNT The **weather** is the condition of the atmosphere in one area at a particular time, for example if it is raining, hot, or windy. ❑ *The weather was bad.* ❑ *I like cold weather.* 🄰 V-T/V-I If something such as wood or rock **weathers** or **is weathered**, it changes color or shape as a result of the wind, sun, rain, or cold. ❑ *Unpainted wooden furniture weathers to a grey color.* 🄱 V-T If you **weather** a difficult time or a difficult situation, you survive it and are able to continue normally after it has passed or ended. ❑ *The company has weathered the recession.* 🄲 PHRASE If you say that you are **under the weather**, you mean that you feel slightly ill. ❑ *I was still feeling a bit under the weather.* →see **forecast**, **storm**
→see Word Web: **weather**

철학은 단지 유행에 불과했으며, 신선함은 서서히 사라져 버렸다.

🄸 구동사 낡아 없어지다; 낡아 없어지게 하다 ❑ 그녀는 시계를 볼 때마다 배터리가 다 닳아 가고 있는 것이 아닐까 생각했다. ❑ 장거리 승마용 말은 편자가 더 빨리 닳는 경향이 있다. 🄰 구동사 기진맥진하게 만들다 [비격식체] ❑ 지난 며칠은 정말 그를 기진맥진하게 만들었다. ❑ 젊은이들이 기진맥진할 때까지 공을 차면서 뛰어다닌다.

불가산명사 마손, 마모 ❑ 거친 사막 환경에서 장비의 마모 문제

🄸 형용사 지친 ❑ 레이첼은 창백하고 지쳐 보였다. 🄰 형용사 -에 싫증난 ❑ 그들은 이 어리석은 전쟁에 넌더리가 나고 있다.

🄸 불가산명사 날씨, 기상 ❑ 날씨가 나빴다. ❑ 나는 추운 날씨를 좋아한다. 🄰 타동사/자동사 풍화되다, (색 등이) 기후 때문에 변하다 ❑ 칠을 하지 않은 나무 가구는 풍상을 맞아 회색으로 변한다. 🄱 타동사 견디어 내다, 뚫고 나가다 ❑ 그 회사는 불경기를 견디어 냈다. 🄲 구 몸이 안 좋은 ❑ 나는 여전히 몸이 좀 좋지 않았다.

Word Partnership   weather의 연어

ADJ.	**bad** weather, **clear** weather, **cold** weather, **cool** weather, **dry** weather, **fair** weather, **good** weather, **hot** weather, **mild** weather, **nice** weather, **rainy** weather, **rough** weather, **severe** weather, **stormy** weather, **sunny** weather, **warm** weather, **wet** weather 🄸
N.	weather **conditions**, weather **prediction**, weather **report**, weather **service** 🄸

weath|er fore|cast (**weather forecasts**) N-COUNT A **weather forecast** is a statement saying what the weather will be like the next day or for the next few days.

가산명사 일기 예보

weave /wiːv/ (**weaves**, **weaving**, **wove**, **woven**)

The form **weaved** is used for the past tense and past participle for meaning 🄱.

weaved는 🄱 의미의 과거 및 과거 분사로 쓰인다.

🄸 V-T If you **weave** cloth or a carpet, you make it by crossing threads over and under each other using a frame or machine called a loom. ❑ *They would spin and weave cloth, cook and attend to the domestic side of life.* ● **wo|ven** ADJ ❑ *...woven cotton fabrics.* ● **weav|ing** N-UNCOUNT ❑ *When I studied weaving, I became intrigued with natural dyes.* 🄰 V-T If you **weave** something such as a basket, you make it by crossing long plant stems or fibers over and under each other. ❑ *Jenny weaves baskets from willow she grows herself.* ● **wo|ven** ADJ ❑ *The floors are covered with woven straw mats.* 🄱 V-T/V-I If you **weave** your way somewhere, you move between and around things as you go there. ❑ *The cars then weaved in and out of traffic at top speed.* ❑ *He weaved around the tables to where she sat with Bob.* →see **industry**

🄸 타동사 (피륙을) 짜다 ❑ 그들은 실을 자아 천을 짜고, 요리하고, 가사를 돌보곤 했다. ● 직조한 형용사 ❑ 면직물 ● 직조 불가산명사 ❑ 나는 직조를 공부할 때, 천연 염색에 큰 흥미를 갖게 되었다. 🄰 타동사 엮다, 짜다 ❑ 제니는 자신이 직접 기르는 버드나무로 바구니를 엮는다. ● 엮은 형용사 ❑ 바닥에는 짚으로 엮은 돗자리가 깔려 있다. 🄱 타동사/자동사 이리저리 빠져나가다, 누비며 나가다 ❑ 그 차들이 그러고는 최고 속도로 차량 사이를 요리조리 빠져나갔다. ❑ 그는 테이블 사이를 누벼 그녀가 밥과 함께 앉아 있는 곳으로 갔다.

weav|er /wiːvər/ (**weavers**) N-COUNT A **weaver** is a person who weaves cloth, carpets, or baskets.

가산명사 직조공, 베 짜는 사람

web /wɛb/ (**webs**) 🄸 N-COUNT A **web** is the thin net made by a spider from a sticky substance which it produces in its body. ❑ *...the spider's web in the window.* 🄰 N-COUNT A **web** is a complicated pattern of connections or relationships, sometimes considered as an obstacle or a danger. ❑ *He's forced to untangle a complex web of financial dealings.* 🄱 N-PROPER **The Web** is the same as the **World-Wide Web**. [COMPUTING]

🄸 가산명사 거미줄 ❑ 창문의 거미줄 🄰 가산명사 거미줄처럼 얽힌 상황 ❑ 그는 금융 거래의 복잡한 상황을 어쩔 수 없이 해결해야만 한다. 🄱 고유명사 월드 와이드 웹 [컴퓨터]

Word Web   weather

Researchers believe the **weather** affects our bodies and minds. When barometric **pressure** drops before a **storm**, some people get migraine headaches. The difference in pressure may change the blood flow in the brain. **Damp, humid** weather leads to increased problems with arthritis. A sudden heat wave can produce heatstroke. Seasonal affective disorder or SAD occurs during the short, **gloomy** days of winter. As the word "sad" suggests, people with this condition feel depressed. The bitter cold of a **blizzard** can cause frostbite. The **hot, dry** Santa Ana winds* in southern California create confusion and depression in some people.

Santa Ana winds: strong, hot, dry winds that blow in southern California in fall and early spring.

web|cam /wɛbkæm/ (**webcams**) also **Webcam** N-COUNT A **webcam** is a video camera that takes pictures which can be viewed on a website. The pictures are often of something that is happening while you watch. [COMPUTING]

가산명사 웹 캠, 인터넷 화상 카메라 [컴퓨터]

web|cast /wɛbkæst/ (**webcasts**) also **Webcast** N-COUNT A **webcast** is an event such as a musical performance which you can listen to or watch on the Internet. [COMPUTING] ❑ ...a Webcast of the Saturday and Sunday concerts.

가산명사 인터넷 방송 [컴퓨터] ❑ 토요일과 일요일 연주회의 인터넷 방송

web|master /wɛbmæstər/ (**webmasters**) also **Webmaster** N-COUNT A **webmaster** is someone who is in charge of a website, especially someone who does that as their job. [COMPUTING] →see **Internet**

가산명사 웹 마스터 (웹 사이트 관리자) [컴퓨터]

web page (**web pages**) also **Web page** N-COUNT A **web page** is a set of data or information which is designed to be viewed as part of a website. [COMPUTING] ❑ The company also has a Web page for small businesses and a hotline. →see **Internet**

가산명사 웹 페이지 [컴퓨터] ❑ 그 회사는 소기업을 위한 웹 페이지와 전화 상담 서비스도 하고 있다.

web ring (**web rings**) also **Web ring** also **webring** N-COUNT A **web ring** is a set of related websites that you can visit one after the other. ❑ Log on to the Hammer Web ring, with 12 more sites devoted to macabre movies. [COMPUTING]

가산명사 웹 링 (연관된 웹 사이트들의 모음) ❑ 엽기 영화만 전문으로 다루는 12개 이상의 사이트가 있는 해머 웹 링에 접속하세요. [컴퓨터]

web|site /wɛbsaɪt/ (**websites**) also **Web site, web site** N-COUNT A **website** is a set of data and information about a particular subject which is available on the Internet. [COMPUTING] ❑ ...a website devoted to hip-hop music. →see **Internet**

가산명사 웹 사이트 [컴퓨터] ❑ 힙합 음악 전문 웹 사이트

web|space /wɛbspeɪs/ N-UNCOUNT **Webspace** is computer hard disc space that you can use to create web pages. ❑ There's also 5Mb of webspace so that you can create your own personal web site. [COMPUTING]

불가산명사 웹 스페이스, 웹 공간 ❑ 5메가의 웹 공간도 있어서 자신의 개인 웹 사이트를 만들 수 있다. [컴퓨터]

web|zine /wɛbzin/ (**webzines**) N-COUNT A **webzine** is a website which contains the kind of articles, pictures, and advertisements that you would find in a magazine. [COMPUTING] ❑ The Dismal Scientist, a webzine dedicated to economic news, is fun.

가산명사 웹진 [컴퓨터] ❑ 경제 뉴스 전문 웹진인 '더 디스말 사이언티스트'는 재미있다.

wed /wɛd/ (**weds, wedded**)

> The form **wed** is used in the present tense and is the past tense. The past participle can be either **wed** or **wedded**.

wed는 현재 및 과거로 쓰인다. 과거 분사는 wed 또는 wedded를 쓸 수 있다.

V-RECIP If one person **weds** another or if two people **wed** or **are wed**, they get married. [OLD-FASHIONED] [no cont] ❑ In 1952 she wed film director Roger Vadim.

상호동사 결혼하다 [구식어] ❑ 1952년에 그녀는 영화감독인 로저 바딤과 결혼했다.

Wed.

> The spelling **Weds.** is also used.

철자 Weds.도 쓰인다.

Wed. is a written abbreviation for **Wednesday**.

수

we'd /wɪd, STRONG wid/ **1** **We'd** is the usual spoken form of "we had," especially when "had" is an auxiliary verb. ❑ Come on, George, we'd better get back now. **2** **We'd** is the usual spoken form of "we would." ❑ If we smoked, we'd light a cigarette and let her try it out.

1 we had의 축약형 ❑ 자, 조지, 우리 이제 돌아가는 게 좋겠다. **2** we would의 축약형 ❑ 우리가 담배를 피운다면, 불을 붙여 그녀에게 피워 보게 할 텐데.

wed|ding ♦♢♢ /wɛdɪŋ/ (**weddings**) N-COUNT A **wedding** is a marriage ceremony and the party or special meal that often takes place after the ceremony. ❑ Most Britons want a traditional wedding. ❑ ...the couple's 22nd wedding anniversary. →see Word Web: **wedding**

가산명사 결혼식 ❑ 대부분의 영국인들은 전통적인 결혼식을 원한다. ❑ 그 부부의 결혼 22주년 기념일

> Do not confuse **wedding** and **marriage**. A **wedding** is a ceremony in which a man and woman get married. It usually includes a meal or other celebration that takes place after the ceremony itself. ❑ It wasn't a formal wedding. This ceremony can also be called a **marriage**. ❑ ...the day of my marriage. **Marriage** can also be used to refer to the relationship between a husband and wife. ❑ It has been a happy marriage.

wedding과 marriage를 혼동하지 않도록 하라. wedding은 남자와 여자가 결혼하는 예식이다. 이는 보통 예식 그 자체가 끝난 후에 열리는 식사와 다른 축하 행사를 포함한다. ❑ 그것은 격식을 차린 결혼식이 아니었다. 이러한 결혼 예식을 marriage라고 부를 수도 있다. ❑ ...내 결혼식 날. marriage는 남편과 아내 사이의 관계를 지칭할 때도 쓸 수 있다. ❑ 행복한 결혼생활이었다.

wedge /wɛdʒ/ (**wedges, wedging, wedged**) **1** V-T If you **wedge** something, you force it to remain in a particular position by holding it there tightly or by fixing something next to it to prevent it from moving. ❑ I shut the shed door and wedged it with a log of wood. **2** V-T If you **wedge** something somewhere, you fit it there tightly. ❑ Wedge the plug into the hole. **3** N-COUNT A **wedge** is an object with one pointed edge and one thick edge, which you put under a door to keep it firmly in position. ❑ ...the wooden wedge which held the heavy door open. **4** N-COUNT A **wedge** of something such as fruit or cheese is a piece of it that has a thick triangular shape. ❑ Serve with a wedge of lime.

1 타동사 (-에 쐐기를 박아) 고정시키다 ❑ 나는 헛간 문을 닫고 통나무를 놓아 문이 열리지 않게 고정시켰다. **2** 타동사 (단단히) 끼워 넣다 ❑ 마개를 구멍에 끼워 넣으세요. **3** 가산명사 쐐기 ❑ 그 무거운 문이 열려 있도록 받치고 있던 나무 쐐기 **4** 가산명사 (치즈 등의) 쐐기 모양 ❑ 쐐기 모양으로 자른 라임 쪽과 함께 차려 내세요.

Wednes|day ♦♦♢ /wɛnzdeɪ, -di/ (**Wednesdays**) N-VAR **Wednesday** is the day after Tuesday and before Thursday. ❑ Come and have supper with us on Wednesday, if you're free. ❑ Did you happen to see her leave last Wednesday?

가산명사 또는 불가산명사 수요일 ❑ 시간이 되면, 수요일에 우리 집에서 저녁을 함께 합시다. ❑ 혹시 지난 수요일에 그녀가 떠나는 것 보았니?

wee /wi/ ADJ **Wee** means small in size or extent. [SCOTTISH, INFORMAL] [ADJ n] ❑ He just needs to calm down a wee bit.

형용사 작은; 조금 [스코틀랜드영어, 비격식체] ❑ 그는 그냥 조금 진정해야 돼.

Word Web   wedding

Some **weddings** are fancy, like the one in this picture. Most ceremonies include a similar group of attendants. The maid of honor or matron of honor helps the **bride** get ready for the ceremony. She also signs the **marriage certificate** as a legal **witness**. The **bridesmaids** plan the bride's wedding **shower**. The best man arranges for the bachelor party the night before the wedding. He also helps the groom dress for the wedding. After the **ceremony**, the guests gather for a **reception**. When the party is over, many couples leave on a **honeymoon** trip.

weed /wid/ (**weeds, weeding, weeded**) ◼ N-COUNT A **weed** is a wild plant that grows in gardens or fields of crops and prevents the plants that you want from growing properly. ❑ *With repeated applications of weedkiller, the weeds were overcome.* ◼ V-T/V-I If you **weed** an area, you remove the weeds from it. ❑ *Caspar was weeding the garden.*

▶**weed out** PHRASAL VERB If you **weed out** things or people that are useless or unwanted in a group, you find them and get rid of them. ❑ *He is keen to weed out the many applicants he believes may be frauds.*

week ◆◆◆ /wik/ (**weeks**) ◼ N-COUNT A **week** is a period of seven days. Some people consider that a week starts on Monday and ends on Sunday. ❑ *I had a letter from my mother last week.* ❑ *This has been on my mind all week.* ◼ N-COUNT A **week** is a period of about seven days. ❑ *Her mother stayed for another two weeks.* ❑ *Only 12 weeks ago he underwent major heart transplant surgery.* ◼ N-COUNT Your working **week** is the hours that you spend at work during a week. ❑ *It is not unusual for women to work a 40-hour week.* ◼ N-SING **The week** is the part of the week that does not include Saturday and Sunday. ❑ *...the hard work of looking after the children during the week.* ◼ N-COUNT You use **week** in expressions such as "Monday week," "a week next Tuesday," and "tomorrow week" to mean exactly one week after the day that you mention. [mainly BRIT] ❑ *The 800 meter final is on Monday week.* ◼ N-COUNT You use **week** in expressions such as "a week last Monday," "a week ago this Tuesday," and "a week ago yesterday" to mean exactly one week before the day that you mention. ❑ *"That's the time you weren't well, wasn't it?" — "Yes, that's right, that was a week ago last Monday."* →see **year**

week|day /wikdeɪ/ (**weekdays**) N-COUNT A **weekday** is any of the days of the week except Saturday and Sunday. ❑ *If you want to avoid the crowds, it's best to come on a weekday.*

week|end ◆◆◇ /wikend/ (**weekends**) N-COUNT A **weekend** is Saturday and Sunday. ❑ *She had agreed to have dinner with him in town the following weekend.*

week|ly ◆◆◇ /wikli/ (**weeklies**) ◼ ADJ A **weekly** event or publication happens or appears once a week or every week. [ADJ n] ❑ *Each course comprises 10-12 informal weekly meetings.* ❑ *We go and do the weekly shopping every Thursday.* ● ADV **Weekly** is also an adverb. [ADV after v] ❑ *The group meets weekly.* ◼ ADJ **Weekly** quantities or rates relate to a period of one week. [ADJ n] ❑ *Of course, in addition to my weekly wage, I got a lot of tips.* ◼ N-COUNT A **weekly** is a newspaper or magazine that is published once a week. ❑ *Two of the four national daily papers are to become weeklies.*

weep /wip/ (**weeps, weeping, wept**) V-I If someone **weeps**, they cry. [LITERARY] ❑ *She wanted to laugh and weep all at once.* ❑ *The weeping family hugged and comforted each other.* →see **cry**

weigh ◆◇◇ /weɪ/ (**weighs, weighing, weighed**) ◼ V-T If someone or something **weighs** a particular amount, this amount is how heavy they are. [no cont] ❑ *It weighs nearly 27 kilos (about 65 pounds).* ❑ *This little ball of gold weighs a quarter of an ounce.* ◼ V-T If you **weigh** something or someone, you measure how heavy they are. ❑ *The scales can be used to weigh other items such as parcels.* ◼ V-T If you **weigh** the facts about a situation, you consider them very carefully before you make a decision, especially by comparing the various facts involved. ❑ *She weighed her options.* ❑ *He is weighing the possibility of filing criminal charges against the doctor.*

Word Partnership	*weigh*의 연어
ADV.	weigh **less**, weigh **more** ◼
N.	weigh **ten pounds** ◼
	weigh **alternatives**, weigh **benefits**, weigh **costs**, weigh **the evidence**, weigh **risks** ◼

▶**weigh down** PHRASAL VERB If something that you are wearing or carrying **weighs** you **down**, it stops you moving easily by making you heavier. ❑ *He wrenched off his sneakers. If he had to swim, he didn't want anything weighing him down.*

weight ◆◆◇ /weɪt/ (**weights, weighting, weighted**) ◼ N-VAR The **weight** of a person or thing is how heavy they are, measured in units such as kilograms, pounds, or tons. ❑ *What is your height and weight?* ● PHRASE If someone **loses weight**, they become lighter. If they **gain weight** or **put on weight**, they become heavier. ❑ *I'm lucky really as I never put on weight.* ❑ *The boy appeared anxious, had lost weight and was not sleeping well.* ◼ N-UNCOUNT A person's or thing's **weight** is the fact that they are very heavy. ❑ *His weight was harming his health.* ◼ N-SING If you move your **weight**, you change position so that most of the pressure of your body is on a particular part of your body. ❑ *He shifted his weight from one foot to the other.* ◼ N-COUNT **Weights** are objects which weigh a known amount and which people lift as a form of exercise. ❑ *I was in the gym lifting weights.* ◼ N-COUNT **Weights** are metal objects which weigh a known amount and which are used on a set of scales to weigh other things. ◼ N-COUNT You can refer to a heavy object as a **weight**, especially when you have to lift it. ❑ *Straining to lift heavy weights can lead to a rise in blood pressure.* ◼ V-T If you **weight** something, you make it heavier by adding something to it, for example in order to stop it from moving easily. ❑ *It can be sewn into curtain hems to weight the curtain and so allow it to hang better.* ◼ N-VAR If something is given a particular **weight**, it is given a particular value according to how important or significant it is. ❑ *The scientists involved put different weight on the conclusions of different models.* ◼ N-UNCOUNT If someone or something gives **weight** to what a person says, thinks, or does, they emphasize its significance. ❑ *The fact that he is gone has given more weight to fears that he may try to launch a civil war.* ◼ N-UNCOUNT If you give something or someone **weight**, you consider them to be very important or influential in a particular situation. ❑ *Consumers generally place more weight on negative information than on the positive when deciding what to buy.* ◼ →see also **weighting** ◼ PHRASE If a person or their opinion **carries weight**, they are respected and are able to influence people. ❑ *Senator Kerry*

◼ 가산명사 잡초 ◼ 제초제를 거듭 뿌려서, 잡초가 제거되었다. ◼ 타동사/자동사 잡초를 제거하다 ❑ 카스파는 정원의 잡초를 뽑고 있었다.

구동사 제거하다 ❑ 그는 자기가 보기에 엉터리라고 생각되는 많은 지원자들을 제외시키고 싶어 한다.

◼ 가산명사 주 ❑ 나는 지난주 어머니로부터 편지를 받았다. ❑ 이게 한 주 내내 내 마음에 걸렸다. ◼ 가산명사 1주간, 7일간 ❑ 그녀의 어머니는 2주일을 더 묵었다. ❑ 겨우 12주 전에 그는 심장 이식 대수술을 받았다. ◼ 가산명사 (노동 시간의) 1주 ❑ 여자들이 1주에 40시간 일하는 것은 드문 일이 아니다. ◼ 단수명사 평일, 주중 ❑ 주중에 아이들을 돌보는 힘든 일 ◼ 가산명사 한 주 [주로 영국영어] ❑ 8백 미터 결승은 다음 월요일부터 한 주 후에 있다. ◼ 가산명사 한 주 "그게 네가 아팠던 때지, 그렇지?" "그래, 맞아, 그 때가 지난주 월요일에서 한 주 전이었어."

가산명사 평일 ❑ 사람이 붐비는 것을 피하려면, 평일에 오는 것이 가장 좋다.

가산명사 주말 ❑ 그녀는 그 다음 주말에 그와 함께 시내에서 저녁 식사를 하기로 했었다.

◼ 형용사 매주의, 주 1회의 ❑ 각 과정은 10-12번의 주 1회 비공식 회합으로 구성되어 있다. ❑ 우리는 매주 목요일 주 1회 장을 보러 간다. ● 부사 매주, 주 1회씩 ❑ 그 모임은 매주 한 번씩 만난다. ◼ 형용사 일주일분의 ❑ 물론, 나는 주급 외에 팁을 많이 받았다. ◼ 가산명사 주간지 ❑ 네 개의 전국 지 일간 신문 중 두 개가 주간지가 될 예정이다.

자동사 울다, 눈물을 흘리다 [문예체] ❑ 그녀는 동시에 웃고 울고 싶었다. ❑ 눈물을 흘리면서 가족들이 서로 부둥켜안고 위로했다.

◼ 타동사 무게가 -이다, 무게가 - 나가다 ❑ 그것은 무게가 거의 27킬로(약 65파운드) 나간다. ❑ 이 작고 동그란 금덩이는 무게가 1/4온스이다. ◼ 타동사 -의 무게를 달다 ❑ 그 저울은 소포와 같은 다른 물건의 무게를 재는 데 사용할 수 있다. ◼ 타동사 심사숙고하다, 비교 검토하다 ❑ 그녀는 자신이 선택할 수 있는 사항들을 저울질해 보았다. ❑ 그는 그 의사를 형사 고발할 수 있는 가능성에 대해 심사숙고하고 있다.

구동사 짐이 되다, 무겁게 누르다 ❑ 그는 운동화를 비틀어 벗었다. 만일 헤엄쳐야 한다면, 그는 자기에게 짐이 되는 것은 아무것도 원치 않았다.

◼ 가산명사 또는 불가산명사 체중, 무게 ❑ 당신의 키와 몸무게가 얼마입니까? ● 구 체중이 줄다, 살이 빠지다; 체중이 늘다, 살이 찌다 ❑ 난 정말 운 좋게도 결코 살이 찌지 않는다. ❑ 그 소년은 불안해 보였고, 체중이 줄었으며, 잠을 잘 못 자고 있었다. ◼ 불가산명사 체중, 과다체중 ❑ 그의 과체중이 건강을 해치고 있었다. ◼ 단수명사 체중 ❑ 그는 한 쪽 발에서 다른 쪽 발로 체중을 옮겨 실었다. ◼ 가산명사 웨이트, 역기 ❑ 나는 체육관에서 역기를 들고 있었다. ◼ 가산명사 저울추 ◼ 가산명사 무거운 것 ❑ 무거운 것을 들기 위해 힘을 쓰면 혈압이 올라갈 수 있다. ◼ 타동사 무겁게 하다 ❑ 커튼 밑에 그것을 꿰매어 넣으면 커튼에 무게를 주어 더 보기 좋게 늘어지게 해 준다. ◼ 가산명사 또는 불가산명사 중요성, 무게 ❑ 관련된 과학자들은 모델마다 다른 결론에 다른 무게를 두었다. ◼ 불가산명사 중요성, 무게 ❑ 소비자들은 일반적으로 무엇을 살 것인가를 결정할 때 긍정적인 것보다는 부정적인 정보에 더 무게를 둔다. ◼ 구 영향력이 있다 ❑ 케리 상원의원은 워싱턴에서 상당히 영향력이 있다. ◼ 구 천금과 같은, 매우 쓸모 있는 [강조] ❑ 성공한 관리자는 누구라도 천금 같이 소중하다. ◼ 구 제 역할을 다하다 ❑ 그는 팀이 제 역할을 다하지 못한다고 비난했다.

carries considerable weight in Washington. 🔢 PHRASE If you say that someone or something is **worth** their **weight in gold**, you are emphasizing that they are so useful, helpful, or valuable that you feel you could not manage without them. [EMPHASIS] ❑ *Any successful manager is worth his weight in gold.* 🔢 PHRASE If you **pull** your **weight**, you work as hard as everyone else who is involved in the same task or activity. ❑ *He accused the team of not pulling their weight.* 🔢 **a weight off** your **mind** →see **mind**
→see **diet**

Word Partnership   weight의 연어

V.	**add** weight, **gain/lose** weight, **put on** weight 🔢
N.	weight **gain/loss**, **height and** weight, **size and** weight 🔢
	body weight 🔢
	weight **training** 🔢
ADJ.	**excess** weight, **healthy** weight, **ideal** weight, **normal** weight 🔢
	heavy weight, **light** weight 🔢 🔢

---

weight|ed /wéɪtɪd/ ADJ A system that is **weighted** in favor of a particular person or group is organized so that this person or group has an advantage. ❑ *The current electoral law is still heavily weighted in favor of the ruling party.*

형용사 편중된 ❑ 현재의 선거법은 여당에 유리하게 여전히 심하게 편중되어 있다.

weight|ing /wéɪtɪŋ/ (**weightings**) 🔢 N-COUNT A **weighting** is a value which is given to something according to how important or significant it is. ❑ *The CBI said the poll gave a heavy weighting to smaller firms and was very unrepresentative of CBI members.* 🔢 N-COUNT A **weighting** is an advantage that a particular group of people receives in a system, especially an extra sum of money that people receive if they work in a city where the cost of living is very high. ❑ *I get an extra £2,700-a-year London weighting.* 🔢 →see also **weight**

🔢 가산명사 가중치 ❑ 영국 산업연맹은 그 여론 조사에 소규모 회사에 심한 가중치를 두고 있어서 연맹의 회원사를 대표하기엔 크게 부족하다고 말했다. 🔢 가산명사 지역 수당 ❑ 나는 런던 지역 수당으로 연간 2,700파운드를 더 받는다.

weight|lifting /wéɪtlɪftɪŋ/ also **weight-lifting** N-UNCOUNT **Weightlifting** is a sport in which the competitor who can lift the heaviest weight wins.

불가산명사 역도

weight train|ing N-UNCOUNT **Weight training** is a kind of physical exercise in which people lift or push heavy weights with their arms and legs in order to strengthen their muscles. ❑ *I used to do weight-training years ago.*

불가산명사 웨이트 트레이닝 ❑ 나는 수년 전에 웨이트 트레이닝을 했었다.

weighty /wéɪti/ (**weightier, weightiest**) ADJ If you describe something such as an issue or a decision as **weighty**, you mean that it is serious or important. [FORMAL] ❑ *Surely such weighty matters merit a higher level of debate?*

형용사 중대한 [격식체] ❑ 분명 그처럼 중대한 사안들은 고위급에서 협의해야 되겠지요?

weir /wɪər/ (**weirs**) N-COUNT A **weir** is a low barrier which is built across a river in order to control or direct the flow of water.

가산명사 둑, 댐

weird /wɪərd/ (**weirder, weirdest**) ADJ If you describe something or someone as **weird**, you mean that they are strange. [INFORMAL] ❑ *That first day was weird.* ❑ *Drugs can make you do all kinds of weird things.*

형용사 이상한, 기묘한 [비격식체] ❑ 그 첫날은 이상했다. ❑ 마약은 사람들로 하여금 온갖 이상한 짓을 하게 만들 수 있다.

wel|come ♦♦◇ /wélkəm/ (**welcomes, welcoming, welcomed**) 🔢 V-T If you **welcome** someone, you greet them in a friendly way when they arrive somewhere. ❑ *Several people came by to welcome me.* ❑ *She was there to welcome him home from war.* ● N-COUNT **Welcome** is also a noun. ❑ *There would be a fantastic welcome awaiting him back here.* 🔢 CONVENTION You use **welcome** in expressions such as **welcome home, welcome to Boston,** and **welcome back** when you are greeting someone who has just arrived somewhere. [FORMULAE] ❑ *Welcome to Washington.* 🔢 V-T If you **welcome** an action, decision, or situation, you approve of it and are pleased that it has occurred. ❑ *She welcomed this move but said that overall the changes didn't go far enough.* ● N-COUNT **Welcome** is also a noun. ❑ *Environmental groups have given a guarded welcome to the Prime Minister's proposal.* 🔢 ADJ If you describe something as **welcome**, you mean that people wanted it and are happy that it has occurred. ❑ *Any progress in reducing chemical weapons is welcome.* 🔢 V-T If you say that you **welcome** certain people or actions, you are inviting and encouraging people to do something, for example to come to a particular place. ❑ *We would welcome your views about the survey.* 🔢 ADJ If you say that someone is **welcome** in a particular place, you are encouraging them to go there by telling them that they will be liked and accepted. ❑ *New members are always welcome.* 🔢 ADJ If you tell someone that they are **welcome** to do something, you are encouraging them to do it by telling them that they are allowed to do it. [v-link ADJ, usu ADJ to-inf] ❑ *You are welcome to visit the hospital at any time.* 🔢 ADJ If you say that someone is **welcome to** something, you mean that you do not want it yourself because you do not like it and you are very willing for them to have it. [v-link ADJ to n] ❑ *If women want to take on the business world they are welcome to it as far as I'm concerned.* 🔢 →see also **welcoming** 🔢 PHRASE If you **make** someone **welcome** or **make** them **feel welcome**, you make them feel happy and accepted in a new place. ❑ *Here are six Mediterranean hotels where children are made to feel welcome.* 🔢 CONVENTION You say "**You're welcome**" to someone who has thanked you for something in order to acknowledge their thanks in a polite way. [FORMULAE] ❑ *"Thank you for the information." — "You're welcome."*

🔢 타동사 환영하다, 기쁘게 맞이하다 ❑ 여러 명의 사람들이 나를 환영하려고 들렀다. ❑ 그녀는 전쟁에서 집으로 돌아오는 그를 맞이하려고 거기에 가 있었다. ● 가산명사 환영 ❑ 이곳으로 돌아오는 그를 위한 굉장한 환영이 준비되어 있을 것이다. 🔢 관용 표현 어서 오십시오, 환영합니다 [의례적인 표현] ❑ 워싱턴에 오신 것을 환영합니다. 🔢 타동사 환영하다 ❑ 그녀는 이 조처를 환영하지만, 전반적으로 변화가 충분히 이루어지지 않았다고 말했다. ● 가산명사 환영 ❑ 환경 보호 단체들은 수상의 제안에 조심스러운 환영을 표했다. 🔢 형용사 환영받는 ❑ 화학 무기의 감축에 있어서 어떤 진전도 환영이다. 🔢 타동사 기꺼이 받아들이다 ❑ 우리는 그 조사에 관한 당신의 견해를 기꺼이 받아들이겠습니다. 🔢 형용사 환영받는 ❑ 신입 회원은 언제든지 환영합니다. 🔢 형용사 자유로이 -해도 좋은 ❑ 병원은 아무 때나 방문해도 좋습니다. 🔢 형용사 - 할 대면 하시오 ❑ 여성들이 재계에 발을 들여놓고 싶어 한다면 나로서는 언제든 기꺼이 환영한다. 🔢 🔢 구 -을 환영하다 ❑ 여기에 아이들이 편하게 지낼 수 있는 여섯 군데의 지중해식 호텔이 있다. 🔢 관용 표현 천만에요 [의례적인 표현] ❑ "알려주셔서 감사합니다." "천만에요."

Word Partnership   welcome의 연어

N.	welcome **guests**, welcome **visitors** 🔢
ADV.	welcome **home** 🔢
	always welcome 🔢 🔢
ADJ.	**warm** welcome 🔢 🔢

---

wel|com|ing /wélkəmɪŋ/ ADJ If someone is **welcoming** or if they behave in a **welcoming** way, they are friendly to you when you arrive somewhere, so that you feel happy and accepted. ❑ *When we arrived at her house Susan was very welcoming.*

형용사 환영의, 환영하는 ❑ 우리가 수잔의 집에 도착했을 때 수잔은 아주 환영하는 태도였다.

weld /wɛld/ (**welds, welding, welded**) V-T/V-I To **weld** one piece of metal to another means to join them by heating the edges and putting them together so that they cool and harden into one piece. ❑ *It's possible to weld stainless steel to ordinary steel.* ❑ *Where did you learn to weld?*

wel|fare ◆◇◇ /wɛlfeər/ **1** N-UNCOUNT The **welfare** of a person or group is their health, comfort, and happiness. ❑ *I do not think he is considering Emma's welfare.* **2** ADJ **Welfare** services are provided to help with people's living conditions and financial problems. ❑ *Child welfare services are well established and comprehensive.* **3** N-UNCOUNT In the United States, **welfare** is money that is paid by the government to people who are unemployed, poor, or sick. ❑ *States such as Michigan and Massachusetts are making deep cuts in welfare.*

> The American government has a variety of programs to help people who are poor. They may receive a monthly unemployment check, food stamps, subsidized housing, health care, and other services. This system is called **welfare** and is funded by taxes.

Word Partnership	welfare의 연어
ADJ.	**social** welfare **1**
N.	**animal** welfare, **child** welfare, **health and** welfare **1**
	welfare **programs**, welfare **reform**, welfare **system 2**
	welfare **benefits**, welfare **checks 3**

wel|fare state N-SING In some countries, the **welfare state** is a system in which the government provides free social services such as health and education and gives money to people when they are unable to work, for example because they are old, unemployed, or sick. ❑ *...the future of the welfare state.*

well

① DISCOURSE USES
② ADVERB USES
③ PHRASES
④ ADJECTIVE USE
⑤ NOUN USES
⑥ VERB USES

① **well** ◆◆◆ /wɛl/

> **Well** is used mainly in spoken English.

→Please look at category **9** to see if the expression you are looking for is shown under another headword. **1** ADV You say **well** to indicate that you are about to say something. [ADV cl] ❑ *Sylvia shook hands. "Well, you go get yourselves some breakfast."* **2** ADV You say **well** just before or after you pause, especially to give yourself time to think about what you are going to say. [ADV cl] ❑ *Look, I'm really sorry I woke you, and, well, I just wanted to tell you I was all right.* **3** ADV You say **well** when you are correcting something that you have just said. [ADV cl/group] ❑ *The comet is going to come back in 2061 and we are all going to be able to see it. Well, our offspring are, anyway.* **4** ADV You say **well** to express your doubt about something that someone has said. [FEELINGS] [ADV cl] ❑ *"But finance is far more serious." — "Well I don't know really."* **5** EXCLAM You say **well** to express your surprise or anger at something that someone has just said or done. [FEELINGS] ❑ *"Imelda," said Mrs. Kennerly. "That's my name, Tom." — "Well," said Tom. "Imelda. I never knew."* **6** CONVENTION You say **well** to indicate that you are waiting for someone to say something and often to express your irritation with them. [FEELINGS] ❑ *"Well?" asked Barry, "what does it tell us?"* **7** CONVENTION You use **well** to indicate that you are amused by something you have heard or seen, and often to introduce a comment on it. [FEELINGS] ❑ *Well, well, well, look at you. Ethel, look at this little fat girl.* **8** CONVENTION You say **oh well** to indicate that you accept a situation or that someone else should accept it, even though you or they are not very happy about it, because it is not too bad and cannot be changed. [FEELINGS] ❑ *Oh well, it could be worse.* **9** PHRASE **may well** →see **may**

② **well** ◆◆◆ /wɛl/ (**better, best**) **1** ADV If you do something **well**, you do it to a high standard or to a great extent. [ADV after v] ❑ *All the Indian batsmen played well.* ❑ *He speaks English better than I do.* **2** ADV If you do something **well**, you do it thoroughly and completely. [ADV after v] ❑ *Mix all the ingredients well.* **3** ADV If you speak or think **well of** someone, you say or think favorable things about them. [ADV after v] ❑ *"He speaks well of you." — "I'm glad to hear that."* **4** COMB IN ADJ **Well** is used in front of past participles to indicate that something is done to a high standard or to a great extent. ❑ *Helen is a very well-known novelist in Australia.* ❑ *People live longer nowadays, and they are better educated.* **5** ADV You use **well** to ask or talk about the extent or standard of something. ❑ *How well do you remember your mother, Franzi?* ❑ *He wasn't dressed any better than me.* **6** ADV You use **well** in front of a prepositional phrase to emphasize it. For example, if you say that one thing happened **well before** another, you mean that it happened a long time before it. [EMPHASIS] [ADV prep] ❑ *Franklin did not turn up until well after midnight.* ❑ *There are well over a million Muslims in Britain.* **7** ADV You use **well** before certain adjectives to emphasize them. [EMPHASIS] [ADV adj] ❑ *She has a close group of friends who are very well aware of what she has suffered.* **8** ADV You use **well** after adverbs such as "perfectly," "jolly," or "damn" in order to emphasize an opinion or the truth of what you are saying. [EMPHASIS] ❑ *You know perfectly well I can't be blamed for the failure of that mission.* **9** ADV You use **well** after verbs such as "may" and "could" when you are saying what you think is likely to happen. [EMPHASIS] [modal ADV] ❑ *Ours could well be the last generation for which moviegoing has a sense of magic.*

③ **well** ◆◆◆ /wɛl/ →Please look at category **7** to see if the expression you are looking for is shown under another headword. **1** PHRASE You use **as well**

타동사/자동사 용접하다 ❑ 스테인리스 철을 보통 철에 용접하는 것이 가능하다. ❑ 용접하는 것을 어디서 배웠나요?

1 불가산명사 복리 ❑ 내 생각에는 그가 에마의 복리를 고려하고 있지 않다. **2** 형용사 복지, 후생 ❑ 어린이 후생 서비스가 잘 확립되어 있으며 종합적이다. **3** 불가산명사 (실업 또는 생활) 보조금 ❑ 미시간이나 매사추세츠와 같은 주는 보조금을 크게 삭감하고 있다.

> 미국 정부는 가난한 사람들을 돕기 위한 다양한 프로그램을 두고 있다. 가난한 사람들은 월별 실업 수당, 식량 배급표, 주택 보조, 의료, 기타 서비스를 받을 수 있다. 이런 제도를 welfare(복지)라고 하며 그 기금은 세금으로 지원된다.

단수명사 복지 국가 ❑ 복지 국가의 미래

---

well은 주로 구어체 영어에서 쓰인다.

1 부사 자, 그래 ❑ 실비아는 악수를 했다. "자, 가서 아침 식사를 좀 하지." **2** 부사 글쎄, 저어 ❑ 이봐, 깨워서 정말 미안해, 그리고, 저어, 나는 그냥 내가 괜찮았다는 걸 말해 주고 싶었어. **3** 부사 아니 ❑ 그 혜성은 2061년에 돌아올 것이고 우리 모두 그것을 보게 될 수 있을 것이다. 아니, 어쨌거나 우리 후손들은 말이야. **4** 부사 글쎄, 그런데 [감정 개입] ❑ "하지만 재정이 훨씬 더 심각하지." "글쎄, 저는 정말 잘 몰라요." **5** 감탄사 저런 [감정 개입] ❑ "이멜다"라고 케널리 부인이 말했다. "그게 제 이름이죠, 톰." "저런," 하고 탐이 말했다. "이멜다라고요. 전혀 몰랐어요." **6** 관용 표현 저어, 그래서 [감정 개입] ❑ "그래서?"라고 배리가 물었다. "우리가 거기서 뭘 알 수 있는데?" **7** 관용 표현 그래 [감정 개입] ❑ 그래, 그래, 그래, 요것 봐. 에텔, 작고 통통한 이 꼬마 아가씨 좀 봐. **8** 관용 표현 아 그래 [감정 개입] ❑ 아 그래, 더 나쁠 수도 있겠군.

1 부사 잘 ❑ 인도 타자들이 모두 경기를 잘했다. ❑ 그는 나보다 영어를 더 잘한다. **2** 부사 충분히, 완전히 ❑ 모든 재료를 충분히 섞으세요. **3** 부사 좋게, 호의를 가지고 ❑ "그가 당신에 대해 좋게 말합니다." "그 말을 들으니 기쁩니다." **4** 복합형-형용사 상당히 ❑ 헬렌은 호주에서 아주 잘 알려진 소설가이다. ❑ 사람들이 요즘 더 오래 살고, 교육을 더 잘 받는다. **5** 부사 잘 ❑ 네 어머니를 얼마나 잘 기억하니, 프랜지? ❑ 그가 나보다 옷을 더 잘 차려 입은 것도 아니다. **6** 부사 훨씬, 상당히 [강조] ❑ 프랭클린은 자정이 훨씬 지나도록 나타나지 않았다. ❑ 영국에는 백만 명을 훨씬 넘는 이슬람교도가 있다. **7** 부사 매우, 상당히 [강조] ❑ 그녀에게는 자기가 어떤 고생을 했는지를 아주 잘 아는 친한 친구들이 있다. **8** 부사 충분히, 잘 [강조] ❑ 그 임무의 실패가 내 책임이 아니라는 것을 당신이 아주 잘 알고 있지요. **9** 부사 분명히, 마땅히 [강조] ❑ 우리 세대가 분명히 영화 보러 가는 마력에 끌리는 마지막 세대가 될 것이다.

1 구 게다가, -도 또한 ❑ 더 젊은 여성들에게서도 또한 많이 보았지만, 그것은 삼사십 대 여성들에게 아주

when mentioning something which happens in the same way as something else already mentioned, or which should be considered at the same time as that thing. ❑ *It is most often diagnosed in women in their thirties and forties, although I've seen it in many younger women, as well.* ❑ *"What do you like about it then?" — "Erm, the history, the shops – people are quite friendly as well.* ❑ PHRASE You use as well as when you want to mention another item connected with the subject you are discussing. ❑ *She published historical novels, as well as a non-fiction study of women in the British Empire.* ❸ PHRASE If you say that something that has happened **is just as well**, you mean that it is fortunate that it happened in the way it did. ❑ *Blue asbestos is far less common in buildings, which is just as well because it's more dangerous than white asbestos.* ❹ PHRASE If you say that something, usually something bad, **might as well** be true or **may as well** be true, you mean that the situation is the same or almost the same as if it were true. ❑ *The couple might as well have been strangers.* ❺ PHRASE If you say that you **might as well** do something, or that you **may as well** do it, you mean that you will do it although you do not have a strong desire to do it and may even feel slightly unwilling to do it. ❑ *If I've got to go somewhere I may as well go to Birmingham.* ❑ *Anyway, you're here; you might as well stay.* ❻ PHRASE If you say that something is **well and truly** finished, gone, or done, you are emphasizing that it is completely finished or gone, or thoroughly done. [mainly BRIT, EMPHASIS] ❑ *The war is well and truly over.* ❼ all very well →see all. to know full well →see full

④ **well** ♦♦♦ /wɛl/ ADJ If you are **well**, you are healthy and not ill. ❑ *I'm not very well today, I can't come in.*

⑤ **well**/wɛl/ (**wells**) ❶ N-COUNT A **well** is a hole in the ground from which a supply of water is extracted. ❑ *I had to fetch water from the well.* ❷ N-COUNT A **well** is an oil well. ❑ *About 650 wells are on fire.*

⑥ **well**/wɛl/ (**wells, welling, welled**) V-I If liquids, for example tears, **well**, they come to the surface and form a pool. ❑ *Tears welled in her eyes.* ● PHRASAL VERB **Well up** means the same as **well**. ❑ *Tears welled up in Anni's eyes.*

we'll /wɪl, STRONG wil/ **We'll** is the usual spoken form of "we shall" or "we will." ❑ *Whatever you want to chat about, we'll do it tonight.*

well-balanced also **well balanced** ❶ ADJ If you describe someone as **well-balanced**, you mean that they are sensible and do not have many emotional problems. ❑ *...a fun-loving, well-balanced individual.* ❷ ADJ If you describe something that is made up of several parts as **well-balanced**, you mean that the way that the different parts are put together is good, because there is not too much or too little of any one part. ❑ *...a well-balanced diet.*

well-behaved also **well behaved** ADJ If you describe someone, especially a child, as **well-behaved**, you mean that they behave in a way that adults generally like and think is correct. ❑ *...well-behaved little boys.*

well-being also **wellbeing** N-UNCOUNT Someone's **well-being** is their health and happiness. ❑ *Singing can create a sense of wellbeing.*

well-built also **well built** ADJ A **well-built** person, especially a man, has quite a big body and quite large muscles. ❑ *Mitchell is well built, of medium height, with a dark complexion.*

well-connected also **well connected** ADJ Someone who is **well-connected** has important or influential relatives or friends. ❑ *Mr. Guber and Mr. Peters aren't universally loved in Hollywood but they are well connected.*

well-defined also **well defined** ADJ Something that is **well-defined** is clear and precise and therefore easy to recognize or understand. ❑ *Today's pawnbrokers operate within well-defined financial regulations.*

well done ❶ CONVENTION You say "**Well done**" to indicate that you are pleased that someone has done something good. [FEELINGS] ❑ *"Daddy! I came second in history!" — "Well done, sweetheart!"* ❷ ADJ If something that you have cooked, especially meat, is **well done**, it has been cooked thoroughly. ❑ *Allow an extra 10-15 min if you prefer lamb well done.*

well-dressed also **well dressed** ADJ Someone who is **well-dressed** is wearing fashionable or elegant clothes. ❑ *She's always well dressed.*

well-established also **well established** ADJ If you say that something is **well-established**, you mean that it has been in existence for quite a long time and is successful. ❑ *The University has a well-established tradition of welcoming postgraduate students from overseas.*

well-informed (**better-informed**) also **well informed** ADJ If you say that someone is **well-informed**, you mean that they know a lot about many different subjects or about one particular subject. ❑ *...a lending library to encourage members to become as well informed as possible.*

well-intentioned also **well intentioned** ADJ If you say that a person or their actions are **well-intentioned**, you mean that they intend to be helpful or kind but they are unsuccessful or cause problems. ❑ *He is well-intentioned but a poor administrator.*

well-known ♦♦♦ also **well known** ❶ ADJ A **well-known** person or thing is known about by a lot of people and is therefore famous or familiar. If someone is **well-known** for a particular activity, a lot of people know about them because of their involvement with that activity. ❑ *Hubbard was well known for his work in the field of drug rehabilitation.*

A **famous** person or thing is known to more people than a **well-known** one. A **notorious** person or thing is famous because they are connected with something bad or undesirable. **Infamous** is not the opposite of **famous**. It has a similar meaning to **notorious**, but is a stronger word.

흔하게 진단되는 병이다. ❑ "그러면 그곳에 대해 어떤 점이 좋습니까?" "음, 역사, 상점, 게다가 사람들이 아주 친절해요." ❑ 구 ~은 물론, ~뿐만 아니라 ... 또 ❑ 그녀는 대영 제국의 여성에 관해 실화적 연구서뿐만 아니라 역사 소설도 출판했다. ❸ 구 아주 운이 좋은, 때마침 잘된 ❑ 푸른 석면은 건물에 훨씬 드물게 사용되는데, 그것이 흰 석면보다 더 위험하기 때문에 마침 잘된 셈이다. ❹ 구 ~하는 거나 마찬가지이다 ❑ 그 한 쌍의 남녀는 이방인이나 마찬가지였다. ❺ 구 차라리 ~하는 편이 낫다 ❑ 내가 만약 어디론가 가야만 한다면, 차라리 버밍엄으로 가는 편이 낫겠다. ❻ 구 완전히, 철저히 [주로 영국영어, 강조] ❑ 전쟁은 완전히 끝났다.

형용사 건강한 ❑ 오늘 몸이 좋지 않아서 출근할 수가 없어요.

❶ 가산명사 우물 ❑ 나는 우물에서 물을 길어 와야 했다. ❷ 가산명사 유정 ❑ 약 650개의 유정이 불타고 있다.

자동사 (눈물 등이) 괴이다 ❑ 그녀의 두 눈에 눈물이 고였다. ● 구동사 (눈물 등이) 괴이다 ❑ 애니의 두 눈에 눈물이 고였다.

we shall 또는 we will의 축약형 ❑ 당신이 하고 싶은 얘기가 뭐든 간에 오늘밤에 합시다.

❶ 형용사 정신이 건강한 ❑ 재미를 즐기고 정신적으로 건강한 사람 ❷ 형용사 균형이 잡힌 ❑ 균형 잡힌 식사

형용사 품행이 단정한 ❑ 품행이 단정한 어린 소년들

불가산명사 건강과 행복, 웰빙 ❑ 노래를 부르면 행복감을 가져 올 수 있다.

형용사 체격이 좋은 ❑ 미첼은 체격이 좋고, 중키에, 구릿빛 얼굴을 하고 있다.

형용사 유력한 친지가 있는, 연줄이 든든한 ❑ 구버 씨와 피터스 씨는 할리우드에서 두루 사랑받지는 못하지만 연줄이 든든하다.

형용사 명확한 ❑ 요즘의 전당포 업자들은 명확하게 규정된 금융 법규를 지키며 영업한다.

❶ 관용 표현 잘 하다 [감정 개입] ❑ "아빠! 나 역사 과목에서 2등했어요." "잘 했구나, 애야!" ❷ 형용사 푹 익은, 바짝 구운 ❑ 양고기가 푹 익은 걸 좋아하면 10-15분 정도 더 익히세요.

형용사 잘 차려 입은 ❑ 그녀는 항상 잘 차려입는다.

형용사 확립된, 정착된 ❑ 그 대학은 해외에서 오는 대학원생을 환영하는 전통이 확립되어 있다.

형용사 박식한, 정통한 ❑ 회원들에게 가능한 한 많은 지식을 쌓도록 장려하기 위한 공공 도서 대여 도서관

형용사 선의의, 선의에서 한 ❑ 그는 호의적이지만 어설픈 행정관이다.

❶ 형용사 유명한, 잘 알려진 ❑ 허바드는 마약 갱생 분야 연구로 잘 알려져 있다.

famous한 사람이나 사물은 well-known한 사람이나 사물보다 더 많은 사람들에게 알려져 있다. notorious한 사람이나 사물은 나쁘거나 바람직하지 않은 것과 연관되어 있기 때문에 유명하다. infamous는 '유명하다(famous)'의 반대말이 아니라, '악명 높다(notorious)'와 비슷한 뜻이며 더 강한 말이다.

2 ADJ A **well-known** fact is a fact that is known by people in general. ❑ *It is well known that bamboo shoots are a panda's staple diet.*

2 형용사 주지의, 잘 알려진 ❑ 죽순이 팬더의 주식이라는 것은 잘 알려져 있다.

well-meaning also well meaning ADJ If you say that a person or their actions are **well-meaning**, you mean that they intend to be helpful or kind but they are unsuccessful or cause problems. ❑ *He is a well-meaning but ineffectual leader.*

형용사 선의의, 선의에서 한 ❑ 그는 선의는 있으나 지도자로는 무능하다.

well-off also well off ADJ Someone who is **well-off** is rich enough to be able to do and buy most of the things that they want. [INFORMAL] ❑ *My grandparents were quite well off.*

형용사 부유한, 유복한 [비격식체] ❑ 우리 조부모님께서는 아주 부자셨다.

well-paid also well paid ADJ If you say that a person or their job is **well-paid**, you mean that they receive a lot of money for the work that they do. ❑ *Kate was well paid and enjoyed her job.*

형용사 보수가 좋은 ❑ 케이트는 보수가 좋았고 자기 일을 즐겼다.

well-to-do ADJ A **well-to-do** person is rich enough to be able to do and buy most of the things that they want. ❑ *...a rather well-to-do family of diamond cutters.*

형용사 부유한, 유복한 ❑ 꽤 유복한 다이아몬드 세공사 가족

well-wisher (well-wishers) also wellwisher N-COUNT **Well-wishers** are people who hope that a particular person or thing will be successful, and who show this by their behavior. ❑ *The main street was lined with well-wishers.*

가산명사 지지자 ❑ 중앙 도로에는 지지자들이 줄지어 서 있었다.

wel|ly /wɛli/ (wellies) N-COUNT **Wellies** are long rubber boots which you wear to keep your feet dry. [BRIT, INFORMAL] ❑ *...a pair of green wellies.*

가산명사 고무장화 [영국영어, 비격식체] ❑ 초록색 고무장화 한 켤레

went /wɛnt/ **Went** is the past tense of **go**.

go의 과거

wept /wɛpt/ **Wept** is the past tense and past participle of **weep**.

weep의 과거 및 과거 분사

were /wər, STRONG wɜr/ **1 Were** is the plural and the second person singular of the past tense of **be**. **2 Were** is sometimes used instead of "was" in certain structures, for example in conditional clauses or after the verb "wish." [FORMAL] ❑ *He told a diplomat that he might withdraw if he were allowed to keep part of a disputed oil field.* **3 as it were** →see **as**

1 be동사의 2인칭 단수 및 복수의 과거 **2** 조건절 또는 wish 동사 다음에 was 대신 쓰임 [격식체] ❑ 그는 문제의 유전 일부를 소유하게 해 준다면 철수할 수도 있다고 한 외교관에게 말했다.

we're /wɪər/ **We're** is the usual spoken form of "we are." ❑ *I'm married, but we're separated.*

we are의 축약형 ❑ 난 기혼이지만 별거 중이다.

weren't /wɜrnt, wɛrənt/ **Weren't** is the usual spoken form of "were not."

were not의 축약형

west ♦♦♦ /wɛst/ also West **1** N-UNCOUNT The **west** is the direction which you look toward in the evening in order to see the sun set. [also the N] ❑ *I pushed on towards Flagstaff, a hundred miles to the west.* **2** N-SING The **west of** a place, country, or region is the part of it which is in the west. ❑ *...physicists working at Bristol University in the west of England.* **3** ADV If you go **west**, you travel toward the west. [ADV after v] ❑ *We are going West to California.* **4** ADV Something that is **west of** a place is positioned to the west of it. ❑ *...their home town of Paisley, several miles west of Glasgow.* **5** ADJ The **west** part of a place, country, or region is the part which is toward the west. [ADJ n] ❑ *...a small island off the west coast of South Korea.* **6** ADJ **West** is used in the names of some countries, states, and regions in the west of a larger area. [ADJ n] ❑ *Mark has been working in West Africa for about six months.* ❑ *...his West London home.* **7** ADJ A **west** wind blows from the west. [ADJ n] ❑ *...the warm west wind.* **8** N-SING The **West** is used to refer to the United States, Canada, and the countries of Western, Northern, and Southern Europe. ❑ *...relations between Iran and the West.*

1 불가산명사 서쪽 ❑ 나는 서쪽으로 100마일 떨어져 있는 플래그스태프를 향해 계속 갔다. **2** 단수명사 서부, 서방 ❑ 잉글랜드 서부에 있는 브리스틀 대학교에 근무하는 물리학자들 **3** 부사 서쪽으로 ❑ 우리는 서부 캘리포니아로 간다. **4** 부사 서쪽에 있는 ❑ 글래스고우에서 몇 마일 서쪽에 있는 그들의 고향 마을 페이슬리 **5** 형용사 서부의 ❑ 한국 서해안의 작은 섬 **6** 형용사 서부의 ❑ 마크는 약 6개월 동안 서아프리카에서 일했다. ❑ 서 런던에 있는 그의 집 **7** 형용사 서쪽에서 부는 ❑ 따뜻한 서풍 **8** 단수명사 서구, 서양 ❑ 이란과 서구의 관계

west|er|ly /wɛstərli/ **1** ADJ A **westerly** point, area, or direction is to the west or toward the west. ❑ *...Finisterre, Spain's most westerly point.* **2** ADJ A **westerly** wind blows from the west.

1 형용사 서쪽의 ❑ 스페인의 서쪽 끝인 피니스터 **2** 형용사 서쪽에서 부는 ❑ 압도적인 서풍

west|ern ♦♦◇ /wɛstərn/ (westerns) also Western **1** ADJ **Western** means in or from the west of a region, state, or country. [ADJ n] ❑ *...hand-made rugs from Western and Central Asia.* **2** ADJ **Western** is used to describe things, people, ideas, or ways of life that come from or are associated with the United States, Canada, and the countries of Western, Northern, and Southern Europe. ❑ *Mexico had the support of the big western governments.* **3** N-COUNT A **western** is a book or movie about life in the west of America in the nineteenth century, especially the lives of cowboys. ❑ *John Agar starred in westerns, war films, and low-budget science fiction pictures.*

1 형용사 서부의 ❑ 서부 및 중앙 아시아에서 만든 수제 융단 **2** 형용사 서구의, 서양의 ❑ 멕시코는 서방 강대국 정부들의 지원을 받았다. **3** 가산명사 서부 소설, 서부 영화 ❑ 존 아가는 서부 영화, 전쟁 영화, 저비용의 공상과학 영화에서 주연을 했다.

west|ern|er /wɛstərnər/ (westerners) also Westerner N-COUNT A **westerner** is a person who was born in or lives in the United States, Canada, or Western, Northern, or Southern Europe. ❑ *It's the first time a Westerner has been convicted for a drug-related offence in recent years in China.*

가산명사 서구인, 서양인 ❑ 서양 사람이 최근 중국에서 마약 관련 범죄로 유죄 판결을 받은 것은 처음이다.

west|ern|iza|tion /wɛstərnɪzeɪʃ°n/ [BRIT also westernisation] N-UNCOUNT The **westernization** of a country, place, or person is the process of them adopting ideas and behavior that are typical of Europe and North America, rather than preserving the ideas and behavior traditional in their culture. ❑ *...fundamentalists unhappy with the westernization of Afghan culture.*

[영국영어 westernisation] 불가산명사 서구화, 서양화 ❑ 아프가니스탄 문화의 서구화에 불만인 원리주의자들

west|ern|ized /wɛstərnaɪzd/ [BRIT also westernised] ADJ A **westernized** country, place, or person has adopted ideas and behavior typical of Europe and North America, rather than preserving the ideas and behavior that are traditional in their culture. ❑ *Rapid urbanization brings with it a more westernized and generally more sugary diet.*

[영국영어 westernised] 형용사 서구화된, 서양화된 ❑ 급속한 도시화와 함께 더욱 서구화되고 전반적으로 설탕이 더 많이 든 식사가 도입된다.

west|ward /wɛstwərd/

The form **westwards** is also used.

westwards도 쓰인다.

ADV **Westward** or westwards means toward the west. ❑ *He sailed westward from Palos de la Frontera.* ● ADJ **Westward** is also an adjective. [ADJ n] ❑ *...the one-hour westward flight over the Andes to Lima.*

부사 서쪽으로 ❑ 그는 팔로스 드 라 프론테라에서 서쪽으로 항해했다. ● 형용사 서쪽으로 향하는 ❑ 안데스 산맥을 넘어 리마까지 서쪽으로 한 시간 비행

wet ♦◇◇ /wɛt/ (wetter, wettest, wets, wetting, wetted)

The forms **wet** and **wetted** are both used as the past tense and past participle of the verb.

wet와 wetted 모두 동사의 과거 및 과거 분사로 쓰인다.

a b c d e f g h i j k l m n o p q r s t u v w x y z

A
B
C
D

Word Web   wetlands

Saltwater **wetlands** protect beaches from erosion. These **tidal flats** also provide homes for shellfish and migrating birds. In some areas, mangrove swamps form along the shore. They shelter many species of fish and help filter groundwater before it reaches the ocean. Inland wetlands also form along rivers and streams. They become **marshes** and **freshwater** swamps. A **bog** is an unusual type of freshwater wetland. In a bog, a layer of **peat** forms on the surface of the water. This layer can support shrubs, trees, and small animals. In some places people dry peat and use it for cooking and heating.

E
F
G
H

1 ADJ If something is **wet**, it is covered in water, rain, sweat, tears, or another liquid. ❑ *He toweled his wet hair.* ❑ *I lowered myself to the water's edge, getting my feet wet.* **2** V-T To **wet** something means to get water or some other liquid over it. ❑ *When assembling the pie, wet the edges where the two crusts join.* **3** ADJ If the weather is **wet**, it is raining. ❑ *If the weather is wet or cold choose an indoor activity.* ● N-SING **The wet** is used to mean wet weather. ❑ *They had come in from the cold and the wet.* **4** ADJ If something such as paint, ink, or cement is **wet**, it is not yet dry or solid. ❑ *...leaves dipped in wet paint then pressed on white paper.* **5** V-T If people, especially children, **wet** their beds or clothes or **wet** themselves, they urinate in their beds or in their clothes because they cannot stop themselves. ❑ *A quarter of 4-year-olds frequently wet the bed.*

1 형용사 젖은 ❑ 그는 젖은 머리를 수건으로 말렸다. ❑ 나는 물가까지 내려가 발을 적셨다. **2** 타동사 적시다 ❑ 파이를 만들 때는, 파이 껍질이 서로 붙게 되는 가장자리에 물을 바르세요. **3** 형용사 비가 내리는, 축축한 ❑ 비가 오거나 추우면 실내 활동을 선택하세요. ● 단수명사 비 ❑ 그들은 추위와 비를 피해 안으로 들어와 있었다. **4** 형용사 마르지 않은 ❑ 마르지 않은 물감에 담갔다가 흰 종이 위에 눌러 놓은 잎들 **5** 타동사 (이불 등에) 오줌을 싸다 ❑ 4살짜리 아이들의 4분의 1은 자주 이불에 오줌을 싼다.

Word Partnership   wet의 연어

V.	**get** wet **1**
ADJ.	**soaking** wet **1**
	cold and wet **1** **3**
N.	wet **clothes**, wet **feet**, wet **grass**, wet **hair**, wet **sand** **1**
	wet **snow**, wet **weather** **3**
	wet **the bed** **5**

I
J
K

wet|land /wɛtlænd/ (**wetlands**) N-VAR A **wetland** is an area of very wet, muddy land with wild plants growing in it. You can also refer to an area like this as **wetlands**. ❑ *...a scheme that aims to protect the wilderness of the wetlands.* →see Word Web: **wetlands**

가산명사 또는 불가산명사 습지, 습지대 ❑ 그 습지대의 자연 보호를 목적으로 하는 계획

L

we've /wiv, STRONG wiːv/ **We've** is the usual spoken form of "we have," especially when "have" is an auxiliary verb. ❑ *It's the first time we've been to the cinema together as a family.*

we have의 축약형 ❑ 우리 가족이 함께 영화를 보러 간 것은 이번이 처음이다.

M

whack /wæk/ (**whacks, whacking, whacked**) V-T If you **whack** someone or something, you hit them hard. [INFORMAL] ❑ *You really have to whack the ball.* ● N-COUNT; SOUND **Whack** is also a noun. ❑ *He gave the donkey a whack across the back with his stick.*

타동사 세게 치다 [비격식체] ❑ 공을 정말 세게 쳐야 한다. ● 가산명사; 소리 세게 치기 ❑ 그는 막대기로 당나귀의 등을 한 대 세게 쳤다.

N

whacky /wæki/ →see **wacky**

O

whale /weɪl/ (**whales**) **1** N-COUNT **Whales** are very large mammals that live in the sea. **2** PHRASE If you say that someone **is having a whale of a time**, you mean that they are enjoying themselves very much. [INFORMAL] ❑ *I had a whale of a time in Birmingham.* →see Word Web: **whale**

1 가산명사 고래 **2** 구 무척 즐거운 시간을 보내고 있다 [비격식체] ❑ 나는 버밍엄에서 무척 즐거운 시간을 보냈다.

P

whal|ing /weɪlɪŋ/ N-UNCOUNT **Whaling** is the activity of hunting and killing whales. ❑ *...a ban on commercial whaling.*

불가산명사 포경업, 고래잡이 ❑ 상업용 포경의 금지

Q

wharf /wɔrf/ (**wharves** or **wharfs**) N-COUNT A **wharf** is a platform by a river or the sea where ships can be tied up.

가산명사 부두, 선창

R

what ♦♦♦ /wʌt, wɒt/ **1** QUEST You use **what** in questions when you ask for specific information about something that you do not know. ❑ *What do you want?* ❑ *What did she tell you, anyway?* ● DET **What** is also a determiner. ❑ *What time is it?* ❑ *What crimes are the defendants being charged with?* ❑ *"The heater works." — "What heater?"* **2** CONJ You use **what** after certain words, especially verbs and adjectives, when you are referring to a situation that is unknown or has not been specified. ❑ *You can imagine what it would be like driving a car into a brick wall at 30 miles an hour.* ❑ *I want to know what happened to Norman.* ● DET **What** is also a determiner. ❑ *I didn't know what college I wanted to go to.* ❑ *I didn't know what else to say.* **3** CONJ You use **what** at the beginning of a clause in structures where you are changing the order of the information to give special emphasis to something. [EMPHASIS] ❑ *What precisely triggered off yesterday's riot is still unclear.* ❑ *What I wanted, more than anything, was a few days' rest.* **4** CONJ You use **what** in

1 의문사 무엇 ❑ 무엇을 원하시나요? ❑ 그런데, 그녀가 당신에게 뭐라고 했나요? ● 한정사 어느, 무슨, 몇 ❑ 몇 십니까? ❑ 피고들은 무슨 죄로 기소되고 있습니까? ❑ "히터가 작동하네요." "어느 히터요?" **2** 접속사 무엇, 무슨 일 ❑ 시속 30마일로 자동차를 벽돌담에 충돌하는 것이 어떨지 상상할 수 있겠지요. ❑ 노먼에게 무슨 일이 일어났는지 알고 싶다. ● 한정사 어느, 무슨 ❑ 나는 내가 어느 대학에 가고 싶은지 몰랐다. ❑ 나는 무슨 말을 더 해야 할지 몰랐다. **3** 접속사 무엇, -하는 것 [강조] ❑ 정확하게 무엇이 어제의 폭동을 유발했는지는 아직 분명하지 않다. ❑ 내가 원했던 것은, 무엇보다도 며칠간의 휴식이었다. **4** 접속사 -하는 바; 소위, 이른바 ❑ 그녀는 5년 동안

S
T
U
V

Word Web   whale

Whales are part of a group of animals called cetaceans. This group also includes **dolphins** and porpoises. Although whales live in the water, they are **mammals**. They breathe air and are warm-blooded. Whales have adapted to life in the open **ocean**. They have a 2-inch thick layer of blubber just under their skin. This insulates them from the cold ocean water. They sing beautiful songs that can be heard miles away. Blue whales are the largest animals in the world. They can become almost 100 feet long and weigh up to 145 tons.

W
X
Y
Z

expressions such as **what is called** and **what amounts to** when you are giving a description of something. ❑ *She had been in what doctors described as an irreversible vegetative state for five years.* ⑤ CONJ You use **what** to indicate that you are talking about the whole of an amount that is available to you. ❑ *He drinks what is left in his glass as if it were water.* ● DET **What** is also a determiner. ❑ *They had had to use what money they had.* ⑥ CONVENTION You say "**What?**" to tell someone who has indicated that they want to speak to you that you have heard them and are inviting them to continue. [SPOKEN, FORMULAE] ❑ *"Dad?" — "What?" — "Can I have the car tonight?"* ⑦ CONVENTION You say "**What?**" when you ask someone to repeat the thing that they have just said because you did not hear or understand it properly. "What?" is more informal and less polite than expressions such as "Pardon?" and "Excuse me?". [SPOKEN, FORMULAE] ❑ *"They could paint this place," she said. "What?" he asked.* ⑧ CONVENTION You say "**What**" to express surprise. [FEELINGS] ❑ *"Adolphus Kelling, I arrest you on a charge of trafficking in narcotics." — "What?"* ⑨ PREDET You use **what** in exclamations to emphasize an opinion or reaction. [EMPHASIS] ❑ *What a horrible thing to do!* ● DET **What** is also a determiner. ❑ *What ugly things; throw them away, throw them away.* ⑩ ADV You use **what** to indicate that you are making a guess about something such as an amount or value. [ADV n] ❑ *It's, what, eleven years or more since he's seen her.* ⑪ CONVENTION You say **guess what** or **do you know what** to introduce a piece of information which is surprising, which is not generally known, or which you want to emphasize. ❑ *Guess what? I'm going to dinner at Mrs. Combley's tonight.* ⑫ PHRASE In conversation, you say **or what?** after a question as a way of stating an opinion forcefully and showing that you expect other people to agree. [EMPHASIS] ❑ *Look at that moon. Is that beautiful or what?* ⑬ CONVENTION You say **so what?** or **what of it?** to indicate that the previous remark seems unimportant, uninteresting, or irrelevant to you. [FEELINGS] ❑ *"I skipped off school today." — "So what? What's so special about that?" / "You're talking to yourself." — "Well, what of it?"* ⑭ PHRASE You say "**Tell you what**" to introduce a suggestion or offer. ❑ *Tell you what, let's stay here another day and go to the fair.* ⑮ PHRASE You use **what about** at the beginning of a question when you make a suggestion, offer, or request. ❑ *What about going out with me tomorrow?* ⑯ PHRASE You say **what about** or **what of** when you introduce a new topic or a point which seems relevant to a previous remark. ❑ *Now you've talked about work on daffodils, what about other commercially important flowers, like roses?* ⑰ PHRASE You say **what about** a particular person or thing when you ask someone to explain why they have asked you about that person or thing. ❑ *"This thing with the Corbett woman." — "Oh, yeah. What about her?"* ⑱ PHRASE You say **what if** at the beginning of a question when you ask about the consequences of something happening, especially something undesirable. ❑ *What if this doesn't work out? / What if he was going to die!* ⑲ **what's more** →see **more**

what|ev|er ♦♦◇ /wɒtɛvər, wɒt-/ ① CONJ You use **whatever** to refer to anything or everything of a particular type. ❑ *Franklin was free to do pretty much whatever he pleased. / When you're older I think you're better equipped mentally to cope with whatever happens.* ● DET **Whatever** is also a determiner. ❑ *Whatever doubts he might have had about Ingrid were all over now.* ② CONJ You use **whatever** to say that something is the case in all circumstances. ❑ *We shall love you whatever happens, Diana. / She runs on average about 15 miles a day every day, whatever the circumstances, whatever the weather.* ③ ADV You use **whatever** after a noun group in order to emphasize a negative statement. [EMPHASIS] [with brd-neg, n ADV] ❑ *There is no evidence whatever that competition in broadcasting has ever reduced costs.* ④ QUEST You use **whatever** to ask in an emphatic way about something which you are very surprised about. [EMPHASIS] ❑ *Whatever can you mean?* ⑤ CONJ You use **whatever** when you are indicating that you do not know the precise identity, meaning, or value of the thing just mentioned. [VAGUENESS] ❑ *I thought that my upbringing was "normal," whatever that is.* ⑥ PHRASE You say **or whatever** to refer generally to something else of the same kind as the thing or things that you have just mentioned. [INFORMAL] ❑ *You may like a malt whisky that is peatier, or smokier, or sweeter, or whatever.* ⑦ PHRASE You say **whatever** you **do** when giving advice or warning someone about something. [EMPHASIS] ❑ *Whatever you do, don't look for a pay increase when you know the company is going through some difficulty.*

what's /wɒts, wɒts/ **What's** is the usual spoken form of "what is" or "what has," especially when "has" is an auxiliary verb.

what|so|ev|er /wɒtsoʊɛvər, wɒt-/ ADV You use **whatsoever** after a noun group in order to emphasize a negative statement. [EMPHASIS] ❑ *My school did nothing whatsoever in the way of athletics.*

wheat /wiːt/ (**wheats**) N-MASS **Wheat** is a cereal crop grown for food. **Wheat** is also used to refer to the grain of this crop, which is usually ground into flour and used to make bread. ❑ *...farmers growing wheat, corn, or other crops.* →see **grain**

wheel ♦◇◇ /wiːl/ (**wheels**, **wheeling**, **wheeled**) ① N-COUNT The **wheels** of a vehicle are the circular objects which are fixed underneath it and which enable it to move along the ground. ❑ *The car wheels spun and slipped on some oil on the road.* ② N-COUNT A **wheel** is a circular object which forms a part of a machine, usually a moving part. ❑ *The wheels are usually fairly large.* ③ N-COUNT The **wheel** of a car or other vehicle is the circular object that is used to steer it. The **wheel** is used in expressions to talk about who is driving a vehicle. For example, if someone is **at the wheel** of a car, they are driving it. ❑ *My co-pilot suddenly grabbed the wheel. / Curtis got behind the wheel and they started back toward the cottage.* ④ V-T If you **wheel** an object that has wheels somewhere, you push it along. ❑ *He wheeled his bike into the alley at the side of the house.* ⑤ N-PLURAL People talk about **the wheels of** an organization or system to mean the way in which it operates. ❑ *He knows the*

소위 의사들이 말하는 회복 불능의 식물인간이었다. ⑤ 접속사 -하는 모두 ❑ 그는 자기 잔에 남아 있는 것을 모두 마시듯 마신다. ● 한정사 -하는 모두 ...❑ 그들은 가지고 있던 모든 돈을 다 써야만 했었다. ⑥ 관용 표현 무슨 일인데, 왜? [구어체, 의례적인 표현] ❑ "아빠?" "왜?" "오늘밤 차 좀 써도 되요?" ⑦ 관용 표현 뭐라고? (Pardon?이나 Excuse me?보다 공손하지 못한) [구어체, 의례적인 표현] ❑ "그들이 이 집을 칠할 수 있대요."라고 그녀가 말했다. "뭐라고?"하고 그가 물었다. ⑧ 관용 표현 뭐라고, 이런, 아니 [감정 개입] ❑ "아돌푸스 켈링, 마약 거래 혐의로 당신을 체포한다." "뭐라고?" ⑨ 전치 한정사 얼마나, 참으로 [강조] ❑ 얼마나 끔찍한 일인가. ● 한정사 정말 ❑ 정말 몰사나운 것들이야. 없애 버려, 버리라니까. ⑩ 부사 뭐냐, 뭐지 ❑ 그가 그녀를 본 것은, 뭐냐, 11년 이상 되었다. ⑪ 관용 표현 이게 말야요, 이것저것 ❑ 이거 알아요? 오늘밤 컴블리 여사 집에 저녁 식사하러 가요. ⑫ 구 그렇지 않아? [강조] ❑ 저 달 좀 봐. 아름답지, 그렇지 않아? ⑬ 관용 표현 그래서?, 그래서 어쨌단 말이야? [감정 개입] ❑ "나 오늘 학교 빼 먹었어" "그래서? 그게 뭐가 그렇게 특별한데?" "너 혼잣말을 하고 있구나." "그래, 그래서 어때?" ⑭ 구 좋은 생각이 있는데 ❑ 좋은 생각이 있는데, 우리 여기 하루 더 있으면서 놀이 기구 타러 가자. ⑮ 구 -하는 것은 어때요 ❑ 내일 나와 함께 데이트하는 것은 어때요? ⑯ 구 -은 어떻게 되고 있는가 ❑ 지금 당신이 수선화에 대한 작업을 이야기했는데, 장미와 같이 상업적으로 중요한 다른 꽃들은 어떻게 되어 가고 있나요? ⑰ 구 -가 뭐 ❑ 이건 그 코르벳이라는 여자와 관련된 건데. "아, 그래, 그 여자가 뭐?" ⑱ 구 -하면 어떻게 될까 ❑ 이게 잘 되지 않으면 어떻게 되지요? ❑ 그가 죽어 가고 있으면 어떻게 되나요!

① 접속사 -하는 것은 무엇이나 ❑ 프랭클린은 자기가 하고 싶은 것은 무엇이나 상당히 자유롭게 할 수 있었다. ❑ 나이가 더 들면, 무슨 일이 생기든 대처할 수 있는 정신적 무장이 더 잘 된다고 생각한다. ● 한정사 어떤 -라도 ❑ 그가 잉그리드에 대해 가졌을지도 모를 어떤 의혹도 이제는 다 없어졌다. ② 접속사 어떤 일이 -이라도, 어떤 것이 -이라도 ❑ 우리는 어떤 일이 일어나더라도 다이애나 너를 사랑할 거야. ❑ 상황이 어떻든 날씨가 어떻든, 그녀는 매일 하루 평균 약 15마일씩 달린다. ③ 부사 조금의 -도 [강조] ❑ 여태까지 방송 경쟁이 비용을 절감했다는 증거는 조금도 없다. ④ 의문사 도데체 무엇 [강조] ❑ 도데체 무슨 뜻이에요? ⑤ 접속사 그 내용이 뭐든 [짐작투] ❑ 내 양육 과정을, 그 내용이 뭐든 간에 '정상적'이었다고 나는 생각했다. ⑥ 구 그 밖에 무엇이든지, 기타 등등 [비격식체] ❑ 이탄이 더 많고, 훈향이 더 나고, 더 달콤하고, 기타 등등의 이유로 몰트 위스키를 좋아할 수도 있다. ⑦ 구 어쨌든 간에 [강조] ❑ 어쨌든 간에, 회사가 어려움을 겪고 있는 것을 알고 있으니 임금 인상은 생각하지 마세요.

what is 또는 what has의 축약형

부사 조금의 -도, 하등의 -도 [강조] ❑ 우리 학교는 운동에 관한 것이라고는 전혀 아무것도 하지 않았다.

물질명사 밀, 소맥 ❑ 밀, 옥수수, 또는 다른 작물들을 재배하는 농민들

① 가산명사 바퀴 ❑ 자동차 바퀴가 도로의 기름 위를 헛돌면서 미끄러졌다. ② 가산명사 바퀴 모양의 기계 ❑ 바퀴 모양의 기계는 대개 상당히 크다. ③ 가산명사 (자동차 등의) 핸들; 핸들을 잡음, 운전을 하는 일 ❑ 내 동승 조종사가 갑자기 핸들을 붙잡았다. ❑ 커티스가 운전을 하고 그들은 시골집을 향해 돌아가기 시작했다. ④ 타동사 (바퀴 달린 것을) 움직이다 ❑ 그는 자전거를 끌고 집 옆 골목으로 들어갔다. ⑤ 복수명사 (조직의) 운영 체계 ❑ 그는 행정부 체계는 천천히 돌아간다는 것을 안다.

wheels of administration turn slowly. **6** →see also **steering wheel**, **bicycle**, **skateboarding**

Word Partnership	*wheel*의 연어
N.	wheel **of a car/truck/vehicle** **1** **3**
V.	**grip the** wheel, **slide behind the** wheel, **spin the** wheel, **turn the** wheel **3**

wheel and deal (**wheels and deals, wheeling and dealing, wheeled and dealed**) V-I If you say that someone **wheels and deals**, you mean that they use a lot of different methods and contacts to achieve what they want in business or politics, often in a way which you consider dishonest. ❑ *He still wheels and deals around the globe.* ● **wheel|ing and deal|ing** N-UNCOUNT ❑ *He hates the wheeling and dealing associated with conventional political life.*

자동사 수완을 부리다, 술책을 부리다 ❑ 그는 여전히 세계를 돌아다니며 술수를 부린다. ● 권모술수 불가산명사 ❑ 그는 전통적인 정치 생활과 관련된 권모술수를 싫어한다.

wheel|chair /wiːltʃɛər/ (**wheelchairs**) N-COUNT A **wheelchair** is a chair with wheels that you use in order to move about in if you cannot walk properly, for example because you are disabled or sick.

가산명사 휠체어

wheeze /wiːz/ (**wheezes, wheezing, wheezed**) V-I If someone **wheezes**, they breathe with difficulty and make a whistling sound. ❑ *He had quite serious problems with his chest and wheezed and coughed all the time.*

자동사 (천식 등으로) 숨을 씨근거리다 ❑ 그는 흉부에 상당히 심각한 문제가 있어서 내내 숨을 씨근거리고 기침을 했다.

when ♦♦♦ /wɛn/ **1** QUEST You use **when** to ask questions about the time at which things happen. ❑ *When are you going home?* ❑ *When did you get married?* **2** CONJ If something happens **when** something else is happening, the two things are happening at the same time. ❑ *When eating a whole cooked fish, you should never turn it over to get at the flesh on the other side.* **3** CONJ You use **when** to introduce a clause in which you mention something which happens at some point during an activity, event, or situation. ❑ *When I met the Gills, I had been gardening for nearly ten years.* **4** CONJ You use **when** to introduce a clause where you mention the circumstances under which the event in the main clause happened or will happen. ❑ *When he brought Imelda her drink she gave him a genuine, sweet smile of thanks.* **5** CONJ You use **when** after certain words, especially verbs and adjectives, to introduce a clause where you mention the time at which something happens. ❑ *I asked him when he'd be back to pick me up.* **6** PRON-REL You use **when** to introduce a clause which specifies or refers to the time at which something happens. ❑ *He could remember a time when he had worked like that himself.* **7** CONJ You use **when** to introduce the reason for an opinion, comment, or question. ❑ *How can I love myself when I look like this?* **8** CONJ You use **when** in order to introduce a fact or comment which makes the other part of the sentence rather surprising or unlikely. ❑ *Our mothers sat us down to read and paint, when all we really wanted to do was to make a mess.*

1 의문사 언제 ❑ 언제 집에 갈거니? ❑ 언제 결혼했습니까? **2** 접속사 -한 때 ❑ 통째 요리한 생선을 먹을 때는, 절대로 다른 면의 살을 먹으려고 생선을 뒤집지 마세요. **3** 접속사 (- 하자) 그때 ❑ 내가 질 씨 가족을 만났을 무렵에, 나는 거의 십 년 가까이 원예를 해 온 참이었다. **4** 접속사 -할 때, -하자 ❑ 그가 이멜다에게 마실 것을 가져다주자, 그녀는 진심 어린, 감미로운 감사의 미소를 그에게 건넸다. **5** 접속사 언제 ❑ 나는 그에게 언제 날 데리러 오겠냐고 물었다. **6** 관계대명사 -하는 (때), -했던 (때) ❑ 그는 자기 자신이 그처럼 일했던 때를 기억할 수 있었다. **7** 접속사 -은 생각하면, -한데 ❑ 내가 이렇게 생겼는데 어떻게 나 자신을 좋아할 수 있겠는가? **8** 접속사 (-하면) 그때에 ❑ 우리 어머니들은 우리를 앉혀 놓고 책을 읽고 그림을 그리게 하셨는데, 그때 우리가 정말 하고 싶었던 것은 마구 어질러 놓는 것이었다.

when|ever ♦♢♢ /wɛnɛvər/ **1** CONJ You use **whenever** to refer to any time or every time that something happens or is true. ❑ *She always called at the vicarage whenever she was in the area.* ❑ *You can have my cottage whenever you like.* **2** CONJ You use **whenever** to refer to a time that you do not know or are not sure about. ❑ *He married Miss Vancouver in 1963, or whenever it was.*

1 접속사 -한 때는, 언제나 ❑ 그녀는 근방에 올 때면 언제나 목사관에 들렀다. ❑ 필요할 때는 언제나 제 시골집을 사용하셔도 좋습니다. **2** 접속사 뭐 그 때쯤 ❑ 그는 미스 밴쿠버와 1963년인가, 뭐 그 때쯤 결혼을 했다.

where ♦♦♦ /wɛər/

Usually pronounced /wɛər/ for meanings **2** and **3**.

1 QUEST You use **where** to ask questions about the place something is in, or is coming from or going to. ❑ *Where did you meet him?* ❑ *Where's Anna?* **2** CONJ You use **where** after certain words, especially verbs and adjectives, to introduce a clause in which you mention the place in which something is situated or happens. ❑ *People began looking across to see where the noise was coming from.* ❑ *He knew where Henry Carter had gone.* ● PRON-REL **Where** is also a relative pronoun. ❑ *Conditions which apply to your flight are available at the travel agency where you book your holiday.* **3** QUEST You use **where** to ask questions about a situation, a stage in something, or an aspect of something. ❑ *If they get their way, where will it stop?* **4** CONJ You use **where** after certain words, especially verbs and adjectives, to introduce a clause in which you mention a situation, a stage in something, or an aspect of something. ❑ *It's not hard to see where she got her feelings about herself.* ❑ *She had a feeling she already knew where this conversation was going to lead.* ● PRON-REL **Where** is also a relative pronoun. ❑ *The government is at a stage where it is willing to talk to almost anyone.*

2와 **3** 의미로는 대개 /wɛər/로 발음된다.

1 의문사 어디에, 어디서, 어디로 ❑ 어디서 그를 만났니? ❑ 애너가 어디 있지? **2** 접속사 -하는 곳에, -하는 곳으로 ❑ 사람들이 소리가 나는 곳을 건너다보기 시작했다. ● 관계대명사 -하는 (장소) ❑ 비행기 탑승에 적용되는 조건은 휴가여행을 예약한 여행사에서 알 수 있습니다. **3** 의문사 어떤 상황에, 어떤 단계에, 어떤 상태에 ❑ 만일 그들이 마음대로 한다면, 어떤 상황이 될까요? **4** 접속사 어디에, 어떤 상황에 ❑ 그녀가 자신에 대해 갖고 있는 감정이 어디서 유래된 것인지는 쉽게 알 수 있다. ❑ 그녀는 이 대화가 어디로 이어질 지 이미 알고 있다는 느낌이 들었다. ● 관계대명사 -한 (상황) ❑ 정부는 거의 아무나 붙잡고 기꺼이 상의하고 싶은 단계에 놓여 있다.

where|abouts

Pronounced /ʰwɛərəbaʊts/ for meaning **1**, and /ʰwɛərəbaʊts/ for meaning **2**.

1 N-SING-COLL If you refer to the **whereabouts** of a particular person or thing, you mean the place where that person or thing may be found. ❑ *The police are anxious to hear from anyone who may know the whereabouts of the firearms.* **2** QUEST You use **whereabouts** in questions when you are asking precisely where something is. ❑ *"Whereabouts in France?" — "Normandy," I said.* ❑ *Whereabouts are you living?*

1의 의미일 때는 /ʰwɛərəbaʊts/로, **2**의 의미일 때는 /ʰwɛərəbaʊts/로 발음된다.

1 단수명사-집합 소재, 행방 ❑ 경찰은 누구든 그 총기의 소재를 아는 사람의 제보를 간절히 기다리고 있다. **2** 의문사 (정확히) 어디에, 어느 곳에 ❑ "프랑스 어디?" "노르망디"라고 내가 말했다. ❑ 어디서 살고 있니?

where|as ♦♢♢ /wɛəræz/ CONJ You use **whereas** to introduce a comment which contrasts with what is said in the main clause. ❑ *Pensions are linked to inflation, whereas they should be linked to the cost of living.*

접속사 그러나 (사실은), -인 데 반하여 ❑ 연금은 인플레와 연계되어 있는데, 사실은 생활비와 연계되어야 한다.

where|by /wɛərbaɪ/ PRON-REL A system or action **whereby** something happens is one that makes that thing happen. [FORMAL] ❑ *The system whereby Britons choose their family doctors and the government pays those doctors, has been reasonably successful.*

관계대명사 (그것에 의하여) -하는 [격식체] ❑ 영국인이 가정 주치의를 선택하고 정부가 그 의사에게 지불하는 제도는 상당히 성공적이었다.

where|upon /wɛərəpɒn/ CONJ You use **whereupon** to say that one thing happens immediately after another thing, and usually as a result of it. [FORMAL] ❑ *Mr. Jones refused to talk to them except in the company of his legal colleagues, whereupon the police officers departed.*

접속사 (-하면) 그 결과로 [격식체] ❑ 존스 씨가 자신의 변호사 없이는 그들과 말하기를 거부함에 따라, 경찰관들이 떠났다.

wher|ever /wɛrˈɛvər/ ■ CONJ You use **wherever** to indicate that something happens or is true in any place or situation. ❑ *Some people enjoy themselves wherever they are.* ■ CONJ You use **wherever** when you indicate that you do not know where a person or place is. ❑ *I'd like to leave as soon as possible and join my children, wherever they are.* ■ QUEST You use **wherever** in questions as an emphatic form of "where," usually when you are surprised about something. [EMPHASIS] ❑ *Wherever did you get that idea?*

where|with|al /ˈwɛrwɪðɔːl, -wɪθ-/ N-SING If you have **the wherewithal** for something, you have the means, especially the money, that you need for it. ❑ *Some of the companies illegally sent the wherewithal for making chemical weapons.*

wheth|er ♦♦♦ /ˈwɛðər/ ■ CONJ You use **whether** when you are talking about a choice or doubt between two or more alternatives. ❑ *To this day, it's unclear whether he shot himself or was murdered.* ❑ *Whether it turns out to be a good idea or a bad idea, we'll find out.* ■ CONJ You use **whether** to say that something is true in any of the circumstances that you mention. ❑ *This happens whether the children are in two-parent or one-parent families.* ❑ *Whether they say it aloud or not, most men expect their wives to be faithful.*

which ♦♦♦ /wɪtʃ/

Usually pronounced /wɪtʃ/ for meanings ■, ■ and ■.

■ QUEST You use **which** in questions when there are two or more possible answers or alternatives. ❑ *"You go down that passageway over there." — "Which one?"* ❑ *Which vitamin supplements are good value?* ■ DET You use **which** to refer to a choice between two or more possible answers or alternatives. ❑ *I wanted to know which school it was you went to.* ❑ *I can't remember which teachers I had.* ● CONJ **Which** is also a conjunction. ❑ *In her panic she couldn't remember which was Mr. Grainger's cabin.* ■ PRON-REL You use **which** at the beginning of a relative clause when specifying the thing that you are talking about or when giving more information about it. ❑ *Soldiers opened fire on a car which failed to stop at an army checkpoint.* ❑ *He's based in Banja Luka, which is the largest city in northern Bosnia.* ■ PRON-REL You use **which** to refer back to an idea or situation expressed in a previous sentence or sentences, especially when you want to give your opinion about it. ❑ *They ran out of drink. Which actually didn't bother me because I wasn't drinking.* ● DET **Which** is also a determiner. ❑ *The chances are you haven't fully decided what you want from your career at the moment, in which case you're definitely not cut out to be a boss yet!* ■ PHRASE If you cannot tell the difference between two things, you can say that you do not know **which is which**. ❑ *They all look so alike to me that I'm never sure which is which.*

which|ever /wɪtʃˈɛvər/ ■ DET You use **whichever** in order to indicate that it does not matter which of the possible alternatives happens or is chosen. ❑ *Whichever way you look at it, nuclear power is the energy of the future.* ● CONJ **Whichever** is also a conjunction. ❑ *If you are unhappy with anything you have bought from us, we will gladly exchange your goods, or refund your money, whichever you prefer.* ■ DET You use **whichever** to specify which of a number of possibilities is the right one or the one you mean. ❑ *Learning to relax by whichever method suits you best is a positive way of contributing to your overall good health.* ● CONJ **Whichever** is also a conjunction. ❑ *He has been extraordinarily fortunate or clever, whichever is the right word.*

whiff /wɪf/ (**whiffs**) N-COUNT If there is a **whiff of** a particular smell, you smell it only slightly or only for a brief period of time, for example as you walk past someone or something. ❑ *He caught a whiff of her perfume.*

while
① CONJUNCTION USES
② NOUN AND VERB USES

① while ♦♦♦ /waɪl/

Usually pronounced /ʰwaɪl/ for meaning ■. The form **whilst** is also used in formal or literary English, especially British English.

■ CONJ If something happens **while** something else is happening, the two things are happening at the same time. ❑ *They were grinning and watching while one man laughed and poured beer over the head of another.* ❑ *I sat on the settee to unwrap the package while he stood by.* ■ CONJ If something happens **while** something else happens, the first thing happens at some point during the time that the second thing is happening. ❑ *The two ministers have yet to meet, but may do so while in New York.* ■ CONJ You use **while** at the beginning of a clause to introduce information which contrasts with information in the main clause. ❑ *Marianne was tempted to turn the large rooms into traditional French-style salons, while Howard was in favor of a typically English look.* ■ CONJ You use **while**, before making a statement, in order to introduce information that partly conflicts with your statement. ❑ *While the news, so far, has been good, there may be days ahead when it is bad.*

② while ♦♦♦ /waɪl/ (**whiles**, **whiling**, **whiled**) →Please look at category ■ to see if the expression you are looking for is shown under another headword.
■ N-SING A **while** is a period of time. ❑ *They walked on in silence for a while.* ❑ *He was married a little while ago.* ■ PHRASE You use **all the while** in order to say that something happens continually or that it happens throughout the time when something else is happening. ❑ *All the while the people at the next table watched me eat.* ■ once a while →see **once**. worth your while →see **worth**

▶**while away** PHRASAL VERB If you **while away** the time in a particular way, you spend time in that way, because you are waiting for something else to happen, or because you have nothing else to do. ❑ *Miss Bennett whiled away the hours playing old films on her video-recorder.*

■ 접속사 -하는 곳은 어디든 ❑ 어떤 사람들은 어디에 있든 즐겁게 지낸다. ■ 접속사 어디에서 -하든지 ❑ 나는 가능한 한 빨리 떠나서, 아이들이 어디에 있든지, 그들과 만나고 싶다. ■ 의문사 도대체 어디에, 도대체 어디서 [강조] ❑ 도대체 어디서 그런 아이디어를 얻었는가?

단수명사 필요한 자금, 필요한 수단 ❑ 몇몇 회사들이 화학 무기를 만드는 데 필요한 자금을 불법으로 보냈다.

■ 접속사 -인지 어떤지 ❑ 오늘날까지, 그가 자살했는지 살해당했는지 분명하지 않다. ❑ 그게 좋은 생각인지 나쁜 생각인지는 두고 보면 알게 될 것이다. ■ 접속사 -이든 아니든 ❑ 이런 일은 아이들이 양쪽 부모가 다 있든지 한쪽만 있든지 상관없이 일어난다. ❑ 대부분의 남자들은, 내놓고 말을 하든 안 하든, 자신의 아내가 정절을 지키기를 기대한다.

■, ■과 ■ 의미로는 대개 /wɪtʃ/로 발음된다.

■ 의문사 어느 "저기 저 통로를 따라 내려가세요." "어느 것 말인가요?" ❑ 어느 비타민 보충제가 값어치가 있나요? ■ 한정사 어느, 어떤 ❑ 나는 네가 어느 학교에 다녔는지 알고 싶었다. ❑ 난 어느 선생님께 배웠는지 기억이 나지 않는다. ● 접속사 어느 것 ❑ 너무 놀라서 그녀는 어느 것이 그레인저 씨의 오두막집인지 기억할 수 있었다. ■ 관계대명사 -하는 (것) ❑ 그런데 그것을, 그런데 그것을 ❑ 군인들은 부대 검문소에서 멈추지 않은 차에 발포를 했다. ❑ 그는 반자 루카에 자리를 잡고 있는데, 그곳은 북부 보스니아의 최대 도시이다. ■ 관계대명사 그러나 그것을 ❑ 그들은 술이 떨어졌다. 그러나 내가 술을 안 마셨기 때문에 그것은 사실 나하고는 상관이 없었다. ● 한정사 그런데 그것, 그런데 그것 ❑ 현재 당신이 직장 생활을 통해 성취하고자 하는 것이 무엇인지 완전히 결정되지 않은 것 같은데, 그런 경우라면 당신은 분명히 아직 사장이 될 준비가 되어 있지 않다. ■ 구 어느 것이 어느 것인지 ❑ 그것들은 모두 너무나 비슷해서 나는 어느 것이 어느 것인지 전혀 확실하지 않다.

■ 한정사 어느 쪽의 -이든 ❑ 당신이 어느 측면에서 바라보든지, 원자력은 미래의 에너지이다. ● 접속사 어느 쪽이든지 ❑ 저희에게서 구입한 것이 마음에 들지 않으면, 어느 쪽이든지 원하시는 대로, 기꺼이 물건을 교환하거나 환불해 드리겠습니다. ■ 한정사 어느 쪽이든 그것 ❑ 어떤 방식이든지 당신에게 가장 적합하게 긴장을 푸는 법을 알아내는 것이 당신의 전반적인 건강 증진에 좋은 방법이다. ● 접속사 어느 쪽이든지, 어느 쪽이든지 ❑ 운이 좋았는지 아니면 영리했는지 모르겠지만, 그는 특별히 운이 좋았거나 영리했다.

가산명사 살짝 풍기는 냄새 ❑ 그는 그녀에게서 살짝 풍기는 향수 냄새를 맡았다.

■ 의미로 대개 /ʰwaɪl/로 발음된다. whilst도 특히 영국영어에서 격식체 또는 문예체로 쓰인다.

■ 접속사 -하는 동안, -하는 사이 ❑ 한 남자가 웃으며 다른 남자의 머리 위에 맥주를 붓는 동안 그들은 싱글싱글 웃으며 바라보고 있었다. ❑ 그가 옆에 서 있는 동안 나는 포장을 풀기 위해 소파에 앉았다. ■ 접속사 -하는 동안, -하는 사이 ❑ 그 두 장관은 아직 만나지 못했지만, 뉴욕에 있는 동안 만나게 될 지도 모른다. ■ 접속사 -인 데 반하여 ❑ 매리앤은 큰 방들을 전통 프랑스식 살롱으로 바꾸고 싶어 했는데 반하여, 하워드는 전형적인 영국풍을 선호했다. ■ 접속사 -할지라도, -이긴 하지만 ❑ 비록 지금까지의 소식은 좋았지만, 향후 좋지 않은 날도 있을지 모른다.

■ 단수명사 한동안, (짧은) 동안 ❑ 그들은 한동안 말없이 계속 걸었다. ❑ 그는 얼마 전에 결혼했다. ■ 구 그 동안 내내 ❑ 그 동안 내내 옆 테이블 사람들은 내가 먹는 것을 지켜보았다.

구동사 (시간을) 한가하게 보내다 ❑ 베넷 양은 비디오로 옛날 영화를 보면서 그 시간을 때웠다.

whilst ◆◇◇ /waɪlst/ CONJ **Whilst** means the same as the conjunction **while**. [mainly BRIT, FORMAL or LITERARY]

접속사 -하는 동안, -하는 사이 [주로 영국영어, 격식체 또는 문예체]

whim /wɪm/ (**whims**) N-VAR A **whim** is a wish to do or have something which seems to have no serious reason or purpose behind it, and often occurs suddenly. ❑ We decided, more or less on a whim, to sail to Morocco.

가산명사 또는 불가산명사 일시적인 기분, 변덕 ❑ 우리는 다소 일시적인 기분에 끌려 모로코로 항해하기로 결정했다.

whim|per /wɪmpər/ (**whimpers, whimpering, whimpered**) V-I If someone **whimpers**, they make quiet unhappy or frightened sounds, as if they are about to start crying. ❑ She lay at the bottom of the stairs, whimpering in pain. ● N-COUNT **Whimper** is also a noun. ❑ David's crying subsided to a whimper.

자동사 울먹이다, 훌쩍거리다 ❑ 그녀는 아파서 울먹이며 계단 맨 아래에 누워 있었다. ● 가산명사 울먹임, 훌쩍거림 ❑ 데이비드의 울음은 훌쩍거림으로 잦아들었다.

whim|si|cal /wɪmzɪkəl/ ADJ A **whimsical** person or idea is unusual, playful, and unpredictable, rather than serious and practical. ❑ McGrath remembers his offbeat sense of humor, his whimsical side.

형용사 엉뚱한, 기발한 ❑ 맥그라스는 그의 엉뚱한 측면인 색다른 유머 감각을 기억하고 있다.

whine /waɪn/ (**whines, whining, whined**) **1** V-I If something or someone **whines**, they make a long, high-pitched noise, especially one which sounds sad or unpleasant. ❑ He could hear her dog barking and whining in the background. ● N-COUNT **Whine** is also a noun. ❑ ...the whine of air-raid sirens. **2** V-T/V-I If you say that someone **is whining**, you mean that they are complaining in an annoying way about something unimportant. [DISAPPROVAL] ❑ They come to me to whine about their troubles. ❑ ...children who whine that they are bored.

1 자동사 낑낑거리다, 징징거리다 ❑ 그는 뒤편에서 그녀의 개가 짖고 낑낑거리는 소리를 들을 수 있었다. ● 가산명사 낑낑대는 소리, 징징거리는 소리 ❑ 공습 사이렌이 앵앵거리는 소리 **2** 타동사/자동사 투덜거리다, 징징거리다 [탐탁찮음] ❑ 그들은 자기들 문제에 대해 불평하러 내게 온다. ❑ 지루하다고 징징거리는 아이들

whinge /wɪndʒ/ (**whinges, whingeing** or **whinging**) (**whinged**) V-I If you say that someone **is whingeing**, you mean that they are complaining in an annoying way about something unimportant. [BRIT, INFORMAL, DISAPPROVAL] ❑ All she ever does is whinge and complain.

자동사 징징거리다 [영국영어, 비격식체, 탐탁찮음] ❑ 그녀가 하는 일이라고는 징징거리며 불평하는 것뿐이다.

whip ◆◇◇ /wɪp/ (**whips, whipping, whipped**) **1** N-COUNT A **whip** is a long thin piece of material such as leather or rope, fastened to a stiff handle. It is used for hitting people or animals. **2** V-T If someone **whips** a person or animal, they beat them or hit them with a whip or something like a whip. ❑ Eye-witnesses claimed Mr. Melton whipped the horse up to 16 times. ● **whip|ping** (**whippings**) N-COUNT ❑ He threatened to give her a whipping. **3** V-T If someone **whips** something out or **whips** it off, they take it out or take it off very quickly and suddenly. ❑ Bob whipped out his notebook. ❑ Players were whipping their shirts off. **4** V-T When you **whip** something liquid such as cream or an egg, you stir it very fast until it is thick or stiff. ❑ Whip the cream until thick. ❑ Whip the eggs, oils and honey together. **5** V-T If you **whip** people **into** an emotional state, you deliberately cause and encourage them to be in that state. ❑ He could whip a crowd into hysteria.

1 가산명사 채찍 **2** 타동사 매질하다, 채찍질하다 ❑ 목격자들은 멜튼 씨가 16번씩이나 그 말에 채찍질을 했다고 주장했다. ● 채찍질 가산명사 ❑ 그는 그녀에게 채찍으로 때리겠다고 위협했다. **3** 타동사 휙 움직이다 ❑ 밥은 자기 노트를 휙 꺼냈다. ❑ 선수들은 셔츠를 휙휙 벗어 던지고 있었다. **4** 타동사 (크림 등을) 휘젓다 ❑ 크림이 걸쭉해질 때까지 저으세요. ❑ 계란, 기름, 꿀을 함께 섞어 저으세요. **5** 타동사 -를 ... 상태로 몰아가다 ❑ 그가 군중을 히스테리 상태로 몰아갈 수도 있다.

▶**whip up** PHRASAL VERB If someone **whips up** an emotion, especially a dangerous one such as hatred, or if they **whip** people **up** into an emotional state, they deliberately cause and encourage people to feel that emotion. ❑ He accused politicians of whipping up anti-foreign sentiments in order to win right-wing votes.

구동사 (감정을) 부추기다 ❑ 그는 정치인들이 우익 표를 얻기 위하여 반외국인 정서를 부추겼다고 비난했다.

whip|lash /wɪplæʃ/ N-UNCOUNT **Whiplash** is a neck injury caused by the head suddenly moving forward and then back again, for example in a car accident. ❑ His wife suffered whiplash and shock.

불가산명사 목뼈 골절상 ❑ 그의 부인은 목뼈가 골절되었고 충격을 받았다.

whir /wɜr/ →see **whirr**

whirl /wɜrl/ (**whirls, whirling, whirled**) **1** V-T/V-I If something or someone **whirls** around or if you **whirl** them around, they move around or turn around very quickly. ❑ Not receiving an answer, she whirled round. ❑ He was whirling Anne around the floor. ● N-COUNT **Whirl** is also a noun. ❑ ...the barely audible whirl of wheels. **2** N-COUNT You can refer to a lot of intense activity as a **whirl** of activity. ❑ In half an hour's whirl of activity she does it all. **3** PHRASE If you decide to **give** an activity **a whirl**, you do it even though it is something that you have never tried before. [INFORMAL] ❑ Why not give acupuncture a whirl?

1 타동사/자동사 빙빙 돌다; 빙빙 돌리다 ❑ 대답을 듣지 못해서 그녀는 주변을 빙빙 돌았다. ❑ 그는 앤을 플로어로 이리저리 빙빙 돌리고 있었다. ● 가산명사 회전, 선회 ❑ 거의 들리지 않는 바퀴의 회전 소리 **2** 가산명사 후딱 하기, 빠른 일 처리 ❑ 반시간 정도만 후딱 하면 그녀는 그것을 다 해낸다. **3** 구 시도하다, 한 번 해 보다 [비격식체] ❑ 침을 한 번 맞아 보지 그래?

whirl|wind /wɜrlwɪnd/ (**whirlwinds**) **1** N-COUNT A **whirlwind** is a tall column of air which spins around and around very fast and moves across the land or sea. **2** N-COUNT You can describe a situation in which a lot of things happen very quickly and are very difficult for someone to control as a **whirlwind**. ❑ I had been running around southern England in a whirlwind of activity. **3** ADJ A **whirlwind** event or action happens or is done much more quickly than normal. [ADJ n] ❑ He got married after a whirlwind romance.

1 가산명사 회오리바람 **2** 가산명사 정신없이 돌아가는 상황 ❑ 나는 정신없이 일을 하며 영국 남부 지방을 이리저리 뛰어다니고 있었다. **3** 형용사 급작한, 황급한 ❑ 그는 질풍같은 연애 끝에 결혼했다.

whirr /wɜr/ (**whirrs, whirring, whirred**) also **whir** V-I When something such as a machine or an insect's wing **whirrs**, it makes a series of low sounds so quickly that they seem like one continuous sound. ❑ The camera whirred and clicked. ● N-COUNT; SOUND **Whirr** is also a noun. ❑ He could hear the whirr of a vacuum cleaner.

자동사 윙윙거리다 ❑ 카메라가 윙윙거리더니 찰칵했다. ● 가산명사; 소리 윙윙거리는 소리 ❑ 그는 진공청소기가 윙윙거리는 소리를 들었다.

whisk /wɪsk/ (**whisks, whisking, whisked**) **1** V-T If you **whisk** someone or something somewhere, you take them or move them there quickly. ❑ He whisked her across the dance floor. **2** V-T If you **whisk** something such as eggs or cream, you stir it very fast, often with an electric device, so that it becomes full of small bubbles. ❑ Just before serving, whisk the cream. **3** N-COUNT A **whisk** is a kitchen tool used for whisking eggs or cream. ❑ Using a whisk, mix the yolks and sugar to a smooth paste.

1 타동사 휙 데려가다 ❑ 그가 댄스 플로어를 휙 가로질러 그녀를 이끌고 갔다. **2** 타동사 (빨리 저어) 거품을 내다 ❑ 차려 내기 바로 전에 크림을 휘저어 거품을 내세요. **3** 가산명사 거품기 ❑ 거품기를 사용하여 계란 노른자와 설탕을 섞어 부드러운 반죽을 만드세요.

whisk|er /wɪskər/ (**whiskers**) **1** N-COUNT The **whiskers** of an animal such as a cat or a mouse are the long stiff hairs that grow near its mouth. **2** N-PLURAL You can refer to the hair on a man's face, especially on the sides of his face, as his **whiskers**. ❑ ...wild, savage-looking fellows, with large whiskers, unshaven beards, and dirty faces.

1 가산명사 (고양이 등의) 수염 **2** 복수명사 구레나룻 ❑ 면도 안 한 콧수염에 긴 구레나룻이 있는 지저분한 얼굴을 한 거칠고 험상궂어 보이는 녀석들

whis|key /wɪski/ (**whiskeys**) N-MASS **Whiskey** is a strong alcoholic drink made, especially in the United States and Ireland, from grain such as barley or rye. ❑ ...a tumbler with about an inch of whiskey in it. ● N-COUNT A **whiskey** is a glass of whiskey. ❑ Stark took two whiskeys from a tray.

물질명사 (미국과 아일랜드산) 위스키 ❑ 약 1인치 정도의 위스키가 든 위스키 잔 ● 가산명사 위스키 한 잔 ❑ 스타크는 쟁반에서 위스키 두 잔을 집었다.

whis|ky /wɪski/ (**whiskies**) N-MASS **Whisky** is whiskey that is made especially in

물질명사 (스코틀랜드와 캐나다산) 위스키 ❑ 위스키

Scotland and Canada. ❑ ...*a bottle of whisky.* ● N-COUNT A **whisky** is a glass of whisky. ❑ *She handed him a whisky.*

whis|per ◆◇◇ /wɪspər/ (**whispers, whispering, whispered**) V-T/V-I When you **whisper**, you say something very quietly, using your breath rather than your throat, so that only one person can hear you. ❑ *"Keep your voice down," I whispered.* ❑ *She sat on Rossi's knee as he whispered in her ear.* ❑ *He whispered the message to David.* ● N-COUNT **Whisper** is also a noun. ❑ *Men were talking in whispers in every office.*

whis|tle /wɪsᵊl/ (**whistles, whistling, whistled**) **1** V-T/V-I When you **whistle** or when you **whistle** a tune, you make a series of musical notes by forcing your breath out between your lips, or your teeth. ❑ *He whistled and sang snatches of songs.* ❑ *He was whistling softly to himself.* **2** V-I When someone **whistles**, they make a sound by forcing their breath out between their lips or their teeth. People sometimes whistle when they are surprised or shocked, or to call a dog, or to show that they are impressed. ❑ *He whistled, surprised but not shocked.* ❑ *Jenkins whistled through his teeth, impressed at last.* ● N-COUNT **Whistle** is also a noun. ❑ *Jackson gave a low whistle.* **3** V-I If something such as a train or a kettle **whistles**, it makes a loud, high sound. ❑ *Somewhere a train whistled.* **4** V-I If something such as the wind or a bullet **whistles** somewhere, it moves there, making a loud, high sound. ❑ *The wind was whistling through the building.* **5** N-COUNT A **whistle** is a loud sound produced by air or steam being forced through a small opening, or by something moving quickly through the air. ❑ *...the whistle of the wind.* ❑ *...a shrill whistle from the boiling kettle.* **6** N-COUNT A **whistle** is a small metal tube which you blow in order to produce a loud sound and attract someone's attention. ❑ *On the platform, the guard blew his whistle.* **7** PHRASE If you **blow the whistle on** someone, or on something secret or illegal, you tell another person, especially a person in authority, what is happening. ❑ *Companies should protect employees who blow the whistle on dishonest workmates and work practices.* **8** PHRASE If you describe something as **clean as a whistle**, you mean that it is completely clean. ❑ *The kitchen was clean as a whistle.*

whistle-blowing also **whistleblowing** N-UNCOUNT **Whistle-blowing** is the act of telling the authorities or the public that the organization you are working for is doing something immoral or illegal. ❑ *It took internal whistle-blowing and investigative journalism to uncover the rot.*

white ◆◆◆ /waɪt/ (**whiter, whitest, whites**) **1** COLOR Something that is **white** is the color of snow or milk. ❑ *He had nice square white teeth.* ❑ *Issa's white beach hat gleamed in the harsh lights.* **2** ADJ A **white** person has a pale skin and belongs to a race which is of European origin. ❑ *Working with white people hasn't been a problem for me or for them.* ● N-COUNT **Whites** are white people. ❑ *It's a school that's brought blacks and whites and Hispanics together.* **3** ADJ **White** wine is pale yellow in color. ❑ *Gregory poured another glass of white wine and went back to his bedroom.* **4** ADJ **White** coffee has had milk or cream added to it. [BRIT] ❑ *Wayne has a Coca-Cola and a large white coffee in front of him.* **5** ADJ **White** blood cells are the cells in your blood which your body uses to fight infection. [ADJ n] ❑ *...an AIDS drug that helps restore a patient's white blood cells.* **6** N-VAR The **white** of an egg is the transparent liquid that surrounds the yellow part called the yolk. ❑ *As soon as the whites of the eggs have set, remove the cover.* **7** N-COUNT The **white** of someone's eye is the white part that surrounds the colored part called the iris. ❑ *Susanne stared at me, the whites of her eyes gleaming in the streetlight.*

white|board /waɪtbɔːrd/ (**whiteboards**) N-COUNT A **whiteboard** is a shiny white board on which people draw or write using special pens. Whiteboards are often used for teaching or giving talks.

white-collar also **white collar** **1** ADJ **White-collar** workers work in offices rather than doing physical work such as making things in factories or building things. [ADJ n] ❑ *White-collar workers now work longer hours.* **2** ADJ **White-collar** crime is committed by people who work in offices, and involves stealing money secretly from companies or the government, or getting money in an illegal way. [ADJ n] ❑ *...a New York lawyer who specializes in white-collar crime.*

white goods N-PLURAL People in business sometimes refer to refrigerators, washing machines, and other large pieces of electrical household equipment as **white goods**. Compare **brown goods**. ❑ *...the third largest manufacturer of white goods in Europe.*

White House ◆◇◇ N-PROPER The **White House** is the official home in Washington DC of the President of the United States. You can also use **the White House** to refer to the President of the United States and his or her officials. ❑ *He drove to the White House.*

white knight (**white knights**) N-COUNT A **white knight** is a person or an organization that rescues a company from difficulties such as financial problems or an unwelcome takeover bid. [BUSINESS] ❑ *...a white-knight bid.*

white|wash /waɪtwɒʃ/ (**whitewashes, whitewashing, whitewashed**) **1** N-UNCOUNT **Whitewash** is a mixture of lime or chalk and water that is used for painting walls white. **2** V-T If a wall or building **has been whitewashed**, it has been painted white with whitewash. ❑ *The walls had been whitewashed.* **3** V-T If you say that people **whitewash** something, you are accusing them of hiding the unpleasant facts or truth about it in order to make it acceptable. [DISAPPROVAL] ❑ *The administration is whitewashing the regime's actions.*

whit|tle /wɪtᵊl/ (**whittles, whittling, whittled**) V-T If you **whittle** something from a piece of wood, you carve it by cutting pieces off with a knife. ❑ *He whittled a new handle for his ax.*

▶ **whittle away** PHRASAL VERB To **whittle away** something or **whittle away** at it means to gradually make it smaller, weaker, or less effective. ❑ *I believe that the Government's general aim is to whittle away the Welfare State.*

한 병 ● 가산명사 위스키 한 잔 ❑ 그녀는 그에게 위스키 한 잔을 건넸다.

타동사/자동사 속삭이다, 귓속말하다 ❑ "목소리를 낮춰."라고 내가 속삭였다. ❑ 그녀는 로시의 무릎에 앉아 있고 그는 그녀의 귀에 대고 말을 속삭이고 있었다. ❑ 그는 데이비드에게 전갈을 속삭였다. ● 가산명사 속삭임, 수군거림 ❑ 사무실마다 남자들이 수군거리고 있었다.

1 타동사/자동사 휘파람을 불다 ❑ 그는 휘파람을 불고 노래를 이것저것 조금씩 흥얼거렸다. ❑ 그는 혼자서 나직이 휘파람을 불고 있었다. **2** 자동사 휘파람 소리를 내다 ❑ 그는 충격을 받지는 않았지만 놀라서 '휴우' 하는 휘파람 소리를 냈다. ❑ 젠킨스는 마침내 감동을 받아서 이빨 사이로 휘파람 소리를 냈다. ● 가산명사 휘파람 소리 ❑ 잭슨은 낮은 휘파람 소리를 냈다. **3** 자동사 (기차 등이) 삑삑 소리를 내다 ❑ 어디선가 기차가 기적을 울렸다. **4** 자동사 (바람 등이) 쌩 하고 지나가다 ❑ 건물 안에는 바람이 휘휘 불고 있었다. **5** 가산명사 (증기가 나오는) 삑삑 소리, (바람의) 쌩쌩 소리 ❑ 바람이 윙윙대는 소리 ❑ 물이 끓는 주전자에서 나오는 날카로운 삑삑 소리 **6** 가산명사 호각, 호루라기 ❑ 플랫폼에서 승무원이 호각을 불었다. **7** 구 고발하다, 알리다 ❑ 회사는 정직하지 않은 직장 동료와 업무 행위를 고발하는 직원을 보호해야 한다. **8** 구 아주 깨끗한 ❑ 부엌은 아주 깨끗했다.

불가산명사 고발, 폭로 ❑ 내부 고발과 부정을 조사하는 언론이 있어서 그런 사정 악화가 밝혀졌다.

1 색채어 흰, 백색의 ❑ 그는 치아가 멋진 사각형으로 희었다. ❑ 이사의 하얀색 해변용 모자가 강렬한 햇빛에 반짝거렸다. **2** 형용사 백인의 ❑ 백인과 함께 일하는 것이 내게나 그들에게 문제가 되지 않았다. ● 가산명사 백인 ❑ 흑인과 백인과 라틴 아메리카인을 모두 한자리에 불러 모은 것이 학교였다. **3** 형용사 (포도주가) 백색의 ❑ 그레고리는 또 한 잔의 백포도주를 따라서 침실로 돌아갔다. **4** 형용사 우유나 크림을 넣은 [영국영어] ❑ 웨인의 앞에는 코카콜라와 커다란 밀크 커피 한 잔이 놓여 있다. **5** 형용사 (혈구가) 백색의 ❑ 환자의 백혈구를 회복시키는 데 도움이 되는 에이즈 약 **6** 가산명사 또는 불가산명사 (계란의) 흰자위 ❑ 계란의 흰자가 익자마자 덮개를 여세요. **7** 가산명사 (눈의) 흰자위 ❑ 수잔이 나를 노려보았는데, 그녀 눈의 흰자위가 가로등 불빛을 받아 번득였다.

가산명사 흰색 칠판, 화이트보드

1 형용사 사무직의 ❑ 이제는 사무직 근로자가 더 장시간 일한다. **2** 형용사 (범죄가) 사무직과 관련된 ❑ 화이트칼라 범죄를 전문으로 다루는 뉴욕 변호사

복수명사 (냉장고 등) 백색 가전제품 ❑ 유럽에서 세 번째로 큰 백색 가전제품 제조사

고유명사 백악관; 미국 정부 ❑ 그는 백악관으로 차를 몰았다.

가산명사 구세주, 경영권 위기에 처한 회사를 구하는 사람이나 회사 [경제] ❑ 경영권 방어를 위한 입찰

1 불가산명사 회반죽, 백색 도료 **2** 타동사 회칠이 되어 있다 ❑ 벽은 회칠이 되어 있었다. **3** 타동사 호도하다 [탐탁잖음] ❑ 정부가 정권의 행위를 호도하고 있다.

타동사 깎아 만들다 ❑ 그는 새 도끼 자루를 깎았다.

구동사 줄이다, 약화시키다 ❑ 나는 정부의 전반적인 목표가 복지 국가 정책을 약화시키려는 것이라고 믿는다.

whiz /wɪz/ (**whizzes, whizzing, whizzed**) also **whizz** v-i If something **whizzes** somewhere, it moves there very fast. [INFORMAL] ❑ *They heard bullets continue to whiz over their heads.*

자동사 쌩 하고 움직이다 [비격식체] ❑ 그들은 머리 위로 총탄이 계속 핑핑 지나가는 소리를 들었다.

who ♦♦♦ /hu/

Usually pronounced /hu/ for meanings ② and ③.

② 와 ③ 의미로는 대개 /hu/로 발음된다.

Who is used as the subject or object of a verb. See entries at **whom** and **whose**.

who는 동사의 주어나 목적어로 쓰인다. 표제어 whom과 whose 참조.

❶ QUEST You use **who** in questions when you ask about the name or identity of a person or group of people. ❑ *Who's there?* ❑ *Who is the least popular man around here?* ❑ *"You reminded me of somebody." — "Who?"* ❷ CONJ You use **who** after certain words, especially verbs and adjectives, to introduce a clause where you talk about the identity of a person or a group of people. ❑ *Police have not been able to find out who was responsible for the forgeries.* ❑ *I went over to start up a conversation, asking her who she knew at the party.* ❸ PRON-REL You use **who** at the beginning of a relative clause when specifying the person or group of people you are talking about or when giving more information about them. ❑ *There are those who eat out for a special occasion, or treat themselves.*

❶ 의문사 누구 ❑ 거기 누구십니까? ❑ 여기서 가장 인기가 없는 남자가 누구인가요? ❑ "당신을 보면 누군가가 생각이 나요." "누구요?" ❷ 접속사 누구 ❑ 경찰은 누가 위조지폐를 만들었는지 아직 알아내지 못했다. ❑ 나는 대화를 시작하려고 그녀에게 가서 파티에 온 사람 중 누구를 아느냐고 물었다. ❸ 관계대명사 –하는 (사람) ❑ 특별한 날이거나 아니면 그냥 잘 먹으려고 외식을 하는 사람들이 있다.

Who is now commonly used where it used only to be considered to be correct to use **whom**. Who, however, cannot be used directly after a preposition, for example, you cannot say "...the woman to who I spoke." Instead you can say "...**the woman to whom I spoke**" or "...**the woman I spoke to**." There are some types of sentence in which **who** cannot be used, for example when you are talking about quantities. ❑ *...twenty masked prisoners, many of whom are armed with makeshift weapons.*

과거에는 whom을 써야만 옳다고 여겨지던 위치에 이제는 who가 흔히 사용된다. 하지만, 전치사 바로 뒤에는 who를 쓸 수 없다. 예를 들어, "...the woman to who I spoke"라고 하면 안 된다. 대신, "...the woman to whom I spoke"라고 하거나 "...the woman I spoke to"라고 할 수 있다. who를 쓸 수 없는 문장 형식이 몇 가지 있는데, 예를 들면 수량에 대해 말할 때이다. ❑ ...마스크를 쓴 스무 명의 죄수들, 그 중 다수가 조잡한 무기로 무장하고 있다..

who'd /hud, hud/ ❶ **Who'd** is the usual spoken form of "who had," especially when "had" is an auxiliary verb. ❷ **Who'd** is a spoken form of "who would."

❶ who had의 축약형 ❷ who would의 축약형

who|ever /huevər/ ❶ CONJ You use **whoever** to refer to someone when their identity is not yet known. ❑ *Whoever did this will sooner or later be caught and will be punished.* ❑ *Whoever wins the election is going to have a tough job getting the economy back on its feet.* ❷ CONJ You use **whoever** to indicate that the actual identity of the person who does something will not affect a situation. ❑ *You can have whoever you like to visit you.* ❸ QUEST You use **whoever** in questions as an emphatic way of saying "who," usually when you are surprised about something. [EMPHASIS] ❑ *Whoever thought up that joke?*

❶ 접속사 –하는 누구든지, 누가 –하든 ❑ 누구든 이것을 한 사람은 조만간 잡혀서 처벌을 받을 것이다. ❑ 누가 선거에서 이기든지 경제를 회복시켜야 하는 힘든 임무를 맡게 될 것이다. ❷ 접속사 –하는 누구나, –하는 누구든 ❑ 당신이 부르고 싶은 사람은 누구나 초대해도 좋다. ❸ 의문사 도대체 누가 [강조] ❑ 도대체 누가 그 농담을 생각해 냈지?

whole ♦♦♦ /houl/ ❶ QUANT If you refer to **the whole of** something, you mean all of it. [QUANT of def-n] ❑ *He has said he will make an apology to the whole of Asia for his country's past behavior.* ❑ *I was cold throughout the whole of my body.* ● ADJ Whole is also an adjective. [ADJ n] ❑ *We spent the whole summer in Italy that year.* ❷ N-COUNT A **whole** is a single thing which contains several different parts. ❑ *An atom itself is a complete whole, with its electrons, protons and other elements.* ❸ ADJ If something is **whole**, it is in one piece and is not broken or damaged. [v-link ADJ, v n ADJ] ❑ *I struck the glass with my fist with all my might; yet it remained whole.* ❹ ADV You use **whole** to emphasize what you are saying. [INFORMAL, EMPHASIS] [ADV adj] ❑ *It was like seeing a whole different side of somebody.* ● ADJ Whole is also an adjective. [ADJ n] ❑ *That saved me a whole bunch of money.* ❺ PHRASE If you refer to something **as a whole**, you are referring to it generally and as a single unit. ❑ *He described the move as a victory for the people of South Africa as a whole.* ❻ PHRASE You use **on the whole** to indicate that what you are saying is true in general but may not be true in every case, or that you are giving a general opinion or summary of something. ❑ *On the whole, people miss the opportunity to enjoy leisure.*

❶ 수량사 (~의) 전부, 전체 ❑ 그는 자기 나라의 과거 행위에 대해 아시아 전체에 사과하겠다고 말했다. ❑ 난 온몸이 추웠다. ● 형용사 전체의, 온 ❑ 우리가 그 해는 이탈리아에서 온 여름을 다 보냈다. ❷ 가산명사 완전체, 통합체 ❑ 원자 자체는 전자, 양자, 중성자와 다른 요소를 가진 하나의 통합체이다. ❸ 형용사 온전한 ❑ 나는 유리잔을 온 힘을 다해 주먹으로 쳤으나 잔은 온전했다. ❹ 부사 완전히 [비격식체, 강조] ❑ 그것은 누군가의 완전히 다른 면을 보는 것과 같았다. ● 형용사 완전한 ❑ 그것으로 나는 완전히 엄청난 돈을 절약했다. ❺ 구 전체로서, 대체로 ❑ 그는 그 조처를 남아프리카 공화국 국민 전체의 승리라고 표현했다. ❻ 구 전체적으로 보아, 대체로 ❑ 대체로 사람들은 여가를 즐길 기회를 놓친다.

Whole is often used to mean the same as **all** but when used in front of plurals, **whole** and **all** have different meanings. For example, if you say "**Whole buildings have been destroyed**," you mean that some buildings have been destroyed completely. If you say "**All the buildings have been destroyed**," you mean that every building has been destroyed.

whole은 흔히 all과 같은 뜻으로 쓰이지만 복수 앞에 쓰이면 whole과 all은 다른 뜻을 갖는다. 예를 들어, "Whole buildings have been destroyed."라고 하면, 일부 건물들이 완전히 파괴되었음을 의미한다. 그런데 "All buildings have been destroyed."라고 하면, 모든 건물들이 하나하나 다 파괴되었다는 뜻이다.

whole|heart|ed /houlhɑrtɪd/ also **whole-hearted** ADJ If you support or agree to something in a **wholehearted** way, you support or agree to it enthusiastically and completely. [EMPHASIS] ❑ *The Government deserves our wholehearted support for having taken a step in this direction.* ● **whole|heart|ed|ly** ADV ❑ *That's exactly right. I agree wholeheartedly with you.*

형용사 전폭적으로, 전적인 [강조] ❑ 정부는 이 방향으로 조치를 취한 것에 대해 우리의 전폭적인 지지를 받을 만하다. ● 전폭적으로, 전적으로 부사 ❑ 바로 그거예요. 당신의 말에 전적으로 동의합니다.

whole|sale /houlseɪl/ ❶ N-UNCOUNT **Wholesale** is the activity of buying and selling goods in large quantities and therefore at cheaper prices, usually to stores who then sell them to the public. Compare **retail**. [BUSINESS] ❑ *Warehouse clubs allow members to buy goods at wholesale prices.* ❷ ADV If something is sold **wholesale**, it is sold in large quantities and at cheaper prices, usually to stores. [BUSINESS] [ADV after v] ❑ *The fabrics are sold wholesale to retailers, fashion houses, and other manufacturers.* ❸ ADJ You use **wholesale** to describe the destruction, removal, or changing of something when it affects a very large number of things or people. [EMPHASIS] [ADJ n] ❑ *They are only doing what is necessary to prevent wholesale destruction of vegetation.*

❶ 불가산명사 도매 [경제] ❑ 창고형 도매점은 회원들이 도매가격으로 물건을 산다. ❷ 부사 도매로 [경제] ❑ 그 직물은 도매로 소매상, 의상실, 다른 제조업자들에게 팔린다. ❸ 형용사 대량의, 대규모의 [강조] ❑ 그들은 초목의 대량 파괴를 막는 데 꼭 필요한 일만을 하고 있다.

whole|sal|er /houlseɪlər/ (**wholesalers**) N-COUNT A **wholesaler** is a person whose business is buying large quantities of goods and selling them in smaller amounts, for example to stores. [BUSINESS] ❑ *Under state law, bar owners must buy their booze from wholesalers.*

가산명사 도매업자, 도매상 [경제] ❑ 주법에 따라 술집 주인들은 술을 도매상으로부터 구매해야 한다.

whole|sal|ing /houlseɪlɪŋ/ N-UNCOUNT **Wholesaling** is the activity of buying or selling goods in large amounts, especially in order to sell them in stores or

불가산명사 도매업 [경제] ❑ 사업이 번창하여 그는 도매업을 시작했다.

supermarkets. Compare **retailing**. [BUSINESS] ❑ *The business thrived and he turned to wholesaling.*

whole|some /hoʊlsəm/ ❑ ADJ If you describe something as **wholesome**, you approve of it because you think it is likely to have a positive influence on people's behavior or mental state, especially because it does not involve anything sexually immoral. [APPROVAL] ❑ *Ironically, given its wholesome, family image, Disney has always been a notoriously tough place to work.* ❑ ADJ If you describe food as **wholesome**, you approve of it because you think it is good for your health. [APPROVAL] ❑ *...fresh, wholesome ingredients.*

who'll /hʊl, hul/ **Who'll** is a spoken form of "who will" or "who shall."

whol|ly /hoʊlli/ ADV You use **wholly** to emphasize the extent or degree to which something is the case. [EMPHASIS] ❑ *While the two are only days apart in age they seem to belong to wholly different generations.*

wholly-owned subsidiary (**wholly-owned subsidiaries**) N-COUNT A **wholly-owned subsidiary** is a company whose shares are all owned by another company. [BUSINESS] ❑ *The Locomotive Construction Company Ltd is a wholly-owned subsidiary of the Trust.*

whom ♦♦◇ /hum/

> **Whom** is used in formal or written English instead of "who" when it is the object of a verb or preposition.

❑ QUEST You use **whom** in questions when you ask about the name or identity of a person or group of people. ❑ *"I want to send a telegram." — "Fine, to whom?"* ❑ *Whom did he expect to answer his phone?* ❑ CONJ You use **whom** after certain words, especially verbs and adjectives, to introduce a clause where you talk about the name or identity of a person or a group of people. ❑ *He asked whom I'd told about his having been away.* ❑ PRON-REL You use **whom** at the beginning of a relative clause when specifying the person or group of people you are talking about or when giving more information about them. ❑ *One writer in whom I had taken an interest was Immanuel Velikovsky.* →see **who**

whoop /hup, BRIT ʰwuːp/ (**whoops, whooping, whooped**) V-I If you **whoop**, you shout loudly in a very happy or excited way. [WRITTEN] ❑ *She whoops with delight at a promise of money.* ● N-COUNT **Whoop** is also a noun. ❑ *Scattered groans and whoops broke out in the crowd.*

who're /huər, huər/ **Who're** is a spoken form of "who are." ❑ *I've got loads of friends who're unemployed.*

who's /huz, huz/ **Who's** is the usual spoken form of "who is" or "who has," especially when "has" is an auxiliary verb.

whose ♦♦♦ /huz/

> Usually pronounced /huz/ for meanings ❑ and ❑.

❑ PRON-REL You use **whose** at the beginning of a relative clause where you mention something that belongs to or is associated with the person or thing mentioned in the previous clause. ❑ *I saw a man shouting at a driver whose car was blocking the street.* ❑ *...a speedboat, whose fifteen-strong crew claimed to belong to China's navy.* ❑ QUEST You use **whose** in questions to ask about the person or thing that something belongs to or is associated with. ❑ *"Whose is this?" — "It's mine."* ❑ *"It wasn't your fault, John." — "Whose, then?"* ❑ *Whose car were they in?* ❑ *Whose daughter is she?* ❑ DET You use **whose** after certain words, especially verbs and adjectives, to introduce a clause where you talk about the person or thing that something belongs to or is associated with. ❑ *I'm wondering whose mother she is then.* ● CONJ **Whose** is also a conjunction. ❑ *I wondered whose the coat was.*

who've /huv, huv/ **Who've** is the usual spoken form of "who have," especially when "have" is an auxiliary verb.

why ♦♦♦ /waɪ/

> The conjunction and the pronoun are usually pronounced /waɪ/.

❑ QUEST You use **why** in questions when you ask about the reasons for something. ❑ *Why hasn't he brought the whiskey?* ❑ *Why didn't he stop me?* ❑ CONJ You use **why** at the beginning of a clause in which you talk about the reasons for something. ❑ *He still could not throw any further light on why the elevator could have become jammed.* ❑ *Experts wonder why the U.S. government is not taking similarly strong actions against AIDS in this country.* ● ADV **Why** is also an adverb. ❑ *I don't know why.* ❑ *It's obvious why.* ❑ PRON-REL You use **why** to introduce a relative clause after the word "reason." ❑ *There's a reason why women don't read this stuff; it's not funny.* ● ADV **Why** is also an adverb. [N ADV] ❑ *He confirmed that the city had been closed to foreigners, but gave no reason why.* ❑ QUEST You use **why** with "not" in questions in order to introduce a suggestion. ❑ *Why not give Claire a call?* ❑ QUEST You use **why** with "not" in questions in order to express your annoyance or anger. [FEELINGS] ❑ *Why don't you look where you're going?* ❑ CONVENTION You say **why not** in order to agree with what someone has suggested. [FORMULAE] ❑ *"Want to spend the afternoon with me?" — "Why not?"* ❑ EXCLAM People say "**Why**" at the beginning of a sentence when they are surprised, shocked, or angry. [mainly AM, FEELINGS] ❑ *Why hello, Tom.*

wick|ed /wɪkɪd/ ADJ You use **wicked** to describe someone or something that is very bad and deliberately harmful to people. ❑ *She described the shooting as a wicked attack.*

wick|et ♦♦◇ /wɪkɪt/ (**wickets**) ❑ N-COUNT In cricket, a **wicket** is a set of three upright sticks with two small sticks on top of them at which the ball is bowled. There are two wickets on a cricket field. ❑ *The bowler took his run-up, the batsman lifted his bat and allowed the ball to hit his wicket.* ❑ N-COUNT In cricket, a **wicket** is the area of grass in between the two wickets on the field. ❑ *White walked to the wicket on Tuesday with England 180-5.* ❑ N-COUNT In cricket, when a

wicket falls or is taken, a batsman is out. ❑ *Matthew Hoggard took three wickets in six balls.*

wide ♦♦♦ /waɪd/ (**wider, widest**) **1** ADJ Something that is **wide** measures a large distance from one side or edge to the other. ❑ *All worktops should be wide enough to allow plenty of space for food preparation.* **2** ADJ If you open or spread something **wide**, you open or spread it as far as possible or to the fullest extent. ❑ *"It was huge," he announced, spreading his arms wide.* **3** ADJ You use **wide** to talk or ask about how much something measures from one side or edge to the other. [amount ADJ, as ADJ as, ADJ-compar than, how ADJ] ❑ *...a corridor of land 10 kilometres wide.* ❑ *The road is only one track wide.* **4** ADJ You use **wide** to describe something that includes a large number of different things or people. ❑ *The brochure offers a wide choice of hotels, apartments and holiday homes.* ● **widely** ADV ❑ *He published widely in scientific journals.* **5** ADJ You use **wide** to say that something is found, believed, known, or supported by many people or throughout a large area. ❑ *The case has attracted wide publicity.* ● **widely** ADV [ADV with v] ❑ *At present, no widely approved vaccine exists for malaria.* **6** ADJ A **wide** difference or gap between two things, ideas, or qualities is a large difference or gap. ❑ *Research shows a wide difference in tastes around the country.* ● **widely** ADV ❑ *The treatment regime may vary widely depending on the type of injury.* **7** ADJ **Wider** is used to describe something which relates to the most important or general parts of a situation, rather than to the smaller parts or to details. [ADJ n] ❑ *He emphasized the wider issue of superpower cooperation.* **8** **wide awake** →see **awake**. **wide of the mark** →see **mark**. **wide open** →see **open** →see **ratio**

Thesaurus   wide의 참조어

ADJ.	broad, large; (*ant.*) narrow **1** **4**-**6**

Word Partnership   wide의 연어

N.	wide **grin/smile**, wide **shoulders 1**
	arms/eyes/mouth open wide **2**
	wide **selection**, wide **variety 4**

---

wid|en /waɪdᵊn/ (**widens, widening, widened**) **1** V-T/V-I If you **widen** something or if it **widens**, it becomes greater in measurement from one side or edge to the other. ❑ *He had an operation last year to widen a heart artery.* **2** V-T/V-I If you **widen** something or if it **widens**, it becomes greater in range or it affects a larger number of people or things. ❑ *U.S. prosecutors have widened a securities-fraud investigation.* **3** V-T/V-I If a difference or gap **widens** or if something **widens** it, it becomes greater. ❑ *Wage differences in the two areas are widening.*

wide-ranging ADJ If you describe something as **wide-ranging**, you mean it deals with or affects a great variety of different things. ❑ *...a package of wide-ranging economic reforms.*

wide|screen /waɪdskrin/ ADJ A **widescreen** television has a screen that is wide in relation to its height.

wide|spread ♦♢♢ /waɪdspred/ ADJ Something that is **widespread** exists or happens over a large area, or to a great extent. ❑ *But while there is widespread support for the new proposals, there are also a lot of question marks about how they will translate into practice.*

wid|ow /wɪdoʊ/ (**widows**) N-COUNT A **widow** is a woman whose husband has died and who has not married again. ❑ *She became a widow a year ago.*

wid|owed /wɪdoʊd/ V-T PASSIVE If someone is **widowed**, their husband or wife dies. ❑ *More and more young men are widowed by cancer.*

wid|ow|er /wɪdoʊər/ (**widowers**) N-COUNT A **widower** is a man whose wife has died and who has not married again. ❑ *He is a widower and lives in Croydon.*

width /wɪdθ, wɪtθ/ (**widths**) N-VAR The **width** of something is the distance it measures from one side or edge to the other. ❑ *Measure the full width of the window.* ❑ *The road was reduced to 18ft in width by adding parking bays.* →see **ratio**

wield /wild/ (**wields, wielding, wielded**) **1** V-T If you **wield** a weapon, tool, or piece of equipment, you carry and use it. ❑ *He was attacked by a man wielding a knife.* **2** V-T If someone **wields** power, they have it and are able to use it. ❑ *He remains chairman, but wields little power at the company.*

wife ♦♦♦ /waɪf/ (**wives**) N-COUNT A man's **wife** is the woman he is married to. ❑ *He married his wife Jane 37 years ago.* →see **family, love**

wig /wɪg/ (**wigs**) N-COUNT A **wig** is a covering of false hair which you wear on your head, for example because you have little hair of your own or because you want to cover up your own hair. ❑ *Jo wore a long wig that made her look very sexy.*

wig|gle /wɪgᵊl/ (**wiggles, wiggling, wiggled**) V-T/V-I If you **wiggle** something or if it **wiggles**, it moves up and down or from side to side in small quick movements. ❑ *She wiggled her finger.* ● N-COUNT **Wiggle** is also a noun. ❑ *...a wiggle of the hips.*

wild ♦♦♢ /waɪld/ (**wilds, wilder, wildest**) **1** ADJ **Wild** animals or plants live or grow in natural surroundings and are not taken care of by people. ❑ *We saw two more wild cats creeping towards us in the darkness.* **2** ADJ **Wild** land is natural and is not used by people. ❑ *Elmley is one of the few wild areas remaining in the South East.* **3** N-PLURAL The **wilds** of a place are the natural areas that are far away from cities and towns. ❑ *They went canoeing in the wilds of Canada.* **4** ADJ **Wild** is used to describe the weather or the sea when it is stormy. ❑ *The wild weather did*

개로 세 타자를 아웃시켰다.

1 형용사 넓은 ❑ 모든 조리대는 음식 준비를 위한 여유 있는 공간을 확보할 수 있도록 충분히 폭이 넓어야 한다. **2** 형용사 충분히 열린, 활짝 열린 ❑ "그것은 거대했어."라고 그가 팔을 크게 벌려 보이며 말했다. **3** 형용사 폭이 -인 ❑ 폭이 10킬로미터인 회랑 지대 ❑ 길은 겨우 차 한 대 지나갈 정도의 폭이었다. **4** 형용사 폭넓은, 다양한 ❑ 안내 책자에는 다양하게 선택할 수 있는 호텔, 아파트, 휴가용 주택들이 나와 있다. **5** 형용사 광범위한, 폭넓은 ❑ 그 사건은 폭넓은 관심을 모았다. ● 일반적으로, 널리 부사 ❑ 현재 일반적으로 공인된 말라리아 백신이 없다. **6** 형용사 (차이 등이) 큰 ❑ 조사에 의하면 전국적으로 취향이 크게 다르다. ● 크게 부사 ❑ 치료 요법은 부상의 종류에 따라 크게 다를 수 있다. **7** 형용사 전반적인 ❑ 그는 초강대국의 협력이라는 더욱 포괄적인 쟁점을 강조했다.

1 타동사/자동사 넓히다, 확장시키다; 넓어지다 ❑ 그는 작년에 심혈관 확장 수술을 받았다. **2** 타동사/자동사 (범위를) 확대하다; 확대되다 ❑ 미국 검찰은 증권사기 수사의 범위를 확대했다. **3** 타동사/자동사 커지다, 벌어지다; 벌리다 ❑ 두 지역 간의 임금 격차가 벌어지고 있다.

형용사 광범위한 ❑ 광범위한 경제 개혁 종합정책

형용사 화면이 넓은, 와이드 스크린의

형용사 광범위한, 널리 퍼진 ❑ 새 계획안에 대한 폭넓은 지지가 있는 반면에, 그것이 어떻게 실행될 수 있을지에 대해 많은 의문이 또한 제기되고 있다.

가산명사 과부, 미망인 ❑ 그녀는 일 년 전에 남편을 잃고 홀로 되었다.

수동 타동사 배우자를 잃다 ❑ 더욱 더 많은 젊은 남자들이 암으로 배우자를 잃는다.

가산명사 홀아비 ❑ 그는 홀아비로 크로이든에 살고 있다.

가산명사 또는 불가산명사 넓이, 폭 ❑ 창문의 전체 폭을 재세요. ❑ 그 도로는 주차 공간을 설치하면서 폭이 18피트로 줄었다.

1 타동사 휘두르다, 사용하다 ❑ 그는 칼을 휘두르는 한 남자로부터 피습당했다. **2** 타동사 (권력을) 행사하다, 휘두르다 ❑ 그는 회장으로 남아 있지만 회사에 거의 영향력이 없다.

가산명사 부인, 아내 ❑ 그는 자기 아내 제인과 37년 전에 결혼했다.

가산명사 가발 ❑ 조우는 무척 섹시해 보이는 긴 가발을 썼다.

타동사/자동사 (위 아래 또는 좌우로) 뒤흔들다, 꿈틀거리다 ❑ 그녀는 손가락을 꼼지락거렸다. ● 가산명사 (몸을) 뒤흔듦, 꿈틀거림 ❑ 엉덩이 흔들기

1 형용사 야생의 ❑ 우리는 어둠 속에서 우리를 향해 살금살금 기어오는 들고양이 두 마리를 더 보았다. **2** 형용사 자연 그대로의 ❑ 엘름리는 남동부에서 자연 그대로 보전되어 있는 몇 안 되는 지역 중 하나이다. **3** 복수명사 미개척지, 대자연 ❑ 그들은 캐나다의 대자연 속으로 카누를 타러 갔다. **4** 형용사 거친, 사나운 ❑ 사나운 날씨에도 불구하고 몇몇 사람들은

not deter some people from taking an unseasonable dip in the sea. **5** ADJ **Wild** behavior is uncontrolled, excited, or energetic. ❑ *The children are wild with joy.* ❑ *As George himself came on stage they went wild.* ● **wild|ly** ADV [ADV with v] ❑ *As she finished each song, the crowd clapped wildly.* **6** ADJ If you describe someone or their behavior as **wild**, you mean that they behave in a very uncontrolled way. ❑ *The house is in a mess after a wild party.* ● **wild|ly** ADV [ADV with v] ❑ *Five people were injured as Reynolds slashed out wildly with a kitchen knife.* **7** ADJ A **wild** idea is unusual or extreme. A **wild** guess is one that you make without much thought. [ADJ n] ❑ *Browning's prediction is no better than a wild guess.* ● **wild|ly** ADV ❑ *"Thirteen?" he guessed wildly.* **8** →see also **wildly** **9** PHRASE Animals that live **in the wild** live in a free and natural state and are not taken care of by people. ❑ *Fewer than a thousand giant pandas still live in the wild.* **10** **beyond** your **wildest dreams** →see **dream**. **in** your **wildest dreams** →see **dream**. **to sow** your **wild oats** →see **oats**

바다에 때 아닌 수영을 하러 갔다. **5** 형용사 광란의, 흥분한 ❑ 아이들은 기뻐서 난리였다. ❑ 조지가 직접 무대에 나오자 그들은 흥분했다. ● 격렬하게, 열광적으로 부사 ❑ 그녀가 노래를 마칠 때마다, 관중들은 열광적으로 박수를 쳤다. **6** 형용사 광란의, 제멋대로의 ❑ 그 집은 광란의 파티를 치르고 나서 난장판이다. ● 미친 듯이, 걷잡아서 부사 ❑ 레이놀즈가 미친 듯이 부엌칼을 휘둘러서 다섯 명이 부상당했다. **7** 형용사 엉뚱한, 엉뚱무모한 ❑ 브라우닝의 예견은 얼토당토않게 추측한 것이나 다름없다. ● 얼토당토 부사 ❑ "열 셋?"하고 그는 제멋대로 추측했다. **9** 구 야생 상태에 ❑ 천 마리가 안 되는 거대한 팬더들이 아직 야생 상태로 살고 있다.

Thesaurus   wild의 참조어

ADJ.   desolate, natural, overgrown **2**
       stormy **4**
       excited, rowdy, uncontrolled **5** **6**

Word Partnership   wild의 연어

N.   wild **animal**, wild **beasts/creatures**, wild **game**, wild **horse**, wild **mushrooms** **1**
      wild **pitch**, wild **swing** **5**
V.   go wild **5** **6**

wild card (**wild cards**) also **wildcard** **1** N-COUNT If you refer to someone or something as a **wild card** in a particular situation, you mean that they cause uncertainty because you do not know how they will behave. ❑ *The wild card in the picture is eastern Europe.* **2** N-COUNT A **wildcard** is a symbol such as * or ? which is used in some computing commands or searches in order to represent any character or range of characters. [COMPUTING]

1 가산명사 예측 불가능한 사람, 예측 불가능한 요인 ❑ 그 상황에서 예측 불가능한 요인은 동유럽이다. **2** 가산명사 와일드카드, 임의 문자 기호 [컴퓨터]

wil|der|ness /wɪldərnɪs/ (**wildernesses**) N-COUNT A **wilderness** is a desert or other area of natural land which is not used by people. ❑ *...the icy Canadian wilderness.*

가산명사 황야, 황무지 ❑ 얼어붙은 캐나다의 황무지

wild|fire /waɪldfaɪər/ PHRASE If something, especially news or a rumor, **spreads like wildfire**, it spreads extremely quickly. ❑ *These stories are spreading like wildfire through the city.* →see **fire**

구 (소문 등이) 삽시간에 퍼지다 ❑ 이 이야기들은 삽시간에 온 도시에 퍼지고 있다.

wild|life /waɪldlaɪf/ N-UNCOUNT You can use **wildlife** to refer to the animals and other living things that live in the wild. ❑ *People were concerned that pets or wildlife could be affected by the pesticides.* →see **zoo**

불가산명사 야생동물 ❑ 사람들은 애완동물이나 야생 동물이 살충제에 해를 입을까 우려했다.

wild|ly /waɪldli/ ADV You use **wildly** to emphasize the degree, amount, or intensity of something. [EMPHASIS] ❑ *Here again, the community and police have wildly different stories of what happened.* →see also **wild**

부사 완전히, 터무니없이 [강조] ❑ 여기서 또다시, 지역 사회와 경찰은 일어난 사건에 관해 서로 완전히 다른 말을 하고 있다.

wil|ful /wɪlfʊl/ →see **willful**

will

① MODAL VERB USES
② WANTING SOMETHING TO HAPPEN

① **will** ♦♦♦ /wɪl/

Will is a modal verb. It is used with the base form of a verb. In spoken English and informal written English, the form **won't** is often used in negative statements.

will은 조동사이며 동사 원형과 함께 쓰인다. 구어체 영어와 비격식 문어체 영어의 부정문에서는 종종 won't가 쓰인다.

1 MODAL You use **will** to indicate that you hope, think, or have evidence that something is going to happen or be the case in the future. ❑ *I'm sure we will find a wide variety of choices available in school cafeterias.* ❑ *Will you ever feel at home here?* ❑ *The ship will not be ready for a month.* **2** MODAL You use **will** in order to make statements about official arrangements in the future. ❑ *The show will be open to the public at 2pm; admission will be 50p.* **3** MODAL You use **will** in order to make promises and threats about what is going to happen or be the case in the future. ❑ *I will call you tonight.* ❑ *Price quotes on selected product categories will be sent on request.* **4** MODAL You use **will** to indicate someone's intention to do something. ❑ *I will say no more on these matters, important though they are.* ❑ *In this section we will describe common myths about cigarettes, alcohol, and marijuana.* ❑ *"Dinner's ready." — "Thanks, Carrie, but we'll have a drink first." ❑ *Will you be remaining in the city?* **5** MODAL You use **will** in questions in order to make polite invitations or offers. [POLITENESS] ❑ *Will you stay for supper?* ❑ *Will you join me for a drink?* **6** MODAL You use **will** in questions in order to ask or tell someone to do something. ❑ *Will you drive me home?* ❑ *Will you listen again, Andrew?* **7** MODAL You use **will** to say that someone is willing to do something. You use **will not** or **won't** to indicate that someone refuses to do something. ❑ *All right, I will forgive you.* →see also **willing** **8** MODAL You use **will** to say that a person or thing is able to do something in the future. ❑ *How the country will defend itself in the future has become increasingly important.* **9** MODAL You use **will** to indicate that an action usually happens in the particular way mentioned. ❑ *The thicker the material, the less susceptible the garment will be to wet conditions.* **10** MODAL You use **will** in the main clause of some "if" and "unless" sentences to indicate something that you consider to be fairly likely to happen. ❑ *If you overcook the pancakes they will be difficult to roll.* **11** MODAL You use **will** to say that someone insists on behaving or doing something in a particular way and

1 법조동사 -할 것이다, -일 것이다 ❑ 나는 교내 식당에 아주 다양한 먹거리가 있을 것이라고 확신한다. ❑ 당신이 여기서 편하게 느낄 날이 있을까요? ❑ 배가 한 달 안에는 준비되지 않을 것이다. **2** 법조동사 -한다 ❑ 그 공연은 오후 2시에 일반 관람이 됩니다. 입장료는 50펜스입니다. **3** 법조동사 -하겠다 ❑ 오늘밤 네게 전화할게. ❑ 선별된 상품 종류에 따른 가격은 요청할 경우 보내 드리겠습니다. **4** 법조동사 -하고자 한다, -하겠다 ❑ 비록 이 문제들이 중요하긴 하지만, 나는 더 이상 거기에 관해 언급하지 않겠다. ❑ 이 절에서는 담배, 술, 대마초에 관한 일반적인 통념에 대해 기술하겠다. ❑ "저녁 다 됐어." "고마워, 캐리, 하지만 우린 술부터 한 잔 할게." ❑ 너 시내에 계속 있을 거니? **5** 법조동사 -하지 않겠습니까? [공손체] ❑ 저녁 먹고 가지 않을래? ❑ 같이 한 잔 하지 않겠니? **6** 법조동사 -해 주시겠어요? ❑ 차로 집에 데려다 주시겠어요? ❑ 다시 한 번 들어볼래, 앤드류? **7** 법조동사 기꺼이 -하려고 한다, -하지 않으려 한다 ❑ 좋아, 내가 용서해 줄게. **8** 법조동사 -할 수가 있다 ❑ 나라가 앞으로 어떻게 자주국방을 할 수가 있을 것인가가 더욱 더 중요해졌다. **9** 법조동사 -하기 마련이다, -하는 경향이 있다 ❑ 원단이 두터울수록, 옷이 쉽게 젖지 않기 마련이다. **10** 법조동사 -하기 쉽다 ❑ 팬케이크를 너무 익히면 동그랗게 말기 어려워진다. **11** 법조동사 -하게 된다, 항상 -한다 ❑ 그는 항상 양말을 아무 데나 벗어 두는 데 난 그것 때문에 미치겠다. **12** 법조동사 -하게 될 것이 분명하다 ❑ 2010년까지 천만 명이나

a b c d e f g h i j k l m n o p q r s t u v w x y z

you cannot change them. You emphasize **will** when you use it in this way. ❑ *He will leave his socks lying all over the place and it drives me mad.* ⓬ MODAL You use **will have** with a past participle when you are saying that you are fairly certain that something will be true by a particular time in the future. ❑ *As many as ten-million children will have been infected with the virus by the end of the decade.* ⓭ MODAL You use **will have** with a past participle to indicate that you are fairly sure that something is the case. ❑ *The holiday will have done him the world of good.*

되는 어린이들이 그 바이러스에 감염될 것이 분명하다. ⓭ 법조동사 틀림없이 ‐한 것이다 ❑ 휴가가 분명 그에게 도움이 될 것이다.

② **will** ♦♦◇ /wɪl/ (**wills, willing, willed**) ❶ N-VAR **Will** is the determination to do something. ❑ *He was said to have lost his will to live.* →see also **free will** ❷ N-SING If something is **the will of** a person or group of people with authority, they want it to happen. ❑ *He has submitted himself to the will of God.* ❸ V-T If you **will** something **to** happen, you try to make it happen by using mental effort rather than physical effort. ❑ *I looked at the telephone, willing it to ring.* ❹ N-COUNT A **will** is a document in which you declare what you want to happen to your money and property when you die. ❑ *Attached to his will was a letter he had written to his wife just days before his death.* ❺ PHRASE If something is done **against** your **will**, it is done even though you do not want it to be done. ❑ *No doubt he was forced to leave his family against his will.*

❶ 가산명사 또는 불가산명사 의욕, 결의 ❑ 그가 삶에 대한 의욕을 잃어버린 것으로 알려졌었다. ❷ 단수명사 의지, 뜻 ❑ 그는 자신을 신의 뜻에 맡겼다. ❸ 타동사 (의지의 힘으로) ‐하게 하다, ‐하기를 염원하다 ❑ 나는 전화기를 바라보며, 벨이 울리기를 염원했다. ❹ 가산명사 유언장 ❑ 그의 유언장에는 죽기 바로 며칠 전 그가 아내에게 쓴 편지가 첨부되어 있었다. ❺ 구본의 아니게 ❑ 필시 그는 본의 아니게 가족과 헤어져야만 했을 것이다.

will|ful /wɪlfəl/ ❶ ADJ If you describe actions or attitudes as **willful**, you are critical of them because they are done or expressed deliberately, especially with the intention of causing someone harm. [ADJ n] ❑ *The sergeant faces a lesser charge of willful neglect of duty.* ❷ ADJ If you describe someone as **willful**, you mean that they are determined to do what they want to do, even if it is not sensible. ❑ *Molly was at times impatient and willful.*

❶ 형용사 고의의, 계획적인 ❑ 그 하사관은 고의적 직무 유기라는 좀 더 가벼운 혐의를 받게 된다. ❷ 형용사 고집 센, 막무가내의 ❑ 말리는 때로 참을성이 없었고 고집을 부렸다.

will|ing ♦♦◇ /wɪlɪŋ/ ❶ ADJ If someone is **willing to** do something, they are fairly happy about doing it and will do it if they are asked or required to do it. [v-link ADJ to-inf] ❑ *The military now say they're willing to hold talks with the political parties.* ❷ ADJ **Willing** is used to describe someone who does something fairly enthusiastically and because they want to do it rather than because they are forced to do it. ❑ *Have the party on a Saturday, when you can get your partner and other willing adults to help.* ❸ **God willing** →see **god**

❶ 형용사 기꺼이 ‐하는 ❑ 군부는 이제 정당들과 기꺼이 대화를 하겠다고 말한다. ❷ 형용사 자발적인, 자진해서 하는 ❑ 그 파티는 토요일에 열자. 그 때는 네 파트너와 기꺼이 도와줄 다른 어른들의 도움을 받을 수 있으니까.

will|low /wɪloʊ/ (**willows**) N-COUNT A **willow** or a **willow tree** is a type of tree with long branches and long narrow leaves that grows near water.

가산명사 버드나무

will|power /wɪlpaʊər/ also **will-power, will power** N-UNCOUNT **Willpower** is a very strong determination to do something. ❑ *He came in for help after his attempts to stop smoking by willpower alone failed.*

불가산명사 의지력, 결단력 ❑ 그는 의지만 가지고 담배를 끊으려다 실패하고서 도움을 구하러 왔다.

wilt /wɪlt/ (**wilts, wilting, wilted**) V-I If a plant **wilts**, it gradually bends downward and becomes weak because it needs more water or is dying. ❑ *The roses wilted the day after she bought them.*

자동사 시들다 ❑ 장미는 그녀가 산 다음날 시들었다.

wily /waɪli/ (**wilier, wiliest**) ADJ If you describe someone or their behavior as **wily**, you mean that they are clever at achieving what they want, especially by tricking people. ❑ *His appointment as prime minister owed much to the wily maneuvering of the president.*

형용사 약삭빠른, 교활한 ❑ 그가 총리로 임명된 데에는 대통령의 교활한 술수가 큰 몫을 했다.

wimp /wɪmp/ (**wimps**) N-COUNT If you call someone a **wimp**, you disapprove of them because they lack confidence or determination, or because they are often afraid of things. [INFORMAL, DISAPPROVAL] ❑ *I was a wimp, because I had spent my life being bullied by my Dad.*

가산명사 겁쟁이, 약골 [비격식체, 탐탁잖음] ❑ 나는 아빠에게 평생 괴롭힘을 당하며 살았기 때문에 겁쟁이다.

win ♦♦♦ /wɪn/ (**wins, winning, won**) ❶ V-T/V-I If you **win** something such as a competition, battle, or argument, you defeat those people you are competing or fighting against, or you do better than everyone else involved. ❑ *He does not have any realistic chance of winning the election.* ❑ *The top four teams all won.* ● N-COUNT **Win** is also a noun. ❑ *...Arsenal's dismal league run of eight games without a win.* ❷ V-T If something **wins** you something such as an election, competition, battle, or argument, it causes you to defeat the people competing with you or fighting you, or to do better than everyone else involved. ❑ *The Conservative Party will face the choice of who can best hope to win them the next general election against the present odds.* ❸ V-T If you **win** something such as a prize or medal, you get it because you have defeated everyone else in something such as an election, competition, battle, or argument, or have done very well in it. ❑ *She won bronze for Great Britain in the European Championships.* ❹ V-T If you **win** something that you want or need, you succeed in getting it. [BRIT also **win round**] ❑ *...moves to win the support of the poor.* ❺ →see also **winning** ❻ to **win hands down** →see **hand**

❶ 타동사/자동사 이기다 ❑ 그가 현실적으로 선거에서 이길 가망이 전혀 없다. ❑ 상위 네 팀이 모두 이겼다. ● 가산명사 승리 ❑ 한번도 이기지 못하고 여덟 경기를 치른 아스날의 비참한 리그전 ❷ 타동사 이기게 해 주다 ❑ 보수당은 누구를 선택하면 현재의 역경을 딛고 일어나 다음 총선에서 자기 당이 이길 가망성이 가장 높을지 결정해야 한다. ❸ 타동사 (상금 등을) 획득하다 ❑ 그녀는 유럽 챔피언쉽에서 영국에 동메달을 선사했다. ❹ 타동사 얻다, 얻어 내다 [영국영어 win round] ❑ 빈곤층의 지지를 얻어 내려는 조치들

Thesaurus	win의 참조어
V.	conquer, succeed, triumph; (ant.) defeat, lose ❶
N.	conquest, success, victory; (ant.) defeat ❶

▶ **win over** PHRASAL VERB If you **win** someone **over** or **win** them **round**, you persuade them to support you or agree with you. ❑ *He has won over a significant number of the left-wing deputies.*

▶ **win round** →see **win over**

구동사 (설득하여) 자기편으로 만들다 ❑ 그는 상당한 수의 좌익 의원을 자기편으로 만들었다.

wince /wɪns/ (**winces, wincing, winced**) V-I If you **wince**, the muscles of your face tighten suddenly because you have felt a pain or because you have just seen, heard, or remembered something unpleasant. ❑ *Every time he put any weight on his left leg he winced in pain.*

자동사 얼굴을 찡그리다 ❑ 그는 왼쪽 다리에 무게가 실릴 때마다 아파서 얼굴을 찡그렸다.

winch /wɪntʃ/ (**winches, winching, winched**) ❶ N-COUNT A **winch** is a machine which is used to lift heavy objects or people who need to be rescued. It consists of a drum around which a rope or chain is wound. ❷ V-T If you **winch** an object or person somewhere, you lift or lower them using a winch.

❶ 가산명사 윈치 ❷ 타동사 윈치로 감아올리다 ❑ 그는 그 차의 차대에 케이블을 연결해서 윈치로 차를 운하 제방 위로 들어올리려고 했다.

❏ He would attach a cable around the chassis of the car and winch it up on to the canal bank.

Word Partnership　　wind의 연어

ADJ.	**cold** wind, **hot** wind, **icy** wind, **warm** wind ① ■
N.	**desert** wind, **gust** of wind, **wind** power, **winter** wind ① ■
V.	wind **blows**, wind **whips** ① ■
	get wind of *something* ① ⑥

---
wind
---

① AIR
② TURNING OR WRAPPING

① **wind** ♦♦◇ /wɪnd/ (**winds, winding, winded**) ■ N-VAR A **wind** is a current of air that is moving across the earth's surface. ❏ There was a strong wind blowing. ■ N-COUNT Journalists often refer to a trend or factor that influences events as a **wind of** a particular kind. ❏ The winds of change are blowing across the country. ■ V-T If you **are winded** by something such as a blow, the air is suddenly knocked out of your lungs so that you have difficulty breathing for a short time. ❏ He was winded and shaken. ■ N-UNCOUNT **Wind** is the air that you sometimes swallow with food or drink, or gas that is produced in your intestines, which causes an uncomfortable feeling. ❏ I suffer terribly with wind and it really can be very embarrassing if I am in company. ■ PHRASE If someone **breaks wind**, they release gas from their intestines through their anus. ❏ If I break wind at table, should I say "Pardon," or pretend nothing has happened? ⑥ PHRASE If you **get wind of** something, you hear about it, especially when someone else did not want you to know about it. [INFORMAL] ❏ I don't want the public, and especially not the press, to get wind of it at this stage.
→see beach, electricity, erosion, storm, wave
→see Word Web: wind

Thesaurus　　wind의 참조어

N.	air, current, gust ① ■
V.	bend, loop, twist; (*ant.*) straighten ② ■ ■

② **wind** ♦♦◇ /waɪnd/ (**winds, winding, wound**) ■ V-T/V-I If a road, river, or line of people **winds** in a particular direction, it goes in that direction with a lot of bends or twists in it. ❏ The Moselle winds through some 160 miles of tranquil countryside. ❏ ...a narrow winding road. ■ V-T When you **wind** something flexible around something else, you wrap it around it several times. ❏ The horse jumped forwards and round her, winding the rope round her waist. ■ V-T When you **wind** a mechanical device, for example a watch or a clock, you turn a knob, key, or handle on it several times in order to make it operate. ❏ I still hadn't wound my watch so I didn't know the time. ● PHRASAL VERB **Wind up** means the same as **wind**. ❏ I wound up the watch and listened to it tick. ■ V-T To **wind** a tape or film **back** or **forward** means to make it move towards its starting or ending position. ❏ The camcorder winds the tape back or forward at high speed.
▶**wind down** ■ PHRASAL VERB When you **wind down** something such as the window of a car, you make it move downwards by turning a handle. ❏ Glass motioned to him to wind down the window. ■ PHRASAL VERB If you **wind down**, you relax after doing something that has made you feel tired or tense. [INFORMAL] ❏ I regularly have a drink to wind down. ■ PHRASAL VERB If someone **winds down** a business or activity, they gradually reduce the amount of work that is done or the number of people that are involved, usually before closing or stopping it completely. ❏ Foreign aid workers have already begun winding down their operation.
▶**wind up** ■ PHRASAL VERB When you **wind up** an activity, you finish it or stop doing it. ❏ The President is about to wind up his visit to Somalia. ■ PHRASAL VERB When someone **winds up** a business or other organization, they stop running it and close it down completely. [BUSINESS] ❏ The Bank of England seems determined to wind up the company. ■ PHRASAL VERB When you **wind up** something such as the window of a car, you make it move upwards by turning a handle. ❏ He started winding the window up but I grabbed the door and opened it. ■ PHRASAL VERB If you **wind** someone **up**, you deliberately say things which annoy them. [BRIT, INFORMAL] ❏ This woman really wound me up. She kept talking over me. ■ →see also **wind 3, wound up**

windfall /wɪndfɔl/ (**windfalls**) N-COUNT A **windfall** is a sum of money that you receive unexpectedly or by luck, for example if you win a lottery. ❏ ...the man who received a £250,000 windfall after a banking error.

■ 가산명사 또는 불가산명사 바람 ❏ 강한 바람이 불고 있었다. ■ 가산명사 바람, 동향, 동향 ■ 변화의 바람이 온 나라에 불고 있다. ■ 타동사 (턱 하게) 숨이 막히다 ❏ 그는 턱 하고 숨이 막히며 몸이 흔들렸다. ■ 불가산명사 공기; 가스 ❏ 나는 배에 가스가 차서 너무 힘들기 때문에 사람들과 함께 있으면 정말로 아주 민망할 수 있다. ■ 구 방귀를 뀌다 ❏ 식탁에서 방귀를 뀌면 "미안합니다."라고 말해야 되나요, 아니면 아무 일도 없었던 것처럼 해야 되나요? ⑥ 구 ~을 알아채다, ~을 눈치 채다 [비격식체] ❏ 이 단계에서 국민, 특히 언론이 그것을 눈치 채지 않았으면 좋겠다.

■ 타동사/자동사 구불구불하다 ❏ 모젤 강은 평온한 시골 지방을 160마일 정도 굽이져서 흐른다. ■ 좁고 구불구불한 길 ■ 타동사 감다, 동이다 ❏ 말이 그녀를 향해 뛰어올라 그녀의 허리에 로프를 감으면서 돌았다. ■ 타동사 (시계태엽 등을) 감다 ❏ 아직 내 시계태엽을 감아 놓지 않아서 시간을 몰랐다. ● 구동사 (시계태엽 등을) 감다 ❏ 나는 시계태엽을 감고 째깍거리는 소리를 들었다. ■ 타동사 (테이프 또는 필름을) 되로 되감다; 진행 방향으로 감다 ❏ 그 캠코더는 테이프를 고속으로 앞뒤로 감는다.

■ 구동사 (자동차의 창문 등을) 감아 내리다 ❏ 글라스가 그에게 창문을 내리라는 동작을 취했다. ■ 구동사 긴장을 풀다 [비격식체] ❏ 나는 긴장을 풀기 위해 규칙적으로 한 잔 한다. ■ 구동사 서서히 일을 줄이 나가다, 서서히 규모를 축소하다 ❏ 외국 구호 단원들은 이미 활동을 축소해 나가기 시작했다.

■ 구동사 마치다 ❏ 대통령의 소말리아 방문이 마무리 단계에 접어들고 있다. ■ 구동사 폐업하다, 해산하다 [경제] ❏ 영국 은행은 그 회사를 폐업시키려고 결심한 것 같다. ■ 구동사 (자동차의 창문 등을) 감아올리다 ❏ 그가 창문을 올리기 시작했으나 내가 문을 잡고 열었다. ■ 구동사 약올리다 [영국영어, 비격식체] ❏ 이 여자가 나를 정말 약올렸다. 그녀는 계속 내 얘기를 했다.

가산명사 뜻밖의 횡재 ❏ 은행의 실수로 25만 파운드의 횡재를 한 남자

Word Web　　wind

The earth's surface **temperature** isn't the same everywhere. This temperature difference causes **air** to flow from one area to another. We call this airflow **wind**. As warm air expands and rises, air pressure goes down. Then denser cool air **blows** in. The amount of difference in air pressure determines how strong the wind will be. It can be anything from a **breeze** to a **gale**. The earth's geography creates prevailing winds. For example, air in the warmer areas near the Equator is always rising, and cooler air from polar regions is always flowing in to take its place.

wind|mill /wɪndmɪl/ (**windmills**) N-COUNT A **windmill** is a building with long pieces of wood on the outside which turn around as the wind blows and provide energy for a machine that crushes grain. A **windmill** is also a similar structure that is used to convert the power of the wind into electricity.

가산명사 풍차; 풍력 발전기

win|dow ♦♦◇ /wɪndoʊ/ (**windows**) ■ N-COUNT A **window** is a space in the wall of a building or in the side of a vehicle, which has glass in it so that light can come in and you can see out. □ *He stood at the window, moodily staring out.* □ *The room felt very hot and she wondered why someone did not open a window.* ■ N-COUNT A **window** is a glass-covered opening above a counter, for example in a bank, post office, train station, or museum, which the person serving you sits behind. □ *The woman at the ticket window told me that the admission fee was $17.50.* ■ N-COUNT On a computer screen, a **window** is one of the work areas that the screen can be divided into. [COMPUTING] □ *Yahoo! Pager puts a small window on your screen containing a list of your "friends."* ■ PHRASE If you say that something such as a plan or a particular way of thinking or behaving **has gone out of the window** or **has flown out of the window**, you mean that it has disappeared completely. □ *By now all logic had gone out of the window.*

■ 가산명사 창문, 유리창 □ 그는 창가에 서서 우울하게 창밖을 응시하고 있었다. □ 방이 무척 더워서 그녀는 왜 아무도 창문을 열지 않았는지 의아했다. ■ 가산명사 창구, 매표구 □ 매표구 안의 여자가 입장료가 17달러 50센트라고 내게 말했다. ■ 가산명사 (컴퓨터) 창, 윈도우 [컴퓨터] □ '야후! 페이저'는 화면에 '친구들' 목록이 들어 있는 작은 창을 열어 준다. ■ 구 이미 사라져 버리다, 이미 날아가 버리다 □ 이제는 모든 논리가 사라져 버렸다.

Word Partnership	*window*의 연어
ADJ.	**open** window ■
	broken window, **dark** window, **large/small** window, **narrow** window ■ ■
V.	**close/open** a window ■
	look in/out a window, **peer in/into/out/through** a window, **watch through** a window ■ ■
N.	**car** window, window **curtains**, **kitchen** window, window **screen** ■ window **display**, **shop** window, **store** window ■

wind|screen /wɪndskriːn/ (**windscreens**) N-COUNT The **windscreen** of a car or other vehicle is the glass window at the front through which the driver looks. [BRIT; AM **windshield**]

가산명사 (자동차 등의) 전면부 유리 [영국영어; 미국영어 windshield]

wind|screen wip|er (**windscreen wipers**) N-COUNT A **windscreen wiper** is the same as a **windshield wiper**. [BRIT] [usu pl]

가산명사 앞유리 와이퍼 [영국영어]

wind|shield /wɪndʃiːld/ (**windshields**) N-COUNT The **windshield** of a car or other vehicle is the glass window at the front through which the driver looks. [AM; BRIT **windscreen**]

가산명사 (자동차 등의) 전면부 유리 [미국영어; 영국영어 windscreen]

wind|shield wip|er (**windshield wipers**) N-COUNT A **windshield wiper** is a device that wipes rain from a vehicle's windshield. [AM; BRIT **windscreen wiper**]

가산명사 (자동차 등의) 와이퍼 [미국영어; 영국영어 windscreen wiper]

wind|surf|ing /wɪndsɜːrfɪŋ/ N-UNCOUNT **Windsurfing** is a sport in which you move along the surface of the sea or a lake on a long narrow board with a sail on it.

불가산명사 윈드서핑, 파도타기

windy /wɪndi/ (**windier, windiest**) ADJ If it is **windy**, the wind is blowing a lot. □ *It was windy and Jake felt cold.*

형용사 바람이 많이 부는 □ 바람이 많이 불어 제이크는 추위를 느꼈다.

wine ♦♦◇ /waɪn/ (**wines**) N-MASS **Wine** is an alcoholic drink which is made from grapes. You can also refer to alcoholic drinks made from other fruits or vegetables as **wine**. □ *...a bottle of white wine.*

물질명사 포도주; 과실주 □ 백포도주 한 병

wine bar (**wine bars**) N-COUNT A **wine bar** is a place where people can buy and drink wine, and sometimes eat food as well.

가산명사 와인 바

wing ♦♦◇ /wɪŋ/ (**wings**) ■ N-COUNT The **wings** of a bird or insect are the two parts of its body that it uses for flying. □ *The bird flapped its wings furiously.* ■ N-COUNT The **wings** of an airplane are the long flat parts sticking out of its side which support it while it is flying. □ *The plane made one pass, dipped its wings, then circled back.* ■ N-COUNT A **wing** of a building is a part of it which sticks out from the main part. □ *We were given an office in the empty west wing.* ■ N-COUNT A **wing** of an organization, especially a political organization, is a group within it which has a particular function or particular beliefs. □ *...the military wing of the African National Congress.* →see also **left-wing, right-wing** ■ N-PLURAL In a theater, **the wings** are the sides of the stage which are hidden from the audience by curtains or scenery. □ *Most nights I watched the start of the play from the wings.* ■ PHRASE If you say that someone is waiting **in the wings**, you mean that they are ready and waiting for an opportunity to take action. □ *There are now more than 20 big companies waiting in the wings to take over some of its business.* ■ PHRASE If you **spread your wings**, you do something new and rather difficult or move to a new place, because you feel more confident in your abilities than you used to and you want to gain wider experience. □ *I led a very confined life in my village so I suppose that I wanted to spread my wings.* ■ PHRASE If you **take** someone **under** your **wing**, you look after them, help them, and protect them. □ *Her boss took her under his wing after fully realizing her potential.* →see **bird**

■ 가산명사 날개 □ 그 새는 날개를 힘차게 퍼덕였다. ■ 가산명사 (비행기의) 날개 □ 그 비행기는 한 번 지나가서, 급강하한 다음, 선회하여 되돌아왔다. ■ 가산명사 (본관에 연결된) 부속 건물, 윙 □ 우리는 비어 있는 서쪽 윙의 사무실을 받았다. ■ 가산명사 (조직의) 단 □ 아프리카 국민 회의의 군사단 ■ 복수명사 (무대의) 좌우 열 □ 거의 밤마다 나는 무대 옆에서 연극이 시작되는 것을 지켜보았다. ■ 구 대기하고 있는 □ 지금 20개 이상의 큰 회사들이 그 사업의 일부를 인수하려고 대기하고 있다. ■ 구 (비유적으로) 날개를 펴다 □ 내가 고향 마을에 갇혀 살았기 때문에 날개를 한 번 펼쳐 보고 싶었던 것 같다. ■ 구 (~을) 보호 육성하다 □ 사장은 그녀의 잠재력을 완전히 깨닫고 나서 그녀를 보호하며 키웠다.

Word Partnership	*wing*의 연어
N.	**aircraft** wing ■
ADJ.	**military/political** wing ■

winged /wɪŋd/ ADJ A **winged** insect or other creature has wings. □ *Flycatchers feed primarily on winged insects.*

형용사 날개가 있는 □ 딱새는 주로 날개 달린 곤충을 먹고 산다.

wink /wɪŋk/ (**winks, winking, winked**) ■ V-I When you **wink at** someone, you look toward them and close one eye very briefly, usually as a signal that something is a joke or a secret. □ *Brian winked at his bride-to-be.* ● N-COUNT **Wink** is also a noun. □ *I gave her a wink.* ■ PHRASE If you say that you **did not**

■ 자동사 윙크하다 □ 브라이언은 자기 신부가 될 사람에게 윙크를 했다. ● 가산명사 윙크 □ 나는 그녀에게 윙크를 했다. ■ 구 한숨도 못 자다 [비격식체] □ 나는 비행기에서 한숨도 자지 못했다.

sleep a wink or **did not get a wink of sleep**, you mean that you tried to go to sleep but could not. [INFORMAL] ❑ *I didn't get a wink of sleep on the aeroplane.*

win|ner ♦♦◇ /wɪnər/ (**winners**) N-COUNT The **winner** of a prize, race, or competition is the person, animal, or thing that wins it. ❑ *She will present the trophies to the award winners.* →see **lottery**

win|ning ♦◇◇ /wɪnɪŋ/ **1** ADJ You can use **winning** to describe a person or thing that wins something such as a competition, game, or election. [ADJ n] ❑ *The leader of the winning party took her oath of office as prime minister.* **2** ADJ You can use **winning** to describe actions or qualities that please other people and make them feel friendly toward you. [ADJ n] ❑ *She gave him another of her winning smiles.* **3** →see also **win**

win|nings /wɪnɪŋz/ N-PLURAL You can use **winnings** to refer to the money that someone wins in a competition or by gambling. ❑ *I have come to collect my winnings.*

win|ter ♦♦◇ /wɪntər/ (**winters**) N-VAR **Winter** is the season between fall and spring. In the winter the weather is usually cold. ❑ *In winter the nights are long and cold.* ❑ *...the late winter of 1941.*

win-win ADJ A **win-win** situation is one where you are certain to do well or be successful. ❑ *It is surprising that it has taken people so long to take advantage of what is a win-win opportunity.*

wipe ♦♦◇ /waɪp/ (**wipes, wiping, wiped**) **1** V-T If you **wipe** something, you rub its surface to remove dirt or liquid from it. ❑ *I'll just wipe the table.* ❑ *When he had finished washing he began to wipe the basin clean.* ● N-COUNT **Wipe** is also a noun. ❑ *Tomorrow I'm going to give the toys a good wipe as some seem a bit greasy.* **2** V-T If you **wipe** dirt or liquid from something, you remove it, for example by using a cloth or your hand. ❑ *Gleb wiped the sweat from his face.* **3** N-COUNT A **wipe** is a small moist cloth for cleaning things and is designed to be used only once. ❑ *...antiseptic wipes.*

▶**wipe out** PHRASAL VERB To **wipe out** something such as a place or a group of people or animals means to destroy them completely. ❑ *Experts say if the island is not protected, the spill could wipe out the Gulf's turtle population.*

wip|er /waɪpər/ (**wipers**) N-COUNT A **wiper** is a device that wipes rain from a vehicle's windshield.

wire ♦♦◇ /waɪər/ (**wires, wiring, wired**) **1** N-VAR A **wire** is a long thin piece of metal that is used to fasten things or to carry electric current. ❑ *...fine copper wire.* **2** N-COUNT A **wire** is a cable which carries power or signals from one place to another. ❑ *I ripped out the telephone wire that ran through to his office.* **3** V-T If you **wire** something such as a building or piece of equipment, you put wires inside it so that electricity or signals can pass into or through it. ❑ *...learning to wire and plumb the house herself.* ❑ *Each of the homes has a security system and is wired for cable television.* ● PHRASAL VERB **Wire up** means the same as **wire**. ❑ *He was helping wire up the Channel Tunnel last season.* **4** PHRASE If something goes **to the wire**, it continues until the last possible moment. [MAINLY JOURNALISM] ❑ *Negotiators again worked right down to the wire to reach an agreement.* **5** →see also **barbed wire** →see **metal**

wire|less /waɪərlɪs/ (**wirelesses**) **1** ADJ **Wireless** technology uses radio waves rather than electricity and therefore does not require any wires. ❑ *...the fast-growing wireless communication market.* **2** N-COUNT A **wireless** or **wireless set** is a radio. [BRIT, OLD-FASHIONED] →see **cellphone**

wir|ing /waɪərɪŋ/ N-UNCOUNT The **wiring** in a building or machine is the system of wires that supply electricity to the different parts of it. ❑ *Faulty wiring is the major cause of house fires.*

wiry /waɪəri/ **1** ADJ Someone who is **wiry** is rather thin but is also strong. ❑ *His body is wiry and athletic.* **2** ADJ Something such as hair or grass that is **wiry** is stiff and rough to touch. ❑ *Her wiry hair was pushed up on top of her head in an untidy bun.*

wis|dom /wɪzdəm/ **1** N-UNCOUNT **Wisdom** is the ability to use your experience and knowledge in order to make sensible decisions or judgments. ❑ *...the patience and wisdom that comes from old age.* **2** N-SING If you talk about **the wisdom of** a particular decision or action, you are talking about how sensible it is. ❑ *Many Lithuanians have expressed doubts about the wisdom of the decision.*

wise ♦♦◇ /waɪz/ (**wiser, wisest**) **1** ADJ A **wise** person is able to use their experience and knowledge in order to make sensible decisions and judgments. ❑ *She has the air of a wise woman.* ● **wise|ly** ADV [ADV with v] ❑ *The three of us stood around the machine nodding wisely.* **2** ADJ A **wise** action or decision is sensible. ❑ *It's never wise to withhold evidence.* ❑ *She had made a very wise decision.* ● **wise|ly** ADV ❑ *They've invested their money wisely.*

wish ♦♦◇ /wɪʃ/ (**wishes, wishing, wished**) **1** N-COUNT A **wish** is a desire or strong feeling that you want to have something or do something. ❑ *She was sincere and genuine in her wish to make amends for the past.* ❑ *The decision was made*

가산명사 우승자, 수상자 ❑ 그녀가 수상자들에게 트로피를 수여할 것이다.

1 형용사 이긴, 승리한 ❑ 승리한 당의 총재가 수상 취임 선서를 했다. **2** 형용사 마음을 끄는, 애교 있는 ❑ 그녀가 그에게 한 번 더 매력적인 미소를 보냈다.

복수명사 (경기의) 상금; (도박에서) 딴 돈 ❑ 나는 상금을 찾으러 왔다.

가산명사 또는 불가산명사 겨울 ❑ 겨울에는 밤이 길고 춥다. ❑ 1941년의 늦겨울

형용사 승산이 확실한 ❑ 사람들이 승산이 확실한 기회를 이용하는 데 시간이 그렇게 오래 걸리는 것이 놀랍다.

1 타동사 닦다, 훔치다 ❑ 탁자를 닦기만 할게. ❑ 그는 세안을 마치고 세면대를 깨끗이 닦기 시작했다. ● 가산명사 닦기 ❑ 장난감 일부가 기름기가 조금 묻은 것 같아서 내일 내가 잘 닦으려고 한다. **2** 타동사 닦아내다 ❑ 글렙은 얼굴의 땀을 닦아냈다. **3** 가산명사 일회용 물휴지 ❑ 일회용 항균 물휴지

구동사 완전히 없애다 ❑ 전문가들은 그 섬을 보호하지 않으면 그 기름 유출로 인해서 걸프 만의 거북이 개체군이 완전히 없어질 것이라고 말한다.

가산명사 (자동차의) 와이퍼

1 가산명사 또는 불가산명사 철사, 전선 ❑ 가는 구리선 **2** 가산명사 전선, 전선선 ❑ 나는 그의 사무실로 통하는 전화선을 잡아 뜯어 버렸다. **3** 타동사 전선을 가설하다, 배선하다 ❑ 그녀가 직접 집에 배선을 하고 배관을 하는 것을 배우고 ❑ 집집마다 보안 장치가 되어 있고 유선 텔레비전이 설치되어 있다. ● 구동사 전선을 가설하다 ❑ 그는 지난 시즌에 영불 해협 해저 터널의 전선 가설을 돕고 있었다. **4** 구 마지막 순간까지 [주로 언론] ❑ 교섭자들은 합의에 이르기 위해 또 다시 바로 마지막 순간까지 일했다.

1 형용사 무선의 ❑ 급속히 성장하는 무선 통신 시장 **2** 가산명사 라디오 [영국영어, 구식어]

불가산명사 배선망 ❑ 배선 결함이 가옥 화재의 주요 원인이다.

1 형용사 마르고도 강인한 ❑ 그의 몸은 말랐지만 강인하고 운동 능력이 뛰어나다. **2** 형용사 억센, 뻣뻣한 ❑ 그녀의 억센 머리털은 머리 위로 틀어 올려 대충 쪽을 찌고 있었다.

1 불가산명사 지혜, 현명 ❑ 노년에서 오는 인내와 지혜 **2** 단수명사 -의 현명함 ❑ 많은 리투아니아 사람들이 그 결정이 현명한 것인지에 대해서 의구심을 보였다.

1 형용사 현명한 ❑ 그녀에게는 현명한 여인의 분위기가 있다. ● 현명하게 부사 ❑ 우리 셋은 그 기계 주위에 둘러서서 아는 듯이 고개를 끄덕였다. **2** 형용사 분별 있는, 사려 깊은 ❑ 증거를 제시하지 않고 보류해 두는 것은 분별 있는 처사다. ❑ 그녀는 아주 현명한 결정을 내렸었다. ● 분별 있게 부사 ❑ 그들은 자기들의 돈을 분별 있게 투자했다.

1 가산명사 소망, 희망 ❑ 그녀가 과거에 대한 보상을 하려는 소망은 진지하고 진실했다. ❑ 그 결정은 당 총재의 소망과 반대 방향으로 내려졌다.

against the wishes of the party leader. **2** V-T/V-I If you **wish** to do something or to have it done for you, you want to do it or have it done. [FORMAL] ❑ *If you wish to go away for the weekend, our office will be delighted to make hotel reservations.* ❑ *We can dress as we wish now.* **3** V-T If you **wish** something were true, you would like it to be true, even though you know that it is impossible or unlikely. [no cont] ❑ *I wish I could do that.* ❑ *Pa, I wish you wouldn't shout.* **4** V-T If you **wish for** something, you express the desire for that thing silently to yourself. In fairy tales, when a person wishes for something, the thing they wish for often happens by magic. ❑ *We have all wished for men who are more like women.* ● N-COUNT **Wish** is also a noun. ❑ *The custom is for people to try and eat 12 grapes as the clock strikes midnight. Those who are successful can make a wish.* **5** V-T If you say that you would not **wish** a particular thing on someone, you mean that the thing is so unpleasant that you would not want them to be forced to experience it. [no cont, with brd-neg] ❑ *It's a horrid experience and I wouldn't wish it on my worst enemy.* **6** V-T If you **wish** someone something such as luck or happiness, you express the hope that they will be lucky or happy. ❑ *I wish you both a very good journey.* **7** N-PLURAL If you express your good **wishes** toward someone, you are politely expressing your friendly feelings toward them and your hope that they will be successful or happy. [POLITENESS] ❑ *I found George's story very sad. Please give him my best wishes.*

> Note that **wish** and **want** have similar meanings, but are used differently. If you **want** something, you feel a need for it or a desire to have it. You can say that you **want** to do something, that you **want** someone to do something, or that you **want** something to happen. If you use **wish** with a "to" infinitive, this has the same meaning as **want** but is more formal. ❑ *I want to get out of here... She wished to consult him about her future.* **Wish** is normally followed by a "that"-clause, although the word "that" is often omitted from the clause. If you **wish** that something was the case, you would like it to be the case, even though this is unlikely or impossible. ❑ *I wish I lived near Miami... He wished he had phoned for a cab.* Note the use of the tenses in the examples; when **wish** is in the present tense, the past tense is used in the clause, and when **wish** is in the past tense, the past perfect tense is used in the clause.

Word Partnership   *wish*의 연어

V.	**get your** wish, **grant a** wish, **have a** wish, **make a** wish **1 4** wish **come true 4**
N.	wish *someone* **the best**, wish *someone* **luck 6**

wish|ful think|ing N-UNCOUNT If you say that an idea, wish, or hope is **wishful thinking**, you mean that it has failed to come true or is unlikely to come true. ❑ *It is wishful thinking to expect deeper change under his leadership.*

wist|ful /ˈwɪstfəl/ ADJ Someone who is **wistful** is rather sad because they want something and know that they cannot have it. ❑ *I can't help feeling slightly wistful about the perks I'm giving up.*

wit /wɪt/ (**wits**) **1** N-UNCOUNT **Wit** is the ability to use words or ideas in an amusing, clever, and imaginative way. ❑ *Boulding was known for his biting wit.* **2** N-SING If you say that someone has **the wit to** do something, you mean that they have the intelligence and understanding to make the right decision or take the right action in a particular situation. ❑ *The information is there and waiting to be accessed by anyone with the wit to use it.* **3** N-PLURAL You can refer to your ability to think quickly and cleverly in a difficult situation as your **wits**. ❑ *She has used her wits to progress to the position she holds today.* **4** N-PLURAL You can use **wits** in expressions such as **frighten** someone **out of their wits** and **scare the wits out of** someone to emphasize that a person or thing worries or frightens someone very much. [EMPHASIS] ❑ *You scared us out of our wits. We heard you had an accident.*

witch /wɪtʃ/ (**witches**) **1** N-COUNT In fairy tales, a **witch** is a woman, usually an old woman, who has evil magic powers. Witches often wear a pointed black hat, and have a pet black cat. **2** N-COUNT A **witch** is a man or woman who claims to have magic powers and to be able to use them for good or bad purposes.

witch|craft /ˈwɪtʃkræft/ N-UNCOUNT **Witchcraft** is the use of magic powers, especially evil ones. ❑ *This week Sabrina uses witchcraft to overcome her fear of giving a speech.*

witch-hunt (**witch-hunts**) N-COUNT A **witch-hunt** is an attempt to find and punish a particular group of people who are being blamed for something, often simply because of their opinions and not because they have actually done anything wrong. [DISAPPROVAL] ❑ *...U.S. Senator Joe McCarthy, who led the witch-hunt against alleged communists in the 1950s.*

with ♦♦♦ /wɪð/ /wɪθ/ /wɪð, wɪθ/

> In addition to the uses shown below, **with** is used after some verbs, nouns and adjectives in order to introduce extra information. **With** is also used in most reciprocal verbs, such as "agree" or "fight," and in some phrasal verbs, such as "deal with" and "dispense with."

1 PREP If one person is **with** another, they are together in one place. ❑ *With her were her son and daughter-in-law.* **2** PREP If something is put **with** or is **with** something else, they are used at the same time. ❑ *Serve hot, with pasta or rice and French beans.* **3** PREP If you do something **with** someone else, you both do it together or are both involved in it. ❑ *Parents will be given reports on their child's progress and the right to discuss it with a teacher.* **4** PREP If you fight, argue, or compete **with** someone, you oppose them. ❑ *About a thousand students*

2 타동사/자동사 희망하다, 원하다 [격식체] ❑ 주말에 어디론가 떠나고 싶으시면, 저희 회사에서 기꺼이 호텔 예약을 해 드리겠습니다. ❑ 우리는 이제 원하는 대로 옷을 입을 수 있다. **3** 타동사 −이면 좋겠다고 생각하다 ❑ 내가 그것을 할 수 있으면 좋겠는데. ❑ 아빠, 소리 좀 지르지 말았으면 좋겠어요. **4** 자동사 소망을 하다, 소원을 빌다 ❑ 우리 모두는 더 여자 같은 남자를 소망한다. ● 가산명사 소망, 소원 ❑ 시계가 자정을 알릴 때 포도 12알을 먹는 풍습이 있다. 그렇게 한 사람은 소원을 빌 수 있다. **5** 타동사 −에게 ...을 강요하다 ❑ 그것은 끔찍한 경험이었고 나는 내 철천지원수라도 그것을 겪게 하고 싶지 않다. **6** 타동사 (−에게 ...을) 빌다, 기원하다 ❑ 두 분 모두 아주 좋은 여행되시기를 빕니다. **7** 복수명사 축원, 안부 [공손체] ❑ 조지의 일은 정말 안됐군요. 그에게 제 축원을 전해 주시기 바랍니다.

> wish와 want가 비슷한 뜻을 가졌지만 다르게 쓰인다는 것을 유의하라. 만일 무엇을 want하면, 그것을 필요로 하거나, 갖고 싶어 하는 것이다. want to do something, want someone to do something이나 want something to happen이라고 쓴다. 만일 wish를 부정사와 같이 사용하면, 이것은 want와 같은 뜻이지만 좀 더 격식적이다. ❑ 나는 여기서 벗어나고 싶다... 그녀는 자신의 미래에 관해서 그와 상의하기를 희망했다. wish 뒤에는 보통 that 절이 따라온다. 절에서 that은 흔히 생략되기도 한다. 만일 무엇이 어떠하기를 wish하면, 비록 그것이 일어날 법하지 않거나 불가능할지라도 일이 그렇게 되기를 원하는 것이다. ❑ 나는 마이애미에 근처에 살고 있으면 좋겠다... 그는 전화로 택시를 불렀더라면 좋았을텐데 하고 생각했다. 이 예문들에서의 시제에 주의하라. wish가 현재시제이면, 그 뒤에 오는 절에는 과거시제를 쓰고, wish가 과거시제이면, 뒤의 절에 과거완료시제를 쓴다.

불가산명사 희망 사항 (에 불과한 일) ❑ 그의 치하에서 심각한 변화를 기대하는 것은 희망 사항일 뿐이다.

형용사 동경하는, 아쉬운 듯한 ❑ 나는 내가 포기해야 하는 특전에 대해 조금은 아쉬워하지 않을 수 없다.

1 불가산명사 재치, 위트 ❑ 보울딩은 신랄한 위트로 유명하다. **2** 단수명사 이해력, 분별력 ❑ 그 정보는 그것을 사용할 만한 분별이 있는 사람에게는 누구나 접근이 가능하도록 되어 있다. **3** 복수명사 기지 ❑ 그녀는 기지를 발휘해서 현재 차지하고 있는 지위에 올랐다. **4** 복수명사 제정신, 분별; (놀라서 해서) 제정신이 아니게 만들다 [강조] ❑ 우리는 너 때문에 놀라서 정신이 나갔었다. 우리는 네가 사고를 당했다고 들었다.

1 가산명사 마녀, 마귀할멈 **2** 가산명사 마법사

불가산명사 마법 ❑ 이번 주에는 사브리나가 마법을 사용해서 연설에 대한 두려움을 극복합니다.

가산명사 마녀 사냥 [탄핵찾음] ❑ 1950년대에 공산주의 혐의자에 대한 마녀 사냥을 이끌었던 미국 상원 의원 조 맥카시

> with는 아래 용법 외에도 추가 정보를 나타내기 위해 일부의 동사, 명사, 형용사 뒤에 쓴다. 또한 'agree', 'fight'과 같은 상호 동사와 'keep on at', 'play at'과 같은 구동사에도 쓰인다.

1 전치사 −와 함께 ❑ 아들과 며느리가 그녀와 함께 있었다. **2** 전치사 −와 같이, −와 함께 ❑ 파스타나 밥과 강낭콩을 곁들여 뜨겁게 차려내세요. **3** 전치사 −와 함께 ❑ 부모는 자녀의 학업진전에 대한 성적표를 받고, 그것에 대해 선생님과 상의할 권리도 갖게 될 것입니다. **4** 전치사 −을 상대로, −와 ❑ 약 천 명의 학생이 수도에서 폭동 진압 경찰을 상대로 싸웠다.

fought with riot police in the capital. **5** PREP If you do something **with** a particular tool, object, or substance, you do it using that tool, object, or substance. ❑ *Remove the meat with a fork and divide it among four plates.* ❑ *Pack the fruits and nuts into the jars and cover with brandy.* **6** PREP If someone stands or goes somewhere **with** something, they are carrying it. ❑ *A young woman came in with a cup of coffee.* **7** PREP Someone or something **with** a particular feature or possession has that feature or possession. ❑ *He was in his early forties, tall and blond with bright blue eyes.* **8** PREP Someone **with** an illness has that illness. ❑ *I spent a week in bed with flu.* **9** PREP If something is filled or covered **with** a substance or **with** things, that substance or those things is in it or on it. ❑ *His legs were caked with dried mud.* **10** PREP If you are, for example, pleased or annoyed **with** someone or something, you have that feeling toward them. [adj/n PREP n] ❑ *He was still a little angry with her.* **11** PREP You use **with** to indicate what a state, quality, or action relates to, involves, or affects. ❑ *Our aim is to allow student teachers to become familiar with the classroom.* ❑ *He still has a serious problem with money.* **12** PREP You use **with** when indicating the way that something is done or the feeling that a person has when they do something. ❑ *...teaching her to read music with skill and sensitivity.* **13** PREP You use **with** when indicating a sound or gesture that is made when something is done, or an expression that a person has on their face when they do something. ❑ *With a sigh, she leant back and closed her eyes.* **14** PREP You use **with** to indicate that someone have a particular appearance or type of behavior. ❑ *Gil was white and trembling with anger.* **15** PREP You use **with** when mentioning the position or appearance of a person or thing at the time that they do something, or what someone else is doing at that time. [PREP n prep/-ing] ❑ *Joanne stood with her hands on the sink, staring out the window.* **16** PREP You use **with** to introduce a current situation that is a factor affecting another situation. ❑ *With all the night school courses available, there is no excuse for not getting some sort of training.* **17** PREP You use **with** when making a comparison or contrast between the situations of different people or things. ❑ *We're not like them. It's different with us.* **18** PREP If something increases or decreases **with** a particular factor, it changes as that factor changes. [v PREP n] ❑ *The risk of developing heart disease increases with the number of cigarettes smoked.* **19** PREP If something moves **with** a wind or current, it moves in the same direction as the wind or current. ❑ *...a piece of driftwood carried down with the current.* **20** PREP If someone says that they are **with** you, they mean that they understand what you are saying. [INFORMAL] [v-link PREP n] ❑ *Yes, I know who you mean. Yes, now I'm with you.* **21** PREP If someone says that they are **with** you, they mean that they support or approve of what you are doing. [v-link PREP n] ❑ *"I'm with you all the way." — "Thank you."*

Word Link

with ≈ against, away : with**draw**, with**hold**, with**stand**

---

with|draw ♦♢◇ /wɪθˈdrɔ, wɪθ-/ (**withdraws**, **withdrawing**, **withdrew**, **withdrawn**) **1** V-T If you **withdraw** something from a place, you remove it or take it away. [FORMAL] ❑ *He reached into his pocket and withdrew a sheet of notepaper.* **2** V-T/V-I When groups of people such as troops **withdraw** or when someone **withdraws** them, they leave the place where they are fighting or where they are based and return nearer home. ❑ *He stated that all foreign forces would withdraw as soon as the crisis ended.* ❑ *The United States has announced it is to withdraw forty-thousand troops from Western Europe in the next year.* **3** V-T If you **withdraw** money from a bank account, you take it out of that account. ❑ *Open a savings account that does not charge ridiculous fees to withdraw money.* **4** V-I If you **withdraw from** an activity or organization, you stop taking part in it. ❑ *The African National Congress threatened to withdraw from the talks.*

Word Partnership   withdraw의 연어

N.   withdraw **an offer**, withdraw **support** **1**
    decision to withdraw **1** **4**
    deadline to withdraw, **forces/troops** withdraw **2**
    withdraw **money** **3**

---

with|draw|al ♦♢◇ /wɪθˈdrɔəl, wɪθ-/ (**withdrawals**) **1** N-VAR The **withdrawal** of something is the act or process of removing it, or ending it. [FORMAL] ❑ *If you experience any unusual symptoms after withdrawal of the treatment then contact your doctor.* **2** N-UNCOUNT Someone's **withdrawal from** an activity or an organization is their decision to stop taking part in it. ❑ *...his withdrawal from government in 1946.* **3** N-COUNT A **withdrawal** is an amount of money that you take from your bank account. ❑ *I went to the machine to make the withdrawal and it told me to see someone inside the bank.* **4** N-UNCOUNT **Withdrawal** is the period during which someone feels ill after they have stopped taking a drug which they were addicted to. ❑ *Withdrawal from heroin is actually like a severe attack of gastric flu.*

with|drawn /wɪθˈdrɔn, wɪθ-/ **1** **Withdrawn** is the past participle of **withdraw**. **2** ADJ Someone who is **withdrawn** is very quiet, and does not want to talk to other people. [v-link ADJ] ❑ *Her husband had become withdrawn and moody.* →see **bank**

with|drew /wɪθˈdru, wɪθ-/ **Withdrew** is the past tense of **withdraw**.

with|er /wɪðər/ (**withers**, **withering**, **withered**) **1** V-I If someone or something **withers**, they become very weak. ❑ *When he went into retirement, he visibly withered.* ● PHRASAL VERB **Wither away** means the same as **wither**. ❑ *To see my body literally wither away before my eyes was exasperating.* **2** V-I If a flower or plant **withers**, it dries up and dies. ❑ *The flowers in Isabel's room had withered.*

---

5 전치사 -을 사용하여, -으로 ❑ 포크로 고기를 들어내어 접시 네 개에 나눠 담으세요. ❑ 과일과 견과류를 병에 채워 넣고 가득 잠기도록 브랜디를 부으세요. **6** 전치사 -을 가지고 ❑ 젊은 여자가 커피 한 잔을 가지고 들어왔다. **7** 전치사 -을 가진 ❑ 그는 사십 대 초반에, 키가 크고, 반짝이는 푸른 눈에 금발이었다. **8** 전치사 -때문에, -으로 인해 ❑ 나는 독감으로 일주일을 누워 있었다. **9** 전치사 -으로 ❑ 그의 다리는 마른 진흙으로 범벅이 되어 있었다. **10** 전치사 -에, -에 대하여 ❑ 그는 여전히 그녀에게 조금 화가 나 있었다. **11** 전치사 -에 관해서 ❑ 우리의 목표는 교생들이 학급에 익숙해지도록 하는 것이다. ❑ 그에게는 여전히 심각한 금전 문제가 있다. **12** 전치사 -로, -하게, -하며 ❑ 그녀에게 음악을 기교와 감수성을 가지고 이해하도록 가르치기 **13** 전치사 -하면서, -하며 ❑ 한숨을 쉬면서 그녀가 뒤로 기대며 눈을 감았다. **14** 전치사 -으로 인해 ❑ 질은 화가 나서 하얗게 질려 몸을 떨고 있었다. **15** 전치사 -으로, -한 채 ❑ 조앤은 양손을 싱크대에 올려놓은 채로 창밖을 응시하며 서 있었다. **16** 전치사 -인 상황에서 ❑ 그 많은 야간 학교 강좌들이 있는 상황에서, 어느 정도 교육을 받지 못하는 것에 대해서는 변명이 있을 수 없다. **17** 전치사 -에 있어서는, -의 경우는 ❑ 우리들은 그들과 같지 않다. 그건 우리 경우에는 다르다. **18** 전치사 -에 따라서, -와 비례하여 ❑ 심장병에 걸릴 위험은 피운 담배의 개수에 비례해서 증가한다. **19** 전치사 -와 같은 방향으로, -을 타고 ❑ 조류를 타고 떠내려 온 부목 한 조각 **20** 전치사 -을 이해하여 [비격식체] ❑ 네, 누구를 뜻하는지 알겠어요. 그래요, 이제 알아듣겠어요. **21** 전치사 -을 지지하여 ❑ "저는 언제까지나 당신 편입니다." "고맙습니다."

1 타동사 꺼내다, 빼내다 [격식체] ❑ 그는 주머니에 손을 넣어 메모지 한 장을 꺼냈다. **2** 타동사/자동사 (군대 등이) 철수하다; (군대 등을) 철수시키다 ❑ 그는 모든 외국 군대는 위기가 끝나자마자 철수할 것이라고 말했다. ❑ 미국은 내년에 서유럽에서 4만 명의 병력을 철수시킬 예정이라고 발표했다. **3** 타동사 (계좌에서) 인출하다 ❑ 돈을 인출하는 데 터무니없는 수수료를 부과하지 않는 저축 계좌를 만드세요. **4** 자동사 탈퇴하다 ❑ 아프리카 민족 회의는 회담에서 빠지겠다고 위협했다.

1 가산명사 또는 불가산명사 철수, 중단 [격식체] ❑ 치료를 중단한 다음에 조금이라도 이상한 증상이 있으면 의사에게 연락하세요. **2** 불가산명사 탈퇴, 물러남 ❑ 1946년에 그가 정부에서 물러남 **3** 가산명사 인출; 인출액 ❑ 나는 기계로 가서 돈을 인출하려고 했는데 기계가 은행 안에 가서 문의해 보라고 알려주었다. **4** 불가산명사 금단 증상; 금단 증상 기간 ❑ 헤로인 금단 증상은 실제로 배가 아픈 독감에 심하게 걸린 것과 비슷하다.

1 withdraw의 과거 분사 **2** 형용사 내성적인 ❑ 그녀의 남편은 내성적이 되었고 감정의 기복이 심해졌다.

withdraw의 과거

1 자동사 약해지다, 시들다 ❑ 그는 은퇴하자 눈에 띄게 쇠약해졌다. ● 구동사 약해지다, 시들다 ❑ 내 몸이 내 눈앞에서 문자 그대로 시들어 가는 것을 보니 분통이 터졌다. **2** 자동사 시들다, 말라 죽다 ❑ 이사벨의 방에 있는 꽃들이 시들어 죽어 있었다.

with|ered /wɪðərd/ ADJ If you describe a person or a part of their body as **withered**, you mean that they are thin and their skin looks old. □ *Diana grasped his face in her withered hands.*

형용사 마르고 쭈글쭈글한 □ 다이애나는 마르고 쭈글쭈글한 두 손으로 그의 얼굴을 잡았다.

Word Link   with ≈ against, away : with**draw**, with**hold**, with**stand**

---

with|hold /wɪðhoʊld, wɪθ-/ (withholds, withholding, withheld /wɪðheld, wɪθ-/) V-T If you **withhold** something that someone wants, you do not let them have it. [FORMAL] □ *Police withheld the dead boy's name yesterday until relatives could be told.*

타동사 억제하다, 보류하다 [격식체] □ 경찰은 어제 사망한 소년의 이름을 친척에게 알릴 때까지 공개하지 않았다.

with|hold|ing tax (withholding taxes) N-VAR A **withholding tax** is an amount of money that is taken in advance from someone's income, in order to pay some of the tax they will owe. [mainly AM, BUSINESS]

가산명사 또는 불가산명사 원천 과세, 원천 과세액 [주로 미국영어, 경제]

with|in ♦♦♦ /wɪðɪn, wɪθ-/ ■ PREP If something is **within** a place, area, or object, it is inside it or surrounded by it. [FORMAL] □ *Clients are entertained within private dining rooms.* ● ADV **Within** is also an adverb. □ *A small voice called from within. "Yes, just coming."* ■ PREP Something that happens or exists **within** a society, organization, or system, happens or exists inside it. □ *...the spirit of self-sacrifice within an army.* ● ADV **Within** is also an adverb. □ *The Church of England, with threats of split from within, has still to make up its mind.* ■ PREP If something is **within** a particular limit or set of rules, it does not go beyond it or is not more than what is allowed. □ *Troops have agreed to stay within specific boundaries to avoid confrontations.* ■ PREP If you are **within** a particular distance of a place, you are less than that distance from it. □ *The man was within a few feet of him.* ■ PREP **Within** a particular length of time means before that length of time has passed. [PREP amount] □ *About 40% of all students entering as freshmen graduate within 4 years.* ■ PREP If something is **within sight**, **within earshot**, or **within reach**, you can see it, hear it, or reach it. □ *His twenty-five-foot boat was moored within sight of West Church.* ■ **within reason** →see reason

■ 전치사 -의 안에 [격식체] □ 고객들은 내실 만찬장 안에서 접대를 받는다. ● 부사 안쪽에서 □ 안에서 작은 목소리가 들려 왔다. "네, 나갑니다." ② 전치사 -의 내부에 □ 군대 내부의 자기희생 정신 ● 부사 내부에서 □ 영국 국교회는, 내부적인 분열의 위협을 받으며, 아직 결단을 내리지 못하고 있다. ③ 전치사 -의 범위 내에서 □ 군대끼리 맞서게 되는 상황을 피하기 위해 특정한 경계선 내에 머물기로 합의했다. ④ 전치사 (거리가) - 이내에 □ 그 남자는 그로부터 몇 피트 이내에 있었다. ⑤ 전치사 (시간이) - 이내에 □ 신입생으로 들어오는 모든 학생의 약 40퍼센트가 4년 이내에 졸업한다. ⑥ 전치사 보이는 곳에; 들리는 곳에; 닿는 곳에 □ 그의 25피트짜리 보트는 웨스트 교회가 보이는 곳에 정박되어 있었다.

with|out ♦♦♦ /wɪðaʊt, wɪθ-/

In addition to the uses shown below, **without** is used in the phrasal verbs "do without," "go without," and "reckon without."

without은 아래 용법 외에도 'do without', 'go without', 'reckon without'과 같은 구동사에 쓰인다.

■ PREP You use **without** to indicate that someone or something does not have or use the thing mentioned. □ *I don't like myself without a beard.* □ *She wore a brown shirt pressed without a wrinkle.* ■ PREP If one thing happens **without** another thing, or if you do something **without** doing something else, the second thing does not happen or occur. [PREP n/-ing] □ *He was offered a generous pension provided he left without a fuss.* □ *They worked without a break until about eight in the evening.* ■ PREP If you do something **without** a particular feeling, you do not have that feeling when you do it. □ *Janet Magnusson watched his approach without enthusiasm.* ■ PREP If you do something **without** someone else, they are not in the same place as you are or are not involved in the same action as you. □ *I told Franklin he would have to start dinner without me.*

■ 전치사 -없이, -없는 □ 나는 수염이 없는 내 모습이 마음에 들지 않는다. □ 그녀는 주름 하나 없이 다린 갈색 셔츠를 입고 있었다. ② 전치사 -하지 않고 □ 그는 조용히 떠날 경우 넉넉한 연금을 주겠다는 제안을 받았다. □ 그들은 저녁 8시경까지 쉬지 않고 일했다. ③ 전치사 - 없이 □ 자넷 매그너슨은 그가 다가오는 것을 별 감흥 없이 바라보았다. ④ 전치사 - 없이 □ 나는 프랭클린에게 나 없이 저녁을 시작해야 할 것이라고 말했다.

with-profits ADJ A **with-profits** savings plan or financial plan is one in which the people who put money into the plan receive extra money each year based on how successful the investment has been. [BUSINESS] [ADJ n] □ *Returns on with-profits bonds have improved.*

형용사 추가 배당 [경제] □ 추가 배당 보장 공채의 수익이 나아졌다.

with|stand /wɪðstænd, wɪθ-/ (withstands, withstanding, withstood /wɪðstʊd, wɪθ-/) V-T If something or someone **withstands** a force or action, they survive it or do not give in to it. [FORMAL] □ *...armoured vehicles designed to withstand chemical attack.*

타동사 견디 내다, 이겨 내다 [격식체] □ 화학무기 공격에 견디도록 고안된 장갑 차량

wit|ness ♦♢♢ /wɪtnɪs/ (witnesses, witnessing, witnessed) ■ N-COUNT A **witness** to an event such as an accident or crime is a person who saw it. □ *Witnesses say the crash say they saw an explosion just before the disaster.* ② V-T If you **witness** something, you see it happen. □ *Anyone who witnessed the attack should call the police.* ③ N-COUNT A **witness** is someone who appears in a court of law to say what they know about a crime or other event. □ *In the next three or four days, eleven witnesses will be called to testify.* ④ N-COUNT A **witness** is someone who writes their name on a document that you have signed, to confirm that it really is your signature. □ *The codicil must first be signed and dated by you in the presence of two witnesses.* ⑤ V-T If someone **witnesses** your signature on a document, they write their name after it, to confirm that it really is your signature. □ *Ask a friend, (not your spouse), to witness your signature.* ⑥ V-T If you say that a place, period of time, or person **witnessed** a particular event or change, you mean that it happened in that place, during that period of time, or while that person was alive. □ *India has witnessed many political changes in recent years.* →see trial, wedding

■ 가산명사 목격자 □ 충돌 사고 목격자들은 사고 직전 폭발이 일어나는 것을 보았다고 말한다. ② 타동사 목격하다 □ 그 폭행을 목격한 사람은 누구든 경찰에 전화해야 한다. ③ 가산명사 증인, 참고인 □ 다음 3-4일간, 11명의 참고인들이 증언을 위해 소환될 것이다. ④ 가산명사 연서인, 입회인 □ 연서하는 두 명의 입회인 하에 당신이 먼저 유언 보충서에 서명하고 날짜를 기입해야 한다. ⑤ 타동사 (증인으로) 서명하다, 인서하다 □ 당신의 서명에 증인으로 연서하도록 (배우자 말고) 친구에게 부탁하세요. ⑥ 타동사 (사건 등을) 목격하다 □ 인도는 최근 몇 년 동안 많은 정치적 변화를 목격했다.

Word Partnership   witness의 연어

v.	**call** a witness, witness **tells**, witness **testifies** ③
N.	**defense** witness, **key** witness, **prosecution** witness, **star** witness ③

---

wit|ty /wɪti/ (wittier, wittiest) ADJ Someone or something that is **witty** is amusing in a clever way. □ *His plays were very good, very witty.*

형용사 재치 있는 □ 그의 희곡 작품들은 매우 훌륭하고 아주 재치가 있었다.

wives /waɪvz/ **Wives** is the plural of **wife**.

wife의 복수형

wiz|ard /wɪzərd/ (wizards) ■ N-COUNT In legends and fairy tales, a **wizard** is a man who has magic powers. ② N-COUNT If you admire someone because they are very good at doing a particular thing, you can say that they are a **wizard**. [APPROVAL] □ *...a financial wizard.* ③ N-COUNT A **wizard** is a computer program

■ 가산명사 마법사 ② 가산명사 달인, 귀재 [마음에 듦] □ 금융의 귀재 ③ 가산명사 (컴퓨터 프로그램) 마법사 [컴퓨터] □ 마법사와 템플릿이 안내 책자, 달력, 웹 페이지를 제작하는 데 도움이 될 수 있다.

that guides you through the stages of a particular task. [COMPUTING] ❑ *Wizards and templates can help you create brochures, calendars, and Web pages.* →see **fantasy**

wk (wks) **wk** is a written abbreviation for **week**.

wob|ble /wɒbªl/ (**wobbles, wobbling, wobbled**) V-I If something or someone **wobbles**, they make small movements from side to side, for example because they are unsteady. ❑ *A gravitational wave made the spacecraft wobble.* ● N-VAR **Wobble** is also a noun. ❑ *We might look for a tiny wobble in the position of a star.*

wob|bly /wɒbli/ ADJ Something that is **wobbly** moves unsteadily from side to side. ❑ *I was sitting on a wobbly plastic chair.* ❑ *...a wobbly green jelly.*

woe /woʊ/ N-UNCOUNT **Woe** is very great sadness. [LITERARY] ❑ *He listened to my tale of woe.*

woe|ful /woʊfəl/ ❶ ADJ If someone or something is **woeful**, they are very sad. ❑ *...a woeful ballad.* ● **woe|ful|ly** ADV [ADV with v] ❑ *He said woefully: "I love my country, but it does not give a damn about me."* ❷ ADJ You can use **woeful** to emphasize that something is very bad or undesirable. [EMPHASIS] ❑ *...the woeful state of the economy.* ● **woe|ful|ly** ADV ❑ *Public expenditure on the arts is woefully inadequate.*

woke /woʊk/ **Woke** is the past tense of **wake**.

wok|en /woʊkən/ **Woken** is the past participle of **wake**.

wolf /wʊlf/ (**wolves, wolfs, wolfing, wolfed**) ❶ N-COUNT A **wolf** is a wild animal that looks like a large dog. ❷ V-T If someone **wolfs** their food, they eat it all very quickly and greedily. [INFORMAL] ❑ *I was back in the changing-room wolfing tea and sandwiches.* ● PHRASAL VERB **Wolf down** means the same as **wolf**. ❑ *He wolfed down the rest of the biscuit and cheese.*

| Word Link | man ≈ human being : fore**man**, hu**mane**, wo**man** |

wom|an ◆◆◇ /wʊmən/ (**women**) ❶ N-COUNT A **woman** is an adult female human being. ❑ *...a young Lithuanian woman named Dayva.* ❑ *...men and women over 75 years old.* ❷ N-UNCOUNT You can refer to women in general as **woman**. ❑ *...the oppression of woman.* ❸ →see also **career woman** →see **age**

wom|an|hood /wʊmənhʊd/ ❶ N-UNCOUNT **Womanhood** is the state of being a woman rather than a girl, or the period of a woman's adult life. ❑ *Pregnancy is a natural part of womanhood.* ❷ N-UNCOUNT You can refer to women in general or the women of a particular country or community as **womanhood**. ❑ *She symbolized for me the best of Indian womanhood.*

womb /wuːm/ (**wombs**) N-COUNT A woman's **womb** is the part inside her body where a baby grows before it is born. ❑ *...the development of the foetus in the womb.*

wom|en /wɪmɪn/ **Women** is the plural of **woman**.

won /wʌn/ **Won** is the past tense and past participle of **win**. →see **election**

won|der ◆◆◇ /wʌndər/ (**wonders, wondering, wondered**) ❶ V-T/V-I If you **wonder** about something, you think about it, either because it interests you and you want to know more about it, or because you are worried or suspicious about it. ❑ *I wondered what that noise was.* ❑ *"He claims to be her father," said Max. "We've been wondering about him."* ❷ V-I If you **wonder at** something, you are very surprised about it or think about it in a very surprised way. ❑ *Walk down Castle Street, admire our little jewel of a cathedral, then wonder at the castle.* ❸ N-SING If you say that it is a **wonder that** something happened, you mean that it is surprising and unexpected. ❑ *It's a wonder that it took almost ten years.* ❹ N-UNCOUNT **Wonder** is a feeling of great surprise and pleasure that you have, for example when you see something that is very beautiful, or when something happens that you thought was impossible. ❑ *"That's right!" Bobby exclaimed in wonder. "How did you remember that?"* ❺ N-COUNT A **wonder** is something that causes people to feel great surprise or admiration. ❑ *...a lecture on the wonders of space and space exploration.* ❻ ADJ If you refer, for example, to a young man as a **wonder** boy, or to a new product as a **wonder** drug, you mean that they are believed by many people to be very good or very effective. [ADJ n] ❑ *Mickelson was hailed as the wonder boy of American golf.* ❼ PHRASE You can say "I **wonder**" if you want to be very polite when you are asking someone to do something, or when you are asking them for their opinion or for information. [POLITENESS] ❑ *I was just wondering if you could help me.* ❽ PHRASE If you say "**no wonder**", "**little wonder**", or "**small wonder**," you mean that something is not surprising. ❑ *No wonder my brother wasn't feeling well.* ❾ PHRASE You can say "**No wonder**" when you find out the reason for something that has been puzzling you for some time. ❑ *Brad was Jane's brother! No wonder he reminded me so much of her!* ❿ PHRASE If you say that a person or thing **works wonders** or **does wonders**, you mean that they have a very good effect on something. ❑ *A few moments of relaxation can work wonders.*

Word Partnership	*wonder*의 연어
V.	**begin to** wonder, wonder **what happened**, **make** *someone* wonder ❶
CONJ.	wonder **how**, wonder **what**, wonder **when**, wonder **where**, wonder **whether**, wonder **who**, wonder **why** ❶ wonder **that** ❸

won|der|ful ◆◆◇ /wʌndərfəl/ ADJ If you describe something or someone as **wonderful**, you think they are extremely good. ❑ *The cold, misty air felt wonderful on his face.* ❑ *It's wonderful to see you.* ● **won|der|ful|ly** ADV ❑ *It's a system that works wonderfully well.*

---

week의 준임말
자동사 기우뚱거리다 ❑ 중력파 때문에 우주선이 기우뚱거렸다. ● 가산명사 또는 불가산명사 기우뚱거림 ❑ 우리는 어쩌면 별 위치가 미세하게 기우뚱거리는 것도 찾을 수 있을 것이다.

형용사 기우뚱한 ❑ 나는 기우뚱한 플라스틱 의자에 앉아 있었다. ❑ 흐늘거리는 녹색 젤리

불가산명사 비애, 비통 [문예체] ❑ 그는 내 비통한 사연에 귀 기울였다.

❶ 형용사 슬픈, 비통한 ❑ 슬픈 연가 ● 비통하게 부사 ❑ 그는 비통하게 말했다: "나는 조국을 사랑하지만, 조국은 나 같은 건 안중에도 없다." ❷ 형용사 한심한, 비참한 [강조] ❑ 비참한 경제 상태 ● 한심하게 부사 ❑ 예술에 대한 공공 지출이 한심할 정도로 부족하다.

wake의 과거

wake의 과거 분사

❶ 가산명사 늑대 ❷ 타동사 게걸스레 먹어 치우다 [비격식체] ❑ 나는 탈의실로 돌아와서 차와 샌드위치를 게걸스레 먹어 치웠다. ● 구동사 게걸스레 먹어 치우다 ❑ 그는 남은 비스킷과 치즈를 게걸스레 먹어 치웠다.

❶ 가산명사 (성인) 여성, 여자 ❑ 다이바라는 이름의 젊은 리투아니아 여성 ❑ 일흔다섯 살 이상의 남녀 ❷ 불가산명사 (집합적) 여성 ❑ 여성 탄압

❶ 불가산명사 여자임, 성인 여성의 생애 ❑ 임신은 여성의 삶의 자연스런 일부이다. ❷ 불가산명사 여성 일반, (한 국가나 지역의) 여성 ❑ 그녀가 내게는 인도 여성 중 최고의 상징이었다.

가산명사 자궁 ❑ 자궁 내 태아의 발육

woman의 복수형

win의 과거, 과거 분사

❶ 타동사/자동사 궁금해하다 ❑ 나는 그 소음이 무엇일까 궁금했다. ❑ "그가 그녀의 아버지라고 주장해."라고 맥스가 말했다. "우리는 내내 그 사람에 대해 궁금했었다." ❷ 자동사 놀라다, 경탄하다 ❑ 캐슬 스트리트를 걸어 내려가서, 우리의 작은 보물인 대성당을 감상하고, 그 다음에 성을 보고 경탄하세요. ❸ 단수명사 경이로운 일, 이상한 일 ❑ 그것이 십 년 가까이 걸렸다는 것은 이상한 일이다. ❹ 불가산명사 경이, 놀라움 ❑ "맞아." 보비가 놀라서 외쳤다. "어떻게 그걸 기억해 냈니? ❺ 가산명사 경이로운 것, 놀라운 일 ❑ 우주와 우주 탐험의 경이에 관한 강연 ❻ 형용사 경이로운, 놀라운 ❑ 미켈슨은 미국 골프계의 신동으로 갈채를 받았다. ❼ 구 혹시 ~할까 생각한다, ~이 아닐까 생각한다 [공손체] ❑ 혹시 절 좀 도와주실 수 있지 않나요? ❽ 구 전혀 이상하지 않다; 별로 이상하지 않다 ❑ 우리 형이 몸이 좋지 않은 게 전혀 이상한 일이 아니지. ❾ 구 ~하는 것이 당연하다 ❑ 브래드가 제인의 오빠라고! 그러니 그를 보면 제인이 그렇게 생각났지. ❿ 구 (사람이) 기적을 이루다; (약 등이) 신통하게 듣다 ❑ 잠깐의 휴식은 놀랄 만한 효과를 가져올 수 있다.

형용사 아주 멋진, 훌륭한 ❑ 그의 얼굴에 와 닿는 차갑고 촉촉한 공기가 상쾌하게 느껴졌다. ❑ 네를 보게 되어 정말 기쁩니다. ● 훌륭하게, 놀랄 만큼 부사 ❑ 그것은 놀랄 만큼 잘 돌아가는 체제이다.

won't /woʊnt/ **Won't** is the usual spoken form of "will not." ❑ *The space shuttle Discovery won't lift off the launch pad until Sunday at the earliest.*

will not의 축약형 ❑ 우주 왕복선 디스커버리 호는 빨라야 일요일에나 발사대에서 이륙할 것이다.

woo /wu/ (**woos, wooing, wooed**) V-T If you **woo** people, you try to encourage them to help you, support you, or vote for you, for example by promising them things which they would like. ❑ *They wooed customers by offering low interest rates.* →see **love**

타동사 얻으려고 애쓰다 ❑ 그들은 낮은 금리를 내세워 고객을 유치하려 했다.

wood ♦♦♢ /wʊd/ (**woods**) **1** N-MASS **Wood** is the material which forms the trunks and branches of trees. ❑ *There was a smell of damp wood and machine oil.* **2** N-COUNT A **wood** is a fairly large area of trees growing near each other. You can refer to one or several of these areas as **woods**, and this is the usual form in American English. ❑ *After dinner Alice slipped away for a walk in the woods with Artie.* **3** PHRASE If something or someone is **not out of the woods** yet, they are still having difficulties or problems. [INFORMAL] ❑ *The nation's economy is not out of the woods yet.* **4** CONVENTION You can say "**knock on wood**" in American English, or "**touch wood**" in British English, to indicate that you hope to have good luck in something you are doing, usually after saying that you have been lucky with it so far. ❑ *I got it all taken care of, knock on wood.* →see **energy**, **fire**, **forest**

1 물질명사 나무, 목재 ❑ 그들의 접시는 목재였다. ❑ 젖은 나무와 기계유 냄새가 났다. **2** 가산명사 숲, 삼림 ❑ 저녁 식사 후에 엘리스는 아티와 숲으로 산책을 가려고 조용히 빠져 나왔다. **3** 구 곤경을 벗어나지 못한 [비격식체] ❑ 나라의 경제가 아직 어려움을 벗어나지 못했다. **4** 관용 표현 행운을 빌다 ❑ 나는 그걸 모두 처리했지, 잘 되길 빌어야지.

wood|ed /wʊdɪd/ ADJ A **wooded** area is covered in trees. ❑ *...a wooded valley.*

형용사 수목이 우거진 ❑ 수목이 우거진 계곡

wood|en ♦♢♢ /wʊdᵊn/ ADJ **Wooden** objects are made of wood. [ADJ n] ❑ *...the shop's bare brick walls and faded wooden floorboards.*

형용사 목재의 ❑ 그 가게의 맨 벽돌 벽과 빛이 바랜 마룻바닥

wood|land /wʊdlənd/ (**woodlands**) N-VAR **Woodland** is land with a lot of trees. ❑ *...an area of dense woodland.*

가산명사 또는 불가산명사 삼림지 ❑ 울창한 삼림 지역

wood|work /wʊdwɜrk/ **1** N-UNCOUNT You can refer to the doors and other wooden parts of a house as the **woodwork**. ❑ *I love the living room, with its dark woodwork, oriental rugs, and chunky furniture.* **2** N-UNCOUNT **Woodwork** is the activity or skill of making things out of wood. ❑ *I have done woodwork for many years.*

1 불가산명사 (가옥의) 목조부 ❑ 나는 짙은 색 목재를 쓴, 동양풍 융단과 큼직한 가구가 있는 거실을 아주 좋아한다. **2** 불가산명사 목공 ❑ 나는 수년 동안 목공 일을 해 왔다.

wool /wʊl/ (**wools**) **1** N-UNCOUNT **Wool** is the hair that grows on sheep and on some other animals. ❑ *A new invention means sheep do not have to be sheared – the wool just falls off.* **2** N-MASS **Wool** is a material made from animal's wool that is used to make things such as clothes, blankets, and carpets. ❑ *...a wool overcoat.* **3** →see also **cotton wool**

1 불가산명사 양털, 양모 ❑ 새로운 발명으로 양들이 털을 깎을 필요가 없어지게 된다. 양털이 그냥 빠진다. **2** 물질명사 모직물, 울 ❑ 모직 코트

wool|en /wʊlən/ [BRIT **woollen**] ADJ **Woolen** clothes or materials are made from wool or from a mixture of wool and artificial fibers. ❑ *...thick woolen socks.*

[영국영어 woollen] 형용사 모직의 ❑ 두터운 모직 양말

wool|ly /wʊli/ [AM also **wooly**] ADJ Something that is **woolly** is made of wool or looks like wool. ❑ *She wore this woolly hat with pompoms.*

[미국영어 wooly] 형용사 양털의, 양털 같은 ❑ 그녀는 털 방울이 달린 이 양털 모자를 쓰고 있었다.

word ♦♦♦ /wɜrd/ (**words, wording, worded**) **1** N-COUNT A **word** is a single unit of language that can be represented in writing or speech. In English, a word has a space on either side of it when it is written. ❑ *The words stood out clearly on the page.* ❑ *The word "ginseng" comes from the Chinese word "Shen-seng."* **2** N-PLURAL Someone's **words** are what they say or write. ❑ *I was devastated when her words came true.* **3** N-PLURAL The **words** of a song consist of the text that is sung, in contrast to the music that is played. ❑ *Can you hear the words on the album?* **4** N-SING If you have **a word** with someone, you have a short conversation with them. [SPOKEN] ❑ *I think it's time you had a word with him.* **5** N-COUNT If you offer someone **a word** of something such as warning, advice, or praise, you warn, advise, or praise them. ❑ *A word of warning. Don't stick too precisely to what it says in the book.* **6** N-SING If you say that someone does **not** hear, understand, or say **a word**, you are emphasizing that they hear, understand, or say nothing at all. [EMPHASIS] ❑ *I can't understand a word she says.* **7** N-UNCOUNT If there is **word** of something, people receive news or information about it. ❑ *There is no word from the authorities on the reported attack.* **8** N-SING If you give your **word**, you make a sincere promise to someone. ❑ *...an adult who gave his word the boy would be supervised.* **9** N-SING If someone gives **the word** to do something, they give an order to do it. ❑ *I want nothing said about this until I give the word.* **10** V-T To **word** something in a particular way means to choose or use particular words to express it. ❑ *If I had written the letter, I might have worded it differently.* ● **-worded** COMB in ADJ ❑ *...a strongly-worded statement.* →see also **wording** **11** PHRASE If you say that people consider something to be a **dirty word**, you mean that they disapprove of it. ❑ *So many people think feminism is a dirty word.* **12** PHRASE If you do something **from the word go**, you do it from the very beginning or start of a period of time or situation. ❑ *It's essential you make the right decisions from the word go.* **14** PHRASE You can use **in their words** or **in their own words** to indicate that you are reporting what someone said using the exact words that they used. ❑ *Even the Assistant Secretary of State had to admit that previous policy did not, in his words, produce results.* **15** PHRASE If someone has **the last word** or **the final word** in a discussion, argument, or disagreement, they are the one who wins it or who makes the final decision. ❑ *She does like to have the last word in any discussion.* **16** PHRASE If news or information passes by **word of mouth**, people tell it to each other rather than it being printed in written form. ❑ *The story has been passed down by word of mouth.* **17** PHRASE You say **in other words** in order to introduce a different, and usually simpler, explanation or interpretation of something that has just been said. ❑ *The mobile library services have been reorganized – in other words, they visit fewer places.* **18** PHRASE If you say something **in your own words**, you express it in your own way, without copying or repeating someone else's description. ❑ *Now tell us in your own words about the events of Saturday.* **19** PHRASE If you say to someone "**take** my **word for it**," you mean that they should believe you because you are telling the truth. ❑ *You'll buy nothing but trouble if you buy that house, take my word for it.* **20** PHRASE If you repeat something **word for word**, you repeat it exactly as it was originally said or written. ❑ *I don't try to memorize speeches word for word.* **21** **the operative word** →see **operative** →see **English**

1 가산명사 단어 ❑ 그 단어들이 지면에서 선명하게 두드러졌다. ❑ '진생'이라는 단어는 중국어인 '센-셍'에서 왔다. **2** 복수명사 (-의) 말 ❑ 나는 그녀가 한 말이 현실이 되자 망연자실했다. **3** 복수명사 (노래의) 가사 ❑ 앨범의 가사가 들리나요? **4** 단수명사 이야기, 대화 [구어체] ❑ 내 생각엔 이제 당신이 그와 얘기해 봐야 될 것 같네요. **5** 가산명사 (충고 등의) 말 ❑ 한 마디 경고하게. 꼭 책에 나와 있는 그대로 할 필요는 없어. **6** 단수명사 한 마디 말 [강조] ❑ 나는 그녀가 하는 말을 한 마디도 이해할 수 없다. **7** 불가산명사 소식, 기별 ❑ 보도된 공격에 관해 당국으로부터는 아무런 언급이 없다. **8** 단수명사 언질, 약속 ❑ 그 소년을 지도하겠다고 언질을 준 한 성인 **9** 단수명사 지시, 명령 ❑ 내가 지시할 때까지 이것에 대해 언급하지 마세요. **10** 타동사 말을 골라 쓰다 ❑ 내가 그 편지를 썼더라면 아마도 달리 표현했을지도 모르겠다. ● -어조의 복합형 형용사 ❑ 강한 어조의 진술 **11** 구 기분 나쁜 단어, 듣기 싫은 말 ❑ 아주 많은 사람들이 페미니즘을 듣기 싫은 말로 생각한다. **12** 구 맨 처음부터 ❑ 맨 처음부터 올바른 결정을 하는 것이 가장 중요하다. **14** 구 -의 말에 의하면, - 자신의 말에 의하면 ❑ 심지어 국무차관보도 이전 정책이, 그의 말에 의하면, 결실이 없었다는 것을 인정해야만 했다. **15** 구 (마지막) 결정적인 한 마디 ❑ 그녀는 어떤 토론에서나 결정적인 발언을 하는 것을 정말로 좋아한다. **16** 구 구두, 입소문 ❑ 그 이야기는 구두로 전해져 왔다. **17** 구 바꾸어 말하면 ❑ 이동도서관 서비스가 재구성되었다. 바꾸어 말하면, 방문 장소가 줄어들었다. **18** 구 자신의 말로 ❑ 자, 이제 토요일에 있었던 일에 대해 당신이 직접 얘기해 보세요. **19** 구 -의 말을 믿다 ❑ 만약 저 집을 사면 근심거리만 사는 게 되지, 내 말을 믿어. **20** 구 한 마디 한 마디, 문자 그대로 ❑ 나는 연설을 한 마디 한 마디 다 암기하려고 하지 않는다.

word|ing /wɜrdɪŋ/ N-UNCOUNT The **wording** of a piece of writing or a speech are the words used in it, especially when these are chosen to have a particular effect. ❑ *The two sides failed to agree on the wording of a final report.*

불가산명사 자구, 어휘 선택 ❑ 양측은 최종 보고서의 자구에 합의하지 못했다.

word pro|cess|ing also **word-processing** N-UNCOUNT **Word processing** is the work or skill of producing printed documents using a computer. [COMPUTING] ❑ *Many job agencies offer word processing courses to those with rusty office skills.*

불가산명사 워드 프로세싱 [컴퓨터] ❑ 많은 직업소개소에서 사무 능력이 무뎌진 사람들에게 컴퓨터 문서 작성 훈련 과정을 제공한다.

word pro|ces|sor (**word processors**) N-COUNT A **word processor** is a computer program or a computer which is used to produce printed documents. [COMPUTING]

가산명사 워드 프로세서 [컴퓨터]

word wrap|ping N-UNCOUNT In computing, **word wrapping** is a process by which a word which comes at the end of a line is automatically moved onto a new line in order to keep the text within the margins. [COMPUTING]

불가산명사 단어 정렬 (워드 프로세서에서 행의 끝을 맞추기 위해 마지막 단어를 다음 줄로 넘기는 것) [컴퓨터]

wore /wɔr/ **Wore** is the past tense of **wear**.

wear의 과거

work ♦♦♦ /wɜrk/ (**works, working, worked**) **1** V-I People who **work** have a job, usually one which they are paid to do. ❑ *I started working in a recording studio.* ❑ *He worked as a bricklayer's mate.* ❑ *I want to work, I don't want to be on welfare.* **2** N-UNCOUNT People who have **work** or who are in **work** have a job, usually one which they are paid to do. ❑ *Fewer and fewer people are in work.* ❑ *I was out of work at the time.* **3** V-I When you **work**, you do the things that you are paid or required to do in your job. ❑ *I can't talk to you right now – I'm working.* ❑ *He was working at his desk.* **4** N-UNCOUNT Your **work** consists of the things you are paid or required to do in your job. ❑ *We're supposed to be running a business here. I've got work to do.* ❑ *I used to take work home, but I don't do it any more.* **5** V-I When you **work**, you spend time and effort doing a task that needs to be done or trying to achieve something. ❑ *Linda spends all her time working on the garden.* ❑ *The government expressed hope that all the sides will work towards a political solution.* ● N-UNCOUNT **Work** is also a noun. ❑ *There was a lot of work to do on their house.* **6** N-UNCOUNT **Work** is the place where you do your job. ❑ *Many people travel to work by car.* **7** N-UNCOUNT **Work** is something which you produce as a result of an activity or as a result of doing your job. ❑ *It can help to have an impartial third party look over your work.* **8** N-COUNT A **work** is something such as a painting, book, or piece of music produced by an artist, writer, or composer. ❑ *In my opinion, this is Rembrandt's greatest work.* **9** V-I If someone **is working on** a particular subject or question, they are studying or researching it. ❑ *Professor Bonnet has been working for many years on molecules of this type.* ● N-UNCOUNT **Work** is also a noun. ❑ *Their work shows that one-year-olds are much more likely to have allergies if either parent smokes.* **10** V-I If you **work with** a person or a group of people, you spend time and effort trying to help them in some way. ❑ *She spent a period of time working with people dying of cancer.* ● N-UNCOUNT **Work** is also a noun. ❑ *She became involved in social and relief work among the refugees.* **11** V-I If a machine or piece of equipment **works**, it operates and performs a particular function. ❑ *The pump doesn't work and we have no running water.* **12** V-I If an idea, system, or way of doing something **works**, it is successful, effective, or satisfactory. ❑ *95 per cent of these diets do not work.* **13** V-I If a drug or medicine **works**, it produces a particular physical effect. ❑ *I wake at 6am as the sleeping pill doesn't work for more than nine hours.* **14** V-I If your mind or brain **is working**, you are thinking about something or trying to solve a problem. ❑ *My mind was working frantically, running over the events of the evening.* **15** V-I If you **work on** an assumption or idea, you act as if it were true or base other ideas on it, until you have more information. ❑ *We are working on the assumption that it was a gas explosion.* **16** V-T If you **work** someone, you make them spend time and effort doing a particular activity or job. ❑ *They're working me too hard. I'm too old for this.* **17** V-T When people **work** the land, they do all the tasks involved in growing crops. ❑ *Farmers worked the fertile valleys.* **18** V-T If you **work** a machine or piece of equipment, you use or control it. ❑ *Many adults still depend on their children to work the video.* **19** V-I If something **works** into a particular state or condition, it gradually moves so that it is in that state or condition. ❑ *It's important to put a locking washer on that last nut, or it can work loose.* **20** N-COUNT-COLL A **works** is a place where something is manufactured or where an industrial process is carried out. **Works** is used to refer to one or to more than one of these places. ❑ *The steel works, one of the landmarks of Stoke-on-Trent, could be seen for miles.* **21** N-PLURAL **Works** are activities such as digging the ground or building on a large scale. ❑ *...six years of disruptive building works, road construction and urban development.* **22** →see also **working** **23** PHRASE If someone is **at work** they are doing their job or are busy doing a particular activity. ❑ *The salvage teams are already hard at work trying to deal with the spilled oil.* **24** PHRASE If a force or process is **at work**, it is having a particular influence or effect. ❑ *It is important to understand the powerful economic and social forces at work behind our own actions.* **25** PHRASE If you **put** someone **to work** or **set** them **to work**, you give them a job or task to do. ❑ *By stimulating the economy, we're going to put people to work.* **26** PHRASE If you **get to work**, **go to work**, or **set to work** on a job, task, or problem, you start doing it or dealing with it. ❑ *He promised to get to work on the state's massive deficit.* **27** PHRASE If you **work** your **way** somewhere, you move or progress there slowly, and with a lot of effort or work. ❑ *Rescuers were still working their way towards the trapped men.* →see **factory**

1 자동사 일하다, 근무하다 ❑ 나는 녹음 스튜디오에서 일을 시작했다. ❑ 그는 벽돌공의 조수로 일했다. ❑ 나는 일하고 싶지, 정부 보조금에 의존하고 싶지 않다. **2** 불가산명사 일, 직장, 일이 있는, 직장이 있는 ❑ 점점 더 일자리를 가진 사람들이 줄고 있다. ❑ 나는 당시에 직장이 없었다. **3** 자동사 일하다 ❑ 지금 너하고 이야기를 할 수 없어. 일하는 중이야. ❑ 그는 자기 책상에서 일하고 있었다. **4** 불가산명사 (해야 할) 일, 직무 ❑ 우리 여기 사업하러 왔잖아. 난 할 일이 있어. ❑ 나는 예전에 집으로 일거리를 가져가곤 했지만, 더 이상 그러지 않는다. **5** 자동사 노력해 일하다 ❑ 린다는 정원 가꾸느라 시간을 다 보낸다. ❑ 정부는 모든 측들이 정치적 해결을 위해 노력했으면 하는 희망을 표현했다. ● 불가산명사 (한) 일 ❑ 그들의 집은 손볼 데가 많았다. **6** 불가산명사 직장 ❑ 많은 사람들이 차로 출근한다. **7** 불가산명사 결과물 ❑ 당신의 작업 결과물을 공평한 제삼자가 한 번 보도록 하는 것이 도움이 될 수 있다. **8** 가산명사 (예술 등의) 작품 ❑ 내 생각엔 이것이 렘브란트의 최고 걸작이다. **9** 자동사 ∼에 관해 연구하다 ❑ 보네트 교수는 이런 유형의 분자에 관해 수년 동안 연구해 오고 있다. ● 불가산명사 연구 ❑ 그들의 연구는 부모 중 한 사람이 담배를 피우면 한 살짜리 아이들이 알레르기를 갖게 될 가능성이 더 높아진다는 것을 보여 준다. **10** 자동사 ∼를 도우며 일하다 ❑ 그녀는 한동안 암으로 죽어 가는 사람들을 돕는 일을 했다. ● 불가산명사 봉사 ❑ 그녀는 난민들을 돕는 사회 및 구호 봉사 일에 참가하게 되었다. **11** 자동사 작동하다 ❑ 펌프가 작동하지 않아서 우리는 수돗물이 안 나온다. **12** 자동사 잘 되어 가다, 효과가 있다 ❑ 이런 다이어트들의 95퍼센트는 효과가 없다. **13** 자동사 (약이) 듣다, 효과가 있다 ❑ 수면제가 아홉 시간 이상 효과가 지속되지 않기 때문에 나는 오전 6시에 잠이 깨어난다. **14** 자동사 (머리가) 회전하다 ❑ 내 머릿속은 저녁 행사들을 점검하며 미친 듯이 바삐 돌고 있었다. **15** 자동사 ∼을 근거로 행동하다 ❑ 우리는 그것이 가스 폭발이라는 가정하에 움직이고 있다. **16** 타동사 일을 시키다 ❑ 그들은 나를 혹사시킨다. 난 이 일을 하기에는 너무 늙었다. **17** 타동사 경작하다 ❑ 농부들은 골짜기의 비옥한 땅을 경작했다. **18** 타동사 작동시키다 ❑ 많은 성인들이 아직도 비디오를 작동시킬 때 아이들에게 기댄다. **19** 자동사 차차 ∼이 되다 ❑ 저 마지막 너트에는 풀림 방지 와셔를 끼워 두는 것이 중요하다. 그렇게 하지 않으면 너트가 차츰 풀릴 수 있다. **20** 가산명사-집합 공장, 공장들 ❑ 스토크온트렌트의 대표적 상징물의 하나인 제철소들은 수 마일에 걸쳐 보인다. **21** 복수명사 (토목) 공사 ❑ 6년 동안 계속되며 문제를 일으키는 건축 공사, 도로 공사, 그리고 도시 개발 **22** 구 일하는 있는 **23** 구 해난 구조대들이 유출된 기름을 처리하기 위해 벌써부터 열심히 일하고 있다. **24** 구 (힘이) 작용하는 ❑ 우리 자신의 행위 이면에 작용하고 있는 강력한 경제적, 사회적 힘을 이해하는 것이 중요하다. **25** 구 ∼에게 일을 주다 ❑ 우리는 경제를 활성화해서 사람들이 일을 할 수 있게 하려고 한다. **26** 구 일을 시작하다, 일에 착수하다 ❑ 그는 국가의 엄청난 적자에 대한 조치를 취하겠다고 약속했다. **27** 구 (∼로) 애써 나아가다 ❑ 구조대가 갇혀 있는 사람들을 향해서 아직도 힘겹게 나아가고 있었다.

The verb **work** has a different meaning in the continuous tenses than it does in the simple tenses. You use the continuous tenses, with the "-ing" form, to talk about a temporary job, but the simple tenses to talk about a permanent job. For example, if you say "I'm working in Boston," this suggests that the situation is temporary and you may soon move to a different place. If you say "I work in Boston", this suggests that Boston is your permanent place of work.

동사 work는 진행시제로 쓰면 단순시제로 쓸 때와 뜻이 다르다. 임시로 하는 일에 대해 말하려면 -ing형으로 진행시제를 사용하지만, 장기적으로 하는 일에 대해 말하려면 단순시제를 쓴다. 예를 들어, "I'm working in Boston."이라고 하면, 그 상황이 일시적이고 곧 다른 곳으로 옮겨갈지도 모른다는 것을 나타낸다. "I work in Boston."이라고 하면, 보스턴이 장기적인 직장이 있는 곳이라는 뜻이다.

Thesaurus   *work*의 참조어

   v.   labor **1** **3** **5**
            function, go, operate, perform, run **11** **12**
   N.   business, craft, job, occupation, profession, trade, vocation; (ant.)
            entertainment, fun, pastime **1** **4**

▶**work off** PHRASAL VERB If you **work off** energy, stress, or anger, you get rid of it by doing something that requires a lot of physical effort. ❑ *Cleaning my kitchen really works off frustration if I've had a row with someone.*

구동사 (스트레스 또는 화를) 해소하다, 발산하다 ❑ 누군가와 언쟁을 하고 나서 부엌 청소를 하면 정말 내 좌절감이 싹 해소된다.

▶**work out** **1** PHRASAL VERB If you **work out** a solution to a problem or mystery, you manage to find the solution by thinking or talking about it. ❑ *Negotiators are due to meet later today to work out a compromise.* ❑ *It took me some time to work out what was causing this.* **2** PHRASAL VERB If you **work out** the answer to a mathematical problem, you calculate it. ❑ *It is proving hard to work out the value of bankrupt firms' assets.* **3** PHRASAL VERB If something **works out** at a particular amount, it is calculated to be that amount after all the facts and figures have been considered. ❑ *The price per pound works out at £3.20.* **4** PHRASAL VERB If a situation **works out** well or **works out**, it happens or progresses in a satisfactory way. ❑ *Things just didn't work out as planned.* ❑ *The deal just isn't working out the way we were promised.* **5** PHRASAL VERB If a process **works** itself **out**, it reaches a conclusion or satisfactory end. ❑ *People involved in it think it's a nightmare, but I'm sure it will work itself out.* **6** PHRASAL VERB If you **work out**, you do physical exercises in order to make your body fit and strong. ❑ *Work out at a gym or swim twice a week.* **7** →see also **workout**

1 구동사 (해결책 등을) 찾다 ❑ 교섭자들이 절충안을 찾기 위해 오늘 늦게 만날 예정이다. ❑ 이것의 원인을 찾아내는 데 시간이 좀 걸렸다. **2** 구동사 (해답을) 산출하다 ❑ 파산한 회사의 자산 가치 산출이 어렵다는 것이 입증되고 있다. **3** 구동사 (금액 등이) 산정되다 ❑ 파운드 당 가격이 3파운드 20펜스로 산정된다. **4** 구동사 잘 되어 가다 ❑ 일이 계획한 대로 잘 풀리지 않았다. ❑ 그 거래는 우리가 약속받은 대로 되고 있지 않다. **5** 구동사 (일이) 풀리다 ❑ 그것에 관련된 사람들은 그게 악몽이라고 생각하지만, 나는 그게 저절로 잘 풀릴 것이라고 확신한다. **6** 구동사 운동하다 ❑ 일주일에 두 번씩 체육관에서 운동하거나 수영하세요.

▶**work up** **1** PHRASAL VERB If you **work** yourself **up**, you make yourself feel very upset or angry about something. ❑ *She worked herself up into a bit of a state.* →see also **worked up** **2** PHRASAL VERB If you **work up** the enthusiasm or courage to do something, you succeed in making yourself feel it. ❑ *Your creative talents can also be put to good use, if you can work up the energy.* **3** PHRASAL VERB If you **work up** a sweat or an appetite, you make yourself sweaty or hungry by doing exercise or hard work. ❑ *Even if you are not prepared to work up a sweat three times a week, any activity is better than none.*

1 구동사 흥분하다 ❑ 그녀는 흥분해서 조금 신경과민이 되어 있었다. **2** 구동사 (용기 등을) 불러일으키다, 북돋우다 ❑ 원기를 불러일으키기만 한다면, 당신의 창조적 재능 또한 잘 활용될 수 있다. **3** 구동사 (운동을 해서 땀을) 내다, (운동을 해서 식욕을) 북돋우다 ❑ 일주일에 세 번 땀이 날 만큼 운동할 태세는 되어 있지 않더라도, 뭐라도 하는 것이 하지 않는 것보다는 낫다.

work|able /wɜ́rkəbᵊl/ ADJ A **workable** idea or system is realistic and practical, and likely to be effective. ❑ *Investors can simply pay cash, but this isn't a workable solution in most cases.*

형용사 실현 가능한, 현실적인 ❑ 투자자가 그냥 현금으로 지불할 수도 있지만, 그것은 대부분의 경우 현실적인 해결책이 못 된다.

work|a|hol|ic /wɜ́kəhɔ̀lɪk, BRIT wɜ́ːkəhɒ̀lɪk/ (**workaholics**) N-COUNT A **workaholic** is a person who works most of the time and finds it difficult to stop working in order to do other things. [INFORMAL] ❑ *Eighteen per cent of 30-year-olds claim they are workaholics.*

가산명사 일 중독자, 일 벌레 [비격식체] ❑ 서른 살의 18퍼센트가 자신이 일 중독자라고 주장한다.

work|book /wɜ́rkbʊk/ (**workbooks**) N-COUNT A **workbook** is a book to help you learn a particular subject which has questions in it with spaces for the answers. ❑ *...the new Aromatherapy Workbook by top aromatherapy expert Shirley Price.*

가산명사 학습장 ❑ 방향 요법의 최고 전문가 셜리 프라이스가 쓴 새 방향 요법 학습장

work|day /wɜ́rkdeɪ/ (**workdays**) also **work day** **1** N-COUNT A **workday** is the amount of time during a day which you spend doing your job. [mainly AM; BRIT usually **working day**] ❑ *His workday starts at 3.30 a.m. and lasts 12 hours.* **2** N-COUNT A **workday** is a day on which people go to work. ❑ *What's he doing home on a workday?*

1 가산명사 근무 시간 [주로 미국영어; 영국영어 대개 working day] ❑ 그의 근무 시간은 새벽 3시 30분에 시작해서 12시간 동안 계속된다. **2** 가산명사 근무일, 평일 ❑ 그가 근무일에 집에서 뭘 하고 있는 건가요?

worked up ADJ If someone is **worked up**, they are angry or upset. [v-link ADJ] ❑ *Steve shouted at her. He was really worked up now.*

형용사 화가 난 ❑ 스티브가 그녀에게 고함을 질렀다. 그는 이제 정말로 화가 나 있었다.

work|er ♦♦♦ /wɜ́rkər/ (**workers**) **1** N-COUNT A particular kind of **worker** does the kind of work mentioned. ❑ *She ate her sandwich alongside several other office workers taking their break.* **2** N-COUNT **Workers** are people who are employed in industry or business and who are not managers. ❑ *Wages have been frozen and workers laid off.* **3** N-COUNT You can use **worker** to say how well or badly someone works. ❑ *He is a hard worker and a skilled gardener.* →see also **social worker** →see **factory**

1 가산명사 근로자, 직원 ❑ 그녀는 휴식을 취하는 다른 몇 명의 사무실 직원들과 함께 샌드위치를 먹었다. **2** 가산명사 근로자들 ❑ 임금은 동결되었고 근로자들은 해고를 당했다. **3** 가산명사 일하는 사람 ❑ 그는 열심히 일하는 사람이며 숙련된 원예가이다.

Thesaurus   *worker*의 참조어

   N.   employee, help, laborer **2**

work|force /wɜ́rkfɔ̀rs/ (**workforces**) **1** N-COUNT The **workforce** is the total number of people in a country or region who are physically able to do a job and are available for work. ❑ *...a country where half the workforce is unemployed.* **2** N-COUNT The **workforce** is the total number of people who are employed by a particular company. ❑ *...an employer of a very large workforce.*

1 가산명사 노동력, 노동 인구 ❑ 노동 인구의 절반이 실직 상태인 나라 **2** 가산명사 전 종업원 ❑ 아주 많은 종업원을 고용한 업주

work|ing ♦♦♦ /wɜ́rkɪŋ/ (**workings**) **1** ADJ **Working** people have jobs which they are paid to do. [ADJ n] ❑ *Like working women anywhere, Asian women are buying convenience foods.* **2** ADJ **Working** people are ordinary people who do not have professional or very highly paid jobs. [ADJ n] ❑ *The needs and opinions of ordinary working people were ignored.* **3** ADJ A **working** day or week is the amount of time during a normal day or week which you spend doing your job. [mainly BRIT; AM usually **workday**, **work week**] [ADJ n] ❑ *For doctors the working day often has no end.* **4** ADJ A **working** day is a day on which people go to work. [mainly BRIT; AM usually **workday**] [ADJ n] ❑ *The full effect will not be apparent until Tuesday, the first working day after the three day holiday weekend.* **5** ADJ Your **working** life is the period of your life in which you have a job or are of a suitable age to have a job. [ADJ n] ❑ *He started his working life as a truck driver.* **6** ADJ The **working** population of an area consists of all the people in that area who have a job or who are of a suitable age to have a job. [ADJ n] ❑ *Almost 13 per cent of the working population is*

1 형용사 일하는, 직업이 있는 ❑ 전 세계의 근로 여성들과 마찬가지로 아시아 여성들도 편의 식품을 구입한다. **2** 형용사 근로의, 노동의 ❑ 일반 근로자의 요구와 의견이 무시되었다. **3** 형용사 일하는, 근무하는 [주로 영국영어; 미국영어 대개 workday, work week] ❑ 의사에게는 종종 근무 시간이 끝이 없다. **4** 형용사 일하는, 근무하는 [주로 영국영어; 미국영어 대개 workday] ❑ 3일간 연휴 주말 이후 첫 근무일인 화요일이 되어서야 완전한 효과가 눈에 띄게 드러날 것이다. **5** 형용사 근로 활동을 하는 ❑ 그는 트럭 기사로 사회생활을 시작했다. **6** 형용사 사회 활동을 하는 ❑ 사회 활동 인구의 거의 13퍼센트가 이미 무직이다. **7** 형용사 근로의 ❑ 파업자들은 더 높은 임금과 더 나은 근로 조건을 요구하고 있다. **8** 형용사

already unemployed. ◻ ADJ **Working** conditions or practices are ones which you have in your job. [ADJ n] ◻ *The strikers are demanding higher pay and better working conditions.* ◻ ADJ A **working** farm or business exists to do normal work and make a profit, and not only for tourists or as someone's hobby. [ADJ n] ◻ *...a holiday spent on a working farm.* ◻ ADJ The **working** parts of a machine are the parts which move and operate the machine, in contrast to the outer case or container in which they are enclosed. [ADJ n] ◻ *The reel comes complete with a set of spares for all the working parts.* ◻ ADJ A **working** knowledge or majority is not very great, but is enough to be useful. [ADJ n] ◻ *This book was designed in order to provide a working knowledge of finance and accounts.* ◻ N-PLURAL The **workings of** a piece of equipment, an organization, or a system are the ways in which it operates and the processes which are involved in it. ◻ *Neural networks are computer systems which mimic the workings of the brain.* ◻ **in working order** →see **order**

영업의, 실제의 ◻ 실제 농장에서 보낸 휴가 ◻ 형용사 (실제) 작동하는 ◻ 그 낚싯대 릴은 작동하는 모든 부품에 대한 예비 부품 세트를 완비하고 있다. ◻ 형용사 직질한, 실용적인 ◻ 이 책은 재정과 회계에 관한 실용적인 지식을 제공하기 위해 기획되었다. ◻ 복수명사 작용 ◻ 신경 회로망은 뇌의 작용을 본 뜬 컴퓨터 시스템이다.

work|ing capi|tal N-UNCOUNT **Working capital** is money which is available for use immediately, rather than money which is invested in land or equipment. [BUSINESS] ◻ *He borrowed a further £1.5 m from conventional sources to provide working capital.*

불가산명사 운전 자본, 유동 자산 [경제] ◻ 그는 운전 자본을 마련하려고 기존 금융권에서 추가로 150만 파운드를 빌렸다.

work|ing class (working classes) N-COUNT-COLL The **working class** or the **working classes** are the group of people in a society who do not own much property, who have low social status, and who do jobs which involve using physical skills rather than intellectual skills. ◻ *A quarter of the working class voted for him.* ● ADJ **Working class** is also an adjective. ◻ *...a self-educated man from a working class background.*

가산명사-집합 노동자 계층 ◻ 노동자 계층의 4분의 1이 그에게 투표했다. ● 형용사 노동자 계층의 ◻ 노동자 계층 출신으로 독학으로 공부한 남자

work|load /wɜːrkloʊd/ (workloads) also **work load** N-COUNT The **workload** of a person or organization is the amount of work that has to be done by them. ◻ *The sudden cancellation of Mr. Blair's trip was due to his heavy workload.*

가산명사 업무, 업무량 ◻ 블레어 총리의 갑작스런 여행 취소는 그의 과중한 업무 때문이었다.

work|man /wɜːrkmən/ (workmen) N-COUNT A **workman** is a man who works with his hands, for example building or repairing houses or roads. ◻ *In University Square workmen are building a steel fence.*

가산명사 (공사판) 노동자 ◻ 유니버시티 스퀘어에서 노동자들이 철제 담장을 세우고 있다.

work|man|ship /wɜːrkmənʃɪp/ N-UNCOUNT **Workmanship** is the skill with which something is made and which affects the appearance and quality of the finished object. ◻ *The problem may be due to poor workmanship.*

불가산명사 솜씨, 기량 ◻ 그 문제는 기량이 부족한 탓일 것이다.

work|mate /wɜːrkmeɪt/ (workmates) N-COUNT Your **workmates** are the people you work with. [mainly BRIT, INFORMAL] ◻ *My workmates, and, even more, the management, didn't want me to leave.*

가산명사 동료 [주로 영국영어, 비격식체] ◻ 내 동료들과 심지어 경영진도 내가 그만두는 것을 원하지 않았다.

work of art (works of art) N-COUNT A **work of art** is a painting or piece of sculpture which is of high quality. ◻ *...a collection of works of art of international significance.* →see **drawing**

가산명사 미술품, 예술품 ◻ 국제적 중요성을 지닌 미술 소장품

work|out /wɜːrkaʊt/ (workouts) N-COUNT A **workout** is a period of physical exercise or training. ◻ *Give your upper body a workout by using handweights.* →see **muscle**

가산명사 운동 ◻ 아령을 이용하여 상체 운동을 하세요.

work|place /wɜːrkpleɪs/ (workplaces) also **work place** N-COUNT Your **workplace** is the place where you work. ◻ *...the difficulties facing women in the workplace.*

가산명사 직장 ◻ 직장에서 여성이 직면하는 어려움

work|sheet /wɜːrkʃiːt/ (worksheets) N-COUNT A **worksheet** is a specially prepared page of exercises designed to improve your knowledge or understanding of a particular subject. ◻ *Complete this worksheet before you decide on the model you want.*

가산명사 평가지 ◻ 당신이 원하는 모델을 정하기 전에 이 평가지를 다 푸세요.

work|shop /wɜːrkʃɒp/ (workshops) ◻ N-COUNT A **workshop** is a period of discussion or practical work on a particular subject in which a group of people share their knowledge or experience. ◻ *Trumpeter Marcus Belgrave ran a jazz workshop for young artists.* ◻ N-COUNT A **workshop** is a building which contains tools or machinery for making or repairing things, especially using wood or metal. ◻ *...a modestly equipped workshop.*

◻ 가산명사 연수회, 워크숍 ◻ 트럼펫 연주가 마커스 벨그레이브는 젊은 음악인들을 위해 재즈 연주회를 열었다. ◻ 가산명사 작업장 ◻ 장비가 별로 많지 않은 작업장

work|sta|tion /wɜːrksteɪʃən/ (workstations) also **work station** N-COUNT A **workstation** is a screen and keyboard that are part of an office computer system. ◻ *Or you can set up databases on any number of servers and access them from particular workstations.*

가산명사 워크스테이션, 단말기 ◻ 아니면 데이터베이스를 여러 대의 서버에 구축하여 특정한 단말기에서 사용할 수 있다.

work|week /wɜːrkwiːk/ (workweeks) N-COUNT A **workweek** is the amount of time during a normal week when you spend doing your job. [mainly AM; BRIT usually **working week**] ◻ *The union had sought a wage increase, a shorter workweek.*

가산명사 1주 근로 시간 [주로 미국영어; 영국영어 대개 working week] ◻ 노동조합은 임금 인상과 주당 근로 시간 단축을 요구했다.

world ◆◆◆ /wɜːrld/ (worlds) ◻ N-SING The **world** is the planet that we live on. ◻ *The satellite enables us to calculate their precise location anywhere in the world.* ◻ N-SING The **world** refers to all the people who live on this planet, and our societies, institutions, and ways of life. ◻ *The world was, and remains, shocked.* ◻ *He wants to show the world that anyone can learn to be an ambassador.* ◻ ADJ You can use **world** to describe someone or something that is one of the most important or significant of its kind on earth. [ADJ n] ◻ *China has once again emerged as a world power.* ◻ N-SING You can use **world** in expressions such as **the Arab world**, **the western world**, and **the ancient world** to refer to a particular group of countries or a particular period in history. ◻ *Athens had strong ties to the Arab world.* ◻ N-COUNT Someone's **world** is the life they lead, the people they have contact with, and the things they experience. ◻ *His world seemed so different from mine.* ◻ N-SING You can use **world** to refer to a particular field of activity, and the people involved in it. ◻ *The publishing world had certainly never seen an event quite like this.* ◻ N-SING You can use **world** to refer to a particular group of living things, for example **the animal world**, **the plant world**, and **the insect world**. ◻ *When it comes to dodging disaster, the champions of the insect world have to be cockroaches.* ◻ →see also **real world, Third World** ◻ PHRASE If you say that someone has the **best of both worlds**, you mean that they have only the benefits of two things and none of the disadvantages. ◻ *Her living room provides the best of both worlds, with an office at one end and comfortable sofas at the other.*

◻ 단수명사 지구 ◻ 그 인공위성은 우리가 지구 어느 곳에서든 그들의 정확한 위치를 계산해 낼 수 있게 해 준다. ◻ 단수명사 세계, 전 세계 ◻ 전 세계가 충격을 받았고, 여전히 충격 상태에 빠져 있다. ◻ 그는 누구나 대사가 될 수 있다는 것을 전 세계에 보여 주고 싶어 한다. ◻ 형용사 세계적인 ◻ 중국이 다시 한 번 세계적인 강대국으로 부상했다. ◻ 단수명사 (특정한 지역, 시대의) 세계 ◻ 아테네는 아랍 세계와 강한 유대가 있었다. ◻ 가산명사 (한 개인의) 세계, 세상 ◻ 그의 세계는 내 세계와는 너무도 달라 보였다. ◻ 단수명사 -계(界) ◻ 분명 출판계가 이와 같은 행사를 결코 본 적이 없었다. ◻ 단수명사 (동식물 등의) 세계; 동물 세계; 식물세계 ◻ 곤충 세계 ◻ 재난을 피하는 데 있어서 곤충 세계의 최고 고수는 바퀴벌레임이 틀림없다. ◻ 구 서로 다른 두 가지의 장점, 금상첨화 ◻ 그녀의 거실은 한쪽에는 사무 공간이 있고 다른 한쪽에는 안락한 소파가 있어 금상첨화이다. ◻ 구 기분을 좋게 하다 [비격식체] ◻ 한잠 자고 나면 기분이 좋아질 것이다. ◻ 구 도대체; 도대체 무엇이; 도대체 누가 [강조] ◻ 도대체 그가 무엇을 하고 있나요? ◻ 구 이상적으로는, 완전하게는 ◻ 캐런 스티븐스가

10 PHRASE If you say that something **has done** someone **the world of good** or **a world of good**, you mean that it has made them feel better or improved their life. [INFORMAL] ❑ *A sleep will do you the world of good.* **11** PHRASE You can use **in the world** in expressions such as **what in the world** and **who in the world** to emphasize a question, especially when expressing surprise or anger. [EMPHASIS] ❑ *What in the world is he doing?* **12** PHRASE You can use **in an ideal world** or **in a perfect world** when you are talking about things that you would like to happen, although you realize that they are not likely to happen. ❑ *In an ideal world Karen Stevens says she would love to stay at home with her two-and-half-year old son.* **13** PHRASE You can use **the outside world** to refer to all the people who do not live in a particular place or who are not involved in a particular situation. ❑ *For many, the post office is the only link with the outside world.* **14** **not be the end of the world** →see **end**. **the world is** your **oyster** →see **oyster**. **on top of the world** →see **top**

말하기를 이상적으로는 자기가 두 살 반짜리 아들과 집에 있으면 참 좋겠다고 한다. **13** 구 외부 세계, 바깥 세계 ❑ 많은 사람들에게 우체국은 바깥 세계와의 유일한 연결 고리이다.

Word Partnership	*world*의 연어
PREP.	**all over the** world, **anywhere in the** world, **around the** world **1**
V.	**travel the** world **1**
N.	world **history**, world **peace**, world **premiere 2**
	world **record 3**
	world **of *something* 2 6 7**

world-class ADJ A **world-class** athlete, performer, or organization is one of the best in the world. [JOURNALISM] ❑ *He was determined to become a world-class player.*

형용사 세계적 수준의 [언론] ❑ 그는 세계적 수준의 선수가 되려는 결의가 굳었다.

world-famous ADJ Someone or something that is **world-famous** is known about by people all over the world. ❑ *...the world-famous Hollywood Bowl.*

형용사 세계적으로 유명한 ❑ 세계적으로 유명한 할리우드 원형 극장

world|ly /wɜ͟rldli/ **1** ADJ Someone who is **worldly** is experienced and knows about the practical or social aspects of life. ❑ *He was different from anyone I had known, very worldly, everything that Dermot was not.* **2** ADJ You can refer to someone's possessions as their **worldly** goods or possessions. [LITERARY] [ADJ n] ❑ *...a man who had given up all his worldly goods.*

1 형용사 세속적인 ❑ 그는 내가 알았던 어떤 사람과도 달랐다. 매우 세속적이었고, 더멋과는 완전히 판판이었다. **2** 형용사 속세의 [문예체] ❑ 자기가 가진 모든 속세의 재물을 포기했던 사람

World Trade Or|gani|za|tion N-PROPER The **World Trade Organization** is an international organization that encourages and regulates trade between its member states. The abbreviation **WTO** is also used. ❑ *... institutions such as the World Bank and the World Trade Organization.*

고유명사 세계 무역 기구 ❑ 세계은행이나 세계 무역 기구와 같은 기구들

world view (**world views**) also **world-view** N-COUNT A person's **world view** is the way they see and understand the world, especially regarding issues such as politics, philosophy, and religion. ❑ *...their Christian world view.*

가산명사 세계관 ❑ 그들의 기독교적 세계관

world war ♦♢♢ (**world wars**) N-VAR A **world war** is a war that involves countries all over the world. ❑ *Many senior citizens have been through two world wars.*

가산명사 또는 불가산명사 세계 대전 ❑ 많은 노년층들이 두 차례의 세계 대전을 겪었다.

world|wide ♦♢♢ /wɜ͟rldwaɪd/ also **world-wide** ADV If something exists or happens **worldwide**, it exists or happens throughout the world. ❑ *His books have sold more than 20 million copies worldwide.* ● ADJ **Worldwide** is also an adjective. ❑ *Today, doctors are fearing a worldwide epidemic.*

부사 전 세계에 ❑ 그의 책은 전 세계에 2천만 부 이상 팔렸다. ● 형용사 전 세계에 미치는 ❑ 오늘날, 의사들은 전 세계에 퍼지는 전염병을 두려워하고 있다.

World-Wide Web N-PROPER The **World Wide Web** is a computer system which links documents and pictures into a database that is stored in computers in many different parts of the world and that people everywhere can use. The abbreviations **WWW** and the **Web** are often used. [COMPUTING] →see **Internet**

고유명사 월드 와이드 웹 [컴퓨터]

worm /wɜ͟rm/ (**worms, worming, wormed**) **1** N-COUNT A **worm** is a small animal with a long thin body, no bones and no legs. **2** V-T If you say that someone **is worming** their **way** to success, or **is worming** their **way** into someone else's affection, you disapprove of the way that they are gradually making someone trust them or like them, often in order to deceive them or gain some advantage. [DISAPPROVAL] ❑ *She never misses a chance to worm her way into the public's hearts.* **3** N-COUNT A **worm** is a computer program that contains a virus which duplicates itself many times in a network. [COMPUTING] ❑ *...a new computer worm that disables security software.* **4** PHRASE If you say that someone is opening **a can of worms**, you are warning them that they are planning to do or talk about something which is much more complicated, unpleasant, or difficult than they realize and which might be better left alone. ❑ *You've opened up a whole new can of worms here I think. We could have a whole debate on student loans and grants.*

1 가산명사 벌레 **2** 타동사 교묘히 ~로 파고 들다 [탐탁잖음] ❑ 그녀는 교묘히 대중의 마음속에 파고들 기회를 절대 놓치지 않는다. **3** 가산명사 웜 [컴퓨터 바이러스] [컴퓨터] ❑ 보안 소프트웨어를 무력화시키는 새로운 컴퓨터 바이러스 **4** 구 (비유적) 벌레 ❑ 내 생각에 당신은 여기서 새 벌집을 통째로 건드린 것 같습니다. 우리는 학자금 대여와 장학금에 대해 전체적으로 토의해야 할지도 모릅니다.

worn /wɔ͟rn/ **1** **Worn** is the past participle of **wear**. **2** ADJ **Worn** is used to describe something that is damaged or thin because it is old and has been used a lot. ❑ *Worn rugs increase the danger of tripping.* **3** ADJ If someone looks **worn**, they look tired and old. [V-LINK ADJ] ❑ *She was looking very haggard and worn.*

1 wear의 과거 분사 **2** 형용사 써서 낡은 ❑ 낡은 융단은 걸려 넘어질 위험성이 높다. **3** 형용사 지치고 수척한 ❑ 그녀는 아주 지치고 수척해 보였다.

worn out also **worn-out** **1** ADJ Something that is **worn out** is so old, damaged, or thin from use that it cannot be used anymore. ❑ *Car buyers tend to replace worn-out tyres with the same brand.* **2** ADJ Someone who is **worn out** is extremely tired after hard work or a difficult or unpleasant experience. ❑ *Before the race, he is fine. But afterwards he is worn out.*

1 형용사 낡아 해진 ❑ 자동차 구매자들은 다 닳은 타이어를 상표가 같은 것으로 교체하는 경향이 있다. **2** 형용사 기진맥진한 ❑ 경주 전에 그는 멀쩡하다. 그러나 나중이 되면 그는 기진맥진한다.

wor|ried ♦♢♢ /wɜ͟rid, BRIT wʌ͟rid/ ADJ When you are **worried**, you are unhappy because you keep thinking about problems that you have or about unpleasant things that might happen in the future. ❑ *He seemed very worried.*

형용사 걱정스러운, 걱정하는 ❑ 그는 아주 걱정스러워 보였다.

wor|ri|some /wɜ͟risəm, BRIT wʌ͟risəm/ ADJ Something that is **worrisome** causes people to worry. [mainly AM; BRIT usually **worrying**] ❑ *It's Houston's injury that is now the most worrisome.*

형용사 걱정되는 [주로 미국영어; 영국영어 대개 worrying] ❑ 지금 가장 걱정되는 것은 휴스턴의 부상이다.

wor|ry ♦♦♢ /wɜ͟ri, BRIT wʌ͟ri/ (**worries, worrying, worried**) **1** V-T/V-I If you **worry**, you keep thinking about problems that you have or about unpleasant things that might happen. ❑ *Don't worry, your luggage will come on afterwards by taxi.* ❑ *I worry about her constantly.* **2** V-T If someone or something **worries** you, they make you anxious because you keep thinking about problems or

1 타동사/자동사 걱정하다, 근심하다 ❑ 걱정 마, 네 짐은 나중에 택시로 올 거야. ❑ 난 자꾸 그녀가 걱정된다. **2** 타동사 걱정시키다, 괴롭히다 ❑ 난 아직도 회복 초기 단계라서 그게 걱정스럽다. **3** 타동사 괴롭히다, 성가시게 하다 [구어체] ❑ 난

unpleasant things that might be connected with them. ❑ *I'm still in the early days of my recovery and that worries me.* ❸ V-T If someone or something does not **worry** you, you do not dislike them or you are not annoyed by them. [SPOKEN] [oft with neg] ❑ *The cold doesn't worry me.* ❹ N-UNCOUNT **Worry** is the state or feeling of anxiety and unhappiness caused by the problems that you have or by thinking about unpleasant things that might happen. ❑ *The admission shows the depth of worry among the Tories over the state of the economy.* ❺ N-COUNT A **worry** is a problem that you keep thinking about and that makes you unhappy. ❑ *My main worry was that Madeleine Johnson would still be there.*

Word Partnership	*worry*의 연어
N.	**analysts** worry, **experts** worry, **people** worry ❶ no need **to** worry ❶ ❷
V.	**begin to** worry, **don't** worry, **have things/nothing to** worry **about,** **not going to** worry ❶ ❷

wor|ry|ing /wɜːriɪŋ, BRIT wʌriɪŋ/ ADJ If something is **worrying**, it causes people to worry. [mainly BRIT; AM usually **worrisome**] ❑ *It is very worrying that petrol bombs have been brought into a fight between two secondary schools.*

추위는 상관없다. ❹ 불가산명사 우려, 걱정 ❑ 그렇게 자인하는 것은 토리당 내에서 경제 상태에 대해 얼마나 우려하는지를 보여 준다. ❺ 가산명사 걱정거리, 근심거리 ❑ 내 가장 큰 걱정거리는 매들린 존슨이 아직 거기 있을지도 모른다는 것이었다.

형용사 걱정되는, 우려되는 [주로 영국영어; 미국영어 대개 worrisome] ❑ 두 중학교 간의 싸움에 화염병이 등장했다는 것이 무척 우려된다.

worse /wɜːs/ ❶ **Worse** is the comparative of **bad.** ❷ **Worse** is the comparative of **badly.** ❸ PHRASE If a situation changes **for the worse,** it becomes more unpleasant or more difficult. ❑ *The grandparents sigh and say how things have changed for the worse.*

wors|en /wɜːsən/ (**worsens, worsening, worsened**) V-T/V-I If a bad situation **worsens** or if something **worsens** it, it becomes more difficult, unpleasant, or unacceptable. ❑ *The security forces had to intervene to prevent the situation worsening.*

wor|ship /wɜːʃɪp/ (**worships, worshiping, worshiped**) [BRIT, sometimes AM **worshipping, worshipped**] ❶ V-T/V-I If you **worship** a god, you show your respect to the god, for example by saying prayers. ❑ *...disputes over ways of life and ways of worshiping God.* ● N-UNCOUNT **Worship** is also a noun. ❑ *...the worship of the ancient Roman gods.* ● wor|ship|er (**worshipers**) N-COUNT ❑ *She burst into tears and loud sobs that disturbed the other worshipers.* ❷ V-T If you **worship** someone or something, you love them or admire them very much. ❑ *She had worshiped him for years.*

❶ bad의 비교급 ❷ badly의 비교급 ❸ 구 한층 더 나쁘게, 나쁜 쪽으로 ❑ 조부모들은 한숨을 쉬며 세상이 얼마나 나빠졌는지 얘기한다.

타동사/자동사 악화되다; 악화시키다 ❑ 사태가 악화되는 것을 막기 위해 보안군이 개입해야 했다.

[영국영어, 미국영어 가끔 worshipping, worshipped] ❶ 타동사/자동사 숭배하다, 신을 섬기는 방식에 대한 논쟁 ● 불가산명사 숭배, 예배 ❑ 고대 로마 신들에 대한 숭배 ● 예배자, 참배자 가산명사 ❑ 그녀가 눈물을 쏟으며 큰 소리로 흐느껴서 다른 예배자들에게 방해가 되었다. ❷ 타동사 흠모하다, 열애하다 ❑ 그녀는 수년 동안 그를 흠모해 왔다.

worst /wɜːst/ ❶ **Worst** is the superlative of **bad.** ❷ **Worst** is the superlative of **badly.** ❸ N-SING **The worst** is the most unpleasant or unfavorable thing that could happen or does happen. ❑ *Though mine safety has much improved, miners' families still fear the worst.* ❹ **Worst** is used to form the superlative of compound adjectives beginning with "bad" and "badly." For example, the superlative of "badly-affected" is "worst-affected." ❑ *The worst-affected areas were in Scotland.* ❺ PHRASE You say **worst of all** to indicate that what you are about to mention is the most unpleasant or has the most disadvantages out of all the things you are mentioning. ❑ *The people most closely affected are the passengers who were injured and, worst of all, those who lost relatives.* ❻ PHRASE You use **at worst** or **at the worst** to indicate that you are mentioning the worst thing that might happen in a situation. ❑ *At best Nella would be an invalid; at worst she would die.* ❼ PHRASE When someone is **at their worst,** they are as unpleasant, bad, or unsuccessful as it is possible for them to be. ❑ *This was their mother at her worst. Her voice was strident, she was ready to be angry at anyone.* ❽ PHRASE You use **if worst comes to worst** to say what you might do if a situation develops in the most unfavorable way possible. The form **if the worst comes to the worst** is used in British English and sometimes in American English. ❑ *If worst comes to worst, Europe could withstand a trade war.*

❶ bad의 최상급 ❷ badly의 최상급 ❸ 단수명사 최악, 최악의 것 ❑ 비록 광산의 안전 수준이 많이 향상되었지만, 광부 가족들은 여전히 최악의 상황을 우려한다. ❹ 최악의, 가장 심한 ❑ 가장 심한 타격을 받은 지역들이 스코틀랜드 내에 있었다. ❺ 구 최악의 경우는, 무엇보다도 나쁜 것은 ❑ 가장 직접적으로 피해를 입은 사람들은 부상당한 승객들이며 또, 최악의 경우는, 친지를 잃은 사람들이다. ❻ 구 최악의 경우는 ❑ 최상의 경우라도 넬라는 불구가 되고, 최악의 경우는 사망할 수도 있다. ❼ 구 최악의 상태에 ❑ 이게 그들 어머니의 최악의 상태였다. 그녀의 목소리는 귀에 거슬렸고, 아무한테나 화를 낼 태세였다. ❽ 구 최악의 경우에는, 그것도 안 된다면 ❑ 최악의 경우라도, 유럽은 무역 전쟁에 대항할 수 있을 것이다.

worth ♦♦◇ /wɜːθ/ ❶ V-T If something is **worth** a particular amount of money, it can be sold for that amount or is considered to have that value. [v-link worth amount] ❑ *A local jeweler says the pearl is worth at least $500.* ❑ *His mother inherited a farm worth 15,000 dollars a year.* ❷ COMB in QUANT **Worth** combines with amounts of money, so that when you talk about a particular amount of money's **worth** of something, you mean the quantity of it that you can buy for that amount of money. [QUANT of n] ❑ *I went and bought about six dollars' worth of potato chips.* ● PRON **Worth** is also a pronoun. ❑ *Gold reserves had fallen to less than $3 billion worth.* ❸ COMB in QUANT **Worth** combines with time expressions, so you can use **worth** when you are saying how long an amount of something will last. For example, a week's **worth of** food is the amount of food that will last you for a week. [QUANT of n] ❑ *You've got three years' worth of research money to do what you want with.* ● PRON **Worth** is also a pronoun. ❑ *There's really not very much food down there. About two weeks' worth.* ❹ V-LINK **worth -ing** If you say that something is **worth** having, you mean that it is pleasant or useful, and therefore a good thing to have. ❑ *He's decided to get a look at the house and see if it might be worth buying.* ❑ *Most things worth having never come easy.* ❺ V-LINK **worth n/-ing** If something is **worth** a particular action, or if an action is worth doing, it is considered to be important enough for that action. ❑ *I am spending a lot of money and time on this boat, but it is worth it.* ❑ *This restaurant is well worth a visit.* ❻ PHRASE If an action or activity is **worth** someone's **while,** it will be helpful, useful, or enjoyable for them if they do it, even though it requires some effort. ❑ *It might be worth your while to go to court and ask for the agreement to be changed.* ❼ **worth** your **weight in gold** →see **weight**

❶ 타동사 -의 가치가 있는 ❑ 동네 보석상은 그 진주가 적어도 5백 달러의 가치가 있다고 한다. ❑ 그의 어머니는 연간 15,000달러 상당 수입이 있는 농장을 상속받았다. ❷ 복합형-양화사 -어치의 ❑ 나는 가서 약 6달러어치의 감자튀김을 샀다. ● 대명사 -어치, - 상당 ❑ 금 보유고가 30억 달러 상당 이하로 떨어졌다. ❸ 복합형-양화사 -치의, -분의 ❑ 당신에게는 원하는 것을 할 수 있는 3년 치의 연구비가 있다. ● 대명사 -치, -분 ❑ 거기에는 정말 식량이 별로 많지 않다. 대략 2주치 정도다. ❹ 연결동사 worth -ing -한 가치가 있는, -할 만한 ❑ 그는 그 집을 한 번 보고 구매할 만한 가치가 있는지 알아보기로 결정했다. ❑ 가질 만한 가치가 있는 것은 대부분 쉽게 얻을 수 없다. ❺ 연결동사 worth 명사/-ing -할 가치가 있는 ❑ 나는 이 배에 많은 돈과 시간을 들이고 있지만, 그것은 그럴 만한 가치가 있다. ❑ 이 식당은 정말 한 번 가볼 만하다. ❻ 구 (노력을 들일) 가치가 있는, (노력을 들일) 보람이 있는 ❑ 당신이 법정에 가서 그 합의를 변경해 달라고 요청할 만한 가치가 있다.

Word Partnership	*worth*의 연어
N.	worth **five dollars,** worth **a fortune,** worth **money,** worth **the** **price** ❶ worth **the effort,** worth **the risk,** worth **the trouble,** worth **a try** ❺

worth|less /wɜːθləs/ ❶ ADJ Something that is **worthless** is of no real value or

❶ 형용사 쓸모없는, 소용없는 ❑ 보증은 회사가 망하면

use. ❏ *The guarantee could be worthless if the firm goes out of business.* ❏ *Training is worthless unless there is proof that it works.* ❷ ADJ Someone who is described as **worthless** is considered to have no good qualities or skills. ❏ *You feel you really are completely worthless and unlovable.*

worth|while /wɜ̃rθwaɪl/ ADJ If something is **worthwhile**, it is enjoyable or useful, and worth the time, money, or effort that is spent on it. ❏ *The President's trip to Washington this week seems to have been worthwhile.*

Thesaurus	*worthwhile*의 참조어
ADJ.	beneficial, helpful, useful; *(ant.)* worthless

wor|thy /wɜ̃rði/ (**worthier, worthiest**) ADJ If a person or thing is **worthy of** something, they deserve it because they have the qualities or abilities required. [FORMAL] ❏ *The bank might think you're worthy of a loan.*

would ♦♦♦ /wəd STRONG wʊd/

Would is a modal verb. It is used with the base form of a verb. In spoken English, **would** is often abbreviated to **'d**.

❶ MODAL You use **would** when you are saying what someone believed, hoped, or expected to happen or be the case. ❏ *No one believed the soldiers stationed at the border would actually open fire.* ❏ *Would he always be like this?* ❷ MODAL You use **would** when saying what someone intended to do. ❏ *The statement added that although there were a number of differing views, these would be discussed by both sides.* ❸ MODAL You use **would** when you are referring to the result or effect of a possible situation. ❏ *Ordinarily it would be fun to be taken to fabulous restaurants.* ❏ *It would be wrong to suggest that police officers were not annoyed by acts of indecency.* ❹ MODAL You use **would**, or **would have** with a past participle, to indicate that you are assuming or guessing that something is true, because you have good reasons for thinking it. ❏ *You wouldn't know him.* ❏ *His fans would already be familiar with Caroline.* ❺ MODAL You use **would** in the main clause of some "if" and "unless" sentences to indicate something you consider to be fairly unlikely to happen. ❏ *If only I could get some sleep, I would be able to cope.* ❏ *I think if I went to look at more gardens, I would be better on planning and designing them.* ❻ MODAL You use **would** to say that someone was willing to do something. You use **would not** to indicate that they refused to do something. ❏ *They said they would give the police their full cooperation.* ❏ *He wouldn't say where he had picked up the information.* ❼ MODAL You use **would not** to indicate that something did not happen, often in spite of a lot of effort. ❏ *He kicked, pushed, and hurled his shoulder at the door. It wouldn't open.* ❽ MODAL You use **would**, especially with "like," "love," and "wish," when saying that someone wants to do or have a particular thing or wants a particular thing to happen. ❏ *She asked me what I would like to do and mentioned a particular job.* ❏ *Ideally, she would love to become pregnant again.* **would rather** →see **rather** ❾ MODAL You use **would** with "if" clauses in questions when you are asking for permission to do something. ❏ *Do you think it would be all right if I smoked?* ❿ MODAL You use **would**, usually in questions with "like," when you are making a polite offer or invitation. [POLITENESS] ❏ *Would you like a drink?* ❏ *Would you like to stay?* ⓫ MODAL You use **would**, usually in questions, when you are politely asking someone to do something. [POLITENESS] ❏ *Would you do me a favor and get rid of this letter I've just received?* ❏ *Would you come in here a moment, please?* ⓬ MODAL You say that someone **would** do something when it is typical of them and you are critical of it. You emphasize the word **would** when you use it in this way. [DISAPPROVAL] ❏ *Well, you would say that: you're a man.* ⓭ MODAL You use **would**, or sometimes **would have** with a past participle, when you are expressing your opinion about something or seeing if people agree with you, especially when you are uncertain about what you are saying. [VAGUENESS] ❏ *I think you'd agree he's a very respected columnist.* ❏ *I would have thought it a proper job for the Army to fight rebellion.* ⓮ MODAL You use **I would** when you are giving someone advice in an informal way. ❏ *If I were you I would simply ring your friend's bell and ask for your bike back.* ⓯ MODAL You use **you would** in negative sentences with verbs such as "guess" and "know" when you want to say that something is not obvious, especially something surprising. ❏ *Chris is so full of artistic temperament you'd never think she was the daughter of a banker.* ⓰ MODAL You use **would have** with a past participle when you are saying what was likely to have happened by a particular time. ❏ *Within ten weeks of the introduction, 34 million people would have been reached by our television commercials.* ⓱ MODAL You use **would have** with a past participle when you are referring to the result or effect of a possible event in the past. ❏ *My daughter would have been 17 this week if she had lived.* ⓲ MODAL If you say that someone **would have** liked or preferred something, you mean that they wanted to do it or have it but were unable to. ❏ *I would have liked a life in politics.*

would-be ADJ You can use **would-be** to describe someone who wants or attempts to do a particular thing. For example, a **would-be** writer is someone who wants to be a writer. [ADJ n] ❏ *...a book that provides encouragement for would-be writers who cannot get their novel into print.*

wouldn't /wʊdⁿt/ **Wouldn't** is the usual spoken form of "would not." ❏ *They wouldn't allow me to smoke.*

would've /wʊdəv/ **Would've** is a spoken form of "would have," when "have" is an auxiliary verb. ❏ *I knew deep down that my mom would've loved one of us to go to college.*

---
wound

① VERB FORM OF "WIND"
② INJURY
---

① **wound** /waʊnd/ **Wound** is the past tense and past participle of **wind** 2.

쓸모없는 것이 될 수도 있다. ❏ 훈련은 그것이 효과가 있다는 증거가 없다면 소용없다. ❷ 형용사 가치 없는, 쓸모없는 ❏ 당신은 스스로가 정말 완전히 쓸모없고 사랑스럽지 않다고 느끼고 있다.

형용사 보람이 있는 ❏ 대통령의 이번 주 워싱턴 방문은 보람이 있었던 것으로 보인다.

형용사 -할 가치가 있는, -할 자격을 갖춘 [격식체] ❏ 은행에서는 네가 대부받을 만한 요건을 갖추었다고 생각할지 모른다.

would는 조동사이며 동사 원형과 함께 쓰인다. 구어체 영어에서 would는 종종 'd로 축약된다.

❶ 법조동사 -일 것이다 ❏ 아무도 국경에 배치된 군인들이 실제로 발포할 것이라고 생각하지 않았다. ❏ 그가 항상 이럴까요? ❷ 법조동사 -할 것이다 ❏ 그 성명서는 비록 많은 이견이 있지만 양측이 이것에 대해 논의할 것이라고 덧붙였다. ❸ 법조동사 -일 것이다 ❏ 대개는 누가 멋진 식당에 데려가 주면 즐거울 것이다. ❏ 경찰관이 음란 행위에 기분 나빠하지 않는다고 시사하는 것은 잘못일 것이다. ❹ 법조동사 -일 것이다, -할 것이다; -였을 것이다, -했을 것이다 ❏ 너는 그를 모를 것이다. ❏ 그의 팬들은 이미 캐럴라인을 잘 알고 있을 것이다. ❺ 법조동사 -일 텐데, -할 생각인데 ❏ 내가 잠을 좀 잘 수만 있다면, 대처할 수 있을 텐데. ❏ 내가 다른 정원들을 좀 더 본다면, 정원의 계획과 설계를 더 잘 할 것이라고 생각한다. ❻ 법조동사 -하려고 하다; -하려고 하지 않다 ❏ 그들은 경찰에 최대한 협조하겠다고 말했다. ❏ 그는 어디서 그 정보를 입수했는지 말하려 하지 않았다. ❼ 법조동사 (아무리 애써도) - 하지 않았다 ❏ 그가 문을 발로 차고, 손으로 밀고, 어깨로 밀어 보았다. 문은 열리지 않았다. ❽ 법조동사 -하고 싶다 ❏ 그녀는 내게 하고 싶은 것이 무엇인지 묻고 나서 특정한 일자리를 언급했다. ❏ 이상적으로 그녀는 다시 아기를 갖고 싶어 한다. ❾ 법조동사 -해도 될까요 ❏ 제가 담배를 피워도 괜찮겠습니까? ❿ 법조동사 -하시겠습니까 (정중한 제의나 초대) [공손체] ❏ 한 잔 하시겠습니까? ❏ 여기 계시겠어요? ⓫ 법조동사 -해 주시겠습니까 [공손체] ❏ 부탁 좀 드릴 게 있는데, 방금 제가 받은 편지를 좀 없애 주시겠습니까? ❏ 여기로 잠깐만 들어와 주시겠습니까? ⓬ 법조동사 으레 -하다 [탐탁찮음] ❏ 글쎄, 넌 으레 그렇게 말하지. 넌 남자니까. ⓭ 법조동사 -일 것이다 ❏ 크리스는 예술적 기질이 넘치기 때문에 너는 그녀가 은행가의 딸이라고는 전혀 생각지 못할 것이다. ⓮ 법조동사 나라면 -하겠다 ❏ 내가 너라면, 그냥 네 친구네 초인종을 누르고 네 자전거를 돌려 달라고 하겠다. ⓯ 법조동사 너는 -일 것이다 ❏ 크리스는 예술적 기질이 넘치기 때문에 너는 그녀가 은행가의 딸이라고는 전혀 생각지 못할 것이다. ⓰ 법조동사 (아마) - 했을 것이다 ❏ 10주 내에, 3,400만 명의 사람이 우리 텔레비전 광고를 접했을 것이다. ⓱ 법조동사 (결과적으로) - 했을 것이다 ❏ 내 딸이 살아 있었다면 이번 주에 열일곱 살이 되었을 것이다. ⓲ 법조동사 -했으면 했다 ❏ 나는 정치 생활을 해보았으면 했다.

형용사 -이 되려고 하는, -을 지망하는 ❏ 소설을 출판하지 못하는 작가 지망생들에게 용기를 주는 책

would not의 축약형 ❏ 그들은 내가 담배를 피도록 허락해 주려고 하지 않았다.

would have의 축약형 ❏ 나는 우리 엄마가 우리들 중 한 명이 대학에 간다면 기뻐했을 거라는 것을 내심 알고 있었다.

wind의 과거, 과거 분사

② **wound** ♦♦◇ /wund/ (wounds, wounding, wounded) **1** N-COUNT A **wound** is damage to part of your body, especially a cut or a hole in your flesh, which is caused by a gun, knife, or other weapon. ❏ *The wound is healing nicely and the patient is healthy.* **2** V-T If a weapon or something sharp **wounds** you, it damages your body. ❏ *A bomb exploded in a hotel, killing six people and wounding another five.* ● N-PLURAL The **wounded** are people who are wounded. ❏ *Hospitals said they could not cope with the wounded.* **3** V-T If you **are wounded** by what someone says or does, your feelings are deeply hurt. ❏ *He was deeply wounded by the treachery of close aides.*

1 가산명사 상처, 부상 ❏ 상처가 잘 낫고 있으며 환자는 건강하다. **2** 타동사 부상을 입히다 ❏ 한 호텔에서 폭탄이 폭발해서 여섯 명이 사망했고 다섯 명이 부상을 입었다. ● 복수명사 부상자들 ❏ 병원에서는 부상자들을 더 이상 감당할 수 없다고 말했다. **3** 타동사 감정이 상하다 ❏ 그는 측근의 배신으로 깊은 상처를 받았다.

> Note that when someone is hurt accidentally, for example, in a car crash or when they are playing sports, you do not use the word **wound**. You use **injury** instead. ❏ *A man and his baby were injured in the explosion... Many of the deaths that occur in cycling are due to head injuries.* In more formal English, **injury** can also be an uncount noun. ❏ *Two teenagers escaped serious injury when their car rolled down an embankment.* **Wound** is normally restricted to soldiers who are injured in battle, or to deliberate acts of violence against a particular person. ❏ *...stab wounds*

> 누가 사고로, 예를 들어 자동차 충돌사고나 운동을 하다가, 다친 경우, wound를 쓰지 않고 injury를 쓰는 것을 유의하라. ❏ 남자 한 명과 그의 아기가 폭발사고로 부상당했다... 자전거를 타다가 생기는 사망사고 중 많은 경우가 머리 부상 때문이다. 좀 더 격식을 갖춘 영국 영어에서는, injury는 불가산명사이다. ❏ 십대 두 명이 탄 차가 강둑에서 굴렀지만 중상을 면했다. wound는 보통 전투에서 부상당한 군인이나 특정인에 대한 고의적인 폭력행위에 국한되어 쓰인다. ❏ ...칼에 찔린 상처

Word Partnership   *wound*의 연어

N.	**bullet** wound, **chest** wound, **gunshot** wound, **head** wound ② **1**
V.	**die from a** wound, wound **heals**, **inflict a** wound ② **1**
ADJ.	**fatal** wound, **open** wound ② **1**

wound up /waʊnd ʌp/ ADJ If someone is **wound up**, they are very tense and nervous or angry. ❏ *"My caddie got so wound up I had to calm him down," Lancaster said.*

형용사 긴장한, 흥분한 ❏ 랭커스터는 "내 캐디가 너무 흥분해서 내가 진정시켜야만 했다."라고 말했다.

wove /woʊv/ **Wove** is the past tense of **weave**.

weave의 과거

woven /woʊvⁿ/ **Woven** is a past participle of **weave**.

weave의 과거 분사

wow /waʊ/ EXCLAM You can say "wow" when you are very impressed, surprised, or pleased. [INFORMAL, FEELINGS] ❏ *I thought, "Wow, what a good idea."*

감탄사 와, 아 [비격식체, 감정 개입] ❏ 나는 "와, 참 좋은 생각이다."라고 생각했다.

wrangle /ræŋgᵊl/ (wrangles, wrangling, wrangled) V-RECIP If you say that someone is **wrangling** with someone **over** a question or issue, you mean that they have been arguing angrily for quite a long time about it. ❏ *The two sides have spent most of their time wrangling over procedural problems.*

상호동사 언쟁을 벌이다 ❏ 양측은 절차상의 문제로 언쟁을 벌이느라 그들의 시간 대부분을 써버렸다.

wrap ♦◇◇ /ræp/ (wraps, wrapping, wrapped) **1** V-T When you **wrap** something, you fold paper or cloth tightly around it to cover it completely, for example in order to protect it or so that you can give it to someone as a present. ❏ *Harry had carefully bought and wrapped presents for Mark to give them.* ● PHRASAL VERB **Wrap up** means the same as **wrap**. ❏ *Diana is taking the opportunity to wrap up the family presents.* **2** V-T When you **wrap** something such as a piece of paper or cloth around another thing, you put it around it. ❏ *She wrapped a handkerchief around her bleeding hand.* **3** →see also **wrapping** **4** PHRASE If you keep something **under wraps**, you keep it secret, often until you are ready to announce it at some time in the future. ❏ *The bids were submitted in May and were meant to have been kept under wraps until October.*

1 타동사 싸다, 포장하다 ❏ 해리는 마크가 그들에게 줄 수 있도록 정성을 들여 선물을 구입하여 포장했다. ● 구동사 싸다, 포장하다 ❏ 다이애나는 기회를 잡아 가족에게 줄 선물을 포장하고 있다. **2** 타동사 싸다, 감싸다 ❏ 그녀는 피가 나는 손바닥을 손수건으로 감쌌다. **3** 구 비밀로 ❏ 입찰 서류들은 5월에 제출되었고 10월까지는 비밀에 부쳐 두기로 되어 있었다.

▶ **wrap up** **1** PHRASAL VERB If you **wrap up**, you put warm clothes on. ❏ *Markus has wrapped up warmly in a woolly hat.* ❏ *Kids just love being able to romp around in the fresh air without having to wrap up warm.* **2** PHRASAL VERB If you **wrap up** something such as a job or an agreement, you complete it in a satisfactory way. ❏ *NATO defense ministers wrap up their meeting in Brussels today.* **3** →see also **wrap 1, wrapped up**

1 구동사 (따뜻하게) 단단히 차려입다 ❏ 마커스는 따뜻하게 양털 모자를 챙겨 썼다. ❏ 아이들은 따뜻하게 옷을 차려 입지 않은 채 바깥에서 그저 뛰어 놀 수 있는 것만 좋아한다. **2** 구동사 (성공리에) 마치다 ❏ 나토 국가들의 국방 장관들이 오늘 브뤼셀에서 회의를 마쳤다.

wrapped up ADJ If someone is **wrapped up** in a particular person or thing, they spend nearly all their time thinking about them, so that they forget about other things which may be important. [v-link ADJ in/with n] ❏ *He's too serious and dedicated, wrapped up in his career.*

형용사 몰두한, 완전히 빠진 ❏ 그는 자기 일에 완전히 빠져 너무도 진지하고 열심이다.

wrapper /ræpər/ (wrappers) N-COUNT A **wrapper** is a piece of paper, plastic, or thin metal which covers and protects something that you buy, especially food. ❏ *I emptied the sweet wrappers from the ashtray.*

가산명사 포장지 ❏ 내가 재떨이에 있던 사탕 포장지들을 비웠다.

wrapping /ræpɪŋ/ (wrappings) N-VAR **Wrapping** is something such as paper or plastic which is used to cover and protect something. ❏ *Nick asked for the tile to be delivered in waterproof wrapping.*

가산명사 또는 불가산명사 포장지 ❏ 닉은 타일을 방수 포장하여 배달해 달라고 부탁했다.

wrath /ræθ, BRIT rɒθ/ N-UNCOUNT **Wrath** means the same as anger. [LITERARY] ❏ *He incurred the wrath of the authorities in speaking out against government injustices.*

불가산명사 분노, 노여움 [문예체] ❏ 그는 정부의 부당 행위에 반대하는 의견을 말해서 당국의 노여움을 샀다.

wreak /rik/ (wreaks, wreaking, wreaked)

> Some people use **wrought** as the past tense and past participle of **wreak**, but many people consider this to be wrong.

> 일부 사람들이 wreak의 과거 및 과거 분사로 wrought를 쓰지만 많은 사람들이 이를 틀린 것으로 본다.

V-T Something or someone that **wreaks** havoc or destruction causes a great amount of disorder or damage. [LITERARY] ❏ *Violent storms wreaked havoc on the French Riviera, leaving three people dead and dozens injured.*

타동사 (피해 등을) 입히다, 가하다 [문예체] ❏ 거센 폭풍우가 프랑스 리비에라 지역에 엄청난 피해를 입혀 세 명이 죽고 수십 명이 다쳤다.

wreath /riθ/ (wreaths) **1** N-COUNT A **wreath** is an arrangement of flowers and leaves, usually in the shape of a circle, which you put on a grave or by a statue to show that you remember a person who has died or people who have died. ❏ *The coffin lying before the altar was bare, except for a single wreath of white roses.* **2** N-COUNT A **wreath** is a circle of leaves which some people hang on the front door of their house at Christmas. ❏ *A Christmas wreath exclaiming PEACE ON EARTH hangs on the restaurant door.*

1 가산명사 화환 ❏ 제단 앞에 놓여 있는 관에는 백장미 화환 하나를 제외하고는 아무것도 없었다. **2** 가산명사 화환 ❏ '지구에 평화를'이라고 주장하는 글귀가 적힌 성탄절 화환이 식당 문에 걸려 있다.

wreck /rɛk/ (wrecks, wrecking, wrecked) **1** V-T To **wreck** something means to completely destroy or ruin it. ❏ *He wrecked the garden.* ❏ *His life has been wrecked by the tragedy.* **2** N-COUNT A **wreck** is something such as a ship, car, plane, or

1 타동사 망가뜨리다, 파괴하다 ❏ 그가 정원을 망가뜨렸다. ❏ 그의 인생은 그 비극적인 사건으로 엉망이 되었다. **2** 가산명사 (사고로 파괴된) 잔해

building which has been destroyed, usually in an accident. □ ...*the wreck of a sailing ship.* □ *The car was a total wreck.* ⬛ N-COUNT A **wreck** is an accident in which a moving vehicle hits something and is damaged or destroyed. [mainly AM; BRIT usually **crash**] □ *He was killed in a car wreck.* ⬛ N-COUNT If you say that someone is a **wreck**, you mean that they are very exhausted or unhealthy. [INFORMAL] □ *You look a wreck.*

□ 난파된 범선 □ 그 자동차는 완전히 망가져 있었다. ⬛ 가산명사 (교통) 사고 [주로 미국영어; 영국영어 대개 crash] □ 그는 자동차 사고로 죽었다. ⬛ 가산명사 (사나운) 몰골 [비격식체] □ 네 몰골이 말이 아니구나.

wreck|age /rɛkɪdʒ/ N-UNCOUNT When something such as a plane, car, or building has been destroyed, you can refer to what remains as **wreckage** or **the wreckage**. [also the N] □ *Mark was dragged from the burning wreckage of his car.*

불가산명사 잔해 □ 마크는 불타고 있는 자기 차의 잔해에서 끌려 나왔다.

wrench /rɛntʃ/ (**wrenches, wrenching, wrenched**) ⬛ V-T If you **wrench** something that is fixed in a particular position, you pull or twist it violently, in order to move or remove it. □ *He felt two men wrench the suitcase from his hand.* ⬛ V-T/V-I If you **wrench** yourself free from someone who is holding you, you get away from them by suddenly twisting the part of your body that is being held. □ *She wrenched herself from his grasp.* □ *He wrenched his arm free.* ⬛ N-COUNT A **wrench** or a **monkey wrench** is an adjustable metal tool used for tightening or loosening metal nuts of different sizes. ⬛ PHRASE If someone **throws a wrench** or **throws a monkey wrench** into a process, they prevent something happening smoothly by deliberately causing a problem. [AM; BRIT **throw a spanner in the works**] □ *Their delegation threw a giant monkey wrench into the process this week by raising all sorts of petty objections.*

⬛ 타동사 비틀어 떼다, 잡아 떼어 내다 □ 그는 두 남자가 자기 손에서 여행 가방을 잡아 빼는 것을 느꼈다. ⬛ 타동사/자동사 (빠져 나오려고 몸을) 비틀다 □ 그녀는 그의 손아귀에서 몸을 비틀어 빠져나왔다. □ 그는 자기 팔을 비틀어 뺐냈다. ⬛ 가산명사 렌치, 멍키 스패너 ⬛ 구 (문제를 일으켜) 방해하다 [미국영어; 영국영어 throw a spanner in the works] □ 그들 대표단은 이번 주에 온갖 사소한 것에 이의를 제기함으로써 일의 진행을 크게 방해했다.

wres|tle /rɛsəl/ (**wrestles, wrestling, wrestled**) ⬛ V-I When you **wrestle with** a difficult problem, you try to deal with it. □ *Delegates wrestled with the problems of violence and sanctions.* ⬛ V-I If you **wrestle** with someone, you fight them by forcing them into painful positions or throwing them to the ground, rather than by hitting them. Some people wrestle as a sport. □ *They taught me to wrestle.* ⬛ V-T If you **wrestle** a person or thing somewhere, you move them there using a lot of force, for example by twisting a part of someone's body into a painful position. □ *We had to physically wrestle the child from the man's arms.* ⬛ →see also **wrestling**

⬛ 자동사 (문제를 붙들고) 씨름하다 □ 대표단은 폭력과 제재 문제들을 붙들고 씨름을 했다. ⬛ 자동사 레슬링을 하다 □ 그들이 내게 레슬링을 가르쳐 주었다. ⬛ 타동사 맞붙어 싸우다, 몸싸움을 하다 □ 우리는 그 아이를 남자의 팔에서 빼내려고 몸싸움을 해야 했다.

wres|tler /rɛslər/ (**wrestlers**) N-COUNT A **wrestler** is someone who wrestles as a sport, usually for money.

가산명사 레슬링 선수

wres|tling /rɛslɪŋ/ N-UNCOUNT **Wrestling** is a sport in which two people wrestle and try to throw each other to the ground. □ ...*a championship wrestling match.*

불가산명사 레슬링 □ 레슬링 선수권 대회

wretch|ed /rɛtʃɪd/ ⬛ ADJ You use **wretched** to describe someone or something that you dislike or feel angry with. [INFORMAL, FEELINGS] [ADJ n] □ *Wretched woman, I thought, why the hell can't she wait?* ⬛ ADJ Someone who feels **wretched** feels very unhappy. [FORMAL] □ *I feel really confused and wretched.*

⬛ 형용사 형편없는, 재수없는 [비격식체, 감정 개입] □ 형편없는 여자 같으니라고, 도대체 왜 못 기다리는 거야? 하고 그는 생각했다. ⬛ 형용사 비참한, 불쌍한 [격식체] □ 나는 정말 혼란스럽고 비참한 기분이다.

wrig|gle /rɪgəl/ (**wriggles, wriggling, wriggled**) V-T/V-I If you **wriggle** or **wriggle** part of your body, you twist and turn with quick movements, for example because you are uncomfortable. □ *The babies are wriggling on their tummies.*

타동사/자동사 꿈틀거리다; (몸을) 비비 꼬다 □ 아기들이 엎드려서 꼼지락거리고 있다.

▶ **wriggle out of** PHRASAL VERB If you say that someone has **wriggled out of** doing something, you disapprove of the fact that they have managed to avoid doing it, although they should have done it. [DISAPPROVAL] □ *The Government has tried to wriggle out of any responsibility for providing childcare for working parents.*

구동사 요리조리 빠져나가다, 회피하다 [탐탁찮음] □ 정부는 직장이 있는 부모들에게 육아 혜택을 제공할 책임을 회피할 궁리만 해 왔다.

wring /rɪŋ/ (**wrings, wringing, wrung**) ⬛ V-T If you **wring** something **out of** someone, you manage to make them give it to you even though they do not want to. □ *Buyers use different ruses to wring free credit out of their suppliers.* ⬛ PHRASE If someone **wrings** their **hands**, they hold them together and twist and turn them, usually because they are very worried or upset about something. You can also say that someone is **wringing** their **hands** when they are expressing sorrow that a situation is so bad but are saying that they are unable to change it. □ *The Government has got to get a grip. Wringing its hands and saying it is a world problem just isn't good enough.*

⬛ 타동사 -로부터 ...을 우려내다 □ 구매자들은 공급자들로부터 무조건 신용 판매를 얻어내기 위해 다양한 책략을 사용한다. ⬛ 구 (걱정 등으로) 두 손만 비벼대다 □ 정부가 통제권을 움켜쥐어야 한다. 두 손만 비비대면서 그건 전 세계적인 문제라고 말만 해서는 안 된다.

▶ **wring out** PHRASAL VERB When you **wring out** a wet cloth or a wet piece of clothing, you squeeze the water out of it by twisting it strongly. □ *He turned away to wring out the wet shirt.*

구동사 (젖은 옷 등을) 비틀어 짜다 □ 그가 돌아서서 젖은 셔츠를 비틀어 짰다.

wrin|kle /rɪŋkəl/ (**wrinkles, wrinkling, wrinkled**) ⬛ N-COUNT **Wrinkles** are lines which form on someone's face as they grow old. □ *His face was covered with wrinkles.* ⬛ V-T/V-I When someone's skin **wrinkles** or when something **wrinkles** it, lines start to form in it because the skin is getting old or damaged. □ *The skin on her cheeks and around her eyes was beginning to wrinkle.* ● **wrin|kled** ADJ □ *I did indeed look older and more wrinkled than ever.* ⬛ N-COUNT A **wrinkle** is a raised fold in a piece of cloth or paper that spoils its appearance. □ *He noticed a wrinkle in her stocking.* ⬛ V-T/V-I If cloth **wrinkles**, or if someone or something **wrinkles** it, it gets folds or lines in it. □ *Her stockings wrinkled at the ankles.* ● **wrin|kled** ADJ □ *His suit was wrinkled and he looked very tired.* ⬛ V-T/V-I When you **wrinkle** your nose or forehead, or when it **wrinkles**, you tighten the muscles in your face so that the skin folds. □ *Frannie wrinkled her nose at her daughter.* →see **skin**

⬛ 가산명사 주름 □ 그의 얼굴은 주름살이 가득했다. ⬛ 타동사/자동사 주름살이 생기다; 주름살이 지게 하다 □ 그녀의 볼과 눈가 피부에는 주름살이 생기기 시작하고 있었다. ● 주름이 진 형용사 □ 나는 정말 어느 때보다도 더 늙고 주름이 많아 보였다. ⬛ 가산명사 구김살, 주름 □ 그는 그녀의 스타킹에 주름이 져 있는 것을 보았다. ⬛ 타동사/자동사 주름지다, 구겨지다; 구기다, 구김살을 만들다 □ 그녀의 스타킹이 발목 부분에 주름이 잡혀 있었다. ● 구겨진 형용사 □ 그는 양복이 구겨져 있었고 아주 피곤해 보였다. ⬛ 타동사/자동사 찡그리다; 찡그려지다 □ 프래니는 딸을 보고 코를 찡그렸다.

wrist /rɪst/ (**wrists**) N-COUNT Your **wrist** is the part of your body between your hand and your arm which bends when you move your hand. □ *He broke his wrist climbing rocks for a cigarette ad.* →see **body, hand**

가산명사 손목 □ 그는 담배 광고를 찍기 위해 암벽을 오르다 손목이 부러졌다.

writ /rɪt/ (**writs**) N-COUNT A **writ** is a legal document that orders a person to do a particular thing. □ *He issued a writ against one of his accusers.*

가산명사 명령서 □ 그가 자기 고소인 중 한 사람에게 명령서를 발부했다.

write ♦♦♦ /raɪt/ (**writes, writing, wrote, written**) ⬛ V-T/V-I When you **write**, you use something such as a pen or pencil to produce words, letters, or numbers on the surface. □ *Simply write your name and address on a postcard and send it to us.* □ *They were still trying to teach her to read and write.* ⬛ V-T If you **write** something such as a book, a poem, or a piece of music, you create and record it on paper or perhaps on a computer. □ *I had written quite a lot of orchestral music in my student days.* □ *Thereafter she wrote articles for papers and magazines in Paris.* ⬛ V-I Someone who **writes** creates books, stories, or articles, usually for

⬛ 타동사/자동사 (글씨를) 쓰다 □ 우편엽서에 그냥 이름과 주소만 써서 우리에게 보내세요. □ 그들은 여전히 그녀에게 읽기와 쓰기를 가르치려고 애쓰고 있었다. ⬛ 타동사 작곡하다, 쓰다 □ 나는 학창 시절에 상당히 많은 오케스트라 곡을 작곡했다. □ 그 이후 그녀는 파리에서 신문과 잡지에 글을 썼다. ⬛ 자동사 글을 쓰다 □ 제이는 글을 쓰고 싶어 했다. ⬛ 타동사/자동사 (편지를) 쓰다 □ 분명히 그녀가

a
b
c
d
e
f
g
h
i
j
k
l
m
n
o
p
q
r
s
t
u
v
w
x
y
z

publication. ❑ *Jay wanted to write.* ◳ V-T/V-I When you **write to** someone or **write** them a letter, you give them information, ask them something, or express your feelings in a letter. In American English, you can also **write** someone. ❑ *Apparently she had written to her aunt in Holland asking for advice.* ❑ *She had written him a note a couple of weeks earlier.* ❑ *I wrote a letter to the car rental agency, explaining what had happened.* **nothing to write home about** →see **home** ◳ V-T When someone **writes** something such as a check, receipt, or prescription, they put the necessary information on it and usually sign it. ❑ *Snape wrote a receipt with a gold fountain pen.* ◳ V-I If you **write** to a computer or a disk, you record data on it. [COMPUTING] ❑ *You should write-protect all disks that you do not usually need to write to.* ◳ →see also **writing, written**

Thesaurus   *write*의 참조어

v.   jot down, note down, scribble ◳
      author, compose, draft ◳

▶**write back** PHRASAL VERB If you **write back** to someone who has sent you a letter, you write them a letter in reply. ❑ *Macmillan wrote back saying that he could certainly help.*

▶**write down** PHRASAL VERB When you **write** something **down**, you record it on a piece of paper using a pen or pencil. ❑ *On the morning before starting the fast, write down your starting weight.*

▶**write in** PHRASAL VERB If you **write in** to an organization, you send them a letter. ❑ *What's the point in writing in when you only print half the letter anyway?*

▶**write into** PHRASAL VERB If a rule or detail **is written into** a contract, law, or agreement, it is included in it when the contract, law, or agreement is made. ❑ *They insisted that a guaranteed supply of Chinese food was written into their contracts.*

▶**write off** PHRASAL VERB If you **write off** to a company or organization, you send them a letter, usually asking for something. ❑ *He wrote off to the New Zealand Government for these pamphlets about life in New Zealand.* ◳ PHRASAL VERB If someone **writes off** a debt or an amount of money that has been spent on a project, they accept that they are never going to get the money back. [BUSINESS] ❑ *It was the president who persuaded the West to write off Polish debts.* ◳ PHRASAL VERB If you **write** someone or something **off**, you decide that they are unimportant or useless and that they are not worth further serious attention. ❑ *He is fed up with people writing him off because of his age.* ❑ *His critics write him off as too cautious to succeed.* ◳ PHRASAL VERB If you **write off** a plan or project, you accept that it is not going to be successful and do not continue with it. ❑ *We decided to write off the rest of the day and go shopping.* ◳ PHRASAL VERB If someone **writes off** a vehicle, they have a crash in it and it is so badly damaged that it is not worth repairing. [BRIT] ❑ *John's written off four cars. Now he sticks to public transport.* ◳ →see also **write-off**

▶**write out** PHRASAL VERB When you **write out** something fairly long such as a report or a list, you write it on paper. ❑ *We had to write out a list of ten jobs we'd like to do.* ◳ PHRASAL VERB If a character in a drama series **is written out**, he or she is taken out of the series. ❑ *Terry's character has been written out of the show.*

▶**write up** PHRASAL VERB If you **write up** something that has been done or said, you record it on paper in a neat and complete form, usually using notes that you have made. ❑ *He wrote up his visit in a report of over 600 pages.*

write-off (write-offs) ◳ N-SING If you describe a plan or period of time as a **write-off**, you mean that it has been a failure and you have achieved nothing. [INFORMAL] ❑ *Today was really a bit of a write-off for me.* ◳ N-COUNT Something such as a vehicle that is a **write-off** has been so badly damaged in an accident that it is not worth repairing. [BRIT] ❑ *The car was a write-off, but everyone escaped unharmed.*

writ|er ◆◇◇ /ˈraɪtər/ (writers) ◳ N-COUNT A **writer** is a person who writes books, stories, or articles as a job. ❑ *Turner is a writer and critic.* ❑ *...detective stories by American writers.* ◳ N-COUNT The **writer** of a particular article, report, letter, or story is the person who wrote it. ❑ *No-one is to see the document without the permission of the writer of the report.*

writhe /raɪð/ (writhes, writhing, writhed) V-I If you **writhe**, your body twists and turns violently backward and forward, usually because you are in great pain or discomfort. ❑ *He was writhing in agony.*

writ|ing ◆◇◇ /ˈraɪtɪŋ/ ◳ N-UNCOUNT **Writing** is something that has been written or printed. ❑ *If you have a complaint about your holiday, please inform us in writing.* ◳ N-UNCOUNT You can refer to any piece of written work as **writing**, especially when you are considering the style of language used in it. ❑ *The writing is brutally tough and savagely humorous.* ◳ N-UNCOUNT **Writing** is the activity of writing, especially of writing books for money. ❑ *She had begun to be a little bored with novel writing.* ◳ N-UNCOUNT Your **writing** is the way that you write with a pen or pencil, which can usually be recognized as belonging to you. ❑ *It was a little difficult to read your writing.*
→see Word Web: **writing**

writ|ten ◆◇◇ /ˈrɪtᵊn/ ◳ **Written** is the past participle of **write**. ◳ ADJ A **written** test or piece of work is one which involves writing rather than doing something practical or giving spoken answers. ❑ *Learners may have to take a written exam before they pass their driving test.* ◳ ADJ A **written** agreement, rule, or law has been officially written down. [ADJ n] ❑ *The newspaper broke a written agreement not to sell certain photographs.*

wrong ◆◆◇ /rɒŋ, BRIT rɒŋ/ (wrongs) ◳ ADJ If you say there is something **wrong**, you mean there is something unsatisfactory about the situation,

화관에 있는 이모에게 조언을 요청하는 편지를 썼던 것 같다. ❑ 그녀가 그에게 2주쯤 전에 간단한 서신을 보냈었다. ❑ 나는 일어났던 일을 설명하는 편지를 써서 자동차 대여 사무소에 보냈다. ◳ 자동사 (체물 등을) 쓰다, 기입하다 ❑ 스네이프는 금장 만년필로 영수증을 썼다. ◳ 자동사 (컴퓨터 또는 디스켓에) 쓰다, 입력하다 [컴퓨터] ❑ 평소 입력할 필요가 없는 모든 디스켓에는 쓰기 잠금 처리를 해야 한다.

구동사 회신을 쓰다 ❑ 맥밀런은 자기가 확실히 도울 수 있다고 하는 회신을 썼다.

구동사 써 두다, 적어 두다 ❑ 금식을 시작하기 전 아침에 시작 당시의 몸무게를 적어 두세요.

구동사 편지를 보내다 ❑ 귀사에서 편지를 반 쪽밖에 실어주지 않는데 편지를 써 보내야 무슨 소용이 있나요?

구동사 -에 포함되다, -에 명시되다 ❑ 그들은 중국 식품의 공급 보증을 자기들의 계약에 명시할 것을 고집했다.

◳ 구동사 서면으로 부탁하다, 서면으로 요청하다 ❑ 그는 뉴질랜드 정부에 서면으로 뉴질랜드 생활에 관한 이런 팜플릿을 요청했다. ◳ 구동사 (빚 등을) 탕감하다 [경제] ❑ 서방에 폴란드의 빚을 탕감해 주도록 설득한 것은 대통령이었다. ◳ 구동사 고려 대상에서 제외하다 ❑ 그는 나이 때문에 자기를 고려 대상에서 제외시키는 사람들에게 넌더리가 났다. ❑ 그를 비판하는 사람들은 그가 성공하기에는 너무 신중하다고 고려 대상에서 제외한다. ◳ 구동사 단념하다 ❑ 우리는 그날 남은 일정을 포기하고 쇼핑을 가기로 했다. ◳ 구동사 (사고로) 박살내다, 대파하다 [영국영어] ❑ 존은 지금까지 자동차 네 대를 사고로 박살냈다. 이제 그는 대중교통만을 고집한다.

◳ 구동사 (상당히 긴 내용을) 써내다 ❑ 우리는 하고 싶은 일 열 가지를 써내야만 했다. ◳ 구동사 (배역에서) 빠지다 ❑ 테리의 배역이 그 프로에서 빠졌다.

구동사 기록하다 ❑ 그는 자기의 방문에 관해 6백 쪽이 넘는 분량의 보고서를 썼다.

◳ 단수명사 허탕; 공치는 시기 [비격식체] ❑ 오늘은 내게는 정말 좀 되는 일이 없는 날이었다. ◳ 가산명사 박살 [영국영어] ❑ 차는 완전히 박살이 났지만, 사람들은 모두 다치지 않고 빠져나왔다.

◳ 가산명사 작가, 저술가 ❑ 터너는 작가이자 비평가이다. ❑ 미국 작가들이 쓴 탐정 소설들 ◳ 가산명사 저자 ❑ 아무도 그 보고서를 쓴 저자의 허락 없이는 그 문서를 볼 수 없다.

자동사 몸부림치다, 몸을 뒤틀다 ❑ 그는 고통스러워 하며 몸부림쳤다.

◳ 불가산명사 쓰여 있는 것, 문서 ❑ 여러분의 휴가에 대해 불만 사항이 있으시면, 저희에게 서면으로 알려주시기 바랍니다. ◳ 불가산명사 글 ❑ 그 글은 무지막지하게 거칠고 통렬하게 해학적이다. ◳ 불가산명사 글쓰기, 집필 ❑ 그녀는 소설 쓰는 것이 조금 싫증나기 시작한 참이었다. ◳ 불가산명사 필적, 필체 ❑ 당신의 필체를 읽기가 조금 어려웠습니다.

◳ write의 과거 분사 ◳ 형용사 필기로 된 ❑ 운전을 배우는 사람은 운전면허 실기시험을 보기 전에 필기시험을 보아야 할 것이다. ◳ 형용사 문서상의, 성문의 ❑ 그 신문사는 특정한 사진은 팔지 않겠다는 문서상의 협약을 어겼다.

◳ 형용사 잘못된, 고장 난 ❑ 통증은 몸이 우리에게 무언가 이상이 생겼다고 알려주는 것이다. ❑ 아무도

Word Web · writing

Writing began about 6,000 years ago. People used pictograms carved in clay to record transactions involving food and possessions. About 3,000 years later, the Egyptians used modified pictograms called hieroglyphs. Some of these pictures represent verbs. Later still, people in Northern Europe carved letters of an alphabet called **runes** on wood or stone. Chinese ideograms represent whole ideas or words. Today's computers have introduced a new set of language symbols. **Icons** represent processes. For example, the button with scissors on it means "cut." **Emoticons** such as the smiley face show how the writer is feeling.

pictogram

hieroglyph

rune

ideogram

icon

:-)
emoticon

person, or thing you are talking about. [v-link ADJ, oft ADJ with n] ❑ *Pain is the body's way of telling us that something is wrong.* ❑ *Nobody seemed to notice anything wrong.* ❑ *What's wrong with him?* ❷ ADJ If you choose the **wrong** thing, person, or method, you make a mistake and do not choose the one that you really want. ❑ *He went to the wrong house.* ❑ *The wrong man had been punished.* ● ADV **Wrong** is also an adverb. [ADV after v] ❑ *You've done it wrong.* ❸ ADJ If something such as a decision, choice, or action is **the wrong** one, it is not the best or most suitable one. [ADJ n] ❑ *I really made the wrong decision there.* ❑ *The wrong choice of club might limit your chances of success.* ❹ ADJ If something is **wrong**, it is incorrect and not in accordance with the facts. ❑ *How do you know that this explanation is wrong?* ❑ *...a clock which showed the wrong time.* ● ADV **Wrong** is also an adverb. [ADV after v] ❑ *I must have added it up wrong, then.* ❑ *It looks like it's spelled wrong.* ● **wrongly** ADV [ADV with v] ❑ *A child was wrongly diagnosed as having a bone tumor.* ❺ ADJ If something is **wrong** or goes **wrong with** a machine or piece of equipment, it stops working properly. [v-link ADJ, usu ADJ with n] ❑ *We think there's something wrong with the computer.* ❻ ADJ If you are **wrong** about something, what you say or think about it is not correct. [v-link ADJ, oft ADJ about n, ADJ in -ing, it v-link ADJ to-inf, ADJ to-inf] ❑ *I was wrong about it being a casual meeting.* ❑ *I'm sure you've got it wrong. Kate isn't like that.* ❼ ADJ If you think that someone was **wrong to** do something, you think that they should not have done it because it was bad or immoral. [ADJ to-inf] ❑ *She was wrong to leave her child alone.* ● N-UNCOUNT **Wrong** is also a noun. ❑ *...a man who believes that he has done no wrong.* ❽ ADJ **Wrong** is used to refer to activities or actions that are considered to be morally bad and unacceptable. [v-link ADJ, oft v-link ADJ to-inf/that] ❑ *Is it wrong to try to save the life of someone you love?* ❑ *They thought slavery was morally wrong.* ● N-UNCOUNT **Wrong** is also a noun. ❑ *Johnson didn't seem to be able to tell the difference between right and wrong.* ❾ N-COUNT A **wrong** is an unfair or immoral action. ❑ *I intend to right that wrong.* ❿ ADJ You use **wrong** to describe something which is not thought to be socially acceptable or desirable. [ADJ n] ❑ *If you went to the wrong school, you won't get the job.* ⓫ PHRASE If a situation **goes wrong**, it stops progressing in the way that you expected or intended, and becomes much worse. ❑ *It all went horribly wrong.* ⓬ PHRASE If someone who is involved in an argument or dispute has behaved in a way which is morally or legally wrong, you can say that they are **in the wrong**. ❑ *He didn't press charges because he was in the wrong.* ⓭ **to get off on the wrong foot** →see **foot**. **to get hold of the wrong end of the stick** →see **stick**

Thesaurus · *wrong*의 참조어

ADJ.	incorrect; (*ant.*) right ❹
	corrupt, immoral, unjust ❽
N.	abuse, offense, sin ❾

wrong|doing /rɔ́ŋduɪŋ, BRIT rɒ́ŋduːɪŋ/ (**wrongdoings**) N-VAR **Wrongdoing** is behavior that is illegal or immoral. ❑ *The city attorney's office hasn't found any evidence of criminal wrongdoing.*

wrong|ful /rɔ́ŋfəl, BRIT rɒ́ŋfʊl/ ADJ A **wrongful** act is one that is illegal, immoral, or unjust. ❑ *He is on hunger strike in protest at what he claims is his wrongful conviction for murder.* ● **wrong|ful|ly** ADV [ADV with v] ❑ *The criminal justice system is in need of urgent reform to prevent more people being wrongfully imprisoned.*

wrote /roʊt/ **Wrote** is the past tense of **write**.

wrought /rɔt/ V-T If something has **wrought** a change, it has made it happen. [LITERARY] [only past] ❑ *Events in Paris wrought a change in British opinion towards France and Germany.*

wrung /rʌŋ/ **Wrung** is the past tense of **wring**.

wry /raɪ/ ❶ ADJ If someone has a **wry** expression, it shows that they find a bad situation or a change in a situation slightly amusing. ❑ *Matthew allowed himself a wry smile.* ❷ ADJ A **wry** remark or piece of writing refers to a bad situation or a change in a situation in an amusing way. ❑ *There is a wry sense of humor in his work.*

WTO /dʌ́bəlyu ti oʊ/ N-PROPER **WTO** is an abbreviation for **World Trade Organization**. ❑ *The world desperately needs an effective WTO.*

무언가 잘못된 것이 있는지 알아차리지 못한 것 같았다. ❑ 그에게 무슨 일이 있나요? ❷ 형용사 그릇된, 틀린 ❑ 그는 다른 집으로 잘못 갔다. ❑ 다른 사람이 잘못 처벌을 받았다. ● 부사 잘못 ❑ 네가 그것을 잘못했어. ❸ 형용사 잘못된, 부적절한 ❑ 나는 거기서 정말 부적절한 결정을 내렸다. ❑ 클럽을 제대로 선택하지 않으면 너의 성공 가망성이 낮아질지도 모른다. ❹ 형용사 틀린, 잘못된 ❑ 이 설명이 틀리다는 것을 어떻게 아시나요? ❑ 시간이 틀린 시계 ● 부사 틀리게 ❑ 그럼 내가 합산을 잘못한 게 틀림없어. ❑ 그것이 철자가 틀린 것 같다. ● 잘못 부사 ❑ 한 아이가 골종양이라는 오진을 받았다. ❺ 형용사 고장 난, 이상이 있는 ❑ 컴퓨터에 뭔가 이상이 있는 것 같다. ❻ 형용사 판단이 틀린 ❑ 나는 그걸 가벼운 모임으로 잘못 생각했다. ❑ 틀림없이 네가 잘못 판단하는 거야. 케이트는 그렇지 않아. ❼ 형용사 나쁜, 부당한, 잘못된 ❑ 그녀가 아이를 혼자 내버려둔 것은 잘못이었다. ● 불가산명사 잘못 ❑ 자기가 잘못한 것이 없다고 믿는 남자 ❽ 형용사 나쁜, 잘못된 ❑ 사랑하는 사람의 생명을 구하려고 하는 게 잘못인 건가요? ❑ 그들은 노예 제도가 도덕적으로 나쁘다고 생각했다. ● 불가산명사 그릇됨 ❑ 존슨은 옳고 그른 것의 차이를 구별하지 못하는 것 같았다. ❾ 가산명사 잘못된 것 ❑ 나는 그 잘못된 일을 바로잡으려고 한다. ❿ 형용사 나쁜, 좋지 않은 ❑ 만약 네가 안 좋은 학교에 간다면 그 직업을 갖지 못할 것이다. ⓫ 구 잘못되다, 엉망이 되다 ❑ 모든 게 끔찍하게 엉망이 되었다. ⓬ 구 잘못이 있는 ❑ 그는 자기에게 잘못이 있었기 때문에 고발을 안 했다.

가산명사 또는 불가산명사 비행, 범죄 ❑ 시 검찰은 형사상 범죄의 증거를 찾지 못했다.

형용사 불법의, 사악한, 부당한 ❑ 그는 그의 주장에 따르면 자신에 대한 부당한 살인 유죄 판결에 항의하여 단식 투쟁 중이다. ● 부당하게 부사 ❑ 더 많은 사람들이 부당하게 수감되지 않도록 형사 사법 제도를 당장 개혁할 필요가 있다.

write의 과거

타동사 일으키다 [문예체] ❑ 파리에서 있은 행사들이 프랑스와 독일에 대한 영국인들의 생각에 변화를 일으켰다.

wring의 과거

❶ 형용사 비뚤한, 비뚤어진 ❑ 매튜는 일그러진 미소를 지었다. ❷ 형용사 빈정대는, 비꼬는 ❑ 그의 작품에는 빈정대는 듯한 해학이 있다.

고유명사 세계 무역 기구, World Trade Organization의 약자 ❑ 세계는 효율적인 세계 무역 기구를 꼭 필요로 한다.

wuss /wʊs/ (**wusses**) N-COUNT If you call someone a **wuss**, you are criticizing them for being afraid. [INFORMAL, DISAPPROVAL] ❑ *My girlfriend is taking me to a nude beach. I'm getting cold feet. She says I'm a wuss.*

가산명사 겁쟁이 [비격식체, 탐탁찮음] ❑ 내 여자 친구가 나를 나체 해변으로 데리고 간다. 나는 겁을 먹는다. 그녀는 내가 겁쟁이라고 말한다.

WWW /dʌbᵊlyu dʌbᵊlyu dʌbᵊlyu/ **WWW** is an abbreviation for "World-Wide Web." It appears at the beginning of website addresses in the form **www**. [COMPUTING] ❑ *Check out our website at www.collins.co.uk.*

월드 와이드 웹, World-Wide Web의 약자 [컴퓨터] ❑ 우리 웹사이트인 www.collins.co.uk에서 확인해 보세요.

WYSIWYG /wɪziwɪg/ **WYSIWYG** is used to refer to a computer screen display which exactly matches the way that a document will appear when it is printed. **WYSIWYG** is an abbreviation for "what you see is what you get." [COMPUTING] ❑ *WYSIWYG editing makes your word processing smoother and more flexible.*

위지위그 (출력 문서와 일치하는 컴퓨터 화면 표시), what you see is what you get의 약자 [컴퓨터] ❑ 위지위그 편집을 이용하면 문서 작성이 더 원활하고 유연하게 된다.

X, x /ɛks/ (X's, x's) N-VAR X is the twenty-fourth letter of the English alphabet.

xeno|pho|bia /zɛnəfoʊbiə/ N-UNCOUNT **Xenophobia** is strong and unreasonable dislike or fear of people from other countries. [FORMAL] ❑ ...a just and tolerant society which rejects xenophobia and racism.

xeno|pho|bic /zɛnəfoʊbɪk/ ADJ If you describe someone as **xenophobic**, you disapprove of them because they show strong dislike or fear of people from other countries. [FORMAL, DISAPPROVAL] ❑ Xenophobic nationalism is on the rise in some West European countries.

Xer|ox /zɪərɒks/ (Xeroxes, Xeroxing, Xeroxed) **1** N-COUNT A **Xerox** is a machine that can make copies of pieces of paper which have writing or other marks on them. [TRADEMARK] ❑ The rooms are crammed with humming Xerox machines. **2** N-COUNT A **Xerox** is a copy of something written or printed on a piece of paper, which has been made using a Xerox machine. ❑ I got a Xerox of the lyrics, handed them out, and then we had the rehearsals. **3** V-T If you **Xerox** a document, you make a copy of it using a Xerox machine. ❑ I should have simply Xeroxed this sheet for you.

Xmas **Xmas** is used in informal written English to represent the word Christmas. ❑ It would be nice to have my Dad home for Xmas.

X-ray (X-rays, X-raying, X-rayed) also x-ray **1** N-COUNT **X-rays** are a type of radiation that can pass through most solid materials. X-rays are used by doctors to examine the bones or organs inside your body and are also used at airports to see inside people's luggage. ❑ ...a narrow beam of X-rays. **2** N-COUNT An **X-ray** is a picture made by sending X-rays through something, usually someone's body. ❑ She was advised to have an abdominal X-ray. **3** V-T If someone or something **is X-rayed**, an X-ray picture is taken of them. ❑ All hand baggage would be x-rayed. →see **wave**

가산명사 또는 불가산명사 영어 알파벳의 스물네 번째 글자

불가산명사 외국인 혐오 [격식체] ❑ 외국인 혐오와 인종 차별을 거부하는 정의롭고 관용적인 사회

형용사 외국인을 혐오하는 [격식체, 탐탁찮음] ❑ 외국인을 혐오하는 국수주의가 일부 서유럽 국가에서 팽배하고 있다.

1 가산명사 복사기 [상표] ❑ 방마다 응응거리는 복사기들이 꽉 차 있다. **2** 가산명사 복사물 ❑ 내가 노랫말을 복사해서 나누어 준 다음 우리는 리허설을 했다. **3** 타동사 복사하다 ❑ 내가 그냥 이걸 한 장 네게 복사해 주었어야 했는데.

크리스마스 ❑ 성탄절에 아빠가 집에 오시면 좋겠다.

1 가산명사 엑스선, 엑스레이 ❑ 길쭉한 엑스레이 광선 **2** 가산명사 엑스선 사진, 엑스레이 사진 ❑ 그녀는 복부 엑스레이 촬영을 해 보라는 권유를 받았다. **3** 타동사 엑스레이 촬영을 받다 ❑ 모든 수하물은 엑스레이 검색을 받을 것이다.

Yy

Y, y /waɪ/ (**Y's, y's**) N-VAR Y is the twenty-fifth letter of the English alphabet.

yacht ♦◇◇ /yɒt/ (**yachts**) N-COUNT A **yacht** is a large boat with sails or a motor, used for racing or pleasure trips. ❑ *His 36ft yacht sank suddenly last summer.*

yacht|ing /yɒtɪŋ/ N-UNCOUNT **Yachting** is the sport or activity of sailing a yacht. ❑ *...the joys of yachting.*

yank /yæŋk/ (**yanks, yanking, yanked**) V-T/V-I If you **yank** someone or something somewhere, you pull them there suddenly and with a lot of force. ❑ *She yanked open the drawer.* ● N-COUNT **Yank** is also a noun. ❑ *Grabbing his ponytail, Shirley gave it a yank.*

yard ♦◇◇ /yɑrd/ (**yards**) ❶ N-COUNT A **yard** is a unit of length equal to thirty-six inches or approximately 91.4 centimeters. ❑ *The incident took place about 500 yards from where he was standing.* ❑ *...a long narrow strip of linen two or three yards long.* ❷ N-COUNT A **yard** is a flat area of concrete or stone that is next to a building and often has a wall around it. ❑ *I saw him standing in the yard.* ❸ N-COUNT You can refer to a large open area where a particular type of work is done as a **yard**. ❑ *...a railway yard.* ❹ N-COUNT A **yard** is a piece of land next to someone's house, with grass and plants growing in it. [AM; BRIT **garden**] ❑ *He dug a hole in our yard on Edgerton Avenue to plant a maple tree when I was born.*

> In the USA and Australia, when people need to clear out their cupboards, basements or attics (for example if they are moving house), they sometimes hold **yard sales** or **garage sales**, where they set up stalls in the yard or garage and sell unwanted items. In the UK, **car boot sales** are a very popular way of selling unwanted items. The organizers charge a small fee and in return, sellers come together, usually in a car park or a field to set out their goods in the open trunks of their cars.

yard|stick /yɑrdstɪk/ (**yardsticks**) N-COUNT If you use someone or something as a **yardstick**, you use them as a standard for comparison when you are judging other people or things. ❑ *There has been no yardstick by which potential students can assess individual schools before signing up for a course.*

yarn /yɑrn/ (**yarns**) N-MASS **Yarn** is thread used for knitting or making cloth. ❑ *She still spins the yarn and knits sweaters for her family.*

yawn /yɔn/ (**yawns, yawning, yawned**) V-I If you **yawn**, you open your mouth very wide and breathe in more air than usual, often when you are tired or when you are not interested in something. ❑ *She yawned, and stretched lazily.* ● N-COUNT **Yawn** is also a noun. ❑ *Rosanna stifled a huge yawn.* →see **sleep**

yd (**yds**)

> The spelling **yd.** is also used.

yd is a written abbreviation for **yard**. ❑ *The entrance is on the left 200 yds further on up the road.*

yeah ♦♦♦ /yɛə/ CONVENTION **Yeah** means yes. [INFORMAL, SPOKEN] ❑ *"Bring us something to drink."* — *"Yeah, yeah."* →see also **yes**

year ♦♦♦ /yɪər/ (**years**) ❶ N-COUNT A **year** is a period of twelve months or 365 or 366 days, beginning on the first of January and ending on the thirty-first of December. ❑ *The year was 1840.* ❑ *We had an election last year.* →see also **leap year** ❷ N-COUNT A **year** is any period of twelve months. ❑ *The museums attract more than two and a half million visitors a year.* ❑ *She's done quite a bit of work this past year.* ❸ N-COUNT **Year** is used to refer to the age of a person. For example, if someone or something is twenty **years** old or twenty **years** of age, they have lived or existed for twenty years. ❑ *He's 58 years old.* ❑ *I've been in trouble since I was eleven years of age.* ❹ N-COUNT A school **year** or academic **year** is the period of time in each twelve months when schools or colleges are open and students are studying there. In the United States and England, the school year starts in September. ❑ *...the 1990/91 academic year.* ❺ N-COUNT You can refer to someone who is, for example, in their first year at a school or university as a first **year**. [BRIT] ❑ *The first years and second years got a choice of French, German, and Spanish.* ❻ N-COUNT A financial or business **year** is an exact period of twelve months which businesses or institutions use as a basis for organizing their finances. [BUSINESS] ❑ *He announced big tax increases for the next two financial years.* ❼ N-PLURAL You can use **years** to emphasize that you are referring to a long time. [EMPHASIS] ❑ *I haven't laughed so much in years.* ❽ →see also **calendar year**, **fiscal year** ❾ PHRASE If something happens **year after year**, it happens regularly every year. ❑ *Regulars return year after year.* ❿ PHRASE If something

가산명사 또는 불가산명사 영어 알파벳의 스물다섯 번째, 'y'자

가산명사 요트 ❑ 지난 여름 그의 36피트 길이의 요트가 갑자기 가라앉았다.

불가산명사 요트 놀이 ❑ 요트 놀이의 즐거움

타동사/자동사 홱 잡아당기다 ❑ 그녀는 서랍을 홱 잡아당겨 열었다. ● 가산명사 홱 잡아당김 ❑ 셜리가 그의 뒤로 묶은 머리를 움켜잡더니 홱 잡아당겼다.

❶ 가산명사 야드 ❑ 그 사건은 그가 서 있던 곳에서 약 500야드 떨어진 장소에서 일어났다. ❑ 2에서 3야드 길이의 길고 가는 아마포(亞麻布) 조각 ❷ 가산명사 구내 ❑ 나는 그가 구내에 서 있는 것을 보았다. ❸ 가산명사 ~장(場) ❑ 조차장 ❹ 가산명사 마당, 뜰 [미국영어; 영국영어 garden] ❑ 그분은 내가 태어났을 때 에저턴 가에 있던 우리 집 마당에 구멍을 파고 단풍나무를 한 그루 심었다.

> 미국과 호주에서는 사람들이 (예를 들어, 이사를 갈 경우) 찬장, 지하실, 다락방을 청소할 필요가 있을 때 가끔 yard sale(마당 세일) 또는 garage sale(차고 세일)을 하는데, 마당이나 차고에 판매대를 세우고 필요 없는 물건을 판다. 영국에서는 필요 없는 물건을 파는 흔한 방법으로 car boot sale(자동차 트렁크 세일)이 있다. 주최측에서는 소액의 자릿세를 받고, 그 대신 판매자들은 대개 주차장이나 들판에 모여서 자기 자동차의 트렁크를 열어놓고 가져온 물건을 진열한다.

가산명사 기준, 척도 ❑ 지금까지 미래의 학생들이 수강 신청 전에 개별 학교들을 평가하는 데 적용할 수 있는 기준이 없었다.

물질명사 (직물, 편물용의) 실 ❑ 그녀는 아직도 실을 자아서 가족들을 위해 스웨터를 뜬다.

자동사 하품하다 ❑ 그녀는 하품을 하고 나른하게 기지개를 켰다. ● 가산명사 하품 ❑ 로재너는 하품이 크게 나오는 것을 참았다.

> 철자 yd.도 쓰인다.

야드 (yard의 축약형) ❑ 입구는 그 도로 위로 200야드 더 왼쪽에 있다.

관용 표현상 응, 그래 [비격식체, 구어체] ❑ "마실 것 좀 갖다 줘." "응, 그래."

❶ 가산명사 해, 연(年) ❑ 그해는 1840년이었다. ❑ 지난해 선거가 있었다. ❷ 가산명사 일 년 ❑ 일 년 동안 박물관들은 2백 5십만 명의 방문객들을 끌어모은다. ❑ 그녀는 지난 일년간 꽤 많은 일을 해냈다. ❸ 가산명사 ~살, ~세(歲) ❑ 그는 쉰여덟 살이다. ❑ 나는 열한 살 이후로 문제점을 안고 살아 왔다. ❹ 가산명사 학년도 ❑ 1990/1991학년도 ❺ 가산명사 학년생 [영국영어] ❑ 1학년생과 2학년생들은 프랑스어, 독일어, 스페인어 중 하나를 선택했다. ❻ 가산명사 연도 [경제] ❑ 그는 차기 2년간의 회계 연도에 대해 대규모 세금 인상을 발표했다. ❼ 복수명사 긴 세월, 다년간 [강조] ❑ 그렇게 많이 웃어 본 건 몇 년 만에 처음이다. ❽ 구 해마다, 매년 ❑ 단골들은 해마다 찾아온다. ❿ 구 해마다, 매년 ❑ 이 문제는 매년 증가하고 있다. ⓫ 구 일 년 내내 ❑ 읍내 정원이 거의 일 년 내내 꽃이 피니까 이상적이다.

Word Web   year

A **year** is the time it takes the earth to orbit around the sun—about 365 **days**. The exact time is 365.242199 days. To adjust for this, every four years there is a **leap year** with 366 days. The **months** on a **calendar** were inspired by the phases of the moon. The Greeks had a 10-month calendar, but there were about 60 days left over. So the Romans added two months. The idea of seven-day **weeks** came from the Bible. The Romans named the days. We still use three of these names: Sunday (sun day), Monday (moon day), and Saturday (Saturn day).

December

January

changes **year by year**, it changes gradually each year. ❑ *This problem has increased year by year.* ◧ PHRASE If you say something happens **all year round** or **all the year round**, it happens continually throughout the year. ❑ *Town gardens are ideal because they produce flowers nearly all year round.*
→see Word Web: **year**

year|ly /yɪərli/ ◧ ADJ A **yearly** event happens once a year or every year. [ADJ n] ❑ *The seven major industrial countries will have their yearly meeting in London.* ● ADV **Yearly** is also an adverb. [ADV after v] ❑ *Clients normally pay fees in advance, monthly, quarterly, or yearly.* ◨ ADJ You use **yearly** to describe something such as an amount that relates to a period of one year. [ADJ n] ❑ *In Holland, the government sets a yearly budget for health care.* ● ADV **Yearly** is also an adverb. [ADV after v] ❑ *Novello says college students will spend $4.2 billion yearly on alcoholic beverages.*

◧ 형용사 연례의 ❑ 서방 선진 7개국이 런던에서 연례 회의를 개최할 것이다. ● 부사 일 년에 한 번, 매년 ❑ 고객들은 일반적으로 월별로, 분기별로 또는 일년에 한 번 회비를 선납한다. ◨ 형용사 연간의 ❑ 네덜란드 정부는 보건 분야에 대한 연간 예산을 책정한다. ● 부사 연간으로 ❑ 노벨로는 대학생들의 연간 술값이 42억 달러에 이른다고 말한다.

Thesaurus   yearly의 참조어
ADJ.   annual ◧ ◨

yearn /yɜrn/ (yearns, yearning, yearned) V-T/V-I If someone **yearns for** something that they are unlikely to get, they want it very much. ❑ *He yearned for freedom.*

타동사/자동사 갈망하다 ❑ 그는 자유를 갈망했다.

-year-old /-yɪər-oʊld/ (-year-olds) COMB in ADJ **-year-old** combines with numbers to describe the age of people or things. [ADJ n] ❑ *She has a six-year-old daughter.* ● COMB in N-COUNT **-year-old** also combines to form nouns. ❑ *Snow Puppies is a ski school for 3 to 6-year-olds.*

복합형-형용사 - 살 난 ❑ 그녀에게는 여섯 살 난 딸이 있다. ● 복합형-가산명사 -세 된 사람, -년 된 것 ❑ 스노우 파피스는 3세에서 6세까지의 아이들을 위한 스키 학교이다.

yeast /yist/ (yeasts) N-MASS **Yeast** is a kind of fungus which is used to make bread rise, and in making alcoholic drinks such as beer. →see **fungus**

물질명사 효모

yell /yɛl/ (yells, yelling, yelled) ◧ V-T/V-I If you **yell**, you shout loudly, usually because you are excited, angry, or in pain. ❑ *"Eva!" he yelled.* ❑ *I'm sorry I yelled at you last night.* ● PHRASAL VERB **Yell out** means the same as **yell**. ❑ *"Are you coming or not?" they yelled out after him.* ◨ N-COUNT A **yell** is a loud shout given by someone who is afraid or in pain. ❑ *Something brushed past Bob's face and he let out a yell.*

◧ 타동사/자동사 소리치다 ❑ "에바!"라고 그는 소리쳤다. ❑ 지난밤에 네게 소리쳐서 미안해. ● 구동사 소리치다 ❑ "올 거야, 안 올 거야?"라고 그들이 그의 뒤에 대고 소리쳤다. ◨ 가산명사 고함 (소리) ❑ 밥의 얼굴에 뭔가가 스치자 그는 고함을 질렀다.

Thesaurus   yell의 참조어
V.   cry, scream, shout; (ant.) whisper ◧ ◨

yel|low ◆◆◆ /yɛloʊ/ (yellows) COLOR Something that is **yellow** is the color of lemons, butter, or the middle part of an egg. ❑ *The walls have been painted bright yellow.* →see **rainbow**

색채어 노랑, 노란색 ❑ 그 벽들은 밝은 노란색으로 칠해져 있다.

yellow card (yellow cards) N-COUNT In soccer or rugby, if a player is shown the **yellow card**, the referee holds up a yellow card to indicate that the player has broken the rules, and that if they do so again, they will be ordered to leave the field. ❑ *Sheringham was then shown a yellow card for dissent.*

가산명사 (축구 등에서) 옐로카드, 경고 ❑ 그리고 나서 쉐링엄은 심판에 대한 항의 때문에 옐로카드를 받았다.

yen ◆◇◇ /yɛn/

Yen is both the singular and the plural form.

yen은 단수형 및 복수형이다.

N-COUNT The **yen** is the unit of currency used in Japan. ❑ *She's got a part-time job for which she earns 2,000 yen a month.* ● N-SING The **yen** is also used to refer to the Japanese currency system. ❑ *...sterling's devaluation against the dollar and the yen.*

가산명사 엔 (일본 화폐 단위) ❑ 그녀는 시간제 직장에 다녀 한 달에 2,000엔을 번다. ● 단수명사 엔화 ❑ 달러화와 엔화 대비 파운드화의 평가 절하

yep /yɛp/ CONVENTION **Yep** means yes. [INFORMAL, SPOKEN] ❑ *"Did you like it?" — "Yep."*

관용 표현 그럼 (yes의 구어적 표현) [비격식체, 구어체] ❑ "그거 좋아해?" "그럼."

yes ◆◆◆ /yɛs/

In informal English, **yes** is often pronounced in a casual way that is usually written as **yeah**.

yes는 비격식체 영어에서 종종 격 없이 yeah로 쓰고 발음된다.

◧ CONVENTION You use **yes** to give a positive response to a question. ❑ *"Are you a friend of Nick's?" — "Yes."* ❑ *"You actually wrote it yourself, didn't you?" — "Yes."*

◧ 관용 표현 네, 응, 그래 ❑ "너는 닉의 친구니?" "응." ❑ "너 정말 그것을 썼구나, 그지?" "그래."

There are many other informal ways of expressing agreement. Yeah is common in everyday speech. People also say **Yep, Yup, Uh-huh**, and **Mm-hmm** in informal situations. Body language for agreement is a forward nod of the head. This gesture is different in other cultures.

yes 외에도 격식을 차리지 않고 동의를 표현하는 방식으로 여러 가지가 있다. 일상 대화에서는 yeah가 흔하다. 격식을 차리지 않는 상황에서는 Yep, Yup, Uh-huh, Mm-hmm도 사용한다. 동의를 나타내는 몸짓 언어는 머리를 앞으로 끄덕이는 것이다. 이 몸짓은 문화에 따라 다르다.

◨ CONVENTION You use **yes** to accept an offer or request, or to give permission. ❑ *"More wine?" — "Yes please."* ❑ *"Will you take me there?" — "Yes, I will."* ◧ CONVENTION You use **yes** to tell someone that what they have said is correct. ❑ *"Well I suppose it is based on the old lunar months, isn't it?" — "Yes, that's right."* ◪ CONVENTION You

◨ 관용 표현 네, 응 ❑ "와인 더 할래?" "네, 주세요." ❑ "그곳에 데려다 줄래요?" "네, 그럴게요." ◧ 관용 표현 그래요, 그래 ❑ "음, 난 그것이 오래된 음력 월에 근거한다고 봐, 맞지?" "그래, 맞아." ◪ 관용 표현 (노크

use **yes** to show that you are ready or willing to speak to the person who wants to speak to you, for example when you are answering a telephone or a knock at your door. ❑ *He pushed a button on the intercom. "Yes?" came a voice.* ⑤ CONVENTION You use **yes** to indicate that you agree with, accept, or understand what the previous speaker has said. ❑ *"A lot of people find it very difficult indeed to give up smoking." — "Oh yes. I used to smoke nearly sixty a day."* ⑥ CONVENTION You use **yes** to encourage someone to continue speaking. ❑ *"I remembered something funny today." — "Yeah?"* ⑦ CONVENTION You use **yes**, usually followed by "but," as a polite way of introducing what you want to say when you disagree with something the previous speaker has just said. [POLITENESS] ❑ *"She is entitled to her personal allowance which is three thousand pounds of income'" — "Yes, but she doesn't earn any money."* ⑧ CONVENTION You use **yes** to say that a negative statement or question that the previous speaker has made is wrong or untrue. ❑ *"That is not possible," she said. — "Oh, yes, it is!" Mrs. Gruen insisted.* ⑨ CONVENTION You can use **yes** to suggest that you do not believe or agree with what the previous speaker has said, especially when you want to express your annoyance about it. [FEELINGS] ❑ *"There was no way to stop it." — "Oh yes? Well, here's something else you won't be able to stop."* ⑩ CONVENTION You use **yes** to indicate that you had forgotten something and have just remembered it. ❑ *What was I going to say. Oh yeah, we've finally got our second computer.* ⑪ CONVENTION You use **yes** to emphasize and confirm a statement that you are making. [EMPHASIS] ❑ *He collected the £10,000 first prize. Yes, £10,000.* ⑫ CONVENTION You say **yes and no** in reply to a question when you cannot give a definite answer, because in some ways the answer is yes and in other ways the answer is no. [VAGUENESS] ❑ *"Was it strange for you, going back after such a long absence?" — "Yes and no."*

yes|ter|day ♦♦♦ /ˈyɛstərdeɪ, -di/ ① ADV You use **yesterday** to refer to the day before today. [ADV with cl] ❑ *She left yesterday.* ● N-UNCOUNT **Yesterday** is also a noun. ❑ *In yesterday's games, Switzerland beat the United States two-one.* ② N-UNCOUNT You can refer to the past, especially the recent past, as **yesterday**. [also N in pl] ❑ *The worker of today is different from the worker of yesterday.*

yet ♦♦♦ /yɛt/ ① ADV You use **yet** in negative statements to indicate that something has not happened up to the present time, although it probably will happen. You can also use **yet** in questions to ask if something has happened up to the present time. In British English the simple past tense is not normally used with this meaning of "yet." ❑ *They haven't finished yet.* ❑ *No decision has yet been made.* ❑ *She hasn't yet set a date for her marriage.* ② ADV You use **yet** with a negative statement when you are talking about the past, to report something that was not the case then, although it became the case later. ❑ *There was so much that Sam didn't know yet.*

In British English, **yet** and **already** are usually used with the present perfect tense. ❑ *Have they said sorry or not yet?... I have already started knitting baby clothes.* In American English, a past tense is commonly used. ❑ *I didn't get any sleep yet... She already told the neighbors not to come.*

③ ADV If you say that something should not or cannot be done **yet**, you mean that it should not or cannot be done now, although it will have to be done at a later time. [with brd-neg, ADV with v] ❑ *Don't get up yet.* ❑ *The hostages cannot go home just yet.* ④ ADV You use **yet** after a superlative to indicate, for example, that something is the worst or the best of its kind up to the present time. ❑ *This is the BBC's worst idea yet.* ❑ *Her latest novel is her best yet.* ⑤ ADV You can use **yet** to say that there is still a possibility that something will happen. [ADV before v] ❑ *Like the best stories, this one may yet have a happy end.* ⑥ ADV You can use **yet** after expressions which refer to a period of time, when you want to say how much longer a situation will continue for. [n ADV] ❑ *Unemployment will go on rising for some time yet.* ❑ *Nothing will happen for a few years yet.* ⑦ ADV If you say that you have **yet to** do something, you mean that you have never done it, especially when this is surprising or bad. [ADV to-inf] ❑ *She has yet to spend a Christmas with her husband.* ⑧ CONJ You can use **yet** to introduce a fact which is rather surprising after the previous fact you have just mentioned. ❑ *I don't eat much, yet I am a size 16.* ⑨ ADV You can use **yet** to emphasize a word, especially when you are saying that something is surprising because it is more extreme than previous things of its kind, or a further case of them. [EMPHASIS] ❑ *I saw yet another doctor.* ❑ *They would criticize me, or worse yet, pay me no attention.* ⑩ PHRASE You use **as yet** with negative statements to describe a situation that has existed up until the present time. [FORMAL] ❑ *As yet it is not known whether the crash was the result of an accident.*

yield ♦♦◊◊ /yild/ (**yields, yielding, yielded**) ① V-I If you **yield to** someone or something, you stop resisting them. [FORMAL] ❑ *Carmen yielded to general pressure and grudgingly took the child to a specialist.* ② V-T If you **yield** something that you have control of or responsibility for, you allow someone else to have control or responsibility for it. [FORMAL] ❑ *He may yield control.* ③ V-I If something **yields**, it breaks or moves position because force or pressure has been put on it. ❑ *He reached the massive door of the barn and pushed. It yielded.* ④ V-T If an area of land **yields** a particular amount of a crop, this is the amount that is produced. You can also say that a number of animals **yield** a particular amount of meat. ❑ *Last year 400,000 acres of land yielded a crop worth $1.75 billion.* ⑤ N-COUNT A **yield** is the amount of food produced on an area of land or by a number of animals. ❑ *...improving the yield of the crop.* ⑥ V-T If a tax or investment **yields** an amount of money or profit, this money or profit is obtained from it. [BUSINESS] ❑ *It yielded a profit of at least $36 million.* ⑦ N-COUNT A **yield** is the amount of money or profit produced by an investment. [BUSINESS] ❑ *...a yield of 4%.* ❑ *The high yields available on the dividend shares made them attractive to private investors.* ⑧ V-T If something **yields** a result or piece of

등에 대한 대답으로) 네 ❑ 그는 인터폰의 단추를 눌렀다. "네?" 하는 목소리가 들려 왔다. ⑤ 관용 표현 그래요, 맞아요 ❑ "많은 사람들이 금연이 참으로 어렵다는 걸 알게 돼요." "정말 그래요. 저도 하루에 거의 60개비를 피운 적이 있어요." ⑥ 관용 표현 그래 (상대방에게 말을 계속하라고 할 때), 그래요? ❑ "오늘 웃긴 일이 생각났는데." "그래서?" ⑦ 관용 표현 그래, 맞아 [공손체] ❑ "그녀는 소득 중 3,000파운드를 개인 용돈으로 가질 자격이 있어." "맞아, 하지만 그녀는 전혀 돈을 벌지 않아." ⑧ 관용 표현 (상대방의 부정적 의견을 반박할 때) "그것은 불가능해요."라고 그녀가 말했다. "아, 아니. 가능해!"라고 그루엔 부인이 주장했다. ⑨ 관용 표현 그래 (상대방이 말한 것이 어렵다는 듯) [감정 개입] ❑ "그것을 멈출 방법이 없었어." "아, 그랬단 말이야? 음, 여기 네가 멈출 수 없는 것이 또 있어." ⑩ 관용 표현 그래 (뭔가가 막 기억났을 때), 그래 ❑ 내가 막 말 하려던 것은. 아, 그래, 우리는 드디어 두 번째 컴퓨터를 구입했어. ⑪ 관용 표현 그래 (자기가 할 말을 강조) [강조] ❑ 그는 우승으로 10,000파운드를 받았어. 그래, 10,000파운드. ⑫ 관용 표현 그렇기도 하고 안 그렇기도 해 [짐작투] ❑ "그렇게 오랜 공백 후에 다시 돌아가는 것이 이상했나?" "그렇기도 하고 안 그렇기도 했어."

① 부사 어제 ❑ 그녀는 어제 떠났다. ● 불가산명사 어제 ❑ 어제 경기에서 스위스가 미국을 2대 1로 물리쳤다. ② 불가산명사 이제, 과거 ❑ 요즘 근로자는 과거의 근로자와는 다르다.

① 부사 아직 ❑ 그들은 아직 마치지 못했다. ❑ 어떤 결론도 아직 내려지지 않았다. ❑ 그녀는 아직 결혼식 날짜를 정하지 않았다. ② 부사 아직 ❑ 샘이 아직 모르는 것들이 아주 많았다.

영국 영어에서는 already와 yet이 대개 현재완료 시제와 함께 쓰인다. ❑ 그들이 이미 미안하다고 했나요?... 나는 이미 아기 옷을 뜨기 시작했다. 미국 영어에서는 흔히 과거시제가 쓰인다. ❑ 나는 아직 한잠도 못 잤다... 그녀는 이미 이웃들에게 오지 말라고 말했다.

③ 부사 아직 ❑ 아직 일어나지 마. ❑ 인질들은 아직 집으로 갈 수 없다. ④ 부사 이제까지, 지금까지 ❑ 이것은 이제까지 비비시 방송국의 생각 중 최악이다. ❑ 그녀의 최근 소설은 이제까지 나온 소설 중 가장 훌륭하다. ⑤ 부사 그래도, 아직 ❑ 다른 훌륭한 이야기들처럼, 이것도 아직 해피엔드로 끝날 수도 있다. ⑥ 부사 앞으로 ❑ 실업률이 앞으로 한동안 계속 증가할 것이다. ❑ 앞으로 몇 년 동안은 아무 일도 일어나지 않을 것이다. ⑦ 부사 아직 ❑ 그녀는 아직 남편과 함께 크리스마스를 보내 본 적이 없다. ⑧ 접속사 그런데도 ❑ 나는 많이 먹지 않는, 그런데도 난 16사이즈다. ⑨ 부사 또; 훨씬 [강조] ❑ 나는 또 다른 의사와 상담을 했다. ❑ 그들이 나를 비난할 수도 있고, 아니면 훨씬 더 나쁘게 내게 아무런 주의를 기울이지 않을 수도 있다. ⑩ 구 아직까지는 [격식체] ❑ 아직까지는 추락이 사고로 인한 것인지는 알려지지 않았다.

① 자동사 굴복하다 [격식체] ❑ 카멘은 모두의 압력에 굴복해서 마지못해 그 아이를 전문의에게 데리고 갔다. ② 타동사 양보하다 [격식체] ❑ 그가 통제권을 양보할지도 모른다. ③ 자동사 (가해지는 힘에) 따르다 ❑ 그가 거대한 헛간 문에 손을 뻗어 문을 밀었다. 문이 열렸다. ④ 타동사 산출하다 ❑ 지난 해 40만 에이커의 토지에서 17억 5천만 달러 상당의 곡식을 거두었다. ⑤ 가산명사 수확 ❑ 곡물의 수확을 늘리는 ⑥ 타동사 (이익 등을) 내다 [경제] ❑ 그것이 적어도 3천 6백만 달러의 이익을 가져왔다. ⑦ 가산명사 수익률 [경제] ❑ 4퍼센트의 수익률 ❑ 그것들은 배당금 분배 시 받을 수 있는 수익률이 높아 투자가들에게 매혹적이었다. ⑧ 타동사 (결과 등을) 낳다 ❑ 이 연구는 1961년 이후로 진행되고 있고 아주 많은 긍정적인 결과를 낳았다.

information, it produces it. ❑ *This research has been in progress since 1961 and has yielded a great number of positive results.*

Thesaurus   yield의 참조어

V.	give in, submit, succumb, surrender; *(ant.)* resist **1** bear, produce, supply **4**

Word Partnership   yield의 연어

N.	yield **to pressure**, yield **to temptation 1** yield **a profit 6-8** yield **information**, yield **results 8**
V.	**refuse to** yield **1-3**
ADJ.	**annual** yield, **high/higher** yield **6 7**

yoga /yoʊgə/ N-UNCOUNT **Yoga** is a type of exercise in which you move your body into various positions in order to become more fit or flexible, to improve your breathing, and to relax your mind. ❑ *I do yoga twice a week.*

불가산명사 요가 ❑ 나는 일주일에 두 번 요가를 한다.

yogurt /yoʊgərt, BRIT yɒgəⁱt/ (**yogurts**) also **yoghurt** N-VAR **Yogurt** is a food in the form of a thick, slightly sour liquid that is made by adding bacteria to milk. A **yogurt** is a small container of yogurt. ❑ *...a tub of yogurt.*

가산명사 또는 불가산명사 요구르트 ❑ 요구르트 통

yolk /yoʊk/ (**yolks**) N-VAR The **yolk** of an egg is the yellow part in the middle. ❑ *Only the yolk contains cholesterol.*

가산명사 또는 불가산명사 노른자위 ❑ 노른자위에만 콜레스테롤이 있다.

you ♦♦♦ /yu/

You is the second person pronoun. **You** can refer to one or more people and is used as the subject of a verb or the object of a verb or preposition.

you는 2인칭 대명사이다. you는 한 사람 또는 두 사람 이상을 지칭할 수 있으며, 동사의 주어 또는 동사나 전치사의 목적어로 쓰인다.

1 PRON A speaker or writer uses **you** to refer to the person or people that they are talking or writing to. It is possible to use **you** before a noun to make it clear which group of people you are talking to. ❑ *When I saw you across the room I knew I'd met you before.* ❑ *You two seem very different to me.* **2** PRON In spoken English and informal written English, **you** is sometimes used to refer to people in general. ❑ *Getting good results gives you confidence.* ❑ *In those days you did what you were told.*

1 대명사 당신, 당신들, 너, 너희들 ❑ 내가 방 건너편에서 당신을 봤을 때 전에 당신을 만났다는 것을 알았어요. ❑ 너희 둘은 내게 아주 다른 것 같아. **2** 대명사 (일반적인) 사람들 ❑ 좋은 결과를 얻으면 사람들은 확신을 갖게 된다. ❑ 그 당시에는 사람들은 시키는 대로 했다.

you'd /yud/ **1** **You'd** is the usual spoken form of "you had," especially when "had" is an auxiliary verb. ❑ *I think you'd better tell us why you're asking these questions.* **2** **You'd** is the usual spoken form of "you would." ❑ *With your hair and your beautiful skin, you'd look good in red and other bright colors.*

1 you had의 축약형 ❑ 나는 네가 왜 이런 질문들을 하는지 우리에게 설명해야 한다고 생각해. **2** you would의 축약형 ❑ 네 머리카락과 아름다운 피부에는 붉은색과 다른 밝은 계통의 색깔이 잘 어울릴 것 같아.

you'll /yul/ **You'll** is the usual spoken form of "you will." ❑ *Promise me you'll take very special care of yourself.*

you will의 축약형 ❑ 특별히 몸조심하겠다고 내게 약속하세요.

young ♦♦♦ /yʌŋ/ (**younger** /yʌŋgər/ **youngest** /yʌŋgɪst/ **1** ADJ A **young** person, animal, or plant has not lived or existed for very long and is not yet mature. ❑ *In Scotland, young people can marry at 16.* ❑ *I crossed the hill, and found myself in a field of young barley.* ● N-PLURAL **The young** are people who are young. ❑ *The association is advising pregnant women, the very young and the elderly to avoid such foods.* **2** ADJ You use **young** to describe a time when a person or thing was young. [ADJ n] ❑ *In her younger days my mother had been a successful fashionwear saleswoman.* **3** ADJ Someone who is **young** in appearance or behavior looks or behaves as if they are young. ❑ *I was twenty-three, I suppose, and young for my age.* **4** N-PLURAL The **young** of an animal are its babies. ❑ *The hen may not be able to feed its young.* →see **age**

1 형용사 젊은, 어린, 덜 익은 ❑ 스코틀랜드에서는 어린 사람도 16세가 되면 결혼할 수 있다. ❑ 언덕을 넘어가니, 덜 익은 보리밭이 나왔다. ● 복수명사 젊은이들 ❑ 협회는 임신부들 및 노약자들은 그런 음식을 피하라고 충고한다. **2** 형용사 젊은 ❑ 어머니께서는 젊으셨을 때 패션복 판매원으로 성공하셨었다. **3** 형용사 어려 보이는 ❑ 난 23세였는데 생각해 보니 나이에 비해 어려 보였던 것 같다. **4** 복수명사 새끼들 ❑ 그 닭은 새끼들에게 먹이를 줄 수 없을 것이다.

Thesaurus   young의 참조어

ADJ.	childish, immature, youthful; *(ant.)* mature, old **1**
N.	family, litter **4**

youngster ♦◊◊ /yʌŋstər/ (**youngsters**) N-COUNT Young people, especially children, are sometimes referred to as **youngsters**. ❑ *Other youngsters are not so lucky.*

가산명사 어린이 ❑ 다른 어린이들은 그렇게 운이 좋지 않다.

your ♦♦♦ /yɔr, yʊər/

Your is the second person possessive determiner. **Your** can refer to one or more people.

your는 2인칭 소유 한정사이다. your는 한 사람 또는 두 사람 이상을 지칭할 수 있다.

1 DET A speaker or writer uses **your** to indicate that something belongs or relates to the person or people that they are talking or writing to. ❑ *Emma, I trust your opinion a great deal.* ❑ *I left all of your messages on your desk.* **2** DET In spoken English and informal written English, **your** is sometimes used to indicate that something belongs to or relates to people in general. ❑ *Pain-killers are very useful in small amounts to bring your temperature down.* **3** DET In spoken English, a speaker sometimes uses **your** before an adjective such as "typical" or "normal" to indicate that the thing referred to is a typical example of its type. ❑ *Stan Reilly is not really one of your typical Brighton Boys.*

1 한정사 당신의, 당신들의, 너의, 너희들의 ❑ 에마, 나는 당신의 의견을 확실히 믿어요. ❑ 네 책상에 네게 온 메시지를 모두 놔 두었어. **2** 한정사 (일반) 사람들의 ❑ 진통제는 소량으로 사람의 체온을 낮추기 때문에 매우 유용합니다. **3** 한정사 바로 그 ❑ 스탠 레일리는 사실 바로 그 전형적인 브라이턴 보이스들 중의 한 명은 아니다.

you're /yɔr, yʊər/ **You're** is the usual spoken form of "you are." ❑ *Go to him, tell him you're sorry.*

you are의 축약형 ❑ 그에게 가서 미안하다고 말하세요.

yours ♦◊◊ /yɔrz, yʊərz/

Yours is the second person possessive pronoun. **Yours** can refer to one or more people.

yours는 2인칭 소유 대명사이다. yours는 한 사람 또는 두 사람 이상을 지칭할 수 있다.

1 PRON-POSS A speaker or writer uses **yours** to refer to something that belongs or relates to the person or people that they are talking or writing to. ❑ *I'll take my coat upstairs. Shall I take yours, Roberta?* ❑ *I believe Paul was a friend of yours.*

1 소유대명사 당신의 것, 당신들의 것, 네 것, 너희들의 것 ❑ 위층에서 외투를 가져올게요. 로버타, 당신 것도 가져올까요? ❑ 폴이 당신 친구 중 한 명이었던 것

2 CONVENTION People write **yours**, **yours sincerely**, or **yours faithfully** at the end of a letter before they sign their name. ❑ *With best regards, Yours, George.*

your|self ♦♦◇ /yɔrsɛlf, yʊər-/ (**yourselves**)

> **Yourself** is the second person reflexive pronoun.

1 PRON-REFL A speaker or writer uses **yourself** to refer to the person that they are talking or writing to. **Yourself** is used when the object of a verb or preposition refers to the same person as the subject of the verb. [V PRON, prep PRON] ❑ *Have the courage to be honest with yourself and about yourself.* **2** PRON-REFL-EMPH You use **yourself** to emphasize the person that you are referring to. [EMPHASIS] ❑ *They mean to share the business between them, after you yourself are gone, Sir.* **3** PRON-REFL-EMPH You use **yourself** instead of "you" for emphasis or in order to be more polite when "you" is the object of a verb or preposition. [POLITENESS] [V PRON, prep PRON] ❑ *A wealthy man like yourself is bound to make an enemy or two along the way.* **by yourself** →see **by**

youth ♦♦◇ /yuθz, yuðz/ (**youths**) /yuðz/ **1** N-UNCOUNT Someone's **youth** is the period of their life during which they are a child, before they are a fully mature adult. ❑ *In my youth my ambition had been to be an inventor.* **2** N-UNCOUNT **Youth** is the quality or state of being young. ❑ *The team is now a good mixture of experience and youth.* **3** N-COUNT Journalists often refer to young men as **youths**, especially when they are reporting that the young men have caused trouble. ❑ *A 17-year-old youth was remanded in custody yesterday.* **4** N-PLURAL The **youth** are young people considered as a group. ❑ *He represents the opinions of the youth of today.*

Word Partnership	*youth*의 연어
N.	youth **center**, youth **culture**, youth **groups**, youth **organizations**, youth **programs**, youth **services** **4**

youth club (**youth clubs**) N-COUNT A **youth club** is a club where young people can go to meet each other and take part in various leisure activities. Youth clubs are often run by a church or local authority. ❑ *...the youth club disco.*

youth|ful /yuθfəl/ ADJ Someone who is **youthful** behaves as if they are young or younger than they really are. ❑ *I'm a very youthful 50.* ❑ *...youthful enthusiasm and high spirits.*

youth hos|tel (**youth hostels**) N-COUNT A **youth hostel** is a place where people can stay cheaply when they are traveling.

you've /yuv/ **You've** is the usual spoken form of "you have," especially when "have" is an auxiliary verb. ❑ *You've got to see it to believe it.*

yo-yo /yoʊ yoʊ/ (**yo-yos**) N-COUNT A **yo-yo** is a toy made of a round piece of wood or plastic attached to a piece of string. You play with the yo-yo by letting it rise and fall on the string. ❑ *...a competition to find the boy or girl who could do the most tricks with a yo-yo.*

yr (**yrs**) also **yr**. **yr** is a written abbreviation for **year**. ❑ *Their imaginations are quite something for 2 yr olds.*

yuan /yuɑn, BRIT yuːæn/ (**yuan**) N-COUNT The **yuan** is the unit of money used in the People's Republic of China. ❑ *For most events, tickets cost one, two or three yuan.* ● N-SING The **yuan** is also used to refer to the Chinese currency system. [the N] ❑ *The yuan recovered a little; it now hovers around 8.2 to the dollar.*

yup|pie /yʌpi/ (**yuppies**) N-COUNT A **yuppie** is a young person who has a well-paid job and likes to show that they have a lot of money by buying expensive things and living in an expensive way. [DISAPPROVAL] ❑ *The Porsche 911 reminds me of the worst parts of the yuppie era.*

같은데요. **2** 관용 표현 예절 (편지의 끝맺는 말), 세배, 올림, 드림 ❑ 그럼 건강하시길 빕니다. 조지 올림

> yourself는 2인칭 재귀 대명사이다.

1 재귀대명사 당신 자신, 그대들 자신, 당신 자신, 당신 자신 ❑ 당신 자신에게 그리고 당신 자신에 대해 정직할 수 있는 용기를 가지세요. ❑ 당신이 임신 중일 때 당신의 아기는 당신이 자신을 적절히 보살피느냐에 달려 있다. **2** 강조 재귀대명사 바로 당신 [강조] ❑ 그들은 바로 당신이 떠난다면 그 사업을 나눠 가질 작정입니다. **3** 강조 재귀대명사 강조하거나 공손해지 나타내기 위해 you 대신 사용 [공손체] ❑ 당신처럼 부자인 사람은 살다 보면 한두 명의 적을 만들게 되어 있습니다.

1 불가산명사 청년기, 젊은 시절 ❑ 젊었을 때 내 야망은 발명가가 되는 것이었다. **2** 불가산명사 젊음 ❑ 그 팀은 이제 노련한 선수들과 젊은 선수들의 조합이 잘 이루어져 있다. **3** 가산명사 젊은이 ❑ 17세의 젊은이가 어제 다시 구류에 처해졌다. **4** 복수명사 젊은 세대, 젊은이들 ❑ 그는 요즘 젊은 세대의 의견을 대표한다.

가산명사 유스 클럽 ❑ 유스 클럽 디스코

형용사 쾌활한, 청년 특유의 ❑ 나는 50세이지만 아주 팔팔하다. ❑ 청년 특유의 열정과 사기

가산명사 유스 호스텔

you have의 축약형 ❑ 믿기 위해서는 봐야 한다.

가산명사 요요 ❑ 요요를 이용한 가장 멋진 묘기를 부릴 줄 하는 소년·소녀를 찾아내려는 대회

year의 축약형 ❑ 그들의 상상력은 2세 된 아이들로서는 대단한 것이다.

가산명사 위안 (중국 화폐 단위) ❑ 대부분의 경우, 표 값은 일, 이 또는 삼 위안이다. ● 단수명사 위안화 ❑ 위안화가 조금 회복했다. 현재는 달러 대비 8.2위안을 약간 상회한다.

가산명사 여피 [탐탁찮음] ❑ 포르쉐 911을 보면 여피 시대 최악의 요소들이 생각난다.

Zz

Z, z /ziː/, BRIT **zed** (**Z's, z's**) N-VAR Z is the twenty-sixth and last letter of the English alphabet.

zap /zæp/ (**zaps, zapping, zapped**) **1** V-T To **zap** someone or something means to kill, destroy, or hit them, for example with a gun or in a computer game. [INFORMAL] ❏ *A guard zapped him with the stun gun.* **2** V-T To **zap** something such as a computer file or document means to delete it from the computer memory or to clear it from the screen. [INFORMAL, COMPUTING] ❏ *"We zap millions and millions of spam mails a day from our servers," AOL spokesman Nicholas Graham said.*

zeal /ziːl/ N-UNCOUNT Zeal is great enthusiasm, especially in connection with work, religion, or politics. ❏ *...his zeal for teaching.*

zeal|ous /zɛləs/ ADJ Someone who is **zealous** spends a lot of time or energy in supporting something that they believe in very strongly, especially a political or religious ideal. ❏ *She was a zealous worker for charitable bodies.*

Thesaurus	*zealous*의 참조어
ADJ.	eager, enthusiastic

zeb|ra /ziːbrə/

The plural can be either **zebras** or **zebra**.

N-COUNT A **zebra** is an African wild horse which has black and white stripes.

zen|ith /ziːnɪθ, BRIT zɛnɪθ/ N-SING The **zenith** of something is the time when it is most successful or powerful. ❏ *His career is now at its zenith.*

zero /zɪəroʊ/ (**zeros** or **zeroes**) **1** NUM Zero is the number 0. ❏ *Visibility at the city's airport came down to zero, bringing air traffic to a standstill.* **2** N-UNCOUNT Zero is a temperature of 0°. It is freezing point on the centigrade and Celsius scales, and 32° below freezing point on the Fahrenheit scale. ❏ *It's a sunny late winter day, just a few degrees above zero.* **3** ADJ You can use **zero** to say that there is none at all of the thing mentioned. ❏ *This new ministry was being created with zero assets and zero liabilities.*
→see Word Web: zero

As a number, **zero** is used mainly in scientific contexts, or when you want to be precise. In spoken American English, different informal words stand for **zero**, such as **zip**. ❏ *...from zip to 60 in a fraction of one second.* However, when you stating a telephone number, you say **o** (/oʊ/). In some sports contexts, especially in football scores, **nothing** is used. ❏ *Dallas beat San Diego 18 to nothing.* In tennis, **love** is the usual word. ❏ *...a two-games-to-love lead.*

Thesaurus	*zero*의 참조어
NUM.	none, nothing **1 3**

zero-sum game N-SING If you refer to a situation as a **zero-sum game**, you mean that if one person gains an advantage from it, someone else involved must suffer an equivalent disadvantage. ❏ *They believe they're playing a zero-sum game, where both must compete for the same paltry resources.*

zero tol|er|ance N-UNCOUNT If a government or organization has a policy of **zero tolerance** of a particular type of behavior or activity, they will not tolerate it at all. ❏ *They have a policy of zero tolerance for sexual harassment.*

가산명사 또는 불가산명사 영어 알파벳의 스물여섯 번째 글자

1 타동사 제압하다; 죽이다 [비격식체] ❏ 경비원 한 명이 전기 충격 총으로 그를 제압했다. **2** 타동사 (컴퓨터 파일 등을) 삭제하다 [비격식체, 컴퓨터] ❏ "우리는 서버에서 하루에 수백만 통의 스팸 메일을 삭제합니다." 에이오엘 대변인 니콜라스 그레이엄이 말했다.

불가산명사 열의, 열성 ❏ 교육에 대한 그의 열의

형용사 열심인, 열성적인 ❏ 그녀는 자선 단체의 열성 일꾼이었다.

복수는 zebras 또는 zebra이다.

가산명사 얼룩말

단수명사 정점, 절정 ❏ 그는 지금 활동의 정점에 이르러 있다.

1 수사 영, 제로 ❏ 도시 공항의 시계가 제로 상태에 빠져 항공 운항이 정지되었다. **2** 불가산명사 (온도) 0도 ❏ 기온이 영상 몇 도 정도 되는 늦겨울의 어느 맑은 날이었다. **3** 형용사 걸어있거나 있는, 빠져서 없는 ❏ 이 새 부처는 자산도 부채도 전혀 없는 상태에서 만들어지고 있었다.

숫자로서, zero는 주로 과학과 관련해서거나, 정확한 것을 원할 때 쓴다. 미국식 구어에서는, zip과 같은 다른 비격식적인 단어들이 zero대신 쓰인다. ❏ ...0에서 60까지 1초도 안 되는 동안. 그렇지만, 전화번호를 말할 때는 'o'([오])라고 한다. 일부 스포츠와 관련해서, 특히 미식축구 점수에서는, nothing을 쓴다. ❏ 댈러스가 샌디에고를 18대 0으로 이겼다. 테니스에서는 love가 통상적으로 쓰인다. ❏ ...게임 스코어 2대 0으로 이기고 있음.

단수명사 제로섬 게임 (한쪽이 득을 보면 상대방은 그만큼 손실을 보게 되는 상황) ❏ 그들은 서로가 얼마 안 되는 동일한 자원을 얻기 위해 겨루는 제로섬 게임을 하고 있다고 생각한다.

불가산명사 절대 묵인 불가 ❏ 그들은 성희롱에 대해 절대 묵인 불가 방침을 세워 놓고 있다.

Word Web   zero

The **number zero** developed after the other numbers. Ancient peoples first used numbers in concrete situations—to **count** two children or four sheep. It took a while to move from "four sheep" to "four things" to the abstract concept of "four." The use of a **place** holder like zero came from the Babylonians*. Originally, they wrote numbers like 23 and 203 the same way. The reader had to figure out the difference based on the context. The use of zero later came to include the concept of **null** value. It shows that there is no amount of something.

Babylonians: people who lived in the ancient city of Babylon.

Word Web ZOO

Zoos are not just places where people enjoy looking at animals. They perform another very important function. As increasing numbers of **species** become extinct, zoos help preserve **biological diversity**. They do this through educational programs, **breeding** programs, and **research** studies. The Smithsonian National Zoological Park in Washington, DC, provides training for **wildlife** managers from 80 different countries. A breeding program at the Wolong Reserve in China has produced 38 **pandas** since 1991. And the Tama Zoo in Hino, Japan, is conducting research studies of **chimpanzee** behavior. Surprisingly, one chimp has learned to use a vending machine.

zest /zɛst/ (**zests**) **1** N-UNCOUNT **Zest** is a feeling of pleasure and enthusiasm. [also a N, oft N for N] ❑ *He has a zest for life and a quick intellect.* **2** N-UNCOUNT **Zest** is a quality in an activity or situation which you find exciting. ❑ *Live interviews add zest and a touch of the unexpected to any piece of research.*

zig|zag /zɪgzæg/ (**zigzags, zigzagging, zigzagged**) also **zig-zag** **1** N-COUNT A **zigzag** is a line which has a series of angles in it like a continuous series of "W"s. ❑ *They staggered in a zigzag across the tarmac.* **2** V-T/V-I If you **zigzag**, you move forward by going at an angle first to one side then to the other. ❑ *I zigzagged down a labyrinth of alleys.*

zinc /zɪŋk/ N-UNCOUNT **Zinc** is a bluish-white metal which is used to make other metals such as brass, or to cover other metals such as iron to stop a brown substance called rust from forming.

zip /zɪp/ (**zips, zipping, zipped**) **1** V-T When you **zip** something, you fasten it using a zipper. ❑ *She zipped her jeans.* **2** N-COUNT A **zip** or **zip fastener** is the same as a **zipper**. [mainly BRIT] ❑ *He pulled the zip of his leather jacket down slightly.*

▶ **zip up** **1** PHRASAL VERB If you **zip up** something such as a piece of clothing or if it **zips up**, you are able to fasten it using its zipper. ❑ *He zipped up his jeans.* **2** PHRASAL VERB To **zip up** a computer file means to compress it so that it needs less space for storage on disk and can be transmitted more quickly. [COMPUTING] ❑ *These files have been zipped up to take up less disk space so they take less time to download.*

zip code (**zip codes**) N-COUNT Your **zip code** is a short sequence of letters and numbers at the end of your address, which helps the post office to sort the mail. [AM; BRIT **postcode**] ❑ *Type your street address and zip code.*

zip disk (**zip disks**) N-COUNT A **zip disk** is a computer disk, similar to a floppy disk but capable of storing greater amounts of data. [COMPUTING] ❑ *Zip disks could be used to store the equivalent of three music CDs.*

zip drive (**zip drives**) N-COUNT A **zip drive** is a piece of computer equipment that you use for storing large amounts of data. [COMPUTING] ❑ *Zip drives help people to organize their important information.*

zip file (**zip files**) N-COUNT A **zip file** is a computer file containing data that has been compressed. [COMPUTING] ❑ *When you download the font it may be in a compressed format, such as a zip file.*

zip|per /zɪpər/ (**zippers**) N-COUNT A **zipper** is a device used to open and close parts of clothes and bags. It consists of two rows of metal or plastic teeth which separate or fasten together as you pull a small tag along them. [mainly AM; BRIT usually **zip**] ❑ *...the metal zipper on his jacket.*

zo|di|ac /zoʊdiæk/ N-SING The **zodiac** is a diagram used by astrologers to represent the positions of the planets and stars. It is divided into twelve sections, each of which has its own name and symbol. The zodiac is used to try to calculate the influence of the planets, especially on someone's life. ❑ *...the twelve signs of the zodiac.*

zone ♦♢♢ /zoʊn/ (**zones, zoning, zoned**) **1** N-COUNT A **zone** is an area that has particular features or characteristics. ❑ *Many people have stayed behind in the potential war zone.* ❑ *The area has been declared a disaster zone.* **2** V-T If an area of land **is zoned**, it is formally set aside for a particular purpose. [usu passive] ❑ *The land was not zoned for commercial purposes.* ● **zon|ing** N-UNCOUNT ❑ *...the use of zoning to preserve agricultural land.*

Thesaurus zone의 참조어

N. area, region, section **1**

zoo /zu/ (**zoos**) N-COUNT; N-IN-NAMES A **zoo** is a park where live animals are kept so that people can look at them. ❑ *He took his son Christopher to the zoo.*
→see **park**
→see Word Web: **zoo**

zo|ol|ogy /zoʊɒlədʒi/ N-UNCOUNT **Zoology** is the scientific study of animals.

zoom /zum/ (**zooms, zooming, zoomed**) V-I If you **zoom** somewhere, you go there very quickly. [INFORMAL] ❑ *We zoomed through the gallery.*

Thesaurus zoom의 참조어

V. dart, rush, speed; (ant.) slow

---

1 불가산명사 열의, 열정 ❑ 그는 삶에 대한 열정과 영민한 지성을 가지고 있다. **2** 불가산명사 흥취 ❑ 실황 면접은 어떤 것이든 연구 조사에 흥취와 의외성의 묘미를 더해 준다.

1 가산명사 지그재그, 갈지자 꼴 ❑ 그들은 갈지자로 비틀거리며 아스팔트 도로를 가로질러 갔다. **2** 타동사/자동사 지그재그로 나아가다, 갈지자로 걷다 ❑ 나는 미궁 같은 골목을 따라 지그재그로 내려갔다.

불가산명사 아연

1 타동사 지퍼로 잠그다 ❑ 그녀는 바지 지퍼를 잠갔다. **2** 가산명사 지퍼 [주로 영국영어] ❑ 그는 가죽 재킷의 지퍼를 살짝 내렸다.

1 구동사 지퍼로 잠그다; 지퍼로 잠기다 ❑ 그는 바지 지퍼를 잠갔다. **2** 구동사 (컴퓨터 파일을) 압축하다 [컴퓨터] ❑ 이 파일들은 디스크 공간을 덜 차지하여 내려받는 데 시간이 덜 걸리도록 압축되어 있다.

가산명사 우편 번호 [미국영어; 영국영어 postcode] ❑ 집 주소와 우편 번호를 입력하세요.

가산명사 집 디스크 (데이터 압축 저장용) [컴퓨터] ❑ 집 디스크를 쓰면 음악 시디 세 장에 상당하는 분량을 저장할 수도 있다.

가산명사 집 드라이브 (데이터 압축 저장용 장치) [컴퓨터] ❑ 집 드라이브는 사람들이 중요한 정보를 체계화하는 것을 돕는다.

가산명사 집 파일 (압축된 파일) [컴퓨터] ❑ 그 서체를 내려 받았을 때 그것이 집 파일과 같은 압축된 형식으로 되어 있을 수도 있다.

가산명사 지퍼 [주로 미국영어; 영국영어 대개 zip] ❑ 그의 재킷에 달린 금속 지퍼

단수명사 십이궁도, 황도대 ❑ 십이궁도의 열두 개 궁

1 가산명사 지역, 지구 ❑ 많은 사람들이 뒤에 처져서 잠재적 전쟁 지역에 머물러 왔다. ❑ 그 지역은 재해 지구로 선포되었다. **2** 타동사 (특정 지구로) 구획되다 ❑ 그 땅은 상업 목적으로 구획되지 않았다. ● 구획 설정 불가산명사 ❑ 농업 용지를 보존하기 위한 구획 설정 활용

가산명사; 이름명사 동물원 ❑ 그는 아들 크리스토프를 동물원에 데려갔다.

불가산명사 동물학

자동사 재빨리 이동하다 [비격식체] ❑ 우리는 재빨리 화랑 속을 훑어 나갔다.

►**zoom in** PHRASAL VERB If a camera **zooms in on** something that is being filmed or photographed, it gives a close-up picture of it. ❑ ...*a tracking system which can follow a burglar round a building and zoom in on his face.*

구동사 줌 렌즈로 피사체를 확대하다 ❑ 건물 모퉁이를 돌아가는 강도를 뒤쫓아 줌 렌즈로 그 얼굴을 확대해 볼 수 있는 추적 시스템

zuc|chi|ni /zukini/

The plural can be either **zucchini** or **zucchinis**.

복수는 zucchini 또는 zucchinis이다.

N-VAR **Zucchini** are long thin vegetables with a dark green skin. [mainly AM; BRIT usually **courgette**]

가산명사 또는 불가산명사 (오이 모양의) 서양 호박 [주로 미국영어; 영국영어 대개 courgette]

Index

This is an alphabetical index of the translations found in this dictionary. English references in the text are given in alphabetical order following the Korean word. The order of the English words does not imply any order of importance and words with similar senses are not grouped together.

The index directs you to the relevant English entry in the dictionary through the medium of Korean. The index is not a dictionary as such, although the English words to which you are referred can function as translations of the Korean in many cases. For example, the English word *moment* appears in the index against the Korean word 금방이라도. To find 금방이라도 look up *moment* in the dictionary and you will find that 금방이라도 relates to the phrase *at any moment*.

찾아보기

다음은 이 사전의 가나다 순 번역 색인이다. 한국어 단어 오른쪽에 사전 본문에 나오는 영어 어구가 알파벳 순서로 제시된다. 영어 단어의 순서는 중요도 순이 아니며 비슷한 의미의 단어끼리 묶어진 것도 아니다.

이 색인은 한국어를 매개로 사전의 해당 영어 단어 항목으로 안내한다. 여러분들에게 제시된 영어 단어들은 많은 경우에 한국어의 번역으로도 볼 수 있지만 이 색인은 그 자체로서 사전이 아니다. 예를 들어, 한국어 '금방이라도'에 해당하는 색인 항목에 영어 단어 'moment'가 있다. 사전에서 'moment'를 찾아보면 '금방이라도'가 'at any moment'와 관련이 있음을 알게 된다.

0, nought
1, one
1,000, thousand
1,000분의 1, thousandth
10, ten
100, hundred
100만 분의 1, millionth
100분의 1, hundredth
100년, century
100주기, centenary
100주년, centennial
10분의 1, tenth
10억, billion
10월, Oct., October
10종 경기, decathlon
11, eleven
11월, Nov., November
12, twelve
12분의 1, twelfth
12월, Dec., December
13, thirteen
14, fourteen
14행시, sonnet
15, fifteen
15분, quarter
16, sixteen
16분의 1, sixteenth
17, seventeen
17분의 1, seventeenth
180도 전환, U-turn
19, nineteen
1분기, quarter
1월, Jan., January
1인 1시간 노동량, man-hour
1인극, monologue
1인당, head, per capita
1인당의, per capita
1인분, portion, serving
1인실, single
1인용의, single
1점, run
1조, trillion
1종 우편으로, first-class
1종의, first-class
1주, week
1주 근로 시간, workweek
1주간, week
1주일 내내 매일 24 시간 동안, 24-7
1차적인, line
1층, first floor, ground floor
1층 무대 앞좌석, stall
1쿼터짜리 동전, quarter
1파운드, quid
1페니, penny
1페니(1/12 실링)짜리 동전, penny
1회 복용량, dose
1회분, installment
1회분 이야기, episode
2, two
2 등급, second
20, twenty
20대의, twenty
20분의 1, twentieth
24시간 내내, clock
2급품, second
2류, second
2분의 1, half
2세, junior

2월, Feb., February
2인용의, double
2인조, duo
2주일, fortnight
2진 코드, binary code
2진법, binary
2차 소견, second opinion
2차적인, secondary
2층, first floor, upstairs
2층에, upstairs
3, three
30, thirty
30대, thirty
30분, half
3등급, third
3배가 되다, treble, triple
3배의, treble, triple
3부작, trilogy
3분의 1, third
3월, Mar., March
3인조 그룹, trio
3중의, triple
3차원의, three-dimensional
3학년생, junior
4, four
40대, forty
40번째의, fortieth
4개 한 조, foursome
4등분하다, quarter
4륜 구동차, four-wheel drive
4륜 마차, carriage
4분의 1, fourth, quarter
4분의 1로 줄이다, quarter
4분의 3, three-quarters
4월, Apr., April
4인조 그룹, foursome
4중주곡, quartet
5, five
50, fifty
5달러짜리 지폐, fiver
5분의 1, fifth
5센트짜리 동전, nickel
5월, May
5파운드짜리 지폐, fiver
6, six
60, sixty
60년대, sixty
60분의 1, sixtieth
6각형, hexagon
6각형의, hexagonal
6분의 1, sixth
6월, Jun., June
7, seven
70, seventy
70년대, seventy
70분의 1, seventieth
75퍼센트, three-quarters
7분의 1, seventh
7월, Jul., July
8, eight
80년대, eighty
80번째의, eightieth
8강, quarter-final
8분의 1, eighth
8월, Aug., August
9, nine
90, ninety
90년대, ninety

9분의 1, ninth
9월, Sept., September
가, corner
가(街), lane, St.
가가호호, door
가건물, hut
가게, parlor, shop, store
가게 주인, shopkeeper
가격, cost, price, price tag, rate, value
가격 인상, mark-up
가격 책정, pricing
가격 할인 경쟁, price war
(~의) 가격에 팔리다, sell
가격을 내리다, mark, undercut
가격을 부르다, quote
가격을 올리다, mark
가격이 ~다, cost
(~로) 가격이 책정되다, price
가격표, price tag
가계, ancestry
가계비, housekeeping
가고 없는, gone
가공, processing
가공되다, process
가공업자, processor
가공하다, machine
가공하지 않은, crude, raw, untreated
가교, bridge
가구, furniture
가구를 들여놓다, furnish
가구주, householder
가극, opera
가극의, operatic
가금, fowl, poultry
가금 고기, poultry
가급적이면, preferably
가기 쉽게, conveniently
가까스로, barely, narrowly, scarcely
가까스로 이기다, scrape
가까스로 합격하다, scrape
가까스로 해낸, narrow
가까운, close, near
가까운 시일 내에, near
가까움, proximity
가까워지고 있다, get
가까워지다, get
가까이, closely, near, way
가까이에, close, conveniently, hand, near, off, side
가까이에서, close
(~에) 가깝다, verge
가꾸다, plant
가끔, often, sometimes
가끔씩, once
가난하게 하다, impoverish
가난한, poor
가난해진, impoverished
가내 수공업, cottage industry
가냘프게, feebly
가냘픈, slight
가는, fine, thin
가는 것, sharpener
(~로) 가는 길에, route
가는 세로줄 무늬, pinstripe
가는 줄기, thread
가는 중이다, way

(~로) 가는 통로, gateway
가늠하다, fathom, judge, size
가능성, chance, contingency, likelihood, odds, possibility, promise
가능성에 대비한, contingency
가능성이 높은, probable
가능성이 있는, promising
(~할) 가능성이 있다, liable
가능성이 희박하다, stack
(~을) 가능케 하다, permit
가능하게 하다, enable
가능한, likely, possible, potential
가능한 모든 걸 기울여, possibly
가능한 한 빨리, asap
가다, cover, go, last, travel, visit, way
가닥, funnel, strand, thread
가담하다, join, party
가당찮게, outrageously
가당찮은, outrageous
가던 길을 딱 멈추다, track
가동 중인, stream
가동되는, service
가동되다, life
가동되지 않는, service
가동시키다, drive
가동하는, line
가동하다, run
가두 행진, march
가두 행진 시위자, marcher
가두 행진을 벌이다, march
가두다, captive, shut, trap
가두리, hem
가두어 놓다, captive
가둬 놓다, lock
가득 메우다, crowd, jam
가득 몰려들다, crowd
가득 안은, full
(~으로) 가득 차 있다, full
가득 차다, bathe, brim, bulge, choke, inform, pervade
가득 찬, crowded, fraught, full, packed, thick
가득 채우다, pack
가득 채운, crammed
가득하다, reign
(~로) 가득하여, awash
(~로) 가득한, loaded
가득히, across
가라데, karate
가라앉는 배를 떠나다, abandon
가라앉다, dip, settle, sink, subside
가라앉은, subdued
가라앉히다, damp, quieten, settle, sink, subdue
가락, tune
가랑이, crotch, crutch
가량의, near
가려운, itchy
가려움, itch, itching
가려져 있다, shroud
가려지다, screen
가려진, veiled
가렵다, itch
가로대, rail, rung
가로로 된, horizontal
가로막다, forbid, hold, interrupt

가로세로 ~의, square
가로지르다, intersect, span, straddle
(~을) 가로질러, across
가로질러 가다, cross, cut
가로질러서, across
가루, dust, powder
가루로 빻다, grind
가루반죽, pastry
가르고 돌진하다, rip
가르다, divide, separate
가르랑거리는 소리, gurgle
가르랑거리다, gurgle, purr
가르마, part, parting
가르마 타다, part
가르쳐 주다, show
가르치는 것, instruction
가르치다, bring, guide, instruct, school, take, teach
가르침, teaching
가리개, screen
가리다, block, blot, cover, eclipse, hide, mask, obscure, obstruct, shield
가리지 않는, open
가리지 않은, bare
가리키다, indicate, point, refer, say
가만히 있는, inactive, still
가만히 있다, hold, sit, stay
가망, chance, odds, probability, prospect
가망 없는, bleak, forlorn
가망 없음, bleakness, fat
(~의) 가망은 전혀 없다, hope
가망이 없는, doomed
(~할) 가망이 없다, chance, odds
(~할) 가망이 있다, chance
가맹 단체, affiliate
가맹점, franchisee
가맹하다, affiliate
가면, mask
가면을 쓴, masked
가명, alias
가문, dry, origin
가문비나무, spruce
가물거리다, glimmer
가뭄, drought
가미하다, inject, lace
가발, wig
가방, bag
가버린, gone
가벼운, light, lighthearted, lightweight, mild
가벼운 먹을거리, bite
가벼운 입맞춤, peck
가벼움, lightness
가벼워지다, lighten
가변성의, variable
가볍게, lightly, mildly
가볍게 깨물다, nibble
가볍게 누르다, dab
가볍게 닿다, kiss
가볍게 두드리기, pat
가볍게 문지르다, dab
가볍게 여행하다, travel
가볍게 입을 맞추다, peck
가볍게 처벌하다, let
가볍게 치다, pat
가볍게 하다, lighten
가붕을 하다, fit
가사, household, housekeeping, housework, lyric, word
가사의, domestic
가산 명사, countable noun, count noun
가상, fiction
가상 메모리, virtual memory, virtual storage
가상 세계, virtuality
가상공간, cyberspace
가상의, imaginary, virtual
(~라고) 가상하다, pretend
가상현실, virtual reality
가석방, parole
가석방되다, parole
가석방되어, parole
가설, hypothesis
가설적으로, hypothetically

가소성의, plastic
가속도, acceleration
가속시키다, gun
가속하다, accelerate
가속화, acceleration
가솔린, gasoline, petrol
가수, singer, vocalist
가스, fume, gas, wind
가스 굴착 플랫폼, platform
가스통, cylinder
가슴, breast, bust, chest
가슴 깊이, deep
가슴 부분, breast
가슴 아프게 하는, heartbreaking
가슴 아픈 경험, trauma
가슴살, breast
가슴에 사무치는, poignant
가슴에 십자가를 긋는, heart
가슴을 드러낸, topless
가슴을 에는, poignant
가슴을 찢어 놓다, heart
가슴을 펴고 다니다, tall
가슴이 답답한, pit
가슴이 에이다, cut up
가시, spine, thorn
가시가 많은, thorny
가시가 많은 식물, nettle
가시게 하는, disarming
가시게 하다, disarm
가시게 하도록, disarmingly
가시나무, thorn
가시다, drain
가시덤불, thorn
가시성, visibility
가시철사, barbed wire
가식, pantomime
가식을 부리고, posture
가식이 없는, genuine
가식적으로, falsely
가식적인, false
가십 신문, scandal sheet
가여워 하는 마음을 갖다, spare
가연성의, flammable, inflammable
가열하다, heat
가옥, house
가운, dressing gown, robe
가운데, center, midst
가운데에, midst
가운데의, middle
가위, scissors
가을, autumn, fall
가입, admission, entry, initiation
가입시키다, admit, recruit
가입자, subscriber
가입하다, enter, initiate, join, subscribe
가자미, plaice
가장, best, guise, mask, most, very, way
가장 ~한, possible
가장 ~할 것 같지 않은, last
가장 가까운 친척, next of kin
가장 기본적인, bare
가장 나이가 많은, eldest
가장 많은, most
가장 먼, farthest
가장 멀리 떨어진, furthest
(~와) 가장 비슷한, near
가장 빨리, quick
가장 심한, worst
가장 인기 있는 사람, golden
가장 잘 나가는, best-selling
가장 적게, least
가장 적합하게 하다, optimize
가장 전형적인 특징, hallmark
가장 좋아하는, favorite
가장 좋아하는 것, favorite
가장 좋은 것, jewel, very
가장 중시하는, first
가장 중요한, cardinal, chief, essence, first, prime, principal, the, top
가장 중요한 것, flagship
가장 최근에 작성한 유언장, testament
가장 큰 몫, lion's share
가장 큰 피해를 보다, brunt
가장 흥미 있는 부분, highlight

가장자리, border, edge, margin, rim, side
(~의) 가장자리에, fringe
(~을) 가장하다, feign, masquerade, pose
가전 제품, appliance
가정, assumption, home, presumption
가정 폭력, battering
가정 폭력을 당하다, batter
가정부, housekeeper
가정상, hypothetically
가정용의, family
가정의, domestic, home, hypothetical
가정적인, homely, homey
가정하다, postulate, presume, say, suppose
(~라고) 가정한다면, assuming
가져가기 위한, go
가져가다, get, take
가져오다, bring, get, import, retrieve, spell
가족, family, folk, house, household
가족계획, birth control, family planning
가족의, domestic, family
가죽, hide, leather, pelt, skin
가죽을 벗기다, skin
가중치, weighting
가증권, scrip
가지, aubergine, bit, branch, eggplant
가지각색, multiplicity
가지각색의, diverse, riot, various
(~을) 가지고, with
가지고 다니다, carry
(~을) 가지고 따지다, confront
가지고 오다, bring, fetch
가지고 있다, got, hold
(~을) 가지고 태어나다, born
가지다, bear, have, take
가지러 가다, pick
가지런히 짧게 자른 앞머리, bang
가지치기하다, prune
가진 것을 모두 팔아 치우다, sell
가짜, fake, sham
가짜의, bogus, fake, phoney
가차 없는, unrelenting
가차 없이, implacably
가차없는, relentless, ruthless
가차없음, ruthlessness
가차없이, relentlessly, ruthlessly
가축, livestock
가축의, domestic
가출 청소년, runaway
가출하다, run
가치, meaning, merit, value
가치 기준, value
가치 상승, appreciation
가치 없는, value, worthless
가치 있는, deserving, value
가치 있는 것, prize
가치 평가, valuation
가치가 없는, unworthy
가치가 있는 생각, garbage
가치가 오르다, appreciate
(~의) 가치가 있는, worth, worthy
가치관, value
가치관이 혼동된, mixed up
(~의) 가치를 입증하는 것, tribute
가택 연금, house arrest
가택 침입, break-in
가터벨트, suspender
가톨릭교, Catholicism
가톨릭교도, Catholic, Roman Catholic
가톨릭교의, Catholic
가파르게, steeply
가파른, steep
가판대, stall
가판점, stand
가하다, apply, deal, deliver, inflict, put, wreak
가학적 변태 성욕, sadism
가학적 변태 성욕자, sadist
가학적인, sadistic

가해자, assailant, attacker
가혹하게, hard, harshly
가혹한, cruel, draconian, hard, harsh, oppressive, scathing, unkind
가혹한 통치, iron
가혹함, harshness
각, angle
각각, apiece, each, respectively
각각 다른, separate
각각의, each, either, respective
각광을 받는, spotlight
각기, each
각기 제 갈 길을 가다, separate
각도, angle
각별한, particular, particularly
각별히 ~하다, way
각본, play, scenario
각색, adaptation, dramatization
각색되다, dramatize
각성, awakening
각성시키다, wake
각성제, speed
각양각색, variety
각양각색의, sundry
각오가 된, prepared
각인되다, imprint
각자, apiece, each
각종 가게가 즐비한 거리, strip
각종 모음, assortment
각주, footnote
각진, angular
각축을 벌이다, vie
각하, honor, lord
각하하다, dismiss
간, ground, liver
간격, distance, gap, interval
간격 두기, spacing
(~의) 간격으로, interval
간격을 두다, space
간결하게, briefly
간결한, brief, economical
간결하게 말하는, brief
간계함, cunning
간과되는 것, invisibility
간과된, neglected
간과하다, ignore, neglect, overlook, sight
간극, gap
간극을 메우다, bridge
간단명료하게, concisely, succinctly
간단명료한, concise, succinct
간단한, basic, simple, straightforward, terse
간단한 먹을거리, refreshment
간단한 묘사, snapshot
간단한 식사, snack
간단함, simplicity
간단히 말하면, briefly
간단히 말하자면, brief
간담을 서늘하게 하다, chill, frighten
간담이 서늘한, chilling
간병인, caregiver, carer, caretaker
간부의, executive
간선, artery
간선 도로, main road
간섭, interference, intervention
간섭하다, interfere, intervene, intrude, meddle
(~에) 간섭하지 않다, hand
간소하게, simply
간소한, austere, simple
간소화하다, streamline
간수, guard, warder
간식, snack
간식을 먹다, snack
간신히, just, only
간신히 ~하다, manage
간신히 모으다, scrape
간염, hepatitis
간이 상점, kiosk
간이 연장 창고, hut
간이식당, diner, snack bar
간이침대, cot
간절한, pleading
간절함, eagerness
간절히, anxiously, desperately,

eagerly
간절히 바라는, eager
간절히 바라다, pine
간절히 원하는, desperate
간절히 원하다, long
간접 경험의, armchair
간접 목적어, indirect object
간접 화법, indirect discourse,
    indirect speech
간접으로, second
간접적으로, indirectly
간접적인, coded, indirect,
    secondhand
(~로) 간주되다, count
(~으로) 간주하다, call, look, rate,
    regard
간직하다, cherish, keep
간질, epilepsy
간질 환자, epileptic
간질병의, epileptic
간질이다, tickle
간첩, spy
간청, appeal, plea, pleading,
    solicitation
간청하다, appeal, beg, implore,
    plead, solicit
간추린 소식, roundup
간통, adultery, infidelity
간파당하다, rumble
간파하다, see
간판, hoarding
간행, publication
간헐적으로, intermittently
간헐적인, intermittent
간호, nursing
간호사, nurse
간호하다, attend, nurse
갇혀 있는, captive
갇히다, box, catch, pen, trap
(~에) 갇힌, confined, trapped
갇힌 상태, captivity
갈 데까지 가다, hog
갈 수 있는 거리, reach
갈가리 찢다, shred
갈가리 찢은 조각, shred
갈가마귀, raven
갈고리, hook
갈고리 모양의, hooked
갈구, craving
갈기, mane
갈기갈기 찢다, rip
갈기다, lash
갈다, change, grate, grind, mince,
    plow, shed
갈대, reed
갈등, conflict, tension
갈등스러운, agonizing
갈라놓다, cut, part, separate, split
갈라서다, split
갈라져 나오다, branch
갈라지다, break, crack, diverge,
    fork, separate, split
갈라진, chapped
갈라진 금, split
갈라진 틈, crevice, rift, slit
갈리다, diverge, divide
갈림길, fork
갈망, craving, hunger, longing
(~을) 갈망하는, hungry
갈망하다, crave, hunger, starve,
    yearn
갈망하듯, hungrily
갈매기, seagull
갈비, chop, rib
갈비뼈, rib
갈색, brown
갈색 피부의, brown
갈색으로 만들다, brown
갈색이 되다, brown
갈아입다, change
갈아입을 옷, change
갈아타다, change
갈아탐, connection
갈증, thirst
갈지자 꼴, zigzag
갈지자로 걷다, zigzag
갈채, acclaim, cheer
갈채를 받은, acclaimed

갈채를 보내다, acclaim, cheer
갈퀴, rake
갈피를 못 잡게 만들다, disorient
갉다, gnaw
갉아먹다, gnaw, nibble
감각, feeling, sensation, sense,
    taste
감각을 잃게 만들다, numb
감각을 잃은, numb
감각의, sensory
감각이 둔한, insensitive
감각적으로, sensuously
감각적인, sensual, sensuous
감각적임, sensuality
감귤류, citrus
감금, confinement,
    imprisonment, incarceration
감금되다, imprison, incarcerate
감기, cold
감기다, close
감기에 걸리다, cold
감긴, shut
감내, acceptance
감다, close, shut, wind
감당하다, cope, face
감당할 수 있는, affordable, up
감도는, air
감독, coach, director, foreman,
    manager, supervision
감독자, supervisor
감독하다, direct, monitor, oversee,
    shot, supervise
감돌다, hang
감동 받은, impressed, moved,
    touched
감동시키다, impress, move, touch
감동을 받지 않은, unimpressed
감동적으로, movingly
감동적인, moving, stirring,
    touching, unbelievable
감명 받은, impressed
감명을 주다, impress
감미로운, fruity, mellow, sweet
감미롭게, sweetly
감미료, sweetener
감봉하다, dock
감사, appreciation, audit,
    gratitude, inquest, inspection
감사 결의, vote of thanks
감사관, comptroller, controller
감사기도, grace
감사원장, comptroller
감사의 뜻, thank
감사의 뜻을 표하다, thank
감사의 말, acknowledgment
감사장, citation
감사하는, grateful, pleased,
    thankful
감사하다, appreciate, audit,
    inspect, thank
감사하여, gratefully
감사한, nice
감상, appreciation, sentiment
감상자, audience
감상적으로, sentimentally
감상적이고 과장된, melodramatic
감상적인, corny, sentimental
감상적임, sentimentality
감상하다, appreciate
감색, navy
감성, emotion, sensibility
감성적인, moody
감세 수단, tax shelter
감소, decline, decrease, fall,
    lessening, reduction
감소시키다, push
감소하게 된, decline
감소하고 있는, decline
감소하다, decrease, fall
감소하여, downward
감속, slowdown
감수성, sensibility
(~을) 감수하게 하다, involve,
    reconcile
감수하는, reconciled
감수하다, face, submit
감시, surveillance
감시를 받는 중, guard

감시원, ranger
감시인, lookout, watchdog
감시자, monitor
감시하다, guard, tab
감식가, connoisseur
감식력, taste
감싸다, cover, wrap
감아 내리다, wind
감아올리다, hoist, wind
감안을 해서 받아들이다, salt
감안하다, allow
(~을) 감안하면, given, view
감염, attack, infection
감염되다, infect
감염된 상태로, carry
감염시키다, attack, infect
감염을 받다, strike
감염자, carrier
감옥, jail
감옥에 갇혀, bar, inside
감원, downsizing
감원이 있는, head
감원하다, downsize
감을 잡기 시작하다, hang
감자, potato
감자칩, chip
감자튀김, French fries, fry, potato
    chip
감전, electric shock
감전시키다, electrocute
감점하다, dock
감정, appraisal, emotion, feeling,
    heart, sensibility, sentiment,
    temperature
감정 상해하다, offense
감정 이입, identification
감정 이입을 하다, identify
감정 표출, expression
감정상의, sentimental
감정을 건드리는 부분, sore
감정을 상하게 하는, cutting, hurtful
감정을 상하게 하다, hurt
감정의, emotional
감정의 조용한 표출, murmur
감정이 격해서, emotionally
감정이 상하다, wound
감정이 상한, hurt, injured
감정적으로, emotionally
감정적인, emotional
감지기, sensor
감지하다, detect, feel, notice,
    perceive, sense
감질나게 하다, tantalize
감질나는, tantalizing
감촉, feel, texture
감추다, camouflage, conceal,
    cover, disguise, hide, mask, tuck
감축, cut
감축하다, cut, slim
감춤, camouflage
감춰진, hidden
감탄하다, admire
감탄할 만한, admirable
감행, dare
감행하다, carry
감히, venture
감히 ~을 하다, dare
감히 ~하지 못하다, daren't
감히 말하다, hazard
갑, cape
갑각류, shellfish
갑옷, armor, harness
갑자기, abruptly, moment, once,
    sudden, suddenly
갑자기 ~하기 시작하다, break
갑자기 ~하다, erupt, fly, up
갑자기 나타나다, catch
갑자기 덤비다, lunge
갑자기 떠나다, take
갑자기 떨어지다, plunge
갑자기 뛰어듦, plunge
갑자기 멈추게 하다, dead
갑자기 멈추다, cut, dead, short,
    stall
갑자기 멍해지다, blank
갑자기 병에 걸리다, ill
갑자기 생각나다, enter

갑자기 세우다, stall
갑자기 속도를 내다, spurt
갑자기 움직이는, jerky
갑자기 움직이다, jerk
갑자기 움직이며, jerkily
갑자기 일어나다, come
갑자기 자취를 감추다, trace
갑자기 작동을 멈추다, crash
갑자기 죽다, dead
갑자기 터지다, erupt
갑작스러운, abrupt, sharp, sudden
갑작스러움, suddenness
갑작스런, overnight
갑작스런 흔들림, jolt
갑작스레, overnight
(~보다) 갑절로, twice
갑판, deck
값비싼, expensive, valuable, value
값비싼 유광지로 만든, glossy
값싸고 큰, economy
값싼, inexpensive, value
값싼 비지떡, economy
(~의) 값에 팔리다, go
(~의) 값으로, for
값을 끈질기게 깎다, haggle
값을 매기다, set
값을 비교하며 여기저기를 둘러보다,
    shop
값이 ~가 되다, equal
(~의) 값이 되다, buy
값지게, richly
갓, freshly
갓 나온, new
갓 만든, fresh
갓 수확한, fresh
갓 태어난, newborn
갓 태어난 새끼, newborn
갓난아기, infant, newborn
강, river
강간, rape
강간범, rapist
강간하다, rape
강건한, athletic, virile
강건한 사람, athlete
강경, hardening
강경 노선, hardline
강경론자, hawk
강경파, militant
강경하게 나가다, foot
강경하게 말하는, vocal
강경한, militant, strong, tough
강경해지다, harden
강경히, strongly
강당, auditorium
강대국, power, superpower
강도, depth, raider, robber,
    robbery, strength
강도가 낮아지다, water
강등, demotion
강등되다, demote, downgrade
강등시키다, demote
강력하게, forcefully, powerfully,
    strongly, violently
강력한, hard, hot, mighty,
    powerful, ringing, strong,
    vigorous, violent
강력히, fervently, hotly, vigorously
강력하게, intensely, powerfully,
    strongly, vibrantly
강렬한, blinding, high, intense,
    keen, overpowering, powerful,
    strong, vibrant
강렬함, intensity
강령, plank, platform
강매, hard sell
강박 관념, obsession
강박감에 사로잡힌, compulsive
강박에 사로잡힌 사람, obsessive
강박적으로, obsessively
강박적인, obsessive
강변, riverside
강사, instructor, tutor
강설, fall
강세, emphasis, stress
강세를 두다, stress
강세의, bullish, strong
강아지, pup, puppy
강압, force

강어귀, estuary
강연자, lecturer
강요., coercion, compulsion, imposition, insistence
강요된, forced
강요하는, insistent
강요하다, coerce, compel, exact, force, impose, insist, peddle, pin, throat, wish
강우, fall
강우량, rainfall
강의, lecture
강의대, lectern
강의자, lecturer
강의하다, lecture
강인하게 만들다, toughen
강인한, tough
강인함, toughness
강장제, tonic
강점, strength
강제, coercion, compulsion
강제 이주, displacement
강제 퇴거, eviction
강제로, kick
강제로 ~하다, force
강제로 끌려가다, snatch
강제로 말하게 하다, corner
강제로 열다, force
강제적인, compulsory, forcible, mandatory
강제하다, compel, slap
강조, emphasis, stress
강조하다, accentuate, emphasize, highlight, play, ram, stress, underline, underscore
강좌, class, course
강철, steel
강철 같은, iron, steely
강타, blow, clout
강타하다, bash, hammer
강탈당하다, snatch
강탈하다, hijack, hold, usurp
강판, grater
강풍, gale
강하게, powerfully, strongly
강하게 몰아치다, drive
강하게 밀려오다, overpower
강한, forceful, heavy, hefty, powerful, strong
강한 논박, polemic
강한 신념, commitment, conviction
강한 영향, imprint
강한 영향을 끼치다, grip
강한 인상을 주는, impressive
강한 충동, compulsion
강한 확신, hope
강행하다, bulldoze
강화, build-up, reinforcement
강화되다, strengthen, tighten
강화된, fortify
강화하다, beef, bolster, build, consolidate, fortify, intensify, reinforce, shore, step, stoke, strengthen, tighten, toughen
갖가지, variety
갖가지 물건, assortment
갖게 되다, develop
(~을) 갖고 싶다, care
갖고 있다, hold, offer
갖기 시작하다, get
갖다, get, hold
갖추다, equip, stock
갖춰 주다, equip
(~까지) 갖춰진 채로, complete
같다, equal
같은, equal, -like, same, such
같은 것으로, same
(~와) 같은 그런, such
같은 나라 사람, countryman
같은 말을 되풀이하여 말하다, harp
같은 모양의, twin
같은 방법으로, kind
같은 방식으로, way
(~와) 같은 방향으로, with
같은 생각인, mind
같은 식으로, token
(~와) 같이, as, like, together, with

같이 묶여지다, lump
같이 자다, sleep
갚다, pay, repay
개, cake, dog
개 목걸이, collar
개 사육장, kennel
개 집, kennel
개간하다, reclaim
개개의, every, single
개과천선하다, act
개관, overview, panorama
개괄, recap
개괄하다, recap
개구리, frog
개굴개굴 우는 소리, croak
개굴개굴 울다, croak
개념, concept, conception, idea, umbrella
개다, brighten, clear, mix
개당, apiece
개똥지빠귀, thrush
개략적인, approximate
개량, upgrade
개량 장치, refinement
개량하다, refine, upgrade
개론서, introduction
개막, opening
개막식, opening
개막하다, open
개머리판, butt
개미, ant
개발, development, exploitation, mobilization
개발 도상의, developing
개발된, developed
개발은행, development bank
개발자, developer
개발하다, develop, exploit
개방, openness
개방되다, open
개방된, open
개방적인, expansive, inclusive, liberal, open
개방하다, open
개방형 신탁 투자, unit trust
개방형 투자 신탁 회사, unit trust
개별 지도, tutorial
개별 지도의, tutorial
개별적으로, individually, separately
개별적인, separate
개봉 시사회, premiere
개봉되다, premiere
개봉하다, open
개봉한, open
개뿔도, damn
개선, advance, improvement, upgrade
개선되다, improve, pick, refine, upgrade
개선시키다, improve
개선의 여지가 없는, redemption
개선책, corrective
개선하는, remedial
개선하다, better, boost, mend, perk, remedy
개설하다, open
개성, identity, individuality, personality
개성 없는, colorless
개성 있는, individual
(~에) 개성을 주다, individualize
개시, initiation, kickoff, onset
개시의, start-up
개시하다, inaugurate
개암나무, hazel
개업, opening
개업 중이다, practice
개업의, practitioner
개업하다, start
개연성, probability
개요, abstract, outline, overview, sketch, synopsis
개요를 말하다, outline, sketch
개운하게 하는, refresh
개울, stream
개의, canine
개의치 않고, regardless

개의치 않는, unconcerned
개인, individual
개인 교사, coach, tutor
개인 교습을 하다, coach
개인 비서, PA, personal assistant
개인 소유 의상, wardrobe
개인 용무, affair
개인 정보를 알 수 없는, impersonal
개인에 대한 배려가 없는, impersonal
개인용 수첩, personal organizer
개인용 컴퓨터, PC, personal computer
개인용 휴대 정보 단말기, PDA
개인으로서의, private
개인의, individual, personal
개인적으로, personally, privately
개인적인, personal
개인적으로는, personally
개인적인 일, business
개입, intervention
개입하다, intervene, move, step
개자식, son of a bitch
개장, opening
개장(改裝), refit
개장(改裝)되다, refit
개장(改裝)하다, refurbish
개장하다, open
개정, session
개정하다, amend
개조, modification
개조하다, adapt, convert, modify, reconstruct, revamp
개종, conversion
개종시키다, convert
개종자, convert
개줄, lead, leash
개중, lot
개집, doghouse
개척자, pioneer
개척하다, pioneer
개체 수, population
개최국, host
개최하다, give, host
개탄하다, deplore
개판, dog
개편, flat
개편, reorganization, revamp
개혁, reform, revamp
개혁가, innovator, reformer
개혁하다, reform, revamp
개화, flowering
개화된, civilized
개화시키다, civilize
개회, opening, session
개회시키다, open
개회하다, open
객관성, objectivity
객관식, multiple choice
객관적으로, objectively
객관적인, objective
객석, auditorium, seating
객실, cabin, room
객실 사용료, single supplement
객실용 소형 냉장고, minibar
객차, carriage, coach
갠, clear, fair, nice
갤런, gallon
갤리선, galley
갱, pit, shaft
갱단, gang
갱생, rehab, rehabilitation
갱생시키다, rehabilitate
갱신, renewal
갱신하다, break, renew, update
갹출하다, pool
거금, fortune
거금을 들이다, pocket
거기, over, place
거기까지, there
거기에, there
거꾸로, back, backward, conversely, over, reverse, upside down
거꾸로 하다, reverse
거꾸로인, upside down
거닐다, ramble, stroll

거대 기업, giant, major
거대하게, extensively, immensely
거대한, colossal, enormous, extensive, giant, gigantic, huge, immense, mammoth, monster, monstrous, monumental, vast
거동하다, carry
거두다, chalk, score, take
거드름, pomposity
거드름 피우는, pompous
거들다, assist, help
거듭, again, continually
거듭 주장하다, reassert
거듭거듭, time
거듭되는, continual
거듭된, repeated
거듭해서, over, repeatedly
거래, bargain, bargaining, deal, dealings, trade, trading, trade, transaction
거래 정지, freeze
거래를 정지하다, freeze
거래소, dealing room
거래자, trader
거래하다, bargain, business, deal, trade
거룩한, hallowed, heavenly
거룻배, barge
거류지, colony
거르다, filter, skip, strain
거름, manure
거름을 주다, fertilize
거리, distance, street, way
거리 불문, object
(~와는) 거리가 먼, far, nowhere
거리가 멀다, divorced
거리감, distance
거리낌, qualm
거리낌 없는, outspoken
거리낌 없음, outspokenness
거리낌 없이 말하다, speak
거리는 문제가 안 된다, object
거리를 두는, detached
거리를 두다, detach, distance, pull
거리를 유지하다, distance
(~의) 거리에서, range
거만하게, pompously
거만한, arrogant, insolent, lofty, pompous, proud, superior
거만함, arrogance, self-importance
거명, mention
거명하다, identify
거무스름하게, darkly
거무죽죽한, dingy
거물, baron, fat cat, king, magnate
거미, spider
거미줄, cobweb, web
거미줄처럼 얽힌 상황, web
거부, denial, refusal, rejection
거부 반응을 보이는, reject
거부권, veto
거부권을 행사하다, veto
거부되다, defeat
(~을 거부하다, none, refuse, reject, resist
거북, tortoise, turtle
거북한, awkward, uncomfortable
거세, castration
거세게 요동치다, tumble
거세하다, castrate
거세한 수퇘지, hog
거세한 어린 수소, bullock
거스르다, buck
거스름돈, change
(~에게) 거스름돈을 덜 주다, short-change
(~을) 거슬러, against
거슬러 올라가다, date
거슬리는, harsh
거슬리다, grate
거슬림, harshness
거시 경제의, macroeconomic
거식증, anorexia
거식증 환자, anorexic
거식증의, anorexic
거실, living room, lounge, sitting

room
거역, revolt
거역하다, revolt
거울, mirror
거위, goose
거위 고기, goose
거의, all, almost, close, good, half, just, nearly, next, virtually
거의 ~ 아닌, hardly, little
거의 ~한, near
거의 ~한 뻔한, brush
거의 ~ 않는, scarcely
거의 다, way
거의 맞먹다, run
거의 언제나, time
거의 없는, hardly, little, poor
거의 틀림없이, arguably
거의 파탄나다, knee
거의 폐허가 된, ruin
거의 호각으로, closely
거의 호각의, close
거인, giant
거장, virtuoso
거저 주는 것, handout
거절, refusal, rejection
거절하다, decline, deny, nose, rebuff, refuse, reject, scorn, turn
거점, flagship, foothold
거주, residence
거주권, tenure
거주시키다, house, populate
거주인, occupier
거주자, dweller, inhabitant, occupant
거주지, dwelling, place, residence
거주하고 있는, residence, resident
거주하는, living, populated
거주하다, inhabit, occupy, populate, reside
거지, beggar, panhandler
거짓, hoax
거짓 구실, pretense
거짓 없는, honest
거짓 증거에 의한, unsafe
거짓된, false, mock
거짓말, lie, lying, story
거짓말이다, nothing
거짓말쟁이, liar
거짓말투성이, pack
거짓말하고 있다, lie
거짓의, bogus, untrue
거짓임을 드러내다, belie
거창하게, rhetorically
거창한, big, grandiose, rhetorical
거처를 제공하다, shelter
(~을) 거처, via
(~를) 거처서, through
거친, coarse, harsh, heavy-handed, laddish, rough, stormy, turbulent, wild
거친 천, sacking
거친 털, bristle
거친 행동, roughness
거칠거칠한, rough
거칠거칠함, roughness
거칠게, coarsely, harshly, roughly
거칠게 뜯어내다, tear
거칠게 항의하다, curse
거칠게 흔들다, jolt
거칠다, abrasive
거침, harshness
거침없이, riot
거침없이 쏟아 놓는 말, patter
거트, gut
거푸집, mold
거품, bubble, fizz, froth
거품 목욕탕, Jacuzzi
거품기, whisk
거품을 내다, froth, whisk
거품이 많은, bubbly
거품이 이는, fizzy, sparkling
거품이 일다, bubble
거품제, foam
거행되다, place
거점, anxiety, care, dread, unease, uneasiness, worry
걱정 없는, carefree, secure
걱정거리, concern, headache,

trouble, worry
걱정되는, fraught, worrisome, worrying
걱정스러운, scared, troubling, worried
걱정스럽게, anxiously
걱정스러워 하는, troubled
걱정시키다, concern, eat, trouble, unnerve, worry
걱정을 끼치는, hang
걱정하게 하는, unnerving
걱정하는, afraid, anxious, worried
걱정하다, dread, fear, fret, worry
걱정하지 말아라, mind
건, key
건(腱), tendon
건강, constitution, health
건강 진단, checkup, medical
건강과 행복, well-being
건강성, health
건강에 좋은, wholesome
건강에 좋지 않은, unhealthy
건강을 회복하다, convalesce, recuperate
건강이 안 좋은, shape
건강이 좋지 않은, unhealthy
건강이 좋지 않음, ill health
건강이 증진되다, improve
건강하게, healthily, powerfully
건강하지 못한, shape, unhealthy
건강하지 않은, unfit
건강한, fine, fit, healthy, powerful, shape, sound, well
건강한 상태, health
(~을) 건너, across, over
건너다, cross
건너뛰다, skip
(~의) 건너편에, across, past
건너편으로, across
건널목, crossing
건네주다, give, hand, pass, surrender
건드리기, knock
건드리다, agitate, knock, touch
건드리지 않은, undisturbed
건립하다, erect
건망증이 심한, forgetful
건물, building
건물 안에서, indoors
건물 잔해, rubble
건물이 밀집된, built-up
건반, keyboard
건반 악기, keyboard
건방진, cocky, impertinent, presumptuous
건방짐, cheek
건배, cheer
건배하다, drink, toast
건설, building, construction, erection
건설적인, constructive
건설하다, construct
건성으로, half-heartedly
건성으로 하는, half-hearted
건실하지 못한, unhealthy
건장한, burly, robust, rugged
건재하다, strong
건전성, health
건전지, battery
건전한, clean, healthy, right, wholesome
건조기, dry, dryer
건조된, dried
건조시키다, dehydrate
건조한, dry
건조한 상태, dryness
건초, hay
건초열, hay fever
건축 관련해서, architecturally
건축 양식, architecture
건축가, architect
건축물, structure
건축술, architecture
건축업자, builder
건축의, architectural
건포도, raisin
걷기, walk, walking
걷는 속도, pace

걷다, collect, draw, tread, walk
걷어 내다, skim
걷어 올리다, roll
걷잡을 수 없는, rampant
걷히다, clear
걸다, back, bet, hang, hitch, play, risk, stake, wager
걸레, rag
(~에) 걸려 비틀거리다, trip
걸려 오는, incoming
걸려 있다, hang
걸려 찢어지다, snag
걸리기 쉬운, susceptible, vulnerable
(~에) 걸리다, catch, come, contract, go, pick, snag, take
걸림, entanglement
걸림돌, snag
걸맞게, decently
걸쇠, clasp
걸어서, foot
걸어서 바래다주다, walk
걸음, pace, step
걸음걸이, gait, step, walk
걸음마 단계의, fledgling
걸음마를 배우는 아기, toddler
걸이, rack
걸이못, peg
걸인, beggar
걸작, masterpiece
걸쭉하게 되다, pulp
걸쭉하게 하다, thicken
걸쭉한, thick
걸쭉한 물질, pulp
걸쳐놓다, drape
(~에) 걸쳐서, across
걸쳐져 있다, sling
걸치다, drape, sling
걸터앉다, perch
걸터앉아, astride
검게 하다, blacken
검댕, soot
검문소, checkpoint
검붉은 색, ruby
검사, exam, examination, inspection, prosecutor, screening, survey, test
검사관, controller
검사기, checker
검사받다, test
검사소, control
검사인, checker
검사하다, examine, inspect, probe, screen, survey
검색, retrieval, search
검색 엔진, search engine
검색자, surfer
검색하다, browse, retrieve, search
검소하고 엄격한, spartan
검소한, frugal
검소함, frugality, thrift
검시, postmortem
검시관, coroner
검안사, optician
검열, censorship, inspection
검열관, censor, inspector
검열을 통과하다, clear
검열하다, censor, inspect
검은, black
검은 딸기, blackberry
검은 잉크로 지우다, black
검은 점, mole
검정, certification
검정색 계통의, dark
검정색의, dark
검증, identification
검증 각인, hallmark
검진, test
검찰 당국, prosecution
검출기, detector
검토, examination, review
검토되다, examine
검토하다, review, stock
겁, foot, scare
겁 많은, chicken
겁나는, frightening, terrifying
겁내는, nervous
겁먹게 하다, terrify

겁먹다, cow
겁먹은, cowed, intimidated, scared, terrified
겁먹지 않는, undaunted
겁에 질리다, nerve
(~에) 겁을 먹은, frightened
겁쟁이, chicken, coward, wimp, wuss
겁주는, intimidating
겁주다, frighten, intimidate, scare
것, affair, anything, case, one, stuff, that, thing, way, what
겉만 번지르르한, glossy
겉모습, persona, presentation
겉모습만 봐서는, look
겉모양, guise
겉발림으로, glibly
겉발림의, glib
겉보기, facade, semblance
겉보기에는, seemingly
겉보기의, seeming
겉으로 보기에는, outwardly
겉의, right
겉창, shutter
겉치레, gloss, masquerade
겉치장, veneer
게, crab
게걸스러운, greedy, voracious
게걸스럽게, greedily
게걸스럽게 많이 먹다, gorge
게걸스럽게 먹다, devour, gobble
게걸스레 먹다, tuck
게걸스레 먹어 치우다, wolf
게걸증, bulimia
게다가, addition, bargain, besides, indeed, more, moreover, plus, that, then, well
게릴라, guerrilla
게살, crab
게시판, board, bulletin board, noticeboard
게시하는, post, put
게양하다, raise
게우다, vomit
게으른, idle, lazy
게으름, inaction, laziness
게으름 피우다, slack
게이트웨이, gateway
게일어, Gaelic
게일족의, Gaelic
게임, game, play
게임 쇼 프로그램, game show
게임카드, card
게임판, board
게재되다, run
게재하다, print, publish, run
겨, bran
겨냥되다, level
겨냥하다, direct, target
겨누다, aim, fix
겨드랑이, armpit
겨우, barely, just, matter, merely, only, out
겨우 몇 주일, matter
겨우 빛을 면하다, head
겨우 이해하다, head
겨울, winter
겨자, mustard
겨자색, mustard
격, case
격노, furor, fury, rage
격노하게 만들다, enrage
격노하다, rage, red
격노하여, wildly
격노한, furious
격노해서, furiously
격동, surge, turbulence
격동의, tumultuous, turbulent
격려, encouragement, pat, prompting, stimulation
격려 연설, pep talk
격려가 되는, cheering
격려하다, cheer, encourage, pat, stimulate
격려하듯이, encouragingly
격려하여 ~하도록 하다, encourage
격렬하게, bitterly, fiercely, furiously, heatedly, keenly,

madly, vehemently, violently, wildly
격렬하게 움직이다, jig
격렬한, bitter, fierce, furious, grueling, heavy, intense, keen, strenuous, towering, vehement, vigorous, violent
격렬한 항의, outcry
격렬함, bitterness, vehemence, violence
격렬해지다, flare
격렬히, vigorously
격리, insulation, quarantine
격리되다, insulate, quarantine
격리하다, isolate
격발, burst
격변, upheaval
격변하다, burst
격분, exasperation, fury, outrage
격분시키다, infuriate
격분하다, flare
격분한, livid
격상되다, upgrade
격상하다, upgrade
격식에 맞추어, correctly
격식을 갖춘, correct, formal
격식을 갖춤, correctness
격식을 갖춰, formally
격식을 차리지 않고, informally
격식을 차리지 않은, informal
격심한, acute, keen
격심한 활동, exertion
격앙, furor
격앙되다, run
격앙된, heated, overheated
격언, maxim, proverb, saying
격의, distance
격자, lattice
격자 모양, grid
격자무늬, tartan
격자무늬의 모직물, tartan
격정, misgiving
격주로, biweekly, fortnightly
격주로 시행되는, fortnightly
격주의, biweekly
격차, gap
격차를 벌리다, pull
격찬하다, extol
격추되다, down
격추하다, bring, shoot
격통, pang
격퇴하다, fight, repel, see
격투하다, grapple
격하, relegation
격하되다, relegate
격하시키다, lower, relegate
격한, explosive, heated, mad
겪다, endure, experience, go, have, meet, pass, suffer, undergo
겪은 사람, survivor
겪을 만큼 겪다, enough
겪음, experience
견고하게, solidly
견고한, rugged, solid, steady
견고함, solidity
견과, nut
견디 내다, ride, stand, withstand
견디기 힘든, oppressive, trying
견디다, abide, bear, face, hang, hold, stand, stomach, survive, tolerate
(~을) 견디어 내는, -proof
(~을) 견디어 내다, get, hold, persevere, weather
견딜 만하게, tolerably
견딜 만한, bearable, tolerable
견딜 수 없는, unbearable
견딜 수 없을 만큼, unbearably
견문이 넓은, informed
견본, sample, specimen
견습 기간, internship
견실하게, reliably
견실한, stout
견인 차량 보관소, pound
견인차, tractor
견적, costing, estimate, quotation, quote
견적가, quote

견적사(見積士), quantity surveyor
견적서, quotation
견적을 뽑다, quote
견적이 나오다, cost
견제되다, check
견주다, bay
견주다, liken
(~과) 견줄 만하다, compare
견줄 상대가 없는, unrivaled
견지, angle, point of view, standpoint
견진 성사, confirmation
견진 성사를 받다, confirm
견책, censure
견책하다, censure
견학, tour
견학하다, tour
견해, opinion, outlook, perspective, point of view, position, pulse, version, view
결과, consequence, effect, finding, outcome, result
(~한) 결과가 되다, result
(~의) 결과로서, wake
(~한) 결과를 낳다, culminate
결과물, work
결과적으로, consequence, consequently
결과적으로 ~하게 되다, come
결과적으로는, event
결과적인, consequent
결국, come, end, there
결국 ~로 끝나다, end
결국 ~에 이르다, get
결국에는, eventually
결단력, decision, determination, resolution, resolve, willpower
결단력 있게, decisively
결단력 있는, decisive
결렬, breakdown, collapse
결렬되다, break, collapse
결론, conclusion
결론에 이르지 못한, inconclusive
결론으로, conclusion
결론적으로, ultimately
결론짓다, conclude, decide
결말, conclusion, end, ending
결말을 내다, clinch, end
결말이 나다, end
결말이 나지 않은 부분, loose end
결백, innocence
결백하여, clear
결백한, clear, innocent
결별, break, breakup
결별하다, break
(~와) 결부되다, couple
결부된, twin
결부하다, link
결산, accounting, bottom line
결석, stone
결석한, absent
결속력, cohesion, solidarity
결속을 굳히다, rank
결손, deficit
결손의, broken
결승 푯말, post
결승전, final
결승전 진출자, finalist
결실 맺기, fruition
결실을 맺다, fruit, pay
결심, resolution
결심이 서지 않은, undecided
결심하다, determine, mind, resolve
(~하려고) 결심한, bent, determined, resolved
결여되어 있는, zero
결여되어 있다, lack
(~이) 결여된, devoid
결원, vacancy
결원의, vacant
결의, determination, will
결의가 강한, purposeful
결의가 굳은, determined
결의가 되어 있는, resolved
결의안, resolution
결의에 차서, purposefully
결이 거친, coarse
결장, colon

결점, failing, fault, flaw, imperfection, shortcoming, weakness
결점이 없는, impeccable
결정, decision, determination
결정권, casting vote
결정되다, govern, settle
결정을 못 내리다, waver
결정을 못 하는, hung
결정을 보류하다, option
결정적으로, critically, crucially, decisively
결정적이지 않은, indecisive
결정적인, conclusive, critical, decisive
결정적인 요소, bottom line
결정적인 한 마디, word
결정짓다, decide, determine, shape
결정체, crystal
결정체가 되다, crystallize
결정체를 만들다, crystallize
결정타를 가할 준비를 하다, kill
결정판인, definitive
결정하다, decide, determine, thrash
결집하다, marshal
결코, ever, shot
결코 ~ 않다, way
결코 ~가 아니다, exactly
결코 ~이 아닌, anything
결코 ~하지 않아, never
결코 ~이 아니다, scarcely
결코 ~하지 않을 사람, last
결탁, collusion
결탁하다, collude
결투, duel
결투 신청, challenge
결판, showdown
결핍, deficiency, deprivation, lack, poverty, scarcity
결핍된, deficient
결함, defect, fault, flaw, hole
(~에서) 결함을 찾아내다, hole
결함이 있는, defective, faulty, imperfect
결합, fusion
결합 구조, geometry
결합된, combine
결합된, knit, together
결합시키다, bond, knit, string, unite
결합하다, bond, combine, join, unite
결합하여, together
결핵, TB, tuberculosis
결혼, marriage
결혼 상대로 적합한, eligible
결혼 생활, marriage
결혼 전의 성, maiden name
결혼식, marriage, wedding
결혼의, marital, married
결혼하다, marry, wed
결혼한, married
겸비하다, combine
겸손, humility, modesty
겸손하게, humbly, modestly
겸손하게, humble, modest
겸양, humility
겸용의, -cum-
겸하다, combine
겸허하게, humbly
겸허하게 만드는, humbling
겸허하게 만들다, humble
겸허한, humble
겹쳐지다, overlap, superimpose
겹치게 하다, overlap
겹치다, clash, couple, overlap
겹침, overlap
경(卿), sir
경각심, alarm
경감, alleviation, captain, inspector
경감시키다, alleviate, relieve
경건하게, piously
경건한, devout, pious
경건함, piety
경계, alertness, boundary, edge,

limit, line, vigilance
경계선, borderline
경계선상의, borderline
경계의, cautionary
경계하고 있는, alert, vigilant
경계하는, alert, jealous, wary, watchful
경계하여, guard, jealously, warily
경고, caution, warning, yellow card
경고의, warning
경고하다, alert, caution, warn
경공업, light industry
경과, lapse, passage, passing
경과하다, elapse, go, lapse, pass
경관, view
경구, phrase
경기, competition, contest, event, fight, game, leg, match, play, sport
경기 시작 시간, kickoff
경기 종료, full-time
경기 중단, stoppage
경기 침체, recession
경기 하향, downturn
경기 활성, boom, buoyancy
경기를 시작하다, kick
경기자, player
경기장, arena, course, court, field, pitch, playing field, ring, stadium
경도, longitude, rigidity
경도의, longitude
경량의, lightweight
경력, career, record
경련, convulsion, cramp, spasm, twitch
경례, salute
경례하다, salute
경로, line, route
경마, race
경마장 경주로, racetrack
경마장의 경주로, racecourse
경매, auction, sale
경매로 팔다, auction
경매인, auctioneer
경매장, salesroom
경멸, contempt, scorn, sneer
경멸적인, derogatory
경멸하는, contemptuous, scornful
경멸하다, despise, look, nose, scorn, sneer
경모의 대상이 되는 여자, heroine
경박한, dizzy
경범죄, misdemeanor
경보, alert
경보기, alarm
경비, budget, cost, outlay, sentry
경비 중, guard
경비대, guard
경비를 세우다, guard
경비원, security guard
경사, grade, sergeant, slant
경사도, slope
경사로, ramp
경사면, incline, slope
경사지다, slope
경사진, sloping
경솔하게, brashly, carelessly, rashly
경솔한, brash, careless, frivolous, inconsiderate, rash
경솔함, carelessness
경시, disregard, subordination
경시하다, disregard, minimize, play, subordinate, undervalue
경악, astonishment, consternation, fright
경악스러운, staggering
경악하게 하다, shock
경야(經夜), wake
경영, business, management, running
경영 대학, business school
경영 합리화, rationalization
경영 합리화가 이뤄지다, rationalize
경영 효율화, rationalization
경영권 위기에 처한 회사를 구하는 사람이나 회사, white knight

경영권 인수, takeover
경영상의, managerial
경영의, operating
경영인, administrator
경영자, proprietor
경영자 인수, management buyout
경영자에 의한 회사 인수, MBO
경영진, administration, management
경영하다, run
경의, awe
경외심을 느끼다, awe
경우, case, occasion, part
(~하는) 경우에는, event
(~을) 경유하여, via
경의, deference, homage
(~에게) 경의를 표하는, honor
경의를 표하다, hat, honor, salute
경이, marvel, wonder
경이로운, wonder
경이로운 것, wonder
경이롭게도, miraculously
경이적인, phenomenal
경이적인 일, miracle
경작, cultivation, land
경작하는, arable
경작하다, cultivate, farm, plow, work
경작할 수 있는, arable
경쟁, battle, competition, fight, race, rivalry, stake
경쟁 상대, rival
경쟁 상품, competition
경쟁력, competitiveness
경쟁력 있게, competitively
경쟁력 있는, competitive, keen
경쟁사, competitor
경쟁심, competitiveness
경쟁심이 강한, competitive
경쟁에 참가하다, contest
경쟁의, competitive
경쟁자, antagonist, competition, contender, contestant
경쟁하는, opposing
경쟁하다, compete, vie
경쟁하여, competitively
경적, honk, horn
경적 소리, hoot
경전, scripture
경정, superintendent
경제, economy
경제의, economic
경제적으로, economically
경제적인, economical, economy
경제학, economics
경제학자, economist
경주, race, racing, running
경주로, circuit, racetrack, track
경주마, racehorse, racer, runner
경주마 훈련소, stable
경주에 내보내다, race
경주용 차량, racer
경주용 차와 성능이 비슷한, sporty
경주하다, race
경직되게, stiffly
경직되다, stiffen
경직된, inflexible, rigid, stiff
경직성, inflexibility
경직시키다, stiffen
경직함, rigidity
경찰, copper, force, police
경찰 순찰차, cruiser
경찰관, cop, officer, police, policeman, police officer, policewoman
경찰력, police force
경찰봉, billy
경찰서, police station
경찰서 자치 구역, precinct
경찰시장, Chief Constable, superintendent
경첩, hinge
경청, ear, hearing
경축하다, celebrate
경치 좋은, scenic
경치가 아름다운, scenic
경칭, title
경쾌한, brisk

경탄하다, marvel, wonder
경향, current, propensity, tendency
(~하는) 경향을 갖게 하다, predispose
(~할) 경향이 있는, liable, prone
경향이 있다, tend, will
경험, encounter, experience, taste
경험 세계, universe
경험 없는, raw
경험에서 얻은 법칙, rule
경험이 없는, inexperienced, new
경험이 있는, experienced
경험이 풍부한, seasoned
경험이 풍부한 사람, veteran
경험적으로, empirically
경험적인, empirical
경험하다, experience, expose, go, pass, taste
경호원, bodyguard, heavy, minder, security guard
경화(硬貨), hard currency
곁들이다, add
곁들인 것, accompaniment
(~의) 곁에, alongside, next, side
곁에 있는, handy
(~의) 곁을 지키다, stand, stick
계, scene, squad
계간지, quarterly
계고, caution
계고를 받다, caution
계곡, valley
계급, class, echelon, grade, rank
계급 차별이 없는, classless
계급의, hierarchical
계기, catalyst
계기반, dash, dashboard
계단, flight, ladder, stair, staircase, stairway, step
계단식 논밭, terrace
계란, egg
계란 세례를 받다, egg
계략, ploy, ruse, set-up
계량기, meter
계량적인 면, arithmetic
계량하다, meter
계류 중인, pending
계류장, mooring
계모, stepmother
계몽적인, enlightening, illuminating
계몽하다, enlighten
계보의, genealogical
계보학, genealogy
계부, stepfather
계산, arithmetic, calculation, count, mathematics
계산기, calculator
계산대, cash desk, cashier's desk, checkout, till
(~꼴으로) 계산되다, reckon
계산된, calculated
계산서, bill, check, tab
(~을) 계산에 넣다, factor
계산에 넣지 않고, exclusive
계산을 잘하는 사람, mathematician
계산적인, calculating
계산하다, calculate, count, settle
계상하다, account
계선설비, mooring
계속, ever-, forward, inexorably, on, persistently, through
계속 ~이다, stay
계속 ~인 채로 있다, remain
계속 괴롭히다, haunt
계속 나아가다, continue
계속 이어서, onward
계속 이어지는, continuous
계속 진행하다, proceed
계속되는, inexorable, on, perennial, running
계속되다, bubble, continue, go, last, proceed
계속하다, carry, continue, get, go, keep, persist, push, stick, sustain
계속하여, end
계속해 나가다, hang

계속해서, away, onward, running
계속해서 ~하다, go, keep
계승, inheritance, succession
계시, revelation
계약, bargain, contract, covenant, engagement, signing
계약 가수, signing
계약 기간, term
계약 선수, signing
계약금, down payment
계약금으로, down
계약상으로, contractually
계약상의, contractual
계약하는, contract, sign
계엄령, martial law
계열, classification
계율, precept
계절, season
계절적으로, seasonally
계절적인, seasonal
계좌, account
계좌 이체, credit transfer
계주, relay
계층, echelon, layer, rank, sector
계통이 같은 것, relative
계피, cinnamon
계획, blueprint, intention, plan, planning, proposal, scheme, strategy
계획 수립, planning
계획가, planner
계획대로, according to
계획되다, slate
계획된, pipeline
계획안, protocol
계획을 마련하다, lay
계획을 세우다, plan, scheme
계획적인, willful
계획표, timetable
계획하다, design, engineer, mean, mind, plan, put
고(故), late
고(高)~, high
고가 도로, flyover, overpass
고가의, valuable
고갈, depletion
고갈되다, drain, run
고갈된, depleted, dry
고갈시키다, deplete, exhaust
고갈의 근원, drain
고개, head
고개를 들다, head
고객, client, clientele, customer, patron, punter
(~의) 고객이 되다, patronize
고결하게, nobly
고결한, noble, virtuous
고결함, nobility
고고학, archaeology
고고학자, archaeologist
고고학적인, archaeological
고국, homeland
고귀한, exalted
고급 조제 식품 가게, delicatessen
고급으로, upmarket, upscale
고급의, advanced, exclusive, executive, fine, gourmet, high-class, higher, lifestyle, premium, prestige, select, superior, upmarket, upscale, vintage
고기, meat
고기가 많은, meaty
고기구이, roast
고기기름, grease
고난, tribulation
고뇌, angst, distress, pain, torment
고다, simmer
고달픈, tough
고대, antiquity
고대 그리스·로마 문명의, classical
고대 그리스·로마풍의, classically
고대 로마의, Roman
고대 유물, antiquity
고대 이집트의 왕, pharaoh
고대의, ancient

고도, altitude, height
고독, isolation, loneliness, solitude
고독한, alone, desolate, lonely
고동, beat, beating
고동치다, pulsate
고되고 단조로운 일, grind
고된, arduous, demanding, hard
고됨, hardness, rigor
고드름, icicle
고등 교육, higher education, tertiary
고등어, mackerel
고등의, higher
고등학교, high school
고딕 양식의, Gothic
고랑, furrow
고래, whale
고래잡이, whaling
고려, consideration
고려 대상에서 제외하다, write
고려 중인, consideration
(~을) 고려에 넣다, reckon
고려하고 있다, term
고려하다, cater, consider, consideration, contemplate
(~을) 고려하면, considering
(~을) 고려하여, view
고루 잘 섞인, smooth
고루한, staid
고르게, evenly
고르다, choose, opt, pick, select
고르지 않게, irregularly
고르지 않은, irregular, patchy, uneven
고르지 않음, irregularity
고른, even
고리, coil, eye, hoop, link, ring
고리 모양, loop
고리로 걸다, hook
고릴라, gorilla
고립, isolation
고립되다, maroon
고립되어, isolation
고립된, cut off, isolated
고립된 지역, ghetto
고립된 채, vacuum
고립시키다, isolate
고마운 것, blessing
고마운 일, mercy
고마움, thank
고마워하는, appreciative
고막, eardrum
고막이 터질 것 같은, deafening
고맙게 생각하는, thankful
고맙게 여기는, grateful
고맙게도, thankfully
고맙겠습니다, oblige
고맙습니다, thank
고매한, lofty
고명, garnish
고명한, celebrated
고모, aunt, auntie
고모부, uncle
고무, rubber, stimulus
고무 밴드, elastic band
고무 젖꼭지, dummy, nipple, pacifier
고무도장, rubber stamp
고무보트, raft
고무시키는 것, inspiration
고무시키는 사람, inspiration
고무시키다, inspire
고무장화, welly
고무적인, encouraging, heartening, inspiring
고무줄, elastic, rubber band
고무줄 새총, slingshot
고무풀, gum
고문, adviser, consultant, torture
고문 의사, consultant
고문서에 관한, archive
고문을 당하는, torture
고문의, advisory
고민거리, torment
고민상담 칼럼리스트, advice columnist
고민케 하다, distress

고민하는, torn
고발, accusation, charge, denunciation, indictment, whistle-blowing
고발된 상태에 있다., accuse
고발하다, accuse, charge, denounce, inform, press, prosecute, report, whistle
고백, confession
고백하다, confess, profess
고분고분, submissively
고분고분하게, obediently
고분고분하지 않은, unruly
고분고분한, obedient, submissive
고비, mountain
고비를 넘긴, danger
고삐, bridle, rein
고삐 풀린, runaway
(~은) 고사하고, let
고산성의, alpine
고상, elegance
고상한, taste, tasteful
고생, trouble
고생하다, languish, struggle, toil
고성능의, high-powered
고성이 오가는, stormy
고소, charge, prosecution
고소득자를 겨냥한, upmarket
고소인, plaintiff
고소하다, accuse, prosecute, sue
고소해하는, gleeful
고소해하며, gleefully
고소함, glee
고속도로, freeway, motorway, superhighway
고속도로 휴게소, rest area
고수머리, curl
고수하다, hold, keep, stand, stick
고슴도치, hedgehog
고심하다, brood
(~을) 고심하여 도출하다, hammer
고심하여 만들다, elaborate
고아, orphan
고아가 되다, orphan
고아원, institution, orphanage
고안되다, design
고안하다, devise, dream, think
고압적인, heavy-handed
고액의, highly
고약한, miserable
고약한 냄새, stink
고약한 냄새가 나다, stink
고양, enhancement
고양시키다, enhance
고양이, cat, pussy
고양이과 동물, cat
고여 있는, stagnant
고역, grind
고요, calm, stillness, tranquillity
고요하게, serenely, silently
고요한, serene, still, tranquil
고요함, quietness
고용, employment
고용주, employer
고용하다, employ, engage, hire, take
고운, fine
고원, highlands, plateau
고위 인사, dignitary
고위의, high, senior
고위직에, high
고위층에 속한, place
고유 명사, proper noun
고유 영역, preserve
고유성, identity
고유의, intrinsic
고유하게, uniquely
(~에) 고유한, unique
고음의, high, high-pitched
고의가 아닌, inadvertent, unintentional, unwitting
고의로, purpose
고의의, willful
고의적으로, intentionally
고의적으로 방해하다, sabotage
고의적인, intentional
고이 간직한, cherished
고이다, well

고인, deceased
고작, miserable
고장, area, breakdown, failure, town
고장 난, down, wrong
고장나다, break
고장내다, break
고장이 난, order
고장이 잦은, temperamental
고전, classic, classical
고전 문학, classic
고전적 구형의, vintage
고전적인, classical
고정 코너, spot
고정 핀, pin
고정되다, fix, peg
고정되어, back
고정된, fixed, -mounted, set
고정시키다, anchor, fix, lock, mount, steady, wedge
고정하다, pin
고조, wave
고조되다, build, heighten, simmer
고조시키다, heighten
고지, height
고지대, elevation
고지의, high
고질적인, deep-seated, endemic
고집, obstinacy, persistence, tenacity
고집 센, obstinate, willful
고집 있는, persistent
고집스러운, intractable
고집스럽게, insistently, persistently
고집이 센, headstrong, tenacious
고집하다, insist, persist
고착되다, solidify
고착된, entrenched, stuck
고착시키다, entrench, solidify
고철, scrap
고체, solid
고체로 만들다, solidify
고체로 변하다, solidify
고체의, solid
고쳐 말하다, restate
고쳐 쓰다, rewrite
고초, patch, rigor
고충, complaint
고취되다, imbue
고취하다, inspire
고층 건물, high-rise
고층 빌딩, tower
고층의, high-rise
고치, cocoon
고치기 어려운, incurable
고치다, clear, correct, fix, rectify, repair, rework
고통, affliction, anguish, suffering, torment
(~에) 고통 받는, -ridden, stricken
고통 받다, suffer
(~로) 고통받는 사람, martyr
고통스러운, agonizing, pained, painful
(~로) 고통스러워하다, rack
고통스러워하는, pain
고통스럽게, painfully
고통에 찬, anguished
고통을 받는, stricken
고투, slog, struggle
고투하다, battle, struggle
고풍의, archaic
고함, bellow, cry, holler, rant, shout
고함 소리, ranting
고함지르다, bellow, holler
고함치다, bark, bawl, cry, rant, shout
고해, confession
고해하다, confess
고향, birthplace, home
고형, solid
고형의, solid
고환, testicle
곡, number
곡괭이, pick, pickax
곡류, cereal
곡물, grain

곡물 가루, flour
곡선, curve
곡선을 그리다, curve
곡식 열매, ear
곡조, melody, tune
곡해하다, twist
곤경, plight, predicament, strait, trap
곤경에 빠진, high
곤경에 처하여, water
곤경에 처한, difficulty
곤경을 모면하다, day
곤경을 벗어나지 못한, wood
곤두박질로, headlong
곤두박질치듯, headlong, over
곤두세우다, ruffle
곤란, hardship, hurdle
곤란하게, awkwardly
곤란한, awkward, thorny, tricky
곤란한 입장인, difficulty
곤란한 처지의, water
곤봉, baton, club
곤죽이 되도록 맞다, pulp
곤충, bug, insect
곤충 세계, world
곤혹스러운, devastated
곤혹스럽게 하다, puzzle
곤혹하게 하는, puzzling
곧, immediately, long, momentarily, presently, shortly, soon, time, upon
곧 마련될, forthcoming
(~이) 곧 발생하려는, about
곧 부모가 되는, expectant
곧 살 수 있어, shelf
곧 있을, prospective
곧 찾아올, forthcoming
곧게, straight
곧바로, quick, right, straight away
곧은, straight
곧이듣다, swallow
곧장, direct, directly, straight away, through
곧추서서, end
곧추세우다, straighten
골, goal, trough
골격, skeleton
골고루 돌아가다, go
골대, goalpost, post
골동품, antique
골드 카드, gold card
골똘히 생각하는, rack
골라내다, cut, separate
골목, alley, side street
골목의, cross
골반, pelvis
골반의, pelvic
골자, bone, gist
골절, break, fracture
골조, foundation, frame, skeleton
골짜기, valley
골치 아파질 것이다, hell
골치 아픈, maddening, prickly, thorny, vexed
골치 아픈 사항, sticking point
골치 아픈 일, bugger
골칫거리, curse, embarrassment, headache, irritation, menace, puzzle, trouble, worry
골칫거리가 되다, nuisance
골칫거리인, troublesome
골칫덩이, nuisance, pest
골키퍼, goalie, goalkeeper, keeper
골탕 먹임, trick
골판지의, corrugated
골프, golf
골프 선수, golfer
골프 치기, golfing
골프 코스, golf course
골프 클럽, club, golf club
골프의, golfing
골프장, golf course
골프채, club, golf club
곪다, fester
곪아떨어지게 만들다, knock
곰, bear
곰곰이 생각하다, digest, play
곰곰이 생각한 후에, reflection

곰팡이, mold
곱게, finely
곱빼기의, double
곱셈, multiplication
곱슬곱슬하게 말다, curl
곱슬곱슬한, curly, fuzzy
곱슬곱슬한, curl
곱슬머리, curl
곱은, numb
곱하다, multiply
곳, place, way
곳곳에, everywhere, place
공, ball
공간, room, space
공간을 다 차지하다, fill
공간이 넓은, roomy
공간적인, spatial
공갈, racketeering
공갈 협박, blackmail
공갈 협박자, blackmailer
공갈 협박하다, blackmail
공감, empathy, sympathy, understanding
공감대, chemistry
공감하다, identify, relate, sympathize
공개, disclosure, openness, release
공개 시장, open market
공개되다, go
공개의, open
공개의, public
공개적으로, openly, publicly
공개적으로 분명히, record
공개적으로 비난하다, denounce
공개하다, disclose, release, voice
공격, aggression, attack, offensive, strike
공격당하다, savage
공격받기 쉬운, vulnerable
공격성, aggression, belligerence
공격수, forward, striker
공격자, assailant
공격적으로, aggressively
공격적인, aggressive, belligerent, confrontational, strident
공격하다, attack, bat, come, fly, mug, strike, turn
공경할 만한, venerable
공고, announcement, bulletin, notice
공고히 하다, cement, consolidate, strengthen
공공 기관의, institutional
공공 기물 파괴, vandalism
공공 기물 파괴자, vandal
공공 부문, public sector
공공 서비스, service
공공사업, public utility, service
공공연한, open, overt
공공연히, explicitly, overtly, public
공공의, civil, public
공교롭게도, happen
공군, air force
공군 기지, air base
공군 대장, marshal
공급, provision, supply
공급 과잉, glut
공급 과잉이다, glut
공급 회사, purveyor
공급업자, supplier
공급이 부족한, supply
공급자를 찾다, source
공급자들, supply
공급하다, feed, provide, supply
공기, air, atmosphere, wind
공기 조절, air-conditioning
공기로 운반되는, airborne
공단, satin
공동, cavity
공동 대표, partner
공동 생활체, commune
공동 숙소, dormitory
공동 작업, collaboration
공동 적립금, kitty
공동 제작의, collaborative
공동 제작자, collaborator
공동 주연, costar
공동 주연시키다, costar

공동 주택, tenement
(~와) 공동으로, association, collectively, jointly
공동으로 부담하다, share
공동으로 일하다, collaborate
공동의, collective, communal, concerted, joint
공동체, collective
공들인, elaborate
공들임, refinement
공략하다, conquer
공로를 인정하다, credit
공룡, dinosaur
공리주의의, utilitarian
공리주의자, utilitarian
공립학교, grant-maintained, public school, state school
공명성, fairness
공명정대하게, board
공모, collusion, complicity, conspiracy
공모자, conspirator
공모하다, collude, conspire
공무, public service
공무원, civil servant, officer
공무의, official, public
공문, notice
공민의, civic
공백, gap, vacuum
공백 기간, gap
공백의, blank
공범, accessory, accomplice
공보, bulletin, gazette
공보 담당 비서, press secretary
공보 담당관, press officer
공보 비서관, spin doctor
공복, civil servant
공복감, hunger
공부, study
공부하다, do, study
공사, envoy, minister, work
공산주의, communism
공산주의자, communist
공산품, manufacture
공상, daydream, fantasy
공상 과학적 이야기, science fiction, sci-fi
공상 소설, fantasy
공상가, romantic
공상에 잠기다, daydream
공상하다, fantasize
공석인, open, vacant
공세, offensive
공세를 취하는, offensive
공손하게, politely
공손한, polite, respectful
공손함, politeness
공손히, respectfully
공수, airlift
공수도, karate
공수되다, airlift
공수된, airborne
공수병, rabies
공습, air raid, assault, strike
공습을 받다, blitz
공식, formula
공식 기록에 의하면, record
공식 만찬, dinner, function
공식 발표, communiqué
공식 연회, function
휴식을 취해 다시 생기가 도는, rested
공식 절차, formality
공식 행사, formal
공식적으로, formally, officially, record
공식적으로 말하다, sound
공식적인, ceremonial, formal, official, state
공식화하다, formalize
공약하다, pledge
공업, industry
공업 단지, industrial estate, industrial park
공업의, industrial
공업이 발달한, industrial
공업화, industrialization
공업화되다, industrialize
공연, display, performance, run

공연 예술가, artist
공연단, troupe
공연장, auditorium
공연하다, perform
공연히, vainly
공영의, council
공원, garden, park
공유된, between
공유의, common
공유지, common
공유하다, pool, share
공익 시설, utility
공익사업, public service
공인, certification
공인된, chartered
공인을 받다, certify
공인하다, certify
공작, duke
공작 부인, duchess
공작원, operative
공장, factory, plant, work
공장 설비, plant
공장 폐쇄, lockout
공장들, work
공장이나 사무실을 폐쇄하다, lock
공적, exploit
공적으로, publicly
공적인, official, public
공전의, all-time
공정, impartiality, process
공정 무역, fair trade
공정선, line
공정장, playing field
공정하게, cleanly, impartially, justly
공정한, clean, impartial, independent, just
공제, deduction
공제액, credit
공제하다, deduct
공조, liaison
공조하다, liaise
공주, princess
공중, mid-air
공중 급유기, tanker
공중에 떠 있다, hover
공중에 붕 뜬 기분인, kite
공중위생, sanitation
공중으로 퉁기다, flip
공중의, aerial, public
공중전화, payphone
공중전화 박스, kiosk
공중전화실, phone booth, phone box
공중제비, somersault
공중제비를 하다, somersault
공지, announcement
공직, office, public service
공직자, official
공짜 비슷한 것, nothing
공짜로, free
공차기, kick
공천하다, field
공치는 시기, write-off
공터, clearing
공통으로, common
공통의, common, mutual
공평, impartiality
공평무사한, disinterested
공평무사함, detachment
공평하게, fairly, impartially
공평한, equitable, impartial
공포, scare, terror
공포감, fright
공포물의, horror
공포의 대상, terror
공포의 도가니로 몰아넣다, terrorize
공포증, phobia
공포탄, blank
공포하다, issue
공표, declaration, publication
공표하다, break, give, publicize
공학, engineering
공항, airport
공항세, airport tax
공허, emptiness
공허감, emptiness, void
공허하게 느껴지다, ring

공허하게 울리는, hollow
공허한, empty, hollow
공헌, hollowness
공헌, contribution, service
공헌하다, contribute
공화국, commonwealth, republic
공화당, republican
공화당의, republican
공화제의, republican
공황, panic
공황에 빠지다, panic
공회전하다, idle
공훈, exploit, feat
곶, cape
과, family, unit
과감하게, heroically
과감한, drastic, heroic
과감함, boldness
과감히 하다, plunge
과거, past, yesterday
과거지사, water
과격론의, extremist
과격론자, radical
과격한, extreme, radical
과다, excess, overdose, plethora
과다 복용하다, OD
과다 활동의, hyperactive
과다한 무게, weight
과다한 양, excess
과단성, decisiveness
과대 광고, hype
과대 광고하다, hype
과대평가, overestimate
과대평가된, overrated
과대평가하다, overestimate, overrate
과대한, extortionate
과도, binge
과도기의, caretaker, transitional
과도적인, transitional
과도하게, excessively, inordinately, unduly
과도하게 하다, overboard, overdo, overdose
과도한, excessive, exorbitant, extravagant, inordinate, intolerable, undue
과도한 추산, overestimate
과로, overwork
과로하다, overwork
과목, discipline, subject, syllabus
과묵한, reticent
과묵함, reticence
과민 반응을 보이다, overreact
과민한, hyperactive, touchy
과부, widow
과부하를 걸다, overload
과분한, extravagant
과세, taxation
과세 대상의, chargeable
과세 대상인, taxable
과세 연도, tax year
과세되다, tax
과소 지출, underspend
과소비하다, binge
과소평가된, underrated
과소평가하다, underestimate, underrate, undervalue
과수원, orchard
과시, exhibition, show
과시하는, ostentatious
과시하다, flaunt, parade
과시하듯, ostentatiously
과식하다, binge, overeat
과식한, bloated
과실, error
과실 치사, manslaughter
과실이 있는, guilty
과실주, wine
과업, task, undertaking
과열되다, overheat
과열된, overheated
과열시키다, overheat
과오, misconduct
과육, flesh, pulp
과음하다, binge
과일, fruit
과일 맛이 나는, fruity

과잉, plethora, surplus
과잉 투여, overdose
과잉 투여하다, overdose
과잉수용, overcrowding
과잉의, surplus
과장, exaggeration, magnification
과장되게, dramatically, theatrically
과장되게 보여 주다, exaggerate
과장되어, top
과장된, exaggerated, OTT, theatrical
과장된 묘사, caricature
과장하다, blow, exaggerate, inflate, magnify, overstate
과장하여 떠벌리다, gush
과장해서 표현하는, gushing
과정, course, process, road, study
과제, assignment, paper, project
과중한 부담, overload
과중한 부담을 지우다, overload
과중한 부담을 진, overloaded
과체중, weight
과체중의, overweight
과학, science
과학 기술, technology
과학 기술의, technical
과학과 관련해서, scientifically
과학의, scientific
과학자, scientist
과학적으로, scientifically
과학적인, scientific
곽, carton
관, canal, coffin, passage, pipe, piping, tube
관(觀), outlook
관개, irrigation
관개하다, irrigate
관객, audience, spectator
관계, bond, connection, link, relation, relationship
관계 서적 목록, bibliography
(~와) 관계 있는, connected
관계가 없는, immaterial, unrelated
(~와) 관계가 있다, concern, do
(~와) 관계가 화목한, peace
관계되다, pertain, relate
관계된, concerned
관계를 끊다, break, ditch, hand
(~와 ~의) 관계를 보여 주다, connect
(~와의) 관계를 부인하다, dissociate
(~에) 관계없이, irrespective, regardless
관계에 빠진, involved
관계절, relative clause
관광, excursion, sightseeing, tour
관광 안내원, guide
관광객, tourist
관광업, tourism
관광지, sight
관광하다, tour
관념, sense
관능미, sensuality
관능적인, luscious, sensual, sultry
관대하게, generously, leniently
관대하게 대하다, easy
관대한, charitable, forgiving, generous, lenient, permissive, soft, tolerant
관대함, generosity, permissiveness
관람하다, see
관련, connection, link, relationship, relevance
관련 상품, merchandising
관련 없는, irrelevant
관련되다, relate
관련된, about, associated, connected, involved, pertinent, related, -related, relevant
관련성, relevance
관련시키다, associate, involve
관련이 없는, unconnected
(~와) 관련이 있는, allied
관련이 있다, bearing, relate
관련이 있다고 주장하다, link
관련짓다, link, relate
(~와) 관련하여, relation, respect
(~와) 관련해, connection
(~와) 관련해서, further

관례, convention, institution, rule
관례대로 행하다, practice
관례적, institutional
관료, bureaucrat
관리, care, management, official
관리 소홀, neglect
관리의, managerial
관리인, caretaker, custodian, ranger, superintendent, warden
관리자, manager
관리직인, executive
관리하다, care, control, man, manage
관목, bush, scrub, shrub
관문, barrier
관보, gazette
관사, article
관상 기관, tube
관상식물, greenery
관성의 힘으로 달리다, coast
관세, duty, tariff
관세의, customs
관습, convention, custom, ritual
관습법, common law
관습적인, customary
관심, attention, caring, concern, focus, interest
관심 있는, concerned
관심을 가지다, concern
관심을 갖다, care
관심을 끄는, interesting
관심을 끌다, interest
관심을 두지 않다, notice
관심의 초점, focal point, glare
관여, involvement, part, stake
관여자, participant
관여하게 되다, come
관여하다, come, concern, engage, hand, participate
관여하지 않기로 하다, opt
(~에) 관여하지 않다, stay
관용, generosity, tolerance
관용어구, idiom
관자놀이, temple
관장되다, curate
관장약, laxative
관절, joint
관절염, arthritis
관절염에 걸린, arthritic
관절염의, arthritic
관점, angle, point of view, side, standpoint, view, viewpoint
관제사, air traffic controller
관중, audience, spectator
관중석, auditorium, seating, stand
관직, title
관찰, observation
관찰력, eye, observation
관찰력이 예리한, observant
관찰자, observer, viewer
관찰하다, observe, study
관철시키다, carry, push
관측, observation
관측자, observer
관측하다, observe
관통, penetration
관통하다, run
(~을) 관통하여, through
관통할 수 없는, impenetrable
(~에) 관하다, concern
(~에) 관하여, on, re, reference, regard, regarding
(~에) 관한, concerned, into
(~에) 관한 최근 소식을 전하다, update
(~의) 관할 아래 있는, responsible
관할권, jurisdiction
관할지, territory
관할하다, police
(~에) 관해, concerning
관행, practice
관현악 편곡, orchestration
관현악단, orchestra
관현악의, orchestral
괄태충, slug
괄호, bracket, parenthesis
광견병, rabies
광경, sight

광고, ad, advert, advertisement, commercial, publicity
광고 게시판, billboard
광고 대행사, advertising agency
광고 전단, circular, flyer
광고 출연, endorsement
광고되다, herald, parade
광고를 내다, place
광고업, advertising
광고업자, adman
광고에 출연하다, endorse
광고주, advertiser
광고하다, advertise, sponsor
광고하여 구하다, advertise
광년, light year
광대뼈, cheekbone
광대역, broadband
광대한, extensive, immense, vast
광란의, wild
광물, mineral
광범위하게, extensively
광범위한, Catholic, extensive, wide-ranging, widespread
광범한, wide
광부, miner
광분, frenzy
광산, mine
광산업, mining
광상, deposit
광석, ore
광선, beam, ray
광섬유, fiber optics
광섬유의, fiber optics
광신도, fanatic, maniac
광우병, BSE
광장, plaza, square
광적인, fanatic, fanatical, frenzied
광채, radiance, sparkle
광채 나는, bright
광천, spa
광천수, mineral water
광택, gloss, sheen, shine
광택제, enamel, polish, varnish
광택제를 칠하다, varnish
광학의, optical
광화, blaze, brilliance, glitter
광희(狂喜), rapture
광희에 찬, rapturous
괘도, flipchart
괜찮게, all right, decently
괜찮아, forget, matter
괜찮아요, mind
괜찮으시다면, mind
괜찮은, acceptable, all right, bad, decent, okay
괜히 성내다, knickers
괭이, hoe
괭이질하다, hoe
괴기적인, Gothic
괴로운, agonizing, bitter, distressing, harassed, harrowing, pained, painful
괴로운 시간을 보내다, languish
괴로울 정도로, distressingly, painfully
괴로움, anguish
괴로움을 주는, upsetting
괴로워하는, anguished, distressed
괴로워하다, agonize, smart
괴롭게, painfully
괴롭다, hurt
괴롭히기, harassment
괴롭히다, afflict, bother, bully, distress, get, gnaw, harass, hassle, nag, niggle, pain, pester, pick, prey, spite, torment, torture, trouble, worry
괴롭힘, bullying
괴롭힘을 당하다, besiege
괴롭힘을 받지 않는, undisturbed
괴리, discrepancy, split
괴물, freak, monster
괴물 같은, monstrous
괴상하게, morbidly
괴상한, grotesque, morbid
괴이한, queer
괴저, gangrene
괴짜, crank, freak

괴팍한, temperamental
괴팍함, temperament
괴한, attacker
굉음, crash, roar
굉음을 내다, roar
굉음을 내며 가다, roar
굉장한, amazing, devastating, fabulous, great, hell, monstrous, phenomenal, smashing, super, terrific
굉장히, damned, monstrously, phenomenally, super, terribly, tremendously
굉장히 멋진, stunning
교감, communion
교과 과정, curriculum
교과서, course book, textbook
교과서적인, textbook
교구, parish
교구 목사, vicar
교단, order
교대, rotation
교대 근무, shift
교대로, alternately, rotation
교대로 하다, turn
교대시키다, rotate
교대조, shift
교대하다, relieve, rotate
교도소, jail, prison
교도소장, warden
교류, exchange, interaction
교류하다, interact
교리, doctrine, teaching
교리상의, doctrinal
교묘하게, subtly
교묘한, subtle
교묘함, subtlety
교묘히 ~로 파고 들다, worm
교배, breeding
교복, uniform
교사, instructor, teacher
교살하다, strangle
교섭, bargaining, negotiation
교수, lecturer, professor
교수대, scaffold
교수요목, syllabus
교수진, faculty
교수하다, teach
교수형을 당하다, hang
교신, communication
교실, classroom
교양, breeding, sophistication
교양 있는, cultivated, cultured, educated, refined
교역, barter, trade, trading
교역하다, barter, trade
교외, outskirts, suburb, suburbia
교외의, suburban
교우 관계, companionship
교육, education, instruction, teaching, training
교육 과정, curriculum
교육 받은, educated
교육 위원회, school board
(~) 교육받은, -trained
교육을 받다, educate
교육의, educational
교육적인, educational
교육하다, educate, instruct, school, teach, train
교육학의, pedagogical
교의, tenet
교장, head, headmaster, headmistress, principal
교장 선생님, head teacher
교재, text, textbook
교전, action, engagement
교전 행위, warfare
교정, correction, manipulation, revision
교정(矯正) 시설, custody
교정의, corrective, penal
교정하다, correct, manipulate, remedy, revise
교제, intercourse
교제를 피하다, keep
교직원, faculty
교차 도로의, cross

교차된, criss-cross
교차로, interchange, intersection
교차점, crossing, intersection, junction
교차하다, criss-cross, cross, intersect, meet
교착 상태, deadlock, gridlock, stalemate
교체, change, interchange, replacement
교체 선수, sub, substitute
교체되다, interchange
교체자, relief
교체하다, change, interchange, replace, switch
교통, communication, traffic, transport, transportation
교통 위반 딱지, ticket
교통 정체, gridlock, hold-up, jam
교통 차단선, cordon
교통 혼잡 시간, rush hour
교통마비 상태, gridlock
교통수단, transport, transportation
교통하다, communicate
교파, church, denomination, sect
교향곡, symphony
교향악단, symphony orchestra
교화되다, reform
교화된, reformed
교화시키다, reform
교환, change, exchange, interchange, swap, trade
교환 가능 통화, hard currency
교환권, token
교환대, switchboard
교환하다, exchange, swap, trade
(~와) 교환하여, exchange
교활하게, cunningly
교활한, crafty, cunning, devious, manipulative, sly, wily
교활함, cunning
교황, pope
교황의, papal
교회, church
교회에 관한, ecclesiastical
교훈, lesson, moral, precept
교훈적인, instructive
구, former, phrase, sphere
구-, old
구간, stretch
구강으로, orally
구강의, oral
구개, palate
구걸하다, beg
구겨지다, crease, crumple, wrinkle
구겨진, creased, crumpled, wrinkled
구경거리, spectacle, spectacular
구경꾼, bystander, onlooker
구근, bulb
구금, detention
구금되다, intern
구금자, detainee
구금하다, detain
구급차, ambulance
(~을) 구기다, crease, crumple, screw, scrunch, wrinkle
구김, crease
구김살, fold, wrinkle
구내, compound, ground, premise, yard
구내 영업 허가, concession
구내식당, canteen
구단, club
구더기, grub, maggot
구덩이, hole, pit
구독료, subscription
구독자, subscriber
(~을) 구독하다, subscribe
구동사, phrasal verb
구두, word
구두 언어, speech
구두로, orally
구두법, punctuation
구두의, oral, spoken
구두점, punctuation, punctuation mark

구렁텅이, depth
구레나룻, whisker
구르다, roll
구름, cloud
구릉, hill
구릉이 많은, hilly
구리, copper
구릿빛의, brown, copper
구매, purchase
구매 권유, sales pitch
구매 담당자, buyer
구매력, purchasing power
구매자, buyer, purchaser
구매자 시장, buyer's market
구매하다, purchase
구멍, cavity, hole, opening, puncture, socket, vacuum
구멍내다, breach
구멍을 내다, puncture
구멍을 뚫다, gouge, pierce, punch
구멍이 숭숭한, pitted
구명정, lifeboat
구문, construction
구미가 당기게, temptingly
구별, differentiation
구별하다, distinguish, separate, tell
구별해 내다, pick
구부러지다, bend, curve, turn
구부러진, bent, curved
구부려 걸다, hook
구부리다, bend, buckle, crook, flex, get, hunch
구부정하다, stoop
구부정한, bowed
구부정한 자세를 취하다, slouch
구부정함, stoop
구분 짓다, separate
구분되다, section
구분짓다, differentiate
구분하다, apart, differentiate, separate
구분하여, apart
구불거리다, wind
구불구불하다, meander
구불구불한, tortuous
(~의) 구사력, command
구사하다, speak
구상 명사의, concrete
구상하다, plot
구상해 내다, formulate
구석, corner
구석구석, high
구석에 몰아넣다, corner
구석진 곳, recess
구성, composition, configuration, line-up, organization, set-up
구성 단위, unit
구성 요소, component, constituent, ingredient
구성되다, comprise, consist, staff
구성원, member, rank
구성하고 있는, component
구성하다, compose, configure, constitute, construct, field, make, put
구세주, savior, white knight
구속, bondage
구속력 있는, binding
구속복, straitjacket
구속을 받지 않는, unrestricted
구속하다, cramp, restrict
구술로, orally
구술시험, oral, viva
구술의, oral
구슬, bead, marble
구슬리다, cajole, coax
구슬치기, marble
구슬프게, mournfully
구슬픈, melancholy, mournful, plaintive
구슬픈 소리, wail
구식의, obsolete, old-fashioned, out, out of date
구실, cover, plea, pretext
구심점, nucleus
구어의, spoken
구어체의, colloquial

구역, area, block, neighborhood
구역질 나는, sickening
구역질이 나다, gag
구운, roast
구운 식빵, toast
구워삶다, cajole, get
구워지다, cook, grill
구원, redemption, salvation
구원자, salvation, savior
구원하다, redeem
구인 광고, situation
구입, purchase
구입품, purchase
구제, mercy, salvation
구제 불능의, incurable
구제 불능인, impossible
구제 불능일 만큼, incurably
구제역, foot-and-mouth disease
구제하다, bail
구제할 수 없는, redemption
구조, construction, fabric, framework, make-up, rescue, salvage, structure
구조 기술자, structural engineer
구조 신호, SOS
구조 조정, delayering, downsizing, restructuring
구조 조정하다, downsize, restructure
구조대원, rescuer
구조되다, salvage
구조된 물건, salvage
구조물, construction, framework, structure
구조상의, structural
구조적으로, structurally
구조적인, organizational
구조하다, rescue
구조화하다, structure
구좌에 돈이 들어 있는, credit
구직 시장, market
구체, ball, globe, sphere
구체적인, concrete, specific
구체적인 계획을 세우다, map
구체화되다, gel
구축하다, build, model
구치되는, custody
구치된, custody
구타, beating, belt, blow
구타당한, battered
구타하다, batter, beat
구토하는, sick
(~을) 구하다, go, procure, save, seek
구할 수 있는, available
구할 수 있음, availability
구현, embodiment
구현물, representation
구현하다, embody, realize, represent
구호, slogan
구호 물품, relief
구호 활동, charity
구호금, charity
구혼자, suitor
구획, section
구획 설정, zoning
구획되다, zone
구획된 택지, subdivision
구획하다, divide
국, bureau, desk
국가, country, nation, state
국가 간의, international
국가 대표 마크, cap
국가 번호, dialling code
국가 보조금을 받는, GM
국가 원수, head of state
국가 의료 보험 제도, National Health Service
국가 주석, head of state
국가 지배 경제, command economy
국가 직업 자격시험, GNVQ
국가의, state
국가의 군비, armory
국가의 보호를 받고 있는, care
국가적인, national, state
국경, border, frontier
국고의, fiscal

국내 총생산, GDP, gross domestic product
국내에서, internally
국내에서 생산된, home-grown
국내의, civil, domestic, internal
국립공원, national park
국립의, GM
국면, phase
국면을 바꾸다, tip
국무장관, Secretary of State
국민, citizen, country, nation, people, populace, subject
국민 건강 보험, NHS
국민 기본 인권 선언, Bill of Rights
국민 연금 제도, national insurance
국민 총생산, GNP, gross national product
국민 투표, referendum
국민성, character
국방, defense
국부의, local
국세청, Inland Revenue, IRS
국수, noodle
국수주의, chauvinism, nationalist
국수주의자, chauvinist, nationalist
국수주의적인, nationalistic
국영의, state
국왕, king, sovereign
국외 거주자, expatriate
국외에 거주하는, expatriate
국외의, outside
국유화, nationalization
국유화하다, nationalize
국자, scoop
국장, commissioner, director
국적, nationality
국제 경기, international
국제 경기 출전자, international
국제 수지, balance of payments
국제 연합, UN, United Nations
국제 통화 기금, IMF
국제적으로, internationally
국제적인, cosmopolitan, external, international
국토를 횡단하는, cross-country
국한되다, limit
(~에) 국한된, confined
국한시키다, confine
국회, parliament
국회 의사당, Houses of Parliament
국회의원, AM, legislator
국회의원의, parliamentary
군 당국, military
군단, legion
군대, armed forces, defense, force, service, troop
군대의, military
군더더기 없는, neat
군더더기를 붙이다, pad
(~을) 군락지이다, colonize
군무, service
군번, serial number
군법회의, court martial
군법 회의에 회부되다, court martial
군복, fatigue
군부, military
군비, armaments, arsenal
군비 축소, disarmament
군사 훈련, drill, exercise
군사력, force
군사적으로, militarily
군사적인, military
군살을 빼다, slim
군살을 뺀, lean
군살이 없는, lean
군소리 많은 패자, loser
군수품, munitions
군에 입대하다, join
군의, martial
군인, serviceman, soldier
군인다운, military
군주, monarch, prince, sovereign
군주국, monarchy
군주국의 정부, crown
군주제, monarchy
군주제를 주장하는, monarchist
군주제주의자, monarchist
군중, crowd, mob, multitude,

swarm, throng
군침 도는, appetizing
군침을 흘리다, water
굳건한, firm, rugged
굳건히 하다, strengthen
굳게, firmly, securely
굳게 닫힌, secure
굳게 지키다, secure
굳다, seize
굳센, invincible, tough
굳셈, toughness
굳어서 돌이 된, petrified
굳어지다, harden, set, solidify
굳은, iron
굳히다, confirm, harden, solidify
굴, burrow, cave, den, hole, oyster, tunnel
굴뚝, chimney, funnel
굴러 들어오다, roll
굴러 떨어지다, roll, tumble
굴러가다, roll, run, trundle
굴리다, roll, run
굴복, surrender
굴복하다, bow, cave, give, submit, succumb, yield
굴복하지 않다, gun
굴욕, humiliation
굴욕감을 느끼는, humiliated
굴욕감을 주다, humiliate
굴욕을 참다, humble
굴욕적인, humiliating
굴을 파다, burrow
굴절형의, articulated
굴종, subservience
굴종하는, subservient
굴착, excavation
굴하지 않고 해내다, persevere
굴하지 않다, hold
굵게, coarsely
굵은, bold
굶기다, starve
굶어 죽다, starve
굶주리다, hungry, starve
(~에) 굶주린, hungry
굶주림, hunger, starvation
굼뜬, slow, sluggish
굼벵이, grub
굽다, bake, broil, burn, cook, grill, roast, twist
굽실거리다, grovel
굽어지다, bend
굽은 길, corner
굽이, bend, turn, twist
굽이 낮은 신발, flat
굽이치다, twist
굽히다, bake, bend
궁, palace
궁극적으로, ultimately
궁극적으로 가능한 사태, eventuality
궁극적인, ultimate
궁금해 죽겠는 것을 알려 주다, misery
궁금해 하는, curious
궁금해하다, wonder
궁색한, flimsy
궁전, palace
궁정, court
궁지는 면하다, head
궁지에 몰린, beleaguered
궁지에 빠뜨리다, corner
궁지에 빠져 있는, hole
궁지에서 벗어난, hook
궁핍, strait
궁핍한, needy
궁형의, arched
권, copy, ticket, vol., volume
권고, recommendation
권고하다, recommend
권력, power
권력 공조, power-sharing
권력층, establishment
권리, claim, right
권리 강화, empowerment
권리 포기, waiver
권리가 없다, business
(~할) 권리가 있는, right
(~할) 권리나 자격을 주다, enable
권리를 주장하다, stake

권모술수, wheeling and dealing
권위, authority
권위 있는, authoritative, important
권위자, authority, pundit
권위적인, authoritarian
권유하다, induce
권장하다, recommend
권총, pistol
권투, boxing
권투 선수, boxer
권투 시합, fight
권투 연습을 하다, spar
권투 하다, box
권하다, counsel
권한, authority, brief, mandate, power
권한 부여, empowerment
권한 이양, devolution
(~할) 권한을 부여받다, empower, mandate
권한을 부여하다, empower
(~에게) 권한이 있다, belong
궤도, orbit
궤도를 돌다, orbit
궤도에 올리다, motion
궤양, ulcer
귀, ear
귀가 들리지 않는, deaf
귀가 멍멍해지다, deafen
귀가 안 들림, deafness
귀감, paragon
귀걸이, earring
귀결, implication
(~로) 귀결되다, boil
귀국, homecoming
귀뚜라미, cricket
귀띰, tip-off
귀띰을 해 주다, prime
(~에게) 귀띰하다, tip
귀를 기울이다, listen
귀를 멍멍하게 만드는, deafening
귀를 멍멍하게 하다, deafen
귀리, oats
귀빈, VIP
귀신이 나오는, haunted
귀신이 나올 듯한, spooky
귀에 거슬리는, strident
귀에 거슬리는 소리, rasp
귀에 거슬리는 소리를 내다, rasp
귀에 쏙쏙 들어오는, catchy
귀에 쟁쟁하게, just
귀엣말하다, whisper
귀여운, cute, pretty
귀여운 악당, rogue
귀재, wizard
귀족, aristocrat, lord, peer
귀족 계급, aristocracy, nobility, peerage
귀족의, noble
귀족적인, aristocratic
귀중품, valuables
귀중품 금고, safe deposit box
귀중한, precious, treasured, valuable
귀지, wax
(~에) 귀착되다, come
귀찮게 하다, bother, nose, put
귀찮은, unwelcome
귀찮은 것, bore
귀찮은 놈, bugger
귀청을 찢는 듯한, piercing
귀퉁이, corner
귀하, honor
귀하게 여겨지다, prize
귀한, premium
귀향, homecoming
귀환, return
귓병, earache
귓볼, earlobe
규격품이어서, shelf
규명하다, identify
규모, dimension, magnitude, proportion, scale, size
규모를 줄이다, slim
규모의 경제, economies of scale
규범, code, law, norm, standard

규범에 맞게 행동하다, conform
규소, silicon
규약, covenant
규정, law, provision, regulation
규정식, diet
규정하다, define, lay, prescribe, provide, set
규제, regulation, restraint, restriction
규제 기관, regulator
규제 철폐, deregulation
규제자, regulator
규제하는, regulatory
규제하다, regulate
규칙, rule
규칙성, regularity
규칙을 바꾸다, goalpost
규칙을 융통성 있게 적용시키다, rule
규칙적으로, regularly
규칙적인, regular
규탄, condemnation
균등하게, equally, evenly
균등하게 하다, equalize
균등한, even
균등화, equalization
균류(菌類), fungus
균열, aperture, chasm
균일성, uniformity
균일하게, uniformly
균일하게 하다, even
균일한, flat, uniform
균질의, homogeneous
균형, balance, equilibrium, symmetry
균형 잡다, balance
균형 잡힌, balanced, trim
균형 잡힌 시각으로, perspective
균형을 맞추다, balance
균형을 잃은, balance, off-balance
균형을 잃은 시각으로, perspective
균형을 잡다, pivot
균형이 맞지 않는, disproportionate
(~에) 균형이 안 맞는, proportion, scale
균형이 잡힌, well-balanced
균형추, counter
그 결과, therefore
그 결과로, whereupon
그 결과로 생긴, resultant
그 경우에는, event
그 기간 내내, duration
그 놈의 것, thing
그 다음, ensuing
그 다음에, then
그 다음으로, next, place
그 다음의, subsequent
그 대신, alternatively
그 동안 내내, while
그 동안은, meantime
그 뒤에, subsequently
그 때문에, thereby
그 때조차도, second
그 밖에, else
그 밖에 무엇이든지, whatever
그 반대도 마찬가지임, vice versa
그 사이에, interim, meanwhile, way
그 상황에서는, circumstance
그 외, else
그 위에, additionally
그 자체, itself
그 자체는, such
그 자체로서, per se
그 정도로, extent
그 후, subsequently
그 후 줄곧, ever
그 후에, thereafter
그건 그렇고, anyway
냥 보기에, apparently
냥 지나치다, overlook
냥 한번 해보다, try
그녀, swing
그녀, she
그녀 자신, herself
그는, he
그늘, shade, shadow
그늘지게 하다, overshadow

그늘지다, shade
그늘진, shady
그다지 중요하지 않은, peripheral
그대로 반영하다, echo
그대로 있다, stay
그대로 전하다, repeat
그들, them, they, those
그들 자신, themselves
그때그때의, casual
그라인더, grinder
그라피티, graffiti
그래, all right, okay, quite, right, well, yeah, yes
그래도, even, same, still, yet
그래머 스쿨, grammar school
그래요, yes
그래프, graph
그래픽, graphic
그래픽 디자인, graphic design
그래픽 아트 작품, graphic
그래픽의, graphic
그랜드, grand
그램, gm, gram
그러나, but, whereas
그러는 동안, meanwhile
그러므로, accordingly, hence, so, therefore
그럭저럭 살아가다, get
그럭저럭 해내다, muddled up
그런데, now, way, well
그런데도, still, yet
그럴 듯하게, glibly
그럴 듯한 얼버무리다, gloss
그럴 듯한, glib
그럴 듯한 포장, gloss
그럴 리 없음, fat
그럴듯하게, plausibly
그럴듯하지 않은, improbable
그럴듯한, plausible
그럴듯함, plausibility
그럴싸한, spurious
그럼, and, certainly, right, sure, yep, yes
그럼에도 불구하고, nevertheless, nonetheless
그렁그렁하다, brim
그렇게 함으로써, thereby
그렇게 됐지, bet
그렇군, see
그렇습니다, exactly
그렇지만, however, nonetheless, though, time
그레이비, gravy
그레이프프루트, grapefruit
그레이하운드, greyhound
그려 내다, portray
그려 보다, envisage
그로스, gross
그루터기, stubble, stump
그룹, group, lot
그룹 지도, tutorial
그릇, dish
그릇되게, erroneously
그릇된, erroneous, wrong
그릇된 통념, myth
그릇됨, wrong
(~의) 그릇됨을 증명하다, disprove
그리고, and
그리고 나서, then
그리기, painting
그리니치 표준시, GMT
그리다, draw, paint
그리스, grease
그리스 정교회의, orthodox
그리스도를 십자가에 못 박음, crucifixion
(~에) 그리스를 치다, grease
그리움, longing
그리워하다, miss
그린벨트, green belt
그릴, grill
그릴 음식 전문 식당, grill
그릴에 굽기, grilling
그림, drawing, painting, picture, portrayal
그림 같은, picturesque
그림 같은 것, picturesque
그림 그리기, drawing

그림의, pictorial
그림자, shadow
그림자를 드리우다, shadow
그림자처럼 따라다니다, shadow
그만 두다, leave
그만 말하다, drop
그만 믿다, lapse
그만두게 만들다, deflect
그만두기, retreat
그만두기로 하다, quit
그만두다, break, cease, cut, forsake, go, head, pull, quit, retreat, stop, walk
그만하다, drop
그물, net
그물로 잡다, net
그슬리다, scorch
그에 따른, resultant
그에 반하는, contrary
그에 상응하여, correspondingly
그에 알맞게, accordingly
그와 마찬가지로, equally
그와 연관지어, implication
그와는 반대로, contrary
그을린, scorched
그을린 피부, tan
그저, only, simply
그저 ...뿐인, bare
그저 ~만, only
그저 그런, indifferent, mediocre, merely
그저 그렇게, indifferently
그저 아무 ~가 아닌, any
그치다, cease, stop
그칠 줄 모르는, interminable
극, pole
극 중에서, on-screen
극 중의, on-screen
극단, company, troupe
극단론, extremism
극단론의, extremist
극단으로 몰다, extreme
극단으로 치닫다, extreme
극단의, utmost
극단적 숭배, cult
극단적 채식주의자, vegan
극단적으로, radically
극단적인, extreme, far, radical
극단주의자, extremist
극대화하다, maximize
극도로, extremely, super, supremely
극도의, extreme, heroic, supreme
극도의 곤경에 처한, eyeball
극동 지역, Far East
극복, conquest
(~을) 극복하다, come, conquer, cope, get, overcome, recover, rise
극비의, top secret
극빈한, destitute
극심하게, chronically, stiff, violently
극심한, chronic, intense, raging, stiff, violent
극심한 경쟁, rat race
극심한 고통을 주다, scourge
극심한 인플레이션, hyperinflation
극악무도하게, monstrously
극악무도한, flagrant, monstrous
극악무도한 사람, monster
극에 달하다, head
극으로, theatrically
극작가, dramatist, playwright
극장, theater
극장의, theatrical
극장의 발코니, gallery
극적으로, dramatically, spectacularly
극적으로 보이게 만들다, dramatize
극적인, dramatic, sharp, spectacular
극적인 상황, drama
극지, pole
극지방의, polar
극찬하다, rave
극치, height, sublime
극한, limit

극한 상황, breaking point
극형, capital punishment
극히 개인적인, intimate
극히 드문, few
극히 미세한, microscopic
극히 작은 조각, particle
근거, basis, foundation, ground, rationale
근거 없는, mythical
근거 없는 믿음, mythology
근거 없는 안도감, security
근거 없는 통념, fable
근거가 되다, underlie
근거가 없는, groundless
근거가 확실한, valid
(~을) 근거로, basis
근거를 둔, based
근거리 통신망, LAN
근거지, base
(~에) 근거하다, ground
(~에) 근거하여, founded
근교, suburb
근근이 먹고 살다, hand
근로 활동을 하는, working
근로의, working
근로자, worker
근로자 연금, stakeholder pension
근로자들, worker
근면, diligence, industry
근면한, diligent, hard
근무, duty
근무 당번 표, roster, rota
근무 시간, hour, office hours, workday
근무 시간 외에, hour
근무 중, line
근무 중에, job
근무 중인, duty
근무일, workday
근무하는, working
근무하다, serve, work
근본, origin, root
근본적으로, fundamentally
근본적인, fundamental
근본주의, fundamentalism
근본주의자, fundamentalist
근사, approximation
근사한, cool, gorgeous, tremendous
근삿값, approximation
근성, grit
근소한, narrow
근소한 차로 앞서다, edge
근소한 차의, close
근소한 차이로, pip
근시안적인, short-sighted
근시의, nearsighted, short-sighted
근심, care, concern, insecurity
근심하는, concerned
근심하다, worry
근엄하게, primly
근엄한, grave, prim, Victorian
근원, germ, root, seed
근원적인, primal, ultimate
근육, muscle
근육의, muscular
근육이 발달한, muscular
근육이 파열되다, rupture
근육질의, muscular
근육통, RSI
근절, eradication, extermination
근절하다, eradicate, exterminate, root, stamp
근접, proximity
근접 촬영, close-up
근질거리다, itch
근질근질함, itch, itching
근처에, near, nearby, neighborhood
근처에도, near
(~의) 근처에만 머무르다, stick
근처의, nearby, round
근처의 사람들, neighborhood
근친상간, incest
근해, water
글, text, writing
글라이더, glider
글레이즈, glaze

글레이즈를 바르다, glaze
글쎄, know, maybe, mean, well
글쓰기, writing
글을 쓰다, write
글을 읽고 쓸 줄 아는, literate
글을 팔아먹는 사람, hack
글자, letter
글자 그대로, verbatim
글자 그대로의, literal, verbatim
글자 뜻 그대로, literally
글자 쓰기, lettering
글자체, font
긁는 복권, scratch card
긁다, nick, paw, scrape, scratch
긁어 들이다, rake
긁어내다, scrape
긁어모으다, rake
긁히다, nick, scrape
긁힌 자국, nick, scratch
금, chink, crack, Fri., gold
금고, safe
금고실, vault
금관 악기부, brass
금광, goldmine
금괴, bullion
금기, taboo
금기된, forbidden, illicit
금기시하는 말, dirty
금기의, taboo
금단 증상, withdrawal
금단 증상 기간, withdrawal
금단의, forbidden
금리, interest rate
금메달, gold, gold medal
금박 장식, sequin
금발, blonde
금발의, blonde, fair
금발의 여인, blonde
금방, right, time
금방 올 거야, long
금방이라도, moment
금붕어, goldfish
금빛, gold
금빛의, golden
금상첨화, icing, world
금세, that
금세 친해지다, house
금속, metal
금속 느낌이 나는, metallic
금속 용기, canister
금속성의, metallic
금속판, plate
금시초문이다, news
금액, money, sum
금요일, Friday
금욕, abstinence
금융, finance
금융 회사, finance company
금융인, banker
금으로 된, golden
금을 긋다, score
금의, golden
금이 가게 하다, crack
금이 가다, crack, fracture
금작화, broom
금전, money
금전 대출, borrowing
금전 등록기, cash register, till
금전 등록기에 금액을 입력하다, ring
금전 출납원, teller
금전의, pecuniary
금제품, gold
금지, ban, prohibition
금지 명령, injunction
금지당하다, bar
(~이) 금지된, ban, forbidden
금지법, prohibition
금지하다, ban, embargo, interdict, prohibit, veto
금태 중권, gilt
금테를 입힌, gilt-edged
금하다, forbid, inhibit
금후, henceforth
급강하다, dive
급격하게, steeply
급격한, sharp, steep, tight, whirlwind
급격한 동작, jerk

급격한 충격, jolt
급격히, sharply
급격히 늘리다, multiply
급격히 늘어나다, mushroom
급격히 떨어지다, dive
급격히 증가하다, multiply
급격히 치솟다, roof
급경사, drop
급등, surge
급등하다, surge
급료, pay packet
급료 명세표, payslip, paystub
급료 지급 명부, payroll
급류, rapids, torrent
급발진하다, leap
급변, leap
급변하다, leap
급부상하다, catapult
급상승, spiral
급상승하다, spiral
급선무, priority
급성의, acute, invasive
급성장하다, shoot
급소를 찌르다, home
급속한 흐름, rush
급속히 흐르다, rush
급습, foray, storming, swoop
급습당하다, storm
급습하다, bust, swoop
급여, paycheck
급여 소득이 없는 사람, unwaged
급여 수표, paycheck
급여 인상, award, rise
급우, classmate
급전환하다, swerve
급조하다, cobble
급증, bulge, jump, leap, proliferation, upsurge, wave
급증하다, balloon, jump, leap, proliferate, soar
급진적인, radical
급진파, radical
급하게, sharp, sharply
(~을) 급하게 먹다, gobble
급하게 해치운, rushed
급한, hasty, sharp
급함, hurry
급행, express
급히, haste
급히 가다, dash
급히 끌려 다니다, sweep
급히 달려들다, dive
급히 달아나다, run
급히 대다, clap
급히 데려가다, rush
급히 먹다, bolt
급히 쓰다, dash
급히 해치우다, rush
긍정문의, affirmative
긍정적 측면, positive
긍정적 평가를 받다, press
긍정적으로, affirmative, positively
긍정적인, affirmative, positive
기, banner, flag
기가 차다, biscuit
기가바이트, gigabyte
기각되다, defeat
기각하다, overrule, quash, throw
기간, period, space, span, stint, stretch, term, timescale
기갑 부대, armor, cavalry
기거하다, shelter
기결함, out tray
기계, instrument, machine
기계 장치, machine, mechanism
기계 정비 기사, mechanic
기계공, machinist
기계류, machinery
기계에 대해 잘 아는, mechanical
기계적으로, mechanically
기계적인, automatic, mechanical
기계화, mechanization
기계화하다, mechanize
기고가, columnist
기관, authority, institution, organ, service
기관 내의, internal
기관사, engineer

기관지, organ
기관차, engine
기관총, machine gun
기관포, cannon
기괴하게, bizarrely, grotesquely
기괴한, bizarre, grotesque
기교가, technician
기구, apparatus, appliance, body, fitting, gear, instrument, machine
기권, abstention
기권하다, abstain
기근, famine
기금, fund, funding
기금 모금, appeal, fund-raising
기금 조달자, fundraiser
기꺼이, freely, gladly, happily, joyously, kindly, pleased
기꺼이 ~하는, glad, happy, willing
기꺼이 받아들이다, welcome
기꺼이 하는, ready
기꺼이 하려는 자세, readiness
기껏해야, most
기내 난동, air rage
기념, commemoration
기념관, memorial
기념물, memorial, monument
기념비, monument
기념비적인, monumental
기념석, stone
기념식, testimonial
기념일, anniversary, jubilee
기념제, jubilee
기념품, memorabilia, souvenir
기념하는, commemorative
기념하다, mark
(~을) 기념하여, honor
기능, function
기능 선택표, menu
기능적인, functional
기능키, function key
(~로) 기능하다, serve
기다, crawl, grovel
기다리다, await, hang, wait
기다림, waiting
기대, anticipation, expectancy, expectation, hope
기대 이상의 것, bonus
기대다, count, lean, prop, resort, rest
기대를 하며, hopefully
(~에) 기대어, against
기대어 눕다, nestle
기대에 미치다, measure
기대에 부응하는, par
기대에 부응하다, mustard
기대에 차서, expectantly
기대에 찬, expectant
기대주, hopeful
기대치, hope
기대하고 있는, hopeful
기대하고 있다, expect
(~을) 기대하다, bank, bargain, count, expect, hope, look
기도, attempt, bouncer, prayer
기도문, mantra
기도식, prayer
기도실, oratory
기도하다, pray, propose
기독교, Christianity
기독교인, Christian
기동 훈련, maneuver
기둥, column, pillar, plume, post
기득 권익, vested interest
기듯이 간신히 나아가다, claw
기량, skill, workmanship
기력, energy
기력이 다하다, steam
기로, crossroads
기로에 서다, hover
기록, memorandum, minute, record, registry, text
기록 문서, archive
기록기, recorder
기록된, black and white
기록물 보관소, archive
기록부, register
기록원, registrar

기록을 올리다, clock
기록적인, record
기록하다, chart, document, log, note, record, score, set, write
기류, current
기르다, breed, bring, grow, keep, rear
기를 살리다, build
기를 쓰고 공부하다, swot
기를 쓰다, struggle
기름, fat, oil
기름 같은, oily
기름기, grease, richness
기름기 있는, greasy
기름기가 별로 없는, lean
기름기가 있는, oily
기름띠, oil slick
기름막, slick
(~에) 기름을 두르다, grease
기름진, fatty, heavy, rich
기리다, commemorate
기린, giraffe
기마로, horseback
기마병, trooper
기막힌, super
기만, deceit
기만 행위, deception
기만적인, deceitful, deceptive, devious, treacherous
기묘한, odd, weird
(~의) 기미, glimmer, sign, suggestion, touch
기미가 보이다, reek
기민한, agile, astute
기민함, agility
기밀로, confidentially
기밀성, confidentiality
기밀의, classified, confidential, sensitive
기반, footing, foundation, ground, keystone, matrix
(~을) 기반으로 발전시키다, build
(~의) 기반을 조성하다, ground
기발한, whimsical
기발한 착상, inspiration
기백, spirit
기법, technique
기법상의, technical
기법되으로, technically
기벽, eccentricity
기벽(奇癖), quirk
기변(奇變), quirk
기별, news, word
기병대, cavalry
기복, high
기본, basics, bone, fundamentals
기본 금리, base rate
기본 방침, platform
기본 설정의, default
기본 원칙, ground rule
기본 전제, premise
기본의, elementary
기본적으로, basically, essentially, fundamentally
기본적인, basic, common, fundamental, standard
기본적인 것, fundamentals
기부, donation, endowment
기부 기관, donor
기부 약속, pledge
기부금, contribution, donation
기부서약, covenant
기부자, contributor, donor
기부하다, contribute, donate, endow
기분, feeling, frame of mind, humor, inclination, mood, sensation, spirit, temper
기분 나쁘게, nastily, unpleasantly
기분 나쁘게 더듬다, paw
(~을) 기분 나쁘게 받아들이다, personally
기분 나쁜, eerie, sick, unpleasant
기분 전환, recreation, relaxation
기분 전환용 마약, recreational drug
기분 전환을 위해, change
기분 좋게, fondly, pleasingly
기분 좋게 들리다, music

기분 좋게 하는, pleasing
기분 좋다, cheer
기분 좋은, agreeable, congenial, fond
기분을 상하게 하는 것, offense
기분을 상하게 하다, offend
기분을 좋게 하는, feelgood, uplifting
기분을 좋게 하다, world
(~할) 기분이 나는, mood
(~한) 기분이 들다, feel
(~할) 기분이 상한, aggrieved, offended
기분이 안 좋은, mood, rotten
기분이 잡치게 만들다, joint
기분이 좋은, high
기분이 최고인, top
기쁘게, blessedly, happily, joyfully
기쁘게 맞이하다, welcome
기쁘게 하다, please
기쁜, blessed, delighted, glad, joyful, nice, pleased
기쁨, delight, joy, pleasure, rejoicing
기쁨에 차서, delightedly
기쁨을 얻다, delight
기사, article, engineer, item, knight, machinist, news, story
기사 작위를 수여받다, knight
기사의 작위, knighthood
기사형 광고, advertorial
기상, weather
기상의, meteorological
기상학, meteorology
기상학자, meteorologist
기색, note, tinge
기생 동물, parasite
기생 식물, parasite
기생충, parasite
기생충 같은 인간, parasite
기생충에 의한, parasitic
기생하는, parasitic
기성품의, ready-made
기세, edge
기세 좋게 시작하다, launch
기세를 꺾다, edge
기소, indictment, prosecution
기소 배심, grand jury
기소되다, indict
기소자 측, prosecution
기소하다, lay, prosecute
기수, horseman, jockey, rider
기숙사, dormitory, hall, hall of residence, residence hall
기숙학교, boarding school
기술, account, art, attainment, craft, description, mechanic, portrayal, skill, story, technique
기술 지원, technical support
기술 혁신, innovation
기술의, technological
기술자, engineer, technician
기술적, technical
기술적으로, technically, technologically
기술적인, descriptive, technical
기슭, shore
기습하다, surprise
기아, hunger, starvation
기악의, instrumental
기압, pressure
기압계, barometer
기압골, trough
기어 내려오다, climb
기어가다, crawl
기어를 바꾸다, change
기어오르다, clamber, climb, scramble
기억, memory, picture, recollection
기억 상실증, amnesia
기억 장치, memory
기억나게 하다, jog
기억력, memory, recall
기억력이 좋은, long
기억을 되살리다, jog
기억을 떠올리다, dredge
기억을 잃다, memory

기억하다, memorize, remember
기억할 만한, memorable
기억할 만한 것, memorabilia
기억해 내다, recall
기억해 두다, commit
기업 경영, enterprise
기업 농업, agribusiness
기업 대 고객, B2C
기업 대 기업, B2B
기업 매수자, corporate raider
기업 비밀, trade secret
기업 연합, syndicate
기업 인수 희망자, suitor
기업 인수자, acquirer
기업가, entrepreneur
기업가의, entrepreneurial
기업매수 방어책, poison pill
기업의 간부, exec, executive
기업체, enterprise
기여, contribution
기여하다, contribute
기온, temperature
기와, tile
기우뚱거리다, teeter, wobble
기우뚱거림, wobble
기우뚱한, wobbly
기운, aura
기운 나게 하다, perk
기운 넘치는, fresh
기운 빠지게 하는, demoralizing
기운 없는, dull, low
기운을 돋우는, cheering, refreshing
기운을 북돋우는, invigorating
기운을 북돋우다, lighten
기운을 차리다, rouse
기운이 나는, encouraged
기운이 나게, encourage
기운차게, briskly
기울기, tilt
기울다, tip
기울어지게 하다, tilt
기울어지다, slant, slope, tilt
기울이다, give, spend, tilt, tip
기울임, tilt
기웃거리는 사람, snooper
기웃거리다, snoop
기웃거림, snoop
기원, beginning, birth, germ, origin
기원전, BC
기원하다, wish
기이한, curious, freak, improbable
기이한 광경, spectacle
기이한 버릇, quirk
기이한 사람이나 물건, oddity
기이할 정도로, improbably
기이함, oddity
기인, eccentric
기인하다, arise, result, stem
기입 사항, entry
기입하다, enter, put, write
기자, correspondent, journalist, press, reporter
기자 회견, news conference, press conference
기장, captain
기재하다, enter
기저귀, diaper, nappy
기저귀를 갈다, change
(~의) 기저에는, bottom
기적, miracle
기적을 이루다, wonder
기적적인, miraculous
기절, faint
기절하다, faint, pass
기조, keynote, thread
기존의, established, existing, traditional
기존의 것과 다른, alternate
기준, basis, criterion, norm, standard, yardstick
기준에 달하는, mustard
기중기, crane
기증, donation, endowment
기증물, donation
기증자, donor
기증하다, contribute, donate
기증한, donor

기지, base, wit
기지개를 켜다, stretch
기진맥진, exhaustion
기진맥진하게 만들다, wear
기진맥진하게 하다, exhaust
기진맥진한, exhausted, worn out
기질, character, disposition, humor, make-up, temperament, tendency
기질을 지녔다고 착각하다, fancy
기차, train
기차 차장, conductor
기차로, rail
기체, gas
기체역학적, aerodynamic
기초, base, basics, cornerstone, groundwork
기초 작업, groundwork
기초 지식, grounding
기초를 둔, based
기초를 마련하다, lay
기초를 세우는, founding
기초적인, basic, rudimentary
(~의) 기치 아래, banner
기침, cough, coughing
기침 감기, cough
기침하다, cough
기타, etc., guitar
기타 논의 사항, AOB
기타 등등, rest, whatever
기타 연주가, guitarist
기통, cylinder
기포, bubble
기포가 생기다, bubble
기품, class, dignity, grace, panache
기품 있는, dignified
기풍, ethos
기피, dodge
기피하다, dodge
기하학, geometry
기하학의, geometric
기한, deadline
기한이 지난, overdue
기함, flagship
기항하다, call
기형, deformity
기형의, deformed
기형이 되게 하다, deform
기호, character, like, liking, sign, symbol, taste
기호 풀이, key
기호로 바꾸다, encode
기호를 사용한, symbolic
(~의) 기호에 비추어 볼 때, liking
기혼의, married
기회, chance, go, occasion, opportunity, place, scope
기회 균등 실행 고용주, equal opportunity employer
기회를 만들다, way
기회주의자, opportunist
기회주의자인, opportunist
기회주의적인, opportunistic
기후, climate
기후 때문에 변하다, weather
긴, lengthy, long
긴 못, spike
긴 세월, year
긴 소리, wail
긴 안목을 가진, farsighted
긴 여행, voyage
긴 의자, settee
긴 이야기, saga
긴 항해, voyage
긴급, urgency
긴급 직통 전화, hotline
긴급하게, urgently
긴급한, emergency, pressing, urgent
긴급한 과제, imperative
긴밀하게, closely
긴밀한, close
긴박한, tense
긴장, agitation, nerve, strain, tension
긴장감, suspense, tension
긴장된, taut, tense
긴장시키다, tense

긴장을 풀다, loosen, relax, wind
긴장이 풀리다, loosen
긴장하다, knot, tense
긴장한, strained, tense, uptight, wound up
긴축 정책, squeeze
긴축 정책을 펴다, squeeze
긴축의, austere
길, lane, line, passage, path, pathway, road, route, way
길가, roadside
길가 풀밭, verge
길가에 멈추다, pull
길거리, street
길거리 강도, mugger
길게 느껴지는, long
길게 베다, slit
길게 벤 자국, slit
길게 빼다, crane
길고 가는 조각, strip
길고 복잡한, tortuous
길길이 뛰다, roof
길다, grow
길들여진, tame
길들이다, break, tame
길모퉁이, corner
길어지다, lengthen
길을 걷다, tread
(~의) 길을 막다, obstruct
길을 벗어나다, stray
길을 안내하다, way
길을 알려 주다, direct
길을 열다, clear
길을 잃다, astray, lose
길을 잃은, lost
길을 찾아가다, navigate
길을 트다, way
길이, extent, length
길이가 ~인, long
길이로, lengthwise
길쭉하게 돋은 선, ridge
김, vapor
(~하는) 김에, passing
김을 내다, steam
김을 빼다, deflate
김이 빠진, deflated, flat
김이 서리다, cloud, mist, steam
김칫국부터 마신다, chicken
깁스를 한, plaster
깃, collar
깃발, color
깃을 단, feathered
깃털, feather, plume
깃털로 장식된, feathered
깊게, deep, deeply, heavily
깊게 갈라진 틈, chasm
깊게 파다, deepen
깊고 넓게 패인 자국, furrow
깊숙이 들어간 곳, depth
깊숙이 박혀 있다, embed
깊어지게 하다, deepen
깊어지다, deepen
깊은, deep, heavy, intimate, sound
깊은 골, depth
깊은 곳, depth, recess
깊은 관계, involvement
깊은 관계를 맺다, commit
깊은 관계의, intimate
깊은 상처, gash
(~에) 깊은 상처를 입히다, gash
깊은 상처를 주는, traumatic
깊은 우려, preoccupation
깊은 주름살, furrow
깊이, deeply, depth, intimately, profusely, richness, sound, soundly
깊이 들어가다, sink
깊이 박아 넣다, sink
깊이 배어든, ingrained
깊이 빨아들이다, drag
깊이 생각하다, ponder, reflect
깊이 생각함, reflection
깊이 자리 잡은, deep-seated
깊이 잠든, asleep, fast
깊이가 없는, superficial
깊이가 있는, deep
깊지 않은, superficial
까다로운, complicated, demanding, difficult, fiddly, grumpy, particular, tough
까다롭게 만들다, complicate
까닥이다, nod
까닭, reason
까딱거리다, wag
까마귀, crow
까막까치밥 나무 열매, blackcurrant
까맣게 탄, charred
까실까실한, crisp
까치, magpie
까치발, bracket
까탈 부리는, fussy
깍두기 모양으로 썰다, dice
깍둑썰기 하다, cube
깍듯이, courteously
깎기, cut
깎다, carve, clip, cut, shave
깎아 낸 부스러기, shaving
깎아 만들다, whittle
깎아내리다, devalue, diminish
깎아낸 조각, clipping
깎아지른 듯한, sheer
깎은 면, facet
깎음, cut
깔개, rug
깔끔하게, neatly, tidily
깔끔하게 잘라 다듬은, clipped
깔끔하지 못한, messy, untidy
깔끔한, austere, clean, neat, slick, tidy, tidiness
깔끔함, cleanliness, neatness, tidiness
깔다, lay
깔때기, funnel
깔려 죽다, mow
깔보는 태도로 대하다, patronize
깔보다, look, nose
깜박거리다, flicker
깜박거림, blink, flicker
깜박이, turn signal
깜박이다, blink
깜빡 잊고 안 함, oversight
깜빡 잊다, mind
깜빡하다, forget
깜빡함, lapse
깜짝 놀라게 하다, amaze, astonish, astound, electrify, stagger, startle, surprise
깜짝 놀라다, darn
깜짝 놀란, amazed, astonished, staggered, startled, surprised
깜짝 놀랄 만한, astounding
깜짝 놀람, amazement
깜찍하게, daintily
깜찍한, cute, dainty
깡마른, skinny
깡충 뜀, skip
깡충거리다, hop, scamper
깡충거림, hop
깡충깡충 뛰다, hop, skip
깡통, can, canister, tin
깡통에 든 것, tin
깡패, bully
깨끗이 비우다, clean
깨끗이 승복하는 패자, loser
깨끗이 하다, cleanse
깨끗하게 하는 기구, cleaner
깨끗하게 하다, clean
깨끗한, clean, clear, pure
깨끗함, clarity, purity
깨다, beat, break, crack, rouse, wake
깨닫게 하는 계기, reminder
깨닫다, catch, eye, find, head, realize, see
깨달음, realization
깨뜨리다, break
깨물다, bite, chew
깨어 있는, awake, up
깨어지다, break
깨우다, rouse, wake
깨지기 쉬운, frail
깨지다, break
깨지락거리다, toy
꺼끌꺼끌한, rough
꺼끌꺼끌한 수염, bristle
꺼끌꺼끌함, roughness
꺼내다, broach, extract, pull, take, withdraw
꺼리게 만들다, scare
꺼리는, reluctant, shy, unwilling
(~을) 꺼리다, shy
꺼림, reluctance, unwillingness
꺼져, get, off, sod
꺼지다, bugger, cave, go, piss
꺾꽂이 순, cutting
꺾다, blight, dash, pick
껄끄러운, strained
껌, gum
껍데기, shell
껍데기를 벗기다, shell
껍질, jacket, peel, rind, shell, skin
껍질을 벗기다, pare, peel
껍질이 딱딱한, crusty
껴안기 좋은, cuddly
껴안다, cuddle, embrace, hold, hug
껴안아 주고 싶은, cuddly
껴안음, cuddle, hug
꼬다, cross, twist
꼬르륵 소리, rumbling
꼬르륵 소리를 내다, rumble
꼬리, tail
꼬리말, footer
꼬리에 꼬리를 문, bumper
꼬리에 꼬리를 물고, nose
꼬리표, label, tag
꼬리표를 달다, tag
꼬박꼬박 저축을 하는 사람, saver
꼬집기, pinch
꼬집다, pinch
꼬집어 내다, pin
꼬챙이, spit
꼬치, skewer, spit
꼬치꼬치 따지다, hair
꼬치꼬치 알려고 하는, inquisitive
꼬치꼬치 캐다, pry
꼬투리, pod
꼬투리를 잡다, pounce
꼬투리를 잡히게 만들다, catch
꼭, firmly, tight, tightly
꼭 ~하도록 하다, see
꼭 ~하시오, sure
꼭 달라붙게 하다, mold
꼭 달라붙다, mold
(~을) 꼭 닮다, image
꼭 닮은 것, clone, likeness
꼭 닮은 사람, clone
꼭 들어맞는, fitted
꼭 마치, just
꼭 맞게, fittingly
(~에) 꼭 맞는, cut out, snug
꼭 맞다, glove
꼭 어울리게, fittingly
(~에) 꼭 어울리다, fit
(~을) 꼭 잡고 있다, hold
꼭 집어내다, pinpoint
꼭 짜다, squeeze
꼭 짬, squeeze
꼭대기, apex, brow, top
꼭두각시, puppet
꼭지, faucet
꼭지가 돈, pissed
꼭지가 돌다, nut
꼴도 보기 싫어하다, gut
꼴사나움, ugliness
꼼꼼하게, carefully, conscientiously, meticulously
꼼꼼한, careful, conscientious, meticulous, particular, scrupulous
꼼꼼히 살피다, dig, stock
꼼꼼히 찾다, comb
꼼짝 못하는, stuck
꼼짝 않다, stick
꼼짝달싹 못 하는, bogged down
꼼짝하게 하다, budge
꼼짝하다, budge, muscle
꼿꼿이 하다, brace
꼿꼿하게, bolt
꼿꼿한, upright
꽁꽁 언, frozen
꽁무니 빼다, back
꽁초, butt, stub
꽂다, dig, pin
꽂히다, lodge
꽃, bloom, blossom, flower
꽃가루, pollen
꽃과 열매를 맺다, seed
꽃무늬의, floral
꽃병, vase
꽃봉오리, bud
꽃송이, flower
꽃양배추, cauliflower
꽃을 피우는, flowering
꽃을 피우다, bloom, blossom, flower
꽃의, floral
꽃이 피다, bloom, flower
꽃잎, petal
꽃장수, florist
꽃집, florist
꽉, tight, tightly, tight
꽉 끼게, tightly
꽉 끼는, tight
꽉 들어찬, tight
꽉 들어찬 상태, squash
꽉 막힌, jammed
꽉 붙들다, seize
꽉 붙이다, clamp
꽉 잡다, grip, hold
꽉 잡으세요!, hold
꽉 쥐다, clench
꽉 짜인, crowded
꽉 찬, jammed, packed
꽉꽉, tightly
꽉꽉 찬, full up
꽝 하는 소리를 내다, bang
꽤, fairly, pretty, quite, rather, reasonably
꽤 괜찮은, reasonable
꽤 많은, bit
꽤 신나는 일, laugh
꽤 잘하는, reasonable
꽤 큰, sizeable
꽤나, halfway
꽥 하는 소리, squeak
꾀다, seduce
꾀바른, nimble
꾀죄죄한, grotty, scruffy
꾀하다, propose
꾐에 빠져 ~을 하다, rope
꾸러미, bale, package
꾸며 내다, cook, fabricate, invent
꾸며내다, fake
꾸며진, glorified
꾸물거리다, lag
꾸미기, decorating
꾸미다, concoct, cook, decorate, design, glorify
꾸미지 않은, bare
꾸민, mock
꾸밈, act, frill
꾸밈없는, candid, unaffected
꾸불꾸불 나아가다, snake
꾸준한, abiding, steady, unrelenting
꾸준히, steadily
꾸준히 노력하다, slog
꾸준히 해내다, keep
꾸짖다, chide, scold
꾹 참다, fight
꿀, honey
꿀꺽꿀꺽 마시다, gulp
꿀꿀거리다, grunt
꿀떡꿀떡 먹다, gulp
꿀벌통, hive
꿈, dream
꿈꾸는 듯한, distant, dreamy
꿈꾸다, dream
꿈만 같은, dreamy
꿈틀거리다, squirm, stir, wiggle, wriggle
꿈틀거림, wiggle
꿩, pheasant
꿩고기, pheasant
꿰다, thread
꿰뚫다, penetrate
꿰뚫어 보는 듯한, penetrating
꿰뚫어 보다, see
꿰매다, darn, stitch
끄다, extinguish, flip, put, shut, turn
끄덕이다, nod

끄덕임, nod
끄집어내다, extract
끄트머리, end
끈, braid, cord, lace, line, strap, string, tape
끈기, doggedness, perseverance, persistence, tenacity
끈덕지게, persistently
끈덕지게 괴롭힘, tease
끈덕진, persistent
끈을 매다, lace
끈적거리는, sticky
끈적끈적한, slimy, tacky
끈적끈적한 물질, slime
끈질기게, doggedly, insistently, obstinately, relentlessly
끈질긴, dogged, relentless
끈질긴 판매, hard sell
끊기다, cut
끊다, break, kick, sever
끊어진, broken
끊어지지 않는, perennial
끊임없는, eternal, incessant, perpetual, persistent, 24-7, unrelenting
끊임없는 변화, flux
끊임없이, continuously, incessantly, perpetually
끊임없이 떠오르는, haunting
끊임없이 변하는, transient
끊임없이 오는, hook
끊임없이 이어지는, continuous
끊임없이 이어지다, stream
끊지 않고 기다리다, hold
끌, chisel
끌고 가다, drag, march
끌기, pull
끌다, attract, draw, grab, hold, pull, tout, tow
끌려 들어가다, hook
끌로 다듬다, chisel
끌리기 시작하다, fancy
끌리는, attracted, taken
끌리다, go, gravitate
끌어 모으다, draw, gather, pull
끌어가다, tow
끌어내다, drag, draw
끌어내리다, take
끌어당겨 않다, pull
끌어당기다, collect, draw, haul
끌어들이다, draw, involve
끌어안다, absorb
끌어오다, run
끓다, boil
끓어 넘치다, boil
끓이다, boil
끔찍스럽게, dreadfully
끔찍이, dearly
끔찍이 위하다, fuss
끔찍하게, appallingly, horrendously, horribly, monstrously, terribly
끔찍하게 여기다, recoil
끔찍한, appalling, awful, catastrophic, dire, dreadful, ghastly, grisly, horrendous, horrible, horrific, horror, lurid, nasty, terrible
끔찍한 일, horror
끔찍함, nastiness
끔찍해 하다, horrify
끝, conclusion, edge, end, finish, pad, point, top
끝 부분, ending
끝까지, way
끝까지 해 내다, follow
끝나다, cease, conclude, draw, end, finish, stop, terminate
끝난, done, finished, over, up
끝내 주는 것, dynamite
끝내다, close, conclude, end, finish, lift, terminate
끝마치다, complete
끝맺다, conclude
끝없는, never-ending
끝없이, endlessly
끝없이 계속되어, interminably
끝에서 네 번째, last

끝에서 두 번째, last
끝에서 두 번째의, penultimate
끝에서 세 번째, last
끝을 내다, finish
끝의, top
끝이 난, way
끝이 안 보일 정도로, eye
끝이 없는, endless
끝장, death
끝장난, finished
끼고 있다, wear
끼다, cross, fold
끼어들다, barge, break, butt, intervene, intrude, muscle, push
끼얹다, splash
끼워 넣다, insert, slot, wedge
(~에) 끼워 맞추다, fit
끼워져 들어가다, slot
(~에) 끼이다, catch
끼익 하는 소리를 내다, screech
끼적이다, scrawl, scribble
끼익 소리 나다, squeal
끽 하는 소리, squeal
끽끽거리는 소리, squeak
끽끽거리다, squeak
낄낄 웃음, giggle
낄낄거리고 웃다, giggle
낄낄대다, snigger
낄낄댐, snigger
킴새를 채다, rat
낑낑거리다, whine
낑낑대는 소리, whine
나 자신, myself
나가는, outgoing
나가다, exit, fuse, go, nip
나가떨어지게 만들다, fly
나가떨어지다, fly
나감, exit
나누다, divide, separate, split
나누어 쓰다, share
나누어 주다, dish, hand
나눌 수 없는, inseparable
나눗셈, division
나눠 갖다, share, split
나눠 주다, divide, give
나뉘다, divide, separate, split
나는, I
나다, break, emanate, go, run, sprout
나돌아다니는, about
나들이, outing
나라, country, land
나라면 ~하겠다, would
나락, abyss
나란히, abreast, alongside, side, tandem
나루, dock, marina
나룻배, ferry
나르다, bear, carry, hump
나른하게, dully, languidly, lazily
나른한, dull, languid, lazy
나른한 분위기의, sleepy
나른함, dullness
나름의 쓸모가 있다, use
나머지, other, remainder, rest
나무, tree, wood
나무 껍질, bark
나무 메, mallet
나무나 식물이 많은, leafy
나무라다, accuse, blame, chide, criticize
나무랄 데 없는, impeccable
나무랄 데 없이, impeccably
(~해도) 나무랄 수 없다, forgive
나무옹이, knot
나무의 몸통, trunk
나무토막, stick
나뭇가지, stick
나뭇결, grain
나뭇잎, leaf
나방, moth
나부끼다, wave
나비, butterfly
나비로, across
나비매듭, bow
나빠지다, deteriorate, suffer
나쁘게, badly, ill

나쁘게 작용하다, bite
나쁜, bad, ill, sinful, wrong
나쁜 길로 이끌리다, astray
나쁜 버릇, vice
나쁜 사람, villain
나쁜 영향을 주다, hard
나쁜 편으로, worse
나쁠 건 없다, harm, hurt
나사, bolt, screw
나사 홈, thread
나사로 고정시키다, bolt
나사로 고정하다, screw
나삿니, thread
나서다, come, stir
나선, spiral
나선형, curl
나선형 움직임, spiral
나선형으로 움직이다, spiral
나선형의, curly, spiral
나아가게 하다, propel
나아가는, onward
나아가다, do, fight, go, head, pass, pull, way
나아가게 하다, lift, turn
나아가고 있는, mend
나아가다, lift, mend, perk, turn
나열하다, list
나오다, appear, arrive, come, distill, emerge, figure, get
나온, out
나온 것, distillation
(~보다) 나은, superior
나이, age
나이 든, aging, old
나이가 ~대인, in
나이가 ~인, old
나이가 더 많은, senior
나이가 지긋한, elderly
나이트, knight
나이트클럽, club, nightclub
나이프, knife
나일론, nylon
나중에, afterward, later
나중에 도움이 되다, dividend
나중에 생각나는 묘안, hindsight
나중의, later
나체화, nude
나치, Nazi
나치의, Nazi
나치의 유태인 대학살, holocaust
나침반, compass
나침반의 32방위, point
나타나는, manifest
나타나다, appear, come, emerge, face, haunt, manifest, occur, present, register, show, turn
나타남, manifestation
나타내다, denote, exhibit, indicate, read, refer, register, represent, signify
나트륨, sodium
나팔, horn
나풀거리다, flutter
나풀거림, flutter
낙관, feelgood, optimism
낙관적으로, optimistically, positively
낙관적인, positive, upbeat
낙관하는, optimistic
낙관하다, hope
낙농의, dairy
낙담시키는, disheartening
낙담시키다, dash
낙담하게 만들다, discourage
낙담하게 하는, discouraging
낙담하다, dash
낙담한, despondent, discouraged, disheartened
낙서, doodle
낙서하다, deface, doodle, scribble
낙수홈통, gutter
낙승하다, romp, sweep
낙심하다, sink
낙오자, dropout
낙원, heaven, paradise
낙인, brand
낙인을 찍다, brand
낙인이 찍히다, stigmatize

낙제, fail
낙제점을 주다, fail
낙세하다, fail, flunk
낙진, fallout
낙천적인, lighthearted
낙천주의, optimism
낙천주의자, optimist
낙타, camel
낙태, abortion, termination
낙태하다, abort, terminate
낙하, fall
낙하산, chute, parachute
낙하산 부대, paratrooper
낙하산으로 낙하시키다, parachute
낙하산으로 투하하다, parachute
낙하산을 타다, parachute
낚시, fishing
낚시꾼, angler
낚시질, angling
낚시하다, fish
(~을) 낚싯바늘로 낚다, hook
낚아채다, snatch
난, column
난(欄), field
난간, rail, railing
난감한, embarrassing, overwhelming, sticky
난감할 정도로, overwhelmingly
난관, patch
난관을 뚫고 성공하다, break
난국, impasse
난국에 대처하다, occasion
난국에 처한, water
난국을 타개하는, challenge
난기류, turbulence
난기류의, turbulent
난데없이, nowhere
난도질하다, hack
난독증, dyslexia
난동, hooliganism
난동을 부리다, riot
난로, stove
난리, hassle
난리가 나다, hell
난민, displaced person, refugee
난방, heating
난방 장치, heating
난방기, fire, heater
난방열, heat
난소, ovary
난입, storming
난입당하다, storm
난입하다, barge, break
난자, egg
난잡, disarray
난잡한, untidy
난장판, shambles
난쟁이, dwarf
난쟁이의, dwarf
난제, embarrassment, riddle, sticking point
난처하게, awkwardly
난처하게 하다, confound, embarrass
난처한, awkward, unfortunate
난처한 실수를 하다, foot
난초, orchid
난타하다, batter
난투, scuffle
난투극, brawl
난투극을 벌이다, brawl
난투를 벌이다, scuffle
난파, shipwreck
난파선, shipwreck
난폭하게, violently
난폭하게 부딪치다, barge
난폭한, brutal, disorderly, reckless, tough, violent
난폭함, recklessness
난해한, inaccessible, unintelligible
낟알, grain
날, blade, edge
날개, blade, wing
날개 같은 부분, flap
날개가 있는, winged
날개를 펴다, wing
날갯짓 하듯 움직이다, flap
날것의, raw

날다, fly
날뛰다, buck, riot, tear
날렵하게, deftly
날렵한, deft
날리다, blow, throw
날림, puff
날마다, day
날쌔게 움직이다, dart, leap
날씨, weather
날씬한, slender, slim
날아다니는, flying
날아다니다, flit
날아오르다, soar
날염 무늬, print
날염 옷감, print
날을 듯한 기쁨, exhilaration
날이 넓은 큰 칼, machete
날조, invention
날조하다, concoct, cook, fake, invent, make, manufacture
날짜, date
날짜를 기입하다, date
날짜를 바꾸다, move
날짜를 밝히다, date
날카로운, incisive, penetrating, piercing, sharp, shrill
날카로운 고함, screech
날카로운 소리, crack, screech, shriek
날카로운 소리가 나다, crack
날카로운 소리로 말하다, screech
날카로운 소리를 내다, screech, shriek
날카로운 쇳소리, feedback
날카로움, edge
날카로워지다, fray, sharpen
날카롭게, sharply
날카롭게 만들다, sharpen
날카롭게 하다, fray, sharpen
낡다, age, date
낡아빠진, provincial
낡은, old, outdated
낡을 대로 낡은, battered
남 이야기를 지껄이다, gossip
남겨 두다, leave
남극, Antarctic
남기고, behind
남기다, leave
남녀 공용의, mixed, unisex
남녀 공학의, mixed
남다, left, remain, spare
남다른, ordinary, remarkable, unorthodox
남달리, unusually
남동부 지역의, southeastern
남동쪽, southeast
남동쪽에, southeast
남동쪽으로, southeast
남루한 차림의, ragged
남반구 개발도상국들, south
남부 사람, southerner
남부 지방, south
남부의, south, southern
남서부의, southwest, southwestern
남서쪽, southwest
남서쪽에, southwest
남성, male
남성 우월적인, macho
남성 하원의원, congressman
남성복 재단사, tailor
남성성, masculinity, virility
남성용 수영복, trunk
남성의, male
남성의류, menswear
남성적인, masculine, virile
남성형의, masculine
남아 있는, remaining
남아 있다, remain, stand
남아서, behind
남용, abuse, misuse
남용하다, abuse, misuse
남은, go, hand, left
남은 부분, trimming
남은 음식, leftover
남은 평생 동안, life
남을 따라다니며 괴롭히는 사람, stalker

남을 못살게 구는 사람, tease
남을 의식하지 않는, uninhibited
남의 떡이 커 보이다, grass
남의 말을 잘 들어 주는 사람, listener
남의 불행을 이용해 먹는 사람, vulture
남의 손에 넘어가다, hand
남의 이목을 꺼리는, furtive
남이 하는 대로 따라 하다, suit
남자, boy, guy, male, man
남자 분들, gentleman
남자 친구, boyfriend
남자 화장실, gent
남자다운, manly
남자다움, manliness, masculinity
남자다움을 과시하는, macho
남자애, boy
남자용 팬티, short
남자의, male
남자임, masculinity
남작, baron
남작 부인, baroness
남쪽, south
남쪽의, south, southerly, southward
남편, husband, man
남학생, schoolboy
남학생 사교 클럽, fraternity
납, lead
납골당, vault
납득시키다, convince, get, persuade, satisfy, sell
납득이 가게 하는, convincing
납득이 가도록, convincingly
납득하는, satisfied
납세자, taxpayer
납작 엎드린, flat
납작하게 만들다, flatten
납작한, flat
납작한 냄비, pan
납치, abduction, hijack, hijacking, kidnapping
납치되다, hostage
납치범, hijacker, kidnapper
납치죄, kidnap
납치하다, abduct, hijack, kidnap
낫게 하다, mend
낫다, clear, compare, heal, improve
낭독, reading
낭독하다, read
낭떠러지, cliff
낭랑한, rich
낭만적인, romantic
낭보, news
낭비, extravagance, wastage, waste
낭비되다, waste
낭비벽이 있는, extravagant
낭비적인, wasteful
낭비하다, dissipate, squander, throw, waste
낭비할 시간이 없다, time
낭송, reading
낭송회, recital
낭종(囊腫), cyst
낭패를 보게 하다, upset
낭포(囊胞), cyst
낮, day
낮 공연, matinee
낮 시간, day, daytime
낮게 날다, buzz
낮은, badly, deep, gentle, inferior, low, lowly
낮은 목소리로, breath
낮은 소리, murmur
낮은 온도에, gently
낮은 위치의 사람, inferior
낮잠, nap, snooze
낮잠 자다, nap
낮추다, drop, knock, lower, turn
낮춤, lowering
낯 뜨거운, rude
낯선, alien, new, strange, unfamiliar
낯선 사람, stranger
낳다, birth, lay, produce, yield
내 견해로는, view
내 말 뜻은, mean

내 생각에는, ask, mind, opinion, view
내가 직접, myself
내가 처리할 수 있다, manage
내가 추측하는 바로는, gather
내각, cabinet
내걸다, fly
내구 소비재, durable goods
내구력, strength
내구성, durability
내구성 있는, durable
내구재, consumer durable
내기, bet, wager
내기 도박, betting
내기를 걸다, place
내기에 거는 돈, bet
내기에 건 돈, stake
내기에 걸린 물건, stake
내기하다, bet
내내, all, long, solidly, through, way
내놓다, bring, float, proffer, serve
내다, cut, emit, find, let, put, send, summon, turn, work, yield
내다 널다, hang
내다보다, see
(~가) 내다보이다, look, overlook
(~에) 내던져지다, pitch
내던지다, dash, fling, sling, throw
내동댕이치다, fling, throw
내레이션, narration
내레이션을 하다, narrate
내레이터, narrator
내려 주다, drop
내려가기, descent
내려가다, descend, dip, go
내려감, dip
내려놓다, lay
내려앉다, subside
내려주다, drop
내력, history
내륙, interior
내륙의, inland, onshore
내리다, fall, lower, mete, pass, return, roll
내리막 경사, descent
내리막의, downhill
내리받이, descent
내막에 밝은 사람, insider
(~하도록) 내몰다, drive
내몰리다, throw
내무 장관, Home Secretary
내무부, interior
내무부의, interior
내밀다, hold, jut, proffer, stick
내밀한, inside
내밀히, private
내뱉다, spout
(~에) 내버려 두다, consign, leave
내버려 둔, unattended
내벽, lining, wall
내보내다, discharge, let, put
내보냄, discharge
내보이다, dangle
내보임, show
내부, inside, interior
내부 통화 장치, intercom
내부로, inside
내부를 파괴하다, gut
(~의) 내부에, inside, within
내부의, inner, inside, interior, internal, inward
내부자, insider
내부자 거래, insider trading
(~끼리) 내부적으로, among
내빈, guest
내뻗다, stretch
내뿜다, belch, emit, give, puff, spout
내선, ext., extension
내성, tolerance
내성적인, withdrawn
내성적인 사람, violet
내세, eternity
(~를) 내세우다, make, purport, put
내숭 떠는 사람, prude
내숭떠는, coy
내숭을 떨며, coyly

내쉬다, exhale
내습, invasion
내실이 없는, hollow
내심, inside
내심으로는, heart
내야 하는, payable
내역, breakdown
내연 기관이 달린, motor
내연의, common law
(~) 내외, o.n.o.
내용, content
내용을 부풀리다, pad
내용이 충실한, meaty
내음, aroma
내일, tomorrow
내장, bowel, gut, offal
내장된, built-in
내장을 빼내다, gut
내재하는, implicit
내적인, inner
내전, civil war
내정한, impersonal
내주다, part, surrender
내쫓기다, hound
내쫓다, pack, throw
내키지 않는, grudging
내통, sell-out
내팽개치다, fling, throw
내포, bay
내포(內浦), inlet
내포되다, embed
내포된, embedded, implicit
내포된 의미, connotation
(~를) 내포한, fraught
내핍, austerity
내한성의, hardy
낼 수 있는, payable
냄비, pot, saucepan
냄새, odor, smell
냄새가 고약한, smelly
냄새가 나다, reek, smell
냄새를 맡다, scent, smell
냅킨, napkin
냉각 장치, radiator
냉기, chill, coldness
냉담, apathy
냉담하게, coolly
냉담한, aloof, apathetic, cool, distant, icy, unsympathetic
냉동 보관하다, freeze
냉동고, freezer
냉동된, frozen
냉소적으로, cynically
냉소적인, cynical, sardonic
냉소주의, cynicism
냉장 보관하다, refrigerate
냉장고, fridge, refrigerator
냉정, nerve
냉정을 잃다, head
냉정하게, blood, coldly, coolly, soberly, starkly
냉정한, cold, cool, sober, stark
냉정함, coldness
냉큼 받아들이다, jump
냉큼 사다, snap
냉혈 동물의, cold-blooded
냉혹한, cold-blooded
냉혹하게, blood, callously
냉혹한, callous, iron
냉혹함, callousness
너, you
너 자신, yourself
너그러운, benevolent, generous, permissive
너그러움, benevolence
너그럽게, generously
너머, beyond
(~) 너머로, over, past
너무 많이 먹다, overeat
너무 작은, skimpy
너무 차분한, staid
너무나, only, outstandingly, so, too
너무나 ~해서 . . . 하다, so, such
너비, breadth
너스레, quip
너울거리다, wave, waver
너저분함, squalor
너트, nut

너희들, you
너희들 자신, yourself
넉넉하게, generously
넉넉한, ample, generous
넉넉함, fullness
넋이 나가다, carry
넌더리가 나는, damned
넌지시 말하다, imply
넌지시 비치다, hint
넌지시 알리다, intimate
(~이) 널려 있는, scattered
널리, widely
널리 미치는, pervasive
널리 알려진, public
널리 퍼지다, pervade
널리 퍼진, prevalent, widespread
널리 퍼짐, prevalence
널브러지다, flop
(~이) 널브러진, strewn
널빤지, plank
널찍한, roomy, spacious
널찍함, space
넓고 긴, sweeping
넓어지다, broaden, dilate, enlarge, widen
넓은, broad, dilated, spacious, wide
넓이, extent, width
넓히다, broaden, deepen, dilate, enlarge, widen
넘겨받다, take
넘겨주다, hand, pass, turn
(~을) 넘기다, hand, keep, turn, wash
넘다, cross, exceed, turn
넘어, beyond, over
넘어가다, go, pass
넘어뜨리다, bring, tip
넘어서다, cross, pass
넘어선, beyond
넘어야 할 산, mountain
넘어지다, fall
넘어짐, fall
넘쳐 나다, overflow
넘쳐 나도록, overflow
넘치나게 하다, flood
(~이) 넘쳐나다, drip, flood
넘쳐남, overflow
넘치게, over
(~가) 넘치는, lack
(~이) 넘치다, full, glow, overflow, slop
넘칠 정도로 가득 차다, brim
넙치, plaice
(~에) 넣다, drop, feed, get, load
넣어 두다, tidy
(~에) 넣어지다, encase
네, yes
네 발로 기어, four
네 배로 늘리다, quadruple
네 배의, quadruple
네 번째의, fourth
네 부분으로 이루어진, quadruple
네거리, crossroads
네모, box
네온, neon
네트볼, netball
네트워크, network
네트워킹, networking
넥타이, tie
녀석, bloke, chap, fellow, thing
녀석들, lad
노, oar, paddle
노 젓기, row, stroke
노 젓다, row
노 코멘트, comment
노(爐), furnace
노고, labor
노골적으로, baldly, blatantly, face, outright, plainly, pointedly
노골적인, bald, blatant, explicit, outright, pointed, vulgar
노끈, braid
노년, old age, ripe
노다지, bonanza
노동 시장, labor market, market
노동 이동률, turnover
노동 인구, workforce

노동 쟁의, industrial action
노동당, labor, Labour Party
노동력, labor force, manpower, workforce
노동의, working
노동자, labor, laborer, shop floor, workman
노동자 계층, working class
노동조합, labor union, union
노동집약적, labor-intensive
노란색, yellow
노래, number, song, tune
노래 부르기, singing
노래로 만들다, set
노래를 시작하다, song
노래하다, sing, warble
노려보다, glare, glower
노려봄, glare
노력, effort, energy, try
노력을 기울이다, effort
노력을 요하는, exacting
노력하다, exert, strive, try
노력해 일하다, work
노련한, expert
노령 연금 수령자, OAP, old age pensioner
노령의, aged
노령자, senior citizen
노르스름한 녹색, olive
노른자위, yolk
노를 젓다, paddle
노름꾼, gambler
노릇하게 굽다, toast
(~을) 노리다, aim, sight
노망, senility
노망든, senile
노발대발한, livid
노변, roadside
노사 관계, industrial relations, labor relations
노상, always, street
노새, mule
노선, course, line, path, route
노쇠한, infirm
노숙, homelessness
노숙자, homeless
노심초사하는, sick
노심초사하다, brood
노여움, wrath, anger
노역, labor
노예, slave
노예 제도, slavery
노예의 신분, bondage
노예처럼 고되게 일하다, slave
노인, aged, geriatric, senior citizen
노인들, elderly, infirm, old
노인병 환자, geriatric
노인병의, geriatric
노점상인, vendor
노정, journey
노조, trade union
노조에 속하지 않은, nonunion
노조원, trade unionist
노조원을 고용하지 않는, nonunion
노천의, open-air
노출, exposure
노출되다, expose
노크, knock, knocking
노크하다, knock
노트, knot
노트북, notebook
노트북 컴퓨터, laptop
노티가 나는, middle-aged
노하게 하다, anger
노한, irate
노화, aging
노후한, antiquated
녹, rust
녹갈색, khaki
녹는, soluble
녹다, dissolve, melt, thaw
녹말, starch
녹말 성분, starch
녹색, green
녹색당원, green
녹슨, rusty
녹슬다, rust

(~로) 녹아들다, melt
녹아웃, knockout
녹은, molten
녹음, greenness, recording
녹음기, recorder, tape recorder
녹음실, studio
녹음테이프, cassette
녹음하다, record, tape
녹음한 것, recording
녹이다, dissolve, melt
녹지, green
녹지대, green, green belt
녹초로 만드는, exhausting, grueling
녹화, recording
녹화기, recorder
녹화하다, record, tape
논, paddy
논객, commentator
논거, case, ground
논거가 불안정한, ground
논고, discussion
논리, case, logic
논리 폭탄, logic bomb
논리적으로, logically
논리적인, logical
논리학, logic
논문, dissertation, paper
논밭, field
논설, leading article
논설의, editorial
논의, discussion
논의 되고 있는, focus
논의 중인, discussion
논의하다, confer, debate, discuss
논쟁, argument, controversy, debate, dispute
논쟁 중의, dispute
(~와) 논쟁을 벌이다, issue
논쟁의 소지가 많은, controversial
논쟁의 여지가 있는, debatable
논쟁점, bone of contention
논쟁하고 있는, dispute
논쟁하다, argue, debate, horn
논전, controversy
논점, bullet point, contention, issue
논조, tone
논지, thesis
논평, comment, review
논평가, reviewer
논평기사, commentary
논평하다, comment, review
논하다, deal, talk
놀고 있는, idle
놀다, play
놀라 죽을 뻔한, death
놀라게 하다, alarm, surprise
놀라다, aback, marvel, wonder
놀라서 입을 딱 벌리고 바라보다, gape
놀라운, alarming, extraordinary, miraculous, surprising, wonder
놀라운 능력, magic
놀라운 사람, surprise
놀라운 소식, surprise
놀라운 일, magic, wonder
놀라움, surprise, wonder
놀란, alarmed
놀랄 만큼, astonishingly, remarkably, wonderfully
놀랄 만한 일, eye-opener
놀랄 정도로, amazingly, incredibly
놀랄 정도로 멋진, incredible
놀랄 정도의, amazing
놀람, alarm, astonishment
놀랍게, alarmingly, extraordinarily
놀랍게도, surprisingly
놀려 대다, tease
놀리다, fun, idle, kid, leg, name, piss, taunt
놀림, taunt
놀이, play
놀이 기구, amusement, ride
놀이를 하다, play
놀이터, play park
놈, bloke, chap
놋쇠, brass

농가, farmhouse, homestead
농가 마당, farmyard
농구, basketball
농구공, basketball
농담, gag, joke, tone
농담이 아니다, mean
농담조의, tongue
농담하다, joke, kid
농도, concentration, strength
농부, farmer, peasant
농산물, produce
농약, pesticide
농어류의 식용 담수어, perch
농업, agriculture, farming
농업의, agricultural
농작물, crop
농장, farm
농장주, farmer
농지, farmland
농지거리, banter
농축된, concentrated
농축액, essence
높아지다, build, mount, rise
(~보다) 높은, above, exalted, high
높은 곳, height
높은 곳에 강하다, head
높은 곳의, high
높은 산의, alpine
높은 지위에, highly
(~보다) 높이, above, height, high, level
높이 차서 올리다, kick
높이 치솟은, towering
높이 평가하다, rate, value
높이 평가하여, highly
높이가 ~인, high
높이가 같은, level
높이다, bolster, build, enhance
놓다, lay, locate, place, position, put, rest, set
놓아 주다, let, release
놓아두다, stand
놓아먹인, free-range
놓여 있다, lie, rest
놓이게 하다, place
놓이다, go, land
놓인, set
놓치다, give, lose, miss, pass, track, waste
놓침, miss
놔두다, leave, let
뇌, brain
뇌리를 떠나지 않다, haunt
뇌리에서 잊혀지지 않는, haunting
뇌막염, meningitis
뇌물, bribe, payoff
뇌물 증여, bribery
뇌물을 주다, bribe
뇌성, clap
뇌우, thunderstorm
뇌의, cerebral
뇌졸중, stroke
뇌진탕, concussion
누, base
누계의, running
누구, somebody, someone, who
누구나, any, whoever
누그러뜨리다, lighten, mitigate, moderate, soften, soothe, tone
누그러지다, melt, soften
누더기, rag, tatters
누더기가 된, tattered
누덕누덕한, ragged
누드화, nude
누락, omission
누락된, missing
누락하다, omit
(~를) 누르기만 하면, touch
누르다, dial, press, punch
누름, press
누리게 되다, develop
누리다, enjoy, reap
누명을 쓰다, set
누비고 다니다, criss-cross
누비다, weave
누비며 가다, weave
누비이불, quilt
누설, leak, revelation
누설하다, divulge, give, leak, talk

누워 있다, lie
누이, sister
누적되는, cumulative
누추한, sleazy, squalid
누추한 상태, squalor
누출, leak, seep
누출되다, leak
누출량, leakage
눅눅한, damp, humid, soggy
눅눅함, humidity
눈, bud, eye, snow
눈 깜짝할 사이, split second
눈 덮인, snowy
눈 뭉치, snowball
눈 주위의 멍, black eye
눈가리개, blindfold
눈감아 주다, overlook
눈금, scale
눈금판, dial
눈길, gaze
눈길을 끄는, eye-catching
눈길을 끌다, eye
눈길을 보내다, cast
눈길이 마주치다, meet
눈길이 머무르다, fall
눈꺼풀, eyelid
눈더미, drift
눈덩이, snowball
눈덩이처럼 불어나다, snowball
눈독을 들이다, eye
눈동자, pupil
눈멀게 하다, blind
눈물, tear
눈물 어린, tearful
눈물을 흘리다, weep
눈물을 흘리지 않는, dry
눈물이 나다, water
눈물이 흐르는, runny
눈보라, blizzard, flurry
눈부시게, dazzlingly
눈부시게 빛나다, glare
눈부시게 하다, dazzle
눈부신, blinding, dazzling,
  flamboyant, gaudy
눈부신 빛, glare
눈부심, dazzle
눈사태, avalanche
눈살을 찌푸리다, frown
눈썹, brow, eyebrow
눈썹을 뽑다, pluck
눈썹을 치켜 올리다, eyebrow
눈앞에 다가온, sight
눈에 거슬리는 것, eyesore
눈에 띄게, conspicuously, notably,
  remarkably, visibly
눈에 띄는, conspicuous,
  outstanding
눈에 띄다, evidence, eye, stick
눈에 띄지 않게, unobtrusively
눈에 띄지 않는, gray
눈에 보이지 않는, invisible
눈에 보임, visibility
눈에 안 보이게, invisibly
눈에 잘 띄는, catchy
눈을 가늘게 뜨고 보다, squint
눈을 가리다, blindfold
눈을 깜박이다, blink
눈을 뗄 수 없는, compulsive,
  riveting
눈을 뜨자마자, thing
눈을 찡그리고 보다, squint
눈을 휘둥그래지게 하는 것,
  eye-opener
눈의, optic
눈이 내리는, snowy
눈이 먼, blind
눈이 덞, blindness
눈이 부시도록, dazzlingly
눈이 오다, snow
눈이 퉁퉁 붓도록 울다, eye
눈치, tact
눈치 빠르게, tactfully
눈치 빠른, astute, tactful
(~을) 눈치 채다, wind
눌러서 닦아내다, blot
눌어붙지 않는, nonstick
눕다, lie
눕히다, lay

뉘앙스, nuance
뉘우치는, repentant
뉘우치다, repent
뉘우치지 않는, unrepentant
뉴스, news
뉴스 그룹, newsgroup
뉴스 단신, bulletin
뉴스 진행자, newscaster,
  newsreader
느긋하게, leisure, leisurely
느긋하게 만들다, slow
느긋하게 즐기다, hair
느긋한, easygoing, laid-back,
  leisurely, relaxed
느긋해지다, slow
(~을) 느끼다, come, feel, find,
  suffer
느낌, experience, feeling, idea,
  ring, sensation, sense, sound,
  suspicion, vibe
느낌표, exclamation point
느닷없이 ~하다, plunge
느릅나무, elm
느릅나무 목재, elm
느리게, slowly, slow
느리게 하다, slow
느린, sedate, slow
느린 구보, canter
느린 구보로 나아가다, canter
느린 동작, slow motion
느린 말투, drawl
느림, slowness
느릿느릿 말하다, drawl
느슨하게, loosely
느슨하게 하다, loosen, relax
느슨한, loose, slack
느슨해지다, ease, slacken
늑골, rib
늑대, wolf
늘, always, ever
늘 그런 식의, typical
늘 먹는 것, usual
늘 하는 일, usual
늘그막의, later
늘다, gain, increase, put
늘리다, increase, run, stretch
늘리지 않다, keep
늘어나다, add, expand, mount,
  stretch
늘어뜨리다, drape
늘어뜨린, loose
늘어선 열, bank
늘어지다, hang, sag
늘어진 부분, flap
늙다, age
늙은, old
능가하다, outdo, outstrip, surpass
능글능글한, smooth
능글맞게 웃다, smirk
능동태, active
능란한, slick
능력, ability, capability, capacity,
  competence, power
능력껏, ability
능력을 증가시키다, envelope
능력을 최대한 발휘하게 하다,
  stretch
(~할) 능력이 없는, incapable, inept,
  unable
능률, efficiency
능률화하다, streamline
능수능란하게, stuff
능수능란한, shrewd
능숙하게, expertly, skillfully
능숙하게 하다, fine art
능숙한, adept, crack, expert, good,
  proficient, skilled, skillful
능숙함, finesse, proficiency
(~에) 능하다, head
늦게, late
늦게 잠, night
늦게까지 안 자다, sit
늦어도, latest
늦은, late
늦지 않는, punctual
늦추다, loosen, put
늦춰지다, loosen

늪, marsh, swamp
니스, varnish
니켈, nickel
니코틴, nicotine
니트, jersey
니트의, knit
다 끝난, dead
다 떨어지다, run
다 빠지다, drain
다 써 버리다, swallow, use
다 써버리다, exhaust
다 자란, fully-fledged
다 자란 짐승, adult
다 채우다, complete
다 팔리다, sell
다가가다, approach, get, near
다가서다, close
다가오는, forthcoming, upcoming,
  way
다가오다, approach, beckon, come,
  draw, face, loom, near
다가올, ahead of, come, coming
다가옴, approach
다각화, diversification
다각화하다, diversify
다갈색의, dark
다과, hospitality, refreshment
다국적의, multinational
다그치다, push, railroad
다급하게, urgently
다급한, urgent
다급함, urgency
다년간, year
다년생의, perennial
다니다, attend, go, travel
다단계 판매, pyramid selling
다듬기, trim
다듬다, clip, trim
다락, loft
다락방, attic
다람쥐, squirrel
다량, heap, quantity, stack
다량으로, profusely
다량의, galore, profuse
다루기 쉬운, manageable
다루기 어려운, cumbersome,
  stubborn
다루기 어렵게, stubbornly
다루기 힘든, impossible,
  intractable, nasty, unwieldy
다루기 힘든 사람, handful
(~을) 다루는 사람, handler
다루다, care, cover, deal, handle,
  take, touch
다르게, differently, unlike
다르다, differ, diverge, vary
다른, another, different, dissimilar,
  distinct, else, other, unlike
다른 게 섞이지 않은, pure
다른 곳에, elsewhere, out
다른 곳으로 새다, stray
다른 길로 들다, branch
다른 내막, story
다른 데로 가다, wander
다른 두 지역을 잇는 땅덩어리,
  bridge
다른 목적으로 사용하다, redirect
다른 역할도 하다, double
다른 일을 벌이다, branch
다른 일을 시작하다, move
다른 측면, coin
다른 한쪽 편, end
다른 한편으로는, hand
다름, difference
다름 아닌 그, very
다리, bridge, leg
다리다, iron, press
다리를 놓다, bridge
다리미, iron
다림질, ironing
다림질하다, iron
다만, only
다목적성, versatility
다목적의, versatile
다문화적인, multicultural
다물다, shut
다민족의, multinational
다박나룻, stubble

다발, bunch, bundle, pack
다부진, rugged, stocky
다산의, prolific
다섯, five
다섯 번째, fifth
다세대 주택, flat
다소, extent, more, rather,
  somewhat, way
다소 숙련을 요하는, semiskilled
다소의, certain, few
다수, array, battery, heap
다수를 점하는, majority
다수의, majority, multitude,
  numerous
다스려 활용하다, harness
다스리다, curb, govern, nurse
다스릴 수 없는, uncontrollable
다시, again, anew, back
다시 갖다 놓다, return
다시 나타나다, reappear
다시 말하면, or
다시 맞붙게 되는 경기, rematch
다시 맞추다, readjust
다시 발휘되다, reassert
다시 분명히 말하다, reaffirm
다시 불을 붙이다, rekindle
다시 생각해 보니, second thought
다시 시작하다, get, relaunch
다시 악화되다, relapse
다시 유행하다, comeback
다시 적응하다, readjust
다시 정상 궤도에 오른, rail
다시 제자리에 놓다, replace
다시 조정하다, readjust
다시 찾아가다, revisit
다시 찾아오다, return
다시 채우다, refill, restock
다시 채움, refill, top-up
다시 체포하다, recapture
다시 하다, repeat, return
다시 한 번, once
다시 한 번 말씀해 주십시오, pardon
다시 한 번 알려 드릴게요, remind
다시는 ~하지 않아, never
다양성, diversity, portfolio, variety
다양하게, broadly
다양하게 갖춘, rich
다양한, broad, diverse, multiple,
  myriad, varied, various, wide
다양한 인종과 문화가 뒤섞인 장소,
  melting pot
다양한 종류의 사람으로 구성된,
  mixed
다양함, diversity, richness, spread
다양화, diversification
다양화하다, diversify
다용도의, versatile
다우닝 가, Downing Street
다운로드 하다, download
다원주의, pluralism
다음 것, next
다음과 같다, follow
다음번에, next
다음번으로 미루기, rain check
다음에 오는, following, next
다음의, following, next
다의성, ambiguity
다이너마이트, dynamite
다이빙, dive, diving
다이빙대, springboard
다이아몬드, diamond
다이아몬드 패, diamond
다이어트, diet
다이어트 중이다, diet
다이어트의, diet
다이얼, dial
다이제스트, digest
다인종의, multiracial
다임, dime
다자간의, multilateral
다작의, prolific
다재다능한, versatile
다재다능함, versatility
다정하게, affectionately, fondly,
  genially, lovingly
다정한, fond, genial, kind, loving,
  nice
다중의, multiple

다지다, chop, mince
다진 고기, mince
다채로운, assorted, colorful, eventful, riot
다치게 하다, hurt, injure
다치다, hurt
다치지 않은, unhurt, unscathed
다친, injured
다큐멘터리, documentary
다큐멘터리 드라마, docusoap
다투다, argue, compete, contend, dispute, fight, squabble
다툼, conflict, contest, squabbling, strife
다트 던지기 놀이, dart
다행, mercy
다행스러운, blessed
다행히, blessedly, fortunately, happily, luckily
다행히도, mercifully, thankfully
다혈질의, foul
닥쳐오는, around
닥쳐오다, happen
닥치는 대로, randomly, random
닥치는 대로의, random
닥치다, strike
닦기, wipe
닦다, brush, clean, cultivate, mop, polish, rub, wipe
닦달하다, badger
닦아내다, mop, wipe
단, column, corps, only, platform, rung, sweet, tier, unit, wing
단 것, sweet
단 것을 좋아함, tooth
단 음식, sweet
단 하나의, single
단가, unit cost
단거리 경주, sprint
단거리 주자, sprinter
단거리의, short-haul
단검, dagger
단결, solidarity
단결시키다, bind, rally
단결하다, band, rally, stick
단계, notch, phase, rung, scale, stage, step
단계적으로, gradually
단계적으로 도입되다, phase
단계적인, gradual
단골, regular
단골 거래, custom
단골 거래처, account
단골 장소, haunt
단골의, regular
단과 대학, college
단기 금융 시장, money market
단기 여행용의, overnight
단기 융자, bridge loan
단기 체류, stopover
단기 휴가, getaway
단기간의 심한 변화, roller-coaster
단기의, short-term
단기적으로, term
단기적으로 보면, run
단념시키는, deterrent
단념시키다, deter, discourage, dissuade
단념하다, despair, give, kiss, write
단단하게 하다, toughen
단단한, firm, hard, rigid, solid, tight, tough
단단함, hardness, rigidity
단단히, fast, firmly, securely, tightly, tight, tightly
단단히 고정된, secure
단단히 고정시키다, secure
단단히 놓다, plant
단단히 붙잡다, clasp
단단히 잡다, clench
단단히 지켜지는, secure
단단히 처려입다, wrap
단단히 혼을 내다, riot
단도직입적으로, point-blank
단도직입적으로 말해서, put
단독, detached
단독으로 재вы다하는, stand-up
단독의, sole, solitary, unilateral

단락, paragraph
단리, simple interest
단말기, terminal, workstation
단맛, sweetness
단맛이 없는, dry
단면, facet
단면도, cross-section, section
단명의, short-lived
단발성, isolated
단백질, protein
단번에, swoop
단상, platform
단색의, plain
단서, clue, lead
단서(但書), qualification
단속, bust
단속적으로, off, spurt
단속하다, bust
단수의, singular
단수형, singular
단순 기술의, low-tech
단순시제의, simple
단순한, mere, primitive, simple
단순한 것, simplification
단순함, simplicity
단순화, simplification
단순화된, simplistic
단순화하다, simplify
단순히 ~가 아닌, merely
단숨에, gallop
단식, fast, single
단식 투쟁, hunger strike
단식하기, fasting
단식하다, fast
단어, word
단어 정렬, word wrapping
단언하다, affirm, assert, profess, protest
단역 배우, extra
단연코, emphatically, far, foremost, way
단열재, insulation
단열하다, insulate
단원, unit
단위, unit
단위 원가, unit cost
단자, terminal
단장, cane
단절, chasm
단절시키다, cocoon
단절체, cocoon
단절하다, sever
단점, downside, drawback, imperfection, shortcoming
단정치 못하게, untidily
단정치 못한, groomed
단정한, groomed
단조로운, flat, monotonous, pedestrian, prosaic
단조로움, dullness
단지, development, estate, jar, just, merely, park, pot, simply
단지 ~만, alone
단지 ~일 뿐, only
단체, corps, fellowship, organization, society
단체 협상, collective bargaining
단체로 행동하다, gang
단체의, organizational
단추, button
단추 구멍, buttonhole
단추를 잠그다, button
단추를 풀다, open
단축, cut
단축 다이얼, speed dial
단축되다, compress, shorten
단축시키다, cut
단축키, hot key, short cut
단축하다, shorten
단축형, contraction
단층, fault
단편, snatch
단편적인, piecemeal
단풍나무, maple
단호하게, resolutely, ruthlessly
단호한, categorical, emphatic, firm, flat, gritty, resolute, ringing, set, strong,

uncompromising
단호히, categorically, determinedly, emphatically, firmly, flatly
닫다, close, exit, shut
닫집 모양의 차양, canopy
닫히다, close, shut
닫힌, shut
달, month, moon
달갑지 않은, unwelcome
달걀 모양, egg
달게 하다, sweeten
달관하여, philosophically
달관한, philosophical
달그락거리는 소리, rattle
달그락거리다, rattle
(~을) 달다, fit
달라붙는, sticky
달라붙다, adhere, latch, stick
(~에) 달라붙은, plastered
달라지다, diverge, vary
달랑거리다, dangle
달래기, appeasement
달래는, calming, conciliatory
달래다, appease, calm, humor, placate, soothe
달랠 수 없는, implacable
달러, buck, dollar
달려 있다, depend, hang, rest, ride
달려들다, pounce, snap
달력, calendar
(~와는) 달리, distinct, otherwise
달리게 하다, run
달리기, run, running
달리는 사람, runner
달리다, run
달리하다, vary
달빛, moonlight
달성, achievement, attainment
달성하다, accomplish, attain, effect, fulfill, pull, rack
달아나다, flee, get, run
달아오르다, flame, flush
달의, lunar
달인, master, wizard
달콤한, sweet
달콤함, sweetness
달팽이, snail
달팽이같이 느리게, snail
(~에) 달하다, come, creep, reach, run
닭, chicken
닭고기, chicken
닮다, resemble, take
(~을 닮으려 노력하다, mimic
닮은, twin
닮은 점, similarity
닮음, likeness
닳다, wear
닳아 없어지게 하다, wear
닳아 없어지다, wear
닳아 해어짐, wear
닳아 해진, worn out
담, wall
담갈색의, hazel
담겨 있다, enclose
(~을 담고 있다, contain, hold
담그다, immerse, soak
담금, dip
담낭, gall bladder
담담한, neutral
담담함, neutrality
담당, charge
담당 구역, area, beat
담당자게, sir
담당하는, responsible
담당하다, serve
담력, nerve
담론, discourse
담배, cigarette, tobacco
담배 피우기, smoke
담백한, mild
담뱃대, pipe
담보, collateral, guarantee, security, surety
담보가 붙은, bonded
담보를 잡다, secure
담수의, freshwater

담요, blanket
담으로 둘러싸인, walled
담쟁이덩굴, ivy
담합하다, fix
담화, discourse, speech
담황갈색, oatmeal
담황색, buff
답답한, brooding, close, restless, stifling, stuffy
답답함, restlessness
답례로, back, return
답변, plea
답변 바랍니다, RSVP
답변 없는, unanswered
답사, exploration
답사의, exploratory
답사하다, explore
답을 표시하다, check
답장, answer
답장하다, answer
닷컴 기업, dot-com
당구, billiards
당국, administration, authority
당근, carrot
당기는 힘, pull
당기다, pull
당나귀, ass, donkey
당뇨병, diabetes
당뇨병 환자, diabetic
당뇨병의, diabetic
당당하게, majestically
당당한, distinguished, majestic
당당함, majesty
당당히 비판하는, music
당돌하게, boldly
당돌한, bold, cheeky
당면한, immediate
당분, sugar
당분간, interim, present
당분간의, foreseeable, time
당선, election
당선된, elect
당시, day, then
당시의, then
당신, darling, you
당신 자신, yourself
당신들, you
당신의, your
당신의 것, yours
(~을) 당연시하다, grant
당연하게도, understandably
당연하다는 듯이, course
당연한, natural
당연히, absolutely, duly, logically, naturally, nature, of course, reasonably, rightfully
당연히 ~이 되다, follow
당의(糖衣), frosting, icing
당의(糖衣)를 입히다, ice
당장, right
당장은, meantime
당장이라도, minute
당좌 예금, current account
당좌 예금 구좌, checking account
당치 않은, obscene
당파, faction
당파심이 강한, partisan
당파적인, factional
당하게 하다, subject
당하기 쉬운, susceptible
당해도 싸다, serve
당혹, consternation
당혹감, bewilderment, dismay, embarrassment
당혹스러운, bewildering
당혹스러워 하는, dismayed, perplexed
당혹하게 하는, baffling, embarrassing
당혹하게 하다, baffle
당혹하게 하다, dismay
당황스러운, disconcerting
당황스럽게, disconcertingly
당황하게 만들다, rattle, unnerve
당황하게 하다, confound, fluster
당황하는, overwhelmed
당황하다, aback

당황한, perplexed, rattled, sheepish
닻, anchor
닻고리, eye
닻을 내리다, anchor
닿게 하다, touch
닿는 곳에, within
닿다, finish, meet, reach, touch
닿을 수 없는, range
닿을 수 있는, range
대, grand, range, stick
(~) 대(對), versus
대~, great
대가, authority, penalty, price, queen
대가를 치르고, price
대가를 치르다, pay
대가의, virtuoso
대각선으로, diagonally
대각선의, diagonal
대강, crudely
(~을) 대강 훑어 보다, eye
대강의, sketchy
대강의 정의, justice
대개, chiefly, generally, largely, mostly, normally, usually
대개는, main
대개의, general
대건축물, edifice
대걸레, mop
대걸레로 닦다, mop
대견하게도, credit
대결하다, confront
(~에) 대고 몸을 지탱하다, brace
대관식, coronation
대구, cod
대규모 탈출, exodus
대규모로, massively
대규모의, ambitious, epic, extensive, large-scale, massive, wholesale
대기, atmosphere
대기 중인, call, standby
대기 행렬, queue
대기업, big business, conglomerate
대기의, atmospheric
대기자, standby
대기자 명단, waiting list
대기자로, standby
대기하고 있는, wing
대기하다, stand
대나무, bamboo
대놓고, bluntly
대다수, bulk, majority, mass
대다수의 사람, many, multitude
대단원, finale
대단하게, extraordinarily
대단하다고 생각하다, think
대단한, great, keen, quite, some, towering, tremendous
대단한 것, something
대단한 인물, someone
(~라는 대단한 자리, dizzy
대단히, astonishingly, awfully, eminently, extremely, far, indeed, keenly, much, supremely, unusually, vastly
대단히 값진, priceless
대단히 귀중한, priceless
대단히 비싸게, price
대담, interview
대담무쌍한, fearless
대담하게, valiantly
대담한, audacious, bold, daring, intrepid, valiant
대담함, audacity, boldness
대답, answer, reply, response
대답하다, answer, reply
대대, battalion
대대적으로, force
대대적으로 개혁하다, shake
대대적인, far-reaching
대대적인 개혁, shakeup
대대적인 조사를 하다, trawl
대대적인 캠페인, blitz
대도시, metropolis
대도시의, metropolitan

대동하다, parade
대등하게, evenly
대등하다, match
대등한 것, parallel
대략, about, like, neighborhood, roughly, round, somewhere
대략의, rough
대략적으로, approximately
대략적인, approximate, ballpark, crude
대량 비축, stockpile
대량 살육하다, decimate
대량 생산, mass production
대량 생산의, mass-produced
대량 생산하다, mass-produce
대량 우편물, mailshot
대량 학살, genocide
대량 학살하다, decimate
대량으로, bulk
대량으로 계산을 처리하다, crunch
대량으로 비축하다, stockpile
(~을) 대량으로 소비하는, heavy
대량의, heavy, mass, wholesale
대령, captain, colonel
대로, avenue, boulevard
대류, continent, mainland
대륙 간의, intercontinental
대륙의, continental
대리, surrogate
대리 교사, sub, substitute teacher
대리모, surrogate mother
대리석, marble
대리의, surrogate
대리인, agent, alternate, caretaker, delegate, pp, relief, stand-in, sub
대리인을 통해, proxy
대리점, agency, dealership
대립, collision, confrontation
대립 상황, gridlock
대립되는, opposing
대립하다, conflict
대마초, marijuana, pot
대망, expectancy
대머리, baldness
대머리의, bald
대면하다, face
대명사, pronoun
대목, place
대목장, ranch
대못, spike
대문, gateway
대문자, capital, uppercase
대문자의, uppercase
대미를 장식하다, cap
대박을 터뜨리다, big time
대배심, grand jury
대번에, glance
대법원장, Chief Justice
대변 액수, credit
대변동, upheaval
대변인, mouthpiece, spokesman, spokesperson, spokeswoman
대변자, advocate
대변하다, speak
대본, script
대본을 쓰다, script
대부대, battalion
대부분, bulk, majority, most
대부분은, extent
대부분의, most
대비, provision, readiness, to
대비시키다, contrast
(~에) 대비하는, prepared
대비하다, guard, hedge, provide, scene
(~에) 대비하여, against, contrast, versus
(~을) 대비해서, case
대사, ambassador
대사관, embassy
대사관 직원, embassy
대사를 알려주다, prompt
대상, butt, object, subject
대상 포진, shingle
대상(隊商), caravan
대상이 되다, receive
대상자, claimant

대서양, pond
대서양을 횡단하는, transatlantic
대서특필하다, splash
대성공, bonanza
대성공을 거두다, jackpot
대성공의, roaring
대성공하다, far
대성당, cathedral
대성당 참사회 의원, canon
대소동, ferment, uproar
대수도원, abbey
대수롭지 않게, blithely
대수롭지 않은, little, minor
대수학, algebra
대시 기호, dash
대신 받다, hold
대신 일하다, cover
(~) 대신에, behalf, exchange, instead, lieu, place
대신의, alternative
대신하는 것, substitute
(~을) 대신하다, place, replace, represent, shoe, stand, substitute
(~을) 대신하여, for
(~을) 대신할 수 있는 것, substitute
대실업가, baron
대실패, debacle, fiasco
대안, alternative
대안 의학의, complementary
대안적인, alternative
대야, basin, washbasin
대양, ocean
대여섯, dozen
대역, band
대역폭, bandwidth
대열, line
대외비의, privileged
대외의, foreign
대외적인, external
대용, substitution
대용물, surrogate
대우, treatment
대위, captain
대유행, craze
대응책, counter
대응하다, respond
대의, cause
대의원, deputy
대의원회, caucus
대인 관계의, interpersonal
대자연, wild
대장장이, blacksmith
대저택, hall
(~와) 대적하다, contend
대접, reception
대접하다, entertain, treat
대조, contrast
대조시키다, contrast
대조적으로, contrast, opposed
대조하다, collate, draw
대주교, archbishop, primate
대중, many, mass, public
대중 매체, media
대중에 영합하는, gallery
대중의, public
대중의 시선을 받고 있는, gaze
대중의 평판, public relations
대중적 지지, popularity
대중적인, popular
대중화, popularization
대중화하다, popularize
대지, property
대차 대조표, balance sheet
대참사, catastrophe, disastrous
대처, attention
대처하다, deal, play
대체, displacement
대체되다, supersede
대체로, large, mainly, typically, whole
대체물, alternate, alternative
대체적으로, broadly
대체하다, replace, take
대초원, prairie
대추, date
대축척의, large-scale
대출, loan

대출 기관, lender
대출 이자율, lending rate
대출자, lender
대출하다, lend
대충, roughly
대충 놓다, stick
대충 만든, rough
대충 보다, dip
대충 읽다, look
대충 해치우다, corner
대충 훑어보다, glance
대충의, rough
대치 상황, stand-off
대치하다, substitute
대칭, symmetry
대칭적으로, symmetrically
대칭적인, symmetrical
대통령, president
대통령 임기, presidency
대통령 직위, presidency
대통령의, presidential
대퇴이두근, hamstring
대파, leek
대파하다, write
대판 싸움, bust-up
대패, plane
대패질하다, plane, shave
대패하여, run
대팻밥, shaving
대포, artillery, cannon
대폭 낮추다, slash
대폭 줄이다, hack, slash
대폭락, crash
대폭락하다, crash
대표, delegate, representation, representative
대표 선수로 출전하다, represent
대표단, contingent, delegation
대표자, rep, representative
대표작, masterpiece, showpiece
대표적 인물, exponent
대표적인, typical
대표적인 단면, cross-section
대표적인 예, advertisement
대표하다, represent, stand
(~) 대표해서, behalf
대피, evacuation
대피시키다, evacuate
대피처, shelter
대피하다, cover, evacuate
대하, prawn
대하다, regard, treat
대하소설, saga
대학, college, school, university
대학 강사, lecturer
대학 교수의 직, chair
대학 교육, higher education
대학 교정, campus
대학 진학 적성 검사, SAT
대학살, carnage, holocaust, massacre
대학생, undergraduate
대학원, graduate school, postgraduate
대학원생, graduate student, postgraduate
대학원의, postgraduate
(~에) 대한, for, of, over
(~에) 대한 공포, horror
(~에) 대한 기호, penchant
(~에) 대한 내성이 있는, tolerant
(~에) 대한 대가를 치르다, answer
(~에) 대한 반발, reaction
(~에) 대한 반작용을 보이다, react
(~에) 대한 방지책, hedge
(~에) 대한 비난, swipe
(~에) 대한 선호, penchant
(~에) 대한 시도, shot
(~에) 대한 심취, preoccupation
(~에) 대한 안목이, eye
(~에) 대한 열중, passion
(~에) 대한 염려, fear
(~에) 대한 요구, call
(~에) 대한 이야기를 그만두다, rest
(~에) 대한 지배권을 가진, control
(~에) 대한 책임, responsibility
(~에) 대한 책임이 크다, answer

(~에) 대한 추구, pursuit
(~에) 대한 추모비, memorial
(~에) 대한 필요, use
대항, rivalry
대항하다, counter
(~에) 대항하여, against
(~에) 대항해 싸우다, combat
(~에) 대해, about, for, regard, return, to
(~에) 대해 고삐를 바짝 죄다, rein
(~에) 대해 곰곰이 생각하다, meditate
(~에) 대해 끊임없이 지껄이다, go
(~에) 대해 노심초사하다, fear
(~에) 대해 들어 봤다, know
(~에) 대해 불평하다, groan
(~에) 대해 상술하다, enlarge
(~에) 대해 생각하다, think
(~에) 대해 알고 있다, know
(~에) 대해 열려 있는, open
(~에) 대해 책임이 있어, fault
(~에) 대해 최신 정보를 파악하다, track
(~에) 대해 흥분한, heated
(~에) 대해서, as, for, of, onto
대행사, agency
대행의, acting
대형 도매 매장, cash-and-carry
대형 보온통, urn
대형 슈퍼마켓, superstore
대형 쓰레기 수거통, skip
대형 쓰레기 컨테이너, Dumpster
대형 여객기, airliner
대형 천막, pavilion
대형유조 트럭, tanker
대형을 이뤄, formation
대혼란, chaos, havoc, mayhem
대화, conversation, dialog, talk, word
대화가, master
대화방, chatline
대화의, conversational
대화창, dialog box
대화체의, conversational
대화하다, converse, engage, talk
대회, competition, congress, contest, convention, event, game, rally
댐, barrage, dam, weir
더, better, more
(~보다) 더 가치 있다, outweigh
더 공부하다, brush
더 나아가, further
더 나은, better, preferable
더 낫다, beat
더 단단해지다, tighten
더 단단히 잡다, tighten
더 돋우다, stoke
더 많아지다, thicken
더 먼, farther
더 멀리, further
더 못한, lesser
더 빠른, quick
더 빨리 진행시키다, fast track
더 빽빽해지다, thicken
더 위의, upper
더 이상, any, anymore, further
더 적은, lesser
더 좋게는, preferably
더 좋아하다, prefer
더 좋았던 옛날, old
더 좋은, better, favorable
더 중요하다, override
더 큰 소리로 말하다, voice
(~을) 더 흥미롭게 하다, perk
더껑이, scum
더덕더덕 바르다, plaster
(~가) 더덕더덕 발린, plastered
더듬어 나아가다, grope
(~을) 더듬어 찾다, feel, fumble
더듬이, antenna
더디게, slowly
더딘, slow
더딤, slowness
더러운, dirty, filthy, foul, grimy, grubby
더러운 것, mess

더러운 성질, nastiness
더러운 일을 대신하다, dirty
더러워지다, taint
더럽혀진, tainted, tarnished
더럽히다, compromise, dirty, smudge, tarnish
더미, bale, heap, huddle, mass, pile, stack
더미로 묶다, bale
(~와) 더불어, together
더블, double
더블룸, double
더블베이스, double bass
더빙되다, dub
더없이 행복하게, blissfully
더없이 행복한, blissful
더욱, extra, further, more
더욱 더, increasingly, more
더욱이, furthermore, more
더운, hot
더위, heat
더하다, add, gather
더하여, and, over, top, upon
더할 나위 없이, perfectly
(~에) 더해, besides
덕망 있는, venerable
덕목, virtue
(~) 덕분에, thank, virtue
덕분이다, owe
(~) 덕분이라 생각하다, credit
(~의) 덕택인, indebted
던지기, toss
던지다, fling, pelt, pitch, pose, shoot, throw, toss
던지듯 내려놓다, dump
던짐, throw
덜, less
덜 익은, rare, young
덜다, soften
덜덜 떠는, dizzy
덜어 주다, relieve
덜어 줌, relief
덜커덕거리며 가다, bump
덜컥거리는, bumpy
덜컹거리는 소리, rumble, rumbling
덜컹거리다, jar
덜컹거리며 가다, rumble
덤벼들다, come, go, tackle, wade
덤불, brush, clump, scrub, underbrush, undergrowth
덤비다, take
덤핑으로 팔다, dump
덥석덥석 받아들이다, lap
덧대다, pad
덧댄, padded
덧붙다, add
덧붙여, addition, additionally
덧붙여 말하면, parenthesis
덧붙여 말하자면, incidentally
덧붙이는 말, postscript
덧붙이다, add
덧셈, addition
덧씌워지다, superimpose
덧없는, short-lived
덧창, shutter
덩굴 식물, climber, vine
덩어리, billow, block, bundle, chunk, clot, loaf, lump, mass
덩어리진, lumpy
덩치, heavy
덫, snare, trap
덫으로 잡다, snare
덫을 놓아 잡다, trap
덮개, hood
덮개 모양의 것, canopy
덮개가 달린, hooded
덮개가 없는, naked, open
덮개를 벗기다, uncover, unveil
덮다, close, cover, hide
(~을) 덮어, top
덮어 가리는 것, cloak
덮어 가리다, conceal, smother
덮어 감추다, obscure
덮어 끄다, smother
덮어주다, cover
덮이다, drape
(~으로) 덮인, clad
덮치다, pounce

더님, denim
데다, burn, scald
데려 가다, take
데려가다, bring, collect, get
데리고 가다, carry, get, lead, take
데리고 오다, bring, fetch
데리러 가다, call, collect, pick
데모, demo
데뷔, debut
데스크, desk
데시벨, decibel
데우다, heat, warm
데워지다, warm
데이지, daisy
데이터, data, information, input
데이터 뱅크, data bank
데이터 처리, data processing
데이터를 오염시키다, infect
데이터베이스, database
데이트, date
데이트 상대자, date
데이트 중이다, date
데치다, poach
데침, poaching
델리, delicatessen
덴, scald
도, bound, degree
도가 지나친, OTT
도관, duct
도구, implement, tackle, tool
도구 모음, toolbar
도구 한 벌, kit
도금한, gilt, -plated
도급을 맡은, contract
도급자, contractor
도기, pottery
도기 제조소, pottery
도끼, ax
도난당한, stolen
도넛, doughnut
도달하다, arrive, come, get, hit, reach
도대체, earth, ever, god, hell, how, world
도대체 누가, whoever, world
도대체 무엇, whatever
도대체 어디서, wherever
도대체 어디에, wherever
도덕, ethic, morality
도덕관념, moral
도덕군자인 척하는, righteous
도덕성, ethic, morality
도덕의, moral
도덕적 승리, victory
도덕적으로, ethically, morally
도덕적인, ethical, moral, righteous, virtuous
도둑, burglar, robber, thief
도둑맞다, rob
도둑이 들다, burglarize, burgle
도둑질, burglary
도드라지다, stand
도랑, ditch, trench
도래, advent, arrival, coming, dawning
도래하다, arrive, come
도량이 넓은, open-minded
도량이 넓음, open-mindedness
도려내다, cut
도로, road, route
도로 공사, roadworks
도로에 진입하다, pull
도리를 아는, reasonable
도리어, contrary
도리에 맞게, reasonably
도리에 맞음, reasonableness
도마뱀, lizard
도망, getaway
도망 다니는 범법자, outlaw
도망 중인, run
도망가다, flee
도망자, fugitive
도망치다, get, make
도망친, loose
도매, wholesale
도매상, wholesaler
도매상인, merchant
도매업, wholesaling

도매업자, wholesaler
도메인, domain
도메인 네임, domain name
도미노, domino
도미노 놀이, domino
도미노 효과, domino effect
도박, gamble, gambling, gaming
도박꾼, gambler, punter
도박업자, bookmaker
도박을 하다, gamble
도발, provocation
도발적인, challenging, provocative, suggestive
도배공, decorator
도배하다, paper, wallpaper
도보 여행, hike, hiking
도보 여행 하다, hike
도보 여행자, hiker
도보로 이동하는, foot
도산, failure
도산한, business
도살, slaughter
도살하다, destroy, slaughter
도살되다, put
도살하다, butcher
도서관, library
도선, lead
도선사, pilot
도수의, proof
도스, DOS
도시, city
도시 외곽 순환도로, beltway
도시락, box lunch
도시의, urban
도심, downtown
도심부, inner city
도심에서, downtown
도심을 벗어난, uptown
도심의, downtown
도심의 빈민 지역, inner city
도안, graphic
도안의, graphic
도야하다, hone
도약, bound, jump, leap
도약판, springboard
도약하는 사람, jumper
도약하다, leap
도어맨, porter
도예, ceramic
도와주다, hand, help
도용하다, plagiarize, poach, steal
도우미, helper
도움, aid, assistance, hand, help, turn
도움 전화 서비스, helpline
도움말, help
(~의) 도움을 바라다, lean
도움을 받도록 보내다, refer
도움을 얻다, enlist
도움을 주다, service
(~에) 도움이 되는, conducive, helpful, helpfully, helpful, instrumental, use
도움이 되다, assist, assistance, good, handy, help
도움이 되어 주다, oblige
도움이 되지 않는, unhelpful
도입, introduction
도입 부분, prologue
도입부, beginning
도입하다, bring, inject, introduce
도자 장신구, ceramic
도자 제품, ceramic
도장, seal, stamp
도장(塗裝), painting
도저히, possibly
도저히 상상할 수 없는, stretch
도적, bandit
도전, challenge, dare
도전권, shot
도전받지 않은, unchallenged
도전에 응하다, gauntlet
도전자, challenger
도전장을 던지다, gauntlet
도전적인, adventurous, bold, challenging
도전하다, challenge, dare, take
도제, apprentice

(~의) 도제가 되다, apprentice
도제살이, apprenticeship
도주, escape, getaway
도주하다, escape
도중에, process, way
도중에 멈추지 않는, nonstop
도착, arrival
도착적인, perverted
도착하는, incoming
도착하다, arrive, come, get, make, reach
도처에, everywhere, throughout
도처에 널려 있는, place
도청, tap
도청기, bug
도청하다, bug, eavesdrop, tap
도축, slaughter
도축하다, slaughter
도출하다, extract
도취감, euphoria
도취된, entranced, intoxicated
도취시키다, entrance
도취된, euphoric
도킹하다, dock
도토리, acorn
도표, chart, diagram, fig., figure, graph
도표로 그리다, plot
도피구, escape
도형, figure
도화선, fuse
독, dock, poison, venom
독가스, gas
독가스로 죽이다, gas
독감, flu
독단, dogma
독단적으로, dogmatically
독단적인, dogmatic
독단주의, dogmatism
독려하다, push
독립, independence
독립 영화, indie
독립 영화사, indie
독립 영화사가 만든, indie
독립구, borough
독립된, separate, sovereign
독립심, independence
독립의, independent
독립적으로, independently
독립적인, independent, self-sufficient, stand-alone
독립한, independent
독립해서 시작하다, strike
독립형의, stand-alone
독무, solo
독무를 추는 무용수, soloist
독백, monologue
독보적인, leading-edge
독불장군, maverick
독살, poisoning
독살하다, poison
독서, read, reading
독서가, reader
독선, self-righteousness
독선적인, self-righteous
독수리, eagle, vulture
독신의, single
독신주의자, celibate
독실하게, piously
독실한, devout, pious, religious
독실한 신자, devout
독액, venom
독을 가진, poisonous
독을 넣다, poison
독이 있는, poisonous, venomous
독자, audience, reader
독자 수, readership
독자적으로, independently
독자적인, independent, maverick
독자층, readership
독재 국가, dictatorship
독재 정권, dictatorship
독재자, dictator
독재적인, authoritarian, dictatorial
독점, monopolization, monopoly
독점 기사, exclusive
독점 기업, monopoly

독점 재산의, proprietary
독점권, franchise
독점의, exclusive
독점적으로, exclusively
독점적인, exclusive
독점하다, monopolize
독주곡, solo
독주자, soloist
독주회, recital
독직 사건, scandal
독차지, monopoly
독차지하다, monopolize
독창, solo
독창력, initiative
독창성, ingenuity, invention, inventiveness, originality
독창자, soloist
독창적으로, cleverly
독창적인, clever, ingenious, inventive, original
독촉장, reminder
독특하게, distinctively
독특한, different, distinctive, own, peculiar, unique
독특한 스타일, chic
독특함, peculiarity
독학, self-study
독한, strong
독한 증류주, liquor
독해 문제, comprehension
돈, dosh, dough, money
돈독한, strong
돈만 밝히는, mercenary
돈방석에 앉은, money
돈벌이 되는 일, moneymaker, moneyspinner
돈세탁, money laundering
돈세탁하다, launder
돈에 파묻힌, money
돈을 들이다, invest
돈을 모으다, save
돈을 받다, pay
돈을 벌다, money
(~에) 돈을 뿌리다, splash
돈을 쓰다, invest
돈을 추렴하다, chip
돈을 퍼붓다, money
돈을 함부로 쓰는, extravagant
돈이 남아도는, money
돈이 되는, lucrative
돈이 되다, pay
돈이 부족한, badly off, bad off
돈이 힘이다, money
돈보이게 하는, flattering
돋보이게 하다, adorn, highlight
(~보다) 돋보이다, upstage
돋우다, arouse
돌, rock, stone
돌 부스러기, grit
돌개바람, twister
돌게 만들다, piss
돌격, charge
돌격하다, charge
돌고래, dolphin
돌다, circulate, spin, turn
돌돌 말다, curl, roll
돌돌 말리다, curl
돌돌 말아 놓은 것, roll
돌려 따는, screw
돌려받다, reclaim
돌려서 고정하다, screw
돌려주다, give, return
돌리기, twist
돌리다, avert, deal, dial, divert, revolve, spin, turn, twist
돌멩이, rock, stone
돌발, flare-up, outburst
(~로) 돌변하다, mutate
돌보는, caring
돌보는 사람, caregiver, carer, caretaker
돌보다, attend, care, look, mind
돌봄, attention, care
돌아, around, back
돌아가는, indirect
돌아가다, loop, return, roll, round, turn
돌아다니다, circulate, flit, knock,

roam, travel, wander
돌아다님, wander
돌아버리다, crack
돌아서, around, round
돌아선, disaffected
돌아오는, around, return
돌아오다, resume
돌아옴, return
돌연변이, mutant, mutation
돌을 던지다, stone
돌이 많은, stony
돌이켜 보면, retrospectively
돌이키다, turn
돌이킬 수 없게, irrevocably
돌이킬 수 없는, irrevocable
돌진, charge, dash, lunge
돌진하다, charge, dash, lunge, rocket
돌출된, buck
돌출된 부분, bump
돌출하다, jut, protrude
돌파 공격, breach
돌파구, breakthrough
돌파하다, break, penetrate, smash
돌풍, blast, gust, sensation
돔, dome
돕다, aid, assist, help, there
동, copper, east
동강이, stub
동거하는, live-in
동결, freeze
동결시키다, freeze
동결하여, ice
동경, adoration
동경하는, wistful
동경하다, adore
동공, pupil
동굴, cave
동물같이 내부가 넓은, cavernous
동그라미, circle
동그라미를 치다, circle
동그랗게 말다, roll
동그랗게 볼록한 부분, ball
동기, cause, incentive, motivation, motive
동기 부여, motivation
동기(同氣), sibling
동기가 되다, spur
동기를 부여받다, motivate
동기를 부여하다, motivate
동기생, class
동남부, southeast
동등, parity
동등하게 간주하다, equate
동등한, equal, equivalent, tantamount
동등한 것, equivalent
동등한 사람, equal
동등한 조건에서, term
동등화, equalization
동떨어져 있다, divorced
동떨어진, remote, removed
동력 조향 장치, power steering
동력설비를 갖춘, motorized
(~을 동력원으로 하여 작동하다, run
동력을 공급하다, power
동료, associate, brother, colleague, companion, comrade, fellow, mate, peer, workmate
동료들, lad
동류, bird
동맥, artery
동맹, alliance
동맹국, ally
동맹을 맺은, allied
동메달, bronze medal
동명사, gerund
동물, animal
동물 보호 구역, sanctuary
동물 보호소, pound
동물 사육, farming
동물 세계, world
동물군, fauna
동물원, zoo
동물의, animal
동물학, zoology
동반 상승효과, synergy
동반 출마자, running mate

동반자, escort
동반자 정신, companionship
동방의, eastern
동봉하다, enclose
동부, east
동부의, eastern
동사, verb
동사의, verbal
동산, goods
동석, company
동성애, homosexuality
동성애 혐오, homophobia
동성애를 하는, homosexual
동성애를 혐오하는, homophobic
동성애의, gay, homosexual, pink
동성애자, gay, homosexual, queer
동성애자가 아닌, straight
동성애자의, queer
동성애의, gayness
동성연애자라고 폭로하다, out
동성연애자임을 밝힘, outing
동숙자, roommate
동시 발생, conjunction
동시대의, contemporary
(~와) 동시에, accompaniment, concurrently, once, simultaneously, tandem, time, together
동시에 다루다, juggle
동시에 말하다, chorus
동시에 발생하다, parallel
동시에 벌어지다, accompany
동시에 일어나게 하다, synchronize
동시에 일어나는, concurrent
동시에 일어나다, coincide
동시의, parallel, simultaneous
(~) 동안, during, for, in, while
(~) 동안 계속되다, extend
(~) 동안 내내, through
동양, east
동양의, eastern, oriental
동양풍의, oriental
동업 조합, guild
동업자, partner
동여매다, tie
동요, commotion, disquiet, ferment
동요되다, sway
동요시키는, unsettling
동요시키다, destabilize, rock, shake
동요하고 있는, unsettled
동요한, disturbed
동원, mobilization
동원 가능 인력, pool
동원 가능 자금, pool
동원되다, mobilize
동원하다, marshal, mobilize
동의, agreement, assent, motion, sympathy
동의어, synonym
동의어의, synonymous
동의하다, accept, agree, assent, buy, consent, go, move, share, subscribe
동이다, bind, wind
동일 업무를 시간제로 분담해서 근무하다, job share
동일성, uniformity
동일시, equation, identification
동일시하다, equate, identify, match
동일하게, uniformly
동일한, identical, same, uniform
동일한 근거, ground
동작, motion
동전, change, coin, piece
동전 넣는 구멍, slot
동전지갑, change purse
동점, all, draw, tie
동점을 만들다, equalize
동정, sympathy
동정심, pity
동정적으로, sympathetically
동정적인, sympathetic
동정하다, pity, sympathize
동조, alignment, blessing, sympathy

동조자, sympathizer
동조하다, align
동족의, related
동종 요법, homeopathy
동종 요법 치료사, homeopath
동종 요법의, homeopathic
동지, comrade, fellow
동지애, fraternity
동질의, homogeneous
동쪽, east
동쪽에서 부는, east, easterly
동쪽으로, east, eastward
동쪽으로의, eastward
동창, school friend
동체, body, fuselage
동틀 녘, sunrise
동포, brother, compatriot, countryman
동함, stirring
동행, company
동행하다, accompany, come, follow
동향, movement, pulse, wind
동화, assimilation, fairy tale
동화되다, assimilate
동화시키다, assimilate
돛, sail
돛대들, mast
돼지, hog, pig
돼지 같은 인간, pig
돼지고기, pork
됐어, thank
됐어.., all right
됐어요?, all right
되감기다, rewind
되감다, rewind
되는 대로의, random
되는 대로인, haphazard
되는대로, anyhow
되다, become, come, get, go, grow, make, reduce, such, turn
되돌려, back
되돌려 주다, return
되돌릴 수 없는, irreversible
되돌아가게 하다, turn
되돌아가다, go, reclaim, relapse, restore, return, revert, turn
되돌아감, relapse, return
되돌아보면, retrospect
되돌아오다, bounce, get, rebound
(~이) 되려고 하는, would-be
되받아, back
되받아치다, retort, volley
되사기, buy-back
되살리다, bring, refresh, revive
되살아나게 하다, rekindle
되살아나다, revive
되살아남, revival
되어 가다, fare
(~이라고) 되어 있다, go, in, meant, supposed
되짚어가다, retrace
되찾다, get, recapture, reclaim, recover, regain, salvage
되찾아, back
되찾을 수 있는, redeemable
되찾음, recovery
되튀다, rebound
되팔기, resale
되팔기하다, resell
되팔다, sell
되풀이하여, again
되풀이하여 외치다, chant
될 수 있는 대로, possible
(~해도) 될까요, could, would
두 가지로 해석될 수 있는, double-edged
두 가지의, twofold
두 개 언어의, bilingual
두 개의, double
두 나라 말을 하는, bilingual
두 눈 부릅뜨고 지켜보다, eye
두 달에 한 번, other
두 달에 한 번씩의, bimonthly
두 배, double, twice
두 배로, doubly
두 배로 하다, double
두 배의, double, twice

두 번, twice
두 번씩이나, over
두 번째, second
두 번째로, place
두 번째로 가장 좋은, second best
두 사람, pair
두 삼주문 사이, wicket
두 손만 비비대다, wring
두 얼굴의, two-faced
두 요소의, twofold
두 줄로 횡선을 긋다, cross
두각을 나타내다, distinguish, mark
두개골, skull
두건, hood
두건을 뒤집어쓴, hooded
(~을) 두고 머리를 싸매다, puzzle
(~을) 두고 머리를 짜다, puzzle
두고 보다, wait
두고 뵈, watch
두근거리다, pound, pulsate, thud, thump
두꺼비, toad
두꺼운, fat, thick
두꺼운 커튼, drape
두껍게, thickly
두껍고 평평한 조각, slab
두께, thickness
두께가 ~인, thick
두뇌, brain, head
두다, deposit, leave, locate, place, position, put, set, stand
두더지, mole
두드러지게, markedly, noticeably, strikingly
두드러지는, noticeable, outstanding
두드러지다, shine, show, stand
두드러진, bold, dominant, marked, prominent, striking
두드리다, beat, rap
두드림, rap
두들겨 패다, thump
두들기다, punch
두려운, afraid
두려운 것, specter
두려움, fear, horror
두려워하는, fearful
두려워하다, dread, fear
두려워하지 않는, undaunted
두루두루 영향을 미치다, cut
두루마리, roll, scroll
두루미, crane
두르다, skirt
두름수술, bypass
두리번거리다, wander
두문자 어, acronym
두서없는, discursive
두서없는 말, waffle
두서없이 쓰다, ramble
두서없이 지껄이다, waffle
두어 개, couple
두통, headache
두툼한, chunky
두피, scalp
둑, bank, dike, embankment, weir
둑처럼 쌓은 것, bank
둔각의, obtuse
둔감, insensitivity
둔감한, insensitive
둔기, club
둔기로 때리다, bludgeon, club
둔덕, bank
둔탁하게, dully
둔탁한, dull
둔한, slow, thick
둔화, slowdown
둘, two
둘 다, both
둘 중 하나, either
둘러, around
둘러대는, evasive
둘러댐, evasion
둘러보기, browse
둘러보는 손님, browser
둘러보다, browse, look
둘러싸는 것, cocoon
둘러싸다, circle, surround
(~에) 둘러싸이다, bound, frame,

hem, mob, ring, surround
둘레, circumference, perimeter
둘레가 ~인, round
둘레에, about, around, round
둘로 나누다, cut
둘의, dual
둘째, second, secondly
둥근, round, rounded
둥근 테, hoop
둥글게 말아 놓은 것, coil
(~을) 둥글게 굽히다, arch
둥글게 만들다, ball
둥글게 잘라내다, gouge
둥글게 파내다, gouge
둥글어지다, ball
둥둥 떠다니다, bob
둥둥 소리를 내다, drum
둥둥 치다, drum
둥우리, nest
둥지, nest
뒤, back
뒤꿈치, heel
뒤늦은, belated
뒤덮다, cover, shroud
(~로) 뒤덮이다, colonize, shower
뒤돌아보다, look
뒤따라, behind
뒤따르다, ensue, follow
뒤따른, ensuing
(~보다) 뒤떨어져, behind, touch
뒤떨어지지 않고, touch
뒤떨어진, backward, weak
뒤로 나앉다, seat
뒤로 되감다, wind
뒤로 물러서다, back
뒤로 젖혀지다, recline
뒤로 젖히다, recline
뒤로 하나로 묶은 머리, ponytail
뒤로의, backward
(~의) 뒤를 따라, behind
뒤를 밟다, track
뒤를 잇다, follow
뒤범벅, jumble
뒤섞다, jumble, muddle
뒤섞인, muddled up
뒤얽힌, entangled, involved
뒤엎다, overturn, upset
(~한) 뒤에, after, back, behind, following, time
뒤이어 하다, follow
뒤적거리다, rummage
뒤죽박죽, muddle
(~에만) 뒤지는, second
뒤지다, dig, go, hunt, ransack, root, search
뒤지지 않다, hold
뒤집다, invert, overturn, reverse, turn
(~을) 뒤집어엎다, tip
뒤집어져, over
뒤집어져서, inside
뒤집혀, upside down
뒤집히다, overturn, turn
뒤쪽, rear
뒤쪽에, aft
뒤쪽의, hind, rear
(~을) 뒤쫓는, pursuit
뒤쫓다, chase, follow
뒤처지다, fall, lag, leave
뒤처지지 않다, keep
뒤척이다, stir, toss, turn
뒤척거리다, toss
뒤통수를 긁적이며 고민하다, scratch
뒤통수를 치다, stab
뒤통수치기, stab
뒤틀다, distort
뒤틀리다, distort, twist
뒤틀린, distorted, perverse
뒤흔들다, ruffle, shake, surge, wiggle
뒤흔들다, shake
뒤흔들어 놓다, rock
뒤흔듦, wiggle
뒷거울, rear-view mirror
뒷걸음질, recoil
뒷걸음질치다, back
뒷걸음치다, recoil

뒷굽, heel
뒷다리로만 서다, rear
뒷마당, backyard
뒷말, gossip
뒷면, back, reverse, tail
뒷면에, overleaf
뒷면에 계속, PTO
뒷면이 인접하다, back
뒷문으로, door
뒷바닥, backing
뒷받침, credence, support
뒷받침하다, back, bear, prop, strengthen, support
뒷부분, back
뒷조사하다, check
뒷좌석의, backbench
뒹굴다, wallow
듀엣, duo
듀엣 곡, duet
드디어, finally, last
드라마, drama, soap, soap opera
드라이버, driver, screwdriver
드라이브, drive, ride, spin
드라이브스루, drive-through
드라이어, dryer
드라이클리닝하다, dry-clean
드래그, drag
드래프트, draughts
드러나다, come, emerge, express, light, prove, show, turn
드러내 놓고, eye, pointedly
드러내 놓고 하는, pointed
드러내 주는, telling
드러내다, bare, betray, display, expose, release, reveal, show, unlock
드러내어 보이다, expose
드러내지 않다, conceal
드러냄, display, release
드러머, drummer
드럼, drum
드럼통, drum
드레스, dress, gown
드리다, offer
드리블하다, dribble
드리워지다, fall, hang
드릴, drill
드릴로 구멍을 뚫다, drill
드림, yours
드문, rare, unusual
드문드문, sparsely
드문드문 섞인, interspersed
드문드문하게, thinly
드문드문한, sparse
드물게, rarely
드잡이, scuffle, tussle
드잡이하다, scuffle, tussle
득시글거리는, infested, overrun
득시글거리다, infest
득실거리다, crawl
득이 되는, rewarding
득점, goal, run, score
득점 게시판, scoreboard
득점을 막아 내다, save
득점자, scorer
득점하다, score
득표 차, majority
득표하다, poll
듣기 싫은, word
듣다, catch, hear, listen, work
듣자하니, apparently
들것, stretcher
들것으로 옮겨지다, stretcher
들게 하다, throw
들고 있다, hold
들고일어나다, rise
들끓는, infested, overrun
들끓다, infest, smolder, teem
들다, carry, drop, hold, lift, make, pick, take
들떠서, merrily
들뜨게 하다, buoy
들뜨다, buoy
들뜬, buoyant, electric, giddy, high
들뜬 기분, buoyancy
들러, around
들러 보다, try
들러붙다, latch

들려오다, drift
들르다, call, go, stop, visit
들름, stop
들리는, audible
들리는 곳에, within
들리도록, audibly
(~처럼) 들리다, sound
들보, beam
들볶다, hassle
들썩거리다, heave
들쑤시다, ransack
들어 보지도 못한, unknown
들어 본 기억을 살려 연주하다, ear
들어 본 일이 없는, unheard of
들어 봐, listen
들어 올리다, raise
들어 옮기다, scoop
(~에) 들어 있는, present
들어 있음, presence
들어가는 길, entry
(~에) 들어가다, enter, get, go
들어가서 머물다, jack
들어가지 못하게 하다, lock, shut
들어감, entrance
들어내다, cut
들어맞다, answer
들어맞음, fit
들어본 적이 있다, mean
들어서 알고 있다, hear
들어서다, go
들어오다, come
들어오지 못하게 하다, block
들어올려지다, hoist
들어올리는 기계, jack
들어올리는 장치, hoist
들어올리다, elevate, heave, hoist
들어올림, heave
들여다보다, check
들여보내 주다, let
들여보내다, admit, let
들여오다, import
들이다, develop, put, spend
들이닥치다, descend
들이마시다, inhale
들이밀다, poke
들이받다, run, slam, smash
들이쉬다, draw, gulp, take
들쭉날쭉한, inconsistent,
　　ragged
들추다, dredge
들치기, shoplifting
들치기범, shoplifter
들치기하다, shoplift
들통, bucket
들통 나다, rumble
들판, field
들판으로, country
(~인) 듯이, seemingly
등, back
등 뒤에서, back
등 짚고 뛰어넘기, leapfrog
등가, parity
등가물, equivalent
등가의, equivalent
등고선, contour
등급, grade, notch, rating, scale,
　　tier
등급을 매기다, place
등급이 매겨지다, grade
등기, registry
등기 서류, deed
등기관, registrar
등대, beacon, lighthouse
(~) 등등, etc., so
등딱지, shell
등록, enrollment, registration
등록 번호, registration number
등록부, register, roster
등록소, registry
등록시키다, enroll, enter
등록하다, enroll, join, register, sign
등반, ascent, climb, climbing
등반가, mountaineer
등받이, back
등변 등각의, regular
등불, beacon, lamp
등불용 석유, kerosene
등뼈, spine, vertebra

등산, climbing
등산가, climber
등성이, ridge
등용, elevation
등용하다, elevate
등위, number, position
등유, kerosene, paraffin
(~에게) 등을 돌리다, turn
등이 굽은, bent
등장, appearance, emergence,
　　entrance, entry
등장인물, character
등장하다, emerge
등쳐먹다, fleece
등호, equal sign
등화관제, blackout
디 아이 와이, DIY
디디다, step
디렉터리, directory
디브이디, DVD
디비전, division
디스인플레이션, disinflation
디스켓, diskette
디스코, disco
디스크, disk
디스크 드라이브, disk drive
디스크 자키, disc jockey, DJ
디스플레이, display
디엔에이, DNA
디자이너, designer
디자인, design, style
디자인하다, design, style
디저트, dessert, pudding
디저트용 단 음식, sweet
디젤엔진, diesel engine
디젤유, diesel
디지털 라디오, digital radio
디지털 방식의, digital
디지털 카메라, digicam, digital
　　camera
디지털 텔레비전, digital television,
　　digital TV
디폴트 값, default
디플레이션, deflation
디플레이션의, deflationary
딜레마, dilemma
따가운, sore
따각거리는 소리, rattle
따끔거리는, prickly
따끔거리다, sting, tingle
따끔거림, tingling
따끔하게 하다, sting
따끔하게 혼내다, lesson
따끔함, prick, sting
따다, pick, pluck
따돌리다, outwit, shake
따돌림 받는 사람, outcast
따뜻하게, cordially, warmly
따뜻하게 하다, warm
따뜻한, cordial, warm
따뜻한 느낌을 주는, warm
따뜻해지다, warm
(~에) 따라, according to, along, at,
　　by, conformity, depend, down,
　　up
(~을) 따라 나 있다, hug
따라 나아가다, keep
따라 부르다, sing
(~을) 따라 죽 늘어서다, line
따라 하다, follow, imitate, repeat
따라가다, follow, tag
따라다니며 괴롭히다, hound
따라서, accordingly, after, so, with
(~을) 따라서 가다, follow
따라오다, follow
따라잡다, catch, close
따로, aside
따로 남겨 두다, put
따로 떼어 두다, set
따로 떼어서, isolation
따로 마련해 두다, set
따로 배정하다, earmark
따로 불러서 이야기하다, side
따로 표시해 두다, mark
따로따로, separately
따르다, accept, bind, comply,
　　conform, fill, follow, go, listen,
　　obey, pour, yield

따르지 않다, rank
따분하게 웅웅거리다, drone
따분한, gray, loose end, prosaic,
　　routine
따옴표, inverted commas,
　　quotation mark, quote
(~) 따윈 상관없다, hell
따져 보다, debate
(~라더니) 딱 그 짝이다, talk
딱 부러지게, briskly
딱 부러지는, brisk
딱 부러지는 말투의, clipped
딱 소리를 내다, snap
딱딱 부딪치다, chatter
딱딱거리다, snap
딱딱하게, primly, stiffly
딱딱하지 않은, light
딱딱한, hard, prim, serious, stiff
딱딱한 껍질, crust, rind
딱딱한 표지로 제본한 책, hardback
딱딱함, hardness
딱정벌레, beetle
딱지, scab
딱하게도, pitifully
딱한, pitiful, sorry
딱한 일, shame
딴 돈, winnings
(~와) 판in이다, belie, buck
딸, daughter, girl
딸기, strawberry
딸꾹질, hiccup
딸꾹질하다, hiccup
딸랑딸랑 소리, jingle
딸랑딸랑 울리다, jingle
딸랑이, rattle
땀, perspiration, sweat
땀에 젖은, sweaty
땀을 흘리다, sweat
땅, earth, ground, soil
땅거미, twilight
땅딱딱한, chunky, squat
땅뙈기, patch
땅바닥, ground
땅속의, underground
땅에 닿다, land
땅콩, peanut
땋다, braid, plait
땋은 머리, braid, plait
(~할) 때, as, dirt, hour, in,
　　occasion, on, time, when
때 묻지 않은, innocent
때 묻지 않음, innocence
때 이르게, prematurely
때 이른, premature
때가 늦기 전에, going
때가 되어, due
(~할) 때가 된, ready
(~할) 때까지, pending, till, until
(~할) 때는 언제나, whenever
때때로, every, occasionally,
　　sometimes
때때로 끊기는, intermittent
때때로의, occasional
때려 부수다, smash
때려눕히다, flatten, knock
때려부수다, bust
때려치우다, chuck
때로는, maybe, time
때를 가리지 않고, hour
때를 기다리다, hold
때리다, beat, clout, hit, strike
때림, beat, beating, clout
때마침, happen
때마침 잘된, well
때맞추어 해내다, keep
(~) 때문에, account, as, because,
　　being, due, out, owe, since,
　　virtue, with
(~) 때문에 압박을 받는, pressed
(~) 때문인, due
때우다, patch
떠가다, float
떠나, off
떠나가다, go, vacate
떠나게 되다, uproot
떠나고 싶어 발바닥이 근질거림,
　　itchy
떠나기 시작하다, move

떠나는 것으로 반대 의사를 표시하다,
　　vote
떠나다, abandon, desert, get, go,
　　leave, make, move, quit, uproot
떠내려 가다, wash
떠내려 보내다, wash
떠다니다, float
떠돌다, drift
떠돌이, tramp
떠드는 소리, ranting
떠들썩하기만 한 일, circus
떠들썩한, boisterous, tumultuous
떠들썩한 파티, rave
떠들어 대다, rant
떠맡기다, land
떠맡다, account, assume, shoulder,
　　take
떠밀기, shove
떠밀다, bundle, jostle, shove
떠밀어 넘어뜨리다, push
떠받치다, hold, support
떠벌리다, boast
떠서, afloat
떠안기다, press
떠오르게 하다, invoke
떠오르는, budding,
　　up-and-coming
떠오르다, come, hit, occur, rise,
　　think
떠올리다, conjure, head, reflect
떡 벌어진, burly
떡구다, lower
떨다, quake, quiver, shake,
　　tremble, vibrate
떨리는, shaky
떨리다, quiver, shake, tremble
떨림, quiver, shiver, tremble,
　　vibration
떨어뜨리다, depress, detract,
　　dilute, drop, shed
떨어져, apart, away, off
떨어져 나간, missing
떨어져 있는, far
떨어지다, break, come, detach,
　　drop, fall, separate, sink, slip
떨어진, back, clear, out, separated
떨어질 수 없는, inseparable
떨어짐, separation, tumble
떨쳐 버리고, aside
떨쳐 버리다, banish, shake, shrug
떨치다, shake
떳떳하지 못한, guilty
떳떳한 마음, conscience
떼, cluster, colony, flock, herd,
　　horde, shoal, swarm
떼 지어 다니다, swarm
떼 지어 모여들다, crowd
떼다, detach
떼를 지어 이동하다, swarm
떼어 내다, break, disconnect
떼어 놓다, separate
떼어 놓을 수는 없는, together
떼어 두다, reserve
떼어 주고 남은 쪽, stub
떼어서 생각하다, dissociate
뗏목, raft
뗏장, turf
또, and, yet
또 하나의, another
또는, or
또는 그 반대, otherwise
또는 그에 가까운 값으로, o.n.o.
또다른, another
또래, peer
또렷하게, clearly
또렷한, clear
또한, also, either, so, together, well
(~도) 또한 아니다, neither, nor
똑 떨어지는, no-nonsense
똑같은, double, identical, same,
　　uniform
똑같이, equally, identically,
　　likewise, uniformly
똑같이 닮은 사람, double
똑딱거리는 소리, ticking
똑딱거리다, tick
똑딱똑딱 소리, tick
똑똑 떨어뜨리다, drip

똑똑 떨어지다, dribble, drip
똑똑 흐르다, dribble
똑똑하게, intelligently
똑똑한, clever, smart
똑똑한 체하는 사람, know-it-all
똑똑히, distinctly, specifically
똑똑히 말하다, articulate
똑바로, bolt, squarely, straight
똑바로 선, erect
똑바로 앉다, sit
똑바르게 하다, straighten
똑바른, straight, upright
똥, crap, shit
똥 누다, shit
뚜껑, cap, lid, top
뚜렷이, distinctly, sharply, tellingly
뚜렷이 나타내다, show
뚜렷이 내세우다, assert
뚜렷이 드러나다, show
뚜렷하게, palpably, starkly, unequivocally
뚜렷하지 않은, indecisive
뚜렷한, bold, clear-cut, distinct, evident, palpable, pronounced, sharp, stark, unequivocal
뚜렷한 우승 후보자가 없는, open
뚜쟁이, pimp
뚫고 나가다, weather
뚫고 나오다, thrust
뚫고 들어가다, blast, breach
뚫고 들어갈 수 없는, impenetrable
뚫고 지나가다, rip
뚫고서, through
뚫다, bore, breach, open, pierce
뚫리다, open
뚫어져라, hard
뚫어지게 보다, gaze, peer
뚱뚱한, gross, obese, stout
뚱하게, morosely, sourly
뚱한, dour, morose, sour, sullen
뛰놀다, romp
뛰다, beat, jump, leap, run
뛰어 들어오다, storm
뛰어가다, chase
뛰어나게 잘하다, shine
뛰어나다, excel
뛰어난, accomplished, outstanding, prize, strong, top
뛰어난 재능이 있는, gifted
뛰어내리다, bail, jump
뛰어넘다, better, hurdle, jump, leapfrog, surpass, vault
뛰어들다, dive, plunge
뛰어듦, plunge
뛰어오르다, jump, leap, spring
뛰쳐나가다, storm
뛸 듯이 기뻐하다, joy
뜨개질감, knitting
뜨개질하기, knitting
뜨거운, hot, missionary
뜨거운 감자, potato
뜨거운 논란거리, hot button
뜨거운 정도, heat
뜨다, carve, float, knit, open, rise
뜬, open
뜯다, break, pluck
(~을) 뜯어내다, screw, strip, take
뜯어먹다, graze
뜯어지다, break
뜰, ground, yard
뜻, will
뜻밖에, unexpectedly
뜻밖에 찾아듦, stroke
뜻밖의, surprise, unexpected
뜻밖의 사실, revelation
뜻밖의 일, surprise
뜻밖의 횡재, windfall
(~의) 뜻에 따르는, disposal
뜻풀이, definition
뜻하다, get, intend, translate
뜻하지 않은, casual
띄엄띄엄, interval, spurt
띄우다, float
띠, band, ribbon, strap
띠 같이 생긴 것, band
띠다, in, take
라거, lager
라디에이터, radiator

라디오, radio, wireless
라디오 방송, radio
라디오 프로그램, radio
라벤더, lavender
라벨, label
라벨이 붙어 있다, label
라운드, round
라운지, lounge
라이브 공연, gig
라이브 공연의, concert
라이브로, live
라이터, lighter
라이트급, lightweight
라일락, lilac
라켓, racket
라틴 아메리카 사람, Hispanic
라틴 아메리카 출신의, Hispanic
라틴 아메리카의, Latin American
라틴 아메리카인의, Latin American
라틴계의, Latin
라틴어, Latin
란제리, lingerie
랍스터, lobster
랍스터 요리, lobster
래커, lacquer
래퍼, rapper
랜, local area network
랠리, rally
램, RAM
램프, ramp
랩, film, plastic wrap, rap
랩을 하다, rap
러닝메이트, running mate
러시아워, rush hour
러비, rugby
런던의 금융 중심가, City
럼주, rum
레게, reggae
레깅스, leggings
레드카드, red card
레모네이드, lemonade
레몬, lemon
레버, lever
레뷔, revue
레슬링, wrestling
레슬링 선수, wrestler
레슬링을 하다, wrestle
레이더, radar
레이서, racer
레이스, lace
레이스로 된, lacy
레이아웃, layout
레이저, laser
레이저 프린터, laser printer
레인, lane
레인지, range
레인코트, raincoat
레저용 차량, RV
레즈비언, dyke, lesbian
레즈비언의, lesbian
레지던트, resident
레코드, record
레코드 재킷, sleeve
레코드판, vinyl
레퍼토리, repertoire, repertory
렌즈, lens
렌치, wrench
로고, logo, marking
로그아웃하다, log
로그인하다, log
로데오, rodeo
로드, Rd.
로마 교황의 교서, bull
로마 교황청, Vatican
로마 숫자, Roman numeral
로마 시민, Roman
로마의, Roman
로마인, Roman
로맨스, romance
로밍 서비스, roaming
로봇, robot
로비, foyer, lobby
로비 단체, lobby
로비하다, lobby
로션, lotion
로스트, roast
로열티, royalty

로우, row
로제, rosé
로케이션, location
로켓, rocket
로켓 미사일, rocket
로큰롤, rock and roll
로터리, roundabout, traffic circle
록 음악, rock
롤러, roller
롤러블레이드, Rollerblade
롤러블레이드 타기, rollerblading
롤러스케이트, roller-skate, skate
롤러스케이트를 타다, roller-skate
롤러스케이트장, rink
롤러코스터, roller-coaster
롤빵, roll
롬, ROM
루비, ruby
루비빛, ruby
루틴, routine
룰렛 게임, roulette
룸 서비스, room service
룸메이트, flatmate, roommate
룸메이트이다, room
르네상스, renaissance
리그, league
리넨, linen
리넨 제품, linen
리더보드, leaderboard
리더십, leadership
리드, reed
리드미컬하게, rhythmically
리드미컬한, rhythmic
리드타임, lead time
리듬, beat, rhythm
리모컨, remote control
리무진, limousine
리바이벌, revival
리바이벌하다, revive
리베이트, rake-off
리본, ribbon
리본 모양의 상, rosette
리본 모양의 장식, rosette
리볼버, revolver
리셉션, reception
리얼리즘, realism
리얼리티 텔레비전 프로, reality TV
리코더, recorder
리콜하다, recall
리큐어, liqueur
리터, liter
리필제품, refill
리허설, rehearsal
린치, lynching
린치를 가하다, lynch
릴, reel, spool
릴레이 경주, relay
립스틱, lipstick
립싱크하다, mime
링, ring
링바인더, ring binder
링크, link
링크하다, link
마가린, margarine
마감, cut-off
마감 기한, deadline
마감재, binding
마개, plug, top
마구 두드리다, pound
마구 때리다, knock, thrash
마구 부리다, order
마구 설레다, tingle
마구 설렘, tingle
마구 쏘아 대다, spray
마구 자르다, hack
마구 지껄이다, rave
마구 질문을 퍼붓다, grill
마구 차다, knock
마구 퍼부음, torrent
마구 퍼붓다, pelt
마구 흔들다, flail
마구 흔들리다, flail, shudder
마구(馬具), harness
마구간, stable
마구를 달다, harness
마구잡이로, haphazardly
마귀할멈, witch

마그네틱의, magnetic
마네킹, dummy
마녀, witch
마녀 사냥, witch-hunt
마늘, garlic
마다할 리가 없다, say
마당, yard
마디, bar
마땅한, logical
마땅하게, logically, richly, rightfully, well
마땅히 있어야 할, rightful
마땅히 지급되어야 할, due
마라톤, marathon
마라톤 같은, marathon
마력, horsepower
마련하다, arrange, find, lay, organize, raise
마련해 두다, fit, fix
마루, deck
마룻장, floorboard
마르고 쭈글쭈글한, withered
마르고도 강인한, wiry
마르는, dry
마르다, dry, run
마르지 않은, tacky, wet
마르크스주의, Marxism
마르크스주의자, Marxist
마른, dry, thin
마름, dryness
마름모꼴, diamond
마름병, blight
마름질 되다, cut
마리화나, cannabis, marijuana
마리화나 담배, joint
마멀레이드, marmalade
마모, wear, wear and tear
마모되다, wear
마모된, bald
마모시키다, wear
마무리, conclusion, finish
마무리 손질, finish
마무리하다, finish
마법, magic, spell, witchcraft
마법과 같은, magic
마법사, witch, wizard
마법을 지닌 낱말, magic
마법의, magic, magical
마법의 숫자, magic
마법처럼, magically
마부, groom
마분지, cardboard
마비, paralysis
마비되다, paralyze
마비된, paralyzed
마비시키다, numb
마사지, massage
마사지하다, massage
마손, wear and tear
마수, clutch
마술, magic
마술사, magician
마스카라, mascara
마스코트, mascot
마스크, mask
마스크를 쓴, masked
마시다, down, drink
마약, dope, drug, narcotic
마약 거래자, dealer
마약 중독자, junkie
마약에 취한, stoned
마약을 먹이다, dope
마요네즈, mayonnaise
마우스, mouse
마우스 버튼을 누르다, click
마우스 패드, mouse mat, mouse pad
마우스의 오른쪽 버튼을 클릭하다, right-click
마우스피스, mouthpiece
마운드, mound
마을, town, village
마음, feeling, heart, imagination, psyche
마음 내키지 않는, faint
마음 설레게 하는, exciting
마음 터놓고, freely
마음 편히, home

마음껏, heart, heartily
마음껏 ~하게 하다, spoil
마음껏 즐기다, feast
마음대로 가져가다, help
마음대로 주무르다, manipulate
마음속 가장 깊은 곳에서부터, heart
마음속에, heart
마음속에 그리다, picture, visualize
마음속에 떠오르다, mind
마음속에 뚜렷이 남아 있다, mind
마음속으로, inside, inwardly, mind
마음속을 터놓다, heart
마음속해, inward
마음씨, heart
마음씨가 따뜻한, warm
마음에 걸리는, mind
(~을) 마음에 두다, heed
마음에 드는, likeable, liking
마음에 드는 사람, darling
(~의) 마음에 들도록, satisfaction
마음에 새겨지다, register
마음에 안 드는, unsympathetic
마음에 품다, entertain, imagine
마음에서 우러난, heartfelt
마음으로부터의, hearty
마음은 착한, heart
마음을 굳게 먹다, steel
마음을 끄는, engaging, inviting, magnetic, tempting, winning
마음을 끄는 것, magnet
마음을 끄는 힘, magnetism
마음을 끌 만큼, temptingly
마음을 끌다, draw, engage
마음을 돌리다, come
마음을 바꾸게 하다, mind
마음을 바꾸다, mind
마음을 사로잡는, riveting
마음을 상하게 하다, sting
마음을 숨김, reserve
(~에) 마음을 쓰다, mind
(~의) 마음을 어지럽히다, disturb
(~에) 마음을 열다, mind, open
마음을 움직이다, chord
마음을 잘 드러내지 않는, private
마음을 좋이게 하다, suspense
마음을 찢어 놓다, tear
마음을 흔들어 놓다, affect
마음의, moral
마음의 울림, resonance
마음의 준비를 하다, brace
마음의 짐을 덞, mind
마음의 평화, peace
(~에) 마음이 끌리는, warm
마음이 내키게 하다, incline
(~할) 마음이 내키는, inclined
마음이 내키다, incline
마음이 내키지 않는, unprepared
마음이 누그러지다, relent
(~할) 마음이 들다, inclined
마음이 빼앗긴, preoccupied
마음이 어수선하여, distractedly
마음이 잘 맞는, wavelength
마음이 잘 통하는, compatible
마음이 잘 통함, compatibility
마음이 좁은, narrow-minded, petty
마음이 편안한, ease
마음이 편치 못한, uncomfortable
마음이 홀가분한, mind
마음이 홀림, fascination
마이너스, minus
마이너스의, minus, negative
마이크, microphone, mike
마이크로 파이버, microfiber
마이크로칩, microchip
마이크로프로세서, microprocessor
마일, mile
마임, mime
마임으로 보여 주다, mime
마조히스트, masochist
마조히즘, masochism
마조히즘적인, masochistic
마주 보고, face
(~와) 마주 보다, face
마주치다, meet, run
(~와) 마주침, encounter
마중 나가다, meet
마지막, end, finish, gasp, last
마지막 남은, last

마지막 남은 것, last
마지막 부분의, later
마지막 사람, last
마지막 순간, moment
마지막 순간까지, wire
(~을) 마지막까지 놔두다, last
마지막에, lastly
마지막으로, conclusion, finally, for, last, lastly
마지막의, closing, dying, final, last
마지못해, grudgingly, reluctantly, unwillingly
마지못해 내놓다, cough
마지못해 하는, grudging, unwilling
마진, spread
마차, coach
마찬가지, same
마찬가지로, again, like, likewise, token, way
마찬가지의, same
마찰, friction, misunderstanding
마천루, skyscraper
마취사, anesthetist
마취성의, narcotic
마취의, anaesthetist, anesthesiologist
마취제, anesthetic, narcotic
마치 ~인 것처럼, if, like
마치 ~처럼, as
(~에서) 마지다, end, knock, wind, wrap
마침내, end, eventually, last
마침표, full stop, period
마케팅, marketing
마케팅 전문가, marketeer, marketer
마케팅하다, market
마크, marking
마호가니, mahogany
막, act, covering, curtain, film, just, skin
막 ~하려는, ready
막 ~하려고 할 때, point
막 대하는, familiar
막 대하며, familiarly
막 대함, familiarity
막 싹트기 시작한, budding
(~을) 막 하려고 하는, about
막가는 사람, cowboy
막간, interlude
막다, avert, avoid, bar, block, break, clog, close, counter, counteract, fend, hold, jam, keep, obstruct, plug, preclude, shield, shut, snuff, stand, stem, stop, ward
막다른 골목, dead end, impasse
막다른 끝, end
막다른 지경에 이른, tether
막대그래프, bar chart, bar graph
막대기, pole, rod, stick
막대기 모양의 것, stick
막대하게, extensively
막대한, bumper, huge, untold
막대한 양, ocean
막무가내의, willful
막바지에 이르다, come
막사, camp
막상막하로, neck
막상막하의, even
막연한, indefinite
막자사발, mortar
막중함, enormity
막판 대결, showdown
막판으로 내몰린, last-ditch
막혀 있는 것, blockage
막히지 않은, uninterrupted
막힌, stuck
막힘, blockage
만, bay, cove, gulf
만곡, arch, twist
만기, maturity
만기가 되다, expire, mature, run
만끽하다, savor, soak
만나는 장소, rendezvous
만나다, catch, cope, intersect, join, meet, rendezvous, see
만남, meeting, rendezvous

만년, ripe
만년의, later
만능의, all-around
만담꾼, comic
만든, built, of
만들다, build, fix, force, form, make, model, render, set
만들어 내다, make, present, put
만들어 낸, made-up
(~에) 만들어 넣다, build
만들어지다, form
만료되다, run
만류, discouragement
만류하다, discourage
만만찮은, challenging, formidable
만반의 준비를 갖추다, kit
만병통치약, panacea
만사가 잘되면, god
만사를 잘 알고 있다, stuff
만성적으로, chronically
만성적인, chronic
만시지탄의 감을 주는, overdue
만신창이, tatters
만신창이가 되다, mutilate
만약, if
만약 ~이면, provided, providing
만약을 대비해서, safe
만연하는, infest
만연한, infested, rampant, rife
만용, heroic
만원의, full
만일, if
만일을 위하여, case
만장의 갈채를 받다, house
만장일치, unanimity
만장일치로, man, unanimously
만장일치의, unanimous
만져 보다, explore, feel
만족, contentment, gratification, joy, satisfaction
만족감, glow
만족감을 주는, fulfilling, satisfying
만족스러운, fine, fulfilled, gratifying, pleased, right, satisfactory
만족스러워 하는, content
만족스럽지 못한, unsatisfactory
만족시키다, fulfill, gratify, satisfy, suit
만족을 모르는, insatiable
만족을 못 느끼는, unfulfilled
만족하는, satisfied
만족하다, fulfill, settle
만족한, content, contented, happy
만족해하다, gratify
만지기, touch
만지다, finger, touch
만지면 느껴지는 통증, tenderness
만지면 아픈, tender
만지작거리다, fiddle, fidget, play
만질 수 없는, intangible
만질 수 있는, tangible
만찬, dinner, supper
(~할) 만하다, deserve, fit
(~할) 만한, worth
만행, brutality, savagery
만화, strip
만화 영화, cartoon
만화가, cartoonist
만화영화의, animated
만화책, comic, comic book
만회하다, recoup, recover, retrieve
많아야, most
많은, body, cascade, deal, deep, galore, generous, great, heavy, hefty, high, host, hundred, large, load, lot, many, much, plenty, rich
많은 것, lot, many
많은 것을 말해 주는, volume
많은 돈을 쓰다, fork
많은 사람, multitude
많은 사람들이 갖고 싶어 하는, sought-after
많은 수, plague
많은 양, deal, mass, much
많은 주목을 받는 위치, foreground
많은 질문, grilling

많음, stack
많이, deeply, end, far, hard, heartily, lot, more, much
많이 모이다, roll
(~가) 많이 있는, litter
많이 있다, teem
(~보다) 많이 판매되다, outsell
많지 않은, thin
말, end, expression, horse, jumper, mouth, piece, speech, story, talk, tongue, word
말 그대로, literally, verbatim
말 더듬기, stammering, stammer, stutter, stuttering
말 등의, horseback
말 잘 듣는, obedient
말굽종, groom
말굽, hoof
말기의, advanced, terminal
말끔히 치우다, clean
말다툼, argument, quarrel
말다툼하는, bickering
말다툼하다, bicker, quarrel, row
말단, end
말대꾸, retort
말대꾸하다, answer, retort
말도 안 되게, ridiculously
말도 안 되는, insane
말뚝, pile, stake
말라 죽다, wither
말라리아, malaria
말라붙다, dry, run
말라붙은, dry
말랑말랑한, soft
말려 들어가다, mixed up
말려들게 하다, entangle, implicate
말려들다, catch, involve
말로 바꾸다, phrase
말로 표현할 수 없는, untold
말리다, dry
말린 자두, prune
말만 번지르르한, slick
말만 하지 말고 돈을 써서 일이 되게 하다, money
말문이 막히다, dry
말문이 막힌, dumb
말벌, wasp
말뿐인 말, talk
말살, obliteration
말살하다, obliterate
말소, cancellation
말소되다, dissolve
말소하다, cancel
말실수하다, slip
말싸움, fight
말썽, trouble
말썽 많은, vexed
말썽거리, complication
말썽꾸러기, trouble
말썽문, troublemaker
말썽을 부리지 않을 것 같은, harmless
말쑥하게, smartly
말쑥하게 단장한, groomed
말쑥하게 하다, smarten
말쑥한, smart, spruce
말씨, language, phrase, tone, tongue
말아 올리다, roll
말없는, mute, silent
말없이, mute
말에 두서가 없는, incoherent
(~의) 말에 의하면, word
말을 걸다, chat
말을 계속하게 만들다, prompt
말을 계속하다, continue
말을 골라 쓰다, word
말을 더듬다, fumble, splutter, stammer, stutter
(~의) 말을 듣다, obey
(~의) 말을 따르다, defer
말을 못 하는, speechless
(~의) 말을 믿다, word
말을 시작하다, begin
말을 아끼는, mysterious
말을 아끼며, mysteriously
말을 안 듣는, uncontrollable
말을 안 듣다, seize

말을 잘 안 듣는, temperamental
말을 타고, horseback
말을 탄, mounted
말을 하다, noise
말의, verbal
말의 움직임, move
말이 난 김에, incidentally, way
말이 되다, sense
말이 전속력으로 달리다, gallop
말장난, nonsense, pun
말주변이 좋은, plausible
말참견하다, break
말투, speech
말풍선, bubble
말하기, speaking
말하기 거려하며, coyly
말하기 거리는, coy
(~하게) 말하는, -mouthed
말하는 사람, speaker
말하다, draw, go, impart, mention,
  mouth, observe, pass, put,
  remark, say, speak, suggest,
  talk, tell, utter
(~하게) 말하면, speaking
말하자면, as, speak, that
말하지 않다, keep
말하지 않은, unspoken
말할 나위도 없다, say
맑게 하다, clear
맑은, clear, fine
맑음, clarity
맘에 걸리다, heart
맘에 쏙 들다, fancy
맙소사, god, Jesus, lord, no, sake
맛, flavor, -flavored, taste
맛과 향이 강함, body
맛보기, taste
맛보다, sample, taste
맛없는, tasteless, unpalatable
맛없어 보이는, unappetizing
(~의) 맛을 느끼다, taste
맛을 보다, taste
맛이 간, screwed up
맛이 강한, pungent
(~한) 맛이 나다, taste
맛이 없는, bland
맛이 있는, palatable
맛있게, deliciously
맛있는, delicious, luscious, tasty
망, mesh, network
망가뜨리다, wreck
망가진, dud
망가질 듯한, rickety
망각, oblivion
망고, mango
망고나무, mango
망나니, lout
망령, ghost, senility
망루, lookout
망막, retina
망명, asylum, defection, exile
망명 희망자, asylum seeker
망명자, exile, refugee
망명하다, defect
망보는 사람, lookout
망보다, lookout
망사, net
망상, delusion
망상조직, network
망설이게 하다, hold
망설이는, hesitant, tentative
망설이다, dither, hang, hesitate,
  hold
망설이며, hesitantly, tentatively
망설이지 말고 연락하세요, hesitate
망설임, hesitancy, hesitation
망신거리, disgrace
망신시키다, shame
망신을 당한, disgraced
망신을 주다, snub
망아지, colt, foal
망연자실하다, stun
망연자실한, devastated, stunned
망원경, telescope
망을 보다, watch
(~을) 망쳐 놓다, hash, mess, upset
망쳐지는, drain
망쳐지다, mutilate

망측한, shocking
망치, hammer
망치다, botch, mar, poison, ruin,
  screw, scupper, spoil
망치로 치다, hammer
망토, cloak
망하다, bust, fold
망한, bust
망할 것, sod
망할 놈, sod
맞는, correct, keep, right
(~에) 맞다, fit, know, square, suit
맞닥뜨리다, cope, let
맞먹는, equivalent
맞먹는 것, equivalent
맞먹다, equal, rival
맞물리게 하다, mesh
맞물리다, conspire, mesh
(~와) 맞붙는, pit
맞붙어 싸우다, grapple, wrestle
맞비난, recrimination
(~에) 맞서, face
맞서다, confront, stand
맞수, rival
맞아, heaven, right, yes
맞아떨어지도록 하다, balance
맞아요, yes
(~의) 맞은편에, opposite
맞은편에서, opposite
(~을) 맞이하다, host, receive
맞장구를 치다, noise
맞추다, hit, set, square, tune
맞추어 만들다, tailor
맞추어 보다, collate
(~에) 맞추어지다, gear
(~에) 맞춘, accordance,
  tailor-made
맞춤 아기, designer baby
맞춤법, spelling
맞춤법 검사, spellcheck
맞춤법 검사 프로그램, spellchecker
맞춤법 검사를 하다, spellcheck
맞춤법을 알다, spell
맞춤형으로 만든, tailor-made
맡겨 두다, leave
맡기다, check, deposit, entrust,
  leave
(~을) 맡다, handle, take, undertake
맡아 키우다, foster
맡은 사람, charge
매, every, hawk
매 맞다, flog
매 시 정각에, hour
매 시간의, hourly
매각, sell-off
매각 처분하다, hive
매개, vehicle
매국노, traitor
매끄러운, satin, seamless, sleek,
  slick, smooth, soft
매끄럽게, seamlessly
매끄럽게 하기, lubrication
매끄럽게 하다, soften
매끈하게 하다, smooth
매끈함, softness
매너, manner
매년, after, p.a., year, yearly
매니저, manager
매다, fasten, hitch, knot, strap, tie
매달다, dangle, hang
매달려 있다, suspend
매달리다, cling, dangle, hang
매도인, bear, vendor
매도자 시장, market
매도호가, offer price
매듭, knot
매듭을 묶다, knot
매듭을 짓다, clinch
매듭짓다, loop
매력, allure, appeal, attraction,
  attractiveness, beauty, call,
  charm, desirability, glamor, lure
매력 없는, unattractive
매력 있는, desirable, magnetic
매력을 느끼다, attract, fancy
매력적으로, charmingly,
  seductively
매력적인, appealing, attractive,

charming, glamorous,
  gorgeous, magic, magical,
  seductive
(~에) 매료되다, enchant, fancy,
  hypnotize, mesmerize
매를 맞다, batter
매립지, landfill
매립하다, reclaim
매만지다, fix
매매, marketplace, transaction
매매의, commercial
매머드, mammoth
매몰하다, bury
매물로 나와, offer
매번, turn
매복 습격, ambush
매복하여 습격하다, ambush
매사 똑같은 방식의, typical
매서운, acrimonious, bitter,
  virulent
매섭게, bitterly, virulently
매섭게 지켜보다, hawk
매수, bribery
매수 호가, bid price
매수되다, buy
매수인, bull
매수자 시장, market
매스미디어, mass media
매스컴, media
매시, hourly
매어 있지 않은, loose
매우, eminently, exceedingly,
  exceptionally, greatly, half,
  highly, hugely, much, so, very,
  well
매우 고맙게 여기다, honor
매우 귀중한, invaluable
매우 기쁜, overjoyed
매우 놀라운, astonishing
매우 높은, lofty
매우 다양한, Catholic
매우 당당한, brazen
매우 뜨거운, boiling, red-hot
매우 많은, copious
매우 많이, copiously
매우 목마른, parched
매우 밝게, brilliantly
매우 밝은, brilliant
매우 밝음, brilliance
매우 분주한, hectic
매우 빠르게, hell
매우 성공적인, brilliant
매우 쉽다, nothing
매우 쓸모 있는, weight
매우 어려운 일, struggle
매우 위험한, perilous
매우 유쾌한, delightful
매우 재미있는, compulsive
매우 좋아하다, adore, love
매우 중요한, essential
매우 착한 사람, angel
매우 추운, arctic, frosty
매우 튼튼한, heavy-duty
매우 행복한, elated, joyful, joyous
매우 화난, incensed
매우 훌륭한, devastating,
  sensational
매우 힘든, exacting, punishing
매우 힘든 요구, tall
매운, hot
매월의, monthly
(~에) 매이다, bind
매이지 않은, free
(~에) 매인, confined
매일, after, daily, everyday
매일매일, day
매일의, daily
매장, point of sale
매장 지대, field
매장하다, bury
매점하다, buy, corner
매주, weekly
매주의, weekly
매직펜, marker
매진, sell-out
매진되다, sell
매진된, sold out
매진하다, apply

매질, flogging
매질하다, whip
매체, medium
(~을) 매체로 하여, via
매춘, prostitution
매춘부, hooker, prostitute
매춘하다, sell
매출액, takings
매트리스, mattress
매파, hawk
매표구, window
매표소, box office
(~나) 매한가지이다, amount
매형, brother-in-law
매혹, fascination
(~에) 매혹되다, enchant
매혹된, fascinated, taken
매혹시키다, attract, fascinate
매혹적으로, seductively
매혹적으로 만들다, sweeten
매혹적인, enchanting, enticing,
  fascinating, gorgeous, magical
매혹하다, charm
맥, vein
맥락, context, thread
맥락 안에서, context
맥박, beat, beating, pulse
맥아, malt
맥아 분유, malt
맥없는, limp
맥없이 침울해하다, mope
맥주, beer
맥주 한 잔, beer
맨 끝 쪽의, end
맨 끝의, extreme
맨 뒤, rear
맨 뒤에 오다, rear
맨 먼저, first
맨 아래 부분, base
맨 앞, head
맨 앞에 있다, head
맨 앞의, front
맨 위, top
맨 위에 있다, head
맨 위의, top
맨 위층 관람석, gallery
맨 처음부터, word
맨 첫, first
맨발의, barefoot
맨손으로, bare
맴돌다, buzz, hover, mill
맵시 나는, sleek
맵시 있게, smartly
맵시 있는, dashing, smart
맹공격, onslaught
맹꽁이자물쇠, padlock
맹꽁이자물쇠로 잠그다, padlock
맹도견, seeing-eye dog
맹렬한, blistering, ferocious,
  knockout, raging, vehement
맹렬함, vehemence, violence
맹렬히, hammer, hotly, mad,
  vengeance
맹목적으로, blindly, implicitly
맹목적으로 사랑하는, doting
맹목적인, blind, implicit
맹비난을 받고, fire
맹세, oath, pledge, vow
맹세코, heaven, honest
맹세하다, heart, pledge, swear,
  vow
맹세한, sworn
맹위를 떨치다, rage
맹장, appendix
맺다, bear, enter, forge
머그잔, mug
머리, brain, hair, head
머리 모양, hairstyle
머리 받침, headrest
머리 부분, head
머리 스타일, haircut
머리 위로, overhead
머리 위의, overhead
머리 컷, haircut
머리 타래, lock
머리가 돈, screwed up
머리가 벗겨지는, balding
머리가 좋은, bright, intelligent

머리글, header
머리글자, initial
머리글자로 서명하다, initial
머리기사, leading article
머리끝에서 발끝까지, top
머리끝이 쭈뼛해지게 하다, hair
머리로 들이받다, butt
머리로 받다, head
머리를 감다, shampoo
머리를 써서, mentally
머리를 쓰는, mental
머리말, introduction, prologue
머리에 쓰는 관, crown
머리카락, hair
머리카락 색, coloring
머리핀, bobby pin
머무르다, stay, stick
머물다, rest
머뭇거리다, falter
머지않아, long
머천트 뱅크, merchant bank
머천트 뱅크 직원, merchant banker
먹, ink
먹고 먹히는, dog
(~을) 먹고 살다, live
(~을) 먹고 자라다, feed
먹는 사람, eater
먹다, down, eat, feed, have, help, take
먹다 남은, leftover
먹어 치우다, devour
먹여 살려야 할 사람, mouth
먹여 살리다, keep
먹을 것을 주다, feed
먹을 것을 찾아다니는 동물, scavenger
먹을 수 없는, inedible
먹이, prey
먹이다, feed
먹이를 찾아다니다, forage
먹칠을 할 내용, dirt
먹칠하다, blacken
먹통이 된, dead
먹혀들지 않다, ice
먼, distant, far, faraway, long, remote
먼 거리, distance
먼 곳에, distance, way
먼 옛날을 되돌아보면, further
먼 친척 관계로, distantly
먼 훗날을 생각해 보면, further
먼저, ahead, before, begin
먼저 가세요., after
먼저 행동하는, proactive
먼지, dirt, dust, grime
먼지가 쌓이다, dust
먼지가 쌓인, dusty
먼지를 닦아내다, dust
먼지투성이의, dusty
멀리, away, back, distantly, remotely, way
멀리 떨어져, afield
멀리 떨어져 있는, spread out
멀리 떨어져서, far off
멀리서, distance
멀리하다, arm, bay, pull, shun
멀어지게 하다, alienate, distance
멀어지다, recede, turn
멀어진, distanced, estranged
멀찍이, back
멀티미디어, multimedia
멈추게 하다, stop
멈추다, break, die, halt, pull, seize, stop
멈출 수 없는, inexorable
멈춤, standstill, stop
멈춰 서다, pull, rest
멈춰서, halt
멈춰서 꼼짝하지 않다, freeze
멋, style
멋대로의, arbitrary
멋들어진, cool
멋없는, vulgar
멋없음, vulgarity
멋있는, striking
멋지게, artistically, beautifully, prettily, stylishly
멋진, artistic, beautiful, classy,

glamorous, glorious, gorgeous, heavenly, hip, magnificent, noble, pleasant, pretty, splendid, stylish, super, terrific
멍, bruise
멍든, bruised
멍든 눈, black eye
멍들다, bruise
멍청이, bugger, dope, idiot
멍청하게, blankly, dully
멍청한, blank, crazy, dim, dumb
멍하게, listlessly
멍하니, absently, absent-mindedly, vacantly
멍한, absent, listless, vacant
멍한 상태, blank, daze
멍한 상태의, dazed
멎게 하는, stop
멎다, go, pull, settle, stop
메가바이트, megabyte
메뉴, menu
메뉴판, menu
메달, medal
메뚜기, grasshopper, locust
메론, melon
메리 크리스마스, merry
메마른, barren, infertile
메모, memo, note
메모하다, jot
메스꺼운, sickly
메스꺼움, nausea, sickness
메시지, message
메아리, echo
메아리치다, echo
메우다, compensate, fill, jam, make, pad, redeem
메워 주다, fill
메이저리그, major, major league
메이저리그의, major league
메인프레임, mainframe
메일 머지, mail merge
메일 박스, mailbox
메커니즘, mechanism
메탄, methane
멜로 영화, romance
멜로드라마, melodrama
멜로드라마 같은, melodramatic
멜빵, brace
멜빵 작업복, dungarees
멜빵바지, overall
멧돼지, boar
며느리, daughter-in-law
면, end, page, plane, side, way
(~와) 면담하다, meet
면도, shave, shaving
면도기, razor, shaver
면도하는, shave
면목 없는, humiliating
면밀하게, painstakingly
면밀한, close, painstaking
면밀한 관찰, scrutiny
면밀히, closely
면밀히 관찰하다, scrutinize
면사, cotton
면사포, veil
면세의, duty-free, tax-free
면세점, duty-free shop
면식, acquaintance
면식이 있다, know
면역, immunity
면역 체계, immune system
면역되게 함, immunization
면역성, immunity
면역성이 있는, immune
면역의, immune
면적, area
면전에 대고, face
(~의) 면전에서, front, nose, presence
면접, interview
면접관, interviewer
면접을 보다, interview
면제, exemption, immunity
(~이) 면제되는, free
면제되다, excuse
면제된, exempt, immune
면제하다, exempt, waive

면직당하다, depose
면직물, cotton
면책 조항, escape
면하게 하다, free, release
면해 주다, save
면허, license
면허증, certificate, permit
면회를 요청하다, ask
멸시, disdain
멸시하다, despise, disdain
멸종, disappearance, extinction
멸종되다, vanish
멸종된, extinct
명가, dynasty
명기하다, stipulate
명단, list
명랑하게, brightly, cheerfully, merrily
명랑한, boisterous, bright, cheerful, jolly, lighthearted, lively, merry, playful
명랑한 성격, cheerfulness
명랑함, liveliness, playfulness
명령, command, dictate, injunction, instruction, order, word
명령법, imperative
명령서, writ
명령어, command
명령을 받고, order
명령하다, command, dictate, order
명령형, imperative
명료하게, clearly
명료한, clear, lucid, obvious
명료함, clarity
명망 있는, prestigious
명명하는, name
명명하다, name
명목상 대표, figurehead
명목상으로, nominally
명목상으로, officially
명목상의, nominal, official, token
명문의, prestige
명문집, anthology
명물, speciality, specialty
명민함, brilliance
명백하게, decidedly, evidently, manifestly, overtly
명백한, apparent, clear, clear-cut, decided, definite, explicit, manifest, obvious, overt, patent, plain, transparent, undeniable, undisputed, unequivocal, unmistakable, visible
명백해 보이는, apparent
명백히, clearly, explicitly, patently, plainly, unmistakably
명부, book, roll, roster
(~의) 명분 하에, name
명사, celebrity, name, noun, personality
명사들, great
명상, meditation
명상하다, meditate
명색뿐인, nominal
명석하게, clearly
명석한, clear
명석함, clarity
명성, celebrity, eminence, fame, goodwill, prestige, renown, standing, stature
명성이 나서, reputation
명세, breakdown
명세 사항, specification
명소, attraction, sight
명수, ace
명시되지 않은, unspecified
명시하다, specify
명심하다, mind, register, remember
명암 대비, contrast
명언, phrase
명예, credit, fame, honor
명예 퇴직금, payoff
명예 훼손, injury, libel
명예가 실추된, disgraced
명예로운, honorable
명예를 훼손하는, compromising

명예를 훼손하다, libel
명예상, honor
명예의, honorary
(~의) 명의로, name
명의뿐인 회사, shell company
명인, master, virtuoso
명인의, virtuoso
명중, hit
명중하다, hit, home
명쾌하게, elegantly, lucidly
명쾌한, elegant, lucid
명쾌함, lucidity
명판, plaque
명함, business card, calling card, card
명확성, definition
명확하게, definitively, positively
명확한, blinding, definite, definitive, distinct, express, positive, specific, well-defined
몇 ~, many
몇몇, certain, few, several, some
몇몇의, few, several, some
모공, pore
모국의, native
모금 운동, collection
모금하다, collect, raise
모기, mosquito
모기지론, mortgage
모나지 않은, rounded
모난, angular
모노 방식의, mono
모노의, mono
모눈종이, graph paper
모니터, monitor
모니터 요원, monitor
모니터하는, monitor
모닝콜, wake-up call
모닥불, bonfire
모델 일, modeling
모델을 하다, model
모뎀, modem
모독하는, desecrate
모두, all, everybody, everyone, everything, what
모두 ~이 되다, number
모두 다, man
모두 통틀어, told
모두 합친, gross
모두가 알게 하다, known
모두가 인정하는, undisputed
모듈, module
모듈식의, modular
모드, mode
모든, all, every, full
모든 가능한 방법, trick
모든 것, all, everything
모든 것을 태울 듯이 더운, scorching
모든 것을 고려하여, balance
모든 것을 말해 주다, say
모든 것을 포함한, all-inclusive
모든 곳, everywhere
모든 곳에, high
모든 부류, sort
모든 사람, everyone
모든 사람들, sundry
모든 수단을 동원하는, jockey
모든 일상에서 벗어나다, get
모든 점을 고려해 볼 때, considering
모든 종류, sort
모든 주의를 집중하다, home
모든, 전적으로, all
모라토리엄, moratorium
모래, sand
모래 언덕, dune
모래로 덮인, gritty
모래밭, sand
모래의, sandy
모르는, out of touch, unconscious
모르는 사이에 긴행되는, insidious
모르는 척하고, innocently
모르다, god, might
모르모트, guinea pig
모르핀, morphine
모면, escape
모면하게 하다, spare
모면하다, escape, evade, get
모면할 수 없는, inescapable

모반, rebellion
모방, imitation
모방하다, copy, emulate
모방한 것, imitation
모범, example, paragon
모범을 보이다, example
모범의, model
모병, recruiting
모빌, mobile
모사, copy
모사하다, copy
모서리, corner
모서리가 궤매진, fitted
모성상, figure
모순, contradiction, paradox
모순되는, variance
모순되지 않는, compatible
모순된, contradictory, inconsistent
모순되다, contradict
모순이 없는, consistent
모순점, inconsistency
모슬린, muslin
모습, appearance, figure, image, look, shape
모습을 나타내다, turn
모습을 드러내다, face, loom
모습을 드러내지 않고, invisibly
모습을 드러내지 않는, invisible
모습을 보이다, shape
모아 두다, hoard
모양, formation, look, pattern, shape
모양내다, spruce
모양을 마음대로 만들 수 있는, plastic
모양을 만들다, shape
모여, together
모여들다, roll, throng
모욕, affront, indignity, insult, offense, snub
모욕감을 주다, affront
모욕당한, insulted
모욕적 언동, insult
모욕하다, insult
모유, milk
모으다, accumulate, amass, assemble, collect, gather, get, mass, muster, put, round
모음, vowel
모의훈련을 하다, simulate
모의고사, mock
모의실험, simulation
모의실험을 하다, simulate
모의훈련, simulation
모이다, accumulate, assemble, collect, congregate, convene, gather, get, huddle, mass
모임, gathering, get-together, group, society
모자, cap, hat, hood
모자가 달린, hooded
모자를 푹 내려쓴, hooded
모자이크, mosaic
모조 화폐, counter
모조리, all, barrel
모조품, counterfeit, fake, imitation
모직물, wool
모직의, woolen
모진, bitter
모집, recruiting
모집하다, recruit
모체, matrix
모체가 되는, parent
모충, caterpillar
모터, motor
모터가 달린, motor
모텔, motel
모토, motto
모퉁이, corner
모티브, motif
모피, fur
모피 목도리, fur
모피 코트, fur
모피같이 부드러운, furry
모험, adventure, risk

모험가, gambler
모험심, adventure
모험심이 강한, adventurous
모험적 사업, venture
모험적인, enterprising, risky
모형, dummy, model
모형의, model
모호하게, vaguely
모호하게 만들다, obscure
모호한, hazy, vague
목, neck, throat, Thurs.
목 부분, neck
목 조르기, stranglehold
목 졸라 죽이다, choke, strangle
목가의, idyllic
목가적인, pastoral
목걸이, chain, necklace
목격, sighting
목격자, eyewitness, witness
목격하다, catch, sight, witness
목공, woodwork
목록, catalog, inventory, list
목록에 올리다, list
목마른, thirsty
목발, crutch
목뼈 골절상, whiplash
목사, minister, Reverend
목소리, voice
목소리를 낮추다, voice
목소리를 내다, say, voice
목소리를 높이다, raise, voice
목소리의, vocal
목수, carpenter
목숨, life
목숨을 앗아가는 것, killer
목숨을 잃다, kill
목숨이 경각에 달려 있다, life
목쉰, hoarse
목에까지 차 있는, eye
목요일, Thursday
목욕, bath, soak
목욕 가운, robe
목욕 수건, washcloth
목욕시키기, bath
목욕시키다, bath, bathe
목욕용 수건, flannel
목욕을 즐기다, soak
목욕탕, bath
목욕하다, bath, bathe
목을 조르다, throttle
목을 조이다, strangle
목의, cervical
목이 메임, lump
목이 잘려 나가다, decapitate
목장, pasture
목재, lumber, wood
목적, cause, end, goal, idea, intent, motive, object, objective, purpose
목적 없는, aimless
목적 없이, aimlessly
(~할) 목적으로, order, view
목적을 가지고, purposefully
목적을 달성하다, trick
(~) 목적을 충족시키다, serve
목적의식, purpose
목적의식이 있는, purposeful
목적지, destination
목제의, wooden
목조부, woodwork
목차, content
목청껏, top, voice
목초지, pasture
목탄, charcoal
목표, aim, goal, object, objective, target
(~을) 목표로 삼다, aim, go
목표로 하다, go
목표를 향하여 나아가다, home
목표하다, aim
목화, cotton
목회의, pastoral
몫, cut, quota, rake-off, share
몬순, monsoon

몬순 때 오는 비, monsoon
몰고 가다, drive, herd
몰골, wreck
(~에 대한) 몰두, preoccupation
몰두하는, devoted
몰두하다, grip, immerse
몰두한, engrossed, immersed, wrapped up
몰라, ask, dunno
몰락, descent, downfall, fall
몰락의 원인, downfall
몰락하다, fall
몰래, back, door, quiet, secretly
몰래 가지고 가다, sneak
몰래 감시하다, snoop, spy
몰래 데리고 들어오다, smuggle
몰래 두다, plant
몰래 장치하다, plant
몰래 접근하다, stalk
몰래 함, stealth
몰려가다, flock
몰려오다, pour
몰살, extermination
몰수, confiscation, seizure
몰수당하다, forfeit
몰수하다, confiscate, seize
(~를 ...상태로) 몰아가다, whip
몰아내다, chase, dislodge, eject, flush, remove
몰아넣다, ejection
몰아넣다, put, strike
몰아붙이다, push
몰아세우다, lash, pin
몰아치게 하다, blast
몰아치는, driving
몰아침, blast
몰이해, blindness
(~에) 몰이해한, blind
몰인정, unkindness
몰인정하게, unkindly
몰인정한, inhumane
몰입하다, lose
몰입한, busy
몰취미한, tasteless
몸, anatomy, body, flesh, person, system
몸 상태가 좋지 않은, run-down
몸값, ransom
몸값을 치르고 되찾다, ransom
몸매, figure
몸부림치다, squirm, thrash, writhe
몸서리, shudder
몸서리쳐지는, hideous
몸서리치다, shudder
몸소, person, personally
몸싸움을 벌이다, tussle
몸싸움을 하다, wrestle
몸에 꼭 맞는, fitted
몸에 나쁜, unhealthy
몸에 좋은, healthy
몸에 지니고, on
몸에 지니다, bear
몸을 구부리다, double, stoop
몸을 굽히다, lean
몸을 낮추다, get
몸을 낮게 만들다, duck
몸을 던지다, fling
몸을 뒤틀다, writhe
몸을 뒹굴다, turn
몸을 떨다, quiver, shiver
몸을 바짝 붙이다, flatten
몸을 수색하다, search
몸을 씻다, clean
몸을 움직이다, pull
몸을 일으키다, pick, raise
몸을 제대로 펴지 못하는, bent
몸을 쭉 뻗다, stretch
몸을 팔다, sell
몸을 푹 담그기, soak
몸을 푹 담그다, soak
몸을 풀다, loosen
몸의 피로, ache
몸이 굳다, stiffen
몸이 아픈, rotten
몸이 안 좋은, lousy, par, weather
몸이 편치 않은, unwell
몸이 풀어지다, loosen

몸짓, gesture, sign
몸통, torso, trunk
몸통 둘레, girth
몹시, badly, bitterly, blatantly, dead, deadly, dreadfully, hell, madly, sorely, stiff
몹시 괴로운, bitter, excruciating
몹시 나쁜, vile
몹시 놀라다, heart
몹시 놀란, off-balance
몹시 두려운, petrified
몹시 배고픈, starving
몹시 불쾌한, vile
몹시 슬퍼하다, grieve
몹시 싫어하다, detest
몹시 원하다, crave
몹시 탐내다, covet
몹시 피곤한, run-down
몹시 화나게 하는, incense, wall
몹시 화난, mad
몹시 흥분하여, deliriously
몹시 흥분한, delirious, thrilled
못, nail, peg
못 같은 것으로 고정하다, peg
못 고치게, incurably
못 맞히다, miss
(~에) 못 미치는, short
(~을) 못 보는, blind
못 쓰게 되다, perish
못 쓰게 된, impaired
못 쓰게 만드는, crippling
못 하게 막다, inhibit
못뽑이, pincer
못살게 굴다, goad, tease
못생긴, unattractive
못쓰게 되다, mutilate
못을 박다, nail
(~에) 못지않게, outdo
못하는, weak
(~보다) 못하다, compare, fail, omit
(~보다) 못한, less
못했던 일을 하다, catch
몽롱한, high
몽상가, dreamer, romantic
몽상적인, romantic
몽유병이 있다, sleepwalk
묘, grave, tomb
묘기, trick
묘목, seedling
묘미를 더하다, spice
묘비명, inscription
묘사, description, picture, portrayal
(~라고) 묘사하다, characterize, depict, describe, paint, portray, represent
묘상, nursery
묘지, cemetery, graveyard
묘책, maneuver
묘하게, oddly
묘한, uncanny
묘한 성적 매력을 풍기다, smolder
무, nil
무가치한, meaningless
무감각, insensitivity, numbness
무감각하게 만들다, harden, numb
무감각한, insensitive
무감각해지다, harden
무감각해진, numbed
무감해진, numb
무개화차, truck
무거운, heavy, hefty, serious
무거운 것, weight
무거움, heaviness
무겁게 누르다, weigh
무겁게 하다, weight
무게, weight
무게가 ~이다, weigh
무게가 ~인, heavy
(~의) 무게를 달다, weigh
무경험, inexperience
무경험자, stranger
무계획적으로, haphazardly
무계획적인, haphazard
무고한, innocent
무관심, apathy, disinterest, indifference

무관심하게, indifferently
무관심한, careless, disinterested, indifferent
무관한, irrelevance
무구(武具), harness
무균, sterility
무균의, sterile
무급의, unpaid
무기, ammunition, arm, hardware, weapon
무기고, armory, arsenal
무기력, lethargy
무기력하게, weakly
무기력한, lethargic, weak
무기력함, dullness, weakness
무기류, weaponry
무기를 들다, arm
무기를 버리다, disarm
무기를 소유하다, arm
무기성의, inorganic
무기질, mineral
무기한으로, indefinitely
무너뜨리다, break, tear
무너져 가는, dilapidated
무너지다, collapse, fall, give, way
무너짐, fall
무능, impotence, inability, inadequacy
무능력, incompetence
무능력자, incompetent
무능력한, impotent
무능한, inadequate, incapable, incompetent, useless
무능한 사람, bum
무늬, design, ornament, pattern
무늬가 없는, plain
무늬가 있는, patterned
무단 입주자, squatter
무단 침입, trespass
무단 침입하다, trespass
무단결석생, truant
무단결석하다, truant
무단이탈하는, desert
무담보 소액 대출, microcredit
무담보의, unsecured
무대, setting, stage
무대 뒤로, backstage
무대 뒤에서, scene
무대 뒤의, backstage
무대 바로 앞 좌석, orchestra
무대 장치, scenery, set
무대에 올리다, put, stage
무더기, mound, stack
무더운, sticky
무덤, grave, tomb
무도회, ball, dance
무독성의, innocuous
무득점의, goalless
무디게 하다, blunt
무딘, blunt
무량대세, expanse
무려, many, much
무력, force, impotence
무력 충돌, warfare
무력(無力), weakness
무력감, inertia, powerlessness
무력을 쓰는, forcible
무력하게 하다, neutralize
무력한, helpless, impotent, powerless
무력함, helplessness
무렵, hour, near
(~) 무렵에, toward
무례, indecency
무례하게, coarsely, rudely, unpleasantly
무례하게 대하다, insult
무례한, coarse, ignorant, impertinent, impolite, impudent, insolent, insulting, offensive, rude, unpleasant
무례한 표현, flame
무례함, manner, rudeness, vulgarity
무료로, charge, gratis, house
무료의, complimentary, courtesy, free, gratis
무른, runny

(~을) 무릅쓰고, risk
무릅쓰다, brave
무릎, knee, lap
무릎 덮개, rug
무릎 뒤의 건(腱), hamstring
무릎 위에, knee
무릎으로 치다, knee
무릎을 꿇고, knee
무릎을 꿇다, go, knee, kneel
무리, army, band, cluster, colony, gang, herd, horde, huddle, pack, swarm, troop
무리를 주다, strain
무리를 짓다, group
무리지어, en masse
무리지어 걸어가다, troop
무리하다, overdo
무리한, much
무마하다, quiet
무명, obscurity
무명의, unknown
무명인, unknown
무모하게, brashly, recklessly
무모한, mad, reckless
무모함, audacity, recklessness
무방비 상태의, defenseless
무방비의, unprotected
무방하게, safely
무방하다, harm
무방한, safe
무법, lawlessness
무법의, lawless, tough
무법자, outlaw
무법천지의, lawless
무보수의, honorary
무분별하게, indiscriminately
무분별한, mindless, senseless
무사 평온한, uneventful
무사한, safe
무사히, piece, safely, safe
무사히 끝내는, blow
무산되다, fall
무산된, abortive
무산시키다, derail, scuttle
무상 소프트웨어, freeware
무색의, colorless
무색하게 만들다, shame
무색해지다, eclipse, pale
무생물의, inorganic
무서운, frightening, horrible, scary, terrifying
무서운 속도로, breakneck
무서울 정도로, frighteningly
무서워 하는, terrified
무서워서 혼이 나간, mind
무서워하는, scared
무선 응용 통신 규약, WAP
무선 전신, radio
무선 전신기, radio
무선 호출기, beeper
무선의, wireless
무섭게 치솟는, runaway
무섭게 하다, terrify
무성의, silent
무성하게, thickly
무성한, bushy, lush, overgrown, thick
무소속 정치인, independent
무소속의, independent
무쇠, cast iron
무수한, countless, innumerable, myriad
무술, martial art
무스, moose, mousse
무슨 일이야?, matter
무슨 일이지?, up
무슨 일인데?, what
무시, dismissal, disregard, disrespect, slight, snub
무시 못할 정도이다, sneeze
무시당하는, invisible
무시당하는 것, invisibility
무시당하다, slight
무시당한, neglected
무시되다, board
무시무시하게, horrifically
무시무시한, dreaded, dreadful, fearsome, horrific

무시무시함, horror
무시하는, dismissive
무시하다, attention, brush, discount, dismiss, disregard, ignore, light, rubbish, scorn, set, shrug, sniff, snub
무시하듯이, dismissively
무시할 수 없다, sniff
무시해도 좋은, negligible
무식한, ignorant
무신경, insensitivity
무신경한, insensitive
무신론, atheism
무신론자, atheist
무심결의, casual
무심코, absent-mindedly, spite
무심코 입 밖에 내다, slip
무심하게, nonchalantly, thoughtlessly
무심한, blithe, impassive, nonchalant, thoughtless
무심함, nonchalance
무아경, ecstasy
무안케 하는, embarrassing
무안하게 하다, embarrass, show
무안할 정도로, embarrassingly
무안함, embarrassment
무안해 하는, embarrassed
무알코올음료, soft drink
무어인, moor
무언가, anything
무언으로, tacitly
무언의, tacit, unspoken
무엇, something, what
무엇보다, all, best
무엇보다도, first, most, other, principally
무엇보다도 나쁜 것은, worst
무엇이든, anything
무엇이든지, any
무역, commerce, trade, trading
무역 박람회, trade fair
무역 수지, balance of trade
무역 외 수입의, invisible
무역 전쟁, war
무역 흑자, trade surplus
무역상인, merchant
무역의, merchant
무역적자, trade gap
무역하다, trade
무연 휘발유, unleaded
무연의, unleaded
무용, dance, dancing
무용단, company
무용담, saga
무용수, dancer
무의미, insignificance
무의미하게, pointlessly
무의미하게 만들다, nonsense
무의미한, empty, pointless, senseless
무의식적으로, unconsciously
무의식적인, automatic, unconscious
무의식중에, involuntarily
무이자로, interest-free
무이자의, interest-free
무익, point
무익하게, avail, pointlessly
무익한, barren, pointless, unprofitable
무일푼의, penniless
무자비, ruthlessness
무자비하게, mercilessly, ruthlessly
무자비한, harsh, inhumane, merciless, relentless, ruthless, unrelenting
무자비함, brutality
무작위로, randomly, random
무 각위로 뽑이, hat
무작위의, random
무장, intensity, hold-up
무장 괴한, gunman
무장 조직, militia
무장 해제시키다, disarm
무장시키다, arm
무장하지 않은, unarmed
무장한, armed

무적의, invincible, unbeatable, unrivaled
무전, radio
무전기, radio
무전으로 연락하다, radio
무정부 상태, anarchy
무정부 상태의, anarchic
무정부주의, anarchism
무정부주의자, anarchist
무정한, stony
무제한의, unlimited
무제한의 권한, blank check
무조건, absolute
무조건으로, unconditionally
무조건의, unconditional
무조건적인, unqualified
무죄, innocence
무죄 선고, acquittal
무죄를 선언하다, acquit
무죄를 주장하다, plead
무죄의, innocent
무죄임이 밝혀지다, clear
무지, blindness, ignorance
무지개, rainbow
무지무지하게, appallingly
무지무지한, appalling
무지한, ignorant
무직의, jobless
무진 애를 쓰다, drag, strain
무질서, chaos, disorder
무질서 상태, anarchy
무질서한, anarchic, chaotic, disorderly
무찌르다, beat
무참하게, cruelly
무참한, violent
무참히, violently
무책임하게, irresponsibly
무책임하게 행동하다, game
무책임한, irresponsible
무책임한 사람, bum
무책임함, irresponsibility
(~을) 무척 좋아하는, fond, keen
무척 즐거운 시간을 보내고 있다, whale
무턱대고, headlong
무패의, unbeaten
무표정하게, impassively
무표정한, impassive
무한대, infinity
무한정한, unlimited
무한한, infinite, limitless
무한히, infinitely
무해한, benign, harmless, innocent, innocuous
무형 자산, intangible
무형의, intangible
무화과 열매, fig
무화과나무, fig
무효 표시를 하다, cancel
무효로 하다, invalidate, negate, void
무효의, invalid, void
무효한, null
무효화, override
무효화하다, annul, override
묵다, lodge, put, stay
묵묵히, silently
묵살되다, ear
묵살하다, ear, shelve
묵상, musing
묵인하다, condone, countenance
묶는 줄, band
묶다, bind, fasten, lash, loop, strap, tie
묶어 두다, tie
묶음, bunch, lot, pack, pad
문, door
문간, doorway
문간채, lodge
문구류, stationery
문단을 정렬하다, justify
문득 떠오르다, flash, hit
문란한, promiscuity
문맥, context
문맥 없이, context
문맹의, illiterate

문맹자, illiterate
문명, civilization
문명화된, civilized
문법, grammar
문법적인, grammatical
문서, document, note, paper, text, writing
문서 업무, paperwork
문서상의, written
문신, tattoo
문신을 새기다, tattoo
문양, motif, ornament
문어, octopus
문어적인, literary
문외한, layman, stranger
문외한의, lay
문을 닫다, close, shut
문을 열다, door, open
문을 열러 가다, answer
문을 잠그다, lock
문의, inquiry, query
문의하다, hatch, inquire, query
문자, character, script
문자 그대로, word
문자 메시지, text, text message
문자 메시지 전송, SMS, texting, text messaging
문자 메시지를 보내다, text
문자 인식, character recognition
문자반, face
문장, sentence
문장(紋章), crest
(~의) 문제, case, difficulty, hitch, matter, problem, proposition, question, trouble
문제 삼지 않은, unchallenged
문제 해결 능력, resourcefulness
문제 해결 능력이 탁월한, resourceful
문제가 많은, troubled
문제가 생기다, tell
문제가 생긴, trouble
문제가 있는, problematic
문제거리, complication
(~을) 문제로 삼다, issue
문제를 내다, set
문제를 일으키는 사람, troublemaker
문제를 풀다, answer
문제를 해결하다, house
문제의 소지, liability
문젯거리, offender
문지기, janitor
문지르기, scrub
문지르다, rub, scrub
문지방, threshold
문질러 닦다, scour
문질러 닦아내다, scrub
문질러 바르다, rub
문질러 털다, rub
문집, collection
문체, language
문패, plate
문하생, pupil
문학, literature
문학의, literary
문헌, literature
문호 개방, open-door
문호 개방의, open-door
문화, culture
문화 시설, amenity
문화 예술의 파괴, vandalism
문화권, culture
문화의, cultural
문화재로 등록된, listed
문화적으로, culturally
문화적인, cultural
묻다, ask, bury, inquire, query
묻히다, smudge
물, water
물 내리기, flush
물 만난 고기 같은, element
물 밑바닥을 훑다, dredge
물 속에 사는, aquatic
물 한 통, bucket
물가, shoreline, waterfront
물가 지수 연동제의, index-linked
물가로, ashore

물거품, foam
물건, stuff, thing
물건을 사다, shop
물결, flow, wave
물결 모양의, corrugated, wavy
물결치다, wave
물고기, fish
물구나무를 서다, head
물기 없는, dry
물기가 빠지다, drain
물기를 닦아내다, dry
물기를 빼다, drain
물다, bite
물러가도 좋다는 허락을 받다, dismiss
물러나다, back, bow, climb, recede, retire, retreat, stand, step
물러남, retreat, withdrawal
물러서다, back, stand, step
물러서지 않다, ground
물려 들어가다, bite
물려고 하다, snap
물려받다, inherit
물려받음, inheritance
물론, absolutely, among, certainly, course, doubt, means, of course, well
물론 아니다, of course
(~은) 물론이고, let
물론이지, sure
물론입니다, of course
물리 치료, physiotherapy
물리 치료사, physiotherapist
물리적으로, physically
물리적인, physical
물리치다, defeat, fight, trump
물리학, physics
물리학자, physicist
물린 상처, bite
물마루, crest
물물 교환, barter
물물교환하다, barter
물밀듯이 밀려오다, flood
물바다가 되다, flood
물바다로 만들다, flood
물방울, drip, trickle
물방울을 떨어뜨리다, drip
물보라, spray
물세탁이 가능한, washable
물속에 잠그다, submerge
물속에 잠기다, submerge
물속으로, underwater
물속으로, overboard
물속의, underwater
물안개, spray
물약, drop, potion
물어뜯다, bite, chew
물에 띄우다, launch
물에 잠기게 하다, swamp
물에 잠긴, awash
물을 끓이다, boil
물을 내리다, flush
물을 대다, irrigate
물을 댐, irrigation
물을 뿌리다, douse
물을 주다, water
물을 퍼내다, bail
물음표, question mark
물의, aquatic, watery
물의를 일으키는, controversial
물이 나오고 있다, run
물이 들어오지 못하는, watertight
물이 불어난, swollen
물이 새지 않는, watertight
물장난, paddle
물장난을 하다, paddle
물질, material, matter, substance
물질 만능주의, materialism
물질적으로, materially, physically
물질적인, material, physical
물집, blister
물집이 생기다, blister
물체, object
물통, bucket
물품, article
물품세, excise
물품으로, kind
물품을 채우다, stock

묽은, dilute, thin, watery, weak
묾, bite
뭉개다, sit
뭉개다, mangle
뭉근한 불로 끓이다, stew
뭉근히 끓는 상태, simmer
뭉근히 끓다, simmer
뭉근히 끓이다, simmer
뭉치, bundle, clump, wad
뭉치다, band, bunch
뭉친, tight
뭍으로 밀려오다, beach
뭐든지 다 해 주는, subservient
뭐라고?, what
뭐라고요?, pardon, sorry
뭔가 대단한 것, something
뭔가를 숨기고 있는, sly
뭔가를 숨기고 있는 듯이, slyly
뮤지컬, musical
뮤추얼펀드, mutual fund
뮬, mule
미, beauty
미 국무성, State Department
미 항공 우주국, NASA
미 해병대, corps
미각, palate, taste
미개, barbarism
미개발의, virgin
미개척지, wild
미결 서류함, in box, in tray
미경험자, virgin
미국, state, US
미국 달러, dollar
미국 대학원 진학을 위한 시험, GRE
미국 본토의, continental
미국 악어, alligator
미국 정부, White House
미국 흑인, African-American
미국방성, Pentagon
미끄러뜨리듯 움직이다, slide
미끄러운, slippery
미끄러져 가다, skim, slide, slither
미끄러지다, skid, slip
미끄러지듯 움직이다, glide
미끄러짐, skid
미끄럼틀, slide
미끈미끈한, slimy
미끼, bait
미끼를 놓다, bait
미끼를 물다, bite
미끼를 물, bite
미끼상품, loss leader
미납, nonpayment
미납의, unpaid
미니 바, minibar
미니멀리스트, minimalist
미니멀리즘, minimalism
미니어처, miniature
미답의, virgin
미답의 영역, virgin
미덕, virtue
미래, future
미래를 배경으로 하는, futuristic
미래상, vision
미래의, future
미량, grain
미려한, glorious
미로, jungle, labyrinth, maze
미로 같이 복잡한 것, maze
미루다, delay, leave, postpone, put
미루다가 제때를 놓치다, leave
(~으로) 미루어 보아, judge
미리, ahead, ahead of, beforehand, time
미리 짜고 하다, fix
미리 탐색해 보다, water
(~) 미만, under
미망인, widow
미묘(美妙)한, subtle
미묘하게, delicately, subtly
미묘한, delicate, subtle
미묘한 차이, nuance, shade, subtlety
미묘함, delicacy, subtlety
미미하게, modestly
미미한, modest
미발달 단계의, embryo, embryonic

미발달한, immature
미봉책, Band-Aid, quick fix
미불, nonpayment
미사, mass
미사여구, rhetoric
미사일, missile
미생물, microbe, microorganism
미성년자, minor
미세한, fine
미소, smile
미소 띤, smiley
미소 짓다, smile
미소 표시, smiley
미수의, attempted
미숙, inexperience
미숙한, bad, immature, inexperienced, naive, raw, tender, unskilled, untrained
미술, art
미술 활동, art
미술가, artist
미술관, gallery
미술품, fine art, work of art
미스 ~, Miss
미스터리, mystery
미식가, gourmet
미식축구, American football, football
미식축구 공, American football
미신, superstition
미신을 믿는, superstitious
미신적인, superstitious
미심쩍게, dubiously
미심쩍게 생각하다, doubt
미심쩍어, doubt
미심쩍어하는, dubious
미심쩍어하듯, dubiously
미안, oops
미안해요, sorry
미안해하는, apologetic
미안해하며, apologetically
미역 감기, bathe, bathing
미연에 방지하다, forestall
미온적인, lukewarm
미완성의, unfinished
미용, hairdressing
미용사, hairdresser
미용실, hairdresser, salon
미용의, beauty
미움을 사다, doghouse
미이라, mummy
미인, beauty
미인 대회, pageant
미적거리다, sit
미적인 측면, aesthetic
미적지근한, lukewarm
미정, tba, tbc
미정의, pending, uncertain
미증유의, unprecedented
미지, unknown
미지근한, lukewarm, tepid
미지급의, outstanding
미지수, question mark
미진(微震), tremor
미처 날뛰는, rampage
미치광이, loony, lunatic, maniac
미치다, crack, crazy, extend, mind, span
미친, crazy, deranged, insane, mad, nut
미친 듯이, crazily, frantically, insanely, madly, mad, madly, wildly
미친 듯이 날뛰다, rampage
미친 듯한, frantic, insane, mad, maniac
미친 사람, crazy
미친 짓, insanity
미침, madness
미터, meter
미터기, clock
미터법의, metric
미학의, aesthetic
미학적으로, aesthetically
미합중국, US, USA
미해결의, outstanding, unresolved, unsettled

미행하다, tail
미화, glorification
미화된, glorified
미화하다, glorify
미확인의, unconfirmed, unidentified
믹서, mixer
믹스, mix
민간 기업, private enterprise
민간 부문, private sector
민간 피해, collateral damage
민간용으로, commercially
민간용의, commercial
민간의, civil, civilian, private
민간인, civilian
민감성, sensitivity
민감한, emotive, keen, sensitive, susceptible
민감한 부분, sore
민감함, sensitivity
민권, civil rights
민달팽이, slug
민들레, dandelion
민병, militia
민병대원들, paramilitary
민병대의, paramilitary
민속, folklore
민속의, folk
민영, commercial
민영화, privatization
민영화되다, privatize
민요, folk
민원 처리 감찰관, ombudsman
민족, nationality
민족 특유의, ethnic
민족성, character
민족의, ethnic
민족적, national
민족주의, nationalism
민족주의자, nationalist
민주당원, democrat
민주적으로, democratically
민주주의, democracy
민주주의의, democratic
민주주의자, democrat
민첩성, agility
민첩한, agile, nimble
민첩함, quickness
민초, grassroots
믿게 하다, make
믿고 맡기다, rely, trust
믿고 맡김, trust
믿고 안심하다, assured
믿기 어려운, unbelievable
믿기 어려울 정도로, deceptively
(~라고) 믿는, opinion
믿다, believe, buy, follow, pin, trust
믿어지지 않게, unbelievably
믿어지지 않는, incredible
믿어지지 않는 듯이, incredulously
믿을 만한, authentic, believable, reliable, solid, sound, trustworthy
믿을 수 없는, deceptive, dodgy, unreliable
믿을 수 없을 만큼, incredibly
믿을 수 없을 정도로, belief, unbelievably
믿을 수 없을 정도인, unreal
믿을 수 있는, credible, dependable
믿을 수 있는 소식통으로부터, horse
믿음, belief, faith, trust
믿음직스러운, solidity
믿음직스럽게, solidly
믿음직하게, reliably
믿음직한, secure, solid
밀, wheat
밀가루, flour
밀고 나아가다, push
밀고 들어가다, push
밀고자, grass
(~를) 밀고하다, grass, rat
밀기, push
밀다, press, push, shove, trundle
밀도, consistency, density
밀도가 높은, dense
밀랍, wax
밀레니엄, millennium

밀려나다, crush, displace
밀려들다, pour, surge
밀려오다, wash
밀렵 행위, poaching
밀렵꾼, poacher
밀렵하다, poach
밀리그램, mg, milligram
밀리리터, milliliter, ml
밀리미터, millimeter, mm
밀림, jungle
밀매, peddling, traffic, trafficking
밀매상, pusher
밀매자, trafficker
밀매하다, peddle, push, traffic
밀봉 부분, seal
밀봉하다, seal
밀수, smuggling
밀수업자, runner
밀수자, smuggler
밀수하다, smuggle
밀실, den
밀실에서, door
밀어 내다, displace
밀어 넣다, ram, squash, squeeze, tuck
밀어 올리다, push
밀어닥치다, invade
밀어붙이다, bulldoze, pin, press, push
밀월, honeymoon
밀입국자, stowaway
밀접성, identification
밀접하게, closely, inseparably, intimately
밀접하게 관련되다, hand
밀접한, close, intimate
밀집, squeeze
밀집된, massed
밀집하게, densely
밀집한, dense
밀착력, grip
밀착시키다, knit
밀쳐 올리다, propel
밀쳐지다, crush
밀치고 가다, thrust
밀치고 나아가다, force
밀치다, push, shove, thrust
밀침, shove, thrust
밀폐된, airtight, close
밀항, smuggling
밀항자, stowaway
밉살스러운, horrid, obnoxious
밋밋하게, soberly
밋밋한, monolithic, sober
밍크, mink
밍크 모피, mink
밍크로 만든 옷, mink
밍크코트, mink
밑면, underneath, underside
밑면에, underneath
밑면의, underneath
밑바닥, bottom, floor, rock bottom
(~) 밑에, after, beneath, under
밑에 숨은, underlying
밑에 있는, underlying
밑에서, under
밑으로, below, down
밑으로 던지는, underhand
밑의, below, beneath
밑줄을 치다, underline, underscore
밑장이 고무로 된, sole
밑천, capital
바, bar, barroom, what
바 여급, barmaid
바가지 쓴 것, rip-off
바가지 씌우다, overcharge, rip
바가지를 썼다, had
바가지를 쓰다, nose
바구니, basket
바깥 세계, world
바깥에, out, outside
(~의) 바깥쪽에, outside
바깥쪽의, outer, outside
바꾸다, alter, change, flip, leave, move, revise, shift, swap, swing, switch, trade, transform
바꾸어, round
바꾸어 놓다, reverse

바꾸어 말하면, word
바꿈, move
바뀌 말하면, i.e.
바뀌다, alter, break, convert, shift, switch, turn, way
바나나, banana
바느질, sewing
바느질감, sewing
바느질하다, sew, stitch
바늘, needle, pointer, stitch
바늘귀, eye
바늘땀, stitch
바닐라, vanilla
바다, ocean, sea, water
바다거북, turtle
바다표범, seal
바닥, base, bed, bottom, floor
바닥 매트, mat
바닥까지 내려오는, full-length
바닥나다, run
바닥을 드러내다, dry
바닥재, flooring
바닷가, shore
바닷가재, lobster
비닷물 든 방울, ocean
바닷물이 빠지다, ebb
바디랭귀지, body language
(~하기를) 바라는, concerned, desired, hopeful
바라다, desire, hope, trust, want
바라보다, eye, look
바라봄, look, view
바람, hope, wind
바람결에, bird
바람둥이, flirt
바람맞히다, stand
바람을 빼다, deflate
바람이 거세다, blow
바람이 많이 부는, windy
바람이 빠지다, deflate
바람이 빠진, flat
바람이 빠진 타이어, flat
바람이 없는, calm
바람직하지 못한, unhappy
바람직하지 못한 실상, multitude
바람직하지 않은, undesirable
바람직한, desirable
바람직함, desirability
바래다, fade
바래다주다, escort, see
바로, directly, exact, immediately, just, precisely, right, straight, there
바로 가기, short cut
바로 가까이의, range
바로 그, very, your
바로 그 순간, instant
바로 그 자체, itself
바로 그거야, say
바로 그것이다, precisely
바로 근처에, corner
바로 눈앞에 있다, stare
바로 눈앞에서, eye
바로 되받아 말하다, chime
(~의) 바로 뒤를 이어, heel
바로 뒤의, immediate
바로 말씀대로입니다., exactly
바로 서다, right
바로 쓸 수 있는, handy
바로 앞에 나오다, precede
바로 앞의, immediate
바로 옆에, next door
바로 이웃의, immediate
바로 전의, previous
바로 지금, here, just, right
바로 코앞에, doorstep, nose
바로잡는, corrective
바로잡다, adjust, correct, rectify, redress, right, smooth
바륨, Valium
바르게, right, way
바르다, apply, daub, glue, smear
바른, right
바리케이드, barricade
(~에) 바리케이드를 치다, barricade
바리톤, baritone
바보, ass, fool, idiot, mug
바보 같은, foolish, mad, silly,

stupid
바보같이, foolishly
바보같이 굴다, play
바보짓, fool, madness
바비큐 하다, barbecue
바쁘게 ~을 하다, occupy
바쁘고 활동적인, go
(~하느라) 바빠는, busy, go, hand
바쁜, busy, occupied
바삭 하는 소리를 내다, crunch
바삭바삭 썹어 먹다, crunch
바삭바삭 하는 소리, crunch
바삭바삭한, crisp, crunchy
바삭하게 구워지다, crisp
바삭하게 굽다, crisp
바스락거리는 소리, rustle, rustling
바스락거리다, rustle
바싹, hotly
바싹 구운, well done
바싹 달라붙다, snuggle
(~을) 바싹 뒤쫓아, heel
바싹 따라붙다, run
바싹 마르다, dry
바싹 마른, parched
바싹 마르붙게 하다, dry
바싹 말라붙다, dry
바싹 말리다, dry
바싹 파고들다, snuggle
바운드, bounce
바위, boulder, rock
바위턱, ledge
바위투성이의, rocky, rugged
바이러스, virus
바이러스 검사를 받다, scan
바이러스성의, viral
바이스, vise
바이올린, fiddle, violin
바이올린 연주자, violinist
바이트, byte
바지, pants, trousers
바지 가랑이, leg
바지 멜빵, suspender
바지 정장, trouser suit
바지선, barge
바짝, tightly
바짝 당기다, tighten
바치는 것, tribute
바치다, devote, give, invest, offer
바코드, bar code
바퀴, wheel
바퀴 모양의 기계, wheel
바퀴 자국, rut
바퀴 자물쇠, clamp, Denver boot
바퀴 자물쇠를 걸다, clamp
바퀴벌레, cockroach, roach
바퀴통, hub
바탕화면, desktop
바텐더, barman, bartender
바티칸 시국, Vatican
박격포, mortar
박다, bury, drive, stick
박람회, expo, fair
박력, punch
박력 있게, jauntily
박력 있는, jaunty
박멸, eradication, extermination
박멸하다, eradicate, exterminate
박물관, museum
박물학자, naturalist
박사, doctor, Dr., Ph.D.
박사 학위, doctorate, Ph.D.
박살, write-off
박살내다, smash, write
박살이 나다, smash
박수, clap, hand
박수갈채, applause, ovation
박수갈채를 보내다, applaud
박수를 치다, clap
박스, box
박스 오피스, box office
박식한, knowledgeable, sophisticated, well-informed
박엽지, tissue
박자, beat, pulse, tempo
박자에 맞춰, time
박자에 어긋나게, time
박장대소, gale
박장대소를 하다, roar

박제되다, stuff
박쥐, bat
박차, spur
박차고 나가다, walk
박차를 가하다, spur
박탈, deprivation
박탈하다, deprive
박테리아, bacteria
박테리아의, bacterial
박하, mint, peppermint
박하사탕, mint, peppermint
박해, persecution
박해를 받다, persecute
박혀 있는, embedded
박혀 있다, stick
박히다, bury, embed, lodge
밖에, out
밖으로, out, outside, outward
밖을 향한, outward
밖의, outside
반, class, squad
반감, antipathy, dislike, grudge, objection
반값의, half-price
반격, counterattack
반격하다, counterattack, fight
반경, radius
반구, hemisphere
반구형, dome
반날, half-day
반납하다, take
반년 동안의, half-yearly
반년마다, biannually
반년마다의, biannual, half-yearly
반단독 주택, semi, semidetached
반단독 주택형의, semidetached
반달, vandal
반대, argument, converse, disagreement, disapproval, dissent, hostility, no, objection, opposition, rebellion, repudiation, reverse
반대 세력, opponent
반대 심문, cross-examination
반대 심문하다, cross-examine
반대 의견을 가진 정치인, rebel
반대 의견을 말하다, argue
반대되는, contrary, opposed
반대로, conversely, way
반대로 하다, reverse
반대의, reverse
반대자, dissenter, dissident, no
반대자들, opponent
반대쪽, side
반대파, rebel
반대편, side
반대하는, hostile, opposing
반대하다, disagree, dissent, go, object, oppose, opposed, rebel, repudiate
(~에) 반대하여, against
반도, peninsula
반도체, semiconductor
반도체 집적 회로 소자, microchip
반독점, antitrust
반드시, fail, necessarily
반드시 ~을 필요로 하다, cry
반드시 ~일 것이다, bound
반드시 ~할, sure
반드시 ~할 것이다, intention
반드시 그렇지는 않다, necessarily
반드시 필요한 것, must
반들반들한, shiny, slippery
반듯하게 접다, fold
반등, rally
반등하다, rally
반란, insurgency, insurrection, mutiny, rebellion, revolt, uprising
반란군, rebel
반란을 일으키다, mutiny, revolt
반란의, rebellious
반복, antagonism, feud
(~와) 반목하다, feud
반바지, short
반박, defense, retort
반박하다, contradict, dispute,

refute
반반한, even
반발, backlash
(~에) 반발하다, react
반복, duplicate, recurrence, repetition
반복되는, recurrent, repetitive
반복되다, recur, repeat
반복적인, repetitive
반복하다, duplicate, repeat
반복하여 주입시키다, drum
반복해서, over
반사, reflection
반사 신경, reflex
반사 작용, reflex
반사되다, bounce, reflect
반사하는, reflective
반사하다, reflect
반사회적인, antisocial
반성, repentance
반성하는, repentant
반시계 방향의, counterclockwise
반시계 방향으로, counterclockwise
반신반의하는, dubious
반신반의하며, doubtfully
반액의, half-price
반어, irony
반어적으로, ironically
반어적인, ironic
반역, revolt
반역자, rebel, traitor
반역죄, treason
반영, reflection
반영하는, reflective
반영하다, mirror, reflect
반원, semicircle
반원형의 물체, semicircle
반으로 줄이다, halve
반음 낮은, flat
반응, answer, reaction, response, responsiveness
반응력, reaction
반응을 보이다, react, respond, take
반응하는, react, respond
반작용, reaction
반전, reversal
반점, blotch, speck, spot
반주, accompaniment, backing
(~의) 반주를 받다, back
반주하다, accompany
반죽, batter, dough, paste
반죽하다, knead
반지, ring
반지름, radius
반짝 떠오름, stroke
반짝거리다, glisten, twinkle
반짝거리며 나타나다, flash
반짝거림, twinkle
반짝반짝 빛나다, glitter, twinkle
반짝이, glitter, sequin
반짝이는, shiny
반짝이는 작은 장신구, glitter
반짝이다, brighten, glint, shimmer, shine, sparkle, twinkle
반짝임, glint, sparkle
반쯤, way
(~을) 반쯤 끝내고, through
반쯤 정신이 나간, distraught
반창고, plaster
반체제 인사, dissident
반체제적인, dissident
반칙, foul
반칙의, foul
반칙하다, foul
반투명한, translucent
반품하다, take
(~에) 반하다, contradict, enamored, fall
(~에) 반하여, against, contrary
반항, defiance, revolt
반항심, rebelliousness
반항적으로, defiantly
반항적인, defiant, rebellious
반항하는, rebellious
반항하다, defy, rebel, revolt
반향, echo, resonance
반향을 불러일으키다, resonate,

reverberate
반환, return
반환 가능한, refundable
(~을) 받고 있는, under
(~을) 받기 쉬운, open
(~을) 받는, on, receipt
받다, attract, catch, come, get, have, meet, receive, take, undergo
받아 적다, take
받아넘기다, fend
(~하게) 받아들여지다, go, greet, receive
받아들이게 하다, face, sell
받아들이는, resigned
받아들이다, accept, adopt, assimilate, board, face, make, resign, take, term, tolerate
받아들이도록 강요하다, impose
받아들일 수 있는, acceptable
받아들임, acceptance, resignation
받아쓰기, dictation
받아쓰다, transcribe
(~을) 받을 만하다, deserve, merit, rate
받음, receipt
받치다, prop
받침, mat, rest
받침 부위, base
받침 접시, saucer
받침대, pedestal, prop, stand
받침대 아래로, pedestal
받침대 위에, pedestal
받침판, clipboard
발, blind, curtain, foot, paw
발 구르기, stamp
발 디딤, footing
발가락, toe
발가벗은, nude
발견, detection, discovery, find
발견되다, discover
발견하다, catch, come, detect, discover, pick, sight, spot, strike, turn
발견하려고 하다, onto
발광한, crazed
발굴, excavation
발굴하다, excavate, unearth
발기, erection
발기 부전, impotence
발기 부전의, impotent
발길질, kick
발길질하다, kick
발끈 하다, huff
발끈 하여, huff
발끈함, tantrum
발끝으로, tiptoe
발끝으로 걷다, tiptoe
발단, beginning
발달, formation, growth, march
발달 중의, making
발달된, developed
발달하다, develop, grow
발동하다, invoke
발라드, ballad
발랄하게, cheerfully, cheerily
발랄한, bubbly, cheerful, cheery
발레, ballet
발령, posting
발령 나다, post
발령하다, move
발로 밟아 돌리는 기구, treadmill
발로 조작하는, foot
발로 짓밟다, stamp
발리, volley
발리 하다, volley
발매되다, come
발매품, release
발매하다, release
발명, invention
발명가, inventor
발명품, invention
발명하다, devise, invent
발목, ankle
발목까지 내려오는, full-length
(~에) 발목이 잡힘, hostage
발바닥, pad, sole
발바닥의 움푹 들어간 부분, arch

발발, eruption, outbreak
발발하다, erupt
발병, attack
발사, launch, shot
발사대, pad
발사하다, launch
발산, emission
발산되다, emanate
발산시키다, exude
발산하다, project, radiate, rip, vent, work
발상지, home
발생, occurrence
발생률, incidence
(~을) 발생시키는 물건, generator
(~을) 발생시키는 사람, generator
발생시키다, engender, generate
발생지, birthplace
발생하다, come, develop, spring, transpire
발생하지 않는, unknown
(~이) 발생하지 않는다면, absent
발성의, vocal
발소리, footstep
발송, dispatch
발송 서류함, out tray
발송되는, outgoing
발송인, sender
발송하다, dispatch, send
발신음, dialling tone, dial tone
발아, germination
발언, observation, utterance
발언권, say
발육, development
발을 걸어 넘어뜨리다, trip
발을 구르다, stamp
발을 내딛다, foot
발을 들여놓음, door
발을 맞춰, step
발을 안 맞춰, step
발을 절기, limp
발을 질질 끌며 걷기, shuffle
발을 질질 끌며 걷다, shuffle
발을 쿵쾅거리다, stamp
발을 헛디디다, stumble
발을 헛디딤, stumble
발음, pronunciation
발음하기 어려운, mouthful
발음하다, pronounce
발의, initiative, motion
발이 묶이다, strand
발자국, footprint, footstep, print, track
발자취, track
발작, attack, fit, seizure
발작적인, hysterical
발작하듯이, hysterically
발전, advance, development, evolution, extension, stride
발전기, dynamo, generator
발전된, advanced, developed
발전소, plant, power plant, power station
발전시키다, carry, develop, evolve, further
발전하다, come, develop, evolve
발제문, discussion
발족, initiation
발진, rash, spot
발진하다, blast
발췌되다, extract
발췌문, excerpt, extract
발치, bottom, foot
발코니, balcony
발톱, claw, toenail
발톱으로 할퀴다, claw
발파하다, blast
발판, foothold, springboard, steppingstone
발포, firing, fire, firing, gunshot, shot
발포 소리, gunshot
발포를 멈추다, fire
발포하다, fire
발포할 때를 기다리다, fire
발표, announcement, presentation, publication
발표하다, announce, bring, issue,

present, publish, release, unveil
발한, sweating
발행, release
발행 가격, issue price
발행 부수, circulation
발행하다, publish
발현, manifestation
발화, ignition
발효, fermentation
발효되는, effective
발효되다, ferment
발효하다, ferment
밝게, brightly
밝게 비추다, illuminate
밝게 빛나는, radiant
밝게 빛나다, blaze
밝게 하다, lighten
밝기, brightness, lightness
밝아지다, brighten, lighten
밝은, bright, light, vivid
밝은 색 부분, splash
밝은 청록색, turquoise
밝은 초록색, emerald
밝음, brightness
밝혀내다, determine, unearth
밝혀지다, emerge, prove
밝히다, brighten, disclose, divulge, get, light, reveal, unveil
밟다, press, step, tread
밟아 뭉개다, trample
밤, chestnut, night
밤나무, chestnut
밤낮없이, night
밤낮없이, morning
밤늦게까지 일하다, midnight
밤마다, nightly
밤마다의, nightly
밤새, overnight
밤새 지키다, vigil
밤색, chestnut
밤샘 파티, slumber party
밤을 새는, overnight
밤의, nocturnal
밤중에, night
밥, rice
밥상을 차리다, lay
밥을 먹다, eat
밧줄, rope
밧줄로 묶다, rope, tether
방, chamber, room
방갈로, bungalow
방공호, shelter
방과 후 남게 하기, detention
방관자, bystander, sideline
방광, bladder
방귀를 뀌다, wind
방금, just, now, only
(~에서) 방금 나온, fresh
방금 지난, past
방대한, mass
방독면, gas mask
방랑하는, nomadic
방만한, discursive
방목되다, graze
방목의, free-range
방목장, paddock
방문, call, visit
방문자, caller
방문하다, call, come, look, pay, visit
방법, grille
(~하는) 방법, fashion, instrument, method, road, route, way
방법론, methodology
방법론적인, methodological
방벽, barrier
방부제, preservative
방비, hedge
방사능, radiation, radioactivity
방사능의, radioactive
방사성, radioactivity
방사성의, radioactive
방송, airing, broadcast, broadcasting, transmission
방송 내용 목록, playlist
방송 시스템, PA
방송 예정 녹음 목록에 오르다, playlist

방송 전파, airwaves
방송 중인, air
방송국, channel, station
방송대학, Open University
방송되는, on
방송되다, beam, go, transmit
방송인, network
방송실, studio
방송원, announcer
방송인, broadcaster
방송하다, air, broadcast
방수의, waterproof
방식, delivery, light, manner, style, system, way
방심하다, guard
(~에게) 방심하지 못하게 하다, toe
방심하지 않고 지켜보다, eye
방심하지 않는, vigilant, watchful
방심한 화면 사이 당하네, nap
방아쇠, trigger
방어, defense
방어 태세를 취하는, defensive
방어선, line
방어용의, defensive
방어적으로, defensively
방어적인, defensive
방어책, defense
방어하다, defend, fend
방어할 수 없는, untenable
방언, dialect
방에 딸린, en suite
방열기, radiator
방영, run, screening
방영되고 있는, on
방영되다, screen
방영하다, show
방울, bead, bell, drop
방위, security
방음하다, insulate
방이나 집을 함께 쓰다, room
방전된, flat
방정식, equation
방종, self-indulgence
방종한, self-indulgent
방지, prevention
방지하는, preventive
방지하다, preclude, prevent
방청 금지로, camera
방청객, floor
방출, discharge, emission, release
방출되다, discharge
방출하다, emit, expel, give, radiate, release
방충제, repellent
방충제를 뿌리다, spray
방치된, unattended
방침, course, line, orientation, path, policy, tack
방탄의, bullet-proof
방패, shield
방패 꼴 우승패, shield
방패막이를 만들다, cover
방편, expedient, medium, tool
방학, holiday, vacation
방해, barrier, hindrance, impediment, interception, interference, interruption, intrusion, obstruction, setback
방해가 되다, hinder, way
방해를 받지 않는, undisturbed
방해물, irritant
방해받지 않는, private, unchecked
방해하다, disturb, frustrate, hamper, hinder, hold, hurt, impede, intercept, interfere, interrupt, intervene, intrude, jam, keep, obstruct, put, stand, stunt, thwart, wrench
방향, aspect, direction, orientation, side, way
방향 감각을 잃게 만들다, disorient
방향 감각을 잃다, bearing
방향 감각을 찾다, bearing
방향 요법, aromatherapy
방향 지시등, indicator, turn signal
방향 지시등을 켜다, indicate
방향을 돌리다, turn

방향을 바꾸게 하다, deflect
방향을 바꾸다, turn, veer
(~의) 방향을 수정하다, redirect
방향을 잃다, way
방향을 조정하다, guide
방향이 바뀌다, turn
방향타, rudder
방화, arson
방화의, incendiary
방황하는, adrift
밭, bed
밭떼기, patch
배, belly, factor, gut, inside, pear, ship, stomach, time, tummy, vessel
배 밖으로, overboard
배가 잔뜩 부른, bloated
배경, background, pedigree
배경 화면, wallpaper
(~을) 배경으로, against
배경음, background
(~) 배경, set
배고픈, hungry
배고픔, hunger
배관, plumbing
배관 작업, plumbing
배관공, plumber
배관재, tubing
배구, volleyball
배급, distribution, issue
배급 식량, ration
배급권, distributorship
배급량, ration
배급받다, issue
배급사, distributor, distributorship
배급제, rationing
배급제가 되다, ration
배급하다, distribute
배기가스, exhaust
배기관, exhaust, tailpipe
배꼽, navel
배낭, knapsack, rucksack
배달, route
배달되다, arrive
배달시키다, send
배달원, courier, messenger
배달을 주문하다, send
배달의, delivery
배달하다, deliver
배당, allocation
배당금, dividend, payout
배당되다, allocate, allot
배란, ovulation
배란하다, ovulate
배럴, barrel
배려, concern, consideration, regard
배려하는, considerate
배를 불리다, fatten
배반, betrayal, sell-out, treachery
배반하다, betray, rat, sell
배부른, full, full up, hearty
배분, distribution
배분하다, dish
배불리 먹다, stuff
배상, faithfully, indemnity, redress, reimbursement, yours
배상금, award, compensation, payout
배상하다, indemnify, reimburse
배선망, wiring
배선하다, wire
배설물, crap, dung, feces
배설하다, excrete, foul
배속되다, assign
배송, delivery
배송료, delivery charge
배송물, delivery
배수, factor, multiple
배수 장치, drainage
배수관, drain
배수구, gutter
배스, bass
배스 요리, bass
배신자, rat, traitor
배신하다, stab
배심원, juror
배심원단, jury

배심원장, foreman
배양, culture
배양 세포, culture
배양토, compost
배역, role
배열, arrangement
배열하다, arrange
배영, backstroke
배우, actor
배우다, familiarize, learn, study, train
배우자, partner, spouse
배우자 몰래 바람을 피우다, cheat
배우자가 없는, lone
배우자를 잃은, widowed
배웅하다, see
배율, magnification
배은망덕한, ungrateful
배임 행위, malpractice
배전반, panel
배제, exclusion
배제하다, exclude, rule, shut
배지, badge, button
배짱, gut
배짱 있게, boldly
배짱 있는, bold
배척당하다, ostracize
배출구, outlet
배출하다, excrete
배치, alignment, clash, configuration, layout, placement, posting, siting
배치되다, assign, clash, post, site, station
배치하다, set
배타적으로, exclusively
배턴, baton
배트, bat
배포, circulation
배포하다, distribute
배회하다, hover, prowl, roam
배후 조종자, mastermind
배후에 있다, lie
백, hundred
백 년, century
백 번째, hundredth
백과사전, encyclopedia
백금, platinum
백내장, cataract
백랍, pewter
백리향, thyme
백마 탄 왕자, knight
백만, mil, million
백만 번째의, millionth
백만장자, millionaire
백미러, rear-view mirror
백배 사죄하다, humble
백분율, percentage
백색 가전제품, white goods
백색 도료, whitewash
백색 인종의, Caucasian
백색의, white
백수, bum
백신, vaccine
백악, chalk
백악관, White House
백업, back
백열광, glow
백열광을 내다, glow
백인, Caucasian, white
백인의, white
백일몽, daydream
백일몽을 꾸다, daydream
백작, earl
백조, swan
백지 상태, blank
백지 상태가 되다, blank
백지 수표, blank check
백지 신탁, blind trust
백지위임, carte blanche
백합, lily
백혈병, leukemia
백화점, department store
밴, van
밴드, band, Band-Aid, plaster
밸브, valve
뱀, serpent, snake
뱀장어, eel

뱃놀이, boating
뱃머리, bow
뱃멀미, seasickness
뱃멀미가 난, seasick
뱃속, inside
뱉다, spit
버거, burger
버그, bug
버금가는, comparable
버너, burner, ring
(~을) 버는, on
버둥거리다, struggle
버드나무, willow
버려지다, dump
버려진, abandoned, derelict, waste
버릇, habit, way
버릇없는, impolite, naughty, sassy
버릇없는 놈, brat
버릇없이 굴다, misbehave
(~하는) 버릇이 생기다, take
버리게 하다, wean
버리고 떠나다, walk
버리기, dumping
버리다, abandon, bin, cast, desert, discard, dispense, ditch, give, jettison, junk, throw
버림, abandonment, desertion
버림받은 자, outcast
버섯, mushroom
버스, bus
버스 차장, conductor
버스로 가다, bus
버스로 옮겨지다, bus
버저, buzzer
버젓하게, virtuously
버젓한, virtuous
버캐, scum
버클, buckle, clasp
버클을 채우다, buckle
버터, butter
버터를 만드는 통, churn
버터를 바르다, butter
버티다, hang, hold, stick
버팀대, strut, support
버팔로, buffalo
버퍼, buffer
(~을) 벅차게 하다, top
번, time
번갈아, alternately
번갈아 일어나는, alternate
번갈아 일어나다, alternate
번개, lightning
번개 같은, lightning
번개처럼, flash
번거로운 일, bother
번득임, spark
번들, bundle
번민, agony
번복하다, overturn
번복할 수 없는, irrevocable
번식, breeding, reproduction
번식기의, season
번식력, fertility
번식력이 있는, fertile
번식시키다, propagate
번식하다, multiply, reproduce
번역, translation
번역 녹음되다, dub
번역가, translator
번역되다, translate
번영, prosperity
번영하다, bloom, prosper
번지게 하다, spread
번지다, bleed, lead, run, spread
번지르르한, flashy
번짐, spread
번쩍 비추다, flash
번쩍 빛나다, flash
번쩍 하는 불빛, flash
번쩍거리다, blaze
번쩍거림, blaze
번쩍번쩍, brilliantly
번쩍번쩍한, sleek
번창, prosperity
번창하는, flourishing, strong
번창하다, blossom, flourish, prosper, thrive

번창한, prosperous
번호, code, No., number
번호를 매기다, number
번호판, number plate
번화가, high street
번화가의, high street
벌, bee, pack, pair
벌거벗기다, strip
벌거벗은, bare, naked
벌거벗음, nakedness
벌거숭이, nudity
벌건 대낮에, daylight
벌금, fine, forfeit
벌금을 물다, fine
벌꿀, honey
벌다, buy, earn, get, make, realize
벌떡 일어서다, spring
벌레, bug, insect, worm
벌리다, open, widen
벌써, already, early
벌어들이다, take
벌어지다, broaden, gape, part, widen
벌을 가볍게 받다, get
벌을 면하다, get
벌이다, mount, stage, wage
벌주다, punish
벌집, worm
벌집을 만들다, riddle
벌집이 된, riddled
벌채, deforestation
벌채되다, deforest
벌충하다, compensate, make, recoup
벌컥 성을 내다, huff
벌컥 성을 내며, huff
벌컥 열리다, burst
범람하다, burst, flood, inundate
범위, bound, dimension, horizon, parameter, range, scope, spectrum
(~의) 범위 내에서, within
범위가 ~이다, range
(~의) 범위를 넘어서, out, outside
범유럽 디지털 통신 방식, GSM
범인, culprit
범죄, crime, offense, wrongdoing
범죄 조직, gang
범죄의, criminal
범죄자, offender, perpetrator, villain
범주, category, classification
범퍼, bumper
범포, canvas
범하다, commit, perpetrate
법, law
법관, court
법규, statute
법랑질, enamel
법령, act, ordinance, statute
법령의, statutory
법률, law
법률 고문, counsel
법률 제정, legislation
법무 장관, Attorney General
법무관, solicitor
법복, gown
법안, bill
법에 명시된, statutory
법에서 정한, mandatory
법원, court
법원 청사, courthouse
법으로 금지되다, outlaw
법을 제정하다, legislate
법을 준수하는, law-abiding
법의, legal
법의 심판을 받다, justice
법의학의, forensic
법의학의, forensic
법인, Corp., corporation
법인세, corporation tax
법인의, corporate
법적 섹스 동의 가능 연령, age of consent
법적으로, legally
법적인, legal
법전, code
법정, court, courtroom

법정 밖에서, court
법정 변호사, barrister
법정 싸움을 하다, fight
법정 재산 관리, receivership
법정 통화, legal tender
법조계, bar, law
법질서, law and order
법칙, dictate, law, rule
법학, law
벗겨 버리다, strip
벗겨져 떨어지다, flake
벗겨지다, peel
벗기다, peel, strip, undress
벗다, remove, shed, strip, take, undress
벗어, off
벗어나게 하다, pervert, pull, release
벗어나다, break, deviate, elude, emerge, escape, get, outgrow, pull, rid
벗어나지 않고 따라가다, keep
벗어나지 않다, keep
벗어난, beyond, deviant, loose, out, outside
벗어남, release
병병한, disoriented
병병함, disorientation
벙어리의, dumb, mute
벙커, bunker
베 짜는 사람, weaver
베개 받침대, bolster
베게, pillow
베기, cut, slash
베껴 쓰다, copy
베니어판, veneer
베다, chop, cut, slash
베란다, porch, veranda
베스트셀러, bestseller
베스트셀러의, best-selling
베이다, cut, fell
베이스, base
베이스 가수, bass
베이스 기타, bass
베이스의, bass
베이지색, beige
베이컨, bacon
베인 상처, cut
베일, veil
베일에 싸여 있는 것[사람], book
베일에 싸인, mystery
베일을 쓴, veiled
베테랑, veteran
베틀, loom
벤처, venture
벤처 투기 자본, venture capital
벤치, bench
벨, gong
벨 소리, ring tone
벨벳, velvet
벨트, belt
벼락부자, upstart
벼락출세한 사람, upstart
벼락치기 공부, cramming
벼락치기 공부하다, cram
벼랑, cliff
벼룩, flea
벼르고 있는, intent
벼슬, crest
벽, face, wall
벽감, niche, recess
벽난로, fireplace
벽난로 위의 선반, mantelpiece
벽돌, brick, masonry
벽에 부딪히다, brick
벽의 움푹 들어간 곳, recess
벽장, closet, cupboard
벽지, wallpaper
벽지를 바르다, paper
벽촌, backwater
벽화, mural
변경, border, frontier
변기, toilet
변기 속에 넣고 씻어 내리다, flush
변덕, whim
변덕스러운, erratic, fickle, inconsistent, moody, temperamental, unsettled, volatile

변동, fluctuation
변동 없는, flat
변동 환율제를 시행하다, float
변동하다, fluctuate
(~의) 변두리에, fringe
변론하다, plead
변명, excuse
변명의 여지가 없음, excuse
변명하다, excuse, plead
변모, metamorphosis, transformation
변변찮게, lamely
변변찮은, humble, lame
변비, constipation
변비약, laxative
변상하다, compensate
변색되게 하다, stain
변색되다, tarnish
변색된, stained
변색시키다, tarnish
변소, can
변속 레버, gear lever, gearshift
변속기, gear
변수, variable
변신, metamorphosis, transformation
변신시키다, transform
변이, mutation, variant
변이를 일으키다, mutate
변이성, variability
변이하다, mutate
변장, disguise
변장하다, disguise, masquerade
변장한, disguised
변절, defection
변절자, renegade
변절하다, defect
변제 불능, insolvency
변조하다, doctor
변종, variant
(~의) 변주, variation
변천, transition
변치 않는, fixed
변태의, perverted
변통하다, make, manage
변하게 하다, turn
변하기 쉬운, fickle, variable
변하다, break, change, move, turn
변함없는, same, steadfast, unchanged
변함없이, ever, invariably
변함없이 지지하다, stand
변혁, revolution
(~의) 변형, variation, version
변호, defense
변호사, advocate, attorney, counsel, lawyer
변호사업, bar
변호인, defense
변호하다, defend, plead
변호할 수 없는, untenable
변화, adjustment, alteration, change, move, shift, transformation, transition, variation, variety
변화가 심하다, fluctuate
변화가 없는, settled, static
변화를 위해, change
변화를 주다, vary
변화성, variability
변화하다, vary
변화하여, away
변환, conversion
변환시키다, export
변환하다, convert, decode
별, star
별 말씀을요, nothing
별 문제, kettle
별 볼일 없는 곳, nowhere
별 볼일 없는 존재, irrelevance
별 장식 없는, stark
별 장식 없이, starkly
별 힘들이지 않고 하다, duck
별개의, different
별개의 문제, matter
별개이다, thing
별거, separation
별거 중인, estranged, separated

별난, eccentric, freak, wacky
별난 사람, eccentric
별똥별, meteor
별로, really, very
별로 ~하고 싶지 않다, rather
별로 내키지 않는, half-hearted
별로 내키지 않아서, half-heartedly
별로 이상하지 않다, wonder
별명, aka, nickname
(~에게) 별명을 붙이다, nickname
별미, delicacy
별쇄 삽화, plate
별스러움, quirkiness
별안간, rudely
별자리, constellation, sign
별장, villa
별점, horoscope
별종, rebel
별첨, appendix
별칭을 붙이다, dub
별표, asterisk
병, ailment, bottle, bug, complaint, condition, illness, jar, trouble
병 말기에, terminally
병가, sick leave
병균, germ
병기, hardware
병동, ward
병든, ill, sick
병든 사람들, ill, sick
병들게 하다, affect
병력, history, troop
병리상의, pathological
병리학, pathology
병리학자, pathologist
병리학적, pathological
병사, GI, soldier
병상, bed, bedside
병아리, chick
병약자, invalid
병약한, sickly
병에 걸린, diseased
병에 담긴, bottled
병에 담다, bottle
병원, hospital, infirmary
병원균, microbe
병적 과식, bulimia
병적 흥분 상태, hysteria
병적으로, morbidly
병적인, morbid, pathological
병적인 공포, phobia
병치, juxtaposition
병치하다, juxtapose
병행하다, parallel
볕에 탄, brown
보강, reinforcement
보강하다, brace, reinforce, strengthen
보고, goldmine, report
(~을) 보고 ...을 떠올리다, connect
(~을) 보고 비웃다, laugh
(~을) 보고도 못 본 체하다, blind
보고서, paper, report
보고하다, report
보관, storage
보관소, home, repository
보관용 부분, stub
보관용 통, bin
보관하다, keep, store
보관해 두다, save
보궐 선거, by-election
보균자, carrier
보금자리, nest, roost
보금자리를 짓다, nest
보금자리에 깃들이다, nest
보급, diffusion, dissemination, spread
보급되다, diffuse
보급시키다, disseminate
보급하다, distribute
보기, sight
보기 드문, uncommon
보기 싫은, ugly
보기 흉한, unsightly
보내다, funnel, kill, pass, send, spend
보내지다, commit, refer, shunt

보낸 사람, sender
보너스, bonus
보는 각도, angle
보는 방향, angle
보는 사람, observer, viewer
보닛, bonnet, hood
보다, catch, look, make, observe, put, regard, see, show, sit, still, take, view, visit, watch
보답, reward
(~의) 보답으로, recognition
보답을 받다, reward
보답하다, recompense
보도, coverage, report, reporting, sidewalk, walkway
보도 관제, blackout
보도 관제를 받다, black
보도 자료, news release, press release
보도하다, report
보드카, vodka
보듬다, cradle
보라색, violet
보란 듯이, ostentatiously
보람 없이, avail
보람 있는, rewarding
보람이 있는, worthwhile
보류 상태로, hold
보류하다, shelve, withhold
보류하여, ice
보름달의, full
보리, barley
보리수, lime
(~을) 보며 즐기다, feast
(~을) 보면 ...가 생각나다, remind
보모, childminder, minder, nanny
보물, treasure
보물처럼 소중히 여기다, treasure
보물처럼 여기는 것, treasure
보배, jewel
보병, infantry
보복, reprisal, retaliation, retribution, revenge
보복의, punitive
보복하다, retaliate, revenge
보살피다, care
보상, compensation, recompense, reward, satisfaction
보상 판매, trade-in
보상금, bounty, compensation, reward
보상을 보장하다, protect
보상하다, amend, compensate, recompense, right
보석, bail, gem, jewel, stone
보석 가게, jeweler
보석 같은 것, gem
보석 상인, jeweler
보석 세공인, jeweler
보석 중에 잠적했다, bail
보석금, bail
보석금을 내 주다, bail
보석되다, bail
보석처럼 소중한 사람, gem
보송보송한, crisp, fluffy
보수, pay, pay packet, remuneration
보수가 적은, underpaid
보수가 좋은, well-paid
보수를 받는, paid
보수를 받다, pay, remunerate
보수성, reaction
보수적으로, traditionally
보수적인, conservative, reactionary, traditional
보수주의, conservatism
보수주의자, conservative, reactionary
보수파, right-wing, right-winger
보스, boss
보스 행세하는, bossy
보슬비, drizzle
보슬비가 내리다, drizzle
보안, security
보안 카메라, security camera
보안관, marshal, sheriff
보여 주다, chart, demonstrate, display, illustrate, indicate,

record, say, show, tell
보여주다, capture
보온 내의, thermal
보온력, warmth
보온성의, warm
보온성이 좋은, thermal
보완 의학의, complementary
보완물, complement
보완적인, complementary
보완하다, compensate, complement
보유, retention
보유 지분, holding
보유 차량, carpool
보유량, reservoir
보유자, bearer, holder
보유하다, hang, hold, retain
보육원, home
보이기, show
보이는, discernible, sight, view, visible
보이는 곳에, within
(~처럼) 보이다, appear, exhibit, less, look, manifest, seem, show
보이지 않게, away
보이지 않는, hidden, unseen
보이콧, boycott
보이콧하다, boycott
보일러, boiler
보자기, cloth
보자마자, sight
보자마자 죽이 맞다, hit
보잘것없는, humble, nominal, tenuous
보잘것없는 사람, nobody
보장, indemnity
보장하다, assure, ensure, indemnify, vouch
보조, auxiliary
보조 기구, aid
보조금, benefit, grant, subsidy, welfare
보조금을 주다, subsidize
보조금을 지원받는, subsidized
보조를 맞추다, keep, pace
(~와) 보조를 맞추어, coordination
보조의, ancillary, auxiliary, subsidiary
보조익, flap
보존, conservation, preservation, upkeep
보존 처리되다, cure
보존하다, hang, keep, preserve
보좌 신부, curate
보좌관, aide
보증, assurance, certification, guarantee, insurance
보증금, deposit
보증서, guarantee
보증인, guarantor, underwriter
(~의) 보증인이 되다, vouch
보증하다, assure, certify, guarantee, vouch
보초, guard, sentry
보초 서다, guard
보충, supplement
보충 설명, footnote
보충의, remedial, supplementary, top-up
보충재, supplement
보충하다, replenish, supplement
보컬, vocalist
보컬 부분, vocals
보통, generally, ordinarily
보통 명사, common noun
보통밖에 안 됨, mediocrity
보통 수준, average
보통 우편, surface mail
보통 우편의, second-class
보통의, average, common, fair, mediocre, medium, moderate, normal, ordinary, regular, standard, unremarkable, usual
보통주, common stock, equities, ordinary shares
보트, boat
보트타기, row, sailing

보편적인, cosmic, universal
보푸라기, fluff
보풀로 덮인, fuzzy
보행, walk
보행거리, walk
보행자, pedestrian
보험, assurance, insurance
보험 계약자, policyholder
보험 손해 사정인, insurance adjuster
보험 적용, cover
보험 증권, policy
보험 회사, insurer
보험료, premium
보험배상조정관, loss adjuster
보험업자, underwriter
보험에 적용하다, cover
보험을 들다, insure
보호, protection, sanctuary
보호 구역, reservation, reserve
보호 목적의, sheltered
보호 무역론자, protectionist
보호 무역주의, protectionism
보호 무역주의의, protectionist
보호 수단, insurance
보호 수단을 쓰지 않는, unprotected
보호 육성하다, wing
보호관찰관, probation officer
보호구, protector
보호대, brace, guard, protector
보호령, dependency, territory
보호막, cocoon
보호무역, protection
보호물, shield
보호색, camouflage
보호소, refuge
보호용의, protective
보호자, guardian, protector, shield
보호하는, protective
보호하다, cocoon, conserve, protect, safeguard, shield
복고풍의, retro
복구, reconstruction, restoration
복구하다, restore
복권, lottery
복귀, comeback
복도, corridor, hall, hallway, passageway
복리, compound interest, welfare
복면, mask
복면한, masked
복무하다, serve
복반침, fit
복부, abdomen, stomach
복부의, abdominal
복사, duplicate
복사 에너지, radiation
복사기, photocopier, Xerox
복사물, Xerox
복사본, photocopy
복사하다, copy, duplicate, reproduce, Xerox
복사한, duplicate
복수, revenge, vendetta, vengeance
복수를 가하다, exact
복수의, plural
복수하다, avenge, own, pay, revenge
복수형, plural
복숭아, peach
복숭아색, peach
복습, review, revision
복습하다, review, revise
복식 경기, double
복용량, dosage
복용시키다, dose
복용하는, on
복용하다, take
복원, restoration
복원하다, restore
복음, gospel
복음 성가, gospel
복음서, gospel
복잡성, complexity
복잡하게, intricately
복잡하게 만들다, complicate
복잡하게 하다, confuse

복잡하기 짝이 없는, messy
복잡하지 않은, uncomplicated
복잡한, complex, complicated, confused, elaborate, intricate, involved, mixed, sophisticated
복잡한 길, maze
복잡한 상황, jigsaw
복잡한 일들, complexities
복잡한 장치, gadget
복잡함, intricacy, labyrinth
복장, costume
복장과 장비, kit
복장을 갖추다, dress
복장을 하다, go
복점(複占), duopoly
복제 생물, clone
복제물, duplicate
복제품, replica, reproduction
복제하다, clone, reproduce
복제한, duplicate
복종, obedience, submission
복층시키다, line
복지, welfare
복지 국가, welfare state
복직, reinstatement
복직시키다, reinstate
복합 건물, complex
복합 제제, formulation
복합의, compound
복합적인, multiple
본, pattern, template
본 적이 없는, unseen
본거지, home, stronghold
본격적으로, earnest
본격적으로 다루다, grip
본격적으로 진행하다, stride
본격적으로 착수하다, settle
본격적인, full-blown
본고장, home, turf
본관, body, main
본국, home, homeland
본국 송환, repatriation
본국 투자, inward investment
본국으로 송환하다, repatriate
본국의, home
본능, instinct
본능의, instinctive
본능적으로, instinctively
본능적인, gut, instinctive
본떠 만들다, model
본뜨다, model, patterned
본래, essentially
본래 그대로의, untouched
본래 모습을 잃은, shape
본래부터, inherently
본래의, intrinsic, proper
본론으로 들어가다, chase
본문, body, text
본받다, emulate, follow, model
(~을) 본보기로 들다, hold
(~을) 본보기로 징계하다, example
본부, administration, headquarters, HQ
본분을 다하는, bit
본색을 드러내게 만들다, catch
본선, main
본성, inside, nature, self
본성(本城), keep
(~의) 본을 뜨다, example
본의 아니게, unwillingly, will
본의 아닌, involuntary, unwilling
본인 스스로의, personal
본전을 건지다, money
본전을 뽑다, money
본전이다, even
본정신, lucidity
본질, essence, heart, nature, substance
본질적 요소, essential
본질적으로, definition, essence, essentially, inherently, intrinsically, per se
본질적인, essential, inherent
본체, body
본토, mainland
볼, cheek
볼드체, bold
볼링, bowling

(~의) 볼모, hostage
볼장 다 본 거다, had
볼트, bolt, volt
볼품없는, gaunt, grotty, miserably, nasty, unattractive
봄, look, sight, spring
봉, rod
봉건 제도의, feudal
봉건주의, feudalism
봉급, salary, wage packet
봉급 인상액, increment
봉급을 받는, salaried
봉기, uprising
봉기하다, rise
봉사, work
봉사료, service charge
봉사하는, caring
봉사하다, serve
봉쇄, blockade
봉쇄되다, seal
봉쇄하다, block, blockade, seal
봉우리, peak
봉인, seal
봉인된 부분, seal
봉지, bag, packet
(~에) 봉착하다, run
봉투, bag
봉하다, seal
봉합부, seal
봉합하다, stitch
봉화, beacon
봐주다, allowance, bear, mind
부, copy, division, edition, ministry, rich, wealth
부(副)~, assistant
부~, deputy
부가, addition
부가 가치, added value
부가 가치세, value added tax, VAT
부가 급부, fringe benefit
부가 번호, prefix
부가 서비스, facility
부가 약호, prefix
부가되다, tack
부가물, addition
부가세, surtax
부가적으로, additionally
부검, autopsy, postmortem
부고 기사, obituary
부과, imposition
부과액, levy
부과하다, impose, levy, slap
부국의, rich
부근, vicinity
부글부글 끓는 상태, simmer
부글부글 끓다, boil, simmer
부기, bookkeeping, float
부기 계원, bookkeeper
부끄러운, small
부끄러운 줄 모르고, unashamedly
부끄러운 척하여, coyly
부끄러움, shyness
부끄러워하는, ashamed
부끄러워하며, shyly
부끄러워하지 않는, unashamed
부끄럼 타는, shy
부끄럽게 만들다, shame
부끄럽게 하다, embarrass
부닥치다, encounter
부단한, perpetual
부담, strain
부담금, levy
부담을 주다, stretch
부담이 큰, taxing
부담하다, bear
부당 이득 행위, profiteering
부당하게, unfairly, unjustly, wrongfully
부당하게 놓치다, pass
부당한, bum, unfair, unjust, unwarranted, wrongful
부당한 대우, victimization
부당한 대우를 받다, short-change
부당한 대우를 하다, injustice
부당한 대접, deal
부당한 취급을 받다, victimize
부대, contingent, corps, sack,

troop, unit
부대 본부, armory
부대 품목, extra
부대자루 같은, baggy
부도덕한, immoral, improper, unscrupulous
부동산, property, real estate, real property
부동산 공인 중개사, Realtor
부동산 중개소, estate agency
부동산 중개업자, estate agent
부두, dock, jetty, quay, waterfront, wharf
부두 선창, pier
부두에 닿다, dock
부드러운, creamy, feminine, fluid, mellow, silky, smooth, soft, subdued, tender
부드러운 털이 있는, furry
부드러움, softness
부드러워지다, soften
부드럽게, gently, smoothly, softly
부드럽게 말하다, croon
부드럽게 하다, soften, tone
부득불, necessity
부딪다, strike
부딪치다, bang, clash, collide, crack, hit, meet, run, strike
부딪침, bang
부라리다, roll
부랑자, down-and-out, tramp
부러뜨리다, break
부러운, enviable
부러운 듯이, enviously
부러움, envy
부러워하는, envious
부러워하다, envy
부러지다, break, fracture, way
부려먹는, bossy
부려먹다, boss
부력, buoyancy
부력이 있는, buoyant
부록, appendix, supplement
부루퉁하다, sulk
부루퉁함, sulk
부류, category, class, fraternity, kind, league, sort
(~라고) 부르다, call, refer
부르릉거리는 소리, purr
부르릉거리다, purr
부르면 들리는 곳에, earshot
부리, beak, bill
부리다, throw
부모, folk, parent
부모로서의 신분, parenthood
부모를 잃다, orphan
부모의, parental
부목사, vicar
부문, branch, section
부벽, buttress
부부, couple
부분, area, end, fraction, fragment, part, piece, portion, proportion, section, segment, slice, tranche, unit, way
부분 삭제, cut
부분 삭제하다, cut
부분의, way
부분적으로, part, partially, partly
부분적인, half, partial, qualified
부사, adverb
부산, fuss
부산물, by-product, spin-off
부산을 떨다, fuss
부산하다, bustle, buzz
부산함, bustle, hustle
부산히 움직이다, bustle, buzz
부상, rise, wound
부상당한, injured
부상을 입은, hurt
부상을 입히다, wound
부상자들, injured, wound
부서, department, unit
부서의, departmental
부서지기 쉬운, brittle
부서지다, break, crumble, fall, fragment
부서짐, fragility

부속 건물, annex, wing
부속 기구들, fitting
부속 예배당, chapel
부속 예배당 신부, chaplain
부속물, attachment, trappings
부속품, fitting
부수다, break, crumble, demolish, destroy, fragment, tear
부수적인, ancillary, subordinate, subservient
부수적인 것, footnote
부스, booth
부스러기, chip, crumb, scrap
부식, corrosion, decay, rot
부식 동판화, etching
부식되다, corrode
부식된, corroded
부식하다, decay, eat, rust
부실 채권, bad debt
부실한, flimsy
부양, boost, kick-start, provision, stimulation, upkeep
부양하는, stimulative
부양하다, boost, feed, keep, kick-start, maintain, provide, stimulate, support
부어오르다, swell
부어오른 것, swelling
부업, sideline
부업으로, side
부업으로 하다, double
부업하다, moonlight
부엌, kitchen
부여받다, endow
부여하다, concede, confer, endow, entitle, give, impart, invest
부연하다, expand
부위, cut, region
부유, affluence
부유층, affluent
부유층의, smart
부유하게 만들다, enrich
부유하게 하기, enrichment
부유한, affluent, rich, wealthy, well-off, well-to-do
부유한 사람들, wealthy
부은, bloated, swollen
부응하다, cater, live
부인, dame, denial, lady, ma'am, wife
부인 성명, disclaimer
부인과 의사, gynecologist
부인과 의학, gynecology
부인과 의학의, gynecological
부인하다, deny, negate
부인할 수 없는, undeniable
부인할 수 없이, undeniably
부임, arrival
부자, rich
부자연스러운, artificial
부자의, rich
부작용, side-effect
부재, absence
부재의, unavailable
부재자, absentee
부재한, absent
부적, charm
부적당하게, improperly
부적당한, improper, inappropriate, unsuitable
부적응자, misfit
부적절하게, improperly
부적절한, faulty, improper, inappropriate, order, wrong
부적합한, inadequate, unfit, unsuitable
부적합함, inadequacy
부정, denial, rigging, wrong
부정 관사, indefinite article
부정 사건, scandal
부정 자금, slush fund
부정 출발, false start
부정(不貞), infidelity
부정사, infinitive
부정어, negative
(~에서) 부정을 저지르다, rig
부정의, negative
부정이 없는, clean

부정적 평가를 받다, press
부정적으로, badly, negatively
부정적인, negative, unfavorable
부정적임, negativity
부정직, dishonesty
부정직하게, dishonestly
부정직한, bent, crooked, dishonest
부정하는, negative
부정하다, negate
부정하게, negatively, negative
부정한, irregular, wrong
부정한 돈벌이, racket
부정한 수단으로 돈을 벌다, hustle
부정할 수 없는, hard
부정행위, cheating, irregularity
부정행위를 하다, cheat
부정행위자, cheat
부정확하게, incorrectly
부정확한, inaccurate, incorrect, mark
부정확함, inaccuracy
부제, subtitle
부제가 붙다, subtitled
부조리, absurdity
부조리한, incongruous
부조리한 것, absurd
부족, gap, lack, scarcity, shortage, tribe
부족분, shortfall
부족의, tribal
부족하게, inadequately
(~이) 부족하다, lacking, short
부족한, inadequate, low, pressed, scant, scarce, short, wanting
부주의, carelessness, negligence
부주의로, inadvertently
부주의하게, carelessly, negligently
부주의한, careless, negligent
부지, compound, lot, site
부지 밖에, site
부지깽이, poker
부지런함, industry
부지런히, busily, diligently
부지런히 일하다, beaver
부지불식간에, unconsciously, unwittingly
부지불식간의, involuntary
부진, stagnation
부진하다, languish
부진한, stagnant
부진해지다, stagnate
부질없는, futile
부질없음, futility
부차적으로, incidentally
부차적인, incidental, secondary, side, subordinate
부착, insertion
(~에) 부착되어 있는, on
부착하다, attach, fasten
부채, fan, liability
부채가 있는, indebted
부채가 있다, owe
부채질하다, fan, fuel
부처, office
부추기다, egg, instigate, tempt, whip
부추김, instigation
부츠, boot
부치다, post
부침(浮沈), high
부케, bouquet
부탁, favor
부탁하다, ask, call
부티 나는, sleek
부티크, boutique
부패, corruption, decay
부패하다, rot
부패한, corrupt
부표, buoy
부푼, buoyant
부풀게 하다, buoy
부풀게 할 수 있는, inflatable
부풀다, buoy, inflate
부풀려 말하다, talk
부풀리다, blow, inflate
부풀린, inflated
부풀릴 수 있는 물건, inflatable
부풀어 오른, fluffy

부품, part, piece
부품 시장, aftermarket
부피, volume
부피가 큰, unwieldy
부하, load, protégé, subordinate
부하 직원들까지, downward
부하의, subordinate
부합, correspondence
(~에) 부합하다, conform, consistent
(~에) 부합하여, conformity
부호, character, code, sign
부화하다, hatch
부활, rebirth, reinstatement, resurgence, resurrection, revival
부활시키다, reinstate, resurrect, resuscitate
부활절, Easter
부흥, renaissance, revival
북, drum
북극, arctic
북대서양 조약 기구, NATO
북돋우다, bolster, boost, work
북돋움, boost
북동부, northeast
북동쪽, northeast
북동쪽의, northeast, northeastern
북미 원주민, Native American
북받침, rush
북부, north
북새통, hive
북서부, northwest
북서쪽, northwest
북서쪽의, northwest, northwestern
북적거리다, hum
북적대는 군중, crush
북쪽, north
북쪽에, north, up
북쪽으로, north, northward, up
북쪽의, northerly, northern
북향의, northward
분, min., minute
분가, branch
분간하다, discriminate, tell
분간할 수 없는, indistinguishable
분개, indignation
분개하여, indignantly
분개하여 시위하는, arm
분개한, indignant, outraged
분과, branch
분과 위원회, subcommittee
분광, spectrum
분권, decentralization
분권화하다, decentralize
분기별의, quarterly
분기점, watershed
분납, installment
분노, indignation, rage, wrath
분노하다, outrage
분노하여, indignantly
분노한, indignant
분량, volume
분류, categorization, classification
분류되다, bracket, class, fall, group
분류하다, categorize, classify, sort
분리, breakup, divorce, segregation, separation
분리 신설하다, spin
분리되다, come, disengage, separate
분리될 수 있다, divorce
분리시키다, dislodge, isolate
분리주의, separatism
분리주의자, separatist
분리하다, disconnect, disengage, dissociate, isolate, segregate, separate
분리하여, apart, isolation
분만, childbirth, delivery
분만하다, deliver
분말 형태의, powdered
분명하게, evidently, explicitly, unequivocally
분명하지 않은, unclear
분명한, articulate, emphatic, evident, explicit, express,

manifest, positive
분명해지다, dawning
분명히, doubt, doubtless, evidently, expressly, manifestly, obviously, plainly, specifically, surely, visibly, well
분명히 ~이다, mistake
분명히 나타내다, underline
분명히 말하다, articulate
분명히 보여 주는, illuminating
분명히 보여 주다, underscore
분명히 하다, clarify, clear
분무기, aerosol, spray
분발, push
분배, division, spread
분배하다, dispense, distribute, divide, share, split, spread
분별, sense, wit
분별 있게, wisely
분별 있는, practical, sane, sensible, wise
분별력, discrimination, wit
분별없는, indiscriminate
분별없이, unreasonably
분별이 없는, unreasonable
분별하다, distinguish
분비, secretion
분비물, secretion
분비선, gland
분비하다, secrete
분사, participle
분산, decentralization
분산시키다, diffuse, disperse
분산하다, decentralize
분석, analysis
분석가, analyst
분석적인, analytic, analytical, critical
분석하다, analyze, break, unpack
분석하듯, critically
분쇄기, grinder, mill
분쇄하다, smash
분쇄한, ground
분수, fountain, fraction
분수령, watershed
분식 회계, creative accounting
분실, disappearance
분실물, lost and found
분실물 센터, lost and found
분야, area, branch, domain, field, front, line, province, realm, scene, sector, sphere
분열, disintegration, divide, division, fragmentation, split
분열되다, disintegrate, split, tear
분열된, split
분열시키다, divide, split, tear
분열을 초래하는, divisive
분위기, ambience, atmosphere, aura, climate, feeling, mood, note, tone, vein
분위기가 꽁꽁 얼어 있다, knife
분위기가 무르익은, ripe
분위기에 흠뻑 젖다, soak
분을 바르다, powder
분자, molecule
분자로 된, molecular
분자의, molecular
분장, make-up
분쟁, conflict, contention
분쟁 중재자, troubleshooter
분지, basin
분출, burst, eruption, gush, jet, spurt
분출되다, boil, spew
분출하는, erupt, gush, spew, spurt
분투, effort, fight, push, struggle
분투하다, fight, strain, strive, struggle
분파, fragmentation, offshoot, sect
분포, distribution
분필, chalk
(~을) 분필로 쓰다, chalk
분한, resentful
분할, breakup, demerger, division, partition, subdivision
분할 상환하다, amortize

분할되다, demerge, partition, section, split
분할하다, carve, demerge, divide, split
분함, resentment
분해되다, break, come, decompose
분해시키다, decompose
분해하다, break, dismantle, pull, resent, strip, take
분홍색, pink
불, fire, heat, light
불가능, impossibility
불가능하게, impossibly
불가능하게 만들다, rule
불가능한, impossible, on, question
불가능한 일, impossible
불가분의, inseparable
불가사의, mystery
불가사의하게, enigmatically, mysteriously
불가사의한, inexplicable, mysterious
불가산 명사, uncountable noun, uncount noun
불가지론, agnosticism
불가지론자, agnostic
불가피성, inevitability
불가피하게, inescapably, inevitably
불가피한, inescapable
불가항력, circumstance, force
불가항력적으로, irresistibly
불가해하게, inexplicably
불가해한, incomprehensible
불결한, squalid
불경, disrespect
불경기, recession
불경기의, sluggish
불공평, injustice
불공평한, partial, uneven, unfair
(~에) 불과하여, only
(~에) 불과한, but, mere
불교, Buddhism
불교도, Buddhist
불교의, Buddhist
불구, deformity
불구가 되다, cripple, mutilate
불구가 된, disabled
불구대천의, sworn
불구로 만드는, crippling
불구로 만들다, disable
불구속 입건되다, remand
불구자, cripple
불구자로 만들다, maim
(~에도) 불구하고, all, despite, notwithstanding, spite
불굴, perseverance
불굴의, dogged, invincible
불규칙 변화의, irregular
불규칙하게, irregularly
불규칙한, irregular, unsteady
불규칙함, irregularity
불균형, imbalance, inequality
불균형하게, disproportionately
불그스레한, reddish, ruddy
불길하게, darkly, ominously
불길한, brooding, dark, ominous, unlucky
불길한 예감, doom
불길해 보이다, look
불꽃, rocket, spark
불꽃이 없이 타는 빛, glow
불꽃이 튀다, spark
불다, blow, gust
불도저, bulldozer
불도저로 밀다, bulldoze
불똥, spark
불량 납부자, payer
불량 식품, junk food
불량배, bully, hooligan
불량품, reject
불량한, rogue
(~를) 불러 세우다, grab, hail
불러 주어 받아쓰게 하다, dictate
불러내다, call
불러도 들리지 않는 곳에, earshot
불러들이다, call
불러일으키는, evocative
불러일으키다, arouse, draw, evoke,

excite, muster, work
불렀다, lead
불로 소득, handout, unearned income
불룩하게 만들다, plump
불룩하다, bulge
불룩한 부분, bulge
불륜, affair
불리, disadvantage
불리다, label, term
불리하게, adversely, against, disadvantage, unfavorably
불리하게 작용하다, count
불리한, adverse, unfavorable
불리한 입장에 두다, handicap
불리한 입장에 있는, disadvantage
불리한 점, minus
불리한 조건, handicap, small print
불리한 조건의, disadvantaged
불만, discontent, displeasure, dissatisfaction, grievance, gripe, quarrel, quibble, unrest
불만 제기, complaint
불만스러운, dissatisfied, unhappy
불만에 찬, disgruntled
불만을 사다, frown
불만을 제기하다, complain
불만족, unhappiness
불만족스러운, good, unhappy
불면증, insomnia
불면증의, sleepless
불멸, immortality
불명예, disgrace, reflection
불명예를 씻다, live
불명예스러운, scandalous
불명예스럽게, scandalously
불명확한, indefinite
불모의, bare, barren, infertile
불모지, wasteland
불문의, unwritten
불미스러운, unsavory
불법, lawlessness
불법 거래, racket
불법 거주지, squat
불법 거주하다, squat
불법 복제, piracy
불법 복제된, pirate
불법 복제를 하다, pirate
불법 점거자, squatter
불법 체류자, illegal
불법 침입자, hacker
불법거래, traffic
불법으로, unlawfully
불법의, hard, illegal, improper, unlawful, wrongful
불법적으로, illegally, improperly
불법적으로 이익을 얻다, hustle
불복종, disobedience
불복종하다, disobey
불분명하게 발음되어 나오다, slur
불분명하게 발음하다, slur
불분명한, murky, opaque, sketchy, unclear
불붙은, alight
불사, immortality
불사신, immortal
불사의, immortal
불상사, mishap
불성실, disloyalty
불성실한, disloyal
불소 화합물, fluoride
불손한, irreverent
불손함, irreverence
불순물, impurity
불순물이 든, impure
불순분자, subversive
불순한, impure, rogue
불시 단속, raid
불시 단속하다, raid
불시착시키다, ditch
불시착하다, ditch
불식시키다, demolish, quash
불신, disbelief, distrust, mistrust
불신하는, suspicious
불신하다, distrust, mistrust
불쌍하게, pathetically
불쌍한, pathetic, poor, wretched
(~을) 불쌍히 여겨 도와주다, pity

불쑥 나가다, burst
불쑥 나타나다, crop, materialize, pop
불쑥 달려들다, dive
불쑥 들어오다, burst
불쑥 말하다, blurt
불쑥 알려주다, spring
불쑥 움직이게 하다, shoot
불쑥 움직이다, shoot
불쑥 튀어나오다, protrude
불쑥 튀어나와 있다, stick
불안, apprehension, disquiet, fear, insecurity, jitters, suspense, tension, unease, uneasiness
불안감, angst, tremor, uneasiness
불안정, insecurity, instability
불안정하게, precariously, uneasily
불안정하게 하다, destabilize
불안정한, insecure, off-balance, precarious, rocky, shaky, unbalanced, uneasy, unsettled, unstable, unsteady
불안하게, nervously, uneasily
불안하게 하는, disturbing
불안하여, edge
불안한, apprehensive, edgy, haunted, insecure, nervous, uneasy, unsafe, unsettled
불안한 정도로, disturbingly
불안할 정도로 가까운, comfort
불안함, nervousness, trepidation
불안해하는, jittery
불어 끄다, blow
불어 날리다, blow
불어넣다, implant, infuse, inspire
불어서 만들다, blow
불에 구워내다, fire
불에 타서 사라지다, smoke
불완전한, half, imperfect, incomplete, partial
불용해성의, insoluble
불우한, bad off, deprived, disturbed
불운, luck, misfortune
불운한, doomed, hapless, ill-fated, unfortunate
불을 내는, incendiary
불을 내다, spark
불을 때다, stoke
불을 붙이다, fire, ignite, light
불을 커다, light
불의, injustice
불이 나다, fire
불이 나서, fire
불이 붙다, light
불이 붙어, ignite
불이 켜지다, light
불이행, default, failure
불이행하다, default
불일치, conflict
불임, infertility, sterility
불임 시술, sterilization
불임 시술을 받다, sterilize
불임의, infertile, sterile
불참, desertion
불참자, absentee
불청객, gatecrasher
불충, disloyalty
불충분하게, inadequately, insufficiently
불충분한, inadequate, incomplete, insufficient, short
불충분함, inadequacy
불충한, disloyal
불치병에 걸려, terminally
불치의, incurable, terminal
불친절, unkindness
불친절하게, unkindly
불친절한, unfriendly, unkind
불친화성, incompatibility
불쾌, displeasure
불쾌감을 주다, jar
불쾌하게, nastily, unpleasantly
불쾌하게 여겨 받을 빼다, blanch
불쾌하여, sick
불쾌한, unpalatable, unpleasant
불쾌함, harshness
불타 버린, burned-out

불타기 쉬운, inflammable
불타는, ablaze, burning, flaming
불타는 듯한, fiery
불투명한, opaque
불편, discomfort, inconvenience
불편을 끼치다, inconvenience
불편하게, awkwardly, uncomfortably
불편하게 하는, unnerving
불편한, awkward, inconvenient, uncomfortable
불편한 요소, discomfort
불평, complaint, grievance, griping, gripe, groan, grumble, moan, mutter, muttering, quarrel
불평 소리, grunt
불평거리, complaint
불평등, inequality
불평하다, complain, gripe, grumble, moan
불평하지 않고, murmur
불필요하게, gratuitously, needlessly, unnecessarily
불필요한, gratuitous, needless, superfluous, unnecessary, unwarranted
불필요한 것, frill
불필요한 부분을 제거하다, prune
불필요해진, redundant
불합격, rejection
불합격되다, reject
불합리, irrationality
불합리한, illogical, irrational, unreasonable
불행, misery, misfortune, unhappiness
불행하게도, unfortunately
불행한, unfortunate, unhappy, unlucky
불행한 사람, unfortunate
불행히도, unhappily
불현듯 떠오르다, strike
불현듯이 이해되다, click
불화, blood, breach, division, feud, friction, quarrel, rift, rupture, split, strife
불화하는, odds
불화하는 인물, sword
불확실성, question mark, uncertainty
불확실한, doubt, uncertain, unsettled
불황, depression, slump
불후의, immortal
불후의 명성, immortality
불후의 명성을 남기다, immortalize
불후의 인물, immortal
붉은, red
붉은빛을 띤, reddish
붐비는, busy
붐비다, swarm
붐빔, rush
붓, brush
붓다, pour, swell, tip
붓으로 칠하다, brush
붕괴, collapse, fall
붕괴되다, fall, tear
붕괴시키는, disruptive
붕대, bandage, dressing
붕대를 감다, bandage, dress
붙다, hook
붙들고 늘어지다, cling
붙들다, catch, detain
붙들어 두다, keep
붙박이 설비, fixture
붙박이로 만들다, build
붙박이의, fitted
붙어 있다, hang
붙여지다, apply
붙은, gum
붙이다, attach, post, stick
붙임성 있는, amiable, sociable
붙잡고 늘어지다, hang
붙잡다, catch, clutch, detain, grasp, seize
붙잡아 놓다, hold
붙잡으려고 하다, grab

붙잡음, hold
(~에) 붙잡혀, grip
붙잡혀 있는, stuck
붙잡히다, seize
뷔페, buffet
브라우저, browser
브래지어, bra
브래킷, bracket
브랜드, brand
브랜드 이미지, brand image
브랜디, brandy
브랜디 한 잔, brandy
브뤼셀 스프라우트, brussels sprout
브레이크, brake
브레이크를 밟다, brake
브레인스토밍, brainstorming
브레인스토밍 하다, brainstorm
브로일러, broiler
브로치, brooch, pin
브로커, broker
브로콜리, broccoli
브리지, bridge
브리핑, briefing
브리핑을 하다, brief
블라우스, blouse
블라인드, blind
블랙리스트, blacklist
블랙리스트에 오르다, blacklist
블레이저, blazer
블록, bloc, block
블록버스터, blockbuster
블루베리, blueberry
블루스, blues
블루칼라의, blue-collar
비, broom, rain, wet
비가 갑자기 쏟아지다, heaven
비가 내리는, wet
비가 많이 오는, rainy
비가 억수같이 쏟아지다, piss
비가 오다, rain
비겁한, cowardly
비겁함, cowardice
비결, formula, key, secret, trick
비계, scaffold, scaffolding
비공개로, camera, privately, private
비공개의, private
비공식의, informal
비공식적으로, informally, unofficially
비공식적인, unofficial
비과세의, tax-free
비관론, pessimism
비관론자, pessimist
비관적인, pessimistic
비교, comparison
비교 검토하다, weigh
비교급, comparative
비교급의, comparative
비교되는, comparable
비교에 의한, comparative
비교적, comparatively, relatively
비교적인, comparative, relative
비교하다, compare, draw
(~와) 비교하여, compared, comparison
비군사화하다, demilitarize
비굴한 짓을 하다, stoop
비극, tragedy
비극의, tragic
비극적으로, tragically
비극적인, tragic
비기다, compare, draw, tie
비길 데 없는, incomparable, unparalleled, unprecedented
비꼬는, sarcastic, wry
비꼬는 말, innuendo
비꼬면서, sarcastically
비꼼, sarcasm
비난, accusation, condemnation, criticism, indictment, rap, reproach
비난받기 쉬운, limb
비난하다, accuse, attack, blame, condemn, fault, finger, go, lay, rap, reproach, snipe
비논리적인, illogical, spurious
비누, soap

비늘, scale
비능률, inefficiency
비능률적으로, inefficiently
비능률적인, inefficient
비닐, vinyl
비닐 랩, plastic wrap
비단, silk
비단결 같은, silky
비단뱀, python
비대, obesity
비대한, unwieldy
비도덕적인, sordid
비둘기, dove, pigeon
비듬, dandruff
비등하다, nothing
비디오, video, video recorder
비디오 게임, video game
비디오 녹화기, VCR, video recorder
비디오 영상물, video
비디오 폰, videophone
비디오로 녹화하다, video,
　　videotape
비디오테이프, video cassette,
　　videotape
비딱한, wry
비뚤어져, perversely
비뚤어진, bent, crooked, perverse,
　　perverted, wry
비례 대표제, proportional
　　representation
(~에) 비례하는, proportional,
　　proportionate, pro rata
비록 ~이지만, albeit, though
비록 ~한다 해도, even
비롯되다, originate
비료, fertilizer, manure
비릿한, metallic
비만, obesity
비명, cry, scream, shriek
비명 소리, squeal
비명을 지르다, scream, shriek,
　　squeal
비명횡사하다, perish
비무장인 상태로, unarmed
비민주적인, undemocratic
비밀, confidence, secrecy, secret
비밀경찰 요원, secret police
비밀 번호, PIN
비밀 정보, tip-off
비밀로, confidentially, undercover,
　　wrap
비밀로 하다, conceal, hat, keep
비밀로 행해지는, undercover
비밀리에, covertly, quiet, scene,
　　secretly, secret
비밀스러운, mysterious, secretive,
　　sly
비밀스럽게, mysteriously, slyly
(~을) 비밀에 부치는, sweep
비밀에 붙여진, undisclosed
(~에게) 비밀을 이야기하다,
　　confidence
비밀을 지키다, mouth, secret, shut
비밀을 털어놓다, confide
비밀의, clandestine, confidential,
　　covert, inside, secret,
　　underhand
비밀인데, confidentially
비바람, element, flurry
비바람을 피하는, shelter
비바람이 들이치지 않는, sheltered
비방, slander, slur, smear
비방하다, slander, smear
비버, beaver
비번의, off-duty
비번인, duty
비번일, day off
비범한, exceptional, unusual
비법, trick
비벼 끄다, stub
비비 꼬다, wriggle
비비다, grind, rub
비비시 방송, BBC
비상 경계선, cordon
비상 구호대, emergency services
비상 브레이크, emergency brake
비상계단, fire escape
비상근의, part-time

비상사태, emergency
비상시의, emergency, forced
비생산적인, unproductive
비서, secretary
비서의, secretarial
비숍, bishop
비수기의, off-peak
비술(秘術), occult
비술의, occult
비스듬한, sideways
비스듬해지다, slant
비스듬히, angle, diagonally,
　　sideways
비스듬히 눕다, recline
비스듬히 앉다, recline
비스킷, biscuit
비슷하게, alike, similarly
비슷하다, approximate, resemble
비슷한, alike, line, nature, near,
　　par, similar
비슷한 부류, kind
비슷한 사람, like
비슷한 생각의, like-minded
비슷한 위치의, sideways
비슷한 유형, bird
비슷한 점, similarity
비슷한 취미의, like-minded
비슷함, likeness, similarity
비실용적인, impractical
비싸게, expensively
(~보다) 비싸게 값을 부르다, outbid
비싼, costly, dear, pricey, steep
비애, lament, woe
비약적인 발전, quantum
비어 있는, free, vacant
비열하게, dirty
비열한, despicable, dirty, grubby,
　　mean, vicious
비영리의, nonprofit,
　　nonprofit-making
비옥하게 하다, enrich, fertilize
비옥한, fertile, rich
비옥함, fertility
비올라, viola
비용, charge, cost, expense, price
　　tag, spend
비용 물문, object
비용 효율성, cost-effectiveness
비용 효율이 높은, cost-effective
비용 효율적으로, cost-effectively
(~의) 비용으로, expense
비용을 ~로 청구하다, charge
비용을 물리다, set
비용을 절감하다, retrench
비용이 들다, cost
비용이 안 드는, inexpensive
비우다, clear, empty, evacuate
비우호적인, hostile
비웃는, mocking
비웃다, deride, ridicule, scoff,
　　sneer, sniff
비웃을 수 없다, sniff
비웃음, jibe, ridicule, sneer
비워지다, empty
비위, stomach
비위 맞추다, court
비위가 약한, squeamish
비위를 건드리다, rub
비위를 맞추다, humor
비유, comparison, metaphor
비유에 비유를 섞어 쓰다, metaphor
비유적으로, figuratively,
　　metaphorically
비유적인, figurative, metaphorical
비유하다, compare, liken
비윤리적인, unethical
비율, part, percentage,
　　proportion, rate, ratio
비율을 맞춰, scale
비음의, nasal
비이성적으로, irrationally
비이성적인, irrational
비인간적인, impersonal, inhuman
비인격적인, impersonal
비자, visa
비자금, handout
비장(秘藏), hoard
비장애인, able-bodied

비장애인의, able-bodied
비장의 수, trump
비전(秘傳)의, esoteric
비전문의, general practitioner
비정규병, guerrilla
비정규직으로 대체하다, casualize
비정규직화, casualization
비정상적으로, abnormally
비정상적인, abnormal, unhealthy,
　　unnatural
비정상적인 것, abnormality
비정하게, callously
비정한, callous
비정함, callousness
비조직적인, disorganized
비좁은, confined, cramped
비좁은 상태, squash
비종교적인, secular
비주류의, fringe
(~에서) 비죽이 나오다, poke
(~에서) 비죽이 내밀다, poke
비준, ratification, validation
비준하다, ratify, validate
비중이 적은, minor
비즈니스 석, business class
비집어 열다, pry
비쩍 곯은, scrawny
비쩍 마른, skinny
비참하게, miserably
비참하게도 ~하게 되다, condemn
비참한, abject, dismal, harrowing,
　　miserable, sorry, unhappy,
　　woeful, wretched
비참함, misery
비천한, humble
비추다, allude, cast, mirror,
　　project, shine
비축된 것, store
비축량, reservoir
비축물, hoard, reserve, stock
비축물을 채워 넣다, stock
비축용으로, reserve
비축하다, stock, store
비축해 두다, hold
(~에) 비춰 볼 때, light
비춰지다, fall, light
비취, jade
비취색, jade
비치다, reflect
비친 모습, reflection
비커, beaker
비켜서다, stand
비키니, bikini
비키다, move
비타민, vitamin
비타협적 태도, intransigence
비타협적인, intransigent
비탄, distress, grief, heartache
비탄에 잠기게 하다, heart
비탄에 젖은, heartbroken
비탈, ascent, grade, gradient,
　　incline, slope
비탈 위로, uphill
비탈의 경사도, gradient
비탈지다, slope
비터, bitter
비통, woe
비통하게, woefully
비통한, woeful
비트, beat, bit
비트맵, bitmap
비트맵 형식으로 만들다, bitmap
비틀거리다, reel, stagger, stumble,
　　totter
비틀거림, stumble
비틀다, wrench
비틀어 돌리다, twist
비틀어 떼다, wrench
비틀어 열다, prize
비틀어 짜다, wring
비판, attack, commentary,
　　criticism
비판을 하다, judgment
비판적으로, critically
비판적인, critical
비판하다, knock
비평, criticism, critique
비평가, critic

비평문, notice
비폭력의, passive
(~에) 비하면, relation
비하하는, degrading, demeaning
비하하다, degrade, demean
비할 바 없는, incomparable
비합법의, illegitimate
(~에) 비해, compared, for,
　　proportion, relative
(~에) 비해 지나친, proportion
비핵의, conventional
비행, delinquency, flight, flying,
　　misdemeanor, vice, wrongdoing
비행 아동, delinquent
비행 작전, mission
비행 중대, squadron
비행 청소년, delinquent
비행 청소년 집단, gang
비행기, aeroplane, airplane, plane
비행기 스튜어디스, air hostess
비행기 승객, flyer
비행기로 나르다, fly
비행기로 수송하다, lift
비행기를 타고 가다, fly
비행기를 타고 목적지로 가서
　　렌터카로 여행하는, fly-drive
비행을 저지른, delinquent
비행장, airfield
비현실성, unreality
비현실적인, academic, impractical,
　　romantic, unconvincing, unreal,
　　unrealistic, utopian
비효율, inefficiency
비효율적으로, inefficiently
비효율적인, inefficient
비흡연가, nonsmoker
빅토리아 여왕 시대의, Victorian
빅토리아조 풍의, Victorian
빈, blank, empty
빈 방, vacancy
빈 자리, opening
빈곤, poverty
빈곤의 올가미, poverty trap
빈곤한, need, needy
빈곤한 사람들, needy
빈도, frequency, incidence, rate
빈둥거리는, idle
빈둥거리다, loiter, mess, round
빈둥거리며, idly
빈둥대며, round
빈민가, ghetto
빈민굴, gutter, slum
빈발, spate
빈속에, stomach
빈손의, empty-handed
빈약한, flimsy, meager, scant,
　　skimpy, slender, tenuous
빈정거리다, dig
빈정대는, wry
빈정대는 말, innuendo
빈정댐, sarcasm
빈칸, blank
빈털터리, down-and-out
빈털터리의, broke, down-and-out
빈틈없는, airtight, keen, solid,
　　watertight
빈틈없는 협상, horse-trading
빈혈증, anemia
빈혈증이 있는, anemic
빌다, pray, wish
빌딩, building
빌려 주다, advance, lending, lend,
　　loan, rent
빌리다, borrow, bum, hire, rent
빌린, loan, rental
빌릴 수 있는, rent
빌림, loan
빌미, fodder
빌붙다, sponge
빌어먹을, bloody, bugger, damn,
　　darn
빌어먹을!, hell
빗, brush, comb
빗나가게 하다, deflect
빗나가다, skew
빗나간, mark, stray
빗다, comb
빗대어 말하다, hint

빗맞히다, miss
빗맞힘, miss
빗발침, shower
빗방울, raindrop
빗어 내리다, brush
빗어 넘기다, sweep
빗장, bolt, latch
빗장을 걸다, bolt
(~에) 빗장을 질러 잠그다, bar
빗질, brush
빙 돌다, swing
빙 돌리다, swing
빙 돌아, round
빙 돎, swing
빙 두르다, circle
(~에) 빙 둘러, round
빙 둘러선 모양, ring
빙고, bingo
빙글빙글, around
빙빙 돌다, spin, swirl, twirl, whirl
빙빙 돌리다, twirl, whirl
빙산, iceberg
빙산의 일각, tip
빙점, freezing, freezing point
빙판의, icy
빙하, glacier
빙하의, glacial
빚, debt
빚다, mold, shape
빚을 갚다, debt
빚을 지다, debt, owe
빚지고 있는, red
빛, light, radiance, ray
빛깔이 바랜, faded
빛나게, brightly
빛나는, alight, bright, shining
빛나다, burn, glow, shine
빛남, brightness
빛내다, brighten
빛을 반사하다, gleam
빛을 받다, catch
빛을 잃다, overshadow
빠듯한, tight
빠뜨리다, land, miss, plunge
빠르게, rapidly
빠르게 가다, speed
빠르게 달리는, fast
빠르게 돌아가다, race
빠르게 이동하다, zoom
빠르게 진행되다, gallop
빠르게 하다, quicken
빠르게도, early
빠르기, tempo
빠른, fast, quick, rapid, speedy
빠른 걸음, trot
빠른 걸음으로 걷다, trot
빠른 길, fast track
빠른 대응, responsiveness
빠른 반응을 보이는, responsive
빠른 배달의, first-class
빠른 일 처리, whirl
빠른 펀치, jab
빠름, quickness, speed
(~에) 빠져 있다, drown, wallow
빠져나가다, elude, navigate
빠져나갈 수 없는, stuck
빠져나오다, dig
빠져든, immersed
빠져들기 쉬운, addictive
빠져들다, descend, slip
빠져서 없는, zero
(~에) 빠지다, blunder, drain, fall,
    go, indulge, land, miss, plunge,
    reduce, run, subside, turn, walk,
    write
빠진, stuck
빠짐, plunge
빡빡한, heavy, stiff, tight
빤한, corny, obvious, patent
빤히 보이게, glaringly
빤히 보이는, glaring
빨간, red
빨갛게 부어오르다, inflamed
빨개진, red
빨다, puff, suck
빨대, straw
빨라도, earliest
빨라지다, accelerate, quicken

빨래, laundry
빨래집게, clothes peg, clothespin,
    peg
빨리, fast, quickly, soon
빨리 걷게 하다, trot
빨리 걷다, trot
빨리 달리다, hare
빨리 뛰다, race
빨리 집어넣다, pop
빨아들이다, draw, soak, suck
빨치산, partisan
빳빳한, rigid
빵, bread
빵 굽기, baking
빵 굽는 기구, toaster
빵 껍질, crust
빵과자, pastry
빵집, baker, bakery
빻다, pound
(~을 빼고, except
빼기, subtraction
빼내다, eject, siphon, withdraw
빼다, deduct, drain, knock, leave,
    lose, omit, remove, sap,
    subtract, take
빼앗기다, lose, rob
빼앗김, loss
빼앗다, deprive, strip, take, usurp
빼어난, ethereal
빽빽이 들어가다, cram
빽빽이 들어찬, crammed
빽빽이 채우다, cram
빽빽하게, thickly
빽빽한, thick
뺀, minus
뺏기다, lose
뺑소니, hit-and-run
뺨, cheek
뻐꾸기, cuckoo
뻐드러진, buck
뻔뻔스러운, brazen, impudent
뻔뻔스러운, cheek, gall
뻔뻔스럽게, brazenly
뻔뻔스럽게도 ~하다, nerve
뻔뻔하게, shamelessly
뻔뻔한, shameless
뻔한, transparent
뻔한 결과, foregone
뻔한 속임수, charade
뻔한 이야기이다., story
뻗다, extend, run, spread, stretch
뻗어 나가다, spread
뻗어 있다, extend, stretch
뻗은 지역, stretch
뻣뻣하게, stiffly
뻣뻣하게 만들다, stiffen
뻣뻣한, stiff, wiry
뻣뻣한 털, bristle
뻣뻣해지다, stiffen, tighten
뻥, pop
뻥 뚫린, gaping
뼈, bone
뼈 빠지게 열심히 일하다, gut
뼈가 앙상한, bony, skeletal
뼈가 있는, bony
뼈대, frame, skeleton
뼈로 만든, bone
뼈를 바르다, fillet
뼈를 발라내다, bone
뼈의, skeletal
뽐내다, show
뽐내며 걷다, strut
뽑다, extract, pick, pluck, run,
    select
뽑아 들다, draw
뽑아내다, extract
뽑아냄, extraction
뽀루지, rash
뾰족구두, spike heels, stiletto
뾰족뾰족한, spiky
뾰족한, pointed, sharp
뾰족한 끝, tip
뾰족한 방울 모양의 열매, cone
뿌듯해 하는, pleased
뿌려주다, spray
뿌리, root
뿌리 깊은, ingrained, rooted
뿌리 뽑다, root

뿌리다, distribute, douse, dust,
    plant, spray, sprinkle
뿌리를 내리다, root
(~에) 뿌리를 둔, rooted
뿌리를 먹는, root
뿌리박힌, embedded
뿌리의, root
뿌리째 뽑다, uproot
뿌연, matt, murky
(~할) 뿐인, just
뿔, horn
뿔뿔이, apart
뿔뿔이 흩어지게 하다, scatter
뿔뿔이 흩어지다, scatter
(~의) 뿔에 받히다, gore
뿜어 나오다, spurt
뿜어내다, puff, spew
뿜어져 나오다, puff, spew
삐거덕거리는 소리, grind
삐거덕거리며 움직이다, grind
삐걱거리는 소리, creak
삐걱거리다, creak, grate, groan,
    squeak
삐걱거리며 멈추다, grind
삐다, sprain, strain, twist
삐삐, beeper
삐죽거리다, pout
삐죽이다, pout
삐치다, resent
삐침, tantrum
삑 소리, whistle
삑 소리를 내다, whistle
삠, sprain, strain
사각형 모양의, square
사각형 폭 빠진, square
사건, accident, case, episode, event,
    happening, incident,
    occurrence
사건이 없는, uneventful
사건이 지난 후 생기는 통찰력,
    hindsight
사격을 개시하다, fire
사격장, range
사견, theory
사고, accident, thinking, wreck
사고력 차단, block
사고방식, mind
사고하다, think
사과, apology, apple, satisfaction
사과 주스, cider
사과주, cider
사과하다, apologize
사교가, mixer
사교계, society
사교생활을 하다, socialize
사교적으로, socially
사교적인, outgoing, sociable
사귀다, go, see
사그라들다, ebb
사그라뜨리다, dim
사그라지다, dim, evaporate
사기, con, morale, racketeering,
    swindle
사기가 저하된, demoralized
사기꾼, crook, fake, fraud, vulture
사기로, fraudulently
사기를 저하시키다, demoralize
사기의, fraudulent
사기죄, fraud
사기치다, con
사나운, ferocious, fierce, foul, wild
사나움, ferocity
사나이, fellow
사납게, fiercely
사내, guy
사내 특유의, laddish
사내아이 같은, boyish
사내의, in-house
사냥, hunt, hunting, shooting
사냥 여행, safari
사냥감, game
사냥개, hound
사냥꾼, hunter
사냥하다, hunt
사다, buy
사다리, ladder
사단, division
사들이다, buy
사디스트, sadist

사디즘, sadism
사라져 가는, dying
사라지고 있는, way
사라지다, disappear, dust, melt,
    piss, vanish
사라진, extinct, lost
사라짐, disappearance
사람, character, dude, man,
    person, soul, spirit, we
사람 좋은, generous
사람들, folk, one, oneself, people,
    person, public, those, you
사람들 눈에 잘 띔, profile
사람들 눈에 잘 안 띔, profile
사람들 앞에서, public
사람들과 사귀다, socialize
사람들과 어울리지 않다, keep
사람들로 가득 찬, crowded
사람들의 기억에 남아, memory
(~한) 사람들이 거주하다, people
사람을 너무 많이 태우는, overload
사람을 너무 많이 태운, overloaded
사람을 빼내다, poach
사람을 사로잡는, consuming
사람을 칼로 찌른 사건, stabbing
사람의, human
사람이 없는, deserted
사랑, affection, caring, love
사랑 이야기를 담은, romantic
(~에게) 사랑받게 하다, endear
사랑스러운, adorable, darling,
    endearing, lovable, lovely
사랑에 빠지다, love
사랑에 푹 빠진, head
사랑의 도피를 하다, run
사랑하는, beloved
사랑하다, love
사려, understanding
사려 깊게, thoughtfully
사려 깊은, considerate, thoughtful,
    wise
사려가 없는, inconsiderate
(~을) 사려고 하는, market
사례, case, instance
사례 연구, case study
사례금, gratuity
사로잡는, absorbing
사로잡다, absorb, attract, capture,
    catch, come, grip, hold, obsess,
    overtake
(~에) 사로잡힌, grip
사로잡히다, captivate, grip, obsess,
    rivet
사로잡힌, absorbed, captive,
    obsessed
사료, feed, fodder
사료 짐마차, wagon
사리, coil
사리 추구, self-interest
사리사욕, self-interest
사리에 맞게 말하다, talk
사립 고등학교, prep school
사립 중등학교, college
사립 초등학교, prep school
사립의, independent
사립학교, private school, public
    school
사마귀, mole, wart
사막, desert
사망, demise, fatality
사망률, death rate, mortality
사망자 수, death toll
사망하다, die
사망한, late
사면, amnesty, pardon
사면되다, pardon
사멸, extinction
사멸한, extinct
사명, mission
사명감, vocation
사모님, lady, ma'am, madam
사무 변호사, solicitor
사무국, secretariat
사무소, office
사무실, office
사무원, clerk
사무원으로 근무하다, clerk
사무적인, brisk, businesslike,

matter-of-fact
사무적인 투로, matter-of-factly
사무직과 관련된, white-collar
사무직의, clerical, white-collar
사무총장, secretary-general
사물, object
사물함, locker
사발, bowl
사발처럼 생긴 부분, bowl
사방으로 뻗다, radiate
사방의, near
사법, justice
사법권, jurisdiction
사법부, judiciary
사법의, judicial
사법적으로, judicially
사별의 슬픔, bereavement
사병, rank
사보타주, sabotage
사복 차림의, plain
사본, copy, duplicate
사사오입하다, round
사산된, stillborn
사상, thought
사상가, thinker
사상자, casualty
사색, thought
사색이 된, deathly
사생아인, illegitimate
사생활, privacy
사서, librarian
사서 고생을 하다, ask
사서함, box, PO Box, post office box
사서함 번호, box number
사선(斜線), slash
사설, editorial
사설로, privately
사설의, editorial, private
사소한, insignificant, little,
　marginal, minor, petty, small
사소한 다툼을 벌이다, quibble
사소한 실수, slip
사소한 일, trifle
사슬, chain, tether
사슬로 매다, chain
사슬로 묶다, tether
사슴, deer
사슴고기, venison
사시, squint
사실, actually, all, bottom, fact,
　realistically, reality, truth
사실 같지 않은, improbable
사실 같지 않음, improbability
사실 그대로의, bare
사실 무근의, unfounded
사실과 다르게, erroneously
사실과 다른, mythical
사실로 인정되다, stand
사실무근의, groundless
사실상, effect, effectively, intent,
　practically, virtually
사실상의, effective, virtual
사실에 입각한, factual
사실은, actually, fact, matter,
　reality
사실을 말하자면, truth
사실이 아니다, nothing
사실이 확인되지 않은, alleged
사실이 확인되지 않은 주장에 의하면,
　allegedly
사실이다, case
사실인, true
사실적으로, realistically
사실적인, realistic
사실주의, realism
사실주의자, realist
사실혼의, common law
사심 없는, disinterested, selfless
사악한, evil, sinister, wicked,
　wrongful
사악한 것, evil
사암, sandstone
사양, model
사양(仕樣), spec
사양하다, decline
사업, business, enterprise,
　undertaking
사업 계획, business plan, project

사업가, businessman,
　businessperson
사업권, concession
사업체, operation, practice
사열, parade
사외의, nonexecutive
사외이사, nonexecutive
사용, occupancy, usage, use, wear
사용 설명서, manual
사용 중이다, occupy
사용 중인, engaged
사용권, tenure, use
사용되고 있는, use
사용되는, service
사용되지 않는, use
사용법, direction, usage
사용하기 쉬운, user-friendly
사용하다, employ, get, touch, use,
　wield
사용하지 않는, free, idle
사용하지 않은, unused
사우나, sauna
사운드 시스템, sound system
사운드 카드, soundcard
사운드 트랙, soundtrack
사원, temple
사위, son-in-law
사유의, private
사유지, land
사육, breeding, feeding
사육사, keeper
사육자, breeder
사육장, farm
사육제, carnival
사육하다, raise
사은품, giveaway
사의, gratitude
사이, interlude, while
(~와) 사이가 좋지 않다, foul
사이가 틀어지다, fall
사이가 틀어짐, rupture
사이드라인, sideline
사이렌, siren
사이버 섹스, cybersex
사이비 종교 집단, cult
(~의) 사이에, among, between,
　during
(~) 사이에 끼어 있다, catch
사이에 끼우다, sandwich
(~) 사이에서 갈등하다, catch
사이의, between, intervening
사이좋은, side
사이좋은, harmonious, term
사이클, cycle
사이클론, cyclone
사이키델릭한, psychedelic
사이펀, siphon
사인, autograph
사인 심리, inquest
(~에) 사인하다, autograph
사임하다, give, resign, stand
사자, lion
사장, boss
사재기하다, buy
사적 자유, privacy
사적인, personal, private
사전, dictionary
사전 단계, precursor
사전 조사, homework
사전 준비, preliminary
사전 준비를 하다, set
사전에, advance
사전에 준비된, prepared
사전에 준비된 것, preparation
사전에 차단하다, preempt
사전의, advance, preliminary, prior
사전적인, literal
사절단, mission
사정, assessment, condition,
　matter, thing
사정거리, fire, range
사정거리 내의, range
사정거리 밖의, range
사정을 알다, score
사정이 ~에게 불리하다, stack
사정인, assessor
사정하다, assess
사제, priest

사제장, dean
사조, thought
사중주단, quartet
사중창단, quartet
사증, visa
사직을 허용하다, let
사직하다, resign
사진, image, photo, photograph,
　photography, picture, portrayal,
　print, shot, snap
사진 기사, photographer
사진 설명, caption
사진을 찍다, photograph
사진의, photographic
사진0l나 그림에 등장하다, picture
사진작가, photographer
사진처럼 정확한, photographic
사진첩, album
사창가, brothel
사촌, cousin, uncle
사춘기, adolescence, puberty
사춘기 청소년, adolescent
사춘기의, adolescent
사취, swindle
사취하다, swindle
사치, luxury
사치스러운, luxurious
사치스럽게, expensively
사치품, extravagance, luxury
사치광인, luxury
사칭(詐稱), impersonation
사타구니, groin
사탄, devil, Satan
사탕, candy, sweet
사탕무, beet
사탕옥수수, sweetcorn
사태 진전, development
사태가 진정되다, dust
사퇴하다, vacate
사투를 벌이다, death, fight
사파리, safari
사파이어, sapphire
사파이어색, sapphire
사팔뜨기, squint
사포, sandpaper
사포로 문지르다, sand
사표, resignation
사표를 내다, notice
사학자, historian
사항, point, way
사형, capital punishment, death
　penalty
사형 선고, death sentence
사형 집행, execution
사형수 사동, death row
사형시키다, execute
사형에 처할 만한, capital
사형을 선고받은, condemned
사환, page
사회, community, society
사회 규범, moral, morality
사회 기반 시설, infrastructure
사회 보장 제도, social security
사회 복지, social services
사회 복지사, social worker
사회를 보다, host
사회봉사, community service,
　public service
사회사업, social work
사회사업가, social worker
사회의, social
사회자, chairman, host
사회적 약자 우대 정책, positive
　discrimination
사회적 약자를 돕기 위한, sheltered
사회적으로, socially
사회적인, social
사회정치적인, sociopolitical
사회주의, socialism
사회주의 성향의, socialist
사회주의자, socialist
사회학, sociology
사회학의, sociological
사회학자, sociologist
사회학적인, sociological

사후 검토, postmortem
사훈(社訓), mission statement
삭감, cutback, deduction, drop
삭감하는 사람, cutter
삭감하다, cut
삭구, rigging
삭제하다, censor, cross, cut, delete,
　erase, strike, uninstall, zap
산, acid, mountain
산 물건, purchase
산간 무지, moorland
산길, pass, trail
산꼭대기, peak
산더미, mountain
산더미 같은, mountainous
산도, acidity
산들바람, breeze
산딸기, raspberry
산뜻하게, pleasingly
산뜻하게 하다, smarten
산뜻한, fresh
산란하게 만들다, distract
산란한, distracted
산림학, forestry
산마루, crest
산만해지다, wander
산맥, range
산문, prose
(~의) 산물, product
산발적으로, sporadically
산발적인, scattered, sporadic
산봉우리, pinnacle
산부인과 의사, obstetrician
산사태, landslide
산산이, apart
산산이 부서지다, shatter
산산이 부서짐, shattering
산산조각, piece
산산조각 나다, shatter
산산조각 내다, shatter
산산조각이 나다, fall
산성비, acid rain
산성의, acid
산소, oxygen
산수, arithmetic, sum
산아 제한, birth control
산악 지역, highlands
산악성의, mountainous
산악자전거, mountain bike
산업, industry
산업 단지, industrial park,
　industrial estate
산업 박람회, trade fair
산업 폐기물, sludge
산업의, industrial
산업이 발달한, industrial
산업화, industrialization
산업화되다, industrialize
산이 들어 있는, acidic
산이 많은, mountainous
산장, chalet, lodge
산재하다, sprinkle
산재한, interspersed
산재한 것, scattering
산정되다, work
산정하다, calculate
산줄기, range
산중턱, mountainside
산책, ramble, stroll, walk
산책길, walk
산책하다, ramble, stroll
산출량, run
산출하다, work, yield
산탄총, shotgun
산허리, mountainside
산호, coral
산호빛의, coral
살, bar, flesh, year
살 곳을 찾아 주다, place
살 수 없을 정도로, prohibitively
살 수 없을 정도인, prohibitive
살 수 있는, sale
살갗을 태우다, burn
살갗이 벗겨진, raw
살갗이 튼, chapped
살결이 흰, fair
살구, apricot
살구색의, apricot

살균, sterilization
살균제, disinfectant
살균하다, disinfect, sterilize
살균한, sterile
살금살금 가다, sneak
살금살금 걷다, creep
살다, lead, live
살랑거리게 하다, stir
살랑이다, stir
살림, housekeeping
살살 달래서 얻어내다, coax
살살 밀기, nudge
살살 밀다, nudge
살살 설득하다, nudge
살살 설득함, nudge
살상부, hit list
살아 있는, alive, live
살아가게 하다, sustain
살아가다, exist
살아남다, live, survive
살아남음, survival
살얼음 위를 걷고 있다, ice
살얼음을 밟고, ice
살을 붙이다, flesh
살을 빼다, slim
살을 에는 듯한, piercing
살을 에이듯이 추운, biting
살이 빠지다, weight
살이 찌게 하는, fattening
살이 찌다, weight
살인, homicide, killing, murder
살인을 저지를 것 같은, homicidal
살인자, killer, murderer
살인적인, cut-throat
살짝, discreetly, thinly
살짝 건드리다, jog
살짝 깨물기, nip
살짝 꼬집기, nip
살짝 꼬집다, nip
살짝 담그다, dip
살짝 물다, nip
살짝 보이다, peep
살짝 찔러 작은 구멍을 내다, prick
살짝 튀기다, saute
살짝 풍기는 냄새, whiff
살찌는, fattening
살찐, fat, obese
살충제, insecticide
살충제를 뿌리다, spray
살코기, fillet
살펴보다, go, look, see, study, view
살펴봄, look
살포하다, distribute
살해, killing
살해 대상자 명단, hit list
살해범, killer
살해하다, murder
삶, incarnation, life
삶다, boil
삶의 양식, way of life
삶의 질을 개선하는, lifestyle
삼가는, understated
삼가서 하는 말, understatement
삼각건, sling
삼각대, tripod
삼각의, triangular
삼각주, delta
삼각형, triangle
삼림, wood
삼림지, woodland
삼목, cedar
삼목재, cedar
삼삼오오 모이다, cluster
삼주문, wicket
삼키다, keep, swallow
삼킴, swallow
삽, shovel, spade
삽시간에 퍼지다, wildfire
삽으로 푸다, shovel
삽입, insertion
삽입 광고물, insert
삽입하다, insert
삽화, illustration
삽화를 그리다, illustrate
상, award, prize, reward
상(像), figure, image, statue
상감 세공을 한, inlaid
상공, mid-air

상공 회의소, chamber of commerce
상관, senior, superior
상관관계, correlation, equation
상관없는, point
상관의, senior
상관하다, correlate, mind
상근, full-time
상근직의, full-time
상금, winnings
상급생, senior
상급의, pile, superior
상기시키다, bring, invoke, prod, remind, take
상기의 것, above
상냥하게, sweetly, tenderly
상냥하고 매력적인, suave
상냥한, affable, amiable, attentive, caring, feminine, friendly, gracious, pleasant, sweet, tender
상냥함, friendliness, geniality, tenderness
상다리가 휘어질 지경이다, groan
상단, header
상담, consultation, counseling
상담원, counselor
상담하다, counsel
상당 부분을 차지하다, soak
상당하게, considerably
상당하는, equivalent
(~에) 상당하다, amount
상당한, bit, considerable, fair, great, handsome, healthy, mass, quite, reasonable, significant, sizeable, some, substantial
상당한 값어치, value
상당한 거리, mile
상당한 양, measure
상당한 양의, cascade
상당한 양의 것, chunk
상당한 정도, degree
상당히, deal, enough, fairly, fantastically, pretty, quite, reasonably, significantly, something, substantially, well
상당히 떨어진 곳에, way
상당히 많은, fair, fantastic
상당히 많은 양, diet
상당히 많이, measure
상당히 큰, measurable
상대, opponent, partner
상대 선수, opponent, opposition
상대하다, distribute
상대 팀, opposition
상대 회사, partner
상대국, partner
상대되는 것, counterpart
상대자, adversary
상대적으로, relatively
상대적인, relative
상대편 사람, counterpart
상동, ditto
상동병, corporal
상록수, evergreen
상록의, evergreen
상류 사회, society, upper class
상류 사회에 속한, posh
상류로, upstream
상류의, exclusive, high-class, upstream
상류층, upper class
상류층용의, select
상류층을 겨냥한, upscale
상류층의, genteel, upper class
상륙, landing
상륙시키다, land
상륙하다, land
상반, incompatibility
(~와) 상반되는, inconsistent
상반되는 태도를 가진, ambivalent
상반된 효과를 가져오는, double-edged
상반신, trunk
상부의, upper
상사, boss, Messrs
상상, imagination, vision
상상력, imagination
상상력이 뛰어난, imaginative
상상의, imaginary, mythical,

phantom
상상하다, conceive, envisage, envision, fancy, imagine, picture, see, visualize
상상할 수 없는, unimaginable, unthinkable
상상할 수 없이, unimaginably
상상할 수 있는, conceivable, imaginable
상세 정보, detail
상세하게, detail, intimately
상세한, detailed, intimate
상세한 내용, particulars
상세한 정보를 주다, fill
상세히, full
상세히 설명하다, expound, spell
상소, appeal
상소하다, appeal
상속 받다, inherit
상속세, inheritance tax
상속인, beneficiary, heir
상쇄되다, offset
상쇄시키다, counter
상쇄하다, cancel
상술, discussion, elaboration
상술하다, detail, elaborate, recount, specify
상스러운, bad, coarse, crude, indecent, vulgar
상스러움, vulgarity
상스럽게, coarsely, crudely, indecently
습관적인, chronic, habitual
상승, ascent, upturn
상승 온난 기류, thermal
상승세, uptrend
상승세의, bullish
상승시키다, better
상승하는, climb, move, rise
상승하여, up, upward
상시 평가, continuous assessment
상식, common sense, sense
상식적인, sensible
상실, loss
상실감, loss
(~을) 상실한, bereft
상심, heartbreak
상심시키다, heart
상심하다, smart
상심한, heartbroken
상아, ivory
상아로 만든, bone
상아색의, ivory
상어, shark
상업 은행, commercial bank
상업의, commercial
상업적으로, commercially
상업적인, commercial
상업주의, commercialism
상업화, commercialization
상업화되다, commercialize
상업화된, commercialized
상여금, bonus
상연물, act
상연하다, enact, present
상영, screening
상영되다, screen
상영하다, show
상용의, commercial
상원, House of Lords, lord, Senate
상원 또는 하원, house
상원 의사당, House of Lords
상원 의원, senator
상위의, pile, senior
상을 당한, bereaved
상을 받다, honor
상을 보다, lay
상응하는, corresponding
상응하다, correspond
상의, jacket
상의도 없이, head
상이, disparity, divergence
상이한, disparate
상인, merchandiser, merchant, trader
상자, box, carton, chest, crate, package
상자에 넣다, crate

상장 폐지하다, delist
상장 회사, listed company
상장(上場), quotation
상장되다, list
상장되지 않은, unlisted
상장하다, float
상전벽해의 변화, sea change
상점, merchandiser, shop, store
상점 카운터, POS
상점하다, table
상주하지 않는, roving
상징, emblem, icon, metaphor, symbol
상징성, symbolism
상징적으로, symbolically
상징적인, symbolic
상징주의, symbolism
(~을) 상징하는, symbolic
상징하다, capture, embody, mark, symbolize
상처, bruise, scar, sore, wound
상처나다, bruise
상처를 내다, gouge
상처를 입히다, injure
상처를 주다, scar
상처받기 쉬운, vulnerable
상처받기 쉬움, vulnerability
상처받은, injured
상추, lettuce
상충, collision
상충하는, variance
상충하다, collide
상층 원형 관람석, circle
상쾌한, bracing, crisp, fresh, refreshed, refreshing
상태, condition, going, state
상태가 양호한, order
(~한) 상태로 만들다, drive
(~한) 상태를 유지하다, stay
(~한) 상태에 빠지다, lapse
(~한) 상태에 있다, find, lie
상투어, commonplace
상투적인, stock
상투적인 말, platitude
상투적인 문구, cliché
상표, make, trademark
상표 없는 것, generic
상표명, brand name, trade name
상품, commodity, goods, merchandise, offering
상품 전시장, salesroom
상품권, token, voucher
상품명, trade name
상품의 장점, selling point
상하게 하다, spoil
상하다, go, spoil
상한, bad, off, sour
상해, harm, injury
상호 대체 가능하게, interchangeably
상호 대체 가능한, interchangeable
상호 연관성, interconnection
상호 의존성, interdependence
상호 의존적인, interdependent
상호 작용, interaction
상호 작용하다, interact
상호 회사의, mutual
상호간에, mutually
상호간의, reciprocal
상호의, mutual
상환, payment, redemption, repayment, settlement
상환금, payment, repayment
상환의, payback
상환하다, redeem
상환할 수 있는, redeemable
상환해야 할, repayable
상황, affair, circumstance, condition, context, going, matter, picture, position, situation, state of affairs, thing
상황 설명을 하다, picture
상황에 따라 다르다, depend
상황에 맞춰 말을 하다, noise
(~한) 상황으로 빠져들다, drift
상황을 악화시키다, matter
상황이 그러하니, circumstance
상황이 아직 좋을 때, going

상황이 안 좋은, badly off
상황이 어려워지면, shove
상흔, scar
살, crotch
살살이, inside, top
살살이 뒤지다, rifle, scour
살살이 조사하다, trawl
살살이 훑다, comb
새, bird, new
새 단장, facelift
새 발의 피, ocean
새 사육장, aviary
새 인물, new blood
새 천년, millennium
새 출발, slate
새겨지다, etch, fix, impress
새기다, carve, inscribe
새김글, inscription
새김눈, notch
새끼, baby, calf, cub, pup
새끼 고양이, kitten
새끼 사슴, fawn
새끼 새, chick
새끼 양, lamb
새끼 양의 고기, lamb
새끼 염소, kid
새끼들, young
새끼를 낳다, breed, foal
새는 곳, leak
새다, break, escape, leak, seep, spill
새된, high-pitched, shrill
새로, anew, newly
새로 고치다, refresh
새로 꾸미다, refurbish
새로 나온, new
새로 발견된, new, newfound
새로 발생한, fresh
새로 온, new
새로 온 사람, intake, newcomer
새로 진출하다, move
새로운, adventurous, fresh, new, novel
새로운 것, change, novelty
새로운 지평을 열다, ground
새로운 활력을 주다, revitalize
새로운 흐름, new wave
새로움, novelty
새로워진, new
새로이, afresh
새롭게 선보이다, rebrand
새롭게 하다, refresh, update
새벽, dawn, daylight
새벽 급습, dawn raid
새 색시, bride
새소리, song
새싹, shoot
새어 나오는, chink
새어들다, filter
새우, shrimp
새우 칵테일, shrimp cocktail
새의 수컷, cock
새장, cage
새장에 갇힌, caged
새총, catapult
새치기하다, jump
새파래지다, blanch
새해, New Year
색, color
색깔, coloring
색다른, different
색다른 물건, novelty
색색의, colorful
색소, pigment
색소폰, sax, saxophone
색소폰 연주자, saxophonist
(~한) 색의, colored
색인, index
색인을 달다, index
색인표, tab
색정, lust
색정적인, erotic
색조, shade, tint, tone
(~) 색조를 띤, tinged
색채, color, palette
색칠, coloring
색칠하다, color
샌드위치, sandwich

샌드위치 과정, sandwich course
샌들, sandal
샐러드, salad
샐러드 드레싱, dressing
샘, spring
샘물, spring
샘플, sample
샛강, creek
샛길, side road
생, incarnation
생가, home
생각, conception, idea, image, mind, notion, sense, think, thought
생각 없는, mindless
생각 없이, mindlessly
생각 없이 행동하다, hip
생각나게 하다, remind
생각나다, hit, mind, remember
생각만 하다, flirt
생각만 함, flirtation
생각만 해도 걱정이다, dread
생각보다 안 좋은, joke
생각에 잠겨 말하다, muse
생각에 잠겨 쓰다, muse
생각에 잠겨서, thoughtfully
생각에 잠긴, reflective, thoughtful
생각을 묻어 두다, block
생각을 시로잡다, preoccupy
생각을 하다, feel, think
생각이 같은, step
생각이 나다, occur
생각이 다른, step
생각이 들다, enter, head
생각이 이랬다저랬다 하다, waffle
(~할) 생각이다, intend
(~할) 생각인데, would
생각조차 못 할, inconceivable
생각조차 할 수 없는, question
생각하고 싶지 않다, hate
생각하고 싶지도 않다, hate
생각하다, believe, conceive, feel, figure, guess, hope, imagine, look, reckon, say, see, sense, spare, suppose, think
(~을) 생각하면, when
(~라고) 생각하여, belief
생각하지 않으려 하다, block
(~라고) 생각한다, find
생각할 거리, food
생각할 수 없는, unthinkable
생각할 수 있는, conceivable, imaginable
생각함, second thought
(~라고) 생각합니까, suppose
생각해 내다, conceive, think
생각해 보니, think
생각해 보면, come
생강, ginger
생강빛, ginger
(~을) 생겨나게 하다, birth
생겨나다, spring
생계, livelihood, living
생계 수단, living
생계비, cost of living
생계비 지수, cost of living index
생글거리는, smiley
생기, life, sparkle
생기 없는, lifeless, limp
생기 있는, alive
생기가 돌다, life
생기가 있다, sparkle
(~을) 생기게 하다, breed
생기다, form, grow, happen, originate, sprout
생기를 돋우는, exhilarating
생기를 띠다, liven
생기를 불어넣다, alive, animate, life, liven
생기에 찬, sparkling
생김새, look
생나무 울타리, hedge, hedgerow
생년월일, date of birth
생도, cadet
생동감이 없는, inert
생략, omission
생략 없는, full-length
생략하다, omit

생략함, omission
생리, period, physiology
생리 기능, physiology
생리대, sanitary napkin, sanitary towel
생리적인, physiological
생리학, physiology
생리학의, physiological
생명, life
생명 공학, biotechnology
생명 보험, life assurance, life insurance
생명력, vitality
생명선, lifeline
생명을 앗다, life
생명의 주기, life cycle
생명이 없는, lifeless
생명이 있는, animate
생명체, creature
생물, being, life
생물학, biology
생물학의, biological
생물학자, biologist
생물학적으로, biologically
생물학적인, biological
생방송으로, live
생방송의, live
생분해성의, biodegradable
생시기 걸린, death
생산, manufacture, manufacturing, production
생산 과잉, overcapacity
생산 능력, capacity
생산 라인, production line
생산량, output, production
생산성, productivity
생산업체, manufacturer
생산자, grower, producer
생산적인, fruitful, productive
생산품, product
생산하다, manufacture, produce
생생하게, graphically, vividly
생생하게 떠올림, flashback
생생한, graphic, vivid
생선, fish
생선살, fillet
생성하다, produce
생식기, genital
생식기의, genital
생식력, virility
생식의, reproductive
생애, lifetime
생일, birthday
생장, growth
생장하다, grow
생존, existence, survival
생존 가능한, viable
생존 능력, viability
생존자, survivor
생존하다, exist
생지옥, hell
생짜의, raw
생체 검사, biopsy
생체 해부, vivisection
생태, biology
생태 보호의, ecological
생태 환경, ecology
생태계, ecosystem
생태상의, ecological
생태적으로, ecologically
생태학, ecology
생태학자, ecologist
생포, capture
생포하다, capture
생화학, biochemistry
생화학 작용, biochemistry
생화학자, biochemist
생화학적인, biochemical
생활, life, living
생활 방식, lifestyle, way of life
생활 지도, pastoral
생활비, cost of living, housekeeping, keep, maintenance
생활수준, standard of living
생활양식, culture
생활을 편하게 하는 것들, comfort
생활하는, living

(~으로) 생활하다, live
샤워, shower
샤워기, shower
샤워장, shower
샤워하다, shower
샬레, chalet
샴페인, champagne
샴푸, shampoo
샹들리에, chandelier
섀시, chassis
서 있는 자세, stance
서 있다, stand
서(書), book
서곡, overture
서광, ray
서구, west
서구의, western
서구인, westerner
서구화, westernization
서구화된, westernized
서기, AD
서까래, rafter
서늘한, cool
서다, halt, join, stand, stop
서두, introduction, opening
서두르는, hurried
서두르다, hasten, hurry
서두르지 않다, easy
서두를 시작하다, preface
서두를 필요는 없다, hurry
서두름, hurry, rush
서둘러, come, haste, hurriedly
서둘러 ~하다, rush
서둘러 가다, hurry, hustle, rush
서둘러 떠나다, dash
서둘러 하는, rustling
서둘러 하게 하다, hurry
서둘러 하다, hurry, hustle
서둘러서, hastily
서랍, drawer
서랍장, bureau
서로, another, each, mutually
서로 관련시키다, correlate
서로 다른, different, divergent, diverse
서로 다투다, feud
서로 모르는 사이, stranger
서로 배타적인, exclusive
서로 비벼 대다, rub
서로 시간 차를 두다, stagger
서로 엇갈리게 배열하다, stagger
서로 연결하다, interconnect
서로 운이 맞는 시행, rhyme
서로 으르렁대는, throat
서로 이야기하다, converse
서로의, mutual
서류, document, paper
서류 가방, briefcase
서류 일체, dossier
서류 작업, paperwork
서류상으로는, paper
서류철, folder
서른, thirty
서른 번째, thirtieth
서리, frost
서리 덮인, frosty
서먹서먹한 분위기를 없애다, ice
서면으로 요청하다, write
서면의, paper
서명, signature, signing
서명인, signatory
서명하고 들어가다, sign
서명하다, dotted, sign, witness
서문, foreword, preface
서민, mass
서버, server
서부, west
서부 소설, western
서부 영화, western
서부의, west, western
서브, serve
서브 넣을 차례, service
서브 득점, ace
서브 실패, fault
서브를 넣다, serve
서브하는 사람, server
서비스, service
서비스 산업, service industry

서비스 업종, service
서비스 제공업체, service provider
서비스를 제공하다, serve
서사시, epic
서사시적 작품, epic
서사시적인, epic
서서히 ~에 떨어지다, drift
서서히 규모를 축소하다, wind
서서히 그러나 분명히, surely
서서히 멈추다, grind
서서히 바뀌다, transition
서서히 불어넣다, instill
서서히 시작하다, dawn
서서히 일을 줄여 나가다, wind
서서히 작동하다, tick
서서히 퍼지다, seep
서성거리다, hover, pace
서성서리다, shuffle
서술, narration
서술자, narrator
서술하다, narrate
서슴없다, hesitation
서슴없이, hesitation
서식, format
서식지, habitat
서식하는, populated
서식하게 하다, colonize, inhabit,
    populate
서신, correspondence
서약, commitment, declaration,
    oath, pledge, vow
서약하다, pledge, vow
서양, west
서양 방풍나물, parsnip
서양 자두, plum
서양 호박, courgette, zucchini
서양의, western
서양인, westerner
서양화, westernization
서양화된, westernized
서열, hierarchy, line
서열의, hierarchical
서재, study
서적, title
서점, bookstore
서정적인, lyric
서쪽, west
서쪽에서 부는, west, westerly
서쪽으로, west, westward
서쪽의, west, westerly
서체, handwriting, typeface
서커스, circus
서투르게, awkwardly, clumsily
서투른, awkward, clumsy, inept
서투름, clumsiness
서툰, hopeless
서품, ordination
서핑, surfing
서행, crawl
서혜부, groin
석공, mason
석면, asbestos
석방, release
석방되다, release
석방시키다, free
석사 학위, master, master's degree
석쇠, grill
석영, quartz
석유, oil, petroleum
석유 굴착 장치, oil rig
석유 굴착 플랫폼, platform
석유 수출국 기구, OPEC
석탄, coal
석판, tablet
석호, lagoon
석화(石化)된, petrified
석회, lime
석회암, limestone
섞다, beat, blend, mix
섞어서 만들다, concoct
섞이다, blend, mingle, mix
선, good, line, virtue
선 두르는 재료, binding
선거, election, fight, poll, polling
선거 운동을 하다, canvass
선거구, constituency
선거구민, constituent
선거권, franchise, vote

선거권을 박탈하다, disenfranchise
선거로, electorally
선거의, electoral
선거인, elector
선견지명, foresight
선견지명이 없는, short-sighted
선고, sentence
선고받다, condemn
선고하다, declare, pass, sentence
선교, mission
선교 활동, missionary
선교사, missionary
선구자, forerunner, pioneer,
    precursor
선구적인, modern, pioneering
선글라스, sunglasses
선금, advance
선단, fleet
선도, lead
선도적인, leading, pioneering
선도하는, initiative, way
선동, incitement, instigation
선동자, instigator
선동적인, inflammatory
선동하다, incite
선두, forefront, head, leader, top
선두 주자, brand leader,
    front-runner, leader
선두에, front
선두에 있는, leading
선두에 있다, head
선뜻, readily
선량함, goodness
선례, precedent
선례를 따르다, footstep
선로, line, railroad, railway, track
선로 바꿈틀, point
선로 변환기, switch
선루프, sunroof
선망의 대상, envy
선망의 대상인, coveted
선명도, definition
선명하게, brightly, strongly,
    vibrantly, vividly
선명한, bright, palpable, strong,
    vibrant, vivid
선명함, brightness
선물, gift, present
선물 바구니, hamper
선물(先物), future
선박, craft, vessel
선박 여행, sailing
선박의, marine
선반, lathe, rack, shelf
선발, selection
선발하다, single
선방, save
선방하다, save
선배, senior
선배의, senior
선별 도태, cull
선별 도태시키다, cull
선별하다, cherry-pick
선보이다, stage
선봉, vanguard
(~의) 선봉에, vanguard
선봉에 서다, spearhead
선불, advance
선불된, prepaid
선불로, up front
선불의, up front
선불하다, advance
선사 시대의, prehistoric
선상의, aboard
선생, mason
선생님, Miss, sir
선서, oath
선수, player
선수권, championship, title
선수권 대회, championship
선수권 보유자, champion
선수단, squad
선수들, field
선수를 치다, beat
선수용 탈의실, pavilion
선실, cabin
선심(線審), linesman
선언, proclamation,

pronouncement
선언하다, announce, come,
    declare, proclaim, pronounce
선원, crew, sailor, seaman
선율, melody, tune
선의에서 한, well-intentioned,
    well-meaning
선의의, well-intentioned,
    well-meaning
선이 부드러운, soft
선인장, cactus
선임료, retainer
선입견, preconception
선입관, prejudice
선잠, snooze
선장, captain, skipper
선장이 되다, captain
선적, shipment
선전, plug
(~으로) 선전하다, bill, pitch, plug,
    tout
선정적이고 통속적인, pulp
선정적인, sensational
선제하는, preemptive
선제하다, preempt
선조, ancestor, family
선진국의, north
선진의, advanced, developed
선창, dock, quay, wharf
선창가, waterfront
선천적으로, innately
선체, hull
선출, election
선출하다, choose, elect
선취권을 주다, preference
선택, choice, option, selection
선택 과목, option
선택 그룹, focus group
선택권, option
선택의, optional
선택의 여지가 없는, captive
선택의 여지가 없다, choice
선택의 폭, choice
선택의 폭이 무진장한, spoil
선택적 근로 시간제, flextime
선택적으로, selectively
선택적인, selective
선택하다, choose, elect, go, opt,
    select
선탠, suntan
선탠용의, suntan
선풍기, fan
선풍적으로, sensationally
선풍적인, sensational
선행, virtue
선행하다, precede
선형의, linear
선호, preference
선호되는, choice
선호하다, favor, give, prefer
선회, whirl
선회하다, circle, orbit
섣부른 판단의, judgmental
설거지, washing-up
설거지 거리, washing-up
설거지하다, dish, wash
설계, design
설계 명세서, specification
설계, 건조되다, engineer
설계도, blueprint, design, plan
설계자, architect, planner
설계하다, design, plan
설교, sermon
설교단, pulpit
설교자, preacher
설교하다, preach
설교하려 들다, preach
설날, New Year
설득, persuasion
설득력, eloquence
설득력 없는, weakly
설득력 없는, feeble, unconvincing
설득력 없이, unconvincingly
설득력 있게, convincingly,
    eloquently, persuasively
설득력 있는, compelling,
    convincing, eloquent, forceful,
    persuasive

설득력이 없는, unconvincing, wea
설득력이 있는, eloquent
설득시키다, peddle
설득하다, convince, persuade, talk
설레게 하다, thrill
설렘, anticipation, romance, thril
설립, establishment, foundation,
    institution, setting up
설립자, founder
설립하다, establish, set
설명, clarification, explanation,
    instruction, interpretation,
    run-down, version
설명 프로그램, tutorial
설명서, covering letter, cover lette
설명이 필요 없는, self-explanatory
설명적인, descriptive, explanatory
설명하다, account, clarify,
    describe, explain, illuminate,
    illustrate, lay, light, present,
    put, set, talk
설문에 응하다, poll
설문지, questionnaire
설비, convenience, device, facility
설사, diarrhea
설상가상으로, insult
설정, setting
설정하다, set
설치, installation, setting up,
    set-up
설치 동물, rodent
설치된, -mounted
설치하다, install, lay, mount, put,
    set
설탕, sugar
설탕 조림, preserve
설탕엿, caramel
설탕을 넣다, sweeten
설파하다, preach
섬, island, isle
섬 주민들, islander
섬광, bolt, flash
섬기다, worship
섬뜩하게 하는, repelled
섬뜩하게 하다, repel
섬뜩한, appalled, gruesome, hairy,
    macabre, repellent
섬세하게, delicately
섬세한, delicate
섬세함, delicacy
섬유, fiber
섬유 산업, textile
섬유소, fiber
섭리, providence
섭씨, Celsius, centigrade
섭씨 0도, freezing point
섭씨의, Celsius, centigrade
섭취, consumption, intake
섭취하다, consume, take
성, castle, château, fort, gender
성 차별적인, sexist
성 차별주의, sexism
성 차별주의자, sexist
성(姓), surname
성(聖) ~, St.
성가, chant, hymn
성가 소리, chanting
성가를 부르다, chant
성가시게 굴다, pester
성가시게 하다, trouble, vex, worry
성가신, prickly, stupid, tiresome,
    vexing
성가신 것, bore
성가신 일, annoyance
성가심, irritation
성격, character, personality,
    quality, sort
성격 묘사, characterization
성격을 형성하다, mold
(~) 성격의, nature
성경, Bible
성경의, biblical
성공, coup, success
성공 가능성이 있는, credible
성공가도를 달리기 시작하다, take
성공시키다, go
성공을 거둔, home
성공이 확실한, home

성공적으로, successfully
성공적인, successful
성공하다, come, get, grade, hit, major league, nicely, succeed
성공하지 못하여, unsuccessfully
성공하지 못한, unsuccessful
성공한, big time, healthy, high-flying, prosperous, successful
성공한 것, success
성공한 사람, success
성공할 것이 확실하다, made
성공할 것이다, place
성공회 부목사, curate
성과, coup, fruit, performance, success
성과급, commission, performance-related pay
성과를 거두다, succeed
성과표, report card
성관계, sexual intercourse
성관계가 문란한, promiscuous
성관계를 가지다, love
성관계를 갖다, bed, sleep
성관계를 갖지 않는, celibate
성교, intercourse, sex, shag
성교 불능의, impotent
성교하다, make, screw, shag
성급하게, hastily, headlong, rashly
성급한, hasty, headlong, precipitate, rash, snap
성급한 언동을 하다, hip
성급함, haste, impatience
성급히 덤비다, rush
성급히 떠밀린, rushed
성긴, sparse
성깔, nastiness
성깔 있는, 급한, 불과 같은, 성미가 급한, quick
성나게 하는, provocative
성나게 하다, exasperate, madden, provoke
성나서, angrily
성난, angry, irate, vexed
성냥, match
성년, majority, manhood
성대모사, impression
성대하게, lavishly
성대하게 축하받다, fete
성대한, lavish
성대한 파티, bash
성도착자, pervert
성립시키다, constitute, establish
성마르게, irritably
성마른, brash, hot, impatient, irritable, petulant, short, touchy
성마름, irritability
성매매 제의 행위, soliciting
성명, communiqué
성명서, announcement, manifesto, statement
성문의, written
성문화되지 않은, unwritten
성미, temper
성미에 맞지 않다, grain
성벽, propensity
성별, gender, sex
성별에 의해, sexually
성별의, sexual
성분, component, constituent, ingredient
성분을 이루는, component
성사 가능한, grasp
성상(聖像), icon
성생활, sexuality
성숙, maturity
성숙하다, grow, mature
성숙하지 못한, immature
성숙한, grown, grown-up, mature
성스러운, hallowed, sacred
성실, diligence, integrity
성실 납부자, payer
성실하게, dutifully
성실한, diligent
성악, song
성역, sanctuary
성욕, desire
성욕을 자극하는, erotic

성을 내다, fume
성인, adult, grown-up, manhood
성인 교육, further education
성인 여성의 생애, womanhood
성인(聖人), saint
성인기, adulthood
성인용, adult
성인용의, grown-up
성인의, adult
성자 같은, saintly
성자와 같은 사람, saint
성장, development, growth, maturity
성장 중인, growth
성장시키다, grow
성장을 방해당한, stunted
성장하다, develop, grow
성적, form, grade, performance, result
성적 도착, perversion
성적 매력을 느끼다, hot
성적 취향, sexuality
성적 학대, sexual abuse
성적 흥분의 절정, orgasm
성적으로, sexually
성적으로 흥분되다, arouse
성적을 매기다, mark
성적인, physical, sexual, steamy
성적표, report card
성화, star sign
성지, shrine
성직 임명, ordination
성직의, ecclesiastical
성직자, clergyman, cleric, priest, priesthood, Reverend
성직자들, clergy
성직자로 임명되다, ordain
성직자로서 보낸 기간, priesthood
성직자의, clerical
성직자의 지위, priesthood
성질, humor, make-up, nature, property, temper, temperament
성질 더러운, nasty
성질을 부리다, temper
(~한) 성질의, disposed
성질이 나쁜, bad-tempered
성질이 다른, alien
성질이 맞지 않는, incompatible
성찬, feast
성찬식, communion
성추행하다, molest
성취, achievement
성취감, fulfillment
성취하다, achieve
성큼성큼 걷다, stride
성큼성큼 뛰다, bound
성패를 건 모험, gamble
성품, quality
성향, disposition, orientation, predisposition, tendency
성향을 띠다, tend
(~) 성향을 타고나다, inclined
성향이 있는, bent, inclined, predisposed
성형 수술, cosmetic surgery, plastic surgery
성희롱, sexual harassment
성희롱하다, molest
세 끼 식사가 딸린 숙박, full board
세 번째의, third
세 쌍둥이, triplet
세간, furnishings
세간의 주목을 받는, high-profile
세계, hard
세계 닫다, slam
세계 당기다, tug
세계 당김, tug
세계 묶다, bale
세계 부딪다, smash
세계 부딪치다, crash, impact
세계 자다, boot
세계 충돌하다, smash
세계 치기, whack
세계 치다, belt, pound, whack
세계, globe, world
세계 대전, world war
세계 무역 기구, World Trade Organization, WTO

세계관, world view
세계적 수준의, world-class
세계적으로 유명한, world-famous
세계적인, world
세계화, globalization
세계화하다, globalize
세관, customs
세균, germ
세금, duty, tax
세금 경감, tax relief
세금 우대 조치, tax break
세금이 붙는, taxable
세기, century
세기가 바뀌는 시기, turn
세내다, hire
세뇌하다, brainwash
세다, count
세단, sedan
세단형 승용차, saloon
세대, generation, home
세라믹, ceramic
세력, force, potency
세력권, territory
세력을 잃다, ground
세련, polish, sophistication
세련된, chic, classy, polished, refined, sophisticated
세련됨, flair
세련미, chic, class, grace
세례, baptism, hail
세례를 받다, baptize, christen, shower
세례식, christening
세로의, lengthwise
세로줄, bar
세면 용품, toiletries
세면기, washbasin
세면대, basin
세목, detail, fine print, small print
세미나, seminar
세밀하게 구별하다, hair
세밀화, miniature
(~을) 세밀히 조사하다, go
세부 사항, detail, in, specifics
세상, world
세상 일반의, general
세상에, earth, Jesus, my, no
세상을 소란스럽게 하는 사람, scaremongering
세상의 이목, limelight
세상의 주목을 받게 된, fore
세세하게, finely
세세한, fine
세세히 조정하다, fine-tune
세속적인, material, secular, worldly
세수, taxation
세습의, hereditary
세심하게, attentively, sensitively
세심한, attentive, fastidious, prudent, scrupulous, sensitive
세심함, delicacy, prudence, sensitivity
세심히 조사하다, scrutinize
세안제, cleanser
세액 공제, tax credit
세어 놓다, count
세우다, erect, found, put, set, stop
세워 두다, stand
세워지다, found, go
세이지, sage
세인의 주목을 받는, spotlight
세일, sale
세입, revenue
세입자, tenant
(~의) 세전 총수익을 올리다, gross
세전의, pretax
세제, cleaner, detergent, taxation
세제곱, cube
세제상 특전, tax break
세시나, rise
세차게 흘러나오다, gush
세찬, raging
세척제, cleanser
세척하다, cleanse
세탁, wash
세탁 중이다, wash
세탁기, washer, washing machine

세탁물, laundry, washing
세탁물 건조기, tumble dryer
세탁소, cleaner, laundry
세탁실, laundry
세탁업자, launderer
세탁하다, launder
세트, set
세트장, set
세포, cell
세포의, cellular
세후 임금, take-home pay
섹스, sex
섹스 심벌, sex symbol
섹스하다, sex
섹시한, cute, sensual, sexy
섹시한 남자, hunk
센, hefty
센세이션, sensation
센터, center
센트, cent
센티미터, centimeter, cm
셀 수 없이 많은, innumerable
셀 프로그램, shell program
셀러리, celery
셀룰라이트, cellulite
셀프서비스의, self-service
셈, count
셋, three
셋째로, third, thirdly
셋톱박스, set-top box
셔츠, shirt
셔터, shutter
셰리주, sherry
셰이크, sheikh
소, cattle, filling, stuffing
소각, burning, incineration
소각로, furnace, incinerator
소각하다, incinerate
소강, remission
소강상태, lull
소개, evacuation, induction, introduction, placement, recommendation, referral
소개된 주민, evacuee
소개서, covering letter, cover letter
소개의, introductory
소개하다, bring, introduce, present
소계, subtotal
소고기 국거리, steak
소관, concern, remit
소구획지, plot
소굴, den
소규모 접전, skirmish
소규모의, small, small-scale
소극, farce
소극성, negativity
소극적인, passive
소금, salt
소금을 넣다, salt
소금을 넣은, salted
소급 적용되는, retrospective
소급되다, backdate
소급하여, retrospectively
소나기, shower
소나무, pine
소나무 재목, pine
소나타, sonata
소네트, sonnet
소녀, girl
소년, boy, lad
소년 같은, boyish
소년 같이, boyishly
소년기, boyhood
소다수, soda, soda water
소도시, town
소도시 주민, town
소독, sterilization
소독면, swab
소독약, antiseptic
소독제, disinfectant
소독하나, disinfect, sterilize
소동, commotion, disturbance, row, scare, scene, stink, stir
소득, earnings, income
소득 공제의, tax-deductible
소득 신고서, tax return
소득 없이, vain
소득 지원, income support

소득세, income tax
소득이 없는, fruitless
소란, racket, uproar
소란스러운, disorderly, stormy
소량, bit, dash, handful, morsel, ounce, trace
소량의, little
소량의 액체, splash
소령, major
소론, essay
소를 넣다, stuff
소름 끼치게 하다, appall
소름 끼치는, appalled, appalling
소름끼치게, hideously
소름끼치게 하는, creepy
소름끼치는, frightful, gruesome, hideous, sickening
소름이 끼치게 하다, flesh
소리, noise, note, sound
소리 내어, loud
소리 내어 부르다, call
소리 내어 읽다, read
소리 높여, vociferously
소리 높여 외치는, vociferous
소리 높여 요구하다, bay
소리 없이 입 모양으로 말하다, mouth
소리 지르다, scream
소리가 나다, sound
소리가 들리는지 귀를 기울이다, listen
소리가 울리다, echo
소리가 크게, loud
소리가 큰, loud
소리를 꽥 지르다, squeak
소리를 낮추다, mute
소리를 내다, sound, wail
소리를 내어, aloud
소리를 죽이다, muffle
소리를 지르다, roar
소리의, sonic
소리의 높낮이, pitch
소리의 크기, volume
소리치다, shout, yell
소리침, yell
소립자, particle
소망, dream, wish
소망을 하다, wish
소매, arm, retail, retailing, sleeve
소매 물가 지수, retail price index
소매 없는 원피스, pinafore
소매가격, list price
소매로, retail
소매상, retailer
소매상인, shopkeeper
소매치기, pickpocket
소매치기하다, pocket
소맥, wheat
소맷단, cuff
소맷부리, cuff
소멸, cancellation
소멸되다, lapse
소멸시키다, cancel, extinguish
소멸하고 있는, way
소멸한, defunct
소명 의식, vocation
소모성의, consumable
소모적인, exhausting
소모품, consumable
소문, grapevine, report, rumor
(~라고) 소문나다, rumored
소문에 ~라고 하다, have
소문에 의하면, reportedly
소문자, lowercase
소박하게, plainly, simply
소박한, frugal, plain, rustic, simple
소방관, fire fighter, fireman
소방대, fire brigade
소방대장, captain
소방서, fire department
소방서장, marshal
소방차, fire engine, fire truck
소변, urine
소변을 보다, urinate
소비, consumption, expenditure
소비 중심 사회, consumer society
소비세, excise
소비자, consumer, spender

소비자 대출, consumer credit
소비재, consumer goods
소비하다, consume, expend, spend
소생, resuscitation
소생시키다, resurrect, resuscitate, revitalize, revive
소설, fiction, novel
소설가, novelist
(~에) 소속된, attached, to
소속의, from, inside, of
소송, action, lawsuit, litigation, suit
소송 비용, cost
소송 사건, case
소송 절차, proceeding
소송을 제기하다, court, sue
소수, decimal, few, handful, minority
소수 민족, minority
소수 민족의, ethnic
소수 민족적으로, ethnically
소수 집단인, minority
소수에게만 전해지는, esoteric
소수의, few
소수의 사교(邪敎) 집단, cult
소수점, decimal point, dot, point
소수점 아래 한 자리, place
소스, sauce
소시민의, bourgeois
소시지, sausage
소식, communication, news, word
소식을 듣다, hear
소식지, bulletin
소식통, source
소식통의, informed
소실되다, burn, lose
소심하게, timidly
소심한, timid
소심함, timidity
소아, infant
소아과, pediatrics
소아과 의사, pediatrician
소아마비, polio
소아애, pedophilia
소아애자, pedophile
소아용 변기, potty
소액 지급 준비금, petty cash
소요, disorder, turmoil
소요 경비, expense
소요 경비 계정, expense account
소요 사태, rioting, trouble
소용, point
소용돌이, spiral, swirl
소용돌이 모양, swirl
소용돌이무늬, scroll
소용돌이치게 하다, curl, swirl
소용돌이치다, curl, spiral, swirl
소용없는, good, useless, vain, worthless
소용돌을, use
소용없이, ineffectually, vain
소울 뮤직, soul
소원, wish
소원을 빌다, wish
소원하게 만들다, alienate
소원한, estranged
소원해지다, grow
소위, so-called, what
소위원회, subcommittee
소유, ownership, possession
소유격의, possessive
소유권, ownership
소유권 주장, claim
소유권을 주장하다, claim
소유를 나타내는, possessive
소유물, goods, possession
소유욕, possessiveness
소유욕이 강한, possessive
(~의) 소유이다, belong
소유자, bearer
소유주, proprietor
소유지, estate
소유하다, own, possess
소유하려고 하는, possessive
소음, din, noise, racket
소이탄, incendiary
소인(素人), predisposition
소인을 찍다, cancel

소인이 되다, predispose
소인이 있는, predisposed
소일거리, pastime
소일하다, potter
소작농, peasant
소장, governor, intestine
소장품, collection
소재, location, material, whereabouts
소재지, seat
소절, measure
소제하다, clear
소중한, cherished, dear, heart, precious, valuable
소중한 사람, jewel
소중히 받들다, cherish
소중히 여기다, cherish, value
(~할) 소지를 심어 주다, predispose
소지인, holder
소지품, belongings, effect
소지품들, thing
소지하다, hold
소질, instinct
소질이 있는, bent
소질이 있다, have, making
소집하다, call, convene
소책자, booklet, pamphlet
소총, rifle
소켓, socket
소통된, open
소파, couch, sofa
소파 세트, suite
소포, package, parcel
소품, prop
소풍, excursion, outing, picnic
소풍 가다, picnic
소프라노, soprano
소프트웨어, software
소형 구축함, frigate
소형 기기, hand-held
소형 디스크, minidisc
소형 버스, minibus
소형 빵, biscuit
소형 오토바이, motorbike, scooter
소형 위성 안테나, minidish
소형 트럭, pick-up
소형이고 경제적인, compact
소홀한, careless
소홀히 여기는, ignore
소홀히 하다, neglect
소화, digestion
소화 기관, digestion
소화 불량, indigestion
소화기, fire extinguisher
소화되다, digest
소화의, digestive
소화하다, absorb, digest
소환, extradition, recall
소환당하다, cite
소환되다, call, extradite, haul, summons
소환장, citation, subpoena, summons
소환장을 발부하다, subpoena
소환하다, haul, recall, subpoena
속, core, filling, tummy
속(屬), genus
속개하다, kick
속기, shorthand
속내를 보이는, game
속눈썹, eyelash, lash
(~에) 속다, deceive, fall, lull, nick, ride, take
속달, express
속달로, express
속담, proverb, saying
속담 투의, proverbial
속도, pace, rapidity, rate, speed, tempo, velocity
속도가 늘다, speed
속도가 줄다, slow
속도계, clock, speedometer
속도를 높이다, speed
속도를 늦추다, slow
속도를 맞추다, pace
속도위반, speeding
속도위반을 하다, speed
속력을 내다, pick

속마음을 드러내지 않는, reserved
속물, snob
속물근성, snobbery
속박, bondage
속박되다, hem
속박하다, hem, restrict
속보, trot
속삭이다, whisper
속삭임, whisper
속상한, upset
속상함, hurt
속설, fable
속세의, temporal, worldly
속속 만들어 내다, churn
속속들이, inside, round
속속들이 말하다, exhaust
속수무책으로, helplessly
속수무책인, helpless
속수무책임, helplessness
속아 넘어간 사람, dupe
속어, slang
(~의) 속에, inside, into, under, underneath
(~이) 속에 든, -centered
속여 빼앗다, swindle
속여 팔다, mis-sell
속여서 빼앗다, cheat
속옷, underwear
속옷 윗도리, undershirt, vest
(~) 속으로, into
속을 빼다, core
속이 꽉 찬, solid
속이 들여다보이는, obvious
속이 비치는, see-through
속이 빈, hollow
속이 상하다, heart
속이다, con, deceive, delude, dupe, fool, kid, trap, trick
속임, hoax
속임수, deceit, masquerade, trap, trick
속임수를 쓰는, underhand
속편, sequel
(~에) 속하다, belong, go, number, pertain
(~에) 속한다고 생각하다, ascribe
(~에) 속하여, among
속행되다, continue
속행하다, continue
숱다, thin
숱아 내기를 하다, cull
숱아내기, cull
숱아지다, thin
손, hand
손 관리, manicure
손가락, finger
손가락 관절, knuckle
손가락 모양, finger
손가락 부분, finger
손가락 하나 까딱하다, finger
손가락에 장을 지지다, damned
손가락을 꼬다, finger
손가락을 딱 튕기기, snap
손가방, purse
손길이 닿다, touch
손끝, fingertip
손녀, granddaughter
손님, guest, punter, visitor
손님용 숙소, guest house
손님이 손수 갖다 먹는 식의, self-service
손닿는 곳에, hand
(~을) 손대지 않다, hand
손대지 않은, undisturbed
손도 대지 않은, untouched
손목, wrist
손목까지 내려오는, full-length
손목시계, watch
손바닥, palm
손발, limb
손발이 맞다, gel
손발이 맞음, chemistry
손보다, do
손뼉을 치다, clap
손상, damage, erosion, harm, injury
손상되다, erode
손상되지 않은, intact, untouched

손상된, impaired, tarnished
(~을) 손상시켜, detriment
손상시키다, damage, detract, eat, erode, impair, rupture, tarnish, undermine
(~을) 손상하지 않고, detriment
손수 만들기, do-it-yourself
손수건, handkerchief
손수레, trolley
손수레식 탁자, trolley
손실, cost, damage, loss
손아귀, grasp, jaw
손아귀 안에, palm
손아랫사람, junior
(~의) 손에 넘겨져, mercy
손에 넣다, clinch, come, hand, hold, pocket, secure
손에 넣을 수 있는, grab
손에 들고 사용하는, hand-held
(~의) 손에 있는, hand
손에 잡힐 듯한, grasp
손위, big
손위의, elder
손으로, hand
손으로 더듬어 찾다, grope
손으로 만든, handmade
손으로 빛을 가리다, shade
손으로 쓴, handwritten
(- 을) 손으로 쥐다, handle
손으로 찌르다, poke
손을 관리하다, manicure
손을 내밀다, put
손을 대다, dip, finger, touch
손을 대보다, hand
(~의) 손을 떠난, hand
손을 떼다, back, get, opt, pull, retreat
손을 빌다, enlist
손을 빌려 주다, hand
손을 뻗다, reach
손을 쑥 넣다, dip
손을 씻다, hand
손을 잔 모양처럼 만들어 받치다, cup
손을 잡고, hand
손을 잡다, hand
손을 흔들다, wave
손을 흔들어 지시하다, wave
손의, manual
손이 닿을 수 있는 곳, reach
손이 묶이다, hand
손자, grandson
손잡이, handle, knob
손잡이의 굵은 쪽 끝, butt
손전등, flash, flashlight, lantern, torch
손주, grandchild
손질, touch
손질이 잘 된, trim
손질하다, fiddle, groom, style
손짓, gesture, sign
손짓으로[고갯짓으로] 부르다, beckon
손짓하다, motion
손톱, fingernail, nail
손톱 손질, manicure
손톱을 손질하다, manicure
손해, harm
손해 배상금, damage
손해 볼 건 없다, hurt
손해 사정인, claims adjuster
(~에) 손해 없이, detriment
손해도 이익도 없다, even
손해되는, detrimental
손해를 보는 사람, loser
손해를 보며, loss
손해를 입다, lose
솔, brush
솔기, seam
솔깃한, tempting
솔선, initiative
솔선수범, lead
솔직 담백하게, brutally
솔직 담백한, brutal
솔직하게, directly, frankly, outright, straight
솔직하게 따지다, tackle
솔직하게 말하면, honest
솔직한, blunt, candid, direct,

earthy, frank, honest, open, outright, straight, straightforward, up front
솔직한 심정, piece
솔직함, bluntness, candor, directness, frankness, openness
솔직히, honestly
솔직히 말해서, honesty
솔질, brush
솜사탕, cotton candy
솜씨, knack, touch, workmanship
솜을 넣은, padded
솜털, fluff
솟구쳐 올리다, throw
솟구치다, soar, spout, spurt
솟다, climb
솟아 나옴, gush
송곳니, fang
송금액, remittance
송금하다, remit
송달하다, serve
송수신용의, two-way
송신기, transmitter
송신탑, mast, tower
송아지, calf
송아지고기, veal
송어, trout
송어요리, trout
송이, bunch
송장, corpse, invoice
송전선, power line
송전선망, grid
송전하다, send
송화기, mouthpiece
솥, kettle
쇄, issue
쇄골, collarbone
쇄도, bombardment, deluge, influx, invasion, rush, shower, torrent
쇄도당하다, deluge
쇄도하다, inundate
쇄신, regeneration
쇄신하다, innovate, regenerate
쇠고기, beef
쇠락하다, decay
쇠살대, grate
쇠스랑, fork
쇠약, breakdown
쇠약해지다, fail, rot, waste
쇠창살, grille
쇠퇴, decay, decline
쇠퇴하고 있는, decline
쇠퇴하다, decay, decline
쇠퇴한, run-down
쇠하다, languish
쉿소리, rasp
쉿소리를 내다, rasp
쇼, show, spectacle, spectacular
쇼비니스트, chauvinist
쇼비니즘, chauvinism
쇼윈도에, in
쇼크, shock
쇼핑, shopping
쇼핑 몰, shopping mall, retail park
쇼핑객, shopper
쇼핑센터, plaza, shopping center
쇼핑용 카트, cart
쇼핑하다, shop
쇼핑한 물건, shopping
숄, shawl
수, move, number, stitch, Wed.
(~할) 수 없는, hardly, incapable, unable
(~할) 수 있게 하다, enable
(~할) 수 있는, be, capable, possible
(~할) 수 있는 입장인, position
(~보다) 수가 많다, outnumber
수간호사, sister
수감되다, jail
수감의, custodial
수갑, handcuff
수갑을 채우다, handcuff
수강하다, take
수거, collection
수건, towel
수건으로 닦다, towel

수고, effort, trouble
수고하다, trouble
수공예, craft
수군거림, whisper
수그러들다, cave, fade, let
수그러지다, abate
수금, collection
수금원, collector
수긍하다, take
수녀, nun, sister
수녀원, convent
수놓다, embroider
수다, chat, chatter, gossip
수다 떨다, chat, gossip, talk
수다스러운, talkative
수다쟁이, gossip
수단, channel, instrument, means, medium, move, tool, vehicle, way
수당, allowance
수도, capital
수도꼭지, tap
수도사, monk
수도원, monastery
수도원의 작은 방, cell
수돗물의, running
수동 변속기, stick shift
수동으로, manually
수동의, manual
수동적으로, passively
수동적인, passive
수동태, passive
수락, acceptance
수락하다, accept
수락할 수 있는, open
수레, cart
수력의, hydraulic
수련 과정, internship
수련 수녀, novice
수련 수사, novice
수련을 받다, groom
수련의, resident
수렴, convergence
수렴하다, canvass
수렵, hunting
수령액, receipt
수령을 통지하다, acknowledge
수령인, recipient
수령증, receipt
수로, canal, channel, course, waterway
수로 안내인, pilot
수료증, certificate
수류탄, grenade
수리, refit, renovation, repair
수리공, repairer
수리되다, refit
수리하다, do, mend, renovate, repair
수립, construction, formulation
수립하다, erect
수막염, meningitis
수많은, flock, regiment, score
수면, sleep
수면 위로 올라오다, surface
수명, life, life cycle, lifespan
수명이 다하다, go
수모, indignity
수목이 우거진, wooded
수문식 독, lock
수반되는, involved
수반하다, carry, entail, involve
수배 중인, wanted
수백, hundred
수백만의, million, one
수법, gimmick
수분, moisture
수분시키다, fertilize
수분을 공급하다, moisturize
수비, defense
수비대, garrison
수비수, defender, fielder
수비하다, field
수사, brother, investigation, monk, rhetoric
수사관, investigator
수사슴, stag

수사적으로, rhetorically
수사적인, rhetorical
수사하다, investigate
수사학, rhetoric
수상, Chancellor, PM, premier, Prime Minister
수상 임기, premiership
수상기, receiver, set
수상자, winner
수상쩍어 하는, suspicious
수상쩍은, questionable
수상하게, dubiously, suspiciously
수상한, dubious, shady, suspect, suspicious
수색, hunt, search
수색 영장, search warrant
수색대, search party
수색하다, search, sweep
수석의, first
수선하다, patch
수선화, daffodil
수소, hydrogen, ox
수송, shipment, shipping, transit, transport, transportation
수송 물자, traffic
수송 중인, transit
수송 체계, transit
수송량, traffic
수송관, duct, pipeline
수송되다, ship
수송차, carrier
수송하다, transport
수수께끼, enigma, puzzle, riddle
수수께끼 같은, cryptic, enigmatic
수수께끼같이, enigmatically
수수료, commission, fee
수수하게, soberly
수수한, homely, low-key, modest, restrained, sober
수술, operation, surgery
수술로, surgically
수술실, operating room, operating theatre, surgery, theater
수술을 통한, invasive
수술의, surgical
수술하다, operate
수습, article
수습 기간, probation
수습 직원, trainee
수습직, placement
수습하다, patch, salvage
수신 상태, reception
수신기, earphone, receiver, set
수신음, reception
수신자 부담 전화, collect call
수신자 부담 전화를 하다, collect
수신하다, pick, receive
수심, pain
수심 측정 단위, fathom
수십 개, dozen
수십억, billion
수십억 개의, billion
수십의, dozen
수압, pressure
수액, sap
수업, course work, lesson, teaching, tuition
수업 시간표, class schedule, schedule
수업 중에, class
수업료, tuition
수여, presentation
수여받다, award
수여식, presentation
수여하다, bestow, confer
수역, body
수염, whisker
수영, bathing, swim, swimming
수영 선수, swimmer
수영법, stroke
수영복, swimming trunks, swimsuit
수영장, pool, swimming pool
수영하다, swim
수완, finesse
수완 좋게, diplomatically
수완을 부리다, wheel and deal
수완이 좋은, diplomatic

수요, demand
수요일, Wednesday
수용 공간, accommodation
수용 능력, capacity
수용되다, commit
수용성의, soluble
수용소, concentration camp
수용적인, receptive
수용하다, accommodate, hold, house, seat, take
수원, source
수월하게 들어가다, breeze
수월하게 따내다, walk
수월하게 받아들이다, stride
수월하게 해내다, sail
수월한, downhill
수위, janitor, level
수위가 조절되다, water
수위실, water
수은, mercury
수의, shroud
수의사, doctor, vet, veterinarian
수의사의, veterinary
수의학의, veterinary
수익, gain, payback, return, take
수익금, proceed
수익률, rate of return, yield
수익성, profitability
수익원, earner
수익을 내다, earn
수익을 올리다, ring
수익자, earner
수임료, fee
수입, earnings, import, importation, income, revenue
수입업자, importer
수입이 생기다, bring
수입이 충분하게, comfortably
수입이 충분한, comfortable
수입품, import
수입하다, import
수작을 걸다, chat
수저류, cutlery, flatware
수정, adjustment, amendment, crystal, fertilization, modification, revision
수정같이 맑은, crystal clear
수정시키다, fertilize
수정안, amendment
수정체, lens
수정판, reprint
수정하다, amend, edit, modify, qualify, revise
수제의, handmade
수족, limb
수준, mark, pitch, standard, threshold
수준 높은, creditable, polished
(~한) 수준에 맞춰지다, pitch
(~한) 수준으로 설정되다, pitch
수줍게, shyly, timidly
수줍어하는, sheepish
수줍은, diffident, shy, timid
수줍음, diffidence, shyness, timidity
수중, clutch, way
수중에 든 새, bird
수중에서, underwater
수중용의, underwater
수중으로 들어가다, fall
수중의, underwater
수지, resin
수지 타산, budget
수지를 겨우 맞추다, end
수지맞는, lucrative
수직 기둥, upright
수직 등판만 있는, upright
수직 안정판, fin
수직 통로, shaft
수직으로, vertically
수직의, vertical
수집, collecting, collection
수집가, collector
수집품, collection
수집하다, collect, gather, glean
수채화, watercolor
수채화 물감, watercolor
수척한, gaunt

수천, thousand
수천 번의, thousandth
수천의, one, thousand
수첩, notebook
수축, contraction
수축시키다, contract, retract
수축하는, constrict, contract, retract
수출, export
수출 회사, exporter
수출국, exporter
수출용의, exportable
수출품, export
수출하는 사람, exporter
수출하다, export
수취, receipt
수취인, payee
수취인 서명을 하다, sign
(~를) 수취인으로 하는, payable
수치, count, disgrace, figure, humiliation, level, reading
수치를 모르는, unashamed
수치스러운, disgraceful, humiliated
수치스러운 것, disgrace
수치스러운 상황, humiliation
수치스럽게, disgracefully
수치심, shame
수칙, regime
수컷, buck, bull, male
수컷의, male
수탉, cock
수태, conception, fertilization
수통, canteen
수퇘지, boar
수평, horizontal
수평 건널목, grade crossing
수평 비행하다, level
수평선, horizon
수평으로, horizontally
수평의, flat, horizontal
수포, blister
수포로 돌아가다, smoke
수표, check, cheque
수표 보증 카드, cheque card
수표를 작성하다, make
수표책, checkbook, cheque book
수풀, clump
수프, broth, soup
수플레, soufflé
수하물, hand luggage
수학, math, mathematics, maths
수학을 잘하는, mathematical
수학자, mathematician
수학적으로, mathematically
수학적인, mathematical
수행, execution, implementation, performance, pursuit
수행 방법, conduct
수행원들, entourage
수행하다, conduct, discharge, implement, perform, pursue, wage
수행해 내다, fill
수험생, candidate
수혈, transfusion
수혜자, beneficiary, claimant, recipient
수호자, guardian
수호하다, guard
수화, signing, sign language
수화기, handset, phone, receiver
수화하다, sign
수확, harvest, yield
수확 연도와 장소, vintage
수확 기, mower
수확량, harvest
수확물, crop
수확하다, harvest, reap
숙고, deliberation, musing, reflection
숙고하다, appraise, deliberate, mull, reflect, turn
숙녀, lady
숙녀연하는 사람, prude
숙달, mastery
숙달되다, master
숙달된, practiced

숙련된, adept, expert, master, skilled
숙련을 요하는, skilled
숙맥, mug
숙모, aunt, auntie
숙박, lodging
숙박 업소, bed and breakfast
숙박객, guest
숙박시키다, accommodate, house
숙박업소, guest house
숙성하다, mature
숙성한, mature
숙소, accommodation, lodging
숙소를 제공하다, house
숙식을 함께 하는, residential
숙어, idiom
숙이다, bend, bow, hunch, incline, lower
숙제, homework
숙지시키다, acquaint
숙청, purge
숙청하다, purge
숙취, hangover
순간, hour, instant, moment, second
순간적으로, instantaneously
순간적인, instant, instantaneous, momentary
순간적인 충동에서, spur
순결, celibacy, virginity
순결주의의, celibate
순경, constable, PC
순교자, martyr
순교자인 척하는 사람, martyr
순교하다, martyr
순도, purity
순례, pilgrimage
순례자, pilgrim
순록, reindeer
순무, turnip
순번, turn
순서, order, sequence
순수 연극, art
순수주의자, purist
순수하게, net
순수한, innocent, net, pure, solid, stark
순수함, innocence, purity
순식간, moment
순식간에, flash, fleetingly, instantly
순식간에 지나가는, fleeting
순양함, cruiser
순위, place
순위를 매기다, rank
순응, compliance
순익을 얻다, net
순자산 총액, equity
순전한, downright, flat, sheer, simple
순전히, purely
순조로운, course, flawless, smooth
순조롭게, flawlessly, smoothly
순조롭지 않은, unfavorable
순종, obedience, pedigree
순종적인, dutiful, submissive
순진하게, innocently, naively
순진한, childlike, naive
순진한 사람, innocent
순진함, naivety
순찰, patrol, route
순찰 중인, patrol
순찰대, patrol
순찰하다, cruise, patrol
순한, mild
순화하다, tone
순환, circulation
순환하는, circular
순회, circuit, round, tour
순회 중인, tour
순회지, circuit
순회하는, roving
순회하다, tour
숟가락, spoon
술, alcohol, booze, drink, liquor
술 마시기, booze
술 장식, fringe
술 장식이 달린, fringed
술 취하지 않은, sober

술 취한, drunken, intoxicated
술 한 잔, drink
술김에, drunkenly
술렁거림, stir
술술 늘어놓다, reel
술에 취한, drunk
술에 취함, drunkenness
술에 취해, drunkenly
술을 마시다, drink
술이 깨다, sober
술집, bar, pub, saloon
술책, intrigue
술책을 부리다, wheel and deal
숨, breath
숨 돌릴 여유, breathing space
숨 막힐 듯한, oppressive
숨 막힐 정도로 애정을 퍼붓다, smother
숨 막힐 정도의, breathtaking
숨겨 가지고 있다, sleeve
숨겨 두다, stash, tuck
숨겨진, veiled
숨결, breath
숨기고 있다, sleeve
숨기는, secretive
숨기다, conceal, harbor, hide, hold, keep, secrete, suppress
숨기지 않다, secret
숨김, concealment, suppression
숨김없는, explicit
숨다, cover, ground, hide, tuck
숨막히게 하다, suffocate
숨막히는, breathless
숨막히다, suffocate
숨막힐 정도의, stifling
숨쉬다, breathe
숨어 있는, latent
숨은, hidden, ulterior
숨은 의도, hidden agenda
숨을 곳, cover
숨을 내쉬다, breathe
숨을 들이쉬다, breathe
숨을 씨근거리다, wheeze
숨을 죽여, breath
숨을 죽인, hushed
숨을 헐떡이며, breath, breathlessly
숨음, concealment
숨이 가쁜, breath
숨이 막히는 듯한 소리, gasp
숨이 막히다, wind
숨이 참, breathlessness
숨죽인, hushed
숨찬, breathless
숫기 없는, diffident
숫양, ram
숫자, figure, number
숫자로, numerically
숫자에 능하다, head
숫자에 밝은 사람, mathematician
숫자의, numerical
숫자판, keypad
숭고한, noble, sublime, venerable
숭고한 것, sublime
숭배, reverence, worship
숭배를 받는, cult
숭배의 대상, cult
숭배하다, idolize, revere, worship
숯, charcoal, coal
숯이 적은, thin
숲, forest, wood
숲 속의 빈터, opening
숲 파괴, deforestation
숲이 파괴되다, deforest
쉐어웨어, shareware
쉬는, free
쉬다, break, heave, rest, take
쉬쉬하다, hush
쉬운, comfortable, easy, effortless, simple
쉬운 일, sailing
쉬이 하는 소리를 내다, hiss
쉬익 하는 소리, hiss, hissing
쉰 목소리, rasp
쉰 목소리로, hoarsely
쉰 목소리로 말하는, rasp
쉰 목소리의, hoarse
쉴 새 없는, incessant
쉴 새 없이, incessantly

섬 없이 이어지는, solid
쉼터, shelter
쉼표, comma
쉽게, comfortably, ease, easily,
   effortlessly, readily, simply
쉽게 고치다, dumb
쉽게 넘어가는, responsive
쉽게 눈에 띄다, stand
쉽게 눈에 띄지 않는, unobtrusive
쉽게 번 돈, rope
쉽게 사용할 수 있는, fingertip
쉽게 얻은, plate
쉽게 영향을 받는, susceptible
쉽게 이기다, hand, romp
쉽게 차지하다, walk
쉽게 찾을 수 있는, fingertip
쉽게 흥분하는, foul
쉽고 편한 일로 바꾸다, downshift
쉽고 편한 일로 전업, downshifting
쉽고 편한 일로 전업한 사람,
   downshifter
쉽사리 믿지 않는, incredulous
쉽지 않은 문제, matter
쉿, hush, sh
쉿 하며 거품을 내다, fizz
슈퍼 모델, supermodel
슈퍼마켓, supermarket
숏, shot
숏하다, shoot
스낵 바, snack bar
스냅 사진, snapshot
스노보드, snowboard
스노보드 타기, snowboarding
스노클, snorkel
스노클을 물고 수영하다, snorkel
스누커, snooker
스르르 기어가다, slither
스릴러물, thriller
스릴을 맛보려고, kick
스마일리, smiley
스마트 카드, smart card
스며 나오게 하다, ooze
스며 나오다, exude, ooze
(~로) 스며들다, distill, merge,
   permeate, soak
스모그, smog
스무 번째의, twentieth
스물, twenty
스미다, seep
스산한, bleak, bleakly
스스로, itself
스스로 부과한, self-imposed
스스로 자초한, making
스스로 하는, own
스스로를 드러내다, present
스스로에게 가한, self-inflicted
스스로의 길을 개척하다, strike
스웨이드 천, suede
스웨터, jersey, jumper, pullover,
   sweater
스웨터 셔츠, sweatshirt
스위치, knob, switch
스위치를 끄다, switch
스위치를 켜다, switch
스위트룸, suite
스윙, swing
스쳐 가는, passing
스쳐 가다, run
스쳐 지나가다, skim, sweep
스치게 하다, sweep
스치다, brush, cross, graze
스카우트되다, headhunt
스카이라인, skyline
스카치위스키, Scotch
스카프, scarf
스캐너, scanner
스캐너로 읽히다, scan
스캔, scan
스캔들, affair, scandal
스캔들이 될 만한 것, dynamite
스커트, skirt
스케이트 타기, skating
스케이트를 타는 사람, skater
스케이트를 타다, ice-skating, skate
스케이트보드, skateboard
스케이트보드 타기, skateboarding
스케이트장, rink
스케이트화, ice-skate

스케일, scale
스케줄, schedule
스케치, sketch
스케치하다, sketch
스코틀랜드 의회 의원, MSP
스쿠버다이빙, scuba diving
스쿠터, motorbike, scooter
스쿼시, squash
스크램블하다, scramble
스크램블한, scrambled
스크랩북, scrapbook
스크롤바, scroll bar
스크롤하다, scroll
스키, ski
스키 타기, skiing
스키를 타다, ski
스키어, skier
스타, star
스타디움, stadium
스타의 지위, stardom
스타일, idiom, mode, style, vein
스타킹, stocking
스타트를 먼저 하다, gun
스태그플레이션, stagflation
스태미나, stamina
스탬프, stamp
스탬프를 찍다, stamp
스턴트, stunt
스테레오, hi-fi, stereo
스테레오의, stereo
스테로이드, steroid
스테이션 왜건, station wagon
스테이크, steak
스테이플러, stapler
스테인드글라스, stained glass
스테인리스 스틸, stainless steel
스텐실, stencil
스텐실로 찍다, stencil
스텝, step
스토브, stove
스토커, stalker
스토킹하다, stalk
스톡옵션, share option, stock
   option
스톤, stone
스톱워치, stopwatch
스튜, stew
스트레스, stress
스트레스로 지친, stressed out
스트레스를 받은, stressed
스트레스를 주는, stressful
스트레이트의, neat
스트리퍼, stripper
스티커, sticker
스틸 사진, still
스파게티, spaghetti
스파르타식의, spartan
스파링 하다, spar
스파이, mole, spy
스파이 노릇을 하다, spy
스파크, spark
스패너, spanner
스팸 메일, spam
스팸 메일을 보내다, spam
스펀지, sponge
스펀지 고무, foam
스펀지로 닦다, sponge
스펀지케이크, sponge
스페이드, spade
스페이드 카드, spade
스펙트럼, spectrum
스포츠, sport
스포츠 경기, fixture
스포츠 실용차, SUV
스포츠 용품의, sporting
스포츠를 위한 스포츠, sake
스포츠맨, sportsman
스포츠우먼, sportswoman
스포츠의, sporting
스포츠카, sports car
스포츠카의, sporty
스포트라이트, spotlight
스포트라이트를 비추다, spotlight
스폰서, sponsor
스폰서가 되다, sponsor
스푼, spoon
스푼으로 떠 넣다, spoon
스프레드시트, spreadsheet

스프레이, spray
스프레이로 칠해지다, spray
스프린터, sprinter
스프린트, sprint
스피커, loudspeaker
스핀, spin
슬그머니 가다, slip
슬그머니 놓다, slip
슬라이드, slide, transparency
슬럼가, slum
슬레이트, slate
슬로 모션, slow motion
슬로건, slogan
슬로프, run
슬리퍼, slipper
슬며시 나타나다, creep
슬며시 다가가다, creep
슬슬 가다, draw
슬슬 떠나다, move
슬슬 움직여 보다, move
슬슬 움직이다, draw
슬쩍 건네다, slip
슬쩍 빠져나가다, scarce
(~을) 슬쩍하다, help
슬프게, sadly
슬프게 하다, sadden
슬픈, moody, sad, saddened,
   woeful
슬픈 일, sorrows
슬픔, heartache, sadness, sorrow
슬픔을 술로 달래다, drown
습격, raid
습격하다, raid, strike
습관, custom, force, habit, ritual,
   way
(~의) 습관을 고치다, break
습관을 버리다, break
(~하는) 습관이 있는, habit
습관적으로, habitually
습관적인, customary, habitual
습관적인 행동, reflex
습기, damp, dampness, humidity,
   moisture
습기가 있는, moist
습도, humidity
습득, acquisition
습득하다, acquire, pick
습지, bog, marsh, swamp, wetland
습지대, wetland
습진, eczema
습한, humid
승강구, hatch
승강기, lift
승강이하다, haggle
승강장, platform, rank
승객, passenger
승객용의, passenger
승격, promotion
승격되다, promote
승격시키다, elevate
승계, succession
승계하다, succeed
승낙 연령, age of consent
(~에) 승낙하다, agree, assent
승리, triumph, victory, win
승리를 거두다, triumph
승리의 기쁨, triumph
승리자, victor
승리하다, prevail
승리한, victorious, winning
승마, riding
승마의, equestrian
승무원, crew, steward, stewardess
승무원으로 일하다, crew
승산 없는 일, shot
승산(勝算), odds
승산이 없는, running
승산이 없는 상황, no-win situation
승산이 없는 선수, outsider
승산이 있는, hunt, running
(~의) 승산이 있다, odds
승산이 확실한, win-win
승선권, boarding card
승선하다, embark
승선해서 되다, aboard
승인, approval, endorsement,
   go-ahead, ratification,
   recognition, sanction

승인되다, grant
승인하다, approve, dotted,
   endorse, grant, ratify, recognize,
   sanction, underwrite, validate
(~의) 승인하에, auspices
승자 진출 시합, tie
승자만이 진출하는, knockout
승진, advancement, promotion
승진되다, upgrade
승진시키다, elevate
승진하다, graduate, promote, rise
승차권, pass
승차하여, on
시, poem, poetry, rhyme, verse
시가, cigar
시가를 매기다, quote
시각, hour, perspective, time,
   viewpoint, vision
시각 자료, visual
시각 장애인, blind
시각의, optical, visual
시각적으로, visually
시간, hour, period, session, space,
   span, time
시간 기록, time
시간 기록계, clock
시간과의 싸움, race
시간당, hourly
시간대, slot
시간마다, hourly
시간에 맞춰, time
시간을 내다, fit, time
시간을 다투어, clock
시간을 때우다, fill, time
시간을 맞추어, punctually
시간을 보내다, fill
시간을 상당히 들이다, plod
시간을 앞당기다, forward
시간을 재다, time
시간을 지키는, punctual
시간의, temporal
시간이 걸리다, time
시간이 금방 가다, time
시간이 넉넉하게 미리, time
시간이 많이 걸리는,
   time-consuming
시간이 오래 걸리는, slow
시간이 정확하다, time
(~에) 시간이나 마음을 쏟다, occupy
시간표, timeline, timetable
시계, clock, view
시계 바늘, hand
시계 반대 방향으로, anticlockwise
시계 반대 방향의, anticlockwise
시계 방향으로, clockwise
시계 방향의, clockwise
시계(視界), visibility
시계같이, clockwork
시골, country, countryside,
   province
시골길, trail
시골의, provincial, rural
시골풍의, rural
시굴하다, prospect
시금석, test
시금치, spinach
시기, chapter, hour, jealousy,
   period, stage, time, timing
시기를 맞추다, time
시기상조의, premature,
   prematurely
시기상조이다, early
시기적절한, timely
시기하는, jealous
시기하여, jealously
시끄러운, loud, noisy, rowdy
시끄러운 소리를 내며 가다, clatter
시끄럽게, noisily
시끄럽게 울다, blast
시끄럽게 울리다, blast
시끄럽게 울림, blast
(~을) 시끄럽게 주장하는, clamor
시나리오, scenario, screenplay
시나리오 작가, screenwriter
시내, high street, town
시내 전차, tram, trolley
시내의, high street
시누이, sister-in-law

시늉, act, pretense
시늉만 하다, mime, motion
시달리는, harassed, laden, stricken
시달리다, beset, buffet, plague
시달린, haunted
시대, age, era, generation, period, time
시대극의, costume
시대를 앞선, time
시대를 초월한, timeless
시대에 뒤떨어지다, date
시대에 뒤떨어진, middle-aged, old-fashioned, time
시대에 뒤진, dated, outdated
시대에 발맞추다, time
시대의, period
시대의 흐름을 따라가는, abreast
시도, attempt, bid, endeavor, go, stab, try
시도하다, attempt, bid, hand, seek, try, whirl
시동 장치, ignition
시동 생, brother-in-law
시동을 걸다, kick-start, start
시동이 걸리다, fire
시드를 배정받다, seed
시들게 하다, dampen
시들다, wilt, wither
시들해지다, flag
시디, CD
시디라이터, CD burner, CD writer
시디롬, CD-ROM
시디롬 드라이브, CD-ROM drive
시디플레이어, CD player
시럽, syrup
시렁, shelf
시력, eyesight, sight, vision
시력의, optic
시련, ordeal, trial
시련 없는, sheltered
시료, sample, specimen
시류, bandwagon
시리얼, cereal
시리얼 포트, serial port
시리즈, series
시리즈 중 한 편, edition
시멘트, cement
시무룩하게, glumly, moodily
시무룩한, glum
시뮬레이션, simulation
시뮬레이션 게임, sim
시민, citizen, national
시민권, citizenship
시민으로서의, civic
시민의, civic, civil
시민임, citizenship
시범, demonstration
시범 경기, exhibition game
시범 계획, pilot
시범운영을 하다, pilot
시범을 보이는 사람, demonstrator
시범을 보이다, demonstrate
시보, trial
시보로 일하는, trial
시뻘겋게 단, red-hot
시사, current affairs
시사 문제의, topical
시사 풍자극, revue
시사만화, cartoon
(~을) 시사하는, suggestive
시사하다, signal, suggest
시사회, preview
시상식, presentation
시선, gaze
시선 끌기, plug
시선을 던지다, cast, dart
시선이 ~에 집중되다, fix
시설, establishment, facility, installation, institution
시설에 수용되다, institutionalize
시설의, institutional
시소, seesaw
시속, kph
시속 ~마일, mph
시스템, system
시스템 분석가, systems analyst
시스템 중단 시간, downtime
시시한, small

시식, taste
시신, body
시아버지, father-in-law
시아주버니, brother-in-law
시안화물, cyanide
시야, field, view, vision
시야가 넓은, cosmopolitan
시야가 흐려지다, blur
시어머니, mother-in-law
시연, rehearsal
시연회, preview
시외로 향하는, outbound
시원스러운, cool
시원스러움, space
시원시원한, breezy
시원찮은, wrong
시원하게, merrily
시원한, cool
시원해지다, cool
시위, assertion, demo, demonstration
시위자, demonstrator, protester
시위하다, assert, demonstrate
시의, poetic
시인, poet
시인하다, concede
시작, beginning, commencement, kickoff, onset, start
(~로) 시작되다, begin, kick, set, start
시작된, stream
시작하다, begin, commence, get, going, initiate, institute, introduce, open, originate, set, start, strike, take
시장, bazaar, market, marketplace, mart, mayor
시장 선두 주자, market leader
시장 원리, market forces
시장 점유율, market share
시장 조사, market research
시장성이 있는, marketable
시장에 나와 있는, market
시장의, market
시장의 힘, market forces
시장한 듯이, hungrily
시적인, poetic
시절, day
시점, point
시정하다, redress
시제, tense
시제품, prototype
시중들다, serve, wait
시즌, season
시차로 인한 피로, jet lag
시책, scheme
시청, town hall
시청각 교재, visual aid
시청률, rating
시청자, audience, viewer
시청자 전화 참여 프로, call-in
시청자 전화 참여 프로그램, phone-in
(~을) 시청하다, tune, view
시체, body, carcass, corpse
시체 공시소, morgue, mortuary
시쳇말로, coin
시초, beginning, birth
시추하다, drill
시치다, tack
시침질하다, tack
시크교, Sikhism
시크교도, Sikh
시큼한, tart
시키는 대로 하게 하다, line
시키다, boss, have
시트를 갈다, change
시폰, chiffon
시합, bout, competition, game, leg, play
시합의 전후반전, half
(~와) 시합하다, play
시행, administration, enforcement, operation
시행 중인, force, place
시행되기 시작하다, play
시행되다, operation
시행착오, trial

시행하다, administer, enforce, operation
시험, exam, examination, test, testing, trial
시험 문제, question
시험 중에 있는, trial
시험 판매, market test, market testing
시험 판매되다, market test
시험관, examiner
시험관 아기 시술, IVF
시험대, test
시험을 보다, examine
시험을 거스르는 것, irritant
시험작, pilot
시험적으로, experimentally
시험적인, experimental
시험지, paper
시험하는, trial
시험하다, test
시험해보다, experiment, test, try
(~하는) 식, fashion
식견, insight
식견이 있는, discerning
식구, household
식기 및 수저류, utensil
식기 세척기, dishwasher
식기류, crockery
식다, chill, cool
식단표, menu
식당, dining room, house, restaurant
식료품, foodstuff, grocery
식료품 가게, grocer, grocery
식료품 상인, grocer
식물, plant, vegetation
식물군, flora
식물세계, world
식물의, vegetable
식물학, botany
식물학의, botanical
식물학자, botanist
식민지, colony
식민지 개척자, colonist
식민지 시대의, colonial
식민지로 만들다, colonize
식민지의, colonial
식민주의, colonialism
식민통치, colonialism
식별, diagnosis
식별력, discrimination
식별하다, discern, discriminate, distinguish, identify, know, tell
식별할 수 있는, discernible
식사, board, dinner, feed, meal
식사를 직접 해 먹으며 보내는 휴가, self-catering
식사를 직접 해 먹을 수 있는 숙소, self-catering
식사하는 사람, diner
식사하다, dine
식상한, overworked
식성, operator
식욕, appetite
식용 뱀장어, eel
식용 조류, fowl
식용에 적합하지 않은, inedible
식용의, edible
식은땀을 흘리는, sweat
식이 요법, diet
식이 요법의, dietary
식인 풍습, cannibalism
식인종, cannibal
식초, vinegar
식초나 소금물에 절이다, pickle
식초나 소금물에 절인 음식, pickled
식탁, table
식탁보, tablecloth
식품, food
식히다, chill, cool
신, almighty, deity, god, providence, shoe, sour
신 포도, grape
신개발품, innovation
신경, nerve
신경 끼, hell
신경 쇠약, nervous breakdown
신경 쇠약에 걸리다, crack

신경 쇠약이 되다, piece
신경 써서, care
신경 쓰는, concerned
(~에) 신경 쓰다, mind, sleep
신경 쓰이게 하다, niggle
신경 쓰임, niggle
신경 쓰지 말아라, mind
신경 안정제, tranquilizer
신경계, nervous system
신경과민, nerve
신경과민의, neurotic
신경에 거슬리는, annoying, jarring
신경을 거스르는 것, irritant
신경을 거스르다, jar, nerve
신경을 끄다, switch
신경을 많이 씀, preoccupation
(~에) 신경을 쓰는, -conscious
신경의, nervous
신경이 쇠약해지다, fall
신경증 환자, neurotic
신경질, temperament
신경질적인, nervous
신고 있다, wear
신고서, declaration
신고하다, declare, register, report
신관을 제거하다, defuse
신교도, Protestant
신교도의, Protestant
신교의, Protestant
신규 모집, recruitment
신규 업체, start-up
신규의, start-up
신기술, innovation
신기원, epoch
신기원을 이루다, ground
신기한 듯이, curiously
신나 하는, gleeful
신나는, exciting
신나는 일, laugh
신념, belief, bent, idea, persuasion
신다, put
신도석, pew
신동, prodigy
신디케이트, syndicate
신랄하게, virulently
신랄한, acrimonious, biting, blistering, scathing, tart, virulent
신랄함, edge
신랑, bridegroom, groom
신뢰, confidence, credence, trust
신뢰도, reliability
(~을) 신뢰하다, put, trust
신뢰할 수 없는, treacherous
신뢰할 수 있는, credible, reliable
신만이 안다, heaven
신맛이 나는, sour
신망, respectability
신문, journal, newspaper, paper, press
신문 1면에 실을 만한, front-page
신문 가판대, newsagent
신문 가판대 주인, newsagent
신문 인쇄용 잉크, newsprint
신문 인쇄용지, newsprint
신문사, newspaper
신문에 실린 글, newsprint
신문지, newspaper
신발, shoe
신발류, footwear
신변을 정리하다, house
신병, recruit
신병 모집, recruitment
신봉되어 온, cherished
신봉자, believer, faithful, follower
신봉자들, following
신봉하다, cherish, espouse, follow
신부, bride
신부 들러리, bridesmaid
신부의, bridal
신분, place, status
신분 제도, caste
신분상으로 높은, above
신분증, ID, identification, identity card, paper
신비, mystery, secret
신비로운, mystic, mystical, occult
신비로운 분위기, mystique

신비에 싸인, mystery
신비주의, mysticism
신비주의자, mystic
신비한 매력, magic
신빙성, reliability
신빙성 없는, spurious
신빙성이 떨어지는, patchy
신사, gent, gentleman
신상 기록, record
신상 명세, profile
신상(神像), idol
신생의, newborn
신선미가 없는, stale
신선하지 않은, stale
신선한, fresh
신선한 것, change
신선한 공기, fresh air
신선한 공기를 마시러, breath
신성 모독, blasphemy, desecration
신성한, hallowed, holy, sacred
신성함, sanctity
신세, case
신세 많이 졌어., debt
신세를 지다, owe
(~에게) 신세를 진, indebted
신속하게, swiftly
신속한, prompt, quick, speedy, swift
신속함, haste, speed
신속히 장악하다, overrun
신시사이저, synthesizer
신식의, modern
신식인, modern
신실한, genuine
신앙, faith
신앙심, piety
신앙심이 깊은, religious
신어 보다, try
신에 대한 불경, blasphemy
신에 의하여, divinely
신예의, budding
신용, goodwill
신용 등급, credit rating
신용 사기, scam
신용 상태, creditworthiness
신용 카드, charge card, credit card, plastic
신용도, creditworthiness
신용도가 좋은, creditworthy
신원, background, identity
신원 미상의, unknown
신원 보증인, referee, reference
신원 조회, vetting
신원 조회를 받다, vet
신원 증명서, reference
신원 확인, identification
신원을 밝히다, identify
신원을 확인할 수 있는, identifiable
신음, moan
신음 소리, groan
신음하다, groan, moan
신음하듯 말하는, groan
신의, divine
신의 가호가 있기를, heaven
신이 나서, excitedly, gleefully
신이 난, excited
신인 선수, rookie
신임, credibility
신입의, incoming, new
신입장, credentials
신입 회원, entrant, intake, recruit
신입생, entrant
신자, believer
신장, gain, kidney, stature
신전, temple
신조, belief, creed, persuasion
신조어를 만들다, coin
신주 인수권, rights issue
신중, caution
신중을 요하는, sensitive
신중하게, carefully, cautiously, deliberately, discreetly, gingerly, prudently
신중하게 고르는, selective
신중하게 골라, selectively
신중한, careful, cautious, deliberate, discreet, guarded,

prudent
신중함, discretion, prudence
신진대사, metabolism
신진대사의, metabolic
신참, arrival, rookie
신청, application
신청을 취소하다, unsubscribe
신청하다, challenge, petition, put
신체, person, system
신체 건강한, able-bodied
신체 상해, mutilation
신체 접촉이 많은, physical
신체 치수, measurement
신체검사, physical
신체의, bodily, personal, physical
신체의 각 부위를 조화롭게 사용하는 능력, coordination
신체적 악영향, exposure
신체적으로, physically
신탁, trust
신탁 관리자, trustee
신탁 기관, trust
신탁 자금, trust fund
신통력을 가진, psychic
신통력의, psychic
신통력이 있는, clairvoyant
신통하게 듣는, wonder
신통한 생각, inspiration
신품의, brand-new, new
신하, subject
신학, theology
신학의, theological
신호, cue, signal
신호등, light, stoplight, traffic light
신호를 보내는, motion, signal
신호음, tone
신호탄, rocket
신혼여행, honeymoon
신혼여행을 하다, honeymoon
신화, myth, mythology
신화의, mythical, mythological
신화적인, mythological
싣기, pick-up
싣다, carry, load, take
실, thread, yarn
실격, disqualification
실격시키다, eliminate
실격하다, disqualify
실권, fall
실권하다, fall
실기 시험, practical
실내 장식, decoration
실내 장식가, decorator
실내 장식을 하다, decorate
실내의, indoor
실내화, slipper
실눈을 뜨다, narrow
실눈이 되다, narrow
실례, instance
실례(實例), illustration
실례하다, excuse
실례합니다, excuse, pardon
실로, indeed
실루엣, silhouette
실룩거리다, twitch
실룩거림, twitch
(~을) 실룩대다, twitch
실리적인, economic
실리콘, silicon, silicone
실리콘 칩, silicon chip
실린더, cylinder
실마리, clue
실망, disappointment
실망스러운, disappointing, discouraging
실망스럽게, disappointingly
실망시키다, disappoint, fail, let
실망한, disappointed, let down
실명, blindness
실물, reality
실물 크기의, full-scale
실물로, person
실생활, real life
실생활에서의, real life
실성, madness
실성한, mad
실속 없는, idle

실속 있는, solid
실수, bungle, fault, mistake
실수로, accidentally, error
실수를 인정하다, error
실수를 하다, slip
실수투성이의, bungling
실수하다, err, foot
실습, practical
실시, holding, operation
실시간의, real-time
실시되다, effect, operation
실시하다, action, operation
실신시키다, stun
실어 나르다, cart, ferry
실업, unemployment
실업 수당, dole, unemployment benefit, unemployment compensation
실업 수당을 받는, dole
실업자, jobless, unemployed, unwaged
실업자 수, dole queue
실업자인, unemployed
실없는, empty
실용적으로, practically, sensibly
실용적인, no-nonsense, practical, sensible, utilitarian, working
실용주의, pragmatism
실용주의자, pragmatist
실용주의적으로, pragmatically
실용주의적인, pragmatic
실은, actually, honesty, such, thing
실을 꿰다, thread
실재, entity, existence
실재의, objective
실적, track record
실적 카드, loyalty card
실제 날짜보다 늦게 적은, postdated
실제 크기의, full-size
실제로, actually, fact, flesh, practice, real, really, so
실제로 참가하는, hands-on
실제로 해봄, experiment
실제로는, as, heart, intent, such
실제의, actual, concrete, factual, hands-on, real, working
실제적인 지식, know-how
실종, disappearance
실종된, missing
실직 소득, take-home pay
실직의, jobless
실직자, jobless
실직한, out of work, unemployed
실질상의, virtual
실질적으로, practically
실질적으로 보면, real
실질적인, actual, practical, real, substantive
실질적인 측면, practicality
실책, mishandling
실책을 인식하다, error
실천에 옮기다, practice
실천하는, practicing
실천하다, practice
실체, substance
실체가 없는, intangible, phantom
실체가 있는, tangible
실추되는, drain
실추된, discredited
실추시키다, discredit
실컷, heartily
실크, silk
실탄의, live
실패, bungle, defeat, failure, reel
실패로 끝내다, fail
실패의 원인, undoing
실패자, failure, flop, loser
실패작, disaster, failure, flop
실패하다, botch, bungle, founder, go, grief, lose, mess
실패한, unsuccessful
실행, execution
실행 가능한, practicable, viable, workable
실행 불가능한, unworkable
실행 시간, run time
실행으로 옮기다, carry
실행하다, action, effect, execute,

pursue
실험, experiment, experimentation, test, trial
실험 대상, guinea pig, subject
실험실, lab, laboratory
실험적으로, experimentally
실험적인, experimental
(~으로) 실험하다, experiment, test
실현, fruition, fulfillment, realization
실현 가능성, feasibility
실현 가능한, feasible, possible, realizable
실현되다, materialize, realize, true
실현되지 않은, unfulfilled
실현된, prophetic
실현하다, realize
실황으로, live
실효가 없는, neutral
실효성, efficacy
싫어도 ~할 수밖에 없는, captive
(~이) 싫어져, off
(~이) 싫어지다, go
싫어하게 되다, dislike
(~을) 싫어하게 하다, put
(~하기) 싫어하는, loath, unwilling
싫어하는 것, dislike
싫어하다, against, dislike, hate, mind
싫어함, unwillingness
싫은, distasteful
싫은 소리, piece
싫은 일을 떠맡게 됨, straw
싫음, distaste
싫증나는, tedious
(~에) 싫증나다, tire
(~에) 싫증난, tired, weary
싫증이 난, fed up
싫지만 어쩔 수 없는 일, pill
심, lead
심각성, depth, seriousness
심각하게, critically, gravely, seriously, severely
심각하게 받아들이다, seriously
심각하게 잘못된, criminal
심각한, acute, critical, deep, explosive, grave, grievous, heavy, massive, serious, severe, solemn
심각한 피해를 입다, batter
심각함, severity
심금을 울리다, chord
심다, implant, plant
심드렁하게, languidly
심드렁한, languid
심란하게 만드는, distracting
심란하게 하는, unsettling
심란하여, distractedly
심란한, distracted
심령의, psychic
심리, hearing, inquiry, psychology
심리 기제, mechanism
심리 상태, state of mind
심리 요법, psychotherapy
심리 치료사, psychotherapist
심리받다, try
심리적으로, psychologically
심리적인, psychological
심리하는, hear
심리학, psychology
심리학자, psychologist
심리학적인, psychological
심문, interrogation, questioning
심문하다, interrogate, interview, question
심미적으로, sensuously
심미적인, aesthetic, sensuous
심복, right-hand man
심부름, errand
심부름 가다, errand
심부전, heart failure
심부정맥 혈전증, DVT
심사 위원, judge
심사 위원단, jury
심사 위원회, tribunal
심사숙고, contemplation, dissection
심사숙고하다, contemplate, think

심사숙고한, thoughtful
심사숙고해서, thoughtfully
심사하다, judge, screen
심상, image, imagery
심상하게, blithely, casually
심상한, blithe, casual
심술궂게, grumpily, maliciously, sourly
심술궂은, grumpy, malicious, mean, sour
심신을 단련하다, discipline
심심한, profuse
심심히, profusely
심야의, midnight
심약한, weak
심약함, weakness
심연, abyss
심오한, profound
심의, deliberation
심의를 보류하다, table
심장, heart
심장 마비, heart attack, heart failure
심장 박동, heartbeat
심장 잡음, murmur
심장의, cardiac, coronary
심지가 굳은, strong
심지어, even
심취한 사람, junkie
심카드, SIM card
심판, judge, official, ref, referee, umpire
심판을 보다, referee, umpire
심포지엄, symposium
심하게, acutely, badly, grievously, hard, heavily, mortally, profusely, terribly
심하게 때림, thrashing
심하게 피를 흘리다, hemorrhage
심한, bad, grievous, gross, hard, heavy, high, mortal, nasty, profuse, stiff, terrible, unbelievable
심한 고통, agony
심한 고통을 주다, kill
심한 구속, straitjacket
심한 비판, polemic
심한 손상을 입히는, crippling
심한 타격을 받은, hard
심함, heaviness
심해지다, fester
심히, grossly
십, ten
십 대, teen, teenager
십 대의, teenage
십이궁도, zodiac
십자가에 못 박음, crucifixion
십자가에 못 박히다, crucify
십자로, crossroads
십자말풀이, crossword
십자의, criss-cross
십자형, cross
십장, foreman
십중팔구, bet, likely, time
십중팔구는, probability
십진법, decimal
싱거운, bland, watery
싱글 곡, single
싱글 레코드, single
싱글 시디, single
싱크대, sink
(~하고) 싶다, fancy, like, would
(~하고) 싶어 근질거리다, itch
(~하고) 싶어 안달인, impatient
(~하고) 싶어 하는, disposed
(~하고) 싶어 하다, mind, want
(~하고) 싶은, ready, tempted
(~하고) 싶은 생각이 들다, feel
싸게, cheaply, keenly
싸게 삼, bargain
싸구려 술집, dive
싸구려의, cheap, tacky
싸다, pack, wrap
(~에) 싸여 있다, encase, shroud
싸우다, battle, fight, pit, skirmish, struggle
싸움, battle, bust-up, combat, fight, run-in, struggle

싸움꾼, fighter
(~에게) 싸움을 걸다, pick
싸워서 결판을 짓다, battle
싹둑 자르다, ax, chop, snip
싹싹한, accommodating
싹양배추, sprout
싹을 잘라 버리다, bud
싹트게 하다, germinate, sow
싹트다, germinate, sprout
싼, cheap, keen
쌀, rice
쌀쌀맞은, brusque, remote
쌀쌀한, chill, chilly, distant, icy
쌈지, pouch
쌍, couple, pair
쌍둥이, twin
쌍둥이의, twin
쌍반점, semicolon
쌍방에서, bilaterally
쌍방의, bilateral
쌍방향성, interactivity
쌍방향의, interactive
쌍수를 들고, arm
쌍안경, binoculars
쌓다, build, pile, stack
쌓아올리다, heap, pile, stack
쌓아올린 더미, pile
쌓이다, collect, drift, pile
쌩 하고 가다, swish
쌩 하고 지나가다, whistle
쌩 하는 소리, swish
써내다, write
써넣다, insert
써레, rake
써레질을 하다, rake
써서 낡은, used, worn
썩 좋지 않게, indifferently
썩 좋지 않은, indifferent
썩다, decay, rot
썩어 나가다, rot
썩어 없어지다, decompose
썩은, decayed, rotten
썩음, rot
썰다, cut
썰매, sled, sledge, sleigh
썰매를 타다, sled, sledge
썰물, ebb
쏘다, bite, fire, let, shoot, sting, tab
쏘아보다, glower
쏘아붙이다, snap
(~에) 쏙 들어가다, fit
(~을) 쏙 빼닮다, spit
쏜살같이, shot
쏜살같이 가다, fly, streak
쏜살같이 달려가다, belt
(~에) 쏟다, channel, devote, spill
쏟아 내다, dispense, pump
쏟아 붓다, pour, pump, throw
쏟아져 나가다, pour
쏟아져 나오다, spill
쏟아져 들어오다, pour
쏟아지다, flood, pour, spill, stream
쏟은 액체, spill
쏠리다, graze, lurch
쏠림, lurch
쐐기, peg, wedge
쐐기 모양, wedge
쐐기풀, nettle
쑤셔 넣다, cram, jam, ram, squash, squeeze, stuff, tuck
쑤시는 느낌, stab
쑤시다, pick, smart
쑥 들어가 있다, stick
쑥 들어가다, dive
쓰게, bitterly
쓰고 남은, leftover
쓰고 있다, wear
쓰다, compose, keep, pen, play, put, spend, write
쓰다듬다, caress, pet, stroke
쓰라린, bitter, kick
쓰러드리다, topple
쓰러지다, collapse, down, drop, fall, keel, pitch, strike, topple
쓰러진, fallen
쓰러질 듯한, ramshackle
쓰러짐, collapse, fall

쓰레기, crap, garbage, junk, litter, refuse, rubbish, trash, waste
쓰레기 같은, crap
쓰레기 같은 것, rubbish, shit, trash
쓰레기 더미, scrapheap
쓰레기 더미를 뒤지다, scavenge
쓰레기 매립, landfill
쓰레기 처리장, garbage dump
쓰레기 하치장, dump, tip
쓰레기더미, scrapheap
쓰레기장, dump
쓰레기장 같은 곳, tip
쓰레기통, bin, dustbin, garbage can, trash can
쓰리다, smart
쓰이지 않는, disused
쓴, bitter
쓴웃음 지으며 참다, grin
쓸 만한, acceptable, decent, order
쓸 수 있는, usable
쓸다, sweep
쓸데없이, gratuitously, vain
쓸데없이 참견하다, mess
쓸모 있게 되다, useful
쓸모 있는, handy, usable, use
쓸모가 없어진, sell-by date
쓸모없게 된, out of date
쓸모없는, dead, good, unwanted, use, useless, worthless
쓸모없는 것, dud
쓸어 가다, wash
쓸어 내다, brush, sweep
쓸어 모으다, sweep
쓰여 있다, read
씨, Mr., Ms., pip, pit, seed, stone
(~) 씨 부인, Mrs.
씨를 뺀, pitted
(~에) 씨를 뿌리다, seed, sow
씨름하다, grapple, tackle, wrestle
씨앗, seed
씩 웃다, grin
씩씩거리며 가다, march
씰룩거리는, jerky
씰룩거리며, jerkily
씹다, bitch, chew
씻기, wash
씻다, bathe, wash
씻어 내기, rinse
씻어 내다, flush, rinse
씻어 내리다, flush, wash
씽씽 소리, whistle
아, ah, oh
아가씨, bird, girl, lass
아구창, thrush
아귀를 맞추는, piece
아기, baby
아기 침대, crib
아기방, nursery
아껴 쓰다, stretch
아껴서, sparingly
아끼는, careful, devoted, sparing
아끼다, conserve
아낌없이, freely
아나운서, announcer
아날로그, analogue
아내, wife
아내의 출산 시에 남편이 받는 휴가, paternity leave
아노락, anorak
아늑하게 자리 잡다, nestle
아늑한, cozy, intimate, mellow, snug
아는 듯이, knowingly
아는 듯한, knowing
아는 사람, acquaintance
(~와) 아는 사이가 되다, acquaintance, meet
(~와) 아는 사이인, acquainted
아는 체를 했다, acknowledge
아는 체하는 사람, know-it-all
아는 체함, acknowledgment
아니, nope, or, well, what, yes
아니, why
아니다, hardly, neither, no, nor
(~이든) 아니든, or, whether
(~뿐만) 아니라 ~도, well
아니라고, negative
(~가) 아니라면, be, but, only

아니면, alternatively, else, or
아니면 ~이거나, else
(~는) 아니었지만, if
(~이) 아닌, no, not
(~은) 아닌 것 같군요, say
아닌 것 같다, doubt, suppose
(~이) 아닌 한, unless
(~인지) 아닌지, if
(~이) 아닐까 생각한다, wonder
(~이) 아닐까 싶다, suspect
아담하게, neatly
아담한, compact, little, neat, petite
아동, infant
아드레날린, adrenalin
아들, boy, son
아라비아 숫자, digit
아랍의, Arab
아랍인, Arab
아랑곳없다는 듯, cynically
아래로, below, down, downward, under
아래로 던져, underhand
(~) 아래에, under
아래위로, up
아래의, below, lower
아래쪽, underside
아래쪽의, downward
아래층, downstairs
아래층에, downstairs
아량, tolerance
아량 있는, tolerant
아로새겨진, engraved
아로새긴, inlaid
아름다운, beautiful, lovely, romantic
아름다움, beauty, loveliness
아름답게, beautifully, exquisitely, romantically
아름답게 꾸미는, grace
아마, likely, maybe, perhaps, presumably, probably
아마도게, easily, maybe, possibly, probably, supposedly
아마추어, amateur
아마추어의, amateur
아마포, linen
아멘, amen
아몬드, almond
아몬드 나무, almond
아무 거나, old
아무 거나 좋다, mind
아무 곳에나 분류해 넣다, pigeonhole
아무 데나 두다, lie
아무 데도 없다, nowhere
아무 때나, anytime
아무 일도 없다는 듯, business
아무 제약을 받지 않는, uninhibited
아무 짝에도 쓸모없는, useless
아무 표가 없는, unmarked
아무 흔적이 없는, unmarked
아무것, any
아무것도, anything
아무것도 모르는, dark
아무것도 쓰여 있지 않은, clean
아무것도 아닌 것, nothing
아무나, anyone
아무도, any, anybody, anyone
아무도 ~이 아니다, no one
아무도 ~하지 않는, nobody
(~은) 아무도 모른다, god, heaven, know
아무도 없는 상태에서, scratch
아무런 이유 없이, reason
아무런 조건 없이, string
아무렇게나, anyhow, randomly
아무렇게나 걷다, blunder
아무렇게나 대하다, mess
아무렇게나 만든, ramshackle
아무렇게나 하다, game
아무렇지도 않게, course
아무렇지도 않게 생각하다, think
아무를 돕다, assistance
아무리 ~라 할지라도, matter
아무리 ~해도, however
아무리 강조해도 지나치지 않다, overestimate

아무리 생각해도, stretch
아무리 해도, possibly
아무짝에도 못쓸, rotten
아무튼, anyway, anyways, somehow
아무하고나 자다, sleep
아방가르드의, avant-garde
아버지, father
아버지 쪽의, paternal
(~의) 아버지가 되다, father
아버지로서의, paternal
아버지임, fatherhood
아보카도, avocado
아부하다, flatter
아빠, dad, daddy, papa, pop
아뿔싸!, gracious
아삭아삭 섭어 먹다, crunch
아삭아삭한, crisp, crunchy
아쉬운 듯한, wistful
아쉬워하다, mourn
아스파라거스, asparagus
아스팔트 포장, blacktop
아스피린, aspirin
아슬아슬하게, narrowly
아슬아슬한, narrow, racy
아슬아슬한 순간, shave
아슬아슬함, narrowness
아시아 사람, Asian
아시아의, Asian
아야, ouch, ow
아연, zinc
아연실색하게 하다, shock
아연실색한, aghast
아우르는, collective
아우르다, blend, embrace, extend, straddle, stretch
아웃된, out
아웃렛, outlet
아웃소싱, outsourcing
아웃소싱을 주다, outsource
아이, child, kid
아이 돌보듯 하다, mother
아이 방, nursery
아이가 없는, childless
아이고, gee
아이고!, grief
아이러니, irony
아이를 낳다, have
아이를 낳을 수 없는, infertile
아이를 봐 주다, babysit
아이스 바, Popsicle
아이스 스케이팅, ice-skating
아이스스케이트, skate
아이스크림, ice cream
아이스크림콘, cone
아이스하키, hockey, ice hockey
아이싱, icing
아이콘, icon
아이쿠!, gosh
아저씨, mister
아주, altogether, blatantly, crucially, downright, much, perfectly, quite, very
아주 가까운, point-blank
아주 가까이에서, point-blank, quarter
아주 곤란한, nasty
아주 괜찮은, respectable
아주 기본적인, rudimentary
아주 기분 좋게, luxuriously
아주 기분 좋은, luxurious
아주 깔끔하게, immaculately
아주 깔끔한, immaculate
아주 깨끗하게, immaculately
아주 깨끗한, pristine, whistle
아주 놀라운, startling
아주 다른, apart
아주 먼, far off
이주 멀리 떨어진, far off
아주 멋진, fantastic, smashing, wonderful
아주 명료한, crystal clear
아주 분명하게, uncertain
아주 분명하다, stare
아주 불쾌한, obnoxious
아주 빨리, flash
아주 상쾌한, exhilarating

아주 성숙한 태도, behavior
아주 솔직히, heart
아주 쉬운, foolproof
아주 싫은, horrible
아주 아름다운, exquisite
아주 약간, subtly
아주 얌전한, gold
아주 예절 바른, gold
아주 오래 된, ancient
아주 운이 좋은, well
아주 웃기게, hysterically
아주 웃기는, hilarious, hysterical
아주 유용한, ready-made
아주 인기 있는, red-hot
아주 작은, minute, tiny
아주 잘, ideally
아주 잘하는, dream
아주 잠시, split second
아주 재미있게, hilariously
아주 재미있는, hilarious
아주 적은, mean
아주 조금, shred
아주 조금씩 다가가다, edge
아주 조심스럽게, gingerly
아주 조심해서 행동하다, tread
아주 좋아하게 되다, love
아주 좋은, fine
아주 중요하게, critically
아주 짜증스럽게 하는, infuriating
아주 짧은, brief
아주 착한, gold
아지랑이, haze
아직, still, yet
아직 나타나지 않음, sign
아직 안 쓴, new
아직 태어나지 않은, unborn
아직까지는, yet
아찔할 정도의, bewildering
아치, arch
아치형의, arched
아침, morning
아침 식사 포함 숙박, bed and breakfast, B&B
아침 일찍 일어나는 사람, early bird
아침밥, breakfast
아침밥을 먹다, breakfast
아침에, morning
아케이드, arcade
아크릴 소재, acrylic
아티초크, artichoke
아파르트헤이트, apartheid
아파서 결근한, sick
아파트, apartment, flat, tenement
아파트 건물, apartment building
아파하는, pain
아편, opium
아포스트로피, apostrophe
아프게, painfully
아프게 하다, hurt
아프다, ache, hurt
아프지 않게, painlessly
아프지 않은, painless
아픈, ill, painful, poorly, rough, sick, sore, unwell
아픈 사람들, sick
아픈 상태, sickness
아홉, nine
아홉 번째, ninth
아흔 번째, ninetieth
악, evil
악감정, blood, feeling
악귀, devil
악기, instrument, musical instrument
악담을 퍼붓다, curse
악당, rogue, villain
악대, band
악독하게, viciously
악령, demon
악마, devil, Satan
악마 같은, evil
악마의, demonic, satanic
악명, notoriety
악명 높게, notoriously
악명 높은, infamous, notorious
악몽, nightmare
악몽 같은 일, nightmare

악물다, clench
악물리다, clench
악보, music, score
악성 부채, debt burden
악성의, malignant, virulent
악센트 부호, accent
악수, handshake
악수하다, shake
악순환, vicious circle
악쓰다, howl
악어, crocodile
악영향을 끼치다, prejudice
악용, exploitation
악용하다, bend, exploit
악을 쓰다, bawl
악의, malice, spite
악의 없는, innocent
악의 있는, malicious, malignant, vicious
악의에 찬, venomous
악의적으로, maliciously, mischievously
악의적인, mischievous
악질인, wicked
악취, reek, stench, stink
악취가 나는, smelly
악취가 나다, smell, stink
악취를 풍기다, reek
악평하다, damn
악필, scribble
악한, rogue
악화, deterioration, exacerbation, flare-up, rot
악화 일로로, downhill
악화되다, deteriorate, fester, turn, worsen
악화된, unmitigated
악화시키다, aggravate, degrade, exacerbate, inflame, worsen
안, proposal
안 보이는, sight
안 좋게, badly
안 좋은, bad
안 좋은 감정, feeling
안 좋은 일을 계속 상기시키다, nose
(~을) 안 하게 되다, outgrow
(~을) 안 해도 되다, need
안감, backing, lining
안개, fog, haze, mist
안개가 낀, foggy, misty
안겨 주다, leave
안경, eyeglasses, glass, spec, spectacle
안경 제작자, optician
안경 판매상, optician
안경점, optician
안경테, frame
안경테의 가운데 연결 부위, bridge
안과 밖이 같은 재료인, solid
안구, eyeball
안내, guidance, induction, information
안내 책자, prospectus
안내문, notice
안내서, guide, handbook
안내원, attendant
안내장, circular
안내하다, guide, lead, show, usher
안녕, bye, farewell, goodbye, hi
안녕하세요, good evening, good morning
안녕하세요, hello
안녕히 계십시오, goodbye, regard
안다, hug
안달, impatience
안달하는, impatient
안달하며, impatiently
안대, patch
안도, relief
안도감, reassurance, security
안도의 한숨, sigh
안됐군요, sorry
안됐다고 느끼는, sorry
안뜰, courtyard
안락, comfort, ease
안락사, euthanasia
안락사시키다, misery

안락사하다, sleep
안락의자, armchair
안락한, cozy, easy, snug
안락한 생활, rose
안마, manipulation, rub
안마당, courtyard
안마하다, manipulate
안면 주름 제거 수술, facelift
안목, eye
안목 없는, vulgar
안목 없음, vulgarity
안무, choreography
안무하다, choreograph
안부, love, regard, wish
안부를 묻다, respect
안색, complexion
안성맞춤인, perfect, tailor-made
안식 휴가, sabbatical
안식일, Sabbath
안식처, den, haven, oasis
안심, complacency, reassurance, security
안심시키는, reassuring
안심시키는 말, reassurance
(~을) 안심시키다, mind, reassure, rest
안심시키듯, reassuringly
안심하는, complacent, reassured, relieved, secure
(~을) 안쓰러워하다, feel
(~) 안에, in, into, within
안에 있는 사람, occupant
안으로, in, into
안을 대다, line
안을 바르다, line
안이한 해결책, way
안장, saddle
안장을 얹다, saddle
안전, safety
안전 담당관, safety officer
안전 보장 이사회, Security Council
안전 요원, lifeguard
안전 조치, safeguard
안전띠, seat belt
안전망, safety net
안전벨트, safety belt
안전성, safety
안전을 꾀하다, safe
안전의, safety
안전핀, safety pin
안전하게, safely
안전하게 하다, insure, secure
안전하지 않은, unsafe
안전한, safe
안전한 곳, safety
안전한 곳에, safe
안전한 선택, option
안전한 성행위, safe sex
안전한 장소에, harm
안전한 피신처, safe haven
안절부절 못하는, ease
안절부절 못하다, shuffle
안절부절못하겠다는 듯이, restlessly
안절부절못하는, hot, jittery, restless
안절부절못하다, fidget, squirm
안절부절못함, restlessness
안정, equilibrium, moderation, stability
안정기, plateau
안정되다, calm, level, stabilize
안정되어, keel
안정된, comfortable, safe, settled, stable, steady
안정성, stability
안정성 있는, stable
안정시키다, calm, stabilize, tranquilize
안정적인, secure
안정화, stabilization
안중에도 없는, cavalier
안쪽, inside
안쪽 면, side
안쪽 부분, crook
(~의) 안쪽에, inside
안쪽에서, within
안쪽으로, inside, inward
안쪽으로 향하는, inward

안쪽의, inner, inside, outside
안치되다, state
안타까운, tragic
안타까워하다, lament
안테나, aerial, antenna
앉는 부분, seat
앉는 자리, saddle
앉다, perch, seat, settle, sit
앉아 쉬다, roost
앉아 있다, sit
앉히다, sit
(~하지) 않게 되다, cease
(~하지) 않겠습니까?, will
(~하지) 않겠지요, suppose
(~하지) 않고, without
(~하지) 않다, fail
(~하지) 않다면, only
(~하지) 않도록 설득하다, talk
(~하지) 않으려 한다, will
(~답지) 않은, unlike
(~하지) 않을 수 없다, help
알, egg
알 만한, understandable
알 수 없는, mysterious, shadowy
알 수 없는 것, quantity
알 수 없는 사람, quantity
(~) 알갱이, grain
알게 되다, find, know
알게 뭐야, care
알게 하다, teach
알겠니?, clear
알겠지, see
알고 보니 ~이다, transpire
알고 싶어 하는, inquiring
알고 있는, aware
(~가) 알고 있는 한, knowledge
(~을) 알고 있다, in, keep, know,
    understand
알고 있음, understanding
알고서도, knowingly
알기 쉬운, clear, plain, transparent
알기 어렵게 하다, obscure
알다, find, know, see, tell
알다시피, know, obviously
알뜰한, economical
알라, Allah
알레르기가 있는, allergic
알레르기성, allergic
알려 주다, inform, say, tell
알려져 있기로, reputedly
알려져 있다, know, reputed,
    understand
알려지다, break, get, travel
알려지지 않은, dark, unknown
알려지지 않은 사람, unknown
알려진, known
알루미늄, aluminum
알리다, announce, break, bring,
    familiarize, give, impart, let,
    signify, strike, tell, whistle
알리바이, alibi
알맞다, fit, lend
알맞은, ripe
알몸 상태, nudity
알몸의, naked
알선, placement
알아 볼 수 있는, readable
알아내다, discover, figure, find,
    learn, nail, see, uncover
알아듣게 이야기하다, reason
알아듣다, catch, make, understand
알아맞히기 게임, puzzle
알아보기 쉽게 하다, identify
알아보다, check, discern, know,
    look, make, pick, recognize, see
알아볼 수 없는, unrecognizable
알아볼 수 있는, recognizable,
    visible
알아봄, acknowledgment,
    recognition
알아봄, recognition
알아차리다, detect
알아차리지 못 하다, miss
알아채다, catch, find, hint, notice,
    sense, spot, wind
알았어, okay, see
알았지?, okay

알약, pill, tablet
알을 품음, incubation
알지 못하는, unaware
알차게, solidly
알찬, solid
알코올, alcohol
알코올 중독, alcoholism
알코올 중독에서 벗어나게 하다, dry
알코올 중독에서 벗어나다, dry
알코올 중독자, alcoholic
알코올의, alcoholic
알파벳, alphabet
알파벳순의, alphabetical
앓다, have, suffer
암, cancer
암기하다, memorize
암기하여, heart
암담한, black
암모니아, ammonia
암묵적으로, implicitly
암묵적인, unspoken
암살, assassination
암살하다, assassinate
암살자, assassin
암석, rock
암송하다, recite
암시, allusion, hint, implication,
    indication, pointer, suggestion
암시장, black market
암시적으로, implicitly
암시적인, implicit
(~을) 암시하는, indicative
암시하다, allude, imply, indicate,
    infer, intimate, signal, suggest
암실, darkroom
암암리에, covertly
암양, ewe
암울한, gloomy, grim
암울해하는, gloomy
암의, cancerous
암중모색하다, grope
암초, reef
암캐, bitch
암컷, cow, female
암컷의, female
암탉, hen
암퇘지, sow
암페어, amp, ampere
암페타민, amphetamine
암표 장사를 하다, scalp
암표를 팔다, tout
암표상, scalper, tout
암호, code, password
암호로 바꾸다, encode
암호화된, coded
암흑가, underworld
압도당하다, overcome, swamp
압도적으로, decisively,
    overwhelmingly
압도적인, decisive, overwhelming
압도하다, better, drown,
    overpower
압력, pressure, strain
압력 단체, caucus, pressure group
압력 때문에 ~하게 되다, pressurize
압력을 가하다, pressure
압력을 넣다, ransom
압력을 받는, pressured, pressurized
압류, foreclosure
압류하다, foreclose
압박, pressure
압박감, pressure
압박하다, press, top
압수, confiscation, seizure
압수되다, impound
압수품, haul
압수하다, confiscate, seize
압승, landslide
압승을 거두다, sweep
압승하다, hammer
압운, rhyme
압인을 찍다, stamp
압정, drawing pin, tack,
    thumbtack
압정으로 붙이다, tack
압제, repression
압축, compression
압축 파일을 풀다, unzip

압축되다, compress
압축하다, compress, encapsulate,
    zip
(~을) 압축해서 보여 주다, sum
앗다, claim
앗아갔다, cost
앙갚음, retaliation, vendetta,
    vengeance
앙갚음하다, retaliate
앙상블, ensemble
앙심, animosity, spite, venom,
    vindictiveness
앙심을 품다, have, in
앙심을 품은, vindictive
앙코르, encore
(~) 앞, FAO, front
앞 뒤 분간이 안 되는, disoriented
앞 지퍼, fly
앞다리를 들어 올리다, rear
앞당기다, advance, bring
앞뒤가 들어맞다, place
앞뒤가 맞다, add
앞뒤로, back, backward, to
앞뒤를 분간하다, head
앞뜰, forecourt
앞면, front, head
앞부분, nose
앞부분의, fore
앞서, ahead of, before, earlier,
    previously
앞서 가는, front
앞서 말한, aforementioned,
    aforesaid
앞서 언급한 책, op. cit.
앞서고 있다, lead
앞서다, precede
앞선, ahead, ahead of
앞선, lead
앞에, ahead, before, front
앞에 놓여 있다, lie
앞에서, above, ahead of, before
(~) 앞에서 입을 다물다, door
앞으로, ahead, forth, forward,
    onward, yet
앞으로 감다, fast forward
앞으로 겪게 될, store
앞으로 나아가는, onward
앞으로 몰다, bowl
앞으로는, future
앞을 내다보는, forward
앞을 내다보다, forward
앞의, ahead of, prior
앞이 안 보여, blindly
(~로) 앞이 안 보이는, blind
앞잡이, puppet
앞장서 가다, way
앞지르다, leapfrog, outwit,
    overtake
앞지른, ahead
앞쪽, front
앞쪽 자리에, forward
앞쪽의, early
앞치마, apron
애 봐 주는 사람, childminder
애가, lament
애교 있는, winning
애국심, nationalism, patriotism
애국자, patriot
애국적인, patriotic
애니메이션, animation
애니메이션 제작, animation
애도, condolence, lament,
    memory, remembrance
애도자, mourner
애도하다, lament, mourn
애를 봐 주는 사람, babysitter
애매모호, confusion
애매모호한, confusing, vague
애매하게, ambiguously, cryptically,
    vaguely
애매한, ambiguous, fuzzy, hazy,
    murky, vague
애매한 부분, gray area
애매한 상태, no-man's land
애매한 상황, gray area
애매함, ambiguity
애먹는, uphill
애무하다, pet

애벌레, caterpillar, larva
애석하게도, alas
애석한, sad
애석한 일, pity
애석해 하며, sadly
애석해하는, sorry
애송이의, green
애써 ~하다, way
애써 나아가다, work
애써 일하다, toil
애쓰는, out
(~하려고) 애쓰다, endeavor,
    exert, labor, pain, struggle,
    try
애완동물, pet
애완동물의, domestic
애원하다, appeal, implore
애인, girl, girlfriend, man
애정, affection, attachment,
    fondness, love
애정 생활, love life
애정 표현, romance
애정어린, affectionate, loving
애정을 갖고, lovingly
애지중지하는, doting
애지중지하다, dote
애착, affection, attachment,
    involvement
애착이 강한, attached
애처로운, sad
애처롭게도, sadly
애칭, nickname
애타게 그리워하다, pine
애통해하다, grieve
애프터마켓, aftermarket
애프터쉐이브 스킨, aftershave
애플릿, applet
애호, fondness, keenness
애호가, lover
애호품, love
액, amount
액면 그대로, face value
액면 금액, denomination
액면 상으로는, paper
액면가, face value
액세서리, accessory
액셀러레이터, accelerator
액션, action
액수, sum
액운, luck
액자에 끼워지다, frame
액정 화면, LCD
액체, fluid, liquid
액체 같은, runny
액체의, liquid
액화 석유 가스, LPG
앰프, amp, amplifier
앵무새, parrot
앵무새처럼 되뇌다, parrot
앵초, primrose
앵커, anchor
앵커로 진행하다, anchor
야, boy, wow
야!, why
야간, night
야간 수업, evening class
야간 명소, nightlife
야간 통행 금지령, curfew
야간에, night
야광의, luminous
야구, baseball
야구공, baseball
야구장, ballpark
야금거리다, nibble
야기하다, export, pose, provoke,
    start, trigger
야단, hassle
야단났다, god
야단맞다, reprimand
야단법석, fuss, uproar
야단법석을 떨다, fuss
야단스러운 몸짓, flourish
야단을 피우다, big deal
(~에게) 야단치다, go, tell
야당, opposition
야당 내각, shadow
야당 내각 각료, shadow
야드, yard, yd

야만, barbarism
야만성, brutality
야만인들, savage
야만적으로, savagely
야만적인, barbaric, savage, uncivilized
야망, ambition
야무지지 못하게, limply
야무지지 못한, limp
야비한, despicable
야생 상태의, wild
야생동물, wildlife
야생의, wild
야심 있는, ambitious
야심이 있는, aspiring
야심적인, ambitious
야영, camping
야영단, camp
야영자, camper
야영하다, camp
야외, open-air
야외 바비큐 틀, barbecue
야외 바비큐 파티, barbecue
야외 촬영지, location
야외 활동, outdoors
야외극, pageant
야외에서, open, outdoors
야외에서 식사하다, picnic
야외에서의 간단한 식사, picnic
야외의, open-air, outdoor
야유, boo, booing, heckle, heckling, jeering, jeer
야유 소리, hoot
야유꾼, heckler
야유하다, boo, heckle, hoot, jeer
야자수, palm
야채, vegetable
야채만의, vegetarian
야행성의, nocturnal
야회복, dinner jacket, DJ, wear
약, around, drug, maybe, neighborhood, pharmaceutical, précis, region, résumé, round, some
약간, bit, crack, dash, faintly, hint, kind, lightly, little, marginally, mildly, moderately, partially, pinch, quite, slightly, some, somewhat, vaguely
약간 곱슬거리는, wavy
약간 바꿔 표현한 것, paraphrase
약간 바꿔서 인용하는, paraphrase
약간 숙련된, semiskilled
약간 제 정신이 아닌, unbalanced
약간의, discreet, few, little, mild, moderate, slight, some, vague
약골, weakling, wimp
약국, chemist, druggist, drugstore, pharmacist, pharmacy
약물, medication
약물 과다 복용, OD
약물 남용, overdose
약물 중독자, drug addict
약사, chemist, druggist, pharmacist
약삭빠른, cute, slippery, wily
약세, weakness
약세의, bearish, weak
약소, weak
약속, appointment, arrangement, commitment, engagement, promise, undertaking, word
약속 어음, promissory note
약속하다, arrange, pledge, promise, undertake
약솜, swab
약식 차용 증서, IOU
약어, abbreviation, acronym
약어표, key
약에 취해 정신이 나간, mind
약올리다, wind
약을 먹이다, dose, drug
약을 타다, dope, drug
약자, weak
약점, frailty, weakness
약점을 악용하다, kick
약진(躍進), quantum
약진하다, bound

약초, herb
약초의, herbal
약칭, shorthand
(~의) 약칭인, short
약탈, looting, plunder
약탈자, predator
약탈하는, predatory
약탈하다, loot, plunder
약하게, dully, weakly
약하게 하다, soften
약하여, short
약학, pharmacy
약한, dull, feeble, gentle, low, muted, thin, weak
약해지다, abate, cool, fade, go, recede, thin, wither
약해짐, fragility
약혼, engagement
약혼 기간, engagement
약혼녀, fiancée
약혼한, engaged
약화, fatigue
약화되다, moderate, weaken
약화시키다, dent, mute, tone, weaken, whittle
얄팍하게, thinly
얄팍한, superficial
얇게, thinly
얇게 썬 감자튀김, chip
얇게 썬 조각, slice
얇게 썰다, slice
얇은, flimsy, sheer, slim, thin
얇은 조각, flake, sliver
얇은 층, sheet
얌전하게 있다, nose
얌전한, meek
얌전히, meekly
양, amount, foster, lady, Miss, quantity, sheep, volume
양 끝, end
양 방향의, two-way
양고기, mutton
양귀비, poppy
양극단, extreme, pole
양극화, polarization
양극화되다, polarize
양극화시키다, polarize
양날의 검, sword
양념, seasoning, spice
양념 맛이 강한, spicy
양념을 넣은, spiced
양념을 하다, season
양념장, marinade
양념장에 재다, marinade, marinate
양단 간의, straight
양단간에 결정을 못 내리는, mind
양대 주도권, duopoly
양도 서명을 하다, sign
양도 소득, capital gains
양도되다, pass
양도하다, assign, cede, pass, surrender
양도할 수 있는, transferable
양로 보험 증권, endowment
양로원, nursing home
양립, reconciliation
양립성, compatibility
양립시키다, reconcile
양립치 않는, contradictory
양립하는, compatible
양립할 수 없는, exclusive, incompatible, irreconcilable
양말, sock
양면 기사, spread
양면에 걸쳐 실린 내용, spread
양면적인, ambivalent
양모, fleece, wool
양물푸레나무, ash
양물푸레나무 재목, ash
양반, gentleman
양반 계층, nobility
양배추, cabbage
양보, compromise, concession
양보와 협조, give
양보하다, budge, concede, give, yield
양보하지 않는, intransigent
양산, umbrella

양상, biology
양상추, lettuce
양성애의, bisexual
양성애자, bisexual
양성의, benign, positive
양성하다, nurture
양수의, positive
양식, common sense, form, mode, pattern, style
양식장, bed, farm, fishery
양식적인, stylistic
양식화된, stylized
양심, conscience, scruple
양심에 걸리는, conscience
양심의 가책, conscience
양심적인, scrupulous
양어장, fishery
양에 관한, quantitative
양육, childcare, nurture, parenting, upbringing
양육권, custody
양육권의, custodial
양육하다, nurture
양을 말하다, quantify
양을 재다, quantify
양음 악센트의, acute
양자 간의, straight
양자 간의, adoptive
양자(量子), quantum
양적인, quantitative
양조 회사, brewer
양조자, brewer
양조장, brewery
양조하다, brew
양쪽에 걸치다, straddle
양초, candle
양치기, shepherd
양치식물, fern
양치하다, gargle
양탄자, carpet
양털, fleece, wool
양털 같은, woolly
양털의, woolly
양파, onion
양해, understanding
양해를 구하는, excuse
양호실, infirmary
얕보는, disparaging
얕보다, disparage, light
얕봄, slight
얕은, shallow
얕잡아 볼 수 없다, sneeze
어, eh
어귀, mouth
어기다, breach, break, cheat, flout, infringe, rat, violate
어기적어기적 걷다, lumber
어김, breach
어김없이, fail
어깨, shoulder
어깨 망토, cape
어깨로 밀다, shoulder
어깨를 나란히 하여, shoulder
어깨를 으쓱하기, shrug
어깨를 으쓱하다, shrug
어깻살, shoulder
어느, either, one, what, which
어느 것, which
어느 것이든지, whichever
어느 곳에, whereabouts
어느 모로 보나, appearance
어느 정도, degree, halfway, how, more, part, sense, way
어느 정도까지는, extent, point
어느 정도로, extent
어느 정도의, certain, degree
어느 쪽, either
어느 쪽도 ~않다, neither
어느 쪽의 ~이든, whichever
어느 한쪽의, either
어느새 ~이 되다, slide
어는점, freezing point
어두운, black, dark, dim, shadowy
어두움, darkness
어두워지다, darken, dim
어두침침한, gloomy
어두침침함, gloom
어두컴컴한, murky, somber

어둑한, dim
어둠, dark
어둡게, darkly
어둡게 하다, blacken, darken, dim
어디, anyplace
어디로 튈지 모르는 사람, cannon
어디서, anywhere, where
어디서나, universally
어디서든지, anywhere
어디에, where, whereabouts
어디에나, everywhere
어디에나 있는, ubiquitous
어디에도, anywhere
어디에서 ~하든지, wherever
어딘가, somewhere
어딘가 이상하게, suspiciously
어딘가에, someplace
(~은) 어떠세요?, how
어떠한, every, how
어떠한 ~라도, any
어떠한 대가를 치르더라도, price
어떤, certain, one, particular, some, which
어떤 ~라도, whatever
어떤 것, something
어떤 것에 열중하게 된 사람, convert
어떤 것이 ~이라도, whatever
어떤 대가를 치르고서라도, cost
어떤 면에서는, sense, way
어떤 사람, one, somebody, someone
어떤 상황에서도, circumstance
어떤 식으로, how
어떤 식으로 ~하더라도, however
어떤 일도 서슴지 않다, stop
어떤 일에 생소한, game
어떤 형태는, shape
(~은) 어떤가요?, how
(~인지) 어떤지, whether
어떻게, how
(~하면) 어떻게 될까, what
어떻게 해서든, cost
어떻게든지, somehow
어떻든, all, way
어려 보이는, young
어려운, difficult, hard, hostile, lean, stiff, taxing
어려운 상태, going
어려움, difficulty, job
어려움에 처한, ailing
어려움이 있는, hard-pressed
어렴풋이, dimly, vaguely
어렴풋이 생각나다, bell
어렴풋한, dim, faint, vague
어렵고 힘든, hard
어렵지 않게 해치우는, breeze
어뢰, torpedo
어뢰에 맞아 격침되다, torpedo
어루만지다, caress, stroke
어루만짐, caress
어른거리는 빛, shimmer
어른거리다, shimmer
어른스러운, grown-up
어른이 되다, grow
어리둥절하게 하는, mystifying
어리둥절하다, mystify
어리둥절한, confused, puzzled
어리석게, mindlessly, unwisely
어리석게 굴다, mess
어리석게도, stupidly
어리석은, foolish, mindless, silly, stupid, unwise
어리석은 짓, folly, insanity
어리석음, foolishness, stupidity
어린, baby, little, small, tender, young
어린 새, fledgling
어린 새들, brood
어린 시절, beginning, childhood
어린 학생들, schoolchild
어린애 같은, childish, childlike
어린이, child, kid, youngster
어릴 때, boyhood
어림도 없는, near
어림수의, round
어림잡다, estimate, judge
어림짐작으로 한 추측, guesstimate
어릿광대, clown

어릿광대짓을 하다, clown
어마어마하게, monstrously
어마어마한, staggering
어마어마함, enormity
어머나, goodness
어머니, mother
어머니 같은, motherly
어머니 쪽의, maternal
어머니가 되다, mother
어머니다운, maternal
어머니의, maternal
어머니임, motherhood
어미, ending
어법, grammar, usage
어부, fisherman
어색하게, awkwardly
어색한, awkward
어색해하다, squirm
어서, come, now
어서 오십시오, welcome
어설프게, awkwardly, clumsily,
    limply
어설프게 손보다, tinker
어설픈, awkward, clumsy, limp,
    poor
어설픔, clumsiness
어수선하게 함, disturbance
어수선하다, disorderly, untidy
어수선함, mess
어스, ground
어슬렁거리다, loiter
어슬렁어슬렁 거닐기, stroll
어슴푸레한, shadowy
어슴푸레한 빛, gleam
어우러지다, mix
어우러짐, mix
어울려 다니다, associate
어울리게, appropriately, suitably
어울리게 하다, mesh
어울리는, appropriate, keep,
    matched, matching
어울리다, become, befit,
    coordinate, fit, go, interact,
    match, mesh, mingle, mix,
    move, rub, suit, together
어울리지 않게, incongruously
어울리지 않는, inappropriate,
    incongruous, place
어울리지 않다, clash
어음 교환 은행, clearing bank
어음 교환소, clearinghouse
어이, hey, man
어이없는, dumb
어장, fishery
어정거리다, hang
어정쩡한, neutral
어정쩡한 상태, limbo
어제, yesterday
어조, inflection, note, tone
(~) 어조의, -worded
어지럽게 널려 있다, litter
어지럽게 널린, littered
어지럽게 만듦, disturbance
어지럽게 메우다, clutter
어지럽다, spin
어지럽히다, clutter, disturb
어질러 놓은 물건, clutter
(~으로) 어질러진, strewn
어질어질한, faint
어쨌든, anyhow, anyway, anyways,
    event, hell, rate
어쩌다, unintentionally
어쩌면, just, maybe, perhaps
어쩔 수 없는, impossible
어쩔 줄 몰라 하는, overwhelmed
어찌할 바를 모르는, bewildered,
    loss, lost
어처구니없게, ludicrously,
    pathetically
어처구니없는, ludicrous, pathetic
어처구니없는 실수, blunder
어처구니없는 실수를 하다, blunder
어투, accent, phrase
어학의, linguistic
어휘, vocabulary
어휘 선택, wording
억누르다, grind, push, quell,
    repress, restrain, smother, stifle

억눌린, inhibited, pent-up
억류되다, intern
억류자, detainee
억류하다, detain, hold
억만장자, billionaire
억센, sturdy, wiry
억센 털, bristle
억수같은, torrential
억압, oppression, repression
억압감, inhibition
억압되다, repress
억압된, inhibited, repressed
억압받는, oppressed
억압적인, oppressive
억압하는, repressive
억압하다, clamp, hold, keep,
    oppress, stifle
억양, accent, inflection
억울하게 생각하다, resent
억울한, resentful
억울함, resentment
억제, control, curb, repression,
    suppression
억제감, inhibition
억제되다, check, suppress
억제되지 않는, unchecked
억제책, control
억제하는, deterrent
억제하다, check, control, curb,
    deter, hold, inhibit, keep,
    restrain, smother, stifle, subdue,
    suppress, withhold
억제할 수 없는, overpowering,
    uncontrollable
억제할 수 없이, uncontrollably
억지, deterrence, imposition
억지 해석, travesty
억지력, deterrent
억지로, kick
억지로 ~하다, manage
(~을) 억지로 떠맡다, lumber
(~로부터) 억지로 떼어 놓다, tear
억지로 젊어 보이려는 여자, mutton
억지로 쥐어 주다, press
억지로 참다, repress
억지로 하는, fixed
억지를 부리다, impose
억지의, forced
억측, conjecture
억측하다, conjecture
언급, allusion, mention, reference,
    remark
언급하다, cite, mention, pick,
    point, refer, touch
언급하지 않는, pass
언더핸드의, underhand
언덕, hill
언뜻 보기에는, face
언뜻 보면, sight
언뜻 웃다, flash
언론, press
언론 그룹, syndicate
언론 담당자, spin doctor
언론계, journalism
언명하다, commit
언변이 좋은, slick
언어, language, tongue
언어 능력, speech
언어 장애를 가진, dumb
언어 행위, speech
언어의, linguistic, verbal
언어학의, linguistic
언어학자, linguist
언쟁, exchange, row, run-in
언쟁을 벌이다, row, wrangle
언저리, periphery
언제, when
언제나, always
언제나 끊임없이, 24-7
언제쯤, sometime
언젠가, day, sometime, time
언질, word
언짢은, sour
언행을 삼가는, discreet
얹어 놓다, perch
(~에게) 얹혀살다, live
얻다, acquire, buy, command,
    derive, earn, extract, find, gain,

get, take, win
얻어내다, draw, win
얻었다, garner
얻으려고 노력하다, pitch
얻으려고 애쓰다, woo
얻으려고 하다, seek
얻을 것 같다, stand
얼간이의, daft
얼굴, face, mug
얼굴 생김새, feature
얼굴 팩, mask
얼굴[정면]을 아래/위로 하고,
    face
얼굴을 보이지 않는, invisible
얼굴을 붉히다, blush, color
얼굴을 찌푸리다, face, frown,
    grimace, scowl
얼굴을 찌푸림, grimace
얼굴을 찡그리다, wince
얼굴을 찡그림, frown
얼굴의, facial
얼굴이 붉어진, flushed
얼굴이 빨개지다, pink
얼다, freeze
얼레, spool
얼룩, blot, blotch, fleck, smear,
    smudge, speck, stain
얼룩말, zebra
얼룩지게 하다, smudge, stain
얼룩진, stained, -stained
얼리다, freeze
얼마 안 되는, paltry, slender
얼마나, how, what
얼마의 가격으로 내놓다, ask
얼버무리고 넘어가다, explain
얼버무리다, fudge
얼버무림, evasion
얼빠진, vacant
얼어 붙은, frozen
얼어 붙을 듯 추운, freezing
얼어 죽을 듯하다, freeze
얼어붙다, rooted
얼어붙은, petrified
얼얼하게 하다, sting
얼얼하다, sting
얼음, ice
얼음으로 차게 한, iced
얼음처럼 차가운, icy
얼토당토않은, extravagant, wild
얼핏 보기에는, glance
얼핏 보다, catch, glance, glimpse
얽다, tangle
얽매이다, tie
얽매인, bound, bogged down,
    bound, trapped
얽은, pitted
얽히게 하다, entangle
얽히다, tangle
얽힌, inextricably
얽힘, entanglement, tangle
엄격하게, rigidly, rigorously,
    severely, strictly, tightly
엄격한, austere, draconian, hard,
    puritanical, rigid, rigorous,
    severe, stern, strict, stringent,
    tight, Victorian
엄격한 의미의, proper
엄격함, rigidity, rigor, severity
엄격히, strictly
엄격히 따지면, technically
(~을) 엄격히 통제하다, rein
엄니, tusk
엄마, mom, mommy, mother,
    mum, mummy
엄명, edict
엄밀한, strict
엄밀히, strictly
엄밀히 말해서, exact
엄선된 것, choice
엄선된 것들, selection
엄선된 사람들, selection
엄선한, select
엄숙, solemnity
엄숙하게, gravely, soberly
엄숙한, sober, solemn
엄숙함, solemn
엄습하다, wash
엄연한, hard

엄연한 현실의 자각, awakening
엄정 단속, crackdown
엄중하게, sternly
엄중한, stern, stringent, strong
엄중히 단속하다, crack
엄지손가락, thumb
엄청, awfully, infinitely
엄청나게, dramatically, drastically,
    dreadfully, enormously,
    extravagantly, horrendously,
    horrifically, hugely, immensely,
    incredibly, massively,
    prodigiously, ridiculously, vastly
엄청나게 많은, hell
엄청나게 비싸게, prohibitively
엄청나게 비싼, prohibitive
엄청난, awful, colossal, dramatic,
    drastic, dreadful, enormous,
    gigantic, gross, horrendous,
    horrific, huge, incredible,
    infinite, massive, mighty,
    monumental, prodigious, super,
    terrific, tremendous
엄청난 대가를 치르다, dearly
엄청난 양, blaze
엄청난 충격을 받다, shatter
엄청난 충격을 받은, shattered
엄청남, enormity
엄포, bluff
엄포를 놓다, bluff
엄하게, strictly
엄하게 다스리다, crack
엄한, strict
엄호, cover
업계, profession
업무, business, duty, practice,
    workload
업무 수행 요령을 가르쳐 주다, rope
업무량, load, workload
업무를 보다, sit
업무용 차량, company car
업무용의, service
업신여기다, dirt
업적, accomplishment,
    achievement, deed, track record
업종, business
업체, business
(~이) 없기 때문에, want
(~이) 없는, free, minus, no, void,
    without
(~이) 없다면, barring, be, for
없애 버리다, finish, flatten
없애다, dispense, do, dump, kill,
    lift, purge, relieve, rid, shed
없어도 되는, dispensable
(~이) 없어서 섭섭해 하다, miss
없어서는 안 될, essence
없어지다, astray, go
없어진, missing
(~) 없이, without
(~이) 없이 지내다, go, short
엇비슷한, comparable, matched
엉긴 피, gore
엉덩이, arse, ass, backside,
    bottom, bum, butt, buttock,
    hip, rump
엉덩이 부분, seat
엉덩이 뼈, hip
엉덩이를 때리다, spank
엉덩잇살, rump
엉뚱한, whimsical, wild
엉뚱한 짓을 하다, fool
엉뚱한 행동, antics
엉망, mess, muddle
엉망으로, shoddily
(~을) 엉망으로 만들다, hell
엉망이 되다, wrong
엉망인, crap, rubbish
엉망진창, dog
엉망진창으로 만들다, mess
엉성한, ramshackle, sloppy
엉키다, tangle
엉킴, tangle
엉터리의, broken
엎드리다, go
엎드린, prone
엎어져/바로, face
엎지르다, spill

얼질러지다, spill
엎어 데 덮치기로, insult
엎친 데 덮치다, kick
에나멜, enamel
에나멜 도료, enamel
에너지, energy, power
에누리해서 듣다, salt
에두르는, oblique
에로틱한, steamy
에메랄드, emerald
에세이, essay
에센스, essence
에스컬레이터, escalator
에어로빅, aerobics
에어로졸, aerosol
에어백, airbag
에어컨이 장착된, air-conditioned
에에, er
에워싸다, encircle, encompass, envelop
에워싸여 있다, enclose
에이-레벨 시험, A level
에이스, ace
에이스 서브, ace
에이전트, agent
에이즈, AIDS
에이치 아이 브이 양성이다, HIV
에이치 아이 브이 음성이다, HIV
에이커, acre
에이펙스 티켓, Apex
에칭, etching
에칭 기법으로 새겨지다, etch
에티켓, etiquette
엑스레이, X-ray
엑스레이 사진, X-ray
엑스레이 촬영을 받다, X-ray
엑스선, X-ray
엑스선 사진, X-ray
엑스트라, extra
엑스포, expo
엑스포, cross
엔, yen
엔진, engine
엔진이 달린, motorized
엔화, yen
엘리베이터, elevator
엘리트, elite
엘리트주의, elitism
엘리트주의자, elitist
엠피3, MP3
여가, leisure
여가 시간, spare time
여가의, free
여객 항공사, carrier
여객선, boat
여걸, heroine
여겨지다, deem, supposed
여과 장치, filter
여과지, filter
여관, bed and breakfast, inn
여권, passport
여권 신장의, feminist
여권 신장주의, feminism
여권주의자, feminist
여기, here, over
(~라고) 여기다, consider, regard, see, think, view
여기에, here
여기저기, round
여기저기 돌아다니다, get
(~이) 여기저기 흩어져 있는, dotted
여기저기에, around, here
여기저기의, round
여남은, dozen
여남작, baroness
어느 때보다도 더, usually
어느 때처럼, usual
여단, brigade
여단장, brigadier
여당 대표, First Minister, First Secretary
여덟, eight
여덟 번째의, eighth
여드름, acne, spot
여든, eighty
여러 가지, multiplicity, sundries
여러 가지 해석이 가능한, ambiguous

여러 가지로, variously
여러 가지의, sundry
여러 개의, various
(~에) 여러 군데를 맞추다, pepper
여러 면에서, respect
여러 번, time
여러 번 나눠 하다, spread
여러 사람과 성관계를 갖다, sleep
여러 사람에게 전화를 돌리다, ring
여러 인종이 섞여 있는, mixed
여러 종류로 된, assorted
여러분, folk, guy
여론, opinion, public opinion
여론 조사, opinion poll, poll
여론 조사에 응하다, poll
여름, summer
여름 캠프, summer camp
여린, soft
여명, dawn
여물통, trough
여배우, actress
여백, margin, space
여보, darling, honey
여보게, mate, son
여보세요, hello
여분의, extra, hand, spare, surplus
(~) 여사, Mrs.
여생 동안, life
여섯, six
여섯 번째, sixth
여성, female, woman, womanhood
여성 동지, sister
여성 사업가, businesswoman
여성 성직자, priestess
여성 소유주, proprietress
여성 속옷류, lingerie
여성 영업 사원, saleswoman
여성 일반, womanhood
여성 정장 한 벌, pantsuit
여성 판매원, saleswoman
여성 하원의원, congresswoman
여성다운, feminine
여성다움, femininity
여성성, femininity
여성에게 자상한, gallant
여성용 예복, gown
여성의, female, feminine
여성의 가슴, bosom
여신, goddess
여왕, queen
여왕벌, queen
여우, fox
여우 사냥, hunt
여우 사냥을 하다, hunt
여울, rapids
여원, thin
여유, respite, space
여유 있게, comfortably
여유 있는, comfortable, more
여유가 없다, afford
여유로운, leisurely
여유롭게, leisure, leisurely
여유를 두다, spare
여윳돈이 거의 없는, shoestring
여의다, bury, lose
여임, loss
여자, woman
여자 동성애자, dyke
여자 바텐더, barmaid
여자 사제, priestess
여자 상속인, heiress
여자 의장, chairwoman
여자 친구, girl, girlfriend
여자 화장실, lady
여자 후계자, heiress
여자분, lady
여자애, girl
여자의, female
여자인, womanhood
여장(女裝), drag
여장부, heroine
여장을 한, drag
여전히, same
여전히 ~한 상태로 있다, remain
여정, journey, lap, pilgrimage
여정의 일부, leg
여주인, hostess

여주인공, heroine
여지, margin, room, space
여지가 있는, open
여지배인, manageress
여차여차한, such
여차여차해서, anyway
여파, fallout, ripple
여피, yuppie
여학생, schoolgirl
여행, foray, journey, pilgrimage, tour, travel, trip
여행 가방, case
여행 안내서, guide, guidebook
여행 일정, itinerary
여행사, travel agent
여행사 직원, travel agent
여행용 가방, suitcase
여행용 대형 가방, carryall
여행자, traveler
여행자 수표, traveler's check
여행하고 싶은 욕망, itchy
여행하다, journey, tour, travel
역, converse, part, reverse
역(驛), station
역겨운, disgusting, gross, horrid, horrifying, nasty, obscene, revolting, sick
역겨움, revulsion
역겨워 하는, disgusted
역겹게 하다, sicken
역경, adversity, hardship
역기, weight
역년, calendar year
역대, time
역도, weightlifting
역동성, dynamism
역동적으로, dynamically
역동적인, dynamic
역량, capability
역량 있는, capable
역량을 충분히 발휘하다, justice
역량이 미치지 못하는, depth
(~의) 역량이 있는, competent
역력한, glaring
역법, calendar
역사, history, story
역사가, historian
역사상의, historical
역사에 남다, history
역사적으로, historically
역사적인, historic, monumental
역사적인 일을 하다, history
역사학, history
역설, irony, paradox
역설적으로, ironically, paradoxically
역설적인, ironic, paradoxical
역설하다, press, stress
역시, also, so, too
역전, reversal
역학, dynamic, mechanic
역학 관계, politics
역할, hat, role
역할 모델, role model
(~로서) 역할을 수행하다, act
(~한) 역할을 하다, part, play
역행, setback
역행하는, backward
(~에) 역행하여, against
역화하다, backfire
역효과를 가져오다, backfire
역효과의, counterproductive
엮다, weave
엮은, woven
엮은이, editor
연, kite, verse
연 4회의, quarterly
연(年), year
연간, p.a., per annum
연간의, yearly
연감, annual
연결, connection, join, link, link-up
연결 고리, bridge, link
연결 부분, connection
연결되다, connect, forward, interface, lead, link
연결되어, through

연결부, hinge
(~와 ...을 연결시키다, connect, interface, match
연결을 끊다, disconnect
연결, connection
연결하다, connect, hook, join, link, plug, run
연계, affiliation, connection
(~와) 연계되다, connect
연고, balm, ointment
연골, cartilage
연공서열, seniority
연관, relationship, tie
연관되다, tie
연관이 없는, disconnected
연구, research, study, work
연구 개발, R&D
연구소, institute, lab
연구실, laboratory
연구원, researcher
연구하다, pursue, research
연극, theater
연극의, dramatic, theatrical
연극조로, theatrically
연극조의, theatrical
연극하듯, dramatically
연금, annuity, pension
연금 불입금, superannuation
연금 수령자, pensioner
연금 제도, pension plan, pension scheme
연금을 받을 수 있는, pensionable
연기, acting, fog, fume, performance, portrayal, postponement, smoke, suspension
연기가 자욱한, smoky
연기를 뿜다, smoke
연기만 피워 올리다, smolder
연기자, performer
연기처럼 사라지다, smoke
연기하다, act, adjourn, defer, play, postpone, put, suspend
연단, platform, podium
연달아, after, another
연달아 치이다, buffet
연달아 크게 울리는 북소리, roll
연대, regiment
연대감, bond
연대기, chronicle, history, timeline
연대순으로, chronologically
연대순으로 기록하다, chronicle
연대순의, chronological
연대의, regimental
연도, year
(~에) 연동되다, index
연락, communication
연락선, ferry
연락을 받다, hear
연락을 주고받다, communicate
(~와) 연락을 취하여, touch
연락이 끊긴, out of touch
연락이 닿다, catch
(~와) 연락이 두절되다, contact
연락처, contact
연락하다, contact, get, hold, reach
연례 동창회, homecoming
연례 총회, AGM
연례의, yearly
연료, fuel
연료 보충, refueling
연료 창고, bunker
연료를 보충받다, refuel
연료를 보충하다, refuel
연루, complicity, entanglement, implication
연루되다, hook, involve
연루시키다, implicate, involve
연립 정부, coalition
연립 주택, row house, terrace
연립 주택 한 채, terraced house
연마, cultivation
연마제, abrasive
연마하다, cultivate, grind, hone, polish, train
연맹, federation, league
연맹의, federal
연못, pond, pool

연미복, tail
연민, compassion, pity
연방, commonwealth
연방 국가, federation
연방 정부에 의해, federally
연방의, federal
연방주의자, federalist
연보, annual
연보라색, lilac
연비, mileage
연사, speaker
연삭기, grinder
연상, association
연상시키다, invoke
(~을) 연상케 하다, smack
연상하게 하는, reminiscent
연상하다, associate
연서인, witness
연서하다, witness
연석, curb, kerb
연설, address, speaking, speech
연설 기회, platform
(~에게) 연설하다, address, speak
연소, combustion
연소한, little
연속, catalog, chain, continuity, run, sequence, series, streak, stream, succession, train
연속 폭격을 가하다, bombard
연속극, serial, soap, soap opera
연속극으로 방영되다, serialize
연속극화, serialization
연속된, uninterrupted
연속으로, straight
연속의, consecutive, straight, unbroken
연속적인, successive
연속해서, row
연쇄, sequence, series
연쇄의, serial
연쇄적인, knock-on
연수, training
연수의, soft
연수하다, train
연수회, workshop
연습, practice
연습 문제, exercise
연습하다, practice, rehearse, run
연안에, offshore
연안의, offshore
연애, love affair, romance
연애 감정, romance
연애 소설, romance
연애의, romantic
연애하며, romantically
연약한, delicate, vulnerable
연약함, vulnerability
연어, salmon
연역법, deduction
연연하다, dwell
연예, entertainment
연예계, show business
연예인, artist, entertainer
연인, bird, love, lover
연인 사이, item
연자(連字) 부호, hyphen
연장, continuation, extension, implement, renewal, tool
연장 가능한, renewable
연장 코드, extension
연장선, extension
연장자, elder
연장전, playoff
연장전의 우승 결정 골, golden goal
연장하다, extend, prolong, renew
연재, serialization
연재되다, serialize
연재물, serial
연좌, implication
연좌 농성, sit-in
연주되다, play
연주자, performer, player
연주하다, perform, play
연출로 얻은 자리, job
연줄이 든든한, well-connected
연착륙, soft landing
연체금, arrears
연체된, arrears, overdue

연체하다, fall
연초, New Year
연출하다, present
연필, pencil
연한, muted
연한을 채우다, serve
연합, coalition, confederation, link-up, union
연합군, ally
연합된, associated, united
연합의, federal
연합체, syndicate, union
연합하다, join, link, unite
연합한, united
연해의, coastal
연행, pick
연행해 가다, take
연혁, history
연호 소리, chanting
연호하다, chant
연화 차관, soft loan
연회, banquet
열, fever, heat, rank, row, ten
열 받은, pissed
열 번째의, tenth
열거하다, detail, list
열광, frenzy, love affair, mania
열광시키다, thrill
열광자, enthusiast, freak
열광적으로, enthusiastically, wildly
열광적인, enthusiastic, euphoric, rapturous
열광하게 만들다, enthuse
열광하는, crazy, nut
열기, heat
열기가 고조되다, heat
열기구, balloon
열네 번째의, fourteenth
열다, give, hold, mount, open, present, throw, unlock
열다섯 번째, fifteenth
열대 우림, rainforest
열대 지방, tropics
열대 지방의, tropical
열대성의, tropical
열두 개, dozen
열두 번째, twelfth
열둘, twelve
열등, inferiority
열등체, junk bond
열등한, inferior, second-class, second-rate
열띤, feverish, hot
열렬한, ardent, avid, devout, ecstatic, fervent, impassioned, keen, passionate, strong
열렬한 찬사의, glowing
열렬히, fervently, passionately, strongly, warmly
열리다, open
열린, open
열린 마음, mind
열망, ambition, aspiration, eagerness, hunger, keenness
열망어린, eager
열망하는, anxious, keen
열망하다, aspire, heart
열매, bean
열매를 맺다, fruit
열변을 토하다, enthuse, harangue
열성, fervor, zeal
열성적인, zealous
열성팬, fanatic, maniac
열세 번째, thirteenth
열셋, thirteen
열쇠, key
열심인, avid, keen, zealous
열심히, avidly, diligently, feverishly, hard
열심히 쫓아다니다, chase
(~을) 열심히 찾다, seek
열심히 하는, keen
열아홉 번째, nineteenth
열악한, bad, poor
열애, devotion
열애하는, devoted

열애하다, worship
열어 보다, try
열어 젖히다, open
열어 젖힌, open
열여덟, eighteen
열여덟 번째, eighteenth
열여섯, sixteen
열여섯 번째, sixteenth, sixth
열을 식히다, chill
열을 지어 늘어선 것, string
열의, thermal, zeal, zest
열의 없는, listless
열의 없이, listlessly
(~할) 열의가 없다, heart
열의에 찬, passionate
열이 나는, hot
열이 나다, temperature
열이 있는, feverish
열이 있다, temperature
열일곱, seventeen
열일곱 번째, seventeenth
열정, ebullience, energy, enthusiasm, fervor, keenness, passion, zest
열정이 넘치는, ebullient
열정적으로, energetically, furiously
열정적으로 일하다, overtime
열정적인, furious, impassioned, intense, keen
열중, addiction, keenness
(~에) 열중하는, keen, mad
(~에) 열중하다, glue
(~에) 열중하여, into
열중한, involved, mad
열차, train
열판, hob
열풍, mania
열한 번째의, eleventh
엷게 염색되다, tint
엷은, neutral
엷은 색, tint
엷은 색조, tinge
엷은 색조를 띠게 만들다, tint
엷은 황갈색, fawn
염(鹽), salt
염가 판매, sale
(~을 염두에 두고, mind
염두에 두는, mindful
염려, fear, misgiving
염려스러운, uneasy
염려하는, concerned
염료, color, dye
염료가 빠지지 않는, fast
염불, mantra
염색, coloring
염색체, chromosome
염색하다, color, dye
염세적인, pessimistic
염세주의, pessimism
염세주의자, pessimist
염소, chlorine, goat
염원, prayer
염원하는, sought-after
염좌, sprain
염주, bead
염증, inflammation
염증성의, inflammatory
염증이 생긴, septic
염치가 있다, decency
염탐, snoop
염탐꾼, snooper
염탐하다, snoop, spy
염화불화탄소, CFC
엽서, card
엽총, shotgun
엿 먹다, screw
엿기름, malt
엿듣다, eavesdrop, listen
엿보다, peek, peep
엿봄, peek, peep
영, nil, nought, zero
영가적 음악, gospel
영감, brainwave, inspiration
영감을 받다, inspire
(~에) 영감을 받은, -inspired
영감을 불어넣다, inspire
영감을 불어넣어 주는, inspiring
영감의 근원, inspiration

영공, airspace
영광, glory, privilege
영광스럽게 여기다, honor
영광을 누리다, honor
영광의 날들, glory
영구, permanence
영구적으로, permanently, perpetually
영구적인, permanent, perpetual
영구화하다, perpetuate
영구히 계속되는, interminable
영국, UK
영국 건축 조합, building society
영국 공군, RAF
영국 법정 표준의, imperial
영국 사람들, English
영국 연방, commonwealth
영국 정부, Downing Street
영국 화폐 제도, sterling
영국의, English
영국의 보수당, Conservative Party
영국인, Briton
영글나, crop
영락하다, descend
영리를 위한, profit-making
영리하게, cleverly
영리한, bright, clever, cute, nimble, shrewd, smart
영리함, cleverness
영매, medium
영보다 큰, plus
영사, consul
영사(映寫), projection
영사관, consulate
영사기, projector
영사의, consular
영상, film, picture, reflection
영상의, optical
영생, immortality
영세한, shoestring
영속, permanence
영속시키다, perpetuate
영속적인, standing
영속하는, perpetual
영수증, receipt, sales slip
영안실, morgue, mortuary
영양 공급, nourishment
영양 섭취, nutrition
영양가 있는, nourishing
영양가가 있는, nourishing
영양분을 공급하다, nourish
영양소, nutrient
영양실조, malnutrition
영양을 공급하다, feed
영양의, nutritional
영양적으로, nutritionally
영어, English
영어 교육, ELT
영업, sale, service
영업 비밀, trade secret
영업 사원, salesman, salesperson
영업 중인, business, open
영업부 직원들, sales force
영업시간, business hours, opening hours
영업의, operating, working
영업하다, operate
영역, domain, spectrum, sphere, territory
영역과 다룸과 관련된, territorial
영예, distinction, glory, honor
영예로운, glorious
영예롭게, gloriously
영예의, coveted
영웅, hero
영웅상, figure
영웅적으로, heroically
영웅적인, heroic
영원, eternity
영원의 세계, eternity
영원한, eternal, immortal
영원히, eternally, forever, good, time
영원히 떠나다, leave
영입하다, bring, sign
영장, warrant
영장류, primate
영점, love

영주권, green card
영토, dominion, territory
영토의, territorial
(~에) 영합하다, pander
영해, water
영향, effect, impact, influence, operation, ramification
영향력, clout, force, hand, importance, influence, leverage, muscle, strength
영향력 있는, influential, powerful
영향력을 행사하다, string
영향력이 있다, weight
영향력이 큰, high-powered, seminal
영향을 끼치다, hit, mold, play
(~에) 영향을 미치다, act, affect, color, operate
(~의) 영향을 받는, subject
(~의) 영향을 받는, condition
(~의) 영향을 받아, influence
영향을 받지 않는, immune, unaffected
영향을 받지 않은, untouched
영향을 주다, dictate, difference, impact, impression, influence, move, touch
영향을 행사하다, influence
영혼, soul, spirit
영혼을 팔다, sell
(~한) 영혼의 소유자, spirit
영화, cinema, film, motion picture, movie, picture
영화 관람, cinema, movie, picture
영화 대본, screenplay
영화 산업, film
영화 음악, soundtrack
영화 제작, filming
영화 화면, shot
영화관, cinema, movie theater, theater
영화를 찍다, film
영화배우, movie star
영화사, studio
영화의, cinematic
영화팬, moviegoer
옅게, lightly
옅은, light, pale, watery
옅은 막, veil
옆, side
옆 사람, neighbor
옆구리, flank, side
옆구리가 땅김, stitch
옆길, side street
옆길로 새다, stray
옆면, side
옆모습, profile
옆모습으로, profile
옆에, beside, by, close
(~의) 옆에 있는, next door
(~) 옆에 있다, adjoin
옆으로, by, sideways
옆으로 나란한, level
옆으로 나란히, level
옆의, next, sideways
옆집의, next door
예, example
예각의, acute
예감, feeling, hunch, premonition
예견가, visionary
예견력 있는, visionary
예견하다, foresee
예견할 수 있는, foreseeable
예고, herald, notice
예고 없는, unannounced
예고되다, herald
예고편, trailer
예고하다, herald
예금, deposit, saving
예금 세좌, deposit account
예금하다, deposit
예기치 못한, rude, unforeseen
예기치 않은, unexpected
예능인, entertainer
예를 들다, illustrate
예를 들면, instance
예를 들어, e.g., example
예를 들어 ~와 같은, such

예리하게, keenly
예리한, acute, incisive, keen, penetrating, piercing, sharp
예리함, subtlety
예명, aka
예민하여, edge
예민한, sensitive, tender
예민함, sensitivity, subtlety
예방, prevention
예방 접종, immunization, jab, vaccination
예방 접종 주사를 맞다, immunize
예방 접종하다, vaccinate
예방 조치, precaution
예방 조치하다, guard
예방의, preventive
예배, chapel, service, worship
예배당, chapel, oratory
예배자, worshiper
예보, forecast
예보하다, forecast
예복, robe
예비, contingency
예비 된, store
예비 부품, spare part
예비 선거, primary
예비 자원, backup
예비 장치, backup
예비 행위, preliminary
예비용, spare
예비용의, auxiliary
예비의, preliminary, spare
예비적인, exploratory
예비품, standby
예쁘게, prettily
예쁘장한, dainty
예쁘지 않은, plain
예쁜, pretty, sweet
예사로 생각하다, think
예산, budget
예산 세우기, budgeting
예산상의, budgetary
예산안 발표, budget
예산에 감안하다, budget
예산을 세우다, budget
예상, forecast, prospect
예상 밖의 진전, twist
예상되는, prospective
예상되는 대로, predictably
예상외로, unexpectedly
(~을) 예상하고, anticipation
예상하다, anticipate, expect, forecast
예상할 수 있는, predictable
예상했던 대로, unnaturally
예선, heat
예선 통과자, qualifier
예선을 통과하다, qualify
예선전, qualifier
예수, Christ, Jesus
예순, sixty
예순 번째, sixtieth
예술, art
예술 영화, art
예술가, artist
예술성, artistry
예술을 위한 예술, sake
예술의, artistic
예술적으로, artistically
예술적인, artistic
예술품, work of art
예스러운, quaint
예시하다, exemplify
예식, ceremony
예약, booking, reservation
예약하다, speak
예약된, reserved
예약을 통한, appointment
예약이 꽉 찬, book, booked up
예약하다, book, reserve
예언, prophecy
예언자, prophet
예언적인, prophetic
예언하다, prophesy
예열시키다, warm
예열하다, preheat, warm
예외, exception
예외 없이, exception

예외가 아닌, exception
예외로, excepted
예외적으로, exceptionally
예외적인, exceptional, ordinary
예의, civility, courtesy
예의 바르게, properly
예의 바른, courteous, polite, proper
예의 바름, manner
예의 주시하다, watch
예의를 갖추어, graciously
예의를 갖춘, gracious
예의를 표하는, courtesy
예의범절, breeding, etiquette
예전에, back, once
예전의, form, old, one-time
예절 바르게 처신하다, behave
예정, schedule
예정대로, schedule
예정대로 가는, target
예정되어 있다, schedule
예정된, appointed, due
예정보다 길어지다, overrun
예정이다, slate
예정인, due
예증, illustration
예증하다, illustrate
예초기, mower
예출금 내역서, statement
예측, prediction, projection
예측 가능성, predictability
예측 불가능한 사람, wild card
예측 불가능한 요인, wild card
예측 불허의 인물, joker
예측되다, project
예측하다, calculate, predict
예측할 수 없는, unpredictable
예측할 수 없음, unpredictability
예건대, say
예행연습, dry run, rehearsal
예행연습하다, rehearse
예후, prognosis
옐로카드, yellow card
옛 공장 지대, brownfield
옛 주택 지대, brownfield
옛날, back
옛날에는, old
옛날의, old
오, oh
오감, sense
오게 하는, bring
오그라든, shriveled
오그라들다, curl, shrivel
오그라시다, curl
오그리다, curl
오금이 저리다, quake
오기, grape
오냐오냐하는, indulgent
오냐오냐하다, indulge
오냐오냐하며, indulgently
오냐오냐하며 대함, indulgence
오는 중이다, way
오늘, today
오늘날, present, today
오늘날의, present-day
오늘밤, tonight
오다, come
오도 가도 못하게 되다, strand
오도된, misguided
오도하다, mislead
오두막, cabin, hut
오디션, audition
오디션을 보다, audition
오디오 테이프, audiotape
오디오의, audio
(~을) 오라고 하다, call
오락, amusement, pleasure
오락거리, amusement, pleasure
오락성 정보 프로그램, infotainment
오래, long
오래 가게 하다, stretch
오래 가다, stretch
오래 걸리는, drawn-out, long
오래 끄는, protracted
오래 끌다, drag
오래 남는, abiding
(~보다) 오래 남다, outlive

오래 동안 계속된, age-old
오래 머무르다, linger
(~보다) 오래 살다, outlive, survive
오래가게 하다, spin
오래가다, wear
오래도록 유용하다, wear
오래된, aging, old
오랜, long, old
오랜 세월에도 불구하고 건재하다, test
오랜 시간, eternity, haul, hour
오랫동안, age, long
오랫동안 계속된, long-standing
오랫동안 보지 못한, long-lost
오랫동안 사랑을 받아 온 것, favorite
오랫동안의, long-time
오렌지, orange
오려 내다, clip
오려 낸 기사나 사진, clipping
오려내다, cut
오로지, purely, solely
오로지 ~만, only
오로지 본인 탓이다., blame
오류, bug
오류 하나 없는, immaculate
오르가슴, orgasm
오르간 연주자, organist
오르는, upward
오르다, climb, go, make, mount, rise, scale
오르막, ascent
오르막의, uphill
오르막이 되다, rise
오른손으로, right-handed
오른손잡이의, right-handed
오른쪽, right
오른쪽으로, right
오른쪽의, right, right-hand
오른팔 같은 사람, right-hand man
오른편의, right-hand
오름, climb
오름세, uptrend
오름차순의, ascending
오리, duck
오리무중이다, foggy
오리엔테이션, orientation
오만, pride
오명, stigma
오명을 뒤집어 쓰다, brand
오명을 쓰다, stigmatize
오명을 안기다, shame
오명을 얻다, taint
오명을 얻은, tainted
오묘하게, subtly
오묘한, subtle
오물, filth, muck, sewage, sludge
오므리다, purse
오믈렛, omelet
오버롤, overall
오버헤드 프로젝터, overhead projector, OHP
오븐, oven
오산, miscalculation
오소리, badger
오솔길, lane, path
오십 대, fifty
오십 대 오십, fifty-fifty
오십 번째, fiftieth
오싹하게, chillingly
오싹한, chilling
오아시스, oasis
오염, contamination, pollution
오염 물질, pollutant, pollution
오염 물질을 배출하지 않는, clean
오염 요인을 없애다, clean
오염된, contaminate, polluted
오염시키다, infect, poison, pollute, taint
오용, abuse, misuse
오용하다, abuse, misuse
오이, cucumber
(~으로) 오인되다, pass
오일, oil
오작동, malfunction
오전, a.m., morning
오전에, morning
오점, blemish, blot, taint

오존, ozone
오존 친화적인, ozone-friendly
오존층, ozone layer
오줌 싸다, piss
오줌을 싸다, wet
오지, bush, depth, outback
오지 안내원, guide
오지 여행, trek
오직, only
오직 ~만, all
오직 ~뿐, nothing
오징어, squid
오케스트라, orchestra
오케스트라의, orchestral
오크 재목, oak
오크나무, oak
오토매틱 자동차, automatic
오토바이, cycle, motorbike, motorcycle
오토바이 운전자, motorcyclist
오토바이 폭주족, biker
오트밀, oatmeal
오판하다, miscalculate, misjudge
오페라, opera
오페라의, operatic
오페어, au pair
오프라인으로, offline
오프라인의, offline
오프사이드, offside
오프사이드의, offside
오한, chill
오합지졸, rabble
오해, misconception, misinterpretation, misunderstanding
오해를 받는, misunderstood
오해를 살 수 있게, misleadingly
오해를 살 수 있는, misleading
오해하다, misinterpret, misunderstand, stick
오호라, alas
오후, afternoon, p.m.
오후 간식, tea
오히려, anything, more, rather
옥(玉), jade
옥수수, corn, maize
옥신각신, haggling
옥신각신하다, quibble
옥에 티, ointment
옥외에서, door, open, outdoors
옥외의, outdoor
온, whole
온 마음을 사로잡다, enthrall
온갖 궁리를 하다, play
온갖 악조건에도 불구하고, odds
온갖 재주를 부리다, hoop
온갖 종류의, kind
온건파, dove, moderate
온건한, moderate
온건한 판매 방식, soft sell
온기, warmth
온당하게, correctly
온당한, correct, proper
온도, heat, temperature
온도계, thermometer
온라인의, online
온몸으로, bodily
온몸이 오싹하게 만들다, flesh
온순하게, mildly
온순한, mild
온스, ounce
온스의 약어, oz
온실, conservatory, greenhouse
온실 효과, greenhouse effect
온실 효과를 일으키는, greenhouse
온전한, whole
온천, spa
온천의, thermal
(~에) 온통, through
온통 덮다, blanket
온통 살얼음판이다, knife
온화하게, genially, gently
온화한, benign, genial, gentle, mild, temperate
온화함, geniality, gentleness
온후한, good-natured
올가미, noose, snare
올곧은, straight

올곧은 사람, straight arrow
올라 있는, up
올라가는, upward
올라가다, ascend, go, move, rise
올라서서, astride
올리다, inflate, notch, post, put, rack, raise, turn, up, upload
올리브 나무, olive
올리브 열매, olive
올리브기름, olive oil
올리브색, olive
올림, faithfully, sincerely, yours
올림표, sharp
올림픽 경기, Olympic, Olympic Games
올바르게 인식하다, appreciate
올바르지 않게, incorrectly
올바르지 않은, incorrect
올바른, accurate, fair, good, right, righteous, sound
올바른 방향으로, track
올바름, right
올빼미, owl
올이 굵은, coarse
올이 풀린 길, ladder
올케, sister-in-law
옮아매기 시작하다, catch
옮기다, bring, dump, flip, move, remove, shift, transfer
옳게, right
옳다, water
옳은, correct, good, right
옴부즈맨, ombudsman
옵서버, observer
옵션, option
옷, clothes, clothing, garment
옷 입다, dress
옷 한 벌, suit
옷감, material, textile
옷걸이, coat hanger, hanger
옷깃, lapel
옷단, hem
옷을 벗다, kit, strip
옷을 벗은, undressed
옷을 벗지 않다, kit
옷을 입다, dress
옷을 입은, clothed, dressed
옷을 입히다, dress
옷을 차려 입다, dress
옷을 차려입히다, dress
옷장, wardrobe
옷차림이~한 사람, dresser
옹송그리고 붙어 있다, huddle
옹알거리다, gurgle
옹졸한, intolerant, narrow-minded
옹호, advocacy
옹호자, champion, defender, proponent
옹호하다, champion, defend, stand, stick
옻칠, lacquer
와, wow
와락 잡다, snatch
와서, washer
와이드 스크린의, widescreen
와이퍼, windshield wiper, wiper
와인 바, wine bar
와일드카드, wild card
와전된, garbled
와전시키다, twist
와트, watt
와해, breakup, disintegration
와해되다, fall, fracture, seam
와해시키다, dismantle, fracture
왁스, wax
왁스로 윤을 내다, wax
완강하게, stubbornly
완강한, adamant, invincible, obstinate, stubborn
완강함, stubbornness
완강히, adamantly, obstinately
완강히 반대하다, foot
완결하다, complete
완고하게, obstinately, stubbornly
완고한, inflexible, intractable, obstinate, rigid, stubborn
완고함, inflexibility, obstinacy, stubbornness

완곡어법, euphemism
완곡하게, euphemistically, obliquely
완곡한, euphemistic, oblique
완두콩, pea
완료된, complete, done
완만하게, gently
완만하게 펼쳐지는, rolling
완만한, gentle
완벽, perfection
완벽주의자, perfectionist
완벽하게, ideally, immaculately, inch
완벽하게 활용하는, command
완벽한, exhaustive, immaculate, perfect, pure, resounding, watertight
완벽함, purity
완비된, complete
완성, completion, perfection
완성된, done
완성하다, complete
완수하다, carry, execute, get, go
완수해 내다, deliver
완전, perfection
완전 새것인, pristine
완전 소멸, oblivion
완전 처음부터, scratch
완전 출자 자회사, wholly-owned subsidiary
완전무결하게, flawlessly
완전무결한, faultless, flawless
완전물, whole
완전하게 개선하다, perfect
완전하게는, world
완전한, absolute, complete, dead, full, outright, perfect, pure, thorough, total, utter, whole
완전한 변모, sea change
완전히, altogether, barrel, clean, completely, comprehensively, downright, entirely, fully, hundred, literally, outright, perfectly, right, soundly, thoroughly, through, top, totally, way, well, whole, wholly, wildly
완전히 ~는 아니다, exactly
완전히 갖춰진, fully-fledged
완전히 구기다, screw
완전히 끝낸, through
완전히 멈추다, halt
완전히 무너져, ruin
완전히 미쳐서, raving
완전히 빠진, wrapped up
완전히 실패하다, flat, flop
완전히 없애다, wipe
완전히 이해되다, sink
완전히 자라다, mature
완전히 제거되다, tear
완전히 제압하다, floor
완전히 지우다, obliterate
완전히 지친, shattered
완전히 파괴하다, annihilate
완충 장치, buffer
완충기, bumper
완충제, cushion, padding
완쾌하다, pull
완파, thrashing
완파하다, thrash
완패, beating
완패시키다, annihilate, rout
완화, loosening, moderation, relaxation
완화되다, ease, let, loosen, relax, slacken
완화시키는, soothing
완화시키다, ease, soothe
완화하다, cushion, defuse, loosen, mitigate, moderate, relax, slacken, soften
왈츠, waltz
왈츠를 추다, waltz
왕, king
왕관, crown
왕국, empire, kingdom, realm
왕다운, regal
왕립의, royal

왕모래, grit
왕복 여행, round trip
왕복 운행되다, shuttle
왕복의, return, round trip
왕복표, return
왕복하다, shuttle
왕비, queen
왕새우, prawn
왕성하게 먹다, tuck
왕실, court
왕실 사람들, courtier
왕실의, royal
왕에 걸맞은, regal
왕위, throne
왕위에 오르다, crown
왕자, prince
왕정주의자, royalist
왕조, dynasty
왕족, monarchy, royal, royalty
왕좌, throne
왕짜증 나는 일, pain
왜, why
왜?, how, what
왜곡, distortion
왜곡되다, skew
왜곡된, distorted, garbled
왜곡하다, distort, falsify, rewrite
왜냐면, 'cos
왜냐하면, because
(~) 외, et al.
외가, side
외견, exterior
외견상으로, officially
외견상의, outward
외계인, alien
외골집의, wayward
외골수인, single-minded
외과 의사, surgeon
외과용 메스, scalpel
외과의, surgical
외과적으로, surgically
외곽, outside
외곽으로, uptown
외곽의, outlying
외관, guise, presentation, semblance, surface
외관상의, seeming
외관이 손상되다, disfigure
외관이 손상된, disfigured
외교, diplomacy
외교 사절, envoy
외교관, diplomat
외교단, diplomatic corps
외교의, diplomatic
외교술, diplomacy
외교적 수완이 있는, diplomatic
외교적인 수단으로, diplomatically
외국어로서 영어 교육, EFL
외국어에 능한 사람, linguist
외국에서 온, overseas
외국의, alien, foreign
외국인, alien, foreigner
외국인 혐오, xenophobia
외국인을 혐오하는, xenophobic
외국행의, outbound
외다, learn
외도를 한, unfaithful
외도하지 않는, faithful
외동의, only
외딴, isolated, secluded
외딴 곳에서, nowhere
외람된 말씀이지만, respect
외람됩니다만, due
외래 환자, outpatient
외로운, isolated, lonely
외로움, loneliness
외면하다, eye, walk
외모, appearance, exterior, look
외모 가꾸기, grooming
외모의, personal
외무부, Foreign Office
외박하다, stay
외부, exterior, outside
외부 구조, shell
외부 세계의, outward
외부 위탁, outsourcing
외부 자원을 활용하다, outsource
외부에 위탁하다, outsource

외부에서, externally, outside
외부와 절연된 상태인, vacuum
외부의, exterior, external,
   externally, external, outside
외부인, outsider
외부적으로, externally
외삼촌, uncle
외상 거래, credit
외상으로, account
외설, indecency, obscenity
외설스러운, naughty
외설의, indecent
외설적인, dirty, obscene
외설적인 언사, obscenity
외설죄, indecency
외양, front, persona
(~) 외에, top
(~) 외에는, exception, other
(~) 외에는 모두, all
(~) 외에는 second, second
외워서, heart, memory
외주를 주다, contract
외진, remote
외출을 시켜 주다, take
외출하다, get, go
외출하여, out
외치다, cry, exclaim, howl, shout
외침, cry, exclamation, holler,
   outcry, rant, roar, shout
외투, overcoat
외판원, rep, representative
외풍, draft
외피, shell
외향적인, extrovert, extroverted,
   outgoing
외향적인 사람, extrovert
외형, exterior
외형의, outward
외화, foreign exchange
외환, foreign exchange, forex
외환 시장, foreign exchange
왼손잡이의, left-handed
왼쪽, left
왼쪽 여백을 맞추다, left-justify
왼쪽 클릭, left-click
왼쪽으로, left
왼쪽의, left, left-hand
요가, yoga
요구, call, claim, demand
요구 사항, demand, requirement
요구르트, yogurt
요구사항을 늘리다, ante
요구에 맞추다, tailor
요구자, claimant
요구하다, ask, call, claim, demand,
   exact, necessitate, press,
   require, take
요금, charge, fare, fee, rate, tariff
요금이 부과되는, chargeable
요동, fluctuation, surge
요동하다, jar
요란하게, raucously
요란하게 발산되다, blaze
요란한, garish, loud, lurid, raucous
요란한 소리를 내다, crack
요람, cradle
요령, maneuver, trick
요령 있게, tactfully
요령 있게 처리하다, maneuver
요령 있는, tactful
요령껏 움직이다, maneuver
요령껏 움직임, maneuver
요령을 알다, rope
요령을 터득하다, rope
요리, cooking, cookery, cooking,
   cuisine, dish, menu
요리 기구, cooker, utensil
요리 조달자, caterer
요리법, cuisine, recipe
요리사, chef, cook
요리에 고명을 얹다, garnish
요리용의, cooking
요리의, culinary
요리조리 빠져나가다, thread,
   wriggle
요리책, cookbook
요리하는 사람, cook
요리하다, cook

요법, therapy
요새, bastion, castle, fortress
요소, element, ingredient, streak
요술을 걸다, enchant
요술을 부리다, juggle
요술을 부리듯 생기게 하다, conjure
요술의, magical
요술이나 재주를 부리는 사람,
   juggler
요시찰인 명부, blacklist
요식, red tape
요식 행위, bureaucracy
요식에 따른, bureaucratic
요실금, incontinence
요실금의, incontinent
요약, recapitulation, roundup,
   summary
요약 보고, briefing
요약 설명하다, brief
요약문, sketch
요약판 자료 책자, fact sheet
요약하다, condense, encapsulate,
   recap, recapitulate, sum,
   summarize
요약하면, summary
요양, convalescence
요양소, home
요양하다, convalesce
요오드, iodine
요요, yo-yo
요율, tariff
요인, factor, ingredient,
   parameter, VIP
요전의, other
요점을 말하는, point
요점을 벗어난, point
요점을 정리하다, sum
요정, fairy
요주의 인물, joker
요즘, day, nowadays
요즘에는, these
요지, gist, keynote
요지부동이다, heel
요직의, high
요청, request
요청받는 대로, demand
요청받다, invite
(~의) 요청에 따라, request
요청이 있으면, request
요청하다, ask, put, request
요컨대, all, altogether, brief, short
요트, yacht
요트 놀이, yachting
요트 타기, sailing
요행, fluke
요행수를 바라고, spec
욕구, appetite, desire, impulse,
   need
욕망, appetite, desire, urge
욕설, abuse, curse, language
욕설의, abusive, foul
욕실, bathroom
욕실 세트, suite
욕을 하다, curse, swear
욕정, lust
욕조, bath, bathtub, tub
욕지기, nausea
욕하다, abuse, name, run
용, dragon
용감하게, bravely, gallantly,
   valiantly
용감하게 굴다, neck
용감한, brave, daring, gallant,
   intrepid, valiant
용감한 행위, bravery
용골, keel
용광로, furnace, melting pot
용구 한 세트, kit
용기, bravery, carton, case,
   container, courage, daring, gut,
   heroism, holder, nerve, spirit,
   strength
용기 있는, courageous, spirited
용기 있는 행위, heroic
용기를 내다, pluck
용기를 북돋우다, encourage
용기를 얻다, heart, hearten
용기를 얻은, heartened

요납되지 않는, on
용납하다, allow
용납할 수 없는, disgusting
용도, use
용도를 설명하다, account
용돈, allowance, pocket money
용량, capacity
용매, solvent
용무, business
용법, usage, use
용변을 보다, bathroom
용병, mercenary
용서, forgiveness, mercy
용서하다, excuse, forgive
용솟음침, spurt
용수철, spring
용암, lava
용액, preparation, solution,
   solvent
용액조, bath
용어, language, term, terminology,
   vocabulary
용어 해설 목록, glossary
용역, service
용융, meltdown
(~할) 용의가 있는, game
용의자, suspect
용이하게 하는 사람, facilitator
용이함, ease
용인, acceptance
용인되는, acceptable, palatable
용인될 수 있게, acceptably
용인성, acceptability
용인할 수 없는, unacceptable
용적, capacity
용접하다, weld
용지, ground
용케 헤어나다, get
용해, meltdown
용해된, molten
용해성의, soluble
우거진, lush
우격다짐으로 하다, hustle
우기, rain
우기다, insist
우는 소리, call
우단, velvet
우대 금리, prime rate
우대 조건, sweetener
우대 조건을 달다, sweeten
우대받는, preferential
우대의, complimentary
우두머리, chief, head
우둔살, rump
우등 학위, honor
우뚝 솟다, dominate
우뚝 솟아오르다, rise
우뚝 솟은, towering
우라늄, uranium
우량 증권, gilt
우량의, gilt-edged
우량주, blue chip
우러러보다, look
우렁찬 소리로 말하다, boom
우레, storm
우레 같은, thunderous
우려, concern, fear, worry
우려내다, scrounge, wring
우려낸 차, brew
우려되는, worrying
우려하는, disturbed, fearful
우르르 내리다, pile
우르르 몰려가다, stampede
우르르 몰려감, stampede
우릉거리는 소리, grumble,
   rumble
우릉거리다, grumble, rumble
우리, cage, pen, us, we
우리 자신, ourselves
우리다, brew
우리에 갇힌, caged
우리에게, us
우리의, our
우리의 것, ours
우묵한, hollow
우묵한 곳, hollow
우물, well
우물쭈물하다, hesitate

우박, hail
우박이 쏟아지다, hail
우방, friend
우산, umbrella
우상, god, hero, heroine, icon, idol,
   role model
우상시하다, idolize
우선, begin, first, instance, place,
   start
우선 사항, priority
우선 첫째로, thing
우선권을 주다, preference
우선순위, precedence
우선순위를 매기다, prioritize
우선순위의, high
(~보다) 우선시되다, priority
(~보다) 우선시하다, place,
   prioritize, priority
우선적인, prior
우선주, preference shares,
   preferred stock
우선하다, override
우세, balance, dominance, edge,
   superiority, upper
우세를 보이다, lead
우세하게, predominantly
우세하다, predominate, prevail
우세한, dominant, predominant,
   ruling, superior
우세해지다, ground
우송, mailing
우수, excellence
우수리 없는, round
우수성, merit
우수하게, excellently
우수한, excellent, first-class,
   outstanding, superior
우수함, distinction, quality
우스개, joke
우스개조의, tongue
우스갯소리를 하다, joke
우스꽝스러운 일, farce
우스꽝스러움, humor
우스꽝스럽게, humorously
우스꽝스럽게 묘사하다, caricature
우스운, comical, funny
우스워 죽는, hysterics
우스워 죽다, kill
우승, championship
우승 결정전 시리즈, playoff
우승 후보, favorite
우승배, cup
우승자, winner
우승컵, cup, trophy
우아, elegance
우아하게, elegantly, gracefully,
   tastefully
우아한, chic, elegant, graceful,
   refined, tasteful
우아함, grace, refinement
우연, accident, chance
우연의 일치, coincidence
우연의 일치인, coincidental
우연적, accidental
우연한, chance
우연히, accidentally, chance
우연히 ~을 하다, happen
우연히 듣다, overhear
우연히 마주치다, encounter
우연히 만나다, bump, run
우연히 발생하다, come
우연히 부딪치다, bump
우연히 찾아내다, stumble
우연히도, coincidentally
우우 하고 야유하다, hiss
우우 하는 야유, hiss
우울증, depression
우울하게, darkly, depressingly
우울하게 하는, depressing
우울하게 하다, depress, get
우울한, blue, dark, depressed,
   desolate, gloomy, low,
   melancholy, moody
우울함, gloom
우월, supremacy
우월감, superiority
우월의식, snobbery
우위, advantage, dominance,

superiority, supremacy, upper
우위를 점하다, jump, predominate
우유, milk
우유나 크림을 넣은, white
우유나 크림을 넣지 않은, black
우유를 넣은, milky
우유부단, indecision
우유부단한, indecisive
우윳빛의, milky
우의, raincoat
우익, right, right-wing
우익 인사, conservative
우익의, conservative, right-wing
우적우적 먹다, munch
우정, friendship
우주, cosmos, creation, outer
  space, space, universe
우주 비행사, astronaut
우주 왕복선, shuttle, space shuttle
우주 정거장, space station
우주선, craft, spacecraft, spaceship
우주의, cosmic
우중(愚衆), herd
우중충한, dull, gray, miserable
우지끈 하는 소리, crack
우쭐하게, flattering
우쭐해진, flattered
우체국, post office
우체통, mailbox
우파, left, right
우파의, right-wing
우편, mail, post
우편 광고, direct mail, direct
  marketing
우편 번호, postcode, zip code
우편료, postage
우편물, mail, mailing, post
우편물 발송함, out box
우편물 수취인 명부, mailing list
우편물 집배원, mailman
우편물 투입구, letterbox
우편배달, post
우편엽서, coupon, postcard
우편으로 보내다, mail
우편의, postal
우편함, mailbox, postbox
우편환, money order, postal order
우표, stamp
우표 첨부 회신용 봉투, stamped
  addressed envelope
우현, starboard
우현 쪽이, starboard
우호, friendship
우호 관계, rapport
우호적인, amicable, friendly
우화, fable, parable
우환 없는, sheltered
우회, detour
우회로, bypass, detour, diversion
우회적으로, indirectly
우회적인, indirect, roundabout
우회하는, roundabout
우회하다, bypass
욱신거리다, throb, tingle
욱신거림, tingling
운, destiny, fortune
운동, athletics, campaign,
  crusade, exercise, motion,
  movement, sport, workout
운동가, activist, campaigner,
  crusader
운동량, momentum
운동복, sweatsuit, tracksuit
운동선수, athlete
운동시키다, exercise
운동을 벌이다, crusade
운동을 좋아하는, sporty
운동을 하다, agitate, campaign
운동의, athletic
운동장, playground, playing field
운동하다, exercise, work
운동화, sneaker, trainer
운명, destiny, doom, fate, lot
운명의 장난, quirk
(~할) 운명이다, doomed
운명짓다, doom
운문, rhyme, verse
운반 도구, sling

운반 장치, conveyor belt
운반원, porter
운반하다, haul
운석, meteorite
운세, horoscope, star
운송, carriage, haulage, transport,
  transportation
운송 수단, transport,
  transportation, vehicle
운송 화물, freight
운송 회사, hauler, haulier
운송되다, route, ship
운송료, carriage
운송하는 사람, hauler, haulier
운송하다, transport
운수 회사, line
운수대통, bonanza
운에 맡기고 해 보다, chance
운영, admin, administration,
  management, operation,
  running
운영 위원, governor
운영 중인, open
운영 체계, wheel
운영 체계, operating system
운영되다, function
운영비, running costs
운영상으로, operationally
운영상의, administrative,
  operational
운영자, operator
운영하다, operate, run
운용 가능한, operational
운용 중인, operational
운용되다, function
운용하다, invest
운을 걸다, gamble
운이 나쁜, unlucky
운이 맞는 단어, rhyme
운이 맞다, rhyme
운이 없다, luck
운이 좋다, foot, luck
운이 좋은, fortunate, lucky
운전, driving
운전 자본, working capital
운전과 관련된, motoring
운전면허증, driver's license,
  driving licence
운전석, cab
운전을 하는, wheel
운전자, driver, motorist
운전하다, drive, operate
운치, atmosphere
운치 있는, atmospheric
운하, canal
운항로, course
운행, operation, service, traffic
운행 시각표, schedule
운행하다, run
울, wool
울다, chatter, crow, weep
울렁거리게 하다, churn
울렁거리다, churn, heave
울려 퍼지는, resounding, ringing
울려 퍼지다, blare, echo, resonate,
  reverberate, ring
울로 둘러싼, enclosure
울리는, ringing
울리는 소리, peal, ringing
울리다, blow, chime, go, honk,
  hoot, peal, reduce, reverberate,
  toll
울림, blare, ring
울림을 주다, resonate
울먹이다, whimper
울먹임, whimper
울부짖다, bay, cry, howl, wail
울부짖음, howl
울음, crying, tear
울음소리, chatter, crying, cry
울타리, fence, fencing
울타리를 치다, fence
울퉁불퉁한, bumpy, ragged,
  uneven
움직이게 하다, drive, send
움직이고 있다, move
움직이는, moving
움직이다, behave, bounce, bring,

budge, get, go, move, pass,
  sway, throw, veer, wheel
움직이지 않는, inert, motionless,
  still
움직이지 않다, jam
움직일 수 없는, action
움직일 수 있는, mobile, movable
움직임, behavior, motion, move,
  movement
움직임이 없는, static
움찔하다, cringe, flinch, recoil,
  start
움찔함, recoil, start
움츠러들다, shrink
움츠리다, huddle
움켜잡기, grab, grasp, grip
움켜잡다, grab, grasp, hold
움켜잡으려고 하다, claw
움켜쥐다, hold
움푹 꺼지다, hollow
움푹 내려앉은, cave
움푹 들어가게 하다, dent
움푹 들어가다, dip
움푹 들어간, sunken
움푹 들어간 곳, dent
움푹 들어감, dip
움푹 파인 곳, depression
웃기는, ridiculous
웃다, laugh
웃어넘기다, joke, laugh
웃을 일이 아닌, joke
웃음, laugh
웃음거리, joke
웃음거리가 되다, fool
(~을) 웃음거리로 만들다, fool
웃음소리, laughter
웃음을 참는 얼굴, face
웃자란, overgrown
웅대함, magnificence
웅덩이, pool, puddle
웅변, eloquence, oratory
웅변술, eloquence, oratory
웅변적으로, eloquently
웅변적인, eloquent
웅성거림, buzz, rumbling
웅웅거리는 말투, drone
웅웅거리듯 말하다, drone
웅장하게, majestically
웅장한, epic, grand, majestic
웅장함, grandeur, majesty
웅크리다, crouch, curl, huddle
워드 프로세서, word processor
워드 프로세싱, word processing
워커, boot
워크맨, Walkman
워크숍, workshop
워크스테이션, workstation
원, chamber, circle
원가, cost, cost price
원가 계산, cost accounting,
  costing
원격, distance
원격 접속, remote access
원격 조종, remote control
원격 회의, teleconference,
  teleconferencing
원고, plaintiff, transcript
원고, manuscript
원곡의, original
원광, halo
원금, capital
원기, vitality
원기 왕성하게, energetically
원기 왕성한, energetic, exuberant,
  vibrant
원기를 잃다, heart
원기를 회복시키다, refresh
원대한, grand
원동력, dynamic, motivation, spur
원동력이 되는, driving
원래, intrinsically, originally
원래 모습을 잃지 않은, unspoiled
원래의, original
원로, elder
원료, material
원룸, studio
원룸 아파트, studio
원리, principle

원만하게 하다, mellow
원만한, rounded
원만해지다, mellow
원문, text
원문 그대로의, sic
원반, disk
원본, original
원본의, master, original
원뿔, cone
원산의, native
원상을 회복하다, right
원상태로 돌리다, undo
원상태로 되돌리다, reinstate
원소, element
원수, foe
원숙하게 하다, mellow
원숙한, mellow
원숙해지다, mellow
원숭이, ape, monkey
원시 생물의, primitive
원시적인, primitive
원예, gardening, horticulture
원예가, gardener
원예의, horticultural
원예의 재능, green
원예학, horticulture
원예학의, horticultural
원유, crude, crude oil
원인, cause, culprit, origin, recipe,
  source, trigger
(~에) 원인을 돌리다, attribute
원인이 되다, account, cause,
  dictate
원자, atom
원자력의, atomic
원자로, nuclear reactor, reactor
원자의, atomic
원작의, original
원점으로 돌아가다, square
원정, expedition
원정 경기에서, away
원정 경기의, away
원정대, expedition
원조, aid, assistance
(~의) 원조를 받은, -aided
원조를 중지하다, rug
원주민, native
원주민의, native
원천, source
원천 과세, withholding tax
원초적인, raw
원추형, cone
원치 않는, unwanted
원칙, basis, line, principle
원칙대로라면, right
원칙상, theoretically, theory
원칙상의, doctrinal
원칙에 따라, principle
원칙을 저버리다, sell
원칙적으로, principle
원통, cylinder
원통하게, bitterly
원통한, bitter
원통함, bitterness
원피스, dress
원하건대, hopefully
(~가) 원하는, choice, desired, for
원하는 것, want
원하는 것은 무엇이든 할 수 있다,
  oyster
원하는 대로, please
(~가) 원하는 조건으로, term
원하다, desire, want, wish
원한, enmity, venom
원한을 갚다, score
원형, archetype
원형 도표, pie chart
원형의, archetypal, circular
원호, arc
원활하, keel
월, Mon.
월가, Wall Street
월간의, monthly
월경, menstruation, period
월경을 치르다, menstruate
월경의, menstrual
월계수, laurel
월급날, pay day

월급봉투, pay envelope
월드 와이드 웹, web, World-Wide Web, WWW
월식, eclipse
월요일, Monday
웜, worm
웨이브, wave
웨이브가 있는, wavy
웨이터, waiter
웨이트, weight
웨이트 트레이닝, weight training
웨이트리스, waitress
웨이퍼, wafer
왝왝거리다, heave
웰빙, well-being
웹 공간, webspace
웹 디렉터리, directory
웹 링, web ring
웹 마스터, webmaster
웹 사이트, website
웹 스페이스, webspace
웹 캠, webcam
웹 페이지, web page
웹사이트, site
웹사이트 주제별 분류, directory
웹진, webzine
위, stomach
위계질서, hierarchy
위기, crisis, edge, menace
(~의) 위기에 처하다, teeter
위대한, great
위대한 업적, greatness
위대함, greatness
위도, latitude
위도의, latitude
위독하여, critically
위독한, critical, death
위력적인, potent
위로, across, comfort, on, onto, over, up
(~) 위로 다리를 벌려 걸치다, straddle
(~) 위로 비쭉 튀어나오다, overhang
위로 치켜들다, hold
위로 향한, upward
위로가 되는, comforting
위로를 주는 것, comforter
위로부터, above
위로자, comforter
위로하다, comfort, console
위반, breach, contravention, infringement, violation
위반자, offender
위반하다, contravene, rat, violate
위법의, illegitimate, illicit
위생, hygiene
위생의, sanitary
위생적인, hygienic, sanitary
위선, hypocrisy
위선자, hypocrite
위선적인, hypocritical, insincere, two-faced
위성, moon, satellite
위성 국가, satellite
위성 방송 수신용 안테나, satellite dish
위성 지역, satellite
위성의, satellite
위세, grandeur
위세적으로 하다, pump
위스키, whiskey, whisky
위스키 한 잔, whiskey, whisky
위신, face, prestige
위아래로 뛰다, bounce
위아래로 움직이다, bounce
위안, comfort, consolation, pleasure, refuge, solace, yuan
위안의 장소, oasis
위안제, balm
위안화, yuan
위압당하다, overawe
위압적인, overpowering
위압하다, daunt
위엄, dignity, grandeur
위엄 있는, dignified
위업, feat
(~) 위에, above, on, over, top, up, upon

위원, commissioner
위원단, panel
위원장, chair, chairman, chairperson, president
위원회, commission, committee, council
위의, above, gastric
위인들, great
위임, commission, delegation
위임받다, delegate
위임하다, commission, delegate
위장, camouflage, cover, pretense
위장 단체, front
위장된, disguised
위장하다, camouflage, disguise
위조된, counterfeit
위조범, forger
위조의, fake
위조죄, forgery
위조품, counterfeit, forgery
위조하다, counterfeit, falsify, forge
(~) 위주의, oriented
위증, perjury
위지위그, WYSIWYG
(~의) 위쪽에, up
(~의) 위쪽으로, up, upward
위축되다, contract
위축된, daunted
위축시키다, daunt
위층, upstairs
위층으로, upstairs
위층의, upstairs
위치, alignment, location, position, seat, walk of life
위치를 바꾸다, place
위치를 보여 주다, mark
위치를 알아내다, locate
위치하다, lie, rank
위치한, located, set, situated
위탁, referral
위탁하다, entrust
위태로운, jeopardy, precarious, stake
위태로운 상황에, limb
위태롭게, dangerously, precariously
위태롭게 하다, jeopardize
위트, wit
위풍당당한, commanding
(~를) 위하여, account, favor, interest, sake, toward
(~를) 위한, for, meant
(~를) 위해, benefit, for
(~을) 위해 건배하다, toast
(~을) 위해 일하다, serve
(~하기) 위해서, order
위헌의, unconstitutional
위험, danger, hazard, peril, risk, specter
위험 관리, risk management
위험 분자, risk
위험 요소, danger
위험 요인, risk
위험 투자가, venture capitalist
위험성, risk
위험에 빠뜨리다, endanger
위험에 빠져, jeopardy
위험에 처한, stake
위험을 무릅쓰고 ~을 하다, venture
위험을 무릅쓰고 하다, risk
위험을 무릅쓰다, neck, risk
위험을 알리다, alarm
위험을 줄이다, hedge
(~할) 위험이 있다, risk
위험인물, security risk
위험하게, dangerously, perilously
위험한, dangerous, dodgy, hairy, hazardous, risky, rough, treacherous
위험한 비탈길, slippery
위험한 상태에 있는, risk
위협, intimidation, menace
위협받는, threat
위협을 느끼다, cow
위협적인, intimidating, menacing, threatening
위협적인 것, menace
위협적인 사람, menace

위협적인 존재, threat
위협하다, menace, terrorize, threaten
위협하듯, menacingly
위협하여 쫓아버리다, frighten
윈도우, window
윈드서핑, windsurfing
윈치, winch
윈치로 감아올리다, winch
윗도리, top
윗몸 일으키기, sit-up
윗옷, top
윗옷을 입지 않은, topless
윙, wing
윙윙거리는 소리, buzz, drone, hum, whirr
윙윙거리다, buzz, drone, howl, hum, whirr
윙윙거림, buzz
윙크, wink
윙크하다, wink
유가 증권, portfolio, security
유가 증권 일람표, portfolio
유감스러운, regrettable, sad
유감스럽게, regrettably
유감스럽게 생각하다, regret
유감스럽지만 ~입니다, regret
유개 운반차, van
유골, ash, remain
유골 단지, urn
유광 페인트, gloss, gloss paint
유괴, kidnapping
유괴범, kidnapper
유괴죄, kidnap
유괴하다, kidnap
유권자, elector, electorate
유권자들, voter
유급의, paid
유기, abandonment, abdication
유기 재배로, organically
유기된, derelict
유기의, organic
유기체, organism
유기체의, organic
유기하다, abdicate
유난히, particularly
유년 시대, infancy
유능하게, capably, competently, skillfully
유능한, able, capable, competent, skillful
유니버설 뱅크, universal bank
유니폼, uniform
유달리, especially, specially
유대 관계를 형성하다, bond
유대가 강한, tight
유대감, bond, fellowship, loyalty
유대교, Judaism
유대교 율법 학자, rabbi
유대교 지도자, rabbi
유대교 회당, synagogue
유대인, Jew
유대인의, Jewish
유도, judo
유도하다, lead, tempt
유도해 내다, elicit
유독성의, toxic
유독한, poisonous
유동 자산, working capital
유동성, liquidity, mobility
유동적으로, loosely
유동적인, liquid, loose, mobile
유두, nipple
유람, excursion
유람선, cruiser
유람선 여행, cruise
유람선을 타고 여행하다, cruise
유람하다, swan
유래하다, derive
유럽 본토, continent
유럽 본토의, continental
유럽 연합, European Union
유럽 의회 의원, MEP
유럽사람, European
유럽연합, EU
유럽의, European
유력 인사, mover, power broker
유력자, heavyweight

유력한, dominating, important, major league, probable, strong
유력한 친지가 있는, well-connected
유력함, importance
유령, ghost, phantom, spirit
유령 같은, ghostly, phantom
유령의, ghostly
유례없는, unparalleled
유로, euro
유로랜드, Euroland
유료, subscription
유리, edge, glass
유리 제품, glass
유리 천장, glass ceiling
유리된, out of touch
유리를 끼운, glazed
유리잔, glass
유리창, window
유리컵, glass
(~에게) 유리하게, advantage, favor
유리한, advantageous, benign, favorable, one, side
유리한 스타트, head start
유리한 위치, vantage point
유리한 입장, advantage, vantage point
유리한 입장에 서려고 획책하다, jockey
유린, ravages
유린당하다, ravage
유린하다, devastate, violate
유망주, hopeful
유망한, high-flying, hot, promising
유망함, promise
유머, humor
유머 감각, sense of humor
유명 상표의, branded
유명 상품, brand-name product
유명 스타, superstar
유명인, celebrity
유명하게, famously
유명한, celebrated, famed, famous, illustrious, public, well-known
유명해지다, splash
유모차, baby carriage, pram, pushchair, stroller
유목민의, nomadic
유물, artifact, hangover, monument, relic
유물론, materialism
유발시키다, create
유발하다, provoke, spark
유방, breast
유별나게, unusually
유별난, kind
유별난 사람, kind, odd
유별하다, categorize
유복한, well-off, well-to-do
유사 관계, analogy
유사물, analogue
유사성, parallel, resemblance, similarity
유사하다, parallel
유사한, analogous, close, parallel, tantamount
유산, estate, heritage, inheritance, legacy, miscarriage, termination
유색 인종의, color, colored
유서, testament
유서 깊은, venerable
유선형의, streamlined
유성, meteor
유성 물감, oil paint
유세지, trail
유스 클럽, youth club
유스 호스텔, youth hostel
유식한, informed
유심히 보다, peer, study
유심히 살피다, survey
유아, infant
유아 놀이방, playgroup
유아 반, infant
유아기, infancy
유아용 침대, cot
유아용의, infant
유아원, crèche
유약, enamel

유약을 칠한, glazed
유약칠, glaze
유언비어를 퍼뜨리는 사람, scaremongering
유언으로 증여하다, bequeath
유언장, will
유에스비, USB
유엔, United Nations
유역, basin
유연성, flexibility
유연성 있는, supple
유연한, flexible, fluid, pliable, soft, supple
유예 결정, reprieve
유용, diversion
유용성, usefulness, value
유용하게, usefully
유용하다, siphon
유용한, helpful, useful
유의어 사전, thesaurus
유익하게, profitably
유익한, beneficial, fruitful, good, informative, profitable, wholesome
유익한 목적으로, cause
유인, incentive, invitation
유인물, handout
유인의, manned
유인책, decoy, inducement
유인하다, beckon, lure
유일하게, alone, solely, uniquely
유일한, alone, only, sole, unique
유일함, uniqueness
유입, influx
유적, ruin
유전 공학, genetic engineering
유전되다, run
유전성의, hereditary
유전의, genetic
유전자, gene
유전자 변형 물질, GMO
유전자 변형의, genetically modified, GM
유전자 지도, blueprint
유전적 성질, inheritance
유전적으로, genetically
유전학, genetics
유정, well
유정 굴착 장치, rig
유제, milk
유제품 판매점, dairy
유제품의, dairy
유조선, tanker
유족, survivor
유죄 선고, conviction
유죄 선고를 받다, convict
유죄가 입증되다, convict
유죄를 인정하다, plead
유죄의, guilty
유지, maintenance, preservation, retention, upkeep
유지 가능한, sustainable
유지되다, keep
유지하다, hold, keep, maintain, preserve, retain, uphold
유창성, fluency
유창하게, fluently
유창한, fluent
유출, outflow, spillage
유출되다, escape
유출물, spillage
유출을 막다, guard
유치, detention
유치원, infant, kindergarten, nursery, nursery school
유치한, childish, immature
유쾌하게, delightfully, merrily
유쾌하게 하는, pleasing
유쾌한, good, gratifying, merry
유쾌한 기분, exhilaration
유대인의, Hebrew
유턴, U-turn
유토피아, utopia
유토피아적인, utopian
유통 기한, expiration date, sell-by date
유통되는, circulation
유통되다, flow

유통되지 않는, circulation
유포, circulation, dissemination, flow, propagation, spread
유포되다, circulate, flow
유포하다, disseminate, propagate
유품, effect
유한 책임 회사, Inc.
유한 책임의, Incorporated, limited
유해한, detrimental, pernicious
유행, fashion, prevalence, trend, vogue
유행병, epidemic
유행어, buzzword
유행에 맞춰서, fashionably
유행을 따라, stylishly
유행을 따른, stylish
유행이 돌아오다, come
유행하게 되다, come
유행하는, vogue
유행하는, fashion, fashionable, in, vogue
유행하다, catch, prevail
유행하지 않는, fashion, unfashionable
유혈 사태, bloodshed
유혈의, bloody, gory
유형, mold, strain, type
(~한) 유형의 사람이다, mark
유혹, call, seduction, temptation
유혹물, temptation
유혹적인, inviting, seductive
유혹하다, beckon, entice, seduce, tempt
유혹하듯, invitingly
유화, canvas, oil painting
유화 정책, appeasement
유황, sulfur
유효성, validity
유효하다, hold, stand
유효한, valid
유휴지, place
육감, hunch
육감적으로, sensuously
육감적인, sensuous
육군, army
육군 대장, marshal
육군 준장, brigadier
육로로, overland
육로의, overland
육상, athletics
육상 경기, track and field
육상선수, athlete
육수, stock
육식 동물, predator
육식의, predatory
육아, parenting
육아 시설, childcare
육아 휴가, parental leave
육중한, bulky
육즙, juice
육즙 소스, gravy
육지, land
육지에, onshore
육체관계, intimacy
육체관계를 가지며, romantically
육체관계의, intimate, romantic
육체노동의, manual
육체의, bodily, physical
육체적으로, physically
육체적인, physical
육필의, handwritten
윤, polish, sheen, shine
윤곽, contour, figure, form, outline, profile, silhouette
윤곽을 따라가다, trace
윤곽이 드러나다, outline
윤기 있는, sleek
윤년, leap year
윤리, ethic
윤리의, moral
윤리적으로, ethically, morally
윤리적인, ethical
윤리학, ethic
윤번, rotation
윤색하다, embellish, embroider
윤을 내다, polish
윤이 나는, glossy, polished
윤활유, grease

윤활유를 바르다, lubricate
윤활유를 치다, oil
율, rate
융기, bump
융기선, ridge
융통성, adaptability, flexibility
융통성 없는, inflexible, rigid
융통성 없이, rigidly
융통성 있는, adaptable, flexible
융합, fusion
융합되다, fuse
융합시키다, fuse
융합하다, amalgamate
융화, integration
으깨다, crush, mash, pound
으뜸 패, trump
으뜸가는, foremost
으레, routinely
으레 그렇듯이, typically
으르렁거리는 소리, growl, roar
으르렁거리다, growl, roar, snarl
으르렁거리듯 말하다, growl
으르렁거림, snarl
으리으리한, opulent, pompous
으리으리함, opulence
으스대는, condescending
으스대다, condescend
으스대며 걷기, swagger
으스대며 걷다, swagger
으스러지다, mangle
으스스한, chill, eerie, raw, spooky
으스스할 정도로, eerily
으슬으슬한, raw
으쓱하게 만드는, flattering
으쓱한, flattered
은, silver
은괴, bullion
은근히 깔보는, patronizing
은근히 무시하다, patronize
은닉물, cache
은닉처, stash
은둔, seclusion
은둔자, recluse
은둔지, retreat
은둔한, reclusive
은메달, silver medal
은밀한, covert, inner, private
은밀히, privately
은박지, foil
은색, silver
은색의, silvery
은식기류, silver, silverware
은신, hiding
은신처, retreat, safe haven
은신처를 제공하다, harbor
은어, slang
은연 중 나타내다, indicate
은유, metaphor
은유적으로, metaphorically
은유적인, metaphorical
은은하게, delicately, softly
은은한, delicate, soft
은자(隱者), hermit
은제 식기류, silverware
은제 우승컵, silverware
은제품, silver
은총, grace
은퇴 생활, retirement
은퇴하다, retire
은퇴한, retired
은폐, concealment, cover-up
은폐 수단, cloak
은폐하다, cover
은하, galaxy
은하계, galaxy
은하수, galaxy
은행, bank
은행 간부 직원, banker
은행 건물, bank
은행 발행 신용 카드, bank card
은행 업무, banking
은행 예금 계좌, bank account
은행 예금 잔고, bank balance
은행 잔고 증명서, bank statement
은행 어음, bank draft, banker's draft
은행권, banknote
은행에 계좌를 트고 이용하다, bank

은행의 할인율, bank rate
은혜를 모르는, ungrateful
은혜를 베풀다, oblige
은혜를 원수로 갚다, bite
은화, silver
음, eh, note, oh, sound
음감, ear
음경, penis
음계, scale
음극의, negative
음담패설, filth
음란물, filth, pornography
음란하게, dirty
음란하지 않은, clean
음란한, obscene
음란한 말, obscenity
음량, volume
음료, beverage
음매 하고 울다, bellow
음모, conspiracy, intrigue, plot
음모하다, plot
음미하다, savor
음반, album, record
음반 재킷, jacket
음반사, studio
음색, tone
음성, tone, voice
음성 사서함, voice mail
음성의, negative
음수의, negative
음식, food, grub, meal
음식 바구니, hamper
음식 분배용의, serving
음식을 만드는 사람, caterer
음식을 제공하다, cater
음식을 차리다, dish
음식의, dietary
음악, music, score
음악 스타일, sound
음악 연주, busking
음악 학교, conservatory
음악가, musician
음악에 재능이 있는, musical
음악을 연주하다, busk
음악의, musical
음악이 나오다, play
음악적으로, musically
음악적인, musical
음악처럼 듣기 좋은, musical
음영, shade
음울한, black, dark, dismal, gray
음이 맞지 않는, tune
음이 잘 맞는, tune
음전기로, negatively
음전기의, negative
음절, syllable
음조, pitch
음주, drinking
음주 운전자, drink-driver, drunk driver
음주가, drinker
음주측정기, Breathalyzer
음주측정을 하다, breathalyze
음침한, dingy, dismal, grim, murky
음탕한, filthy, saucy
음향 영상의, audiovisual
음향 효과, acoustic
음향학, acoustic
음화, negative
음흉하게 웃다, leer
음흉한, murky, sly
읍, town
읍사무소, town hall
응, yeah, yes
응고하다, clot
응급 처치, first aid
응급 처치 요원, paramedic
응급실, A & E, accident and emergency, casualty, emergency room, ER
응급의, emergency
응답 시간, response time
응답 없는, unanswered
응답하다, respond
응모 가담자, conspirator
응모권, coupon
응분의 대가를 받는 순간, payback
응사하다, fire

응석꾸러기의, pampered
응석을 다 받아 주다, pamper, spoil
응석을 다 받아 주듯, indulgently
응수하다, reply
응시, contemplation, gaze, stare
응시하다, contemplate, gaze, stare
응용, application
응용의, applied
응원, cheer
응원하다, cheer, support
응접실, drawing room
응집력, cohesion
응축되다, condense
의견, comment, idea, observation, opinion, point of view, reflection, sentiment, theory, thinking, thought, verdict, voice, way
의견 대립, disagreement
의견 차, difference
(~의) 의견에 따라, favor
의견을 같이하다, share
(~와) 의견을 교환하다, consult
의견을 말하다, judgment
(~에게) 의견을 묻다, run
의견을 싹 바꾸었다, tune
의견의 일치, consensus
의견이 다르다, disagree
의견이 엇갈리다, differ
의기소침한, down
의기양양, elation
의기양양하게, triumphantly
의기양양한, crest, elated, flushed, triumphant
의기투합하여, wavelength
의도, idea, intent, intention, meaning, message, thought
의도되다, intend
의도를 드러내다, game
의도를 품다, mean
의도적으로, consciously, deliberately, intentionally, purpose
의도적으로 하다, mean
의도적인, conscious, deliberate, intentional
의도치 않게, unintentionally
의도하다, mean
의도하지 않은, inadvertent
의례, protocol, rite
의례적인, ceremonial, ritual
의뢰, commission, recourse
의뢰받은 일, commission
의뢰하다, commission, refer
의료, medicine
의료의, medical
의류, clothing
의무, duty, job, obligation, onus
의무가 없는, obligation
의무를 다하는, dutiful
의무인, incumbent
의무적인, compulsory, mandatory, obligatory
의무하다, mandate
의문을 제기하다, cast
의문의 여지가 없는, indisputable, unquestionable
의문의 여지없이, unquestionably
(~의) 의미, by, meaning, sense, status, usage
의미 없는, meaningless
의미 있는, meaningful
의미 있는 듯이, expressively
의미론, semantics
의미를 갖다, mean
의미를 잘못 이해하다, read
의미심장하게, meaningfully, significantly
의미심장한, meaningful, pregnant, significant
의미하다, denote, mean, represent, signify, spell, stand
의복, dress, garment, wear
의붓동생, stepbrother, stepsister
의붓딸, stepdaughter
의붓아들, stepson
의붓아버지, stepfather
의붓어머니, stepmother

의붓언니, stepsister
의붓자매, half-sister
의붓형, stepbrother
의붓형제, half-brother
의사, doctor, physician, practitioner
의사 소통, communication
의사 전달 수단, language
의사(議事), debate
(~할) 의사가 전혀 없다, intention
의사록, minute, proceeding
의사를 타진하다, bounce
의사소통하다, communicate
의상, costume, gear, outfit
의석, bench, seat
의식, ceremony, consciousness, idea, practice, rite, ritual, service
의식 구조, consciousness
의식 불명, unconsciousness
의식을 되찾다, consciousness, revive
의식을 잃게 하다, knock
의식을 잃다, consciousness, pass
의식을 잃은, senseless
의식을 차리다, come
의식을 찾다, come
의식의, ceremonial, ritual
의식이 깨어 있는, conscious
의식이 없는, cold, unconscious
의식적으로, consciously
의식적인, conscious
의식하고 있는, conscious
의식하지 못하는, oblivious
의식하지 못한, unwitting
의심, distrust, doubt, question, suspicion
의심스러운, doubtful, dubious, questionable, suspect
의심의 여지없이, uncertain
의심치 않는, unsuspecting
의심하는, suspicious
의심하는 듯한, incredulous
의심하다, distrust, doubt, question, suspect
의심하듯, suspiciously
의심하여, doubt
의심할 바 없는, undisputed
의심할 바 없이, doubt
의심할 여지없는, clear, undoubted
의심할 여지없이, doubt, doubtless, undoubtedly
의아해하는, questioning
의약의, medicinal
의약품, medication, medicine
의욕, morale, motivation, will
의욕 있는, motivated
의욕을 못 느끼다, mope
의욕이 생기게 하다, motivate
의욕이 없는, loose end
의욕적인, aggressive
의원, deputy, doctor, doctor's office, member
의의, significance
의자, chair, stool
의장, chair, chairman, chairperson, president, speaker
의장 임기, chairmanship
의장의, presidential
의장직, chairmanship, presidency
(~의) 의장직을 맡다, chair
의전, protocol
의절하다, disown
의정서, protocol
의제, agenda
의존, dependence, dependency, reliance, resort
의존증, dependency
의존하는, dependent, reliant
의존하다, depend, hang, rely, resort, rest
의지, recourse, will
의지력, willpower
(~에) 의지하다, bank, count, depend, fall, look, turn
의지할 대상, crutch

의학, medicine
의학의, medical
의학적으로, medically
(~에) 의해, by
의향, inclination
의혹, suspicion
의혹을 가지는, suspicious
의혹을 없애다, air
의혹을 제기하다, question
의회, chamber, Congress, house, Houses of Parliament, parliament
의회의, congressional, parliamentary
이, louse, these, this, tooth
이 모양, tooth
이(異)문화, subculture
이가 빠진, chipped
이거 알아, guess
이거 알아요, what
이것, this
이것들, these
이것저것, this
이것저것 바꾸다, skip
이게 아닌데 싶으면서도, judgment
이겨 내다, fight, withstand
이곳, this
이교, heresy
이교도, pagan
이교도의, pagan
이국적으로, exotically
이국적인, exotic
이권, interest
이기, convenience
이기게 해 주다, win
이기다, beat, better, defeat, overpower, prevail, see, win
이기적으로, selfishly
이기적인, selfish
이기적인 일, selfishness
이긴, winning
이길 승산이 제일 없는 사람, underdog
이끌다, bring, captain, head, initiate, lead, steer
이끌어 내다, bring, derive, elicit
이끌어 내어, forth
이끼, moss
이내, presently
(~) 이내에, inside, within
이념, ideology, spirit
이념의, ideological
이념적으로, ideologically
이다, be
이단, heresy
이대로 나가면, rate
이대로라면, rate
이데올로기, ideology
이동, drift, flow, migration, movement, passage, relocation, transfer, transit
이동 능력을 가진, mobile
이동 방향, path
이동 유원지, carnival
이동 주택, caravan
이동 주택 주차장, caravan site
이동 중인, move, transit
이동되다, shift
이동성, mobility
이동시키다, move, taxi
이동식 무대차, float
이동식 주택, trailer
이동식 침대, gurney
이동식의, mobile
이동이 용이한 물건, portable
이동하기 쉬운, portable
이동하다, flow, shift, taxi, transfer, travel
이득, interest, payoff
이득을 보다, gain, profit
이득이 되다, pay
이등급의, second-class
이등병, private
이등석, second-class
이등석으로, second-class
이등석의, second-class
이따금, interval, now, occasionally, sporadically

이따금 일어나는, sporadic
이따금씩, off
이따금씩의, occasional
(~) 이래, since
이래라저래라 하다, order
(~) 이래로, as
이랬다저랬다 하다, flit, hot
이러이러한 것, so-and-so
이러이러한 사람, so-and-so
이러저러한, another, such
이러지도 저러지도 못 하는, torn
이럭저럭 ~해내다, manage
이런, dear, gracious, oops, these, what
이런 것들, these
이런 데에서, respect
이런 사람들, these
이런 식으로, like
이런저런, odd
이런저런 일, thing
이럴 수도 저럴 수도 없는 상황, no-win situation
이렇게, like, so, thus, way
이렇게 하면, way
이력, credentials
이력서, curriculum vitae, CV, résumé
이력의, past
이례적으로, run
이례적인 것, anomaly
이례적인 일, aberration
이로운, advantageous
이론, theory
이론가, theorist
이론상, theoretically, theory
이론의, theoretical
이론적으로, pure, theoretical
이루 말로 다 할 수 없는, unspeakable
이루 말로 다할 수 없이, unspeakably
이루다, achieve, form, make, realize
이룩하다, build
이류의, second-class, sort
이륙, takeoff
이륙이 금지되다, ground
이륙하다, take
이륙한, airborne
이륙했다, lead
(~에) 이르는 길, gateway
(~로) 이르는 길에서, road
이르다, approach, arrive, come, find, get, go, hit, range, reach
이른, early
이른 새벽에, hour
이른 저녁 식사, tea
이른바, so-called, what
이를 갈다, grind, grit
이를 악물고 참다, bullet
이를 악물고 하다, grit
이를테면 ~와 같은, like
이름, Christian name, first name, forename, name
(~라고) 이름 짓다, call
(~의) 이름으로, name
이름을 떨치다, name
이름을 적다, book
이름이 밝혀지지 않은, unnamed
이름이 언급되다, mention
이름이 없는, unnamed
이리저리, about, around, round, to
이리저리 걷다, meander
이리저리 빠져나가며, weave
이마, brow, forehead
이마가 벗어지다, recede
이마를 맞대고 상의하다, head
이마에 드리운 앞머리, fringe
이만큼, this
이메일, e-mail, mail
이메일 주소록, address book
이메일을 보내다, e-mail
이면, coin, reverse
(~) 이면에, behind
이면의, ulterior
이모, aunt, auntie
이모부, uncle
이모티콘, emoticon
이복을 끌기 위한 행위, stunt

이목이 집중되다, eye
이물, bow
이물질을 섞다, adulterate
이미, already
이미 날아가 버리다, window
이미 들은 얘기이나., hear
이미 만들어 놓은, ready-made
이미 사라져 버리다, window
이미 지나간, behind
이미 지나간 일, water
이미지, image
이미지 쇄신, rebranding
이미지들, imagery
이민, emigrant, emigration, immigrant, immigration
이민 가다, emigrate
이민국, Home Office
이바지, service
(~에) 이바지하는, conducive
(~에) 이바지하다, make, serve
이발, haircut, hairdressing
이발사, barber, hairdresser
이발소, barber, hairdresser
이방의, alien
이방인, outsider
이번 한 번만, once
이번에는, around, round, turn
이별, parting
이복 자매, half-sister
이복형제, half-brother
이봐, listen, man
이불, duvet
이불을 잘 덮어 주다, tuck
이사, commissioner, director, executive, move, removal
이사 가다, move
이사 오다, move
이사직, directorship
이사하다, move
이사회, board, board of directors, directorate, Senate
이사회의, executive
이삭, ear
이산화탄소, carbon dioxide, greenhouse gas
이상, abnormality, above, condition, deviance, dream, ideal, over, than, upward
이상가, visionary
이상이 있는, wrong
이상적으로, ideally
이상적으로는, world
이상적인, dream, ideal, perfect, utopian, visionary
이상적인 것, ideal
이상주의, idealism
이상주의의, idealistic
이상주의자, idealist
이상하게, oddly, strangely, uncannily, unnaturally
이상하게도, curiously, strangely, suspiciously
이상한, odd, queer, strange, uncanny, unnatural, weird
이상한 일, wonder
이상함, strangeness
이상향, utopia
이상화하다, idealize
이성, opposite sex, reason
이성 친구, sweetheart
이성애, heterosexuality
이성애의, heterosexual, straight
이성애자, heterosexual, straight
이성에 의거한, reasoned
이성을 잃은, beside
이성의 소리에 귀 기울이다, reason
이성적으로, rationally
이성적인, rational, rationalist
이성주의자, rationalist
이슬, dew
이슬람 사원, mosque
이슬람교, Islam
이슬람교도, Muslim
이슬람교의, Islamic, Muslim
이슬비, drizzle
이승의, earthly
이식, implant, transplant
이식용 조직, graft

(~에) 이식하다, graft, implant, transplant
이심전심의, unspoken
이십원, score
이야기, account, narrative, story, tale, talk, word
이야기를 꺼내다, approach
이야기에 ~라고 되어 있다, go
이야기의 서술, narrative
이야기하기, telling
이야기하다, recount, speak, talk, tell
이양, transfer
이양되다, devolve, transfer
이양하다, devolve
이어 주다, lead
이어지다, follow, lead, mean, pass, run, stretch, succeed, take
이어폰, earphone
이와 비슷하게, similarly
이완되다, relax
이완시키다, relax
이외에, outside, plus
이용 가능한, about, available, hand
이용 가능함, availability
이용당하다, ride
이용되다, function
이용자, user
이용하다, advantage, capital, capitalize, cash, exploit, play, use, utilize
이용할 수 없는, inaccessible
이용해 먹다, prey
이웃 사람, neighbor
이웃에, next door
이웃에 있는 것, neighbor
이웃의, neighboring, next door
이웃집 남자, next door
이웃집 여자, next door
이유, explanation, ground, rationale, reason
이유 없이, reason
이유가 밝혀지지 않은, unexplained
(~의) 이유로, account, ground, reason, through
이유로 내세우다, plead
이윤, mark-up
이윤 폭, profit margin
이의, dissent, objection, protest
이의 없는, undisputed
이의 제기, challenge
이의가 제기되지 않은, unchallenged
이의를 말하다, object
이의를 제기하다, challenge, contest, dissent, issue, protest, refute
이익, benefit, good, interest, mileage, payback, plus, profit
이익 가산의, cost-plus
이익 단체, caucus, interest
이익 배당금, bonus
이익 분배, profit-sharing
이익을 거두다, profit
이익을 내는, profitable
이익을 내다, money
이익을 내며, profitably
이익을 얻다, benefit
이익을 주다, benefit, profit
(~에) 이익이 되는, good
이익이 되다, pay
이익이 없는, unprofitable
(~에게) 이익인, benefit
이자, interest
이자가 붙다, bear
이자율, interest rate
이적 행위, collaboration
이적 행위자, collaborator
이전, move, relocation
이전 모델, predecessor
이전 비용, relocation expenses
이전과 같은 책의, ibid.
이전만 못한, rusty
이전시키다, relocate
(~) 이전에, before, earlier, formerly, previously
이전의, former, previous
이전하다, move, relocate
이전할 수 있는, transferable

이점, advantage, merit, virtue
이점이 많다, going
이제, moment, now, then
이제까지, yet
이제부터, henceforth
이젤, easel
이종의, disparate
이주, emigration, immigration, migration
이주민, immigrant
이주시키다, transplant
이주자, emigrant, migrant
이주하다, emigrate, migrate
이중 유리, double-glazing
이중 유리를 끼우다, double-glaze
이중 유리의, double-glazed
이중으로, doubly
이중의, double, dual
이중창 곡, duet
(~) 이지만, though
이직률, turnover
이질의, foreign
이착륙장, pad
이채로운, colorful
이층 버스, double-decker
이치를 따져 설득하다, reason
이치에 닿는 말을 하다, sense
이치에 맞는, sense
이치에 맞는, fair
이치에 맞다, water
이퀄 사인, equal sign
이타심, altruism
이타적인, selfless
이탈, departure
이탈하다, depart, rank
이탈한, breakaway
이탤릭체, italic
이탤릭체의, italic
이테일링, etailing
이해, appreciation, comprehension, grasp, understanding
이해 당사자, stakeholder
이해가 더딘, slow
(~의) 이해관계, stake
이해관계가 있는, interested
이해되다, construe, get, receive, sense
이해되지 않는, head
이해력, comprehension, wit
이해시키다, get, put
이해심, understanding
이해심 있는, understanding
이해하기 쉬운, accessible, understandable
이해하기 쉬움, accessibility
이해하기 어려운, enigmatic, obscure
이해하기 어려운 사람, puzzle
이해하기 힘든, inaccessible
이해하기 힘든 것, obscurity
이해하기 힘듦, obscurity
이해하다, appreciate, board, catch, comprehend, follow, get, head, interpret, know, make, relate, see, sense, sympathize, take, understand
이해하지 못하다, miss, mistake
이해할 수 없는, impenetrable, unintelligible
이해할 수 있게, understandably
이해할 수 있는, intelligible, understandable
이해할 수가 없다, know
이행, implementation, movement, passage, performance, transition
이행하다, fulfill, honor, implement
이혼, divorce
이혼하다, divorce
이혼한, divorced
이혼한 사람, divorcee
이후, beyond, since
이후까지, beyond
(~) 이후에, after, since
익게 하다, ripen
익다, cook, ripen
익명, anonymity

익명 동업자, sleeping partner
익명성, anonymity
익명으로, anonymously
익명의, anonymous, faceless
익명의 동업자, silent partner
익사시키다, drown
익사하다, drown
익살극, farce
익살꾼, clown
익살맞은 일, clown
익살스러운, humorous
익살스럽게, humorously
익숙지 않은, unfamiliar
익숙케 하다, accustom
익숙하다, know, used
(~에) 익숙하지 않은, unused
익숙한, accustomed, familiar
익숙함, familiarity
(~에) 익숙해지다, swing, used
익숙해진, accustomed
익은, ripe
익히다, boil, cook, pick, poach
익힘, poaching
인가, go-ahead, recognition
인가된, licensed
인가받지 않은, unauthorized
인가하다, recognize
인간, flesh, human, human being, humanity, man, mortal
인간관계 형성, networking
인간관계를 형성하다, network
인간성, humanity
인간쓰레기, scum
인간애, humanity
인간의, human
인간의 감정이 없는, impersonal
인간의 본성, human nature
인간의 손이 미치지 않는, untouched
인간의 천성, human nature
인격, character, personality
인격이 형성되는, formative
인계받다, inherit
인계하다, hand
인공 지능, artificial intelligence
인공 기관, crown
인공림, plantation
인공물, artifact
인공위성, satellite
인공의, artificial, man-made
인공적으로, artificially
인공적인, plastic, unnatural
인구, population
인구 조사, census
인구 집단, demographic
인구 통계, demographic
인구가 많은, crowded
인권, human rights
인근, neighborhood
인기, popularity
인기 없는, favor, unpopular
인기 없음, unpopularity
인기 있는, demand, favor, hot, popular
인기도, standing
(~에게서) 인기를 가로채다, upstage
인기를 얻다, catch
인내, patience
인내력, endurance, tolerance
인내심을 시험하다, patience
인내심이 강한, long-suffering
인내심이 있는, patient
인대, ligament
인도, extradition, pavement, sidewalk, surrender
인도되다, extradite, shepherd
인도적으로, humanely
인도적인, humane
인도주의적인, humanitarian
인도하다, guide, lead, steer, turn
인디, indie
인디 밴드, indie
인디 음반사, indie
인력, manpower
인력 빼내기, poaching
인류, humanity, human race, mankind
인류학, anthropology

인류학자, anthropologist
인명 구조원, lifeguard
인문학, art, humanity
인물, character
인본주의, humanism
인본주의자, humanist
인부, laborer
인사, bow, greeting, hello
인사 관리, human resources, man management
인사과, personnel
인사불성, oblivion
인사하다, bow, greet
인산, phosphate
인산비료, phosphate
인상, appearance, feeling, hike, impression, sound, vibe
인상 깊게 생각하다, strike
인상을 주다, come, impress, impression, reflect, strike
인상적으로, impressively
인상적인, dramatic, imposing, impressive, striking
인상하다, hike, lift, raise
인색한, cheap, mean, stingy
인색함, meanness
인생철학, philosophy
인세, royalty
인쇄, printing
인쇄 매체의, print
인쇄 출력한 문서, printout
인쇄기, press
인쇄되다, print
인쇄되지 않은, unwritten
인쇄된, black and white
인쇄된 글자, print
인쇄물, handout, literature
인쇄본, type
인쇄소, printer
인쇄업자, printer
인쇄에 들어가다, press
인쇄하다, print, run
인수, acquisition
인수하다, take
인슐린, insulin
인스턴트, instant
인습에 얽매이지 않는, unconventional
인식, awareness, consciousness, perception, realization, recognition, sense
인식되다, impress
인식시키다, project
인식의, cognitive
인식이 박히다, stereotype
인식하고 있는, aware
인식하다, discern, perceive
인신공격적인, personal
인양, salvage
인양되다, salvage
인양물, salvage
인어, mermaid
인용, citation, quotation, quote
인용 부호, inverted commas, quote
인용 부호로, inverted commas
인용구, quote, reference
인용문, quotation, reference
인용하다, cite, quote
인원, personnel, strength
인원 수, head count
인위적으로, artificially, unnatural, unnaturally
인위적인, artificial, contrived
인장, seal
인재 스카우트 담당자, headhunter
인적 구성, staffing
인적 자원 관리, HR, human resources
인적이 드문, beaten, lonely
인접하다, adjoin, border
인접한, adjacent, neighboring
인정, acknowledgment, admission, approval, heart, recognition
인정 많은, kindly
인정 받다, hail
인정 없는, unkind, unsympathetic
인정되지 않다, disallow

인정받은, approved
인정사정없는, dog, ruthless
인정하다, acknowledge, admit, approve, concede, grant, own, recognize
(~을 인정하여, recognition
인정하지 않다, opposed
(~을 인정한다 해도, admittedly
인정할 건 인정해 주다, due
인조 모피, fur
인조 양모, fleece
인조의, false, synthetic
인종, color, race
인종 간의 관계, race relations
인종 말살, ethnic cleansing
인종 차별을 하지 않는, integrated
인종 차별이 철폐되다, integrate
인종 차별주의, racism
인종 차별주의자, racist
인종 청소, ethnic cleansing
인종 통합, integration
인종 통합적인, integrated
인종 통합형, integrated
인종의, ethnic, racial
인종적으로, ethnically, racially
인증, authorization
인지, cognitive
인지하다, observe, recognize
인지한, alert
인지할 수 없는, unrecognizable
인지할 수 있는, visible
인질, hostage
(~을) 인질로 잡고 몸값을 요구하다, ransom
인질로 잡히다, hostage
인척, in-laws
인체, anatomy, body
인체 면역 결핍 바이러스, HIV
인출, withdrawal
인출액, withdrawal
인출하다, draw, withdraw
인치, inch
인칭, person
인터넷, Internet, net
인터넷 거래, e-business
인터넷 검색, surfing
인터넷 릴레이 채팅, IRC
인터넷 방송, webcast
인터넷 사업, e-business
인터넷 상거래, etailing
인터넷 상거래 회사, etailer
인터넷 상거래인, etailer
인터넷 서비스 제공자, ISP
인터넷 연결이 안 되는, offline
인터넷 잡지, e-zine
인터넷 주소, URL
인터넷 카페, cybercafé, Internet café
인터넷 화상 카메라, webcam
인터넷에 올린 글, posting
인터넷을 이용한, online
인터넷을 이용해서, online
인터뷰, interview
인터페이스, interface
인터폰, intercom
인턴, intern
인테리어, decoration
인테리어업자, decorator
인트라넷, intranet
인파, throng
인포테인먼트, infotainment
인품 있는, fine
인플레이션, inflation
인플레이션을 일으키는, inflationary
인플레이션의, inflationary
인하, reduction
(~로) 인하여, reason
인하하다, knock
(~로) 인해, out, with
인형, doll
인형극용 인형, puppet
인화하다, print
일, affair, business, career, commitment, concern, goings-on, job, occupation, occurrence, proposition, service, Sun., task, trade, work
일 년, year

일 년 내내, year
일 년 동안에, annually
일 년간의, annual
일 년에 한 번, yearly
일 벌레, workaholic
일 이야기만 하다, shop
일 중독자, workaholic
일가, clan
일거에 얻다, shoot
일견, glimpse
일곱 번째, seventh
일관성, coherence, consistency
일관성 있게, consistently
일관성 있게 효율적으로 행동하다, act
일관성 있는, coherent, cohesive, consistent
일관성이 없는, incoherent, inconsistent
일관성이 없음, inconsistency
일광욕, sunbathing
일광욕하다, sunbathe
일그러지다, contort
일급의, first-class
일기, diary, journal
일기 예보, weather forecast
일년 내내, long, round
일년생 식물, annual
일다, rise
일단 ~하자, once
일단의, body
일당, clan, ring
일대일, one-to-one
일대일 대응의, one-to-one
일대일로, one-to-one
일등석, first-class
일등석의, first-class
일람표, schedule
일련, chain, list, string, train
일련번호, serial number
일련의 군사 행동, campaign
일련의 무리, crop
일련의 사건들, turn
일련의 연중행사, calendar
일련의 작업, routine
일련의 정책, package
일련의 치료, course
일렬, file
일렬로, file, line
일렬의, linear
일루미네이션, illumination
일류의, big time, first-rate, major league, top
일률성, uniformity
일률적으로, board
일리, sense
일리가 있는, reasonable
일리가 있다, point
일말, faintest
일말의 가능성도 없는, question
일말의 의심, shadow
일면, face
일몰, sunset
일반 경비, overhead
일반 공립학교, comprehensive
일반 공립학교의, comprehensive
일반 공휴일, bank holiday
일반 국민, people
일반 대중, general public, grassroots
일반 보통 사람의, lay
일반 사람들, they, us
일반 상식, general knowledge
일반 수요자, mass market
일반 수요자용의, mass market
일반 의사, general practitioner, GP
일반 직원, rank
일반 판매 약의, counter
일반 판형의 신문, broadsheet
일반 학교, day school
일반명의, generic
일반석, economy class
일반석의, economy
일반인, multitude, public
일반인에 공개된, open
일반인의 접근이 불허된, private
일반적으로, commonly, generally, popularly, rule, typically,

universally, usually, widely
일반적인, common, general, generalized, popular, standard, universal
일반화, generalization
일반화시키다, generalize
일반화하여 말하다, generalize
일방적인, one-sided, unbalanced, unilateral
일방적인 대화, monologue
일방통행의, one-way
일별, glance, glimpse
일부, certain, fraction, part, some
일부러 ~하다, bother
일부러 관심이 없는 체하다, hard
일부분, patch, snippet, subdivision
일부에 한정되지 않은, general
일부의, part
일부일처의, monogamous
일부일처제, monogamy
일비(日費), per diem
일사병, sunstroke
일산화탄소, carbon monoxide
일상사, daily
일상의, day-to-day
일상적인, household, mundane, routine
일상적인 것, mundane
일상적인 일, day, routine
일석이조의 효과를 보다, bird
일소하다, dispel
일시 중단, moratorium
일시 중지, respite
일시 하락하다, dip
일시 해고, furlough
일시 해고되다, furlough
일시불, lump sum
일시적 유행, fad
일시적 의식 상실, blackout
일시적 정지, pause
일시적으로, temporarily
일시적인, passing, temporary, transient
일시적인 고요, lull
일시적인 기분, whim
일시적인 문제, hiccup
일식, eclipse
일신상의, intimate
일어나 있는, up
일어나게 하다, bring
일어나기 시작한, motion
일어나다, arise, break, get, happen, occur, place, present, rise, stir, transpire
일어나려 하여, horizon
일어나려고 하다, brew
일어나지 않을, against
일어난 일, incident
일어날 것 같지 않은, improbable
일어남직하지 않음, improbability
일어서다, get, rise, stand
일어서서, foot
일어선, foot
일에 익숙해지다, rope
일에 착수하다, work
일요일, Sunday
일원, member, part
일원이 되다, include, sit
(~의) 일원인, on
일으켜, up
일으켜 보내다, blast
일으켰다, wrought
일으키다, bring, cause, generate, induce, present, raise, set, stir
일을 그만두고 떠나다, chuck
일을 마치다, day
일을 보다, service
(~의) 일을 생각하니, account
일을 시작하다, work
일을 시키다, work
(~에게) 일을 주다, work
(~로) 일을 키우다, blow
일이 단순 작업화 되다, deskill
일이 없는, idle
일이 있는, work
일인 일표주의, vote
일일이 감시하다, neck
일자리, employment

일자리를 알선하다, place
일정, schedule, timeline
일정량, measure, ration
일정을 다시 잡다, reschedule
일정이 꽉 찬, booked up
일정하게 반복되는, regular
일정한, constant, even, uniform
일정한 비율로, scale
일정한 정도의, degree
일제 사격, volley
일제히, unison
일제히 함, round
일조하다, hand
일종의, kind, sort
일주일 분의, weekly
일지, log
일찌감치 나가떨어진, burned-out
일찍, early
일찍 잠, night
일찍이, ever
일차적인, primary
일체 설비가 완비된, self-contained
일체를 포함한, inclusive
일촉즉발의, volatile
일축하다, spurn
일출, sunrise
일치, correspondence, overlap
(~와) 일치되게, line
일치시키다, square, synchronize
일치하다, agree, coincide, concur, consistent, correspond, jibe, overlap, square, tally
(~라고) 일컫다, call
일탈, deviance, deviation, lapse
일탈하다, deviate
일탈한, deviant
일하고 있는, work
일하는, working
일하는 곳에서 숙식하는, resident
일하는 사람, worker
일하다, labor, work
일행, party
일화, anecdote, episode
일화성의, anecdotal
일회성의, one-off
일회성의 일, one-off
일회용 물휴지, wipe
일회용 반창고, Band-Aid
일회용의, disposable
일회용품, disposable
읽고 쓰는 능력, literacy
읽고 이해하다, read
읽다, look, read
읽을 수 있는, readable
읽을거리, read
(~을) 잃게 만들다, knock
잃다, lose
잃도록 하다, lose
잃어버리다, lose
잃어버린, lost
잃어버린 시간을 보완하다, time
잃은, lost
잃을 것 같다, stand
임금, wage, wage packet
임금 격차, differential
임금 인상, raise
임기, mandate, tenure, term
임대, hire, rental
임대 계약, lease
임대된, leasehold
임대용의, hire
임대하다, hire, lease, let, rent
임명, appointment, installation, nomination
(~에) 임명되다, install
임명하다, appoint, designate, make, name, nominate
임무, assignment, brief, mission
(~의) 임무를 맡다, man
임박하여, corner
임박한, imminent, impending, pending, sight
임산부를 위한, maternity
임상의, clinical
임상적으로, clinically
임시 구조물, pavilion
임시 직원, temp
임시 직원으로서 일하다, temp

임시 파견, secondment
임시로, provisionally, temporarily
임시로 배치되다, second
임시방편, quick fix
임시변통, makeshift
임시의, acting, ad hoc, caretaker, casual, interim, provisional, temporary
임신, conception, pregnancy
임신 기간, term
임신 중이다, expect
임신하다, conceive, have
임신한, pregnant
임의 문자 기호, wild card
임의로, arbitrarily, randomly, random
임의의, arbitrary, random
임차, tenancy
임차료, rent, rental
임차인, tenant
임차하다, rent
임차한, rental
임차할 수 있는, rent
임펄스, impulse
입, mouth
입 다물게 하다, shut
입 다물다, mouth, shut
입 맞추다, kiss
입 밖에 내다, utter
입 안 세척제, rinse
입건하다, book
입고, on
(~을) 입고 있는, clad, in
입고 있다, wear
입구, doorway, mouth
입구가 ~한, -mouthed
입국 심사, immigration
입금되다, credit
입금액, credit
입금액을 기록하다, credit
입금하다, pay
입김을 불다, blow
입다, bask, put, receive, sustain, take
입대시키다, enlist
입대하다, enlist
입력 장치, input device
입력하다, enter, feed, input, key, type, write
입맛을 쩝쩝 다시다, smack
입맞춤, kiss
입문, initiation, introduction
입문서, introduction
입문시키다, introduce
입문의, introductory
입방체, cube
입방체의, cubic
입법부, legislature
입법의, legislative
입법자, legislator
입사하다, enter
입상자, runner-up
입소문, word
입수 가능성, reach
입수하다, obtain
입수할 수 없는, unavailable
입술, lip
입씨름, exchange, haggling
입안을 헹굼, rinse
입양, adoption
입양하다, adopt
입어 보기, fitting
입어 보다, try
입에 맞는, palatable
입에 맞지 않는, unpalatable
입욕, bath
입원, hospitalization
입원 환자, inmate
입원하다, admit, hospitalize
입으로, orally
(~을) 입은, clad, -coated
입을 다물 수 없게 만드는, jaw-dropping
입을 다물다, bite, quiet
입을 못 열게 만들다, silence
입을 열다, mouth
입을 헹구다, rinse
입이 ~한, -mouthed

입자, dust, speck
입장, admission, entry, stand, take
입장 불가, entry
입장료, admission
(~의) 입장에서, part
(~) 입장에서 말하면, speaking
입장을 고수하다, ground, gun
입장을 바꾸다, ground, place
입장을 분명히 하다, commit
입장을 취하다, stand
(~의) 입장이 되다, shoe
(~할) 입장이 아닌, position
입증, corroboration, validation, verification
입증되지 않은, unsubstantiated
입증하다, corroborate, prove, substantiate, verify
입지, footing
입지가 편리한, convenient
입질, bite
입찰, bid, tender
입찰자, bidder
입찰하다, bid, tender
입천장, palate
입출력, input/output
입출력 기재, input/output
입출력 통제 프로그램, input/output
입학, admission, entrance
입학의, admission
입학하다, get
입혀 보다, fit
입회, entrance, initiation
입회인, observer, witness
(~에) 입회하다, initiate
입후, nomination
입후보, candidacy, run
입후보하다, run, stand
입후보한, up
입히다, coat, wreak
(~을) 입힌, -coated
입힌 것, coating
잇다, carry, connect, link
잇달아, running
잇따른, continual
잇따름, succession
잇몸, gum
(~에게) 있는, in, present
있는 그대로, person
있는 그대로 보자, face
있는 그대로의, unaffected
(~가) 있는 데서, presence
있다, be, find, get, have, here, in, lie, reside
있어야 할 곳, place
있을 수 있는, possible
있음, presence
있음직한, likely
있음직한 일, likelihood
있잖아, guess, know, what
잉글랜드의, English
잉크, ink
잊고 안 가져가다, forget
잊다, forget
잊어버리다, erase
잊을 수 없는, unforgettable
잊지 않게 알려 주다, remind
잊지 않다, remember
잊혀지다, escape, slip
잊혀지지 않다, stick
잊혀진 상태이다, lie
잊혀짐, oblivion
잎, blade, foliage, leaf, needle
잎맥, vein
잎이 무성한, bushy, leafy
잎이 없는, bare
자, now, okay, right, ruler, well
자가용으로 데려다 주다, chauffeur
자각, awakening
자각하지 않은, unconscious
자간, spacing
자갈, cobble, cobblestone, gravel, rubble
자갈 채취장, pit
자격, capacity, entitlement, place, qualification, status
자격 박탈, disqualification
자격 증명, credentials
자격 취득, qualification

자격을 갖게 하다, qualify
자격을 갖추다, qualify
자격을 갖춘, qualified, worthy
(~에게) 자격을 갖춰 주다, fit
자격을 박탈당하다, disqualify
자격을 취득하다, qualify
자격이 되다, bill
자격이 없는, unqualified, unworthy
자격이 있는, deserving, fit
자격이 있다, qualify
자격이 정지되다, strike
자결(自決), self-determination
자경단원, vigilante
자고 가기, sleepover
자구, wording
자국, impression, imprint, mark, speck, trail
자국어, vernacular
자국을 남기다, mark
자국이 생기다, scar
자궁, uterus, womb
자궁 경부, cervix
자궁 경부암 검사, smear
자궁 경부의, cervical
자궁 수축, contraction
자궁 절제, hysterectomy
자그마한, diminutive, discreet
자그마한 부지, plot
자극, goad, incitement, irritation, kick, provocation, spur, stimulation, stimulus
자극받다, motivate
자극성 물질, irritant
자극을 받은, stimulate
자극을 주는, stimulating
자극적인, pungent, stimulating, titillating
자극제, irritant
자극하는, irritating
자극하다, galvanize, goad, incite, inflame, irritate, prompt, provoke, rouse, spur, stimulate, titillate
자금, cash, finance, pocket
자금 부족 사태, crunch
자금 사정, finance
자금 이체, credit transfer
자금 흐름, cash flow
자금난을 겪고 있는, cash-starved
자금원, financier
자금을 공급하다, finance
자금을 제공하다, fund
자금을 지원하다, bankroll
자금자족, self-sufficiency
자금자족할 수 있는, self-sufficient
자금적, subsistence
자기, china, honey, love, magnetism, porcelain
자기 규제, self-regulation
자기 뜻대로 하다, way
자기 마음대로 하다, way
자기 발로 서다, foot
자기 방어, self-defense
자기 본위의, self-centered
자기 생각대로 하다, way
자기 연민, self-pity
자기 의견을 말하다, speak
자기 자본 확충, recapitalization
자기 자본을 확충하다, recapitalize
자기 자신, oneself
자기 자신의 것, own
자기 존중, self-respect
자기 집 같은, homely, homey
자기 책임으로, account
자기 편, ally
자기 학대, masochism
자기 학대의, masochistic
자기 혼자만의, private
자기가 태어난, native
자기의, own
자기만족의, smug
자기보다 못한, beneath
자기의, magnetic
자기장, field
자기주장에 유리한 정보, ammunition

자기주장을 뚜렷이 내세우는, assertive
자기주장을 뚜렷이 내세움, assertiveness
자기중심의, self-centered
자기편으로 만들다, win
자녀, child
자다, roost
자동 권총, automatic
자동 배급기, dispenser
자동 이체, direct debit, standing order
자동 잠금장치, latch
자동 현금 인출기, ATM
자동사의, intransitive
자동응답 녹음기, answerphone
자동응답기, answering machine
자동의, automatic
자동적으로, automatically, mechanically
자동적인, automatic, mechanical
자동차, auto, automobile, car
자동차 배터리, battery
자동차 번호판, plate
자동차 사고, crash
자동차 전용, drive-in
자동차 정비소, garage
자동차 탈취 폭주족, joyrider
자동차 편승자, hitchhiker
자동차 함께 타기, carpool
자동차를 탄 채로 이용 가능한, drive-through
자동차와 관련된, motoring
자동차의, motor
자동판매기, vending machine
자동화, automation
자동화된, automated
자동화하다, automate
자라나다, sprout
자라나, burgeon, grow
자라서 ~을 못 입게 되다, outgrow
자라서 옷이 몸에 맞다, grow
자라서 옷이 몸에 맞지 않다, grow
자랑, boast
자랑거리, credit
자랑꾼, show-off
자랑스러운, proud
자랑스러움, pride
(~을) 자랑스러워하다, pride
자랑스럽게, proudly
자랑스레 보이다, show
자랑하다, boast, brag
자력, magnetism
자력의, magnetic
자로 재다, measure
자료, data, input, matter
자료철, file
자루, shaft
자르는 사람, cutter
자르다, amputate, chop, crop, cut, sack, sever
자른 면, facet
자름, cut
자리, place, post, seat, seating
자리 잡기 시작하다, set
(~에) 자리 잡다, install, locate, perch, set
(~할) 자리가 아니다, place
자리를 내주다, move, way
자리를 비운, absent
자리를 잡다, foot, settle
자리를 좁히다, move
자립, self-help
자립정신, independence
자립하다, foot
자릿수, figure
자막, subtitle
자막이 있는, subtitled
자만심, pride
자만심이 강한, self important, vain
자만하게 하다, head
자만하지 마, flatter
자매, sister
자매 관계의, sister
자면서 생각해 보다, sleep
자명종, alarm, alarm clock
자명하다, speak
자명한, self-evident,

self-explanatory
자모, alphabet
사몽, grapefruit
자문관, adviser
자문을 구하다, advice, consult
자문을 구함, consultation
자문의, advisory, consultative
자물쇠, lock
자물쇠를 따다, pick
자물쇠를 채워 보관하다, lock
자바 언어, Java
자발적으로, bat, spontaneously, voluntarily
자발적인, spontaneous, voluntary, willing
자백, confession
자백하다, confess, own
자본, capital
자본 계정, capital account
자본 수지, capital account
자본 이득, capital gains
자본 집약적, capital-intensive
자본가, capitalist, industrialist
자본금, capital
자본재, capital goods
자본주의, capitalism
자본주의자, capitalist
자본화하다, capitalize
자부심, pride, self-esteem
자비, humanity, mercy
자비로운, charitable, humane
자비롭게, humanely
자사 상표 제품, own brand, own label
자산, asset
자산 박탈, asset-stripping
자살, suicide
자살 충동을 느끼는, suicidal
자살의, suicidal
자살하다, commit, end, life
자상하게, obligingly
자상한, obliging
자생 식물, native
(~에) 자생하는, native
자서전, autobiography
자서전의, autobiographical
자석, magnet
자석과 같은 것, magnet
자선 단체, charity
자선 바자, jumble
자선 바자회, bazaar
자선 사업, charity
자선의, charitable
자성을 띤, magnetic
자세, gesture, pose, position, posture, spirit
자세를 낮추다, go
자세를 취한, poised
자세하게, finely, graphically
자세한, fine, full, graphic
자세한 논의, discussion
자세히, detail
자세히 다루다, discuss
자세히 말하다, detail, expand
자세히 밝히다, specify
자세히 살펴보다, pore, scan
자세히 조사하다, dissect, inquire
자손, descendant, offspring
자수, embroidery
자수 놓기, embroidery
자수하다, give
자술서, confession
자승, square
자식, family, offspring
자식들, brood
자식을 낳다, reproduce
자신, assurance, himself, self
자신 없는, tentative, unsure
자신 없어 하며, tentatively
자신 있게, confidently
자신 있는, assured, self-assured
자신감, confidence,
self-confidence
자신감 있는, self-confident
자신감을 잃다, grip
자신감을 주는, encouraging
자신도 모르게, spite
자신만만하게, confidently

자신만만한, confident
자신만의, own
자신만의 것으로 삼다, own
자신을 학대하는 사람, masochist
자신의 말로, word
(~) 자신의 말에 의하면, word
자신의 의지가 분명하다, mind
자신이 없는, doubtful, insecure
자신이 책임지고, risk
자신하는, confident
자신하다, flatter
자아, ego, self
자아내다, raise, rouse
자아도취의, smug
자아상, self-image
자애로운, compassionate
자양분, nourishment
자업자득의, making
자업자득이, roost
자연, nature
자연 감축, natural wastage
자연 과학, science
자연 그대로의, wild
자연 자원, natural resources
자연 증가로 생기다, accrue
자연 환경, environment
자연 환경의, environmental
자연발생적의, spontaneous
자연스러운, natural
자연스러운 모습을 담은, fly-on-the-wall
자연스러운 행동거지, spontaneity
자연스러움, naturalness
자연스럽게, naturally
자연스럽게 다가오다, naturally
자연스럽게 터득하다, go
자연의, natural
자연적으로, naturally
자연적인 이유로, natural
자연연식물분, accrual
자연히, naturally, spontaneously
자영업의, self-employed
자영업자, self-employed, tradesman
자외선 차단제, sunscreen
자외선의, ultraviolet
자욱한, thick
자원, resource
자원 봉사의, voluntary
자원 봉사자, volunteer
자원을 갖춘, resourced
자원의, voluntary
자원행위를 하다, masturbate
자유, freedom, liberty
자유 계약으로, freelance
자유 계약의, freelance
자유 기업 제도, free enterprise
자유 민주당, Liberal Democrat Party
자유 시장, free market
자유 시장 지지자, free-marketeer
자유 의지, free will
자유 의지로, free will
자유 행동권, blank check
자유가 있는, liberty
자유로운, free, liberal
자유로워, clear
자유로이 ~해도 좋은, welcome
자유롭게, freely
자유롭게 ~하는, free
자유롭게 움직이는, loose
자유롭게 해 주다, free
자유방임주의, laissez-faire
자유의사에 의해, account
자유인의, free
자유재량, hand
자유재량의, discretionary
자유주의자, liberal
자유항, free port
자유학, liberalization
자유화하다, liberalize
자율, autonomy
자율 학습의, self-access
(~에게) 자율권을 주다, rein
자율적인, autonomous
자음, consonant
자의가 아닌, involuntary
자의식이 강한, self-conscious

자인하는, self-confessed
자임하는, self-styled
자작 농장, homestead
자작나무, birch
자잘한 물건들, bob
자재, material
자전거, bicycle, bike, cycle
자전거 이용자, biker
자전거 타기, cycling
자전거 타는 사람, cyclist
자전거를 타다, bike, cycle
자전적인, autobiographical
자정, midnight
자제, restraint, suppression
자제된, controlled
자제력, control, self-control
자제력을 잃게 하다, run
자제력을 잃다, break
자제심을 잃다, handle
자제하는, restrained
자제하다, abstain, control, grip, hold, refrain, suppress
자조, self-help
자족적인, self-contained
자존심, pride, self-esteem, self-respect
자존심이 있는, proud
자주, freely, frequently, independence, much, often, regularly
자주 ~하는, prone
자주 우울해 함, moodiness
자주 일어나는, common, frequent, regular
자주 하는 질문, FAQ
(~을) 자주 하다, habit
자주색, purple
자주의, independent
자주적인, free, sovereign
자지 않고 기다리다, wait
자지 않고 깨어 있다, stay
자진 신고 기간, amnesty
자진 신고 납세, self-assessment
자진하여, free will, voluntarily
자진하여 하다, volunteer
자진해서, accord
자진해서 말하다, volunteer
자진해서 하는, self-imposed, willing
자질, caliber, competence, faculty, gift
자질, 자격, qualification
자질들 갖춘, equal
자책하다, reproach
자철, magnet
자체 정보 처리 능력을 갖춘, intelligent
자초, invitation
자초하다, court
자초한, self-inflicted
자취, echo, trace, vestige
자취를 더듬다, trace
자치, autonomy
자치 도시, borough
자치구, borough
자치의, autonomous
자칭하는, self-styled
자택, home
자판, keyboard
자폐증, autism
자포자기하다, piece
자행하다, practice
자화상, self-portrait
자화자찬, spin
자활하는, independent
자활하다, fend
자회사, subsidiary
작가, author, writer
작게 말하다, voice
작곡가, composer
작곡하다, compose, write
작동, operation
작동되다, function, go
작동시키다, crank, run, set, trigger, work
작동하는, operative, working
작동하다, activate, come, go, operate, run, work

작동하지 않다, fail
작문, essay
작문하다, compose
작별 인사, farewell, goodbye
작별을 고하다, goodbye
작별의, parting
작성하다, complete, draw, fill, make
작아 보이다, dwarf
작업, effort
작업 대기열, queue
작업 대기열로 보내다, queue
작업 라인, line
작업 중단, downtime
작업 중인, site
작업량, load
작업복, overall
작업을 중단하다, walk
작업장, studio, workshop
작업장 밖에 있는, site
작업조, team
작열하는, fiery
작용, behavior, operation, working
작용하는, work
(~에) 작용하다, act, behave, operate
작위, peerage
작은, little, low, marginal, small, wee
작은 가지, twig
작은 감방, cell
작은 구멍이 많은, porous
작은 글자 부분, print
작은 기계, gadget
작은 덩어리, knob
작은 덩이, pat
작은 도끼, hatchet
작은 만, creek, inlet
작은 물방울, droplet
작은 밭, bed
작은 별장, lodge
작은 보트, dinghy
작은 봉지, sachet
작은 부분, bit, detail
작은 소란, flurry
작은 소리로, confidentially
작은 소리의, muted
작은 소포, packet
작은 시골집, cottage
작은 시내, creek
작은 식당이나 술집, bistro
작은 알갱이, speck
작은 언덕, foothills, hump
작은 장식물, charm
작은 전동차, cart
작은 전투, skirmish
작은 조각, bit
작은 지역, locality, pocket
작은 카펫, rug
작은 통, packet
작은 호텔, guest house
작은 화살, dart
작음, modesty
작전, operation, tactic
작전 중 실종, missing
작전상의, tactical
작전적으로, tactically
작정이다, intend, plan
작지만 단단한, compact
작품, composition, piece, production, work
작품 관리자, curator
작품 속 광고, product placement
작품 해석, interpretation
작품집, portfolio
잔, cup
잔가지, twig
잔고, balance
잔금, balance
잔당, rump
잔돈, change
잔돈으로 바꾸어 주다, change
잔디, grass, turf
잔디 깎는 기계, lawnmower, mower
잔디를 깎다, mow
잔디밭, lawn

잔뜩 든, full
잔뜩 술렁거림, build-up
잔뜩 실은, laden
잔뜩 올려놓다, load
잔뜩 채우다, saturate
잔뜩 흐린, dull
잔류파, ripple
잔물결, ripple
잔물결을 일으키다, ripple, ruffle
잔물결이 일다, ripple
잔소리, lecture, nagging
잔소리꾼, nag
잔소리하다, lecture, nag
잔심부름꾼, runner
잔여 업무, backlog
잔인하게, brutally, cruelly, savagely, viciously
잔인한, brutal, cruel, inhuman, vicious
잔인한 짓, cruelty
잔인함, viciousness
잔잔한, calm, placid
잔잔해지다, calm
잔재, legacy, remnant
잔치, feast, festival, fete
잔치를 벌임, feasting
잔치에 참석하다, feast
잔학 행위, atrocity
잔학한, gory
잔해, remain, ruin, wreck, wreckage
잘, capably, easily, fine, nicely, okay, well
잘 ~하는, prone
(~을) 잘 견디다, tolerant
잘 되다, crop
잘 되어 가다, fast lane, right, work
잘 듣는, receptive
(~을) 잘 모르는, unfamiliar
잘 못하는, bad, poor
잘 못하다, perform
잘 못하여, poorly
잘 보이지 않는 부분, recess
잘 부서지는, crumbly, fragile
잘 분별하여, eye
잘 산 물건, buy
잘 생긴, good-looking
잘 섞어하는, flourishing
잘 속는, gullible
잘 속음, gullibility
잘 알고 있는, familiar, know
잘 알려지지 않은, obscure
잘 알려지지 않음, obscurity
잘 알려진, familiar, household, renowned, well-known
잘 알지 못하는, uncertain
잘 어울리는 것, complement
(~와) 잘 어울리다, complement, harmonize
잘 이겨진, smooth
잘 익은, done
잘 읽히는, readable
잘 자라는, flourishing
잘 자라다, flourish
잘 잡히지 않는, elusive
잘 지내다, fine
(~와) 잘 지내다, get
잘 지지 않는, stubborn
잘 차려 입은, well-dressed
잘 찾다, find
잘 처리하다, master, top
잘 통과하다, negotiate
잘 팔리는 상품, seller
잘 하다, well done
잘 해 나가다, go, nicely
잘 해내다, get
잘 헤쳐 나가다, manage, thrive
잘 훈련된, crack
잘게, finely
잘나가다, fast lane
잘난 척 하는 사람, snob
잘난 체하는, cocky, condescending
잘난 체하다, condescend
잘도 빠져나가는, elusive
잘라 내다, cut
잘라 버리다, cut
잘라내다, censor
잘라낸 것, cutting

잘리다, boot, can
잘못, error, falsely, mistakenly, sin, slip, wrong, wrongly
잘못 관리하다, mismanage
잘못 관리함, mismanagement
잘못 다루다, mishandle
잘못 묘사하다, misrepresent
잘못 묘사함, misrepresentation
잘못 보다, misjudge
잘못 사용되다, misspend
잘못 읽다, misread
잘못 주어진, misplaced
잘못 파악하다, misread
잘못 파악함, misreading
잘못 해석하다, misinterpret
잘못 헤아리다, miscalculate
잘못되게 만들다, sour
잘못되다, sour, wrong
잘못된, amiss, erroneous, irregular, misguided, mistaken, perverted, wrong
잘못된 것, wrong
잘못된 방향으로, track
잘못된 생각, fallacy, misconception
잘못된 시작, false start
잘못된 판단을 하게 만들다, astray
잘못된 해석, misinterpretation
잘못에 대한 책임을 지다, music
잘못을 ~에게 돌리다, pin
잘못을 깨닫게 하다, sort
잘못을 깨닫다, see
잘못이 있는, wrong
잘못한, wrong
잘못해서, inadvertently
잘생긴, handsome
잘하는, strong
잘하다, perform
잘했다, good
잠, sleep, slumber
잠 못 이루는, sleepless
잠결에 걸어 다니다, sleepwalk
잠귀 떼어 내다, lock
잠그다, fasten, lock, shut
잠금장치, catch
잠긴 목소리, croak
잠긴 목소리로 말하다, croak
잠깐, awhile, bit, fleetingly, moment, momentarily, sec, short
잠깐 ~하다, lapse
잠깐 기다려, minute
잠깐 남의 일을 보아 주다, fort
잠깐 동안 의식을 잃다, black
잠깐 동안의, brief
잠깐 들르다, drop, pop
잠깐 들름, stopover
잠깐 멈추다, pause
잠깐 손을 대다, dabble
잠깐 자다, doze
잠깐 중단, time out
잠깐만, just
잠깐만 기다려, wait
잠깐씩 ~함, lapse
잠든, asleep
잠들다, asleep, sleep
잠마, jumper
잠복하다, lurk
잠복한 상태의, dormant
잠수, dive, diving
잠수부, diver
잠수하다, dive
잠수함, sub, submarine
잠시, briefly
잠시 기다리다, hold
잠시 동안, little
잠시 머무르다, stop
잠시 머묾, stop
잠시 후, wait
잠시 시도해 보다, sample
잠시 제쳐 두다, side
잠시 중단하다, break, suspend
잠시의, little
잠식하다, eat, encroach, inroads, nibble, undermine
잠옷, pajamas
잠옷 바람의, undressed
잠으로 떨치다, sleep

잠을 못 자는, sleepless
잠을 자서 낫게 하다, sleep
잠이 오게 하는, hypnotic
잠입, infiltration, penetration
잠입시키다, infiltrate
잠입하다, infiltrate, penetrate
잠자는 사람, sleeper
잠자는 시간, sleep
잠자다, sleep, slumber
잠자리, bed, dragonfly
잠자리에 들다, settle
잠자리와 아침 식사, B&B
잠자코 있는, quiet
잠잠해지다, quiet
잠잠해짐, hush
잠재된, latent
잠재력, potential
잠재우다, mute, quash, quell, quiet, scotch
잠재의식, subconscious
잠재의식적으로, subconsciously
잠재의식적인, subconscious, subliminal
잠재적으로, potentially
잠재적인, potential, underlying
잠재해 있다, lurk
잠정적으로, provisionally, tentatively
잠정적인, provisional, tentative
잠행, stealth
잠행성의, insidious
(~를) 잡고 있다, stall
잡곡, corn
잡기, catch
잡년, bitch, tramp
잡다, allow, catch, have, take, trap
잡다한, miscellaneous
잡다한 것, sundries
잡담, chatter
잡동사니, bit, bob, clutter
잡동사니 우편물, junk mail
잡석, rubble
잡아 떼어 내다, wrench
잡아 뜯다, pluck
잡아당기기, pull
잡아매다, moor, secure
(~을) 잡아먹고 살다, prey
잡아먹다, absorb
잡아채다, grab, snatch, tear
잡용의, general
잡음, static
잡종, hybrid
잡종의, hybrid
잡지, journal, mag, magazine, periodical
잡초, weed
잡초를 제거하다, weed
잡히지 않은, large
잣다, spin
장, ground, page
장(章), chapter, page
장갑, armor, gauntlet, glove
장갑의, armored
장거리 버스, coach
장거리의, long-distance, long-haul, long-range
장과(漿果), berry
장관, minister, secretary, Secretary of State, spectacle, splendor
장관(壯觀), pomp
장관을 이루는, spectacular
장관을 이루는 것들, splendor
장관의, ministerial
장관직, portfolio
장광설, tirade
장교, captain, commander, officer
장군, admiral, general
장기, organ
장기 기증, donation
장기간에 걸친, long-running
장기를 기증하다, donate
장기적으로, long-term, run, term
장기적인, long-range, long-term
장기적인 영향을 미치다, mark
장기화된, prolonged
장난, giggle, mischief, play, prank
장난감, toy
장난꾸러기, monkey

장난삼아 하다, play
장난스러움, playfulness
장난스런, playful
장난스럽게, mischievously
장난스레, playfully
장난으로, fun
장난을 좋아하는, mischievous
장난이 아닌 일, joke
장난치며 놀다, frolic
장난하다, play
장난하지 마, kid
장단, beat
장단을 맞추다, time
장단점, pro
장대한, imposing
장대한, grandeur
장래, future, tomorrow
장래를 내다보다, forward
장래성이 없는, dead end
장려, encouragement
장려하다, encourage
장려한 것을, splendor
장력, tension
장례, burial
장례식, funeral
장르, genre
장르 혼합, crossover
장막, veil
장만하다, set
장면, footage, picture, scene
장모, mother-in-law
장미, rose
장미 덩굴, rose
장밋빛, rose
장밋빛의, rosy
장방형의, rectangular
장벽, bar, barrier, glass ceiling
장부, book
장부 가격, book value
장부 작성자, bookkeeper
장비, equipment, gear, paraphernalia
장선, gut
장성, maturity
장성하다, mature
장소, ground, location, place, setting, site, space, spot, venue
장소를 제공하다, house
장수, seller
장시간에 걸친, marathon
장식, decor, decoration, trim, trimming
장식 못, stud
장식 핀, pin
(~로) 장식되다, embellish, trim
(~로) 장식된, paneled
장식띠, sash
장식물, decoration, trappings
장식용 금속 단추, stud
장식용 금속 단추가 박힌, studded
장식용 꽃, buttonhole
장식용의, decorative, ornamental
장식이 화려한, ornate
장식품, ornament
장식하다, adorn
장식한, plastered
장신구, jewelry
장악, command, grasp, grip, seizure
장악력을 잃다, grip
장악하다, command, corner, hold, seize, tune
장애, bar, barrier, disability, disturbance, handicap, hitch, hurdle, impairment, impediment, obstacle
장애가 있는, handicapped
장애물, barrier, drag, fence, impediment, obstacle, obstruction, stumbling block
장애물이 없는, clear
장애인, disabled
장애자, handicapped
장엄, solemnity
장엄하게, majestically
장엄한, awesome, majestic, solemn, sublime
장엄함, grandiose, majesty, pomp

장외의, counter
장의사, mortician, undertaker
장인, craftsman, father-in-law
장인의 솜씨, craftsmanship
장작, firewood
장전하다, load
장점, advantage, beauty, strength, virtue
(~의) 장점을 늘어놓다, tout
장정, binding
장정되다, bind
장조의, major
장중, solemnity
장중한, resonant
장중함, resonance
장착하다, equip, load
장치, apparatus, device, gimmick, system, unit
장터, fair, fairground, marketplace
장편 영화, feature
장학금, grant, scholarship
장화, boot
장황하게, ponderously
장황하게 지껄이다, hold
장황한, ponderous
잦아들다, abate, die, fade
잦아지다, die
재, ash
재가, sanction
재가하다, sanction
재간, caliber
재간꾼, operator
재갈, gag, muzzle
재갈을 물리다, gag, muzzle
재갈이 물리다, muzzle
재개, renewal, resumption, resurgence, return
재개발, redevelopment, renewal
재개시, relaunch
재개시하다, relaunch
재개표, recount
재개하다, renew, resume, return
재건, reconstruction, regeneration
재건하다, rebuild, reconstruct, regenerate
재검토, reexamination
재검토하다, reexamine
재검표, recount
재경기, replay
재경기를 갖다, replay
재계의 거물, tycoon
재고, rethink, second thought, stock
재고 관리, stock control
재고 조사, stocktaking
재고가 없는, stock
재고가 있는, stock
재고품, inventory, stock
재고하다, reconsider, rethink, think, twice
재교육, reskilling, retraining
재교육 과정, refresher course
재교육받다, retrain
재교육시키다, reskill
재교육을 받다, reskill
재교육하다, retrain
재구류, remand
재구류되다, remand
재구매의, repeat
재구성의, reconstruction
재구성하다, reconstruct
재기, sparkle
재기 넘치는, brilliant, sparkling
재기 발랄하다, sparkle
재기 발랄함, brilliance
재기 불능의, crushing
재기가 넘치게, brilliantly
재난, calamity, disaster, distress, doom
재능, ability, capacity, talent
재능 있는, talented
재다, debate, take
재단, foundation
재단되다, cut
재담꾼, joker
재떨이, ashtray
재래식 우편 제도, snail mail
재래식의, conventional

재량권, discretion, latitude
재량껏 쓸 수 있는, disposable
(~의) 재량에 따라, discretion
(~의) 재량에 맡겨진, disposal
(~을) 재료로 하여, from
재목, timber
재무 상태, budget
재무 장관, Chancellor, Chancellor of the Exchequer
재무부, Exchequer, treasury
재무부 비밀 검찰국, secret service
재물, wealth
재미, amusement, fun, giggle
재미 삼아, kick, laugh
재미 삼은, lighthearted
재미로, fun
재미없고 피곤한 일, treadmill
재미없는, bland, dry, dull, tame
재미있게, amusingly
재미있는, amusing, funny, juicy
재미있는 사람, fun
재미있는데, alive
재발, recurrence, relapse
재발매, relaunch
재발하다, recur, relapse, repeat
재방송, repeat
재배, yours
재배 농장, plantation
재배열하다, rearrange
재배자, grower
재배하다, grow, raise
재배된, cultivated
재보급하다, replenish
재분배, redistribution
재분배되다, redistribute
재빠르게, swiftly
재빠르게 퍼 넣다, shovel
재빠른, nimble, quick, swift
재빨리 달려가다, jump
재빨리 반응하는 능력, reflex
재빨리 붙잡다, snatch
재빨리 비키다, dodge
재빨리 이동하다, hop
재빨리 피하다, dodge
재빨리 하다, snatch
재산, means, possession, property, purse, rich
재산 관리인, receiver
재산이 많은, wealthy
재상연, revival
재상연하다, revive
재생, regeneration, renewal, replay
재생 가능한, renewable
재생되다, regenerate, renew
재생시키다, regenerate
재생하다, play, replay
재선, re-election
재선되다, reelect
재소자, inmate
재소집되다, reconvene
재소집하다, reconvene
재수없는, bum, wretched
재시합, playoff, rematch
재앙, blight, calamity, catastrophe, curse, disaster, scourge
재앙을 안겨 주다, scourge
재앙의, catastrophic
재앙의 씨앗, disaster
재외 기지, outpost
재워 주다, put
재원, cash cow, purse
재원을 특별한 목적에 사용하다, channel
재원이 부족한, underfunded
재임 기간, tenure
재잘거리다, chatter
재적응, readjustment
재정, finance
재정 상태, balance sheet
재정비, overhaul
재정비하다, overhaul
재정의, monetary
재정적으로, financially
재정적인, financial
재조정, rearrangement

재조정하다, readjust, rearrange, reschedule
재주, craft, knack
재주 부리기, juggling
재주 부리다, juggle
재주넘기, somersault
재주를 넘다, somersault
재즈, jazz
재직자, incumbent
재차 말하다, reiterate
재채기, sneeze
재채기하다, sneeze
재청, encore
재청하다, second
재촉, prompting
재촉하다, hasten, hurry, urge
재출현, reappearance
재치, wit
재치 있는, witty
재치 있는 말, quip
재킷, jacket
재택근무, telecommuting, teleworking
재통일, reunification
재통합하다, reunite
재투자되다, plow
재판, judgment, reprint, trial
재판(再版), reprint
재판관, judge
재판관석, bench
재판받다, trial, try
재판소, courthouse
재판을 받는 중인, trial
재판을 받다, commit
재판이 발행되다, reprint
재판장, Chief Justice
재편, reorganization
재편성되다, regroup
재편성하다, regroup, reorganize
재평가, reassessment
재평가하다, reassess, revalue
재향 군인, vet, veteran
재현, duplicate, reconstruction, recreation
재현하다, duplicate, recreate, reproduce
재확인하다, double-check, reaffirm
재활, rehab, rehabilitation
재활시키다, rehabilitate
재활용, recycling
재활용하다, recycle
재회, reunion
재회하다, reunite
잭, jack
잼, jam, jelly
잽, jab
쟁기, plow
쟁반, tray
쟁의, dispute
쟁점, issue
쟁점이 되고 있는, issue
쟁취하다, take
쟁탈전, scramble
쟁탈전을 벌이다, scramble
저, please, that, those
저 멀리, distance
저 악센트의, grave
저-, low
저가의, budget, downmarket
저가주, penny shares
저개발의, underdeveloped
저것, that
저것들, those
저격수, sniper
저격하다, snipe
저기, over
저기, 있잖아요, look
저기압, depression
저기에, there
저녁, evening, night
저녁 식사, supper
저당 잡히다, mortgage, pledge
저도 모르게, involuntarily
저도 모르는, involuntary
저런, gee, oops, well
저런!, almighty, goodness, grief, heaven

저렴하게, cheaply
저렴하고 좋은 물건, snip
저렴한, budget, cheap
저렴한 유흥업소, joint
저류(低流), undercurrent
저명, eminence, prominence
저명한, distinguished, eminent, grand, great, illustrious, note, prominent, public
저물다, set
저미다, carve, slice
저버리다, betray, forsake, renege
저벅저벅 밟다, crunch
저벅저벅 하는 소리, crunch
저소득 지역의, sink
저속한, cheap, sleazy, vulgar
저속한 말, language
저속함, sleaze, vulgarity
저수지, reservoir
저술가, writer
저습지, flat
저열한, belt
저예산으로, shoestring
저울, scale
저울되는, balance, weigh
저울추, balance, weight
처음 조절 손잡이, bass
저음역, bass
저음의, bass
저의(底意), undercurrent
저의가 있는, loaded
저인망 어선, trawler
저인망으로 고기를 잡다, trawl
저임금의, low-paid
저자, author, writer
저작권, copyright
저작권 사용료, royalty
저작권 침해, piracy
저작권을 침해하다, pirate
저장, storage
저장 식품으로 만들다, preserve
저장물, hoard
저장소, bank, store
저장하다, hoard, keep, save, store
저절로, accord
저점, low, trough
저조한, ebb, low
저주, curse
저지르다, commit, perpetrate
저지하다, arrest, check, defeat, foil, oppose, set, snuff, stop
저쪽 끝, bottom
저축 대부, savings and loan
저축과 융자, S & L
저축인, saver
저축하다, save
저칼로리의, diet
저택, château, house, manor, mansion, villa
저하, slip, slippage
저하시키다, impoverish
저항, defiance, resistance
저항력, resistance
저항력이 약한, vulnerability
저항력이 없는, vulnerable
저항력이 있는, resistant
저항하는, resistant
저항하다, hold, resist
저항할 수 없는, irresistible
적, adversary, enemy, foe
적갈색, auburn, maroon, rust
적갈색의, bay, copper, red
적게 지출하다, underspend
적격성, eligibility
적격의, eligible
적격인, tailor-made
적군, enemy
적군의, hostile
적극적으로, actively, aggressively
적극적인, active, aggressive
적나라한, gritty, naked, uncompromising
적다, note, put, set
적당하게, medium, moderately
적당한, adequate, appropriate, fair, medium, moderate, proper, reasonable
적당한 선에서 그만두다, stop

적당한 속도로 운행하다, cruise
적당한 수준의, modest
적당히, acceptably, moderation
적당히 ~하다, easy
적대 행위, hostility
적대감을 느끼게 하다, antagonize
적대자, antagonist
적대적, hostile
적대적인, adversarial, hostile
적도, equator
적령기의, eligible
적막한, silent
적발하다, nail, uncover
적성, aptitude
적소, niche
적수, opponent
적시다, wet
적어 넣다, inscribe, put
적어 두다, commit, jot, mark, write
적어도, least
적에게 협력하다, collaborate
적용, application
적용 가능한, applicable
적용되는, effect, true
적용되다, apply, cover, go, hold, true
적용하다, apply, enforce
(~보다) 적은, less, low
적은 양, dab
적응, adaptation
적응된, accustomed
적응성, adaptability
적응시키다, adapt, break
적응하다, acclimatize, adapt, adjust, settle
적응할 수 있는, adaptable
적의, hostile, malice
적의 있는, unfriendly
적의를 노골적으로 드러내다, knife
적임의, competent
적자, deficit
적자 상태의, deficit
적자의, red
적재 공간, compartment
적절치 못하게, hopelessly
적절치 못한, hopeless
적절치 않은, incorrect, unfortunate
적절하게, aptly, reasonably
적절한, apt, correct, decent, due, fitting, point, proper, right, working
적절히, adequately, correctly, properly
적정한, fair, moderate, reasonable
적중률이 높은, accurate
적포도주, red
적합성, suitability
적합하게, suitably
적합하다, befit, fit
적합한, adapted, equal, good, suitable, suited
적합함, fit, fitness
적혀 있는, writing
적화장, dock
전 ~, over
전 국민적인, popular
전 세계, world
전 세계에, worldwide
전 세계에 미치는, worldwide
전 세계적으로, globally
전 세계적인, global, universal
전 종업원, workforce
전 직원, personnel
전가하다, shift
전갈, message
전개 과정, line
전개되다, unfold
전경, foreground, panorama
전공, major, speciality, specialty
전공자, major, specialist
전공하다, major, specialize
전과, record
전광석화처럼, lightning
(~) 전교, c/o
전교 학생 및 교직원, school
전구, bulb, light bulb
전국적으로, nationally, nationwide

전국적인, national, nationwide
전권 위임, carte blanche
전극, electrode, element, terminal
전근, transfer
전근하다, transfer
전기, biography, electricity, turning point
전기 공급의, electric
전기 기사, electrician
전기 문학의, biography
전기 쇼크, electric shock
전기 작가, biographer
전기 충격, shock
전기가 통하는, electric
전기가 흐르고 있는, live
전기로, electrically
전기로 움직이는, electric
전기를 통하게 하다, electrify
전기와 관련된, electrical
전기의, electric, electrical
전기의자, chair, electric chair
전기의자 사형, electrocution
전기의자로 처형하다, electrocute
전기장, field
전기적인, biographical
전나무, fir
전날, eve
전념, application, concentration, devotion
전념하고 있는, intent
전념하다, dedicated
전념하다, dedicate
전념하여, intently
전능한 존재처럼 행세하다, god
전단지, leaflet
전달자, bearer
전달하다, communicate, deliver, hand, pass, relay, transmit
전당포 주인, pawnbroker
전당포에 잡히다, pawn
전도가 유망한, up-and-coming
전도시키다, invert
전도체, conductor
전도하다, conduct
전동 자전거, moped
전등, lamp
전등 장식, illumination
전락, descent
전락하다, descend
전람 중에, view
전람회, exhibition
전략, strategy
전략가, strategist
전략적, tactical
전략적으로, strategically
전략적인, strategic
전력, power
전력 공급, electrification
전력 질주, sprint
전력 질주하다, sprint
전력으로 작동하는, power
전력을 더하여, might
전력을 다해서, flat
전력을 총동원하여, gun
(~의) 전력이 있다, history
전령, messenger
전례 없는, all-time, unprecedented
전례가 없는, unheard of
전류, current
전리품, trophy
전망, outlook, prospect, view, vision, vista
전매 상품이 붙은, proprietary
전매(轉買), resale
전매(轉買)하다, resell
전면부 유리, windscreen, windshield
전면을 덮는 것, blanket
전면적인, all-out, full-scale, sweeping
전멸, annihilation, extinction
전멸시키다, annihilate
전무, nil
전무이사, MD
전문, speciality, specialty
전문 부장, editor
전문 분야, specialization
전문 용어, term, terminology

전문가, expert, guru, money, professional, pundit, specialist
전문가답지 않은, unprofessional
전문가에 의한, expert
전문가의, professional
전문성, professionalism
전문어, jargon
(~을) 전문으로 다루다, specialize
(~만) 전문으로 취급하는, devoted
전문의, dedicated, specialized, technical
전문적 기술, expertise
전문적 사항, technicality
전문적 절차, technicality
전문적 지식, expertise
전문적 활동, technicality
전문적으로, professionally
전문적인, expert, professional, scholarly
전문적인 지식, know-how
전문화, specialization
전문화된, specialized
전반에 걸친, all-around
전반의, early
전반적으로, board, general, overall
전반적인, general, overall, rough, wide
전방에 있는, front
전방의, forward
전법, tactic
전보, telegram
전복, overthrow, subversion
전복되다, overthrow
전복시키는, subversive
전복시키다, bring, capsize, overturn, subvert, topple
전복하다, capsize
전부, all, altogether, everything, sum, together, total, whole
전부 갖춘, complete
전부의, complete
전부이거나 아니거나, nothing
전사, transfer, warrior
전사되다, transfer
전산망으로, line
전산화된, computerized
전산화하다, computerize
전선, cable, flex, front, line, wire
전선을 가설하다, wire
전설, legend
전설상의, legendary
전설에 의하면 ~하고 한다, have
전설적인, legendary
전설적인 인물, legend
전성기, heyday, prime
전성기를 지난, hill
전세 내다, charter
전세의, charter
전소하다, ground
전속 기사, chauffeur
전속되어 있는, contract
전속력으로, hell, steam
전속력으로 달리다, spurt
전속력으로 말 타기, gallop
전속력을 내다, foot
전송, transfer, transmission
전송되어 오다, transfer, transmit
전송하다, upload
전수하다, hand, initiate
전시, display, exhibition, wartime
전시되다, exhibit, parade
전시실, showroom
전시품, exhibit
전시하다, display, show
전시하여, view
전시회, exhibit, exhibition, show
전시회를 열다, exhibit
전신, ancestor, forerunner, telegram
전신선, wire
전신의, full-length, generalized
전압, voltage
전언, communication
전에, ago, before, previously, prior, route
(~) 전에 일을 끝내다, beat
전역, campaign
(~의) 전역에서, across

전염, transmission
전염병, infection
전염성의, contagious
전염성이 강한, contagious, infectious
전염시키다, transmit
전염의, infectious
전용(轉用)하다, reallocate, redirect
전용의, dedicated
전용하다, divert
전원, country, main
전원 지역의, greenfield
전원 집결, strength
전원을 켜다, power
전원의, rural
전원풍의, idyllic
(~의) 전위에, vanguard
전위적인, avant-garde
전유, monopoly
전율, quiver, shudder, thrill, tremor
전율을 느끼게 하는, electrifying
전율하다, shudder
전이, transfer
전이되다, transfer
전입, transfer
전입되다, transfer
전임자, predecessor
전자, electron, former
전자 공학, electronics
전자 공학적으로, electronically
전자 상거래, e-commerce
전자 우편, electronic mail, e-mail
전자 음향 합성 장치, synthesizer
전자 장치를 쓰지 않은, acoustic
전자 출판, desktop publishing, DTP, electronic publishing
전자 카드, swipe card
전자레인지, microwave
전자레인지에 넣고 돌리다, microwave
전자의, electronic
전자책, e-book, electronic book
전자통신, messaging
전자통신을 하다, message
전장, battlefield
전쟁, battle, war, warfare
전쟁 이전의, prewar
전쟁 중인, warring
전쟁을 시작하다, war
전쟁의, martial
전쟁터, battleground
전적으로, absolutely, entirely, purely, squarely, totally, utterly, wholeheartedly, wholly
(~에) 전적으로 달려있다, hinge
(~을) 전적으로 찬성하는, for
전적인, pure, total, utter, wholehearted
전제 정치, tyranny
전제 조건, precondition
전조, herald
전주곡, prelude
전직 알선, outplacement
전직의, former
전진하다, advance, go
전집, complete
전차, streetcar, tank
전철기, point
전체, entirety, whole
전체 내용의 일부분에 불과한, story
전체로서, whole
전체론, holism
전체론적인, holistic
전체의, all-, entire, full-length, whole
전체적으로 보아, whole
전체적인, global
전체주의의, totalitarian
전초 기지, outpost
전초전, dress rehearsal
전축, record player
전치사, preposition
전통, custom, tradition
전통의상, costume
전통적으로, traditionally
전통적인, conventional, traditional

전투, action, battle, combat, fighting, hostilities, struggle
전투기, fighter
전투용의, assault
전투원, combatant
전투하다, fight
전파, beam, diffusion, transmission
전파 방해, interference, jamming
전폭적으로, wholehearted, wholeheartedly
전하, charge, Highness
전하가 없는, neutral
전하다, carry, convey
전함, battleship, warship
전해지다, filter, travel
전향, conversion
전향시키다, convert
전향자, convert
전혀, all, altogether, blissfully, earth, earthly, emphatically, not, remotely, slight, very
전혀 가망이 없는, hiding
전혀 가망이 없다, hope
전혀 관심 없다, care
전혀 관심이 없다, give
전혀 그렇지 않다, far
전혀 뜻밖의, stunning
전혀 모르는, blissful
전혀 모르다, clue, foggy
전혀 영향을 끼치지 못하는, duck
전혀 이상하지 않다, wonder
전혀 잠이 안 오는, awake
전형, classic, epitome, ideal, personification
전형(典型), stereotype
전형이 되다, typify
(~의) 전형이다, epitomize
전형적으로, typically
전형적이지 않은, uncharacteristic
(~에) 전형적인, characteristic, classic, prime, representative, textbook, typical
전화, line, phone, phone call, telephone
전화 거는 사람, caller
전화 교환원, operator
전화 받다, answer
전화 상담 서비스, hotline
전화 연락을 돌리다, call
전화 카드, phonecard
전화 판매, telesales
전화 판촉, telemarketing
전화 회선, line
전화 회의, conference call
전화기, phone, telephone
전화로 병가를 내다, phone
전화로 부르다, call
전화로 이야기하다, telephone
전화로 주문을 하다, phone
(~에게) 전화를 걸다, call, phone, telephone
전화를 끊다, hang, ring
전화를 연결하다, put
전화번호, number
전화번호 안내, directory assistance
전화번호부, phone book
전화번호부에 실리지 않은, ex-directory, unlisted
전화벨, ring
전화벨 소리, ringing
전화벨이 울리다, ring
전화하다, call, phone, ring
전환, conversion, diversion, reversal, switch, transformation, turn, turning
전환기, turn, turning point
전환시키다, transform
전환하다, change, move, reverse, switch
전후(戰後), postwar
전희 순서, routine
절, bow, clause, temple, verse
절감, cut, economy
절감하다, cut, pare
절교하다, break, finish
절규하다, cry, rave
절단 수술, amputation

절단기, cutter
절단하다, amputate, chop
절대 묵인 불가, zero tolerance
절대 아니다, hell
절대로, account, ever, possibly
절대로 ~ 아니다, way
절대적으로, absolutely, implicitly
절대적인, absolute, implicit, unqualified
절대적인 것, absolute
절대적인 사실, gospel
절도, theft
절뚝거리다, limp
절뚝거림, limp
절룩거리는, lame
절름거리다, hobble
절름발이, lame
절망, despair, desperation, hopelessness
절망감, desolation
절망적으로, hopelessly
절망적이다, hope
절망적인, desperate, hopeless
절망하다, despair
절멸하라, kill
절묘한 사례, masterpiece
절박, urgency
절박한, imminent, pressing
절반, half
절반씩 부담하다, half
절반의, half
절반의 성공, qualified
절반쯤의, medium
(~을) 절실히 느끼게 하다, home
(~가) 절실히 필요함, crying
절약, conservation, economy, saving
절약하는, economical
절약하다, conserve, economize, save
절연, break
절연되다, insulate
절정, height, peak, pinnacle, zenith
절정에 이르다, peak
절정에 이르러, height
절제, constraint, discipline, moderation
절제되지 않은, uncontrolled
절제된, understated
절제된 표현, understatement
절제력이 있는, disciplined
절조가 있는, principled
절차, mechanism, procedure, process
절차상의, procedural
절충, negotiation
절충을 하다, strike
절충하다, compromise
절하, depreciation
절하다, bow
젊은, young
젊은 세대, youth
젊은 시절, youth
젊은 피, blood
젊은이, lad, son, youth
젊은이들, young, youth
젊음, youth
점, dot, fleck, spot, way
점거하다, hold
점거하여 입구를 봉쇄하다, barricade
점검, check
점검하다, check, monitor
점두의, counter
점령, capture, occupation
점령지, conquest
점령하다, capture, occupy, seize
점보기, jumbo
점선으로 된, broken
점선의, dotted
점성가, astrologer
점성술, horoscope
점성학, astrology
점수, mark, point, score
점수 기록원, scorer
점수를 얻다, score
점수판, scoreboard

점심, lunch
점심 만찬, luncheon
점심 시간, lunchtime
점심 식사하다, lunch
점액, mucus, slime
점원, assistant, clerk, shop assistant
점유, occupancy
점유인, occupier
점유자, occupant
점유하다, occupy
점으로 표시해 연결하다, plot
점잖게, conservative, conservatively, decently, graciously
점잖은, decent, gracious
점점, increasingly
점점 가늘게 만들다, taper
점점 가늘어지는, tapered
점점 가늘어지다, taper
점점 강해지다, strength
점점 더, more
점점 더해 가는, gathering
점점 사라져, away
점점 사라져 없어지다, wear
점점 사라지다, dissolve
점점 약해져, away
점점 유명해지다, gain
(~이) 점점 좋아지다, grow
점점 커지는 소리, crescendo
점점이 흩어져 있다, dot
점증적인, cumulative
점진적으로, gradually, progressively
점진적인, gradual, organic, progressive
점차, bit
점차 감소하다, tail
점차 사라지다, die
점차 소멸하다, peter
점차 우세해지다, gain
점차 확대되다, escalate
점치다, fortune
점토, clay, pottery
점퍼스커트, jumper
점포, shop
점프 스타트, jump-start
점프 스타트를 하다, jump-start
점화, ignition
점화 장치, ignition
점화구, ring
점화되다, ignite
점화하다, ignite
접견권, access
접경하다, border
접근, access, approach
접근 불가능한, inaccessible
접근 시간, access time
접근 용이성, accessibility
접근권, access
접근로, approach
접근법, approach
접근이 금지된, bound
접근이 용이한, accessible
접근하기 어려운, inaccessible
접근하다, access, approach, tread
접근할 수 없는, inaccessible
접다, close, fold
접대, service
접대하는, entertaining
접대하다, entertain
접두사, prefix
(~에) 접목하다, graft
접미사, suffix
접사, affix
접속, connectivity
접속 보안 장치, firewall
접속된, online
접속사, conjunction
접속하다, hook, log
접수계원, desk clerk, receptionist
접수처, reception
접수하다, take
접시, dish, plate
접어 넣다, tuck
접어들다, enter
접전 지역, marginal
접전을 벌이다, skirmish

접전의, marginal
접점, interface
접지, earth, ground
접지 면, tread
접지르다, strain
접질림, strain
접착, bond
접착성의, adhesive
접착제, adhesive, cement, glue
접착제가 발라져 있는, self-adhesive
접착제로 붙이다, glue
접촉, contact, touch
(~와) 접촉 중인, contact
접하다, expose, meet
접합, join
접합 부분, connection, joint
접합되다, cement, knit
접합하다, join
접히다, fold
접힌 자국, crease
젓기, shake, stroke
젓다, shake, stir
젓다, shake, stir
정가표, tag
정각에, dot, promptly, sharp
정강이, shin
정거장, depot, stop
정곡을 찌르다, home
정관사, definite article
정교하게, delicately, elaborately, exquisitely
정교하게 만들어지다, craft
정교한, delicate, elaborate, exquisite, refined, sophisticated
정권, power, regime
정권을 잡은, power
정규, formal
정규직으로, permanently
정규직의, permanent
정기 간행물, periodical
정기 이용권, season ticket
정기 장, fair
정기 휴가, vacation
정기선, liner
정기적으로, regularly
정기적인, regular
정년, retirement
정년 이후, retirement
정당, party
정당방위, self-defense
정당성 입증, vindication
정당하게, duly, justifiably, legitimately
정당하지 않은, unjustified
정당한, legitimate, rightful
정당한 이유, justification
정당함, justice, legitimacy, rightness
정당함이 입증되다, vindicate
정당화, justification
정당화하다, justify, warrant
정당화할 수 있는, justifiable
(~) 정도, anything, degree, extent, magnitude, so, way
(~) 정도까지, extent, far
(~) 정도로만 하겠다, suffice
정도에서 벗어남, aberration
정돈되다, order
정돈된, order, orderly
정돈하다, straighten, tidy
정떨어지게, horribly
정략적 계책, game
정략적인, expedient
정력, energy
정력적으로, vigorously
정력적인, vigorous
정렬, array
정렬시키다, line
정렬하다, align, lay, line
정례적으로, routinely
정례적인, routine
정류장, depot, stand, station, stop
정리, clearance
정리 대상 명단, hit list
정리 대상 사항, hit list
정리 대상의, chop
정리 해고, layoff, redundancy
정리 해고당하다, lay

정리 해고되는, redundant
정리된, order
정리하다, clear, fix, liquidate, order, organize, sort, straighten
정말, chance, damn, indeed, only, really, truly, what
정말 끔찍한, untold
정말 심각한, real
정말 우습게도, funnily
정말 작은, minuscule
정말 중요한, real
정말 한, honestly
정말로, actually, darn, genuinely, honest, how, literally, positively, real, really, so, sure, thoroughly, truly
정말이야, seriously
정말이지, hell, seriously, tell
정말인, genuine
정맥, vein
정맥 내의, intravenous
정맥 주사로, intravenously
정맥 주사의, intravenous
정면, facade, front
정면으로, ahead, head-on, squarely
정면으로 반(反)하다, face
정면의, frontal, head-on
정물화, still life
정밀, accuracy
정밀 검사하다, scan
정밀 검토, dissection
정밀 조사, scrutiny
정밀 촬영, scan
정밀성, sensitivity
정밀하게, accurately, finely
정밀한, accurate, close, sensitive
정박 위치, berth
정박시키다, anchor, moor
정박지, mooring
정박하다, anchor, berth
정박해 있는, anchor
정반대, antithesis, opposite
정반대의, opposite, polar
정반대인, pole
정보, code, info, information, input, intelligence, pointer, tip
정보 기술, information technology, IT
정보 센터, clearinghouse
정보 제공자, informant, informer
정보를 주다, surf
정보를 종합하여 결론을 내리다, two
정보를 주는, informative
(~에게) 정보를 주지 않다, hold
정보에 입각한, informed
정보원, informant, informer, source
정보지, literature
정보통의, informed
정화 과정, data processing
정복, conquest
정복자, conqueror
정복하다, conquer
정부, government, mistress, state
정부 기관, agency
정부 예산안, budget
정부의, governmental
정비, maintenance, overhaul, service
정비되다, overhaul, tune
정비를 받다, service
정비하다, maintain, tune
정사, affair, love affair
정사각형, square
정사각형 모양의, square
정상, normality, pinnacle, summit
정상 가동 중인, running
정상 궤도에 오른, track
정상 작동되는, functional
정상 회담, summit
정상적으로, normally
정상적인, normal
정상화, normalization
정상화하다, normalize
정색한 얼굴, face
정서, emotion, mood, sentiment, temperature
정서 장애의, disturbed

정설, orthodoxy
정성(연구)의, qualitative
정세, affair
정수, essence, ultimate
정수리, crown
정숙, quiet
정숙함, modesty
정시에, punctually
정식 절차, proceeding
정식으로, formally
정식의, full, solemn
정신, ethos, spirit
정신 감응, telepathy
정신 감응 능력이 있는, telepathic
정신 나간, crazed, lunatic, mind, raving
정신 나간 듯한, manic
정신 못 차리게 하다, fluster
정신 못 차리는, flustered
정신 병원, asylum, institution
정신 분석, psychoanalysis
정신 분석가, analyst, psychoanalyst
정신 분열증, schizophrenia
정신 분열증 환자, schizophrenic
정신 분열증의, schizophrenic
정신 상태, mentality
정신 요법, psychotherapy
정신 요법 의사, psychotherapist
정신 의학, psychiatry
정신 의학의, psychiatric
정신 이상, insanity, psychosis
정신 이상의, psychotic
정신 착란, brainstorm
정신과 의사, psychiatrist, shrink
정신력, strength
정신병, psychosis
정신병의, psychiatric
정신병자, lunatic, psychopath
정신성, spirituality
정신세계, psyche
정신없는, frantic, hectic
정신없이, frantically, manically
정신없이 늘어나는, runaway
정신없이 돌아가는, frenetic
정신없이 돌아가는 상황, whirlwind
정신없이 돌아감, merry-go-round
정신없이 비명을 지르다, head
정신없이 설명하다, rave
정신없이 움직이는, manic
정신없이 웃다, head
정신을 산만하게 만드는, distracting
정신을 산만하게 하는 것, distraction
정신을 잃게 만들다, knock
정신을 잃다, faint
정신을 차리게 하다, wake
정신을 차리다, earth, pull
정신의, mental, spiritual
정신이 건강한, well-balanced
정신이 다른 곳에 팔린, absent-minded
정신이 또렷한, awake
정신이 말짱한, sober
정신이 맑은, lucid
정신이 번쩍 드는, sobering
정신이 아득해짐, disorientation
정신적 단절, block
정신적 승리, victory
정신적 외상, trauma
정신적으로, mentally, psychologically, spiritually
정신적인, moral, platonic, psychological, spiritual
정신적인 충격을 받다, traumatize
정액, semen, sperm
정액제의, unmetered
정어리, sardine
정연한, neat
정연함, neatness, orderliness
정열적으로, dynamically, passionately
정열적인, passionate
정예의, elite
정오, midday, noon
정욕, desire, passion
정원, garden
정원사, gardener

정원을 가꾸다, garden
정육면체, cube
정육점, butcher
정육점 주인, butcher
정의, definition, justice
정의를 내리다, define
정자, sperm
정장, suit
정전, blackout, ceasefire, outage, power cut
정전기, static
정전되다, black
정절, fidelity
정점, climax, culmination, peak, zenith
정점에 달하게 하다, climax
정점에 달하다, climax
정정, correction
정정당당하게, fair
정정하다, correct
정제, refining
정제 설탕, confectioners' sugar
정제되다, refine
정제된, refined
정제소, refinery
정중하게, gallantly
정중하고 합리적인, civilized
정중한, attentive, civil, courteous, formal
정중한 행동, courtesy
정중함, formality, refinement
정중히, courteously, formally
정지, standstill, stop
정지되다, dry
정지시키다, disable
정지하다, halt
정지한, stationary, still
정직, honesty, suspension
정직을 당하다, suspend
정직하게, honestly, truthfully
정직하게 말하면, honest
정직한, candid, honest, truthful, up front, upright
정직함, candor, truthfulness
정차하다, call
정착되다, root
정착된, well-established
정착민, settler
정착시키다, settle
정착지, settlement
정착하다, arrive, root, settle
정찬, dinner
정찰, reconnaissance
정찰병, scout
정찰을 하다, spy
정찰하다, scout
정책, policy
정체, identity
정체기, plateau
정체를 드러내다, give
정체불명의, unidentified
정취, atmosphere
정치, government, politics
정치 경제학, political economy
정치 선전, propaganda
정치 활동을 하는, political
정치에 관심이 있는, political
정치인, politician, statesman
정치적 망명, political asylum
정치적 성향, politics
정치적으로, politically
정치적으로 정당한, politically correct
정치적으로 정당한 사람들, politically correct
정치적인, political
정치학, politics
정크 푸드, junk food
정통, orthodoxy
정통으로, smack
정통의, orthodox
정통이 아닌, unorthodox
정통적으로, classically
정통한, knowledgeable, well-informed
정평, reputation
정하다, decide, fix, ordain, set, settle

정해지지 않은, indefinite
정해진, given, set
정향, clove
정형(定形) stereotype
정형되다, stereotype
정형화된, stereotypical
정화, purification
정화 처리되지 않은, raw
정화하다, clean, cleanse, purify
정확, accuracy
정확성, accuracy, precision
정확하게, accurately, dead, exactly
정확하게 제 모습을 보여 주다, justice
정확한, accurate, correct, exact, flat, good, precise
정확한 위치를 집어내다, pinpoint
정확함, correctness
정확히, clockwork, correctly, day, exactly, precisely
정확히 규명하다, pinpoint
정확히 말해서, exactly
정확히 밝히다, finger
정확히 알다, finger
정황, circumstance
정황으로 보아, nature
젖가슴, breast
젖꼭지, nipple
젖병, bottle
젖소, cow
젖어 있다, wallow
젖은, wet
젖을 떼다, wean
젖을 먹다, feed
젖을 먹이다, feed
젖을 짜다, milk
젖히다, tilt
젖힘, tilt
제 1 야당의, shadow
제 1인자, ace
제 2언어, second language
제 3차의, tertiary
제 모습을 갖추게 하다, shape
제 몸 이상을 갖다, hog
제 소견으로는, humble
제 역할을 다하다, weight
제 위치에, position
제 잇속을 챙기다, fatten
제 정신의, sane
제 정신이 아닌, beside, distraught
제1선매권, refusal
제1차 세계 대전 때의 전장, trench
제2언어로서 영어, ESL
제2의 천성, nature
제각각, each
제값을 하는, salt
제거, clearance, elimination, purge, removal
제거된, missing
제거하다, clear, eliminate, knock, mop, purge, remove, rid, take, weed
제곱, sq, square
제곱근, square root
제곱하다, square
(~) 제공, courtesy, injection, provision
제공하다, arm, furnish, lend, offer, provide, put
제국, empire
제국의, imperial
제국주의, imperialism
제국주의자, imperialist
제기랄, darn, fuck
제기하다, lodge, raise, suggest
제단, altar, shrine
제대로, correctly, right
제대로 다루다, justice
제대로 돌보지 않다, neglect
제대로 알다, straight
제대로 알리다, straight
제대로 작동하는, order
제대로 작동하지 않다, malfunction
제도, institution
제도적, institutional
제도화하다, institutionalize
제동, brake

제동을 걸다, spanner
제등, lantern
제때를 만나다, moment
제로, zero
제로섬 게임, zero-sum game
제막식을 하다, unveil
제멋대로, erratically, wildly
제멋대로 구는, self-indulgent
제멋대로 굶, self-indulgence
(~을) 제멋대로 하게 놔두다, indulge
제멋대로 하다, murder
제멋대로 하도록 내버려 두다, rope
제멋대로의, crass, wild
제멋대로인, unruly, wayward
제명되다, expel
제모, cap
제목, heading, re, title
제목을 부여하다, entitle
제목을 붙이다, title
제물, offering, prey, sacrifice
제물로 바치다, sacrifice
제물의, sacrificial
(~에게) 제반 편의를 제공하다, cater
제발, please, sake
제방, bank, dike, embankment
제복, uniform
제복을 입는, uniformed
제본되다, bind
제분소, mill
제분하다, mill
제비, swallow
제비꽃, violet
제비뽑기 하다, lot
제비뽑다, draw
제빵사, baker
제삼자, outsider
제설차, snowplow
제수, sister-in-law
제시, presentation
제시 가격, asking price, offer
제시간에 맞춘, time
제시되어, forward
제시하다, give, offer, present, produce, proffer, put, set
(~을) 제시하여, production
제안, offer, proposition, suggestion
제안하다, move, offer, propose, suggest
제압하다, defeat, overpower, overwhelm, zap
제약, constraint, limit, limitation, restriction
제약업, pharmacy
제약의, pharmaceutical
제약하다, constrain
제어, control
제어력을 잃은, runaway
제어하기 힘든, obstinate
제어하다, contain, control
제어할 수 없는, control
제외, exception, exclusion
제외되다, leave, sideline
제외된, out
(~을) 제외하고, apart, bar, but, except, excepting, excluding, exclusion, exclusive, short
(~을) 제외하고는, barring, beyond, exception
제외하다, exclude, shut
제의, offer, suggestion
제의하다, dangle, offer
제이페그 파일, JPEG
제일 중요한, overriding
제일선, cutting edge
제일의, number one
제자, disciple, pupil
제자리, place
제자리를 벗어난, place
제자리를 찾다, place
제자리에 안 놓여, hook
제자리에 있는, place
제자리에 있다, belong
제작, construction, making, production
제작 과정, making
제작에 참여한 사람들, credit
제작자, maker, producer

제작하다, construct, create, produce
제재, sanction, subject matter
제정, enactment, institution
제정신, sanity, wit
제정신으로, mind
제정신을 잃다, mind
제정신이 아니게 만들다, wit
제정신이 아닌, insane, mind
제정하다, enact, establish, institute, make, ordain
제조, manufacture, manufacturing
제조 공장, mill
제조사, make, maker
제조업, industry
제조업체, manufacturer
제조하다, manufacture
제지, deterrence
제지하다, hold, inhibit
제철보다 빨리, early
제쳐 두다, lay
제쳐놓다, put
제쳐두고, aside
제초기, lawnmower
제출하다, file, hand, lodge, propose, send, submit
제치다, humble
제트 스키, jet ski
제트 엔진, jet engine
제트기, jet
제트기로 가다, jet
제품, product
제품 계열, product line
제한, limitation, restriction
제한 속도, speed limit
제한 없는, open-ended
제한 조치, control
제한되다, control
제한된, confined, restricted
제한을 받지 않는, unrestricted
제한적 관행, restrictive practice
제한적인, qualified, restrictive
제한하는, limiting
제한하다, box, confine, constrict, keep, limit, restrict
제휴, association, cooperation, link-up
제휴하는, affiliate, cooperate
젠체하는, self-important
젠체함, self-importance
젤, gel
젤로, Jell-O
젤리, jelly
젤리 상태, jelly
조, key, team
조가비, shell
조각, carving, cut, fragment, likeness, morsel, patch, piece, scrap, sculpture, segment
조각 그림 맞추기, jigsaw
조각가, sculptor
조각그림 맞추기, puzzle
조각나다, splinter
조각내다, carve, splinter
조각되다, sculpt
조각보 깁기 식의, patchwork
조각상, carving
조각술, sculpture
조각이 떨어져 나간, chipped
조각조각 떨어져 나가다, flake
조각조각 자르다, cut
조각하다, carve, sculpt
조개, clam
조개껍데기, shell
조개류, shellfish
조건, condition, qualification, stipulation, term
조건 짓다, determine
조건 형성, conditioning
조건부 유급 휴직, gardening leave
(~을) 조건으로, condition, provided, providing
(~을) 조건으로 하여, subject
(~을) 조건으로 한, conditional
조건으로서 지정하다, specify
조건을 달다, qualify, stipulate

조건절의, conditional
(~이라는) 조건하에, understanding
조경, landscaping
조경하다, landscape
조금, bit, crack, dab, little, one, ounce, slightly, snatch, snippet, some, spot, touch, trifle, vaguely, wee
조금 깎다, trim
조금 떨어진 곳에, way
조금 마시다, sip
조금 흐르다, trickle
조금도, any, earth, none, slight
조금도 ~ 아닌, half
조금도 ~하지 않다, bit
조금도 ~하지 않은, none
조금도 개의치 않다, hoot
조금씩, bit, piecemeal, sparingly
조금씩 따오다, cull
조금씩 뜯어먹다, nibble
조금씩 베어 먹기, nibble
조금씩 베어 먹다, nibble
조금씩 움직이다, inch, trickle
조금씩 움직임, trickle
조금씩 지치게 하다, wear
조금씩 해치다, undermine
조금씩 허물어지다, crumble
조금씩 흘러나오다, ooze
조금씩 흘리다, ooze
조금씩의, piecemeal
조금의, little, mere, slight, some
조금의 ~도, whatever, whatsoever
조급증, impatience, mania
조급하게, impatiently
조급하게 굴다, gun
조급한, impatient
조급함, impatience
조기퇴직 특별우대조치, golden parachute
조기에, prematurely
조기의, early, premature
조깅, jog, jogging
조깅하는 사람, jogger
조깅하다, jog
조끼, vest, waistcoat
조난, distress
조난 사고, shipwreck
조난 신호, SOS
조난당하다, shipwreck
조달, procurement
조달하다, procure, raise
조동사, auxiliary, modal
조랑말, pony
조력자, facilitator
조련사, handler, trainer
조례, act, ordinance
조롱, derision, jibe, mockery, ridicule, taunt
조롱거리, mockery
조롱하는, derisive, mocking
조롱하다, deride, jibe, mock, piss, ridicule, taunt
조류, algae, tide
조리, coherence, cookery
조리 있게 잘 받아치다, field
조리 있는, coherent
조리가 없는, disjointed
조리개, aperture
조리대, countertop
조리법, recipe
조리의, culinary
조리하다, cook
조립, assembly, construction
조립용품 한 벌, kit
조립하다, assemble, build, compose, put
조만간, now
조망, panorama, vista
조망점, viewpoint
조망하는, panoramic
조명, illumination, lighting
조명탄, flare
조명등, floodlight
조명등으로 밝히다, floodlight
조명하다, illuminate
조목, clause
조목별로 작성하다, itemize

조문, condolence
조문객, mourner
조부모, grandparent
조사, examination, inquest, inquiry, inspection, investigation, probe, survey
조사관, surveyor
조사의, investigative
조사자, investigator
조사하다, ascertain, check, examine, go, inspect, investigate, look, probe, survey
조산사, midwife
조산하여, prematurely
조산한, premature
조상, ancestor
조상 대대로의, ancestral
조상(彫像), statue
조생종의, early
조선소, shipyard
조성지, development
조세 우대의, offshore
조세 피난지, tax haven
조세액, taxation
조소, jeering
조소하다, jeer
조속한, quick
조수, assistant, auxiliary, tide
조수의, tidal
조숙한, precocious
조식과 석식이 포함된 숙박시설, half board
조심, caution
조심성 있는, guarded
조심스러운, careful, conservative, sedate
조심스런, controlled
조심스럽게, carefully, cautiously, conservatively, discreetly
조심스럽게 말하면, mildly
조심하는, cautious, wary
(~에) 조심하다, mind, step, watch
조심하여, care, guard, warily
조심해, look, watch
조약, pact, treaty
조약돌, pebble, shingle
조언, advice, counsel, counseling, hint, pointer, tip
조언자, mentor
조언하다, advise, counsel, mentor
조여 붙이다, clamp
조용한, low, private, quiet, sedate, serene, silent, soft, subdued
조용한 공간, den
조용함, quietness
조용해지다, quiet, quieten
조용해진, hushed
조용해짐, hush
조용히, hush, quietly, serenely, silently, softly
조용히 걷다, pad
조용히 시키다, hush, quiet, quieten
조용히 하다, hush
조우하다, come
조율하다, tune
조의, condolence
조이 스틱, joystick
조이는 듯한 느낌, knot
조이다, knot
조인, signing
조인국, signatory
조인기관, signatory
조작, fabrication, fix, manipulation, operation, rigging
조작자, operator
조작하다, fabricate, fiddle, fix, manipulate, massage, operate, program, rig, tamper
조잡하게, shoddily
조잡한, shoddy
조장하는, fertile
조절 가능한, adjustable
조절 장치, mixer
조절판, throttle
조정, adjustment, coordination, reconciliation
조정(漕艇), rowing
조정실, cockpit

조정자, coordinator
조정책, corrective
조정하다, adjust, calibrate, coordinate, fiddle, revise, rework, set
조제, preparation
조제해 주다, dispense
조조할인, early bird
조종, manipulation, navigation
조종 장치, control
조종사, airman, navigator, pilot
조종석, cockpit
조종하다, fly, manipulate, navigate, pilot, steer
조준, aim
조준하다, aim
조증(躁症), mania
조지 왕조 시대의, Georgian
조지 왕조풍의, Georgian
조직, apparatus, composition, logistics, machine, machinery, make-up, orchestration, organization, outfit, texture, tissue
조직 내의, in-house
조직 체계, scheme
조직 폭력배, gangster
조직망, network, system
조직상의, organizational
조직적, organizational, systemic
조직적으로, methodically
조직적인, methodical
조직적인 운동, drive
조직책, coordinator, organizer
조직체, structure
조직하는, organizational
조직하다, assemble, compose, coordinate, form, get, mount, orchestrate, organize, stage, structure
조직화된, organized
조짐, rumbling, sign, symptom
조짐을 보이다, threaten
조짐이 보여, horizon
조차도, even
조치, action, measure, move, step
조치를 취하다, do, move
조카, nephew
조카딸, niece
조커, joker
조폐국, mint
조합, association, brotherhood
조항, article, clause, provision
조형, figurative
조화, harmony, match, reconciliation
조화되지 않는, irreconcilable
조화롭게 움직이도록 하다, coordinate
조화를 이루다, blend, go, harmonize, interface
(~와) 조화를 이루어, coordination
조화시키다, coordinate, harmonize, interface, reconcile
조회, assembly
조회수, hit
족보의, genealogical
족속, lot
족쇄, chain
족장, chief
족집게, pincer
족하다, do
존경, esteem, regard, respect, reverence
존경받는, prestigious, revered
존경받을 만하게, honorably
존경을 받는, respected
존경하다, look, respect, revere, think
존경할 만한, creditable, honorable, respectable
존속하다, persist, stand
존엄성, dignity
존재, being, entity, existence, presence
존재하는, around
존재하다, exist, find, occur, reside
존재하여, there

존재하지 않는, nonexistent
존중, esteem, respect
존중하다, respect
졸, pawn
졸다, doze, nod, snooze
졸도하다, keel
졸려서, sleepily
졸리는, drowsy
졸린, sleepy
졸린 듯이, sleepily
졸아들다, reduce
졸업, graduation
졸업생, graduate
졸업식, commencement, graduation
졸업장, diploma
졸업하다, graduate
졸음, drowsiness
졸이게 하다, guess
졸이다, knot, reduce
졸작, trash
졸필, scrawl
좀, quite
좀 많이 어림잡다, overestimate
좀 신나는 일, laugh
좀 이른 감이 있다., early
좀이 쑤시다, tingle
좀이 쑤심, tingle
좀처럼 ~ 않는, seldom
좀처럼 ~하지 않는, rarely
좀처럼 없어지지 않는다, die
좀처럼 없어지지 않다, linger
좀처럼 진에이 없는, hard
좁고 긴 지역, strip
좁아지다, narrow
좁아짐, narrowing
좁은, narrow
좁은 길, footpath, track
좁은 통로 다리, catwalk
좁음, narrowness
좁히다, narrow
종, bell, servant
종(種), species
종가, closing price
종가가 ~이 되다, close
종결, closure, ending, end, termination
종결시키다, terminate
종결짓다, finalize
종결하다, close
종교, creed, faith, religion
종교의, religious
종교적인, sacred, spiritual
종국의, eventual
종기, boil
종렬, column
종료된, up
종류, class, description, genus, kind, sort, strain, type, variety
종마, stallion, stud
종말, death
종목, description
종묘원, nursery
종사자, servant
종사하게 되다, go
종사하는, engaged
종사하다, engage
종소리, peal
종속, dependence, subordination
(~에) 종속된, subject
(~에) 종속시키다, subordinate
종속적으로, dependent, subsidiary
종신형, life
종아리, calf
종양, growth, tumor
종언, demise
종업원, clerk, servant, waiter, waitress
종이, paper
종이 끼우개, folder
종이 올리다, ring
종이 클립, paper clip
종이로 인쇄된 문서, hard copy
종이를 따라 그리다, trace
종이에, paper
종잇조각, slip
종자돈, seed money
종족, tribe

종종, time
종종걸음으로 걷다, trot
종종걸음으로 달리다, scuttle
종지, end
종지부를 찍다, stamp
종착하다, terminate
종파의, sectarian
종합, synthesis
종합 계획, master plan
종합 시설, center
종합 정보 통신망, ISDN
종합 정책, package
종합하다, piece, synthesize
종합한, put
좇다, comply
(~를) 좇아 행동하다, act
좋게, nicely, well
좋게 안내해 주다, flatter
(~했으면) 좋겠다, do, like, mind
(~이면) 좋겠다고 생각하다, wish
좋기만 한, sweetness
좋다, better, excellent, fine
좋다고 했다가 싫다고 하곤 하다, hot
좋아, all right, good
좋아 봤자, best
좋아!, great
좋아서 미치는, crazy
좋아하는, fond, partial
좋아하는 것, like
좋아하다, care, like, take
좋아하지 않음, dislike
좋아함, fondness, liking, taste
좋으실 대로 하세요, guest
좋은, good, high, lovely, nice, superior, unbelievable
좋은 기회, break, opening
좋은 기회를 놓치다, boat
좋은 냄새가 나는, scented
좋은 뜻으로, cause
좋은 생각, brainstorm
좋은 품질, quality
좋을 대로 하다, suit
좋지 않게, unfavorably
좋지 않게 생각하다, disapprove
좋지 않은, bad, negative, unfavorable, wrong
좋지 않은 영향을 미치다, tell
좌경화, left
좌석, place, seat
좌석 배치, seating
좌석 안내원, usher
좌시하다, stand
좌우 열, wing
좌우간에, rate
좌우되다, govern
(~에) 좌우되어, mercy
좌우로, side
좌우명, motto, watchword
좌우의, lateral
좌우하다, guide, influence
좌익, leftist
좌익의, left-wing
좌절, collapse, frustration, upset
좌절감을 주는, frustrating
좌절감을 주다, deflate
좌절되다, collapse
좌절시키다, frustrate, let, thwart
좌절하다, crush
좌절한, deflated, frustrated, upset
좌우지 하다, roost
좌천, demotion, relegation
좌천되다, downgrade
좌천시키다, demote, relegate
좌초되다, ground
좌초하다, beach, ground
좌초하여, aground
좌파, left, left-wing
좌표, coordinate
좌현, port
좌현의, port
죄, blame, charge, guilt, sin, vice
죄 많은, sinful
죄 없는, innocent
죄값, penalty
죄다, tighten
죄다 팔아 치우다, sell
죄를 뒤집어씌우다, frame
죄를 범함, guilt

죄를 씌우다, incriminate
죄를 저지르다, offend
죄를 짓다, sin
죄목, count
죄송하지만, afraid
죄송합니다, excuse, forgive, pardon
죄송합니다만, hate, sorry
죄수, convict, prisoner
죄수가 아닌, free
죄악, sin, sinfulness
죄의식, guilt
죄인, criminal, sinner
죄책감, remorse
죄책감을 느끼는, guilty
죄책감을 느끼며, guiltily
죔쇠, clamp
주, week
주 1회의, weekly
주 경찰관, trooper
주 사이의, interstate
주 활동 무대, turf
주(州), state
주가 지수, share index
주간 고속도로, interstate
주간 보호 시설, day care
주간의, daytime
주간지, weekly
주거 부정의, fixed
주거의, residential
주거지, residence
주격, scoop
주고받기, interchange
주고받다, exchange, trade
주고받음, give
주관성, subjectivity
주관적으로, subjectively
주관적인, subjective
주교, bishop
주교에 임명되다, consecrate
주근깨, freckle
주급 봉투, pay packet
주기, cycle
주기적으로, periodically
주기적인, cyclical, periodic,
 periodical
주기적임, regularity
주다, accord, assign, award,
 concede, confer, do, give, hand,
 hold, impart, invest, offer,
 present, serve
주도, initiative
주도권, initiative
주도하다, initiative, lead
주동자, instigator
주된, basic, main, predominant,
 predominantly, principal, ruling
주된 요소, base
주둔, presence
주둔되다, station
(~에) 주둔시키다, garrison
주둔지, camp, garrison
(~에) 주둔하다, garrison
주둥이, mouth, spout
주둥이가 ~한, -mouthed
주례를 맡다, marry
주로, chiefly, largely, main, mainly,
 mostly, primarily, principally
주로 앉아 지내는, sedentary
주로 앉아서 일하는, sedentary
주루 코치, coach
주류, mainstream
주류 판매 허가를 받은, licensed
주류 판매점, off-licence
주름, crease, fold, line, pleat,
 wrinkle
주름 장식, frill, ruffle
주름살이 생기다, wrinkle
주름을 펴다, smooth
주름이 잡힌, pleated
주름이 진, wrinkled
주름지게 만들다, wrinkle
주름지다, wrinkle
주름진, creased
주립 대학, state school, state
 university
주말, weekend
주머니, pocket, pouch
주머니 사정, pocket

주머니 사정이 안 좋은, pocket
주머니 속에 집어넣다, pocket
주먹, fist
주먹으로 치다, punch
주먹질, punch
주목, attention, publicity
주목받는, noted
주목을 받다, discover
주목하다, attention, note, notice,
 pay
주목할 만한, notable, remarkable
주무르다, knead, manipulate, rub
주무름, manipulation
주문, charm, mantra, order, spell
주문 대장, order book
주문 제작 기간, lead time
주문되어 있는, order
주문을 받아서, order
주문품, order
주문하다, order, place
주물, cast
주민, inhabitant, people, resident
주방, galley, kitchen
주방장, chef
주변, margin, periphery
주변 장치, peripheral
주변부, fringe
주변에, round
주변의, around, peripheral
주변의 모양, ambience
주변적인, marginal, peripheral
주부, housewife
주사, injection, jab
주사기, syringe
주사위, dice
주사하다, inject
주석, note, tin
주석을 달다, annotate, gloss
주선하다, sponsor
주성분, base
주소, address
주소록, address book, directory
주술적 행위, charm
주스, juice
주시받고 있는, watch
주시하다, follow, rest, watch
주식, staple, stock
주식 공모 회사, public company,
 public limited company
주식 매점, buyout
주식 발행, share issue
주식 시장, market, stock market
주식 시장 강세, bull market
주식 시장 약세, bear market
주식 자본금, share capital
주식 처분액, stock
주식을 공개하다, public
주식의 매점, greenmail
주식회사, Corp., Inc., plc
주안점, bullet point
주어, subject
주어지다, fall, go
(~이) 주어지면, given
주어진, given
(~에서) 주역을 맡다, star
주연으로 등장시키다, star
주연의, leading
주연하다, feature
주요 간선 도로, highway
주요 관심사, forefront
주요 뉴스, headline
주요 대회, major
주요 역할자, player
주요 지형물, landmark
주요소, staple
주요한, arch-, basic, main, major,
 staple
주위, perimeter
주위 환경의, environmental
(~의) 주위를 회전하다, revolve
주위에, around, round
주유기, pump
주유소, gas station, petrol station,
 service station
주의, attention, caution, doctrine,
 line, NB, tenet, warning
주의 깊게, attentively, hard
주의 깊게 살펴보다, eye

주의 깊은, attentive, hard
주의 사항, do, rule
(~에) 주의를 기울이다, heed
주의를 끌다, attention
주의를 끌지 않은, unnoticed
주의를 딴 데로 돌리게 하는 것,
 diversion
주의를 딴 데로 쏠리게 하는,
 diversionary
주의를 주다, warn
주의를 환기시키다, spotlight
주의보, advisory
주의시키다, caution
주의의, cautionary
주의하다, beware, mind
주인, host, master, owner
주인 없는, stray
주인공, hero, protagonist
주인공의, heroic
주인이 바뀌다, hand
주입하다, hammer, inject, instill
주자, racer, runner
주장, argument, assertion,
 captain, case, claim, insistence,
 pretension, proposition, skipper
주장 임기, captaincy
주장 지위, captaincy
주장을 바꾸다, ground
주장을 입증하다, point
주장을 철회하다, climb
주장의 요지, contention
주장이 되다, captain
주장하는, insistent
주장하다, allege, argue, assert,
 claim, contend, insist,
 maintain, make, press, pretend,
 protest
주재하다, chair, preside
주저, hesitancy, hesitation,
 indecision
주저하다, collapse
주저하는, hesitant, reluctant
주저하다, hesitate, waver
주저하며, hesitantly
주저하며 말하다, venture
주저하지 마시고 전화하세요,
 hesitate
주저하지 않는, quick
주저함, reserve
주전론자, hawk
주전자, jug, kettle, pitcher
주절대다, babble
주제, subject, subject matter,
 theme, topic
주제넘게 ~하다, presume
주제넘은, presumptuous
(~을) 주제로 하다, concern
주제를 바꾸다, move
주제를 알게 해 주다, place
주조하다, cast, mint
주주, shareholder, stakeholder,
 stockholder
주중, week
주지의, well-known
주차, parking
주차 건물, parking garage
주차 공간, parking
주차 요금 계산기, parking meter
주차 요금 징수기, meter
주차장, car park, parking lot
주차하다, park
주창, advocacy
주창자, advocate, exponent,
 protagonist
주창하다, advance, advocate
주체스러운, cumbersome
주최자, host, organizer
주최하다, host
주축, pivot
주춤거리다, falter, hang
주춤하다, flinch
주택, house, housing
주택 담보 대출, mortgage
주택단지, housing estate
주파수, frequency, wavelength
(~에) 주파수가 맞추어지다, tune
주파수대, channel
주파수대를 변환하다, scramble

주행 거리, mileage
주형, mold
주황색의, orange
죽, ever, throughout
죽 뻗어 있다, sprawl
죽 찢긴 자국, slit
죽 찢다, slit
죽 펼쳐져 있다, sprawl
죽기보다 싫어하다, dead
죽는, dying
죽다, die, pass, perish, snuff
죽도록 ~하고 싶다, die
죽도록 ~하다, kill
죽도록 고생시키다, hell
죽도록 고생하다, hell
죽도록 두들겨 맞다, pulp
죽어 가는, dying
죽어도, dead, kill
죽어라고, kill
죽어야 할 운명, mortality
죽어야 할 운명의, mortal
죽여버리다, kill
죽은, dead, lifeless
죽은 듯이, deathly
죽은 듯한, dead, lifeless
죽은 사람들, dead
죽을 지경이 되게 하다, kill
(~해서) 죽을 지경이다, die
죽을 지경인, death
죽음, death, passing
(~의) 죽음에 책임이 있다, blood
죽음을 초래하는, fatal
죽음의 덫, death trap
죽이기, kill
(~을) 죽이다, do, life, zap
준 대로 돌아오다, reciprocate
준~, associate
준결승, semi, semifinal
준공식, inauguration
준공식을 거행하다, inaugurate
준군사 조직, paramilitary
준군사 조직 대원들, paramilitary
준법 투쟁을 하다, rule
준비, arrangement, logistics,
 preparation
준비 없는, impromptu
준비 없이, hand, top
준비 없이 첨병 뛰어들다, end
준비 없이 홀로 내던져지다, end
준비 운동, warm-up
준비 운동을 하다, warm
(~할) 준비가 되어 있는, poised
(~할) 준비가 되어 있다, gear
준비가 되지 않은, unprepared
준비하고 있다, wait
준비된, ready, set
준비를 갖추다, ready
(~할) 준비를 하다, gear
준비시키다, prime
준비의, preparatory
준비하다, arrange, fix, line,
 organize, prepare, see
준비해 두다, put
(~을) 준비해 주다, fix
준수, compliance, observance,
 respect
준수하다, adhere, observe, respect
준엄한, stern
준의료 활동 종사자, paramedic
준준결승, quarter-final
줄, cord, file, line, queue, rank,
 row, streak, stream, string,
 stripe, tether
줄거리, plot
줄곧, along, always, right, solidly,
 straight, through
줄기, cane, funnel, shaft, stalk,
 stem, stream
줄기세포, stem cell
줄기처럼 길게 뻗어 나온 땅덩이나 물,
 arm
줄넘기, skipping
줄넘기를 하다, skip
줄다, decline, decrease, diminish,
 fall, lessen, shorten
줄무늬, streak, stripe
줄무늬가 있는, striped
(~에) 줄무늬를 그리다, streak

줄어들다, come, dwindle, shrink, wane
줄어 쓰다, abbreviate
줄어서, short
줄어지다, thin
줄을 긋다, rule, streak
(~와) 줄을 맞추어, line
줄을 서다, queue
줄이다, compress, cut, decrease, diminish, knock, lessen, narrowly, pare, reduce, roll, run, shorten, shrink, slim, thin, whittle
줄일 대로 줄어, bone
줄자, tape measure
줄줄 이어지다, stream
줄줄 흐르다, ooze
줄질하다, file
줄표, dash
줌 렌즈로 피사체를 확대하다, zoom
중간, cross
중간 가격의, mid-range
중간 관리자, middle management
중간 광고, commercial break
중간 기착지의, transit
중간 상인, middleman
중간 상태, limbo
중간 정도의, moderately
중간 지대, no-man's land
중간 지점에, halfway
중간 크기의, regular
중간 휴식, half-time
중간 휴식 시간, intermission, interval
중간값, mean
중간색의, medium
중간에, halfway
중간에 낀, intervening
중간의, average, halfway, intermediate, intervening, medium
중간적 시기, no-man's land
중간점, interface
중간쯤, midway
중간쯤의, midway
중개소, agency
중개업체, brokerage
중개인, agent, broker
중개자, go-between, intermediary
중계하다, relay
중고의, secondhand, used
중고품을 파는, secondhand
중공업, heavy industry
중괄호, brace
중급의, intermediate
중급자, intermediate
중기, medium-term
중기적으로, term
중년, middle age
중년의, mature, middle-aged
중단, cut, disruption, interruption, suspension, termination, withdrawal
중단 없는, unbroken
중단되다, beat, discontinue, punctuate, stall, track
중단되지 않은, uninterrupted
중단시키다, arrest, disrupt, interrupt, plug, scotch, stall
중단하다, abort, cease, cut, discontinue, drop, halt, head, quit, shut, stop, track
중대, company
중대성, importance
중대하게, vitally
중대한, critical, crucial, fateful, grave, grievous, important, large, momentous, serious, vital, weighty
중대한 갈림길, crossroads
중대한 시기, crunch
중대함, gravity
중도, ground, middle
중도 탈락자, wastage
중도 탈락하다, drop
중도 해약 반환금, surrender value
중도에 좌파하다, day
중도의, middle-of-the-road

중도파, center
중독, addiction, habit, poisoning
중독되다, poison
중독된, addicted, hooked, married
중독성이 약한, soft
중독자, addict
중동, Middle East
중등, secondary
중등 교육 자격시험, GCSE
중등학교, high school, secondary school
중력, gravity
중력의, gravitational
중력장, field
중립, neutrality, neutral
중립국, neutral
중립의, neutral
중립적, neutral
중립적인 태도를 취하다, fence
중매인, go-between
중반에, midway
중반의, midway
중복, duplication
중부지방, Midlands
중뿔난, nosy
중산층, Main Street, middle class
중산층의, middle class
중상, slander, slur, smear
중상하다, slander, smear
중성의, neutral
중세의, medieval
중심, center, eye, focus, heart
중심 되는, central
중심 탑, keep
중심가, center, Main Street
중심도시, metropolis
중심부, core, heartland
중심부에, centrally
중심부의, central
(~를 중심에 두다, revolve
중심으로, centrally, round
(~) 중심의, -centered
중심적인, central
중심적인 인물, pillar
중심지, capital, center, hive, hub, stronghold
중압, strain
중압하는, strain
중앙, center, middle
중앙 분리대 쪽의, outside
중앙 분리대가 있는 고속도로, divided highway
중앙 집권, centralization
중앙 집권적으로, centrally
중앙 집권화하다, centralize
중앙 처리 장치, CPU
중앙난방, central heating
중앙에, centrally
중앙의, central
중언부언하다, repeat
중얼거리다, mumble, murmur, mutter
중얼거림, mumble, murmur, mutter, muttering
(~) 중에, course, during, middle
중에서, between, out
중요도, status
중요성, emphasis, import, importance, magnitude, significance, validity, weight
중요성을 인식시키다, impress
(~보다) 중요시하다, place
중요하게, importantly, prominently, significantly
중요하게 여기다, care
중요하다, count, matter, outweigh
중요하지 않은, account, immaterial, irrelevant, meaningless, unimportant
중요하지 않은 것, nothing
중요한, big, dear, heart, high, imperative, important, precious, primary, prior, prominent, significant, strong, valid
중요한 단어, operative
중요한 부분, parcel

중요한 사람, someone
중요한 역할을 하다, feature
중요한 요소이나, way
중요한 일, business
중용, ground, moderation
중위, lieutenant
중장비의, heavy
중재, arbitration, mediation
중재관, negotiator
중재자, mediator, middleman
중재하다, arbitrate, broker, mediate
중점, stress
중점을 두다, center
중죄, felony
중지시키다, stop
중진, heavyweight
중추, hub
중추부, inner circle
중추적인, pivotal
중퇴자, dropout
중퇴하다, drop
중퇴한, dropout
중학교, junior high, junior high school
중화하다, neutralize
쥐, cramp, mouse, rat, spasm
쥐 죽은 듯이, deathly
쥐고 아무 짓도 안 하다, sit
쥐고 흔들다, roost, sway
쥐다, take
쥐뿔도, bugger all, sod
쥐새끼 같은 놈, rat
쥐어뜯다, tear
쥐어짜다, arm
(~에게) 쥐어사는, thumb
즈음, near
즉, i.e., namely, say, that, viz.
즉각, spot
즉각의, immediate
즉각적인, instant, prompt, ready
즉결의, summary
즉사하다, outright
즉석 식품, fast food
즉석에서, hand, spot, top
즉석에서 만들다, improvise
즉석에서 하다, improvise
즉석의, impromptu
즉시, bat, fast, hand, hat, immediately, instantly, instantaneously, once, promptly, right, there
즉시 사용할 수 있는, ready
즉시의, immediate, instantaneous
즉위식, coronation
즉위하다, crown
즉흥 연주를 하다, improvise
즉흥적으로, spontaneously
즉흥적인, cuff, spontaneous
즐거운, enjoyable, fun, good, happy, jolly, pleasant, pleasurable, upbeat
즐거운 시간, quality time
즐거운 일, pleasure
즐거움, amusement, delight, enjoyment, pleasure, relish
즐거워하는, amused
즐거워하다, enjoy
즐겁게, pleasantly
즐겁게 보내다, amuse
즐겁게 하다, amuse, delight, entertain, please
즐겁게 해 주는, entertaining
즐긴다는, appreciative
(~를) 즐겨 마시는 사람, drinker
즐겨찾기, bookmark
즐기다, appreciate, enjoy, relish
즐김, appreciation
즙이 많은, juicy, luscious, succulent
증가, boom, build-up, growth, increase, increment, rise
증가시키다, augment, elevate, increase, perk, push, step, swell
증가하고 있는, increase
증가하는, upward
증가하다, explode, increase, perk,

rise, swell
증가하여, up, upward
증강시키다, beef
증거, evidence, proof, testament, testimony
증거 서류, documentary, documentation
증거 자료, documentation
증거가 없는, unsubstantiated
증거물, exhibit
증권 거래소, stock exchange
증권 인수인, underwriter
증권 중개업, stockbroking
증권 중개인, stockbroker
증권 회사, share shop
증기, steam, vapor
증대, enlargement, growth, increase, increment
증대시키다, augment, magnify
증대하고 있는, increase
증대하다, grow, intensify
증류, distillation
증류기, still
증류되다, distill
증류주, spirit
증명, certification, demonstration, testimony
증명서, certificate, testimonial
증명하다, attest, demonstrate, prove, show
증발, evaporation
증발되다, evaporate
증발하다, evaporate
증보판, supplement
증상, symptom
증서, deed
증설, extension
증식, multiplication
증언, testimony
증언하다, attest, evidence, testify
증오, animosity, hate, hatred
증오하다, hate
증원 병력, reinforcement
증원하다, reinforce
증인, witness
증인석, stand
증정, presentation
증정하다, present
증진, advancement, enhancement
증축, extension
증축하다, extend
증폭, amplification
증폭기, amp, amplifier
증폭시키다, amplify
증폭하다, amplify
증후군, syndrome
지 알 이, GRE
지각, crust, lateness, perception, sense
지각하다, perceive
지갑, billfold, pocketbook, purse, wallet
지게 하다, hold
지겨운, jaded
지겨운 것, drag
지겨워 죽겠는, death
지구, district, earth, globe, neighborhood, quarter, world, zone
지구 대기권 밖, outer space
지구 온난화, global warming
지구(地區), sector
지구의, globe, terrestrial
지구촌 마을, global village
지국, branch
지그재그, zigzag
지그재그로 나아가다, zigzag
지그춤, jig
지극한 행복, bliss
지글거리다, sizzle
지금, now
지금까지는, hitherto
지금껏, time
지금부터, hence
지금으로서는, moment, time
지급, issue
지급받다, issue
지긋지긋하다, had

지긋지긋한, damned, dreaded, fucking, ghastly, hell, horrid, sick
지절이다, crack, spout
지끈거리다, throb
지나가게 하다, funnel, run
지나가는, passing
지나가는 사람, passer-by
지나가는 차에 편승하다, hitch
지나가다, funnel, go, pass
지나간, bygone, lost, past
지나갈 공간, passage
지나감, passing
지나다, pass, turn
지나서, past
지나치게, excess, extravagantly, inordinately, much, overly, painfully
지나치게 관대한, indulgent
지나치게 낙관하다, hope
지나치게 돈을 쓰다, overspend
지나치게 많은 보수를 받는, overpaid
(~에) 지나치게 우호적인, loaded
(~에) 지나치게 적대적인, loaded
지나치게 좋아함, weakness
지나치게 화려한, garish, ostentatious
지나치다, sight
지나친, bit, disproportionate, excessive, extravagant, inordinate, much
지나친 관용, indulgence
지나친 취재 열기, media circus
지난, gone, last
지난번, earlier
지난번 것, last
지난번의, last
지난한, tortuous
(~없이) 지내다, forego, keep, spend
지느러미, fin
지능, intellect, intelligence
지능 지수, IQ
지능을 가진, intelligent
(~을) 지니고, with
지니고 있다, hold
지니고 있다고 믿다, credit
지니다, bear, carry, have
(~을) 지닌, blessed, of
지다, go, lose, set
지대, belt
지대하게, profoundly
지대한, profound, supreme
지도, guidance, map, supervision, tuition
지도력, leadership
지도록 만들다, lose
지도를 만들다, chart, map
지도부, leadership
지도에 표시하다, plot
지도자, guru, leader, trainer
지도적인, leading
지도 책, atlas
지도층, hierarchy
지도하다, direct, guide, supervise
지독하게, appallingly, deadly, dreadfully, feverishly, hell
지독한, awful, dire, fearful, frightful, hell, horrible, intense, perfect, terrible
지독함, intensity
지독히, horribly
지독히도, deadly
지렛대, lever
지력, intellect
지력의, intellectual
지령, directive
지뢰, mine
지뢰가 매설되다, mine
지뢰밭, minefield
지루하게, tediously
지루하게 기다리다, heel
지루하다, bore
지루한, bland, bored, boring, dry, flat, slow, tedious, tiresome
지루한 사람, bore
지루함, boredom
지루해서 죽으려 하는, mind
지름, diameter

지름길, short cut
지름으로, across
지리, geography
지리적인, geographical
지리학, geography
지리학의, geographical
지리학적으로, geographically
(~을)지망하는, would-be
지면, ground
지명도, stature
지명되다, nominate
지명된, designate
지명수배를 받다, want
지명하다, designate, name
지목하다, single
지문, fingerprint, print
지문을 채취당하다, fingerprint
지문을 채취하다, fingerprint
지만, ground
지방, country, fat, province, region
지방 당국, municipality
지방 시민들, Main Street
지방 의회, council
지방 의회 의원, councilor
지방 자치, local government
지방 자치 단체, local government
지방 자치의, municipal
지방 자치체, municipality
지방 정부, local authority, local government
지방 청사, courthouse
지방 제거 수술, tuck
지방분, grease
지방을 함유한, fatty
지방의, fatty, local, provincial, regional, rural
지배, domination, hold
지배권, control
(~에) 지배받는, -ridden
지배력, grip
(~의) 지배를 받는, subject
지배인, controller, manager
지배적인, dominating
지배하는, ruling
지배하다, command, control, dominate, rule, sway, tune
지부, affiliate, arm, bureau
지분, interest, share, shareholding, tranche
지분거리다, bait
지분을 사다, buy
지불, payment, settlement
지불 능력, solvency
지불 능력이 있는, solvent
지불 불능, insolvency
지불 불능의, insolvent
지불 승인을 받다, clear
지불 완료, pd
지불을 거절하다, bounce
지불을 승인하다, clear
지불자, payer
지불하다, meet, pay, settle, tab
지붕, roof
지붕이 떠나가라 박수갈채를 받다, house
지붕이 있는 길거리 상가, arcade
지사, governor
지상에, ground
지상에서, ground
지상의, terrestrial
지선도로, side road
지성, intellect, mind
지성에 호소하는, cerebral
지성의, intellectual
지성인, mind
지세, feature
지속, continuation, maintenance, persistence
지속 기간, duration
지속되는, persistent
지속되다, hold, last, run, span
지속시키다, hold
지속적으로, constantly, continually, permanently, persistently
지속적으로 수정 가능한, open-ended
지속적인, constant, continual,

insistent, lasting, permanent, running
지속하는, enduring
지속하다, carry, endure, keep, maintain, sustain
지수, factor, index
지시, direction, instruction, order, word
지시봉, pointer
지시하다, dictate, instruct, order, prescribe, tell
지식, idea, knowledge, understanding
지식인, intellectual
지양하다, turn
지역, area, country, district, province, region, terrain, territory, zone
지역 번호, area code, dialling code
지역 사람들, community
지역 사회, community
지역 수당, weighting
(~) 지역 출신인 사람, native
지역구, county
지역민, local
지역에서, locally
지역의, local, regional
지역적인, spatial
지연, delay, hold-up, lag
지연 없이, quick
지연되다, stall
지연시키다, delay, drag, fall, set, stall
지연하다, fall
지엽, detail
지엽적으로, incidentally
지엽적인, incidental
지옥, hell
지용성의, soluble
지우개, eraser, rubber
지우다, black, blot, dismiss, erase, impose
지워 버리다, erase, rub
지원, application, assistance, support
지원병, volunteer
지원자, applicant, bidder, volunteer
지원하다, apply, sponsor, support, volunteer
지위, place, position, rank, rung, standing, status
지은, built
지인, acquaintance
지장을 주다, interfere
지저귀다, chatter, warble
지저귐, chatter
지저분하게, dirty
지저분한, dirty, messy, seedy, sordid
지저분한 곳, dump
지적, point
지적 능력, intelligence, mind
지적 호기심이 강한, lively
지적으로, intellectually
지적인, cerebral, intellectual
(~을) 지적하는, point
지점, branch, mark, point
지정되다, designate, earmark
지정된, set
지정하다, designate, earmark, name
지주, stake, strut
지주(支柱), prop
지주로 받치다, shore
지주회사, holding company
지중해, Mediterranean
지중해 연안, Mediterranean
지지, advocacy, backing, endorsement, favor, support
지지 않고 버티다, hold
(~에) 지지 않도록, outdo
지지난 밤, last
지지난 선거, last
지지난번 지도자, last
지지대, pole
지지자, friend, protagonist, supporter, well-wisher

지지직 소리 나다, crackle
지지층, constituency
(~을) 지지하는, for, side
지지하다, advocate, ally, back, come, espouse, prop, second, sponsor, stick, support, uphold
(~을) 지지하여, behind, favor, for, with
지지하지 않는, unsympathetic
지진, earthquake, quake
지진에 의한, seismic
지진의, seismic
지질, geology
지질학, geology
지질학의, geological
지질학자, geologist
지체, delay, lag, lateness
지체시키다, hold
지체하다, delay
지출, expenditure, outgoings, outlay
지층, bed
지치게 만들다, drain
지치게 하는, draining, punishing, tiring
지치게 하다, take
지치고 수척한, worn
지친, drained, jaded, tired, weary
지칠 대로 지친, exhausted
지칠 줄 모르고, tirelessly
지칠 줄 모르는, tireless
지침, directive, guide, guideline
지침(指針), pointer
지침서, tutorial
지켜보다, follow, look, watch
지키게 하다, hold
지키다, abide, defend, good, guard, hold, honor, insure, keep, observe, protect, salvage, stick, watch
지킴, observance
지탱, support
지탱하다, bear, hold, support, sustain
지팡이, cane, crook, stick
지퍼, zip, zipper
지퍼가 열리다, unzip
지퍼나 단추, fastening
지퍼로 잠그다, zip
지퍼로 잠기다, zip
지퍼를 내리다, open
지퍼를 내린, open
지퍼를 열다, unzip
지평선, horizon
지폐, banknote, bill, note
지표, barometer, benchmark, guideline, indicator
지푸라기도 잡으려 하다, straw
지프, Jeep
지하, below
지하 감옥, dungeon
지하 경제, black economy
지하 조직의, underground
지하가, restrain
지하도, underpass
지하보도, subway
지하실, cellar
지하에, ground, underground
지하의, subterranean, underground
지하철, metro, subway, tube, underground
지하층, basement
지형, geography, terrain
지혜, wisdom
(~와) 지혜를 겨루다, pit
지휘, command
지휘관, commandant, commander
지휘권, command
지휘봉, baton
지휘부, command
지휘자, conductor, director
지휘하는, commanding
지휘하다, command, conduct, head, lead, mastermind, shot
직각, right angle
직각 삼각형, right triangle
직각으로, right angle

직감, instinct
직감을 따르다, nose
(~을) 직감하는 능력이 있다, nose
직경, diameter
직계의, immediate
직공, operative
직관, instinct, intuition
직관적으로, intuitively
직관적인, intuitive
직립의, erect
(~에) 직면하다, come, confront, face
직면하여, face
직면해 있는, up
직모의, straight
직무, duty, work
직무 내용 설명서, job description
직물, fabric, textile
직분, province
직불 카드, debit card
직사 거리에서, point-blank
직사 거리의, point-blank
직사각형, rectangle
직사각형의, rectangular
직사각형의 물건, bar
직선의, linear
직선적으로, bluntly, directly
직선적인, blunt, direct, linear
직선적임, bluntness, directness
직설적인, straight
직속 상사, line manager
직시하게 하다, face
직시하다, face
직업, career, hat, line, occupation, profession, trade
직업상의, occupational, vocational
직업소개소, employment agency
직업여성, career woman
직업의, career, professional
직업이 있는, working
직업인, professional
직업인으로서, professionally
직업적으로, professionally
직업적인, professional
직역의, literal
직원, employee, staff, worker
직원 수, staffing
직원용의, service
(~을) 직원으로 두다, staff
직원이 ~한, staffed
직위, grade, post, title
직장, job, work, workplace
직장 생활을 시작하다, start
직장이 없는, out of work
직장이 있는, work
직전, eve
(~) 직전 기간, run-up
직전에, right, verge
(~하기) 직전인, brink
직접, direct, directly, first, first hand, immediately, ourselves, person, personally
직접 목적어, direct object
직접 얻은, first hand
직접 화법, direct discourse, direct speech
직접세, direct tax
직접의, direct, personal
직접적으로, immediately, personally
직접적이 아닌, indirect
직접적인, direct
직조, weaving
직조공, weaver
직조한, woven
직진하다, nose
직책, appointment, position
직통의, direct
직판점, outlet
직함, title
직항으로, nonstop
직행의, direct, directly, nonstop
직행의, direct
직후, aftermath
직후에, directly, right
진, gin, jeans
진가를 발휘하다, own
진격, advance, push

진격하다, advance, push
진공 상태, vacuum
진공청소기, hoover, vacuum cleaner
진공청소기로 청소하다, hoover, vacuum
진공청소기로 청소함, hoovering
진군, advance
진귀한, rare
진기한 것, curiosity, rarity
진기한 사람, rarity
진눈깨비, sleet
진단, assessment, diagnosis
진단받다, diagnose
진단용의, diagnostic
진단하다, assess
진동, vibration
진동 소리를 내다, throb
진동시키다, vibrate
진동하다, pulsate, pulse, tremble, vibrate
진두지휘하다, spearhead
진드기, mite
진력, exertion
진력이 난, fed up
진로, line, path, way
진로의, career
진료 상담소, clinic
진료 시간, surgery
진료소, clinic, surgery
진료실, doctor, doctor's office, office, surgery
진료의, clinical
진리, truth
진법, base
진보, advance, march, progress
진보당, liberal
진보당의, liberal
진보적인, progressive
진보주의자, liberal, progressive
진보하다, advance
진보한, enlightened
진부한, banal, commonplace, corny, stale
진부한 말, commonplace
진부한 문장, platitude
진부한 생각, cliché
진상, fact, truth
진상을 밝히다, bottom
진수, launch
진수시키다, launch
진술, proposition, statement
진술 조서, deposition
진술서, affidavit, declaration, statement
진술하다, state
진실, truth
진실 같다, ring
진실된, genuine, true
진실로, truly
진실성, sincerity
진실한, sincere
진심, seriousness
진심 어린, hearty
진심으로, god, heart, heartily, seriously, sincerely
진심으로 말하는, mean
진심인, serious
진압, crushing, suppression
진압하다, contain, crush, put, quash, quell, squash, subdue, suppress
진열대, stall
진열실, showroom
진열장, cabinet
진열하다, set
진영, camp
진용, line-up
진용을 짜다, line
진입로, drive, driveway
(~에) 진입하다, break
진자, pendulum
진저리나는, horrid, horrifying
진저리나다, horrify
진저리날 정도로, hideously
진저리치다, recoil
진전되는, forward

진전되다, come, progress
진정, remission, seriousness
진정되다, settle, subside
진정서, petition
진정시키는, calming, soothing
진정시키다, allay, calm, cool, placate, soothe, sort, steady, tranquilize
진정으로, genuinely, seriously
진정의, serious
진정제, sedative, tranquilizer
진정제를 투여 받다, sedate
진정제를 투여받은, sedation
진정하다, calm, cool
진정한, authentic, raw, real, true, veritable
진주, pearl
진지하게, earnestly, seriously, soberly
진지하게 받아들이다, seriously
진지한, earnest, serious, sober
진지력, gravity
진짜, actual, really
진짜 같은, authentic
진짜가 아닌, plastic
진짜로, truly
진짜의, authentic, genuine, real
진짜임, authenticity
진짜처럼 만든 가짜, dummy
진찰, exam, examination
진찰대, couch
진찰하다, examine
진창, sludge, slush
진척, progress
진척되는, forward
진척되다, get, headway
진출, entrance
진출로, exit
진출하다, foray
진취력, enterprise
진취적인, enterprising, go-ahead
진탕 마시고 놀기, orgy
진통, labor
진통제, painkiller
진품, article
진품 같은, authentic
진하게, darkly, richly
진한, strong
진행, passage, progress, progression, way
진행 방법, conduct
진행 방향으로 감다, wind
진행 요원, marshal
진행 정도, way
진행 중에 있는, hand
진행 중인, afoot, motion, ongoing, pipeline, progress, underway, way
진행되고 있는, on
진행되고 있다, move
진행되다, go, progress
(~을) 진행시키다, go
진행원, steward
진행자, host, presenter
진행하다, conduct, go, host, present
진행형의, continuous
진홍색, crimson, scarlet
진화, evolution
진화되다, go
진화하는, evolutionary
진화하다, evolve, extinguish
진흙, mud
진흙으로 더럽히다, muddy
진흙투성이의, muddy
질, vagina
질 나쁜, shoddy
질 낮은, low, second-class, second-rate
질 좋은, fine
질(質), quality
질감, texture
질기게 하다, toughen
질긴, tough
질량, mass
질리게 하다, appall
질리는, sick
질문, inquiry, question

질문을 받다, quiz
(~에게) 질문하다, put, question
질병, disease, illness, sickness
질병 수당, sick pay
질산염, nitrate
질색, loathing
질색하다, loathe
질서, order
질서 정연하게, methodically
질서 정연한, methodical, orderly
질서가 잡히다, order
질소, nitrogen
질식, suffocation
질식되다, overcome
질식하게 하다, suffocate
질식하다, suffocate
질식시켜 죽이다, smother
질식시키다, choke, suffocate
질식하다, choke, suffocate
질식할 듯한, stifling
질의, vaginal
질의응답, Q & A
질이 떨어지는, inferior
질적인, qualitative
질주하다, career, gallop, race, tear
질질 끌다, drag, linger, trail
질질 끌리다, trail
질책, rebuke, reprimand
질책받다, reprimand
질책하다, rap, rebuke
질타하다, hammer, round
질투, jealousy
질투심이 가득하여, jealously
질투하는, jealous
질펀한 잔치, orgy
질풍, gale
질환, affliction, disorder
싫어지다, shoulder
짐, baggage, burden, load, luggage
짐 꾸리기, packing
짐꾼, porter
짐승, beast
짐승 같은 사람, brute
짐을 내리다, unload
짐을 너무 많이 싣다, overload
짐을 너무 많이 실은, overloaded
짐을 지우다, burden
짐을 진, burdened
짐이 되다, weigh
짐작, guess
짐작으로, guess
짐작하다, guess, presume
짐칸, hold
집, door, home, house, nest, place, shelter
집 드라이브, zip drive
집 디스크, zip disk
집 밖에서, rough
집 파일, zip file
집게, clip
집게발, claw, pincer
(~을) 집게벌레, earwig
집게손가락, forefinger
집결, concentration
집다, pick
집단, army, battalion, bracket, circle, cluster, collection, collective, colony, community, element, group, grouping
집단 거주지, colony
집단 사육의, battery
집단으로, collectively
집단의, collective, communal, mass
집단적으로 공격하다, gang
집배원, postman
집사, butler
집세, rent
집시, gypsy
집시의, gypsy
집안, birth, clan, family, household
집안 내력이다, blood
집안 식구, house
집안의, domestic
집안일, housework
집약적으로, intensively
집약적인, intensive
집어 올리다, pick

(~안에) 집어넣다, poke, stow
집어삼켜지다, swallow
집어삼키다, engulf
(~을) 집어치워라, hell
집에, home
집에 안 들어오다, stay
집에 있다, stay
집에서 기다리다, wait
집에서 기른, home-grown
집에서 만든, home-made
집에서 함께 사는, live-in
집요하게, tenaciously
집요한, tenacious
집으로, home
집적거리는 사람, tease
집적거리다, tease
집적거림, tease
집전하다, celebrate
집주인, landlady, landlord
집중, concentration
집중 공격, barrage
(~의) 집중 공격을 받다, barrage
집중 공세, onslaught
집중 사격, barrage
집중 치료, intensive care
집중되다, center, direct
집중된, concentrated
집중되어 있다, concentrate
집중적으로, intensively
집중적인, concerted, intensive
집중적인 관심, limelight
집중하다, concentrate, focus, revolve
집중하여, intently
집중할 수 없다, hear
(~을) 집중해서 보다, fix
집집마다, door
집착, obsession
집착하다, obsess
집찰원, collector
집필, writing
집필되지 않은, unwritten
집필하다, write
집합, set
집합시키다, muster
집합하다, muster
집행 유예, probation, reprieve
집행 유예를 받다, reprieve
집행관, bailiff
집행부의, executive
집행하다, administer, serve
집회, assembly, convention, rally
집회자, assembly
깃, goings-on
깃궂은, saucy
깃누르다, grind
깃눌리다, squash
깃다, build
깃밟다, trample
깃밟히다, trample
깃이겨진 것, pulp
싱, gong, stud
징검돌, steppingstone
징계, correction, punishment
징계를 받다, discipline
징계의, disciplinary
징벌, retribution
징역을 살다, serve
징역의, custodial
징조, omen, signal
징조가 보이다, promise
(~의) 징조를 나타내다, indicate
징조를 보이다, bode, shape
징집, conscription, draft
징집되다, call, conscript, draft
징집병, conscript
징징거리는 소리, whine
징징거리다, whine, whinge
징후를 보이는, symptomatic
짖는 소리, bark, howl
짖다, bark, howl
짙게, richly
짙은, deep, dense, murky, rich, thick
짙은 자색의, plum
짙음, richness
짚, straw
짜깁기하다, patch

짜내다, squeeze
짜다, knit, weave
짜증, annoyance, irritation
짜증나게 하다, annoy, irritate, wall
짜증나는, aggravating, irritated
짜증나는 일, aggravation
짜증내는, irritable
짜증내며, irritably
짜증냄, irritability
짜증스러운, irritating
짜증스럽게, irritatingly
짜증을 내는, cross
짜증을 내며, crossly
짜증이 난, annoyed
짝, mate, pair
짝수의, even
짝이 안 맞는, odd
짝지어지다, pair
짝짓기하다, mate
짠, salty
짠!, boo
짤랑거리는 소리, jingle
짤랑거리다, jingle
짧게, tersely
짧게 자르다, crop
짧게 하다, shorten
짧아지다, shorten
짧은, little, short
짧은 공식 문서, memorandum
짧은 광고 문구, jingle
짧은 수염, stubble
짧은 수영, dip
짧은 여행, expedition, hop
짧은 이동, run
짧은 편지, note
짧은 헤어스타일, crop
짧은 휴가, break, getaway
짧은 휴식, break
짭짤한, fat, savory
짭짤한 스낵, savory
째다, split
째지다, split
째진 틈, tear
쨍그랑거리다, jangle
쩔쩔매다, stump
쩨쩨한, petty
쩨쩨함, pettiness
쪼개다, break, splinter, split
쪼개지다, divide, splinter, split
쪼개진 조각, splinter
쪼개진 틈, split
쪼그려 앉다, crouch
쪼그려 앉아 있다, crouch
쪼그리고 앉다, squat
쪼그리고 앉은 자세, squat
쪼그림, crouch
쪼글쪼글해지다, shrivel
쪼글쪼글해진, shriveled
쪼다, peck
쪼들리는, hard-pressed, pushed
쪼들리다, pinch
쪼아 먹다, peck
쪽, page, segment, side, way
(~) 쪽에, toward
(~) 쪽으로, at, onto, toward
(~) 쪽으로 마음이 기우는, disposed
쫄바지, leggings
쫓겨나다, banish, exile, expel, oust
쫓겨남, eviction
쫓아 버리다, turn
쫓아내다, chase, door, kick
쫓아다니며 괴롭히다, stalk
쫓아다님, chase
(~를) 쫓아버리다, drive
쬐다, bask
쭉, along, always, right
쭉 뻗친, outstretched
찌, float
찌그러뜨리다, crush
찌꺼기, residue, scrap
찌꺼기의, residual
찌는 듯이 더운, baking, boiling, sweltering
찌는 듯한, blistering, boiling, muggy
찌다, put, steam
찌르는 듯한, stabbing
찌르는 듯한 아픔, stab

찌르다, plunge, prick, prod, spear, stab, sting, thrust
찌뿌드드한, awful
찌푸린 얼굴, scowl
찍 나오는 줄기, squirt
찍 싸다, squirt
(~을) 찍 뿌리다, squirt
찍 짜기, squirt
찍 싸다, squirt
찍기, dip
찍다, dip, shoot
(~가) 찍혀 있다, imprint
찍히다, capture, print
찔러 넣다, dig, stab, stick
찜통 같은, steamy
찡그려지다, wrinkle
(~을) 찡그리다, screw, wrinkle
찢다, rip, tear
찢어지다, rip, tear
찢어진 곳, tear
찢어진 부분, rip
찧다, strike
차, car, difference, margin, tea
차 없는 거리, precinct
차가운, cold
차가움, coldness
차갑게, coldly
차게 하다, chill
차고, depot, garage
차고 건조한, brisk
차관, deputy, loan
차근차근, step
차근차근 설명하다, talk
차기, kick
차다, chuck, ditch, fill, kick
차단, cut-off, insulation, interception
차단하다, disconnect
차단되다, insulate
차단된, cut off
차단물, obstruction
차단하다, block, close, cut, exclude, intercept, interdict, obstruct, shut
차대, chassis
차대(車隊), fleet
차도, carriageway
차라리, first, more, or
차라리 ~ 하려 하다, soon
차라리 ~하고 싶다, rather
차라리 ~하는 편이 낫다, well
차량, car, carriage, traffic, vehicle
차량 경보기, car alarm
차량 번호, license number
차량 번호판, license plate
차량들, fleet
차량을 세우다, pull
차려 자세를 취하다, attention
차려입다, do
차례, go, sequence, turn
차례가 된, order
차례로, one, turn
차례로 돌아가게, round
차례로 들르다, round
차로 데려다 주다, drive, run
차를 갈아 대다, pull
차를 멈추다, pull
차를 몰고 가다, run
차를 몰아 들어가서 세우다, pull
차를 몰아 도로에 진입하다, pull
차를 세우다, pull
차를 타고 가며, drive-by
차리다, set
차마 ~하지 못하다, heart
차버리다, dump
차별, differentiation, segregation
차별 대우, discrimination
차별을 두다, distinction
차별적이 아닌, PC
차별적인, discriminatory
차별하다, differentiate, discriminate, segregate
차별화 특성, USP
(~을) 차별화하다, individualize
차분한, gentle, placid, quiet, relaxed, sedate, serene
차분히, gently, serenely

차서 벗다, kick
차선, carriageway, lane
차선의, second best
차선책, second best
차액, difference, spread
차액 거래, arbitrage
차양, shade
차용, loan, tenancy
차용자, borrower
차원, dimension
차이, chasm, difference, differential, disparity, distance, distinction, divergence, margin, split, variation
(~의) 차이를 나타내다, distinguish
차이를 보이다, contrast
차익 거래, profit-taking
차임벨, chime
(~에) 차입금을 이용하여 투자하다, leverage
차장, guard
차점자, runner-up
차지 카드, charge card
차지하다, account, claim, hold, occupy, take
차질, snag
차차 ~이 되다, work
차차 두고 보자, see
차체, hull
차츰 확대시키다, escalate
(~은) 차치하고, apart
차트, chart
차환하다, refinance
차후의, subsequent
착각, delusion
착각하다, delude, mistake, take
착륙, landing
착륙시키다, land
착륙하다, land, touch
착복, embezzlement
착복하다, cream, pocket
착상되다, implant
착색제, coloring
착수, launch
착수 자금, seed money
착수하는, start-up
착수하다, attack, embark, hand, initiate, launch, set, start, turn
착수하여, ground
착오, mistake
착용, wear
착용하는, on
착잡한, mixed
착착 진행 중인, course, track
착취, exploitation
착취당하다, bleed
착취하다, exploit, milk, prey
착한, good-natured
찬가, hymn
찬동, blessing
찬동하는, associate
찬란하게, gloriously
찬란하게 빛나는, brilliant
찬란한, glorious, gorgeous
찬물을 끼얹다, water
찬반 의사 표시를 하다, vote
찬사, accolade, celebration, compliment, credit
찬사를 보내다, congratulate
찬성, approval, assent
찬성 의견을 말하는, argue
찬성을 못 받다, frown
(~에) 찬성하는, for, pro
(~에) 찬성하다, agree, approve, countenance, second, subscribe
(~을) 찬성하여, favor
찬송가, hymn
찬양하는, complimentary
찬연히, brilliantly
찬장, closet, cupboard, dresser
찰과상, graze
찰과상을 내다, scrape
찰과상을 입다, graze
찰깍, snap
찰나, instant
찰싹 때리기, slap
찰싹 때리다, slap, swat
찰싹거리는 소리, lapping

찰싹거리다, lap
찰칵 하고 울리게 하다, click
찰칵 하는 소리, click
찰흙, clay
참가, entry, involvement, participation
참가시키다, enter
참가자, competitor, entrant, field, participant
참가자 수, entry, turnout
참가하다, come, compete, enter, join, part, participate
(~에) 참가하, in
참견하다, mess, nose, put
참고, reference
참고 문헌 목록, bibliography
참고 봐주다, stand
참고로, record
참고용의, reference
참고인, witness
참고하다, account, refer
참고하라고 하다, refer
참관하다, sit
참다, abide, bear, put, stand, stifle, tolerate
참담하게, disastrously
참담한, kick
참담할 정도로, disastrously
참뜻, spirit
참모총장, Chief of Staff
참배자, worshiper
참사, disaster, tragedy
참새, sparrow
참석, appearance, attendance
참석자 수, attendance
참석하다, attend, make
참석하지 못하다, miss
(~에) 참석한, present
참수되다, decapitate
참신하게, refreshingly
참신한, fresh, refreshing
참아 주다, bear
참여, participation
참여하다, associate
참여해서 돕다, pitch
참으려고 안간힘을 쓰다, fight
참으로, enough, how, indeed, tell, what
참을 수 없는, intolerable, unbearable
참을 수 없는 욕망, itch
참을 수 없이, intolerably
참을 수 있는, tolerable
참을성, patience
참을성 있게, patiently
참을성 있는, long-suffering, patient
참작하다, account, allowance
참작할, mitigating
참전 용사, vet, veteran
참전하다, fight
참조, cc, cf., reference
참조 기호, reference
참조 번호, ref
(~을) 참조하다, consult, refer
참조하시오, see
참지 못하는, impatient
참치, tuna
참패, beating, rout
참패한, disastrous
참호, trench
참화, devastation, ravages
참화를 입다, ravage
찻숟가락, teaspoon
찻잎, tea
찻주전자, pot, teakettle, teapot
창, spear, window
창고, depot, shed, store, warehouse
창구, window
창궐, epidemic
창꼬치, pike
창녀, tart
창립, founding
창립하다, found
창문, window
창문턱, ledge, sill
창백한, colorless, pale

창설자, founder
창시자, father
창유리, pane
창의력, creativity
창의력이 있는, creative
창의력이 풍부한, fertile
창의적인, creative, inventive
창자, gut, intestine
창작물, brainchild, creation
창작하다, create
창조, creation
창조자, creator
창조주, god
창조하다, create
창출, creation
창출되다, open
창출하다, create, open
창피, shame
창피를 주다, humiliate, shame
창피스러운, shameful
창피스럽게, shamefully
창피한 줄 알아라, shame
찾기, hunting
(~을) 찾는 사람, hunter
찾다, find, grub, hunt, search, seek, work
(~을) 찾아, search
찾아내다, catch, dig, look, recover, track, turn, unearth
(~을) 찾아다니다, forage, scout
찾아보기, index
찾아보다, check, look
찾아봄, look
찾아서 보다, look
찾아오다, collect
찾으러 가다, collect
채, shred, stick
채 마르지 않은, fresh
채광, lighting
채광되다, mine
채권, bond, debenture
채권 소유자, bondholder
채권으로 보증되는, bonded
채권자, creditor
채널, channel
채널을 돌리다, turn
채를 썰다, shred
채무 기관, debtor
채무 연장을 하다, reschedule
채무국, debtor
채무자, debtor
채비를 하다, ready
채비하다, see
채색된, colored
채석장, quarry
채석하다, quarry
채식주의자, vegetarian
채우다, complete, do, fill, make, take
채워 넣다, fill, stuff
채워 주다, fill
(~로) 채워지다, imbue
채워진, filled
채이다, stub
채점, marking
채점하다, mark
채찍, lash, whip
채찍질, whipping
채찍질하다, whip
채택, adoption
채택하다, adopt
채팅방, chat room
책, book, text
책 속 부록, covermount
책 속의 상호 참조, cross-reference
책갈피표, bookmark
책꽂이, shelf
책등, spine
책략, ruse
책략가, operator
책망, censure, reproach
책망하다, censure, reproach, tell
책무, accountability, commitment, obligation, responsibility
책상, bureau, desk
책임, accountability, blame, fault, liability, obligation, onus, responsibility

책임 있는, accountable
책임감 있게, responsibly
책임감 있는, responsible
(~의) 책임으로, hand
(~의) 책임으로 돌리다, blame
책임을 ~에게 지우다, pin
책임을 묻다, book
책임을 전가하다, buck, scapegoat
책임을 져야 마땅하다, blame
책임을 지다, account
(~의) 책임을 추궁받다, account
(~의) 책임이 끝난, hand
책임이 무거운, responsible
책임이 있는, liable, responsible
(~의) 책임인, down, up
책임자, controller, director, hand, superintendent
책임지고 있는, charge
책임지다, bear, look
책임짐, charge
책자, brochure
책장, bookcase, leaf
책장을 주욱 넘기다, leaf
챈트, chant
챔피언, champ, champion
챙, brim, peak
챙기다, extract
처남, brother-in-law
처넣다, plunge
처넣어버리다, throw
처녀, girl, lass, maiden, virgin
처녀성, virginity
처량하다, forlorn
처리, disposal, handling, processing, treatment
처리 과정, process
처리 방안, prescription
처리 장치, processor
처리기, processor
처리되다, process
처리되지 않은, raw
처리하다, action, care, cope, deal, dispose, fix, go, handle, process, run, see, treat
처리하지 않은, untreated
처리해야 할, reckon
처마, eaves
처마 같은 것, overhang
처방, formula, prescription
처방약, prescription
처방전, prescription
처방전 없이, counter
처방전이 있어야만, prescription
처방하다, prescribe, treat
처벌, penalty, punishment
처벌도 안 받고, scot-free
처벌을 받다, penalize
처벌의, punitive
처벌이 있다, head
처벌하다, punish
처분하다, dispose, rid
처세법, philosophy
처소, shelter
처신하다, behave, carry, conduct
처음, first
처음 경험하게 하다, introduce
처음 만나다, meet
처음부터, outset
처음부터 다시, over
처음부터 다시 시작하다, start
처음부터 또 다시, over
처음에, initially, outset, place
처음에는, begin, first, start
처음으로, first, for
처음의, first, opening
처제, sister-in-law
처지, case, circumstance, position
(~하는 처지가 되다, reduce
처지다, sag
처지에 있다, stand
처지에 처하다, come
(~의) 처지였다면, place
처진 살, bag
처참하게, miserably
처참한, catastrophic, miserable
처하다, reduce
처형, sister-in-law

처형되다, death
처형하다, execute
척, chuck
척도, barometer, gauge, measure, yardstick
척박한, arid, barren
척추, backbone, spine, vertebra
척추의, spinal
(~) 척하다, fake, feign
천, cloth, fabric, thousand
천 달러, grand
천 번째, thousandth
천 파운드, grand
천공기, punch
천국, heaven, paradise
천국 같은, heavenly
천국의, heavenly
천금과 같은, weight
천년, millennium
천당, heaven
천도복숭아, nectarine
천둥, thunder
천둥 치다, thunder
천막, tent
천만에, certainly, hell, not
천만에요, welcome
천문대, observatory
천문학, astronomy
천문학의, astronomical
천문학자, astronomer
천문학적인, astronomical
천박한, cheap, common, kitsch, naughty, shallow, tacky, taste, tasteless, vulgar
천박한 것, kitsch
천박함, vulgarity
천부적 재능, flair
천부적으로, innately, naturally
천부적인, effortless, natural
천부적인 재능, gift
천사, angel
천사 같은, angelic
천사의, angelic
천성, nature
천식, asthma
천식 환자, asthmatic
천식 환자의, asthmatic
천식의, asthmatic
천연덕스러운, dry
천연덕스러움, dryness
천연의, natural
천연적으로, naturally
천의무봉으로, seamlessly
천의무봉의, seamless
천장, ceiling, roof
천재, genius
천재성, genius
천주교, Catholicism
천주교도, Roman Catholic
천주교의, Catholic, Roman Catholic
(~) 천지의, bursting
천직, vocation
천진하게, innocently
천진한, childlike
천착하다, pursue
천천히, slowly, slow
천천히 가다, trek
천천히 걷다, saunter
천천히 나아가다, roll
천천히 내려가다, sink
천천히 뛰다, jog
천천히 움직이다, nose
천천히 이동하다, drift
천천히 하다, easy, time
천체도, chart
천체의, celestial
천하를 다 얻은 것 같은, top
천한, gross, menial
철, iron, season
철 따라 이동하다, migrate
철 이른, early
철거, demolition
철거하기로 결정하다, condemn
철도, rail, railroad, railway
철도 신호기, signal
철도 회사, railroad, railway

철도로, rail
철두철미, inch
철두철미한, saturation, thorough
철두철미함, thoroughness
철렁하다, sink
철면피, gall
철물, hardware
철사, wire
철새, migrant
철석 같은, adamant
철수, withdrawal
철수시키다, pull, withdraw
철수하다, pull, withdraw
철썩 때리기, smack
철썩 때리다, smack
철썩철썩 치다, thrash
철야 기도, vigil
철야 기도하다, vigil
철야 농성, vigil
철야 농성하다, vigil
철없는, overgrown, silly
철이 들다, grow
철자, spelling
철자를 말해 주다, spell
철자를 쓰다, spell
철자를 알다, spell
철저하게, carefully, exhaustively, rigorously
철저한, careful, dead, deafening, downright, rigorous, thorough
철저함, thoroughness
철저히, comprehensively, depth, home, thoroughly, well
철저히 논의하다, talk, thrash
철저히 망라된, exhaustive
철저히 읽다, go
철저히 조사하다, sift
철천지한을 품은, implacable
철폐하다, deregulate
철하다, file
철학, philosophy
철학의, philosophical
철학자, philosopher
철학적으로, philosophically
철회, retraction
철회하다, back, go, retract, revoke, take, waive
첨가물, additive
첨가하다, add
첨단, leading edge, tip
첨단 기술, high technology
첨단 기술의, high-tech
첨병 하는 소리, splash
첨벙거리다, splash
첨부 파일, attachment
첨부하다, attach
첨예한, contentious
첨탑, spire
첩, book
첩보, intelligence
첩보 활동, espionage, spying
첩보 활동을 하다, spy
첩보부, secret service
첩보원, agent, operative, spy
첩보의, spy, undercover
첩자를 심다, plant
첫 번째로, place
첫 번째의, first
첫 코스, starter
첫 할부금, down payment
첫눈에, glance, sight
첫발을 잘못 내딛다, foot
첫째로, firstly, instance
첫째의, first, primary
청, directorate, favor
청각, hearing
청각장애인, deaf
청결, cleanliness
청교도, puritan
청교도의, puritanical
청교도적인, puritan
청구, claim
청구서, bill, invoice
청구서를 보내다, invoice
청구하다, bill, charge, claim
청년 특유의, youthful
청년기, youth

청동, bronze
청동색, bronze
청량음료, soft drink
청력, hearing
청문회, hearing
청바지, dungarees, jeans
청부인, contractor
청사진, blueprint
청산, liquidation
청산유수, patter
청산인, liquidator
청산칼리, cyanide
청산하다, liquidate
청산해야 할, reckon
청소, clean, cleaning
청소기, cleaner
청소년, juvenile
청소년의, juvenile
청소부, cleaner
청소하다, clean, clear, sweep
청승맞게, pathetically
청승맞은, pathetic
청신호, light
청약하다, subscribe
청어, herring
청어 살, herring
청원, petition
청원하다, petition
청원휴가, compassionate leave
청자, listener
청자색, violet
청정한, pure
청취자, audience, listener
청취자 전화 참여 프로그램, phone-in
청취하다, hear, tune
청하지 않은, unsolicited
청해 문제, comprehension
청혼, proposal
청혼하다, propose, question
체, sieve
체격, build, frame, physique
체격이 좋은, well-built
체결, conclusion
체계, structure, system
체계가 없는, disorganized
체계적으로, scientifically, systematically
체계적으로 기술하다, formulate
체계적인, organized, scientific, systematic
체계적인 기술, formulation
체계화하다, organize
체내에서, internally
체내의, internal
체념, resignation
체력, fitness, stamina
체로 거르다, sieve, sift
체류, stay
체리, cherry
체리나무, cherry
체면, decency, face
체모, hair
체불 임금, back pay
체불된, overdue
체스, chess
체신청, post office
체온, temperature
체온을 재다, temperature
체외 수정, IVF
체육, athletics, gym
체육관, gym, gymnasium
체육의, athletic
체인, chain
체인점, multiple
체인점 영업권, franchise
체재, format
체제, fabric, machinery, regime, system
체제 전복적인, subversive
체제가 싫어 망명하다, vote
체조, gymnastics
체조 선수, gymnast
체중, weight
체중을 풀이다, slim
체중이 늘다, weight
체중이 줄다, weight
체증, congestion

체증이 심한, congested
(~가) 체질에 맞는, cut out
체커, checker
체크 표시, tick
체크 표시를 하다, tick
체크무늬, check, tartan
체크무늬의, checked
체크아웃하다, check
체크인하다, check
체크하다, check
체포, arrest
체포되다, bust, seize
체포하는, arrest, nick, round
(~인) 체하다, act, impersonate, play, pretend
체험, experience
체형, corporal punishment
첼로, cello
첼로 연주가, cellist
처들다, brandish
초, sec., second
초가의, thatched
초고를 쓰다, draft
초고속 정보 통신망, superhighway
초과, overrun
초과 근무, overtime
초과 인출하다, overdrawn
초과 지출, overspend
초과액, excess
초과하다, exceed, overrun, surpass
(~을) 초과하여, excess
초극세사, microfiber
초기, beginning, early
초기 투입 자본, seed capital
초기 투자금, seed corn
초기에, early, infancy, initially
초기의, early, embryo, embryonic, infant, initial
초단기 매매가, day trader
초당 비트 전송률, bps
초대, invitation, invite
초대받지 않고 들어가다, gatecrash
초대장, invitation
초대하다, ask, invite
초대형 히트작, blockbuster
초등 교육의, primary
초등학교, elementary school, grade school, grammar school, junior school, primary school
초라한, sleazy
초래하다, bring, effect, incur, invite, leave, produce, result, rise
초록빛, green
초만원이나, seam
초목, growth, vegetation
초미세 합성 섬유, microfiber
초미의, burning
초반에, early
초반에 막다, bud
초법적인, law
초보의, fledgling
초보자, beginner, virgin
초보자용의, entry-level
초보적인, entry-level, rudimentary
초상, figure, likeness
초상화, portrait
초석, cornerstone, keystone
초소형 중앙 처리 장치, microprocessor
초소형 컴퓨터, hand-held
초승달 모양, crescent
초시계, stopwatch
초심자, newcomer, novice
초안, draft
초연, premiere
초연되다, premiere
초연함, detachment
초원, meadow
초월하다, transcend
(~을) 초월하여, across
초월한, beyond
초음속의, supersonic
초음파, ultrasound
초인플레이션, hyperinflation
초읽기, countdown
초자연적인, mystic, mystical, supernatural

초자연적인 것, supernatural
초점, focus, issue
초점 맞추기, focus
초점을 맞추다, adjust, focus
초점을 잃다, glaze
초점을 잃은, glazed
초점이 맞는, focus
초점이 맞다, adjust, focus
초점이 맞지 않는, focus
초조, jitters
초조하게, impatiently
초조하게 하다, agitate
초조한, agitated, edgy, state
초조함, agitation
초조해 하는, uptight
초장기 문제, teething problems
초청, invitation
초청 손님, guest
초청장, invitation
초청하다, invite
초췌한, drawn
초콜릿, chocolate
초콜릿빛, chocolate
초크, choke
초현대적인, futuristic
초현실적인, surreal
촉각, touch
촉감, feel
촉구하다, urge
촉매, catalyst
촉매제, catalyst
촉박한, urgent
촉발, eruption
촉발시키다, precipitate, spark
촉수, tentacle
촉진, promotion
촉진시키다, foster
촉진하다, encourage, facilitate, further, promote
촉촉하게 하다, moisten
촉촉한, moist
촌극, sketch
촌스러운, provincial
총, all, collective, general, grand, gun
총 ~명의, strong
총각, bachelor
총검, bayonet
총격, blast, shooting
총격전, exchange
총계, count, tally
총계~이 되다, add, amount
총계의, gross, total
총괄의, general
총기, firearm
총기 휴대자, gunman
총독, governor
총림, bush
총매상고, turnover
총명하게, intelligently
총무, secretary
총무부장, company secretary
총부리, muzzle
총살하다, mow
총선거, general election
총수, total
총신, barrel
총알, bullet, pellet
총알같이, shot
총알을 퍼붓다, spray
총액으로, gross
총액의, gross
총연습, dress rehearsal
총열, barrel
총으로 쏘다, blast, shoot
총으로 위협받고, gunpoint
총을 맞고 쓰러지다, gun
총장, dean
총재, head
총체, umbrella
총체적인, generalized
총칭적인, generic
총칭하는, collective
총칭하여, collectively
총탄, gunshot
총파업, general strike
총판, franchisee
총판권을 허가하다, franchise

총판업자, franchiser
총합, sum
촬영, shoot, shooting
촬영 기사, cameraman
촬영 장면, take
촬영 카메라 앞에서, camera
촬영되고 있는, camera
최고, best, golden, maximum
최고 경영자, CEO, chief executive officer, managing director
최고 권력을 가진, sovereign
최고 기록, record
최고 상금, jackpot
최고 수준, high
최고 지위에 올라, top
최고 학년, senior
최고 한도, ceiling
최고가의, high-end
최고급의, fancy, first-class, superb, top-end
최고로, best, superbly
최고로 숙련된, consummate
최고상, star prize
최고에 오르다, top
최고에서 최악으로, sublime
최고위, top
최고위의, top
최고의, ace, best, chief, fancy, golden, max., paramount, peak, premier, prime, second, sovereign, supreme, top, ultimate, utmost
최고의 것, pick
최고의 기량, best
최고의 사람, pick
최고의 찬사, superlative
최고인, definitive
최고점, peak
최고점에 달하다, peak
최고조, climax, crescendo, culmination, heat
최고조에 오른, crest
(~로) 최고조에 이르다, culminate
최고치, high
최근까지, date
최근에, lately, newly, recently
최근에 두드러진, newfound
최근에 사망한, deceased
최근에 사망한 사람, deceased
최근의, last, latest, recent
최근의 것, last
최근친, next of kin
최대, maximum
최대 출력, blast
최대로 하다, maximize
최대의, full, max., maximum
최대한, full, most
최대한 이익을 뽑아내다, milk
최대한 활용하다, most
최대한으로, maximum
최대의, capacity, maximum
최대화하다, maximize
최루 가스, tear gas
최면, hypnosis, trance
최면 상태, hypnosis
최면 상태의, hypnotic
최면술, hypnosis, hypnotism
최면술사, hypnotist
최면에 걸린, hypnotic
최면을 걸다, hypnotize
최상급, superlative
최상급의, superlative
최상위, top
최상위의, top
최상으로, superbly
최상의, ideal, superb, superlative, ultimate
최선, best, utmost
최선을 다하다, best, shot
최선을 위해, best
최선의, right
최소, least, min., minimum
최소 인원의, skeleton
최소로, least, minimum
최소의, minimal, minimum
최소한, least
최소한의, minimum
최소화하다, minimize

최신 소식을 아는, up-to-date
최신 유행, buzz
최신 유행에 정통한, hip
최신 유행의, designer, trendy
최신 정보, update
최신식의, state-of-the-art
최신의, hot, latest, red-hot, up-to-date
최신판, update
최악, worst
최악의, deadly, ultimate, worst
최악의 경우에, worst
최우선의, top
최우선이다, first
최우선하는, paramount
최저, rock bottom
최저 경매 가격, reserve price
최저 생활, subsistence
최저가, reserve price
최저의, rock bottom
최저임금, minimum wage
최적의, optimum
최전방, front line
최전선에서, front line
최정점, apex
최종 결과, end result, upshot
최종 사용자, end user
최종 산출물, end product
최종 심사 대상자, shortlist
최종 후보 명단, shortlist
최종 후보자 명단에 오르다, shortlist
최종적인, final, net
최첨단, cutting edge
최첨단의 기술, state-of-the-art
최초로 성관계를 가지다, consummate
최초의, originally
최초의, initial
최하부, foot
최후, gasp
최후의, last-ditch, minute, ultimate
최후의 결정타, straw
최후의 수단으로, resort
최후통첩, ultimatum
추, pendulum
추가, addition
추가 기기, add-on
추가 배당, with-profits
추가 비용, supplement
추가 사항, addition
추가 요금, extra, surcharge
추가 요금의, extra
추가 통지가 있을 때까지, notice
추가로, extra, plus
추가의, added, additional, another, fresh, further, more, top-up
추가하다, add
추간 연골, disk
추격, chase
추구, chase, hunting
추구하는 사람, seeker
추구하다, chase, court, pursue
(~을) 추구하는, after, pursuit
추궁하다, book
추근거리다, flirt
추근거림, flirtation
추기경, cardinal
추다, dance
추도, commemoration, remembrance
추도의, memorial
추락, fall, nosedive, tumble
추락하다, crash, go, nosedive, plunge
추려 낸, select
추론, deduction, inference
추론 과정, reasoning
추론하다, deduce, infer
추리, inference
추리 소설, mystery
추모, memory
추모의, memorial
추모지, shrine
추문, scandal
추문에 얽힌, scandalous
추방, deportation, exile
추방당하다, banish

추방되다, exile, expel
추방하다, deport
추산, reckoning
추산된, estimated
추상의, abstract
추상적 개념, abstraction
추상적인, abstract
추상화, abstract
추세, current, trend
추세에 뒤떨어지다, touch
추수, harvest
추수 감사절, Thanksgiving
추수하다, harvest
추신, postscript, PS
추악한, hideous
추억, memory, reminiscence
추억에 잠기다, reminisce
추운, chilly, cold
추워 죽겠는, freezing
추월 차선, fast lane
추월하다, overtake
추위, cold
추위에 강한, hardy
추이, development
추잡한, gross, sleazy, ugly
추잡함, sleaze, ugliness
추장, chief
추적, chase, hunt
추적 중인, trail
추적자, pursuer
(~을) 추적하는, pursuit
추적하다, hunt, pursue, trace, track, trail
추적하여 잡다, hunt
추정, estimate, estimation, extrapolation, guess
추정된, estimated
추정상의, supposed
추정하다, assume, calculate, estimate, extrapolate, guess, infer
추종자, follower
추종자들, following
(~으로) 추진되는, propel
추진력, drive, impetus, thrust
추진하다, pilot, push
추천, recommendation
추천되어, forward
추천받는, recommended
추천받다, nominate
추천서, reference, testimonial
추천하다, commend, propose, recommend, suggest
추첨, draw
추첨식 복권, raffle
추첨을 해 주다, raffle
추첨하다, draw
추출, distillation, extraction, ousting
추출되다, distill
추출물, extract
추출하다, extract
추측, conjecture, guess, speculation, surmise
추측에 근거한, speculative
추측으로, guess
추측하는, conjecture, gather, guess, presume, speculate, suppose, surmise
추태, scene
추파를 던지다, hit
추하게, scandalously
추한, scandalous, ugly, unsightly
추함, ugliness
추후 공고, tba
추후 확정, tbc
축, axis, pivot, shaft
축 처지다, droop, hang
축 처짐, droop
축구, football, soccer
축구 선수, footballer, soccer player
축구공, football
축복, blessing
축복하다, bless
축산을 하다, farm
축성되다, consecrate
축소, decrease
축소 모형, miniature

축소 모형의, scale
축소술, tuck
축소판, microcosm
축소판의, miniature
축소하다, curtail, run, scale, trim
축소해 말하다, understate
축약한, concise
축약하다, shorten
축연, fete
축우, cattle
축원, blessing, wish
축음기, record player
축이다, moisten
축일의, festive
축적, accumulation
축적물, accumulation
축적하다, accumulate, amass
축전, celebration
축제, feast, festival, festivity, fete, gala
축제 기간, festival
축제의, festive
축제일, festival
축척, scale
축축한, damp, soggy, wet
축출, expulsion, overthrow
축출되다, oust, overthrow
축출하다, remove
축하, congratulation, festivity
축하 파티, shower
축하 행사, celebration, festivity
축하인사, congratulations
축하하다, celebrate, congratulate
(~을) 축하하여, honor
축하합니다, congratulations, happy
출간하다, publish
출격, sortie
출구, exit
출국, exodus
출국 사증, exit visa
출근 시각을 기록하다, clock
출근 카드를 찍다, clock
출근하다, clock
출금 기록, debit
출금되다, debit
출납 장부, account
출납원, cashier
출두시키다, call
출두 명령, summons
출두하다, appear, present
출력된 정보, output
출력하다, print
출마시키다, put
출몰하는, fight, put
출몰하다, haunt
출발, departure
출발 대기장, lounge
출발 라운지, departure lounge
출발 신호용 총, gun
출발선, grid
출발이 아주 좋다, flying
출발점, springboard, starting point
출발지, starting point
출발지에서 도착지까지, door
출발하는, outgoing
출발하다, depart, going, set, start
출범, launch
출산 예정 시기, term
출산 전의, prenatal
출산력, fertility
출산율, birth rate
출산하다, birth
출산할 수 있는, fertile
출생, birth
출생 증명서, birth certificate
출생지, birthplace
출생지인, native
출석, attendance
출세, advancement, rise
출세의 수단, ladder
출세하다, major league, rise
출시, appearance, launch
출시 기념의, introductory
출시 할인의, introductory
출시되다, arrive
출시된, out

출시품, introduction, release
출시하다, bring, launch, release
출신, descent
출신 배경, background
(~) 출신의, from, native
(~의) 출신이다, come, hail
(~) 출신인 사람, son
출연, exposure
출연시키다, cast
출연이 예정되다, bill
출연자 명단, bill
출연자 홍보 우선순위, billing
출연진, cast
출연하다, appear, go
출입 금지의, limit
출입 불가, entry
출입 및 사용의 자유, run
출입구, doorway, entrance
출입국 관리, immigration
출입문, gate
출입이 금지된, bound
출입이 제한된, restricted
출자, investment
출장, visit
출전 등록, entry
출전이 어려울 것 같은, doubtful
출중한, preeminent
출중함, preeminence
출처, origin, source
출판, publication
출판되다, go
출판되지 않은, unpublished
출판물, publication, title
출판사, publisher, publishing
  house
출판업, publishing
출판업자, publisher
출판하다, publish
출품자, exhibitor
출항하다, sail
출현, advent, emergence
출혈, bleeding, hemorrhage,
  hemorrhaging
출혈이 있다, hemorrhage
춤, dance, dancing
춤을 추는 무대, dance floor
춤을 추다, dance
춤추기 시작하다, floor
춤추는 사람, dancer
춤추다, dance, flicker
춥게 하다, chill
충격, blow, impulse, jolt, shock
충격받은, staggered
충격을 받은, shocked
충격을 완화하는, cushion
(~에게) 충격을 주다, jolt, shock,
  stagger
충격의 여파, shock wave
충격적으로, shockingly
충격적인, devastating, lurid,
  outrageous, shocking, stunning
충격적인 소식, bombshell
충격적인 일, outrage
충격파, shock wave
충고, advice, recommendation
충고하다, advise, recommend, tell,
  warn
충당하다, cover, give
충돌, bump, clash, collision,
  conflict, impact
충돌시키다, strike
충돌하다, clash, collide, conflict,
  crash, hit, impact, ram, strike
충동, drive, impulse, urge
충동적으로, impulse, impulsively,
  spur
충동적인, impulsive
충만하다, fill, permeate
충복, stalwart
충분하게, sufficiently
충분하다, do, suffice
충분한, adequate, ample, due,
  enough, full, good, plenty,
  sufficient, the, to
충분한 고려 없이 승인해 주다,
  rubber stamp
충분한 생각, second thought
충분한 증거가 없는, unsafe

충분함, enough, plenty
충분히, adequately, amply,
  enough, well
충분히 상의하다, talk
충분히 생각하다, think
충분히 알고 있다, full
충분히 연구하다, read
충분히 열린, wide
충분히 이해하다, mean
충성, allegiance, fidelity, homage,
  loyalty
충성스런, faithful, loyal
충성스레, loyally
충성심, spirit
충실하게, faithfully,
  staunchly
충실한, faithful, full, loyal,
  staunch, steady, true
충실한 신봉자, stalwart
충실히, faithfully, loyally
충심으로, heart
충원하다, fill
충전기, charger
충전물, padding
충전시키다, charge
충전재, filling, stuffing
충족되지 않은, unfulfilled
충족된, fulfilled
충족시키다, meet, satisfy
취급, handling
취급 품목, selection
취급하다, deal, sell
취기, drunkenness
취득, acquisition, realization
취득하다, acquire, come
취미, hobby, liking, pastime
취미 활동, pursuit
취사용 화덕, range
취소, cancellation, retraction
취소되어, off
취소하다, call, cancel, go, retract,
  revoke, take
취약성, vulnerability
취약점, deficiency, weakness
취약한, fragile
취약함, failing
취옥, emerald
취임, arrival, inauguration,
  installation
취임 선서를 하다, swear
취임의, inaugural
취임하다, inaugurate
취중의, drunken
취지, drift, message, substance
취지를 이해하다, point
취하, dropping
취하게 하는, heady
취하게 하다, head
취하다, assume, grab, strike, take
취향이나 필요에 맞게 개조하다,
  customize
측, side
측량, survey
측량 장치, instrument
측량관, surveyor
측량하다, survey
측면, aspect, dimension, flank,
  side
(~의) 측면에 두다, flank
(~) 측면에서, term
측면의, lateral
측은지심, compassion
측은한, pathetic, pitiful
측은해하는, compassionate
측은히 여기다, sympathize
측정, measurement
측정 계기, gauge
측정기, counter
측정하다, gauge, measure, take
측정할 수 있는, measurable
층, base, deck, floor, layer, seam,
  story, tier
층계참, landing
층위, layer
치고 빠지는, hit-and-run
치고 지나가다, clip
치과, dentist
치과 의사, dentist, doctor

치과 진료실, dentist's office
치과의, dental
치기, knock
치는 소리, stroke
치다, beat, catch, clip, clout, draw,
  hit, knock, ram, run, strike,
  strum
치달다, race
치러지다, pass
치료, remedy, therapy, treatment
치료 자문 회의, consultation
치료 중인, recovery
치료를 돕는, therapeutic
치료법, cure
치료사, healer, therapist
치료의, therapeutic
치료하다, cure, patch, treat
치료하지 않은, untreated
치뤄야 할, hand
치를 떨다, blanch
치마, skirt
치매, dementia
치명적으로, fatally, mortally
치명적인, deadly, fatal, fateful,
  lethal, mortal, pernicious,
  virulent
치사한, cheap
치석, plaque
치솟다, rocket, soar
치수, dimension, measurement,
  size
치아, tooth
치아의, dental
치안, order
치안 판사, magistrate
치안관, constable
치안을 유지하다, police
치약, toothpaste
치열 교정기, brace
치열한, fierce, hot
치욕스럽게 만들다, disgrace
치우다, clear, remove, tuck
치우치게 하는, bias
(~에) 치우치다, err
(~쪽으로) 치우친, biased
치워 두다, put, set, tidy
치워서, away
치유 가능한, curable
치유되다, heal
치유할 수 없게, incurably
치이다, knock
치장하다, dress, spruce
치즈, cheese
치즈버거, cheeseburger
치질, pile
치켜세우다, build
치핵, pile
치명, edict
칙칙 소리를 내며 가다, chug
칙칙한, dingy, drab, somber
칙칙함, drabness
친가, side
친교, community, intercourse,
  intimacy
친구, buddy, dude, friend, pal
친구 사이, friendship
친구가 되다, befriend, friend
친구들, gang, guy
친구와 밀린 이야기를 하다, catch
친근감, affinity
친근한, informal
친목, community
친목의, social
친목회, reunion
친밀감이 드는, intimate
친밀하게, intimately
친밀한, close, intimate
친밀한 관계, association
친밀함, closeness, intimacy
친분, link
친분을 쌓다, cultivate
친선, goodwill
친선 경기, friendly
친선 관계, rapport
친선의, friendly
친숙한, intimate
친숙함, familiarity
친애하는, dear, dearest

친절, hospitality, kindness, turn
친절하게, benignly, cordially,
  kindly, nicely, obligingly,
  tenderly
친절한, accommodating, benign,
  caring, congenial, cordial,
  gentle, good, gracious, kind,
  nice, obliging, tender
친절함, tenderness
친족, kin
친족인, related
친척, kin, relation, relative
친척이 아닌, unrelated
친필의, manuscript
친하게, socially
(~와) 친하게 지내다, get
친한, friendly, good
(~에) 친화적인, -friendly
친환경 관광 여행, ecotourism
친환경 여행자, ecotourist
친환경적인, eco-friendly
칠, coating
칠리, chili
칠면조, turkey
칠면조 고기, turkey
칠십, seventy
칠십 번째, seventieth
칠판, blackboard, board,
  chalkboard
칠하다, daub
침, needle, saliva, spit, sting
침 치료, acupuncture
침구, bedclothes, bedding
침낭, sleeping bag
침대, bed, berth, bunk
침대 시트, sheet
침대 커버, bedclothes, cover
침대를 정돈하다, bed
침대맡, bedside
침대차, sleeper
침략, invasion
침략군, invader
침략군, invader
침략자, aggressor
침략하다, invade
침례, baptism
침로, course
침로를 벗어나, course
침몰하다, go
침몰한, sunken
침묵, quiet, silence
침묵을 깨다, silence
침묵하게 만들다, silence
침범하다, attack, intrude
침상, bed
침수시키다, swamp
침술, acupuncture
침식, erosion
침식되다, erode
침식하다, eat
침실, bedroom
침울하게, gloomily, morosely,
  unhappily
침울한, morose, somber
침울함, gloom, unhappiness
침을 꿀꺽 삼키다, gulp, swallow
침을 뱉다, spit
침을 흘리다, dribble, drool
침입, invasion, raid
침입자, intruder, raider
침입하다, break, hack, infect,
  inroads, raid
침적토, silt
침전물, sediment
침착, composure, serenity
침착하게, calmly, steadily
침착하게 대처하다, stride
침착하다, head
침착한, calm, cool, poised, steady
침착한 태도, poise
침착함, calm
침체, stagnation
침체 상태, doldrums
침체되다, stagnate
침체된, depressed, flat, stagnant
침체된 곳, backwater
침침한, blurred, hazy, smoky

침침해지다, blur
침투, infiltration, penetration
침투시키다, infiltrate
침투하다, infiltrate, penetrate
침팬지, chimpanzee
침하되다, subside
침해, encroachment, infringement, injury, intrusion, invasion
(~을) 침해하다, encroach, infringe, violate
칩, chip
칫솔, toothbrush
칭송 받다, hail
칭송하다, acclaim
칭찬, celebration, commendation, compliment, praise
칭찬받다, applaud
칭찬의, complimentary
칭찬하다, build, commend, compliment, hat, plug, praise, speak
칭찬할 만한, commendable
칭호, title
카네이션, carnation
카누, canoe
카니발, carnival
카드, card, playing card
카드 키, key card
카드놀이, card
카드를 섞다, shuffle
카드를 섞고 퇴근하다, clock
카드식 색인, card index
카디건, cardigan
카레, curry
카르텔, cartel
카리브 사람, Caribbean
카리브 사람의, Caribbean
카리브 제도의, Caribbean
카리브 해, Caribbean
카리브 해의, Caribbean
카리스마, charisma
카리스마 있는, charismatic
카메라, camera
카메라 맨, cameraman
카메라 앞에서 벗어나, camera
카메오, cameo
카바레, cabaret
카세트테이프, tape
카스트, caste
카스트 제도, caste
카오스, chaos
카우보이, cowboy
카운슬러, counselor
카운터, bar, counter
카운트다운, countdown
카운티, county
카지노, casino
카키색, khaki
카키색 군복용 천, khaki
카탈로그, catalog
카트, cart
카트리지, cartridge
카페, café
카페인, caffeine
카페인을 제거한, decaffeinated
카페테리아, cafeteria
카펫, carpet
카펫이 깔리다, carpet
카폰, car phone
카풀, carpool
칵 소리 나다, click
칵테일, cocktail
칸, stall
칸(막이), compartment
칸막이, partition, screen
칸막이 공간, cubicle
칸막이 벽을 없애다, knock
칸막이가 없는, open-plan
칸막이로 분할하다, partition
칸막이를 한 곳, stall
칼, sword
칼라, collar
칼럼니스트, columnist
칼로 찌르다, knife
칼로리, calorie
칼리지, college
칼새, swift

칼슘, calcium
칼슘 함량이 낮은, soft
칼집, sheath
칼집을 내다, score
깜깜하게 되다, black
캐내려고 하다, fish
캐드, CAD
캐러멜, caramel
캐럴, carol
캐럿, carat
캐리커처, caricature
캐묻기 좋아하는, inquisitive
캐비닛, cabinet, filing cabinet
캐비아, caviar
캐서롤, casserole
캐스팅보트, casting vote
캐스팅하다, cast
캐시 메모리, cache
캐시미어, cashmere
캐시플로, cash flow
캐주얼의, casual
캐주얼하게, casually
캔버스, canvas
캔버스 천, canvas
캠코더, camcorder
캠프 지도원, counselor
캠프용 트레일러, camper
캠프장, camp, campsite
캠핑, camping
캡션, caption
캡슐, capsule
캣워크, catwalk
캥거루, kangaroo
커다란, huge, mortal
커리큘럼, curriculum
커밍아웃 하다, come
커버, cover, jacket, upholstery
커브, corner
커브를 돌다, corner
커서, cursor
커스터드, custard
커스터드 소스, custard
커지다, dilate, grow, widen
커튼, curtain
커플, couple
커피, coffee
커피숍, coffee shop
커피점, café
컨버터블, convertible
컨베이어 벨트, conveyor belt
컨설팅, consultancy
컨설팅 회사, consultancy
컨소시엄, consortium
컨테이너, container
컨트리 뮤직, country
컬러, color
컬러로, color
컬렉션, collection
컬트, cult
컬트적인, cult
컴백, comeback
컴퓨터, computer
컴퓨터 게임, computer game
컴퓨터 문서, document
컴퓨터 사용, computing
컴퓨터 사용 능력이 있는, computerate, computer-literate
컴퓨터 설계, CAD
컴퓨터 응용 프로그램, application
컴퓨터 프로그램의 오류를 수정하다, debug
컴퓨터 합성의자 사진, e-fit
컴퓨터로 처리하다, computerize
컴퓨터를 사용하는, computational
컴퓨터에 저장된, computerized
컴퓨터의, computing
컵, cup
컷, cut
케이, carat
케이블, cable
케이블 방송, cable
케이블카, tram
케이스, case
케이오, knockout
케이크, cake
케이크 팬, cake pan
케이터링, catering
케이프, cape

켜, base, layer
켜다, flip, put, strike, turn
켜지다, come, turn
켜진, on, up
켜켜로 쌓다, layer
코, nose, stitch
코골기, snore
코끼리, elephant
코끼리의 코, trunk
코냑, cognac
코냑 한 잔, cognac
코너 히트, corner
코너킥, corner
코담배, snuff
코드, chord, code, cord
코드 번호, code
코드로 표시하다, code
코드화, coding
코드화된, coded
코란, Koran, Quran
코로 흡입하다, snort
코르크, cork
코르크 마개, cork
코르크 마개 따개, corkscrew
코를 골다, snore
코를 킁킁거리다, sniff
코를 풀다, blow
코를 훌쩍거리다, sniff
코미디, comedy
코미디 같은 일, farce
코미디언, comedian
코미디의, comic
코브라, cobra
코뿔소, rhino, rhinoceros
코스, course, run
코스 요리, course
코와 주둥이 부분, muzzle
코웃음, snort
코웃음 치다, snort
코의, nasal
코일, coil
코치, coach, trainer
코치하다, coach
코카인, cocaine, coke
코카인 마약, crack
코코넛, coconut
코코아, cocoa
코크스, coke
코트, coat, court
콘도르, vulture
콘돔, condom, rubber
콘돔을 사용하지 않은, unprotected
콘서트, concert
콘센트, outlet, plug, point, socket
콘솔, console
콘체르토, concerto
콘크리트, cement, concrete
콘크리트 조각, masonry
콘크리트를 깔다, concrete
콘택트렌즈, contact lens
콜 센터, call center
콜라, cola
콜라주, collage
콜레라, cholera
콜레스테롤, cholesterol
콜론, colon
콜리플라워, cauliflower
콤비, duo
콤팩트디스크, CD, compact disc
콧구멍, nostril
콧김, snort
콧김을 내뿜다, snort
콧노래를 부르다, hum
콧대, bridge
콧대를 꺾다, humble
콧물이 흐르는, runny
콧방귀, sniff, snort
콧방귀 뀌다, sniff, snort
콧방귀를 뀌다, nose
콧수염, mustache
콩, bean, pulse
콩류, pulse
콩팥, kidney
쾅, bump
쾅 내려놓다, bang
쾅 닫다, bang, slam
쾅 치다, bang
쾅 하고 내려놓다, slam

쾅 하는 소리, bang
쾅 하며 닫히다, bang
쾌락주의, hedonism
쾌락주의의, hedonistic
쾌속으로 달리다, barrel
쾌적한, agreeable, cheerful, congenial, hospitable
쾌적한 설비, amenity
쾌활하게, jauntily
쾌활한, jaunty, vivacious
쾌히, kindly
쾌히 받아들이는, amenable
쿠데타, coup, coup d'état
쿠션, cushion
쿠키, cookie
쿠폰, coupon, voucher
쿡 찌르기, dig
쿡 찌르다, jab, poke
쿨렁쿨렁 하는 소리, gurgle
쿨렁쿨렁 하는 소리를 내다, gurgle
쿵, bump
쿵 소리를 내다, boom
쿵 하고 부딪치다, bang
쿵 하는 소리, boom
쿵쾅거리다, thump
쿵쿵거리는 소리, tramp
쿵쿵거리며 걷다, stomp, tramp
쿼터, quota
쿼트, quart
쿼티 자판의, QWERTY
퀭한, sunken
퀴즈, quiz
퀴퀴한, stale
퀵서비스로 보내다, courier
퀸, queen
큐, cue
큐레이터, curator
큐를 보내다, cue
크게, big time, greatly, grossly, loudly, mile, mortally, strongly, widely
크게 기뻐하다, rejoice
크게 다치다, maul
크게 당황한, off-balance
크게 도움이 되다, stead
크게 동요하다, reel
크게 되다, big
크게 생각하다, big
크게 울리다, boom
크게 위축시키다, decimate
크게 읽다, read
크게 하다, dilate, turn
크게 흔들리다, jolt
크기, dimension, extent, magnitude, proportion, size
크래커, cracker
크랭크, crank
크레디트, credit
크레바스, crevice
크레센트, crescent
크레용, crayon
크로뮴, chromium
크로스, cross
크로스오버, crossover
크로스컨트리 경주, cross-country
크루와상, croissant
크로켓, croquet
크롤, crawl
크롬, chrome
크리스마스, Christmas, Christmas Day, Xmas
크리스마스 전야, Christmas Eve
크리스털, crystal
크리켓, cricket
크리켓 선수, cricketer
크림, cream
크림 같은, creamy
크림 성분이 들어 있는 것, cream
크림색의, cream
크림을 함유한, creamy
(~보다) 큰, above, big, dilated, extensive, great, gross, hefty, large, powerful, strong, wide
큰 가위, shear
큰 간격, gulf
큰 걸음, stride
큰 고깃덩이, joint
큰 관심과 인기의 대상, sensation

(~에) 큰 관심을 보이다, seize
큰 구멍, crater
큰 그릇, basin
큰 기대, hope
큰 냄비, casserole
큰 노력과 결심을 요하는, challenging
큰 대자로 눕다, sprawl
큰 덩어리, hunk
큰 도로를 이용하지 않고, country
큰 변동, swing
큰 부분을 차지하는, strong
큰 부상 없음, harm
큰 불, blaze
큰 사슴, moose
큰 사업, big business
큰 소리, blare
큰 소리 내며 급히 움직이다, hurtle
큰 소리로, loud, loudly
큰 소리로 늘어놓다, recite
큰 소리로 말하다, shout
큰 소리로 외치다, hoot
큰 소리로 울다, bawl
큰 소리로 웃다, roar
큰 소리를 내며 질주하다, thunder
큰 솥, cauldron
큰 수요, run
큰 수익원, moneymaker, moneyspinner
큰 스푼, tablespoon
큰 슬픔, grief
큰 실수, crime
큰 웃음, howl
큰 웃음소리, roar
큰 일, big deal
큰 접시, platter
큰 차이, conflict, gulf
큰 채구, bulk
큰 충격, trauma
큰 키, height
큰 통, butt
큰 한 모금, slug
(~에) 큰돈을 쓰다, shelling
큰소리로 껄껄 웃다, howl
클라리넷, clarinet
클러치, clutch
클럽, club, mess
클럽 한 잔, club
클럽 회관, club, clubhouse
클레이 코트, clay
클로즈, Close
클로즈드 숍, closed shop
클로즈업, close-up
클로즈업으로, close-up
클릭, click
클릭하다, click
클립, clip
클립보드, clipboard
클립으로 고정시키다, clip
킁킁거림, sniff
킁킁대며 냄새 맡다, sniff
키, height, key, rudder
키 높이보다 깊은 곳에 빠진, depth
키 누르기, keystroke
키 작은, dwarf
키가 ~인, tall
키가 작은, short
키가 큰, tall, upright
키가 훨씬 크다, tower
키득거리다, snigger
키득거림, snigger
키보드, keyboard
키스, kiss
(~에게) 키스를 불어 보내다, kiss
키스하다, kiss
키오스크, kiosk
키우다, build, nurture, raise, rear
키위, kiwi, kiwi fruit
키퍼, keeper
킥, kick
킥 웃음, chuckle
킥 하고 웃다, chuckle
킥보드, scooter
킥오프, kickoff
킬로, kilo
킬로그램, kilogram
킬로미터, kilometer, km
킬로바이트, kilobyte

킬로와트, kilowatt, KW
킬로헤르츠, kilohertz
킹, king
킹 메이커, power broker
타개, break
타개하다, break
타격, blow, knock
타격받다, bruise
타격을 입히다, toll
타격을 주다, hit
(~을) 타고 가다, ride
타고 있는, board, burn, burning
타고난, born, effortless, innate, natural
타고난 것, inheritance
타고난 명수, natural
타고난 재능, instinct
타고난 재능이 있는, gifted
타기, ride
타는 듯이, burning
타는 듯이 더운, blazing
타는 듯한, burning, searing
타는 사람, rider
타다, board, burn, catch, get, lace, mount, ride, take
타닥타닥 하는 소리, crackle
타당성, adequacy, validity
타당성을 입증하다, validate
타당성이 없는, invalid
타당하게, reasonably, soundly
타당하다, add, hold
타당한, advisable, good, justified, legitimate, logical, reasonable, sound, valid
타도, overthrow
타도되다, overthrow
타동사의, transitive
타락, corruption, degradation, perversion
타락시키다, corrupt, degrade
타락한, corrupt, degenerate
타락한 상태, perversion
타르, tar
타맥, tarmac
타맥 포장 도로, tarmac
타박상, bruise
타블로이드판 신문, tabloid
타석에 서다, bat
타성, force
타악기, percussion
타오르게 하다, ignite
타오르는, burn, burning
타오르다, blaze, flame
타워, tower
타원, oval
타원형의, oval
타의 추종을 불허하는, unbeatable
타이밍, timing
타이어, tire
타이츠, tights
타이틀, title
타이프 치기, typing
타이프 치다, type
타인의 시선을 의식하는, self-conscious
타일, tile
타임아웃, time out
타자, batter, typing
타자 기술, typing
타자기, typewriter
타자기로 치다, type
타자수, typist
타조, ostrich
타진하다, sound
타트, tart
타파하다, explode
타협, compromise, conciliation
타협을 보다, strike
타협이 불가능한, irreconcilable
타협적인, conciliatory
타협하다, compromise, halfway, term
타협하지 않는, uncompromising
타협하지 않음, intransigence
탁, snap
탁 소리 나게, thump
탁 소리 나게 놓다, thump
탁 치기, thump

탁 터놓은, informal
탁 트인, open
탁상공론의, academic
탁상용 컴퓨터, desktop
탁상용의, desktop
탁송품, consignment
탁아소, day nursery
탁월한, eminent, great
탁월함, distinction
탁탁 소리를 내며, thud
탁한, cloudy
(~을) 탄, aboard, burnt
탄갱, colliery
탄광, pit
탄두, warhead
탄력, elasticity, momentum, resilience, tone
탄력 있는, resilient
탄력성, flexibility
탄력성 있는, elastic
탄력적인, flexible
탄막, barrage
탄산, soda, soda water
탄산을 첨가한, sparkling
탄산음료, pop, soda, soda pop
탄산음료 한 잔, soda pop
탄산의, carbonated
탄산이 안 든, still
탄생, birth
탄생하다, born
탄소, carbon
탄수화물, carbohydrate, starch
탄수화물 식품, carbohydrate
탄식, sigh
탄식하다, grave, sigh
탄알, pellet
탄약, ammunition, munitions
탄약통, cartridge
탄원, plea, pleading
탄원서, petition
탄창, magazine
탄탄하게, solidly
탄탄하게 하다, tone
탄탄한, firm, healthy, powerful, solid
탄탄함, solidity, tone
탄핵, denunciation
탈, upset
(~을) 탈 잡다, niggle
탈구시키다, dislocate
탈라, exit
탈락되다, drop, knock
탈바꿈시키다, transform
탈색되다, bleach
탈색하다, bleach
탈선, deviation
탈선하다, derail, rail
탈세, tax evasion
탈수, dehydration
탈수되다, dehydrate
탈수시키다, dehydrate
탈영병, deserter
탈영하다, desert
탈옥, breakout
탈옥하다, break
탈이 난, upset
탈장, hernia
탈지 우유, skim milk
탈지면, cotton, cotton wool
탈출, escape, flight
탈출구, escape
탈출하다, escape
탈취, takeover
탈취범, hijacker
탈취제, deodorant
탈퇴, withdrawal
탈퇴하다, leave, withdraw
탈피하다, grow
탈환, recapture
탈환하다, recapture
탐구, exploration, quest
탐구자, seeker
탐구하다, explore, pore
탐닉, addiction, binge
탐닉하다, indulge
탐독하다, devour
탐문, inquiry

탐사, exploration
탐사하다, explore, probe, prospect
탐색, quest
탐색하는, searching
탐색하다, explore
탐욕, greed
탐욕스러운, greedy, insatiable
탐욕스럽게, greedily
탐정, detective
탐정의, detective
탐조등, searchlight
탐지, detection
탐지기, detector
탐지하다, detect, scan, track
탐침(探針), probe
탐탁지 않게 생각하다, disapprove
탐탁지 않다는 듯이, disapprovingly
탐탁지 않은, undesirable
탐탁지 않음, disapproval
탐탁해 하지 않는, disapproving
탐폰, tampon
탐험, expedition
탐험가, explorer
탐험대, expedition
탑, tower
탑승 수속대, check-in
탑승 수속을 밟다, check
탑승구, gate
탑승권, boarding card
탑승해서, aboard
탓, fault
(~의) 탓으로 돌리다, ascribe, door, put
(~을) 탓하다, fault
탕, snap
탕 하는 소리, bang
탕감하다, write
탕진하다, blow, get
태도, attitude, bearing, behavior, front, gesture, manner, position, posture, spirit, stance, stand
(~한) 태도의, -mannered
태도의 변화, heart
태만, negligence
태만하게, negligently
태만한, negligent, slack
태만히 하다, neglect
태생, birth
태생의, birth
(~할) 태세의, set
태아, embryo, fetus, unborn
태양, sun
태양계, solar system
태양열의, solar
태양의, solar
태어나다, born
(~가) 태어난, birth, native
태업, go-slow, slowdown
태연한, unconcerned
태엽 장치, clockwork
태우기, pick-up
태우다, burn
태워 줌, lift
태중의, unborn
태클, tackle
태클하다, tackle
태평스러운, carefree
태평스러움, complacency
태평한, complacent, easygoing
태풍, hurricane, typhoon
태피스트리, tapestry
태형, corporal punishment, flogging
태환성, convertibility
태환할 수 있는, convertible
택시, cab, taxi
택시 승차장, taxi rank, taxi stand
택지 개발업자, developer
택하다, take
탱크, tank
터, site
터널, tunnel
터널을 파다, tunnel
터놓고, explicitly
터놓고 말하는, open
터득하다, digest
터뜨리다, burst, rupture, vent

터무니없게, unreasonably
터무니없는, absurd, exorbitant, extortionate, extraordinary, extravagant, farcical, far-fetched, fond, indecent, ludicrous, preposterous, ridiculous, unreasonable
터무니없는 돈을 요구받다, nick
터무니없이, absurdly, indecently, ludicrously, outrageously, preposterously, wildly
터무니없이 비싸게, extravagantly
터무니없이 비싼, overpriced
터미널, terminal
터벅터벅 걷기, trudge
터벅터벅 걷는 소리, tramp
터벅터벅 걷다, plod, tramp, trudge
터부, taboo
터부시된, forbidden
터빈, turbine
터전, backyard
터져 나갈 지경이다, seam
터져 나오는, hysterical
터지는 소리, peal
터지다, break, burst, erupt, rupture
(~으로) 터질 듯한, bursting
터치스크린, touchscreen
터치톤식의, touch-tone
터키옥색, turquoise
턱, chin, jaw
턱뼈, jaw
턱수염, beard
턱수염을 기른, bearded
턱시도, tuxedo
털, coat, fleece, fur, hair
털 깎기, shearing
털끝만큼 하다, stroke
털끝만한 관심도 두지 않다, damn
털다, brush, shake
털실로 짠, knit
털썩, heavily
털썩 내리다, dump
털썩 놓다, slap, smack
털썩 던지다, smack
털썩 주저앉다, flop, slump
털어놓다, tell, unlock
털을 깎다, shear
털이 많은, hairy
털이 없는, naked
털털거리다, splutter
텁수룩한, shaggy
텅 빈, bare
텅 빈 큰 공간, void
텅 빔, emptiness
(~) 테가 달린, edged
(~로) 테가 둘러진, border
테너, tenor
테너의, tenor
테니스, tennis
테두리, border, circumference, rim
테라스, patio, terrace
테라코타, terracotta
테러, terror
테러 행위, terrorism
테러리스트, terrorist
테러리즘, terrorism
테마, theme
테마 음악, theme
테스토스테론, testosterone
테스트를 통해 효능이 입증된, tried
테스트하다, pilot, test
테이블, booth
테이블스푼, tablespoon
테이크아웃 음식, takeaway, takeout
테이크아웃 전문점, takeaway, takeout
테이프, tape
테이프 스트리머, tape streamer
테이프로 붙이다, tape
텐트, tent
텔레마케팅, telemarketing
텔레비전, box, television, telly, tube, TV
텔레비전 관련 산업, television
텔레비전으로 방송되다, televise
텔레파시, telepathy

토, Sat.
토끼, bunny, hare, rabbit
토너먼트, tournament
토너먼트의, knockout
토닉, tonic
토닥이다, pat
토대, base, basis, foundation, template
(~을) 토대로 하다, build
토론, consultation, debate, dialog
토론식의, interactive
토론장, forum
토론회, forum
토리당, Tory
토리당의, Tory
토마토, tomato
토막, block
토사물, sick, vomit
토속 신앙인, pagan
토속신앙의, pagan
토스터, toaster
토스트, toast
토실토실한, plump
토양, earth
토요일, Saturday
토의, debate
토지, land
토지 관리인, bailiff
토착어, vernacular
토착의, indigenous
토치램프, torch
토크 쇼, chat show
토큰, token
토탄, peat
토피, taffy, toffee
토피 한 개, toffee
토하다, throw, vomit
토하려고 하다, gag
톡 쏘는, pungent
톡톡 치다, tap
톡톡 침, tap
톤, ton, tonne
톱, saw
톱날같은, jagged
톱밥, sawdust
톱으로 켜다, saw
통, barrel, holder, pot, tub, tube
통계, statistic
통계적으로, statistically
통계적인, statistical
통계학, statistic
통곡, wail
통곡하다, wail
통과되다, carry, get
통과시키다, pass
통과하게 하다, let
통과하다, cross, get, go, navigate, pass, penetrate
(~를) 통과하여, through
통관 검사대, customs
통근 거리, commute
통근권, commuter belt
통근자, commuter
통근하다, commute
통념대로, popularly
통달, mastery
통달하다, master
통렬하게, keenly
통렬한, blistering, incisive, sharp, stabbing
통례를 벗어난, unconventional
통례의, current
통로, aisle, channel, gangway, hall, line, passage, passageway
통밀로 된, brown
통보, notice
통보하다, communicate
통상 금지, embargo
통상의, conventional
통상적으로, conventionally
통속극, melodrama
통속적 문필가, hack
통신, communication, telecommunications
통신 교육, correspondence course
통신 규약, protocol
통신 판매, mail order
통신 판매 상품, mail order

통신사, news agency
통역, interpreter, translation
통역되다, translate
통역사, interpreter, translator
통역하다, interpret
통용되는, accepted
통일, unification, unity
통일된, cohesive, unified, united
통일성, coherence, uniformity
통일하다, unify
통제, grasp, hold, restriction
통제 불능의, maniac
통제 불능인 사람, cannon
통제가 안 되는, hand
통제권, rein
통제되고 있는, hand
통제되는, control
통제되지 않은, uncontrolled
(~의) 통제를 받고 있는, control
(~의) 통제를 받다, come
통제하다, hand, rein, restrict
통제할 수 없는, uncontrollable
통조림, tin
통조림으로 만든, tinned
통조림으로 만들다, can
통증, ache, pain, prick
통지, notice, notification
통지하다, notify
통째로 삼키다, bolt, gobble
통찰, insight
통찰거리다, insight, perception
통찰력이 있는, perceptive
통치, domination, government, reign, rule
통치권, sovereignty
통치의, governmental
통치자, ruler
통치하는, ruling
통치하다, administer, dominate, govern, reign, rule
통쾌한, sweet
통탄할, deplorable
통통 튀는, bouncy
통통한, chubby, full
통틀어, together
통풍구, vent
통풍이 잘 되는, airy
통하다, open, pass
통합, amalgamation, fusion, integration, integrity, unity
통합되다, incorporate, integrate, unify
통합된, integrated, unified
통합체, whole
통합하다, absorb, consolidate, integrate, unify
(~을) 통해, from, means, over
(~을) 통해서, by, care, through, via
통행 허가, passage
통행료, toll
통행증, pass
통화, call, currency
통화 공급량, money supply
통화 수축, deflation
통화 수축의, deflationary
통화 연결, line
통화 요금을 수신인 부담으로 하다, reverse
통화 중 대기, call waiting
통화 중인, busy, engaged, phone, telephone
통화의, monetary
통화주의, monetarism
통화주의의, monetarist
통화주의자, monetarist
퇴각, retreat
퇴각하다, retreat
퇴거시키다, evict
퇴근 시각을 기록하다, clock
퇴근하다, clock
퇴락, degradation
퇴락하다, degenerate
퇴락한, disused, run-down
퇴보, regression
퇴보하다, regress
퇴비, compost
퇴위, abdication
퇴위하다, abdicate

퇴임하는, outgoing
퇴장, exit
퇴장 명령 카드, red card
퇴장당하다, send
퇴적물, sediment
퇴조, erosion
퇴직, severance
퇴직하여 연금을 받다, pension
퇴진, exit
퇴짜, rebuff, rejection
퇴짜 놓다, rebuff, reject, spurn
퇴출, expulsion
퇴치제, repellent
퇴폐, decadence
퇴폐적인, decadent
퇴학, expulsion
퇴행, regression
퇴행하다, regress
퇴화, degeneration
퇴화하다, degenerate
투과성의, porous
투광 조명, floodlight
투광 조명을 밝히다, floodlight
투구, bowling
투구공, wicket
투구하다, bowl
투기자, speculator
투기적으로, spec
투기적인, speculative
투기하다, speculate
투덜거리다, grumble, whine
투덜대다, gripe, mutter
투덜댐, grumble
투매하다, dump
투명도, transparency
투명성, transparency
투명한, clear, invisible, transparent
투박하게, crudely
투박한, crude, primitive
투사, champion, fighter
투사 환등기, OHP
투사로서 활동하다, champion
투수, bowler, pitcher
투여하다, administer
투영, projection
투영하다, project
투옥, imprisonment, incarceration
투옥되다, imprison, incarcerate
투입, deployment, injection, investment
투입하다, deploy, inject
투자, investment
투자 대상, investment
투자액, investment
투자자, investor
투자하다, invest, put, sink
투쟁, battle, fight, war
투쟁력, fight
투지, fight, grit
투창, javelin
투창 경기, javelin
투표, ballot, vote, voting
투표권, vote
투표로 뽑다, vote
투표소, poll
투표수, vote
투표에 부치다, ballot
투표용지, ballot
투표하다, cast, vote
투하, dropping
툭, snap, thud
툭 부러드리다, snap
툭 부러지다, snap
툭 소리 나게 놓다, snap
툭 틴, unrestricted
툭 하고 움직이다, snap
툴툴거리다, grunt
퉁명스러운, abrupt, blunt, brusque, curt, terse
퉁명스럽게, bluntly, curtly, tersely
퉁명스레, abruptly
튀게 하다, bounce
튀기다, fry, spatter, splash, splatter
튀는 사람, odd
튀다, bounce, spatter, splash, splatter, stick
튀어 나오다, bulge
튀어나가다, bolt

뛰어나오다, eject, jut, project, stand
펑겨 나가다, catapult
핑깅, bounce
튜닉, tunic
튜브, tube
튤립, tulip
트다, break
트라이, try
트라이앵글, triangle
트라이플, trifle
트래커 펀드, tracker fund
트랙, track
트랙터, tractor
트랙터트레일러, tractor-trailer
트럭, lorry, truck
트럭 운전사, trucker
트럭 화물칸, trailer
트럭으로 운반되다, truck
트럼펫, trumpet
트렁크, boot, trunk
트레이너, trainer
트레이드마크, trademark
트레일러, caravan, trailer
트롤 어업을 하다, trawl
트롤선, trawler
트롬본, trombone
트림, belch
트림하다, belch
트위드 천, tweed
특가, offer
특공대, commando
특공대원, commando
특권, prerogative, privilege
특권층, privileged
특급의, deluxe
특기할 점, distinction
특대의, jumbo
특무 비행, mission
특무 상사, sergeant major
특별 공연, gala
특별 관람석, grandstand
특별 사은품, offer
특별 상영 기간, season
특별 상품, special
특별 선물, treat
특별 연구원직, fellowship
특별 위원회, tribunal
특별 제공품, special offer
특별 지도하다, cream
특별 직책의, special
특별 출연자, guest
특별 퇴직금, golden handshake
특별 프로그램, feature, special
특별 할인기, concession
특별 회원, fellow
특별석 구역, box
특별하게, extraordinarily, uniquely
특별한, ad hoc, express, extraordinary, particular, special
특별한 목적을 위해 세워진, purpose-built
특별한 이유 없이, apparent
특별한 훈련이 필요치 않은, unskilled
특별히, additionally, expressly, extra, particularly, specially, specifically
(~에) 특별히 관련된, specific
특별히 아끼는, pet
특사, amnesty, pardon
특산물, native
특산품, speciality
특색, character, touch
특성, attribute, characteristic, edge, peculiarity, property, trait
특성상, nature
(~한) 특성에 넘치는, steeped
특성에 맞지 않게, uncharacteristically
특성에 맞지 않는, uncharacteristic
특수 병과, corps
특수 용어, jargon
특수 효과, effect, special effect
특수한, special, technical
특수한 인종이나 집단에 한정된, segregated

특유의, particular, special
특유하게, peculiarly, uniquely
특유한, peculiar, unique
특이하게, peculiarly, unusually
특이한, peculiar, quirky
특이한 행동 방식, eccentricity
특이함, peculiarity
특전, perk, privilege
특정 상표의 제품, brand
특정 양조 연도의 포도주, vintage
특정 언어 구사자, speaker
특정 종류, brand
특정한, particular, specific
특정한 상태가 되게 하다, set
특정한 상황에서 꼭 하는 일, ritual
특제품, specialty
특종, exclusive
특종 기사, scoop
특집 기사, feature
(~을) 특집으로 다루다, feature
특징, attribute, beauty, character, feature, mark, quality, trait
(~을) 특징으로 하다, characterize
특징을 나타내다, typify
(~한) 특징이 있다고 생각하다, attribute
(~에) 특징적인, characteristic
특징적인 면, cross-section
특파원, correspondent
특허, patent
특허권, patent
특허권 사용료, royalty
특허권을 얻다, patent
특혜, privilege, privileged
특혜를 누리는 자들, privileged
특혜의, preferential
특히, especially, particular, particularly, specifically
튼튼하게, solidly, strongly, sturdily
튼튼한, robust, secure, solid, sound, stable, stout, strong, sturdy
튼튼함, solidity
틀, crate, frame, framework, mold, tin
틀니, dentures
틀다, play, put, run
틀리게, incorrectly, wrong
틀린, inaccurate, incorrect, mistaken, out, wrong
틀림없는, unmistakable
(~임에) 틀림없다, got, must
틀림없이, assure, exactly, honest, surely
틀림없이 ~할 것이다, will
틀림없이 성공할, sure-fire
틀어지게 만들다, sour
틀어지다, sour
틀어진, sour
틀에 넣다, crate
틀에 박힌 생활, routine
틀에 박힌 일, routine
틀을 깨다, mold
틈, aperture, chink, crack, gap
틈새시장, niche
틈새의, niche
(~을) 틈타, cover
티 없이 깨끗하게, spotlessly
티 없이 깨끗한, spotless
티 하나 없이 깨끗한, immaculate
(~) 티가 나는, tinged
티격태격, squabbling
티격태격하다, squabble
티셔츠, T-shirt
티크, teak
팀, side, team
팀 동료, teammate
팀워크, teamwork
팀원들, crew
팀을 이루다, team
팁, gratuity, service charge, tip
팁을 주다, tip
파, par
파견, dispatch
파견되다, draft
파견하다, dispatch, send
파고들다, bite, burrow, delve, dig
파괴, destruction

파괴 행위, sabotage
파괴되다, knock, sabotage, vandalize
파괴적인, destructive, devastating, disruptive, lethal
파괴하다, blight, destroy, havoc, wreck
파국, meltdown
파기, excavation
파내다, dig, excavate, unearth
파는 쪽 사람, seller
파다, dig, inscribe, sink
파도, surf, wave
파도타기, surfing, windsurfing
파도타기를 하는 사람, surfer
파도타기를 하다, surf
파동, pulse, wave
파라오, pharaoh
파라핀, paraffin
파란색, sapphire
파랑, blue
파렴치한, shameless, unscrupulous
파리, fly
파리 한 마리도 못 죽이는, fly
파마, perm, permanent
파마하다, perm
파멸, destruction
파멸시키다, destroy
파멸하다, dog
파문, ripple
파묻다, bury
파벌, clique, faction
파벌의, factional
파벌적인, sectarian
파산, bankruptcy, failure, ruin
파산시키다, bankrupt, ruin
파산자, bankrupt
파산하다, broke, fail, go
파산하지 않고, afloat
파산한, bankrupt, insolvent
파생 상품, spin-off
파생 효과, spin-off
파생물, derivative
파생하다, derive
파스닙, parsnip
파스타, pasta
파스텔풍의, pastel
파스텔풍의 색조, pastel
파슬리, parsley
파시스트, fascist
파시즘, fascism
파시즘의, fascist
파악, fix, grasp
파악하다, discern, gauge, grasp, hold, pick, take
파악하지 못 하다, mistake
파안대소하게 하다, crack
파안대소하다, crack
파업, strike, walkout
파업 참가자, striker
파업하다, come, strike, walk
파열, rupture
파열되다, rupture
파열시키다, rupture
파운데이션, foundation
파운드, pound
파운드화, pound
파워 스티어링, power steering
파이, pie
파이 껍질, crust
파이 차트, pie chart
파이프, pipe
파이프 담배, pipe
파이프 오르간, organ
파이프 오르간의 음반, pipe
파이프라인, pipeline
파이프로 전달되다, pipe
파인애플, pineapple
파인트, pint
파일, file, pile
파일럿, pilot
파장, ramification, wave, wavelength
파종, planting
파충류, reptile
파탄, breakdown
파탄 나다, break

파탄난, broken
파탄에 이른, bankrupt
파탄을 초래하다, break
파테, pâté
파트너, escort, partner
(~의) 파트너가 되다, partner
파트타임으로, part-time
파트타임의, part-time
파티, do, get-together, party
파티를 열다, party
파티에서 즐겁게 놀다, party
파편, debris, fragment
파헤치다, dig
판, arena, board, edition, landscape, rut, slab
판결, decree, judgment, ruling, verdict
판결에 큰 영향을 주는, material
판결을 받다, find
판결하다, rule
판권, copyright, right
판단, judge, judgment, reading
판단력, acumen, judgment
판단을 흐리다, blind
판단을 유보하다, judgment
판단이 안 서는 점, reservation
판단을 유보하다, jury
판단이 틀린, wrong
(~으로) 판단하건대, judge
판단하다, judge, look, reason
판독기에 넣다, swipe
판독하다, decipher
판돈, kitty
판례가 되는 소송 사건, test case
판매, sale
판매 가격, selling price
판매 관리, point of sale
판매 사원, sales clerk
판매 수량, unit sales
판매 촉진 방안, merchandising
판매되어 발표되다, syndicate
판매량, sale
(~의) 판매를 촉진시키다, sell
판매세, seller
판매세, sales tax
판매원, clerk, salesperson
판매인, dealer, seller
판매자, seller, stockist
판매자 부담으로, house
판매자 시장, seller's market
판명되다, emerge
판사, judge, justice
판에 박힌, routine, stereotypical
판자, board, panel
판자로 막다, board
판잣집, shack
판지, card, cardboard
판촉, promotion
판촉을 벌이다, promote
판화, print
팔, arm
팔 굽혀 펴기, press-up, push-up
팔걸이, arm
팔과 같은 부분, arm
팔꿈치, elbow
팔꿈치로 밀치다, elbow
팔꿈치로 슬쩍 찌르는 것, nudge
팔꿈치로 슬쩍 찌르다, nudge
팔다, sell
팔다리 운동, stretch
팔다리를 아무렇게나 벌리고 앉다, sprawl
팔다리를 쭉 뻗고, full-length
팔뚝, forearm
팔랑거리다, flutter
팔레트, palette
팔려고 내놓은, sale
(~에) 팔리다, fetch, realize, retail, sell
팔아 치우다, sell
팔을 쭉 뻗어, arm
팔짝 뜀, skip
팔짝팔짝 뛰다, skip
팔짱을 끼고, arm
팔짱을 끼다, link
팔찌, bracelet
팔팔한, playful, youthful

팜, cut
팜탑 컴퓨터, palmtop
팝, pop, POP
팝콘, popcorn
팡파르, fanfare
패, circle, hand
패거리, crowd, gang, pack
패거리들, crony
패권, supremacy
패기, dynamism
패널, panel
패널로 된, paneled
패널로 장식된, paneled
패닝하다, pan
패돔 (1.8미터), fathom
패드, pad
패러다임, paradigm
패러디, parody
패러디하다, parody
패러프레이즈, paraphrase
패러프레이즈하다, paraphrase
패배, defeat
패배를 모르는, unbeaten
패배를 선언하다, concede
패배를 인정하다, concede
패배자, loser
패션, fashion
패션쇼의 돌출 무대, catwalk
패스, pass
패스트푸드, fast food
패스하다, pass
패자, loser
패치, patch
패치워크, patchwork
패치워크 식의, patchwork
패키지, package
패킹, packing
패턴, pattern
팩 하고 화를 잘 내는, prickly
팩스, fax
팩시밀리, fax
팩시밀리로 보내다, fax
(~) 팬, buff, fan, pan
팬케이크, pancake
팬터마임, pantomime
팬티, brief, knickers, panties, pants, underpants
팬티스타킹, pantyhose, tights
팸플릿, brochure, pamphlet
팽개치다, chuck
팽창시키다, swell
팽창하다, expand, swell
팽팽한, taut, tight
팽팽해지다, tighten
퍼 주다, ply
퍼내다, scoop
퍼덕거리다, flap, flutter
퍼덕이다, flap
퍼드리다, spread, waft
퍼레이드, parade
퍼부음, bombardment
퍼붓다, bombard, fire, heap, hurl, ply, rain, unleash
퍼센트, percent
퍼지, fudge
퍼지고 있다, go
퍼지기 쉬운, infectious
퍼지다, carry, diffuse, get, infect, permeate, ripple, run, spread, waft
퍼짐, spread
퍼트, putt
퍼트하다, putt
퍼팅 그린, green
퍽, thud
퍽 하는 소리를 냄, thump
퍽 하며, thud
펀치, punch
펄떡거리다, pulse
펄럭이게 하다, flap
펄럭이다, billow, flap
펄럭임, flutter
펄롱, furlong
펄쩍 뛰어, jump
펄프, pulp
펌프, pump
펌프로 공기를 넣다, pump
펑, pop

펑 소리를 내다, pop
펑크, puncture
펑크 나다, puncture
펑크 록, punk
펑크를 내다, puncture
펑크족, punk
펑키한, funky
페널티, penalty
페니실린, penicillin
페달, pedal
페달을 밟다, pedal
페미니스트, feminist
페미니스트의, feminist
페미니즘, feminism
페스트, plague
페이소스, pathos
페이스트, paste
페이지, page, pp
페이퍼, paper
페이퍼백, paperback
페이퍼뷰, pay-per-view
페인트, paint
페인트가 벗겨지다, peel
페인트공, painter
페인트칠, paint
페인트칠하다, paint
펜, pen
펜더, fender
펜던트, pendant
펜싱, fencing
펜치, pliers
펜트하우스, penthouse
펠트, felt
펠트 펜, felt-tip
펭귄, penguin
펴 바르다, spread
펴다, flatten, flex, open, spread, turn, unfold
펴지다, flatten, open, unfold
편, side
편(篇), book
편견, bias, prejudice
편견 없음, open-mindedness
편견을 가지게 하다, prejudice
편견을 가진, biased, prejudiced
편견을 갖게 하다, bias
편견이 없는, open-minded
편곡, arrangement
편곡되다, arrange
편대를 이뤄, formation
편도 차표, single
편도로, one-way
편도의, one-way, single
편두통, migraine
편들다, side
편람, handbook
편리, convenience
편리하게, conveniently
편리하게, handy, suit
편리한, convenient, expedient, soft
편리한 것, convenience
편리함, ease
편법, expedient
편성, organization
편승하다, hitchhike
편안하게, casually, comfortably
편안하게 생각하는, casual
편안한, comfortable, comfy, cozy, easy, smooth
편안함, comfort
편안히, peacefully
편안히 쉬다, lounge
편안히 앉다, settle
편애, favoritism
편애하다, favor
(~의) 편을 들다, defense
편의, convenience, expediency, facility
(~의) 편의를 위한, -friendly
편의에 따라, selectively
편의적인, selective
편익, convenience
편익을 제공하다, service
(~의) 편인, side
편자, editor, horseshoe
편자 모양의 물건, horseshoe

편재하는, ubiquitous
편중된, weighted
편지, correspondence, letter
편지 봉투, envelope
편지 쓰기, correspondence
편지를 보내다, write
(~와) 편지를 주고받다, correspond
편집 프로그램, editor
편집물, compilation
편집의, editorial
편집인, editor
편집장, editor
편집증, paranoia
편집증 환자, paranoid
편집증의, paranoid
편집증적인, paranoid
편집하다, compile, edit
편찬물, compilation
편찬하다, compile
편취하다, defraud
편파적인, one-sided, partial
편평한, flat
편평한 모양의, flat
편평한 부분, flat
편하게, comfortably, easily, sensibly
편하고 튼튼한, sensible
편한, comfortable, convenient, plush, relaxing, soft
편한 속도로, pace
편향, slant
편향되다, slant
편협하게, narrowly
편협한, bigoted, insular, intolerant, narrow, narrow-minded, parochial
편협한 사람, bigot
편협함, bigotry, insularity, intolerance, narrowness
편히 몸을 눕히다, nestle
편히 쉬다, foot
펼쳐지다, unfold, unfurl
펼쳐진, open
펼치다, spread, unfold, unfurl
평가, appraisal, assessment, estimate, estimation, evaluation, feedback, opinion, rating
평가 절상하다, revalue
평가 절하, devaluation
평가 절하되다, depreciate
평가 절하하다, depreciate, devalue
평가되다, rate
평가인, assessor
평가지, worksheet
평가하다, appraise, assess, evaluate, place, rank, rate, set, value
평결, finding, verdict
평균, average
평균 ~이다, average
평균 가치, basket
평균 미달인, par
평균의, average
평균적으로, average
평균치, average
평등, equality
평등하게 하다, equalize
평등한, equal
평론, critique
평론가, critic
평론가들의, critical
평면, flat, plane
평면 교차, level crossing
평발의, flat
평방, sq
평방의, square
평범하게, conventionally
평범하게 생긴, homely
평범하지 않은, quirky
평범한, common, commonplace, conventional, middle-of-the-road, mundane, ordinary, plain, unremarkable
평범한 것, mundane
평범함, mediocrity
평사원들, rank and file
평상복으로, informally

평상복의, casual, informal
평상시 먹는 음식, diet
평상시에, ordinarily
평생 교육, continuing education
평생의, lifelong
평생토록, long
평소의, regular
평안, peace
평영, breaststroke
평온, calm, peace, serenity, tranquillity
평온하게, peacefully, serenely
평온한, calm, gentle, peace, peaceful, serene, tranquil, undisturbed
평온함, calm
평원, plain
평의원의, backbench
평의회, Senate
평이한, pedestrian
평일, week, weekday, workday
평정, composure, equilibrium, poise
평정을 되찾다, recover
평정을 잃지 않는, balanced
평지풍파, storm
평탄한, flat
평판, name, reputation, tablet
평판 있는, reputable
평판에, reputedly
평판을 듣고, reputation
평판이 나빠지는, disrepute
평판이 나쁜, seedy
평평하지 않은, uneven
평평한, even, flat, level
평하다, describe
평행한, parallel
평형, equilibrium
평화, peace
평화로운, peaceful
평화롭게, peacefully
평화를 유지하다, peace
평화적으로, amicably, peacefully
평화적인, amicable, peaceful
평화주의, pacifism
평화주의자, pacifist
평화주의적인, pacifist
폐, lung
폐경기, menopause
폐경기의, menopausal
폐기되다, pulp
폐기물, waste
폐기하다, break, ditch, dump, jettison, kill, scrap
폐렴, pneumonia
폐로 여기다, mind
폐물, junk
폐물이 된, obsolete
폐색, obstruction
폐쇄, closing, closure, shutdown
폐쇄 회로, closed-circuit
폐쇄 회로 텔레비전, CCTV
폐쇄되다, shut
폐쇄하다, close, shut
폐업, closing, closure, shutdown
폐쇄하다, close, wind
폐점 후에, hour
폐점되다, shut
폐점하다, close
폐지, abolition, repeal
폐지하다, abolish, do, repeal
폐품인, scrap
폐하, majesty
폐허, ruin
폐허가 된, ruined
폐허로 만드는, devastating
폐허로 만들다, devastate
포, artillery
포개지다, superimpose
포격, bombardment, shelling
포격하다, shell
포경업, whaling
포고, declaration
포고령, decree
포고령을 내리다, decree
포괄적인, blanket, comprehensive, extensive, generic, global, sweeping

포괄하다, span, stretch
포기, abandonment, surrender
포기를 공표하다, renounce
포기하다, abandon, forfeit, give, jettison, quit, relinquish, sacrifice, surrender, towel, waive
포도, grape
포도나무, vine
포도당, glucose
포도원, vineyard
포도주, wine
포도주 공장, vineyard
포도주 저장실, cellar
포동포동한, plump
포로, captive, prisoner
포로로 잡다, captive
포르노, porn
포르노그래피, pornography
포르노의, pornographic
포리지, porridge
포만감, fullness
포만감을 주는, filling
포만감을 주다, fill
포맷, format
포맷하다, format
포병대, artillery
포복절도하는, hysterics
포상, distinction
포스터, poster
포식자, predator
포식하는, predatory
포식하다, stuff
포악한, vicious
포옹, cuddle, embrace, hug
포옹하다, embrace, hug
포용, acceptance, embrace
포용력 있는, expansive
포용하다, embrace
포위, siege
포위되다, surround
포위하다, besiege, close, siege
포유동물, mammal
포일, foil
포장, packing, packaging
포장 용기, package
포장도로, pavement
포장되다, package, pave
포장지, wrapper, wrapping
포장하다, pack, wrap
포주, pimp
포주 노릇을 하다, pimp
포즈, pose
포즈를 취하다, pose
(~을) 포진시키다, surround
포착하다, pick, seize
포커, poker
포커스 그룹, focus group
포켓볼, billiards
포켓형의, pocket
포크, fork
포크로 먹다, fork
포탄, shell
포털사이트, portal
포테이토칩, crisp
포트, port
포트 와인, port
포트폴리오, portfolio
포학, tyranny
포함, inclusion, insertion
포함되다, include, write
(~에) 포함되어 있다, embody
포함된, included
포함시키다, add, build, count
포함하다, add, comprise, contain, embrace, encompass, extend, include, incorporate, insert
(~을) 포함하여, including, inclusive
포함한, inclusive
포회, gunfire
포화 상태, saturation
포화 상태를 만들다, saturate
포화를 받는, fire
포효, roar
폭, breadth, span, width
폭격, bombing, bombardment
폭격기, bomber
폭군, tyrant

폭넓게, broadly, widely
폭넓은, broad, eclectic, wide
폭넓은 의미로, broadly
폭넓은 의미의, broad
폭넓음, spread
폭도, mob, rioter
폭동, insurrection, riot, rioting
폭동을 일으키다, riot
폭락, dive, nosedive, plunge, slump, tumble
폭락하다, dive, nosedive, plummet, slump, tumble
폭력, violence
폭력 강도, mugging
폭력 사태, rage
폭력 장면이 많은, violent
폭력단, gang
폭력이 난무하는, tough
폭력적인, violent
폭로, exposure, revelation, whistle-blowing
폭로 보도의, investigative
폭로된 것, revelation
폭로적인, revealing
폭로하다, expose, give, reveal
폭리 취득 행위, profiteering
폭발, blast, eruption, explosion, gust, outburst
폭발 직전의, volatile
폭발로 생기다, blast
폭발물, explosive
폭발시키다, detonate, explode, let, set, unleash
폭발의, explosive
폭발적 증가, explosion
폭발적인, explosive
폭발적인 반응, sensation
폭발하다, blast, detonate, erupt, explode, go, snap
폭발하듯이, hysterically
폭삭 타 버리다, ground
폭소, gale
폭식증 환자, bulimic
폭식하는, bulimic
폭언, abuse
폭언을 하다, strike
폭우, downpour
폭우가 쏟아지다, pour
폭이 ~인, wide
폭죽, firework
폭탄, bomb
폭탄 파편, shrapnel
폭탄선언, bombshell
폭탄선언 하다, bombshell
폭파, blast, explosion
폭파 장치, trigger
폭파되다, blow
폭파범, bomber
폭파시키다, bomb
폭파하다, blow
폭포, fall, waterfall
폭포처럼 쏟아지다, cascade
폭풍, storm
폭풍우, storm
폭풍우가 몰아치는, stormy
폭행, assault
폭행하다, assault, attack
폴더, folder
폴로, polo
폴리스티렌, polystyrene
폴리에스테르, polyester
폴리에틸렌, polyethylene, polythene
폴트, fault
표, table, ticket
표결, vote
표류하다, drift
표류하여, adrift
표면, surface
표면상, face
표면상의, cosmetic, superficial
표면으로 떠오르다, surface
표면의, right
표명, statement
표명하다, declare, profess, voice
표백제, bleach
표백하다, bleach
표범, leopard

표본, example, sample, specimen
(~의) 표본이 되다, exemplify
표상, emblem, poster child
표시, indication, mark, show, signal
표시 도구, marker
표시를 달다, tag
표시를 안 한, unmarked
(~을) 표시하는, indicative
표시하다, indicate, mark, record, signify
표적, target
표적으로 삼다, target
표절 행위, plagiarism
표절하다, plagiarize
표정, expression, face, look
표정 없는, blank
(~한) 표정으로 찡그리다, screw
표정의, expressive
표제, heading, headline, title
표제가 붙다, head, headline
표제를 장식하다, headline
표준, criterion, norm
표준 키보드의, QWERTY
표준시, standard time
표준적인, standard
표준화, standardization
표준화하다, standardize
표지, binding, cover, jacket
표지판, sign
표찰, plate
표창장, citation
표창하다, recognize
표출, release
표출되다, exude
표출하다, release
표피상의, superficial
(~을) 표해야 한다, owe
표현, demonstration, expression, statement
표현 수단, outlet
표현의, expressive
표현하다, express, offer, phrase, put
표현한 것, representation
푸드덕거리다, beat
푸들, poodle
푸딩, pudding
푸주한, butcher
푸짐한 식사, meal
푹 누르다, jab
푹 들어간 곳, socket
푹 빠지게 하는, irresistible
푹 빠지다, carry, crazy
푹 빠진, addicted, deep, hooked, mad, married
푹 쓰러지다, drop, fall, flat, slump
푹 익은, well done
푹신한 이불, comforter
풀, paste, starch
풀다, clear, crack, loosen, solve, undo, unpack, unravel, untie, unwind, unwrap
풀려고 애쓰다, grapple
풀려나다, release
풀려난, free
풀로 붙이다, paste
풀리다, fray, unravel, work
풀리지 않은, unsolved
풀린, loose
풀무, bellow
풀숲, grass
풀썩 내려놓다, drop
풀어 내리다, roll
풀어 주다, free
풀어내다, figure
풀어지다, loosen
풀오버, pullover
풀을 뜯어 먹다, browse
풀이 무성한, grassy
풀이 죽은, down
품격, style
품격 있는, gracious
품귀의, premium
품다, conceive, harbor, hold, incubate, nurse
품목, item
품성, character

품에 안다, hug
품위, decency, dignity
품위 없는, common
품위 있게, gracefully
품위 있는, genteel, graceful
품이 넉넉한, full
품종, breed
품질, caliber, grade
품질 관리, quality control
품질 보증서, warranty
품질을 떨어뜨리다, adulterate
품질이 떨어지는, doubtful
품행, demeanor
품행이 단정한, well-behaved
풋내기의, green
풍경, landscape, scenery, sight
풍경화, landscape
풍기다, emanate
풍랑이 거센, stormy
풍력, force
풍력 발전기, windmill
풍문, grapevine, rumor
풍부, richness
풍부한, abound, abundant, copious, full, plentiful, rich
풍부한 자원, rich
풍부함, abundance
풍선, balloon
풍성하게, liberally
풍성한, liberal, rich
풍성함, bounty, richness
풍요로움, bounty
풍우, element
풍자, irony, satire
풍자극, satire
풍자적인, satirical
풍작의, bumper
풍조, bandwagon
풍차, windmill
풍채, presence
풍취를 곁들이다, spice
풍화되다, weather
퓌레, puree
퓌레로 만들다, puree
퓨전, fusion
퓨즈, fuse
프라이팬, frying pan
프랜차이저, franchiser
프랜차이즈, franchise
프런트, front desk, reception
프런트 직원, receptionist
프레임, frame
프렌치프라이, potato chip
프로, pro, professional
프로그래머, programmer
프로그래밍, programming
프로그램, program, show
프로그램을 넣다, program
프로그램을 짜다, program
프로로서, professionally
프로모터, promoter
프로의, professional
프로젝터, projector
프로젝트, project
프로토콜, protocol
프로펠러, propeller
프로필, profile
프루프의, proof
프리랜스로, freelance
프리랜스의, freelance
프리미엄을 붙여, premium
프린터, printer
플라스크, flask
플라스크에 가득한 양, flask
플라스틱, plastic, vinyl
플라스틱 물질, PVC
플라스틱 솔, bristle
플라크, plaque
플라타너스, plane
플란넬, flannel
플랫, flat
플래시, flash
플래시백, flashback
플래카드, placard
플랫의, flat
플랫폼, platform
플러그, plug
플러그 앤 플레이식의,

plug-and-play
플러그 접속식의, plug-in
플러그를 뽑다, unplug
플러그인, plug-in
플러스, plus
플레이어, deck
플레이오프, playoff
플레임, flame
플로 차트, flow chart
플로피 디스크, floppy disk
플루토늄, plutonium
플루트, flute
피, blood
(~에) 피가 났다, bloody
피격당한, fire
피고, defendant
피고석, dock
피고용인, employee
피고인, accused
피난, refuge
피난민, evacuee
피난처, haven
피날레, finale
피다, open
피도 눈물도 없는, cold-blooded
피드백, feedback
피디에이, personal digital assistant
피딱지, gore
피라미드, pyramid
피라미드 모양의 것, pyramid
피라미드 조직, pyramid
피라미드식 판매, pyramid selling
피로, exhaustion, fatigue, tiredness
피로감, fatigue
피로하게 하다, tire
피로하다, tire
피로한, tired
피를 흘리다, bleed
피를 흘리며 죽게 만들다, shed
피를 흘리며 죽다, shed
피리, pipe
피막, membrane
피망, bell pepper, pepper
피면접자, interviewee
피보호자, protégé
피부, skin
피부가 벗겨지다, rub
피부색, color, coloring, complexion
피부양자, dependent
피비린내 나는, bloody
피사체, subject
피상적인, superficial
피스톤, piston
피스트, piste
피시방, Internet café
피신, escape, flight, refuge
피신시키다, get
피신처, cover, refuge, safe haven, sanctuary
피실험자, subject
피아노, piano
피아니스트, pianist
피어, out
피어 오르다, billow
피어싱을 하다, pierce
피억압자들, oppressed
피우다, bear, puff, smoke
피위 올리다, throw
피임, contraception
피임 링, coil
피임약을 복용 중인, pill
피임용 격막, diaphragm
피임의, contraceptive
피임제, contraceptive
피자, pizza
피처, pitcher
피켓 농성, picket
피켓 농성 대열, picket line
피켓 농성 시위자, picket
피켓 농성을 벌이다, picket
피크, peak
피클, pickle
피클 소스, pickle
피클을 만들다, pickle
피투성이의, bloody
피트, foot, ft, pit

피폐시키다, impoverish
피하 주사, hypodermic
피하 주사의, hypodermic
피하다, avert, avoid, berth, deflect, duck, elude, escape, evade, keep, shrink, shun, shy, steer, ward, way
피학적 성향, masochism
피학적인, masochistic
피할 수 없는, inevitable, unavoidable
피할 수 없는 것, inevitable
(~을) 피할 수 없다, help
피해, damage, off, out
피해 가다, bypass
피해 보상 보장, protection
피해 최소화 대책, damage control
피해로부터 보호받다, buffer
피해를 입기 쉬운, vulnerable
피해를 주다, toll
피해망상증, paranoia
피해자, casualty, survivor, victim
픽셀, pixel
픽업트럭, pick-up
핀, out, pin
핀업, pin-up
필기로 된, written
필기록, transcript
필기체, script
필레, fillet
필름, film
필름의 한 컷, exposure
필름통, canister, cassette
필멸, mortality
필멸의, mortal
필명, pseudonym
필사적으로, desperately
필사적인, cut-throat, desperate
필사적임, desperation
필사하다, transcribe
필수, must
(~에) 필수 불가결한, fundamental
필수 요소, essential
필수 조건, prerequisite
필수의, indispensable, integral, obligatory
필수적인, basic, essential, imperative, vital
필수품, basics, necessity
필연, necessity
필연성, inevitability
필연적으로, inevitably
필연적인, inevitable, necessary
필요, necessity, need, requirement
필요 이상으로, unduly
필요 이상의, overly, undue
(~할) 필요가 있다, occasion, want
(~을) 필요로 하다, call, exact, involve, necessitate, need, require, take
필요조건, requisite
필요치 않은, superfluous
(~이) 필요하다, need, require, want
필요하면, need
필요하면 ~할 수 있다, right
필요한, involved, necessary, ready, requisite
필요한 것을 공급하다, serve
필요한 수단, wherewithal
필요한 자금, wherewithal
필요한 절차를 마치다, motion
필적, handwriting, writing
필적할만한 것이 없는, parallel
필적하는, matched, near
필적하다, equal, match, rival
필적할 만한 상대, rival
필체, writing
필터, filter
핑계, excuse, fodder, pretext
핑크색, pink
하강, descent
하강하다, swoop
(~) 하게 되다, mean, reduce
(~을) 하고 싶다, care, want
하고 싶은 대로, please
하고 싶은 말을 참다, shut

(~를) 하고 있는 중의, act
(~을) 하고자 하다, aim
하급의, junior, lower, pile
하급자, junior, subordinate
(~을) 하기 시작하다, get, start
(~) 하기로 되어 있는, meant
하나, one
하나 걸러의, alternate
하나도 급할 게 없는, hurry
하나도 빠짐없이, each
하나도 빠짐없이 모두, round
하나로 이어 주다, bond
하나의, roll
하나씩, one
하나의 경매물품, lot
하나의 원인, contributor
하나하나, each, through
하나하나 살피다, look
하나하나 확인하다, check
하녀, maid
하느님, god, lord
하느님 맙소사, my
(~을) 하는 것이 좋다, better
하는 사람, performer
하는 중이다, go
하늘, sky
하늘거리다, billow, stir
하늘의, celestial
(~하도록) 하다, bring, confine, deliver, dish, do, get, give, have, hold, instigate, lead, leave, make, must, oblige, owe, persuade, play, proceed, put, run, should, take, trouble, will, would
하단, bottom, crotch
하단의, bottom
하도급 업자, subcontractor
하도급을 주다, subcontract
(~가) 하도록 내버려 두다, leave
(~을) 하도록 하다, let
하드 디스크, hard disk
하드웨어, hardware
하드커버, hardback
하등의 ~도, whatsoever
(~을) 하라고 촉구하다, prod
하락, dip, downswing, fall, slide, slip
하락하다, go, slide
하루, day
하루 걸러, other
하루 벌어 하루 먹는, hand-to-mouth
하루 종일, long
하루살이 생활을 하다, hand
하루살이로, hand-to-mouth
하루살이의, hand-to-mouth
하루의, daily
하룻밤 묵다, stay
하룻밤 사이의, overnight
하룻밤 새에, overnight
하룻밤 생각해 보다, sleep
하류로, downstream
하류의, downstream
(~을) 하리라 예상되다, tip
하릴없는, idle
하릴없이, around, idly
하릴없이 머물다, around
하릴없이 앉아 있는, around
하반신불수 환자, paraplegic
하반신불수의, paraplegic
하버드출신 남자, man
하부, underneath
하부 구조, infrastructure
하사관, sergeant
하소연할 곳, shoulder
하수, sewage
하수 처리, sanitation
하수도, sewer
하숙인, lodger
하숙하다, lodge
(~) 하시겠습니까, would
하에, under
하원, common, house, House of Commons, House of Representatives
하원 의사당, House of Commons

하원의원, common, Member of Congress, Member of Parliament, MP, representative
하위, inferiority
하위문화, subculture
하위의, pile
하의, bottom
하이라이트, highlight
하이라이트 처리하다, highlight
하이커, hiker
하이킹, hike, hiking
하이킹하다, hike
하이파이 장치, hi-fi
하이퍼링크, hyperlink
하이퍼링크 되다, hyperlink
하이퍼텍스트, hypertext
하이픈, hyphen
하인, servant
하자마자, minute
하자면, coin
하제, laxative
하중, load
하지 않다, line, neglect, short, would
(~을) 하지 않도록, fear
(~) 하지 않으면, unless
하지만, again, although, but, however, if, much, while
하찮게 생각하다, dirt
하찮게 여기다, trivialize
하찮아지다, pale
하찮은, account, empty, frivolous, insignificant, lightweight, negligible, paltry, small, trivial, unimportant
하찮은 것, home, nothing, trivia
하찮은 사람, lightweight
하찮음, insignificance
하키, field hockey, hockey
하트, heart
하트 놀이, heart
하품, yawn
하품하다, yawn
하프, harp
하프타임, half-time
하한선, bottom line
하향 조정되다, downgrade
하향의, downward
하향추세, downtrend
학, crane
학과, study, subject
학교, school
학교 공부를 마친 사람, school leaver
학교 교사, schoolteacher
학교 교육, schooling
학교의, academic
학구적인, academic, scholarly
학급, class
학기, semester, term
학년, grade
학년도, year
학대, abuse, cruelty, punishment
학대하는, abusive
학대하다, abuse
학문, science
학문 분야, discipline
학문적으로, academically
학문적인, academic, scholarly, scholastic
학부, faculty, school
학부생, undergraduate
학사, graduate
학살, slaughter
학살당하다, massacre, slaughter
학살하다, butcher
학생, pupil, student
학설, theory
학술계의, scholarly
학술지, journal
학습, learning, study
학습 곡선, learning curve
학습자, learner
학습장, workbook
학식, attainment, scholarship
학식이 있는, learned
학원, academy, school
학위, degree
학위 논문, thesis

학위 수여식, commencement
학위 취득 희망자, candidate
학위복, gown
학자, academic, scholar, student
학장, dean, principal
학적 담당자, registrar
학점, credit
학창 시절, schooldays
학파, school
학회, academy, institute, society
(~하는) 한, far, long
한 가지 원인이 되다, contribute
한 개, article
한 개의, single, single-
한 걸음 앞선, step
한 겨울에, dead
한 경기, round
한 곡, track
한 냄비, pot
한 단계, lap
한 달, month
한 달에 한 번 있는, monthly
한 달의, monthly
한 대야 가득한 분량, basin
한 동, block
한 동안, time
한 때, once
한 떼, batch
한 마디 말, word
한 마디 한 마디, word
한 모금, drink, nip, puff, sip
한 목소리로 말함, chorus
한 묶음, batch
한 바구니 분량, basket
한 바퀴, lap
한 바퀴 앞서다, lap
한 바탕, bout
한 발, round
한 발 물러서다, stand
한 방울, blob
한 방향으로 쭉, along
한 번, once
한 번 더, again
(~할까) 한 번 생각해 보다, toy
한 번 입힌 막, coat
한 번 찔린 곳을 또 찌르는 격이다,
  knife
한 번 치기, stroke
한 번 투어, shot
한 번 해 보다, whirl
(~에) 한 번씩, once
한 번의 실수, move
한 벌, deck, service
한 벌의 기구, battery
한 봉지, packet
한 부모, single parent
한 부분, passage
한 사람당, head
한 사람이 한 시합에서 3점을 넣기,
  hat-trick
한 세트, service
한 손에 들어오는, hand-held
한 순간 무너지다, snap
한 시간, hour
한 시간마다, hourly
한 움큼, handful
한 입, bite
한 입 가득, mouthful
한 입으로, breath
한 잔, drink, glass, shot
한 장, frame, sheet
한 점에 모이다, converge
한 접시, plate
한 주, week
한 주 중반의, midweek
한 주전자, kettle, pot
한 주전자 분량의 것, jug
한 줄기, beam
한 줄로 꿴 것, string
한 줄로 늘어놓다, line
한 줄로 늘어선 것, chain
한 줄로 서다, line
한 줄로 세우다, line
한 줌, handful
한 지붕 아래, roof
한 집안의 생계를 책임진 사람,
  breadwinner
한 쪽, clove, one

한 쪽 편을 들다, side
한 쪽으로, aside
한 쪽의, one
한 차례, round
한 차례 더 먹는 음식, second
한 차에 탄 사람들, carpool
(~) 한 컵, glass
한 컵 분량, cup
한 통, packet, pot
한 통조림 분량의 것, tin
한 편의 시와 같은 것, poetry
한 푼, penny
한가운데, middle
(~의) 한가운데에, amid
(~의) 한가운데에서, midst
한가하게 보내다, while
한가한, available
한결같은, even, steady
한계, frontier, horizon, limit,
  limitation, threshold
한계의, marginal
한계점, breaking point, restriction
한곳에 정체하다, hang
한곳에만 총력을 모으다, egg
한기, chill
한껏, possibly
한껏 즐기다, revel
한낮, half-day
한낮의, midday
한낮의, noon
한눈팔지 않는, faithful
(~해야) 한다, got, gotta, have,
  must, ought, should, will
한담, chat
한담을 나누다, chat
한대 지역 같은, arctic
한데 모이다, converge, rally
한데 묶다, bind
한데 어우러지다, blend
한데서, rough
한도, limit, limitation
한도량, quota
한동안, spell, while
한때에는, time
한몫, action
한몫 끼다, act
한몫 잡다, killing
한물가다, seed
한물간, dead
한물간 사람, has-been
한바탕, fit
한바탕 달리기, spin
한바탕 사건들, turn
한밤중에, dead
한배 새끼, litter
한번, once
한번도 ~하지 않아, never
한번에, time
한산한, slack
한산한 때의, off-peak
한숨, sigh
한숨 돌리기, breather
한숨 쉬다, sigh
한숨도 못 자다, wink
한심하게, pitifully, woefully
한심한, pitiful, sad, woeful
(~하는) 한에 있어서, insofar as
(~하는) 한은, inasmuch as
한입 가득 들어가는 양, gulp
한적하게, quietly
한적하고 고풍스러운, genteel
한적한, quiet, secluded
한정된, finite, limited
한정사, determiner
한정판, limited edition
한쪽 끝, end
한쪽 끝을 깨뜨리다, chip
한쪽 끝이 떨어져 나가다, chip
한쪽 벽이 옆집에 붙은,
  semidetached
한쪽 옆으로 기울다, bank
한쪽 편, party
한쪽으로, aside
한쪽으로 기울어진, lopsided
한쪽으로 비켜, aside
한쪽으로 샌, stray
한차례의 동요, flurry
한참, way

한참 모자라는, near
한창, peak, spurt
한창 ~하는 중, way
한창 ~하는 중에, amid
한창 ~하는 중인, midst
한창 잘 나가는, moment
한창 진행 중인, flow, swing
한창때, middle
한창때가 지나다, seed
한창때가 지난, hill
한창때의, height
한창의, full
한촌, backwater
한층 더, still
한층 더 나쁘게, worse
한탄하는, sorry
한탄하다, mourn
한턱, treat
한턱 내다, lay
한패, associate, bunch, clan
한패인, league
한편, hand
한편으로는, hand, meanwhile,
  time
한풀 꺾이게 하다, dampen
(~) 할 가치가 있는, worth
할 말을 못하게 하다, gag
할 일을 잃다, floor
(~) 할 보람이 있는, worth
(~) 할 수 없음, inability
(~) 할 수 있는 상태가 아니다, state
할 일이 많다, plate
할 테면 해 보라고 한다, defy
(~을) 할 필요가 없다, need
(~을) 할 필요가 있다, need
할당 인원, quota
할당량, quota
할당하다, assign
할례, circumcision
할례를 받다, circumcise
할머니, gran, grandma,
  grandmother, granny
할부, HP, installment
할부 구입, hire purchase
할부로, account
할아버지, grandad, grandfather,
  grandpa
할애하다, commit, devote,
  manage, spare
할양하다, cede
할인, discount
할인 가격, cut-price
할인가의, cut-rate
할인점, outlet
할인되는, sale
할인하다, discount
(~에서) 할인하여, off
할증료, premium
할퀴다, scratch
핥기, lick
핥다, lick
핥아먹다, lap
함, job
함교, bridge
함구하다, quiet
(~와만) 함께, alone, along,
  alongside, to, together, with
함께 가지고, along
(~와) 함께 걷다, walk
함께 넣어, inclusive
함께 데리고, along
함께 묶치다, stick
(~와) 함께 있어 주다, company
함께 지내는, together
함께하는, concerted, together
함께하여, together
함대, fleet
함락, fall
함락되다, fall
함부로 만지다, paw
함부로 장난치다, fool
함선, ship
함성, cry, roar
함유량, content
함유하다, contain
함의, implication
함정, catch, pitfall, snare, trap
함축, overtone

함축적 의미, connotation
함축적으로, implication
함축적인, loaded
함축하다, imply, infer
합격, pass
합격하다, get, pass
합계, total
합계 ~이 되다, total
합계의, combined, total
합계하여, altogether, total
합당하게, justly
합당하게 여기고 따르다, reason
합당한, right
합당한 정도인, reason
합동의, combined, joint
합류하다, join
합리성, rationality
합리적으로, rationally, sensibly
합리적인, rational, rationalist,
  sensible
합리주의자, rationalist
합리하다, rationalize
합법성, legality, legitimacy
합법적으로, lawfully, legitimately
합법적인, lawful, legal, legitimate,
  valid
합법화되다, legalize
합병, absorption, amalgamation,
  annexation, integration,
  merger, union
합병되다, incorporate, merge
합병증, complication
합병하다, amalgamate, annex,
  combine, merge
합본, volume
합산하다, add
합산한, aggregate
합성, synthesis
합성물, composite
합성수지, plastic, resin
합성의, composite, compound,
  synthetic
합성하다, synthesize
합심하여, unison
합심한, united
합의, accord, agreement,
  settlement, understanding
합의로, court
합의를 보다, settle
합의점, ground
합자 회사, joint-stock company
합작, collaboration
합작품, collaboration
합창, chorus
합창곡, chorus
합창단, choir, chorus, company
합창을 하다, chorus
합창의, choral
합쳐, between
합쳐서, collectively, together
합쳐지다, combine, merge
합치다, combine, merge
합친, collective
합판, plywood
핫도그, hot dog
핫링크, hot link
핫초코, chocolate
항공, air, aviation
항공 우편, airmail
항공기, aircraft, craft
항공기 승무원, flight attendant
항공기 조종사, flyer
항공기에 의한, aerial
항공기의 격납고(格納庫), hangar
항공사, airline
항공편, flight
항구, harbor, port
항구 도시, port
항구적인, lasting, permanent
항로, channel, course, lane
항명, mutiny
항명하다, mutiny
항목, item
항목별 광고, classified ad,
  classifieds
항문, anus
항문의, anal
항변, plea

항복, submission, surrender
항복하다, capitulate, give, surrender, towel
항상, always, invariably, morning, time, turn
항상 그러하듯이, usual
항상 따라다니다, dog
항생제, antibiotic
항의, cry, opposition, protest
항의 퇴장, walkout
항의자, protester
항의하다, protest
항체, antibody
항해, navigation, passage
항해 선수상(船首像), figurehead
항해사, navigator
항해의, nautical
항해하다, navigate, sail
해, sun, work
해 보다, chance, see
해 보이다, show
해 지기 전에, dark
해가 되지 않다, harm
해가 떠 있는, light
해가 바뀌는 시기, turn
해결, settlement
해결 방안, antidote
해결책, answer, cure, fix, formula, remedy, resolution, solution
해결하다, clear, cure, iron, mop, resolve, settle, smooth, solve, sort
해결할 수 없는, insoluble
해결해야 할 문제들, iron
해고, dismissal, sack
해고 대상의, chop
해고당하다, can
해고를 통지하다, notice
해고하다, dismiss, fire, let, sack
해고함, sacking
해군, navy
해군의, naval
해내다, hang, hat, succeed
해답, answer, solution
해당되는, question
해당하는, equivalent
해당하다, correspond
해덕, haddock
해도, chart
해독제, antidote
해독하다, break, decipher, decode
해동시키다, thaw
해로운, damaging, evil, harmful, poisonous
(~에) 해롭지 않은, -friendly, harmless
해류, current
해를 끼치다, harm
해를 끼침, mischief
해를 입지 않다, harm, spare
해를 입지 않은, unharmed, unhurt
해마다, annually, per annum, year
해마다의, annual
해머, hammer
해머 던지기, hammer
해명, answer, clarification, explanation
해명을 요구받다, account
해명하다, explain, unravel
해명할 의무가 있는, accountable
해바라기, sunflower
해바라기 정치인, hack
해발, altitude, elevation
해방, emancipation, freedom, liberation, release
해방시키다, emancipate
해방하는, liberating
해방하다, liberate
해변, beach, seaside
해변으로, ashore
해병 대원, marine
해볼 테면 해보라고 하다, bluff
해부, dissection
해부의, anatomical
해부하다, dissect
해부학, anatomy
해부학적인, anatomical
해빙기, thaw

해산, childbirth, demobilization, dissolution
해산되다, dissolve
해산물, seafood
해산시키다, break, disperse
해산하다, break, demobilize, disband, disperse, wind
해상의, marine, maritime
해석, interpretation, reading, spin
해석되다, read, translate
해석하다, interpret
해설, commentary, talk
해설서, commentary
해설의, explanatory
해설자, commentator
해설자의 목소리, voice-over
해설하다, commentate, introduce
해소하다, break, diffuse, heal, quench, work
해수면, sea level
해수욕, bathe
해악, ill, mischief
해안, coast, seashore
해안 경비 대원, Coast Guard
해안 도로, seafront
해안 수비 대원, Coast Guard
해안 수비대, Coast Guard
해안 지구, seafront
해안선, coastline, shoreline
해안의, coastal
해야 할 일, bet
해양의, marine
해어진, ragged
해외로, abroad, overseas
해외에서, overseas
해외의, foreign, overseas
해운, shipping
해이한, lax
해이함, laxity
해일, tidal wave
해임, ousting
해임되다, relieve
해저, seabed
해적, pirate
해적판의, pirate
해적행위, piracy
해제, dissolution
해제하다, disable
해조류, seaweed
해질 후에, dark
해질 녘, sunset
해질녘, dusk
해체, disintegration
해체되다, disintegrate
해체하다, strip
해초, seaweed
해충, pest
해치, hatch
해치는 것, blight
해치다, damage, harm, impair
해커, hacker
해킹, hacking
해킹하다, hack
해트 트릭, hat-trick
해학, humor
해학적인, humorous
해협, strait
핵, nucleus
핵무기, bomb
핵심, core, crux, focus, heart, issue, nucleus, pillar, point, root
핵심 인물, figure
핵심 지역, heartland
핵심을 짚다, nail
핵심의, key
핵심적인, salient
핵심층, inner circle
핵의, nuclear
핸드백, bag, handbag, pocketbook, purse
핸드세트, handset
핸들, steering wheel, wheel
핸들을 잡은, wheel
핸디캡, handicap
핸디캡이 붙는 경우, handicap
핸즈프리의, hands-free
핼쑥한, gaunt
햄, ham

햄버거, hamburger
햄스터, hamster
햇, new
햇볕, sun
햇볕에 타다, tan
햇볕에 탄, sunburned, tanned
햇볕에 탐, sunburn
햇볕에 태우다, tan
햇볕에 피부를 태우기, suntan
햇빛, daylight, sun, sunlight, sunshine
햇빛이 잘 드는, sunny
햇살, sunshine
햇수, age
행, line
행간, spacing
행군, march
행군시키다, march
행군하다, march
행동, bearing, behavior
행동 연구의, behavioral
행동의, behavioral
행동주의자, activist
행동하다, act, behave, conduct, go, move, take, tread
행락객, vacationer
행렬, matrix, pageant, parade, procession, train
행로, path
행방, whereabouts
행복, happiness
행복감, euphoria, high
행복하게, happily, joyously
행복한, happy
행복한 시기, honeymoon
행사, event, exercise, occasion
행사장, fairground
행사하다, exercise, exert, wield
행상하다, peddle
행성, planet
행성의, planetary
행실, conduct, demeanor, goings-on
행실을 고치다, mend
행실이 단정치 못한 여자, tart
행실이 바른, good
행운, joy, luck
행운을 빌다, wood
행운을 빌어 luck
행운의, lucky
행위, act, action, deed
행인, passer-by
행적, movement
행정, admin, administration
행정 교구, parish
행정 체제, bureaucracy
행정관, administrator
행정부, administration, Civil Service, executive
행정상의, administrative
행정적인, executive
행주, cloth
행진곡, march
행진하다, parade
행하다, perform
행해지다, pass
향, incense
향긋하게 하다, scent
향기, aroma, bouquet, fragrance, scent
향기로운, aromatic, fragrant, sweet
향락, decadence
향료, flavoring, incense, perfume
향료를 넣다, flavor
향상, advancement, improvement
향상되는, onward
향상되다, improve
향상되어, onward
향상시키다, brush, improve, raise
향수, fragrance, nostalgia, perfume, scent
향수를 불러일으키는, nostalgic
향수병, homesickness
향수병에 걸린, homesick
향수에 젖어서, nostalgically
향수에 젖은, nostalgic
향신료, spice

향연, fete
향유, balm
(~에) 향을 내다, perfume
향주머니, sachet
향초, herb
향하게 하다, direct, turn
(~을 향하는, bound
향하다, bear, direct, face, head, level
(~을 향하여, after, toward
(~을 향하여 가다, make
(~을 향하여 단숨에 내달리다, dash
(~를 향해, at, for
(~을 향해 돌진하다, rush
(~을 향해 얼굴을 돌리다, face
(~쪽으로 향해 있다, point
향후 몇 년, hence
허가, approval, authority, authorization, clearance, concession, license, permission
허가 소유자, concessionaire
허가된, licensed
허가를 받다, clear
허가서, pass
허가증, permit
허가하다, authorize, license, permit
허공, air
허공의, space
허구, fiction, invention
허구의, fictitious
허구적인, fictional
허깨비를 보다, thing
허둥거리는, hop
허둥대다, scramble, scurry
허둥지둥 달리다, scurry
허둥지둥하는, hop
허드렛일, chore
허들, hurdle
허락, consent, okay
허락을 구하다, square
허락하다, have, okay, permit
(~을 허락하지 않다, hear
허락할 수 없다, have
(~의) 허를 찌르다, guard
허름한 옷을 입다, dress
허리, waist
허리 부분, waist
허리띠를 졸라매다, belt
허리를 곧추세우다, straighten
허리를 펴다, straighten
허리의 잘록한 부분, small
허리케인, hurricane
허무맹랑한, fanciful
허물, niggle
허물다, demolish, knock, pull, take
허물어지다, crumble
허벅지, thigh
허브, herb
허비된, lost
허비하다, squander
허섭스레기, shit
허세, bravado, pretension
허세 부리는, ostentatious, pretentious
허세를 부리며, ostentatiously
허수아비, scarecrow
허술한, lax
허술함, laxity
허식, veneer
허식이 없는, no-nonsense
허식이 지나친, ostentatious
허약, weakness
허약자, weakling
허약한, delicate, frail, infirm, rickety, weak
허약한 상태, frailty
허영심, vanity
허영심 많은, vain
허용되는, permissible
허용되다, allow
허용량, allowance
허용하다, accord, allow, concede, let
허용하지 않다, defy, stand
허우적대다, flounder
허울, facade

허울만의, hollow
허위, mythology
허위 정보, false alarm
허위 정보, misinformation
허위의, false, fictitious, phoney, untrue
허점, loophole
허탕, write-off
허투루 하지 않는, no-nonsense
허튼 짓, nonsense
허풍, pretension
허풍스러운, pretentious
헉 하는 소리, gasp
헌, old
헌금, collection
헌법, constitution
헌법에 위배되는, unconstitutional
헌법의, constitutional
헌사(獻辭), inscription
헌신, dedication, devotion
헌신적인, dedicated, devoted
헌신적인 애정, devotion
헌신하다, dedicate
헌장, charter
헌정하다, dedicate
헌혈, donation
헌혈하다, donate
헐거운, loose
헐겁게, loosely
헐떡거리다, gasp, pant, puff
헐뜯다, knock, run, speak
헐렁하게, loosely
헐렁한, floppy, loose
험난한, testing
험담, gossip
험담거리, dirt
험담꾼, gossip
험상궂은, grim
험악한, rough, stormy, ugly
험한, rough
험한 꼴, ride
헛간, barn, shed
헛것을 듣다, thing
헛기침하다, throat
헛되게, ineffectually
헛되이, needlessly, vainly, vain
헛된, barren, ineffectual, needless, vain
헛된 기대를 하다, hope
헛디디 넘어지다, trip
헛소리, nonsense
헝겊, cloth, rag
헝클어 놓다, ruffle
헝클어진, disheveled, ruffled
헤더, heather
헤드, head
헤드라이트, headlight
헤드라인, headline
헤드셋, headset
헤드폰, headphones, headset
헤딩하다, head
헤로인, heroin, smack
헤르니아, hernia
헤매다, wander
헤브라이 사람의, Hebrew
헤브라이 어, Hebrew
헤브라이 어의, Hebrew
헤비급 권투 선수, heavyweight
헤아리다, fathom
(~에서) 헤어나지 못하다, overwhelm
헤어롤, roller
헤어스타일, hairstyle
헤어져, apart
헤어지게 만들다, split
헤어지다, part, separate
헤어진, separated
헤어짐, parting, separation
헤엄, swim
헤엄을 치는 사람, swimmer
헤엄쳐 건너다, swim
헤엄쳐 나아가다, swim
헤엄치다, bathe, swim
헤지 펀드, hedge fund
헤지다, fray
헤집다, burrow
헤쳐 나가다, make, wade
(~을) 헤치고 나아가다, break

헤치며 걷다, wade
헤프게, lavishly
헤프게 주다, lavish
헤픈, lavish
헥타르, hectare
헬기 이착륙장, helipad
헬리콥터, chopper, helicopter
헬멧, helmet
헷갈리는, confusing
헹구기, rinse
헹구다, flush, rinse
혀, reed, tongue
혁대, belt
혁명, revolution
혁명가, revolutionary
혁명의, revolutionary
혁명적 변화, revolution
혁명적으로 바꾸다, revolutionize
혁명적인, revolutionary
혁신, innovation
혁신가, innovator
혁신시키다, revolutionize
혁신적인, innovative
혁신하다, innovate
현, string
현가장치, suspension
현관, foyer, hall, hallway, porch
현관 안내인, doorman
현관 앞 계단, doorstep
현관 홀, entrance hall
현관까지 배웅하다, door
현금, cash, hard cash
현금 서랍, till
현금 인출 카드, cash card
현금 지급기, cash dispenser, cashpoint
현금 카드, bank card
현금으로 바꾸다, cash
현금화하기 쉬운, liquid
현금화하다, cash
현금화할 수 있는, realizable
현기증, dizziness
현기증 나는, dizzy, giddy
현기증이 나다, swim
현대의, modern, present-day
현대적인, contemporary
현대판, descendant
현대화, modernization
현대화하다, modernize
현란한, flamboyant
현명, wisdom
현명하게, judiciously, sensibly, wisely
현명하지 못한, unwise
현명한, advisable, judicious, sensible, wise
현물로, kind
현미경, microscope
현미경을 사용하는, microscopic
현미로 된, brown
현상, phenomenon
현상금, bounty, reward
현상하다, develop
현세의, earthly, temporal
현시점에서, here
현실, reality, real life
현실 같은, real
현실 도피, escapism
현실 도피적인, escapist
현실 세계, real world
현실 인식, grip
현실감을 잃지 않다, foot
현실로 돌아오다, earth
현실을 직시하자, face
현실이 되다, realize
현실이 됨, realization
현실적으로, realistically
현실적으로 가능한, realistic
현실적인, down-to-earth, earthy, practical, realistic, workable
현실주의, realism
현실주의자, realist
현실화되다, true
현악기부, string
현안, agenda
현자, philosopher
현장, field, scene, site
현장 급습, raid

현장에, scene
현장에 있을 때, site
현장으로부터, scene
현장을 포착하다, act
현재, currently, moment, present, presently, today
현재까지는, far
현재로서는, present
현재로서는 만족스러운, going
현재의, current, immediate, present
현재의 상황, status quo
현저하게, markedly, strikingly
현저한, emphatic, marked, striking
(~와는) 현저히 다른, contrast
현존하는, existing
현지에서, locally
현지의, local
현지인, local
현직의, incumbent, in-service
현직자, incumbent
현찰, cash
현학적인, pedantic
현행의, going
현혹되다, take
현혹하다, dazzle
현황, status, status quo
혈관, blood vessel
혈기, heat
혈류, bloodstream
혈색, bloom
혈색이 좋은, rosy
혈압, blood pressure
혈액 검사, blood test
혈액 순환, circulation
혈우병, hemophilia
혈우병 환자, hemophiliac
혈육, flesh
혈장, plasma
혈청, serum
혈청 주사액, serum
혈통, blood, descent, origin, pedigree
혈통서, pedigree
혐오, aversion, distaste, loathing
혐오감, disgust, revulsion
혐오감을 느끼는, disgusted
혐오감을 주다, disgust
혐오스러운, abominable, disgusting, distasteful, repulsive, revolting
혐오스럽게, horribly
혐오스럽다는 듯이, disgustedly
혐오하다, detest, hate, loathe
혐의, allegation, suspicion
혐의 제기, accusation
혐의를 씌우다, allege
혐의를 입증하는, incriminating
혐의에 따르면, allegedly
협곡, canyon, gorge, gully, ravine
협동의, cooperative
협동조합, cooperative
협력, collaboration, cooperation
협력 관계, partnership
협력자, ally, collaborator
협력적인, cooperative, supportive
협력하는, cooperative
협력하다, collaborate, cooperate, force
협력하여, cooperatively, shoulder
협력하여 일하다, pull
협박, intimidation, threat
협박하다, intimidate, threaten
협박하여 ~하게 하다, bully
협상, negotiation
협상 테이블, negotiating table
협상용 대상, chip
협상자, negotiator
협상하다, negotiate. talk
협상할 수 있는, negotiable
협소한 통로, track
협약, convention, deal
협의, conference
협의하다, confer, talk
협잡, con
협정, accord, agreement, convention

협정하다, negotiate
협조, assistance, cooperation
협조적인, cooperative, forthcoming
협조하다, assist, cooperate
협주곡, concerto
협찬, sponsorship
협회, association, brotherhood, fellowship
형광등의, fluorescent
형광색의, fluorescent
형벌, punishment, sentence
형법, law
형사, detective
형상, geometry, imagery, shape
형상화되다, crystallize
형상화하다, crystallize
형성, formation
형성되다, form, sculpt
형성하다, form
형세, face
형수, sister-in-law
형식, form
형식적인, ceremonial, token
형식적인 것, formality
형언, description
형언하기 어려운, unspeakable
형용사, adjective
형제, brethren, brother
형제애, brotherhood
형제자매, sibling
형체, shape
형태, form, format, mode, shape
형태가 망가진, disfigured
형태로, in
형태를 갖추다, shape
형태의, shaped
형판, template
형편, convenience
형편 좋은, convenient
형편없게, abysmally
형편없는, abysmal, atrocious, dire, lousy, miserable, poor, shocking, some, terrible, wretched
형편없는 것, rubbish
형편없다, stink
형편없이, miserably, poorly, shockingly
(~할) 형편이 아니다, ill
형편이 안 좋은, badly off
형평을 잃은, unbalanced
혜성, comet
혜성처럼 나타나다, burst
(~의) 혜택, benefit, boon, inducement
혜택 받지 못한, deprived, disadvantaged
호, arc, issue
호각, whistle
호각을 이루는, neck
호감 가는, pleasant
호감을 주다, appeal
호감이 가는, desirable, likeable
호감을 시키다, pamper
호객 행위를 하다, solicit
호구지책, subsistence
호기, occasion
호기를 놓치지 않다, hay
호기심, curiosity
호기심 어린 눈초리로, curiously
호기심에 가득 차서, inquiringly
호기심에 찬, inquiring
호기심을 자극하게, intriguingly
호기심을 자극하는, intriguing
호기심을 자극하다, intrigue
호기심이 생긴, interested
호기심이 있는, curious
호도하다, whitewash
호된, tart
호두, walnut
호랑가시나무, holly
호랑이, tiger
호루라기, whistle
호르몬, hormone
호르몬의, hormonal
호른, horn
호리다, enchant

호리호리한, slender, slim
호명하여, name
호모, queer
호모의, queer
호밀, rye
호밀빵, rye
호박, pumpkin
호박색, amber
호버크라프트, hovercraft
호사스러운, lifestyle
호소, appeal
호소하는 듯한, appealing
호소하다, complain, invoke
호송 대열, convoy
호송자, escort
호수, lake, loch
호스, hose
호스로 물을 뿌리다, hose
호스텔, hostel
호스트 컴퓨터, host
호스피스, hospice
호위 하에, escort
호위대, guard
호의, courtesy, friendliness,
  goodwill, kindness
호의를 가지고, well
호의적으로, sympathetically
호의적이다, sympathize
호의적인, favorable, friendly,
  sympathetic
호이스트, hoist
호전, pick-up, upturn
호전되다, pick, turn
호전되어, mend
호전된, better
호전성, militancy
호전적인, combative
호젓함, solitude
호주 원주민, aboriginal, Aborigine
호주 원주민의, aboriginal
호출, summons
호출 받다, page
호출기, pager
호출장, subpoena, summons
호출하다, summon
호치키스, stapler
호치키스로 철하다, staple
호치키스의 철침, staple
호텔, hotel
호텔 경영자, hotelier
호텔 여종업원, maid
호통, bellow
호통치다, blow
호혜적인, reciprocal
호화, luxury
호화 쇼, extravaganza
호화로운, lush, luxurious, posh
호화롭게, lavishly, luxuriously
호화스러운, sumptuous
호화스런, plush
호환되지 않는, incompatible
호환성 있는, compatible
호환성이 있는, interchangeable
호황, boom
호황과 불황의 반복, boom-bust
  cycle
호황을 타다, boom
호흡, breathing
호흡 곤란, breathlessness
호흡을 가다듬다, breath
호흡의, respiratory
호흡이 잘 맞는, compatible
호흡하다, breathe
혹, bump, hump, lump, wart
혹독하게, harshly
혹독한, crushing, harsh, hostile,
  searing
혹독한 훈련, iron
혹독함, harshness
혹사, punishment
혹사당하는, overworked
혹사시키다, overwork
혹시 ~할까 생각한다, wonder
혹시 모르니까, case
혹심한 공격을 받다, gauntlet
혹평, flak, rap
혹평을 받다, gauntlet, pan, slate
혹평하다, castigate, crucify, lash,

rap, slam
혹한, freeze
혼내 주다, crucify
혼동, confusion
혼동된, muddled up, muddled
혼동하다, confuse, mix, muddle
혼란, confusion, disarray, disorder,
  disorganization, disruption,
  mess, turmoil, upset
혼란스러운, bemused, chaotic,
  confused, disconcerting,
  disorganized, muddled, puzzled
혼란스럽게 만들다, dislocate
혼란스럽게 하다, confuse, muddy,
  upset
혼란스럽다, reel
혼란시키다, disrupt, havoc, throw
혼령, ghost
혼례의, bridal
혼미한, delirious
혼비백산하게 만들다, scare
혼비백산하다, heart
혼선, interference
혼성의, composite, hybrid
혼수, coma
혼인 여부, marital status
혼자, by, fiancé, own
혼자 있는 것을 즐기는 사람, loner
혼자 잘 지내는, solitary
혼자 틀어박히다, shut
혼자 힘으로, alone, by
혼자 힘으로 행하다, alone
혼자만 알다, keep
혼자서, isolation, own,
  single-handed, solo
혼자서 하는, solo
혼자서도 잘 사는, self-sufficient
혼자서만, alone, privately
혼자의, lone, sole, solitary
혼자인, single
혼잡, congestion
혼잡한, congested, overcrowded
혼잡한 곳, jungle
혼잣말하다, say
혼합, blend, combination, mixture
혼합 경제, mixed economy
혼합 비료, compost
혼합기, mixer
혼합물, cocktail, composite,
  compound, concoction, hybrid,
  mixture
혼합의, hybrid, mixed
혼혈의, mixed
홀, hall, hole
홀딱 반하게 하는, irresistible
홀딱 반할 만큼, irresistibly
홀딱 반함, crush
홀로, alone, single-handed
홀로 버려진, isolated
홀로인, alone
홀로코스트, holocaust
홀리는, bewitching
홀리다, bewitch
홀수의, odd
홀아비, widower
홀인원, hole
홀짝이다, sip
홀쭉하게, slightly
홀쭉한, slight
홈, groove, home
홈그라운드의, home
홈쇼핑, home shopping
홈쇼핑 채널, shopping channel
홈페이지, homepage
홉, hop
홍당무, beet, beetroot
홍보, PR, promotion, publicity
홍보 담당자, publicist
홍보 활동, advertising campaign,
  public relations
홍보의, promotional
홍보하다, drum, promote,
  publicize
홍수, flood, flooding
홍역, measles, rash
홍조, bloom, blush, flush, glow
홍조를 띠다, glow
홍채, iris

홍합, mussel
화, anger, Tues.
화가, painter
화가 끓어오르다, seethe
화가 난, angry, exasperated,
  temper, worked up
화가 날 정도로, maddeningly
화가 많이 난, overheated
화가(畵架), easel
화강암, granite
화끈거리다, burn
화나게 만들다, ruffle
화나게 하는, maddening, vexing
화나게 하다, aggravate, gall, piss,
  vex
화나다, nettle
화난 얼굴, dirty
화내다, blow, handle
화단, bed
화답하다, return
화랑, gallery
화려하게, richly
화려한, gaudy, gorgeous
화려함, flamboyance, glamor
화력, firepower
화로, hearth
(~에) 화를 내다, exception, offense
화를 잘 내는, excitable, hot
화면, screen
화면 내용, display
화면 모양, view
화면보호기, screensaver
화면에 나오는, on-screen
화면이 넓은, widescreen
화목, peace
화목하게, harmoniously
화목한, harmonious
화물, cargo, load
화물 수송기, freighter
화물 운송, freight
화물선, freighter
화물용 선반, luggage rack
화물차, freight car
화물칸, baggage car
화법, speech
화산, volcano
화산 작용에 의한, volcanic
화산의, volcanic
화살, arrow
화살표, arrow
화상, burn
화상 전화, videophone
화상 표시기, VDT, VDU
화상 회의의, video-conference
화상 회의 시스템, video
  conferencing
화색, radiance
화석, fossil
화석 연료, fossil fuel
화성, harmony
화성의, harmonic
화소, pixel
화신, embodiment, incarnation,
  personification, reincarnation
(~의) 화신이 되다, personify
화씨 온도계, Fahrenheit
화씨의, Fahrenheit
화약통, cartridge
화염, flame
화염에 휩싸여, flame
화염에 휩싸이다, flame, go
화요일, Tuesday
화음, chord, harmony
화이트보드, whiteboard
화장, make-up
화장(火葬), cremation
화장(火葬)되다, cremate
화장대, dresser
화장실, bathroom, cloakroom,
  lavatory, loo, restroom, toilet,
  WC
화장실에 가다, toilet
화장지, tissue
화장판, veneer
화장품, cosmetic, make-up
화장한, made-up

화재, fire
화재경보기, fire alarm
화재를 촉발시키다, spark
화제, topic
화제가 되는, sensational
화제를 모으며, sensationally
화제를 바꾸다, subject
화차, wagon
화창한, sunny
화초, flower
화폐제도, coinage
화포, canvas
화필, paintbrush
화학, chemistry
화학 물질, agent, chemical
화학 분자식, formula
화학 약품, chemical
화학 작용으로, chemically
화학 작용의, chemical
화학의, chemical
화학자, chemist
화학적 성격, chemistry
화학적으로, chemically
화학적인, chemical
화합, harmony, unity
화합물, compound
화해, conciliation, reconciliation
화해시키다, heal, reconcile
화형, hatchet, make, reconcile
화형당하다, burn
화환, garland, wreath
확 뜯어내다, rip
확 타오르다, flame, flare
확고하게, firmly, staunchly
확고한, absolute, firm, forthright,
  inflexible, robust, set, staunch,
  steadfast, strong, unmoved
확고한 신념에, faith
확고함, inflexibility
확고히, fast, strongly
확고히 자리 잡다, establish
확고히 하다, entrench
확대, enlargement, escalation,
  expansion, magnification
확대되다, blow, enlarge, widen
(~로) 확대하다, blow, carry, enlarge,
  extend, magnify, scale, widen
확률, probability
확립된, established,
  well-established
확산, diffusion, escalation,
  proliferation, rise, spread
확산되다, diffuse, proliferate,
  spread
확산시키다, spread
확성, amplification
확성 장치, PA
확성기, bullhorn, microphone,
  speaker
확신, assurance, certainty,
  confidence, conviction
확신시키다, convince
확신에 찬, definite, sure
확신을 가진, convinced
확신이 서지 않는, uneasy
확신이 없는, doubtful, uncertain
확신이 없이, uncertainly
확신이 있는, assured
확신하는, certain, confident,
  positive, sure
(~라고) 확신하다, bet
확신하지 못하는, unsure
확실하게, unquestionably
확실하게 하다, certain
확실한, assured, cast iron, certain,
  definite, distinct, firm,
  foolproof, reliable, secure, solid,
  strong, sure, undoubted
확실성, certainty
확실한 결과, foregone
확실한 출처에서, horse
확실히, certain, certainly,
  confidently, definitely,
  distinctly, fact, once, plainly,
  reliably, safely, sure, surely
확실히 ~할 것 같은, destined
확실히 말하다, clear
(~을) 확실히 믿다, swear

확실히 이해한, clear
확실히 쥔 이득, bird
확실히 하다, sure
확약하다, commit
확언, affirmation, confirmation
확언하다, confirm, guarantee, verify
확연하게, distinctly
확연히 드러나다, register
확인, affirmation, check, confirmation, identification, validation, verification
확인되다, check
확인하다, affirm, ascertain, certain, check, confirm, sure, validate, verify
확인해 보다, check
확인해 주다, verify
확장, enlargement, expansion
확장되다, expand, spread
확장시키다, widen
확장하다, extend
확정, confirmation
확정 짓다, nail
확정된, definite
확정이 나지 않은, inconclusive
확정하다, confirm, seal
확증, confirmation
확증된, established
확증하다, confirm, establish
환각, hallucination, illusion, vision
환각에 빠지다, hallucinate
환각제, ecstasy
환각제를 사용한, psychedelic
환각제의, psychedelic
환경, climate, environment, milieu, surroundings
환경 보호, conservation
환경 보호의, green
환경 보호주의자, conservationist, environmentalist
환경 친화, greenness
환경 친화적인, green
환경 파괴 없이 지속 가능한, sustainable
환경의 변화, scene, scenery
환경적으로, environmentally
환금하다, cash
환기, ventilation
환기시키다, evoke
환기하다, ventilate
환대, hospitality
환대하는, hospitable
환대하다, entertain
환멸, disenchantment, disillusion, disillusionment
환멸을 느끼게 하다, disillusion
환멸을 느끼는, disenchanted
환멸을 느낀, disillusioned
환불, rebate, refund
환불증, credit note, credit slip
환불하다, refund
환산하다, convert
환상, fantasy, illusion, vision
환상을 깨다, disillusion
환상적으로, sensationally
환상적인, sensational
환생, reincarnation
환성, whoop
환성을 지르다, whoop
환시시키는, evocative
환심을 사다, curry
환어음, draft
환영, illusion, vision, welcome
환영받는, welcome
환영받지 못하는, unwelcome
환영하는, welcoming
환영하다, welcome
환영회, reception
환율, exchange rate
환자, case, patient
환자 운반용 침대, trolley
환자 이동 도우미, porter
환전하다, change
환풍구, vent
환풍기, fan
환하게 웃다, beam
환하게 하다, brighten

환한 얼굴의, radiant
환해지다, light
환희, glee
환희에 넘친, jubilant
환히 빛나는, ablaze
활, bow
활강로, chute
활강하다, glide
활공하다, glide
활기, liveliness, punch, spirit, vigor
활기 없는, lackluster, sleepy, tame
활기 있는, active, vivacious
활기가 넘치는, vibrant
활기가 넘치다, hum
활기를 되찾다, alive, perk
활기를 띠다, hot, liven
활기를 불어넣다, alive, liven
활기차게, briskly, vigorously
활기차게 하다, enliven
활기찬, alive, bouncy, brisk, hearty, lively, spirited, vigorous
활기참, vibrancy
활꼴, segment
활동, activity
활동 기간, career
활동 무대, stage
활동 정지, inactivity
활동 중인, active
활동을 그친, extinct
활동적으로, energetically
활동적이지 않은, passive
활동적인, active, energetic, sporty
활동하기 시작하다, play
활동하는, alive
활동하다, move
활동하지 못하게 되다, hand
활동하지 않는, inactive
활력, exuberance, impetus, vigor, vitality
활력을 주다, rejuvenate
활력이 넘치는, exuberant, vigorous
활발하게, exuberantly
활발한, animated, brisk, buoyant, lively, playful, spirited
활발한 움직임, activity
활발함, liveliness
활발히, briskly
활보하다, swagger
활성이 있는, active
활성화, boost
활성화되다, boom
활성화된, clickable
활성화하다, rejuvenate
활용, utilization
활용 용이성, accessibility
활용이 용이한, accessible
활용하다, advantage, draw, exploit, utilize
활자, print, type
활자체, typeface
활자체로 쓰다, print
활자화되어, print
활주로, runway
활주부, runner
활짝, broadly
활짝 열린, open, wide
활짝 웃는, broad
활짝 웃다, grin
활짝 웃음, grin
활활 타오르는, raging, roaring
황, sulfur
황갈색, buff, ginger
황갈색의, olive
황금 시간대, peak time, prime time
황금률, golden rule
황금색, gold
황금색의, golden
황급하게, hurriedly
황급한, hurried, whirlwind
황급히 벗다, tear
황당하게도, fondly
황당한, fond
황도대, zodiac
황량한, bleak, desolate, dreary
황량함, desolation
황무지, wasteland, wilderness
황색, amber
황소, bull, ox

황송하게, humbly
황야, moor, wilderness
황제, emperor
황제의, imperial
황족, monarchy
황토의, earthy
황폐한, desolate, dilapidated, run-down
황폐한 산간 지대, moor
황폐함, desolation
황폐해지다, dog
황폐화, devastation, ruin
황폐화시키다, blight, impoverish
황혼, twilight
황홀감, rapture
황홀경, ecstasy
황홀하게 하다, entrance
황홀한, heady, high
황후, empress
홰, roost
(~을) 홱 움직이다, jerk, whip
홱 잡아당기다, pluck, yank
홱 잡아당김, jerk, yank
홱 젖히기, toss
홱 젖히다, toss
홱 하고 움직이다, whiz
횃대, perch
횃불, torch
회, order
회개, repentance
회개하다, repent
회견, interview
회견을 하다, interview
회계, accounting
회계 감사원, auditor
회계 담당자, treasurer
회계 사무, accountancy
회계 연도, financial year, fiscal year
회계 장부, ledger
회계사, accountant
회계의, fiscal
회계학, accountancy
회고적인, retrospective
회고전, retrospective
회고하다, think
회관, auditorium, hall, house
회교, Islam
회교국, Islam
회교국 군주, sultan
회교국의, Islamic
회기, parliament, session
회담, talk
회담하다, meet
회당 목사, vicar
회람되다, circulate
회랑 지대, corridor
회로, circuit
회 반죽, mortar, plaster, whitewash
회반죽을 칠하다, plaster
회백색, silver
회백색의, silvery
회보, newsletter
회복, convalescence, rally, recovery, recuperation, restoration, return
회복되다, return
회복력, resilience
회복력이 강한, resilient
회복시키다, restore
(~에서) 회복하다, get, pull, rally, recover, redeem, renew, repair, restore
회복하여, foot
회복한, up
(~에) 회부되다, come
회비, subscription
회사, company, corporation, firm, house, Ltd, operation, service
회사 차량, company car
회사법, law
회사의, corporate
회사채 발행, flotation
회상, recollection, reminiscence
회상의, retrospective
(~을) 회상하다, mind, recollect, relive, replay

회색, gray
회색시장, gray market
회선을 마비시키다, jam
회수, recovery, repossession, retrieval
회수당하다, repossess
회수하다, recall, retrieve
회신용 봉투, s.a.e., SASE
회신을 쓰다, write
회오리바람, tornado, twister, whirlwind
회원, member
회원 자격, membership
회원국, member
회원제의, private
회유책, carrot
회의, conference, consultation, council, doubt, meeting, session
회의 참석자들, meeting
회의론, skepticism
회의론자, skeptic
회의실, boardroom
회의장, chamber, floor
회의적인, skeptical
회자되다, echo
회장, director general
회전, rotation, round, spin, whirl
회전목마, merry-go-round, roundabout
회전시키다, rotate, spin, swivel, turn
회전식 연발 권총, revolver
회전식 원형 컨베이어, carousel
회전식의, rotary
회전축, pivot
회전하는, rotary
회전하다, pivot, revolve, rotate, spin, swivel, turn, work
회전하여, round
회중, congregation
회중시계, watch
회진, round
회칠이 되어 있다, whitewash
회피, dodge, evasion
회피하는, evasive
회피하다, avoid, bypass, dodge, duck, evade, evasive, run, sidestep, skirt, wriggle
회피하려 하다, stall
회피하며, evasively
회한, remorse
회합, assembly
회합자, assembly
회합하다, convene
획, stroke
획 숙이다, duck
획기적인 사건, landmark, milestone
획기적인 진전, breakthrough
획득, acquisition, attainment
획득물, haul
획득하다, acquire, attain, chalk, earn, gain, get, net, obtain, pull, secure, win
획득했다, garner
획일성, uniformity
획일적인, monolithic
획일적인 행동, conformity
획책하다, contrive, plot
횟수, frequency
횡격막, diaphragm
횡단 여행, crossing
횡단보도, crossing
횡령, embezzlement
횡령하다, embezzle
횡설수설, babble
횡설수설인, disjointed
횡설수설하다, babble
횡포, tyranny
효과, effect, impact
효과가 극대화되는, strategic
효과가 극대화되도록, strategically
효과가 없는, ineffective, ineffectual
효과가 다른, difference
효과가 있는, operative
효과가 있다, come, difference, trick, way, work

효과를 노리고, effect
효과음으로 녹음된, canned
효과적으로, effect, effectively
효과적인, effective
효과적임, effectiveness
효능, potency
효능이 입증되어 믿을 수 있는, tried
효력을 내다, effect
효력을 상실한, sell-by date
효모, yeast
효소, enzyme
효율성, effectiveness
효율적으로, efficiently
효율적인, efficient
효자 상품, cash cow
효험, efficacy
후, after-
후각, nose, smell
후견인, guardian
후계자, heir
후광, halo
후닥닥하는, feverish
후드득거리다, patter
후드득거림, patter
후들거리는, unsteady
후딱 벗다, slip
후딱 입다, slip
후딱 하기, whirl
후려갈기다, bash
후려치다, lash, swing, swipe
후려들다, swing, swipe
후렴, chorus, refrain
후루룩 마시다, slurp
후루룩 하고 들이키기, slurp
후루룩 하는 소리, slurp
후무리다, shoplift
후미, back
후미에, back
후반의, latter
후보, nominee
후보 지명, nomination
후보에 오르다, nominate
후보의, possible
후보자, candidate, possible
후불의, arrears
후비다, pick
후생, welfare
후세, posterity
후세에 전하다, hand
후속 작업, follow-up
후속 조치, follow-up
후속 조치를 취하다, follow
(~의) 후손인, descended
(~한) 후에, after, afterward, away,
    in, later
후예, descendant
후원, backing, patronage,
    sponsorship
후원자, backer, benefactor, patron,
    promoter, sponsor, supporter
후원하다, back, patronize, sponsor
(~의) 후원하에, auspices
후의, later
후임자, replacement, successor
후자, latter
후자의, latter
후줄근한, shabby
후진 기어, reverse
후진시키다, reverse
후진하다, back, reverse
후추, pepper
후텁지근한, heavy, muggy,
    oppressive, sultry
후퇴, retreat
후퇴하는, backward
후퇴하다, ground, retreat
후폭풍, battering
후하게, lavishly
후하게 주는, lavish
후한, generous, lavish
후회, regret
후회하는, sorry
후회하다, regret
혹, hook
훈계, lecture
훈계하다, lecture
훈련, discipline, drill, training
훈련받는 사람, trainee

훈련받다, train
(~) 훈련받은, -trained
훈련받지 않은, untrained
훈련사, trainer
훈련받지 않은, untrained
훈련시키다, train
훈련하다, train
훈령, injunction
훈육, discipline, upbringing
훈장, honor, medal
훈제 처리되다, smoke
훈제한 듯한, smoky
훌륭하게, admirably, beautifully,
    brilliantly, honorably,
    splendidly, wonderfully
훌륭한, admirable, beautiful,
    brilliant, distinguished,
    exemplary, extraordinary, fine,
    golden, good, magnificent,
    marvelous, prize, rare,
    respectable, shining, splendid,
    sterling, terrific, wonderful
훌륭한 것, beauty, prize
훌륭한 솜씨, prowess
훌륭함, magnificence,
    respectability
훌륭히, ably, brilliantly,
    magnificently, marvelously,
    nicely
훌리건, hooligan
훌쩍거리다, whimper
훌쩍거림, whimper
훌쩍임, sniff
훑다, drag
훑어 나아가다, pan
훑어보기, scan
훑어보다, browse, run, scan, skim
훔쳐보다, peek, peep, sneak
훔쳐봄, peek, peep
훔치다, nick, pinch, steal, sweep,
    swipe, take, wipe
훨씬, even, ever, far, mile, shot,
    still, way, well, yet
훨씬 높은, tower
훨씬 더, all
훨씬 뛰어난, shoulder
훼방 놓다, impede
훼방을 놓는, intrusive
훼방하다, hamper, knock
훼손, desecration, violation
훼손되다, vandalize
훼손하다, compromise, desecrate,
    violate
휑뎅그렁한, bare, barren
휘갈겨 쓰다, scrawl, scribble
휘갈겨 쓴 글씨, scrawl
휘다, curve, warp
휘두르다, brandish, slash, swing,
    wave, wield
휘두름, swing
휘둥그레지다, pop
(~에) 휘말리다, embroiled, entangled
휘몰아치다, lash
휘발성의, volatile
휘발유, gas, gasoline
휘어지다, buckle
휘어진, bowed, curved
휘장, drape
휘저으며 익히다, scramble
휘저으며 익힌, scrambled
휘젓다, beat, churn, whip
휘청거리는, unsteady
휘청거리다, lurch, reel
휘청거리며, unsteadily
휘청거림, lurch
휘청함, lurch
휘파람 소리, whistle
휘파람 소리를 내다, whistle
휘파람을 불다, whistle
휘황찬란하게, dazzlingly
휙 끄다, flick
휙 내리치기, flick
휙 내리치다, flick
휙 넘기기, flick
휙 던지다, hurl
휙 떨어대리는, whisk
휙 돌다, swing
휙 돌리다, swing
휙 몸을 돌리다, swing

휙 방향을 틀다, swerve
휙 보다, flash
휙 보여 주다, flash
휙 소리 내며 지나가게 하다, swish
휙 소리 내며 지나가다, swish
휙 움직이게 하다, sweep
휙 움직이다, bob, flick, fling, shoot,
    spring, sweep
휙 움직임, flick, sweep
휙 지나가다, flash, sweep
휙 켜다, flick
휙 털다, flick
휙 튀기기, flick
휙 하는 소리, swish
휙 휘두르다, swish
휙휙 넘기다, flick, flip
휠체어, wheelchair
휩싸다, engulf
휩쓸고 지나가는, rampage
휩쓸고 지나가다, rampage
휩쓸다, board, storm, sweep
휩쓸려 들어가다, suck
휩쓸려 버리다, engulf
휴가, holiday, leave, vacation
휴가객, holidaymaker, vacationer
휴가를 보내다, holiday, vacation
휴게소, service, service station
휴게실, lounge
휴대 가능한 물건, portable
휴대 전화, cellphone, cellular
    phone
휴대용 병, flask
휴대용 음향기기, personal stereo
휴대용 카세트 플레이어, Walkman
휴대용 컴퓨터, laptop, palmtop
휴대용의, portable
휴대폰, mobile, mobile phone
휴대품 보관소, cloakroom
휴식, recess, respite, rest, time out
휴식년, gap year
휴식하다, break
휴양, recreation
휴양 시설, spa
휴양 시설의 공동 사용권, time-share
휴양객, holidaymaker
휴양의, recreational
휴양지, resort
휴업, shutdown, stoppage
휴업하는, idle
휴일, day off, holiday
휴전, truce
휴정, adjournment, recess
휴지, pause
휴지 상태의, dormant
휴지 시간, downtime
휴직, leave
휴회, adjournment, recess
휴회하다, adjourn
흉, reflection
흉금을 털어놓는, bosom
흉내, imitation, impression
흉내 내는 사람, mimic
흉내 내다, ape, imitate, mimic,
    simulate
흉내 내며 놀리다, mock
흉내 냄, impersonation
흉내내다, copy
흉보, news
흉상, bust
흉악범, thug
흉악한, atrocious, tough
흉측하게, grotesquely
흉측한, grotesque
흉터, scar
흉터가 남다, scar
흉포한, ferocious
흉포함, ferocity
흉하게 생긴 사람, grotesque
흉한, nasty
흐느껴 욺, cry
흐느끼다, sob
흐느낌, sobbing, sob
흐려지게 하다, dull
흐려지다, dull, tarnish
흐려진, blurred
흐르는, running
흐르다, flow, run, spill
흐름, flow, tide

흐름을 막다, trap
흐리게 하다, blur, muddy, tarnish
흐리다, cloud
흐리멍덩한, glazed
흐린, cloudy, gray
흐릿하게, dimly
흐릿하게 보이는 것, blur
흐릿하게 하다, dim
흐릿한, blurred, dim, dull, hazy,
    smoky, vague
흐릿한 김, haze
흐릿한 열기, haze
흐릿한 형상, blob
흐릿해지다, blur, dim, glaze
흐트러뜨리다, diffuse
흐트러진, disheveled
흑백, black and white
흑백의, black and white
흑백이 분명한, black and white
흑사병, plague
흑색 가전제품, brown goods
흑연, graphite
흑인, black
흑인 음악, soul
흑인 자치구, homeland
흑인의, black
흑자, surplus
흑자의, black
흑자를 낳다, pay
흔들거리는, unsteady
흔들기, wave
흔들다, agitate, rock, shake,
    swing, wag, wave, weaken
흔들리다, dance, move, rock, sway,
    swing, teeter, waver, weaken
흔들리지 않은, unmoved
흔들릴 없는, stable
흔들어 대다, flourish
흔듦, shake, swing
흔적, echo, impression, imprint,
    mark, remain, stamp, trace,
    trail, vein, vestige
흔적도 없이 사라지다, trace
흔적도 없이, air
흔적을 남기다, mark
흔하다, prevail
흔한, common, prevalent
흔히, commonly, popularly
흔히 말하는, proverbial
흔히 반복되는 말, refrain
흔히 생각하듯, popularly
흔히 있는, usual
흘끗 보다, glance
흘끗 봄, glance
흘러나오게 하다, exude
흘러나오다, stream
흘러내리다, roll, run
흘러넘치다, ooze
(~에) 흘러들다, empty
흘려보내다, pump
흘리게 하다, draw
흘리다, funnel, run, shed, spill
흘린 것, mess
흙, dirt, soil
흙 같은, earthy
흙 채취장, pit
흙먼지, dust
흙받이, fender
흙으로 된, dirt
흠, blemish, chip, flaw, hole,
    imperfection
흠 없이, piece
흠 잡을 데 없는, faultless
흠 하나 없이, immaculately
흠모, admiration, adoration
흠모하는 사람, admirer
흠모하다, admire, adore, worship
흠뻑 땀이 나는 상태, sweat
흠뻑 적시다, drench, soak
흠뻑 젖다, saturate
흠뻑 젖은, soaked, soaking, sodden
(~에) 흠을 내다, blemish, damage
흠이 있는, flawed
흠이 전혀 없는, perfect
흡수, absorption, assimilation
흡수되다, swallow
흡수성의, absorbent
흡수하다, absorb, assimilate, soak

흡연, smoking
흡연용의, smoking
흡연자, smoker
흡인력 있는, compelling
흡입, intake
흡입관, siphon
흡입관으로 빼내다, siphon
흡입하다, sniff
흡족한, good
흡족해하다, gloat
흡혈귀, vampire
흥건한 곳, pool
흥겨운, festive
흥미, interest
흥미 없는, inert, unattractive
흥미로운, interesting, intriguing
흥미로운 사건, news
흥미로운 인물, news
흥미롭게도, interestingly
흥미를 가진, interested
흥미를 갖게 하다, interest
흥미를 끌다, imagination, interest
흥미를 느끼는, intrigued
흥미를 느끼도록 만들다, fire
흥미를 불러일으키다, excite
(~에) 흥미를 잃다, go
흥미진진한, gripping, racy, stirring,
    thrilling
흥밋거리, interest
흥분, arousal, excitement, kick
흥분거리, excitement
흥분시키다, rouse, titillate, turn
흥분을 잘 하는, excitable
흥분제, stimulant
흥분하다, work
흥분하여, excitedly
흥분한, excited, state, wild, wound
    up
흥분해서, excitedly
흥얼거리다, croon
흥정, horse-trading
흥정을 하다, bargain
흥청망청, extravagantly

흥청망청하기, spree
흥취, zest
흩날리다, fly, spray
흩다, disturb
흩뜨리다, dissipate, scatter
흩뿌리다, scatter, spray
흩어져 사라지다, dissipate
(~주변에) 흩어져 있는, dotted,
    scattered
(~에) 흩어져 있다, litter
흩어지다, disperse, fan, spread
흩어진, loose, scattered
희곡, drama, play
희귀성, rarity
희귀한, rare, unusual
희극의, comic
희극적인, comic
희롱, banter, harassment
희망, hope, wish
희망 사항, wishful thinking
희망을 갖고, hopefully
희망을 걸고 하는, hopeful
희망을 걸다, bet, pin
희망을 잃지 않다, hope
희망을 주는 것, hope
희망을 품고 살다, hope
희망이 없는, down-and-out,
    hopeless
희망적으로, positively
희망적인, hopeful, positive,
    rosy
희망하다, hope, wish
희미하게, dimly, distantly, dully,
    faintly, vaguely, weakly
희미하게 빛나다, glimmer
희미한, dim, faint, fuzzy, vague,
    watery, weak
희미한 빛, gleam, glimmer,
    shimmer
희미해지다, fade
희박하게, sparsely
희박한, remote, slim, sparse
희생, cost, sacrifice

(~의) 희생 아래, detriment
희생되다, victimize
(~을) 희생시켜, expense
희생시키다, cost
희생양, scapegoat
희생양으로 삼다, scapegoat
희생자, casualty, prey,
    victim
희생자 수, toll
희생하다, sacrifice
희석되다, dilute
희석시키다, dilute
희석용 음료, mixer
희석하다, dilute
희석한, dilute
희열, gratification
희열에 넘친, ecstatic
희열에 넘칠 정도로,
    ecstatically
희화, caricature
희화(戱畵), caricature
희화하다, caricature
흰, white
흰색 칠판, whiteboard
흰자위, white
히스테리, frenzy, hysteria
히스테리 상태의, hysterics
히스테리를 부리는, hysterics
히스테리의, hysterical
히스테리적으로, hysterically
히스패닉, Hispanic
히스패닉의, Hispanic
히죽히죽 웃다, smirk
히치하이크를 하다, hitch,
    hitchhike, thumb
히터, heater
히트 치다, hit
히피, hippie
힌두교, Hinduism
힌두교 지도자, guru
힌두교도, Hindu
힌두교의, Hindu
힌트, clue

힌트를 주다, drop
힐끗 보다, glimpse
힐난하다, jump
힘, energy, force, might, potency,
    power, strength
힘 있는 나라, power
힘겨운, testing, uphill
힘겨운 일, slog
힘겹게 해 나가다, slog
힘껏, full, might
힘든, awkward, hard, heavy,
    laborious, onerous, rocky,
    rough, tough
힘든 노력, graft
힘든 상태, going
힘들게, laboriously
힘들게 끌다, lug
힘들게 여행하다, trek
힘들어지다, flounder
힘들여 움직이다, lever
힘들여 해내다, wade
힘들지 않게, painlessly
힘들지 않은, painless
힘듦, hardness
힘없는, muted
힘없이, feebly, weakly
힘에 부친, daunting
힘을 과시하다, muscle
힘을 더하다, reinforce
힘을 불어넣기, jump-start
힘을 불어넣다, jump-start
(~에) 힘을 쏟다, put
힘을 주다, empower
힘이 나다, cheer
힘이 많이 드는, strenuous
힘이 센, strong
힘이 없는, weak
힘이 풀리다, buckle
(~에) 힘입어, strength
힘줄, tendon
힘차게, forcefully
힘차게 춤추다, jig
힘찬, forceful, rousing

영문 쓰기 안내

구두점

아포스트로피

- '아포스트로피+s'는 단수명사나 복수명사와 함께 쓰여 소유를 나타낸다.
  [명사가 s로 끝날 때는 아포스트로피만 쓴다.]
- '아포스트로피+s'가 소유권을 나타낸다.
  [두 번째 이름에 's가 붙은 것은 그들이 이 CD들을 공동으로 소유하고 있음을 나타낸다.]
  [두 사람 다의 이름에 's가 붙은 것은 그들 각자가 다른 모자를 소유하고 있음을 나타낸다.]
- 아포스트로피는 축약형에 쓰인다.

각괄호

- 각괄호는 인용되는 내용 속에 자기 자신의 정보를 덧붙일 때 쓴다.
- 점 세 개를 묶은 각괄호는 인용문 속에서 내용을 생략할 때 쓴다.

콜론

- 콜론은 시계상의 시간을 나타낼 때 쓴다.
- 콜론은 목록을 도입할 때 쓴다.
- 콜론은 업무적인 편지에서 인사말 뒤에 쓴다.

콤마

- 콤마는 날짜와 주소에 쓰인다.
- 콤마는 문장의 도입 부분에 해당하는 구나 절 뒤에 쓴다.
- 콤마는 일련의 요소를 하나씩 나열할 때 쓴다.
- 콤마는 비한정적인 구나 절을 통해 정보를 덧붙일 때 쓴다.
- 콤마는 비격식적인 편지의 인사말과 맺음말 뒤에 쓴다.

대시

- 대시는 뒤에 추가되는 정보 속에 콤마가 들어 있을 경우, 원래 콤마를 쓸 자리에 그 대신 쓴다.

느낌표

- 느낌표는 강한 감정을 나타내는 단어나 어구 뒤에 쓴다.

하이픈

- 하이픈은 합성어나 숫자에 쓴다.
- 하이픈은 글의 행 끝에서 단어를 나눌 때 쓴다.

(둥근) 괄호

- 둥근 괄호는 꼭 필요하지 않은 정보나, 열거에 쓰인 숫자나 글자를 나타낼 때 쓴다.

마침표

- 마침표는 의문문이나 감탄문이 아닌 모든 문장의 끝에 쓴다.
- 마침표는 많은 약어들 뒤에 쓴다.

물음표

- 물음표는 질문을 나타내는 단어나 문장 뒤에 쓴다.

따옴표

- 따옴표는 말하는 내용을 직접 인용할 때 쓴다. 간접적으로 인용할 때는 쓰지 않는다.

- 따옴표는 시나 단편소설이나 책 속의 장이나 노래, 잡지 기사들과 같은 짧은 글의 제목을 나타 낼 때 쓴다.

세미콜론
- 세미콜론은 독립된 절들 사이에 (and, but, or, nor, for 같은) 등위접속사가 없을 때 그 절들을 이어 주기 위해 쓴다.
- 세미콜론은 또 독립된 절을 이어 주기 위해 접속부사(however, furthermore 등) 앞에 쓴다.

사선
- 사선은 서로 대체 가능한 것들을 구분할 때 쓴다.
- 사선은 날짜에 쓰인 숫자를 구분하거나 분수의 분자와 분모를 구분할 때 쓴다
- 사선은 시의 구절을 인용할 때, 각 행이 끝나는 부분에 쓴다.

대문자 쓰기
고유 명사와 고유 형용사의 첫 글자는 대문자로 쓴다.
- 제목 속의 주요 단어들
- 사람 이름
- 도시, 국가, 주, 국적, 언어
- 지리적 요소
- 회사 및 조직체
- 부서, 정부 부처
- 건물
- 등록된 상표의 제품
- 요일, 달, 공휴일
- 마침표가 없는 일부 약어
- 종교 및 관련어
- 역사적 기간, 사건, 문서
- 직함, 칭호
- 인쇄물의 제목

이탤릭체로 쓰기
손으로 쓰거나 타자를 친 글에서는 이탤릭체 부분을 밑줄로 표시한다.
다음과 같은 요소들은 이탤릭체로 쓴다.
- 강조하고자 하는 단어나 구절.
- 무엇의 일부로서가 아니라 독립적으로 출간되는 인쇄물.
- 영어 문장 속에 쓰인 외래어[외국어].
- 대수 방정식에 쓰인 글자.

철자

철자 오류가 빈번히 발생하는 단어들

다음과 같은 단어들은 철자가 혼동되는 경우가 종종 있다:

accept, except	discreet, discrete	peace, piece
access, excess	dyeing, dying	personal, personnel
advice, advise	elicit, illicit	plain, plane
affect, effect	emigrate, immigrate	pray, prey
aisles, isles	envelop, envelope	precede, proceed
alley, ally	fair, fare	presence, presents
already, all ready	faze, phase	principle, principal
altar, alter	fine, find	prophecy, prophesy
altogether, all together	formerly, formally	purpose, propose
always, all ways	forth, fourth	quiet, quit, quite
amoral, immoral	forward, foreword	raise, rise
angel, angle	gorilla, guerrilla	respectfully, respectively
ask, ax	have, of	right, rite, write
assistance, assistants	hear, here	road, rode
baring, barring, bearing	heard, herd	sat, set
began, begin	heroin, heroine	sense, since
believe, belief	hole, whole	shown, shone
board, bored	holy, wholly	stationary, stationery
break, brake	horse, hoarse	straight, strait
breath, breathe	human, humane	than, then
buy, by, bye	its, it's	their, there, they're,
capital, capitol	later, latter	there're
censor, censure, sensor	lay, lie	threw, through,
choose, chose	lead, led	thorough
cite, site, sight	lessen, lesson	throne, thrown
clothes, cloths	lightning, lightening	to, too, two
coarse, course	lose, loose	tract, track
complement, compliment	marital, martial	waist, waste
conscience, conscious	maybe, may be	weak, week
council, counsel	miner, minor	weather, whether
diary, dairy	moral, morale	were, wear, where, we're
decent, descent, dissent	of, off	which, witch
desert, dessert	passed, past	who's, whose
device, devise	patience, patients	your, you're

NOTE: 아래 요약한 내용은 철자와 관련된 많은 질문들에 대한 답이 되어 줄 것이다. 그러나 이 외에도 더 많은 규칙들이 있고 또 예외들도 많다. 의심스러울 때는 항상 사전을 보고 확인하라.

ei와 ie

다음과 같은 옛말이 있다: "c 뒤에 오거나, neighbor와 weigh에서처럼 ay[ei]로 발음 나는 경우 외에는 i가 e 앞에 온다."

- i가 e보다 앞에 오는 경우:
- c 뒤에서 e가 i보다 앞에 오는 경우:
- ay[ei]로 발음되면서 e가 i보다 앞에 오는 경우:

접두사

접두사는 한 단어의 뜻을 바꿔놓는다. 이 때 따로 추가되거나 삭제되는 철자는 없다.

접미사

- 모음으로 시작되는 접미사가 붙을 때는 기본형 마지막에 나오는 e를 삭제한다
- 자음으로 시작되는 접미사가 붙을 때는 기본형에서 묵음으로 발음되는 e는 그대로 둔다
- 기본형이 (1) 자음으로 끝나고, (2) 단음절어이거나 강세 음절일 때 또 (3) 마지막 자음이 모음 다음에 올 때는, 마지막 자음을 한 번 더 쓴다
- 기본형이 y로 끝날 때는 접미사 –ing를 붙이는 경우 외에는 모두 y를 i로 바꾼다

문법

접속사

접속사는 단어, 어구, 절을 연결하는 말이다.

등위접속사

등위접속사는 and, but, for, nor, or, so, yet이 있다.

- Sarah **and** Michael
- on vacation **for** three weeks
- You can borrow the book from a library **or** you can buy it at a bookstore.

상관접속사

상관접속사는 짝을 이뤄 쓰인다.

상관접속사로는 both . . . and, either . . . or, neither . . . nor, not only . . . but also, whether . . . or가 있다.

- **Neither** Sam **nor** Madeleine could attend the party.
- The singer was **both** out of tune **and** too loud.
- Oscar **not only** ate too much, **but also** fell asleep at the table.

종속접속사

종속접속사는 종속절을 주절과 연결시키는 데 쓴다.

- Antonia sighed loudly **as if** she were really exhausted.
- Uri arrived late **because** his car broke down.

다음은 종속접속사들의 목록이다.

after	before	no matter how	than	where
although	even if	now that	though	wherever
as far as	even though	once	till	whether
as if	how	provided that	unless	while
as soon as	if	since	until	why
as though	in as much as	so that	when	
because	in case	supposing that	whenever	

접속 부사

두 개의 독립된 절은 '세미콜론＋접속 부사＋콤마(,)'로 연결할 수 있다. 접속 부사는 흔히 세미콜론 바로 다음에 온다.

- Kham wanted to buy a car; **however**, he hadn't saved up enough money.
- Larry didn't go right home; **instead**, he stopped at the health club.

일부 접속 부사는 두 번째 절 속에서 다른 위치에 나타날 수도 있다.

- Kham wanted to buy a car; he hadn't, **however**, saved up enough money.
- Larry didn't go right home; he stopped at the health club **instead**.

다음은 접속 부사들의 목록이다:

also	finally	indeed	nevertheless	then
anyhow	furthermore	instead	next	therefore
anyway	hence	likewise	otherwise	thus
besides	however	meanwhile	similarly	
consequently	incidentally	moreover	still	

연결 어구

글 속에 나오는 모든 문장이 '주어＋동사'로 시작한다면 지루할 것이다. 다양성을 줄 수 있도록 일부 문장에서는 서두를 '연결 어구＋콤마(,)'로 시작하라.

- Rita needed to study for the test. **On the other hand**, she didn't want to miss the party.
- Yuki stayed up all night studying. **As a result**, he overslept and missed the test.

다음은 연결 어구들의 목록이다:

after all	for example
as a result	in addition
at any rate	in fact
at the same time	in other words
by the way	on the contrary
even so	on the other hand

전치사

전치사는 다른 품사와의 관계를 묘사한다. 전치사는 보통 명사나 대명사 앞에 쓰인다.

- Sancho was waiting **outside** the club.
- I gave the money **to** him.

다음은 흔히 쓰이는 전치사들의 목록이다.

about	by	out
above	concerning	outside
across	despite	over
after	during	past
against	down	regarding
among	except	round
around	for	since
as	from	through
at	in	to
before	inside	toward
behind	into	under
below	lie	unlike
beneath	near	until
beside	of	up
between	off	upon
beyond	on	with

구 전치사

다음은 구 전치사들의 목록이다.

according to	by way of	in spite of
along with	due to	instead of
apart from	except for	on account of
as for	in addition to	out of
as regards	in case of	up to
as to	in front of	with reference to
because of	in lieu of	with regard to
by means of	in place of	with respect to
by reason of	in regard to	with the exception of

참고문헌 작성법

대학에서 연구 과제나 에세이를 작성할 때는 보통 세 가지 양식(APA, Chicago, MLA) 중 한가지로 작성을 하도록 요구한다. 이어지는 내용은 이들 세 가지 양식의 가장 중요한 점들을 비교, 대조한 것이다.

APA 스타일(American Psychological Association Style)

1. 전반적인 미주 양식

   제목은 'References(참고문헌)'로 한다. 행간은 더블스페이스로 하고 저자의 성(姓)을 알파벳 순서로 정리하여 이름을 적은 다음 괄호 속에 연도를 표시하고 그 뒤에 다른 출간 관련 정보를 쓴다.

2. 단일 저자 인용

   Moore, (1992). *The care of the soul*. New York: HarperPerennial.

3. 복수 저자 인용

   각 저자의 성을 먼저 쓰고 이름은 두음자만 적는 방식으로 저자명을 나열하고, 맨 마지막 저자 이름 앞에 &를 써라.

   Spinosa, C., Flores, F., & Dreyfus, H.L. (1997). *Disclosing new worlds: Entrepreneurship, democratic action, and the cultivation of solidarity*. Cambridge: MA: MIT Press.

4. 편저자 인용

   Wellwood, J. (Ed.). (1992). *Ordinary magic: Everyday life as a spiritual path*. Boston: Shambhala Publications.

5. 정기간행물에 실린 논문[글] 인용

   성(姓)이 먼저 오게 저자명을 적고 간행물의 출간 연도와 달을(찾을 수 있으면 날짜도) 적는다. 그 뒤에 논문의 제목(밑줄 없이), 정기간행물명(발행 호수도 있으면 그 뒤에 붙여서), 페이지 수를 적는다.

   Gibson, S. (2001, November). Hanging wallpaper. *This Old House*, 77.

6. 온라인 자료 인용

   독자가 관련 정보를 찾을 수 있도록 충분한 정보를 제공하라. 게시 날짜, 제목, 원래 인쇄된 출처(있는 경우에 한해), 그 정보를 찾은 곳에 대한 기술, 자료를 찾은 날짜를 포함시키도록 하라.

   Arnold, W. (April 26, 2002). "State senate announces new tax relief." *Seattle Post-Intelligencer*. Retrieved May 1, 2002, from http://seattle.pi.nwsource.com/printer2/index.asp?ploc=b

7. 본문 속 인용 표기 양식

   다음의 두 가지 정보를 포함시켜라: 저자(들)의 성과 발표 연도.
   (Moore, 1992).

Chicago 스타일(The Chicago Manual of Style에서)

1. 전반적인 미주 양식

   페이지 제목은 'Notes'로 한다. 행간은 더블스페이스로 한다. 각 항목에 번호를 붙이고 첫 행은 들여 쓴다. 저자 이름은 두음자가 아니라 모두 다 쓴다. 관련 페이지는 항목 끝에 붙인다.

2. 단일 저자 인용

   Thomas Moore, *The Care of the Soul* (New York: HarperPerennial, 1992), 7–9.

3. 복수 저자 인용

   Charles Spinosa, Ferdinand Flores, and Hubert L. Dreyfus, *Disclosing New Worlds: Entrepreneurship, Democratic Action, and the Cultivation of Solidarity* (Cambridge: MIT Press, 1997), 66.

4. 편저자 인용

   John Wellwood, ed. 1992. *Ordinary Magic: Everyday Life as Spiritual Path* (Boston: Shambhala Publications).

5. 정기간행물에 실린 논문(글) 인용

   성(姓)이 먼저 오게 저자명을 쓴다. 그 뒤에 논문 제목을 따옴표 속에 넣어 쓰고, 간행물명, 권번호(주어져 있는 경우), 연도, 페이지 번호를 쓴다.

   Gibson, Stephen, "Hanging Wallpaper," *This Old House* 53 (2001): 77.

6. 온라인 자료 인용

   각 항목에 번호를 붙이고 첫 행을 들여 쓴다. 독자가 관련 정보를 찾을 수 있도록 충분한 정보를 제공한다. 저자명(이름을 먼저 오게), 게시 날짜(괄호 속에 넣어), 제목, 원래 인쇄된 출처(있는 경우에 한해), 그 정보를 찾은 곳에 대한 기술, 인터넷 서버 주소(URL), 자료를 찾은 날짜(괄호 속에 넣어)를 포함시키도록 하라.

   William Arnold, "State Senate Announces New Tax Relief," *Seattle Post-Intelligencer*, April 26, 2002, http://seattle.pi.nwsource.com/printer2/index.asp?ploc=b

7. 본문 속 인용 표기 양식

   모든 본문 속 주석에 번호를 붙인다. 본문 속에 인용 저서를 처음 언급할 때는 위 2에서 말한 내용을 모두 적는다. 동일 저작물을 다시 인용할 때에는 저자(들)의 성만 쓰고 관련 페이지 번호만 적는다.

   (Moore, 8)

MLA 스타일(Modern Language Association Style)

1. 전반적인 미주 양식

   페이지 제목은 'Works Cited'로 한다. 행간은 더블스페이스로 하고 저자의 성(姓)을 알파 벳순으로 배열한 뒤 다음과 같은 나머지 출간 정보를 쓴다.

2. 단일 저자 인용

   Moore, Thomas. *The Care of the Soul*. New York: HarperPerennial, 1992.

3. 복수 저자 인용

   제1저자의 이름을 제목 페이지에 나와 있는 것과 동일한 순서로 나열한다. 제1저자만 성 (姓)을 먼저 적는다.

   Spinosa, Charles, Ferdinand Flores, and Hubert L. Dreyfus. *Disclosing New Worlds: Entrepreneurship, Democratic Action, and the Cultivation of Solidarity*. Cambridge: MIT, 1997.

4. 편저자 인용

   Wellwood, John, ed. *Ordinary Magic: Everyday Life as Spiritual Path*. Boston; Shambhala, 1992.

5. 정기 간행물에 실린 논문[글] 인용

   저자명(성(姓)이 먼저 오도록), 논문 제목(인용 부호를 써서), 잡지명(마침표 없이), 권 번호, 연도(뒤에 콜론을 찍음), 페이지 번호 순으로 쓴다.

   Gibson, Stephen "Hanging Wallpaper." *This Old House* 53 (2001): 77.

6. 온라인 자료 인용

   독자가 관련 정보를 찾을 수 있도록 충분한 정보를 제공한다. 게시 날짜, 제목, 원래 인쇄된 출처(있는 경우에 한해), 자료를 찾은 날짜, (가능한 경우에 한해) 인터넷 서버 주소(URL)를 적는다.

   Arnold, William. "State Senate Announces New Tax Relief." Seattle Post-Intelligencer 26 Apr. 2002 http://seattle.pi.nwsource.com/printer2/index.asp?ploc=b

7. 본문 속 인용 표기 방식

   항목에 번호를 붙이지 않는다. 'Work Cited'에 나열된 저작물을 인용할 때는 저자(들)의 성 (姓)과 관련 페이지 번호만 적는다.

   (Moore 7-8)

블록 서신 양식
블록 서신 양식에서는 안으로 들여 쓰는 행이 없다.

회신[발신자] 주소	77 Lincoln Avenue Wellesley, MA 02480
날짜	May 10, 2007
내부[수신자] 주소	Dr. Rita Bennett Midland Hospital Senior Care Center 5000 Poe Avenue Dayton, OH 45414
인사말	Dear Dr. Bennett:
서신 본문	I am responding to your advertisement for a dietitian in the May 5 edition of the *New York Times*. I graduated from Boston University two years ago. Since graduation, I have been working at Brigham and Women's Hospital and have also earned additional certificates in nutritional support and diabetes education. I am interested in locating to the Midwest and will be happy to arrange for an interview at your convenience.
맺는 말	Sincerely,
서명	*Daniel Chin*
타자한 이름	Daniel Chin

들여 쓴 서신 양식

회신 주소, 날짜, 맺는 말을 종이 오른쪽 끝 부분에 붙여 쓴다. 각 단락의 첫 행도 들여 쓴다.

회신[발신자] 주소	77 Lincoln Avenue Wellesley, MA 02480
날짜	May 15, 2007
내부[수신자] 주소	Dr. Rita Bennett Senior Care Center 5000 Poe Avenue Dayton, OH 45414
인사말	Dear Dr. Bennett:
서신 본문	It was a pleasure to meet you and learn more about the programs offered at the Senior Care Center. I appreciate your taking time out to show me around and introduce me to the staff. I am excited about the possibility of working at the Senior Care Center and I look forward to talking with you again soon.
맺는 말	Sincerely,
서명	*Daniel Chin*
타자한 이름	Daniel Chin

이력서
성공적인 이력서 작성 전략

- 길이: 1페이지
- 정직성: 사실이 아닌 내용은 절대 쓰지 마라
- 내용: 경력과 자격에 대한 정보를 포함시킨다. 연령, 종교, 혼인 여부, 인종이나 국적은 쓰지 않는다. 사진을 첨부할 필요도 없다.

서두
성명, 주소, 이메일, 전화번호를 쓴다.

목적
자신의 목표나 기술 또는 이 둘을 쓴다.

능력
지원하는 업무에 도움이 될 기술을 가진 게 있으면 적는다.

경력
지금까지 거친 직장들에 대해 쓴다. 업적이나 수상 내력도 포함시킨다. 강한 의미를 갖는 동사들과 함께 적극적이고 행동 지향적인 말을 사용하라. 현 직장에 대해서는 동사를 현재시제로 쓰고 과거에 거친 직장들에 대해서는 과거 시제로 써라. 맡았던 직책 이름들도 포함시켜라.

학력
다닌 학교들을 적어라. 대학 졸업자의 경우에는 고등학교는 포함시키지 말아라. 가장 최근에 취득한 학위부터 먼저 적어라.

취미
이 부분은 반드시 써야 하는 것은 아니지만 장차 고용주가 될 측에게 자신이 폭넓은 인성을 갖춘 사람임을 보여주는 데 도움이 될 수 있다.

이력서 견본

사용 가능한 이력서 양식은 몇 가지가 있다. 다음은 그 한 예이다.

Maria Gonzales

9166 Main Street, Apartment 3G
Los Angeles, CA 93001
gonzales@email.com
213-555-9878

OBJECTIVE: Experienced manager seeks a management position in retail sales

EXPERIENCE:

Assistant Director of Retail

2005 – Present   Shopmart, Los Angeles CA
Manage relationships with vendors to complete orders, create accounts, and resolve issues. Maintain inventory and generate monthly inventory reports. Plan weekly promotions. Communicate with all retail employees to improve product knowledge and selling techniques. Implemented new customer service procedures.

Server

2005 – Present   Chuy's Grill, San Monica, CA
Greet and seat guests. Bus tables. Answer phones and take and prepare in-house, phone, or fax orders. Train new and existing employees. Awarded Employee of the Month five times for exceeding company expectations for quality and service.

Store Supervisor

1999 – 2005   Impact Photography Systems, Waco, TX
Oversaw daily operations, including customer and employee relations, counter sales, inventory management, maintaining store appearance, banking transactions, and equipment maintenance. Managed, trained, and scheduled staff of 35.

SKILLS: Fluent in English and Spanish. Expert in MS Word and Excel.

EDUCATION:

Associate of Arts Degree

1997 – 2000   Los Angeles Community College, Los Angeles, CA
Coursework in business management, marketing, studio art, communication, psychology, and sociology.

Study Abroad

2000 – 2001   University of Valencia, Valencia, Spain
Coursework in Spanish and international business.

INTERESTS: Backpacking, playing softball, and volunteering as a tutor for Literacy First.

교정 부호

교사들이 학생들의 과제를 검토할 때는 다음과 같은 약어와 부호를 흔히 쓴다.

문제점	부호	예시
일치	**agr**	He **go** to work at 8:oo.
대문자	**cap**	the United states
분철	**div**	disorientati
	hy	**-on**
불완전한 문장	**frag**	**Where she found the book.**
문법	**gr**	It's the **bigger** house on the street.
이탤릭체 필요	**ital**	I read it in **The Daily News.**
소문자 필요	lc	I don't like Peanut Butter.
구두점 오류	p	Where did you find that coat.
복수형 필요	pl	I bought the **grocery** on my way home.
철자 오류	sp	Did you reci**e**ve my letter yet?
틀린 시제	t	I **see** her yesterday.
틀린 단어	**ww**	My family used to **rise** corn and wheat.
아포스트로피 필요	⌄	I don⌄t know her name.
콤마 필요	⌃	However⌃we will probably arrive on time.
일부 삭제	⟋	We had the most best meal of our lives.
새 단락으로 시작	¶	. . . since last Friday.
		¶ Oh, by the way . . .
단어 순서 바꾸기	⌒	They live on the floor first.

abate	aim	arrival	bond
abbreviate	albeit	article	book
above	alleviate	ascend	boorish
abroad	allocation	ascertain	border
abrupt	allow	aspect	bothersome
absence	allowance	assert	bottom
absolute	alter	assimilate	boundary
absurd	amaze	assortment	brand
abuse	ambiguous	assume	break
abyss	ambivalence	assure	breakthrough
accelerate	amenity	astounding	brevity
accentuate	amiable	astute	brief
accept	amicable	atom	brilliant
acceptable	amorous	atone	brink
access	ample	attendance	broaden
accident	amplify	attest	bud
acclaim	amusement	attract	budget
accord	analogous	attractive	bulk
account	analogy	auction	burgeon
accounting	analyze	audacious	cabinet
accredited	anchor	audible	caliber
accretion	ancient	auditorium	calisthenics
accurate	animal	augment	callous
acknowledge	animate	auspicious	candid
acquiesce	animosity	author	capable
acquire	annals	authorize	capital
active	annex	autograph	captive
actually	anniversary	autonomous	capture
addict	annoying	avail	card
adept	annual	avarice	career
adhere	annuity	average	carpet
adjacent	antecedent	avoid	carry
adjust	anterior	background	categorize
admiration	anthropology	backup	caution
admit	anticipate	baffle	celebrated
admonish	antipathy	baked	cement
adopt	antiquated	balanced	certificate
advance	antisocial	bankrupt	challenge
advanced	apart	barometer	chaotic
advantage	apathy	bear	characteristic
advent	apology	become	charisma
adverse	apparel	bellicose	chiefly
advertisement	apparent	benefit	chilly
advice	appeal	benevolent	chore
affable	appealing	benign	chronic
affliction	apprehensive	bibliography	chronicle
affluent	appropriate	bill	chronological
afford	approximately	biology	circle
affordable	aptly	bisect	circulate
agenda	aqueous	blame	circumstance
agent	arbiter	bland	citizenship
aggravating	arbitrary	blind	clamor
aggregate	archaic	block	clarify
agile	arduous	bloom	classify
agitate	arid	blossom	clear
agnostic	aroma	blur	clerk
agoraphobia	arrest	bold	clever

clock
coarse
code
coherent
collateral
colleague
collect
collection
college
colloquial
colonist
command
commemorate
commonplace
compatible
compel
complex
comply
conceal
concede
conceive
concept
concoct
condense
condition
conducive
conduct
confide
confidential
confirm
conform
conjure
conscientious
conscious
consecutive
consent
conservation
consider
considerate
consideration
consistently
consortium
constant
constraint
constrict
construe
consumption
contact
contemplate
contemporary
contend
content
contentment
contingent
continue
contort
contradictory

controversial
convene
convenience
convenient
conventional
convert
convey
convince
cook
copy
core
corner
corporate
corpse
corrupt
cost
counsel
couple
courageous
courier
course
court
cowardly
crack
crate
create
credible
credit
creed
creep
crescent
critical
criticize
crop
crucial
crush
cultivate
curb
curious
currency
current
custom
cyclone
damp
dangle
dash
deadline
deceased
deceive
decent
declare
decline
decompose
decorate
deduce
deduct
deep

default
deflate
defy
degenerate
degree
dehydrate
delegate
delicate
delighted
deluge
demand
demolish
demonstration
demure
dense
dentistry
dependent
depict
deplete
depreciate
deprive
describe
description
desiccated
despise
destroy
destruction
detail
detect
determined
develop
deviate
diagnose
dial
dichotomy
dictate
dictionary
diet
difficult
diffident
dignitary
dignity
diligent
dim
diminish
diminutive
direct
disapproval
discard
discernible
discount
discourse
discreditable
discuss
disguise
disintegrate
dismiss

disorient
disparate
disparity
disperse
display
dispose
disregard
disrobe
disruptive
dissimilar
dissociate
dissuade
distinct
distinguish
distort
distribute
disturb
disturbing
diverse
docile
doctor
doctrine
document
dogma
doleful
domestic
dominant
dormant
download
downturn
drab
dramatic
drastic
draw
droop
drought
dubious
due
dumbfound
dweller
dwelling
dwindle
dynamic
dysentery
dysfunction
dyslexia
dyspepsia
dystrophy
eager
earnest
educate
efface
effect
effective
effigy
egregious
eject

elaborate	examiner	firm	grumble
elect	exceed	flaw	guess
election	exceedingly	flimsy	harass
element	exceptional	floor	harmful
elementary	exchange	florist	harmless
elevator	excite	flourish	harvest
elicit	exclaim	fluctuate	hasten
eligible	exclude	fluent	hazardous
eliminate	exclusively	fluid	haze
elucidate	excursion	forbearance	head
elude	exemplify	forbid	heave
emit	exhaust	forecast	heighten
empathy	exhibit	forfeit	henceforth
emphasize	exit	formal	heretic
employee	expand	format	hero
employment	expansion	formerly	hesitate
emulate	expel	formidable	hidden
enact	experience	formulate	highlight
enchant	explain	fortify	hit
encircle	exploit	fortune	homophone
encompass	export	found	honor
encourage	express	founder	host
endeavor	exquisite	fracture	hue
endorse	extensive	fragment	humane
endorsement	extent	frail	humid
endure	exterminate	frame	hyperactive
energetic	extol	fraud	hyperbole
engine	extract	freezing	hypersensitive
enhance	extradite	frequently	hypertension
enormous	extremely	freshly	ideal
enrich	fabricate	frigid	identical
ensue	face	frontier	illuminate
enthrall	facet	fulfillment	illustrate
enthuse	facsimile	function	illustration
entirely	fact	fundamental	immense
envision	factory	further	immigrant
equal	fail	gain	impact
equity	faint	gather	impede
equivalent	fallacy	gaudy	impediment
erode	familiar	generally	implicate
erratic	famous	generous	import
espionage	fantasy	geography	impossible
essence	fare	get	impressive
essential	fashion	ghastly	improper
establish	fathom	gigantic	inaccessible
eternal	feasible	gingerly	inactive
eugenics	feature	glove	inconvenience
eulogize	fee	goal	incorporate
euphemism	feign	good	increase
euthanasia	fertile	government	incredible
evade	fiction	grade	incredulity
evaporate	fidelity	gradually	incredulous
even	figment	graffiti	incumbent
eventually	figure	grant	indeed
evident	final	graphic	indicate
evolution	finance	gratitude	indigenous
exaggerate	finit	grimace	indiscriminate

indispensable	know	mental	novelty
indivisible	labor	mention	novice
induce	lachrymose	merchandise	nuance
induct	lack	merciless	number
inert	lasting	metropolitan	obese
inevitable	launch	microbe	oblige
infancy	lawyer	microcosm	observe
infant	layman	microfilm	obsolete
infer	lead	micrometer	obstruct
influence	league	microscope	obtain
inhabitant	lease	microsecond	obviously
initiate	leash	microwave	occasion
injury	leather	midday	occupancy
innovate	legal	mild	occur
innovative	legible	miniature	odd
inordinate	legitimate	minimal	offense
inquire	library	minimum	offensive
insensitive	likelihood	ministry	offer
insipid	limber	minor	office
inspire	limit	minuscule	omit
institution	litter	minute	ongoing
instrument	loafer	mirror	operate
intensify	lobotomy	mirth	opposition
intent	logic	misanthropy	opus
intentionally	logo	misconstrue	order
interact	loom	misogyny	orthodox
intercept	lose	missive	otherwise
interchangeable	lounge	mistake	outlandish
intermediate	lucrative	misunderstand	overcome
intermittent	luggage	mobile	overlook
interpret	lustrous	moist	owner
interrelate	macrocosm	monotone	ownership
interrupt	macroeconomics	morphology	package
intersperse	magnificent	mortgage	pad
intervene	magnitude	motion	page
intolerable	mail	motivate	paradox
intrepid	maintain	multiply	parallel
intricate	malign	must	parched
intrigue	manage	mutable	partially
intrinsic	management	naïve	participate
introduction	manhood	narrate	particle
intrude	manly	narrow	particular
inundate	manual	nascent	partisan
invent	manufacture	native	party
invention	margin	nausea	pass
investment	marvel	necessarily	passage
involuntarily	maternity	neglect	passion
involve	matriarch	negligible	patch
irate	maximum	neurology	paternal
irrelevant	mayor	nevertheless	pathetic
irritation	mean	nocturnal	pathological
isolate	meanwhile	nominal	pathology
itinerant	meddle	nonsense	patient
jeopardy	medieval	normally	patriarch
jettison	mediocre	note	pattern
judge	memory	notion	peace
junction	mend	novel	peculiar

pedal	precede	radiant	retrieve
pedestal	precedent	raise	retrospect
pedestrian	precious	range	reveal
pedicure	preconception	rate	reverberate
perceive	precondition	react	reverse
percent	predecessor	reaction	revert
perch	predict	readily	review
perennial	predictably	reason	revive
perfect	predominant	rebellion	revoke
persistent	preference	rebound	revolt
perspective	pregnant	recede	revolve
persuade	prestige	receive	rhythm
pervade	presumably	receptionist	ridge
petition	presumptuous	recess	rigid
petrified	pretense	recession	rigor
petty	prevail	recognize	rivalry
petulant	prevalent	record	robust
phantom	prevent	recover	route
pharmacist	previously	reduce	routine
phenomena	primary	refer	routinely
philanthropic	prime	refine	rudimentary
philanthropy	privacy	reflect	rupture
philharmonic	procedure	reflection	rush
philology	process	refurbish	ruthless
philosopher	proclaim	regard	sacrifice
philosophy	produce	regulate	salvage
phobia	production	reject	saturated
photograph	proficient	rejoicing	savory
pier	programmer	relate	scarce
pillage	progress	relation	scarcely
pioneer	prohibit	release	scattered
place	project	reliable	scene
placid	proliferate	relinquish	scenic
plaid	prolong	remarkable	science
plentiful	prominent	remind	scorching
ply	promise	reminisce	score
pocket	promontory	remove	scribble
podiatrist	promote	renew	script
podium	prompt	renown	scrupulous
point	prone	repel	scrutinize
policy	propel	replace	season
poll	prophetic	replay	security
pollution	propose	reply	seduce
polygamy	prospective	reportedly	seedling
polytechnic	prosperous	representative	segment
ponder	protection	requisite	selective
population	protrude	rescue	selfish
portray	provision	research	seminar
position	proximity	resident	senior
post	psychology	resilient	sensation
postpone	psychopathic	resource	sense
postscript	publication	respected	sensitive
posture	publisher	respiration	sentimental
potent	pulse	restore	sequence
practical	pungent	restrain	serve
practice	query	retain	settle
precarious	quest	reticent	settler

severe
shallow
shatter
shed
shelf
sheltered
shift
ship
shipment
shipping
shoot
shortage
shrink
sideways
significance
significant
signify
sinecure
singular
site
situated
sketchy
skin
soaked
society
sociology
solid
solitary
soluble
solve
sometimes
somewhat
sound
source
spacious
span
specimen
spectator
spectrum
speculate
spiteful
spontaneous
sporadic
spread
sprout
spurn
square
stack
stagnant
stake
stance
static
stationary
stature
steady

stem
step
stipulate
stock
store
stream
strengthen
stress
stretch
strike
striking
stringent
strive
submit
subscribe
subsequent
subside
subsidize
substantiate
succeed
successive
succumb
suffer
suitable
sum
superficial
superfluous
superior
supervise
supplement
supply
supposition
surmise
surveillance
suspect
suspend
swift
switch
symbols
sympathetic
sympathy
synonym
synthesis
taciturn
talk
tangible
task
teacher
technology
tedious
telegram
telepathy
temper
temporize
tempt

tenacious
tentative
terminal
terrain
terrifying
territory
testify
theology
theoretically
thermal
thermometer
thrive
thrust
ticket
timid
title
topic
torment
torpid
torsion
total
tour
toxic
tradition
trail
train
transcend
translucent
transmit
transport
trap
trash
treacherous
treasury
treaty
tremor
tremulous
triangle
triple
tripod
triumph
trivial
trouble
truculent
tyro
ultrasonic
unbiased
undeniable
undercut
underestimated
underline
unfavorably
uniform
unique
unison

unite
unlikely
unmistakable
unravel
unwarranted
update
uproar
vacancy
vacant
vacuum
value
vanity
varied
vast
vegetable
vehemence
veil
veracity
verbalize
verify
versatile
verve
vibrant
viewpoint
vigorous
vindicate
virtual
visible
vital
vivid
vocal
vogue
volume
voluptuous
wait
wane
wanton
weak
weakness
wealth
weapon
weigh
wide
widespread
wilt
wisdom
wither
withstand
witticism
woo
worthwhile
wrinkle
xenophobia
zenith

USA States, Abbreviations, and Capitals

State	Capital
Alabama (AL)	Montgomery
Alaska (AK)	Juneau
Arizona (AZ)	Phoenix
Arkansas (AR)	Little Rock
California (CA)	Sacramento
Colorado (CO)	Denver
Connecticut (CT)	Hartford
Delaware (DE)	Dover
Florida (FL)	Tallahassee
Georgia (GA)	Atlanta
Hawaii (HI)	Honolulu
Idaho (ID)	Boise
Illinois (IL)	Springfield
Indiana (IN)	Indianapolis
Iowa (IA)	Des Moines
Kansas (KS)	Topeka
Kentucky (KY)	Frankfort
Louisiana (LA)	Baton Rouge
Maine (ME)	Augusta
Maryland (MD)	Annapolis
Massachusetts (MA)	Boston
Michigan (MI)	Lansing
Minnesota (MN)	Saint Paul
Mississippi (MS)	Jackson
Missouri (MO)	Jefferson City
Montana (MT)	Helena
Nebraska (NE)	Lincoln
Nevada (NV)	Carson City
New Hampshire (NH)	Concord
New Jersey (NJ)	Trenton
New Mexico (NM)	Santa Fe
New York (NY)	Albany
North Carolina (NC)	Raleigh
North Dakota (ND)	Bismarck
Ohio (OH)	Columbus
Oklahoma (OK)	Oklahoma City
Oregon (OR)	Salem
Pennsylvania (PA)	Harrisburg
Rhode Island (RI)	Providence
South Carolina (SC)	Columbia
South Dakota (SD)	Pierre
Tennessee (TN)	Nashville
Texas (TX)	Austin
Utah (UT)	Salt Lake City
Vermont (VT)	Montpelier
Virginia (VA)	Richmond
Washington (WA)	Olympia
West Virginia (WV)	Charleston
Wisconsin (WI)	Madison
Wyoming (WY)	Cheyenne

Capital of the United States of America (USA)

District of Columbia (DC)	Washingon (commonly abbreviated: Washington, D.C.)

지리적인 장소와 국적

아래 목록은 지리적인 장소의 철자와 발음을 나열한 것이다. 국가의 국가명과 형용사형, 그 나라 사람을 나타내는 말이 각각 다를 때에는 그 단어들을 모두 제시했다. 이 목록에 포함되었다고 해서 각 나라가 모두 주권 국가라는 의미는 아니다.

Af|ghani|stan /æfgænɪstæn/; Af|ghan, Af|ghani /æfgæn/, /æfgæni, -gani/

Af|ri|ca /æfrɪkə/; Af|ri|can /æfrɪkən/

Al|ba|nia /ælbeɪniə/; Al|ba|ni|an /ælbeɪniən/

Al|ge|ria /æljɪəriə/; Al|ge|ri|an /æljɪəriən/

An|dor|ra /ændɔrə/; An|dor|ran /ændɔrən/

An|go|la /æŋgoʊlə/; An|go|lan /æŋgoʊlən/

Ant|arc|ti|ca /æntɑrktɪkə, -ɑrtɪ-/; Ant|arc|tic /æntɑrktɪk, -ɑrtɪk/

An|ti|gua and Bar|bu|da /æntigə ən barbudə/; An|ti|guan, Bar|bu|dan /æntigən/, /barbudən/

(the) Arc|tic Ocean /(ði) ɑrktɪk oʊʃən, ɑrtɪk/; Arc|tic /ɑrktɪk, ɑrtɪk/

Ar|gen|ti|na /ɑrjəntinə/; Ar|gen|tine, Ar|gen|tin|ian, or Ar|gen|tin|ean /ɑrjəntin, -taɪn/, /ɑrjəntɪniən/

Ar|me|nia /ɑrminiə/; Ar|me|nian /ɑrminiən/

A|sia /eɪʒə/; A|sian /eɪʒən/

(the) Atlantic Ocean /(ði) ætlæntɪk oʊʃən/

Aus|tral|ia /ɔstreɪlyə/; Aus|tral|ian /ɔstreɪlyən/

Aus|tria /ɔstriə/; Aus|trian /ɔstriən/

Azer|bai|jan /æzərbaɪdʒan, ɑzər-/; Azer|bai|jani, Azeri /æzərbaɪdʒani, ɑzər-, /əzɛri/

(the) Ba|ha|mas /(ðə) bəhɑməz/; Ba|ha|mian /bəheɪmiən, -hɑ-/

Bah|rain /bareɪn/; Bah|raini /bareɪni/

Ban|gla|desh /bɑŋglədɛʃ, bæŋ-/; Ban|gla|deshi /bɑŋglədɛʃi, bæŋ-/

Bar|ba|dos /barbeɪdoʊs/; Bar|ba|dian /barbeɪdiən/

Bela|rus /bɛlərus, byɛl-/; Bela|rus|sian /bɛlərʌʃən, byɛl-/

Bel|gium /bɛldʒəm/; Bel|gian /bɛldʒən/

Be|lize /bəliz/; Be|liz|ean /bəliziən/

Be|nin /bənin/; Be|ni|nese /bənɪniz/

Bhu|tan /butɑn, -tæn/; Bhu|tani, Bhu|ta|nese /butɑni, -tæni/, /butʰniz/

Bo|liv|ia /bəlɪviə/; Bo|liv|ian /bəlɪviən/

Bos|nia and Her|ze|go|vina /bɒzniə ən hɛrtsəgoʊvinə/; Bosnian, Her|ze|go|vinian /bɒzniən/, /hɛrtsəgoʊvɪniən/

Bot|swana /bɒtswɑnə/; Mot|swana (person), Bat|swana (people) /mɒtswɑnə/, /batswɑnə/

Bra|zil /brəzɪl/; Bra|zil|ian /brəzɪlyən/

Bru|nei Da|rus|salam /brunaɪ dɑrusɑləm/; Bru|nei, Bru|nei|an /brunaɪ/, /brunaɪən/

Bul|garia /bʌlgɛəriə/; Bul|gar|ian /bʌlgɛəriən/

Bur|kina Faso /bərkinə fɑsoʊ/; Bur|kin|abe, Bur|kinese /bərkinabeɪ/, /bərkɪniz/

Bur|ma--See Myanmar /bɜrmə/; Bur|mese— /bɜrmiz/

Bu|rundi /bʊrundi/; Bu|run|dian /bʊrundiən/

Cam|bo|dia /kæmboʊdiə/; Cam|bo|dian /kæmboʊdiən/

Cam|eroon /kæmərun/; Cam|eroo|nian /kæməruniən/

Can|ada /kænədə/; Ca|na|dian /kəneɪdiən/

Cape Verde /keɪp vɜrd/; Cape Ver|dean /keɪp vɜrdiən/

Cen|tral Af|ri|can Re|pub|lic /sɛntrəl æfrɪkən rɪpʌblɪk/; Cen|tral Af|ri|can /sɛntrəl æfrɪkən/

Chad /tʃæd/; Chad|ian /tʃædiən/

Chi|le /tʃɪli, -leɪ/; Chil|ean /tʃɪliən, tʃɪleɪ-/

Chi|na /tʃaɪnə/; Chi|nese /tʃaɪniz/

Co|lom|bia /kəlʌmbiə/; Co|lom|bian /kəlʌmbiən/

Co|mo|ros /kɒmərouz/; Co|mor|an /kəmɔrən/

Co|sta Ri|ca /kɒstə rikə/; Co|sta Ri|can /kɒstə rikən/

Côte d'Ivoire /koʊt divwɑr/; Ivoir|ian /ivwɑriən/

Croa|tia /kroʊeɪʃə/; Croatian /kroʊeɪʃən/

Cu|ba /kyubə/; Cu|ban /kyubən/

Cy|prus /saɪprəs/; Cyp|riot /sɪpriət/

(the) Czech Re|pub|lic /(ðə) tʃɛk rɪpʌblɪk/; Czech /tʃɛk/

Demo|cratic Re|pub|lic of the Congo, or (the) Congo /dɛməkrætɪk rɪpʌblɪk əv ðə kɒŋgoʊ/, /(ðə) kɒŋgoʊ/; Con|go|lese /kɒŋgəliz, -lis/

Den|mark /dɛnmark/; Da|nish, Dane /deɪnɪʃ/, /deɪn/

Dji|bouti /dʒɪbuti/; Dji|bou|tian /dʒɪbutiən/

Domi|nica /dɒmɪnɪkə, dəmɪnɪkə/; Domi|ni|can /dɒmɪnɪkən/

(the) Do|mi|ni|can Re|pub|lic /(ðə) dəmɪnɪkən rɪpʌblɪk/; Dominican /dəmɪnɪkən/

East Ti|mor /ist timɔr/; East Ti|mor|ese /ist timɔriz/

Ecua|dor /ɛkwədɔr/; Ecua|dor|ian /ɛkwədɔriən/

Egypt /idʒɪpt/; Egyp|tian /ɪdʒɪpʃən/

El Sal|va|dor /ɛl sælvədɔr/; Sal|va|do|ran, Sal|va|do|rean /sælvədɔrən/, /sælvədɔriən/

Eng|land /ɪŋglənd/; Eng|lish /ɪŋglɪʃ/

Equi|to|rial Guinea /ɛkwɪtɔriəl gɪni/; Equi|to|rial Guin|ean, Equito|guinean /ɛkwɪtɔriəl gɪniən/, /ɛkwɪtoʊgɪniən/

Eri|trea /ɛrɪtriə/; Eri|trean /ɛrɪtriən/

Es|to|nia /ɛstoʊniə/; Es|to|nian /ɛstoʊniən/

Ethio|pia /iθioʊpiə/; Ethio|pian /iθioʊpiən/

Eu|rope /yuərəp/; Euro|pean /yuərəpiən/

Fiji /fidʒi/; Fi|jian /fidʒiən, fiji-/

Fin|land /fɪnlənd/; Fin|nish, Finn, Fin|lander /fɪnɪʃ/, /fɪn/, /fɪnləndər, -lændər/

France /fræns/; French /frɛntʃ/

Ga|bon /gaboʊn/; Gabo|nese /gæbəniz/

(the) Gam|bia /(ðə) gæmbiə/; Gam|bian /gæmbiən/

Geor|gia /dʒɔrdʒə/; Geor|gian /dʒɔrdʒən/

Ger|many /dʒɜrməni/; Ger|man /dʒɜrmən/

Ghana /gɑnə/; Gha|naian /gɑniən, gəneɪən/

Greece /gris/; Greek /grik/

Gre|nada /grɪneɪdə/; Gre|nadian /grɪneɪdiən/

Gua|temala /gwɑtəmɑlə/; Gua|temalan /gwɑtəmɑlən/

Guinea /gɪni/; Guin|ean /gɪniən/

Guinea-Bissau /gɪni bɪsaʊ/; Guin|ean /gɪniən/

Guy|ana /gaɪænə, -ɑnə/; Guy|anese /gaɪəniz/

Haiti /heɪti/; Hai|tian /heɪʃən/

Hon|du|ras /hɒndʊərəs/; Hon|du|ran /hɒndʊərən/

Hungary /hʌŋgəri/; Hungarian /hʌŋgɛəriən/

Ice|land /aɪslənd/; Ice|lan|dic, Ice|lander /aɪslændɪk/, /aɪsləndər, -lændər/

In|dia /ɪndiə/; In|dian /ɪndiən/

(the) In|dian Ocean /(ði) ɪndiən oʊʃən/

In|do|ne|sia /ɪndəniʒə/; In|do|ne|sian /ɪndəniʒən/

Iran /ɪrɑn, ɪræn, aɪrɑn/; Ira|nian, Irani /ɪreɪniən, ɪrɑ-, aɪreɪ-/, /ɪrɑni/

I|raq /ɪræk, ɪrɑk/; I|raqi /ɪræki, ɪrɑki/

Ire|land /aɪərlənd/; Ir|ish /aɪrɪʃ/

Is|rael /ɪzriəl, -reɪəl/; Is|raeli /ɪzreɪli/

Ita|ly /ɪtəli/; Ital|ian /ɪtælyən/

Ja|maica /dʒəmeɪkə/; Ja|mai|can /dʒəmeɪkən/

Ja|pan /dʒəpæn/; Japa|nese /dʒæpəniz/

Jor|dan /dʒɔrdən/; Jor|danian /dʒɔrdeɪniən/

Kaza|khstan /kɑzakstan, -stæn/; Kaza|khstani, Kazakh /kɑzakstɑni, -stæni/, /kɑzak, kəzæk/

Kenya /kɛnyə, kin-/; Ken|yan /kɛnyən, kin-/

Kiri|bati /kɪərəbati, -bæs/; I-Kiri|bati /i kɪərəbati, -bæs/

Ko|rea, South Ko|rea, North Ko|rea /kəriə, kɔ-/, /saʊθ kəriə, kɔ-/, /nɔrθ kəriə, kɔ-/; Ko|rean /kəriən, kɔ-/, /saʊθ kəriən, kɔ-/, /nɔrθ kəriən, kɔ/

Ku|wait /kuweɪt/; Ku|waiti /kuweɪti/

Kyr|gyz|stan /kɪərgɪstan, -stæn/; Kyr|gyz|stani /kɪərgɪstɑni, -stæni/

Laos /laʊs, laʊs/; Lao, Laotian /laʊ, laʊ/, /leɪoʊʃən/

Lat|via /lætviə, lɑt-/; Lat|vian /lætviən, lɑt-/

Leba|non /lɛbənɒn, -nɒn/; Leba|nese /lɛbəniz/

Le|so|tho /ləsoʊtoʊ, -sutu/ Sotho, Mo|so|tho (person), Ba|so|tho (people) /soʊtoʊ, sutu/, /məsoʊtoʊ, -sutu/, /basoʊtoʊ, -sutu/

Li|beria /laɪbɪəriə/; Li|berian /laɪbɪəriən/

Libya /lɪbiə/; Lib|yan /lɪbiən/

Liech|ten|stein /lɪktənstaɪn/; Liech|ten|stein, Liech|ten|steiner /lɪktənstaɪn/, /lɪktənstaɪnər/

Lithua|nia /lɪθueɪniə/; Lithua|nian /lɪθueɪniən/

Luxem|bourg /lʌksəmbɜrg/; Luxem|bourg, Luxem|bourger /lʌksəmbɜrg/, /lʌksəmbɜrgər/

Mac|edo|nia /mæsɪdoʊniə/; Mac|edo|nian /mæsɪdoʊniən/

Mad|agas|car /mædəgæskər/; Mada|gas|can, Mala|gasy /mædəgæskən/, /mæləgæsi/

Ma|lawi /məlɑwi/; Ma|la|wian /məlɑwiən/

Ma|lay|sia /məleɪʒə/; Ma|lay|sian /məleɪʒən/

Mal|dives /mɔldivz, -daɪvz/; Mal|div|ian /mɔldɪviən/

Mali /mɑli/; Ma|lian /mɑliən/

Malta /mɔltə/; Mal|tese /mɔltiz/

(the) Marshall Islands /(ðə) mɑrʃəl aɪləndz/; Marshallese /mɑrʃəliz/

Mau|ri|ta|nia /mɔrɪteɪniə/; Mau|ri|ta|nian /mɔrɪteɪniən/

Mau|ri|tius /mɔrɪʃəs/; Mau|ri|tian /mɔrɪʃən/

Mexi|co /mɛksɪkoʊ/; Mexi|can /mɛksɪkən/

Mi|cro|nesia /maɪkrəniʒə/; Mi|cro|nesian /maɪkrəniʒən/

Mol|dova /mɔldoʊvə/; Mol|do|van /mɔldoʊvən/

Mon|aco /mɒnəkoʊ/; Mon|acan, Mon|egasque /mɒnəkən/, /mɒnɪgæsk/

Mon|go|lia /mɒŋgoʊliə/; Mon|go|lian /mɒŋgoʊliən/

Mo|rocco /mərɒkoʊ/; Mo|roc|can /mərɒkən/

Mo|zam|bique /moʊzæmbik, -zəm-/; Mo|zam|bi|can /moʊzæmbikən, -zəm-/

Myan|mar (Burma) /myanmɑr (bɜrmə)/; Bur|mese /bɜrmiz/

Na|mibia /nəmɪbiə/; Na|mib|ian /nəmɪbiən/

Na|uru /naʊru/; Na|uruan /naʊruən/

Ne|pal /nəpɔl/; Nepa|lese /nɛpəliz/

(the) Nether|lands /(ðə) nɛðərləndz/; Dutch /dʌtʃ/

New Zea|land /nu zilənd/; New Zea|land, New Zea|lander /nu zilənd/, /nu ziləndər/

Nica|ra|gua /nɪkərɑgwə/; Nica|ra|guan /nɪkərɑgwən/

Ni|ger /naɪdʒər, niʒɛər/; Ni|ge|rien, Nigerois /naɪdʒɪəriən, niʒɛryɛn/, /niʒɛrwɑ/

Ni|geria /naɪdʒɪəriə/; Ni|gerian /naɪdʒɪəriən/

Nor|way /nɔrweɪ/; Nor|we|gian /nɔrwidʒən/

Oman /oʊmɑn/; Omani /oʊmɑni/

(the) Pa|cific Ocean /(ðə) pəsɪfɪk oʊʃən/

Paki|stan /pækɪstæn, pɑkɪstɑn/; Paki|stani /pækɪstæni, pɑkɪstɑni/

Pa|lau /palaʊ, pə-/; Pa|lauan /palaʊən, pə-/

Pan|ama /pænəmɑ, -mɔ/; Pan|ama|nian /pænəmeɪniən/

Pap|ua New Guinea /pæpyuə nu gɪni, papua/; **Pap|ua
New Guin|ean, Pap|uan** /pæpyuə nu gɪniən, papua/,
pæpyuən, papuən/

Para|guay /pærəgwaɪ, -gweɪ/; **Para|guayan** /pærəgwaɪən,
-gweɪən/

Peru /pəru/; **Pe|ru|vian** /pəruviən/

(the) Phil|ip|pines /(ðə) fɪlɪpinz/; **Phil|ip|pine, Fili|pino,
Fili|pina** /fɪlɪpin, /fɪlɪpinou/, /fɪlɪpinə/

Po|land /poulənd/; **Po|lish, Pole** /poulɪʃ/, /poul/

Por|tu|gal /pɔrchəgəl/; **Por|tu|guese** /pɔrchəgiz/

Qa|tar /kətɑr/; **Qa|tari** /kətɑri/

Ro|ma|nia /roumeɪniə/; **Ro|ma|nian** /roumeɪniən/

Rus|sia /rʌʃə/; **Rus|sian** /rʌʃən/

Rwanda /ruɑndə/; **Rwan|dan** /ruɑndən/

Saint Kitts–Ne|vis /seɪnt kɪts nivɪs/; **Kittitian, Ne|visian**
/kɪtɪʃən/, /nɪvɪʒən/

Saint Lu|cia /seɪnt luʃə/; **Saint Lu|cian** /seɪnt luʃən/

Saint Vin|cent and the Grena|dines /seɪnt vɪnsənt
ən ðə grɛnədinz/; **Saint Vin|cen|tian, Vin|cen|tian**
/seɪnt vɪnsɛnʃən/, /vɪnsɛnʃən/

Sa|moa /səmouə/; **Sa|moan** /səmouən/

San Ma|rino /sæn mərinou/; **Sam|mari|nese,
San Mari|nese** /sæmmæriniz/, /sæn mæriniz/

Sao Tome and Prin|cipe /soun təmeɪ ən prɪnsipi/;
Sao Tomean /soun təmeɪən/

Saudi Arabia /soudi əreɪbiə/; **Saudi Arabian** /soudi
əreɪbiən/

Scot|land /skɒtlənd/; **Scot|tish, Scot(s)** /skɒtɪʃ/, /skɒts/

Sen|egal /sɛnɪgɔl, -gal/; **Sen|egal|ese** /sɛnɪgəliz/

Ser|bia and Mon|te|negro /sɜrbiə ən mɒntɪnegrou/
Ser|bian, Serb, Mon|te|negrin /sɜrbiən/, /sɜrb/,
/mɒntɪnegrɪn/

(the) Sey|chelles /(ðə) seɪʃɛlz/; **Sey|chel|lois** /seɪʃɛlwɑ/

Si|erra Le|one /siɛrə lioun/; **Si|erra Le|onean**
/siɛrə liouniən/

Sin|ga|pore /sɪŋəpɔr, sɪŋə-/; **Sin|ga|porean** /sɪŋəpɔriən,
sɪŋə-/

Slo|va|kia /slouvɑkiə, -vækiə/; **Slo|vak, Slo|va|kian**
/slouvæk/, /slouvɑkiən, -væk-/

Slo|ve|nia /slouviniə/; **Slo|ve|nian** /slouviniən/

Solo|mon Is|lands /sɒləmən aɪləndz/; **Solo|mon Is|lander**
/sɒləmən aɪləndər/

So|ma|lia /səmɑliə, sou-/; **So|ma|li, So|ma|lian** /səmɑli,
sou-/, /səmɑliən, sou-/

South Af|rica /souθ æfrɪkə/; **South Af|ri|can** /souθ æfrɪkən/

(the Re|pub|lic of) Spain (ðə rɪpʌblɪk əv) /speɪn/;
Span|ish, Span|iard /spænɪʃ, /spænyərd/

Sri Lanka /sri lɑŋkə, ʃri/; **Sri Lan|kan** /sri lɑŋkən, ʃri/

Su|dan /sudæn, -dɑn/; **Su|da|nese** /sudᵊniz/

Su|ri|name /suərɪnɑm/; **Su|ri|na|mer, Su|ri|na|mese**
/suərɪnɑmər/, /suərɪnəmiz/

Swazi|land /swɑzilænd/; **Swazi** /swɑzi/

Swe|den /swidᵊn/; **Swe|dish, Swede** /swidɪʃ/, /swid/

Switzer|land /swɪtsərlənd/; **Swiss** /swɪs/

Syria /sɪəriə/; **Syr|ian** /sɪəriən/

Tai|wan /taɪwɑn/; **Tai|wan|ese** /taɪwɑniz/

Ta|jiki|stan /tɑdʒɪkɪstæn, -stɑn/; **Ta|jiki|stani, Tajik**
/tɑdʒɪkɪstæni, -stɑni/, /tɑdʒɪk, -dʒik/

Tan|za|nia /tænzəniə/; **Tan|za|nian** /tænzəniən/

Thai|land /taɪlænd, -lənd/; **Thai** /taɪ/

Togo /tougou/; **To|go|lese** /tougəliz/

Tonga /tɒŋə/; **Ton|gan** /tɒŋən/

Trini|dad and To|bago /trɪnɪdæd ən təbeɪgou/;
Trini|dadian, To|bago|nian /trɪnɪdeɪdiən/,
/toubəgouniən/

Tu|ni|sia /tuniʒə/; **Tu|ni|sian** /tuniʒən/

Tur|key /tɜrki/; **Tur|kish, Turk** /tɜrkɪʃ/, /tɜrk/

Turk|meni|stan /tɜrkmɛnɪstæn, -stɑn/; **Turk|men**
/tɜrkmɛn, -mən/

Tu|valu /tuvɑlu, tuvəlu/; **Tu|va|luan** /tuvəluən/

Uganda /yugændə, ugan-/; **Ugan|dan** /yugændən, ugan-/

Ukraine /yukreɪn/; **Ukran|ian** /yukreɪniən/

(the) United Arab Emir|ates /(ðə) yunaɪtɪd ærəb ɛmərɪts,
-əreɪts/; **Emir|ati** /ɛmərɑti/

**(the) United King|dom of Great Brit|ain and
North|ern Ire|land** /(ðə) yunaɪtɪd kɪŋdəm əv greɪt brɪtᵊn
ən nɔrðərn aɪərlənd/; **Brit|ish** /brɪtɪʃ/

(the) United States of America /(ðə) yunaɪtɪd steɪts
əv əmɛrɪkə/; **Ameri|can** /əmɛrɪkən/

Uru|guay /yuərəgweɪ, -gwaɪ/; **Uru|guayan**
/yuərəgweɪən, -gwaɪən/

Uz|beki|stan /uzbɛkɪstæn, -stɑn, uz-/; **Uz|beki|stani,
Uz|bek** /uzbɛkɪstæni, -stɑni, uz-/, /uzbɛk, uz-/

Van|uatu /vænwɑtu/; **Ni-Van|uatu** /ni vænwɑtu/

Vat|ican City /vætɪkən sɪti/

Ven|ezuela /vɛnɪzweɪlə/; **Ven|ezue|lan** /vɛnɪzweɪlən/

Vi|et|nam /vietnɑm, vyɛt-/; **Vi|et|nam|ese** /vietnəmiz,
vyɛt-/

Wales /weɪlz/; **Welsh** /wɛlʃ/

Yemen /yɛmən/; **Yem|eni, Yem|en|ite** /yɛməni/, /yɛmənaɪt/

Zam|bia /zæmbiə/; **Zam|bian** /zæmbiən/

Zim|ba|bwe /zɪmbɑbweɪ, -wi/; **Zim|ba|bwean**
/zɪmbɑbweɪən, -wiən/

CREDITS

Illustrations

Richard Carbajal: pp. 52, 250, 424, 844, 861, 898, 985, 1266, 1360, 1374, 1514; © Richard Carbajal / illustrationOnLine.com
Todd Daman: pp. 35; © Todd Daman / illustrationOnLine.com
Dick Gage: pp. 101, 157, 428 (top); © Dick Gage / illustrationOnLine.com
Patrick Gnan: pp. 67 (top), 449, 744, 944 (right), 1177; © Patrick Gnan / illustrationOnLine.com
Sharon and Joel Harris: pp. 145, 328, 367, 538, 622, 913, 1158, 1274; © Sharon and Joel Harris / illustrationOnLine.com
Philip Howe: pp. 182, 238, 488, 901, 987, 1212, 1551; © Philip Howe / illustrationOnLine.com
Robert Kayganich: pp. 109, 132, 363, 428 (bottom), 436, 568 (top), 559, 651, 860, 1325, 1572; © RobertKayganich / illustrationOnLine.com
Robert Kemp: pp. 286, 305, 429, 443, 600, 940; © Robert Kemp / illustrationOnLine.com
Stephen Peringer: pp. 240, 360, 537, 576, 1568; © Stephen Peringer / illustrationOnLine.com
Mark Ryan: pp. 1461; © Mark Ryan / illustrationOnLine.com
Simon Shaw: pp. 128, 437, 574, 796, 1106; © Simon Shaw / illustrationOnLine.com
Daniel M. Short: pp. 450; © Daniel M. Short
Gerard Taylor: pp. 30, 113, 495, 726, 1299, 1527, 1528; © Gerard Taylor / illustrationOnLine.com
Ralph Voltz: pp. 70, 497, 539, 668, 845, 852, 960, 1182, 1274, 1291, 1401; © Ralph Voltz / illustrationOnLine.com
Cam Wilson: pp. 296, 384, 448, 539, 549, 604, 755, 771, 1134, 1293 (bottom); © Cam Wilson / illustrationOnLine.com

Photos

23: ImageState / Alamy; **81:** © Louie Psihoyos / CORBIS; **172:** Frank Siteman / Index Stock Imagery; **190;** Craig Lovell / Eagle Visions Photography / Alamy; **194:** Phil Talbot / Alamy; **227:** Robert Harding Picture Library Ltd / Alamy; **228:** © William Manning / Corbis; **236:** © Jonathan Blair / CORBIS; **244:** Holt Studios International Ltd / Alamy; **261:** © Royalty-Free / Corbis; **269:** Redferns Music Picture Library / Alamy; **295:** Image Source / Alamy; **311:** © Tim Wright / CORBIS; **322:** Blend Images / Alamy; **324:** (right) BananaStock / Alamy, (center) Kimball Hall / Alamy, (left) Digital Archive Japan / Alamy; **331:** © Bettmann / CORBIS; **369:** (top) Dinodia Images / Alamy; **371:** BananaStock / Alamy; **379:** Dinodia Images / Alamy; **377:** Frances Roberts / Alamy; **400:** Owe Andersson / Alamy; **409:** © Alinari Archives / CORBIS; **416:** Adams Picture Library t/a apl / Alamy; **417:** Dynamic Graphics Group / Creatas / Alamy; **425:** (bottom) David Butow / CORBIS SABA; **458:** © Herbert Spichtinger / zefa / Corbis; **490:** © CORBIS; **524:** Pam Fraser / Alamy; **524:** Dennis MacDonald / Alamy; **544:** Bill Marsh Royalty Free Photography / Alamy; **563:** (top) © Jean Louis Atlan / Sygma / Corbis , (bottom) nagelestock.com / Alamy; **598:** (bottom) Medioimages / Alamy; **617:** Image Source / Alamy; **643:** © Alexander Burkatovski / CORBIS; **664:** BananaStock / Alamy; **666:** Jeff Greenberg / Alamy; **676:** Bubbles Photolibrary / Alamy; **704:** (left) image100 / Alamy, (right top) Trevor Smithers ARPS / Alamy; **732:** © Alinari Archives / CORBIS; **759:** © CORBIS; **766:** © Bettmann / CORBIS; **768:** MONSERRATE J. SCHWARTZ / Alamy; **791:** Dynamic Graphics Group / IT Stock Free / Alamy; **818:** © Royalty-Free / Corbis; **825:** ImageState / Alamy; **842:** © Hulton-Deutsch Collection / CORBIS; **882:** (right) Craig Lovell / Eagle Visions Photography / Alamy; **885:** © NASA / Roger Ressmeyer / CORBIS; **888:** numb / Alamy; **897:** BananaStock / Alamy; **907:** (right) Comstock Images / Alamy; **1003:** Nikreates / Alamy; **1014:** (left) foodfolio / Alamy; **1016:** (left) © Araldo de Luca / CORBIS, (center) © The Art Archive / Corbis; (right) © Bettmann / CORBIS; **1018:** Stockbyte Platinum / Alamy ; **1029:** Wildscape / Alamy; **1036:** © Royalty-Free / Corbis; **1042:** oote boe / Alamy; **1066:** © Bettmann / CORBIS; **1068:** © Bettmann / CORBIS; **1102:** © Bohemian Nomad Picturemakers / CORBIS; **1108:** AM Corporation / Alamy; **1114:** (left) nagelestock.com / Alamy, (right) © Gianni Dagli Orti / CORBIS; **1160:** Brand X Pictures / Alamy; **1169:** Food Features / Alamy; **1200:** PHOTOTAKE Inc. / Alamy; **1247:** ImageState / Alamy; **1251:** Stock Connection Distribution / Alamy; **1267;** © Mark Peterson / CORBIS; **1278:** Blend Images / Alamy; **1337:** AGStockUSA, Inc. / Alamy; **1396:** © Kim Kulish / Corbis; **1398:** (top) Mark Hamilton / Alamy, (bottom, right) Rex Argent / Alamy, (bottom left) Leslie Garland Picture Library / Alamy; **1408:** North Wind Picture Archives / Alamy; **1423:** © Richard T. Nowitz / CORBIS; **1443:** © HASHIMOTO NOBORU / CORBIS SYGMA; **1446:** © Bettmann / CORBIS; **1451:** Comstock Images / Alamy; **1459:** Digital Archive Japan / Alamy; **1480:** © Robert Galbraith / Reuters / Corbis; **1501:** Stockbyte Platinum / Alamy; **1515:** Bettmann / CORBIS; **1522:** ©Stapleton Collection / CORBIS; **1534:** (bottom) Purestock / Alamy; **1540:** (bottom) Stephen Frink Collection / Alamy; **1577:** John Sturrock / Alamy

Photos on the following pages are from JUPITER IMAGES. © 2006 Jupiterimages Corporation: 48, 50, 69, 103, 110, 189, 221, 244, 302, 323, 332, 369 (bottom), 410, 421, 442, 520, 529, 532, 559, 674, 774, 796, 830, 851, 856, 860, 882, 907 (left, center), 917, 944 (left), 946, 983, 990, 1014 (right), 1050, 1143, 1203, 1216, 1285, 1290, 1309, 1393, 1502

Photos on the following pages are from IndexOpen. © 2006 IndexOpen: 66, 190, 194, 207, 220, 267, 409, 519, 851, 1533